W9-BLF-327
WITHDRAWN

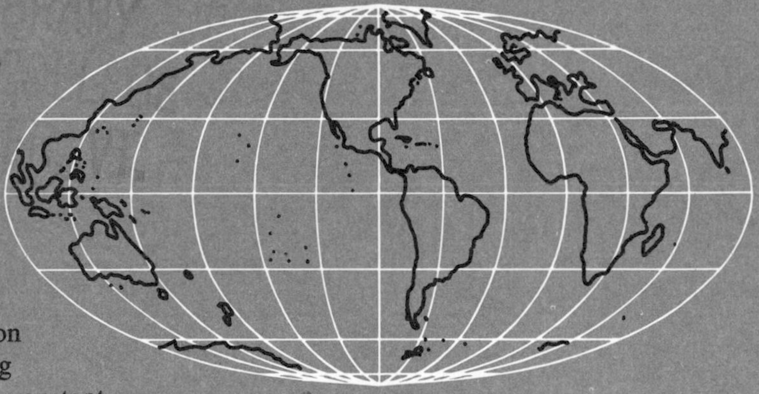

MOLLWEIDE

An equal-area projection in ellipse form; scales along equator and parallels constant and equal; outer areas progressively distorted.

VERMONT COLLEGE
MONTPELIER, VERMONT
WITHDRAWN

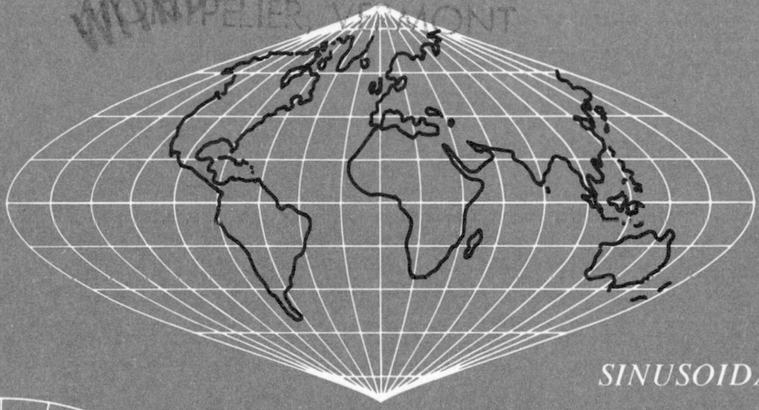

SINUSOIDAL

An equal-area projection; equator and central meridian are straight lines, parallels correct to scale; other meridians are curved lines.

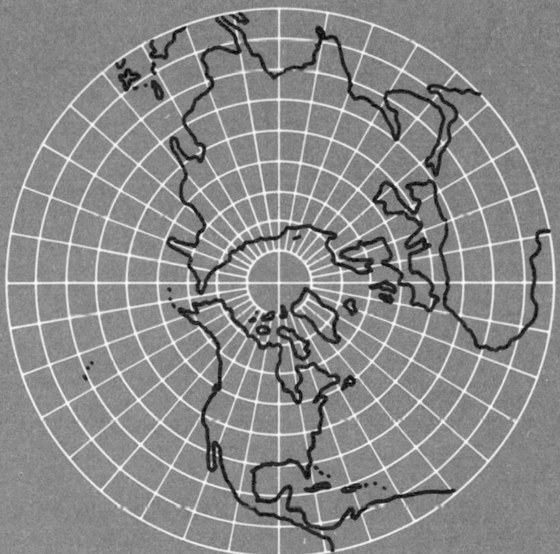

POLAR AZIMUTHAL EQUIDISTANT

Constructed around a central point; the scale along radii from this center is constant, while scale expands along parallels of latitude.

MAP PROJECTIONS

SEE PAGES XXV-XXVI FOR FURTHER INFORMATION

VERMONT COLLEGE
MONTPELIER, VERMONT
WITHDRAWN

WEBSTER'S NEW GEOGRAPHICAL DICTIONARY

WITHDRAWN

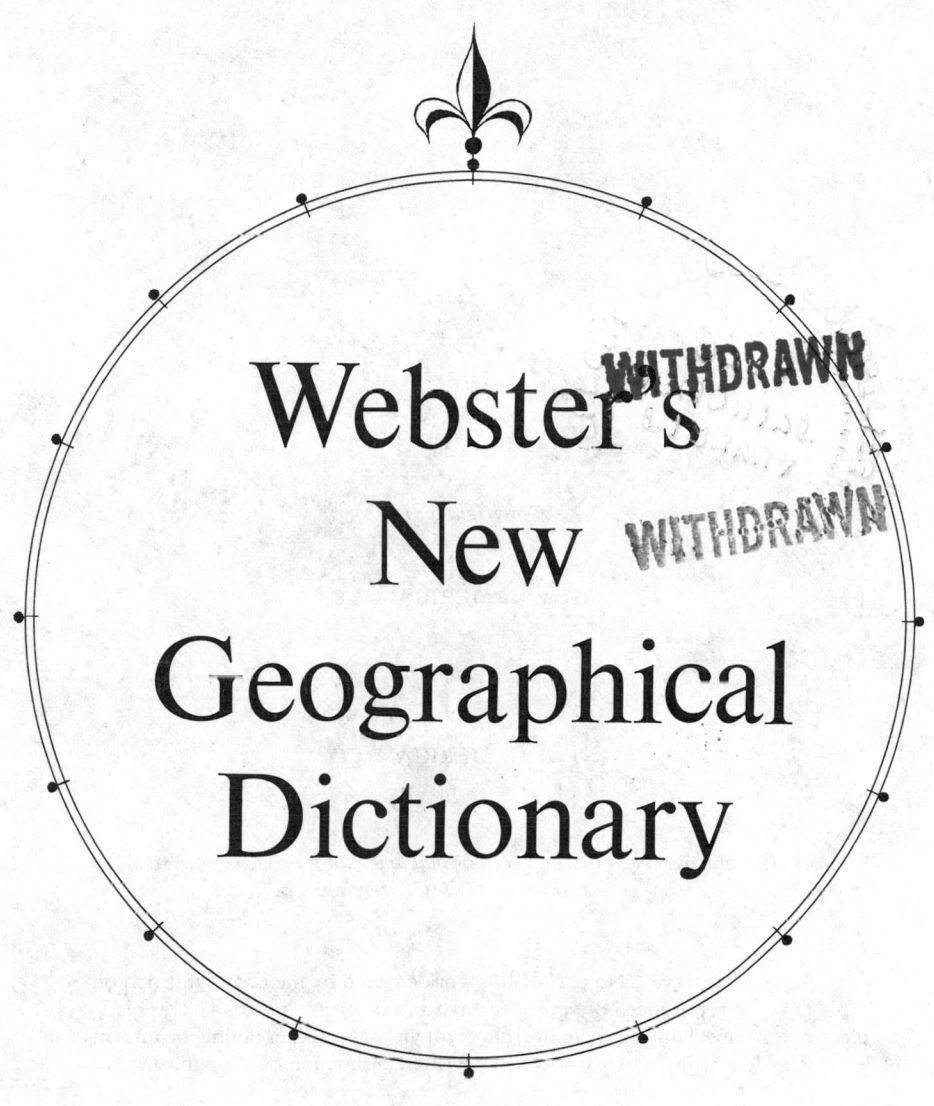

Webster's New Geographical Dictionary

WITHDRAWN
WITHDRAWN

A Merriam-Webster®

G. & C. MERRIAM COMPANY, *Publishers*
SPRINGFIELD, MASSACHUSETTS

Copyright © 1972

BY

G. & C. MERRIAM CO.

Philippines copyright 1972

BY

G. & C. MERRIAM CO.

All rights reserved under international and Pan-American copyright conventions by G. & C. Merriam Co.

All rights reserved. No part of this work covered by the copyrights hereon may be reproduced or copied in any form or by any means — graphic, electronic, or mechanical, including photocopying, recording, taping, or information and retrieval systems — without written permission of the publisher.

Library of Congress Cataloging in Publication Data
Main entry under title:

Webster's New geographical dictionary.

Previous editions published under title: Webster's geographical dictionary.
"A Merriam-Webster."
1. Geography — Dictionaries.

G103.W45 1972 910'.3 72-6103

ISBN 0-87779-146-5

COMPOSED, PRINTED, AND BOUND IN THE UNITED STATES OF AMERICA

910.3
W385
1972

CONTENTS

27812

PREFACE

More than two decades have passed since *Webster's Geographical Dictionary* first appeared. During this time the world has witnessed a number of significant political developments, shifts in population, and a reorientation of economies at both the national and the regional levels. The editors attempted to record the more important changes in a number of revisions of the initial work, but the limitations of revisions and the magnitude of change made it desirable to review critically the entire work and recompose the book.

Webster's New Geographical Dictionary consists of more than 47,000 entries, as compared with some 40,000 in the original work, and contains 217 maps prepared for this edition by Hammond Incorporated, as compared with 159 in its predecessor work. The objectives of the new work are to provide briefly essential information on spelling, pronunciation, and, depending on the nature of the entry, location, population, size (*e.g.*, area, height, length), economy, and history. Entries have been selected on the basis of their usefulness and interest to the general reader and include the world's independent states, dependencies, major administrative subdivisions, largest cities, and significant natural physical features. In addition, a large number of entries of historical interest have been included.

Alphabetization of entries has been governed in most instances by the use of conventional spelling. But a significant number of alternate and former names have been included, which, together with foreign-language variants, produce some 15,000 cross-references.

Inasmuch as *Webster's New Geographical Dictionary* will have its widest distribution in the United States and Canada, entries for those two countries, and to a lesser extent for other English-speaking states, have been included on a scale considerably broader than that used for other parts of the world. In the United States and Canada, for example, all incorporated places with a population of more than 2500 have been included; examples of minimum figures for other areas are: Australia and New Zealand 8000; Africa—Algeria 30,000, Egypt 50,000, Ethiopia 20,000, Ivory Coast 20,000, Kenya 20,000, Nigeria 50,000, South Africa 8000, Tanzania 15,000; Asia—China 100,000, India 50,000, Indonesia 50,000, Iran 30,000, Japan 50,000, Malaysia 20,000, Pakistan 50,000, Turkey 30,000; Europe—United Kingdom 10,000, U.S.S.R. 40,000, other states 20,000; Latin America—municipalities in Brazil and Mexico 50,000 and 30,000 respectively, other states 20,000.

A large number of communities with populations below the minima indicated above have been included because of their regional importance or historical interest. In addition, all county seats in the United States have been included irrespective of their population size.

Population figures were taken from the most recent available official sources. In a number of instances, the figures given in the book were not available during the planning stages and, as a result, cut-off points had to be based on earlier figures. More recent figures were entered as they became available up to the time of going to press.

STAFF

The editorial research and preparation of the text for *Webster's New Geographical Dictionary* were directed by Arthur J. Stevenson, assisted by Roland J. Green, Romas Kinka, and María B. Masó Fernández. Copy editing was supervised by Necia Brown, assisted by Charles M. Cegielski, Rama Deva, Marilyn Klein, and Lois C. Lantz. Cross-referencing was supervised by Frances Latham, assisted by Grace Lord and Mary Neumann. Editorial coordinators were William S. Jarrett and Margaret Sutton. Pronunciations were prepared by Dolores R. Harris and Raymond R. Wilson under the direction of Edward Artin. The Hammond maps were prepared under the direction of Martin A. Bacheller, Robert Laughlin, and Ashley F. Talbot.

ACKNOWLEDGMENTS

The number of individuals, organizations, and government agencies providing data used in this book is large, and only an abbreviated list is given below. The editors acknowledge with thanks permission to make use of various published reports, and are happy to record their debt to the many persons whose assistance in various ways greatly facilitated their work.

Arab Information Center, Washington, D.C.; Australian News and Information Bureau, New York City; Board on Geographic Names, Washington, D.C.; British Information Services, New York City; Bureau of Census and Statistics, Manila, The Philippines; Bureau of Mines, Washington, D.C.; Bureau of Reclamation, Washington, D.C.; Bureau of Statistics, Office of the Prime Minister, Tokyo, Japan; Bureau of Statistics, Dar es Salaam, Tanzania; Bureau of the Census, Washington, D.C.; Canadian Permanent Committee on Geographical Names, Ottawa, Canada; Central Agency for Public Mobilisation and Statistics, Cairo, Egypt; Central Bureau of Statistics, Jerusalem, Israel; Central Bureau of Statistics, The Hague, The Netherlands; Central Bureau of Statistics, Oslo, Norway; Central Statistical Authority under the Council of Ministers of the U.S.S.R., Moscow, U.S.S.R.; Central Statistical Board, Bucharest, Romania; Central Statistical Office, Addis Ababa, Ethiopia; Central Statistical Office, Helsinki, Finland; Central Statistical Office, Warsaw, Poland; Commonwealth Bureau of Census and Statistics, Canberra, Australia; Department of Agriculture, Washington, D.C.; Department of Community Services, Charlottetown, Prince Edward Island, Canada; Department of Highways, Carson City, Nevada; Department of Indian Affairs and Northern Development, Ottawa, Canada; Department of Lands, Forests, and Water Resources, Victoria, British Columbia, Canada; Department of Municipal Affairs, Halifax, Nova Scotia, Canada; Department of Municipal Affairs, Toronto, Ontario, Canada; Department of State, Washington, D.C.; Department of Statistics, Kabul, Afghanistan; Department of Statistics, Wellington, New Zealand; Department of Statistics, Pretoria, Rep. of South Africa; Eidgenössisches Statistisches Amt, Bern, Switzerland; Environmental Science Services Administration, Washington, D.C.; William O. Field, American Geographical Society, New York City; Geological Survey of Canada, Ottawa, Canada; Information Service of South Africa, New York City; Institut für Landeskunde, Bad Godesberg, West Germany; Institut National de la Statistique, Kinshasa, Zaire; Institut National de la Statistique et des Études Économiques, Paris, France; Institut National de Statistique, Brussels, Belgium; Instituto Brasileiro de Estatística, Rio de Janeiro, Brazil; Instituto Centrale di Statistica, Rome, Italy; Instituto Nacional de Estadística, Madrid, Spain; Instituto Nacional de Estadística y Censos, Buenos Aires, Argentina; Legislative Counsel Bureau, Carson City, Nevada; National Central Bureau of Statistics, Stockholm, Sweden; National Information Office to the Council of Ministers, Sofia, Bulgaria; National Park Service, Washington, D.C.; National Statistical Institute, Lisbon, Portugal; National Statistical Service of Greece, Athens, Greece; Office of Population Censuses and Surveys, London, England; Österreichisches Statistisches Zentralamt, Vienna, Austria; Staatliche Zentralverwaltung für Statistik, East Berlin, East Germany; State Institute of Statistics, Ankara, Turkey; Statistical Centre of Iran, Tehran, Iran; Statistics Canada, Ottawa, Canada; Statistisches Bundesamt, Wiesbaden, West Germany; Tennessee Valley Authority, Knoxville, Tennessee; Union Research Institute, Kowloon, Hong Kong; United States Army Engineer Topographic Data Center, Washington, D.C.; United States Geological Survey, Washington, D.C.; United States Naval Oceanographic Office, Washington, D.C. Population figures for cities in the People's Republic of China were taken with permission from *World Urbanization 1950–1970 Volume I: Basic Data for Cities, Countries, and Regions,* (1969) University of California, Berkeley, by Kingsley Davis, to whom special thanks are due.

EXPLANATORY NOTES

In preparing *Webster's New Geographical Dictionary,* the objective has been clarity of presentation rather than absolute uniformity or rigid consistency in the arrangement of information. Thus the basic patterns of arrangement that are used in general throughout the book have been modified to suit the needs of particular entries. The basic patterns of the entries and the principal details of arrangement are described below.

1. General arrangement and kinds of information.

(*a*) The principal details of each entry (or numbered part of an entry) treating a political division are given usually in the following order: the entry word in bold faced type with syllabic division plainly indicated; pronunciation (where not given in a preceding entry); alternative forms and names in bold-faced type (with syllabic division and pronunciation); identification; location; area and population; geographical and physical features; economic data; items of general interest, such as names of colleges and universities and historical information. If the historical information is of sufficient length or relative importance, it is placed in a separate paragraph introduced by the label *History*.

Obviously, not all of the details of the basic pattern described above are included at each entry, since in some entries certain details are not applicable or are not of sufficient importance to warrant inclusion.

(*b*) In entries treating natural features, besides the identifying description and the location, the following kinds of information are included: physical features, such as lengths of rivers, heights of mountains, lengths and areas of islands and of lakes; economic data, such as navigability of rivers, mineral wealth of mountains, agricultural and industrial products of islands; and historical information, as date of discovery, colonization, or acquisition.

(*c*) Details of information of the states of the United States usually follow a definite basic pattern: the entry word with its syllabic division and pronunciation; identification; geographical location; rank in area and the area; rank in population and the population; capital; date of admission to the Union; nickname; state flower; motto; rivers; mountains; chief products; chief cities; political divisions listed in tabular form; and history.

(*d*) The treatment of long entries of major countries, political divisions, etc., follows more or less closely the general arrangement used for states of the United States (see *c,* above). Sometimes, however, an entry may contain special information that requires treatment in a separate paragraph with an introductory word (as at Antarctica a paragraph headed *Ownership*).

(*e*) Many political divisions, such as departments, provinces, and counties, are entered with only a cross reference to a table at the main entry at which information about the political division can be found. See **7,** below. Others are described briefly at their own entries, following the general arrangement of information (see *a,* above). Similar treatment is accorded to United States dams, national parks and monuments, and other such entries.

(*f*) Population data are presented in one of three ways: as estimates (e); as preliminary census figures (p); as final census figures (c). With the abbreviation is given the year to which it applies. In entries containing more than one population figure for the same year, the year is given only once.

2. Alphabetical arrangement of entries.

(*a*) For entries in this dictionary, the ordinary rules of alphabetical sequence govern: (1) the single name; (2) this name with a preceding modifier—necessarily represented for alphabetical purposes with the modifier, preceded by a comma, following the name; (3) this name followed by another word or words. Thus:

George
George, Cape
George, Lake
George Bay
George V Coast
George Hill

A name containing a numeral, as **George V Coast,** above, is alphabetized as if the numeral were spelled out.

A name spelled as a solid word or a hyphenated word precedes the same name when spelled as two words; thus **Georgetown** precedes **George Town.**

(*b*) Names beginning with the prefix **Mc** or **M'** are all alphabetized as if spelled with the full form of this prefix, **Mac.** In alphabetizing, no distinction is made between these and other names (such as **Macclesfield**) in which the initial letters **M a c** are not a prefix.

(*c*) Names of natural features, such as capes, lakes, points, and straits, are generally entered at the significant part of the full name; thus, **Cape Malea** is entered at **Malea, Cape; Point Barrow** is entered at **Barrow, Point; Lake Michigan** is at **Michigan, Lake; Strait of Malacca** is at **Malacca, Strait of; Paso del Inca** is at **Inca, Paso del.**

(*d*) As a general rule, the words Bay, Island, Lake, Mount, etc., have been included as part of the bold-faced vocabulary entry. With rare exceptions, the word River has been omitted, so that the consultant looking for the Amazon River should look at **Amazon.**

(*e*) Names beginning with **Al, El, De, Du, Des, L', La, Le, Les,** etc., are alphabetized at **Al, El, De,** etc., respectively. Names containing "the" are at the main word; thus, **The Everglades** is at **Everglades, The.**

(*f*) Two or more names identical in spelling and pronunciation usually are combined in a single entry. Thus:

Bex·ley \ˈbek-slē\. **1** City, Franklin co., cen. Ohio, surrounded by Columbus; pop. (1970c) 14,888.
2 Borough of Greater London, SE England. See table at LONDON 4.

(*g*) Names with identical spelling that differ in pronunciation or etymology are often entered separately, as the entries at **Acre, Bayonne,** and **Tigre.**

3. Arrangement of parts within entries.

For numbered parts within an entry, the order described below has been followed:

(*a*) An alphabetical arrangement by country, except that places in the United States precede all others. Territories and dependencies of the United States and dependencies of other countries are treated as if independent countries.

When, however, the entry name applies to a country, this application of the name has generally been made the first item under the entry, followed by the remaining items in the order described above. See the entry at DENMARK.

(*b*) An arrangement of geographical and political categories under the countries, placing natural features ahead of political entities (arranged in descending order, e.g., state or province, county, city, town or village).

4. Composite entries.

It has occasionally been found desirable to treat in a single entry names that are related to each other or that form parts of a whole, in order to give the consultant a more complete geographical and historical picture. Such names are printed in bold-faced type. Thus, at **Gaul** are included the early divisions of the ancient country, at **Nile** are described the several sections of the river, at **Taimyr Peninsula** are included the similarly named **Taimyr River, Taimyr Lake, Taimyr Bay,** and **Taimyr Island.**

5. Tables.

To make more usable the information provided, entries of certain classes of names are given in the form of tables, and each name in the table (with the exception of UNITED STATES, *Population of Standard Metropolitan Statistical Areas*) has been made a cross entry at its own alphabetical place in the vocabulary. For example, the counties of the state of California are listed in a table at **California,** and each county name has been cross-entered at its own alphabetical place in the vocabulary; the metropolitan boroughs of London are given in tabular form at **London** and each name has been cross-entered to the table at London. Other examples are the tables of ranges at **Alps** and of dams at **Tennessee Valley Authority** and the several tables at **Canada** and **United States.**

6. Syllabic division and pronunciation.

(*a*) *Syllabic division.* The syllabic division shown for a bold-faced name indicates, for the guidance of printers, proofreaders, writers, and others, those points at which the name may be divided at the end of a line. A name may be divided wherever a centered period or a hyphen appears in the bold-faced name. The rules for such division, established for each language by long and widespread practice, are in some respects more or less arbitrary; accordingly, the division of a name sometimes differs from that of its respelled pronunciation, which attempts to show how the word is syllabified when spoken.

(*b*) *Pronunciation.* Pronunciation is indicated by respelling the name in symbols used in Merriam-Webster dictionaries. A full key to those symbols is given on page xvi, and a guide key appears at the bottom of each odd-numbered text page in the dictionary. The pronunciation is enclosed within slant lines immediately following the bold-faced name.

Effort has been made to secure accurate information on the pronunciation of all names included in the dictionary, and the pronunciations included are in large measure based on information supplied by native speakers and by consulting specialists. Where usage has established one, an anglicized pronunciation has been given in addition to the local pronunciation.

Where there is more than one entry with the same bold-faced name, the pronunciation and syllabication usually appear at the first bold-faced entry. See **Admiralty Bay.** If there are two or more forms of the entry word with different spellings but the same pronunciation, the single pronunciation usually appears after all forms are given. See **Abukir.** In entries in which no syllabication and pronunciation are given, the syllabication and pronunciation are those of the nearest preceding entry or, in the case of differing pronunciations, those of the matching language. See **Florida.** A hyphen that precedes or follows a pronunciation indicates a previously pronounced element or an unpronounced generic term.

7. Cross references.

Two general types of cross references are found in this dictionary: cross entries in the vocabulary and cross references in the body of an article. The name to which the consultant is directed is indicated by the use of special type (SMALL CAPITALS) or by placing after the name the letters *q.v.* (for Latin *quod vide = which see*) or, if reference is to more than the one name, *qq.v.* (for Latin *quae vide = which* [plural] *see*). Thus:

Eger. 1 River, West Germany and Czechoslovakia. See OHRE.
2 City, Czechoslovakia. See CHEB.

Euxine Sea. See BLACK SEA.

Fauquier. County in Virginia. See table at VIRGINIA.

Federation of Malaya. See MALAYA, FEDERATION OF.

Finger Lakes . . . including notably lakes Seneca, Cayuga, Keuka, Canandaigua, Owasco, and Skaneateles (*qq.v.*).

Gomera . . . One of the Canary Is. (*q.v.*)

Grand Coulee Dam. See UNITED STATES, *Dams and Reservoirs.*

Cross references with "see" are frequently used in the body of an article. "See" leads to additional information. See the articles at **American Samoa, Florida Keys, Germany, Hawaii.**

Throughout this dictionary, the words UNITED STATES only are used in cross entries and cross references that refer to the entry **United States of America.**

8. Abbreviations and symbols.

Abbreviations are used throughout the book, in vocabulary entries, tables, and maps, wherever it is felt that their use permits little or no difficulty of understanding. A few unconventional abbreviations are used on some maps due to space considerations. Points of the compass when used as directional points only usually are set in sans serif type with no following period (thus: SW Maine). A complete list of the abbreviations used in the text is given on pages xiv–xv. For symbols used on the maps, see the list on page xxvii.

ABBREVIATIONS & SYMBOLS

ab.	about
abbr.	abbreviated, abbreviation
Acad.	Academy
A.D.	Anno Domini (*Latin,* in the year of our Lord)
Ala.	Alabama
Alb.	Albania, Albanian
alt.	altitude
Alta.	Alberta
Amer.	America, American
anc.	ancient
angl.	anglicized
ANZUS	Australia–New Zealand–United States Treaty
approx.	approximate, approximately
Apr.	April
A.R.	Autonomous Region, Autonomous Republic
Arab.	Arabic
Arch.	Archipelago
Argen.	Argentine
Ariz.	Arizona
Ark.	Arkansas
AS.	Anglo-Saxon
Assoc.	Association
A.S.S.R.	Autonomous Soviet Socialist Republic
Aug.	August
Auton.	Autonomous
av.	average
A.V.	Authorized Version
B.C.	Before Christ, British Columbia
Belg.	Belgian, Belgium
bet.	between
Bib.	Biblical
bor.	borough
bpl.	birthplace
Braz.	Brazilian
Brit.	British
Bulg.	Bulgaria, Bulgarian
c	census (after a date)
c.	circa (before a date; *Latin,* about)
C.	Cabo, Cape, Centigrade
Calif.	California
Can.	Canada, Canadian
cen.	center, central
cent(s).	century (centuries)
Chin.	Chinese
Chron.	Chronicles
co.	county
Col.	Colombia, Colonel, Colossians
Coll.	College
Colo.	Colorado
COMECON	Council for Mutual Economic Assistance
comm.	commune
Conn.	Connecticut
Cor.	Corinthians
cos.	counties
Croat.	Croatian
cu.	cubic
C.Z.	Canal Zone
d.	died
Dak.	Dakota
Dan.	Daniel, Danish
D.C.	District of Columbia
Dec.	December
Del.	Delaware
Den.	Denmark
dept(s).	department(s)
Deut.	Deuteronomy
dist(s).	district(s)
div.	division
Dom. Rep.	Dominican Republic
Dr.	Doctor
Du.	Dutch
e	estimate (after a date)
E	east, eastern
Eccles.	Ecclesiastes
EEC	European Economic Community
EFTA	European Free Trade Association
e.g.	exempli gratia (*Latin,* for example)
elev.	elevation
Eng.	England, English
Eph., Ephes.	Ephesians
esp.	especially
est.	estimate, estimated
Est.	Estonia, Estonian
estab.	established
Esth.	Esther
et al.	et alii (*Latin,* and others)
etc.	et cetera (*Latin,* and so forth)
excl.	excludes, excluding, exclusive
Exod.	Exodus
Ez., Ezr.	Ezra
Ezek.	Ezekiel
f.	founded
Fahr.	Fahrenheit
Feb.	February
Fed.	Federation
ff.	following
Fin.	Finland
Finn.	Finnish
Fla.	Florida
Flem.	Flemish
form.	former, formerly
fr.	from
Fr.	French
ft.	foot, feet
Ft.	Fort
Ga.	Georgia
Gal.	Galatians
Gen.	General, Genesis
Geo.	George
Ger.	German, Germany
Gk.	Greek
Glos.	Gloucestershire
gov.	governorate, governorship
govt(s).	government(s)
Hab.	Habakkuk
Hag.	Haggai
Heb.	Hebrew(s)
Hind.	Hindustani
Hon.	Honduras
Hos.	Hosea
Hung.	Hungarian
I.	Indian, Isla, Island, Isle
Î.	Île (*French,* Island, Isle)
Icel.	Icelandic
i.e.	id est (*Latin,* that is)
Ill.	Illinois
in.	inch(es)
incl.	included, includes, including
incorp.	incorporated
Ind.	Indian, Indiana
Inst.	Institution, Institute
Ir.	Irish
Ire.	Ireland
Is.	Islands, Islas, Isles
Isa.	Isaiah
Ital.	Italian, Italy
Jan.	January
Jap.	Japan, Japanese
Jas.	James
Jer.	Jeremiah
Josh.	Joshua
Jr.	Junior
Judg.	Judges
Kans.	Kansas
Ky.	Kentucky

L. .... Lago, Lagoa, Lake, Latin, Little
La. .... Louisiana
Lam. .... Lamentations
lat. .... latitude
Lat. .... Latin
Lev. .... Leviticus
Lith. .... Lithuania, Lithuanian
long. .... longitude
m. .... mile(s)
Mal. .... Malachi
Man. .... Manitoba
Mar. .... March
Mass. .... Massachusetts
Matt. .... Matthew
max. .... maximum
Md. .... Maryland
Me. .... Maine
Medit. .... Mediterranean
met. .... metropolitan
Mex. .... Mexican, Mexico
Mic. .... Micah
Mich. .... Michigan
Mil. .... Military
Minn. .... Minnesota
Miss. .... Mississippi
Mo. .... Missouri
mod. .... modern
Mongol. .... Mongolian
Mont. .... Montana
MS(S). .... Manuscript(s)
Mt(s). .... Mount(s), Mountain(s)
munic. .... municipality, municipal
N .... north, northern
Nah. .... Nahum
Nat. .... National
NATO .... North Atlantic Treaty Organization
Naut. .... Nautical
naut.m. .... nautical mile(s)
N.B. .... New Brunswick
N.C. .... North Carolina
NE .... northeast, northeastern
Nebr. .... Nebraska
Neh. .... Nehemiah
Neth. .... Netherlands
Nev. .... Nevada
Nfld. .... Newfoundland
N.H. .... New Hampshire
Nic. .... Nicaragua
N.J. .... New Jersey
N. Mex. .... New Mexico
Norw. .... Norway, Norwegian
Nov. .... November
nr. .... near
N.S. .... Nova Scotia
N.T. .... New Testament, Northern Territory
Num. .... Numbers
NW .... northwest, northwestern
N.Y. .... New York
N.Z. .... New Zealand
Ob. .... Obadiah
obs. .... obsolete
occas. .... occasional, occasionally
Oct. .... October
O.E. .... Old English
Okla. .... Oklahoma
Ont. .... Ontario
opp. .... opposite
Ore. .... Oregon
org. .... organized
orig. .... original, originally
O.T. .... Old Testament
p .... preliminary census (after a date)
p. .... page
Pa. .... Pennsylvania
Pal. .... Palestine
par. .... parish
P.E.I. .... Prince Edward Island
penin. .... peninsula
Pers. .... Persian
Pet. .... Peter
Phil. .... Philippines
P.O. .... Post Office
Pol. .... Poland, Polish
polit. .... politically
pop. .... population
Port. .... Portugal, Portuguese
pp. .... pages
P.R. .... Puerto Rico
pron. .... pronounced, pronunciation
prov(s). .... province(s)
Prov. .... Proverbs
Ps., Psa. .... Psalms
Pt. .... Point, Punta
pub. .... published
qq.v .... quae vide (*Latin*, which [plural] see)
Que. .... Quebec
q.v. .... quod vide (*Latin*, which see)
R. .... Río, Rio, River
Ra. .... Range
reincorp. .... reincorporated
Rep. .... Republic
Res. .... Reservation, Reservoir
Rev. .... Revelation
R.I. .... Rhode Island
riv(s). .... river(s)
Rom. .... Romania, Romanian
Rom. Cath. Roman Catholic
R.R. .... Railroad
Russ. .... Russian
Ry(s). .... Railway(s)
S .... south, southern
Sam. .... Samuel
Sask. .... Saskatchewan
S.C. .... South Carolina
Scot. .... Scotland, Scottish
Sd. .... Sound
SE .... southeast, southeastern
sep. .... separate, separated
Sept. .... September
Serb. .... Serbian
S.F.S.R. .... Soviet Federated Socialist Republic
Sol. .... Solomon
Somal. .... Somaliland
Span. .... Spanish
sq. .... square
sq.m. .... square miles
Sr. .... Senior
S.R. .... Socialist Republic
S.S.R. .... Soviet Socialist Republic
St. .... Saint, Sint
Sta. .... Station
Ste. .... Sainte
Str. .... Strait
sub. .... suburb
SW .... southwest, southwestern
Swed. .... Swedish
Switz. .... Switzerland
Tasm. .... Tasmania
Tenn. .... Tennessee
Terr. .... Territory
Tex. .... Texas
Thess. .... Thessalonians
Tim. .... Timothy
trib(s). .... tributary (tributaries)
Turk. .... Turkish
U.K. .... United Kingdom
Ukrain. .... Ukrainian
UN .... United Nations
unincorp. .... unincorporated
Univ. .... University
U.S. .... United States
U.S.A. .... United States of America
U.S.S.R. .... Union of Soviet Socialist Republics
usu. .... usual, usually
Va. .... Virginia
var(s). .... variant(s)
Ven. .... Venezuela
V.I. .... Virgin Islands
Vol. .... Volcano
Vt. .... Vermont
W .... west, western
Wash. .... Washington
Wis. .... Wisconsin
W.Va. .... West Virginia
Wyo. .... Wyoming
yd(s). .... yard(s)
Yorks. .... Yorkshire
Zech. .... Zechariah
Zeph. .... Zephaniah

* .... capital
⊗ .... county seat, parish seat, borough seat (Alaska), district seat (Ontario)

PRONUNCIATION SYMBOLS

ə . . . . . banana, collect, abut

ˈə, ˌə humdrum, abut

^{ə} . . . . . immediately preceding \l\, \n\, \m\, \ŋ\, as in battle, mitten, eaten, and sometimes cap and bells \-^{ə}m-\, lock and key \-^{ə}ŋ-\; immediately following \l\, \m\, \r\, as often in French table, prisme, titre

ər . . . . operation, further, urger

ˈər-, ˈə-r as in two different pronunciations of hurry \ˈhər-ē, ˈhə-rē\

a . . . . . mat, map, mad, gag, snap, patch

ā . . . . . day, fade, date, aorta, drape, cape

ä . . . . . bother, cot, and, with most American speakers, father, cart

ȧ . . . . . father as pronounced by speakers who do not rhyme it with bother

au̇ . . . now, loud, out

b . . . . . baby, rib

ch . . . chin, nature \ˈnā-chər\ (actually, this sound is \t\ + \sh\)

d . . . . . did, adder

e . . . . . bet, bed, peck

ˈē, ˌē beat, nosebleed, evenly, easy

ē . . . . easy, mealy

f . . . . . fifty, cuff

g . . . . go, big, gift

h . . . . hat, ahead

hw . . whale as pronounced by those who do not have the same pronunciation for both *whale* and *wail*

i . . . . . tip, banish, active

ī . . . . site, side, buy, tripe (actually, this sound is \ä\ + \i\, or \ȧ\ + \i\)

j . . . . . job, gem, edge, join, judge (actually, this sound is \d\ + \zh\)

k . . . . . kin, cook, ache

k̲ . . . . German ich, Buch

l . . . . . lily, pool

m . . . . murmur, dim, nymph

n . . . . . no, own

^{n} . . . . indicates that a preceding vowel or diphthong is pronounced with the nasal passages open, as in French *un bon vin blanc* \œ^{n}-bō^{n}-va^{n}-blä^{n}\

ŋ . . . . sing \ˈsiŋ\, singer \ˈsiŋ-ər\, finger \ˈfiŋ-gər\, ink \ˈiŋk\, thing \ˈthiŋ\

ō . . . . bone, know, beau

ȯ . . . . saw, all, gnaw

œ . . . . French bœuf, German Hölle

œ̄ . . . French feu, German Höhle

ȯi . . . . coin, destroy, sawing

p . . . . pepper, lip

r . . . . . rarity

s . . . . . source, less

sh . . . with nothing between, as in shy, mission, machine, special (actually, this is a single sound, not two); with a hyphen between, two sounds as in death's-head \ˈdeths-ˌhed\

t . . . . . tie, attack

th . . . . with nothing between, as in thin, ether (actually, this is a single sound, not two); with a hyphen between, two sounds as in knighthood \ˈnīt-ˌhu̇d\

t̲h̲ . . . then, either, this (actually, this is a single sound, not two)

ü . . . . rule, youth, union \ˈyün-yən\, few \ˈfyü\

u̇ . . . . pull, wood, book

ue . . . German füllen, hübsch

u̅e̅ . . . French rue, German fühlen

v . . . . vivid, give

w . . . . we, away; in some words having final \(ˌ)ō\ a variant \ə-w\ occurs before vowels, as in \ˈfäl-ə-wiŋ\, covered by the variant \ə(-w)\ at the entry word

y . . . . yard, young, cue \ˈkyü\, union \ˈyün-yən\

^{y} . . . . indicates that during the articulation of the sound represented by the preceding character the front of the tongue has substantially the position it has for the articulation of the first sound of *yard*, as in French *digne* \dēn^{y}\

yü . . . youth, union, cue, few, mute

yu̇ . . . curable, fury

z . . . . zone, raise

zh . . . with nothing between, as in vision, azure \ˈazh-ər\ (actually, this is a single sound, not two); with a hyphen between, two sounds as in gazehound \ˈgāz-ˌhau̇nd\

\ . . . . slant line used in pairs to mark the beginning and end of a transcription: \ˈpen\

ˈ . . . . . mark preceding a syllable with primary (strongest) stress: \ˈpen-mən-ˌship\

ˌ . . . . . mark preceding a syllable with secondary (next-strongest) stress: \ˈpen-mən-ˌship\

- . . . . . mark of syllable division

( ) . . . indicate that what is symbolized between is present in some utterances but not in others: \ˈfak-t(ə-)rē\ at *factory* =\ˈfak-tə-rē, ˈfak-trē\

GEOGRAPHICAL TERMS

A selection of geographical terms in various languages and their equivalents in English is provided in the following lists for the convenience of users of the dictionary. The terms have been selected on the basis of their usefulness to the average consultant. In addition to the names of physical features and of political divisions, the lists contain a number of words (such as *old* and *new*; *eastern, western*, and *central*; *upper* and *lower*) that are often used in compound proper names.

Each list is arranged in alphabetical sequence. The first, List I, gives foreign-language terms and their equivalents in English; the second, List II, gives English-language terms with their foreign-language equivalents. Names of languages are indicated by abbreviations, which, if not self-evident, may be identified in the list of abbreviations on pages xiv–xv.

LIST I

ab	Pers.	water
-abad	Hind.	city, town
abajo	Span.	lower
acqua	Ital.	water
ada, adasi	Turk.	island
agua	Port., Span.	water
ain	Arab.	spring, well
ákra, akrotírion	Gk.	cape, point
alt	Ger.	old
altipiano	Ital.	plateau
altiplano	Span.	plateau
alto	Ital., Port., Span.	high, upper
ao	Thai	bay
archipel	Du., Fr.	archipelago
archipiélago	Span.	archipelago
arkhipelag	Russ.	archipelago
austral	Span.	southern
ayer	Malay	water
baai	Du.	bay
bab	Arab.	strait, gate
bælt	Dan.	strait
bahía	Span.	bay
bahr	Arab.	sea, river
bai	Ger.	bay
baía	Port.	bay
baie	Fr.	gulf, bay
baixo	Port.	low, lower
bajo	Span.	low, lower
bana	Jap.	cape
banco	Span.	shoal
band	Pers.	mountain range
bandar	Pers.	port, harbor
baru	Malay	new
bas, basse	Fr.	low
basso	Ital.	low
batu	Malay	rock
bel	Turk.	pass
belyi	Russ.	white
ben	Gaelic	mountain
bereg	Russ.	shore, coast
berg	Du., Ger.	mountain
besar	Malay	great, big
bir	Arab.	spring, well
birket, birkat	Arab.	lake
boca	Span.	mouth, estuary
bogaz, boğaz, boğazı, boghaz	Turk.	strait
bois	Fr.	forest, wood
bolshoi	Russ.	big, great
bucht	Ger.	bay, bight
bugt	Dan.	bay, bight
bukhta	Russ.	bay, bight
bukit	Malay	hill
burnu	Turk.	cape
burun	Turk.	cape
cabo	Port., Span.	cape
campo	Port., Span.	plain
canal	Fr., Span.	channel, canal
canale	Ital.	channel, canal
cap	Fr.	cape
capo	Ital.	cape
cascada	Span.	waterfall
cascata d'acqua	Ital.	waterfall
cataracta	Port.	waterfall
central	Fr., Span.	middle, central
centrale	Ital.	middle, central
cerro	Span.	hill
chaîne	Fr.	mountain range
champ	Fr.	plain, field
chico	Span.	little, small
chiisai	Jap.	little, small
chott	Arab. (Fr. transliteration)	(salt) lake
chute d'eau	Fr.	waterfall
cidade	Port.	city, town
cima	Ital.	peak
cime	Fr.	peak
cité	Fr.	city, town
città	Ital.	city, town
ciudad	Span.	city, town
col	Fr.	pass
colline	Fr.	hill
cordillera	Span.	mountain range
costa	Span.	coast
côte	Fr.	coast
cumbre	Span.	peak
dağ, dagh	Turk.	mountain
dağlari	Turk.	mountain range
dal	Du.	valley
darya	Pers.	river
dasht	Pers.	plain, desert
deniz	Turk.	sea, lake
derbent	Pers.	pass
dere	Turk.	valley
désert	Fr.	desert
deserto	Ital.	desert
desht	Pers.	plain, desert
desierto	Span.	desert
détroit	Fr.	strait
djebel	Arab. (Fr. transliteration)	mountain
dlinny	Russ.	long

dolina	Slavic	valley
eau	Fr.	water
eiland	Du.	island
erg	Arab.	desert
est	Fr., Ital.	east
este	Port., Span.	east
estrecho	Span.	strait
estreito	Port.	strait
estuaire	Fr.	estuary
estuario	Span.	estuary
étang	Fr.	lake, lagoon
falaise	Fr.	cliff
feld	Ger.	field, plain
fels	Ger.	cliff
fertő	Hung.	lake
fiume	Ital.	river
fleuve	Fr.	river
fluss	Ger.	river
fokani	Arab.	upper
fonn	Norw.	glacier
forêt	Fr.	forest
foz	Port.	estuary
garh	Hind.	hill
gawa	Jap.	river
gebel	Arab.	mountain
gebergte	Du.	mountain range
gebirge	Ger.	mountain range
gegend	Ger.	region
ghat	Hind.	pass
gherb	Arab.	west
gletscher	Dan., Ger.	glacier
gobi	Mongol.	desert
goenoeng	Malay (Du. transliteration)	mount, mountain
göl	Turk.	lake
golf	Dan., Du., Ger.	gulf
golfe	Fr.	gulf
golfo	Ital., Port., Span.	gulf
gölü	Turk.	lake
gora	Russ.	mountain
gorod	Russ.	city
gory	Russ.	mountain range
góry	Pol.	mountains
grand	Fr.	big
grande	Span.	big
groot	Du.	big
gross	Ger.	big
grosso	Ital., Port.	big
guba	Russ.	gulf, bay
gunong	Malay	mountain
guntō	Jap.	archipelago
gunung	Indonesian	mountain
hafen	Ger.	port
haff	Ger.	lagoon
hai	Chin.	sea
halbinsel	Ger.	peninsula
hamada, hammada	Arab.	desert
hāmūn	Pers.	lake
hantō	Jap.	peninsula
hara	Jap.	plain, field
haut	Fr.	high
higashi	Jap.	east
ho	Chin.	river
hoch	Ger.	high
hochebene	Ger.	plateau
hoek	Du.	cape
hoku	Jap.	north
hoog	Du.	high
hor	Arab.	lake
hsiao	Chin.	little, small
hu	Chin.	lake
île	Fr.	island
ilha	Port.	island
inférieur	Fr.	lower

inferiore	Ital.	lower
insel	Ger.	island
ırmak	Turk.	river
isla	Span.	island
isola	Ital.	island
itadaki	Jap.	peak
jabal	Arab.	mountain
järvi	Finn.	lake
jebel	Arab.	mountain
jezira, jeziret	Arab.	island
jima	Jap.	island
jökull	Icel.	glacier
kaap	Du.	cape
kai	Jap.	sea
kaikyō	Jap.	channel, strait
kaku	Jap.	point
kali	Malay	river
kam	Korean	cape
kap	Dan., Norw., Swed.	cape
kapu	Turk.	pass
kawa	Jap.	river
kebir	Arab.	big
kechil	Malay	small
khrebet	Russ.	mountain range
kiang	Chin.	river
kiao	Chin.	cape, point
kidul	Malay	south
kita	Jap.	north
klein	Du., Ger.	small
ko	Siamese	island
ko	Jap.	lake
koh	Pers.	mountain
koh	Siamese	island
kol	Mongol.	lake
kolpos, kólpos	Gk.	gulf
kong	Chin.	river
kop	Afrikaans	hill
körfez, körfezi	Turk.	gulf, bay
kosui	Jap.	lake
krai	Russ.	territory
kuh	Pers.	mountain
kul	Mongol.	lake
kulon	Malay	west
kum	Turk.	desert
kyst	Dan.	coast
laag	Du.	low
lac	Fr.	lake
lago	Ital., Port., Span.	lake
lagoa	Port.	lagoon
laguna	Span.	lagoon
land	Ger.	country
lang	Du., Ger.	long
largo	Span.	long
laut	Malay	sea
lembah	Malay	valley
les	Russ.	forest
levante	Ital.	east
límni	Gk.	lake
litoral	Port.	coast
llano	Span.	plain
long	Fr.	long
longo	Port.	long
lungo	Ital.	long
ma	Arab.	water
maha	Hind.	big, great
maidan	Hind.	plain, field
mali	Russ.	small
mar	Port., Span.	sea
mare	Ital.	sea
massif	Fr.	mountain group
medio	Span.	middle
meer	Du.	lake
meer	Ger.	sea
meio	Port.	middle

mer	Fr.	sea
meridional	Span.	southern
méridional	Fr.	southern
middelst, midden	Du.	middle
midi	Fr.	south
minami	Jap.	south
misaki	Jap.	cape
mittel	Ger.	middle
mizu	Jap.	water
mont	Fr.	mountain
montagna	Ital.	mountain
montagnes	Fr.	mountain range
monte	Ital., Port., Span.	mountain
monti	Ital.	mountain range
more	Russ.	sea
mori	Jap.	mount
moyen	Fr.	middle
mündung	Ger.	river mouth, estuary
mys	Russ.	cape
nada	Jap.	gulf, sea
nagai	Jap.	long
nahr	Arab.	river
naka	Jap.	middle
nan	Chin.	south
negri	Malay	country
neu	Ger.	new
nieder	Ger.	lower
niedrig	Ger.	low
nieuw	Du.	new
nishi	Jap.	west
nizhni	Russ.	lower
noord	Du.	north, northern
nor	Mongol.	lake
nord	Fr.	north
nord-	Ger.	north
nördlich	Ger.	northern
norte	Ital., Port., Span.	north
nos	Russ.	cape
nouveau, nouvelle	Fr.	new
novo	Port.	new
novy	Russ.	new
nuevo	Span.	new
nuovo	Ital.	new
nuur	Mongol.	lake
o	Jap.	big
ø (ö)	Dan., Norw.	island
ö	Swed.	island
ober	Ger.	upper
oblast	Russ.	region
occidental	Fr., Span.	western
occidentale	Ital.	western
occidente	Ital.	west
oceaan	Du.	ocean
océan	Fr.	ocean
oceano	Ital., Port.	ocean
océano	Span.	ocean
oedjoeng	Malay (Du. transliteration)	cape
oeste	Port., Span.	west
okrug	Russ.	district
oost	Du.	east
oostersch	Du.	eastern
opper	Du.	upper
oriental	Fr., Span.	eastern
orientale	Ital.	eastern
oriente	Span.	east
orta	Turk.	middle
ost-	Ger.	east
östlich	Ger.	east, eastern
ostrov	Russ.	island
oud	Du.	old
ouest	Fr.	west
over	Du.	upper
ozean	Ger.	ocean
ozero	Russ.	lake
padang	Malay	plain
paese	Ital.	country
país	Port., Span.	country
paiz	Port.	country
panchang	Malay	long
paso	Span.	pass
pass	Ger.	pass
passo	Ital., Port.	pass
pays	Fr.	country
peh, pei	Chin.	north
peninsula	Span.	peninsula
penisola	Ital.	peninsula
pequeno	Port.	small
pequeño	Span.	small
pereval	Russ.	pass
petit	Fr.	small
pic	Fr.	peak
picco	Ital.	peak
piccolo	Ital.	small
pico	Port., Span.	peak
pinhal	Port.	forest
piz	Romansh	peak
plaine	Fr.	plain, field
planalto	Port.	plateau
plateau	Fr.	plateau
ploskogorie	Russ.	plateau
poelau	Malay (Du. transliteration)	island
pointe	Fr.	point
poluostrov	Russ.	peninsula
ponta	Port.	point
port	Fr.	port
porthmós	Gk.	strait
porto	Ital., Port.	port
poulo	Malay	island
presqu'île	Fr.	peninsula
prezhni	Russ.	old (former)
prokhod	Russ.	pass
proliv	Russ.	strait
puerto	Span.	port
pulau	Indonesian, Malay	island
punta	Ital., Span.	point
pustnya	Russ.	desert
qum	Turk.	desert
ras, ra's	Arab.	cape
ravnina	Russ.	plain, field
rayon	Russ.	region
região	Port.	region
région	Fr.	region
región	Span.	region
regione	Ital.	region
reka	Russ.	river
rettō	Jap.	island (chain)
rio	Port.	river
río	Span.	river
rivier	Du.	river
rivière	Fr.	river
rud	Pers.	river
sabaku	Jap.	desert
sahra (*pl.* sahara)	Arab.	desert
saki	Jap.	cape
san	Jap.	hill, mountain
saut	Fr.	waterfall
schiereiland	Du.	peninsula
see	Ger.	sea, lake
seghir	Arab.	little, small
selat	Malay	channel
selva	Span.	wood, forest
septentrional	Fr., Port., Span.	northern
serra	Port.	mountain range
seto	Jap.	strait
settentrionale	Ital.	northern

shan	Chin.	hill, mountain mountain range
shang	Chin.	upper
shat, shatt	Arab.	river, (salt) lake
shemal	Arab.	north
sherk	Arab.	east
shima	Jap.	island
shimo	Jap.	lower
shotō	Jap.	archipelago
shott	Arab.	(salt) lake
shui	Chin.	water
si	Chin.	west
sierra	Span.	mountain range
sopka	Russ.	mountain (extinct volcano)
spitze	Ger.	peak
sredni	Russ.	middle
stad	Du.	city, town
stadt	Ger.	city, town
-stan	Pers.	country
step	Russ.	plain
straat	Du.	strait
strasse	Ger.	strait
stretto	Ital.	strait
strom	Ger.	river
su	Turk.	water, river
sud	Fr., Ital., Span.	south
süd-	Ger.	south
südlich	Ger.	southern
suid	Afrikaans	south
suidō	Jap.	strait
sul	Port.	south
supérieur	Fr.	upper
superior	Port., Span.	upper
superiore	Ital.	upper
sur	Span.	south
suyu	Turk.	water, river
sziget	Hung.	island
tafelland	Du.	plateau
takai	Jap.	high
tal	Ger.	valley
tandjoeng	Malay (Du. transliteration)	cape, point
tani	Jap.	valley
tanjong	Malay	cape, point
tao	Chin.	island
taung	Burmese	hill
tel, tell	Arab.	hill
temin	Arab.	south
tepe	Turk.	hill
t'ien	Chin.	plain, field
tinggi	Malay	high
tó	Hung.	lake
tō	Jap.	island
tōge	Jap.	pass
tua	Malay	old
tung	Chin.	east
udjung	Indonesian	cape
ue-no	Jap.	upper
ulu	Turk.	big, great
umi	Jap.	sea
unter	Ger.	lower
ura	Jap.	bay
utan	Malay	forest, woods
utara	Malay	north
val	Ital.	valley
valle	Ital., Port., Span.	valley
vallée	Fr.	valley
vecchio	Ital.	old
veld	Afrikaans	plain (grassland)
velho	Port.	old
veliki	Russ.	great, big
verkhni	Russ.	upper
vershina	Russ.	peak
viejo	Span.	old
vieux, vieille	Fr.	old
vik	Swed.	bay
ville	Fr.	city, town
voda	Russ.	water
vostochni	Russ.	eastern
vostok	Russ.	east
wadi	Arab.	valley (dry watercourse)
wald	Ger.	forest, woods
wan	Chin., Jap.	gulf, bay
wasser	Ger.	water
wasserfall	Ger.	waterfall
water	Du.	water
waterval	Du.	waterfall
west	Du., Ger.	west
westlich	Ger.	western
wetan	Malay	east
wüste	Ger.	desert
yama	Jap.	mountain
yug	Russ.	south, southern
zaki	Jap.	cape, point
zalew	Pol.	gulf
zaliv	Russ.	gulf
zapad	Russ.	west
zapadni	Russ.	western
zee	Du.	sea
zemlya	Russ.	country, land
zuid	Du.	south

LIST II

archipelago:	
Du., Fr.	archipel
Jap.	guntō, shotō
Russ.	arkhipelag
Span.	archipiélago
bay:	
Chin.	wan
Dan.	bugt
Du.	baai
Fr.	baie
Ger.	bucht, bai
Jap.	ura, wan
Port.	baía
Russ.	guba, bukhta
Span.	bahía
Swed.	vik
Thai	ao
Turk.	körfez, körfezi
big: see GREAT	
bight:	
Dan.	bugt
Ger.	bucht
Russ.	bukhta
cape:	
Arab.	ras, ra's
Chin.	kiao
Dan., Norw., Swed.	kap
Du.	hoek, kaap
Fr.	cap
Gk.	ákra, akrotírion
Indonesian	udjung
Ital.	capo
Jap.	bana, saki, misaki, zaki
Korean	kam
Malay	tandjoeng (Du. transliteration), tanjong, oedjoeng (Du. transliteration)
Port.	cabo
Russ.	mys, nos
Span.	cabo
Turk.	burnu, burun

channel: (see also STRAIT)	
Fr., Span.	canal
Ital.	canale
Jap.	kaikyō
Malay	selat
city, town:	
Du.	stad
Fr.	ville, cité
Ger.	stadt
Hind.	-abad
Ital.	città
Port.	cidade
Russ.	gorod
Span.	ciudad
cliff:	
Fr.	falaise
Ger.	fels
coast:	
Dan.	kyst
Fr.	côte
Russ.	bereg
Span.	costa
country, region, land:	
Fr.	pays; région; terre
Ger.	land; gegend
Ital.	paese; regione; terra
Malay	negri
Pers.	-stan (as in Hindustan)
Port.	país, paiz; região; terra
Russ.	zemlya; oblast; rayon; okrug (district)
Span.	país; región; tierra
desert:	
Arab.	sahra (*pl.* sahara), hamada, hammada, erg
Fr.	désert
Ger.	wüste
Ital.	deserto
Jap.	sabaku
Mongol.	gobi
Pers.	dasht, desht
Russ.	pustnya
Span.	desierto
Turk.	kum, qum
east:	
Arab.	sherk
Chin.	tung
Du.	oost
Fr.	est
Ger.	ost-; östlich
Ital.	est, levante
Jap.	higashi
Malay	wetan
Port.	este
Russ.	vostok
Span.	este, oriente
eastern:	
Du.	oostersch
Fr., Span.	oriental
Ger.	östlich
Ital.	orientale
Russ.	vostochni
estuary, river mouth:	
Fr.	estuaire
Ger.	mündung
Port.	foz
Span.	boca, estuario
field: see PLAIN	forêt, bois
forest, wood:	wald
Fr.	utan
Ger.	les

Malay	selva
Russ.	les
Span.	selva
glacier:	
Dan., Ger.	gletscher
Icel.	jökull
Norw.	fonn
great, big:	
Arab.	kebir
Du.	groot
Fr.	grand
Ger.	gross
Hind.	maha
Ital., Port.	grosso
Jap.	o
Malay	besar
Russ.	bolshoi; veliki
Span.	grande
Turk.	ulu
gulf:	
Chin.	wan
Dan., Du., Ger.	golf
Fr.	golfe, baie
Gk.	kolpos, kólpos
Ital., Port., Span.	golfo
Jap.	nada, wan
Pol.	zalew
Russ.	guba, zaliv
Turk.	körfez, körfezi
high:	
Du.	hoog
Fr.	haut
Ger.	hoch
Ital., Port., Span.	alto
Jap.	takai
Malay	tinggi
hill:	
Afrikaans	kop
Arab.	tel, tell
Burmese	taung
Chin.	shan
Fr.	colline
Hind.	garh
Jap.	san
Malay	bukit
Span.	cerro
Turk.	tepe
island:	
Arab.	jezira, jeziret
Chin.	tao
Dan., Norw.	ø (ö)
Du.	eiland
Fr.	île
Ger.	insel
Hung.	sziget
Indonesian	pulau
Ital.	isola
Jap.	jima, shima, tō; rettō (chain)
Malay	poulo, poelau (Du. transliteration), pulau
Port.	ilha
Russ.	ostrov
Siamese	ko, koh
Span.	isla
Swed.	ö
Turk.	ada, adasi
lagoon:	
Fr.	étang
Ger.	haff
Port.	lagoa
Span.	laguna

lake:	
Arab.	birket, birkat, hor; (salt lake) shat, shatt, shott, or, Fr. transliteration, chott
Chin.	hu
Du.	meer
Finn.	järvi
Fr.	lac, étang
Ger.	see
Gk.	límni
Hung.	fertő, tó
Ital., Port., Span.	lago
Jap.	ko, kosui
Mongol.	kol, kul; nor, nuur
Pers.	hāmūn
Russ.	ozero
Turk.	deniz, göl, gölü
land: see COUNTRY	
little, small:	
Arab.	seghir
Chin.	hsiao
Du., Ger.	klein
Fr.	petit
Ital.	piccolo
Jap.	chiisai
Malay	kechil
Port.	pequeno
Russ.	mali
Span.	pequeño, chico
long:	
Du., Ger.	lang
Fr.	long
Ital.	lungo
Jap.	nagai
Malay	panchang
Port.	longo
Russ.	dlinny
Span.	largo
low:	
Du.	laag
Fr.	bas, basse
Ger.	niedrig
Ital.	basso
Port.	baixo
Span.	bajo
lower:	
Fr.	inférieur
Ger.	nieder, unter
Ital.	inferiore
Jap.	shimo
Port.	baixo
Russ.	nizhni
Span.	bajo, abajo
middle:	
Du.	middelst, midden
Fr.	central, moyen
Ger.	mittel
Ital.	centrale
Jap.	naka
Port.	meio
Russ.	sredni
Span.	medio, central
Turk.	orta
mount, mountain:	
Arab.	jebel, gebel, jabal, djebel (Fr. transliteration)
Chin.	shan
Du., Ger.	berg
Fr.	mont, massif (group)
Gaelic	ben
Indonesian	gunung
Ital.	montagna, monte

Jap.	mori, san, yama
Malay	goenoeng (Du. transliteration), gunong (Du. transliteration)
Pers.	kuh, koh
Pol.	góry (mountains)
Port., Span.	monte
Russ.	gora; sopka (extinct volcano)
Turk.	dağ, dagh
mountain range:	
Chin.	shan
Du.	gebergte
Fr.	montagnes, chaîne
Ger.	gebirge
Ital.	monti
Pers.	band
Port.	serra
Russ.	khrebet, gory
Span.	cordillera, sierra
Turk.	dağları
new:	
Du.	nieuw
Fr.	nouveau, nouvelle
Ger.	neu
Ital.	nuovo
Malay	baru
Port.	novo
Russ.	novy
Span.	nuevo
north:	
Arab.	shemal
Chin.	peh, pei
Du.	noord
Fr.	nord
Ger.	nord-
Ital., Port., Span.	norte
Jap.	hoku, kita
Malay	utara
northern:	
Du.	noord
Fr., Port., Span.	septentrional
Ger.	nördlich
Ital.	settentrionale
ocean:	
Du.	oceaan
Fr.	océan
Ger.	ozean
Ital., Port.	oceano
Span.	océano
old:	
Du.	oud
Fr.	vieux, vieille
Ger.	alt
Ital.	vecchio
Malay	tua
Port.	velho
Russ.	prezhni (former)
Span.	viejo
pass:	
Fr.	col
Ger.	pass
Hind.	ghat
Ital., Port.	passo
Jap.	tōge
Pers.	derbent
Russ.	prokhod, pereval
Span.	paso
Turk.	kapu, bel
peak:	
Fr.	pic, cime
Ger.	spitze
Ital.	picco, cima
Jap.	itadaki
Port.	pico

Romansh	piz
Russ.	vershina
Span.	pico, cumbre
peninsula:	
Du.	schiereiland
Fr.	presqu'île
Ger.	halbinsel
Ital.	penisola
Jap.	hantō
Russ.	poluostrov
Span.	península
plain, field:	
Afrikaans	veld (grassland)
Chin.	t'ien
Fr.	plaine, champ
Ger.	feld
Hind.	maidan
Jap.	hara
Malay	padang
Pers.	dasht, desht
Port.	campo
Russ.	step, ravnina
Span.	llano, campo
plateau:	
Du.	tafelland
Fr.	plateau
Ger.	hochebene
Ital.	altipiano
Port.	planalto
Russ.	ploskogorie
Span.	altiplano
point: (see also CAPE)	
Chin.	kiao
Fr.	pointe
Ital., Span.	punta
Jap.	kaku, zaki
Malay	tandjoeing, tanjong
Port.	ponta
port:	
Fr.	port
Ger.	hafen
Ital., Port.	porto
Pers.	bandar
Span.	puerto
region: see COUNTRY	
river:	
Arab.	bahr, shat, shatt, nahr
Chin.	kiang, ho, kong
Du.	rivier
Fr.	fleuve, rivière
Ger.	fluss, strom
Ital.	fiume
Jap.	kawa, gawa
Malay	kali
Pers.	darya, rud
Port.	rio
Russ.	reka
Span.	río
Turk.	ırmak, su, suyu
river mouth: see ESTUARY	
sea:	
Arab.	bahr
Chin.	hai
Du.	zee
Fr.	mer
Ger.	meer, see
Ital.	mare
Jap.	kai, nada, umi
Malay	laut
Port., Span.	mar
Russ.	more
Turk.	deniz
small: see LITTLE	
south:	
Afrikaans	suid
Arab.	temin
Chin.	nan
Du.	zuid
Fr.	sud, midi
Ger.	süd-
Ital.	sud
Jap.	minami
Malay	kidul
Port.	sul
Russ.	yug
Span.	sud, sur
southern:	
Fr.	méridional
Ger.	südlich
Russ.	yug
Span.	meridional, austral
strait:	
Arab.	bab
Dan.	bælt
Du.	straat
Fr.	détroit
Ger.	strasse
Gk.	porthmós
Ital.	stretto
Jap.	kaikyo, seto, suido
Port.	estreito
Russ.	proliv
Span.	estrecho
Turk.	bogaz, boğaz, boğazı, boghaz
town: see CITY	
upper:	
Arab.	fokani
Chin.	shang
Du.	opper, over
Fr.	supérieur
Ger.	ober
Ital.	alto, superiore
Jap.	ue-no
Port., Span.	alto, superior
Russ.	verkhni
valley:	
Arab.	wadi (dry water-course)
Du.	dal
Fr.	vallée
Ger.	tal
Ital.	val, valle
Jap.	tani
Malay	lembah
Port., Span.	valle
Slavic	dolina
Turk.	dere
water:	
Arab.	ma
Chin.	shui
Du.	water
Fr.	eau
Ger.	wasser
Ital.	acqua
Jap.	mizu
Malay	ayer
Pers.	ab
Port., Span.	agua
Russ.	voda
Turk.	su, suyu
waterfall:	
Du.	waterval
Fr.	chute d'eau, saut
Ger.	wasserfall
Ital.	cascata d'acqua
Port.	cataracta

west:	
Arab.	gherb
Chin.	si
Du., Ger.	west
Fr.	ouest
Ital.	occidente
Jap.	nishi
Malay	kulon
Port., Span.	oeste
Russ.	zapad
western:	
Du.	westersch
Fr., Span.	occidental
Ger.	westlich
Ital.	occidentale
Russ.	zapadni
wood: see FOREST	
Span.	cascada

MAP PROJECTIONS

One of the most difficult problems in map making is projection — the representation of the round surface of the earth on a flat surface such as a page or chart. Although before the Christian era it was known that the earth was round and certain methods of map projection were formulated and carried into execution, most maps remained comparatively crude by modern standards until the age of discovery in the 15th and 16th centuries began to supply the considerable gaps that had up to then existed in man's knowledge of the world as a whole. This widening knowledge in turn stimulated cartographers to devise improved methods of projection.

Although maps of small areas may be true enough to scale throughout so that the distortion is for practical purposes of no consequence, maps of large areas — for example, a continent or a hemisphere — involve distortion of some degree, and this distortion varies throughout the area mapped. The extent that this distortion can reach is vividly brought out by one projection (Mercator) of the world, wherein the poles, which are actually mere points without any dimension, have the same dimension as the equator.

There is no one method of projection that is best for all purposes. All involve distortion of some sort, and what projection is best for a given case is determined by weighing the advantages against the disadvantages of each method in the light of the use to which the map is to be put and the size, configuration, and orientation of the area to be mapped. Not all projections would produce a desirable route map for long-distance airplanes. A country long from north to south and narrow from east to west (e.g., Chile) is not represented to best advantage by the projection that serves best for a country broad from east to west in relation to its depth from north to south (e.g., the United States or the Union of Soviet Socialist Republics).

Reference data employed by projectionists are the parallels of latitude, the meridians of longitude, the poles, and the equator.

The following brief description of some of the more commonly used projections is provided as a complement to the pictures of various projections on the end papers of this book. For those who would like a much fuller treatment, clarified by more detailed illustrations, Erwin J. Raisz, *Principles of Cartography* (McGraw-Hill, 1962) and Arthur H. Robinson and Randall D. Sale, *Elements of Cartography,* 3rd. ed. (John Wiley, 1969), may be suggested.

Hollow rubber balls painted as globes and generously lined with meridians and parallels of latitude can be used to advantage in explaining projections, and an imagined globe of this sort is used in a few of the explanations that follow.

Orthographic. This projection, conceived by Hipparchus about 125 B.C., presents the earth as it would appear to an observer a great distance above it. A sharp picture made by a camera held at a considerable distance from a globe would approximate such a projection. The center is satisfactorily true to scale, but the scale contracts as the distance from the center is increased. Hence this projection is not commonly used for extensive areas.

Azimuthal Equidistant ("azimuthal" means that true direction from the center of the map is preserved). A modern projection that serves well for continents or other large areas. Any point on the globe can be used as a center. (If one of the poles is used, the projection is called *polar azimuthal equidistant.* Like the orthographic, the polar azimuthal equidistant projection is constructed around a central point, and the scale changes with the distance from this point. However, in the azimuthal equidistant, the scale along radii from this center is constant while the scale expands along circles (parallels of latitude) having this point as center, in proportion to the increasing size of the circles (in a polar projection of the whole world, the antipole is grotesquely exaggerated, appearing as the outermost circle); whereas in the orthographic the scale along such circles is constant, while the scale along the radii contracts in proportion to the distance from the center.

A hemispheric polar azimuthal equidistant projection can be roughly demonstrated by slicing a hollow rubber globe at the equator, cutting along the meridians of one of the halves almost up to the pole, pasting the sections on a flat surface (taking care that all the angles between sections are equal), and painting in the gaps between sections to make the broken land masses continuous.

Lambert's Azimuthal Equal-Area (devised by the German cartographer Johann Heinrich Lambert [1728–1777]). In this projection — which is best used for large areas, such as continents — the quadrilaterals formed by intersecting parallels and meridians are kept equal in area by decreasing the scale in the radial direction from the center inversely as it increases along the parallel circles about the center, with the result that at the edge of the map the quadrilaterals are considerably distorted in shape. (Among the projections that are not equal-area are *conformal* projections. In these the distortion of shape that is necessary to keep the quadrilaterals equal in area is not practiced, with the result that, although there is variation in the area of the quadrilaterals, elementary areas anywhere on the map have their correct shapes.)

Mercator. One of the best-known conformal projections, developed by the Flemish geographer Gerhardus Mercator (1512–1594) and first used in his chart of 1569. Such a projection of the earth as a whole is printed as a rectangle on which parallels and meridians appear as straight lines intersecting at right angles. All parallels of latitude have the same length as the central one, the equator (whereas actually they get progressively smaller toward the poles), and all meridians are parallel throughout their entire length (whereas actually they converge to a point at each pole). The presentation of areas not too distant from the equator is satisfactory, but there is great distortion, in scale, of the polar regions.

The construction of a Mercator projection of the world can be roughly demonstrated in this manner: Cut along one meridian of a hollow rubber globe all the way from north to south pole; cut along all the other meridians from the north pole almost to the equator, and then along all the meridians from the south pole almost to the equator. Flatten out the sectioned globe on a flat surface so that the equator lies directly over a straight line on the surface and the pointed section ends are separated from each other by a space equal to that between two adjacent meridians at the equator. Then paint in the gaps between sections to make the broken land masses continuous.

Mollweide (devised by the German mathematician and astronomer Karl Mollweide [1774–1825]). An equal-area projection of the world as an ellipse whose longer axis is twice the length of its shorter axis. The distortion in shape of the equatorial belt and particularly of the outer regions is the chief defect of this projection.

Sinusoidal. An equal-area projection somewhat similar to the elliptical Mollweide projection, but cone-shaped at the poles rather than flattened, the meridians being sine curves.

Conic and *Polyconic*. The conic projection, which originated with Ptolemy, is well suited to areas of wide spread from east to west lying between the equator and one of the poles, such as the United States or the Mediterranean area. In this projection use is made of the concept of a "standard parallel"—a circle of latitude at all points of which a hollow cone dropped down over a globe is tangent to the globe. With a paper cone and a hollow rubber globe, both with this circle of tangency marked on them, we may roughly demonstrate a conic projection in this manner: The standard parallel should pass about midway through the area being projected. Cut this area out of the rubber globe. Cut along each of the meridians from the north almost up to the standard parallel, and then do the same thing from the south. Unfasten the pasted-together or pinned-together cone so that it will lie flat. Then superimpose the sectioned area from the rubber globe on the cone (taking care that the standard parallel on the globe is lined up with the standard parallel on the cone), paste the globe sections to the cone, and paint in the gaps between the sections so as to make the broken land masses continuous.

The *polyconic* projection, which is well suited to areas long from north to south and narrow from east to west, is accomplished by imagining a number of coaxial cones of varying height, each tangent to the sphere at a different parallel. It was devised in the United States by the first superintendent of the Coast and Geodetic Survey, in whose maps it has been used for more than a century. The central meridian is a straight line, the other meridians are curved; the parallels of latitude are arcs of circles, not concentric, and are true to scale.

Other projections often used but not described above are the *gnomonic, stereographic, parabolic, Albers conical, Lambert conformal conic,* and *Bonne*. A *transverse* projection is one in which the orientation of its axis is not normal; e.g., the axis of a transverse Mercator projection may be a meridian or any oblique great circle instead of the equator, which is its normal axis construction. A *transverse Mercator projection* has been used to chart routes between distant points (e.g., international air routes). A *transverse polyconic projection* was used by the National Geographic Society for its large map (1944) of the Union of Soviet Socialist Republics.

MAP SYMBOLS

Capitals of countries	*Banks, shoals*
Capitals of internal divisions	*Reefs*
Towns	*Glaciers and ice shelves*
International boundaries	*Deserts*
Internal boundaries	*Passes*
Drainage	*Elevations (in feet)* 5,344 ▲
Intermittent drainage	*National parks, monuments, recreation areas, seashores*
Canals	*Historical sites, memorials, monuments*
Intermittent or dry lakes	*Military or government posts*
Swamps, marshes	*Ruins*
Dams	*Indian reservations*
Falls	

LIST OF MAPS

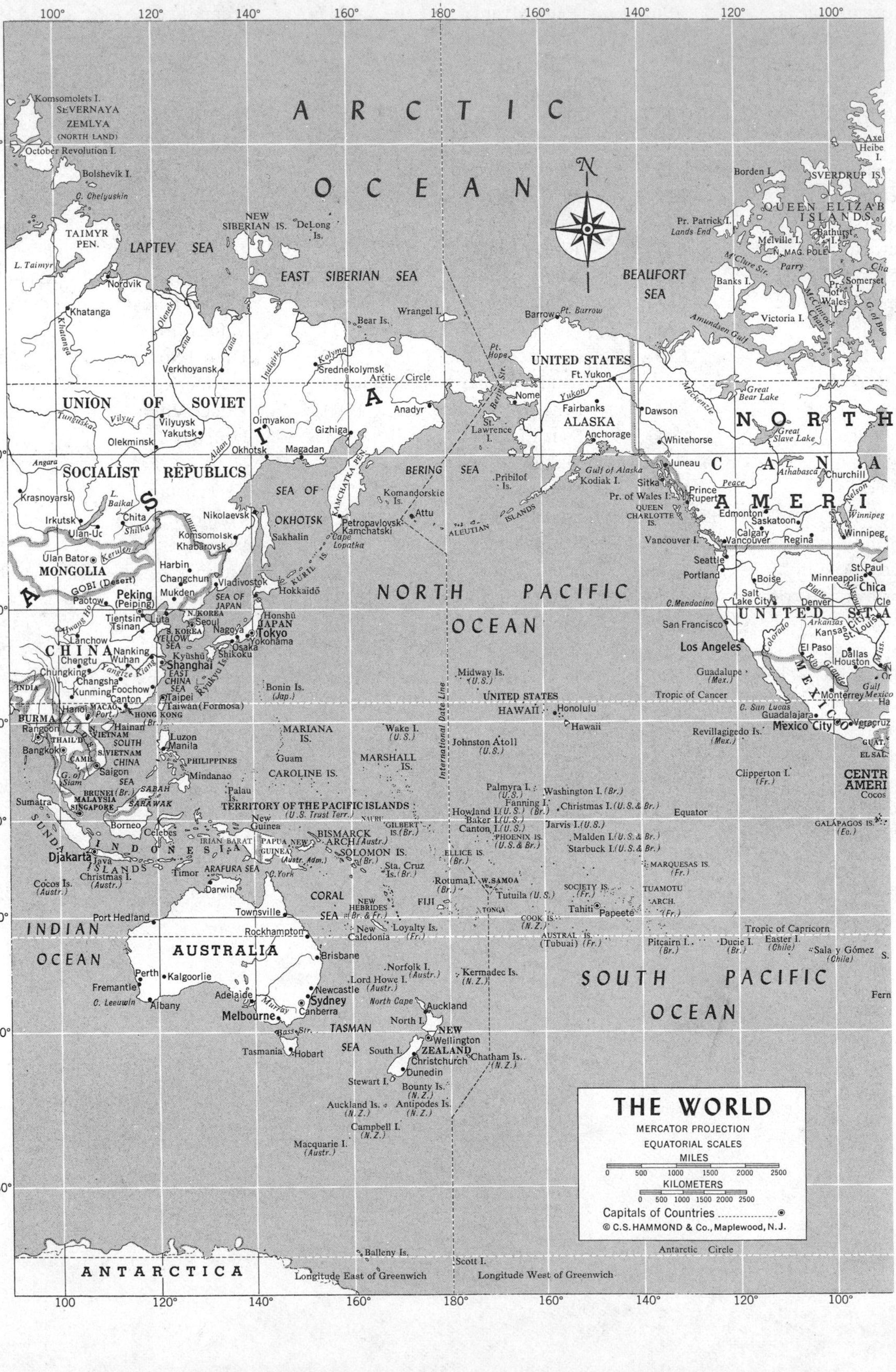
THE WORLD
MERCATOR PROJECTION
EQUATORIAL SCALES
MILES
0 500 1000 1500 2000 2500
KILOMETERS
0 500 1000 1500 2000 2500
Capitals of Countries
© C.S. HAMMOND & Co., Maplewood, N.J.
100° 120° 140° 160° 180° 160° 140° 120° 100°
80° 60° 40° 20° 0° 20° 40° 60°
ARCTIC OCEAN
Komsomolets I.
SEVERNAYA ZEMLYA (NORTH LAND)
October Revolution I.
Bolshevik I.
C. Chelyuskin
TAIMYR PEN.
L. Taimyr
LAPTEV SEA
NEW SIBERIAN IS.
DeLong Is.
EAST SIBERIAN SEA
Nordvik
Khatanga
Olenek
Lena
Yana
Indigirka
Kolyma
Verkhoyansk
Srednekolymsk
Arctic Circle
Bear Is.
Wrangel I.
UNION OF SOVIET SOCIALIST REPUBLICS
ASIA
Tunguska
Vilyui
Vilyuysk
Yakutsk
Olekminsk
Aldan
Oimyakon
Gizhiga
Anadyr
Okhotsk
Magadan
Angara
Krasnoyarsk
L. Baikal
Irkutsk
Chita
Shilka
Ulan-Ude
Amur
SEA OF OKHOTSK
KAMCHATKA PEN.
Nikolaevsk
Komsomolsk
Khabarovsk
Sakhalin
Petropavlovsk-Kamchatski
Cape Lopatka
KURIL IS.
Komandorskie Is.
Attu
BERING SEA
Pribilof Is.
ALEUTIAN ISLANDS
Ulan Bator
Kerulen
MONGOLIA
GOBI (Desert)
Harbin
Changchun
Mukden
Vladivostok
Hokkaido
Peking (Peiping)
Paotow
Hwang Ho
Tientsin
Tsinan
Lüta
N. KOREA
Seoul
S. KOREA
YELLOW SEA
SEA OF JAPAN
Honshu
JAPAN
Tokyo
Nagoya
Osaka
Yokohama
Kyushu
Shikoku
Lanchow
CHINA
Nanking
Wuhan
Chengtu
Shanghai
Yangtze Kiang
Chungking
Changsha
EAST CHINA SEA
Ryukyu Is.
Kunming
Foochow
Canton
Taipei
Taiwan (Formosa)
INDIA
Hanoi
MACAO (Port.)
HONG KONG (Br.)
Hainan
BURMA
Rangoon
THAILAND
Bangkok
N. VIETNAM
S. VIETNAM
LAOS
CAMB.
G. of Siam
Saigon
SOUTH CHINA SEA
Luzon
Manila
PHILIPPINES
Mindanao
Bonin Is. (Jap.)
MARIANA IS.
Guam
CAROLINE IS.
Palau Is.
Wake I. (U.S.)
MARSHALL IS.
BRUNEI (Br.)
SABAH
MALAYSIA
SARAWAK
SINGAPORE
Sumatra
Borneo
Celebes
SUNDA
INDONESIA
Djakarta
Java
ISLANDS
Christmas I. (Austr.)
Timor
Cocos Is. (Austr.)
TERRITORY OF THE PACIFIC ISLANDS (U.S. Trust Terr.)
New Guinea
NAURU
IRIAN BARAT
PAPUA NEW GUINEA (Austr. Adm.)
BISMARCK ARCH. (Austr.)
SOLOMON IS. (Br.)
GILBERT IS. (Br.)
ARAFURA SEA
C. York
Darwin
Sta. Cruz Is. (Br.)
NEW HEBRIDES (Br. & Fr.)
CORAL SEA
FIJI
New Caledonia
Loyalty Is. (Fr.)
Townsville
Rockhampton
Port Hedland
INDIAN OCEAN
AUSTRALIA
Brisbane
Perth
Kalgoorlie
Fremantle
C. Leeuwin
Albany
Adelaide
Murray
Newcastle
Sydney
Canberra
Melbourne
Bass Str.
Tasmania
Hobart
TASMAN SEA
Norfolk I. (Austr.)
Lord Howe I. (Austr.)
North Cape
Auckland
North I.
NEW ZEALAND
Wellington
South I.
Christchurch
Dunedin
Stewart I.
Chatham Is. (N.Z.)
Bounty Is. (N.Z.)
Antipodes Is. (N.Z.)
Auckland Is. (N.Z.)
Campbell I. (N.Z.)
Macquarie I. (Austr.)
Kermadec Is. (N.Z.)
Balleny Is.
Scott I.
ANTARCTICA
Longitude East of Greenwich
Longitude West of Greenwich
Antarctic Circle
International Date Line
NORTH PACIFIC OCEAN
SOUTH PACIFIC OCEAN
Midway Is. (U.S.)
UNITED STATES
HAWAII
Honolulu
Hawaii
Johnston Atoll (U.S.)
Palmyra I. (U.S.)
Washington I. (Br.)
Fanning I. (Br.)
Christmas I. (U.S. & Br.)
Howland I. (U.S.)
Baker I. (U.S.)
Jarvis I. (U.S.)
Canton I. (U.S.)
PHOENIX IS. (U.S. & Br.)
Malden I. (U.S. & Br.)
Starbuck I. (U.S. & Br.)
ELLICE IS. (Br.)
Rotuma I. (Br.)
W. SAMOA
Tutuila (U.S.)
TONGA
COOK IS. (N.Z.)
SOCIETY IS. (Fr.)
Tahiti
Papeete
TUAMOTU ARCH. (Fr.)
MARQUESAS IS. (Fr.)
AUSTRAL IS. (Tubuai) (Fr.)
Pitcairn I. (Br.)
Ducie I. (Br.)
Easter I. (Chile)
Sala y Gómez (Chile)
Tropic of Capricorn
Equator
Tropic of Cancer
Clipperton I. (Fr.)
Revillagigedo Is. (Mex.)
Guadalupe (Mex.)
GALÁPAGOS IS. (Ec.)
Cocos
BEAUFORT SEA
Pt. Barrow
Barrow
Pt. Hope
Bering Str.
UNITED STATES
Ft. Yukon
Yukon
Nome
Fairbanks
ALASKA
St. Lawrence I.
Anchorage
Gulf of Alaska
Kodiak I.
Dawson
Whitehorse
Mackenzie
Juneau
Sitka
Pr. of Wales I.
QUEEN CHARLOTTE IS.
Prince Rupert
Vancouver I.
Vancouver
Seattle
Portland
Borden I.
SVERDRUP IS.
Axel Heiberg I.
QUEEN ELIZABETH ISLANDS
Pr. Patrick I.
Lands End
Melville I.
Bathurst I.
N. MAG. POLE
M'Clure Str.
Parry
Banks I.
Pr. of Wales I.
Somerset I.
Victoria I.
Amundsen Gulf
Great Bear Lake
Great Slave Lake
L. Athabasca
Peace
Churchill
Nelson
NORTH AMERICA
CANADA
Edmonton
Saskatoon
Calgary
Regina
Winnipeg
L. Winnipeg
St. Paul
Minneapolis
Boise
Salt Lake City
Denver
Platte
C. Mendocino
San Francisco
UNITED STATES
Colorado
Arkansas
Kansas City
St. Louis
Los Angeles
El Paso
Dallas
Houston
Rio Grande
Gulf of Mexico
MEXICO
Monterrey
C. San Lucas
Guadalajara
Mexico City
Veracruz
GUAT.
EL SAL.
CENTRAL AMERICA
OCEAN

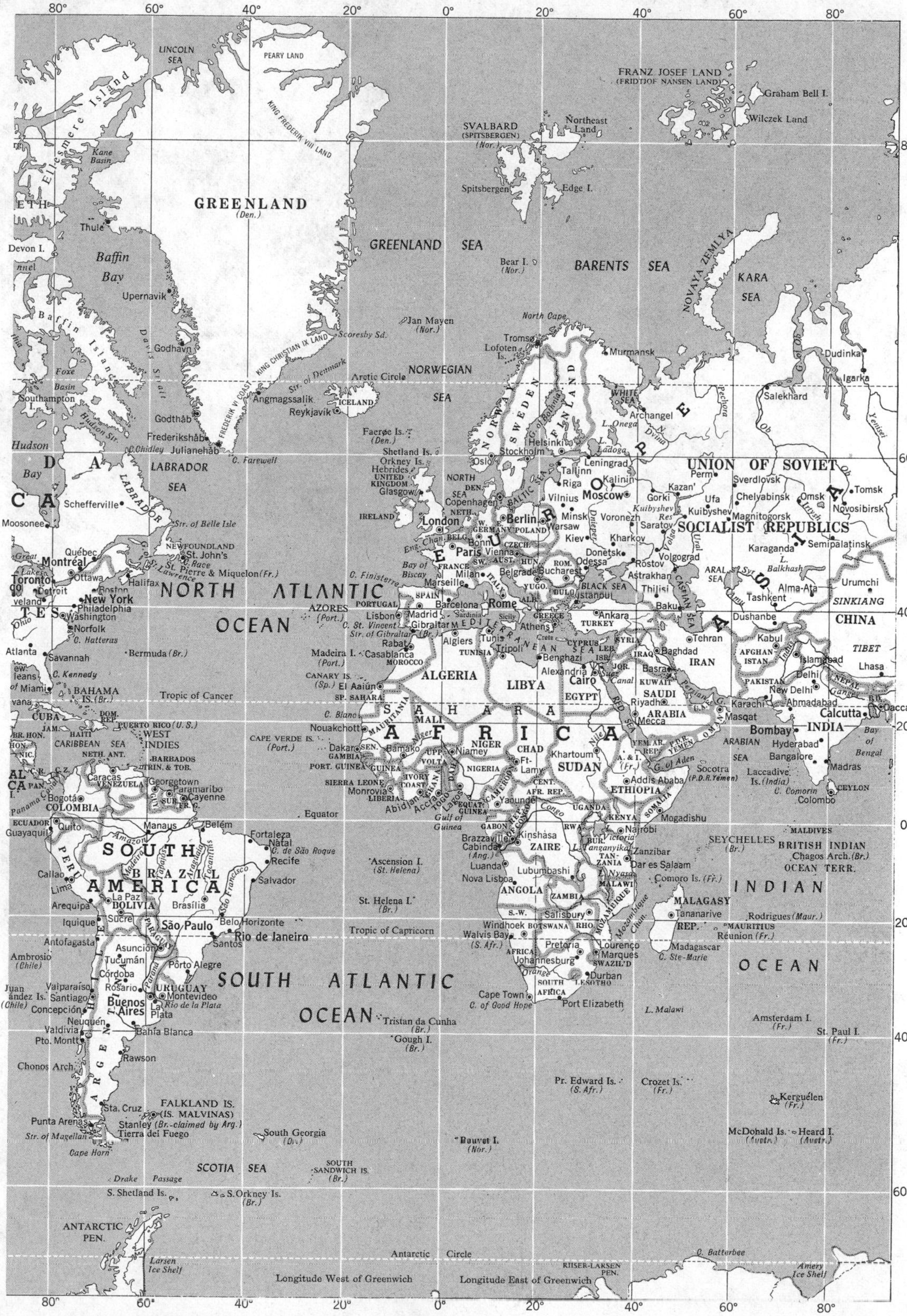

80°
60°
40°
20°
0°
20°
40°
60°
80°
LINCOLN SEA
PEARY LAND
KING FREDERIK VIII LAND
Ellesmere Island
Kane Basin
GREENLAND
(Den.)
Thule
Devon I.
Baffin Bay
Upernavik
Baffin Island
Davis Strait
Godhavn
KING CHRISTIAN IX LAND
Scoresby Sd.
Foxe Basin
Southampton I.
Godthåb
FREDERIK VI COAST
Angmagssalik
Str. of Denmark
Frederikshåb
Julianehåb
C. Chidley
C. Farewell
Hudson Str.
Hudson Bay
LABRADOR SEA
LABRADOR
Schefferville
Moosonee
Str. of Belle Isle
NEWFOUNDLAND
St. John's
C. Race
St. Pierre & Miquelon (Fr.)
G. of St. Lawrence
Québec
Montréal
Ottawa
Halifax
Toronto
Boston
Detroit
New York
Philadelphia
Washington
Norfolk
C. Hatteras
Atlanta
Savannah
C. Kennedy
Miami
BAHAMA IS. (Br.)
Bermuda (Br.)
Tropic of Cancer
CUBA
JAM.
HAITI
DOM. REP.
PUERTO RICO (U. S.)
WEST INDIES
CARIBBEAN SEA
NETH. ANT.
BARBADOS
TRIN. & TOB.
Caracas
VENEZUELA
Georgetown
Paramaribo
Cayenne
Bogotá
COLOMBIA
Panama Canal
ECUADOR
Quito
Guayaquil
Equator
Manaus
Belém
Fortaleza
Natal
C. de São Roque
Recife
Amazon
SOUTH AMERICA
BRAZIL
PERU
Callao
Lima
Salvador
La Paz
BOLIVIA
Brasília
São Francisco
Arequipa
Sucre
Iquique
São Paulo
Belo Horizonte
Rio de Janeiro
Santos
Antofagasta
Asunción
Tucumán
Pôrto Alegre
Córdoba
Rosario
URUGUAY
Montevideo
Rio de la Plata
Buenos Aires
La Plata
Valparaíso
Santiago
Concepción
Neuquén
Valdivia
Pto. Montt
Bahía Blanca
Rawson
Chonos Arch.
ARGENTINA
Sta. Cruz
FALKLAND IS. (IS. MALVINAS)
Stanley (Br.-claimed by Arg.)
Punta Arenas
Str. of Magellan
Tierra del Fuego
Cape Horn
Drake Passage
SCOTIA SEA
S. Shetland Is.
S. Orkney Is. (Br.)
South Georgia
SOUTH SANDWICH IS. (Br.)
ANTARCTIC PEN.
Larsen Ice Shelf
GREENLAND SEA
Jan Mayen (Nor.)
Arctic Circle
NORWEGIAN SEA
ICELAND
Reykjavík
Faeroe Is. (Den.)
Shetland Is.
Orkney Is.
Hebrides
UNITED KINGDOM
Glasgow
IRELAND
London
NORTH ATLANTIC OCEAN
AZORES (Port.)
C. Finisterre
Bay of Biscay
PORTUGAL
SPAIN
Lisbon
Madrid
C. St. Vincent
Str. of Gibraltar
Gibraltar (Br.)
Madeira I. (Port.)
Casablanca
MOROCCO
CANARY IS. (Sp.)
El Aaiún
SP. SAHARA
C. Blanc
Nouakchott
MAURITANIA
CAPE VERDE IS. (Port.)
Dakar
SEN.
GAMBIA
PORT. GUINEA
GUINEA
SIERRA LEONE
Monrovia
LIBERIA
IVORY COAST
Abidjan
Accra
GHANA
TOGO
Lagos
Gulf of Guinea
Bamako
MALI
Niamey
NIGER
UPPER VOLTA
NIGERIA
CHAD
Ft. Lamy
CAMEROON
Yaoundé
EQUAT. GUINEA
GABON
CONGO
Brazzaville
Kinshasa
Cabinda (Ang.)
Luanda
Nova Lisboa
ANGOLA
Ascension I. (St. Helena)
St. Helena I. (Br.)
Tropic of Capricorn
S.-W. AFRICA
Windhoek
Walvis Bay (S. Afr.)
BOTSWANA
Cape Town
C. of Good Hope
SOUTH ATLANTIC OCEAN
Tristan da Cunha (Br.)
Gough I. (Br.)
Bouvet I. (Nor.)
SAHARA
AFRICA
ALGERIA
Algiers
TUNISIA
Tunis
Tripoli
LIBYA
Benghazi
Alexandria
Cairo
EGYPT
Suez Canal
Nile
SUDAN
Khartoum
RED SEA
ETHIOPIA
Addis Ababa
SOMALIA
Mogadishu
UGANDA
KENYA
Nairobi
L. Victoria
RWA.
BUR.
ZAIRE
Congo
L. Tanganyika
TANZANIA
Zanzibar
Dar es Salaam
Lubumbashi
ZAMBIA
MALAWI
L. Nyasa
MOZAMBIQUE
Mozambique Chan.
RHO.
Salisbury
Pretoria
Johannesburg
Lourenço Marques
SWAZIL'D
Durban
LESOTHO
SOUTH AFRICA
Orange
Port Elizabeth
Comoro Is. (Fr.)
MALAGASY REP.
Tananarive
Madagascar
C. Ste-Marie
MAURITIUS
Réunion (Fr.)
Rodrigues (Maur.)
L. Malawi
Pr. Edward Is. (S. Afr.)
Crozet Is. (Fr.)
SVALBARD (SPITSBERGEN) (Nor.)
Spitsbergen
Northeast Land
Edge I.
Bear I. (Nor.)
FRANZ JOSEF LAND (FRIDTJOF NANSEN LAND)
Graham Bell I.
Wilczek Land
BARENTS SEA
NOVAYA ZEMLYA
KARA SEA
North Cape
Tromsø
Lofoten Is.
Murmansk
WHITE SEA
Archangel
Pechora
NORWAY
SWEDEN
FINLAND
G. of Bothnia
Helsinki
Stockholm
Oslo
NORTH SEA
DEN.
Copenhagen
BALTIC SEA
NETH.
W. GERMANY
E. GERMANY
Berlin
POLAND
BELG.
Eng. Chan.
Bonn
Paris
FRANCE
SW.
CZECH.
AUST.
Vienna
HUN.
Milan
Marseille
ITALY
Barcelona
Sardinia
Rome
Sicily
YUGO.
Belgrade
ROM.
Bucharest
BUL.
ALB.
GREECE
Athens
Crete
MEDITERRANEAN SEA
Tallinn
Riga
Leningrad
L. Ladoga
L. Onega
Dvina
Vilnius
Minsk
Warsaw
Kalinin
Moscow
Kiev
Kharkov
Voronezh
Dnieper
Donetsk
Odessa
Rostov
BLACK SEA
Istanbul
Ankara
TURKEY
CYPRUS
SYRIA
LEB.
ISR.
JOR.
Gorki
Kazan'
Kuibyshev Res.
Kuibyshev
Saratov
Volga
Volgograd
Astrakhan
Tbilisi
CASPIAN SEA
Baku
Ural
Perm
Sverdlovsk
Ufa
Chelyabinsk
Magnitogorsk
UNION OF SOVIET SOCIALIST REPUBLICS
EUROPE
ASIA
Ob
Yenisei
Salekhard
Dudinka
Igarka
Omsk
Irtysh
Tomsk
Novosibirsk
Karaganda
Semipalatinsk
L. Balkhash
ARAL SEA
Syr
Amu
Tashkent
Alma-Ata
Urumchi
SINKIANG
Dushanbe
CHINA
TIBET
Lhasa
Tehran
IRAN
IRAQ
Baghdad
Basra
KUWAIT
SAUDI ARABIA
Riyadh
Mecca
Persian G.
OMAN
Masqat
YEM. AR. REP.
P.D.R. YEMEN
G. of Aden
F. T. A. & I. (Fr.)
Socotra (P.D.R. Yemen)
Kabul
AFGHANISTAN
PAKISTAN
Islamabad
Indus
Delhi
New Delhi
NEPAL
Ganges
Karachi
Ahmadabad
Calcutta
Dacca
INDIA
Bombay
Hyderabad
Bangalore
Madras
ARABIAN SEA
Bay of Bengal
Laccadive Is. (India)
C. Comorin
CEYLON
Colombo
MALDIVES
SEYCHELLES (Br.)
BRITISH INDIAN OCEAN TERR.
Chagos Arch. (Br.)
INDIAN OCEAN
Amsterdam I. (Fr.)
St. Paul I. (Fr.)
Kerguélen (Fr.)
McDonald Is. (Austr.)
Heard I. (Austr.)
Antarctic Circle
RIISER-LARSEN PEN.
C. Batterbee
Amery Ice Shelf
Longitude West of Greenwich
Longitude East of Greenwich

A

DICTIONARY OF NAMES OF PLACES

WITH GEOGRAPHICAL AND HISTORICAL INFORMATION, AND PRONUNCIATIONS

Aa \ˈä\. **1** Small river, N France; rises in Pas-de-Calais dept., flows into North Sea at Grand-Fort-Philippe.

2 *or* **Sar·ner–Aa** \ˈzär-nər-ˌä\. River, Unterwalden canton, cen. Switzerland; flows N through Lakes Lungern and Sarnen into Lake of Lucerne.

3 River, N cen. Switzerland; rises in Lucerne canton, flows N into Aargau canton, expanding into Lakes Baldegg and Hallwil, and continues into Aare river.

4 Two rivers, Latvian S.S.R., U.S.S.R. See GAUJA and LIELUPE.

Aabenraa. See ÅBENRÅ.

Aa·chen \ˈäk-ən, ˈäḵ-\. **1** Administrative district, North Rhine-Westphalia, West Germany; 1208 sq. m.; formerly part of Prussia.

2 *or Fr.* **Aix–la–Cha·pelle** \ˌäk-ˌslä-shə-ˈpel\; *anc.* **Aquae Gra·ni** \ˌak-wē-ˈgrā-ˌnī, ˌäk-\ *or* **Aquis·gra·num** \-wəs-ˈgrā-nəm\. City, its ✱, 40 m. WSW of Cologne; pop. (1969e) 176,781; chemicals, glass, textiles; railroad junction; tourist resort; mineral springs and baths; town hall built 1333–70 on ruins of Charlemagne's palace; cathedral founded by Charlemagne c. 800; technical univ. (1870).

History: Site of Roman baths 1st cent. A.D.; second capital of empire of Charlemagne, who was probably born there; favorite residence of Charlemagne after 768; center of Carolingian culture and site of Charlemagne's great palace (practically destroyed by Northmen 881 but restored 983); given rights of an imperial city 1166 and 1215; coronation city of Holy Roman Empire 813–1531; treaties of Aix-la-Chapelle drawn up here to provide for peace terminating War of Devolution 1668 and War of Austrian Succession 1748; given to France by Peace of Lunéville 1801; returned to Prussia 1815; scene of Conference of Holy Alliance (also called Congress of Aix-la-Chapelle) 1818; Prussian military base in Franco-Prussian War 1870–71; air base in World War I; captured by Allied armies Oct. 1944; over half the city was destroyed during World War II, but has since been rebuilt.

Aa·iún \ä-ˈyün\. Town, ✱ of Spanish Sahara, NW Africa; pop. (1970p) 24,519.

Aalborg. See ÅLBORG.

Aa·len \ˈäl-ən\. Industrial city, Baden–Württemberg, West Germany, 44 m. E of Stuttgart; pop. (1968e) 34,773; chemicals, iron goods, textiles; free imperial city 1360–1803.

Aalesund. See ÅLESUND.

Aals·meer \ˈäls-ˌme(ə)r\. Commune, North Holland prov., Netherlands, 8 m. SW of Amsterdam; pop. (1970e) 18,666; horticultural center.

Aalst \ˈälst\ *or Fr.* **Alost** \ä-ˈlöst\. City, East Flanders prov., Belgium, 14 m. NW of Brussels; pop. (1969e) 46,616; beer, textiles, textile machinery; a former capital of the counts of Flanders; held by France 1667–1706; under German control Sept. 1914–Nov. 1918, and May 1940–Sept. 1944.

Aa·rau \ˈär-ˌaů\. Commune, ✱ of Aargau canton, N Switzerland, on Aare river 23 m. W of Zurich; pop. (1970c) 16,881; footwear, optical and scientific instruments; founded in 13th century; taken from Hapsburgs by Bern 1415; became capital of Helvetic Republic 1798 (see SWITZERLAND), capital of Aargau canton 1803.

Aa·re \ˈär-ə\ *or* **Aar** \ˈär\ *or anc.* **Obrin·ga** \ō-ˈbriŋ-gə\. River, cen. and N Switzerland; 183 m. long; flows NW from Bernese Alps, traversing Hasli Tal (valley) and passing through the Gorge of the Aare (**Aar·esch·lucht** \ˈär-ə-ˌshlůkt\) then through Lakes of Brienz and Thun, past Bern, thence NE past Solothurn and Aarau to Rhine; navigable to Thun; connected by canal with Lake of Biel.

Aar·gau \ˈär-ˌgaů\ *or Fr.* **Ar·go·vie** \ˌär-gə-ˈvē\. Canton, N Switzerland; 542 sq. m.; pop. (1970c) 433,284; ✱ Aarau; dairy products, fruit; precision instruments; tourism.

History: Anciently part of Helvetia; conquered by Franks in 6th cent.; under Hapsburgs 1264–1415; taken by Cantonal League and divided bet. Bern and Lucerne; in part to Helvetic Republic 1798; member of Swiss Confederation 1803; constitution fixed by Congress of Vienna 1815, replaced 1831.

Aarhus. See ÅRHUS.

Aath. See ATH.

Aba \ä-ˈbä\. Town, East-Central State, Nigeria, ab. 40 m. NE of Port Harcourt; pop. (1969e) 151,923; furniture, soap, textiles.

Ab·a·co \ˈab-ə-ˌkō\. Two of the Bahama Islands, **Great Abaco** (80 m. long) and **Little Abaco,** in Atlantic Ocean E of S Florida; 776 sq. m.; pop. (with adjacent cays; 1970c) 6501.

Ābā·dān \ˌäb-ə-ˈdän, ˌab-; ˌab-ə-ˈdan\. **1** Island, Khūzestān prov., W Iran, on the Shatt-al-Arab; 42 m. long, from 2 to 12 m. wide; probably settled before time of Herodotus; long disputed bet. Persia and Turkey, but assigned to Persia by treaty 1847.

2 Town on Ābādān I., on the Shatt-al-Arab, 33 m. from Persian Gulf; pop. (1971e) 280,000; large oil refineries.

Ābā·deh \äb-ə-'dä\. Town, Fārs prov., SW Iran, 110 m. N of Shīrāz; pop. (1966c) 10,888.

Abae \'ā-ˌbē\. Ancient town, Phocis, cen. Greece, on Boeotian border 10 m. SE of Elateia; famous for oracle of Apollo; pillaged by Persians, partially restored through Emperor Hadrian.

Abae·te·tu·ba \ə-ˌbī-tə-'tü-bə\. Municipality, Pará state, N Brazil; pop. (1968e) 54,473.

Abai. See NILE.

Abai·ang \ə-'bī-ˌäŋ\. Island (atoll), NW Gilbert Is., W Pacific Ocean, just N of the equator; 16 m. long by 5 m. wide; first residence of American missionaries 1857, under Hiram Bingham.

Aba·kan \äb-ə-'kän\. 1 River, Khakass Autonomous Oblast, Russian S.F.S.R., U.S.S.R.; 350 m. long; rises at W end of Sayan Mts. and flows NE to Yenisei river.

2 Town, ✱ of Khakass Autonomous Oblast, Russian S.F.S.R., U.S.S.R., on the Yenisei at confluence of the Abakan; pop. (1970p) 90,000; food products, lumber, textiles; metalworking.

Aba·los Point \ə-ˌbäl-əs-\. Cape, W coast of Cuba, N of Guadiana Bay.

Abana *or* **Abanah.** See BARADA.

Aban·cay \ˌäb-äŋ-'kī\. Town, ✱ of Apurímac dept., Peru, 80 m. W of Cuzco in valley of Andes; pop. (1961c) 9053; alt. 7200 ft.; sugar; mining center.

Aba·no Ter·me \äb-ə-nō-'te(ə)r-mā\. Commune, Padova prov., Veneto, N Italy, 5 m. SW of Padua; pop. (1968e) 13,059; resort; hot springs and mud baths.

Ab·a·rim Mountains \ˌab-ə-rəm-\. Ancient name (*Num.* xxxiii. 47, 48) of low mountain range or bluffs overlooking Dead Sea from NE, now in Jordan; highest point Mt. Nebo (see PISGAH, MOUNT 2) 2644 ft.

Aba·shi·ri \ˌäb-ə-'shi(ə)r-ē\. Town, Hokkaidō prefecture, Japan, NE coast of Hokkaidō I.; pop. (1970c) 43,904; railroad terminus on **Abashiri Bay;** fishing.

Aba·ya, Lake \-ə-'bī-ə\. Lake, SW Ethiopia, E Africa; 485 sq. m.

Abbai. See NILE.

Ab·be·ville \'ab-ē-ˌvil\. 1 County in South Carolina. See table at SOUTH CAROLINA.

2 City, ⊗ of Henry co., SE Alabama; pop. (1970c) 2996; sawmills, cotton gins.

3 City, ⊗ of Wilcox co., S cen. Georgia, on Ocmulgee river; pop. (1970c) 781.

4 Town, ⊗ of Vermilion parish, S Louisiana, in rice-growing region 20 m. SSW of Lafayette; pop. (1970c) 10,996; rice mills, cotton gins, sugar factory.

5 City, ⊗ of Abbeville co., W South Carolina, 14 m. W of Greenwood; pop. (1970c) 5515; in agricultural and dairy-farming region; settled by Huguenots in 18th cent.; scene of last Confederate cabinet meeting of Jefferson Davis 1865.

Abbeville \ˌab-(ə-)'vē(ə)l\ *or anc.* **Ab·ba·tis Vil·la** \ə-ˌbāt-əs-'vil-ə\. Commune, Somme dept., N France, on Somme river 25 m. NW of Amiens; pop. (1968c) 23,999; beer, sugar, textiles; late-Gothic church of St. Wulfran begun 1488. Dependent upon St-Riquier abbey 9th cent. A.D.; capital of Ponthieu (*q.v.*); received charter as a commune 1184; under English rule from 1272 to 1369. Allied base in World War I; under German control May 1940–Sept. 1944.

Ab·bia·te·gras·so \ä-ˌbyät-ē-'gräs-(ˌ)ō\. Commune, Milano prov., Lombardy, N Italy, 13 m. SW of Milan; pop. (1968e) 25,903; market and industrial town.

Ab·bots·ford \'ab-əts-fərd\. Estate, Roxburgh co., SE Scotland, on Tweed river 2½ m. W of Melrose; residence 1812–32 of Sir Walter Scott.

Ab·bott·abad \'ab-ət-ə-ˌbäd\. Town and military cantonment, Pakistan, 35 m. N of Islamabad; pop. (1961c) 31,036; alt. 4120 ft.; hill resort; founded 1853.

Abd al–Ku·ri \ˌab-ˌdal-'ku̇(ə)r-ē\. Rock and coral reef in Arabian Sea, halfway between Cape Asir, Somalia, and the island of Socotra; ab. 1 m. long; belongs to Yemen (✱ Aden).

Āb·dā·nān \ˌäb-də-'nän\. Town, ✱ of Īlām gov., W Iran.

Ab·de·ra \ab-'dir-ə\. 1 *or Gk.* **Av·di·ra** \äv-'dir-ə\. City of ancient Thrace, on Aegean Sea E of the mouth of the Nestos, nearly opp. Thasos; now in ruins. First settled 7th cent. B.C.; colonized second time by inhabitants of Teos in Ionia c. 544 B.C.; birthplace of several famous Greeks, esp. Democritus and Protagoras. Its inhabitants gained reputation for stupidity, whence the term *Abderite* became one of reproach.

2 Seaport, Spain. See ADRA.

Abé·ché \ˌab-ā-'shā\ *or* **Abeshr** \ə-'besh-ər\. Town, E cen. Chad, 400 m. NE of Fort-Lamy; pop. (1968e) 25,564.

Abela. See ÁVILA 2.

Abellinum. See AVELLINO 2.

Abel–Me·ho·lah \ˌā-bəl-mə-'hō-lə\. Ancient town, now an archaeological site, Jordan, 35 m. NNW of Amman; birthplace of Elisha (*1 Kings* xix. 16).

Ab·e·ma·ma \ˌab-ə-'mäm-ə\ *or* **Ap·a·ma·ma** \ˌap-ə-'mäm-ə\. Island (atoll), cen. Gilbert Is., W Pacific Ocean, 0°21′N, 173°51′E; 12 m. long by 5 m. wide; good anchorage; seized by Japanese 1942; recaptured by American Marines Nov. 21, 1943.

Aben·rå *or* **Aa·ben·raa** \'ȯ-bən-ˌrȯ\ *or Ger.* **Apen·ra·de** \ˌäp-ən-'räd-ə\. Town, ⊗ of Sønderjylland co., Denmark, at head of fjord opening on Little Belt, 15 m. S of Haderslev; pop. (1970e) 20,264; received civic rights 1335; formerly German, passed to Denmark by plebiscite 1920.

Abens·berg \'ab-ənz-ˌbərg, äb-ənz-ˌbe(ə)rg\. City, Bavaria, West Germany, 18 m. SW of Regensburg; pop. (1964e) 2500; founded ab. 1040; scene of Austrian defeat by Napoleon April 20, 1809.

Abe·o·ku·ta \ˌab-ē-'ō-kət-ə\. Town, Western State, SW Nigeria, on railroad ab. 60 m. N of Lagos; pop. (1969e) 217,201; center of palm kernel and cocoa-producing region; established ab. 1830 as refuge from slave hunters; chief town of the Egbas, who made treaty with the British 1893.

Aberbrothock. See ARBROATH.

Ab·er·carn \ˌab-ər-'kärn\ *or formerly* **New·bridge** \'n(y)ü-brij\. Urban district, Monmouthshire, SE Wales, in coal-mining region 26 m. WNW of Bristol; pop. (1971p) 18,468; iron and tinplate works.

Abercorn. See MBALA.

Ab·er·crom·bie, Mount \-'ab-ər-ˌkräm-bē, -ˌkrəm-\. Peak, Stevens co., NE Washington; 7308 ft.

Ab·er·dare \ˌab-ər-'da(ə)r, -'de(ə)r\. Urban district, Glamorganshire, S Wales, 20 m. NNW of Cardiff; pop. (1971p) 37,760; beer, bricks, coal.

Aberdare Range *also* **Aberdare Mountains.** Mountain range, W Kenya; av. height 11,000 ft.; S part established as **Aberdare National Park.**

Ab·er·deen \'ab-ər-ˌdēn\. 1 Residential town, Harford co., NE Maryland, 29 m. ENE of Baltimore; pop. (1970c) 12,375. Nearby is **Aberdeen Proving Ground,** a testing ground for shells, mines, and other military matériel; a Federal reservation comprising a flat tract of 35,000 acres along W side of upper Chesapeake Bay S of the town.

2 City, ⊗ of Monroe co., NE Mississippi, 24 m. N of Columbus; pop. (1970c) 6507; cotton, dairy products.

3 City, ⊗ of Brown co., NE South Dakota, ab. 90 m. W of Big Stone Lake; pop. (1970c) 26,476; railroad and wholesale distributing center in agricultural region; flour mills, grain elevators, stockyards and packing plants; dairy products, farm implements; Northern State Coll. (1899); settled 1880.

4 City and port of entry, Grays Harbor co., W Washington, at E end of Grays Harbor 46 m. W of Olympia; pop. (1970c) 18,489; lumber center; dairying, fishing; canning industries; Grays Harbor Coll. (1930); founded 1867, incorp. 1890.

5 Lake, N cen. Keewatin dist., Northwest Territories, Canada; 475 sq. m.

Aberdeen \ˌab-ər-ˈdēn\. 1 *or* **Ab·er·deen·shire** \-ˌshi(ə)r, -shər\. County, NE Scotland; area 1971 sq. m.; pop. (1971p) 319,887; rivers Dee, Don, Ythan; Grampian Hills in SW; fishing, agriculture (esp. cattle raising), quarrying; tourism.

2 *or anc.* **De·va·na** \di-vā-na\. Burgh and commercial and industrial center, its ⊗, on the North Sea; part in Kincardine co.; pop. (1971p) 182,006; fishing port; chemicals, granite, paper, textiles; Univ. of Aberdeen (1860).

History: Royal burgh and seat of a bishopric from 12th cent.; a Scottish royal residence 12th–14th cents.; supported Robert Bruce in wars for Scottish independence, captured and for a time made headquarters of Edward I; burned by Edward III 1336; welcomed Charles II 1650; occupied by Gen. Monck and Cromwellians 1651; garrisoned by English until 1659; declared for Stuarts 1715 and 1745.

Ab·er·fel·dy \ˌab-ər-ˈfel-dē\. Burgh, W Perth co., Scotland, on Tay river 25 m. NW of Perth; pop. (1971p) 1539; supposed scene of Burns's *Birks of Aberfeldy;* Black Watch regiment raised here 1725.

Ab·er·foyle \ˌab-ər-ˈfȯil\. Parish and village, SW Perth co., Scotland, ab. 6 m. SE of Loch Katrine; parish pop. (1961c) 1316; immortalized by Scott's *Rob Roy;* summer resort for residents of Glasgow.

Ab·er·ga·ven·ny \ˌab-ər-gə-ˈven-ē\ *or anc.* **Go·ban·ni·um** \gō-ˈban-ē-əm\. Municipal borough, Monmouthshire, SE Wales, at confluence of Gavenny and Usk rivs.; pop. (1971p) 9388; iron founding, printing; cattle market.

Ab·er·nathy \ˈab-ər-ˌnath-ē\. City, Hale and Lubbock cos., NW Texas, 21 m. N of Lubbock; pop. (1970c) 2625; agriculture.

Abert, Lake \-ˈā-bərt\. Lake, cen. Lake co., S Oregon; ab. 20 m. long and 5 m. wide; has no outlet and is sometimes dry.

Ab·er·til·lery \ˌab-ər-tə-ˈle(ə)r-ē\. Urban district, Monmouthshire, SE Wales, ab. 30 m. NW of Bristol; pop. (1971p) 21,140; coal mining.

Ab·er·yst·wyth \ˌab-ə-ˈris-ˌtwəth\. Municipal borough, Cardiganshire, W Wales, on Cardigan Bay; pop. (1971p) 10,680; seaside resort; boatbuilding, brewing; Univ. Coll. of Wales (1872), Welsh National Library (completed 1955). Castle said to have been built 1109; town built around fortress of Edward I 1277.

Abeshr. See ABÉCHÉ.

a–Bhuird, Ben–. See BEN-A-BHUIRD.

Abi·a·thar Peak \ə-ˈbī-ə-thər-\. Mountain, Yellowstone National Park, NW Wyoming; 10,928 ft.

Ab–i–Diz. See DEZ, AB-I-.

Ab·i·djan \ˌab-i-ˈjän\. City, ✱ of Ivory Coast, W Africa; pop. (1963e) 285,000; beer, lumber, soap; exports bananas, cocoa, coffee; univ. (1963); port facilities established 1951.

Abila. See MUSA, JEBEL.

Ab·i·lene \ˈab-ə-ˌlēn\. 1 City, ⊗ of Dickinson co., E cen. Kansas, on Smoky Hill river 25 m. E of Salina; pop. (1970c) 6661; distributing center for cattle, grain, and dairy products; Eisenhower Center; former frontier town, railhead 1867–71 for cattle-raising region to SW.

2 City, ⊗ of Taylor co., NW cen. Texas, 145 m. WSW of Fort Worth; pop. (1970c) 89,653; distributing center for agricultural region; food products, oil field equipment, soap; Hardin-Simmons Univ. (1891), Abilene Christian Coll. (1906), McMurry Coll. (1923).

Ab·i·le·ne \ˌab-ə-ˈlē-nē\. Region in Syria, E of Anti-Lebanon Mts.; c. 29 A.D. comprised Tetrarchy of Lysanias (*Luke* iii. 1).

Abindonia. See ABINGDON 3.

Ab·ing·don \ˈab-iŋ-dən\. 1 City, Knox co., W Illinois, in agricultural region 11 m. S of Galesburg; pop. (1970c) 3936.

2 Town, ⊗ of Washington co., SW Virginia, in farming and dairying region of Blue Ridge Mts. 15 m. NE of Bristol; pop. (1970c) 4376; lumber, flour, tobacco; site of Black's Fort 1776; settled c. 1770.

3 *or anc.* **Ab·in·do·nia** \ˌab-ən-ˈdō-nē-ə, -ˈdōn-yə\. Municipal borough, Berkshire, S England, on the Thames 6 m. S of Oxford; pop. (1971p) 18,596; automobiles, scientific instruments; has many interesting antiquities; site of a Benedictine abbey founded 675; received charter 1556.

Abingdon Island. See PINTA ISLAND.

Ab·ing·ton \ˈab-iŋ-tən\. 1 Town, Plymouth co., SE Massachusetts, 4 m. ENE of Brockton; pop. (1970c) 12,334.

2 Urban township, Montgomery co., SE Pennsylvania, N of Philadelphia; pop. (1970c) 62,899.

Ab–i–Pandj. See PANDJ, AB-I-.

Ab·i·shim \ˌab-ə-ˈshēm\. Mountain, West Azerbaijan prov., NW Iran, SW of Lake Urmia; 8392 ft.

Ab·i·tibi \ˌab-ə-ˈtib-ē\. County of Quebec, Canada. See table at QUEBEC.

Abitibi Lake. Lake on E boundary of Ontario, Canada; 369 sq. m. (313 sq. m. in Ontario, 56 sq. m. in Quebec); source of **Abitibi River** (340 m. long), E Ontario, flowing N to Moose river near James Bay.

Ab–i Wakhan. See WAKHAN 2.

Ab·kha·zian Autonomous Soviet Socialist Republic \ab-ˈkā-zhən-, -ˈkäz-ē-ən-\ *also* **Ab·kha·zia** *or* **Ab·kha·sia** \ab-ˈkā-zh(ē-)ə, -ˈkäz-ē-ə\. Autonomous republic, NW Georgian S.S.R., U.S.S.R., on Black Sea coast at W end of Caucasus Mts.; 3320 sq. m.; pop. (1970p) 487,000; ✱ Sukhumi; citrus fruit, tea, timber, tobacco, silk; major mineral is coal; became Christian under Justinian in 6th cent.; Russian protectorate formally established 1810; annexed by Russia 1864; created an autonomous republic 1919.

Ablain–Saint–Na·zaire \ä-ˈbla^{n}-sa^{n}-nə-ˈze(ə)r\. Commune, Pas-de-Calais dept., N France, near Vimy Ridge 7 m. N of Arras; pop. (1962c) 1295; completely destroyed in second battle of Artois May 21, 1915.

Åbo. See TURKU.

Ab·o·mey \ˌab-ə-ˈmā, ə-ˈbō-mē\. Town, S Dahomey, W Africa, 65 m. NNW of Porto-Novo; pop. (1970e) 34,000; palm oil; former slave center; capital of former native kingdom of Dahomey (*q.v.*); fired and abandoned to French 1892; rebuilt by French and connected with coast by rail 1905.

Abo·ny \ˈȯ-ˌbōn-yə\. Commune, Pest co., cen. Hungary, 10 m. E of Cegléd; pop. (1970p) 15,640.

Aboukir. See ABUKIR.

Abra \ˈäb-rə\. 1 River, NW Luzon, Phil.; ab. 100 m. long; rises in S cen. part of Mountain Prov. in Cordillera Central, flows N then W to South China Sea; third longest river on the island.

2 Inland mountainous province, NW Luzon, Phil.; 1535 sq. m.; pop. (1970p) 149,397; chief town and ✱ Bangued; corn, rice, timber; traversed by middle course of Abra river and its many tributaries N and E; greatly broken by mountain ranges and groups of the Cordillera Central, and by hills; highest point Mt. Manmanoc 6634 ft. on E border. Little settlement attempted by Spanish; suffered serious uprising latter half of 18th cent.; province created 1846; came under American control 1899; civil government established Aug 19, 1901.

Abra·ham, Mount \-ˈā-brə-ˌham\. 1 Mountain, Franklin co., W Maine; 4049 ft.

2 Peak, Addison co., W Vermont; 4052 ft.

Abran·tes \ə-ˈvrä^{n}(n)t-ish\ *or anc.* **Au·ran·tes** \ȯ-ˈrant-ēz\. Commune, Santarém dist., W cen. Portugal, on Tagus river 32 m. ENE of Santarém; munic. pop. (1970p) 48,161;

founded c. 300 B.C.; captured Nov. 24, 1807 by Napoleon's general Junot, who assumed title of duc d'Abrantès.

Abre·us \ä-ˈbrā-üs\. Town and municipality, Las Villas prov., W cen. Cuba, 12 m. NW of Cienfuegos; munic. pop. (1967e) 15,090.

Abro·lhos \ə-ˈbrōl-yəs\. Group of pointed rocky islands off Caravelas, S Bahia state, Brazil, bet. 17° and 18°S lat.

Abrotonum. See SABRATA.

Abruz·zi \ä-ˈbrüt-sē, ə-\. Autonomous region, cen. Italy; 4168 sq. m.; pop. (1968e) 1,205,142; ✱ Aquila; grapes, tobacco, wheat; formerly part of Abruzzi e Molise.

Abruzzi Apennines. See table at APENNINES.

Abruzzi e Mo·li·se \-ā-ˈmō-li-ˌzā\. Former administrative region, cen. Italy, bet. Adriatic Sea and Apennines (which attain their greatest height here) and Tronto and Sangro rivers; now divided into Abruzzi and Molise. See table at ITALY.

History: District formed part of duchy of Spoleto in Lombard times and of Apulia under Normans; in 1240 made a single province by Frederick II, who founded Aquila; province of Angevin kingdom of Naples, to which it was of strategic importance; incorporated in kingdom of Italy as part of Naples 1860; administrative region established 1948, dissolved 1965.

Ab·sa·ro·ka Range \ab-ˈsär-ə-kə-, -ˈsȯ(ə)r-kē-\. Range of Rocky Mts., from S Montana across NE corner of Yellowstone Park into NW Wyoming; ab. 175 m. long; highest point Franks Peak 13,140 ft.; others Mt. Crosby 12,435 ft. and Dead Indian Peak 12,216 ft.

Ab·se·con \ab-ˈsē-kən\. City, Atlantic co., SE New Jersey, 6 m. NW of Atlantic City; pop. (1970c) 6094.

Absecon Inlet. Narrow strait leading from Atlantic Ocean through barrier reefs in Atlantic co., SE New Jersey; its S shore is the N end of **Absecon Beach,** the island (10 m. long) on which Atlantic City is situated.

Abu, Mount \-ˈäb-ˌü\. 1 Hill, Aravalli Range, Rajasthan, NW India; 5650 ft.

2 Hill station, on Mt. Abu, Rajasthan, NW India, 115 m. N of Ahmadabad; pop. (1961c) 8076; site of Dilwara Jain temples (11th–13th cent.) and Achalgarh temples (15th cent.); was administrative center of former Rajputana Agency.

Abuam. See TAFILALT.

Abu·cay \ə-ˈbü-(ˌ)kī\. Municipality near E coast of Bataan prov., Luzon, Phil., 3 m. N of Balanga; pop. (1969e) 17,700. In Japanese attack on Philippines 1941–42 it was anchor point of E end of first line of American defense; scene of Japanese drive Jan. 10–17, 1942 and of strong American counterattack Jan. 25.

Abu Dha·bi \ˌäb-ü-ˈdab-ē\. 1 Sheikhdom on S coast of Persian Gulf; 26,000 sq. m.; pop. (1968c) 46,375; ✱ Abu Dhabi; petroleum. See UNITED ARAB EMIRATES.

2 *or Arab.* **Abū Za·bi** \-ˈzäb-ē\. Town, its ✱, also provisional ✱ of the United Arab Emirates; pop. (1968c) 22,023.

Abu Do·khān, Ge·bel \ˈjeb-əl-ˌab-ü-də-ˈkän\. Mountain, E Egypt, near coast at N end of Red Sea; 5492 ft.; porphyry quarries, source of the red building stone used by the Romans.

Ab·u·kir *or* **Ab·ou·kir** *or* **Abū Qīr** \ˌab-(ˌ)ü-ˈki(ə)r, ˌäb-\. 1 Bay, Egypt, bet. Rosetta mouth of Nile and Alexandria.
2 Village, 13 m. NNE of Alexandria, Egypt, on Abukir Bay; approximate site of ancient Canopus (*q.v.*). In the bay was fought the "Battle of the Nile" Aug. 1–2, 1798, in which Nelson completely defeated French fleet under Brueys; near the village Napoleon defeated Turks 1799 and Sir Ralph Abercromby landed and defeated French 1801.

Abu Klea \ˌab-ü-ˈklā\. Locality, N Sudan, W of the Nile, 63 m. SW of Ed Damer; scene of battle Jan. 17, 1885 in which large force of Mahdists was repulsed by British.

Abu·ku·ma \ə-ˈbü-kə-mə\. River, N Honshū, Japan; 122 m. long; flows NNE into Pacific Ocean ab. 15 m. S of Sendai.

Abu Kurkas. See ABU QURQĀS.

Abulliont. See APULYONT.

Abu Mu·sa \ˌäb-ü-ˈmü-sə\. Small island, Persian Gulf, 25°52′N, 55°03′E; belongs to Sharjah, which concluded an agreement with Iran 1971 permitting stationing of Iranian troops on island.

Abu·ná \ˌä-bü-ˈnä\. River, N Bolivia; ab. 200 m. long; flows NE forming a section of Brazil-Bolivia boundary and empties into Madeira river at N point of Bolivia.

Abū Qīr. See ABUKIR.

Abu Qur·qās *or* **Abu Kur·kas** \ˌä-bü-kůr-ˈkäs\. Town on Nile river, Egypt, 13 m. SSW of Al-Minya.

Abury. See AVEBURY.

Abus. See HUMBER 2.

Abu Sim·bel \ˌäb-ˌü-ˈsim-bəl\ *or* **Abu Sun·bul** \ˌäb-ü-ˈsům-bəl\ *or* **Ip·sam·bul** \ˌip-səm-ˈbül\. Locality, Egypt, 22°22′N, 31°38′E; site of two rock temples of Ramses II (c. 1250 B.C.), discovered 1812, opened 1817; larger temple had four colossi of the king more than 65 ft. high; colossi cut apart and reassembled on higher ground due to flooding of area 1966.

Abu·ye Me·da *or* **Abu·ya Mye·da** \ˌə-ˌbü-yə-ˈmād-ə, -mē-ˈäd-ə\. Peak, cen. Ethiopia, ab. 130 m. NE of Addis Ababa; 13,120 ft.

Abu·yog \ä-ˈbü-ˌyōg\. Municipality on east coast of Leyte, Phil., 34 m. S of Tacloban; pop. (1969e) 51,100.

Abū Zabi. See ABU DHABI 2.

Aby·dos \ə-ˈbīd-əs\. 1 Ancient town, Mysia (*q.v.*), on the Hellespont; site of town NE of modern Çanakkale, NW Turkey; scene of crossing of Xerxes' army when he invaded Greece 480 B.C.; resisted Philip V of Macedon 200 B.C.; scene of story of Hero and Leander; toll station until late Byzantine times.

2 Town, anc. Egypt, on left bank of Nile ab. 100 m. below Thebes; one of oldest Egyptian cities, mentioned in early inscriptions; site of temples built from Ist to XXVth dynasty; especially prosperous in XIXth dynasty when temples dedicated to Osiris were built by Seti I and Ramses II; has many tombs of rulers; site near modern Araba al-Madfuna.

Abyla. 1 Mountain, Morocco. See MUSA, JEBEL.

2 City, Spain. See ÁVILA 2.

Abyssinia. See ETHIOPIA.

Aca·dia \ə-ˈkād-ē-ə\. 1 Parish in Louisiana. See table at LOUISIANA.

2 *or Fr.* **Aca·die** \a-ka-ˈdē\. Original name, of Micmac origin, of Nova Scotia (*q.v.*), first used 1603 in commission to Sieur de Monts, who made first settlement 1604; in early 17th cent. region extended to include all territory bet. St. Lawrence river and gulf and Atlantic Ocean, with indefinite W boundary, but included New Brunswick and E Maine. Settled 1632–1713 by French, who formed peaceful farming community in the Grand Pré district; fought over by England and France in colonial wars of 18th cent.; its inhabitants (ab. 10,000 Acadians) deported by English 1755 and scattered from Maine to Louisiana (see ACADIAN COAST).

Acadia National Park. See UNITED STATES, *National Parks.*

Aca·di·an Coast \ə-ˈkād-e-ən-\. District, S Louisiana, W of lower Mississippi river and WNW of New Orleans; settled 1760 and later by exiled Acadians from Nova Scotia; now chiefly in St. James parish.

Aca·hay *or* **Aca·haí** \ˌäk-ə-(h)ä-ˈē\. Town, Paraguarí dept., S Paraguay; pop. (1970e) 20,415.

Aca·je·te \ˌäk-ə-ˈhāt-ē\. Municipality, Puebla state, Mexico, 80 m. SE of Mexico City; pop. (1970p) 27,103; cattle raising.

Aca·jut·la \ˌäk-ə-ˈhüt-lə\. Seaport town, Sonsonate dept., SW El Salvador; pop. (1961c) 3662; breakwaters and new port facilities constructed 1956–61; oil refineries, cement and chemical fertilizer factories.

Acám·ba·ro \ə-ˈkäm-bə-ˌrō\. Municipality, Guanajuato state, cen. Mexico, 90 m. NW of Mexico City; pop. (1970p) 80,259; railroad junction.

Acan·thus \ə-'kan(t)-thəs\. Ancient town, N Greece, on E coast at base of Acte penin., Chalcidice, ab. 4 m. W of site of Xerxes' canal cut across the isthmus of Acte 480 B.C.

Aca·po·ne·ta \ˌäk-ə-pə-'nāt-ə\. Municipality, Nayarit state, W Mexico, on **Acaponeta River;** pop. (1970p) 29,829.

Aca·pul·co \ˌäk-ə-'pu̇l-(ˌ)kō, ˌak-, -'pül-\ *or in full* **Acapulco de Juá·rez** \-t͟hā-'hwär-ˌes, -'wär-əz\. Seaport, Guerrero state, Mexico, on Pacific Ocean, 190 m. SSW of Mexico City; munic. pop. (1970p) 234,866; international resort; shipping point for cotton, fruit, hides, and tobacco. For 250 years (1565–1815) chief port for Spanish trade with Philippines (the "Manila galleons" making yearly voyages across the Pacific to and from Manila) and for transshipment across Mexico.

Acarahy Serra. See SERRA ACARAÍ.

Acaraí, Serra. See SERRA ACARAÍ.

Aca·raú \ˌak-ə-rə-'ü\. Municipality, Ceará state, NE Brazil, on north coast, 130 m. NW of Fortaleza; pop. (1968e) 58,705.

Aca·ri·gua \ˌäk-ə-'rē-gwə\. Town, Portuguesa state, W cen. Venezuela, 165 m. WSW of Caracas; pop. (1970e) 46,262.

Ac·ar·na·nia *also* **Akar·na·nía** \ˌak-ər-'nā-nē-ə\. Mountainous country of ancient Greece, in W part, W of Aetolia and on Ionian Sea, separated from Aetolia by the Achelous river; chief town Stratus. Loosely organized into Acarnanian League; dominated by Sparta 391 B.C. and by Thebes 371 B.C.; allied with Philip of Macedon against Rome; required to give up federal capital and submit to Rome 167 A.D.

Acate \ə-'kät-ē\ *or formerly* **Bis·ca·ri** \bis-'kär-ē\. Village, Ragusa prov., SE Sicily, Italy, 15 m. E of Gela; pop. (1968e) 6233; in World War II its airfield captured by U.S. Army July 14, 1943.

Aca·te·nan·go \ˌäk-ə-tə-'näŋ-(ˌ)gō\. Volcano, Guatemala, ab. 31 m. SW of the city of Guatemala; 13,044 ft.

Aca·tlán de Oso·rio \ˌäk-ə-'tlän-dā-ə-'sȯr-ē-ˌō\. Municipality, Puebla state, SE cen. Mexico, 58 m. S of Puebla; pop. (1970p) 20,507.

Aca·yu·cán \ˌäk-ə-yü-'kän\. Municipality, SE Veracruz state, E Mexico, 37 m. SE of San Andrés Tuxtla; pop. (1970p) 36,352.

Accad. See AKKAD.

Accho. Seaport city, Israel. See ACRE.

Ac·co·mac \'ak-ə-ˌmak\. **1** *or officially* **Ac·co·mack** \'ak-ə-ˌmak\. County in Virginia. See table at VIRGINIA.

2 Town, its ⊗, on N part of Delmarva Penin.; pop. (1970c) 373; twice a refuge of Gov. Berkeley during Bacon's rebellion 1675–76.

Ac·cra \ə-'krä\. Seaport city, ✱ of Ghana, W Africa; pop. (1970p) 562,220, met. area pop. 736,718; apparel, food products, footwear; has anchorage with breakwater and wharves; terminus of railroad to Kumasi; Univ. of Ghana (1961).

History: Site of trading forts, James and Crèvecœur, founded by English and Dutch 17th century, and of Danish Fort Christiansborg; Fort Crèvecœur ceded to British 1850, Fort Christiansborg ceded 1871; became ✱ of Gold Coast Colony 1876, ✱ of Ghana 1957.

Ac·cring·ton \'ak-riŋ-tən\. Municipal borough, Lancashire, NW England, 20 m. N of Manchester; pop. (1971p) 36,838; coal mines, textile mills; dyestuffs and textile machinery.

Acelum. See ASOLO.

Acer·ra \ä-'cher-ə\. Commune, Napoli prov., Campania, S Italy, 9 m. NE of Naples; pop. (1968e) 29,149; site of ancient city, **Acer·rae** \ə-'ser-(ˌ)ē\, which received Latin rights 332 B.C.; destroyed by Hannibal 216 B.C.; restored 210 B.C.; Roman headquarters in Social War 90 B.C.

Acesines. See CHENAB.

Achaea \ə-'kē-ə\ *or* **Acha·ia** *or Gk.* **Akhaïa** \ə-'kī-ə, -'kā-(y)ə\. **1** Region, anc. Greece, N part of the Peloponnesus, bordering on Gulfs of Corinth and Patras on N and bounded by Elis, Arcadia, and Sicyonia on SW, S, and SE respectively; chief towns Patrae, Helice, and Aigion.

History: Region presumably settled by the Achaeans, an early Greek people; first given loose political unity by the formation of the Achaean League of twelve Achaean cities, which allied with Athens against Sparta 362 B.C.; aided Greek efforts to stop invasions by Philip and Alexander the Great of Macedon 4th cent. B.C.; renewed 280 B.C. the Achaean League, which supported the wars against Macedon until the Roman defeat of Philip V 197 B.C. and was dissolved by Rome 146 B.C. for assisting Macedon. As a Roman imperial province 146 B.C.–c. 4th cent. A.D. included all of Greece S of Thessaly; a province of the Eastern Roman (Byzantine) Empire until made a Latin principality 1204; overrun by Turks 1460.

2 Department of Greece; approx. coextensive with historical region. See table at GREECE.

Achaea Phthi·o·tis \ə-ˌkē-ə-thī-'ōt-əs\. Region, S part of ancient Thessaly, Greece, N of Mt. Othrys, extending E to the Pagasaean Gulf.

Achal·pur \'äch-əl-ˌpu̇(ə)r\; *formerly* **El·lich·pur** *or* **El·ich·pur** \'el-ich-\. Town, N Maharashtra, cen. India, 110 m. W of Nagpur; pop. (1961c) 36,500; active trade, chiefly in timber and cotton. Supposedly founded 11th cent.; became seat of Imad Shah dynasty of Berar 1484; hereditary ruler in 1803 received the title of nawab; family died out in 19th cent.

Achard Point \ä-ˌshär-\. Cape, W San Cristóbal I., SE British Solomon Is., W Pacific Ocean.

Achar·nae \ə-'kär-(ˌ)nē\ *or Gk.* **Akhar·naí** \ˌäk-ər-'nā\. Village, Attica, Greece, ab. 6 m. N of Athens; charcoal burners of the village gave their name to a play of Aristophanes, *The Acharnians,* performed 425 B.C.

Acheen. See ATJEH.

Ach·e·lo·us *or Gk.* **Akhe·ló·os** \ˌak-ə-'lō-əs\ *also* **As·pro·pot·a·mos** \ˌas-prō-'pät-ə-məs\. River, W Greece; 137 m. long; rises in Pindus Mts., NW Thessaly, and flows S to Ionian Sea; longest river in Greece.

Acherusia, Palus. See FUSARO.

Achi Ba·ba \ˌäch-ē-bä-'bä\ *or Turk.* **Al·çı Te·pe** \ˌäl-chē-te-'pā\. Height dominating tip of Gallipoli Penin., Turkey in Europe; main position of Turkish defense in Gallipoli fighting of 1915.

Ach·ill \'ak-əl\. Island, W coast of Eire, NW of Clew Bay; ab. 15 m. long; 56 sq. m.; at W end is cape, **Achill Head.**

Achin. See ATJEH.

Achinsk \ə-'chin(t)sk\. Town, SW Krasnoyarsk Krai, Russian S.F.S.R., U.S.S.R., on Chulym river and on Trans-Siberian R.R. 90 m. W of Krasnoyarsk; pop. (1968e) 85,000.

Achmetha. See HAMADAN 2.

Achray, Loch \-ə-'krā\. Lake, Perth co., Scotland; 1¼ m. long; max. depth 97 ft.; connects with Loch Katrine.

Acht·kar·spe·len \'äkt-'kär-spə-lən, ˌäkt-\. Commune, Friesland prov., N Netherlands; pop. (1970e) 21,725.

Aci·re·a·le \ˌäch-ē-rā-'äl-ē\. Seaport, Catania prov., E Sicily, Italy, on E coast 10 m. N of Catania; pop. (1968e) 47,581; resort with sulfur baths; earthquake 1693.

Ack·er·man \'ak-ər-mən\. Town, ⊗ of Choctaw co., cen. Mississippi, 44 m. WSW of Columbus; pop. (1970c) 1502; sawmills.

Ack·er Peak \ˌak-ər-\. Mountain in Sierra Nevada, E Tuolumne co., cen. California; 10,918 ft.

Ack·ley \'ak-lē\. Town, Franklin and Hardin cos., N cen. Iowa, 38 m. W of Waterloo; pop. (1970c) 1794.

Ack·lins Island \ˌak-lənz-\. One of the Bahama Islands in Atlantic Ocean, adjoining Crooked Island and W of Mayaguana I.; 120 sq. m.

Ac·o·ma \'ak-ə-ˌmȯ\. Pueblo of Acoma Indians, on reservation 60 m. W of Albuquerque, Valencia co., New Mexico; situated on rock mesa **(Acoma Rock)** 357 ft. high with steep sides and difficult trail. Discovered by Coronado's men 1540; captured by Juan de Oñate 1599; joined in Pueblo revolts against Spanish 1680, 1696; subdued 1692, 1699.

Acon·ca·gua \ˌak-ən-ˈkäg-wə, ˌäk-\. 1 Mountain, W Argentina, near Chilean border at Uspallata Pass; 22,834 ft.; highest peak of Andes and of Western Hemisphere; first climbed 1897.

2 River, cen. Chile; ab. 120 m. long; rises on slopes of Aconcagua Mt.; flows W into Pacific Ocean 12 m. N of Valparaíso.

3 Province of cen. Chile. See table at CHILE.

Acon·qui·ja \äk-ən-ˈkē-ə\. Peak in the Andes, Tucumán prov., N Argentina; ab. 16,400 ft.

Açores. See AZORES.

Ac·qui Ter·me \ˌak-wē-ˈte(ə)r-mē\; *anc.* **Aq·uae** \ˈak-wē; ˈäk-\ *or* **Aquae Sta·ti·el·lae** \ˌak-wē-ˌstā-shē-ˈel-ē, ˌäk-\. Commune, Alessandria prov., Piedmont, NW Italy, 17 m. SSW of Alessandria; pop. (1968e) 20,934; sulfurous waters and mud baths, known in Roman times.

Acrae. See PALAZZOLO ACREIDE.

Acragas. See AGRIGENTO 2.

Acre \ˈäk-ər, ˈā-kər, ˈäk-rə\ *or* **ʻAk·ko** \ä-ˈkō\ *or Fr.* **Saint-Jean-d'Acre** \saⁿ-zhäⁿ-dȧ-krᵊ\; **Ac·cho** \ä-ˈkō\ *of O.T. or* **Ptol·e·ma·ïs**\ˌtäl-ə-ˈmā-əs\ *of N.T.* Seaport city, Israel, on promontory 13 m. N of Mt. Carmel; pop. (1970e) 33,900; light industries; steel rolling mills; fishing.

History: As a city of Phoenicia, known as Ptolemaïs; captured by Arabs 638 A.D.; a Syrian town under the Seljuk Turks when attacked by Crusaders 12th cent.; as Saint-Jean-d'Acre, included in the Kingdom of Jerusalem set up by Crusaders 1104–87, 1191–1291; conquered by Saladin 1187, reconquered by Philip Augustus 1191; residence of Knights of St. John 13th cent.; became Muslim again at fall of Jerusalem 1291; captured by Turks 1517; declined until 18th cent.; besieged by Napoleon 1799; as part of Syria captured by Mehemet Ali 1832; taken by British 1840 and restored to Ottoman Empire; again taken by British Sept. 23, 1918; part of Israel 1948.

Acre \ˈäk-rə, ˈä-(ˌ)krā\ *or formerly* **Aqui·ry** \ˌäk-ə-ˈrē\. 1 River, W cen. South America; ab. 400 m. long; chief tributary of Purús; forms part of boundary bet. Brazil and Bolivia, and bet. Brazil and Peru.

2 State, W Brazil; 58,915 sq. m.; pop. (1970p) 203,900; ✱ Rio Branco; coffee, rice, sugar; rubber production important 1895–1910; formerly territory of Bolivia; encroachment of Brazilian traders led to trouble with Bolivia; revolt 1899 and independence declared; annexed by Brazil by treaty (1903), with payment of about $10,000,000 to Bolivia.

Acri \ˈäk-rē\. Commune, Cosenza prov., Calabria, S Italy, 15 m. NE of Cosenza; pop. (1968e) 22,810.

Acro·ce·rau·nia \ˌak-rō-sə-ˈrȯ-nē-ə\. Promontory, NW Epirus, ancient Greece, opp. SE point of Italy. To S along coast and inland heights sometimes called **Ac·ro·ce·rau·ni·an Mts.** \-nē-ən-, -nyən-\ *also* **Ka·na·lit Mts.** \kə-ˈnä-lēt-\. Promontory now known as Cape Gjuhëzës in SW Albania.

Ac·ro·co·rin·thus \ˌak-rō-kə-ˈrin(t)-thəs\. Acropolis of Corinth, Greece, a rock 1887 ft. high on which was anciently a citadel, also a temple of Aphrodite; at its foot the Pirene spring; in Middle Ages site of Byzantine fortifications.

Acro·ï·num \ə-ˈkrō-ə-nəm\ *or* **Akro·i·non** \ə-ˈkrō-ə-ˌnän\. Ancient town, S Phrygia, Asia Minor, near the modern Afyonkarahisar, W cen. Turkey; battle 739 A.D. in which Leo III defeated the Muslims.

Ac·te \ˈak-(ˌ)tē\ *or Gk.* **Ak·tí** \äk-ˈtē\. Most easterly of the three peninsulas of Chalcidice, Macedonia, NE Greece, extends SE into Aegean Sea bet. Strymonic Gulf on the N and Singitic Gulf on the S; ab. 35 m. long; at its tip is Mount Athos (see ATHOS). Its narrow isthmus, where it joins the mainland near Acanthus, was cut by a canal by orders of the Persian king Xerxes 480 B.C.

Ac·ti·um \ˈak-shē-əm, ˈak-tē-\. Promontory and ancient town, W cen. Greece, on S side of entrance to Ambracian Gulf; scene of naval battle 434 B.C. preliminary to Peloponnesian War and of famous naval victory of Octavius over Antony and Cleopatra 31 B.C. by which he became emperor of Rome.

Ac·ton \ˈak-tən\. 1 Town, Middlesex co., NE Massachusetts, 13 m. SSE of Lowell; pop. (1970c) 14,770.

2 Town, Halton co., SE Ontario, Canada, 35 m. W of Toronto; pop. (1968e) 4604.

3 Former municipal borough, SE England; now part of London borough of Ealing; known as a center of Puritanism during the Commonwealth.

Acton Vale. Town, Bagot co., S Quebec, Canada, 36 m. NW of Sherbrooke; pop. (1971p) 4572.

Ac·to·pan \ak-ˈtō-ˌpän\. Municipality, Hidalgo state, cen. Mexico, 80 m. ENE of Mexico City; pop. (1970p) 26,270.

Açúcar, Pão de. See PÃO DE AÇÚCAR.

Acunum Acusio. See MONTÉLIMAR.

Acush·net \ə-ˈku̇sh-nət\. Town, Bristol co., SE Massachusetts, on inlet of Buzzards Bay 3 m. N of New Bedford; pop. (1970c) 7767; settled c. 1659; devastated during King Philip's War; scene of battle Sept. 1776 bet. Minutemen and British troops.

Ac·worth \ˈak-wərth\. City, Cobb co., NW Georgia; pop. (1970c) 3929.

Ada \ˈād-ə\. 1 Mountain, E side of Baranof I., Alaska; 4536 ft.

2 County in Idaho. See table at IDAHO.

3 City, ⊗ of Norman co., NW Minnesota, 32 m. NNE of Moorhead; pop. (1970c) 2076; dairy products, potatoes.

4 Village, Hardin co., NW cen. Ohio, 15 m. E of Lima; pop. (1970c) 5309; farm implements; Ohio Northern Univ. (1871).

5 City, ⊗ of Pontotoc co., S cen. Oklahoma, 65 m. SE of Oklahoma City; pop. (1970c) 14,859; bricks, cement, glassware; agriculture (corn, dairy products); oil refining; East Central State College (1909); settled 1889, incorp. 1910.

Adabazar. See ADAPAZARI.

Adai Khokh. See UILPATA.

Adair \ə-ˈda(ə)r, -ˈde(ə)r\. 1 Name of counties in four states of the U.S. See tables at IOWA, KENTUCKY, MISSOURI, OKLAHOMA.

2 Bay at NE end of Gulf of California, extending into NW Sonora state, Mexico.

Adak \ˈā-ˌdak\. Island, central Andreanof Is., Aleutian Is., SW Alaska; 289 sq. m.; treeless and barren but has several good harbors. In World War II, after Japanese seizure of W Aleutians, occupied 1942 by Americans and developed as air base for attack on Kiska 250 m. W.

Ada·lar \ˌad-ᵊl-ˈär\. District, comprising group of small islands, E Sea of Marmara, İstanbul prov., Turkey in Asia; pop. (1965c) 15,219.

Adalia. See ANTALYA 2.

Adam \ˈad-(ˌ)am\. Inland town, E Oman, SE Arabian Penin., W of Sur.

Ad·am, Mount \-ˈad-əm\. Peak, N West Falkland, Falkland Is.; 2297 ft.

Ad·a·mana \ˌad-ə-ˈman-ə\. Village, Apache co., Arizona, 20 m. E of Holbrook; gateway to Petrified Forest National Park.

Ad·a·ma·wa \ˌad-ə-ˈmä-wə\. Region in W Africa, bet. Bight of Biafra and Lake Chad; ab. 50,000 sq. m.; largely a plateau (1500 to 2000 ft.) with highest point about 6000 ft.; crossed by Benue river and tributaries; inhabited by Fulah and Hausa tribes. First explored by Germans, then by French. From about 1900 divided by France, Germany, and Great Britain. German sector (former Kamerun) divided 1919 into British and French mandates: French mandate now part of Cameroon, British mandate part of Nigeria.

Ada·mel·lo, Mon·te \ˈmȯn-tē-ˌad-ə-ˈmel-(ˌ)ō\. Mountain, Rhaetian Alps, N Italy, 27 m. WNW of Trent and N of Lake Garda; 11,657 ft.

Ad·ams \'ad-əmz\. 1 Name of counties in twelve states of the U.S. See tables at COLORADO, IDAHO, ILLINOIS, INDIANA, IOWA, MISSISSIPPI, NEBRASKA, NORTH DAKOTA, OHIO, PENNSYLVANIA, WASHINGTON, WISCONSIN.
2 Town, N Berkshire co., W Massachusetts, 14 m. NNE of Pittsfield; pop. (1970c) 11,772; chemicals, paper. Settled 1762, incorp. as town 1778.

Adams, Mount. 1 Peak in White Mts., Coos co., New Hampshire, in Presidential Range N of Mt. Washington; 5798 ft., second highest peak of White Mts.
2 Peak, Essex co., NE New York; 3584 ft.
3 Peak in Cascade Range, SW Yakima co., Washington, S of Mt. Rainier; 12,307 ft.

Adams, Point. Cape at mouth of Columbia river, NW Oregon.

Adam's Bridge. Chain of shoals bet. Ceylon and SE coast of India (Tamil Nadu); ab. 30 m. long; traditionally, the remains of a causeway built by Rama, hero of the *Ramayana*, to allow the passage of his army from India to Ceylon in order to rescue his wife Sita.

Adam's Peak *or Singhalese* **Sa·ma·na·la** \'səm-ə-nə-lə\. Mountain, S cen. Ceylon; 7360 ft.; sacred as place of pilgrimage for Hindus, Buddhists, and Muslims —named, according to the Muslim legend, after a large hollow (5 ft. long), resembling a footprint, in rock on its summit, said to have been made by Adam, standing there on one foot for 1000 years as an act of penance for his expulsion from Paradise.

Ad·ams·town \'ad-əmz-ˌtau̇n\. Village on Pitcairn Island (*q.v.*).

Adana. See ADEN.

Ada·na \'äd-ə-nə, -ˌnä\ *or formerly* **Sey·han** \sā-'hän\. 1 Province of S Turkey. See table at TURKEY.
2 City, its ✱, on left bank of Seyhan river about 30 m. from its mouth; met. area pop. (1970p) 529,926; explosives, soap, textiles, tobacco.
History: Roman military station; after decline, restored by Harun-al-Rashid c. 782 A.D.; held by Egyptians 1832–40; scene of Armenian massacres of 1909; occupied by French army 1919–21; scene of conference Jan. 30–31, 1943 bet. Prime Minister Churchill for Allies and Turkish officials.

Ada·pa·za·rı \ˌäd-ə-ˌpäz-ə-'rē\ *or formerly* **Ada·ba·zar** \ˌäd-ə-bə-'zär\. Town, ✱ of Sakarya prov., NW Turkey in Asia, ab. 80 m. E of İstanbul; pop. (1970p) 152,171; textile and tobacco industries; has rail connections with Üsküdar.

Adare \ə-'da(ə)r, -'de(ə)r\. Cape, NE Victoria Land, Antarctica, in Ross Dependency, 71°17′S, 170°14′E.

Ad·da \'äd-ə, 'ad-ə\. River, Lombardy, N Italy; 194 m. long; flows S through Lake Como into Po river 7 m. W of Cremona.

Ad Da·bah \ad-'dab-ə\ *or* **Al–Da·ba** \al-\. Village on coastal road, NW Egypt, E of Matrūh and 30 m. W of Al-Alamein; seized by Germans June 1942 in their advance to Al-Alamein.

Ad Dabbah. See ED DEBBA.

Addagalla. See ADIGALA.

Ad Damir. See ED DAMER.

Ad–Dawhah. See DOHA.

Ad·ding·ton \'ad-iŋ-tən\. See *Lennox and Addington* in table at ONTARIO.

Ad Dir'īyah. See DERAIYEH.

Ad·dis Ab·a·ba *or Ital.* **Addis Abe·ba** \ˌad-ə-'sab-ə-bə\. City, ✱ of Ethiopia and ✱ of Shewa prov., in cen. part; pop. (1970e) 795,900; altitude over 8000 ft.; footwear, textiles; food processing; univ. (1961); site of headquarters of Organization of African Unity. Scene of peace treaty by which Italy recognized the independence of Ethiopia 1896; capital of Ethiopia since 1896; occupied by Italians May 5, 1936 signaling end of Ethiopian resistance to invasion; restored by British April 1941.

Ad·di·son \'ad-ə-sən\. 1 County in Vermont. See table at VERMONT.
2 Village, Du Page co., NE Illinois, 19 m. W of Chicago; pop. (1970c) 24,482; foundries, industrial heating equipment; residential.

Ad Diwaniya. See DIWANIYAH.

Ad·do Elephant National Park \ˌad-ō-\. National park, S Cape Province, Rep. of South Africa; 26½ sq. m.; habitat for rare Addo elephant and Cape buffalo; established 1931.

Ad Duwaym. See ED DUEIM.

Adel \ā-'del\. 1 City, ⊗ of Cook co., S Georgia; pop. (1970c) 4972; corn, tobacco.
2 Town, ⊗ of Dallas co., S cen. Iowa, 24 m. W of Des Moines; pop. (1970c) 2419; bricks, tiles.

Ad·e·laide \'ad-ᵊl-ˌād\. 1 City, ✱ of South Australia, in SE part on Torrens river and 7 m. by rail from its port, Port Adelaide; pop. (1969e) 16,800, met. area pop. 808,600; farm implements, furniture, textiles; large export trade; Univ. of Adelaide (1874), Flinders Univ. of South Australia (1966), two cathedrals; founded 1837; first municipality in Australia to be incorporated (1840).
2 Town, E Cape Prov., Rep. of South Africa, 94 m. NNE of Port Elizabeth; pop. (1967e) 7600; wool center.

Adelaide Island. Island, W of Antarctic Penin., British Antarctic Territory, Antarctica; ab. 68 m. long, 20 m. wide.

Adelaide Peninsula. Peninsula, NW Keewatin dist., Northwest Territories, Canada, 68°09′N, 97°45′W, opp. King William Island.

Adé·lie Coast *or* **Adélie Land** \ə-'dā-lē-\ *or Fr.* **Terre Adélie** \ter-á-dā-lē\. Part of Antarctica, bet. 66° and 67°S, 136° and 142°E; estimated area ab. 150,000 sq. m. First sighted by Capt. d'Urville of French navy 1840; explored by Mawson in his expeditions of 1911–14, 1929–31; placed under French sovereignty by decree Apr. 1, 1938. See WILKES LAND.

Adelsberg. See POSTOJNA.

Aden \'äd-ᵊn, 'ād-, 'ad-\ *or anc.* **Ad·a·na** \'äd-ə-nə, -ˌnä\. 1 Former British colony on coast of SW Arabian Penin., now part of Yemen (✱Aden); 75 sq. m., with Perim I. 80 sq. m.
2 Seaport, ✱ of the People's Democratic Republic of Yemen, and ✱ of former Aden Protectorate, on Gulf of Aden; pop. (1970e) 250,000; cigarettes, salt, soap; refueling port.
History: Trading port in Roman times; chief port on medieval Arab trade route between the Red Sea and the Persian Gulf and India; unsuccessfully attacked by Portuguese under Albuquerque 1513; captured by Turks 1538; ruled by Sultan of San'a from 17th century; held by British and governed as part of India 1839–1937; increased greatly in importance as coaling station and transshipment point after opening of Suez Canal 1869; separated from India and made crown colony 1937; a fortified naval base during World War II; member of Federation of South Arabia 1963–67; became ✱ of independent republic 1968.

Aden, Gulf of. Arm of Indian Ocean bet. S coast of Arabian Penin. and Somalia, E Africa; ab. 550 m. long; connecting on W through Bab al-Mandab with the Red Sea. Controlled by British after their occupation of Aden 1839, Perim 1857, and Socotra 1876 (*qq.v.*).

Ade·na \ə-'dē-nə\. Village, Harrison and Jefferson cos., E Ohio, 15 m. SW of Steubenville; pop. (1970c) 1134.

Aden Protectorate. Former British protectorate, S coast of Arabian Penin., extending from Aden to border of Oman; 112,000 sq. m.; now part of Yemen (✱ Aden); consisted of a number of states whose rulers had entered into treaty relations with Great Britain 1882–1914; states in W region formed Federation of South Arabia Feb. 1959, joined by other states 1959–65; became part of independent Yemen 1967.

Adernò. See ADRANO.

Ad·i·a·be·ne \ˌad-ē-ə-ˈbē-nē\. Region of ancient Assyria in N part, E of the Tigris and bet. the Great Zab and the Little Zab; later much extended.

Ad·i·ga·la *also* **Ad·da·gal·la** \ˌäd-ə-ˈgäl-ə\. Town, E Ethiopia, ab. 80 m. N of Harer.

Adi·ge \ˈäd-ə-ˌjā\ *or Lat.* **Ath·e·sis** \ˈath-ə-səs\ *or Ger.* **Etsch** \ˈech\. River, NE Italy; 255 m. long; rises in Rhaetian Alps, flows SE and S past Merano, Trent, and Verona to Adriatic Sea bet. Venice and mouths of Po; navigable for 170 m. Changed its course 587 A.D.; scene of many battles, the best known of which occurred 1799, when General Schérer defeated the Austrians, and in the Austrian-Italian campaign of 1916.

Adigey Autonomous Oblast. See ADYGEI AUTONOMOUS OBLAST.

Adi·grat \ˌäd-i-ˈgrät\. Town, N Ethiopia, 82 m. SSE of Asmara; pop. (1970e) 9071.

Ad·i·ron·dack Mountains \ˌad-ə-ˈrän-ˌdak-\. Mountain group, chiefly in Clinton, Essex, Hamilton, and Franklin cos., NE New York; highest Mt. Marcy 5344 ft.; others Algonquin Peak 5114 ft., Skylight 4926 ft., and Haystack 4960 ft.; includes many lakes, as Saranac, Placid, Tupper, Long, and Raquette; source of Hudson and Ausable rivers; noted for fine scenery; has many resorts, esp. for winter sports. In center of mountain region is the **Adirondack Forest Preserve,** area over 5,000,000 acres, set aside by state with camp sites for public recreation and to conserve forests and water supply.

Adı·ya·man \ˌäd-ē-ə-ˈmän\. 1 Province of SE Turkey, Asia. See table at TURKEY.
2 Town, its ✱; pop. (1965c) 22,153.

Adjar. See ADZHAR AUTONOMOUS SOVIET SOCIALIST REPUBLIC.

Ad·jun·tas \äd-ˈhünt-əs\. Town and municipality, W cen. Puerto Rico; pop. (1970p) 5309 (town), 18,584 (munic.); summer resort.

Ad·mi·ral·ty Bay \ˈad-m(ə-)rəl-tē-\. See SOUTH SHETLAND ISLANDS.

Admiralty Inlet. 1 Branch of Puget Sound, NW Washington, bet. Whidbey I. and mainland (Island and Jefferson cos.).
2 Fjord, NW Baffin I., Franklin dist., Northwest Territories, Canada, opening into Lancaster Sound; 180 m. long; cuts off Brodeur Peninsula to the W.

Admiralty Island. Island, N Alexander Archipelago, SE Alaska, bet. mainland on E and Chichagof and Baranof Islands on W; ab. 90 m. long; 1650 sq. m.

Admiralty Islands *or often* **Ad·mi·ral·ties** \ˈad-m(ə-)rəl-tēz\. Island group, W Pacific Ocean, N of the island of New Guinea and ab. 260 m. W of New Hanover I.; 800 sq. m.; pop. (1969e) 21,588; comprises Manus, the only large island, Rambutyo, and ab. 16 small islands; part of Bismarck Archipelago, constituting with Northwestern Is. the Manus district of Papua New Guinea; ✱ Lorengau; copra; fishing. First seen by Schouten and Le Maire 1616; became part of German protectorate 1884; occupied by Australian forces 1914; mandated to Australia 1920. Seized by Japanese 1942; liberated by Allied forces 1944.

Admiralty Mountains. Mountains on coast, N part of Victoria Land, Antarctica.

Admiralty Sound. Deep inlet, SW coast of Tierra del Fuego, Chile.

Ado·na·ra *or* **Adu·na·ra** *or* **Adoe·na·ra** \ˌad-ə-ˈnär-ə\. Island, Lesser Sunda Is., Indonesia; bet. E end of Flores and Lomblen Islands; ab. 23 m. long by 11 m. wide; 224 sq. m.; main settlement Sagu on N coast.

Ado·ni \ə-ˈdō-nē\. Town, W Andhra Pradesh, S India, 142 m. SW of Hyderabad; pop. (1961c) 69,951; cotton.

Adour \ə-ˈdu̇(ə)r\ *or anc.* **At·u·rus** \ˈach-ə-rəs\. River, SW France; 208 m. long; flows NW and W from Pyrenees to Bay of Biscay near Biarritz.

Adowa. See ADWA.

Adra \ˈäd-rə\ *or anc.* **Ab·de·ra** \ab-ˈdir-ə\. Seaport, Almería prov., SE Spain, 30 m. W of Almería; pop. (1970p) 16,283. Ancient town, Abdera, in Baetica, S Hispania, at foot of hill below present town; a maritime city founded by Carthaginians, taken by Romans.

Adramyttium. See EDREMİT.

Adramyttium, Gulf of. See EDREMİT, GULF OF.

Adra·no \ə-ˈdrän-(ˌ)ō\ *or* **Ader·nò** \ˌäd-ər-ˈnȯ\ *or anc.* **Ha·dra·num** \hə-ˈdrā-nəm\. Commune, Catania prov., E Sicily, Italy, at foot of Mt. Etna and 24 m. NW of Catania; pop. (1968e) 32,475; founded c. 400 B.C. by Dionysius the Elder; parts of ancient walls still standing; has Norman castle built in 1157.

Adranos. See ATRANOS.

Adrar \ä-ˈdrär\. Name of several mountainous regions in Sahara desert region of NW Africa: (1) Region, W Mauritania, bordering on SE Spanish Sahara; (2) *or in full* **Adrar des Ifo·ras** \-dā-ˌzē-fō-ˈrä\. Region, cen. Sahara, NE of Tombouctou, Mali.

Adria. See ADRIATIC SEA.

Adria \ˈäd-rē-ə\; *anc.* **Ha·dria** \ˈhā-drē-ə\ *also* **Ha·tria** \ˈhāt-rē-a\ *or* **Atria** \ˈā-trē-ə\. Commune, Rovigo prov., Veneto, NE Italy, 15 m. E of Rovigo; pop. (1968e) 22,703; orig. on Adriatic Sea but now 13 m. inland. Ancient Etruscan settlement which gave its name to Adriatic Sea; in Roman times, a port and naval station.

Adri·an \ˈā-drē-ən\. City, ⊗ of Lenawee co., SE Michigan, on Raisin river 59 m. SW of Detroit; pop. (1970c) 20,382; center of agricultural and truck-garden region; auto accessories, chemicals, paper; Adrian Coll. (1845), Siena Heights Coll. (1919); settled 1825, incorp. as city 1853.

Adrianople *or* **Adrianopolis.** See EDİRNE.

Adri·at·ic Sea \ˌā-drē-ˈat-ik-, ˌad-rē-\ *or* **Gulf of Venice** *or Ital.* **Ma·re Adri·a·ti·co** \ˌmär-ē-ˌäd-rē-ˈät-i-ˌkō\; *anc.* **Adria** \ˈā-drē-ə\ *or* **Mare Adri·at·i·cum** \ˌma(ə)r-ē-ˌā-drē-ˈat-i-kəm, ˌme(ə)r-, -ˌad-rē-\. Arm of Mediterranean Sea between Italy and Balkan Penin.; ab. 500 m. long, av. width ab. 110 m.

Adua. See ADWA.

Adu·la \ˈäd-ə-lə\. Mountain group, Lepontine Alps, SE Switzerland; highest peak Rheinwaldhorn 11,158 ft.

Adul·lam \ə-ˈdəl-əm\. Ancient village, Israel, 15 m. SW of Jerusalem; now an archaeological site; a cave in its vicinity was from early times a place of refuge (*1 Sam.* xxii. 1, 2).

Adunara. See ADONARA.

Aduwa. See ADWA.

Ad·vent Bay \ˌad-ˌvent-, -vənt-\. Bay in Ice Fjord, Spitsbergen, Svalbard, Norway; settlements at Longyear City and Advent City.

Advent City. Mining settlement on Advent Bay, Spitsbergen, Norway.

Ad·wa \ˈäd-wə, ˈad-\ *also* **Adu·wa** *or* **Ado·wa** *or Ital.* **Adua** \ˈäd-ə-wə, ˈad-\. Town, Tigre prov., N Ethiopia, ab. 80 m. S of Asmara; pop. (1970e) 15,712; scene of disastrous defeat of Italians March 1, 1896 by Emperor Menelik II, because of which Ethiopia secured recognition of her independence; captured by Italians soon after invasion of Ethiopia Oct. 1935; included in Eritrea 1935–41; retaken by British 1941.

Ad·wick le Street \ˈad-ik-lə-ˈstrēt\. Urban district, West Riding, Yorkshire, England, 20 m. NE of Sheffield; pop. (1971p) 18,000.

Ady·gei Autonomous Oblast *or* **Adi·gey Autonomous Oblast** \ˌäd-ə-ˈgā . . . ˈō-bləst, -ˌblast\. Autonomous subdivision, Russian S.F.S.R., U.S.S.R., NE of Black Sea, entirely surrounded by Krasnodar Krai; 2934 sq. m.; pop. (1970p) 386,000; Kuban river marks N border; land partly river basin, partly hilly; corn, potatoes, tobacco, wheat; livestock raising; lumber, petroleum. Formerly part of Kuban prov., inhabited by a Circassian people who had been Christianized in 6th cent. and converted to Islam 17th cent.; created an autonomous area 1922 and a region 1936. In World War II occupied by Germany in Caucasus drive Aug. 9, 1942, but recaptured by U.S.S.R. Jan. 31, 1943.

Adzhar Autonomous Soviet Socialist Republic \ə-ˈjär-\; *frequently* **Adzhar** *or* **Adjar** \ə-ˈjär\ *also* **Adzhar·ia** \ə-ˈjärē-ə\ *or* **Adzhar·i·stan** \ə-ˈjär-ə-ˌstan\. Autonomous republic, SW Georgian S.S.R., U.S.S.R., on Black Sea coast; on S borders on NE Turkey; 1158 sq. m.; pop. (1970p) 310,000; ✱ Batumi; mountainous with dense forests; has heavy rainfall; watered in SW by lower course of Çoruh (Chorokh) river; plain along Black Sea has subtropical vegetation; avocados, citrus fruits, tea, tobacco; livestock rearing; oil refining. Controlled 17th and 18th cents. by Turks who introduced Islamic influences; greater part of region annexed by Russia middle of 19th cent. and Batumi acquired 1877–78; after Revolution of 1917 held by Turks for a time but restored to Russia Oct. 1921.

Aea. See KUTAISI.

Aeaea. See CIRCEO, MONTE.

Ædua. See AUTUN.

Aegadian Isles. See EGADI ISLANDS.

Ae·ga·le·os, Mount \-ē-ˈgā-lē-əs\. Mountain, W Attica, Greece, just W of Athens; overlooks the Bay of Eleusis and the island of Salamis; 1573 ft.; on it sat Xerxes watching the defeat of his fleet by the Greeks in the battle of Salamis 480 B.C.

Aegates. See EGADI ISLANDS.

Ae·ge·an Islands \i-ˈjē-ən-\. **1** Islands of the Aegean Sea, including the Cyclades, Sporades, Dodecanese, etc.

History: Cyclades and southern islands probably part of Aegean civilization 2d millennium B.C. (see AEGEAN SEA); colonized by Aeolian, Dorian, and Ionian Greeks from mainland c. 1000–700 B.C.; during Greek wars with Persia, islands in Thracian Sea helped Persia, but eastern islands were under influence of revolting Ionian cities; allied with or dependent upon Athens, the leader of the Delian League (see ATHENS 10), 5th cent. B.C.; except for Cyclades, chiefly controlled by Macedonian empire until they were conquered by Rome 2d cent. B.C.; ruled by Byzantine Empire 5th–13th cents.; ravaged and seized by Roger II of Sicily during Second Crusade 1147; Naxos became center of duchy of Naxos which was established 1207 by Venice from her acquisitions in the Fourth Crusade; in 13th cent., politically controlled by leading Venetian families and commercially dominated by Venetian traders; Imbros, Samothrace, Lesbos recovered by Eastern Empire 1261; western islands remained under Venetian Duchy of the Archipelago; Chios held by Genoese 1261–1329; Rhodes belonged to Knights of St. John of Jerusalem (Hospitalers) 1310–1522; in a series of Venetian wars with Ottoman Turks during 15th and 16th cents., gradually conquered by Turks; part of Ottoman Empire from death of Suleiman I 1566 until joined Greek revolt 1821; most of islands became part of independent Greece by Treaty of Adrianople 1829.

2 *or Gk.* **Ní·soi Ai·yaí·ou** \ˌnē-sòi-ā-ˈyā-ˌü\. Administrative region of Greece, comprising five departments; constituted 1931. See table at GREECE.

3 *or Ital.* **Iso·le Ita·li·a·ne dell'Egeo** \ˈē-zə-ˌlā-ē-ˌtäl-ē-ˈän-ā-ˌdel-ā-ˈjā-ō\. The Italian Aegean Is. (Dodecanese, Rhodes, and Castelrosso) 1923–47.

Aegean Sea *or Gk.* **Ai·gai·on Pe·la·gos** \ˌā-ˌyòn-ˈpel-ə-ˌgòs\. Arm of Mediterranean Sea bet. Greece and Turkey; ab. 400 m. long by 200 m. wide. It was the center of earliest European civilization, formerly called Mycenean or Minoan but in broader aspects now termed Aegean (c. 3000–1100 B.C.).

Ae·ge·ri, Lake of \-ˈā-gə-rē\ *or Ger.* **Äge·ri·see** \ˈā-gə-re-ˌzā\. Lake, Zug canton, Switzerland, E of Lake of Zug; ab. 3 sq. m.

Ægidia. See KOPER.

Ae·gi·na \i-ˈjī-nə\ *or Gk.* **Aí·yi·na** \ˈa-yi-nä\. **1** Island in the Saronic Gulf, attached to Attica dept., Greece; off SE coast of Greece; 9 m. long.

2 Commune, Attica dept., Greece, on W coast of Aegina I.; pop. (1961c) 6092; sponge fishing.

History: Greek state of maritime importance even in pre-Dorian times; first state in European Greece to coin money in the standard which came to prevail in ancient times; a leading commercial state at the beginning of 5th cent. B.C., but gradually eclipsed by Athens; ravaged Attica on behalf of Thebes; gave submission to Persia 491 B.C.; scene of battle in the so-called First Peloponnesian War in which Aeginetans, allies of Sparta, were defeated by Athens 457 B.C. and forced to join the Delian League; lost its greatness after Athens expelled its people 431 B.C.; destroyed by the Romans 210 B.C. Center of the rebel Greek government after its defeat by the Turks at Mesolóngion 1826.

Aegina, Gulf of. See SARONIC GULF.

Aegium. See AIGION.

Ae·gos·pot·a·mi \ˌē-gə-ˈspät-ə-ˌmī\ *or* **Ae·gos·pot·a·mos** \-məs\. Small river and town, ancient Thrace, in the Chersonese. Mouth of river on the Dardanelles scene of Spartan victory under Lysander over Athenian fleet 405 B.C., the last battle of the Peloponnesian War.

Aegusa. See LINOSA.

Aegyptus. See EGYPT.

Aelana. See 'AQABA.

Aelia Capitolina. See JERUSALEM 2.

Æmilia. See EMILIA–ROMAGNA.

Æmilianum. See MILLAU.

Aenaria. See ISCHIA.

Aenos. See ENEZ.

Aenus. See INN.

Aeoliae Insulae. See LIPARI ISLANDS.

Ae·o·lis \ˈē-ə-ləs\ *or* **Ae·o·lia** \ē-ˈō-lē-ə, -ˈōl-yə\. Ancient country, NW Asia Minor; included island of Lesbos; settled by Aeolian Greeks, a Thessalian people, who founded a number of cities along the coast before 1000 B.C. Religious center was at Gryneion, near Cyme. Later formed a district of Mysia and Lydia, overcome by Croesus.

Aequum Tuticum. See ARIANO IRPINO.

A–erh–chin Shan–mo \ˌä-ˌe(ə)r-ˈchin-shän-ˈmō\ *also* **As·tin Tagh** \ˌas-tən-ˈtä(g)\ *or* **Al·tin Tagh** *or* **Al·tyn Tagh** \ˌal-ˌtin-\. Mountain range (*tagh*), N Tibet and S Sinkiang Uighur, W China; highest peak ab. 25,000 ft.; branch of the Kunlun Shan.

Ærø \ˈa(ə)r-ˌə(r), ˈe(ə)r-\. Island in the Baltic, Fyn co., Denmark, S of Fyn I.; ab. 15 m. long; 34 sq. m.; pop. (1965c) 9656.

Æsernia. See ISÉRNIA.

Æsis. See IESI.

Aethalia. See ELBA 2.

Ae·thi·o·pia \ˌē-thē-ˈō-pē-ə\. Ancient name for the region of NE Africa, incl. modern Egypt, Ethiopia, Sudan, and as far S as the knowledge of the ancients extended.

Aetna. See ETNA.

Ae·to·lia \ē-ˈtōl-yə, -ˈtō-lē-ə\ *also* **Ai·to·lia** \ˌāt-ə-ˈlē-ə\. Ancient district, cen. Greece, N of Gulf of Patras and Locris, and E of Acarnania, now part of Aetolia and Acarnania dept. from which it is separated by the Achelous river; a mountainous region.

History: In early times home of a backward group of tribes; first given unity by the formation of the Aetolian League 290 B.C., a military confederation which at its height included most of central Greece and separated Sparta from the Achaean League (see ACHAEA); driven out of area of Peloponnesus by Achaeans and Philip V of Macedon 3d cent. B.C.; helped Rome defeat Macedonians at Cynoscephalae 197 B.C.; punished by Rome for aiding Antiochus III of Syria 189 B.C.; incorporated into the Roman province of Achaea 146 B.C.; became part of Eastern (Greek) Empire 1204 A.D.; under Scanderbeg (see ALBANIA), Venetians, and Turks in the course of 15th cent.

Aetolia and Ac·ar·na·nia \-ˌak-ər-ˈnā-nē-ə, -ˈnā-nyə\ *or Gk.* **Ai·to·lía kai Akar·na·nía** \ˌat-ō-ˈlē-ə-ˌkā-ˌäk-ˌär-nä-ˈnē-ə\. Department of Greece. See table at GREECE.

Afars and Is·sas \ˈäf-ˌärz . . . ē-ˈsäz\; *officially* **French Territory of the Afars and the Issas** *or Fr.* **Ter·ri·toire fran·çaise des Afars et des Issas** \ter-i-twär-fräⁿ-säz-dāz-ä-får-zā-dāz-ē-sä, -sez-\; *formerly* **French So·ma·li·land** \-sō-ˈmäl-ē-ˌland\; *Fr.* **Côte fran·çaise des So·ma·lis** \kōt-fräⁿ-säz-dā-sȯ-må-lē, -sez-\. Overseas territory of France, E Africa, on Gulf of Aden at entrance to Red Sea; 8880 sq. m.; pop. (1970e) 95,000; ✱ Djibouti. Chief exports: Hides, skins, salt; derives revenues from port of Djibouti.

History: Obock acquired by French 1862; small strip of hinterland added to establish French protectorate of Somaliland 1884–85; capital transferred to Djibouti on trade route to Ethiopia 1892; rail connection with Addis Ababa completed during World War I; by treaty with Italy 1935, France ceded 309 sq. m. to Eritrea; had status of a colony until 1946 when it became a territory within French Union; became a member of French Community 1958; voted to retain links with France 1967.

Af·ghan·i·stan \af-ˈgan-ə-ˌstan\. Kingdom, cen. Asia, bounded on N by U.S.S.R., on NE by China, on E and S by Pakistan, and on W by Iran; 250,775 sq. m.; pop. (1970e) 16,519,677; ✱ Kabul. *Physical features:* Has Helmand river in center and SW, flowing into Lake Helmand, Hari Rud in NW, Amu Darya on NE boundary, and Kabul in E, flowing to Indus; very mountainous in cen. and N sections, Hindu Kush ranges 15,000 to 25,000 ft.; many fertile plains and valleys; desert regions in S; Khyber Pass on E border to Pakistan. *Major products:* Barley, corn, sugar, wheat; livestock; cement, textiles. *Chief towns:* Kabul, Kandahār, Bāghlān, Chārikār, Kundūz, Qala Nau. Divided into the following provinces (for pronunciation of their names, see their individual entries):

NAME	AREA (sq. m.)	POP.[1] (1970e)	CAPITAL
Badakhshān	16,844	344,495	Faizābād
Bādghis	9,544	320,103	Qala Nau
Bāghlān	5,219	733,483	Bāghlān
Balkh	5,849	353,722	Mazār-i-Sharīf
Bāmiān	11,197	346,017	Bāmiān
Farah	22,306	314,297	Farah
Faryab	7,874	434,710	Maimāna
Ghazni	12,587	1,205,492	Ghazni
Ghor	13,387	323,464	Qala Āhangarān
Helmand	19,909	317,557	Lashkar Gah
Herāt	15,616	685,846	Herāt
Jowzjan	8,132	430,473	Shibarghān
Kabul	1,228	1,293,364	Kabul
Kandahār	17,156	742,257	Kandahār
Kāpīsā	1,744	344,726	Tagāb
Konarhā	3,628	329,710	Chigha Sarāi
Kundūz	3,026	405,446	Kundūz
Laghmān	3,120	222,531	Tigri
Logar	1,622	309,182	Barakī Barak
Nangarhār	2,686	817,905	Jalālābād
Nimroze	20,339	121,887	Zaranj
Paktīā	6,564	732,779	Gardez
Parwān	3,351	887,127	Chārikār
Samāngan	5,904	207,310	Haibak
Takhar	8,031	494,279	Taliqan
Uruzgān	12,179	527,821	Uruzgān
Wardak	3,996	415,630	Maidan
Zabul	7,737	358,074	Qalat

[1]Exclusive of ab. 2,500,000 nomads.

History: In early times formed part of Persian and Alexander's empires; little known until Turkoman dynasty set up at Ghazni (*q.v.*) in 10th century; conquered by Mongol emperor Tamerlane c. 1400; part, including Kabul, added to the Mogul Empire of India by its founder, Babur (1483–1530); Kandahār became independent 1709; with western India, seized by Persian Nadir Shah 1737; consolidated as a separate unit by Ahmad Shah Durrani, at whose death (1773) the Afghan empire included eastern Persia, Afghanistan, Baluchistan, Kashmir, and the Punjab; under successive rulers soon lost Punjab and other territory; in 1809 entered first agreement with the British against the Persians and Russians; invaded by British in First Afghan War 1839–42, thereafter throughout 19th century much disturbed; subject of the jealousy and misunderstanding between British and Russians which resulted in the Second Afghan War 1878–79; maintained a degree of independence under Abd-er-Rahman Khan (1880–1901) who confirmed the cession of the Khyber Pass (*q.v.*) to the British; settled boundaries with India 1893, with Russia 1895. Neutral in World War I; recognized as independent by the British in the Treaty of Rawalpindi 1919; entered treaties with Persia, Turkey, and U.S.S.R., 1921; under the modernizing influence of Amanullah Khan (1919–29), adopted constitution 1923; at the overthrow of Amanullah, established new line of rulers under Nadir Shah (1929–33) whose son joined Turkey, Iraq, and Iran in forming an Oriental Entente 1937. Neutral in World War II; first Afghan minister to U.S. sent to Washington 1943; initiated its first five-year economic plan 1956; adopted new constitution 1964; has followed neutralist foreign policy since World War II.

Af·ghan Turkistan \ˌaf-gən-\. Region, part of Turkistan (*q.v.*), NE Afghanistan, about coextensive with the district around Mazār-i-Sharīf. Some include also the province of Badakhshān to the E. Long under Uzbek influence and claimed by Russia; settled in favor of Afghanistan by Anglo-Russian Agreement 1859.

Af·goi \äf-ˈgȯi\. Town, SE Somalia, E Africa, ab. 20 m. NW of Mogadisho.

Afiun Karahissar. See AFYONKARAHİSAR.

Afog·nak \ə-ˈfȯg-ˌnak, -ˈfäg-\. Island, W side of Gulf of Alaska, N of Kodiak I. and separated from mainland by Shelikof Strait; 47 m. long; 721 sq. m.

Afon·so Cláu·dio \ˈə-ˈfōⁿ-(ˌ)sü-ˈklaůd-ē-ˌü\. Municipality, Espírito Santo state, E Brazil, ab. 50 m. WNW of Vitória; pop. (1968e) 63,768.

Afra·go·la \ˌä-frə-ˈgō-lə\. Commune, Napoli prov., Campania, S Italy; pop. (1968e) 51,437.

Af·ri·ca \ˈaf-ri-kə\. Second largest continent on the globe, in both N and S hemispheres with greater part N of the equator; 4970 m. long, 4600 m. broad (max. E-W extent); 11,677,239 sq. m. (including offshore islands); coastline ab. 16,100 m. long; pop. (1968e) 335,916,000. *Boundaries:* On N, Mediterranean Sea; most northerly point Ras ben Sekka, 37°21′N; on NW separated from Europe by Strait of Gibraltar; joined on NE to Asia at Sinai Peninsula. On E, Red Sea and Indian Ocean (chief subdivisions Gulf of Aden and Mozambique Channel); chief island Malagasy Republic (Madagascar), and several small groups; most easterly point Cape Hafun, 51°26′E. On S, Indian and Atlantic Oceans (with arbitrary separation line at 20th meridian E long.); most southerly point Cape Agulhas, 34°52′S. On W, Atlantic Ocean (subdivision Gulf of Guinea); chief islands St. Helena and Ascension in South Atlantic and Cape Verde, Canary, and Madeira Is. groups in North Atlantic; most westerly point Cape Almadies, 17°32′W. *Mountains:* Atlas Mts. in NW (highest peak 13,671 ft.); high plateau region of Ethiopia in NE, Mts. Kenya and Kilimanjaro (its peak Mt. Kibo, highest in Africa 19,340 ft.) and Ruwenzori in E, and the Drakensberg in E part of Rep. of South Africa. Other notable physical features are the great desert of the Sahara in the N, partly desert region of the Sudan, the smaller Libyan and Nubian Deserts of Egypt bordering the Nile valley, and the Kalahari Desert in the S; nearly all the S third of the continent is plateau region. *Rivers:* Nile in NE, Niger and Senegal in W, Congo in cen. part, and Zambezi, Orange, and Limpopo in S. *Lakes:* Victoria, Tanganyika, Albert, and Rudolf in E, sources of the Nile or Congo, and Nyasa in SE with outlet to the Zambezi; in cen. Sudan (region) is Chad, with area much reduced in dry season.

Political divisions: (1) Mainland: Afars and Issas, Algeria, Angola, Botswana, Burundi, Cameroon, Central African Republic, Chad, Congo, Dahomey, Egypt, Equatorial Guinea, Ethiopia, Gabon, Gambia, Ghana, Guinea, Ivory Coast, Kenya, Lesotho, Liberia, Libya, Malawi, Mali, Mauritania, Morocco, Mozambique, Niger,

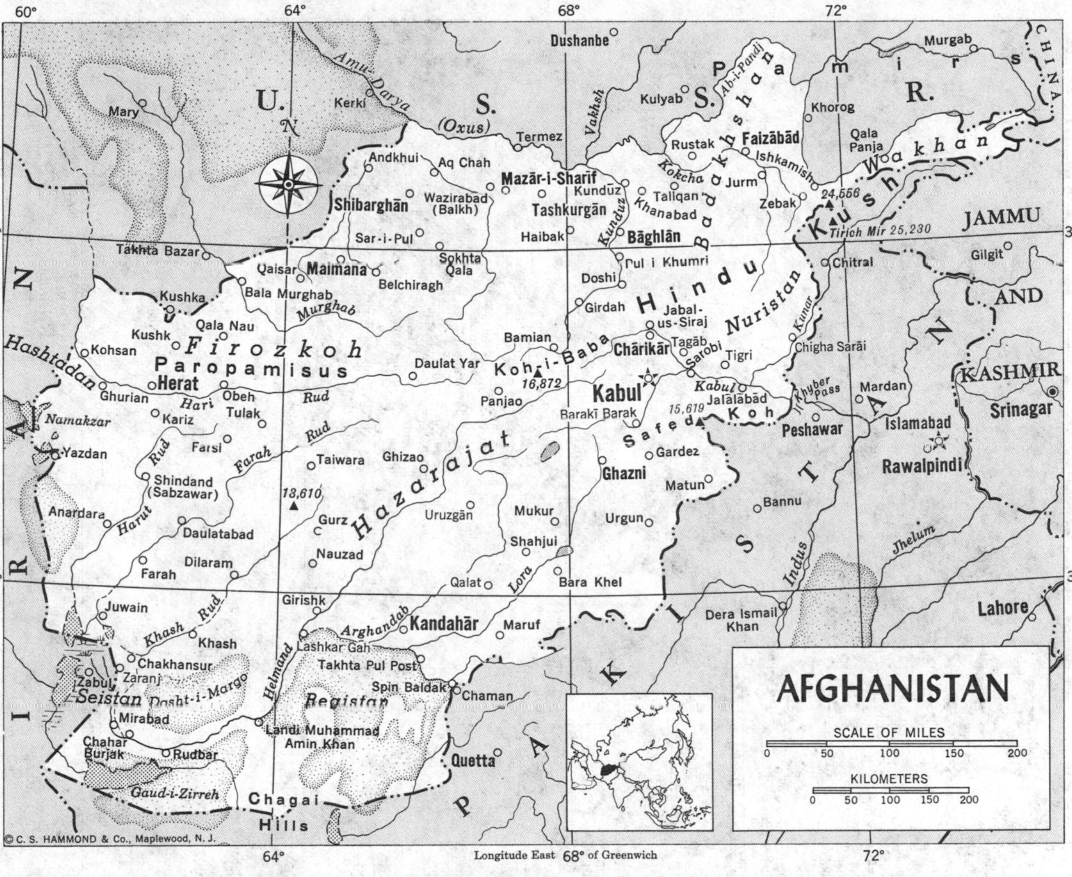

Nigeria, Portuguese Guinea, Rhodesia, Rwanda, Senegal, Sierra Leone, Somalia, Rep. of South Africa, South-West Africa, Spanish Plazas (Ceuta, etc.), Spanish Sahara, Sudan, Swaziland, Tanzania, Togo, Tunisia, Uganda, Upper Volta, Zaire, Zambia. (2) Offshore islands: British Indian Ocean Territory, Canary Is., Cape Verde Is., Comoro Is., Madeira Is., Malagasy Republic, Mauritius, Réunion, St. Helena and dependencies, São Tomé e Principe, Seychelles. The majority of these states achieved independence during the period 1957–68; see their individual entries for description and history.

Africa, Roman. Proconsular Roman province (*Lat.* **Africa Pro·con·su·la·ris** \-ˌprō-ˌkän(t)-sə-ˈlar-əs\) formed after 146 B.C. from territory around Carthage, extended to include Numidia and N part of modern Libya. Later (bet. 30 B.C. and A.D. 180) Egypt, Cyrenaica, Marmarica, and Mauretania became parts of Roman Empire; lost to Vandals in 5th cent. except for Egypt which was part of Byzantine Empire, later 641 conquered by Muslims.

Africa Orientale Italiana. See ITALIAN EAST AFRICA.

Afrine \ä-ˈfrēn\. River, S Turkey and NW Syria; 100 m. long; rises in Gaziantep prov., S Turkey, flows S and SW through swamp region to join the Orontes at Antakya (Antioch).

Afrique, Cape \-a-ˈfrēk\. Cape, E Tunisia, N Africa.

Afrique Equatoriale française. See FRENCH EQUATORIAL AFRICA.

Afrique Occidentale française. See FRENCH WEST AFRICA.

Af·ton \ˈaf-tən\. 1 Town, Lincoln co., SW Wyoming; pop. (1970c) 1290.

2 River, SE Ayrshire, Scotland, flowing N to the Nith; 9 m. long.

ʻAfu·la \ä-ˈfü-lə\. Town, N Israel, 6 m. S of Nazareth; pop. (1970e) 16,900; railway junction; built 1925.

Af·yon·ka·ra·hi·sar \ä-ˈfyōn-ˌkär-ə-his-ˈär\ *or formerly* **Afiun Ka·ra·his·sar** \ä-ˈfyün-\. 1 Province of W cen. Turkey, Asia. See table at TURKEY.

2 City, its ✱, on railroad 128 m. NW of Konya; pop. (1965c) 44,026; barley, wheat; carpets; captured by Greeks March 1921, and retaken by Turks August 1921 during Greco-Turkish war.

Agade. See AKKAD 2.

Aga·dez \ˌag-ə-ˈdez\ *or* **Aga·dès** \-ˈdes\. City, Niger, W Africa; pop. (1962e) 6882.

Aga·dir \ˌäg-ə-ˈdi(ə)r, ˌag-\. Seaport, SW Morocco, ab. 123 m. SW of Marrakech; pop. (1970e) 34,000.

History: Founded in early 16th cent. by Portuguese; later became important port of Morocco; second Moroccan crisis precipitated by visit of German gunboat *Panther* 1911 (see MOROCCO); opened to commerce as a projected port Jan. 1, 1930. In World War II Allied forces landed here Nov. 1942; destroyed by earthquakes Feb. 29–Mar. 1, 1960, since largely rebuilt.

Aga·le·ga Islands \ˌäg-ə-ˌlā-gə-\. Group of small islands in Indian Ocean, 540 m. ENE of Malagasy Republic; dependency of Mauritius.

Ag·a·men·ti·cus, Mount \-ˌag-ə-ˈment-i-kəs, -ˌad-ə-ˈmat-i-\. Elevation, S York co., SW Maine, ab. 5 m. from coast, 43°13′N lat.; 692 ft.; a sailors' landmark.

Aga·na \ə-ˈgän-yə\. Town, ✱ of Guam, on W coast of island, on **Agana Bay** ab. 8 m. NE of Apra Harbor, Mariana Islands, W Pacific Ocean; pop. (1970p) 2131.

Agar·ta·la \ˌəg-ər-tə-ˈlä\. Town, ✱ of Tripura territory, NE India, 125 m. SSW of Shillong; pop. (1961c) 54,878.

Ag·as·siz, Mount \-ˈag-ə-(ˌ)sē\. Peak, Duchesne co., NE cen. Utah; 12,433 ft.

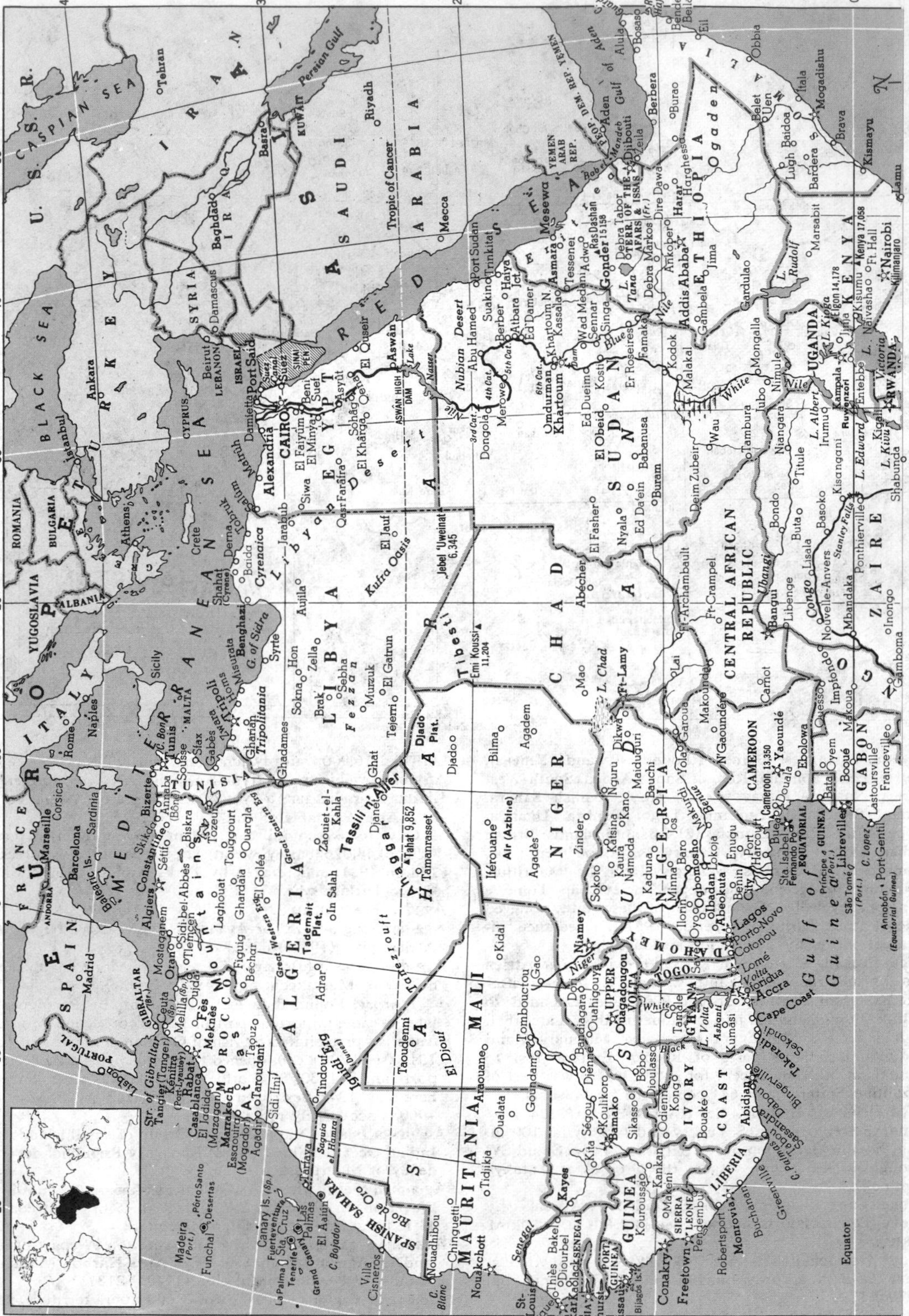
SPAIN
PORTUGAL
FRANCE
ITALY
YUGOSLAVIA
ALBANIA
BULGARIA
ROMANIA
TURKEY
BLACK SEA
CASPIAN SEA
U.S.S.R.
IRAN
IRAQ
SYRIA
LEBANON
ISRAEL
SAUDI ARABIA
KUWAIT
Persian Gulf
MEDITERRANEAN SEA
MOROCCO
ALGERIA
TUNISIA
LIBYA
EGYPT
RED SEA
SUDAN
ETHIOPIA
SOMALIA
KENYA
UGANDA
RWANDA
ZAIRE
CHAD
NIGER
MALI
MAURITANIA
SPANISH SAHARA
SENEGAL
GAMBIA
PORT. GUINEA
GUINEA
SIERRA LEONE
LIBERIA
IVORY COAST
UPPER VOLTA
GHANA
TOGO
DAHOMEY
NIGERIA
CAMEROON
CENTRAL AFRICAN REPUBLIC
GABON
EQUATORIAL GUINEA
YEMEN ARAB REP.
PEOP. DEM. REP. YEMEN
TERR. OF THE AFARS & ISSAS (Fr.)
SAHARA
Gulf of Guinea
Tropic of Cancer
Equator

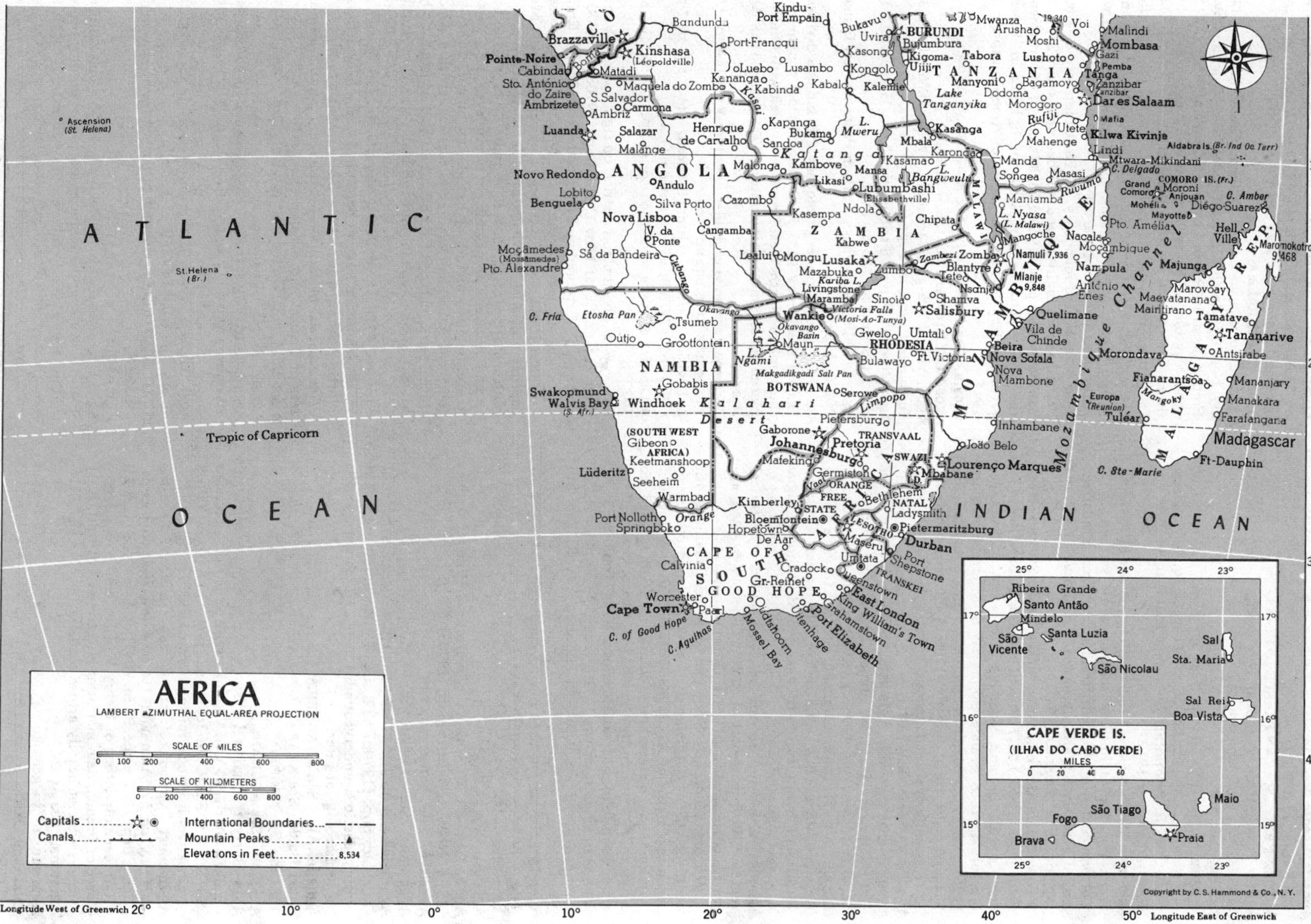

Copyright by C. S. Hammond & Co., N. Y.

Agassiz Needle. Peak in Sierra Nevada, E Fresno co., S cen. California; 13,882 ft.

Agassiz Peak. See SAN FRANCISCO PEAKS.

Agate Fossil Beds National Monument. See UNITED STATES, *National Monuments.*

Agatha. See AGDE.

Ag·at·tu \ˌag-ə-ˈtü\. Island, Near Is. group at W end of Aleutian Is., SW Alaska, SE of Attu; 85 sq. m.; highest point 3089 ft.; temporarily occupied by Japanese from ab. June to October 1942.

Ag·a·wam \ˈag-ə-ˌwäm\. **1** Indian village on site of Ipswich, Essex co., Massachusetts; sold to white settlers 1638. Cultural center in 17th cent.; residence of Anne Bradstreet and of Nathaniel Ward, author of *The Simple Cobbler of Aggawam in America* (1645).

2 Town, Hampden co., Massachusetts, 4 m. SW of Springfield; pop. (1970c) 21,717; settled 1636, incorp. 1885.

Agde \ˈagd\ *or anc.* **Ag·a·tha** \ˈag-ə-thə\. Commune, Hérault dept., S France, 30 m. SW of Montpellier; pop. (1968c) 10,184; settled 6th cent. B.C. by Phocaeans; held by Visigoths; episcopal see 400–1790; 12th cent. medieval fortress cathedral (St-Étienne).

Agedabia. See AJDĀBIYAH.

Agen \á-zhaⁿ\ *or anc.* **Agin·num** \ə-ˈjin-əm\. City, ✱ of Lot-et-Garonne dept., SW France, on Garonne river 74 m. SE of Bordeaux; pop. (1968c) 34,949; textiles; trade center for agricultural region. Capital of Agenais (*q.v.*); a bishopric since 4th cent. A.D.; at end of Albigensian Crusade, location of an inquisition tribunal; joined Catholic League against Huguenots 1589.

Age·nais \ˌäzh-ə-ˈnā\ *or* **Age·nois** \ˌäzh-ən-ˈwä\. Historical region, SW France; part of ancient Guienne; ✱ Agen; approx. coextensive with Lot-et-Garonne dept.

History: Home of Nitiobriges in ancient Gaul; in 4th cent. A.D. *Civitas Agennensium* which formed diocese of Agen (*q.v.*); part of Aquitaine (*q.v.*); acquired by dukes of Aquitaine as a hereditary countship 1038; passed to England 1152; given by Richard I as part of dowry of his sister Joan who married Raymond VI of Toulouse 1196; lapsed to French crown 1271; restored to England 1279; changed hands frequently in Hundred Years' War, but French after 1444; reunited to French crown 1615.

Agen·cy Lake \ˌa-jən-sē-\. Inlet, Klamath co., S Oregon, at N end of Upper Klamath Lake.

Agendicum. See SENS.

Agenois. See AGENAIS.

Ageo \ˈäg-ā-ˌō\. City, Saitama prefecture, Honshū, Japan, 25 m. NNW of Tokyo; pop. (1970c) 110,792.

Ägerisee. See AEGERI, LAKE OF.

Aggershus. See AKERSHUS.

Agg·te·lek \ˈäk-tə-ˌlek\. Village, N Hungary, 25 m. NNW of Miskolc; pop. (1970p) 882; site of great limestone grotto with stalactites, underground stream, and many passages, of archaeological interest.

Agheila, Al–. See AL-AGHEILA.

Aghri Dagh. See ARARAT 3.

Aghrim. See AUGHRIM.

Agiguan. See AGUIJAN.

Agin–Bur·yat National Okrug \ə-ˈgēn-bu̇r-ˈyät- . . . ˈō-ˌkrük, -ˌbu̇r-ē-ˈät-\. Administrative district, Russian S.F.S.R., U.S.S.R.; 7336 sq. m.; pop. (1970p) 66,000; ✱ Aginskoye; livestock raising; formed 1937.

Ag·in·court \ˈaj-ən-ˌkō(ə)rt, ˈā-jən-, -ˌkȯ(ə)rt; ˈäzh-ən-ˌku̇(ə)r\ *or Fr.* **Azin·court** \á-zaⁿ-kür\. Village, Pas-de-Calais dept., N France, 33 m. WNW of Arras; pop. (1962c) 106; scene of victory of Henry V of England over a larger force of French, demonstrating effectiveness of warfare by archers against heavily armed feudal array Oct. 25, 1415.

Aginnum. See AGEN.

Agin·sko·ye \ə-ˈgēn-skə-yə\. Town, ✱ of Agin-Buryat National Okrug, Russian S.F.S.R., U.S.S.R., ab. 70 m. SE of Chita.

Agi·ra \ə-ˈjir-ə\ *or anc.* **Agyr·i·um** \ə-ˈjir-ē-əm\. Commune, Enna prov., cen. Sicily, Italy, 15 m. ENE of Enna; pop. (1968e) 12,634; ancient Siculian city colonized with Greeks by Timoleon 339 B.C. In World War II taken by Americans and Canadians July 29, 1943.

Aglar. See AQUILEIA.

Agna·del·lo \ˌän-yə-ˈdel-ˌō\. Village, Cremona prov., N Italy; pop. (1968e) 2011; scene of defeat of Venetians by the French (as members of League of Cambrai) May 14, 1509.

Ag·no \ˈäg-(ˌ)nō\. River, NW Luzon, Phil.; 128 m. long; flows S and SW through Pangasinan prov., then N to Lingayen Gulf near Lingayen; course is through flood plain of rich soil; one of the important rivers of Luzon. In World War II much fighting on its banks 1942 and when Americans landed January 1945.

Agoo \ˌäg-ˈō\. Municipality, S La Union prov., Luzon, Phil., on main highway and railroad near coast 21 m. S of San Fernando; pop. (1969e) 28,900; one of oldest towns in the Malay Archipelago. Scene of fighting in Japanese invasion Dec. 1941 and on return of American forces Jan. 1945.

Agosta. Commune, Italy. See AUGUSTA.

Agostini, Cordillera de. See ANDES.

Agou, Mount \-ˈä-gü\. Mountain, SW Togo, W Africa; 3937 ft.; highest peak in Togo.

Agout \a-ˈgü\. River, S tributary of Tarn, Hérault and Tarn depts., S France; 112 m. long.

Ago·yan Falls \ä-gə-ˌyän-\. Falls in Pastaza river, Ecuador; 200 ft. high.

Agra \ˈäg-rə\. **1** Former presidency, NE India; a division of Bengal Presidency 1833–35; became 1835 a province with the name of North-West Provinces, which with Oudh was placed under one administrator 1877; now part of Uttar Pradesh (*q.v.*).

2 Former province of India; now the W portion of Uttar Pradesh; 82,176 sq. m.

3 Division, W cen. Uttar Pradesh; 8662 sq. m.; pop. (1961c) 7,179,264; wheat, cotton.

4 District of Agra div.; 1861 sq. m.; pop. (1961c) 1,862,-142.

5 City, ✱ of division and district, on right bank of Yamuna river 115 m. SE of New Delhi; pop. (1970e) 628,070.

History: Captured by Babur, founder of Mogul Empire, 1526; present city created by Muslim conquerors of northern India; stone fort begun by Akbar 1564; Mogul capital until 1658; visited by John Miedenhall, first representative of English East India Company to reach capital 1603; site of magnificent examples of Indo-Saracenic architecture, including Taj Mahal, built c. 1631–45 as tomb of Shah Jahan's empress, the Fort (within which is the imperial palace of Akbar, the Pearl Mosque or Moti Masjid of Shah Jahan, and the Hall of Private Audience or Diwan-i-Khas) and the Tomb of Itmad-ud-Daulah; captured 1784 by Sindhia, a Maratha dynasty; taken 1803 by British under Lake in Second Maratha War; capital of North-West Provinces 1835–62; besieged by sepoys 1857; after removal of capital to Allahabad, became headquarters of district and division of Agra.

Agra and Oudh, United Provinces of. See UTTAR PRADESH.

Agram. See ZAGREB.

Agra·mon·te \ˌäg-rə-ˈmȯn-(ˌ)tā\. Town and municipality, Matanzas prov., W cen. Cuba, SE of Matanzas; munic. pop. (1967e) 9150.

Agri \ˈäg-rē\. River, Basilicata, S Italy; 68 m. long; flows E into the head of Gulf of Taranto.

Ağ·rı \ä(g)-ˈrē\. Province of E Turkey, Asia. See table at TURKEY.

Ağrı Dağı. See ARARAT 3.

Ag·ri Dec·u·ma·tes \ˈag-rī-ˌdek-yə-ˈmāt-ēz\. Roman district, E and N of the upper Rhine and N of the Danube (now lies within Baden-Württemberg, West Germany); taken from Germans as they retired eastward; later given to Gauls and to Roman veterans as tithe lands (Lat. *agri decumates*); incorporated in the Empire 2d cent. A.D.

Agri·gen·to \ˌäg-ri-ˈjen-(ˌ)tō\ *or formerly* **Gir·gen·ti** \jer-ˈjent-ē\. **1** Province of S Sicily, Italy. See table at ITALY.

2 *anc.* **Ag·ri·gen·tum** \ˌag-rə-ˈjent-əm\ *or* **Ac·ra·gas** *or Gk.* **Ak·ra·gas** \ˈak-rə-gəs\. Commune, its ✱, near SW coast 60 m. SSE of Palermo; pop. (1968e) 51,682; archaeological ruins; exports sulfur. Founded by colonists from Gela c. 580 B.C.; destroyed by Carthage 406 B.C.; rebuilt by Timoleon, a leader of Syracuse; scene of defeat of Carthaginian general Hanno by Romans 262 B.C. In World War II taken by Americans July 22, 1943.

Agri·han \ˌäg-rē-ˈhän\ *or* **Agri·gan** \-ˈgän\. Volcanic island, N end of Mariana Is., W Pacific Ocean, 18°46′N lat. and 145°40′E long.; ab. 6 m. long by 2 m. wide; 18 sq. m.; highest point 3166 ft. American and Hawaiian colony formed here 1810, but destroyed by Spanish. Taken by U.S. forces Aug. 1945.

Agri·ni·on \ä-ˈgrēn-ˌyȯn\ *or formerly* **Vra·kho·ri** \vrä-ˈkōr-ē, -ˈkȯr-\. Town, part of Greater Athens, E Greece; pop. (1971p) 32,415; in tobacco-growing region.

Agua \ˈä(g)-wə\. Volcano, SW of Guatemala City, Guatemala; 12,388 ft.

Agua·ca·te \ˌä(g)-wə-ˈkät-ē\. Town and municipality, La Habana prov., W Cuba, 36 m. E of Havana; munic. pop. (1967e) 11,560.

Agua·chi·ca \ˌä(g)-wə-ˈchē-kə\. Municipality, El Cesar dept., N Colombia, 90 m. NNW of Bucaramanga; pop. (1968e) 37,430.

Agua Cla·ra \ˌä(g)-wə-ˈklar-ə, -ˈkler-\. River in Panama E of the Panama Canal.

Agua·da \ə-ˈgwäth-ə\. Town and municipality, NW Puerto Rico, near S shore of Aguadilla Bay; munic. pop. (1970p) 25,166; founded 1511 and claims to be oldest settlement on island; raises sugarcane.

Aguada de Pa·sa·je·ros \-thā-ˌpäs-ə-ˈher-(ˌ)ōs\. Municipality, SW Las Villas prov., Cuba, 30 m. NW of Cienfuegos; pop. (1967e) 37,850.

Agua·das \ə-ˈgwäth-əs\. Town, Caldas dept., W cen. Colombia, 50 m. S of Medellín; munic. pop. (1964c) 37,130.

Agua·dil·la \ˌä(g)-wə-ˈthē-(y)ə\. Seaport and municipality, NW Puerto Rico; pop. (1970p) 21,087 (town), 51,332 (munic.); has extensive trade in fruit and sugar; site of park and memorial. Founded 1775; probably visited by Columbus 1493.

Aguadilla Bay. Bay on W coast of Aguadilla municipality, NW Puerto Rico.

Agua·dul·ce \ˌä(g)-wə-ˈdül-sē\. Town, S cen. Panama; pop. (1970p) 8192.

Agua Fria \ˌä(g)-wə-ˈfrē-ə\. River in Arizona; 120 m. long; rises in cen. Yavapai co., flows S to empty into Gila river in cen. Maricopa co. W of Phoenix.

Aguán \a-ˈgwän\. River, N Honduras; ab. 150 m. long; flows E and NE into Caribbean Sea.

Agua Pri·e·ta \ˌä(g)-wə-prē-ˈät-ə\. Town, Sonora state, NW Mexico; munic. pop. (1970p) 21,627; plan of Agua Prieta 1920 was formal statement of aims of revolutionists seeking to depose Carranza.

Agua·ri·co \ˌä(g)-wə-ˈrē-(ˌ)kō\. River, N Ecuador; ab. 240 m. long; flows ESE into Napo river.

Aguas Bue·nas \ˌä(g)-wəs-ˈbwā-nəs\. Town and municipality, E cen. Puerto Rico; munic. pop. (1970p) 18,702.

Aguas·ca·lien·tes \ˌä(g)-wə-ˌskal-ˈyen-ˌtās\. 1 State, cen. Mexico. See table at MEXICO.

2 City, its ✱, by rail 364 m. NW of Mexico City; munic. pop. (1970p) 222,105; alt. 6193 ft.; mineral springs; built above intricate system of tunnels, probably work of unknown early race; founded 1575; made capital 1835.

Agui·jan \ˌäg-ē-ˈhän\ *or* **Agi·guan** \-ˈgwän\. Small island, S Mariana Islands, W Pacific Ocean, off S end of Tinian I.

Agui·lar \ˌäg-i-ˈlär\ *or* **Aguilar de la Fron·te·ra** \-ˌdel-ə-ˌfrən-ˈter-ə\. Commune, Córdoba prov., S Spain, ab. 25 m. S of Córdoba; pop. (1970p) 13,934; olive groves and vineyards; in Middle Ages on border of Moorish lands.

Agui·las \ˈäg-i-ˌläs\. Seaport, Murcia prov., SE Spain, 40 m. SW of Cartagena; pop. (1970p) 17,389.

Agu·ja, Cape \-ä-ˈgü-hä\ *or Span.* **Ca·bo de la Aguja** \ˈkäb-ō-thā-lä-\. Cape extending into Caribbean Sea on N coast of Colombia, E of Santa Marta.

Aguja, Point *or Span.* **Pun·ta de Aguja** \ˌpün-tə-thā-\. Cape on NW coast of Peru, extending W into the Pacific Ocean.

Agu·je·re·a·da, Point \-ˌäg-ü-ˌhā-rē-ˈäth-ə\. Cape on NW extremity of Puerto Rico, 18°31′N, 67°08′W.

Agul·has, Cape \-ə-ˈgəl-əs\. Most S point of Africa, Cape Province, Rep. of South Africa, 120 m. ESE of Cape Town, at 34°52′S lat., 20°E long. (the meridian that serves as dividing line bet. Atlantic and Indian Oceans); lighthouse.

Agulhas Current. See MOZAMBIQUE CURRENT.

Agulhas Ne·gras, Pi·co das \ˈpē-kō-däs-ə-ˈgül-yəs-ˈnā-grəs\. Peak in Mantiqueira range, SE Brazil, at junction of boundaries of the states of São Paulo, Minas Gerais, and Rio de Janeiro; 9141 ft.

Agung, Gu·nung \ˈgü-ˌnüŋ-ˈäg-üŋ\ *or Du.* **Goe·noeng Agoeng** \ˈgü-ˌnüŋ-ˈäg-ˌüŋ\ *or* **Peak of Ba·li** \-ˈbäl-ē\. Volcano, NE Bali, Indonesia; 10,308 ft.; erupted 1963.

Agu·san \ä-ˈgü-ˌsän\. 1 River, E Mindanao, Phil.; 240 m. long; rises in highlands of SE Davao del Norte and flows N to Butuan Bay; forms fertile valley 40 to 50 m. wide; navigable in lower course.

2 Former province, NE Mindanao, Phil.; ✱ Butuan; now divided into two provs., **Agusan del Nor·te** \-del-ˈnȯrt-ē\ and **Agusan del Sur** \-del-ˈsü(ə)r\ (see table at PHILIPPINES); largely coextensive with wide fertile valley of Agusan river; in NE includes ab. two thirds of Lake Mainit; mountainous along E and W boundaries, esp. Diuata Mts., highest Mt. Hilonghilong 6599 ft.; in S is large marsh and lake region in middle course of Agusan river; produces abaca, coconuts, corn, timber. In Spanish times a part of Surigao prov.; established as separate province by Americans Sept. 1914; missionaries active on lower Agusan in 17th and 18th cents.; later often suffered from raids of Moros; divided into two provinces 1967.

Agu·ta·ya \ˌäg-ü-ˈtī-ə\. Island in Cuyo group, Palawan prov., Phil., N of Cuyo I.; 6 sq. m.

Agylla. See CERVETERI.

Agyrium. See AGIRA.

Ahag·gar Mountains \ə-ˈhag-ər-, ˌä-hə-ˈgär-\ *or* **Hog·gar Mountains** \ˈhäg-ər-, hə-ˈgär-\. High plateau region in cen. Sahara, S Oasis dept., S Algeria; highest peak 9842 ft.

Ahi·pa·ra Bay \ī-ˌpär-ə-\. Bay on extreme NW coast of N extension of North Island, New Zealand.

Ah·len \ˈäl-ən\. City, North Rhine-Westphalia, West Germany, 17 m. SE of Münster; pop. (1969e) 45,175; enamelware, shoes; coal mining.

Ah·mad·a·bad *or* **Ah·med·a·bad** \ˈäm-əd-ə-ˌbäd\. 1 District, Gujarat state, NW India; 3461 sq. m.; pop. (1961c) 2,231,534.

2 City, its ✱ and ✱ of Gujarat state, on left bank of Sabarmati river 290 m. N of Bombay; pop. (1970e) 1,550,779; cotton, glass, silk, tobacco; univ. (1949); many well-known monuments and buildings, including: Jama Masjid (Great Mosque) and Tomb of Ahmad Shah, Hathi Singh Jain temple (built 1848).

History: Founded in 1411 by Ahmad I of Gujarat on site of previous Hindu cities; built 1411–42; at height in 15th cent. as capital of Gujarat kingdom; declined 1512–72 with Gujarat dynasty; revived under Mogul emperors 1572–1707; reverted to British with other holdings of Peshwa 1818; became modern manufacturing and trading center, esp. noted for cotton textiles; associated with Indian nationalist cause as scene of an anti-British rebellion 1918 and of beginning of Gandhi's efforts 1930 and his arrest 1933.

Ahmadi, Al–. See AL-AHMADI.

Ah·mad·na·gar *or* **Ah·med·na·gar** \ˌäm-əd-ˈnəg-ər\. 1 District, Maharashtra state, W cen. India; 6591 sq. m.; pop. (1961c) 1,771,066.

2 City, its ✱, 130 m. E of Bombay; pop. (1970e) 133,529; textiles.

History: Founded 1490 as one of the five Muslim kingdoms of the Deccan (*q.v.*); conquered by Shah Jahan 1636 when it became part of Mogul Empire; exchanged several times between British and Marathas in wars of 18th cent.; seized by Gen. Wellesley 1803; ceded to British by Treaty of Poona 1817; has fort and cantonment.

Aho·me \ä-ˈ(h)ōm-ē\. Municipality, Sinaloa state, W Mexico; pop. (1970p) 165,612.

Ahos·kie \ə-ˈhäs-kē\. Town, Hertford co., NE North Carolina, 44 m. W of Elizabeth City; pop. (1970c) 5105; cotton, lumber, peanuts, tobacco.

Ah·rens·burg \ˈär-ənz-ˌbərg, -ˌbu̇(ə)rg\. City, Schleswig-Holstein, West Germany, 22 m. SW of Lübeck; pop. (1969e) 25,599; cigarettes; printing; founded in 13th cent.

Ahua·cha·pán \ˌä-wə-chə-ˈpän\. 1 Department of SW El Salvador. See table at EL SALVADOR.

2 Town, its ✱, near Guatemala border; pop. (1968e) 25,556; alt. 2470 ft.; has trade in coffee and tobacco; hot mineral waters nearby.

Ahua·lul·co de Mer·ca·do \ˌä-wə-ˈlül-ˌkō-ˌdā-mər-ˈkäd-ˌō\. Town, Jalisco state, W cen. Mexico, 38 m. W of Guadalajara; munic. pop. (1970p) 15,439.

Ahu·ri·ri \ˌä-hü-ˈri(ə)r-ē, au̇-\. River, S cen. South Island, New Zealand; one of the headstreams of the Waitaki.

Ah·vāz \ä-ˈväz\ *or* **Ah·waz** \ä-ˈwäz\. Town, ✱ of Khūzestān prov., SW Iran, on the Kārūn river ab. 70 m. NNE of Khorramshahr; pop. (1971e) 215,000; connected by rail with Persian Gulf port of Bandar-e Shāhpūr; has oil pipelines; important commercially, esp. in oil business. Under the Arabs in 12th and 13th cents. was a trade center for sugar, rice, and silk; modern town laid out on extensive ruined area of ancient Persian city.

Ah·ve·nan·maa \ˈä(k)-və-nän-ˌmä\ *or* **Åland Islands** \ˌō-ˌländ-\. Archipelago in S Gulf of Bothnia bet. Sweden and Finland, constituting a province of Finland (see table at FINLAND); ✱ Maarianhamina; of ab. 300 total islands and rocky islets, ab. 80 inhabited; chief island **Ahvenanmaa** *or* **Åland.**

History: Colonized early (12th cent.) by Swedes; Swedish fleet defeated and islands seized by Peter the Great 1714; restored by Russia to Sweden 1721; ceded with Finland by Sweden to Russia 1809; subject of international disputes and treaties in 19th cent.; part of independent Finland 1917; neutralized and demilitarized by treaty 1921–22.

Ahwaz. See AHVĀZ.

Ai \ˈā-ˌī, ˈī\. Town in mountains of E Canaan, ancient Palestine, SE of Bethel; destroyed by Joshua (*Josh.* vii–viii).

Ai·bo·ni·to \ˌī-bə-ˈnēt-(ˌ)ō\. Town and municipality, SE cen. Puerto Rico, 30 m. NW of Guayama; pop. (1970p) 7564 (town), 19,834 (munic.).

Ai·chi \ˈī-ˌchē\. Prefecture, Honshū, Japan; 1955 sq. m.; pop. (1970c) 5,386,163; ✱ Nagoya; important industrial area; automobiles, ceramics, cotton textiles.

Aidin. See AYDIN.

Ai·ea \ī-ˈā-ə\. City, Honolulu co., S Oahu, Hawaii, on E shore of Pearl Harbor; pop. (1970c) 12,560.

Aigaion Pelagos. See AEGEAN SEA.

Ai·gi·on \ˈā-ˌyōn\ *or* **Ae·gi·um** \ˈē-jē-əm\ *or Gk.* **Aí·yion** \ˈā-ˌyōn\. Seaport town, Achaea dept., NW Peloponnesus, Greece, on Gulf of Corinth.

Aigues–Mortes \eg-ˈmȯ(ə)rt\ *or, anc.* **Aq·uae Mor·tu·ae** \ˌak-wē-ˈmȯr-chə-ˌwē, ˌäk-\. Commune, Gard dept., S France, in Rhone estuary 25 m. SSW of Nîmes; pop. (1968c) 3776. Founded by St. Louis who connected it by canal with Gulf of Lions and used it as embarkation point for Sixth Crusade 1248 and Seventh Crusade 1270; fortified 1272 by Philip the Bold; of little importance today except for Tour de Constance and fine medieval military ramparts.

Aiguille d'Argentière. See ARGENTIÈRE, AIGUILLE D'.

Aiguille de Chambeyron. See CHAMBEYRON, AIGUILLE DE.

Ai–hui \ˈī-ˈhwē\ *also* **Ta·hei·ho** \ˈtä-ˈhā-ˈhə\ *or Jap.* **Hei·ho** \ˈhā-ˈhə\. Town, NE Heilungkiang prov., NE China, on the Amur river; ✱ of former Heiho prov.

Ai–hun \(ˌ)ī-ˈhün\ *or* **Ai·gun** \(ˌ)ī-ˈgün\. City, NE Heilungkiang prov., NE China, on the Amur river 20 m. below and S of Blagoveshchensk, U.S.S.R. By treaty signed here 1858 China ceded left bank of Amur and right bank below the Ussuri to Russia; destruction by fire 1900 followed by decline in trade.

Ai·ja·lon \ˈā-jə-ˌlän, ˈī-\ *or* **Aj·a·lon** \ˈaj-ə-\. Town in valley of Aijalon, anc. Palestine, 13 m. NW of Jerusalem. On frontier of kingdoms of Ephraim and Judah; valley scene of Biblical episode in which Joshua commanded the sun and moon to stand still (*Josh.* x. 12); assigned to tribe of Dan.

Ai·ken \ˈā-kən\. 1 County in W South Carolina. See table at SOUTH CAROLINA.

2 City, its ⊗, 52 m. SW of Columbia; pop. (1970c) 13,436; winter resort; textile and lumber mills; fertilizers; in farming region. Scene of battle bet. Union and Confederate troops Feb. 1865.

Ai·lette \ā-ˈlet\. River, Aisne dept., N France, tributary of Oise from SE near Laon; ab. 40 m. long; in World War I severe fighting along its banks Oct. 1917 and Sept. 1918.

Aimorés, Serra dos. See SERRA DOS AIMORÉS.

Ain \a^n\. 1 River, E France; 118 m. long; rises in Jura Mts. and flows S into Rhone river.

2 Department of E France. See table at FRANCE.

Aïn Beï·da \(ˈ)īn-ˈbād-ə, (ˈ)ān-\. Commune, Constantine dept., NE Algeria, 50 m. SE of Constantine; pop. (1966c) 30,757; founded 1848.

Ain Ja·lut *or Arab.* **ʻAyn Jā·lūt** \ˌīn-jə-ˈlüt, ˌān-\. Locality near Nazareth, N Israel; here in 1260 Mongol army of Hulagu destroyed by the Mamelukes of Egypt, and Syria recovered.

Aïn Se·fra \ˌīn-sə-ˈfrä, ˌān-\. Commune in Atlas Mts., NW Algeria, 200 m. S of Oran; pop. (1966c) 16,818.

Ains·worth \ˈānz-ˌwərth\. City, ⊗ of Brown co., N Nebraska, 65 m. W of O'Neill; pop. (1970c) 2073; trade center for agricultural region.

Aintab. See GAZİANTEP 2.

Aïn Té·mou·chent \ˈīn-ˌtā-mü-ˈshä^n\. Commune, Oran dept., NW Algeria, ab. 45 m. SW of Oran; pop. (1966c) 30,462.

Ain·tree \ˈān-trē\. Locality, 5 m. N of Liverpool, Lancashire, England; racecourse where Grand National steeplechase is run every March.

Ai–pi \ˈī-ˈpē\ *also* **Ebi Nor** \ˌā-bē-ˈnȯ(ə)r\. Salt lake (*nor*), W Dzungaria, NW Sinkiang Uighur, W China, bet. the Dzungarian Ala Tau Mts. and N ranges of Tien Shan; alt. 2300 ft.

Aïr \ä-ˈi(ə)r, ˈi(ə)r\ *also* **Az·bine** \az-ˈbēn\ *or* **As·ben** \az-ˈben\. Mountainous region, N cen. Niger, W Africa; ab. 30,000 sq. m.; highest peaks ab. 5000 ft.; former native kingdom; main products dates, millet, and senna. Inhabited by Tuaregs; a native kingdom, called Asben, until conquered by Berbers; recognized as in French sphere from 1890.

Air, Point of \-ˈa(ə)r, -ˈe(ə)r\. Point at mouth of Dee river, Flintshire, NE Wales.

Aira Force \ˌar-ə-ˈfō(ə)rs, ˌer-, -ˈfȯ(ə)rs\ *or* **Air·ey Force** \ˌar-ē-, ˌer-ē-\. Waterfall (Scot. *force*), Cumberland, NW England; 80 ft. high; in small stream flowing into Ullswater Lake, in the Lake District.

Air·drie \ˈa(ə)r-drē, ˈe(ə)r-\. Burgh, Lanark co., S cen. Scotland, 11 m. E of Glasgow; pop. (1969e) 36,188; deposits of coal and iron nearby; cotton mills, engineering works.

Aire \ˈa(ə)r, ˈe(ə)r\. 1 River, W Yorkshire, England; 70 m. long; flows SE and E through Leeds and industrial region to Ouse river; navigable to Leeds. **Aire·dale** \-ˌdāl\, valley of the Aire, original home of the Airedale terrier.

2 River, Meuse and Ardennes depts., NE France; ab. 80 m. long; flows NW through the Argonne to Aisne river near Vouziers; severe fighting on its banks in World War I.

3 *anc.* **Vi·cus Ju·lii** \ˌvī-kəs-ˈjü-lē-ˌī\ *or later* **Atu·ra** \ə-ˈtu̇r-ə\. Commune, Landes dept., SW France, on left bank of Adour ab. 20 m. SE of Mont-de-Marsan; pop. (1962c) 5528; residence of the kings of the Visigoths; bishopric in 5th cent., later an episcopal town.

Aire·bor·ough \ˈa(ə)r-ˌbər-ə, ˈe(ə)r-, -ˌbə-rə, -b(ə-)rə\. Urban district, West Riding, Yorkshire, N England; pop. (1971p) 29,477.

Airey Force. See AIRA FORCE.

Ai·ro·lo \ī-ˈrō-(ˌ)lō, -ˈrȯ-\. Commune, Ticino canton, SE cen. Switzerland, at S end of St. Gotthard Tunnel in valley of Ticino river; pop. (1970c) 2140.

Aisén. See AYSÉN.

Ai·shi·hik \ˈā-shi-ˌhik\. Lake, SW Yukon, Canada; 107 sq. m.; outlet through Alsek river to the Pacific.

Aisne \ˈān\ *or anc.* **Ax·o·na** \ˈak-sə-nə\. 1 River, N France; 165 m. long; rises in Meuse dept., flows NW and W from Argonne Forest to Oise near Compiègne. Four major battles in valley in World War I: (1) Defeat of Germans Sept. 15–18, 1914 in their retreat from the Marne; (2) French seizure Apr.–July 1917 of heights (Chemin des Dames) N of Aisne; (3) German capture of heights May–June 1918; (4) Final defeat of Germans by French and Americans Sept.–Oct. 1918. In World War II crossed Aug. 1944 by American troops in pursuit of Germans.

2 Department of N France. See table at FRANCE.

Ai·ta·pe *also* **Ei·ta·pe** \ˌī-tä-ˈpā, ī-ˈtä-pā\. Seaport town, Papua New Guinea, on N coast of New Guinea; pop. (1966p) 540; government station. American forces landed here and at Hollandia April 22, 1944; airfields taken; large Japanese force cut off.

Ait·kin \ˈā-kən\. 1 County, E cen. Minnesota. See table at MINNESOTA.

2 Village, its ⊗, on Mississippi river 26 m. ENE of Brainerd; pop. (1970c) 1553; shipping center for dairy products, turkeys, and small fruits.

Aitolia. See AETOLIA.

Aitolía kai Akarnanía. See AETOLIA AND ACARNANIA.

Ai·tu·ta·ki \ˌīt-ə-ˈtäk-ē\. Island, NW Cook Islands (*q.v.*), S Pacific Ocean, NW of Rarotonga; 18°52′S lat., 159°45′W long.; 7 sq. m.; pop. (1968e) 2834; has wide surrounding reef and large lagoon (5 m. across); second to Rarotonga in importance.

Aiud \ˈä-ˌyüd\ *or Hung.* **Nag·yen·yed** \nȯj-ˈen-yed\ *or Ger.* **Strass·burg** \ˈs(h)träs-ˌbu̇(ə)rg\. Town, Alba co., Romania, on Mureşul river 20 m. NNE of Alba Iulia; pop. (1966c) 19,534.

Aivali. See AYVALIK.

Aix \ˈāks\ *or* **Aix–en–Pro·vence** \ˌāk-ˌsäⁿ-prō-ˈväⁿs\ *or anc.* **Aquae Sex·ti·ae** \ˌak-ˌwē-ˈsek-stē-ˌē, ˌäk-\. City, Bouches-du-Rhône dept., SE France, 19 m. N of Marseilles; pop. (1968c) 89,556; tourism; cathedral, palace, univ. (1413, reconstituted 1896).

History: Founded as military colony by Romans 123 B.C.; scene of defeat 102 B.C. of the Teutones by Marius; chief city of E Narbonensis (4th cent.); occupied by Visigoths 477, by Saracens 731; in Middle Ages as capital of Provence reached high cultural levels; became part of France 1487; seat of parlement of Provence 1501–1789.

Aix–la–Chapelle. See AACHEN 2.

Aix–les–Bains \e(k)s-lā-baⁿ\ *or anc.* **Aquae Gra·ti·a·nae** \ˈak-(ˌ)wē-ˌgrā-shē-ˈan-(ˌ)ē, -ˈän-, -ˈān-; ˈäk-(ˌ)wē-ˌgrät-ē-ˈän-(ˌ)ē\. Commune, Savoie dept., E France, on SE shore of Lake Bourget 9 m. N of Chambéry; pop. (1968c) 20,627; resort; its sulfur baths famous in Roman times.

Ai·yá·leo \ā-ˈyäl-ē-ˌō\. City, part of Greater Athens, E Greece; pop. (1961c) 57,840.

Aíyina. See AEGINA.

Aíyion. See AIGION.

Ai·zu·wa·ka·mat·su \ˈī-(ˌ)zü-ˌwäk-ə-ˈmät-(ˌ)sü\. City, cen. Fukushima prefecture, Honshū, Japan; pop. (1970c) 104,065.

Ajac·cio \ä-ˈyäch-(ˌ)ō\. Seaport commune, ✱ of Corse dept. (coextensive with island of Corsica), France, on N side of **Gulf of Ajaccio** on W coast of Corsica; pop. (1968c) 40,834; tourist center; exports fruit and timber; episcopal see; became French 1768 (see CORSICA); birthplace of Napoleon; departmental capital 1810; Allied naval base in World War I.

Ajai·garh \ə-ˈjī-ˌgär, -gər\. Former Indian state, cen. India; 788 sq. m.; now part of Madhya Pradesh.

Ajalon. See AIJALON.

Ajan·ta \ə-ˈjənt-ə\. Village in hills of cen. Maharashtra, S cen. India, NNE of Aurangabad; nearby are ab. 30 remarkable caves, the earliest dating from 200 B.C. to 200 A.D. and the latest from 7th cent. A.D., comprising halls and dormitories with walls covered with fresco paintings; caves discovered 1817, excavated by Buddhists.

Ajanta Range. Range of hills, cen. India, extending across N cen. Maharashtra; watershed for tributaries of Tapti and Godavari rivers.

Ajax \ˈā-ˌjaks\. Town, Ontario co., SE Ontario, Canada, on Lake Erie 27 m. NE of Toronto; pop. (1971p) 12,509; chemicals, electronic equipment, pumps; dairy farming.

Ajax Mountain. Peak in Bitterroot Range on Montana-Idaho state boundary; 10,900 ft.

Aj·dā·bi·yah \äj-ˈdäb-ē-(y)ə\ *also* **Ag·e·da·bia** \ˌäj-ə-ˈdäb-ē-ə\. Road junction, near E coast of Gulf of Sidra, N Libya; battle Jan. 1942 bet. British and Germans in first retreat of Rommel's Afrika Korps.

Aj·dir, Cape \-aj-ˈdi(ə)r\ *or Arab.* **Ras Ajdīr** \räs-\. Cape extending into the Mediterranean Sea, on border between Tunisia and Libya.

Aji·ka·wa \äj-i-ˈkä-wə\. See YODO 2.

Aj·man \aj-ˈman\. 1 Sheikhdom. See UNITED ARAB EMIRATES.

2 Coastal town, its ✱; pop. (1968c) 3725.

Aj·mer \ˌəj-ˈmi(ə)r, -ˈme(ə)r\ *or* **Aj·mere** \-ˈmi(ə)r\. 1 *or formerly* **Ajmer–Mer·wa·ra** \-mer-ˈwär-ə\. District, Rajasthan, NW India; 3283 sq. m.; pop. (1961c) 976,547.

2 City, Rajasthan, NW India, 84 m. SW of Jaipur; pop. (1970e) 269,233; situated at base of rocky hill Taragarh (3000 ft.); conducts large trade in salt; manufactures oils and cotton cloths, and is noted for its dyeing of the latter.

History: Founded c. 145 A.D.; stronghold of Chauhan Rajputs until 12th cent.; conquered 1193 by the Muslim dynasty at Delhi (*q.v.*); feudal state dependent upon Delhi until 1365; ruled by Udaipur (*q.v.*) until captured by Mogul emperor Akbar 1556; in 1770 given to Marathas under whom it was scene of violent upheavals until ceded to British 1818 by Maratha ruler of Gwalior after the Pindari War; has notable ruins, esp. dargah (tomb) of famous Muslim saint.

Ajmer–Merwara. See AJMER 1.

Aj·na·da·in \ˌaj-nə-ˈdā-ən\ *or* **Jan·na·ba·ta·in** \ˌjän-ə-bə-ˈtā-ən\. Village, anc. Palestine, just SW of Jerusalem; scene of victory 634 A.D. by Arabs over Theodorus, brother of Byzantine emperor Heraclius, which opened way for Muslim conquest of Syria.

Ajo \ˈä-(ˌ)hō\. Town (unincorporated), Pima co., S Arizona; pop. (1970c) 5881; mining.

Ajodh·ya *also* **Ayodh·ya** \ə-ˈyōd-yə\. Former town, United Provs., N India, on right bank of Ghaghara river 6 m. E of Faizābād; now part of that city (now in Uttar Pradesh). In ancient times one of the greatest of Indian cities; capital of kingdom of Kosala, as described in the *Ramayana;* a revived Brahmanism under King Vikramaditya restored it c. 57 B.C. and ab. 400 A.D. it became capital of Chandragupta II; birthplace of founder of Jainism and center of pilgrimages. From it modern Oudh derives its name.

Ajus·co \ä-ˈhüs-(ˌ)kō\. Volcanic mountain, Federal District, Mexico, S of Mexico City and just N of Cuernavaca; 12,887 ft.

Akaba. See ʻAQABA.

Aka·gi \ä-ˈkäg-ē\ *or Jap.* **Aka·gi·san** \-ˈsän\. Group of peaks, cen. Honshū, Japan; highest point 5996 ft.; surrounds a volcanic crater, **Lake Akagi**.

Akai·shi \ä-ˈkīsh-ē\. Peak, N part of Shizuoka prefecture, cen. Honshū, Japan; 10,234 ft.

Aka·koa Point \ˌäk-ə-ˌkō-ə-\. Cape on N coast of Hawaii I., Hawaii.

Akal·kot \ˈək-əl-ˌkōt, ə-ˈkəl-\. 1 Former state, W India; 473 sq. m.; now part of Maharashtra.
2 Town, 25 m. SE of Sholapur, Maharashtra, India.

Akamagaseki. See SHIMONOSEKI.

Aká·mas, Cape \-ə-ˈkäm-əs\. Cape, most westerly part of Cyprus.

Akarnanía. See ACARNANIA.

Aka·roa \ˌäk-ə-ˈrō-ə\. Borough and administrative co., E South Island, New Zealand, 30 m. SSE of Christchurch on **Akaroa Harbor,** an inlet in Banks Peninsula; co. pop. (1968e) 1550; claimed by British 1840 a few days before arrival of French; some of French immigrants remained and descendants still live here.

Aka·shi \ä-ˈkäsh-ē\. City, Hyōgo prefecture, W Honshū, Japan, on coast 12 m. W of Kōbe; pop. (1970c) 206,525; electrical equipment, farm implements; separated from N end of Awaji I. by **Akashi Strait,** E end of Inland Sea; its meridian 135°E is standard time meridian for Japan.

Akas·sa \ə-ˈkäs-ə\. Village, East-Central State, Nigeria, at mouth of Niger. See BRASS.

Ak·dağ *or* **Ak Dağ** \ˈäk-ˈdä(g)\. Name of several mountains in Turkey in Asia, esp.: (1) Range in cen. part W of Sıvas, highest point 8860 ft. (2) Peak 10,125 ft., SW of Antalya near coast. (3) Peak 9350 ft., in Taurus Mts. E of Cilician Gates. (4) Peak 8186 ft., SSW of Afyonkarahisar.

Ak·dar, Je·bel \ˌjeb-əl-ak-ˈdär\. Mountain range, Oman, SE Arabian Penin.; highest peak Jebel Sham, 9927 ft.

Akers·hus *also* **Ag·gers·hus** \ˈäk-ərs-ˌhüs\. County of E Norway. See table at NORWAY.

Ak Göl \ˌäk-ˈgə(ə)l\. Salt lake (*göl*), S cen. Turkey in Asia, N of Taurus Mts.

Akhaïa. See ACHAEA.

Akhal·tsi·khe \ə-ˈkält-si-ˌka\. Town, S Georgian S.S.R., U.S.S.R., near left bank of upper Kura river 65 m. E of Batumi; pop. (1967e) 18,000; trades in silk and, especially, in silver filigree work. Capital of Turkish Armenia 1579–1828; chief town of a pashalik of Ottoman Empire and center of slave trade; district ceded to Russia by Treaty of Adrianople 1829.

Akharnaí. See ACHARNAE.

Akhelóos. See ACHELOUS.

Akhi·nou, Lake \-ˌäk-i-ˈnü\ *also* **Lake Ta·khi·no** \-ˈtäk-i-ˌnō\ *or anc.* **Ker·ki·ni·tis** \ˌkər-kə-ˈnīt-əs\. Drained lake, E cen. Macedonia, Greece; town of Serrai is near its N end.

Ak·hi·sar \ˌäk-(h)is-ˈär\ *or anc.* **Thy·a·ti·ra** \ˌthī-ə-ˈtī-rə\. Town, N Manisa prov., W Turkey in Asia, 52 m. NE of İzmir; pop. (1965c) 46,167; exports cotton, tobacco, wool. Ancient Greek city of Thyatira in Lydia was colonized and named 280 B.C. by Seleucus Nicator; its inhabitants famous for skill in dyeing purple; one of the Seven Churches of Asia Minor (*Rev.* i. 4, ii. 18–24).

Akh·mīm *or* **Ekh·mīm** \ˌək-ˈmēm\; *anc.* **Chem·mis** \ˈkem-əs\ *or later* **Pa·nop·o·lis** \pə-ˈnäp-ə-ləs\. Town on right bank of Nile river, Sawhaj gov., Egypt, 66 m. S of Asyūt; pop. (1966c) 44,800; textiles. Chemmis an important city of the Thebais; famous for its manufacture of linen and its limestone quarries; religious center, with temple of Pan.

Akhtiar. See SEVASTOPOL.

Akh·tyr·ka \äk-ˈti(ə)r-kə\. Town, Sumy Oblast, N Ukrainian S.S.R., U.S.S.R., ab. 65 m. WNW of Kharkov; pop. (1967e) 39,000; cathedral (1753).

Aki \ˈäk-ē\. Former province, SW Honshū, Japan; now part of Hiroshima prefecture.

Ak·i·mis·ki Island \ˌak-ə-ˌmis-kē-\. Island in James Bay, Northwest Territories, Canada, opp. mouth of Attawapiskat river, S Hudson Bay, Keewatin dist.; 1137 sq. m.

Aki·shi·ma \ˌäk-i-ˈshē-mə, ä-ˈkē-shi-mə\. City, Tokyo prefecture, Honshū, Japan, 23 m. WNW of Tokyo; pop. (1970c) 75,662.

Aki·ta \ä-ˈkēt-ə\. 1 Prefecture, Honshū, Japan; 4482 sq. m.; pop. (1970c) 1,241,376; rice, lumber.
2 City, its ✱, on right bank of Omono river near its mouth; pop. (1970c) 235,873; univ. (1949); petroleum products.

Ak·kad *or* **Ac·cad** \ˈak-ˌad, ˈäk-ˌäd\. 1 The northern division of ancient Babylonia. From about 4th millennium B.C., inhabited by a leading Semitic people called the Akkadians; after a period of Sumerian rule (see SUMER) under Sargon I and Naram-Sin, developed empire which included Sumer, Elam, the upper Tigris, and northern Syria to the Mediterranean c. 2600–2420 B.C.; adopted Sumerian culture and developed great art (relief of Naram-Sin); lost supremacy after invasion by Gutians c. 2420 B.C.; united with Sumer under latter's leadership; invaded by Amorites (see BABYLON 2).
2 *or anc.* **Aga·de** \ə-ˈgäd-ə\. Ancient city, its ✱, in cen. Mesopotamia, placed by some near Sippar, Sargon's capital.

Akkerman. See BELGOROD-DNESTROVSKI.

ʻAkko. See ACRE.

Aklan \ä-ˈklän\. Province, Panay I., Phil. (see table at PHILIPPINES); rice; formed 1957.

Akla·vik \ə-ˈkläv-ik, -ˈklav-\. Community on left bank of Mackenzie river near its mouth, NW Mackenzie dist., Northwest Territories, Canada; pop. (1966c) 611.

Ak Mechet. See SIMFEROPOL.

Akmolinsk. See TSELINOGRAD.

Akmolinsk Oblast. See TSELINOGRAD OBLAST.

Ako·bo \ə-ˈkō-(ˌ)bō\. 1 River on border bet. Ethiopia and SE Sudan, E cen. Africa; 270 m. long; flows NW into Pibor river.
2 Town, Upper Nile prov., SE Sudan, at confluence of Akobo and Pibor rivers on border of Ethiopia.

Ako·la \ə-ˈkō-lə\. 1 District, Maharashtra, India; 4095 sq. m.; pop. (1961c) 1,189,354.
2 City, its ✱, 140 m. WSW of Nagpur; pop. (1970e) 147,293; center of cotton trade.

Ak·pa·tok Island \ˌak-pə-ˌtäk-\. Island at mouth of Ungava Bay, SE Franklin dist., E Northwest Territories, Canada; 296 sq. m.

Akragas. See AGRIGENTO 2.

Ákra Sidhirókastron. See SIDEROKASTRON.

Akrítas. See GALLO, CAPE.

Akroïnon. See ACROÏNUM.

Ak·ron \ˈak-rən\. 1 Town, ⊗ of Washington co., NE Colorado; pop. (1970c) 1775; dairy products.
2 Village, Erie co., W New York, ab. 22 m. ENE of Buffalo; pop. (1970c) 2863; cement factory.
3 Manufacturing and industrial city, ⊗ of Summit co., NE Ohio, 35 m. SE of Cleveland on Little Cuyahoga river; pop. (1970c) 275,425; on old Indian Portage Trail bet. Cuyahoga and Tuscarawas rivers; rubber, chemicals, aircraft; trucking center; Univ. of Akron (1913); settled ab. 1825, incorporated as village 1836, made county seat 1842, granted charter as city 1865; first rubber factory estab. 1869 by Dr. B. F. Goodrich; after 1910 began phenomenal growth due to demand for tires and other rubber goods.
4 Borough, Lancaster co., SE Pennsylvania, 11 m. NE of Lancaster; pop. (1970c) 3149.

Akro·te·ri Peninsula \ˌak-rə-ˈti(ə)r-ē-\. Peninsula, on N coast of Crete near W end, Greece; Canea is at its base on the W and Suda Bay enclosed by it on SE; ab. 10 m. long.

Akro·ti·ri Bay \ˌäk-rə-ˌti(ə)r-ē-\. Inlet of Mediterranean Sea on S coast of Cyprus; Limassol is on it.

Ak·sa·ray \ˌäk-sə-ˈrī\. Town, N Niğde prov., S cen. Turkey, 85 m. NE of Konya; highway junction point SE of Tuz Lake; pop. (1965c) 24,414.

Ak·şe·hir \ˌäk-shə-ˈhi(ə)r\ *or formerly* **Ak·shehr** \äk-ˈshe(ə)r\ *or anc.* **Phil·o·me·li·on** \ˌfil-ə-ˈmē-lē-ən\. Town, Konya prov., SW cen. Turkey, on railroad 70 m. NW of Konya; pop. (1965c) 25,269; on ancient highway in fertile plain S of Akşehir Gölü; known to Cicero and important as frontier town under Byzantine emperors; became a Seljuk town ab. 1400.

Akşehir Gö·lü \-gə-ˈlue̅\. Lake, W cen. Turkey in Asia, E of Afyonkarahisar.

Ak·su \ˈäk-ˈsü\. **1** River, SW Turkey; ab. 80 m. long; flows S into Gulf of Antalya.

2 *also* **Aq·su** \ˈäk-ˈsü\ *or Chin.* **Wen–su** \ˈwən-ˈsü\. Town, Sinkiang Uighur, W China, at foot of Tien Shan range; Mongol capital in 14th cent.

Ak·sum *or* **Ax·um** \ˈäk-ˌsüm\. Town, Tigre prov., N Ethiopia, 5 m. WSW of Adwa; pop. (1970e) 12,804.

History: Capital of ancient Ethiopian kingdom known as the Axumite Empire which was ruled by Himyaritic emigrants from Arabia, 1st and 2d cents. A.D.; religious center which contained, according to tradition, the Ark of the Covenant brought from Jerusalem by descendant of Solomon and Queen of Sheba.

Aktí. See ACTE.

Ak·tyu·binsk \äk-ˈtyü-bin(t)sk\. Town, ✻ of Aktyubinsk Oblast, W cen. Kazakh S.S.R., U.S.S.R.; pop. (1970p) 150,000; engineering works, flour mills, stockyards; founded 1869.

Aktyubinsk Oblast. Subdivision of Kazakh S.S.R., U.S.S.R., in W cen. part; 115,753 sq. m.; pop. (1970p) 550,000; ✻ Aktyubinsk; livestock rearing; chrome and nickel; steppe region traversed by Emba and Irgiz rivers, by the Orenburg-Tashkent R.R. and by oil pipelines.

Akun \ˈäk-ˌün\. Island, Aleutian Is., Alaska, just NE of Akutan I.; 63 sq. m.; separated on NE from Unimak I. by Unimak Pass.

Aku·re \ä-ˈku̇(ə)r-ē\. Town, Western State, Nigeria, ab. 130 m. NE of Lagos; pop. (1969e) 82,461.

Akur·ey·ri \ˈäk-ə-ˌrā-rē\. Town on Eyja Fjord, N Iceland; pop. (1970c) 10,755; 3d largest town in Iceland; incorporated 1786.

Aku·tan \ə-ˈkü-tan\. One of the Fox Islands, Aleutian Is., Alaska; 127 sq. m.; an active volcano 4244 ft. high; separated on SW from Unalaska I. by **Akutan Pass.**

Akyab. See SITTWE.

Al·a·bama \ˌal-ə-ˈbam-ə\. **1** Navigable river, Alabama; 315 m. long; formed by confluence of Tallapoosa and Coosa rivers, flows SW from cen. Alabama to join the Tombigbee and form the Mobile and Tensaw rivers flowing into Mobile Bay at Mobile.

2 A southern state of U.S.A., bounded on N by Tennessee, on E by Georgia, on S by Florida and the Gulf of Mexico, and on W by Mississippi; 29th state in area, 51,609 sq. m. (land area 50,851 sq. m.); 21st state in population, (1970c) 3,444,165; ✻ Montgomery; 22d state admitted to Union (1819).

Nicknames: The Cotton State; Yellowhammer State; Heart of Dixie. *State flower:* Camellia. *Motto:* We Dare Defend Our Rights. *Rivers:* Mobile, formed by Alabama and Tombigbee; Alabama (see 1, above); Tombigbee, formed by junction of E and W forks in NE Mississippi; Tennessee, flowing W across N counties (for great dams, see TENNESSEE river and TENNESSEE VALLEY AUTHORITY); Chattahoochee forming SE boundary with Georgia; Conecuh and Pea, in S and SE part. Mobile and Tensaw (part of its estuary) flow into Mobile Bay, arm of Gulf of Mexico. Martin lake in E is expansion of Tallapoosa river.

Mountains: S end of Appalachian Mts. (chief ranges Raccoon and Lookout) in NE corner extending as far as Birmingham. Highest point Cheaha Mt. 2407 ft., in Cleburne co. *Chief products:* Cotton, corn, soybeans, peanuts; livestock; coal, iron ore, limestone, bauxite, petroleum; manufacturing: iron and steel, chemicals, textiles, paper. *Chief cities:* Birmingham, Mobile, Huntsville, Montgomery, Tuscaloosa, Prichard. See *Table of States* at UNITED STATES. Divided into the following 67 counties (for pronunciation of their names, see their individual entries):

NAME	LOCATION	AREA[1] (sq. m.)	POP. (1970c)	CO. SEAT
Autauga	cen.	599	24,460	Prattville
Baldwin	SW; coastal	1,758	59,382	Bay Minette
Barbour	SE	899	22,543	Clayton
Bibb	cen.	625	13,812	Centerville
Blount	N cen.	640	26,853	Oneonta
Bullock	SE	615	11,824	Union Springs
Butler	S	773	22,007	Greenville
Calhoun	NE	611	103,092	Anniston
Chambers	E	599	36,356	Lafayette
Cherokee	NE	600	15,606	Centre
Chilton	cen.	699	25,180	Clanton
Choctaw	W	918	16,589	Butler
Clarke	SW	1,238	26,724	Grove Hill
Clay	E	603	12,636	Ashland
Cleburne	NE	574	10,996	Heflin
Coffee	SE	677	34,872	Elba
Colbert	NW	596	49,632	Tuscumbia
Conecuh	S	850	15,645	Evergreen
Coosa	E cen.	650	10,662	Rockford
Covington	S	984	34,079	Andalusia
Crenshaw	S	611	13,188	Luverne
Cullman	N	743	52,445	Cullman
Dale	SE	559	52,938	Ozark
Dallas	SW cen.	976	55,296	Selma
De Kalb	NE	778	41,981	Fort Payne
Elmore	E cen.	624	33,661	Wetumpka
Escambia	S	962	34,912	Browton
Etowah	NE	555	94,144	Gadsden
Fayette	NW	627	16,252	Fayette
Franklin	NW	644	23,933	Russellville
Geneva	SE	577	21,924	Geneva
Greene	W	640	10,650	Eutaw
Hale	W	662	15,888	Greensboro
Henry	SE	565	13,254	Abbeville
Houston	SE corner	577	56,574	Dothan
Jackson	NE corner	1,079	39,202	Scottsboro
Jefferson	cen.	1,116	644,991	Birmingham
Lamar	NW	605	14,335	Vernon
Lauderdale[2]	NW corner	662	68,111	Florence
Lawrence	N	685	27,281	Moulton
Lee	E	612	61,268	Opelika
Limestone	N	545	41,699	Athens
Lowndes	S cen.	715	12,897	Hayneville
Macon	E	616	24,841	Tuskegee
Madison	N	803	186,540	Huntsville
Marengo	W	978	23,819	Linden
Marion	NW	743	23,788	Hamilton
Marshal[1]	NE	571	54,211	Guntersville
Mobile[3]	SW corner; coastal	1,240	317,308	Mobile
Monroe	SW	1,032	20,883	Monroeville
Montgomery	SE cen.	790	167,790	Montgomery
Morgan	N	570	77,306	Decatur
Perry	W cen.	734	15,388	Marion
Pickens	W	887	20,326	Carrollton
Pike	SE	673	25,038	Troy
Randolph	E	581	18,331	Wedowee
Russell	E	639	45,394	Seale and Phenix City
Saint Clair	NE cen.	640	27,956	Pell City
Shelby	cen.	798	38,037	Columbiana
Sumter	W	915	16,974	Livingston
Talladega	E cen.	750	65,280	Talladega
Tallapoosa	E	705	33,840	Dadeville
Tuscaloosa	W cen.	1,338	116,029	Tuscaloosa
Walker	NW cen.	808	56,246	Jasper
Washington	SW	1,066	16,241	Chatom
Wilcox	SW cen.	899	16,303	Camden
Winston	NW	633	16,654	Double Springs

[1] Area = land area.
[2] Bounded by Tennessee river, including Wilson Dam.
[3] Includes Dauphin Island.

History: Explored by Spaniards, notably by De Soto 1539–40; first permanent settlement established 1711 by French at site of Mobile on Mobile Bay; became English 1763; southern part included in West Florida, retroceded to Spain in 1783 and claimed by U.S. as part of Louisiana Purchase 1803; rest of Alabama became part of United States 1783, with dividing line under dispute until 1795 when Spain ceded claim north of 31°; included in territory of Mississippi (*q.v.*) 1798; created a territory 1817; 1st constitutional convention July 1819; admitted to Union Dec. 14, 1819; 2d constitutional convention Jan. 7–Mar. 20, 1861 passed ordinance of secession Jan. 11, 1861; government of Confederate States of America organized at Montgomery Feb. 4, 1861; 3d constitutional convention Sept. 12–30, 1865 declared secession null and void, and abolished slavery; readmitted to Union 1868; present constitution, formulated by 6th constitutional convention, adopted 1901 (see BIRMINGHAM 1).

Al·a·bas·ter \ˈal-ə-ˌbas-tər, ˌal-ə-ˈ\. Town, Shelby co., cen. Alabama, 20 m. S of Birmingham; pop. (1970c) 2642.

Ala·bat \ˌäl-ə-ˈbät\. Long narrow island, at S end of Lamon Bay off Luzon, Phil.; 74 sq. m.; ab. 15 m. long; pop. (1969e) 11,700.

Ala·chua \ə-ˈlach-ə-wə, -ˈlä-chə-ˌwä\. **1** County in Florida. See table at FLORIDA.

2 City, Alachua co., N Florida; pop. (1970c) 2252.

Ala·cra·nes \ˌäl-ə-ˈkrän-ās\. Town and municipality, Matanzas prov., W cen. Cuba, 18 m. S of Matanzas; munic. pop. (1967e) 8820.

Ala·dağ *or* **Ala Dağ** \ˌäl-ə-ˈdä(g)\. Name of several mountains in Turkey, esp.: (1) Mountain 60 m. N of Adana, 11,066 ft. (2) Mountain N of Lake Van, 10,994 ft. (3) Mountain ab. 60 m. SSW of Kars, 10,282 ft.

Al–Aghei·la *or* **El Agheila** \ˌal-ə-ˈgā-lə, el-\ *or* **Al–ʻUqay·lah** \ˌal-ə-ˈkī-lə, -ˈkā-\. Town on coastal road, N Libya, near SE end of the Gulf of Sidra; starting point for caravans S; scene of several battles of World War II; reached by British Feb. 1941 during offensive against the Italian army and again in Dec. 1941 during retreat of Germans; site of first blow of Rommel's offensive against British Jan. 23, 1942; again reached by Allies Nov. 13, 1942 and captured Dec. 17.

Ala·go·as \ˌal-ə-ˈgō-əs\. State of E Brazil; 10,707 sq. m.; pop. (1970p) 1,606,165; ✱ Maceió; cotton, rice, sugar, tobacco.

Ala·goi·nhas \ˌal-ə-ˈgwēn-yəs\. City, Bahia state, E Brazil, 70 m. N of Salvador; munic. pop. (1968e) 75,516.

Ala·gón \ˌäl-ə-ˈgōn\. River, W Spain; ab. 120 m. long; flows SW into Tagus river 2 m. NE of Alcántara.

Al–Ah·madi \ˌal-ä-ˈmäd-ē\. Town, Kuwait, ab. 22 m. SSE of Al-Kuwait; pop. (1970c) 21,244.

Alai \ˈä-ˌlī\. **1** Mountain range in SW Kirgiz S.S.R., U.S.S.R., running E and W; average height 16,000 ft.; highest peak 19,554 ft. See TRANS ALAI.

2 Valley of Kyzyl-Su (a N tributary of the Amu Darya), S of Alai Mts.

Alais. See ALÈS.

Ala·jue·la \ˌäl-ə-ˈhwā-lə\. **1** Province, cen. Costa Rica (see table at COSTA RICA); plateau region; produces sugar, coffee, hides.

2 Town, its ✱, 14 m. W of San José; pop. (1970p) 29,171; center of sugar industry.

Ala·kol *or* **Ala Kul** \ˌäl-ə-ˈkōl, -ˈkə(r)l\. Lake, E Kazakh S.S.R., U.S.S.R., E of Lake Balkhash; 803 sq. m.

Ala·la·kei·ki \ə-ˌläl-ə-ˈkā-kē\. Channel bet. SW Maui and Kahoolawe, Hawaii; 6 m. wide.

Al–Ala·mein *or* **El Alamein** *or* **Al–ʻAla·mayn** \ˌal-ˌal-ə-ˈmān, ˌel-\. Village on coastal road, N Egypt, ab. 65 m. W of Alexandria and N of NE corner of Qattara Depression; farthest German advance July 1, 1942 in campaign to seize Alexandria, Cairo, and the Suez Canal; scene of battle Oct. 19–Nov. 3, 1942 in which Allies defeated Germans. See AL-AQQAQIR.

Alalia. See ALERIA.

Al·a·ma·gan \ˌal-ə-mə-ˈgan\. One of the Mariana Islands (*q.v.*), W Pacific Ocean, 165 m. N of Saipan, 17°36′N, 145° 50′E; included in Japanese mandate 1919; taken by U.S. Aug. 1945.

Al·a·mance \ˈal-ə-ˌman(t)s\. **1** Small stream (**Alamance Creek,** a headstream of Cape Fear river), N cen. North Carolina; on its banks ab. 20 m. W of Hillsboro colonial forces of British governor, William Tryon, decisively defeated Regulators May 16, 1771.

2 County in North Carolina. See table at NORTH CAROLINA.

Al·a·man·nia \ˌal-ə-ˈman-ē-ə\. Region, on both sides of Upper Rhine (modern E France and SW West Germany), W Europe; home of the Alamanni; in time of Clovis, a Frankish province; later (c. 1000) a duchy.

Al·a·me·da \ˌal-ə-ˈmēd-ə\. **1** County in California. See table at CALIFORNIA.

2 City, Alameda co., W California, on island near E shore of San Francisco Bay, 6 m. E of San Francisco, separated from Oakland by estuary; pop. (1970c) 70,968; port of entry; naval air base and commercial airports, starting point for first China Clipper flight Nov. 22, 1935; shipping center; manufactures pumps, borax, aircraft parts, diesel engines, pottery; shipbuilding yards; fish canneries; incorp. 1854.

3 Former city, Bannock co., SE Idaho; now part of Pocatello.

Alameda–Oak·land Tunnel \-ˈōk-lənd-\. Vehicular tunnel under an inlet of San Francisco Bay, California, connecting Alameda with Oakland; 4500 ft. long.

Alamein, Al–. See AL-ALAMEIN.

Ala·mi·nos \ˌal-ə-ˈmē-nəs\. Municipality, NW Pangasinan prov., Luzon, Phil., near W shore of Lingayen Gulf; pop. (1969e) 41,300.

Al·a·mo \ˈal-ə-ˌmō\. **1** Town, ⊗ of Wheeler co., SE cen. Georgia; pop. (1970c) 833; cotton.

2 Town, ⊗ of Crockett co., W Tennessee; pop. (1970c) 2499.

3 City, Hidalgo co., S Texas, in agricultural area 10 m. E of McAllen; pop. (1970c) 4291.

Alamo, The. Fort in San Antonio, Texas; Spanish Franciscan mission built c. 1722; converted to a fort 1793; in the Texan war of independence from Mexico, besieged by the Mexicans under Santa Anna Feb. 23–Mar. 6, 1836; defended to the last man of the Texan garrison of 187; became a symbol of Texan fortitude as used in Houston's cry "Remember the Alamo!" at the battle of San Jacinto 46 days later.

Al·a·mo·gor·do \ˌal-ə-mə-ˈgȯrd-(ˌ)ō\. City, ⊗ of Otero co., S New Mexico, W of Sacramento Mts. 60 m. NE of Las Cruces; pop. (1970c) 23,035; alt. 4350 ft.; to the SW are White Sands National Monument (ab. 20 m.) and (11 m.) **Hol·lo·man Air Force Base** \ˈhäl-ə-mən-\ *or formerly* **Alamogordo Air Base;** ab. 55 m. to the NW at N end of the desert which extends between the Rio Grande and the San Andres Mts. is site of the first man-made atomic explosion July 16, 1945.

Alamogordo Dam. Dam, N De Baca co., New Mexico, across Pecos river; height 148 ft.; completed 1938; impounds water, **Alamogordo Reservoir,** for irrigation.

Alamo Heights \ˌal-ə-ˌmō-\. City, Bexar co., S cen. Texas, 5 m. NE of San Antonio; pop. (1970c) 6933; suburb of San Antonio.

Alamos, Los. See LOS ALAMOS.

Al·a·mo·sa \ˌal-ə-ˈmō-sə, -ˈmü-\. **1** County in S Colorado. See table at COLORADO.

2 City, its ⊗, on Rio Grande 84 m. WNW of Trinidad; pop. (1970c) 6985; industrial, shipping, and retail center for San Luis Park; flour mill, oil refinery, stockyards; Adams State Coll. (1921); founded 1878.

Ala·mut, Rock of \-ˌal-ə-ˈmüt\. Elevation, N Iran, W end of Elburz Mts., ab. 70 m. NW of Tehran; stronghold of the Assassins, a secret order of the Ismailians, in medieval ages.

Åland. See AHVENANMAA.

Åland Islands. See AHVENANMAA.

ALABAMA
MILES
0 20 40 60
KILOMETERS
0 20 40 60
State Capitals
County Seats
TENNESSEE
GEORGIA
FLORIDA
MISSISSIPPI
GULF OF MEXICO
88° 87° 86° 85°
35° 34° 33° 32° 31°
Longitude West of Greenwich
LAUDERDALE
LIMESTONE
MADISON
JACKSON
COLBERT
FRANKLIN
LAWRENCE
MORGAN
MARSHALL
DE KALB
MARION
WINSTON
CULLMAN
ETOWAH
CHEROKEE
LAMAR
FAYETTE
WALKER
BLOUNT
ST. CLAIR
CALHOUN
CLEBURNE
JEFFERSON
PICKENS
TUSCALOOSA
SHELBY
TALLADEGA
RANDOLPH
CLAY
BIBB
GREENE
HALE
PERRY
CHILTON
COOSA
TALLAPOOSA
CHAMBERS
SUMTER
AUTAUGA
ELMORE
LEE
MARENGO
DALLAS
LOWNDES
MONTGOMERY
MACON
RUSSELL
BULLOCK
CHOCTAW
WILCOX
BUTLER
CRENSHAW
PIKE
BARBOUR
CLARKE
MONROE
WASHINGTON
CONECUH
COFFEE
DALE
HENRY
ESCAMBIA
COVINGTON
GENEVA
HOUSTON
MOBILE
BALDWIN
Birmingham
Montgomery
Mobile
Huntsville
Tuscaloosa
Gadsden
Anniston
Florence
Sheffield
Tuscumbia
Decatur
Athens
Scottsboro
Guntersville
Cullman
Jasper
Bessemer
Selma
Dothan
Chattanooga
Atlanta
Columbus
Rome
Pensacola
PICKWICK LANDING DAM
WILSON DAM
WHEELER DAM
GUNTERSVILLE DAM
REDSTONE ARSENAL
RUSSELL CAVE N.M.
CHICKAMAUGA AND CHATTANOOGA NAT'L MIL. PK.
KENNESAW MT. NAT'L BATTLEFIELD PK.
ANNISTON ARMY DEPOT
FT. McCLELLAN
HORSESHOE BEND NAT'L MIL. PK.
MAXWELL A.F.B.
GUNTER A.F.B.
CRAIG A.F.B.
FT. RUCKER
BROOKLEY A.F.B.
WALTER F. GEORGE DAM
Cheaha Mtn. 2,407
Wheeler Lake
Guntersville L.
Weiss Res.
L. M. Smith L.
Bankhead L.
Logan Martin Lake
Martin L.
West Point Res.
L. Harding
Lake Eufaula
Lake Seminole
Demopolis Lake
Mobile Bay
Mississippi Sound
Santa Rosa Island
Dauphin Island
Tennessee R.
Tombigbee R.
Black Warrior R.
Alabama R.
Coosa R.
Tallapoosa R.
Chattahoochee R.
Cahaba R.
Conecuh R.
Escambia R.
Choctawhatchee R.
Pea R.
© Copyright HAMMOND INCORPORATED, Maplewood, N.J.

Åland Sea \'ō-ˌländ-\. Body of water bet. Ahvenanmaa archipelago at the entrance to the Gulf of Bothnia and the mainland of Sweden.

Alang·a·lang \'äl-ˌäŋ-'äl-ˌäŋ\. Municipality, N Leyte prov., Phil., 12 m. W of Palo; pop. (1969e) 30,300.

Ala·o·tra \ˌäl-ə-'ō-trə\. Lake, NE cen. Malagasy Republic; 70 sq. m.; the republic's largest lake.

Alaouites, Territory of the. See LATAKIA.

Ala·pa·yevsk \ˌäl-ə-'pī-ˌəfsk\. Town, Sverdlovsk Oblast, Russian S.F.S.R., U.S.S.R., ab. 80 m. NNE of Sverdlovsk; pop. (1967e) 49,000; steel works.

Ala·pii Point \ˌäl-ə-'pē-\. Cape on W coast of Kauai I., Hawaii.

Al–'Aqabah. See 'AQABA.

Al–Aq·qa·qir *or* **El Aqqaqir** \ˌal-ə-'käk-ˌi(ə)r, ˌel-\. Village, N Egypt, near Al-Alamein; scene of tank battle Nov. 2–3, 1942 in which Germans were severely beaten; closing phase of battle of Al-Alamein.

Al–Aqsur. See LUXOR.

Al–Ar·ba \al-'är-bə\ *also* **L'Ar·ba** \'är-'bä\. Commune, Alger dept., N Algeria, ab. 18 m. SE of Algiers; pop. (1966c) 14,415.

Alar·cos \ə-'lär-kəs\. Hill and former village, Ciudad Real prov., S cen. Spain, 7 m. W of Ciudad Real; scene of battle 1195 in which the Almohades under al-Mansur defeated Alfonso VIII of Castile.

Al–'Arīsh *or* **El 'Arīsh** \ˌal-ə-'rēsh, ˌel-\ *or anc.* **Rhi·no·co·lu·ra** \ˌrī-(ˌ)nō-kə-'lu̇(ə)r-ə\. Town, ✻ of Sinai gov., NE Egypt, on Mediterranean Sea; pop. (1970e) 43,000; in World War I important point in advance of British toward Palestine, taken Dec. 20, 1916; occupied by Israel 1967.

Ala·şe·hir \ˌal-ə-shə-'hi(ə)r, ˌäl-\ *or formerly* **Ala·shehr** \-'she(ə)r\ *or anc.* **Phil·a·del·phia** \ˌfil-ə-'del-fē-ə, -'del-fyə\. City, Manisa prov., W Turkey in Asia, on Alaşehir river (tributary of Gediz) and on railroad 75 m. E of İzmir; pop. (1965c) 16,012.

History: Site of ancient city of Philadelphia founded c. 150 B.C. by Attalus II (Philadelphus) of Pergamum; one of the Seven Churches of Asia Minor (*Rev.* i–iii); after a long period of resistance, the last city of Asia Minor to fall to the Turks 1390; said to have been conquered by Tamerlane 1402; largely destroyed by the Greeks 1922.

A–la Shan \ˌäl-(ˌ)ä-'shän\ *or* **Ho–lan Shan** \ˌhō-ˌlän-'shän\.
1 Mountain range, W Inner Mongolia, N China, W of the Yellow river; highest peak ab. 12,000 ft.
2 Desert region of Inner Mongolia, N China, W of A-la Shan mountain range.

Al–Ash·mū·nein *or* **El Ashmūnein** \ˌal-ˌash-mu̇-'nān, -'nīn, (ˌ)el-\. Village, Egypt, near W bank of the Nile; site of **Her·mop·o·lis Mag·na** \(ˌ)hər-ˌmäp-ə-ləs-'mag-nə\, in ancient times center of the worship of Anubis or Thoth.

Al–'Āṣī, Nahr. See ORONTES 2.

Alas·ka \ə-'las-kə\ *or earlier name* (*to 1867*) **Russian America.** A state of U.S.A., the NW part of North America, bounded on N by Arctic Ocean, on E by Canada, on SW by Pacific Ocean, and on W by Bering Sea and Arctic Ocean; 1st state in area, 586,400 sq. m. (land area 571,065 sq. m.); 50th state in population, (1970c) 302,173; ✻ Juneau; 49th state admitted to Union (1959).

Nicknames (unofficial): The Last Frontier; Land of the Midnight Sun. *State flower:* The forget-me-not. *Motto* (unofficial): North to the Future. *Capes and Islands:* Most northerly point is Point Barrow 71°23′N; Cape Prince of Wales, W point of Seward Penin., separated by Bering Strait (53 m. wide) from Asia; Alaska Penin. and Aleutian Is. in SW extend 1200 m. toward Asia enclosing Bering Sea on S (furthest point W Attu I. 172°30′E); many other islands off coast: St. Lawrence, Nunivak, and Pribilof in Bering Sea, Kodiak and Afognak E of Alaska Penin., and islands of Alexander Archipelago off narrow strip of mainland in SE bordering Brit. Columbia. *Rivers:* Yukon (lower course) crosses from E to W (tributaries: Porcupine, Tanana, Koyukuk), Noatak in N, Kuskokwim in SW, Susitna and Copper in S. *Mts.:* Wrangell Mts. in SE extending to Yukon border, Chugach Mts. along S coast, Alaska Range in S cen. part, Brooks Range in N, and Aleutian Range on Alaska Penin. Highest point Mt. McKinley 20,320 ft. Has one national park, Mount McKinley in Alaska Range, and 3 national monuments, Glacier Bay, Katmai, Sitka. *Chief industries:* Mining (gold, platinum; oil), fishing; timber, furs. *Chief cities:* Anchorage, Fairbanks, Ketchikan, Juneau, Kodiak. See *Table of States* at UNITED STATES. Contains nine organized boroughs (for pronunciation of their names, see their individual entries):

NAME	LOCATION	AREA[1] (sq. m.)	POP. (1970c)	BOROUGH SEAT
Bristol Bay	SW	1,200	1,147	Naknek
Fairbanks North Star	cen.	7,500	30,618	Fairbanks
Greater Anchorage Area	cen.	1,500	102,994	Anchorage
Greater Sitka	SE	2,900	6,109	Sitka
Haines	SE	2,200	1,351	Haines
Juneau[2]	SE	3,108	13,556	Juneau
Kenai Peninsula	S cen.	15,000	13,500	Soldotna
Kodiak Island		4,500	6,357	Kodiak
Matanuska-Susitna	S cen.	23,000	6,509	Palmer

[1]Approximate.
[2]Full name is City and Borough of Juneau.

History: Discovered by Russian voyages, esp. of Vitus Bering 1741; first permanent settlement 1792 on Kodiak I.; visited by British explorers Cook, Vancouver, and Mackenzie and by Hudson Bay traders 1778–1847; under trade monopoly of Russian-American Fur Company 1799–1861, first managed by Aleksandr Baranov; ownership claimed by Russia; region south to 54°40′ ceded by Russia to U.S. for $7,200,000 by treaty of 1867 negotiated by Secretary of State Seward (hence early nickname of Alaska, "Seward's Folly"); organized 1884, received final U.S. territorial status 1912; gold discoveries, including Klondike 1896; disputed boundary with British Columbia arbitrated in favor of U.S. 1903; restriction of seal fisheries by treaties with Great Britain, Russia, and Japan 1911; in World War II Aleutian islands of Attu and Kiska occupied by Japanese June 1942–Aug. 1943; present constitution adopted 1956; was granted statehood 1959; suffered severe earthquake damage 1964; large oil reserves discovered 1968.

Alaska, Gulf of. Gulf, S Alaska, bet. Alaska Penin. and Alexander Archipelago.

Alaska Highway. Military and commercial road, extending from Dawson Creek, E British Columbia, Canada, NW across N British Columbia; 1519 m. long; built as **Al·can Highway** \'al-ˌkan-\ (*Al*aska and *Can*ada) by U.S. Army engineers Mar.–Nov. 1942; later, improved and partly relocated; passes through Fort St. John, Fort Nelson, and Lower Post, then through Teslin, Whitehorse, and Kluane in SW Yukon, and Tanacross, Big Delta (where it meets the Richardson Highway, *q.v.*), and Richardson in E Alaska, to Fairbanks. Highest point 4212 ft. bet. Fort Nelson and Watson Lake.

Alaska Peninsula. Peninsula, SW Alaska, extending from Iliamna Lake to Unimak I.; ab. 475 m. long; geographically a unit with Aleutian Is.

Alaska Range. Mountain range, S Alaska, extending in semicircle from Alaska Penin. to Yukon boundary; highest Mt. McKinley. See MCKINLEY, MOUNT and UNITED STATES, *National Parks* (Mount McKinley National Park).

Al–As·nam \ˌal-as-'nam\. 1 Department of N Algeria. See table at ALGERIA.
2 Town, its ✻; pop. (1966c) 49,109.

Alas Strait \ə-'läs-\. Channel bet. Lombok and Sumbawa Is., Lesser Sunda Is., Indonesia, connecting W Flores Sea with Indian Ocean; 10 to 15 m. wide.

Ala Tau \ˌal-ə-'tau̇, ˌäl-\. Several ranges of the Tien Shan mountain system, E Kazakh and Kirgiz S.S.Rs., U.S.S.R., around and NE of Issyk-Kul; max. elev. ab. 18,000 ft. See DZUNGARIAN ALA TAU.

Ala·tri \ə-'lä-trē\ *or anc.* **Ale·tri·um** \ə-'lē-trē-əm\. Commune, Frosinone prov., Latium, cen. Italy, 6 m. N of Frosi-

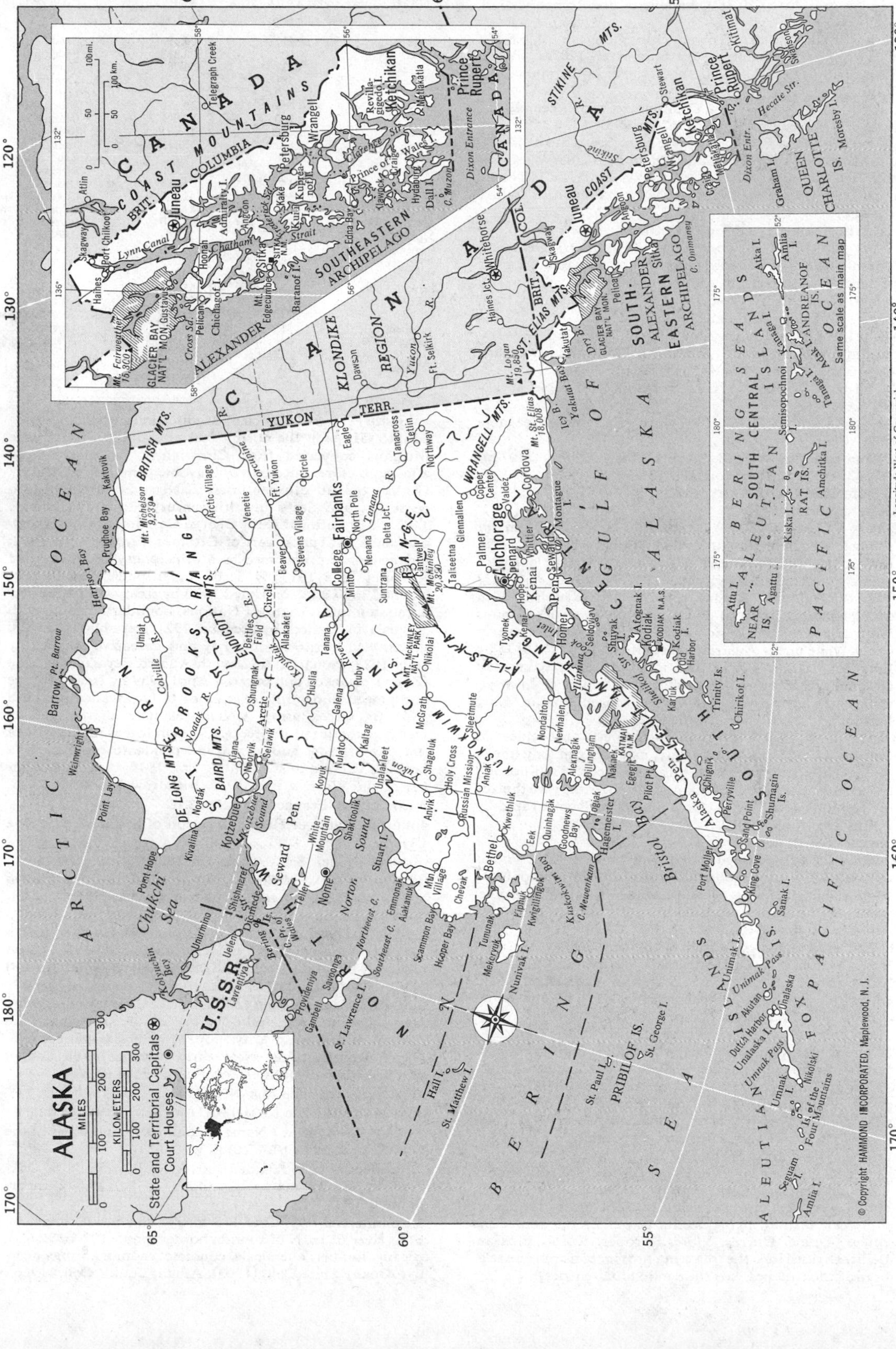
ALASKA
MILES
0 100 200 300
KILOMETERS
0 100 200 300
State and Territorial Capitals
Court Houses
ARCTIC OCEAN
BERING SEA
PACIFIC OCEAN
GULF OF ALASKA
CANADA
U.S.S.R.
YUKON TERR.
BRIT. COL.
Chukchi Sea
Norton Sound
Bristol Bay
Seward Pen.
Alaska Pen.
BROOKS RANGE
ALASKA RANGE
KUSKOKWIM MTS.
WRANGELL MTS.
ST. ELIAS MTS.
COAST MTS.
ALEUTIAN ISLANDS
PRIBILOF IS.
SOUTHEASTERN ARCHIPELAGO
ALEXANDER ARCHIPELAGO
KLONDIKE REGION
Mt. McKinley 20,320
Mt. Logan 19,850
Mt. St. Elias 18,008
Barrow
Fairbanks
Anchorage
Juneau
Nome
Kodiak
Sitka
Ketchikan
Whitehorse
Prince Rupert
Same scale as main map
Longitude West of Greenwich
© Copyright HAMMOND INCORPORATED, Maplewood, N.J.

none; pop. (1968e) 20,869; remains of pre-Roman wall of cyclopean masonry.

Ala·tyr \äl-ə-'ti(ə)r\. Town, SW Chuvash A.S.S.R., U.S.S.R., on left bank of the Sura river 120 m. SW of Kazan; pop. (1967e) 43,000; shoes, tobacco; thermal power station.

Alau·sí \ˌäl-aů-'sē\. Town, Chimborazo prov., cen. Ecuador, S of Riobamba; pop. (1962c) 8993.

Ala·va \'äl-ə-və\. Province of N Spain. See table at SPAIN.

Al·a·va, Cape \-'al-ə-və\. Cape, Clallam co., NW Washington, just S of Cape Flattery, 124°43′W long., 48°10′N lat.; most westerly point of United States mainland excluding Alaska.

Alawiya *or* **Alawiyya.** See LATAKIA.

Al–'Ay·zar·ī·yah \ˌal-ˌī-zə-'rē-(y)ə\ *or formerly* **Beth·a·ny** \'beth-ə-nē\. Village, Jordan, on Mt. of Olives ab. 2 m. E of Jerusalem (Israel); in area occupied by Israel 1967.

Al–'Azi·zi·ya \al-ˌaz-ē-'zē-(y)ə\. Town on Tigris river, Iraq, ab. 50 m. below Baghdad.

Al·ba. 1 \'äl-ba\ *or anc.* **Alba Pom·pe·ia** \-päm-'pē-(y)ə\. Commune, Cuneo prov., Piedmont, NW Italy, on Tanaro river 33 m. NE of Cuneo; pop. (1968e) 26,462.

2 \'äl-bə\. County, W cen. Romania. See table at ROMANIA.

Al·ba·ce·te \ˌal-bə-'sāt-ē\. 1 Province of SE Spain. See table at SPAIN.

2 Commune, its ✱, 138 m. SE of Madrid; pop. (1970p) 93,233; cutlery, flour; founded 1365.

Al–Bahnasā. See OXYRHYNCHUS.

Al–Bahr. See NILE.

Alba Iu·lia \ˌäl-bə-'yül-yə\ *or Lat.* **Apu·lum** \ə-'pyü-ləm\ *or Hung.* **Gyu·la·fe·hér·vár** \'jü-ˌlò-'fā-her-ˌvär\ *or Ger.* **Karls·burg** \'kärlz-ˌbů(ə)rg\. Town, ⊗ of Alba co., Romania, on Mureşul river; pop. (1968e) 84,074.

History: Site of Roman colony; bishopric since 11th cent.; contains tomb of Hungarian national hero, János Hunyadi; 16th cent. residence of princes of Transylvania (*q.v.*); while under Austria, upper citadel built 1716–35 by Emperor Charles VI; as traditional center of Romanian nationalism, scene of proclamation of union of Transylvania with Romania 1918 and of coronation of King Ferdinand I and Queen Marie 1922.

Alba Lon·ga \ˌal-bə-'lòŋ-gə\. Ancient city, the oldest in Latium, 12 m. SE of Rome, Italy, extending in long line in Alban Hills to E shore of Albanus Lacus. Traditionally founded by Ascanius, son of Aeneas; legendary birthplace of Romulus and Remus, the founders of Rome; razed by Tullus Hostilius 665 B.C.

Albana. See DERBENT.

Al·ban Hills \ˌòl-bən-, ˌal-\ *or Ital.* **Mon·ti Al·ba·ni** \'mòn-tē-äl-'bän-ē\ *or anc.* **Al·ba·nus Mons** \äl-ˌbän-ə-'smòn(t)s\. Mountain group near Albano Laziale, Italy, SE of Rome; a part of the Lower Apennines.

Al·ba·nia \al-'bā-nē-ə, -nyə *also* òl-\. 1 Ancient country of E Caucasus region on W side of Caspian Sea, extending N from Cyrus and Araxes rivers and corresponding largely to NE Azerbaijan S.S.R. and S Dagestan A.S.S.R., U.S.S.R. Inhabited by fierce Scythian tribe who fought under Mithridates VI against Pompey.

2 *or officially* **People's Republic of Albania;** *Albanian* **Shqip·ni** \shkip-'nē\ *or* **Shqip·ri** \ˌshkēp-rē\ *or* **Shqi·pë·ri** \ˌshkyēp-ə-'rē\. Republic, W Balkan Penin., bet. Yugoslavia and Greece, on E coast of Adriatic; 11,100 sq. m.; pop. (1970e) 2,170,000; ✱ Tiranë. *Physical features:* Very mountainous country; North Albanian Alps in N (highest peak 9026 ft.). *Rivers:* Drin in N, Shkumbin and Seman in center, Vijosë in S; SE part of Lake Scutari on N border, outlet Buenë river; parts of Lakes Ohrid and Prespa in SE. *Chief products:* Corn, cotton, tobacco, wheat; coal, chrome, copper, oil; manufacturing: chemicals, fertilizers, footwear, textiles; hydroelectric power production. *Chief towns:* Tiranë, Durrës, Vlorë, Shkodër, Korçë, Elbasan, Berat. Divided into the following provinces (for pronunciation of their names, see their individual entries):

NAME	AREA (sq. m.)	POP. (1967e)	CAPITAL
Berat	412	104,390	Berat
Dibër	606	93,812	Peshkopi
Durrës	332	155,780	Durrës
Elbasan	581	130,430	Elbasan
Fier	460	139,175	Fier
Gjirokastër	439	49,170	Gjirokastër
Gramsh	270	24,095	Gramsh
Kolonjë	310	18,685	Kolonjë
Korçë	842	159,115	Korçë
Krujë	236	55,325	Krujë
Kukës	604	58,880	Kukës
Lesh	182	33,225	Lesh
Librazhd	391	42,730	Librazhd
Lushnje	275	81,595	Lushnje
Mat	397	45,340	Burrel
Mirditë	269	22,465	Rrëshen
Përmet	362	30,340	Përmet
Pogradec	280	42,775	Pogradec
Pukë	374	27,568	Pukë
Sarandë	424	58,135	Sarandë
Shkodër	978	150,350	Shkodër
Skrapar	278	23,035	Corovodë
Tepelenë	315	30,850	Tepelenë
Tiranë	446	72,600	Tiranë
Tiranë[1]	12	169,300	
Tropojë	403	25,570	Bajram Curri
Vlorë	621	119,995	Vlorë

[1]Capital city, constituting a separate administrative unit.

History: Home of ancient Mediterranean people, divided into Ghegs in the north, Tosks in south; later became Muslims converted from Christianity; as a race little affected by Greco-Roman or Slavonic penetration; held by Goths 4th and 5th centuries, Eastern Empire 6th–13th centuries, and Serbs in 14th century; despite resistance 1443–68 of national hero, George Castriota (Scanderbeg), overcome by Turks; part of Ottoman Empire until 1912; independence proclaimed as a principality 1912; invaded for brief time 1913 by Serbs; independence again proclaimed 1917 and confirmed 1920 by treaty with Italy and admission into League of Nations; boundary dispute with Yugoslavia settled by League 1921; republic 1925–28; guaranteed territorial integrity and defensive alliance by Italy 1927; monarchy 1928 with Ahmed Bey Zogu as king (Zog I); attacked and overrun April 1939 by Italian troops and placed under rule of king of Italy; invaded in south 1941 by Greek army, which was later driven out by German conquest of Greece. German forces finally driven out Nov. 1944 and again independent; established a people's (Communist) republic Jan. 1946; became a member of the Warsaw Pact 1955, withdrew 1968.

3 Commune, France. See AUBAGNE.

4 Ancient name of Highland region of Scotland, N of the Clyde.

Albaniae Pylae. See CASPIAN GATES.

Al·ba·no, Lake \-al-'bän-(ˌ)ō, -äl-\ *or Ital.* **La·go di Albano** \'läg-(ˌ)ō-(ˌ)dē-\ *or anc.* **Al·ba·nus La·cus** \al-'bā-nəs-ˌlā-kəs\. Lake, in crater of extinct volcano near Albano Laziale, Italy; 3 sq. m.; max. depth 558 ft.; its outlet a rock-hewn tunnel ab. 1 m. long made 398–397 B.C., on advice of Delphic Oracle, still in use. Castel Gandolfo and many beautiful villas on its shores.

Albano La·zia·le \al-'bän-(ˌ)ō-lä-'tsyä-lə\. Commune, Roma prov., Latium, cen. Italy, 14 m. SE of Rome on Lake Albano and Appian Way; pop. (1968e) 24,393; summer resort; Roman ruins. Near early town of Alba Longa, established by Septimius Severus c. 195 A.D.

Albanus Lacus. See ALBANO, LAKE.

Albanus Mons. See ALBAN HILLS.

Al·ba·ny \'òl-bə-nē\. 1 Name of counties in two states of the U.S. See tables at NEW YORK, WYOMING.

2 Residential city, Alameda co., W California, N of Oakland on San Francisco Bay; pop. (1970c) 14,672; incorporated 1908.

3 Commercial city, ⊗ of Dougherty co., SW Georgia, on Flint river 65 m. N of Florida border; pop. (1970c) 72,623; pecans, lumber, chemicals, concrete; radium springs nearby; Albany State Coll. (1903), Albany Junior Coll. (1966).

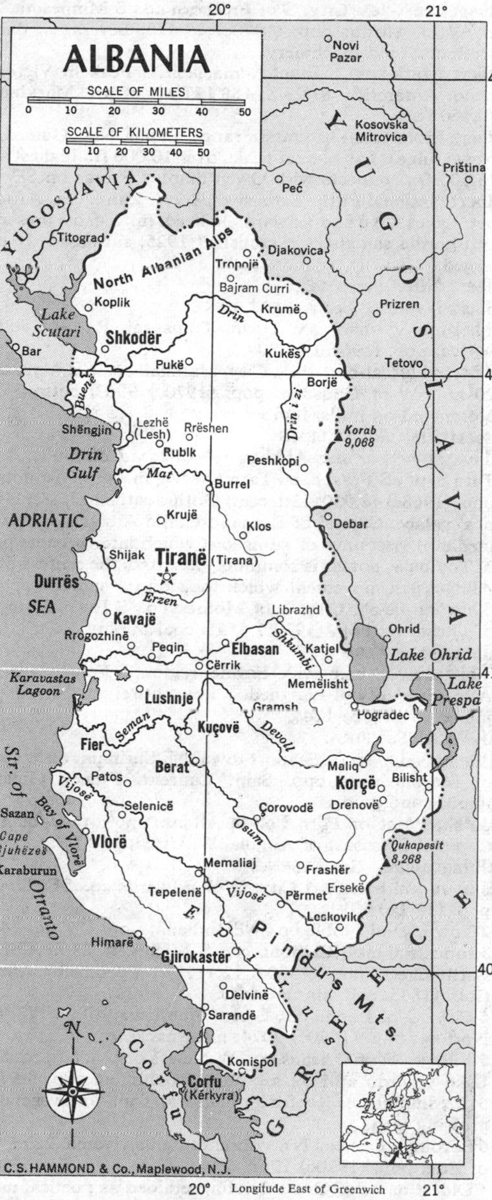

4 Town, Delaware co., E cen. Indiana, 12 m. NE of Muncie; pop. (1970c) 2293; corn, wheat.

5 City, ⊗ of Clinton co., S Kentucky; pop. (1970c) 1891.

6 City, ⊗ of Gentry co., NW Missouri, 45 m. NE of St. Joseph; pop. (1970c) 1804; soybeans; livestock.

7 City, ✱ of New York state and ⊗ of Albany co., on W bank of Hudson river 145 m. N of New York; pop. (1970c) 114,873; chemicals, paper, pharmaceuticals, steel; State Univ. at Albany (1844), a unit of the State Univ. of New York (1848), state capitol (1871), Schuyler Mansion (1761).

History: Second oldest permanent settlement within thirteen colonies, begun 1614 by establishment of Dutch trading post; actual colonization 1624 when Fort Orange was founded by Dutch West India Company; village, granted independence from the patroon, became Beverwyck 1652; after surrender of Fort Orange to English 1664, Beverwyck became Albany; received charter 1686; long a center for fur trade and contact with Indians; scene of the Albany Congress of the seven English colonies and the Iroquois 1754 when Albany Plan of Union was drafted; seriously menaced by British attack during Revolutionary War, especially in 1777; became capital of state of New York 1797; expanded as a commercial center after opening of Erie Canal 1825 and of Albany-Schenectady R.R. 1831.

8 City, ⊗ of Linn co., W Oregon, on Willamette river 10 m. NE of Corvallis; pop. (1970c) 18,181; furniture, leather goods, lumber, meat products; estab. 1848.

9 City, ⊗ of Shackelford co., N cen. Texas, 30 m. NE of Abilene; pop. (1970c) 1978; ships livestock; oil wells.

10 Seaport municipality, on King George Sound, SW Western Australia, ab. 260 m. SE of Perth; pop. (1968e) 12,050; a military settlement 1825. Possesses good harbor; popular vacation and health resort.

11 River, N cen. Ontario, Canada; 610 m. long; rises in chain of lakes (largest St. Joseph) in W Ontario and flows E and NE into W James Bay at Fort Albany; chief tributaries the Kenogami and Ogoki rivers.

Alba Pompeia. See ALBA 1.

Al–Basrah. See BASRA.

Al·ba·tross Point \al-bə-ˌtrȯs-, -ˌträs-\. Cape on NW cen. coast of North Island, New Zealand, at S entrance to Kawhia Harbor.

Al·bay \äl-ˈbī\. **1** Province, SE Luzon, Phil. (see table at PHILIPPINES); includes the islands of Batan, Cagraray, Rapu-Rapu, and San Miguel; very mountainous, includes among other peaks the perfect volcanic cone of Mt. Mayon; watered by many small streams; very fertile, esp. well adapted to hemp (abacá) and rice, its main crops; other agricultural products coconuts, sugar, fruits; coal, copper. Chief towns Legaspi, Tabaco, Ligao, and Guinobatan.

History: A populous region before coming of Spaniards but infrequently visited by them before 18th century; became prosperous after 1750 but suffered from great eruption of Mayon 1815; territory decreased 1846 by loss of islands of Masbate and Ticao and by cession of towns to Camarines Sur; civil government established by Americans Apr. 1901. Invaded by Japanese Dec. 1941.

2 Municipality on Albay Gulf, now part of Legaspi (*q.v.*).

Al–Ba·ya·di·ya *or* **El Bayadiya** \ˌal-ˌbī-ə-ˈdē-(y)ə, ˌel-\. Town, Qena gov., Upper Egypt, just S of Luxor.

Al–Bayda. See BEIDA.

Albay Gulf. Inlet of Pacific Ocean in SE Luzon, Phil., on E coast of Albay prov.; ab. 30 m. long by 8 to 12 m. wide; its N shore formed by islands of Cagraray, Batan, and Rapu-Rapu. Port of Legaspi is at its head.

Al·be·marle \ˈal-bə-ˌmärl\. **1** County in Virginia. See table at VIRGINIA.

2 Town, ⊗ of Stanly co., S cen. North Carolina, 26 m. SE of Salisbury; pop. (1970c) 11,126; bricks, cottonseed oil, lumber, textiles.

Albemarle Island. See ISABELA ISLAND.

Albemarle Sound. Inlet of Atlantic Ocean, in NE North Carolina; 52 m. long; forms parts of Currituck, Camden, Pasquotank, Perquimans, and Chowan cos. on the N, Bertie co. on W, and Washington, Tyrrell, and Dare cos. on S; receives the Chowan river in the NW.

Al·ben·ga \äl-ˈbeŋ-gə\ *or anc.* **Al·bum In·gau·num** \ˌal-bəm-iŋ-ˈgȯ-nəm\ *or* **Al·bin·gau·num** \ˌal-bəŋ-ˈgȯ-nəm\. Seaport, Savona prov., Liguria, NW Italy, on Ligurian Sea 22 m. SW of Savona; pop. (1968) 18,150; Gothic cathedral and well-preserved Roman bridge.

Al·ber·che \äl-ˈbe(ə)r-(ˌ)kā\. River, cen. Spain; 113 m. long.

Al·bères, Monts \mōⁿ-zál-ˈbe(ə)r\. Easternmost section of the Pyrenees, bet. SW France and NE Spain; highest peak Pic Noulos 4128 ft.

Al·ber·ga \al-ˈbər-gə\. Intermittent river, N South Australia; ab. 350 m. long; flows E from Musgrave Range and in rainy season joins with Finke river.

Al·ber·ni \al-ˈbər-nē\. City, E cen. Vancouver I., British Columbia, Canada, on Alberni Canal near Port Alberni and 95 m. NW of Victoria; pop. (1966c) 4783; both towns practically destroyed by fire Aug. 1947.

Alberni Canal. Narrow fjord, S cen. Vancouver I., SW British Columbia, Canada; ab. 30 m. long; an inlet of the Pacific opening into Barkley Sound. Port Alberni is at its head.

Al·bert \ˈal-bərt\. County in New Brunswick, Canada. See table at NEW BRUNSWICK.

Albert \al-ˈbe(ə)r\ *or formerly* **An·cre** \äⁿ(ŋ)krᵊ\. Commune, Somme dept., N France, ab. 17 m. NE of Amiens; pop. (1968c) 10,960; on edge of Battle of the Somme 1916, almost completely destroyed in battles of 1918.

Albert, Lake *or* **Albert Nyan·za** \ˌal-bərt-ˈnyan-zə, -nē-ˈan-, -nī-ˈan-\. Lake (*nyanza*) bet. Uganda and Zaire, cen. Africa, ab. 135 m. NW of Lake Victoria; 100 m. long by 20 m. wide; 2075 sq. m.; max. depth 168 ft.; elevation 2030 ft. It receives at SW end the Semliki; outlet of Lake Edward; at NE corner just below Murchison Falls it receives Victoria Nile from Lake Victoria. Its outlet at N end is Albert Nile section of Nile. Discovered by Sir Samuel Baker 1864; circumnavigated by Gessi Pasha 1876 and by Emin Pasha 1884; initially part of Uganda (*q.v.*), but northwest shores leased to Congo Free State 1894 (see ZAIRE 1).

Al·ber·ta \al-ˈbərt-ə\. 1 Province, W Canada, most westerly Prairie Province, bounded on N by Mackenzie dist., on E by Saskatchewan, on S by U.S. (Montana), and on W by British Columbia; 255,285 sq. m. (incl. 6485 sq. m. of water); pop. (1970e) 1,600,000; ✱ Edmonton. *Physical features:* An extensive plateau with higher portion in S; main range of the Canadian Rockies along its SW border; many peaks 8000 to 11,000 ft.; its eastern slopes have been in large part set aside as national recreation areas, noted for their scenery (see *Jasper, Banff,* and *Waterton Lakes National Parks* in table at CANADA); in N is the S half of Wood Buffalo National Park; contains also two other smaller national parks and ab. 50 provincial parks. Prairie lands well watered, in N by Athabaska and Peace river systems, in center by the North Saskatchewan, and in S by the South Saskatchewan. In NE corner is Lake Claire and W end of Lake Athabaska; in cen. part is Lesser Slave Lake. *Chief products:* Wheat, barley, sugar beets; livestock raising; petroleum, natural gas, coal, gypsum; manufacturing: processing of raw materials; chemicals, paper. *Chief cities:* Edmonton, Calgary, Lethbridge, Red Deer, Medicine Hat.

History: Part of territory ruled by Hudson's Bay Company until 1870; as part of Northwest Territories, under the Dominion of Canada 1870–82; S part set up as a district, bet. Rocky Mts. and 112°W and S of 55°N, 105,300 sq. m., with capital at Calgary; developed by an increasing number of "homesteaders" after completion of Canadian Pacific R.R. 1886; dominated by ranching until ab. 1900; became famed for its wheat and mineral production; received provincial status 1905; important oil reserves discovered 1947.

2 Mountain, Rocky Mt. range, SW Alberta, at S end of Jasper National Park; 11,874 ft.

Albert Canal \ˌal-bərt-\. Canal, NE Belgium, from Liége to Antwerp; 80 m. long, 140 ft. wide; crossed by Germans May 11, 1940; retaken by British Sept. 7, 1944.

Albert Ed·ward \-ˈed-wərd\. Peak in the Owen Stanley Range, Papua New Guinea, SE New Guinea, N of Port Moresby; 13,097 ft.

Albert Edward Nyanza. See EDWARD, LAKE.

Albert Lea \-ˈlē\. City, ⊗ of Freeborn co., S Minnesota, 20 m. W of Austin; pop. (1970c) 19,418; beverages, dairy products, road machinery.

Albert Mark·ham, Mount \-ˈmär-kəm\. Peak in Victoria Land, Antarctica, 81°23′S, 158°12′E, N of Mt. Markham; 10,460 ft.

Albert Mountains. Mountain range, Papua New Guinea, E New Guinea; has several peaks over 10,000 ft., highest ab. 13,600 ft.; connects with Owen Stanley Range on SE.

Albert National Park. Extensive park, E Zaire, cen. Africa, bet. Lakes Kivu and Edward; 3088 sq. m.; a game preserve and gorilla sanctuary established 1925, subsequently enlarged.

Albert Nile. See NILE.

Albert Nyanza. See ALBERT, LAKE.

Al·ber·ton \ˈal-bərt-ᵊn\. Town, Transvaal, Rep. of South Africa; pop. (1967e) 44,800.

Al·bert·ville \ˈal-bərt-ˌvil\. City, Marshall co., NE Alabama, 20 m. NW of Gadsden; pop. (1970c) 9963; cotton and cottonseed-oil mills; lumber.

Albertville. See KALEMI.

Al·bi \al-ˈbē\ *or anc.* **Al·bi·ga** \al-ˈbī-gə\. Commune, ✱ of Tarn dept., S France, on Tarn river 42 m. NE of Toulouse; pop. (1968c) 42,930; 13th cent. Gothic cathedral; archbishops' palace. Capital of Romano-Gallic Albigenses and of medieval viscounty of Albigeois, which later became part of Toulouse; not, as is commonly asserted, the center of the Albigensian movement which took on its name.

Al·bia \ˈal-bē-ə\. City, ⊗ of Monroe co., S Iowa, 22 m. W of Ottumwa; pop. (1970c) 4151; coal mining.

Albiga. See ALBI.

Al·bi·geois \ˌal-bizh-ˈwä\. Former region, S France, around Albi, viscounty of Languedoc, now entirely in Tarn dept.; joined to France 1247.

Al–Bika. See BIKA.

Al·bi·na \al-ˈbē-nə\. Seaport town, NE Surinam, on W bank of Maroni river opp. Saint Laurent, French Guiana; lumber and gold.

Albina, Point *or Port.* **Pon·ta Albina** \ˌpōⁿn-tə-äl-ˈbē-nə\. Cape on SW coast of Angola, W Africa; 15°51′S, 11°44′E.

Albingaunum. See ALBENGA.

Al·bi·on \ˈal-bē-ən\. 1 City, ⊗ of Edwards co., SE Illinois; pop. (1970c) 1791.

2 Town, ⊗ of Noble co., NE Indiana; pop. (1970c) 1498.

3 Industrial city, Calhoun co., S Michigan, 23 m. ESE of Battle Creek; pop. (1970c) 12,112; iron products; Albion Coll. (1835, coll. status 1861).

4 City, ⊗ of Boone co., E cen. Nebraska, 40 m. WSW of Norfolk; pop. (1970c) 2074; meat-packing.

5 Village, ⊗ of Orleans co., W New York, ab. 10 m. S of Lake Ontario and 32 m. W of Rochester; pop. (1970c) 5122; shipping center for agricultural, fruit- and vegetable-growing area.

6 Borough, Erie co., NW corner of Pennsylvania, 22 m. SW of Erie; pop. (1970c) 1768.

7 Oldest name of Great Britain; retained as poetical name of England.

Al–Biqa. See BIKA.

Albis. See ELBE.

Al·blas·ser·dam \ˈäl-ˌbläs-ər-ˌdäm\. Commune, South Holland prov., Netherlands, 9 m. SE of Rotterdam; pop. (1970e) 17,342.

Albona. See LABIN.

Al·bo·rán \ˌal-bə-ˈrän\. Island in W Mediterranean Sea, part of Almería prov., Spain, N of Melilla and 45 m. off coast of Spain.

Ålborg *or* **Aal·borg** \ˈól-ˌbó(ə)rg\ *or anc.* **Al·burg·um** \al-ˈbər-gəm\. Commercial seaport, ⊗ of Nordjylland co., Denmark; pop. (1970e) 154,737; cement, textiles, tobacco, shipbuilding; castle (1539); founded 1342.

Al·box \äl-ˈvōks, -ˈvōk\. Commune, Almería prov., SE Spain, ab. 41 m. NE of Almería; pop. (1970p) 10,036.

Al·brook Field \ˌól-ˌbru̇k-\. Airfield in Canal Zone, near Ancon and the Pacific terminus of the Panama Canal.

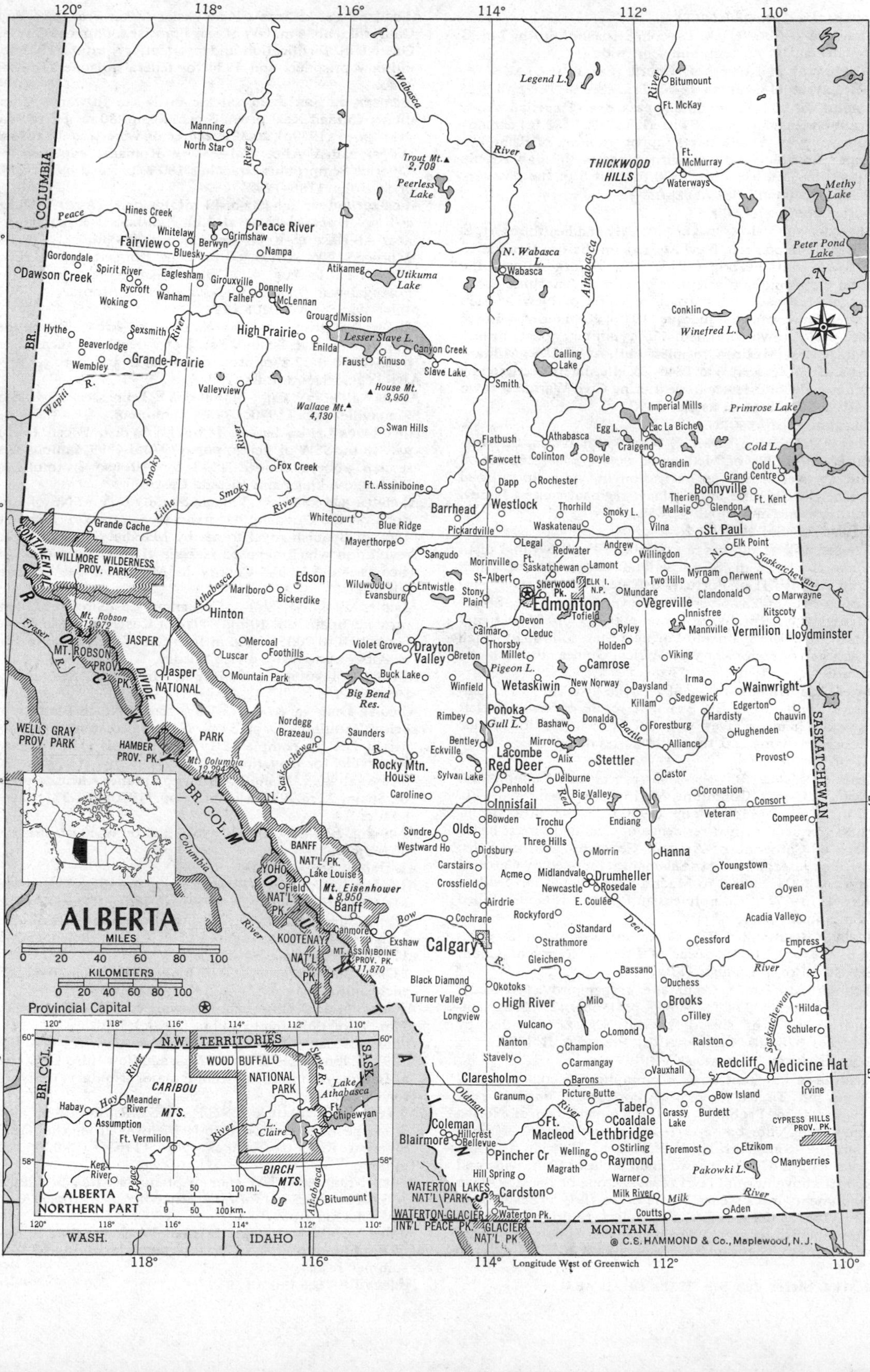
ALBERTA
MILES
0 20 40 60 80 100
KILOMETERS
0 20 40 60 80 100
Provincial Capital
120°
118°
116°
114°
112°
110°
56°
54°
52°
50°
BR. COLUMBIA
SASKATCHEWAN
MONTANA
WASH.
IDAHO
Longitude West of Greenwich
© C.S. HAMMOND & Co., Maplewood, N.J.
Legend L.
Bitumount
Ft. McKay
Ft. McMurray
Waterways
THICKWOOD HILLS
Methy Lake
Peter Pond Lake
Wabasca
River
Athabasca
Trout Mt. 2,700
Peerless Lake
Manning
North Star
Peace
Hines Creek
Whitelaw
Peace River
Grimshaw
Fairview
Berwyn
Bluesky
Nampa
Gordondale
Dawson Creek
Spirit River
Eaglesham
Girouxville
Rycroft
Wanham
Falher
Donnelly
McLennan
Woking
Atikameg
Utikuma Lake
N. Wabasca L.
Wabasca
Conklin
Winefred L.
Grouard Mission
Hythe
Sexsmith
High Prairie
Enilda
Lesser Slave L.
Canyon Creek
Beaverlodge
Grande-Prairie
Wembley
Faust
Kinuso
Slave Lake
Calling Lake
Wapiti R.
Valleyview
House Mt. 3,950
Smith
Wallace Mt. 4,130
Swan Hills
Imperial Mills
Primrose Lake
Egg L.
Lac La Biche
Athabasca
Craigend
Cold L.
Flatbush
Colinton
Boyle
Fawcett
Grandin
Cold L.
Grand Centre
Smoky
Little
Fox Creek
Dapp
Rochester
Bonnyville
Ft. Kent
Ft. Assiniboine
Therien
Glendon
Mallaig
Thorhild
Smoky L.
Vilna
St. Paul
Elk Point
Barrhead
Westlock
Waskatenau
Grande Cache
Whitecourt
Blue Ridge
Pickardville
CONTINENTAL
WILLMORE WILDERNESS PROV. PARK
Mayerthorpe
Legal
Redwater
Andrew
Willingdon
Sangudo
Morinville
Ft. Saskatchewan
Lamont
Myrnam
Derwent
Two Hills
Edson
Wildwood
Entwistle
Evansburg
St-Albert
Stony Plain
Sherwood Pk.
ELK I. N.P.
Edmonton
Mundare
Vegreville
Clandonald
Marwayne
Marlboro
Bickerdike
Hinton
Mt. Robson 12,972
Fraser R.
JASPER
Devon
Tofield
Innisfree
Kitscoty
Calmar
Leduc
Mannville
Vermilion
Lloydminster
Mercoal
Thorsby
Ryley
Luscar
Foothills
MT. ROBSON PROV. PK.
Violet Grove
Drayton Valley
Millet
Holden
Breton
Viking
Jasper NATIONAL
Mountain Park
Pigeon L.
Camrose
DIVIDE
Buck Lake
Winfield
Wetaskiwin
New Norway
Daysland
Irma
Wainwright
Big Bend Res.
Killam
Sedgewick
Edgerton
Chauvin
WELLS GRAY PROV. PARK
Nordegg (Brazeau)
Rimbey
Ponoka
Gull L.
Bashaw
Donalda
Hardisty
Forestburg
Hughenden
Saunders
PARK
Bentley
Mirror
Battle
Alliance
HAMBER PROV. PK.
Eckville
Lacombe
Alix
Stettler
Provost
Mt. Columbia 12,294
Rocky Mtn. House
Sylvan Lake
Red Deer
Delburne
Castor
Saskatchewan
Penhold
Big Valley
Coronation
Caroline
Innisfail
Consort
BR. COL.
Bowden
Trochu
Endiang
Veteran
Compeer
Sundre
Olds
Three Hills
Westward Ho
Didsbury
Morrin
Hanna
Columbia
BANFF NAT'L PK.
Carstairs
Acme
Midlandvale
Drumheller
Youngstown
YOHO
Lake Louise
Field
NAT'L PK.
Mt. Eisenhower 8,950
Banff
Crossfield
Newcastle
Rosedale
Cereal
Oyen
Airdrie
E. Coulee
Rockyford
Acadia Valley
Canmore
Bow
Cochrane
Standard
KOOTENAY NAT'L PK.
Exshaw
Calgary
Strathmore
Cessford
Empress
MT. ASSINIBOINE PROV. PK. 11,870
Gleichen
Deer
Bassano
Black Diamond
Okotoks
Duchess
Turner Valley
High River
Brooks
Longview
Milo
Tilley
Hilda
Vulcan
Lomond
Schuler
Nanton
Champion
Ralston
Stavely
Carmangay
Vauxhall
Redcliff
Medicine Hat
Claresholm
Barons
Irvine
Granum
Picture Butte
Bow Island
Oldman
Taber
Grassy Lake
Burdett
Coleman
Ft. Macleod
Coaldale
Lethbridge
CYPRESS HILLS PROV. PK.
Blairmore
Hillcrest
Bellevue
Stirling
Pincher Cr
Welling
Raymond
Foremost
Etzikom
Manyberries
Magrath
Hill Spring
Warner
Pakowki L.
Cardston
WATERTON LAKES NAT'L PARK
Milk River
Milk
WATERTON-GLACIER INT'L PEACE PK.
Waterton Pk.
Coutts
Aden
GLACIER NAT'L PK
ROCKY MOUNTAINS
N.W. TERRITORIES
WOOD BUFFALO NATIONAL PARK
SASK.
Slave R.
Lake Athabasca
Ft. Chipewyan
CARIBOU MTS.
Hay
Meander River
Habay
Assumption
Ft. Vermilion
L. Claire
BIRCH MTS.
Keg River
Bitumount
ALBERTA NORTHERN PART
0 50 100 mi.
0 50 100 km.
60°
58°

Albuera, La. See LA ALBUERA.

Al·bu·fe·ra \ˌal-bu̇-ˈfer-ə\. Lagoon, E coast of Spain, 7 m. S of Valencia; 11 m. long and 4 m. wide.

Al–Buhayrah al–Murrah al–Kubrā. See BITTER LAKES.

Al–Buhayrah al–Murrah as–Sughrā. See BITTER LAKES.

Al·bu·la \ˌäl-bə-lə\. Mountain pass over Rhaetian Alps, Graubünden canton, SE Switzerland; alt. 7583 ft.; extends from valley of **Albula River** (upper tributary of Rhine) to Upper Engadine Valley; railroad passes through **Albula Tunnel** (3⅔ m. long, alt. 5970 ft.) just S of the pass.

Album Ingaunum. See ALBENGA.

Al–Bunbah. See BOMBA.

Al·bu·quer·que \ˈal-b(y)ə-ˌkər-kē\. City and health resort, ⊗ of Bernalillo co., cen. New Mexico, on the Rio Grande 55 m. SW of Santa Fe; pop. (1970c) 243,751; largest city in the state; electronic and scientific equipment, machine tools, textiles; railroad shops; tourism; Univ. of New Mexico (1889), Univ. of Albuquerque (1940); Kirtland Air Force Base. Old town founded 1706; military post during Spanish and Mexican regimes; outpost of U.S. Military Dept. after Mexican War 1846–70; alternately occupied by Union and Confederate forces during Civil War; new town platted 1880, incorp. as city 1890.

Alburgum. See ÅLBORG.

Al·bury \ˈal-bə-rē\. Town, S New South Wales, SE Australia, 170 m. NE of Melbourne; pop. (1968e) 26,210; on Murray river at head of navigation and on main railroad line bet. Melbourne and Sydney; regional center; honey, wool; became municipality 1859.

Al–Buseira. See BOZRAH 2.

Al·cá·cer do Sal \äl-ˌkas-ər-du̇-ˈsäl\. Village, Setúbal dist., Portugal, ab. 25 m. SE of Setúbal; battle 1217 in which King Alfonso II of Portugal defeated the Moors.

Al·ca·ço·vas \äl-ˈkas-ə-vəs(h)\. Town, Évora dist., S cen. Portugal, ab. 19 m. SW of Évora; pop. (1970p) 2640; treaty signed here bet. Spain and Portugal Mar. 6, 1480 in which possession of regions in West Africa, Guinea, and Atlantic islands was settled.

Al·ca·lá de Gua·dai·ra \ˌal-kə-ˈlä-t͟hā-gwə-ˈt͟hī-rə\. Commune, Sevilla prov., SW Spain, 10 m. SE of Seville on left bank of Guadaira river; pop. (1970p) 33,999; flour mills; Moorish remains, esp. the castle (surrendered to Ferdinand III of Castile 1244).

Alcalá de He·na·res \-t͟hā-ə-ˈnär-əs\ *or anc.* **Com·plu·tum** \kəm-ˈplüt-əm\. Commune, Madrid prov., cen. Spain, ab. 20 m. ENE of Madrid; pop. (1970p) 59,783; after reconquest frequently royal residence of Castilian kings; birthplace of Catherine of Aragon, Cervantes, and de Solis; university, second only to Salamanca, founded by Cardinal Jiménez 1508 (moved to Madrid 1846); noted for production (1513–17) of Complutensian Polyglot Bible, so called from ancient name of city.

Alcalá la Re·al \-lä-rē-ˈäl\. Commune, Jaén prov., S Spain; pop. (1970p) 21,349; scene of French victory of Count Sebastiani over Spanish 1810.

Al·ca·mo \ˈäl-kä-ˌmō\. Commune, Trapani prov., NW Sicily, Italy, 25 m. E by S of Trapani; pop. (1968e) 42,758; agricultural trade; near site of ancient Segesta; founded by Saracens 828 A.D.; site moved by Frederick II 1233.

Alcan Highway. See ALASKA HIGHWAY.

Al·cán·ta·ra \al-ˈkant-ə-rə\. Commune, Câceres prov., W Spain, on Tagus river near Portuguese border; pop. (1970p) 4636. Probably not the Roman town of **Nor·ba Cae·sa·rea** \ˈnȯr-bə-ˌsē-zə-ˈrē-ə, -ˌses-ə-, -ˌsez-\. Named from the Roman bridge built here by Hadrian 105 A.D. (total length 670 ft.; its two main arches 110 ft. wide and 210 ft. above normal level of river), one of finest Roman monuments in existence; home of knightly order (organized 1156, as the Knights of St. Julian, to drive the Moors from Spanish territory) which changed its name to Order of Alcántara when the town was given it 1217 by Alfonso IX.

Alcaraz, Sierra de. See SIERRA DE ALCARAZ.

Al·ca·traz \ˈal-kə-ˌtraz\. Rocky island, San Francisco Bay, California, ab. 4 m. NW of San Francisco, opp. the Golden Gate; U.S. fortification and penitentiary, estab. 1868 for military prisoners and 1934 for federal prisoners, closed 1963.

Al·cá·zar de San Juan \al-ˈkäz-ər-də-san-ˈ(h)wän\. Commune, Ciudad Real prov., S cen. Spain, 80 m. SE of Madrid; pop. (1970p) 26,391; center of wine trade; railroad shops; called **Al·ce** \ˈal-sē\ by Romans; captured by Tiberius Sempronius Gracchus 180 B.C.; ruled by Knights of St. John 1186–1292.

Al·ca·zar·qui·vir \al-ˌkäz-ər-ki-ˈvi(ə)r\ *or* **Al·cá·zar** \al-ˈkäz-ər\ *or Arab.* **Al–Qsar al–Kbir** \ˌal-kə-ˌsär-ˌal-kə-ˈbi(ə)r\ *also* **Al–Kasr al–Kebir** \al-ˌkas-ər-al-kə-ˈbi(ə)r\. City, N Morocco, NW Africa, 60 m. S of Tangier; pop. (1960c) 34,035; battle Aug. 4, 1578 in which King Sebastian of Portugal was defeated and slain by the Moors.

Alchevsk. See KOMMUNARSK.

Al·ci·ra \al-ˈsir-ə\ *or anc.* **Su·cro** \ˈsü-ˌkrō\. Commune, Valencia prov., E Spain, 23 m. S of Valencia on Júcar river; pop. (1970p) 32,876; produces oranges and rice.

Alçı Tepe. See ACHI BABA.

Al·coa \al-ˈkō-ə\. City, Blount co., E Tennessee, 15 m. S of Knoxville; pop. (1970c) 7739; aluminum.

Al·co·ba·ça \ˌal-kə-ˈbas-ə\. Town, Leiria dist., W cen. Portugal, 18 m. SSW of Leiria; pop. (1970p) 4799; famous Cistercian abbey founded 1148 by Alfonso I; tombs of Portuguese kings and Inés de Castro.

Al·co·lea \ˌäl-kə-ˈlā-ə\. Village, Spain, ab. 5 m. NE of Córdoba on the Guadalquivir river; scene of defeat Sept. 28, 1868 of Spanish royal forces by Marshal Serrano during revolution which deposed Isabella II from throne.

Al·co·na \al-ˈkō-nə\. County in Michigan. See table at MICHIGAN.

Al·co·ra \äl-ˈkōr-ə, -ˈkȯr-\. Commune, Castellón de la Plana prov., E Spain, ab. 10 m. WNW of Castellón de la Plana; pop. (1970p) 7005; noted in 18th cent. for its manufacture of Alcora porcelain, a rich faïence.

Al·corn \ˈȯl-ˌkȯ(ə)rn\. County in Mississippi. See table at MISSISSIPPI.

Al·co·va Dam \al-ˌkō-və-\. Dam across North Platte river below Pathfinder Dam, S cen. Natrona co., cen. Wyoming; height 265 ft.; completed 1938; impounds water, **Alcova Reservoir,** for irrigation.

Al·coy \äl-ˈkȯi\. Manufacturing commune, Alicante prov., SE Spain, 22 m. N of Alicante; pop. (1970p) 61,371; paper, textiles.

Al·cu·dia, Bay of \-äl-ˈkü-t͟hyə\. Bay on N coast of island of Majorca.

Al–Daba. See AD DABAH.

Al·dab·ra \al-ˈdab-rə\. **1** Island group in Indian Ocean N of Malagasy Republic, part of British Indian Ocean Territory; includes Aldabra and Assumption; unusual flora and fauna; visited by Portuguese 1511; French dependency in 17th cent.; became British 1810.

2 Chief island in group; 20 m. long; 60 sq. m.; an oval atoll enclosing a lagoon.

Al·dan \ˈȯl-dən\. Borough, Delaware co., SE Pennsylvania, 7 m. W of Philadelphia; pop. (1970c) 5001.

Aldan \äl-ˈdän\. **1** River, SE Yakutsk A.S.S.R., U.S.S.R.; 1393 m. long; rises in Aldan Mts. and flows into Lena river at Batamay, forming its second major tributary; navigable for 800 m.

2 Town, SE Yakutsk A.S.S.R., U.S.S.R., in Aldan valley S of the river and on S-to-N highway from the Trans-Siberian R.R. to Yakutsk; pop. (1967e) 15,000; gold mining.

Aldan Mountains. NW spur of Stanovoi Mts., S Yakutsk A.S.S.R., U.S.S.R., forming watershed bet. upper Aldan and Olekma rivers.

Al·den \ˈȯl-dən\. Village, Erie co., W New York, 20 m. E of Buffalo; pop. (1970c) 2651; paper products; agriculture; summer resort.

Aldenville. See CHICOPEE 2.

Alder, Ben *or* **Mount Alder.** See BEN ALDER.

Al·der·ney \ˈȯl-dər-nē\ *or Fr.* **Au·ri·gny** \ō-rē-nyē\ *or anc.* **Ri·du·na** \ri-ˈd(y)ü-nə\. Northernmost of Channel Is., in Guernsey bailiwick; 4½ m. long; 3 sq. m.; pop. (1971p) 1686; ✱ St. Anne; separated from Cape La Hague, France, by dangerous 8 m.-wide tidal channel, **Race of Alderney.** Agriculture and cattle raising.

Al·der·shot \ˈȯl-dər-ˌshät\. Municipal borough, Hampshire, S England, 32 m. SW of London; pop. (1971p) 33,311; its permanent military camp (estab. 1855) became 1904–14 center for English military training. See BISLEY.

Aldrich Deep. See KERMADEC TRENCH.

Al·dridge–Brown·hills \ˌȯl-drij-ˈbrau̇n-ˌhilz\. Urban district, Staffordshire, England; pop. (1971p) 88,475; electrical and light engineering.

Ale·do \ə-ˈlēd-ˌō\. City, ⊗ of Mercer co., NW Illinois, 25 m. SSW of Rock Island; pop. (1970c) 3325.

Ale·gre \ə-ˈleg-rə\. Municipality, Espírito Santo state, E Brazil, 90 m. SW of Vitória; pop. (1968e) 67,473.

Ale·gre·te \ˌäl-ə-ˈgrāt-ə\. Municipality, Rio Grande do Sul state, S Brazil, 260 m. W of Pôrto Alegre; pop. (1968e) 63,945.

Alejandro Selkirk. See MÁS AFUERA.

Ale·ksan·dra Land \ˌal-ik-ˈsan-drə-, -ig-ˈzan-\. See FRANZ JOSEF LAND.

Alek·san·dri·ya \ˌal-ik-ˈsan-drē-(y)ə, ˌel-, -ig-ˈzan-\. Town, Kirovograd Oblast, Ukrainian S.S.R., U.S.S.R., ab. 45 m. ENE of Kirovograd; pop. (1969e) 70,000; coal deposits.

Aleksandropol. See LENINAKAN.

Alek·san·drov \ˌal-ik-ˈsan-drəf, ˌel-, -ig-ˈzan-\. Town, Vladimir Oblast, Russian S.F.S.R., U.S.S.R., ab. 60 m. WNW of Vladimir; pop. (1967e) 46,000; textiles; founded by Ivan the Terrible 1564.

Ale·ksan·drovsk \ˌal-ik-ˈsan-drəfsk, ˌel-, -ig-ˈzan-\. **1** *or* **Aleksandrovsk–Grushevski.** City, Russian S.F.S.R., U.S.S.R. See SHAKHTY.

2 City, Ukrainian S.S.R., U.S.S.R. See ZAPOROZHYE.

Aleksandr Range. See KIRGIZ RANGE.

Alek·sin \ə-ˈlek-sən\. Town, Tula Oblast, Russian S.F.S.R., U.S.S.R., 30 m. NW of Tula; pop. (1969e) 54,000.

Alek·si·nac \ə-ˈlek-sə-ˌnäts\. Town, E Yugoslavia, on Morava river, 18 m. NNW of Niš; battle 1876 in which Serbs and Russians were defeated by Turks.

Alemtejo. See ALENTEJO.

Alen·çon \ˌal-ä^{n}-ˈsō^{n}\. City, ✱ of Orne dept., NW France, on Sarthe river 28 m. N of Le Mans; pop. (1968c) 31,656; lacemaking center.

History: Town, center of medieval territory of Alençon, successively a lordship, county, and duchy, the title to which usually belonged to member of royal house 13th–16th cents.; after 1525 seat of court of Margaret of Navarre, sister of Francis I; lace introduced by Colbert as part of effort to develop French industry (in second half of 17th cent.). In World War II reached by American forces Aug. 1944.

Alen·te·jo *or formerly* **Alem·te·jo** \ə-lā(^{n})n-ˈtā-zhü\. Ancient province of SE Portugal; 9083 sq. m.; ✱ Évora; now consists of Beja, Évora, and Portalegre dists.; drained by Tagus, Sado, and Guadiana rivers; region occupied by province now produces rice, fruit, olives; sometimes called "Granary of Portugal"; manufactures olive and other oils, woolens, leather.

Ale·nu·i·ha·ha \ˌäl-ə-ˌnü-ē-ˈhä-(ˌ)hä\. Channel, Hawaiian Is., bet. Hawaii and Maui; 26 m. wide.

Alep·po \ə-ˈlep-(ˌ)ō\ *or* **Alep** \ä-ˈlep\; *Arab.* **Ha·leb** *or* **Ha·lab** \hə-ˈleb\. **1** Former Turkish province, now largely in N Syria.

2 *or anc.* **Be·roea** \bə-ˈrē-ə\. City, NW Syria; pop. (1970e) 639,000; cotton printing, silk weaving; cement, wool; univ. (1960).

History: Ancient city, capital of a kingdom, first taken by Hittites as early as 2000 B.C.; scene of conflict between Hittites and Egyptians, especially in 15th century B.C.; an independent Hittite principality until conquered by Assyrian king 853 B.C.; enlarged by Seleucus Nicator (306–280 B.C.) and named Beroea; see SYRIA for events of significance up to Muslim conquest; taken by Muslim Arabs 638 A.D.; temporarily recovered by Greeks under Nicephorus Phocas 969; held by Seljuks 1090–1117; unsuccessfully besieged by Crusaders 1118, 1124; sacked by Mongols 1260 and by Tamerlane 1401; after capture by Ottoman Turks 1517, experienced revival of trade with East; a flourishing trade center in 16th century, gradually declined because of use of sea route to India and later opening of Suez Canal (1869); largely destroyed by earthquakes 1822, 1830; taken by Ibrahim Pasha 1832; in 1918 captured by British and Arabs under Allenby as part of World War I campaign against Turkey; organized as state of French mandate of Syria 1920; united with Damascus to form state of Syria 1925.

Ale·ria \ə-ˈlir-ē-ə\ *or* **Ala·lia** \ə-ˈlā-lē-ə\. One of the chief cities of ancient Corsica, near E coast; modern commune is **Alé·ria** \ə-ˈlir-ē-ə, -ˈler-\, pop. (1962c) 1200.

Alert Bay \ə-ˌlərt-\. Village and port on island off NE coast of Vancouver I., British Columbia, Canada, at S end of Charlotte Strait; pop. (1971p) 743; steamer stop on route from Vancouver to northern ports.

Alès \a-ˈles\ *or formerly* **Alais** \á-les\. City, Gard dept., S France, 27 m. NNW of Nîmes; pop. (1968c) 42,818; metallurgical workshops; tourism.

Ale·sia \ə-ˈlē-zh(ē-)ə\. Town, NE Celtic Gaul, on a hill, near source of Sequana; site of successful siege of Vercingetorix by which Caesar put down Gallic revolt 52 B.C.

Ales·san·dria \ˌal-ə-ˈsan-drē-ə\. **1** Province of Piedmont, NW Italy. See table at ITALY.

2 Commune, its ✱, on the Tanaro river 35 m. ESE of Turin; pop. (1968e) 99,023; railroad and commercial center.

History: Founded 1168; became member of the Lombard League; besieged unsuccessfully by Frederick Barbarossa 1174; seized by Francesco Sforza 1522; attacked by French 1657; captured by Prince Eugene 1707; ceded to Savoy 1713; citadel built 1728; occupied by French 1800–14.

Alessio. See LESH.

Ale·sund *or* **Aa·le·sund** \ˈō-lə-ˌsu̇n\. Seaport city, Møre og Romsdal co., W Norway, on an island bet. Bergen and Trondheim; munic. pop. (1970e) 39,390; trading center, esp. for Norwegian W coast cod and herring fisheries; headquarters for Arctic sealing fleet.

Aletrium. See ALATRI.

Aletsch·horn \ˈäl-ich-ˌhȯrn\. Mountain, Bernese Alps, Valais canton, Switzerland, ab. 5 m. SSE of the Jungfrau; 13,763 ft.

Aleu·tian Islands \ə-ˈlü-shən-\ *or commonly* **Aleu·tians** \-shənz\ *or formerly* **Cath·er·ine Archipelago** \ˌkath-(ə-)rən-\. Chain of volcanic islands, extending 1700 m. W from Alaska Penin. 163°W to 172°30′E (but E of Date Line); 6821 sq. m.; islands separate Bering Sea from North Pacific Ocean; coextensive with Aleutian Islands district of Alaska; chief islands and groups from E to W are Fox Is. (including Unimak and Unalaska), Islands of the Four Mountains, Andreanof Is., Rat Is., and Near Is. (including Attu, only 500 m. E of Kamchatka); chief town Dutch Harbor on Unalaska; several volcanoes still active (highest Shishaldin, on Unimak, 9370 ft.); even climate but much fog and rain; fertile soil; industries fishing, raising furbearing animals, and some agriculture.

History: Eastern part discovered by Chirikov and several of western group by Bering 1741 (see ALASKA); exploited by Siberian fur traders; served as approach for Russian expansion to mainland of Alaska; purchased with

Alaska by U.S. from Russia 1867; basis of U.S. claim in controversy over seal fisheries that Bering Sea (*q.v.*) was a *mare clausum;* W islands (Attu and Kiska) occupied by Japanese June 1942; Attu retaken by U.S. forces May 1943; Kiska abandoned by Japanese Aug. 1943; site of U.S. airfields and radar stations.

Aleutian Range. Mountain range along E coast of N Alaska Penin.; includes Mt. Katmai (6715 ft.) and Katmai National Monument.

Aleutian Trench *or* **Aleutian Trough.** Deep, in North Pacific Ocean at W end of Aleutian Is.; max. depth 26,574 ft.

Al·ex·an·der \ˌal-ig-ˈzan-dər, ˌel-\. Name of counties in two states of the U.S. See tables at ILLINOIS, NORTH CAROLINA.

Alexander, Cape. Cape, NW Choiseul I., British Solomon Islands, W Pacific Ocean, 6°35′S, 156°30′E.

Alexander Archipelago. Group of ab. 1100 islands, SE Alaska, made up of tops of submerged mountains, with irregular coastlines and deep channels between them; from N to S chief islands are Chichagof, Admiralty, Baranof, Kupreanof, Prince of Wales, and Revillagigedo; chief towns Sitka and Ketchikan.

Alexander Bay. Bay on extreme NW coast of Cape Province, Rep. of South Africa, at the mouth of the Orange river.

Alexander City. City, Tallapoosa co., E Alabama, 5 m. N of Martin Lake; pop. (1970c) 12,358; cotton goods, lumber; Alexander City State Junior Coll. (1965); incorporated 1873.

Alexander Graham Bell National Historic Park. See CANADA, *National Historic Parks.*

Alexander Island *or formerly* **Alexander I Island.** Island in Antarctica, W of base of Antarctic Penin., British Antarctic Territory; ab. 235 m. long; 16,700 sq. m.; formerly considered part of Antarctic continent; discovered and named by Bellingshausen on expedition 1819–21.

Alexander Range. See KIRGIZ RANGE.

Alexandra, Mount. See RUWENZORI, MOUNT.

Al·ex·an·dra Land \ˌal-ig-ˈzan-drə-, ˌel-\. Island, W part of Franz Josef Land, 80°45′N, 46°E; belongs to U.S.S.R.

Al·ex·an·dret·ta \ˌal-ig-(ˌ)zan-ˈdret-ə, ˌel-\ *or Turk.* **İs·ken·de·run** \(ˌ)is-ˌken-də-ˈrän, -ˈrün\. **1** Formerly an administrative district of Turkey; after World War I (1920) a semiautonomous region of NW Syria extending ab. 100 m. along Gulf of İskenderun and E Mediterranean; ab. 5000 sq. m. Set up as a state with limited autonomy 1925 and as the Republic of Hatay 1938; incorporated in Turkish republic by agreement bet. France and Turkey June 23, 1939. Contains Nur Mountains, with Musa Dagh at its S end, Orontes and Afrine rivers, and the port of Süveydiye, N of mouth of Orontes.

2 *or Fr.* **Alex·an·drette** \á-lek-säⁿ-dret\. City. See İSKENDERUN.

Alexandretta, Gulf of. See İSKENDERUN, GULF OF.

Al·ex·an·dria \ˌal-ig-ˈzan-drē-ə, ˌel-\. **1** City, Madison co., cen. Indiana, in agricultural section 17 m. WNW of Muncie; pop. (1970c) 5168; canned goods.

2 City, ⊗ of Campbell co., N Kentucky; pop. (1970c) 3844.

3 City, ⊗ of Rapides parish, cen. Louisiana, 100 m. NW of Baton Rouge; pop. (1970c) 41,557; chemicals, fertilizers, lubricating oil; cotton ginning, meat-packing.

4 City, ⊗ of Douglas co., W cen. Minnesota, 60 m. WNW of Saint Cloud; pop. (1970c) 6973; resort center in lake region.

5 City, ⊗ of Hanson co., SE South Dakota; pop. (1970c) 598.

6 Independent city, Virginia, on Potomac river 6 m. S of Washington, D.C.; 15 sq. m.; pop. (1970c) 110,938; residential; beverages, chemicals, fertilizers, lumber; port of entry; Episcopal Theological Seminary (1825), Luther Rice Coll. (1967); home of George Washington; founded 1749; ⊗ of Fairfax co. 1752; incorp. as town 1779; became part of District of Columbia 1791, but was returned to Va. as free city 1847; ⊗ of Alexandria (now Arlington) co. 1847–98; became city 1852; occupied by Union forces during Civil War; seat of Unionist Alexandria government 1863–65.

7 Commune, ⊗ of Teleorman co., S Romania, on lower Vedea river; pop. (1969e) 21,687.

Alexandria *or Arab.* **Al–Is·kan·da·rī·yah** \ˌal-(ˌ)is-ˌkan-də-ˈrē-(y)ə\. **1** Governorate of N Egypt. See table at EGYPT. **2** Seaport, its ✱, on strip of land bet. the Mediterranean and Lake Mareotis; pop. (1970e) 2,032,000; approx. coextensive with Alexandria gov.; car-assembly workshops, oil refinery; food processing; exports cotton, cereals, vegetables; univ. (1942). Ancient island (Pharos), on which was famous lighthouse, now a peninsula connected with mainland by sandy isthmus filled in around ancient mole; modern harbor is W of peninsula and formed partly by a breakwater.

History: Founded by Alexander the Great after his capture of Egypt 332 B.C.; a trading center, also became a center of Hellenistic culture, famed as meeting ground of Greek, Arab, and Jewish ideas; site of greatest library of ancient times which was founded by Ptolemy I (323–285 B.C.) and was alleged to have contained 700,000 rolls of papyri; library lost in a conflagration which occurred when Caesar captured city 48 B.C.; captured by Arabs 640 A.D. and by Turks 1517; occupied by French 1798–1801 during Napoleon's Egyptian campaign (see ABUKIR); after a long period of decline in its significance because of rise of Cairo and neglect to dredge the silted harbor, revived commercially when Mehemet Ali joined it by a canal to the Nile early 19th century; bombarded and occupied by British 1882, after a series of nationalist riots against foreign domination of Egypt; temporarily taken over by British troops because of riots 1921. British naval base in World War II; saved from capture by Rommel by battle of Al-Alamein Oct.–Nov. 1942; evacuated by British forces 1946.

Alexandria Arachosiorum. See KANDAHĀR 2.

Alexandria Bay. Village, Jefferson co., N New York, on St. Lawrence river 25 m. N of Watertown; pop. (1970c) 1440; summer resort and tourist center for Thousand Islands region.

Alexandria Troas. See TROAS 2.

Al·ex·an·dri·na, Lake \-ˌal-ig-(ˌ)zan-ˈdrē-nə, -ˌel-\. Lake, SE South Australia, at mouth of Murray river; 220 sq. m.; actually a lagoon with shallow outlet, a fact that hinders navigation of the Murray; its S arm is the Coorong (*q.v.*).

Alexandropol. See LENINAKAN.

Ale·xan·droú·po·lis \ˌal-ig-zan-ˈdrü-pə-ləs\ *or Turk.* **De·de Ag·ach** \ˌdad-ə-ä-ˈ(g)äch\. Seaport city, ✱ of Evros dept., Western Thrace, Greece, on Aegean 10 m. NW of mouth of Maritsa river; pop. (1971p) 25,124; episcopal see; a trading town. Annexed by Bulgaria 1915–18; by treaty after World War I returned to Greece. Occupied by Bulgaria 1941–44.

Al–Fai·yūm *also* **El Faiyūm** *or* **El Fa·yum** \ˌal-fā-ˈ(y)üm, ˌel-\. Town, ✱ of Faiyūm gov., N Upper Egypt, ab. 70 m. SW of Cairo; pop. (1970e) 150,900; cotton ginning, tanning; important modern town on the Bahr Yusef bet. the Nile and Birket Qārūn; lies in bed of ancient Lake Moeris near site of Arsinoë, in region rich in archaeological objects and papyri.

Al·fal·fa \al-ˈfal-fə\. County in Oklahoma. See table at OKLAHOMA.

Al–Fal·lu·ja *or* **Al–Fal·lu·jah** \ˌal-fə-ˈlü-jə\. Town, cen. Iraq, on left bank of Euphrates 35 m. W of Baghdad and E of Lake Habbaniya; pop. (1965c) 38,072.

Al·fa·ro \äl-ˈfär-(ˌ)ō\ *or formerly* **Du·rán** \dü-ˈrän\. Railroad center, Guayas prov., W Ecuador, on Guayas river opp. Guayaquil; starting point of Guayaquil-Quito railroad, completed 1908.

Al–Fash·ir \al-ˈfash-ˌi(ə)r\ *or* **El Fash·er** \el-ˈfash-ər\. Town, ✱ of Darfur prov., W Sudan; pop. (1969e) 46,380.

Alfiós. See ALPHEUS.

Al·föld, Great \-ˈöl-ˌfə(r)ld\. Great central plain of Hungary, traversed by Danube and Tisza rivers. The **Little**

Alföld *also* **Kis–Alföld** \'kish-\ is a plain in NW Hungary and S Czechoslovakia, near Bratislava.

Al·fort·ville \ˌal-ˌfȯr-'vēl\. Commune, Val-de-Marne dept., N France, on Seine and Marne rivers 4 m. SE of Paris; pop. (1968c) 35,023; separated from Maisons-Alfort 1885.

Al·fred \'al-frəd, -fərd\. 1 Town, ⊗ of York co., SW Maine; pop. (1970c) 1211.

2 Village, Allegany co., SW New York, ab. 9 m. SW of Hornell; pop. (1970c) 3804; Alfred Univ. (1836).

Alfred, Mount. Peak, Coast Mountains, SW British Columbia, Canada, 80 m. NE of Vancouver; 8450 ft.

Al·fre·ton \'ȯl-frət-ᵊn\. Urban district, Derbyshire, N cen. England, 14 m. NNE of Derby; pop. (1971p) 21,670; foundation traditionally ascribed to King Alfred.

Alfsborg. See ÄLVSBORG.

Al–Fung *or* **El Fung** \al-'fu̇ŋ, el-\. Former province, E Anglo-Egyptian Sudan, now part of Blue Nile prov., Sudan.

Al–Furāt. See EUPHRATES.

Al–Fustāt. See CAIRO, Egypt.

Al·gar·ro·bo, Point \-ˌal-gə-'rō-(ˌ)bō\. Cape on W coast of Puerto Rico.

Algarrobo Bay. Inlet of Pacific Ocean on W cen. coast of Chile below Valparaíso.

Al·gar·ve \äl-'gär-və, al-\. Ancient kingdom, S Portugal; ✱ Faro; forms modern district of Faro; Serra do Monchique (highest point 2959 ft.) in N; fish, fruit; mining. Medieval Moorish kingdom (capital Silves) conquered 1253 by Alfonso III and title King of Algarve added to Portuguese crown 1253; later reduced to a province.

Al·gäu *or* **All·gäu** \'äl-ˌgȯi\. Region, SW Bavaria, West Germany; noted for dairy products. In its widest sense, the territory extending N to the Danube, S to the Inn, and W to the Lech.

Algäu Alps *or* **Allgäu Alps;** *Ger.* **Al·gau·er Al·pen** *or* **All·gäu·er Alpen** \ˌäl-ˌgȯi-ər-'äl-pən\. Mountains bet. Bavaria, West Germany, and Tirol, Austria, including such peaks as Hohes Licht (8706 ft.), Mädelegabel (8689 ft.), Hochvogel (8505 ft.); they extend E from Lake of Constance forming W section of Bavarian Alps, and contain sources of the Lech and Iller rivers. See ALPS.

Al–Ga·za·la *or* **El Gazala** \ˌal-gə-'zal-ə, ˌel-\. Village, NE Libya, on coast W of Tobruk; in World War II an Axis supply port; in early part of 1942 part of British defense line, evacuated in June.

Al·ge·ci·ras \ˌal-jə-'sir-əs, -hā-\. Seaport, Cádiz prov., SW Spain, 6 m. W of Gibraltar; munic. pop. (1970p) 81,662; exports leather, cork, stone, spirits.

History: Held by Moors 711–1344; after famous siege conquered by Alfonso XI of Castile; Moorish city destroyed and site reoccupied by Spanish 1704 who erected the modern town 1760; station for Spanish fleet during siege of Gibraltar 1780–82; scene of conference of the European Powers called to settle first Moroccan crisis 1906; gave name to Act of Algeciras which, in substance, gave France and Spain control of Morocco (*q.v.*).

Algeciras, Bay of. See GIBRALTAR, BAY OF.

Al·ge·me·sí \äl-ˌhā-mə-'sē\. Commune, Valencia prov., E Spain, ab. 6 m. N of Alcira; pop. (1971p) 22,123.

Al–Ge·nei·na *or* **El Geneina** \ˌal-jə-'nā-nə, ˌel-\. Town, W Darfur prov., W Sudan, on border W of Al-Fashir.

Al·ger \'al-jer\. County in Michigan. See table at MICHIGAN.

Alger \al-'zhā\. 1 Department of N Algeria, between Constantine and Oran depts.; 1312 sq. m.; pop. (1970e) 1,839,000; ✱ Algiers; has mountain ranges along coast and high plateau in interior. Chief towns Algiers and Blida.

2 City, Algeria. See ALGIERS 2.

Al·ge·ria \al-'jir-ē-ə\ *or officially* **Democratic and Popular Republic of Algeria;** *Fr.* **Al·gé·rie** \ál-zhā-rē\. Republic, N Africa, bounded on N by the Mediterranean Sea, on E by Tunisia and Libya, on S by Niger and Mali, and on W by Mauritania, Spanish Sahara, and Morocco; 896,588 sq. m.; pop. (1970e) 13,547,000; ✱ Algiers. *Physical features:* N part traversed by Atlas Mts. and Saharan Atlas; highest peak is Djebel Chélia 7648 ft., in NE; cen. and S parts occupy a large section of N Sahara Desert, including the Ahaggar massif and part of the Adrar des Iforas; coastline has few inlets and rivers are small. *Chief products:* Wheat, barley, grapes, figs, olives; livestock; oil, natural gas, iron ore, phosphates; manufacturing: cement, fertilizers, footwear. *Chief cities:* Algiers, Oran, Constantine, Annaba, Sétif. Divided into the following 15 departments (for pronunciation of their names, see their individual entries):

NAME	AREA (sq. m.)	POP. (1970e)	CAPITAL
Al Asnam	4,734	885,000	Al Asnam
Alger	1,312	1,839,000	Algiers
Annaba	9,560	1,056,000	Annaba
Batna	14,355	856,000	Batna
Constantine	7,560	1,682,000	Constantine
Médéa	23,654	979,000	Médéa
Mostaganem	4,290	874,000	Mostaganem
Oasis	780,617[1]	573,000	Ouargla
Oran	6,486	1,075,000	Oran
Saïda	21,784	268,000	Saïda
Saoura		238,000	Béchar
Sétif	6,995	1,382,000	Sétif
Tiaret	9,907	404,000	Tiaret
Tizi-Ouzou	2,208	936,000	Tizi-Ouzou
Tlemcen	3,135	500,000	Tlemcen

[1] Includes area of Saoura.

History: Territory known to Romans as Numidia; conquered by Vandals 430–31 A.D., by Eastern Roman Empire 531–34, and by Arabs in 7th century; nominally under rule of Ottoman Empire until 1705; repudiated Turkish rule and controlled by tribal organizations under dey of Algiers until occupied by French 1830; hinterland not subjugated until 1847 after a series of intermittent wars by French against Abd-al-Kader; placed under military rule by Napoleon III; in 1863 given a land law which helped break up tribal organization; after 1879 under civil rule as a part of France; scene of an uprising during French difficulties with Tunis 1881; under a reorganized government after 1898. In World War II under Vichy control until Nov. 1942; occupied by Allied forces Nov. 8–12, 1942; nationalist revolt against French rule 1954–61; granted independence following referendum of July 1, 1962; government overthrown in *coup d'état* 1965; settled boundary dispute with Morocco 1970.

Al–Gha·raq as–Sul·ta·ni \al-'gär-ˌäk-ˌas-su̇l-'tän-ē\. Town, Upper Egypt, just SW of Al-Faiyūm.

Al·ghe·ro \äl-'ge(ə)r-(ˌ)ō\. Seaport, Sassari prov., NW Sardinia, Italy, 17 m. SSW of Sassari; pop. (1968e) 30,697; exports fruit, wine, oil, coral, preserves; founded by Doria family (Genoese) ab. 1102; settled by Catalonians 14th cent.; under House of Aragon 1354–1720 and subsequently under House of Savoy.

Al·giers \al-'ji(ə)rz\ *or Fr.* **Al·ger** \ál-zhā\ *or Arab.* **Al–Ja·zā'·ir** \ˌal-jə-'zā-i(ə)r\. 1 Former Barbary state, N Africa, now Algeria.

2 *or anc.* **Ico·si·um** \ī-'kō-sē-əm\. Seaport city, ✱ of Algeria and of Alger dept., on W side of **Bay of Algiers;** pop. (1966c) 897,352, met. area pop. 1,106,990; exports iron ore, phosphates, wine, vegetables; univ. (1859, reorganized 1909), cathedral, National Library, astronomical observatory.

History: Founded in the 10th century on site of a Roman town; held by Spain 1509–17; invaded disastrously by Charles V 1541; chief among the Barbary States which exacted tribute from European shipping; included in U.S. wars against the Barbary States 1801–05, 1815; encouraged by the absence of U.S. naval vessels to attack American shipping in the Mediterranean, finally forced to cease exaction of tribute after defeated by Decatur's punitive expedition 1815; bombarded by British 1816 in effort to force the dey to end Christian slavery; dey

deposed by French 1830; became an important trading center as capital of the French colony of Algeria (*q.v.*). Allies landed Nov. 8, 1942.

Al–Gizeh. See GIZA.

Al·goa Bay \al-ˌgō-ə-\. Bay on SE coast of Cape Prov., Rep. of South Africa, ab. 420 m. E of Cape Town; discovered by Portuguese 15th cent.; Port Elizabeth (*q.v.*) founded by British on its shores 1820.

Al·go·ma \al-ˈgō-mə\. 1 City, Kewaunee co., E Wisconsin, on Lake Michigan 28 m. NE of Green Bay (city); pop. (1970c) 4023; dairy products, plywood, veneer.

2 District, Ontario, Canada. See table at ONTARIO.

Al·go·na \al-ˈgō-nə\. City, ⊗ of Kossuth co., N Iowa, 38 m. N of Fort Dodge; pop. (1970c) 6032; machine tools.

Al·go·nac \ˈal-gə-ˌnak\. Village, St. Clair co., SE Michigan, on St. Clair river 24 m. S of Port Huron; pop. (1970c) 3684; boatbuilding center; summer resort.

Al·gon·quin \al-ˈgän-kwən, -ˈgäŋ-\. Village, McHenry co., N Illinois, 40 m. NW of Chicago; pop. (1970c) 3515; hampers, caskets; diversified agriculture.

Algonquin Park. Canadian provincial park in SE Ontario, 180 m. N of Toronto; 2910 sq. m.; game preserve; noted for its fishing waters and beautiful scenery; contains more than 1200 lakes; camping facilities. Covers watershed bet. Ottawa river and streams to Georgian Bay.

Algonquin Peak. Mountain in Adirondack Mountains, Essex co., NE New York; 5114 ft.

Al–Guet·tar *or* **El Guettar** \al-gə-ˈtär, ˌel-\. Village, S cen. Tunisia, ab. 12 m. SE of Gafsa; pop. (1966c) 2700; taken by American troops Mar. 17, 1943.

Al–Habbāniyah, Hawr. See HABBANIYA, LAKE.

Al–Habesha. See ETHIOPIA.

Al–Hadhr \al-ˈhäd-ər\ *or anc.* **Hat·ra** \ˈhat-rə\. Ancient town and fortress, Mesopotamia, in desert W of the Tigris 55 m. SW of Mosul; now village and archaeological site in NW Iraq; Trajan repulsed by the Parthians 117 A.D.; scene of revolt 240 A.D. crushed by Shapur I.

Al–Hadithah. See HADITHA.

Al–Haffah. See HAFFE.

Al–Hajara. See HAJARA, AL-.

Al–Halfāyah, Nagb. See HALFAYA PASS.

Al–Hamad. See SYRIAN DESERT.

Al·ham·bra \al-ˈham-brə\. 1 Residential city, Los Angeles co., SW California, 5 m. ENE of Los Angeles; pop. (1970c) 62,125; steel tanks; incorporated 1903.

2 Hill in Granada, Spain; site of remains of Moorish palace and fortifications.

Al–Ham·ma *or* **El Hamma** \al-'ham-ə, el-\. Town, cen. Tunisia, on E shore of Chott Djerid 16 m. W of Gabès; pop. (1966c) 3800.

Al–Ham·mām *or* **El Hammām** \ˌal-hə-'mam, el-\. Village on coastal road, N Egypt, bet. Al-Alamein and Alexandria; pop. (1966c) 1700.

Al–Ha·sa \al-'hä-sə\ *also* **El Hasa** \el-\. Province, E Saudi Arabia, on W coast of Persian Gulf; 41,200 sq. m.; pop. (1961e) 500,000; a steppe region with oases, producing oil, dates, wheat, and rice; chief towns Hofuf and Mubarraz and the ports of Qatif and Jubail. In early times a semi-independent principality; Turkish 1875 to 1914 when it was taken by the Wahabis.

Al·hau·rín el Gran·de \äl-ˌ(h)aù-'rēn-el-'gränd-ē\. Commune, Málaga prov., S Spain, 20 m. SW of Málaga; pop. (1970p) 11,847; marble quarries, oil.

Al–Hawtah. See HAUTA.

Al–Hijarah. See HAJARA, AL-.

Al–Hindiyah. See HINDIYA 2.

Al–Hīrah. See HIRA.

Al–Hou·ta \ˌal-hü-'tä\; *formerly* **La·hej** *or* **La·hij** \'lä-(ˌ)hij\. Town, Yemen (✱ Aden), SW Arabian Penin., ab. 25 m. NNW of Aden; pop. (1970e) 35,000; formerly the capital of a sultanate (sultanate abolished 1967).

Al·hu·ce·mas \ˌäl-ü-'sā-məs\. Name of bay and three small islands on Mediterranean coast of Morocco, ab. 50 m. W of Melilla; bombarded 1923 by Moors in Moroccan revolt against Spanish rule.

Al–Hudaydah. See HODEIDA.

Al–Hufuf. See HOFUF.

Alia·ga \äl-'yä-gə\. Municipality, W Nueva Ecija prov., Luzon, Phil.; pop. (1969e) 25,700.

Aliákmon. See VISTRITSA.

Ali·bag \'al-i-ˌbag\. See KOLABA.

Al·i·ba·tes Flint Quarries and Texas Panhandle Pueblo Culture National Monument \ˌal-ə-'bät-ēz-\. See UNITED STATES, *National Monuments.*

Ali·can·te \ˌal-ə-'kant-ē, ˌäl-ə-'känt-ē\. **1** Province of SE Spain. See table at SPAIN.
2 Seaport city, its ✱, 77 m. S of Valencia; pop. (1970p) 184,716; commercial port of Madrid; metalworking; bricks, cigarettes, fertilizers, wine; tourism. Said to be ancient Roman city of **Lu·cen·tum** \lü-'sent-əm\ and, previous to that a Greek colony; captured by Moors 713; recaptured 1265 by James I of Aragon; besieged by French 1709 and 1812 and by federalists of Cartagena 1873.

Al·ice \'al-əs\. City, ⊗ of Jim Wells co., S Texas, 40 m. W of Corpus Christi; pop. (1970c) 20,121; railroad division point; oil, cotton, farm crops, livestock.

Alice, Mount. Peak in Front Range of Rocky Mts. on boundary bet. Boulder and Grand cos., N cen. Colorado; 13,310 ft.

Alice Springs *or formerly* **Stu·art** \'st(y)ü-ərt, 'st(y)u̇(-ə)rt\. Town, S cen. Northern Territory, Australia, on highway line from Adelaide (994 m.) to Darwin (1105 m.); pop. (1968e) 7810; virtually the central point of the continent; in Macdonnell Ranges with altitude of 1926 ft.; center of pastoral and mining region; popular winter resort. Site discovered 1860 by J. McDouall Stuart; capital (1927–31, under the name Stuart) of former Central Australia terr.

Al·ice·ville \'al-əs-ˌvil, -vəl\. City, Pickens co., W Alabama, 35 m. WSW of Tuscaloosa; pop. (1970c) 2851.

Ali·garh \ˌal-i-'gär\. **1** District, Uttar Pradesh, N India; 1941 sq. m.; pop. (1961c) 1,765,275.
2 *or* **Koil–Aligarh** \'kō-əl-, 'kȯi(ə)l-\. City, its ✱, 43 m. N of Agra; pop. (1970e) 237,954; a joint municipality consisting of fortress of Aligarh and the native city of **Koil** *or* **Kol** \'kōl\; trade and industrial center; metal works; carpets; Aligarh Muslim Univ. (1920). Became key Maratha fort under Sindhia 1759; stormed by British Aug. 28, 1803, during Second Maratha War (1803–05).

Ali Khel \ˌal-ī-'kā(ə)l, -'kel\. Village in Safed Koh, E Afghanistan, on border of Pakistan, at W end of Peiwar Pass 50 m. SE of Kabul; scene of fighting 1879 when occupied by Lord Roberts.

Ali Masjid. See KHYBER PASS.

Al·ine, Loch \-'al-ən\. Inlet of Atlantic Ocean on coast of W cen. Scotland, in Argyll co.; 3½ m. long.

A–ling Mountains \äl-(ˌ)iŋ-\ *or* **A–ling Gan·gri** \-'gäŋ-(g)rē\. Mountain range, W Tibet, China, incl. **A–ling Mountain** (24,000 ft.) near its W end.

Alings·ås \ˌal-iŋ-'sōs\. Town, Älvsborg co., SW Sweden, on lake 25 m. NE of Göteborg; pop. (1970e) 20,053.

Al·i·quip·pa \ˌal-ə-'kwip-ə\. Borough, Beaver co., W Pennsylvania, on Ohio river 19 m. WNW of Pittsburgh; pop. (1970c) 22,277; concrete; steelworks.

Ali·raj·pur \ˌäl-i-'räj-ˌpu̇(ə)r\. **1** Former state in SW Central India Agency, cen. India; now part of Madhya Pradesh.
2 Town, its ✱, in SW Madhya Pradesh 100 m. WSW of Indore; pop. (1961c) 10,161.

Ali·şar Hü·yük \ˌäl-i-ˌshär-hə-'yük\. Ruins of ancient town on Konak river (tributary of Delice river), cen. Turkey in Asia, ab. 35 m. SE of Yozgat; archaeological site of Hittite town.

Al–Iskandarīyah. Governorate and seaport, Egypt. See ALEXANDRIA.

Al–Ismā'īlīyah, Tur'at. See ISMAILIA CANAL.

Al–Ittihad. See MADINAT ASH SHA'B.

Ali·wal North \ˌäl-ī-ˌwäl-\. Town, NE Cape Prov., Rep. of South Africa, on Orange river 231 m. NNE of Port Elizabeth; pop. (1967e) 10,700; founded 1849; health resort with sulfur springs; cheese, furniture.

Al–Jabal ash Sharqī. See ANTI-LEBANON.

Al–Ja·di·da \ˌal-jə-'dē-də\ *or formerly* **Maz·a·gan** \ˌmaz-ə-'gan\. Seaport, W Morocco, ab. 60 m. SW of Casablanca; pop. (1960c) 40,302; founded 1502 by Portuguese and held by them until 1769.

Al–Jawf. See JAUF.

Al–Jazā'ir. See ALGIERS.

Al–Jazira. See JAZIRA, AL-.

Al–Jazirah. See GEZIRA.

Al–Jem *or* **El Djem** \al-'jem, el-\. Town, NE Tunisia, 40 m. S of Sousse; pop. (1966c) 3000.

Al–Jīzah. See GIZA.

Al·ju·bar·ro·ta \ˌäl-zhu̇-bə-'rōt-ə\. Village, Leiria dist., W cen. Portugal, in Liz valley 16 m. SSW of Leiria. Scene of most important battle in Portuguese history in which invading Castilian forces under John I were defeated 1385 by John I of Portugal; battle established Portuguese independence. See BATALHA.

Al–Juf *or* **El Juf** *or* **El Djouf** \ˌal-'jüf, el-\. Desert region in E Mauritania and W Mali, W Africa; at W end of the Sahara.

Al–Jumhūrīyah al–'Arabīyah as–Sūrīyah. See SYRIA 3.

Al–Kadhimain *or* **Al–Kazimīyah.** See KADHIMAIN.

Al–Kan·ta·ra *or* **El Kantara** \ˌal-'kant-ə-rə, el-\. Oasis, N of Biskra, Algeria, at S end of gorge through Atlas Mts. on edge of Sahara Desert.

Al–Ka·rak \al-'kär-ək, ˌal-kə-'rak\ *or* **El Ke·rak** \ˌal-'ker-ək, el-\ *or* **Kerak;** *anc.* **Kir Mo·ab** *or* **Kir of Moab** \'kər . . . 'mō-ˌab\. Town, W Jordan, E of S end of Dead Sea; fortified 1136 by Crusaders who called it **Le Crac** \lə-'krak\; taken by Saladin 1188; taken by Turks 13th cent.; suffered considerably in World War I.

Al–Kasr al–Kebir. See ALCAZARQUIVIR.

Al–Kef. See LE KEF.

Al–Khābūrah. See KHABURA.

Al–Khalīl. See HEBRON 4.

Al–Khār·ga *or* **El Khārga** \al-'kär-gə, el-\ *also* **Al–Khār·i·jah** \-'kär-i-jə\. Town in the Khārga oasis, New Valley gov., Lower Egypt; pop. (1970e) 16,800.

Al–Khums. Seaport, Libya. See HOMS.

Alk·maar \'alk-ˌmär\. Commune, North Holland prov., W Netherlands, on North Holland canal 20 m. NNW of Amsterdam, intersected by canals; pop. (1970e) 52,091; specially noted for its cheese market; exports also butter and grain; buildings include the town hall, church (Groote Kerk, built 1470–98), and a weigh-house (1582). First Dutch city successfully to resist Spanish 1573; Duke of York forced to capitulate by French under Brune 1799 and permitted to evacuate Russian-English forces.

Al–Ku·fa \al-'kü-fə\. Town on W bank of the Euphrates, S cen. Iraq, ab. 90 m. S of Baghdad; pop. (1965c) 30,862.
History: Founded 638 A.D. by Caliph Omar I at the same time as Basra, became one of the two Islamic centers of the early Ommiad caliphs; in 7th and 8th centuries A.D. prosperous capital of perhaps 200,000 population, a Muslim literary, theological, and political center. Overwhelmed by Karmathians 890. Developed the Kufic angular script of Arabic used almost exclusively for the Koran and on monuments and coins.

Al–Ku·frah \al-'kü-frə\ *or* **Oases of Cu·fra** *or* **Oases of Ku·fra** \-'kü-frə\ *also* **Ku·fa·ra** \'kü-fə-re\. Group of five oases in cen. Libyan Desert, Libya; ab. 7000 sq. m.; stronghold of the Senusi, overcome by Italians 1930–31.

Al–Ku·nei·tra *or* **El Kuneitra** *also* **El Qu·nei·tra** \ˌal-kü-'nā-trə, ˌel-\ *or Arab.* **Al–Qu·nay·ṭi·rah** \-'nāt-ə-rə, -'nīt-\. Town, SW Syria, ab. 40 m. SW of Damascus in region occupied by Israel 1967.

Al–Kūt. See KUT 1.

Al–Ku·wait \ˌal-kə-'wāt\ *or* **Kuwait.** Seaport, ✻ of Kuwait, at head of Persian Gulf; pop. (1970c) 80,008, met. area 217,364; has good harbor and considerable trade; petrochemical plants; univ. (1966).

Al·la·da \ˌal-ə-'dä\. Town, Dahomey, W Africa, about 25 m. N of Ouidah; in 17th and 18th centuries chief town of an extensive kingdom of same name.

Al·la·gash \'al-ə-ˌgash\. River, in Piscataquis and Aroostook cos., N Maine; flows N into St. John river; outlet of many lakes incl. **Allagash Lake** in N Piscataquis co.

Al·lah·a·bad \'al-ə-hə-ˌbad, -ˌbäd\. 1 Division, Uttar Pradesh, N India; 10,096 sq. m.; pop. (1961c) 8,339,947.
2 District of Allahabad division; 2800 sq. m.; pop. (1961c) 2,422,558.
3 City, ✻ of the division and the district, SE Uttar Pradesh, on the Ganges at its junction with the Yamuna; pop. (1970e) 534,676; administrative, legal, and transportation center; trades in cotton and sugar. Has historic Jama Masjid (Great Mosque), various public buildings, and Univ. of Allahabad (1887).
History: Ancient city, a Holy City of India, long sacred to Hindu pilgrims; under Muslim rule 1194–1801; a residence of Mogul emperor, Akbar, who built fort there 1575; taken by British under Clive 1765; restored to ruler of Oudh 1771 in political bargains arranged by Hastings; finally ceded to British 1801; scene of a serious outbreak in Sepoy Mutiny 1857; site of Pillar of Asoka (erected 240 B.C.).

Al·laire \ə-'la(ə)r, -'le(ə)r\. Deserted iron-industry village, Monmouth co., E cen. New Jersey, ab. 8 m. SW of Asbury Park; now Camp Burton, gift of Arthur Brisbane to Boy Scouts of America.

Al–Lajā. See AL-LEDJA.

Al·la·lin·horn \ˌäl-ə-'lēn-ˌhò(ə)rn\. Mountain, Pennine Alps, Valais canton, Switzerland, ab. 8 m. NNE of Monte Rosa and ab. 8 m. ENE of Zermatt; 13,213 ft.

Al·la·ma·kee \ˌal-ə-mə-'kē\. County in Iowa. See table at IOWA.

All–American Canal. See IMPERIAL VALLEY.

Al·lan Mountain \ˌal-ən-\. Peak in Bitterroot Range, NE Lemhi co., E cen. Idaho; 9154 ft.

Al·lan·myo \ə-'län-myō\. Town, Burma, on Irrawaddy river opp. Thayetmyo; pop. (1953c) 15,580.

Al·lan·ridge \'al-ən-rij\. Town, Orange Free State, Rep. of South Africa; pop. (1967e) 10,900.

Al·la·too·na \ˌal-ə-'tü-nə\. Hamlet and creek, SE Bartow co., Georgia; battle (**Allatoona Pass**) at creek 12 m. NW of Marietta Oct. 5, 1864 in Sherman's march on Atlanta.

Alle. See LAVA.

Al–Led·ja \al-'lej-ə\ *or* **Al–La·jā** \-laj-ə\ *also* **El Ledja** \el-\ *or* **Ledja.** Region of lava wilderness, containing many caves, on W frontier of Jebel ed Druz, SW Syria, S of Damascus.

Al·le·gan \'al-i-gən\. 1 County in SW Michigan. See table at MICHIGAN.
2 City, its ⊗, 22 m. NNW of Kalamazoo; pop. (1970c) 4516; in agricultural, dairy, and fruit-growing section; drugs, flour, paper.

Al·le·ga·ny \ˌal-ə-'gā-nē, -'gen-ē\. 1 Name of counties in two states of the U.S. See tables at MARYLAND, NEW YORK.
2 Village, Cattaraugus co., SW New York, on Allegheny river 4 m. W of Olean; pop. (1970c) 2050; in agricultural region. St. Bonaventure College and Seminary (f. 1859, chartered 1875) in nearby **St. Bon·a·ven·ture** \-ˌbän-ə-'ven-chər\. Nearby is **Allegany State Park,** 60,400 acres.

Al·le·gha·ny \ˌal-ə-'gā-nē, -'gen-ē\. Name of counties in two states of the U.S. See tables at NORTH CAROLINA, VIRGINIA.

Alleghany Mountains. See ALLEGHENY MOUNTAINS.

Al·le·ghe·ny \ˌal-ə-'gā-nē, -'gen-ē\. 1 River, Pennsylvania and New York; 325 m. long; navigable for ab. 200 m.; rises in Potter co., Pa., loops NW into SW New York state, turns S across Pa. border in Warren co., flows S through W Pa., and unites with Monongahela river to form Ohio river at Pittsburgh; chief tributaries the Clarion, French Creek, and the Kiskiminetas.
2 County in Pennsylvania. See table at PENNSYLVANIA.

Allegheny Heights. Elevation, Garrett co., NW corner of Maryland; 3187 ft.

Allegheny Mountain. Peak, Pendleton co., E West Virginia; 4017 ft.

Allegheny Mountains *also* **Alleghany Mountains** *or* **Al·le·ghe·nies** \-'gā-nēz, -'gen-ēz\. Ranges of Appalachian system in Pennsylvania, Maryland, Virginia, and West Virginia, W of and generally parallel with the Blue Ridge; varying in height from 2000 to over 4800 ft.; E slope sometimes called **Allegheny Front** and the entire upland area from Cumberland Plateau on S to Mohawk valley in N.Y. is known as the **Allegheny Plateau.**

Al·len \'al-ən\. Name of a parish in Louisiana and of counties in four states of the U.S. See tables at INDIANA, KANSAS, KENTUCKY, LOUISIANA, OHIO.

Allen, Bog of. Series of peat bogs, cen. Eire, from ab. 17 m. W of Dublin almost to the Shannon; ab. 370 sq. m.; in Kildare, Offaly, Laoighis, and Westmeath; source of the Brosna, Boyne, and Barrow rivers; cut by Grand and Royal canals.

Allen, Lough \'läk-\. Lake (*lough*), Eire, 8½ m. N of Carrick; ab. 14 sq. m.; the Shannon river flows through it.

Allen, Mount. 1 Peak in Glacier National Park, NW Montana; 9355 ft.
2 Peak in Adirondack Mts., Essex co., NE New York; 4345 ft.

Al·len·dale \'al-ən-ˌdāl\. 1 County in South Carolina. See table at SOUTH CAROLINA.
2 Borough, Bergen co., NE corner of New Jersey, 8 m. N of Paterson; pop. (1970c) 6240.
3 Town, ⊗ of Allendale co., SW South Carolina, 43 m. SW of Orangeburg; pop. (1970c) 3620; cotton, melons, lumber; settled in mid-18th cent.

Allende. See SAN MIGUEL DE ALLENDE.

Allen Park \ˌal-ən-\. City, Wayne co., SE Michigan, 10 m. WSW of Detroit; pop. (1970c) 40,747.

Allenstein. See OLSZTYN 2.

Al·lens·town \'al-ənz-ˌtau̇n\. Town, Merrimack co., S cen. New Hampshire, E of Concord; pop. (1970c) 2732.

Al·len·town \'al-ən-ˌtau̇n\. City, ⊗ of Lehigh co., E Pennsylvania, on Lehigh river 48 m. N of Philadelphia; pop. (1970c) 109,527; manufactures electronic equipment, textiles, machine tools, trucks; Muhlenberg Coll. (1848),

Cedar Crest Coll. (1867), Eastern Pilgrim Coll. (1921), Lehigh County Community Coll. (1966); first platted 1762; sheltered Liberty Bell during Revolution; incorp. as borough 1811 and made ⊗; incorp. as city 1867.

Al·lep·pey *also* **Al·lep·pi** \ə-'lep-ē\. Town, cen. Kerala, S India, on Malabar Coast 130 m. S of Calicut; pop. (1970e) 163,977; coconut oil, carpets; exports copra; good harbor.

Al·ler \'äl-ər\. River, rises near Magdeburg, East Germany, flows NW into Weser river SE of Bremen, West Germany; 131 m. long.

Aller \äl-'ye(ə)r\. Commune, Oviedo prov., NW Spain, 20 m. SE of Oviedo; pop. (1971p) 22,812; agricultural produce; coal, iron, and lead mines; coke.

Allgäu. See ALGÄU.

Al·lia \'al-ē-ə\. Small river of ancient Italy ab. 11 m. N of Rome, flowing into the Tiber on the left bank; identified by some with modern Fosso della Bettina, by others with Fosso di Marcigliana. According to Livy, scene of battle in which Romans were defeated by Gauls under Brennus 390 B.C. and the way opened for sack of Rome.

Al·li·ance \ə-'lī-ən(t)s\. 1 City, ⊗ of Box Butte co., NW Nebraska, 45 m. ENE of Scottsbluff; pop. (1970c) 6862; trade center for agricultural region.

2 Industrial city, Stark co., NE Ohio, on Mahoning river 16 m. ENE of Canton; pop. (1970c) 26,547; electric traveling cranes, milling machinery, castings; coal mines nearby; Mount Union Coll. (1846); settled by Quakers 1805; incorp. as village 1854, as city 1889.

Al·lier \al-'yā\ *or anc.* **Ela·ver** \i-'lā-vər\. 1 Navigable river, S cen. France; ab. 4 m. W of Nevers; 255 m. long; flows NNW into Loire river.

2 Department of cen. France. See table at FRANCE.

Al·li·ga·tor Lake \ˌal-ə-ˌgāt-ər-\. Lake in Alligator Swamp, NW Hyde co., E North Carolina.

Alligator Point. Point on E coast of Orleans parish, SE Louisiana, extending into Lake Borgne.

Alligator Swamp. Great swamp, E North Carolina, extending bet. Albemarle Sound and Pamlico Sound and surrounding **Alligator River**, inlet of Albemarle Sound.

Al·li·son \'al-ə-sən\. Town, ⊗ of Butler co., NE cen. Iowa; pop. (1970c) 1071; dairy products, poultry.

Al·lis·ton \'al-əs-tən\. Town, Simcoe co., SE Ontario, Canada, 20 m. SSW of Barrie; pop. (1971p) 3174.

Al–Līṭānī, Nahr. See LITANI.

Al·loa \'al-ə-wə\. Seaport burgh, Clackmannan co., Scotland, 25 m. NE of Glasgow near mouth of Forth river; pop. (1971p) 14,110; ale, hosiery, tiles; exports coal; seat of the Earls of Mar and the Erskines.

Al·lo·way \'al-ə-ˌwā\. Hamlet, S Ayr co., Scotland, 2¼ m. S of Ayr near mouth of the Doon; pop. (1961c) 997; birthplace of Robert Burns and the scene of his *Tam O'Shanter.*

All Saints Bay *or Port.* **Ba·ía de To·dos os San·tos** \bə-'ē-ə-thə-ˌtō-thə-zü-'sant-əs\. Bay on E coast of Bahia state, E Brazil; ab. 100 m. in circumference; at its E entrance is the city of Salvador.

Allsch·wil \'älsh-ˌvil\. Commune, Basel-Land demicanton, Basel canton, NW Switzerland, 3 m. W from Basel; pop. (1970c) 17,638; bricks, chemicals, leather.

Al–Luhayyah. See LUHAIYA.

Al·lu·mette \ˌal-ə-'met\. Island in Ottawa river, SW Quebec, Canada, opp. Pembroke, Ont.; 70 sq. m.; the expansion of Ottawa river SW of island sometimes known as **Allumette Lake.**

Al·ma \'al-mə\. 1 City, ⊗ of Bacon co., SE Georgia; pop. (1970c) 3756.

2 City, ⊗ of Wabaunsee co., E Kansas, 35 m. W of Topeka; pop. (1970c) 905; poultry farms.

3 City, Gratiot co., cen. Michigan, 17 m. S of Mt. Pleasant; pop. (1970c) 9790; beet sugar and oil refineries; Alma Coll. (1886).

4 City, ⊗ of Harlan co., S Nebraska; pop. (1970c) 1299.

5 City, ⊗ of Buffalo co., W Wisconsin; pop. (1970c) 956.

6 Island, East Lake St. John co., S Quebec, Canada, bet. the outlets of Lake St. John.

7 City, East Lake St. John co., Quebec, Canada, on Saguenay river, 33 m. WNW of Chicoutimi; pop. (1971p) 22,353; paper mills.

8 Small river, SW Crimean Oblast, U.S.S.R.; enters Black Sea 17 m. N of Sevastopol. Scene of defeat of Russians under Prince Menshikov by English and French Sept. 20, 1854, one of earliest battles of Crimean War.

Alma–Ata \ˌal-mə-ə-'tä\ *or formerly* **Ver·nyi** \'ve(ə)rn-yē\ *also* **Vyer·nyi** \'vye(ə)rn-yē\. City, ✱ of Kazakh S.S.R. and ✱ of Alma-Ata Oblast, U.S.S.R., in SE part N of Issyk-Kul; pop. (1970p) 730,000; heavy machinery, lumber, tobacco; univ. (1934); founded by Russians as a fort 1855; developed as trading center, esp. after building of Turkistan-Siberian R.R.

Alma–Ata Oblast \-'ō-bləst, -ˌblast\. Subdivision of Kazakh S.S.R., U.S.S.R., bounded on N by Lake Balkhash, on NE by Taldy-Kurgan Oblast, on SE by Sinkiang Uighur, China, on S by Kirgiz S.S.R., and on W by Dzhambul Oblast; 40,425 sq. m.; pop. (1970p) 1,443,000; ✱ Alma-Ata; largely desert, traversed by the I-li river, except in S along N slope of Ala Tau Mts.; sugar beets, tobacco, wheat.

Al·ma·da \äl-'mäd-ə\. City, Setúbal dist., W Portugal, on Tagus estuary, opp. Lisbon; pop. (1970p) 43,537.

Alma Dağ. See NUR MOUNTAINS.

Al·ma·dén \ˌäl-mə-'dān\ *or anc.* **Sis·a·pon** \'sis-ə-ˌpän\. Commune, Ciudad Real prov., S cen. Spain, 50 m. WSW of Ciudad Real; pop. (1970p) 10,774; bet. two mountains of the Sierra Morena; site of mercury mines, hence the name **Almadén del Azo·gue** \-del-ə-'sō-gə\ [Span. *azogue,* "mercury"]; also produces lead and sulfur. Mercury mines known to Romans and Moors, leased to Fuggers of Augsburg in 16th cent., worked by the Rothschilds of London in 19th cent.

Al·ma·di·es, Cape \-ˌal-mə-'dē-əs\. The extreme tip of the peninsula forming Cape Vert (*q.v.*), Senegal, W Africa, near Dakar, 17°32′W; the westernmost point of Africa.

Al–Madīnah. See MEDINA 6.

Al–Madrakah, Ras. See MADRAKA, CAPE.

Al–Majdal. See MAGDALA.

Al–Makīlī. See AL-MECHILI.

Al·ma·lyk \ˌal-mə-'lik\. Town, Tashkent Oblast, Uzbek S.S.R., U.S.S.R., 40 m. SE of Tashkent; pop. (1969e) 76,000; building materials; mining (copper, zinc, molybdenum).

Al–Mamlakah al–'Arabīyah as–Su'ūdīyah. See SAUDI ARABIA.

Al–Mamlakah al–Maghribīyah. See MOROCCO 1.

Al–Manamah. See MANAMA.

Almanor, Lake. See BIG MEADOWS DAM.

Al·man·sa \äl-'män(t)-sə\ *or formerly* **Al·man·za** \-'män-zə\. Commune, Albacete prov., SE Spain, 43 m. ESE of Albacete; pop. (1970p) 16,695; linen and cotton fabrics, leather, soap. Scene of decisive victory 1707 by French under Duke of Berwick over English, Spanish, and Portuguese under Earl of Galway (War of the Spanish Succession).

Al–Man·sū·ra *or* **El Mansūra** \ˌal-(ˌ)man-'su̇r-ə, ˌel-\. Commercial and industrial city, ✱ of Daqahlīya gov., Lower Egypt, on right bank of Damietta branch of the Nile SW of Lake Manzala; pop. (1970e) 212,300; scene of battle Feb. 8, 1250 in which Crusaders (Sixth Crusade) under King Louis IX of France were severely defeated and Louis was captured.

Al–Manzilah, Buḥayrat. See MANZALA, LAKE.

Al·man·zor, Pla·za de \'pläz-ə-dā-ˌäl-mən-'zȯ(ə)r\. Highest peak in Sierra de Gredos, W cen. Spain; 8501 ft.

Al·man·zo·ra \ˌal-mən-ˈzōr-ə, -ˈzȯr-\. River, SE Spain; 65 m. long; flows E through cen. Almería prov. into Mediterranean Sea.

Al–Marj. See BARKA 3.

Al–Ma·ta·rī·ya *or* **El Matarīya** \ˌal-ˌmat-ə-ˈrē-(y)ə, ˌel-\. Town, Daqahlīya gov., Lower Egypt, a NE suburb of Cairo; pop. (1966c) 41,000; near ruins of Heliopolis.

Al–Mawṣil. See MOSUL.

Al–Me·chi·li *or* **El Mechili** *or* **Al–Ma·kī·lī** \ˌal-mə-ˈkē-lē, ˌel-\. Town, Libya, N Africa, ab. 50 m. SSW of Derna on road connecting Salūm, Egypt and Benghazi, Libya; set up as a gasoline depot by the British Dec. 1940; taken by Germans in advance on Egypt but retaken Nov. 1942.

Al·mei·da \al-ˈmād-ə\. Fortified commune, Guarda dist., NE Portugal; pop. (1970p) 1191; sulfur waters; formerly one of chief strongholds against Spain; captured 1762 by Spain, but shortly afterward reverted to Portuguese; in Peninsular War captured by French 1810, recaptured by British and Portuguese 1811.

Al·me·lo \ˈäl-mə-ˌlō\. Industrial commune, Overijssel prov., E Netherlands, 9 m. NW of Hengelo; pop. (1970e) 58,941; cotton, furniture; seat of the Barons van Rechteren 1350 ff. and Counts Limpurg 1711 ff.

Al·me·nar \ˌäl-mə-ˈnär\. Commune, Lérida prov., NE Spain, ab. 11 m. NNE of Lérida; pop. (1970p) 3784; scene of defeat of Spanish ruler Philip V by Austrians 1710 during War of Spanish Succession.

Al·me·na·ra \ˌäl-mə-ˈnär-ə\. Commune, S Castellón de la Plana prov., Spain, 20 m. NNE of Valencia; pop. (1970p) 4091; scene of defeat of Moors 1238 by James I.

Al·men·dra·le·jo \ˌäl-ˌmen-drə-ˈle-(ˌ)hō\. Commune, Badajoz prov., SW Spain, 27 m. ESE of Badajoz; pop. (1970p) 21,929; wheat, wine.

Al·me·ría \ˌal-mə-ˈrē-ə\. 1 Province of S Spain. See table at SPAIN.
2 *anc.* **Un·ci** \ˈən-ˌsī\ *also* **Por·tus Mag·nus** \ˌpōrt-ə-ˈsmag-nəs, ˌpȯrt-\. Seaport, its ✻, 65 m. ESE of Granada at head of Gulf of Almería; pop. (1970p) 114,510; chemicals; metalworking.
History: One of chief Roman harbors after 19 A.D.; after fall of Ommiads as rulers of Spain, became head of small independent Moorish state, then a petty kingdom dependent on Granada; a leading seaport for Moors from which they preyed on Christian commerce; captured by Alfonso VII of Castile 1147, but retaken and held by Moors until 1489.

Almería, Gulf of. Inlet of Mediterranean Sea in S Almería prov., Spain; one of leading harbors in Spain.

Almesbury. See AMESBURY 2.

Al·me·tyevsk \ˌäl-mi-ˈt(y)efsk\. Town, Tatar A.S.S.R., Russian S.F.S.R., U.S.S.R., ab. 140 m. ESE of Kazan; pop. (1969e) 77,000; oil refinery; founded 1950.

Al·mi·na, Point \-al-ˈmē-nə\. Point of land extending into the Mediterranean Sea at extremity of peninsula on which Ceuta is situated, NE Morocco, NW Africa; at SE entrance to Strait of Gibraltar.

Al–Min·ya *or* **El Minya** \ˌal-ˈmin-yə, el-\. City, ✻ of Minya gov., Upper Egypt, on left bank of the Nile 90 m. S of Al-Faiyūm; pop. (1970e) 122,100; food processing, cotton ginning.

Al·mi·ran·te \ˌal-mə-ˈränt-ē\. Port on NW side of Chiriquí Lagoon, NW Panama; pop. (1970p) 6591; a headquarters of the United Fruit Company.

Almirante Brown \-ˈbraủn\. City, S suburb of Buenos Aires, Argentina; pop. (1960c) 136,924.

Almissa. See OMIŠ.

Al·mo·dó·var del Cam·po \ˌäl-mə-ˈdō-(ˌ)vär-del-ˈkäm-(ˌ)pō\. Commune, Ciudad Real prov., S cen. Spain, 22 m. SW of Ciudad Real; pop. (1970p) 11,637; old Moorish fortress.

Al·mond \ˈäm-ənd\. River, Lanark, West Lothian and Midlothian cos., SE Scotland; 24 m. long; flows E and NE to Firth of Forth.

Al·monte \ˈal-ˌmänt\. Industrial town, Lanark co., SE Ontario, Canada, on Mississippi river 32 m. WSW of Ottawa; pop. (1968e) 3518.

Al·mo·ra \äl-ˈmōr-ə, -ˈmȯr-\. 1 District, Uttar Pradesh, N India, in W Himalayas; 2713 sq. m.; pop. (1961c) 633,407.
2 Town and hill station, its ✻, 160 m. NE of Delhi; pop. (1961c) 16,004; alt. 5494 ft.

Al·mu·ñé·car \ˌäl-mün-ˈyā-ˌkär\ *or anc.* **Sexi** \ˈsek-ˌsī\. Mediterranean seaport, Granada prov., S Spain, ab. 32 m. S of Granada; pop. (1970p) 13,251; landing place 756 of Abd-er-Rahman I, founder of the emirate of Córdoba.

Aln *or* **Alne** \ˈaln\. River, N Northumberland, N England; 16 m. long; flows E into North Sea at Alnmouth.

Aln·wick \ˈan-ik\. Urban district, Northumberland, N England, on Aln river 37 m. N of Newcastle upon Tyne; pop. (1971p) 7113; breweries, grain mills, tobacco factories; feudal fortress (Alnwick Castle, seat of Dukes of Northumberland) stands at N entrance of town; besieged by Scots 1093, 1135, 1174, 1328, 1448.

Al–Obeid. See AL-UBAYYID.

Alo·fi \ə-ˈlō-fē\. 1 One of the Futuna Islands (*q.v.*).
2 Chief village of Niue I., Cook Is., on W coast.

Alónnisos. See ILIODHRÓMIA.

Alor \ˈal-ˌȯ(ə)r, ˈäl-\ *or formerly* **Om·bai** \ˈȯm-ˌbī\. Island, E end of Lesser Sunda Is., Indonesia, 20 m. N of Timor and WSW of Wetar; ab. 60 m. long; 810 sq. m.; chief town Kalabahi; very mountainous, highest point 6033 ft. at E end; has harbor (Kalabahi Bay) at W end. With Pantar forms the **Alor Islands** group (1126 sq. m.).

Álo·ra \ˈäl-ə-(ˌ)rä\. Commune, Málaga prov., S Spain, 18 m. WNW of Málaga; pop. (1970p) 15,602; grain, dates, and fruit, esp. oranges; mineral springs.

Alor Se·tar \ˌal-ˌȯ(ə)r-sə-ˈtär, ˌäl-\ *also* **Alor Star** \-ˈstär\. Town, ✻ of Kedah state, Malaysia, near coast 50 m. N of Penang; pop. (1970p) 66,179; on highway and railroad N to Thailand.

Alor Strait. Channel bet. Lomblen and Pantar Islands in the Lesser Sundas, Indonesia; ab. 10 m. wide; connects Flores Sea with Savu Sea.

Alor·ton \ə-ˈlȯrt-ᵊn\. Village, St. Clair co., SW Illinois; pop. (1970c) 3573.

Alost. See AALST.

Alo·te·nan·go \ˌäl-ə-tə-ˈnäŋ-(ˌ)gō\. Town, Sacatepéquez dept., S cen. Guatemala; munic. pop. (1964p) 6437.

Al–Oued *or* **El Oued** \al-ˈwed, el-\ *also* **Al–Wad** \-ˈwad\. Town and oasis, NE Algeria, on highway 50 m. NE of Touggourt; pop. (1966c) 11,429.

Al·pen \ˈäl-pən\. German form of *Alps*. See table at ALPS.

Al·pe·na \al-ˈpē-nə\. 1 County in NE Michigan. See table at MICHIGAN.
2 City, its ⊗, on Thunder Bay, Lake Huron, at mouth of Thunder Bay river 50 m. N of mouth of Saginaw Bay; pop. (1970c) 13,805; beverages, cement, paper; summer resort; Alpena Community Coll. (1952).

Al·pes \ˈal-(ˌ)pēz\. Latin form of *Alps*. See table at ALPS.

Alpes \älp\. French form of *Alps*. See table at ALPS.

Alpesa. See ELVAS.

Alpes–de–Haute Pro·vence \ˌalp-də-ˌōt-prə-ˈvänˢs\ *or formerly* **Basses–Alpes** \bäs-ˈzalp\. Department of SE France. See table at FRANCE.

Alpes–Mar·i·times \ˌalp-ˌmär-i-tēm\. Department, France. See table at FRANCE.

Al·pha \ˈal-fə\. Borough, Warren co., NW New Jersey, 3 m. SSE of Phillipsburg; pop. (1970c) 2829.

Al·phen \ˈäl-fən\ *or in full* **Alphen aan den Rijn** \-ˌän-dən-ˈrīn\. Commune, South Holland prov., Netherlands, ab. 19 m. NE of Rotterdam; pop. (1970e) 33,430; metalworking.

Al·phe·us \al-ˈfē-əs\ *or Gk.* **Al·fi·ós** \äl-ˈfyȯs\ *also* **Rou·fi·ás** \rü-ˈfyäs\. River, W Peloponnesus, S Greece; ab. 75 m. long; rises in Arcadia, flows NW through S Elis into Ionian Sea near Pyrgos; Olympia is on its N bank.

Alp·hu·bel \ˈälp-ˌhü-bəl\. Mountain and pass in the Alps, Valais canton, SW cen. Switzerland, ab. 6 m. NE of Zermatt; 13,799 ft.

Al·pi \'äl-pē\. Italian form of *Alps*. See table at ALPS.

Alpi Apuane. See table at APENNINES.

Al·pine \'al-ˌpīn\. 1 County in California. See table at CALIFORNIA.

2 Town, ⊗ of Brewster co., W Texas, 130 m. SE of El Paso; pop. (1970c) 5971; in mountainous region; livestock raising; granite quarries and mineral deposits nearby; Sul Ross State Coll. (1920).

Alportel, São Brás de. See SÃO BRÁS DE ALPORTEL.

Alps \'alps\ *or anc.* **Al·pes** \'al-(ˌ)pēz\. Mountain system of S cen. Europe, extending in crescent shape ab. 660 m. from Mediterranean coast bet. France and Italy into Switzerland and along N boundary of Italy, through SW Austria and into NW and W Yugoslavia; area occupied estimated at ab. 80,000 sq. m.; highest point Mont Blanc (*q.v.*) 15,771 ft.; geologically of many rock types and varied folds and thrusts; noted for magnificent scenery with many glaciers, valleys (Chamonix, Interlaken, Engadine, Lauterbrunnen, Grindelwald, Zermatt) and lakes (Geneva, Thun, Lucerne, Brienz, Zug, Zurich, Constance, Maggiore, Como, Garda, Iseo); source of major rivers or their tributaries (Danube, Rhine, Rhone, Po). See also NORTH ALBANIAN ALPS, AUSTRALIAN ALPS.

The principal ranges (all of which have offshoot ranges and subsidiary groups) are shown in the table on page 38.

Famous passes and tunnels are:

Arl·berg \'är(ə)l-ˌbərg, -ˌbe(ə)rg\. Pass, SW Austria; alt. 5881 ft.; connects Vorarlberg and the Tirol; railroad tunnel beneath pass 6¼ m. long, on road from Bludenz to Landeck, opened 1884, electrified 1923.

Bren·ner \'bren-ər\ *or Ital.* **Bren·ne·ro** \'bren-ə-ˌrō\. Pass bet. Austria and Italy; 59 m. long; highest point at Brenner, alt. 4497 ft.; the lowest of any of the important Alpine passes; much frequented from earliest times; crossed by Teutonic invaders of Italy; carriage road built 1772 and railroad 1864–67 (22 tunnels and 60 large bridges).

Great Saint Ber·nard \-ˌsānt-bə(r)-'närd\ *or Fr.* **Grand–Saint–Bernard** \grän-san-ber-nár\. Pass bet. Valais, SW cen. Switzerland and Aosta prov., Piedmont, N Italy, 53 m. by road from Martigny to Aosta; alt. 8098 ft.; known to Celts and Romans in early times (*Lat.* Mons Jo·vis \ˌmänz-'jō-vəs\); much frequented by pilgrims and clerics on visits to Rome and later often crossed by medieval armies; used May 14–20, 1800 by Napoleon for his 40,000 troops for campaign in N Italy; named after the hospice at the summit of the pass, founded in 11th cent. by Saint Bernard of Menthon (923–1008); hospice is a stone building dating from 16th cent. kept by Augustinian monks who, with their St. Bernard dogs, give aid to travelers.

Little Saint Bernard \-ˌsānt-bə(r)-'närd\ *or Fr.* **Pet·tit–Saint–Bernard** \pə-tē-san-ber-nár\. Pass from Bourt-Saint-Maurice, Savoie dept., France, over Savoy Alps 39 m. to La Thuile, Aosta prov., Piedmont, Italy; alt. 7178 ft.; known in Roman times, has hospice founded in 11th cent. now administered by Order of St. Maurice and St. Lazarus.

Mont Ce·nis \mōn-sə-nē\ *or Ital.* **Mon·te Ce·ni·sio** \ˌmōn-tā-chā-'nē-zyō\. Pass (*col*) bet. Modane, Savoie dept., France, and Susa, Torino prov., Piedmont, Italy; alt. 6831 ft.; ab. 46 m. over the Mont Cenis massif in Graian Alps, known since 4th cent. A.D.; crossed by many armies; has been surmised but not proved that it was the pass used by Hannibal; carriage road constructed 1803–13 by order of Napoleon; hospice (at 6332 ft.). **Mont Cenis Tunnel** is 16 m. SW of pass and pierces Massif du Fréjus, 8½ m. from Modane to near Bardonnecchia, Italy; highest point 4246 ft.; constructed 1857–70, opened 1871, first of the great tunnels through the Alps.

Saint Gott·hard *or* **Saint Got·hard** \sānt-'gät(h)-ərd\ *or Fr.* **Saint–Go·thard** \san-gò-tár\. Pass bet. Altdorf in Uri canton and Bellinzona in Ticino canton, Switzerland; actual pass ab. 19 m. over Saint Gotthard group of Lepontine Alps, Göschenen to Airolo; alt. 6916 ft.; road over pass open since early 13th cent.; named after the hospice in the pass, dedicated to St. Gotthard or Godehardus, bishop of Hildesheim (d. 1038); hospice first built in 14th cent. but has often been destroyed by avalanches; carriage road built 1820–30 but not much used since completion of **Saint Gotthard Tunnel,** 9½ m., highest point 3788 ft., constructed 1872–80.

Sim·plon \'sim-ˌplän\ *or Ital.* **Sem·pio·ne** \sem-'pyō-nā\. Pass bet. Brig, Valais canton, SW cen. Switzerland, and Iselle, NE Piedmont, Italy; 29 m. over Alps; alt. 6590 ft.; marks dividing line bet. Pennine and Lepontine Alps; named from village of Simpeln or Simplon in the pass; hospice at summit founded 1802 by Napoleon (not completed until 1825); carriage road built by Napoleon 1800–07; pass less used since completion of **Simplon Tunnel,** 12½ m., longest in the world, from Brig to Iselle under Monte Leone at W end of Lepontine Alps, alt. at highest point 2313 ft., constructed 1898–1905.

Splü·gen \'s(h)plü-gən\ *or Ital.* **Splu·ga** \'splü-(ˌ)gä\. Pass bet. Splügen, Graubünden canton, E Switzerland, and Chiavenna, Lombardy, Italy, near head of Lake Como, 25 m. over Rhaetian Alps; alt. 6946 ft.; road built by Austrian government 1818–23.

See also Mont Blanc Tunnel at BLANC, MONT.

Al·pu·jar·ras, Las \läs-ˌal-pü-'här-əs\. Mountainous region, Granada and Almería provs., S Spain, S of the Sierra Nevada and parallel to it, bet. Motril and Almería; extremely fertile valleys; populated by colonists, esp. from Estremadura, and descendants of Moors who took refuge there after fall of Granada; scene of Moorish uprisings 1500–70.

Al–Qaḍārif. See GEDAREF.

Al–Qāhirah. See CAIRO, Egypt.

Al–Qan·ta·ra *or* **El Qantara** \al-'känt-ə-rə, el-, -'kant-\. Village on E bank of Suez Canal, Sinai gov., NE Egypt, bet. Port Said and Ismailia; occupied by Israel 1967.

Al–Qasr \al-'käs-ər\ *or* **El Qasr** \el-\ *also* **Al–Kasr** \al-'kas-ər\ *or Lat.* **Cas·trum** \'kas-trəm\. Chief town of Dakhla oasis, New Valley gov., Egypt; pop. (1966c) 3300.

Al–Qas·rayn \ˌal-käs-'rīn\ *also* **Kas·ser·ine** \ˌkas-ə-'rēn\. Village, N cen. Tunisia, ab. 135 m. SW of Tunis; pop. (1966c) 9847; scene of U.S. victory during World War II, Feb. 1943.

Al–Qa·tra·ni \ˌal-kä-'trä-nē\ *or* **Al–Qa·trā·nah** \-kə-'trä-nə\ *or* **El Qatrani** \ˌel-\. Town, W cen. Jordan, on railroad ab. 50 m. S of Amman.

Al–Qsar al–Kbir. See ALCAZARQUIVIR.

Al·quí·zar \al-'kē-ˌzär\. Town and municipality, La Habana prov., Cuba, 33 m. SW of Havana; munic. pop (1967e) 16,830.

Al–Qunayṭirah. See AL-KUNEITRA.

Al–Qur·na \al-'kúr-nə\ *also* **Kur·na** \'kúr-nə\. Town, SE Iraq, on right bank of the lower Tigris river where it joins the Euphrates to form the Shatt-al-Arab, ab. 45 m. NNW of Basra; captured by British 1914 in World War I.

Al–Qu·seir *or* **Al–Qu·ṣayr** *or* **El Quseir** *or* **El Qo·seir** \ˌal-kü-'se(ə)r, ˌel-, -'sī(ə)r\ *or formerly* **Kos·seir** \kə-'se(ə)r\. Seaport, E Egypt, on the Red Sea E of Qena; pop. (1966c) 5500; on ancient caravan route to the Nile.

Al–Qusur. See LUXOR.

Als \'äls\ *or Ger.* **Al·sen** \'äl-zən\. Island off E coast of S Jutland, Sønderjylland co., Denmark; 124 sq. m.; pop. (1965c) 48,676; in the Little Belt, separated from mainland

ALPS—PRINCIPAL RANGES

NAME English	Classical[1]	Native	LOCATION	HIGHEST POINT
WESTERN				
Maritime Alps	Al·pes Ma·ri·ti·mae \ˈal(ˌ)-pēz-mə-ˈrit-ə-ˌmē\	*Fr.* Alpes Ma·ri·times \ȧl-pə-mȧ-rē-tēm\; *Ital.* Al·pi Ma·rit·ti·me \ˈäl-pē-mä-ˈrēt-tē-mā\	In S bet. France and Italy	Punta Argentera 10,817 ft.
Li·gu·ri·an Alps \lə-ˈgyu̇r-ē-ən-\		*Ital.* Al·pi Li·gu·ri \ˌäl-pē-ˈlē-gü-rē\	E extension of Maritime Alps along coast of NW Italy	Saccarello 7,216 ft.
Cot·ti·an Alps \ˈkät-ē-ən-\	Alpes Cot·ti·ae \ˈkät-ē-ˌē\	*Fr.* Alpes Cot·ti·ennes \ȧl-pə-kȯ-tyen\; *Ital.* Al·pi Co·zie \ˌäl-pē-ˈkȯts-yā\	N of Maritime Alps bet. Basses-Alpes and Hautes-Alpes depts., France, and Torino prov., Italy	Mount Viso 12,602 ft.
Gra·ian Alps \ˈgrā-(y)ən-, ˈgrī-ən-\	Alpes Gra·iae \-ˈgrā-(ˌ)(y)ē, -ˈgrī-(ˌ)ē\	*Fr.* Alpes Graies \ȧl-pə-grā\; *Ital.* Alpi Graie \ˌäl-pē-ˈgrä-yā\	Savoie dept., France, and NW Piedmont, Italy	Gran Paradiso 13,323 ft.
Dau·phi·né Alps \ˌdō-fi-ˈnā-\		*Fr.* Alpes du Dau·phi·né \ȧl-pə-dü̅e-dō-fē-nā\	In old prov. of Dauphiné (*q.v.*), France, W of Cottian Alps	Barre des Écrins 13,461 ft.
Sa·voy Alps \sə-ˈvȯi-\		*Fr.* Alpes de Sa·voie \ȧl-pə-də-sȧv-wȧ\	In Haute-Savoie dept., France	Mont Blanc 15,771 ft.
CENTRAL: *Southern*				
Pen·nine Alps \ˈpen-ˌīn-\	Alpes Pen·ni·nae \-pə-ˈnī-(ˌ)nē\	*Fr.* Alpes Pen·nines \ȧl-pə-pe-nēn\; *Ital.* Al·pi Pen·ni·ne \ˌäl-pē-pān-ˈnē-nā\	In Valais canton, SW cen. Switz., and N Piedmont, Italy, NE of Graian Alps	Monte Rosa 15,203 ft.
Le·pon·tine Alps \li-ˈpän-ˌtīn-, ˈlep-ən-\		*Fr.* Alpes Lé·pon·ti·ennes \ȧl-pə-lā-pōⁿ-tyen\; *Ital.* Al·pi Le·pon·ti·ne \ˈäl-pē-ˌlā-pōn-ˈtē-nā\	On boundary bet. Switzerland and Italy and in Ticino and Graubünden cantons, Switz.	Monte Leone 11,654 ft.
Rhae·tian Alps \ˈrē-sh(ē-)ən-\	Alpes Rae·ti·cae \-ˈrēt-ə-ˌsē\	*Fr.* Alpes Rhé·tiques \ȧl-pə-rā-tēk\; *Ital.* Al·pi Re·ti \ˌäl-pē-ˈrā-tē\; *Ger.* Rä·ti·sche Al·pen \ˌrā-ti-shə-ˈäl-pən\	E Graubünden canton, Switz.	Piz Bernina 13,284 ft.
CENTRAL: *Northern*				
Bern·ese Alps \ˌbər-ˈnēz-, ˈbər-ˌ\		*Fr.* Alpes Ber·noises \ȧl-pə-bern-wȧz\; *Ger.* Ber·ner Ober·land \ˌber-nər-ˈō-bər-ˌlänt\ *or* Berner Al·pen \-ˈäl-pən \	S cen. Switz.—Bern, Valais, and Uri cantons	Finsteraarhorn 14,022 ft.
EASTERN				
Nor·ic Alps \ˈnȯr-ik-, ˈnär-\	Alpes No·ri·cae \-ˈnȯr-ə-ˌsē, ˈnär-\	*Ger.* No·ri·sche Al·pen \ˌnō-ri-shə-ˈäl-pən\	Austria, bet. valleys of Mur and Drava	Eisenhut 8,006 ft.
Ho·he Tau·ern \ˌhō-ə-ˈtau̇-ərn\		*Ger.* Hohe Tauern	Bet. Carinthia and Tirol, W Austria	Grossglockner 12,470 ft.
Car·nic Alps \ˈkär-nik-\	Alpes Car·ni·cae \-ˈkär-nə-ˌsē\	*Ger.* Kar·ni·sche Al·pen \ˌkär-ni-shə-ˈäl-pən\; *Ital.* Al·pi Car·ni·che \ˌäl-pē-ˈkär-ni-kā\	Bet. S Austria and NE Italy and in Carniola	Kellerwand 9,217 ft.
Do·lo·mites \ˈdō-lə-ˌmīts, ˈdäl-ə-\(Tri·den·tine Alps \trī-ˈden-tīn-, ˈtrīd-ᵊn-\	Alpes Ve·ne·tae \-ˈven-ə-ˌtē\	*Ital.* Do·lo·mi·ti \ˌdō-lə-ˈmē-tē\	NE Italy, bet. valleys of Adige and Piave	Marmolada 10,965 ft.
Ju·lian Alps \ˈjül-yən-\	Alpes Ju·li·ae \-ˈjü-lē-ˌē\	*Ital.* Al·pi Giu·lie \ˌäl-pē-ˈjül-yā\; *Ger.* Ju·li·sche Al·pen \ˌyü-li-shə-ˈäl-pən\	In Slovenia, NW Yugoslavia	Triglav 9,395 ft.
Ka·ra·wan·ken \ˌkär-ə-ˈväŋ-kən\	Ca·ra·van·ca Mons \ˌkar-ə-ˌvaŋ-kə-ˈmänz\	*Ital.* Ca·ra·van·che \ˌkä-rə-ˈväŋ-kā\	S of the valley of the Drava bet. S Austria and NW Yugoslavia	Hochstuhl 7,341 ft.
Di·nar·ic Alps \də-ˈnar-ik-\	Alpes Di·nar·i·cae \-də-ˈnar-ə-ˌsē\	*Ital.* Al·pi Di·na·ri·che \ˈäl-pē-dē-ˈnä-ri-kā\; *Serbo-Croat.* Di·na·ra Pla·ni·na \ˌdē-nə-rä-plä-ˈnē-nə\	Parallel to W coast of Yugoslavia, S to Albania	Voljnac 7,800 ft.

[1] Latin names given of those ranges known by name to the ancients.

by Sound of Alsen (**Al·sen·sund** \-ˌzünt\); fertile, producing esp. apples and grain; lake and sea commercial fishing. Under Danish government to 1864, Prussian 1864–1919, Danish (by plebiscite) from 1919.

Al·sace \al-ˈsas, -ˈsās, ˈal-ˌ\ *or Ger.* **El·sass** \ˈel-ˌzäs\ *or anc.* **Al·sa·tia** \al-ˈsā-sh(ē-)ə\. Old German and later French province, NE France, bet. Rhine river and Vosges Mts., in modern depts. of Bas-Rhin and Haut-Rhin.

History: Ruled by Rome (see STRASBOURG); gradually penetrated by Germanic peoples; created a Frankish duchy; part of Middle Kingdom (see LORRAINE) assigned to Lothair I by Treaty of Verdun 843 A.D.; belonged to Holy Roman Empire 870–1648; united to duchy of Swabia 925; broken up into feudal principalities controlled chiefly by Bishop of Strasbourg and Hapsburg family in 14th century; Upper Alsace given to Burgundy 1469, but soon broke free; a center of the Peasants' Revolt of 1525; occupied by French in Thirty Years' War; linked with France by means of Louis XIV's "Chambers of Reunion" 1680; consolidated into provinces of Bas-Rhin and Haut-Rhin after 1789 and under Napoleon; ceded to Germany by Treaty of Frankfurt 1871. For recent history, see ALSACE-LORRAINE.

Alsace–Lor·raine \-lə-ˈrān, -lȯ-\ *or Ger.* **El·sass–Lo·thring·en** \ˌel-ˌzäs-ˈlō-triŋ-ən\. Frontier region bet. France, West Germany, Belgium, and Switzerland; except for Rhine on E has had indefinite boundaries.

History: Formed from French province of Alsace, French department of Moselle, and some subdivisions (*arrondissements*) of the former dept. of Meurthe which were ceded to Germany by Treaty of Frankfurt 1871; administered in three divisions, Upper Alsace (*Ger.* Ober-el·sass \ˈō-bər-ˌel-ˌzäs\), Lower Alsace (Un·ter·el·sass \ˈün-tər-ˌel-ˌzäs\), and Lorraine (Lothringen), under the German Empire 1871–1918; subject to unsuccessful attempts to Germanize 1880–1910; restored to France by Treaty of Versailles 1919. In World War II held by Germany 1940–44; retaken by French and American armies and again restored to France.

Al·sa·ger \ˈȯl-si-jər, ȯl-ˈsā-\. Urban district, Cheshire, NW England; pop. (1971p) 10,202.

Alsatia. See ALSACE.

Als·dorf \ˈäls-ˌdȯrf\. City, North Rhine-Westphalia, West Germany, 8 m. NNE of Aachen; pop. (1969e) 31,420; chemicals, textiles, coal mining.

Al·sek \ˈal-ˌsek\. River, SW Yukon and SE Alaska; 260 m. long; rises in Aishihik Lake and flows S through E end of St. Elias Mts. and Alaska to the Pacific.

Alsen *and* **Alsensund.** See ALS.

Al·sip \ˈal-səp\. Village, Cook co., NE Illinois, 15 m. SSW of Chicago; pop. (1970c) 11,141.

Alt. See OLT 1.

Al·ta \ˈäl-tə\. Winter sports area, Salt Lake co., N Utah, in Wasatch Range SE of Salt Lake City.

Alta. See ALTEELVA.

Alta California *also* **Upper California.** Spanish name for the present state of California, used to differentiate it from Baja California (*q.v.*).

Al·ta·de·na \ˌal-tə-ˈdē-nə\. Urban community (unincorporated), Los Angeles co., California, NE of Pasadena; pop. (1970c) 42,380.

Al·ta·gra·cia \ˌäl-tə-ˈgräs-ē-ə\. Town, Zulia state, NW Venezuela, on NE shore of Lake Maracaibo and opp. Maracaibo; pop. (1961c) 7362.

Al·ta Gra·cia \ˌäl-tə-ˈgräs-ē-ə\. Mountain resort, W Córdoba prov., N cen. Argentina, ab. 30 m. SSW of Córdoba; pop. (1960c) 11,628.

Al·tai \ˈal-ˌtī\. Mountain system bet. W Mongolian People's Republic and NE Sinkiang Uighur, W China, and bet. Kazakh S.S.R. and Gorno-Altai Autonomous Oblast, U.S.S.R.; highest peak ab. 15,000 ft.; source of Irtysh and Ob rivers.

Altai Krai \-ˈkrī\. Administrative territory, Russian S.F.S.R., U.S.S.R.; 101,042 sq. m.; pop. (1970p) 2,670,000; ✱ Barnaul; formerly included at its E end the Gorno-Altai Autonomous Oblast; traversed by the upper Ob, flowing generally N into Novosibirsk Oblast; corn, oats, wheat; barium, copper, lead, zinc.

Al·ta·ma·ha \ˈȯl-tə-mə-ˌhȯ\. River, SE Georgia; 137 m. long; formed by junction of Ocmulgee and Oconee rivers at SE tip of Wheeler co.; flows SE to Atlantic ab. 12 m. N of Brunswick.

Altamaha Sound. Inlet of Atlantic Ocean on SE coast of McIntosh co., SE Georgia, receiving the Altamaha river on the W.

Al·ta·mi·ra \ˌal-tə-ˈmir-ə\. Caverns (*cuevas*) in Santander prov., N Spain, ab. 13 m. WSW of Santander; discovered 1879; prehistoric drawings and paintings of animals, assigned to Upper Magdalenian Age.

Al·ta·mont \ˈal-tə-ˌmänt\. 1 City, Effingham co., SE cen. Illinois; pop. (1970c) 1929.

2 Urban community (unincorporated), Klamath co., S Oregon, E of Klamath Falls; pop. (1970c) 15,746.

3 Town, ⊗ of Grundy co., S cen. Tennessee; pop. (1970c) 546.

Al·ta·monte Springs \ˌal-tə-ˌmänt-\. City, Seminole co., cen. Florida, 6 m. N of Orlando; pop. (1970c) 4391.

Al·ta·mu·ra \ˌäl-tə-ˈmu̇r-ə\ *or anc.* **Lu·pa·tia** \lü-ˈpā-sh(ē-)ə\. Commune, Bari prov., Apulia, SE Italy, at foot of the Apennines 28 m. SW of Bari; pop. (1968e) 45,988; oil, wine, wool; walled city rebuilt 1232 by Emperor Frederick II.

Al·tan·bu·lag \ˌäl-tän-ˈbü-läk\ *or* **Kiach·ta** *or* **Kyakh·ta** \ˈkyäk-tä\ *or* **Al·tan Bu·lak** \ˌäl-tän-ˈbü-läk\ *or formerly* **Mai·ma·chin** \ˌmī-ˌmä-ˈchēn\. Commercial town, N Mongolian People's Republic, opp. Kyakhta in Buryat A.S.S.R., Russian S.F.S.R., U.S.S.R., and just E of Orhon river; on caravan and motor highway 150 m. N of Ulan Bator.

Altan–Nor. See ELTON, LAKE.

Alta Peak \ˈal-tə-\. Mountain in Sierra Nevada, NE Tulare co., S cen. California; 11,204 ft.

Al·tar \äl-ˈtär\ *or formerly* **Ca·pac–Ur·cu** \ˌkäp-ˌäk-ˈu̇(ə)r-(ˌ)kü\. Mountain in the Andes, cen. Ecuador, E of Riobamba; 17,725 ft.

Alta Ve·ra·paz \ˈäl-tə-ˌver-ə-ˈpäz\. Department of cen. Guatemala. See table at GUATEMALA.

Al·ta·vis·ta \ˌal-tə-ˈvis-tə\. Town, Campbell co., S cen. Virginia, on Roanoke river 23 m. S of Lynchburg; pop. (1970c) 2708; rayon, cedar chests.

Altbreisach. See BREISACH AM RHEIN.

Alt·dorf \ˈalt-ˌdȯrf, ˈält-\ *or* **Al·torf** \ˈal-ˌtȯrf, ˈäl-\. Commune, ✱ of Uri canton, cen. Switzerland, near SE tip of Lake of Lucerne 20 m. SE of Lucerne; pop. (1970c) 8647; rubber works; connected with William Tell legend, having a colossal statue of Tell (by Kissling) on the supposed site of the apple-shooting episode, and a theater for the production of Schiller's *William Tell;* site of oldest Capuchin monastery (1581) in Switzerland.

Al–Teb *or* **El Teb** \al-ˈteb, el-\. Locality, NE Sudan, near coast of Red Sea S of Port Sudan; scene of two battles Feb. 1884.

Al·te·el·va \ˌäl-tə-ˈel-və\ *or formerly* **Al·ta** \ˈäl-tə\. River, N Norway; flows N in Finnmark co. into **Alta** (**Al·ten** \ˈält-ᵊn-\) **Fjord,** inlet of Arctic Ocean at 70°N, hiding place of German fleet in World War II.

Al·te·na \ˈäl-tə-ˌnä\. Manufacturing city, North Rhine-Westphalia, West Germany, 47 m. S of Münster; pop. (1969e) 31,391; metalware and wire; site of ancestral castle of Counts von der Marck.

Al·ten·burg \ˈält-ᵊn-ˌbu̇(ə)rg\. 1 Manufacturing city, Leipzig dist., East Germany, in valley of the Pleisse 49 m. E of Weimar; pop. (1970e) 46,737; hats, playing cards, sewing machines; processing.

History: One of oldest German cities east of Saale river (mentioned as early as 976); seat of a burgrave from 12th century; given to Wettin family as fief of Holy Roman Empire 1329; burned by Hussites 1430; held by Ernestine branch of family 1485–1547 and from 1554; scene 1568–69 of conference between Lutherans and Philippists, two groups of German Protestants; from 1603–72 and 1826–1918 capital of independent duchy of Saxe-Altenburg.

2 Town, Hungary. See MOSONMAGYARÓVÁR.

Alten Fjord. See ALTEELVA.

Al·ten·kir·chen im Wes·ter·wald \ˌält-ᵊn-ˈki(ə)r-kən-im-ˌves-tər-ˈvält\. Town, Rhineland-Palatinate, West Germany, 22 m. N of Koblenz; pop. (1964e) 4600; scene of two battles bet. Austrians and French during War of the First Coalition 1796.

Al–Tih *or* **El Tih** \al-ˈtē, el-\ *also* **Ja·bal at Tīh** \ˌjəb-əl-at-ˈtē\. Plateau, cen. Sinai Penin., NE Egypt, just N of the Egma Plateau; 1800 to 3600 ft.

Altin Tagh. See A-ERH-CHIN SHAN-MO.

Alt·kirch \ˈält-ˌki(ə)rk\. Commune, Haut-Rhin dept., NE France, 29 m. SSW of Colmar; pop. (1962c) 4246; scene of several battles 1914.

Alt·mühl \ˈält-ˌmu̅e̅l, -ˌmyü(ə)l\. River, West Germany; 137 m. long; flows E in Bavaria to join the Danube river at Kelheim.

Al·to, Pi·co \ˌpē-kü-ˈäl-(ˌ)tü\. Volcanic peak on Pico I. in the Azores; 7713 ft.; highest point in the Azores.

Alto Adi·ge \ˌäl-(ˌ)tō-ˈäd-i-ˌjā\ *or* **South Ti·rol** \-tə-ˈrōl; -ˈtī-ˌrōl, -tī-ˈ; -ˈtir-əl\. Former administrative district, now N part of Trentino-Alto Adige, N Italy; language rights of its German-speaking residents object of pact signed by Austria and Italy 1969.

Al·ton \ˈȯlt-ᵊn\. 1 City, Madison co., SW Illinois, on Mississippi river 22 m. N of East St. Louis; pop. (1970c) 39,700; industrial center and shipping point; oil refineries, limestone quarries, flour mills, foundries.

2 City, ⊗ of Oregon co., S Missouri; pop. (1970c) 715.

3 Urban district, Hampshire, England, on the Wey river ab. 24 m. NE of Southampton; pop. (1971p) 12,686; hops, corn, cattle; paper.

Al·to·na \ˈäl-tə-ˌnä\. Former city, now part of Hamburg, West Germany.

History: Fishing village when passed to Denmark 1640; granted customs privileges with intention of making it rival Hamburg, its neighbor; burned by Swedes 1713; despite Napoleonic Wars, prospered until 1853 when it lost privileges; occupied 1864 in name of North German Confederation; became Prussian 1867; with Hamburg joined *Zollverein* 1888; became part of Hamburg 1937. See HAMBURG 4.

Al·too·na \al-ˈtü-nə\. 1 Industrial city, Blair co., S cen. Pennsylvania, near source of Juniata river in bituminous coal region 90 m. E of Pittsburgh; pop. (1970c) 63,115; extensive manufacturing and repair shops of Pennsylvania R.R.; auto and machine parts; 5 m. W is scenic Horseshoe Curve of railroad; settled 1849, incorp. as city 1868.

2 City, Eau Claire co., W Wisconsin, 5 m. E of Eau Claire; pop. (1970c) 2718.

Alto Pa·ra·ná \ˌal-ˌtō-ˌpar-ə-ˈnä\. 1 River. See PARANÁ 1.

2 Department of E Paraguay. See table at PARAGUAY.

Altorf. See ALTDORF.

Al·tos \ˈäl-ˌtōs\. Town, Cordillera dept., cen. Paraguay; munic. pop. (1970e) 9963.

Alto Son·go \ˌal-tō-ˈsȯŋ-gō\. Town and municipality, Oriente prov., Cuba, NE of Santiago; munic. pop. (1967e) 107,870.

Al·to·ton·ga \ˌal-tə-ˈtäŋ-gə\. Municipality, Veracruz state, Mexico, 80 m. NW of Veracruz; pop. (1970p) 31,231; diversified agriculture.

Alt·ran·städt \ˈält-ˈrän-ˌs(h)tet\. Village, East Germany, ab. 15 m. W of Leipzig. Gave name to two treaties: (1) treaty of 1706, during Great Northern War, by which Augustus II, king of Poland and elector of Saxony, was forced by Charles XII of Sweden to renounce claim to Polish crown in favor of Stanislas I Leszczyński; (2) treaty of 1707, in which Austrian Emperor Joseph I guaranteed to Charles XII religious toleration and freedom for Protestants in Silesia.

Al·trinc·ham \ˈȯl-triŋ-əm\. Municipal borough, Cheshire, NW England, 8 m. SW of Manchester; pop. (1971p) 40,752; typesetting machinery; noted for its market gardens; its annual fair dates from Edward I (1290).

Altsohl. See ZVOLEN.

Alt·stät·ten \ˈält-ˌs(h)tet-ᵊn\. Commune, St. Gall canton, NE Switzerland, in fertile Rhine valley 8 m. S of Lake Constance; pop. (1970c) 9084; textiles; rebuilt after 1410 fire.

Al·tu·ras \al-ˈtu̇r-əs\. City, ⊗ of Modoc co., NE corner of California, on Pit river 138 m. NE of Chico; pop. (1970c) 2799; grain, lumber; livestock; foundry; settled 1869; called **Dor·ris Bridge** \ˈdȯr-əs-, ˈdär-\ until 1874.

Al·tus \ˈal-təs\. City, ⊗ of Jackson co., SW Oklahoma, 58 m. W of Lawton; pop. (1970c) 23,302; food processing; Altus Junior Coll. (1926); founded 1891.

Altyn Tagh. See A-ERH-CHIN SHAN-MO.

Al–Ubay·yid \ˌal-ü-ˈbā-(y)əd\ *or* **Al–Obeid** *or* **El Obeid** \-ō-ˈbād, ˌel-\. Town, ✱ of Kardofan prov., cen. Sudan; pop. (1969e) 66,270; battle fought nearby Nov. 1–4, 1883 in which Gen. William Hicks and Egyptian army were defeated by Mahdi.

Al·u·la \a-ˈlü-lə\. Small port on Gulf of Aden, NE Somalia, W of Ras (cape) Asir.

Al·um Rock \ˈal-əm-\. Urban community (unincorporated), Santa Clara co., California, NE of San Jose; pop. (1970c) 18,355.

Al–ʿUqaylah. See AL-AGHEILA.

Al–ʿUqayr. See OQAIR.

Al–Uqsor. See LUXOR.

Aluta. See OLT 1.

Al·va \ˈal-və\. City, ⊗ of Woods co., NW Oklahoma, 53 m. WNW of Enid; pop. (1970c) 7440; business center in stock-raising, wheat, and dairy-farming region; Northwestern State Coll. (1897).

Al·va·ra·do \ˌal-və-ˈräd-(ˌ)ō\. 1 Seaside resort, Argentina. See GENERAL ALVARADO.

2 Town, Veracruz state, E Mexico, on coast 33 m. SE of Veracruz; munic. pop. (1970p) 33,152.

Alvarado, Pa·so de \ˈpä-sō-dā-\. Andean mountain pass on Argentina-Chile border, bet. W Mendoza prov., Argentina and E Santiago prov., Chile; alt. 12,484 ft.

Álvaro Obregón. See FRONTERA.

Al·ver·stone, Mount \-ˈal-vər-ˌstōn\. Mountain, St. Elias Mts., Yukon, Canada; 14,500 ft.

Al·vin \ˈal-vən\. City, Brazoria co., SE Texas, in agricultural region 25 m. S of Houston; pop. (1970c) 10,671; Alvin Junior Coll. (1949); oil wells.

Älvs·borg *also* **Alfs·borg** *or* **Elfs·borg** \ˈelfs-ˌbȯr-ē\. County of SW Sweden. See table at SWEDEN.

Al–Wad. See AL-OUED.

Al·wand, Mount \-al-ˈwänd\ *or* **Mount El·vend** \-ˈel-ˌvend\ *or Pers.* **Kuh–i–Alwand** \ˌkü-(h)ē-\ *or anc.* **Oron·tes** \ō-ˈrän-ˌtēz\. Mountain, W Iran, just SW of Hamadān; 11,640 ft.

Al·war *also* **Al·wur** \ˈəl-wər\. 1 Former Indian state, now part of Rajasthan, NW India; 3158 sq. m.; founded by Rajput chieftain Pratap Singh in 1771; joined British against Marathas 1803.

2 City, its ✱, ab. 80 m. SW of Delhi; pop. (1961c) 72,707; surrounded by wall and moat; has several palaces and temples.

Al–Zallāqah. See ZALLAKA.

Al·zette \al-ˈzet\. River, cen. Luxembourg; 43 m. long; flows N into Sauer river.

Ama·cu·ro \ˌäm-ə-ˈkü(ə)r-(ˌ)ō\ *also* **Ama·ku·ra** \-ˈkür-ə\. Small river, NE Venezuela, flowing NE then NW to Orinoco delta; along its middle course forms short section of Venezuela-Guyana boundary (as drawn 1835 by Schomburgk but not accepted by Venezuela until confirmation of British claims by arbitration 1899).

Am·a·de·us, Lake \-ˌam-ə-ˈdē-əs\. Large lake, cen. Australia, in SW corner of Northern Territory, S of Macdonnell Ranges; E-W extent ab. 90 m.; very shallow; discovered 1872 by Ernest Giles, Australian explorer.

Ama·di·ya \ə-ˈmad-ē-(y)ə\. Town, S Kurdistan, N Iraq, ab. 55 m. NNE of Mosul.

Amadj·uak Lake \ə-ˌmaj-ə-ˌwak-\. Lake in S Baffin Island, E Franklin dist., Northwest Territories, Canada.

Am·a·dor \ˈam-ə-ˌdȯ(ə)r\. County in California. See table at CALIFORNIA.

Amador, Fort. United States fort in the Canal Zone at the Pacific terminus of the Panama Canal.

Ama·do·ra \ˌam-ə-ˈdōr-ə, -ˈdȯr-\. City, Lisbon dist., W Portugal, ab. 6 m. NW of Lisbon; munic. pop. (1970p) 109,965.

Ama·ga·sa·ki \ˌam-ə-gə-ˈsäk-ā\. City, Hyōgo prefecture, W Honshū, Japan, on NE shore of Osaka Bay; pop. (1970c) 553,696; a suburb of Ōsaka and an important chemical and iron and steel center in the Ōsaka-Kōbe industrial area; heavily bombed by American planes 1945.

Ama·ger \ˈäm-ə-gər\. Island forming a part of Denmark, lying in Øresund off the NE cen. coast of the island of Sjælland and separated from Sjælland by the harbor of Copenhagen; 25 sq. m.; pop. (1965c) 177,818; includes a section of the city of Copenhagen; inhabitants are largely descendants of 16th cent. Dutch colonists.

Amak·nak \ə-ˈmak-ˌnak\. Small island, Unalaska Bay, Unalaska I., E Aleutian Is.; ab. 4 m. long; highest point 1640 ft.

Amakura. See AMACURO.

Ama·ku·sa \ä-ˈmäk-ə-ˌsä\. Island group off W coast of Kyūshū, Japan, E of **Amakusa Sea** and S of Nagasaki; 342 sq. m.; in Kumamoto prefecture; comprises two large islands and ab. 65 small islands.

Amal·fi \ə-ˈmäl-fē\. Town, Salerno prov., Campania, Italy, on north coast of Gulf of Salerno, ab. 22 m. SE of Naples; pop. (1968e) 7162; built on mountain slope; archiepiscopal see; cathedral of Sant'Andrea (11th cent.) with bronze doors cast at Constantinople before 1066.

History: Originally a Byzantine settlement, became important commercial port in 9th century equal to Venice and Genoa; by 839 succeeded in freeing itself from Naples and Benevento; as a leading naval power, helped Pope Leo IV against Saracens 848; one of first Italian cities to become independent republic (under rule of doges) near beginning of 11th century; captured by Normans under Roger II of Sicily 1131; sacked by Pisans 1135, 1137; declined gradually until inundation of 1373 destroyed much of town and harbor. Notable particularly for the *Tabulae Amalphitanae,* its maritime code, recognized on the Mediterranean until 1750.

Ama·li·as \ˌäm-əl-ˈyäs\. City, Elis dept., NW Peloponnesus, Greece, near W coast; in fertile region producing wine grapes and currants.

Amal·ner \ə-ˈməl-nər, -ˈmäl-\. Town, Gujarat, India, on tributary of Tapti river 145 m. E of Surat; pop. (1961c) 46,963.

Amambaí, Serra de. See SERRA DE AMAMBAÍ.

Amam·bay \ˌäm-əm-ˈbī\. Department of E Paraguay. See table at PARAGUAY.

Amambay, Cordillera de. See SERRA DE AMAMBAÍ.

Ama·mi \ə-ˈmäm-ē\ *also, officially* **Oshi·ma** \ˈō-shi-mə, ō-ˈshē-\. Island group (**Amami Gun·to** \-ˈgün-(ˌ)tō\), N Ryukyu Is., Japan, NE of Okinawa; 498 sq. m.; includes Amami-Ō-shima, or Ō-shima (largest), Tokuno Shima, Okierabu, Kikai Shima, and others.

Amana \ə-ˈman-ə\. Village, Iowa co., Iowa, 18 m. SW of Cedar Rapids; oldest of seven villages in Iowa co. founded by a religious communal society under Christian Metz, originating in a German Pietist sect, which became established near Buffalo, N.Y. 1842–54 and migrated to Iowa in 1855. Communities incorporated as Amana Society 1859.

Ama·na \ˌam-ə-ˈnä\. Peak, S French Guiana, in the Tumuc-Humac Mountains; 1950 ft.

Amanus. See NUR MOUNTAINS.

Aman·zim·to·ti \ə-ˌmän-zim-ˈtōt-ē\. Coastal town, Natal, Rep. of South Africa; pop. (1967e) 26,600.

Ama·pá \ˌam-ə-ˈpä\. **1** Territory of N Brazil; 54,161 sq. m.; pop. (1970p) 116,481; ✱ Macapá; timber, nuts; fishing; formed 1943.

2 *or formerly* **Mon·te·ne·gro** \ˌmōn-tə-ˈneg-(ˌ)rü, -(ˌ)rō\. Municipality, Rio Grande do Sul, S Brazil, 60 m. NW of Porto Alegre; pop. (1968e) 52,151.

Ama·pa·la \ˌam-ə-ˈpä-lə\. Seaport on Tigre Island, Gulf of Fonseca, Honduras, ab. 70 m. SSW of Tegucigalpa; pop. (1961c) 2368; only good anchorage on Pacific coast of Honduras.

ʻAma·ra \ə-ˈmär-ə\. Town, Iraq, on E bank of Tigris river 100 m. NW of Basra; pop. (1965c) 64,847; taken by Gen. Townshend as part of Mesopotamian campaign (part of British advance to Baghdad) June 1915. See KUT.

Ama·ran·te \ˌam-ə-ˈra(ⁿ)nt-ə\. Town, Piauí state, Brazil, on Parnaíba river 240 m. SSW of Parnaíba; munic. pop. (1968e) 12,683; trade center for sugar, cotton, cereals, hides, etc.

Ama·ra·pu·ra \ˌəm-ə-ˌräp-ə-ˈrä, ˌäm-\. Town on E bank of Irrawaddy river, Mandalay div., Burma; a S suburb of Mandalay; pop. (1962e) 71,015. Founded 1782 as new capital of kingdom of Burma; destroyed by fire 1810; declined after removal of native court to Ava 1823; capital again 1837–60, when it was abandoned for Mandalay; suffered from earthquake 1839.

Ama·ra·va·ti \ˌəm-ə-ˈräv-ət-ē, ˌäm-\. Ruined city, cen. Andhra Pradesh, E India, on S bank of Krisha river ab. 60 m. from its mouth; ancient capital of Vengi, Buddhist kingdom of the Andhras; has tope with elaborate carvings of life of Buddha.

Am·ar·go·sa \ˌam-är-ˈgō-sə\. River, S Nevada and E California; flows into Death Valley, E California.

Amargosa Range. Mountains in SE California, E of Death Valley; highest point 6397 ft.

Am·a·ril·lo \ˌam-ə-ˈril-(ˌ)ō, -ˈril-ə\. City, Potter and Randall cos., NW Texas, ⊗ of Potter co., 65 m. E of New Mexico border; pop. (1970c) 127,010; alt. 3658 ft.; commercial and industrial center of Texas panhandle; supply center for oil and helium gas (U.S. helium plant); zinc smelters, grain elevators, oil refineries; Amarillo Coll. (1929).

ʻAmarna, Tell al–. See TELL AL-ʻAMARNA.

Ama·ro \ə-ˈmär-(ˌ)ō\. Peak in the Apennines, Abruzzi, SE cen. Italy; 9170 ft.

Ama·roú·sion \ˌäm-ə-ˈrüs-ˌyōn\. City, Greece, part of Greater Athens; pop. (1971p) 26,645.

Ama·sya \ˌäm-ə-ˈsyä\. **1** Province of N Turkey, Asia. See table at TURKEY.

2 *or anc.* **Am·a·sia** \ˌam-ə-ˈsī-ə, -ˈsē-ə\. Commercial city, its ✱, 50 m. SSW of Samsun; pop. (1965c) 34,168; fruit gardens.

History: Ancient town capital of kingdom of Pontus (*q.v.*); site of rock-cut tombs of Pontine kings; base of Mithridates' operations against Romans 89, 72, 67 B.C.; made free city by Pompey 65 B.C.; one of chief cities of Greek empire of Trebizond (see TRABZON) and of the Seljuks; withstood siege by Tamerlane; an early residence of Ottoman (Turkish) sultans; birthplace of the geographer Strabo.

Am·a·tig·nak \ˌam-ə-ˈtig-ˌnak\. Small island, most southwesterly of the Andreanof Is., Aleutian Is., Alaska.

Ama·ti·que, Gulf of \-ˌäm-ə-ˈtē-(ˌ)kā\. Arm of Gulf of Honduras, NE Guatemala and SE British Honduras.

Ama·ti·tlán \ˌäm-ə-tē-ˈtlän\. 1 Lake in mountains of SE Guatemala; ab. 8 m. long and 3 m. broad; a tourist resort noted for beautiful scenery.
2 Town on the lake, ab. 12 m. SW of Guatemala City; munic. pop. (1964e) 19,430; coffee and sugar plantations.

Amatongaland. See TONGALAND.

Amay \a-ˈmā\. Commune, Liège prov., Belgium, on the Meuse ab. 12 m. SW of Liège; pop. (1969e) 7581; quarries, tile and ceramics works, dried fruits.

Am·a·zon \ˈam-ə-ˌzän, -zən\ *or Port.* **Rio Ama·zo·nas** \ˈrē-ü-ˌam-ə-ˈzō-nəs\ *or Span.* **Río de las Amazonas** \ˈrē-ō-(ˌ)dā-läs-ˌäm-ə-ˈzō-nəs\ *or originally* **Orel·la·na** \ˌōr-ā-ˈ(y)än-ə, ˌȯr-\. Largest river in the world by volume (exceeded in length by the Nile river), South America; length of Amazon including Marañón, which rises ab. 100 m. from Pacific Ocean and is usually considered the Amazon proper, 4000 m.; length including Ucayali and its headstream, the Apurímac, 3915 m.; flows N in the Peruvian Andes, then E through N Brazil to Atlantic Ocean; its basin ab. 2,053,318 sq. m. (including Tocantins, ab. 2,722,000 sq. m.) extends through 25° of latitude from source of Rio Branco near Mt. Roraima (5°N) to source of a headstream of the Madeira in S Bolivia (ab. 20°S); formed in Peru by union of its two headstreams, the Marañón and Ucayali, just above Iquitos; in Brazil called Solimões from Peruvian border to mouth of Negro.

Chief tributaries: On N receives the Napo from N Ecuador and Peru and the Içá (Putumayo), Japurá, Negro, Trombetas, Paru, and Jari in Brazil; on S the Huallaga in N Peru, Javarí forming part of boundary bet. Peru and Brazil, Jutaí, Juruá, Purus, Maderia, Tapojós, Xingu, and Tocantins (strictly not a tributary). At its mouth has two branches around island of Marajó (*q.v.*); N branch (at the equator) has Caviana and many smaller islands in it; S and E branch, known as Pará, receives Tocantins; has tidal phenomenon, known as bore, reaching far upstream and at times 16 ft. in height; discharge at its mouth averages 7,000,000 cu. ft. per second; volume of river so great that its discharge can be detected 200 m. out in ocean; navigable for ocean steamers 2300 m. up to Iquitos; its most important port Manaus, at mouth of Negro, 1000 miles from mouth; its high water floods occur in June causing width to vary from 5 to 400 m.; has extremely low gradient, alt. 35 ft. at 2000 m. from the sea. In S Venezuela confluence of Negro and Casiquiare unites Amazon and Orinoco systems.

History: Discovered by Spanish adventurer Vicente Yáñez Pinzón 1500; first descended (from Andes) by Orellana 1541 and ascended by Pedro Teixeira 1637–39; except for occasional ascents in search of slaves, little explored until mid-19th century; steam navigation authorized by Emperor Pedro II of Brazil 1850, and a company, formed 1852, began to operate vessels 1853; opened to world shipping by decree 1866; valley of Amazon and its tributaries center of crude-rubber industry which reached height in 1910–11 but declined by 1915 after shift of market to East Indies rubber; explored by scientific expeditions of Roosevelt and Rondon 1913–14, Rice 1910–24, American Geographical Society, and others; perpetual free navigation of Amazon guaranteed by treaty bet. Colombia and Brazil (ratified by Colombia 1929).

Ama·zo·nas \ˌam-ə-ˈzō-nəs\. 1 State of NW Brazil; 604,032 sq. m.; pop. (1970p) 714,803; ✱ Manaus; rubber, jute, cattle; made a province 1852, a state 1889.
2 Commissary of SE Colombia. See table at COLOMBIA.
3 Department of N Peru. See table at PERU.
4 Territory of S Venezuela. See table at VENEZUELA.

Am·a·zo·nia \ˌam-ə-ˈzō-nē-ə\. The regions about the Amazon river in South America, including the greater part of Brazil and parts of bordering countries, esp. Colombia, Ecuador, Peru, and Bolivia; so called because Orellana and early Spanish explorers thought they saw female warriors on its banks.

Ambacia. See AMBOISE.

Am·ba·la \əm-ˈbäl-ə\. 1 Division, Haryana, N India.
2 District of Ambala division; 1436 sq. m.; pop. (1961c) 895,000; wheat, corn, peanuts.
3 City, ✱ of division and of dist., 115 m. NNW of Delhi; pop. (1967e) 87,750; glass, paper; trades in grain and sugar.

Am·ba·ra·wa \ˌäm-bə-ˈrä-wə\. Town, Central Java prov., Indonesia, ab. 20 m. S of Semarang; scene of fighting by British troops against Indonesian nationalists Aug.–Dec. 1945.

Am·ba·to \äm-ˈbät-(ˌ)ō\. Manufacturing and commercial city, ✱ of Tungurагua prov., cen. Ecuador, ab. 70 m. S of Quito and near N base of Mt. Chimborazo; pop. (1970e) 75,300; alt. 8435 ft.; known as "garden city" of Ecuador; raises much fruit; manufactures boots, shoes, and textiles.

Am·ber \ˈəm-bər, ˈäm-\. Ruined city, ancient ✱ of Jaipur state, now in E Rajasthan, NW India, 5 m. N of Jaipur, picturesquely situated at mouth of a mountain gorge by lake; made famous by Rajput structures including the old palace (begun 1600) and the Diwan-i-ʻAm, richly decorated with sculpture; seized by Rajputs 1037; supplanted by Jaipur 1728.

Amber, Cape \-ˈam-bər\ *or Fr.* **Cap d'Am·bre** \kȧp-däⁿbrᵊ\. N point of Malagasy Republic, 11°57′S, 49°17′E.

Am·berg \ˈäm-ˌbe(ə)rg\. City, Bavaria, West Germany, 35 m. E of Nürnberg; pop. (1969e) 42,300; formerly capital of Upper Palatinate; enamels, earthenware; blast furnaces, breweries; iron and coal mined in the vicinity. Scene of defeat of French Aug. 24, 1796 by Archduke Charles (of Austria) during War of the First Coalition (1792–97).

Am·ber·gris Cay \ˌam-bər-ˌgris-, -ˌgrēs-\. Island in Caribbean Sea off NE British Honduras; encloses S part of Chetumal Bay.

Ambergris Cays. Group of islets (keys) in Caicos Is., West Indies.

Am·ber·ley \ˈam-bər-lē\. Village, Hamilton co., SW Ohio, 8 m. NNE of Cincinnati; pop. (1970c) 5574.

Ambianum. See AMIENS.

Am·bler \ˈam-blər\. Borough, Montgomery co., SE Pennsylvania, N of Philadelphia; pop. (1970c) 7000; asbestos, pharmaceuticals, sheet-metal products.

Am·blève \äⁿ-blev\. River, E Belgium; ab. 53 m. long; flows NW into Ourthe river a few miles S of Liège; Stavelot is on it. Its banks reached in German offensive Dec. 1944.

Am·bo·di·fo·to·tra \am-ˌbōd-i-fə-ˈtō-trə\. Town, Sainte-Marie I., off NE coast of Malagasy Republic.

Am·boi·na \am-ˈbȯi-nə\. 1 Island, Indonesia. See AMBON 1.
2 District, Indonesia. See CENTRAL MALUKU.
3 Town, Indonesia. See AMBON 3.

Am·boise \äⁿ-ˈbwäz\ *or Lat.* **Am·ba·cia** \am-ˈbā-sh(ē-)ə\. Commune, Indre-et-Loire dept., NW cen. France, on left bank of Loire river 15 m. E of Tours; pop. (1962c) 7332; optical instruments, plastic goods, photographic equipment, shoes; notable particularly for its castle.

History: Lordship under counts of Anjou in 11th century, united to royal domain by Charles VII 1431; castle, rebuilt and beautified by Charles VIII and successors, became a residence of French kings and later a state prison, Abd-al-Kader having been confined there 1848–52; castle's chapel of St. Hubert said to be burial place of Leonardo da Vinci; gave name to conspiracy of Amboise 1560, an unsuccessful plot of Huguenots to remove Francis II from influence of Guise family, and to edict of Amboise 1563, a pacification, concluded by Catherine de Médicis with Huguenots, which guaranteed liberty of worship to Protestant nobility and gentry; castle, confiscated in French Revolution, finally restored to house of Orléans 1872.

Amboland. See OVAMBOLAND.

Am·bon \'am-ˌbän\ *also* **Am·boi·na** *or* **Am·boy·na** \am-'bȯi-nə\. 1 Island of the Moluccas, Indonesia, Malay Archipelago, off SW coast of Ceram I.; 31 m. long by 10 m. wide; 314 sq. m.; pop. (1957e) 72,679; formed by two long strips of land connected by narrow isthmus; has high peaks that are active volcanoes (highest Salhutu 3360 ft.); main products tropical fruits and spices.

2 District, Indonesia. See CENTRAL MALUKU.

3 Seaport, its chief town and ✱ of Maluku prov., on harbor (**Ambon Bay**); by air 1150 m. ENE of Surabaja and 425 m. SE of Manado; pop. (1961c) 56,000; univ. (1962).

History (town and island): Discovered by Portuguese 1510 and settled 1521; source of Portuguese clove monopoly until Portuguese were ousted by Dutch East India Company 1605; settlement made on the island by English traders 1615; scene of incident known as "massacre of Amboina" 1623 when Dutch killed English on pretext of latter's treachery (until 1654, a bitter issue of Anglo-Dutch relations); entire island claimed by Dutch when they took over suzerainty of Moluccas (1683); captured by British 1796, 1810, but finally restored to Dutch 1814; a separate residency until united with Ternate to form Government of the Moluccas 1927; in 1930 census a division of Moluccas residency; under Japanese control 1942–45.

Am·bos Ca·ma·ri·nes \'äm-ˌbōs-ˌkäm-ə-'rē-nəs\. Former province, Phil., now divided into the provs. Camarines Norte and Camarines Sur. See CAMARINES NORTE.

Am·bo·si·tra \ˌam-bə-'sē-trə\. Inland town, S cen. Malagasy Republic, S of Antsirabe; pop. (1969e) 15,131; road junction.

Amboyna. See AMBON.

Ambracia. City, Greece. See ARTA 3.

Am·bra·cian Gulf \am-ˌbrā-shən-\ *also* **Gulf of Ar·ta** \-'ärt-ə\. Inlet of Ionian Sea, S Epirus, on W coast of Greece; 25 m. long and from 4 to 10 m. wide; on its shores are ruins of several cities important in ancient Greece; battle of Actium (*q.v.*) fought near its entrance 31 B.C.

Ambre, Cap d'. See AMBER, CAPE.

Am·bridge \'am-brij\. Borough, Beaver co., W Pennsylvania, on Ohio river 17 m. WNW of Pittsburgh; pop. (1970c) 11,342; steel, wrought iron; built on site of German communistic settlement called Economy (estab. 1825).

Am·brim *or* **Am·brym** \'am-ˌbrim\. Island, NE part of the New Hebrides, SW Pacific Ocean, E of Malekula I.; 24 m. long by 16 m. wide; pop. (1967c) 4246; has active volcano Minnei Peak that had disastrous eruption 1913.

Am·briz \am-'brēz\. Seaport, NW Angola, Africa, 75 m. N of Luanda; munic. pop. (1961c) 38,967.

Am·brose Channel \ˌam-ˌbrōz-\. Channel across Sandy Hook bar, entrance to New York harbor SSE of the Narrows; 7½ m. long, 40 ft. deep, and from 1850 to 2000 ft. wide; dredged 1899–1913. **Ambrose Channel Lightship,** marking its entrance, is ab. 9 m. E of Sandy Hook.

Am·bur \əm-'bu̇(ə)r, äm-\. Town, Tamil Nadu, S India, ab. 107 m. WSW of Madras on Palar river; pop. (1961c) 39,455; commands pass into the Carnatic; scene of battle 1749.

Am·bu·ra·yan \ˌäm-bu̇-'rä-ˌyän, -'rī-ˌän\. 1 River, Luzon, Phil.; ab. 60 m. long; rises in the Cordillera Central, flows W then NW through S Ilocos Sur to South China Sea near Tagudin.

2 Region, NW Luzon; former Spanish military district (*comandancia*), later a subprovince of Mountain Prov.; joined 1920 with Lepanto to form Lepanto-Amburayan subprovince; later divided bet. Ilocos Sur, La Union, and Mountain Prov.

Am·chit·ka \am-'chit-kə\. Island in the Aleutian Is., at E end of Rat Is. group 69 m. SE of Kiska; ab. 15 m. long and 5 m. wide; 121 sq. m.; occupied 1942 by U.S. task force and air base set up for operations against Japanese on Kiska and Attu Jan.–May 1943.

Ame·ca \ä-'mā-kə\. 1 River, W cen. Mexico; ab. 140 m. long; flows W into Banderas Bay.

2 Town, Jalisco state, W cen. Mexico, on Ameca river 45 m. W of Guadalajara; munic. pop. (1970p) 42,016.

Ame·ca·me·ca \ä-ˌmā-kə-'mā-kə\ *or in full* **Amecameca de Juá·rez** \-dā-'hwär-ˌes, -'wär-əz\. Town, México state, cen. Mexico, 36 m. SE of Mexico City; munic. pop. (1970p) 21,753; alt. 7600 ft. Important center of pre-Spanish civilization; has shrine Sacro Monte, hill built over a cave where one of earliest Christian missionaries in Mexico lived, which is visited by thousands of Indians during Holy Week. Starting point for ascents of Popocatépetl and Iztaccíhuatl.

Ame·land \'äm-ə-ˌlänt\. Island, Friesland prov., Netherlands, in North Sea, belongs to West Frisian Is.; ab. 13 m. long and 2 m. wide; pop. (1970e) 2899.

Ame·lia \ə-'mēl-yə\. County in Virginia. See table at VIRGINIA.

Amelia \ə-'māl-yə\ *or anc.* **Ame·ria** \ə-'mir-ē-ə\. Commune, Terni prov., Umbria, cen. Italy, 12 m. W of Terni; pop. (1968e) 10,793; episcopal see since 340; well preserved remains of ancient polygonal city walls.

Amelia Courthouse \ə-ˌmēl-yə-\. Village, ⊗ of Amelia co., SE cen. Virginia.

Amelia Island. Island in Atlantic Ocean off coast of Nassau co., NE Florida; ab. 15 m. long and 4 m. wide; 24 sq. m.

History: Part of Spanish, later of American, Florida; resort of smugglers during U.S. embargo on trade with Europe 1807; scene of incident known as "Amelia Island Affair" in which U.S. sent naval expedition to remove forces of Luis Aury, a South American adventurer, who had set up a government on the island and invited Florida to throw off Spanish rule 1817; captured by U.S. Union forces from Confederates during American Civil War 1862.

Ameria. See AMELIA.

Amer·i·ca \ə-'mer-ə-kə\ *or Span. or Port.* **Amé·ri·ca** \ä-'mer-ē-kä\. A name derived from *Americus* Vespucius, Latinized form of name of Amerigo Vespucci (1451–1512), Italian navigator, and first used in a popular account of his travels in the New World published 1507 by the German geographer Martin Waldseemüller. Originally (as applied by Waldseemüller), the lands discovered by Columbus, *i.e.* South America and the West Indies; later (as used 1538 by Mercator), the New World, *i.e.* the lands of the Western Hemisphere. In current use: either continent of the Western Hemisphere (North America or South America); often, specifically, the United States of America (*q.v.*); also, although in this application the plural form **the Americas** is the usual one, all the lands of the Western Hemisphere including North America, South America, and the West Indies.

History: Earliest European discovery of any part of the Americas was of NE coast of North America by the Norse (Leif Ericsson 1000, Thorfinn Karlsefni 1004–06); general European knowledge of the Americas dates from the voyages of Columbus, whose first landfall was at San Salvador (island in the Bahamas) Oct. 12, 1492, and who later (voyages of 1495, 1498, 1502) touched coasts of Central and South America; in Europe until 16th and 17th centuries known as *the Indies, West Indies,* or *New World;* separation of North America from Asia established by voyage of Magellan 1519–21. For more detailed information, see NORTH AMERICA, SOUTH AMERICA, CENTRAL AMERICA, WEST INDIES.

America Islands. Name sometimes applied to a group of islands in N part of the Line Is. (*q.v.*), 5°50′N to 2°N, including Palmyra, Washington, Fanning, and Christmas Islands (*qq.v.*).

Amer·i·can \ə-ˈmer-ə-kən\. River, N cen. California; ab. 30 m. long; formed by three forks, flows SW into Sacramento river at Sacramento.

American Fall. See NIAGARA FALLS 1.

American Falls. 1 Falls, Niagara river. See NIAGARA FALLS 1.

2 City, ⊗ of Power co., SE Idaho; pop. (1970c) 2769; shipping point for wheat and potatoes.

American Fork. City, Utah co., N cen. Utah, on Utah Lake 14 m. NNW of Provo; pop. (1970c) 7713; beets, poultry, sugar.

American River. See AMERICAN.

American Samoa *also* **Eastern Samoa.** Group of islands of Samoa (*q.v.*), SW cen. Pacific Ocean, E of long. 171°W and ab. 14°S lat.; 76 sq. m.; pop. (1970p) 27,769; ✱ Pago Pago; includes islands of Tutuila, Manua Is. (Tau, Olosega, Ofu), Aunuu, Rose, and Swains; exports: canned tuna and copra. See WESTERN SAMOA.

History: Ruled by native chiefs until ab. 1860; object of American interest since expedition of Commodore Wilkes 1839; visited by Commander Richard W. Meade, U.S.N., 1872; Pago Pago and trading and extraterritorial rights granted to U.S. 1878; under joint administration of U.S., Germany, and England 1889–99 and by treaty of 1899 granted to U.S.; Swains I. annexed 1925.

Administered by U.S. Department of the Navy before 1951 and by U.S. Department of the Interior since then. Constitution, setting up a local legislature, adopted April 1960.

American Virgin Islands. See VIRGIN ISLANDS.

Amer·i·cus \ə-ˈmer-ə-kəs\. Industrial city, ⊗ of Sumter co., SW cen. Georgia; pop. (1970c) 16,091; shirt factories, lumber mills, canneries; Georgia Southwestern Coll. (1906).

Ame·rong·en \ˈäm-ə-ˌrȯŋ-ən\. Commune, Utrecht prov., cen. Netherlands, near the Lower Rhine 23 m. SE of Utrecht; pop. (1970e) 5773; its castle of Count Bentinck was first refuge of Kaiser William II of Germany 1918.

Amers·foort \ˈäm-ərz-ˌfō(ə)rt, -ərs-, -ˌfȯ(ə)rt\. Commune, Utrecht prov., cen. Netherlands, 12 m. NE of Utrecht; pop. (1970e) 78,189; railroad junction; chemicals, foodstuffs; metalworking; has 13th cent. church, Jansenist college, and 312-ft. Gothic tower built c. 1450.

Ames \ˈāmz\. City, Story co., cen. Iowa, 28 m. N of Des Moines; pop. (1970c) 39,505. Iowa State Univ. of Science and Technology (1858); incorp. 1870.

Ames·bury \ˈāmz-ˌber-ē, -b(ə-)rē\. 1 Town, Essex co., NE Massachusetts, on Merrimack river 24 m. NE of Lowell; pop. (1970c) 11,388.

2 *or formerly* **Almes·bury** \ˈämz-bə-rē\. Town, Wiltshire, England, 8 m. N of Salisbury on Avon river; pop. (1961c) 1530; market and fair (grant dating from 1317); known particularly for Stonehenge (1½ m. W), principal surviving megalithic structure in British Isles (see AVEBURY); notable in 17th cent. for production of pipe clay and pipes. Scene of a witenagemot 932; site of nunnery built ab. 980.

Amestratus. See MISTRETTA.

Am·ga \äm-ˈgä\. River, SE Yakutsk A.S.S.R., U.S.S.R.; ab. 800 m. long; rises in Aldan Mts. and flows NE to Aldan river ab. 175 m. E of Yakutsk.

Am·gun \ˈäm-ˌgün\. River, Khabarovsk Krai, U.S.S.R.; 490 m. long; rises in mountains NW of Khabarovsk and flows NE to the Amur near its mouth above Nikolayevsk-na-Amure.

Am·hara \am-ˈhar-ə, -ˈhär-ə\. Former kingdom, NW Ethiopia; 76,235 sq. m.; ✱ Gonder; a province (1936–41) of Italian East Africa; gave name (*Amharic*) to official and court language of Ethiopia.

Am·herst \ˈam-(ˌ)ərst, -ˌhərst\. 1 County in Virginia. See table at VIRGINIA.

2 Town, Hampshire co., W Massachusetts, 19 m. N of Springfield; pop. (1970c) 26,331; Amherst Coll. (1821), Univ. of Massachusetts (1863).

3 Town, Hillsborough co., S New Hampshire, 11 m. SW of Manchester; pop. (1970c) 4605; settled 1733.

4 Village, Lorain co., N Ohio, 27 m. WSW of Cleveland; pop. (1970c) 9902; sandstone quarries.

5 Town, ⊗ of Amherst co., cen. Virginia; pop. (1970c) 1108.

6 District, Tenasserim division, Burma; 2649 sq. m.; pop. (1962e) 582,279; ✱ Moulmein.

7 Seaport in Amherst dist., Burma, on **Amherst Peninsula,** 30 m. S of Moulmein; pop. (1962e) 59,050; has good harbor. Founded 1826.

8 Town, ⊗ of Cumberland co., N Nova Scotia, Canada, 5 m. E of NE end of Chignecto Bay; pop. (1971p) 9898. A thriving Acadian village, then known as **Les Planches,** prior to English occupation; refounded as English town 1760 and named after Jeffrey, Lord Amherst. The inland gateway to Nova Scotia; noted as geographical center of Maritime Provinces; ruins of Forts Lawrence and Beauséjour nearby.

Am·herst·burg \ˈam-ərst-ˌbərg\. Town, Essex co., SE Ontario, Canada, on Detroit river in fertile agricultural section 14 m. S of Windsor; pop. (1971p) 5115. Founded 1796 on site of old French settlement, visited by La Salle 1679; contains remains of **Fort Malden,** built 1797–99 and used as a frontier post in War of 1812.

Amherst Island. 1 Island at NE end of Lake Ontario, Ontario, Canada, SW of Kingston.

2 Chief island of the Magdalen Is. in the Gulf of St. Lawrence, Quebec, E Canada.

Amherst Mountain. Peak, La Plata co., SW Colorado; 13,100 ft.

Amida. See DIYARBAKIR 2.

Am·i·don \ˈam-ə-ˌdän\. Village, ⊗ of Slope co., SW North Dakota; pop. (1970c) 54.

Amiens \am-ˈyaⁿ\ *or anc.* **Sam·a·ro·bri·va** \ˌsam-ə-rō-ˈbrī-və\ *or later* **Am·bi·a·num** \ˌam-bē-ˈā-nəm\. Manufacturing city, ✱ of Somme dept., N France, on Somme river 72 m. N of Paris; pop. (1968c) 117,888; a major center of the French textile industry (since 16th cent.), chemicals; trades in agricultural products; univ. (1965); site of world-famous cathedral of Notre Dame, largest church in France and one of leading representatives of Gothic architecture in Europe.

History: Capital (as Samarobriva) of the Ambiani; became Roman stronghold; chief city of medieval county **Amié·nois** \ˌam-(ˌ)yān-ˈwä\, which became crown land 1185; passed to Burgundy by Peace of Arras 1435, but returned to France at death of Duke Charles the Bold 1477; captured by Spanish 1597 and recovered by Henry IV; capital of Picardy to 1790; scene of signing 1802 of Peace of Amiens bet. France and Britain; captured by Prussians 1870; held by Germans for a short time in 1914; gave name to World War I battle (August 1918) which was part of successful Allied counteroffensive against Germany. In World War II occupied by Germans May 1940–Aug. 1944. Birthplace of Peter the Hermit.

Amindivi Islands. See LACCADIVE ISLANDS.

Am·i·rante Islands \ˌam-ə-ˌrant-\ *or* **Am·i·rantes** \ˈam-ə-ˌran(t)s\. British island group in Indian Ocean E of Tanzania and SW of Seychelles Is., 6°00′S, 53°10′E; administratively a dependency of Seychelles Is.

Amisia. See EMS 1.

Amisus. See SAMSUN 2.

Amite \ā-ˈmēt\. County in Mississippi. See table at MISSISSIPPI.

Amite City. Town, ⊗ of Tangipahoa parish, SE Louisiana, in agricultural region 45 m. ENE of Baton Rouge; pop. (1970c) 3593; cotton, corn, lumber.

Am·i·ter·num \ˌam-ə-ˈtər-nəm\. Ancient town ab. 58 m. NE of Rome, Italy, 5 m. N of modern Aquila in valley of Aterno river; birthplace of Sallust; ruins of imperial Roman structures; Christian catacombs in vicinity.

Am·i·ty·ville \ˈam-ət-ē-ˌvil\. Village, Suffolk co., SE New York, on dividing line bet. Nassau and Suffolk cos., on Great South Bay on Long Island 32 m. E of New York;

pop. (1970c) 9857; residential suburb and seaside summer resort.

Am·lia \'am-lē-ə\. Island at E end of Andreanof Is., Aleutian Is., SW Alaska; 169 sq. m.

Am·man \a-'män, -'man\ *or Bib.* **Rab·bah Am·mon** *or* **Rab·bath Ammon** \ˌrab-ə-'(th)am-ən\ *anc.* **Phil·a·del·phia** \ˌfil-ə-'del-fyə, -fē-ə\. Town, ❋ of Jordan, 25 m. NE of the Dead Sea; pop. (1970e) 570,000; administrative and commercial center; exports building stone, phosphates, vegetables; univ. (1962).

History: Chief city of the Ammonites; besieged and captured by Joab and David (2 *Sam.* xi–xii); improved by Ptolemy II Philadelphus (285–246 B.C.) and named Philadelphia after him; was most southerly of ten cities of the Decapolis; attained greatest prosperity under Eastern Roman Empire; made ❋ 1921; parts of city damaged in Jordanian civil war 1970.

Am·man·ford \'am-ən-fərd\. Urban district, Carmarthenshire, S Wales, 17 m. ESE of Carmarthen; pop. (1971p) 5795; coal mining.

Am·mer \'äm-ər\ *or* **Am·per** \-pər\. River, Bavaria, West Germany; 104 m. long; rises in Tirol and flows through Ammer Lake into Isar river 2 m. N of Moosburg; Oberammergau is near its source.

Ammer Lake *or Ger.* **Am·mer·see** \'äm-ər-ˌzā\. Lake, Bavaria, West Germany, 21 m. WSW of Munich; 10 m. long; 18 sq. m.; in glacial region characterized by irregular moraine.

Ammin. See AMNYŎN.

Ammoedara. See HAÏDRA

Ammonium. See SIWA.

Am·mo·noo·suc \ˌam-ə-'nü-sik, -sək\. River, Coos and Grafton cos., New Hampshire; ab. 100 m. long; flows W and SW from White Mts. to Connecticut river.

Am·ne Ma·chin Shan \ˌam-nē-mə-ˌjin-'shän\. Range of the Kunlun Mts. in E cen. Tsinghai, W cen. China; highest peak, **Amne Machin** *also* **An·ye Machin** \ˌan-yē-mə-'jin\, 99°45′E, 34°25′N, 23,490 ft.

Amnok. See YALU.

Amo–chu \ˌäm-ō-'chü\. River, W Bhutan and NE India; flows through Ch'u-mu-pi valley in S Tibet, W China, then SE across SW corner of Bhutan to the Brahmaputra river.

Āmol \ä-'mōl, ȯ-\ *also* **Amul** \-'mül\. City, Māzanderān prov., N Iran, 23 m. W of Bābol; pop. (1966c) 40,076.

Amor·gos \ə-'mȯr-gəs\ *or Gk.* **Amor·gós** \ˌäm-(ˌ)ȯr-'gȯs\. Island of the Cyclades, S Aegean Sea, 18 m. SE of Naxos; 47 sq. m.; pop. (1961c) 2096; part of Cyclades dept., Greece. Birthplace of Simonides, Greek poet of 7th cent. B.C.

Amo·ry \'ām-(ə-)rē\. City, Monroe co., NE Mississippi, 22 m. SSE of Tupelo; pop. (1970c) 7236; shipping point for cotton, grain, dairy products, timber; gas wells.

Amos \'ā-məs\. Town, ⊗ of Abitibi co., SW Quebec, Canada, on Harricanaw river 50 m. NE of Rouyn; pop. (1971p) 6845; large sawmills.

Amour Mountains \ä-'mu̇(ə)r-\. Range of the Atlas Mts., N Algeria; highest point ab. 5800 ft.

Amoy \ä-'mȯi, a-, ə-\ *or* **Hsia–men** \'shä-'mən\. Seaport, Fukien prov., SE China, on Amoy I. and smaller Ku-lang island, 1/2 m. distant; 140 m. W of Taiwan; pop. (1970e) 400,000; trades in sugar, tobacco, and timber; univ. (1921); good natural harbor.

History: In 18th cent. monopolized Chinese junk trade to Java; first port through which English and Dutch traded with China (former in 1670); occupied by British 1841; opened as treaty port by Treaty of Nanking at close of first British war against China 1842; occupied by Taiping rebels 1853–55; gradually declined as center of tea export; captured by Japanese in 1938 campaign against China and held till end of World War II.

Am·pa·to \äm-'pät-(ˌ)ō\. Peak, Arequipa dept., S Peru; 20,702 ft.

Amper. See AMMER.

Am·phip·o·lis \am-'fip-ə-ləs\. Ancient city, E Macedonia, on Struma river ab. 3 m. above its mouth; colonized by Athens 437 B.C.; in 424 captured by Spartans during Peloponnesian War; became independent after Peace of Nicias 421; occupation by Philip of Macedon caused war with Athens 337 B.C.; headquarters of Roman governor of Macedonia.

Am·phis·sa \am-'fis-ə\ *or* **Sa·lo·na** \sə-'lō-nə\. Town, Phocis dept., Greece, at foot of W slope of Mt. Parnassus, 85 m. NNW of Athens; pop. (1961c) 6076; chief town of ancient Western Locris (see LOCRIS); its rebuilding of Crisa (*q.v.*) was cause of the Fourth Sacred War (339–338 B.C.).

Am·qui \äⁿ-'kē\. Town, ⊗ of Matapédia co., on Gaspé Penin., SE Quebec, Canada, on Matapédia river 25 m. S of Matane; pop. (1971p) 3777; an agricultural community.

Am·ran \am-'rän\. Town, N cen. Yemen (❋ San'a), SW Arabian Penin., 38 m. NW of San'a.

Am·ra·va·ti \ˌəm-'räv-ət-ē, äm-\ *or formerly* **Am·rao·ti** \-'rau̇t-\. 1 District, Maharashtra, cen. India; 4723 sq. m.; pop. (1961c) 1,232,780.

2 Town, NE Maharashtra state, cen. India, on branch of Purna river 85 m. WSW of Nagpur; pop. (1970e) 181,774; important cotton center. Has a fine stupa dating from 2d cent. A.D., whose rich relief decorations are preserved in British Museum (London) and in Madras.

Am·re·li \äm-'rā-lē\. 1 District, SW Gujarat, S Kathiawar penin., W India; 1545 sq. m.; pop. (1961c) 667,823; millet, peanuts.

2 Town, its ❋, 135 m. SW of Baroda; pop. (1961c) 34,699.

'Am·rit \am-'rēt\ *or anc.* **Mar·a·thus** \'mar-ə-thəs\. Town on coast, SW Latakia, Syria, 45 m. S of Latakia and opp. Arwad I.

Am·rit·sar \ˌəm-'rit-sər, äm-\. 1 District, Punjab, N India; 1978 sq. m.; pop. (1961c) 1,534,916; cotton, corn, wheat.

2 Manufacturing city, its ❋; pop. (1970e) 430,783; chemicals, electric fans, textiles.

History: Founded by Ram Das 1574 on site granted by Akbar; site of Golden Temple, center of worship of Sikhs; part of Sikh confederacy under Ranjit Singh (d. 1839); as part of Punjab (*q.v.*), annexed by British 1846; scene of incident known as Amritsar affair April 13, 1919 when British, under Gen. Reginald E. H. Dyer, fired on and killed about 400 and wounded many others in a riot caused by Rowlatt Acts (antisedition laws).

Am·ro·ha \äm-'rō-(ˌ)hä\. Town, Uttar Pradesh, India, 78 m. E of Delhi; pop. (1961c) 68,965; carpet weaving; site of tomb of Muslim saint, Sheikh Saddu, the object of pilgrimages.

Am·rum \'äm-ˌru̇m\. Island, North Frisian Is., SW of Föhr; 8 sq. m.; belongs to West Germany.

Am·stel·veen \'äm-stəl-ˌvān\. Commune, North Holland prov., Netherlands; pop. (1970e) 69,167; suburb of Amsterdam.

Am·ster·dam \'am-stər-ˌdam\. 1 Manufacturing city, Montgomery co., E New York, on New York State Barge Canal and Mohawk river 28 m. NW of Albany; pop. (1970c) 25,524; industrial and shipping center in agricultural district; carpets and rugs, brooms, sweaters, gloves, silk and rayon textiles. Settled 1783, named Veedersburg; renamed Amsterdam 1804; incorporated as city 1885.

2 City, ❋ of the Netherlands, North Holland prov., on S side of IJ (or Y) river, connected with North Sea by ship canal; pop. (1970e) 820,406, met. area 1,035,999; a major port; chemicals, foodstuffs, textiles; diamond cutting, metalworking; Univ. of Amsterdam (1632), Free Reformed Univ. (1880); Royal Palace (1648–55), Rembrandt House.

ə abut; ᵊ kitten, Fr. table; ər further; a back; ā bake; ä cot, cart, ȧ Fr. bac; au̇ out; ch chin; e less; ē easy; g gift; i trip; ī life; j joke; k̲ Ger. ich, Buch; ⁿ Fr. vin; ŋ sing; ō flow; ȯ flaw; œ Fr. bœuf; œ̄ Fr. feu; ȯi coin; th thin; th̲ this; ü loot; u̇ foot; ue Ger. füllen; ue̅ Fr. rue; y yet; ʸ Fr. digne \dēnʸ\, nuit \nwʸē\; yü few; yu̇ furious; zh vision

History: Originally a fishing hamlet, developed by Giesebrecht II and III of Amstel, who built a castle nearby and dammed up the sea (early 13th cent.); received charter as town 1300; joined Hanseatic League 1369; grew steadily in 14th and 15th cents. as evidenced by extent of its walls erected in 1482; received an influx of wealthy merchants from Brabant, and a stream of Portuguese Jews, esp. after decline of Antwerp 1585; with vastly increased population and wealth, became source of the growing Dutch commercial and naval power in 17th cent.; center of Dutch East India and West India Companies (founded in 1602 and 1621) and of Bank of Amsterdam (1609); became leading financial and trade metropolis of Europe, esp. after closure of the Schelde by Treaty of Westphalia (1648) had sealed the fate of its rival Antwerp; opened its dikes against Louis XIV 1672; attracted French Huguenots after revocation 1685 of the Edict of Nantes; after a partial commercial decline in 18th cent., increased its prosperity when connected with North Sea by a canal 1875; capital of the Batavian Republic erected by Napoleon, later of the kingdom of Holland; became part of French Empire 1810; as part of Holland, entered kingdom of the Netherlands 1815; under German occupation 1940–45; Amsterdam-Rhine Canal officially opened 1952.

3 *or* **New Amsterdam.** Volcanic island, S Indian Ocean, 37°52′S, 77°32′E, near St. Paul I.; 18 sq. m.; part of French Southern and Antarctic Territories.

Amsterdam Ship Canal. See NORTH SEA CANAL.

Amu Dar·ya \ˌäm-ü-ˈdär-yə\ *or anc.* **Ox·us** \ˈäk-səs\ *or Arab.* **Jay·hun** \jī-ˈhün\. River, cen. and W Asia, from Pamir plateau to the Aral Sea; ab. 1578 m. long; rises in lakes and mountains of high Pamirs in two headstreams: Vakhsh and Pandj; flows NW down Hindu Kush slope, forming boundary bet. Tadzhik S.S.R. and NE Afghanistan, then generally W and NW through E Turkmen S.S.R. and W of Uzbek S.S.R. into marshes on S shore of Aral Sea in Kara-Kalpak A.S.S.R., where it forms delta 100 m. long; area of basin ab. 180,000 sq. m.; chief tributaries on N are Vakhsh, Kafirnigan, and Surkhab, on S Kundūz; in middle course a source of wide irrigation systems (Kara-Kum Canal system completed 1962); navigable for ab. 900 m.; in lower course flows through great expanse of sandy desert. In mid-19th cent., part of course came to be recognized as boundary bet. Afghanistan and Russia. For its history as site of campaigns by Alexander the Great, see SOGDIANA and BACTRIA.

Amuk·ta \ä-ˈmük-tə\. Volcanic island in Aleutian Is., W of the Islands of the Four Mountains; separated by **Amukta Pass** from Seguam I. on W; 36 sq. m.

Amul. See ĀMOL.

Amund Ring·nes Island \ˌäm-ən-ˈriŋ-ˌnās-\. One of the Sverdrup Is. (*q.v.*), SW of Axel Heiberg I.; 2515 sq. m.

Amund·sen Bay \ˌäm-ən-sən-, ˌam-\ *or formerly* **Ice Bay** \ˈīs-\. Inlet of Indian Ocean, Antarctica, bet. Enderby Land on E and Queen Maud Land on W, ab. 66°55′S and 50°E; ab. 30 m. wide.

Amundsen Gulf. Body of water bet. the NW coast of Mackenzie dist., Northwest Territories, Canada, the S coast of Banks I., and the W coast of Victoria I.; ab. 250 m. long.

Amundsen Sea. Arm of South Pacific Ocean off Marie Byrd Land, Antarctica, bet. Thurston I. on E and Cape Dart on W; 72°S and bet. 123°W and 98°W; explored 1928–29.

Amur \ä-ˈmü(ə)r\ *or Chin.* **Hei–lung chiang** \ˈhā-ˈlüŋ-jē-ˈäŋ\. River, NE Asia; length with Argun and Kerulen ab. 2705 m., from junction ab. 1786 m.; formed by junction of Shilka and Argun rivers (*qq.v.*) at ab. 53°20′N, 121°28′E; forms boundary bet. N Manchuria and two subdivisions of Russian S.F.S.R. (Chita Oblast and Khabarovsk Krai), U.S.S.R.; flows E, SE, and NE to N end of Tatar Strait bet. mainland and Sakhalin I.; below Khabarovsk wholly in Russian territory; est. area of basin 770,000 sq. m.; below junction receives N tributaries Zeya and Bureya, and on S Kumara, Sungari, and Ussuri; chief cities on it: Blagoveshchensk, Khabarovsk, Komsomolsk-na-Amure and Nikolayevsk-na-Amure (near mouth); navigable for ab. 2000 m. up to Sretensk on the Shilka.

History: Region of Amur valley in contact with Russia from 17th cent.; Russia compelled by China to withdraw from valley in Treaty of Nerchinsk (*q.v.*) 1689; settled by Russians from 1847; by Treaty of Ai-hun (*q.v.*) 1858, left bank of Amur yielded by China to Russia, and Ussuri region by Treaty of Peking 1860; occupied by Russians and developed economically, esp. after building of Trans-Siberian R.R.; Blagoveshchensk (*q.v.*) became chief cultural and commercial center; after Japanese occupation of Manchuria, scene of Soviet-Japanese clashes 1937; also scene of Sino-Soviet border clashes during the late 1960s. See also JEWISH AUTONOMOUS OBLAST.

Amur Bay *or Russ.* **Amur·ski Za·liv** \ə-ˌmůr-skē-zəl-ˈ(y)ēf\. Northwest arm of Peter the Great Bay, U.S.S.R.; ab. 42 m. long; Vladivostok is on inlet of its E shore.

Amur Oblast \-ˈō-bləst, -ˌblast\. Subdivision of the Russian S.F.S.R., U.S.S.R.; 140,425 sq. m.; pop. (1970p) 793,000; ✱ Blagoveshchensk; grain, timber; formed 1932 from Khabarovsk Krai; region incorporated into Russia 1858.

Amurski Zaliv. See AMUR BAY.

Amy·clae \ə-ˈmī-(ˌ)klē\. Ancient town, Laconia, SE Peloponnesus, S Greece, ab. 3 m. S of Sparta; chief city of Laconia under the Achaeans and before rise of Dorian Sparta; ultimately conquered by Sparta.

An. See AN PASS.

ʻAna \ˈan-ə\. Town, W bank of Euphrates, W Iraq, ab. 75 m. NW of Hit; pop. (1957c) 11,070. An old town, dating from before 1000 B.C.; in medieval period controlled transport on the river and was starting point for caravan routes across the desert to Syrian cities.

Anaa Island \ä-ˈnä(-ˌä)-\ *or* **Chain Island** \ˈchān-\. Atoll in the Tuamotu Archipelago, French Polynesia, S Pacific Ocean; 17°25′S, 145°30′W; 10 sq. m.; has 11 islets around a lagoon; called Chain I. by Captain Cook, who visited it 1769.

An·a·capa Islands \ˌan-ə-ˌkap-ə-\. Small group of islands in cen. Santa Barbara group, Pacific Ocean; part of Ventura co., SW California; part of group included in Channel Islands National Monument (see UNITED STATES, *National Monuments*).

Anacapa Pass. Strait off NW Los Angeles co., SW California; bet. Anacapa Is. and Santa Cruz I.

Ana·co \ə-ˈnäk-(ˌ)ō\. Town, Anzoátegui state, N Venezuela, ab. 50 m. SSE of Puerto La Cruz; pop. (1970e) 35,432.

An·a·con·da \ˌan-ə-ˈkän-də\. City, ⊗ of Deer Lodge co., SW Montana, 23 m. WNW of Butte; pop. (1970c) 9771. City started with erection 1884, by Anaconda Copper Mining Company of Butte, of a copper-smelting plant, later expanded to contain largest nonferrous production plant in world.

Anaconda Mountain. Peak in Glacier National Park, NW Montana; 8300 ft.

An·a·cor·tes \ˌan-ə-ˈkȯrt-əs\. City, Skagit co., NW Washington, on island in Puget Sound 19 m. S of Bellingham; pop. (1970c) 7701; port of call for several steamship companies; commercial fisheries, oil refineries; incorp. 1889.

An·a·cos·tia \ˌan-ə-ˈkäs-tē-ə, -ˈkȯs-\. 1 River in the District of Columbia; 12 m. long; flows into Potomac river immediately S of the city of Washington.

2 Southeastern suburb of Washington, D.C., on left bank of Anacostia river; site of U.S. Naval Air Station.

An·a·dar·ko \ˌan-ə-ˈdär-(ˌ)kō\. City, ⊗ of Caddo co., W cen. Oklahoma, on Washita river 18 m. W of Chickasha; pop. (1970c) 6682; trading center for agricultural region (alfalfa, cotton, corn); stock raising, cotton ginning, dairying, meat packing; founded 1901.

Anadir Range. See CHUKOT RANGE.

Anadolu. See ANATOLIA.

Ana·dyr *or* **Ana·dir** \ən-ə-ˈdi(ə)r, ˌän-\. River, Chukot National Okrug, U.S.S.R.; rises in mountains S of Chukot Range and flows S and E to Gulf of Anadyr; 694 m. long; area of drainage basin 57,915 sq. m.

Anadyr, Gulf of *or* **Gulf of Anadir.** Inlet of N Bering Sea, S of Chukotski Penin., Chukot National Okrug, U.S.S.R.

Anadyr Range. See CHUKOT RANGE.

Ana·far·ta Bay \ä-ˌnä-fär-ˌtä-\ *also* **Su·vla Bay** \ˌsü-vlä-\. Small bay, W coast of Gallipoli Penin., Turkey, Europe; landing of Anzacs and battle Aug. 6, 1915.

Anafarta Heights. Group of hills, W Gallipoli Penin., Turkey in Europe, ab. 4 m. E of Anafarta Bay; highest 882 ft.; scene of British attacks 1915 during battle of Suvla Bay, a part of operations in Gallipoli campaign.

Anáfi. See ANAPHE.

Ana·gni \ä-ˈnän-yē\ *or anc.* **Anag·nia** \ə-ˈnag-nē-ə\. Commune, Frosinone prov., Latium, cen. Italy, on 1500-ft. hill 12 m. NW of Frosinone; pop. (1968e) 16,487; episcopal see since 487; sulfur mines and springs; 11th cent. cathedral. Principal town of the Hernici; conquered by Rome 306 B.C.; besieged by Saracens 877 A.D.; scene of the imprisonment and humiliation of Pope Boniface VIII by the emissaries of Philip IV of France.

An·a·heim \ˈan-ə-ˌhīm\. City, Orange co., SW California, 16 m. E of Long Beach; pop. (1970c) 166,408; aircraft parts, electronic equipment, farm machinery; fruit canning; site of Disneyland amusement park. Founded 1857 on communal basis by 50 German families; incorporated 1878.

Ana·ho Bay \ä-ˌnä-(ˌ)hō-\. Bay, N coast of Nuku Hiva I., Marquesas Is., S Pacific Ocean.

An·a·huac \ˈan-ə-ˌwak\. City, ⊗ of Chambers co., Texas, 35 m. NE of Galveston on NE shore of Galveston Bay; pop. (1970c) 1881; formerly a Mexican military post, attacked 1832 by American settlers in Texas in effort to release William B. Travis and others, thus furnishing issue preliminary to Texan War of Independence.

Aná·huac \ə-ˈnä-ˌwäk\. Great central plateau in Mexico bet. the Sierra Madre Occidental and the Sierra Madre Oriental; includes valley in which Mexico City is located; elevation 5000 to 9000 ft. in states of Puebla and México, sloping to 3700 ft. at El Paso on U.S. border; center of pre-Columbian Aztec civilization.

Anai·za *also* **Anei·za** *or* **Unay·zah** \ə-ˈnī-zə, -ˈnā-\. Town, N cen. Nejd, cen. Saudi Arabia; pop. (1959e) 25,000.

Analostan Island. See THEODORE ROOSEVELT ISLAND.

Anam. See ANNAM.

Ana Ma·ría, Gulf of \-ˌan-ə-mə-ˈrē-ə, -ˌän-\. Gulf in SW coast of Camagüey prov., E cen. Cuba.

Anam·bas Islands \ə-ˌnäm-bəs-\. Group of islands of Indonesia, 200 m. NE of Singapore in the South China Sea, bet. SE Malay Penin. and W Borneo; 260 sq. m.; administratively a part of Riau province, Sumatra; chief islands Djemadja and Siantan.

An·a·mo·sa \ˌan-ə-ˈmō-sə\. City, ⊗ of Jones co., E Iowa, 23 m. ENE of Cedar Rapids; pop. (1970c) 4389.

Ana·mur, Cape \-ˌän-ə-ˈmu̇(ə)r\ *or Turk.* **Anamur Bur·nu** \-bər-ˈnü\. Cape on S coast of Turkey in Asia, projecting into Mediterranean Sea opp. Cape Kormakítis on N coast of island of Cyprus.

An·an \ˈän-ˌän\. City, Tokushima prefecture, Shikoku, Japan, 14 m. SE of Tokushima; pop. (1970c) 58,467.

Anan·ta·pur \ə-ˈnənt-ə-ˌpu̇(ə)r\. 1 District, Andhra Pradesh, India; 7385 sq. m.; pop. (1961c) 1,767,464; in 18th cent. a stronghold of Marathas.

2 Town, its ✱, ab. 117 m. N of Bangalore; pop. (1961c) 52,280; peanut milling.

Ana·pa \ə-ˈnäp-ə\. Seaport town, W Krasnodar Krai, U.S.S.R., 20 m. NW of Novorossisk; pop. (1967e) 23,000. Turkish fortress founded to maintain Turkish relations with Caucasus region 1781; twice captured and restored by Russia, finally remained Russian by terms of Treaty of Adrianople 1829.

An·a·phe \ˈan-ə-ˌfē\ *or Gk.* **Aná·fi** \ə-ˈnäf-ē\. Island, SE Cyclades, S Aegean Sea, 85 m. N of Crete; 7 m. long by 2 m. wide; has no harbor.

An·á·po·lis \ə-ˈnap-ə-ləs, -ˈnäp-\. City, Goiás state, cen. Brazil, at end of railroad N from São Paulo; munic. pop. (1968e) 83,848; coffee, meat products.

Anapurna. See ANNAPURNA.

Anas. See GUADIANA.

Añas·co \än-ˈyäs-(ˌ)kō\. Town and municipality, W Puerto Rico, 6 m. N of Mayagüez; munic pop. (1970p) 19,296.

Anasquam. See ANNISQUAM.

An·as·ta·sia Island \ˌan-ə-ˌstā-zh(ē-)ə-\. Island off coast of St. Johns co., NE Florida, S of St. Augustine, bet. Matanzas river (*q.v.*) and the Atlantic; ab. 14 m. long and 3 m. wide; 13 sq. m.

Ana·ta·han \ˌän-ə-tə-ˈhän\. Small island, cen. Mariana Is., 80 m. N of Saipan, 16°22′N, 145°40′E; highest point 2585 ft.; taken by U.S. Army 1945.

An·a·to·lia \ˌan-ə-ˈtō-lē-ə, -ˈtōl-yə\ *or Turk.* **Ana·do·lu** \ˌän-ə-dō-ˈlü\. The part of Turkey in Asia equivalent to the Peninsula of Asia Minor (*q.v.*) up to indefinite line on E from Gulf of İskenderun to Black Sea, comprising ab. three fifths of Turkey's provinces.

Ana·yac·si \ˌän-ə-ˈyäk-sē\. Peak, Oruro dept., W Bolivia; 18,380 ft.

An·cash *or formerly* **An·cachs** \ˈäŋ-ˌkäsh\. Department of W Peru. See table at PERU.

An–ch'ing *or* **An·king** \ˈän-ˈkiŋ\; *formerly* **Hwai·ning** \ˈhwī-ˈniŋ\ *or* **Ngan·king** \ˈgän-ˈkiŋ\. City, Anhwei prov., E China, on N bank of Yangtze; pop. (1970e) 160,000; iron and steel; wool, rice; ravaged by Taipings 1852; occupied by Japanese 1938.

An·chor·age \ˈaŋ-k(ə-)rij\. Seaport city, ⊗ of Greater Anchorage Area borough, S Alaska, at head of Cook Inlet near base of Kenai Penin.; pop. (1970c) 48,081; connected by railroad with Fairbanks 470 m. to N and with Seward 114 m. to S; salmon canneries; supply center for the state's oil industry; Alaska Methodist Univ. (1957); founded 1914 as construction camp for railroad; now important army post and airport; headquarters of Alaska Defense Command during World War II; severely damaged in 1964 earthquake.

An·co·hu·ma \ˌaŋ-kə-ˈh(y)ü-mə\. The higher peak of Mt. Sorata, Bolivia; 20,958 ft. See ILLAMPU.

An·con \ˈaŋ-kən\ *or Span.* **An·cón** \äŋ-ˈkōn\. Town, Balboa dist., Canal Zone, NW suburb of Panama; pop. (1970p) 1148; site of American Gorgas Hospital.

An·cón \äŋ-ˈkōn\. 1 Town, S coast of Santa Elena Penin., Ecuador; ab. 60 m. SSW of Guayaquil; oil fields.

2 Town and bathing resort, 22 m. N of Lima, Lima dept., cen. Peru; as a port, superseded by Callao; has Inca remains.

History: Scene of treaty which terminated War of Pacific (1879–83) bet. Chile and Peru Oct. 1883 (for treaty bet. Bolivia and Chile see VALPARAÍSO 2) and by which Peru ceded Tarapacá and Chile was to remain in occupation of Tacna and Arica (*qq.v.*) for 10 years until plebiscite should determine final ownership. Failure to carry out plebiscite provision caused Tacna-Arica dispute.

An·co·na \aŋ-ˈkō-nə, äŋ-\. 1 Province of Marches, Italy. See table at ITALY.

2 Seaport, its ✱ and ✱ of Marches, cen. Italy, on Adriatic coast ab. 125 m. ESE of Florence; pop. (1968e) 108,326; bricks, chemicals, foodstuffs, furniture; metalworking, shipbuilding; transportation center. Ancient mole designed by Trajan topped by triumphal arch by Apollodorus (erected 115 A.D.); modern mole by Pope Clement II has lighthouse and triumphal arch by Vanvitelli.

History: Founded by Greek refugees from Syracuse c. 390 B.C.; purple factory founded by Greek merchants; occupied as naval station by Romans during Illyrian war 178 B.C.; taken by Caesar after his crossing Rubicon 49 B.C.; after improvement of harbor by Emperor Trajan who departed from it on second expedition to Moesia and Dacia

105 A.D., became important seaport and naval station; attacked by Goths, Lombards, Saracens; one of the Pentapolis (*q.v.*) under exarchate of Ravenna; chief town of **Mark of Ancona** (in extent about equivalent to modern Marches region), attached to Holy Roman Empire 1138–1254; later a municipal republic under papal protection until taken by Federigo Gonzaga for Clement VII 1532; scene of death of Pope Pius II on eve of a crusade against Turks 1464; taken by French 1797, by Russians 1799; restored to Pope 1816; occupied by French 1832–39, by Austrians 1849–59; captured by Italian troops soon after Castelfidardo (*q.v.*) victory over papal forces 1860; scene of riots leading to strike 1914; bombed by Austrian fleet 1915. In World War II captured by Polish forces July 19, 1944.

An·cre \ä^{n}kr^{ə}\. 1 River, Somme dept., France; 25 m. long; from NE flows into Somme river near Corbie ab. 9 m. E of Amiens; scene of several battles 1916–18, esp. of successful Allied advance against Germans Nov. 1916, in which tanks were first used.

2 Commune, France. See ALBERT.

An·cud \äŋ-ˈküd, -ˈküth\ *or in full* **San Car·los de Ancud** \sän-ˌkär-lōs-ˌdā-, -ˌthā-\. Seaport, ❋ of Chiloé prov., S cen. Chile, on N Chiloé I. 60 m. SW of Puerto Montt; pop. (1960c) 7390; settled 1768; surrendered to Chile by Spaniards 1826; trading center.

Ancud, Gulf of. Inlet of Pacific Ocean on S cen. coast of Chile, E of N Chiloé I.

Ancyra. See ANKARA.

An·da·col·lo \ˌän-də-ˈkō-(ˌ)yō\. Town, Coquimbo prov., cen. Chile, 10 m. S of Coquimbo; pop. (1960c) 5381.

Ån·dals·nes \ˈȯn-dəls-ˌnās\. Village and railhead port, Møre og Romsdal co., W Norway, at head of Romsdalsfjord, in mountain resort region ab. 55 m. E of Ålesund; pop. (1960c) 2202; occupied by Allied forces Apr. 14–20, 1940; evacuated in May.

An·da·lu·sia \ˌan-də-ˈlü-zh(ē-)ə\. 1 City, ⊗ of Covington co., S Alabama, 65 m. W of Dothan; pop. (1970c) 10,092.

2 *or Span.* **An·da·lu·cía** \ˌän-də-lü-ˈsē-ə, -ˈthē-\. Region, S Spain; 33,695 sq. m.; comprises the modern provinces of Almería, Granada, Jaén, Málaga, Cádiz, Córdoba, Huelva, and Sevilla; traversed by mountain ranges, among them the Sierra Morena (forming the N boundary) and the Sierra Nevada, and including the Mulhacén (11,407 ft.) and Picacho de Veleta (11,125 ft.) peaks; watered by the Guadalquivir and its principal affluents, the Guadalimar, Guadiato, and Genil rivers; wide range of difference in climate, vegetation, and people; divided into **Upper Andalusia,** valley of upper Guadalquivir, and **Lower Andalusia,** valley of lower Guadalquivir; celebrated for its fertility (often called the "granary" of Spain) and for its picturesque beauty; mountainous regions abound in mineral wealth, esp. copper, lead, mercuric sulfide (cinnabar), coal, silver; agricultural products include wheat, corn, barley, grapes, olives, oranges, lemons, sugar.

History: As kingdom of Tartessus (the Biblical Tarshish, *q.v.*), served as outlet for Spanish minerals and tin from the north in latter half of 2d millennium B.C.; colony of Gadir (see CÁDIZ 2) established by Phoenicians c. 1100 B.C.; settled by Carthaginians who destroyed the Tartessian kingdom 480 B.C.; under Romans its W part comprised most of province of Baetica; invaded by Vandals and Visigoths 5th cent. A.D.; subjugated by Moors 711–1492; under Muslim Ommiad dynasty of Spain (756–1031), resident at Córdoba (*q.v.*), became intellectual and political center of the peninsula; Lower Andalusia reconquered by Christians 1212; Upper Andalusia, the ancient Moorish kingdom of Granada, reconquered by Ferdinand and Isabella 1492; declined with subjugation of Moors; restored to some importance through discovery of New World and consequent commercial rise of Seville and Cádiz; remained a Spanish province until divided 1833 into eight modern provinces.

An·da·man and Nic·o·bar Islands \ˌan-də-mən . . . ˌnik-ə-ˌbär-, -ˌman-\ *also* **An·da·mans and Nic·o·bars** \ˈan-də-mənz . . . ˈnik-ə-ˌbärz, -ˌmanz-\. Centrally administered territory of India, comprising two groups of islands in the Bay of Bengal, ab. 400 m. directly W of Coast of Lower Burma; 3202 sq. m.; pop. (1971p) 115,090; ❋ Port Blair; copra, timber. United for administrative purposes 1872. See ANDAMAN ISLANDS and NICOBAR ISLANDS.

Andaman Islands *also* **Andamans** \ˈan-də-mənz\. North group of islands in E part of Bay of Bengal; 2461 sq. m.; pop. (1961c) 48,985; part of territory of Andaman and Nicobar Islands, India. Chief islands North Andaman, Middle Andaman, and South Andaman, close together in a group (known as Great Andaman) and separated from Little Andaman on the S by Duncan Passage; separated from SW Burma by Preparis Channels and from the Nicobars by Ten Degree Channel.

History: First settled by British 1789; settlement transferred to Port Cornwallis 1792 but abandoned 1796; Port Blair established as Indian penal settlement by Government of India 1858; scene of murder of Viceroy Mayo 1872; joined to Nicobar group to form administrative division of Andaman and Nicobar Islands (*q.v.*); under Japanese control 1942–45.

Andaman Sea. That part of the Bay of Bengal E of the Andaman and Nicobar Is.; bounded on N and E by coast of Burma, on E and SE by Malay Penin., and on S by Strait of Malacca and Sumatra; 218,000 sq. m.

An·da·va·ka, Cape \-ˌan-də-ˈväk-ə\. Cape extending into Indian Ocean on SE coast of Malagasy Republic, S of Fort-Dauphin.

An·de·an Group \ˌan-dē-ən-, an-ˌdē-\. Economic organization, consisting of Bolivia, Chile, Colombia, Ecuador, and Peru; has proposed adoption of a common external tariff and establishment of other common market institutions; formed 1969.

Andelys, Les. See LES ANDELYS.

Andematunnum. See LANGRES.

An·denne \ä^{n}-ˈden\. Industrial commune, Namur prov., Belgium, on right bank of Meuse river, ab. 22 m. SW of Liége; pop. (1969e) 8234; in region abounding in lead, iron, zinc, and coal mines, marble quarries, and, esp., clay pits; refractory earthenware, brick, porcelain, paper. Grew up around abbey founded by Saint Bregga; taken and burned by inhabitants of Liége ab. 1159; partially burned by Germans Aug. 1914.

An·der·lecht \ˈän-dər-ˌlekt\. Industrial commune, WSW suburb of Brussels, Brabant prov., Belgium, on Senne river; pop. (1969e) 104,157; spinning, weaving, esp. of calicoes and prints; dyeing works; 15th cent. Gothic church.

An·der·lues \än-dər-ˈlü, ˌä^{n}-der-ˈlue\. Commune, Hainaut prov., Belgium, ab. 30 m. S of Brussels; pop. (1969e) 12,217; coal mines, metallurgical works, breweries.

An·der·matt \ˈän-dər-ˌmät\ *also* **Ur·se·ren** \ˈu̇r-zə-rən\ *or Ital.* **Or·se·ra** \ȯr-ˈser-ə\. Commune, Uri canton, cen. Switzerland, 17 m. S of Altdorf; on route over St. Gotthard Pass; pop. (1970c) 1589; tourist resort, particularly for winter sports; church (1695).

An·der·nach \ˈän-dər-ˌnäk\ *or anc.* **An·tun·na·cum** \ˌan-tə-ˈnā-kəm\. City, Rhineland-Palatinate, West Germany, on the left bank of the Rhine 10 m. NW of Koblenz; pop. (1969e) 22,319; lumber, textiles; has 12th cent. watchtower, 13th cent. late-Romanesque parish church.

History: Founded as a castle by Drusus Senior 12 B.C.; scene of defeat 876 of Charles the Bald by Louis III, son of Louis the German; member of Hanseatic League 1253; burned by the French 1689; to France 1795; ceded to Prussia 1815. In World War II taken by Allies March 1945.

An·der·son \ˈan-dər-sən\. 1 Name of counties in five states of the U.S. See tables at KANSAS, KENTUCKY, SOUTH CAROLINA, TENNESSEE, TEXAS.

2 City, Shasta co., N California, 10 m. S of Redding; pop. (1970e) 5492.

3 City, ⊗ of Madison co., cen. Indiana, 17 m. WSW of Muncie; pop. (1970c) 70,787; automobile accessories, castings, paper board products; prehistoric Indian mounds. Anderson Coll. (1917); founded 1823, incorp. as town 1838, as city 1865.

4 Industrial city, ⊗ of Anderson co., NW South Carolina, 28 m. SSW of Greenville; pop. (1970c) 27,556; commercial and shipping center for agricultural region (cotton, corn, wheat); fertilizers, glass, lumber, textiles; Anderson Junior Coll. (1911); site of branch of Confederate treasury 1864–65.

5 Town, ⊗ of Grimes co., E cen. Texas.

6 River, NW Mackenzie dist., Northwest Territories, Canada; 430 m. long; rises in lakes N of Great Bear Lake and flows W and N into Beaufort Sea.

Anderson, Mount. Mountain, Antarctica, 78°09′S, 86°13′W; 13,957 ft.

Anderson Ranch Dam. See UNITED STATES, *Dams and Reservoirs.*

An·der·son·ville \ˈan-dər-sən-ˌvil\. Village, Sumter co., Georgia, ab. 55 m. SW of Macon; pop. (1970c) 274; large national cemetery; site of large Confederate military prison 1864–65, where conditions were so bad that many Union soldiers died.

Andes. See VIRGILIO.

An·des \ˈan-(ˌ)dēz\; *Span.* **Los Andes** \lō-ˈsän-(ˌ)dās\ *or less correctly* **Cor·dil·le·ra de los Andes** \ˌkȯrd-ᵊl-ˈ(y)er-ə-ˌdā-, ˌkȯrd-ē-ˈer-\. Great mountain system of South America; extends entire length along W coast from Tierra del Fuego to Panama, 4500 m.; has many volcanoes; source of Cauca, Magdalena, Orinoco Amazon (Marañón and Ucayali), Pilcomayo, and all large rivers of Argentina except Paraná; in places, esp. N Argentina, Bolivia, Peru, and Colombia, spreads out over high plateaus in several parallel ranges (cordilleras); highest summit Aconcagua, 22,834 ft.

Divisions: (1) Range in Tierra del Fuego runs E and W along S shore (highest ab. 7600 ft.). (2) Range from S point of Chile runs due N bet. Chile and Patagonia, Argentina, (**Cordillera de Agos·ti·ni** \-dā-ˌäg-ə-ˈstē-nē\) with many lakes and peaks bet. 6000 and 12,000 ft. (3) Range from ab. 42°S lat. N to Bolivia, bet. Chile and Argentina, contains highest peaks of system (many bet. 17,000 and 23,000 ft.); entirely in Chile: Pular 20,423 ft. and Pili 19,849 ft.; entirely in Argentina: Aconcagua, Mercedario 22,211 ft., Bonete 22,546 ft., Nevada 20,023 ft.; on boundary line bet. Chile and Argentina: Ojos del Salado 22,539 ft., Tupungato 22,310 ft., Incahuasi 21,720 ft., Tres Cruces 20,853 ft.; many beautiful lakes (resorts) at S end on both sides bet. 39° and 42°S (Nahuel Huapí, Llanquihue, Ranco, Todos los Santos, etc.); passes (*pasos*) at intervals, esp. Uspallata or La Cumbre bet. Mendoza, Argentina, and Santiago, Chile (with the scenic Puente del Inca and the Transandine R.R., tunnel nearly 2 m. long at highest point 10,469 ft.); in N (ab. 23° to 28°S) is Puna de Atacama, desolate plateau region with average height of 11,000 to 13,000 ft., flanked on W in Chile by **Cordillera Do·mey·ko** \-də-ˈmā-(ˌ)kō\. (4) Central part in Bolivia covers nearly 2/5 of country in elevated plateau (*altiplano*) 10,000 to 12,000 ft. and encloses Lakes Poopó and Titicaca (part in Peru); main range is **Cordillera Re·al** \-rā-ˈäl\ with highest peaks Ancohuma 20,958 ft., Illimani 21,201 ft., Illampu 20,867 ft. (5) From Bolivian Andes direction turns NW extending full length of Peru in many ranges covering territory from 200 to 300 m. wide; includes **Cordillera Orien·tal** \-ˌōr-ē-ˌen-ˈtäl, -ˌȯr-\ (in SE Peru), **Cordillera Oc·ci·den·tal** \-ˌäk-sə-ˌden-ˈtäl\ (along the coast), **Cordillera de Ca·ra·ba·ya** \-dā-ˌkär-ə-ˈbī-ə\ (extension of Cordillera Real in SE Peru), **Cordillera Huay·huash** \-ˈwī-ˌwäsh\ (cen. Peru, N of Lima, watershed bet. Marañón and Pacific streams); highest peaks: Coropuna 21,079 ft., Huascarán 22,205 ft., Solimana 20,068 ft., Salcantay 20,574 ft. (6) In Ecuador, system (**Cordillera Real**) narrows and runs nearly due N; highest peaks: Chimborazo 20,561 ft., Cotopaxi 19,347 ft., Cayambe 18,996 ft., Antisana 18,228 ft. (7) In Colombia, system spreads out into 3 great ranges: **Cordillera Occidental** near coast; **Cordillera Cen·tral** \-sen-ˈträl\ bet. valleys of Cauca and Magdalena rivers; **Cordillera Oriental** in interior (extending as **Cordillera Mé·ri·da** \-ˈmer-əd-ə\ into W Venezuela); highest peaks: Tolima 18,425 ft., Huila 18,865 ft., Puracé 15,604 ft.; connecting range in E Panama and NW Colombia, Serranía del Darién.

Andes \ˈän-ˌdas\. Town, Antioquia dept., NW Colombia; munic. pop. (1968e) 35,759.

Andes, Lake \-ˈan-(ˌ)dēz\. Lake, Charles Mix co., S South Dakota.

Andes, Los. See LOS ANDES.

An·de·vo·ran·to \ˌän-di-və-ˈrän-(ˌ)tō\. Coastal town, E cen. Malagasy Republic; ab. 100 m. E of Tananarive.

An·dhra Pra·desh \ˌän-drə-prə-ˈdāsh, -ˈdesh\. State, SE India, bordering on Bay of Bengal; 106,272 sq. m.; pop. (1971p) 43,394,951; ✱ Hyderabad; rice, wheat, cotton; largest cities: Hyderabad, Vijawada, Secunderabad. Formed 1953 from part of Madras state; enlarged 1956 by addition of part of abolished Hyderabad state.

Andíkaros. See ANTIPAROS.

Andípaxoi. See ANTIPAXOS.

An·di·zhan \ˌan-di-ˈzhan, ˌän-di-ˈzhän\ *or* **An·di·jan** \ˌan-di-ˈjan, ˌän-di-ˈjän\. City, ✱ of Andizhan Oblast, E Uzbek S.S.R., U.S.S.R., 155 m. ESE of Tashkent on upper Syr Darya; pop. (1970p) 188,000; cotton; railroad center.

Andizhan Oblast \-ˈō-bləst, -ˌblast\. Subdivision of the Uzbek S.S.R., U.S.S.R.; 1660 sq. m.; pop. (1970p) 1,060,000; ✱ Andizhan; oil and natural gas.

And·khūi \änd-ˈkü-ē\. Town, N Afghanistan, ab. 100 m. W of Balkh near Turkmen S.S.R. border; chief town of former khanate.

An·dong \ˈän-ˌdȯŋ\. Town, South Korea, 115 m. SE of Seoul; pop. (1970e) 76,434.

An·dor·ra \an-ˈdȯr-ə, -ˈdär-ə\ *or in full* **the Valleys of Andorra** *or Fr.* **An·dorre** \äⁿ-dȯr\. **1** Principality on S slope of E Pyrenees, bet. Ariège dept., France, and Lérida prov., Spain; 180 sq. m.; pop. (1971c) 20,550; ✱ Andorra; consists of gorges, narrow valleys, and many high peaks, highest point Pic d'Etats, 10,295 ft.; contains six parishes and has good highway connections with both France and Spain; has excellent pasture land (cattle and sheep raising); produces some tobacco and fruits; tourism. Language spoken is Catalan. Of Carolingian origin; placed under joint suzerainty of French counts of Foix and Spanish bishops of Urgel 1278; French rights passed to ruler, Henry IV, 1589, and ultimately to president of France.

2 Town, its ✱; pop. (1963e) 4038.

An·do·ver \ˈan-ˌdō-vər, -də-\. **1** Town, Essex co., NE Massachusetts, 9 m. E of Lowell; pop. (1970c) 23,695; site of Phillips Academy (preparatory school for boys, estab. 1778, oldest incorporated school in U.S.; see EXETER 2, N.H.), Abbot Academy (preparatory school for girls, founded 1829, oldest incorporated school for girls in New England). Andover Theological Seminary (1808; affiliated with Harvard University since 1908).

2 Town, ⊗ of Victoria co., New Brunswick, Canada; pop. (1966c) 755.

3 Municipal borough, Hampshire, S England, on the Anton 22 m. N of Southampton; pop. (1971p) 20,688.

And·ø·ya \ˈän-ˌ(d)ə(r)-yə\. Northernmost island of the Vesterålen in the Norwegian Sea off NW coast of Norway; 188 sq. m.; pop. (1969e) 7907; hilly and marshy; has coal beds; fishing.

An·dre·a·nof Islands \ˌan-drē-ˌan-əf-, -ˌȯf-\. One of main groups of Aleutian Is., Alaska, extending from 172°W (Se-

ə abut; ᵊ kitten, Fr. table; ər further; a back; ā bake; ä cot, cart; à Fr. bac; au̇ out; ch chin; e less; ē easy; g gift; i trip; ī life; j joke; k̲ Ger. ich, Buch; ⁿ Fr. vin; ŋ sing; ō flow; ȯ flaw; œ Fr. bœuf; œ̄ Fr. feu; ȯi coin; th thin; t͟h this; ü loot; u̇ foot; ue Ger. füllen; ue̅ Fr. rue; y yet; ʸ Fr. digne \dēnʸ\, nuit \nwʸē\; yü few; yu̇ furious; zh vision

guam I.) to 179°E (Amchitka I. in Rat Is.); chief islands Atka, Tanaga, Adak, Kanaga. In World War II occupied by American army forces and several military bases developed, esp. on Adak I.

An·dre·as, Cape \-an-'drā-əs, -än-\. Cape at end of long narrow peninsula of NE Cyprus, 35°40′N, 34°35′E.

An·dré Fé·lix National Park \ˌäⁿ-ˌdrā-fā-'lēks-\. National park, Central African Republic; 656 sq. m.; grassland; varied wildlife; established 1959.

An·drew \'an-(ˌ)drü\. County in Missouri. See table at MISSOURI.

Andrew Jackson, Mount. See JACKSON, MOUNT 4.

An·drews \'an-(ˌ)drüz\. 1 County in Texas. See table at TEXAS.
2 Town, Cherokee co., W tip of North Carolina, 78 m. WSW of Asheville; pop. (1970c) 1384; lumber.
3 Town, Georgetown and Williamsburg cos., E South Carolina, 17 m. W of Georgetown; pop. (1970c) 2839.
4 City, ⊗ of Andrews co., NW Texas; pop. (1970c) 8625.

An·dria \'än-drē-ə\. Commune, Bari prov., Apulia, SE Italy, 31 m. WNW of Bari; pop. (1968e) 76,482; old Gothic cathedral; trades in olives, grain, and almonds. Founded by Peter, first Norman count of Andria, 1046; favorite residence of Emperor Frederick II who built Castel del Monte (9 m. S).

An·dros \'an-drəs\. Chief island of a western group of the Bahamas; 1600 sq. m.; largest island of the Bahamas; with other islands constitutes an electoral district (2300 sq. m.; pop. [1970c] 8845).

Andros \'an-drəs, 'än-ˌdròs\. 1 Island, part of Cyclades dept., Greece, S Aegean Sea; separated from SE Euboea by narrow strait; ab. 25 m. long; 147 sq. m.; pop. (1961c) 12,928. Populated chiefly by Ionian Greeks; in mid-7th cent. B.C. sent colonies to Chalcidice; revolted from Athens 411 B.C.; important as naval post, conquered by Macedonian, Ptolemaic, and Pergamene rulers; annexed to Rome as part of Pergamum 133 B.C.; part of Greece 1829.
2 Town, its ✱, on E coast; pop. (1961c) 2032.

An·dros·cog·gin \ˌan-drə-'skäg-ən\. 1 River, NE New Hampshire and SW Maine; ab. 157 m. long; rises in Umbagog Lake on Maine-New Hampshire boundary, flows S in New Hampshire, turns E across Maine border and SE into Kennebec river near Bath, S Maine.
2 County in Maine. See table at MAINE.

An·dru·so·vo \än-'drü-sə-və\. Village a few miles S of Smolensk, W Russian S.F.S.R., U.S.S.R. Scene of treaty Jan. 20, 1667 terminating war bet. Poland and Russia (1654–67) and by which Smolensk and E Ukraine, including Kiev, were ceded to Russia.

An·dú·jar \än-'dü-ˌhär\ *or anc.* **Il·li·tur·gis** \ˌil-ə-'tər-jəs\. Commune, Jaén prov., S Spain, on right bank of Guadalquivir 24 m. NW of Jaén; pop. (1970p) 31,464; known esp. for its mineral springs and for the production of pottery.

Ané·cho \ˌan-ə-'kō\. Town, S Togo, W Africa, near border of Dahomey, 30 m. E of Lomé; pop. (1969e) 13,300.

Ane·cón Gran·de \ˌan-ə-ˌkòn-'grän-(ˌ)dā\. Peak, SW Río Negro prov., S cen. Argentina; 6593 ft.

An·e·ga·da \ˌan-ə-'gäd-ə\. Island, British Virgin Is., West Indies; ab. 10 m. long.

Anegada Bay \ˌan-ə-ˌgäd-ə-, -'gäth-\. Inlet of Atlantic Ocean on SE coast of Buenos Aires prov., E Argentina, S of Bahía Blanca.

Anegada Passage \ˌan-ə-'gäd-ə-\. Channel in the British Virgin Is., West Indies, E of Anegada I. and Virgin Gorda I.; ab. 40 m. wide.

Anei·tyum \ä-'nā-ˌtyüm\. Most southerly island of the New Hebrides Is., SW Pacific Ocean, 20°12′S, 169°45′E; ab. 55 sq. m.; pop. (1967c) 320; central peak 2788 ft.

Aneiza. See ANAIZA.

Ane·to, Pi·co de \ˌpē-(ˌ)kō-ˌdā-ə-'nät-(ˌ)ō\ *or Fr.* **Pic de Né·thou** \pēk-də-nā-'tü\. Peak in the Maladeta range, Lérida prov., NE Spain, just S of French border; 11,168 ft.; highest in the Pyrenees.

Anfa. See CASABLANCA.

An·ga \'əŋ-gə, 'äŋ-\. Ancient name of E Bihar, NE India; under the rule of Magadha c. 6th to 8th cent.

An·ga·da·nan \ˌäŋ-gə-'dä-nən\. Municipality, SW Isabela prov., Luzon, Phil., on left bank of Cagayan river 28 m. S of Ilagan; pop. (1969e) 26,800.

An·ga·mos, Point \-äŋ-'gäm-əs\. Cape extending into Pacific Ocean from W cen. Antofagasta prov., N Chile, S of Bay of Mejillones del Sur.

An·ga·ra \ˌäŋ-gə-'ra\. 1 Navigable river, U.S.S.R.; 1151 m. long; area of its drainage basin ab. 400,000 sq. m.; flows from SW corner of Lake Baikal N past Irkutsk and then W to Yenisei river, Irkutsk Oblast; formerly called Upper (Verkhnyaya) Tunguska in its lower course in Krasnoyarsk Krai; chief tributaries Oka and Ilim.
2 *or Russ.* **Verkh·nyaya Angara** \'verk-nə-yə-\ *or* **Upper Angara.** River, N Buryat A.S.S.R., U.S.S.R.; ab. 200 m. long; flows SW into N end of Lake Baikal.

An·garsk \än-'gärsk\. Town, Irkutsk Oblast, Russian S.F.S.R., U.S.S.R., ab. 25 m. NW of Irkutsk; pop. (1970p) 204,000; mining equipment; thermal power station.

An·gat \äŋ-'gät\. River, Bulacan prov., Luzon, Phil.; rises in mountains on Quezon border; utilized for production of hydroelectric power.

An·ga·tho·ní·si \ˌäŋ-ˌgäth-ə-'nē-sē\ *or formerly* **Gai·da·ro** \'gīd-ə-ˌrō\. Small island in the E Aegean Sea, S of Samos, Greece; included in the Dodecanese group.

Ang·aur \äŋ-'aù(ə)r\. Small island at S end of Palau Is., W Pacific Ocean, 6°54′N, 134°09′E; phosphate deposits; chief village Saipan, on W coast. Taken by American forces Sept. 17–Oct. 13, 1944.

An·ge·di·va \ˌan-jə-'dē-və\ *or formerly* **An·ji·div** \'ən-jə-ˌdēv, 'än-\. Island off W coast of India, S of Goa; near Karwar in Mysore state; formerly Portuguese.

Án·gel de la Guar·da \'äŋ-ˌhel-dā-lə-'gwärd-ə\. Island off NE cen. Baja California, in upper Gulf of California; ab. 43 m. long.

An·ge·les \'äŋ-hā-ˌlās\. Chartered city, NW cen. Pampanga prov., Luzon, Phil., on Manila-Dagupan R.R. 10 m. NW of San Fernando; pop. (1970e) 106,600.

Angeles, Mount \-'an-jə-ləs\. Peak, Clallam co., NW Washington; 6454 ft.

An·gel Falls \ˌān-jəl-\. Waterfall, SE Venezuela, on side of large (ab. 20 m. long) flat-topped mountain E of Caroní river; 3212 ft. high; world's highest waterfall.

An·ge·li·na \ˌan-jə-'lē-nə\. 1 River, E Texas; 119 m. long; flows from Smith co. SSE to Neches river on E boundary of Tyler co.
2 County in Texas. See table at TEXAS.

Angel Island \ˌān-jəl-\. Island in San Francisco Bay, California, 2 m. E of Sausalito; ab. 1 sq. m.; belongs to Marin co.

Ang·eln \'äŋ-əln\. Region, NE Schleswig-Holstein, West Germany; area 320 sq. m.; bounded on the N by the Flensburger Förde, on E by Kiel Bay, and on S by Schlei Inlet; ground moraine; fertile farm lands; cattle and pig raising; traditionally home of Angles, a people who are supposed to have migrated in 5th cent. A.D. to E, central, and N parts of England (see EAST ANGLIA).

Angerapp. See ANGRAPA.

Angerburg. See WĘGORZEWO.

Ång·er·man \'òŋ-ər-mən\. River, cen. Sweden; 279 m. long; rises on W boundary of Sweden, flows SE and S into Gulf of Bothnia just N of Härnösand; navigable for ab. 31 m.; course marked by cataracts and waterfalls; noted for beauty of landscape.

Ång·er·man·land \'òŋ-ər-mən-ˌland\. Region, formerly a province of E Sweden, on Gulf of Bothnia, ab. coextensive with modern Västernorrland and Västerbotten cos.

Ang·er·mün·de \ˌäŋ-(g)ər-'myün-də, ˌäŋ-ər-'mœn-\. City, Frankfurt dist., East Germany, ab. 45 m. NNE of Berlin; pop. (1970e) 11,682; 13th cent. Gothic church; scene of defeat of Pomeranians by Elector Frederick I of Brandenburg 1420.

An·gers \äⁿ-ˈzhā\ *or anc.* **Ju·li·om·a·gus** \ˌjü-lē-ˈäm-ə-gəs\. City, ✱ of Maine-et-Loire dept., W France, on Maine river 48 m. ENE of Nantes; pop. (1968c) 128,533; cables, woolen goods, electrical equipment, machinery; episcopal see from 3d cent.; 13th cent. Gothic cathedral of Saint Maurice; university (closed by French Revolution; reorganized 1875); important slate quarries—whence its sobriquet "Black Angers" or the "Black City."

History: Ancient capital of the Andecavi tribe; invaded by Northmen in 9th cent. and by English in 12th and 15th cents.; became seat of counts of Anjou in 9th cent. and later the capital of the duchy (see ANJOU 2); taken by Huguenots 1585; scene of defeat of Vendean royalists 1793.

An·ghia·ri \ˌäŋ-gē-ˈär-ē\. Village, E Tuscany, Italy, ab. 10 m. NE of Arezzo; victory of Florentines over Milanese 1440.

Ang·kor \ˈaŋ-ˌkō(ə)r, ˈäŋ-\ *or orig.* **Angkor Thom** \-ˈtōm\. Ruined ancient city, Cambodia, SE Asia, NW of Tonle Sap ab. 4 m. from Siem Reap; old capital of the Khmers. Founded 1st cent. A.D. by Khmers from NE Burma who transplanted Indian civilization and flourished for several centuries; Angkor Thom built c. 850–900 A.D., a city of 5 sq. m. having moat and walls, and within, palaces, temples, and a great tower (Bayon), richly carved, esp. with four faces of Siva. About 1 m. S is **Angkor Wat** *or* **Vat** \-ˌwät\, rectangular temple of three stories, with towers, porticoes, galleries, stairways, etc., the entire structure covered with exquisite bas-reliefs. After Siamese conquest of the Khmers in 14th cent. city and temples in ruins and buried in jungle; discovered by French botanist 1860 and later cleared and partially restored by government. See CAMBODIA.

An·glem, Mount \-ˈaŋ-gləm\. Peak, N Stewart I., New Zealand; 3208 ft.

An·gle·sey *or* **An·gle·sea** \ˈaŋ-gəl-sē\. **1** *or anc.* **Mo·na** \ˈmō-nə\. Island, NW Wales, separated from mainland by Menai Strait; 276 sq. m.; pop. (1961c) 51,744; most of land given over to cattle and sheep pastures; produces wheat, barley, oats; fishing, quarrying; copper formerly an important export. Notable druidic ruins, esp. dolmens; subdued by Suetonius Paulinus 61 A.D. who demolished sacred groves of the druids; ruled by princes of North Wales 9th–13th cents.; conquered by Edward I 1282.

2 County in Wales, including Anglesey I. and Holyhead I. See table at WALES.

An·glet \äⁿ-ˈglā\. Commune, Pyrénées-Atlantiques dept., SW France, W suburb of Bayonne; pop. (1968c) 21,190.

An·gle·ton \ˈaŋ-gəl-tən\. City, ⊗ of Brazoria co., SE Texas, 36 m. W of Galveston; pop. (1970c) 9770; oil wells.

An·gleur \äⁿ-ˈglər\. Industrial commune, Liège prov., Belgium, 2½ m. SE of Liège near Meuse and Ourthe rivers; pop. (1969e) 12,931; coal mines and foundries.

Anglia. See ENGLAND 1.

Anglo–Egyptian Sudan. See SUDAN 2.

Ang·mags·sa·lik \ä-ˈmäs-ə-ˌlik, äŋ-, -ˈmäks-\. Settlement and trading post, E coast of Greenland, just below Arctic Circle; pop. (1967e) 820; U.S. air base in World War II.

An·gol \äŋ-ˈgōl\. City, ✱ of Malleco prov., S cen. Chile, in agricultural and fruit-growing district 325 m. S of Santiago; pop. (1966e) 21,561.

An·go·la \aŋ-ˈgō-lə, an-\. **1** *or* **Portuguese West Africa.** Portuguese overseas province, SW Africa, bounded on N and NE by Zaire, on SE by Zambia, on S by South-West Africa, and on W by the Atlantic Ocean; 481,351 sq. m.; pop. (1970c) 5,466,600, includes exclave of Cabinda (*q.v.*), N of the Congo river; ✱ Luanda. *Physical features:* Interior forms part of Central African Plateau, alt. 4000 to 6000 ft.; coastal plain ab. 1000 m. long, varies in width from 30 to 100 m.; highest point Mt. Moco 8397 ft., in W. *Chief rivers:* Congo, which for nearly 100 m. forms part of N boundary; many S tributaries of Kasai, notably the Kwango, which have their source in NE; Cuanza in cen. part, flowing NW to Atlantic; Cunene in S, in part forming boundary with South-West Africa; Cubango (Okavango) and Cuíto in SE, flowing into the Okavango Basin; Kwando (or Cuando), an upper tributary of the Zambezi, in SE. *Chief products:* Coffee, corn, sisal, peanuts, cotton, sugarcane; iron ore, oil, diamonds. *Chief towns:* Luanda, Lobito, Nova Lisboa, Benguela.

History: Coast reached by Portuguese sailors 1483; São Paulo de Loanda (now Luanda) settled by Portuguese 1575; Portuguese rule established over coastal area bet. 1575 and 1680, extended south to Moçâmedes 1840; given Cabinda exclave by agreement with Belgian Congo 1886; frontiers determined by Portuguese treaties with France 1886, Germany 1886, Great Britain 1890, 1891; native uprisings 1902, 1907; settled boundary with South-West Africa 1926; status changed from colony to overseas province 1951; outbreak of fighting between Portuguese forces and anti-Portuguese nationalists 1961.

2 City, ⊗ of Steuben co., NE Indiana, 40 m. N of Fort Wayne; pop. (1970c) 5117; die castings, flour; Tri-State Coll. (1884).

3 Village, Erie co., W New York, near Lake Erie 20 m. S of Buffalo; pop. (1970c) 2676; canned goods.

Angora. See ANKARA 2.

An·gos·tu·ra \ˌaŋ-gə-ˈst(y)u̇r-ə, ˌäŋ-gə-ˈstu̇r-\. **1** Town, Sinaloa state, W Mexico; munic. pop. (1970p) 29,709.

2 River port, Venezuela. See CIUDAD BOLÍVAR.

An·gou·lême \ˌäⁿ-gü-ˈlām, -ˈlem\ *or anc.* **Ic·u·lis·ma** \ˌik-yü-ˈliz-mə\. City, ✱ of Charente dept., W France, on Charente river 64 m. NNE of Bordeaux; pop. (1968c) 47,822; papermaking is a major industry; bricks, tiles, refrigerators; episcopal see from 379; Byzantine Romanesque cathedral of St. Pierre (11th and 12th cents.).

History: Taken from Visigoths by Clovis, King of Franks, 507 A.D. in which year he built its first cathedral; from 9th cent. center of countship, held by Lusignan family from 1220; ceded to England by Peace of Bretigny 1360 but restored to France by Charles V 1373; passed to house of Orléans 1394; center of duchy (1515–1844) created by Francis I; united to crown 1714; capital of pre-Revolutionary province of Angoumois (*q.v.*).

An·gou·mois \ˌäⁿ-güm-ˈwä\. Historical region of W cen. France, bounded on N by Poitou, E by Limousin, SE by Guienne, SW by Gironde estuary, NW by Aunis; ✱ Angoulême; watered by Charente river. Medieval county ceded to England by Peace of Bretigny 1360 and restored 1373 to France by Charles V; appanage of royal crown to 1515; raised to rank of duchy by Francis I 1515.

An·gra do He·ro·ís·mo \ˈaŋ-grə-dü-ˌer-ü-ˈēzh-(ˌ)mü\. **1** District of Portugal, Azores. See table at PORTUGAL.

2 Seaport, its ✱, at head of deep bay on S coast of Terceira I., Azores; pop. (1960c) 13,929; episcopal see; harbor protected by promontory; exports wine, fruit (esp. pineapples), grain, flax. Founded 1534; until 1832 capital of Azores; refuge for Portuguese regency 1830–33.

An·gra·pa \äŋ-ˈgräp-ə\ *or Ger.* **Ang·er·app** \ˈäŋ-ə-ˌräp\. River in N Poland and E Kaliningrad Oblast, U.S.S.R.; ab. 106 m. long; flows N from Masurian Lakes into Pregolya river at Chernyakhovsk.

Angra Pequena. See LÜDERITZ.

An·gren \äŋ-ˈgren\. Town, Tashkent Oblast, Uzbek S.S.R., U.S.S.R., ab. 50 m. ESE of Tashkent; pop. (1969e) 94,000; cement; thermal power plant.

An·gri \ˈäŋ-grē\. Commune, Salerno prov., Campania, S Italy, 11 m. WNW of Salerno; pop. (1968e) 23,155; manufactures textiles, esp. silk and cotton goods. Ancient Mons Lactarius (S of Angri) scene of defeat of Ostrogoths 553 by Narses.

Ang Thong *or* **Ang·thong** \äŋ-ˈtōŋ\. **1** Province, S Thailand; 379 sq. m.; pop. (1966c) 197,865.

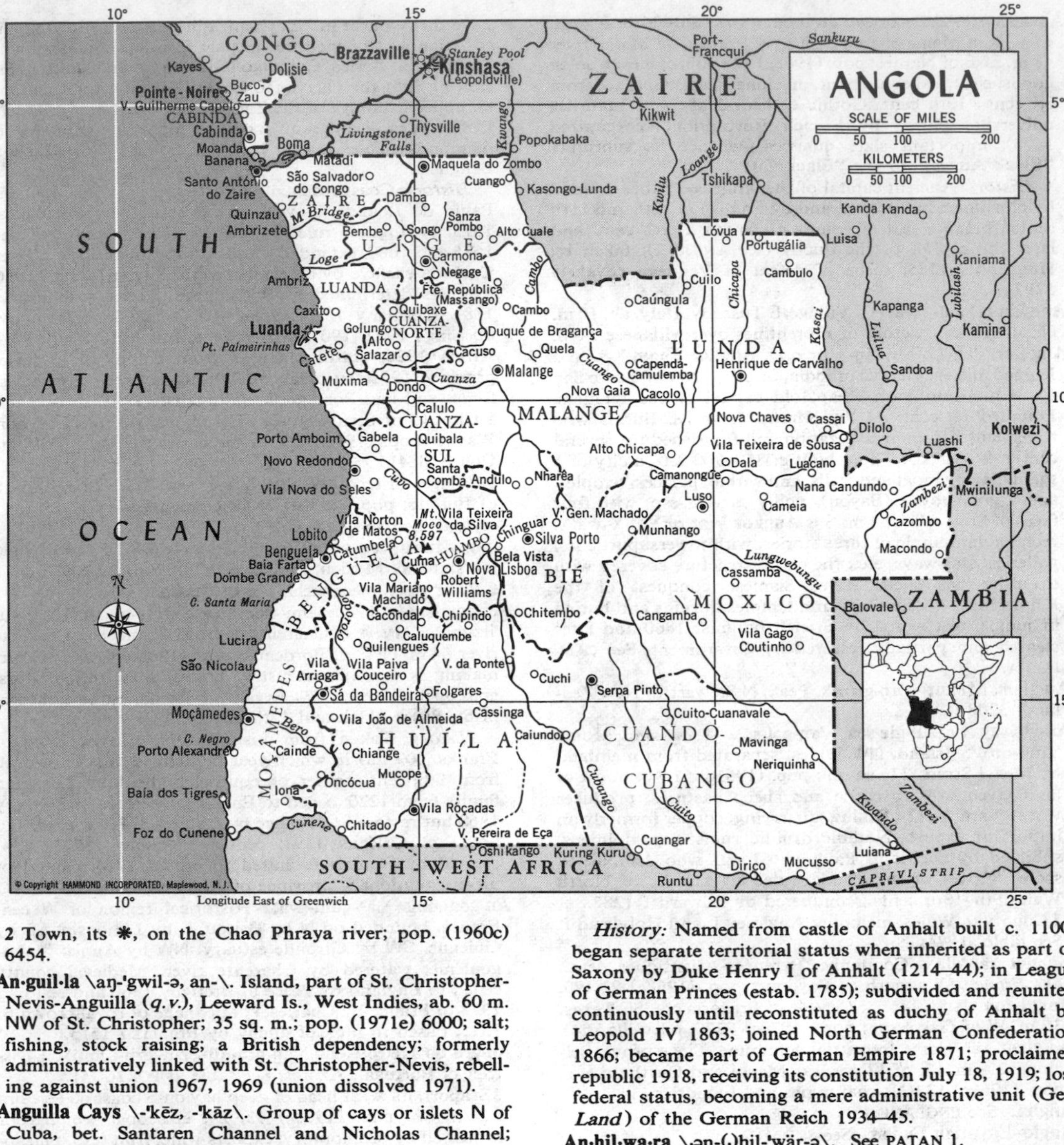

2 Town, its ✻, on the Chao Phraya river; pop. (1960c) 6454.

An·guil·la \aŋ-ˈgwil-ə, an-\. Island, part of St. Christopher-Nevis-Anguilla (*q.v.*), Leeward Is., West Indies, ab. 60 m. NW of St. Christopher; 35 sq. m.; pop. (1971e) 6000; salt; fishing, stock raising; a British dependency; formerly administratively linked with St. Christopher-Nevis, rebelling against union 1967, 1969 (union dissolved 1971).

Anguilla Cays \-ˈkēz, -ˈkāz\. Group of cays or islets N of Cuba, bet. Santaren Channel and Nicholas Channel; belong to the Bahama Is.

An·guille, Cape \-aŋ-ˈgwil\. Cape, SW Newfoundland, Canada, S of entrance to St. George Bay.

An·gus \ˈaŋ-gəs\; *formerly* **For·far** \ˈfȯr-fər\ *or* **For·far·shire** \-ˌshi(ə)r, -shər\. County, E Scotland, bounded on the N by Aberdeen and Kincardine cos., on E by North Sea, on S by Firth of Tay, and on W by Perth co.; 874 sq. m.; pop. (1971p) 279,396; ⊗ Forfar; irregular, hilly land; cut by North Esk, South Esk, and Isla rivers; agriculture (wheat, potatoes, oats); sheep and cattle raising; salmon fishing; jute and linen manufactures. Chief towns Dundee, Forfar, Montrose, Arbroath.

An·gwin \ˈaŋ-(g)wən\. Town (unincorp.), Napa co., California, ab. 20 m. NNW of Napa; pop. (1970c) 2690; fruit; Pacific Union Coll. (1882).

An·halt \ˈän-ˌhält\. Former German state, now part of Magdeburg and Halle districts, East Germany; 893 sq. m.; ✻ Dessau; included part of Harz Mts.; watered by Elbe, Mulde, and Saale rivers.

History: Named from castle of Anhalt built c. 1100; began separate territorial status when inherited as part of Saxony by Duke Henry I of Anhalt (1214–44); in League of German Princes (estab. 1785); subdivided and reunited continuously until reconstituted as duchy of Anhalt by Leopold IV 1863; joined North German Confederation 1866; became part of German Empire 1871; proclaimed republic 1918, receiving its constitution July 18, 1919; lost federal status, becoming a mere administrative unit (Ger. *Land*) of the German Reich 1934–45.

An·hil·wa·ra \ˌən-(ˌ)hil-ˈwär-ə\. See PATAN 1.

An·holt \ˈan-ˌhōlt, -ˌhōlt\. Island, Århus co., Denmark, in middle of Kattegat ab. 45 m. E of Jutland; 8 sq. m.; pop. (1969e) 203; lighthouse.

An–hsi \ˈän-ˈshē\ *also* **An·si** \ˈän-ˈsē\. Town, NW Kansu prov., N cen. China.

An·hwei *or* **An·hui** \ˈän-ˈ(h)wā\. Province, E China, bounded on N by Kiangsu, on E by Kiangsu and Chekiang, on S by Kiangsi, and on W by Hupeh and Honan; 54,015 sq. m.; pop. (1968e) 35,000,000; ✻ Ho-fei; crossed by lower course of Yangtze (ab. 1/3 of province S of river) and in N by Huai and new course of Yellow river; contains Ch'ao lake and part of Hung-tse lake; lowland in N and in valley of Yangtze, mountainous in S; chief products: beans, cotton, rice, tea, wheat; mining (esp. coal, iron ore); hydroelectric power; chief towns: Ho-fei, Wu-na-mu, An-ch'ing, She-hsien. Under Ming dynasty (14th–17th cents.), part of province of Kiang-nan (Kiangsu the other part); made separate province in 17th cent. under Manchu (Ch'ing) dynasty.

An·i·ak·chak Crater \ˌan-ē-ˈak-ˌchak-\. Crater, Alaska Penin., SW Alaska; 6 m. in diameter; one of the largest known explosion craters.

Aniche \a-ˈnēsh\. Commune, Nord dept., N France, 8 m. ESE of Douai; pop. (1968c) 10,190; coal beds.

Anicium. See LE PUY.

Anie·ne \än-ˈyā-nā\ *also* **Te·ve·ro·ne** \ˌtā-və-ˈrō-nā\ *or anc.* **An·io** \ˈan-(ˌ)yō\. River, cen. Italy; 67 m. long; flows into the Tiber river just above Rome.

Ani·na \ˈän-i-nə\; *formerly* **Ştai·er·dorf–Anina** \ˈshtī-ər-ˌdȯrf-\ *or Ger.* **Stei·er·dorf–Anina** \ˈshtī-\. Commune, Caraş-Severin co., SW Romania, ab. 55 m. SE of Timişoara; pop. (1966c) 14,063.

Ani·va, Cape \-ə-ˈn(y)ē-və\. Cape, SE extremity of Sakhalin I., U.S.S.R.

Aniva Bay *or Jap.* **Ani·wa Wan** \än-ē-ˌwä-ˈwän\. Bay, U.S.S.R., E Asia, at S end of Sakhalin I.

An·jen·go \ˌən-ˈjeŋ-(ˌ)gō\. Village on coast of Kerala, SW India, ab. 20 m. NW of Trivandrum; one of the earliest (1684) English settlements in India.

Anjidiv. See ANGEDIVA.

An·jō \an-ˈjō\. City, Aichi prefecture, Honshū, Japan, 22 m. SE of Nagoya; pop. (1970c) 94,307.

An·jou \ˈan-ˌjü, äⁿ-ˈzhü\. 1 Town, Montreal and Jesus Islands co., S Quebec, Canada, 5 m. N of Montreal; pop. (1971p) 33,842.

2 Historical region of NW France, bounded on N by Maine, E by Touraine, SE by Saumurois, S by Poitou, and W by Brittany; ✱ Angers; watered by Loire river.

History: County erected as a fief by the Capetian kings; under Fulk III Nerra (987–1040) and his successors, Angevin house acquired Touraine 1044 and Maine 1110; became English 1154 at accession of Henry II (who had inherited it 1151 from his father, Duke Geoffrey of Anjou); returned to French crown when taken from King John 1204; inherited in 1246 by Prince Charles, who became king of Naples and Sicily; raised to a duchy 1297, returned to royal domain through accession of Philip VI 1328; from 1350 to 1480 under third house of Anjou, founded by Louis I (Count of Provence 1339–84 and Duke of Anjou 1360–84), second son of John II (1350–64); became duchy 1360; annexed to French crown by Louis XI 1480.

An·jou·an \äⁿ-ˈzhwäⁿ\ *or* **Jo·han·na** \jō-ˈhan-ə\. One of Comoro Is., 80 m. SE of Great Comoro, 12°15′S, 44°25′E; 89 sq. m.

An·ju \ˈän-ˈjü\ *or formerly* **An·shu** \ˈän-ˈshü\. Town, North Korea, ab. 38 m. N of P'yŏngyang; coal mines.

An·ka·ra \ˈaŋ-kə-rə, ˈäŋ-\. 1 Province, W cen. Turkey, Asia. See table at TURKEY.

2 *or formerly* **An·go·ra** \aŋ-ˈgōr-ə, an-\ *or anc.* **An·cy·ra** \an-ˈsī-rə\. City, ✱ of Turkey and of Ankara prov., ab. 220 m. ESE of İstanbul; pop. (1970e) 1,162,000; met. area 1,440,779; built on a hill 500 ft. above a plain and on **Ankara River** (ab. 115 m. long), a tributary of Sakarya river; commercial center; building materials, foodstuffs, textiles; metalworking; Univ. of Ankara (1946), Middle East Technical Univ. (1956), Hacettepe Univ. (1967).

History: Important commercial center (Ancyra) from early times; capital of Celtic kingdom of Galatia (*q.v.*) in 3d cent. B.C., of Roman province of Galatia after 25 B.C.; conquered in succession by Persians, Arabs, Seljuk Turks, Latin Crusaders, and finally 1360 by Ottoman Turks; nearby occurred victory of Mongol conqueror, Tamerlane, over Sultan Bajazet I 1402; part of Ottoman Empire after recovery by Turks 1431; center in which Turkish Nationalists set up provisional government 1920 which in 1923 proclaimed the republic of Turkey (*q.v.*); made capital of Turkey 1923; name officially changed from Angora to Ankara 1930; scene of treaty by which Turkey and Greece recognized territorial status quo and agreed to naval equality in Mediterranean 1930.

An·ka·ra·tra \ˌaŋ-kə-ˈrä-trə\. Mountain group, cen. Malagasy Republic; highest peak 8674 ft.

Anking. See AN-CH'ING.

An·klam \ˈäŋ-ˌkläm\. City, Neubrandenburg dist., East Germany, on right bank of Peene river, 40 m. SE of Greifswald; pop. (1970e) 19,615; foundries, machinery works, mills (esp. wool and linen), sugar manufacturing. Settled in 11th cent.; joined Hanseatic League 1283; sacked during Thirty Years' War and Seven Years' War; acquired by Prussia 1720.

An·ko·ber \aŋ-ˈkō-bər, än-\. Town, Shewa prov., cen. Ethiopia, on E slope of mountains 85 m. NE of Addis Ababa; pop. (1970e) 2000.

An·ko·bra \aŋ-ˈkō-brə\. River, W Ghana, W Africa; 130 m. long; enters Gulf of Guinea just W of Axim; navigable for 50 miles.

An·ko·le \aŋ-ˈkō-lē\. Plateau region in SW Uganda, bet. Lake Victoria and Lake Edward; formerly a native kingdom.

An·myŏn \ˈän-ˈmyȯn\ *or formerly* **Am·min** \ˈäm-ˈmin\. Island in the Yellow Sea off W coast of South Ch'ungch'ŏng prov., South Korea.

Ann, Cape \kā-ˈpan\. 1 Eastern peninsula of Essex co., Massachusetts; N of Massachusetts Bay.

2 Cape on coast of Enderby Land, Antarctica, extending into Indian Ocean, 66°10′S, 51°22′E.

An·na \ˈan-ə\. City, Union co., SW Illinois, 28 m. SW of Marion; pop. (1970c) 4766; fruit-shipping center; granite works.

An·na·ba \an-ˈnäb-ə\. 1 Department of NE Algeria. See table at ALGERIA.

2 *or formerly* **Bône** \ˈbōn\; *known as* **Bo·na** \ˈbō-nə\ *down to French occupation.* Seaport, its ✱, 70 m. NE of Constantine; pop. (1966c) 150,161; large trade in phosphates, iron, zinc, and barley; railway workshops, chemical works.

History: Identified with **Aph·ro·di·si·um** \ˌaf-rə-ˈdiz-ē-əm, -ˈdizh-(ē-)əm\, the port of ancient **Hip·po** *or* **Hippo Re·gi·us** \ˌhip-ō-ˈrē-j(ē-)əs\, whose ruins are 1 m. to the S, a rich city of Roman Africa to c. 300 A.D. and the bishopric and home 396–430 of St. Augustine. Hippo and its port severely damaged by Vandals 431 and Arabs 646 and Bona built on latter site by Arabs in 7th cent. Held in medieval times by Italians, Spaniards, Genoese, Algerines; occupied by French 1832; entered by Allies Nov. 12, 1942.

An·na·berg–Buch·holz \ˌän-ə-ˌbe(ə)rg-ˈbük-ˌhōlts\ *or formerly* **Annaberg.** City, Karl-Marx-Stadt dist., East Germany, near Czech border in Erzgebirge 18 m. S of Karl-Marx-Stadt; pop. (1970e) 27,892; electrical appliances; metalworking; former center of German lace, braid, and ribbon industry founded by Barbara Uttmann 1550; gained first importance through the mining of silver, tin, bismuth, and cobalt; marble quarries.

An Nabk. See EN NEBK.

An Na·fud \ˌan-nə-ˈfüd\ *also* **Ne·fud** \nə-ˈfüd\. A desert of red sand in N Saudi Arabia; 140 m. wide at max. extent.

An Na·jaf \an-ˈnaj-ˌaf\. Town, S cen. Iraq, on lake W of the Euphrates 35 m. S of Hilla; pop. (1965c) 128,096; starting point of pilgrimage route to Mecca; contains Ali's shrine.

An·nam \a-ˈnam, ə-\ *or* **Anam** \ˈan-ˌam\. Historic kingdom situated on E coast of Indochina, now a region lying partly in North Vietnam and partly in South Vietnam; 56,974 sq. m.; ✱ Hue; coastline ab. 850 m. long; mountain range extending entire length with max. elevation ab. 7900 ft.

History: Conquered c. 214 B.C. by Chinese; became independent 1428; came under French influence in late 18th cent., but ruled by emperor of Annam at beginning of 19th cent.; French control extended by various treaties until established as protectorate 1883; partitioned between North and South Vietnam 1954; its last emperor was deposed 1955. See INDOCHINA 2.

An·nan \'an-ən\. 1 River, S Scotland; 49 m. long; flows S in Dumfries co. into Solway Firth.
2 Burgh, Dumfries co., S Scotland, on Annan river 2 m. from its mouth; pop. (1971p) 6053; chemicals, machinery; nearby are several atomic reactors.

An·nan·dale–on–Hud·son \'an-ən-ˌdāl-ȯn-'həd-sən, -än-\. Village, Dutchess co., New York, on E bank of Hudson river 21 m. N of Poughkeepsie; Bard Coll. (1860).

An·na Pau·low·na \ˌan-ə-pə-'lō-nə, ˌän-\. Commune, North Holland prov., Netherlands, 33 m. N of Amsterdam; pop. (1970e) 7544.

An·nap·o·lis \ə-'nap-(ə-)ləs\. 1 Seaport, ✱ of Maryland and ⊗ of Anne Arundel co., on S bank of Severn river near its mouth at Chesapeake Bay, 22 m. SSE of Baltimore; pop. (1970c) 29,592; boat yards; concrete products, plastics; site of United States Naval Academy (founded 1845 by George Bancroft) and of St. John's Coll. (1696).

History: Settled as town of **Prov·i·dence** \'präv-əd-ən(t)s, -ə-ˌden(t)s\ by Puritans from Virginia 1649, later known as **Anne Arundel Town** \ˌan-ə-'rən-dᵊl-\; became capital of Maryland and renamed Annapolis in honor of Princess (later Queen) Anne 1694; received city charter 1708; scene of meeting of Continental Congress Nov. 26, 1783–June 3, 1784; seat of the Annapolis Convention 1786 in which delegates from five states met but took no action (precursor of Constitutional Convention of 1787).
2 County, Nova Scotia, Canada. See table at NOVA SCOTIA.

Annapolis Basin. Inlet of Bay of Fundy on W coast of Annapolis co., W Nova Scotia, Canada; receives **Annapolis River** (75 m. long) from NE.

Annapolis Roy·al \-'rȯi(-ə)l\. Town, ⊗ of Annapolis co., W Nova Scotia, Canada, on S shore of Annapolis Basin 70 m. N of Yarmouth; pop. (1971p) 723.

History: One of the oldest settlements in North America N of the Gulf of Mexico; founded as **Port Royal** 1605 by Sieur de Monts and Champlain; several times captured by English in 17th cent. and restored to France; became seat of French government in Acadia 1684; finally seized 1710 and became permanently British 1713 by Treaty of Utrecht; name changed in honor of Queen Anne; until 1750 was capital of Nova Scotia.

An·na·pur·na *or* **Ana·pur·na** \ˌan-ə-'pu̇r-nə\. Mountain range in the Himalayas, Nepal; highest peak 26,504 ft.; first climbed 1950 by French expedition.

An Nāqūrah. See EN NAQURA.

Ann Ar·bor \a-'när-bər\. City, ⊗ of Washtenaw co., SE Michigan, in agricultural section 36 m. W of Detroit; pop. (1970c) 99,797; ball bearings, photographic equipment, precision instruments; Univ. of Michigan (founded 1817 in Detroit, reorganized as college in Ann Arbor 1841), Concordia Lutheran Coll. (1963), Washtenaw Community Coll. (1965); settled 1824.

An Na·si·ri·ya \ˌan-ˌnäs-ə-'rē-(y)ə\. Town, SE Iraq, on left bank of Euphrates river ab. 100 m. NW of Basra; pop. (1965c) 60,405; in World War I taken by British July 25, 1915.

Anne, Mount \-'an\. Mountain, Antarctica, 83°48′S, 168°30′E; 12,703 ft.

Anne Arun·del \ˌan-ə-'rən-dᵊl\. County in Maryland. See table at MARYLAND.

Anne Arundel Town. See ANNAPOLIS 1.

An·ne·cy \ˌan-(ə-)'sē\ *or Lat.* **An·ne·ci·a·cum** \ˌan-ə-'sī-ə-kəm\. City, ✱ of Haute-Savoie dept., E France, at NW end of Lake Annecy 63 m. ENE of Lyons; pop. (1968c) 54,484; linens, cotton yarn, precision instruments, paper; tourism; noted bell foundry in vicinity, **Annecy–le–Vieux** \-lə-'vyœ̄\ *or anc.* **Anneciacum Ve·tus** \-'vēt-əs\, 1½ m. N. Ancient castle, cathedral, and church of St. Francis. Ruled by counts of the Genevois; under dukes of Savoy 1401–1860.

Annecy, Lake. Lake in the Alps, Haute-Savoie dept., E France, 22 m. S of Geneva; 9 m. long, 2 m. wide; 10 sq. m.; connected with Fier river by Thiou canal which runs through Annecy; surrounded by steep, scenic mountains.

Annesley Bay. See ZULA, GULF OF.

An·nette \a-'net, ə-\. Small island S of Revillagigedo I., SE Alaska; 132 sq. m.; Metlakatla is on it; inhabitants, chiefly Indians and Eskimos, engaged in salmon fishing.

An Nhon \'än-'nōn\ *or formerly* **Binh Dinh** \'bin-'din\. Town near coast, South Vietnam, ab. 152 m. SSE of Da Nang; pop. (1965e) 112,050; its port is Qui Nhon.

An·nis·quam *or earlier* **An·as·quam** \'an-ə-ˌskwäm\. Village and summer resort, N suburb and part of Gloucester, Essex co., NE Massachusetts, on Annisquam Harbor.

Annisquam Harbor. Inlet of Atlantic Ocean on N shore of Cape Ann, E Essex co., NE Massachusetts.

An·nis·ton \'an-ə-stən\. Manufacturing city, ⊗ of Calhoun co., NE Alabama, 28 m. SE of Gadsden; pop. (1970c) 31,533; cast iron soil pipes, chemicals, textiles; iron ore mines; founded as private industrial village; incorporated as city 1879; opened to public 1883.

An·no·bón \ˌan-ə-'bän\. Small mountainous island in Gulf of Guinea, 120 m. SW of São Tomé; 4 m. long; 7 sq. m.; pop. (1965e) 1436; part of Equatorial Guinea; a Spanish possession 1778–1968.

An·nœul·lin \ˌan-ˌə(l)-'yaⁿ\. Commune, Nord dept., N France, 9 m. SSW of Lille; pop. (1962c) 5976; coal, brickworks, tanneries.

An·no·nay \ˌan-(ˌ)ō-'nā\ *or anc.* **An·no·ni·a·cum** \ˌan-ə-'nī-ə-kəm\. Commune, Ardèche dept., SE France, on Cance river 36 m. N of Privas; pop. (1968c) 20,757; paper, kid gloves, woolen hosiery; tanneries, dyeworks, silk mills; 14th cent. Gothic church; birthplace of Montgolfier brothers.

An·not·to Bay \ə-ˌnät-ō-\. Town on NE coast of Jamaica, West Indies, 22 m. N of Kingston.

An Nuhūd. See EN NAHUD.

Ann·ville \'an-ˌvil\. Locality in Annville township, Lebanon co., SE cen. Pennsylvania, ab. 4 m. W of Lebanon; pop. (1970c) 4704; shoes, hosiery; dairying; limestone quarries; Lebanon Valley Coll. (1866); platted 1762.

Ano·ka \ə-'nō-kə\. 1 County in E Minnesota. See table at MINNESOTA.
2 City, its ⊗, on Mississippi river 17 m. NNW of Minneapolis; pop. (1970c) 13,489; trade center in agricultural region.

An Pass \'än-, 'an-\. Mountain pass in cen. part of Arakan Yoma, W Burma; alt. ab. 5000 ft.; leads from Sittwe and coast towns to Magwe and Minbu on the Irrawaddy.

Ans \'äⁿs\. Commune, Liège prov., E Belgium, NW suburb of Liège; pop. (1969e) 16,445; coal mines, brickworks, railroad equipment, mine cables.

An·sa·ri·ya, Dje·bel \ˌjeb-əl-ˌan(t)-sə-'rē-(y)ə\. Mountain range, Syria, running N and S ab. 70 m. along W bank of the Orontes river; highest point ab. 5100 ft.; N extension of Lebanon Mts.

Ans·bach \'än(t)s-ˌbäk, -ˌbäk\ *or in English often* **Ans·pach** \'anz-ˌpak\. 1 Former principality, now part of Bavaria, West Germany; ruled by Franconian branch of Hohenzollern family of Brandenburg until its transference to Prussia 1791–92; with Bayreuth (forming margraviate of Ansbach-Bayreuth), ceded to Bavaria by Prussia 1806, confirmed by Congress of Vienna 1815.
2 City, Bavaria, West Germany, 25 m. SW of Nürnberg; pop. (1968e) 30,768; electronic equipment, machinery; meat processing; built around Benedictine monastery founded in 8th cent. by Saint Gumbertus; capital of former Ansbach principality.

An·se·ba \an-'sā-bə\. River, N Ethiopia; rises in cen. Eritrea E of the Barka, flows N and joins the Barka S of Sudan border.

An·ser·ma \än-'ser-mə\. Town, Caldas dept., W cen. Colombia, 50 m. WSW of Manizales; munic. pop. (1968e) 32,800.

An–shan \'än-'shän\. Town, Liaoning prov., NE China, on railroad 55 m. SSW of Mukden; pop. (1970e) 1,500,000; iron and steel, cement, chemicals; steelworks established 1918; bombed by U.S. aircraft July and Sept. 1944.

An·shan \ˈan-ˌshan\ *or* **An·zan** \ˈan-ˌzan\. Region of ancient Persia, NE of Babylonia; a small kingdom, probably in southern Elam (*q.v.*), closely connected with or inclusive of Susa; seat of authority of early Achaemenian kings, predecessors of Cyrus who founded Persian Empire 6th cent. B.C.

Anshu. See ANJU.

An–shun \ˈän-ˈshün\. City, Kweichow prov., S China.

Ansi. See AN-HSI.

An·son \ˈan(t)-sən\. **1** County in North Carolina. See table at NORTH CAROLINA.

2 Residential town, Somerset co., W Maine, on Kennebec river 20 m. NW of Waterville; pop. (1970c) 2168.

3 City, ⊗ of Jones co., NW cen. Texas, 25 m. NNW of Abilene; pop. (1970c) 2615; cotton-shipping center.

Anson Bay. Inlet of Timor Sea on NW coast of Northern Territory, Australia; receives Daly river.

An·son·go \an-ˈsȯŋ-(ˌ)gō\. Town on left bank of Niger, SE Mali, 50 m. SE of Gao; above this point Niger is navigable for 1000 miles.

An·so·nia \an-ˈsō-nē-ə, -ˈsōn-yə\. Manufacturing city, New Haven co., S Connecticut, on Naugatuck river 8 m. WNW of New Haven; pop. (1970c) 21,160; copper, brass, iron castings, electrical supplies, machinery and machine tools, plastics; settled 1651 as part of Derby, independently organized 1845, became borough 1864, city 1893; the town (incorp. 1889) is coextensive with the city.

Anspach. See ANSBACH.

An·ta·kya \ˌant-ə-ˈkyä\ *or* **An·ta·ki·yah** \-ˈkē-(y)ə\ *or anc.* **An·ti·och** \ˈant-ē-ˌäk\ *or Lat.* **An·ti·o·chia** \ˌant-ē-ō-ˈkī-ə\ *or Gk.* **An·ti·o·chea** \-ˈkē-ə\. City, Hatay prov., S Turkey, 27 m. S of İskenderun; pop. (1965c) 57,855; olives, tobacco.

History: Antioch founded by Seleucus Nicator 300 B.C.; became commercial rival of Alexandria; capital of Syria (see SYRIA 1) until 64 B.C. when Pompey conquered the province; a mission center for early Christianity; ancient city destroyed by earthquake 526 A.D.; conquered by Arabs 638; captured by Byzantine Empire under Nicephorus Phocas 969; taken by the Seljuk Turks 1085, regained by the Crusaders 1097–98, and as a principality given to Bohemund; subject of dispute bet. Normans and Byzantine emperor whose suzerainty Bohemund agreed to recognize 1099; Latin Christian principality destroyed by Baybars, Mameluke sultan of Egypt and Syria, 1268. For later history, see SYRIA 3.

An·tal·ya \ˌant-ᵊl-ˈyä\. **1** Province of SW Turkey, Asia. See table at TURKEY.

2 *or formerly* **Ada·lia** \ˌäd-ᵊl-ē-ˈ(y)ä\ *or anc.* **At·ta·leia** \ˌat-ᵊl-ˈī-ə\ *or Bib.* **At·ta·lia** \ˌat-ᵊl-ˈī-ə\. Seaport, its ✱, on Gulf of Antalya; pop. (1965c) 71,833; fruit, timber. Ancient city founded c. 150 B.C. on seacoast of Pamphylia by Attalus II Philadelphus, King of Pergamum; from this port Paul sailed with Barnabas to Antioch on his first missionary journey (*Acts* xiv. 25).

Antalya, Gulf of *or* **Gulf of Adalia** *or Turk.* **Antalya Kör·fe·zi** \-ˌkər-fə-ˈzē\. Inlet of Mediterranean Sea, SW coast of Turkey; ab. 130 m. wide.

Antananarivo. See TANANARIVE.

Ant·arc·ti·ca \ant-ˈärk-ti-kə, -ˈärt-i-\ *or* **Ant·arc·tic Conti·nent** \-ˌärk-tik-, -ˌart-ik-\. A continent lying around the South Pole. *Physical features:* Ab. 5,500,000 sq. m.; covered by ice cap having average thickness of 1 mile; divided into **West Antarctica** (includes Antarctic Penin.) and **East Antarctica** by the **Transantarctic Mountains** \ˌtran(t)s-ˌant-, ˌtranz-\, a mountain range running from Victoria Land (*q.v.*) to Coats Land (*q.v.*); max. ice thickness in West Antarctica ab. 14,000 ft., in East Antarctica ab. 9000 ft.; highest of the continents, with av. elevation of ab. 8000 ft.; highest peak Vinson Massif 16,860 ft.; existence of coal indicative of warmer climate in earlier age; surrounding seas support whaling industry.

Ownership: Claims advanced by several nations: Norway (Queen Maud Land) from 20°W to 45°E; Australia (Enderby Land, Wilkes Land, George V Coast, part of Oates Coast) from 45°E to 136°E and from 142°E to 160°E; France (Adélie Coast) from 136°E to 142°E; New Zealand from 160°E to 150°W; Chile from 90°W to 53°W; Great Britain from 80°W to 20°W; Argentina from 74°W to 25°W; claims not recognized by U.S.

History: Reference to large S continent found in writings of ancient Greeks, including Ptolemy; its presumed area considerably reduced through voyages of Vasco da Gama 1497, Magellan 1520, Drake 1579, and Tasman 1642; significant exploration of region begun with voyages of Capt. James Cook who proved 1768 that New Zealand was not part of the southern continent, and who first crossed Antarctic Circle in circumnavigation of continent 1772–75; region visited by British and American whalers 1778–1839; first land within Antarctic Circle sighted by Bellingshausen 1819–21; Weddell Sea, Graham Coast, Enderby Land, Adélie Coast discovered during period 1823–40; Ross Sea and Ross Ice Shelf discovered 1841 by Capt. Ross, who established 1842 record of 78°9′S, not surpassed until 1902; discovery of region and scientific study of mainland carried on by successive German, Norwegian, Belgian, and British expeditions, especially after 6th International Geographical Congress of 1895; first landing on continent made by member of Norwegian expedition 1895; Ross Ice Shelf to 82°17′S crossed by Scott 1902–04; southern end of Ross Ice Shelf passed by Shackleton's expedition 1908, and South Magnetic Pole reached by other members of his group 1909; South Pole discovered by Capt. Roald Amundsen Dec. 17, 1911; continuity of coast from George V Coast to Enderby Land demonstrated by land explorations of Sir Douglas Mawson's expeditions 1911–14, 1929–31; explored and mapped from air by Sir Hubert Wilkins 1928–29 and by Commander Richard Byrd 1928–30, 1933–35; part of Pacific coast explored by Byrd's third expedition 1939–40 and fourth 1946–47; Ronne (U.S.) expedition 1946–48 determined Antarctica to be a single continent; Fuchs (Brit.) expedition 1957–58 made first land crossing of the continent; establishment of continent as demilitarized zone by treaty 1959; creation of several areas for conservation of flora and fauna 1966–67.

Antarctic Archipelago. See PALMER ARCHIPELAGO.

Antarctic Peninsula *or formerly* **Palm·er Peninsula** \ˌpäm-ər-, ˌpäl-mər-\. Peninsula, Antarctica, extending ab. 700 m. from lat. 73°S to approx. 63°S, and lying between long. 59°W and 67°W; part of British Antarctic Territory; N part known as Graham Land, S part as Palmer Land; separated from South Shetland Is. by Bransfield Strait; near its base on W are Alexander I. and Charcot I. and further N on the W lies the Palmer Archipelago; British and Chilean scientific stations destroyed by volcanic activity 1969.

Antarctic Regions. Antarctica (*q.v.*) and the S waters of the Atlantic, Pacific, and Indian Oceans (sometimes inappropriately termed **Antarctic Ocean**); greatest depth recorded in these S waters is 21,043 ft. (66°58′S, 176°14′W); subpolar conditions extend to lat. 55°S and reach 45°S in area S of Africa. See POLAR REGIONS; ARCTIC, THE.

An·te·lope \ˈant-ᵊl-ˌōp\. **1** County in Nebraska. See table at NEBRASKA.

2 Island, SE Great Salt Lake, Utah; forms part of Davis co.; 15 ½ m. long.

Antelope Peak. **1** Mountain in Sierra Nevada on boundary bet. Mono and Alpine cos., E cen. California; 10,200 ft.

2 Mountain, SW Eureka co., cen. Nevada; 10,220 ft.

Antelope Range. Range in White Pine and Elko cos., NE Nevada.

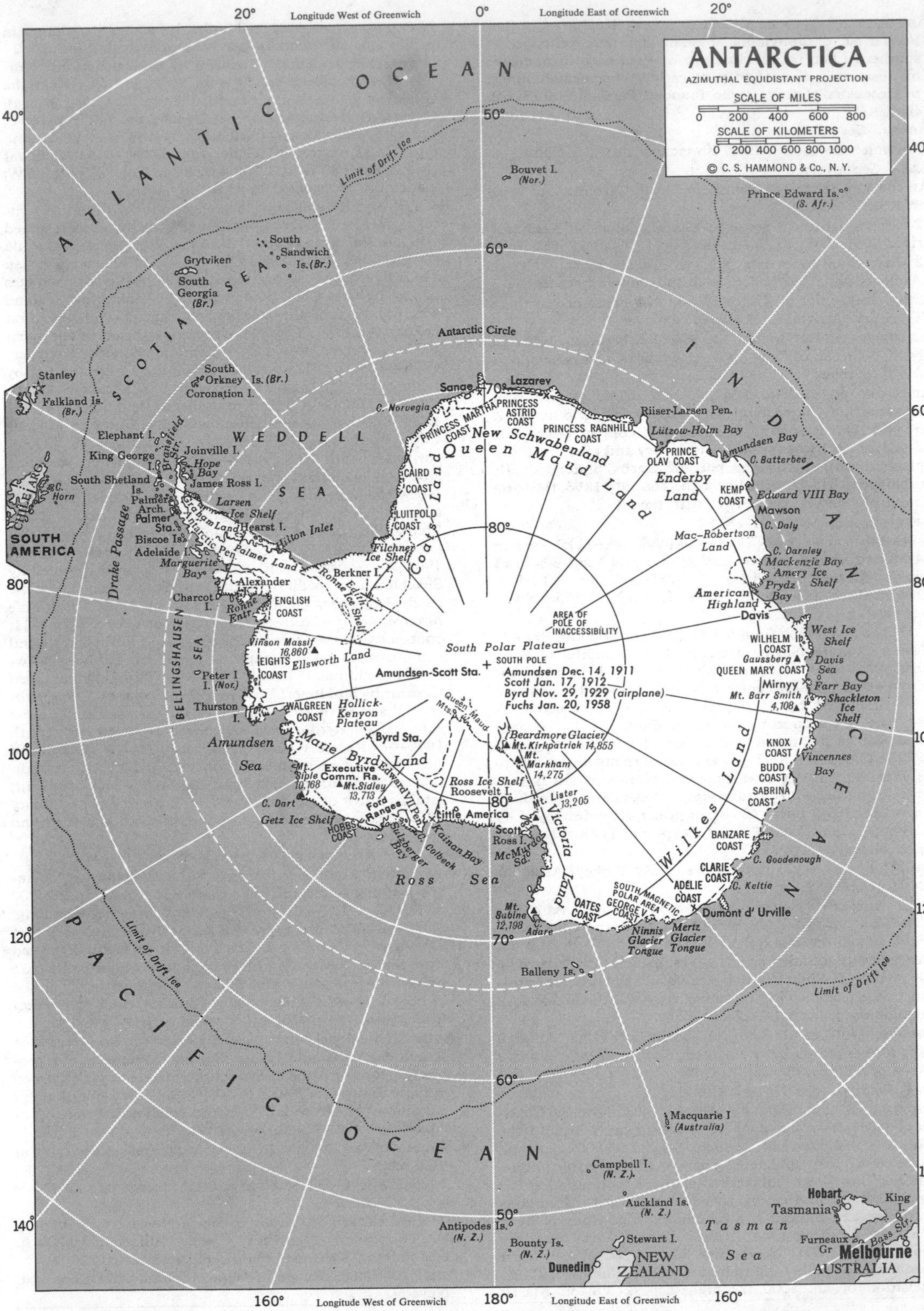
ANTARCTICA
AZIMUTHAL EQUIDISTANT PROJECTION
SCALE OF MILES
0 200 400 600 800
SCALE OF KILOMETERS
0 200 400 600 800 1000
© C. S. HAMMOND & Co., N. Y.
Longitude West of Greenwich
Longitude East of Greenwich
20°
0°
20°
40°
60°
80°
100°
120°
140°
160°
180°
50°
60°
70°
80°
ATLANTIC OCEAN
INDIAN OCEAN
PACIFIC OCEAN
Limit of Drift Ice
Bouvet I. (Nor.)
Prince Edward Is. (S. Afr.)
South Sandwich Is. (Br.)
Grytviken
South Georgia (Br.)
SCOTIA SEA
Antarctic Circle
Stanley
Falkland Is. (Br.)
South Orkney Is. (Br.)
Coronation I.
WEDDELL SEA
Elephant I.
King George I.
Bransfield Str.
Joinville I.
Hope Bay
James Ross I.
South Shetland Is.
C. Horn
CHILE
ARG.
SOUTH AMERICA
Drake Passage
Palmer Arch.
Palmer Sta.
Biscoe Is.
Adelaide I.
Marguerite Bay
Larsen Ice Shelf
Hearst I.
Graham Land
Antarctic Pen.
Palmer Land
Hilton Inlet
Alexander
Charcot I.
Ronne Entr.
ENGLISH COAST
BELLINGSHAUSEN SEA
Peter I I. (Nor.)
Thurston I.
Vinson Massif 16,860
EIGHTS COAST
Ellsworth Land
WALGREEN COAST
Hollick-Kenyon Plateau
Amundsen Sea
Marie Byrd Land
Byrd Sta.
Mt. Siple 10,168
Executive Comm. Ra.
Mt. Sidley 13,713
C. Dart
Getz Ice Shelf
HOBBS COAST
Ford Ranges
Edward VII Pen.
Sulzberger Bay
Colbeck
Kainan Bay
Little America
Ross Ice Shelf
Roosevelt I.
Ross Sea
Queen Maud Mts.
Beardmore Glacier
Mt. Kirkpatrick 14,855
Mt. Markham 14,275
Mt. Lister 13,205
Scott
Ross I.
McMurdo Sd.
Victoria Land
Mt. Sabine 12,198
C. Adare
OATES COAST
GEORGE V COAST
SOUTH MAGNETIC POLAR AREA
Ninnis Glacier Tongue
Mertz Glacier Tongue
ADÉLIE COAST
Dumont d' Urville
C. Keltie
CLARIE COAST
BANZARE COAST
C. Goodenough
Wilkes Land
SABRINA COAST
BUDD COAST
KNOX COAST
Vincennes Bay
Shackleton Ice Shelf
Mt. Barr Smith 4,108
Farr Bay
Mirnyy
Davis Sea
QUEEN MARY COAST
Gaussberg
WILHELM II COAST
West Ice Shelf
Davis
American Highland
Prydz Bay
Amery Ice Shelf
Mackenzie Bay
C. Darnley
Mac-Robertson Land
C. Daly
Mawson
Edward VIII Bay
KEMP COAST
Enderby Land
C. Batterbee
Amundsen Bay
PRINCE OLAV COAST
Lützow-Holm Bay
Riiser-Larsen Pen.
PRINCESS RAGNHILD COAST
PRINCESS ASTRID COAST
PRINCESS MARTHA COAST
Lazarev
Sanae
C. Norvegia
New Schwabenland
Queen Maud Land
CAIRD COAST
LUITPOLD COAST
Coats Land
Filchner Ice Shelf
Berkner I.
Edith Ronne Ice Shelf
AREA OF POLE OF INACCESSIBILITY
South Polar Plateau
SOUTH POLE
Amundsen Dec. 14, 1911
Scott Jan. 17, 1912
Byrd Nov. 29, 1929 (airplane)
Fuchs Jan. 20, 1958
Amundsen-Scott Sta.
Balleny Is.
Macquarie I (Australia)
Campbell I. (N. Z.)
Auckland Is. (N. Z.)
Antipodes Is. (N. Z.)
Bounty Is. (N. Z.)
Stewart I.
Dunedin
NEW ZEALAND
Tasman Sea
Hobart
Tasmania
King I.
Furneaux Gr
Bass Str.
Melbourne
AUSTRALIA

An·te·que·ra \ˌän-tā-ˈker-ə\. 1 Municipality, SW Bohol prov., Phil., 12 m. NNE of Tagbilaran; pop. (1969e) 16,500.
2 *or anc.* **An·ti·quar·ia** \ˌant-ə-ˈkwer-ē-ə\. Commune, Málaga prov., S Spain, 22 m. NNW of Málaga; pop. (1970p) 40,908; textiles; trades in oil, grain; captured from Moors 1410. Caves in vicinity.

An·tero, Mount \-an-ˈte(ə)r-(ˌ)ō\. Peak in Sawatch Range, Chaffee co., cen. Colorado; 14,269 ft.

Antero Peak. Mountain in Sawatch Range, Saguache co., S cen. Colorado; 13,245 ft.

An·tho·ny \ˈan(t)-thə-nē\. 1 City, ⊗ of Harper co., S Kansas, 62 m. S of Hutchinson; pop. (1970c) 2653; flour.
2 Village in Coventry town, Kent co., cen. Rhode Island, ab. 7 m. SW of Cranston; settled c. 1805.

Anthony Peak. Mountain in Sierra Nevada, SE Alpine co., E cen. California; 10,200 ft.

An·tho·nys Nose \ˌan(t)-thə-nēz-\. 1 Promontory, E side of Hudson river, New York, in Putnam co. near Peekskill; 900 ft.
2 Peak, Washington co., E New York; 1048 ft.

Anti–Atlas. See ATLAS MOUNTAINS.

An·tibes \ä^{n}-ˈtēb\ *or anc.* **An·tip·o·lis** \an-ˈtip-ə-ləs\. Seaport, Alpes-Maritimes dept., SE France, on Mediterranean 11 m. SW of Nice; pop. (1968c) 47,547; winter resort; trades in dried fruit, olives, oil, tobacco, perfumery, wine. Founded c. 340 B.C. by the Phocaeans; became Roman municipium, Roman remains still being extant; episcopal see 400–1244; sacked by Saracens in 9th cent.; heavily fortified, withstanding sieges 1746, 1815. The **Cap d'Antibes** \ˌkap-(ˌ)dä^{n}-ˈtēb\, 3 m. SSW, is also a noted winter resort.

Anticithera. See ANTIKÝTHĒRA.

An·ti·cos·ti Island \ˌant-ə-ˈkò-stē-\. Island in St. Lawrence estuary and Gulf of St. Lawrence, Quebec, E Canada; ab. 130 m. long; 3043 sq. m.; has well-developed fisheries and extensive forests. Discovered 1534 by Cartier; purchased 1895 by Henri Menier, French chocolate manufacturer; ownership transferred to Consolidated Paper Corporation 1926.

An·tie·tam Creek \an-ˈtēt-əm-\. Creek in N Maryland, rising in Franklin co., S Pennsylvania, and flowing S through Washington co., Md., to empty into Potomac river 7 m. N of Harpers Ferry. Near its confluence with Potomac is village of **Antietam,** 3 m. N of which, at Sharpsburg, was fought 1862 the battle of Antietam. See SHARPSBURG; UNITED STATES, *National Historical Parks.*

An·ti·fer, Cape \-ˌant-i-ˈfe(ə)r\ *or Fr.* **Cap d'Antifer** \kȧp-dä^{n}-tē-fer\. Cape, Normandy, N coast of France, 15 m. NNE of Le Havre; marks W terminus of chalk cliffs of French coast stretching WSW from the Somme and also the NE point of the Bay of the Seine.

An·ti·go \ˈant-i-ˌgō\. City, ⊗ of Langlade co., NE Wisconsin, 25 m. NE of Wausau; pop. (1970c) 9005; dairy products, canned goods, shoes, lumber; founded after the Civil War.

An·ti·go·nish \ˌant-i-gə-ˈnish\. 1 County, N Nova Scotia, Canada. See table at NOVA SCOTIA.
2 Town, its ⊗, on George Bay 35 m. E of New Glasgow; pop. (1971p) 5403; St. Francis Xavier Univ. (1853), Mount St. Bernard Coll. (1883); first British settlement made 1784 by disbanded officers and men of Nova Scotian regiment.

An·ti·gua \an-ˈtēg-(w)ə, -ˈtig-\. Island, E part of Leeward Is., E West Indies, 5260 m. SE of Puerto Rico; 108 sq. m.; together with Barbuda and Redonda Is. constitutes a self-governing state in association with Great Britain, with total area 171 sq. m.; pop. (1970e) 60,000; ✻ St. Johns. Mountainous, partly volcanic and partly of coral formation; many natural harbors, esp. St. Johns on NW, 2 m. long by $\frac{3}{4}$ m. wide; produces and refines sugar; also raises cotton, fruit, and vegetables; tourism.
History: Discovered by Columbus 1493; settled by English from St. Christopher 1632; occupied by French troops in 1666; returned to England by Treaty of Breda 1667; became self-governing 1967. Two areas (Parham Harbour on N coast, 430 acres, and shoreline strip on Judge's Bay, $1\frac{2}{5}$ sq. m.) leased to U.S. for seaplane base Mar. 27, 1941; 900 acres released 1960.

Antigua *or* **Antiqua Guatemala.** City, ✻ of Sacatepéquez dept., S cen. Guatemala; munic. pop. (1964p) 21,984; former ✻ of Guatemala; twice wrecked by earthquakes; coffee plantations.

An·ti·ký·thē·ra \ˌant-i-ˈkē-thə-ˌrä, -kə-ˈthir-ə\ *or formerly* **An·ti·ci·the·ra** \ˌant-ə-ˈsith-ə-rə\. Small island, midway in passage from Sea of Crete to Mediterranean, Greece, SE of Cerigo and NW of the NW point of Crete (Cape Busa).

An·ti–Leb·a·non \ˌant-i-ˈleb-ə-nən, -ˌnän\ *or* **Anti–Li·ban** \ˌä^{n}-tē-lē-ˈbä^{n}\ *or anc.* **An·ti·lib·a·nus** \ˌant-i-ˈlib-ə-nəs\ *or Arab.* **Al–Ja·bal ash Shar·qī** \al-ˌjab-əl-ash-ˈshär-kē\. Mountain range, running N and S bet. Lebanon and Syria; highest point Mt. Hermon 9232 ft.

An·ti·lla \än-ˈtē-(y)ə\. Coastal town and municipality, Oriente prov., E Cuba; munic. pop. (1967e) 38,890; sugar.

An·til·les, Greater *and* **Lesser Antilles** \-an-ˈtil-ēz\. Two groups of islands in the West Indies, bounding the Caribbean Sea on the N and E. See WEST INDIES.

Antilles françaises. See FRENCH WEST INDIES.

An·ti·och \ˈant-ē-ˌäk\. 1 City, Contra Costa co., W California, on S bank of San Joaquin river near mouth of the Sacramento; pop. (1970c) 28,060; shipping point for fertile agricultural region producing asparagus, celery, lettuce, almonds, grapes, apricots, wheat; vegetable canneries, fruit-packing plants, lumber mills, steelworks; settled 1849, incorp. 1890.
2 Village, Lake co., NE Illinois, on Wisconsin border 15 m. WNW of Waukegan; pop. (1970c) 3189; lake resort.
3 Ancient city, Pisidia, Asia Minor; at certain periods within boundaries of Phrygia; its ruins lie near Yalvaç in N İsparta prov., Turkey, 80 m. WNW of Konya. Visited by St. Paul (*Acts* xiii. 14–52).
4 *or* **Antiochea** *or* **Antiochia.** City, Turkey. See ANTAKYA.

An·ti·o·quia \ˌant-ē-ˈō-kē-ə\. 1 Department of NW Colombia. See table at COLOMBIA.
2 Town, Antioquia dept., Colombia; munic. pop. (1968e) 25,464; founded 1541.

An·tip·a·ros \an-ˈtip-ə-ˌräs, ˌant-i-ˈpa(ə)r-ˌäs\ *or Gk.* **An·dí·ka·ros** \än-ˌdē-ˈkär-ȯs\. One of the Cyclades Is., S Aegean Sea, SW of Paros I.; 13 sq. m.; pop. (1961c) 631; part of Cyclades dept., Greece.

Antipatria. See BERAT 2.

An·ti·pax·os \ˌant-i-ˈpak-ˌsäs\ *or Gk.* **An·di·pax·oi** \än-ˈdē-päk-sē\. Small island, S of Paxos, in the Ionian Sea off NW coast of Greece.

An·tip·o·des \an-ˈtip-ə-ˌdēz\. 1 Australia and New Zealand — a colloquial use originating in England but now found also in North America.
2 Group of rocky islands, 458 m. SE of Dunedin, New Zealand, 49°30′S, 177°30′E; belongs to New Zealand. Almost the exact antipodes of London, England.

Antipolis. See ANTIBES.

An·ti·po·lo \ˌänt-i-ˈpō-(ˌ)lō\. Municipality, S Rizal prov., Luzon, Phil., 12 m. E of Manila; pop. (1969e) 30,100; mecca for pilgrims who come to view miracle-working image of Our Lady of Peace brought from Mexico and placed in the church 1626. Fighting in region during latter part of World War II; captured Mar. 10, 1945 by Americans.

Antipyrgos. See TOBRUK.

Antiquaria. See ANTEQUERA 2.

An·ti·que \än-ˈtē-(ˌ)kā\. Province, W Panay, Phil.; 974 sq. m.; pop. (1970p) 289,627; ✻ San Jose de Buenavista; has long narrow coast bordering on NE Sulu Sea facing Cuyo

Is.; on N bounded by Capiz prov. and on E by Capiz and Iloilo provs.; comprises the plain, valleys, and W mountain slopes of range separating it from the rest of Panay; highest peak, on Capiz border, Mount Nangtud 6724 ft. Lacks good harbors; fishing important but agriculture main industry with sugarcane and copra chief export crops.

History: Probably first settled by peoples from Borneo; Spanish influence not felt until ab. 1600; for a long time troubled by Moro incursions; created a military province 1790 and a province 1798, reorganized 1860, and granted civil government by Americans April 1901.

An·ti·sa·na \ˌant-i-ˈsän-ə\. Volcano in the Andes Mts., N cen. Ecuador, just SE of Quito; 18,228 ft.

An·ti–Tau·rus Mountains \ˌant-i-ˌtȯr-əs-\. Range in E Turkey in Asia, NE of Taurus Mts. of which it is an extension toward the mountains of Armenia.

Antium. See ANZIO.

Antivari. Town, Yugoslavia. See BAR.

Ant·lers \ˈant-lərz\. Town, ⊗ of Pushmataha co., SE Oklahoma, 17 m. N of Hugo; pop. (1970c) 2685; corn, cotton; lumbering.

An·to·fa·gas·ta \ˌant-ə-fə-ˈgäs-tə\. 1 Province of N Chile. See table at CHILE.

2 Seaport, its ✱, 680 m. N of Santiago; pop. (1970p) 125,081; terminus of the international railroad to Oruro and La Paz, Bolivia; ore concentrating; fish meal, sulfuric acid; univ. (1956). Town founded on Bolivian territory 1870; became important as outlet for Chilean nitrate mines; occupied by Chile 1879 and ceded to her by Treaty of Valparaíso 1884 which followed War of the Pacific with Bolivia.

An·to·fa·lla \ˌant-ə-ˈfī-ə\. Volcanic peak, NW Argentina, near Chile border; 20,013 ft.

An·ton·gil Bay \äⁿ-tōⁿ-ˌzhēl-\. Inlet of Indian Ocean on NE coast of Malagasy Republic; 50 m. long and 25 m. wide; settled temporarily by French 1642.

An·to·ny \ˌäⁿ-tə-ˈnē\. Commune, Hauts-de-Seine dept., N France, 5 m. S of Paris; pop. (1968c) 56,638.

An·tra·tsit \ˌän-trət-ˈsit\. Town, Voroshilovgrad Oblast, Ukrainian S.S.R., U.S.S.R., 33 m. SSW of Voroshilovgrad; pop. (1969e) 54,000.

An·trim \ˈan-trəm\. 1 County in Michigan. See table at MICHIGAN.

2 Town, Hillsborough co., S New Hampshire, on Contoocook river 22 m. W of Manchester; pop. (1970c) 2122; Nathaniel Hawthorne Coll. (1962); first settled 1741, incorp. 1777.

3 County, NE Northern Ireland; 1200 sq. m.; pop. (1971p) 353,417 (including Belfast county borough, 712,408); ⊗ Belfast; bounded on N by Atlantic, NE and E by North Channel, SE by Belfast Lough, S by Lagan river (dividing it from co. Down), SW by Lough Neagh, and on W and NW by Bann river (dividing it from co. Londonderry); coastal area widely covered by basalt, the perpendicular basalt column known as Giant's Causeway being notable; greater part of interior is arable; produces oats, potatoes, flax; livestock rearing; linen, cement; shipbuilding, fishing, esp. for salmon; tourism.

4 Town, S co. Antrim, Northern Ireland, near NE shore of Lough Neagh; pop. (1961c) 1448; linen manufacturing, sawmilling; has a round tower 93 ft. high, the finest in Ulster.

Ant·si·ra·be \ˌänt-si-ˈräb-(ˌ)ā\ *or Fr.* **Ant·si·ra·bé** \äⁿt-sē-rä-bā\. Commune, Ankaratra Mts., cen. Malagasy Republic; pop. (1968e) 29,914; thermal springs.

Antsirane. See DIÉGO-SUAREZ.

An·tu·co \an-ˈtü-(ˌ)kō\. Volcanic peak in the Andes Mts., Bío-Bío prov., S cen. Chile, near border of Argentina; 9060 ft.

An·tung \ˈän-ˈdůŋ\. 1 Former province, S Manchukuo; 16,202 sq. m.; ✱ Tan-tung; formed 1932, dissolved 1945.

2 City, China. See TAN-TUNG.

Antunnacum. See ANDERNACH.

Ant·werp \ˈant-(ˌ)wərp\. 1 Agricultural and manufacturing province, N Belgium, adjoins Dutch frontier; 1104 sq. m.; pop. (1970e) 1,535,680; ✱ Antwerp; consists of extensive, sandy, but fertile, plain with tracts of heath and morass in N and NE; watered by Schelde river and its tributaries, the Rupel, Nèthe, and Dijle.

2 *or Fr.* **An·vers** \äⁿ-ver(s)\ *or Flem.* **Ant·wer·pen** \ˈänt-ˌver-pə(n)\. Commercial and manufacturing city, its ✱, on right bank of Schelde river 23 m. N of Brussels; pop. (1970e) 226,570; Belgium's major port; large volume of trade; shipyards, sawmills, automobile assembly plants, oil refineries; food processing, diamond cutting; State Univ. Center (1965), Royal Museum of Fine Arts (1880–90), zoological garden; improved and modernized, its ancient walls having been extended (now ab. 8 m.) and converted into boulevards; vestiges of ancient city remain in the 14th cent. cathedral of Notre Dame (largest Gothic structure in the Low Countries, containing three celebrated paintings by Rubens), the church of St. Jacques, the hôtel de ville, the Bourse, the Vieille Boucherie, and the Steen (part of ancient castle); fortified by 8 outlying forts, and later, by a second row of 15 forts.

History: By 11th cent., center of margraviate later attached to duchy of Brabant (*q.v.*); received municipal rights 1291; member of Hanseatic League 1315; gradually superseded Bruges as center for cloth trade with England in 15th cent.; part of Burgundian inheritance of Emperor Charles V (see BELGIUM); as distribution center for Spanish and Portuguese colonial trade, became commercial and financial capital of Europe in 16th cent.; attacked in "Spanish Fury" 1576; captured by duke of Parma 1585; declined because of these destructive invasions, eviction of Protestants, and finally, provision in Treaty of Westphalia (1648) closing Schelde to navigation (see AMSTERDAM 2); center of famous schools of painting (Massys in 16th cent., Van Dyck and Rubens in 17th cent.); began to revive after Napoleon's improvement of harbor c. 1803; part of kingdom of the Netherlands 1815–30; capture by French 1832 and cession to Belgian nationalists meant success of Belgian revolt from Netherlands; with expanded harbor and dock facilities and aided by free navigation of Schelde 1863, became one of world's leading ports; a fortified city, besieged Sept.–Oct. 1914 by Germans who held it until 1918. In World War II taken by Germans May 18, 1940; recaptured by British Sept. 4, 1944; port almost undamaged but, because of German resistance on Walcheren I. and along Schelde river, proved difficult and costly to open to meet Allied supply problems; port not finally free until Nov. 3.

Antwerp Island. See ANVERS ISLAND.

An Uaimh. See NAVAN.

Anu·da Island \ä-ˌnüd-ə-\ *or* **Cher·ry Island** \ˌcher-ē-\. One of the Santa Cruz Is., SW Pacific Ocean, in E part of group on 170°E long.

Anu·ra·dha·pu·ra \ˌən-ə-ˌräd-ə-ˈpůr-ə, ˌän-\. Town, ✱ of North Central Province, Ceylon, 106 m. NNE of Colombo; pop. (1968e) 30,000.

History: Ancient capital of Singhalese kings of Ceylon; traditionally founded in 5th cent. B.C.; sacred to Buddhists as site of conversion to Buddhism of Ceylonese ruler by Mahinda, son of Asoka, who visited the island ab. 251–246 B.C.; contains sacred Bo Tree, oldest existing historical tree, grown from a slip of the original sacred tree at Buddh Gaya (*q.v.*); abandoned as capital of Singhalese line 11th cent. A.D. in order to escape Tamil invasions; discovered in ruins and reopened by British in 19th cent.

Anvers. See ANTWERP 2.

An·vers Island \ˌäⁿ-ˌver(s)-\ *or formerly* **Ant·werp Island** \ˌant-(ˌ)wərp-\. Largest island of the Palmer Archipelago, off W coast of Antarctic Penin., Antarctica, 64°33′S, 63°35′W. Visited and named 1898 by a Belgian expedition.

Anxur. See TERRACINA.

An–yang \ˈän-ˈyäŋ\. Town, NE Honan prov., E cen. China, 90 m. N of K'ai-feng; pop. (1970e) 225,000; archaeological site and an ancient capital of Shang or Yin dynasty.

Anye Machin. See AMNE MACHIN SHAN.

Anyui \ə-ˈnyü-ē\. River, N Khabarovsk Krai, Russian S.F.S.R., U.S.S.R.; ab. 420 m. long; rises in Chukot Range and flows in two branches W to lower Kolyma river.

An·zac Cove \ˌan-ˌzak-\. Small bay, an inlet of the Aegean Sea, on Gallipoli Peninsula S of Anafarta Bay, Turkey in Europe, 14 m. from its S tip. Anzacs (Australian and New Zealand troops) landed here April 25, 1915, and engaged in actions up to June 30 to retain hold; battle of Sari Bair followed Aug. 6–10, 1915; all troops withdrawn Jan. 1916.

Anzan. See ANSHAN, Persia.

An·zhe·ro–Sud·zhensk \än-ˌzher-ə-sü-ˈjen(t)sk\. Town, Kemerovo Oblast, Russian S.F.S.R., U.S.S.R., in the Kuznetsk Basin 50 m. E of Tomsk on Trans-Siberian R.R.; pop. (1970p) 106,000; chemicals, mining machinery; coal, limestone.

An·zin \äⁿ-ˈzaⁿ\. Commune, Nord dept., N France, on Schelde river 26 m. SE of Lille; pop. (1968c) 15,634; center of richest coal-mining area in France. Destroyed in large part by Germans 1914–18.

An·zio \ˈan-zē-ˌō, ˈän(t)-sē-ˌō\ *or formerly* **Por·to d'Anzio** \ˌpōrt-ō-ˈdän(t)-sē-ˌō, ˌpȯrt-\ *or anc.* **An·ti·um** \ˈan-shē-əm\. Mediterranean seaport, Roma prov., Latium, Italy, 33 m. SSE of Rome; pop. (1968e) 22,108; fishing industry; detergent factory; seaside resort, with **Net·tu·no** \ne(t)-ˈtü-nō, nā(t)-\ (1½ m. E), the favorite of the Romans.

History: In ancient times, a pirate stronghold under the Volscians; lost independence after rising with Latium against Rome 341 B.C.; colonized by Nero who also improved harbor; sacked by Saracens in 9th and 10th cents.; modern town dates from restoration of harbor 1698 by Innocent XII; site of discovery of ancient artifacts, among them the statue often called *Maiden of Anzio;* birthplace of Nero and probably of Caligula. In World War II site of amphibious landing Jan. 22, 1944 of U.S. and British troops, with purpose of disrupting rear communications of Germans at Cassino; after much severe fighting Allied drive on Rome begun May 25, 1944.

An·zo·á·te·gui \ˌän(t)-sō-ˈät-i-gē\. State of N Venezuela. See table at VENEZUELA.

Aoba. See OBA.

Ao·la \ä-ˈō-lə\. Village and government station, N coast of Guadalcanal, E of the cen. part of the island, British Solomon Is., W Pacific Ocean; at mouth of **Aola River,** a short stream flowing N.

Ao·mo·ri \ˈaù-mə-(ˌ)rē, aù-ˈmōr-ē, -ˈmȯr-\. 1 Prefecture, Honshū, Japan; 3712 sq. m.; pop. (1970c) 1,427,520; ✻ Aomori; fishing; apples, rice.

2 Seaport city, its ✻, on Mutsu Bay; pop. (1970c) 240,063; has most important harbor and trading center of N Honshū; important transportation center; ships lumber and fish.

Aonia \ā-ˈō-nē-ə, -nyə\. A district of Boeotia, E cen. Greece, containing the mountains Helicon and Cithaeron, and hence sacred to the Muses.

Aóös. See VIJOSË.

Ao·raï, Mount \-ˈaù-ˌrī\. Peak in center of Tahiti I., Society Is., French Polynesia, near Mt. Orohena; 6788 ft.

Aorangi. See COOK, MOUNT 2.

Aor·nos \ā-ˈȯr-nəs\. 1 Town, Afghanistan. See TASH-KURGHĀN.

2 A great rock, thought to be in Swat, Pakistan, W of the Indus and NE of Peshawar; successfully stormed by Alexander the Great 326 B.C.

Ao·sta \ä-ˈō-stə\. 1 Province of Piedmont, Italy. See table at ITALY.

2 *or anc.* **Au·gus·ta Prae·to·ria** \ȯ-ˌgəs-tə-pri-ˈtōr-ē-ə, ə-ˌgəs-, -ˈtȯr-\. Commune, its ✻, also ✻ of Valle d'Aosta, NW Italy, 48 m. NNW of Turin, at junction of Great and Little St. Bernard Passes; pop. (1968e) 35,257; aluminum, iron and steel; tourism; cathedral said to have been founded by St. Eusebius; Roman remains, including triumphal arch of Augustus, city walls, ruins of amphitheater. Erected c. 24 B.C. as Roman military post by Augustus to celebrate Terentius Varro Murena's victory over the Salassi (25 B.C.).

Apa \ˈäp-ə\. River forming part of E boundary of Paraguay; 125 m. long; flows W into Paraguay river.

Apache \ə-ˈpach-ē\. County in Arizona. See table at ARIZONA.

Apache Mountains. Mountain group S of Guadalupe Mts., W Texas, bet. Pecos river and the Rio Grande; highest peak 5657 ft.

Ap·a·lach·ee Bay \ˌap-ə-ˌlach-ē-\. Inlet of Gulf of Mexico, N Florida, on S coast of Wakulla and Jefferson cos., receiving the Aucilla river on the NE.

Ap·a·lach·ia Dam \ˌap-ə-ˌlach-(ē-)ə-, -ˌläch-\. See table at TENNESSEE VALLEY AUTHORITY.

Ap·a·lach·i·co·la \ˌap-ə-ˌlach-ə-ˈkō-lə\. 1 Navigable river, NW Florida; 90 m. long; flows S into Apalachicola Bay (Gulf of Mexico). Former boundary bet. East and West Florida (see FLORIDA history). E terminus of Gulf Intracoastal Waterway (*q.v.*) is near its mouth.

2 Seaport city, ⊗ of Franklin co., NW Florida, on Apalachicola Bay at mouth of Apalachicola river; pop. (1970c) 3102; oyster beds; sport-fishing center; timber; founded c. 1821 as West Point, incorp. 1827, renamed 1831.

Apalachicola Bay. Inlet of Gulf of Mexico, NW Florida, on S coast of Franklin co., receiving the Apalachicola river on the N.

Apa·lit \ə-ˈpäl-ət\. Municipality, SE Pampanga prov., Luzon, Phil., on right bank of Pampanga river ab. 7 m. SE of San Fernando; pop. (1969e) 35,000; near the Manila-Dagupan R.R. at SW corner of Candaba swamp.

Apam \ä-ˈpäm\. 1 Town, Central Region, S Ghana, just E of Saltpond; pop. (1970p) 8828.

2 Town, SE Hidalgo state, E Mexico, N of Tlaxcala; munic. pop. (1970p) 21,550; in center of finest maguey region of Mexico and noted for its pulque.

Apamama. See ABEMAMA.

Ap·a·mea \ˌap-ə-ˈmē-ə\. Name of several ancient cities, esp.: (1) City, NW Mesopotamia, on left bank of Euphrates river W of Edessa. (2) **Apamea ad Oron·tem** \-ad-ə-ˈrän-təm\, city of W Syria on Orontes river, built by Seleucus Nicator; destroyed by Khosrau II of Persia 7th cent. A.D.; rebuilt, but completely ruined by earthquake 1152. (3) **Apamea Ci·bo·tus** \-si-ˈbō-təs\, city on the Maeander near its source and adjoining Celaenae, S Phrygia, built by Antiochus Soter 3d cent. B.C.; conquered 133 B.C. by Rome which kept control only after Mithridatic Wars (1st cent. B.C.); declined with rise of Constantinople as trade center; taken by Turks 1070.

Apa·pa \ə-ˈpäp-ə\. Town, Lagos State, SW Nigeria, across channel W of Lagos; has modern docks, with good anchorage for large vessels.

Apa·po·ris \ˌäp-ə-ˈpōr-(ˌ)ēs, -ˈpȯr-\. River, S Colombia; ab. 550 m. long; flows SE to Brazilian border and empties into Japurá river on Colombia-Brazil boundary of which it forms a small section.

Apar·ri \ə-ˈpär-ē\. Municipality on N coast of Cagayan prov., Luzon, Phil., on E side of Cagayan river near its mouth, 55 m. N of Tuguegarao; pop. (1969e) 45,700; has best harbor on N coast of Luzon with active coast and river trade; fishing, cattle raising; ships copra, corn, timber; first visited by Spaniards 1572; under Japanese control Dec. 1941–June 1945.

Apa·seo el Gran·de \ˌä-pə-ˈsā-ō-el-ˈgrän-dē\. Town, Guanajuato state, cen. Mexico, 20 m. WSW of Queretaro; munic. pop. (1970p) 34,523.

APENNINES—PRINCIPAL RANGES

NAME — English	NAME — Italian	LOCATION AND DESCRIPTION	HIGHEST POINT
NORTHERN			
Li·gu·ri·an Apennines \lə-'gyůr-ē-ən-\	Appennino Li·gu·re \-'lē-gů-rā\	From upper Bormida river near Savona SE to La Cisa Pass above La Spezia; along coast of Ligurian Sea; many hydraulic plants	Monte Bue (*or* Maggiorasca) 5,840 ft.; on N border of Liguria
Tus·can Apennines \'təs-kən-\	Appennino Tos·ca·no \-tòs-'kän-ō\ *or* Tos·co-E·mi·lia·no \-'tòs-kō-ˌā-mēl-'yän-ō\	From La Cisa Pass SE to sources of the Tiber, 43°50′N; detached range to SW, the Ap·u·an Alps \'ap-yə-wən-\ (*Ital.* Al·pi Apua·ne \äl-pē-ä-'pwän-ā\, W of the valley of the Serchio and containing marble quarries of Carrara	Monte Cimone 7,103 ft.; in S Emilia-Romagna, SW of Bologna
Um·bri·an Apennines \'əm-brē-ən-\	Appennino Um·bro \-'üm-brō\	From sources of the Tiber SSE to Scheggia Pass above Gubbio and near Cagli	Monte Nerone 5,007 ft.; in NW Marches
CENTRAL			
Roman Apennines	Appennino Um·bro-Mar·chi·gia·no \-'üm-brō-ˌmär-ki-'jän-ō\	From near Cagli SSE to Tronto river, 42°50′N; comprise many parallel ranges with low passes	Monte Vettore 8,130 ft.; on SW border of Marches
Abruz·zi Apennines \ä-'brüt-sē-, ə-\	Appennino Abruz·ze·se \-ˌäb-rüt-'sā-sā\	From the Tronto river SSE to the Sangro; consist of 3 parallel chains and include mountain knot of Gran Sasso d'Italia	Monte Corno 9,560 ft.; NNE of Aquila in Abruzzi
SOUTHERN			
Neapolitan Apennines	Appennino Na·po·le·ta·no \-ˌnäp-ō-lā-'tän-ō\	From the Sangro and Volturno valleys S to the Ofanto river; include the Ma·te·sian Mts. \mə-ˌtē-zhən-\ (*Ital.* Ma·te·se \mä-'tā-sā\	Monte Miletto 6,726 ft.; on N border of Campania
Lu·ca·ni·an Apennines \lü-'kā-nē-ən-\	Appennino Lu·ca·no \-lü-'kän-ō\	From the Ofanto river S to the Crati; mark roughly S limit of limestone Apennines	Monte Pollino 7,375 ft.; on border bet. Calabria and Basilicata
Ca·la·bri·an Apennines \kə-'lā-brē-ən-, -'läb-rē-\	Appennino Ca·la·bre·se \-ˌkäl-ə-'brā-sā\	From the Crati river to S tip of toe of peninsula; include granite plateau of Si·la·gian Mts. \sə-ˌlā-j(ē-)ən-\ (*Ital.* La Si·la \lä-'sē-lä\	Aspromonte 6,417 ft.; S Calabria, E of Reggio di Calabria

NOTABLE PASSES AND TUNNELS

NAME	PRONUNCIATION	DESCRIPTION AND LOCATION
Boc·chet·ta	\bō-'ket-ə\	Pass, Liguria, NW Ligurian Apennines, N of Genoa, 2,532 ft.; through it passes highway from Genoa to Alessandria; old Roman road, Genua (Genoa) to Dertona (Tortona)
Ci·sa *or* La Cisa	\(lä-)'chē-zä\	Pass, marking division bet. Ligurian and Tuscan Apennines, N Tuscany near source of Magra river, 3,414 ft.; railroad from La Spezia to Parma passes under it through tunnel
Fu·ta *or* La Futa	\(lä-)'füt-ə\	Pass, S Emilia, in Tuscan Apennines, 2,962 ft.; in valley of the Reno; highway and railroad, Florence to Bologna
Gio·vi	\'jō-vē\	Pass and railroad tunnel (5 m. 250 ft. long, alt. 1,080 ft.), NW Ligurian Apennines, N of Genoa; railroad, Genoa to Turin and Milan
Pe·sca·ra	\pe-'skär-ə\	Pass through Abruzzi Apennines along Pescara river, S of Gran Sasso d'Italia; railroad, Pescara to Rome, passes through several tunnels; old Roman road (Valerian Way)
Scheg·gia	\'skej-ə\	Pass, N Umbria, marking division bet. Northern and Central Apennines, 1,886 ft.; lies bet. Gubbio and Cagli

Apa·ta·ki \ˌap-ə-ˈtäk-ē\. Atoll, Tuamotu Archipelago, French Polynesia, S Pacific Ocean, ab. 65 m. NW of Fakarava atoll; 6 sq. m.; pop. (1967e) 108; has lagoon 18 m. long by 15 m. wide; pearl fishing.

Apa·tin \ˈä-pə-ˌtēn\. Town, NE Yugoslavia, on left bank of Danube, ab. 50 m. NW of Novi Sad; pop. (1965e) 17,000.

Apat·zin·gan \ə-ˌpät-sēŋ-ˈgän\. Town, Michoacán state, SW Mexico, 30 m. SW of Uruapan; munic. pop. (1970p) 63,-384.

Apa·yao \ə-ˈpä-ˌyau̇\. Former subprovince, N Luzon, Phil.; now part of Kalinga-Apayao (*q.v.*).

Apel·doorn \ˈap-əl-ˌdō(ə)rn, ˈäp-, -ˌdō(ə)rn\. Commune, Gelderland prov., Netherlands, ab. 17 m. N of Arnhem; pop. (1970e) 123,628; railroad junction; connected by canals with Zwolle and Zutphen; garden city; noted paper mills; chemicals, furniture; nearby is the Loo (Du. *Het Loo*), summer residence of royal family, originally a hunting lodge of the dukes of Gelder.

Ap·en·nines \ˈap-ə-ˌnīnz\ *or Ital.* **Ap·pen·ni·no** \ˌäp-ə-ˈnē-(ˌ)nō\ *or Lat.* **Ap·en·ni·nus Mons** \ˌap-ə-ˌnī-nəs-ˈmänz\. Mountain range, cen. Italy, arbitrarily divided from the Ligurian Alps in the NW, extending the full length of the peninsula in a bow-shaped range from near Savona in the NW to Reggio di Calabria in the S; ab. 838 m. long, 25 to 80 m. wide; highest peak Monte Corno 9560 ft. Source of most of the rivers of Italy— many short streams on steep slopes of E side and of longer rivers (Arno, Tiber, Volturno, Garigliano) on W. Crossed by many passes, ab. 13 of main importance. Climate severe in higher areas; vegetation includes (to 1500 ft.) olives, garden plants, and winter pasturage, (to 3000 ft.) chestnut and oak trees and agricultural products, (to 6000 ft.) beech and coniferous trees, and (above 6000 ft.) shrubs, Alpine plants, and summer pasturage; resemble Alps in geological structure. Famous for hill towns Pistoia, Florence, Arezzo, Aquila, Benevento, etc. See LOWER APENNINES.

For the principal ranges and notable passes and tunnels, see table on page 60.

Apenrade. See ÅBENRÅ.

Apeú \ˌap-ē-ˈü\. Island in Atlantic Ocean off NE coast of Pará state, Brazil.

Aph·ro·dis·i·as \ˌaf-rə-ˈdiz-ē-əs\. Ancient town, NE Caria, Asia Minor, S of the Maeander and ab. 50 m. ESE of modern Aydın; now in ruins; important as Byzantine town; home of Alexander of Aphrodisias, Greek philosopher, c. 200 A.D.

Aphrodisium. See ANNABA 2.

Api \ˈäp-ē\. Peak in the Himalayas, NW corner of Nepal, near source of Kali river; 23,399 ft.

Api. See EPI.

Apia \ə-ˈpē-ə, ä-\. Seaport, * of Western Samoa, SW cen. Pacific Ocean, on N coast of island of Upolu; pop. (1971e) 30,593; connects by steamship lines with Australia, New Zealand, and the United States; scene 1899 of naval disaster (see SAMOA).

Apiskigamish, Lake of. See BIENVILLE, LAKE OF.

Ap Iwan \ä-ˈpē-(ˌ)wän\. Peak in NW tip of Santa Cruz prov., S Argentina, on Chile border; 7600 ft.

Apo, Mount \-ˈäp-(ˌ)ō\. Highest mountain in the Philippines, SE Mindanao, ab. 24 m. WSW of City of Davao; 9690 ft.; an active volcano with three peaks on its summit; its slopes and immediate vicinity have been established as **Mount Apo National Park,** partly in Cotabato prov.

Apol·da \ä-ˈpōl-də\. City, Erfurt dist., East Germany, 81 m. ENE of Weimar; pop. (1970e) 29,087; knitted and woven goods (esp. hosiery), chemicals.

Apo·li·ma \ˌap-ə-ˈlē-mə\. Small island, Western Samoa, SW cen. Pacific Ocean, in middle of **Apolima Strait** (10 m. wide) bet. E Savai'i and W Upolu I.

Apol·lo \ə-ˈpäl-(ˌ)ō\. Borough, Armstrong co., W Pennsylvania, 25 m. ENE of Pittsburgh; pop. (1970c) 2308; beverages, cement; coal mines, gas wells, limestone quarries.

Ap·ol·lo·nia \ˌap-ə-ˈlō-nē-ə\. **1** Lake, Turkey. See APULYONT. **2** Name of numerous ancient towns, esp.:(1) Town on N coast of Cyrenaica, E of Cyrene and its port; belonged to the Pentapolis. (2) Town, Illyria, near coast of Adriatic S of Dyrrhachium; a Greek colony important commercially and culturally; Octavius studied here. (3) Town, E Macedonia, 30 m. SW of Amphipolis; visited by St. Paul (*Acts* xvii. 1). (4) Town, NE Thrace, on Pontus Euxinus coast; *mod.* **So·zo·pol** \sə-ˈzȯ-pəl, -ˈzō-\, village on Black Sea SSE of Burgas, Bulgaria.

Apop·ka \ə-ˈpäp-kə\. City, Orange co., cen. Florida penin., 10 m. NNW of Orlando; pop. (1970c) 4045; citrus fruit; truck farms. Settled 1856 on site of Seminole Indian village; incorp. 1929.

Apopka, Lake. Lake on W boundary of Orange co., cen. Florida penin.

Apos·tle Islands \ə-ˌpäs-əl-\. Group of islands in SW Lake Superior, off NW coast of Wisconsin; known also as the **Twelve Apostles,** but there are ab. 20 islands; they belong chiefly to Ashland co., Wisconsin, esp. islands of Madeline (with only settlement, La Pointe), Outer, Stockton, Oak, Michigan, and Long; Sand Island and two smaller islands belong to Bayfield co.

Apostolic See. See VATICAN CITY.

Ap·pa·lach·ia \ˌap-ə-ˈlach-(ē-)ə\. Mining town, Wise co., SW Virginia, 40 m. WNW of Bristol; pop. (1970c) 2161.

Ap·pa·la·chia \ˌap-ə-ˈlā-ch(ē-)ə, -ˈlach-(ē-)ə\ *or* **Ap·pa·la·chian America** \-ˌlā-chən-\. Region of SE United States including the various ranges of the Appalachian Mts., with no definite boundaries but generally comprising the Southern Tier of New York, most of Pennsylvania and the mountainous parts of Virginia, West Virginia, Kentucky, Tennessee, North Carolina, South Carolina, Georgia, and Alabama; historically (c. 1690–1756) included also early settlements beyond the colonies of the Atlantic seaboard.

Ap·pa·la·chian Mountains \ˌap-ə-ˌlā-chən-, -ˌlach-ən-\ *or* **Ap·pa·la·chians** \-ˈlā-chənz, -ˈlach-ənz\. Mountain system of E North America, extending from the Canadian provinces of Newfoundland, Quebec, and New Brunswick SW to cen. Alabama; it includes the White Mts. in New Hampshire, the Green Mts. in Vermont, the Catskills in New York, the Alleghenies in Pennsylvania, the Blue Ridge in Virginia and North Carolina, and the Cumberland Mts. in Tennessee; highest peak Mount Mitchell (6684 ft.) in Yancey co., North Carolina.

Appalachian Trail. Footpath extending from Mt. Katahdin in Maine to Springer Mountain, N Georgia; over 2000 m. long; traverses mountains of the Appalachian range; highest point on the trail Clingmans Dome (6643 ft.) in Great Smoky Mts.

Ap·pa·noose \ˈap-ə-ˌnüs\. County in Iowa. See table at IOWA.

Ap·pe·kun·ny Mountain \ˌap-ə-ˌkü-nē-\. Peak in Glacier National Park, NW Montana; 9053 ft.

Appennino. Italian form of *Apennines.* See APENNINES.

Ap·pen·zell \ˈap-ən-ˌzel, ˌäp-ən(t)-ˌsel\. **1** Swiss canton; subdivided into demicantons: **Appenzell In·ner Rhodes** \-ˈin-ə(r)-ˌrōdz, -ˌrȯd\ *or Ger.* **Appenzell Inner Rho·den** \-ˌrōd-ᵊn\, almost wholly Catholic, and **Appenzell Outer Rhodes** *or Ger.* **Appenzell Aus·ser Rhoden** \-ˈau̇-sə(r)-\, almost wholly Protestant. Agricultural and manufacturing canton, notable for scenic beauty; highest point the Säntis 8205 ft. Originally part of dominions of princely abbots of St. Gallen; formed alliance with Swabian imperial cities and adopted own constitution 1377; under protection of

Swiss Confederation 1411, becoming a member 1513; divided 1597 into demicantons; assumed present status 1803; known for its institution of the Landsgemeinde. See table at SWITZERLAND.

2 Commune, ✱ of Appenzell Inner Rhodes demicanton, NE Switzerland, 7 m. S of St. Gallen; pop. (1970c) 5217; resort; embroidery, textiles; sheep raising; ancient chapel of abbots of St. Gallen, who made summer home here; Capuchin convent and monastery; 2 m. to the SE is **Weissbad** \ˈvīs-(ˌ)bät\, a summer resort, site of one of oldest whey cure establishments in Switzerland.

Ap·pi·an Way \ˌap-ē-ən-\ *or Lat.* **Via Ap·pia** \ˌvī-ə-ˈap-ē-ə, ˌvē-ə-\. First paved Roman road; extended 132 m. straight SE from Rome past Lake Albanus to Tarracina, thence along the coast and inland to Capua; built 312 B.C. by Appius Claudius Caecus, censor; later extended through Benevenum to Brundisium, total of 366 m.; near Rome lined with tombs and monuments.

Ap·pi·sto·ki Peak \ˌap-ə-ˌstō-kē-\. Mountain in Glacier National Park, NW Montana, near Two Medicine Lake; 8135 ft.

Ap·ple·by \ˈap-əl-bē\. Municipal borough, ⊗ of Westmorland, NW England, on the Eden 26 m. SE of Carlisle; pop. (1971p) 1946; trade center in agricultural area; baronial castle (rebuilt in 17th cent.).

Ap·ple·gate Peak \ˌap-əl-ˌgāt-\. Mountain, W Klamath co., SW Oregon, on S rim of Crater Lake; 8135 ft.

Ap·ple·ton \ˈap-əl-tən, -əlt-ᵊn\. 1 Village, Swift co., W Minnesota, on Minnesota river 23 m. NW of Montevideo; pop. (1970c) 1789; dairy products, flour.

2 Commercial and industrial city, ⊗ of Outagamie co., E Wisconsin, on Fox river 17 m. N of Oshkosh; pop. (1970c) 57,143; canned goods, paper and paper products, flour, knit goods, farm implements; Lawrence Univ. (1847); incorporated 1857.

Ap·ple Valley \ˌap-əl-\. Village, Dakota co., SE Minnesota; pop. (1970c) 8502; residential suburb of St. Paul.

Ap·pling \ˈap-liŋ\. 1 County in Georgia. See table at GEORGIA.

2 Town, ⊗ of Columbia co., E Georgia; pop. (1970c) 2216.

Ap·po·mat·tox \ˌap-ə-ˈmat-əks\. 1 River, SE cen. Virginia; 137 m. long; rises in Appomattox co., flows E into James river at Hopewell; navigable to Petersburg.

2 County in Virginia. See table at VIRGINIA.

3 Town, its ⊗, 18 m. E of Lynchburg; pop. (1970c) 1400; at old Appomattox Courthouse (county town) on April 9, 1865 Confederates under Gen. Robert E. Lee surrendered to Union army under Gen. Ulysses S. Grant; site now a national historical park: see UNITED STATES, *National Historical Parks* (Appomattox Court House).

Ap·po·naug \ˈap-ə-ˌnȯg\. Village, Kent co., cen. Rhode Island, W of Warwick; shopping center of Warwick; textile bleaching and printing.

Apra Harbor \ˌäp-rə-\ *also* **Port Apra** *or formerly (Span.)* **San Lu·is d'Apra** \ˌsän-lü-ˌēs-ˈdäp-rə\. Harbor on W coast of island of Guam, W Pacific Ocean; best anchorage in the island, protected on S by Orote Penin. and on N by Cabras I. and reefs; Piti, the port of entry, is on its NE shore. Scene of Allied landing in invasion of Guam July 20, 1944.

Apre·mont \ˌap-rə-ˈmōⁿ, ˈap-rə-ˌmänt\. 1 Village, Ardennes dept., NE France, on Aire river ab. 20 m. NW of Verdun; pop. (1962c) 221; scene of advance of U.S. division Sept.–Oct. 1918 in battle of the Argonne.

2 *or in full* **Apremont–la–For·êt** \-ˌläf-ō-ˈrā\. Village, Meuse dept., NE France, 4 m. SE of St-Mihiel; pop. (1962c) 179; landmark of American front 1918.

Apri·lia \ə-ˈprēl-yə\. Commune, Latina prov., SW Latium, W Italy, near Anzio and ab. 22 m. S of Rome; pop. (1968e) 24,441; founded on reclaimed land of Agro Pontino 1937. Occupied by American patrols Jan. 25, 1944.

Ap·she·ron \ˌäp-shə-ˈrȯn\. Peninsula projecting into the Caspian Sea, E Azerbaijan S.S.R., U.S.S.R.; 400 sq. m.; extensive oil fields; Baku is on SW coast.

Apt \ˈapt\ *or anc.* **Ap·ta Ju·lia** \ˌap-tə-ˈjül-yə\. Commune, Vaucluse dept., SE France, 29 m. E of Avignon; pop. (1968c) 9623; ocher and sulfur mines; meteorological station; episcopal see 3d–18th cents.; 8th cent. church (former cathedral); Roman remains. Capital city of Vulgientes; beautified by Julius Caesar (who added to its name the epithet *Julia*); became French 1481.

Apuan Alps. See table at APENNINES.

Apuania. 1 Province, Italy. See MASSA-CARRARA.

2 Commune, Italy. See CARRARA.

Apu·ca·ra·na \ˌap-ə-kə-ˈran-ə\. Municipality, Paraná state, S Brazil, 300 m. W of São Paulo; pop. (1968e) 79,645.

Apu·lia \ə-ˈpyül-yə\; *Ital.* **Pu·glia** \ˈpül-(ˌ)yä\ *or* **Le Pu·glie** \lā-ˈpül-(ˌ)yā\. Autonomous region, SE Italy, bet. Adriatic on N and Apennines and Gulf of Taranto on S; 7469 sq. m.; pop. (1968e) 3,616,086; ✱ Bari; vast coastal plain; watered by Ofanto river; wine, wheat, oats, olives, fruits, tobacco; livestock raising, production of salt and niter from coastal lakes; fishing.

History: Home of ancient Apulians, a people allied to Rome in second Samnite War (322–304 B.C.), but unfriendly during Punic Wars; scene of fighting during Punic Wars (see CANNAE); came under rule of republican Rome by end of 3d cent. B.C.; united with Calabria (under this name) to form administrative unit (Regio II) of Roman Empire; conquered by Lombards 668 A.D.; recovered by Byzantine Empire 9th cent.; became county after conquest by Normans 1042; raised to duchy 1059 by Pope Nicholas II who gave it to Robert Guiscard; united with kingdom of the Two Sicilies 1130; invaded by papal forces 1228–29 in struggle bet. Frederick II and Pope Gregory IX. For later history, see NAPLES 3.

Apulum. See ALBA IULIA.

Apul·yont \ˌäp-ˌu̇l-ˈyȯnt\ *also* **Abul·liont** \ˌäb-ˌu̇l-ˈyȯnt\ *or Lat.* **Ap·ol·lo·nia** \ˌap-ə-ˈlō-nē-ə\. Lake, NW Turkey in Asia, W of Bursa and S of Sea of Marmara; 18 m. long, 12 m. wide; traversed by Atranos river.

Apu·re \ə-ˈpu̇(ə)r-(ˌ)ā\. 1 River, W Venezuela; 509 m. long; rises on E slopes of N Andes, flows E into Orinoco river; navigable for over 300 m.

2 State of W Venezuela. See table at VENEZUELA.

Apu·rí·mac \ˌäp-ə-ˈrē-ˌmäk\. 1 River, S and cen. Peru; 428 m. long; rises in Lake Villafro in Andes Mts. in Arequipa dept., less than 100 m. from the Pacific, flows N to unite with Urubamba river and form Ucayali river, an upper tributary of the Amazon; its lower course for short stretches called the Perené and Tambo.

2 Department of S Peru. See table at PERU.

'Aqa·ba *or* **Aka·ba** \ˈäk-ə-bə, ˈak-\ *or* **Al–'Aqa·bah** \al-\; *anc.* **Elath** \ˈē-ˌlath\ *or later* **Ae·la·na** \ē-ˈlā-nə\. Seaport town, SW Jordan, at head of the Gulf of 'Aqaba and on highway S from Ma'an, at S end of great valley of the Wadi al-'Araba; pop. (1964e) 10,000; Jordan's only seaport.

History: As ancient Elath was on the caravan route from Egypt to Arabia and just E of Ezion-geber; a chief city of the Edomites. Called Aelana by the Romans and made a strong military post. In medieval times an important port of Palestine; later held by Egypt, then by Turkey; part of Hejaz 1917–25 and in 1925 taken over by Jordan; occupied by Israel Nov. 1956–Jan. 1957.

'Aqaba, Gulf of *or anc.* **Si·nus Ae·la·nit·i·cus** \ˌsī-nə-ˌsē-lə-ˈnit-i-kəs\. Northeast extension of the Red Sea, bet. NW Saudi Arabia and the Sinai Penin., Egypt; 100 m. long.

Aqqaqir, Al–. See AL-AQQAQIR.

Aqsu. Town, China. See AKSU 3.

Aqsur, Al–. See LUXOR.

Aquae. See ACQUI TERME.

Aquae Augustae. See DAX.

Aquae Calidae. See BATH 6.

Aquae Flaviae. See CHAVES.

Aquae Grani. See AACHEN 2.

Aquae Gratianae. See AIX-LES-BAINS.

Aquae Mortuae. See AIGUES-MORTES.

Aquae Panoniae. See BADEN 1.

Aquae Sextiae. See AIX.

Aquae Solis. See BATH 6.

Aquae Statiellae. See ACQUI TERME.

Aquae Tarbellicae. See DAX.

Aqui·da·ban *or Span.* **Aqui·da·bán** \ˌäk-ē-də-ˈbän\. River, N cen. Paraguay; ab. 150 m. long; flows W to Paraguay river. Scene of battle ending war (1865–70) of Paraguay with Argentina, Brazil, and Uruguay, in which Paraguayan forces were completely crushed and Francisco Solano López was killed 1870.

Aquid·neck Island \ə-ˈkwid-ˌnek-\. Rhode Island (the island), in Narragansett Bay, R.I.; 39 sq. m.

Aqui·la \ˈäk-wi-lə, ˈak-\ *or* **L'Aquila** \ˈläk-, ˈlak-\ *or in full* **Aquila de·gli Abruz·zi** \-ˌdāl-yē-ä-ˈbrüt-sē, -yē-ə-\. 1 Province of Abruzzi, Italy. See table at ITALY. 2 Commune, its ✱ and ✱ of Abruzzi, cen. Italy, in valley of the Aterno 54 m. NE of Rome; pop. (1968e) 58,631; summer resort; 2362 ft. above sea level; bricks, radio equipment; tourism; univ. (1952). Founded by Conrad IV in 1253–54; episcopal see 1257; part of kingdom of Italy 1860.

Aqui·le·ia *or* **Aqui·le·ja** \ˌäk-wə-ˈlā-(y)ə\ *or anc.* **Aqui·le·ia** \ˌak-wə-ˈlē-(y)ə\ *or medieval* **Aglar** \ə-ˈglär\. Town, Udine prov., Friuli-Venezia Giulia, Italy, 6 m. inland at head of Adriatic and 22 m. WNW of Trieste; pop. (1968e) 3149; ancient cathedral; formerly in Austria.

History: Founded by Romans as strongly fortified outpost against Illyrian peoples 181 B.C.; became most flourishing commercial city of northern Italy; ravaged by Attila and Huns 452 A.D., whereupon inhabitants fled to lagoons (see VENICE 3); seat of patriarch who refused allegiance to Roman see (6th cent.); belonged to Carolingian march of the Friuli in 9th line and to march of Verona and Aquileia (fief of Holy Roman Empire); came under authority of Venice in 15th cent.

Aquin·cum \ə-ˈkwiŋ-kəm\. Ancient town, Pannonia, on the Danube; the modern Buda (see BUDAPEST).

Aquiry. See ACRE.

Aquisgranum. see AACHEN 2.

Aq·ui·taine \ˈak-wə-ˌtān\. Historical region of SW France; originally roughly equivalent in extent to Roman Aquitania at time of its conquest by Clovis, later shrinking in size; ✱ Toulouse.

History: For earlier history, see AQUITANIA. After Frankish conquest 507 A.D., became semiautonomous duchy until subjugated by Pepin the Short 768; made subkingdom by Charlemagne and given to his son Louis 781; reunited to French crown 877; after Carolingian decline, became powerful feudal duchy which by 11th cent. controlled most of France south of Loire; passed to Capetian line when Eleanor of Aquitaine married Louis VII 1137, and later to English Plantagenets on Eleanor's second marriage to Henry II 1152; from about 10th cent. called Guienne, a corruption of Aquitaine. For later history, see GUIENNE and GASCONY.

Aq·ui·ta·nia \ˌak-wə-ˈtā-nyə, -nē-ə\. A Roman division of SW Gaul; under Caesar consisted of country bet. Pyrenees Mts. and Garonne river peopled by an Iberic race or races, the Aquitani, whom he conquered 56 B.C.; under Augustus made one of 5 divisions of Gaul with capital at Bourges and expanded to include all of Gaul S and W of the Loire (Liger) and Allier (Elaver) rivers; in 3d cent. A.D. subdivided into: **Aquitania Pri·ma**\-ˈprī-mə\, E part of district bet. Loire and Garonne rivers, with capital at Bourges; **Aquitania Se·cun·da** \-sə-ˈkən-də\, W part of district, with capital at Bordeaux; became the Guienne of medieval France; **Aquitania Ter·tia** \-ˈtər-shē-ə, -shə\ *or* **No·vem·pop·u·la·na** \ˌnō-vəm-ˌpäp-yə-ˈlā-nə\, the original Aquitania bet. the Pyrenees and the Garonne, with capital at Éauze. Conquered by Visigoths c. 419; became part of Frankish kingdom on defeat of Visigoth king, Alaric II, by Clovis, king of the Franks, in battle near Poitiers 507. For later history, see AQUITAINE and GUIENNE.

Aquitanicus Sinus. See BISCAY, BAY OF.

Ar·ab \ˈā-ˌrab\. Town, Marshall co., NE Alabama, 28 m. S of Huntsville; pop. (1970c) 4399; diversified agriculture.

Arab, Shatt–al–. See SHATT-AL-ARAB.

'Ara·ba, Wa·di al– \ˌwäd-ē-al-ˈar-ə-bə, -ˈär-\ *or Bib.* **Ar·a·bah** \ˈar-ə-bə\. Large valley extending S from the Dead Sea to the Gulf of 'Aqaba, on the border bet. SE Israel and SW Jordan.

Ara·ba al–Mad·fu·na \ə-ˈräb-ə-ˌal-mad-ˈfü-nə\. Village, Egypt; site of ancient Abydos. See ABYDOS 2.

Ara·bat \ˌar-ə-ˈbät, ˌär-\ *or* **Tongue of Arabat** *or Russ.* **Ara·bat·ska·ya Strel·ka** \-ˌbät-skə-yə-ˈstrel-kə\. Narrow sandy peninsula on W side of Sea of Azov; part of NE Crimean Oblast, Ukrainian S.S.R., U.S.S.R.; ab. 70 m. long.

Arabia. See ARABIAN PENINSULA.

Arabia Deserta. See ARABIAN PENINSULA.

Arabia Felix. See ARABIAN PENINSULA.

Ara·bi·an Desert \ə-ˌrā-bē-ən-\ *or* **Eastern Desert.** Desert area, E Egypt, E of Nile and bordering Gulf of Suez and N Red Sea; from ab. 22°N to the Mediterranean; 86,000 sq. m.

Arabian Gulf. See PERSIAN GULF 1.

Arabian Peninsula *or* **Ara·bia** \ə-ˈrā-bē-ə\ *or Turk.* **Ara·bi·stan** \är-ə-bi-ˈstän, ə-ˈräb-i-ˌ\. Great peninsula of SW Asia, extending N and S bet. 12° and 32°N lat. and 35° and 60°E long.; length (along Red Sea) ab. 1200 m., max. breadth (from S Yemen [✱ San'a] to NE Oman) 1300 m.; ab. 1,000,000 sq. m. In early times divided into: **Arabia Pe·traea** \-pə-ˈtrē-ə\, the NW part including Sinai Peninsula (not part of modern Arabian Peninsula), the only part ever conquered, which became a Roman province; **Arabia De·ser·ta** \-di-ˈzərt-ə\, the N part bet. Syria and Mesopotamia; **Arabia Fe·lix** \-ˈfē-liks\ the main part of the peninsula, but by some geographers restricted to Yemen (✱ San'a).

Bounded on N by Jordan and Iraq, on E by Persian Gulf and Gulf of Oman, on SE by Arabian Sea, on S by Gulf of Aden, on W by Red Sea; fertile in some coastal regions, but arid plateau in its central part; no rivers, but many short wadis; only a few islands along its coast; important oil-producing region. *Political divisions:* Bahrain (islands in Persian Gulf), Kuwait, Oman, Qatar, Saudi Arabia, United Arab Emirates, Yemen (✱ Aden), Yemen (✱ San'a).

History: Seat of little-known southern Minaean and Sabaean kingdoms in 1st millennium B.C.; invaded or crossed by Assyrians, Hebrews, and at different times by Romans; part held by Persians 575 A.D.; before Mohammed, occupied by Semitic tribes; consolidation begun by Mohammed and extended after his death 632; center of orthodox caliphate 632–661; under Ommiad caliphate, ruled from Damascus 661–750; lapsed into tribal warfare following Muslim disintegration in 8th cent.; dominated by Karmathians in 10th cent.; in general dominated by Mamelukes and after 1517 by the Ottoman Turks but subdivisions of Al-Hasa, Oman, Yemen, and Nejd were practically independent; influenced by rise of Wahabi movement centered in Nejd which organized resistance against the Turks (18th–19th cents.); reconquered for Turks by Egyptian Mehemet Ali 1811–20; Wahabi empire reestablished 1843–65; internally divided bet. tribes and sects (see HEJAZ and NEJD); in revolt against Turks 1916; resistance directed by Col. Lawrence 1917; gradual consolidation by 1932 of Saudi Arabia under ibn-Saud; for recent history, see individual states.

Arabian Sea. The section of the Indian Ocean lying bet. India on the E and Arabian Peninsula on the W.

Arabistan. 1 Peninsula, Asia. See ARABIAN PENINSULA.

2 Province, Iran. See KHŪZESTĀN.

Arabkir. See ARAPKİR.

Arab League. Political organization, consisting of Algeria, Bahrain, Egypt, Iraq, Jordan, Kuwait, Lebanon, Libya, Morocco, Oman, Qatar, Saudi Arabia, Syria, Tunisia, United Arab Emirates, Yemen (✱ San'a); headquarters at Cairo, Egypt; purpose is to improve cooperation among Arab states. Formed 1945; boycotted by Egypt 1962–63 and by Tunisia after 1965; has coordinated members' policies with regard to economic boycott of Israel and oil deliveries to the West.

Arabos, Los. See LOS ARABOS.

Arab Republic of Egypt. See EGYPT.

Arab Republics, Confederation of. Confederation, consisting of Egypt, Libya, and Syria; formed 1971.

Ar·abs Gulf \ˌar-əbz-\. Inlet of Mediterranean Sea, W of Alexandria, N Egypt.

Ar·a·by \ˈar-ə-bē\. Archaic or poetic for ARABIAN PENINSULA.

Ara·ca·ju \ˌar-ə-kə-ˈzhü\. City, ✱ of Sergipe state, E Brazil, on the right bank at the mouth of the Cotinguiba river; munic. pop. (1970p) 183,333; in region producing cotton and sugar; univ. (1967).

Ara·ca·ti \ˌar-ə-kə-ˈtē\. Seaport, Ceará state, NE Brazil, at mouth of Jaguaribe river; munic. pop. (1968e) 43,850.

Ara·ça·tu·ba \ˌar-ə-sə-ˈtü-bə\. City, São Paulo state, SE Brazil; munic. pop. (1968e) 95,946.

Ar·a·cho·sia \ˌar-ə-ˈkō-zh(ē-)ə\. Ancient province, E part of Persian Empire and of the empire of Alexander; about equivalent to S part of modern Afghanistan.

Arachthus. See ARAKHTHOS.

Arad \ä-ˈräd\. 1 County, W Romania. See table at ROMANIA.

2 City, W Romania, on Mureşul river; pop. (1969e) 115,468; transportation and commercial center; machine tools, textiles, railway cars, alcohol, cattle, timber. A Turkish fort in 17th cent.; belonged to Hungary after 1699 and figured prominently in Hungarian struggle for independence 1848–49; passed to Romania 1919 after World War I.

Ara·da \ə-ˈräd-ə\. Town, Chad, N cen. Africa, N of Abéché.

Ara·duey \ˌär-ə-ˈdwā\ *also* **Val·de·ra·duey** \ˌväl-də-rä-ˈdwā\. River, NW cen. Spain; ab. 100 m. long; tributary of Duero river.

Aradus. See ARWAD.

Ara·fat \ˌär-ə-ˈfat\. Granite hill 15 m. SE of Mecca, Saudi Arabia; object of pilgrimages.

Ar·a·fu·ra Sea \ˌar-ə-ˌfu̇r-ə-\. Sea bet. N Australia and Indonesia; 800 m. long by ab. 350 m. wide; W New Guinea touches it on NE and several groups of islands (Tanimbar, Kai, and Aru) lie along its N border.

Ar·a·gats \ˌar-ə-ˈgats\. Mountain, Armenian S.S.R., U.S.S.R.; 13,418 ft.

Ar·a·gon \ˈar-ə-ˌgän, -gən\ *or Span.* **Ara·gón** \ˌär-ə-ˈgȯn\. 1 River, N Spain; ab. 80 m. long; rises in the Pyrenees and flows SW into Ebro river in Navarra prov.

2 Region and ancient kingdom, NE Spain; 18,405 sq. m.; bounded on N by the Pyrenees, E by Catalonia, SE by Valencia, SW by New Castile, W by Old Castile, and NW by Navarre; comprises the modern provinces of Huesca, Zaragoza, and Teruel; mountainous in N and S portions.

History: After overthrow of Carthaginian power in Spain, became part of Roman province of Hispania Tarraconensis; conquered by Visigoths in 5th cent. A.D. and by Moors in 8th cent.; became Carolingian county, emerging from Navarrese rule as independent kingdom 1035; ruled Navarre 1076–1134, Saragossa 1118; united with Catalonia 1137 and 1164, with county of Barcelona 1150; lost Provence 1196; conquered Balearic Is. 1229–35, Valencia 1238; ruler of Aragon obtained kingdom of the Two Sicilies (1282–85) which he later surrendered for Sardinia and Corsica; held duchy of Athens 1311–88; conquered Naples 1435; united with Castile 1479. See SPAIN.

Ara·go·na \ˌär-ə-ˈgō-nə, ˌar-\. Commune, Agrigento prov., SW Sicily, Italy, 7 m. N of Agrigento; pop. (1968e) 13,722; sulfur mines; near mud volcano **Mac·ca·lu·ba** \ˌmäk-ə-ˈlü-bə\, 135 ft. high, 860 ft. above sea level.

Ara·gua \ə-ˈräg-wə\. 1 State of N Venezuela. See table at VENEZUELA.

2 *or* **Aragua de Bar·ce·lo·na** \-də-ˌbär-sə-ˈlō-nə\. Town, Anzoátegui state, N Venezuela, 62 m. SSW of Barcelona; pop. (1961c) 8241.

Ara·guaia *or* **Ara·guaya** \ˌar-ə-ˈgwī-ə\. River, cen. Brazil; 1366 m. long; rises in S cen. Mato Grosso state and flows N into Tocantins river.

Ara·gua·ri \ˌar-ə-gwə-ˈrē\. 1 River, NE Brazil; ab. 240 m. long; flows into Atlantic N of Amazon river.

2 Municipality, W Minas Gerais state, E Brazil, 290 m. WNW of Belo Horizonte; pop. (1968e) 59,798.

Arahal, El. See EL ARAHAL.

Araish, Al–. See LARACHE.

Araito. See ATLASOVA.

Ara Jovis. See ARANJUEZ.

Arāk \ə-ˈräk\ *or formerly* **Sul·tan·a·bad** \ˌsu̇l-ˌtän-ə-ˈbäd\. City, W cen. Iran; pop. (1966c) 72,930; on highway N from Ahvāz, junction point ab. equally distant (80 m.) from Hamadān to NW and Qom to NE; pottery and metalwork.

Ara·ka·ka \ˌar-ə-ˈkäk-ə\. Town, W Guyana, on Barima river 140 m. NW of Georgetown; goldfields.

Ara·kan \ˌär-ə-ˈkän, ˌar-ə-ˈkan\. Division of Burma along the coast of NE Bay of Bengal; 14,194 sq. m.; pop. (1969e) 1,847,000; ✱ Sittwe; contains Mayu, Kaladan, and Lemro rivers; E border formed by the Arakan Yoma range; rice, tobacco. Conquered by Burmese 1784; ceded to British 1826 by Treaty of Yandabu (*q.v.*); scene of much fighting bet. Japanese and Allied forces 1942–45.

Arakan Hill Tracts. Former district of Arakan division, Burma; 1901 sq. m.; now part of Chin Special division.

Arakan Yo·ma \-ˈyō-mə\. Mountain range in W cen. Burma, extending from Manipur state in Assam, NE India, S to Cape Negrais; highest peak Saramati 12,663 ft.; includes the Naga Hills, Chin Hills, and Lushai Hills and forms barrier between Burma and India.

Arakh·thos \ˈär-äk-ˌthȯs\ *or* **Ar·ta** \ˈärt-ə\ *or anc.* **Arach·thus** \ə-ˈrak-thəs\. River, W Greece; ab. 80 m. long; chief river of Epirus; flows S to Ambracian Gulf; navigable to Arta.

Araks \ə-ˈräks\ *or Turk.* **Aras** \ə-ˈräs\ *or anc.* **Arax·es** \ə-ˈrak-(ˌ)sēz\. River, Turkey and U.S.S.R.; 568 m. long; rises in mountains of Turkish Armenia S of Erzurum, flows E to join the Kura, about 60 m. from its mouth, and also since 1897 flows by its own mouth into the Caspian Sea; for about half its course, 43°45'E to 48°E, forms the boundary bet. the Armenian and Azerbaijan S.S.Rs. on the N and Turkey and NW Iran on the S; has a very rapid current; chief tributaries Razdan from the N and Qareh Sū from the S.

Ar·al Sea \ˌar-əl-\ *or Russ.* **Aral·sko·ye Mo·re** \ə-ˌral-skə-yə-ˈmȯr-(y)ə\ *or formerly* **Lake Aral;** *anc.* **Ox·i·a·nus La·cus** \ˌäk-sē-ˌā-nə-ˈslā-kəs, -sē-ˌan-ə-\. Inland sea, bet. Kazakh S.S.R. and Uzbek S.S.R., SW U.S.S.R.; 280 m. long; 25,659 sq. m.; max. depth 223 ft.; salinity 10.7 percent; second to Caspian Sea in size in Asia, and fourth largest inland body of water in the world; except on S its shores are steppe or desert and uninhabited; on NE receives the Syr Darya and on S the Amu Darya; its level varies greatly over a period of years.

Ar·am \ˈar-əm, ˈer-\. Ancient country in SW Asia extending from the Lebanon Mts. to beyond the Euphrates river; the Hebrew name of ancient Syria; named from a northern Semitic people, the Aramaeans, who emerged from Syrian Desert to invade Syria and Upper Mesopotamia (c. 14th cent. B.C.–1100 B.C.) and who (esp. in 10th cent. B.C.) built up numerous highly civilized city-kingdoms, best known of which was Damascus (*q.v.*); gave its name to Aramaic language. See SYRIA 1.

Ar·an \'ar-ən\. Island, co. Donegal, Eire, in Atlantic Ocean off NW coast of Ireland; 7 sq. m.

Aran·das \ə-'rän-dəs\. Town, Jalisco state, W cen. Mexico, 70 m. E of Guadalajara; munic. pop. (1970p) 41,958.

Aran Islands \ˌar-ən-\ *or Irish* **Arana Naomh** \ˌar-ə-nə-'nyüv\ (literally, "Aran of the Saints"). Group of small islands, co. Galway, W Eire, off W coast of Ireland at entrance to Galway Bay; 18 sq. m.; pop. (1961c) 1648; comprises Inishmore or Aranmore (the largest), Inishmaan, Inisheer, and (off W of Inishmore) an islet, Eeragh; oats, potatoes, fish; chief town Kilronan, on Inishmore; pre-Christian remains.

Aran·juez \ˌär-äŋ-'hwäth\ *or anc.* **Ara Jo·vis** \ˌar-ə-'jō-vəs\. Commune, Madrid prov., cen. Spain, 26 m. SSE of Madrid; pop. (1970p) 29,548; planned and built by Ferdinand VI; known chiefly as site of royal summer palace built by Philip II, rebuilt and expanded by Ferdinand VII and Charles III; treaties bet. France and Spain 1745, 1779, 1805; abdication of Charles IV 1808.

Aran Mawdd·wy *or* **Aran Mowdd·wy** \ˌar-ən-'mau̇th-wē\. Peak, Merionethshire, W Wales, ab. 30 m. NE of Aberystwyth; 2970 ft.; highest in Cambrian Mts.

Aranmore. See INISHMORE and ARAN ISLANDS.

Aran·sas \ə-'ran(t)-səs\. County in Texas. See table at TEXAS.

Aransas Bay. Inlet of Gulf of Mexico NE of Corpus Christi Bay, S Texas, bet. mainland and St. Joseph I.

Aransas Pass. 1 Passage to Aransas Bay and Corpus Christi Bay, S Texas.
2 City, Aransas, Nueces, and San Patricio cos., S Texas, on Aransas Bay; pop. (1970c) 5813; fishing; oil shipping. **Port Aransas** is a fishing resort on nearby Mustang I.

Arao \ə-'rä-ˌō, -'rau̇\. City, Kumamoto prefecture, Kyūshū, Japan, 40 m. S of Fukuoka; pop. (1970c) 55,452.

Arap·a·ho \ə-'rap-ə-ˌhō\. Town, ⊗ of Custer co., W Oklahoma; pop. (1970c) 531.

Arap·a·hoe \ə-'rap-ə-ˌhō\. County in Colorado. See table at COLORADO.

Arapahoe Peak. Mountain in Front Range of Rocky Mts., Grand and Boulder cos., N cen. Colorado; 13,506 ft.

Ara·pi·les \ˌär-ə-'pē-ləs\. Village, Salamanca prov., W Spain, 4 m. SE of Salamanca; site of battle of Salamanca 1812 in which allied troops under Wellington defeated French under Marmont.

Ara·pi·ra·ca \ˌar-ə-pi-'rak-ə\. Municipality, Alagoas state, E Brazil, 60 m. WSW of Maceió; pop. (1968e) 57,209.

Arap·kir *or formerly* **Arab·kir** \ˌär-(ˌ)äp-'ki(ə)r\. Town, E Turkey in Asia, ab. 50 m. N of Malatya; pop. (1965c) 7056.

Ara·pon·gas \ˌar-ə-'pȯŋ-gəs\. Municipality, Paraná state, S Brazil, 300 m. W of São Paulo; pop. (1968e) 63,905.

Arar. See SAÔNE.

Ara·ra \ə-'rär-ə\. Village on N coast of Irian Barat, Indonesia, nearly opp. Wakde Is. and ab. 125 m. W of Djajapura; scene of landing of Allied troops May 17, 1944.

Ara·ra·qua·ra \ˌär-ə-rə-'kwär-ə\. City, cen. São Paulo state, SE Brazil, 150 m. NE of São Paulo; munic. pop. (1968e) 93,009.

Ar·a·rat \'ar-ə-ˌrat\. 1 Ancient kingdom. See URARTU.
2 Town, W cen. Victoria, Australia, 115 m. WNW of Melbourne; pop. (1966c) 8233.
3 *or Armenian* **Ma·sis** \mä-'ses\; *Turk.* **Ağ·ri Da·ği** *or* **Agh·ri Dagh** \ˌä(g)-rē-dä(g)-'ē\; *Pers.* **Koh–i–nuh** \ˌkō-i-'nü\. Isolated mountain in Ağri province, in E extremity of Turkey, near Iranian border; has two peaks, Great Ararat (16,945 ft.) and Little Ararat (12,877 ft.); legendary landing place of Noah's Ark (*Gen.* viii. 4); first climbed in modern times 1829.

Aras. See ARAKS.

Arau·ca \ə-'rau̇-kə\. 1 Intendancy of E Colombia. See table at COLOMBIA.
2 Town, its ✱, on Arauca river; pop. (1968e) 4429.
3 River, W Venezuela; ab. 430 m. long; flows E forming a part of Venezuela-Colombia boundary; empties into Orinoco.

Ar·au·ca·nía \ə-ˌrau̇-'kän-ē-ə, ˌär-ˌau̇-\. Former region of S Chile, S of Bío-Bío river, now included in Arauco, Bío-Bío, Malleco, and Cautín provinces; home of the Araucanian Indians.

Arau·co \ə-'rau̇-(ˌ)kō\. 1 Province of S cen. Chile. See table at CHILE.
2 Commune on coast of Arauco prov., S cen. Chile, 35 m. S of Concepción; pop. (1960c) 16,721.

Arauco, Gulf of. Inlet of Pacific Ocean in coast of S cen. Chile, S of Concepción.

Arausio. See ORANGE, France.

Ara·val·li Range *or* **Aravalli Hills** \ə-ˌräv-ə-lē-\. Mountain range, NW India, in cen. and S Rajasthan; ab. 300 m. long; average height 1000 to 3000 ft., highest Mt. Abu 5650 ft.; generally bare and thinly inhabited.

Ara·wa Harbour \ə-'rä-wə-\ *or formerly* **Ra·wa Harbour** \'rä-wə-\. Anchorage on E coast of Bougainville I., NW Solomon Is.

Ara·we \ə-'rä-we\. Village and peninsula (ending in Cape Merkus) on S coast at W end of New Britain I.; first point of Allied invasion of island Dec. 20, 1943.

Ara·xá \ˌar-ə-'shä\. Town, Minas Gerais state, E Brazil, 65 m. E of Uberaba; munic. pop. (1968e) 32,798.

Araxes. See ARAKS.

Araxos *or* **Araxus.** See PAPAS.

Ara·yat \ə-'rī-ət\. 1 Isolated extinct volcano, NE Pampanga prov., Luzon, Phil.; 3867 ft.
2 Municipality, NE Pampanga prov., Luzon, Phil., at S foot of Mt. Arayat 11 m. N of San Fernando; pop. (1969e) 45,000.

Arba, Al–. See AL–ARBA.

Ar·ba Minch \ˌär-bə-'minch\. Town, ✱ of Gemu Gefa prov., SW Ethiopia; pop. (1970e) 6677.

Arbe. See RAB.

Arbela. See ERBIL.

Ar·ber \'är-bər\. Highest peak in Bohemian Forest, Bavaria, West Germany, E of Regensburg; 4780 ft.

Arbil. See ERBIL.

Ar·bo·ga \är-'bü-gə, -'bō-\. Town, Västmanland co., E Sweden, 8 m. N of Lake Hjälmaren on **Arboga River** 9 m. W of its mouth in Lake Mälaren; pop. (1970e) 12,254; iron foundries; site of first diet in Sweden 1435 and of diet of 1561 at which Arboga Articles were adopted enabling Eric XIV to curb power of nobility.

Ar·bon \är-'bōⁿ\ *or anc.* **Ar·bor Fe·lix** \ˌär-bər-'fē-liks\. Commune, Thurgau canton, NE Switzerland, on SW coast of Lake Constance 16 m. SE of Konstanz; pop. (1970c) 13,122; steel pipes, trucks, textile machinery; neolithic pile dwellings.

Ar·broath \är-'brōth\ *or* **Ab·er·bro·thock** \ˌab-ər-brə-'thäk\. Seaport and manufacturing burgh, Angus co., E Scotland, 45 m. SSW of Aberdeen; pop. (1971p) 22,585; site of meeting of Robert Bruce with Scottish nobles to resist claims of Edward II 1320.

Ar·buck·le Mountains \ˌär-ˌbək-əl-\. Low mountain region, S cen. Oklahoma.

Ar·ca·chon \ˌär kə 'shōⁿ\. Commune, Gironde dept., SW France, on S coast of the **Bas·sin d'Ar·ca·chon** \ˌbä-ˌsaⁿ-ˌdär-\ (inlet of Bay of Biscay), 32 m. WSW of Bordeaux; pop. (1968c) 14,986; resort; oyster culture.

Ar·cade \är-'kād\. Village, Wyoming co., W New York, 33 m. SE of Buffalo; pop. (1970c) 1972; in dairying region.

Ar·ca·dia \är-'kād-ē-ə\. 1 Residential city, Los Angeles co., SW California, 13 m. ENE of Los Angeles; pop. (1970c) 43,237.
2 City, ⊗ of De Soto co., SW cen. Florida penin., 43 m. ESE of Sarasota; pop. (1970c) 5658; cattle; winter resort.

3 Town, ⊗ of Bienville parish, NW Louisiana, 52 m. E of Shreveport; pop. (1970c) 2970; cotton; lumber; salt deposits.
4 City, Trempealeau co., W Wisconsin; pop. (1970c) 2159.
5 Ancient country in cen. Peloponnesus, Greece; mountainous, highest peak ab. 8000 ft.; chief cities Tegea, Mantinea, Orchomenus, and Megalópolis.

History: Home of Arcadians, an ancient Greek people who never attained full political unity; Tegea fought against Sparta c. 800 B.C. but c. 560 B.C. became its subject ally; Arcadian cities later allied with Argos, but were forced to return to Sparta 469 B.C.; formed leagues against Sparta 420 B.C. and 370 B.C.; Megalópolis founded 370 B.C. as federal capital. Suffered in medieval period under Frankish barons, recovered under Turkish rule, again devastated during War of Independence 1821–29.

6 *or Gk.* \ˌär-kə-ˈthē-ə\. Department of Greece, nearly coextensive with ancient country. See table at GREECE.

Ar·ca·dy \ˈär-kəd-ē\. Archaic and poetic for ARCADIA.

Arcae Remorum. See CHARLEVILLE-MÉZIÈRES.

Ar·ca·ta \är-ˈkāt-ə\. City, Humboldt co., NW California, on N end of Humboldt Bay 8 m. NE of Eureka; pop. (1970c) 8985; Humboldt State Coll. (1913).

Arc Dome \ˈärk-\. Peak, Nye co., cen. Nevada; 11,788 ft.

Ar·ce·lia \är-ˈsāl-ē-ə\. Municipality, Guerrero state, S Mexico; pop. (1970p) 25,631.

Ar·ce·tri \är-ˈchā-trē\. Village, Firenze prov., Tuscany, cen. Italy, near Florence; home of Galileo 1634–42.

Ar·ce·via \är-ˈchā-vē-ə\. Commune, Ancona prov., Marches, cen. Italy; pop. (1968e) 7770.

Archangel. See ARKHANGELSK.

Archangel, Gulf of. See DVINA GULF.

Arch·bald \ˈärch-ˌbȯld\. Borough, Lackawanna co., NE Pennsylvania; pop. (1970c) 6118; anthracite coal mines.

Arch·bold \ˈärch-ˌbōld\. Village, Fulton co., NW Ohio, 42 m. WSW of Toledo; pop. (1970c) 3047; furniture; diversified agriculture.

Arch·dale \ˈärch-ˌdāl\. Town, Randolph co., cen. North Carolina, 19 m. SW of Greensboro; pop. (1970c) 4844.

Ar·cher \ˈär-chər\. County in Texas. See table at TEXAS.

Archer City. City, ⊗ of Archer co., N Texas, 25 m. S of Wichita Falls; pop. (1970c) 1722.

Arch·es National Park \ˈär-chəz-\. See UNITED STATES, *National Parks.*

Ar·chi·pel·a·go \ˌär-kə-ˈpel-ə-ˌgō, ˌär-chə-\ *or Turk.* **Je·za·iri–Bahri–Se·fid** \ˌjez-ə-ˈi(ə)r-ē-ˌbär-ē-sə-ˈfēd\. Former Turkish province in Asia Minor; composed of islands off W coast; 2660 sq. m.; now mostly Greek.

Archipiélago de Colón. See GALÁPAGOS ISLANDS.

Archipiélago de los Chonos. See CHONOS ARCHIPELAGO.

Ar·chu·leta \ˌär-chə-ˈlet-ə\. County in Colorado. See table at COLORADO.

Ar·cis–sur–Aube \är-ˈsē-ˌsu̇(ə)r-ˈōb\. Commune, Aube dept., NE France, 17 m. N of Troyes; pop. (1962c) 2856; battle Mar. 20–26, 1814 in which allied forces under Schwarzenberg defeated Napoleon.

Ar·co \ˈär-(ˌ)kō\. 1 Village, ⊗ of Butte co., Idaho; pop. (1970c) 1244.
2 Commune, Trentino-Alto Adige, NE Italy, 4 m. N of Lake Garda; pop. (1968e) 10,769.

Arcobriga. See ARCOS DE LA FRONTERA.

Ar·co·la \är-ˈkō-lə\. City, Douglas co., E cen. Illinois, 37 m. ESE of Decatur; pop. (1970c) 2276.

Ar·co·le \ˈär-kə-ˌlā\. Village, Verona prov., N Italy, 15 m. SE of Verona; pop. (1968e) 3983; critical battle in Napoleon's early career in which he defeated the Austrians 1796.

Ar·cos de la Fron·te·ra \ˈär-ˌkōz-ˌdel-ə-frən-ˈter-ə, -frän-\ *or Lat.* **Ar·co·bri·ga** \ˌär-kə-ˈbrī-gə\. Commune, Cádiz prov., SW Spain, 31 m. NE of Cádiz; pop. (1970p) 25,966; Gothic church; ancient fortifications; ruled by Moors under name of **Me·di·na–Ar·kosh** \mə-ˌdē-nə-ˈär-ˌkȯsh, -ˌku̇sh\; captured by Alfonso el Sabio in 13th cent.

Ar·cot \är-ˈkät, ˈär-ˌ\. Town, E Tamil Nadu, S India, on Palar river 65 m. W of Madras; pop. (1961c) 25,029; capital of the Nawabs of the Carnatic (*q.v.*) from 1712; seized by Robert Clive 1751 during struggle of English against French domination of Carnatic; retaken by French 1760; passed to British with Carnatic 1801.

Arc·tic, The \-ˈärk-tik, -ˈär-tik\ *also* **Arctic Regions.** The Arctic Ocean and lands in it and adjacent to it, about to lat. 70°N; including Point Barrow in Alaska, most of Franklin dist. in Canada, two thirds of Greenland, Svalbard, Franz Josef Land, Novaya Zemlya, N Siberia. See POLAR REGIONS.

History: Areas within Arctic Circle first explored 9th–12th cents. A.D. by Norse, who discovered White Sea, Iceland, Greenland, NE North America, and probably Spitsbergen; exploration advanced 16th and 17th cents. by English and Dutch as by-product of search for Northeast or Northwest Passage (*qq.v.*) to China; S part of Baffin I. discovered and Hudson Strait entered by Frobisher 1576–78; Davis Strait explored by John Davis 1585–87; W coast of Novaya Zemlya, Yamal Peninsula, and Spitsbergen discovered by Barents and Nay 1594–97; Hudson Strait and E coast of Hudson Bay navigated by Hudson 1610–11; knowledge of N Canadian coast advanced by servants of Hudson's Bay Company and of Siberian coast by Russian merchant expeditions and government expeditions (from 18th cent.); area near Spitsbergen and Greenland frequented by whaling expeditions; in 19th cent. its exploration became scientific rather than commercial; as result of loss of Sir John Franklin, who had proved route of Northwest Passage 1845–47, more than 7000 miles explored by 40 relief expeditions 1848–59; Franz Josef Land discovered by Austrians 1871–74, carefully explored by Russian scientists, annexed by U.S.S.R. 1928; Northeast Passage first made by Nordenskjöld 1878–79 and Northwest Passage by Amundsen 1903–06; drift across Polar Basin accomplished by Nansen 1893–96; North Pole reached by Peary 1909; Canadian Arctic explored by extensive sledge expeditions (MacMillan, Stefansson, Rasmussen); first explored from air by Byrd and Bennett 1926; traversed from Spitsbergen to Alaska in flight of Amundsen, Nobile, and Ellsworth 1926; floating scientific station (Soviet) first utilized 1937; first submerged transit of North Pole (*USS Nautilus* and *Skate*) 1958.

Arctic Archipelago *also* **Canadian Arctic Islands.** Large group of islands in Arctic Ocean; area ab. 550,000 sq. m.; nearly coextensive with Franklin dist., Northwest Territories, Canada; includes the large islands of Baffin, Ellesmere, Victoria, Banks, Prince of Wales, Devon, Somerset, and the Parry and Sverdrup groups, and many smaller islands.

Arctic Current. See LABRADOR CURRENT.

Arctic Ocean. The ocean N of the Arctic Circle; 5,427,000 sq. m.; max. depth 17,880 ft. (82°23′N, 19°31′E), av. depth ab. 4300 ft.; various sections are known by specific names, as Barents Sea, Beaufort Sea, Chukchi Sea, East Siberian Sea, Greenland Sea, Kara Sea, Laptev Sea, Lincoln Sea, Norwegian Sea.

Arctic Red. River, NW Northwest Territories, Canada; 310 m. long; flows NW to the Mackenzie at **Arctic Red River,** post on the Mackenzie SE of Aklavik.

Ar·cueil \är-ˈkəi\ *or Lat.* **Ar·cu·li** \ˈär-kyü-(ˌ)lī\. Commune, Val-de-Marne dept., N France, 4 m. S of Paris; pop. (1968c) 21,877; stone quarries; notable for its aqueducts, the first (Arcus Julianus, now in ruins) built by Julian in 4th cent., the second by Marie de Médicis 1613–24, the third, superimposed on the second, 1868–72.

Ard, Loch \-ˈärd\. Small lake in Perth co., cen. Scotland, 2 m. W of Aberfoyle; max. depth 107 ft.

Ar·da \ˈärd-ə\. River, S Bulgaria and Turkey in Europe; 180 m. long; rises on S slopes of Rhodope Mts. and flows E joining Maritsa opp. Edirne in NW Turkey.

Ar·da·bīl *or* **Ar·de·bil** \ˌärd-ə-ˈbē(ə)l\. City, East Azerbaijan prov., NW Iran, on the Qareh Sū 30 m. W of the Caspian Sea; pop. (1971e) 88,000; carpets and rugs; cereals, melons;

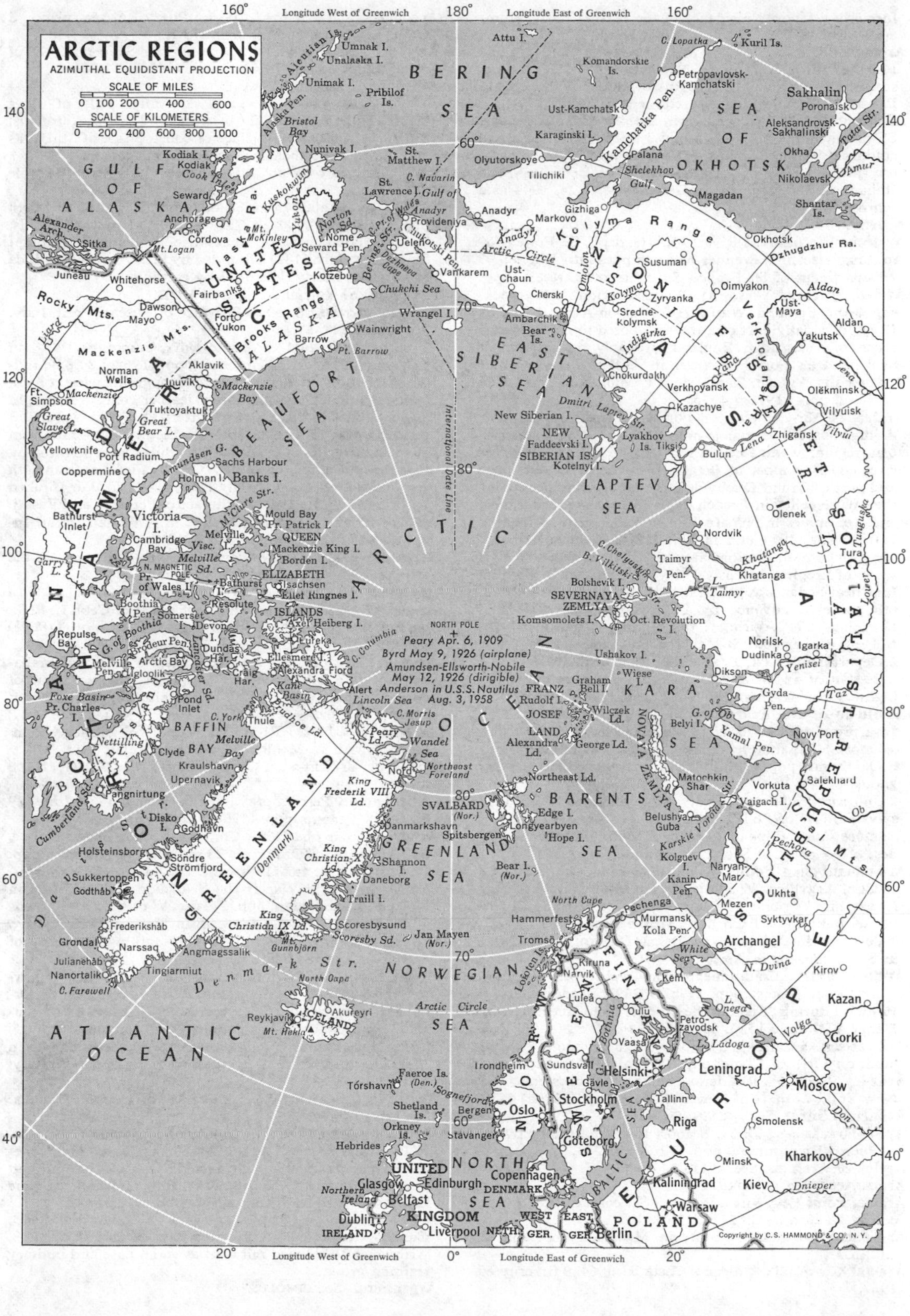
ARCTIC REGIONS
AZIMUTHAL EQUIDISTANT PROJECTION
SCALE OF MILES
0 100 200 400 600
SCALE OF KILOMETERS
0 200 400 600 800 1000
160°
Longitude West of Greenwich
180°
Longitude East of Greenwich
160°
140°
120°
100°
80°
60°
40°
20°
0°
Longitude West of Greenwich
Longitude East of Greenwich
BERING SEA
GULF OF ALASKA
SEA OF OKHOTSK
UNITED STATES
ALASKA
AMERICA
NORTH AMERICA
UNION OF SOVIET SOCIALIST REPUBLICS
ARCTIC OCEAN
BEAUFORT SEA
EAST SIBERIAN SEA
LAPTEV SEA
KARA SEA
BARENTS SEA
GREENLAND SEA
NORWEGIAN SEA
NORTH SEA
BALTIC SEA
ATLANTIC OCEAN
BAFFIN BAY
GREENLAND (Denmark)
EUROPE
NORWAY
SWEDEN
FINLAND
UNITED KINGDOM
IRELAND
POLAND
NETH.
WEST GER.
EAST GER.
DENMARK
Aleutian Is.
Umnak I.
Unalaska I.
Unimak I.
Pribilof Is.
Alaska Pen.
Bristol Bay
Nunivak I.
St. Matthew I.
St. Lawrence I.
Attu I.
Komandorskie Is.
C. Lopatka
Kuril Is.
Petropavlovsk-Kamchatski
Kamchatka Pen.
Ust-Kamchatsk
Karaginski I.
Olyutorskoye
Tilichiki
Palana
Shelekhov Gulf
Sakhalin
Poronaisk
Aleksandrovsk-Sakhalinski
Okha
Nikolaevsk
Tatar Str.
Amur
Magadan
Shantar Is.
Okhotsk
Dzhugdzhur Ra.
Kodiak I.
Kodiak
Cook Inlet
Seward
Anchorage
Cordova
Kuskokwim
Yukon
Alaska Ra.
Mt. McKinley
Mt. Logan
Norton Sd.
Nome
Seward Pen.
Bering Str.
C. Pr. of Wales
Uelen
Dezhneva Cape
Chukotski Pen.
Gulf of Anadyr
C. Navarin
Providenlya
Anadyr
Markovo
Gizhiga
Kolyma Range
Arctic Circle
Vankarem
Ust-Chaun
Omolon
Susuman
Oimyakon
Aldan
Ust-Maya
Yakutsk
Kotzebue
Chukchi Sea
Wrangel I.
Wainwright
Barrow
Pt. Barrow
Brooks Range
Fairbanks
Fort Yukon
Alexander Arch.
Sitka
Juneau
Whitehorse
Dawson
Mayo
Rocky Mts.
Mackenzie Mts.
Liard
Aklavik
Inuvik
Norman Wells
Ft. Simpson
Mackenzie
Mackenzie Bay
Tuktoyaktuk
Great Slave L.
Great Bear L.
Yellowknife
Port Radium
Coppermine
Amundsen G.
Sachs Harbour
Banks I.
Holman I.
M'Clure Str.
Victoria I.
Bathurst Inlet
Cambridge Bay
Mould Bay
Pr. Patrick I.
Melville I.
Visc. Melville Sd.
QUEEN ELIZABETH ISLANDS
Mackenzie King I.
Borden I.
N. MAGNETIC POLE
Pr. of Wales I.
Bathurst I.
Isachsen
Ellef Ringnes I.
Resolute
Boothia Pen.
Somerset I.
Devon I.
Axel Heiberg I.
Eureka
Garry L.
Repulse Bay
G. of Boothia
Brodeur Pen.
Dundas Har.
Arctic Bay
Ellesmere I.
Alexandra Fiord
Craig Har.
Melville Pen.
Igloolik
Lancaster Sd.
Foxe Basin
Pr. Charles I.
Pond Inlet
C. York
Thule
Kane Basin
Alert
Lincoln Sea
C. Columbia
Prudhoe Ld.
Baffin Island
Nettilling L.
Clyde
Melville Bay
Kraulshavn
Upernavik
Pangnirtung
Cumberland Sd.
Davis Str.
Disko I.
Godhavn
Holsteinsborg
Söndre Strömfjord
Sukkertoppen
Godthåb
Frederikshåb
Grondal
Narssaq
Julianehåb
Nanortalik
C. Farewell
Tingiarmiut
Angmagssalik
King Christian IX Ld.
Mt. Gunnbjörn
Denmark Str.
North Cape
Scoresbysund
Scoresby Sd.
King Christian X Ld.
Shannon I.
Daneborg
Traill I.
Danmarkshavn
King Frederik VIII Ld.
Nord
Northeast Foreland
Wandel Sea
Peary Ld.
C. Morris Jesup
NORTH POLE
Peary Apr. 6, 1909
Byrd May 9, 1926 (airplane)
Amundsen-Ellsworth-Nobile
May 12, 1926 (dirigible)
Anderson in U.S.S. Nautilus
Aug. 3, 1958
International Date Line
New Siberian I.
NEW SIBERIAN IS.
Faddeevski I.
Kotelnyi I.
Dmitri Laptev Str.
Lyakhov Is.
Tiksi
Bear Is.
Ambarchik
Cherski
Kolyma
Zyryanka
Sredne-Kolymsk
Indigirka
Chokurdakh
Yana
Verkhoyansk
Verkhoyansk Ra.
Kazachye
Lena
Olëkminsk
Vilyuisk
Vilyui
Zhigansk
Bulun
Olenek
Nordvik
Khatanga
Taimyr Pen.
L. Taimyr
Tura
Lower Tunguska
C. Chelyuskin
B. Vilkitski Str.
Bolshevik I.
SEVERNAYA ZEMLYA
Komsomolets I.
Oct. Revolution I.
Norilsk
Igarka
Dudinka
Yenisei
Ushakov I.
Dikson
Wiese I.
Graham Bell I.
FRANZ JOSEF LAND
Rudolf I.
Wilczek Ld.
Alexandra Ld.
George Ld.
NOVAYA ZEMLYA
Gyda Pen.
Taz
G. of Ob
Belyi I.
Yamal Pen.
Novy Port
Salekhard
Ob
Matochkin Shar
Vorkuta
Vaigach I.
Ural Mts.
Pechora
Belushya Guba
Karskie Vorota Str.
Kolguev I.
Naryan-Mar
Ukhta
Kanin Pen.
Mezen
Syktyvkar
Northeast Ld.
SVALBARD (Nor.)
Edge I.
Longyearbyen
Spitsbergen
Hope I.
Bear I. (Nor.)
North Cape
Pechenga
Hammerfest
Murmansk
Kola Pen.
Tromsö
Archangel
White Sea
N. Dvina
Kirov
Lofoten Is.
Kiruna
Narvik
Kem
Luleå
Oulu
L. Onega
Petro-zavodsk
Kazan
Volga
Gorki
G. of Bothnia
Vaasa
L. Ladoga
Leningrad
Moscow
Jan Mayen (Nor.)
Arctic Circle
ICELAND
Akureyri
Reykjavik
Mt. Hekla
Trondheim
Sundsvall
Helsinki
Gävle
Tallinn
Faeroe Is. (Den.)
Tórshavn
Sognefjord
Shetland Is.
Bergen
Oslo
Stockholm
Don
Smolensk
Orkney Is.
Stavanger
Riga
Hebrides
Göteborg
Minsk
Kharkov
Glasgow
Edinburgh
Copenhagen
Kaliningrad
Kiev
Dnieper
Northern Ireland
Belfast
Warsaw
Dublin
Liverpool
Berlin
Copyright by C. S. HAMMOND & CO., N. Y.

formerly a favorite residence of the Persian court. Home and shrine of Persian saint, Safi-al-Din (1252–1334).

Ar·da·han \ˌärd-ə-ˈhän\ *or Russ.* **Ar·da·gan** \ˌärd-ə-ˈgän\. Fortified town, Kars prov., NE Turkey, 45 m. N of Kars; stormed by Russians 1877 in Russo-Turkish War; ceded to Russia 1878 but with Kars returned to Turkey 1921.

Ar·dea \ˈärd-ē-ə\. Ancient town, Latium, Italy, near coast SE of Lavinium; chief town of the Rutuli; conquered and colonized by the Romans 442 B.C. In area N of the modern village in caves (**Ar·de·a·tine Caves** \ˌär-dē-ə-ˌtīn-\) 336 Italians were massacred by Germans Mar. 24, 1944 as a reprisal measure.

Ardebil. See ARDABĪL.

Ar·dèche \är-ˈdesh\. 1 River, Ardèche dept., SE France; 69 m. long; rises in Cévennes Mts., empties into Rhone.
2 Department of SE France. See table at FRANCE.

Ar·den, Forest of \-ˈärd-ᵊn\. Wooded region, N Warwickshire, cen. England, W of Stratford-upon-Avon; 17 m. by 12 m.; originally part of a tract supposed to have covered much of cen. and E England; probably the original of Shakespeare's Forest of Arden in *As You Like It.*

Arden Hills. Village, Ramsey co., E Minnesota, 5 m. N of St. Paul; pop. (1970c) 4975.

Ar·dennes \är-ˈden\. 1 *or* **Forest of Ardennes** *or anc.* **Ar·du·en·na Sil·va** \ˌär-jə-ˌwen-a-ˈsil-və\. Wooded plateau region, average height less than 1600 ft., E of Meuse river covering most of Belgian province of Luxembourg and part of Grand Duchy of Luxembourg, and occupying the Meuse valley in French department of Ardennes; coal and iron mines in NW. In World War I scene of frontier battles Aug. 1914 and in Nov. 1918 of the severing of German communications around Sedan. In World War II scene of German offensive May 1940 in which Maginot Line near Sedan was penetrated and Allied forces to N cut off; scene of advance by U.S. troops Sept. 1944 and Dec.–Jan. 1945 during bitter fighting ("Battle of the Bulge") esp. around St-Vith and Bastogne.
2 Department of NE France. See table at FRANCE.

Ar·de·stān *or* **Ar·di·stan** \ˌär-də-ˈstän\. Town, cen. Iran, on highway bet. Kāshān and Yazd; pop. (1966c) 6645.

Ar·dju·no *or Du.* **Ar·djoe·no** \är-ˈjü-(ˌ)nō\. Volcano, East Java prov., Indonesia, N of Malang; 9968 ft.

Ard·more \ˈärd-ˌmō(ə)r, -ˌmȯ(ə)r\. 1 City, ⊗ of Carter co., S Oklahoma; pop. (1970c) 20,881; dairy products, leather goods; oil.
2 Unincorporated community, Montgomery co., SE Pennsylvania, NW of Philadelphia; pop. (1970c) 5801.

Ardmore Point. Cape on N coast of Mull I. in Inner Hebrides, off W coast of Scotland; lighthouse.

Ard·na·mur·chan Point \ˌärd-nə-ˌmər-kən-\. Cape on NW coast of Argyll co., W Scotland, N of Mull I. and S of Eigg I.; extreme W point of mainland of Great Britain; lighthouse, built 1849, fixed light, visible 18 m.

Ar·dost \är-ˈdȯst\. Peak in the Bulgar Dağları, Taurus Mts., in S cen. Turkey in Asia; 11,444 ft.

Ar·dres \ˈärdrᵊ\. Commune, Pas-de-Calais dept., N France, 9 m. SE of Calais; pop. (1962c) 2997; headquarters of Francis I during "Field of the Cloth of Gold" meeting with Henry VIII June 1520. See GUÎNES.

Ard·ros·san \är-ˈdräs-ᵊn\. Seaport burgh, Ayr co., SW Scotland, on Firth of Clyde; pop. (1971p) 10,569; resort.

Ards·ley \ˈärdz-lē\. Residential village, Westchester co., SE New York, 21 m. N of New York City; pop. (1970c) 4470.

Arduenna Silva. See ARDENNES 1.

Are·ci·bo \ˌär-ə-ˈsē-(ˌ)bō\. Seaport town and municipality, N Puerto Rico; munic. pop. (1970p) 73,283.

Arelas *or* **Arelate.** See ARLES 2.

Aremorica. See ARMORICA.

Are·na, Point \-ə-ˈrē-nə\. Point on SW coast of Mendocino co., W California, 38°57′N, 123°44′W.

Ar·e·nac \ˈar-ə-ˌnak\. County in Michigan. See table at MICHIGAN.

Are·nal \ˌär-ə-ˈnäl\. Volcano, Costa Rica; 6429 ft.; erupted 1968.

Are·na·les \ˌär-ə-ˈnäl-əs\. Peak, Puerto Aysén prov., S Chile, E of Gulf of Penas; 11,273 ft.

Aren·dal \ˈär-ən-ˌdäl\. Seaport on the Skagerrak, ⊗ of Aust-Agder co., S Norway; pop. (1970e) 11,831.

Arensburg. See KURESSAARE.

Ar·e·op·a·gus \ˌar-ē-ˈäp-ə-gəs\. Literally, Hill of Ares (Mars' Hill); rocky height in Athens W of the Acropolis; 377 ft.; ancient meeting place of court. Scene of St. Paul's address to the Athenians recorded in *Acts* xvii.

Are·qui·pa \ˌar-ə-ˈkē-pə\. 1 Department of S Peru. See table at PERU.
2 City, its ✱, ab. 475 m. SE of Lima, at foot of El Misti; pop. (1970e) 194,700; alt. 7557 ft.; steel plant, textile mills; leather, nylon, plastics; tourism; chief distributing point for S Peru; univ. (1821); founded by Pizarro on site of Inca town 1540; nearly destroyed by earthquake 1868.

Arequipa, El Volcán de. See EL MISTI.

Arez·zo \ə-ˈret-(ˌ)sō, ä-\. 1 Province of Tuscany, cen. Italy. See table at ITALY.
2 *or anc.* **Ar·re·tium** \ə-ˈrē-sh(ē-)əm\. Commune, its ✱, on the Arno 39 m. SE of Florence; pop. (1968e) 84,839; railroad junction; in district producing grain, wine, olives, fruits; manufactures silk fabrics, leather goods, textiles. In ancient times, noted esp. for pottery (Arretine ware) and copper work; 13th cent. Gothic cathedral; city-state from 1098; in struggles of Guelphs and Ghibellines, defeated by Florence at Campaldino 1289; ruled by Florence from 16th cent. until unification of Italy 1860; in World War II taken by British July 16, 1944. Birthplace of Petrarch and Vasari.

Ar·fak \ˈär-ˌfäk\. Mountain range in NW Irian Barat, Indonesia; highest point Kwoka 8042 ft.

Ar·ga \ˈär-gə\. River, N Spain; ab. 60 m. long; rises in the Pyrenees, flows S into Aragón river.

Argaeus. See ERCİYAS DAĞI.

Ar·gao \är-ˈgau̇\. Municipality on E coast of Cebu I., Phil., on Bohol Strait 36 m. SSW of City of Cebu; pop. (1969e) 43,800; seized by Japanese 1942; retaken 1945.

Ar·gaon \ˈär-ˌgau̇n\ *or* **Ar·gaum** \-ˌgau̇m\. Village, N Maharashtra state, cen. India, 137 m. W of Nagpur; scene of decisive defeat Nov. 29, 1803 of Marathas by British under Gen. Wellesley.

Ar·gens \är-ˈzhäⁿs\. River, Var dept., SE France; 72 m. long; flows E to Mediterranean near Fréjus.

Ar·gen·ta \är-ˈjent-ə\. 1 City, Arkansas. See NORTH LITTLE ROCK.
2 Commune, Ferrara prov., Emilia-Romagna, N Italy, 19 m. SE of Ferrara; pop. (1968e) 26,259.

Ar·gen·tan \ˌär-ˌzhäⁿ-ˈtäⁿ\. Commune, Orne dept., France, on right bank of Orne river 23 m. NNW of Alençon; pop. (1968c) 14,558; two 15th cent. churches and 15th cent. castle. In World War II the S anchor of Allied line in Normandy campaign, opp. Falaise; W of these two towns six German divisions trapped in Falaise pocket Aug. 18–23, 1944 met disastrous defeat, marking beginning of withdrawal to the Seine.

Ar·gen·ta·rio \ˌär-jən-ˈtär-ē-ˌō\ *or anc.* **Ar·gen·tar·i·us** \ˌär-jən-ˈtar-ē-əs, -ˈter-\. Mountain, W Italy, off coast at Orbetello 36 m. NW of Civitavecchia; 2081 ft.; on a promontory, connected with mainland by two tongues of land.

Ar·gen·te·ra, Pun·ta \ˈpünt-ə-ˌär-jən-ˈter-ə\. Peak, highest in Maritime Alps, Cuneo prov., SW Piedmont, NW Italy; 10,817 ft.

Ar·gen·teuil \ˌär-zhən-ˈtəi\. 1 County of Quebec, Canada. See table at QUEBEC.
2 City, Val-d'Oise dept., N France, on Seine river 5 m. NNW of Paris; pop. (1968c) 90,480; residential area; vineyards; metallurgical and chemical industries. Built around nunnery founded 656 by Charlemagne which became famous in 12th cent. through its abbess, Héloïse.

Ar·gen·tia \är-ˈjen-chə\. Peninsula, SE Newfoundland, Canada, extending into Placentia Bay; leased 1940 for U.S. Army and Navy base and used as aerial base and military training ground.

Argentiera. See CIMOLUS.

Ar·gen·tière, Ai·guille d' \ā-'gwē-ˌdär-zhən-tē-'e(ə)r\. Peak in the Mont Blanc massif, Pennine Alps, E France, ab. 8 m. ENE of Chamonix-Mont-Blanc; 12,800 ft.

Ar·gen·ti·na \ˌär-jən-'tē-nə\ *or* **Ar·gen·tine Republic** \ˌär-jən-ˌtēn-\. Federal republic, S cen. and S South America, bounded on N by Bolivia and Paraguay, on E by Brazil, Uruguay, and the Atlantic Ocean, and on S and W by Chile; 1,072,156 sq. m.; pop. (1970p) 23,364,443; ❋ Buenos Aires. *Physical features:* Subtropical lowlands characterize the N (see CHACO 1); Patagonia and Tierra del Fuego (*qq.v.*) in S; in cen. region are temperate plains. Main rivers: Río de la Plata (estuary of the Paraná and Uruguay); Bermejo, tributary of the Paraguay, and Salado, tributary of the Paraná, which as the Alto Paraná forms the NE boundary; Colorado, Negro, Chubut. There are many lakes, esp. on slopes of S Andes; among them famous resorts, as Nahuel Huapí. Chief mountains: Aconcagua (22,834 ft.), highest peak of Western Hemisphere, Mercedario, Llullaillaco (volcano), Incahuasi, Tupungato (volcano), and Maipo (volcano), all in W part, near or on the Chilean boundary line, all except Maipo above 21,000 ft. Near Aconcagua is Uspallata Pass (see ANDES). *Chief products:* Wheat, corn, cotton, rice, sugarcane; livestock; oil, natural gas, lead, zinc; manufacturing: meat processing; cement, chemicals, automobiles, steel, textiles. *Chief cities:* Buenos Aires, Rosario, Córdoba, La Plata, San Miguel de Tucumán, Mar del Plata, Santa Fe, Salta, and Mendoza; large suburbs of Buenos Aires include: La Matanza, Morón, Avellaneda, and Quilmes. Divided into a Federal District, 22 provinces, and one territory (for pronunciation of their names, see their individual entries):

NAME	AREA (sq. m.)	POP. (1970p)	CAPITAL
Federal District[1]	77	2,972,453	
Provinces			
Buenos Aires	118,843	8,774,529	La Plata
Catamarca	38,540	172,323	Catamarca
Chaco	38,468	566,613	Resistencia
Chubut	86,751	189,920	Rawson
Córdoba	65,161	2,060,065	Córdoba
Corrientes	34,054	564,147	Corrientes
Entre Ríos	29,428	811,691	Paraná
Formosa	27,825	234,075	Formosa
Jujuy	20,548	302,436	Jujuy
La Pampa	55,382	172,029	Santa Rosa
La Rioja	35,649	136,237	La Rioja
Mendoza	58,239	973,075	Mendoza
Misiones	11,506	443,020	Posadas
Neuquén	36,324	154,570	Neuquén
Río Negro	78,383	262,622	Viedma
Salta	59,759	509,803	Salta
San Juan	33,257	384,284	San Juan
San Luis	29,632	183,460	San Luis
Santa Cruz	94,186	84,457	Gallegos
Santa Fe	51,354	2,135,583	Santa Fe
Santiago del Estero	52,222	495,419	Santiago del Estero
Tucumán	8,697	765,962	San Miguel de Tucumán
National Territory			
Tierra del Fuego	7,873	15,658	Ushuaia

[1]Comprises capital city of Buenos Aires.

History: Río de la Plata discovered by Solís 1516; explored by Sebastian Cabot 1526–30; permanent colonization undertaken by Pedro de Mendoza at Buenos Aires (*q.v.*) 1536; Asunción, Santa Fe, Buenos Aires settled by 1580; attached to viceroyalty of Peru 1620; included with regions of modern Uruguay, Paraguay, and Bolivia in viceroyalty of La Plata or Buenos Aires 1776; Buenos Aires attacked by British 1806–07; with setting up of United Provinces of the Plate River 1816, accomplished its independence from Spain; recognized as independent by U.S. 1823, Great Britain 1825; with its recognition of an independent Uruguay, settled dispute with Brazil 1828; torn by warfare bet. Federalists and Unitarians; after dictatorship of Rosas (1835–52), set up federal constitution 1853; allied with Brazil and Uruguay in war against Paraguay 1865–70; finally resolved struggle bet. Buenos Aires and provinces 1880; represented at first Pan-American Congress 1890; settled boundaries with Brazil by arbitration 1895, with Chile 1899, 1902; participated in ABC (Argentina, Brazil, and Chile) mediation of U.S. dispute with Mexico 1914; neutral in World War I; among first to join League of Nations 1920; withdrew 1921 at failure of its proposals for compulsory arbitration; returned to League 1933; participant in all Pan-American conferences; neutral in World War II; government overthrown by army 1943; army leader, Juan Perón, elected president 1946; Perón overthrown by army 1955 and civilian rule restored; military government reestablished 1966.

Ar·gen·ti·no, Lake \-ˌär-jən-'tē-(ˌ)nō\. Lake, W Santa Cruz prov., S Argentina; 546 sq. m.

Argentoratum. See STRASBOURG.

Ar·geş \'är-ˌjesh\. **1** River, S Romania; flows S into Danube river at Olteniţa; utilized for hydroelectric power production; battle Dec. 1–5, 1916 in which Austro-German army defeated the Romanians.

2 County of S cen. Romania. See table at ROMANIA.

Ar·gi·nu·sae \ˌär-jə-'n(y)ü-ˌsē\. Group of small islands off SE coast of island of Lesbos in E Aegean Sea; naval battle in Peloponnesian War 406 B.C., last victory of Athens over Sparta in the war.

Argirocastro. See GJIROKASTËR.

Ar·go \'är-(ˌ)gō\. **1** Island in Nile river, Northern Province, Sudan; 25 m. long, 5 m. wide.

2 Town on the Nile opp. N end of Argo I.

Ar·go·lis \'är-gə-ləs\. **1** A district of E Peloponnesus, ancient Greece, forming a peninsula; under Mycenaean influence until invaded by Dorians; dominated, although never completely united, by Argos.

2 Department of Peloponnesus, Greece. See table at GREECE.

Argolis, Gulf of *also* **Gulf of Nau·plia** \-'nȯ-plē-ə\. Inlet of Aegean Sea on E coast of Peloponnesus, S Greece, SE of Argos; Nauplia is at its N end.

Argolis and Cor·inth \-'kȯr-ən(t)th, -'kär-\ *or Gk.* **Argolis kai Ko·rin·thia** \ˌär-gəl-'yēs-kā-ˌkȯr-ən-'thē-ə\. Former department of Greece, now divided into Argolis and Corinth depts.

Ar·gonne \är-'gän, 'är-ˌ\ *or* **Argonne Forest.** Wooded plateau, NE France, in Meuse, Ardennes, and Marne depts. near Belgian border S of Ardennes, ab. 25 m. long and 10 m. wide, lying bet. the Meuse and the Aisne, with Verdun at its S end; alt. ab. 1150 ft. Scene of campaign of Dumouriez against Prussians before battle of Valmy 1792; also scene of Allied offensive in World War I Sept.–Nov. 1918, often known as the Meuse-Argonne offensive, in which an American army under Pershing advanced from a line S and E of Argonne Forest to Sedan and Stenay by time of Armistice; in World War II overrun by German armies June 1940; crossed by Americans Aug. 30–31, 1944.

Ar·gos \'är-ˌgäs, -gəs\. City, Argolis dept., NE Peloponnesus, Greece, 7 m. NNW of Nauplia; railroad junction.

History: As a city-state under King Pheidon c. 680 B.C., claimed hegemony over Peloponnesus; a weak state in continual conflict with Sparta after latter's rise; entered alliances with Spartan enemies, esp. the Quadruple Alliance (Corinth, Mantinea, Elis, and Argos) against Sparta 421 B.C. and the alliance with Corinth, Athens, and Thebes in Corinthian War 395–387 B.C.; joined Achaean League 229 B.C., headquarters of Achaean power under Rome; remained under Byzantine Empire until captured by Franks 1210; held in fief to Athens 1246–61; part of Byzantine Empire 1261–1460 and of Ottoman Empire 1460–1830; seat of national assembly in movement for Greek independence 1822; destroyed by Ibrahim Pasha 1825.

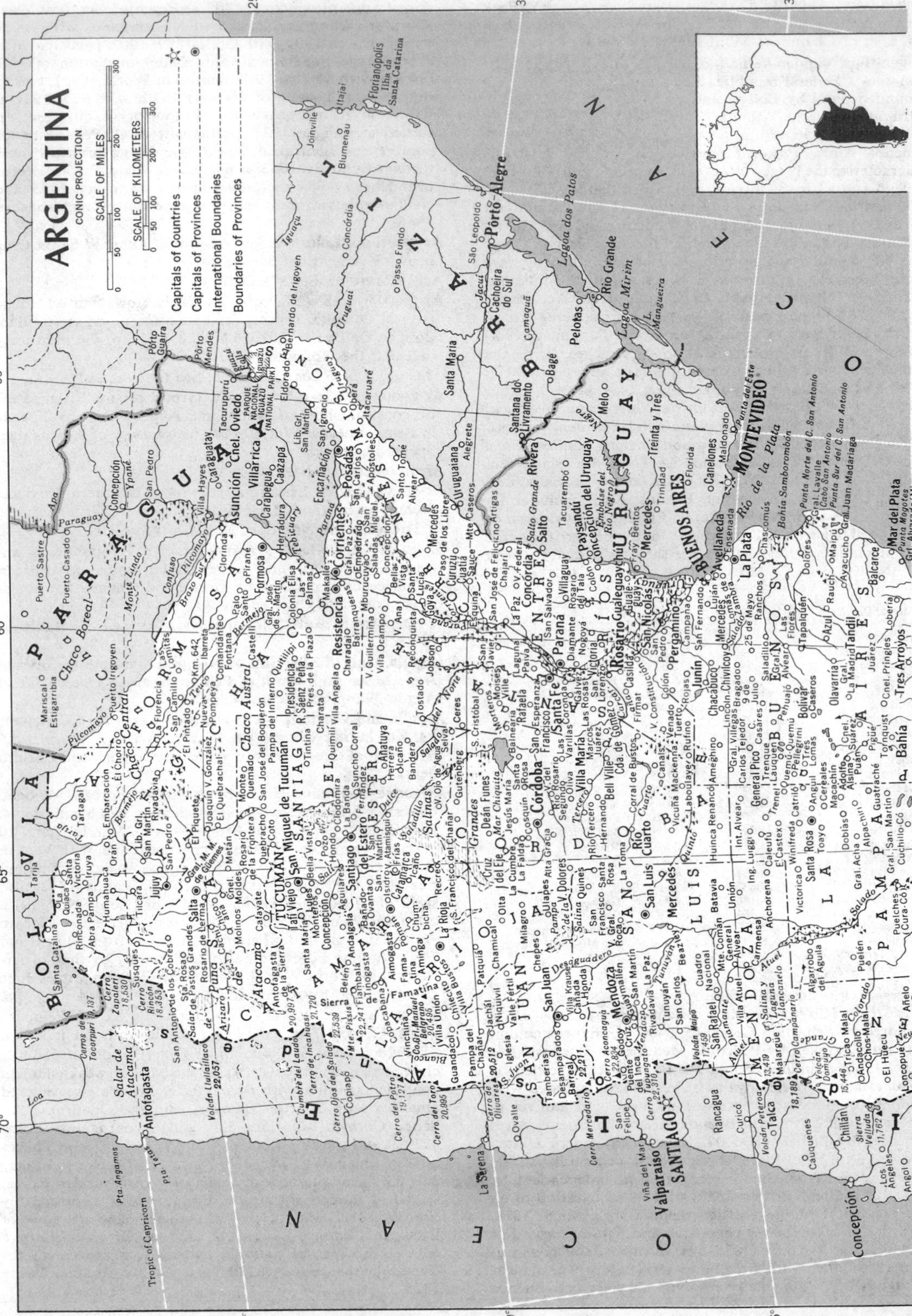
ARGENTINA
CONIC PROJECTION
SCALE OF MILES
0 50 100 200 300
SCALE OF KILOMETERS
0 50 100 200 300
Capitals of Countries
Capitals of Provinces
International Boundaries
Boundaries of Provinces

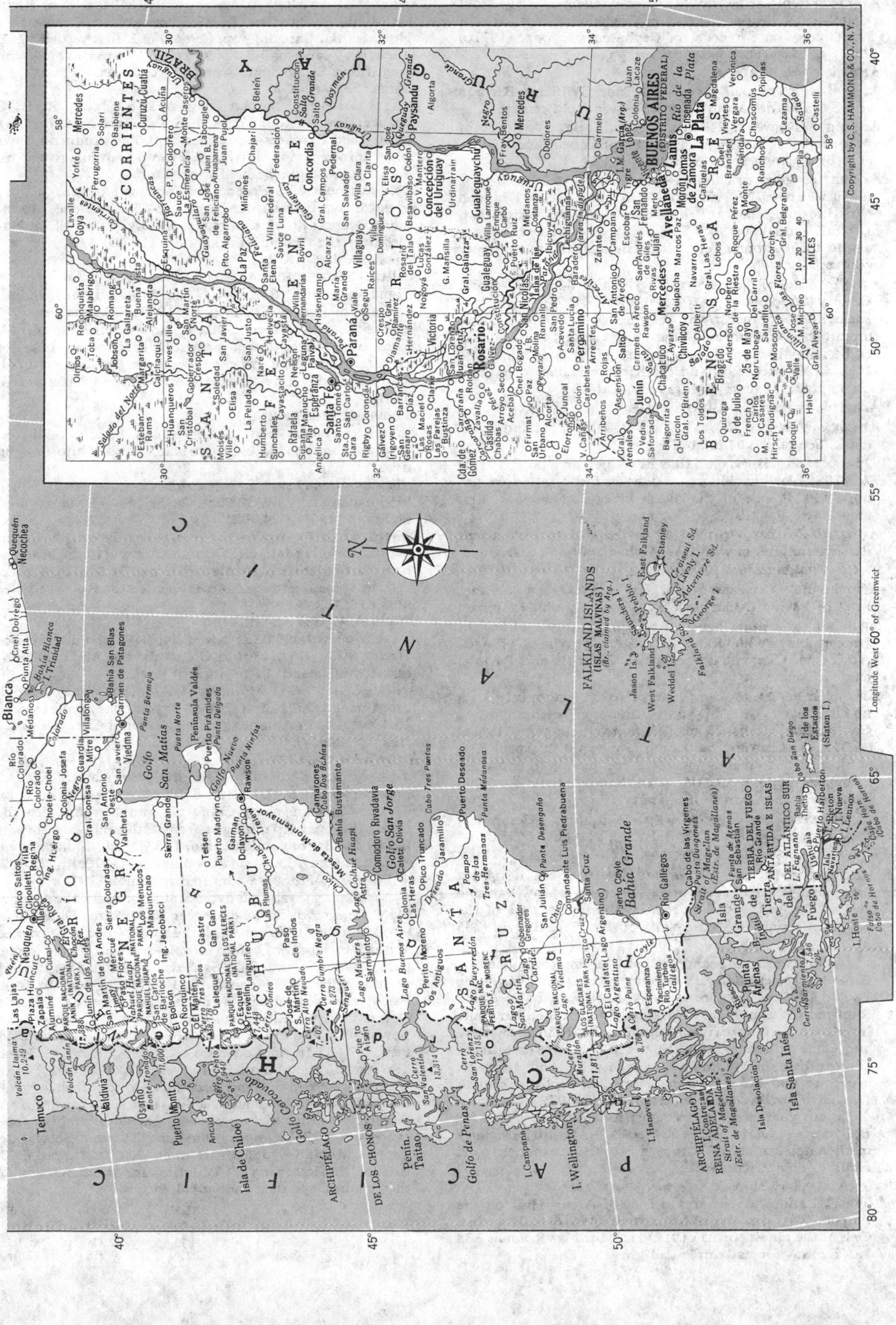
FALKLAND ISLANDS
(ISLAS MALVINAS)
(Br., claimed by Arg.)
West Falkland
East Falkland
Stanley
Jason Is.
Weddel I.
Falkland Sd.
Lively I.
Adventure Sd.
George I.
Choiseul Sd.
Saunders I.
Golfo San Matías
Península Valdés
Puerto Pirámides
Golfo Nuevo
Punta Ninfas
Punta Norte
Punta Delgada
Punta Bermeja
Rawson
Trelew
Gaiman
Puerto Madryn
Viedma
Carmen de Patagones
Bahía San Blas
Bahía Blanca
I. Trinidad
Punta Alta
Cnel. Dorrego
Necochea
Quequén
Médanos
Río Colorado
Choele-Choel
Colonia Josefa
Guardia Mitre
Gral. Conesa
San Antonio Oeste
San Javier
Valcheta
Sierra Grande
Neuquén
Cipolletti
Cinco Saltos
Villa Regina
Allen
Ing. Huergo
Plaza Huincul
Zapala
Las Lajas
Aluminé
Junín de los Andes
San Martín de los Andes
San Carlos de Bariloche
El Bolsón
Norquinco
El Maitén
Esquel
Trevelín
Languiñeo
Gastre
Telsen
Gan Gan
Paso de Indios
Las Plumas
Dolavon
Meseta de Montemayor
Camarones
Cabo Dos Bahías
Bahía Bustamante
Comodoro Rivadavia
Golfo San Jorge
Caleta Olivia
Pico Truncado
Cabo Tres Puntas
Puerto Deseado
Jaramillo
Punta Médanosa
Pampa de las Tres Hermanas
Colonia Las Heras
Perito Moreno
Los Antiguos
Lago Buenos Aires
Lago Musters
Lago Colhué Huapí
Sarmiento
Alto Río Senguerr
Lago Pueyrredón
Lago San Martín
Lago Viedma
Lago Argentino
El Calafate
Gobernador Gregores
San Julián
Punta Desengaño
Comandante Luis Piedrabuena
Santa Cruz
Puerto Coyle
Bahía Grande
Río Gallegos
Cabo de las Vírgenes
Punta Dungeness
Strait of Magellan
(Estr. de Magallanes)
Punta Arenas
Río Turbio
La Esperanza
Isla Grande de Tierra del Fuego
TIERRA DEL FUEGO
ANTÁRTIDA E ISLAS DEL ATLÁNTICO SUR
San Sebastián
Río Grande
Punta de Arenas
Ushuaia
Puerto Harberton
Bahía Thetis
Cabo San Diego
I. de los Estados
(Staten I.)
I. Picton
I. Nueva
I. Lennox
Isla Navarino
I. Hoste
Cabo de Hornos
Falso Cabo de Hornos
Cape Horn
L. Fagnano
Isla Santa Inés
Isla Desolación
ARCHIPIÉLAGO REINA ADELAIDA
I. Hanover
I. Wellington
I. Campana
Golfo de Penas
Penín. Taitao
ARCHIPIÉLAGO DE LOS CHONOS
Isla de Chiloé
Golfo Corcovado
Ancud
Puerto Montt
Osorno
Valdivia
Temuco
Volcán Llaima
Volcán Lanín
Monte Tronador
Cerro San Valentín
Cerro San Lorenzo
Cerro Fitz Roy
Cerro Murallón
Cerro Paine
Puerto Aisén
Longitude West 60° of Greenwich
SANTA FE
ENTRE RÍOS
CORRIENTES
BUENOS AIRES
URUGUAY
BRAZIL
Santa Fe
Paraná
Rosario
Concordia
Gualeguaychú
Concepción del Uruguay
Paysandú
Mercedes
Salto
Fray Bentos
Colonia
Buenos Aires (DISTRITO FEDERAL)
La Plata
Lanús
Avellaneda
Morón
Lomas de Zamora
Ensenada
Río de la Plata
Junín
Pergamino
Chivilcoy
Mercedes
San Nicolás
Campana
Zárate
Luján
Chascomús
Bragado
9 de Julio
25 de Mayo
Goya
Reconquista
Esquina
Curuzú Cuatiá
Copyright by C. S. HAMMOND & CO., N.Y.
MILES

Ar·go·sto·lion \ˌär-gə-ˈstȯl-ˌyȯn\ *or sometimes* **Ar·go·sto·li** \-ˈstȯl-(y)ē\. Seaport city, ✱ of Cephalonia dept., Ionian Is., Greece, on SW coast of Cephalonia I.; pop. (1971p) 7521; good harbor; episcopal see.

Argovie. See AARGAU.

Ar·guel·lo, Point \-ˌär-ˈgwel-(ˌ)ō\. Cape, SW Santa Barbara co., SW California; site of missile-launching center.

Ar·guin \är-ˈgwēn\. Island in **Arguin Bay,** N coast of Mauritania, W Africa, ab. 50 m. SE of Cape Blanc; discovered by Portuguese 15th cent.

Ar·gun \är-ˈgün\ *or Chin.* **O–erh–ku–na** \ˌō-ˌe(ə)r-ˌkü-ˈnä\. Navigable river, NE Asia; ab. 450 m. long; rises in Khingan Mts., forming part of boundary bet. NE China and U.S.S.R., and unites with Shilka river on extreme N boundary to form Amur river; called Hailar (*q.v.*) in its upper course.

Ar·gyll \är-ˈgī(ə)l, ˈär-ˌgīl\ *or* **Ar·gyll·shire** \-ˌshi(ə)r, -shər\. County, W Scotland; 3110 sq. m.; pop. (1971p) 59,909; ⊗ Lochgilphead; other towns Campbeltown, Dunoon, Oban; mountainous region, a popular tourist resort; coast indented by many lochs and includes many islands (Mull, Islay, Jura, Coll, Tiree, etc.) and the Kintyre Penin.; sheep and cattle grazing, quarrying (granite, slate).

Argyrokastron. See GJIROKASTËR.

År·hus *or* **Aar·hus** \ˈȯ(ə)r-ˌhüs\. 1 County, E Jutland, Denmark. See table at DENMARK.

2 Seaport city, its ⊗, on **Århus Bay;** met. area pop. (1971c) 238,138; beer, machinery, textiles; transportation center; univ. (1928); one of the oldest cities in Denmark, first mentioned 948 A.D.

Ar·ia \ˈar-ē-ə, ˈer-; ə-ˈrī-ə\. 1 An eastern province of ancient Persian Empire, now in NW Afghanistan and E Iran.

2 City, Afghanistan. See HERĀT 2.

Ari·a·ke Bay \ˌär-ē-ˌäk-ē-\ *or Jap.* **Ariake Wan** \-ˈwän\. Inlet of Pacific Ocean on SE coast of Kyūshū I., Japan.

Ar·i·a·na \ˌar-ē-ˈä-nə, -ˈan-ə\. An extensive region of ancient Persian Empire including the eastern provinces of Aria, Arachosia, Carmania, Drangiana, Gedrosia and Parthia; named from Aria.

Aria·no Ir·pi·no \ˌär-ē-ˈän-(ˌ)ō-ir-ˈpē-(ˌ)nō\ *or formerly* **Ariano di Pu·glia** \-dē-ˈpül-yə\. Commune, Avellino prov., Campania, S Italy, 23 m. NE of Avellino; pop. (1968e) 25,012; earthenware; built on rocky height in Apennines; subject to earthquakes; episcopal see; many old churches. Occupies supposed site of ancient Samnite town **Ae·quum Tu·ti·cum** \ˌē-kwəm-ˈt(y)üt-i-kəm\.

Ariano nel Po·le·si·ne \-ˌnel-pə-ˈlā-zi-(ˌ)nā\. Commune, Rovigo prov., Veneto, NE Italy; pop. (1968e) 6698.

Aria Palus. See HAMUN-I-MASHKEL.

Ari·ca \ə-ˈrē-kə, ä-\ *or in full* **San Mar·cos de Arica** \ˌsän-ˌmär-kəs-ˌdā-\. Seaport city, Tarapacá prov., extreme N Chile; pop. (1966e) 63,160; northernmost port of the republic; terminus of railroad from La Paz, Bolivia (285 m.).

History: Peruvian seaport in colonial times; occupied by Chile 1880 after boundary disputes resulting in War of the Pacific 1879–84; by Treaty of Ancón (*q.v.*) 1883, which followed Chilean victory, awarded (with Tacna) to Chile for 10 years with provision for plebiscite; claimed by Peru and Chile in Tacna-Arica dispute which long embittered Chilean-Peruvian relations and came to head 1921–29; access to sea through Arica claimed by Bolivia through League of Nations 1920; by settlement of 1929 awarded to Chile but guaranteed as free port for Peru and outlet for Bolivia via Arica-La Paz R.R. (see TACNA); with its vicinity made a department of Tarapacá prov. 1930; modern port facilities completed 1965.

Aric·cia \ä-ˈrē-chä\ *or formerly* **Ari·cia** \ə-ˈrish-(ē-)ə\. Town, Latium, cen. Italy, at foot of Alban Hills on the Appian Way 16 m. SE of Rome; pop. (1968e) 9504; resort. One of the oldest towns of Italy; subdued by Romans 338 B.C.; famous for its temple and grove of Diana.

Ar·i·chat \ˈar-ə-ˌshat\. Unincorporated village, ⊗ of Richmond co., on Madame I. off S coast of Cape Breton I., Nova Scotia, Canada; pop. (1966c) 652; first settled 1713.

Ari·chu·na \ˌär-ə-ˈchü-nə\. River, W Venezuela; 240 m. long; flows E and joins Arauca river in Apure state.

Aricia. See ARICCIA.

Ariège \ˌar-ē-ˈezh\ *or* **La Riège** \ˌlär-ē-ˈezh\. 1 River, S France; 106 m. long; rises in E Pyrenees Mts. forming border bet. Pyrénées-Orientales dept. and Andorra; flows NNW through wide alluvial valley into Garonne river 5 m. S of Toulouse; navigable for ab. 26 m.

2 Department of S France. See table at FRANCE.

Ari·en·zo San Fe·li·ce \ˌär-ē-ˌen(t)-sō-ˌsän-fə-ˈlē-chē\. Commune, Napoli prov., Campania, S Italy, 18 m. NE of Naples near the Caudine Forks; pop. (1968e) 4781.

Arīhā. See JERICHO 2.

Arilica. See PESCHIERA DEL GARDA.

Ari·ma \ə-ˈrē-mə\. Borough, N cen. Trinidad, West Indies, 16 m. E of Port of Spain; pop. (1960c) 10,982.

Ar·i·ma·thea *also* **Ar·i·ma·thaea** \ˌar-ə-mə-ˈthē-ə\. Greek form of Ramah; town, probably in Samaria but not definitely identified, whence came the councillor Joseph who placed the body of Jesus in his own tomb (*Matt.* xxvii. 57 ff.).

Ariminum. See RIMINI.

Ari·nos \ə-ˈrē-nəs, -ˌnüs\. River, W cen. Brazil; ab. 400 m. long; rises in cen. Mato Grosso state, flows N into Juruena river.

Ario de Ro·sa·les \ˈär-ē-ˌō-ˌdā-rō-ˈsäl-əs, -ˈzäl-\. Town, Michoacán state, SW Mexico, 20 m. SE of Uruapan; munic. pop. (1970p) 24,302.

Ari·pua·nã \ˌar-əp-wə-ˈnaⁿ\. River, W cen. Brazil; ab. 400 m. long; rises in N Mato Grosso state, flows N to the Madeira river; in SE Amazonas state it is joined by the Rio Roosevelt; by some the lower course is named the Roosevelt. See ROOSEVELT, RIO.

ʻArīsh, Al–. See AL–ʻARISH.

Ar·is·taz·a·bal Island \ˌar-ə-ˈstaz-ə-ˌbal-\. Island, E side of Hecate Strait, off W British Columbia, Canada, W of Princess Royal Island; 27 m. long.

Ari·tao \ˌär-ə-ˈtau̇\. Municipality, Nueva Vizcaya prov., cen. Luzon, Phil., 15 m. SW of Bayombong; pop. (1969e) 15,400; taken in American advance toward Cagayan valley June 6, 1945.

Arius. See HARI RUD.

Ar·i·zo·na \ˌar-ə-ˈzō-nə\. A southwestern state of U.S.A., bounded on N by Utah, on E by New Mexico, on S by Mexico, and on W by California and Nevada with the Colorado river separating it from California and in part from Nevada; 6th state in area, 113,909 sq. m. (land area, 113,563 sq. m.); 33d state in population, (1970c) 1,772,482; ✱ Phoenix; 48th state admitted to Union (1912).

Nickname: Grand Canyon State, formerly the Copper State. *State flower:* Saguaro cactus. *Motto:* Ditat Deus (God Enriches). *Rivers:* Colorado on W border, widened at north by Hoover Dam to form Lake Mead; Verde in cen. part flowing SE into Salt; Salt, rising in E region, flowing W into Gila and widened by Roosevelt Dam to form Roosevelt Lake in cen. Arizona; Gila, flowing SW into Colorado river; Little Colorado, rising in E region and flowing NW into the Colorado. *Highest point:* Humphreys Peak, 12,633 ft., in Coconino co. *Scenic features:* Grand Canyon of the Colorado river in N; Petrified Forest National Park in E. *Chief products:* Cotton, fruit, vegetables; copper, molybdenum, gold, sand and gravel; manufacturing: electronic equipment, machine tools; food processing. *Chief cities:* Phoenix, Tucson, Scottsdale, Tempe, Mesa. See table of states at UNITED STATES. Divided into the following 14 counties (for pronunciation of their names, see their individual entries):

NAME	LOCATION	AREA[1] (sq. m.)	POP. (1970c)	CO. SEAT
Apache[2]	NE corner	11,171	32,304	St. Johns
Cochise	SE corner	6,256	61,918	Bisbee

NAME	LOCATION	AREA[1] (sq. m.)	POP. (1970c)	CO. SEAT
Coconino[3]	N	18,562	48,326	Flagstaff
Gila[4]	E cen.	4,748	29,255	Globe
Graham[5]	SE	4,618	16,578	Safford
Greenlee	SE	1,879	10,330	Clifton
Maricopa	SW cen.	9,238	968,487	Phoenix
Mohave[6]	NW corner	13,227	25,857	Kingman
Navajo	NE	9,910	47,559	Holbrook
Pima	S	9,240	351,667	Tucson
Pinal	S	5,386	68,579	Florence
Santa Cruz	S	1,246	13,966	Nogales
Yavapai	cen.	8,091	36,837	Prescott
Yuma	SW corner	9,991	60,827	Yuma

[1] Area = land area.
[2] Its NE point the only point in U.S. common to 4 states (Ariz., N. Mex., Colo., and Utah).
[3] Painted Desert in E; many high plateaus and peaks, highest Humphreys Peak 12,633 ft.
[4] Bounded on S by Gila river, including Coolidge Dam and San Carlos Lake; Roosevelt Dam and Lake on cen. W border.
[5] Bounded on NW by San Carlos river, including San Carlos Lake.
[6] Hoover Dam (Boulder Dam) and Lake Mead on part of NW boundary.

History: Spanish exploration began with expedition of Franciscan friar Marcos de Niza 1539; ruled by Spain as part of New Spain 1598–1821; inauguration of Spanish missions to Hopis 1638; region acquired by United States by Treaty of Guadalupe Hidalgo 1848 and Gadsden Purchase 1853; organized as separate territory 1863; subjugation of Apaches 1877; with New Mexico refused statehood 1906; submitted a constitution for congressional approval 1911; congressional resolution accepting this constitution vetoed by President Taft chiefly because of provision allowing recall of judges by popular vote; after objectionable matter withdrawn from constitution, admitted to Union Feb. 14, 1912; by state constitutional amendment restored the provision allowing recall of judges Nov. 1912.

Ar·jo·na \är-ˈhō-nə\. 1 Town, Bolívar dept., N Colombia, just SE of Cartagena; munic. pop. (1968e) 21,900.
2 Commune, Jaén prov., S Spain, 19 m. WNW of Jaén; pop. (1970p) 8171.

Ar·ka·del·phia \ˌär-kə-ˈdel-fē-ə\. City, ⊗ of Clark co., SW Arkansas, on Ouachita river 28 m. S of Hot Springs; pop. (1970c) 9841; in cotton-growing area; flour, lumber, and cotton mills; Ouachita Baptist Univ. (1886), Henderson State Coll. (1929); founded 1839.

Ar·ka·dhía \ˌär-kə-ˈdē-ə\. Greek form of *Arcadia,* department of Greece. See table at GREECE.

Ar·kaig, Loch \-är-ˈkāg\. Lake, W Inverness co., NW Scotland, 10 m. N of Fort William; 12 m. long; 6 sq. m.; trout fishing.

Ar·kan·sas. 1 \är-ˈkan-zəs *is usual in Kansas and frequent in Colorado,* ˈär-kən-ˌsȯ *is usual elsewhere*\. River, 1450 m. long, rising in Lake co., cen. Colorado, and flowing E through S Kansas and SE across NE corner of Oklahoma; bisects Arkansas and empties into Mississippi river in Desha co., SE Arkansas; navigable 650 m.; its largest tributaries are the Canadian and Cimarron rivers. See ROYAL GORGE.

2 \ˈär-kən-ˌsȯ\. A south central state of U.S.A., bounded on N by Missouri, on E by Mississippi river separating it from Tennessee and Mississippi, on S by Louisiana, on W by Texas and Oklahoma; 27th state in area, 53,104 sq. m. (land area 52,175 sq. m.); 32d state in population, (1970c) 1,923,295; ✱ Little Rock; 25th state admitted to Union (1836). *Nickname:* Land of Opportunity. *State flower:* Apple blossom. *Motto:* Regnat Populus (The People Rule). *Rivers:* Arkansas, bisecting state from W to E and flowing into the Mississippi; Red, flowing E and S in extreme SW area, forming part of boundary with Texas; Ouachita rising in W area and flowing E and then S; White, flowing from N to SE into Arkansas river near confluence with Mississippi. *Highest point:* Magazine Mt. in Logan co., 2753 ft. *Chief products:* Soybeans, cotton, rice; livestock; oil, bauxite, manganese; manufacturing: wood products, electrical machinery, chemicals. *Chief cities:* Little Rock, Fort Smith, North Little Rock, Pine Bluff, Hot Springs. See table of states at UNITED STATES. Divided into the following 75 counties (for pronunciation of their names, see their individual entries):

NAME	LOCATION	AREA[1] (sq. m.)	POP. (1970c)	CO. SEAT
Arkansas	E	1,015	23,347	De Witt and Stuttgart
Ashley	SE	928	24,976	Hamburg
Baxter	N	537	15,319	Mountain Home
Benton	NW corner	886	50,476	Bentonville
Boone	N	593	19,073	Harrison
Bradley	S	651	12,778	Warren
Calhoun	S	629	5,573	Hampton
Carroll	NW	634	12,301	Berryville and Eureka Springs
Chicot	SE corner	643	18,164	Lake Village
Clark	SW	878	21,537	Arkadelphia
Clay	NE corner	639	18,771	Corning and Piggott
Cleburne	N cen.	539	10,349	Heber Springs
Cleveland	S	601	6,605	Rison
Columbia	SW	768	25,952	Magnolia
Conway	cen.	561	16,805	Morrilton
Craighead	NE	716	52,068	Jonesboro and Lake City
Crawford	NW	596	25,677	Van Buren
Crittenden	E	608	48,106	Marion
Cross	E	625	19,783	Wynne
Dallas	S cen.	672	10,022	Fordyce
Desha	SE	736	18,761	Arkansas City
Drew	SE	832	15,157	Monticello
Faulkner	cen.	641	31,595	Conway
Franklin	NW	613	11,301	Charleston and Ozark
Fulton	N	608	7,699	Salem
Garland	W cen.	658	54,131	Hot Springs[2]
Grant	S cen.	631	9,711	Sheridan
Greene	NE	579	24,765	Paragould
Hempstead	SW	736	19,308	Hope
Hot Spring	SW cen.	621	21,963	Malvern
Howard	SW	600	11,412	Nashville
Independence	NE cen.	752	22,723	Batesville
Izard	N	574	7,381	Melbourne
Jackson	NE	629	20,452	Newport
Jefferson	SE cen.	873	85,329	Pine Bluff
Johnson	NW	673	13,630	Clarksville
Lafayette	SW	523	10,018	Lewisville
Lawrence	NE	590	16,320	Powhatan and Walnut Ridge
Lee	E	608	18,884	Marianna
Lincoln	SE	563	12,913	Star City
Little River	SW	541	11,194	Ashdown
Logan	W	718	16,789	Booneville and Paris
Lonoke	cen.	796	26,249	Lonoke
Madison	NW	832	9,453	Huntsville
Marion	N	584	7,000	Yellville
Miller	SW corner	623	33,385	Texarkana
Mississippi	NE	904	62,060	Blytheville and Osceola
Monroe	E	607	15,657	Clarendon
Montgomery	W	775	5,821	Mount Ida
Nevada	SW	616	10,111	Prescott
Newton	NW	822	5,844	Jasper
Ouachita	S	736	30,896	Camden
Perry	cen.	551	5,634	Perryville
Phillips	E	686	40,046	Helena
Pike	SW	600	8,711	Murfreesboro
Poinsett	NE	760	26,822	Harrisburg
Polk	W	860	13,297	Mena
Pope	NW cen.	812	28,607	Russellville
Prairie	E cen.	661	10,249	Des Arc and De Valls Bluff
Pulaski	cen.	765	287,189	Little Rock
Randolph	NE	647	12,645	Pocahontas
Saint Francis	E	635	30,799	Forrest City
Saline	cen.	724	36,107	Benton
Scott	W	898	8,207	Waldron
Searcy	N	664	7,731	Marshall
Sebastian	W	527	79,237	Fort Smith and Greenwood
Sevier	SW	585	11,272	De Queen
Sharp	N	598	8,233	Evening Shade and Hardy
Stone	N	608	6,838	Mountain View
Union	S	1,050	45,428	El Dorado
Van Buren	N cen.	619	8,275	Clinton
Washington	NW	962	77,370	Fayetteville
White	NE cen.	1,041	39,253	Searcy
Woodruff	NE cen.	591	11,566	Augusta

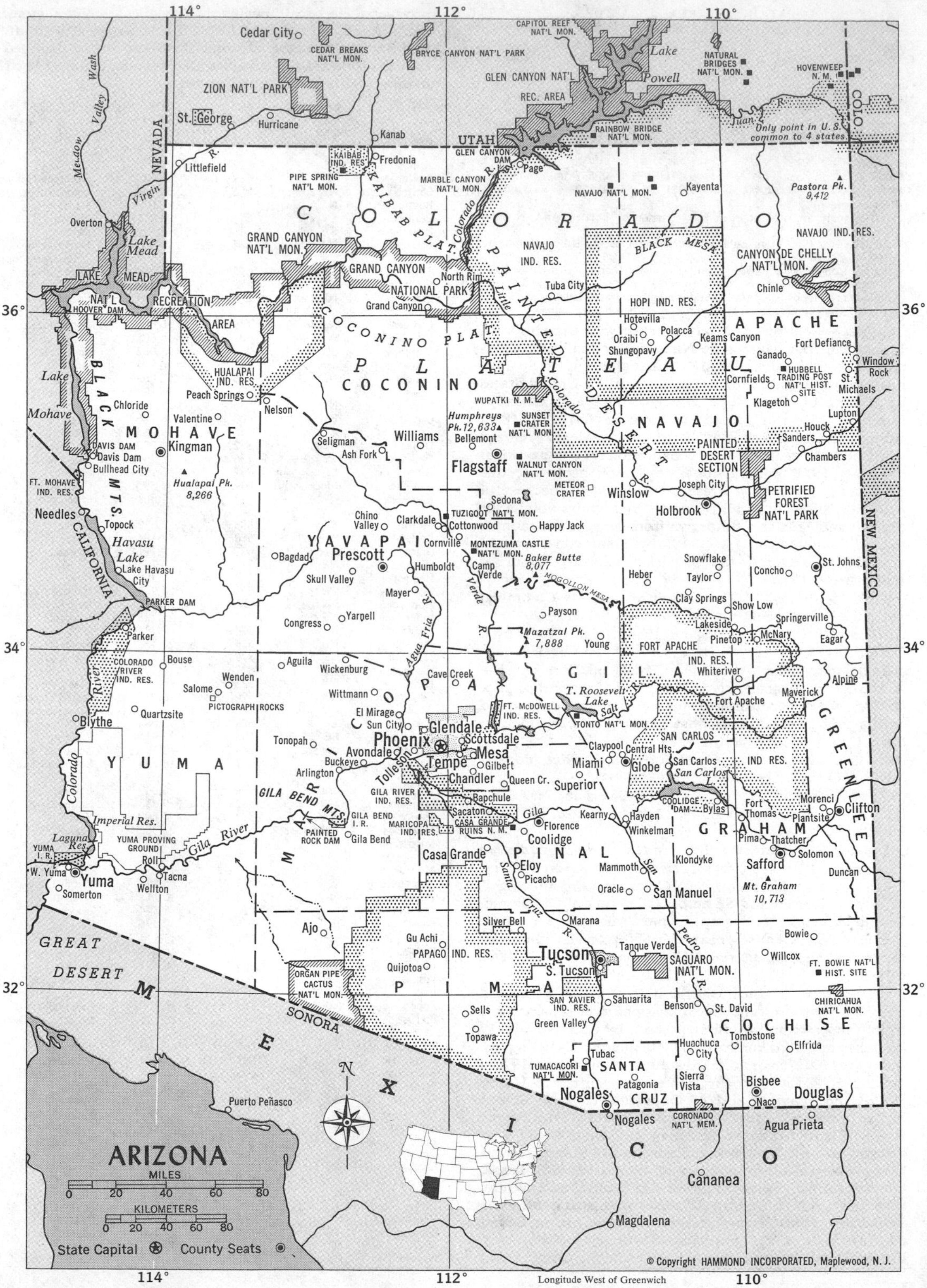
114°
112°
110°
36°
34°
32°
Cedar City
CEDAR BREAKS NAT'L MON.
BRYCE CANYON NAT'L PARK
CAPITOL REEF NAT'L MON.
Lake Powell
NATURAL BRIDGES NAT'L MON.
HOVENWEEP N. M.
COLO.
ZION NAT'L PARK
GLEN CANYON NAT'L REC. AREA
St. George
Hurricane
Kanab
RAINBOW BRIDGE NAT'L MON.
San Juan R.
Only point in U.S. common to 4 states.
UTAH
NEVADA
Meadow Valley Wash
Virgin R.
Littlefield
KAIBAB IND. RES.
Fredonia
PIPE SPRING NAT'L MON.
GLEN CANYON DAM
Page
MARBLE CANYON NAT'L MON.
NAVAJO NAT'L MON.
Kayenta
Pastora Pk. 9,412
Overton
Lake Mead
KAIBAB PLAT.
Colorado R.
C O L O R A D O
GRAND CANYON NAT'L MON.
NAVAJO IND. RES.
BLACK MESA
NAVAJO IND. RES.
CANYON DE CHELLY NAT'L MON.
LAKE MEAD NAT'L RECREATION AREA
GRAND CANYON NATIONAL PARK
North Rim
Tuba City
Chinle
HOOVER DAM
Grand Canyon
HOPI IND. RES.
APACHE
Little Colorado
PAINTED DESERT
Hotevilla
Polacca
Keams Canyon
Oraibi
Shungopavy
Fort Defiance
COCONINO PLAT.
Ganado
Window Rock
HUBBELL TRADING POST NAT'L HIST. SITE
P L A T E A U
Cornfields
St. Michaels
HUALAPAI IND. RES.
COCONINO
Peach Springs
WUPATKI N. M.
Klagetoh
Lake Mohave
Chloride
Nelson
Humphreys Pk. 12,633
SUNSET CRATER NAT'L MON.
NAVAJO
Lupton
BLACK MTS.
Valentine
MOHAVE
Kingman
Seligman
Williams
Bellemont
Houck
Sanders
DAVIS DAM
Davis Dam
Bullhead City
Ash Fork
Flagstaff
PAINTED DESERT SECTION
Chambers
WALNUT CANYON NAT'L MON.
FT. MOHAVE IND. RES.
Hualapai Pk. 8,266
METEOR CRATER
Winslow
Joseph City
PETRIFIED FOREST NAT'L PARK
Sedona
Holbrook
Needles
CALIFORNIA
Topock
Chino Valley
Clarkdale
TUZIGOOT NAT'L MON.
Cottonwood
Happy Jack
NEW MEXICO
Havasu Lake
YAVAPAI
Cornville
MONTEZUMA CASTLE NAT'L MON.
Lake Havasu City
Bagdad
Prescott
Camp Verde
Baker Butte 8,077
Snowflake
Concho
St. Johns
Humboldt
Heber
Taylor
Skull Valley
MOGOLLON MESA
Mayer
Verde R.
Clay Springs
Show Low
PARKER DAM
Agua Fria R.
Payson
Lakeside
Springerville
Parker
Congress
Yargell
Pinetop
McNary
Mazatzal Pk. 7,888
Young
FORT APACHE IND. RES.
Eagar
COLORADO RIVER IND. RES.
Bouse
Aguila
Wickenburg
Whiteriver
Wenden
Cave Creek
GILA
Alpine
Colorado River
Salome
Wittmann
FT. McDOWELL IND. RES.
T. Roosevelt Lake
Maverick
PICTOGRAPH ROCKS
El Mirage
Salt
Fort Apache
Quartzsite
Sun City
Glendale
TONTO NAT'L MON.
GREENLEE
Blythe
Tonopah
Phoenix
Scottsdale
SAN CARLOS IND. RES.
Avondale
Mesa
Claypool
Central Hts.
YUMA
Buckeye
Tolleson
Tempe
Gilbert
Miami
Globe
San Carlos
San Carlos L.
Arlington
Chandler
Queen Cr.
Superior
MARICOPA
Colorado
GILA BEND MTS.
GILA RIVER IND. RES.
Bapchule
COOLIDGE DAM
Bylas
Fort Thomas
Morenci
Clifton
Plantsite
GILA BEND I. R.
Sacaton
MARICOPA IND. RES.
CASA GRANDE RUINS N. M.
Gila
Florence
Kearny
Hayden
Winkelman
GRAHAM
PAINTED ROCK DAM
Gila Bend
Coolidge
Pima
Thatcher
Imperial Res.
Laguna Res.
YUMA I. R.
YUMA PROVING GROUND
Gila River
Casa Grande
PINAL
Klondyke
Safford
Solomon
Roll
Eloy
San
Mammoth
W. Yuma
Yuma
Tacna
Picacho
Duncan
Somerton
Wellton
Santa Cruz R.
Oracle
San Manuel
Mt. Graham 10,713
GREAT DESERT
Ajo
Silver Bell
Marana
Pedro
Bowie
Gu Achi
PAPAGO IND. RES.
Tanque Verde
Willcox
Quijotoa
Tucson
S. Tucson
SAGUARO NAT'L MON.
FT. BOWIE NAT'L HIST. SITE
ORGAN PIPE CACTUS NAT'L MON.
P I M A
R.
M E X I C O
SONORA
SAN XAVIER IND. RES.
Sahuarita
Benson
St. David
CHIRICAHUA NAT'L MON.
Sells
Green Valley
COCHISE
Topawa
Tombstone
Huachuca City
Elfrida
Tubac
TUMACACORI NAT'L MON.
SANTA CRUZ
Patagonia
Sierra Vista
Bisbee
Douglas
Naco
Nogales
CORONADO NAT'L MEM.
Puerto Peñasco
N
Agua Prieta
ARIZONA
MILES
0 20 40 60 80
KILOMETERS
0 20 40 60 80
Cananea
Magdalena
State Capital
County Seats
© Copyright HAMMOND INCORPORATED, Maplewood, N. J.
Longitude West of Greenwich

NAME	LOCATION	AREA[1] (sq. m.)	POP. (1970c)	CO. SEAT
Yell	W cen.	929	14,208	Danville and Dardanelle

[1]Area = land area.
[2]City includes Hot Springs National Park, created 1921.

History: Visited by de Soto 1541, Marquette and Joliet 1673, La Salle and de Tonti 1682; Arkansas Post first permanent settlement (1686); in region claimed by France and yielded to Spain 1762; retroceded to France 1800; included in Louisiana Purchase 1803; parts of Louisiana and Missouri territories before becoming Arkansas Territory 1819; adopted first constitution 1836 and admitted to Union June 15 of same year; seceded 1861; capture of Arkansas Post from Confederates 1863; readmitted into Union 1868.

3 \ˈär-kən-ˌsȯ\. County in Arkansas. See table at ARKANSAS.

Arkansas City. 1 \ˌär-kən-ˌsȯ-\. Town, ⊗ of Desha co., SE Arkansas, on Mississippi river; pop. (1970c) 615.

2 \är-ˌkan-zəs-\. City, Cowley co., S Kansas, at confluence of Arkansas and Walnut rivers 47 m. S of Wichita; pop. (1970c) 13,216; flour; oil refineries; Cowley County Community Junior Coll. (1922).

Arkansas Post. Village and oldest white settlement (1686) in Arkansas and in lower Mississippi valley, on N bank of Arkansas river just above its junction with the Mississippi; established by Henry de Tonti, one of La Salle's expedition; colonized by John Law 1719; became part of Louisiana Territory 1763; capital of Arkansas Territory 1819–21; captured by Union troops Jan. 12, 1863; declined after Civil War. Nearby is **Arkansas Post National Memorial,** 62 acres, created 1960.

Arkansas River Navigation System *or officially* **Mc·Clel·lan–Kerr Arkansas River Navigation System** \mə-ˌklel-ən-ˈkər-\. Waterway consisting of sections of the Arkansas and Verdigris rivers, extending from Catoosa (suburb of Tulsa, Oklahoma) to junction of Arkansas and Mississippi rivers, Arkansas; 440 m. long; 17 locks; dedicated 1971.

Ar·khan·gelsk \är-ˈkan-ˌgelsk\ *or Eng.* **Arch·an·gel** \ˈär-ˌkān-jəl\. City, ✱ of Arkhangelsk Oblast, Russian S.F.S.R., U.S.S.R., on right bank of Northern Dvina near its mouth ab. 460 m. NE of Leningrad; pop. (1970p) 343,-000; major export is timber; shipbuilding, paper and pulp making. At head of Dvina Gulf with very large harbor, closed by ice sometimes as much as 190 days in a year, but this handicap now much reduced by icebreakers; has much river and canal traffic and is terminus of rail lines to Moscow and Leningrad; has a monastery dedicated to the Archangel Michael, from which it received its name.

History: Vicinity settled by Northmen 10th cent. A.D.; harbor discovered by English trading expedition under Richard Chancellor who had been sent to discover Northeast Passage 1553; town began with establishment there of first factory (trading station) of Muscovy Company; opened to trade of other European nations by Boris Godunov (1598–1605); flourished as sole Russian seaport until building of St. Petersburg (see LENINGRAD) 1703; a scene of Allied (British, French, and American) support of north Russian government which resisted Bolshevist government of Russia 1918–19; of great importance in World War II, receiving convoys of lend-lease goods from England and United States 1941–45.

Arkhangelsk Oblast \-ˈȯ-blast, -ˌblast\. Subdivision of the Russian S.F.S.R., U.S.S.R., bordering on Barents Sea; its W coast extends along the White Sea; 226,795 sq. m.; pop. (1970p) 1,402,000; ✱ Arkhangelsk. Includes also two large island groups in the Arctic, Novaya Zemlya and Franz Josef Land. Chief rivers Northern Dvina, Onega, and lower course of Mezen. Climate is severe and coastal waters are frozen from late October for an average of 140 days; lumbering, fishing; chief towns Arkhangelsk, Onega, Severodvinsk, Mezen, Kotlas; formed 1937.

Ark·low \ˈär-(ˌ)klō\. Market town and seaport, co. Wicklow, SE Eire, on E coast at mouth of Avoca river 37 m. S by SE of Dublin; pop. (1971p) 6750; oyster and herring fisheries; ancient castle of the Ormondes captured and demolished by Cromwell 1649; Irish insurgents defeated by British 1798.

Ar·ko·na \är-ˈkō-nə\. Promontory on N coast of Rügen I., East Germany, in Baltic Sea, 148 ft. above sea level; remains of foundation of ancient temple, destroyed 1168 by Danes and Pomeranians, found 1921.

Arl·berg \ˈär(ə)l-ˌbərg, -ˌbe(ə)rg\. Alpine valley, pass, and tunnel in the Tirol, W Austria. In the valley the "Arlberg technique" in skiing was perfected. See ALPS.

Arles \ˈär(ə)l\. 1 Medieval kingdom, also called kingdom of Burgundy (*q.v.*), formed from union by Rudolf II in 933 of kingdoms of Cisjurane Burgundy and Transjurane Burgundy; attached to Holy Roman Empire under Emperor Conrad II 1033–34; kingdom had only nominal unity in 11th and 12th cents., although title King of Arles was assumed by German emperors, notably by Frederick Barbarossa 1178; gradually split up, Provence passing to house of Anjou 1246 and to French Crown 1481, and Dauphiné 1349, Franche-Comté 1678, and Savoy 1860 being annexed to France.

2 *or anc.* **Ar·e·las** \ˈa(ə)r-ə-ləs\ *or* **Ar·e·la·te** \ˌar-ə-ˈlā-tē\. City, Bouches-du-Rhône dept., SE France, on left bank of Rhone 45 m. NW of Marseilles; pop. (1968c) 45,774; chemicals, paper; shipbuilding; grapes, olive trees; connected with Mediterranean by canal; ancient Romanesque cathedral; ancient remains, including Roman burial place and ruins of palace of Constantine.

History: Began to prosper as trading center after consul Marius had built canal connecting it with sea 103 B.C., and some of Caesar's legions had settled there; as outlet for commerce of Gaul, surpassed Massilia (see MARSEILLES) and became, next to Rome, wealthiest city of early Roman Empire; episcopal see from 1st cent. A.D.; residence of Emperor Constantine; seat of Council of Arles which decided Donatist controversy 314 A.D. and of several later ones 353, 452, 475; in 5th and 6th cents. captured by Visigoths, besieged by Franks, and taken by Ostrogoths; sacked by Saracens in 8th cent.; capital of kingdom of Arles 933–1246; besieged by Emperor Charles V 1526; archiepiscopal see suppressed by 1790.

Ar·leux \är-ˈlə(r), -ˈlœ\. Commune, Nord dept., N France, 15 m. E of Arras; pop. (1962c) 1961; battle Sept.–Oct. 1918 in advance of Canadians upon Cambrai.

Arleux–en–Go·helle \-äⁿ-ˈgwī\. Commune, Pas-de-Calais dept., N France, 7 m. NE of Arras; pop. (1962c) 564; seized by Canadians Apr. 1917 in one of the battles around Arras.

Ar·ling·ton \ˈär-liŋ-tən\. 1 County in Virginia. See table at VIRGINIA. Suburb of Washington, D.C., across Potomac river; officially, a county governed as a unit, without districts or other subdivisions and classified as urban with no incorporated place. Site of Arlington National Cemetery (on former estate of Robert E. Lee), containing memorial amphitheater (dedicated 1920) and Tomb of the Unknown Soldier; Marymount Coll. (1950); Pentagon Building, headquarters of U.S. Dept. of Defense; Fort Myer nearby. Alexandria located in county but independent of it.

2 Locality, Riverside co., SE California, SW part of city of Riverside.

3 Town, Middlesex co., NE Massachusetts, 6 m. NW of Boston; pop. (1970c) 53,524; residential suburb of Boston.

4 Manufacturing and residential town, Hudson co., NE New Jersey, on Passaic river ab. 3 m. NNE of Newark; unincorporated, part of Kearny town.

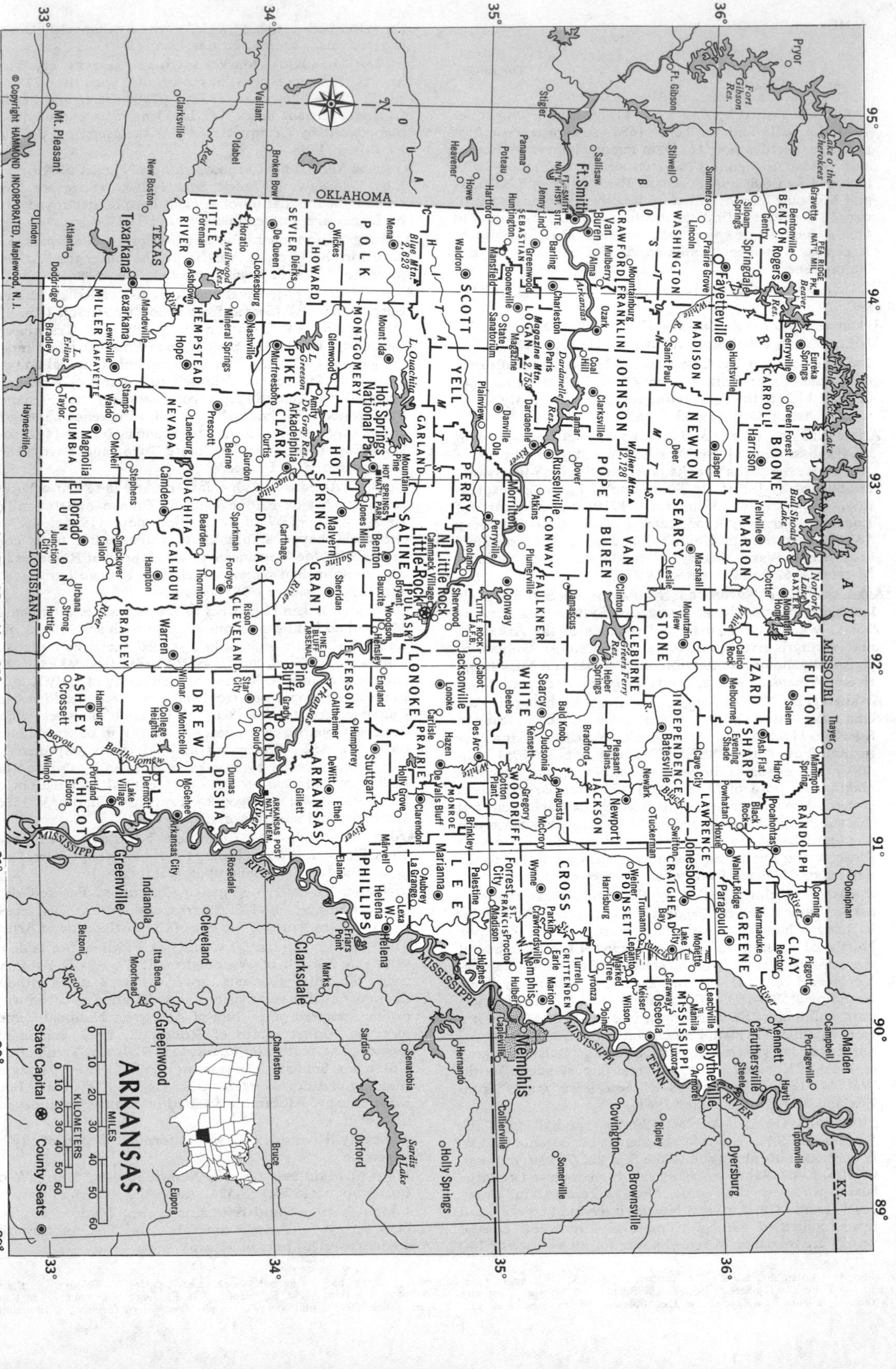
ARKANSAS
MILES
0 10 20 30 40 50 60
KILOMETERS
0 10 20 30 40 50 60
State Capital
County Seats
© Copyright HAMMOND INCORPORATED, Maplewood, N.J.
Longitude West of Greenwich
OKLAHOMA
MISSOURI
TEXAS
LOUISIANA
TENN.
KY.
MISSISSIPPI
BENTON
CARROLL
BOONE
MARION
BAXTER
FULTON
RANDOLPH
CLAY
WASHINGTON
MADISON
NEWTON
SEARCY
STONE
IZARD
SHARP
LAWRENCE
GREENE
CRAWFORD
FRANKLIN
JOHNSON
POPE
VAN BUREN
CLEBURNE
INDEPENDENCE
JACKSON
CRAIGHEAD
MISSISSIPPI
SEBASTIAN
LOGAN
YELL
CONWAY
FAULKNER
WHITE
WOODRUFF
CROSS
POINSETT
CRITTENDEN
SCOTT
PERRY
PULASKI
LONOKE
PRAIRIE
MONROE
ST. FRANCIS
LEE
POLK
MONTGOMERY
GARLAND
SALINE
GRANT
JEFFERSON
ARKANSAS
PHILLIPS
SEVIER
HOWARD
PIKE
CLARK
HOT SPRING
DALLAS
CLEVELAND
LINCOLN
DESHA
LITTLE RIVER
HEMPSTEAD
NEVADA
OUACHITA
CALHOUN
BRADLEY
DREW
CHICOT
MILLER
LAFAYETTE
COLUMBIA
UNION
ASHLEY
Little Rock
N. Little Rock
Ft. Smith
Fayetteville
Springdale
Rogers
Jonesboro
Pine Bluff
Hot Springs National Park
Texarkana
El Dorado
Blytheville
Memphis
West Memphis
Helena
Greenville
Clarksdale
Greenwood
Conway
Russellville
Camden
Magnolia
Arkadelphia
Searcy
Benton
Stuttgart
Harrison
Batesville
Paragould
Forrest City
Osceola
Magazine Mtn. 2,753
Blue Mtn. 2,623
Walker Mtn. 2,128
Bull Shoals Lake
Norfork Lake
Beaver Res.
Greers Ferry Res.
Dardanelle Res.
L. Ouachita
Millwood Res.
Lake o' the Cherokees
Fort Gibson Res.
Sardis Lake
Arkansas
White
Red
Ouachita
Saline
Black
St. Francis
Bayou Bartholomew
MISSISSIPPI RIVER
PEA RIDGE NAT'L MIL. PK.
FT. SMITH NAT'L HIST. SITE
HOT SPRINGS NAT'L PARK
PINE BLUFF ARSENAL
LITTLE ROCK A.F.B.
ARKANSAS POST NAT'L MEM.

5 Residential community (unincorporated), Dutchess co., New York, E of Poughkeepsie; pop. (1970c) 11,203.
6 City, Kingsbury co., E South Dakota; pop. (1970c) 954.
7 City, Tarrant co., N Texas, 13 m. E of Fort Worth; pop. (1970c) 89,723; Univ. of Texas at Arlington (1895).
8 City, ⊗ of Arlington co., Virginia.

Arlington Heights. 1 Village, Cook and Lake cos., NE Illinois, 25 m. NW of Chicago; pop. (1970c) 64,884; racecourse.
2 Village, Hamilton co., SW Ohio; pop. (1970c) 1476; N suburb of Cincinnati.

Ar·lon \är-ˈlōⁿ\ *or anc.* **Or·o·lau·num** \ˌȯr-ə-ˈlō-nəm, ˌär-\. Commune, ✱ of Luxembourg prov., SE Belgium, near border of Grand Duchy of Luxembourg; pop. (1970e) 14,343; wool factories, iron and pottery works; museum of Roman antiquities. Fortified 1671; occupied by French 1684–97; victories of Jourdan over Imperial forces 1793, 1794; Belgian since 1831. In World War II on edge of German advance Dec. 1944–Jan. 1945.

Ar·ma \ˈär-mə\. City, Crawford co., SE Kansas, 10 m. N of Pittsburg; pop. (1970c) 1348.

Ar·ma·ged·don \ˌär-mə-ˈged-ᵊn\. Greek form of Hebrew name of place, probably Megiddo (*q.v.*), where, according to *Revelation* xvi. 16, a great battle is to be fought.

Ar·magh \är-ˈmä, ˈär-ˌ\. 1 County, S Northern Ireland, touches S shore of Lough Neagh; 512 sq. m.; pop. (1971p) 131,441; ⊗ Armagh; other towns Portadown, Lurgan; rich agricultural land; electrical equipment, synthetic fabrics; food processing; tourism.
2 Urban district, its ⊗, 33 m. SW of Belfast; pop. (1971p) 11,724; linen; seat of Roman Catholic and Protestant archbishops. According to tradition, founded by St. Patrick; seat of famous medieval school of theology; metropolis of Ireland and a leading intellectual center of the western world from 5th to 9th cents.

Ar·ma·gnac \ˌär-mən-ˈyak\. Small territory in the old province of Gascony, SW France, now included in department of Gers; capitals successively Auch and Lectoure. Known particularly for viticulture, producing famous Armagnac brandy.
History: Region near Auch (*q.v.*) part of Roman province of Aquitania; part of Gascon county of Fézensac (erected in 9th cent.) until it became separate countship of Armagnac c. 960; under Count Gerald III annexed Fézensac 1140; in 15th cent. countship extended from the Garonne to the Adour; first annexed to French Crown 1497, but returned finally by descent through Navarre family 1607; countship granted 1645 by Louis XIV to Henry of Lorraine, Count of Harcourt, by whose family it was held until 1789.

Ar·ma·vir \ˌär-mə-ˈvi(ə)r\. City, Krasnodar Krai, U.S.S.R., 100 m. E of Krasnodar, NE of Maikop oil fields; pop. (1970p) 146,000; center of fertile agricultural region; food processing; footwear; under German control Aug.–Dec. 1942; founded 1848.

Ar·me·nia \är-ˈmē-nē-ə, -nyə\. 1 *or Bib.* **Min·ni** \ˈmin-ˌī\. Ancient country in W Asia, now divided bet. the U.S.S.R., Turkey, and Iran. It centered in the mountainous region (highest point Mt. Ararat) SE of Black Sea and SW of Caspian Sea; included sources of Euphrates and Araks rivers and lakes Van and Sevan.
History: Equivalent to ancient kingdom of Van c. 1270–850 B.C. bet. Caucasus and Lake Van; residence of Vannic peoples, skilled in industrial arts and metallurgy; repeatedly attacked by Assyrians who called it Urartu (*q.v.*); conquered by Medes 612 B.C.; occupied by Armenian peoples and under kings of Media 612–549 B.C.; administered as a Persian satrapy 549–331 B.C.; under Alexander and successors 331–317 B.C.; following independence and division into two, reunited with Artaxata as capital by Tigranes (95–55 B.C.), most powerful ruler of Asia; after defeat by Lucullus 69 B.C., became allied to Rome; first to adopt Christianity as national religion 303 A.D.; persecution of Christians 4th–5th cents.; separated from Greek rite 491; changed hands frequently in wars bet. Neo-Persian and Roman Empires 3d–7th cents.; under caliphates, scene of strife bet. Arabs, Seljuks, Byzantines, and Mongols; ruled by Ottoman Turks from 1514; eastern part ceded to Persia 1620; its northern boundary contiguous with Russia 1802 after latter's occupation of Georgia; two districts ceded to Russia 1828, 1829; rise of Armenian nationalism among its scattered peoples 19th cent.; subject of "Armenian question" which plagued European powers after Ottoman Empire failed to carry out reforms first promised in Treaty of Berlin 1878; part ceded to Russia by Turkey by Treaty of San Stefano 1878; scene of a series of massacres which began 1893–94 and continued spasmodically throughout World War I; suffering aggravated as scene of Russo-Turkish hostility during war; after Turkish defeat, Russian part set up as Soviet republic 1921, rest remaining under Turkey (see ARMENIA, TURKISH).
2 Republic, U.S.S.R. See ARMENIAN SOVIET SOCIALIST REPUBLIC.

Armenia \är-ˈmän-yə\. City, ✱ of Quindío dept., W cen. Colombia, W of Ibagué; pop. (1968e) 142,191; univ. (1960); in rich coffee district.

Armenia, Greater. Name sometimes given, esp. in medieval times, to region of Armenia.

Armenia, Lesser. See CILICIA.

Armenia, Turkish. The NE part of Turkey in Asia, comprising the whole or parts of 9 provinces; ab. 57,000 sq. m.; chief towns Kars, Erzurum, Erzincan. For history, see ARMENIA 1.

Armenia Minor. In Roman times, an E district of province of Pontus, bordering W Armenia.

Armenian Soviet Socialist Republic *or frequently* **Armenia** *or Armenian* **Ha·yas·dan** \ˌhī-ə-ˈstän, ˌhä-yəs-ˈdän\. A constituent republic of the U.S.S.R., in S Transcaucasia, bounded on N by Georgian S.S.R., on E by Azerbaijan S.S.R., on S by Iran and Nakhichevan A.S.S.R., and on W by Turkey; 11,506 sq. m.; pop. (1970p) 2,493,000; ✱ Yerevan. Mountainous, with many peaks above 10,000 ft., highest Aragats 13,418 ft. Contains Lake Sevan with its outlet the Razdan river, a tributary of the Araks which forms boundary with Turkish Armenia on SW; in Araks valley chief products raised are cotton, mulberry, fruits, rice, and tobacco; copper, zinc, lead. *Chief cities:* Yerevan, Leninakan, Kirovakan. Set up as Soviet republic Apr. 2, 1921; joined Georgian S.S.R. and Azerbaijan S.S.R. Mar. 12, 1922 to form the Transcaucasian S.F.S.R. which on Dec. 30, 1922 became part of the U.S.S.R.; on abolition of the Transcaucasian S.F.S.R. Dec. 5, 1936, became a constituent republic of U.S.S.R.

Ar·men·tières \ˌär-mən-tē-ˈe(ə)r, -ˈti(ə)rz\. Commune, Nord dept., N France, 8 m. WNW of Lille; pop. (1968c) 26,916; textiles; near British front line in World War I; taken and destroyed by Germans April 10, 1918; retaken by British Oct. 1–2, 1918; rebuilt after the war.

Ar·me·ro \är-ˈme(ə)r-(ˌ)ō\. Town, Tolima dept., W cen. Colombia; munic. pop. (1968e) 27,491.

Ar·mi·dale \ˈär-mə-ˌdāl\. Town, NE New South Wales, SE Australia, 240 m. N of Sydney; pop. (1968e) 15,890; in agricultural area; Univ. of New England (1954).

Ar·mor·i·ca \är-ˈmȯr-ə-kə, -ˈmär-\ *or older* **Ar·e·mor·i·ca** \ˌar-ə-\. Ancient name for region in NW France comprising the coast of Gaul bet. Seine and Loire rivers. Inhabited by Cymric Celts; with Caesar's subjugation of Veneti 56 B.C., came under Roman rule; organized as Roman province of Lugdunensis; extreme NW part invaded in 5th cent. A.D. by Britons (Celtic peoples from Britain) and thereafter called Brittany (*q.v.*); E part became Normandy.

Ar·mour \ˈär-mər\. City, ⊗ of Douglas co., S South Dakota; pop. (1970c) 925; grain farms.

Arm·strong \ˈärm-ˌstrȯŋ\. 1 Name of counties in two states of the U.S. See tables at PENNSYLVANIA, TEXAS.

2 Former county in South Dakota; annexed to Dewey co. 1954.

Ar·nett \är-ˈnet\. Town, ⊗ of Ellis co., NW Oklahoma; pop. (1970c) 711; dairy farms.

Arn·hem \ˈärn-ˌhem, ˈär-nəm\. Commune, ✱ of Gelderland prov., E Netherlands, on right bank of Rhine near confluence with IJssel 33 m. ESE of Utrecht; pop. (1970e) 132,531; electrical equipment, rayon fiber; metalworking, shipbuilding; tourism.

History: First mentioned 893 A.D.; home of the dukes of Gelderland 13th–16th cents.; formerly member of the Hanseatic League; has town hall, Groote Kerk, museum of antiquities. Conquered 1473 by Charles the Bold; came under States-General 1585; taken by French 1672 and 1795 and by Prussians 1813. In World War II captured by Germans 1940; scene of heroic fight Sept. 17–25, 1944 by British 1st Airborne Division encircled by Germans in unsuccessful attempt to secure Rhine bridges, about only one quarter escaping; finally captured Apr. 13, 1945.

Arnhem, Cape \-ˈär-nəm\. Point, NE Arnhem Land, Australia, on NW coast of Gulf of Carpentaria.

Arnhem Land *also* **Arn·hem·land** \ˈär-nəm-ˌland\. Region on N coast of Northern Territory, Australia; bauxite, manganese; discovered 1623 by expedition of Jan Carstensz.

Ar·no \ˈär-(ˌ)nō\ *or anc.* **Ar·nus** \-nəs\. River, Tuscany, cen. Italy; 150 m. long; rises in Monte Falterona, flows W from the Apennines through Florence into Ligurian Sea 7 m. below (W of) Pisa; navigable up to Florence; near Arezzo connected with Tiber by its canalized tributary, the Chiani; subject to sudden rises and disastrous floods. In World War II reached by Allied armies in advance N from Rome June–Aug. 1944.

Ar·nold \ˈärn-ᵊld\. 1 City, Westmoreland co., SW Pennsylvania, on Allegheny river 16 m. NE of Pittsburgh; pop. (1970c) 8174; manufactures window glass.

2 Urban district, Nottinghamshire, N cen. England, 5½ m. NE of Nottingham; pop. (1971p) 33,254; textiles.

Arnon. See MAWJIB, WADI AL-.

Arn·øya \ˈärn-ˌə(r)-yə\. Island in Arctic Ocean off N coast of Norway, ab. 50 m. NE of Tromsø.

Arn·pri·or \ˈärn-ˌprī(-ə)r\. Town, Renfrew co., SE Ontario, Canada, at confluence of Madawaska and Ottawa rivers 37 m. W of Ottawa; pop. (1971p) 6017; industrial town.

Arns·berg \ˈärnz-ˌbərg, ˈärn(t)s-ˌbe(ə)rg\. City, North Rhine-Westphalia, West Germany, on Ruhr river 42 m. SSE of Münster; pop. (1969e) 22,794; paper, textiles; brewery; ancient capital of Westphalia; founded 1077; received municipal charter 1237; joined Hanseatic League; became Prussian 1815.

Arn·stadt \ˈärn-ˌs(h)tät\. City, Erfurt dist., East Germany, S of Erfurt; pop. (1970e) 28,762; engineering works; ancient capital of principality of Schwarzburg-Sondershausen; first mentioned 704 A.D.; received municipal rights 1266; bought by counts of Schwarzburg 1306 whose seat it was till 1716.

Arnswalde. See CHOSZCZNO.

Arnus. See ARNO.

Aro \ˈär-(ˌ)ō\. River, cen. Venezuela; ab. 100 m. long; flows N into the Orinoco.

Aroe Islands. See ARU ISLANDS.

Arol·sen \ˈär-əl-zən\. Town, ✱ of former Waldeck principality, now in Hesse, West Germany; pop. (1964e) 5800.

Aromata. See ASIR, RAS.

Aroos·took \ə-ˈrüs-tək, -ˈru̇s-, -tik\. 1 River, N Maine; 140 m. long; rises in NE Piscataquis co., flows NE across New Brunswick (Canada) border and into St. John river. This region was scene of "Aroostook War" Feb.–May 1839, a clash bet. authority of Maine and New Brunswick over territory near the river, a preliminary to determining the boundary of Maine in Webster-Ashburton Treaty 1842.

2 County in Maine. See table at MAINE.

Aro·roy \ˌär-ə-ˈrȯi\. Municipality, port on N coast of Masbate I., Masbate prov., Phil.; pop. (1969e) 24,500.

Arpachiya. See TELL ARPACHIYA.

Ar·pi·no \är-ˌpē-(ˌ)nō\ *or anc.* **Ar·pi·num** \är-ˈpī-nəm\. Commune, Frosinone prov., Latium, cen. Italy, 13 m. E of Frosinone; pop. (1968e) 8322; textiles; marble quarries. Ancient town of the Volsci and, later, of the Samnites; conquered by Romans 305 B.C.; given Roman civic privileges 188 B.C. Birthplace of Marius, Cicero, and Marcus Vipsanius Agrippa.

Ar·qua Pe·trar·ca \är-ˌkwä-pə-ˈträr-kə\. Village, Veneto, NE Italy, on SE slope of Euganean Hills ab. 15 m. SW of Padua; Petrarch died here 1374.

Arques \ˈärk\ *or in full* **Arques–la–Ba·taille** \-ˌläb-ə-ˈtī\. Village and castle, Seine-Maritime dept., France, just S of Dieppe, Normandy; scene of battle Sept. 21, 1589 in which Henry IV defeated forces of the Holy League under duc de Mayenne.

Ar·rah \ˈär-ə\. Town, W Bihar, NE India, 35 m. W of Patna; pop. (1961c) 38,092; scene of defense against overwhelming odds by small body of British troops during Sepoy Mutiny 1857.

Ar Ramāḍī. See RAMADI.

Ar Ramal. See RAMLEH.

Ar·ran \ˈar-ən\. Island, Bute co., in Firth of Clyde, off SW coast of Scotland; 166 sq. m.; pop. (1961c) 3705; harbors at Brodick and Lamlash; prehistoric and Danish relics; hideout for Robert Bruce (King's Caves); seat of the dukes of Hamilton (Brodick Castle).

Ar Raqqah. See RAKKA.

Ar·ras \ə-ˈräs, ˈar-əs\ *or anc.* **Nem·e·to·cen·na** \ˌnem-ət-ə-ˈsen-ə\. City, ✱ of Pas-de-Calais dept., N France, 25 m. SW of Lille; pop. (1968c) 49,144; administrative and trading center; episcopal see from 390; famous cathedral, abbey of St. Vaast, and city hall ruined by shells in World War I.

History: Principal town of the Atrebates; destroyed by Attila 451 A.D. and by Northmen 800; ruled by county of Flanders; noted as medieval center for manufacture of tapestries; scene of two treaties: (1) bet. Burgundians and Armagnacs 1435, and (2) terminating war bet. Maximilian I of Austria and Louis XI of France 1482; ceded to France by latter treaty and its name changed (temporarily) by Louis XI to **Fran·chise** \fräⁿ-ˈshēz\; ceded to Maximilian of Austria 1493 and held by Spanish branch of Hapsburgs to 1640; gave name to league of Catholic provinces of Netherlands which were loyal to Spain 1579; taken by Louis XIII of France 1640, and, as part of Artois (*q.v.*), ceded to France 1659; scene of fierce battles 1914–18, during which city almost completely razed by shellfire; largely rebuilt. Captured by British Aug. 31, 1944.

Ar·re·ci·fe \ˌär-ə-ˈsē-(ˌ)fā\ *or* **Puer·to Arrecife** \ˌpwert-ō-\. Seaport, Las Palmas prov. (E Canary Is.), Spain, on SE coast of Lanzarote I. 129 m. NE of Las Palmas; pop. (1970p) 21,906.

Arretium. See AREZZO 2.

Arriaca. See GUADALAJARA 2.

Ar Rimal. See RUBʻ AL-KHALI.

Arroe Islands. See ARU ISLANDS.

Ar·ro·manches–les–Bains \ˌar-ō-ˈmäⁿsh-lā-ˈbaⁿ\. Coast village, Calvados dept., N France, 5 m. NNE of Bayeux; site of one of the two portable harbor installations used by Allies June 1944 in invasion of Normandy.

Ar·row, Lough \ˌläk-ˈar-(ˌ)ō\. Lake, SE co. Sligo, Eire; 4 m. long, 2½ m. wide; its outlet flows ab. 12 m. NW into Owenboy river S of Sligo.

Arrow Lake \ˌar-ō-\. Reservoir, a widening of Columbia river in SE British Columbia, Canada; ab. 93 m. long; 199 sq. m.; often divided into **Upper Arrow Lake** (to the N) ab. 36 m. long, and **Lower Arrow Lake** (to the S) ab. 51 m. long.

Arrow Peak. Mountain in San Juan Mts., San Juan co., SW Colorado; 13,810 ft.

Ar·royo \ə-'rȯi-(ˌ)ō\. Town and municipality, on the coast, SE Puerto Rico; munic. pop. (1970p) 13,093.

Arroyo Gran·de \ə-ˌrȯi-ə-'gran-dē\. City, San Luis Obispo co., SW California, 11 m. SSE of San Luis Obispo; pop. (1970c) 7454; truck farming.

Ar·roy·os y Es·te·ros \ə-'rȯi-ōs-ˌē-e-'ster-əs\. Town and district, Cordillera dept., cen. Paraguay; district pop. (1962c) 20,484.

Ar Ruṭbah. See RUTBA.

Arsanias. See MURAT NEHRI.

Arsenaria. See ARZEW.

Ar·se·nyev \är-'shen-yəf\ *or before 1952* **Se·me·nov·ka** \səm-'yȯn-əf-kə\. Town, Primorski Krai, Russian S.F.S.R., U.S.S.R., ab. 100 m. NE of Vladivostok; pop. (1967e) 41,000.

Ar·sie·ro \ärs-'ye(ə)r-(ˌ)ō\. Commune, Vicenza prov., Veneto, NE Italy, 20 m. NNW of Vicenza; pop. (1968e) 3760; marble quarries; burned by Austrians 1916.

Ar·sin·oë \är-'sin-ə-ˌwē\. 1 Ancient town, one of the Pentapolis of Cyrenaica, on the coast NE of Berenice (*or mod.* Benghazi, Libya).

2 *or older* **Croc·o·di·lop·o·lis** \ˌkräk-ə-də-'läp-ə-ləs\. City of ancient Egypt, on Birket (lake) Qārūn near the site of modern Al-Faiyūm; said to have been founded ab. 2300 B.C.; chief seat of early Egyptian worship of the crocodile; received its later name from sister and wife of Ptolemy II Philadelphus.

Arta \'ärt-ə\. 1 River, Greece. See ARAKHTHOS.

2 Department of Greece. See table at GREECE.

3 *or anc.* **Am·bra·cia** \am-'brā-sh(ē-)ə\. City, its ✱, S Epirus, NW Greece, on Arakhthos river N of Ambracian Gulf; pop. (1971p) 20,333; episcopal see.

History: Ambracia founded by Corinthians 7th cent. B.C.; became capital of Pyrrhus, king of Epirus, 295 B.C.; after its decline, new town of Arta founded on its site and became important fortification in Byzantine times; seat of despot of Epirus in 13th and 14th cents.; taken 1449 by Turks, by Ali Pasha 1798, by Reshid Pasha 1822; to Greece 1881.

Arta, Gulf of. See AMBRACIAN GULF.

'Ar·ta·wi·ya \ˌärt-ə-'wē-(y)ə\. Town, N Saudi Arabia, in NE Nejd; founded since 1912 as first Ikhwan colony in Wahabi revival.

Ar·tax·a·ta \är-'tak-sət-ə\. Ruined city, ancient ✱ of Armenia, on left bank of Araks river 17 m. S of Yerevan, Armenian S.S.R., U.S.S.R.; destroyed 58 A.D. by Roman general Corbulo.

Ar·tei·jo \är-'tā-(ˌ)hō\. Commune, La Coruña prov., Spain, 6 m. SW of La Coruña; pop. (1970p) 12,166.

Ar·tem \är-'tyȯm\. Town, Primorski Krai, Russian S.F.S.R., U.S.S.R., ab. 20 m. NE of Vladivostok; pop. (1969e) 65,000; porcelain factory, thermal power station; founded 1924.

Ar·te·mi·sa \ˌärt-ə-'mē-sə\. Town and municipality, E Pinar del Río prov., W Cuba; town pop. (1967e) 27,300.

Ar·te·mi·sium \ˌärt-ə-'miz(h)-ē-əm, -'mizh-əm\ *or Gk.* **Ar·te·mí·si·on** \-'mēs-ˌyȯn\. Promontory forming NE point of Greek island of Euboea, Aegean Sea; scene of naval victory of the Greeks over the Persians 480 B.C.

Ar·te·movsk \är-'tem-əfsk\ *or formerly* **Bakh·mut** \'bäk-mu̇t, 'bäk̲-\. City, N Donetsk Oblast, Ukrainian S.S.R., U.S.S.R., 45 m. N of Donetsk in the Donets Basin; pop. (1969e) 81,000; industrial town and railroad junction; extensive salt mines; coal and mercury.

Ar·te·sia \är-'tē-zhə\. 1 City, Los Angeles co., California, NE of Long Beach; pop. (1970c) 14,757.

2 City, Eddy co., SE New Mexico, 38 m. S of Roswell; pop. (1970c) 10,315; Coll. of Artesia (1966).

Artesium. See ARTOIS.

Ar·tha·bas·ka \ˌär-thə-'bas-kə\. 1 County, S Quebec, Canada. See table at QUEBEC.

2 Town, its ⊗, 38 m. SE of Three Rivers; pop. (1971p) 4483.

Ar·thing·ton \'är-thiŋ-tən\. Town, W Liberia, W Africa, 30 m. NNE of Monrovia.

Ar·thur \'är-thər\. 1 County in W Nebraska. See table at NEBRASKA.

2 Village, its ⊗; pop. (1970c) 175.

3 River, NW Tasmania, Australia; ab. 100 m. long; rises in NW part of central highland and flows WNW to Indian Ocean S of Cape Grim.

Arthur Kill \-'kil\. Channel, NE New Jersey, bet. New Jersey and Staten I., New York; connects Newark Bay with Raritan Bay.

Arthur Peak. 1 Mountain, E boundary of Yellowstone National Park, NW Wyoming; 10,426 ft.

2 Peak, N South I., New Zealand; 8800 ft.

Ar·thur's Pass \ˌär-thərz-\. Mountain pass through Otira Gorge in Southern Alps, cen. South I., New Zealand.

Arthur's Seat. Hill in Edinburgh, Scotland, overlooking SE section of city; elev. 823 ft.; from it King Arthur is said to have watched the defeat of the Picts by his army.

Ar·ti·bo·nite \ˌärt-i-bə-'nēt\. River, Haiti, flowing W into Gulf of Gonave.

Ar·ti·gas \är-'tē-gəs\. 1 Department of NW Uruguay. See table at URUGUAY.

2 *or* **San Eu·ge·nio** \ˌsän-eu̇-'hā-(ˌ)nyō\ *also* **San Eugenio del Cua·reim** \-ˌdel-kwä-'rām\. Town, its ✱, near Brazil border, ab. 304 m. N of Montevideo; pop. (1963c) 23,781.

Ar·tois \är-'twä\ *or Lat.* **Ar·te·sium** \är-'tē-zhē(-ə)m, -zē-əm\ *or Flemish* **Atrecht** \'ä-ˌtrekt\. Historical region of N France, bounded on N by the Strait of Dover, E by Flanders, S and W by Picardy; ✱ Arras.

History: Western part of county of Flanders, given as dowry to Isabella of Hainaut on her marriage to Philip Augustus 1180; inherited by Louis VIII who made it part of royal domain 1222; returned to count of Flanders 1382; passed to dukes of Burgundy who held it 1384–1477; with marriage 1477 of Mary of Burgundy to Hapsburg Maximilian I, passed to Austria, ultimately to Philip IV of Spain 1640; France received final sovereignty over it by Treaties of the Pyrenees 1659 and of Nijmegen 1678; scene of three battles of World War I, Sept. 27–Oct. 10, 1914, May 9–June 18, 1915, and Sept. 25–Oct. 15, 1915.

Art·vin \ärt-'vēn\. 1 Province of NE Turkey, Asia. See table at TURKEY.

2 Town, its ✱; pop. (1965c) 9847.

Aru·ba *also* **Oru·ba** \ə-'rü-bə\. Island off coast of NW Venezuela; administratively part of Netherlands Antilles; 19 m. long by ab. 5 m. wide; 69 sq. m.; pop. (1969e) 59,813; chief town Oranjestad; barren; no oil deposits, but has important refineries where oil from Venezuela is processed; phosphates. In World War II the refineries were shelled by German submarines Feb. and Apr. 1942 and some damage done.

Aru·cas \ə-'rü-kəs\. Commune, Las Palmas prov. (E Canary Is.), Spain, on Grand Canary I. 6 m. W of Las Palmas; pop. (1970p) 24,030; sugarcane.

Aru Islands; *formerly* **Aroe Islands** *also* **Ar·roe Islands** \ˌär-(ˌ)ü-\. Group of one large and ab. 90 small islands off SW coast of island of New Guinea, Maluku prov., Indonesia; 3305 sq. m.; pop. (1961c) 29,604. Chief island Tanahbesar, ab. 122 m. long by 58 m. wide, divided into six sections by narrow channels; chief town Dobo on small island on W coast of Tanahbesar I.

Ar·un \'ar-ən\. River, Sussex, S England; 37 m. long; flows S into the English Channel at Littlehampton.

Aru·na·chal Pra·desh \ˌär-ə-ˌnäch-əl-prə-'desh\ *or formerly* **North East Frontier Agency.** Union territory, NE India; ab. 35,000 sq. m.; ✱ Ziro; established 1972.

Ar·un·del \'ar-ən-dᵊl\. 1 Municipal borough, West Sussex, England, on Arun river 5 m. from its mouth; pop. (1971p)

2382; formerly a flourishing seaport connected 1813 by canal with London; now small market town; site of Arundel Castle, seat of dukes of Norfolk.
2 Small island of the New Georgia Is., cen. Solomon Is., off NW tip of New Georgia and at SW end of Kula Gulf. Occupied by U.S. forces Aug. 1943.

Aru·sha \ə-'rü-shə\. 1 Region of NE Tanzania. See table at TANZANIA.
2 Town, its ✻; pop. (1967c) 32,452; seat of secretariat of East African Community.

Aru·si \ə-'rü-sē\. Province of cen. Ethiopia. See table at ETHIOPIA.

Aru·tanga \ˌär-ə-'täŋ-gə\. Chief village of Aitutaki, Cook Is., S Pacific Ocean, on W coast.

Aru·wi·mi \ˌär-ə-'wē-mē\. River, cen. Africa; 620 m. long; rises in NE Zaire near Lake Albert, flows SW and W across N Zaire into Congo river; called the Ituri in its upper course.

Arva. See ØRAVA.

Arvad. See ARWAD.

Ar·va·da \är-'vad-ə, -'väd-\. Town, Adams and Jefferson cos., Colorado, W of Denver; pop. (1970c) 46,814.

Ar·vi·da \är-'vīd-ə\. City, Chicoutimi co., S Quebec, Canada, 5 m. W of Chicoutimi on the Saguenay; pop. (1971p) 18,433; important aluminum plant.

Ar·vi·ka \är-'vē-kə\. Town, Värmland co., W Sweden, ab. 30 m. NW of Lake Vänern; pop. (1970e) 15,998.

Ar·vin \'är-vən\. City, Kern co., S California, 16 m. SE of Bakersfield; pop. (1970c) 5199; grapes and peaches.

Ar·wad \är-'wad, -'wäd\ *or Fr.* **Île Rou·ad** \ēl-rü-åd\ *or Bib.* **Ar·vad** \'är-ˌvad\ *or anc.* **Ar·a·dus** \'ar-əd-əs\. Island ab. 2 m. off the coast of Syria, near Tartūs; seaport of ancient Phoenicia (*Ezek.* xxvii. 8) and a flourishing city during Phoenician ascendancy (see TRIPOLI 3). In World War I first point on Syrian coast occupied by French; made postal station 1916; at end of war became part of French mandate of Latakia.

Ar·za·mas \ˌär-zə-'mäs\. Town, S Gorki Oblast, U.S.S.R., ab. 60 m. S of Gorki; pop. (1969e) 62,000; a junction point on railroad bet. Moscow and Kazan.

Ar·za·no \är(d)-'zän-(ˌ)ō\. Commune, Napoli prov., Campania, S Italy, 3 m. N of Naples; pop. (1968e) 19,989.

Ar·zew *or* **Ar·zeu** \är-'zeü\ *or anc.* **Ar·se·nar·ia** \ˌär-sə-'nar-ē-ə\. Seaport, NW Algeria, N Africa, 22 m. NE of Oran near Cape Ferrat; pop. (1966c) 11,499; one of the landing places of American army Nov. 8, 1942.

Ar·zi·gna·no \ˌär(d)-zi-'nyän-(ˌ)ō\. Commune, Vicenza prov., Veneto, NE Italy, 10 m. W of Vicenza; pop. (1968e) 19,439.

Aš *or Ger.* **Asch** \'äsh\. Town, Czech S.R., W Czechoslovakia; pop. (1968e) 11,555; textile mills. One of the first towns occupied by Germans in their seizure of Sudetenland Oct. 1938.

Asa·han \ˌäs-ə-'hän\. River, N Sumatra, Indonesia; ab. 75 m. long; outlet of Lake Toba flowing ENE into cen. Strait of Malacca.

Asa·hi Da·ke \ˌä-ˌsä-hē-'däk-(ˌ)ā\ *or formerly* **Ishi·ka·ri Dake** \ˌish-i-ˌkär-ē-\. Mountain, cen. Hokkaidō I., Japan; 7513 ft.

Asa·hi·ka·wa \ˌä-ˌsä-hē-'kä-wə\ *or* **Asa·hi·ga·wa** \-'gä-\. City, cen. Hokkaidō I., Japan; pop. (1970c) 288,492; textiles, wood products, brewing.

Asa·ma \ə-'säm-ə\ *or* **Asa·ma·ya·ma** \ə-ˌsäm-ə-'yäm-ə\. Active volcano on W border of Gumma prefecture, cen. Honshū, Japan, 85 m. NW of Tokyo; 8340 ft.; one of the largest active volcanoes in Japan; had disastrous explosion 1783.

Asan·sol \'äs-ᵊn-ˌsōl\. City, West Bengal, NE India, 120 m. NW of Calcutta; pop. (1970e) 137,725; coal-mining center and rail junction.

Asben. See AÏR.

As·best \ˌäz-'best\. Town, Sverdlovsk Oblast, Russian S.F.S.R., U.S.S.R., ab. 40 m. ENE of Sverdlovsk; pop. (1969e) 76,000; important asbestos deposits.

As·bes·tos \as-'bes-təs, az-\. Town, Richmond co., S Quebec, Canada, 26 m. N of Sherbrooke; pop. (1966c) 10,534; site of asbestos mines.

As·bury Park \ˌaz-ˌber-ē-, -b(ə-)rē-\. City and summer resort, Monmouth co., E cen. New Jersey, on Atlantic Ocean 24 m. SSE of Perth Amboy; pop. (1970c) 16,533; orig. developed as summering place chiefly for temperance advocates 1870; became city 1897; oceanside auditorium, convention hall, pier, and boardwalk; summer theater center.

Ascalon. See ASHQELON 1.

Ascania. See İZNİK LAKE.

As·cen·sion \ə-'sen-chən\. 1 Parish in Louisiana. See table at LOUISIANA.
2 British island in S Atlantic Ocean, 7°57'S lat. and 14°22'W long., 700 m. NW of St. Helena; 9 m. long, 6 m. wide; 34 sq. m.; pop. (1968e) 1363; since 1922 administratively a part of British colony of St. Helena; only settlement Georgetown. Of volcanic origin, its extinct crater (Green Mt.) 2817 ft. Discovered by Portuguese navigator João da Nova on Ascension Day 1501; visited by Dampier 1701. In World War II airfield built by American engineers Apr. 28–July 10, 1942, used as refueling base in transatlantic flights to S Europe, North Africa, and Near East.
3 Island, Caroline Is. See PONAPE.

Asch. See AŠ.

Aschaf·fen·burg \ä-'shäf-ən-ˌbu̇(ə)rg\. City, Bavaria, West Germany, on right bank of Main river 21 m. ESE of Frankfurt am Main; pop. (1969e) 55,772; colored paper, clothing, electrical apparatus, machine and precision tools. Castle built on site of Roman castrum; scene of imperial diet 1447 which produced the Aschaffenburg Concordat; taken several times in Thirty Years' War; part of grand duchy of Frankfurt 1806; ceded with Lower Franconia to Bavaria 1814; taken by U.S. forces Apr. 1945.

Aschers·le·ben \'äsh-ərs-ˌlā-bən\. City, Halle dist., East Germany, 26 m. SSW of Magdeburg; pop. (1970e) 37,196; potash, coal, and salt mining; machine tools, paper, beet sugar. Founded probably in 11th cent. by Count Esico, ancestor of house of Anhalt; under episcopal see of Halberstadt 1315 and of Brandenburg 1648; to Prussia 1813.

Asco·li Pi·ce·no \ˌäs-kə-lē-pi-'chā-(ˌ)nō\. 1 Province of Marches, cen. Italy. See table at ITALY.
2 *or Lat.* **As·cu·lum Pi·ce·num** \ˌas-kyə-ləm-(ˌ)pī-'sē-nəm\. Commune, its ✻, 87 m. NE of Rome; pop. (1968e) 54,536; in rich agricultural region; chemicals, silks, glass; episcopal see; Roman and medieval remains, including bridges still in use.
History: One of most ancient cities of Italy; capital of ancient Picenum; taken 268 B.C. by Rome; all Roman citizens within its walls massacred 90 B.C. during Social War; recaptured by Rome 89 B.C.; occupied by Caesar, after crossing the Rubicon 49 B.C.; taken by Totila 545 A.D.; ruled by bishops from 8th cent., became free republic in 12th cent., and joined papal possessions in 15th cent.

Ascoli Sa·tria·no \-ˌsä-trē-'än-(ˌ)ō\ *or anc.* **Aus·cu·lum Ap·u·lum** \ˌós-kyə-ləm-'ap-yə-ləm\ *or* **As·cu·lum** \'as-kyə-ləm\. Commune, Foggia prov., Apulia, SE Italy, on E slope of Apennines 18 m. S of Foggia; pop. (1968e) 8779; episcopal see; site of Roman defeat by Pyrrhus, king of Epirus, 279 B.C. when Pyrrhus lost a large part of his army.

As·cot \'as-kət\. Village, Berkshire, England, 6 m. SSW of New Windsor, 29 m. SW of London by rail; fashionable two-mile race track (at **Ascot Heath**) established 1711 by Queen Anne.

Asculum. See ASCOLI SATRIANO.

Asculum Picenum. See ASCOLI PICENO 2.

As·cut·ney, Mount \-ə-'skət-nē\. Peak, SE Windsor co., E Vermont; 3320 ft.

Aseb *also* **As·sab** \'äs-əb\. Seaport, Eritrea, N Ethiopia; pop. (1970e) 14,900; acquired by Italian government 1882.

Ase·la \ä-ˈsal-ə\. Town, ✻ of Arusi prov., cen. Ethiopia; pop. (1970e) 17,106.

Ase·nov·grad \ä-ˈsen-əf-ˌgrad\ *or before 1934* **Sta·ni·ma·ka** \ˌstän-i-ˈmäk-ə\. Town, S Bulgaria, 10 m. SE of Plovdiv; pop. (1968e) 38,147; cigarettes.

Ashan·ti \ə-ˈshant-ē, -ˈshänt-\. Region, cen. Ghana; 9417 sq. m.; pop. (1970p) 1,477,397; ✻ Kumasi.

History: Originally a Negro kingdom with capital at Kumasi (*q.v.*); expanded towards Gold Coast and came into conflict with British from early 19th cent.; waged four wars with British, 1824–27, 1873–74, 1893–94, 1895–96; claimed as British protectorate 1894; after capture of Kumasi by Sir Francis Scott 1896 again declared protectorate; rose against British 1900 and besieged Kumasi but repressed; annexed to British Gold Coast Colony 1901; administration reorganized 1934; became an administrative region of Ghana 1957; greatly reduced in area 1959.

Ash·bourne \ˈash-ˌbō(ə)rn, -ˌbȯ-\. Urban district, Derbyshire, England, on a branch of the Dove 11 m. NW of Derby; pop. (1971p) 5577; cotton and lace manufacturing; iron and copper foundries; site of a defeat of Charles I by Parliamentary party 1644.

Ash·burn \ˈash-bərn\. City, ⊗ of Turner co., S Georgia, 30 m. ENE of Albany; pop. (1970c) 4209.

Ash·burn·ham \ˈash-bərn-ˌham\. Town, Worcester co., cen. Massachusetts, 7 m. WNW of Fitchburg; pop. (1970c) 3484.

Ash·bur·ton \ˈash-ˌbərt-ᵊn\. **1** River, NW Western Australia; ab. 400 m. long; flows NW to Indian Ocean near Exmouth Gulf.

2 Urban district, Devonshire, England, 19 m. NE of Plymouth; pop. (1971p) 3495; market town; tourism; 15th cent. church.

3 River, E cen. South I., New Zealand; 56 m. long; flows SE into Canterbury Bight.

Ash·by de la Zouch \ˈash-bē-də-lä-ˈzüsh\. Urban district, Leicestershire, England, 15 m. NW of Leicester; pop. (1971p) 8291; coal mining; soap; castle, known through Scott's *Ivanhoe* and as prison for Mary, Queen of Scots (1569, 1586), lies S of town; fine late-Perpendicular church.

Ash·dod \ˈash-ˌdäd\ *or anc. Gk.* **Azo·tos** \ə-ˈzōt-əs\ *or Lat.* **Azo·tus** \ə-ˈzōt-əs\. City, Israel, ab. 3 m. inland from the Mediterranean, 35 m. W of Jerusalem; pop. (1970e) 37,600; synthetic fiber plant; important harbor facilities constructed on coast; one of five Philistine city-kingdoms and a center of worship of Dagon (*1 Sam.* v). Besieged for 29 years by Psamtik I of Egypt.

Ash·down \ˈash-ˌdau̇n\. City, ⊗ of Little River co., SW Arkansas, 18 m. NNW of Texarkana; pop. (1970c) 3522.

Ashe \ˈash\. County in North Carolina. See table at NORTH CAROLINA.

Ashe·boro \ˈash-ˌbər-ə, -ˌbə-rə\. Industrial town, ⊗ of Randolph co., cen. North Carolina, 25 m. S of Greensboro; pop. (1970c) 10,797; hosiery, lumber, furniture.

Ash·er·ton \ˈash-ərt-ᵊn\. City, Dimmit co., S Texas, 51 m. S of Uvalde; pop. (1970c) 1645.

Ashe·ville \ˈash-ˌvil, -vəl\. City, ⊗ of Buncombe co., W North Carolina, near E entrance to Great Smoky Mountains National Park; pop. (1970c) 57,681; alt. 1985 ft.; health and tourist resort; electrical equipment, cellophane, paper, wool, tobacco; feldspar, copper, and mica mines. Asheville-Biltmore Coll. (1927); founded 1794; incorp. 1797; chartered as city 1835.

Ash·ford \ˈash-fərd\. Urban district, Kent, SE England, on Stour river 20 m. W of Dover; pop. (1971p) 35,560; bricks, iron foundries; marble quarries; breweries.

Ashi·bet·su \ˌäsh-i-ˈbet-(ˌ)sü\. City, Hokkaidō, Japan, 50 m. NE of Sapporo; pop. (1970c) 42,730.

Ashi·ka·ga \ˌäsh-i-ˈkäg-ə\. Commercial city, cen. Honshū, Japan, in Tochigi prefecture 50 m. N of Tokyo; pop. (1970c) 156,004; center of weaving industry, probably established several centuries ago; nylon. As the ancestral home of Ashikaga shoguns, gave its name to a Japanese dynasty (1338–1573).

Ash·ing·ton \ˈash-iŋ-tən\. Urban district, Northumberland, N England, 13 m. N of Newcastle upon Tyne; pop. (1971p) 25,645; collieries.

Ashi·ya \ˈäsh-ē-ˌ(y)ä\. City, Hyōgo prefecture, Honshū, Japan, 13 m. NW of Ōsaka; pop. (1970c) 70,938.

Ashi·zu·ri, Cape \-ä-ˈshē-zə-(ˌ)rē, -ˌäsh-i-ˈzu̇(ə)r-ē\ *or formerly* **Cape Sa·da** \-ˈsäd-ə\. Cape, W extremity of Shikoku I., Japan, at N end of Bungo Strait, 32°44′N, 133°01′E.

Ashkelon. See ASHQELON.

Ashkh·a·bad \ˈash-kə-ˌbad, -ˌbäd\ *or formerly* **Pol·to·ratsk** \ˌpäl-tə-ˈrätsk\. City, ✻ of Turkmen S.S.R., U.S.S.R., in S part on Iran border; pop. (1970p) 253,000; situated in fertile oasis; food processing, silk spinning; univ. (1950); founded 1881.

Ash·land \ˈash-lənd\. **1** Name of counties in two states of the U.S. See tables at OHIO and WISCONSIN.

2 Town, ⊗ of Clay co., E Alabama; pop. (1970c) 1921.

3 City, ⊗ of Clark co., S Kansas; pop. (1970c) 1244.

4 Industrial city, Boyd co., NE Kentucky, on Ohio river; pop. (1970c) 29,245; chemicals, lumber, coke, steel; oil refining.

5 Town, Aroostook co., N Maine, on Aroostook river 20 m. W of Presque Isle; pop. (1970c) 1761; shipping center for potatoes and lumber.

6 Town, Middlesex co., NE Massachusetts, 20 m. E of Worcester; pop. (1970c) 8882.

7 Village, ⊗ of Benton co., N Mississippi; pop. (1970c) 348.

8 City, Saunders co., E Nebraska; pop. (1970c) 2176.

9 City, ⊗ of Ashland co., N cen. Ohio, in agricultural region 13 m. NE of Mansfield; pop. (1970c) 19,872; automobile parts, farm implements, rubber goods, pumps; Ashland Coll. (1878); platted 1815, became city 1844, ⊗ 1846.

10 City, Jackson co., SW Oregon, in farming area 8 m. SSE of Medford; pop. (1970c) 12,342; canned goods, lumber; gold mines, granite quarries nearby; Southern Oregon Coll. (1926).

11 Borough, Schuylkill and Columbia cos., E cen. Pennsylvania, 11 m. NE of Pottsville; pop. (1970c) 4737; coal mining, farming; mine pumps, knit goods; platted 1847.

12 Town, Hanover co., E cen. Virginia, 16 m. N of Richmond; pop. (1970c) 2934; flour, lumber; began as health resort 1848. Randolph-Macon Coll. (1830; moved from Boydton 1868).

13 City and port of entry, ⊗ of Ashland co., N Wisconsin, on Lake Superior 58 m. E of Superior; pop. (1970c) 9615; lumber; foundry, granite quarries; Northland Coll. (1892), Ashland County Teachers Coll. (1914).

Ashland City. Town, ⊗ of Cheatham co., NW cen. Tennessee; pop. (1970c) 2027; wood products.

Ash·ley \ˈash-lē\. **1** River, SE South Carolina; ab. 40 m. long; rises in Berkeley co. and flows SE into Charleston harbor where it joins the Cooper river.

2 County in Arkansas. See table at ARKANSAS.

3 City, ⊗ of McIntosh co., S North Dakota; pop. (1970c) 1236; poultry, wheat.

4 Borough, Luzerne co., E Pennsylvania, 3 m. SW of Wilkes-Barre; pop. (1970c) 4095; settled 1810; coal mines.

Ash·more and Car·tier Islands \ˈash-ˌmō(ə)r . . . ˈkärt-ē-ˌā-, -ˌmȯ(ə)r-\. Uninhabited islands, constituting an external territory of Australia, ab. 200 m. N of N Western Australia, ab. 2 sq. m.; administratively part of Northern Territory.

Ash·mūn \ash-ˈmün\. Town, Minūfīya gov., Egypt, on railroad in Nile delta 25 m. NW of Cairo.

Ashmūnein, Al–. See AL-ASHMŪNEIN.

Asho·kan Dam \ə-ˌshō-kən-\ *or* **Ol·ive Bridge Dam** \ˌäl-iv-, -əv-\. Dam across Esopus Creek, N Ulster co., SE New York; height 252 ft.; completed 1912; forms **Ashokan**

ATLANTIC OCEAN
ARCTIC OCEAN
PACIFIC OCEAN
North Pole
Arctic Circle
Greenland
Iceland
Spitsbergen
Svalbard (Spitsbergen) (Nor.)
Franz Josef Ld.
Novaya Zemlya
Severnaya Zemlya
New Siberian Is.
Wrangel I.
BARENTS SEA
KARA SEA
LAPTEV SEA
BERING SEA
SEA OF OKHOTSK
SEA OF JAPAN
E. CHINA SEA
NORTH SEA
BALTIC SEA
BLACK SEA
CASPIAN SEA
MEDITERRANEAN SEA
ADRIATIC SEA
AEGEAN SEA
RED SEA
UNITED STATES
ALASKA
Aleutian Is.
Kamchatka Pen.
Kuril Is.
Sakhalin
Hokkaido
Honshu
JAPAN
TOKYO
Yokohama
Osaka
Kobe
Kyoto
Nagoya
UNION OF SOVIET SOCIALIST REPUBLICS
RUSSIAN SOVIET FEDERATED SOCIALIST REPUBLIC
SIBERIA
KAZAKH S.S.R.
UZBEK S.S.R.
TURKMEN S.S.R.
MONGOLIA
MANCHURIA
INNER MONGOLIA
SINKIANG
TIBET
CHINA
KOREA
AFGHANISTAN
PAKISTAN
KASHMIR
IRAN (PERSIA)
IRAQ
SYRIA
TURKEY
SAUDI ARABIA
KUWAIT
QATAR
ISRAEL
JORDAN
LEB.
CYPRUS
Kolyma Range
Gt. Khingan
Sikhote-Alin
Altai Mts.
Tien Shan
Kunlun
Altyn Tagh
Trans-Himalayas
Caucasus
Ural
Gobi
Taklamakan
L. Baikal
L. Balkhash
Aral Sea
Lena
Yenisei
Ob
Irtysh
Amur
Volga
Kolyma
Indigirka
Yana
Khatanga
Lower Tunguska
Hwang Ho
MOSCOW
Leningrad
LONDON
Paris
Berlin
Warsaw
Vienna
Budapest
Bucharest
Sofia
Belgrade
Rome
Athens
Istanbul
Ankara
Cairo
Alexandria
Baghdad
Tehran
Kiev
Volgograd (Stalingrad)
Sverdlovsk
Chelyabinsk
Omsk
Novosibirsk
Krasnoyarsk
Irkutsk
Tashkent
Alma-Ata
PEKING
Shanghai
Nanking
Wuhan
Chungking
Mukden
Harbin
Vladivostok
Khabarovsk
Stockholm
Oslo
Copenhagen
Helsinki
Riga
Hamburg
Amsterdam
Brussels
Edinburgh
Glasgow
Dublin
Belfast
Milan
Prague

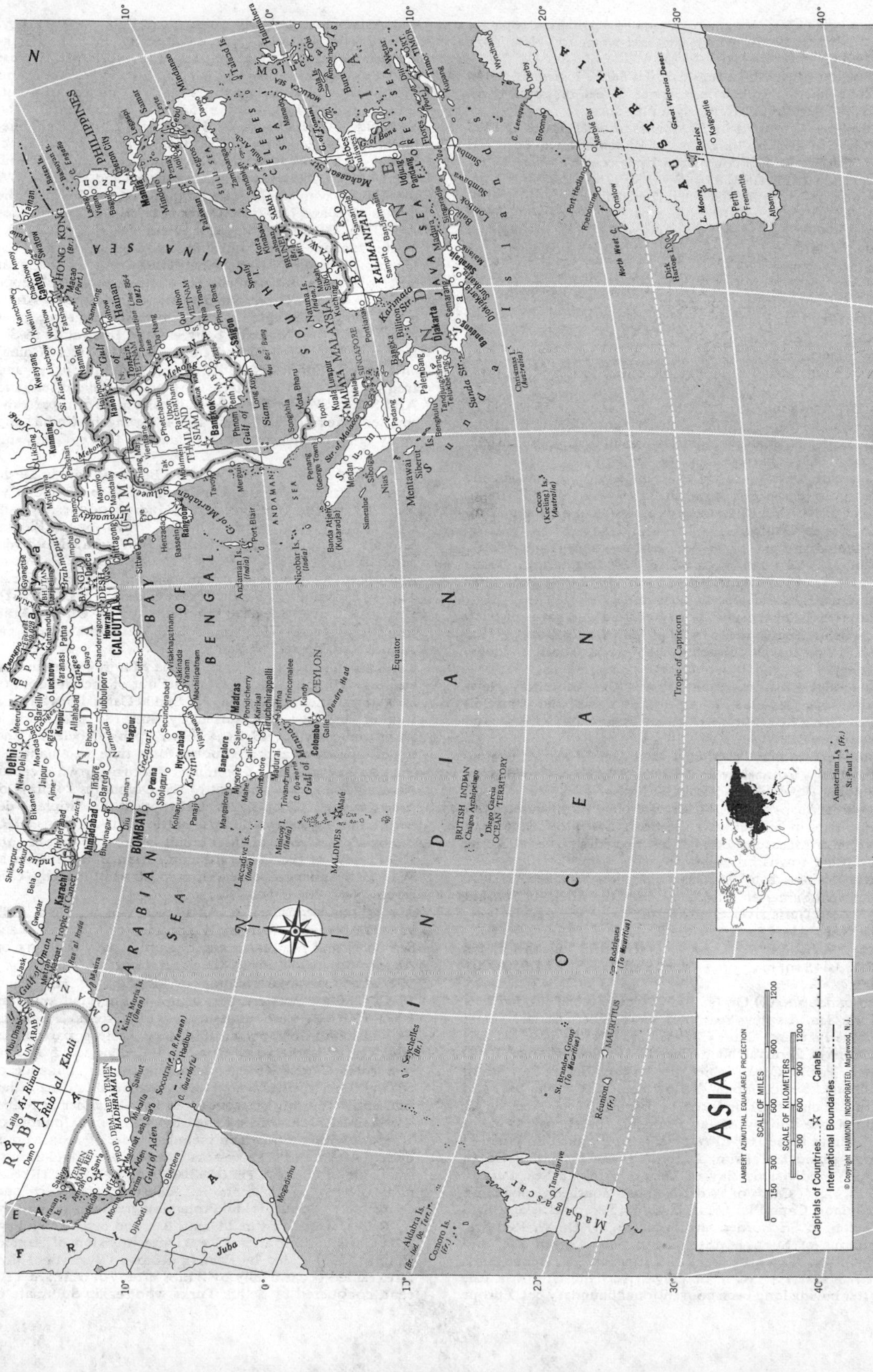
ASIA
LAMBERT AZIMUTHAL EQUAL-AREA PROJECTION
SCALE OF MILES
0 150 300 600 900 1200
SCALE OF KILOMETERS
0 300 600 900 1200
Capitals of Countries
Canals
International Boundaries
© Copyright HAMMOND INCORPORATED, Maplewood, N.J.
Longitude East of Greenwich
INDIAN OCEAN
ARABIAN SEA
BAY OF BENGAL
SOUTH CHINA SEA
ANDAMAN SEA
SULU SEA
CELEBES SEA
MOLUCCA SEA
JAVA SEA
FLORES SEA
INDIA
BURMA
THAILAND (SIAM)
MALAYSIA
INDONESIA
PHILIPPINES
KALIMANTAN
BORNEO
CEYLON
MALDIVES
AUSTRALIA
ARABIA
AFRICA
Madagascar
NEPAL
BHUTAN
BANGLADESH
HONG KONG
Tropic of Cancer
Equator
Tropic of Capricorn
Delhi
BOMBAY
CALCUTTA
Madras
Karachi
Rangoon
Bangkok
Saigon
Hanoi
Manila
Djakarta
SINGAPORE
Colombo
Canton
Gulf of Aden
Gulf of Oman
Gulf of Mannar
Str. of Malacca
Sunda Str.
Makassar Str.
Andaman Is.
Nicobar Is.
Laccadive Is.
Cocos (Keeling) Is. (Australia)
Christmas I. (Australia)
Seychelles (Br.)
MAURITIUS
Réunion (Fr.)
Amsterdam I. (Fr.)
St. Paul I.
BRITISH INDIAN OCEAN TERRITORY
Chagos Archipelago
Diego Garcia
Great Victoria Desert
Perth
Socotra (P.D.R. Yemen)
Hainan
Timor
Sumatra
Java

Reservoir, 12 m. long, ab. 13 sq. m., estimated capacity 130 billion gallons, which supplies water for New York City.

Ash·qe·lon *also* **Ash·ke·lon** \'ash-kə-ˌlän\. 1 *also* **As·ca·lon** \'as-kə-ˌlän\. Archaeological site, Israel, on coast 41 m. WSW of Jerusalem; formerly a city-state.

History: Captured by Egyptians under Ramses II 1285 B.C.; one of five city-kingdoms of Philistines who occupied it c. 1200–900 B.C.; conquered by successive ancient empires (see PALESTINE) but never by Israelites and Jews; conquered by Arabs 636 A.D.; scene of victory of Crusaders under Godfrey of Bouillon and Tancred over sultan of Egypt 1099; captured by Baldwin III 1153; retaken by Saladin 1187 and demolished 1191; finally destroyed by Sultan Baybars I 1270.

2 City, Israel, ab. 38 m. WSW of Jerusalem; pop. (1970e) 40,100; cement; founded 1949.

Ash Shām. 1 Ancient country. See SYRIA.

2 City, Syria. See DAMASCUS.

Ash–Shaqrā. See SHAQRA.

Ash·ta·bu·la \ˌash-tə-'byü-lə\. 1 County in Ohio. See table at OHIO.

2 City, Ashtabula co., NE Ohio, on Lake Erie 55 m. NE of Cleveland; pop. (1970c) 24,313; automobile forgings, chemicals, farm implements; shipbuilding; settled 1803, incorp. 1831, chartered as city 1892.

Ash·ta·roth \'ash-tə-ˌrōth\. Ancient city of Bashan, in the Decapolis region, SW Syria, ab. 32°50'N lat. and 36°E long.; a seat of worship of Astarte. Now ruins at a village 22 m. E of Sea of Galilee.

Ash·ton \'ash-tən\ *or in full* **Ashton–under–Lyne** \-'līn\. Municipal borough, Lancashire, NW England, on Tame river 6 m. E of Manchester; pop. (1971p) 48,865; filter equipment, leather goods; coal mines.

Ashton–in–Ma·ker·field \-'mā-kər-ˌfēld\. Urban district, Lancashire, England, 15 m. W of Manchester; pop. (1971p) 26,271; extensive collieries; iron goods, cotton goods, pottery.

Ash·ua·nipi \ˌash-wə-'nip-ē\. Lake, SW Labrador, Newfoundland, Canada; 319 sq. m.; source of the Churchill river (see CHURCHILL 4), called **Ashuanipi River** in its upper course.

Ashuap·mu·chuan \ə-ˌshä(p)-məsh-'wän\ *or* **Cha·mou·chouane** \ˌshäm-əsh-'wän\. River, S Quebec, Canada; 165 m. long; flows SE into Lake St. John.

Ash·ue·lot \ash-'wil-ət\. River, SW New Hampshire; 75 m. long; rises in SE Sullivan co., flows SW into Connecticut river near Massachusetts border; provides power at Keene and other towns in its course.

Ashur \'äsh-ər, 'ash-\. 1 Ancient empire, Asia. See ASSYRIA.

2 Ancient Sumerian settlement; now the village of Sharqat (*q.v.*) on Tigris river S of Mosul.

'Āsī, Nahr Al–. See ORONTES 2.

Asia \'ā-zhə, -shə\. 1 Largest continent on the globe; 17,139,445 sq. m.; pop. (1969e, excl. U.S.S.R.) 1,950,000,-000.

Boundaries: (1) On N, Arctic Ocean (chief subdivisions Kara Sea, Laptev Sea, and East Siberian Sea); most northerly point Cape Chelyuskin 77°45'N; chief islands Severnaya Zemlya, New Siberian Is., and Wrangel I. (2) On E, Pacific Ocean (chief subdivisions Bering Sea, Sea of Okhotsk, Sea of Japan, Yellow Sea, East China Sea, and South China Sea); marked by peninsulas of Kamchatka and Korea and by Malay Peninsula; most easterly point Dezhneva Cape 169°40'W; chief islands Sakhalin, Japan (4 large islands), Taiwan, Luzon. (3) On S, Indian Ocean (chief subdivisions Bay of Bengal, Arabian Sea, Persian Gulf, and Gulf of Aden); most southerly point on mainland Cape Piai (Malaysia), 1°15'N; chief island in S Ceylon, in SE Borneo and Sumatra. (4) On W, Red Sea, Isthmus of Suez, Mediterranean Sea, Aegean Sea, and Black Sea, Caucasus Mts., NW Caspian Sea, steppe lands of W Kazakh S.S.R. (E of Volga river) and Ural Mts., the latter having long been conventional boundary bet. Europe and Asia; most westerly point Cape Baba, NW Turkey, 26°04'E; chief island Cyprus. *Mountains, etc.:* The Himalayas in S containing highest peak in the world Mt. Everest 29,028 ft., with branches of Hindu Kush to W, Pamir and Tien Shan to NW, and on the N the great plateau of Tibet, China, (average height above 15,000 ft.) with Kunlun Mts. on N side; Altai Mts. in W Mongolian People's Republic, Greater Khingan Mts. in NE China, and Verkhoyansk, Stanovoi, Cherskogo, and Kolyma ranges in E Siberia; many high volcanic peaks in Kamchatka and Japan; in SW the Elburz Mts. of N Iran (highest 18,934 ft.) and the ranges of W and NW Iran. Other notable physical features are Gobi Desert of the Mongolian People's Republic, Takla Makan Desert of Sinkiang Uighur, China, the Deccan plateau of S India, the plateau of Iran, the great deserts of Syria and Arabian Penin., and the Kirgiz Steppe of SW U.S.S.R. *Rivers:* Ob, Yenisei, Lena in the N, Amur in NE, Yellow, Yangtze, and Hsi in the E (the three great rivers of China), Mekong, Salween, and Irrawaddy in SE, Brahmaputra, Ganges, and Indus in S (in Tibet [China] and India), Euphrates and Tigris in SW (in Turkey and Iraq), and Ural in W. *Lakes:* Caspian Sea (inland sea) and Aral Sea in SW, Baikal in N, Balkhash in W cen. part, the smaller lakes of Tung-t'ing and P'o-yang in China, and many other comparatively large lakes in Turkey, Iran, and China.

Political divisions: Afghanistan, Bahrain, Bangla Desh, Bhutan, Brunei, Burma, Cambodia, Ceylon, China, Cyprus, Egypt (part), Hong Kong, India, Indonesia, Iran, Iraq, Israel, Japan, Jordan, North Korea, South Korea, Kuwait, Laos, Lebanon, Macao, Malaysia, Maldives, Mongolian People's Republic, Nepal, Oman, Pakistan, Philippines, Qatar, Saudi Arabia, Sikkim, Singapore, Syria, Taiwan, Thailand, Timor (Portuguese), Turkey (part), Union of Soviet Socialist Republics (part), United Arab Emirates, North Vietnam, South Vietnam, Yemen (✱ Aden), and Yemen (✱ San'a).

2 A Roman province, W part of Asia Minor; ✱ Pergamum, and later Ephesus; formed 133 B.C. out of the kingdom of Pergamum and included Mysia, Lydia, Caria, Phrygia, and smaller districts; reorganized by Sulla 84 B.C.; made a senatorial province 27 B.C.; broken up by Diocletian and under Byzantine Empire known for a time as Asiana.

Asia·go \äz-'yä-(ˌ)gō\. Commune, Vicenza prov., Veneto, NE Italy, on plateau at foot of the Dolomites 24 m. N of Vicenza; pop. (1968e) 6726; chief town of the Altipiano dei Sette Comuni; scene of famous battle with Austrians 1916.

Asia Islands. Group of three small islands, Indonesia, ab. 130 m. NW of the Doberai Penin., Irian Barat; in World War II a Japanese observation post; captured by U.S. forces Nov. 20, 1944.

Asia Mi·nor \-'mī-nər\ *or* **An·a·to·lia** \ˌan-ə-'tō-lē-ə, -'tōl-yə\. The peninsula forming W extremity of Asia, bet. Black Sea on N and Mediterranean Sea on S and bordering on Aegean Sea on W; forms the greater part of Turkey.

History: Original location of kingdom of Hittites c. 1900–1200 B.C.; western part center of Phrygian kingdom 1000–750 B.C.; west coast settled by Greeks (Aeolians, Dorians, and Ionians) c. 1000 B.C.; western part under kingdom of Lydia (*q.v.*) 670–546 B.C.; conquered by Persian ruler Cyrus 546 B.C.; despite temporary alliance of coastal (Greek) cities with Athens, remained under Persian rule until 4th cent. B.C.; conquered by Alexander of Macedon 333 B.C. who was followed by Antigonus, founder of a separate kingdom which included most of Asia Minor; under Alexander's successors (Diadochi), divided into small kingdoms (see PERGAMUM, CAPPADOCIA, BITHYNIA, and PONTUS) 3d–1st cents. B.C.; coast and southern part contested by Seleucids and Ptolemies; gradually conquered by Rome, west coast in 2d cent. B.C., and rest by 1st cent. A.D.; Christianized after 33 A.D.; after division of Roman Empire (395), ruled by Eastern Roman (Byzantine) Empire; raided occasionally by Arabs after 7th cent.; in 11th cent. conquered by Seljuk Turks who set up Sultanate of

Rum (*q.v.*); reconquered in 12th cent. with help of Crusaders who set up Latin Empire and empires of Nicaea and Trebizond (*qq.v.*); overrun by Mongols in 13th cent.; gradually overcome in 14th and 15th cents. by Ottoman Turks, Karaman (*q.v.*) being last state to succumb. For later history, see OTTOMAN EMPIRE and TURKEY.

Asian and Pacific Council. Consultative organization, consisting of Australia, Japan, South Korea, Malaysia, New Zealand, Philippines, Taiwan, South Vietnam; Laos has observer status; purpose is to promote economic and technical cooperation among the members; formed 1966.

Asid Gulf \ä-ˈsēd-\. Arm of Visayan Sea on S coast of Masbate I., Phil.

Asinalunga. See SINALUNGA.

Asi·na·ra \ˌäs-ə-ˈnär-ə\. Small Italian island in Mediterranean Sea off NW extremity of the island of Sardinia.

Asinara, Gulf of. Inlet of Mediterranean Sea on N coast of Sardinia, Italy, E of Asinara I.; ab. 35 m. wide.

As·i·ne \ˈas-ə-(ˌ)nē\. Ancient town on E coast of the Gulf of Argolis, E Peloponnesus, S Greece; an archaeological site near Nauplia.

Asi Nehri. See ORONTES 2.

Asing·an \ä-ˈsēŋ-(ˌ)än\. Municipality, W cen. Luzon, Phil., 28 m. E of Lingayen; pop. (1969e) 36,300.

Asir \a-ˈsi(ə)r\. Province, SW coast of Saudi Arabia; 40,130 sq. m.; bounded on N by Hejaz, on E by Nejd, on S by Yemen (✱ San'a), and on W by the Red Sea. A maritime plain ab. 230 m. along the coast with mountain range (average height 6000 to 7000 ft.) and plateau inland; cereals, dates; cattle; salt. Under Turkish rule control only nominal; became politically active in early part of 20th cent.; acknowledged ibn-Saud 1926; made a division of Saudi Arabia 1930.

Asir, Ras *or* **Ras As·sir** \ˌräs-ə-ˈsi(ə)r\ *or formerly* **Cape Guar·da·fui** \-ˌg(w)ärd-əf-ˈwē, -ə-ˈfü-ē\ *or anc.* **Aro·ma·ta** \ə-ˈrō-mə-tə\. Cape extending into Indian Ocean from NE tip of Somalia, S of entrance to Gulf of Aden.

'Asīr Tihāmat. See TIHAMA.

Asisium. See ASSISI.

Ask·ja \ˈäsk-(ˌ)yä\. Volcanic peak, E cen. Iceland, 65°N, 16°48'W; ab. 4750 ft.; largest crater in Iceland.

As·ma·ra \az-ˈmär-ə, -ˈmar-ə\ *also* **As·me·ra** \az-ˈmer-ə\. Town, ✱ of Eritrea prov., N Ethiopia, ab. 40 m. SW of Mesewa; pop. (1970e) 218,360; alt. 7765 ft.; ceramics, footwear, textiles; univ. (1964); in 19th cent. under Egypt; occupied by Italy 1889; capital of a province of Italian East Africa 1936–41; under British military administration 1941–52.

As·nelles \ä-ˈnel\. Village on Normandy coast, France. See CALVADOS REEF.

Ås·nen \ˈȯs-nən\. Lake, Kronoberg co., S Sweden, 56 m. W of Kalmar; 20 m. long; 58 sq. m.

As·nières \an-ˈye(ə)r\ *or in full* **Asnières–sur–Seine** \-sü(ə)r-ˈsän, -ˈsen\. Commune, Hauts-de-Seine dept., N France, on left bank of Seine river 3 m. NW of Paris; pop. (1968c) 80,530; boating center notable for its summer regattas; perfumery, dyes.

Aso \ˈäs-(ˌ)ō\ *or* **Aso·san** \ˌäs-ō-ˈsän\. Volcanic mountain, cen. Kyūshū I., Japan, ab. 25 m. E of Kumamoto; highest of its five peaks 5223 ft.; has huge crater, one of the largest in the world, from 10 to 15 m. in diameter with walls ab. 2000 ft. high.

Aso·la \ˈäz-ə-(ˌ)lä\. Commune, Mantova prov., Lombardy, N Italy, on Chiese river 18 m. WNW of Mantua; pop. (1968e) 9015.

Aso·lo \ˈäz-ə-ˌlō\ *or anc.* **Ac·e·lum** \ˈas-ə-ləm\. Commune, Treviso prov., Veneto, NE Italy, 18 m. NW of Treviso; pop. (1968e) 6326; made episcopal see in 6th cent.; remains of Roman baths, theater, and aqueduct; residence of Caterina Cornaro 1489–1510.

Asor. See ULITHI.

Asosan. See ASO.

Aso·tin \ə-ˈsōt-ᵊn\. 1 County in SE Washington. See table at WASHINGTON.

2 Town, its ⊗; pop. (1970c) 637.

Aspadana. See EŞFAHĀN 2.

As·pen \ˈas-pən\. City, ⊗ of Pitkin co., W cen. Colorado, 30 m. W of Leadville; pop. (1970c) 2437; resort; silver.

Aspen Butte. Mountain, SW Klamath co., S Oregon; 8210 ft.

As·per·mont \ˈas-pər-ˌmänt\. Town, ⊗ of Stonewall co., NW Texas; pop. (1970c) 1198; fruit farms.

As·pern \ˈas-pərn, ˈäs-\. Former village, Austria, 5 m. ENE of Vienna, in the Marchfeld; here and at the nearby village of Essling, May 21–22, 1809, the French under Napoleon were defeated by the Austrians under Archduke Charles Louis; since 1905 part of Vienna.

As·phal·ti·tes, La·cus \ˌlā-kəs-ˌas-fȯl-ˈtīt-ēz\. The Dead Sea, so called by Josephus.

As·pin·wall \ˈas-pən-ˌwȯl\. 1 Borough, Allegheny co., SW Pennsylvania, on Allegheny river; pop. (1970c) 3541; residential suburb of Pittsburgh.

2 City, Panama. See COLÓN 5.

As·pir·ing, Mount \-ə-ˈspī(ə)r-iŋ\. Peak, SW South I., New Zealand, ab. 20 m. W of Lake Wanaka; 9960 ft.

As·pro·mon·te \ˌas-prə-ˈmänt-ē, ˌäs-prə-ˈmȯn-(ˌ)tā\. Mountain ridge of S Apennines, Reggio di Calabria, Italy, E of Strait of Messina and Reggio; over 30 m. long; 6417 ft. high at Montalto peak; sharp, heavily wooded slopes. Scene of skirmish Aug. 29, 1862 in which Garibaldi, in his attempt against wishes of Victor Emmanuel II to secure Rome (papal territory) for kingdom of Italy, was wounded and captured by the latter's troops under Pallavicino.

Aspropotamos. See ACHELOUS.

As·pull \ˈas-pəl\. Urban district, Lancashire, NW England, 2 m. NE of Wigan; pop. (1971p) 7510; steel.

Assab. See ASEB.

As·saí \ˌa-sä-ˈē\. Municipality, Paraná state, S Brazil, 260 m. W of São Paulo; pop. (1968e) 53,525.

As–Sallūm. See SALŪM.

As·sam \ə-ˈsam, a-; ˈas-ˌam\. State, NE India; 69,867 sq. m.; pop. (1971p) 14,857,314; ✱ Shillong. *Physical features:* E Himalayas lie along N border; Brahmaputra enters through gorges at NE corner; in W cen. part S of Brahmaputra valley are Garo Hills and Khasi Hills; on E and SE various hill ranges (Patkai and Naga on N, Lushai on S) form boundary with Burma. *Chief products:* Rice, tea, jute, timber. *Chief towns:* Shillong, Gauhati, Nowgong.

History: Strong independent kingdom first founded by Ahoms, invaders from Burma and Chinese frontier, 13th cent.; fought with Muslim governor of Bengal 17th cent., but never came under his rule; became dependency of Burmese 1822 and thus a partial cause of First Burmese War (1824–26); ceded to British by Treaty of Yandabu (*q.v.*) 1826; under chief commissioner 1874–1905 and 1912–19; part of province of Eastern Bengal and Assam 1905–12 (see BENGAL), separate province 1919. In World War II a British-American base in Burma campaign against the Japanese 1943–45. In division of India in August 1947 lost most of Sylhet district to Pakistan; was constituted a state 1950; scene of border clash between Indian and Chinese troops 1962.

As–Samāwah. See SAMAWA.

As·sa·teague Island \ˌas-ə-ˌtēg-\. Island, Worcester co., SE Maryland, and Accomac co., N part of E peninsula, Virginia, separating Chincoteague Bay throughout its length from Atlantic Ocean; 28 sq. m.

As·sa·wa·man Island \ˌas-ə-ˌwäm-ən-\. Island, E Virginia, on coast off Accomac county; 4¼ m. long; at the N end is **Assawaman Inlet.**

As·sa·ye \ˈəs-ə-(ˌ)yā, ˈäs-\. Village, cen. Maharashtra state, cen. India, 45 m. NE of Aurangabad; scene of battle Sept.

23, 1803 in which Gen. Wellesley completely defeated Sindhia and Nagpur branches of Marathas.

As·sen \'äs-ᵊn\. Commune, ❋ of Drenthe prov., Netherlands, 16 m. S of Groningen; pop. (1970e) 38,956; connected by canal with Groningen and Meppel and the Wadden Zee; built around old nunnery now serving as group of public buildings; in vicinity are peat bogs, gardens, the "Giants' Caves" mentioned by Tacitus, and prehistoric stone monuments resembling those at Stonehenge; museum of antiquities; founded 1257.

As Sharqāṭ. See SHARQAT.

Asshur. See ASSYRIA.

As·sin·i·boia \ə-ˌsin-ə-'bȯi-ə\. 1 Early region of W Canada, c. 1811–70, with indefinite boundaries; controlled by Hudson's Bay Company with headquarters at Fort Garry; included Red River Settlement.

2 Former district, formed 1882 out of Northwest Territories, Canada, W of Manitoba and S of Saskatchewan dist.; 89,000 sq. m.; ❋ Regina. Greater part of it united Sept. 1, 1905 with Saskatchewan dist. and E part of Athabaska dist. to form Saskatchewan prov.

3 Town, Saskatchewan, Canada, 60 m. SSE of Moose Jaw; pop. (1971p) 2609; lumber; agriculture.

As·sin·i·boine \ə-'sin-ə-ˌbȯin\. River, S Canada; 590 m. long; rises in SE Saskatchewan, flows S and E across S Manitoba into the Red River of the North at Winnipeg; navigable for ab. 300 m.; has two tributaries, the Qu' Appelle, its main headstream, and the Souris on the S. Discovered by the La Vérendryes 1736; its valley was route to the plains by colonists from Red River Settlement.

Assiniboine, Mount. Mountain in Rocky Mts., Canada, on border bet. SE British Columbia and SW Alberta, ab. 25 m. SW of Banff; 11,870 ft.

Assiout. See ASYŪT.

Assir, Ras. See ASIR, RAS.

As·si·si \ə-'sē-sē, -'sē-zē\ *or anc.* **Asi·sium** \ə-'sizh-ē(-ə)m, -'siz-ē-əm\. Commune, Perugia prov., Umbria, cen. Italy, on S slope of Monte Subasio 12 m. E by SE of Perugia; pop. (1968e) 24,755; episcopal see; famous as place of birth and death of St. Francis of Assisi (1182–1226); Gothic Franciscan monastery and Upper and Lower Church of St. Francis, containing paintings by old masters, esp. Giotto.

Assiut. See ASYŪT.

As·siz \ə-'sēs, -'sēz\. City, São Paulo state, SE Brazil, ab. 240 m. WNW of São Paulo; munic. pop. (1968e) 51,479.

Assomption, L'. See L'ASSOMPTION.

As·sos *or Lat.* **As·sus** \'as-əs\. Ancient city of S Troas, in Aeolis, on coast of Gulf of Adramyttium (Edremit) W of Mt. Ida and opp. N shore of Lesbos; founded c. 900 B.C. and long an important city and port. Aristotle taught here 348–345 B.C. Its ruins now an archaeological site and part of village of **Beh·ram·köy** \ˌber-äm-'kü-ē\, Çanakkale prov., NW Turkey.

Assouan *or* **Assuan.** See ASWĀN.

As·suad, Cape \-'as-ˌwäd\. Cape extending into Indian Ocean, cen. part of E coast of Somalia.

As·sump·tion \ə-'səm(p)-shən\. 1 Parish in Louisiana. See table at LOUISIANA.

2 City, Christian co., cen. Illinois; pop. (1970c) 1487.

3 Island, Indian Ocean. See ALDABRA.

Assur. See ASSYRIA.

Assus. See ASSOS.

As Suwaydā. See ES SUWEIDA.

As–Suways. See SUEZ.

As·synt, Loch \-'as-ˌint\. Lake, Sutherland co., N Scotland, draining W into Enard Bay; 6½ m. long.

As·syr·ia \ə-'sir-ē-ə\; *anc.* **As·sur** \'äs-ˌu̇(ə)r, 'as-ər\ *or* **Ashur** *or* **As·shur** \'äsh-ˌu̇(ə)r, 'ash-ər\. One of the great ancient empires of the world, holding dominion in W Asia; early ❋ Calah, later ❋ Nineveh; extended along E bank of middle Tigris and over foothills to the E. Probably originated c. 2700 B.C. in Sumerian settlement of Ashur but later became part of Akkadian empire and from c. 1950 to 1850 B.C. was under Babylonian rule; frequently overrun and much influenced by Hittites and Hurrians; after 1800 B.C. hard pressed by Egyptians. Slowly gained control of trade routes under Tiglath-pileser I (c. 1115–1102 B.C.) but was especially powerful in 884 to 782 B.C. when it reached Mediterranean in its conquests under Ashurnasirpal II and Shalmaneser III and in 745 to 626 B.C. when it conquered Israel 734, Damascus 732, and Babylon and Samaria 722, and conducted successful campaigns against Egypt; its greatest rulers then were Tiglath-pileser III, Sargon II, Sennacherib, Esarhaddon, and Ashurbanipal. Lost power rapidly 626–612 B.C. when Nineveh was destroyed by kings of Media and Babylonia (Chaldea). Made a Roman province for a brief time under Trajan 116 A.D.; invaded 627 A.D. by Roman emperor Heraclius; with other Persian provinces became part of the caliphate by 656. For later history of the region, see MESOPOTAMIA.

Astaboras. See ATBARA.

Asta Colonia. See ASTI 2.

Astacus. See İZMİT.

Asta Pompeia. See ASTI 2.

As·ta·ra \ˌäs-tə-'rä\. Seaport, SE Azerbaijan S.S.R., U.S.S.R., on W coast of Caspian Sea, on border of Iran 20 m. S of Lenkoran.

Astarabad *or* **Asterabad.** See GORGĀN 1.

Asti \'äs-tē\. 1 Province of Piedmont, NW Italy. See table at ITALY.

2 *anc.* **As·ta Pom·pe·ia** *or* **Has·ta Pompeia** \ˌ(h)as-tə-päm-'pē-(y)ə\ *or* **Asta Co·lo·nia** *or* **Hasta Colonia** \-kə-'lōn-yə\. Commune, its ❋, on left bank of Tanaro river 20 m. W of Alessandria; pop. (1968e) 73,211; known for the sparkling wine Asti spumante; silk mills; Gothic cathedral built 1348, 8th cent. and 11th cent. baptisteries. Powerful medieval republic; burned by Frederick Barbarossa 1155; captured by the Visconti of Milan 1348; ceded to France 1387 as part of a dowry of daughter of Gian Galeazzo Visconti; given to dukes of Savoy 1529.

Astigi. See ÉCIJA.

Astin Tagh. See A-ERH-CHIN SHAN-MO.

Astipálaia. See ASTYPALAIA.

As·ton \'as-tən\. 1 Residential township, Delaware co., Pennsylvania, SW of Philadelphia; pop. (1970c) 13,704.

2 Ward, Birmingham borough, Warwickshire, W cen. England.

As·tor, Mount \-'as-tər\. Peak, Antarctica, 86°01′S, 155°30′W; 12,175 ft.

As·tor·ga \ä-'stȯr-gə\ *or anc.* **As·tu·ri·ca Au·gus·ta** \a-'st(y)u̇r-i-kə-ȯ-'gəs-tə, -ə-'gəs-\. Commune, León prov., NW Spain, 28 m. WSW of León; pop. (1970p) 11,794; chocolate, textiles; episcopal see; medieval fortifications; Gothic 15th cent. cathedral. Ancient Roman capital of Asturias and military center; site of church council 446; a famous center of Spanish resistance against Moors in 8th cent.; captured by French 1810 and retaken by Spaniards 1812 (Peninsular War).

As·to·ria \a-'stōr-ē-ə, ə-stōr-, -'stȯr-\. 1 Former village, Queens co., SE New York, on Long Island, on East River, now residential and industrial section of Long Island City (*q.v.*) in borough of Queens, New York City.

2 City and port of entry, ⊗ of Clatsop co., NW Oregon, on S bank and near mouth of Columbia river; pop. (1970c) 10,244; fisheries; Clatsop Community Coll. (1958); near site of Fort Clatsop, estab. by Lewis and Clark expedition 1805. Founded as trading post by John Jacob Astor 1811; taken by British 1813; restored to U.S. 1818.

Astrabad. See GORGĀN 1.

As·tra·khan \'as-trə-ˌkan, -kən\. City, ❋ of Astrakhan Oblast, Russian S.F.S.R., U.S.S.R., on left bank of the Volga at head of its delta ab. 235 m. SE of Volgograd; pop. (1970p) 411,000; altitude 50 ft. below sea level; port frozen for about one third of the year; exports oil, timber; food processing; has fortress, or *kreml* (built ab. 1550 on a hill), univ. (1919).

History: Capital of a Tatar khanate on lower Volga, which became independent of former Kipchak (Golden

Horde) empire (1237–1486; see MONGOLIA and RUSSIA); conquered 1554–56 by Ivan IV who thus gained control for Russia of entire course of Volga, an important route for eastward expansion; town burned by Turks 1569; center of Peter the Great's campaign against Persia; given special trade privileges by Catherine II; has suffered much from flood, fire, famine, and a cholera epidemic 1830. Reached by Germans 1942.

Astrakhan Oblast \-'ò-bləst, -ˌblast\. Subdivision, SE Russian S.F.S.R., U.S.S.R., W and SW of the lower Volga with narrow strip along its E bank; 17,027 sq. m.; pop. (1970p) 868,000; ✻ Astrakhan; fishing, cattle raising; vegetables; formed 1945.

As·tro·labe, Cape \-'as-trə-ˌlāb\. Cape, NW point of Malaita I., E Solomon Is., W Pacific Ocean.

Astrolabe Bay. Inlet of Bismarck Sea on NE cen. coast of New Guinea I., Papua New Guinea, at W end of Vitiaz Strait.

As·tu·ra *Lat.* 'as-chə-rə, *Ital.* ä-'stùr-ə\. Village, Roma prov., Latium, Italy, 36 m. SSE of Rome and near Anzio; formerly an islet, now a peninsula; site of a favorite villa of Cicero from which he embarked on the flight that ended with his murder at Formiae 43 B.C.; site of medieval castle of the Frangipani where Conradin, the last Hohenstaufen, unsuccessfully sought refuge after battle of Tagliacozzo 1268.

As·tu·ri·as \ə-'st(y)ùr-ē-əs, a-\. 1 Municipality on W coast of Cebu I., Phil., 22 m. NW of City of Cebu; pop. (1969e) 38,800.

2 Region and ancient kingdom, NW Spain, bounded on the N by Bay of Biscay, E by Old Castile, S by León and the Cantabrian Mts., and W by Galicia; 4079 sq. m.; now forms modern province of Oviedo; picturesque mountain woodlands, steep chasms, fertile valleys; rich pasturage, producing an excellent breed of horses and cattle; deposits of copper, lead, iron, and other minerals; excellent fisheries; produces barley, wheat, corn, olives.

History: Conquered by Romans under Augustus 25 B.C.; refuge for Goths from Saracen onslaught in 8th cent.; kingdom created by Pelayo (718–737), successor to Visigoth ruler, which he successfully defended against Moors; became part of kingdom of León on accession of Alfonso III 866, and later of kingdom of León and Castile; made principality 1388, held until 1931 by heir apparent to the Spanish throne with title Prince of the Asturias; from 1838 officially the province of Oviedo.

3 City, NW Spain. See OVIEDO 2.

Asturica Augusta. See ASTORGA.

Asty·pa·laia *or Gk.* **Asti·pá·laia** \ˌäs-ti-'päl-ē-ə\ *or Ital.* **Stam·pa·lia** \ˌstäm-pə-'lē-ə\. One of the Dodecanese Is. (*q.v.*), Greece; 37 sq. m.; pop. (1961c) 1539.

Asun·cion \ə-ˌsün(t)-sē-'ōn, ä-\. Small island, N end of Mariana Is., W Pacific Ocean, 19°40′N, 145°24′E; taken by U.S. forces Aug. 1945.

Asun·ción \ə-ˌsün(t)-sē-'ōn, (ˌ)ä-\ *or* **Nues·tra Se·ño·ra de la Asunción**\ˌnwās-trə-sān-'yōr-ə-dā-lä-ˌsün(t)-sē-'on, -'yòr-\. City, ✻ of Paraguay and of Central dept., on E bank of Paraguay river at the confluence of the Pilcomayo; pop. (1970e) 437,136; commercial center; food products, footwear, textiles; national univ. (1889), catholic univ. (1960).

History: Founded 1538 by expedition under Irala sent inland from coast by Mendoza; first permanent settlement in La Plata region; capital of region until Buenos Aires refounded 1580 and developed; seat of revolutionary junta which threw off rule of Buenos Aires 1811 (see PARAGUAY); occupied 1868 by forces of Brazil, Argentina, and Uruguay in war for Greater Paraguay; under Brazilian control 1868–76.

Asunción, La. See LA ASUNCIÓN.

Asunción Mi·ta \-'mēt-ə\. Town, Jutiapa dept., SE Guatemala; munic. pop. (1964p) 25,286.

As·wān *or* **As·wan** *also* **As·souan** *or* **As·suan** \a-'swän, ä-\. 1 Governorate of SE Egypt. See table at EGYPT.

2 *or anc.* **Sy·e·ne** \sī-'ē-nē\. City, its ✻, on right bank of the Nile, ab. 10 m. N of Lake Nasser; pop. (1970e) 206,300; steel, textiles; popular winter health resort; has ruins of temple built by Ptolemy Euergetes; ancient Syene an important town in 1st millennium B.C. Ab. 3½ m. to the S of the city at the beginning of the 1st Cataract is the great **Aswān Dam,** 6400 ft. long, built 1898–1902 to replace 19th cent. barrage; above it is the **Aswān High Dam** (364 ft. in height), dedicated 1971, impounding water (Lake Nasser) which is utilized for irrigation and power production.

As·yūt *also* **As·siout** *or* **As·siut** \ˌas-ē-'üt, ˌäs-\ *or* **Siut** \'syüt\. 1 Governorate of E cen. Egypt. See table at EGYPT.

2 *or anc.* **Ly·cop·o·lis** \lī-'käp-ə-ləs\. City, its ✻, on left bank of the Nile; pop. (1970e) 175,700; noted for its pottery and ornamental wood and ivory work; technical univ. (1957).

Ata·ba·po \ˌät-ə-'bäp-(ˌ)ō\. River, S Venezuela; 140 m. long; flows N to Orinoco river and forms section of boundary bet. Colombia and Venezuela.

Ata·ca·ma \ˌät-ə-'käm-ə\. Province of N cen. Chile. See table at CHILE.

History: While under Bolivian administration, its valuable nitrate deposits were developed by Chilean capital; subject of disagreement bet. Chile and Bolivia which led to War of Pacific (1879–84); control transferred to victorious Chile by Treaty of Valparaíso 1884 (see also ANTOFAGASTA); awarded permanently to Chile 1905.

Atacama, Pu·na de \'pü-nə-dā-\. Highland region in NW Argentina and adjacent region of Chile, with average altitude of 11,000 to 13,000 ft.

Atacama Desert. Arid area extending N from Copiapó in N cen. Chile, covering most of Antofagasta prov. and N part of Atacama prov.; completely barren, with borax lakes and saline deposits and large nitrate deposits; for years a chief source of the world's nitrates.

Ata·fu \ˌat-ə-'fü\ *or* **Duke of York.** Island (atoll) in Tokelau group (*q.v.*), cen. Pacific Ocean, bet. Phoenix Is. and Samoa; pop. (1970c) 600; consists of a reef ab. 1 m. sq. with 62 islets; discovered 1765.

Atak·pa·mé \ˌä-täk-'päm-ˌā\. Town, Togo, W Africa, 103 m. N of Lomé; pop. (1970p) 18,008.

At·a·lan·te \ˌat-^{ə}l-'ant-ē\ *or Gk.* **Ata·lán·tē** \ˌät-ə-'län-dē\. Channel extending bet. the island of Euboea, Aegean Sea, and Greece, N of Evripos Strait.

Ata·lé·ia \ˌat-ə-'lā-(y)ə\. Municipality, Minas Gerais state, E Brazil; pop. (1968e) 52,943.

Ata·mi \ä-'täm-ē\. City on Sagami Sea, on E coast of Izu Penin., Shizuoka prefecture, Honshū, Japan, ab. 55 m. SW of Tokyo; pop. (1970c) 51,281.

Atar \'ä-ˌtär\. Town, W Mauritania, W Africa; pop. (1969e) 10,000.

Atas·ca·dero \ə-ˌtas-kə-'de(ə)r-(ˌ)ō\. Urban community (unincorp.), San Luis Obispo co., California; pop. (1970c) 10,290.

At·a·sco·sa \ˌat-ə-'skō-sə\. County in Texas. See table at TEXAS.

Atáviros. See ATTAIRO.

Atax. See AUDE 1.

At·ba·ra *or* **'At·ba·rah** \'at-bə-rə, 'ät-\ *or anc.* **As·tab·o·ras** \as-'tab-ə-rəs\. 1 River, NE Africa; ab. 500 m. long; its headstream, the Tekeze, rises in N Ethiopia, flows NW through E Sudan into the Nile at Atbara; last tributary of the Nile.

2 Town, Northern Province, NE Sudan, at the junction of Atbara and Nile rivers; pop. (1969e) 53,110; victory of Anglo-Egyptian army over Mahdi's forces April 8, 1898.

Atchaf·a·laya \(ə-)ˌchaf-ə-'lī-ə\. River, S Louisiana; ab. 225 m. long; rises in Avoyelles parish, cen. Louisiana, flows S into Atchafalaya Bay; an additional outlet for Red and Mississippi rivers during periods of high water.

Atchafalaya Bay. Inlet of Gulf of Mexico on S boundary bet. St. Mary and Terrebonne parishes, SE Louisiana, receiving (through Grand Lake) the Atchafalaya river on the N.

Atchin. See ATJEH.

Atch·i·son \'ach-ə-sən\. 1 Name of counties in two states of the U.S. See tables at KANSAS and MISSOURI.

2 City, ⊗ of Atchison co., NE Kansas, on Missouri river 20 m. N of Leavenworth; pop. (1970c) 12,565; incorp. 1855; stopping place of westbound caravans in the Gold Rush and later; railroad shops; flour, industrial alcohol, leather goods; St. Benedict's Coll. (1858), Mount St. Scholastica Coll. (1863).

Ater·no \ä-'te(ə)r-(ˌ)nō\ *or anc.* **Ater·nus** \ə-'tər-nəs\. River, SE cen. Italy; ab. 80 m. long; flows out of the Apennines SE and then NE into Adriatic Sea at Pescara; in its lower course known as the **Pe·sca·ra** \pes-'kär-ə\.

Aternum. See PESCARA 3.

Ates·sa \ə-'tes-ə\. Commune, Chieti prov., Abruzzi, cen. Italy, 24 m. SE of Chieti; pop. (1968e) 9268; cattle and fruit market.

Ateste. See ESTE.

Ath *or* **Aath** \'ät\. Commune, Hainaut prov., SW Belgium, on left bank of Dender river 55 m. SW of Brussels; pop. (1969e) 11,167; medieval tower sole remains of ancient town; railroad junction; linen, wool, lace, and glove factories, ironworks, dye works.

Ath·a·bas·ca *also* **Ath·a·bas·ka** \ˌath-ə-'bas-kə\. 1 River, S tributary of the Mackenzie, in Alberta, W cen. Canada; 765 m. long; rises in Rocky Mts. in Jasper National Park, flows NE and N into Lake Athabaska; chief tributaries Pembina, Lesser Slave, and La Biche; important because of oil sands along its course, believed one of largest oil reservoirs in world.

2 Former district, cen. Canada, formed 1882 out of Northwest Territories bet. 60° N and 55° N, approximately the N part of present Alberta; extended 1885 to include N part of present Saskatchewan. Both parts absorbed 1905 by the modern provinces.

Athabasca, Lake. Lake, W cen. Canada, extending across N section of the Alberta-Saskatchewan boundary; 208 m. long; 3120 sq. m.; on SW receives Athabaska river and on NW discharges into Slave river; connected at its E end by Fond du Lac river with Lake Cree.

Ath·a·ma·nia \ˌath-ə-'mā-nē-ə\. A district of ancient Epirus, NW Greece, W of Pindus Mts.

Ath·el·ney \'ath-əl-nē\. Locality in Somersetshire, SW England, ab. 8 m. ENE of Taunton; in King Alfred's time an isle in W cen. Wessex, surrounded by marshes; Alfred's refuge from the Danes 878–879. Site of monastery founded by Alfred.

Ath·ens \'ath-ənz\. 1 County in Ohio. See table at OHIO.

2 City, ⊗ of Limestone co., N Alabama, 12 m. N of Decatur; pop. (1970c) 14,360; agricultural center; lumber mills; Athens Coll. (1822); occupied by Union troops 1862; site of Campbell's surrender to Confederate General Forrest 1864.

3 City, ⊗ of Clarke co., NE Georgia, 60 m. ENE of Atlanta; pop. (1970c) 44,342; electrical equipment; cotton, cottonseed products, lumber; Univ. of Georgia (chartered 1785, estab. 1801), oldest state university; founded 1785, incorp. 1801.

4 *also* 'āth-\. Village, Greene co., SE New York, on Hudson river near Catskill Mts. 26 m. S of Albany; pop. (1970c) 1718; Columbia-Greene Community Coll. (1967); settled 1686.

5 Commercial city, ⊗ of Athens co., SE Ohio, 32 m. W of Marietta; pop. (1970c) 24,168; steel products, flour; Ohio Univ. (1804); settled c. 1797, became ⊗ 1805.

6 Borough, Bradford co., N Pennsylvania, on Susquehanna river 3 m. S of New York border; pop. (1970c) 4173; foundry products; settled 1778.

7 City, ⊗ of McMinn co., SE Tennessee, 27 m. NNE of Cleveland; pop. (1970c) 11,790; farm implements, flour; Tennessee Wesleyan Coll. (1866); founded 1823, incorp. 1868.

8 City, ⊗ of Henderson co., NE Texas, 30 m. WSW of Tyler; pop. (1970c) 9582; brick, pottery, cottonseed oil; meat processing; oil wells nearby; Henderson County Junior Coll. (1946); settled 1848.

9 Town, Mercer co., S West Virginia, ab. 6 m. NE of Princeton; pop. (1970c) 967; Concord Coll. (1872).

10 *or Gk.* **Athí·nai** \ä-'thē-nā\ *or anc.* **Athe·nae** \ə-'thē-nē\. City, ✱ of Greece and of Attica dept., E Central Greece and Euboea, near the Saronic Gulf, on Attic plain enclosed on three sides by hills; pop. (1971p) 862,133; **Greater Athens** (department) 167 sq. m., pop. 2,530,207; commercial and transportation center; chemicals, textiles; food processing, oil refining, publishing; tourism; national library, national museum, numerous schools of archaeology, technical univ. (1836), univ. (1837). Formerly connected with its harbor Piraeus by the Long Walls; contains the Acropolis, the Areopagus (on which hill Paul preached) and the excavated ancient market place Agora; among the principal ancient structures on the Acropolis were the Odeum, Parthenon, Erechtheum, Propylaea, and Dionysiac theater.

History: Ancient Greek city-state which by the beginning of the 7th cent. B.C. included the territory known as Attica; abolished hereditary kingship 683 B.C.; under Solon's law code of 594 B.C., freed from the Draconian code (published 621 B.C.); ruled by tyrants, the most famous of whom was Pisistratus (560–527 B.C.); largely a democracy after the reforms of Cleisthenes 508 B.C.; under Themistocles, first chosen archon in 493–492 B.C., began building strong fleet in anticipation of Persian invasion; defeated Persia at battle of Marathon (*q.v.*) 490 B.C.; destroyed by Xerxes 480 B.C. in campaign in which Persians were finally defeated by the Peloponnesian League; began fortification of city and Piraeus 479 B.C.; headed the Delian League which was founded in 478 B.C., with headquarters on the island of Delos, as a confederacy against Persia but became the instrument of Athenian empire after subjugation of Naxos 471 B.C. and of Thasos 463 B.C.; at height of its commercial prosperity, leadership in architecture and culture, and of political democracy under Pericles 460–431 B.C.; after a long period of opposition to Sparta, withdrew from Peloponnesian League and entered so-called First Peloponnesian war 460–445 B.C.; transferred treasury of Delian League from Delos 454 B.C.; at height of empire (c. 450 B.C.) allied to Thessaly, Achaea, Argos, Samos, Chios, and Lesbos, and had as dependents Euboea, Andros, Naxos, and the remaining Cyclades, most of the extreme western coast of Asia Minor, the entrances to the Propontis and to the Euxine, the coast and islands of the Thracian Sea, and Chalcidice; built Parthenon 447–432 B.C.; lost supremacy in Greece after being defeated in the renewed (Second) Peloponnesian War 431–404 B.C.; sentenced Socrates to death 399 B.C.; allied against Sparta in Corinthian War 395–387 B.C. and again in 377 B.C.; opposed by her former allies in the Social War 357–355 B.C.; anti-Macedonian under Demosthenes, defeated by Philip of Macedon 338 B.C.; under Macedonian hegemony after 322 B.C.

Established friendly relations with Rome 228 B.C. and was aided by Rome against Macedonians, who were finally defeated at Cynoscephalae 197 B.C.; with Roman destruction of the Achaean League 146 B.C., as part of Greece, became subject to Rome; part of Roman province of Achaea (*q.v.*); visited by St. Paul c. 54 A.D.; taken by the Heruli 267 A.D.; surrendered to Alaric and the Goths 395; became a duchy after the Latin conquest of Greece 1204; conquered by the Ottoman Empire 1456; Parthenon destroyed during siege by Venetians 1687–88; became the capital of modern Greece 1835. In World War II occupied by Germans April 1941 to Oct. 1944.

Ath·er·ton \'ath-ərt-ᵊn\. 1 Residential town, San Mateo co., W California, suburb of Redwood City, 22 m. SE of San Francisco; pop. (1970c) 8085; incorp. 1923.

2 *also* 'ath-\. Urban district, Lancashire, NW England, 13 m. WNW of Manchester; pop. (1971p) 21,758; cotton factories, collieries, ironworks.

Atherton Plateau *or* **Atherton Tableland.** Plateau region, NE coast of Queensland, NE Australia, at N end of Great Dividing Range; ab. 15,000 sq. m.; highest point Mt. Bartle Frere 5287 ft.

Athesis. See ADIGE.

Ath·garh \'ət-ˌgär, 'ät-\. Former Indian state, now part of Orissa, E India, on N bank of Mahanadi river; 163 sq. m.; chief town Athgarh 15 m. NW of Cuttack.

Athi \'ät-ē\. River, Kenya; ab. 200 m. long; rises near Nairobi and flows SE through **Athi Plain,** noted for its numerous wild game, to the Sabaki river. See SABAKI.

Athínai. See ATHENS 10.

Athis–Mons \ˌa-ˌtē-'smōⁿs\. Commune, Essonne dept., N France, on Seine river 8 m. SSE of Paris; pop. (1968c) 27,640; naval and aeronautical construction.

'Ath·lit \at(h)-'lēt\. Ancient town and modern archaeological site, on coast of Israel, ab 8 m. SSW of Haifa; noted for discovery of remarkable fossil specimens. Last place in Holy Land held by Crusaders 1291.

Ath·lone \ath-'lōn\. Urban district, W co. Westmeath, on the Shannon, N cen. Eire; pop. (1971p) 9821; agricultural center; woolen and linen goods; salmon fisheries; successfully stormed 1691 by Gen. Godert de Ginkel, after withstanding siege by William of Orange.

Ath·mal·lik \ˌət-'məl-ik, ät-'mäl-\. Former Indian state, now part of Orissa, E India, on N bank of Mahanadi river; 723 sq. m.

Ath·ol \'ath ˌȯl\. Industrial town, Worcester co., cen. Massachusetts, 21 m. W of Fitchburg; pop. (1970c) 11,185; tools, toys, leather goods, wood products.

Ath·oll *or* **Ath·ole** \'ath-əl\. Mountainous district, N Perth co., Scotland, at S base of Grampian Mts.; ab. 450 sq. m.; includes Tay river and Loch Rannoch; land generally uncultivable; extensive hunting tracts.

Ath·os \'ath-ˌäs, 'ā-ˌthäs\. Mountain occupying E end of Acte Penin., Chalcidice, NE Greece; 6667 ft.; inhabited since 9th cent. A.D. by monastic communities of Greek Rule of St. Basil; the "Holy Mountain" of the Greek Church; as **Mount Athos,** declared a theocratic republic 1927.

Athy \ə-'thī\. Urban district, SW co. Kildare, E Eire, 37 m. SW of Dublin; pop. (1971p) 4262; agricultural center; has two ancient castles; as site of a ford of the Barrow river, strategically important in historic time and scene of many battles.

Ati·mo·nan \ˌät-i-'mō-ˌnän\. Municipality, S Quezon prov., Luzon, Phil., on SW shore of Lamon Bay 21 m. E of Lucena; pop. (1969e) 44,300; harbor; under Japanese control Dec. 1941 to April 1945.

Ati·qui·za·ya \ˌät-i-ki-'zī-ə, -'sī-\. Town, Ahuachapán dept., SW El Salvador, 15 m. W of Santa Ana; pop. (1961c) 6346.

Ati·tlán \ˌät-i-'tlän\. 1 Lake, SW Guatemala, at 4700 ft. altitude; 12 m. long, 6 m. wide; occupies a crater 1000 ft. deep.

2 Volcano, S of the lake; 11,604 ft.

3 Town, Guatemala. See SANTIAGO ATITLÁN.

Atiu \ˌät-ē-'ü\ *also* **Va·tiu** \ˌvät-ē-'ü\. Island in cen. part of Cook Is. group, S Pacific Ocean, 116 m. NE of Rarotonga; 20°S lat. and 158°W long.; 10 sq. m.; pop. (1968e) 1448.

Atjeh \'äch-(ˌ)ā\ *also* **Achin** *or* **Acheen** *or* **Atchin** \ä-'chēn\. Province of Indonesia, N Sumatra; 21,387 sq. m.; pop. (1970e) 2,055,000; ✱ Banda Atjeh; rice, rubber, copra, pepper.

History: Former sultanate; visited by member of da Cunha's fleet 1506; destination of first ventures of Dutch and English East India companies 1599 and 1602; at height of power 1607–37, controlled entire western tip of Sumatra; unsuccessfully attacked Portuguese at Malacca 1615; declined after 17th cent.; treaty with British 1819 to exclude other Europeans lapsed after British ceded Sumatran claims to Dutch; region never brought under total Dutch control; rebelled against central government 1953.

At·ka \'at-kə, 'ät-\. Island, largest of the Andreanof group, Aleutian Is., SW Alaska; 422 sq. m.; chief settlement Atka village. In N is Korovin volcano 4852 ft. Inhabited by the Atka, one of the two dialectic divisions of the Aleut; U.S. Army base in World War II.

At·kin·son \'at-kən-sən\. County in Georgia. See table at GEORGIA.

At·lan·ta \ət-'lant-ə, at-\. 1 Commercial and industrial city, ✱ of Georgia and ⊗ of Fulton co., located in De Kalb and Fulton cos., NW cen. Ga., 55 m. E of Alabama border; pop. (1970c) 497,421; largest city in the state; alt. 1050 ft.; important commercial, financial, and transportation center; iron and steel, chemicals, textiles; food processing; Georgia Institute of Technology (1885), Atlanta Univ. (1865), Clark Coll. (1869), Morehouse Coll. (1867), Morris Brown Coll. (1881), and Spelman Coll. (1881); in nearby suburbs are Oglethorpe Univ. (1835), Emory Univ. (1836), Beulah Heights Coll. (1828), Georgia State Coll. (1913).

History: Region around Atlanta ceded to Georgia by Creek Indians 1821; selected 1836 by railroad as end of line and named **Ter·mi·nus** \'tər-mə-nəs\; incorp. 1843 as town of **Mar·thas·ville** \'mär-thəz-ˌvil\, name changed to Atlanta 1845, reincorporated as city 1847; made county seat of newly created Fulton co. 1853; became market center for its area; Confederate supply depot in Civil War; burned by Sherman Nov. 15, 1864; scene of constitutional convention 1867–68; temporary capital of Georgia 1868, permanent capital from 1887.

2 Village, ⊗ of Montmorency co., NE Michigan.

3 City, Cass co., NE Texas, on Arkansas border 20 m. S of Texarkana; pop. (1970c) 5007; lumbering; oil wells.

At·lan·tic \ət-'lant-ik, at-\. 1 County in New Jersey. See table at NEW JERSEY.

2 City, ⊗ of Cass co., SW Iowa, 47 m. ENE of Council Bluffs; pop. (1970c) 7306; stoves; packing plants.

3 Seaside resort, Accomac co., N part of E peninsula, Virginia, 8 m. SW of Chincoteague.

Atlantic City. City, Atlantic co., SE New Jersey, on Atlantic Ocean ab. 60 m. SE of Philadelphia; pop. (1970c) 47,859; noted seaside resort; built 1852 on Absecon Is. (or Absecon Beach); incorporated as city 1854; railroad terminus; 4-mile-long boardwalk of steel and concrete (built 1896); amusement and recreation piers.

Atlantic Highlands. Borough and summer resort, Monmouth co., E cen. New Jersey, on S shore of Sandy Hook 14 m. ESE of Perth Amboy; pop. (1970c) 5102.

Atlantic In·tra·coast·al Waterway \-ˌin-trə-ˌkō-stᵊl-\. A system of inland waterways including rivers, bays, and canals along the Atlantic coast of the U.S.A. from Cape Cod to Florida Bay; includes the Cape Cod Canal, the Chesapeake and Delaware Canal, and the Dismal Swamp Canal; main points on the system are Trenton, N.J., Norfolk, Va., Beaufort, N.C., Jacksonville, Fla., and Miami, Fla.

At·lán·ti·co \ät-'länt-ə-ˌkō\. Department of N Colombia. See table at COLOMBIA.

Atlantic Ocean \ət-ˌlant-ik-, at-\ *or anc.* **Oce·anus At·lan·ti·cus** \ō-ˌsē-ə-nə-sət-'lant-i-kəs\. Body of water separating North and South America from Europe and Africa; 31,814,640 sq. m. (with its branches 41,081,040 sq. m.); av. depth 12,257 ft. Often divided into **North Atlantic Ocean** (max. depth 28,374 ft. in Puerto Rico Trench at 19°35'N, 68°17'W) and **South Atlantic Ocean** (max. depth 27,113 ft. in South Sandwich Trench at 55°07'S, 26°46'W). Merges with Arctic Ocean N of 60° N; S of South America connects with Pacific Ocean by Drake Passage; S of Africa arbitrarily separated from Indian Ocean by meridian 20°E. See SARGASSO SEA.

Atlantic Peak. Mountain, SW Fremont co., cen. Wyoming; 12,490 ft.

At·lán·ti·da \ət-ˈlänt-əd-ə\. Department of N Honduras. See table at HONDURAS.

At·las Mountains \ˌat-ləs-\. Mountain system, NW and N Africa, extending from Cape Dra on SW Morocco coast to Cape Bon on NE Tunisia coast; highest peak Toubkal in W Morocco 13,671 ft. In ancient times the name Atlas Mountains was restricted to the Grand Atlas range on the S border of Mauretania. Comprises several ranges: **Grand Atlas** *or* **High Atlas** in W and S Morocco containing highest peaks; **An·ti–Atlas** \ˈant-ē-, ˈan-ˌtī-\ to the S and parallel with it, highest point ab. 6750 ft.; **Middle Atlas** *or Fr.* **Moy·en Atlas** \mwȧ-ye-nȧt-läs\ in N cen. Morocco, highest ab. 11,000 ft.; **Mar·i·time Atlas** \ˌmar-ə-ˌtīm-\ *or* **Little Atlas** *also* **Tell Atlas** \ˈtel-\, coastal ranges, generally lower (averaging 5000 ft.) from Ceuta eastward in Morocco and Algeria to Cape Bon in Tunisia; and **Sa·har·an Atlas** \sə-ˈhar-ən-, -ˈher-, -här-\ *or Fr.* **Atlas Sa·ha·rien** \ȧt-läs-sȧ-ȧ-rya^{n}\ including the Aurès range in E Algeria, highest Djebel Chélia 7648 ft. Not explored extensively until 19th cent.

At·la·so·va \ət-ˈläs-ə-və\ *or Jap.* **Arai·to** \ə-ˈrī-(ˌ)tō\. Small island off NW coast of Paramushir I. at N end of Kuril Is., Sakhalin Oblast, Russian S.F.S.R., U.S.S.R.; its peak 7674 ft. highest point in the Kuril chain.

At·lin Lake \ˌat-lən-\. Long, narrow lake, NW British Columbia and SW Yukon, Canada; 299 sq. m.; connects with Tagish Lake to the W. Town of **Atlin** is on E shore.

Atlix·co \ä-ˈtlēs-(ˌ)kō\. Town, Puebla state, SE cen. Mexico, 58 m. SE of Mexico City; munic. pop. (1970p) 72,256.

At·more \ˈat-ˌmō(ə)r, -ˌmȯ(ə)r\. City, Escambia co., Alabama, 35 m. NE of Mobile Bay; pop. (1970c) 8239; fertilizer.

Ato·ka \ə-ˈtō-kə\. 1 County in Oklahoma. See table at OKLAHOMA.
2 City, its ⊗, 43 m. SE of Ada; pop. (1970c) 3346; flour, lumber; founded 1867.

Ato·to·nil·co el Al·to \ˌät-ə-tō-ˈnil-(ˌ)kō-el-ˈäl-(ˌ)tō\. Town, Jalisco state, W cen. Mexico, 57 m. E of Guadalajara; munic. pop. (1970p) 35,297.

Ato·yac, Río \ˌrē-ō-ˌät-ə-ˈyäk\. River, headstream of the Balsas, cen. Mexico; ab. 150 m. long; rises in Tlaxcala and flows S and SW into Guerrero; unnavigable.

Atoyac de Al·va·rez \ät-ə-ˈyäk-dā-äl-ˈvär-əs\. Town, Guerrero state, S Mexico, ab. 43 m. WNW of Acapulco; munic. pop. (1970p) 37,398.

Atraf–i–Bal·da \ə-ˌträf-ē-ˈbəl-də, -ˈbäl-\. Former district, S cen. Hyderabad, S cen. India; 2651 sq. m.; ✱ Hyderabad.

Atrak. See ATREK.

Atra·nos \ä-trə-ˈnȯs\ *also* **Adra·nos** \-drə-\ *or anc.* **Rhyn·da·cus** \ˈrin-də-kəs\. River, NW Turkey in Asia; ab. 150 m. long; flows NW from beyond Kütahya and through Lake Apulyont to the Susıgırlık near the Sea of Marmara.

Atra·to \ə-ˈträt-(ˌ)ō\. River, NW Colombia; ab. 350 m. long; flows N into Gulf of Darien. See TRUANDO.

Atrecht. See ARTOIS.

Atrek \ə-ˈtrek\ *or* **Atrak** \-ˈtrak\. River, NE Iran; ab. 300 m. long; flows W forming section of boundary bet. Iran and the Turkmen S.S.R. and empties into SE Caspian Sea in U.S.S.R.

Atri \ˈä-trē\; *anc.* **Ha·tria Pi·ce·na** \ˌhā-trē-ə-pī-ˈsē-nə\ *or* **Ha·dria Picena** \ˌhā-drē-\. Commune, Teramo prov., Abruzzi, cen. Italy, near Adriatic coast 14 m. ESE of Teramo; pop. (1968e) 12,057; agricultural products; Romanesque-Gothic cathedral; remains of ancient town; became Roman colony 290 B.C.

Atria. See ADRIA.

Atropatene. See AZERBAIJAN 1.

Atsu·gi \ät-ˈsü-gē, ˈät-sü-\. Town, Kanagawa prefecture, SE Honshū, Japan, 15 m. W of Yokohama; pop. (1970c) 82,-888.

Atsu·ta \ˈät-sü-ˌtä\. Former town, Aichi prefecture, S Japan, at head of Ise Bay; now part of Nagoya, in S part of city.

Atsuta Bay. See ISE BAY.

At Tafilah. See ET TAFILA.

At·tai·ro \ə-ˈtī-(ˌ)rō\ *or Gk.* **Atá·vi·ros** \ə-ˈtäv-i-ˌrȯs\. Mountain, highest on Rhodes I., Greece; 3986 ft.

At·tala \ə-ˈtal-ə\. County in Mississippi. See table at MISSISSIPPI.

Attaleia *or* **Attalia.** See ANTALYA 2.

At·tal·la \ə-ˈtal-ə\. Industrial city, Etowah co., NE Alabama, 5 m. W of Gadsden; pop. (1970c) 7510.

At·ta·wa·pis·kat \ˌat-ə-wə-ˈpis-kət\. River, NE Ontario, Canada; 465 m. long; rises in chain of lakes in NW Ontario, flows E and NE into James Bay; at long. 88°W flows through **Attawapiskat Lake.**

At·ter, Lake \-ˈat-ər, -ˈät-\ *or* **Lake Kam·mer** \-ˈkäm-ər\; *Ger.* **At·ter·see** \ˈät-ər-ˌzā\ *or* **Kam·mer·see** \ˈkäm-ər-ˌzā\. Lake, Upper Austria, 40 m. SW of Linz; 12 m. long; 17 sq. m.; its shores form a summer resort region.

At·ti·ca \ˈat-i-kə\. 1 City, Fountain co., W Indiana, on Wabash river 22 m. WSW of Lafayette; pop. (1970c) 4262; steel castings; sandstone quarries nearby.
2 Village, Genesee and Wyoming cos., W New York, 31 m. E of Buffalo; pop. (1970c) 2911; in dairying region.
3 Ancient division and state of E Greece, forming the territory of Athens; bounded on N by Boeotia, on E by Aegean Sea, on S by Saronic Gulf, and on W by Megaris; included the island of Salamis; chief towns were Athens, Piraeus, and Eleusis.
History: In legend divided into 12 independent Pelasgian states; a center of Mycenaean culture 2d millennium B.C.; invaded by Ionian Greeks by c. 1300 B.C.; territory without political unity until gradually unified under Athens by 700 B.C. (traditionally accomplished by King Theseus). For later history, see ATHENS 10.
4 *or Gk.* **At·ti·kí** \ät-i-ˈk(y)ē\. Department of Greece. See table at GREECE.

Attinianum. See VODNJAN.

At·tle·boro \ˈat-ᵊl-ˌbər-ə, -ˌbə-rə\. City, Bristol co., SE Massachusetts; pop. (1970c) 32,907; jewelry, electronic components.

Attock. See CAMPBELLPORE.

At·tu \ˈat-(ˌ)ü\. Rocky island in Near Island group and most westerly of the Aleutian Islands, SW Alaska, 52°55′ N, 172°30′E; 388 sq. m.; highest point more than 3000 ft.; formerly a prosperous Atka Aleut settlement. Occupied by Japanese June 1942; retaken by U.S. forces May–June 1943.

Atuel \ä-ˈtwel\. River, W Argentina; ab. 300 m. long; rises in the Andes, flows E and SSE in Mendoza prov. to unite with the Salado in N La Pampa prov.

Atu·o·na \ˌät-ə-ˈwō-nə\ *or* **Atu·a·na** \-ˈwän-ə\. Village, Hiva Oa I., French Polynesia; formerly ✱ of Marquesas Is.

Atura. See AIRE 3.

Aturus. See ADOUR.

At·wa·ter \ˈat-ˌwȯt-ər, -ˌwät-\. City, Merced co., California, NW of Merced; pop. (1970c) 11,640.

At·wood \ˈat-ˌwu̇d\. City, ⊗ of Rawlins co., NW Kansas; pop. (1970c) 1658.

Atwood Cay. See SAMANA CAY.

Aty·rá \ˌät-ī-ˈrä\. Town, Cordillera dept., cen. Paraguay; pop. (1970e) 8571.

Au·au Channel \ˌau̇-ˌau̇-\. Strait bet. NW Maui I. and Lanai I., Hawaii; 7 m. wide. See LAHAINA.

Au·bagne \ō-ˈban(-yə)\ *or anc.* **Al·ba·nia** \al-ˈbā-nē-ə, -nyə, ȯl-\. Commune, Bouches-du-Rhône dept., SE France, 8 m. E of Marseilles; pop. (1968c) 27,938.

Aube \ˈōb\. 1 River, N cen. France; 154 m. long; rises in Haute-Marne dept., flows NW and W into Seine river 23 m. NNW of Troyes.

2 Department of NE France. See table at FRANCE.

Au·be·nas \ˌōb-(ə-)ˈnä\. Commune, Ardèche dept., SE France, on Ardèche river at foot of Cévennes Mts.; pop. (1968c) 10,763; near several extinct volcanoes.

Au·ber·vil·liers \ˌō-bər-(ˌ)vēl-ˈyā\ *or formerly* **No·tre Dame des Ver·tus** \ˌnò-trə-dàm-dā-ver-tᵫ\. Commune, Seine-St-Denis dept., N France, NNE suburb of Paris 2 m. from right bank of Seine river; pop. (1968c) 73,695; chemical products, perfumes, glass, rubber; battle 1814.

Au·burn \ˈȯ-bərn\. 1 City, Lee co., E Alabama, 8 m. W of Opelika; pop. (1970c) 22,767; textile mills, tire factories; Auburn Univ. (1856).

2 City, ⊗ of Placer co., E California, 36 m. NE of Sacramento; pop. (1970c) 6570; fruit; founded as gold-mining camp 1848, incorp. as city 1888.

3 City, Sangamon co., cen. Illinois, 17 m. S of Springfield; pop. (1970c) 2594; coal mines.

4 City, ⊗ of De Kalb co., NE Indiana, 22 m. NNE of Fort Wayne; pop. (1970c) 7388; automotive parts, foundry products; in agricultural area.

5 City, ⊗ of Androscoggin co., SW Maine, on Androscoggin river opp. Lewiston 30 m. N of Portland; pop. (1970c) 24,151; Auburn Maine School of Commerce (1916).

6 Town, Worcester co., cen. Massachusetts, 5 m. SSW of Worcester; pop. (1970c) 15,347; residential suburb of Worcester.

7 City, ⊗ of Nemaha co., SE Nebraska, 55 m. SE of Lincoln; pop. (1970c) 3650; in fruit-growing region.

8 Manufacturing city, ⊗ of Cayuga co., cen. New York, on outlet of Lake Owasco 25 m. WSW of Syracuse; pop. (1970c) 34,599; electronic equipment, shoes, plastics; Auburn Community Coll. (1953), state prison (1816); founded 1793, became ⊗ 1805, chartered as city 1848.

9 City, King co., W cen. Washington, 11 m. ENE of Tacoma; pop. (1970c) 21,817; sheet metal products, lumber; manufactures pottery, cabinets.

10 Municipality, E New South Wales, SE Australia, W suburb of Sydney; pop. (1966c) 48,691.

Au·burn·dale \ˈȯ-bərn-ˌdāl\. Residential city, Polk co., cen. Florida penin., 10 m. E of Lakeland; pop. (1970c) 5386; fruit, phosphates.

Auburn Dam *and* **Auburn Reservoir.** See UNITED STATES, *Dams and Reservoirs.*

Au·bus·son \ˌō-bə-ˈsōⁿ\. Commune, Creuse dept., cen. France, on Creuse river 20 m. SE of Guéret; pop. (1962c) 5669; long celebrated for its carpets and tapestries, the famous Savonnerie carpets and the Beauvais and Gobelin tapestries still being made on hand looms.

Au·by \ō-ˈbē\. Commune, Nord dept., N France, 3 m. NNW of Douai; pop. (1962c) 9007; coal mines, zinc works; chemical products.

Auch \ˈōsh\ *or anc.* **El·im·ber·rum** \ˌel-əm-ˈber-əm\ *or later* **Au·gus·ta Aus·co·rum** \ȯ-ˌgəs-tə-ȯs-ˈkōr-əm, ə-ˌgəs-, -ˈkȯr-\. City, ✻ of Gers dept., SW France, on Gers river 42 m. W of Toulouse; pop. (1968c) 21,462; tiles, tobacco; late-Gothic cathedral (begun 1489) famous for its stained-glass windows and handworked choir stalls; museum and library. Chief town of the Ausci, a Celtiberian tribe; ravaged by Saracens 732; medieval capital of Armagnac; became capital of the generality of Gascony in the 17th cent.

Au·chel \ō-ˈshel\. Commune, Pas-de-Calais dept., N France, 20 m. NW of Arras; pop. (1968c) 14,091; coal.

Au·chin·leck \ˌȯ-kən-ˈlek, -k̲ən-\. Parish, Ayr co., SW Scotland; family home of James Boswell.

Auchterhouse Hill. See SIDLAW HILLS.

Au·cil·la \ȯ-ˈsil-ə\ *or* **Ocil·la** \ō-\. River, N Florida; ab. 70 m. long; flows S from S Georgia into Apalachee Bay.

Auck·land \ˈȯ-klənd\. Seaport city, on Waitemata and Manukau Harbors, North I., New Zealand; pop. (1971p) 151,588, met. area 581,302; New Zealand's principal port; chemicals, leather goods, building materials; fishing, food processing, metalworking; Univ. of Auckland (1882, reorganized 1957), City Art Gallery (1888), Museum of Transport and Technology (1964); founded 1840 as capital of New Zealand, but replaced by Wellington 1865.

Auckland Islands. Uninhabited group of islands 200 m. S of New Zealand, 50°32′S, 166°13′E; 234 sq. m.; discovered 1806; mountainous; several good harbors.

Aude \ˈōd\. 1 *or anc.* **Atax** \ˈa-ˌtaks\. River, S France; 130 m. long; rises on the slopes of the Pyrenees, flows N and E into Mediterranean Sea near Narbonne.

2 Department of S France. See table at FRANCE.

Au·de·narde \ˌōd-ᵊn-ˈärd\ *or Flem.* **Ou·de·naar·de** \ˌau̇d-ᵊn-ˈärd-ə\. Commune, East Flanders prov., NW cen. Belgium, on Schelde river 31 m. W of Brussels; pop. (1969e) 22,084; cotton, tobacco; railroad junction; notable for its churches and late-Gothic hôtel de ville; scene of defeat July 11, 1708 of French under duke of Vendôme by Prince Eugene and Marlborough during War of the Spanish Succession; captured by French and American troops Nov. 1, 1918.

Au·den·shaw \ˈȯd-ᵊn-ˌshȯ\. Urban district, Lancashire, NW England, 5 m. E of Manchester; pop. (1971p) 11,887; cotton mills.

Au·der·ghem \ˌōd-ər-ˈgem\ *or Flem.* **Ou·der·gem** \ˈau̇d-ər-gəm\. Commune, Brabant prov., cen. Belgium, SE suburb of Brussels (1½ m.); pop. (1969e) 33,410.

Audh. See OUDH.

Au·drain \ȯ-ˈdrān, ˈȯ-ˌ-\. County in Missouri. See table at MISSOURI.

Au·du·bon \ˈȯd-ə-bən, -ˌbän\. 1 County in Iowa. See table at IOWA.

2 City, its ⊗, W Iowa, 59 m. NE of Council Bluffs; pop. (1970c) 2907; in agricultural region; canneries.

3 Borough, Camden co., SW New Jersey, 4 m. SSE of Camden; pop. (1970c) 10,802; suburb of Camden.

Audubon, Mount. Peak in Front Range of the Rocky Mts., Boulder co., N cen. Colorado; 13,223 ft.

Aue \ˈau̇-ə\. Industrial city, Karl-Marx-Stadt dist., East Germany, in the Erzgebirge 13 m. SE of Zwickau; pop. (1970e) 30,930; iron foundries, machine shops, cotton mills, hardware and tool factories; received city charter 1629.

Au·er·bach \ˈau̇(-ə)r-ˌbäk, -ˌbäk̲\. Industrial city, Karl-Marx-Stadt dist., East Germany, 55 m. S of Leipzig; pop. (1970e) 18,903; embroidery, carpets, textiles; founded c. 1144.

Au·er·stedt *or* **Au·er·städt** \ˈau̇(-ə)r-ˌs(h)tet\. Village, East Germany, 14 m. NE of Weimar; scene of defeat of Prussians under duke of Brunswick by French under Davout Oct. 14, 1806, simultaneously with Napoleon's victory over main Prussian army at Jena.

Aufidus. See OFANTO.

Au·ghra·bies Falls *or* **Au·gra·bies Falls** \ȯ-ˌgräb-ēz-\. Falls in the Orange river, NW Cape Province, Rep. of South Africa, ab. 35 m. E of the South-West Africa border; 480 ft. high; discovered 1824.

Augh·rim *or* **Agh·rim** \ˈȯ-grəm\. Parish and town, co. Galway, Eire, 30 m. E of Galway; scene of decisive victory of William III over James II July 12, 1691, which, together with battle of the Boyne (July 1, 1690), is commemorated in Northern Ireland on Orangemen's Day (July 12).

Augila. See AWJIDAH.

Au·glaize \ȯ-ˈglāz\. 1 River, W Ohio; ab. 100 m. long; rises in Auglaize co. and flows W and N to the Maumee river at Defiance.

2 County in Ohio. See table at OHIO.

Augrabies Falls. See AUGHRABIES FALLS.

Au Gres, Point \-ȯ-ˈgrā\. Point on SE coast of Arenac co., E Michigan, at N entrance to Saginaw Bay.

Augs·burg \ˈȯgz-ˌbərg, ˈau̇gz-ˌbu̇(ə)rg, ˈau̇ks-ˌbu̇rk\ *or anc.* **Au·gus·ta Vin·del·i·co·rum** \ȯ-ˈgəs-tə-(ˌ)vin-ˌdel-ə-ˈkōr-əm, ə-'gəs-, -'kȯr-\. Commercial city, Bavaria, West Germany, on the Lech river 30 m. WNW of Munich; pop. (1969e) 212,963; machinery, chemicals, textiles, electronic equipment, aircraft; buildings include the cathedral, the Rathaus with its notable Golden Hall, and the episcopal palace.

History: Roman colony founded by Augustus 14 B.C.; received municipal rights from Hadrian; scene of defeat of Hungarians by Otto I 955 A.D.; recognized as free imperial city 1276; because of location and undertakings of Fugger and Welser families, became center for trade bet. northern and southern Europe in 15th and 16th cents.; scene of diet to which Melanchthon presented Confession of Augsburg 1530, and of drafting of Religious Peace of Augsburg 1555; League of Augsburg against France 1686; lost municipal freedom and became part of Bavaria 1806. In World War II frequently bombed 1940–45; taken by Allied armies April 28, 1945.

Au·gus·ta \ȯ-'gəs-tə, ə-\. 1 County in Virginia. See table at VIRGINIA.

2 City, ⊗ of Woodruff co., NE cen. Arkansas, on White river 56 m. SW of Jonesboro; pop. (1970c) 2777; sawmill, cotton gins.

3 City, ⊗ of Richmond co., E Georgia, on Savannah river 105 m. ENE of Macon; pop. (1970c) 59,864; barge terminal; fertilizer, cotton and cottonseed products; kaolin deposits; Paine Coll. (1882), Augusta Coll. (1925); settled in 1735 by James Oglethorpe; captured by British 1778, but retaken by Americans under "Lighthorse Harry" Lee 1781; capital of Georgia 1786–95, incorporated as city 1798.

4 City, Butler co., S Kansas, 20 m. E of Wichita; pop. (1970c) 5977; dairy farms, oil wells.

5 City, Bracken co., NE Kentucky, on Ohio river 17 m. NW of Maysville; pop. (1970c) 1434; tobacco.

6 City, ✱ of Maine and ⊗ of Kennebec co., SW Maine, on Kennebec river 25 m. NE of Lewiston; pop. (1970c) 21,945; summer resort; cotton goods, timber; at head of navigation on Kennebec river; trading post in 17th cent.; site of Fort Western 1754, incorporated as town 1797, as city 1849; made capital of Maine 1831.

7 City, Eau Claire co., W Wisconsin, 20 m. ESE of Eau Claire; pop. (1970c) 1242.

Au·gu·sta \au̇-'gü-stə\ *or* **Ago·sta** \ä-'gō-stə\. Commune, Siracusa prov., SE Sicily, Italy, 12 m. N of Syracuse; pop. (1968e) 31,602; on small island, formerly the peninsula of Xiphonia, connected by bridge with Sicilian mainland; saltworks; exports wine, cheese, fruits, sardines. Founded by Frederick II 1232; near site of ancient Megara Hyblaea (*q.v.*); sacked 1286; burned by Turks 1551; almost completely destroyed by earthquake 1693. In World War II taken by British July 1943.

Au·gus·ta, Cape \-au̇-'gü-stə\. Cape extending into Caribbean Sea on N coast of Colombia at Barranquilla.

Augusta Auscorum. See AUCH.

Augusta Bay. See EMPRESS AUGUSTA BAY.

Augusta Emerita. See MÉRIDA 2.

Augusta Praetoria. See AOSTA 2.

Augusta Suessionum. See SOISSONS.

Augusta Taurinorum. See TURIN.

Augusta Treverorum. See TRIER.

Augusta Vangionum. See WORMS 2.

Augusta Vindelicorum. See AUGSBURG.

Au·gus·tine \'ȯ-gə-ˌstēn\. Island, SW part of Cook Inlet, Alaska; 41 sq. m.; highest point 3999 ft.; volcano, eruption 1883.

Augustobona Tricassium. See TROYES.

Augustodunum. See AUTUN.

Augustodurum. See BAYEUX.

Augustonemetum. See CLERMONT-FERRAND.

Augustoritum Lemovicensium. See LIMOGES.

Au·gus·tów \au̇-'gü-stüf, -stəf\ *or Russ.* **Av·gus·tov** \äf-'gü-stəf\. Town, N Białystok prov., NE Poland, 50 m. N of Białystok; pop. (1968e) 18,800; founded 1650 by Sigismund II Augustus of Poland. Battle in World War I in which Russians defeated Germans Sept. 29–Oct. 4, 1914; during World War II held by Germans; taken by Soviet troops Oct. 24, 1944; part of Belorussian S.S.R. 1945–46.

Au–ké·na \au̇-'kā-nə\. Small island of Gambier Is., French Polynesia, S Pacific Ocean.

Au·ki \'au̇-kē\. Chief village, on W coast of Malaita I., British Solomon Is., W Pacific Ocean.

Auld·earn \ȯl-'dərn\. Village, Nairn co., NE Scotland, E of Nairn; pop. (1961c) 318; scene of victory of Montrose over the Covenanters under Sir John Urry May 9, 1645.

Aulie Ata. See DZHAMBUL.

Au·lis \'ȯ-ləs\. Harbor in Boeotia on Evripos Strait, E cen. Greece; according to tradition, starting place of Greek fleet sailing against Troy at beginning of the Trojan War, and scene of the sacrifice of Iphigenia.

Aullagas, Lake. See POOPÓ, LAKE.

Aul·nay–sous–Bois \ō-ˌnā-sü-'bwä\. Commune, Seine-St-Denis dept., N France, 6 m. NE of Paris; pop. (1968c) 61,521.

Aulon. See VLORË 2.

Au·male \ō-'mäl\. 1 Commune, Algeria. See SOUR ALGHOZLANE.

2 Commune, Seine-Maritime dept., N France, 40 m. NE of Rouen; has old church of 16th and 17th cents.

History: Its surrounding territory granted to Odo, brother-in-law of William the Conqueror; ruling family important in French nobility as counts (from 11th cent.) and dukes (after 1547); duchy passed 1618 to ducal house of Nemours (Savoy), thence to Louis XIV by purchase 1686, and finally to House of Orléans 1769.

Aundh \'au̇nd\. 1 Former Indian state, now part of Maharashtra state, India.

2 Town, its ✱, 27 m. SE of Satara.

Au·nis \ō-'nēs\. Historical region of W cen. France; bounded on N by Poitou, E by Angoumois, S by Gironde estuary, and W by Bay of Biscay; ✱ La Rochelle. Early became a feudal dependency of Poitou.

Aunus. See OLONETS 1.

Auob \'üb\ *or* **Oup** \'üp\. River bed, SW Africa, extending from S cen. South-West Africa to the Molopo; ab. 300 m. long.

Au·rang·abad *also* **Au·rung·abad** \au̇-'rəŋ-(g)ə-ˌbäd\. 1 District, N Maharashtra, W cen. India; formerly in Hyderabad state and (1956–60) in Bombay state; 6314 sq. m.; pop. (1961c) 1,532,341; ✱ Aurangabad; oil pressing.

2 City, its ✱, 207 m. ENE of Bombay; pop. (1961c) 87,579; tourism; univ. 1958. Founded 1610 by Malik Ambar; Aurangzeb's capital in 17th cent. campaign against southern Indian Muslim states; here he erected to his wife a beautiful mausoleum sometimes compared with the Taj Mahal; later the ✱ of independent Nizams before it was removed to Hyderabad.

Au·ra·ni·tis \ˌȯr-ə-'nīt-əs\. In the time of Herod the Great (37–4 B.C.) that part of Hauran forming NE section of his kingdom, E of the Sea of Galilee.

Aurantes. See ABRANTES.

Au·rar·ia \ȯ-'rer-ē-ə, -'rar-\. First settlement in Colorado, established 1858; soon united (1860) with two other villages to become Denver.

Au·ray \ȯ-'rā\. Commune, Morbihan dept., NW France, on Auray river 11 m. W of Vannes; famed church of Sainte Anne d'Auray (3 m. NW); pilgrimage resort.

Aurelia Aquensis. See BADEN-BADEN.

Aurelianum. See ORLÉANS.

Au·re·lian Way \ȯ-ˌrēl-yən-\ *or Lat.* **Via Au·re·lia** \'vī-ə-ȯ-'rēl-yə, 'vē-ə-\. Roman highway, called the "Great Coast Road," running NW along the coast of Etruria, at first to Pisae (Pisa), but later extended to Genua (Genoa) in Liguria; near Luna (W of Apuania) it was joined by the Cassian Way.

Au·rès Mountains \ȯ-'res-\. Mountain massif in the Saharan Atlas, cen. Batna dept., NE Algeria; highest peak Djebel Chélia 7648 ft.

Au·ri·gnac \ˌō-rēn-ˈyak\. Commune, Haute-Garonne dept., S France, 37 m. SW of Toulouse; tanneries; caves with significant paleolithic remains, the appropriate subdivision of the Stone Age now being called the Aurignacian period.

Aurigny. See ALDERNEY.

Au·ril·lac \ˌō-rē-ˈ(y)ak\. City, ✱ of Cantal dept., S cen. France, 105 m. NNE of Toulouse; pop. (1968c) 28,226; umbrellas, gloves; trade in cattle, horses, cheese; 11th cent. castle. Developed around 9th cent. abbey of St. Géraud; famous seat of medieval learning.

Au·ro·ra \ə-ˈrōr-ə, ȯ-, -ˈrȯr-\. **1** County in South Dakota. See table at SOUTH DAKOTA.

2 Suburban residential city, Adams and Arapahoe cos., NE cen. Colorado, 5 m. E of Denver; pop. (1970c) 74,974.

3 Industrial city, Kane co., NE Illinois, 37 m. W of Chicago; pop. (1970c) 74,182; chemicals, transportation equipment, glass; Aurora Coll. (1893); incorp. as a city 1857.

4 City, Dearborn co., SE Indiana, on Ohio river 54 m. SE of Shelbyville; pop. (1970c) 4293; furniture, castings, coffins.

5 Village, St. Louis co., NE Minnesota, 13 m. E of Virginia; pop. (1970c) 2531; trade center for iron-mining region.

6 City, Lawrence co., SW Missouri, 30 m. SW of Springfield; pop. (1970c) 5359; trade center in dairy and poultry-raising region; zinc and lead deposits nearby.

7 City, ⊗ of Hamilton co., SE cen. Nebraska, 18 m. E of Grand Island; pop. (1970c) 3180; flour mills, dairies.

8 Village, Cayuga co., cen. New York, on E shore of Cayuga Lake ab. 12 m. SSW of Auburn; pop. (1970c) 1072; Wells Coll. (1868); settled 1789.

9 Town, Erie co., New York; pop. (1970c) 14,426; includes East Aurora village (*q.v.*).

10 Town, York co., SE Ontario, Canada, 25 m. N of Toronto; pop. (1971p) 13,534; farm implements, shoes.

11 Island of the New Hebrides. See MAEWO.

Aur·sund·en \ˈau̇(-ə)r-ˌsu̇n-ən\. Lake in cen. Norway, N of Femund Lake; drains into headwaters of Glåma river.

Ausa. See VICH.

Au Sa·ble \ō-ˈsā-bəl\. River, N cen. Michigan; 80 m. long; flowing from Crawford co. E into Lake Huron in NE Iosco co.

Au Sable Forks. Village, Essex and Clinton cos., NE New York; pulp, paper manufacturers.

Au Sable Point. **1** Point on NE coast of Alger co., N Michigan penin., extending into Lake Superior.

2 Point on E coast of Iosco co., NE Michigan, extending into Lake Huron.

Au·san·ga·te, Ne·va·do \nə-ˈväd-ō-ˌau̇-säŋ-ˈgät-ē\ *or Eng.* **Ausangate Knot.** Mountain, Cuzco dept., SE Peru; 20,945 ft.; highest point in the Cordillera de Carabaya.

Auschwitz. See OŚWIĘCIM.

Ausculum Apulum. See ASCOLI SATRIANO.

Aussig. See ÚSTÍ NAD LABEM.

Aust–Ag·der \ˈau̇st-ˌäg-dər\. County of S Norway. See table at NORWAY.

Aus·tell \ō-ˈstel\. City, Cobb and Douglas cos., NW Georgia, 15 m. NW of Atlanta; pop. (1970c) 2632; diversified agriculture.

Aus·ten, Mount \-ˈȯs-tən, -ˈäs-\. Hill and landmark ab. 4 m. S of Henderson Field, cen. Guadalcanal, Solomon Is.; held by Japanese during early part of campaign for the island; taken by U.S. marines Dec. 1942.

Austerlitz. See SLAVKOV.

Aus·tin\ˈȯs-tən, ˈäs-\. **1** County in Texas. See table at TEXAS.

2 Town, Scott co., SE Indiana, 30 m. N of New Albany; pop. (1970c) 4902.

3 City, ⊗ of Mower co., S Minnesota, 34 m. SW of Rochester; pop. (1970c) 25,074; Austin State Junior Coll. (1940).

4 Village, ⊗ of Lander co., cen. Nevada, 145 m. ENE of Carson City; sheep raising, silver, gold mining; founded 1862, became ⊗ 1863; important mining and trading center and post station during early gold-rush period in Nevada.

5 City, ✱ of Texas and ⊗ of Travis co., cen. Texas, on Colorado river 75 m. NE of San Antonio; pop. (1970c) 251,808; electronic equipment, glass, furniture; food processing; real estate, finance, insurance; St. Edward's Univ. (1876), Huston-Tillotson Coll. (1877), Univ. of Texas (1881), Austin Presbyterian Theological Seminary (1902), Concordia Lutheran Coll. (1926), Southwest Episcopal Seminary (1951). Site first settled as Waterloo 1835; chosen as capital of Republic of Texas 1839, incorp., and renamed Austin; government returned to Houston 1842–45 because of marauding Mexicans and Indians; capital of state of Texas from 1845.

Austin, Lake. Lake, Western Australia, 310 m. NNE of Perth; 320 sq. m.

Aus·tral·asia \ˌȯs-trə-ˈlā-zhə, ˌäs-, -ˈlā-shə\. The portion of Oceania bet. the equator and lat. 47°S; ab. 3,300,000 sq. m.; also, by extension, all of Oceania, but in general, and especially in Australia and New Zealand, the term is not commonly used because of confusion with Australia.

Aus·tra·lia \ō-ˈstrāl-yə, ä-\ *or in full* **Commonwealth of Australia.** Independent state, smallest continent on the globe, bounded on N by Timor and Arafura seas, on NE by Coral Sea, on E by South Pacific Ocean, and on S and W by Indian Ocean; 2,967,909 sq. m.; pop. (1970e) 12,551,-700; ✱ Canberra.

Physical features: Entirely in S hemisphere; largely desert; many salt lakes, esp. in S (lowest Lake Eyre) and W; low Artesian Basin in E cen. part. Mountain range (Great Dividing Range), parallel with E coast from N Queensland around to cen. Victoria, highest point Mt. Kosciusko (*q.v.*); also plateau uplands in E New South Wales. Coast indented with extensive Gulf of Carpentaria in NE (Cape York Peninsula on E) and Great Australian Bight and Spencer Gulf in S; coastline rugged with few good harbors, but some excellent: Port Jackson (harbor of Sydney), Newcastle (mouth of Hunter river), Brisbane (Moreton Bay), Darwin (Port Darwin), Fremantle (estuary of Swan river), Port Adelaide, Port Pirie, and Port Lincoln in South Australia, and Melbourne (on Port Phillip Bay). Many islands and reefs along coast, esp. Great Barrier Reef on NE, Thursday I. and others in Torres Strait, Melville I. N of Darwin, Kangaroo I. off South Australia, and Fraser I. off SE Queensland; Tasmania, constituting a state, is separated from mainland by Bass Strait. Chief rivers Murray-Darling system; others Fitzroy, Burdekin, Flinders, Swan, Cooper's Creek. *Chief products:* Wheat, barley, oats, fruit, sugarcane, wool, dairy products; bauxite, gold, silver, lead, zinc, copper, iron, limestone, coal, natural gas; manufacturing: iron and steel, electrical equipment, machine tools, agricultural machinery, chemicals, textiles, paper; food processing. *Chief cities:* Sydney, Melbourne, Brisbane, Adelaide, Perth, Newcastle, Wollongong. Divided into six states and two territories—see table below. Exercises control over the following external territories: Ashmore and Cartier Is., Australian Antarctic Terr., Christmas I., Cocos Is., Coral Sea Islands Terr., Heard and McDonald Is., Norfolk I., and Papua New Guinea.

NAME	AREA (sq. m.)	POP. (1970e)	CAPITAL
States			
New South Wales	309,433	4,567,000	Sydney
Queensland	667,000	1,799,200	Brisbane
South Australia	380,070	1,164,700	Adelaide
Tasmania	26,383	392,500	Hobart
Victoria	87,884	3,443,800	Melbourne
Western Australia	975,920	980,000	Perth
Territories			
Australian Capital Terr.	939	133,100	Canberra
Northern Terr.	520,280	71,400	Darwin

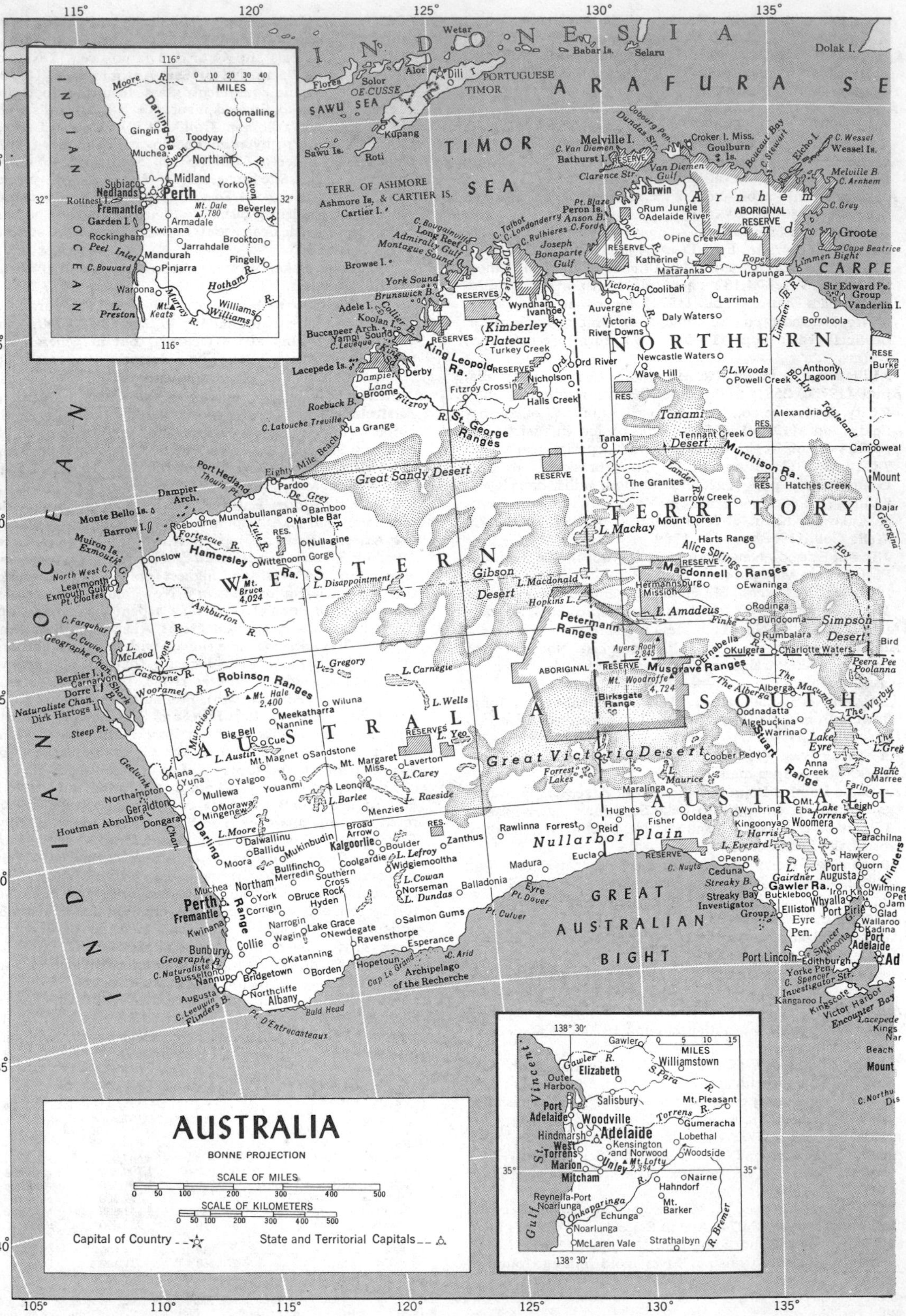
AUSTRALIA
BONNE PROJECTION
SCALE OF MILES
0 50 100 200 300 400 500
SCALE OF KILOMETERS
0 50 100 200 300 400 500
Capital of Country
State and Territorial Capitals
I N D O N E S I A
A R A F U R A S E
TIMOR SEA
SAWU SEA
PORTUGUESE TIMOR
TERR. OF ASHMORE & CARTIER IS.
INDIAN OCEAN
GREAT AUSTRALIAN BIGHT
WESTERN AUSTRALIA
NORTHERN TERRITORY
SOUTH AUSTRALIA
Great Sandy Desert
Gibson Desert
Great Victoria Desert
Nullarbor Plain
Simpson Desert
Tanami Desert
Kimberley Plateau
Arnhem Land
ABORIGINAL RESERVE
Macdonnell Ranges
Musgrave Ranges
Petermann Ranges
Hamersley Ra.
Robinson Ranges
King Leopold Ra.
Darling Range
Perth
Fremantle
Darwin
Adelaide
Alice Springs
Kalgoorlie
Geraldton
Broome
Derby
Port Hedland
Carnarvon
Albany
Esperance
Port Augusta
Whyalla
Port Pirie
Port Lincoln
Woomera
Tennant Creek
Katherine
Ayers Rock 2,845
Mt. Woodroffe 4,724
Mt. Bruce 4,024
Melville I.
Bathurst I.
Groote
L. Eyre
L. Torrens
L. Gairdner
L. Amadeus
L. Mackay
L. Carnegie
Gawler
Elizabeth
Salisbury
Woodville
Port Adelaide
Hindmarsh
West Torrens
Marion
Mitcham
Unley
Mt. Lofty 2,334
Kensington and Norwood
Williamstown
Mt. Pleasant
Gumeracha
Lobethal
Woodside
Nairne
Hahndorf
Mt. Barker
Echunga
Noarlunga
Reynella-Port Noarlunga
McLaren Vale
Strathalbyn
Gulf St. Vincent
Gingin
Toodyay
Northam
Goomalling
Midland
Subiaco
Nedlands
York
Beverley
Armadale
Kwinana
Rockingham
Mandurah
Pinjarra
Brookton
Pingelly
Waroona
Williams
Mt. Dale 1,780
MILES
0 10 20 30 40
0 5 10 15
105° 110° 115° 120° 125° 130° 135°
10° 15° 20° 25° 30° 35° 40°

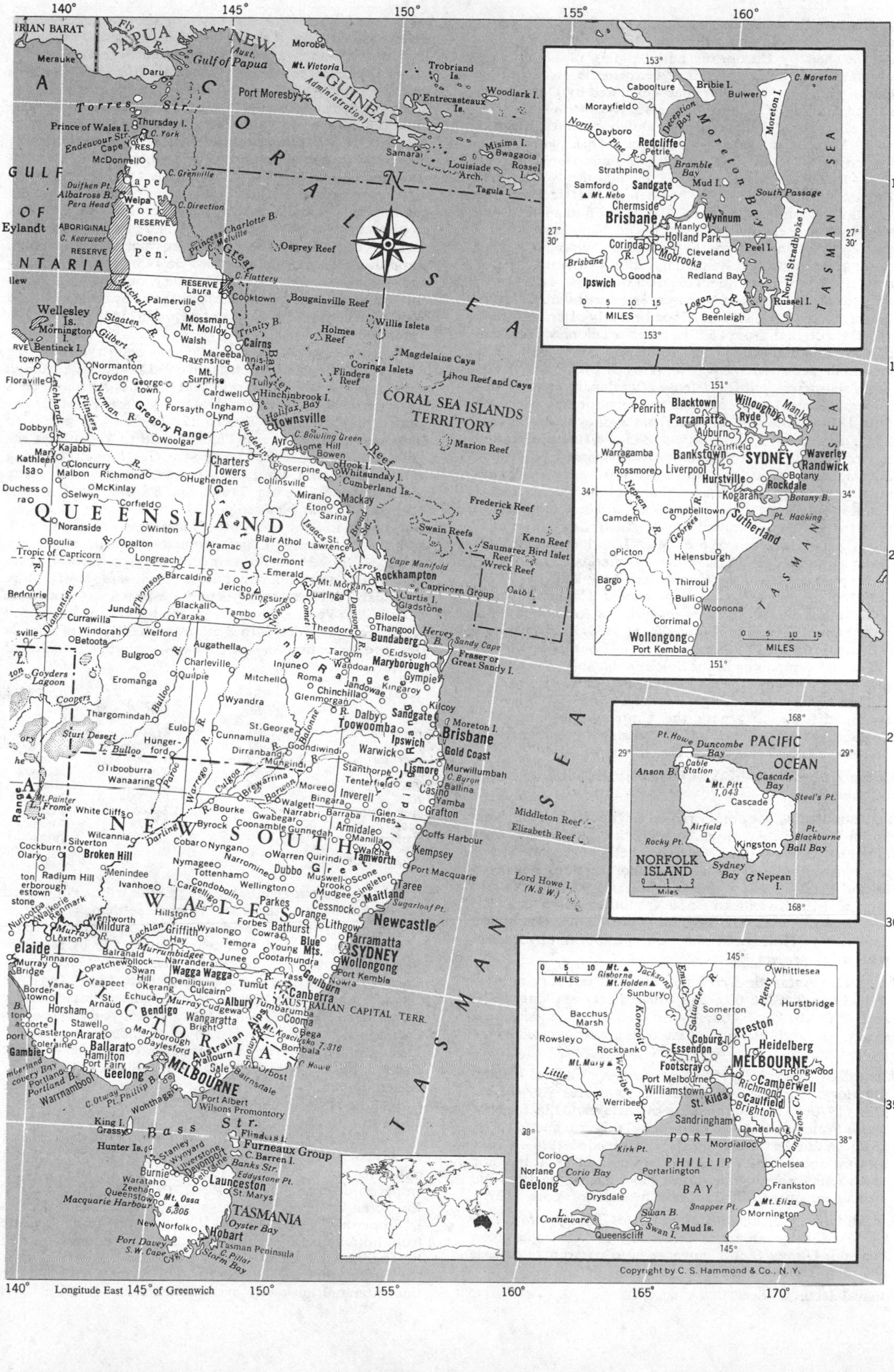

140° 145° 150° 155° 160°
IRIAN BARAT
PAPUA
NEW
GUINEA
(Aust. Administration)
Fly R.
Gulf of Papua
Merauke
Daru
Morobe
Mt. Victoria
Port Moresby
Trobriand Is.
Woodlark I.
D'Entrecasteaux Is.
Samarai
Misima I.
Bwagaoia
Louisiade Arch.
Rossel I.
Tagula I.
Torres Str.
Prince of Wales I.
Thursday I.
C. York
Endeavour Str.
Cape York
RES.
McDonnell
GULF OF CARPENTARIA
Duifken Pt.
Albatross B.
Pera Head
Weipa
Cape York Pen.
RESERVE
ABORIGINAL RESERVE
C. Keerweer
C. Grenville
C. Direction
Coen
Eylandt
Princess Charlotte B.
C. Melville
Osprey Reef
CORAL SEA
C. Flattery
RESERVE
Laura
Cooktown
Palmerville
Bougainville Reef
Willis Islets
Wellesley Is.
Mornington I.
Bentinck I.
Staaten R.
Mitchell R.
Gilbert R.
Mossman
Mt. Molloy
Walsh
Trinity B.
Cairns
Holmes Reef
Normanton
Croydon
Mareeba
Ravenshoe
Innisfail
Mt. Surprise
Georgetown
Tully
Cardwell
Hinchinbrook I.
Magdelaine Cays
Coringa Islets
Flinders Reef
Lihou Reef and Cays
Floraville
Leichhardt R.
Flinders R.
Norman R.
Gregory Range
Forsayth
Ingham
Lynd
Halifax Bay
Townsville
Great Barrier Reef
CORAL SEA ISLANDS TERRITORY
Marion Reef
Dobbyn
Woolgar
Ayr
C. Bowling Green
Home Hill
Bowen
Burdekin R.
Mary Kathleen
Kajabbi
Cloncurry
Mt. Isa
Malbon
Richmond
Charters Towers
Hughenden
Proserpine
Hook I.
Whitsunday I.
Cumberland Is.
Collinsville
Duchess
McKinlay
Selwyn
Corfield
Mirani
Mackay
Eton
Sarina
Frederick Reef
QUEENSLAND
Noranside
Winton
Great Dividing Range
Isaacs R.
Broad Sd.
Swain Reefs
Kenn Reef
Saumarez Reef
Bird Islet
Wreck Reef
Boulia
Opalton
Blair Athol
Clermont
St. Lawrence
Tropic of Capricorn
Longreach
Aramac
Emerald
Cape Manifold
Fitzroy R.
Barcaldine
Thomson R.
Jericho
Springsure
Mt. Morgan
Rockhampton
Capricorn Group
Cato I.
Bedourie
Diamantina R.
Jundah
Blackall
Tambo
Nogoa R.
Comet R.
Duaringa
Dawson R.
Curtis I.
Gladstone
Currawilla
Windorah
Betoota
Yaraka
Theodore
Biloela
Thangool
Bundaberg
Hervey B.
Sandy Cape
Welford
Augathella
Taroom
Eidsvold
Maryborough
Fraser or Great Sandy I.
Bulgroo
Charleville
Wandoan
Injune
Roma
Mitchell
Gympie
Eromanga
Quilpie
Chinchilla
Jandowae
Kingaroy
Goyders Lagoon
Coopers
Glenmorgan
Wyandra
Dalby
Sandgate
Kilcoy
Moreton I.
Thargomindah
Bulloo R.
Sturt Desert
St. George
Toowoomba
Ipswich
Brisbane
Eulo
Cunnamulla
Balonne R.
Gold Coast
L. Bulloo
Hungerford
Dirranbandi
Goondiwindi
Warwick
Mungindi
Murwillumbah
Tibooburra
Wanaaring
Paroo R.
Warrego R.
Culgoa R.
Stanthorpe
Lismore
C. Byron
Tenterfield
Ballina
Casino
Brewarrina
Barwon R.
Moree
Inverell
Yamba
Mt. Painter
L. Frome
White Cliffs
Bourke
Walgett
Bingara
Glen Innes
Grafton
Middleton Reef
Elizabeth Reef
NEW SOUTH WALES
Byrock
Gwabegar
Narrabri
Barraba
Armidale
Coonamble
Gunnedah
Wilcannia
Darling R.
Manilla
Walcha
Coffs Harbour
Cockburn
Olary
Silverton
Broken Hill
Cobar
Nyngan
Warren
Quirindi
Tamworth
Kempsey
Nymagee
Narromine
Dubbo
Port Macquarie
Radium Hill
Menindee
Tottenham
Muswellbrook
Scone
Ivanhoe
Condobolin
Wellington
Singleton
Taree
Lord Howe I. (N.S.W.)
L. Cargelligo
Mudgee
Maitland
Parkes
Cessnock
Sugarloaf Pt.
Renmark
Wentworth
Mildura
Hillston
Orange
Newcastle
Loxton
Murray R.
Lachlan R.
Griffith
Wyalong
Forbes
Bathurst
Lithgow
Cowra
Blue Mts.
Parramatta
SYDNEY
Wollongong
Port Kembla
Temora
Young
Balranald
Hay
Pinnaroo
Murrumbidgee R.
Narrandera
Junee
Cootamundra
Patchewollock
Swan Hill
Wagga Wagga
Yass
Goulburn
Nowra
Murray Bridge
Deniliquin
Culcairn
Tumut
Canberra
AUSTRALIAN CAPITAL TERR.
Yanac
Yaapeet
Kerang
Border-town
Echuca
Albury
Tumbarumba
St. Arnaud
Cudgewa
Horsham
Bendigo
Wangaratta
Cooma
Stawell
Bright
Mt. Kosciusko 7,316
Bega
VICTORIA
Ararat
Maryborough
Casterton
Coleraine
Australian Alps
Bombala
Snowy R.
Ballarat
Hamilton
Daylesford
Yallourn
Gambier
Port Fairy
Sale
Orbost
Geelong
MELBOURNE
Bairnsdale
C. Howe
Portland
Portland B.
Warrnambool
C. Otway
Pt. Phillip B.
Wonthaggi
Port Albert
Wilsons Promontory
King I.
Grassy
Bass Str.
Flinders I.
Furneaux Group
C. Barren I.
Hunter Is.
Stanley
Wynyard
Ulverstone
Devonport
Latrobe
Banks Str.
Eddystone Pt.
Burnie
Launceston
St. Marys
Waratah
Zeehan
Queenstown
Mt. Ossa 5,305
Macquarie Harbour
TASMANIA
Oyster Bay
New Norfolk
Hobart
Port Davey
S.W. Cape
Cygnet
Tasman Peninsula
C. Pillar
Storm Bay
TASMAN SEA
10° 15° 20° 25° 30° 35°
153°
Caboolture
Bribie I.
C. Moreton
Bulwer
Morayfield
Moreton I.
Deception Bay
Moreton Bay
North Pine R.
Dayboro
Redcliffe
Petrie
Bramble Bay
Strathpine
Samford
Mt. Nebo
Sandgate
Mud I.
South Passage
Chermside
Brisbane
Wynnum
North Stradbroke I.
27° 30′
Manly
Holland Park
Corinda
Moorooka
Cleveland
Peel I.
Brisbane R.
Ipswich
Goodna
Redland Bay
Russel I.
0 5 10 15 MILES
Logan R.
Beenleigh
TASMAN SEA
151°
Penrith
Blacktown
Willoughby
Manly
Parramatta
Ryde
Auburn
Strathfield
Warragamba
Bankstown
SYDNEY
Waverley
Randwick
Rossmore
Liverpool
Botany
Hurstville
Rockdale
34°
Nepean R.
Georges R.
Kogarah
Botany B.
Camden
Campbelltown
Pt. Hacking
Sutherland
Picton
Helensburgh
Bargo
Thirroul
Bulli
Woonona
Corrimal
Wollongong
Port Kembla
0 5 10 15 MILES
168°
Pt. Howe
Duncombe Bay
PACIFIC OCEAN
29°
Anson B.
Cable Station
Mt. Pitt 1,043
Cascade Bay
Cascade
Steel's Pt.
Airfield
Pt. Blackburne
Rocky Pt.
Kingston
Ball Bay
NORFOLK ISLAND
Sydney Bay
Nepean I.
0 1 2 Miles
145°
0 5 10 MILES
Mt. Gisborne
Mt. Holden
Jacksons Cr.
Emu Cr.
Saltwater R.
Plenty R.
Whittlesea
Sunbury
Hurstbridge
Bacchus Marsh
Kororoit Cr.
Somerton
Rowsley
Rockbank
Coburg
Preston
Essendon
Heidelberg
Mt. Mary
Werribee R.
Footscray
MELBOURNE
Ringwood
Little R.
Port Melbourne
Richmond
Camberwell
Williamstown
Caulfield
Werribee
St. Kilda
Brighton
Sandringham
Dandenong
Dandenong Cr.
38°
Kirk Pt.
PORT PHILLIP BAY
Mordialloc
Corio
Chelsea
Norlane
Geelong
Corio Bay
Portarlington
Frankston
Drysdale
Snapper Pt.
Mt. Eliza
Mornington
L. Connewarre
Swan B.
Swan I.
Mud Is.
Queenscliff
Copyright by C. S. Hammond & Co., N. Y.
140° Longitude East 145° of Greenwich 150° 155° 160° 165° 170°

History: First sighted by Spanish in early 17th cent.; missed by Torres, who sailed up Torres Strait (*q.v.*) 1606; not reached by Europeans until landing of Dutch ship *Duyfken* on E coast of Gulf of Carpentaria 1606; in first half of 17th cent. N and W coasts explored by Dutch, who named it New Holland (see also TASMANIA and NEW ZEALAND, both discovered by Dutch mariner Tasman 1642); W coast navigated by Dampier 1688; E part claimed for Britain 1770 by Capt. Cook, who discovered Botany Bay (*q.v.*) and named the land New South Wales; first English settlement 1788, by convicts at Port Jackson (see SYDNEY); circumnavigated by Matthew Flinders 1801–03, who thus proved continental unity of New South Wales and New Holland; came to be called Australia in 19th cent.; granted right of free immigration by British government 1816; entire continent claimed by Britain 1829; given limited self-government by passage of Australian Colonies Government Act 1850; developed rapidly after gold rush of 1851; adopted, from 1855 in separate colonies, exclusion of Chinese immigrants, thus beginning policy of "White Australia"; crossed from E to W by J. McDouall Stuart 1862; self-dependent for defense after departure of British imperial forces 1870; opened transcontinental telegraph lines 1872; completed railroad from Sydney to Melbourne 1883; carried out federalization 1885–1901; act federating separate colonies into commonwealth passed by British Parliament 1900 and put into force 1901; adopted federal tariff and woman suffrage 1902; administered federal Territory of Papua (*q.v.*) after 1906 and Northern Territory after 1910; maintained Royal Australian Navy after 1911; participated in World War I and represented at Peace Conference 1919; received mandate of certain German possessions in Pacific (see NEW GUINEA, TRUST TERRITORY OF); occupied new capital Canberra (*q.v.*), 1927; received authority over one third of Antarctica 1933; joined Great Britain in World War II 1939; Darwin and its N coast threatened by Japanese 1941–42 but battle of Coral Sea and campaigns in the Solomon Is. and New Guinea prevented invasion. Placed Terr. of Papua and Trust Terr. of New Guinea under single administration 1949; signed a Pacific defense pact with the United States and New Zealand (ANZUS treaty) 1951; became a member of the Southeast Asia Treaty Organization 1954.

Australia Fe·lix \-ˈfē-liks\. A fertile district of cen. Victoria, SE Australia.

Australian Alps. Mountain range, E Victoria and SE New South Wales, SE Australia, forming the S end of the Great Dividing Range and the watershed bet. the headstreams of the Murrumbidgee river and the short streams flowing S to the Pacific Ocean; average height 2500 to 5000 ft.; highest Mt. Kosciusko 7316 ft.; other peaks are Mt. Jagungul 6754 ft., Mt. Bogong 6508 ft., Mt. Feathertop 6307 ft., Mt. Hotham 6108 ft.; site of important hydroelectric power project.

Australian Antarctic Territory. External territory of Australia lying S of lat. 60°S and situated between long. 160°E and 45°E; ab. 2,360,000 sq. m.; does not include Adélie Coast. Antarctic claims S of lat. 60°S not recognized by the United States.

Australian Capital Territory *or formerly* **Federal Capital Territory.** Territory of Australia; total area 939 sq. m.; pop. (1970e) 133,100; consists of enclaves (1) in SE New South Wales, 911 sq. m. including Canberra, and (2) area, 28 sq. m., at Jervis Bay on the coast (ceded 1917). Ceded by New South Wales to Commonwealth in 1911; building operations for new government buildings begun 1923 and Parliament opened at Canberra by duke of York 1927.

Australia–New Zealand–United States Treaty; *abbr.* **ANZUS.** Military alliance, consisting of Australia, New Zealand, United States; purpose is to coordinate defense planning; formed 1951.

Austral Islands. See TUBUAI ISLANDS.

Aus·tra·sia \ȯ-ˈstrā-zhə, ä-, -shə\ *or* **Os·tra·sia** \ä-\. The eastern dominions of the Merovingian Franks, extending from the Meuse river to the Bohemian Forest.

History: Emerged as eastern part of kingdom of Franks after division of lands which followed death of Clovis (511 A.D.); ruled by Merovingian kings, alternately as separate kingdom and as kingdom in conjunction with rule of Neustria (*q.v.*), 6th cent.; original seat of authority of mayors of palace of house of Pepin who founded Carolingian line of Frankish kings in 8th cent.; although recognized as territorial division in partitions of land which were customary at ruler's death, ceased to exist in Frankish empire as it was consolidated by Charlemagne (768–814).

Aus·tria \ˈȯs-trē-ə, ˈäs-\ *or Ger.* **Öster·reich** \ˈœ̄-stə(r)-ˌrīk\. Republic, cen. Europe, bounded on N by West Germany and Czechoslovakia, on E by Hungary, on S by Yugoslavia and Italy, and on W by Liechtenstein, Switzerland, and West Germany; 32,375 sq. m.; pop. (1971p) 7,459,000; ✱ Vienna.

Physical features: A mountainous country, N of the Alps, containing many of its spurs and branches; bordered on S by Karawanken, Carnic, and Ötztaler Alps and on S Bavarian border by Bavarian Alps; highest point Grossglockner in the Hohe Tauern 12,470 ft. Chief passes to Italy are the Brenner and Plöcken, and to Yugoslavia the Loibl. Chief river is the Danube (*or Ger.* Donau) crossing in N from Bavaria, West Germany, to Hungary with many tributaries, esp. the Inn, Traun, and Enns; in the S are the Mur and Drava; Neusiedler Lake on E border is largest lake; in W and S are many other lakes, many of them health and resort centers. *Chief products:* Wheat, rye, fruit, potatoes, timber; cattle; iron ore, magnesite, coal, lead, salt, petroleum; manufacturing: iron and steel, pulp, chemicals, textiles, transportation equipment; tourism. *Chief cities:* Vienna, Graz, Linz, Salzburg, Innsbruck, and Klagenfurt. Divided into 8 states and the city of Vienna (for pronunciation of their names, see their individual entries):

NAME	AREA (sq. m.)	POP. (1971p)	CAPITAL
Burgenland	1,531	272,000	Eisenstadt
Carinthia	3,681	526,000	Klagenfurt
Lower Austria[1]	7,402	1,411,000	Vienna
Salzburg	2,762	399,000	Salzburg
Styria	6,326	1,191,000	Graz
Tirol	4,883	539,000	Innsbruck
Upper Austria	4,625	1,244,000	Linz
Vienna	160	1,603,000	Vienna
Vorarlberg	1,004	274,000	Bregenz

[1]Excluding Vienna.

History: Territory inhabited by Celtic tribes, conquered by Rome 14 B.C.; included Roman settlement of Vindobona (see VIENNA); invaded by Marcomanni and Quadi 2d cent. A.D., by Huns 5th cent.; settled 590 by Slovenes who later formed kingdom of the Avars; erected by Charlemagne into a border state, East Mark (*or Ger.* Österreich); became part of Holy Roman Empire under Saxon line; after defeat of Magyars 955, reestablished as East Mark by Otto the Great; as an independent duchy 1156, granted to Henry of Austria in return for Bavaria; claimed by Ottokar II, ruler of the Slavic kingdom of Bohemia (1253–78); after defeat of Ottokar by Rudolf of Hapsburg 1278, remained Hapsburg until 1918; failed in effort to enforce control over Swiss cantons; as archduchy, center of imperial authority which also ruled adjacent duchies of Styria, Carinthia, Carniola, and county of Tirol; one of ten circles of empire 1512 organized under first great emperor, Maximilian I (1493–1519); with other central European lands of Hapsburgs, passed to Spanish Charles I (Emperor Charles V 1519–56); continued to be separate from holdings of Spanish Hapsburgs after it was inherited by Ferdinand I 1556; eastern European bulwark against the Turks who besieged Vienna 1529; lost Alsace and more than nominal authority over Holy Roman Empire 1648;

saved from Turks by Poles under John Sobieski 1683; by Peace of Karlowitz 1699, received Slavonia, Transylvania, and most of Hungary; awarded Spanish Netherlands (see BELGIUM), Sardinia, and Naples 1713; entered series of wars against Frederick the Great of Prussia (*q.v.*); lost Silesia 1748; received Galicia in First Partition of Poland 1772; lost Spanish Netherlands 1797, Venice and Tirol 1805 after defeat by Napoleon; became the Austrian Empire at the formal dissolution of the Holy Roman Empire 1806; leading member of the Germanic Confederation formed 1815; in the settlement imposed by the Congress of Vienna 1815, received Lombardy and Venetia, Illyrian provinces, Salzburg and the Tirol, and Galicia; under Metternich, led in maintaining the principle of "legitimacy" against the European nationalistic and liberal revolts up to 1848; with Russian aid put down Hungarian revolt 1848; ruled by Emperor Francis Joseph 1848–1916; in war with Italy and France, lost Lombardy 1859; after defeat by Prussia in 1866, forced to withdraw from German affairs; with Hungary formed "dual monarchy" of Austria-Hungary 1867. (For history of AUSTRIA-HUNGARY, see that entry.) After the collapse of Austria-Hungary, Austria lost its status as a monarchy and was refused permission to unite with Germany; by the Treaty of St-Germain 1919, ceded Bohemia, Moravia, Galicia, Hungary, Bosnia, and the Dalmatian coast, Trieste and the Trentino; as a republic 1919–33, suffered severe economic and social disorder; yielded dictatorial powers to Chancellor Dollfuss 1933; occupied by Nazi Germany and incorporated into the German Reich 1938–45 as an administrative unit (*Land*) under official name **Ost·mark** \'ȯst-ˌmärk\. During World War II its industrial cities severely bombed by Allies 1944–45; invaded by Soviet armies from E in March 1945 and by Allies from W in April and May; reestablished as a republic 1945; occupied by four powers U.S., U.S.S.R., Great Britain, and France 1945–55; declared itself a neutral state 1955.

Austria–Hun·ga·ry \-'həŋ-gə-rē\. Former monarchy, cen. Europe; 261,027 sq. m.; included Austria, Hungary, and Czechoslovakia, Bukovina and Transylvania in Romania, NW half of Yugoslavia, Galicia in Poland, and NE section of Italy.

History: A "dual monarchy" formed in 1867, restoring partial Hungarian autonomy and creating the Austro-Hungarian Empire from the Austrian Empire and the kingdom of Hungary; after the Treaty of Berlin 1878, administered Turkish provinces of Bosnia and Herzegovina which it annexed in 1908; a member of the Triple Alliance with Germany and Italy 1882–1914; up to 1914 maintained a precarious balance bet. its various minorities; after the assassination (June 28, 1914) of Archduke Francis Ferdinand, issued an ultimatum to Serbia which precipitated the outbreak of World War I 1914; collapsed as the result of defeat in the war and of revolutions by the Czechs, Yugoslavs, and Hungarians 1918. For earlier, before 1867, and later, after 1918, history of AUSTRIA and HUNGARY, see those entries.

Aus·tro·ne·sia \ˌȯs-trə-'nē-zhə, ˌäs-, -'nē-shə\. In general, the islands of the South Pacific Ocean; more accurately, the vast island area extending from the Malagasy Republic in the W, through the Malay Penin. and Archipelago, to Hawaii and Easter I. in the E—a name applied by ethnologists to the region where the peoples speak related agglutinative languages (Austronesian languages). Linguistically the region has three subdivisions: Indonesia, Polynesia, and Melanesia, each inhabited by an Austronesian subfamily.

Aust·våg·øy \'au̇st-ˌvȯ-gəi\ *also* **Öst·våg·öy** \'əst-vȯ-ˌgəi\. Island in the Lofoten group off NW coast of Norway; 203 sq. m.

Au·tau·ga \ȯ-'tȯ-gə\. County in Alabama. See table at ALABAMA.

Autesiodorum. See AUXERRE.

Au·teuil \ō-'təi\. District in W part of Paris, France, at SE entrance to Bois de Boulogne (*q.v.*); famous racecourse for steeplechasing; notable in French literary history through Boileau, Molière, and Mme Helvétius, who held a salon here (known as the Société d'Auteuil).

Au·tlán *or* **Autlán de Na·var·ro** \au̇-'tlän-ˌdā-nə-'vär-(ˌ)ō\. Town, SW Jalisco state, W cen. Mexico, 80 m. SW of Guadalajara; munic. pop. (1970p) 30,853.

Autricum. See CHARTRES.

Au·tun \ō-'tən, -'tœⁿ\ *or anc.* **Æd·ua** \'ej-ə-wə, 'ēj-\ *or later* **Au·gus·to·du·num** \ȯ-ˌgəs-tə-'d(y)ü-nəm, ə-ˌgəs-\. Commune, Saône-et-Loire dept., E cen. France, 51 m. NNW of Mâcon; pop. (1968c) 18,398; market for livestock; metal-working; leather goods; 11th cent. Gothic cathedral; 12th cent. castle; Roman remains; residence of Roman prefects of Gaul; economic and educational center under Romans; ruined by barbaric invasions 406–895; under dukes of Burgundy; burned by British 1379.

Au·vergne \ō-'ve(ə)rn(-yə), -'vərn\. Historical region of S cen. France; bounded on N by Bourbonnais, NE by Lyonnais, SE by Languedoc, SW by Guienne, W by Limousin, and NW by Marche; ✱ Clermont (now Clermont-Ferrand); mountains of volcanic origin; medicinal springs.

History: Inhabited by Arverni, Gallic people led by Vercingetorix and defeated by Caesar; yielded to Visigoths 475 A.D.; conquered by Clovis 507; part of Aquitaine; became countship 8th cent.; divided into four lordships, one of which, Terre d'Auvergne, became duchy 1360 (capital Riom), passed to Bourbons 1416, to France 1527.

Auvergne Mountains. Mountain range in cen. France; highest peak Puy de Sancy 6188 ft.

Aux Barques, Pointe \ˌpȯint-ō-'bärk\. Point, S Michigan penin., extending into Lake Huron.

Aux Cayes. See CAYES.

Au·xerre \ō-'se(ə)r\ *or anc.* **Au·te·si·o·do·rum** \ȯ-ˌtē-zē-ə-'dōr-əm, -ˌtē-sē-, -'dȯr-\. Commercial city, ✱ of Yonne dept., NE cen. France, on Yonne river 96 m. SE of Paris; pop. (1968c) 35,784; wine, metal products; 13th cent. cathedral; old abbey; flourished in pre-Roman and Roman days; taken by Clovis; part of kingdom of Burgundy; captured by English 1359; united to France by Louis XI; bombarded by Germans 1870.

Au·xonne \ō-'sȯn\. Commune, Côte-d'Or dept., E France, on left bank of Saône river 18 m. ESE of Dijon; cloth, plaster of Paris. Chartered 1229; under dukes of Burgundy from 13th cent.; surrendered to Austrians 1815.

Aux Sources, Mont \ˌmōⁿ-(ˌ)tō-'sü(ə)rs\. Peak in Drakensberg Mts., N Lesotho, on the Natal border; 10,822 ft.

Ava \'ā-və\. City, ⊗ of Douglas co., S Missouri; pop. (1970c) 2504; lumber.

Ava \'äv-ə\. Ruined city on Irrawaddy river, Sagaing div., Burma, 6 m. SW of Mandalay; founded in 14th cent.; for 400 years capital of Burma; replaced by Amarapura in 1783; again capital 1823–37.

Av·a·lanche Peak \ˌav-ə-ˌlanch-\. Mountain, E boundary of Yellowstone National Park, NW Wyoming; 10,566 ft.

Aval·lon \ˌav-ə-'lōⁿ\. Commune, Yonne dept., NE cen. France, on Cousin river 27 m. SE of Auxerre; pop. (1962c) 6371; on hill of red granite; 12th cent. church. Celtic in origin; sacked by Saracens 731, by Normans 843; viscounty in medieval duchy of Burgundy; joined to French crown 1477; pillaged by forces of the League 1593.

Av·a·lon \'av-ə-ˌlän\. **1** Resort city, Los Angeles co., SW California, at E end of Santa Catalina I. 50 m. S of Los Angeles; pop. (1970c) 1520; recreation center; Indian museum; incorp. 1913.

2 Residential borough, Allegheny co., SW Pennsylvania, on Ohio river 6 m. NW of Pittsburgh; pop. (1970c) 7010.

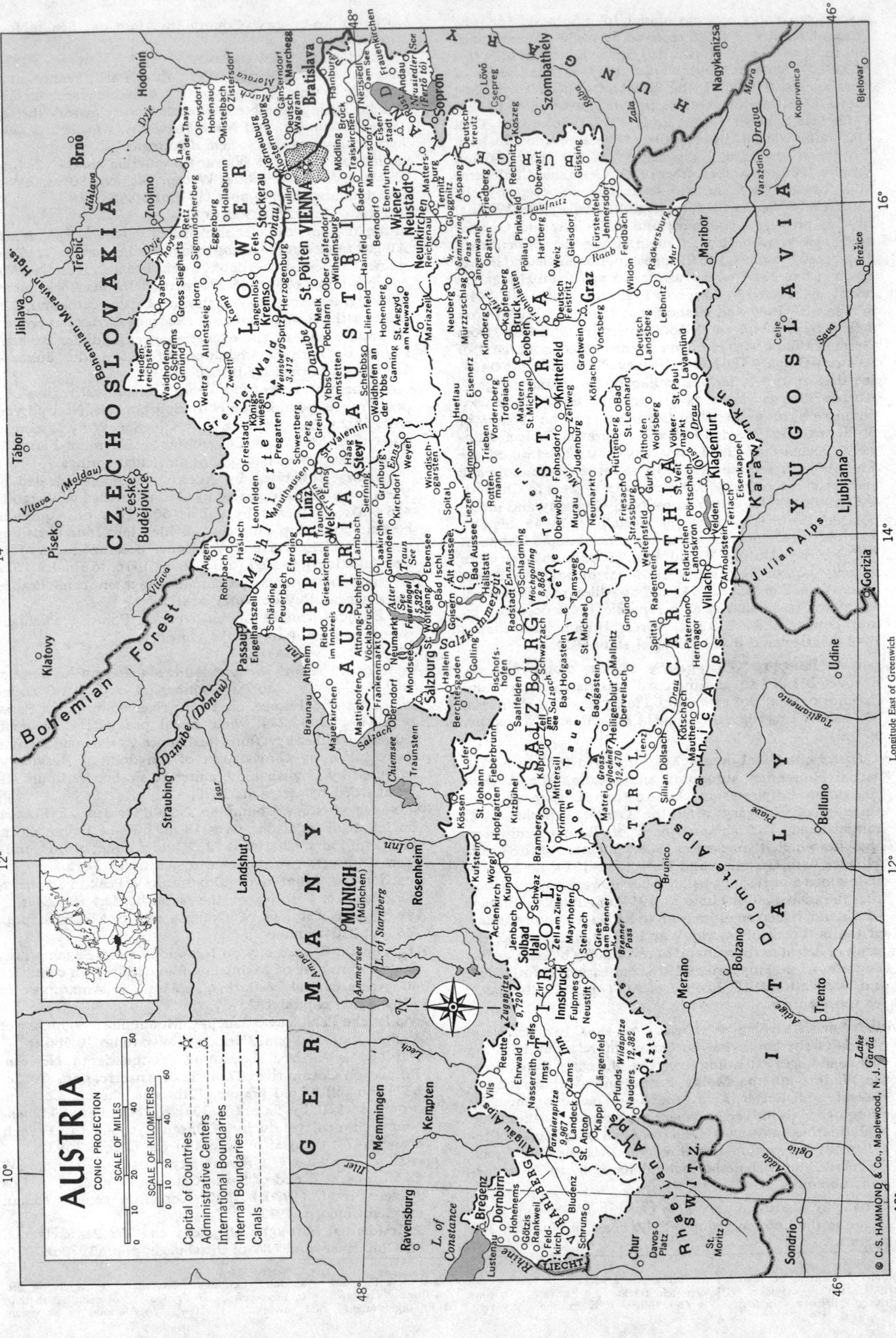
AUSTRIA
CONIC PROJECTION
SCALE OF MILES
0 10 20 40 60
SCALE OF KILOMETERS
0 10 20 40 60
Capital of Countries
Administrative Centers
International Boundaries
Internal Boundaries
Canals
CZECHOSLOVAKIA
GERMANY
LOWER AUSTRIA
UPPER AUSTRIA
SALZBURG
STYRIA
CARINTHIA
TIROL
VORARLBERG
HUNGARY
YUGOSLAVIA
ITALY
SWITZ.
LIECHT.
VIENNA
MUNICH (München)
Linz
Salzburg
Graz
Innsbruck
Klagenfurt
Bregenz
St. Pölten
Wiener-Neustadt
Bratislava
Brno
Ljubljana
Bohemian Forest
Danube
Inn
Drau
Mur
Enns
Bohemian-Moravian Hgts.
Julian Alps
Karawanken
Dolomite Alps
Carnic Alps
Hohe Tauern
Niedere Tauern
Allgäu Alps
Rhaetian Alps
Ötztal Alps
Zugspitze 9,720
Grossglockner 12,470
Wildspitze 12,382
Parseierspitze 9,967
Hochgolling 8,868
L. of Constance
Neusiedler See (Fertő tó)
Longitude East of Greenwich
© C. S. HAMMOND & Co., Maplewood, N. J.

3 Large peninsula of SE Newfoundland, Canada, bet. Trinity and Placentia Bays.

Avalon Dam *and* **Avalon Lake.** See CARLSBAD 2.

Avan·ti \ə-ˈvənt-ē, -ˈvänt-\. Early kingdom of N India 6th–4th cents. B.C., about coextensive with Malwa; ✱ Ujjain.

Avarau. See PALMERSTON.

Ava·ré \ˌav-ə-ˈrā\. Municipality, São Paulo, SE Brazil, 120 m. W of Campinas; pop. (1968e) 38,024.

Avaricum. See BOURGES.

Avar·is \ə-ˈvar-əs, -ˈver-\. City of ancient Egypt in E part of Nile delta, the Hyksos capital; completely destroyed, but has been identified with Tanis or Pelusium.

Ava·rua \ˌäv-ə-ˈrü-ə\. Village, ✱ of the Cook Is., on N coast of the island of Rarotonga, S Pacific Ocean; pop. (1966c) 9907.

Avdira. See ABDERA 1.

Ave·bury \ˈāv-b(ə-)rē\ *or* **Abury** \ˈā-bə-rē\. Village, Wiltshire, England, 29 m. E of Bristol; pop. (1961c) 525; vast megalithic remains of uncertain date and origin.

Avei·ro \ə-ˈvā-(ˌ)rü, -ˈve(ə)r-(ˌ)ü\. **1** Salt lagoon on NW coast of Portugal, S of Pôrto.

2 District of NW Portugal. See table at PORTUGAL.

3 Seaport, its ✱, on Aveiro lagoon 135 m. N by E of Lisbon, connected by canal with Atlantic Ocean; pop. (1960c) 16,430; episcopal see; produces sea salt; fisheries (esp. sardines); kaolin and mercury mines. Said to be Roman **Tal·a·bri·ga** \ˌtal-ə-ˈbrī-gə\; well known through João Afonso's exploitation of Newfoundland dried codfish trade in 16th cent.

Avel·la·ne·da \ˌäv-ə-zhə-ˈnā-də\. City, Buenos Aires prov., E Argentina, a suburb of Buenos Aires (city); pop. (1960c) 326,531.

Avel·li·no \ˌäv-ə-ˈlē-(ˌ)nō\. **1** Province of Campania, S Italy. See table at ITALY.

2 *or anc.* **Ab·el·li·num** \ˌab-ə-ˈlī-nəm\. Commune, its ✱, 29 m. E by N of Naples; pop. (1968e) 49,745; earthquake 1930; ruins of ancient town nearby; convent of Monte Vergine (founded 1119) pilgrim resort.

Avenches \a-ˈvä^{n}sh\ *or anc.* **Aven·ti·cum** \ə-ˈvent-i-kəm\. Commune, Vaud canton, W Switzerland, near Lake of Morat 8 m. NW of Fribourg; pop. (1970c) 2235; one of oldest cities of Switzerland; capital of ancient Helvetia; made Roman colony by Vespasian and Titus, its population then being 60,000; destroyed by Alamanni c. 260 A.D.; refounded 12th cent. by Burkhardt, Bishop of Lausanne. Roman antiquities, including ruins of city walls.

Avenio. See AVIGNON.

Av·en·tine \ˈav-ən-ˌtīn, -ˌtēn\. One of the seven hills of Rome. See SEVEN HILLS.

Ave·reest \ˌäv-ə-ˈrāst\. Commune, Overijssel prov., E Netherlands, 13 m. NE of Zwolle; pop. (1970c) 12,065.

Aver·nus, Lake \-ə-ˈvər-nəs\ *or Ital.* **La·go d'Aver·no** \ˌläg-ō-də-ˈve(ə)r-(ˌ)nō\ *or anc.* **La·cus Aver·nus** \ˌlā-kəs-ə-ˈvər-nəs\. Lake, Napoli prov., Campania, Italy, in crater of extinct volcano 8 m. W of Naples; ab. 2 m. in circumference; because of its dismal aspect and mephitic vapors, considered by the ancients (Homer, Vergil) as entrance to underworld; grove of Hecate, grotto of the Cumaean Sibyl, and home of the Cimmerii placed nearby in ancient legend; transformed by Agrippa into naval base (**Por·tus Iu·li·us** \ˌpōrt-əs-ˈyu-lē-əs, ˌpȯrt-\), and connected with Lacus Lucrinus.

Aver·sa \ä-ˈver-sə\. Commercial commune, Caserta prov., Campania, S Italy, 8 m. N by W of Naples; pop. (1968e) 47,018; known for its sparkling white wine (Asprino); built near site of ancient Atella by Normans 1030, being the first settlement in Italy granted them.

Avery \ˈāv-(ə-)rē\. County in North Carolina. See table at NORTH CAROLINA.

Aves Islands \ˈäv-(ˌ)ās-\ *or* **Bird Islands.** Group of small Venezuelan islands in Caribbean Sea E of Bonaire.

Avesnes \ä-ˈven\. City, Nord dept., N France, 25 m. SE of Valenciennes; built around 11th cent. castle; held by Spain 1559–1659; captured by Prussians 1815; occupied by Germans in World War I.

Aves·ta \ˈäv-ə-ˌstä\. Town, Kopparberg co., Sweden, 92 m. NW of Stockholm; pop. (1970e) 28,545; aluminum, steel.

Avey·ron \ˌav-ā-ˈrō^{n}\. **1** River, S France; ab. 150 m. long; flows W into Tarn river 7 m. NW of Montauban.

2 Department of S France. See table at FRANCE.

Avez·za·no \ˌäv-ə(d)-ˈzän-(ˌ)ō\. Commune, Aquila prov., Abruzzi, cen. Italy, 22 m. S of Aquila; pop. (1968e) 32,111; episcopal see; 15th cent. castle; suffered from earthquake 1915.

Avgustov. See AUGUSTÓW.

Avi·glia·no \ˌäv-ēl-ˈyän-(ˌ)ō\. Commune, Potenza prov., Basilicata, S Italy, 7 m. NNW of Potenza; pop. (1968e) 11,429; marble quarries and mineral springs.

Avi·gnon \ˌav-ēn-ˈyō^{n}\ *or anc.* **Ave·nio** \ə-ˈvē-nē-ˌō\. Commercial and manufacturing city, ✱ of Vaucluse dept., SE France, near confluence of Rhone and Durance rivers 50 m. NNW of Marseilles; pop. (1968c) 86,096; chemicals, leather products, soap; ancient cathedral; papal palace.

History: Founded as Phocaean colony; conquered by Romans, Goths, Burgundians, Ostrogoths, finally Franks; part of kingdom of Arles (*q.v.*); republic 1135–46; part of Venaissin (see COMTAT VENAISSIN); sold by Joanna I of Naples to Pope Clement VI 1348; seat of papacy 1309–77 and of Avignonese popes during Western Schism 1378–1417; united to France 1791.

Ávi·la \ˈäv-i-lə\. **1** Province of cen. Spain. See table at SPAIN.

2 *anc.* **Ab·y·la** *or* **Ab·e·la** \ˈab-ə-lə\. City, its ✱, 53 m. WNW of Madrid; pop. (1970p) 30,938, founded as walled city in late 11th cent.; cathedral; site of university (1455–1807) founded by Ferdinand and Isabella.

Avi·lés \ˌäv-i-ˈlās\. Seaport, Oviedo prov., NW Spain, 14 m. NNW of Oviedo on an inlet of the Bay of Biscay; pop. (1970p) 81,710; steel; coal mines; fishing.

Avion \ˌav-ē-ˈō^{n}\. Commune, Pas-de-Calais dept., N France, 9 m. NNE of Arras; pop. (1968c) 22,422; severe fighting Apr.–June 1917; taken by Canadians.

Aviz \ə-ˈvēsh\. Commune, Portalegre dist., E cen. Portugal, 30 m. SW of Portalegre; gives name to Portuguese and Brazilian Order of Aviz (founded 1147).

Avlona. See VLORË 2.

Avo·ca \ə-ˈvō-kə\. **1** Town, Pottawattamie co., SW Iowa, 34 m. ENE of Council Bluffs; pop. (1970c) 1535.

2 Borough, Luzerne co., E Pennsylvania, 7 m. SW of Scranton; pop. (1970c) 3543; coal mining; silk mills.

3 *or* **Ovo·ca** \ə-ˈvō-kə\. Valley and river in co. Wicklow, E Eire; celebrated in one of Moore's songs.

Avo·court \ˌav-ə-ˈku̇(ə)r\. Commune, Meuse dept., NE France, 11 m. NW of Verdun; pop. (1962c) 219; battles 1916–18, the forest **Bois d'Avocourt** \ˌbwäd-\ being taken by Germans Mar. 1916 and retaken by American forces Sept. 1918.

Avo·la \ˈä-və-lə\. Seaport, Siracusa prov., SE Sicily, Italy, 14 m. SW of Syracuse; pop. (1968e) 29,078; almonds and sugarcane; sugar refineries.

Avon. **1** \ˈā-ˌvän\. Town, W cen. Hartford co., N Connecticut; pop. (1970c) 8352; incorp. 1830.

2 \ˈā-ˌvän\. Town, Norfolk co., E Massachusetts, 4 m. N of Brockton; pop. (1970c) 5295; residential suburb of Brockton.

3 \ˈav-ən\. Village, Livingston co., W New York, on Genesee river 18 m. S of Rochester; pop. (1970c) 3260.

4 \ˈā-ˌvän\. City, Lorain co., N Ohio, 17 m. W of Cleveland; pop. (1970c) 7214.

5 \ˈā-vən\. Upper course of the Swan river (*q.v.*), Western Australia; ab. 200 m. long.

6 *or* **East Avon** \-'ā-vən\. River, S England; 48 m. long; rises near Devizes in Wiltshire, flows S into English Channel.

7 *or* **Lower Avon** \-'ā-vən\. River, SW England; 75 m. long; rises in Gloucestershire, flows S and W through the city of Bristol into Bristol Channel at Avonmouth.

8 *or* **Upper Avon** \-'ā-vən\. River, cen. England; 96 m. long; rises in Northamptonshire, flows WSW into the Severn at Tewkesbury; the "Shakespeare" Avon.

9 \'ā-vən, 'av-ən\. River, cen. Scotland; 18 m. long; flows E into Firth of Forth.

Avon, Ben. See BEN AVON.

Av·on–by–the–Sea \ˌav-ən-\. Borough, Monmouth co., E cen. New Jersey; pop. (1970c) 2163; seaside resort.

Av·on·dale \'av-ən-ˌdāl\. City, Maricopa co., Arizona, W of Phoenix; pop. (1970c) 6304; cotton, grain.

Avon Lake \ˌā-ˌvän-\. Village, Lorain co., N Ohio, on Lake Erie 18 m. W of Cleveland; pop. (1970c) 12,261.

Avon·mouth \'ā-vən-ˌmau̇th\. Suburb of Bristol, Gloucestershire, SW cen. England, at mouth of the Avon; deep-sea docks of port of Bristol.

Avon Park \ˌā-ˌvän-\. City, Highlands co., cen. Florida penin., 43 m. SE of Lakeland; pop. (1970c) 6712; South Florida Junior Coll. (1965).

Avoy·elles \ə-'vȯi-əlz, ˌav-wä-'yel\. Parish in Louisiana. See table at LOUISIANA.

Avranches \ə-'vräⁿsh\. Commune, Manche dept., NW France, on inlet 32 m. E of St-Malo; pop. (1968c) 9775; resort. Taken by Americans July 25–31, 1944; scene of decisive Allied breakthrough.

Avre \'ävrᵊ\. River, Somme dept., N France; 36 m. long; flowing into Somme river near Amiens; battles March–May 1918.

Av·şa \äv-'shä\. Island, SW Sea of Marmara, W of Kapudağ Penin., Çanakkale prov., Turkey in Asia.

Awaj \a-ˌwaj\. See PHARPAR.

Awa·ji \ə-'wäj-ē\. Island of Japan, E of Harima Sea, S of Honshū and NE of Shikoku I.; area 230 sq. m.; part of Hyōgo prefecture; chief town Sumoto.

Awash \'ä-(ˌ)wäsh\ *or* **Ha·wash** \'hä-\. River, E Ethiopia; ab. 500 m. long; flows NE into the Danakil Desert on border of Afar and Issas.

Awe, Loch \-'ȯ\. Lake, Argyll co., cen. Scotland; 24 m. long; 16 sq. m.; max. depth 307 ft.; extends NNE to base of Ben Cruachan; empties by means of **Awe River** into Loch Etive; has several wooded islands on which are numerous old castles; traveled by steamers.

Aw·ji·dah \ȯ-'jē-də\ *or formerly* **Au·gi·la** \au̇-'jē-lə\. Oasis and town, Libya, ab. 200 m. SSE of Benghazi.

Awu, Gu·nung *or Du.* **Goe·noeng Awoe** \ˌgü-ˌnu̇ŋ-'ä-(ˌ)wü\. Volcanic peak on Sangihe I., Sangihe Is. (*q.v.*), Indonesia; eruptions 1856, 1892.

Ax. See DAX.

Ax·ar Fjord \ˌäk-ˌsär-\. Inlet of the Arctic Ocean on N coast of Iceland, E of Eyja Fjord.

Ax·el \'äk-səl\. Commune, Zeeland prov., SW Netherlands, 20 m. SE of Middelburg; pop. (1970e) 8904.

Axel Hei·berg \ˌak-səl-'hī-ˌbərg\. One of the Sverdrup Is. (*q.v.*), W of Ellesmere I.; 15,779 sq. m.

Ax·im \'ak-səm\. Coast town, SW Ghana, W Africa, at mouth of Ankobra river ab. 30 m. W of Takoradi; pop. (1970p) 8107.

Axius. See VARDAR.

Ax·min·ster \'ak-ˌsmin(t)-stər\. Town, Devonshire, England, on Axe river 23 m. ENE of Exeter; pop. (1961c) 2400; formerly (1755–1835) famous for its carpets.

Axona. See AISNE.

Axum. See AKSUM.

Ay \'ī, ȧ-'ē\. Commune, Marne dept., NE France, on Marne river 12 m. S of Reims; pop. (1962c) 6682; produces Ay wine.

Aya·cu·cho \ˌī-ə-'kü-(ˌ)chō\. 1 Town, Buenos Aires prov., E Argentina, S of Buenos Aires; pop. (1960c) 10,004.

2 Department of S Peru. See table at PERU.

3 Town, ✱ of Ayacucho dept., Peru, 200 m. SE of Lima; pop. (1969e) 27,900; textiles, wine, pottery; silver, nickel, copper, and sulfur mined nearby; univ. (1677, closed 1874, reopened 1958); founded 1539 by Pizarro and known as Guamanga or Huamanga until 1825; decisive battle on small plain of Ayacucho, near the village of La Quinua, Dec. 9, 1824, in which the Spanish viceroy La Serna was defeated by Gen. Sucre, won independence for Peru.

Aya·guz \ˌä-yə-'güs\. 1 River, E Kazakh S.S.R., U.S.S.R.; ab. 240 m. long; flows generally SW into NE end of Lake Balkhash.

2 *or formerly* **Ser·gi·o·pol** \ˌsər-gē-'ō-pəl\. Town, E Kazakh S.S.R., U.S.S.R., on Ayaguz river 185 m. S of Semipalatinsk; on Turkistan-Siberian R.R.

Aya·mon·te \ˌī-ə-'mȯnt-ē\. Seaport, Huelva prov., SW Spain, on left bank of Guadiana river near its mouth, 23 m. W of Huelva; pop. (1970p) 13,099; shipbuilding.

Aya·pel \ˌī-ə-'pel\. Municipality, Córdoba dept., N Colombia, ab. 150 m. SSE of Cartagena; pop. (1968e) 43,015.

Aya Soluk. See SELÇUK.

'Aybāl, Jabal. See EBAL, MOUNT.

Ay·den \'ād-ən\. Town, Pitt co., E North Carolina, 35 m. E of Goldsboro; pop. (1970c) 3450.

Ay·dın *or* **Ai·din** \ī-'din\. 1 Province of SW Turkey, Asia. See table at TURKEY.

2 *or anc.* **Tral·les** \'tral-ēz\. Town, its ✱, on Menderes river 55 m. SE of İzmir; pop. (1965c) 43,483; railroad and trading town; olives, figs, grapes, and cotton. In ancient times Tralles was a flourishing city of Lydia.

Ayer \'a(ə)r, 'e(ə)r\. Town, Middlesex co., NE Massachusetts, 10 m. E of Fitchburg; pop. (1970c) 8283; Fort Devens nearby.

Ayer Itam \ˌī-ər-'ē-ˌtäm\. Town, Penang state, Malaysia; pop. (1957c) 22,369.

Ayer's Cliff \'a(ə)rz-, 'e(ə)rz-\. Village, ⊗ of Stanstead co., S Quebec, Canada, 18 m. S of Sherbrooke; pop. (1966c) 798.

Áyios Dhi·mí·tri·os \'ä-ˌyȯs-di-'mē-trē-ˌȯs\. City, Greece, part of Greater Athens; pop. (1971p) 42,904.

Áyios Evstrátios. See HAGIOS EVSTRÁTIOS.

Áyiosilías. See HAGIOS ELIAS, MOUNT.

Ayles·bury \'ā(ə)lz-b(ə-)rē, -ˌber-ē\. Municipal borough, ⊗ of Buckinghamshire, SE cen. England, 32 m. NW of London; pop. (1971p) 41,288; in Thames valley (**Vale of Aylesbury**); noted lace industry.

Ayl·mer \'āl-mər\. 1 Town, Elgin co., SE Ontario, Canada, 11 m. E of St. Thomas; pop. (1971p) 4697.

2 Resort town, Hull co., SW Quebec, Canada, on Ottawa river 7 m. W of Hull; pop. (1971p) 7160.

Aylmer, Lake. Lake, E cen. Mackenzie dist., Northwest Territories, Canada; 340 sq. m.

'Ayn Jālūt. See AIN JALUT.

Ayodhya. See AJODHYA.

Ay·ot Saint Law·rence \'ā-ət-sānt-'lȯr-ən(t)s, -sənt-, -'lär-\. Village, cen. Hertfordshire, England, W of Welwyn Garden City; home of George Bernard Shaw.

Ayr \'a(ə)r, 'e(ə)r\. 1 Town, Queensland, Australia; pop. (1966c) 8674.

2 *or* **Ayr·shire** \-ˌshi(ə)r, -shər\. County, SW Scotland; area 1131 sq. m.; pop. (1971p) 361,074; chief towns Ayr, Kilmarnock, Prestwick, Irvine, Girvan, Troon; rivers Ayr and Doon; dairy farms, coal mines; chemicals, textiles, explosives; engineering.

3 Seaport burgh, its ⊗; pop. (1971p) 47,884; chemicals, shoes; sawmills, shipbuilding and engineering works.

Ayre, Point of \-'a(ə)r, -'e(ə)r\. N extremity of the Isle of Man, Irish Sea; lighthouse.

Ay·sén *or* **Ai·sén** \ī-'sen, -'sān\. 1 Province of S Chile. See table at CHILE.

2 Commune, its ✱. See PUERTO AYSÉN.

Ayu·tla \ä-'yüt-lə\ *or in full* **Ayutla de los Li·bres** \-ˌdā-lōs-'lē-brəs\. Town, Guerrero state, S Mexico, 45 m. E of Acapulco; plan of Ayutla (1854), demanding Santa Anna's removal, framing of new constitution, and establishment of representative government, was program of revolution led by Juan Álvarez 1855.

Ayutthaya. See PHRA NAKHON SI AYUTTHAYA.

Ay·va·lık \ˌī-və-ˈlik\ *also* **Ai·va·li** \ī-və-ˈlē\ *or anc.* **Her·a·clea** \ˌher-ə-ˈklē-ə\. Coastal town, Balıkesir prov., NW Turkey in Asia, on strait opp. Lesbos I.; pop. (1965c) 16,283.

Azam·garh \ˈäz-əm-ˌgär\. 1 District, Gorakhpur division, Uttar Pradesh, N India; 2222 sq. m.; pop. (1961c) 2,408,052.

2 Town, its ✻; pop. (1961c) 32,391.

Aza·na·que \ˌäs-ə-ˈnäk-(ˌ)ā, ˌäz-\. Peak, W Bolivia, on SE shore of Lake Poopó; 16,840 ft.

Azbine. See AÏR.

Az·ca·po·tzal·co \ˌäs-kə-pət-ˈsäl-(ˌ)kō, ˌäz-gə-\. City, Federal District, cen. Mexico, NW of Mexico City; munic. pop. (1970p) 545,513.

Azem·mour *or* **Azi·mur** *or* **Aze·mur** \ˈaz-ə-ˌmu̇(ə)r\. Seaport, NW Morocco, NW Africa; munic. pop. (1960c) 12,449.

Azer·bai·jan \ˌaz-ər-bī-ˈjän, ˌäz-\. 1 *anc.* **At·ro·pa·te·ne** \ˌa-trō-pə-ˈtē-nē\ *or* **Me·dia Atropatene** \ˈmēd-ē-ə-\. Former province, NW Iran, now divided into **East Azerbaijan** and **West Azerbaijan** (see table at IRAN); mountainous country that includes Lake Urmia, and one of the most fertile regions of Iran; scene of revolt against Iranian government 1945–46. Ancient Media Atropatene (see MEDIA) nearly coincided with the former province; it was the N part of Media and for some time after the death of Alexander was an independent kingdom.

2 Constituent republic, U.S.S.R. See AZERBAIJAN SOVIET SOCIALIST REPUBLIC.

Azerbaijan Soviet Socialist Republic *also* **Azer·bai·dzhan Soviet Socialist Republic** \ˌaz-ər-bī-ˈjän-\ *shortened to* **Azerbaijan** *or* **Azerbaidzhan.** A constituent republic of the U.S.S.R., E Transcaucasia, bounded on N by Georgian S.S.R. and Dagestan A.S.S.R., on E by the Caspian Sea, on S by Iran, and on W by the Armenian S.S.R.; 33,436 sq. m.; pop. (1970p) 5,111,000; ✻ Baku. It includes the Nakhichevan A.S.S.R. and the Nagorno-Karabakh Autonomous Oblast. Central part is a plain through which flow the Kura river and its tributaries, esp. the Araks whose upper course forms part of boundary bet. the U.S.S.R. and Iran; N of the plain is E end of Caucasus Mts. *Chief products:* Barley, corn, cotton, rice, tea, fruit; oil, copper. *Chief towns:* Baku, Kirovabad, Sumgait.

History: In ancient times home of Scythian tribes and part of Roman Empire; in medieval times overrun by Turks in 11th cent.; after fall of Tamerlane site of several Tatar khanates, esp. Shirvan; again under Persians in 17th cent.; larger part conquered by Russia 1806, 1813; scene of fighting in World War I; with part of Azerbaijan prov. of Persia set up as a republic May 28, 1918; invaded by Turkish Nationalists and Soviet troops 1919–20; established a Soviet government 1920; as member of Transcaucasian Federation (*q.v.*) joined U.S.S.R. Dec. 30, 1922; became constituent republic 1936.

Azil, Le Mas d'. See LE MAS D'AZIL.

Azimur. See AZEMMOUR.

Azincourt. See AGINCOURT.

ʻAziziya, Al–. See AL-ʻAZIZIYA.

Azle \ˈā-zəl\. City, Parker and Tarrant cos., N Texas, 15 m. NW of Fort Worth; pop. (1970c) 4493; meat packing, machine shops; diversified agriculture.

Azof. See AZOV.

Azo·gues \ə-ˈzō-gəs, -ˈsō-\. City, ✻ of Cañar prov., W cen. Ecuador, 80 m. ESE of Guayaquil; pop. (1970e) 9300; manufactures straw hats.

Azores \ˈā-ˌzō(ə)rz, -ˌzȯ(ə)rz, ə-ˈ-\ *or Port.* **Aço·res** \ə-ˈsōr-is(h)\. Group of nine islands and several islets belonging to Portugal in the N Atlantic Ocean, bet. lat. 36°50′ and 39°44′N and long. 25° and 31°16′W; ab. 800 m. off the coast of Portugal; 905 sq. m.; pop. (1970e) 336,100; chief town Ponta Delgada; other towns Horta and Angra do Heroísmo. Comprises districts of Angra do Heroísmo, Horta, and Ponta Delgada; divided into three groups, the NW group containing Flores and Corvo, the central group containing Terceira, São Jorge, Pico, Faial, and Graciosa, and the E group containing São Miguel and Santa Maria; highest point Pico Alto 7713 ft. Exports fruits, grain, and wines.

History: Date of discovery uncertain, but existence known in Europe in 14th cent.; visited by Portuguese navigator Diogo de Seville 1427–31; known for a time as Flemish Islands owing to Flemish settlement which followed gift of Faial to Isabella of Burgundy 1466; assigned to Portugal by treaty of Alcatçovas 1480; subject to Spain 1580–1640; famous sea fight off Flores 1591 bet. *Revenge* under Sir Richard Grenville and Spanish fleet; contested by rival claimants of Portuguese crown 1830–31. In World War II naval and air bases granted Great Britain Oct. 16, 1943.

Azotos *or* **Azotus.** See ASHDOD.

Azov *or* **Azof** \ˈaz-ˌȯf, ˈāz-, -ˌäv\. Town, SW Rostov Oblast, Russian S.F.S.R., U.S.S.R., near mouth of Don river on S shore of E end of Gulf of Taganrog; pop. (1969e) 59,000; agricultural machinery, textiles; fishing. It is near site of ancient Tanais, a Greek colony. Captured by Vladimir I in 10th cent. and by Genoese in 13th cent., who fortified it and made it a trading port for Oriental goods; sacked by Tamerlane 1395; held alternately by Russians and Turks until 1739 when it was secured to Russia under Empress Anna.

Azov, Sea of *or* **Sea of Azof** *or Russ.* **Azov·sko·ye Mo·re** \ə-ˈzȯf-skə-yə-ˈmȯr-yə\ *or anc.* **Pa·lus Mae·o·tis** \ˌpā-ləs-mē-ˈōt-əs\. Sea, bet. the Ukrainian S.S.R. on the N and Rostov Oblast and Krasnodar Krai on the E, S U.S.S.R.; ab. 200 m. long; 14,517 sq. m.; connected with Black Sea on S by Kerch Strait; shallow, sandy shores (see ARABAT); its NE arm, the Gulf of Taganrog, receives the Don river.

Az·pei·tia \äs-ˈpāt-ē-ə\. Commune, Guipúzcoa prov., N Spain, 17 m. SW of San Sebastián; pop. (1970p) 10,797; mineral springs; site nearby (on road to W) of the Santa Casa, said to be birthplace of St. Ignatius of Loyola.

Az·tec \ˈaz-tek\. City, ⊗ of San Juan co., NW corner of New Mexico; pop. (1970c) 3354; fruit-growing center.

Aztec Mountain. Peak, La Plata co., SW Colorado; 13,200 ft.

Aztec Ruins National Monument. See UNITED STATES, *National Monuments.*

Azua \ˈäs-wə, ˈäz-\. 1 Province, S Dominican Republic. See table at DOMINICAN REPUBLIC.

2 *or* **Azua de Com·pos·te·la** \-dā-ˌkäm-pə-ˈstel-ə\. Town, its ✻, on S coast; pop. (1970e) 17,261.

Azua·ga \ä-ˈswäg-ə\. Commune, Badajoz prov., SW Spain, NW of Córdoba; pop. (1970p) 11,171.

Azuay \ä-ˈswī\. Province of S Ecuador. See table at ECUADOR.

Azúcar, Pan de. See PAN DE AZÚCAR.

Azue·ro Peninsula \ä-ˌswer-ō-\. Peninsula on S Panama coast, W of Gulf of Panama.

Azu·fre \ä-ˈsü-(ˌ)frā\. Volcanic peak, SE corner of Antofagasta prov., N Chile, near Argentina border; 18,635 ft.

Azufre, Pa·so del \ˌpä-sō-del-\. Andean mountain pass bet. San Juan prov., Argentina, and Coquimbo prov., Chile.

Azul \ä-ˈsül\. 1 Peak, S Los Andes prov., NW Argentina; 16,600 ft.

2 City, Buenos Aires prov., E Argentina, 170 m. SW of Buenos Aires; pop. (1960c) 33,535.

Azu·ma \ˈäz-ə-ˌmä\. Volcano, one of a group of peaks on S boundary of Yamagata prefecture, N Honshū, Japan, W of Fukushima; 7654 ft.; eruption 1900.

Azu·sa \ə-ˈzü-sə\. City, Los Angeles co., SW California, 18 m. ENE of Los Angeles; pop. (1970c) 25,217; citrus fruit; Azusa Pacific Coll. (1899); settled 1887.

Az Zahrān. See DHAHRAN.

Az–Zaqāzīq. See ZAGAZIG.

Az–Z̄arqā'. See ZARQA 2.

Az–Zāwiyah. See ZĀWIA.

Az Zuwaytīnah. See EZ ZUETINA.

Ba. See MBA.

Ba·al·bek \ˈbā-əl-ˌbek, ˈbäl-ˌbek\ *or* **Ba·ʻal·bek** \ˈbal-\ *or anc.* **He·li·op·o·lis** \ˌhē-lē-ˈäp-(ə-)ləs\. Village, E Lebanon, 35 m. N of Damascus and on railroad and highway from Beirut to Aleppo; pop. (1956e) 11,700; in ancient times a city of great size and importance, built on the lower W slope of the Anti-Lebanon Mts.; its identification with the worship of Baal as a Semitic sun-god gave rise to its Greek name Heliopolis, "City of the Sun"; made a Roman colony by Julius Caesar. Its ruins cover a great area; most of the buildings erected under the Romans, esp. during reign of Antoninus Pius (138–161).

Baar·le–Her·tog \ˌbär-lə-ˈhe(ə)r-ˌtäg\. Belgian exclave in the Netherlands, ab. 22 m. W of Eindhoven; 3 sq. m.; pop. (1969e) 2185.

Baarn \ˈbärn\. Commune, Utrecht prov., cen. Netherlands, 11 m. NE of Utrecht; pop. (1970e) 24,106; resort.

Ba·ba, Cape \-bä-ˈbä\ *or Turk.* **Baba Bur·nu** \-bər-ˈnü\ *or anc.* **Lec·tum** \ˈlek-təm\. Cape on W coast of Turkey, 39°29′N, 26°04′E, N of entrance to Gulf of Edremit; most westerly point of Asia.

Baba, Koh–i– \ˌkō-(h)ē-bä-ˈbä\. Mountain range, E cen. Afghanistan; a SW extension of the Hindu Kush; highest peak Shah Fulādi 16,872 ft.

Ba·ba·ho·yo \ˌbäb-ə-ˈ(h)ō-(ˌ)yō\ *or formerly* **Bo·de·gas** \bə-ˈdā-gəs\. 1 River, W cen. Ecuador; its estuary known as the Guayas river (*q.v.*); navigable for ab. 200 m.

2 Town, ✱ of Los Ríos prov., W cen. Ecuador, 40 m. NE of Guayaquil; pop. (1970e) 22,500.

Bab al–Man·dab *or* **Bab el Man·deb** \ˌbab-əl-ˈman-ˌdəb\. Strait bet. SW Arabian Penin. and the African coast, uniting Red Sea and Gulf of Aden (Indian Ocean); 20 m. wide.

Bab al–Zakak. See GIBRALTAR, STRAIT OF.

Ba·bar Islands \ˌbäb-ˌär-\. Island group of Maluku prov., Indonesia, on S side of Banda Sea ENE of Timor I. and W of Tanimbar Is.; 314 sq. m.; comprises **Babar Island** (the only large island, 220 sq. m.) and five small islands; densely forested.

Bab·bitt \ˈbab-ət\. Village, St. Louis co., NE Minnesota, 63 m. N of Duluth; pop. (1970c) 3076.

Ba·bel \ˈbā-bəl, ˈbab-əl\. Biblical city in the plain of Shinar (*Gen.* x. 10; xi. 1–9); the same Akkadian word as that for *Babylon.*

Babeldoab. See BABELTHUAP.

Ba·bels·berg \ˈbäb-əlz-ˌbərg, -əls-ˌberg\ *or formerly* **No·wa·wes** \ˌnō-və-ˈves, nō-ˈvä-ves\. Former city, now part of Potsdam, Potsdam dist., East Germany; 19th cent. castle; founded by Frederick the Great 1751.

Ba·bel·thu·ap \ˌbäb-əl-ˈtü-ˌäp\ *also* **Ba·bel·do·ab** \-ˈdō-ˌäp\ *or* **Pa·lau** \pə-ˈlau̇\. Largest island of Palau group in W Pacific Ocean, Trust Territory of the Pacific Islands; ab. 27 m. long and bet. 1 and 8 m. wide; 143 sq. m.; mountainous, well-wooded, and fertile. Included in Japanese mandate 1919; with seizure of Peleliu and Angaur by American forces 1944, its control by air secured.

Ba·bia Gó·ra \ˌbäb-ē-ə-ˈgu̇r-ə\ *or Czech* **Babia Ho·ra** \-ˈhȯr-ə\. Peak, highest of the Beskids, W Carpathian Mts., in West Beskids on border bet. Czechoslovakia and Poland; 5659 ft.

Ba·bine Lake \ba-ˌbēn-\. Long narrow lake, cen. British Columbia, Canada; 194 sq. m.; drains N through **Babine River** (ab. 55 m. long) into Skeena river.

Babine Mountains. Range of the Coast Mts. in W cen. British Columbia, Canada; highest point ab. 8000 ft.

Bā·bol \bä-ˈbōl\ *also* **Ba·bul** \bä-ˈbül\; *formerly* **Bar·fu·rush** \ˌbär-fə-ˈrüsh\ *or* **Bal·frush** \bäl-ˈfrüsh\. City, N Iran, 15 m. S of the Caspian Sea, in Māzandarān prov.; pop. (1971e) 52,000; has considerable trade through its port **Bābol Sar** \-ˈsär\.

Ba·bo·qui·va·ri Mountains \ˌbäb-ō-ki-ˌvär-ē-\. Small range in S Pima co., S Arizona; highest point 7730 ft.

Ba·bor Mountains \bä-ˈbȯ(ə)r-\. Range of Little Atlas Mts., N Algeria; highest point ab. 6560 ft.

Ba·bu·na \ˈbäb-ə-ˌnä\. Mountain range, pass, and small river in S Yugoslavia, N of Bitola.

Ba·bush·kin \ˈbäb-u̇sh-ˌkin\ *or formerly* **Lo·si·no·os·trovsk** \ˌləs-(y)i-nə-ə-ˈstrȯfsk\. Former city, Moscow Oblast, U.S.S.R.; incorporated into Moscow (city) 1960.

Ba·bu·yan \ˌbäb-u̇-ˈyän\. Island in Babuyan group, N of Luzon, Phil.; 28 sq. m.

Babuyan Channel. Passage bet. Babuyan Is. and N Luzon, Phil.; ab. 135 m. long and 25 m. wide.

Babuyan Cla·ro \-ˈklär-(ˌ)ō\. Active volcano, Babuyan I., Phil.; 3569 ft.

Babuyan Islands *or* **Ba·bu·ya·nes** \bäb-u̇-ˈyän-(ˌ)äs\. Island group, N Phil., N of Luzon; belongs to Cagayan prov.; contains 24 islands; ab. 225 sq. m.; of volcanic origin; chief islands Babuyan, Camiguin, Calayan, Fuga, and Dalupiri.

Bab·y·lon \ˈbab-ə-lən, -ˌlän\. 1 Village and summer resort, Suffolk co., SE New York, on Great South Bay on Long I., 37 m. E of New York City; pop. (1970c) 12,588.

2 Ancient city, now in ruins, on Euphrates river ab. 55 m. S of Baghdad, Iraq, near modern Hilla; ✱ of Babylonia.

History: Ancient town probably in existence from 4th millennium B.C.; one of a number of small city-kingdoms of Babylonia, it was seized by Semitic Amorites before 2200 B.C.; under Amoritic line of kings (c. 2050–1750 B.C.) of which Hammurabi was greatest, became capital of Old Empire of Babylonia and chief commercial city of Euphrates-Tigris valley; ruled by Kassites and Assyrians (see BABYLONIA); destroyed by Sennacherib 689 B.C. but rebuilt; capital of Neo-Babylonian Empire (see CHALDEA) 625–538 B.C.; attained greatest glory under Nebuchadnezzar II 605–562 B.C.; captured by Cyrus the Great 539 B.C. and in 331 B.C. by Alexander of Macedon who died there 323 B.C.; gradual commercial decline accelerated by removal of capital to Seleucia (*q.v.*) by Seleucis Nicator (312–280 B.C.).

Bab·y·lo·nia \ˌbab-ə-ˈlō-nyə, -nē-ə\. Ancient country in the lower Euphrates valley, SW Asia, coinciding with the plain between Baghdad, Iraq, and the Persian Gulf. See ʻIRAQ ʻARABI.

History: For earliest historic period, see SUMER and AKKAD. City-kingdom of Babylon attained hegemony under Ist Dynasty (Amoritic) 2050–1750 B.C.; led by Hammurabi (c. 1955–1913 B.C.), sixth and greatest ruler of Ist Dynasty, conquered all of Mesopotamia and spread its administration (Code of Hammurabi) and civilization over entire area; raided by Hittites; conquered and ruled by Kassites, a non-Semitic people, 1750–1180 B.C.; invaded by Arameans in 11th and 10th cents. B.C.; devastated by wars with Assyria (*q.v.*) which ruled Babylon 722–626 B.C., ruled 625–538 B.C. by Chaldea (*q.v.*); under Chaldean (Neo-Babylonian) Empire controlled Mesopotamia and Syria, captured Jerusalem c. 588 B.C.; empire broke up at fall of Babylon 539 B.C.; ruled by Persia 538–331 B.C. when Alexander captured Babylon, by Seleucidae 312–171 B.C., by Parthians 171 B.C.–226 A.D., and by Sassanidae 226–641 A.D. (see IRAN).

Ba·ca \ˈbäk-ə\. County in Colorado. See table at COLORADO.

Ba·ca·bal \ˌbək-ə-ˈbäl\. Municipality, Maranhão state, NE Brazil, ab. 125 m. SSW of São Luís; pop. (1968e) 111,753.

Ba·ca·cay \ˌbäk-ə-ˈkī\. Municipality on E coast of Albay prov., Luzon, Phil., on Tabaco Bay, ab. 10 m. N of Legaspi; pop. (1969e) 39,900.

Ba·cău \bə-ˈkaů\. 1 County of E cen. Romania. See table at ROMANIA.
2 City, its ⊗, on Bistriţa river; pop. (1969e) 65,987; paper, footwear, textiles.

Bachan *or* **Bachian.** See BATJAN.

Ba·cha·rach \ˈbäk-ə-ˌräk, ˈbäk-ə-ˌräk\. Town, Rhineland-Palatinate, West Germany; pop. (1964e) 2100; first mentioned 922.

Bachi Channel. See BASHI CHANNEL.

Bač·ka *or* **Bach·ka** \ˈbäch-kə\. Former subprovince in N Yugoslavia; now represented approximately by W part of Vojvodina autonomous region.

Back Alleghany Mountains. Ridge running N and S in Pocahontas co., E cen. West Virginia.

Back·bone Mountain \ˌbak-ˌbōn-\. Mountain, Garrett co., W extremity of Maryland; 3360 ft.; highest point in the state; extends SW into N West Virginia.

Backergunge. See BAKARGANJ.

Back·nang \ˈbäk-(ˌ)näŋ\. City, Baden-Württemberg, West Germany, 18 m. NE of Stuttgart; pop. (1969e) 27,850; leather products, machine shops, lumber; became city 1245.

Back River *or formerly* **Great Fish River.** River, N Canada; 605 m. long; rises in lakes in E cen. Mackenzie dist., Northwest Territories, flows NE through lakes Pelly, Garry, and Macdougall, across NW Keewatin dist. into Chantrey Inlet.

Back·stairs Passage \ˌbak-ˌsta(ə)rz-, -ˌste(ə)rz-\. Channel bet. E end of Kangaroo I. and mainland of South Australia; ab. 7 m. wide; forms SE entrance to Gulf of St. Vincent.

Bac·ninh \ˈbäk-ˈnin\. Town, North Vietnam, on railroad 16 m. NE of Hanoi.

Ba·co, Mount \-bä-ˈkō\. Mountain, cen. Mindoro I., Phil.; 8163 ft.

Ba·co·lod \bä-ˈkō-ˌlȯd\. Chartered city, ❋ of Negros Occidental, Negros, Phil., on Guimaras Strait opp. Guimaras I.; pop. (1970e) 165,000; univ. (1957).

Ba·co·lor \ˌbäk-ə-ˈlō(ə)r\. Municipality, Luzon, Phil., 3 m. SW of San Fernando; pop. (1969e) 40,800; former ❋ of Pampanga prov.

Ba·con \ˈbā-kən\. County in Georgia. See table at GEORGIA.

Bacon \ˈbä-ˈkȯn\. Municipality, NE Sorsogon prov., Luzon, Phil., on SE shore of Albay Gulf 6 m. across narrow neck of land from Sorsogon; pop. (1969e) 29,700.

Ba·cong \bä-ˈkȯŋ\. Municipality, SE Negros Oriental, Negros, Phil., on coast 4 m. S of Dumaguete, opp. Siquijor I.; pop. (1969e) 14,400; founded 1801.

Ba·co·or \ˌbäk-ə-ˈwȯ(ə)r\. Municipality, NE Cavite prov., Luzon, Phil., on shore of Bacoor Bay SE of City of Cavite and ab. 9 m. SSW of Manila; pop. (1969e) 37,400.

Bacoor Bay. Large inlet of SE Manila Bay, Phil., on Cavite shore S of Cavite Penin.; inner anchorage of Cavite naval base.

Bács·al·más \ˈbäch-ˌȯl-ˌmäsh\. Commune, S Hungary, 43 m. SW of Szeged; pop. (1970p) 9023.

Bács–Kis·kun \ˈbäch-ˌkish-kůn\. County of S cen. Hungary. See table at HUNGARY.

Bactra. See BALKH 2.

Bac·tria \ˈbak-trē-ə\ *also* **Bac·tri·a·na** \ˌbak-trē-ˈan-ə, -ˈän-ə, -ˈā-nə\. Ancient country of SW Asia; ab. 250 m. long by 120 m. wide, bet. Hindu Kush and Oxus river; ❋ Bactra; partly desert; home of nomadic people, the Bactrians; made part of the Persian Empire by Cyrus the Great (550–529 B.C.); conquered by Alexander the Great 328 B.C.; from 302 B.C. ruled as province of Seleucid empire; under its Greek satrap, Diodotus, revolted and became independent kingdom c. 250 B.C.; expanded to include part of Afghanistan and of Punjab; after 135 B.C., kingdom destroyed by invasion of Sacae, mixed Scythian, Tatar, and Chinese tribes. In Christian Era region became known as Balkh (*q.v.*).

Ba·cup \ˈbā-kəp\. Municipal borough, Lancashire, NW England, on the Irwell 21 m. N of Manchester; pop. (1971p) 15,102; coal mines, iron foundries.

Bad \ˈbad\. River, S cen. South Dakota; ab. 110 m. long; rises in E Pennington co., flows E into Missouri river opp. Pierre.

Ba·da·csony \ˈbȯd-ə-ˌchōn-yə\. Plateau region, Hungary, NW of Lake Balaton; produces white wine.

Ba·da·joz \ˌbäth-ə-ˈhōs, ˌbäd-ə-ˈhōz\. 1 Province of SW Spain. See table at SPAIN.
2 *or anc.* **Pax Au·gus·ta** \ˌpak-sȯ-ˈgəs-tə, -sə-\. City, its ❋, 52 m. SW of Cáceres near Portuguese border, on left bank of Guadiana river; pop. (1970p) 101,710; food processing, blankets; 13th cent. cathedral. Center of 11th cent. Moorish kingdom; captured c. 1227 by Alfonso IX of León; besieged by Portuguese 1660 and by Allies 1705 (War of the Spanish Succession); besieged and taken by French during Peninsular War, retaken by Wellington 1812.

Ba·dakh·shān \ˌbäd-äk-ˈshän\. Frontier province, NE Afghanistan; 16,844 sq. m.; pop. (1967e) 344,495; ❋ Faizābād; a mountainous region bet. the upper Amu Darya on the N and the Hindu Kush range on the S, with the Kundūz river as its W boundary; wheat, barley, corn, cotton; livestock; in ancient times a part of the Greek Bactria.

Badakhshan. See GORNO-BADAKHSHAN AUTONOMOUS OBLAST.

Ba·da·lo·na \ˌbäd-ᵊl-ˈō-nə\ *or anc.* **Bae·tu·lo** \ˈbē-chə-ˌlō\. Industrial commune and seaport, Barcelona prov., NE Spain, 5 m. N of Barcelona; pop. (1970p) 162,888.

Ba·da·ri \bə-ˈdär-ē\. Village, Egypt, ab. 19 m. SE of Asyūt; in region where excavations by Sir Flinders Petrie revealed evidences of a predynastic neolithic culture, dated before 4000 B.C.

Bad Axe \ˈbad-ˌaks\. City, ⊗ of Huron co., E Michigan, 15 m. S of mouth of Saginaw Bay; pop. (1970c) 2999.

Bad·deck \bə-ˈdek\. Village (unincorporated), ⊗ of Victoria co., NE Nova Scotia, Canada, on N arm of Bras d'Or Lake 30 m. W of Sydney; pop. (1966c) 718; scene of first airplane flight in British Empire Feb. 23, 1909.

Bad Do·be·ran \ˌbät-ˌdō-bə-ˈrän\. Town, Rostock dist., East Germany, ab. 2 m. from shore of Bay of Mecklenburg 7 m. W of Rostock; pop. (1970e) 12,834; resort; ruins of 12th cent. Cistercian Abbey, 14th cent. Gothic church.

Bad Dürk·heim \bät-ˈdů(ə)rk-ˌhīm, -ˈdœrk-\ *or* **Dürkheim.** Town, Bavaria, West Germany, 15 m. NW of Speyer; pop. (1968e) 15,761; mineral springs; first mentioned 946.

Bad Ems \bäd-ˈemz, bät-ˈem(p)s\ *also* **Ems.** Town, Rhineland-Palatinate, West Germany, on the Lahn river 11 m. SE of Koblenz; pop. (1966e) 10,235; health resort; here on Aug. 25, 1786 the four Roman Catholic archbishops of Cologne, Trier, Mainz, and Salzburg prepared the Punctuation of Ems asserting episcopal rights against the Pope; also scene of interview bet. the King of Prussia and the French ambassador July 13, 1870 resulting in the sending by Bismarck of the famous Ems dispatch, a direct cause of the Franco-Prussian War 1870–71.

Ba·den \ˈbād-ᵊn\. Residential borough, Beaver co., W Pennsylvania, 19 m. NW of Pittsburgh; pop. (1970c) 5536.

Baden \ˈbäd-ᵊn\. 1 *or* **Baden bei Wien** \-bī-ˈvēn\ *or anc.* **Aq·uae Pa·no·ni·ae** \ˈak-(ˌ)wē-pə-ˈnō-nē-ˌē, ˈäk-\. Commune, Lower Austria, 14 m. SSW of Vienna; pop. (1961c) 22,484; famous for warm mineral springs frequented since Roman times.
2 Former German state, now part of Baden-Württemberg state, West Germany; 5817 sq. m.; ❋ Karlsruhe.

History: Became political unit when Frederick, son of Margrave of Verona, took title of Margrave of Baden 1112; split up and reunited many times before final reunion of all territories under Charles Frederick 1771; member of League of German Princes 1785; became new electorate 1803; supported Napoleon against Austria in War of Third

Coalition and received rest of Hapsburg territory in western Germany and rank of grand duchy 1805 (Treaty of Pressburg: see BRATISLAVA); member of Confederation of Rhine until joining Allies against Napoleon 1813; member of Germanic Confederation 1815; received constitution 1818; joined Zollverein 1835; became a leader of German liberal movement and center of action in revolution 1848–49; member of Frankfurt Parliament; supported Austria against Prussia 1866; forced to pay indemnity and become military ally of Prussia; joined North German Confederation 1870 and German Empire 1871; proclaimed republic 1918; became administrative division of the Reich 1933–34; southern part became a state of West Germany 1949, northern part incorporated in Württemberg-Baden state; following a referendum (1951) both states merged to form Baden-Württemberg state (1952).
3 City, West Germany. See BADEN-BADEN.
4 Commune, Aargau canton, N cen. Switzerland, 13 m. ENE of Aarau; pop. (1970c) 14,115; old castle; its sulfur springs and baths known since Roman times.

Baden–Baden \ˌbäd-ᵊn-ˈbäd-ᵊn\ *or* **Baden** *or anc.* **Au·re·lia Aquen·sis** \ȯ-ˌrēl-yə-ə-ˈkwen(t)-səs\. City, Baden-Württemberg, West Germany, 18 m. SSW of Karlsruhe; pop. (1969e) 39,074; tourist resort; its thermal baths frequented by ancient Romans.

Ba·den·wei·ler \ˌbäd-ᵊn-ˈvī-lər\. Village, Baden-Württemberg, West Germany, 28 m. NE of Basel, Switzerland; pop. (1964e) 3100; mineral springs; Roman baths.

Baden–Würt·tem·berg \ˌbäd-ᵊn-ˈwərt-əm-ˌbərg, -ˈwu̇rt-; -ˈvu̇ert-əm-ˌberg\. A state of West Germany; 13,803 sq. m.; pop. (1970e) 8,959,700; ✻ Stuttgart; textiles, glass, pottery; engineering industries; established 1952. For history, see BADEN 2 and WÜRTTEMBERG.

Bad Freienwalde. See FREIENWALDE.

Badgastein. See GASTEIN.

Bad·ger Pass \ˈbaj-ər-\. Mountain pass, cen. California, in Yosemite National Park; alt. 7100 ft.; skiing.

Bād·ghis \ˈbäd-gəs\. Province of NW Afghanistan. See table at AFGHANISTAN.

Bad Go·des·berg \bät-ˈgōd-əs-ˌbərg, -ˌbe(ə)rg\ *also* **Godesberg.** City, North Rhine-Westphalia, West Germany, on left bank of the Rhine 4 m. S of Bonn; pop. (1969e) 73,512; mineral springs; ruins of castle (called the Godesburg, founded 1213, destroyed 1583 by Bavarians) nearby; manufactures pharmaceutical goods; scene of conference Sept. 22, 1938 bet. Neville Chamberlain and Hitler, prior to that at Munich, in regard to Czechoslovakia; site of a number of foreign legations.

Bad Harz·burg \bät-ˈhärts-ˌbərg, -ˌbu̇(ə)rg\ *also* **Harzburg.** Town, Lower Saxony, West Germany, N of the Harz Mts.; pop. (1968e) 11,334; mineral springs.

Bad Hers·feld \ˌbät-ˈhe(ə)rs-ˌfelt\. City, Hesse, West Germany, 32 m. SSE of Kassel; pop. (1969e) 23,551; ruins of 11th cent. abbey church; machine tools, electronic equipment, textiles, leather.

Bad Hom·burg \bät-ˈhäm-ˌbərg, -ˈhȯm-ˌbu̇(ə)rg\ *also* **Homburg** *or in full* **Bad Homburg vor der Hö·he** \-ˌfōr-dər-ˈhœ̄-ə\. City, SW Hesse, West Germany, 18 m. ENE of Wiesbaden; pop. (1969e) 40,485; mineral baths; health and tourist resort; 17th cent. castle with fine tower; manufactures leather goods, hats (first Homburg hats made here), machinery, chocolates, synthetic oil. Ruled by landgraves of Hesse-Homburg 1622–1866; bombed during latter part of World War II.

Ba·di·an \ˌbäd-ē-ˈän\. Municipality on W coast of Cebu I., Phil., at S end of Tanon Strait; pop. (1969e) 24,900.

Ba·dia Po·le·si·ne \bä-ˈdē-ə-pə-ˈlā-zə-ˌnā\. Commune, Rovigo prov., Veneto, NE Italy; pop. (1968e) 10,265.

Badin Lake. See NARROWS DAM.

Bad Ischl. See ISCHL.

Bad Kissingen. See KISSINGEN.

Bad Kreuznach. See KREUZNACH.

Bad Lands \ˈbad-ˌlan(d)z\; *orig. Fr.* **Mau·vaises Terres** \ˌmō-ˌvāz-ˈte(ə)r\ *or* **Terres Mauvaises** \ˈte(ə)r-mō-ˈvāz\. Barren region with eroded surface in SW South Dakota E of the Black Hills and in NW Nebraska; contains extensive fossil deposits; marked by steep hills, deep gullies, and other features of geological interest. From this name comes the generic term *badlands* applied also to similar areas in other western states and in South America and Asia.

Bad·lands National Monument \ˈbad-ˌlan(d)z-\. See UNITED STATES, *National Monuments.*

Bad Nauheim. See NAUHEIM.

Bad Neu·en·ahr–Ahr·weil·er \bät-ˈnȯi-ə-ˌnär-ˈär-ˌvī-lər\. City, Rhineland-Palatinate, West Germany, 13 m. S of Bonn; pop. (1969e) 25,278.

Badnur. See BETUL.

Badoeng Strait. See BADUNG STRAIT.

Bad Reichenhall. See REICHENHALL.

Ba·dri·a·gua·to \ˌbäd-rē-ə-ˈgwät-ˌō\. Municipality, Sinaloa state, Mexico, 50 m. N of Culiacan; pop. (1970p) 28,955; timber; wheat, sweet potatoes.

Ba·dri·nath \ˌbəd-ri-ˈnät, ˌbäd-\. Peak in the Himalayas, N Garhwal, Uttar Pradesh, N India; 23,420 ft.; village and temple on its slope at 10,291 ft.

Bad River. See BAD.

Bad Salz·uf·len \ˈbät-ˈsälts-u̇f-lən, -ˈzalts-\. City, North Rhine-Westphalia, West Germany, 45 m. SW of Hannover; pop. (1969e) 48,436; thermal springs; health resort; woodworking. Founded 1048; became city 1488.

Ba·dul·la \bə-ˈdəl-ə\. Town, SE Ceylon, 85 m. E of Colombo; pop. (1968e) 30,000; in tea-growing region.

Ba·dung Strait *or* **Ba·doeng Strait** \ˌbäd-ˌu̇ŋ-\. Channel bet. SE Bali and the island of Nusa Besar, Indonesia; ab. 9 m. wide; connects with Lombok Strait (*q.v.*).

Bad·wa·ter \ˈbad-ˌwȯt-ər, -ˌwät-\. Small salt pool, Death Valley, California; 282 ft. below sea level; lowest point in North America.

Ba·e·na \bä-ˈā-nə\. Commune, Córdoba prov., S Spain, 32 m. SE of Córdoba; pop. (1970p) 10,781; Roman ruins.

Bær·um \ˈbar-əm\. Commune, Akershus co., suburb of Oslo, SE Norway; pop. (1970e) 74,713; wood pulp.

Baeterrae. See BÉZIERS.

Bae·ti·ca \ˈbēt-i-kə\. A province of the Roman Empire in S Spain, roughly equivalent to W Andalusia.

Baetis. See GUADALQUIVIR.

Baetulo. See BADALONA.

Ba·e·za \bä-ˈā-zə, -sə\. Commune, Jaén prov., S Spain, ab. 24 m. NE of Jaén; pop. (1970p) 14,834; as medieval Moorish city, sacked by Ferdinand III of Castile 1239.

Ba·fa, Lake \-ˈbäf-ə\ *or Turk.* **Bafa Gö·lü** \-gəl-ˈ(y)ü\. Lake in W Turkey in Asia at the mouth of the Menderes river; 22 sq. m.; site of ancient Priene is on its W shore and of Miletus just to S of it.

Baf·fin Bay \ˌbaf-ən-\. 1 Inlet of Laguna Madre, S Texas. 2 Large inlet of Atlantic Ocean bet. W Greenland and E Baffin I.; connected with Atlantic Ocean by Davis Strait; discovered and partly explored by William Baffin 1616.

Baffin Island *or formerly* **Baffin Land.** Largest island of Canadian Arctic Archipelago, E Franklin dist., Northwest Territories, W of Baffin Bay and Davis Strait; 183,810 sq. m.; pop. (1961c) 3387, chiefly Eskimos; 5th largest island in the world; separated from Quebec on the S by Hudson Strait; in NW is Admiralty Inlet, in S part two lakes, Amadjuak and Nettilling, and on SE coast two large inlets, Cumberland Sound and Frobisher Bay; coal, iron ore; its S part first visited by Frobisher 1576–78; its N part explored by Baffin 1616.

Ba·fing \bə-ˈfiŋ\. The upper course of the Senegal river in Guinea and Mali; ab. 350 m. long; rises in the Fouta Djallon highlands and flows NE and N to join the Bakoy at Bafoulabé.

Ba·fou·la·bé *or* **Ba·fu·la·bé** \ˌbaf-ˌü-lə-ˈbā\. Town on Senegal river at confluence of its headstreams, Bafing and Bakoy, W Mali, 13°48′N, 10°50′W.

Ba·fra \bä-ˈfrä\. Town, Samsun prov., N Turkey in Asia, on Kızıl Irmak near its mouth; pop. (1965c) 26,239.

Ba·gac \bä-ˈgäk\. Municipality on W coast of Bataan prov., Luzon, Phil., ab. halfway bet. Subic Bay and Mariveles; pop. (1969e) 9700; fighting nearby Feb. 1942.

Ba·ga·mo·yo \ˌbäg-ə-ˈmȯi-(ˌ)ō\. Seaport town, E Tanzania; pop. (1967p) 5100.

Ba·ga·na \bə-ˈgän-ə\. Volcano, S cen. Bougainville I., Papua New Guinea; 6558 ft.

Bagaria. See BAGHERIA.

Bagdad. See BAGHDAD.

Ba·gé \bə-ˈzhā\. City, S Rio Grande do Sul state, S Brazil; munic. pop. (1968e) 90,593.

Bagh·dad *or* **Bag·dad** \ˈbag-ˌdad\. City, ✻ of Iraq, on both sides of the Tigris; pop. (1970e) 2,183,760; commercial and transportation center; cement, textiles, tobacco products; railroad workshops; two universities (1956).

History: Settlement on site of Baghdad from ancient times; sacked by Muslim Arabs 634 A.D.; rose to importance after its choice 762 A.D. by al-Mansur as capital of Abbasside caliphate; as center of Islam, especially under Caliph al-Mamun (813–833), second only to Constantinople as trade and cultural center (estimated pop. of ab. 2,000,000); though power of Baghdad caliphate declined from about middle of 9th cent., city remained commercially important and continued to rule area corresponding roughly to modern Iraq; almost destroyed when Hulagu, grandson of Genghis Khan (see MONGOLIA), overthrew Abbasside caliphate 1258 and began rule of Il-khans of Persia (1260–1340); conquered by Tamerlane 1401; though captured by Suleiman the Magnificent 1534, did not become part of Ottoman Empire until 1638; objective of British Mesopotamian campaign 1915–17, it was finally captured Mar. 11, 1917; became capital of kingdom of Iraq (*q.v.*) 1921; scene of *coup d'état* against monarchy 1958.

Baghdadi, Khan. See KHAN BAGHDADI.

Ba·ghel·khand \ˈbəg-əl-ˌkənd, ˈbäg-əl-ˌkänd\. Former agency, E division of Central India Agency, India; 14,706 sq. m.

Ba·ghe·ria *or* **Ba·ga·ria** \ˌbäg-ə-ˈrē-ə\. Commune, Palermo prov., NW cen. Sicily, Italy, near Bay of Palermo 8 m. S by E of Palermo; pop. (1968e) 36,553.

Bāgh·lān \ˈbäg-ˌlän\. 1 Province of NE Afghanistan. See table at AFGHANISTAN.

2 Town, its ✻; pop. (1970e) 103,104; beet sugar, cotton.

Bagirmi. See BAGUIRMI.

Ba·ğır·pa·şa Dağ \ˈbä(g)-ˌı(ə)r-pə-ˌshä-ˈdä(g)\. Peak, E Turkey, 70 m. SW of Erzurum; 10,768 ft.

Ba·gi·stan \ˌbag-i-ˈstan\. An occasional term for a region, encompassing Bangla Desh and parts of adjoining Meghalaya and Assam, India, having a Muslim majority. See EAST BENGAL.

Bag·ley \ˈbag-lē\. Village, ⊗ of Clearwater co., NW Minnesota; pop. (1970c) 1314; lake resort.

Ba·gna·ca·val·lo \ˌbän-yə-kə-ˈväl-(ˌ)ō\. Commune, Ravenna prov., Emilia-Romagna, N Italy, 12 m. W by S of Ravenna; pop. (1968e) 17,851; birthplace of the painter Il Bagnacavallo.

Ba·gna·ra Ca·la·bra \bən-ˌyär-ə-ˈkäl-ə-brə\. Commune, Reggio di Calabria prov., Calabria, S Italy, 11 m. NNE of Reggio di Calabria; pop. (1968e) 12,696.

Ba·gnères–de–Bi·gorre \ban-ˈye(ə)r-də-bi-ˈgȯ(ə)r\. Commune, Hautes-Pyrénées dept., SW France, 13 m. SSE of Tarbes; pop. (1968c) 10,216; health resort, known since Roman times; produces barège, a gauzelike fabric containing wool, first made at Barèges ab. 25 m. SSW.

Ba·gneux \ban-ˈyə(r)\. Commune, Hauts-de-Seine dept., N France, S suburb of Paris; pop. (1968c) 42,006; battle during siege of Paris, Oct. 13, 1870.

Ba·gni di Luc·ca \ˌbän-yē-di-ˈlü-kə\. Commune, Lucca prov., Tuscany, cen. Italy, 13 m. NNE of Lucca; pop. (1968e) 9,000; thermal mineral springs.

Bagni San Giuliano. See SAN GIULIANO TERME.

Ba·gno a Ri·po·li \ˈbän-yō-ä-ˈrē-pə-lē\. Commune, Firenze prov., Tuscany, cen. Italy, 4 m. SE of Florence; pop. (1968e) 20,831; remains of ancient Roman bath.

Bagno di Ro·ma·gna \-di-rō-ˈmän-yə\. Commune, Forlì prov., Emilia-Romagna, N Italy, 26 m. S by W of Forlì; pop. (1968e) 7565; summer resort; thermal springs.

Ba·gno·let \ˌban-yə-ˈlā\. Commune, Seine-St-Denis dept., N France, E suburb of Paris; pop. (1968c) 34,038.

Ba·go \ˈbäg-(ˌ)ō\. Chartered city, W Negros Occidental, Negros, Phil., on Guimaras Strait ab. 12 m. SSW of City of Bacolod; pop. (1970e) 81,900.

Bag·ot \ˈbag-ət\. County, Quebec, Canada. See table at QUEBEC.

Bag·ot·ville \ˈbag-ət-ˌvil\. Town, Chicoutimi co., S Quebec, Canada, on S bank of Saguenay river 10 m. ESE of Chicoutimi; pop. (1971p) 6019.

Bagradas. See MEDJERDA.

Ba·gra·ti·o·novsk \bə-ˌgrat-ē-ˈō-nəfsk\; *formerly* **Preus·sisch Ey·lau** \ˌprȯi-sish-ˈī-ˌlau̇\ *or* **Eylau.** Town, Kaliningrad Oblast, Russian S.F.S.R., U.S.S.R., 23 m. S of Kaliningrad; formerly in East Prussia, Germany; scene of indecisive battle Feb. 8, 1807 bet. the allied Russians and Prussians and the French under Napoleon.

Ba·guio \ˈbäg-ē-ˌō\. Chartered city, summer ✻ of the Philippines, W cen. Benguet prov., NW Luzon, ab. 130 m. N of Manila; pop. (1969e) 71,400; elev. 4500 ft.; summer resort; visited by Spaniards 1829 but until 20th cent. of less importance than La Trinidad (*q.v.*) to the N; incorporated as City of Baguio 1909; occupied by Japanese Dec. 1941; retaken by Americans Apr. 29, 1945.

Ba·guir·mi *or* **Ba·gir·mi** \bə-ˈgi(ə)r-mē\. Former sultanate, now part of SW Chad, N cen. Africa, SE of Lake Chad; ✻ before 1898 Massénya; level area ab. 1000 ft. above sea level, traversed by tributaries of the Chari river which forms its W and SW boundary; Fort-Lamy is in NW corner. Explored by Dixon Denham 1823, Heinrich Barth 1855, and Gustav Nachtigal 1872; came under French protection 1897; used as base for operations against Germans in N Cameroons 1914.

Ba·ha·ma Banks \bə-ˌhäm-ə-\. Two areas of shoal water in the Bahama Is.: **Little Bahama Bank,** N of Grand Bahama I. and bet. it and Abaco on E; **Great Bahama Bank,** covering a large curved area some 330 m. long with Andros on its E rim, separated from Cuba on S by Old Bahama Channel and from Florida on W and NW by Straits of Florida.

Bahama Islands *or* **Ba·ha·mas** \bə-ˈhäm-əz\ *or officially* **Commonwealth of the Bahama Islands.** British colony comprising a chain of islands, cays, and reefs lying SE of Florida and N of Cuba; total area 5386 sq. m., area of inhabited island ab. 4404 sq. m.; pop. (1970c) 168,812; ✻ Nassau (on island of New Providence); *Chief islands:* (From N to S) Grand Bahama, Abaco, Eleuthera, New Providence, Andros, Cat I., San Salvador (or Watlings I.), Exuma, Long I., Crooked I., Acklins I., Mayaguana, Inagua; chain of islands terminates in Turks and Caicos Is. (*q.v.*). *Chief exports:* Crayfish, lumber, salt, tomatoes, fruit. A major tourist resort.

History: Islands inhabited by Lucayan Indians at time of discovery by Columbus Oct. 12, 1492 (see SAN SALVADOR 1); assigned to Spain by papal grant but visited only by slave raiders and buccaneers; granted by British crown 1629 to Sir Robert Heath, to whom islands surrendered 1629; suffered from Spanish attacks (as in 1641, 1684, 1719–20) and from use as pirates' base; settlement of islands by company of Eleutherian Adventurers (incorp. 1647) authorized by Parliament 1649; settlements made on Eleuthera and New Providence; islands granted to lords proprietors of Carolina 1670 but civil and military government assumed by crown 1717; piracy in islands ended by Capt. Woodes Rogers, first royal governor, 1718; first meeting of general assembly in Nassau 1729; Nassau seized and disarmed by American force 1776; islands capitulated to Spain 1782 but restored to Great Britain by Treaty of Versailles 1783; influx of American loyalists as settlers 1783–84; proprietary rights of lords proprietors surrendered to crown 1787; Turks Is. under administration of colony 1804–48; abolished slavery 1833; base for blockade running to Southern States 1861–65; site on Mayaguana leased to U.S. for naval base 1940; British air base maintained on New Providence during World War II; adopted new constitution 1964.

Ba·ha·rī·ya *also* **Be·ha·ri·eh** *or* **Ba·ha·ri·eh** \bə-ˈrē-(y)ə, ˌbä-hə-ˈrē-\. Oasis in the Libyan Desert, Matrūh gov., Egypt, ab. 28°15′N, 28°57′E.

Ba·ha·wal·pur \bə-ˈhä-wəl-ˌpu̇(ə)r\ *or* **Bha·wal·pur** \ˈbä-wəl-\. 1 Former Indian state, SW Punjab, now part of Pakistan; 17,494 sq. m.; region stretches more than 300 m. along the Sutlej, Panjnad, and Indus rivers with practically all of its territory in the Thar Desert. Its rulers became independent of Afghans in early 19th cent.; made treaty with British 1838; joined Pakistan 1947; reconstituted into an administrative division 1955; 17,508 sq. m.; pop. (1961c) 2,574,066.

2 Town, its ✱, near Sutlej river ab. 225 m. SW of Lahore; met. area pop. (1969e) 146,800; cotton, pottery, soap.

Ba·hia \bə-ˈhē-ə, bä-ˈē-ə\. 1 State, E Brazil; 216,612 sq. m.; pop. (1970p) 7,420,906; ✱ Salvador; sugar, tobacco, hides.

2 City, Brazil. See SALVADOR.

Ba·hía, Is·las de la \ˈēz-ˌläs-ˌdā-lä-bə-ˈhē-ə, -bä-ˈē-ə\ *also* **Bay Islands** \ˈbā-\. Group of islands in Caribbean Sea off N Honduras coast, including Roatán, largest of the group, and Guanaja; a department of Honduras. See table at HONDURAS.

Bahía Blan·ca \bə-ˌhē-ə-ˈblaŋ-kə, bä-ˌē-ˈbläŋ-\. 1 Large bay in SE Buenos Aires prov., E Argentina.

2 City, Buenos Aires prov., E Argentina, at head of this bay; pop. (1960c) 120,580; naval port; shipping point for La Pampa, Neuquén, and Río Negro provs.; exports cattle, wheat, wool; univ. (1956); dates from fort and trading post 1828.

Bahía Gran·de \bə-ˌhē-ə-ˈgran-dē, bä-ˌē-ə-ˈgrän-(ˌ)dā\. Widemouthed bay on SE coast of Santa Cruz prov., S Argentina.

Ba·ho·ru·co \bau̇-ˈrü-(ˌ)kō, ˌbä-hō-\. 1 Mountain range and its highest peak 5346 ft. in SW Dominican Republic.

2 Province, SW Dominican Republic. See table at DOMINICAN REPUBLIC.

Bah·raich \bə-ˈrīk\. 1 District, E Uttar Pradesh, N India; 2620 sq. m.; pop. (1961c) 1,499,929; ✱ Bahraich; corn, wheat, rice.

2 Town, its ✱, on affluent of Ghāghara river 65 m. NE of Lucknow; pop. (1961c) 56,033; trades in sugar, timber, tobacco; contains tomb of Masaud, a champion of Islam, a place of pilgrimage for both Hindus and Muslims.

Bah·rain *also* **Bah·rein** \bä-ˈrān\; *anc.* **Ty·los** \ˈtī-ˌläs\ *or* **Ty·ros** \-ˌräs\. Independent state, an archipelago in W Persian Gulf, 20 m. off Al-Hasa coast of Arabian Penin., NW of Qatar; 255 sq. m.; pop. (1971p) 216,815; ✱ Manama; comprises low-lying islands of **Bahrain** (the largest, 27 m. long by 10 m. wide), Muharraq, Sitra, and several islets; extensive oil fields; shipbuilding; sailcloth and mats; dates, rice.

History: Occupied by Portuguese 1521–1602, by Arab subjects of Persia to 1783; ruled since 1782 by a member of a Kuwait (*q.v.*) family; its defense a British responsibility 1820–1971; Persian ownership denied by British 1928; oil discovered 1932; established a Council of State 1970; became a member of the United Nations 1971.

Bahr al–Abyad. The White Nile. See NILE.

Bahr al–Arab \ˌba(ə)r-al-ˈär-ˌäb, bär-\. River, S Sudan, NE Africa; flows E to join with the Jur and form the Bahr al-Ghazal.

Bahr al–Azraq. The Blue Nile. See NILE.

Bahr al–Gha·zal \ˌba(ə)r-ˌal-gə-ˈzal, ˌbär-\. 1 River, SW Sudan; 445 m. long; formed by confluence of Bahr al-Arab and Jur rivers in NW Upper Nile prov.; flows E to unite at Lake No with the Bahr al-Jebel and form the White Nile (see NILE).

2 Province of SW Sudan. See table at SUDAN 2.

Bahr al–Je·bel \-ˈjeb-əl\. Section of the Nile in S Sudan. See BAHR AL-GHAZAL.

Bahrein. See BAHRAIN.

Bahr en Nīl. See NILE.

Bahret Lut. See DEAD SEA.

Bahr·gan, Cape \-bär-ˈgän\. Cape on W coast of Iran, projecting into NE corner of the Persian Gulf.

Bahr Yusef. See YUSEF, BAHR.

Ba·ia–Ma·re \ˌbä-yə-ˈmär-ə\ *or Hung.* **Nagy·bá·nya** \ˈnäj-ˈbän-ˌyȯ\. Town, ⊗ of Maramureş co., NW Romania, ab. 65 m. N of Cluj; pop. (1969e) 51,181; lead and zinc smelting plants.

Baibazar. See BEYPAZARI.

Bai·bung, Point \-ˈbī-ˌbu̇ŋ\; *formerly* **Point Ca·mau** \-kə-ˈmau̇\ *or* **Cam·bo·dia Point** \kam-ˌbōd-ē-ə-\. Cape, S end of South Vietnam; extends W into South China Sea and marks the SE corner of Gulf of Siam.

Baiburt. See BAYBURT.

Baie Co·meau \bā-ˈkō-(ˌ)mō, ˌbā-kə-ˈmō\. Town, Saguenay co., SE Quebec, Canada; pop. (1966c) 12,236.

Baie d'Ur·fé \ˌbā-dər-ˈfā\. Town, Montreal and Jesus Islands co., S Quebec, Canada, 9 m. SW of Montreal; pop. (1971p) 3886.

Baie Saint Paul \ˌbā-sānt-ˈpȯl\. Town, ⊗ of West Charlevoix co., S Quebec, Canada, on St. Lawrence river 57 m. NE of Quebec; pop. (1966c) 4702; summer resort; hunting and fishing.

Bai·kal, Lake *or* **Lake Bay·kal** \-bī-ˈkȯl, -ˈkäl\. Lake in S Siberia, U.S.S.R., chiefly within the Buryat A.S.S.R.; 395 m. long; 11,780 sq. m.; max. depth 5715 ft.; the largest freshwater basin in Eurasia. Two thirds of its W shore, with the Baikal Mts., and its S end, with the Angara outlet, lie in Irkutsk Oblast; it receives on the E the Barguzin and Selenga rivers. Island of Olkhon is in its center. Discovered 1643.

Baikal Mountains. Mountain range, U.S.S.R., W shore of Lake Baikal (*q.v.*), mostly in Irkutsk Oblast; highest peak 6890 ft.

Bai·ko·nur \ˌbī-kə-ˈnu̇r\. Locality, Karaganda Oblast, Kazakh S.S.R., U.S.S.R., ab. 150 m. NE of the Aral Sea; site of principal Soviet missile and rocket-testing facility, from which have been launched all major Soviet manned and unmanned earth satellites and interplanetary probes.

Bai·lan *or* **Bei·lan** \ba-ˈlän\ *or anc.* **Syr·i·ae Por·tae** \ˌsir-ē-ˌē-ˈpȯrt-ē, -ˈpȯrt-\ *or Eng.* **Syr·i·an Gates** \ˌsir-ē-ən-\. 1 Mountain pass, Hatay prov., S Turkey, S of İskenderun; cuts through the Nur Mts.; connected ancient Cilicia with Syria.

2 Town, Hatay prov., S Turkey, just S of İskenderun.

Bail·don \ˈbā(ə)l-dən\. Urban district, West Riding, Yorkshire, N England, 7 m. N of Bradford; pop. (1971p) 14,690.

Baile Atha Cliath. See DUBLIN 5.

Bai·lén \bī-ˈlān, -ˈlen\. Commune, Jaén prov., S Spain, 20 m. N of Jaén; pop. (1970p) 13,233; galena and zinc blende mined nearby; Spaniards defeated French July 1808.

Bai·ley \ˈbā-lē\. County in Texas. See table at TEXAS.

Bailey, Mount. Peak, NW of Crater Lake, SW Oregon; 8363 ft.

Bai·ley·ville \ˈbā-lē-ˌvil\. Town, Washington co., SE Maine, on St. Croix river 8 m. SW of Calais; pop. (1970c) 2167.

Bail·leul \bä-'yə(r)l\. Manufacturing city, Nord dept., N France, near Belgian frontier 15 m. NW of Lille; pop. (1968c) 13,077; made free commune by counts of Flanders; became French 1678; devastated in World War I.

Bain·bridge \'bān-brij\. 1 Island in Puget Sound 10 miles directly W of Seattle, Washington, in Kitsap co.; 26 sq. m.
2 City, ⊗ of Decatur co., SW Georgia, on Flint river 13 m. N of Florida border; pop. (1970c) 10,887; barge terminal.

Baird \'ba(ə)rd, 'be(ə)rd\. City, ⊗ of Callahan co., N cen. Texas, 20 m. E of Abilene; pop. (1970c) 1538; cotton, wheat.

Baird Mountains. Mountain range, W end of Brooks Range, NW Alaska, S of Noatak river.

Baireuth. See BAYREUTH.

Bairns·dale \'ba(ə)rnz-ˌdāl, 'be(ə)rnz-\. Town, Victoria, SE Australia, on coast E of Melbourne; pop. (1966c) 7785.

Bai·ro·ko \bī-'rō-(ˌ)kō\. Village on **Bairoko Harbour** (an inlet of Kula Gulf), NW coast of New Georgia I., cen. Solomon Is.; Japanese supply base bombed by Americans July and Aug. 1943; captured Aug. 25.

Ba·is \'bä-ˌēs\. Chartered city, E Negros Oriental, Negros, Phil., on Tanon Strait; pop. (1970e) 47,000.

Bai·ta·ra·ni \bī-'tär-ə-nē\. River, E India; ab. 250 m. long; rises in NE Orissa and flows into the Bay of Bengal.

Ba·ja \'bȯ-(ˌ)yȯ\. City, S Hungary, ab. 60 m. W of Szeged on Danube river; pop. (1970p) 34,360; textiles; trades in corn and cattle; engineering coll. (1962).

Baja Ca·li·for·nia \ˌbä-(ˌ)hä-ˌkal-ə-'fȯr-nyə, -nē-ə\ *or* **Lower California.** Peninsula extending SSE bet. the Pacific Ocean and the Gulf of California, NW Mexico; divided into 2 sections: a state, **Baja California,** to the N, and a territory, **Baja California Sur** \-'sü(ə)r\, to the S (see table at MEXICO). Discovered by Spanish 1533–34; most successfully settled by Jesuit missions (from late 17th cent.); separated from Alta (Upper) California 1772.

Baja Ve·ra·paz \'bä-(ˌ)hä-ˌver-ə-'päz, -'päs\. Department of cen. Guatemala. See table at GUATEMALA.

Baj·ram Cur·ri \bī-'räm-'kü(ə)r-ē\. Town, ✱ of Tropojë prov., N Albania; pop. (1967e) 2415.

Ba·jur Bay \'ba-jər-\ *or formerly* **Ko·ning·in·ne Bay** \ˌkō-niŋ-'in-ə-\. Inlet of Indian Ocean, W coast of Sumatra, Indonesia; on its NW shore is Telukbajur, port of Padang.

Bakan. See SHIMONOSEKI.

Ba·kar·ganj *or* **Back·er·gunge** \ˌbäk-ər-'gənj\. Former district, Bengal prov., Brit. India; now part of Bangla Desh; 3783 sq. m.

Ba·ker \'bā-kər\. 1 Name of counties in three states of the U.S. See tables at FLORIDA, GEORGIA, OREGON.
2 City, E Baton Rouge parish, SE cen. Louisiana, 10 m. N of Baton Rouge; pop. (1970c) 8281; agriculture.
3 City, ⊗ of Fallon co., E Montana; pop. (1970c) 2584.
4 City, ⊗ of Baker co., E Oregon, on fork of Powder river ab. 40 m. SSE of La Grande; pop. (1970c) 9354; lumber; gold, silver, copper mines nearby; Baker Coll. (1957); settled in 1863; became ⊗ 1868, incorp. 1874.

Baker, Mount. 1 Peak, NE Grand co., N Colorado; 12,406 ft.
2 Peak in Cascade Range, cen. Whatcom co., NW Washington; 10,778 ft.

Baker Butte. Butte in cen. Arizona, at S border of the Mogollon Rim; 8077 ft. high.

Baker Island. Small island (atoll) in cen. Pacific Ocean near the equator at long. 176°31′W; less than 1 sq. m. Visited for guano 1850 to 1890; claimed by U.S. and Great Britain; occupied by colonists (Hawaiians) for U.S. 1935 and formally proclaimed U.S. territory 1936. Abandoned by U.S. forces early in 1942; reoccupied without opposition Aug. 1944. See HOWLAND ISLAND.

Baker Lake. Lake, the expansion of upper (W) Chesterfield Inlet, cen. Keewatin dist., Northwest Territories, Canada; 975 sq. m.; receives outlet of Aberdeen Lake at NW and Kazan river in S.

Ba·kers·field \'bā-kərz-ˌfēld\. City, ⊗ of Kern co., S California, on Kern river at S end of San Joaquin valley; pop. (1970c) 69,515; oil wells; oil refining; steel castings, electronic components.

Ba·kers·ville \'bā-kərz-ˌvil\. Town, ⊗ of Mitchell co., W North Carolina; pop. (1970c) 409; mica mines.

Bakh·chi·sa·rai \ˌbäk-chi-sə-'rī\. Town, S Crimean Oblast, Ukrainian S.S.R., U.S.S.R., on railroad 15 m. SSW of Simferopol; copper articles; from 15th cent. to 1783 capital of Tatar khanate.

Bakhmut. See ARTEMOVSK.

Bakh·tī·a·rī \bäk-'tē-ə-rē\. Mountainous region in W Iran; highest peaks above 12,000 ft.

Bakhtīarī va Cha·har Ma·hāll \-ˌvä-'chä-ˌhär-mə-'häl\. Governorship of W cen. Iran. See table at IRAN.

Bakh·ti·gān \ˌbak-ti-'gän\ *or* **Ni·riz** \ni-'rēz\. Salt lake, N cen. Fārs prov., SW Iran; 10 m. long; formerly 60 m. long.

Ba·kır·köy \ˌbäk-ˌi(ə)r-'kȯi, -'kəi\. Suburban district, İstanbul prov., Turkey in Europe; 112 sq. m.; its chief town, Bakırköy, is SW of İstanbul near coast of Sea of Marmara.

Ba·kony Forest \'bȯ-ˌkōn-yə-\ *or Ger.* **Ba·ko·nyer·wald** \'bäk-ən-yər-ˌvält\. Mountain range bet. the Rába (Raab) river and Lake Balaton, Hungary; av. alt. 2000 ft.

Ba·koy *or* **Ba·koye** \bä-'kȯi\. River, W Mali, W Africa; ab. 300 m. long; a headstream uniting with the Bafing to form the Senegal; chief tributary the Baoulé.

Ba·ku \bä-'kü\. City, ✱ of Azerbaijan S.S.R., U.S.S.R., a port on SW shore of the Apsheron Penin. on the W coast of the Caspian Sea; pop. (1970p) 1,261,000; center of one of the most extensive oil-producing regions in U.S.S.R.; oil refineries; cement, chemicals, textiles; food processing; shipbuilding; univ. (1920).

History: Old part of city dates back to 9th cent.; has Arabic and 11th cent. Persian architectural remains; Persian town 1509 to 1723; seized by Russians 1723 but restored 1735; finally incorporated in Russia 1806; suffered from disastrous fires and riots 1901, 1904–05, and during the civil war of 1917–21; made capital of Bolshevist government 1917; occupied by British troops July 1918–Aug. 1919; became capital of new republic of Azerbaijan 1920.

Bakwanga. See MBUJI-MAYI.

Ba·la·bac \bə-'läb-ˌäk\. Island, SW Phil., SW of Palawan I.; 125 sq. m.; part of Palawan prov.; Balabac town (pop. [1969e] 6300) on E coast has good harbor.

Balabac Strait. Passage bet. S end of Balabac I., Phil., and islands off N coast of Sabah, Borneo; 34 m. wide; connects Sulu Sea with South China Sea.

Ba·la·ba·la·gan Islands \ˌbäl-ə-bə-ˌläg-ən-\ *or* **Little Pa·ter·nos·ters** \-'pat-ər-ˌnäs-tərz, -'pät-\. Group of about 30 low coral islets in W cen. Makasar Strait, bet. Borneo and Celebes, Indonesia.

Balaclava. See BALAKLAVA.

Ba·la·ghat \'bäl-ə-ˌgät\. 1 District, Madhya Pradesh, India; 3573 sq. m.; pop. (1961c) 806,702.
2 Town, its ✱, on Wainganga river NE of Nagpur; pop. (1961c) 18,990.

Ba·lah Lakes \ˌbal-ə-\. Contiguous lakes, N Egypt, on W side of Suez Canal at its N end; contain several islands; connected with Lake Manzala.

Ba·lakh·na \bə-'läk-nə\. Town, Gorki Oblast, Russian S.F.S.R., U.S.S.R., ab. 25 m. NW of Gorki; pop. (1967e) 33,000.

Ba·la·kla·va *also* **Ba·la·cla·va** \ˌbal-ə-'klav-ə, -'kläv-; ˌbäl-ə-'kläv-\. Seaport village, SW coast of Crimean Oblast, Ukrainian S.S.R., U.S.S.R., 8 m. SE of Sevastopol; scene Oct. 25, 1854 of indecisive battle of Crimean War memorable for charge of Light Brigade.

Ba·la·ko·vo \bə-'läk-ə-ˌvō\. Town, Saratov Oblast, Russian S.F.S.R., U.S.S.R., ab. 85 m. WNW of Saratov; pop. (1970p) 103,000.

Bala Lake \ˌbal-ə-\. Lake, E Merionethshire, Wales; ab. 4 m. long; source of Dee river; largest natural lake in Wales but smaller than the artificial Lake Vyrnwy (*q.v.*).

Ba·lam·ban \ˌbäl-əm-'bän\. Municipality, W coast of Cebu I., Phil., on Tanon Strait; pop. (1969e) 51,600.

Ba·lam·bang·an \ˌbäl-əm-ˈbäŋ-ən\. Island, N Sabah, East Malaysia, just S of main channel of Balabac Strait; British settlement here 1762–75.

Ba·lan·ga \bə-ˈläŋ-gə\. Municipality, ✱ of Bataan prov., Luzon, Phil., near E coast in central part; pop. (1969e) 24,900; taken by Japanese Feb. 1942.

Ba·lan·guin·gui \ˌbäl-ən-ˈgiŋ-gē\. 1 Former name of Samales (*q.v.*) group of islands, Sulu Archipelago, Phil.
2 Most important island of the group, ab. 18 m. E of E tip of Jolo I.; 1 sq. m.

Ba·la·shi·kha \ˌbal-ə-ˈshē-kə\. Town, Moscow Oblast, Russian S.F.S.R., U.S.S.R., ab. 14 m. ENE of Moscow; pop. (1969e) 78,000; textiles.

Ba·la·shov \ˌbäl-ə-ˈshȯf, -ˈshȯv\. Town, SW Saratov Oblast, Russian S.F.S.R., U.S.S.R., 110 m. W of Saratov; pop. (1969e) 76,000; food processing; heavy machinery.

Ba·la·si·nor \ˌbäl-ə-si-ˈnȯ(ə)r\. 1 Former Indian state, now part of Gujarat state, W India; 195 sq. m.
2 Town, its ✱, 45 m. E of Ahmadabad.

Ba·la·sore \ˈbəl-ə-ˌsō(ə)r, ˈbäl-, -ˌsȯ(ə)r\. 1 District, E Orissa, E India, on coast of Bay of Bengal; 2500 sq. m.; pop. (1961c) 1,415,923.
2 Town, its ✱, SW of Calcutta; pop. (1961c) 33,931.

Ba·las·sa·gyar·mat \ˌbȯ-lə-shə-ˈjä(ə)r-ˌmät\. City, N Hungary, 42 m. N of Budapest; pop. (1970p) 13,745.

Bal·a·ton, Lake \-ˈbal-ə-ˌtän, -ˈbȯl-ə-ˌtōn\ *or Ger.* **Plat·ten·see** \ˈplät-ᵊn-ˌzā\. Lake, W Hungary, 55 m. SW of Budapest; 232 sq. m.; max. depth 35 ft.; largest lake in central Europe; has many resorts on its shores.

Ba·la·ton·fü·red \ˈbal-ə-ˌtän-ˈfyü(ə)r-ˌed, ˈbȯl-ə-ˌtōn-, -ˈfᵫe-ˌred\ *or* **Füred.** Village, W Hungary, on N shore of Lake Balaton.

Ba·la·yan \ˌbäl-ə-ˈyän\. Municipality on SW coast of Batangas prov., Luzon, Phil., on NW shore of Balayan Bay 26 m. NW of Batangas; pop. (1969e) 32,400.

Balayan Bay. Large inlet of South China Sea in SW Batangas prov., Phil.; from 14 to 16 m. wide; Cape Santiago is its SW point and Maricaban I. lies to SE.

Bal·bi \ˈbäl-bē\. Active volcano in Emperor Range, NW Bougainville I., Solomon Is., W Pacific Ocean; 8999 ft.; highest point on the island.

Bal·boa \bal-ˈbō-ə\. 1 District occupying SE part of Canal Zone; 222 sq. m.; pop. (1970p) 33,050.
2 Town, Balboa dist., adjacent to Panama at Pacific entrance to Panama Canal; pop. (1970p) 2568.

Balboa Heights. Suburb of Balboa; location of U.S. administrative center for the Canal Zone.

Bal·brig·gan \bal-ˈbrig-ən\. Seaport and manufacturing town, NE coast of co. Dublin, E Eire, 19 m. NNE of Dublin; pop. (1966c) 3248; linen, cotton, calico.

Bal·car·ce \bäl-ˈkär-(ˌ)sā\. Town, Buenos Aires prov., E cen. Argentina; pop. (1960c) 20,540.

Balch Springs \ˈbȯlch-\. Town, Dallas co., Texas, E suburb of Dallas; pop. (1970c) 10,464.

Bal·clu·tha \bal-ˈklü-thə\. Borough near mouth of Clutha river, SE South I., New Zealand; pop. (1968e) 4570.

Bal·co·nes Heights \bal-ˌkō-nəs-\. City, Bexar co., S cen. Texas, entirely within city limits of San Antonio; pop. (1970c) 2504.

Bal·degg \ˈbäl-ˌdek\. Lake, N cen. Switzerland, in N Lucerne canton; 3½ m. long; 2 sq. m.; formed by expansion of Aa river.

Bald·face Mountain \ˌbȯl(d)-ˌfās-\. Peak in the Adirondack Mts., Essex co., NE New York; 3903 ft.

Bald Hills \ˈbȯld-\. Range in Pennington co., SW South Dakota; alt. 5000 ft.

Bald Mountain. 1 Peak, Summit co., cen. Colorado; 13,694 ft.
2 Peak, cen. Custer co., cen. Idaho; 10,313 ft.
3 Peak, NW Elmore co., SW cen. Idaho; 9389 ft.
4 Peak, Grant co., E cen. Oregon; 8330 ft.
5 Peak, Lawrence co., W South Dakota; 7000 ft.
6 Peak, S Summit co., NE Utah; 11,947 ft.
7 Peak, Big Horn co., N Wyoming; 10,029 ft.
8 Peak, in Wind River Range, W cen. Wyoming; 10,760 ft.

Bald Mountains. Range of the Appalachian Mts. along the Tennessee-North Carolina boundary, NE of Great Smoky Mts.; highest point ab. 5560 ft.

Bal·dwin \ˈbȯl-dwən\. 1 Name of counties in two states of the U.S. See tables at ALABAMA and GEORGIA.
2 Village, ⊗ of Lake co., W Michigan; pop. (1970c) 612.
3 Unincorp. community, Nassau co., SE New York, S shore of Long I. 23 m. E of Brooklyn; pop. (1970c) 34,525.
4 Borough, Allegheny co., Pennsylvania, on Monongahela river S of Pittsburgh; pop. (1970c) 26,729.

Baldwin City. City, Douglas co., E Kansas; pop. (1970c) 2520; gas wells; Baker Univ. (1858).

Baldwin Park. City, Los Angeles co., California, SE of Monrovia; pop. (1970c) 47,285.

Baldwin Peninsula. See KOTZEBUE.

Bal·dwins·ville \ˈbȯl-dwənz-ˌvil\. Village, Onondaga co., cen. New York, on N.Y. State Barge Canal 14 m. NW of Syracuse; pop. (1970c) 6298; natural gas deposits nearby.

Baldy, Mount \-ˈbȯl-dē\. 1 Mountain, California. See SAN ANTONIO PEAK 1.
2 Peak, E Beaver co., SW Utah; 12,000 ft.

Baldy Mountain. Mountain, Manitoba, Canada, ab. 120 m. NNW of Brandon; 2729 ft.; highest peak in Manitoba.

Baldy Peak. 1 Mountain, S Apache co., E Arizona; 11,590 ft. Also known as **Thom·as Peak** \ˌtäm-əs-\.
2 Mountain, New Mexico. See SANTA FE BALDY.
3 Mountain, W Texas. See LIVERMORE, MOUNT.

Ba·le \ˈbäl-ā\. Province of S Ethiopia. See table at ETHIOPIA.

Bâle. See BASEL.

Bal·e·ar·ic Islands \ˌbal-ē-ˌar-ik-\ *or Span.* **Is·las Ba·le·a·res** \ˈēz-(ˌ)läs-ˌbäl-ē-ˈär-əs\. Island group in W Mediterranean Sea near E coast of Spain; 1936 sq. m.; pop. (1970p) 558,287; forms Spanish province of **Baleares** (see table at SPAIN); comprises the islands of Majorca, Minorca, Ibiza, Formentera, Cabrera (*qq.v.*), and 11 smaller islands; popular resort, noted esp. for its picturesque scenery and mild climate; produces fruits, wine, grain, cattle; fishing.
History: Became part of Carthaginian empire 5th cent. B.C.; conquered by Rome c. 123 B.C.; overrun by Vandals 465 A.D.; reconquered for Byzantine Empire by Belisarius 534; raided by Arabs in 9th cent. but not permanently conquered until early 10th cent. by Ommiad line at Córdoba (*q.v.*); kingdom of Mallorca taken by James I of Aragon 1229–35 and made a separate kingdom for his son, united to kingdom of Aragon by Pedro IV 1344; Minorca held by British 1708–56, 1763–82, 1798–1802.

Balearis Major. See MAJORCA.

Ba·ler Bay \bä-ˈle(ə)r-\. Inlet of Pacific Ocean on E coast of Luzon, Phil., 15°50′N, 121°37′E. Near its head on short stream is municipality of **Baler** (pop. [1969e] 14,000), which has one of best harbors on Pacific coast of Luzon; occupied by U.S. troops Apr. 14, 1900; in World War II occupied by Japanese; seized by Americans Feb. 12, 1945.

Balesh. See ELVAS.

Baleswar. See GANGES DELTA.

Ba·le·te Pass \bə-ˌlät-ē-\. Pass in Caraballo Mts., SW Nueva Vizcaya prov., Luzon, Phil., on main highway bet. cen. Luzon and Cagayan valley in the N.

Bal·frin \bäl-ˈfrēn\. Peak in the Pennine Alps, in Valais canton, SW cen. Switzerland; 12,454 ft.

Balfrush. See BĀBOL.

Ba·li \ˈbäl-ē, ˈbal-\. Island, Indonesia, off E end of Java and bet. Bali Sea and Indian Ocean, westernmost of the Lesser Sunda Is.; constitutes with minor adjacent islands, a province (2171 sq. m.; pop. [1970e] 2,247,000; ✱ Denpasar); mountainous, with highest peaks in E (Gunung Agung 10,308 ft.) and N cen. part; at S end has low hook-shaped peninsula; lacks good harbors; its rivers are mostly unnavigable and generally run S from the N plateau; has luxuriant vegetation and grows a great variety of tropical products: rice, sweet potatoes, cassava; copra; meat processing; tourism.

History: Colonized direct from India in early times, its civilization is Hindu; many fine old temples; little contact with Dutch before 19th cent., when Balinese princes recognized Dutch supremacy but retained local autonomy; native piracy overcome by Dutch expedition 1846; bet. 1882 and 1908 came definitely under Dutch government; naval battle Feb. 19, 1942 off SE coast in Badung Strait, won by Allied Nations, did not prevent occupation of island by Japanese, who made landing Feb. 20; surrendered to Allies Sept. 1945.

Bali, Peak of. See AGUNG, GUNUNG.

Bali and Lom·bok \-'läm-ˌbäk\. Residency of the former Neth. Indies, comprising the islands of Bali and Lombok; now part of the Indonesian provs. of Bali and West Nusa Tenggara.

Ba·lı·ke·sir \ˌbäl-i-ke-'si(ə)r\. **1** Province of NW Turkey, Asia. See table at TURKEY.

2 City, its ✱, on tributary of the Simav 50 m. S of Sea of Marmara; pop. (1965c) 69,341; textiles, leather goods.

Ba·likh \bə-'lēk\. River, W Asia; ab. 120 m. long; rises in S Turkey N of Urfa and flows S to the Euphrates in N Syria near Rakka.

Ba·lik·pa·pan \ˌbäl-ik-'päp-ˌän\. Seaport town, SE Borneo, Indonesia, on **Balikpapan Bay** 225 m. NE of Bandjarmasin; pop. (1961c) 91,706; has become one of the major oil centers of Borneo. Naval engagement off the bay Jan. 24, 1942 bet. U.S. destroyers and Japanese warships; occupied by Japanese 1942–45.

Ba·lin·ga·sag \ˌbäl-iŋ-gə-'säg\. Municipality, Mindanao, Phil., on E shore of Macajalar Bay; pop. (1969e) 26,600.

Ba·lin·tang Channel \ˌbäl-ən-ˌtäŋ-\. Strait bet. Batan Is. on the N and Babuyan Is. on the S, N Phil.; 50 m. wide; connects Philippine Sea and South China Sea.

Bali Sea. Body of water bet. Kangean Is. on the N and Bali on the S, Indonesia; forms SW part of Flores Sea; Madura Strait opens into it from the W.

Bali Strait. Channel bet. E end of Java and W end of Bali, Indonesia, connecting Bali Sea with the Indian Ocean; only 1 m. wide at narrowest point just N of Banjuwangi, Java.

Ba·li·uag \bä-'lē-(ˌ)wäg\. Municipality, W Bulacan prov., Luzon, Phil., on right bank of Angat river 10 m. NE of Malolos; pop. (1969e) 51,400; rice market. Taken by American forces May 2, 1899 during Philippine rebellion; lost to Japanese Dec. 1941; retaken Jan. 1945.

Bal·kan Mountains \ˌbȯl-kən-\ *or Bulg.* **Sta·ra Pla·ni·na** \'stär-ə-ˌplän-i-'nä\ *or anc.* **Hae·mus** \'hē-məs\. Range of mountains extending E and W across cen. Bulgaria from Yugoslav border to the Black Sea; highest point Botev Peak 7793 ft.; crossed by Shipka Pass, N of Kazanlŭk.

Balkan Peninsula. Peninsula in SE Europe bet. the Adriatic and Ionian Seas on the W, the Mediterranean Sea on the S, and the Aegean and Black Seas on the E.

Balkan States \'bȯl-kən-\ *or* **Bal·kans** \-kənz\. Countries occupying the Balkan Peninsula: Albania, Bulgaria, Greece, Romania, and Turkey (in Europe).

History: For earlier history, see GREECE and MACEDONIA. Incorporated as Roman provinces 168 B.C.–107 A.D. (see EPIRUS, ACHAEA, MACEDONIA, DALMATIA, MOESIA, PANNONIA, THRACE, DACIA, and ILLYRIA); settled by Slavic invaders, Serbs, Croats, Slovenes, and Slavonized Bulgars, who were pushed into Balkan region in 6th cent.; gradually organized into kingdoms (see BULGARIA, CROATIA, SERBIA, and BOSNIA); except for Montenegro, conquered by Ottoman Turks 14th and 15th cents.; aroused by nationalism and encouraged by decline of Turkish authority, began series of revolts against Turkish rule 1804 (see SERBIA); independence of region, alternately supported and opposed by the Great Powers, was part of issue of European politics known as "Eastern Question"; by 1912, Greece (1829), Serbia, Montenegro, and Romania (all in 1878), and Bulgaria (1908) were recognized as independent states, Croatia, Dalmatia, Bosnia, and Herzegovina belonged to Austria-Hungary, and Macedonia remained in Turkish hands; in First Balkan War 1912–13, Bulgaria, Serbia, Montenegro, and Greece took Macedonia from Turkey, and the independence of Albania (*q.v.*) was proclaimed; in Second Balkan War 1913, former allies and Romania united against Bulgaria; in World War I which was precipitated by Austrian demands on Serbia, only Bulgaria joined Central Powers; Romania, Yugoslavia, Greece, and Turkey signed Balkan Pact 1934, Bulgaria not joining because of desire for revision of boundaries she received by peace treaties of World War I; in World War II, Albania became Italian 1939, Bulgaria joined Axis, Greece was conquered by Germany, and Yugoslavia and Romania were occupied by Axis forces 1941. Yugoslavia 1945, Albania and Bulgaria 1946 proclaimed republics; peace treaties with Bulgaria and Romania signed by United Nations Feb. 10, 1947.

Balkaria. See KABARDINO-BALKARIAN AUTONOMOUS SOVIET SOCIALIST REPUBLIC.

Balkh \'bälk\. **1** Province, N Afghanistan; 5849 sq. m.; pop. (1969e) 353,722; ✱ Mazār-i-Sharīf; approx. coextensive with ancient Bactria (*q.v.*); in medieval times on trade route bet. India and Europe.

2 *or anc.* **Bac·tra** \'bak-trə\. Ancient city, ✱ of Bactria; once a center of Zoroastrianism; twice destroyed, first by Genghis Khan and later by Tamerlane; after great cholera epidemic in 19th cent. reduced to village (Wazīrābād) near Mazār-i-Sharīf.

3 Village, N Afghanistan, just N of Wazīrābād (site of anc. Balkh).

Bal·khash *or Turk.* **Bal·qash** \bal-'kash, bäl-'käsh\. Town on N shore of Lake Balkhash, E Kazakh S.S.R., U.S.S.R.; pop. (1969e) 77,000; metal refining, fish canning.

Balkhash, Lake *or Turk.* **Balqash.** Freshwater lake in SE Kazakh S.S.R., U.S.S.R., 600 m. E of the Aral Sea; 376 m. long; 7115 sq. m.; max. depth 85 ft.; frozen Nov.–March; its chief feeder is the I-li entering at SE in a wide delta.

Ball, Mount \-'bȯl\. Peak in SW Canada, on border bet. Alberta and British Columbia; 10,865 ft.

Bal·la·rat \'bal-ə-ˌrat\. City, S cen. Victoria, SE Australia, 70 m. WNW of Melbourne; pop. (1968e) 41,910; paper, engineering products; school of mines; a former gold-mining town; founded 1851.

Bal·lard \'bal-ərd\. County in Kentucky. See table at KENTUCKY.

Ballari. See BELLARY.

Bal·la·ter \'bal-ət-ər\. Village, Aberdeen co., NE Scotland, on the Dee E of Balmoral; pop. (1971p) 982; medicinal springs (see PANNANICH) nearby.

Bal·le·ny Islands \ˌbal-ə-nē-\. Group of volcanic islands in Ross Dependency, Antarctica, ab. 66°S and 163°E.

Bal·lia \'bäl-ē-ə\. **1** District, Uttar Pradesh, N India; 1183 sq. m.; pop. (1961c) 1,335,863; barley, rice.

2 Town, its ✱, near N bank of Ganges; pop. (1961c) 38,216.

Bal·li·na \'bal-ə-nə\. Urban district, N co. Mayo, NW Eire, on Moy river; pop. (1971p) 6056; trade center; salmon fisheries and fish curing; linen weaving.

Bal·li·na·muck \ˌbal-ə-nə-'mək\. Village, N co. Longford, N cen. Eire; scene of surrender 1798 of Irish insurrectionary forces.

Bal·li·na·sloe \ˌbal-ə-nə-'slō\. Urban district, E co. Galway, W Eire; pop. (1971p) 5958; annual cattle fair.

Bal·lin·ger \'bal-ən-jər\. City, ⊗ of Runnels co., W cen. Texas, 32 m. NE of San Angelo; pop. (1970c) 4203; meat packing; oil wells.

Bal·lin·skel·ligs Bay \ˌbal-ən-ˌskel-igz-\. Inlet of Atlantic on SW coast of Ireland, N of Kenmare river.

Ball's Bluff \'bȯlz-\. Locality in Loudoun co., NE Virginia, on the Potomac 33 m. NW of Washington; battle Oct. 21, 1861 in which Union force was severely defeated, a conflict of no military importance but one which aroused much criticism in the North.

Ball·ston Spa \ˌbȯl-stən-ˈspä, -ˈspȯ\. Village, ⊗ of Saratoga co., E New York, ab. 6 m. SW of Saratoga Springs; pop. (1970c) 4968; resort; mineral springs; founded c. 1787.

Ball·win \ˈbȯl-wən\. City, St. Louis co., Missouri, W of St. Louis; pop. (1970c) 10,656.

Bal·ly \ˈbäl-ē\. Town, West Bengal, India, on Hooghly river across from Calcutta; pop. (1961c) 130,896.

Bal·ly·me·na \ˌbal-ē-ˈmē-nə\. Municipal borough, co. Antrim, NE Northern Ireland; pop. (1971p) 16,485; linen goods, tobacco.

Bal·ly·na·hinch \ˌbal-ə-nə-ˈhinch\. Town, co. Down, SE Northern Ireland, 14 m. S of Belfast; battle 1798 in which United Irishmen were defeated by the yeomanry.

Bal·main \bal-ˈmān\. City, E New South Wales, SE Australia, industrial suburb W of Sydney on Parramatta river; chemical works, shipyards.

Bal·maz·új·vá·ros \ˈbȯl-ˌmȯz-ˌü-ē-ˈvär-(ˌ)ōsh\. Commune, E cen. Hungary, W of Debrecen; pop. (1970p) 17,423.

Bal·mor·al \bal-ˈmȯr-əl, -ˈmär-\. Castle in SW Aberdeen co., Scotland, on the Dee river E of Braemar; Scottish residence of British sovereigns; purchased 1852 by Prince Albert who bequeathed it to Queen Victoria.

Balqash. See BALKHASH.

Bal·quhid·der \bal-ˈhwid-ər\. Village and parish, S Perth co., Scotland, ab. 28 m. NW of Stirling; district won by Macgregor clan 1558; in the churchyard is grave of Rob Roy who died here 1734.

Bal·sam Lake \ˌbȯl-səm-\. Village, ⊗ of Polk co., NW Wisconsin; pop. (1970c) 648.

Balsar. See BULSAR.

Bal·sas, Río de las \ˈrē-(ˌ)ō-ˌdā-läs-ˈbȯl-səs, -ˈbäl-\ *also* **Mex·ca·la** \mäs-ˈkäl-ə\. River, cen. Mexico; 426 m. long; rises in Tlaxcala state, flows S and then W through Guerrero into Petacalco Bay; its lower course forms boundary bet. Michoacán and Guerrero.

Bal·ta \ˈbäl-tə, ˈbȯl-\. Town, Odessa Oblast, Ukrainian S.S.R., U.S.S.R., on a tributary of the Bug river ab. 112 m. NNW of Odessa; pop. (1967e) 20,000; center of an agricultural region raising especially grain and cattle; a Turkish town, formerly in Podolia; became Russian by treaty 1792; capital of Moldavian A.S.S.R. 1924–29; in World War II held by Germans 1941–44.

Bălţi. See BELTSY.

Baltic Port. See PALDISKI.

Bal·tic Provinces \ˈbȯl-tik-\. The former Russian governments of Estonia, Livonia, and Kurland, which in 1918 were formed into the independent republics of Estonia and Latvia. See BALTIC STATES.

Baltic Sea *or Ger.* **Ost·see** \ˈȯst-ˌzā\ *or Russ.* **Bal·ti·sko·ye Mo·re** \bəlt-ˌyē-skə-yə-ˈmȯr-yə\ *or anc.* **Ma·re Sue·vi·cum** \ˌmā-rē-ˈswē-vi-kəm, ˌmär-(ˌ)ā-\. Sea in N Europe, an arm of the Atlantic Ocean connecting with the North Sea through the Skaggerak, Kattegat, and Øresund, and extending roughly NE to SW bet. 54° and 66°N lat. and 9° and 30°E long.; 1056 m. long; 163,050 sq. m.; max. depth 1539 ft.; enclosed by Denmark, Sweden, Finland, U.S.S.R., (Estonian, Latvian, and Lithuanian S.S.Rs.), Poland, East Germany, and West Germany. Has two large arms: Gulf of Bothnia, its N extension bet. Sweden and Finland, and Gulf of Finland bet. Finland and Estonian S.S.R.

Baltic States. The former republics of Estonia, Latvia, and Lithuania on the E shore of the Baltic Sea, which were established as independent states in 1917 out of the Baltic Provinces (*q.v.*) of Russia and the government of Kovno and part of Wilno (later Lithuania); aided by German and Allied forces in forcing out Bolshevist invasion 1919; incorporated in the U.S.S.R. Aug. 3, 1940; overrun by German forces 1941; recovered by Soviet troops in summer and fall of 1944. Name was sometimes applied to include Finland and Poland as well.

Bal·tīm \bal-ˈtēm\. Town, Egypt, near coast in Nile delta midway bet. Rosetta and Damietta mouths and at E end of Lake Burullus; pop. (1966p) 16,100.

Bal·ti·more \ˈbȯl-tə-ˌmō(ə)r, -ˌmȯ(ə)r, -mər\. **1** County in Maryland. See table at MARYLAND.

2 City, Maryland, on Patapsco river at upper end of Chesapeake Bay ab. 40 m. NE of Washington; pop. (1970c) 905,759; geographically in S Baltimore co. but administratively independent (see table at MARYLAND); important seaport; manufactures aerospace equipment, electrical insulators, chemicals, steel, electronic equipment; copper and sugar refining; St. Mary's Seminary and Univ. (1791), Coll. of Notre Dame of Maryland (1848), Loyola Coll. (1852), Peabody Conservatory of Music (1857), Mount Saint Agnes Coll. (1867), Morgan State Coll. (1867), Johns Hopkins Univ. (1876), Coppin State Coll. (1900), Univ. of Baltimore (1925), Baltimore Hebrew Coll. (1919), Easter Coll. (1928), Community Coll. of Baltimore (1947); Mount Providence Junior Coll. (1952), Trinitarian Coll. (1956).

History: Purchased by Maryland legislature 1729 and made a shipbuilding and export center; during American Revolution, meeting place for American Congress during the British occupation of Philadelphia; incorporated as city 1797; bombardment of its Fort McHenry by British Sept. 12–13, 1814 inspired Francis Scott Key to write the *Star Spangled Banner;* in 1827 local merchants organized Baltimore and Ohio R.R. to retain share in trans-Allegheny trade which the Erie Canal threatened to draw entirely to New York; during Civil War, sympathy with the South occasioned riots when Union troops marched through Apr. 19, 1861; suffered from a destructive fire Feb. 7, 1904.

Bal·tisk \bəl-ˈtēsk\ *or Ger.* **Pil·lau** \ˈpil-ˌau̇\. Town, on sandspit at entrance of the Vislinski Zaliv, Russian S.F.S.R., U.S.S.R., formerly in East Prussia, Germany; pop. (1967e) 17,000; shipbuilding, fishing. Site of landing of Gustavus Adolphus 1626. Assigned to U.S.S.R. at Potsdam Conference 1945.

Baltiski. See PALDISKI.

Baltiskoye More. See BALTIC SEA.

Bal·ti·stan \ˌbȯl-tə-ˈstan, ˌbəl-\ *or* **Little Ti·bet** \-tə-ˈbet\. Part of Ladakh frontier district in Pakistani-controlled sector of Jammu and Kashmir state, bet. 34° and 36°N lat. and 75° and 77°E long.; contains some of highest peaks of W Himalayas; inhabited by Baltis, a non-Mongol Muslim people.

Bal·to·ro \bȯl-ˈtō(ə)r-ō, bäl-, -ˈtȯ(ə)r-\. Glacier, Karakoram Range, in region administered by Pakistan; 35 m. long, ab. 2 m. wide near its terminus.

Ba·lū·che·stān va Sīstān \bə-ˌlü-chi-ˈstän-ˌvä-si-ˈstän\. Province of SE Iran. See table at IRAN.

Ba·lu·chi·stan *also* **Be·luch·i·stan** \bə-ˌlü-chi-ˈstan, -ˈstän\. **1** Region, W Asia, encompassing territory lying in E Iran and SW Pakistan. Iranian sector (formerly called **Persian Baluchistan**) part of Kermān prov. until it united with Sīstān (1959) forming Balūchestān va Sīstān prov. For Pakistani sector, see 2 below.

2 Province, SW Pakistan, bounded on N by Afghanistan, on E by provs. of North-West Frontier, Punjab, and Sind, on S by the Arabian Sea, and on E by Iran; 133,107 sq. m.; pop. (1969e) 1,483,999; ✱ Quetta; mountainous, esp. in NE; Sulaiman Range on NE border, Kirthar Range on SE; ranges of 5000 ft. in cen. part; Hamuni-Mashkel marsh and desert in NW; much of land is barren with irregular and scant water supply, but with some fertile valleys. *Rivers:* Mashkel, Dasht, Hingol, Hab. *Chief cities:* Quetta, Kalat.

History: In ancient times, part of Gedrosia; traversed by Alexander the Great 325 B.C.; part of Bactrian kingdom (see BALKH 2); ruled from 7th–10th cents. A.D. by Arabs who overthrew Persia; except for period when part of Mogul Empire 1594–1638, returned to moderate form of Persian rule; under Nasir Khan of Kalat (1739–95), most able of its princes, included several districts of Sind; by treaty of 1876 made virtually a British dependency; districts, assigned at close of Afghan War (1878–79), enlarged; made British province of India 1887; boundaries with Afghanistan and Persia settled 1885 and 1896; its subdivisions (1) **British Baluchistan** (9084 sq. m.; ✱ Quetta), (2) Agency territories (43,613 sq. m.; ✱ Quetta), (3) Kalat (in cen. part; 59,068 sq. m.; ✱ Kalat), (4) Kharan (in NW part; 14,210 sq. m.), and (5) Las Bela (in SE part; 7132 sq. m.) became part of Pakistan 1947–48; **Baluchistan States** (a union of Kalat, Kharan, and Las Bela, formed 1952) lost most of its administrative functions 1955; reconstituted as a separate province 1970.

Baluchistan, Persian. See BALUCHISTAN 1.

Ba·lut \bä-'lüt\. Island, larger and westernmost of the Sarangani Is., SW Davao del Sur prov., Mindanao, Phil.; 22 sq. m.; has volcano 3110 ft.

Bal·zar \bal-'zär, -'sär\. Town, Guayas prov., W Ecuador, 55 m. N of Guayaquil; pop. (1962c) 6588.

Bam \'bam, 'bäm\. Town, Kermān prov., SE Iran, on caravan route SE of Kermān; pop. (1966c) 21,761; its trade more important in Middle Ages than in modern times; has citadel held by Afghans 1719–1801.

Ba·ma·ko \'bam-ə-ˌkō\. Town, ✱ of Mali, W Africa, on Niger river ab. 90 m. NE of the Guinea border; met. area pop. (1970e) 387,650; commercial center; terminus of railroad from Dakar in Senegal.

Bam·ba·ta·na \ˌbam-bə-'tän-ə\. Chief settlement, on cen. part of W coast of Choiseul I., British Solomon Is., W Pacific Ocean.

Bam·berg \'bam-ˌbərg\. 1 County in SW South Carolina. See table at SOUTH CAROLINA.

2 Town, its ⊗, 18 m. SW of Orangeburg; pop. (1970c) 3406; lumber; grain farms.

Bamberg \'bam-ˌbərg, 'bäm-ˌbe(ə)rg\. Manufacturing city, Bavaria, West Germany, on Regnitz river near its confluence with the Main 30 m. W of Bayreuth; pop. (1969e) 69,303; textiles, paper, electronic equipment; cathedral (Romanesque-Gothic transition); bishop's palace (1571–76), seminary, observatory; first mentioned in 902.

Bam·burgh *or earlier* **Bam·bor·ough** \'bam-b(ə-)rə\. Civil parish, E Northumberland co., N England, on coast 17 m. SE of Berwick-upon-Tweed; pop. (1961c) 734; as Bamborough was capital of ancient Bernicia and for a time capital of Northumbria.

Bā·mi·ān \ˌbäm-ē-'än\. 1 Valley and pass in W Hindu Kush Mts., NE Afghanistan, ab. 60 m. NNW of Kabul; alt. 12,500 ft.

2 Province of cen. Afghanistan. See table at AFGHANISTAN.

3 City, its ✱, Bāmiān valley, N of the Koh-i-Baba; pop. (1969e) 47,827; ruins of great towers and numerous cave dwellings in the walls of the valley, also two colossal images of Buddhist figures, described 630 A.D. by Chinese traveler Hsüan Tsang. Its early history obscure, but it flourished in 12th cent. under Ghuri dynasty; besieged and destroyed 1221 by Genghis Khan.

Bam·pur \bäm-'pu̇(ə)r\. Town, Balūchestān va Sīstān prov., SE Iran, in a fertile valley; chief town of former Persian Baluchistan.

Bam·ra \'bäm-rə\. Former Indian state, now part of Orissa, E India; 1974 sq. m.; ✱ Deogarh.

Ba·mu \'bäm-(ˌ)ü\. Island in Stanley Pool (*q.v.*) in Congo river, W Africa; belongs to Congo.

Banaba. See OCEAN ISLAND 1.

Ba·na·hao, Mount \-bə-'nä-ˌhau̇\. Extinct volcano, SW Quezon prov., Luzon, Phil., on Laguna border NW of Lucena; 7103 ft.; last serious eruption 1730.

Ba·nam \bə-'nam\. Town, Cambodia, SE Asia, on left bank of the Mekong 30 m. SE of Pnompenh.

Ba·nana \bə-'nan-ə\. 1 River, actually a wide part of the lagoon bet. Canaveral Penin. and Merritt I., Brevard co., E Florida.

2 Seaport town, W Bas-Zaïre prov., W Zaire, on N side of the mouth of Congo river.

Banana Islands. Group of small islands in Atlantic Ocean off S point of Sierra Leone Penin., Sierra Leone, W Africa, once a station for English slave traders.

Ba·na·nal \ˌban-ə-'näl\. Island in Araguaia river, NW Goiás state, Brazil; over 200 m. long.

Banaras. See VARANASI.

Ba·nas \'bən-ˌäs, 'bän-\. River, S Rajasthan, N cen. India; 330 m. long; rises at S end of Aravalli Range in Udaipur, flows NE to the Chambal.

Banas, Cape \-'ban-əs\ *or Arab.* **Ras Ba·nās** \räs-\ *also* **Ras Be·nas** \-'ben-əs\. Cape (*ras*) on E coast of Egypt, projecting into Red Sea N of Foul Bay; 23°54′N, 35°48′E.

Ba·nat \bə-'nät, 'bän-ˌät\. 1 Agricultural region (also known as the Vojvodina, *q.v.*) formerly in S Hungary E of Tisza river, S of the Mureşul, N of the Danube, and W of the Transylvanian Alps; divided bet. Romania and Yugoslavia, except a small strip near Szeged. In Middle Ages, 9th–14th cents., settled chiefly by Magyars and Serbs; fell into neglect under rule of Turks 1552–1718; reclaimed by Maria Theresa (after 1740), incorporated into Hungary 1779, made an Austrian crownland 1849, and reverted to Hungary 1860. After World War I divided bet. Yugoslavia and Romania 1919; in World War II its W part (in Yugoslavia) seized by Hungary 1944–45.

2 Region, W Romania; 7224 sq. m.; formerly part of the Banat region of Hungary, later a province of Romania.

3 Former subprovince in N Yugoslavia; ✱ Veliki Bečkerek (Petrovgrad); later (1929–45) a part of Dunavska co.; since 1945 forms the autonomous region Vojvodina in Yugoslavia.

Ba·na·ue \bə-'nä-ˌwä\. Municipality, NW Ifugao prov., Luzon, Phil., ab. 10 m. N of Kiangan; pop. (1969e) 24,400; in World War II taken by Americans July 1945.

Ban·bridge \ban-'brij\. Urban district, co. Down, SE Northern Ireland, on the Bann river; pop. (1971p) 6816.

Ban·bury \'ban-ˌber-ē, -b(ə-)rē\. Municipal borough, Oxfordshire, cen. England, on the Cherwell 38 m. SE of Birmingham; pop. (1971p) 29,216; cattle market, aluminum works; famous for its Banbury cakes.

Ban·da \'bän-də, 'ban-\. 1 District, Uttar Pradesh, N India; 2950 sq. m.; pop. (1961c) 953,731; rice, millet, cotton.

2 Town, its ✱, on Ken river 95 m. W of Allahabad; pop. (1961c) 37,744; cotton, moss agates.

Banda, La. See LA BANDA.

Banda At·jeh \ˌbän-də-'ä-chē\; *formerly* **Koe·ta·ra·dja** *or* **Ku·ta·ra·ja** \ˌkü-tə-'rä-jə\. Town, ✱ of Atjeh prov., Sumatra, Indonesia; pop. (1961c) 40,067.

Ban·dai \'bän-ˌdī\ *or* **Ban·tai** \-ˌtī\. Volcano in Fukushima prefecture, N cen. Honshū, Japan, N of Lake Inawashiro; 5968 ft.; had four peaks, one of which was blown off in a destructive eruption July 1888.

Banda Islands \'bän-də-, 'ban-\. Island group of the S cen. Moluccas, Indonesia, Malay Archipelago, 66 m. S of E Ceram; 72 sq. m.; pop. (1956e) 13,686; ✱ Bandanaira; comprises three large islands Great Banda, Bandanaira, and Gunung Api, and seven small islands, all of volcanic origin. For centuries important in the spice trade; soil adapted to growing nutmegs, which are indigenous; also produces other spices, coconuts, fruits. Discovered and annexed by Portuguese 1512; conquered by Dutch 1621; settlement and interference of English led to Amboina massacre 1623; held by British 1796–1800 and during Napoleonic Wars; under Japanese control during World War II.

Ban·da·ma \ban-'däm-ə\. River, cen. Ivory Coast, W Africa; 497 m. long; flows S into Atlantic.

Ban·da·nai·ra *or* **Ban·da Ne·i·ra** \ˌbän-də-'nī-rə\. 1 Small island, most important of the Banda Is., Indonesia.

2 Town on the island, ✻ of the Banda Is.; pop. (1956e) 6000; its harbor is formed by close juxtaposition of Great Banda and Gunung Api (*qq.v.*); from 16th to 19th cents., an important trade center for spices.

Banda Ori·en·tal \ˈbän-də-ˌōr-ē-en-ˈtäl, -ˌȯr-\. Former name of URUGUAY.

Bandar. See MACHILIPATNAM.

Ban·dar ʻAb·bās \ban-ˌdär-ə-ˈbäs\ *or* **Ben·der·ab·bas** \ben-ˌder-\ *or* **Bun·der ʻAbbās** \bən-ˌdər-ə-ˈbäs\ *or formerly* **Gombroon** \gäm-ˈbrün\. Seaport, ✻ of Persian Gulf prov., S Iran, on the Strait of Hormuz; pop. (1971e) 38,000; founded 1623 by Shah Abbas I; has long been one of the chief ports of Iran, English and Dutch factories having been established for trade in 17th cent.; exports rugs, wool, dates.

Bandar Besar. See GREAT BANDA.

Bandar–e Len·geh \bən-ˌdär-ə-liŋ-ˈgā\ *or formerly* **Lin·geh.** Seaport town, Persian Gulf prov., S Iran, on the Persian Gulf, opp. W end of Qeshm I. and ab. 100 m. SW of Bandar ʻAbbās; pop. (1966c) 7218. Old trading port, formerly a center for export of pearls; products now chiefly carpets, fruits, tobacco, hides. Held by Arabia from latter part of 18th cent. to 1887.

Bandar–e Pah·la·vī *also* **Pah·le·vī** \ban-ˌdär-ē-ˈpäl-ə-(ˌ)vē\. Town on Caspian Sea, NW Iran; pop. (1971e) 48,000.

Bandar–e Shāh \ban-ˌdär-ē-ˈshä, -ˈshȯ\. Port, N Iran, at SE corner of Caspian Sea; connected by highway and railroad across the Elburz Mts. with Tehran; N terminus of Trans-Iranian R.R. from Bandar-e Shāhpūr; pop. (1966c) 13,081.

Bandar–e Shāh·pūr \-shä-ˈpu̇(ə)r\. Town, SW Iran, 55 m. ENE of Ābādān; pop. (1966c) 6013; S terminus of Trans-Iranian R.R. and oil port at head of Persian Gulf.

Bandar Ma·ha·ra·ni \ˈbän-ˌdär-ˌmä-hə-ˈrän-ē\ *also* **Mu·ar** \mü-ˈär\. Seaport on the Strait of Malacca, at the mouth of the Muar river, NW Johore state, Malaysia; pop. (1957c) 39,046; chief port of the state.

Bandar Peng·ga·ram \ˈbän-ˌdär-pəŋ-ˈgär-əm\. Seaport on the Strait of Malacca, W Johore state, Malaysia, SE of Bandar Maharani; pop. (1957c) 39,294.

Bandar Se·ri Be·ga·wan \ˈbän-ˌdär-ˌser-ē-bə-ˈgä-wən\; *formerly* **Bru·nei** \ˈbrü-ˌnī, -(ˌ)nā\ *or* **Brunei Town.** Town, ✻ of Brunei; pop. (1971p) 36,574; royal palace, mosque.

Banda Sea \ˌbän-də-, ˌban-\. Body of water in E Malay Archipelago, SE of Celebes I., S of Buru I. and Ceram I., W of Kai Is. and Aru Is., NW of the Tanimbar group, and NE of Timor I.; 285,000 sq. m.; max. depth ab. 21,000 ft.

Ban·dei·ra, Pi·co da \ˈpē-(ˌ)kü-ˌdä-ban-ˈde-rə\. Mountain, E Brazil, on border between Espírito Santo and Minas Gerais; highest peak in Brazil, 9495 ft.

Ban·dei·ran·tes \ˌba(ⁿ)n-də-ˈra(ⁿ)n-təs\. Municipality, Paraná state, S Brazil, ab. 215 m. WNW of São Paulo; pop. (1968e) 50,732.

Ban·de·lier National Monument \ˌban-də-ˈli(ə)r-\. See UNITED STATES, *National Monuments.*

Ban·de·ra \ban-ˈder-ə\. 1 County, SW cen. Texas. See table at TEXAS.

2 City, its ⊗; pop. (1970c) 891; resort.

Ban·de·ras Bay \bän-ˌder-əs-\. Inlet of the Pacific Ocean on W cen. coast of Mexico, chiefly in NW Jalisco state.

Ban·dır·ma \ˌbän-dər-ˈmä\ *or formerly* **Pan·der·ma** \ˈpän-dər-ˌmä\. Town on S shore of Sea of Marmara, Balıkesir prov., NW Turkey in Asia; pop. (1965c) 33,116.

Ban·djar·ma·sin *or* **Ban·jar·ma·sin** \ˌban-jər-ˈmäs-ᵊn, ˌbän-\. Town, ✻ of South Kalimantan prov., Indonesia, on Martapura river near its junction with the Barito, SE Borneo; pop. (1961c) 214,096; about 24 m. from the sea and a port of call for large vessels; trade center for Barito river basin, exporting timber, pepper, rubber; univ. (1961). In early times under Hindu influences; became Muslim ab. 1500 under Javanese; settled by Dutch 1711; held by English 1811–17; bombed by Japanese and seized by them Feb. 13, 1942; retaken by Allies Aug. 1945.

Bandoeng. See BANDUNG.

Ban·don \ˈban-dən\. Town on **Bandon River,** S co. Cork, SW Eire; pop. (1966c) 2294; agricultural center, brewing, distilling; a noted stronghold of Protestantism in the 17th cent.

Ban·dra \ˈbän-drə\. Suburb of Bombay, Maharashtra, W India, at S end of Salsette I.; population includes many native-born Christians who date their religious affiliations back to 16th cent. and 17th cent. Portuguese missionaries.

Ban·dun·du \bän-ˈdün-(ˌ)dü\. 1 Province of W Zaire. See table at ZAIRE 1.

2 Town, its ✻, on Kasai river; pop. (1968e) 107,191.

Ban·dung *or Du.* **Ban·doeng** \ˈbän-ˌdu̇ŋ, ˈban-, -ˌdəŋ\. City, ✻ of West Java prov., Indonesia, on railroad 75 m. SE of Djakarta; pop. (1971e) 1,114,000; elevation 2346 ft.; third largest city in Indonesia; surrounded by volcanoes and high mountains; center of Sundanese cultural life; several universities and colleges; Nuclear Research Center (1964). In World War II was main defense position of Dutch government and Allied headquarters but was captured by Japanese Mar. 7, 1942; site of Asian-African Conference 1955; founded 1810.

Ba·nes \ˈbän-(ˌ)ās\. Seaport and municipality, N Oriente prov., E Cuba; munic. pop. (1967e) 27,900.

Banff \ˈbam(p)f\. 1 Resort town near Lake Louise (*q.v.*) in Banff National Park, SW Alberta, Canada; pop. (1966c) 896.

2 *or* **Banff·shire** \-ˌshi(ə)r, -shər\. County, NE Scotland; area 630 sq. m.; pop. (1971p) 43,501; ⊗ Banff; other large town Buckie; rivers Spey and Deveron; quarrying (granite, limestone, slate), salmon and herring fisheries, dairy farming, whisky distilling.

3 Burgh, ⊗ of Banff co., Scotland; pop. (1971p) 3723; seaside resort; fishing.

Banff National Park. See CANADA, *National Parks.*

Ban·ga·lore \ˈbaŋ-gə-ˌlō(ə)r, -ˌlȯ(ə)r\. 1 District, SE Mysore, S India; 3081 sq. m.; pop. (1961c) 2,504,462; oil seeds.

2 City, its ✻ and ✻ of Mysore state, 183 m. W of Madras; pop. (1970e) 1,041,900; alt. 3113 ft.; transportation center; pharmaceuticals, textiles, paper, agricultural implements; Bangalore Univ. (1964), Univ. of Agricultural Sciences (1964), National Aeronautical Research Laboratory (1960). Founded in 16th cent.; later a possession of the Marathas; became a fief of Haidar Ali 1758; taken 1791 by British under Lord Cornwallis; except for civil and military station restored to raja of Mysore 1881.

Ban·ga·na·pal·le \ˌbəŋ-gə-nə-ˈpəl-ē\. 1 Former Indian state, now part of Tamil Nadu, S India, 210 m. NW of Madras; 259 sq. m.; once under Hyderabad, control ceded to Madras government 1800.

2 Town, its ✻; pop. (1961c) 8000.

Ban·gas·sou \ˌbäŋ-gə-ˈsü\. Town, S Central African Republic, N cen. Africa, on N bank of Bomu river.

Bang·gai Archipelago \ˈbäŋ-ˌgī-\. Group of islands off E coast of Celebes I., Indonesia, Malay Archipelago; 1221 sq. m.; large islands **Banggai Island,** Peleng (*q.v.*), and about 25 small islands.

Bang·gi \ˈbäŋ-gē\. Island, N Sabah, E Malaysia, S of the main channel of Balabac Strait.

Bangi. See BANGUI.

Bang·il \ˈbaŋ-ˌil\. Town, East Java prov., Indonesia, near SW coast of Madura Strait; pop. (1961c) 28,275; on railroad ab. 20 m. S of Surabaja.

Bang·ka \ˈbaŋ-kə\. 1 *or* **Ban·ka** \ˈbaŋ-\. An island of Indonesia, at NW corner of the Java Sea off SE Sumatra; 136 m. long by 69 m. wide; 4609 sq. m.; pop. (1961c) 251,639; separated from Sumatra by the narrow **Bangka Strait** (ab. 10 m. wide); chief town Pangkalpinang; formed greater part of former Bangka residency; an important tin-producing area; rice, coffee, pepper; chief port Muntok at N end of Bangka Strait. Formerly belonged to ruler of Palembang; ceded to British 1812; became Dutch by exchange in 1814 for Cochin in India; under Japanese control 1942–45; part of independent Indonesia 1949.

2 *or officially* **Bangka and Dependencies.** Former residency, SE Sumatra, Neth. Indies, now part of the Indonesian prov. of South Sumatra; ✱ Pangkalpinang; comprised the islands of Bangka (see 1, above) and Belitung.

Bang·ka·lan \ˌbäŋ-kə-ˈlän\. Town, W coast of Madura I., East Java prov., Indonesia; pop. (1961c) 22,514.

Bang·kok \ˈbaŋ-ˌkäk, baŋ-ˈ\ *or Thai* **Krung Thep** \ˈkrüŋ-ˈtep\. City, ✱ of Thailand, on the Chao Phraya 25 m. above its mouth; munic. pop. (1970p) 2,132,000; transportation center; port facilities; cement, paper, textiles; food processing; several universities and colleges, several hundred Buddhist temples; old section of city built on pontoons or piles with many canals. Only an agricultural village and a fort before 1767 when it became a stronghold against the Burmese; became the capital 1782. Seized by Japanese Dec. 8, 1941; frequently bombed by Allied planes 1944–45; since 1955 site of headquarters of Southeast Asia Treaty Organization, also site of headquarters of the UN Economic Commission for Asia and the Far East. See PHETCHABUN 2.

Ban·gla Desh *or* **Bangladesh** \ˌbäŋ-lə-ˈdesh, ˌbaŋ-, -ˈdāsh\ *or formerly* **East Pakistan.** Republic, S Asia, bounded on N and E by India, on SE by India and Burma, on S by the Bay of Bengal, and on W by India; 55,126 sq. m.; pop. (1969e) 59,330,000; ✱ Dacca. *Physical features:* Generally flat, with max. elev. about 660 ft.; characterized by alluvial plains, which are dissected by numerous connecting rivers and streams; S part consists of E sector of Ganges-Brahmaputra Delta; chief rivers Ganges and Brahmaputra (here known as Jamuna), uniting to form Padma; much of area subject to flooding (mean annual rainfall in excess of 60 inches). *Chief products:* Rice, jute, tea, timber. *Chief towns:* Dacca, Chittagong, Narayanganj, Khulna, Barisal. For history of region, see BENGAL; was part of Pakistan 1947–71; scene of defeat (1971) of Pakistani forces by Bengali nationalists (supported by Indians), following Pakistani attempt to suppress Bengali autonomy movement.

Ban·gor \ˈban-ˌgȯ(ə)r, ˈbaŋ-ˌgȯ(ə)r, ˈbaŋ-gər\. 1 City, ⊗ of Penobscot co., E cen. Maine, at head of navigation on Penobscot river 60 m. NE of Augusta; pop. (1970c) 33,168; paper, lumber, electronic equipment; Bangor Theological Seminary (1814), Bangor Business Coll. (1891), Husson Coll. (1898), Northern Conservatory of Music (1929).

2 Borough, Northampton co., E Pennsylvania, 23 m. NE of Allentown; pop. (1970c) 5425; founded 1773.

3 Municipal borough, co. Down, SE Northern Ireland, on S side of entrance to Belfast Lough 12 m. ENE of Belfast; pop. (1971p) 35,105; seaside resort; textile mills.

4 Municipal borough and city, Caernarvonshire, NW Wales; pop. (1971p) 14,526; slate quarries nearby; Univ. College of North Wales (1884).

Bang Phra. See TRAT.

Bang Pla Soi. See CHON BURI.

Ban·gued \bäŋ-ˈged\. Municipality, ✱ of Abra prov., NW Luzon, Phil., on Abra river; pop. (1969e) 26,400.

Ban·gui *also* **Ban·gi** \bäŋ-ˈgē, ˈbäŋ-ˌ\. Town, ✱ of Central African Republic, on Ubangi river; pop. (1968c) 238,579; commercial center; exports coffee, cotton, sisal, timber.

Bangui \ˈbäŋ-(ˌ)gē\. Municipality, N Ilocos Norte, Luzon, Phil., on Bangui Bay 25 m. NNE of Laoag; pop. (1969e) 12,200.

Bangui Bay. Inlet of South China Sea on N coast of Ilocos Norte prov., Luzon, Phil., extending from Dialao Point on NE to Negra Point on SW; ab. 10 m. wide.

Bang·we·u·lu, Lake \-ˌbaŋ-wē-ˈü-(ˌ)lü\ *or* **Lake Bang·we·o·lo** \-ˈō-(ˌ)lō\. Lake, N Zambia, S cen. Africa, SSE of Lake Mweru and SSW of Lake Tanganyika; 45 m. long; 3800 sq. m. (including swamps); its outlet is the Luapula, a

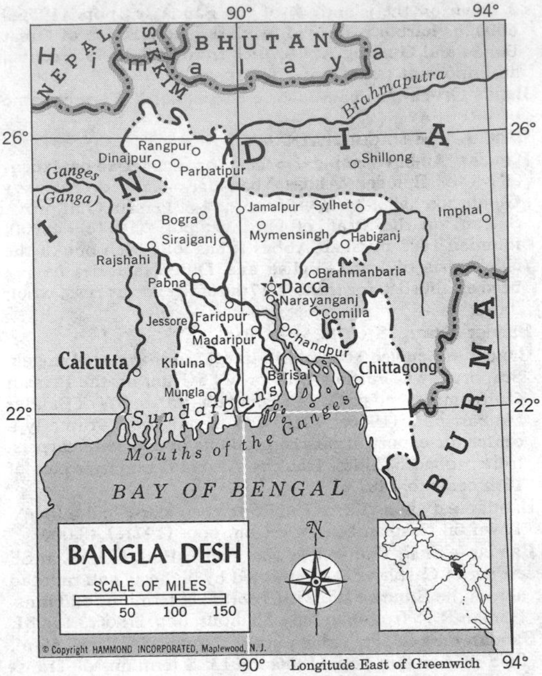

headstream of the Congo. First visited by Livingstone 1868; circumnavigated 1896.

Ba·ní \bä-ˈnē\. City, ✱ of Peravia prov., S Dominican Republic, SW of Santo Domingo; pop. (1970p) 18,860.

Banī Suwayf. See BENI SUEF.

Ba·ni·yas *or* **Ba·ni·as** \ˌban-ē-ˈ(y)as\ *also* **Pa·ne·as** \pə-ˈnē-əs\. 1 Town on coast of Syria, 25 m. S of Latakia.

2 *or anc.* **Cae·sa·rea Phi·lip·pi** \ˌsē-zə-ˌrē-ə-ˈfil-ə-ˌpī, ˌses-ə-, ˌsez-ə-, -fə-ˈlip-ˌī\. Village, SW Syria, in region occupied by Israel 1967; ancient city; has temple which was built by Herod the Great and enlarged by Philip the Tetrarch; important in Roman times.

Ban·jak Islands *or* **Ban·yak Islands** \ˌbän-ˌyäk-\. Island group, Atjeh prov., Indonesia, in the Indian Ocean off NW coast of Sumatra; 123 sq. m.; comprises about 65 islands, most of them very small, **Great Banjak,** the largest, being ab. 20 m. by 7 m.

Ba·nja Lu·ka \ˌbän-yə-ˈlü-kə\. Town, NW cen. Yugoslavia, in Bosnia and Herzegovina on Vrbas river; pop. (1971p) 89,866; iron foundry; leather goods; thermal springs. Probably dates back to a Roman fort; especially important 16th–18th cents. when it was several times a battlefield bet. Austrians and Turks (1527, 1688, and 1737).

Banjarmasin. See BANDJARMASIN.

Ban·ju·mas *also* **Ban·yu·mas** *or Du.* **Ban·joe·mas** \ˌbän-yu̇-ˈmäs\. 1 Former residency, Java, Neth. Indies, now part of the Indonesian prov. of Central Java; 2472 sq. m. First came under Dutch 1705.

2 Town, its ✱.

Ban·ju·wangi *also* **Ban·yu·wangi** *or Du.* **Ban·joe·wangi** \ˌbän-yu̇-ˈwäŋ-ē\. Seaport on Bali Strait, East Java prov., Indonesia; pop. (1961c) 54,408; port for Bali I. and railroad terminus of line from Surabaja.

Banka. See BANGKA 1.

Banks \ˈbaŋks\. County in Georgia. See table at GEORGIA.

Banks, Cape. Point on coast of New South Wales, SE Australia, on N shore of entrance to Botany Bay.

Banks Island. 1 Small island in Torres Strait, N of Cape York, Queensland, NE Australia.

2 Island off W cen. British Columbia, Canada, on E side of Hecate Strait; 50 m. long; 400 sq. m.

3 Island, W Franklin dist., Northwest Territories, Canada, NW of Victoria I.; ab. 250 m. long; 23,230 sq. m.; separated from mainland of Mackenzie dist. by Amundsen Gulf.

Banks Islands. Group of five small islands and a number of islets, SW Pacific Ocean, N of New Hebrides; administered as part of the New Hebrides; chief islands Vanua Lava and Santa María; volcanic and fertile, with luxuriant vegetation; discovered ab. 1595.

Banks Peninsula. Peninsula projecting from E cen. coast of South I., New Zealand; ab. 35 m. long and 25 m. wide; Christchurch is at its base on N side, Akaroa Harbor at its SE extremity.

Banks Strait. Passage separating the Furneaux group of islands from NE coast of Tasmania (*q.v.*); ab. 13 m. wide.

Ban·ku·ra \ˈbäŋ-kə-ˌrä\. 1 District, West Bengal, NE India; 2646 sq. m.

2 Town, its ✱, 95 m. WNW of Calcutta; pop. (1961c) 62,833; silk weaving; four colleges.

Ban Mak Khaeng. See UDON THANI.

Ban·me·thu·ot \ˌbän-mə-ˈtü-ət\. Town, South Vietnam, 160 m. NNE of Saigon; pop. (1968e) 62,092.

Bann \ˈban\. Name of two rivers in Northern Ireland: the **Upper Bann** 25 m. long, rising in co. Down and flowing NW into Lough Neagh; the **Lower Bann** 33 m. long, flowing N out of Lough Neagh into the Atlantic.

Ban·nack \ˈban-ək\. Mountain in Yellowstone National Park, NW Wyoming; 10,300 ft.

Ban·ner \ˈban-ər\. County in Nebraska. See table at NEBRASKA.

Banner Peak. Mountain in Sierra Nevada, in NE Madera co., cen. California; 12,957 ft.

Ban·ning \ˈban-iŋ\. City, Riverside co., SE California, 25 m. ESE of San Bernardino; pop. (1970c) 12,034; electronic components; fruit farms; founded 1883.

Ban·nock \ˈban-ək\. County in Idaho. See table at IDAHO.

Ban·nock·burn \ˈban-ək-ˌbərn, ˌban-ək-ˈ\. Town, Stirling co., cen. Scotland, 2½ m. SSE of Stirling; battle June 23, 1314 in which Robert Bruce routed the English under Edward II and took Stirling Castle.

Bannock Peak. Mountain, W of Bannock Range, cen. Power co., SE Idaho; 8321 ft.

Bannock Range. Mountains on W border of Bannock co., SE Idaho.

Ban·nu \ˈbən-(ˌ)ü, ˈbän-\. 1 District, S cen. North-West Frontier Province, Pakistan; 1695 sq. m.; pop. (1961c) 428,061.

2 *or formerly* **Ed·war·des·abad** \ed-ˈwärd-əs-ə-ˌbäd\. Town, its ✱, on Kurram river 100 m. SSW of Peshawar; pop. (1961c) 31,623; wooden articles; military station.

Ba·ño·las \bän-ˈyō-ləs\. Town, Gerona prov., NE Spain, 10 m. N of Gerona; pop. (1970p) 10,023; skull found here 1887 has been classified as Neanderthal type.

Baños, Los. See LOS BAÑOS.

Bans·da \ˈbänz-də\. 1 Former Indian state, now part of Gujarat, W India; 212 sq. m.

2 Town, its ✱, S Gujarat; pop. (1961c) 5937.

Ban·ská Bys·tri·ca \ˈbän-ˌskä-ˈbis-trit-ˌsä\ *or Hung.* **Besz·ter·cze·bá·nya** \ˌbes-tərt-sə-ˈbän-yȯ\ *or Ger.* **Neu·sohl** \ˈnȯi-ˌzōl\. Commune, Slovak S.R., Czechoslovakia, on Hron river 100 m. NE of Bratislava; pop. (1968e) 38,865.

Ban·stead \ˈban-ˌsted, -stəd\. Urban district, Surrey, S England; pop. (1971p) 44,986; Epsom racecourse borders on **Banstead Downs.**

Bans·wa·ra \bänz-ˈwär-ə\. 1 Former Indian state, now part of Rajasthan, NW India; 1606 sq. m.

2 Town, its ✱; pop. (1961c) 19,600.

Bantai. See BANDAI.

Ban·tam \ˈbant-əm, ˈbän-ˌtäm\. 1 Former residency, Java, Neth. Indies, now part of the Indonesian prov. of West Java; 3067 sq. m.; ✱ Serang; comprised W end of Java bet. Java Sea and Indian Ocean, with W coast on Sunda Strait; region mountainous in S, contains Mt. Karang in midst of N plain; well developed agriculturally.

History: In early 16th cent. became powerful Muslim sultanate which extended its control over parts of Sumatra and Borneo; invaded by Dutch, Portuguese, and English; recognized Dutch sovereigns 1684, annexed by Dutch 1809; scene of several revolts in 19th cent.; suffered severely from volcanic eruption of Krakatau (*q.v.*) 1883.

2 Town, Indonesia. See BANTEN.

Bantam Lake \ˌbant-əm-\. Lake, Litchfield co., NW Connecticut; 25 sq. m.; its outlet is **Bantam River,** a tributary of the Shepaug.

Ban·ta·yan \ˌbänt-ə-ˈyän\. 1 Island, cen. Phil., 9 m. W of N tip of Cebu I. and 20 m. NE of Negros; 45 sq. m.; part of Cebu prov.

2 Municipality on SW coast of Bantayan I.; pop. (1969e) 41,000.

Ban·ten \ˈbän-ˌten\ *or formerly* **Ban·tam** \ˈbant-əm, ˈbän-ˌtäm\. Former town on Banten Bay, N coast of West Java prov., Indonesia; now in ruins. Capital of Muslim sultanate; Portuguese trading station after 1545; site of first Dutch settlement 1596 and of British factory 1603, bet. which great rivalry developed until expulsion of British 1683; under British control 1811–14.

Banten Bay *or formerly* **Bantam Bay.** Inlet of Java Sea on NW coast of Java, Indonesia, E of Sunda Strait.

Ban·ton \bän-ˈtȯn\. Small island, Romblon prov., Phil., NNW of Romblon I. and N of Simara I.; 11 sq. m.; pop. (1969e) 8500.

Ban·try \ˈban-trē\. Town at head of Bantry Bay, SW co. Cork, SW Eire; pop. (1961c) 3159; fishing center.

Bantry Bay. Bay, SW co. Cork, SW Eire; ab. 25 m. long; site of unsuccessful French attempts at landing 1689 and 1796 to help Irish insurrections.

Banyak Islands. See BANJAK ISLANDS.

Ban·yu·mas. See BANJUMAS.

Ban·yu·wangi. See BANJUWANGI.

Ban·zare Coast \ˌban-ˌza(ə)r-, -ˌze(ə)r-\. Section of coast of Wilkes Land, Antarctica, extending along Indian Ocean from ab. 121°E long. to 126°E.

Bao \ˈbaů\. Short stream in NW Leyte I., Phil., flowing S into Ormoc Bay; scene of severe fighting bet. Americans and Japanese Nov.–Dec. 1944.

Ba·ou·lé *or* **Ba·u·le** \ˈbaů-(ˌ)lā\. River, W Mali, W Africa; chief tributary of the Bakoy.

Ba·paume \bä-ˈpōm\. Commune, Pas-de-Calais dept., N France; pop. (1962c) 3274; scene of victory of French general Faidherbe over the Prussians Jan. 2–3, 1871; scene of severe fighting in 1916 and 1917 and of successful assault by British forces on the Hindenburg Line Aug. 21–Sept. 1, 1918, the town being completely destroyed.

Ba·ʻqu·ba *or* **Ba·ʻqū·bah** \bə-ˈkü-bə\. Town, E Iraq, on Diyala river in fertile agricultural region and on railroad 32 m. NE of Baghdad; pop. (1965c) 34,575.

Bar \ˈbär\. Town, W Vinnitsa Oblast, W cen. Ukrainian S.S.R., U.S.S.R., 40 m. W of Vinnitsa.

History: Important town of Podolia, in 16th cent. a Lithuanian possession, later Polish but held for a short time in 17th cent. (to 1683) by the Turks; headquarters of the Confederation of Bar, formed here 1768 as a Polish patriotic and anti-Russian association, suppressed 1770–72; became Russian 1793 in First Partition of Poland.

Bar *or* **An·ti·va·ri** \än-ˈtē-və-rē\. Town, SW Montenegro, S Yugoslavia; pop. (1961c) 2184.

Ba·ra Ban·ki *or* **Ba·ra·ban·ki** \ˌbär-ə-ˈbaŋ-kē, -ˈbäŋ-\. District, Uttar Pradesh, N India; 1714 sq. m.; pop. (1961c) 1,414,547.

Ba·ra·ba Steppe \ˌbär-ə-ˌbä-\. Swamp and steppe region, SW Siberia, U.S.S.R., bet. Ob and Irtysh rivers.

Bar·a·boo \'bar-ə-ˌbü\. 1 River, S cen. Wisconsin; ab. 90 m. long; flows from Juneau co. SE into Wisconsin river below Portage, Columbia co.
2 City, ⊗ of Saulk co., S cen. Wisconsin, 15 m. WSW of Portage; pop. (1970c) 7931; cotton goods; brewery, foundry.

Ba·ra·cal·do \ˌbar-ə-'käl-(ˌ)dō, ˌbär-\. Commune, Vizcaya prov., N Spain; pop. (1970p) 108,757; iron and steel works.

Ba·ra·coa \ˌbar-ə-'kō-ə, ˌbär-\. Seaport and municipality on N coast of E Oriente prov., E Cuba; munic. pop. (1967e) 105,070; exports bananas and coconuts; oldest town in Cuba, settled 1512 by Diego Velásquez.

Ba·ra·da \'bär-əd-ə\; *Bib.* **Ab·a·na** *or* **Ab·a·nah** \'ab-ə-nə\ [*2 Kings* v. 12]; *classical* **Chry·sor·rho·as** \kris-'ór-ə-wəs, -'är-\. One of the chief rivers of Damascus, W Syria, flowing SE ab. 45 m. from Anti-Lebanon Mts. past Damascus to swamps at edge of desert.

Bar·a·ga \'bar-ə-gə\. County in Michigan. See table at MICHIGAN.

Ba·ra·gan Steppe \ˌbär-ə-ˌgän-\. Level open tract on the lower Danube river, E Walachia, Romania.

Ba·ra·ho·na \ˌbar-ə-'hō-nə, ˌbär-ə-'(h)ō-\. 1 Province, SW Dominican Republic. See table at DOMINICAN REPUBLIC.
2 City, its ✱; pop. (1970p) 37,889; sugar, coffee.

Ba·rail Range \bə-'rī(ə)l-\. Mountain range, NE India, along boundary bet. Assam and Manipur; the S continuation of the Naga Hills; highest Mt. Japvo 9890 ft.

Ba·rak \bə-'räk\. Upper course of the Surma river in Manipur, NE India. See SURMA.

Baraka River. See BARKA 1.

Ba·ra·kī Ba·rak \bə-ˌräk-ē-bə-'räk\. Town, ✱ of Logar prov., E Afghanistan; pop. (1969e) 49,520.

Ba·ram *or* **Bar·ram** \'bär-ˌäm\. River, N Sarawak, East Malaysia; ab. 250 m. long; flows NW into South China Sea at Baram Point.

Baram Point *or Malay* **Tan·jong Baram** \ˌtän-ˌjôŋ-'bär-ˌäm\. Cape on N coast of Sarawak, East Malaysia; projects into South China Sea, ab. 4°36′N, 113°58′E.

Ba·ra·mul·la *or* **Ba·ra·mu·la** \ˌbär-ə-'mu̇l-ə\. 1 *also* **Kash·mir North** \ˌkash-ˌmi(ə)r-, 'kazh-, kash-ˌ, kazh-ˌ\. District, Jammu and Kashmir, N India; pop. (1961c) 604,659.
2 Town, Jammu and Kashmir, N India, ab. 30 m. WNW of Srinagar; pop. (1961c) 19,900.

Ba·ra·na·gar \bə-'rän-ə-gər\. Town, West Bengal, India, N suburb of Calcutta on Hooghly river; pop. (1970e) 147,920.

Ba·ra·noa \ˌbar-ə-'nō-ə, ˌbär-\. Town, Atlántico dept., N Colombia, near Barranquilla; munic. pop. (1968e) 20,607.

Bar·a·nof \'bar-ə-ˌnóf, -ˌnäf, bə-'rän-əf\. Island, W Alexander Archipelago, SE Alaska, S of Chichagof I.; ab. 100 m. long; 1597 sq. m.; Sitka is on its W coast.

Ba·ra·no·vi·chi \bə-'rän-ə-ˌvich-ē\ *or Pol.* **Ba·ra·no·wi·cze** \ˌbär-ə-nə-'vē-chə\. City, Brest Oblast, W cen. Belorussian S.S.R., U.S.S.R., 85 m. SW of Minsk; pop. (1970p) 102,000; food processing, metalworking; important railroad junction; was Polish frontier station to Russia; scene of violent fighting bet. Germans and Russians June and July 1916; in World War II seized by Germans July 1941 and held until retaken by Soviet troops July 8, 1944.

Ba·ra·nya \'bór-ən-ˌyō\. County of S Hungary. See table at HUNGARY.

Ba·raque Mi·chel \bə-ˌräk-mē-'shel\. Peak in Hohe Venn Mts., near Spa, E Belgium; 2211 ft.

Bar·a·tar·ia Bay \ˌbär-ə-ˌtar-ē-ə-, -ˌter-\. 1 Inlet of Gulf of Mexico on boundary bet. Jefferson and Plaquemines parishes, SE Louisiana.
2 Bayou and village, SE Louisiana, W of the mouth of the Mississippi; region connected with legends and activities (1810–15) of Jean and Pierre Lafitte, who led a band of privateers and smugglers.

Barataria Pass *or formerly* **Grand Pass.** Narrow strait connecting Barataria Bay, SE Louisiana, with Gulf of Mexico.

Ba·raun·dha \bə-'rau̇n-də\. Former Indian state, now part of Madhya Pradesh, cen. India; 228 sq. m.

Bar·ba \'bär-bə\. Volcano, cen. Costa Rica, N of San José; 9534 ft.

Bar·ba·ce·na \ˌbär-bə-'sā-nə\. City, S Minas Gerais state, E Brazil, 125 m. N of Rio de Janeiro; munic. pop. (1968e) 63,050; center of agricultural district; altitude 3500 ft.

Bar·ba·co·as \ˌbär-bə-'kō-əs\. Municipality and river port, Nariño dept., SW Colombia, 45 m. ESE of Tumaco; pop. (1968e) 18,382.

Bar·ba·dos \bär-'bād-(ˌ)ōz, -əs\. Island in the Lesser Antilles, West Indies, E of cen. Windward Is.; 166 sq. m.; pop. (1970p) 238,000; ✱ Bridgetown. Chiefly of coral formation with no good harbors and only small streams; generally level but with hills in cen. part, highest point Mt. Hillaby 1104 ft.; chief industry sugar; exports molasses and rum; tourism.

History: Probably discovered by Portuguese in 16th cent.; claimed for England in 1605 when it was visited by Leigh's Guiana expedition; first settled under auspices of Courteen 1626; included in grant to earl of Carlisle 1627 whose settlers overcame those of Courteen 1629; leased by Lord Willoughby, a Royalist, who governed until forced to yield to Commonwealth 1652; taken over by Crown 1663; became prosperous as sugar producer, esp. in 17th and 18th cents.; suffered from wars of England with France, Spain, and later with U.S.; abolished slavery 1834; seat of government for Windward Is. 1833 to 1885, when made separate administration; member of West Indies Federation 1958–62; achieved independence 1966; joined Caribbean Free Trade Area 1968.

59°30′

13° 30′

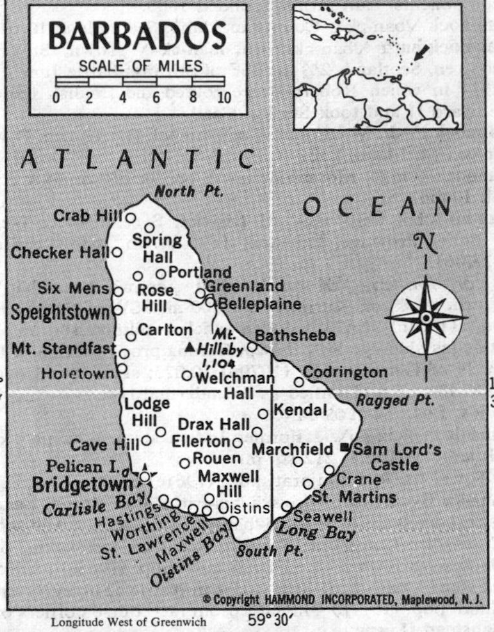

13° 30′

Longitude West of Greenwich 59° 30′

Bar·ba·ry \'bär-b(ə-)rē\. Coastal region in N Africa, extending from Egypt to the Atlantic Ocean.

History: For early history, see MAURETANIA, NUMIDIA, and CYRENAICA. Overrun by Vandals under Genseric 5th cent. A.D.; conquered by Belisarius for Byzantine Empire 533–534; gradually overcome by Islam 7th cent.; broken up into independent Muslim states known as **Barbary States** (see MOROCCO, ALGIERS, TUNIS, TRIPOLI); European penetration begun by occupation of Ceuta by Portuguese 1415; Oran, Bejaïa, and Tripoli conquered by Spanish 1509–11; dominion of corsair Barbarossa reduced by victory 1535 of expedition of Charles V under Andrea Doria, but Algiers held out against Charles until 1541; Tripoli lost to Turks 1551; carried on piracy against European commerce and collected tribute from leading European states; after U.S. war with Tripoli 1801–05, U.S. expedition to Algiers 1815, and bombardment of Algiers by British 1816, ceased exaction of tribute and Christian slavery. For later history, see under separate states.

Bar·bas, Cape \-'bär-bəs\. Cape on SW coast of Spanish Sahara, NW Africa; 22°18′N, 16°41′W.

Bar·bas·tro \bär-'bäs-trō\. Commune, Huesca prov., Spain; pop. (1970p) 13,427; old city, known in Roman times; 16th cent. cathedral.

Bar·ba·te, Río \ˌrē-ō-bär-'bät-ē\. Short stream in Cadiz prov., SW Spain, flowing SW to the Atlantic Ocean just E of Cape Trafalgar; on its banks in 711 A.D. is supposed to have been fought the battle in which Roderick, last king of the Visigoths, was defeated and probably slain by the Muslims under Tariq.

Bar·ber \'bär-bər\. County in Kansas. See table at KANSAS.

Bar·be·ri·no di Mu·gel·lo \ˌbär-bə-'rē-nō-ˌdē-mü-'jel-(ˌ)ō\. Commune, Firenze prov., Tuscany, cen. Italy, 16 m. N of Florence; pop. (1968e) 7612.

Bar·bers Point \ˌbär-bərz-\ *also* **Ka·la·e·loa Point** \kə-ˌlī-ˌlō-ə-\. Cape on SW corner of Oahu I., Hawaii, W of Pearl Harbor, 21°18′N, 158°07′W.

Bar·ber·ton \'bär-bərt-ᵊn\. 1 City, Summit co., NE Ohio, 7 m. SSW of Akron; pop. (1970c) 33,052; automobile tires, chemicals, high tension insulators, steam boilers; founded 1893.

2 Town, E Transvaal, Rep. of South Africa, 180 m. E of Pretoria; pop. (1967e) 13,200; center of De Kaap goldfields; asbestos, magnesite, talc, and nickel in vicinity.

Bar·bi·zon \ˌbär-bə-'zōⁿ\. Village, Seine-et-Marne dept., N France, S of Melun, near forest of Fontainebleau; center of Barbizon School of French painters.

Bar·bour \'bär-bər\. Name of counties in two states of the U.S. See tables at ALABAMA and WEST VIRGINIA.

Bar·bours·ville \'bär-bərz-ˌvil\. Village, Cabell co., W West Virginia, 9 m. E of Huntington; pop. (1970c) 2279; scene of Union victory in Civil War July 13, 1861.

Bar·bour·ville \'bär-bər-ˌvil\. City, ⊗ of Knox co., SE Kentucky, 22 m. NNW of Middlesborough; pop. (1970c) 3549; Union Coll. (1879).

Bar·bu·da \bär-'büd-ə\. Flat coral island in E West Indies, a dependency of Antigua, 25 m. N of Antigua; 62 sq. m.; pop. (1960c) 1145; principal crop sea-island cotton.

Barca. See BARKA.

Barce. See BARKA 3.

Bar·cel·lo·na \ˌbär-chə-'lō-nə\ *or in full* **Barcellona Poz·zo di Got·to** \-ˌpōt-sō-di-'gȯt-(ˌ)ō\. Commune, Messina prov., NE Sicily, Italy on Longano river 18 m. WSW of Messina; pop. (1968e) 34,526; summer resort.

Bar·ce·lo·na \ˌbär-sə-'lō-nə\. 1 Province of NE Spain. See table at SPAIN.

2 *anc.* **Bar·ci·no** \'bär-sə-ˌnō\ *or later* **Bar·ci·no·na** \ˌbär-sə-'nō-nə\. City, its ✱, on the Mediterranean 315 m. ENE of Madrid; pop. (1970p) 1,745,142; important port; textiles; engineering works, oil refinery; Univ. of Barcelona (1450), Autonomous Univ. of Barcelona (1968); 13th cent. Spanish Gothic cathedral; ancient ruins; old Roman wall fortifications destroyed 1868.

History: Traditionally, city founded 3d cent. B.C. by Hamilcar Barca of Carthage; ruled by Romans, Visigoths; taken by Moors 713 A.D.; retaken by Franks for Charlemagne 801 and made capital of Spanish March (see CATALONIA); Frankish county of Barcelona became almost independent in 9th cent.; after Catalonia united with Aragon 1137, city became flourishing commercial center, an originator of deposit banking, and the rival of Italian ports; captured in 1652 as center of resistance in great Catalonian rebellion; abandoned by Allies 1714; in 19th cent. became center of radical social movements and of movement for Catalonian separatism; seized in military coup of Primo de Rivera 1923; loyalist capital 1937–39; its capture in 1939 brought collapse of Catalonian resistance.

3 Town, ✱ of Anzoátegui state, N Venezuela, 150 m. ESE of Caracas; pop. (1970e) 54,916; coal mines nearby; founded 1634.

Bar·ce·lo·ne·ta \ˌbär-sə-lə-'net-ə\. Town and municipality, N Puerto Rico, on the Manatí river and on railroad 28 m. W of San Juan; munic. pop. (1970p) 20,628, town pop. 4486.

Barcino *or* **Barcinona.** See BARCELONA 2.

Barcoo. See COOPER'S CREEK.

Bar·daï \bär-'dī\. Town, N Chad, N cen. Africa, in Tibesti Mts.

Bar·de·jov \'bärd-ə-yȯf\ *or Hung.* **Bárt·fa** \'bärt-ˌfȯ\ *or Ger.* **Bart·feld** \'bärt-ˌfelt\. Town, Slovak S.R., Czechoslovakia, in S foothills of Carpathian Mts. 20 m. N of Prešov; pop. (1968e) 12,033; hot springs.

Bar·de·ra \'bär-der-ə\. Town, S Somalia, E Africa, on the Juba river ab. 250 m. W of Mogadisho; head of steamship service on the Juba.

Bar·dī·yah *or* **Bar·dia** \'bärd-ē-ə, bär-'dē-ə\ *or formerly* **Por·to Bardia** \ˌpȯrt-ō-, pȯrt-\. Town on coastal road, NE Libya, N Africa, near Egyptian border. Several times captured in World War II: starting point of Italian attack Sept. 1940; taken by British Dec. 1940–Jan. 1941; lost to Rommel's forces Apr. 1941; taken and lost again by British 1941–42; finally recaptured Nov. 13, 1942.

Bar·do·li \bär-'dō-lē\. Town, SE Gujarat, India, just SE of Surat; pop. (1961c) 12,400.

Bārdow. See LE BARDO.

Bard·sey \'bärd-zē\. Island, Caernarvonshire, Wales, in the Irish Sea off the W Welsh coast N of entrance to Cardigan Bay; 2 m. long; fishing, farming; ruins of 13th cent. abbey on foundation thought to date from 516; anciently a place of religious pilgrimage.

Bards·town \'bärdz-ˌtau̇n\. City, ⊗ of Nelson co., cen. Kentucky, 36 m. SSE of Louisville; pop. (1970c) 5816.

Barduli. See BARLETTA.

Bardwan. See BURDWAN.

Bard·well \'bärd-ˌwel, -wəl\. City, ⊗ of Carlisle co., SW Kentucky; pop. (1970c) 1049; fertilizers.

Ba·règes \bä-'rezh, -'räzh\. Village, Hautes-Pyrénées dept., SW France, in the Pyrenees Mts.; pop. (1962c) 286; health resort. See BAGNÈRES-DE-BIGORRE.

Ba·reil·ly *or* **Ba·re·li** \bə-'rā-lē\. 1 Division, Uttar Pradesh, India. See ROHILKHAND.

2 District, Uttar Pradesh, N India; 1591 sq. m.; pop. (1961c) 1,478,490; ✱ Bareilly; rice, wheat, sugarcane.

3 City, its ✱, on Ramganga river 130 m. ESE of Delhi; pop. (1970e) 334,064; sugar, rope, furniture; site of a military cantonment; college (1837); important railroad junction. Founded 1537.

Ba·rents Island \ˌbar-ən(t)s-, 'bär-\. Island, E Spitsbergen archipelago, Arctic Ocean, N of Edge I., 78°27′N, 21°15′E; 37 m. long; 514 sq. m.

Barents Sea. Part of Arctic Ocean N of Norway and U.S.S.R. and bet. Spitsbergen and Novaya Zemlya; 529,-096 sq. m.

Bar·fleur \bär-'flər\. Town, Manche dept., NW France, on NE point of Cotentin Penin. 2 m. S of **Point Barfleur** which marks the NW point of the Bay of the Seine; pop. (1962c) 847; resort; fishing; in Middle Ages an important port.

Barfurush. See BĀBOL.

Bar·ga \'bär-gə\. 1 Commune, Lucca prov., Tuscany, cen. Italy, 17 m. N of Lucca; pop. (1968e) 11,131.

2 Region, NE China. See HU-LUN-PEI-ERH.

Barge Canal. See NEW YORK STATE BARGE CANAL.

Bar·gu·zin \ˌbär-gə-ˈzēn\. 1 Mountain range, W Buryat A.S.S.R., U.S.S.R.; parallel with the Barguzin river and bet. it and Lake Baikal; highest point 8862 ft.
2 River, W Buryat A.S.S.R., U.S.S.R.; 437 m. long; flows SW to Lake Baikal.
3 Town on right bank near mouth of the river.

Bar Harbor \bär-\. Town, Hancock co., SE Maine, on Mt. Desert I. on Frenchman Bay; pop. (1970c) 3716; first permanent English settlement 1763; summer resort; greatly damaged by fire 1947.

Ba·ri \ˈbär-ē\ *or in full* **Bari del·le Pu·glie** \-ˌdel-ə-ˈpül-(ˌ)yā\. 1 Province of Apulia, Italy. See table at ITALY.
2 *or anc.* **Bar·i·um** \ˈbar-ē-əm, ˈber-\. Commercial seaport, its ✱ and ✱ of Apulia, SE Italy, on Adriatic Sea 139 m. E by N of Naples; pop. (1968e) 348,914; oil refining, boat building, printing; building materials, textiles, tobacco, wine, machinery; 11th cent. cathedral and church; pilgrim resort; univ. (1924).
History: Leading commercial center of Apulia since 2d cent. B.C.; successively dominated by Goths, Greeks, Saracens, Byzantines, Normans, Germans, and Venetians; became part of kingdom of Naples 1557. In World War II taken by British Sept. 1943; Allied ships in harbor bombed by Germans Dec. 2, 1943.

Ba·ria *or* **Ba·ri·ya** \ˈbär-ē-ə\. Former Indian state, now part of Gujarat, W India; 810 sq. m.

Baria. River in S Venezuela; rises in mountains on border, Serra Curupira, in extreme S tip of Venezuela, flows N into Casiquiare river.

Ba·ri Do·ab \ˌbär-ē-dō-ˈäb\. Plain region, mostly in Punjab, Pakistan, with NE section in India, lying bet. Sutlej and Ravi rivers.

Ba·ri·li \bə-ˈrē-lē\. Municipality near W coast of Cebu I., Cebu prov., Phil., 30 m. SW of City of Cebu; pop. (1969e) 38,500.

Ba·ri·lo·che \ˌbär-i-ˈlō-chē\ *or* **San Car·los de Bariloche** \san-ˈkär-ləs-dā-\. Town, SW Río Negro prov., S cen. Argentina, on S shore of Lake Nahuel Huapí; pop. (1960c) 15,995; resort.

Barīm. See PERIM.

Ba·ri·ma \bə-ˈrē-mə\. River, NW Guyana; ab. 250 m. long; flows SE, then curves to the NW, crosses the Venezuelan border and empties into Atlantic Ocean at the S Orinoco delta; navigable for 52 m.

Ba·ri·nas \bə-ˈrē-nəs\. 1 *or formerly* **Za·mo·ra** \zə-ˈmōr-ə, sə-, -ˈmȯr-\. State of W cen. Venezuela. See table at VENEZUELA.
2 Town, its ✱, 260 m. SW of Caracas; pop. (1970e) 50,576; cattle trading center.

Ba·rin·go, Lake \-bə-ˈriŋ-(ˌ)gō\. Lake, Kenya, E Africa, NE of Lake Victoria; ab. 50 sq. m.

Ba·ri·pa·da \ˌbär-ə-ˈpäd-ə\. Town, Orissa, E India, 115 m. SW of Calcutta; pop. (1961c) 20,300; ✱ of former Mayurbhanj state.

Ba·ri·sal \ˈbar-ə-ˌsȯl\. Town, Bangla Desh, near Tetulia mouth of Ganges river, 73 m. S of Dacca; pop. (1969e) 79,300; river port with active trade; rice market; exports fish; three colleges; noted for natural phenomenon known as "Barisal guns," noises like distant thunder or cannon fire, thought to be of seismic origin.

Ba·ri·san Mountains \ˌbär-i-ˌsän-\. Mountain system extending the length of the island of Sumatra, Indonesia, chiefly along the W coast; ab. 1000 m. long, containing many volcanic peaks from 6000 to more than 12,400 ft.; highest peak Mt. Kerintji 12,483 ft.; for the most part made up of two parallel chains with a series of mountain lakes in the high valley bet. them, largest of which is Toba (*q.v.*).

Ba·ri·to \bə-ˈrēt-(ˌ)ō\. River, SE Borneo, Indonesia; ab. 550 m. long; rises in E ranges of Muller Mts., flows S into Java Sea; its lower course flows through wide marshy region in which cross branches connect with other streams; one of the largest rivers of Borneo, navigable for steamers of moderate size for about 250 m.

Barium. See BARI 2.

Bariya. See BARIA.

Bar·ka *also* **Bar·ca** \ˈbär-kə\. 1 River in NE Africa, chiefly in Ethiopia; ab. 400 m. long; rises in cen. Eritrea, Ethiopia, flows N, receives the Anseba from E; crosses into Sudan where it is called **Ba·ra·ka** \ˈbär-ə-kə\; empties into Red Sea.
2 Region, NE Libya, N Africa, esp. the height of land (**Barka Plateau,** highest point ab. 2340 ft.) surrounding the ancient town of Barca (see 3, below); part of the Pashalik of Tripoli under the Ottoman Turks.
3 *or Ital.* **Bar·ce** \ˈbär(ˌ)chā\ *or Arab.* **Al–Marj** \al-ˈmärj\. Town, N Libya, Africa, ab. 60 m. NE of Benghazi; pop. (1964c) 10,645; in region of fighting 1941–42. Ancient **Barca** in Cyrenaica was founded ab. 550 B.C.; became center for Greek refugees, but was a Libyan, not a Greek, town; plundered by Persians 512 B.C.; declined under the Ptolemies; again important under Muslims.

Bar·king \ˈbär-kiŋ\. Borough of Greater London, SE England. See table at LONDON 4.

Bark·ley Sound \ˌbär-klē-\. Inlet of Pacific Ocean, in SW Vancouver I., SW British Columbia, Canada.

Bark·ly Tableland \ˌbär-klē-\. Plateau region, Australia, mostly in E Northern Territory, but its SE end in Queensland; alt. ab. 1000 ft.; cattle raising.

Barkly West. Town, Cape Province, Rep. of South Africa, on N bank of Vaal river; pop. (1967e) 4300; formerly most important town in Griqualand.

Barkol *or* **Barkul.** See PA-LI-K'UN.

Bârlad. See BÎRLAD.

Bar–le–Duc \ˌbär-lə-ˈd(y)ük\ *or unofficially* **Bar–sur–Ornain** \ˈbär-ˌsu̇(ə)r-ȯr-ˈnaⁿ\. Commune, ✱ of Meuse dept., NE France, 128 m. E of Paris; pop. (1968c) 19,159; iron foundry; hosiery; 14th cent. church; old Roman gate.

Bar·lee, Lake \-ˈbär-lē\. Large salt lake, W Western Australia.

Bar·let·ta \bär-ˈlet-ə\ *or anc.* **Bar·du·li** \ˈbärd-ᵊl-ˌī, -ē; ˈbär-jə-ˌlī\. Seaport, Bari prov., Apulia, SE Italy, on Adriatic coast near mouth of Ofanto river 34 m. WNW of Bari; pop. (1968e) 75,097; automobiles, electrical equipment, chemicals; 12th cent. Romanesque cathedral and 13th cent. Gothic church; college founded by Ferdinand IV.

Bar·lin \bär-ˈlaⁿ\. Commune, Pas-de-Calais dept., N France, NW of Arras; pop. (1962c) 9501; coal mines.

Bar·mouth \ˈbär-məth\. Urban district, Merionethshire, N Wales, on coast of Cardigan Bay; pop. (1971p) 2103; resort nearby is first property acquired by the National Trust (1895).

Bar·nard, Mount \-ˈbär-nərd\. Peak in Sierra Nevada, near Mt. Whitney, SE cen. California; 13,990 ft.

Barnard Castle. Urban district, Durham, N England, on Tees river 17 m. W of Darlington; pop. (1971p) 5228; 13th cent. castle figures in Sir Walter Scott's poem *Rokeby.*

Bar·na·ul \ˌbär-nə-ˈül\. Town, ✱ of Altai Krai, Russian S.F.S.R, U.S.S.R., on the Ob river 110 m. S of Novosibirsk; pop. (1970p) 439,000; engineering works; diesel motors, textiles, timber; located on Turkistan-Siberian railroad; in rich mining region; meteorological observatory (founded 1841), mining school, museums; founded 1738.

Bar·ne·gat Bay \ˌbär-ni-ˌgat-, -gət-\. Inlet of Atlantic Ocean, extending N to S in Ocean co., New Jersey; ab. 30 m. long.

Barnegat Inlet. Strait bet. Long Beach I. and Island Beach leading from Atlantic Ocean into Barnegat Bay.

Barnegat Light *or before 1948* **Barnegat City.** Borough, New Jersey, at N tip of Long Beach I. on Barnegat Inlet; pop. (1970c) 554; site of lighthouse built 1855, abandoned 1930.

Barnes \ˈbärnz\. County in North Dakota. See table at NORTH DAKOTA.

Barnes·boro \ˈbärnz-ˌbər-ə, -ˌbə-rə\. Borough, Cambria co., SW cen. Pennsylvania, 24 m. WNW of Altoona; pop. (1970c) 2708; clothing; coal mines, truck farms.

Barnes·ville \'barnz-ˌvil, -vəl\. **1** City, ⊗ of Lamar co., W cen. Georgia, 35 m. WNW of Macon; pop. (1970c) 4935; hosiery, furniture; cotton mills; pecan processing.

2 Village, Belmont co., E Ohio, 38 m. SW of Steubenville; pop. (1970c) 4292; evaporated milk, mine cars and parts, glass, paper; coal and natural gas deposits nearby; diversified farming.

Bar·net \'bär-nət\. A borough of Greater London, SE England; pop. (1971p) 303,578; scene of decisive Yorkist victory Apr. 14, 1471, in the Wars of the Roses, in which the earl of Warwick was killed. See table at LONDON 4.

Bar·ne·veld \'bär-nə-ˌvelt\. Commune, Gelderland prov., E Netherlands, 10 m. E of Amersfoort; pop. (1970e) 30,046; poultry.

Bar·nolds·wick \bär-'nōl(d)z-ˌwik, 'bär-lik\. Urban district, West Riding, Yorkshire, N England, 9 m. N of Burnley; pop. (1971p) 9937; cotton-spinning works.

Barns·dall \'bärnz-(ˌ)dȯl\. City, Osage co., N Oklahoma, 16 m. SW of Bartlesville; pop. (1970c) 1579; called **Bigheart** \'big-ˌhärt\ until 1921; oil and gas wells; livestock.

Barns·ley \'bärnz-lē\. County borough, West Riding, Yorkshire, N England, on the Dearne 30 m. ENE of Manchester; pop. (1971p) 75,330; textile mills; glass, paper; coal deposits nearby.

Barn·sta·ble \'bärn-stə-bel\. **1** County in SE Massachusetts. See table at MASSACHUSETTS.

2 Town, its ⊗, on S shore of Cape Cod Bay; pop. (1970c) 19,842; summer resort.

Barn·sta·ple \'bärn-stə-pəl, -stə-bəl\. Municipal borough, Devonshire, SW England, on the Taw estuary 50 m. N of Plymouth; pop. (1971p) 17,342; gloves, furniture; tourism; one of the oldest royal boroughs; site of Cluniac priory of 11th cent.; incorp. 1557.

Barnstaple Bay. Bay on NW coast of Devonshire, SW England; receives the Taw river from the E.

Barn·well \'bärn-ˌwel, -wəl\. **1** County in SW South Carolina. See table at SOUTH CAROLINA.

2 City, its ⊗, 36 m. SW of Orangeburg; pop. (1970c) 4439; lumber, watermelons.

Ba·ro \'bär-(ˌ)ō\. River, W Ethiopia; 190 m. long; unites with Pibor river on border of SE Sudan to form Sobat river.

Ba·ro·da \bə-'rōd-ə\. **1** Former Indian state, W India; 8176 sq. m.; had four divisions, three in Gujarat (Kadi, Baroda, and Navsari) and one in peninsula of Kathiawar (Amreli, with Okhamandal). Once a part of Mogul Empire; in 18th cent. its princes belonged to Maratha Confederacy; c. 1721 secured part of Gujarat; in 19th cent. subject to British administrative control until gaekwar (ruler) given full powers 1881; became part of Bombay state 1948 and of Gujarat state 1960.

2 Division of former Baroda state, E of Surat; 1922 sq. m.

3 District, Gujarat; 2955 sq. m.; pop. (1961c) 1,527,044.

4 City, SE Gujarat, India, 244 m. N of Bombay; pop. (1970e) 404,229; chemicals, cotton, wool, tobacco; univ. (1949); noted for its jewelry and silver-interwoven cloth; ✱ of former Baroda state.

Baroda and Gu·ja·rat States Agency \-ˌgüj-ə-'rät-, -ˌgu̇j-\. A political agency of W India (1937–47), consisting of the state of Baroda and a number of smaller states formerly in the Rewa Kantha, Kaira, Surat, Nasik, and Thana agencies; now part of Gujarat, W India.

Ba·ro·ghil Pass \bə-ˌrō-ˌgil-\. Pass over the Hindu Kush bet. Chitral, N Pakistan, and the Wakhan valley; alt. 12,-457 ft.

Ba·ro·tac Nue·vo \ˌbär-ə-ˌtäk-nu̇-'ā-(ˌ)vō\. Municipality, SE Iloilo prov., Panay, Phil., 16 m. NNE of City of Iloilo; pop. (1969e) 31,600.

Ba·rot·se \bə-'rät-sə\. Province, W Zambia, S cen. Africa; 48,798 sq. m.; pop. (1967e) 408,000; ✱ Mongu; crossed by Zambezi river; approx. coextensive with **Ba·rot·se·land** \-ˌland\, region inhabited by the Barotse people. See ZAMBIA.

Bar·qui·si·me·to \ˌbär-ki-sə-'māt-(ˌ)ō\. City, ✱ of Lara state, NW Venezuela, 170 m. WSW of Caracas; pop. (1970e) 291,-353; at N end of Cordillera Mérida at alt. of 1856 ft.; center of agricultural region; cement, lumber, pottery; univ. (1968); founded 1552.

Bar·ra \'bar-ə\. Chief island of S group in the Outer Hebrides, off NW coast of Scotland; ab. 8 m. long and bet. 2 and 3 m. wide; chief village Castlebay, with ruins of Kisamul Castle, seat of the ancient Clan Macneil; with ab. 20 smaller islands (including Vatersay, Sandray, Mingulay, Berneray) constitutes parish of **Barra** or **Barra Islands;** administratively a part of Inverness co.; cockle and herring fisheries; many Norse and Celtic remains.

Barra, Sound of. Channel bet. South Uist I. and Barra I. in the Outer Hebrides, off NW coast of Scotland.

Bar·rack·pore \'bar-ək-ˌpō(ə)r, -ˌpȯ(ə)r\ *also* **Bar·rack·pur** \-ˌpu̇(ə)r\. Town, West Bengal, NE India, 15 m. N of Calcutta on left bank of Hooghly river; pop. (1961c) 63,778; station for troops since 1772; scene of mutiny 1824 which was suppressed; scene of disbandment of first Sepoy regiment to mutiny Mar. 1857.

Ba·rra de São Fran·cis·co \'bär-ə-də-ˌsau̇ⁿ(m)-frən-'sis-(ˌ)kü\. Municipality, Espírito Santo state, E Brazil; pop. (1968e) 114,945.

Barra do Pi·raí \'bär-ə-(ˌ)dü-ˌpir-ə-'ē\. City, Rio de Janeiro state, SE Brazil; munic. pop. (1968e) 60,384; railroad junction point ab. 45 m. NW of Rio de Janeiro.

Bar·ra·fran·ca \ˌbär-ə-'fräŋ-kə\. Commune, Enna prov., cen. Sicily, Italy, 14 m. SSW of Enna; pop. (1968e) 14,879; sulfur mines.

Bar·ra Head \ˌbar-ə-\. Cape on Berneray I., the S point of Barra Is., Outer Hebrides, off W coast of Scotland; lighthouse.

Barram. See BARAM.

Ba·rra Man·sa \ˌbar-ə-'man(t)-sə\. City, Rio de Janeiro state, SE Brazil, NW of Rio de Janeiro; munic. pop. (1968e) 84,937.

Ba·rran·ca·ber·me·ja *or* **Bar·ran·ca Ber·me·ja** \bə-ˌräŋ-kə-bər-'mā-(ˌ)hä\. River port, Santander dept., NW cen. Colombia, on the Magdalena river ab. 50 m. W of Bucaramanga; pop. (1968e) 68,309; oil refinery.

Ba·rran·cas \bə-'räŋ-kəs\. River, SW cen. Argentina; rises near Chilean border, flows SE to unite with Río Grande and form Colorado river.

Ba·rran·co \bə-'räŋ-(ˌ)kō\. Town, S suburb of Lima, Peru, on the coast; pop. (1961c) 42,449.

Ba·rran·que·ras \ˌbar-ən-'ker-əs\. River port, Chaco prov., N Argentina, on Paraná river near Corrientes; pop. (1960c) 19,779; ships hardwood and cotton.

Ba·rran·quil·la \ˌbar-ən-'kē-(y)ə\. City and port, ✱ of Atlántico dept., N Colombia, on Magdalena river 10 m. from its mouth; pop. (1971e) 656,100; cement, flour, textiles; Free Univ. (1956), Univ. of the Atlantic (1956); river channel deepened for ocean-going vessels 1935; founded 1629.

Ba·rran·qui·tas \ˌbar-ən-'kēt-əs\. Town and municipality, cen. Puerto Rico; munic. pop. (1970p) 19,853, town pop. 4399.

Bar·re \'bar-ē\. **1** Town, Worcester co., cen. Massachusetts, 19 m. WNW of Worcester; pop. (1970c) 3825; foundries, dairies.

2 City, Washington co., N cen. Vermont, 7 m. SSE of Montpelier; pop. (1970c) 10,209; extensive granite quarries and works; manufactures machines and tools; settled c. 1788; organized as town 1793, as city 1894.

Barre des Écrins \'bär-dā-zā-'kraⁿ\. Highest peak in the Dauphiné Alps and in the Pelvoux group of that range, SE France; 13,461 ft. See table at ALPS.

Ba·rrei·ro \bä-'rer-ō\. City, Setúbal dist., W Portugal, on Tagus estuary, opp. Lisbon; pop. (1970p) 35,622.

Bar·ren \'bar-ən\. 1 River, S Kentucky; 130 m. long; flows NW out of Monroe co. into Green river.

2 County in Kentucky. See table at KENTUCKY.

Barren Grounds. Low level treeless plains of N Canada, chiefly in Mackenzie dist. E of the Mackenzie basin and in Keewatin dist. NW of Hudson Bay; marked by many lakes, swamps, thin soil; sparsely inhabited by Eskimos and trappers.

Ba·rre·tos \bə-'rāt-(,)üs\. City, N São Paulo state, SE Brazil; munic. pop. (1968e) 69,901.

Bar·rett Dam \,bar-ət-\. Dam across Cottonwood Creek, S San Diego co., SW California; height 213 ft.; completed 1922; impounds water for water supply.

Barr·head \'bär-,hed\. Town, Alberta, Canada, 54 m. NW of Edmonton; pop. (1971p) 2786; lumber, flour mills, creamery.

Barrhead \bär-'hed\. Manufacturing burgh, Renfrew co., SW Scotland, on Levern river; pop. (1971p) 18,281; cotton mills, engineering works; iron and brass founding.

Bar·rie \'bar-ē\. City, ⊗ of Simcoe co., SE Ontario, Canada, on W extremity of Lake Simcoe; pop. (1971p) 26,985; summer resort; electrical equipment; plastics, shoes.

Bar·ri·er, Cape \-'bar-ē-ər\. Cape on S end of Great Barrier I., off NE North I., New Zealand.

Barrier Range. See MAIN BARRIER RANGE.

Barrier Reef. See GREAT BARRIER REEF.

Bar·ri·ga·da, Mount \-,bar-ə-'gäd-ə\. Elevation in E cen. Guam, Mariana Is., 5 m. E of Agana; 674 ft.; taken by Americans Aug. 3, 1944 in reconquest of Guam.

Bar·ring·ton \'bar-iŋ-tən\. 1 Village, Cook and Lake cos., NE Illinois, 33 m. NW of Chicago; pop. (1970c) 8674.

2 Borough, Camden co., SW New Jersey, 6 m. SSE of Camden; pop. (1970c) 8409.

3 Town, Bristol co., E Rhode Island, E of Narragansett Bay and 8 m. ESE of Providence; pop. (1970c) 17,554; residential and resort center; shipbuilding; Barrington Coll. (1900); incorp. by Massachusetts 1717, became part of Rhode Island 1746–47, incorp. by Rhode Island 1770.

Barrington Hills. Village, Cook, Kane, Lake, and McHenry cos., N Illinois, 33 m. NW of Chicago; pop. (1970c) 2712.

Ba·rro Col·o·ra·do \'bar-ō-,käl-ə-rad-(,)ō, 'bär-ō-,käl-ə-'räd-\. Island in Gatun Lake, Canal Zone; 6 sq. m.; biological station; wildlife preserve.

Bar·ron \'bar-ən\. 1 County in NW Wisconsin. See table at WISCONSIN.

2 City, its ⊗, 8 m. SW of Rice Lake (city); pop. (1970c) 2337; creamery products, lumber.

Ba·rro·sa \bä-'rō-sə\. Village, Cádiz prov., Spain, SE of Cádiz; British victory over French nearby 1811.

Bar·row \'bar-(,)ō\. 1 County in Georgia. See table at GEORGIA.

2 City, Alaska. See BARROW, POINT.

3 Island off NW coast of Western Australia, NE of North West Cape.

4 *or* **Barrow–in–Fur·ness** \-'fər-nəs\. County borough, Lancashire, NW England, on Furness Penin. opp. Isle of Walney 52 m. N of Liverpool; pop. (1971p) 63,998; steelworks, smelters, shipbuilding yards; paper.

5 River, SE Eire; 119 m. long; flows S from SE co. Offaly to Waterford Harbour.

Barrow, Point. Most northerly point of Alaska, 71°23′N, 156°30′W, on Arctic Ocean ab. 550 m. NE of Nome and an equal distance NW of Fairbanks; has small Eskimo settlement (Nuvuk). City, **Barrow** (pop. [1970c] 2104) ab. 12 m. S, is government station with post office and radio and weather bureau stations; has been important in explorations and aviation. Barrow Arctic Science Station opened by U.S. Navy 1947.

Barrow Creek. Post and telegraph station in desert region of cen. Northern Territory, Australia.

Bar·row·ford \'bar-ō-fərd, -ə-\. Urban district, Lancashire, NW England, on Leeds and Liverpool Canal 27 m. N of Manchester; pop. (1971p) 5130.

Barrow Strait. Channel bet. Bathurst and Cornwallis Is. on the N and Prince of Wales and Somerset Is. on the S, N Franklin dist., Northwest Territories, Canada; from 40 to 70 m. wide; ab. 150 m. long.

Bar·ry \'bar-ē\. 1 Name of counties in two states of the U.S. See tables at MICHIGAN and MISSOURI.

2 City, Pike co., W Illinois, ESE of Quincy; pop. (1970c) 1444; diversified farming.

3 Municipal borough and seaport, Glamorganshire, SE Wales; pop. (1971p) 41,578; shipping point for coal; resort.

Bar·sac \bär-'sak\. Commune, Gironde dept., SW France, near the Garonne; pop. (1962c) 2347; sauterne wine (see SAUTERNES).

Bar·si \'bär-sē\. Town, S Maharashtra, W India, 200 m. ESE of Bombay; pop. (1961c) 50,389; active trade center, esp. in cotton and oil seeds.

Bar·sing·haus·en \,bär-ziŋ-'haùz-ᵊn\. City, Lower Saxony, West Germany, 12 m. WSW of Hannover; pop. (1969e) 20,752; residential; first mentioned 991.

Bar·stow \'bär-(,)stō\. City, San Bernardino co., California; pop. (1970c) 17,442; railroad shops; Barstow Coll. (1960).

Bar–sur–Aube \,bär-(,)sù(ə)r-'ōb\. Commune, Aube dept., NE France; pop. (1962c) 4631; evidences of Roman occupation found nearby; destroyed by Huns 5th cent.; rebuilt, gained commercial importance; now market center for agricultural region producing wine, grain. Scene of battle Feb. 27, 1814 in which Allies defeated the French.

Bar–sur–Ornain. See BAR-LE-DUC.

Bartenstein. See BARTOSZYCE.

Bártfa *or* **Bartfeld.** See BARDEJOV.

Bar·thol·o·mew \bär-'thäl-ə-,myü\. County in Indiana. See table at INDIANA.

Bartholomew Bayou. River, SE Arkansas and NE Louisiana; 275 m. long; navigable 150 m.; rises in Jefferson co., SE cen. Arkansas, winds SE and S across Louisiana border into the Ouachita river in NE Louisiana.

Bar·ti·ca \bär-'tē-kə\. Town, N Guyana, at confluence of Essequibo, Mazaruni, and Cuyuni rivers 45 m. SW of Georgetown; point of departure for gold and diamond fields.

Bar·tle Frere, Mount \-'bärt-ᵊl-,fri(ə)r\. Mountain in Atherton Plateau, S of Cairns, NE Queensland, Australia; 5287 ft.; highest peak in Queensland.

Bar·tles·ville \'bärt-ᵊlz-,vil\. City, ⊗ of Washington co., NE Oklahoma, 41 m. N of Tulsa; pop. (1970c) 29,683; oil and gas wells; manufactures oil-field equipment; Bartlesville Wesleyan Coll. (1910); founded 1877.

Bart·lett \'bärt-lət\. 1 Village, Cook and Du Page cos., NE Illinois, 28 m. W of Chicago; pop. (1970c) 3501; hardware, vacuum cleaners, electronic equipment.

2 Village, ⊗ of Wheeler co., NE cen. Nebraska; pop. (1970c) 193.

3 Town, Carroll co., E New Hampshire, on Saco river 11 m. NW of Conway; pop. (1970c) 1098; resort in White Mts.

Bartlett Dam. Dam across Verde river in Salt River Indian Reservation, E Maricopa co., S cen. Arizona; height 287 ft.; completed 1939; impounds water for irrigation.

Bart·lett's Ferry Dam \,bärt-ləts-\. Dam across Chattahoochee river, on Georgia-Alabama border, ab. 18 m. N of Columbus, Ga.; height 145 ft.; completed 1926; impounds water for power, forming **Bartlett's Ferry Lake.**

Bar·ton \'bärt-ᵊn\. 1 Name of counties in two states of the U.S. See tables at KANSAS and MISSOURI.

2 Town, Orleans co., N Vermont; pop. (1970c) 2874.

Barton–upon–Hum·ber \-'həm-bər\. Urban district, Parts of Lindsey, Lincolnshire, E England, 8 m. SW of Hull; pop. (1969e) 6720; important port in 14th cent.

Bar·ton·ville \'bärt-ᵊn-,vil\. Village, Peoria co., NW cen. Illinois, 7 m. SW of Peoria; pop. (1970c) 7221.

Bar·to·szy·ce \ˌbärt-ə-ˈshit-sə\ *or Ger.* **Bar·ten·stein** \ˈbart-ᵊn-ˌs(h)tīn\. Town, N Olsztyn prov., N Poland, N of Olsztyn; pop. (1968e) 14,800; founded c. 1325.

Bar·tow \ˈbär-(ˌ)tō\. **1** County in Georgia. See table at GEORGIA.

2 City, ⊗ of Polk co., cen. Florida penin., 15 m. SSE of Lakeland; pop. (1970c) 12,891; phosphate mining, citrus canning, cigar making.

Bar·wa·ni \bər-ˈwän-ē\. **1** Former Indian state, now part of Madhya Pradesh, cen. India, in Satpura Range S of Narmada river; 1189 sq. m.

2 Town, its ✱; pop. (1961c) 17,446.

Bar·won \ˈbär-wən\. Upper course of Darling river in NE New South Wales, SE Australia; rises in SE Queensland and flows SW ab. 400 m.; forms part of boundary bet. Queensland and New South Wales.

Barygaza. See BROACH.

Basarabia. See BESSARABIA 2.

Ba·sau·ri \bä-ˈsau̇(ə)r-ē\. Commune, Vizcaya prov., N Spain, 5 m. SE of Bilbao; pop. (1960c) 23,030.

Bas·co \ˈbäs-(ˌ)kō\ *or in full* **San·to Do·min·go de Basco** \ˌsant-əd-ə-ˈmiŋ-go-dā-\. Municipality, ✱ of Batanes prov., N Phil., on W shore of Batan I. ab. 150 m. N of Aparri; pop. (1969e) 3900.

Bas·cu·ñán, Cape \-ˌbas-kən-ˈyän\. Cape on SW coast of Atacama prov., N cen. Chile.

Ba·sel \ˈbäz-əl\ *or older* **Basle** \ˈbäl\ *or Fr.* **Bâle** \bäl\. **1** Swiss canton; subdivided into demicantons: **Basel–Land** \-ˌlänt\ *also* **Ba·sel·land** \ˈbäz-əl-ˌland\ *or* **Basel (Land),** *and* **Basel–Stadt** \-ˈs(h)tät\ *also* **Ba·sel·stadt** \-ˌshtät\ *or* **Basel (Stadt).** See table at SWITZERLAND.

2 City, ✱ of Basel-Stadt demicanton and of Basel canton, NW Switzerland, on both sides of Rhine river 43 m. N of Bern; pop. (1970c) 212,857, met. area pop. 370,200; transportation center; chemicals, silk; publishing; 11th cent. church, univ. (1460).

History: Scene of famous church council which lasted through 45 sessions from 1431 until 1443; became member of Swiss Confederation 1501; Confession of Basel adopted by Protestants 1534; peace treaties signed here Apr. 5, July 22, and Aug. 28, 1795, bet. Prussia, Spain, and France.

Ba·sey \bä-ˈsā\. Municipality, S Samar, Phil., on N shore of San Pedro Bay; pop. (1969e) 40,300.

Ba·shahr \ˈbəsh-ər, ˈbüsh-\ *also* **Bus·sa·hir** \ˈbu̇s-ə-ˌhi(ə)r\. Former Indian state, now part of Punjab, N India; 3439 sq. m.

Ba·shan \ˈbā-shən\. Northernmost of E Palestine's three anc. divisions; region now in S part of Syria.

Ba·shi Channel \ˌbäsh-ē-\ *or formerly* **Ba·chi Channel** \ˌbäch-ē-\. Strait bet. Batan Is. of the Philippines and S end of Taiwan; ab. 92 m. wide; traversed at approximately 21°25′N by the boundary line as determined by Treaty of Paris Dec. 10, 1898.

Bash·kir Autonomous Soviet Socialist Republic \bash-ˈki(ə)r-\ *also* **Bash·kir·ia** \bash-ˈkir-ē-ə\. Autonomous republic, a subdivision of the Russian S.F.S.R., U.S.S.R., bounded on N by Perm and Sverdlovsk oblasts, on E by Chelyabinsk Oblast, on S and SW by Orenburg Oblast, and on W by Tatar A.S.S.R.; 55,443 sq. m.; pop. (1970p) 3,819,000; ✱ Ufa. A plateau and mountainous (Southern Urals) area, watered by the Belaya and its tributary the Ufa; has Ural river on its E border; has extensive forests and valuable mineral deposits in the mountains (bauxite, coal, copper, manganese); rye, oats, corn, flax; oil production and refining; iron and steel, chemicals, machine tools. Chief towns Ufa, Sterlitamak, Oktyabrski. Bashkirs came under Russian control 1556, but have rebelled several times since.

Ba·si·gon \bə-ˈsē-ˌgän\. River, cen. Camarines Norte prov., Luzon, Phil.; ab. 35 m. long.

Ba·si·lan \bə-ˈsē-ˌlän\. **1** Island group, SW of Mindanao, Phil.; ab. 530 sq. m.; comprises Basilan I. and about 50 small islands.

2 Largest island in Basilan group, separated from Zamboanga by Basilan Strait; 495 sq. m. Mountainous, with highest point **Basilan Peak** 3320 ft.; has valuable timber; inhabitants mainly Moros whose chief occupation is fishing. Occupied by Americans Mar. 18, 1945.

3 *formerly* **Isa·be·la** \ˌiz-ə-ˈbel-ə\ *or* **Isabela de Basilan.** Chartered city, NW Basilan I., Phil.; pop. (1970e) 222,600.

Basilan Strait. Passage bet. Basilan I. and SW Mindanao, S Phil.; connects Moro Gulf with the Sulu Sea; ab. 10 m. wide.

Bas·il·don \ˈbaz-əl-dən\. Urban district, Essex, SE England, 25 m. ENE of London; pop. (1971p) 129,073; chemicals; light engineering.

Ba·si·li·ca·ta \bə-ˈzil-i-ˈkät-ə\ *or formerly* **Lu·ca·nia** \lü-ˈkän-yə\. Autonomous region, S Italy; 3857 sq. m.; pop. (1968e) 633,538; ✱ Potenza; wheat, rye; livestock. For provincial divisions, see table at ITALY.

Bas·i·lisk Harbour \ˌbas-ə-ˌlisk-, ˌbaz-\. Large inlet in Utupua I., Santa Cruz Is., SW Pacific Ocean.

Ba·sin \ˈbās-ᵊn\. Town, ⊗ of Big Horn co., N Wyoming; pop. (1970c) 1145; oil wells.

Ba·sing·stoke \ˈbā-ziŋ-ˌstōk\. Municipal borough, Hampshire, S England, 46 m. WSW of London; pop. (1971p) 52,502; leather goods, precision instruments; an old town with many antiquities; at **Ba·sing** \ˈbāz-iŋ\ parish to the E occurred Ethelred's victory over the Danes 871; first charter granted 1227.

Ba·sir·hat \ˌbəs-ər-ˈhät, ˌbäs-\. Town, West Bengal, NE India, on Kalindi river 30 m. E of Calcutta; pop. (1961c) 53,943.

Ba·sit, Cape \-bə-ˈsēt\ *or Arab.* **Ras al–Basit** \ˌräs-ˌal-\. Cape, N coast of Latakia, Syria, 35°51′N.

Bas·ka·tong \ˈbas-kə-ˌtäŋ, -ˌtȯŋ\. Lake, Gatineau co., SW Quebec, Canada; outlet S through Gatineau river.

Basle. See BASEL.

Ba·so·ko \bə-ˈsō-ˌkō\. Town, Haut-Zaïre prov., NE Zaire, at junction of Aruwimi and Congo rivers.

Basque Provinces \ˈbask-\ *or Span.* **Pro·vin·cias Vas·con·ga·das** \prə-ˈvēn(t)-sē-ˌäs-ˌvas-kən-ˈgäd-əs\. Region, N Spain; bounded N by Bay of Biscay, E by Navarre, S and W by Old Castile; 2800 sq. m.; comprises modern provinces of Vizcaya, Álava, and Guipúzcoa; has Pyrenees on E and E end of Cantabrian Mts. on W; forests, orchards, vineyards; center of iron-mining district; copper mining, marble quarrying; fisheries.

History: Inhabited by Basques, a people of obscure racial and linguistic origin who retained virtual autonomy until 19th cent.; little affected by Moorish conquest of Spain; Álava and Vizcaya successively dependent upon kingdoms of Asturias, Navarre, and Castile; took part in Carlist War 1834–76, but allowed by Alfonso XII to keep only certain amount of administrative autonomy; given autonomy soon after outbreak of Civil War 1936 but occupied by Insurgents 1936–37.

Bas·ra \ˈbäs-rə, ˈbəs-, ˈbas-, ˈbäz-, ˈbəz-, ˈbaz-\ *or Arab.* **Al–Bas·rah** \al-\ *also* **Bus·so·ra** *or* **Bus·so·rah** \ˈbəs-ə-rə\; *formerly* **Bus·ra** *or* **Bus·rah** \ˈbäs-rə, ˈbəs-\. Port, at head of the Shatt-al-Arab, SE Iraq, ab. 75 m. from the Persian Gulf; pop. (1965c) 313,327; connected by rail with Baghdad; administrative and commercial center; univ. (1967). Founded by Caliph Omar I 638; famous under the Abbassides; known in *Arabian Nights* as **Bas·so·rah** \ˈbas-ə-rə\; taken by Turks 1668 but declined as a trade center until World War I; in World War II occupied by British 1941, became important for transshipment of supplies to Turkey and U.S.S.R.

Bas–Rhin \ˈbä-ˈraⁿ\. Department of NE France. See table at FRANCE.

Bassae. See PHIGALIA.
Bassam. See GRAND BASSAM.
Bas·sa·no \bə-'sän-(,)ō\ *or in full* **Bassano del Grap·pa** \-del-'gräp-ə\. Commune, Vicenza prov., Veneto, NE Italy, on left bank of Brenta river 19 m. NE of Vicenza; pop. (1968e) 34,763; has 12th cent. Romanesque church and 13th cent. castle; majolica ware, leather, silk. First mentioned 998; joined Venetian republic 1402; scene of defeat of Austrians by Napoleon Sept. 8, 1796; made duchy by Napoleon and conferred upon Maret 1809.
Bassas da India. See INDIA, BASSAS DA.
Bassée, La. See LA BASSÉE.
Bas·sein \bə-'sān\. 1 River, Bassein dist., Burma; ab. 160 m. long; a navigable outlet of the Irrawaddy in W part of its delta.
2 District, Irrawaddy div., Burma; 4149 sq. m.; pop. (1962e) 914,506; rice.
3 City, its ✱ and ✱ of Irrawaddy division, in the Irrawaddy delta 90 m. W of Rangoon; pop. (1969e) 175,000, met. area pop. 424,000; rice mills, machine shops; badly damaged by Japanese 1942; reoccupied by British May 25, 1945.
Bas·sen·thwaite \'bas-ᵊn-,thwāt\. Lake in the Lake District in Cumberland co., NW England, E of Cockermouth; an expansion of Derwent river.
Basses–Alpes. See ALPES-DE-HAUTE PROVENCE.
Basses–Pyrénées \,bäs-,pir-ə-'nā\. See PYRÉNÉES 2.
Basse·terre \bäs-'te(ə)r\. Seaport on St. Christopher I., Leeward Is., West Indies; pop. (1970e) 14,133; ✱ of St. Christopher-Nevis; sugar refining; founded 1627.
Basse–Terre \,bäs-(ə-)'te(ə)r\. 1 Island, the W part of the French department of Guadeloupe, West Indies, N of Dominica; 35 m. long.
2 Seaport on SW coast of Basse-Terre I., ✱ of the French dept. of Guadeloupe; pop. (1967c) 15,458; founded 1643.
Bas·sett \'bas-ət\. 1 Village, ⊗ of Rock co., N Nebraska; pop. (1970c) 983.
2 Urban community (unincorp.), Henry co., Virginia, NW of Martinsville; pop. (1970c) 3058.
Bass Island \'bas-\. Three islands in W Lake Erie, **North Bass I., Middle Bass I.,** *and* **South Bass I.,** N and E of Ottawa co., N Ohio; Put-in-Bay, scene of Perry's naval victory 1813, is on South Bass Island and is the site of a national monument.
Bassorah. See BASRA.
Bass Rock. Large isolated greenstone rock, S of entrance to Firth of Forth, SE Scotland; lighthouse; site of ruins of 17th cent. castle, seized by Jacobites 1691 and held 3 years before surrendering to William of Orange.
Bass Strait. Strait separating Australia from Tasmania; 80 to 150 m. wide, 185 m. long; av. depth 230 ft.; discovered 1798 by George Bass, British surgeon and navigator.
Bas·tar \'bəs-tər, 'bäs-\. 1 Former Indian state, now part of Madhya Pradesh, E cen. India; 13,701 sq. m.
2 District, S Madhya Pradesh, India; 15,124 sq. m.; pop. (1961c) 1,167,501; ✱ Jagdalpur; iron ore.
Bas·ti \'bəs-tē, 'bäs-\. 1 District, Uttar Pradesh, N India; 2821 sq. m.; pop. (1961c) 2,627,061; rice, sugarcane, barley.
2 Town, its ✱, 115 m. NNE of Allahabad; pop. (1961c) 38,403; textiles; college.
Basti. See BAZA.
Ba·stia \'bas-tē-ə, 'bäs-\. Seaport city, Corse dept., France, on NE coast of island of Corsica 65 m. NE of Ajaccio; pop. (1968c) 49,375; principal commercial and industrial city of Corsica; exports include: wine, asbestos, fish; citadel; cathedral. Taken by British 1745; became French 1768; made capital of Corsica 1791 (later superseded by Ajaccio).
Bas·togne \ba-'stōn(-yə)\. Town, E Luxembourg prov., SE Belgium; pop. (1969e) 6694; an upland town of the Ardennes 43 m. S of Liége; important railroad and highway junction point. In World War II in the German offensive (Battle of the Bulge) of December 1944, an American division surrounded here Dec. 22–27; held after severe fighting until German forces driven back Jan. 1945.
Bas·trop \'bas-trəp\. 1 County in Texas. See table at TEXAS.
2 City, ⊗ of Morehouse parish, N Louisiana, 24 m. NNE of Monroe; pop. (1970c) 14,713; paper mills, gas wells; chemicals.
3 City, ⊗ of Bastrop co., S cen. Texas, on Colorado river 28 m. ESE of Austin; pop. (1970c) 3112; coal mines, oil wells; diversified farming.
Basutoland. See LESOTHO.
Bas–Za·ïre \'bä-zä-'i(ə)r\ *or formerly* **Kon·go–Cen·tral** \ käⁿ-'gō-säⁿ-träl\. Province of W Zaire See table at ZAIRE.
Ba·ta \'bät-ə\. Seaport, chief town of Río Muni, Equatorial Guinea, W Africa; pop. (1960c) 27,024.
Ba·taan \bə-'tan, -'tän\. Province, W Luzon, Phil., forming a peninsula 30 m. long by 15 m. wide on W side of Manila Bay; 530 sq. m.; pop. (1970p) 214,131; ✱ Balanga. Traversed by S end of Zambales Mts., highest point in province 4444 ft.; has many short streams and few indentations on its coast; Mariveles Bay at its S end is best harbor; its NW coast forms E shore of the large safe anchorage of Subic Bay; western half is covered with forests and jungle; eastern coastal plain is most populous; chief towns Dinalupihan, Balanga, Orion, Abucay.
History: Bet. 1600 and 1650 the scene of several conflicts with the Dutch; in early times a part of Pampanga; created separate province by Spanish governor general 1754; civil government established March 1901. In World War II scene of final struggle of American and Filipino forces under Gen. Douglas MacArthur against Japanese conquest of Phil. Northern end occupied about Jan. 10, 1942, after fall of Manila, by American forces, who, after withdrawal southward toward Mariveles, surrendered Apr. 9, 1942; remnant of force retired to Corregidor (*q.v.*), which also gave up May 6. Retaken by Americans Feb. 15–21, 1945.
Ba·ta·ba·nó \,bät-ə-bə-'nō\. Town and municipality, S La Habana prov., W Cuba; town pop. (1967e) 18,190; sponge and turtle fisheries.
Batabanó, Gulf of. Widemouthed gulf S of La Habana and Pinar del Río provs., W Cuba, and N of Isle of Pines.
Ba·tac \'bä-,täk\. Municipality, SW Ilocos Norte prov., Luzon, Phil., 10 m. S of Laoag; pop. (1969e) 36,800.
Ba·taisk \bə-'tīsk\. City, SW Rostov Oblast, Russian S.F.S.R., U.S.S.R., 5 m. S of Rostov-na-Donu; pop. (1969e) 91,000; building materials, furniture; important railroad junction point with main line running SE to Caucasus. Key point in struggle for Rostov-na-Donu 1918 in civil war; seized by German armies July 1942; recaptured Feb. 1943.
Ba·tak·land \'bä-,tak-,land\ *or Du.* **Ba·tak·lan·den** \,bä-,täk-'län-dən\. Region around Lake Toba, N Sumatra, Indonesia; original home of the Batak, an Indonesian people, formerly cannibals, now numbering more than 1,500,000; country not controlled by Dutch until after middle of the 19th cent.
Ba·ta·la \bə-'täl-ə\. Town, NW Punjab, NW India, ab. 25 m. NE of Amritsar; pop. (1961c) 51,300.
Ba·ta·lha \bə-'tal-yə\. Commune, Leiria dist., W cen. Portugal, 6 m. S of Leiria; pop. (1970p) 6673; famous for its Dominican monastery, now a national monument containing tomb of John I of Portugal and other kings, built by John I of Portugal to commemorate his victory 1385 over John I of Castile at Aljubarrota nearby.
Batalpashinsk. See CHERKESSK.
Ba·tam \bə-'täm\. Island in the Riau Archipelago, Indonesia, opp. Singapore; 180 sq. m.; its N shore borders on Singapore Strait.
Ba·tan \bə-'tän\. Island, E Albay prov., Luzon, Phil., in center of chain of three islands N of Albay Gulf and forming part of S shore of Lagonoy Gulf; ab. 13 m. long by 5 m. wide; 35 sq. m.; has valuable coal mines.

Ba·ta·naea \ˌbat-ə-ˈnē-ə\. Roman name of S Bashan, ancient Palestine, forming the SW part of the region ruled over by Philip the Tetrarch (4 B.C.–34 A.D.).

Ba·ta·nes \bə-ˈtän-əs\. Province, comprising the **Ba·tan Islands** \bə-ˈtän-\, N of Luzon, N Phil.; 81 sq. m.; pop. (1970p) 11,425; ✱ Basco, on Batan I.; separated from Taiwan by Bashi Channel and from the Babuyan Is. to the S by Balintang Channel; comprises Itbayat, Batan, and Sabtang Is. and 11 islets; mountainous, with an extinct volcano on Batan I. Long inhabited; first conquered by Spanish 1791; made a province 1909.

Ba·tang \ˈbä-ˌtäŋ\. Town, Central Java prov., Indonesia, just E of Pekalongan.

Ba·tan·gas \bə-ˈtaŋ-gəs, -ˈtäŋ-\. 1 Province, S Luzon, Phil.; 1222 sq. m.; pop. (1970p) 927,290; ✱ Batangas; numerous mountains, esp. in W and NE; many small streams; in cen. part is large Lake Taal with Taal volcano forming an island in its center; three large bays Balayan, Batangas, and Tayabas; main products sugar, lumber, coconut oil. Chief towns Batangas, Lipa, Tanauan, Nasugbu, Rosario.

History: Populous region in pre-Spanish times; explored by Spaniards 1570 and created a province 1581, much larger than at present; in 17th cent. suffered from Moro attacks and in 18th cent. from severe eruptions of Taal volcano; active in revolution against Spanish; civil government established May 1901.

2 Municipality, its ✱, in S part of province on NE coast of Batangas Bay 58 m. S of Manila; pop. (1969e) 113,200; oil refinery; Japanese landed here Dec. 24, 1941.

Batangas Bay. Inlet in S coast of Batangas prov., Luzon, Phil.; ab. 9 m. across at mouth; island of Maricaban on SW; Batangas and Bauan at its head.

Batang Lu·par \ˌbä-ˌtäŋ-ˈlü-ˌpär\. River, SW Sarawak, East Malaysia; 120 m. long; flows W into the South China Sea.

Batan Islands. See BATANES.

Ba·tan·ta \bə-ˈtänt-ə\. Island off N coast of Salawati (*q.v.*) I., Irian Barat, Indonesia; ab. 40 m. long.

Ba·ta·via \bə-ˈtā-vē-ə\. 1 Industrial city, Kane co., NE Illinois, 35 m. W of Chicago; pop. (1970c) 8994; farm implements, engines, and foundry products; nearby is the National Accelerator Laboratory.

2 Manufacturing city, ⊗ of Genesee co., W New York, 33 m. WSW of Rochester; pop. (1970c) 17,338; shoes, farm implements, die castings; gypsum mines; Genesee Community Coll. (1966); settled 1801, incorporated 1914.

3 Village, ⊗ of Clermont co., SW Ohio, 17 m. E of Cincinnati; pop. (1970c) 1894; tobacco, corn, wheat.

4 Former residency, Java, Neth. Indies, now part of the Indonesian prov. of West Java; 3098 sq. m.; included lowlands along NW coast of Java on Java Sea and Djakarta Bay and the Thousand Is. group in SW Java Sea; region has many short streams; densely populated.

5 City, Indonesia. See DJAKARTA.

Batavia Bay. See DJAKARTA BAY.

Ba·ta·vi·an Republic \bə-ˌtā-vē-ən-\. The name given to Holland by the French after its conquest in 1795; lasted until 1806 when kingdom of Holland was established with Louis, brother of Napoleon, as its ruler.

Batdambang. See BATTAMBANG.

Bates \ˈbāts\. County in Missouri. See table at MISSOURI.

Bates·burg \ˈbāts-ˌbərg\. Town, W cen. South Carolina, 32 m. W of Columbia; pop. (1970c) 4036.

Bates·ville \ˈbāts-ˌvil, -vəl\. 1 City, ⊗ of Independence co., NE cen. Arkansas; pop. (1970c) 7209; bottling works; marble and manganese in vicinity. Arkansas Coll. (1872; incorp. 1836 as Batesville Academy); first settled 1812.

2 City, Franklin and Ripley cos., SE Indiana, 31 m. ESE of Shelbyville; pop. (1970c) 3799; furniture manufacturing.

3 Town, a ⊗ of Panola co., NW Mississippi, 35 m. ENE of Clarksdale; pop. (1970c) 3796; cotton gins; timber.

Bath \ˈbath, ˈbäth\. 1 Name of counties in two states of the U.S. See tables at KENTUCKY and VIRGINIA.

2 City, ⊗ of Sagadahoc co., S Maine, on inlet of Atlantic Ocean 28 m. NE of Portland; pop. (1970c) 9679; port of entry and trading center; shipbuilding; incorp. 1781.

3 Village, ⊗ of Steuben co., S New York, 19 m. E of Hornell; pop. (1970c) 6053; diversified farming; settled 1793.

4 Borough, Northampton co., E Pennsylvania, 10 m. NNE of Allentown; pop. (1970c) 1829.

5 Town, West Virginia. See BERKELEY SPRINGS.

6 *anc.* **Aquae Cal·i·dae** \ˌak-(ˌ)wē-ˈkal-ə-ˌdē, ˌäk-\ *or* **Aquae So·lis** \-ˈsō-ləs\. City and county borough, Somersetshire, SW England, on the Avon 12 m. SE of Bristol; pop. (1969e) 84,760; health resort with thermal springs; electrical engineering; printing; Bath Univ. of Technology (1966); Roman remains (baths discovered 1775); received charter 1189.

Bath·gate \ˈbath-ˌgāt, -gət\. Manufacturing burgh, West Lothian co., SE Scotland; pop. (1969e) 14,763; coal mines, stone quarries, whisky distilleries, steel works.

Bath·urst \ˈbath-(ˌ)ərst\. 1 City, E New South Wales, SE Australia, on Macquarie river in Blue Mts., 100 m. WNW of Sidney; pop. (1968e) 17,330; elev. 2206 ft.; center of wheat-growing district; fruit, tobacco, cereals; tourist center; trout fishing; founded 1815.

2 City, ⊗ of Gloucester co., NE New Brunswick, Canada, on Nepisiguit Bay at mouth of Nepisiguit river; pop. (1971p) 16,404; summer resort; important salmon center and shipping port for lumber; Bathurst Coll. (1899).

3 Seaport, ✱ of Gambia, W Africa, on the Island of St. Mary in the Gambia river; pop. (1971e) 36,570; exports peanuts, hides; during World War II developed as important airport.

4 Village, SE Cape Province, Rep. of South Africa, 90 m. ENE of Port Elizabeth; first home and administrative center of British settlers of 1820.

Bathurst, Cape. Cape, NW Mackenzie dist., Northwest Territories, Canada, extending into Beaufort Sea, 70°35′N, 128°W.

Bathurst Inlet. Large inlet of Coronation Gulf, NE Mackenzie dist., Northwest Territories, Canada.

Bathurst Island. 1 Island, NW of Northern Territory, Australia, W of Melville I.; 30 m. long; 786 sq. m.; separated from mainland by Clarence Strait.

2 Island, one of the Parry Is., NW Franklin dist., Northwest Territories, N Canada; 7609 sq. m.

Ba·tis·can \ˌbat-ə-ˈskäⁿ\. River, S Quebec, Canada; ab. 50 m. long; rises in W Quebec co., flows S into St. Lawrence river near Batiscan in Champlain co.

Ba·tjan *also* **Ba·chan** *or* **Ba·chian** \ˈbäch-ˌän\. Largest island of a group in Moluccas, Indonesia, Malay Archipelago, just SW of Halmahera; 50 m. long by ab. 27 m. wide; 914 sq. m.; pop. (1957e) 21,861; irregular in shape, mountainous and volcanic; highest point 6926 ft.; remarkable for its fauna and flora. Formerly a sultanate; seized by Dutch 1609 and put under control of Sultan of Ternate. The group (2268 sq. m.) includes the smaller islands of Kasiruta and Mandioli to the W and the large group of Obi Is. (*q.v.*) to the S.

Bat·ley \ˈbat-lē\. Municipal borough, West Riding, Yorkshire, N England, 6 m. SSW of Leeds; pop. (1971p) 42,004; center of woolen trade; textile equipment, plastics.

Bat·na \ˈbat-nə\. 1 Department of NE Algeria. See table at ALGERIA.

2 City, its ✱, on Toggourt-Annaba railroad, 195 m. SE of Algiers; pop. (1966c) 54,924.

Ba·to, Lake \-bə-ˈtō\. Small lake on S boundary of Camarines Sur prov., Luzon, Phil., partly in NW Albay prov.; total area 15 sq. m.; receives many streams of Albay that rise near the foot of Mt. Mayon; outlet is the Bicol river.

Batoe. See BATU.

Bat·on Rouge \ˌbat-ᵊn-ˈrüzh\. 1 For parishes in Louisiana, see *East Baton Rouge* and *West Baton Rouge* in table at LOUISIANA.

2 City, ✱ of Louisiana and ⊗ of East Baton Rouge parish, SE cen. Louisiana, on Mississippi river 78 m. WNW of New Orleans; pop. (1970c) 165,963; 3d largest city in the state, located on bluffs on E side of the river; deep water port facilities; petroleum refineries; chemicals; distributing center for agricultural region. Louisiana State Univ. and Agricultural and Mechanical Coll. (1860).

History: Transferred from France to Great Britain by Treaty of Paris 1763, and made a part of West Florida; conquered by Spain during American Revolution; ceded by Spain to France 1800; claimed again by Spain at time of Louisiana Purchase 1803; established independence by rebellion 1810, and declared itself county by the name of Feliciana; after admission of Louisiana to the Union 1812, incorporated as a town 1817; state capital 1849–61 and 1882 to date; held by Union forces for greater part of Civil War; consolidation of city and parish governments 1947.

Ba·trun *or Fr.* **Ba·troun** \bə-ˈtrün\. Town, on coast in N Lebanon.

Bat·tam·bang \ˈbat-əm-ˌbaŋ\ *or* **Bat·dam·bang** \-dəm-\. Town, W Cambodia, W of Tonle Sap; pop. (1962p) 38,846; in a fertile plain in large rice-growing area. Ceded to Siam (Thailand) by Cambodia 1809 and by Siam to French Indochina 1907; under Japanese pressure yielded by the French Vichy government to Siam Mar. 1941; returned to Cambodia 1946.

Bat·ten·berg \ˈbat-ᵊn-ˌbərg, ˈbät-ᵊn-ˌbe(ə)rg\. Village, Hesse, West Germany, 15 m. NNW of Marburg; pop. (1964e) 2000; seat of family of counts whose title died out c. 1314 and was revived 1851 for a royal branch, English members of which renounced the title 1917 and assumed the surname Mountbatten.

Bat·ti·ca·loa \ˌbət-i-kə-ˈlō-ə\. Seaport town, Ceylon, on Bay of Bengal; pop. (1968e) 24,000; located on a lagoon noted for its "singing fish," a natural phenomenon, still unexplained, consisting of musical notes rising from the water. Taken from Portuguese 1639 by Dutch, who erected a fort 1682.

Bat·ti·pa·glia \ˌbät-i-ˈpäl-yə\. Commune, Salerno prov., S Campania, S Italy, 12 m. ESE of Salerno; pop. (1968e) 32,465; road junction, taken by Allies Sept. 12, 1943.

Bat·tle \ˈbat-ᵊl\. 1 River, cen. Alberta and Saskatchewan, Canada; ab. 340 m. long; flows E from cen. Alberta into North Saskatchewan at Battleford.

2 Market town and parish, East Sussex, England, 6 m. NW of Hastings; pop. (1961c) 4300; named from the Battle of Hastings that took place 1066 on a hill SE of the town. Site of Battle Abbey, founded by William the Conqueror and consecrated 1094, now mostly in ruins. The "Roll of Battle Abbey," a list of Norman surnames, probably compiled in 14th cent.

Battle Creek. Industrial city, Calhoun co., S Michigan, 22 m. E of Kalamazoo; pop. (1970c) 38,931; manufactures breakfast foods, also printing presses, gas stoves, farm machinery; Kellogg Community Coll. (1956); site of Battle Creek Sanitarium.

Bat·tle·ford \ˈbat-ᵊl-fərd\. Town, W Saskatchewan, Canada, at junction of Battle and North Saskatchewan rivers opposite North Battleford; pop. (1971p) 1792; flour mills and mineral water works. Founded 1875; capital of Northwest Territories 1876–82, and of Saskatchewan dist. 1882–1905; invested by Indians during second Riel rebellion 1885.

Battle Harbour. Village on small island off SE Labrador coast, Canada, N of N end of Strait of Belle Isle, on sheltered roadstead; site of a Grenfell Mission Hospital, estab. 1893, which was destroyed by fire 1923.

Battlement Mountain. Peak, W Park co., NW Wyoming; 11,900 ft.

Battle Mountain. Peak, Fall River co., SW corner of South Dakota; 4431 ft.

Bat·to·nya \ˈbȯt-ən-ˌyȯ\. Commune, SE Hungary, 42 m. ENE of Szeged; pop. (1970p) 9335.

Ba·tu *or Du.* **Ba·toe** \ˈbä-(ˌ)tü\. Island group, Indonesia, in the Indian Ocean off W cen. coast of Sumatra; 464 sq. m.; pop. (1957e) 13,135; crossed by the equator; contains about 48 islands with only three of any size, Tanahmasa, Tanahbala, and Pini.

Batu Anam \ˌbä-(ˌ)tü-ˈän-ˌäm\. Village on railroad, N Johore state, Malaysia, near Gemas; severe fighting bet. Australians and Japanese Jan. 1942.

Ba·tu·da·ka \ˌbät-ü-ˈdäk-ə\. See PENJU ISLANDS.

Batu Ga·jah \-ˈgäj-ə\. Town, cen. Perak state, Malaysia, on railroad just S of Ipoh; headquarters of Kinta Valley tin-producing region.

Ba·tu·lao, Mount \-bə-ˈtü-ˌlaü\. Mountain, NW Batangas prov., Luzon, Phil., W of Lake Taal; 2894 ft.

Ba·tu·mi \bə-ˈtü-mē\ *or formerly* **Ba·tum** \-ˈtüm\. City and seaport, ✱ of Adzhar A.S.S.R., SW Georgian S.S.R., on Black Sea near Turkish border; pop. (1970p) 101,000; has best port at E end of Black Sea; connected by rail and oil pipe line with Tbilisi and Baku; shipyard, oil refineries, engineering works; exports oil, manganese, citrus fruits. Long a possession of Persia and Turkey; acquired by Russia 1878; occupied by British 1918; one of the Black Sea bases of Soviet fleet.

Bat Yam \ˈbät-ˈyäm\. Coastal city, W cen. Israel, suburb of Tel Aviv-Jaffa; pop. (1970e) 83,500; printing and publishing.

Ba·uan \ˈbä-ˌwän\. Municipality on N coast of Batangas Bay, Batangas prov., Luzon, Phil., 4 m. NW of Batangas; pop. (1969e) 55,900; piña cloth embroidery.

Ba·uang \ˈbä-ˌwäŋ\. Municipality, S cen. La Union prov., Luzon, Phil., at river mouth near the coast 6 m. S of San Fernando; pop. (1969e) 35,600.

Bau·chi \ˈbaü-chē\. Town, North-Eastern State, Nigeria, 150 m. SE of Kano; pop. (1963c) 37,778.

Bau·dette \bō-ˈdet\. Village, ⊗ of Lake of the Woods co., N Minnesota, on Rainy river; pop. (1970c) 1547.

Baudh \ˈbaüd\ *or* **Bod** \ˈbōd\. 1 Former Indian state, now part of Orissa, E India; 1156 sq. m.

2 *or* **Baudh Raj** \-ˈräj\. Town, its ✱, on S bank of Mahanadi river 100 m. WNW of Cuttack; pop. (1961c) 6088.

Baudissin. See BAUTZEN.

Bauld, Cape \-ˈbȯld\. Cape at NE tip of Newfoundland, Canada, at N entrance to the Strait of Belle Isle.

Baule. See BAOULÉ.

Bau·res \ˈbaü-rəs\. River in NE Bolivia; flows NW into Guaporé river on Brazilian border; with headstream Blanco ab. 360 m. long.

Bau·ru \baü-ˈrü\. City, S cen. São Paulo state, SE Brazil, 175 m. NW of São Paulo; munic. pop. (1968e) 110,961; trade center.

Bau·ta \ˈbaüt-ə\. Town and municipality, La Habana prov., W Cuba, 14 m. SW of Havana; munic. pop. (1967e) 34,690.

Baut·zen \ˈbaüt-sən\ *or older* **Bu·dis·sin** \ˈbüd-ə-ˌsēn\ *or* **Bau·dis·sin** \ˈbaüd-\. City, Dresden dist., East Germany; on Spree river 32 m. ENE of Dresden; pop. (1970e) 43,670; leather, paper, textiles, radio equipment; iron foundries; became German 1031; scene of defeat of Prussian and Russian armies by Napoleon May 20–21, 1813.

Baux–de–Provence, Les. See LES BAUX-DE-PROVENCE.

Bau·ya \ˈbaü-yə\. Town, W Sierra Leone, W Africa; connected with Freetown by rail.

Bauzanum. See BOLZANO 2.

Ba·var·ia \bə-ˈver-ē-ə, -ˈvar-\ *or Ger.* **Bay·ern** \ˈbī-ərn\. A state of West Germany; 27,239 sq. m.; pop. (1970e) 10,603,200; ✱ Munich; mountains include the Bavarian Alps, the Fichtelgebirge, and the Bohemian Forest (Böhmer Wald); grain, vegetables, fruit; scientific instruments, glass, paper, textiles; tourism; brewing. Largest cities: Munich, Nürnberg, Augsburg.

History: Territory conquered by Romans 1st cent. B.C. (see NORICUM and RAETIA); invaded by Germanic peoples (Marcomanni) who became tributary to Franks in 6th cent. A.D.; conquered by Charlemagne and incorporated in his empire 788; assigned to East Frankish kingdom in divisions of Frankish empire 817, 843; one of great stem duchies of Holy Roman Empire; Bavarian East Mark became separate duchy of Austria (*q.v.*) 1156; taken from Saxony (*q.v.*) and given to house of Wittelsbach by Frederick Barbarossa 1180; divided into Upper and Lower Bavaria 13th cent.; under Louis IV of Upper Bavaria, who was crowned emperor 1328, added temporarily Brandenburg, Tirol, and Netherlandish counties; became electorate 1623; under Maximilian I leader of Catholic League in Thirty Years' War; received Upper Palatinate 1648; allied with France 1701–04, during War of Spanish Succession; after War of Bavarian Succession 1778–79, united with Palatinate; its boundaries and make-up changed several times during Napoleonic era; granted constitution 1818; in 1833 merged its customs union with that of Prussia, laying basis of later Zollverein; joined Austria in war on Prussia 1866; joined North German Confederation 1870 and German Empire 1871; became a republic 1918; constitution abolished by National Socialist regime 1933; part of U.S. occupation zone 1945; adopted new constitution 1946.

Ba·var·i·an Alps \bə-ˌver-ē-ən-, -ˌvar-\. Range of the Alps bet. S Bavaria, West Germany, and Tirol, Austria, extending E and W from Lake Constance to Salzburg; highest point the Zugspitze 9720 ft. The Aulgäuer Alps form its W end.

Bawd·win \ˈbȯd-ˌwin\. Town, N Shan State, E cen. Burma, in mountains 30 m. WNW of Lashio; has wolframite deposits that have been an important source of tungsten; ruby mines.

Ba·we·an \ˈbä-wē-ˌän\. Island in the Java Sea, Indonesia, 100 m. N of Surabaja; area 77 sq. m.; invaded by Japanese Feb. 25, 1942; just NE of the center of the naval battle of Java Sea Feb. 26–28, 1942; surrendered to Allies Sept. 1945.

Baxar. See BUXAR.

Bax·ley \ˈbak-slē\. City, ⊗ of Appling co., SE Georgia, 38 m. N of Waycross; pop. (1970c) 3503; tobacco, pecans.

Bax·ter \ˈbak-stər\. County in Arkansas. See table at ARKANSAS.

Baxter, Mount. Peak in Sierra Nevada, on the boundary between Fresno and Inyo cos., SE cen. California; 13,118 ft.

Baxter Springs. City, Cherokee co., SE corner of Kansas; pop. (1970c) 4489; diversified farming; zinc and lead mines nearby.

Bay \ˈbā\. **1** Name of counties in two states of the U.S. See tables at FLORIDA and MICHIGAN.

2 *or* **Bay Village.** City, Cuyahoga co., N Ohio, on Lake Erie 12 m. W of Cleveland; pop. (1970c) 18,163.

Bay, La·gu·na de \lə-ˌgü-nə-də-ˈbī\. Large crescent-shaped lake, cen. Luzon, Phil., SE of Manila; ab. 32 m. long; 344 sq. m.; largest lake of the Philippines; its outlet is the Pasig at the NW.

Bayadiya, Al–. See AL-BAYADIYA.

Ba·yam·bang \ˌbī-əm-ˈbäŋ\. Municipality, S Pangasinan prov., Luzon, Phil., 21 m. SE of Lingayen on N bank of Agno river; pop. (1969e) 65,600.

Ba·ya·mo \bə-ˈyäm-(ˌ)ō\. Town and municipality, Oriente prov., E Cuba; munic. pop. (1967e) 45,400, on **Bayamo River** (tributary of the Cauto) 27 m. E of Manzanillo; founded 1514. A center of revolutionary movement against Spain 1868–98; here Cuban soldier Calixto García Íniguez received 1898 the "Message to Garcia."

Ba·ya·món \ˌbī-ə-ˈmōn\. **1** River in E cen. Puerto Rico; flows N into Atlantic Ocean.

2 Town and municipality, NE cen. Puerto Rico; munic. pop. (1970p) 154,440, town pop. 146,363; according to tradition, the first municipality in Puerto Rico to be settled; produces fruit, tobacco, sugar, coffee.

Bay·ard \ˈbā-ərd\. **1** City, Morrill co., W Nebraska, on North Platte river 20 m. ESE of Scottsbluff; pop. (1970c) 1338; beet-sugar refinery, grain farms.

2 Village, Grant co., SW New Mexico, 75 m. NW of Las Cruces; pop. (1970c) 2908.

Bay·bay \ˌbī-bī\. Municipality, Leyte prov., on W coast of Leyte I., Phil., on Camotes Sea 42 m. SSW of Tacloban; pop. (1969e) 70,200; important hemp port.

Bay·boro \ˈbā-ˌbər-ə, -ˌbə-rə\. Town, ⊗ of Pamlico co., E North Carolina, near Pamlico Sound; pop. (1970c) 665.

Bay Bulls \ˈbā-ˌbu̇lz\. Seaside resort, SE Newfoundland, Canada, on Atlantic Ocean 20 m. S of St. John's.

Bay·burt *or* **Bai·burt** \bī-ˈbu̇rt\. Town, Gümüşhane prov., NE Turkey, on Çoruh river 60 m. WNW of Erzurum; pop. (1965c) 15,184.

Bay City \ˈbā-\. **1** City, ⊗ of Bay co., E Michigan, at head of Saginaw Bay 13 m. N of Saginaw; pop. (1970c) 49,449; shipyards, iron foundries, oil and sugar refineries; automobile parts, electrical equipment.

2 City, ⊗ of Matagorda co., SE Texas, 70 m. WSW of Galveston; pop. (1970c) 11,733; sulfur mines and oil wells.

Bayda, Al–. See BEIDA.

Bay de Verde \ˌbād-ə-ˈvərd\. Seaport, SE Newfoundland, Canada, at mouth of Conception Bay; pop. (1971p) 810.

Bayern. See BAVARIA.

Ba·yeux \bī-ˈ(y)ü, bā-; bä-ˈyə(r); bá-yœ̄\ *or anc.* **Au·gus·to·du·rum** \ȯ-ˌgəs-tə-ˈd(y)u̇r-əm, ə-\. Town, Calvados dept., Normandy, NW France, ab. 15 m. WNW of Caen and ab. 5 m. inland from the English Channel; pop. (1968c) 11,451. An old town, with bishopric after 4th cent.; taken by Norsemen 890; several times besieged and captured in wars bet. 12th and 16th cents. Has fine 13th cent. Gothic church and a museum containing the famous Bayeux tapestry (probably of 11th cent.), representing in 72 panels incidents in the life of William the Conqueror.

Bay·field \ˈbā-ˌfēld\. County in Wisconsin. See table at WISCONSIN.

Bay Harbor Islands \ˌbā-\. Town, Dade co., SE Florida, on coast 7 m. NW of Miami; pop. (1970c) 4619.

Bayındır. See CAŸSTER.

Bay Islands. See BAHÍA, ISLAS DE LA.

Baykal, Lake. See BAIKAL, LAKE.

Bay·lor \ˈbā-lər\. County in Texas. See table at TEXAS.

Bay Mi·nette \ˌbā-mə-ˈnet\. City, ⊗ of Baldwin co., SW Alabama, 22 m. NE of Mobile; pop. (1970c) 6727; furniture; soybeans, cattle.

Bay of Islands. **1** Inlet of Bering Sea, W coast of Adak I., Andreanof Is., Aleutian Is.

2 Inlet of Gulf of St. Lawrence, W coast of Newfoundland, Canada; receives the Humber river.

3 Inlet of South Pacific Ocean, NE coast of North I., New Zealand.

Bay of Pigs. See COCHINOS BAY.

Bay of Whales. See WHALES, BAY OF.

Ba·yom·bong \ˌbī-əm-ˈbȯŋ\. Municipality, ✻ of Nueva Vizcaya prov., Luzon, Phil., on Magat river; pop. (1969e) 23,900.

Bay·onne \bā-ˈōn\. City, Hudson co., NE New Jersey, on peninsula that separates Upper New York Bay from Newark Bay 5 m. SW of Jersey City; pop. (1970c) 72,743; connected with Staten I. by **Bayonne Bridge** (steel arch, with channel span of 1675 ft.) over Kill van Kull; important petroleum refining and exporting center; manufactures chemicals, paint, radiators, electric motors and generators; extensive docks; motorboat and yacht-building yards; U.S. naval supply depot. Site visited by Henry

Hudson 1609; original grant 1646; incorp. as city of Bayonne 1869.

Ba·yonne \ˌbā-'ōn, bä-'yòn\ *or anc.* **La·pur·dum** \lə-'pərd-əm\. Port town, Pyrénées-Atlantiques dept., SW France, at confluence of the Nive with the Adour near Bay of Biscay 55 m. WNW of Pau; pop. (1968c) 42,743; fishing port; shipbuilding; oil and gas wells nearby; cathedral (13th–16th cents.), citadel, arsenal.

History: Taken by English 1199; held by French since 1451; meeting place of Catherine de Médicis and duke of Alva 1565 where Massacre of St. Bartholomew is said to have been planned; famous in 16th and 17th cents. for manufacture of cutlery and armaments, the bayonet having been invented here (whence its name); meeting of Napoleon, Charles IV of Spain, and Prince of the Asturias 1808 which led to abdication of Spanish monarchs in favor of Napoleon.

Bay·ou La Ba·tre \ˌbī-ə-lə-'ba-trē\. Town, Mobile co., SW Alabama, 20 m. SW of Mobile; pop. (1970) 2664.

Bay·port \'bā-ˌpō(ə)rt, -ˌpȯ(ə)rt\. Village, Washington co., E Minnesota, on St. Croix river 15 m. ENE of St. Paul; pop. (1970c) 2987; state prison.

Bay·reuth *also* **Bai·reuth** \bī-'rȯit, 'bī-ˌ\. Industrial city, Bavaria, West Germany, 41 m. NE of Nürnberg; pop. (1969e) 63,530; 16th cent. and 18th cent. palaces; the Festspielhaus (designed by composer Richard Wagner), where the Wagner festivals have been held at irregular intervals since its opening 1876. Founded 1194 under Bishop Otto II of Bamberg; under burgrave of Nürnberg 1248–1398, margraves of Brandenburg-Kulmbach 1603–1769; to Prussia 1791, Napoleon 1806, Bavaria 1810. In World War II taken by Allies Apr. 1945.

Bay Rob·erts \-'räb-ərts\. Town on W shore of Conception Bay, Newfoundland, Canada, S of Harbour Grace and 27 m. W of St. John's; pop. (1971p) 3629; port of entry.

Bayrut. See BEIRUT.

Bay St. Lou·is \-sānt-'lü-əs, -sənt-\. City, ⊗ of Hancock co., S Mississippi, on Gulf of Mexico 15 m. W of Gulfport; pop. (1970c) 6752; bottling works; winter resort.

Baysān. See BET SHE'AN.

Bay Shore. Town (unincorp.), Suffolk co., SE New York, on S shore of Long I. and Great South Bay ab. 40 m. E of Brooklyn; pop. (1970c) 11,119; resort.

Bay·side \'bā-ˌsīd\. Village, Milwaukee and Ozaukee cos., SE Wisconsin; pop. (1970c) 4461.

Bay Springs. Town, a ⊗ of Jasper co., SE cen. Mississippi; pop. (1970c) 1801; cotton, timber.

Baytīn. See BETHEL 6.

Bayt Jālā. See BEIT JALA.

Bayt Laḥm. See BETHLEHEM 2.

Bay·town \'bā-ˌtaün\. City, Harris co., SE Texas, on Galveston Bay ab. 22 m. ESE of Houston; pop. (1970c) 43,980; oil wells; petrochemicals, synthetic rubber; settled 1864; site of Confederate shipyard 1864.

Bay·ville \'bā-ˌvil\. Village on N shore of Long I., Nassau co., SE New York; pop. (1970c) 6147.

Ba·za \'bäz-ə, 'bäs-\ *or anc.* **Bas·ti** \'bas-ˌtī\. Commune, Granada prov., S Spain, 53 m. NE of Granada; pop. (1970p) 19,990. Besieged by Isabella of Castile 1489; scene of French victory over Spaniards 1810.

Ba·zan·court \ˌbaz-ˌäⁿ-'kü(ə)r\. Town, Marne dept., France, NE of Reims; pop. (1962c) 1545; scene of battle Oct. 7, 1918 when Germans were forced to evacuate it.

Ba·zar·dyu·ze \ˌbäz-ər-'dyü-zə\. Peak in E Caucasus Mts., bet. Dagestan A.S.S.R. and Azerbaijan S.S.R., U.S.S.R.; 14,698 ft.

Bazargic. See TOLBUKHIN 2.

Bazmān, Kūh–e– \ˌkü-(h)ē-baz-'män\. Peak of an extinct volcano, SE Iran; 11,447 ft.

Beach \'bēch\. City, ⊗ of Golden Valley co., W North Dakota; pop. (1970c) 1408; wheat.

Beach Haven Inlet. Narrow strait leading from Atlantic Ocean into S extremity of Barnegat Bay off SE tip of Ocean co., New Jersey.

Beachwood \'bēch-ˌwu̇d\. 1 Borough, Ocean co., E New Jersey, on Toms river 42 m. NNE of Atlantic City; pop. (1970c) 4390.

2 City, Cuyahoga co., Ohio, E of Cleveland; pop. (1970c) 9631.

Beachy Head \ˌbē-chē-\. Headland on S coast of East Sussex, S England, projecting into English Channel; 575 ft. high; lighthouse. Scene July 10, 1690 (new style) of naval victory of French over British and Dutch.

Bea·con \'bē-kən\. City, Dutchess co., SE New York, at foot of Mt. Beacon on Hudson river opp. Newburgh; pop. (1970c) 13,255.

Beacon Falls. Town, New Haven co., S Connecticut; pop. (1970c) 3546; settled 1678, incorp. 1871.

Bea·cons·field \'bē-kənz-ˌfēld\. 1 Municipality, N Tasmania, Australia, on Tamar river 25 m. NW of Launceston; pop. (1970e) 11,100; dairy products, fruit; important goldfields nearby 1877–1919.

2 City, Quebec, Canada, SW suburb of Montreal; pop. (1966c) 15,702.

3 *usu.* 'bek-ənz-\. Urban district, Buckinghamshire, S cen. England, 22 m. NW of London; pop. (1971p) 11,861; noted for its associations with Edmund Burke, Benjamin Disraeli, and G. K. Chesterton.

4 Former town, N Cape Province, Rep. of South Africa, SE suburb of Kimberley; united with Kimberley 1912.

Bea·dle \'bēd-ᵊl\. County in South Dakota. See table at SOUTH DAKOTA.

Bea·gle Channel \ˌbē-gəl-\. Channel bet. S Tierra del Fuego I. and S group of Chilean islands off S tip of South America in Tierra del Fuego archipelago.

Beams·ville \'bēmz-ˌvil\. Town, Lincoln co., SE Ontario, Canada, on Lake Ontario 21 m. E of Hamilton; pop. (1968e) 4047; concrete blocks, canned goods; diversified agriculture.

Bear \'ba(ə)r, 'be(ə)r\. River, SE Idaho and N Utah; ab. 350 m. long; rises in Uinta Mts., N Utah, flows N crossing Wyoming border twice, turns NW into SE Idaho, bends S and empties into Great Salt Lake, N Utah.

Bear Butte. Peak, Meade co., W South Dakota; 4422 ft.

Beard·more Glacier \ˌbi(ə)rd-ˌmō(ə)r-, -ˌmȯ(ə)r-\. Glacier, Queen Maud Mountains, Antarctica; 260 m. long; world's largest glacier.

Beards·town \'bi(ə)rdz-ˌtaun\. City, Cass co., W cen. Illinois, on Illinois river 45 m. WNW of Springfield; pop. (1970c) 6222; railroad workshops; meat processing.

Bearhaven. See BEREHAVEN.

Bear Island \'ba(ə)r-, 'be(ə)r-\. 1 Island, Eire. See BEREHAVEN.

2 Island in Barents Sea 240 m. N of Norway; 69 sq. m.; with Spitsbergen group forms Svalbard, Norway.

Bear Islands *or Russ.* **Med·ve·zhi Os·tro·va** \məd-ˌvā-zhē-ˌäs-trə-'vä\. Group of small islands, opp. mouth of Kolyma river, East Siberian Sea, off NE coast of Yakutsk A.S.S.R., Russian S.F.S.R., U.S.S.R.

Bear Lake. 1 Lake, E Idaho-Utah border; ab. 20 m. long, 7 m. wide; max. depth 36 ft.; outlet is tributary of Bear river.

2 County in Idaho. See table at IDAHO.

Bear Mountain. 1 Peak, San Juan co., SW Colorado; 12,950 ft.

2 Mountain in town of Salisbury, extreme NW Connecticut; 2355 ft.

3 Mountain on Hudson river, New York, in Bear Mountain Park (5066 acres, a section of Palisades Interstate Park); 1305 ft.; Bear Mountain Bridge, opened 1924, crosses Hudson here.

4 Mountain in NE Dauphin co., SE cen. Pennsylvania, on the edge of the Bear Valley coal basin; 2000 ft.

5 Peak, Pennington co., SW South Dakota; 7166 ft.

Bé·arn \bā-'ärn\ *or Lat.* **Ben·e·har·num** \ˌben-i-'här-nəm\. Historical region of SW France; bounded anciently on W, N, and E by Gascony and on S by Pyrenees; ✱ Pau. Part of Aquitania under Romans; devastated by Vandals, Visigoths, and later by Saracens; hereditary viscountship in

11th cent.; countship of Béarn held by Henry IV and retained when he became king of France 1589; united with French crown 1620; province of France 1620–1789.

Bear River. See BEAR.

Bear·wal·low Mountain \ˌba(ə)r-ˌwäl-ō-, ˌbe(ə)r-\. Peak, Yancey co., W North Carolina; 6487 ft.

Be·as *or* **Bi·as** \ˈbē-ˌäs\ *or anc.* **Hyph·a·sis** \ˈhif-ə-səs\. River, one of the "Five Rivers" of the Punjab, N India; 290 m. long; rises in the Himalayas E of Dharmsala, Himachal Pradesh, flows W and SW to the Sutlej river in W Punjab state SW of city of Kapurthala.

Beas de Se·gu·ra \ˈbā-ˌäz-dā-sə-ˈgu̇r-ə\. Commune, Jaén prov., S Spain, 55 m. NE of Jaén; pop. (1970p) 11,162; in region producing wine, oil, fruits, flax.

Be·ata, Cape \-bā-ˈät-ə\. Cape extending into Caribbean Sea from S cen. coast of Hispaniola.

Beata Island \bā-ˌät-ə-\. Small island in the Caribbean Sea off S cen. coast of Hispaniola.

Be·aten·berg \bā-ˈät-ᵊn-ˌbərg, -be(ə)rg\ *or* **Sankt Beaten-berg** \ˌzäŋ(k)t-\. Village, Bern canton, Switzerland, NW of Interlaken; pop. (1970c) 1263; resort.

Be·at·rice \bē-ˈa-trəs\. City, ⊗ of Gage co., SE Nebraska, 35 m. S of Lincoln; pop. (1970c) 12,389; in grain and livestock-raising region; irrigation equipment, farm machinery, gasoline engines, dairy products; Pershing Coll. (1966).

Beat·tie Peak \ˌbēt-ē-, ˌbāt-ē-\. Mountain, San Juan and San Miguel cos., SW Colorado; 13,200 ft.

Beat·ton \ˈbēt-ᵊn\. River, E British Columbia, Canada; ab. 145 m. long; flows E and S into Peace river.

Beat·ty·ville \ˈbāt-ē-ˌvil\. City, ⊗ of Lee co., E Kentucky; pop. (1970c) 923; coal mines, oil wells.

Beau Bas·sin \ˌbō-bə-ˈsa^{n}\. See ROSE HILL.

Beau·caire \bō-ˈka(ə)r, -ˈke(ə)r\; *anc.* **Uger·num** \yü-ˈjər-nəm\ *or later* **Bel·li Quad·rum** \ˌbel-ˌī-ˈkwäd-rəm\. Commune, Gard dept., S France, on right bank of Rhone river (opp. Tarascon) 15 m. E of Nîmes; pop. (1962c) 8243; 14th cent. churches. Formerly famous for great annual fair (founded 1217 by Raymond VI, Count of Toulouse).

Beauce \ˈbōs\. **1** County, Quebec, Canada. See table at QUEBEC.

2 Ancient district of N cen. France, now part of departments of Loir-et-Cher and Eure-et-Loir; ✱ Chartres.

Beauce·ville East \ˈbōs-ˌvil-ˈēst\ *or Fr.* **Beauceville–Est** \bōs-vēl-est\. Town, ⊗ of Beauce co., S Quebec, Canada, on Chaudière river SSE of Quebec; pop. (1971p) 2186.

Beau·court–sur–l'An·cre \bō-ˈku̇(ə)r-su̇(ə)r-ˈlä^{n}krᵊ\. Village, Somme dept., NE France, 5 m. N of Albert; pop. (1962c) 132; scene of fighting Aug. 1918.

Beau·fort. 1 \ˈbō-fərt\. County in North Carolina. See table at NORTH CAROLINA

2 \ˈbyü-fərt\. County in South Carolina. See table at SOUTH CAROLINA.

3 \ˈbō-fərt\. Town and seaside resort, ⊗ of Carteret co., SE North Carolina, on inlet of Atlantic Ocean 35 m. SE of New Bern; pop. (1970c) 3368; port of entry at terminus of an inland waterway; canning plants, commercial fisheries; lumbering, farming; estab. 1722.

4 \ˈbyü-fərt\. City, ⊗ of Beaufort co., S South Carolina, on Port Royal 52 m. SW of Charleston; pop. (1970c) 9434; tourist center; truck farms; commercial fisheries; timber; conquered by British in the Revolution; fell into hands of Union fleet 1861.

5 \ˈbō-fərt\. Town, SW Sabah, East Malaysia, NE of Brunei Bay and on railroad 45 m. SSW of Kota Kinabalu.

Beaufort Sea \ˌbō-fərt-\. That part of the Arctic Ocean NE of Alaska, NW of Canada, and W of Banks I. in the Arctic Archipelago; max. depth ab. 15,000 ft.

Beaufort West. Town, S cen. Cape Province, Rep. of South Africa, 260 m. ENE of Cape Town; pop. (1967e) 16,300; in Great Karroo region; sheep raising; railway workshops; founded 1818.

Beau·har·nois \ˌbō-ˌärn-ˈwä\. **1** County, Quebec, Canada. See table at Quebec.

2 Manufacturing town, its ⊗, on St. Lawrence river 20 m. SW of Montreal; pop. (1971p) 8141.

Beau·lieu \ˈbyü-lē\. Parish, New Forest rural dist., Southampton, S England; ruins of Beaulieu Abbey, wealthy Cistercian house founded by King John 1204.

Beau·ly \ˈbyü-lē\. Small river in N cen. Scotland, flowing NE into Moray Firth W of Inverness.

Beau·mar·is \bō-ˈmar-əs\. Municipal borough, ⊗ of Anglesey co., NW Wales, on **Beaumaris Bay;** pop. (1971p) 2096; 13th cent. castle.

Beau·mont \ˈbō-ˌmänt\. **1** City, Riverside co., SE California, 21 m. SE of San Bernardino; pop. (1970c) 5484; electronic components; fruit canning.

2 *also* bō-ˈmänt\. Industrial city and port of entry, ⊗ of Jefferson co., SE Texas, on Neches river 73 m. E of Houston; pop. (1970c) 115,919; connected with Gulf of Mexico by Sabine-Neches Canal; port of entry; shipyards, oil refineries; chemicals, synthetic rubber, paper; Lamar State Coll. of Technology (1923); settled 1835, ⊗ 1838, incorp. 1881.

Beaumont–Ha·mel \ˈbō-ˌmō^{n}-ä-ˈmel\. Village, Somme dept., NE France, near the Ancre ab. 5 m. N of Albert; pop. (1962c) 273; fighting July–Nov. 1916; taken by British Nov. 13, 1916, a phase of the battle of the Somme.

Beaune \ˈbōn\ *or Lat.* **Bel·na** \ˈbel-nə\. Commercial and manufacturing city, Côte-d'Or dept., E France, 23 m. SSW of Dijon; pop. (1968c) 16,874; 12th cent. church; large hospital (founded 1443); 15th cent. ramparts; school of viticulture; trades in Burgundy wines.

Beau·port \bō-ˈpȯ(ə)r\. City, Quebec co., S Quebec, Canada, NE suburb of Quebec on St. Lawrence river; pop. (1971p) 14,739. Granted to Robert Gifford 1634, became first seigneury established in New France; served as Montcalm's headquarters 1759.

Beau·pré \bō-ˈprā\. Town, Montmorency No. 1 co., S Quebec, Canada, on St. Lawrence river 27 m. NE of Quebec; pop. (1971p) 2853.

Beau·re·gard \ˈbōr-ə-ˌgärd, ˈbȯr-\. Parish in Louisiana. See table at LOUISIANA.

Beau·sé·jour \ˌbō-ˌsā-ˈzhu̇(ə)r, ˈbō-zə-ˌzhu̇(ə)r\. Town, SE Manitoba, Canada, 30 m. ENE of Winnipeg; pop. (1971p) 2225; truck farms; timber.

Beau·so·leil \ˌbō-sə-ˈlā\. Commune, Alpes-Maritimes dept., SE France, near Ligurian Sea 8 m. ENE of Nice; pop. (1968c) 14,144; winter resort.

Beau·vais \bō-ˈvā\; *anc.* **Bel·lov·a·cum** \bə-ˈläv-ə-kəm\ *also* **Cae·sar·om·a·gus** \ˌsē-zə-ˈräm-ə-gəs\. Manufacturing commune, ✱ of Oise dept., N France, 42 m. NNW of Paris; pop. (1968c) 46,777; blankets, carpets, chemicals, tractors; its tapestry factory was destroyed in World War II; 13th cent. cathedral (unfinished); 10th and 12th cent. churches; 12th cent. palace; ancient Roman ramparts. Became commune 1096; made heroic resistance to large army of Burgundians under Charles the Bold 1472; occupied by Germans 1940–44.

Beaux, Les. See LES BAUX-DE-PROVENCE.

Bea·ver \ˈbē-vər\. **1** River, NW Oklahoma; 280 m. long; flows E into Texas for 15 m., then into Oklahoma again; joins Wolf Creek, forming North Canadian river.

2 River, W Pennsylvania; formed by confluence of Shenango and Mahoning rivers in Lawrence co., flows S into Ohio river at Rochester, cen. Beaver co.

3 Name of counties in three states of the U.S. See tables at OKLAHOMA, PENNSYLVANIA, UTAH.

4 Town, ⊗ of Beaver co., NW Oklahoma; pop. (1970c) 1853; dairy and poultry farms.

5 Residential borough, ⊗ of Beaver co., W Pennsylvania, on Ohio river 26 m. NW of Pittsburgh; pop. (1970c) 6100; beverages.

6 City, ⊗ of Beaver co., SW Utah, 42 m. SE of S end of Sevier Lake; pop. (1970c) 1453; livestock.

7 River, tributary of Churchill river in Saskatchewan and Alberta provs., Canada; 305 m. long.

Beaver City. City, ⊗ of Furnas co., S Nebraska; pop. (1970c) 802; butter, wheat.

Beaver Creek. River, NW Kansas and SW Nebraska; 200 m. long; rises in Kit Carson co., E Colorado, flows NE across NW corner of Kansas into Nebraska and joins Sappa river 10 m. before emptying into Republican river in Harlan co., S Nebraska.

Beaver Dam. 1 City, Ohio co., W cen. Kentucky, 34 m. NW of Bowling Green; pop. (1970c) 2622.

2 City, Dodge co., SE cen. Wisconsin, 29 m. SSW of Fond du Lac; pop. (1970c) 14,265; foundry products, outboard motors, shoes.

Beaver Dam Creek. See MECHANICSVILLE.

Beaver Dam Mountains. Range in extreme SW Utah.

Beaver Falls. Industrial city, Beaver co., W Pennsylvania, on Beaver river 18 m. S of New Castle; pop. (1970c) 14,-375; cold-drawn steel, chinaware, metal, paper, cork products, textiles; coal mines, clay pits, cattle farms; Geneva Coll. (1848).

Bea·ver·head \ˈbē-vər-ˌhed\. County in Montana. See table at MONTANA.

Beaverhead Mountains. Mountain range, part of Bitterroot Range, in Continental Divide, forming part of the boundary bet. SW Montana and E Idaho.

Bea·ver·hill Lake \ˌbē-vər-ˌhil-\. Lake in cen. Alberta, Canada, ab. 35 m. E of Edmonton; 80 sq. m.

Beaver Island. 1 Island in N Lake Michigan, W of Emmet co., N Michigan, a part of Charlevoix co.; 56 sq. m.

2 One of the Falkland Is. (*q.v.*).

Beaver Meadows. Borough, Carbon co., E Pennsylvania, 21 m. S of Wilkes-Barre; pop. (1970c) 1274; coal mining.

Beaver River. See BEAVER.

Bea·ver·ton \ˈbē-vərt-ᵊn\. City, Washington co., Oregon, W of Portland; pop. (1970c) 18,577; diversified farming.

Be·a·war \bē-ˈä-wər\. Town, cen. Rajasthan, India, on affluent of Luni river 115 m. SW of Jaipur; pop. (1961c) 53,931.

Beb·ing·ton \ˈbeb-iŋ-tən\. Municipal borough, Cheshire, NW England on the Mersey opp. Liverpool; pop. (1971p) 61,488; soap, margarine; engineering.

Bec. Abbey. See LE BEC-HELLOUIN.

Bé·can·cour \ˌbā-ˌkäⁿ-ˈku(ə)r\. Town, ⊗ of Nicolet co., S Quebec, Canada, on St. Lawrence river; pop. (1971p) 8163.

Bec·cles \ˈbek-əlz\. Municipal borough, East Suffolk, E England, 100 m. NE of London; pop. (1971p) 8015.

Be·čej \ˈbech-ˌā\. Town, Serbia, E Yugoslavia, ab. 60 m. NNW of Belgrade; pop. (1965e) 22,000; leather, textiles.

Be·ce·lae·re \ˌbā-sə-ˈlär-ə\. Small commune, West Flanders prov., NW Belgium; a stronghold in the German front line in World War I.

Bé·char \bā-ˈshär\; *formerly* **Co·lomb** \kō-ˈlōⁿ\ *or* **Colomb–Béchar.** Town, ✱ of Saoura dept., Algeria, ab. 440 m. SW of Algiers; pop. (1966c) 42,090; former French Foreign Legion post.

Bech·a·rof Lake \ˌbech-ə-ˌrȯf-\. Lake, N Alaska Penin., SW of Katmai National Monument; ab. 30 m. long; 458 sq. m.

Bec–Hellouin, Le. See LE BEC-HELLOUIN.

Bech·u·a·na·land \ˌbech-(ə-)ˈwän-ə-ˌland\. 1 Republic, S Africa. See BOTSWANA.

2 Former colony, Africa. See BRITISH BECHUANALAND.

Bechuanaland Protectorate. See BOTSWANA.

Beck·er \ˈbek-ər\. County in Minnesota. See table at MINNESOTA.

Beck·ham \ˈbek-əm\. County in Oklahoma. See table at OKLAHOMA.

Beck·ley \ˈbek-lē\. City, ⊗ of Raleigh co., S West Virginia, 35 m. N of Bluefield; pop. (1970c) 19,884; coal mining; Beckley Coll. (1933).

Beck·um \ˈbek-əm\. Manufacturing city, North Rhine-Westphalia, West Germany, 23 m. SE of Münster; pop. (1969e) 22,189; cement.

Bedd·gel·ert \beth-ˈgel-ərt, bāth-\. Village, Caernarvon, NW Wales, S of Snowdon Mt.; pop. (1961c) 1055; resort, noted for its beautiful location; scene of legend of Prince Llewellyn and his hound.

Bed·ford \ˈbed-fərd\. 1 Name of counties in three states of the U.S. See tables at PENNSYLVANIA, TENNESSEE, VIRGINIA.

2 City, ⊗ of Lawrence co., S Indiana, 20 m. S of Bloomington; pop. (1970c) 13,087; limestone quarries.

3 City, ⊗ of Taylor co., SW Iowa, 73 m. SE of Council Bluffs; pop. (1970c) 1733.

4 City, ⊗ of Trimble co., N Kentucky; pop. (1970c) 780; timber, tobacco.

5 Town, Middlesex co., NE Massachusetts, 10 m. S of Lowell; pop. (1970c) 13,513; truck farms.

6 Agricultural town, Hillsborough co., S New Hampshire, 3 m. SW of Manchester; pop. (1970c) 5859.

7 City, Cuyahoga co., N Ohio, 11 m. SE of Cleveland; pop. (1970c) 17,552; residential suburb of Cleveland.

8 Borough, ⊗ of Bedford co., S Pennsylvania, on branch of Juniata river 30 m. S of Altoona; pop. (1970c) 3302; mineral springs nearby in **Bedford Springs,** a summer resort. Settled as **Rays·town** \ˈrāz-ˌtau̇n\ c. 1750; Fort Bedford, an important frontier station in last half of 18th cent., built 1751; town laid out 1766.

9 City, Tarrant co., N Texas, 15 m. ENE of Fort Worth; pop. (1970c) 10,049.

10 Independent city, ⊗ of Bedford co., SW cen. Virginia, 22 m. WSW of Lynchburg; pop. (1970c) 6011.

11 Town, ⊗ of Missisquoi co., S Quebec, Canada, 40 m. SE of Montreal; pop. (1971p) 2789.

12 County in England. See BEDFORDSHIRE.

13 Municipal borough, ⊗ of Bedfordshire, SE cen. England, on the Ouse 48 m. NNW of London; pop. (1971p) 73,064; commercial center; agricultural implements, diesel engines, transistors. Dates back to 6th cent.; scene of John Bunyan's imprisonment 1660–72 and 1675 (when he is supposed to have written *Pilgrim's Progress,* published 1678).

Bedford Heights. Village, Cuyahoga co., Ohio, S of Cleveland; pop. (1970c) 13,063.

Bed·ford·shire \ˈbed-fərd-ˌshi(ə)r, -shər\ *or* **Bedford** *or* **Beds** \ˈbedz\. County, SE cen. England; area 477 sq. m.; pop. (1971p) 463,493; ⊗ Bedford; other towns Luton, Dunstable; watered by the Ouse; diversified farming; automobiles, ball bearings, electrical equipment.

Bed·ling·ton \ˈbed-liŋ-tən\. Parish, Northumberland, N England; electrical components; known for its terriers; a part of **Bed·ling·ton·shire** \-ˌshi(ə)r, -shər\, urban district (pop. [1971p] 28,167), on the Blyth near its mouth in North Sea 11 m. N of Newcastle upon Tyne.

Bedloe's Island. See LIBERTY ISLAND.

Bed·min·ster \ˈbed-ˌmin(t)-stər\. Locality in Bedminster township, Bucks co., SE Pennsylvania, ab. 20 m. SE of Allentown; pop. (1970c) 3252 (township).

Be·dra·shen \ˌbed-rə-ˈshen\. Village on left bank of the Nile, Egypt, S of Cairo; site of ruins of ancient Memphis.

Beds. See BEDFORDSHIRE.

Bed·was and Ma·chen \ˈbed-ˌwas . . . ˈmak-ən, -ˌmak-ən\. Urban district, Monmouthshire, SE Wales, 27 m. WNW of Bristol; pop. (1971p) 12,548.

Bed·well·ty \bed-ˈwel-tē\. Urban district, Monmouthshire, SE Wales, 31 m. WNW of Bristol; pop. (1971p) 25,326; iron foundry; coal mining.

Bed·worth \ˈbed-(ˌ)wərth\. Urban district, Warwickshire, cen. England; pop. (1971p) 40,535; residential; light engineering.

Bę·dzin \'ben-ˌjēn\ *or Russ.* **Ben·din** \'ben-ˌdēn\ *or Ger.* **Bend·zin** \'bent-ˌsēn\. Commune, Katowice prov., S Poland, ab. 7 m. NW of Katowice; pop. (1970p) 42,800; coal and iron deposits; steelworks.

Bee \'bē\. County in Texas. See table at TEXAS.

Bee·be \'bē-(ˌ)bē\. City, White co., NE cen. Arkansas, 27 m. NE of Little Rock; pop. (1970c) 2805; agriculture; sawmill.

Beech Grove \'bēch-\. City, Marion co., cen. Indiana, 7 m. SE of Indianapolis; pop. (1970c) 13,832; electrical equipment; dairy farms.

Bee·croft Head \ˌbē-ˌkrȯft-\. Peninsula and point of land, SE New South Wales, Australia, enclosing Jervis Bay on the N. See SAINT GEORGE, CAPE 2.

Bee·mer·ang, Mount \-'bē-mə-ˌraŋ\. Mountain, Blue Mts., E New South Wales, Australia; 4100 ft.

Bee·ren·berg \'ber-ən-ˌbərg\. Extinct volcano on Jan Mayen I., Arctic Ocean; 7430 ft.; highest point on island.

Beeroth. See BIRE.

Be·er·she·ba \bi(ə)r-'shē-bə, be(ə)r-, bər-\ *or Heb.* **Be·'er She·va'** \-'shē-və\ *or Arab.* **Bir es Sa·ba** \ˌbi(ə)r-ˌes-'sab-ə\. Town, * of Southern District, S Israel, ab. 45 m. SW of Jerusalem; pop. (1970e) 77,400; chemicals, glass; univ. (1965), Negev Institute for Arid Zone Research. Marked the extreme S limit of Palestine (*Judges* xx. 1): see DAN. Scene of victory of British over Turks Oct. 31, 1917.

Bees·ton and Sta·ple·ford \'bē-stən . . . 'stā-pəl-fərd\. Urban district, Nottinghamshire, N cen. England, 4 m. SW of Nottingham; pop. (1971p) 63,498.

Bee·ville \'bē-ˌvil\. City, ⊗ of Bee co., S Texas, 48 m. NNW of Corpus Christi; pop. (1970c) 13,506; cotton, livestock; oil wells.

Be·gem·dir and Si·men \bə-'gem-ˌdi(ə)r . . . si-'men\. Province of NW Ethiopia. See table at ETHIOPIA.

Bè·gles \begl[ə]\. Commune, Gironde dept., SW France, on Garonne river 4 m. SSE of Bordeaux; pop. (1968c) 27,330.

Beg·na \'beŋ-nə\. River in S Norway; flows S into Tyrifjord Lake, whence it issues as the Dramselva.

Begovat. See BEKABAD.

Bé·hague, Pointe \ˌpwant-bi-'hag\. Cape extending into Atlantic Ocean from E coast of French Guiana.

Behar. See BIHAR.

Beharieh. See BAHARĪYA.

Beh·be·hān \ˌbā-bə-'hän\. Town, Khūzestān prov., SW Iran, E of Bandar-e Shāhpūr; pop. (1971p) 42,000; oil fields nearby; near ruins of an ancient Persian city.

Be·hei·ra \bə-'her-ə\. Governorate, N Egypt. See table at EGYPT.

Behisni. See BESNI.

Behistun. See BĪSITŪN.

Behnesa. See OXYRHYNCHUS.

Behramköy. See ASSOS.

Beibazar. See BEYPAZARI.

Bei·da *or Arab.* **Al–Bay·da** \(al-)'bād-ə\. Town, NE Libya, NE of Benghazi; pop. (1964c) 12,799; elev. ab. 2000 ft.; tomb of Raweifi ibn Thabit.

Bei·jer·land \'bī-(y)ər-ˌlänt\ *or* **Hoek·sche Waard** \'hu̇k-sə-ˌvärt\. Island attached to South Holland prov., Netherlands; 6 m. S of Rotterdam.

Bei Kem \'bā-'kem\. See YENISEI.

Beilan. See BAILAN.

Bei·ra \'bā-rə\. **1** Former province, N cen. Portugal; * Coimbra; soil rocky, except on coast; watered by Douro, Tagus, Mondego, and numerous other rivers; traversed by Serra da Estrela. Region produces grain, oil, wine, chestnuts; coal, iron, salt; marble quarries; in 1835 was divided into the districts of Aveiro, Castelo Branco, Coimbra, Guarda, and Viseu.

2 Seaport, * of Manica and Sofala dist., on SE coast of Mozambique, SE Africa, 120 m. SW of mouth of the Zambezi; pop. (1960c) 58,970; chief port for Rhodesia, Malawi, and cen. Mozambique; exports ores, hides, cotton, sugar.

Beira Al·ta \-'äl-tə\. Province of Portugal; lost most of its administrative functions 1959.

Beira Bai·xa \-'bī-shə\. Province of Portugal; lost most of its administrative functions 1959.

Beira Li·to·ral \-ˌlēt-ə-'räl\. Province of Portugal; lost most of its administrative functions 1959.

Bei·rut *or* **Bay·rūt** \bā-'rüt\ *or Fr.* **Bey·routh** \bā-rüt\ *or anc.* **Be·ry·tus** \bə-'rīt-əs\. City, * of Lebanon, built on a promontory with Lebanon Mts. behind it; pop. (1964e) 131,500, met. area pop. 330,995; financial and commercial center; port facilities; food processing; connected by highway with Damascus and Baghdad; several universities and colleges including American Univ. of Beirut (1866, new charter 1920) and Lebanese Univ. (1951, reorganized 1953).

History: Ancient Phoenician settlement mentioned in Tell al'Amarna tablets; ruled by Romans until Arab capture of Syria (*q.v.*) 635 A.D.; captured for kingdom of Jerusalem (*q.v.*) by Baldwin I 1110; object of struggle bet. Crusaders and Saracens until latter finally captured it 1291; although came to be ruled by Druses, technically belonged to Ottoman Empire; in 1840 bombarded and captured by British and French who intervened in Syria to quell revolt of Mehemet Ali against sultan (see EGYPT); captured by French in campaign against Turkey 1918; capital of Lebanon since 1920.

Beisān. See BET SHE'AN.

Beit·bridge \'bīt-(ˌ)brij\. Town, S Rhodesia, on the Limpopo opp. Messina in Transvaal; pop. (1969c) 1920.

Beit Ja·la \bāt-'jal-ə\ *or* **Bayt Jā·lā** \bāt-'jäl-ə\ *or Bib.* **Gal·lim** \'gal-əm\. Town, Jordan, ab. 1 m. NW of Bethlehem; in area occupied by Israel 1967.

Beit Jibrin. See ELEUTHEROPOLIS.

Be·ja \'bā-zhə\. **1** District of S Portugal. See table at PORTUGAL.

2 *or anc.* **Pax Ju·lia** \'paks-'jül-yə\. Commune, its *, 85 m. SE of Lisbon; pop. (1970p) 37,205; oil, pottery, textiles, leather; copper and manganese mined nearby. Roman ruins, including an aqueduct.

Bé·ja \bā-'zhä\ *or anc.* **Vac·ca** \'vak-ə\ *also* **Va·ga** \'vä-gə\. Town, N Tunisia, N Africa, 65 m. W of the city of Tunis; pop. (1966c) 28,145; exports wheat; fighting on highway running N to Bizerte in final stage of Tunisia campaign Apr. 1943 in World War II.

Be·jaïa \be-'jī-ə\ *or Fr.* **Bou·gie** \bü-zhē\ *or anc.* **Sal·dae** \'sal-(ˌ)dē\. Seaport and commune, NE Algeria, on W shore of **Gulf of Bejaïa**, ab. 115 m. E of Algiers; pop. (1966c) 49,930; has good harbor; trades in oils, wool, hides, and minerals; in 5th cent. a fortified city of Genseric the Vandal; in 11th cent. capital of powerful Berber dynasty; later under the Hafsids, Barbary pirates, and Spaniards; taken by French 1833. Occupied by British troops Nov. 11, 1942.

Bejraburana. See PHETCHABUN.

Bejraburi. See PHET BURI.

Be·ju·cal \ˌbā-hü-'käl\. Town and municipality, La Habana prov., W Cuba; munic pop. (1967e) 14,410.

Be·káa \bi-'kä\. **1** Former sanjak in E Lebanon.

2 Valley, Lebanon. See BIKA.

Bek·abad \'bā-kə-ˌbäd, 'bek-ə-\ *or before 1964* **Be·go·vat** \ˌbeg-ə-'vät\. Town, Tashkent Oblast, Uzbek S.S.R., U.S.S.R., ab. 80 m. S of Tashkent; pop. (1969e) 60,000; metallurgical works; cement, bricks.

Be·ka·si \bə-'käs-ē\. City, West Java prov., Indonesia; pop. (1961c) 32,012; destroyed Dec. 1945 by British in retaliation against Indonesians.

Bek–Budi. See KARSHI.

Bé·kés \'bā-ˌkāsh\. **1** County of SE Hungary. See table at HUNGARY.

2 Commune, Békés co., SE Hungary; pop. (1970p) 21,061; trade center in agricultural region.

Bé·kés·csa·ba \ˈbā-ˌkāsh-ˌchȯ-ˌbȯ\. City, ⊗ of Békés co., SE Hungary, S of Békés; pop. (1970p) 55,408; textiles; food processing.

Be·la \ˈbā-lə\. Town, Baluchistan, Pakistan, 100 m. NW of Karachi; pop. (1961c) 3139.

Bela Crk·va \ˌbel-ət-ˈsərk-və\ *or Hung.* **Fe·hér·tem·plom** \ˌfā-ˌhe(ə)r-ˈtem-(ˌ)plōm\ *or Ger.* **Weiss·kir·chen** \ˈvīs-ˌki(ə)r-kən\. Town, Serbia, E Yugoslavia, 45 m. E of Belgrade near border of Romania; pop. (1965e) 11,000.

Bél·air \bā-ˈla(ə)r, be-, -ˈle(ə)r\. Town, Quebec co., S Quebec, Canada; pop. (1966c) 3408.

Bel Air \bel-ˈa(ə)r, -ˈe(ə)r\. Town, ⊗ of Harford co., NE Maryland, 23 m. NE of Baltimore; pop. (1970c) 6307; Harford Junior Coll. (1957).

Be·la·jan \bə-ˈlä-ˌyän\. River, E Borneo, Indonesia; ab. 150 m. long; a N tributary of the Mahakam.

Be·lal·cá·zar \ˌbel-äl-ˈkä-zər\. Commune, Córdoba prov., S Spain, 51 m. NNW of Córdoba; pop. (1970p) 5425; wheat, barley, wine, oil, fruit; argentiferous lead mining.

Bela–Sla·ti·na \ˌbel-ä-ˈslät-ə-nə\. Town, Vratsa prov., N cen. Bulgaria.

Be·la·wan \bə-ˈlä-ˌwän\ *or* **Belawan–De·li** \-ˈdā-lē\. Town and seaport at mouth of Deli river, Sumatra, Indonesia; pop. (1961c) 35,404; port of Medan.

Be·la·ya \ˈbel-ə-yə\. Navigable river, Bashkir A.S.S.R., Russian S.F.S.R., U.S.S.R.; 882 m. long; rises in Southern Urals S of Zlatoust and flows S, W, and NW to the Kama river S of Sarapul.

Belaya Tser·kov \ˌbel-ə-yət-ˈse(ə)r-kəf\. Town, W Kiev Oblast, N Ukrainian S.S.R., U.S.S.R., on a tributary of the Dnieper 50 m. S of Kiev; pop. (1970p) 109,000; commercial center on railroad. First mentioned 1569; held by Germans in World War II from 1941 until late in 1943.

Belbeis. See BILBEIS.

Bel·cher Islands \ˌbel-chər-\. Island group in SE Hudson Bay, Keewatin dist., Northwest Territories, Canada; 1118 sq. m.

Bel·cher·town \ˈbel-chər-ˌtau̇n\. Town, Hampshire co., W Massachusetts, 15 m. NE of Springfield; pop. (1970c) 5936.

Bel·chi·te \bel-ˈchē-(ˌ)tā\. Commune, Zaragoza prov., NE Spain, 22 m. SSE of Saragossa; pop. (1970p) 2147; in Peninsular War scene of victory of French forces under Suchet over Spanish forces under Blake, June 1809.

Bel·ding \ˈbel-diŋ\. City, Ionia co., S cen. Michigan, 25 m. ENE of Grand Rapids; pop. (1970c) 5121; dies, tools, pumps; diversified farming.

Be·lém \bə-ˈlem\ *or sometimes* **Pa·rá** \pə-ˈrä\. Seaport city, ✱ of Pará state, N Brazil, on Pará river 90 m. from the sea; munic. pop. (1970p) 642,514; distributing center for Amazon valley; exports include nuts and pepper; univ. (1957); founded 1616.

Be·len \bə-ˈlen\. Village, Valencia co., W New Mexico, on the Rio Grande 30 m. S of Albuquerque; pop. (1970c) 4823; alfalfa, cereals, fruit, wool.

Be·lén \bə-ˈlen\. Town and district, Concepción dept., N cen. Paraguay, 125 m. N of Asunción; pop. (1970e) 9260.

Bel·ep Islands \ˌbel-əp-\. Group of small islands bet. parallel coral reefs, SW Pacific Ocean, 28 m. NW of NW tip of New Caledonia.

Be·le·ri·um \bə-ˈlir-ē-əm\. Ancient name of CORNWALL county, SW England.

Bel·fast \ˈbel-ˌfast\. **1** Seaport city, ⊗ of Waldo co., S Maine, on Penobscot Bay 30 m. SSW of Bangor; pop. (1970c) 5957; tourist center; settled 1769.

2 *also* bel-ˈ\. County borough and seaport, ✱ of Northern Ireland and ⊗ of co. Antrim, E Northern Ireland; pop. (1971p) 358,991; shipbuilding, food processing; linen, aircraft, tobacco; Queen's University of Belfast (1908).

History: Site of Norman castle in possession of earls of Ulster, granted to Sir Arthur Chichester 1604 who settled colonists (see ULSTER 2); town incorporated by James I of England (1603–25); settled by Scots from 17th cent., it became center of Irish Protestantism.

3 Town, SE cen. Transvaal, Rep. of South Africa, 125 m. E of Pretoria; pop. (1960c) 3984; summer resort.

Belfast Lough \-ˈläk\. Inlet of the North Channel on E coast of Northern Ireland; the city of Belfast lies at its head.

Bel·fort \bel-ˈfȯ(ə)r, bā-ˈ, ˈbel-ˌ, ˈbā-ˌ\. Fortified commune, ✱ of Territoire de Belfort, E France, 88 m. ENE of Dijon; pop. (1968c) 53,214; commands pass (Belfort Gap, *q.v.*) bet. Vosges and Jura Mts.; electrical and metallurgical industries; textiles. Ceded to France by Austria 1648; fortified by Vauban; unsuccessfully besieged by Allies 1814; besieged by Germans 1870–71; the only part of Alsace left to France after cession of 1871.

Belfort, Ter·ri·toire de \ˌter-i-ˈtwär-də-\. Department of E France. See table at FRANCE.

Belfort Gap *or Fr.* **Trou·ée de Belfort** \tru̇-ād-ə-\. Pass bet. Vosges and Jura Mts., E France, through which passes historic route from Saône valley to the Rhine; highest point 1158 ft. In World War II seized by Germans June 17, 1940; occupied by American and French forces Aug.–Sept. 1944.

Belgard. See BIAŁOGARD.

Bel·gaum \bel-ˈgau̇m\. **1** District, Mysore, SW India; 5163 sq. m.; pop. (1961c) 1,983,811.

2 Town, its ✱, 240 m. SSE of Bombay; pop. (1970e) 159,-485; textiles, pottery.

Belgian Congo. See ZAIRE 1.

Belgian East Africa. See RUANDA-URUNDI.

Bel·gi·ca \ˈbel-ji-kə\. Ancient country, NE Gallia; one of the five administrative areas into which Augustus and Tiberius divided Gaul; corresponds in part with modern Belgium.

Bel·gium \ˈbel-jəm\ *or Fr.* **Bel·gique** \bel-zhēk\ *or Flem.* **Bel·gië** \ˈbel-gē-ə\. Kingdom, NW Europe, bounded on NW by the North Sea (42 m. of coastline), on N by Netherlands, on E by West Germany, on SE by the Grand Duchy of Luxembourg, and on S and W by France; 11,781 sq. m.; pop. (1970e) 9,694,991; ✱ Brussels. *Physical features:* Schelde river and its tributaries (Lys, Dender, Senne, Rupel) in W cen. part and the Meuse in E and SE (also as boundary in NE along Limburg prov. of Netherlands); chief tributaries of the Meuse: Sambre, Ourthe, Amblève; extensive canal system connects many of the streams. Mostly plain with wooded hill region (Ardennes) in S; chief port on North Sea is Oostende, but Antwerp near mouth of Schelde has much greater trade. *Chief products:* Wheat, barley, oats, rye, potatoes, sugar beets; coal; manufacturing: chemicals, textiles, iron and steel, leather and paper goods; shipbuilding, metal refining; one of the world's most industrialized countries. *Chief cities:* Antwerp, Brussels, Gent, Liège, Schaerbeek, Anderlecht. Divided into the following nine provinces (for pronunciation of their names, see their individual entries):

NAME	AREA (sq. m.)	POP. (1970e)	CAPITAL
Antwerp	1,104	1,535,680	Antwerp
Brabant	1,302	2,177,975	Brussels
East Flanders	1,151	1,314,031	Gent
Hainaut	1,463	1,330,789	Mons
Liège	1,497	1,019,309	Liège
Limburg	935	656,477	Hasselt
Luxembourg	1,706	219,186	Arlon
Namur	1,413	384,689	Namur
West Flanders	1,210	1,056,855	Brugge

History: Inhabited in ancient times by Belgae, a people of Celtic stock, who were conquered by Caesar 57 B.C.; Belgica, a Roman province, erected by Augustus; invaded by Germanic peoples, including the Franks who incorporated territory in their kingdom; part of Carolingian kingdom of Lotharingia (see LORRAINE); except for duchy of Flanders which became dependency of France, attached to medieval empire as duchy of Lower Lorraine; broke up into semi-independent territories, such as Brabant, Limburg, Luxembourg (*qq.v.*); by 1484, territories of Netherlands, of which future Belgium was a part, gradually united into Burgundian state which passed to Hapsburgs 1477; the center of European commerce in 16th cent. (see

ANTWERP); allotted to Spanish Hapsburgs 1555; basis of modern Belgium laid in southern Catholic provinces, reclaimed from revolt against Spain and split from northern Protestant provinces after Union of Utrecht 1579 (see NETHERLANDS); Artois, Lille, Maubeuge, and Cambrai lost to France in 17th cent.; Spanish Netherlands became Austrian 1713; overrun by French 1792 (see JEMAPPES) and incorporated in France 1801; reunited to Holland as independent kingdom of the Netherlands 1815; after revolt begun in 1830, recognized (by treaties of 1831 and 1839) as independent kingdom of Belgium, its neutrality guaranteed by the Great Powers; received half of duchies of Limburg and Luxembourg; under Leopold II, Congo Free State in personal union with Belgium 1885 and annexed in 1908 (see ZAIRE 1); invasion by Germany 1914 the occasion of British entrance into World War I; in peace treaty 1919, awarded Moresnet, Eupen-et-Malmédy, and mandate of Ruanda-Urundi (*qq.v.*); by treaty with England and France 1926, abrogated former status of neutrality; in World War II invaded May 1940 and occupied by Germans; cen. and E part overrun by Allied armies Sept. 1944; Battle of the Bulge in E Dec. 1944–Jan. 1945; formed customs union with Netherlands and Luxembourg 1947; became a member of NATO 1949, EEC 1958; granted independence to Congo (now Zaire) 1960; adjusted provincial boundaries in accordance with distribution of the two national languages (Flemish in N, French in S) 1963.

Bel·go·rod *also* **Byel·go·rod** \ˈbel-gə-ˌräd, ˈbyel-gə-rət\. City, ✱ of Belgorod Oblast, Russian S.F.S.R., U.S.S.R., on upper Donets river and on railroad 50 m. N of Kharkov; pop. (1970p) 151,000; food processing; iron ore deposits nearby. Of ecclesiastical importance in 17th cent. and later a fortified point in conflicts with the Tatars. Held by Germans in World War II 1941–42; scene of bitter fighting Feb.–Mar. 1943, retaken by Soviet troops Aug. 5, 1943.

Belgorod–Dnes·trov·ski \-ne-ˈstrôf-skē, -strȯv-\ *or formerly* **Ak·ker·man** \ˌäk-ər-ˈman, -ˈmän\ *or Rom.* **Ce·ta·tea Al·bă** \chə-ˌtät-ē-ə-ˈäl-bə\ *or anc.* **Ty·ras** \ˈtī-rəs\. City, Odessa Oblast, SW Ukrainian S.S.R., U.S.S.R., on right bank of Dniester estuary 28 m. SE of Odessa; pop. (1967e) 29,000; has shallow harbor but considerable trade in salt, fish, wool, tallow, and especially in wine; old fortifications.

History: On site of old Milesian colony of Tyras (founded 7th cent. B.C.); held by Macedonians and Romans; in medieval times under control of Tatars and Genoese, and in 1484 captured by Turks; seized several times by Russians who finally acquired it by treaty 1826; became a Romanian town 1918, a port of Bessarabia; ceded to U.S.S.R. June 1940 but seized by Germany 1941; retaken by U.S.S.R. 1944 and name changed from Akkerman 1946.

Belgorod Oblast \-ˈō-bləst, -ˌblast\. Subdivision, Russian S.F.S.R., U.S.S.R.; 10,463 sq. m.; pop. (1970p) 1,261,000; ✱ Belgorod; winter and spring wheat; iron ore deposits; formed 1954.

Bel·grade \ˈbel-ˌgrād, -ˌgräd, -grad, bel-ˈ\ *or Serbo-Croat.* **Be·o·grad** \ˈbā-ə-ˌgräd\. 1 Former county, E Yugoslavia; 93 sq. m.; ⊗ Belgrade; incorporated 1945 in Serbia, Yugoslavia.

2 *or anc.* **Sin·gi·du·num** \ˌsin-jə-ˈd(y)ü-nəm\. City, ✱ of Yugoslavia and of Serbia, on right bank of Danube river where the Sava joins it; pop. (1971p) 741,613; commercial and transportation center; textiles, electrical equipment, machine tools; food processing; citadel (1725–36), cathedral (1845), univ. (1863); seat of Serbian Academy of Sciences.

History: Roman fortification, Singidunum; destroyed by Avars 6th cent. A.D.; held by Avars to 9th cent., Bulgars in 10th, Byzantines from 11th to 13th, and by Serbs in 14th cent.; saved from siege by Turks when Hunyadi defeated them nearby 1456 (see HUNGARY); captured by Suleiman the Magnificent (see OTTOMAN EMPIRE) 1521; ceded to Austria 1718 by Treaty of Passarowitz and recovered by Turks in Peace of Belgrade 1739; in 19th cent. capital of independent principality of Serbia (*q.v.*); bombardment by Turks 1862 the cause of forced withdrawal of Turkish garrisons 1867; in World War I captured and lost by Austrians 1914, held by Central Powers 1915–18; scene of proclamation of Kingdom of Serbs, Croats, and Slovenes of which it became capital (see YUGOSLAVIA). In World War II devastated and captured by Germans Apr. 1941; retaken by Yugoslav and Soviet forces Oct. 20, 1944.

Bel·gra·no \bel-ˈgrän-(ˌ)ō\. Peak, NW Santa Cruz, S Argentina, NE of **Lake Belgrano;** 7526 ft.

Bel·gra·via \bel-ˈgrā-vē-ə\. A fashionable residential district in the W end of London, SE England, centering at Belgrave Square.

Bel·ha·ven \bel-ˈhā-vən\. Town, Beaufort co., E North Carolina, on Pamlico Sound 38 m. NE of New Bern; pop. (1970c) 2259; lumbering; fisheries.

Be·ling·ton \ˈbē-liŋ-tən\. City, Barbour co., N West Virginia, 8 m. NNW of Elkins; pop. (1970c) 1567.

Be·li·tung \bə-ˈlē-ˌtu̇ŋ\ *or* **Bil·li·ton** \bə-ˈlē-ˌtän\ *or Du.* **Be·li·toeng** \bə-ˈlē-ˌtu̇ŋ, ˈbel-i-\. Island, Indonesia, in the Java Sea off the SE coast of the island of Sumatra; 55 m. long by 43 m. wide; 1866 sq. m.; pop. (1961c) 102,375; chief town Tandjungpandan; tin mines.

Be·lize \bə-ˈlēz\ *or Span.* **Be·li·ce** \bā-ˈlē-sə\. 1 Colony, Central America. See BRITISH HONDURAS.

2 River, British Honduras; 180 m. long; rises in NE Guatemala and flows E into the Gulf of Honduras at Belize.

3 District, E British Honduras; 1623 sq. m.; pop. (1967e) 51,473; ✱ Belize.

4 *also* **Belize City.** Seaport, ✱ of district, at mouth of Belize river; pop. (1970p) 39,257; former ✱ of British Honduras; exports mahogany, cedar, sugar, copra; devastated by hurricane 1961.

Beljak. See VILLACH.

Bel·knap \ˈbel-ˌnap\. County in New Hampshire. See table at NEW HAMPSHIRE.

Belknap Peak. Mountain, Piute co., SW cen. Utah; 12,139 ft.

Bell \ˈbel\. 1 Name of counties in two states of the U.S. See tables at KENTUCKY and TEXAS.

2 Residential city, Los Angeles co., SW California, 5 m. S of Los Angeles; pop. (1970c) 21,836; automobile parts, paints; incorp. 1927.

Bell, Mount. Mountain, Antarctica, 84°04′S, 167°30′E; 14,117 ft.

Bel·la Coo·la \ˌbel-ə-ˈkü-lə\. Short stream in SW British Columbia, Canada; flows W into Burke Channel.

Bel·laire \bə-ˈla(ə)r, -ˈle(ə)r, be-\. 1 Village, ⊗ of Antrim co., NW Michigan; pop. (1970c) 897.

2 City, Belmont co., E Ohio, on Ohio river 26 m. S of Steubenville; pop. (1970c) 9655; coal, clay, limestone deposits; glass, enamelware.

3 City, Harris co., Texas, entirely within city of Houston; pop. (1970c) 19,009.

Bel·la·ry \bə-ˈlär-ē\ *or* **Bal·la·ri** \bə-ˈlär-ē\. Town, SW Mysore, S cen. India, 270 m. NW of Madras; pop. (1961c) 85,673; cotton and sugar trade.

Be·lla·vis·ta \ˌbā-ə-ˈvē-stə\. City, Callao constitutional province, W Peru, W suburb of Lima; pop. (1961c) 43,128.

Bella Vista National Park. National park, Bolivia; 3475 sq. m.; subtropical forest; established 1964.

Belle·air \bə-ˈla(ə)r, -ˈe(ə)r, be-\. Town, Pinellas co., W cen. Florida, 20 m. W of Tampa; pop. (1970c) 2962.

Belle–Alliance, La. See LA BELLE-ALLIANCE.

Bel·leau \be-ˈlō, ˈbe-ˌ\. Village, Aisne dept., N France, 9 m. NW of Château-Thierry; pop. (1962c) 126; American military cemetery (dedicated 1923).

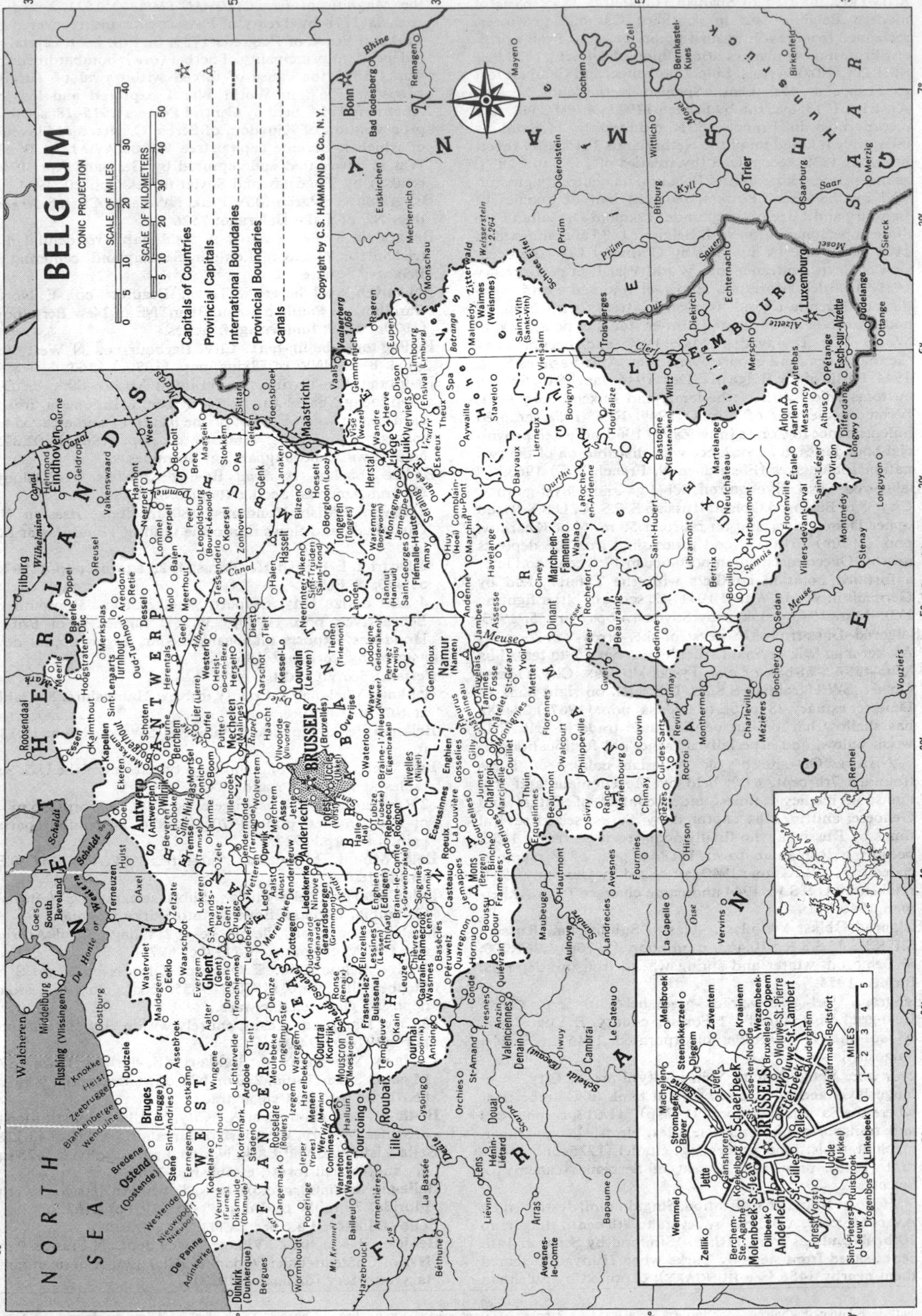
BELGIUM
CONIC PROJECTION
SCALE OF MILES
0 5 10 20 30 40
SCALE OF KILOMETERS
0 5 10 20 30 40 50
Capitals of Countries
Provincial Capitals
International Boundaries
Provincial Boundaries
Canals
Copyright by C.S. HAMMOND & Co., N. Y.
NORTH SEA
NETHERLANDS
GERMANY
FRANCE
LUXEMBOURG
ANTWERP
LIMBURG
LIÈGE
NAMUR
LUXEMBOURG
HAINAUT
BRABANT
EAST FLANDERS
WEST FLANDERS
BRUSSELS
Antwerp (Antwerpen)
Ghent (Gent)
Bruges (Brugge)
Liège (Luik)
Namur (Namen)
Mons (Bergen)
Hasselt
Arlon (Aarlen)
Louvain (Leuven)
Mechelen (Malines)
Ostend (Oostende)
Charleroi
Tournai (Doornik)
Courtrai (Kortrijk)
Maastricht
Lille
Luxemburg
Meuse
Scheldt
Sambre
Ourthe
Semois
Moselle
Rhine
Longitude East 5° of Greenwich
MILES
0 1 2 3 4 5

Belleau Wood *or Fr.* **Bois de Belleau** \bwäd-(ə)-be-lō\ *also* **Bois de la Bri·gade Ma·rine** \-lä-brē-gäd-mə-rēn\. Wood, S of Belleau village, France; scene of battle June 6–25, 1918, in which five German divisions were defeated by 4th U.S. Marine Brigade, stopping German advance on Paris, but with heavy loss to the marines.

Belle·chasse \bel-ˈshas\. County, Quebec, Canada. See table at QUEBEC.

Bel·leek \bə-ˈlēk\. Parish and village, co. Fermanagh, Northern Ireland, on the Erne river; famous for its china.

Belle·fon·taine \bel-ˈfau̇nt-ᵊn, -ˈfänt-\. City, ⊗ of Logan co., W Ohio, 30 m. N of Springfield; pop. (1970c) 11,255; in agricultural region; former site of Shawnee Indian village; settled 1806.

Bellefontaine Neighbors. City, St. Louis co., Missouri, N of St. Louis; pop. (1970c) 13,987.

Belle·fonte \ˈbel-ˌfänt\. Industrial borough, ⊗ of Centre co., cen. Pennsylvania, 25 m. NNW of Lewistown; pop. (1970c) 6828.

Belle Fourche \bel-ˈfüsh\. **1** River, NE Wyoming and W South Dakota; ab. 350 m. long; rises in NE Wyoming, flows NE and E into Cheyenne river in E Meade co., South Dakota. In S Butte co., South Dak., a canal links river with **Belle Fourche Reservoir,** used for irrigation and formed by **Belle Fourche Dam** (completed 1911, height 112 ft. built across Owl Creek, a N tributary).

2 City, ⊗ of Butte co., W South Dakota, on Belle Fourche river 25 m. N of Lead; pop. (1970c) 4236; beet sugar, flour, bricks.

Belle Glade \ˈbel-ˌglād, bel-ˈglād\. City, Palm Beach co., SE Florida, on SE shore of Lake Okeechobee; pop. (1970c) 15,949; built 1925, laid waste by hurricane 1928, rebuilt.

Belle–Île–en–Mer \be-ˈlē(ə)l-äⁿ-ˈme(ə)r\. Island in N Bay of Biscay, off S coast of Morbihan dept. (to which it belongs), NW France; 35 sq. m.

Belle Isle \bel-ˈī(ə)l\. **1** City, Orange co., cen. Florida; pop. (1970c) 2705.

2 Island in Atlantic Ocean at entrance to Strait of Belle Isle; ab. 15 sq. m.; administratively part of Newfoundland, Canada; lighthouse.

Belle Isle, Strait of. Channel bet. N tip of Newfoundland and SE Labrador, Canada, connecting Gulf of St. Lawrence with Atlantic Ocean; 10 to 20 m. wide; ab. 90 m. long.

Bellenz. See BELLINZONA.

Belle Plaine \ˈbel-ˌplān\. City, Benton co., E cen. Iowa, 34 m. W of Cedar Rapids; pop. (1970c) 2810; pottery works.

Belle·rive \ˈbel-ˌrēv\. Residential suburb of Hobart, Tasmania (*q.v.*), directly opp. on left bank of the Derwent.

Belle Ver·non \bel-ˈvər-nən\. Borough, Fayette co., SW Pennsylvania, on Monongahela river 24 m. SSE of Pittsburgh; pop. (1970c) 1496; coal, glass; settled 1791.

Belle·ville \ˈbel-ˌvil\. **1** Industrial city, ⊗ of St. Clair co., SW Illinois, 14 m. SE of East St. Louis; pop. (1970c) 41,699; in coal-mining region; boilers, agricultural implements, stoves, tools; Belleville Junior Coll. (1946); Scott air force base nearby. See SCOTT 2.

2 City, ⊗ of Republic co., N Kansas, 17 m. N of Concordia; pop. (1970c) 3063; poultry and dairy farms.

3 Town, Essex co., NE New Jersey, on Passaic river 4 m. N of Newark; pop. (1970c) 37,629; electrical equipment, fire extinguishers, water pumps, precision instruments; an old Dutch settlement of 17th cent.; originally known as Second River section of Newark; became separate community 1839.

4 Industrial city, ⊗ of Hastings co., SE Ontario, Canada, on Bay of Quinte 47 m. W of Kingston; pop. (1971p) 34,498; electronic products, plastics, dietary food products; fishing; site of Ontario School for the Deaf; founded 1790; became a city 1877.

Belle·vue \ˈbel-ˌvyü\. **1** Town, Jackson co., E Iowa, on Mississippi river 20 m. SSE of Dubuque; pop. (1970c) 2336; pottery works.

2 City, Campbell co., N Kentucky, on Ohio river just above Newport; pop. (1970c) 8847; a suburb of Covington, Ky., and Cincinnati, Ohio.

3 City, Sarpy co., E Nebraska, on Missouri river 8 m. S of Omaha; pop. (1970c) 21,953; oldest town in Nebraska; on site of fur-trading post; missionary station 1833.

4 City, Huron and Sandusky cos., N Ohio, 14 m. SSW of Sandusky; pop. (1970c) 8604; limestone quarries; farm implements, automobile accessories; settled 1815.

5 Borough, Allegheny co., SW Pennsylvania, on Ohio river; pop. (1970c) 11,586; residential suburb of Pittsburgh.

6 City, King co., Washington, E of Seattle; pop. (1970c) 61,102; Bellevue Community Coll. (1966).

Bell·flow·er \ˈbel-ˌflau̇(-ə)r\. City, Los Angeles co., California, N of Long Beach; pop. (1970c) 51,454; truck farms.

Bell Gardens \ˈbel-\. City, Los Angeles co., California, NW of Downey; pop. (1970c) 29,308.

Bel·li·court \ˌbel-i-ˈku̇(ə)r\. Commune, Aisne dept., N France, 8 m. N of Saint-Quentin; pop. (1962c) 609; in World War I part of Hindenburg Line, taken by Americans Sept. 29, 1918; American military cemetery.

Bel·ling·ham \ˈbel-iŋ-ˌham\. **1** Town, Norfolk co., E Massachusetts, 19 m. SE of Worcester; pop. (1970c) 13,967; birthplace of William T. Adams ("Oliver Optic").

2 Commercial and industrial city, ⊗ of Whatcom co., NW Washington, on **Bellingham Bay** ab. 18 m. S of Canadian border; pop. (1970c) 39,375; port of entry; pulp and paper, logging machinery, cement; shipbuilding, fish canning; Western Washington State Coll. (1893); settled 1852 as **What·com** \ˈhwät-kəm, ˈwät-\ and became ⊗ 1854; incorp. with adjoining town of Fairhaven 1890 and named **Fair·haven** \ˈfa(ə)r-ˌhā-vən, ˈfe(ə)r-\; merged with New Whatcom and renamed Bellingham 1903.

Bel·lings·hau·sen Sea \ˌbel-iŋz-ˌhau̇z-ᵊn-\. Inlet of South Pacific Ocean on coast of Antarctica; extends along coast from Alexander I. to Thurston I., ab. long. 75° to 98°W and bet. lat. 70° and 72°S.

Bel·lin·zo·na \ˌbel-ən-ˈzō-nə, -ˈsō-\ *or Ger.* **Bel·lenz** \ˈbel-ˌen(t)s\. Commune, ✱ of Ticino canton, SE cen. Switzerland, near Ticino river 92 m. SE of Bern; pop. (1970c) 16,979; linoleum; railroad junction. Fortified in Roman times; to city of Como 1231, to Milan 1396, to Swiss Confederation 1503.

Belli Quadrum. See BEAUCAIRE.

Bell Island. **1** Island in Atlantic Ocean, off NE coast of Newfoundland, Canada, 50°44′N, 55°35′W.

2 Island in Conception Bay, Newfoundland, Canada, W of city of St. John's, 47°36′N, 52°58′W.

Bell·mawr \bel-ˈmär\. Borough, Camden co., New Jersey, SW of Camden; pop. (1970c) 15,618.

Bell·mead \ˈbel-ˌmēd\. City, McLennan co., Texas, NE suburb of Waco; pop. (1970c) 7698.

Bell·more \ˈbel-ˌmō(ə)r, -ˌmȯ(ə)r\. Urban community (unincorp.), Nassau co., SE New York, on Long I.; pop. (1970c) 18,431.

Be·llo \ˈbā-yō\. Town, Antioquia dept., NW Colombia; munic. pop. (1968e) 108,808.

Bello Horizonte. See BELO HORIZONTE.

Bel·lo·na \bə-ˈlō-nə\. Small island in SE Solomon Is., W Pacific Ocean, ab. 110 m. S of Guadalcanal and ab. 20 m. WNW of Rennell I.

Bellovacum. See BEAUVAIS.

Bel·lows Falls \ˌbel-əz-\. Industrial village, in Rockingham town, Windham co., SE corner of Vermont, on Connecticut river 21 m. N of Brattleboro; pop. (1970c) 3505; paper, farm machinery; settled 1753.

Bell·port \'bel-ˌpō(ə)rt, -ˌpȯ(ə)rt\. Village, Suffolk co., SE New York, on Great South Bay 13 m. ESE of Islip; pop. (1970c) 3046.

Bell Rock. See INCHCAPE ROCK.

Bell Sound \'bel-\. Large inlet on SW coast of Spitsbergen I., Svalbard.

Bel·lu·no \bə-'lü-(ˌ)nō\. 1 Province of Veneto, NE Italy. See table at ITALY.

2 Commune, its ✻, on Piave river 50 m. N of Venice; pop. (1968e) 33,721; furniture; tourism; 16th cent. cathedral. Became Roman 180 B.C.; in Middle Ages became Lombard duchy and later a Frankish countship; part of Venetian Republic 1405–1797; occupied by Austro-German forces 1917.

Bell·ville \'bel-ˌvil\. 1 City, ⊗ of Austin co., SE cen. Texas; pop. (1970c) 2371; furniture; cotton gins.

2 Town, SW Cape Province, Rep. of South Africa, 12 m. ENE of Cape Town; pop. (1967e) 42,500.

Bell Vi·lle \bezh-'vē-(ˌ)zhā\. Town, Córdoba prov., N cen. Argentina, 110 m. WNW of Rosario; pop. (1960c) 19,269.

Bell·wood \'bel-ˌwu̇d\. 1 Residential village, Cook co., NE Illinois, 13 m. W of Chicago; pop. (1970c) 22,096.

2 Borough, Blair co., S cen. Pennsylvania, 8 m. NNE of Altoona; pop. (1970c) 2395; coal mines; farming.

Bel·ly \'bel-ē\. River, SW Alberta, Canada; 180 m. long; rises in Glacier National Park, Montana, and flows NNE to Oldman river.

Bel·mar \'bel-ˌmär\. Borough, Monmouth co., E cen. New Jersey; pop. (1970c) 5782; seashore resort; fishing.

Bél·mez \'bel-ˌmās\. Commune, Córdoba prov., S Spain, 35 m. NW of Córdoba; pop. (1970p) 5832.

Bel·mond \'bel-ˌmänd\. City, Wright co., N cen. Iowa, 28 m. SW of Mason City; pop. (1970c) 2358; beet-sugar plant.

Bel·mont \'bel-ˌmänt\. 1 County in Ohio. See table at OHIO.

2 City, San Mateo co., W California, 10 m. SSE of San Francisco; pop. (1970c) 23,667; Coll. of Notre Dame (1851).

3 Town, Middlesex co., NE Massachusetts, 7 m. WNW of Boston; pop. (1970c) 28,285; residential suburb of Boston.

4 Village, Mississippi co., SE Missouri, 15 m. S of Cairo, Illinois; scene of battle Nov. 7, 1861 in which Gen. Grant's attacking force was driven back by Confederate forces under Gen. Leonidas Polk.

5 Village, ⊗ of Allegany co., SW New York; pop. (1970c) 1102.

6 City, Gaston co., SW North Carolina, 7 m. E of Gastonia; pop. (1970c) 5054; yarn, hosiery, dyes; Belmont Abbey Coll. (1878).

Bel·mo·pan \ˌbel-mō-'pan\. Town, ✻ of British Honduras, 41 m. SW of Belize; pop. (1970e) 1000; became ✻ 1970.

Belna. See BEAUNE.

Bel·oeil \be-'lī(ə)l\. Town, Verchères co., S Quebec, Canada, on Richelieu river NE of Montreal; pop. (1971p) 12,248.

Be·lo·gorsk \ˌb(y)el-ō-'gȯrsk\; *formerly* **Kui·by·shev·ka** \ˌkü-bi-'shef-kə\ *or* **Boch·ka·re·vo** \bəch-kə-'rō-və\. Town, Amur Oblast, Russian S.F.S.R., U.S.S.R., just NE of Blagoveschensk; junction point on Trans-Siberian R.R. for Blagoveshchensk; pop. (1969e) 53,000.

Be·lo·gursk \ˌb(y)el-ō-'gu̇rsk\ *or formerly* **Ka·ra·su·ba·zar** \ˌkär-ə-ˌsü-bə-'zär\. Town, S cen. Crimean Oblast, Ukrainian S.S.R., U.S.S.R., NE of Simferopol; pop. (1956e) 8800.

Be·lo Ho·ri·zon·te *or formerly* **Be·llo Horizonte** \'bā-lō-ˌhȯr-ə-'zänt-ē, 'bel-ō-, -ˌhär-\. City, ✻ of Minas Gerais state, E Brazil, 220 m. N of Rio de Janeiro; munic. pop. (1970p) 1,106,722; alt. 2811 ft.; chemicals, furniture, iron and steel; federal univ. (1927), Catholic Univ. (1959); region important for cotton and cattle.

Be·loit \bə-'lȯit\. 1 City, ⊗ of Mitchell co., N cen. Kansas, on Solomon river 51 m. NW of Salina; pop. (1970c) 4121; trading center in agricultural region.

2 Industrial city, Rock co., S Wisconsin, on Rock river on Illinois border; pop. (1970c) 35,729; diesel engines, shoes; Beloit Coll. (1846); Indian mounds nearby.

Be·lo·morsk \ˌb(y)el-ə-'mȯ(ə)rsk\ *or formerly* **So·ro·ka** \sə-'rō-kə\. Seaport town on W coast of Onega Bay, SW White Sea, E Karelian A.S.S.R., Russian S.F.S.R., U.S.S.R., on railroad S of Kem; pop. (1967e) 16,000.

Be·lo·re·chensk \ˌb(y)el-ō-'rech-ˌin(t)sk\. Town, Krasnodar Krai, Russian S.F.S.R., U.S.S.R., ab. 50 m. ESE of Krasnodar; pop. (1967e) 42,000.

Be·lo·retsk \ˌb(y)el-ə-'retsk\. Town, E Bashkir A.S.S.R., Russian S.F.S.R., U.S.S.R., on Belaya river in Southern Ural Mts.; pop. (1969e) 66,000; metallurgical industries.

Be·lo·rus·sian Soviet Socialist Republic \ˌbel-ō-'rəsh-ən-\ *or* **Bye·lo·rus·sian Soviet Socialist Republic** \bē-ˌel-ō-\ *also* **Be·lo·rus·sia** \-'rəsh-ə\ *or* **Bye·lo·rus·sia** *or* **White Russia.** A constituent republic of the U.S.S.R., bounded on N by Russian S.F.S.R. and Latvian S.S.R., on NW by Lithuanian S.S.R., on W by Poland, on S by Ukrainian S.S.R., and on E by Russian S.F.S.R.; 80,154 sq. m.; pop. (1970p) 9,003,000; ✻ Minsk. *Chief rivers:* The N part is crossed by the Western Dvina; upper course of Dnieper flows through E part from N to S; along the Pripyat in the S extends extensive marshy area (see POLESYE). In the W (former Poland) is upper course of Neman river and its tributaries and on the SW the Bug forms part of the boundary. *Chief products:* Potatoes, flax, barley, timber; manufacturing: textiles, pulp and paper, machine tools; food processing. *Chief towns:* Minsk, Gomel, Vitebsk, Mogilev.

History: In medieval times region was subject to Lithuanians and Poles; small section came under Ivan the Great 1503 but reconquered by Poles and continued as part of Poland until 1656; for the next century a prize of war; E part to Russia in First Partition of Poland 1772 and remainder by Second 1793; continual wars left country devastated and made worse by Napoleon's Campaign 1812 (see BEREZINA); again overrun in World War I and occupied by Poles 1919; in 1921 W part assigned to Poland; in 1922 became part of U.S.S.R.; in 1924 and 1926 E boundary adjusted by U.S.S.R. to include Vitebsk and Gomel; in World War II overrun by German armies in summer of 1941; recovered by Soviet troops 1944; after World War II increased in area through Soviet annexation of part of NE Poland.

Belostok. See BIAŁYSTOK.

Belovar. See BJELOVAR.

Beloye More. See WHITE SEA.

Be·lo·ye Oze·ro \ˌb(y)el-ə-yə-'ō-zə-rə\ *or* **Byel·oze·ro** \byə-'lō-\. Lake (*ozero*) in W Vologda Oblast, Russian S.F.S.R., U.S.S.R.; 433 sq. m.; outlet to Rybinsk Reservoir by Sheksna river; along its W and S shores is a part of the Volga-Baltic Waterway.

Bel·pas·so \bel-'päs-ˌō\. Commune, Catania prov., E Sicily, Italy, on S slope of Mt. Etna; pop. (1968e) 12,142; rebuilt just N of older town destroyed by lava in 1669.

Bel·per \'bel-pər\. Urban district, Derbyshire, N cen. England, on the Derwent 8 m. N of Derby; pop. (1969e) 16,360; cotton, hosiery.

Bel·pre \'bel-ˌprā\. City, Washington co., SE Ohio, on Ohio river 10 m. SSW of Marietta; pop. (1970c) 7189; Blennerhassett I. nearby.

Bel·sen \'bel-zən\ *or in full* **Ber·gen–Belsen** \ˌber-gən-\. Locality in Lower Saxony, West Germany, ab. 12 m. NNW of Celle; site of Nazi concentration camp taken by Allies Apr. 14, 1945.

Belt, Great. See GREAT BELT.

Belt, Little. See LITTLE BELT.

Bel·ton \'belt-ᵊn\. 1 City, Cass co., W Missouri, 12 m. S of Kansas City; pop. (1970c) 12,179; agriculture.

2 Village, Montana. See WEST GLACIER.

3 Town, Anderson co., NW South Carolina, 9 m. E of Anderson; pop. (1970c) 5257; cotton mills.

4 City, ⊗ of Bell co., cen. Texas, W of Temple; pop. (1970c) 8696; Mary Hardin-Baylor Coll. (1845).

Bel·trami \bel-'tram-ē\. County in Minnesota. See table at MINNESOTA.

Belts·ville \'belts-,vil\. Village (unincorp.), Prince Georges co., Maryland, ab. 12 m. NE of Washington; pop. (1970c) 8912; principal experiment station, U.S. Department of Agriculture.

Bel·tsy \'belt-sē\ *or Rom.* **Băl·ţi** \'bəlts(-ē)\. Town, N cen. Moldavian S.S.R., U.S.S.R., on a W tributary of the Dniester 70 m. NW of Kishinev; pop. (1970p) 102,000; formerly in Romania.

Beluchistan. See BALUCHISTAN.

Be·lu·kha \bə-'lü-kə\ *also* **Bye·lu·kha** \byə-\. Highest peak in the Altai mountain system, on border bet. Kazakh S.S.R. and Gorno-Altai Autonomous Oblast, Russian S.F.S.R., U.S.S.R.; 15,157 ft.

Bel·ve·dere \'bel-və-,di(ə)r\. City, Marin co., W California, on San Francisco Bay 8 m. N of San Francisco; pop. (1970c) 2599.

Bel·vi·dere \'bel-və-,di(ə)r\. 1 City, ⊗ of Boone co., N Illinois, 15 m. E of Rockford; pop. (1970c) 14,061.
2 Town, ⊗ of Warren co., NW New Jersey, on Delaware river 11 m. NNE of Phillipsburg; pop. (1970c) 2722.

Bel·yan·do \bel-'yan-(,)dō\. River, E Queensland, NE Australia; ab. 250 m. long; flows N along E slope of Eastern Highlands.

Bel·zo·ni \bel-'zō-nē\. City, ⊗ of Humphreys co., W Mississippi, 28 m. SW of Greenwood; pop. (1970c) 3146.

Be·mid·ji \bə-'mij-ē\. City, ⊗ of Beltrami co., N Minnesota, 28 m. S of Lower Red Lake; pop. (1970c) 11,490; summer resort; lumber, cement, bricks, woolen goods; Bemidji State Coll. (1913).

Bemis Heights. See SARATOGA 3.

Be·na Be·na \,bā-nə-'bā-nə\. Village, on island of New Guinea, Papua New Guinea, ab. 90 m. NW of Lae; held by Japanese in World War II.

Ben–a–Bhuird \,ben-ə-'bu̇(ə)rd\. Mountain on N border of W Aberdeen co., NE Scotland; 3924 ft.

Benacus, Lacus. See GARDA, LAKE.

Ben·a·dir \,ben-ə-'di(ə)r\. Coastal region, S Somalia, E Africa; its chief town is Mogadisho.

Ben Al·der \ben-'ȯl-dər\. Mountain, SE Inverness co., N cen. Scotland, on W side of Loch Ericht; 3757 ft.

Be·nal·la \bə-'nal-ə\. Urban center, Victoria, Australia, 104 m. NE of Melbourne; pop. (1966c) 8640.

Benares. See VARANASI.

Benas, Ras. See BANAS, CAPE.

Ben Av·on \ben-'av-ən\. Borough, Allegheny co., SW Pennsylvania, on Ohio river 7 m. NW of Pittsburgh; pop. (1970c) 2713; suburb of Pittsburgh.

Ben Avon \ben-'än\. Mountain in SW Aberdeen co. on boundary of Banff co., NE cen. Scotland; 3843 ft.

Benbaun. See BENNEBEOLA, TWELVE BENS OF.

Ben·bec·u·la \ben-'bek-yə-lə\. Island of the Outer Hebrides, Inverness co., off NW coast of Scotland, bet. the islands of North Uist and South Uist; ab. 8 m. long.

Ben·bon·yathe, Mount \-,ben-bən-'yath-ē\. Peak in North Flinders Range, E South Australia; 3470 ft.

Ben·brook \'ben-,bru̇k\. Village, Tarrant co., N Texas, 10 m. SW of Fort Worth; pop. (1970c) 8169.

Ben Cleuch. See OCHIL HILLS.

Ben Cru·a·chan \ben-'krü-ə-kən, -k̲ən\. Mountain, N Argyll co., W Scotland, SE of Loch Etive; 3689 ft.

Bend \'bend\. Industrial city, ⊗ of Deschutes co., cen. Oregon, on Deschutes river 95 m. E of Eugene; pop. (1970c) 13,710; lumber; Central Oregon Community Coll. (1949).

Ben Da·vis Point \ben-,dā-vəs-\. Point on SW coast of Cumberland co., SW New Jersey, in Delaware Bay.

Ben Dearg *or* **Ben Derg** \ben-'jer-ək\. Mountain, Ross and Cromarty co., N Scotland, SE of Loch Broom; 3547 ft.

Benderabbas. See BANDAR 'ABBĀS.

Ben·de·ry \ben-'der-ē\ *or* **Ben·der** \ben-'de(ə)r\ *or Rom.* **Ti·ghi·na** \ti-'gē-nə\. Town, Moldavian S.S.R., U.S.S.R., near right bank of the Dniester in its lower course 30 m. SE of Kishinev; pop. (1969e) 68,000; on rail line bet. Kishinev and Odessa; trades in timber, fruits, and tobacco.
History: Genoese trading town in 12th cent.; controlled by many different peoples down to 18th cent.; site of fortress erected 1558 by Suleiman the Magnificent; headquarters of Charles XII for his campaign in Russia 1709 and place where he was held prisoner 1712–14; became part of Bessarabia, Romania, 1918; ceded to U.S.S.R. 1940; held by Axis powers 1941–44.

Ben·di·go \'ben-di-,gō\ *or formerly* **Sand·hurst** \'sand-,hərst\. City, cen. Victoria, SE Australia, 80 m. NNW of Melbourne; pop. (1968e) 31,350; iron foundries, potteries, livestock market; founded 1851; one of earliest places where alluvial gold was discovered (1851).

Bendin. See BĘDZIN.

Ben Dou·ran \ben-'du̇r-ən\ *or* **Ben Do·ran** \-'dōr-ən, -'dȯr-\. Mountain in Grampian Mts., NE Argyll co., W Scotland; 3523 ft.

Bendzin. See BĘDZIN.

Be·ne Be·raq \bə-,nā-bə-'räk\. City, W cen. Israel, NE suburb of Tel Aviv-Jaffa; pop. (1970e) 72,100; textiles; diamond cutting and polishing.

Be·ne·dikt·beu·ern \,bā-nə-,dikt-'bȯi-ərn, ben-ə-\. Village, Bavaria, West Germany, on railroad 30 m. S of Munich in N foothills of Alps; pop. (1964e) 2050; noted Benedictine monastery founded 733 where was discovered 13th cent. MS., the *Carmina Burana,* a collection of goliardic songs, now in Munich.

Beneharnum. See BÉARN.

Be·ne·lux Economic Union \'ben-ᵊl-,əks-\. Economic community, consisting of Belgium, Luxembourg, and the Netherlands; headquarters Brussels, Belgium; purpose is to bring about economic union of members; treaty signed 1958, put into force 1960; border controls between members abolished.

Be·ne·ven·to \,ben-ə-'ven-(,)tō\. 1 Province of Campania, Italy. See table at ITALY.
2 *anc.* **Male·ven·tum** \,mal-ə-'vent-əm\ *also* **Bene·ven·tum** \,ben-ə-'vent-əm\. Commune, its ✻, at confluence of Calore and Sabbato rivers 34 m. NE of Naples; pop. (1968e) 59,578; agricultural machinery, bricks; in agricultural region; antiquities include a 9th cent. Lombard-Saracenic cathedral and the Porta Aurea (*Ital.,* golden gate), a triumphal arch of Trajan, erected 114 A.D.
History: Ancient town of the Samnites; became Roman colony 268 B.C.; became seat of Lombard duchy of Benevento 571 A.D.; fell to Saracens and later to Normans; made a principality by Napoleon 1806 and conferred upon Talleyrand; under papal control 1815 until its unification with the kingdom of Italy 1860.

Ben·e·wah \'ben-,wä, -,wȯ\. County in Idaho. See table at IDAHO.

Ben·fleet \'ben-,flēt\. Urban district, Essex, SE England, on inlet of Thames estuary 29 m. E of London; pop. (1969e) 46,270.

Ben·gal \ben-'gȯl, beŋ-\ *or earlier* **Bengal Presidency.** Former province, NE British India, now a region encompassing West Bengal, India and Bangla Desh; 77,442 sq. m.; ✻ Calcutta; included geographically Indian states of Tripura and Cooch Behar, 5370 sq. m.; total area 82,812 sq. m. Most of S part known as Sundarbans, occupied by delta of Ganges and Brahmaputra (see GANGES DELTA); S ranges of Himalayas in N and hills in Chittagong and Tripura in SE.
History: Ancient Hindu region introduced to Buddhism by Asoka 3d cent. B.C.; NE part of older Bengal (see MAGADHA and BIHAR) nucleus of Maurya and Gupta empires; conquered by an Afghan ruler, Mohammed of

Ghor (see GHOR), c. 1199; E Bengal made province under Tughlak dynasty 1324; Bengal under independent dynasty 1338–1539; in 1576 taken from Afghans by Moguls; first visited by factors of English East India Company 1633; Calcutta (*q.v.*) founded by English 1690 and Bengal made a presidency 1699; soon after Clive's victory at Plassey (*q.v.*) 1757 came to be under the Company's financial and military control; seat of authority of governor-general 1773–1834; Eastern Bengal and Assam separated from Bengal province 1905, but restored in 1912 when the whole was constituted as new presidency; made autonomous province 1937 (see INDIA 1); divided Aug. 15, 1947 into East Bengal, now Bangla Desh, and West Bengal, part of India (see these terms for former divisions and districts of Bengal assigned to each).

Bengal, Bay of. Part of Indian Ocean bet. E India and W coasts of Burma and the Malay Penin.

Bengawan. See SOLO 1.

Ben·gha·zi *also* **Ben·ga·si** *or* **Ben·ga·zi** \ben-'gäz-ē, beŋ-, -'gaz-\. 1 Former province of N (Italian) Libya, N Africa; 58,684 sq. m.; ✱ Benghazi.

2 *or anc.* **Ber·e·ni·ce** \ˌber-ə-'nī-sē\. Coastal city, Libya, on NE shore of Gulf of Sidra; pop. (1970e) 170,000; cement; food processing; exports incl. hides and sponges; univ. (1956); formerly a ✱ of Libya. Under Italian administration developed as seaport and naval and air base. In World War II Italian supply base; captured by British Feb. 7, 1941, by Germans Apr. 4, 1941; again taken by British Dec. 25, 1941; given up Jan. 28, 1942, retaken Nov. 20, 1942.

Beng·ka·lis \beŋ-'käl-əs\. 1 Island, E Sumatra, Indonesia, at S end of Strait of Malacca.

2 Town and fishing port on W side of island, ab. 120 m. W of Singapore; pop. (1961c) 11,673.

Beng·ku·lu \beŋ-'kü-(ˌ)lü\ *or formerly* **Beng·koe·len** \beŋ-'kü-lən\ *or* **Ben·koe·len** *or* **Ben·ku·len** \beŋ-'kü-lən, ben-\. 1 Former residency of Neth. Indies, on the SW coast of Sumatra, now part of the Indonesian prov. of South Sumatra; 10,132 sq. m.; ✱ Bengkulu; comprised the elevated region of the S Barisan Mts. and a narrow coastal strip.

2 Town, its ✱, a port in 3°48′S, 102°16′E, ab. 350 m. NW of Djakarta; pop. (1961c) 25,330. Settlement established by British 1684 and fort built a few years later; in early years a center of pepper and spice trade; ceded to Dutch 1824 in exchange for Malacca.

Ben·go, Bay of \-'beŋ-(ˌ)gō\. Inlet of Atlantic Ocean on NW coast of Angola, W Africa; Luanda is on it.

Ben·gore Head \ˌben-ˌgō(ə)r-, -ˌgȯ(ə)r-\. Cape, E of Giant's Causeway, co. Antrim, Northern Ireland.

Ben·guela *also* **Ben·guel·la** \ben-'g(w)el-ə, beŋ-\. 1 Coastal district, W Angola, SW Africa; 14,598 sq. m.; pop. (1960c) 487,873; ✱ Benguela.

2 Seaport town, its ✱; pop. (1969e) 35,162; railroad terminus; exports cattle, hides. Fort built here 1587; town founded 1617.

Benguela Current *or* **Benguella Current.** A cold ocean current moving northward along the W coast of S Africa.

Ben·gué·rir \ˌben-gā-'ri(ə)r\. Town, W cen. Morocco, NW Africa, ab. 45 m. NNE of Marrakech on railroad and highway to Casablanca; pop. (1960c) 15,881.

Ben·guet \beŋ-'get\. Province, N Luzon, Phil., in mountainous region of S Cordillera Central and Caraballo Mts.; 1025 sq. m.; pop. (1970p) 262,679; ✱ La Trinidad; agriculture; gold mining. Formed by Spanish as a military district (*comandancia*) 1846; made subprovince 1908, province 1968. Baguio, its most important town, administered separately.

Ben·ha \'ben-(h)ə\. City, ✱ of Qalyubīya gov., N Egypt, on railroad E of the Damietta branch of the Nile ab. 28 m. N of Cairo; pop. (1970e) 72,500; in region producing grapes and cotton.

Ben Hill \'ben-'hil\. County in Georgia. See table at GEORGIA.

Be·ni \'bā-nē, 'ben-ē\. 1 River, N and cen. Bolivia; 994 m. long; rises in E cordillera of Andes in Cochabamba dept., flows N to unite with Mamoré river and form Madeira river; near its mouth receives large tributary from the W, the Madre de Dios.

2 *or in full* **El Beni** \el-\. Department of N Bolivia. See table at BOLIVIA.

Bé·ni Ab·bès \ˌbā-nē-ä-'bes\. Town, Saoura dept., Algeria, near Morocco border, ab. 100 m. S of Béchar; pop. (1966c) 2341; dates.

Be·ni·cia \bə-'nē-shə\. City, Solano co., cen. California, on N shore of Carquinez Strait 18 m. NNE of Oakland; pop. (1970c) 7349; fishing, manufacture of dredging machinery; U.S. Army Arsenal. Founded 1848; capital of California 1853–54; chartered as city 1861.

Beni Has·an \ˌben-ē-'has-ˌan\. Village on the Nile river, Egypt, 75 m. N of Asyūt; site of rock tombs (XIIth dynasty, c. 2000 B.C.).

Be·nin \bə-'nin, -'nēn; 'ben-ən\. 1 Formerly part of Upper Guinea, W Africa, bet. the Volta river and Rio del Rey, including all of Slave Coast and the Niger delta region.

2 Name formerly given by French to their possessions on the Guinea coast including Dahomey.

3 Former native kingdom, one of the most highly organized of the Negro states of W Africa before the coming of the Portuguese 1485; exerted great influence in 17th cent., then known to Europeans as **Great Benin;** control taken over by British 1897–99.

4 River, S Nigeria, flowing into Bight of Benin; ab. 100 m. long; connects with W part of Niger delta.

5 *or* **Benin City.** Town, ✱ of Mid-Western State, Nigeria, in W delta of the Niger ab. 150 m. E of Lagos; pop. (1969e) 116,774; brasswork; rubber processing; first visited by Europeans 1472.

Benin, Bight of. Widemouthed bay in N section of the Gulf of Guinea, W Africa.

Be·ni Saf \ˌben-ē-'saf\. Seaport and commune, NE Tlemcen dept., NW Algeria, ab. 50 m. SW of Oran; pop. (1966c) 18,507; fisheries; exports iron ore.

Beni Su·ef *or* **Ba·nī Su·wayf** \ˌben-ē-sü-'āf\. 1 Governorate of Upper Egypt. See table at EGYPT.

2 City, its ✱, on W bank of Nile 22 m. SE of Al-Faiyūm; pop. (1970e) 99,400; trade center; cotton manufacture.

Ben·ja·min \'benj-(ə-)mən\. City, ⊗ of Knox co., N Texas; pop. (1970c) 308.

Ben·kel·man \'beŋ-kəl-mən\. City, ⊗ of Dundy co., S Nebraska; pop. (1970c) 1349.

Benkoelen *or* **Benkulen.** See BENGKULU.

Ben Laoigh. See BEN LUI.

Ben Law·ers \ben-'lȯ(-ə)rz\. Mountain, Perth co., cen. Scotland, NW of Loch Tay; 3984 ft.

Benld \bə-'nel(d)\. City, Macoupin co., SW cen. Illinois, 26 m. NE of Alton; pop. (1970c) 1736.

Ben Ledi \ben-'led-ē\. Mountain in SW Perth co., cen. Scotland, NE of Loch Katrine; 2875 ft.

Ben Lo·mond \ben-'lō-mənd\. 1 Mountain, N Utah, just N of Ogden; 9717 ft.

2 Mountain, NE New South Wales, SE Australia; 4877 ft.; highest peak in New England range.

3 Mountain, NE Tasmania, Australia, bet. the North and South Esk rivers; 5160 ft.

4 Mountain, Stirling co., S cen. Scotland, on E side of Loch Lomond; 3192 ft.; dominating peak of the region.

Ben Lui \ben-'lü-ē\ *also* **Ben Laoigh** \-'lə-ē\. Mountain, on border bet. Perth and Argyll cos., cen. Scotland, N of Ben Lomond; 3708 ft.

Ben Mac·dhui \ˌben-mək-'dü-e\ *also* **Ben Muich·dhui** \-mək-\. Mountain, SW Aberdeen co., NE cen. Scotland; 4296 ft.; one of the Cairngorm group.

Ben More \ben-'mō(ə)r, -'mȯ(ə)r\. 1 Mountain, cen. part of the island of Mull off W coast of Scotland; 3169 ft.

2 Mountain, SW Perth co., cen. Scotland; 3843 ft.

3 Mountain, Sutherland co., N Scotland; 3273 ft.

Ben·more, Lake \-ben-'mō(ə)r, -'mȯ(ə)r\. Lake, South I., New Zealand; 30½ sq. m.; max. depth 315 ft.; largest man-made lake in New Zealand.

Ben·ne·be·o·la, Twelve Bens of \-ˌben-ə-'bē-ə-lə\ *or formerly* **Twelve Bens of Bun·na·be·o·la** \-ˌbən-\. Mountain group in Connemara, W co. Galway, W Eire; highest peak **Ben·baun** \ben-'bōn\ 2395 ft.

Ben·nett \'ben-ət\. County in South Dakota. See table at SOUTH DAKOTA.

Bennett, Lake. Lake, the W arm of Tagish Lake, on border bet. British Columbia and Yukon, Canada.

Bennett Island \ˌben-ət-\. Westernmost island of De Long group in Arctic Ocean, Yakutsk A.S.S.R., U.S.S.R, NE of New Siberian Is., 76°21′N, 148°56′E.

Ben·netts·ville \'ben-əts-ˌvil, -vəl\. City, ⊗ of Marlboro co., NE South Carolina, 30 m. N of Florence; pop. (1970c) 7468; yarn, tire fabrics, lumber.

Ben Nev·is \ben-'nev-əs\. Peak in Grampian Mts., Inverness co., W cen. Scotland, E of N end of Loch Linnhe; 4406 ft.; highest peak in Great Britain.

Ben·ning·ton \'ben-iŋ-tən\. **1** County in Vermont. See table at VERMONT.

2 Village in Bennington town, a ⊗ of Bennington co., SW corner of Vermont, 31 m. W of Brattleboro; pop. (1970c) 7950 (village), 14,586 (town); knit goods, paper, electronic equipment, plastics; Bennington Coll. (1925).

History: Chartered by New Hampshire 1749, settled 1761; claimed by both New York and New Hampshire before Vermont became state; during the Revolution an important supply base for Continental Army; battle of Bennington fought nearby Aug. 16, 1777 in which Americans under Gen. Stark defeated Col. Baum, in command of a raiding force from Gen. Burgoyne's army. See HOOSICK FALLS.

Be·no·ni \bə-'nō-nē\. Town, S Transvaal, NE Rep. of South Africa, in the Witwatersrand 20 m. E of Johannesburg; pop. (1968e) 135,818; alt. 5600 ft.; engineering machinery; mining center with some of the richest gold mines in the world; important industrial town.

Bénoué. See BENUE.

Bens·berg \'benz-ˌbərg, 'ben(t)s-ˌbe(ə)rg\. Mining commune, North Rhine-Westphalia, West Germany, 10 m. ENE of Cologne; pop. (1969e) 40,516; chemicals, pharmaceuticals; atomic research center; ruins of castle (1250).

Ben·sen·ville \'ben(t)-sən-ˌvil\. Village, Cook and Du Page cos., NE Illinois, 18 m. WNW of Chicago; pop. (1970c) 12,956.

Bens·heim \'ben(t)s-ˌhīm\. City, Hesse, West Germany, 16 m. S of Darmstadt; pop. (1969e) 26,975; apparel, paper.

Ben·son \'ben(t)-sən\. **1** County in North Dakota. See table at NORTH DAKOTA.

2 Town, Cochise co., SE corner of Arizona, 42 m. ESE of Tucson; pop. (1970c) 2839; explosives.

3 City, ⊗ of Swift co., W Minnesota, 10 m. N of Montevideo; pop. (1970c) 3484; dairying.

4 Town, Johnston co., E North Carolina, 28 m. S of Raleigh; pop. (1970c) 2267; cotton, timber.

5 *or* **Ben·sing·ton** \'ben(t)-siŋ-tən\. Parish and village, SE Oxfordshire, cen. England, on the Thames; pop. (1961c) 1213; scene of battle 777 A.D. in which Offa of Mercia defeated Cynewulf of Wessex.

Ben Sta·rav \ben-'stär-əv\. Mountain, N Argyll co., W Scotland, E of Loch Etive; 3541 ft.

Bent \'bent\. County in Colorado. See table at COLORADO.

Ben·tinck Island \ˌben-ti(ŋ)k-\. Island, cen. Mergui Archipelago (*q.v.*).

Bent·ley, Mount \-'bent-lē\. Mountain, Antarctica, 78°07′S, 86°14′W; 13,934 ft.

Bent·ley·ville \'bent-lē-ˌvil\. Borough, Washington co., SW Pennsylvania, 23 m. S of Pittsburgh; pop. (1970c) 2714.

Bentley with Ark·sey \'bent-lē . . . 'ärk-sē\. Urban district, West Riding, Yorkshire, N England; pop. (1971p) 22,888.

Ben·ton \'bent-ᵊn\. **1** Name of counties in nine states of the U.S. See tables at ARKANSAS, INDIANA, IOWA, MINNESOTA, MISSISSIPPI, MISSOURI, OREGON, TENNESSEE, WASHINGTON.

2 City, ⊗ of Saline co., cen. Arkansas, 20 m. SW of Little Rock; pop. (1970c) 16,499; founded 1836.

3 City, ⊗ of Franklin co., S Illinois, 25 m. S of Mount Vernon; pop. (1970c) 6833; coal mining, farming.

4 City, ⊗ of Marshall co., W Kentucky, 22 m. SE of Paducah; pop. (1970c) 3652; tobacco, corn, strawberries.

5 Village, ⊗ of Bossier parish, NW Louisiana; pop. (1970c) 1493; cotton gins.

6 Town, ⊗ of Scott co., SE Missouri; pop. (1970c) 640.

7 Town, ⊗ of Polk co., SE Tennessee; pop. (1970c) 749.

Benton Harbor. City, Berrien co., SW corner of Michigan, on Lake Michigan 48 m. WSW of Kalamazoo; pop. (1970c) 16,481; foundry products; fruit packing. Seat of the communistic religious colony known as the House of David (organized 1903).

Ben·ton·ville \'bent-ᵊn-ˌvil\. **1** City, ⊗ of Benton co., NW corner of Arkansas, 22 m. N of Fayetteville; pop. (1970c) 5508; founded 1837.

2 Village, Johnston co., cen. North Carolina, 37 m. SE of Raleigh; indecisive battle Mar. 19, 1865 bet. Confederates under Johnston and left wing of Sherman's army.

Be·nue \'bān-(ˌ)wā, 'ben-\ *or* **Bin·ue** \'bin-(ˌ)wā\ *or* **Bé·noué** \bān-'wā\. River, W Africa, chief tributary of Niger river from E; ab. 870 m. long; rises in N Cameroon, flows W across E cen. Nigeria.

Benue–Pla·teau \-pla-'tō\. State of E cen. Nigeria. See table at NIGERIA.

Ben Ve·nue \ˌben-və-'n(y)ü\. Mountain, SW Perth co., cen. Scotland, just S of Loch Katrine; 2393 ft.

Ben Vor·lich \ben-'vō(ə)r-lik\. Mountain, S Perth co., cen. Scotland, S of Loch Earn; 3224 ft.

Ben·wood \'ben-ˌwu̇d\. City, Marshall co., N West Virginia, on Ohio river 3 m. S of Wheeling; pop. (1970c) 2737; coal mining; steel industries.

Ben Wyv·is \ben-'wiv-əs\. Mountain, E Ross and Cromarty co., N Scotland; 3429 ft.

Ben–y–Gloe \ˌben-ē-'glō\. Mountain, NE Perth co., cen. Scotland; 3671 ft.

Ben·zie \'ben-zē\. County in Michigan. See table at MICHIGAN.

Beo \'bā-(ˌ)ō\. See TALAUD ISLANDS.

Beograd. See BELGRADE.

Bep·pu \'bep-(ˌ)ü\. City, on **Beppu Bay** (an arm of W end of Inland Sea), NE Kyūshū I., Japan, in Ōita prefecture; pop. (1970c) 123,786; hot springs.

Be·quia \'bek-ˌwā\. An island of the Grenadines, E West Indies, S of St. Vincent; administratively a part of St. Vincent.

Be·rar \bā-'rär, bə-\. Division of former Central Provinces and Berar, cen. India, in SW part N of Hyderabad; 17,809 sq. m.; ✱ Amravati; divided into six districts; crossed by Ajanta Range; bordered on E by Wardha river and on S by the Penganga. Founded 1484, one of the five Muslim kingdoms of the Deccan (*q.v.*); lasted until 1572 when it became part of Mogul Empire; overrun by Marathas near end of 17th cent.; with help of Wellesley, territory west of Wardha river acquired by ruler of Hyderabad; taken over by British government as Assigned Districts of Hyderabad 1853; transferred to administration of Central Provinces 1903. In Madhya Pradesh 1947–56; in Bombay state 1956–60; in Maharashtra since 1960.

Be·rat \bə-'rät\ *or formerly* **Be·rati** \-'rät-ē\. **1** Province of S cen. Albania. See table at ALBANIA.

2 *or anc.* **An·ti·pa·tria** \ˌant-i-'pa-trē-ə, -'pā-\. Town, its ✱, ab. 30 m. NE of Vlorë; pop. (1967e) 23,895; food processing.

Berau. See DOBERAI.

Be·rau Bay \bə-'raü-\ *or formerly* **Mc·Cluer Gulf** \mə-'klü(ə)r-\. Inlet on NW coast of New Guinea I., Irian Barat, Indonesia; 125 m. long by 15–30 m. wide; almost cuts off Doberai Penin. from rest of New Guinea, being separated on E from Sarera Bay by isthmus only ab. 15 m. wide.

Beraun. 1 River, Czechoslovakia. See BEROUNKA.

2 Town, Czechoslovakia. See BEROUN.

Ber·ber \'bər-bər\. Town, SE Northern Province, Sudan, on E bank of the Nile river ab. 30 m. N of Ed Damer; in earlier days starting point for caravans going across the Nubian Desert to Suakin; occupied by Mahdists 1884–97.

Ber·be·ra \'bər-bə-rə\. Seaport, Somalia, E Africa, on S shore of Gulf of Aden; pop. (1963e) 12,219; exports hides.

Ber·bé·ra·ti \ˌber-bə-'rät-ē\. Town, SW Central African Republic; pop. (1968c) 37,699.

Ber·bice \ˌbər-'bēs\. 1 River, E Guyana; 370 m. long; flows N into Atlantic Ocean near New Amsterdam; navigable for 125 m.

2 County, E Guyana, divided into two districts, **East Berbice** (pop. [1960c] 115,511) and **West Berbice** (pop. 26,524).

Ber·chem \'be(ə)r-kəm, ber-'kem\. Commune, Antwerp prov., N Belgium, S suburb of Antwerp; pop. (1969e) 50,-767.

Berch·tes·ga·den \'berk-təs-ˌgäd-ᵊn\. Town, SE Bavaria, West Germany, in E Bavarian Alps ab. 10 m. S of Salzburg; pop. (1964e) 4500; alt. 1889 ft.; resort; site of villa built as hideout for Hitler to which he often retired during World War II; scene of important conferences. Bombed by Allies Mar. 1945 and occupied May 7.

Berck \'be(ə)rk\. Commune, Pas-de-Calais dept., N France, on English Channel ab. 50 m. WNW of Arras; pop. (1968c) 13,690; resort.

Ber·di·chev \bər-'dē-chəf\. City, S Zhitomir Oblast, W cen. Ukrainian S.S.R., U.S.S.R., 22 m. S of Zhitomir; pop. (1969e) 61,000; railroad junction; engineering works, sugar refinery; center of district that trades in farm products; first mentioned 1320; assigned to Lithuania 1546 by treaty, to Poland 1569; captured by Russia 1768. Held by Germans 1941–44.

Berdsk \'b(y)e(ə)rtsk\. Town, Novosibirsk Oblast, Russian S.F.S.R., U.S.S.R., 20 m. SSE of Novosibirsk; pop. (1969e) 50,000.

Ber·dyansk \ber-'dyänsk\ *or formerly* **Osi·pen·ko** \ˌäs-ə-'peŋ-(ˌ)kō, ˌəs-\. Seaport town, SE Zaporozhye Oblast, SE Ukrainian S.S.R., U.S.S.R., on N shore of Sea of Azov 45 m. SW of Zhdanov; pop. (1970p) 100,000; has good harbor and carries on export trade in grains, linseed, wool, skins; large salt lagoons in vicinity. In World War II taken by Germany Oct. 1941; retaken by U.S.S.R. Sept. 17, 1943.

Be·rea \bə-'rē-ə\. 1 City, Madison co., E cen. Kentucky, 28 m. E of Danville; pop. (1970c) 6956; pressure gauges; diversified farming; Berea Coll. (1855).

2 City, Cuyahoga co., N Ohio, 12 m. SW of Cleveland; pop. (1970c) 22,396; greenhouses for scientific growing of vegetables; Baldwin-Wallace Coll. (1845).

3 Town, Greece. See VEROIA.

Be·re·go·vo \ˌber-ə-'gȯ-və\ *or Hung.* **Be·reg·szász** \'ber-ˌeg-ˌsäs\. Town, Transcarpathian Oblast, Ukrainian S.S.R., U.S.S.R.; pop. (1967e) 27,000; a Hungarian town included 1918 in Czechoslovakia; returned to Hungary 1939–45.

Bere·ha·ven *or* **Bear·ha·ven** \'ba(ə)r-ˌhā-vən, 'be(ə)r-\ *also* **Cas·tle·town·bere** \ˌkas-əl-ˌtaün-'ba(ə)r, -'be(ə)r\ *or officially* **Castletown Bearhaven.** Small town, co. Cork, SW Eire, on N coast of Bantry Bay; pop. (1966c) 729; has harbor partly enclosed by **Bere Island** \'ba(ə)r-, 'be(ə)r-\; formerly used as a British naval base.

Ber·e·ni·ce \ˌber-ə-'nī-sē\. 1 Ruined city, SE Egypt, on a bay of the Red Sea; ancient seaport sheltered on N by point of land (*mod.* Cape Banas); founded by Ptolemy II 3d cent. B.C.

2 City, Libya. See BENGHAZI 2.

Beres·ford \'bi(ə)rz-fərd\. City, Lincoln and Union cos., SE South Dakota, 35 m. S of Sioux Falls; pop. (1970c) 1655; dairy, stock, grain farms.

Be·re·stech·ko \ˌber-ə-'st(y)ech-kə\ *or Pol.* **Be·re·stecz·ko** \-'stech-(ˌ)kō\. Village, NW Ukrainian S.S.R., U.S.S.R., ab. 30 m. S of Lutsk; defeat July 1, 1651, of Cossack hetman Bogdan Chmielnicki by Poles.

Be·ret·tyó \'ber-ə-ˌtyō\ *or Rom.* **Be·re·tăul** \ˌber-ə-'təl\. River, E Hungary and W Romania; ab. 150 m. long; rises in W Transylvania, flows W and SW to the Körös.

Be·ret·tyó·új·fa·lu \'ber-ə-ˌtyō-'üi-ˌfȯ-(ˌ)lü\. Commune, E Hungary, S of Debrecen; pop. (1970p) 13,767.

Be·re·zha·ny \bər-ə-'zhä-nē\ *or Pol.* **Brze·ża·ny** \bə-zhə-'zhä-nē\. Town, W Ukrainian S.S.R., U.S.S.R. (formerly in Poland), 30 m. WSW of Ternopol. Scene of German breakthrough Aug. 28, 1915, retaken by Russians July 1, 1916.

Be·re·zi·na \bə-'räz-ᵊn-ə, -'rez-\. River, Belorussian S.S.R., U.S.S.R.; 365 m. long; drainage basin 9471 sq. m.; flows SE into Dnieper river W of Gomel. Battle fought at the crossing of the river near Borisov Nov. 26–28, 1812, by Napoleon's army in the retreat from Moscow, when three Russian armies inflicted enormous losses on it. In World War II scene of fierce fighting July 3–8, 1941, during German advance on Smolensk.

Be·rez·ni·ki \bər-'yȯz-nə-kē\. City, cen. Perm Oblast, Russian S.F.S.R., U.S.S.R., at foot of W slope of Ural Mts. on left bank of Kama river; pop. (1970p) 145,000; fertilizers, medicines.

Be·re·zo·vo \bər-'yȯ-zə-və\ *or formerly* **Be·re·zov** \-zəf\. Town, Tyumen Oblast, Russian S.F.S.R., U.S.S.R., on left bank of lower Ob where Sosva joins it; established as Cossack trading post 1593.

Berg \'be(ə)rk, 'be(ə)rg\. Former duchy on the Rhine E of Cologne, Germany, bounded on N by duchy of Kleve and on W by Jülich; ab. 1120 sq. m.; made countship 1108, became duchy 1380, associated with Jülich 1423, with Kleve 1511; became part of Prussia 1815. See DÜSSELDORF.

Ber·ga·ma \bər-'gäm-ə\. Town, İzmir prov., W Turkey, Asia, 50 m. N of İzmir; pop. (1965c) 24,121.

History: Important city, ancient Mysia, Asia Minor, ✱ of the kingdom of Pergamum (*q.v.*) and for a time of the Roman province of Asia, ab. 18 m. inland from Aeolis coast opp. Lesbos. Flourished for ab. four centuries as a political and cultural center of the East, rivaling Ephesus and Smyrna in importance. An early seat of Christianity and one of the Seven Churches; remained a center of commercial activity under Byzantine and Ottoman empires; modern excavations begun 1878.

Ber·ga·mo \'be(ə)r-gə-ˌmō\. 1 Province of Lombardy, N Italy. See table at ITALY.

2 *or anc.* **Ber·go·mum** \'bər-gə-ˌməm\. Commune, its ✱, in foothills of Alps 30 m. NE of Milan; pop. (1968e) 124,626; textiles, cement; 12th cent. Romanesque cathedral, ancient walls. Settled by Gauls; became Roman municipium under Caesar; destroyed by Attila; became Lombard duchy; fell to Milan 1264; ruled by the Visconti of Lombardy 1296–1428, by Venetian Republic 1428–1797; conquered by Napoleon 1796; under Austrian rule 1814–59.

Ber·ge·dorf \'ber-gə-ˌdȯrf\. Section of Hamburg, West Germany, on branch of Elbe river; observatory. Made a city 1275; belonged to Lübeck and Hamburg 1420–1868; became part of Hamburg 1938.

Ber·gen \'bər-gən\. County in New Jersey. See table at NEW JERSEY.

Bergen. See MONS.

Bergen *or* **Bergen auf Rü·gen** \'bər-gən-aüf-'rü-gən, -'rue-\. Chief town of island of Rügen, Rostock dist., East Germany; pop. (1970e) 11,046; fisheries.

Bergen \'bər-gən, 'be(ə)r-\. Seaport city, ⊗ of Hordaland co., SW Norway; pop. (1970e) 115,590; 3d largest city in Norway; formerly constituted a county; after Oslo, Norway's most important port; shipbuilding; steel, electrical equipment, office machinery, textiles; exports include base metals and fish; oil refineries; univ. (1948); founded 1070;

N outpost of Hanseatic League in 15th and 16th cents.; cathedral dating from 13th cent.; damaged by fire 1702, 1855, 1916. Occupied by Germans Apr. 9, 1940, and held until end of World War II.

Bergen–Belsen. See BELSEN.

Ber·gen·field \'bər-gən-ˌfēld\. Borough, Bergen co., NE corner of New Jersey, 9 m. E of Paterson; pop. (1970c) 29,000; machinery, surgical instruments.

Bergen op Zoom \ˌber-gən-ȯp-'zōm\. Commune, North Brabant prov., S Netherlands, at mouth of small stream (Zoom) on Schelde estuary; pop. (1970e) 39,051; engineering works, confectioneries, distillery; captured by Normans in 880; formerly strongly fortified.

Ber·ge·rac \'ber-zhə-ˌrak\. Commune, Dordogne dept., SW cen. France, on Dordogne river 25 m. SSW of Périgueux; pop. (1968c) 27,165; wine; 19th cent. Gothic church; captured by English 1345 and fortified; taken by French 1450.

Ber·gisch Glad·bach \ˌber-gish-'glät-ˌbäk\. Industrial city, North Rhine-Westphalia, West Germany, 9 m. NE of Cologne; pop. (1969e) 49,704; paper and metal goods; made city 1856.

Berg·ka·men \berk-'käm-ən\. City, North Rhine-Westphalia, West Germany, 10 m. NE of Dortmund; pop. (1969e) 43,585; coal mining; chemicals.

Bergomum. See BERGAMO 2.

Bergues \'be(ə)rg\. Town, Nord dept., N France, ab. 5 m. S of Dunkerque; pop. (1962c) 4689; built as a frontier fortress and often besieged in Flemish wars.

Ber·ha·la Strait \bər-ˌhäl-ə-\. Channel bet. the island of Singkep, Lingga Archipelago, and the E cen. coast of Sumatra, Indonesia.

Ber·ham·pore \'ber-əm-ˌpō(ə)r, -ˌpȯ(ə)r\. Town, cen. West Bengal, NE India, on left bank of Bhagirathi river 110 m. N of Calcutta; pop. (1961c) 62,317; founded as military station 1767; scene of first overt act of Sepoy Mutiny 1857. Includes remnant of **Cos·sim·ba·zar** \'käs-əm-ˌbäz-ˌär\, a city formerly important.

Ber·ham·pur \'ber-əm-ˌpu̇(ə)r\. Town, cen. Orissa, E India, 103 m. SW of Cuttack and 9 m. from the Bay of Bengal; pop. (1961c) 76,931; college (1878).

Ber·ing Glacier \ˌbi(ə)r-iŋ-, ˌbe(ə)r-\. Glacier, Chugach-St. Elias Mts., S Alaska; 126 m. long; ab. 30 m. wide near terminus; largest glacier in North America.

Bering Island *or* **Be·rin·ga Island** \ˌber-ən-gə-\. See KOMANDORSKIYE ISLANDS.

Bering Sea. Part of North Pacific Ocean; 885,000 sq. m.; max. depth 15,659 ft.; enclosed on E by mainland of Alaska, on SE and S by Aleutian Is., on SW by Kamchatka Penin., and on NW by E Siberia; connects by Bering Strait with Arctic Ocean; contains St. Lawrence I., Nunivak I., Pribilof Is. (all U.S.) and Komandorskiye Is. (U.S.S.R.); latter two groups famous as fur-seal breeding grounds; receives Yukon river; crossed diagonally by International Date Line. Explorations of its waters and of Bering Strait 1728 and 1741 by Danish navigator Vitus Bering in employ of Russia formed chief basis for Russian claims to Alaska. Bering Sea Controversy bet. Great Britain and U.S. 1886–93 settled by court of arbitration at Paris 1893 in favor of Great Britain, denying U.S. the right to prohibit pelagic hunting of fur seals in Bering Sea.

Bering Strait. Strait connecting Arctic Ocean and Bering Sea (*q.v.*), and separating Asia (U.S.S.R.) from North America (Alaska); at narrowest point 53 m. wide; Diomede Is. (*q.v.*) in middle. Traversed by Vitus Bering 1728.

Be·ris·so \bə-'rēs-(ˌ)ō, -'ris-\. Town, Buenos Aires prov., Argentina, 5 m. NE of La Plata; pop. (1960c) 40,983.

Ber·ja \'be(ə)r-ˌhä\. Commune, Almería prov., SE Spain, 20 m. W of Almería; pop. (1970e) 11,429; viticulture; lead mining; textile industries.

Berke·ley \'bər-klē\. 1 Name of counties in two states of the U.S. See tables at SOUTH CAROLINA and WEST VIRGINIA.
2 Residential and industrial city, Alameda co., W California, on San Francisco Bay N of Oakland; pop. (1970c) 116,716; food products, soaps, engines, serums, vaccines, foundry products; Univ. of California (1868), Armstrong Coll. (1918). Founded 1853, incorporated as city 1909; most of N section of city destroyed by fire 1923 and since rebuilt.
3 Village, Cook co., NE Illinois, 14 m. W of Chicago; pop. (1970c) 6152.
4 City, St. Louis co., E Missouri, NW suburb of St. Louis; pop. (1970c) 19,743; incorp. as a city 1937.
5 Plantation on left bank of the James river, Charles City co., E Virginia, at **Har·ri·son's Landing** \ˌhar-ə-sənz-\; birthplace of Benjamin Harrison, signer of the Declaration of Independence, and of William Henry Harrison, 9th president of the U.S.; plundered by Benedict Arnold 1781; base for Union army after Malvern Hill.

Berkeley Springs *or legally* **Bath** \'bath, 'bäth\. Town and health resort, ⊗ of Morgan co., NE West Virginia, near Potomac river 18 m. NW of Martinsburg; pop. (1970c) 944; mineral springs; chartered 1776.

Berk·hamp·stead \'bər-kəm(p)-stəd, -ˌsted *also* 'bär-\ *or formerly* **Great Berkhampstead.** Urban district, Hertfordshire, SE England, on Grand Union Canal 26 m. NW of London; pop. (1971p) 15,439; chemical works; remains of 11th cent. castle; birthplace of William Cowper.

Berk·ley \'bər-klē\. Residential city, Oakland co., SE Michigan, 12 m. SSE of Pontiac; pop. (1970c) 21,879; in the Detroit suburban area.

Berks \'bərks\. 1 County in Pennsylvania. See table at PENNSYLVANIA.
2 *Brit. usu.* 'bärks\. County in England. See BERKSHIRE 2.

Berk·shire \'bərk-ˌshi(ə)r, -shər\. 1 County in Massachusetts. See table at MASSACHUSETTS.
2 *Brit. usu.* 'bärk-\ *or* **Berks** \'bärks\. County, S England; 725 sq. m.; pop. (1971p) 633,457; ⊗ Reading; largely in the Thames river basin; agriculture and livestock raising (Berkshire hogs); agricultural machinery, paper; two nuclear research centers.

Berkshire Hills *or commonly* **Berk·shires** \'bərk-ˌshi(ə)rz, -shərz\. Highlands in Berkshire co., W Massachusetts; highest peak Mount Greylock 3491 ft.

Bêrlad. See BÎRLAD.

Ber·len·gas \bər-'leŋ-gəsh\. Group of small islands off W coast of Portugal, lat. 39°25′N; lighthouse.

Ber·lin \'bər-lən, -ˌlin\. 1 Industrial town, S Hartford co., cen. Connecticut, 11 m. SSW of Hartford; pop. (1970c) 14,149.
2 City, Coos co., N New Hampshire, in White Mts., at confluence of Dead and Androscoggin rivers 17 m. S of Umbagog Lake; pop. (1970c) 15,256; paper, wood-fiber string, wood pulp; foundries; U.S. government fish hatchery nearby; winter sports.
3 Borough, Camden co., SW New Jersey, 15 m. SE of Camden; pop. (1970c) 4997.
4 Borough, Somerset co., S Pennsylvania, 28 m. S of Johnstown; pop. (1970c) 1766; farm and dairy products.
5 Manufacturing city, Green Lake and Waushara cos., cen. Wisconsin, 20 m. W of Oshkosh; pop. (1970c) 5338.
6 City, Canada. See KITCHENER.
7 Town, SE Cape Province, S Rep. of South Africa, 20 m. WNW of East London; resort.

Berlin \(ˌ)bər-'lin, *Ger.* ber-'lēn\. City, former ✱ of Germany; since 1945 partitioned into East Berlin and West Berlin (*qq.v.*).

History: Kölln and Berlin, both Wendish villages, founded in early 13th cent.; member of Hanseatic League 14th cent.; united under name of Berlin, it became residence of Hohenzollerns and capital of Brandenburg (*q.v.*); from 1701 capital of kingdom of Prussia (*q.v.*); grew to be industrial and commercial center, especially under Frederick II (1740–86); entered by Austrians 1757 and by Russians 1760; occupied by French under Napoleon, who issued there the Berlin decree 1806; capital of German Empire 1871–1918, of Republic 1919–32, of Third Reich 1933–45; scene of Congress of Berlin 1878 and of Berlin Conference 1885; much of city destroyed by Allied bombing 1941 and 1943–45; occupied by Soviet troops Apr.–May 1945; divided June 1945 into four occupation zones (American, British, French, and Soviet); on setting up of independent governments in E and W Germany 1949, West Berlin became part of West Germany (made a state 1950 but not formally incorporated), and East Berlin was made * of East Germany.

Berlin, East. City, * of East Germany, 85 m. ENE of Magdeburg; pop. (1970e) 1,085,441; constitutes a district of East Germany; apparel, chemicals, food products, electronic equipment; German Academy of Sciences (1700), Humboldt Univ. (1810); anti-government demonstrations June/July 1953 suppressed with aid of Soviet forces; wall built along East Berlin-West Berlin boundary 1961 by East Germany to prevent flight of its citizens to West Germany.

Berlin, Mount \-ˈbər-lən\. Peak, N Nye co., cen. Nevada; 9081 ft.

Berlin, West. City, a West German exclave lying wholly within East Germany; 185 sq. m.; pop. (1970e) 2,130,900; chemicals, electronic equipment, machinery, pharmaceutical products; publishing; enjoys close political, economic, and cultural ties with West Germany (but is not a constitutional part of West Germany); Charlottenburg Palace, Technical Univ. (1799, present status 1946); Soviet blockade of city resulted in massive Anglo-American airlift of critical supplies June 26, 1948–Sept. 30, 1949; East German claims to the city have been consistently rejected by the Western Powers.

Ber·me·jo \bər-ˈmā-(ˌ)hō, ber-\ *also* **Ver·me·jo** \vər-ˈmā-(ˌ)hō\. River, N Argentina; 650 m. long; rises on the Bolivian frontier and flows SE into Paraguay river on the Paraguay-Argentina boundary; its middle course known as the Teuco.

Ber·meo \bər-ˈmā-(ˌ)ō, -ˈmeů\. Commune, Vizcaya prov., N Spain, on Bay of Biscay 15 m. NE of Bilbao; pop. (1970p) 17,745.

Ber·mu·da \bər-ˈm(y)üd-ə\ *also* **Bermuda Islands** *or* **Ber·mu·das** \-ˈmyüd-əz\ *or formerly* **Som·ers Islands** \ˌsəm-ərz-\. British colony comprising a group of about 300 islands (of which only some 20 are inhabited), ab. 640 m. ESE of Cape Hatteras in W North Atlantic Ocean; 20 sq. m.; pop. (1970p) 53,000; principal island **Bermuda Island** *also called* **Great Bermuda** *or* **Long Island;** * Hamilton, on Bermuda I.; tourism; ship-repairing.

History: Visited by Spanish 1515 and named for Juan de Bermúdez; English called them Somers Islands after Sir George Somers who was forced to land there while on his way to Virginia 1609; first colonized by English (sent by members of Virginia Company) on St. George's I. 1612; settled and governed under the Somers Island Company 1615–84; taken over by British Crown 1684; capital removed from St. George to Hamilton 1815; sites for military and naval bases leased to U.S. 1940; adopted new constitution 1968.

Bermuda Hundred. Village, a settlement of Jamestown colony 1613, on peninsula, Chesterfield co., SE cen. Virginia, bet. James and Appomattox rivers; a Union base in Grant's campaign against Richmond 1864.

Bern *or* **Berne** \ˈbərn, ˈbe(ə)rn\. **1** Swiss canton. See table at SWITZERLAND.

2 City, * of Switzerland and of Bern canton, on Aare river 59 m. SW of Zurich; pop. (1970c) 162,405, met. area pop. 261,341; chemicals, pharmaceuticals, textiles, precision instruments, chocolate; univ. (1528, univ. status 1834), national library; 15th cent. Gothic cathedral, 15th cent. Gothic town hall, hall of Swiss Federal Council, headquarters of Universal (or International) Postal Union (founded 1874) and of telegraph, railway, and copyright unions.

History: Founded as military post by Duke Berchtold V of Zäringen 1191; became free imperial city 1218; achieved final independence 1339; entered Swiss Confederation 1353 (see SWITZERLAND); accepted Reformation 1528; became powerful in 18th cent. when it ruled Vaud, Fribourg, Aargau, and the region of the Bernese Alps; after French occupation 1798, made member of Helvetic Republic; made capital of Switzerland 1848.

Ber·nal Hill \(ˌ)bər-ˌnäl-\. Peak, SW San Miguel co., NE cen. New Mexico; 7020 ft.

Ber·na·lil·lo \ˌbərn-ᵊl-ˈē-(ˌ)ō\. **1** County in New Mexico. See table at NEW MEXICO.

2 Town, ⊗ of Sandoval co., NW cen. New Mexico, on the Rio Grande 12 m. N of Albuquerque; pop. (1970c) 2016; lumber products; approximate site of Coronado's headquarters 1540–42; settled 1698.

Ber·nam \ˈbe(ə)r-ˌnäm\. River on boundary bet. S Perak and N Selangor states, Malaysia; ab. 120 m. long; flows W into the Strait of Malacca; navigable for steam launches for over 100 m.

Ber·nards·ville \ˈbər-nərdz-ˌvil\. Borough, Somerset co., N cen. New Jersey, 8 m. SW of Morristown; pop. (1970c) 6652.

Ber·nay \ber-ˈnā\. Commune, Eure dept., France, 25 m. WNW of Évreux; pop. (1968c) 10,009; leather, soap, textiles; grew up around Benedictine Abbey (founded 1013).

Bern·burg \ˈbərn-ˌbərg, ˈbe(ə)rn-ˌbů(ə)rg\. Manufacturing city, Halle dist., East Germany, on Saale river 22 m. W of Dessau; pop. (1970e) 45,322; agricultural machinery, salt. Fortified town in 10th cent.; capital of duchy of Anhalt-Bernburg. Site of bomber manufacturing plants, object of British and American air raids 1944–45.

Berne \ˈbərn\. **1** City, Adams co., E Indiana, 32 m. S of Fort Wayne; pop. (1970c) 2988; founded 1852 by Mennonite immigrants from Bern, Switzerland; official publishing house for the Mennonite General Conference.

2 City, Switzerland. See BERN.

Ber·ne·ray \ˈbər-nə-ˌrā\. See BARRA.

Ber·nese Alps \(ˌ)bər-ˌnēz-, -ˌnēs-\ *or* **Bernese Ober·land** \-ˈō-bər-ˌland, -ˌlänt\ *or Ger.* **Ber·ner Al·pen, Berner Oberland** \ˌber-nər-ˈäl-pən, -ˈō-bər-ˌlänt\. See OBERLAND and table at ALPS.

Ber·ni·cia \(ˌ)bər-ˈnish-(ē-)ə\. Anglian kingdom of 6th cent. A.D., located bet. Tyne and Forth, with capital at Bamborough; united with Deira (*q.v.*) to form kingdom of Northumbria (*q.v.*).

Ber·ni·er \ˈbər-nē-ər\. Island off W coast of Western Australia, at entrance to Shark Bay, 24°52′S, 113°08′E.

Ber·ni·na \bər-ˈnē-nə\. Southern extension of the Rhaetian Alps, on border bet. Italy and Switzerland; its highest peak and the highest in the Rhaetian Alps is **Piz Bernina** \ˌpēts-\ 13,284 ft. on the Italian border but in Switzerland. **Bernina Pass** 7621 ft. is E of the peak.

Bern·kas·tel–Kues \ˌbern-ˌkäs-tᵊl-ˈkü(-ə)s\ *or formerly* **Bernkastel.** Town, Rhineland-Palatinate, West Germany, on the Mosel 21 m. NE of Trier; pop. (1964e) 5900; tourism; white wine (Bernkasteler); received charter 1291.

Beroea. 1 Town, Greece. See VEROIA.

2 Town, Jerusalem. See BIRE.

3 City, Syria. See ALEPPO 2.

Be·roun \ˈbe(ə)r-ˌōn\ *or Ger.* **Be·raun** \ˈbā-ˌraůn\. Town, Czech S.R., W Czechoslovakia, ab. 17 m. WSW of Prague; pop. (1968e) 17,766; textiles.

Be·roun·ka \ˈber-ən-ˌkä\ *or Ger.* **Be·raun** \ˈbā-ˌraůn\. River, W Czechoslovakia; ab. 140 m. long; formed by union of several streams near Plzeň, flows E into Vltava river.

Ber·ra \ˈber-ə\. Commune, Ferrara prov., Emilia-Romagna, N Italy; pop. (1968e) 7609.

Berre, Étang de \ā-ˌtä^{n}-də-ˈbe(ə)r\. Lagoon, S Bouches-du-Rhône dept., S France, E of the Rhone; 13 m. long, 3 to 8 m. wide; has narrow outlet to Gulf of Lions.

Ber·ri·en \'ber-ē-ən\. Name of counties in two states of the U.S. See tables at GEORGIA and MICHIGAN.

Berrien Springs. Village, Berrien co., SW Michigan, 47 m. WSW of Kalamazoo; pop. (1970c) 1951; Andrews Univ. (1874).

Ber·ry *or* **Ber·ri** \be-'rē\. Historical region of cen. France, bounded anciently on N by Orléanais, E by Nivernais, SE by Bourbonnais, SW by Marche, W by Touraine; ✱ Bourges. Originally inhabited by the Bituriges Cubi who opposed Vercingetorix; under Romans was part of Aquitania Prima; countship in Carolingian period; fell to Crown in 11th cent.; made duchy 1360; returned to French Crown 1601; province to 1789.

Berry–au–Bac \be-ˌrē-ō-'bȧk\. Village, Aisne dept., N France, 11 m. NW of Reims; crossing of Aisne river here frequently of importance in World War I, esp. in Chemin des Dames battles 1917–18.

Berry Islands \ˌber-ē-\. Group of small islands in the Bahama Is., N of Andros I.; 20 sq. m.; pop. (1963c) 266.

Ber·ry·ville \'ber-ē-ˌvil, -vəl\. 1 City, a ⊗ of Carroll co., NW Arkansas; pop. (1970c) 2271.

2 Town, ⊗ of Clarke co., N Virginia; pop. (1970c) 1569.

Ber·si·mis \ˌber-sə-'mē\. River, tributary of the St. Lawrence river in Quebec, Canada; ab. 240 m. long; flows SSE; enters the St. Lawrence NE of Tadoussac.

Ber·thier \'bert-ē-ˌā\. 1 County, Quebec, Canada. See table at QUEBEC.

2 *or* **Ber·thier·ville** \-ˌvil\. Town, its ⊗, on St. Lawrence river 37 m. WSW of Three Rivers; pop. (1971p) 4076.

Ber·thoud Pass \ˌbər-thəd-\. Mountain pass, Clear Creek and Grand cos., N Colorado, in Front Range of the Rocky Mts.; 11,315 ft.; ski runs; highway.

Ber·tie \bər-'tē, 'bər-ˌ\. County in North Carolina. See table at NORTH CAROLINA.

Ber·tin·court \ˌber-ˌtaⁿ-'kü(ə)r\. Village, Pas-de-Calais dept., N France, ab. 6 m. E of Bapaume; pop. (1962c) 812; fighting Mar. 1917 and Mar. 1918 in World War I.

Be·ru \'bā-(ˌ)rü\. Island (atoll) at S end of Gilbert Is. S of the equator, W Pacific Ocean; 11 m. long.

Ber·wick \'bər-(ˌ)wik\. 1 Town, St. Mary parish, S Louisiana, 53 m. S of Baton Rouge; pop. (1970c) 4168; fishing center; oyster and shrimp works.

2 Town, York co., SW Maine, on New Hampshire border 25 m. SW of Biddeford; pop. (1970c) 3136.

3 Industrial borough, Columbia co., E cen. Pennsylvania, on Susquehanna river 23 m. WSW of Wilkes-Barre; pop. (1970c) 12,274; railroad trucks, silk, garments, foundry and machine-shop products; founded 1786.

Berwick \'ber-ik\ *or* **Ber·wick·shire** \-ˌshi(ə)r, -shər\. County, SE Scotland; area 457 sq. m.; pop. (1971p) 22,523; ⊗ Duns; livestock grazing, wheat, oats, potatoes; fisheries.

Berwick–upon–Tweed \ˌber-ik . . . 'twēd\. Municipal borough, Northumberland, N England, on North Sea at mouth of the Tweed near Scottish border; pop. (1971p) 11,644; herring and salmon fisheries; engineering; English from 1482.

Ber·wyn. 1 \'bər-ˌwin, -wən\. Residential city, Cook co., NE Illinois, 10 m. W of Chicago; pop. (1970c) 52,502.

2 \bər-'win\. Locality, Chester co., SE Pennsylvania, ab. 9 m. NE of West Chester.

Berwyn Heights \ˌbər-wən-\. Town, Prince Georges co., S cen. Maryland, 8 m. NE of Washington, D.C.; pop. (1970c) 3924.

Berwyn Mountains \ˌbe(ə)r-wən-\. Range in N Wales, along the border bet. Merionethshire and Montgomeryshire; highest point Moel Sych 2713 ft.

Berytus. See BEIRUT.

Be·san·çon \bə-'zan(t)-sən, bə-zäⁿ-'sōⁿ\ *or anc.* **Ve·son·tio** \və-'zän-shē-ˌō\. Commercial and manufacturing city, ✱ of Doubs dept. (and, earlier, ✱ of Franche-Comté), E France, 47 m. E of Dijon; pop. (1968c) 113,220; watch and clock industry; textiles, paper; univ. (1423); citadel by Vauban; school of artillery; Roman ruins, including triumphal arch of Marcus Aurelius, aqueduct, and amphitheater; captured by Julius Caesar 58 B.C.

Besi. See SANANA 1.

Be·şik·taş \'besh-ik-ˌtäsh\. District and suburb of İstanbul, Turkey in Europe, on the Bosporus NE of Beyoğlu.

Bes·kids, East *and* **West Beskids** \-'bes-ˌkidz, -be-'skēdz\. Mountain ranges, W Carpathians, on NE boundary of Czechoslovakia; highest peak Babia Góra, in West Beskids; 5659 ft.

Bes·ni \bes-'nē\ *or formerly* **Be·his·ni** \ˌbā-his-'nē\. Town, Adıyaman prov., S Turkey, in mountains 53 m. ENE of Maraş; pop. (1965c) 11,625.

Besoeki. See BESUKI.

Bes·sa·ra·bia \ˌbes-ə-'rā-bē-ə\. 1 Region of SE Europe, bet. Dniester and Prut rivers extending from Black Sea N to Poland. In Roman times a part of the colony of Dacia; later a borderland overrun by barbarian migrations; named after Bassarab dynasty of Walachia, 14th cent. A.D.; became part of principality of Moldavia (*q.v.*) 1367; fought over by Turks and Russians 1711–1812; ceded by Turkey to Russia 1812; part yielded 1856 to Moldavia after Crimean War but most of it recovered by Russia 1878 by Treaty of Berlin; formed a government under Russia 1812–1917 (17,147 sq. m.; ✱ Kishinev).

2 *or Rom.* **Ba·sa·ra·bia** \ˌbäs-ə-'räb-yə\. Former province, E Romania; 17,151 sq. m.; ✱ Chişinău (Kishinev). Proclaimed independence from Russia as Moldavian (Bessarabian) Republic (*q.v.*) 1917; joined Romania Apr. 9, 1918 and recognized as Romanian by Treaty of Versailles 1919 but still claimed by U.S.S.R. Seized by U.S.S.R. June 27, 1940; with Bukovina incorp. Aug. 1940 as Moldavian Federal Soviet Republic, renamed the Moldavian S.S.R. (*q.v.*), a part of the U.S.S.R., SW of the Ukrainian S.S.R. Retaken by Germans and Romanians June 1941; recovered by U.S.S.R. 1944.

Bes·se·mer \'bes-ə-mər\. 1 City, Jefferson co., Alabama, SW of Birmingham; pop. (1970c) 33,428; steel, freight cars, lumber.

2 City, ⊗ of Gogebic co., NW upper Michigan penin., 5 m. E of Ironwood; pop. (1970c) 2805; in iron-mining section.

3 Borough, Lawrence co., W Pennsylvania, 9 m. W of New Castle; pop. (1970c) 1427.

Bessemer City. Town, Gaston co., SW North Carolina, 7 m. W of Gastonia; pop. (1970c) 4991; cotton, tobacco.

Be·su·ki *or Du.* **Be·soe·ki** \bā-'sü-kē\. Former residency, Java, Neth. Indies, now part of the Indonesian prov. of East Java; 3913 sq. m.; ✱ Bondowoso; included E end of Java bet. Madura Strait on the N, Indian Ocean on the S.

Besztercze. See BISTRIŢA 2.

Beszterczebánya. See BANSKÁ BYSTRICA.

Bet Guvrin. See ELEUTHEROPOLIS.

Beth·al \'beth-əl\. Town, Transvaal, Rep. of South Africa; pop. (1967e) 16,600.

Be·thal·to \bə-'thól-(ˌ)tō\. Village, Madison co., SW Illinois, 23 m. NNE of East St. Louis; pop. (1970c) 7074.

Be·tha·ni·en \bə-'tän-ē-ən\; *formerly* **Beth·a·nie** *or* **Beth·a·ny** \'beth-ə-nē\. Town, S South-West Africa, 130 m. E of Lüderitz; pop. (1960c) 1053.

Beth·a·ny \'beth-ə-nē\. 1 Town, New Haven co., S Connecticut, 9 m. NW of New Haven; pop. (1970c) 3857.

2 City, ⊗ of Harrison co., N Missouri, 43 m. NW of Chillicothe; pop. (1970c) 2914.

3 City, Oklahoma co., cen. Oklahoma, 7 m. W of Oklahoma City; pop. (1970c) 21,785; Bethany Nazarene Coll. (1899; removed from Oklahoma City 1909).

4 Town, Brooke co., N West Virginia, ab. 12 m. NE of Wheeling; pop. (1970c) 602; Bethany Coll. (1840).

5 Village, Jordan. See AL-'AYZARĪYAH.

Beth·el \'beth-əl\. 1 City, W Alaska, near mouth of Kuskokwim river; pop. (1970c) 2416.
2 Manufacturing town, N cen. Fairfield co., SW Connecticut; pop. (1970c) 10,945; electronic components, chemicals, tools.
3 Town, Oxford co., W Maine, 36 m. WNW of Lewiston; pop. (1970c) 2220; in the Rangeley Lakes region; resort.
4 Village, Clermont co., SW Ohio; pop. (1970c) 2214.
5 Borough, Allegheny co., Pennsylvania, S of Pittsburgh; pop. (1970c) 34,791.
6 Ancient city of Palestine now an archaeological site and village (*Arab.* **Bay·tīn** \bā-'tēn\), Jordan, in area occupied by Israel 1967, ab. 11 m. N of Jerusalem; in early history of Israel considered a holy place (*Gen.* xii. 8; xxviii. 19).

Be·thes·da \bə-'thez-də\. Residential district, Montgomery co., cen. Maryland; pop. (1970c) 71,621; residential section for Washington, D.C.

Beth–ho·ron, Lower *and* **Upper Beth–horon** \-beth-'hōr-ən, -'hȯr-\. Twin towns, in mountain pass, Jordan, ab. 11 m. NW of Jerusalem, Israel, in region occupied by Israel 1967; in Old Testament times a strategical place where there were often conflicts (*Josh.* x. 11; *1 Kings* ix. 17).

Bé·thin·court \ˌbā-ˌtaⁿ-'ku̇(ə)r\. Village, Meuse dept., NE France, 6 m. NW of Verdun; held by Germans in siege of Verdun 1916–17.

Beth·le·hem \'beth-li-ˌhem, -lē-(h)əm\. 1 City, Lehigh and Northampton cos., E Pennsylvania, on Lehigh river 5 m. E of Allentown; pop. (1970c) 72,686; steel, foundry and machine products, electrical apparatus, textiles, cement; Lehigh Univ. (1865), Moravian Coll. (1807), Northampton County Area Community Coll. (1966); founded by Moravians 1741; housed hospital for Continental soldiers during Revolution; incorp. as borough 1845; became city 1917. Music center (home of annual Bach festival); chief center of Moravian sect in U.S.
2 *or Arab.* **Bayt Laḥm** \bāt-'läm\. Town, Jordan, 5 m. SSW of Jerusalem, Israel, in area occupied by Israel 1967; pop. (1967e) 16,313; ancient town of Judaea, the early home of David. Regarded by Christendom as the site of the Nativity.
3 Town, NE Orange Free State, E cen. Rep. of South Africa, 150 m. ENE of Bloemfontein; pop. (1967e) 31,400; railroad center; large railroad shops, flour mills; furniture; in fertile agricultural region; mountain scenery.

Beth·page \beth-'pāj\. Urban community (unincorporated), Nassau co., New York, in cen. Long I. S of Hicksville; pop. (incl. Old Bethpage; 1970c) 18,555.

Beth·sa·i·da of Galilee \beth-'sā-əd-ə . . . 'gal-ə-ˌlē, -ˌgal-ə-'\ *or* **Bethsaida of Gau·lo·ni·tis** \-ˌgȯ-lə-'nīt-əs\ *also* **Bethsaida Ju·li·as** \-'jü-lē-əs\. Ancient city, thought to have been in Galilee; its site disputed.

Be·thu·lie \bə-'t(y)ü-lē, -'tue̅-\. Town, S Orange Free State, E cen. Rep. of South Africa, near N bank of Orange river 100 m. S of Bloemfontein; pop. (1967e) 4200.

Bé·thune \bā-'tyün, -'tue̅n\. Commune, Pas-de-Calais dept., N France, 17 m. NNW of Arras; pop. (1968c) 27,154; coal mines. During World War I held by British and several times attacked, esp. Apr. 1918.

Be·tio \'bā-chē-ˌō\. Islet and village, S end of Tarawa (*q.v.*) atoll, Gilbert Is., W Pacific Ocean.

Bet·pak–Da·la \ˌb(y)et-ˌpäk-də-'lä\ *or* **Go·lod·na·ya Step** \gə-ˌlȯd-nə-yə-'st(y)āp\ *or* **Hun·ger·steppe** \'həŋ-gər-ˌstep\. Steppe region in SE Kazakh S.S.R., U.S.S.R., W of Lake Balkhash; ab. 300 m. wide; bordered on NW by Sary-su.

Bet She'·an \ˌbāt-shi-'än\; *Arab.* **Bay·sān** *also* **Bei·sān** \bā-'san\; *anc.* **Scy·thop·o·lis** \sith-'äp-ə-ləs\. Town, Northern District, Israel, W of the Jordan ab. 18 m. SE of Nazareth; pop. (1970e) 11,900; in cotton-producing region. Site of settlement of Early Bronze Age (c. 3000–2000 B.C.) and rich in archaeological material of the pre-Israelite period; important in Hittite and early Egyptian history; fell to Arabs 636 A.D. One of the ten cities of Decapolis.

Bet She·mesh \bet-'shē-ˌmesh\. Urban settlement, Israel, ab. 15 m. W of Jerusalem; pop. (1970e) 10,200; manufactures aircraft engines; next to an archaeological site having same name; anc. settlement built bet. 2400 and 2100 B.C., destroyed by Nebuchadrezzar II 6th cent. B.C.

Bet·si·bo·ka \ˌbet-si-'bō-kə\. River, cen. Malagasy Republic, flowing N into Bombetoka Bay.

Bet·ten·dorf \'bet-ᵊn-ˌdȯrf\. Industrial city, Scott co., E Iowa, on Mississippi 5 m. E of Davenport; pop. (1970c) 22,126; steel and foundry products.

Bet·ti·ah \'bet-ē-ə\. Town, NW Bihar, NE India, 100 m. NNW of Patna; pop. (1961c) 39,990.

Bet·tws y Coed \ˌbet-ə-sə-'kȯid\. Urban district, Caernarvonshire, NW Wales, on the Conway river ab. 16 m. S of Llandudno; pop. (1969e) 800; in beautiful glen and river scenery; tourist and artist center.

Be·tul \'bā-ˌtül\ *formerly* **Bad·nur** \'bäd-ˌnu̇(ə)r\. Town, Madhya Pradesh, 103 m. SSE of Bhopal, cen. India; pop. (1961c) 19,860.

Bet·wa \'bā-ˌtwä\. River, cen. India; 360 m. long; rises in W Madhya Pradesh, flows NE and E into Yamuna river near Hamirpur; feeds large irrigation system.

Beu·el \'bȯi-əl\ *or formerly* **Vi·lich** \'fē-lik\. City, North Rhine-Westphalia, West Germany, on Rhine river opp. Bonn; pop. (1969e) 38,668; chemicals.

Beu·lah \'byü-lə\. Village, ⊗ of Benzie co., NW Michigan; pop. (1970c) 461.

Beu·ron \'bȯi-ˌrȯn\. Village and monastery, Baden-Württemberg, West Germany, on the N bank of the Danube ab. 8 m. NE of Tuttlingen; pop. (1964e) 500; monastery founded 1077 by Augustinians, secularized 1802, taken over by Benedictines 1863; library.

Beuthen. See BYTOM.

Be·ve·land \'bā-və-ˌlänt\. Two islands, **North Beveland** (35 sq. m.; pop. [1959e] 9300) and **South Beveland** (144 sq. m.; pop. [1959e] 62,720), of the Netherlands, in Zeeland prov. in the estuary of the Schelde river, separated by narrow channel. In World War II South Beveland occupied by Allies Oct. 10–30, 1944.

Be·ve·ren \'bā-və-ran\. Commune, East Flanders prov., NW cen. Belgium, 6 m. N of Antwerp; pop. (1969e) 15,579.

Bev·er·ley \'bev-ər-lē\. Municipal borough, ⊗ of East Riding, Yorkshire, N England, 7 m. NNW of Hull; pop. (1971p) 17,124; shipbuilding; received first charter 1129.

Bev·er·ly \'bev-ər-lē\. 1 City, Essex co., NE corner of Massachusetts, 16 m. NE of Boston; pop. (1970c) 38,348; electronic tubes, shoes; Endicott Junior Coll. (1939), North Shore Community Coll. (1965).
2 City, Burlington co., S cen. New Jersey, on Delaware river 13 m. NE of Camden; pop. (1970c) 3105.

Beverly Hills. 1 Residential city, Los Angeles co., SW California, W suburb of Los Angeles; pop. (1970c) 33,416.
2 Village, Oakland co., SE Michigan, S of Pontiac; pop. (1970c) 13,598.

Be·ver·wijk \'bā-vər-ˌvīk\. Commune, North Holland prov., W Netherlands; pop. (1970e) 41,357.

Bew·cas·tle \byü-'kas-əl\. Village, Cumberland, NW England, 10 m. NE of Brampton; has remarkable cross of 7th (or 10th) cent., with runic inscriptions.

Bex \'bā\. Commune, Vaud canton, W Switzerland, near the Rhone SE of E end of Lake of Geneva; pop. (1970c) 5069; salt mines, brine baths.

Bexar \'ba(ə)r, 'be(ə)r\. County in Texas. See table at TEXAS.

Bex·hill \'beks-'hil\. Municipal borough, East Sussex, S England, on English Channel; pop. (1971p) 32,849.

Bex·ley \'bek-slē\. 1 City, Franklin co., cen. Ohio, surrounded by Columbus; pop. (1970c) 14,888.
2 Borough of Greater London, SE England. See table at LONDON 4.

Bey Dağ·la·rı \'bā-ˌdä(g)-lä-'rē\. Mountain range in SW Turkey in Asia, W of the Gulf of Antalya; highest point Akdağ 10,125 ft.

Bey·koz \bā-ˈkȯz\. Town, Kocaeli prov., NW Turkey in Asia, on E shore of the Bosporus N of Üsküdar.

Bey·o·ğlu \ˌbā-ə-ˈ(g)lü\ *or formerly* **Pe·ra** \ˈper-ə\. Division of İstanbul, Turkey in Europe; the section N of the Golden Horn.

Bey·pa·za·rı \ˌbā-ˌpäz-ə-ˈrē\; *formerly* **Bei·ba·zar** \ˌbā-bə-ˈzär\ *also* **Bai·ba·zar** \ˌbā-ə-bə-ˈzär\. Town, Ankara prov., W cen. Turkey in Asia, 60 m. W of Ankara; noted for its fruit; important under the Byzantine emperors.

Beyrouth. See BEIRUT.

Bey·şe·hir \ˌbā-shə-ˈhi(ə)r\. Town on SE shore of Lake Beyşehir, Konya prov., Turkey.

Beyşehir Lake *or Turk.* **Beyşehir Gö·lü** \-gəl-ˈ(y)ü\. Lake, SW cen. Turkey, W of Konya; 35 m. long; 250 sq. m.

Be·zen·gi \bə-ˈzeŋ-gē\. Glacier, Kabardino-Balkarian A.S.S.R., Russian S.F.S.R., U.S.S.R.; 8 m. long, ½ m. wide near its terminus.

Be·zhi·tsa \ˈbezh-ət-sə\, *during World War II until Jan. 1944* **Or·dzho·ni·kid·ze·grad** \ˌȯr-ˌjän-ə-ˈkid-zə-ˌgräd\. Former town, Bryansk Oblast, Russian S.F.S.R., U.S.S.R.; incorporated into Bryansk city 1956.

Bé·ziers \bāz-ˈyā\ *or anc.* **Bae·ter·rae** \bē-ˈter-ē\. City, Herault dept., S France, 38 m. SW of Montpellier; pop. (1968c) 80,492; regional trade center; alcohol distilling; chemicals; surrounded by old walls; 12th cent. Gothic cathedral. Ancient Gallic fortress; captured by Romans 120 B.C.; massacre 1209 of 20,000 inhabitants for having harbored (1200) the Albigenses; episcopal see to 1790.

Be·zons \bə-ˈzōⁿ\. Commune, Val-d'Oise dept., N France, NW suburb of Paris; pop. (1968c) 24,475.

Bezwada. See VIJAYAWADA.

Bha·dar \ˈbəd-ər, ˈbäd-\. River, Kathiawar Penin., W India; ab. 120 m. long; flowing WSW into Arabian Sea.

Bhadgaon. See BHAKTAPUR.

Bhad·res·war \bəd-ˈres-wər\. Town, West Bengal, India, on Hooghly river 20 m. N of Calcutta; pop. (1961c) 35,489.

Bha·gal·pur \ˈbäg-əl-ˌpu̇(ə)r\. **1** District, Bihar, NE India; 2183 sq. m.; pop. (1961c) 1,711,136; rice, corn, oilseeds.

2 City, Bihar, NE India, on right bank of Ganges river 205 m. NNW of Calcutta; pop. (1970e) 178,216; rail center; silk; four colleges.

Bha·gi·ra·thi \bə-ˈgir-ət-ē\. **1** The Ganges river at its source, near Gangotri, N India.

2 Upper course of the Hooghly (*q.v.*), West Bengal, NE India, one of the Ganges distributaries. See also GANGES DELTA.

Bha·kra Dam \ˌbək-rə-, ˌbäk-\. Dam in gorge of Sutlej river near village of Bhakra, Himachal Pradesh, N India, NW of Bilaspur; 740 ft. high. With **Nan·gal Dam** \ˌnəŋ-gəl-, ˌnäŋ-\ forms part of Bhakra-Nangal irrigation and hydroelectric project, completed 1954.

Bhak·ta·pur \ˈbək-tə-ˌpu̇(ə)r\ *or formerly* **Bhad·ga·on** \ˈbəd-ˌgau̇n\. Town, cen. Nepal, 8 m. E of Katmandu; pop. (1968e) 35,500; palace (1697).

Bha·mo \bə-ˈmō\. **1** District, Kachin State, N Burma; 4086 sq. m.; pop. (1962e) 167,063; ✱ Bhamo; timber.

2 Town, its ✱, on E bank of upper Irrawaddy river 100 m. S of Myitkyina and 65 m. NW of Namhkam; pop. (1960e) 16,000; about 40 m. from China border; head of navigation of the Irrawaddy, with steamer connections with Rangoon; was an important station on Stilwell Road (earlier Ledo Road) connecting Myitkyina with Burma Road; lost to Japanese Apr. 1942 and scene of much fighting before its recovery Oct.–Dec. 1944.

Bhan·da·ra \bən-ˈdär-ə\. Town, NE Maharashtra, cen. India, on branch of Wainganga river 33 m. E of Nagpur; pop. (1961c) 27,710.

Bharat. See INDIA 2.

Bha·rat·pur \ˈbə-rət-ˌpu̇(ə)r\ *or* **Bhurt·pore** \ˈbərt-ˌpō(ə)r, -ˌpȯ(ə)r\. **1** Former Indian state, now part of Rajasthan, NW India; 1978 sq. m.

2 City, its ✱, 34 m. W of Agra; pop. (1961c) 49,776; known for beauty and workmanship of its chowries, made from sandalwood, ivory, and silver. Strongly fortified; unsuccessfully besieged 1805 by British under Lord Lake; besieged by Lord Combermere 1825–26 and captured.

Bharoch. See BROACH.

Bha·tin·da \bə-ˈtin-də\. Town, Punjab, N India, 100 m. S of Amritsar; pop. (1961c) 52,253; rail center.

Bhat·pa·ra \bät-ˈpär-ə\. City, West Bengal, NE India, on Hooghly river 22 m. N of Calcutta; pop. (1970e) 160,607; jute processing.

Bhav·na·gar *or* **Bhau·na·gar** \bau̇-ˈnəg-ər\. **1** Former Indian state, E Kathiawar, on W shore of Gulf of Cambay, now part of Gujarat, W India; 2961 sq. m. Region first settled by Gohel Rajputs about 1260; came into close relations with Bombay government in 18th cent. and its lands consolidated by British in 1807.

2 Town and seaport, its ✱, on W coast of Gulf of Cambay 200 m. N of Bombay; pop. (1970e) 222,462; spinning mills, brick factories, iron foundry; several colleges; founded 1723; chief seaport of Kathiawar Penin.

Bhawalpur. See BAHAWALPUR.

Bhawanipatna. See KALAHANDI.

Bhe·ra \ˈbā-rə, ˈber-ə\. Town, N Punjab, Pakistan, on Jhelum river 105 m. NW of Lahore; pop. (1961c) 17,992; ancient Indian mounds nearby.

Bhi·lai \bi-ˈlī\. Town, Madhya Pradesh, cen. India, 160 m. E of Nagpur; pop. (1961c) 86,100; steel plant.

Bhi·ma \ˈbē-mə\. River, S India; ab. 400 m. long; rises in Maharashtra state in Western Ghats E of Bombay, flows SE in S Maharashtra, N Mysore, and cen. Andhra Pradesh to Krishna river near Raichur.

Bhir *or* **Bir** \ˈbi(ə)r\. Town, cen. Maharashtra, cen. India, 65 m. SSE of Aurangabad; pop. (1961c) 33,066.

Bhi·wa·ni \bi-ˈwän-ē\. Town, W Haryana, N India, 70 m. W of Delhi; pop. (1961c) 58,194.

Bho·pal \bō-ˈpäl\. **1** Former state, S Central India States, India; 6921 sq. m.; incorporated 1956 in Madhya Pradesh. Chief state of former Bhopal Agency and next to Hyderabad the most important Muslim state in India. Surface broken by Vindhya Mts.; Narmada river formed its S border. Founded 1723 by Dost Mohammed Khan, an Afghan chieftain who had served under Aurangzeb; made treaty arrangements with British government 1817; ruled by female line (Begums of Bhopal) 1844–1926.

2 City, ✱ of Madhya Pradesh, India, ab. 182 m. NW of Nagpur; pop. (1970e) 325,721; heavy electrical equipment; several colleges; ✱ of former Bhopal state.

Bhopal Agency. Formerly, a group of nine Indian states (including Bhopal), a subdivision of Central India Agency; 9073 sq. m.; ✱ Bhopal.

Bhor \ˈbō(ə)r, ˈbȯ(ə)r\. **1** Former Indian state, one of Deccan and Kolhapur States in Western Ghats, now part of Maharashtra, W India; 910 sq. m.

2 Town, its ✱, in S cen. Maharashtra; 25 m. S of Poona.

Bhot \ˈbȯt\ *or* **Bho·ti·ya** \ˈbȯt-ē-(y)ə\ *or* **Bho·ti·yal** \-ē-ˌ(y)äl\. Old names for Tibet.

Bhu·ba·nes·war \ˌbü-bə-ˈnesh-wər\ *also* **Bhu·va·nesh·war** \ˌbü-və-ˈnesh-\. Town, ✱ of Orissa, E India, 30 m. N of Puri; pop. (1961c) 38,211; Utkal Univ. (1943), Orissa Univ. of Agriculture and Technology (1962); has ab. 500 (originally several thousand) temples in Orissan style of architecture, erected bet. 8th and 12th cents. A.D.; the Great Temple one of the finest Hindu shrines in India.

Bhuj \ˈbüj\. Town, ✱ of former Kutch state, now in Gujarat, W India, 190 m. W of Ahmadabad; pop. (1961c) 40,180; known for silverwork.

Bhuket. See PHUKET.

Bhurtpore. See BHARATPUR.

Bhu·sa·wal *or* **Bhu·sa·val** \bu̇-ˈsäv-əl\. Town, N Maharashtra, W India, on Tapti river; pop. (1961c) 79,121.

Bhu·tan \bü-'tan, -'tän\ *or* **Druk–yul** \'drük-'yül\. Kingdom in E Himalayas on NE border of India, bounded on N by Tibet, China, on E by Assam, India, on S by Assam and West Bengal, and on W by Sikkim and Tibet; ab. 16,000 sq. m.; pop. (1970e) 800,000; ❋ Thimbu (Tashi Chho Dzong); crossed for most part by short high mountain ridges (peaks up to 24,000 ft.) running N to S and separated by deep valleys (12,000 to 18,000 ft.). *Chief products:* Rice, corn, wheat, barley. Inhabitants (Bhutanese) are a branch of Tibetan Mongolians (chiefly Buddhists).

History: Came under Chinese domination 1720; relations with British began about 1772; outrages against British subjects 1863 led to invasion 1865 when by treaty portions were annexed to India; since 1907 under rule of hereditary maharaja; responsibility for external relations assumed by Great Britain in treaty 1910; after 1949 accepted Indian guidance in foreign affairs; territorial claims to parts of the country advanced by China 1958; became a member of the United Nations 1971.

Bhuvaneshwar. See BHUBANESWAR.

Biache–Saint–Vaast \bē-ˌash-saⁿ-'vä\. Commune, Pas-de-Calais dept., N France, 7 m. SW of Douai; severe fighting in July 1916 and Aug. 1918.

Biac·na·ba·to *or* **Biak–na–ba·to** \bē-äk-nə-'bät-(ˌ)ō\. Village in mountains of NE Bulacan prov., Luzon, Phil., 28 m. NE of Malolos; noted for its caves. Area NE of village forms **Biacnabato National Park.** Scene Dec. 14, 1897 of signing of Pact of Biacnabato bet. Aguinaldo, head of provisional government, and Spanish governor-general in attempt to terminate the revolution.

Bia·fo Glacier \bē-'äf-(ˌ)ō-\. Glacier, Karakoram Range, Pakistan (in region claimed by India); 36 m. long; ab. 1.2 m. wide near its terminus.

Bi·a·fra \bē-'af-rə, bē-'äf-, bī-'af-\. Name of Nigeria's former Eastern Region during its secession 1967–70; region now divided into the Nigerian states East-Central, Rivers, and South-Eastern.

Biafra, Bight of. Widemouthed bay in E section of the Gulf of Guinea, W Africa.

Bi·ak \bē-'(y)äk\ *also* **Wi·ak** \wē-\. Island, largest of the Schouten Is., off N coast of Irian Barat, Indonesia; 45 m. long by 23 m. wide; 948 sq. m. Northwest part hilly; several populous towns on coast including Bosnik; three airfields. Seized by Japanese 1942; retaken after fierce fighting May 27–June 20, 1944 by Allied forces.

Bia·ła \bē-'äl-ə\. 1 River, E Kraków prov., Poland, a branch of the Dunajec river; 71 m. long; battles May 1915 in German offensive under Mackensen.

2 River, W Kraków prov., Poland, tributary of the upper Vistula; 21 m. long.

Biała Pod·la·ska \-pȯd-'läs-kə\. Commune, Lublin prov., E Poland, 60 m. NNE of Lublin; pop. (1970p) 26,200.

Bia·ło·gard \byä-'lȯg-ˌärt\ *or Ger.* **Bel·gard** \'bel-ˌgärt\. City, Koszalin prov., NW Poland, ab. 15 m. SSW of Koszalin; pop. (1970p) 20,500; food processing; wood products; church (1310); formerly in Pomerania, Germany; assigned to Poland by the Potsdam Conference 1945.

Bia·ło·wie·za National Park \bē-'äl-əv-ˌyezh-ə-\. National park, E Poland; 20 sq. m.; habitat of European bison; established 1947.

Bia·ły·stok \bē-'äl-i-ˌstȯk\; *Russ.* **Be·lo·stok** *also* **Bie·lo·stok** \ˌb(y)el-ə-'stȯk\. 1 Province, NE Poland; 8939 sq. m.; pop. (1970p) 1,737,000; ❋ Białystok; added to Belorussian S.S.R. 1944–45 as Belostok; with Suwałki ceded back to Poland by U.S.S.R. Aug. 1945.

2 Industrial city, its ❋, 105 m. NE of Warsaw; pop. (1970p) 166,600; textile center; important railroad junction. Founded in 14th cent.; annexed to Prussia 1795–1807, then Russian until taken by Germans Aug. 1915; restored to Poland 1919. In World War II overrun by Germans July 1941; retaken by Soviet troops July 1944.

Bian·ca·vil·la \bē-ˌäŋ-kə-'vē-lə\ *or older* **Ines·sa** \ē-'nes-ə\. Commune, Catania prov., E Sicily, Italy, at foot of Mt. Etna; pop. (1968e) 21,251; founded 1480 as Albanian colony.

Bianco, Monte. See BLANC, MONT.

Bi·a·ro \bē-'är-(ˌ)ō\. See SANGIHE ISLANDS.

Biar·ritz \ˌbē-ə-'rits, 'be-ə-ˌ\. Commune, Pyrénées-Atlantiques dept., SW France, on Gulf of Gascogne 5 m. WSW of Bayonne; pop. (1968c) 26,750; fashionable summer and winter resort; mineral baths; sea bathing.

Bi·as \'bē-äs\. See BEAS.

Bias Bay. See TA-YA BAY.

Bi·bai \bē-'bī, 'bē-ˌ\. City, Hokkaidō, Japan, 36 m. NW of Sapporo; pop. (1970c) 47,369.

Bi·bane Mountains \bē-ˌbän-\. Range of the Little Atlas Mts., N Algeria.

Bibb \'bib\. Name of counties in two states of the U.S. See tables at ALABAMA and GEORGIA.

Bibb City. Town, Muscogee co., W Georgia, 5 m. N of Columbus; pop. (1970c) 812.

Bib·bie·na \ˌbib-ē-'ā-nə\. Commune, Arezzo prov., Tuscany, cen. Italy, on Arno river; pop. (1968e) 10,192.

Bi·be·rach \'bē-bə-ˌräk\ *or in full* **Biberach an der Riss** \-än-də-'ris\. Industrial city, Baden-Württemberg, West Germany, 56 m. SE of Stuttgart; pop. (1969e) 25,456; chemicals, machinery; founded 1170; scene of defeat of Austrians by French 1796 and 1800.

Bibi Eibat. See KHANLAR.

Bi·brac·te \bə-'brak-(ˌ)tē\. Ancient town, E Gaul, near modern Autun; capital of the Aedui; battlefield 58 B.C. where Julius Caesar defeated the Helvetii.

Bi·brax \'bī-ˌbraks\. Ancient town of the Remi, Belgica, NE Gaul, near the Aisne on or near site of Laon.

Bices·ter \'bis-tər\. Urban district, Oxfordshire, England, 12 m. NNE of Oxford; pop. (1971p) 12,340.

Bi·cê·tre \bē-'setrᵊ\. South suburb of Paris, France; asylum for the insane founded by Richelieu.

Biche, Lac la. See LA BICHE, LAC.

Bichitra. See PHICHIT.

Bick·nell \'bik-nᵊl\. City, Knox co., SW Indiana, 13 m. ENE of Vincennes; pop. (1970c) 3717; coal mines.

Bi·col *or* **Bi·kol** \'bē-ˌkōl\. River, W cen. Camarines Sur prov., Luzon, Phil.; ab. 75 m. long; flows NW from Lake Bato to San Miguel Bay; fertile valley.

Bicol Peninsula. SE extension of Luzon, Phil., inhabited principally by the Bikol; comprises Camarines Norte, Camarines Sur, Albay, and Sorsogon provs.

Bida. See DOHA.

Bida \ˈbēd-ə\. City, North-Western State, Nigeria, near left bank of the Niger; pop. (1969e) 63,791; noted for its brass and copper work; cloth dyeing. Founded 1859; came under British 1901.

Bi·dar \ˈbēd-ər\. 1 District, N Mysore, S cen. India; 2119 sq. m.; pop. (1961c) 663,172; one of the five Muslim kingdoms of the Deccan 1492–c.1609.
2 Town, its ✱, 68 m. NW of Hyderabad; pop. (1961c) 32,420; dynastic capital of Bidar kingdom in 16th cent.

Bi·das·soa \ˌbed-ə-ˈsō-ə\. Stream, at N frontier of Spain; 41 m. long; rises in Spain and flows W and N to Bay of Biscay at Fuenterrabía; for ab. 7 m. its lower course forms boundary bet. France and Spain.

Bid·de·ford \ˈbid-ə-fərd\. Industrial city, York co., SW Maine, across the Saco river from Saco; pop. (1970c) 19,983; automotive parts, shoes, lumber; Saint Francis Coll. (1953); settled 1630.

Bid·dulph \ˈbid-ˌəlf\. Urban district, Staffordshire, W cen. England, 8 m. N of Stoke-on-Trent; pop. (1971p) 17,372.

Bid·e·ford \ˈbid-ə-fərd\. Municipal borough, Devonshire, SW England, near mouth of Torridge river 45 m. N of Plymouth; pop. (1971p) 11,766.

Bie·brza \bē-ˈeb-(ˌ)zhä\ *or Russ.* **Bobr** \ˈbȯ-bər\. River, N Poland; ab. 102 m. long; flows into Narew river.

Biel \ˈbē(ə)l\ *or Fr.* **Bienne** \byen\. Commune, N Bern canton, Switzerland, near Lake of Biel 17 m. NNW of Bern; pop. (1970c) 64,333; railroad junction; clocks, machinery, earthenware, paper. Founded c. 1200 by bishop of Basel; to France 1798; to Bern canton 1815.

Biel, Lake of *or Fr.* **Lac du Bienne** \läk-dᵫē-byen\ *or Ger.* **Bie·ler See** \ˈbē-lər-ˌzā\. Lake, Bern canton, W Switzerland, 3 m. NE of Lake of Neuchâtel; 10 m. long and bet. 1 and 3 m. wide; 16 sq. m.; contains St. Pierre I., Rousseau's residence 1765.

Bie·la·wa \byä-ˈläv-ə, ˌbē-ə-\ *or Ger.* **Lang·en·bie·lau** \ˌläŋ-ən-ˈbē-ˌlaù\. Town, Wrocław prov., SW Poland, 37 m. SSW of Wrocław; pop. (1970p) 31,000; textiles.

Bie·le·feld \ˈbē-lə-ˌfelt\. City, North Rhine-Westphalia, West Germany, 38 m. E of Münster; pop. (1969e) 168,695; bicycles, machine tools, chemicals, pharmaceuticals; founded c. 1214.

Bieler See. See BIEL, LAKE OF.

Biel·la \bē-ˈel-ə\. Manufacturing commune, Vercelli prov., Piedmont, NW Italy, 25 m. NW of Vercelli; pop. (1968e) 53,839; railroad terminus; in rich agricultural area.

Bielostok. See BIAŁYSTOK.

Biel·sko–Bia·ła \bē-ˌel-(ˌ)skȯ-bē-ˈäl-ə\ *or Ger.* **Bie·litz** \ˈbē-ləts\. Town, Katowice prov., S Poland, at NW foot of Carpathians 26 m. S of Katowice; pop. (1970p) 105,600; textiles.

Bien–hoa \bē-ˈen-ˈ(h)wä\. Town, South Vietnam, 20 m. NNE of Saigon; pop. (1968e) 82,506; industrial town; formerly capital of Cambodia; Buddha statues.

Bienne, Lac du. See BIEL, LAKE OF.

Bi·en·ville \bē-ˈen-ˌvil, -vəl\. Parish in Louisiana. See table at LOUISIANA.

Bienville, Lake of \-bē-ˈen-ˌvil, -byaⁿ-ˈvil\ *or* **Lake of Apis·ki·ga·mish** \-ə-ˌpis-ki-gə-ˈmish\. Lake, N cen. Quebec, Canada; with outlet through Great Whale river into Hudson Bay; 392 sq. m.

Bié Plateau \bē-ˌā-\. Highland region, cen. Angola, SW Africa; alt. ab. 5000 ft.

Bier·stadt, Mount \-ˈbi(ə)r-ˌstat\. Peak, Clear Creek co., N cen. Colorado; 14,060 ft.

Bie·tig·heim \ˈbēt-ig-ˌhīm\. City, Baden-Württemberg, West Germany, 13 m. N of Stuttgart, pop. (1969e) 22,303; worsteds, linoleum; received city charter 1364.

Big An·ne·mes·sex River \-ˌan-ə-ˌmes-iks-\. Inlet of Tangier Sound, Somerset co., SE Maryland.

Big Bay Point. Point on N coast of Marquette co., N Michigan penin., extending into Lake Superior.

Big Bear Lake. Reservoir in San Bernardino Valley, SW San Bernardino co., SW California, formed by damming small natural lake; center of resort area.

Big Bea·ver \-ˈbē-vər\. Borough, Beaver co., W Pennsylvania, 6 m. NNE of Beaver Falls; pop. (1970c) 2739.

Big Bend National Park. See UNITED STATES, *National Parks.*

Big Beth·el \-ˈbeth-əl\. Locality, Warwick co., Virginia, ab. 10 m. NW of Fort Monroe; battle June 10, 1861.

Big Black. 1 *also* **Great Black.** River, NW Maine; ab. 40 m. long; formed by junction of branches in NW Aroostook co., flows NE into St. John river.
2 River, W cen. Mississippi; 330 m. long; rises in Webster co., N cen. Miss., flows SW into the Mississippi river in NW Claiborne co., SW Miss.

Big Blue. River, Nebraska and Kansas; 300 m. long; flowing from Hamilton co., SE cen. Nebraska, SE into Kansas river at Manhattan, Riley co., NE Kansas.

Big Bone Lick. Locality, Boone co., N Kentucky, just E of Ohio river; deposit of mammoth fossils; discovered ab. 1729; visited by Daniel Boone 1770.

Big Creek No. 2 and No. 3. See SAN JOAQUIN 1.

Big Cypress Swamp. Swamp region, W part of the Everglades, S Florida; ab. 2400 sq. m.

Big Delta. Village and post station, E Alaska, on Tanana river and on Alaska Highway at its junction with Richardson Highway, 65 m. SE of Fairbanks.

Big Diomede. See DIOMEDE ISLANDS.

Bi·gej \ˈbē-ˌgej\. Islet, SE Kwajalein atoll, W Marshall Is., ab. 12 m. NNE of Kwajalein I.; taken by Allies Feb. 6, 1944.

Big Elk Peak. Mountain, E Bonneville co., SE Idaho, 9478 ft.

Big·e·low, Mount \-ˈbig-(ə-)(ˌ)lō\. Mountain, Somerset co., W Maine; 4150 ft.

Big Equinox. See EQUINOX MOUNTAIN.

Big Flats. Town, Chemung co., S New York, ab. 9 m. NW of Elmira near Chemung river; pop. (1970c) 2509.

Big Fork. River, N Minnesota; ab. 120 m. long; rises in NW Itasca co., flows N into Rainy river on United States-Canada boundary.

Big·gar \ˈbig-ər\. Town, SW cen. Saskatchewan, Canada, 58 m. W of Saskatoon; pop. (1971p) 2598.

Big·gles·wade \ˈbig-əlz-ˌwād\. Urban district, Bedfordshire, SE cen. England, 42 m. N of London; pop. (1971p) 9598.

Bigheart. See BARNSDALL.

Big Hole National Battlefield Site. See UNITED STATES, *National Historical Parks.*

Big·horn \ˈbig-ˌhȯ(ə)rn\. River, formed by confluence of Popo Agie and Wind rivers in Fremont co., W cen. Wyoming; 336 m. long; flows N into Yellowstone river in SW Treasure co., SE cen. Montana.

Big Horn. Name of counties in two states of the U.S. See tables at MONTANA and WYOMING.

Bighorn Mountain. Peak, Banner co., W Nebraska; 4713 ft.

Big Horn Mountains. Range in N Wyoming extending N and S from Montana border to Natrona co.; highest point Cloud Peak 13,175 ft.

Big Jay Peak. See JAY PEAK.

Big Lake. 1 Lake in cen. Washington co., E Maine.
2 Town, ⊗ of Reagan co., W Texas; pop. (1970c) 2489.

Big Meadows Dam. Dam across N fork of Feather river, NW Plumas co., NE California; height 130 ft.; completed 1927; impounds water, **Lake Al·ma·nor** \-ˈal-mə-ˌnȯ(ə)r\, for water power.

Big Muddy. River, SW Illinois; ab. 100 m. long; rises in S cen. Illinois, flows SW into Mississippi in W Jackson co., SW Illinois.

Big Nemaha. See NEMAHA.

Bigorra. See TARBES.

Bi·gorre \bi-'gȯ(ə)r\. Medieval county in W Pyrenees, SW France, in valley of the Adour; ✱ Tarbes; attached to Béarn 1425.

Big Pine Key. One of the Florida Keys.

Big Rapids. City, ⊗ of Mecosta co., cen. Michigan, 35 m. WNW of Mt. Pleasant; pop. (1970c) 11,995; summer resort; furniture, shoes; natural gas and oil wells; Ferris State Coll. (1884).

Big Sa·ble Point \-'sā-bəl-\. Point on W coast of Mason co., W Michigan, extending into Lake Michigan.

Big Sandy. 1 River, W Arizona; ab. 80 m. long; joins Santa Maria river on SE boundary of Mohave co. to form Williams river.

2 Navigable river, E Kentucky; 22 m. long; formed by confluence of Levisa Fork and Tug Fork (*qq.v.*) in E Lawrence co., E Kentucky, flows N forming N section of Kentucky-West Virginia boundary, and empties into Ohio river near Catlettsburg, NE Kentucky.

Big Sandy Creek. River, E Colorado; 200 m. long; rises in N El Paso co., flows SE into Arkansas river.

Big San·ta Ani·ta Dam \-ˌsant-ə-(ə-)ˌnēt-ə-\. Dam across Big Santa Anita creek, California; height 235 ft.; completed 1927; impounds water for flood control.

Big Sioux \-'sü\. River, South Dakota and Iowa; 420 m. long; rises in W Grant co., NE South Dakota, flows S and SE to form South Dakota-Iowa boundary, and empties into Missouri river at extreme SE corner of South Dakota on W boundary of Sioux City.

Big Slide Mountain \-ˌslīd-\. Peak in the Adirondack Mountains, Essex co., NE New York; 4255 ft.

Big Southern Butte. Peak, S Butte co., SE cen. Idaho; 7576 ft.

Big Spring. City, ⊗ of Howard co., NW Texas, 78 m. NW of San Angelo; pop. (1970c) 28,735; chemicals, fertilizers; oil refineries; Howard County Junior Coll. (1945).

Big Stone. County in Minnesota. See table at MINNESOTA.

Big Stone Gap. Town, Wise co., SW Virginia, in Cumberland Mts. 40 m. WNW of Bristol; pop. (1970c) 4153.

Big Stone Lake. Narrow lake, bet. NE corner of South Dakota and W Minnesota; ab. 30 m. long.

Big Sur \-'sər\. 1 Village, Monterey co., California, near coast SE of Point Sur on **Big Sur River** (ab. 10 m. long).

2 Resort region, Monterey co., California, extending from vicinity of Point Sur ab. 80 m. SE along coast W of Santa Lucia Range.

Big Timber. City, ⊗ of Sweet Grass co., S cen. Montana, on Yellowstone river; pop. (1970c) 1592.

Big Tu·jun·ga No. 1 \-tə-'həŋ-gə-\. Dam across Big Tujunga creek, Los Angeles co., California; height 250 ft.; impounds water for flood control.

Big Tupper Lake. See TUPPER LAKES.

Big Wich·i·ta Dam \-'wich-ə-ˌtȯ-\ *or* **Wichita Falls Dam.** Dam across Wichita river, Baylor co., N Texas; height 100 ft.; completed 1923; impounds water for irrigation, forming **Lake Kemp** \-'kemp\.

Big Wood. River, S Idaho; 95 m. long; rises on S slopes of Sawtooth Range, flows S, then W to Snake river.

Bi·hać \'bē-ˌhäch\. Town, Bosnia and Herzegovina, Yugoslavia, on Una river; pop. (1965e) 19,000; under Turkish rule 1592–1878.

Bi·har *or* **Be·har** \bi-'här\. 1 State, NE India; 67,184 sq. m.; pop. (1971p) 56,387,296; ✱ Patna; plateau region in S (Chota Nagpur) and Ganges valley in N. *Chief products:* Rice, corn, wheat; coal, iron ore. *Largest cities:* Patna, Gaya, Jamshedpur, Muzaffarpur.

History: Its limits nearly the same as ancient kingdoms of Videha and Magadha with records dating back to c. 600 B.C. Under Bimbisara, Gautama began his preaching at Buddh Gaya (*q.v.*). Succeeded by Maurya empire, followed 320 A.D. by Gupta empire, with Pataliputra (Patna) as capital. Native dynasty overcome in 1194 by Muslims and about 1497 annexed to Delhi; came into possession of East India Company 1765 and made a part of Bengal; set up as part of province of Bihar and Orissa 1912 but made a separate province 1936; boundaries readjusted 1956.

2 Former division, Bihar state; 42,633 sq. m.

3 Town, cen. Bihar state, 40 m. SE of Patna; pop. (1961c) 78,581; produces muslins and gold and silver brocades; has many mosques and graves holy to Muslims and is a place of pilgrimage. Capital of Magadha until seat of government moved to Patna in 16th cent.

Bihar and Oris·sa \-ō-'ris-ə\. Former province 1912–36 of British India; 83,054 sq. m.; ✱ Patna; geographically included Indian States, 28,648 sq. m.

Bi·hor \bi-'hȯ(ə)r\. County of NW Romania. See table at ROMANIA.

Bihor Mountains *or Hung.* **Bi·har Mountains** \'bē-ˌhȯ(ə)r-\. Mountains, W cen. Transylvania, Romania, NW of the Transylvanian Alps; highest point ab. 6065 ft.

Biisk. See BISK.

Bi·ja·gós, Ar·qui·pé·la·go dos \ˌär-ki-'pel-ə-(ˌ)gü-(ˌ)düz(h)-ˌvē-zhə-'gȯs(h)\ *also* **Ilhas dos Bijagós** \'ēl-yəz(h)-\ *or Eng.* **Bis·sa·gos Islands** \bis-ˌäg-əs-\. Group of low islands, Portuguese Guinea, W Africa, off coast SW of Bissau; largest are Orango, Formosa, Caravéla; on easternmost island, Bolama, is town and port of Bolama I.

Bijanagar. See VIJAYANAGAR.

Bi·ja·pur \bi-'jäp-ər\. Town, Mysore, W India, 240 m. SE of Bombay; pop. (1961c) 78,854. Adopted 1489 by Yusuf Adil Shah as capital of independent state; one of the five Muslim kingdoms of the Deccan (*q.v.*). Has numerous pre-Muslim ruins and large mosques, palaces, and buildings in Islamic style; also an impressive citadel and fort. Kingdom conquered by Aurangzeb 1686, ceded to Marathas 1760, and taken over by British 1818.

Bi·ja·war \bi-'jä-wər\. Former Indian state, now part of Madhya Pradesh, cen. India; 980 sq. m.

Bi·je·lji·na \bi-'yel-yə-(ˌ)nä\. Town, Bosnia and Herzegovina, cen. Yugoslavia; pop. (1965e) 19,000.

Bij·nor \'bij-ˌnō(ə)r\. Town, NW Uttar Pradesh, N India, 3 m. from left bank of Ganges river 75 m. NE of Delhi; pop. (1961e) 33,821.

Bi·ka \bi-'kä\ *or* **Al–Bika** \ˌal-\ *also* **Be·káa** \bi-'kä\ *or* **Buk·a'a** \bu̇-\ *or Arab.* **Al–Bi·ga'** \ˌal-bi-'kä\; *anc.* **Coe·le–Syr·ia** *or* **Coe·le·syr·ia** \ˌsē-lē-'sir-ē-ə\. Valley in Lebanon, bet. the Lebanon and Anti-Lebanon mountain ranges; 80 m. long, 10 m. wide; traversed by the Upper Orontes (flowing N) and the Litani (flowing S) rivers. During the wars between the Seleucids and Egypt, Coele-Syria encompassed much of S Syria.

Bi·ka·ner \ˌbik-ə-'ne(ə)r, ˌbē-kə-, -'ni(ə)r\. 1 Former Indian state, now part of Rajasthan, NW India; 23,181 sq. m.; desolate tract, part of Thar Desert without a single stream; N part watered by irrigation canals. Founded ab. 1465 by Rajput chief; adhered loyally to Mogul Empire; waged wars with Jodhpur through 18th cent.; received British political agent 1883.

2 City, its ✱, 240 m. W of Delhi; pop. (1970e) 190,868; founded 1485 by Bika, a Rajput chief of Marwar; noted for its carpets and blankets; surrounded by stone wall and overlooked by citadel; its temples and palaces constructed of bright red sandstone.

Bi·ki·ni \bə-'kē-nē\. Atoll with ab. 20 islets, Marshall Is., Micronesia, 11°35′N, 165°23′E; lagoon 21½ m. long by 11 m. wide. Largest islets Bikini, Enyu, and Namu; entrance to lagoon is through Enyu Channel on the SE, 9 m. wide. Population of 167 removed to Rongerik before American tests of atomic bomb July 1 and 25, 1946; hydrogen bomb tested 1954, 1956; inhabitants returned 1969.

Bikol. See BICOL.

Bik·scho·te \'bik-(ˌ)skōt-ə\ *or* **Bix·schoo·te** \'bīk-ˌskō-tə\. Village, West Flanders prov., NW Belgium, 5 m. N of Ieper (Ypres); pop. (1969e) 696; scene of first German gas attack Apr. 22, 1915, in World War I.

Bi·laa Point \(ˌ)bē-ˌlä-\. Most northerly point of Mindanao, Phil., at NE corner, Surigao del Norte prov.

Bilād–es–Sudan. See SUDAN.

Bilá Hora. See WHITE MOUNTAIN 3.

Bi·las·pur \bə-ˈläs-ˌpu̇(ə)r\. Town, NE Madhya Pradesh, cen. India, on tributary of Mahanadi river 210 m. ENE of Nagpur; pop. (1961c) 86,706.

Bilaspur *or* **Kah·lur** \kä-ˈlu̇(ə)r\. 1 Former Indian state, now a district of Himachal Pradesh, N India; 448 sq. m.; pop. (1961c) 158,806.

2 Town, its ✱, on Sutlej river; pop. (1961c) 7424.

Bi·lauk·taung Range \bi-ˌlau̇k-tau̇ŋ-\. Mountain range along boundary bet. SE Burma and SW Thailand; elev. bet. 2000 and 5000 ft.

Bil·bao \bil-ˈbä-ˌō, -ˈbau̇, -ˈbä-(ˌ)ō\. City, ✱ of Vizcaya prov., N Spain, 7 m. from the Bay of Biscay; pop. (1970p) 410,-490; a major Spanish port; chemical and metallurgical industries; shipbuilding, fishing; univ. (1886); founded 1300; besieged by Carlists 1833–35, 1872–76.

Bil·beis *or* **Bel·beis** *or* **Bil·bays** \bil-ˈbās\. Town, Sharqīya gov., NE Egypt, ab. 30 m. NE of Cairo; pop. (1970e) 73,-300.

Bilbilis. See CALATAYUD.

Bildt, de. See DE BILDT.

Bi·le·cik \ˌbē-lə-ˈjek\. 1 Province of NW Turkey, Asia. See table at TURKEY.

2 Town, its ✱, 37 m. NW of Eskişehir; pop. (1965c) 9722.

Bíle Karpaty. See WHITE CARPATHIAN MOUNTAINS.

Bí·li·na \ˈbē-li-(ˌ)nä\ *or Ger.* **Bi·lin** \bi-ˈlēn\. City, Czech S.R., W Czechoslovakia; pop. (1968e) 12,226; glass; mineral springs.

Bi·li·ran \bə-ˈlē-ˌrän\. Island N of Leyte, cen. Phil.; 192 sq. m.; chief town Caibiran.

Bilkas. See BILQĀS.

Bille·rica \(ˈ)bil-ˈrik-ə, ˌbel-ə-\. Town, Middlesex co., NE Massachusetts, 6 m. S of Lowell; pop. (1970c) 31,648.

Bil·linge and Win·stan·ley \ˈbil-inj . . . ˈwin(t)-stən-lē\. Urban district, Lancashire, NW England, 12½ m. NE of Liverpool; pop. (1969e) 10,510.

Bil·ling·ham \ˈbil-iŋ-əm\. Former urban district, Durham, N England; became part of the county borough of Teesside 1968.

Bil·lings \ˈbil-iŋz\. 1 County in North Dakota. See table at NORTH DAKOTA.

2 City, ⊗ of Yellowstone co., S cen. Montana, on Yellowstone river; pop. (1970c) 61,581; alt. 3120 ft.; trading and shipping point for livestock, poultry, and wool; beet-sugar factories, flour mills. Eastern Montana Coll. (1927), Rocky Mountain Coll. (1883).

Billiton. See BELITUNG.

Bill Wil·liams Mountain \ˌbil-ˌwil-yəmz-\. Peak, SW Coconino co., N cen. Arizona; 9256 ft.

Bi·ly–Mon·ti·gny \bē-ˈyē-ˌmō^{n}-ˌtēn-ˈyē\. Commune, Pas-de-Calais dept., N France, 11 m. NE of Arras; pop. (1968c) 10,028; coal mines.

Bil·ma \ˈbil-mə\. Oasis, E Niger, W Africa.

Bi·loxi \bə-ˈlək-sē, -ˈläk-\. City, Harrison co., SE Mississippi, on Gulf of Mexico 13 m. E of Gulfport; pop. (1970c) 48,486; resort; boatbuilding; commercial oyster and shrimp fisheries; Keesler Air Force Base with U.S. Air Force Technical School; first permanent white settlement in the Mississippi valley (1699).

Bil·qās *or* **Bil·kas** \bil-ˈkäs\ *or in full* **Bilqās Qism Aw·wal** \-ˌkis-əm-ə-ˈwäl\. Town, Daqahlīya gov., Egypt, in Nile delta 30 m. SW of Damietta; pop. (1966c) 41,100.

Bi·ma Bay \ˌbē-mə-\. Inlet of Flores Sea on NE coast of Sumbawa I., Lesser Sunda Is., Indonesia; one of best harbors in Indonesia; town of Raba on it.

Bim·i·ni \ˈbim-ə-nē\ *or* **Bim·i·nis** \-nēz\. Two small islands of the Bahama Is., E of S Florida and separated from Florida by the Straits of Florida; 9 sq. m.; named for mythical island of Bimini, supposed site of "fountain of youth" the quest for which led to discovery of Florida 1513 by Ponce de Leon.

Bi·nal·ba·gan \ˌbē-näl-ˈbäg-än\. Municipality, W coast of Negros Occidental prov., Negros, Phil., on Panay Gulf; pop. (1969e) 42,900.

Bi·na·lo·nan \ˌbē-nə-ˈlō-nän\. Municipality, E Pangasinan prov., Luzon, Phil., 23 m. E of Lingayen; pop. (1969e) 35,000; important road center.

Bi·ñan \bin-ˈyän\. Municipality, W Laguna prov., Luzon, Phil., near SW coast of Laguna de Bay; pop. (1969e) 46,-000; important terminus for roads to Cavite.

Bi·nang·o·nan \ˌbē-näŋ-ˈō-nän\. Municipality, S Rizal prov., Luzon, Phil., on W shore of peninsula on Laguna de Bay 10 m. SE of Pasig; pop. (1969e) 42,600; large quarries of building stone nearby.

Binche \ˈba^{n}sh\. Commune, Hainaut prov., SW Belgium, on Haine river 10 m. E of Mons; pop. (1969e) 10,153.

Bindhachal. See MIRZAPUR.

Bindloe Island. See MARCHENA ISLAND.

Bindraban. See VRINDAVAN.

Bin·du·ra \bin-ˈdu̇r-ə\. City, Rhodesia, ab. 40 m. NE of Salisbury; pop. (1969p) 10,290.

Bing·en \ˈbiŋ-ən\. City, Rhineland-Palatinate, West Germany, at confluence of Rhine and Nahe rivers 17 m. W of Mainz; pop. (1969e) 24,350; tourism; wine; 15th cent. Gothic church; Klopp castle nearby; famous Drusus-brücke (bridge; built by Drusus 13 B.C.) over the Nahe river; ancient Mäuseturm (Mouse Tower; according to legend, Archbishop Hatto devoured by mice here c. 970); Rhenish Technical College; inhabited by ancient Belgae; scene of defeat of Gauls by Romans 70 A.D.; Emperor Henry IV imprisoned in nearby castle 1105; burned by French 1689; under French rule 1797–1814; to Hesse 1815.

Bin·ger·ville \ˌba^{n}-zhər-ˈvē(ə)l\. Seaport town, Ivory Coast, W Africa; pop. (1963c) 2500; former territorial ✱ .

Bing·ham \ˈbiŋ-əm\. County in Idaho. See table at IDAHO.

Bingham Canyon. Town, Salt Lake co., N Utah, 20 m. SSW of Salt Lake City; pop. (1970c) 31.

Bing·ham·ton \ˈbiŋ-əm-tən\. City, ⊗ of Broome co., S New York, at confluence of Chenango and Susquehanna rivers 65 m. S of Syracuse; pop. (1970c) 64,123; aircraft parts, cameras and film, small boats; Broome Technical Community Coll. (1946), State Univ. of New York at Binghamton (1946). With Johnson City and Endicott one of so-called Triple Cities; first permanent settlement 1787; incorporated as village 1834, city 1867; site of first farm bureau in U.S. (1911).

Bingian, Slieve. See SLIEVE BINGIAN.

Bing·ley \ˈbiŋ-lē\. Urban district, West Riding, Yorkshire, N England, on the Aire 7 m. NNW of Bradford; pop. (1971p) 26,540; woolen mills, paper mills.

Bin·göl \biŋ-ˈgəl\. 1 Province of E Turkey, Asia. See table at TURKEY.

2 Town, its ✱; pop. (1965c) 11,727.

Bingöl Da·ğı \-dä-ˈ(g)ē\. Mountain range (*dağı*), Armenia, E Turkey, NW of Lake Van; highest point 11,975 ft.

Bin·go Sea \ˌbiŋ-(ˌ)gō-\ *or* **Sea of Bingo.** Expansion of the Inland Sea, Japan, in its central part, N of Shikoku I.

Binh Dinh. See AN NHON.

Bin·ma·ley \ˌbēn-mə-ˈlā\. Municipality, cen. Pangasinan prov., Luzon, Phil., in Agno delta 3 m. E of Lingayen on S shore of Lingayen Gulf; pop. (1969e) 44,100.

Bin·tan \ˈbin-ˌtän\ *or* **Bin·tang** \-ˌtäŋ\. Island, largest of the Riau Archipelago, Indonesia, off S tip of the Malay Peninsula; 415 sq. m.; bauxite mines.

Bin·tu·lu \bin-ˈtü-(ˌ)lü\. Coastal town, W Sarawak, East Malaysia, NW Borneo.

Binue. See BENUE.

Bío–bío \ˌbē-ō-ˈbē-(ˌ)ō\. 1 River, S cen. Chile; 238 m. long; flows from the Andes Mts. into the Pacific Ocean at the city of Concepción.

2 Province of S cen. Chile. See table at CHILE.

Bipontium. See ZWEIBRÜCKEN.

Biqa', Al–. See BIKA.

Bir. See BHIR.

Bir, Cape \-'bi(ə)r\ *or Arab.* **Ras Bir** \räs-\. Cape projecting from E coast of Afars and Issas into the Gulf of Aden at entrance to Bab al-Mandab.

Bīrah. See BIRE.

Bir al–Go·bi \ˌbi(ə)r-al-'gō-bē\. Village and pass in the hills of Libya, N Africa, 37 m. S of Tobruk; fighting 1941–42.

Bi'r al–Hukayyim. See BIR HACHEIM.

Bi·rat·na·gar \bə-'rät-ˌnəg-ər\. Town, SE Nepal, ab. 150 m. SE of Katmandu; pop. (1971p) 44,938.

Bircao. See BUR GAVO.

Bird Islands. See AVES ISLANDS.

Birds·boro \'bərdz-ˌbər-ə, -bə-rə\. Industrial borough, Berks co., SE Pennsylvania, on Schuylkill river 9 m. SSE of Reading; pop. (1970c) 3196; steel castings; founded 1740.

Bir·dum \'bərd-əm\. Settlement, N cen. Northern Territory, Australia, on railroad 270 m. SE of Darwin.

Bi·re *or* **Bi·reh** *or* **Bī·rah** \'bi(ə)r-ə, 'bē-rə\ *or Bib.* **Be·e·roth** \bē-'i(ə)r-ˌōth, 'bi(ə)r-\ *or anc.* **Be·roea** \bə-'rē-ə\. Town, Jordan, 9 m. N of Jerusalem on a rocky hilltop; in region occupied by Israel 1967; battle 161 B.C.

Bi·re·cik *or* **Bi·ri·jik** \ˌbir-ə-'jēk\. Town on left bank of the Euphrates river, Urfa prov. SE Turkey in Asia, 45 m. WSW of Urfa; pop. (1965c) 15,317.

Bir es Saba. See BEERSHEBA.

Bir Ha·cheim \ˌbi(ə)r-hä-'kām\ *or Arab.* **Bi'r al–Hu·kay·yim** \-al-hu̇-'kī-yim\. Village, Libya, N Africa, 40 m. SSW of Tobruk; in World War II scene of much fighting 1942, esp. when taken by Germans under Rommel June 1942.

Bir·han \bi(ə)r-'hän\. Peak, cen. Ethiopia, NNW of Addis Ababa; 13,628 ft.

Birijik. See BIRECIK.

Bīr·jand \bi(ə)r-'jand\. Town, SE Khorāsān prov., NE Iran; pop. (1971p) 28,000; on a plateau (alt. 4440 ft.) and on the highway from Mashhad to Zāhedān; carpets.

Bir·ken·head \'bər-kən-ˌhed, ˌbər-kən-'\. 1 County borough, Cheshire, NW England, on the Mersey estuary opp. Liverpool; pop. (1971p) 137,738; shipbuilding and shipping center; has flour mills; steel manufacturing; abattoirs; technical coll. (1955). Connected with Liverpool by tunnel under the Mersey 2 1/7 m. long. First iron vessel in England built here 1829; new docks opened 1847; Confederate privateer *Alabama* launched 1862; first European town to have streetcars.

2 Borough, North I., New Zealand; pop. (1968e) 12,800; suburb of Auckland on N shore of Waitemata Harbor.

Bir·ket Qā·rūn \ˌbir-kət-kə-'rün\. Shallow lake, along NW boundary of Faiyūm gov., Egypt; ab. 30 m. long, 5 m. wide; 85 sq. m.; occupies part of basin of ancient Lake Moeris (*q.v.*).

Bir·kir·ka·ra \ˌbir-kər-'kär-ə\. Town, Malta, ab. 3 m. W of Valletta; pop. (1969e) 17,763.

Bîr·lad *or formerly* **Bâr·lad** *or* **Bêr·lad** \bər-'läd\. City, E Romania, 60 m. NNW of Galaţi; pop. (1966c) 41,060; food processing; ball bearings.

Bir·ming·ham \'bər-miŋ-ˌham, *Brit. usu.* -miŋ-əm\. 1 Industrial city, ⊗ of Jefferson co., N cen. Alabama; pop. (1970c) 300,910; area rich in coal, hematite, and many other minerals; iron and steel, aircraft, mining machinery, chemicals; electrical equipment, carbide, cotton and cottonseed products; food processing; Samford Univ. (1842), Birmingham-Southern Coll. (1856), Daniel Payne Coll. (1889), Miles Coll. (1907), Southern Bible Coll. (1934), Jefferson State Junior Coll. (1963), Wenonah State Technical Junior Coll. (1963); incorp. 1871.

2 Residential city, Oakland co., SE Michigan, 8 m. SSE of Pontiac; pop. (1970c) 26,170.

3 City and county borough, Warwickshire, Staffordshire, and Worcestershire, W cen. England, 98 m. NW of London; pop. (1971p) 1,013,366; a major manufacturing and transportation center; automobiles, machinery, electrical equipment, rubber products, chocolate; Univ. of Birmingham (1900), Univ. of Aston in Birmingham (1966). Grammar school founded 1552 by King Edward VI. Before 13th cent. a market town; swept by plague 1665; enfranchised by Reform Act 1832; bombed by German planes 1940–41.

Bir·nie \'bər-nē\. Island in center of Phoenix Islands group, cen. Pacific Ocean, S of Canton I.; 1 sq. m.

Bi·ro·bi·dzhan *or* **Bi·ro–Bi·djan** \ˌbir-ō-bi-'jän, -'jan\. 1 See JEWISH AUTONOMOUS OBLAST.

2 Town, ❋ of Jewish Autonomous Oblast, Russian S.F.S.R., U.S.S.R., on Trans-Siberian R.R. ab. 110 m. W of Khabarovsk; pop. (1970p) 56,000.

Birr \'bər\ *or* **Par·sons·town** \'pärs-ᵊnz-ˌtau̇n\. Urban district, W co. Offaly, cen. Eire; pop. (1971p) 3320; shoes; brewing; castle, noted as astronomical observatory.

Birsen. See BIRŽAI.

Bir·žai \'bi(ə)r-ˌzhī\ *or Russ.* **Bir·zhai** \bir-'zhī\ *or Ger.* **Bir·sen** \'bi(ə)rz-ᵊn\. Town, Lithuanian S.S.R., U.S.S.R.; alliance bet. Peter the Great of Russia and Augustus II of Poland formed here 1701 against Sweden.

Bi·sai \bi-'sī, 'bē-ˌsī\. City, Aichi prefecture, Honshū, Japan, 12 m. NW of Nagoya; pop. (1970c) 51,337.

Bisanthe. See TEKİRDAĞ 2.

Bisayas. See VISAYAN ISLANDS.

Bis·bee \'biz-bē\. City, ⊗ of Cochise co., SE corner of Arizona, 58 m. E of Nogales; pop. (1970c) 8328; center of one of richest copper-producing regions in America; also mines gold, silver, lead.

Biscari. See ACATE.

Biscay *or* **Biscaya.** See VIZCAYA.

Biscay, Bay of *or* **Gulf of Gas·co·ny** \-'gas-kə-nē\ *or Fr.* **Golfe de Gas·cogne** \gȯl-fə-də-gȧ-skȯnʸ\; *anc.* **Ma·re Can·tab·ri·cum** \'mā-(ˌ)rē-kan-'tab-ri-kəm, 'mär-(ˌ)ā-\ *or* **Aq·ui·tan·i·cus Si·nus** \ˌak-wə-'tan-i-kə(s)-'sī-nəs\ *also* **Si·nus Can·tab·ri·cus** \'si-nə-skan-'tab-ri-kəs\ *or* **Can·ta·ber Oce·a·nus** \'kant-ə-bər-ō-'sē-ə-nəs\. Large inlet of the Atlantic Ocean on W coast of France and N coast of Spain, from Île d'Ouessant on the N to Cape Ortegal, Spain, on the S; max. depth 15,525 ft.; receives the Loire, Garonne, and Adour rivers on the E.

Bis·cayne Bay \bis-'kān-, 'bis-ˌ\. Inlet of Atlantic Ocean on E coast of Dade co., SE Florida; the city of Miami is on its NW shore and the island of **Biscayne Key** is on the NE.

Biscayne National Monument. See UNITED STATES, *National Monuments.*

Biscayne Park. Village, Dade co., SE Florida; pop. (1970c) 2717.

Bi·sce·glie \bi-'shāl-(ˌ)yā\. Seaport, Bari prov., Apulia, SE Italy, on Adriatic 21 m. WNW of Bari; pop. (1968e) 44,317; engineering shops, sawmills.

Bisch·heim \bē-'shem, 'bish-ˌhīm\. Commune, Bas-Rhin dept., NE France, NW suburb of Strasbourg; pop. (1968c) 14,383.

Bish·en·pur \'bish-ən-ˌpu̇(ə)r\. Town, S cen. Manipur, NE India, ab. 20 m. SSW of Imphal; severe fighting near here Apr. 1944 in which Japanese advance was stopped.

Bish·nu·pur \'bish-nə-ˌpu̇(ə)r\. Town, West Bengal, NE India, 75 m. NW of Calcutta; pop. (1961c) 30,958; in ancient times an important city.

Bish·op \'bish-əp\. 1 City, Inyo co., E California, in Owens river valley 35 m. W of Nevada border; pop. (1970c) 3498; stock raising and tungsten mining.

2 Town, Nueces co., S Texas, 30 m. SW of Corpus Christi; pop. (1970c) 3466.

Bishop and Clerks \-'klärks\. Group of small rocky islands in St. George's Channel, off Pembrokeshire, SW coast of Wales; ab. 5 m. W of St. David's Head.

Bishop Auck·land \ˌbish-ə-'pȯ-klənd\. Urban district, Durham, N England, at confluence of Wear and Gaunless rivers 23 m. S of Newcastle upon Tyne; pop. (1971p) 33,-292; grammar school (1605).

Bish·op's Falls \ˌbish-əps-\. 1 Waterfall in Exploits river, cen. Newfoundland, Canada, ab. 14 m. from its mouth. 2 Lumber town on Exploits river near the falls; pop. (1971p) 4108; pulp and paper mills.

Bishop's Stort·ford \ˌbish-əp(s)-ˈstȯ(ə)r-fərd\. Urban district, Hertfordshire, SE England, on the Stort 28 m. NNE of London; pop. (1971p) 22,084.

Bishop's Wearmouth. See SUNDERLAND.

Bish·op·ville \ˈbish-əp-ˌvil, -vəl\. Town, ⊗ of Lee co., NE cen. South Carolina, 22 m. NNE of Sumter; pop. (1970c) 3404; cottonseed products, lumber.

Bī·si·tūn *or* **Bi·su·tun** \ˌbē-sə-ˈtün\ *or* **Be·his·tun** \ˌbā-his-\. Ruined town in W Iran, Lorestān prov., 22 m. E of Kermānshāhan; on limestone cliff above present village is monument of Darius the Great consisting of sculptures in relief and trilingual (cuneiform) inscriptions, the "Rosetta Stone of Asia"; decipherment by Henry Rawlinson in 1846 furnished key to our knowledge of Assyrian and Babylonian records.

Bisk *or* **Biisk** \ˈbisk, ˈbēsk\. Town, E Altai Krai, Russian S.F.S.R., U.S.S.R., on the Biya river near its junction with the Katun; pop. (1970p) 186,000; electric furnaces; food processing.

Bis·kra \ˈbis-krə, -(ˌ)krä\. Commune, Batna dept., NE Algeria, at an oasis ab. 120 m. SSW of Constantine; pop. (1966c) 53,177; dates, olives; winter resort; in fort here French garrison massacred by Arabs May 12, 1844.

Bis·ley \ˈbiz-lē\. Village, Surrey, S England, ab. 29 m. SW of London and ab. 7 m. NE of Aldershot; pop. (1961c) 1165; scene since 1890 of annual meet of National Rifle Association.

Bis·marck \ˈbiz-ˌmärk\. City, ✱ of North Dakota and ⊗ of Burleigh co., S cen. North Dakota, on Missouri river; pop. (1970c) 34,703; trading center in spring wheat region; farm machinery; oil refinery; Bismarck Junior Coll. (1939), Mary Coll. (1959); Kennedy Memorial Center (dedicated 1971). First settled 1873; became territorial capital 1883, state capital 1889.

Bismarck Archipelago. Island group in W Pacific Ocean N of E end of island of New Guinea; 19,173 sq. m.; pop. (1961c) 176,471; includes islands of New Britain, New Ireland, New Hanover, Admiralty Is., and about 200 other islands and islets; part of Papua New Guinea. Islands are of volcanic origin with active volcanoes, esp. on New Britain; main part of archipelago is circular in form enclosing extensive Bismarck Sea and lies bet. 1° and 6°20'S lat. and 145° and 154°E long.; natives mainly Melanesians, with many different languages; chief products copra, cocoa, and shellfish.

History: First visited in early part of 17th cent.; coasts of New Britain explored by Dampier 1700 and after 1767 other islands by Carteret and others. Proclaimed German protectorate 1884. Occupied by Australians 1914 and included in mandate (Trust Territory of New Guinea) to Australia 1920. Seized by Japanese Jan. 1942; Rabaul, Gasmata, Kavieng frequently bombed by Allied forces 1943–44; parts of New Britain and the Admiralty Is. seized 1944 but Japanese forces in many places bypassed in advance of Allies to Philippines.

Bismarckburg. See KASANGA.

Bismarck Range. Mountain range, Papua New Guinea, E New Guinea I.; highest peak Mt. Wilhelm 14,762 ft.

Bismarck Sea. Part of the W Pacific Ocean enclosed by the islands of the Bismarck Archipelago, ab. 500 m. across from E to W. In battle of Bismarck Sea Mar. 2–3, 1943 Allied planes completely destroyed Japanese fleet of 10 warships, 12 transports, 63 planes.

Bisnulok. See PHITSANULOK.

Bi·son \ˈbīs-ᵊn\. Town, ⊗ of Perkins co., NW South Dakota; pop. (1970c) 406.

Bissagos Islands. See BIJAGÓS, ARQUIPÉLAGO DOS.

Bis·sau *or* **Bis·são** \bis-ˈaù(ⁿ)\. Seaport, ✱ of Portuguese Guinea, W Africa; pop. (1970p) 62,101.

Bis·ti·neau, Lake \-ˈbis-tə-ˌnō\. Lake on boundary bet. Bienville and Bossier parishes, NW Louisiana; ab. 30 m. long and 2 m. wide; navigable for steamboats; connected by outlet stream S with Red river.

Bis·tri·ţa *or* **Bis·tri·tsa** \ˈbēs-trət-ˌsä\. 1 River, NE Romania; 185 m. long; rises in SE Carpathian Mts., flows SE into Siretul river near Bacău in Moldavia.

2 *or Hung.* **Besz·ter·cze** \ˈbes-tərt-ˌsä\. River, N Romania; ab. 60 m. long; an upper tributary of the Someşul.

3 City, ⊗ of Bistriţa-Năsăud co., Romania, on Bristriţa river ab. 40 m. N of Tîrgu-Mureş; pop. (1969e) 23,752; founded by German colonists in 12th cent.

Bistriţa–Nă·să·ud \-ˌnə-sə-ˈüd\. County of N Romania. See table at ROMANIA.

Bisutun. See BĪSITŪN.

Bitche \ˈbēch\ *or Ger.* **Bitsch** \ˈbich\. Commune, Moselle dept., NE France, near Saar border 60 m. NW of Strasbourg; pop. (1962e) 6800. Citadel on rocky hill dominating the town defended in several wars; in World War II a strong point of German defense, taken by U.S. troops Jan. 1945.

Bi·thyn·ia \bə-ˈthin-ē-ə\. Ancient country in NW Asia Minor, bordering on the Propontis and Euxine and adjoining Paphlagonia on the E and Galatia, Phrygia, and Mysia on the S. Mountainous and well-forested; on the W indented by two inlets and crossed by the Sangarius (*or mod.* Sakarya) river. Settled by a Thracian tribe. Its first king, Nicomedes I, founded Nicomedia (*or mod.* İzmit) as capital 264 B.C.; prosperous until overcome by Mithridates of Pontus; became Roman province 74 B.C. with varying boundaries; known as **Bithynia et Pon·tus** \-et-ˈpänt-əs\ 98–117 A.D.; under Byzantine Empire divided into two parts.

Bithynium. See CLAUDIOPOLIS.

Bit·lis \bit-ˈlēs\. 1 Province of E Turkey, Asia. See table at TURKEY.

2 Commercial and manufacturing town, its ✱, ab. 16 m. SW of Lake Van; pop. (1965c) 18,725; at altitude 4700 ft.

Bi·to·la \ˈbēt-ᵊl-ˌyä\ *or Serbo-Croat.* **Bi·tolj** \ˈbē-tōl(-yə), -tȯi\ *or* **Mo·nas·tir** \ˌmän-ə-ˈsti(ə)r\. City, Macedonia, S Yugoslavia; pop. (1971p) 65,851; alt. 2019 ft.; rubber products, carpets; founded by Slavs 1014 near ancient **Her·a·clea Lyn·ces·tis** \ˌher-ə-ˌklē-ə-lin-ˈses-təs\; passed to Turks 1383 and strengthened by them about 1820; taken from Turks in Second Balkan War and assigned to Serbia by Treaty of Bucharest 1913. In World War I taken 1915 by Bulgaria but retaken by Allies; again captured 1941 by Bulgarians in World War II.

Bi·ton·to \bi-ˈtȯn-(ˌ)tō\ *or anc.* **Bu·tun·tum** \byü-ˈtənt-əm\. Commune, Bari prov., Apulia, SE Italy, 11 m. W of Bari; pop. (1968e) 41,749; 12th cent. Romanesque cathedral.

Bitsch. See BITCHE.

Bit·ter·feld \ˈbit-ər-ˌfelt\. Industrial city, Halle dist., East Germany, 45 m. SE of Magdeburg; pop. (1970e) 28,964; lignite works; chemicals, machinery; aluminum, graphite, magnesium. Founded 1143; conquered by landgrave Dietrich von Meissen 1476; under Saxon rule; passed to Prussia 1815.

Bit·ter·fon·tein \ˈbit-ər-ˌfän-ˌtān\. Town, W Cape Province, Rep. of South Africa, 205 m. N of Cape Town.

Bit·ter Lakes \ˈbit-ər-\. Two lakes, Isthmus of Suez, Egypt, just N of Suez; connected and traversed by the Suez Canal (23 m. across). **Great Bitter Lake** (*or Arab.* **Al–Bu·hay·rah al–Mur·rah al–Ku·brā** \ˌal-bu̇-ˈhī-rə-al-ˈmu̇r-ə-al-ˈku̇b-(ˌ)rä\) and **Little Bitter Lake** (*or Arab.* **Al–Buhayrah al–Murrah as–Su·ghrā** \-as-ˈsu̇g(ˌ)rä\). Originally in ancient bed of Red Sea; in modern times marshy depressions until filled by the cutting of the canal.

Bit·ter·root *or* **Bitter Root** \ˈbit-ə(r)-ˌrüt, -ˌru̇t\. River, W Montana; rises in S Ravalli co., flows N and joins Clark Fork near Missoula in cen. Missoula co.

Bitterroot Range *or* **Bitterroot Mountains** *also* **Bitter Root Range** *or* **Bitter Root Mountains.** A range of the Rocky Mts. extending along the Idaho-Montana boundary; 300 m. long; highest point Scott Peak 11,393 ft.; pierced by **Bitterroot Tunnel,** a railroad tunnel nearly 2 m. long.

Biv·ouac Peak \ˌbiv-ˌwak-, -ə-ˌwak-\. Mountain in N Grand Teton National Park, NW Wyoming; 11,045 ft.

Bi·wa \ˈbē-(ˌ)wä\ *or* **Omi** \ˈō-mē\. Lake in W cen. Honshū, Japan, NE of Kyōto; 40 m. long and 12 m. wide; 260 sq. m.; largest lake in Japan; altitude 285 ft.; noted for its scenic beauty and famous in Japanese legends; its outlet is the Yodo.

Bix·by \ˈbiks-bē\. Town, Tulsa co., NE Oklahoma, 15 m. SE of Tulsa; pop. (1970c) 3973; diversified agriculture; oil wells.

Bixschoote. See BIKSCHOTE.

Bi·ya \ˈbē-(y)ə\. River, Gorno-Altai Autonomous Oblast, Russian S.F.S.R., U.S.S.R.; 190 m. long; flows NW, joins the Katun to form the Ob.

Bi·ya·la \bi-ˈyal-ə\. Town, Kafr al-Sheikh gov., Egypt, ab. 14 m. NW of Al-Mansūra; pop. (1966c) 33,000.

Bi·zerte \bə-ˈzərt-ē, bi-ˈze(ə)rt\ *or* **Bi·zer·ta** \bə-ˈzərt-ə\ *or anc.* **Hip·po Za·ry·tus** \ˈhip-(ˌ)ō-zə-ˈrīt-əs\. Fortified seaport, N Tunisia, N Africa; pop. (1966c) 51,708; fishing, oil refining; cement factory, ship repairing yards; northernmost town in Africa; threefold harbor: outer harbor on Mediterranean with breakwater and two jetties, inner harbor (Bay of Sebra) connected with outer by canal, and Lake Bizerte (*q.v.*) with well-developed naval port and arsenal (Sidi Abdallah); military post, Menzel Bourguiba, on S shore of lake.

History: In early times a Roman colony; taken by Arabs 7th cent.; subject for many years to Tunis and Constantine and scene of frequent revolts. Harbor fell into neglect but after French seizure in 1881, remade and opened 1895. In World War II captured by Allies May 7–9, 1943; French naval base evacuated 1963.

Bizerte, Lake *or* **Lake Bizerta.** Deep-water lagoon, forming a landlocked harbor for Bizerte (*q.v.*); 42 sq. m.

Bjarg·tan·gar, Cape \-ˌbyärg-ˈtaŋ-ər\. Cape, W Iceland, N of Breidha Fjord.

Bje·lo·var \ˈbyel-ō-ˌvär\ *also* **Bel·o·var** \ˈbel-ə-ˌvär\. Town, Croatia, N Yugoslavia, 43 m. E of Zagreb; pop. (1965e) 18,000.

Bjeshkët e Nemuna. See NORTH ALBANIAN ALPS.

Björkö \ˈbyər-ˌkər\. Swedish name of Primorsk, fortress and outer port of Vyborg, U.S.S.R. (formerly Viipuri, Finland); scene of signing of treaty July 24, 1905 bet. William II of Germany and Nicholas II of Russia, in an unsuccessful attempt to form a coalition against Great Britain. See PRIMORSK.

Björneborg. See PORI.

Black \ˈblak\. **1** River, E cen. Louisiana; 101 m. long; formed by confluence of Ouachita and Tensas rivers; flows S into Red river forming section of boundary bet. Catahoula and Concordia parishes, E cen. Louisiana.

2 River, SE Missouri and NE Arkansas; 280 m. long; navigable 100 m.; rises in NE Reynolds co., SE Missouri, flows S into White river on boundary of Jackson and Independence cos., NE cen. Arkansas.

3 River, N cen. New York; 120 m. long; navigable for 40 m.; rises in Herkimer co., flows W and NW into Lake Ontario near Watertown, Jefferson co.

4 River, SE North Carolina; 150 m. long; flows S from Sampson co. into Cape Fear river ab. 10 m. above Wilmington.

5 River, E South Carolina; rises in Sumter co., flows SE into Winyah Bay in E Georgetown co.

6 River, N Vermont; rises in S Orleans co., flows N into Lake Memphremagog.

7 River, SE Vermont; 40 m. long; flows S and SE in Windsor co. into Connecticut river.

8 River, W cen. Wisconsin; 160 m. long; rises in Taylor co., flows SW into Mississippi river at La Crosse.

9 *or in China* **Li–hsien** \ˌlē-shē-ˈen\ *or in Vietnam* **Song Da** \ˈsòŋ-ˈdä\. River, SE Asia; ab. 500 m. long; rises in cen. Yunnan, China, flowing SE and uniting with the Red river near Sontay, North Vietnam.

Black Belt. A strip of rolling prairie land extending across cen. Alabama and Mississippi, with black clayey soil, good for growing cotton.

Black Broth·ers \-ˈbrət͟h-ərz\. Mountain, Yancey co., W North Carolina; 6620 ft.

Black·burn \ˈblak-(ˌ)bərn\. County borough, Lancashire, NW England, 21 m. NNW of Manchester; pop. (1971p) 101,672; textiles, electrical equipment; technical coll. (1954); coalfields nearby.

Blackburn, Mount. Mountain, Wrangell Mts., SE Alaska, 120 m. NE of mouth of Copper river; 16,390 ft.

Black Canyon. **1** Canyon of the Colorado river bet. Arizona and Nevada; ab. 15 m. long; site of Boulder Canyon project ab. 25 m. SE of Las Vegas, Nevada. See *Hoover Dam* at UNITED STATES, *Dams and Reservoirs.*

2 Canyon of the Gunnison river in NE Montrose co., W Colorado, where the river cuts through granite, gneiss, and black schist; ab. 50 m. long, averages 1300 ft. wide, walls 3000 ft. at highest point; most picturesque part is now the **Black Canyon of the Gunnison National Monument.** See UNITED STATES, *National Monuments.*

Black Country. The Midland districts of S Staffordshire and N Warwickshire, England — so called because of the grime from industrial pollutants.

Black Di·a·mond \-ˈdī-(ə-)mənd\. Town, King co., W cen. Washington, ab. 22 m. E of Tacoma; pop. (1970c) 1160.

Black Dome. Peak in the Catskill Mts., Greene co., SE New York; 3990 ft.

Black Down. See MENDIP HILLS.

Black·foot \ˈblak-ˌfu̇t\. **1** River, SE Idaho; ab. 100 m. long; flows out of **Blackfoot River Reservoir,** Caribou co., NW and W into Snake river in cen. Bingham co.

2 City, ⊗ of Bingham co., SE Idaho, 23 m. N of Pocatello; pop. (1970c) 8716; farm machinery; sugar beets.

Blackfoot Mountain. Peak in cen. Glacier National Park, NW Montana, SW of St. Mary Lakes; 9597 ft.; has glacier on N slope.

Black·ford \ˈblak-fərd\. County in Indiana. See table at INDIANA.

Black Forest *or Ger.* **Schwarz·wald** \ˈshfärts-ˌvält, ˈshwȯrt-swȯld\. Mountainous region, Baden-Württemberg, West Germany, along E bank of upper Rhine from the Neckar to the Swiss border; highest peak Feldberg 4905 ft.; higher parts thickly forested; has many lakes and mineral springs; contains sources of Neckar and Danube rivers; tourist resort.

Black Hawk \ˈblak-ˌhȯk\. County in Iowa. See table at IOWA.

Black·head \ˈblak-ˌhed\. **1** Peak, San Juan Mts., E Archuleta co., S Colorado; 12,500 ft.

2 Cape on NE coast of Northern Ireland, on N side of entrance to Belfast Lough; lighthouse.

Black Head \ˈblak-ˌhed\. Cape on W coast of Eire, on S side of entrance to Galway Bay.

Black Head Peak. Peak in the Catskill Mts., Greene co., SE New York; 3940 ft.

Black·heath \ˈblak-ˌhēth\. Open common and residential district, SE London, England, mainly in Lewisham and Greenwich boroughs S of the Thames; area of common 267 acres; headquarters of Kentish rebels 1381 under Wat Tyler and again 1450 under Jack Cade; later notorious for its highwaymen. Here golf first introduced into England 1608.

Black Hills. Group of mountains in W South Dakota and NE Wyoming; total area ab. 6000 sq. m.; contains gold, lead, and other mineral deposits; highest mountain 7242 ft.

Harney Peak, South Dakota; drained chiefly by the Belle Fourche and S fork of Cheyenne river.

Blackhope Scar. See MOORFOOT HILLS.

Black Lake. 1 Lake, N Natchitoches parish, NW cen. Louisiana; ab. 13 m. long; outlet is to Red river; part of a large fish and game preserve.

2 Lake, W St. Lawrence co., N New York; ab. 20 m. long; outlet from N end into Oswegatchie river.

3 Town, Megantic co., S Quebec, Canada, 5 m. SSW of Thetford Mines; pop. (1971p) 4140; asbestos mines.

Black Me·sa \-'mā-sə\. Elevation in Cimarron co., extreme NW Oklahoma; 4973 ft.; highest point in the state.

Black·more, Mount \-'blak-ˌmō(ə)r, -ˌmȯ(ə)r\. Peak, cen. Gallatin co., S Montana; 10,196 ft.

Black Mountain. 1 Peak, Dawson and Gilmer cos., N Georgia; 3600 ft.

2 Mountain, Harlan co., SE Kentucky; 4145 ft.; highest peak in the state.

3 Peak, N Grant co., SW New Mexico; 9020 ft.

4 Town, Buncombe co., W North Carolina, 13 m. E of Asheville; pop. (1970c) 3204; summer tourist center.

Black Mountains. 1 Ridge in W Mohave co., NW cen. Arizona, along E bank of Colorado river.

2 Range of Blue Ridge Mts., chiefly in Yancey and Buncombe cos., in W North Carolina; highest peak Mount Mitchell 6684 ft.

3 Range in Brecknockshire, SE Wales, E of the Usk river; highest peak 2660 ft.

Black Pine Peak. Mountain, SE Cassia co., S Idaho; 9385 ft.

Black·pool \'blak-ˌpül\. County borough, Lancashire, NW England, on Irish Sea 28 m. N of Liverpool; pop. (1971p) 151,311; seaside pleasure resort; prefabricated joinery.

Black River. 1 Name of several rivers. See BLACK.

2 Town on SW coast of Jamaica; pop. (1960c) 3077.

Black River Falls. City, ⊗ of Jackson co., W cen. Wisconsin, on falls of Black river 25 m. N of Sparta; pop. (1970c) 3273; lumber and grist mills; dairying; poultry.

Black·rock \'blak-ˌräk\. Residential urban district, co. Dublin, E Eire; a SE suburb of Dublin on the coast near Dun Laoghaire.

Black Rock Desert. Alkaline sink in NW Nevada; ab. 70 m. long and 20 m. wide; 1000 sq. m.; **Black Rock Range** (highest point Pahute Peak 8618 ft.) extends along its W side, in Humboldt co.

Blacks·burg \'blaks-ˌbərg\. 1 Town, Cherokee co., N South Carolina, 27 m. ENE of Spartanburg; pop. (1970c) 1977.

2 Town, Montgomery co., W Virginia, 28 m. W of Roanoke; pop. (1970c) 9384; Virginia Polytechnic Inst. (1872).

Black Sea *also* **Eux·ine Sea** \'yük-sən-, -(ˌ)sīn-\ *or Russ.* **Cher·no·ye Mo·re** \ˌchȯr-nə-yə-'mȯr-yə\; *anc.* **Pon·tus** *or* **Pon·tus Eux·i·nus** \ˌpän-təs-yük-'sī-nəs\. Sea bet. Europe and Asia; ab. 180,000 sq. m.; max. depth 7250 ft.; connected with Aegean Sea through the Bosporus, Sea of Marmara, and Dardanelles, and with the Sea of Azov, its N arm, by Kerch Strait; receives many rivers, esp.: Danube, Dniester, Bug, Dnieper, Kuban (of Europe); Kızıl Irmak and Sakarya (of Turkey in Asia); the Sea of Azov receives the Don.

Black·shear \'blak-ˌshi(ə)r\. City, ⊗ of Pierce co., SE Georgia, 10 m. NE of Waycross; pop. (1970c) 2624.

Black·sod Bay \ˌblak-ˌsäd-\. Inlet of Atlantic Ocean on W coast of Eire, S of Erris Head, enclosed on the W by Mullet penin.

Black·stock Knob \ˌblak-ˌstäk-\. Peak, Buncombe co., W North Carolina; 6386 ft.

Black·stone \'blak-ˌstōn\. 1 River, S cen. Massachusetts and NE Rhode Island; 40 m. long; rises in S cen. Worcester co., Mass., flows SE across NE corner of Rhode Island, becomes the Sekonk at Pawtucket.

2 Town, Worcester co., cen. Massachusetts, 20 m. SE of Worcester; pop. (1970c) 6566.

3 Town, Nottoway co., S cen. Virginia, 36 m. WSW of Petersburg; pop. (1970c) 3412; tobacco market.

Black Stream. See JAPAN CURRENT.

Black·town \'blak-ˌtau̇n\. Town, E New South Wales, SE Australia, on railroad 18 m. NW of Sydney.

Black Volta. See VOLTA, BLACK.

Black War·ri·or \-'wȯr-yər, -'wȯr-ē-ər, -'wär-\. Navigable river, cen. Alabama; 178 m. long; formed by confluence of Locust and Mulberry forks in Jefferson co., flows SW, through coalfields, into Tombigbee river near Demopolis; furnishes water power above Tuscaloosa.

Black·wa·ter \'blak-ˌwȯt-ər, -ˌwät-\. 1 River, W cen. Missouri; ab. 85 m. long; rises in W Johnson co., flows E into Missouri river in N Cooper co.

2 River, SE Virginia; rises in Prince George co., joins Nottoway river on North Carolina boundary to form the Chowan.

3 River, S cen. British Columbia, Canada; ab. 130 m. long; flows E into Fraser river.

4 River, S Eire; 100 m. long; rises 16 m. NE of Killarney, flows E across co. Cork, then S to Youghal Bay.

5 River, co. Meath, E Eire; ab. 40 m. long; flows SE from co. Cavan into the Boyne river at Navan.

6 River, W Essex co., SE England; 40 m. long; rises near Saffron Walden and flows SE into the North Sea.

7 River, SW cen. Northern Ireland; 50 m. long; rises in co. Tyrone and flows along boundary bet. cos. Tyrone and Armagh into SW Lough Neagh.

Blackwater Falls. Falls in Blackwater river (tributary of Cheat river), Tucker co., NE West Virginia, 63 ft. high; above **Blackwater Canyon** (gorge ab. 10 m. long with rugged walls 1000 ft. high) in **Blackwater Falls State Park,** at N end of Monongahela National Forest.

Black·well \'blak-ˌwel\. City, Kay co., N Oklahoma; pop. (1970c) 8645; oil refining, zinc smelting. See WELFARE IS.

Blackwells Island. See WELFARE ISLAND.

Bla·den \'blā-dən\. County in North Carolina. See table at NORTH CAROLINA.

Bla·dens·burg \ˌblā-dənz-ˌbərg\. Town, Prince Georges co., S central Maryland, 7 m. ENE of Washington; pop. (1970c) 7488; site of battle Aug. 21, 1814 in which American defeat by British resulted in the burning of most of the public buildings of Washington Aug. 24–25, 1814.

Blaen·av·on \blīn-'av-ən\. Urban district, Monmouthshire, SE Wales, 31 m. NW of Bristol; pop. (1971p) 7182.

Bla·go·ev·grad \blä-'gȯ-yəf-ˌgräd\. 1 Province of SW Bulgaria. See table at BULGARIA.

2 Town, its ✱; pop. (1968e) 35,334; tobacco processing; mineral springs.

Bla·go·vesh·chensk \ˌbläg-ə-'vesh-ˌ(ch)en(t)sk\. City, ✱ of Amur Oblast, Russian S.F.S.R., U.S.S.R., on Amur river, near junction with Zeya river; pop. (1970p) 128,000; food processing; founded 1856 by Nikolai Muraviëv; scene of Russo-Japanese naval incident 1937; base for Soviet advances into Manchuria Aug. 1945.

Blaina. See NANTYGLO AND BLAINA.

Blaine \'blān\. 1 Name of counties in four states of the U.S. See tables at IDAHO, MONTANA, NEBRASKA, OKLAHOMA.

2 City, Anoka and Ramsey cos., Minnesota, NW of Minneapolis; pop. (1970c) 20,640.

3 City and port of entry, Whatcom co., NW Washington, near Canadian boundary 20 m. NNW of Bellingham; pop. (1970c) 1955; in farming region; tourist center.

Blair \'bla(ə)r, 'ble(ə)r\. 1 County in Pennsylvania. See table at PENNSYLVANIA.

2 City, ⊗ of Washington co., E Nebraska, on Missouri river 22 m. N of Omaha; pop. (1970c) 6106; trade center in agricultural region; Dana Coll. (1884).

Blair·more \ˈbla(ə)r-mōər, ˈble(ə)r-, -mȯ(ə)r\. Coal-mining town, S Alberta, Canada, near British Columbia border 72 m. W of Lethbridge; pop. (1971p) 2041.

Blairs·ville \ˈbla(ə)rz-ˌvil, ˈble(ə)rz-\. 1 Town, ⊗ of Union co., N Georgia; pop. (1970c) 491.
2 Borough, Indiana co., W cen. Pennsylvania, on Conemaugh river 21 m. W of Johnstown; pop. (1970c) 4411.

Bla·kang Ma·ti \ˌbläk-äŋ-ˈmät-ē\. Fortified island in Singapore Strait just SSW of Singapore; ab. 2 m. long; part of the defense of Singapore harbor.

Blake·ly \ˈblā-klē\. 1 City, ⊗ of Early co., SW Georgia, 47 m. WSW of Albany; pop. (1970c) 5267; founded 1821.
2 Borough, Lackawanna co., NE Pennsylvania, 7 m. NE of Scranton; pop. (1970c) 6391; suburb of Scranton; coal.

Blake Point \ˈblāk-\. Point at NE extremity of Isle Royale, Michigan, NW Lake Superior.

Blam·bang·an Peninsula \blam-ˌbäŋ-ən-\. Narrow strip of land forming southernmost point of Java, Indonesia, bet. S end of Bali Strait and Indian Ocean.

Blanc, Cape \-ˈblaŋk, -ˈblä^{n}\. 1 *or* **Cape Blan·co** \-ˈblaŋ-(ˌ)kō\. Cape on NW coast of Africa; a narrow peninsula extending S into Atlantic Ocean; bisected by the boundary bet. Spanish Sahara and Mauritania.
2 Cape on N tip of Tunisia, N Africa, 37°20′N, 9°50′E.

Blanc, Mont \mō^{n}-ˈblä^{n}\ *or Ital.* **Mon·te Bian·co** \ˌmȯn-tē-bē-ˈäŋ-(ˌ)kō\. Highest mountain of the Alps, Savoy Alps, Haute-Savoie dept., SE France, on Italian border; 15,771 ft. Beneath it is **Mont Blanc Tunnel** (7½ m.) connecting Chamonix-Mont-Blanc, France, with Courmayeur, Italy; longest vehicular tunnel in the world.

Blan·ca, La·gu·na \lə-ˌgü-nə-ˈbläŋ-kə\. Large freshwater lake in extreme S Chile, E of Skyring Water.

Blanca Peak \ˌblaŋ-kə-\. Mountain, Castilla, Huerfano, and Alamosa cos., S Colorado; 14,317 ft.; highest peak in the Sangre de Cristo Mts.

Blanche Bay \ˈblanch-\. Inlet of Pacific Ocean on NE coast of New Britain I., Bismarck Archipelago; its inner part is site of Rabaul.

Blanche Harbour. Protected body of water in Treasury Is., S of Bougainville I., British Solomon Is., bet. Mono and Stirling Is.; affords good anchorage.

Blan·ches·ter \ˈblan-ˌches-tər\. Industrial village, Clinton co., SW Ohio, 29 m. ENE of Cincinnati; pop. (1970c) 3080; foundries; settled 1832.

Blanc–Mesnil, Le. See LE BLANC-MESNIL.

Blanc–Nez \ˈblä^{n}-ˈnā\. White chalk cliff forming a cape on Strait of Dover, N France, 5 m. SW of Calais; its companion cape is Gris-Nez (*q.v.*).

Blan·co \ˈblaŋ-(ˌ)kō\. County in Texas. See table at TEXAS.

Blanco \ˈbläŋ-(ˌ)kō\. 1 River, E Bolivia; 330 m. long.
2 River, W Honduras; ab. 45 m. long; flows out of Lake Yojoa (*q.v.*) into the Ulúa river.

Blanco, Cape \-ˈblaŋ-(ˌ)kō\. Cape on NW coast of Curry co., SW corner of Oregon; westernmost point of Oregon, 42°50′N, 124°34′W.

Blanco, Cape \-ˈbläŋ-(ˌ)kō\. 1 Cape, Africa. See BLANC, CAPE 1.
2 Cape at S extremity of Nicoya Penin., on W coast of Costa Rica, at the entrance to the Gulf of Nicoya.
3 Cape at extreme NW tip of Peru.

Blanco, Pi·co \ˌpē-kō-ˈbläŋ-(ˌ)kō\. Mountain, SE Costa Rica, in the Cordillera de Talamanca; 11,693 ft.

Blanc Sa·blon \ˌblä^{n}-sȧ-ˈblō^{n}\. Village, E Quebec, Canada, on **Blanc Sablon Bay,** inlet at S end of Strait of Belle Isle on boundary bet. Labrador and Quebec.

Bland \ˈbland\. 1 County in W Virginia. See table at VIRGINIA.
2 Village, its ⊗.

Blan·ken·ber·ge \ˈbläŋ-kən-ˌbər-gə, -ˌber-k̲ə\. Commune, West Flanders prov., NW Belgium; pop. (1969e) 10,230; resort.

Blan·ken·burg *or* **Blankenburg am Harz** \ˈbläŋ-kən-ˌbərg-äm-ˈhärts, -ˌbu̇(ə)rg-\. City, Magdeburg dist., East Germany, 35 m. SW of Magdeburg; pop. (1970e) 19,603; wooden products; founded c. 1200.

Blan·quil·la \bläŋ-ˈkē-yə\. Venezuelan island in Caribbean Sea 74 m. NNE of La Tortuga I.

Blan·tyre \blan-ˈtī(ə)r\. City, Shire Highlands, S Malawi, SE Africa; pop. (1971e) 169,000; approx. alt. 3600 ft.; combined with Limbe forming single municipality 1956; fruit canning, distilling; cement, textiles; chief commercial center of Malawi; founded 1876.

Blar·ney \ˈblär-nē\. Town, cen. co. Cork, SW Eire, 4 m. NW of Cork; pop. (1966c) 932; in its 15th cent. Blarney Castle is the "Blarney stone," which is said to make anyone who kisses it proficient in blarney (i.e., smooth wheedling talk or flattery).

Blas·dell \ˈbläz-(ˌ)del\. Village, Erie co., W New York, on Lake Erie 7 m. S of Buffalo; pop. (1970c) 3910.

Blas·ket Islands \ˈblas-kət-\. Group of small islands in co. Kerry, off SW coast of Eire, N of entrance to Dingle Bay; largest is Great Blasket.

Blå·vand, Cape \-ˈblȯ-ˌvän\ *or Dan.* **Blå·vands Huk** \ˈblȯ-ˌvän(t)s-ˌhu̇k\. Cape on W cen. coast of Jutland penin., Denmark.

Bla·vet \bla-ˈvā\. River, Brittany, NW France; 87 m. long; rises in Côtes-du-Nord dept., flows SSW to the Bay of Biscay; its estuary forms the harbor of Lorient.

Blaw·nox \ˈblȯ-ˈnäks\. Industrial borough, Allegheny co., SW Pennsylvania, on Allegheny river 9 m. ENE of Pittsburgh; pop. (1970c) 1907; steel and iron manufactures.

Blay·don \ˈblād-ᵊn\. Urban district, Durham, N England, on the Tyne 5 m. W of Newcastle upon Tyne; pop. (1971p) 32,018; iron and steel manufactures, brick kilns; coal.

Bleck·ley \ˈblek-lē\. County in Georgia. See table at GEORGIA.

Bled \ˈbled\. Resort village in mountains of NW Yugoslavia ab. 30 m. NW of Ljubljana.

Bled·soe \ˈbled-(ˌ)sō\. County in Tennessee. See table at TENNESSEE.

Ble·kinge \ˈblā-kiŋ-ə\. County of S Sweden. See table at SWEDEN.

Blencathara. See SADDLEBACK.

Blen·heim \ˈblen-əm\. 1 Town, Kent co., SE Ontario, Canada, 10 m. SE of Chatham; pop. (1971p) 3483.
2 Borough, NE South I., New Zealand; pop. (1968e) 13,950; harbor for smaller vessels.
3 *Eng. and French form of German* **Blind·heim** \ˈblint-ˌhīm\. Village on Danube, W Bavaria, West Germany, 23 m. NNW of Augsburg; pop. (1961e) 900; scene of victory Aug. 13, 1704 of English under Marlborough and Prince Eugene over French and Bavarians under Marshals Tallard and Marsin in War of Spanish Succession; called also battle of Höchstädt (*q.v.*).

Blenheim Park. Civil parish, orig. seat (**Blenheim Palace**) of duke of Marlborough near Woodstock, Oxfordshire, cen. England; granted to duke by government in Queen Anne's reign.

Blen·ner·has·sett Island \ˌblen-ər-ˌhas-ət-\. Island in Ohio river 2 m. below Parkersburg, West Virginia; famous as meeting place 1805 of Aaron Burr and Harman Blennerhassett who had purchased part of island 1798.

Blesae. See BLOIS.

Bletch·ley \ˈblech-lē\. Urban district, Buckinghamshire, SE cen. England, 43 m. NW of London; pop. (1971p) 30,608; electrical engineering; Open Univ. (1969).

Blibba. See BLITTA.

Bli·da \ˈblēd-ə\. City, Alger dept., N Algeria, ab. 10 m. SW of the city of Algiers; pop. (1966c) 85,683; situated on edge of a plain at base of Maritime Atlas Mts.; active trade in oranges and flour. Dates from 16th cent.; important under the Turks; airfield taken by U.S. Nov. 8, 1942.

Blindheim. See BLENHEIM 3.

Blind River \ˌblīnd-\. Town and port, Algoma dist., S Ontario, Canada, on North Channel at mouth of Mississagi river 70 m. E of Sault Ste. Marie; pop. (1971p) 3393; railroad town in mining district; lumber; paper mills.

Bliss·field \'blis-,fēld\. Village, Lenawee co., S Michigan, 32 m. S of Ann Arbor; pop. (1970c) 2753.

Bli·tar \'blē-,tär\. Town East Java prov., Indonesia, ab. 20 m. SE of Kediri; pop. (1961c) 62,972.

Blit·ta \'blē-tə\ *or formerly* **Blib·ba** \'blib-ə\. Town, Togo, W Africa, on railroad ab. 143 m. N of Lomé.

Block Island \,bläk-\. 1 Island in Atlantic Ocean at E entrance to Long Island Sound, ab. 9 m. SW of Point Judith, Rhode Island; 7 m. long, 3½ m. wide; ab. 11 sq. m.; part of Washington co., Rhode Island; coextensive with town of New Shoreham; summer resort and deep-sea fishing center; has two good harbors and two lighthouses. First settlement 1661; admitted to the colony 1664.

2 Village in town of New Shoreham, Washington co., SE Rhode Island; resort.

Block Island Sound. Body of water bet. Washington co., S Rhode Island and Block I., connecting Atlantic Ocean on E with Long Island Sound on W.

Bloe·men·daal \'blü-mən-,däl\. Commune, North Holland prov., W Netherlands, just N of Haarlem; pop. (1970e) 19,253; steel.

Bloem·fon·tein \'blüm-,fän-,tān\. City, ✱ of Orange Free State, Rep. of South Africa, 295 m. W of Durban on a tributary of Modder river; pop. (1967e) 146,200; glassware, furniture, plastics; railway workshops; meat canning; Univ. of the Orange Free State (1855, present status 1950); possesses two observatories: Lamont-Hussey (Univ. of Michigan) and Boyden Station of Harvard Observatory; founded 1846.

Bloem·hof \'blüm-,hȯf\. Town, SW Transvaal, NE Rep. of South Africa, on Vaal river 95 m. NNE of Kimberley; pop. (1967e) 5600; diamond mining; cattle.

Blois \blə-'wä\ *or anc.* **Ble·sae** \'blē-(,)sē\. City, Loir-et-Cher dept., N cen. France, on right bank of Loire river 35 m. SW of Orléans; pop. (1968c) 42,264; aircraft, precision instruments, footwear; 17th cent. cathedral; ancient Roman aqueduct. Famous castle rich in historical associations: residence of counts of Blois; became a favorite residence of French kings.

Blom·i·don, Cape \-'bläm-əd-ən\. Cape and promontory on W coast of Nova Scotia, Canada, S of entrance to Minas Basin; 670 ft. high.

Blön·du·ós \'blən-dü-,ōs\. Village, NW Iceland, on E side of Húna Bay; pop. (1970c) 690.

Bło·nie \'blon-yə\. Village, Warszawa prov., Poland, ab. 17 m. W of Warsaw; in World War I in Russian W defense line, taken by Germans July 20, 1915.

Bloods·worth Island \,blədz-(,)wərth-\. Island in Chesapeake Bay, S Dorchester co., Maryland.

Bloody Nose Ridge. Name given by U.S. Marines to Umurbrogol Mt. on Peleliu I., S Palau Is., W Pacific Ocean; scene of severe fighting Sept. 19–26, 1944 which resulted in isolation of Japanese.

Bloo·mer \'blü-mər\. City, Chippewa co., W Wisconsin, 13 m. NNW of Chippewa Falls; pop. (1970c) 3143.

Bloom·field \'blüm-,fēld\. 1 Residential and agricultural town, cen. Hartford co., N Connecticut, NNW of Hartford; pop. (1970c) 18,301; tobacco raising; incorp. 1835.

2 Town, ⊗ of Greene co., SW Indiana, 24 m. WSW of Bloomington; pop. (1970c) 2565; grain, livestock, lumber.

3 City, ⊗ of Davis co., SE Iowa, 18 m. S of Ottumwa; pop. (1970c) 2718; distributing point in sheep-raising region.

4 City, ⊗ of Stoddard co., SE Missouri; pop. (1970c) 1584.

5 Town, Essex co., NE New Jersey, 4 m. NNW of Newark; pop. (1970c) 52,029; electrical appliances, pharmaceuticals, porcelain enamel; Bloomfield Coll. (1868); orig. part of Newark, made separate township 1812.

Bloomfield Hills. City, Oakland co., SE Michigan, 20 m. NW of Detroit; pop. (1970c) 3672.

Bloom·ing·dale \'blü-miŋ-,dāl\. 1 Village, Du Page co., NE Illinois, 27 m. W of Chicago; pop. (1970c) 2974.

2 Borough, Passaic co., N New Jersey, 9 m. WNW of Paterson; pop. (1970c) 7797.

Bloom·ing Grove \,blüm-iŋ-'grōv\ *or formerly* **Cor·si·ca** \'kȯr-si-kə\. Village, Morrow co., cen. Ohio; birthplace of Warren G. Harding, 29th president of the U.S.

Bloom·ing·ton \'blü-,miŋ-tən\. 1 City, ⊗ of McLean co., cen. Illinois, 35 m. ESE of Peoria; pop. (1970c) 39,992; in coal-mining, farming, and dairy region; ironworks; Illinois Wesleyan Univ. (1850).

2 City, ⊗ of Monroe co., S cen. Indiana, 45 m. SW of Indianapolis; pop. (1970c) 42,890; limestone quarries; Indiana Univ. (1820); settled 1815.

3 City, Hennepin co., SE cen. Minnesota, SW of Minneapolis; pop. (1970c) 81,970; Normandale State Junior Coll. (1968).

Blooms·burg \'blümz-,bərg\. Town, ⊗ of Columbia co., E cen. Pennsylvania, 26 m. NNW of Pottsville; pop. (1970c) 11,652; Bloomsburg State Coll. (1839).

Blooms·bury \'blümz-b(ə-)rē, *U.S. also* -,ber-ē\. A central district of London, SE England; British Museum, Univ. of London; once fashionable but now largely a lodginghouse area.

Blo·ra \'blōr-ə, 'blȯr-\. Town, central Java prov., Indonesia, E of Semarang; pop. (1961c) 29,201; in hilly region producing teak.

Blore Heath \,blō(ə)r-, ,blȯ(ə)r-\. Area in Staffordshire, W England, 3 m. ENE of Market Drayton; site of Yorkist victory 1459.

Bloss·burg \'blȯs-,bərg\. Borough, Tioga co., N Pennsylvania, on Tioga river 30 m. N of Williamsport; pop. (1970c) 1753; iron foundries; coal mines.

Blount \'blənt\. Name of counties in two states of the U.S. See tables at ALABAMA and TENNESSEE.

Blounts·town \'blənts-,taun\. City, ⊗ of Calhoun co., NW Florida, on Apalachicola river 47 m. W of Tallahassee; pop. (1970c) 2384; lumber and naval-stores center.

Blu·cher Point \,blü-chər-\. Point of land on NE coast of Huon Penin., Papua New Guinea, New Guinea I.

Blu·denz \'blü-den(t)s\. Town, Vorarlberg, SW Austria, on the Ill river 25 m. S of Bregenz; pop. (1965e) 11,400; tourist resort; castle (1746); given municipal charter 1296.

Blue \'blü\. 1 River, S Indiana; ab. 40 m. long; rises in Washington co., flows S into Ohio river.

2 Upper course of East Fork of the White river, Indiana, to cen. Bartholomew co. See WHITE 3.

Blue Ash \'blü-,ash\. City, Hamilton co., SW Ohio, NE of Cincinnati; pop. (1970c) 8324.

Blue Earth. 1 County in Minnesota. See table at MINNESOTA.

2 City, ⊗ of Faribault co., S Minnesota, 18 m. E of Fairmont; pop. (1970c) 3965; in agricultural region.

Blue·field \'blü-,fēld\. 1 Town, Tazewell co., SW Virginia, on border adjoining Bluefield, West Virginia, 32 m. WNW of Pulaski; pop. (1970c) 5286.

2 City, Mercer co., S West Virginia, in Blue Ridge Mts. contiguous with Bluefield, Virginia; pop. (1970c) 15,921; near coalfield, also iron, limestone, and silica mines; lumber mills. Bluefield State Coll. (1895).

Blue·fields \'blü-,fēl(d)z\. 1 River in Nicaragua. See ESCONDIDO.

2 Town, ✱ of Zelaya dept., Nicaragua, on SE coast at mouth of the Escondido river; munic. pop. (1970e) 22,910; export center for bananas, coconuts, and cabinet woods.

Blue·grass \'blü-,gras\. Region in central Kentucky where Kentucky bluegrass (*Poa pratensis*) abounds; noted for breeding of fine horses.

Blue Grot·to \-'grät-(,)ō\. Cavern, N shore of island of Capri, in Bay of Naples, Italy; ab. 175 ft. long and 50 ft. high; renowned for the dazzling blue light inside.

Blue·hill Bay \,blü-,hil-\. Inlet of Atlantic Ocean on S coast of Hancock co., Maine, W of Mt. Desert I.

Blue Island. City, Cook co., NE Illinois, 15 m. S of Chicago; pop. (1970c) 22,958; industrial suburb of Chicago.

Blue Knob. Peak, Bedford co., S Pennsylvania, N of Bedford; 3130 ft.

Blue Licks \-ˈliks\. Locality, including mineral springs (**Blue Licks Springs**), Nicholas co., NE Kentucky, on right bank of Licking river ab. 40 m. NE of Lexington; scene of battle Aug. 19, 1782 in which Kentucky pioneers were defeated by a force of Indians and Canadians; site now **Blue Licks Battlefield State Park.**

Blue Me·sa Dam *and* **Blue Mesa Reservoir** \-ˈmā-sə-\. See UNITED STATES, *Dams and Reservoirs.*

Blue Mountain. 1 *or formerly* **Rich Mountain** \ˈrich-\. Peak in Ouachita Mts., Polk and Scott cos., W Arkansas; 2623 ft.; second highest point in state. See MAGAZINE MOUNTAIN.

2 Peak, Franklin co., W Maine; 3600 ft.

3 Peak, N Clallam co., NW Washington; 6007 ft.

4 Town, Tippah co., N Mississippi; pop. (1970c) 677; Blue Mountain Coll. (1873).

Blue Mountains. 1 Mountain range, NE Oregon and SE Washington; highest peak Rock Creek Butte 9105 ft.

2 Range in NE Pennsylvania, part of Kittatinny Mountain (*q.v.*).

3 *or* **Blue Plateau.** Part of Great Dividing Range, E New South Wales, SE Australia; 2000–3600 ft.

4 City, New South Wales, SE Australia; pop. (1968e) 32,-110; formed 1947.

5 Range in E Jamaica, West Indies; highest **Blue Mountain Peak** 7388 ft., on slopes of which is raised Blue Mountain coffee.

Blue Mountains National Park. National park, New South Wales, Australia; 328 sq. m.; mountainous area; established 1959.

Blue Mud Bay. Inlet on W Gulf of Carpentaria on Arnhem Land coast, N Northern Territory, Australia.

Blue Nile. 1 River, Sudan, NE Africa. See NILE.

2 *or* **Ge·zi·ra** \jə-ˈzir-ə\. Province of E Sudan. See table at SUDAN.

Blue Plateau. See BLUE MOUNTAINS 3.

Blue Point. Locality, Suffolk co., Long Island, New York, on Great South Bay, SW of Patchogue; noted for its oyster beds.

Blue Ridge. 1 *also* **Blue Ridge Mountains.** The eastern and southeastern range of the Appalachian Mts., extending from a point near Harpers Ferry, West Virginia, SW across western Virginia and W North Carolina into N Georgia; by some considered to include the N extension into Maryland, Pennsylvania, and New York; its highest peaks are in the Black Mountains (*q.v.*) of North Carolina; average elevation 2000 to 4000 ft.

2 City, ⊗ of Fannin co., N Georgia; pop. (1970c) 1602.

Blue Ridge Dam. See table at TENNESSEE VALLEY AUTHORITY.

Blue River. Name of two rivers in Indiana. See BLUE.

Blue Springs. City, Jackson co., W Missouri, 10 m. SE of Independence; pop. (1970c) 6779; agriculture.

Blue Sulphur Springs. Mineral springs and village, Greenbrier co., SE West Virginia.

Bluff \ˈbləf\ *or formerly* **Camp·bell·town** \ˈkam-(b)əl-ˌtau̇n\. Borough on peninsula (**The Bluff**), S South I., New Zealand, at entrance to **Bluff Harbour,** an inlet of Foveaux Strait; port of Invercargill; pop. (1968e) 3300.

Bluff, Mount. Peak in the Blue Ridge, western Virginia; 3350 ft.

Bluff·ton \ˈbləf-tən\. 1 City, ⊗ of Wells co., NE Indiana, 23 m. S of Fort Wayne; pop. (1970c) 8292; chemicals, farm implements, lumber products.

2 Village, Allen co., NW Ohio, 15 m. NE of Lima; pop. (1970c) 2935; distribution point for crushed stone and limestone of vicinity; Bluffton Coll. (1900).

Blu·me·nau \ˌblü-mə-ˈnau̇\. Town on the Itajaí river, Santa Catarina state, S Brazil; munic. pop. (1968e) 84,139; founded 1851 by German immigrants.

Blüm·lis·alp \ˈblüm-lē-ˌsälp\. Range in the Bernese Alps, S cen. Switzerland; highest peak **Blüm·lis·alp·horn** \-ˌhȯ(ə)rn\ 12,021 ft.

Blunts Reef \ˈblən(t)s-\. Reef just off Cape Mendocino, California; has lightship.

Blyth \ˈblī(th)\. Municipal borough, Northumberland, N England, on North Sea at mouth of the **Blyth River** (20 m. long) 12 m. NNE of Newcastle upon Tyne; pop. (1971p) 34,617; shipbuilding yards; electroplating; exports coal.

Blythe \ˈblīth, ˈblīth\. City, Riverside co., SE California, near the Colorado river; pop. (1970c) 7047; cotton; truck farms; Palo Verde Coll. (1947); settled 1910.

Blythe·ville \ˈblī(th)-ˌvil, ˈblīth-, -vəl\. City, a ⊗ of Mississippi co., NE Arkansas, 5 m. S of Missouri border; pop. (1970c) 24,752; trade center for agricultural region.

Blyth River. See BLYTH.

Bo·ac \ˈbō-ˌak\. Municipality, ✱ of Marinduque prov., Marinduque I., Phil., on river 2 m. from W coast; pop. (1969e) 36,600; an old Spanish-built town.

Bo·a·co \bō-ˈä-(ˌ)kō\. 1 Department of SW cen. Nicaragua. See table at NICARAGUA.

2 Town, its ✱; munic. pop. (1970e) 24,047.

Boa Esperança, Cabo da. See GOOD HOPE, CAPE OF 2.

Bo·a·no \bō-ˈän-(ˌ)ō\. Small island off W end of Ceram I., Indonesia; 18 m. long, 12 m. wide.

Boars Head \ˈbō(ə)rz-, ˈbȯ(ə)rz-\. Peak, Schuylkill co., E cen. Pennsylvania; 2100 ft.

Boa Vis·ta \ˌbō-ə-ˈvēsh-tə\. 1 Town, ✱ of Roraima territory, W Brazil, on right bank of upper Rio Branco; pop. (1970p) 37,062.

2 Easternmost of Cape Verde Is.; 239 sq. m.; pop. (1960c) 3309.

Bo·az \ˈbō-ˌaz\. City, Marshall and Etowah cos., NE Alabama, 17 m. NW of Gadsden; pop. (1970c) 5635; Snead State Junior Coll. (1898).

Bob·bi·li \ˈbäb-ə-lē\. Town, NE Andhra Pradesh, E India, 60 m. N of Vishakhapatnam; pop. (1961c) 25,592; when attacked by French and natives 1756, held out until every man was dead or mortally wounded.

Bober. See BÓBR.

Bo·bi·gny \ˌbȯ-bē-ˈnyē\. Commune, ✱ of Seine-St-Denis dept., N France, NE suburb of Paris; pop. (1968c) 39,453.

Böb·ling·en \ˈbə(r)-bliŋ-ən\. City, Baden-Württemberg, West Germany, 10 m. SW of Stuttgart; pop. (1969e) 35,-869; computer laboratories. Founded c. 1250; heavily bombed in World War II, since rebuilt.

Bo·bo–Diou·las·so \ˈbō-(ˌ)bō-d(y)ü-ˈlas-(ˌ)ō\. Town, W Upper Volta, W Africa; pop. (1970e) 77,385; terminus of railroads from Abidjan and Ouagadougou.

Bo·bon \bō-ˈbȯn\. Municipality, N coast of Samar, Phil., 55 m. N of Catbalogan; pop. (1969e) 17,300.

Bóbr \ˈbȯ-bər\ *or Ger.* **Bo·ber** \ˈbō-\. River, chiefly in W Wrocław prov., SW Poland; flows N to the Odra (Oder) SE of Frankfurt, East Germany; formerly in Silesia, Germany.

Bobr. River, Poland. See BIEBRZA.

Bobriki. See NOVOMOSKOVSK 1.

Bo·bruisk \bä-ˈbrü-isk\. City, Mogilev Oblast, Belorussian S.S.R., U.S.S.R., 90 m. SE of Minsk; pop. (1970p) 138,000; engineering; textiles, shoes; on Berezina river; fortified by Alexander I; withstood attack of French army 1812; nearly destroyed by great fire 1902; seized by Germans July 1, 1941, recovered June 1944.

Boca, La. See LA BOCA.

Bo·ca Chi·ca \ˌbō-kə-ˈchē-kə\. Island in Florida Keys adjacent to Key West; U.S. Naval Air Station.

Boca Chica. See CORREGIDOR and NORTH CHANNEL.

Boca del Río \-del-ˈrē-ō\. Municipality, Veracruz state, Mexico, 6 m. S of Veracruz; pop. (1970p) 27,884; fishing, fruit growing.

Boca Grande. See CORREGIDOR and SOUTH CHANNEL.

Bo·cai·u·va *or* **Bo·cay·u·va** \ˌbü-kī-ˈü-və\. Town, Minas Gerais state, E Brazil, on railroad ab. 190 m. N of Belo Horizonte; munic. pop. (1968e) 29,113; visited by scientists to observe eclipse of the sun May 20, 1947.

Boca Ra·ton \ˌbō-kə-rə-ˈtōn\. City, Palm Beach co., SE Florida, on the coast 17 m. N of Fort Lauderdale; pop. (1970c) 28,506; Marymount Coll. (1963), Florida Atlantic Univ. (1964); radar training center of U.S. Air Force.

Bo·cas del To·ro \ˌbō-kəz-del-ˈtȯr-(ˌ)ō\. 1 Province of W Panama. See table at PANAMA.
2 Atlantic coast port, its ✻, on an island off NW coast of Panama; pop. (1970p) 9636; exports bananas, coffee, cacao.

Boc·ca Ti·gris \ˌbäk-ə-ˈtē-grəs\. Narrow channel bet. the upper and lower Pearl rivers, bet. Canton and Hong Kong. See PEARL 2.

Bocchetta Pass. See table at APENNINES.

Bochkarevo. See BELOGORSK.

Boch·nia \ˈbȯk-nē-ˌä\. Mining commune, Kraków prov., Poland, ab. 20 m. ESE of Kraków; pop. (1968e) 13,800; salt mines; gypsum quarries; trades in agricultural products. Taken 1702 by Charles XII.

Bo·cholt \ˈbȯk-ˌōlt\. Manufacturing city, North Rhine-Westphalia, West Germany, near Dutch border; pop. (1969e) 47,847; cotton and iron goods.

Bo·chum \ˈbō-kəm\. Industrial city, North Rhine-Westphalia, West Germany, in Ruhr valley 37 m. SSW of Münster; pop. (1969e) 346,010; automobiles, chemicals, electrical equipment; metallurgical industries; church (1599), univ. (1961), planetarium (1964); first mentioned 1041; received municipal charter 1321; in World War II bombed by British; rebuilt after 1946.

Bock·um–Hö·vel \ˈbō-kəm-ˈhə(r)-vəl\. City, North Rhine-Westphalia, West Germany, 16 m. NE of Dortmund; pop. (1969e) 25,140; coal mining; metalware. Founded in 12th cent.

Bod. See BAUDH.

Bo·dai·bo \bə-ˌdī-ˈbō\. Town, NE Irkutsk Oblast, Russian S.F.S.R., U.S.S.R., on right bank of Vitim river NE of Lake Baikal.

Bodegas. See BABAHOYO.

Bo·de·le \bō-ˈdā-lē\ *or Fr.* **Bo·dé·lé** \bō-dā-lā\. Low area, N Chad, N cen. Africa, NE of Lake Chad and S of Tibesti Mts.; tobacco, cotton, forage grasses.

Bo·den \ˈbü-dən\. Town, Norrbotten co., N Sweden, on Luleålv river 22 m. NNW of Luleå; pop. (1970e) 24,727.

Bodensee. See CONSTANCE, LAKE.

Bo·derg, Lough \läk-ˈbō-ˌde(ə)rg, -ˌdərg\. Lake in N cen. Ireland, S of Lough Allen; one of the chain of lakes traversed by the Shannon river.

Bod·ie Island \ˌbäd-ē-\. Long narrow island, NE North Carolina, separating Albemarle and Roanoke sounds from the Atlantic Ocean; 37 sq. m.; lighthouse at its S end.

Bo·di·na·yak·ka·nur \ˈbōd-i-nə-ˌyək-ə-ˈnu̇(ə)r\. Town, Tamil Nadu, S India; 55 m. W of Madurai; pop. (1961c) 44,914.

Bodincomagus. See CASALE MONFERRATO.

Bo·djo·ne·go·ro *or* **Bo·jo·ne·go·ro** \ˌbō-jō-nə-ˈgōr-(ˌ)ō, -ˈgȯr-\. 1 Former residency, Neth. Indies, now part of the Indonesian prov. of East Java; 2634 sq. m.; ✻ Bodjonegoro.
2 Town, its ✻, on Solo river 60 m. W of Surabaja.

Bod·kin Point \ˌbäd-kən-\. Point, Anne Arundel co., cen. Maryland, on S side of mouth of Patapsco river.

Bod·min \ˈbäd-min\. Municipal borough, ⊗ of Cornwall, SW England, 26 m. WNW of Plymouth; pop. (1971p) 9204.

Bodø \ˈbō-ˌdər\. Seaport, ⊗ of Nordland co., N Norway, ab. 100 m. SW of Narvik; pop. (1970e) 28,545; trade center; shipping point for copper ore and marble; tourist resort, with the midnight sun from June 1 to July 12.

Bodotria. See FORTH.

Bod·rog \ˈbōd-ˌrōg\. Small river in NE Hungary; flows SW into Tisza river near Tokaj.

Bo·drum \bō-ˈdrüm\ *also* **Bu·drum** \bə-ˈdrüm\ *or anc.* **Hal·i·car·nas·sus** \ˌhal-ə-(ˌ)kär-ˈnas-əs\. Seaport, Muğla prov., SW Turkey in Asia, on S side of **Bodrum Peninsula** on Aegean Sea, opp. Kos Is. See HALICARNASSUS.

Bodza. See BUZĂU.

Boeleleng. See BULELENG.

Bo·èo, Cape \-bō-ˈā-(ˌ)ō\ *or* **Cape Li·li·beo** \-ˌlē-li-ˈbā-(ˌ)ō\. Westernmost point of Sicily, Italy.

Boe·o·tia \bē-ˈō-sh(ē-)ə\. 1 District and ancient republic in E cen. Greece, bounded on N by Locris Opuntia, on E by the Atalante channel and the Evripos, on S by Attica, Megaris, and Gulf of Corinth, on W and NW by Phocis; chief cities Orchomenus and Thebes (*qq.v.*).
History: Inhabited by Boeotians, an Aeolian people from Thessaly; politically significant after formation of Boeotian League under headship of Thebes c. 600–550 B.C.; a Medized state during Greek war with Persia; hostile to Athens which succeeded in breaking up Boeotian League and forcing members, except Thebes, to join Delian League 457 B.C.; revolted against Athens and restored League 447 B.C.; in Peloponnesian War, defeated Athenians at Delium 424 B.C.; after battle of Leuctra (*q.v.*) 371 B.C., led by Thebes, dominated Greece; declined after Philip of Macedon's victory at Chaeronea 338 B.C. and the destruction of Thebes by Alexander the Great 336 B.C.
2 *or Gk.* **Voi·o·tia** \vyō-ˈtē-ə\. Department, Central Greece and Euboea, Greece. See table at GREECE.

Boer·ne \ˈbər-nē\. City, ⊗ of Kendall co., S cen. Texas; pop. (1970c) 2432; tourist and health resort.

Boeroe. See BURU.

Boetoeng. See BUTUNG.

Boeuf River \ˈbəf-, ˈbu̇f-\ *or* **Boeuf Bay·ou** \ˌbəf-ˈbī-(ˌ)(y)ō, -(y)ü\. River, NE Louisiana; ab. 200 m. long; rises just N of Arkansas border, flows SW into Ouachita river in N Catahoula parish.

Bōfu. See HŌFU.

Bo·ga·djim \bō-ˈgäj-əm\. Village and port at head of Astrolabe Bay, Trust Territory of New Guinea, ab. 12 m. S of Madang. Taken by U.S. Apr. 1944.

Bo·ga·lu·sa \ˌbō-gə-ˈlü-sə\. Industrial city, Washington parish, E Louisiana, 60 m. NNE of New Orleans; pop. (1970c) 18,412; paper and lumber mills.

Bo·gaz·köy *or* **Bo·ghaz·keui** \ˌbō-ˌ(g)äz-ˈkȯi\ *or* **Hat·tu·shash** \ˈhat-ə-ˌshash\ *or Gk.* **Pte·ria** \ˈtir-ē-ə\. Village in mountains of N cen. Turkey in Asia, 16 m. NW of Yozgat and ab. 90 m. E of Ankara; containing ancient Hittite ruins; remarkable remains of probable capital of powerful Hattic dynasty (c. 16th–12th cents. B.C.); described by Herodotus.

Bogdo–ola *or* **Bogdo Ula.** See PO-KO-TO.

Bo·gen·fels \ˈbō-gən-(ˌ)felz, ˈbü-gən-(ˌ)fels\. Town, SW South-West Africa, on coast 50 m. S of Lüderitz; has remarkable natural rock archway.

Bog·nor Re·gis \ˌbäg-nər-ˈrē-jəs\. Urban district, West Sussex, S England, on the coast ab. 17 m. E of Portsmouth; pop. (1971p) 34,389; seaside resort.

Bo·go \bə-ˈgō\. Municipality on E coast of Cebu I., Phil., on inlet of Visayan Sea 54 m. N of City of Cebu; pop. (1969e) 40,400; good harbor.

Bo·go·du·khov \ˌbə-gə-ˈdü-kəf\. Town, E Ukrainian S.S.R., U.S.S.R., ab. 30 m. WNW of Kharkov; pop. (1967e) 18,000.

Bo·gong, Mount \-ˈbō-ˌgäŋ\. Mountain, SE Victoria, SE Australia, in Darg Plateau at S end of Great Dividing Range; 6508 ft.; highest point in Victoria.

Bo·gor \ˈbō-ˌgȯ(ə)r\ *or Du.* **Bui·ten·zorg** \ˈbīt-ᵊn-ˌzȯ(ə)rg\. 1 Residency of the Indonesian prov. of West Java; 4484 sq. m.; a residency of the former Neth. Indies; in N of this area are mountains of central range of Java (see SALAK and GEDE); produces tea and coffee, rice, sugar, and rubber.
2 City, its ✻, 36 m. S of Djakarta; pop. (1961c) 154,092; several universities and colleges, incl. Univ. of Bogor (1961); palace, formerly residence of the Dutch governor general; at elevation of ab. 870 ft.; notable botanical garden

(founded 1817) with more than 10,000 kinds of plants. City founded 1745.

Bogorodsk. See NOGINSK.

Bo·go·slof \'bō-gə-ˌsläf, -ˌslȯf\. Small island in Bering Sea ab. 60 m. W of N Unalaska I., Alaska, built up by submarine volcano; uninhabited; first reported by Russian navigators ab. 1796 when it appeared as a single peak. Violent eruptions 1823, 1883, 1900, and 1907 have changed its aspect; now has several peaks joined by a land strip.

Bo·go·ta \bə-'gōt-ə\. Borough, Bergen co., NE corner of New Jersey, 8 m. ESE of Paterson; pop. (1970c) 8960.

Bo·go·tá \'bō-gə-'tȯ, -'tä\. 1 *or formerly* **Fun·za** \'fün-zə\. River in W cen. Colombia; flows into Magdalena river near Bogotá. See TEQUENDAMA FALLS.

2 *orig.* **San·ta Fe** \ˌsant-ə-'fā\ *or later* **Santa Fe de Bogotá.** City, ✱ of Colombia and ✱ of Cundinamarca dept., on plateau (alt. 8563 ft.) of eastern Andes; pop. (1968e) 1,966,341; constitutes, with adjacent area, the Special District (613 sq. m.; pop. 2,148,387); commercial and financial center of Colombia; several universities and colleges, incl. the National Univ. of Colombia (1563); cathedral (rebuilt 1814), observatory.

History: Originally center of Chibcha culture; Spanish settlement founded 1538 by Gonzalo Jiménez de Quesada, conquistador; capital of viceroyalty of New Granada; audiencia established 1549; scene of revolt 1810–11 against Spanish rule; recovered by Spaniards 1816–19; freed by victory of Bolívar at Boyacá 1819; capital of Greater Colombia and later (1831) of New Granada (Colombia); Pan American Conference Mar.–Apr. 1948.

Bog·ra \'bäg-rə\. Town, Bangla Desh, 57 m. NE of Rajshahi; pop. (1961c) 33,784.

Bogue Sound \ˌbōg-\. Sound bet. S mainland of Carteret co., SE North Carolina, and barrier reefs off the coast; connects at W end with Atlantic through the **Bogue Inlet.**

Bo·gu·szów \bȯ-'gü-shüf\ *or Ger.* **Got·tes·berg** \'gät-əs-ˌberg\. Mining and manufacturing city, S Wrocław prov., SW Poland, 47 m. SW of Wrocław; pop. (1968e) 12,600; formerly in Germany; assigned to Poland by Potsdam Conference 1945.

Bo·he·mia \bō-'hē-mē-ə\ *or Czech* **Če·chy** \'chek-ē\ *or Ger.* **Böh·men** \'bœ̄-mən\. Former kingdom, cen. Europe, since 1918 part of Czechoslovakia; ✱ Prague; constitutes W part of Czech S.R. Encircled by mountains: Erzgebirge on NW, Sudetic Mts. on NE, Bohemian-Moravian Highlands on SE, and the Bohemian Forest on SW; highest point 5256 ft. in the Riesengebirge, a range of the Sudetic Mts. Chief rivers the Elbe (here called the Labe) and its tributaries the Vltava (Moldau) and Ohře (Eger); flax, hops, timber; graphite, iron ore, coal; chief towns Prague, Plzeň, České Budějovice, Pardubice.

History: Settled in 5th cent. A.D. by west Slavic people, Czechs; tributary to Charlemagne's empire (see FRANCE); part of kingdom of Moravia (*q.v.*) founded 870; converted to Latin Christianity by German missionaries 9th cent.; after dissolution of Moravia c. 907, became duchy which in 10th cent. was forced to accept German suzerainty; under rule of Přemysl family, expanded to include Moravia, parts of Silesia, Slovakia, and Kraków (forced to yield Polish conquests by Emperor Henry III 1041); in 12th cent. raised to rank of electorate and hereditary kingdom within Holy Roman Empire; at height of power under Ottokar II (1253–78) who conquered Styria from Hungary and Austrian territories but was defeated by Emperor Rudolf (of Hapsburg) 1278; last ruler of Přemysl line (d. 1306) also king of Poland; during reign of Charles I 1347–78 (also Emperor Charles IV) of Luxembourg line (1308–1437) reached "golden age," controlling Upper and Lower Lusatia, Moravia, Silesia, and Brandenburg; alienated by anti-Huss Council of Constance (see KONSTANZ), plunged into Hussite wars 1420–36; from election of Ferdinand as king (see AUSTRIA) 1526, remained under Hapsburg rule to 1918; deposition of ruler (Defenestration of Prague) 1618 inaugurated Thirty Years' War (see GERMANY); Protestantism exterminated and independence lost at battle of White Mountain 1620; by 18th cent. completely incorporated in Austrian Empire; battleground in wars of Frederick II and in 1866 (see PRUSSIA); with Moravia and Slovakia, declared independence 1918 (see CZECHOSLOVAKIA); invaded by Germans and made part of German Protectorate of Bohemia and Moravia Mar. 1939; made a province of Czechoslovakia 1945; province dissolved 1949 and divided into several administrative units; became part of the Czech S.R. 1968.

Bohemia and Mo·ra·via \-mə-'rā-vē-ə\. German protectorate comprising the two western divisions of Czechoslovakia; set up Mar. 1939, dissolved 1945.

Bo·he·mi·an Forest \-'hē-mē-ən-\ *or Ger.* **Böh·mer Wald** \'bœ̄-mər-ˌvält\ *or Czech* **Čes·ký Les** \'ches-kē-'les\. Mountain range along the boundary bet. Bavaria, West Germany, and Bohemia, W Czechoslovakia; highest peak Arber, in Bavaria, 4780 ft.

Bohemian–Mo·ra·vi·an Highlands \-mə-'rā-vē-ən-\ *or Czech* **Čes·ko·mo·rav·ská Vrch·o·vi·na** \ˌches-kə-ˌmȯ-räf-skə-'vər-kȯ-və-nə\. Mountain range forming boundary bet. the former provinces of Bohemia and Moravia, Czechoslovakia; highest point ab. 2700 ft.; runs NE and SW.

Böhmisch–Brod. See ČESKÝ-BROD.

Böhmisch–Leipa. See ČESKÁ LÍPA.

Bo·hol \bō-'hȯl\. Island, one of the Visayan Is., S cen. Phil., N of Mindanao; 1492 sq. m.; with smaller adjacent islands, forms a province, (1590 sq. m.; pop. [1970p] 674,806; ✱ Tagbilaran). Has fairly regular coastline with many islands, largest Panglao on SW and Lapinin on W side of Canigao Channel; few good anchorages; highest peaks ab. 2600 ft.; short rivers; produces rice, sugar, coconuts, hemp, tobacco; weaving an important industry; chief towns, mostly on the coast, Tagbilaran, Loon, Ubay, Talibon. Visited by Legaspi 1565; in early days under jurisdiction of Cebu; suffered from rebellion 1622 and again 1744; made separate province by the Spanish 1854; civil government created Apr. 20, 1901; came under Japanese control 1942; invaded and recovered Apr. 1945 by U.S. forces.

Bohol Strait. Passage bet. SE Cebu and W Bohol, Phil.; from 12 to 25 m. wide; connects Camotes Sea on the N with Mindanao Sea on the S.

Bo·hot·le Wein \bə-ˌhät-li-'vān\. Town, N Somalia, E Africa, SE of Berbera on Ethiopia border.

Boi·ro \'bȯi-(ˌ)rō\. Coastal commune, La Coruña prov., NW Spain, 54 m. SSW of La Coruña; pop. (1970p) 13,867; cattle raising; fishing; sardine canneries.

Bois. See BOIS DE BOULOGNE.

Bois Blanc Island. 1 \ˌbäb-ˌlō—*sic*\. Island in NW Lake Huron, a part of Mackinac co., Michigan; 35 sq. m.

2 \ˌbwä-ˌblaŋk-\. Long, narrow island in Detroit river, SE Michigan opp. Amherstburg, Ontario, Canada.

Bois Brule. See BRULE.

Bois–Co·lombes \ˌbwä-kō-'lōⁿb\. Manufacturing commune, Hauts-de-Seine dept., N France, NW suburb of Paris; pop. (1968c) 28,934.

Bois d'Avocourt. See AVOCOURT.

Bois de Belleau. See BELLEAU WOOD.

Bois de Bou·logne \ˌbwäd-ə-bü-'lōn, -'lȯin\ *or familiarly* **Bois** \'bwä\. Park, formerly a forest, just W of Paris, France, in a loop of the Seine adjoining Neuilly on the N and Boulogne on the W; 2155 acres; acquired by the city of Paris 1852 and transformed into a recreational area; contains the famous race tracks of Longchamp in SW part and Auteuil (steeplechases) in SE.

Bois de la Brigade Marine. See BELLEAU WOOD.

Bois des Fi·li·on \ˌbwä-dā-fēl-'yōⁿ\. Village, Terrebonne co., S Quebec, Canada, 15 m. NW of Montreal; pop. (1966c) 3219.

Bois de Sioux \ˌbȯid-ə-'sü\. River, W Minnesota; flows N out of Lake Traverse, forms S section of North Dakota-

Minnesota boundary, unites with Otter Tail river to form Red River of the North.

Bois–du–Roi \ˌbwäd-ər-ˈwä\. Highest peak in Morvan Mts., E cen. France; 2959 ft.

Boi·se \ˈbȯi-sē, -zē\. 1 River, SW cen. Idaho, below Arrowrock Dam; ab. 60 m. long; formed by forks uniting in NW Elmore co.; flows W through Boise (city) and Canyon co. into Snake river.

2 County in Idaho. See table at IDAHO.

3 City, ❋ of Idaho and ⊗ of Ada co., SW Idaho; pop. (1970c) 74,990; alt. 2704 ft.; largest city in the state; packing houses; food processing; stone quarries; Boise State Coll. (1932); founded 1863 on the site of an army camp; incorporated as city 1864; capital of Idaho Territory 1864, and of the state from 1890.

Boise City \ˌbȯis-\. Town, ⊗ of Cimarron co., NW Oklahoma, 60 m. W of Guymon; pop. (1970c) 1993; oil wells.

Bois–le–Duc. See 'S HERTOGENBOSCH.

Boj·a·dor, Cape \-ˈbäj-ə-ˌdȯ(ə)r\. Cape extending into Atlantic Ocean on W cen. coast of Spanish Sahara, NW Africa, S of Canary Is., 26°08′N, 14°30′W.

Bojana. See BUENË.

Bo·je·a·dor, Cape \-ˌbō-ˌhā-ə-ˈdō(ə)r\. Point on NW coast of Ilocos Norte prov., Luzon, Phil., 18°30′N, 120°34′E; lighthouse.

Boj·nūrd *also* **Buj·nurd** \bōj-ˈnu̇(ə)rd\. Town in mountains of N Khorāsān prov., NE Iran; pop. (1971p) 34,000.

Bo·jo·la·li \ˌbō-yə-ˈlä-lē\. Town, cen. Java, Indonesia, at foot of Mt. Merapi; pop. (1961c) 15,148.

Bojonegoro. See BODJONEGORO.

Bo·ké \bō-ˈkā\. Town on Nunez river, W Guinea, W Africa, 110 m. NW of Conakry.

Bokhara. See BUKHARA.

Bokn Fjord *also* **Bukn Fjord** \ˈbük-ən-\. Inlet of the North Sea on SW coast of Norway, N of Stavanger; ab. 35 m. long; 10 to 15 m. wide.

Bokonka. See MINYA KONKA.

Bo·ko·ro \bə-ˈkōr-ō, -ˈkȯr-\. Town, SW cen. Chad, N cen. Africa, 140 m. E of Fort-Lamy.

Boks·burg \ˈbäks-ˌbərg\. Town, S Transvaal, NE Rep. of South Africa, 15 m. E of Johannesburg; pop. (1968e) 108,850; electrical equipment, freight cars, soap; fruit canning; important gold-mining center.

Bo Kunka. See MINYA KONKA.

Bo·la·ma \bō-ˈläm-ə\ *or* **Bu·la·ma** \bu̇-\. 1 Island of the Arquipélago dos Bijagós (see BIJAGÓS, ARQUIPÉLAGO DOS).

2 Town on Bolama I., former ❋ of Portuguese Guinea, W Africa.

Bolangir. See PATNA 1.

Bo·lan Pass \bō-ˈlän-\. Mountain pass, Pakistan; bet. Sibi and Quetta in N Baluchistan; ab. 60 m. long; elev. at crest 5900 ft.

Bol·bē, Lake \-ˈbäl-(ˌ)bē\ *or Gk.* **Lím·ni Vól·vi** \ˌlim-nē-ˈvȯl-vē\. Lake in N part of Chalcidice, Macedonia, Greece.

Bol·bec \bȯl-ˈbek\. Industrial commune, Seine-Maritime dept., N France; pop. (1962c) 12,492.

Bolbitine, Bolbitinic Mouth. See ROSETTA.

Bolbok. See SAN JUAN 12.

Bol·don \ˈbōl-dən\. Urban district, Durham, NE England, 7 m. SE of Newcastle upon Tyne; pop. (1971p) 23,904.

Bolerium. See LANDS END.

Boleslav, Mladá. See MLADÁ BOLESLAV.

Bo·le·sła·wi·ce \ˌbȯl-ə-slä-ˈvēt-sə\ *or Ger.* **Bun·zel·witz** \ˌbu̇n(t)-zəl-ˌvitz\. Village, Wrocław prov., SW Poland, 7 m. N of Świdnica; formerly in Silesia, Germany; battle 1761 bet. forces of Frederick the Great and combined Austrian and Russian forces.

Bo·le·sła·wiec \ˌbȯl-ə-ˈsläv-yetz\ *or Ger.* **Bunz·lau** \ˈbu̇nts-ˌlau̇\. Town, W Wrocław prov., SW Poland, on Bóbr river; pop. (1970p) 30,500; to Bohemian crown 1392, to Prussia 1742; assigned to Poland by Potsdam Conference 1945.

Bol·ga·tan·ga \ˌbōl-gə-ˈtäŋ-gə\. Town, ❋ of Upper Region, N Ghana; pop. (1970p) 18,719.

Bol·grad \bəl-ˈgrät\. Town, SW Ukrainian S.S.R., U.S.S.R., ab. 25 m. N of Izmail; pop. (1967e) 16,000.

Bo·li·nao \ˌbō-li-ˈnau̇\. 1 Cape, NW point of the peninsula of W Pangasinan prov., Luzon, Phil., 16°20′N, 119°52′E, on South China Sea coast W of Lingayen Gulf.

2 Municipality, NW Pangasinan, just E of the cape and opp. Santiago I.; pop. (1969e) 35,800.

Bo·ling·brook \ˈbōl-iŋ-ˌbru̇k\. Village, Will co., NE Illinois, 25 m. SW of Chicago; pop. (1970c) 7643.

Bo·li·var \ˈbäl-ə-vər\. 1 County in Mississippi. See table at MISSISSIPPI.

2 City, ⊗ of Polk co., SW Missouri; pop. (1970c) 4769; bottling works, flour mills; Southwest Baptist Coll. (1878).

3 Town, ⊗ of Hardeman co., SW Tennessee; pop. (1970c) 6674; cotton gins; timber.

Bo·lí·var \bə-ˈlē-ˌvär\. 1 Town, Buenos Aires prov., E Argentina, ab. 170 m. SW of Buenos Aires; pop. (1960c) 15,750; trading center.

2 Department of N Colombia. See table at COLOMBIA.

3 Municipality, Cauca dept., SW Colombia, 47 m. NNE of Pasto; pop. (1964c) 41,029; mining town at alt. 6435 ft.

4 Province of W Ecuador. See table at ECUADOR.

5 State of SE Venezuela. See table at VENEZUELA.

Bolívar, Cer·ro \ˌser-(ˌ)ō-bə-ˈlē-ˌvär\ *or formerly* **La Pa·ri·da** \ˌläp-ə-ˈrē-thə\. Hill, Bolívar state, Venezuela, S of Ciudad Bolívar; ab. 6 m. long; 2000 ft. high; iron mining.

Bolívar, Pi·co \ˌpē-(ˌ)kō-bə-ˈlē-ˌvär\. Mountain, Mérida state, W Venezuela; highest in the Cordillera Mérida and in Venezuela, 16,427 ft.

Bolivar Peninsula \ˈbäl-ə-vər-\ *or* **Bolivar Point.** Peninsula at E entrance to Galveston Bay, Texas; ab. 23 m. long.

Bo·liv·ia \bə-ˈliv-ē-ə\. Republic, W cen. South America, bounded on N and E by Brazil, on SE by Paraguay, on S by Argentina, and on W by Peru and Chile; 424,162 sq. m.; pop. (1971e) 5,062,500; administrative ❋ La Paz, constitutional ❋ Sucre.

Physical features: In eastern part has low, hot, fertile land, watered by many rivers; in central part on E slope of mountains high plateau region; in W part the central ranges of the Andes, esp. the Cordillera Real E of Lake Titicaca, highest peaks Sorata (Ancohuma and Illampu) 20,958 ft., Sajama 21,391 ft., Illimani 21,201 ft.; many volcanic peaks; in SW in Oruro and Potosí depts. are elevated nitrate deserts, esp. Salar de Uyuni. Chief rivers are large headstreams of the Madeira: Guaporé (along Brazilian border) and its tributaries Baures and Itonamas; Mamoré, with many tributaries draining E slopes of the Andes; Beni and its tributary the Madre de Dios; Abuna (forming in N part of boundary with Brazil); upper Pilcomayo in the S. Includes part of Lake Titicaca (*q.v.*) which receives waters of Lake Poopó in SW cen. part through the Desaguadero river. *Chief products:* Barley, corn, wheat, rice; tin, copper, lead, antimony, oil; manufacturing: cement, textiles; food processing. *Chief cities:* La Paz, Cochabamba, Santa Cruz, Oruro, Potosí, Sucre. Divided into the following nine departments (for pronunciations, see their individual entries):

NAME	AREA (sq. m.)	POP. (1969e)	CAPITAL
Chuquisaca	19,893	450,200	Sucre
Cochabamba	21,479	780,500	Cochabamba
El Beni	82,457	190,600	Trinidad
La Paz	51,732	1,509,100	La Paz
Oruro	20,690	334,600	Oruro
Pando	24,644	31,500	Cobija
Potosí	45,644	850,400	Potosí
Santa Cruz	143,097	455,200	Santa Cruz
Tarija	14,526	201,800	Tarija

History: Home of the Aymaras, Indians with a high pre-Inca culture, who were conquered by Incas in 14th cent.; conquered 1538 by Hernando Pizarro, half brother of conqueror of Peru (*q.v.*); organized as dependency of Charcas or Upper Peru; joined to Viceroyalty of Buenos Aires 1776; although struggles against royalists continuous from 1809, achieved independence from Spain only in 1825 when Sucre invaded Charcas, and called congress to proclaim republic of Bolivia; long troubled by internal strife and series of unsuccessful wars; lost seacoast in War of the Pacific against Chile (*q.v.*) 1879–84; after dispute with Brazil, ceded Acre (*q.v.*) 1903; finally made peace 1904 with Chile which retained Arica (*q.v.*); renewed dispute 1920–29; lost most of Chaco (*q.v.*) by treaty 1938 which settled war with Paraguay (1932–35); period 1952–64 marked by economic and political reforms (incl. land redistribution and nationalization of the largest tin mines); civilian government overthrown 1964; new constitution adopted 1967.

Bol·la·te \bō-'lä-(ˌ)tā\. Commune, Milano prov., Lombardy, N Italy, 6 m. NNW of Milan; pop. (1968e) 39,654.

Bol·li·gen \'bȯl-i-gən\. Town, Bern canton, Switzerland, E suburb of Bern; pop. (1970c) 26,121; ball bearings, artificial fibers.

Bol·lin \'bäl-ən\. River, Cheshire, NW England; 20 m. long; tributary of the Mersey.

Bol·lin·ger \'bō-liŋ-(g)ər, 'bu̇l-iŋ-(g)ər, 'bäl-in-jər\. County in Missouri. See table at MISSOURI.

Bol·ling·ton \'bäl-iŋ-ˌtən\. Urban district, Cheshire, NW England, 25 m. E of Liverpool; pop. (1971p) 6610.

Bo·lo·gna \bə-'lōn-(y)ə\. **1** Province of Emilia-Romagna, N Italy. See table at ITALY.

2 *anc.* **Fel·si·na** \'fel-sə-nə\ *or later* **Bo·no·nia** \bə-'nō-nē-ə\. Commune, its ✻ and ✻ of Emilia-Romagna, at foot of Apennines 51 m. N by E of Florence; pop. (1968e) 488,510; transportation center; food processing; electric motors, agricultural machinery; univ. (11th cent.), Gothic 14th cent. church of San Petronio.

History: Site of Etruscan town Felsina; made Roman military colony 192 B.C.; belonged to Byzantine exarchate of Ravenna (*q.v.*); after short period of Lombard rule became free commune, receiving charter in 12th cent.; seat of oldest European university, founded 1088; joined Lombard League against Frederick Barbarossa 1167; helped break power of Frederick II; in course of 15th cent. ruled temporarily by Bentivoglio and Visconti families; incorporated in States of the Church (*q.v.*) by Pope Julius II 1506; scene of crowning of Emperor Charles V 1530; after French occupation 1796, made capital of Cispadane Republic (*q.v.*); restored to States of the Church 1815; occupied by Austria after revolts 1831, 1848; voted annexation to kingdom of Italy 1860. In World War II after surrender of Italy Sept. 1943, controlled by Germans until April 1945.

Bo·lon·da \bə-'län-də\. Settlement on S coast of Guadalcanal I., British Solomon Is., W Pacific Ocean.

Bo·lon·drón \ˌbō-lən-'drōn\. Municipality, Matanzas prov., W cen. Cuba; pop. (1967e) 11,580.

Bolos. See VOLOS.

Bo·lot·no·ye \bə-'lōt-nə-yə\. Town, E Novosibirsk Oblast, Russian S.F.S.R., U.S.S.R., 75 m. NE of Novosibirsk; pop. (1967e) 22,000.

Bol·se·na \bōl-'sā-nə\ *or anc.* **Vol·sin·ii** \väl-'sin-ē-ˌī\. Commune, Viterbo prov., N Latium, Italy, on Lake Bolsena; pop. (1968e) 4089; 11th cent. church.

Bolsena, Lake. Lake, N Latium, cen. Italy, 10 m. NNW of Viterbo; 10 m. long, 8 m. wide; discharges through Marta river SW into N Tyrrhenian Sea.

Bolshaya. See MCKINLEY, MOUNT.

Bol·sha·ya Ki·nel \bəl-ˌshī-ə-kə-'nel\. River, E Russian S.F.S.R., U.S.S.R.; 220 m. long; rises in N Orenburg Oblast and flows W to join the Samara just E of Kuibyshev.

Bol·she·vik \'bōl-shə-ˌvik, 'bȯl-, 'bäl-, -ˌvek\. Island, SE Severnaya Zemlya, in Arctic Ocean off Taimyr Penin., Russian S.F.S.R., U.S.S.R.

Bol·shoi Be·gich·ev \bōl-ˌshȯi-'b(y)ā-gə-chəv, bȯl-, bäl-\. Island, NW Yakutsk A.S.S.R., Russian S.F.S.R., U.S.S.R., N of Nordvik Bay, at mouth of Khatanga river.

Bolshoi Berezovy Island. See PRIMORSK.

Bolshoi Ir·giz \-ir-'gēz\. River, Russian S.F.S.R., U.S.S.R.; ab. 300 m. long; rises in S Kuibyshev Oblast and flows W into Volga river opp. Volsk; navigable except at low-water season.

Bolshoi Lya·khov \-lē-'äk-əf\. Largest island of the Lyakhov Is. (*q.v.*).

Bolshoi Tyu·ters \-'tyü-tərs\ *or formerly* **Ty·tär·saari** \ˌtü-tər-'sär-ē\. Island, Gulf of Finland, off coast of Estonian S.S.R., U.S.S.R.

Bolshoi Ye·ni·sei \-ˌyen-ə-'sā\. See YENISEI.

Bolsón de Mapimí. See MAPIMÍ, BOLSÓN DE.

Bol·so·ver \'bōl-ˌzō-vər\. Urban district, Derbyshire, N cen. England, 13 m. SSE of Sheffield; pop. (1971p) 10,956.

Bols·ward \'bȯls-värt\. Commune, Friesland prov., Netherlands, 15 m. SW of Leeuwarden; pop. (1970e) 9247.

Bolt Head \'bōlt-\. Headland on S coast of Devonshire, SW England, W of Start Point.

Bol·ton \'bōlt-ᵊn\. **1** Town, Tolland co., N Connecticut; pop. (1970c) 3691.

2 *or in full* **Bolton–le–Moors** \-lə-'mu̇(ə)rz\. County borough, Lancashire, NW England, on the Croal 11 m. NW of Manchester; pop. (1971p) 153,977; textile mills, ironworks, paper mills, chemical manufacturing; coal deposits nearby; one of the oldest centers of the woolen trade, where Richard Arkwright invented the spinning frame (1769) and S. Crompton the spinning mule (1779).

Bolton Brown, Mount \-ˌbōlt-ᵊn-'brau̇n\. Peak in Sierra Nevada, E Fresno co., S cen. California; 13,527 ft.

Bo·lu \bō-'lü\. **1** Province of NW Turkey, Asia. See table at TURKEY.

2 Town, its ✻; pop. (1965c) 21,700; lumber.

Bo·lus Head \ˌbō-ləs-\. Cape on SW coast of Eire, on W side of entrance to Ballinskelligs Bay.

Bol·za·no \bōlt-'sän-(ˌ)ō, bōl-'zän-\. **1** Province of Trentino-Alto Adige, Italy. See table at ITALY.

2 *or Ger.* **Bo·zen** \'bōt-sən\ *or anc.* **Bau·za·num** \bȯ-'zā-nəm\. Commune, its ✻, in S Tirol at confluence of the Isarco river with the Adige 87 m. NNW of Venice; pop. (1968e) 103,479; trade center for region producing wine and fruits; aluminum, steel; 14th cent. Gothic cathedral; Franciscan monastery. Ancient Roman town; fell to Lombards 680 A.D., to Franks 740; seat of Bavarian border countships; fell to episcopate of Trent 1027; under Hapsburgs from 1363 sharing the history of the Tirol; conquered by Italy 1918.

Bo·ma \'bō-mə\. Town, W Zaire, ab. 60 m. from the mouth of the Congo river on N bank; pop. (1967e) 79,230; until 1923 ✻ of Belgian Congo. Founded as a slave market in 16th cent.

Bo·mar·sund \'bü-mər-ˌsənd\. **1** Strait in the Ahvenanmaa Is. in the Gulf of Bothnia.

2 Russian fort on Ahvenanmaa captured Aug. 16, 1854 by British and French (Crimean War).

Bom·ba \'bäm-bə\ *or Arab.* **Al–Bun·bah** \al-'bu̇m-bə\. Town, Libya, N Africa, bet. Derna and Tobruk on the **Gulf of Bomba.**

Bom·ba·la \bäm-'bä-lə\. Town, SE New South Wales, SE Australia, 110 m. S of Canberra and ab. 38 m. W of Eden harbor; pop. (1966c) 1495; one of many sites considered 1903–04 for Commonwealth capital.

Bom·bay \bäm-'bā\. **1** Former state, W India; area (1956) 190,919 sq. m.; ✻ Bombay; a presidency (until 1937) and province (1947) of British India, a province of India 1947–56; reorganized 1956 as state incorporating Kutch and Saurashtra and the Marathi-speaking parts of Hyderabad and Madhya Pradesh, small areas being transferred at that time to Mysore and Rajasthan states; divided 1960 into two states: Gujarat and Maharashtra (*qq.v.*). Extended along W coast from Pakistan boundary on the NW to Mysore on the S, with Western Ghats along most of its

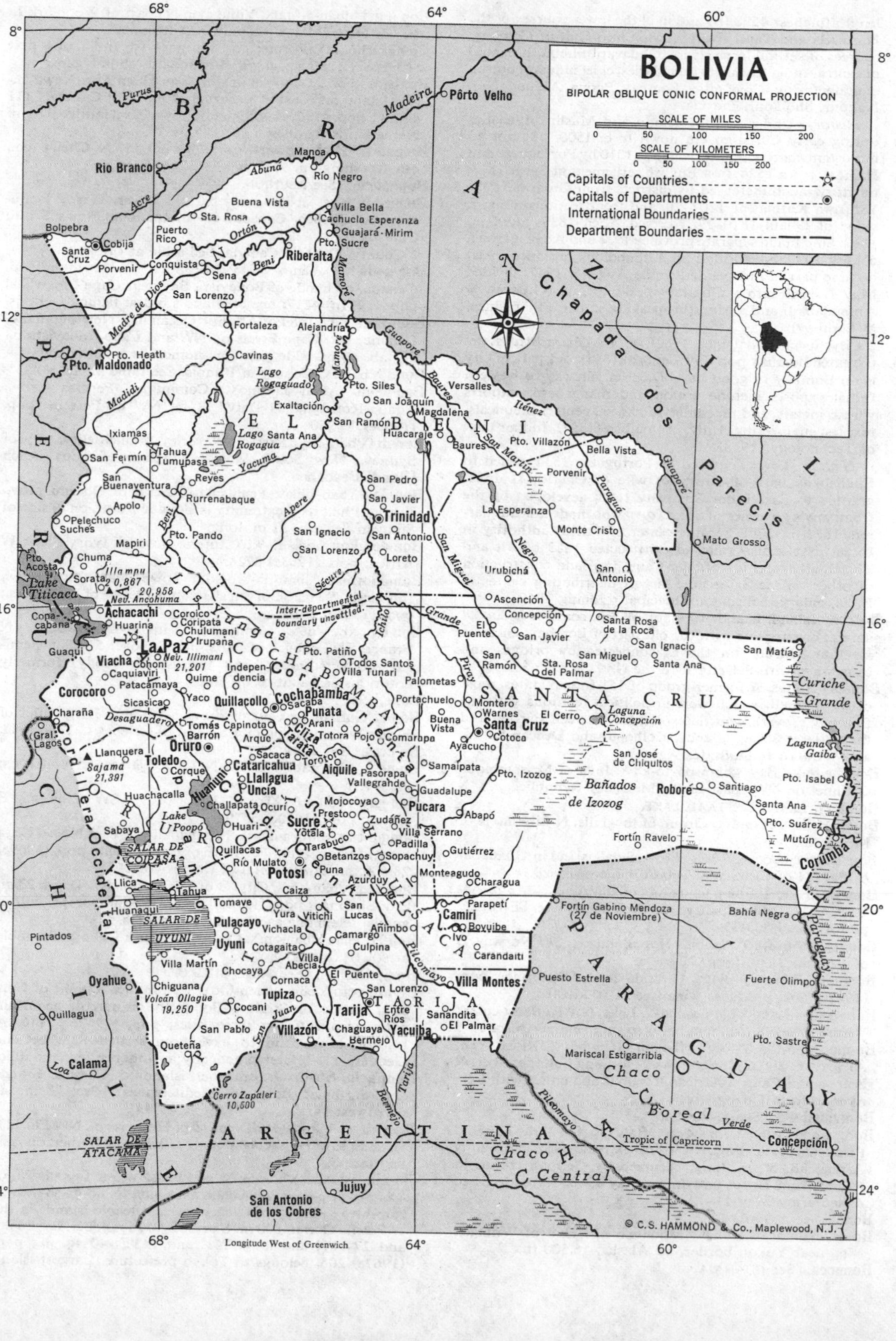
BOLIVIA
BIPOLAR OBLIQUE CONIC CONFORMAL PROJECTION
SCALE OF MILES
0 50 100 150 200
SCALE OF KILOMETERS
0 50 100 150 200
Capitals of Countries
Capitals of Departments
International Boundaries
Department Boundaries
68°
64°
60°
8°
12°
16°
20°
24°
B R A Z I L
P E R U
C H I L E
A R G E N T I N A
P A R A G U A Y
P A N D O
E L B E N I
S A N T A C R U Z
L A P A Z
O R U R O
P O T O S Í
C O C H A B A M B A
C H U Q U I S A C A
T A R I J A
Pôrto Velho
Madeira
Purus
Acre
Abunã
Rio Branco
Manoa
Río Negro
Buena Vista
Villa Bella
Cachuela Esperanza
Guajará - Mirim
Pto. Sucre
Riberalta
Sta. Rosa
Bolpebra
Cobija
Santa Cruz
Puerto Rico
Porvenir
Conquista
Sena
Ortón
Beni
Mamoré
San Lorenzo
Madre de Dios
Fortaleza
Alejandría
Pto. Heath
Pto. Maldonado
Cavinas
Madidi
Lago Rogaguado
Pto. Siles
San Joaquín
Exaltación
San Ramón
Magdalena
Huacaraje
Baures
Versalles
Guaporé
Iténez
Chapada dos Parecis
Lago Rogagua
Santa Ana
Ixiamas
San Fermín
Tahua
Tumupasa
Reyes
Yacuma
San Buenaventura
Rurrenabaque
Apolo
Pelechuco
Suches
Mapiri
Chuma
Pto. Acosta
Sorata
Illampu 20,867
20,958 Nev. Ancohuma
Lake Titicaca
Achacachi
Copacabana
Guaqui
Huarina
Coroico
Coripata
Chulumani
Irupana
La Paz
Nev. Illimani 21,201
Viacha
Cohoni
Caquiaviri
Patacamaya
Quime
Corocoro
Sicasica
Yaco
Charaña
Desaguadero
(Gral. Lagos)
Cordillera Occidental
Llanquera
Sajama 21,391
Tomás Barrón
Oruro
Toledo
Corque
Huachacalla
Challapata
Lake Poopó
Sabaya
SALAR DE COIPASA
Llica
Tahua
Huanaqui
SALAR DE UYUNI
Pintados
Oyahue
Volcán Ollagüe 19,250
Quillagua
Calama
Loa
SALAR DE ATACAMA
Cerro Zapaleri 10,500
Pto. Villazón
Bella Vista
Porvenir
Paraguá
San Martín
San Pedro
San Javier
Trinidad
Apere
San Ignacio
San Antonio
San Lorenzo
Loreto
Pto. Pando
Sécure
Inter-departmental boundary unsettled.
Los Yungas
Ichilo
Grande
La Esperanza
Negro
Monte Cristo
San Miguel
Urubichá
San Antonio
Mato Grosso
Ascención
Concepción
El Puente
San Javier
Santa Rosa de la Roca
San Ignacio
San Miguel
Santa Ana
San Matías
San Ramón
Sta. Rosa del Palmar
Curiche Grande
Pto. Patiño
Todos Santos
Villa Tunari
Indepen-dencia
Cordillera Oriental
Palometas
Piray
Quillacollo
Cochabamba
Sacaba
Arani
Punata
Cliza
Tarata
Capinota
Arque
Totora
Pojo
Comarapa
Portachuelo
Montero
Warnes
Buena Vista
Santa Cruz
Cotoca
El Cerro
Laguna Concepción
Ayacucho
Oruro
Sacaca
Toro Toro
Catarichahua
Llallagua
Uncía
Aiquile
Pasorapa
Vallegrande
Samaipata
Pto. Izozog
San José de Chiquitos
Laguna Gaiba
Pto. Isabel
Bañados de Izozog
Roboré
Santiago
Santa Ana
Guadalupe
Pucara
Mojocoya
Presto
Zudáñez
Ocurí
Huari
Quillacas
Sucre
Yotala
Tarabuco
Villa Serrano
Padilla
Abapó
Gutiérrez
Fortín Ravelo
Pto. Suárez
Mutún
Corumbá
Río Mulato
Betanzos
Sopachuy
Potosí
Puna
Azurduy
Monteagudo
Charagua
Caiza
Tomave
Yura
Vitichi
San Lucas
Parapetí
Camiri
Boyuibe
Ivo
Fortín Gabino Mendoza (27 de Noviembre)
Bahía Negra
Paraguay
Pulacayo
Vichacla
Añimbo
Camargo
Culpina
Uyuni
Cotagaita
Villa Martín
Villa Abecia
Chocaya
Cornaca
El Puente
Carandaiti
Chiguana
Villa Montes
Pilcomayo
Puesto Estrella
Fuerte Olimpo
Tupiza
San Lorenzo
Cocani
Entre Ríos
Sanandita
Tarija
Yacuiba
El Palmar
San Pablo
Villazón
Chaguaya
Bermejo
San Juan
Queteña
Pto. Sastre
Mariscal Estigarribia
Chaco Boreal
Verde
Tropic of Capricorn
Concepción
Chaco Central
Bermejo
Tarija
Jujuy
San Antonio de los Cobres
© C.S. HAMMOND & Co., Maplewood, N.J.
Longitude West of Greenwich

length (highest 4500 ft.) and in N the lower courses of the Narmada and Tapti rivers flowing into Gulf of Cambay; sources of several large rivers (Godavari, Bhima, Krishna) of central India within its boundaries; chief industry cotton manufacturing. Chief cities Bombay, Poona, Ahmadabad, Nagpur, Sholapur, Baroda.

History: Under various Hindu and Muslim dynasties during early Christian era down to c. 1500, but not an important center; Goa (*q.v.*) taken 1510 by Portuguese and Bombay town 1534; first English settlement at Surat 1613; territory much increased by districts from Gujarat 1805–18, from Kathiawar 1807–20, and from sections along E slope of Ghats 1819–27; received Aden 1839 and Sind 1843. Sind made separate province 1936 and Aden a crown colony 1937; constituted an autonomous province 1937; became part of independent India Aug. 15, 1947; divided May 1, 1960 into a Gujarati-speaking state (Gujarat, ❋ Ahmadabad) and a Marathi-speaking state (Maharashtra, ❋ Bombay).

2 City, its ❋ and (since 1960) ❋ of Maharashtra state; (**Greater Bombay** pop. [1970e] 5,700,358); old part of city is on Bombay I.; good harbor, ocean gateway to western India; exports include cotton and manganese; imports wheat, metals, and machinery; financial center; chemicals, textiles; engineering; Univ. of Bombay (1857), Indian Inst. of Technology (1958).

History: Town acquired by Portuguese 1534; ceded to English as part of dowry of wife of Charles II 1661; granted to East India Company 1668; developed by the Company's governor of Surat (*q.v.*) who made it headquarters 1672; in 1708 became center of British authority in India; first Indian railroad constructed 1853 bet. it and Thana; after opening of Suez Canal 1869 and construction of other railroads, became largest distributing center in India; enlarged through municipal rezoning 1950.

Bombay Island. Island, 10 m. off W cen. coast of India; 24 sq. m.; coextensive with the old part of Bombay; encloses **Bombay Harbor** on the E; connected by bridges and causeways with Salsette I. to the N.

Bombay States. A former group of 151 Indian states, most of them small, which were in political relations with the Bombay Government; later divided between Baroda and the Gujarat States Agency, Kolhapur and Deccan States, and Western India States Agency.

Bom·be·to·ka Bay \ˌbäm-bə-ˈtō-kə-\. Inlet of Mozambique Channel on NW coast of the Malagasy Republic.

Bombon, Lake. See TAAL, LAKE.

Bo·mi Hills \ˌbō-mē-\. Group of low hills, N Liberia, N of Monrovia.

Bom Je·sus \ˌbōm-zhi-ˈzüs, ˌbō^{n}-\. Small island in Guanabara Bay, N of the city of Rio de Janeiro, Brazil.

Bom Jesus do Ita·ba·po·a·na \ˌbōm-zhi-ˈzüs-dü-ˌē-tə-bə-pō-ˈän-ə, bō^{n}-\. Municipality, Rio de Janeiro state, SE Brazil; pop. (1968e) 50,604.

Bøm·lo \ˈbəm-(ˌ)lō\. Island, Hordaland co., SW Norway, S of Bergen; 21 m. long; 70 sq. m.

Bommes \ˈbȯm\. Village, Gironde dept., SW France; pop. (1962c) 502; produces wine (see SAUTERNES).

Bom·o·seen Lake \ˈbäm-ə-ˌzēn-\. Lake, NW Rutland co., W Vermont; ab. 8 m. long; ab. 4 sq. m.; summer resort.

Bo·mu \ˈbō-(ˌ)mü\ *or* **Mbo·mu** \əm-ˈbō-\. River, cen. Africa; ab. 500 m. long; flows W forming boundary bet. N Zaire and S Central African Republic and unites with Uele river to form Ubangi river.

Bomvanaland. See TEMBULAND.

Bon, Cape \-ˈbō^{n}\ *or Arab.* **Ra's aṭ Ṭīb** \ˌräs-ät-ˈtēb\. Peninsula extending NE from extreme NE Tunisia, N Africa; ab. 50 m. long; occupied by German troops in retreat from Egypt and Libya May 1943; surrendered to Allied army May 11–12.

Bona. See ANNABA 2.

Bo·na, Mount \-ˈbō-nə\. Mountain at E end of Wrangell Mts. near Yukon border, SE Alaska; 16,500 ft.

Bonacca. See GUANAJA.

Bon·a·gai \ˈbän-ə-(ˌ)gī\. Village on N coast of Woodlark I., off SE New Guinea; its port is Kulamadau.

Bo·nai \ˈbō-ˌnī\. Former princely state, NE India, now part of Orissa; 1280 sq. m.; ❋ **Bo·nai·garh** \ˌbōn-i-ˈgär\.

Bon·aire \bə-ˈna(ə)r, -ˈne(ə)r\ *or Span.* **Buen Ai·re** \bwā-ˈnī-rē\. Island off coast of Venezuela 30 m. E of Curaçao; 111 sq. m.; pop. (1969e) 8099; chief town Kralendijk; part of Netherlands Antilles.

Bo·nan·za Peak \bə-ˌnan-zə-\. Mountain, N Chelan co., cen. Washington; 9511 ft.

Bonaparte. See RÉUNION.

Bon·a·ven·ture \ˌbän-ə-ˈven-chər\. 1 River, Gaspé Peninsula, SE Quebec, Canada; ab. 60 m. long; flows S into Chaleur Bay.

2 County, Quebec, Canada. See table at QUEBEC.

Bon·a·vis·ta \ˌbän-ə-ˈvis-tə\. Seaport, E Newfoundland, Canada, on E side of Bonavista Bay near Cape Bonavista; pop. (1971p) 4217; one of island's oldest fishing stations.

Bonavista Bay. Inlet of Atlantic Ocean in E Newfoundland, Canada, bet. Cape Freels on NW and **Cape Bonavista** on SE; ab. 40 m. wide; contains numerous small islands.

Bond \ˈbänd\. County in Illinois. See table at ILLINOIS.

Bon·de·no \bōn-ˈdā-(ˌ)nō\. Commune, Ferrara prov., Emilia-Romagna, N Italy, 12 m. NW of Ferrara; pop. (1968e) 19,950.

Bon·di \ˈbän-ˌdī\. Part of Waverley municipality, city of Sydney, New South Wales, Australia; famous beach (**Bondi Beach**).

Bon·doc \bän-ˈdäk\. Peninsula, SE end of Quezon prov., Luzon, Phil.; its S extremity is **Bondoc Point,** on N side of Sibuyan Sea; ab. 37 m. long.

Bon·dou·kou \ˌbō^{n}-dü-ˈkü\. Interior town, E Ivory Coast, W Africa; pop. (1963e) 8728.

Bon·do·wo·so \ˌbȯn-də-ˈwō-sō\. Town, East Java prov., Indonesia, 90 m. SE of Surabaja; in valley W of Idjen Mts.; pop. (1961c) 35,760.

Bon·dy \bō^{n}-ˈdē\. Commune, Seine-St-Denis dept., N France, ENE suburb of Paris; pop. (1968c) 51,652; chemical products; near forest (**Forest of Bondy**) formerly notorious as haunt of brigands.

Bône. See ANNABA 2.

Bo·ne, Gulf of *or* **Gulf of Bo·ni** \-ˈbō-nē\. Large inlet of Flores Sea extending into S coast of Celebes I., Indonesia.

Bo'ness. See BORROWSTOUNNESS.

Bo·ne·te \bə-ˈnāt-ē\. Peak, N La Rioja prov., Argentina; 22,546 ft.

Bon·ga \ˈbȯŋ-gə\. Town, Kefa prov., SW Ethiopia, E Africa; pop. (1970e) 5579.

Bong·a·bon \bȯŋ-ˈä-ˌbȯn\. Municipality, E cen. Nueva Ecija prov., Luzon, Phil., 16 m. NE of Cabanatuan; pop. (1969e) 28,600; an early capital of the province.

Bon·ham \ˈbän-əm\. City, ⊗ of Fannin co., NE Texas, 23 m. E of Sherman; pop. (1970c) 7698; gasoline pumps, cotton goods, telephone cables; dairy products.

Bon Homme \ˈbän-əm\. County in South Dakota. See table at SOUTH DAKOTA.

Boni, Gulf of. See BONE, GULF OF.

Bo·ni·fa·cio \ˌbän-ə-ˈfäch-(ˌ)ō\. Commune, S point of Corsica, France, on Strait of Bonifacio, on narrow peninsula with steep cliffs on three sides; pop. (1962c) 2146. A historic town, said to have been settled 828; became Genoese 1187, later practically an independent republic.

Bonifacio, Strait of. Strait bet. islands of Corsica, France and Sardinia, Italy, in Mediterranean Sea; 7 m. at narrowest part.

Bon·i·fay \ˈbän-ə-ˌfā\. Town, ⊗ of Holmes co., NW Florida, 96 m. ENE of Pensacola; pop. (1970c) 2068; timber; diversified farming.

Bo·nin Islands \ˈbō-nən-\ *or* **Oga·sa·wa·ra Islands** \(ˌ)ō-ˌgäs-ə-ˈwär-ə-\ *or Jap.* **Ogasawara–gun·tō** \ˌō-gə-sə-ˌwär-ə-ˈgün-(ˌ)tō\. Group of twenty-seven volcanic islands in the W Pacific Ocean, 600 m. S of Tokyo, Japan, bet. lat. 26°30′ and 27°44′N and long. 141° and 143°E; 40 sq. m.; pop. (1967e) 205; belongs to Tokyo prefecture. Largest island

Chichi-shima in center; other important islands Haha-Jima, Muko-shima, and Yome-shima. First known to Japanese c. 1600; first colonized 1830 by small group of Europeans and Hawaiians; occupied by Japanese 1862, annexed 1876. In World War II attacked by U.S. task force Sept. 1944; frequently bombed by U.S. planes 1944–45. Administered by U.S. 1945–68.

Bo·ni·rau \ˌbō-nə-ˈrau̇\. Mountain, N Doberai Penin., NW Irian Barat, Indonesia; 7546 ft.

Bonn \ˈbän, ˈbȯn\. City, ✱ of West Germany, in North Rhine-Westphalia on the left bank of Rhine river 16 m. SSE of Cologne; pop. (1969e) 138,012; chemicals, office furniture, stoneware, light metal goods; insurance companies, publishing houses; 13th cent. Romanesque cathedral, 18th cent. town hall, univ. (1777, dissolved 1794, refounded 1818). Birthplace of Beethoven. Bombed by Allies 1944–45, captured Mar. 7–8, 1945; meeting place of constituent assembly which drafted constitution, approved May 8, 1949, for West German republic (comprising American, British, and French occupation zones); chosen as capital of the new republic (sometimes called **Bonn Republic**) May 1949.

Bonne Bay \ˈbän-\. Inlet of the Gulf of St. Lawrence, W Newfoundland, Canada.

Bon·ner \ˈbän-ər\. County in Idaho. See table at IDAHO.

Bon·ners Ferry \ˈbän-ərz-\. City, ⊗ of Boundary co., N Idaho, 75 m. NNE of Coeur d'Alene; pop. (1970c) 1909; sawmills.

Bonner Springs \ˌbän-ər-\. City, Wyandotte co., NE Kansas, 15 m. W of Kansas City; pop. (1970c) 3662; wheat, hogs; site of Agricultural Hall of Fame.

Bonne Terre \bän-ˈte(ə)r\. City, St. Francois co., E Missouri, 52 m. SSW of St. Louis; pop. (1970c) 3622; lead.

Bon·ne·ville \ˈbän-ə-ˌvil\. County in Idaho. See table at IDAHO.

Bonneville, Mount. Peak, E Sublette co., W Wyoming; 12,530 ft.

Bonneville Salt Flats *or* **Bonneville Flats.** A stretch of barren salt flat land, Tooele co., NW Utah, E of Wendover; ab. 100 sq. m.; part of bed of the Pleistocene **Lake Bonneville;** several world automobile speed records established here since 1935.

Bon·ny \ˈbän-ē\. Seaport village at mouth of **Bonny River** (one of the mouths of the Niger, *q.v.*), Rivers State, SE Nigeria; formerly important, now its trade taken over by Port Harcourt.

Bononia. 1 City, Bulgaria. See VIDIN.

2 Seaport city, France. See BOULOGNE.

3 Commune, Italy. See BOLOGNA 2.

Bon Se·cour Bay \ˌbän-sə-ˈku̇(ə)r-\. Inlet of Gulf of Mexico on SW coast of Baldwin co., SW Alabama.

Bon·thain \bȯn-ˈtīn\. 1 Port at S end of SW peninsula of Celebes I., Indonesia; pop. (1961c) 9974.

2 Peak, Indonesia. See LOMPOBATANG.

Bon·the \ˈbän-tē\. Seaport town, Sierra Leone, on E coast of Sherbro I.; trading town.

Bon·toc \bän-ˈtäk\. Municipality, ✱ of Mountain Province, Luzon, Phil., on upper Chico river, in W part of province; pop. (1969e) 22,500.

Bo·ny \bō-ˈnē\. Village, Aisne dept., NE France, 10 m. NNW of St-Quentin; pop. (1962c) 152; battle Sept. 29, 1918; American military cemetery.

Book·er T. Wash·ing·ton National Monument \ˌbu̇k-ər-ˌtē-ˈwȯsh-iŋ-tən-, -ˈwäsh-\. See UNITED STATES, *National Monuments.*

Boom \ˈbōm\. Commune, Antwerp prov., N Belgium, on the Rupel 8 m. S of Antwerp; pop. (1969e) 16,770.

Boo·mer \ˈbüm-ər\. Residential town, Fayette co., S cen. West Virginia, SE of Charleston; pop. (1970c) 1261 (with Harewood).

Boom·plaats \ˈbüm-ˌpläts\. Locality, S Orange Free State, Rep. of South Africa, near Jagersfontein, SW of Bloemfontein; scene Aug. 29, 1848 of defeat of Boers under Pretorius by Sir Harry Smith.

Boone \ˈbün\. 1 Name of counties in eight states of the U.S. See tables at ARKANSAS, ILLINOIS, INDIANA, IOWA, KENTUCKY, MISSOURI, NEBRASKA, WEST VIRGINIA.

2 City, ⊗ of Boone co., cen. Iowa, 35 m. NNW of Des Moines; pop. (1970c) 12,468; hydraulic equipment, soap; railroad shops, hatcheries; Indian antiquities discovered nearby; Boone Junior Coll. (1927).

3 Town, ⊗ of Watauga co., NW North Carolina, 22 m. NNW of Lenoir; pop. (1970c) 8754; lumber; Appalachian State Univ. (1903).

Boone Dam. See table at TENNESSEE VALLEY AUTHORITY.

Boones·boro *or earlier* **Boones·bor·ough** \ˈbünz-bər-ə, -bə-rə\. Former village, Madison co., E cen. Kentucky, on Kentucky river; site of a fort founded by Daniel Boone 1775.

Boone·ville \ˈbün-ˌvil\. 1 City, a ⊗ of Logan co., W Arkansas, 34 m. SE of Fort Smith; pop. (1970c) 3239; sawmills; natural gas; tuberculosis sanatorium.

2 City, ⊗ of Owsley co., E Kentucky; pop. (1970c) 126; corn, livestock.

3 Town, ⊗ of Prentiss co., NE Mississippi; pop. (1970c) 5895; lumber mills; shoes; Northeast Mississippi Junior Coll. (1948).

Boons·boro \ˈbünz-bər-ə, -bə-rə\. Town, Washington co., N Maryland, ab. 10 m. S of Hagerstown near a gap in South Mountain (*q.v.*); pop. (1970c) 1410; scene of Union victory Sept. 14, 1862.

Boon·ton \ˈbünt-ᵊn\. Town, Morris co., N New Jersey, 8 m. NNE of Morristown; pop. (1970c) 9261; railway fuses; oil refinery, truck farms; settled 1762, incorp. 1867; important ironmaking center during middle of 19th cent.

Boon·ville \ˈbün-ˌvil\. 1 City, ⊗ of Warrick co., SW Indiana, 17 m. ENE of Evansville; pop. (1970c) 5736; bricks; coal mines.

2 City, ⊗ of Cooper co., cen. Missouri, on Missouri river 25 m. W of Columbia; pop. (1970c) 7514; livestock; Kemper Military School and Coll. (1844); scene June 17, 1861 of first land battle of Civil War in Missouri, in which Union troops under Gen. Nathaniel Lyon defeated Confederate force under Col. John S. Marmaduke.

3 Village, Oneida co., cen. New York, 20 m. N of Rome; pop. (1970c) 2488; in dairy-farming region.

Booth·bay Harbor \ˌbüth-bā-\. Seaport town, Lincoln co., S Maine, on Atlantic Ocean 34 m. ENE of Portland; pop. (1970c) 2320; fishing center and summer resort.

Boo·thia, Gulf of \-ˈbüth-i-ə\. Gulf bet. Boothia Penin. and Melville Penin., S of NW Baffin I., Northwest Territories, Canada.

Boothia Peninsula *or formerly* **Boothia Fe·lix Peninsula** \-ˈfē-liks-\. Peninsula, almost an island, S Franklin dist., Northwest Territories, Canada; separated from Baffin I. on the E by Gulf of Boothia and from Prince of Wales I. on the NW by Franklin Strait. The North Magnetic Pole was formerly located on its W shore (see MAGNETIC POLE). Its N tip is northernmost point of mainland of North America, at 70°30′N.

Boo·tle \ˈbüt-ᵊl\. County borough, Lancashire, NW England, on the Mersey, suburb of Liverpool; pop. (1971p) 74,208; shipping center; metal manufacturing, flour milling; dye works, lumberyards.

Bo·po·lu \bō-ˈpō-lü\. Settlement, NW Liberia, W Africa, ab. 70 m. N of Monrovia.

Bo·que·rón \ˌbō-kə-ˈrōn\. 1 Department of NW Paraguay. See table at PARAGUAY.

2 Port, a barrio of Cabo Rojo municipality, SW Puerto Rico, on **Boquerón Bay.**

Bor \'bȯr\. 1 Town, Gorki Oblast, Russian S.F.S.R., U.S.S.R., ab. 7 m. NNE of Gorki; pop. (1969e) 51,000.
2 Town, Serbia, E Yugoslavia, ab. 95 m. SE of Belgrade; pop. (1965e) 20,000; copper mine.

Bo·ra–Bo·ra *or* **Bo·ra·bo·ra** \ˌbōr-ə-'bōr-ə, ˌbȯr-ə-'bȯr-ə\. One of the Leeward Is. group of the Society Is., French Polynesia, 9 m. W by N of Tahaa; ab 14 sq. m.; pop. (1962c) 1723.

Bo·rah Peak \ˌbōr-ə-, ˌbȯr-\. Mountain in Lost River Range, Custer co., cen. Idaho; 12,662 ft.; highest point in the state.

Bo·ran \'bōr-ən, 'bȯr-\. Region, S Ethiopia, bordering on Kenya.

Bo·rås \bü-'rōs\. Town, Älvsborg co., SW Sweden, 35 m. E of Göteborg; pop. (1970e) 71,227; textile mills; founded 1632 by Gustavus Adolphus.

Bo·rāz·jān \ˌbȯ-räz-'jän, -jün\. Town, SW Iran, ab. 25 m. NE of Büshehr.

Borbetomagus. See WORMS 2.

Bor·bon \bȯr-'bȯn\. Municipality on NE coast of Cebu I., Phil., 38 m. N of City of Cebu; pop. (1969e) 25,300.

Borbonensis Ager. See BOURBONNAIS.

Bor·deaux \bȯr-'dō\ *or anc.* **Bur·dig·a·la** \(ˌ)bər-'dig-ə-lə\. Commercial seaport and industrial city, ✱ of Gironde dept., SW France, 13 m. above confluence of Garonne and Dordogne rivers, 310 m. SSW of Paris; pop. (1968c) 266,-662; shipbuilding and marine engineering; chemicals; oil refining, food processing; archiepiscopal see; famous for its red and white wines; important structures include a 17-arch stone bridge (1821), city gate (Porte de Bourgogne), 8th cent. Gothic church, 10th cent. Romanesque church, 11th cent. Gothic cathedral, univ. (1441).

History: Under Roman rule was capital of Aquitania Secunda; taken by Goths and Normans; passed to King Louis VII of France; held by England 1154–1451; suffered during Revolution as a Girondist center; joined with Bourbon forces 1814; seat of government of National Defense 1870; an American military base 1918; French government temporarily removed here 1918; occupied by Germans 1940–45; relieved Apr. 1945.

Bor·den \'bȯrd-ᵊn\. County in Texas. See table at TEXAS.

Borden Island. Island, N Perry Is., Franklin dist., Northwest Territories, Canada.

Bor·den·town \'bȯrd-ᵊn-ˌtau̇n\. City, Burlington co., S cen. New Jersey, on Delaware river 6 m. SSE of Trenton; pop. (1970c) 4490; diversified farming; settled 1682 by English Quakers; partly destroyed by British 1778; incorporated as city 1867.

Bor·di·ghe·ra \ˌbȯrd-i-'ger-ə\. Commune, Imperia prov., Liguria, NW Italy, ESE of Ventimiglia; pop. (1968e) 12,-172; seaport; winter resort.

Bordj Bou Ar·re·ridj \ˌbȯrj-bü-ə-rā-'rēj\. Commune, Sétif dept., NE Algeria, ab. 110 m. WSW of Constantine; pop. (1966c) 33,780.

Bordj Me·na·ïel \-mā-nä-'yel\. Commune, Tizi-Ouzou dept., N Algeria, ab. 40 m. E of Algiers; pop. (1966c) 14,284.

Bordø \'bȯrd-ˌər\. An island of the Faeroes (*q.v.*).

Borgå. See PORVOO.

Bor·gar·nes \ˌbȯr-gär-'nās\. Village, SW coast of Iceland, just N of Reykjavík; pop. (1970c) 1157.

Bør·ge·fjell National Park \'bər-gə-ˌfyel-\. National park, Norway; 386 sq. m.; alpine area; established 1963.

Bor·gen Bay \ˌbȯr-gən-\. Inlet of Bismarck Sea on N coast of New Britain I., Bismarck Archipelago, at W end just E of Cape Gloucester; strategic Hill 660 on the bay captured by marines Jan. 14, 1944 after a ten-day battle.

Bor·ger \'bȯr-gər\. City, Hutchinson co., NW Texas, in the panhandle; pop. (1970c) 14,195; gas and oil wells; Frank Phillips Coll. (1946).

Bor·ger·hout \'bȯr-gər-ˌhau̇t\. Commune, Antwerp prov., N Belgium, an E suburb of Antwerp; pop. (1969e) 48,766.

Borg·holm \'bȯrg-ˌhōm, 'bȯr-yᵊ-ˌhȯlm\. Seaport, Kalmar co., SE Sweden, on W coast of Öland I.; pop. (1970e) 6917; chief town of island; seaside resort.

Borgne, Lake \-'bȯ(ə)rn\. Inlet of Mississippi Sound in Orleans and St. Bernard parishes, SE Louisiana; connects Lake Pontchartrain with Gulf of Mexico.

Bor·go Grap·pa \ˌbȯr-gō-'gräp-ə\. Village, Latium, W Italy, near Cisterna and ab. 10 m. S of Velletri, where the Anzio and southern armies of U.S. joined May 25, 1944 in advance on Rome.

Bor·go·ma·ne·ro \ˌbȯr-(ˌ)gō-mə-'ne(ə)r-(ˌ)ō\. Commune, Piedmont, NW Italy; pop. (1968e) 18,448.

Borgo San Donnino. See FIDENZA.

Borgo San Lo·ren·zo \'bȯ(ə)r-(ˌ)gō-ˌsan-lə-'ren-(ˌ)zō\. Commune, Firenze prov., Tuscany, cen. Italy, 14 m. NNE of Florence; pop. (1968e) 14,302; sulfur springs; summer resort.

Bor·go·se·sia \ˌbȯ(ə)r-(ˌ)gō-'sā-zhə\. Commune, Vercelli prov., Piedmont, NW Italy, on Sesia river 27 m. NNW of Vercelli; pop. (1968e) 15,675; textiles.

Borgo Val di Ta·ro \ˌbȯ(ə)r-(ˌ)gō-ˌväl-dē-'tär-ō\. Commune, Parma prov., Emilia-Romagna, N Italy, 36 m. SW of Parma; pop. (1968e) 8205; lignite deposits nearby.

Bor·gu \'bȯ(ə)r-(ˌ)gü\ *or Fr.* **Bor·gou** \bȯr-gü\. Region, N Dahomey and North-Western State, Nigeria, W Africa, bounded on NE and E by the Niger; an area contested by France and Great Britain 1894–98; divided by convention of June 1898; chief town Nikki, Dahomey.

Bo·ri·nage \ˌbȯr-i-'näzh\. Coal-mining district surrounding Mons, Hainaut prov., Belgium.

Bo·rin·quén \ˌbōr-ən-'kān, ˌbȯr-\. Early native name of PUERTO RICO.

Borinquén, Point. Cape at NW end of Puerto Rico, at E side of entrance to Mona Passage.

Bo·ri·slav \bə-'rē-sləf\ *or Pol.* **Bo·ry·sław** \-ˌsläv\. City, W Ukrainian S.S.R., U.S.S.R., at N foot of Carpathians 44 m. SW of Lvov; pop. (1967e) 32,000; formerly in Poland; oil field; natural gas deposits.

Bo·ri·so·glebsk \bə-ˌris-ə-'glepsk\. City, E Voronezh Oblast, Russian S.F.S.R., U.S.S.R., at junction of Vorona and Khoper rivers; pop. (1969e) 65,000; foundries; established 1646 as a fort against the Crimean Tatars; center of grain-producing area.

Bo·ri·sov \bə-'rē-səf\. Town, N cen. Belorussian S.S.R., U.S.S.R., on left bank of Berezina river 50 m. NE of Minsk; pop. (1969e) 77,000; metalworking; glass works, sawmills. Held by Germans July 1941 to July 1944. See BEREZINA.

Bo·ri·sov·ka \bə-'rē-səf-kə\. 1 Town, S Kazakh S.S.R., U.S.S.R., on railroad 145 m. NW of Tashkent.
2 Town, SW Belgorod Oblast, Russian S.F.S.R., U.S.S.R., on left bank of Vorskla river near its source 52 m. N of Kharkov; held by Germans 1941–43.

Bor·ja \'bȯr-hə, 'bōr-\. Town, Guairá dept., S Paraguay, S of Villarrica; munic. pop. (1970e) 8861.

Borkhaya. See BUORKHAYA.

Bor·ku \'bȯr-ˌkü\. A region in E Sahara, N Chad, N cen. Africa.

Bor·kum \'bȯr-kəm\. West German island in North Sea at mouth of Ems river 26 m. NW of Emden, the westernmost of the East Frisian Islands; ab. 6 m. long; 14 sq. m.; pop. (1967e) 5744; a favorite summer resort.

Bor·länge \'bȯr-leŋ-ə\. Town, Kopparberg co., cen. Sweden; pop. (1970e) 29,793; iron products.

Bor·mi·da \'bȯr-məd-ə\. River, mostly in Piedmont, NW Italy; ab. 100 m. long; rises at E end of Maritime Alps, flows NE to the Tanaro below Alessandria.

Bor·na \'bȯr-nə\. Mining and manufacturing city, Leipzig dist., East Germany; pop. (1970e) 21,923; leather; became city c. 1200.

Bor·neo \'bȯr-nē-ˌō\. Island in the Malay Archipelago, E of Sumatra, N of Java, and W of Celebes; 290,320 sq. m.; pop. (1970e) 6,800,000; third largest island in the world; northern part includes the Malaysian states of Sabah and Sarawak, and the British protectorate of Brunei; S section

(*Indonesian* **Ka·li·man·tan** \ˌkal-ə-ˈman-ˌtan, ˌkäl-ə-ˈmän-ˌtän\) forms part of Indonesia, and is divided into the provinces of Central Kalimantan, East Kalimantan, South Kalimantan, and West Kalimantan (see table at INDONESIA). Touches South China Sea on W and NW, Sulu Sea on NE, Celebes Sea and Makasar Strait on E, and Java Sea on S. Crossed by the equator in S cen. part; has indented coastline with numerous good harbors. Mountainous throughout N and cen. parts; chief ranges Muller, Schwaner, and Kapuas; highest point Mt. Kinabalu 13,455 ft. in Sabah. Most important rivers are the Barito, Kapuas, Mahakam, and Rajang. Produces rice, tobacco, millet, copra, pepper; bauxite, coal, iron, and oil.

History: Invaded c. 5th cent. A.D. by people from S India; S part influenced in turn by Sumatra and Java (*qq.v.*); sultanate of Brunei (*q.v.*) on N coast probably founded from Malaya and gave its name in corrupted form to entire island; visited by Portuguese, Dutch, and English traders 16th and 17th cents.; Sabah (North Borneo), Sarawak, and Brunei (sometimes called collectively **British Borneo**) declared British protectorates 1888 (see also LABUAN); rest (**Dutch Borneo**) claimed by Dutch who subdued coast, esp. in wars 1850–54, 1859–62; oil discovered in Brunei 1929. In World War II seized by Japanese Dec. 1941–Feb. 1942; frequently bombed by U.S. planes 1944–45; invasion begun at Tarakan by Australian troops May 1, 1945, and operations continued until surrender of Japan Aug. 14, 1945. Dutch Borneo reorganized 1947 as a federation of autonomous provinces to be included in the projected United States of Indonesia; reorganized again as part of Republic of Indonesia 1950; Sabah and Sarawak made states of Malaysia 1963; period 1963–66 marked by hostilities bet. Indonesia and Malaysia.

Borneo, South and East. Former residency of Dutch Borneo, Neth. Indies, now divided into the Indonesian provinces of Central Kalimantan, East Kalimantan, and South Kalimantan (*qq.v.*).

Borneo, West. See KALIMANTAN, WEST.

Born·holm \ˈbȯrn-ˌhō(l)m\. Island, constituting a county of Denmark, in Baltic Sea 25 m. S of Sweden; 227 sq. m.; pop. (1971c) 47,241; ⊗ Rønne. Generally hilly; popular tourist resort. In early times the home of pirates; seized by the Hanseatic League 1510; down to 1660 held for varying periods by Denmark, Lübeck, Sweden; Danish since 1660.

Born·höved \bȯrn-ˈhə(r)ft\. Village, SE Schleswig-Holstein, West Germany, 10 m. E of Neumünster; pop. (1966e) 1940; battle here July 22, 1227, in which Danes under Waldemar II were defeated by Germans, decisively ending Danish dominion over Baltic region.

Bor Nor. See PEI-ERH.

Bor·no·va \ˌbȯr-nə-ˈvä\. Town, İzmir prov., W Turkey, 5 m. NE of İzmir; pop. (1965c) 30,445.

Bor·nu \ˈbȯ(ə)r-(ˌ)nü\. A vast plain, NE Nigeria, sloping toward Lake Chad; inhabited chiefly by Kanuri Negroes; constituted a Muslim kingdom from ab. 11th cent.; together with Kanem formed an empire from ab. 13th cent., at height of its power 1571–1603; came in conflict with Fulahs ab. 1808; after 1835 visited by Europeans and by 1900 French, Germans, and British had spheres of influence; in 1902 became part of Nigeria under British.

Bor·ny \bȯr-ˈnē\. See COLOMBEY.

Bo·ro·bu·dur *or Du.* **Bo·ro·boe·doer** \ˌbōr-ə-bə-ˈdu̇(ə)r, ˌbȯr-\. Ruins of a great Buddhist temple, Central Java prov., Indonesia, ab. 10 m. S of Magelang and 18 m. NW of Jogjakarta; about 1000 years old, built of volcanic lava over a hill, with eight galleries of some 1500 exquisite bas-relief carvings and 430 life-size images of Buddha; rediscovered 1835; under government care.

Bo·ro·di·no \ˌbȯr-ə-ˈdē-(ˌ)nō, ˌbär-\. Village, W Moscow Oblast, Russian S.F.S.R., U.S.S.R., 70 m. WSW of Moscow on the Moscow-Smolensk highway (now on railroad). Scene of great battle of Napoleonic Wars Sept. 7, 1812 in which Napoleon defeated Gen. Kutuzov with heavy losses on both sides. In World War II scene of fighting Oct. 15–16, 1941.

Bo·ron·ga Islands \bə-ˌrȯŋ-gə-\. Group of small islands in Bay of Bengal off W coast of cen. Burma, S of Sittwe.

Bo·rong·an \bə-ˈräŋ-ən\. Municipality, ✱ of Samar Oriental prov., SE Samar, Phil., on coast 36 m. E of Catbalogan; pop. (1969e) 33,100; has extensive coconut plantations.

Bo·ro·vi·chi \bə-ˈro-vi-chē, -rȯv-yi-\. Town, SE Novgorod Oblast, Russian S.F.S.R., U.S.S.R., on Msta river 160 m. SE of Leningrad; pop. (1969e) 56,000; coal mining.

Bor·ro·me·an Islands \ˌbȯr-ə-ˌmē-ən-, ˌbär-\ *or Ital.* **Iso·le Bor·ro·mee** \ˈē-zə-(ˌ)lā-ˌbȯr-ə-ˈmā(-ˌā)\. Four small islands in Lake Maggiore, NW Italy; noted for their scenery.

Bor·row·dale \ˈbär-ō-ˌdāl, ˈbȯr-\. Valley in Cumberland, NW England, near Keswick, famed for its beauty; through it flows the Derwent.

Bor·row·stoun·ness \bō-ˈnes, ˌbär-ə-stō-ˈnes, ˌbȯr-\ *or officially* **Bo'·ness** \bō-ˈnes\. Seaport burgh, West Lothian co., SE Scotland, on Firth of Forth; pop. (1971p) 10,272; coal mining, iron founding.

Bor·sip·pa \bȯr-ˈsip-ə\. Ancient Akkadian city near Babylon; its ruins are just S of Hilla.

Bor·sod–Abaúj–Zemp·lén \ˌbȯr-shȯd-ˌäb-ə-ü(-yə)-zem-ˈplān\. County of N Hungary. See table at HUNGARY.

Bor·stal \ˈbȯrst-ᵊl, ˈbōrst-\. Village near Rochester, Kent, SE England; site of Borstal reformatory (founded 1902) which pioneered the segregation of young offenders from mature criminals, and other reforms (Borstal system).

Bo·rü·jerd *or* **Bu·ru·jird** \ˌbōr-ə-ˈjerd\. City, W Iran, 200 m. SW of Tehran; pop. (1971p) 75,000; alt. ab. 5500 ft.

Borysław. See BORISLAV.

Borysthenes. See DNIEPER.

Bor·zya \ˈbȯr-zhə\. Town, S Chita Oblast, Russian S.F.S.R., U.S.S.R., on Russian-Manchurian R.R. ab. 170 m. SE of Chita; pop. (1967e) 26,000.

Bo·san·ska Gra·diš·ka \ˌbō-sän-skə-ˈgräd-esh-kə\. Town, NW cen. Yugoslavia, on Sava river N of Banja Luka.

Bos·ca·wen \ˈbäs-kwin, -kȯin, -ˌkȯ-ən\. Town, Merrimack co., S cen. New Hampshire, on Merrimack river 9 m. N of Concord; pop. (1970c) 3162.

Boscawen. See TAFAHI.

Bos·co·bel \ˌbäs-kə-ˈbel\. 1 City, Grant co., SW corner of Wisconsin, on Wisconsin river; pop. (1970c) 2510; farm trade center; founding place of the Gideons, society of commercial travelers (1899).

2 Locality, Shropshire, W England, E of Shrewsbury; site of Royal Oak in which Prince Charles (later Charles II) hid in his flight after battle of Worcester 1651.

Bo·sco·re·a·le \ˌbäs-kō-rā-ˈäl-ē\. Commune, Napoli prov., Campania, Italy, at foot of S slope of Vesuvius near Pompeii; pop. (1968e) 19,655; important discoveries of antiquities have been made in vicinity.

Bos·co·tre·ca·se \ˌbäs-kō-trə-ˈkä-zə\. Commune, Napoli prov., Campania, SW Italy, ab. 12 m. SE of Naples; pop. (1968e) 20,215.

Bos·ham \ˈbäz-əm\. Village, South Downs, West Sussex, England, on coast 4 m. W of Chichester; resort and fishing village. A historical site said to have been residence of King Canute and Roman Emperor Vespasian.

Bos·hof \ˈbäs-ˌhäf\. Town, health resort, W Orange Free State, E cen. Rep. of South Africa, 30 m. ENE of Kimberley; pop. (1966e) 3040; a center of wool industry.

Bo·si·le·grad *or* **Bo·silj·grad** \ˈbō-sēl-ə-ˌgräd\. Town, SE Yugoslavia, NE of Skopje; with surrounding district, 320 sq. m., ceded to Yugoslavia by Bulgaria 1920.

Bos·koop \ˈbȯs-ˌkōp\. Commune, South Holland prov., Netherlands, 2 m. NW of Gouda; pop. (1970e) 11,600; famous for its nurseries of roses and other flowering shrubs.

Bos·kop \'bäs-ˌkäp\. Locality in the Transvaal, Rep. of South Africa; site of discovery of fossilized skull 1913.

Bos·na \'bäz-nə\. 1 River, W cen. Yugoslavia; 150 m. long; flows N into Sava river 24 m. E of Slavonski Brod.
2 Region, Yugoslavia. See BOSNIA.

Bos·nia \'bäz-nē-ə\ *or Serbo-Croat.* **Bos·na** \'bäz-nə\. Region, cen. Yugoslavia, separated from Croatia on N by the Sava river, from Serbia on E by the Drina river, borders Montenegro on S, Herzegovina on SW, and Croatia on W; Dinaric Alps along W border.

History: Ruled by Croatian kings c. 958 A.D.; subject to Hungary 1000–1200; organized c. 1200 under a ban who later took province of Herzegovina; after period of Serbian rule, became strong lordship with territory reaching seacoast (Stephen Kotromanić, ban, 1322–53); independent kingdom with its ruler, Stephen Tvrtko, taking title "King of Bosnia and Serbia" 1376; took part in battle of Kosovo (*q.v.*) 1389; kingdom disintegrated from 1391, the S part becoming independent duchy Herzegovina (*q.v.*); conquered by Turks 1463, made Turkish province; scene of insurrections against Turkish rule 1821–51; after rising 1875 which encouraged revolt in Bulgaria (*q.v.*), placed under control of Austria-Hungary 1878 and made part of province of **Bosnia and Her·ze·go·vi·na,** \-ˌhert-sə-gō-'vē-nə, -ˌhərt-\, which was formally annexed to Austria-Hungary 1908 and became a province of Yugoslavia 1918 (ab. 23,000 sq. m.); reunited with Herzegovina as a federated republic (19,741 sq. m.; pop. [1971p] 3,742,852; ✱ Sarajevo) in 1946 constitution.

Bos·nik \'bäz-nek, 'bäs-\. Village on SE coast of Biak I., Schouten Is., Irian Barat, Indonesia; with Mokmer airfield a few miles W taken by Allies May–June 1944.

Bosora. See BUSRA.

Bos·po·rus \'bäs-p(ə-)rəs\ *or Turk.* **Ka·ra·de·niz Bo·ğa·zı** \ˌkär-ə-də-'nēz-ˌbō-(g)ä-'zē\ *or anc.* **Bosporus Thra·ci·us** \-'thrā-sh(ē-)əs\ *also, commonly but incorrectly,* **Bos·pho·rus** \'bäs-fə-rəs\. Narrow strait bet. Turkey in Europe and Turkey in Asia connecting the Sea of Marmara with the Black Sea; 19 m. long and from ab. $1/2$ to $2^3/_4$ m. wide. Noted for its scenery on both banks and on European side lined with many residential suburban villages of İstanbul. From ancient times, important as thoroughfare of commerce bet. Black Sea and Aegean and Mediterranean; of great importance in medieval trade of Constantinople; controlled by Turks since 1452, when they completed fortification of its shores. See also DARDANELLES and, for later history, the STRAITS.

Bosporus, Cimmerian. 1 Strait, U.S.S.R. See KERCH STRAIT.
2 Ancient kingdom. See CIMMERIAN BOSPORUS.

Bos·que \'bäs-kē\. County in Texas. See table at TEXAS.

Bosra. See BUSRA.

Bos·sier \'bō-zhər\. Parish in Louisiana. See table at LOUISIANA.

Bossier City. Industrial town, Bossier parish, NW Louisiana, E suburb of Shreveport; pop. (1970c) 41,595; oil refineries; timber.

Bos·ton \'bȯ-stən\. 1 Seaport city, ✱ of Massachusetts, and ⊗ of Suffolk co., E Massachusetts, on Massachusetts Bay and at mouths of Charles and Mystic rivers; pop. (1970c) 641,071; largest city in the state. Industrial, commercial, financial, and medical center; important fish market, and greatest wool market in U.S.; shipbuilding, publishing; electronic equipment, apparel, chemicals, plastics. Home of the Unitarian movement in U.S.; birthplace of the Christian Science movement. Famous buildings include: Christ Church (Old North Church 1723), from the steeple of which the signal was given to Paul Revere to inform him of the route taken by the British in their march on Concord, Old South Meetinghouse (1729), Faneuil Hall (1742, known as the "Cradle of Liberty"), the old State House (1748), U.S. Custom House, Boston Public Library, Boston Museum of Fine Arts. Massachusetts Coll. of Pharmacy (1823), Boston Univ. (1839), Massachusetts State Coll. at Boston (1852), New England Conservatory of Music (1867), Garland Junior Coll. (1872), Massachusetts Coll. of Art (1873), Burdett Coll. (1879), Emerson Coll. (1880), Wheelock Coll. (1889), Chamberlayne Junior Coll. (1892), Perry Normal School (1898), Fisher Junior Coll. (1903), Wentworth Inst. (1904), Suffolk Univ. (1906), Emmanuel Coll. (1919), Graham Junior Coll. (1950).

History: Settled by Gov. John Winthrop 1630 (see CHARLESTOWN 2); made capital of Massachusetts Bay Colony 1632; began first continuously published colonial newspaper 1704; leader in opposition to British trade restrictions and other policies leading to the outbreak of the American Revolution; scene of the Boston Massacre Mar. 5, 1770, and the so-called Boston Tea Party Dec. 16, 1773; trade shut off by Boston Port Bill 1774; battle of Bunker Hill June 17, 1775; British withdrew from city Mar. 17, 1776; opposed to Jefferson's embargo policy and War of 1812; incorporated as a city 1822; center of antislavery movement 1830–65.
2 Village, ⊗ of Bowie co., NE Texas.
3 *or formerly* **St. Bot·olph's Town** \sānt-'bät-əlfs-, sənt-, -bə-'tälfs-\. Municipal borough, ⊗ of The Parts of Holland, Lincolnshire, E England, on the Witham near its mouth 49 m. E of Nottingham; pop. (1971p) 25,995; shipping, fisheries; trade center in agricultural region.

Boston Bay. Western section of Massachusetts Bay, E Massachusetts; the city of Boston is situated at its W end on **Boston Harbor.**

Boston Corner. Town, Columbia co., New York; $1^1/_2$ sq. m.; former SW corner of Massachusetts ceded to New York 1853.

Boston Mountains. Ridge in Ozark Plateau in NW Arkansas; highest peak over 2800 ft.

Bostra. See BUSRA.

Bos·well \'bäz-ˌwel, -wəl\. Borough, Somerset co., S Pennsylvania, 13 m. SSW of Johnstown; pop. (1970c) 1529.

Bos·worth Field \ˌbäz-(ˌ)wərth-\. Region in rural district of Market Bosworth, Leicestershire, cen. England; site of final battle 1485 in Wars of the Roses in which Richard III was defeated and killed.

Bo·ta·fo·go Bay \ˌbōt-ə-ˌfō-(ˌ)gō-\. Inlet of Guanabara Bay in S section of Rio de Janeiro, Brazil, enclosed on SE by Pão de Açúcar (Sugarloaf Mt.).

Bot·a·ny \'bät-ᵊn-ē, 'bät-nē\. Municipality, E New South Wales, Australia, suburb of Sydney; pop. (1966c) 31,871.

Botany Bay. Inlet of South Pacific Ocean, on S border of city of Sydney, New South Wales, SE Australia, 9 m. S of Port Jackson; ab. 6 m. at greatest width. Scene of first landing on Australian soil by Capt. Cook Apr. 1770; selected 1787 as site for penal settlement; landing made Jan. 1788; settlement transferred later to Port Jackson.

Botany Point. Cape on W end of St. Thomas I., Virgin Is., West Indies.

Bot·e·tourt \'bät-ə-ˌtät, 'bōt-ə-ˌtȯ(ə)rt\. County in Virginia. See table at VIRGINIA.

Bo·tev Peak \'bȯ-tef-\. Mountain, Bulgaria, ab. 81 m. E of Sofia; 7793 ft.; highest peak in Balkan Mountains.

Bo·tha·ville \'bōt-ə-ˌvil\. Town, Orange Free State, Rep. of South Africa; pop. (1967e) 9300.

Both·ell \'bäth-əl\. City, King co., W cen. Washington, 12 m. NE of Seattle; pop. (1970c) 4883; concrete products; diversified agriculture.

Both·nia \'bäth-nē-ə\. Former name of the region about the Gulf of Bothnia.

Bothnia, Gulf of. Northern arm of the Baltic Sea, extending bet. Sweden on the W and Finland on the E.

Both·well \'bäth-ˌwel, -wəl\. Parish and town, Lanark co., Scotland, ab. 7 m. SE of Glasgow; ruins of Bothwell Castle of 13th cent.; at **Bothwell Bridge** over the Clyde the Royalists under Monmouth and Claverhouse defeated the Covenanters June 22, 1679.

Botocan. See PAGSANJAN.

Bo·to·şa·ni *or* **Bo·to·sha·ni** \ˌbät-ə-'shän(-ē)\. 1 County of NE Romania. See table at ROMANIA.

2 Commercial town, its ⊗; pop. (1969e) 31,604; textiles; trade center for agricultural area.

Bo·trange \bō-'trä^nzh\. Peak in Hohe Venn Mts., Liège prov., E Belgium; 2277 ft.; highest peak in Belgium.

Bo·tswa·na \bät-'swän-ə\; *formerly* **Bech·u·a·na·land Protectorate** *or short form* **Bechuanaland** \ˌbech-(ə-)'wän-əˌland\. Republic, S Africa, bounded on W and N by South-West Africa, on NE by Rhodesia, and on SE and S by the Rep. of South Africa; 219,916 sq. m.; pop. (1971e) 667,000; linked with Zambia across Zambezi river; ✱ Gaborone. *Physical features:* Essentially a tableland with mean elev. of ab. 3300 ft.; part of Kalahari Desert is in SW and W, Okavango Basin and salt lakes in N; average yearly rainfall is 18 in. *Chief products:* Economy heavily dependent on the export of cattle; crops include corn, sorghum, peanuts; asbestos, diamonds, copper, manganese, salt. *Chief towns:* Gaborone, Kanye, Molepolole, Mochudi.

History: Region occupied by British at instigation of Cecil Rhodes 1884; organized as British protectorate 1885, divided into British Bechuanaland and Bechuanaland Protectorate (the latter lying N of Molopo river); included in grant to British South Africa Company 1889 but never administered by it; when British Bechuanaland (*q.v.*) was attached to Cape of Good Hope 1895, N part remained a protectorate until it became an independent republic 1966; diamond and copper discoveries 1969–70.

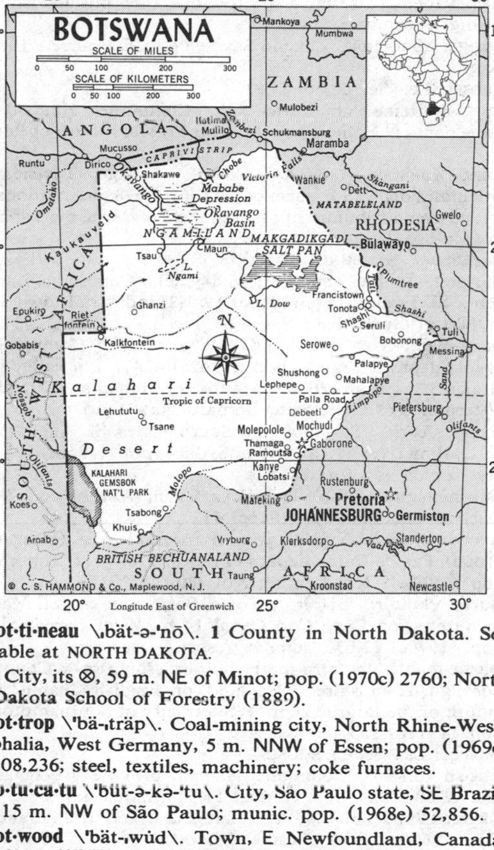

Bot·ti·neau \ˌbät-ə-'nō\. 1 County in North Dakota. See table at NORTH DAKOTA.

2 City, its ⊗, 59 m. NE of Minot; pop. (1970c) 2760; North Dakota School of Forestry (1889).

Bot·trop \'bä-ˌträp\. Coal-mining city, North Rhine-Westphalia, West Germany, 5 m. NNW of Essen; pop. (1969e) 108,236; steel, textiles, machinery; coke furnaces.

Bo·tu·ca·tu \ˌbüt-ə-kə-'tü\. City, São Paulo state, SE Brazil, 115 m. NW of São Paulo; munic. pop. (1968e) 52,856.

Bot·wood \'bät-ˌwu̇d\. Town, E Newfoundland, Canada, 160 m. WNW of St. John's; pop. (1971p) 4109; has large seaplane base and 30 m. to the E is large airport, western terminus for transatlantic planes. See GANDER.

Bötzow. See ORANIENBURG.

Boua·ké *or* **Bwa·ke** \'bwäk-(ˌ)ā\. Commercial town, S cen. Ivory Coast, W Africa, on railroad 180 m. NNW of Abidjan; pop. (1963e) 53,000; cotton and tobacco factories.

Bou-Am. See TAFILALT.

Bou–Aou·kaz, Dje·bel \ˌjab-ᵊl-ˌbü-au̇-'kaz\. Hill, NW cen. Tunisia, N Africa; 2000 ft. high; severe fighting in British attack on Tunis Apr. 27–30, 1943.

Bouar \'bwär\. Town, W Central African Republic, ab. 210 m. NW of Bangui; pop. (1968c) 48,358.

Bou Ara·da \bü-'ər-ə-də\. Town, N Tunisia, ab. 45 m. SW of Tunis; pop. (1966c) 3600; scene of fighting 1943.

Bou·cher·ville \'bü-shər-ˌvil\. Town, Chambly co., S Quebec, Canada, on St. Lawrence river 9 m. NE of Montreal; pop. (1971p) 20,000; chemicals.

Bouches–du–Rhône \ˌbüsh-dü-'rōn\. Department of SE France. See table at FRANCE.

Bou·cle du Baou·lé National Park \'bü-klə-d(y)ü-bau̇-'lā-\. National park, Mali; 2977 sq. m.; wildlife refuge; established 1954.

Bou·fa·rik *or* **Bu·fa·rik** \ˌbü-fə-'rēk\. Commune, Alger dept., N Algeria, ab. 21 m. SSW of Algiers; pop. (1966c) 24,108.

Bou·gain·ville \'bü-gən-ˌvil, 'bō-\. 1 Largest of the Solomon Islands, W Pacific Ocean; ab. 127 m. long by ab. 49 m. wide; 3880 sq. m.; a part of Papua New Guinea. Traversed lengthwise by a mountain range called Emperor Range in N and Crown Prince Range in S, highest peak Mount Balbi 8999 ft. in N section; much of the interior unexplored. Has rich volcanic soil; coconut plantations, other products are coffee, cocoa, and copper. On N is Buka I. separated from it by narrow Buka Passage, and on the S are Shortland Is. Good harbors are at Kieta, Buka Passage, and Buin at S end; on W coast is anchorage in Empress Augusta Bay.

History: Discovered by Louis de Bougainville 1768; came under control of a German trading company 1882 and was a German possession 1899–1914; taken by Australians in World War I and included 1920 in mandated New Guinea. Occupied Jan. 1942 by Japanese who developed harbors and made airfields; bombed by Allied air forces 1943 and landings made by U.S. Marines Nov. 1, 1943 on coast of Empress Augusta Bay, but most of island and Japanese forces bypassed 1944 until campaign by Australians in 1945.

2 *or formerly* **Ki·e·ta** \kē-'āt-ə\. District of Papua New Guinea, comprising Bougainville, Buka, and adjacent small islands in Solomon Is., W Pacific Ocean; 4100 sq. m.; pop. (1969e) 72,661; chief town Kieta. See SOLOMON ISLANDS.

Bougainville Strait. Channel bet. S Bougainville and NW Choiseul Is., W cen. Solomon Is.; ab. 30 m. wide; through it passes boundary line bet. the Solomon Is. of Papua New Guinea and the British Solomon Is.

Bou·ga·roun, Cape \-ˌbü-gə-'rün\. Cape on N coast of Constantine dept., NE Algeria.

Bougie. See BEJAÏA.

Bouil·lon \bü-'yōn, -'yō^n\. Town in the Ardennes, Luxembourg prov., Belgium, on the Semois ab. 7 m. NNE of Sedan; pop. (1969e) 2949; made capital of small duchy (1088) of crusader Godfrey of Bouillon; later attached successively to Liège, Sedan, France, Netherlands, Belgium.

Bou·ï·ra \bü-'ir-ə\. Commune, N Algeria, 58 m. SE of Algiers; pop. (1966c) 16,615.

Boukhara. See BUKHARA.

Boul·der \'bōl-dər\. 1 County in N cen. Colorado. See table at COLORADO.

2 City, its ⊗, 25 m. NW of Denver; pop. (1970c) 66,870; resort; in rich agricultural region; mining; space research industries; National Bureau of Standards, Univ. of Colorado (1876); settled 1858, incorp. 1871.

3 Town, ⊗ of Jefferson co., SW cen. Montana; pop. (1970c) 1342; livestock; lead, zinc.

4 Town, S Western Australia, in gold-mining district 335 m. ENE of Perth; pop. (1961c) 9696.

Boulder Canyon. Former canyon of the Colorado river ab. 20 m. above Black Canyon (site of Hoover Dam), bet. Arizona and Nevada; now covered by Lake Mead.

Boulder City. Model city, Clark co., SE corner of Nevada; pop. (1970c) 5223; built by U.S. government in 1932 as construction headquarters during work on Hoover Dam and as permanent administrative headquarters for Reclamation and National Park Service forces in area.

Boulder Dam. See *Hoover Dam* at UNITED STATES, *Dams and Reservoirs.*

Boulder Peak. Mountain, S Custer co., cen. Idaho; 10,966 ft.

Bou·lin·da, Mount \-bu̇-'lin-də\. Peak in cen. part of island of New Caledonia, SW Pacific Ocean; 4078 ft.

Bou·logne \bü-'lōn, -'lȯin\ *or* **Boulogne–sur–Mer** \-ˌsu̇(ə)r-'me(ə)r\; *anc.* **Ges·o·ri·a·cum** *or* **Ges·so·ri·a·cum** \ˌjes-ə-'rī-ə-kəm\ *or later* **Bo·no·nia** \bə-'nō-nē-ə\. Seaport city, Pas-de-Calais dept., N France, on English Channel 61 m. NW of Arras; pop. (1968c) 49,276; shipbuilding; foundries, cement factories; fishing center; 13th cent. castle; Italian Renaissance cathedral; Roman remains; large English population.

History: Inhabitants massacred by Normans 882 A.D.; taken by Henry VIII of England 1544; sold back to France 1550; demolished by Emperor Charles V 1553; place where Napoleon gathered large army 1803–05 in preparation for attack on England. In World War II taken by Germans May 21, 1940; stormed by Canadians Sept. 18, 1944 after four days of hard fighting.

Boulogne–Bil·lan·court \-ˌbē-ˌ(y)ä^{n}-'ku̇(ə)r\ *or formerly* **Boulogne–sur–Seine** \-ˌsu̇(ə)r-'sān, -'sen\. Commune, Hauts-de-Seine dept., N France, SW suburb of Paris on the Seine river, near Bois de Boulogne; pop. (1968c) 109,008; automobiles, airplanes, chemical products.

Bound·a·ry \'bau̇n-d(ə-)rē\. County in Idaho. See table at IDAHO.

Boundary Bay. Inlet of Strait of Georgia in extreme SW British Columbia on U.S.-Canada border bet. Point Roberts and Blaine, Washington.

Boundary Peak *or* **East Peak.** Mountain, W Esmeralda co., SW Nevada, on Nevada-California boundary; 13,140 ft.; highest point in Nevada.

Bound Brook \'bau̇n(d)-ˌbru̇k\. Borough, Somerset co., N cen. New Jersey, on Raritan river 7 m. NW of New Brunswick; pop. (1970c) 10,263; chemicals, roofing material; settled c. 1660; scene of attack by British force under Cornwallis 1777.

Boun·ti·ful \'bau̇nt-i-fəl\. City, Davis co., N Utah, 8 m. N of Salt Lake City; pop. (1970c) 27,956; truck gardens; fruit (esp. cherry) orchards.

Boun·ty Islands \ˌbau̇nt-ē-\. Group of 13 islets, 415 m. ESE of Dunedin, New Zealand, 48°S, 178°30′E; 1/2 sq. m.; uninhabited; under New Zealand administration; discovered 1788 by Capt. William Bligh in H.M.S. *Bounty.*

Bou·quet Canyon Dam \ˌbō-ˌkā-, ˌbü-\. Dam across **Bouquet Creek,** California; height 225 ft.; completed 1934; impounds water for water power.

Bou·rail \bu̇(ə)r-'ī\. Town, New Caledonia I., SW Pacific Ocean, 80 m. NW of Nouméa; pop. (1969c) 2433.

Bour·bon \'bər-bən\. Name of counties in two states of the U.S. See tables at KANSAS and KENTUCKY.

Bourbon. See RÉUNION.

Bour·bon·nais \bər-'bō-nəs\. Village, Kankakee co., NE Illinois, 5 m. N of Kankakee; pop. (1970c) 5909.

Bourbonnais \ˌbu̇r-bə-'nā\ *or Lat.* **Bor·bo·nen·sis Ager** \ˌbȯr-bə-ˌnen(t)-səs-'ā-jər\. Historical region of cen. France; bounded anciently on NE by Nivernais, E by Burgundy, SE by Lyonnais, S by Auvergne, SW by Marche, and NW by Berry; ✱ (from late 15th cent.) Moulins.

History: Part of Celtic Gaul under Caesar, then of Aquitania under Augustus; began separate existence in 10th cent. A.D. under Aimar, founder of first house of Bourbon (became extinct 1218); ruled by second house of Bourbon until 1272; given in dowry to Robert of Clermont (6th son of Louis IX) who founded the third and most famous house of Bourbon; became part of royal domain 1527 and subsequently a province of France.

Bourbon–Vendée. See LA ROCHE–SUR–YON.

Bou·rem *or* **Bu·rem** \bu̇-'rem\. Town, Mali, W Africa, on Niger river E of Tombouctou.

Bou·resches \bu̇-'resh\. Village, Aisne dept., NE France, 7 m. WNW of Château-Thierry; taken by Americans June 1918 in battle of Belleau Wood.

Bourg \'bu̇(ə)r\ *also* **Bourg–en–Bresse** \ˌbu̇(ə)r-kä^{n}-'bres\. Commune, ✱ of Ain dept., E France, 45 m. W of Geneva, Switzerland; pop. (1968c) 37,887; furniture; iron works; tourism; 16th cent. Gothic church; museum of antiquities. See BRESSE.

Bourges \'bu̇(ə)rzh\ *or anc.* **Avar·i·cum** \ə-'var-i-kəm\. Commune, ✱ of Cher dept., cen. France., 126 m. S of Paris; pop. (1968c) 70,814; aircraft, chemicals, rubber products, leather, textiles; in rich agricultural region; 13th cent. Gothic cathedral; archiepiscopal palace; taken by Caesar 52 B.C.; under Augustus became capital of Roman province of Aquitania; at division of Aquitania in 3d cent. was made capital of Aquitania Prima; site of numerous medieval councils; university founded 1463 but abolished during Revolution.

Bour·get \bu̇r-'zhā\. Lake in Savoie dept., E France; 11 m. long.

Bourget, Le. See LE BOURGET.

Bourg–la–Reine \ˌbu̇(ə)r-lə-'rān\. Commune, Hauts-de-Seine dept., N France; pop. (1962c) 17,908; suburb of Paris.

Bourg–Ma·dame \ˌbu̇(ə)r-ma-'dam\. Village, Pyrénées-Orientales dept., S France; pop. (1962c) 698; international bridge over a tributary of the Segre to Puigcerdá marks the Franco-Spanish frontier.

Bourgogne. See BURGUNDY.

Bour·goin–Jal·lieu \bu̇r-'gwa^{n}-zhä-'yə(r)\. Commune, Isère dept., SE France; pop. (1968c) 19,941; industrial town 34 m. NW of Grenoble.

Bourg–Saint–Mau·rice \ˌbu̇(ə)r-sa^{n}-mȯ-'rēs\. Commune, Savoie dept., E France; pop. (1962c) 4247; in a valley in Graian Alps at alt. 2668 ft.; railroad terminal and French W terminus of Little Saint Bernard Pass; tourism.

Bourke \'bərk\. Town, N New South Wales, SE Australia, on Darling river 410 m. NW of Sydney; pop. (1966c) 3262; first settled as a fort 1835.

Bour·la·maque \ˌbu̇(ə)r-lə-'mak\. Town, Abitibi co., SW Quebec, Canada; pop. (1966c) 4122.

Bour·lon \bu̇r-'lō^{n}\. Village and forested area (**Bourlon Wood**), Pas-de-Calais dept., N France, 5 m. W of Cambrai; pop. (1962c) 1120; fighting Nov. 20–30, 1917.

Bourne \'bō(ə)rn, 'bȯ(ə)rn\. Town, Barnstable co., SE Massachusetts, on Cape Cod Canal 14 m. W of Barnstable; pop. (1970c) 12,636; summer resort.

Bourne·mouth \'bō(ə)rn-məth, 'bȯ(ə)rn-, 'bu̇(ə)rn-\. County borough, Hampshire, S England, on English Channel at mouth of the Bourne 28 m. WSW of city of Southampton; pop. (1971p) 153,425; resort.

Bouscat, Le. See LE BOUSCAT.

Bous·su \bu̇-'sü\. Commune, Hainaut prov., SW Belgium, just W of Mons; pop. (1969e) 11,545; industrial town.

Bou·vet Island \ˌbü-(ˌ)vā-\. Norwegian island in S Atlantic Ocean 1600 m. SSW of Cape of Good Hope, Rep. of South Africa, 54°26′S, 3°24′E.

Bou·vines \bu̇-'vēn\. Village, Nord dept., NE France, 10 m. SE of Lille; battlefield July 27, 1214 where French under Philip Augustus defeated Emperor Otto IV, King John of England, and their allies.

Bow \'bō\. River, SW Alberta, Canada; 315 m. long; rises in Banff National Park on the E slopes of the Rocky Mts., flows SE through the park just E of Lake Louise then E past Calgary to unite with the Oldman and form the South Saskatchewan river.

Bow·bells \'bō-ˌbelz\. City, ⊗ of Burke co., NW North Dakota; pop. (1970c) 584; wheat.

Bow·doin Lake \ˌbōd-ᵊn-\. Lake, N cen. Phillips co., N Montana, 12 m. ENE of Malta; ab. 5 m. long; federal migratory bird refuge.

Bow·en \'bō-ən\. Seaport, E Queensland, NE Australia, 290 m. NW of Rockhampton; pop. (1966c) 5144.

Bow Fell \'bō-'fel\. Mountain, SE Cumberland, NW England, in the Lake District; 2960 ft.

Bow·ie \'bü-ē\. **1** County in Texas. See table at TEXAS.

2 Town, Prince Georges co., Maryland, NE of Washington; pop. (1970c) 35,028; Bowie State Coll. (1867).

3 City, Montague co., N Texas, 42 m. SE of Wichita Falls; pop. (1970c) 5185; oil refineries; cotton.

Bow Island. See HAO.

Bowl·ing \'bō-liŋ\. Village, Dunbarton co., W cen. Scotland, on Clyde river ab. 3 m. SE of Dumbarton; shipbuilding.

Bowling Green \ˌbō-liŋ-'grēn\. **1** City, ⊗ of Warren co., S Kentucky, 64 m. SE of Owensboro; pop. (1970c) 36,253; trade center in agricultural region; tobacco market; auto parts, chemicals; limestone quarries. Western Kentucky Univ. (1906).

2 City, ⊗ of Pike co., E Missouri; pop. (1970c) 2936; diversified farming.

3 City, ⊗ of Wood co., NW Ohio, 18 m. S of Toledo; pop. (1970c) 21,760; meat packing; oil wells; Bowling Green State Univ. (1910).

4 Town, ⊗ of Caroline co., E Virginia; pop. (1970c) 528.

Bow·man \'bō-mən\. **1** County in SW corner of North Dakota. See table at NORTH DAKOTA.

2 City, its ⊗; pop. (1970c) 1762.

Bow·man·ville \'bō-mən-ˌvil\. Industrial town, Durham co., SE Ontario, Canada, on Lake Ontario 42 m. ENE of Toronto; pop. (1971p) 8894; resort; foundry.

Bow River. See BOW.

Box Butte \'bäks-ˌbyüt\. County in Nebraska. See table at NEBRASKA.

Box El·der \'bäk-ˌsel-dər\. County in Utah. See table at UTAH.

Box·ford \'bäks-fərd\. Town, Essex co., NE Massachusetts, 20 m. NNE of Boston; pop. (1970c) 4032.

Box Hill. Town, S Victoria, SE Australia, NE suburb of Melbourne; pop. (1970e) 19,080.

Box·tel \'bäks-tᵊl\. Commune, North Brabant prov., S Netherlands, ab. 12 m. E of Tilburg; pop. (1969e) 18,487.

Bo·ya·cá \ˌbȯi-yə-'kä\. **1** Department of cen. Colombia. See table at COLOMBIA.

2 Town, Boyacá dept., cen. Colombia; munic. pop. (1968e) 7719; battle in which Spanish were defeated by small army under Bolívar Aug. 7, 1819. See BOGOTA 2.

Boyana. See BUENË.

Boyd \'bȯid\. Name of counties in two states of the U.S. See tables at KENTUCKY and NEBRASKA.

Boyd·ton \'bȯid-tən\. Town, ⊗ of Mecklenburg co., S Virginia; pop. (1970c) 541.

Boy·er \'bȯi-ər\. River, W Iowa; 123 m. long; rises in Buena Vista co., NW Iowa, flows SW into Missouri river in W Pottawattamie co., SW Iowa.

Bo·yer Ah·ma·dī–ye Sar·dīr va Koh·kī·lū·yeh \ˌbō-yə-rä-mə-'dē-yə-sär-ˌdir-va-ˌkō-ki-'lü-yə\. Governorship of W cen. Iran. See table at IRAN.

Boy·er·town \'bȯi-ər-ˌtau̇n\. Borough, Berks co., SE Pennsylvania, 16 m. E of Reading; pop. (1970c) 4428; auto bodies, iron castings, footwear.

Boyle \'bȯil\. **1** County in Kentucky. See table at KENTUCKY.

2 Town, N co. Roscommon, N cen. Eire; pop. (1961c) 1739; ruins of Cistercian abbey dating from 12th cent.

Boyls·ton \'bȯilz-tən\. Town, Worcester co., cen. Massachusetts, 7 m. NE of Worcester; pop. (1970c) 2774.

Boyne \'bȯin\. River, E Eire; 70 m. long; rises in the Bog of Allen, co. Kildare, flows NNE into the Irish Sea just below Drogheda; important battle fought on its banks 3 m. W of Drogheda July 1, 1690 in which the forces under King William III of England defeated the Jacobites under King James II. See AUGHRIM.

Boyne City. City, Charlevoix co., NW Michigan, 40 m. SW of Cheboygan; pop. (1970c) 2969; fishing; resort.

Boyn·ton Beach \ˌbȯint-ᵊn-\. City, Palm Beach co., SE Florida, S of West Palm Beach; pop. (1970c) 18,115.

Boz, Cape \-'bōz\ *or Turk.* **Boz·bu·run** \ˌbōz-bə-'rün\. Cape on NW coast of Turkey in Asia, projecting W into the Sea of Marmara, 40°24′N, 26°54′E.

Boz·ca·a·da \ˌbōz-jä-'dä\ *or anc.* **Ten·e·dos** \'ten-ə-ˌdäs\. Turkish island in NE Aegean Sea off W coast of Turkey in Asia, S of the island of İmroz and ab. 12 m. S of the Dardanelles; in the Trojan legend the station of the Greek fleet; used as a base by Xerxes in the Persian War and later an ally of Athens. See GREECE.

Boz Dağ \bōz-'dä(g)\ *or anc.* **Tmo·lus** \(tə-)'mō-ləs\. Mountain range, W Turkey 20 m. E of İzmir; ab. 6200 ft. high; divides valleys of Gediz and Caÿster.

Boze·man \'bōz-mən\. City, ⊗ of Gallatin co., S Montana, 80 m. ESE of Butte; pop. (1970c) 18,670; wheat, barley; cattle; Montana State Univ. (1893; oldest unit of Univ. of Montana).

Bozeman Pass. Mountain pass near Bozeman, S Montana; alt. ab. 6000 ft., on the **Bozeman Trail** which extended from Julesburg, Colorado, on the South Platte river to Virginia City, mining town in SW Montana; traced by John M. Bozeman 1863–65; its use by gold seekers opposed by Indians and abandoned after 1868; after 1877 became important cattle route.

Bozen. See BOLZANO 2.

Boz·rah \'bäz-rə\. **1** Village, Syria. See BUSRA.

2 *or mod.* **Al–Bu·sei·ra** \ˌal-bə-'sī-rə, -'sa(ə)r-ə, -'se(ə)r-ə\. Town, Jordan, SSE of Dead Sea and near Petra; ancient capital of Edom (*Gen.* xxxvi. 33).

Bra \'brä\. Commune, Cuneo prov., Piedmont, NW Italy, 25 m. NE of Cuneo; pop. (1968e) 21,776.

Bra·bant \brə-'bant, -'bänt\. **1** Old duchy of the Netherlands, covering territory of what is now S Netherlands and central and N Belgium.

History: Region settled by Franks in 5th cent. A.D.; in 9th cent. included in kingdom of Lotharingia and after 959 in duchy of Lower Lorraine (see LORRAINE); in late 12th cent. became independent duchy; finally passed to house of Burgundy 1430; inherited by Hapsburgs 1477; from 15th cent. a center of culture and commerce (see ANTWERP and BRUSSELS); northern section took part in revolt from Spain and by treaty of 1609 was awarded to United Provinces (see NETHERLANDS); southern (and larger) section remained part of Spanish, later Austrian Netherlands; united under French rule 1794–1814 and in kingdom of Netherlands 1815–30; provinces of Antwerp and southern Brabant joined revolt of Belgium (*q.v.*) 1830.

2 Province, cen. Belgium; 1302 sq. m.; pop. (1970e) 2,177,975; ✻ Brussels; Belgium's most densely populated province; rivers Senne, Dijle, Demer; chemical and metallurgical industries; tanneries, sawmills; food processing. Formerly, part of the old duchy of Brabant; overrun by the Germans in 1914 and 1940 and occupied by them through World Wars I and II.

Brabant Island. Island, second in size in Palmer Archipelago, Antarctica; 33 m. long.

Brač *or* **Brach** \ˈbräch\ *or Ital.* **Braz·za** \ˈbrät-sə\. Yugoslav island in the Adriatic Sea off the Dalmatian coast; 152 sq. m.; pop. (1961c) 14,227.

Bracara Augusta. See BRAGA 2.

Brac·cia·no, Lake \-bräch-(ē-)ˈän-(ˌ)ō\ *or anc.* **Sab·a·ti·nus** \ˌsab-ə-ˈtī-nəs\. Lake, W cen. Italy, 17 m. NW of Rome; 22 sq. m.; drains SW into the Tyrrhenian Sea.

Brace·bridge \ˈbrās-ˌbrij\. Town, ⊗ of Muskoka dist., SE Ontario, Canada, 5 m. E of S end of Lake Muskoka; pop. (1971p) 6936; boat works; foundry; summer resort.

Brach. See BRAČ.

Brack·en \ˈbrak-ən\. County in Kentucky. See table at KENTUCKY.

Brack·en·ridge \ˈbrak-ən-rij\. Borough, Allegheny co., SW Pennsylvania, on Allegheny river 18 m. NE of Pittsburgh; pop. (1970c) 4796; coke, stainless steel.

Brack·ett·ville \ˈbrak-ət-ˌvil\. City, ⊗ of Kinney co., SW Texas, 28 m. E of Del Rio; pop. (1970c) 1539.

Brack·we·de \ˈbräk-ˌvād-ə\. Town, North Rhine-Westphalia, West Germany, 36 m. E of Münster and just S of Bielefeld; pop. (1969e) 26,448; metal goods, drugs, textiles; first mentioned 1151.

Bra·da·no \brə-ˈdän-(ˌ)ō\. River, S Italy; 73 m. long; flows SE into the head of the Gulf of Taranto.

Brad·dock \ˈbrad-ək\. Industrial borough, Allegheny co., SW Pennsylvania, on Monongahela river 8 m. E of Pittsburgh; pop. (1970c) 8795; steel foundry products; scene of Braddock's defeat July 9, 1755 by French and Indians.

Bra·den·ton \ˈbrād-ᵊn-tən\. City, ⊗ of Manatee co., W Florida penin., at S end of Tampa Bay 11 m. N of Sarasota; pop. (1970c) 21,040; winter resort; travertine quarries.

Brad·ford \ˈbrad-fərd\. **1** Name of counties in two states of the U.S. See tables at FLORIDA and PENNSYLVANIA.
2 Village, Darke and Miami cos., W Ohio, 28 m. NNW of Dayton; pop. (1970c) 2163.
3 Industrial city, McKean co., N Pennsylvania, 18 m. W of Allegheny river as it crosses New York border; pop. (1970c) 12,672; chemicals, explosives; oil refineries.
4 Village in Westerly town, Washington co., S Rhode Island, ab. 4 m. SE of Hopkinton; pop. (1970c) 1333.
5 Town, Simcoe co., SE Ontario, Canada, 30 m. NNW of Toronto; pop. (1971p) 3390; diversified agriculture; flour mills.
6 County borough, West Riding, Yorkshire, N England, near the Aire 10 m. W of Leeds; pop. (1971p) 293,756; center of worsted industry; coal and iron; wool exchange (1867), Univ. of Bradford (1966).

Bradford–on–Avon \-ˈā-vən, -ˈav-ən\. Urban district, Wiltshire, S England, 6 m. ESE of Bath; pop. (1971p) 8001; ancient Saxon church.

Brad·ley \ˈbrad-lē\. **1** Name of counties in two states of the U.S. See tables at ARKANSAS and TENNESSEE.
2 Village, Kankakee co., NE Illinois, 3 m. N of Kankakee; pop. (1970c) 9881.

Bradley, Mount. Peak in Sierra Nevada, NE Tulare co., S cen. California; 13,280 ft.

Bradley Beach. Borough, Monmouth co., E cen. New Jersey, on Atlantic Ocean 2 m. S of Asbury Park; pop. (1970c) 4163; seaside resort; fisheries.

Bra·dy \ˈbrād-ē\. City, ⊗ of McCulloch co., cen. Texas, 46 m. SSW of Brownwood; pop. (1970c) 5557; shipping point for poultry, esp. turkeys; cotton, pecans, wool.

Brae·mar \brā-ˈmär\. **1** District in SW Aberdeen co., NE Scotland, comprising the upper valley of the Dee river; 24 m. long; tourist resort.
2 Village, SW Aberdeen co., NE Scotland, 7 m. W of Balmoral Castle; seat of the earl of Mar; standard of revolt raised here 1715 by 6th earl.

Brae·ri·ach \brā-ˈrē-ək\. Peak, N cen. Scotland, on border bet. Inverness and Aberdeen cos.; 4248 ft.

Bra·ga \ˈbräg-ə\. **1** District of NW Portugal. See table at PORTUGAL.
2 *or anc.* **Brac·a·ra Au·gus·ta** \ˌbrak-ə-rə-ó-ˈgəs-tə\. Commune, its ✱, 30 m. NNE of Oporto; munic. pop. (1970p) 101,877; cutlery, firearms, jewelry; capital of old province of Entre-Douro-e-Minho and ancient capital of Lusitania; said to have been founded by Carthaginians; Roman ruins; 12th cent. cathedral; archiepiscopal see and primacy of Portugal; residence of Portuguese court 1093–1147.

Bra·ga·do \brə-ˈgä-dō\. Town, Buenos Aires prov., E Argentina; pop. (1960c) 20,689.

Bra·gan·ça \brə-ˈga(ⁿ)n-sə\. **1** Town, NE Pará state, N Brazil, ab. 120 m. E of Belém; munic. pop. (1968e) 59,987.
2 City, São Paulo state, SE Brazil, 40 m. N of São Paulo; munic. pop. (1968e) 59,184.
3 *or* **Bra·gan·za** \-ˈgán-zə\. District of NE Portugal. See table at PORTUGAL.
4 Commune, its ✱, near Spanish border 88 m. ENE of Braga; munic. pop. (1970p) 33,928; textiles; former capital of old province of Trás-os-Montes; episcopal see; castle of dukes of Braganza.

Brah·man·ba·ria \ˌbrä-mən-ˈbär-ē-ə\. Town, SE Bangla Desh, 50 m. ENE of Dacca.

Brah·ma·ni \ˈbräm-ə-nē\. River, Orissa, E India; ab. 300 m. long; rises in S Bihar and flows S to join the Mahanadi delta N of Cuttack.

Brah·ma·pu·tra \ˌbräm-ə-ˈp(y)ü-trə\; *anc.* **Dy·ar·da·nes** \ˌdī-ər-ˈdā-(ˌ)nēz\ *or* **Oe·da·nes** \ē-ˈdā-(ˌ)nēz\. River in Tibet, China (where its upper course is called Tsangpo), NE India, and Bangla Desh; ab. 1800 m. long; area of basin 361,000 sq. m.; rises in SW Tibet in the Kailas Range (Himalayas) near 82°E; as the Tsangpo (or **Ma·tsang** \ˈmä-ˈtsäŋ\) flows E 700 m. across S part of Tibet; on its S bank is Jih-k'a-tse. At about 95°E turns abruptly S and breaks through E Himalayas in great gorges (known in this section as the **Di·hang** \ˈdē-ˈhäŋ\) and turns again SSW near Sadiya in NE Assam to flow W through Assam valley and S in Bangla Desh, where it becomes the Jamuna and merges with the Ganges in the Ganges-Brahmaputra Delta (*q.v.*). Navigable for 800 m. to Dibrugarh, India. Its upper course long unknown, esp. its identity with the Tsangpo, first established by exploration 1884–86; the Dihang explored 1913.

Braich–y–Pwll \ˌbrīk-i-ˈpül\. Cape, Lleyn Penin., NW coast of Wales.

Bra·i·la \brə-ˈē-lə\. **1** County of SE Romania. See table at ROMANIA.
2 City, its ⊗, on Danube river, 12 m. S of Galați; pop. (1969e) 122,410; important port; metalworking, food processing; important in wars of Turks, Walachians, and Russians.

Braine–l'Al·leud \ˌbran-lə-ˈlə(r)\. Commune, Brabant prov., cen. Belgium, 11 m. S of Brussels; pop. (1969e) 17,737; manufactures glass.

Braine–le–Comte \ˌbran-lə-ˈkōⁿt\. Commune, Hainaut prov., Belgium; pop. (1969e) 11,918.

Brai·nerd \ˈbrā-nərd\. City, ⊗ of Crow Wing co., cen. Minnesota, on Mississippi river 53 m. N of St. Cloud; pop. (1970c) 11,667; dairy products; Brainerd State Junior Coll. (1938).

Brain·tree \ˈbrān-(ˌ)trē\. Town, Norfolk co., E Massachusetts, 10 m. S of Boston; pop. (1970c) 35,050; residential and industrial suburb of Boston.

Braintree and Bock·ing \-ˈbäk-iŋ\. Urban district, Essex, SE England, on the Blackwater 39 m. NE of London; pop. (1971p) 24,839; textile mills, ironworks; plastics.

Brak·pan \ˈbrak-ˌpan\. Town, S Transvaal, NE Rep. of South Africa, in the Witwatersrand, 23 m. E of Johannesburg; pop. (1968e) 63,997; formerly part of Benoni, became separate municipality 1919; rich gold mines.

Brambanan. See PRAMBANAN.

Bram·ham Moor \ˈbram-əm-\. Locality, Yorkshire, N England, ENE of Leeds; battle Feb. 1408 in which Sir Henry Percy was defeated and killed.

Bramp·ton \ˈbram(p)-tən\. **1** Industrial town, ⊗ of Peel co., SE Ontario, Canada, 20 m. W of Toronto; pop. (1971p) 41,238; metal products, optical lenses, communications equipment.

2 Market town in Brampton parish, Cumberland, NW England, 11 m. NE of Carlisle.

Branch \'branch\. County in Michigan. See table at MICHIGAN.

Bran·co, Rio \ˌrē-ō-'braŋ-(ˌ)kō, -(ˌ)kü\ *or* **Pa·ri·ma** \pə-'rē-mə\. River, N Brazil; 350 m. long; formed by confluence of the Uraricoera and Tacutu; flows S into the Rio Negro.

Bran·den·burg \'bran-dən-ˌbərg\. City, ⊗ of Meade co., NW cen. Kentucky; pop. (1970c) 1651; wheat, tobacco.

Brandenburg \'bran-dən-ˌbərg, 'brän-dən-ˌbu̇(ə)rk\. 1 Historical region and province of Prussia; since 1945 the E section has been part of Poland, the W section part of East Germany.

History: Earliest Germanic inhabitants replaced by Slavic Wends who were unsubdued by Charlemagne; overcome in 12th cent. by Albert the Bear, margrave of Brandenburg, who established order, planted German colonists, and laid basis for expansion of territory secured by co-operation of his successors with Teutonic Knights (see PRUSSIA); recognized as one of seven imperial electorates 1356; declined and lost territory under rule of Wittelsbach and Luxembourg houses 1323–1411; given by emperor to Frederick of Nürnberg who became margrave 1415 and elector 1417; helped Teutonic Knights in war against Poland 15th cent.; extended boundaries and crushed nobility; accepted Reformation c. 1540; acquired Cleves and Ravensberg 1614 by marriage of Elector John Sigismund, who became duke of Prussia 1618; added East Friesland under Great Elector, Frederick William (1640–88), whose successful participation in wars against Sweden made Brandenburg-Prussia a leading power; its elector became king of Prussia 1701; its administration reorganized 1815; following World War II, E part to Poland; W part constitutes (since 1952) the East German districts of Potsdam, Frankfurt, and (in part) Cottbus.

2 *or* **Brandenburg an der Ha·vel** \-ˌän-dər-'häf-əl\. Industrial city, Potsdam dist., East Germany, on Havel river 38 m. WSW of Berlin; pop. (1970e) 93,660; steel, textiles; 12th cent. Romanesque cathedral, 14th cent. town hall; episcopal see 948–1598; seat of Prussian National Assembly 1848; former residence of reigning family of Prussia.

Bran·der, Pass of \-'bran-dər\. Mountain pass, N Argyll co., W Scotland, through which the waters of Loch Awe pass to Loch Etive; ab. 7 m. long.

Bran·don \'bran-dən\. 1 Town, ⊗ of Rankin co., S cen. Mississippi; pop. (1970c) 2685; textiles, timber.

2 Town, Rutland co., W Vermont, 14 m. NNW of Rutland; pop. (1970c) 3697; marble products; lumbering; resort.

3 City, SW Manitoba, Canada, on S bank of Assiniboine river; pop. (1971p) 30,832; railroad divisional point; grain elevators, oil refineries, creameries; chemicals, agricultural implements; Brandon Univ. (1899, univ. status 1967); industrial school for Indians, and a government experimental farm. Founded 1879; named after Brandon House, a Hudson's Bay post 17 m. E, established 1793.

4 Mountain in co. Kerry, near the sea W of Brandon Bay, SW Eire; 3127 ft.

Brandon and By·shot·tles \-'bi-ˌshät-ᵊlz\. Urban district, Durham, N England, on the Deerness 17 m. S of Newcastle upon Tyne; pop. (1971p) 16,849.

Brandon Bay. Inlet of Atlantic Ocean on SW coast of Eire, W of Tralee Bay.

Bran·dy·wine \'bran-dē-ˌwīn\. A creek in Pennsylvania and Delaware uniting with Christina creek (now Christina river) at Wilmington, Delaware; battlefield on the creek in Pennsylvania 10 m. NW of Wilmington where on Sept. 11, 1777 the British under Gen. Howe defeated the Americans under Gen. Washington and entered Philadelphia Sept. 27. See CHADDS FORD.

Bran·ford \'bran-fərd\. Borough, New Haven co., S Connecticut, on Long Island Sound 6 m. ESE of New Haven; pop. (1970c) 2080; resort; boats, wire; fishing; settled 1644, incorp. 1893; in town of Branford (pop. 20,444) incorporated 1930.

Bra·nie·wo \bran-'yā-(ˌ)vō\ *or Ger.* **Brauns·berg** \'braun(t)s-ˌbe(ə)rk\. City, NW Olsztyn prov., N Poland, NE of Elbląg; pop. (1968e) 11,500; founded 13th cent.; to Poland 1466, to Prussia 1772, to Poland 1945.

Brans·field Strait \ˌbran(t)s-ˌfēld-\. Channel bet. South Shetlands on N and Antarctic Penin. on S, Antarctica; ab. 175 m. long, and 52 m. wide.

Brant \'brant\. County, Ontario, Canada. See table at ONTARIO.

Bran·tas \'brant-əs\ *or* **Ke·di·ri** \kə-'di(ə)r-ē\. River, E cen. Java, Indonesia; 195 m. long; flows W, N, and NE into Madura Strait, one branch (Kali Mas) at Surabaja and the other 25 m. S at the town of Bangil.

Brant·ford \'brant-fərd\. City, ⊗ of Brant co., SE Ontario, Canada, on Grand river 22 m. WSW of Hamilton; pop. (1971p) 62,853; agricultural implements, truck bodies; headquarters for the united Iroquois tribes of Six Nations; early home of Alexander Graham Bell; founded 1830.

Brant·ley \'brant-lē\. County in Georgia. See table at GEORGIA.

Bras d'Or \'brä-'dȯ(ə)r\. Salt lake, cen. Cape Breton I., Nova Scotia, Canada; ab. 50 m. long; 360 sq. m. Its N extension is **Little Bras d'Or.**

Brasil. See BRAZIL.

Bra·sí·lia \brə-'zil-yə, -'zēl-\. City, ✱ of Brazil, on the Paraná (a headstream of the Tocantins); pop. (1970p) 272,002; constitutes with surrounding area, the Federal District (2245 sq. m.; pop. 544,862); presidential palace, cathedral, univ. (1961); construction begun 1956; capital moved from Rio de Janeiro 1960.

Bra·şov *or* **Bra·shov** \brä-'shȯv\ *or Hung.* **Bras·só** \'brȯsh-(ˌ)ō\. 1 County of cen. Romania. See table at ROMANIA.

2 *or Ger.* **Kron·stadt** \'krōn-ˌshtät\ *or from 1950 to 1960* **Stalin** \'stäl-ən, 'stal-, -ˌēn\. City, its ⊗, in the foothills of Transylvanian Alps; pop. (1969e) 175,264; chemicals, electrotechnical equipment, tractors; town hall (1420, restored 1777), Gothic church (1385–1425), technical institute (1948); founded by Teutonic Order 1211; a leader in Reformation in Transylvania in 16th cent.

Brass \'bras\. Town at mouth of **Brass River** (100 m. long, a channel of the Niger delta), Nigeria; formerly a flourishing trading settlement, visited by Portuguese and British; traded in slaves; territory taken after massacre of Christians at Akassa 1895.

Bras·schaat *or* **Bras·schaet** \brä-'skät\. Commune, Antwerp prov., N Belgium; pop. (1969e) 28,183.

Brass·town Bald \ˌbras-ˌtau̇n-\ *or* **Mount Eno·tah** \-i-'nōt-ə\. Mountain on boundary of Towns and Union cos., N Georgia; 4784 ft.; highest point in the state.

Bra·ti·sla·va \ˌbrat-ə-'släv-ə, ˌbrät-\ *or Ger.* **Press·burg** \'pres-ˌbərg, -ˌbu̇(ə)rk\ *or Hung.* **Po·zsony** \'pō-ˌzhōn-yə\. City, ✱ of Slovak S.R., S cen. Czechoslovakia, on left bank of Danube ab. 30 m. E of Vienna; pop. (1968e) 285,905; textiles, timber; food processing, oil refining; Comenius Univ. (1919), Technical Univ. (1937); large Gothic cathedral (begun 1090, rebuilt 1845–67) where kings of Hungary were formerly crowned.

History: As Pressburg an old town dating back to 9th cent.; capital of Hungary 1541–1784 and seat of Diet until 1848; scene of signing of Treaty of Pressburg Dec. 26, 1805 bet. France and Austria, by which Austria lost much territory and recognized Napoleon as king of Italy. On formation of Czechoslovakia became capital of province of Slovakia 1918–39; capital of German protected state of Slovakia 1939–45; capital of Slovak S.R. 1969.

Bratsk \'brätsk\. City, Irkutsk Oblast, Russian S.F.S.R., U.S.S.R., on Angara river; pop. (1970p) 155,000; metallurgical industries; important hydroelectric power installations.

Brat·tle·boro \'brat-ᵊl-ˌbər-ə, -ˌbə-rə\. Town, Windham co., SE corner of Vermont, on Connecticut river 8 m. N of Massachusetts border; pop. (1970c) 12,239; wood products, optical lenses, paper; resort; settled by garrison of Fort Dummer 1724, chartered 1753, incorp. as village 1832.

Braunsberg. See BRANIEWO.

Braunschweig. See BRUNSWICK.

Braun·ston \'brȯn-stən, 'brän-\. Village, Northamptonshire, cen. England, 3 m. NW of Daventry; terminus of the Grand Union Canal which here goes through a tunnel 1½ m. long.

Bra·va \'bräv-ə\. 1 Southernmost island of the Cape Verde Islands; 25 sq. m.; pop. (1960c) 8646.
2 Coastal town, SE Somalia, 90 m. SW of Mogadisho; pop. (1965e) 7665.

Brava Point \ˌbräv-ə-\. Cape on S coast of Uruguay near Montevideo extending into the Río de la Plata (56 m. wide here) opp. Piedras Point in Argentina.

Bravo, Río *or* **Río Bravo del Norte.** See RIO GRANDE.

Braw·ley \'brȯ-lē\. City, Imperial co., SE corner of California, in Imperial Valley S of Salton Sea; 115 ft. below sea level; pop. (1970c) 13,746; fruit.

Brax·ton \'brak-stən\. County in West Virginia. See table at WEST VIRGINIA.

Bray \'brā\. 1 Urban district and port, NE co. Wicklow, E Eire; pop. (1971p) 14,458; on wide bay, just N of Bray Head.
2 Civil parish, Berkshire, S England; pop. (1961c) 4858; residence of a vicar who is said to have been twice a Roman Catholic and twice a Protestant in four successive English reigns bet. 1520 and 1560.
3 Small region in Somme dept., N France; chief town Neufchâtel.
4 *or* **Bray–sur–Somme** \'brā-sü(ə)r-'säm, -'səm\. Village, Somme dept., N France, on the Somme SE of Albert; battle in Allied retreat Mar. 25–26, 1918.

Bray Head. 1 Cape at SW end of Valentia I., co. Kerry, SW coast of Eire, S of entrance to Dingle Bay.
2 Point on E coast of Eire, just S of Dublin.

Bra·zeau \brə-'zō\. River, SW Alberta, Canada; ab. 125 m. long; a tributary of the upper North Saskatchewan.

Brazeau, Mount. Peak in Jasper National Park, SW Alberta, Canada, near source of Brazeau river; 11,386 ft.

Bra·zil \brə-'zil\ *or Span.* **Bra·sil** \brä-'sēl\; *officially* **Federative Republic of Brazil** *or Port.* **Re·pú·bli·ca Fe·de·ra·ti·va do Bra·sil** \rə-'pü-bli-kə-fād-ə-rə-'tē-və-dü-brə-'zil\; *from 1891 to 1967* **United States of Brazil** *or Port.* **Es·ta·dos Uni·dos do Brasil** \ish-'täth-ə-zü-'nē-thəz-\. 1 Federal republic, E cen. South America, bounded on NW by Colombia, on N by Venezuela, Guyana, Surinam, and French Guiana, on E by the Atlantic Ocean, on S by Uruguay, and on W by Argentina, Paraguay, Bolivia, and Peru; 3,284,426 sq. m.; pop. (1970p) 93,204,379; ✱ Brasília.

Physical features: Mountain ranges (averaging less than 4000 ft.) and plateau region are chiefly in E and S parts; highest point is the Pico da Bandeira, 9495 ft. high, located in the eastern part on the border between the states of Minas Gerais and Espírito Santo; in northern part on Guyana and Venezuela borders are Tumuc-Humac, Acaraí, Pacaraima, Parima, and other ranges (*serras*). Its entire N and central part is lowland region, occupied by the Amazon (*q.v.*) and its many great tributaries; other rivers: in plateau region in E the São Francisco, Parnaíba, and Jequitinhonha; in the SW the Paraguay, Alto Paraná, and Uruguay (each in part a boundary stream); in the Iguaçu, tributary of the Alto Paraná, are the famous Iguaçu Falls. Has few lakes of any size; largest is Lagoa dos Patos, in Rio Grande do Sul. Except for the large islands of Marajó and Caviana at the mouth of the Amazon and Maracá to the N there are no large islands along the 4603 miles of the Atlantic coastline; ab. 250 m. NE of Cape São Roque, at 3°51′S, 32°25′W, is the important small island of Fernando de Noronha, now a territory. Has good harbors at Belém, Salvador, Rio de Janeiro, Santos, and Pôrto Alegre. Its immense forests (*selvas*) of the Amazon region are source of many forest products (balata, Brazil nuts, vegetable oils); the savannas or grasslands (*campos*) are source of cattle and agricultural products; its plateau region in E and S is of great importance for its coffee, cacao, tobacco, cotton, and yerba maté; also produces sugar, rice, wheat; fishing; large mineral deposits: bauxite, manganese, iron ore, beryllium, chrome, diamonds; manufacturing: food processing, metalworking; chemicals, machinery, textiles, automobiles, electrical equipment, cement, iron and steel. *Chief cities:* Rio de Janeiro, São Paulo, Recife, Belo Horizonte, Salvador, Pôrto Alegre, Belém, Fortaleza, Curitiba, and Santos. Divided into 22 states, 4 territories, and the Federal District (for pronunciation of their names, see their individual entries):

NAME	AREA (Sq. m.)	POP. (1970p)	CAPITAL
Federal District	2,245	544,862	Brasília
States			
Acre	58,915	203,900	Rio Branco
Alagoas	10,707	1,606,165	Maceió
Amazonas	604,032	714,803	Manaus
Bahia	216,612	7,420,906	Salvador
Ceará	57,147	4,440,286	Fortaleza
Espírito Santo	17,605	1,597,389	Vitória
Goiás	247,912	2,989,414	Goiânia
Guanabara	524	4,296,782	Rio de Janeiro
Maranhão	126,897	2,883,211	São Luís
Mato Grosso	475,501	1,475,117	Cuiabá
Minas Gerais	226,707	11,279,872	Belo Horizonte
Pará	481,869	1,984,745	Belém
Paraíba	21,765	2,383,518	João Pessoa
Paraná	77,048	6,741,520	Curitiba
Pernambuco	37,946	5,208,011	Recife
Piauí	96,886	1,735,568	Teresina
Rio de Janeiro	16,568	4,694,089	Niterói
Rio Grande do Norte	20,469	1,603,094	Natal
Rio Grande do Sul	108,951	6,652,618	Pôrto Alegre
Santa Catarina	37,060	2,911,479	Florianópolis
São Paulo	95,713	17,716,186	São Paulo
Sergipe	8,492	900,119	Aracaju
Territories			
Amapá	54,161	116,481	Macapá
Fernando de Noronha[1]	10	1,239	
Rondônia	93,839	95,311	Pôrto Velho
Roraima	88,843	40,855	Boa Vista

[1]Island off E coast.

History: Northern coast discovered by Vicente Pinzón, a Spaniard, 1500; although allotted to Portugal by Treaty of Tordesillas 1494, not formally claimed by discovery until Cabral accidentally touched there 1500; title confirmed to John III of Portugal by Congress of Badajoz 1524; first settled at São Vicente under system of hereditary captaincies 1532; settled for short periods by French at Rio de Janeiro 1555–60 and at Maranhão (São Luís) 1612, by Dutch at Pernambuco 1630–54; neglected during period of Spanish rule of Portugal 1580–1640; fought war which resulted in expulsion of Dutch 1641–54; made viceroyalty with capital at Bahia 1640–1762 and at Rio de Janeiro from 1763; interior opened by Paulistas (people of São Paulo) and others who developed production of mineral wealth, gold and diamonds, and planting of sugar and coffee, especially in 18th cent.; expanded Portuguese boundaries recognized in treaties of Madrid 1750 and San Ildefonso 1777; in 1808 became refuge and seat of government of John VI, prince regent, when Napoleon invaded Portugal; opened to foreign commerce 1808; United Kingdom of Portugal, Brazil, and Algarve proclaimed and ruled from Brazil 1815–21; forced grant of constitution by John VI who returned to Portugal 1821; in 1822 proclaimed independence (see SÃO PAULO 2) under Pedro who became Emperor Pedro I (1822–31); fought war with Argentina over Banda Oriental 1825–28 (see URUGUAY); prosperous and internally peaceful during reign of Emperor Pedro II (succeeded 1831, ruled 1841–89); helped overthrow dictatorship of Rosas 1852 (see

ARGENTINA); allied with Argentina and Uruguay in war against Paraguay 1865–70; deposed Pedro II 1889 and adopted constitution for federal republic; became United States of Brazil 1891; settled peaceably numerous boundary disputes 1895–1909; declared war on Germany 1917; entered League of Nations 1920 but withdrew 1928; under President Getulio Vargas (first term 1930–45) set up constitutions 1934 and 1937, the second of which established dictatorial powers; joined Allies in World War II Aug. 1942; second Vargas term 1951–54; Brasília made capital 1960; civilian government overthrown 1964; new constitution became effective 1969.

2 City, ⊗ of Clay co., W Indiana, 15 m. ENE of Terre Haute; pop. (1970c) 8163; clay products.

Brazil, Plateau of *or* **Plan·al·to Cen·tral** \plə-ˌnal-tə-sen-ˈträl, -ˌnəl-\. Highland region in SE Brazil, chiefly in Minas Gerais and São Paulo states.

Brazil Current. A warm ocean current flowing S along the coast of Brazil.

Bra·zo·ria \brə-ˈzōr-ē-ə\. County in Texas. See table at TEXAS.

Braz·os \ˈbraz-əs\. 1 River, cen. Texas; 840 m. long, navigable 40 m. (300 m. in high water); drainage area 42,800 sq. m.; formed by confluence of Salt Fork and Double Mountain Fork in Stonewall co., N Texas, flows SE into Gulf of Mexico in S Brazoria co.

2 County in Texas. See table at TEXAS.

Brazos Peak. Mountain, NE Rio Arriba co., N New Mexico; 11,274 ft.

Brazza. See BRAČ.

Braz·za·ville \ˈbraz-ə-ˌvil, ˈbräz-ə-ˌvēl\. River port, ✱ of Congo, (see CONGO 3), on NW shore of Stanley Pool in the Congo river; pop. (1970p) 175,000; food processing; textiles; tanneries; connected with Atlantic seaboard by railroad completed 1934; center for river trade for 1000 m. up the Congo; maintains motorboat service with Kinshasa. Founded 1883 by Pierre Brazza, French explorer; used as a base for later claims of France to vast territory to NE; ✱ of former French Equatorial Africa.

Brč·ko \ˈbərch-(ˌ)kō\. Town, Bosnia and Herzegovina, Yugoslavia, ab. 70 m. NNE of Sarajevo; pop. (1965e) 21,-000.

Brea \ˈbrā-ə\. City, Orange co., SW California, 22 m. NE of Long Beach; pop. (1970c) 18,447.

Bread·al·bane \brə-ˈdȯl-bən, -ˈdal-\. District in W Perth co., cen. Scotland; traversed by the Grampians.

Breath·itt \ˈbreth-ət\. County in Kentucky. See table at KENTUCKY.

Breaux Bridge \ˌbrō-ˈbrij\. Town, St. Martin parish, S Louisiana, 8 m. ENE of Lafayette; pop. (1970c) 4942.

Bre·bes \ˈbrā-bəs\. Town, cen. Java, Indonesia, W of Tegal; pop. (1961c) 36,851.

Bré·cey \brā-ˈsā\. Commune, Manche dept., NW France, E of Avranches; pop. (1962c) 2139.

Brèche–de–Ro·land \ˌbresh-də-rō-ˈläⁿ\. Defile, Hautes-Pyrénées dept., SW France, in the Pyrenees on the Franco-Spanish boundary 35 m. S of Tarbes; alt. 9200 ft.; in medieval legend said to have been hewn by the knight Roland with one blow of his sword Durendal.

Bre·chin \ˈbrē-kən\. Burgh, Angus co., E Scotland; pop. (1971p) 7221; paper mills, distilleries; linen weaving.

Bre·chou \brə-ˈshü\. One of the Channel Islands, just W of Sark; 74 acres.

Breck·en·ridge \ˈbrek-ən-(ˌ)rij\. 1 Town, ⊗ of Summit co., cen. Colorado; pop. (1970c) 548.

2 City, ⊗ of Wilkin co., W Minnesota; pop. (1970c) 4200; livestock.

3 City, ⊗ of Stephens co., N cen. Texas, 50 m. ENE of Abilene; pop. (1970c) 5944; grain, cattle; oil and gas wells.

Breckenridge Hills. Village, St. Louis co., Missouri, NW of St. Louis; pop. (1970c) 7011; wheat.

Breck·in·ridge \ˈbrek-ən-rij\. County in Kentucky. See table at KENTUCKY.

Breck·nock \ˈbrek-ˌnäk, -nək\ *or* **Brec·on** \ˈbrek-ən\. 1 County, SE Wales. See BRECKNOCKSHIRE.

2 Municipal borough, ⊗ of Brecknockshire, SE Wales; pop. (1971p) 6283; textiles (woolens, flannels).

Brecknock Beacons *or* **Brecon Beacons.** Two sandstone peaks, Brecknockshire, Wales, S of Usk valley; highest massif in S Wales; highest point 2907 ft.

Brecknock Peninsula. Peninsula extending westward from SW Tierra del Fuego I., Chile.

Breck·nock·shire \ˈbrek-ˌnäk-ˌshi(ə)r, -nək-, -shər\ *or* **Brec·on·shire** \ˈbrek-ən-shi(ə)r, -shər\ *also* **Brecknock** \ˈbrek-ˌnäk, -nək\ *or* **Brecon** \ˈbrek-ən\. County, SE Wales; area 733 sq. m.; pop. (1971p) 53,234; ⊗ Brecknock; mountainous region; rivers Usk and Wye; livestock raising; coal, limestone; tourism.

Brecks·ville \ˈbreks-ˌvil\. Village, Cuyahoga co., N Ohio, 12 m. S of Cleveland; pop. (1970c) 9137.

Břec·lav \bər-ˈzhets-(ˌ)läf\ *or Ger.* **Lun·den·burg** \ˈlün-dən-ˌbu̇(ə)rk\. Town, Czech S.R., cen. Czechoslovakia; pop. (1968e) 12,985.

Brecon. See BRECKNOCK; BRECKNOCKSHIRE.

Bre·da \brā-ˈdä\. Commune, North Brabant prov., S Netherlands, on the Merk river 14 m. W of Tilburg; pop. (1970e) 121,209; artificial silk, chocolate; foundries; Gothic church (15th cent.).

History: An old town (received municipal charter 1252), strongly fortified in early times; Compromise of Breda signed 1566 by the Dutch and Spanish; seized by duke of Parma 1581 but retaken 1590 by Maurice of Nassau; after siege of a year surrendered 1625 to Spaniards; retaken by Dutch 1637; Declaration of Breda (amnesty proclamation) issued Apr. 1660 by Charles II of England; Peace Treaties of Breda concluded 1667 bet. Britain, France, and Netherlands; important in wars of French Revolution 1793–95. In World War II fell to Germans May 1940, retaken by British Oct. 29, 1944.

Bre·das·dorp \brə-ˈdäs-dōrp, -dȯ(ə)rp\. Town, SW Cape Province, S Rep. of South Africa, 105 m. ESE of Cape Town; pop. (1967e) 4700; wool, tobacco, and grain.

Bred·bury and Rom·i·ley \ˈbred-b(e-)rē . . . ˈräm-ə-lē\. Urban district, Cheshire, NW England, 6 m. SE of Manchester; pop. (1971p) 28,472.

Bree \ˈbrā\. River, SW Cape Province, Rep. of South Africa; 165 m. long; flows SE into Indian Ocean.

Breed's Hill. See BUNKER HILL.

Breese \ˈbrēz\. City, Clinton co., SW cen. Illinois, 33 m. E of East St. Louis; pop. (1970c) 2885.

Bre·ga \ˈbrā-gə\. Town, N Libya, bet. Ajdābiyah and Al-Agheila near SE coast of Gulf of Sidra.

Bre·genz \ˈbrā-ˌgen(t)s\ *or anc.* **Bri·gan·ti·um** \brig-ˈan-chē-əm\. City, ✱ of Vorarlberg, Austria, at E end of Lake Constance 78 m. WNW of Innsbruck; pop. (1969e) 24,078; chemicals, electronic equipment, textiles; brewery; lake harbor and tourist resort; has a museum of Roman and Celtic antiquities. Ancient Celtic settlement; important station under Romans; became city c. 1200; in Middle Ages under counts of Bregenz, later under counts of Montfort; passed to Hapsburgs 1523; stormed by Swedes 1647; under Bavarian rule 1805–14.

Brei·dha Fjord \ˌbrā-t͟hä-\. Bay on W coast of Iceland.

Brei·sach am Rhein \ˌbrī-ˌzäk-äm-ˈrīn\ *or formerly* **Alt·brei·sach** \ˌält-ˈbrī ˈzäk\ *or anc.* **Mons Bri·si·a·cus** \ˌmänz-bri-ˈsī-ə-kəs\. Town, Baden-Württemberg, West Germany, on right bank of Rhine W of Freiburg; pop. (1964e) 5400; an old fortified town of the Sequani on left bank of Rhine, captured by Ariovistus c. 61 B.C.; one of chief fortresses of the German Empire during Middle Ages; resisted Protestants during Thirty Years' War but capitulated after siege by French 1638 and ceded to France 1648 by Treaty of

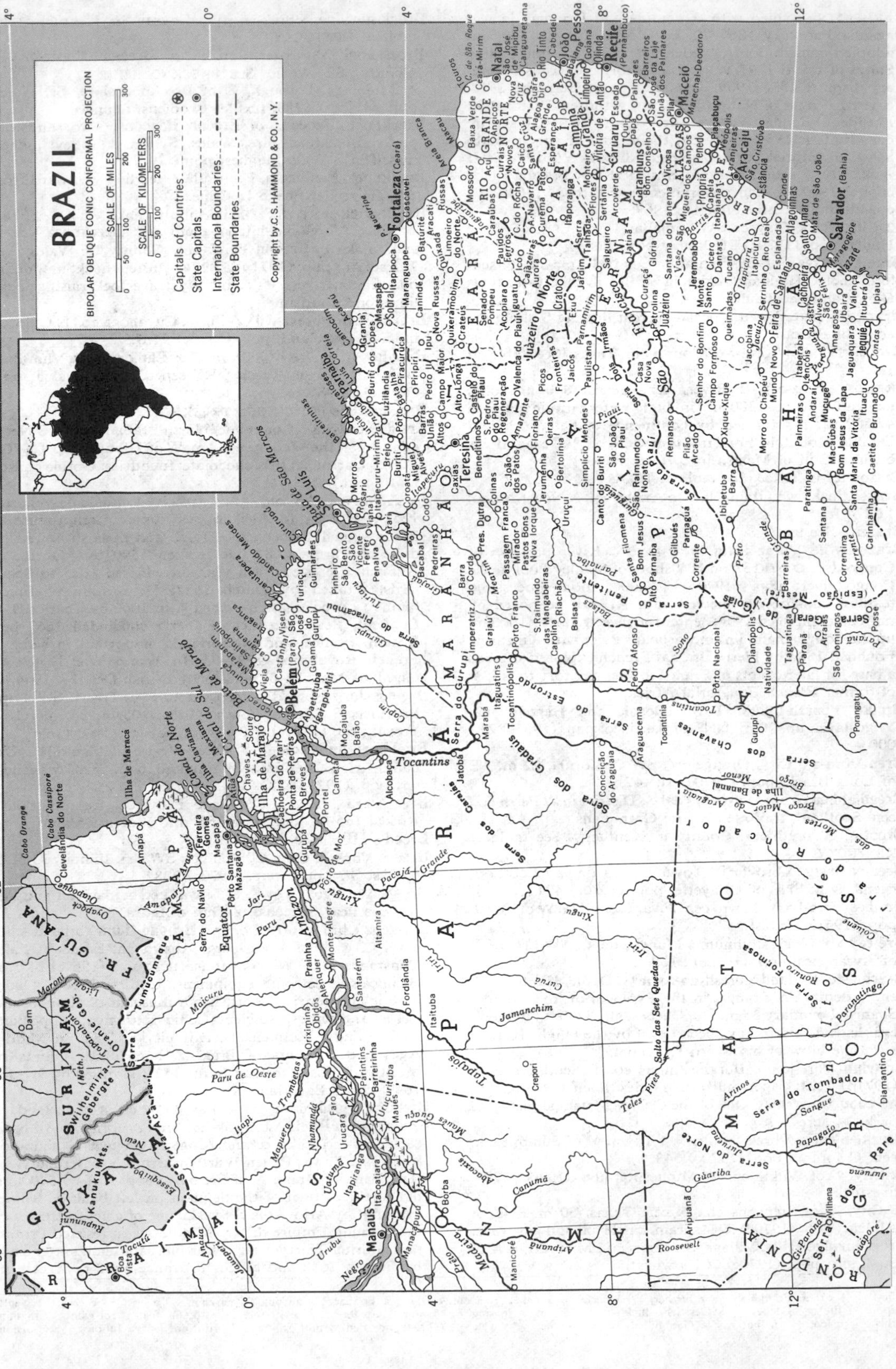
BRAZIL
BIPOLAR OBLIQUE CONIC CONFORMAL PROJECTION
SCALE OF MILES
0 50 100 200 300
SCALE OF KILOMETERS
0 50 100 200 300
Capitals of Countries
State Capitals
International Boundaries
State Boundaries
Copyright by C.S. HAMMOND & CO., N.Y.

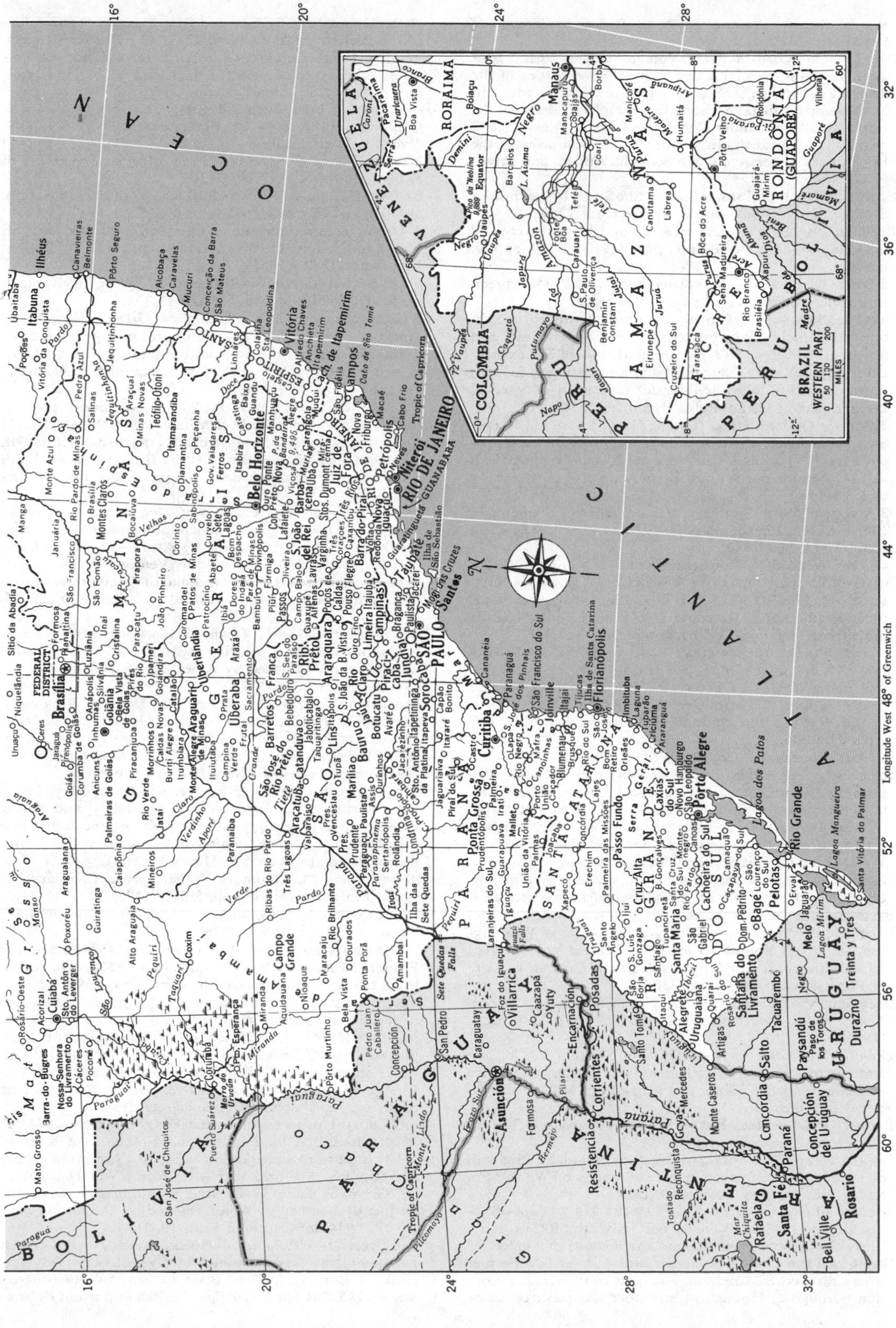
BRAZIL WESTERN PART
MILES
Longitude West 48° of Greenwich
Tropic of Capricorn
COLOMBIA
VENEZUELA
RORAIMA
AMAZONAS
ACRE
RONDÔNIA (GUAPORÉ)
PERU
BOLIVIA
PARAGUAY
URUGUAY
MATO GROSSO
GOIÁS
MINAS GERAIS
ESPÍRITO SANTO
RIO DE JANEIRO
GUANABARA
SÃO PAULO
PARANÁ
SANTA CATARINA
RIO GRANDE DO SUL
FEDERAL DISTRICT
Brasília
Belo Horizonte
Vitória
Niterói
Santos
Curitiba
Florianópolis
Pôrto Alegre
Rio Grande
Pelotas
Goiânia
Cuiabá
Campo Grande
Uberaba
Uberlândia
Campinas
Juiz de Fora
Campos
Petrópolis
Asunción
Concepción
Encarnación
Corrientes
Resistencia
Posadas
Santa Fé
Paraná
Rosario
Manaus
Boa Vista
Pôrto Velho
Rio Branco
Ilhéus
Itabuna
Montes Claros
Teófilo Otoni
Governador Valadares
Ponta Grossa
Joinville
Blumenau
Passo Fundo
Santa Maria
Uruguaiana
Bagé
Paysandú
Salto
Durazno
Concepción del Uruguay
Lagoa dos Patos
Lagoa Mirim

Westphalia; to Austria 1697; to Baden by Treaty of Pressburg 1805.

Brei·ten·feld \'brīt-ᵊn-ˌfelt\. Village, Leipzig dist., East Germany, 6 m. N of Leipzig; scene of two battles of the Thirty Years' War: (1) Sept. 17, 1631 in which Swedes and Saxons under Gustavus Adolphus completely defeated the Imperialist forces under Count von Tilly; (2) Nov. 2, 1642 in which the Swedish army under Torstenson defeated the Imperialists under Archduke Leopold William and Prince Piccolomini.

Breit·horn \'brīt-ˌhȯ(ə)rn\. Peak on the Swiss-Italian border S of Zermatt, Valais canton, Switzerland; 13,685 ft.

Bre·men \'brē-mən\. 1 City, Carroll and Haralson cos., W Georgia, 40 m. W of Atlanta; pop. (1970c) 3484; apples, peaches.

2 Town, Marshall co., N Indiana; pop. (1970c) 3487; precision roller bearings, iron castings; farming.

Bremen \'brem-ən, 'brā-mən\. 1 Former German archbishopric and duchy, covering territory bet. lower Weser and lower Elbe rivers, NW of former duchy of Brunswick-Lüneburg; ab. 2000 sq. m.; made archbishopric in 13th cent.; created a duchy 1648 under supremacy of Sweden; became part of electorate of Hannover 1715.

2 Former German state, NW Germany; 99 sq. m.; ✱ Bremen; comprised district around city of Bremen; lost sovereignty at accession of National Socialist regime 1933; in 1947 became part of new Bremen state, West Germany (see 3 below).

3 A state of West Germany, includes cities of Bremen and Bremerhaven; 156 sq. m.; pop. (1970e) 754,400; ✱ Bremen; state established 1947.

4 Commercial city, ✱ of Bremen state (not a part of earlier duchy), West Germany, on Weser river 59 m. SW of Hamburg; pop. (1969e) 606,500. West Germany's second major port; shipbuilding, iron and steel production; electrical industries; 11th cent. Romanesque cathedral.

History: Became episcopal see 787, seat of an archbishopric 845; one of the important Hanse Towns; became free city under elector of Brunswick; part of French empire 1810–13; joined North German Confederation 1866; in World War II submarine and naval base; taken by British Apr. 27, 1945.

Bre·mer \'brē-mər\. County in Iowa. See table at IOWA.

Brem·er·ha·ven \'brem-ər-ˌhäv-ən, ˌbrā-mər-'häf-ən\. Seaport city, West Germany, at the mouth of the Weser 35 m. N of Bremen, forming an exclave of Bremen state; pop. (1969e) 149,250; shipbuilding; engineering works, fisheries; founded 1827, became a city 1851; in 1938 united with **We·ser·mün·de** \ˌvā-zər-'myün-də\ founded 1924, and known by that name until 1947 when it became, as Bremerhaven, part of the newly created Bremen state.

Bremersdorp. See MANZINI.

Brem·er·ton \'brem-ərt-ᵊn\. City, Kitsap co., W Washington, on Puget Sound 15 m. W of Seattle; pop. (1970c) 35,307; lumber, dairy products; Olympic Coll. (1946); site of Puget Sound Navy Yard (1891).

Bren·ham \'bren-əm\. City, ⊗ of Washington co., SE cen. Texas, 35 m. S of Bryan; pop. (1970c) 8922; Blinn Coll. (1883).

Bren·ner \'bren-ər\ *or Ital.* **Bren·ne·ro** \'bren-ə-ˌrō\. Village and customs station at Italian end of Brenner pass; scene of conferences bet. Hitler and Mussolini 1940–41; surrendered to Allies May 5, 1945.

Brenner Pass *or Ital.* **Pas·so Bren·ne·ro** \ˌpäs-(ˌ)ō-'bren-ə-ˌrō\. Alpine pass. See ALPS.

Brent \'brent\. A borough of Greater London, SE England, consisting of the former munic. boroughs of Wimbledon and Willesden. See table at LONDON 4.

Bren·ta \'brent-ə\ *or anc.* **Me·do·a·cus Ma·jor** \mə-ˌdō-ə-kəs-'mā-jər\. River, Veneto, NE Italy; ab. 100 m. long; flows SE through Venezia into the lagoons of Venice.

Brent·ford and Chis·wick \ˌbrent-fərd . . . 'chiz-ik\. Former urban district, SE England, now part of the Greater London borough of Hounslow; Brentford was scene of defeat of the Danes 1016 by Edmund Ironside, and of the defeat of the Parliamentarians Nov. 12, 1642 by Prince Rupert.

Bren·ton Point \ˌbrent-ᵊn-\ *or* **Bren·ton's Point** \ˌbrent-ᵊnz-\. Southernmost point of the island of Rhode Island, Newport co., SE Rhode Island, SSW of Newport.

Brent·wood \'brent-ˌwu̇d\. 1 City, Contra Costa co., W California, 38 m. E of San Francisco; pop. (1970c) 2649; diversified agriculture.

2 Town, Prince Georges co., S cen. Maryland, 5 m. NE of Washington; pop. (1970c) 3426.

3 City, St. Louis co., E Missouri, 8 m. W of St. Louis; pop. (1970c) 11,248; residential suburb of St. Louis.

4 Urban community (unincorporated), Suffolk co., SE New York, in Islip town, cen. Long I.; pop. (1970c) 27,868; Brentwood Coll. (1955).

5 Residential borough, Allegheny co., SW Pennsylvania, 5 m. S of Pittsburgh; pop. (1970c) 13,732.

6 Urban district, Essex, SE England, 20 m. ENE of London; pop. (1971p) 57,976; agricultural machinery; seat of a grammar school dating from the middle 16th cent.

Bre·scia \'bresh-ə, 'brā-shə\. 1 Province of Lombardy, N Italy. See table at ITALY.

2 *or anc.* **Brix·ia** \'brik-sē-ə\. Walled commune, its ✱, at foot of Alps 54 m. E by N of Milan; pop. (1968e) 204,369; firearms, machinery, linens and silks; railroad junction; 9th cent. and 17th cent. cathedrals; the Broletto palace (12th cent.), and the Palazzo della Loggia; many fine Roman remains.

History: Ancient Celtic town; became seat of Roman colony 27 B.C. and later a Roman municipium; devastated by Goths 412 A.D., plundered by Attila 452; fell to Lombardy; free city 936–1426; held by Venice 1426 ff., France 1796 ff., Austria 1815 ff., Sardinia 1859–60; became part of kingdom of Italy 1860; entered by Allies Apr. 28–29, 1945.

Bres·kens \'bres-kəns\. Town, Zeeland prov., SW Netherlands, on S shore of Schelde estuary; pop. (1970e) 3857; unsuccessfully attacked by Allies Oct. 8–9, 1944.

Breslau. See WROCŁAW 2.

Bres·sa·no·ne \ˌbräs-ə-'nō-nə\ *or Ger.* **Bri·xen** \'brik-sən\. Commune, Bolzano prov., Trentino-Alto Adige, NE Italy, at S end of Brenner Pass in S Tirol on Isarco river, 20 m. NE of Bolzano; pop. (1968e) 15,125; 18th cent. cathedral; health resort; ceded to Italy 1919 by Austria.

Bresse \'bres\. Region, E France; ab. 60 m. long, 20 m. wide; fertile region specializing in poultry and cattle. Ancient countship comprised the plain around Bourg and the Revermont; under house of Savoy from 1272 with Bourg its capital; ceded to Henry IV 1601.

Bres·so \'bres-ō\. Commune, Milano prov., Lombardy, N Italy, 5 m. N of Milan; pop. (1968e) 27,432.

Bres·soux \bre-'sü\. Commune, Liège prov., E Belgium, NE suburb of Liège; pop. (1969e) 13,380.

Bres·suire \ˌbres-ü-'i(ə)r\. Commune, Deux-Sèvres dept., W France, 38 m. N of Niort; pop. (1962c) 8520; a historical town damaged and pillaged in wars 1214, 1598, 1794.

Brest \'brest\. 1 Fortified seaport commune, Finistère dept., NW France on Atlantic Ocean 32 m. NW of Quimper; pop. (1968c) 154,023; a major naval station of France, planned by Richelieu and fortified by Vauban in 17th cent.; manufactures chemicals, shoes, linens; trades in wine, coal, timber, flour, fruit, vegetables; brewing, ship repairing; naval schools; botanical gardens.

History: Unsuccessfully attacked by English and Dutch 1694; blockaded by English, and French fleet defeated 1794; important debarkation point for American troops and supplies in World War I. In World War II occupied by Germans June 1940; used as submarine base and frequently bombed by Allies; reached by U.S. forces Aug. 26–28, 1944 and captured Sept. 19, 1944.

2 *or* **Brest Li·tovsk** \ˌbrest-lə-'tȯfsk, -'tȯvsk\ *or Pol.* **Brześć nad Bu·giem** \bə-'zhests-näd-'büg-ˌyem\. City on right bank of Bug river, ✱ of Brest Oblast, SW Belorussian S.S.R., U.S.S.R.; pop. (1970p) 122,000; important railroad

junction; textiles; metalworking. Taken by Germans 1915; scene of signing of treaty (Brest Litovsk) bet. Germany and Russia Mar. 3, 1918; in World War II taken by Germans Sept. 28, 1939 but after division of Poland by Germany and U.S.S.R. remained in Soviet part 1939–41; taken by Germany June 24, 1941; retaken by U.S.S.R. July 18, 1944.

Brest Oblast \-'ō-bləst, -ˌblast\. Subdivision of SW Belorussian S.S.R., U.S.S.R.; 12,471 sq. m.; pop. (1970p) 1,295,-000; ✱ Brest; hemp, flax; forestry; nearly coextensive with former Polesie dept. of Poland.

Bretagne. See BRITTANY.

Bre·ti·gny *or Fr.* **Bré·ti·gny** \ˌbrā-tin-'yē\. Village of Normandy, Eure-et-Loir dept., N cen. France, just SE of Chartres; treaty May 8, 1360 bet. England and France, closing the first part of the Hundred Years' War.

Bret·on, Cape \-'bret-ᵊn, -'brit-\. 1 Cape, most easterly point of Cape Breton I., NE Nova Scotia, Canada.

2 County, Nova Scotia, Canada. See table at NOVA SCOTIA.

Breton Sound \ˌbret-ᵊn-\. Inlet of Gulf of Mexico off NE coast of Plaquemines parish, SE Louisiana.

Brett, Cape \-'bret\. Cape on NE coast of N extension of North I., New Zealand, E of Bay of Islands.

Bret·ton Woods \ˌbret-ən-\. Fashionable hotel center and resort, Coos co., N New Hampshire, ab. 18 m. SSE of Littleton; site of United Nations Monetary and Financial Conference July 1–22, 1944 at which an International Monetary Fund was established.

Bre·vard \brə-'värd\. 1 County in Florida. See table at FLORIDA.

2 Town and summer resort, ⊗ of Transylvania co., SW North Carolina, 26 m. SSW of Asheville; pop. (1970c) 5243; lumber; Brevard Coll. (1853).

Bré·vent \brā-'väⁿ\. Peak in the Alps, Haute-Savoie dept., E France, near Mount Blanc; 8285 ft.

Brew·er \'brü-ər, 'brů(-ə)r\. Commercial and industrial city, Penobscot co., E cen. Maine, on Penobscot river opp. Bangor; pop. (1970c) 9300; wood pulp, paper; brick.

Brewer, Mount. Peak on boundary bet. Fresno and Tulare cos., S cen. California, in Sierra Nevada; 13,886 ft.

Brew·ster \'brü-stər\. 1 County in Texas. See table at TEXAS.

2 Town, Barnstable co., SE Massachusetts, on Cape Cod Bay; pop. (1970c) 1790.

3 Village, ⊗ of Blaine co., cen. Nebraska; pop. (1970c) 54.

Brewster, Cape. Point on E coast of Greenland, 70°19′N, 22°05′W.

Brewster, Mount. Peak in Panama, E of the Panama Canal; 3018 ft.

Brew·ton \'brüt-ᵊn\. City, ⊗ of Escambia co., S Alabama, 60 m. ENE of Mobile Bay; pop. (1970c) 6747; lumber.

Brey·ten \'brāt-ᵊn\. Town, E Transvaal, Rep. of South Africa, 120 m. E of Johannesburg; pop. (1967e) 11,100; railroad junction point in stock-raising district.

Bri·an·çon \ˌbrē-äⁿ-'sōⁿ\ *or anc.* **Bri·gan·tio** \bri-'gan-shē-ˌō\. Town, Hautes-Alpes dept., SE France, 48 m. SE of Grenoble; pop. (1962c) 10,105; frontier town and tourist resort at N end of Cottian Alps; connects with Italy by the Col de Genèvre (alt. 6102 ft.). Said to have been founded by the Greeks; in Roman times important station on road from N Italy to SE Gaul.

Briansk. See BRYANSK.

Bri·an·za \brē-'än(t)-sə\. Hilly but fertile district S of Lake Como, Lombardy, N Italy.

Bri·ar·cliff Man·or \ˌbrī(-ə)r-klif-'man-ər\. Residential village, Westchester co., SE New York, E of Hudson river 31 m. N of New York; pop. (1970c) 6521; permanent camps of Girl Scouts and Camp Fire Girls; Briarcliff Coll. (1904).

Brices Cross Roads National Battlefield Site \ˌbrī-səz-\. See UNITED STATES, *National Historical Parks.*

Bri·dal·veil \'brīd-ᵊl-ˌvāl\. Waterfall in Yosemite National Park, E cen. California; 620 ft. high.

Bridge·burg \'brij-ˌbərg\. Former town, Welland co., SE Ontario, Canada; joined with Fort Erie village 1932 to form Fort Erie town.

Bridge·hamp·ton \ˌbrij-'ham(p)-tən\. Village, Suffolk co., SE New York, on Long I. near Atlantic Ocean, ab. 19 m. E of Riverhead; settled 1660.

Bridg·end \brij-'end\. Urban district, Glamorganshire, SE Wales; pop. (1971p) 14,531; trade center in agricultural region; brickworks, stone quarries; brewing.

Bridge·port \'brij-ˌpō(ə)rt, -ˌpȯ(ə)rt\. 1 City, Jackson co., NE corner of Alabama, on Tennessee river 3 m. S of Tennessee border; pop. (1970c) 2908; textiles, lumber.

2 Village, ⊗ of Mono co., E California; pop. (1970c) 500.

3 Industrial city, Fairfield co., SW corner of Connecticut, on Long Island Sound at mouth of Pequonnock river, 17 m. SW of New Haven; pop. (1970c) 156,542; manufactures electrical goods, machinery and machine tools, munitions, metal goods and hardware, sewing machines, pharmaceuticals, radios; Bridgeport Engineering Inst. (1924), Univ. of Bridgeport (1927), Sacred Heart Univ. (1963). First settled 1639 as **Pe·quon·nock** \pi-'kwȯn-ək\, later called **New Fair·field** \-'fa(ə)r-ˌfēld, -'fe(ə)r-\, **Strat·field** \'strat-ˌfēld\, and **Fairfield Village;** incorporated as city 1836; industrial development accelerated after Civil War; first high school established 1876; town (incorp. 1821) and city consolidated and made coextensive 1889.

4 City, Lawrence co., SE Illinois, 17 m. E of Olney; pop. (1970c) 2262; in agricultural and oil-producing region.

5 City, ⊗ of Morrill co., W Nebraska, on North Platte river 32 m. ESE of Scottsbluff; pop. (1970c) 1490.

6 Village, Belmont co., E Ohio, on Ohio river opp. Wheeling, West Virginia, 22 m. S of Steubenville; pop. (1970c) 3001; glass, sheet metal, tin.

7 Borough, Montgomery co., SE Pennsylvania, on Schuylkill river 14 m. NW of Philadelphia; pop. (1970c) 5630; iron and coke works.

8 City, Wise co., N Texas, 40 m. NNW of Fort Worth; pop. (1970c) 3614; in agricultural region; incorp. 1913.

9 Town, Harrison co., N West Virginia, 5 m. E of Clarksburg; pop. (1970c) 4777.

Bridgeport Dam. Dam across W fork of Trinity river, Wise co., NE of Fort Worth, N Texas; height 110 ft.; completed 1931; impounds water, **Lake Bridgeport,** for flood control and water supply.

Bridg·er's Pass \ˌbrij-ərz-\. Mountain pass, S Wyoming, SSE of South Pass; discovered by James Bridger and later used by pony express and Union Pacific R.R.

Bridges Creek. See WAKEFIELD 4.

Bridge·ton \'brij-tən\. 1 Town, St. Louis co., Missouri, NW of St. Louis; pop. (1970c) 19,992.

2 City, ⊗ of Cumberland co., SW New Jersey, 10 m. N of mouth of Delaware river; pop. (1970c) 20,435; baskets, glass containers; diversified farming; tomatoes; founded by Quakers c. 1686; made port of entry 1790; incorp. 1865.

Bridge·town \'brij-ˌtaůn\. 1 Commercial port, ✱ of Barbados, West Indies; pop. (1968e) 12,300; exports sugar; tourism; founded 1628.

2 Town, Annapolis co., W Nova Scotia, Canada; pop. (1971p) 1012; farming.

Bridge View. Village, Cook co., NE Illinois, SW of Chicago; pop. (1970c) 12,522; residential.

Bridge·ville \'brij-ˌvil\. Industrial borough, Allegheny co., SW Pennsylvania, 9 m. SW of Pittsburgh; pop. (1970c) 6717; chemicals, glass, steel; coal.

Bridge·wa·ter \'brij-ˌwȯt-ər, -ˌwät-\. 1 Industrial town, Plymouth co., SE Massachusetts, 7 m. S of Brockton; pop. (1970c) 11,829; Massachusetts State Coll. (1840).

2 Residential borough (P.O. **West Bridgewater**), Beaver co., W Pennsylvania, on Ohio river 25 m. NW of Pittsburgh; pop. (1970c) 966.

3 Town, Rockingham co., N Virginia, SW of Harrisonburg; pop. (1970c) 2828; Bridgewater Coll. (1880).

4 Town, Lunenburg co., S Nova Scotia, Canada, on La Have river, 52 m. WSW of Halifax; pop. (1971p) 5197; founded ab. 1812; first school in Canada established 1632 in this vicinity by six Capuchin monks, later moved to Port Royal (Annapolis Royal).

Bridg·north \ˈbrij-ˌnȯ(ə)rth\. Market town, Shropshire, W England, on the Severn 23 m. W of Birmingham; pop. (1961c) 7552.

Bridg·ton \ˈbrij-tən\. Town, Cumberland co., SW Maine, 25 m. W of Lewiston; pop. (1970c) 2967; in resort area.

Bridg·wa·ter \ˈbrij-ˌwȯt-ər, -ˌwät-\. Municipal borough, Somersetshire, SW England, on the Parret 10 m. from Bristol Channel and 28 m. SSW of Bristol; pop. (1971p) 26,598; seaport; Bath brick, cellulose film.

Brid·ling·ton \ˈbrid-liŋ-tən\. Municipal borough, East Riding, Yorkshire, N England, on North Sea 25 m. NNE of Hull; pop. (1971p) 26,729; excellent harbor; summer resort.

Brid·port \ˈbrid-ˌpō(ə)rt, -ˌpȯ(ə)rt\. Municipal borough, Dorsetshire, S England, on English Channel 63 m. WSW of Southampton; pop. (1971p) 6362; ropes, nets, sailcloth.

Brie \ˈbrē\. Agricultural district and medieval county, NE France, E of Paris, now in departments of Aisne, Marne, and Seine-et-Marne; chief town was Meaux; noted for its vineyards and pastures, and esp. for its cheese (Brie cheese).

Brieg. See BRZEG.

Bri·elle \brē-ˈel\. Borough, Monmouth co., E cen. New Jersey, 9 m. SSW of Asbury Park; pop. (1970c) 3594.

Briel·le \ˈbrē-lə\ *also* **Briel** \ˈbrēl\ *or* **Bril** \ˈbril\ *or in English, esp. formerly,* **The Brill** \-ˈbril\. Commune, South Holland prov., W Netherlands, on N coast of Voorne I. on the Nieuwe Maas, 14 m. W of Rotterdam; pop. (1970e) 8314; has good harbor; first mentioned 1280; first place seized by Dutch (the Gueux led by William de la Marck in 1572) in reconquest of Netherlands from the Spanish, and held against attack by land and sea; occupied by British 1585–1616.

Bri·enne \brē-ˈen\. 1 Small former county in the Champagne, NE France, 23 m. NNE of Troyes; held from 10th cent. to end of 18th cent. by Brienne family; its most famous member was the Crusader, John of Brienne (1148–1237), King of Jerusalem (1210–25).

2 *or* **Brienne–le–Châ·teau** \-lə-sha-ˈtō\. Town, Aube dept., France; pop. (1962c) 3676; site of military school at which Napoleon studied 1779–84; partly destroyed in battle Jan. 29, 1814 in which French gained a victory over Prussians.

Bri·enz \brē-ˈen(t)s\. Commune, Bern canton, Switzerland, at NE end of Lake of Brienz; pop. (1970c) 2796; noted for its scenery and for its wood-carving industry.

Brienz, Lake of *or Ger.* **Bri·enz·er See** \brē-ˈen(t)-sər-ˌzā\. Lake, SE Bern canton, Switzerland; 11.5 sq. m.; max. depth 856 ft.; traversed by the Aare river.

Bri·er \ˈbrī(-ə)r\. City, Snohomish co., NW cen. Washington; pop. (1970c) 3093.

Bri·er·field \ˈbrī(-ə)r-ˌfēld\. Urban district, Lancashire, NW England, 23 m. N of Manchester; pop. (1971p) 7572.

Bri·eulles–sur–Meuse \brē-ˌə(r)l-sū(ə)r-ˈmyüz, -ˈmə(r)z\. Village, Meuse dept., NE France, 18 m. NW of Verdun; pop. (1962c) 532; monument marking crossing of Meuse Nov. 1, 1918 by American forces in last phase of World War I.

Bri·ey \brē-ˈē, -ˈā\. Commune, Meurthe-et-Moselle dept., NE France, 12 m. NW of Metz; pop. (1962c) 5396; center of **Briey Basin,** a district containing extensive iron ore deposits, also smelting furnaces.

Brig \ˈbrēk\ *or Fr.* **Brigue** \brēg\ *or Ital.* **Bri·ga** \ˈbrē-gə\. Commune, Valais canton, SW cen. Switzerland, on Rhone river 31 m. ENE of Sion; pop. (1965e) 5200; tourist resort; station at Swiss end of Simplon Tunnel.

Brig·an·tine \ˈbrig-ən-ˌtēn\. City, Atlantic co., SE New Jersey, on Atlantic coast NE of Atlantic City; pop. (1970c) 6741.

Brigantine Beach. Narrow sandy island off N Atlantic co., SE New Jersey.

Brigantinus Lacus. See CONSTANCE, LAKE.

Brigantio. See BRIANÇON.

Brigantium. See BREGENZ.

Bri·ga–Ten·da \ˌbrē-gə-ˈten-də\. Region in Alpes-Maritimes dept., SE France, formerly in NW Italy, near the S end of the French-Italian border, ab. 32 m. NE of Nice; comprises two small towns, **Briga Ma·rit·ti·ma** \-mə-ˈrē-tə-mə\ and **Tenda,** on a small stream (Roja) in mountain area containing important hydroelectric developments. Demanded by France 1946 as reparation from Italy and ceded by treaty 1947.

Brig·ham City \ˈbrig-əm-\. City, ⊗ of Box Elder co., NW Utah, 20 m. N of Ogden; pop. (1970c) 14,007; woolen goods, beet sugar, canning industries; peaches.

Brig·house \ˈbrig-ˌhau̇s\. Municipal borough, West Riding, Yorkshire, N England, 20 m. SW of Leeds; pop. (1971p) 34,111; radio and television equipment.

Brigh·ton \ˈbrīt-ᵊn\. 1 City, ⊗ of Adams co., NE cen. Colorado, 18 m. NE of Denver; pop. (1970c) 8309; sugar-beet center; founded 1889, incorp. as city 1922.

2 Municipality, SE Tasmania, Australia, 12 m. N of Hobart; pop. (1970e) 2330; in agricultural and orchard region.

3 Municipality, S Victoria, SE Australia, on E side of Port Phillip Bay, suburb 8 m. S of Melbourne; pop. (1966c) 40,617.

4 Village, Northumberland co., SE Ontario, Canada, near N shore of Lake Ontario 20 m. WSW of Belleville; pop. (1971p) 2374; resort.

5 County borough, East Sussex, S England, on English Channel 50 m. S of London; pop. (1971p) 166,081; electrical equipment, machine tools; seaside resort, with chalybeate springs; has no harbor; Univ. of Sussex (1961, located ab. 4 m. NE of Brighton). Mentioned in Domesday Book; for several hundred years merely a fishing village.

Bright·wa·ters \ˈbrīt-ˌwȯt-ərz, -ˌwät-\. Village, Suffolk co., SE New York, on Great South Bay on Long Island, 39 m. E of New York; pop. (1970c) 3808.

Brigue. See BRIG.

Brig·us \ˈbrig-əs\. Seaport, SE Newfoundland, Canada, on S shore of Conception Bay 25 m. W of St. John's; pop. (1966c) 707; fishing.

Bri·hue·ga \brē-ˈwā-gə\. Commune, Guadalajara prov., cen. Spain, 17 m. NE of Guadalajara; pop. (1962c) 2287; scene of English defeat by Philip V Dec. 9, 1710.

Bri·ju·ni \brē-ˈ(y)ü-nē\ *or Ital.* **Bri·o·ni** \brē-ˈō-nē\. Island group in the Adriatic Sea, off the coast of Croatia, NW Yugoslavia.

Bril *or* **The Brill.** See BRIELLE.

Bril·liant \ˈbril-yənt\. Village, Jefferson co., E Ohio, on Ohio river 7 m. S of Steubenville; pop. (1970c) 2178.

Bril·lion \ˈbril-yən\. City, Calumet co., E Wisconsin, 22 m. WNW of Manitowoc; pop. (1970c) 2588; dairy farming.

Brindaban. See VRINDAVAN.

Brin·di·si \ˈbrin-də-(ˌ)zē, ˈbrēn-\. 1 Province of Apulia, SE Italy. See table at ITALY.

2 *anc.* **Brun·du·si·um** \ˌbrən-ˈd(y)ü-z(h)ē-əm\ *or* **Brun·di·si·um** \-ˈdiz(h)-\. Fortified seaport, its ✱, on Strait of Otranto in Adriatic, 66 m. SE of Bari; pop. (1968e) 80,357; trades in wine, cereals, olives, vegetables; naval base during World War I; two 11th cent. churches; 12th cent. cathedral; 13th cent. castle. Original settlement captured by Romans 267 B.C.; became Roman naval station; death place of Vergil 19 B.C.; taken by Saracens 836 and Normans 1071; later lost much of its importance until opening of Suez Canal 1869.

Brink·ley \ˈbriŋk-lē\. City, Monroe co., E Arkansas, 64 m. E of Little Rock; pop. (1970c) 5275; cotton and lumber.

Brioni. See BRIJUNI.

Bri·on Island \ˌbrē-ˌän-\. Small island in the Gulf of St. Lawrence, E Canada, N of Magdalen Is.

Bri·oude \brē-ˈüd\ *or anc.* **Bri·vas** \ˈbrī-vəs\. Town, Haute-Loire dept., S cen. France, 36 m. S of Clermont-Ferrand; pop. (1962c) 6900; trade center of a fertile plain; captured by Goths 532; later taken by Burgundians, Saracens (732), and Normans; Romanesque church.

Briovera. See SAINT-LÔ.

Bris·bane \ˈbriz-bən, -ˌbān\. 1 City, San Mateo co., W California, on San Francisco Bay 5 m. S of San Francisco; pop. (1970c) 3003; glass products, shirts, precision tools.
2 River, SE Queensland, Australia; 215 m. long; flows E to Moreton Bay.
3 Seaport city, ✻ of Queensland, Australia, on N bank of Brisbane river 13 m. W of its mouth in Moreton Bay; pop. (1970e) 703,000; agricultural machinery, textiles; sugar and oil refineries; shipbuilding; Parliament House (1869), museum (1855), art gallery (1895), Univ. of Queensland (1909); founded 1824 as a penal colony; made capital of newly created colony of Queensland 1859.

Bris·coe \ˈbris-(ˌ)kō\. County in Texas. See table at TEXAS.

Bri·si·ghel·la \ˌbrē-zə-ˈgel-ə\. Commune, Ravenna prov., Emilia-Romagna, N Italy; pop. (1968e) 9830.

Bris·tol \ˈbrist-ᵊl\. 1 Name of counties in two states of the U.S. See tables at MASSACHUSETTS and RHODE ISLAND.
2 Industrial city, SW Hartford co., N Connecticut, 15 m. SW of Hartford; pop. (1970c) 55,487; automobile parts, tools, springs, clocks, ball bearings; famous in its early history as clockmaking center; settled 1727, incorp. 1911; the town (incorp. 1785) is coextensive with the city.
3 City, ⊗ of Liberty co., NW Florida; pop. (1970c) 626.
4 Town, Grafton co., W New Hampshire, 14 m. WNW of Laconia; pop. (1970c) 1670; summer resort.
5 Industrial borough, Bucks co., SE Pennsylvania, on Delaware river 19 m. ENE of Philadelphia in Bristol township; pop. (1970c) 12,085 (borough), 67,498 (township); carpets, machinery, woolen goods; early port of call for river traffic; settled 1697.
6 Town and port of entry, ⊗ of Bristol co., E Rhode Island, on Narragansett Bay 13 m. ESE of Providence; pop. (1970c) 17,860; residential area; rubber goods, electric cables; yachting; formerly important for whale fishing and shipbuilding; Roger Williams Coll. (1919); settled 1669; figured in King Philip's War; incorp. by Plymouth Colony 1681; annexed to R.I. 1746; bombarded by British ships 1775; burned and pillaged by British 1778.
7 City, Sullivan co., NE Tennessee, 22 m. NNE of Johnson City on Tennessee-Virginia line, contiguous with Bristol, Virginia, the two cities having a common main thoroughfare through which the state line runs; pop. (1970c) 20,064; in mineral and timber region; ships livestock; manufactures rayon, pulp and paper, leather goods, mine cars, furniture; King College (1867).
8 Town, Addison co., W Vermont, 10 m. NNE of Middlebury; pop. (1970c) 2744; settled 1786.
9 City, SW Virginia, contiguous with Bristol, Tennessee; in Washington co. but politically independent; pop. (1970c) 14,857; lumber, textiles, paper, pharmaceuticals; Sullins Coll. (1870), Virginia Intermont Coll. (1884).
10 City and county borough, Gloucestershire, SW cen. England, at confluence of Avon and Frome rivers 119 m. by rail W of London; pop. (1971p) 425,203; important shipping center; shipbuilding; aircraft, pottery, tobacco; chemical and metallurgical industries; imports include food products, oil, zinc concentrates; exports include automobiles, chemicals, clay; Univ. of Bristol (1909), cathedral (1142), library (1613), art gallery, museum, and Clifton Suspension Bridge over the Avon.
History: From early times a place of commerce; received first charter 1155; active in medieval trade; point of departure 1497 of John Cabot; in Civil War taken 1643 by Royalists under Prince Rupert and in 1645 captured by Parliamentarians; scene of Reform riots 1831; in World War II repeatedly bombed by German air force 1940 and 1941.

Bristol Bay. 1 Arm of Bering Sea in its SE part, on W side of N end of Alaska Penin., SW Alaska; one of richest salmon-fishing areas in the world.
2 Borough in Alaska. See table at ALASKA.

Bristol Channel. Arm of Atlantic Ocean extending bet. S Wales and SW England; ab. 85 m. long and bet. 5 and 43 m. wide.

Bris·tow \ˈbris-(ˌ)tō\. City, Creek co., E cen. Oklahoma, 20 m. WSW of Sapulpa; pop. (1970c) 4653; supply and shipping center for oil and gas fields; manufactures cottonseed oil, fuel and lubricating oils.

Brit·ain \ˈbrit-ᵊn\. Anglicized form of Latin **Bri·tan·nia** \brə-ˈtan-yə, -ˈtan-ē-ə\, applied historically to the island of Great Britain especially during its pre-Roman and Roman periods and in the early Anglo-Saxon period until the merging of the Heptarchy into the England of King Alfred. See GREAT BRITAIN.

Britannia. See BRITAIN.

Britannia Minor. See BRITTANY.

British America. 1 *or specifically* **British North America.** Former designation for Canada.
2 Former designation for all British possessions in, or adjacent to, North and South America.

British Ant·arc·tic Territory \-(ˌ)ant-ˈärk-tik-, -ˈärt-ik-\. British colony, Antarctica, consisting of territory lying S of 60°S and bet. 80°W and 20°W; includes South Shetland Is. and South Orkney Is.; ab. 652,000 sq. m.; administered from Falkland Is.; part of Falkland Is. Dependencies 1908, made separate colony 1962.

British Baluchistan. See BALUCHISTAN 2.

British Bech·u·a·na·land \-ˌbech-(ə-)ˈwän-ə-ˌland\ *or sometimes shortened to* **Bechuanaland.** Former British colony, S Africa, lying bet. Orange and Molopo rivers, bordering Griqualand West on SE; organized as part of British protectorate 1885 (see BOTSWANA); attached to Cape of Good Hope 1895 and with it became in 1910 part of the Union (now Rep.) of South Africa; chief towns Mafeking, Vryburg (*q.v.*), Taung, and Kuruman.

British Borneo. See BORNEO.

British Central Africa Protectorate. See MALAWI.

British Columbia. Province, Canada, on Pacific coast; 366,255 sq. m. (incl. 6976 sq. m. of water); pop. (1970e) 2,137,000; ✻ Victoria. *Physical features:* Most mountainous province of Canada; in N crossed by Rocky Mts. which on SE form boundary with Alberta; has several subsidiary ranges, nearly parallel: Cariboo Mts., Selkirk Mts., Monashee Mts., Purcell Mts., etc.; farther W along the coast are the Coast Mts., a continuation of the Cascade Range of U.S. Its chief river is the Fraser which with tributaries waters most of central and S parts; in SE are Columbia and headstreams, and in NE the Liard and Peace rivers and tributaries, each a part of the Mackenzie river system; along the coast are many shorter streams (as Stikine, Skeena, Nass) with lower courses generally long narrow fjords. Lakes, mostly of the finger type, are numerous in all parts. Has 4 national parks, ab. 250 provincial parks. Off its Pacific shores are many islands, notably Vancouver and the Queen Charlotte group; many good harbors; large ocean trade. *Chief products:* Lumber, fruit; livestock raising, fishing; copper, zinc, lead, molybdenum, iron ore, oil, natural gas. *Chief cities:* Vancouver, Victoria, North Vancouver, New Westminster.
History: Its shores visited by Sir Francis Drake 1578–79, by Juan de Fuca 1592, and by Capt. Cook 1778; careful survey of coast made by Capt. George Vancouver 1792–94 and overland explorations made by several (Mackenzie, Lewis and Clark, Thompson, and Fraser) bet. 1793 and

1811; for a time (1849–58) known as **New Caledonia** and formed part of Hudson's Bay Company's concession; part claimed by U.S. (see OREGON); gold discovered in Fraser river basin 1856. Established as British crown colony 1858; united with Vancouver I. 1866, with N boundary extended to 60°N; became a prov. of Canada 1871. Canadian Pacific Railway completed to Vancouver 1885.

British Commonwealth of Nations. See COMMONWEALTH OF NATIONS.

British East Africa. 1 Former name of Kenya (*q.v.*). 2 Name applied to the former British dependencies in E Africa: Kenya, Tanganyika, Uganda, and Zanzibar.

British Empire. See COMMONWEALTH OF NATIONS.

British Guiana. See GUYANA.

British Honduras *also* **Be·lize** \bə-'lēz\. British colony, Central America, bounded on N by Mexico, on E by the Caribbean Sea, and on S and W by Guatemala; 8866 sq. m.; pop. (1970p) 119,645; ✱ Belmopan. *Physical features:* Generally low and marshy along the coast, rising inland, hilly in S with highest point ab. 3681 ft.; separated from Quintana Roo, Mexico, on the N by the Hondo river and from Guatemala on the S by the Sarstoon; traversed in central part by the Belize river which rises in NE Guatemala and flows E to the Caribbean at Belize; off coast are many islets, reefs, and cays; in NE is Ambergris Cay, and opp. Belize are Turneffe Is. *Chief towns:* Belize and Stann Creek. *Chief products:* Sugar, citrus fruits, forest products. Divided into 6 districts: Belize, Cayo, Corozal, Orange Walk, Stann Creek, and Toledo.

History: Settled ab. 1638 by English logwood cutters from Jamaica; maintained existence despite Spanish opposition which was finally defeated 1798; made British superintendency of Belize 1786 to which Great Britain sought to add Bay Islands 1841; intended expansion by British (see also MOSQUITO COAST) part of background of Clayton-Bulwer Treaty bet. England and the U.S. 1850; southern boundary with Guatemala fixed by treaty 1859; declared a colony subordinate to Jamaica 1862; independent of Jamaica since 1884; adopted new constitution 1960; achieved internal self-government 1965.

British India. That part of India formerly under direct British administration. See INDIA 1.

British Indian Ocean Territory. British colony, Indian Ocean; pop. (1971e) 560; copra; formed 1965 from Chagos Archipelago (formerly part of Mauritius) and Aldabra, Farquhar, and Desroches Islands (formerly part of Seychelles).

British Isles. Island group in W Europe, comprising Great Britain, Ireland, and adjacent islands.

British Kaffraria. See KAFFRARIA.

British Malaya. Former British possessions in the Malay Penin. and the Malay Archipelago, SE Asia. See MALAYA, FEDERATION OF and STRAITS SETTLEMENTS.

British New Guinea. See PAPUA, TERRITORY OF.

British North America. See BRITISH AMERICA 1 and CANADA.

British North Borneo. See SABAH.

British Solomon Islands *or in full* **British Solomon Islands Protectorate.** British protectorate comprising the Solomon Islands (except Bougainville, Buka, and adjacent small islands) and the Santa Cruz Islands; 11,500 sq. m.; pop. (1971e) 166,280; ✱ Honiara. See SOLOMON ISLANDS.

British Somaliland *or* **Somaliland Protectorate.** Former British protectorate on S shore of the Gulf of Aden, E Africa; 67,936 sq. m.; ✱ Hargeysa.

History: In Middle Ages a powerful Arab sultanate; broken up in 17th cent.; coast came under British influence in early 19th cent. but remained actually under Egyptian control until 1884; administered by Government of India 1884–98, by British Foreign Office 1898–1905; transferred to British Colonial Office Apr. 1, 1905; occupied by Italian military forces Aug. 16, 1940–Mar. 16, 1941; united with former Italian Somaliland to form independent republic of Somalia (*q.v.*) 1960.

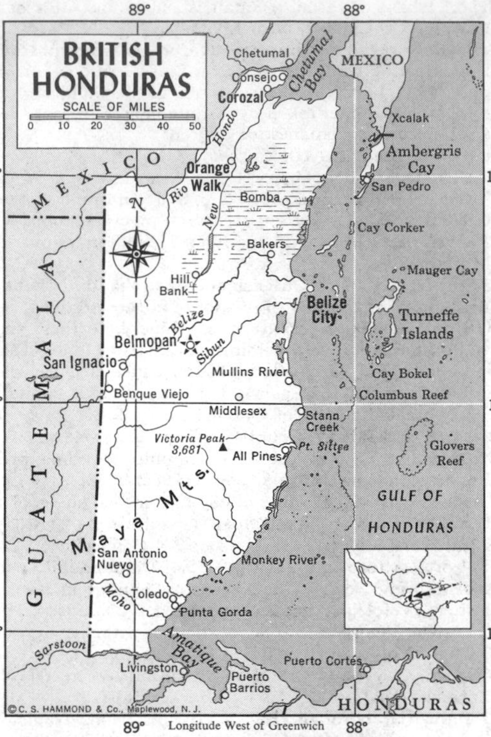

British Virgin Islands. See VIRGIN ISLANDS.

British West Indies. Name applied to the islands of the West Indies (*q.v.*) which were colonies of Great Britain, including Jamaica and its dependencies, the Bahama Is., Leeward Is., Windward Is., Barbados, Trinidad and Tobago. All of the British West Indies except the British Virgin Is. (in the Leeward Is.) and the Bahamas united to form the West Indies Federation 1958–62; variation in political status among the islands: several now fully independent, others remain dependencies of Great Britain.

Bri·to \'brē-tō\. Small port on Pacific coast, SW Nicaragua; proposed as outlet with locks for W end of Nicaragua Canal (see NICARAGUA).

Brit·on Ferry \ˌbrit-ən-\. Seaport, part of the borough of Neath, Glamorganshire, S Wales, at mouth of the Neath river; metallurgical industries; port of Neath, center of export for coal-mining region.

Brits \'brits\. Town, Transvaal, Rep. of South Africa, ab. 28 m. W of Pretoria; pop. (1967e) 11,800.

Britt \'brit\. Town, Hancock co., N Iowa, 30 m. W of Mason City; pop. (1970c) 2069; ships grain.

Brit·ta·ny \'brit-ᵊn-ē\ *or Fr.* **Bre·tagne** \brə-tänʸ\ *or Lat.* **Bri·tan·nia Mi·nor** \bri-ˌtan-yə-'mī-nər, -ˌtan-ē-ə-\. Historical peninsular region of NW France; bounded anciently on N by English Channel, NE by Normandy, E by Maine and Anjou, SE by Poitou, S and W by Atlantic Ocean; exactly equivalent to modern departments of Ille-et-Vilaine, Loire-Atlantique, Côtes-du-Nord, Morbihan, Finistère; ✱ Rennes; numerous short rivers; traditionally divided by Bretons into the *Armor* (coastal regions) and the *Argoat* (hinterland).

History: For early history of region, see ARMORICA; region occupied by Bretons, Celtic people, whom the Anglo-Saxon invasion of Britain drove through SW England to NW corner of France 5th–6th cents. A.D.; subdued by Clovis, King of Franks, but never effectively part of Merovingian or Carolingian kingdoms; at end of 10th cent., Geoffrey I, former count of Rennes, took title of duke of Brittany, unrecognized by France until 1213;

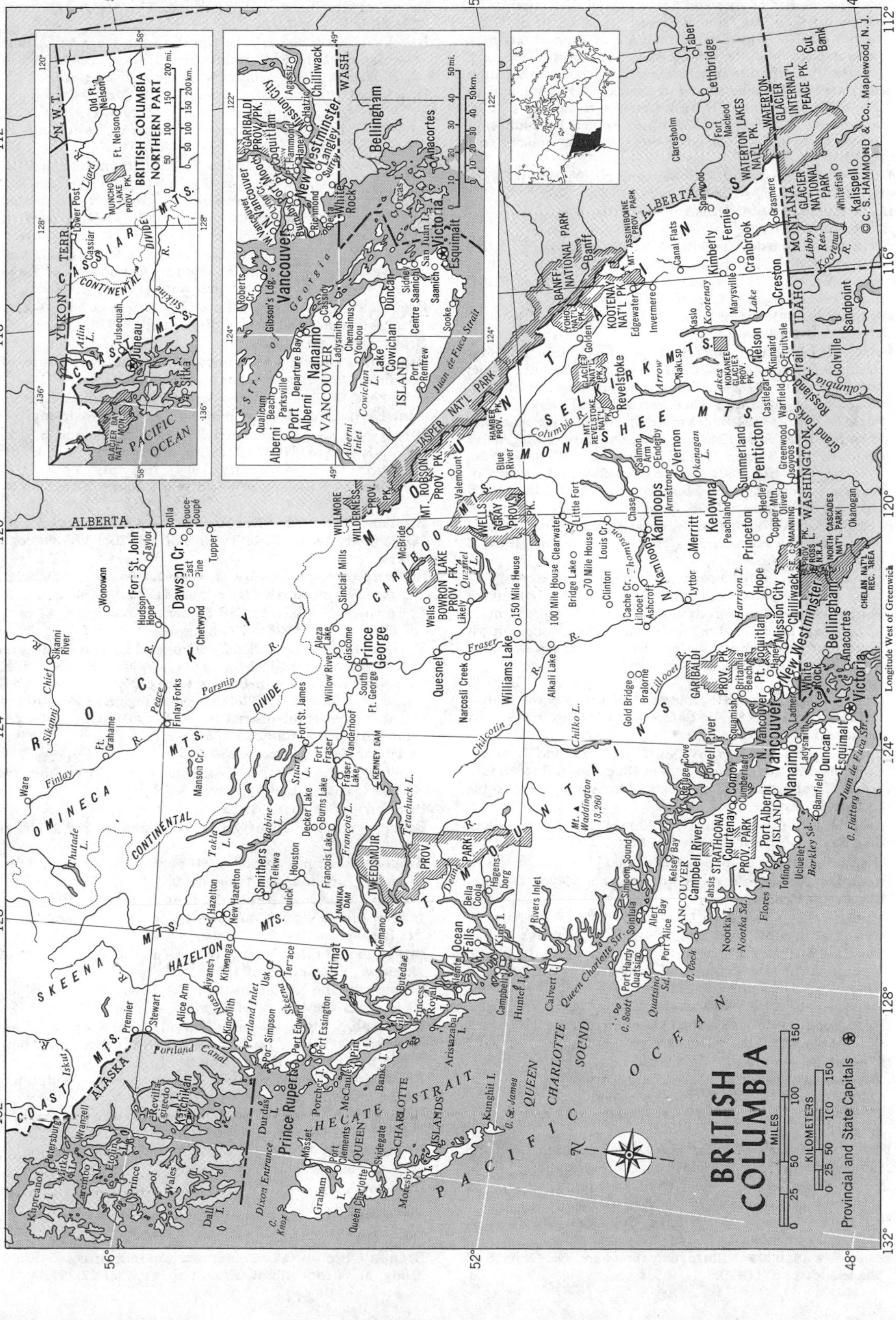
BRITISH COLUMBIA
MILES
0 25 50 100 150
KILOMETERS
0 25 50 100 150
Provincial and State Capitals
BRITISH COLUMBIA NORTHERN PART
PACIFIC OCEAN
QUEEN CHARLOTTE SOUND
HECATE STRAIT
QUEEN CHARLOTTE ISLANDS
VANCOUVER ISLAND
ROCKY MTS.
COAST MOUNTAINS
CARIBOO MTS.
SELKIRK MTS.
MONASHEE MTS.
ALBERTA
WASHINGTON
IDAHO
MONTANA
Prince Rupert
Prince George
Kamloops
Vancouver
Victoria
New Westminster
Nanaimo
Kelowna
Penticton
Vernon
Nelson
Cranbrook
Dawson Cr.
Fort St. John
Williams Lake
Quesnel
Kitimat
Smithers
Revelstoke
Longitude West of Greenwich
© C. S. HAMMOND & Co., Maplewood, N. J.

acquired as fief of England 1169 through betrothal of its heiress to Geoffrey, son of Henry II; at death of Duke Arthur 1203, claimed as vassal state of France; territory expanded to include mouth of Loire; until 15th cent. practically a separate state; came to French crown through marriages of Duchess Anne to Charles VIII 1491 and to Louis XII 1499 and of heiress, Claudia, to Francis I 1514; incorporated in France 1532; up to French Revolution, a French province; involved in Wars of the Vendée (see POITOU).

Brit·ton \'brit-ᵊn\. City, ⊗ of Marshall co., NE South Dakota, 45 m. ENE of Aberdeen; pop. (1970c) 1465.

Briva Isarae. See PONTOISE.

Brivas. See BRIOUDE.

Brive–la–Gail·larde \ˌbrēv-lə-gə-'yärd\ *or formerly* **Brive** *or anc.* **Bri·va Cur·re·tia** \ˌbrī-və-kə-'rē-sh(ē-)ə\. Commune, Corrèze dept., S cen. France, 12 m. SW of Tulle; pop. (1968c) 46,561; 12th cent. church.

Brixen. See BRESSANONE.

Brixia. See BRESCIA 2.

Br·no \'bər-(ˌ)nō\ *or Ger.* **Brünn** \'brün\. Industrial city, Czech S.R., cen. Czechoslovakia, 115 m. SE of Prague; pop. (1968e) 337,247; textiles, machinery, chemicals; trades in sugar and vegetables; technical univ. (1899), Purkyňe Univ. (1919). Founded in 10th cent.; Austrian imperial free city 1243; in various wars besieged or occupied: by Swedes 1645, Prussians 1742 and 1866, French 1805 and 1809; before World War I capital of Austrian crownland of Moravia; capital of Moravia in German protectorate 1938–45.

Broa Bay \ˌbrō-ə-\. Bay on SW coast of Matanzas prov. and SE coast of La Habana prov., W Cuba; enclosed on the S by Zapata Penin.

Broach \'brōch\ *or* **Bha·roch** \bə-'rōch\ *or anc.* **Bar·y·ga·za** \ˌbar-ə-'gā-zə\. City, Gujarat state, India, on N bank of Narmada river 30 m. from Gulf of Cambay and 190 m. N of Bombay; pop. (1961c) 73,639; for centuries one of most important travel and trade centers on India's west coast, noted for its fabrics and ivory work. Annexed to Mogul Empire 1572; under rule of Marathas 1685–1772; English factory established 1616, Dutch 1626; captured by British 1772, but ceded to Sindia of Gwalior 1783, again taken by British 1803.

Broad \'brȯd\. **1** River, W North Carolina and N South Carolina; ab. 220 m. long; rises in Blue Ridge, flows S into South Carolina and unites with Saluda river near Columbia to form Congaree river.

2 River, S South Carolina; ab. 70 m. long; rises in Allendale co., flows SE into the Atlantic Ocean in Beaufort co.

Broad, Mount. Peak in the Himalayas, N India; 26,400 ft.

Broad Haven. Sea inlet on NW coast of co. Mayo, NW Eire, E of Erris Head.

Broads, The \-'brȯdz\. Low-lying district in Norfolk (**Norfolk Broads**) and Suffolk (**Suffolk Broads**), E England, characterized by lakelike expansions of the rivers, esp. along the lower courses of the **Yare** \'ye(ə)r, 'ya(ə)r\, **Bure** \'byu̇(ə)r\, and **Wave·ney** \'wāv-nē\, and by shallow lagoons connected with the rivers by channels.

Broad Sound. Inlet of Pacific Ocean, on E coast of Queensland, Australia, S of Mackay.

Broad·stairs and Saint Pe·ter's \'brȯd-ˌsta(ə)rz . . . sānt-'pēt-ərz, -ˌste(ə)rz-, -sənt-\. Urban district, Kent, SE England, on North Sea 67 m. E of London; pop. (1971p) 19,996; includes **Broadstairs,** a seaside resort near Ramsgate.

Broad·top Mountain \ˌbrȯd-ˌtäp-\. Coalfield in Bedford and Huntingdon cos., S Pennsylvania; 80 sq. m.

Broa·dus \'brȯd-əs\. Town, ⊗ of Powder River co., SE Montana; pop. (1970c) 799.

Broad·view \'brȯd-ˌvyü\. Village, Cook co., Illinois, W of Chicago; pop. (1970c) 9623.

Broadview Heights. Village, Cuyahoga co., NE Ohio, S of Cleveland; pop. (1970c) 11,463.

Broad·wa·ter \'brȯd-ˌwȯt-ər, -ˌwät-\. County in Montana. See table at MONTANA.

Brock·en \'bräk-ən\. Highest peak in the Harz Mts., East Germany, 32 m. S of Brunswick; 3747 ft.; celebrated in legends, esp. in connection with the Faust legend.

Brock·port \'bräk-ˌpō(ə)rt, -ˌpȯ(ə)rt\. Village, Monroe co., W New York, 18 m. W of Rochester; pop. (1970c) 7878; dairy and truck farms; nurseries; canneries; State Univ. of New York Coll. at Brockport (1841).

Brock·ton \'bräk-tən\. Industrial city, Plymouth co., SE Massachusetts, 19 m. S of Boston; pop. (1970c) 89,040; electronic equipment, shoes, machine tools. Land deeded by Indians 1649, settled 1700; until 1821 a part of Bridgewater, name Brockton adopted 1874; incorp. 1881.

Brock·ville \'bräk-ˌvil\. Industrial town, ⊗ of Leeds and Grenville cos., Leeds co., SE Ontario, Canada, on St. Lawrence 48 m. ENE of Kingston; pop. (1971p) 19,707.

Brock·way \'bräk-(ˌ)wā\. Borough, Jefferson co., W cen. Pennsylvania, 9 m. N of DuBois; pop. (1970c) 2529.

Brod. See SLAVONSKI BROD.

Bro·deur Peninsula \(ˌ)brō-ˌdər-\. Northwest section of Baffin I., Northwest Territories, Canada.

Brod·head \'bräd-ˌhed, 'brȯd-\. City, Green co., S Wisconsin, 13 m. E of Monroe; pop. (1970c) 2515; dairying.

Bro·dy \'brȯd-ē\. Commercial city, W Ukrainian S.S.R., U.S.S.R., 40 m. NNW of Ternopol (formerly in Poland); founded 1584; made city 1684; free city 1779–1879; occupied by Russians in World War I; battle 1916; held by Germans 1941–44.

Bro·ken Ar·row \ˌbrō-kən-'ar-(ˌ)ō, -ə\. City, Tulsa co., NE Oklahoma, 14 m. SE of Tulsa; pop. (1970c) 11,789; coal, oil.

Broken Bow \-'bō\. **1** City, ⊗ of Custer co., cen. Nebraska, 65 m. ENE of North Platte; pop. (1970c) 3734; corn.

2 Town, McCurtain co., SE corner of Oklahoma, 47 m. E of Hugo; pop. (1970c) 2980; lumber; farming.

Broken Hill. **1** *or officially* **Broken Hill and Will·yama** \wil-'yam-ə, -'yäm-\. Mining city, W New South Wales, SE Australia, in Main Barrier Range 260 m. NE of Adelaide; pop. (1968e) 30,320; in subarid region at elevation of 1000 ft.; center of district noted for production of lead, zinc, and silver; founded 1884.

2 Town, Zambia. See KABWE.

Bro·lo \'brȯ-lō\. Village, Messina prov., NE Sicily, Italy, on N coast; heavy fighting Aug. 13, 1943.

Bromberg. See BYDGOSZCZ.

Brome \'brōm\. County, Quebec, Canada. See table at QUEBEC.

Brom·ley \'brəm-le, 'bräm-\. A borough of Greater London, SE England. See table at LONDON 4.

Bro·mo \'brō-(ˌ)mō\. Volcano, East Java prov., Indonesia, one of the Tengger Mountains (*q.v.*); 7848 ft.; famous for its frequent activity.

Bromp·ton \'bräm(p)-tən, 'brəm(p)-\. A W cen. district of London, England, S of Hyde Park.

Bromp·ton·ville \'bräm(p)-tən-ˌvil\. Town, Richmond co., S Quebec, Canada, N of Sherbrooke; pop. (1971p) 2766.

Bröm·se·bro \'brəm-sə-ˌbrü\. Town, Kalmar co., SE Sweden, on coast NE of Karlskrona; treaty of peace signed here 1645 bet. Sweden and Denmark.

Broms·grove \'brämz-ˌgrōv\. Urban district, Worcestershire, W cen. England; pop. (1971p) 40,669.

Bron \'brōⁿ\. Commune, Rhône dept., E cen. France, ESE suburb of Lyons; pop. (1968c) 41,619; airfield.

Brong–Aha·fo \'brȯŋ-ə-'hä-fō\. Administrative region of cen. Ghana. See table at GHANA.

Bron·son \'brän-sən\. **1** Town, ⊗ of Levy co., NW Florida penin.; pop. (1970c) 698.

2 City, Branch co., S Michigan, 30 m. S of Battle Creek; pop. (1970c) 2390; auto parts; diversified farming.

Bron·te \'brōn-(ˌ)tā\. Commune, Catania prov., E Sicily, Italy, at W foot of Mt. Etna; pop. (1968e) 22,251.

Bronx \ˈbräŋ(k)s\. 1 River, New York City; rises in Westchester co., flows S into East River Strait, nearly bisecting Bronx borough.

2 County in New York. See table at NEW YORK.

3 *or* **The Bronx.** Residential and industrial borough, forming N part of New York City; ⊗ of Bronx co. and coextensive with the county; 41 sq. m.; pop. (1970c) 1,472,216; only borough of New York City on the mainland, comprising the section NE of Harlem river, with adjacent islands (City, Hart's, Riker's); traversed by Bronx river. Settled 1641; made separate county 1913; park system includes notably Pelham Bay (containing Orchard Beach), Van Cortlandt Park, and Bronx Park (containing N.Y. Zoological Park and Botanical Garden and museum); educational institutions include Fordham Univ. (1841), Hunter College (1870), Herbert H. Lehman Coll. (1931), Bronx Community Coll. (1957). Governed as part of New York City; has a borough president, with local and county functions conducted independently of central municipal government. See also NEW YORK 3.

Bronx·ville \ˈbräŋ(k)s-ˌvil\. Residential village, Westchester co., SE New York, 17 m. NNE of New York; pop. (1970c) 6674; Concordia Junior Coll. (1881), Sarah Lawrence Coll. (1926).

Brooke \ˈbru̇k\. County in West Virginia. See table at WEST VIRGINIA.

Brooke's Point \ˈbru̇ks-\. Coastal town, SE coast of Palawan, Phil., on Sulu Sea; pop. (1969e) 38,600.

Brook Farm. See WEST ROXBURY.

Brook·field \ˈbru̇k-ˌfēld\. 1 Town, Fairfield co., SW Connecticut, 18 m. WSW of Waterbury; pop. (1970c) 9688; electrical equipment; truck farming; resort area.

2 Village, Cook co., NE Illinois, 10 m. W of Chicago; pop. (1970c) 20,284; site of Chicago Zoological Park (Brookfield Zoo).

3 Town, Worcester co., cen. Massachusetts, 15 m. W of Worcester; pop. (1970c) 2063.

4 City, Linn co., N Missouri, 27 m. E of Chillicothe; pop. (1970c) 5491; in agricultural region; coal deposits nearby.

5 City, Waukesha co., SE Wisconsin; pop. (1970c) 32,140; iron foundries.

Brook·ha·ven \bru̇k-ˈhā-vən\. 1 City, ⊗ of Lincoln co., SW Mississippi, 23 m. N of McComb; pop. (1970c) 10,700; electronic equipment; timber; dairying.

2 Town, Suffolk co., Long I., New York, E of Patchogue; pop. (1970c) 245,260; ab. 7 m. to the NE is Upton, site of Brookhaven National Laboratory for Nuclear Research.

3 Borough, Delaware co., SE Pennsylvania, SE of Philadelphia; pop. (1970c) 7370.

Brook·ings \ˈbru̇k-iŋz\. 1 County in South Dakota. See table at SOUTH DAKOTA.

2 City, Curry co., SW Oregon, 75 m. SW of Medford; pop. (1970c) 2720; commercial fishing, lumbering; dairy farming.

3 City, ⊗ of Brookings co., E South Dakota, 53 m. N of Sioux Falls; pop. (1970c) 13,717; dairy farms; South Dakota State Univ. (1881); became city 1883.

Brookland. See WEST COLUMBIA 1.

Brook·lands \ˈbru̇k-ləndz\. Town, S Manitoba, Canada, a suburb of Winnipeg; pop. (1966c) 4181.

Brook·lawn \ˈbru̇k-ˌlȯn\. Borough, Camden co., SW New Jersey, 4 m. S of Camden; pop. (1970c) 2870.

Brook·line \ˈbru̇k-ˌlīn\. Town, Norfolk co., E Massachusetts, 4 m. WSW of Boston; pop. (1970c) 58,689; Hebrew Teachers Coll. (1918), Hellenic Coll. (1937), Cardinal Cushing Coll. (1952); birthplace of John F. Kennedy, 35th president of the U.S.

Brook·lyn \ˈbru̇k-lən\. 1 Residential town, cen. Windham co., NE corner of Connecticut; pop. (1970c) 4965.

2 Village, St. Clair co., SW Illinois; pop. (1970c) 1702.

3 Residential borough, forming part of New York City, ⊗ of Kings co. and coextensive with the county, in SW extremity of Long Island; 71 sq. m.; pop. (1970c) 2,601,852; (largest in pop. of five boroughs of New York City); separated from Manhattan by East river; linked with Staten Island by Verrazano-Narrows Bridge (span 4260 ft.; completed 1964); includes districts of Flatbush, Red Hook, Greenpoint, Bushwick, New Utrecht, Williamsburg, Brownsville, Bay Ridge, Shore Road, Ridgewood, and Brooklyn Heights; brewing, shipbuilding, food processing; manufactures shoes, paint, varnish, machinery, foundry and machine-shop products, building equipment; large grain-shipping facilities. Educational institutions include Brooklyn Coll. (1930), Packer Collegiate Inst. (1845), Polytechnic Institute of Brooklyn (1854), Pratt Institute (1887), Long Island Univ. (1926), St. Francis Coll. (1858, chartered 1884), St. Joseph's Coll. for Women (1916), New York City Community Coll. of Applied Arts and Sciences (1946), Kingsborough Community Coll. (1963). Brooklyn Museum, Prospect Park, Marine Park, Botanical Garden; Coney Island; Greenwood Cemetery; Floyd Bennett Field. Governed as part of New York City; has a borough president, with local and county functions conducted independently of central municipal government. See also NEW YORK 3.

History: Settlements made along Gowanus and Jamaica Bays and at Wallabout Bay (later incorp. as Williamsburg) by Dutch and Walloons 1636 and 1637; settlement established 1645 near present site of borough hall and named *Breuckelen;* New Utrecht settled ab. 1650, Flatbush (at first called Midwout) ab. 1651; scene of battle of Long Island Aug. 27, 1776 in which British under Sir William Howe defeated Americans under Israel Putnam; incorporated as city 1834; annexed Williamsburg and Bushwick 1855, included all of Kings co. by 1896; borough of New York City 1898.

4 City, Cuyahoga co., NE Ohio, SW of Cleveland; pop. (1970c) 13,142.

Brooklyn Center. City, Hennepin co., SE cen. Minnesota, 8 m. NNW of Minneapolis; pop. (1970c) 35,173.

Brooklyn Park. Village, Hennepin co., Minnesota, NW of Minneapolis; pop. (1970c) 26,230.

Brook Park \ˌbru̇k-\. City, Cuyahoga co., NE Ohio, SW of Cleveland; pop. (1970c) 30,774.

Brooks \ˈbru̇ks\. 1 Name of counties in two states of the U.S. See tables at GEORGIA and TEXAS.

2 Town, Alberta, Canada, 100 m. SE of Calgary; pop. (1966c) 3354; alfalfa seed processing; agriculture; gas wells.

Brooks Islands. Former name of MIDWAY.

Brooks Range. Mountain range across N Alaska from Kotzebue Sound to Canadian border, forming watershed bet. Yukon basin on S and Arctic coast on N; highest peak Mt. Michelson 9239 ft.; includes smaller groups or ridges of De Long, Baird, and Endicott Mts.

Brooks·ville \ˈbru̇ks-ˌvil\. 1 City, ⊗ of Hernando co., W Florida penin., 42 m. N of Tampa; pop. (1970c) 4060; East Coast Univ. (1947).

2 City, ⊗ of Bracken co., NE Kentucky; pop. (1970c) 609.

Brook·ville \ˈbru̇k-ˌvil\. 1 Town, ⊗ of Franklin co., E Indiana, 28 m. SSW of Richmond; pop. (1970c) 2864; corn, wheat.

2 Village, Nassau co., SE New York, 5 m. SE of Glen Cove; pop. (1970c) 3212.

3 Village, Montgomery co., SW Ohio, 12 m. WNW of Dayton; pop. (1970c) 4403; tools and dies.

4 Borough, ⊗ of Jefferson co., W cen. Pennsylvania, 18 m. W of Du Bois; pop. (1970c) 4314; structural steel, radio tubes, truck bodies.

Brook·wood \'bru̇k-wu̇d\. Village, Surrey, England, 4 m. SW of Woking and 28 m. SW of London; American military cemetery.

Broom, Loch \-'brüm, -'bru̇m\. Sea inlet in Ross and Cromarty co., on NW coast of Scotland; **Little Loch Broom** is a parallel inlet just to the S.

Broome \'brüm, 'bru̇m\. 1 County in New York. See table at NEW YORK.
2 Seaport town, NW Western Australia, on Roebuck Bay; pop. (1966c) 1570; bombed by Japanese Mar. 1942.

Broom·field \'brüm-fēld\. City, Boulder and Jefferson cos., N cen. Colorado, 12 m. NNW of Denver; pop. (1970c) 7261; diversified agriculture.

Bros·sard \brȯ-'sär(d)\. Town, Laprairie co., S Quebec, Canada; pop. (1971p) 23,421; residential suburb of Montreal.

Broughton Bay. See TONGJOSŎN.

Brough·ty Ferry \'brȯ-tē-\. Suburb of Dundee, Angus co., E Scotland, on Firth of Tay ab. 3½ m. E of main part of the city; castle dating from 1498.

Brow·ard \'brau̇-ərd\. County in Florida. See table at FLORIDA.

Brown \'brau̇n\. Counties in nine states of the U.S. See tables at ILLINOIS, INDIANA, KANSAS, MINNESOTA, NEBRASKA, OHIO, SOUTH DAKOTA, TEXAS, WISCONSIN.

Brown, Mount. Peak in Glacier National Park, NW Montana; 8541 ft.

Brown, Point. Point on SW coast of Grays Harbor co., W Washington, at N entrance to Grays Harbor.

Brown Clee Hill. See CLEE HILLS.

Brown Deer. Village, Milwaukee co., SE Wisconsin, N of Milwaukee; pop. (1970c) 12,582.

Brown·field \'brau̇n-ˌfēld\. City, ⊗ of Terry co., NW Texas, 38 m. SSW of Lubbock; pop. (1970c) 9647; cotton gins, oil wells.

Brown·ing \'brau̇-niŋ\. Town, Glacier co., NW Montana; pop. (1970c) 1700; tourist resort; Museum of the Plains Indians (opened 1941); headquarters of the Blackfeet Indian Reservation.

Brown·lee Dam *and* **Brownlee Reservoir** \ˌbrau̇n-ˌlē-\. See UNITED STATES, *Dams and Reservoirs.*

Browns·burg \'brau̇nz-ˌbərg\. 1 Town, Hendricks co., cen. Indiana, 14 m. NW of Indianapolis; pop. (1970c) 5751.
2 Village, Argenteuil co., SW Quebec, Canada, WNW of Montreal; pop. (1966c) 3596.

Browns·town \'brau̇nz-ˌtau̇n\. 1 Town, ⊗ of Jackson co., S Indiana, 32 m. SE of Bloomington; pop. (1970c) 2376; melons; hatcheries.
2 Borough, Cambria co., SW cen. Pennsylvania, near Johnstown; pop. (1970c) 1035.

Browns·ville \'brau̇nz-ˌvil, -vəl\. 1 City, ⊗ of Edmonson co., cen. Kentucky; pop. (1970c) 542.
2 Borough, Fayette co., SW Pennsylvania, on Monongahela river 13 m. NW of Uniontown; pop. (1970c) 4856.
3 City, ⊗ of Haywood co., W Tennessee, 27 m. W of Jackson; pop. (1970c) 7011; fruit, cotton; sawmills.
4 City and port of entry, ⊗ of Cameron co., S Texas; on Rio Grande opp. Matamoros, Mexico, 25 m. from Gulf of Mexico; pop. (1970c) 52,522; food processing; chemicals; tourism. Began as trading post; Fort Brown (orig. Fort Taylor) established 1846; town founded 1848; scene of Mexican disorders 1859; served as one of principal ports of Confederacy during Civil War.

Brown·ville \'brau̇n-ˌvil\. Town, Piscataquis co., N cen. Maine, 37 m. NNW of Bangor; pop. (1970c) 1490.

Brown Wil·ly \brau̇n-'wil-ē\. Mountain, highest point in Cornwall, SW England, 4½ m. SE of Camelford; 1375 ft.

Brown·wood \'brau̇n-ˌwu̇d\. Industrial city, ⊗ of Brown co., cen. Texas, 64 m. SSE of Abilene; pop. (1970c) 17,368; chemicals, glass; railroad shops; oil wells; pecans; Howard Payne Coll. (1889).

Bru·ay–en–Ar·tois \brü-'ā-äⁿ-när-'twä\. Commune, Pas-de-Calais dept., N France, 17 m. NW of Arras; pop. (1968c) 28,628; chemicals; coal mines.

Bruce \'brüs\. County, Ontario, Canada. See table at ONTARIO.

Bruce, Mount. Mountain in plateau region S of Fortescue river, Western Australia; 4024 ft.; highest point in state.

Bruce Peninsula *also* **Sau·geen Peninsula** \'sȯ-gēn-\. Peninsula of SE Ontario, Canada; extends N bet. Lake Huron and Georgian Bay.

Bruch·sal \'bru̇k-ˌzäl\. City, Baden-Württemberg, West Germany, on a tributary of the Rhine 11 m. NE of Karlsruhe; pop. (1969e) 26,506; electrical equipment; railroad junction; 18th cent. baroque castle. First mentioned 796 A.D.; residence of prince-bishops of Speyer from 12th cent.; to Baden 1803; ab. 80 percent of city destroyed in World War II, now rebuilt.

Bruck \'bru̇k\ *or* **Bruck an der Mur** \-än-dər-'mu̇(ə)r\. Commune, Styria, Austria, at confluence of Mürz and Mur rivers 25 m. NNW of Graz; pop. (1965e) 17,500; old Gothic church; manufactures iron goods, paper, cable.

Brug·ge \'brəg-ə, 'bru̇g-\ *or* **Bruges** \'brüzh\. Commune, ✻ of West Flanders prov., NW Belgium, ab. 55 m. NW of Brussels; pop. (1970e) 51,303; an important commercial city on canals connecting with Zeebrugge and Oostende on the North Sea; shipbuilding, food processing; chemicals, electronic equipment, dies, linens; tourism; has many old buildings; known as "City of Bridges."
History: First mentioned in 7th cent.; a member of Hanseatic League in 13th cent., Bruges developed into chief Hanseatic market; drove out French rulers ("Matins of Bruges") 1302; as center of English wool trade and Flemish cloth industry, became commercial and financial hub of northern Europe; residence of dukes of Burgundy who founded there Order of Golden Fleece 1429; art and cultural center in 15th cent. (Jan van Eyck, Hans Memling, etc.); sanding up of the Zwyn (small stream connecting it with North Sea), falling off of cloth industry, civil strife, and rise of rival Antwerp (*q. v.*) caused its decline from late 15th cent.; occupied by Germans 1914–18 and 1940–44.

Bru·ghe·rio \brü-'gar-ē-ˌō\. Commune, Milano prov., Lombardy, N Italy, 8 m. NE of Milan; pop. (1968e) 20,728.

Brugh na Boinne \ˌbrü-nə-'bȯin\. Locality, co. Meath, NE Eire, on N bank of Boyne river, WSW of Drogheda; site of ancient royal cemetery, includes three great mounds, including Newgrange (*q.v.*).

Brühl \'brül\. City, North Rhine-Westphalia, West Germany, 7 m. S of Cologne; pop. (1969e) 41,475; chemicals, sugar; foundries; became city 1285; its 18th cent. castle used for receptions given by president of West Germany.

Bru·ja Point \ˌbrü-(ˌ)hä-\. Cape at S extremity of Canal Zone, W of the Pacific terminus of the Panama Canal.

Bruk·ka·ros, Mount \-'brək-ə-ˌrōs\. Mountain, S cen. South-West Africa; ab. 5200 ft.; an extinct volcano.

Brule \'brül, 'brü-lē\. County in South Dakota. See table at SOUTH DAKOTA.

Brule \'brül\ *or* **Bois Brule** \'bȯi-\. 1 River, Douglas co., NW corner of Wisconsin; ab. 40 m. long; flows N near E boundary of Douglas co., into Lake Superior.
2 River, NE Wisconsin; rises in N Forest co., flows E and forms section of Wisconsin-Michigan boundary until it joins the Michigamme river to form the Menominee river on N boundary of Florence co.

Bru·nan·burh \'brü-nən-ˌbərg\. Battlefield of uncertain location in S Scotland or N England; site of victory of Athelstan over a league of Welsh, Scots, and Danes 937 A.D.

Brun·didge \'brən-dij\. Town, Pike co., SE Alabama, 60 m. SSE of Montgomery; pop. (1970c) 2709.

Brundusium *or* **Brundisium.** See BRINDISI 2.

Bru·nei \'brü-ˌnī, -(ˌ)nā\. 1 River in Borneo. See LIMBANG.
2 Sultanate under British protection in NE part of Borneo; 2226 sq. m.; pop. (1971p) 135,665; ✻ Bandar Seri Begawan; divided geographically into two parts, each entirely surrounded by Sarawak (Malaysia) and each having coastline on South China Sea and Brunei Bay; the

two sections separated by Limbang river valley. Chief export is oil.

History: In pre-Spanish times a powerful and populous state; visited by Magellan's ships 1521; captured by Spaniards 1580 but not held; declined in influence and became a resort for pirates; its sultan in 1841 handed over Sarawak to Raja James Brooke and in 1846 entered into treaty with Great Britain, ceding Labuan; placed under British protection 1888; in 1906 definitely yielded all administration to a British Resident; oil discovered 1929; occupied by Japanese Dec. 1941, retaken by Australians June 1945; rejected membership in Federation of Malaysia 1963.

3 *or* **Brunei Town.** Town, Brunei. See BANDAR SERI BEGAWAN.

Brunei Bay. Inlet of South China Sea on the NW coast of Borneo; its shores touched by East Malaysia and Brunei; in its N part is Labuan I.; landing place of Australian and Dutch forces June 10, 1945.

Bruni. See BRUNY.

Brü·nig \ˈbrü-nig\. Mountain pass in Bernese Alps, Switzerland, E of Brienz; alt. 3396 ft.; connects valley of the Aare with Lake of Lucerne.

Brun·ke·berg \ˈbrůŋ-kə-ˌbe(ə)rg\. Village, Telemark co., S Norway, ab. 42 m. NW of Skien; battle Oct. 10, 1471 in which Danes were defeated.

Brünn. See BRNO.

Bruns·büt·tel·koog \ˈbrůns-ˌbüt-ᵊl-ˌkōk\. Town, Schleswig-Holstein, West Germany, on Elbe river at S entrance to Kiel Canal; pop. (1966e) 8900; oil pipeline terminal; founded 1762.

Bruns·sum \ˈbrən(t)-səm\. Commune, Limburg prov., SE Netherlands, 11 m. NE of Maastricht; pop. (1969e) 25,943.

Bruns·wick \ˈbrənz-(ˌ)wik\. 1 Name of counties in two states of the U.S. See tables at NORTH CAROLINA and VIRGINIA.

2 Seaport city, ⊗ of Glynn co., SE Georgia, on Atlantic Ocean; pop. (1970c) 19,585; seafood processing; Brunswick Junior Coll. (1964).

3 Town, Cumberland co., SW Maine, 23 m. NE of Portland; pop. (1970c) 16,195; trade center for resort regions; paper, timber; Bowdoin Coll. (1794).

4 Town, Frederick co., N Maryland, on Potomac river 15 m. WSW of Frederick; pop. (1970c) 3566.

5 City, Chariton co., N cen. Missouri, on Missouri river 33 m. SE of Chillicothe; pop. (1970c) 1370.

6 City, Medina co., Ohio, NW of Akron; pop. (1970c) 15,852.

7 City, S Victoria, SE Australia, N suburb of Melbourne; pop. (1966c) 52,012.

Brunswick *or Ger.* **Braun·schweig** \ˈbraůn-ˌshwīg, -ˌshfīk\. 1 Former German state, now part of Lower Saxony, West Germany; 1417 sq. m.; ✱ Brunswick.

2 *or older German* **Bruns·wich** \ˈbrůns-vik\. Manufacturing and commercial city, Lower Saxony, West Germany, on Oker river ab. 90 m. SSE of Hamburg; pop. (1969e) 225,621; automobiles, optical instruments, office machinery; ✱ of free state of Brunswick until its incorporation into Lower Saxony state; has 12th cent. cathedral, numerous fine churches of 12th cent. and later, a 13th to 14th cent. Gothic Rathaus, technical univ. (1745, univ. status 1968).

History (state and city): Reputedly founded by Bruno c. 861; made city 1031; important member of Hanseatic League in 13th cent.; joined Schmalkaldic League during Reformation; in 1671 passed to dukes of **Brunswick–Wol·fen·büt·tel** \-ˈvȯl-fən-ˌbyüt-ᵊl\ who made it their residence 1753; duchy of Brunswick annexed to kingdom of Westphalia 1807–13; member of German Confederation; duchy proclaimed republic Nov. 8, 1918; in World War II important industrial center, esp. in manufacture of fighter airplanes; frequently bombed by Allied air forces 1943–45; taken by Americans Apr. 13, 1945; incorporated into Lower Saxony 1946.

Brunswick–Lü·ne·burg \-ˈlü-nə-ˌbů(ə)rg\. Former duchy, cen. Germany, now part of Lower Saxony, West Germany.

History: An early possession of the Welf family, created 1235 by Frederick II for Otto the Child, who held town of Brunswick and surrounding territory; holdings gradually expanded until its subdivision resulted in several branches of Brunswick house; as younger branch of house of Brunswick, its rulers given electorate of Hannover 1692 (establishing English royal house of Hanover 1714–1901); made part of kingdom of Westphalia 1807–13, but restored as independent state in 1815; joined customs union (*Zollverein*) 1844, North German Confederation 1866, and became state of German Empire 1871; last ruler, Ernest Augustus, abdicated 1918 and duchy declared a republic 1918; lost sovereign rights to Third Reich by law of 1934; region incorporated into Lower Saxony 1946.

Brunswick Peninsula. Peninsula extending S from S tip of mainland of South America (Chile), bet. Strait of Magellan on S and E and Otway Water on NW; Cape Froward, its S tip, is most southerly point of mainland of South America, 53°54′S.

Brunswick–Wolfenbüttel. See BRUNSWICK 2.

Bru·ny *or* **Bru·ni** \ˈbrü-nē\. Island off SE coast of Tasmania, Australia, SW of Storm Bay; its S point is Tasman Head; 149 sq. m.; ab. 32 m. long.

Brusa *or* **Brussa.** See BURSA.

Brush \ˈbrəsh\. Town, Morgan co., NE Colorado, 10 m. E of Fort Morgan; pop. (1970c) 3377.

Brus·sels \ˈbrəs-əlz\ *or Fr.* **Bru·xelles** \brue(k)-sel\ *or Flemish* **Brus·sel** \ˈbrues-əl\. City, ✱ of Belgium and of Brabant prov., on Senne river; pop. (1970c) 161,089, mct. area pop. 1,071,194; commercial and political center; textiles, chemicals, electrical equipment, machinery, rubber goods; brewing; city hall, palaces, cathedral (founded 1010), museums, churches, univ. (1834); site of World's Fair 1958; site of headquarters of executive branch of European Economic Community.

History: Village grew up about chapel on island in Senne; among holdings of Louvain (Leuven) and later of dukes of Brabant (*q.v.*) who made it their residence; slower than Flemish towns to develop cloth industry, it had become, by 14th cent., chief town of Brabant; in 1530 made capital of Netherlands under Hapsburgs; took part in revolt against rulers 1576; won back for Hapsburgs by Alexander of Parma 1585; bombarded by Villeroi during wars of Louis XIV of France; under kingdom of the Netherlands 1815–30; center of Belgian revolution 1830 and capital of Belgium since 1830; scene of several international conferences: 1874 (on usages of war), 1876 (on exploration of central Africa), 1890 (to extirpate African slave trade).

Bruttium. See CALABRIA 2.

Brüx. See MOST.

Bruxelles. See BRUSSELS.

Bry·an \ˈbrī-ən\. 1 Name of counties in two states of the U.S. See tables at GEORGIA and OKLAHOMA.

2 City, ⊗ of Williams co., NW corner of Ohio, 52 m. W of Toledo; pop. (1970c) 7008; truck bodies.

3 City, ⊗ of Brazos co., E cen. Texas, 72 m. SSE of Waco; pop. (1970c) 33,719; chemicals; cotton gins; Allan Military Academy and Junior Coll. (1886).

Bryan·ka \brē ˈän-kə\. Town, Voroshilovgrad Oblast, Ukrainian S.S.R., U.S.S.R., 28 m. WSW of Voroshilovgrad; pop. (1969e) 77,000; founded 1962.

Bryansk *also* **Briansk** \brē-ˈän(t)sk\. City, ✱ of Bryansk Oblast, Russian S.F.S.R., U.S.S.R., on Desna river at head of navigation, W of Orel and 210 m. SW of Moscow; pop. (1970p) 318,000; important railroad junction point; sawmills, flour mills, distilleries, large ironworks, locomotive plant, and glass factories; founded 1146; independent principality to 1356; later subject to Lithuania but became Russian in 17th cent.; in World War II held by Germans Oct. 13, 1941 to Sept. 1943.

Bryansk Oblast \-'ō-bləst, -ˌblast\. Subdivision of the Russian S.F.S.R., U.S.S.R.; 13,475 sq. m.; pop. (1970p) 1,582,000; ✱ Bryansk; created 1946 from Orel Oblast.

Bryce, Mount \-'brīs\. Peak, E British Columbia, Canada, near Alberta border; 11,507 ft.

Bryce Canyon National Park. See UNITED STATES, *National Parks.*

Bryn Ath·yn \brin-'ath-ən\. Residential borough, Montgomery co., SE Pennsylvania, ab. 16 m. NE of Philadelphia; pop. (1970c) 970; seat of Bryn Athyn Cathedral, center of Swedenborgianism in the U.S.

Bryn·mawr \brin-'maůr, -'mȯr\. Urban district, Brecknockshire, S Wales; pop. (1971p) 5930; market town; coal mining and steel manufacture.

Bryn Mawr \brin-'mär\. Unincorporated residential community, Montgomery co., SE Pennsylvania, ab. 7 m. S of Norristown; pop. (1970c) 5737; Bryn Mawr Coll. (1880), Ellen Cushing Junior Coll. (1892), Harcum Junior Coll. (1915).

Bryson City \ˌbrī-sən-\. Town, ⊗ of Swain co., W North Carolina, on edge of Great Smoky Mountains National Park 53 m. W of Asheville; pop. (1970c) 1290; resort.

Brzeg \bə-'zhek\ *or Ger.* **Brieg** \'brēk\ *or anc.* **Civ·i·tas Al·tae Ri·pae** \ˌsiv-ə-təs-ˌal-ti-'rī-pē\. City, Opole prov., SW Poland, on Odra (Oder) river 27 m. SE of Wrocław; pop. (1970p) 30,800; machinery, paper; formerly in Silesia, Germany; 14th cent. Gothic churches, town hall. Received city rights 1250; captured by Prussia in First Silesian War 1741; fortifications destroyed by French 1806; taken by U.S.S.R. Feb. 7, 1945; assigned to Poland by Potsdam Conference 1945.

Brześć nad Bugiem. See BREST 2.

Brzeżany. See BEREZHANY.

Brze·zi·ny \bə-zhə-'zē-nē\. Industrial commune, Łódź prov., cen. Poland, 11 m. E of Łódź; textiles; scene of World War I battle bet. Germans and Russians Nov. 1914.

Bua. See ČIOVO.

Buad \'bwäd\. Island off W coast of Samar, Phil., across entrance to Maqueda and Villareal Bays; 14 sq. m. Town of Zumarraga is on its W coast.

Bu·bas·tis \byü-'bas-təs\. City of anc. Egypt, in Nile delta; its ruins (excavated 1886–87) near modern city of Zagazig, called **Tell Bas·ta** \tel-'bas-tə\; chief seat of worship of the goddess Bast, usually represented as lion-headed or cat-headed; chosen 952 B.C. by Sheshonk I as capital of XXIId (Bubastite) dynasty; destroyed by Persians c. 350 B.C.

Bū·bi·yān \ˌbü-bē-'(y)än\. Island at head of Persian Gulf off N coast of Kuwait and W of mouth of Shatt-al-Arab; administratively a part of Kuwait.

Bu·ca \'bü-kə\. Town, İzmir prov., W Turkey; pop. (1965c) 38,979.

Bu·ca·ra·man·ga \ˌbü-kə-rə-'mäŋ-gə\. City, ✱ of Santander dept., N cen. Colombia; in the Cordillera Oriental of the Andes at alt. of 3340 ft.; pop. (1968e) 249,998; iron products; center of region producing coffee, cacao, tobacco, and cotton; univ. (1947).

Bu·cas Gran·de \bü-'käs-'grän-dē\. Island off NE Mindanao, Phil., a part of Surigao del Norte prov.; 50 sq. m.; highest point 3012 ft.

Buc·ca·neer Archipelago \ˌbək-ə-'ni(ə)r-\. Group of islands off N coast of Western Australia at entrance to King Sound.

Bu·chach *or Pol.* **Bu·czacz** \'bü-chäch\. Town, W Ukrainian S.S.R., U.S.S.R., on Strypa river 34 m. SSW of Ternopol (formerly in Poland); pop. (1959c) 8100. Treaty bet. Poland and Turkey signed here 1672; key point in fighting in World War I Dec. 1915–Jan. 1916 and again in Brusilov's offensive June 1916.

Buch·an \'bək-ən\. Region N of the Ythan river, NE Aberdeen co., Scotland; includes Buchan Ness and the Bullers of Buchan (*qq. v.*).

Bu·chan·an \byü-'kan-ən, bə-\. **1** Name of counties in three states of the U.S. See tables at IOWA, MISSOURI, VIRGINIA.
2 City, ⊗ of Haralson co., W Georgia; pop. (1970c) 800.
3 City, Berrien co., SW corner of Michigan, 53 m. SW of Kalamazoo; pop. (1970c) 4645.
4 Village, Westchester co., SE New York, on Hudson river 37 m. N of New York; pop. (1970c) 2110.
5 *or formerly* **Grand Bas·sa** \-'bas-ə\. Seaport, W Liberia, ab. 70 m. SE of Monrovia; pop. (1962c) 11,909.

Buchanan Dam *or formerly* **Ham·il·ton Dam** \ˌham-əl-tən-\. Dam across Colorado river, Burnet and Llano cos., cen. Texas; height 158 ft.; completed 1937; impounds water for power, forming **Buchanan Lake** (*formerly* **Hamilton Lake**).

Buchan Ness \ˌbək-ən-\. Headland on NE coast of Scotland, S of Peterhead; lighthouse; easternmost point of Scotland.

Bu·cha·rest \'b(y)ü-kə-ˌrest\ *or Rom.* **Bu·cu·reş·ti** \ˌbü-kə-'resht(-ē)\. City, ✱ of Romania, on Dîmboviţa river; the municipality (234 sq. m.) constitutes an administrative district, pop. [1969e] 1,525,591; automobiles, farm implements, textiles; engineering works, oil refineries; univ. (1864), libraries, museums, Floreasca sports complex.

History: Residence of rulers of Walachia (*q. v.*) from 14th cent.; became capital of Romania (*q. v.*) 1862; scene of negotiation of several important treaties: (1) Peace of Bucharest 1812 bet. Russia and Turkey; (2) peace bet. Serbia and Bulgaria 1886 (see EASTERN RUMELIA); (3) Treaty of Bucharest 1913, stripping Bulgaria (*q. v.*) of her conquests. Occupied by Germans 1916–18; under Nazi control 1940–44; occupied by U.S.S.R. Aug. 31, 1944.

Bu·chen·wald \'bü-kən-ˌwȯld, -ˌvält\. Village, Erfurt dist., East Germany, near Weimar; site of concentration camp, taken Apr. 13, 1945 by American forces. One of the worst of German camps for prisoners.

Buchhorn. See FRIEDRICHSHAFEN.

Bück·e·burg \'bü-kə-ˌbů(ə)rg\. Town, Lower Saxony, West Germany; pop. (1968e) 13,088; was ✱ of Schaumburg-Lippe, former German state; received municipal charter 1609.

Buck·eye \'bək-ˌī\. Town, Maricopa co., SW cen. Arizona, 30 m. W of Phoenix; pop. (1970c) 2599; cotton.

Buck·han·non \ˌbək-'(h)an-ən\. **1** River, NE cen. West Virginia; ab. 45 m. long; rises in SW Randolph co., flows N into Tygart river in Barbour co.
2 City, ⊗ of Upshur co., NE cen. West Virginia, on Buckhannon river 14 m. E of Weston; pop. (1970c) 7261; farming and grazing center; coal mines, gas wells; leather, lumber. West Virginia Wesleyan Coll. (1890).

Buck·ha·ven and Meth·il \ˌbək-'hā-vən . . . 'meth-əl\. Burgh comprising two ports, Fife co., E Scotland, 7 to 8 m. NE of Kirkcaldy; pop. (1971p) 21,318.

Buck·ie \'bək-ē\. Seaport burgh, Banff co., NE Scotland, ab. 13 m. E of Elgin; pop. (1971p) 7921; herring fisheries.

Buck·ing·ham \bək-iŋ-əm, *U.S. also* -iŋ-ˌham\. **1** County in Virginia. See table at VIRGINIA.
2 Town, its ⊗, cen. Virginia.
3 Industrial town, Papineau co., SW Quebec, Canada, on Lièvre river 17 m. NE of Ottawa; pop. (1971p) 7267; pulp and paper mills; phosphate, graphite, and mica mines.
4 County in England. See BUCKINGHAMSHIRE.
5 Municipal borough, Buckinghamshire, SE cen. England, 20 m. NE of Oxford; pop. (1971p) 5075; seat (Stowe, with famous gardens) of former dukes of Buckingham.

Buck·ing·ham·shire \'bək-iŋ-əm-ˌshi(ə)r, -shər\ *or* **Buckingham** *or* **Bucks** \'bəks\. County, SE cen. England; area 746 sq. m.; pop. (1971p) 586,211; ⊗ Aylesbury; rivers Thames, Ouse, Thame; wheat, barley, oats; dairying, livestock raising.

Buck Island Reef National Monument \ˌbək-\. See UNITED STATES, *National Monuments.*

Buck·land \'bək-lənd\. Town, Franklin co., NW Massachusetts, 9 m. W of Greenfield; pop. (1970c) 1892.

Buck·ley \'bək-lē\. 1 Town, Pierce and Thurston cos., W Washington, 20 m. ESE of Tacoma; pop. (1970c) 3446; dairying.

2 Manufacturing urban district, Flintshire, NE Wales; pop. (1971p) 11,866.

Buckley, Mount. Peak, W North Carolina; 6599 ft.

Buck Mountain \'bək-\. 1 Peak, Grayson co., SW Virginia; 4630 ft.

2 Peak, S cen. Grand Teton National Park, NW Wyoming; 11,923 ft.

Buckner Bay. See NAKAGUSUKU BAY.

Bucks \'bəks\. 1 County in Pennsylvania. See table at PENNSYLVANIA.

2 County, England. See BUCKINGHAMSHIRE.

Buck·skin, Mount \-'bək-ˌskin\. Peak, Lake and Park cos., cen. Colorado; 13,800 ft.

Bucks·port \'bək-ˌspō(ə)rt, -spȯ(ə)rt\. Town, Hancock co., SE Maine, on Penobscot river 17 m. S of Bangor; pop. (1970c) 3756; lumber.

Bucovina. See BUKOVINA.

Buc·quoy \bü-'kwä\. Village, Pas-de-Calais dept., France, 10 m. S of Arras; pop. (1962c) 1402; scene of fierce fighting July 1918.

Bucureşti. See BUCHAREST.

Bu·cy·rus \byu̇-'sī-rəs\. Industrial city, ⊗ of Crawford co., N cen. Ohio, on Sandusky river 17 m. NNE of Marion; pop. (1970c) 13,111; highway construction machinery, plows, cranes, hoists, steel castings, copper kettles, clay products; settled 1818, became ⊗ 1830.

Buczacz. See BUCHACH.

Bu·da·fok \'büd-ə-ˌfōk\. City, S suburb of Budapest, cen. Hungary, on Danube river.

Bu·da·pest \'büd-ə-ˌpest *also* 'byüd-, 'bu̇d-, -ˌpesht\. City, ✱ of Hungary and ⊗ of Pest co.; 203 sq. m.; pop. (1970p) 1,940,212; includes since 1872 former towns of **Bu·da** \'büd-ə\ on right bank of Danube and **Pest** \'pesht\ on left bank; machinery, precision instruments, textiles, pharmaceuticals, electric locomotives; publishing; several universities and colleges, incl. Eötvös Loránd Univ. (1635, moved to Buda 1745), opera house (1879–84), Academy of Sciences, libraries, theaters, museums.

History: Buda site of Roman camp (*anc.* **Aquin·cum** \ə-'kwin-kəm\) set up in 2d cent. A.D.; Buda and Pest both towns inhabited by Germans in 13th cent.; Buda fortified by Matthias Corvinus in 15th cent. and became capital of Hungary; captured and held by Turks 1541–1686; Buda (Pest almost destroyed earlier) retaken from Turks by Charles of Lorraine 1686; became free imperial city; in 1848–49 both towns disturbed by nationalistic revolt, Pest (which in 18th cent. had outstripped Buda) becoming capital of Kossuth's revolutionary government (see HUNGARY); capital of Hungary under Dual Monarchy 1867 (see AUSTRIA-HUNGARY); united as Budapest 1872, center of revolt for independence of Hungary 1918; occupied by Romanians in war against government of Béla Kun 1919. In World War II an aircraft and supply center for German forces; bombed 1944–45 by U.S. Air Force and Buda badly damaged, taken by U.S.S.R. Feb. 13, 1945 after long bitter fighting; center of anti-communist uprising 1956 and again damaged by Soviet forces.

Bu·daun \bu̇-'dau̇n\. Town, NW cen. Uttar Pradesh, N India, 123 m. ESE of Delhi; pop. (1961c) 58,770; founded ab. 905 A.D.; has ruins of old fort and a splendid mosque converted in 13th cent. from an ancient Hindu temple by Altamsh, King of Delhi; became British 1801.

Budd Coast \'bəd-\. Mountainous section of Antarctica coast, 66°30′S, bet. 110°30′E and 114°E; part of Wilkes Land and part of Australian claim.

Buddh Ga·ya \ˌbu̇d-gə-'yä\. Village, cen. Bihar, NE India, 7 m. S of Gaya; pop. (1961c) 6299. One of the holiest sites of Buddhism; here Gautama Buddha is said to have experienced his Enlightenment under the sacred Bo Tree. A temple and other structures built on the site have been destroyed and a rebuilt temple devoted to Vishnu now marks the place.

Bud·don Ness \ˌbəd-ᵊn-'nes\. Headland on E cen. coast of Scotland, at N entrance to Firth of Tay; lighthouse.

Bude \'byüd\. Coast resort, N Cornwall, England, SW of Bideford on **Bude Bay.**

Budějovice, České. See ČESKÉ BUDĚJOVICE.

Bude–Strat·ton \'byüd-'strät-ən\ *or formerly* **Stratton and Bude.** Urban district, Cornwall, SW England; pop. (1971p) 5629; Stratton scene of battle May 16, 1643 in which Royalists under Sir Ralph Hopton defeated Parliamentarians under the earl of Stamford.

Budge Budge \'bəj-ˌbəj\. Town, West Bengal, NE India, on Hooghly river; pop. (1961c) 39,824.

Budissin. See BAUTZEN.

Bu·drio \'bü-drē-ˌō\. Commune, Bologna prov., Emilia-Romagna, N Italy; pop. (1968e) 16,870.

Budrum. See BODRUM.

Budweis. See ČESKÉ BUDĚJOVICE.

Bue, Mon·te \ˌmȯn-tē-'bü-(ˌ)ā\ *or* **Mag·gio·ra·sca, Monte** \-ˌmäj-ə-'räs-kə\. Highest mountain in the Ligurian Apennines. See APENNINES.

Bu·ea *or* **Bu·ëa** \bü-'ā-ə\. Town, W Cameroon, near the coast at foot of Cameroon Mt.; pop. (1962e) 9000; connected by highway with its port Victoria; formerly ✱ of British Cameroons trust territory and before 1919 ✱ of German Cameroons (Kamerun).

Bued \'bwād\. River, NW Luzon, Phil.; ab. 35 m. long.

Bue·na \'byü-nə\. Borough, Atlantic co., SE New Jersey, 28 m. NW of Atlantic City; pop. (1970c) 3283.

Buen Aire. See BONAIRE.

Buena Park \ˌbwā-nə-\. City, Orange co., California, W of Anaheim; pop. (1970c) 63,646.

Bue·na·ven·tu·ra \ˌbwen-ə-ˌven-'t(y)u̇r-ə, ˌbwā-nə-\. Important Pacific port, Valle dept., W Colombia, 210 m. W of Bogotá on **Buenaventura Bay;** pop. (1968e) 78,655; has steamer connections with Panama and is terminus of railroads in W Colombia; exports coffee, sugar, gold, and platinum; founded 1540.

Buena Vis·ta \ˌbyü-nə-'vis-tə\. 1 County in Iowa. See table at IOWA.

2 City, ⊗ of Marion co., W Georgia; pop. (1970c) 1486.

3 Independent city, Rockbridge co., W cen. Virginia, 25 m. NW of Lynchburg; pop. (1970c) 6425; paper, silk, brick, flour; tannery.

Buena Vista \ˌbwā-nə-'vē-stə\. 1 Mountain, S Costa Rica; 10,820 ft.

2 Battlefield, Coahuila state, NE Mexico, 8 m. S of Saltillo; defeat of Santa Anna by U.S. forces under Zachary Taylor Feb. 1847 ended northern campaign in Mexican War.

3 Island, Solomon Islands. See VATILAU.

Buena Vista Lake *or* **Buena Vista Reservoir** \ˌbyü-nə-'vis-tə-\. Reservoir, in Kern co., S California, SW of Bakersfield, into which the lower course of the Kern river flows.

Buena Vista Peak. Mountain in Sierra Nevada, cen. California, in S part of Yosemite National Park; 9709 ft.

Bue·në \'bwā-nə\; *Serbo-Croat.* **Bo·ja·na** *or* **Bo·ya·na** \'bȯ-yə-'nä\. Small river in NW Albania, the N mouth of the Drin river; flows out of Lake Scutari SW into Adriatic Sea along boundary line bet. Albania and Yugoslavia.

Bue·nos Ai·res \ˌbwā-nə-'sar-ēz, ˌbō-nə-, -'ser-, -'sīr-\. 1 Province of E cen. Argentina. See table at ARGENTINA.

2 Viceroyalty, South America. See LA PLATA 3.

3 City, ✱ of Argentina and itself constituting the Federal District (77 sq. m.), on estuary of the Río de la Plata, E cen. Argentina, ab. 130 m. from the sea; pop. (1970p) 2,972,-

453, met. area pop. 8,352,900; political, commercial and industrial center; meat processing; flour mills, breweries, foundries, tanneries; shallow port; several universities incl. Univ. of Buenos Aires (1821); numerous public buildings, museum, libraries, theaters.

History: First colonized by Pedro de Mendoza 1536 as Santa María del Buen Aire; not permanently settled until 1580; capital of subordinate division of viceroyalty of Peru, it became in 1776 the seat of viceroyalty of La Plata (*q.v.*) or Buenos Aires; blockaded by British in dispute over intervention in Uruguay 1845; drew up constitution separate from provinces in 1854 and began intermittent conflict with them over control of government of Argentina; erection into federal district, as capital of Argentina but separate from province of Buenos Aires, settled war with provinces 1880; seat of Pan-American Congresses 1910, 1936.

Buenos Aires, Lake *or in Chile* **La·go Ge·ne·ral Car·re·ra** \ˌlä-gō-ˌhā-nə-ˌräl-kä-ˈrer-ə\. Lake on the Chile-Argentina boundary, 46°35′S; ab. 75 m. long; 865 sq. m.

Buenos Aires, Point. Cape on NW point of Valdés Penin., enclosing Gulf of San José, NE coast of Chubut prov., S Argentina.

Buer \ˈbu̇(ə)r\. Former city, Germany. See GELSENKIRCHEN.

Bu·et, Mont \mōⁿ-ˈbwā\. Peak in the Pennine Alps, E Haute-Savoie dept., E France; 10,200 ft.

Buey \ˈbwā\. Cape on N coast of Tabasco state, SE Mexico, extending into the Bay of Campeche.

Bufarik. See BOUFARIK.

Buf·fa·lo \ˈbəf-ə-ˌlō\. **1** River, W Tennessee; ab. 100 m. long; rises in N Lawrence co., flows W, then N into Duck river in cen. Humphreys co.

2 Name of counties in three states of the U.S. See tables at NEBRASKA, SOUTH DAKOTA, WISCONSIN.

3 Village, ⊗ of Wright co., S cen. Minnesota, 31 m. WNW of Minneapolis; pop. (1970c) 3275; grain, livestock.

4 City, ⊗ of Dallas co., SW cen. Missouri; pop. (1970c) 1915; poultry.

5 Residential, commercial, and industrial city and port, ⊗ of Erie co., W New York, at NE point of Lake Erie and on Niagara river ab. 16 m. SE of Niagara Falls; pop. (1970c) 462,768; W terminus of N.Y. State Barge Canal and E terminus of Great Lakes; connected with Fort Erie, Canada, by Peace Bridge (opened 1927) across Niagara river; point of departure for Niagara Falls; in agricultural and industrial area; railroad and distributing center; grain and coal elevators; nonferrous foundries, railroad shops, meat-packing plants; steel, electrical motors, automobile and aircraft parts, food products, chemicals; research laboratories. Albright-Knox Art Gallery, Grosvenor Library. Canisius Coll. (1870), State Univ. of New York Coll. at Buffalo (1867), D'Youville Coll. (1908), State Univ. of New York at Buffalo (1846), Medaille Coll. (1937), Erie Community Coll. (1946), Rosary Hill Coll. (1948), Trocaire Coll. (1958), Villa Maria Coll. of Buffalo (1960).

History: Settled by Indians 1780; site platted by Joseph Ellicott 1799; sold in lots 1803; incorporated 1810; military post in War of 1812; burned by British and Indians 1813; rebuilt 1814–15; incorporated as village 1816; became W terminus of Erie Canal (opened 1825); became city 1832; important station on Underground Railroad. Scene of Pan-American Exposition 1901 where President McKinley was assassinated; port on St. Lawrence Seaway since 1957.

6 Town, ⊗ of Harper co., NW Oklahoma; pop. (1970c) 1579; oil and gas wells.

7 Town (unincorporated), Union co., NW South Carolina, ab. 3 m. W of Union; pop. (1970c) 1461.

8 Town, ⊗ of Harding co., South Dakota, on Grand river 36 m. SE of NW corner of state; pop. (1970c) 393.

9 City, ⊗ of Johnson co., N Wyoming, 33 m. S of Sheridan; pop. (1970c) 3394; in livestock-raising region.

10 River, Natal, Rep. of South Africa; ab. 200 m. long; rises in Drakensberg Mts.; flows SE, joining the Tugela river.

Buffalo Bay. Inlet of Lake of the Woods in SE Manitoba, Canada; extends W from the American part of the lake.

Buffalo Bayou. Stream, flowing through Houston, Texas; 45 m. long; lower course is Houston Ship Canal.

Buffalo Fork. River, N Arkansas; 150 m. long; rises in SW Newton co., NW Arkansas, flows E and NE into White river on SE boundary of Marion co., N cen. Arkansas.

Buffalo Grove. Village, Cook and Lake cos., NE Illinois, 25 m. NW of Chicago; pop. (1970c) 11,799.

Buffalo National Park. See *Wood Buffalo National Park* at CANADA, *National Parks.*

Buffalo Peaks. Mountain in Chaffee and Park cos., cen. Colorado; 13,541 ft.

Bu·ford \ˈbyü-fərd\. City, Gwinnett and Hall cos., N Georgia, 35 m. NE of Atlanta; pop. (1970c) 4640; trading center; concrete products.

Bug \ˈbüg\. **1** *or* **Western Bug.** River, E cen. Poland; 481 m. long; rises in W Ukrainian S.S.R., U.S.S.R., flows N to Brest, turns W and NW into Poland to the Vistula river 18 m. NW of Warsaw; navigable below Brest. In World War I several battles fought along its course in 1915. About 200 m. of its central course formed part of the Curzon Line, laid down by the Supreme Council after World War I Dec. 1919 as Poland's eastern frontier; this same section included in the Russo-German boundary of 1939 and retained after World War II in the boundary bet. U.S.S.R. and Poland.

2 *also* **Southern Bug** *or anc.* **Hyp·a·nis** \ˈhip-ə-nəs\. River, SW Ukrainian S.S.R., U.S.S.R.; 532 m. long; rises in Khmelnitski Oblast near former Polish border and flows SE to the Dnieper estuary; has many rapids and is not navigable above Voznesensk; largest tributary is the Ingul, which joins it at Nikolayev; its upper reaches utilized for hydroelectric power production. In World War II crossed by Germans July 1941 and by Soviets Mar. 15, 1944.

Bu·ga \ˈbü-gə\. City, Vallee dept., W Colombia; munic. pop. (1968e) 74,112; trading center for sugar, coffee, and cacao.

Bu·gan·da \b(y)ü-ˈgan-də\. Former native kingdom of SE Uganda, E Africa; ✱ Kampala; included islands in N part of Lake Victoria; monarchy abolished 1967 and kingdom made an integral part of Uganda.

Bu·gul·ma \ˌbu̇g-əl-ˈmä\. Town, SE Tatar A.S.S.R., Russian S.F.S.R., U.S.S.R. on Ulyanovsk-Ufa R.R. 160 m. SE of Kazan; pop. (1969e) 76,000; oil.

Bu·gu·ru·slan \ˌbu̇g-ə-ru̇s-ˈlän\. Town, NW Orenburg Oblast, Russian S.F.S.R., U.S.S.R., on railroad 95 m. NE of Kuibyshev, on N bank of the Bolshaya Kinel river; pop. (1967e) 48,000; natural gas.

Bu·hi \ˈbü-hē\. Municipality, SE Camarines Sur prov., Luzon, Phil., on S shore of **Lake Buhi** (10 m. long by 4 m. wide); pop. (1969e) 52,100.

Buhl \ˈbyül\. **1** City, Twin Falls co., S Idaho, 17 m. W of Twin Falls; pop. (1970c) 2975; diversified farming.

2 Village, St. Louis co., NE Minnesota, 8 m. ENE of Hibbing; pop. (1970c) 1303; iron mining.

Builth Wells \ˈbilth-ˈwelz\. Town, N Brecknockshire, S cen. Wales, on the Wye 14 m. N of Brecknock; pop. (1971p) 1481; spa, market town; notable in Welsh history, dating back to 11th cent.

Bu·in \bü-ˈēn\. Settlement at S end of Bougainville I., NW Solomon Islands, W Pacific Ocean; held by Japanese as base, bypassed by Americans in conquest of the Solomon Is. 1942–43.

Bui·naksk *also* **Buy·naksk** \ˌbü-ē-ˈnäksk\ *or formerly* **Te·mir–Khan–Shu·ra** \ˌtem-ər-ˌkän-shu̇-ˈrä\. Town, N cen. Dagestan A.S.S.R., Russian S.F.S.R., U.S.S.R., on branch railroad 25 m. WSW of Makhachkala; pop. (1967e) 38,000; has large fruit-preserving works.

Buitengewesten. See OUTER PROVINCES.

Buitenzorg. See BOGOR.

Bu·ja·lan·ce \ˌbü-hə-ˈlän-thā, -sə\. Commune, Córdoba prov., S Spain, 23 m. E of Córdoba; pop. (1970p) 8973; manufactures textiles, tile, chinaware, flour; ruins of 10th cent. Moorish castle.

Buj·nurd. See BOJNŪRD.

Bu·jum·bu·ra \ˌbü-jəm-ˈbu̇r-ə\ *or formerly* **Usum·bu·ra** \ˌü-səm-ˈbu̇r-ə\. Town, ✱ of Burundi, E cen. Africa, on E side of N end of Lake Tanganyika; pop. (1970e) 70,000; univ. (1961).

Bu·ka \ˈbü-kə\. One of the Solomon Islands just N of Bougainville I. (*q.v.*) and separated from it by **Buka Passage;** part of Papua New Guinea; 190 sq. m.; contains excellent anchorage. Mostly level with mangrove swamps and some forest and grassland regions. Best anchorage is Queen Carola Harbour. Held by Japanese in World War II but by-passed by U.S. forces Feb. 1944.

Buka'a. See BIKA.

Bu·ka·ma \bü-ˈkäm-ə\. Town, S cen. Katanga, SE Zaire; trading town on navigable Lualaba river.

Bu·ka·vu \bü-ˈkäv-(ˌ)ü\ *or formerly* **Cos·ter·mans·ville** \ˈkäs-tər-mənz-ˌvil\. Town, ✱ of Kivu prov., Zaire, at S end of Lake Kivu; pop. (1968e) 183,025.

Bu·kha·ra *or* **Bo·kha·ra** *or* **Bou·kha·ra** \bü-ˈkär-ə, bō-, -ˈkar-, -ˈhär, -ˈhar-\. 1 Former khanate occupying region around city of Bukhara, W Asia; later, a state in Russian Central Asia. In early times region known as Sogdiana and Transoxiana (*qq.v.*). Ruled effectively by Muslim Arabs from c. 710 A.D.; built up into powerful Islamic kingdom by Samanids (874–999); as capital of Samanid realm, which included territory from Baghdad to borders of India and from Bukhara to Persian Gulf, became intellectual center of Islam and wealthy mart for trade of central Asia; destroyed by Genghis Khan 1219; under various dynasties, the prize of Mongols, Turks, Uzbeks (see TURKISTAN), and others; in 19th cent., its emir controlled khanates of Kokand and Khiva; conquered 1866–68 and made a Russian protectorate; proclaimed a Soviet republic 1920; since 1924 has formed part of Uzbek S.S.R. (*q.v.*).
2 City, ✱ of Bukhara Oblast, W Uzbek S.S.R., U.S.S.R., E of the Amu Darya and ab. 140 m. W of Samarkand; pop. (1970p) 112,000; textiles; chief city of khanate and of Soviet state; has many mosques and minarets and was once second only to Mecca as a holy place of Islam.

Bukhara Oblast \-ˈò-bləst, -ˌblast\. Subdivision of the Uzbek S.S.R., U.S.S.R.; 55,290 sq. m.; pop. (1970p) 934,000; ✱ Bukhara.

Bu·kid·non \bü-ˈkid-ˌnän\. Province, N Mindanao, Phil.; 3202 sq. m.; pop. (1970p) 400,307; ✱ Malaybalay. Mountainous and plateau region with no coastline; highest point is in Katanglad Mts., in W cen. part, ab. 9000 ft.; in N many short streams flowing N and NW to Gingoog and Macajalar bays; largest stream is the Pulangi in E and S forming the upper course of the Mindanao. Has fertile soil esp. suitable for grazing; chief crops corn, coffee, hemp (abacá), rice, and pineapples. Inhabitants are mainly Bukidnons, with some Manobos and Moros. Chief municipalities: Kibawe, Maramag, Malaybalay. Region never adequately explored until recent years; since ab. 1850 a part of Misamis and in 1901 erected as a subprovince; from 1907 to 1914 a subprovince of Agusan.

Bu·kit Mer·ta·jam \ˌbü-kət-mər-ˈtä-jəm\. Town, Penang, West Malaysia; pop. (1957c) 24,663.

Bu·kit·ting·gi \ˌbü-kə-ˈtiŋ-gē\ *or formerly* **Fort de Kock** \ˌfō(ə)rt-də-ˈkòk, fò(ə)rt-, -ˈkäk\. Inland town, W Sumatra, ab. 50 m. N of Padang, Indonesia, in Padang Highlands; pop. (1961c) 51,456; important as a military post; original fortifications erected by Dutch 1825.

Bukn Fjord. See BOKN FJORD.

Bu·ko·ba \bü-ˈkō-bə\. Town, ✱ of West Lake region, Tanzania, on W shore of Lake Victoria; pop. (1967c) 8141; coffee plantations.

Bu·ko·vi·na *or* **Bu·co·vi·na** \ˌbü-kə-ˈvē-nə\. Region, E cen. Europe; 3396 sq. m.; formerly an Austrian crownland; province (1918–40) of N Romania. Occupies foothills of E Carpathian Mts., thickly wooded and source of Dniester, Prut, and Siretul rivers flowing to Black Sea.
History: Inhabited by Ruthenian tribes; part of principality of Moldavia (*q.v.*); occupied by Austria 1774 and formally ceded by Turkey 1777; ruled by Austria as part of Galicia until 1849 when Bukovina was made separate crownland; became independent at collapse of Austria-Hungary 1918 and joined Romania 1918–40; seized by U.S.S.R. June 27, 1940 and incorporated with Bessarabia Aug. 1940 in Moldavian Republic; held by German and Romanian forces 1941–45; N half became part of Ukrainian S.S.R. 1945 (chief town Chernovtsy) and S half, including towns Rădăuţi and Siret, remained in Romania.

Būl, Kūh–e– \ˌkü-(h)ē-ˈbu̇l\. Mountain in SW cen. Iran, 175 m. NE of Büshehr; 13,009 ft.

Bu·la·can \ˌbü-lə-ˈkän\. 1 Province, cen. Luzon, Phil.; 1032 sq. m.; pop. (1970p) 836,714; ✱ Malolos. Western part is in central Luzon plain; hills and mountains in the E, highest Mt. Oryod in SE 3838 ft. Watered by the Angat, a large tributary of the Pampanga; delta of the latter covers a large area of swampy land in SW along shore of Manila Bay. Principal crops corn, rice, sugar, fruit. Chief towns Malolos, Hagonoy, San Miguel.
History: Had large towns before coming of the Spanish; one of earliest provinces created by them 1578; was center of opposition to British 1762–63; increased in population and trade during following century; scene of several notable events of Revolution of 1897 (see BIACNABATO and MALOLOS); civil government established by Americans Feb. 1901. In World War II taken by Japanese Jan. 1942 but recovered Jan.–Feb. 1945.
2 Municipality, SW Bulacan prov., 7 m. SE of Malolos; pop. (1969e) 25,300; former capital of the province.

Bulama. See BOLAMA.

Bu·lan \ˈbü-ˌlän\. Municipality, SW Sorsogon prov., Luzon, Phil.; pop. (1969e) 63,900; port on Ticao Pass 22 m. SSW of Sorsogon; largest town in province.

Bu·land·shahr \ˌbü-lən(d)-ˈshär\. 1 District, Uttar Pradesh, N India; 1887 sq. m.; pop. (1961c) 1,737,397; ✱ Bulandshahr.
2 Town, its ✱, on Kali Nadi river 45 m. SE of Delhi; pop. (1961c) 44,163; taken over by British in 1805.

Bu·laq *or* **Bu·lak** \bü-ˈläk\. Port of Cairo, Egypt, located on the Nile; pop. (1966c) 75,130; originally site of museum (now in Cairo) founded 1863 by the French Egyptologist Mariette.

Bu·lat, Cape \-bu̇-ˈlät\ *or formerly* **Cape Ro·ma·nia** \-rō-ˈmān-ē-ə, -ˈmān-yə\. Cape on SE extremity of the Malay Penin., Johore state, Malaysia, at E end of Singapore Strait.

Bu·la·wa·yo *or* **Bu·lu·wa·yo** \ˌbü-lə-ˈwā-(ˌ)ō, -ˈwī-\. Town, SW Rhodesia, S Africa, 240 m. SW of Salisbury; pop. (1970e) 70,000, met. area pop. 281,000; textiles, radios, vehicle tires; breweries, flour mills; chief town of Matabeleland; important railroad center and trade headquarters for vast grazing area; gold and coal found in region; founded 1893.

Bul·dir \bu̇l-ˈdi(ə)r\. Rocky islet in W Aleutian Is., in channel bet. Kiska on E and Near Is. on W.

Buldur. See BURDUR.

Bu·le·leng *or Du.* **Boe·le·leng** \ˈbü-lə-ˌleŋ\. Seaport town, N coast of Bali I., Lesser Sunda Is., Indonesia; port of Singaradja; harbor unsafe during west monsoon.

Bul·gar Dağ·la·rı \ˈbu̇l-ˌgär-ˌdä(g)-lə-ˈrē\. Range in the Taurus Mts., S Turkey in Asia; highest peak Ardost 11,444 ft. See CILICIAN GATES.

Bul·gar·ia \ˌbəl-ˈgar-ē-ə, bu̇l-, -ˈger-\; *officially* **People's Republic of Bulgaria** *or Bulg.* **Na·rod·na Re·pub·li·ka Būl·ga·ri·ya** \nə-ˌròd-nə-ri-ˈpu̇b-li-kə-bəl-ˈgär-ē-(y)ə\.

Republic, SE Europe, bounded on N by Romania, on E by Black Sea, on SE by Turkey, on S by Greece, and on W by Yugoslavia; 42,823 sq. m.; pop. (1970e) 8,490,000, (1968e) 8,404,080; ✱ Sofia. Crossed in cen. part by Balkan Mts. (locally, the Stara Planina) 3500 to 7793 ft.; in SW and S by Rhodope range; highest point Mt. Musala 9596 ft.; surface varied in plateau, plain, and river valley regions. *Chief rivers:* Maritsa, flowing E into Turkey, and its tributary the Tundzha; Struma and Mesta in SW flowing S into Greece; Danube, forming most of N boundary with Romania. *Chief products:* Wheat, corn, rye, tobacco, vegetables, oats, cotton; coal, copper, zinc; manufacturing: metallurgical and chemical industries; cement, rubber goods, textiles. *Chief towns:* Sofia, Plovdiv, Varna, Ruse, Burgas, Stara Zagora, Pleven. Divided into the following 28 provinces (for pronunciation of their names, see their individual entries):

NAME	AREA (sq. m.)	POP. (1968e)	CAPITAL
Blagoevgrad	2,496	308,999	Blagoevgrad
Burgas	2,929	399,084	Burgas
Gabrovo	799	182,920	Gabrovo
Khaskovo	1,556	290,753	Khaskovo
Kŭrdzhali	1,552	294,253	Kŭrdzhali
Kyustendil	1,159	197,620	Kyustendil
Lovech	1,594	219,947	Lovech
Mikhaylovgrad	1,384	237,666	Mikhaylovgrad
Pazardzhik	1,691	303,932	Pazardzhik
Pernik	909	181,373	Pernik
Pleven	1,615	250,422	Pleven
Plovdiv	2,159	654,782	Plovdiv
Razgrad	1,022	200,111	Razgrad
Ruse	1,013	283,453	Ruse
Shumen	1,303	248,469	Shumen
Silistra	1,111	171,985	Silistra
Sliven	1,440	231,509	Sliven
Smolyan	1,358	173,678	Smolyan
Sofia (city commune)	400	950,676	
Sofia	2,851	316,510	Sofia
Stara Zagora	1,893	368,691	Stara Zagora
Tolbukhin	1,810	238,342	Tolbukhin
Tŭrgovishte	1,063	176,744	Tŭrgovishte
Varna	1,475	387,707	Varna
Veliko Tŭrnovo	1,811	334,841	Veliko Tŭrnovo
Vidin	1,201	176,503	Vidin
Vratsa	1,616	304,220	Vratsa
Yambol	1,714	218,890	Yambol

History: For earlier history of Bulgarian territory, see MOESIA and THRACE. Invaded by Bulgars, a Ural-Altaic people who in 6th cent. A.D. lived bet. Don and Caucasus and in 7th cent. settled in Bessarabia, crossed Danube, became Slavicized, and founded first organized Slavic power in Balkans; soon after baptism of King Boris 865, joined Greek Church; powerful under Tsar Simeon (893–927) who introduced Byzantine culture; invaded by Russians and Byzantines 967–972; western part erected by Samuel (976–1014) into new state but lost independence 1014; part of Byzantine Empire 1018–1185; under Asen family, built second Bulgarian Empire 1185–1366; part of Ottoman Empire from Turkish conquest (1340–96) to 20th cent.; revived nationalism in 19th cent.; premature rising in 1876 caused "massacres" by Turks which made Bulgarian problem a European concern; at close of Russo-Turkish War (1877–78), an autonomous Bulgarian principality (including most of Macedonia) erected by Treaty of San Stefano; divided by Congress of Berlin which returned Macedonia to Turkey and set up autonomous Eastern Rumelia 1878; annexed Eastern Rumelia 1885 thereby invoking war with Serbia; under Prince Ferdinand, reconciled with Russia 1896; declared complete independence from Turkey 1908; took a leading part in First Balkan War and, because of increased territory, caused Second Balkan War (see BALKAN STATES); forced to cede Dobruja to Romania and most of Macedonia to Serbia, Greece, and Turkey 1913; entered World War I on side of Central Powers 1915; by Treaty of Neuilly (see NEUILLY-SUR-SEINE) lost position on Aegean seaboard 1919; by pact with Yugoslavia 1937, began to cooperate with Balkan powers; recovered southern Dobruja from Romania 1940; signed Axis pact 1941; taken over by Germany; invaded by U.S.S.R. Sept. 8, 1944; abolished monarchy and became a people's republic 1946; member of Warsaw Pact and UN 1955; resumed diplomatic relations with U.S. 1959 (broken since 1950); participated with the Soviet Union in the occupation of Czechoslovakia 1968.

Bul·har \'bu̇l-ˌhär\. Seaport town, N Somalia, E Africa, on Gulf of Aden 40 m. W of Berbera.

Bulk·ley \'bəl-klē\. River, W cen. British Columbia, Canada, E of Bulkley Mts.; ab. 130 m. long; flows N into Skeena river.

Bulkley Mountains. Range of the Coast Mts., W cen. British Columbia, Canada, W of Babine Mts.

Bul·lard's Bar Dam \'bu̇l-ərdz-ˌbär-\. Dam across N fork of Yuba river, N Yuba co., N cen. California; height 199 ft.; completed 1924; impounds water, **Bullard's Bar Reservoir,** for waterpower.

Bull Bay \'bu̇l-\. Inlet of Atlantic Ocean on NE coast of Charleston co., SE South Carolina; enclosed on SW by **Bull Island.**

Bul·le·court \bül-'ku̇(ə)r\. Village, Pas-de-Calais dept., N France, 9 m. SE of Arras; pop. (1962c) 290; battles 1917–18, esp. six weeks of severe fighting May–June 1917.

Bul·ler \'bu̇l-ər\. River, N South Island, New Zealand; 110 m. long; flows W to Tasman Sea.

Buller, Mount. Mountain at W end of Great Dividing Range, E Victoria, Australia; 5911 ft.

Bul·lers of Buch·an \'bu̇l-ərz . . . 'bək-ən\. Basin in rocky coast of Buchan region, NE Aberdeen co., Scotland, 6 m. S of Peterhead; ab. 200 ft. deep and 50 ft. wide.

Bull Hill \'bu̇l-\. Peak, Lake co., cen. Colorado; 13,773 ft.

Bull Island. See BULL BAY.

Bul·litt \'bu̇l-ət\. County in Kentucky. See table at KENTUCKY.

Bul·loch \'bu̇l-ək\. County in Georgia. See table at GEORGIA.

Bul·lock \'bu̇l-ək\. County in Alabama. See table at ALABAMA.

Bull Point. Cape on extreme NW point of Devonshire, SW England, S of entrance to Bristol channel; lighthouse.

Bull Run. Stream, NE Virginia; runs SE and forms boundary bet. Fairfax and Prince William cos., E of Manassas, and empties into Occoquan Creek; scene of Civil War battles (1) July 21, 1861 in which Union leader Gen. Irvin McDowell was defeated by Confederate generals J.E. Johnston and P.G.T. Beauregard, and (2) Aug. 29–30, 1862 in which Gen. Lee defeated Union forces under Gen. John Pope. Both battles called Manassas by Confederates; a phase of second battle also known as battle of Groveton.

Bu·lo·lo \bə-'lō-(ˌ)lō\. 1 River, an upper tributary of the Markham river, forming **Bulolo Valley,** part of the Morobe goldfields, SE New Guinea I., Papua New Guinea, in the mountains W of Huon Gulf.
2 Mining town on the Bulolo river.

Bul·sar *or* **Bal·sar** \bəl-'sär\. Seaport town, S Gujarat, W India, 115 m. N of Bombay; pop. (1961c) 37,586; in early days of East India Company an important trading center.

Bulshaia. See MCKINLEY, MOUNT.

Bu·lu·an \bü-'lü-ˌän\. Municipality, E cen. Cotabato prov., Mindanao, Phil., near **Lake Buluan** (24 sq. m.); pop. (1969e) 97,900.

Bu·lu·san \bə-'lü-ˌsän\. Volcano, S cen. Sorsogon prov., Luzon, Phil.; 5118 ft.; 5 m. inland; visible 60 m. at sea and a landmark for ships in San Bernardino Strait; last eruption 1852.

Buluwayo. See BULAWAYO.

Bum·ba \'bu̇m-bə\. Town, Équateur prov., Zaire, on Congo river at its N point; airport.

Bu·na \'bü-nə\. Village on Holnicote Bay, SE coast of Papua New Guinea, New Guinea I.; formerly port for shipment of gold from inland goldfields; after Japanese landings here and at Gona July 1942, used as base for attacks on Port Moresby; captured by Allied forces Jan. 18–20, 1943.

Bunbah, Al–. See BOMBA.

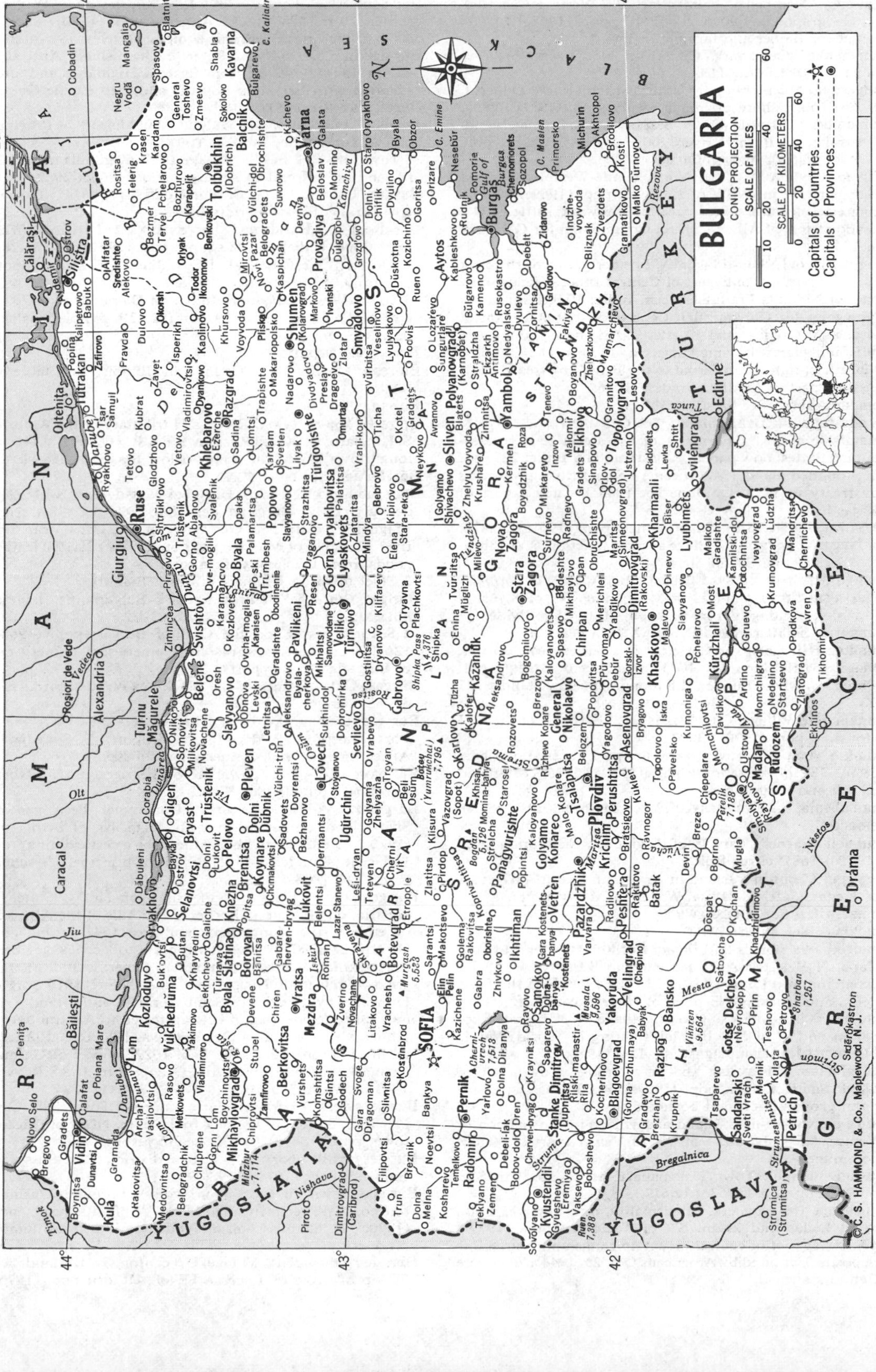
BULGARIA
CONIC PROJECTION
SCALE OF MILES
0 10 20 40 60
SCALE OF KILOMETERS
0 20 40 60
Capitals of Countries
Capitals of Provinces
Longitude East of Greenwich
© C. S. HAMMOND & Co., Maplewood, N. J.

Bun·bury \'bən-bər-ē, -bə-rə\. Port, SW Western Australia, on Geographe Bay 90 m. S of Perth; pop. (1968e) 16,450; outlet for timber and farming region.

Bun·combe \'beŋ-kəm\. County in North Carolina. See table at NORTH CAROLINA.

Bun·cra·na \bən-'kran-ə\. Urban district, NE co. Donegal, N Eire, on E shore of Lough Swilly; pop. (1971p) 2955.

Bun·da·berg \'bən-də-ˌbərg\. Seaport town, E Queensland, Australia, on Burnett river, 200 m. N of Brisbane; pop. (1968e) 26,500; sugar refining.

Bün·de \'byün-də\. City, North Rhine-Westphalia, West Germany, 52 m. WSW of Hanover; pop. (1969e) 40,951; cigarettes, furniture; meatpacking; ironwork; settled 1743; headquarters of Allied Control Commission for Germany in 1945.

Bun·del·khand \'bún-dᵊl-ˌkənd\. Formerly, one of the chief agency divisions, in E part of Central India Agency, now part of Madhya Pradesh, N cen. India; 10,081 sq. m.; ✱ Nowgong (in Chhatarpur). Consisted of 9 states (most important Orchha) and 13 estates. An uneven country of hills and plains; became subject c. 1500 to Delhi and to Marathas; rights transferred to the British by treaty 1817; became part of Madhya Pradesh 1956.

Bunder Abbas. See BANDAR 'ABBĀS.

Bundesrepublik Deutschland. See GERMANY, WEST.

Bun·di \'bün-dē\. 1 Former Indian state in Eastern Rajputana States; now part of Rajasthan, NW India; 2205 sq. m.; founded about 1342, it came under British protection by treaty in 1818. On June 26, 1947 became a part of Rajasthan.

2 Town, its ✱, 95 m. SE of Ajmer; pop. (1961c) 26,478.

Bu Ngem \bün-'gem\. Village at road junction, NW Libya, N Africa, 90 m. SW of Sirte.

Bun·go Strait *or* **Bungo Channel** \ˌbún-(ˌ)gō-\ *or formerly* **Ha·ya·sui Strait** \hä-ˌyäs-wē-\. Channel, NE of Kyūshū, Japan, separating it from Shikoku; 20 to 25 m. wide.

Bunguran Selatan Islands. See NATUNA ISLANDS.

Bun·ker Hill \ˌbeŋ-kər-\. Height in Charlestown, Boston, Mass.; battle June 17, 1775 on adjacent **Breed's Hill** \'brēdz-\, where Bunker Hill monument now stands; 107 ft.

Bunker Hill Village. City, Harris co., SE Texas, 11 m. W of Houston; pop. (1970c) 3977.

Bun·kie \'bəŋ-kē\. Town, Avoyelles parish, cen. Louisiana, 28 m. SSE of Alexandria; pop. (1970c) 5395; cottonseed oil; oil and natural gas.

Bunnabeola, Twelve Bens of. See BENNEBEOLA, TWELVE BENS OF.

Bun·nell \bə-'nel\. City, ⊗ of Flagler co., NE Florida; pop. (1970c) 1687; citrus fruit.

Bun·ting \'bənt-iŋ\. Island in Andaman Sea off NW coast of Kedah state, Malaysia, W side of Malay Penin.

Bunzelwitz. See BOLESŁAWICE.

Bunzlau. See BOLESŁAWIEC.

Bu·or·kha·ya \ˌbü-ór-'kī-(y)ə\ *or* **Bor·kha·ya** \bór-'kī-(y)ə\. Cape, N Yakutsk A.S.S.R., Russian S.F.S.R., U.S.S.R., extending into Laptev Sea at 133°20′E, just E of the Lena delta, and marking NE point of **Buorkhaya Gulf.**

Buq·buq \'búk-(ˌ)búk\. Coastal village, NW Egypt, E of Salūm and W of Sīdī Barrānī; fighting in World War II North African campaigns, esp. Dec. 1940.

Bu·rai·da *or* **Bu·ray·dah** \bə-'rīd-ə, -'rād-\. Town, N cen. Nejd, Saudi Arabia; pop. (1959e) 30,000; has extensive palm groves; important commercially.

Bu·ra·no \bü-'rä-nō\. Island and village in the Lagoon of Venice, NE Italy, ab. 5 m. NE of Venice; part of Venice commune.

Bu·rao \bü-'raú\. Town, N Somalia, E Africa, ab. 80 m. SSE of Berbera; pop. (1963e) 12,617.

Bu·ra·uen \bü-'rä-wān\. Municipality, cen. Leyte I., Phil., W of Dulag and 21 m. SW of Tacloban; pop. (1969e) 43,200; at foot of central mountain range and near sulfur deposits. Captured by Americans Oct. 25, 1944 after severe fighting; airfield.

Bur·bank \'bər-ˌbaŋk\. City, Los Angeles co., SW California, 10 m. NW of Los Angeles; pop. (1970c) 88,871; airplane factories; electronic equipment; television studios.

Bur·de·kin \'bər-di-kən\. River, E Queensland, Australia; 425 m. long; flows SE from Eastern Highlands and after junction with Belyando flows N and E to Pacific Ocean.

Burdigala. See BORDEAUX.

Bur·dur \búr-'dú(ə)r\ *or* **Bul·dur** \búl-'dú(ə)r\. 1 Province of SW Turkey. See table at TURKEY.

2 Town, its ✱, 2 m. SE of Lake Burdur, in hills (alt. 3150 ft.) and on railroad to Antalya; pop. (1965c) 29,268.

Burdur, Lake *or Turk.* **Burdur Gö·lü** \-gəl-'(y)ü\. Lake in SW Turkey, SW of Eğridir Lake.

Bur·dwan *or* **Bar·dwan** \bər-'dwän\. 1 Division, West Bengal, NE India; 16,528 sq. m.; pop. (1961c) 16,165,283.

2 District, West Bengal, NE India; 2716 sq. m.; pop. (1961c) 3,082,846; coal.

3 Town, West Bengal, NE India, on Damodar river 73 m. NW of Calcutta; pop. (1970e) 152,239; temples, palace, univ. (1960).

Bure. See BROADS, THE.

Bu·reau \'byü(ə)r-ō\. County in Illinois. See table at ILLINOIS.

Burem. See BOUREM.

Bu·re·ya \bə-'rā-(y)ə\. River, a N tributary of the Amur in S Khabarovsk Krai, Russian S.F.S.R., U.S.S.R.; 445 m. long; flows SW to the Amur below Blagoveshchensk.

Būr Fu'ād. See PORT FUAD.

Burg \ˌbu(ə)rk\. 1 *also* **Burg bei Mag·de·burg** \-bī-'mäg-də-ˌbú(ə)rk\ *or* **Burg an der Ih·le** \-än-dər-'ē-lə\. City, Magdeburg dist., East Germany, on Ihle Canal near Elbe river 12 m. NE of Magdeburg; pop. (1970e) 29,994; leather goods, iron, machinery, furniture.

2 Chief town on Fehmarn I. See FEHMARN.

Bur·gas \búr-'gäs\. 1 Province of E Bulgaria. See table at BULGARIA.

2 Seaport, its ✱, on the Gulf of Burgas; pop. (1968e) 126,533; engineering works, fish canneries, oil refinery; one of Bulgaria's major ports.

Burgas, Gulf of. Inlet of the Black Sea on the central part of the coast of Bulgaria.

Bur Ga·vo \búr-'gä-vō\ *or* **Bir·cao** \bir-'kaú\ *or formerly* **Port Durn·ford** \-'dərn-fərd\. Seaport, S Somalia, E Africa; in Jubaland, formerly part of Kenya.

Bur·gaw \'bər-ˌgä\. Town, ⊗ of Pender co., SE North Carolina; pop. (1970c) 1744.

Burg·dorf \'bú(ə)rk-ˌdó(ə)rf\. Commune, Bern canton, Switzerland, on Emme river ab. 11 m. NE of Bern; pop. (1970c) 15,888; footwear, textiles; has a castle dating from 11th cent.; founded c. 1175; Pestalozzi principal of a school here 1799–1804.

Bur·gen·land \'bər-gən-ˌland, 'búr-gən-ˌlänt\. State, E Austria, on Hungarian border in foothills of the Alps and on edge of the Hungarian plain; area 1531 sq. m.; pop. (1971p) 272,000; ✱ Eisenstadt; corn, tobacco, sugar beet; coal; textiles, electrical equipment, paper; includes northern two thirds of Neusiedler Lake; before 1919 part of Hungary; by Treaties of Saint-Germain and Grand Trianon entire region was to be transferred to Austria but on Hungary's objection, a plebiscite was held Dec. 1921 and all but Sopron transferred Feb. 1922; as part of German Ostmark, absorbed by Styria. Occupied by U.S.S.R. Apr. 1945 in World War II.

Bur·gers·dorp \'bərg-ərz-ˌdōrp, -ˌdórp\. Town, NE Cape Province, S Rep. of South Africa, 70 m. NNW of Queenstown; pop. (1967e) 10,000; health resort.

Bur·gess Hill \ˌbər-jəs-\. Urban district, East Sussex, S England; pop. (1971p) 19,309.

Bur·getts·town \'bər-jəts-ˌtaún, -gəts-\. Borough, Washington co., SW Pennsylvania, 24 m. W of Pittsburgh; pop. (1970c) 2118; zinc, coal, molybdenum industries; lumber products.

Bürg·len \'búr-glən\. Village, Uri canton, Switzerland, near SE tip of Lake of Lucerne SE of Altdorf; pop. (1970c)

3401; first mentioned 857; legendary birthplace of William Tell.

Bur·gos \ˈbu̇(ə)r-ˌgōs\. **1** Province of N Spain. See table at SPAIN.

2 City, its ✱, 132 m. N of Madrid; pop. (1970p) 119,915; textiles; noted for its old buildings, among them castle of counts of Castile and esp. the cathedral (1221), one of most noted examples of Gothic architecture in Europe; home and burial place of the Cid. Founded 884; made capital of Old Castile; to 1560 a royal residence and capital of kingdom of León and Castile; seat of Falangist government 1936.

Bur·gun·dy \ˈbər-gən-dē\ *or Fr.* **Bour·gogne** \bür-gònʸ\. Region of varying limits in E Gaul and pre-Revolutionary France. Name was originally applied to a kingdom in Rhone valley and W Switzerland (see GENEVA 2) founded by a Germanic people, the Burgundians, who fled from Germany in early 5th cent. It was conquered by the Merovingians c. 534 and incorporated into the Frankish empire; in division of Carolingian empire by the Treaty of Verdun 843, included in Middle Kingdom (see LORRAINE) of Lothair I; region later divided into the kingdoms of Cisjurane (Lower) Burgundy or Provence, founded 879, and Transjurane (Upper) Burgundy, founded 888, which united 933 to form the kingdom of Burgundy or Arles (*q.v.*). After absorption of Arles by the Holy Roman Empire 1032, the name was retained in the Free County of Burgundy or Franche-Comté (*q.v.*) and especially in the duchy of Burgundy which was formed in 9th cent. from lands in NW part of original kingdom S of 48th parallel chiefly bet. Saône and Loire rivers. On death of Philippe de Rouvre 1361, the duchy escheated to French Crown; given as appanage by King John II to his 4th son, Philip the Bold; passed in direct succession to John the Fearless, Philip the Good, and Charles the Bold, before whose death in 1477, the Burgundian house had controlled Nivernais, Franche-Comté, Lorraine (*qq.v.*), and Low Countries; seized from Charles's daughter, Duchess Mary of Burgundy, by King Louis XI and annexed to French Crown; a province until the Revolution.

Bur·han·pur \bər-ˈhän-ˌpu̇(ə)r\. Town, Madhya Pradesh, cen. India, on the Tapti river S of Khandwa and 185 m. W of Nagpur; pop. (1961c) 82,090; known for its brocades, gold and silver embroideries, flowered silks, and gold wire; a walled city of the Moguls, founded 1400, and for two centuries capital of independent Muslim princes; later the capital of the Deccan under the Moguls; captured 1803 by British but not retained; ceded to British 1861.

Bu·rias \ˈbu̇(ə)r-ˌyäs\. Island just SE of Luzon, Phil.; 43 m. long; 164 sq. m.; pop. (1960c) 15,918; forms part of Masbate prov. Long narrow mountainous island, N of Masbate and separated from Luzon on NE by Burias Pass; on NE border of Sibuyan Sea.

Burias Pass. Channel bet. E Burias I. and the mainland of SE Luzon, Phil.; ab. 12 m. wide.

Buriat A.S.S.R. *or* **Buriat–Mongolian A.S.S.R.** See BURYAT AUTONOMOUS SOVIET SOCIALIST REPUBLIC.

Bu·ri·ca, Point \-bü-ˈrē-kə\. Cape on S extremity of Costa Rica, on boundary with Panama, extending S into Pacific Ocean.

Bu·rin \byu̇r-ən\. Fishing town, S Newfoundland, Canada, on W shore of Placentia Bay at its mouth; pop. (1971p) 2580; has land-locked harbor; extensive fisheries.

Bu·ri·ram \ˌbü-rē-ˈräm\ *also* **Pu·ri·ram·ya** \ˌbü-rē-ˈräm—*sic*\. **1** Province, SE Thailand; 4159 sq. m.; pop. (1960c) 583,585; cattle and timber.

2 Town, its ✱; pop. (1960c) 12,579.

Bur·ka·tów \bu̇r-ˈkä-(ˌ)tüf\ *or Ger.* **Bur·kers·dorf** \ˈbu̇r-kərz-ˌdòrf, -ˌdòrf\. Village, S Wrocław prov., SW Poland; formerly in Silesia, Germany; battle July 21, 1762 in which Frederick the Great defeated the Austrians under Daun.

Burk·bur·nett \ˌbərk-bər-ˈnet\. City, Wichita co., N Texas, near Red river 15 m. N of Wichita Falls; pop. (1970c) 9230; livestock; oil wells.

Burke \ˈbərk\. **1** Name of counties in three states of the U.S. See tables at GEORGIA, NORTH CAROLINA, NORTH DAKOTA.

2 City, ⊗ of Gregory co., S South Dakota; pop. (1970c) 892.

Burke Channel. Inlet of Pacific Ocean, W British Columbia, Canada; ab. 52°N; ab. 45 m. long.

Burke Mountain. Peak on boundary bet. Caledonia and Essex cos., NE Vermont; 3267 ft.

Burkersdorf. See BURKATÓW.

Burkes·ville \ˈbərks-ˌvil, -vəl\. City, ⊗ of Cumberland co., S Kentucky; pop. (1970c) 1717.

Bur·kett, Mount \-ˈbər-kət\. Mountain, near Alaska-British Columbia boundary, SE Alaska, 30 m. N of Wrangell; 9600 ft.

Bur·leigh \ˈbər-lē\. County in North Dakota. See table at NORTH DAKOTA.

Bur·le·son \ˈbər-lə-sən\. **1** County in Texas. See table at TEXAS.

2 City, Johnson and Tarrant cos., N Texas, 14 m. S of Fort Worth; pop. (1970c) 7713; diversified agriculture.

Bur·ley \ˈbər-lē\. City, ⊗ of Cassia co., S Idaho, on Snake river 38 m. E of Twin Falls; pop. (1970c) 8279; beet-sugar factory, flour mill, brickyard; livestock.

Bur·lin·game \ˈbər-lən-ˌgām, -liŋ-\. Residential city, San Mateo co., W California, on W shore of San Francisco Bay; pop. (1970c) 27,320; Russell Coll. (1928).

Bur·ling·ton \ˈbər-liŋ-tən\. **1** County in New Jersey. See table at NEW JERSEY.

2 Town, ⊗ of Kit Carson co., E Colorado; pop. (1970c) 2828; sugar beets.

3 Town, W Hartford co., N Connecticut; pop. (1970c) 4070; trout hatchery; settled 1780, incorp. 1806; Nepaug State Forest nearby.

4 City, ⊗ of Des Moines co., SE Iowa, on Mississippi river; pop. (1970c) 32,366; electrical equipment, explosives, tractors; settled 1832 on the site of an Indian village; incorporated as town 1836; temporary seat of government of Iowa Territory 1838.

5 City, ⊗ of Coffey co., E Kansas, 28 m. SE of Emporia; pop. (1970c) 2099; timber; oil field nearby.

6 Town, ⊗ of Boone co., N Kentucky.

7 Town, Middlesex co., NE Massachusetts, 11 m. SSE of Lowell; pop. (1970c) 21,980; in agricultural region.

8 City, Burlington co., S cen. New Jersey, on Delaware river 11 m. SSW of Trenton; pop. (1970c) 11,991; shipping point for farm and dairy products and fruit; manufactures iron pipe, artificial limbs, clothing. Settled by Quakers 1677; became capital of West Jersey and port of entry 1681; alternated with Perth Amboy (*q.v.*) as provincial capital after union of East and West Jersey in 1702; invaded by Hessians 1776; bombarded by British 1778.

9 City, Alamance co., N cen. North Carolina, 20 m. E of Greensboro; pop. (1970c) 35,930; industrial center in agricultural region; manufactures textiles, furniture, chemicals.

10 City and port of entry, ⊗ of Chittenden co., NW Vermont, on Lake Champlain 34 m. WNW of Montpelier; pop. (1970c) 38,633; largest city in the state; industrial center and shipping point; manufactures marble, lumber, and wooden products, electronic equipment, structural steel; summer and winter resort; grave of Ethan Allen. Univ. of Vermont (1791), Trinity Coll. (1925); chartered by Province of New Hampshire 1763; settled 1773, organized 1797; figured as military center and base for naval activity on Lake Champlain in War of 1812; incorp. 1865.

11 City, Skagit co., NW Washington, 20 m. S of Bellingham; pop. (1970c) 3138; fruit canning.

12 City, Racine co., SE Wisconsin, 24 m. W of Racine; pop. (1970c) 7479; food products, beer, brassware; dairying center; Saint Francis Coll. (1930); settled 1833.

13 Town, Halton co., SE Ontario, Canada, on Lake Ontario 7 m. NE of Hamilton; pop. (1971p) 86,125; chemicals, concrete, lumber; fruit.

Bur·ma \'bər-mə\; *officially* **Union of Burma** *or Burmese* **Pyei·taw·in·zu Myan·ma Naing·ngan·daw** \pyā-ˌtä-win-'zü-myän-'mä-nīŋ-ˌu̇ŋ-gän-'dä\. Republic, SE Asia, bounded on N by India and China, on E by China, Laos, and Thailand, on S by Thailand and the Andaman Sea, and on W by the Bay of Bengal, Bangla Desh, and India; extends from lat. 10° to ab. 28°30'N and long. 92° to 101°E, constituting NW section of Indochina peninsula; total area 261,789 sq. m.; pop. (1969e) 26,980,000; ✱ Rangoon. Often divided into **Lower Burma** (the coastal region—Arakan, Irrawaddy, Pegu, and Tenasserim divisions) and **Upper Burma** (the N or inland part—Magwe, Mandalay, and Sagaing divisions). An agricultural country. Inhabitants chiefly Burman groups; others are Shan, Karen, Kachin, Mon, Wa, and Chinese peoples.

Physical features: Mountainous along border with India and Bangla Desh in N part, and in Shan State; other important ranges are the Arakan Yoma, Pegu Yoma, and Dawna and Bilauktaung Ranges. Basin of the Irrawaddy, with its tributaries Chindwin, Shweli, Myitnge, occupies most of country; Salween and Sittang are the main streams of E part. Long coastline and numerous islands provide several good harbors. *Chief products:* Rice, pulses, peanuts, cotton, corn, sugarcane, tobacco; oil, silver, tin, lead, zinc; manufacturing: cement, textiles, sugar; fishing. *Chief cities:* Rangoon in the S, Mandalay in the N, Moulmein, Bassein, Sittwe. Divided into eight administrative divisions, one special division, and four states (for pronunciation of their names, see their individual entries):

NAME	AREA (sq. m.)	POP. (1969e)	CAPITAL
Divisions			
Arakan	14,194	1,847,000	Sittwe
Irrawaddy	13,578	4,264,000	Bassein
Magwe	17,297	2,760,000	Yenangyaung
Mandalay	13,225	3,172,000	Mandalay
Pegu	19,423[1]	3,689,000	Pegu
Rangoon[2]	. . .	1,785,000	Rangoon
Sagaing	38,282	2,933,000	Sagaing
Tenasserim	21,297	1,856,000	Moulmein
Special Division			
Chin	13,903	354,000	Falam
States			
Kachin	33,903	687,000	Myitkyina
Kawthule	11,091	795,000	Pa-an
Kayah	4,506	113,000	Loikaw
Shan	61,090	2,725,000	Taunggyi

[1] Includes Rangoon division.

[2] Area included in Pegu division.

History: Inhabited by people of Mongolian stock and probably of Tibetan origin; in 3d cent. A.D. settled on coast and at river mouths by Hindus; first united in 11th cent. under a dynasty at Pagan which was overthrown by Mongols in 13th cent.; Toungoo, Pegu, and Ava the largest of the petty states which now sprang up; united under Toungoo dynasty assisted by Portuguese who first traded there 1519; short-lived Dutch and English factories were founded in 17th cent.; modern Burmese state founded in 18th cent. by Alaungpaya and his successors who conquered Arakan, Tenasserim coast, Manipur, Assam, and eventually came into conflict with the English East India Company; fought three wars with British: First (1824–26), Second (1852–53), and Third (1885–86); as result of First Burmese War by Treaty of Yandabu (*q. v.*) British acquired Assam, Arakan, Tenasserim, and Pegu; after Second Burmese War Rangoon (*q.v.*) retained by British and Lower Burma formed 1862; as result of Third Burmese War Upper Burma formed 1886, including Mandalay (*q. v.*), a kingdom founded by native dynasty in 19th cent.; as province of British India, under lieutenant governor until 1923 when raised to governor's province; separated from India and made crown colony in 1937. In World War II overcome by Japanese 1942 (Rangoon occupied Mar. 8); government located at Simla; reconquest carried on 1943–45; Sittwe, Myitkyina, and N part retaken by Feb. 1945; Mandalay captured in March. Granted independence by pact signed with Great Britain Oct. 17, 1947, effective Jan. 4, 1948; settled border disputes with China 1960; civilian government overthrown 1962.

Burma Road. Former motor highway from Lashio (at railhead from Mandalay), E Burma, NE to K'un-ming in Yunnan, China; 681 m. long; crossed Burma-China border near Namhkam, Burma, and Wan-t'ing (lowest point on road 3200 ft.), China; then proceeded generally E across Salween and Mekong river valleys through Pao-shan and Tali to K'un-ming; alt. in Salween-Mekong region 6000 to 8500 ft. Extension (often considered a part of the Burma Road) E from K'un-ming to Kuei-yang in Kweichow, then N through Tsun-i to Chungking, ab. 700 m. by road. Total length, Chungking to Rangoon (in Burma by rail from Lashio through Hsipaw, Maymyo, and Mandalay), ab. 2100 m. In early part of World War II a vital transportation connecting link (opened Dec. 1938) for supplies to Chinese government; closed for three months July 18–Oct. 18, 1940; lower part in Burma and Yunnan seized by Japanese Mar. 1942. Reopened Jan. 1945 by completion of Stilwell Road (*q.v.*), earlier Ledo Road (see LEDO), connecting with India through Namhkam, Bhamo, and Myitkyina in Burma. Part in India and Burma abandoned by the military 1946.

Bur·net \'bər-nət\. **1** County in cen. Texas. See table at TEXAS.

2 Town and resort, its ⊗, 43 m. NNW of Austin; pop. (1970c) 2864; in agricultural region.

Bur·nett \bər-'net\. **1** County in Wisconsin. See table at WISCONSIN.

2 River, SE Queensland, NE Australia; 250 m. long; flows NE past Bundaberg and into Hervey Bay.

Burn·ham \'bər-nəm\. **1** Village, Cook co., NE Illinois, 17 m. S of Chicago; pop. (1970c) 3634.

2 Borough, Mifflin co., cen. Pennsylvania, 2 m. N of Lewistown; pop. (1970c) 2607; iron and steel works.

Burnham–on–Sea. Urban district, Somersetshire, SW England, on Bristol Channel 24 m. SW of Bristol; pop. (1971p) 12,281.

Bur·nie \'bər-nē\. Town on N coast of Tasmania, Australia, 75 m. WNW of Launceston; pop. (1970e) 20,060.

Burn·ley \'bərn-lē\. County borough, Lancashire, NW England, at confluence of Burn and Calder rivers 22 m. N of Manchester; pop. (1971p) 76,483; textile mills; light engineering; coal mines nearby.

Burns \'bərnz\. City, ⊗ of Harney co., SE Oregon, 20 m. N of Malheur Lake; pop. (1970c) 3293; capital of old cattle empire, modern livestock center of Oregon including Paiute Indian village within the city boundaries; lumber.

Burns·ville \'bərnz-ˌvil\. Town, ⊗ of Yancey co., W North Carolina; pop. (1970c) 1348.

Burnt·is·land \bərnt-'ī-lənd, brənt-\. Seaport burgh, Fife co., E Scotland, on the Firth of Forth opposite Edinburgh; pop. (1971p) 5694; fisheries, aluminum works; shipbuilding.

Burnt Mountain \'bərnt-\. Peak in Sierra Nevada, E Fresno co., S cen. California; 10,602 ft.

Bur·ra \'bər-ə\ *or* **Koo·rin·ga** \kü-'riŋ-gə\. Town, South Australia, ab. 80 m. NE of Adelaide; pop. (1966c) 1342; nearby copper mines, of rich yield 1847–77, now closed; sheep raising; wheat.

Bur·rard Inlet \bə-'rärd-\. Inlet of the Strait of Georgia, extending E into British Columbia, Canada; 9 m. long; the city of Vancouver is on S side at its mouth and Port Moody at its head. One of the best natural harbors on the Pacific coast of North America.

Bur·rel \'bu̇(ə)r-ˌel\. Town, ✱ of Mat prov., N cen. Albania; pop. (1967e) 3337.

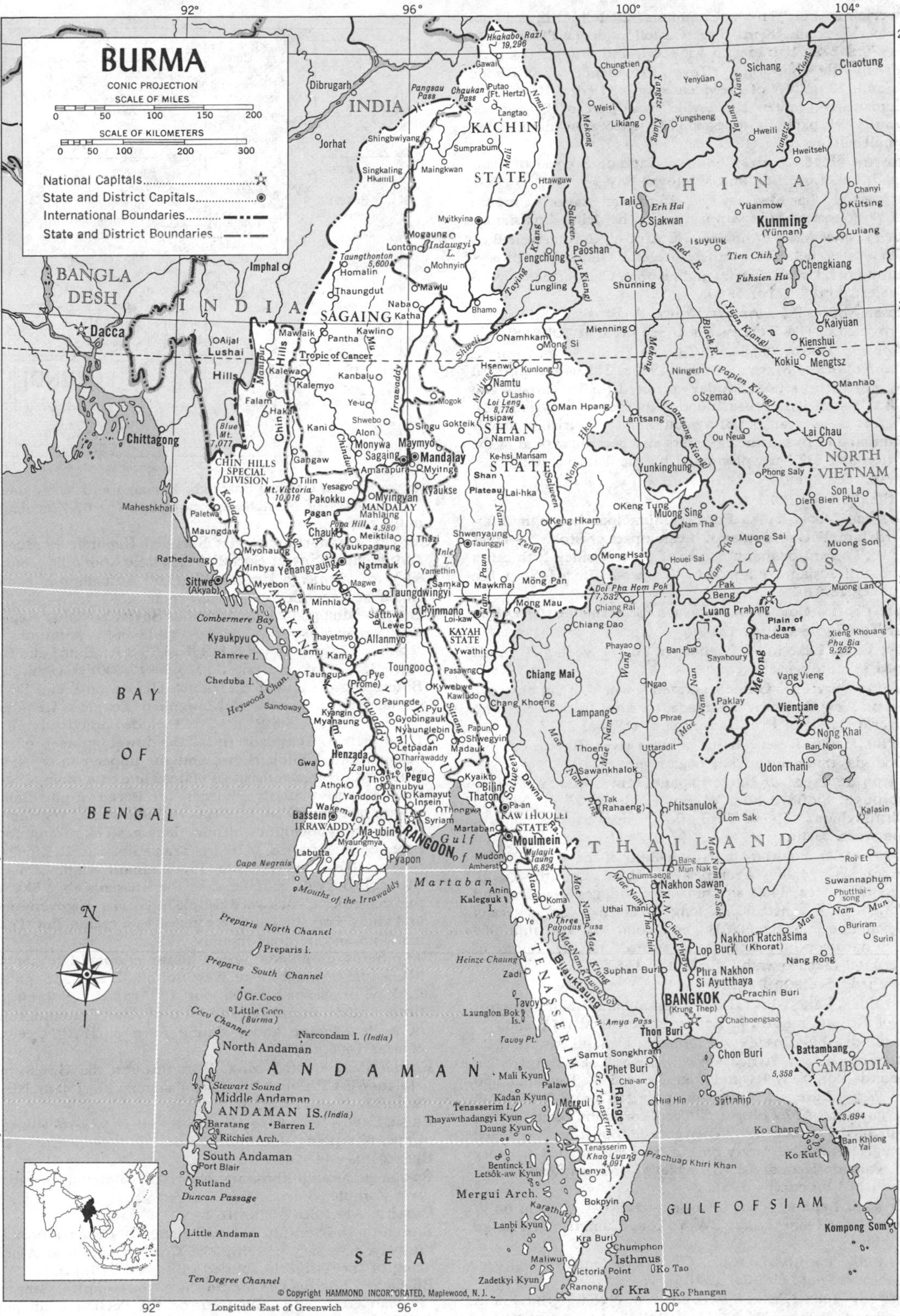
BURMA
CONIC PROJECTION
SCALE OF MILES
0 50 100 150 200
SCALE OF KILOMETERS
0 50 100 200 300
National Capitals
State and District Capitals
International Boundaries
State and District Boundaries
92° 96° 100° 104°
28° 24° 20° 16° 12°
INDIA
BANGLA DESH
Dacca
Chittagong
CHINA
Kunming (Yünnan)
KACHIN STATE
Myitkyina
SAGAING
Tropic of Cancer
SHAN STATE
Mandalay
Maymyo
Sagaing
MANDALAY
Pagan
Taunggyi
CHIN HILLS SPECIAL DIVISION
ARAKAN
Sittwe (Akyab)
KAYAH STATE
PEGU
Pegu
IRRAWADDY
Bassein
RANGOON
KAWTHOOLEI STATE
Moulmein
TENASSERIM
Tavoy
Mergui
Mergui Arch.
NORTH VIETNAM
LAOS
Vientiane
Luang Prabang
THAILAND
BANGKOK (Krung Thep)
Chiang Mai
CAMBODIA
GULF OF SIAM
Isthmus of Kra
BAY OF BENGAL
ANDAMAN SEA
North Andaman
Middle Andaman
ANDAMAN IS. (India)
South Andaman
Little Andaman
Ten Degree Channel
Gulf of Martaban
Mouths of the Irrawaddy
Irrawaddy
Chindwin
Salween
Mekong
Sittang
Hkakabo Razi 19,296
Mt. Victoria 10,016
Popa Hill 4,980
© Copyright HAMMOND INCORPORATED, Maplewood, N. J.
Longitude East of Greenwich

Bu·rria·na \bu̇r-'yän-ə\. Commune, Castellón de la Plana prov., E Spain, 8 m. S of Castellón de la Plana; pop. (1970p) 22,651; trades in wine, oil, and oranges.

Bur·rill·ville \'bər-əl-ˌvil\. Town, Providence co., N Rhode Island, 22 m. NW of Providence; pop. (1970c) 10,087; administrative center Harrisville; was part of Providence until 1731, part of Glocester 1731–1806; now includes ten small villages.

Bur·row Head \ˌbər-ō-, ˌbə-rō-\. Cape on S coast of Scotland, bet. Luce Bay and Wigtown Bay.

Burr·wood \'bər-(ˌ)wu̇d\. U.S. Engineers' station at mouth of W course of Mississippi river in the delta, Louisiana.

Bur·ry Inlet \ˌbər-ē-, ˌbə-rē-\. E arm of Carmarthen Bay, SW Wales, bet. Carmarthenshire and Glamorganshire.

Burry Port. Urban district and seaport, Carmarthenshire, S Wales; pop. (1971p) 5880.

Bur·sa \bu̇r-'sä\; *formerly* **Bru·sa** *or* **Brus·sa** \brü-'sä\. **1** Province of NW Turkey, Asia. See table at TURKEY. **2** *or anc.* **Pru·sa** \'prü-sə\. City, its ✱, ab. 13 m. from SE shore of Sea of Marmara; pop. (1965c) 211,644; connected by rail with its port Mudanya; noted for its carpets and silks. As ancient Prusa founded at foot of (Mysian) Mt. Olympus as seat of Bithynian kings; flourished under Roman and Byzantine emperors and became capital of the Ottomans 1327–61; plundered by the Tatars 1402.

Bursa. See BYRSA.

Būr Sa'īd. See PORT SAID.

Burs·lem \'bərz-ləm\. Former municipal borough, Staffordshire, W cen. England; became part of Stoke-on-Trent 1910; known for manufacture of pottery since 17th cent.; home of Josiah Wedgwood; Wedgwood Inst. (1863). See POTTERIES, THE.

Burt \'bərt\. County in Nebraska. See table at NEBRASKA.

Būr Tawfīq. See PORT TAUFIQ.

Burt Lake. Lake in W Cheboygan co., N Michigan; resort area in state park.

Bur·ton \'bərt-ᵊn\. Unincorporated town, ⊗ of Sunbury co., S cen. New Brunswick, Canada, on right bank of St. John river 18 m. E of Fredericton; pop. (1966c) 2277.

Burton, Lake. Reservoir in Tallulah river, Rabun co., NE Georgia; outlet into Chattooga river.

Burton on Trent *or* **Burton upon Trent** \-'trent\. County borough, Staffordshire, W cen. England, 26 m. NNE of Birmingham; pop. (1971p) 50,175; breweries, chemicals, footwear, castings.

Bu·ru *or Du.* **Boe·roe** \'bu̇r-ü\. Island of the W Moluccas, Indonesia, Malay Archipelago, W of Ceram, 3°24'S, 126°40'E; area 3400 sq. m.; chief villages Namlea and Kajeli, on E coast; 90 m. long by 50 m. wide; generally elevated, esp. in the NW (highest point Mt. Tomahu 7969 ft.); hardwood forests. Long subject to the Sultan of Ternate; taken over by the Dutch 1683.

Burujird. See BORŪJERD.

Bu·rul·lus, Lake \-bə-'rəl-əs\. Coastal lake in Nile delta just E of Rosetta mouth, N Egypt; Baltīm is at its E end.

Bu·run·di \bu̇-'rün-dē\ *or formerly* **Urun·di** \u̇-'rün-dē\. Republic, E cen. Africa, on NE side of Lake Tanganyika, bounded on N by Rwanda, on E and S by Tanzania, and on W by Zaire; 10,759 sq. m.; pop. (1970e) 3,600,000; ✱ Bujumbura. *Chief products:* Corn, sorghum, beans, coffee, bananas; livestock; ab. 95 percent of labor force is engaged in agriculture. Formerly part of the Belgian trust territory of Ruanda-Urundi (*q.v.*); achieved independence 1962; abolished monarchy 1966.

Bur·wash Landing \'bər-(ˌ)wȯsh-, -(ˌ)wäsh-\. Station on W shore of Kluane Lake, SW Yukon, Canada, on Alaska Highway.

Bur·well \'bər-(ˌ)wel, -wəl\. City, ⊗ of Garfield co., cen. Nebraska; pop. (1970c) 1341.

Burwell, Mount. Peak, S Park co., NW Wyoming; 11,738 ft.

Bur·wood \'bər-ˌwu̇d\. Municipality, E New South Wales, SE Australia, W suburb of Sydney; pop. (1966c) 31,843.

Bury \'ber-ē\. County borough, Lancashire, NW England, 10 m. NNW of Manchester; pop. (1971p) 67,776; textile mills; paper.

Bur·yat Autonomous Soviet Socialist Republic *or* **Bur·iat Autonomous Soviet Socialist Republic** \bu̇r-'yät-, ˌbu̇r-ē-'ät-\ *or formerly* **Buryat–Mon·gol Autonomous Soviet Socialist Republic** \-'mäŋ-gəl-, 'män-ˌgōl-, 'mäŋ-ˌgōl-\ *or* **Buryat–Mon·go·lian Autonomous Soviet Socialist Republic** \-män-'gōl-yan-, -mäŋ-, -'gō-lē-ən-\. Autonomous republic of the Russian S.F.S.R., U.S.S.R., E of Lake Baikal; 135,637 sq. m.; pop. (1970p) 812,000; ✱ Ulan-Ude. Bounded on N and W by Irkutsk Oblast, on E and SE by Chita Oblast, on S by Mongolian People's Republic; touches Tuva A.S.S.R. on SW. Includes practically all of Lake Baikal, Barguzin river, the lower courses of the Selenga and Khilok rivers, and the upper course of the Vitim. Main area consists of plateau and mountain ranges, the Yablonovy along E border, the Barguzin and Baikal ranges near the lake. Products include wheat, vegetables, timber, molybdenum, wolfram; fishing, stock raising; food processing. Crossed in S by Trans-Siberian R.R. Chief towns Ulan-Ude, Kyakhta. Predominant ethnic strain is Mongol. Buryats conquered by the Russians ab. 1700; for two centuries a backward people in W part of government known as Transbaikalia; organized as a region Jan. 1922, made an autonomous republic 1923.

Bury Saint Ed·munds \ˌber-ē-(ˌ)sānt-'ed-mən(d)z, -sənt-\. Municipal borough, ⊗ of West Suffolk, E England, on the Lark 63 m. NE of London; pop. (1971p) 25,629; brewery, timber yards; burial place 903 A.D. of King Edmund; ruins of a Benedictine abbey dating from c. 1020; received charter 1606.

Bur·zil Pass \ˌbu̇(ə)r-ˌzil-\. Pass through the Himalayas, North-West Frontier Province, Pakistan, ab. 150 m. NE of Islamabad; alt. 13,775 ft.

Bu·sa, Cape \-'vü-sə\ *or Gk.* **Ák·ra Voú·xa** \ˌäk-rə-'vük-sə\. Cape, NW point of Crete, Greece.

Busaco. See BUSSACO.

Bu·san·ga Swamp \bü-ˌsaŋ-(ˌ)gə-\. Large marsh area in W cen. Zambia, S cen. Africa.

Buseira, Al–. See BOZRAHZ 2.

Bu·sen·to \bü-'sen-(ˌ)tō\. Small stream in Cosenza prov., S Italy, a tributary entering the Crati at Cosenza; Alaric, king of the Visigoths, buried in its bed 410 A.D.

Bü·shehr \bü-'she(ə)r\ *or* **Bu·shire** \bü-'shi(ə)r\. Seaport, Persian Gulf prov., SW Iran, on the Persian Gulf; pop. (1971e) 40,000; one of principal ports of Iran, situated on a peninsula; has good anchorage and steamer connections with many other ports; trade center for inland towns of Shīrāz, Eşfahān, and Tehran; exports carpets, hides, tobacco, fruit and nuts, cotton; founded 1736.

Bush·ey \'bu̇sh-ē\. Urban district, Hertfordshire, SE England, 15 m. WNW of London; pop. (1971p) 23,729; part of Greater London.

Bush·man Land \'bu̇sh-mən-\. Plateau region of NW Cape Province, S Rep. of South Africa, along the left bank of Orange river. **Great Bushman Land** lies chiefly to the west of 20°E long.; **Little Bushman Land** is lower on the course of the Orange; both are semi-desert and rich in minerals.

Bush·nell \'bu̇sh-nəl\. **1** City, ⊗ of Sumter co., cen. Florida penin.; pop. (1970c) 700.
2 City, McDonough co., W Illinois, in agricultural section 29 m. S of Galesburg; pop. (1970c) 3703; stockyards, nurseries; manufactures garden tools.

Bushy Run \ˌbu̇sh-ē-'\. Locality near Greensburg, Westmoreland co., SW Pennsylvania; scene of battle Aug. 5–6, 1763 in Pontiac's War in which Col. Henry Bouquet, on his way to the relief of Fort Pitt (Pittsburgh), defeated the Indians.

Bu·si·ra \bü-'sir-ə\. River, Zaire; 170 m. long; flows W in W cen. Zaire and empties into Ruki river; chief headstream Tshuapa.

Bu·si·ris \byu̇-'sī-rəs\. City of anc. Egypt, in Nile delta ab. 30 m. SW of Tanis; seat of the worship of Osiris as god of nature.

Bus·ke·rud \'bu̇s-kə-ˌrü\. County of S Norway. See table at NORWAY.

Busk–Ivan·hoe Tunnel \'bəsk-'ī-vən-ˌhō-\. Automobile highway tunnel (originally railroad tunnel) through Rocky Mts. in Colorado, near Leadville.

Bus·ra \'bu̇s-rə, 'bəs-\ *or* **Bos·ra** \'bäs-rə\ *also* **Bos·o·ra** \'bäs-ə-rə\ *also* **Boz·rah** \'bäz-\. Ruins of town in the Hauran, now a village in SW Syria on SW border of Jebel ed Druz; not the Bozrah of Edom (*Gen.* xxxvi. 33) or of Moab (*Jer.* xlviii. 24), neither of which, however, has been definitely identified. In the time of the Maccabees a caravan junction point; known to Romans as **Bos·tra** \'bäst-rə\ and became capital of Roman province of Arabia.

Busra *or* **Busrah.** See BASRA.

Bus·sa·co *or* **Bu·sa·co** \bü-'sak-(ˌ)ü\. Mountain on the boundary bet. Viseu and Coimbra districts, NE cen. Portugal; 1795 ft.; site of a Peninsular War battle Sept. 27, 1810 in which Wellington defeated Napoleon's forces under Masséna.

Bussahir. See BASHAHR.

Bus·se·to \bü-'sā-(ˌ)tō\. Town, Parma prov., Emilia-Romagna, N Italy; pop. (1968e) 8049; home of Verdi.

Bussora. See BASRA.

Bussorah. See BASRA.

Bus·sum \'bəs-əm\. Commune, North Holland prov., W Netherlands, SE of Amsterdam; pop. (1970e) 41,787; electronic equipment, rubber goods, furniture.

Bu·sto Ar·si·zio \'bü-(ˌ)stō-är-'sēt-sē-ˌō\. Commune, Varese prov., Lombardy, N Italy, 15 m. S of Varese; pop. (1968e) 75,565; cotton goods; trades in wine; 16th cent. church designed by Bramante.

Bu·su·anga \bü-'swäŋ-ə\. Largest island of Calamian group, Palawan prov., W Phil.; 344 sq. m.; chief town Coron; on SW side of Mindoro Strait.

Busuitan. See MUSU-DAN.

Bu·ta \'bü-tə\. Town, W Haut-Zaïre prov., N Zaire, 160 m. N of Kisangani.

Butaritari. See MAKIN.

Bute \'byüt\. **1** Island in the Firth of Clyde off SW coast of Scotland; ab. 16 m. long and bet. 2 and 5 m. wide; 46 sq. m.; chief town Rothesay.
2 *or* **Bute·shire** \-ˌshi(ə)r, -shər\. County, SW Scotland, comprising Bute, Arran, and Cumbrae Is. in the Firth of Clyde; area 218 sq. m.; pop. (1971p) 14,357; ⊗ Rothesay on Bute; agriculture; fisheries.

Bute Inlet. Deep narrow fjord, SW British Columbia, Canada, lat. 50°37'N and long. 124°53'W; ab. 40 m. long; walls 4000 to 7000 ft. high.

Bu·te·ra \bü-'ter-ə\. Town, Caltanissetta prov., Sicily, Italy, ab. 10 m. NNW of Gela; pop. (1968e) 8488.

Bu·te·re \bü-'ter-ē\. Town, W Kenya, E Africa, NW of Kisumu.

Bu·thi·daung *or* **Bu·the·daung** \ˌbüth-ə-'dau̇ŋ\. Town, Arakan div., Burma, on right bank of Mayu river near the coast 63 m. NW of Sittwe; scene of fighting during Japanese campaign against India.

Bu·thro·tum \byü-'thrōt-əm\ *or Ital.* **Bu·trin·to** \bü-'trēn-(ˌ)tō\. Ancient town of Epirus, NW Greece, on coast opp. N end of Corfu; has fair harbor. Modern town, **Bu·trint** \bü-'trēnt\, is in Albania, on SW coast, and was twice captured in Greek-Italian war of 1941.

But·ler \'bət-lər\. **1** Name of counties in eight states of the U.S. See tables at ALABAMA, IOWA, KANSAS, KENTUCKY, MISSOURI, NEBRASKA, OHIO, PENNSYLVANIA.
2 Town, ⊗ of Choctaw co., W Alabama; pop. (1970c) 2064; plywood.
3 Town, ⊗ of Taylor co., W cen. Georgia; pop. (1970c) 1589; lumber; poultry.
4 City, De Kalb co., NE Indiana, 28 m. NE of Fort Wayne; pop. (1970c) 2394; oats, wheat.
5 City, ⊗ of Bates co., W Missouri, 30 m. N of Nevada; pop. (1970c) 3984; in agricultural region.
6 Borough, Morris co., N New Jersey, 10 m. WNW of Paterson; pop. (1970c) 7051; poultry and truck farms.
7 Industrial city, ⊗ of Butler co., W Pennsylvania, 30 m. N of Pittsburgh; pop. (1970c) 18,691; chemicals, glass, electronic equipment, railroad cars; coal mines, oil wells; platted 1803.

Bu·to \'byü-(ˌ)tō\. City of anc. Egypt, in the Nile delta, S of Coastal Lake (now Lake Burullus); in early (predynastic) times capital of Lower Egypt.

Buton. See BUTUNG.

Bütow. See BYTÓW.

Butrinto. See BUTHROTUM.

Butser Hill. See SOUTH DOWNS.

Butte \'byüt\. **1** Name of counties in three states of the U.S. See tables at CALIFORNIA, IDAHO, SOUTH DAKOTA.
2 City, ⊗ of Silver Bow co., SW Montana, in plateau of Rocky Mts.; pop. (1970c) 23,368; alt. 5765 ft.; 4th largest city in state; located over large mineral deposits (silver, zinc, manganese, and esp. copper). Montana Coll. of Mineral Science and Technology (1893). Founded 1864; copper deposits discovered 1880; incorporated as town 1876, as city 1879.
3 Village, ⊗ of Boyd co., N Nebraska; pop. (1970c) 575.

But·ter·mere \'bət-ər-ˌmi(ə)r\. Lake in the Lake District, NW England, in Cumberland 7 m. SW of Keswick; 1¼ m. long; maximum depth 94 ft.

But·ter·milk Channel \ˌbət-ər-ˌmilk-\. Channel in Upper New York Bay, New York, bet. Governors I. and Brooklyn; ab. 2½ m. long.

But·ter·worth \'bət-ər-(ˌ)wərth\. **1** Town, Penang state, Malaysia, on coast; pop. (1957c) 42,504; tin smelter.
2 Town, E Cape Province, S Rep. of South Africa, 50 m. NNE of East London.

Butt of Lewis. See LEWIS, BUTT OF.

Butts \'bəts\. County in Georgia. See table at GEORGIA.

Bu·tu·an \bə-'tü-ˌän\. City, ✱ of Agusan del Norte prov., NE Mindanao, Phil., on left bank of Agusan river ab. 5 m. from its mouth; pop. (1970e) 116,900.

Butuan Bay. Large inlet of SE Mindanao Sea, NE Mindanao, Phil.; ab. 24 m. wide from Diuata Point to E shore; receives Agusan river.

Bu·tung *or Du.* **Boe·toeng** \ˈbü-ˌtu̇ŋ\ *or formerly* **Bu·ton** \ˈbü-ˌtȯn\. Island off SE coast of Celebes I., Indonesia; ab. 2000 sq. m.; ab. 100 m. long; separated from Muna I. on the W by **Butung Strait** (ab. 65 m. long); chief town Baubau.

Butuntum. See BITONTO.

Bu·tur·li·nov·ka \bu̇-ˈtu̇r-ˈl(y)ē-ˌnəf-kə\. Town, E cen. Voronezh Oblast, Russian S.F.S.R., U.S.S.R., ab. 80 m. SE of Voronezh; pop. (1967e) 23,000; in cattle-raising region.

Bux·ar *or* **Bax·ar** \ˈbək-sər\. Town, W Bihar, NE India, on Ganges 77 m. W of Patna; pop. (1961c) 23,068; victory Oct. 23, 1764 of British under Major Hector Munro over forces of Siraj-ud-daula and Mir Kasim, which established British control over Bengal.

Bux·te·hu·de \ˌbu̇k-stə-ˈhüd-ə\. City, Lower Saxony, West Germany, 14 m. SW of Hamburg; pop. (1969e) 22,646; food processing, metalworking; building materials; developed around Benedictine abbey founded 1197; made city 1237; member of Hanseatic League 1363.

Bux·ton \ˈbək-stən\. **1** Town, York co., SW Maine, 15 m. W of Portland; pop. (1970c) 3135.

2 Municipal borough, Derbyshire, N cen. England, 20 m. SE of Manchester; pop. (1971p) 20,316; resort.

3 Coastal town, N Guyana, 11 m. ESE of Georgetown.

Buynaksk. See BUINAKSK.

Buyr Nuur. See PEI-ERH.

Bü·yük·a·da \ˌbyü-ˌyük-ə-ˈdä\ *or formerly* **Prin·ki·po** \ˌprēŋ-ki-ˈpō\. Island in E Sea of Marmara, W Turkey, SE of entrance to the Bosporus; largest of the Kızıl Is.

Bü·yük·de·re \ˌbyü-ˌyük-də-ˈrā\. Town on the Bosporus, Turkey, 11 m. NE of İstanbul; residential suburb in valley from which İstanbul obtains part of its water supply.

Büyük Menderes Nehri. See MENDERES 1.

Bu·za·chi \bu̇-ˈzäch-ē\. Large peninsula projecting into NE Caspian Sea, N of Mangyshlak Penin., Kazakh S.S.R., U.S.S.R.

Bu·zan·cy \bü-zäⁿ-ˈsē\. **1** Village, Aisne dept., NE France, ab. 3 m. S of Soissons; pop. (1962c) 156; taken by British and French July 28–30, 1918.

2 Village, Ardennes dept., NE France, 12 m. E of Vouziers; pop. (1962c) 455; taken by Americans Nov. 2, 1918.

Bu·zău \bə-ˈzau̇, -ˈzō\ *or Hung.* **Bod·za** \ˈbōd-ˌzȯ\. **1** River, cen. Romania; ab. 150 m. long; rises in Braşov co. and flows SE through **Buzău Pass** in Transylvanian Alps and NE into Siretul river near Galaţi.

2 County of SE Romania. See table at ROMANIA.

3 City, its ⊗, on Buzău river 62 m. NE of Bucharest; pop. (1968e) 55,382; alcohol, textiles; in rich oil-field region.

Bu·zu·luk \ˌbu̇z-ə-ˈlük\. City, W Orenburg Oblast, Russian S.F.S.R., U.S.S.R., on left bank of Samara river and on railroad 90 m. ESE of Kuibyshev; pop. (1969e) 65,000; trading town at the edge of the steppe region; deals esp. in grain and cattle; large Tatar population.

Buz·zards Bay \ˌbəz-ərdz-\. **1** Inlet of Atlantic Ocean, in SE Massachusetts; 30 m. long and 5 to 10 m. wide; the W end of Cape Cod Canal is at its NE extremity.

2 Town, Barnstable co., SE Massachusetts, on Cape Cod Canal near entrance of inlet; pop. (1970c) 2422; Massachusetts Maritime Academy (1891).

Bwa·ga·oia \ˌbwäg-ə-ˈȯi-ə\. See LOUISIADE ARCHIPELAGO.

Bwake. See BOUAKÉ.

Bwa·na M'kub·wa *or* **Bwa·na·mkub·wa** \ˌbwä-näm-ˈku̇b-wä\. Town, cen. Zambia, S cen. Africa; copper mines.

By·am Mar·tin \ˌbī-əm-ˈmärt-ᵊn\. Island in channel bet. Melville and Bathurst Is., Parry Is., Franklin dist., Northwest Territories, Canada.

Byblos. See JUBAYL.

Byd·goszcz \ˈbid-ˌgȯsh(ch)\ *or Ger.* **Brom·berg** \ˈbräm-ˌbərg, ˈbrȯm-ˌbe(ə)rk\. **1** Province of N cen. Poland. See table at POLAND.

2 City, its ✱, 67 m. NE of Poznań; pop. (1970p) 281,000; paper, furniture, electronic equipment, precision instruments. Originally a commercial city of the Teutonic Knights; enlarged and developed by Frederick the Great in 18th cent.; under Prussian rule 1772–1919. In World War II held by Germans 1939–45.

Byel–. Literally "white" in Russian. For names beginning *Byel-*, see BEL-, as *Belgorod, Belomorsk, Belukha.*

Byelorussian Soviet Socialist Republic *or* **Byelorussia.** See BELORUSSIAN SOVIET SOCIALIST REPUBLIC.

Byelozero. See BELOYE OZERO.

Byes·ville \ˈbīz-ˌvil\. Village, Guernsey co., E Ohio, 24 m. E of Zanesville; pop. (1970c) 2097; coal mining.

By·lot Island \ˌbī-ˌlät-\. Island, E Franklin dist., Northwest Territories, Canada, N of Baffin Island and W of Baffin Bay; 4200 sq. m.

Byrds·town \ˈbərdz-ˌtau̇n\. Town, ⊗ of Pickett co., N Tennessee; pop. (1970c) 582.

By·ron \ˈbir-ˌȯn\. City, E Greece, part of Greater Athens; pop. (1971p) 47,025.

Byron. See NIKUNAU.

Byron, Cape \-ˈbī-rən\. Cape, New South Wales, Australia, extreme E point of continent, 28°39′S, 153°38′E.

Byr·sa *or* **Bur·sa** \ˈbər-sə\. The citadel of Carthage.

By·tom \ˈbē-ˌtȯm, ˈbi-\ *or Ger.* **Beu·then** \ˈbȯit-ᵊn\. City, Katowice prov., SW Poland, ab. 8 m. NW of Katowice; pop. (1970p) 187,000; formerly in Silesia, Germany; iron, zinc, and lead works; coal mines. Became part of Prussia 1742. Taken by U.S.S.R. Jan. 1945; in section assigned to Poland by Potsdam Conference 1945.

By·tów \ˈbē-(ˌ)tüf, ˈbi-\ *or Ger.* **Bü·tow** \ˈbü-(ˌ)tō\. Town, Koszalin prov., N Poland, ab. 55 m. E of Koszalin; pop. (1968e) 10,700; iron foundry; railroad junction and market town; founded 1346; Polish town in 15th cent., came under Brandenburg 1657. Assigned to Poland by Potsdam Conference 1945.

Bytown. See OTTAWA 6.

By·za·ci·um \bə-ˈzā-sh(ē-)əm\. The S part of the Roman province of Africa; corresponds to S half of Tunisia.

By·zan·tine Empire \ˌbiz-ᵊn-ˌtēn-, bə-ˌzan-, ˌbiz-ᵊn-; ˌbiz-ᵊn-ˌtīn-; bə-ˌzant-ᵊn-\. Empire of SE and S Europe and W Asia, 4th–15th cents., with boundaries varying greatly; in earliest period generally termed **Eastern Roman Empire,** 395–474, with capital at Constantinople (earlier Byzantium); first Byzantine emperor, so called, Zeno the Isaurian (474–491). Reached its greatest extent under Justinian (527–565), who reconquered large part of Western Empire, erected Church of Saint Sophia, and issued basic codification of Roman law (*Corpus Juris Civilis*); divided into themes for administration; withstood attacks of Persians, Arabs, and Bulgars 7th–10th cents.; ab. 1000 A.D. comprised S Balkans, Greece, Asia Minor, and parts of S Italy. Long controversy over iconoclasm within Eastern Church prepared for break with Roman Church; attained great wealth and cultural supremacy of Mediterranean world because of its control of commerce bet. east and west and its preservation of classical heritage; lost holdings in Italy and, as result of Manzikert (see MALAZGIRT), yielded Asia Minor to Seljuks; declined under Comnenian dynasty and forced to give commercial control to Venice (*q.v.*) which profited most from Crusades; Constantinople sacked by Fourth Crusade 1204 and Empire split up into (1) Latin Empire (*q.v.*), Greek empires of (2) Trebizond and (3) Nicaea, and (4) miscellaneous Venetian, Latin, and Greek holdings (see ACHAEA, ATHENS 10, EPIRUS, SALONIKA); partly restored by capture of Constantinople by Michael VIII 1261; in 14th cent. gradually lost territory to Turks until there remained only Constantinople, Morea, and Salonika; capture of Constantinople in 1453 marked formal end of Byzantine Empire (see OTTOMAN EMPIRE).

By·zan·ti·um \bə-ˈzan-sh(ē-)əm, -ˈzant-ē-əm\. Ancient city, site of modern İstanbul (*q.v.*).

Bzu·ra \bə-ˈzu̇r-ə\. River, Poland, flowing into Vistula river from the S; ab. 90 m. long; its source is just N of Łódź.

Ca·a·cu·pé \ˌkä-ə-kü-ˈpā\. Town, ✱ of Cordillera dept., cen. Paraguay; munic. pop. (1970e) 21,732.

Ca·a·gua·zú \ˌkä-ə-gwä-ˈsü\. Department of E cen. Paraguay. See table at PARAGUAY.

Ca·a·ma·ño Sound \kä-ˌmän-(ˌ)yō-\. Inlet of Hecate Strait, off W coast of British Columbia, Canada, W of Princess Royal I. and N of Aristazabal I.

Ca·a·pu·cú \ˌkä-ə-pü-ˈkü\. Town, Paraguarí dept., S Paraguay, ab. 70 m. SSE of Asunción; pop. (1970e) 8441.

Ca·a·za·pá \ˌkä-ə-sə-ˈpä\. 1 Department of S Paraguay. See table at PARAGUAY.

2 City, its ✱; munic. pop. (1970e) 23,349.

Ca·bad·ba·ran \kə-ˌbäd-bə-ˈrän\. Municipality, Mindanao, Phil., on E shore of Butuan Bay ab. 12 m. N of Butuan; pop. (1969e) 35,900.

Ca·bai·guán \ˌkä-bī-ˈgwän\. Town and municipality, Las Villas prov., W cen. Cuba, 37 m. SE of Santa Clara; munic. pop. (1967e) 38,180.

Ca·ba·llo \kä-ˈbä-(ˌ)yō\ *or* **Pu·lo Caballo** \pü-ˌlō-\. Rocky islet in Corregidor group, ab. 1 m. SE of Corregidor I., in entrance to Manila Bay, Phil.; alt. 420 ft.; lighthouse; site of Fort Hughes. Surrendered to Japanese May 1942; recaptured by U.S. Mar. 1945.

Caballo Dam \kə-ˈbä-(ˌ)yō-\. Secondary dam across Rio Grande river, Sierra co., New Mexico, below Elephant Butte Dam; height 96 ft.; completed 1938; impounds water for irrigation.

Ca·ba·ñas \kə-ˈbän-yəs\. 1 Municipality on NE coast of Pinar del Río prov., W Cuba; pop. (1967e) 38,230.

2 Department, N cen. El Salvador. See table at EL SALVADOR.

Ca·ba·na·tuan \ˌkäb-ə-nə-ˈtwän\. Municipality, ✱ of Nueva Ecija prov., Luzon, Phil., in S cen. part on left bank of Pampanga river; pop. (1970e) 97,000; a highway junction point and trade center. Site of large Japanese prison camp (near Cabu village) for American and Filipino soldiers captured at Bataan and Corregidor, which was taken by U.S. forces Jan. 30, 1945.

Ca·ba·no \ˌkab-ə-ˈnō\. Town, Témiscouata co., S Quebec, Canada, on Lake Témiscouata; pop. (1971p) 3055.

Ca·bar·rus \kə-ˈbar-əs, -ˈber-\. County in North Carolina. See table at NORTH CAROLINA.

Ca·bar·ru·yan Island \ˌkäb-ə-ˈrü-(ˌ)yän-\. Island on NW shore of Lingayen Gulf, Pangasinan prov., Luzon, Phil.; 30 sq. m.; forested; chief town Anda.

Ca·ba·tu·an \ˌkä-bə-ˈtü-(ˌ)wän\. Municipality, W cen. Iloilo prov., Panay, Phil., NW of Iloilo; pop. (1969e) 36,100.

Ca·be·de·lo \ˌkä-və-ˈthā-lü\. Seaport, Paraíba state, E Brazil; munic. pop. (1968e) 13,923; port for João Pessoa.

Cab·ell \ˈkab-əl\. County in West Virginia. See table at WEST VIRGINIA.

Cabellio. See CAVAILLON.

Ca·bes Point \ˌkäb-əs-\. Cape on E coast of St. Thomas I., U.S. Virgin Is., West Indies, W of Pillsbury Sound.

Ca·be·za del Buey \kə-ˌbā-sə-del-ˈbwā\. Commune, Badajoz prov., SW Spain, 90 m. E of Badajoz; pop. (1970p) 9236; lead, galena, and iron mines.

Cabeza del Mo·ro \-ˈmōr-(ˌ)ō, -ˈmȯr-\. Highest peak in the Guadalupe Mts., Cáceres prov., W Spain; 5695 ft.

Cabillonum. See CHALON-SUR-SAÔNE.

Ca·bi·mas \kə-ˈbē-məs\. Town, N Zulia state, NW Venezuela, on NE coast of Lake Maracaibo; pop. (1970e) 147,250.

Ca·bin·da *also* **Ka·bin·da** \kə-ˈbin-də\. 1 District of Angola, N of the mouth of the Congo river; 2807 sq. m.; pop. (1960c) 58,547; oil, timber; exclave attached to Angola, 1886, by agreement with Belgium.

2 Seaport, its ✱; pop. (1960c) 13,499.

Cab·i·net Mountains \ˌkab-(ə-)nət-\. A range of the Rocky Mts. in NW Montana and N Idaho; highest point ab. 9000 ft.

Cabira. See SIVAS 2.

Cabo de Hornos. See HORN, CAPE.

Ca·bo Del·ga·do \ˌkäb-ō-del-ˈgäd-(ˌ)ō\. 1 District, NE Mozambique, SE Africa; 30,260 sq. m.; pop. (1970p) 567,478; ✱ Porto Amélia.

2 Cape, Mozambique, SE Africa. See DELGADO, CAPE.

Cabo Gra·cias a Dios \-ˌgräs-yəs-ä-dē-ˈōs\. Municipality, extreme NE Nicaragua; pop. (1970e) 6166; politically included in Zelaya dept.

Cabo Juby. See TARFAYA.

Ca·bo·ra Bas·sa \kə-ˌbȯr-ə-ˈbäs-ə\. Dam under construction on Zambezi river, NW Mozambique; upon completion will be a major source of hydroelectric power for S Africa.

Ca·bor·ca \kə-ˈbȯr-kə\. City, Sonora state, Mexico, 150 m. NW of Hermosillo; pop. (1970p) 29,486; cotton, wheat.

Cabo Ro·jo \ˌcäb-ō-ˈrō-(ˌ)hō\. Town and municipality, SW Puerto Rico, 7 m. S of Mayagüez; pop. (1970p) 7158 (town), 25,568 (munic.).

Cab·ot \ˈkab-ət\. City, Lonoke co., cen. Arkansas, 18 m. NE of Little Rock; pop. (1970c) 2903; diversified agriculture.

Cabot Head. Cape, SE Ontario, Canada; NE point of Bruce Penin. on Georgian Bay.

Cabot Strait. Channel in Canada, bet. SW Newfoundland and N Cape Breton I.; 68 m. wide; connects the St. Lawrence with the Atlantic Ocean.

Ca·bourg \ká-ˈbu̇(ə)r\. Village, Calvados dept., NW France; adjoins Dives-sur-Mer on the W; pop. (1962c) 2987; one of the finest beaches among the Channel resorts.

Cabo Verde, Ilhas do. See CAPE VERDE ISLANDS.

Cabo Yubi. See TARFAYA.

Ca·bra \ˈkäb-rə\ *or anc.* **Igab·rum** \ig-ˈab-rəm\. Commune, Córdoba prov., S Spain, 37 m. SE of Córdoba; pop. (1970p) 20,428; linen, bricks; captured from Moors by Ferdinand III 1240; recaptured 1311.

Cab·ras Island \ˌkab-rəs-\. Narrow island off W coast of Guam; ab. 2 m. long and 1/4 m. wide; forms part of N shelter of Apra Harbor.

Ca·bre·ra \kə-ˈbrer-ə\ *or anc.* **Ca·prar·ia** \kə-ˈprar-ē-ə, -ˈprer-\. Small island of the Balearic Is., Baleares prov., Spain, 9 m. S of Majorca; a part of Palma commune.

Ca·bri·el \ˌkäb-rē-ˈel\. River, E Spain; ab. 130 m. long; flows S through Cuenca prov. and into Júcar river.

Ca·bril·lo National Monument \kə-ˈbril-ō-\. See UNITED STATES, *National Monuments.*

Ca·bu \ˈkä-(ˌ)bü\. Village, cen. Nueva Ecija prov., Luzon, Phil., ab. 7 m. ENE of Cabanatuan; pop. (1960c) 900. Site 1942–45 of Cabanatuan prison camp (see CABANATUAN).

Ca·bu·gao \kə-ˈbü-(ˌ)gau̇\. Municipality, N Ilocos Sur, Luzon, Phil., on coast 17 m. N of Vigan; pop. (1969e) 24,100.

Ca·ca·hua·mil·pa Caverns \ˌkäk-ə-wə-ˈmil-pə-\. Large natural caverns in NE Guerrero state near Cuernavaca, cen. Mexico.

Ča·čak *or* **Cha·chak** \ˈchä-(ˌ)chäk\. Town, Serbia, Yugoslavia, ab. 62 m. S of Belgrade; pop. (1965e) 33,000; construction materials, electronic equipment, paper.

Ca·ca·pon \kə-ˈkā-pən\. River, NE West Virginia; ab. 130 m. long; rises in S Hardy co., flows N into Potomac river.

Cac·cia, Cape \-ˈkäch-ə\. Cape on NW coast of the island of Sardinia, Italy.

Cá·ce·res \ˈkäs-ə-ˌräs, ˈkäth-\. 1 Province of W Spain. See table at SPAIN.

2 Commune, its ✱, on **Cáceres River** 152 m. SW of Madrid; pop. (1970p) 56,064; pottery, leather goods, cloth; remains of Roman fortifications; held by Moors 1142–1229.

Ca·chan \kȧ-ˈshäⁿ\. Commune, Val-de-Marne dept., N France, S suburb of Paris on Bièvre river; pop. (1968c) 28,187.

Cache \ˈkash\. 1 River, NE Arkansas; ab. 213 m. long; rises in NE Arkansas and flows S into the White river in Monroe co., E cen. Arkansas.
2 County in Utah. See table at UTAH.

Cache la Pou·dre \ˌkash-lə-ˈpü-drə\. River, N Colorado; ab. 125 m. long; flows from a point near Milner Pass N and E to the South Platte near Greeley.

Ca·chí, Ne·va·do de \nə-ˈväd-(ˌ)ō-ˌdā-kə-ˈchē\. Peak in Salta prov., N Argentina; 22,047 ft.

Ca·cho·ei·ra \ˌkash-ə-ˈwe(ə)r-ə\. City, Bahia state, E Brazil, near W coast of All Saints Bay ab. 45 m. W of Salvador; munic. pop. (1968e) 32,432.

Cachoeira do Sul \-də-ˈsül\. City, Rio Grande do Sul state, S Brazil, on Jacuí river 110 m. W of Pôrto Alegre; munic. pop. (1968e) 98,927.

Ca·cho·ei·ro de Ita·pe·mi·rim \ˌkash-ə-ˈwe(ə)r-(ˌ)ō-dā-ˌit-ə-ˌpem-ə-ˈrim\. City, Espírito Santo state, E Brazil, 65 m. SW of Vitória; munic. pop. (1968e) 110,301.

Ca·cou·na \kə-ˈkü-nə\. Village and summer resort, Quebec, Canada; on S shore of St. Lawrence NE of Rivière du Loup; pop. (1966c) 63.

Cad·do \ˈkad-(ˌ)ō\. A parish in Louisiana and a county in Oklahoma. See tables at LOUISIANA and OKLAHOMA.

Caddo Lake. Lake on N Texas-Louisiana boundary; ab. 20 m. long; connected with Soda Lake and Red river; navigable for steamboats.

Ca·de·rey·ta Ji·mé·nez \ˌkä-də-ˌrā-tə-hē-ˈmā-nəs\. Municipality, Nuevo León state, Mexico, 22 m. ESE of Monterrey; pop. (1970p) 30,429; walnuts, oranges.

Ca·der Fron·wen \ˈkäd-ər-frän-ˈwen\. Peak in the Berwyn Mts., N Wales; 2568 ft.

Cader Id·ris \-ˈid-rəs\. Peak, Merionethshire, W Wales, S of Dolgellau; 2927 ft.

Cad·il·lac \ˈkad-ᵊl-ˌak\. City, ⊗ of Wexford co., NW Michigan, 36 m. SSE of Traverse City; pop. (1970c) 9990; automobile tires, malleable iron; poultry; truck farms.

Ca·diz. 1 \ˈkād-(ˌ)iz\. City, ⊗ of Trigg co., SW Kentucky; pop. (1970c) 1987; timber.
2 \ˈkad-(ˌ)iz\. Village, ⊗ of Harrison co., E Ohio, 20 m. WSW of Steubenville; pop. (1970c) 3060; sheet metal; coal.
3 \ˈkäd-(ˌ)ēs\. Chartered city, N Negros Occidental, Negros, Phil., on Visayan Sea NE of Bacolod; pop. (1970e) 125,500.

Cá·diz \ˈkä-ˌthēth, -ˌthēs\ *or angl.* **Ca·diz** \kə-ˈdiz; ˈkād-(ˌ)iz, ˈkäd-, ˈkad-\. 1 Province of SW Spain. See table at SPAIN.
2 *anc.* **Ga·dir** \ˈgād-ər\ *also* **Ga·dire** \gə-ˈdī(ə)r\ *or* **Ga·dier** \-ˈdi(ə)r\ *or later* **Ga·des** \ˈgād-(ˌ)ēz\. Seaport city, its ✱, on Bay of Cádiz 58 m. NW of Gibraltar and 62 m. SSW of Seville; pop. (1970p) 135,743; naval and mercantile shipbuilding yards; exports sherry, salt, olives, fish; 13th cent. and 18th cent. cathedrals (with paintings by Murillo), bullring.

History: Founded as Phoenician trading colony c. 1100 B.C.; outlet for mineral wealth, tin and amber from N; ruled by Carthaginians, Romans, Visigoths; held by Moors from 711 A.D. until captured 1262 by Alfonso of Castile; enjoyed great prosperity as one of two centers for Spanish trade with American colonies (see SEVILLE) 16th–18th cents.; scene of raid of earl of Essex 1596; became seat of Casa de Contratación (clearing house for American trade) 1718; besieged by French 1810–12; seat of national assembly (Span. *Cortes*) which promulgated liberal constitution of 1812; witnessed beginning of revolution which deposed Queen Isabella II 1868.

Cádiz, Bay of. Inlet of the Gulf of Cádiz on SW coast of Spain, affording excellent harbor for the city of Cádiz.

Cádiz, Gulf of. Widemouthed inlet of Atlantic Ocean on SW coast of Spain.

Ca·do·re Alps \kə-ˌdōr-ē-, -ˌdȯr-\ *or* **Ca·dor·ic Alps** \kə-ˌdȯr-ik-, -ˌdär-\. A name of the Dolomites bet. Veneto and Friuli-Venezia Giulia, NE Italy.

Cadurcum. See CAHORS.

Cae·li·an \ˈsē-lē-ən\ *or Lat.* **Cae·li·us Mons** \ˌsē-lē-əs-ˈmänz\. One of the seven hills of Rome. See SEVEN HILLS.

Caen \ˈkäⁿ\. City, ✱ of Calvados dept., Normandy, NW France, on Orne river ab. 9 m. from coast of English Channel and ab. 126 m. WNW of Paris; pop. (1968c) 110,-262; iron and steel; chemicals, electrical equipment; transportation center; notable structures include L'Abbaye-aux-Dames (founded 1066 by Matilda, wife of William the Conqueror), L'Abbaye-aux-Hommes (founded by William the Conqueror 11th cent.), church of Saint-Pierre; university (founded 1432 by Henry VI of England). Under English rule 1346, 1417–50; suffered in religious wars; captured by Protestants 1562. In World War II one of the main objects of Allied invasion; attacked by British on D-day, June 6, 1944; became part of German defense line; again attacked June 25 and taken by British and Canadians July 9; much of the city destroyed.

Caene *or* **Caenepolis.** See QENA 2.

Caere. See CERVETERI.

Caer Gybi. See HOLYHEAD 2.

Caer·le·on \kär-ˈlē-ən\ *or anc.* **Is·ca Sil·u·rum** \ˌis-kə-ˈsil-yə-rəm\. Urban district, Monmouthshire, SE Wales, on Usk river; pop. (1971p) 6235. Thought to be the "Carlion" (where Arthur was crowned and held his court) of Malory's *Morte d'Arthur.*

Caer Luel. See CARLISLE 5.

Caer·nar·von *or* **Car·nar·von** \kär-ˈnär-vən, kər-\. 1 County, Wales. See CAERNARVONSHIRE.
2 Municipal borough and seaport, ⊗ of Caernarvonshire, NW Wales; pop. (1971p) 9253; famous 13th cent. castle, birthplace of Edward II; tourism.

Caernarvon Bay *or* **Carnarvon Bay.** Bay bet. Caernarvonshire and Anglesey, NW Wales; Menai Strait connects it with Beaumaris Bay.

Caer·nar·von·shire *or* **Car·nar·von·shire** \kär-ˈnär-vən-shi(ə)r, kər-, -shər\ *or* **Caenarvon** *or* **Carnarvon.** County, NW Wales; 569 sq. m.; pop. (1971p) 122,852; ⊗ Caernarvon; mountainous area; rivers Conway, Ogwen, Glaslyn; quarrying (esp. slate), livestock raising; tourism.

Caer·phil·ly \kär-ˈfil-ē\. Urban district, Glamorganshire, SE Wales; pop. (1971p) 40,689; trade center in coal-mining region; known esp. for its cheese; has 13th cent. castle.

Caesaraugusta. See SARAGOSSA.

Cae·sa·rea \ˌsē-zə-ˈrē-ə, ˌses-ə-, ˌsez-\. 1 Seaport, Algeria. See CHERCHELL.
2 *or mod.* **Qi·sar·ya** \ki-ˈsär-yə\. Ancient seaport on coast of Samaria and Roman capital of Palestine, ab. 22 m. S of Haifa, Israel; founded by Herod the Great; made Roman capital after Vespasian's reign; site of an early Christian church and frequently mentioned in the New Testament; its fortifications strengthened 1251 by Louis IX; destroyed by Baybars I 1265.

Caesarea Mazaca. See KAYSERİ 2.

Caesarea Philippi. See BANIYAS 2.

Caesarodunum. See TOURS.

Caesaromagus. See BEAUVAIS.

Cae·sar's Head \ˌsē-zərz-\. Range of the Blue Ridge, in N Greenville co., NW South Carolina; the S face is a 1500-ft. precipice; highest peak 3225 ft.

Caesena. See CESENA.

Cae·ti·té *or* **Cai·te·té** \ˌkī-tə-ˈtā\. Municipality, Bahia state, Brazil; pop. (1968e) 36,411.

Ca·ga·rras Islands \kə-ˈgar-əs-\. Islands in Atlantic Ocean off Guanabara state, SE Brazil.

Ca·ga·yan \ˌkäg-ə-ˈyän\. 1 *or* **Rio Gran·de de Cagayan** \ˌrē-ō-ˈgrän-dē-ˌdā-\. River, NE Luzon, Phil.; 220 m. long; flows N to Babuyan Channel; largest river in Luzon; chief tributary the Chico; valley 50 m. wide bet. the Cordillera Central on the W and the Sierra Madre on the E; navigable for much of its course. Near its mouth is the port of Aparri.
2 River, Mindanao, Phil.; ab. 50 m. long; flows N from Bukidnon to Macajalar Bay.

3 Province, NE Luzon, Phil.; 3476 sq. m.; pop. (1970p) 580,810; ✱ Tuguegarao; occupies lower basin of Cagayan river, including part of its tributary the Chico, with Sierra Madre range averaging ab. 3500 ft. E of valley along Pacific Ocean; includes Babuyan Is. (*q.v.*) to the N; northernmost tip is Cape Engaño; valley region fertile, esp. suitable for tobacco. Chief towns Tuguegarao, Aparri, Tuao, Baggao, Gattaran.

History: Visited and explored by Spaniards 1572–81; recognized as a political division by 1583; scene of several uprisings in 17th cent.; suffered from injustices of the tobacco monopoly c. 1782–1830; civil government established Sept. 1901. In World War II Aparri occupied by Japanese Dec. 10, 1941; Cagayan valley reconquered by American forces May–June 1945.

Cagayan de Oro \-də-ˈōr-ō, -ˌȯr-\. Chartered city, ✱ of Misamis Oriental prov., Mindanao, Phil., in E part near S shore of Macajalar Bay ab. 3 m. from mouth of Cagayan river; pop. (1970e) 94,500.

Cagayan Islands *or* **Ca·ga·ya·nes** \ˌkäg-ə-ˈyän-(ˌ)ās\. Group of seven small islands in N part of Sulu Sea, Phil., 70 m. W of SW Negros, 9°40′N, 121°25′E; ab. 5 sq. m.; munic. pop. (1968e) 5300; only settlement **Ca·ga·yan·ci·llo** \ˌkäg-ə-yän-ˈsē(l)-yō\; belong to Palawan prov.

Cagayan Su·lu \-ˈsü-(ˌ)lü\. Small island in SW Sulu Sea, SW Phil., ab. 70 m. off the NE coast of Borneo; 26 sq. m.; surrounded by 13 islets; noted for its scenery, fauna and flora; suffered much in 19th cent. from Moro pirates. With Sibutu I. (*q.v.*) inadvertently omitted from Philippine lands sold by Spain to U.S. by treaty of Dec. 10, 1898; acquired for sum of $100,000 by special agreement of Nov. 7, 1900, proclaimed Mar. 23, 1901.

Ca·gli \ˈkäl-yē\. Commune, Marches, cen. Italy, 29 m. SSW of Pesaro; pop. (1968e) 10,563.

Ca·glia·ri \ˈkäl-yə-(ˌ)rē\. 1 Province of Sardinia, Italy. See table at ITALY.

2 *or anc.* **Car·a·lis** \ˈkar-ə-ləs\. Fortified seaport, its ✱, and ✱ of Sardinia, at head of Gulf of Cagliari on S coast of Sardinia 252 m. SW of Rome; pop. (1968e) 219,852; exports incl. lead, zinc, salt; 14th cent. cathedral; ancient Roman remains; univ. (1606). Founded by Phoenicians; held successively by Romans, Saracens, Pisans, Spain, Austria, and (as kingdom of Sardinia) by Savoy.

Cagliari, Gulf of. Inlet of Mediterranean Sea on S coast of the island of Sardinia.

Cagnes–sur–Mer \ˌkan-(yə-)ˌsu̇(ə)r-ˈme(ə)r\. Commune, Alpes-Maritimes dept., SE France; pop. (1968c) 22,110; resort on the Riviera just W of Nice.

Ca·gra·ray \ˌkäg-rə-ˈrī\. Island, E Albay prov., Luzon, Phil., ab. 11 m. NE of Legaspi; 28 sq. m.; pop. (1960c) 10,000; lies bet. Lagonoy Gulf and Albay Gulf.

Ca·gua \ˈkäg-wə\. Town, Aragua state, N Venezuela; pop. (1961c) 16,233.

Cagua, Mount. Mountain of volcanic origin, NE Cagayan prov., Luzon, Phil., near N end of Sierra Madre range; 3927 ft.

Ca·guas \ˈkäg-ˌwäs\. Town and municipality, E cen. Puerto Rico; pop. (1970p) 62,807 (town), 94,959 (munic.); in fertile agricultural region.

Ca·ha·ba \kə-ˈhȯb-ə, -ˈhäb-\ *also* **Ca·haw·ba** \-ˈhȯb-\. River, cen. Alabama; ab. 200 m. long; rises in St. Clair co., flows S through coalfields into Alabama river in Dallas co. ab. 10 m. SW of Selma.

Ca·ho·kia \kə-ˈhō-kē-ə\. Village, St. Clair co., SW Illinois, just S of East St. Louis; pop. (1970c) 20,649; founded 1699 by the French, one of first permanent white settlements in Illinois. The **Cahokia Mounds,** a group of prehistoric Indian mounds including one which is the largest prehistoric earthwork in the U.S., are not in this village but are located ab. 4 m. NE of East St. Louis.

Ca·hors \kə-ˈ(h)ȯ(ə)r\ *or anc.* **Ca·dur·cum** \kə-ˈdər-kəm\ *or* **Di·vo·na** \ˈdīv-ə-nə, ˈdiv-\. City, ✱ of Lot dept., S cen. France, on Lot river 59 m. N of Toulouse; pop. (1968c) 19,203; episcopal see (from 4th cent.); 12th cent. cathedral; 14th cent. fortified bridge; episcopal palace (now prefecture). Important center of finance in Middle Ages; university (consolidated with Toulouse university 1751) founded 1322 by Pope John XXII, a native; under English rule 1360–1428.

Cahul. See KAGUL.

Cai·ba·rién \ˌkī-ˌbär-ˈyen\. Town and municipality, Las Villas prov., W cen. Cuba; pop. (town [1967e]) 26,400; port on N coast 30 m. E of Santa Clara.

Caicos Islands. See TURKS AND CAICOS ISLANDS.

Cai·cos Passage \ˌkā-kəs-\. Channel in the Bahama Is., West Indies, NW of Caicos Is.; ab. 45 m. wide.

Caieta. See GAETA.

Cail·lou Lake \ˈkā-(ˌ)lü-, kā-ˈlü-\. Lake in S Terrebonne parish, SE Louisiana; 5 m. long; **Grand Caillou Bayou** runs through the lake.

Cai·ma·ne·ra \ˌkī-mə-ˈne(ə)r-ə\. Commune on W side of Guantánamo Bay, SE Oriente prov., E Cuba; pop. (1965e) 8600.

Cainargeava–Mică. See KAYNARDZHA.

Caird Coast \ˈka(ə)rd-, ˈke(ə)rd-\. Ice-covered section of Antarctica, 76°S lat. and 23° to 29°W long., on SE coast of Weddell Sea NE of Luitpold Coast; part of Coats Land; included in British claim.

Cairn Eige \ˈka(ə)rn-ˈā, ˈke(ə)rn-\ *or* **Carn Eige** \ˈkärn-\. Peak, in S Ross and Cromarty co., NW Scotland; 3877 ft.

Cairn·gorm Mountains \ˈka(ə)rn-ˌgȯ(ə)rm-, ˈke(ə)rn-\. Range of the Grampians in NE cen. Scotland; highest peak Ben Macdhui, 4296 ft. high; includes **Cairngorm** 4084 ft., in W Banff co.; chief source of a smoky brown variety of quartz (cairngorm).

Cairn Hill \ˈka(ə)rn-\. Peak in the Cheviot Hills along the border bet. England and Scotland; 2545 ft.

Cairns \ˈka(ə)rnz, ˈke(ə)rnz\. Seaport, NE Queensland, Australia, on Trinity Bay; pop. (1968e) 27,400; on narrow lowland strip E of Atherton Plateau; outlet and supply center for agricultural and mining region; sugar, tobacco, timber; dairying; tin, fluorspar; tourism; founded 1876.

Cairn·toul *also* **Carn·toul** \kärn-ˈtül, -ˈtau̇l\. Peak, SW Aberdeen co., N cen. Scotland, in the Cairngorm group; 4241 ft.

Cai·ro \ˈke(ə)r-(ˌ)ō, ˈkā-(ˌ)rō\. 1 Industrial and commercial city, ⊗ of Grady co., SW Georgia, 50 m. S of Albany; pop. (1970c) 8061; sugarcane syrup; truck farms.

2 City, ⊗ of Alexander co., SW Illinois, at confluence of Ohio and Mississippi rivers; pop. (1970c) 6277; sawmills, flour mills; silica; port of entry; settled c. 1846; incorp. 1857; depot for Union military supplies during Civil War. The "Eden" of Charles Dickens's novel *Martin Chuzzlewit.*

Cairo \ˈkī-(ˌ)rō\. 1 Governorate of N Egypt. See 2, below, and table at EGYPT.

2 *or Arab.* **Al–Qā·hi·rah** \al-ˈkä-hē-ˌrȯ\. City, ✱ of Egypt, on right bank of Nile ab. 9 m. above division into two main branches of the delta; pop. (1970e) 4,961,000, met. area pop. 6,255,000; constitutes the governorate of Cairo; cement, chemicals, leather, textiles; food processing; largest city in Africa; several universities and colleges incl. Univ. of Cairo (1908), Museum of Islamic Art (1869), Egyptian Museum (1902); has ab. 250 mosques (many in ruins), esp. Sultan Hasan Mosque (c. 1361), Mohammed Ali Mosque, and Al-Azhar, one of main educational centers of Islam.

History: Near site of Roman city Babylon which was captured by Arabs 641 A.D.; Old Cairo (**Al–Fus·tāt** \ˌal-fu̇-ˈstät\) built by Arabs as military camp 642; new part (**Al–Qāhirah**) built by Fatimid dynasty (see EGYPT)

968 and made their capital 973, known as "City of Victory"; citadel erected in late 12th cent. by Saladin, ruler of Egypt and Syria at time of Third Crusade; while capital of Mameluke sultans (from 13th cent.), reached greatest prosperity as trade and cultural center; taken by Ottoman Turks 1517; held by French 1798–1801; capital of semi-independent pashalik (province) ruled by Mehemet Ali and of independent kingdom of Egypt (*q.v.*). British and U.S. base in North Africa campaign 1942. Site of conference Nov. 22–26, 1943 of President Roosevelt, Prime Minister Churchill, and Generalissimo Chiang Kai-shek; evacuated by British forces 1946.

Cairo, Mount \-ˈkī-(ˌ)rō\. Mountain dominating Monte Cassino, Italy, on NNW; 5474 ft.

Cai·ro·çu, Point \-ˌkī-rə-ˈsü\. Cape on S coast of Guanabara state, SE Brazil, S of Ilha Grande Bay.

Caiteté. See CAETITÉ.

Caith·ness \ˈkāth-ˌnes, kāth-ˈ\. County, N Scotland; area 686 sq. m.; pop. (1971p) 27,481; ⊗ Wick; oats, turnips; dairy cattle; fisheries; tourism.

Cai·va·no \kī-ˈvän-(ˌ)ō\. Commune, Napoli prov., Campania, S Italy, 8 m. NNE of Naples; pop. (1968e) 26,610; trade center for agricultural area; medieval fortified town.

Ca·ja·bam·ba \ˌkä-hə-ˈbäm-bə\. Town, Chimborazo prov., cen. Ecuador, 9 m. W of Riobamba.

Ca·ja·mar·ca *or formerly* **Ca·xa·mar·ca** \ˌkä-hə-ˈmär-kə\. 1 Department of N Peru. See table at PERU.
2 Town, its ✱, on **Cajamarca River,** ab. 370 m. NW of Lima; pop. (1969e) 27,600; alt. 8597 ft.; in mining region; textiles, leather goods; univ. (1962); hot sulfur springs (known as Baths of the Incas) nearby. Atahualpa, last of the Inca sovereigns, executed here by Pizarro 1533.

Ca·jon Pass \kə-ˌhōn-\. Pass bet. San Gabriel Mts. on W and San Bernardino Mts. on E, S California, N of San Bernardino and ENE of Los Angeles; southeastern gateway for overland travel to the coast since 1831.

Cal·a·bar \ˈkal-ə-ˌbär\. Town, ✱ of South-Eastern State, SE Nigeria, on left bank of **Calabar River** (flows into Cross estuary); pop. (1969e) 88,621; trades in palm oil and palm kernels.

Ca·la·ba·zar de Sa·gua \ˌka-lə-bə-ˌzär-də-ˈsä-gwə\. Town and municipality, Las Villas prov., W cen. Cuba, 15 m. N of Santa Clara; munic. pop. (1967e) 19,370.

Ca·la·bo·zo \ˌkal-ə-ˈbō-(ˌ)zō\. Town, Guárico state, N cen. Venezuela, 110 m. S of Caracas; pop. (1961c) 15,739; cattle and agricultural center in the llanos.

Calabrese, Appennino. See table at APENNINES.

Ca·la·bria \kə-ˈlā-brē-ə, kə-ˈläb-rē-ə\. 1 Region of ancient Italy, a peninsula now forming the S part of Apulia.
2 *or anc.* **Brut·ti·um** \ˈbrət-ē-əm\. Autonomous region, S Italy; 5822 sq. m.; pop. (1968e) 2,067,154; ✱ Catanzaro; consists of marshy coastal flatlands, well-watered and fertile valleys, and a central ridge of granite mountains; heavily forested; subject to severe earthquakes (disastrous ones having occurred 1783–87, 1905, 1908); citrus fruit; stock raising, quarrying.

History: Ancient Bruttium, founded as Greek colony, taken by Romans 268 B.C.; retaken in 9th cent. A.D. by Byzantine Empire; conquered by Normans under Robert Guiscard who became duke of Apulia and Calabria 1059; united to Norman kingdom of Naples and Sicily 11th cent. and with kingdom of Italy 1860; major land reforms carried out after 1951; held elections for regional parliament 1970.

Calabrian Apennines. See table at APENNINES.

Calae. See CHELLES.

Ca·la·fat \ˌkä-lə-ˈfät\. Town, Dolj co., S Romania, on the Danube opp. the Bulgarian city of Vidin; pop. (1966c) 14,507; founded in 14th cent. by colonists from Genoa who developed the ship-repairing industry and whose workmen (*calfats*) gave the town its name; later became grain-trading center; battleground during Russo-Turkish conflicts in 19th cent.

Calagurris. See CALAHORRA.

Ca·lah \ˈkā-lə\ *or mod.* **Nim·rud** \nim-ˈrüd\. Biblical name (*Gen.* x. 11,12) of **Ka·lhu** \ˈkal-(ˌ)(h)ü\, an ancient capital of Assyria, on E bank of Tigris river ab. 20 m. SSE of Mosul. Built probably in 13th cent. B.C.; under Ashurnasirpal II (884–859 B.C.) replaced Nineveh as capital and remained royal residence for 150 years.

Ca·la·ho·rra \ˌkäl-ə-ˈōr-ə\ *or anc.* **Cal·a·gur·ris** \ˌkal-ə-ˈgər-əs\. Commune, Logroño prov., N Spain, on right bank of Ebro 26 m. SE of Logroño; pop. (1970p) 16,340; trades in wine and cattle. Ancient town, Calagurris, taken by Pompey after four years' siege 76–72 B.C.

Cal·ais \ˈkal-əs\. City, Washington co., E Maine, on St. Croix river; pop. (1970c) 4044; port of entry, connected with St. Stephen, New Brunswick, Canada, by International Bridge.

Ca·lais \ka-ˈlā, ˈkal-(ˌ)ā\. Seaport and manufacturing city, Pas-de-Calais dept., N France, on Strait of Dover 64 m. NW of Arras; pop. (1968c) 74,624; lacemaking; chemicals, electrical equipment, paper; 18th cent. and modern town halls; Hôtel de Guise (founded by Edward III of England), Hôtel Dessin; barracks; technical schools. Town of old county of Artois taken 1347 by Edward III of England; after 1450 only remaining English possession in France; recaptured 1558 by duke of Guise; held by Spanish 1596–98; objective, together with Dunkerque, of famous German "drive to the sea" in World War I. In World War II taken by Germans May 22, 1940; launching base for robot bombs June 15–Sept. 1, 1944; surrounded by Canadian Army Sept. 6, 1944 and taken Sept. 30.

Cal·a·mar \ˌkal-ə-ˈmär\. Town, N Bolívar dept., N Colombia, on lower Magdalena river SE of Cartagena; munic. pop. (1964c) 17,985.

Ca·lam·ba \kə-ˈläm-bə\. Municipality on S shore of Laguna de Bay, W Laguna prov., Luzon, Phil.; pop. (1969e) 79,400; birthplace of José Rizal.

Ca·la·mian Islands \ˌkäl-ə-mē-ˌän-\ *or* **Ca·la·mia·nes** \ˌkal-ə-mē-ˈän-(ˌ)ās\. Island group, SW Phil., bet. Mindoro and Palawan Is.; 600 sq. m.; comprises 3 large islands Busuanga, Culion, and Coron, and ab. 95 small ones; part of Palawan prov. Mountainous and well forested; chief town Coron.

Calamine, La. See MORESNET.

Ca·lam·i·ty, Mount \-kə-ˈlam-ət-ē\. Peak in the Adirondack Mts., Essex co., NE New York; 3641 ft.

Cal·a·mus \ˈkal-ə-məs\. River, N cen. Nebraska; ab. 70 m. long; rises in Brown co., flows SE into North Loup river in Garfield co., cen. Nebraska.

Ca·la·ñas \kə-ˈlän-yəs\. Commune, Huelva prov., SW Spain, 32 m. N of Huelva; pop. (1970p) 7796.

Ca·lan·che \kə-ˈläŋ-kē\. Region on W cen. coast of Corsica, France; noted for its red granite formations.

Ca·la·pan \ˌkäl-ə-ˈpän\. Municipality, ✱ of Mindoro Oriental prov., Phil., on NE coast of Mindoro I. at E end of Verde Island Passage; pop. (1969e) 45,800.

Ca·la·pe \kə-ˈläp-ē\. Municipality, W coast of Bohol, Phil., on Bohol Strait N of Tagbilaran; pop. (1969e) 31,100.

Că·lă·ra·şi \kə-lə-ˈräsh(-ē)\. Town, Ialomiţa co., SE Romania, on the Danube ab. 63 m. ESE of Bucharest; pop. (1966c) 35,684; in region producing grapes and tobacco; fisheries.

Ca·lar·cá \ˌkä-lər-ˈkä\. Town, Quindío dept., W cen. Colombia; munic. pop. (1968e) 55,934.

Ca·la·si·ao \ˌkä-lə-sē-ˈaů\. Municipality, cen. Pangasinan prov., Luzon, Phil.; on a branch of the Agno 7 m. E of Lingayen; pop. (1969e) 40,200; hat industry.

Ca·la·ta·fi·mi \kə-ˌlä-tə-ˈfē-mē\. Commune, Trapani prov., NW Sicily, Italy, 21 m. ESE of Trapani; pop. (1968e) 9627; site of Garibaldi's defeat May 15, 1860 of Neapolitans.

Ca·la·ta·gan \ˌkäl-ə-tə-ˈgän\. Municipality on SW coast of Batangas prov., Luzon, Phil.; pop. (1969e) 19,900.

Ca·la·ta·yud \ˌkäl-ə-tə-ˈyüd\. Commune, Zaragoza prov., NE Spain, 45 m. SW of Saragossa; pop. (1970p) 17,217; trade center; sulfur baths; ruins of Moorish forts. Founded in 8th cent.; conquered 1120 by Alfonso I of Aragon.

Birthplace of the Latin epigrammatist Martial 2 m. E at ancient **Bil·bi·lis** \ˈbil-bə-ləs\.

Ca·la·tra·va \ˌkäl-ə-ˈträ-və\. 1 Municipality, NE coast of Negros Occidental prov., Negros, Phil., on Tanon Strait 36 m. E of city of Bacolod; pop. (1969e) 89,700.

2 Ancient fortress, cen. Spain, just ENE of Ciudad Real near Guadiana river; defended against Moors by two Cistercians who presented it to Sancho III of Castile 1158 and instituted Order of Calatrava; captured by Moors 1197, retaken 1212; taken over by Order of Alcántara 1218 when Order of Calatrava built new convent ab. 8 m. S (New Calatrava); only a tower now on site.

Ca·lau·ag \ˌkäl-ə-ˈwäg\. Municipality, Quezon prov., Luzon, Phil.; pop. (1969e) 51,200.

Cal·a·ver·as \ˌkal-ə-ˈver-əs\. 1 River, cen. California; ab. 70 m. long; flows SW into San Joaquin river.

2 County in California. See table at CALIFORNIA.

Ca·la·vi·te, Cape \-ˌkäl-ə-ˈvē-(ˌ)tā\. Northwest point of Mindoro I., Phil., 13°26′N, 120°18′E; just to the E is **Mount Calavite,** 4990 ft.

Ca·la·yan \ˌkäl-ə-ˈyän\. Island in Babuyan group, N of Luzon, Phil.; 73 sq. m.

Cal·ba·yog \käl-ˈbä-ˌyȯg\. Chartered city, W Samar, Phil., on Samar Sea 29 m. NW of Catbalogan; pop. (1970e) 109,000.

Cal·be \ˈkäl-bə\ *or* **Calbe an der Saa·le** \-än-dər-ˈzäl-ə\. City, Magdeburg dist., East Germany, on Saale river 16 m. S of Magdeburg; pop. (1970e) 16,296; electronic equipment, pharmaceuticals; iron work; founded 12th cent.; to Brandenburg 1680.

Cal·ca·sieu \ˈkal-kə-ˌshü\. 1 River, SW Louisiana; ab. 200 m. long; rises in N Vernon parish, flows in wide curve E, SE, and SW, through **Calcasieu Lake** (ab. 15 m. long, in Cameron parish, surrounded by marshes which cover almost entire parish), and into Gulf of Mexico through **Calcasieu Pass** (ab. 5 m. long).

2 Parish in Louisiana. See table at LOUISIANA.

Cal·ce·ta \käl-ˈsā-tə\. Town, Manabí prov., W Ecuador, 100 m. N of Guayaquil.

Calchi. See KHALKĒ.

Cal·cut·ta \kal-ˈkət-ə\. City, ❋ of West Bengal, NE India, on Hooghly river ab. 90 m. from its mouth; pop. (1970e) 3,158,838, met. area pop. 5,100,000; ❋ of former Bengal province and Presidency Division and, until 1912, seat of government of India. Has one of world's most active ports; exports jute and jute manufactures, tea, hides, iron and manganese ores; chemical and glass works, rice mills; Univ. of Calcutta (1857), Jadavpur Univ. (1955), Rabindra Bharati Univ. (1962). Has fine maidan or park (2 sq. m.) which contains Fort William; Jain temple, botanical garden, government buildings.

History: English factory established by Job Charnock on site 1690; Fort William erected 1696; seat of Bengal presidency 1707; captured by Siraj-ud-daula, nawab of Bengal, who imprisoned English (Black Hole of Calcutta) 1756; retaken by Clive 1757; capital of British India 1773–1912 (see DELHI).

Cal·das \ˈkäl-dəs\. Department of W cen. Colombia. See table at COLOMBIA.

Cal·dei·ra \käl-ˈdeɪ-rə\. Mountain peak on Faial I. in the Azores; 3350 ft.

Cal·der \ˈkȯl-dər\. 1 River in Lancashire, NW England; 15 m. long; flows into the Ribble river.

2 River in N cen. England, in SW Yorkshire; flows NE into the Aire river at Castleford below Leeds.

Cal·de·ra \käl-ˈder-ə\. Seaport and commune, Atacama prov., N cen. Chile, ab. 40 m. NW of Copiapó; pop. (1960c) 2715; chief port of province and the port of Copiapó (54 m. by rail); exports nitrate and copper.

Cal·die·ro \käld-ˈyer-(ˌ)ō\. Commune, Verona prov., SW Veneto, NE Italy; pop. (1968e) 3428; scene of battles of Napoleonic Wars in which Masséna defeated the Austrians under Archduke Charles Louis Oct. 30, 1805 but was defeated Nov. 12, 1805.

Çal·di·ran \ˌchäl-də-ˈrän\ *or* **Chal·di·ran** \ˌchäl-\ *or* **Chal·dran** \chäl-ˈdrän\. Town, Turkey, S of Kars; battle Aug. 23, 1514 in which Selim I, Ottoman sultan, defeated Persians.

Cald·well \ˈkȯl-ˌdwel, -dwəl, ˈkäl-\. 1 Name of a parish in Louisiana and of counties in four states of the U.S. See tables at KENTUCKY, LOUISIANA, MISSOURI, NORTH CAROLINA, TEXAS.

2 City, ⊗ of Canyon co., SW Idaho, 25 m. W of Boise; pop. (1970c) 14,219; poultry; stockyards; Coll. of Idaho (1891).

3 City, Sumner co., S Kansas, 33 m. W of Arkansas City; pop. (1970c) 1540; in grazing and wheat region.

4 Borough, Essex co., NE New Jersey, 9 m. NNW of Newark; pop. (1970c) 8719; birthplace of Grover Cleveland.

5 Village, ⊗ of Noble co., SE Ohio, 21 m. N of Marietta; pop. (1970c) 2082; coal mines, oil wells, salt mines.

6 City, ⊗ of Burleson co., E cen. Texas, 20 m. SW of Bryan; pop. (1970c) 2308; manufactures cottonseed oil.

Cal·dy Island *or* **Cal·dey Island** \ˌkäl-de-\. Island, S Wales; at W entrance to Carmarthen Bay; lighthouse; site of 15th cent. monastery at which St. David was a scholar; ancient stone inscribed in ogham and Latin.

Cal·e·don \ˈkal-ə-dən\. 1 River in SE Africa; 240 m. long; rises in the Drakensberg mountain range near the NW boundary of Natal, E Rep. of South Africa, flows WSW forming the boundary bet. Orange Free State and Lesotho, and empties into Orange river.

2 Town, SW Cape Province, S Rep. of South Africa, 70 m. E of Cape Town; pop. (1967e) 4300; thermal springs.

Cal·e·do·nia \ˌkal-ə-ˈdō-nyə, -nē-a\. 1 County in Vermont. See table at VERMONT.

2 Village, ⊗ of Houston co., SE corner of Minnesota, 30 m. S of Winona; pop. (1970c) 2619; agricultural trade center.

3 Town, Haldimand co., SE Ontario, Canada, 13 m. SSW of Hamilton; pop. (1971p) 3184; diversified agriculture; gypsum mines.

4 Ancient name for N Britain; Scotland.

Cal·e·do·nian Canal \ˌkal-ə-ˈdō-nyən-, -ˈdō-nē-ən-\. Ship canal extending diagonally across N Scotland from Loch Linnhe on the SW to Moray Firth on the NE; built by uniting lochs Ness, Oich, Lochy, and Eli with a navigable channel; begun 1805, opened 1822, completed 1847; 60½ m. long, including 22 m. of channel construction and 38½ m. in the lochs; 110 ft. wide at water surface; has 28 locks with an average lift of 8 ft.

Ca·le·ra \kə-ˈler-ə\. Town, Valparaíso prov., cen. Chile, ab. 40 m. NE of Valparaíso; pop. (1960c) 18,134.

Ca·lex·i·co \kə-ˈlek-si-ˌkō, ka-\. City, Imperial co., S California, on Mexican border adjacent to Mexicali, Mexico; pop. (1970c) 10,625; fruit and cotton.

Calf of Man. See MAN, CALF OF.

Cal·ga·ry \ˈkal-gə-rē\. City, S Alberta, Canada, on Bow river; pop. (1971p) 400,154; trading center of an extensive stock raising and wheat region; gas and oil wells nearby; grist and flour mills, grain elevators, brick and cement works, lumber mills, oil refineries, and packing houses; railroad shops. Provincial Institute of Technology and Art (1916), Univ. of Calgary (1945, reorganized 1966). Begun as a fort of the Northwest Mounted Police 1875; city charter 1893; city government reorganized 1952.

Cal·houn \kal-ˈhün\. 1 Name of counties in eleven states of the U.S. See tables at ALABAMA, ARKANSAS, FLORIDA, GEORGIA, ILLINOIS, IOWA, MICHIGAN, MISSISSIPPI, SOUTH CAROLINA, TEXAS, WEST VIRGINIA.

2 City, ⊗ of Gordon co., NW Georgia, 22 m. NNE of Rome; pop. (1970c) 4748; cotton mills, lumber; incorp. 1852; largely destroyed by Sherman 1864 but rebuilt.

3 City, ⊗ of McLean co., W Kentucky; pop. (1970c) 901.

Calhoun Falls. Town, Abbeville co., W South Carolina, 27 m. WSW of Greenwood; pop. (1970c) 2234.

Ca·li \ˈkäl-ē\. City, ✻ of Valle dept., W Colombia; pop. (1971e) 950,500; alt. 3327 ft.; bisected by Cali river; connected by rail with port of Buenaventura 105 m. to W; center of valley trade, esp. livestock, lumber, and mineral products; univ. (1945); founded 1536.

Caliacra, Cape. See KALIAKRA, CAPE.

Ca·li·an Point *also* **Ka·li·an Point** \ˌkä-lē-ˈän-\. Cape on SW coast of Davao del Sur prov., Mindanao, Phil.

Cal·i·cut \ˈkal-i-(ˌ)kət\ *also* **Ko·zhi·kode** \ˈkō-zhə-ˌkōd\. City, cen. Kerala, S India, on the Malabar Coast 170 m. SW of Bangalore; pop. (1970e) 330,225; exports coconuts, coffee, tea, spices; gave its name to the cloth *calico;* several colleges.

History: Visited by Vasco da Gama 1498; unsuccessfully attacked by Albuquerque 1510; site of Portuguese fortified factory 1513–25 (abandoned); visited by British 1615; site of trading posts of British (estab. 1664), French (estab. 1698), Danish (1752–84); occupied by British troops 1790; transferred by treaty to British 1792.

Cal·i·en·te \ˌkal-i-ˈen-tē\. City, Lincoln co., E Nevada, ab. 23 m. S of Pioche; pop. (1970c) 916.

Cal·i·for·nia \ˌkal-ə-ˈfȯr-nyə, -nē-ə\. 1 A western state of U.S.A., bounded on N by Oregon, on E by Nevada and Arizona, on S by Mexican state of Baja California, and on W by the Pacific Ocean; 3d state in area, 158,693 sq. m. (land area 156,537 sq. m.); 1st state in population, (1970c) 19,953,134; ✻ Sacramento; 31st state admitted to Union (1850).

Nicknames: Golden State, also El Dorado. *State flower:* Golden poppy. *Motto:* Eureka (I Have Found It). *Rivers:* Colorado, forming border in extreme SE with Arizona; Sacramento, flowing from near Mt. Shasta into San Francisco Bay; Pit, a tributary of the Sacramento; San Joaquin, flowing NW from Sierra Nevada area to join the Sacramento. *Chief lakes:* Tahoe in E on Nevada border, Owens in SE, and Salton Sea in Imperial Valley in extreme S. *Mts.:* Coast Ranges, in two parts, broken by San Francisco Bay and extending along most of the coast; a higher range, Sierra Nevada, extends along E border and contains Mt. Whitney, highest peak in state 14,494 ft., and at N end Mt. Shasta 14,162 ft.; in this range are Yosemite and Sequoia National Parks, Lassen Peak, and Lassen Volcanic National Park; at its S end is Death Valley, a National Monument and lowest spot in U.S., and Mojave and Colorado deserts. *Chief products:* Vegetables, fruit, cotton, rice; oil, natural gas, lead, magnesium, gypsum; manufacturing: transportation equipment (esp. aircraft and parts), electrical machinery; lumber; food processing; film industry; tourism; has important irrigation systems. *Chief cities:* Los Angeles, San Francisco, San Diego, San Jose, Oakland, Long Beach, Sacramento.

See *Table of States* at UNITED STATES. Divided into the following 58 counties (for pronunciations, see their individual entries):

NAME	LOCATION	AREA[1] (sq. m.)	POP. (1970c)	CO. SEAT
Alameda	W	733	1,073,184	Oakland
Alpine	E	723	484	Markleeville
Amador	cen.	593	11,821	Jackson
Butte	N	1,668	101,969	Oroville
Calaveras	cen.	1,032	13,585	San Andreas
Colusa	N cen.	1,152	12,430	Colusa
Contra Costa	W	733	558,805	Martinez
Del Norte[2]	NW corner; coastal	1,007	14,580	Crescent City
El Dorado	E	1,726	43,833	Placerville
Fresno[3]	S cen.	5,968	413,329	Fresno
Glenn	N	1,319	17,521	Willows
Humboldt[2]	NW; coastal	3,586	99,692	Eureka
Imperial[4]	SE corner	4,241	74,492	El Centro
Inyo[5]	E	10,130	15,571	Independence
Kern	S	8,152	329,271	Bakersfield
Kings	SW cen.	1,396	66,717	Hanford
Lake	W	1,261	19,548	Lakeport
Lassen[6]	NE	4,561	16,796	Susanville
Los Angeles[7]	SW; coastal	4,069	7,036,887	Los Angeles
Madera[8]	cen.	2,145	41,519	Madera
Marin	W; coastal	520	206,758	San Rafael
Mariposa[9]	cen.	1,453	6,015	Mariposa
Mendocino	W; coastal	3,511	51,101	Ukiah
Merced	cen.	1,981	104,629	Merced
Modoc	NE corner	4,097	7,469	Alturas
Mono	E	3,027	4,016	Bridgeport
Monterey	W; coastal	3,324	247,450	Salinas
Napa	W cen.	787	79,140	Napa
Nevada	E	975	26,346	Nevada City
Orange	SW; coastal	782	1,420,248	Santa Ana
Placer	E	1,433	77,632	Auburn
Plumas	NE	2,569	11,707	Quincy
Riverside	SE	7,176	459,074	Riverside
Sacramento	N cen.	975	634,190	Sacramento
San Benito	W	1,397	18,226	Hollister
San Bernardino[10]	SE	20,119	681,535	San Bernardino
San Diego	SW corner; coastal	4,262	1,357,854	San Diego
San Francisco[11]	W; coastal	45	715,674	San Francisco
San Joaquin	cen.	1,415	289,564	Stockton
San Luis Obispo	SW; coastal	3,184	105,690	San Luis Obispo
San Mateo	W; coastal	447	556,601	Redwood City
Santa Barbara[12]	SW; coastal	2,738	264,324	Santa Barbara
Santa Clara	W	1,300	1,066,421	San Jose
Santa Cruz	W; coastal	440	123,790	Santa Cruz
Shasta[13]	N	3,793	77,640	Redding
Sierra	NE	958	2,365	Downieville
Siskiyou	N	6,264	33,225	Yreka
Solano	cen.	826	171,815	Fairfield
Sonoma	W; coastal	1,604	204,885	Santa Rosa
Stanislaus	cen.	1,511	194,506	Modesto
Sutter	N cen.	603	41,935	Yuba City
Tehama	N	2,984	29,517	Red Bluff
Trinity	NW	3,192	7,615	Weaverville
Tulare[14]	S cen.	4,844	188,322	Visalia
Tuolumne[15]	cen.	2,279	22,169	Sonora
Ventura[16]	SW; coastal	1,863	378,497	Ventura
Yolo	N cen.	1,028	91,788	Woodland
Yuba	N cen.	640	44,736	Marysville

[1]Area = land area.
[2]Contains part of Redwood National Park.
[3]SE part occupied by Kings Canyon National Park.
[4]Contains Imperial Valley and (in NW) most of Salton Sea, both below sea level.
[5]Death Valley in E and S.
[6]Part of Lassen Volcanic National Park in SW.
[7]Includes Santa Catalina and San Clemente Is., separated from mainland by San Pedro Channel.
[8]Part of Yosemite National Park in NE.
[9]E portion occupied by part of Yosemite National Park.
[10]Largest county in U.S.
[11]Coextensive with city of San Francisco.
[12]Includes northernmost group of Santa Barbara Is. (San Miguel, Santa Rosa, and Santa Cruz), separated from mainland by Santa Barbara Channel.
[13]SE corner contains part of Lassen Volcanic National Park, including Lassen Peak.
[14]NE portion contains Sequoia National Park.
[15]SE portion occupied by part of Yosemite National Park.
[16]Includes small islands of central part of chain of Santa Barbara Islands.

History: Coast explored by voyage of Cabrillo and Ferrelo who established Spanish claim to region 1542–43; coast reached by Sir Francis Drake 1579; first Franciscan mission established at San Diego 1769; remained under Spanish control, and later under Mexican control until conquered by U.S. forces during Mexican War (1846–47); ceded to U.S. by Treaty of Guadalupe Hidalgo 1848; settlement by Americans begun in 1841, greatly accelerated after discovery of gold at Coloma (Sutter's Mill) in 1848 which brought influx of miners and adventurers (the "forty-niners"); admitted to Union Sept. 9, 1850 as a free state under Compromise Act; present constitution drawn up by constitutional convention Sept. 28, 1878–Mar. 3, 1879, ratified by people, and in force Jan. 1, 1880; large sections of San Francisco destroyed by fire following an earthquake 1906.

2 City, ⊗ of Moniteau co., cen. Missouri, 22 m. W of Jefferson City; pop. (1970c) 3105; dairy farms.

3 Borough, Washington co., SW Pennsylvania, on Monongahela river 15 m. NW of Uniontown; pop. (1970c) 6635; coal mining; California State Coll. (1852).

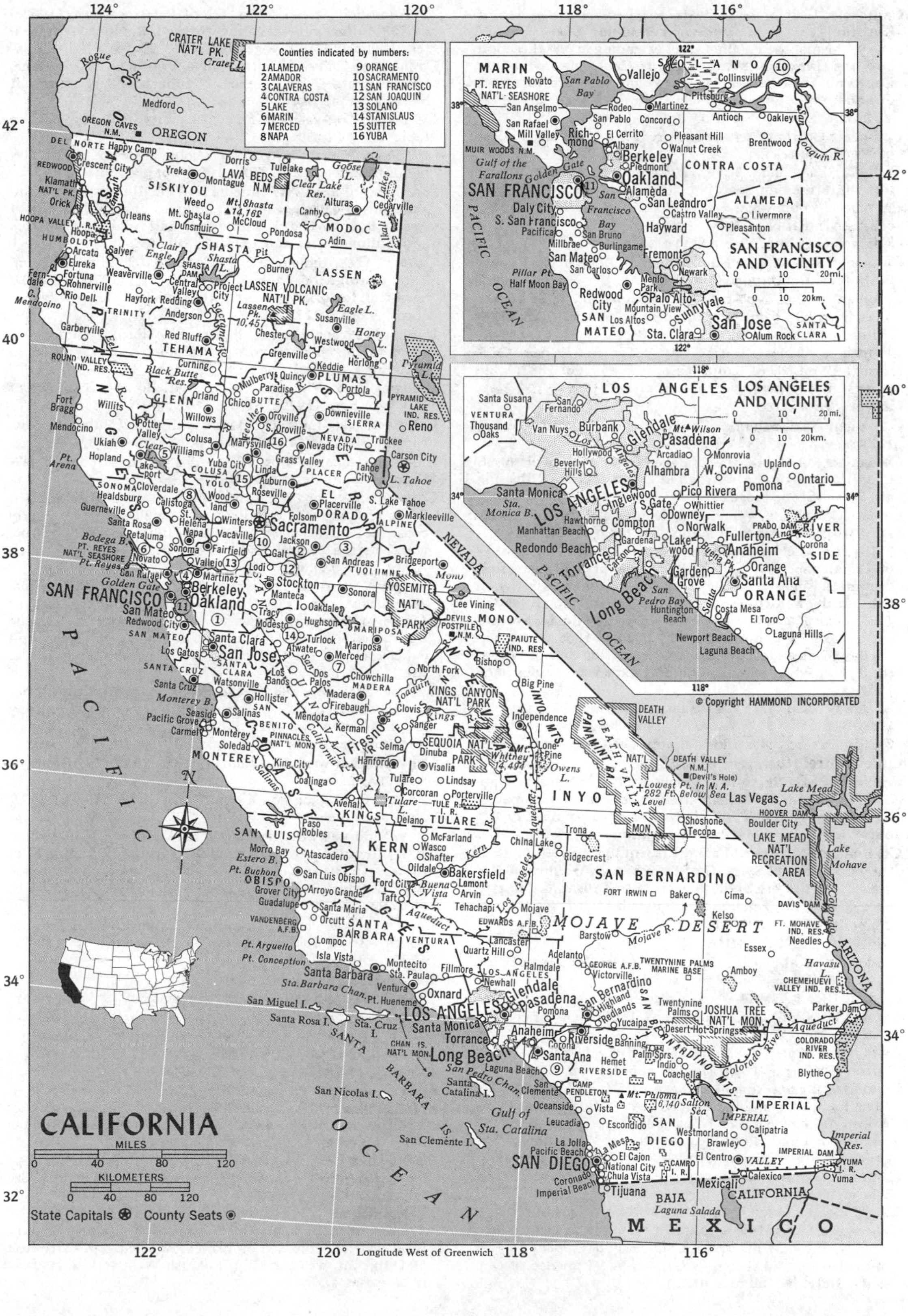
CALIFORNIA
MILES
0 40 80 120
KILOMETERS
0 40 80 120
State Capitals County Seats
Longitude West of Greenwich
124° 122° 120° 118° 116°
42° 40° 38° 36° 34° 32°
Counties indicated by numbers:
1 ALAMEDA
2 AMADOR
3 CALAVERAS
4 CONTRA COSTA
5 LAKE
6 MARIN
7 MERCED
8 NAPA
9 ORANGE
10 SACRAMENTO
11 SAN FRANCISCO
12 SAN JOAQUIN
13 SOLANO
14 STANISLAUS
15 SUTTER
16 YUBA
CRATER LAKE NAT'L PK.
OREGON CAVES N.M.
OREGON
Medford
DEL NORTE
Happy Camp
Crescent City
REDWOOD NAT'L PK.
Klamath
Orick
HOOPA VALLEY I.R.
Hoopa
HUMBOLDT
Arcata
Eureka
Fortuna
Ferndale
Rohnerville
Rio Dell
C. Mendocino
SISKIYOU
Yreka
Montague
Dorris
Weed
Mt. Shasta
Dunsmuir
McCloud
Mt. Shasta 14,162
LAVA BEDS N.M.
Tulelake
Clear Lake Res.
Goose L.
Alturas
Canby
Cedarville
MODOC
Adin
Pondosa
Orleans
Salyer
Weaverville
SHASTA
Shasta L.
Redding
Anderson
Central Valley
Project City
Burney
Hayfork
TRINITY
LASSEN
LASSEN VOLCANIC NAT'L PK.
Lassen Pk. 10,457
Eagle L.
Susanville
Chester
Westwood
Honey L.
Garberville
Red Bluff
TEHAMA
ROUND VALLEY IND. RES.
Corning
Black Butte Res.
Greenville
Keddie
Horlong
Pyramid L.
PYRAMID LAKE IND. RES.
Quincy
PLUMAS
Portola
GLENN
Orland
Willows
Chico
BUTTE
Paradise
Oroville
Downieville
SIERRA
Reno
Fort Bragg
Willits
Mendocino
Ukiah
Potter Valley
Colusa
Williams
Marysville
Nevada City
Grass Valley
Truckee
Carson City
Pt. Arena
Hopland
Lakeport
Yuba City
COLUSA
YOLO
Lincoln
PLACER
Tahoe City
L. Tahoe
Auburn
SONOMA
Healdsburg
Cloverdale
Woodland
Roseville
EL DORADO
Placerville
S. Lake Tahoe
Markleeville
ALPINE
Guerneville
Santa Rosa
Calistoga
St. Helena
Napa
Winters
Vacaville
Folsom
Sacramento
Petaluma
Bodega B.
PT. REYES NAT'L SEASHORE
Pt. Reyes
Sonoma
Fairfield
Jackson
Galt
Novato
Vallejo
Lodi
San Andreas
Bridgeport
San Rafael
Golden Gate
Martinez
Stockton
TUOLUMNE
Mono L.
SAN FRANCISCO
Berkeley
Oakland
Manteca
Sonora
YOSEMITE NAT'L PARK
Lee Vining
MONO
San Mateo
Redwood City
SAN MATEO
Tracy
Oakdale
Modesto
Hughson
Turlock
MARIPOSA
DEVILS POSTPILE N.M.
Santa Clara
San Jose
Los Gatos
SANTA CRUZ
Santa Cruz
SANTA CLARA
Atwater
Merced
Mariposa
PAIUTE IND. RES.
Bishop
Watsonville
Los Banos
Dos Palos
Chowchilla
MADERA
North Fork
Monterey B.
Hollister
Madera
Firebaugh
KINGS CANYON NAT'L PARK
Big Pine
Seaside
Salinas
Mendota
Clovis
Pacific Grove
Carmel
Monterey
SAN BENITO
Kerman
Fresno
Sanger
Independence
INYO MTS.
DEATH VALLEY
PANAMINT RA.
Soledad
PINNACLES NAT'L MON.
Selma
SEQUOIA NAT'L PARK
Mt. Whitney 14,494
Lone Pine
Owens L.
MONTEREY
King City
Hanford
Dinuba
Visalia
Coalinga
Tulare
Lindsay
Corcoran
Porterville
INYO
DEATH VALLEY N.M. (Devil's Hole)
Lowest Pt. in N. A. 282 Ft. Below Sea Level
Las Vegas
Lake Mead
Avenal
KINGS
Tulare L.
TULE R. I. R.
Delano
TULARE
HOOVER DAM
Boulder City
LAKE MEAD NAT'L RECREATION AREA
Shoshone
Tecopa
SAN LUIS OBISPO
Paso Robles
McFarland
Wasco
KERN
Shafter
Trona
China Lake
Ridgecrest
Morro Bay
Estero B.
Atascadero
Pt. Buchon
San Luis Obispo
Oildale
Bakersfield
Lamont
Arvin
SAN BERNARDINO
FORT IRWIN
Baker
Cima
Kelso
Lake Mohave
Grover City
Arroyo Grande
Guadalupe
Santa Maria
Orcutt
Ford City
Taft
Buena Vista L.
Tehachapi
Mojave
DAVIS DAM
VANDENBERG A.F.B.
SANTA BARBARA
EDWARDS A.F.B.
MOJAVE DESERT
FT. MOHAVE IND. RES.
Needles
Pt. Arguello
Pt. Conception
Lompoc
VENTURA
Lancaster
Barstow
Mojave R.
Essex
Quartz Hill
Palmdale
Adelanto
GEORGE A.F.B.
Victorville
TWENTYNINE PALMS MARINE BASE
Amboy
Isla Vista
Montecito
Santa Barbara
Sta. Paula
Fillmore
LOS ANGELES
Newhall
Havasu L.
CHEMEHUEVI VALLEY IND. RES.
ARIZONA
Sta. Barbara Chan.
Ventura
Oxnard
Pt. Hueneme
Glendale
Pasadena
San Bernardino
Highland
Redlands
Twentynine Palms
JOSHUA TREE NAT'L MON.
Parker Dam
San Miguel I.
Santa Rosa I.
Sta. Cruz I.
LOS ANGELES
Pomona
Yucaipa
Desert Hot Springs
Aqueduct
Santa Monica
Torrance
Anaheim
Riverside
Corona
Banning
Palm Sprs.
Indio
COLORADO RIVER IND. RES.
Blythe
Colorado River
CHAN. IS. NAT'L MON.
Long Beach
Santa Ana
Hemet
RIVERSIDE
Coachella
San Pedro Chan.
Laguna Beach
Santa Catalina I.
San Clemente
CAMP PENDLETON
Mt. Palomar 6,140
Salton Sea
IMPERIAL
San Nicolas I.
Oceanside
Vista
Escondido
SAN DIEGO
Gulf of Sta. Catalina
Leucadia
Westmorland
Calipatria
Brawley
Imperial Res.
San Clemente I.
La Jolla
Pacific Beach
La Mesa
El Cajon
El Centro
VALLEY
IMPERIAL DAM
SAN DIEGO
National City
Chula Vista
Coronado
Imperial Beach
CAMPO I. R.
Calexico
YUMA I. R.
Yuma
Tijuana
Mexicali
BAJA CALIFORNIA
Laguna Salada
MEXICO
PACIFIC OCEAN
SANTA BARBARA IS.
COAST RANGES
SIERRA NEVADA
SAN JOAQUIN VALLEY
CASCADE RANGE
SAN BERNARDINO MTS.
MARIN
PT. REYES NAT'L SEASHORE
Novato
San Pablo Bay
Vallejo
SOLANO
Collinsville
Pittsburg
San Anselmo
Rodeo
Martinez
Antioch
Oakley
San Rafael
Mill Valley
San Pablo
Concord
Richmond
El Cerrito
Pleasant Hill
MUIR WOODS N.M.
Albany
Walnut Creek
Brentwood
Gulf of the Farallons
Golden Gate
Berkeley
Piedmont
CONTRA COSTA
Oakland
Alameda
ALAMEDA
San Leandro
Daly City
S. San Francisco
Castro Valley
Livermore
Pacifica
San Bruno
Hayward
Pleasanton
Millbrae
Burlingame
SAN FRANCISCO AND VICINITY
0 10 20 mi.
0 10 20 km.
San Mateo
Fremont
Newark
San Carlos
Pillar Pt.
Half Moon Bay
Menlo Park
Redwood City
Palo Alto
Mountain View
Sunnyvale
SAN MATEO
Los Altos
Sta. Clara
San Jose
Alum Rock
SANTA CLARA
PACIFIC OCEAN
LOS ANGELES
LOS ANGELES AND VICINITY
0 10 20 mi.
0 10 20 km.
Santa Susana
San Fernando
VENTURA
Thousand Oaks
Van Nuys
Burbank
Glendale
Mt. Wilson
Pasadena
Hollywood
Arcadia
Monrovia
Beverly Hills
Alhambra
W. Covina
Upland
Ontario
Pomona
Santa Monica
Sta. Monica B.
LOS ANGELES
Inglewood
Pico Rivera
S. Gate
Whittier
Hawthorne
Downey
Manhattan Beach
Compton
Norwalk
PRADO DAM
RIVERSIDE
Redondo Beach
Gardena
Fullerton
Corona
Lakewood
Anaheim
Torrance
Carson
Orange
Garden Grove
Santa Ana
ORANGE
Long Beach
San Pedro Bay
Huntington Beach
Costa Mesa
El Toro
Laguna Hills
Newport Beach
Laguna Beach
PACIFIC OCEAN
© Copyright HAMMOND INCORPORATED

California, Gulf of *or in Mexico sometimes called* **Sea of Cor·tés** \-'kȯr-ˌtez\; *formerly* **Ver·mil·ion Sea** \vər-'mil-yən-\. Arm of the Pacific Ocean extending in NW direction bet. the Mexican state of Baja California and Baja California Sur (territory) on the W and the Mexican states of Sonora and Sinaloa on the E; ab. 59,000 sq. m.

California, Lower. See BAJA CALIFORNIA.

California Current. An ocean current flowing S off W coast of North America.

Ca·li·ma \kə-'lē-mə\. River, W Colombia; ab. 50 m. long; flows into the San Juan N of Buenaventura.

Cal·i·mere, Point \-'kal-ə-ˌmi(ə)r\. Cape, E Tamil Nadu, SE coast of India, N of Palk Strait.

Calimno *or* **Calino.** See KALYMNOS.

Ca·li·nog \ˌkäl-ə-'nȯg\. Municipality, N Iloilo prov., Panay, Phil., N of Iloilo; pop. (1969e) 40,900.

Cal·i·pa·tria \ˌkal-ə-'pā-trē-ə\. City, Imperial co., SE corner of California, 26 m. N of El Centro; pop. (1970c) 1824; cotton, tomatoes.

Cal·i·sto·ga \ˌkal-ə-'stō-gə\. City, Napa co., W cen. California, 12 m. NE of Santa Rosa; pop. (1970c) 1882; wine grapes; hot springs and geysers; settled 1859.

Calivo. See KALIBO.

Cal·la·han \'kal-ə-ˌhan\. County in Texas. See table at TEXAS.

Cal·lan·der \'kal-ən-dər\. Village, Parry Sound dist., SE Ontario, Canada, on railroad at E end of Lake Nipissing ab. 7 m. SSE of North Bay.

Cal·lao \kə-'yä-(ˌ)ō, -'yau̇\. 1 Constitutional province of W Peru with departmental status. See table at PERU.

2 City, its ✱, chief seaport of Peru on Callao Bay 8 m. W of Lima; pop. (1970e) 335,400; metallurgical industries; breweries, sugar refineries; exports incl. minerals, wool, fish meal; well-equipped maritime terminal. Founded 1537, incorp. as a town 1671; destroyed by tidal wave and earthquake 1746; bombarded by Spanish 1866, and again 1880 by Chilean forces who took possession during War of the Pacific (1879–84); major port expansion undertaken 1958.

Cal·la·way \'kal-ə-ˌwā\. 1 County in Missouri. See table at MISSOURI.

2 City, Bay co., NW Florida; pop. (1970c) 3240.

Calleva Atrebatum. See SILCHESTER.

Cal·lic·u·la \kə-'lik-yə-lə\. Mountain, N of Capua and ab. 4 m. NE of Teanum Sidicinum (*or mod.* Teano), Campania, Italy; here Hannibal on his way back to Apulia 217 B.C. outwitted Fabius Maximus Cunctator.

Cal·li·ni·cum \ˌkal-ə-'nī-kəm\. Ancient town on left bank of the Euphrates, N Syria, S of Edessa; on E frontier of Roman Empire in 6th and 7th cents. A.D.; Belisarius defeated here 531 by the Persian king Kavadh I.

Callipolis. See GELİBOLU.

Callithea. See KALLITHÉA.

Cal·lo·way \'kal-ə-ˌwā\. County in Kentucky. See table at KENTUCKY.

Calmar. See KALMAR.

Cal·no \'kal-(ˌ)nō\ *or* **Cal·neh** \-nə\. Biblical city of N Syria (*Isa.* x. 9).

Ca·lo·o·can \ˌkal-ə-'ō-ˌkän\. Chartered city, NW Rizal prov., Luzon, Phil., just N of Manila; pop. (1970e) 206,600.

Ca·loo·sa·hatch·ee \kə-ˌlü-sə-'hach-ē\. River, S Florida; ab. 75 m. long; rises in Glades co., S cen. Florida penin., flows W into Gulf of Mexico below Fort Myers; connected by canal with Lake Hicpochee, constitutes W portion of the Cross-Florida Waterway (*q.v.*).

Ca·lo·re \kə-'lōr-ē, -'lȯr-\ *or anc.* **Ca·lor** \'kā-ˌlȯ(ə)r\. River, E headstream of the Volturno, S Italy.

Calpe. See PILLARS OF HERCULES; GIBRALTAR, ROCK OF.

Cal·ta·gi·ro·ne \ˌkäl-tə-ji-'rō-nē\. Commune, Catania prov., E Sicily, Italy, 37 m. SW of Catania; pop. (1968e) 43,455.

Cal·ta·nis·set·ta \ˌkäl-tə-ni-'set-ə, ˌkal-\. 1 Province of cen. Sicily, Italy. See table at ITALY.

2 Commune, its ✱, 59 m. SE of Palermo; pop. (1968e) 64,402; sulfur; mineral springs; cathedral; Norman monastery (built 1154 by Roger II).

Ca·luire–et–Cuire \'kal-ˌwi(ə)r-ā-'kwi(ə)r\. Commune, Rhône dept., E cen. France, N suburb of Lyons on left bank of Saône river.

Cal·u·met \'kal-yə-ˌmet, -mət\. 1 County in Wisconsin. See table at WISCONSIN.

2 Village, Houghton co., NW Michigan penin., 70 m. NW of Marquette; pop. (1970c) 1007; copper mines.

3 Industrial area, NW Indiana and NE Illinois, SE of and adjacent to Chicago, Illinois; includes chiefly the cities of East Chicago, Gary, Hammond, and Whiting, Indiana, and Calumet City and Lansing, Illinois.

Calumet City. Industrial city, Cook co., NE Illinois, 20 m. S of Chicago on Indiana border; pop. (1970c) 33,107; chemical factories; meat-packing plants; steelworks; incorp. as city 1925.

Calumet Harbor. Harbor district, SE Chicago, Illinois, on Lake Michigan at mouth of Calumet river (8 m. long) draining **Lake Calumet** in S Chicago.

Calumet Park. Village, Cook co., NE Illinois, S suburb of Chicago; pop. (1970c) 10,069.

Ca·lum·pit \ˌkä-lu̇m-'pēt\. Municipality, SW Bulacan prov., Luzon, Phil., NW of Malolos; pop. (1969e) 38,000.

Cal·va·dos \ˌkal-və-'dȯs, -'dōs, -'däs\. Department of NW France. See table at FRANCE.

Calvados Reef *or Fr.* **Ro·chers du Calvados** \rō-ˌshā-dü-\. Long reef of rocks off village of Asnelles on Normandy coast, Calvados dept., France, W of the mouth of the Orne; was bet. the central and eastern beachheads on which Allies landed June 6, 1944.

Cal·va·ry \'kalv-(ə-)rē\ *or Heb.* **Gol·go·tha** \'gäl-gə-thə, gäl-'gäth-ə\. The place, outside of the ancient city of Jerusalem, where Christ was crucified (*Luke* xxiii. 33); the traditional site is within the walls of modern Jerusalem and is occupied by the Church of the Holy Sepulcher, actual site is uncertain.

Cal·ven \'käl-vən\. Narrow gorge, NE Italy, near the border of Graubünden canton, Switzerland; scene of defeat May 22, 1499 of Maximilian I by the Swiss of the Grisons (Graubünden) who thereby gained their independence.

Cal·vert \'kal-vərt\. 1 County in Maryland. See table at MARYLAND.

2 City, Robertson co., E cen. Texas; pop. (1970c) 2072; cotton; oil field.

Cal·vi \'käl-vē\. Seaport, NW Corsica, France; pop. (1962c) 3087; founded 13th cent.; repulsed forces of Henry II of France 1553; conquered by Nelson 1794 after 7 weeks' siege in which he lost an eye; erroneously claimed to be birthplace of Columbus.

Cal·vin·ia \kal-'vin-ē-ə\. Town, W Cape Province, Rep. of South Africa, 180 m. NNE of Cape Town; pop. (1967e) 6700; center of sheep and wheat region.

Calycadnus. See GÖKSU 1.

Cal·y·don \'kal-ə-ˌdän, -əd-ᵊn\. Ancient city, S Aetolia, cen. Greece, near coast of Gulf of Patras; scene in Greek legend of the Calydonian boar hunt.

Calydon, Gulf of. See PATRAS, GULF OF.

Calymna *or* **Calymnos.** See KALYMNOS.

Cam \'kam\. River, Cambridgeshire and Isle of Ely co., E cen. England; 40 m. long; flows into the Ouse 3½ m. S of Ely; the city of Cambridge, on its banks, derives its name from the river.

Ca·ma·güey \ˌkam-ə-'gwā\ *or formerly* **Puer·to Prín·ci·pe** \ˌpwert-ō-'prin(t)-sə-ˌpā\. 1 Province of E cen. Cuba. See table at CUBA.

2 Municipality and city, its ✱; munic. pop. (1967e) 178,600; distributing center for cattle-raising and agricultural district. Founded on present site 1528; in early part of 19th cent. was capital of Spanish West Indies. Its port is Nuevitas.

Camagüey Archipelago. Group of islands off N coast of Camagüey prov., E cen. Cuba; principal islands are Romano, Sabinal, Coco, and Guajaba.

Ca·ma·io·re \ˌkä-mə-ˈyōr-ə\. Commune, Lucca prov., Tuscany, cen. Italy, 12 m. NW of Lucca; pop. (1968e) 28,393.

Ca·ma·jua·ní \ˌkä-mə-wä-ˈnē\. Town, Las Villas prov., W cen. Cuba, E of Santa Clara; pop. (1967e) 36,610.

Ca·ma·lig \kə-ˈmä-lig\. Municipality, E Albay prov., Luzon, Phil., at S base of Mt. Mayon and on railroad ab. 6 m. W of Legaspi; pop. (1969e) 43,800.

Ca·ma·no Island \kə-ˌmä-nō-\. Island in upper Puget Sound, off W coast of Snohomish co., NW Washington; ab. 14 m. long; a part of Island co., Washington.

Ca·ma·rat, Cape \-ˌkam-ə-ˈrä\. Cape, Var dept., SE France, NE of the Hyères Is.

Ca·ma·ret \ˌkam-ə-ˈrā\ *or in full* **Camaret–sur–Mer** \su̇(ə)r-ˈme(ə)r\. Village, Finistère dept., NW France, at tip of a peninsula ab. 10 m. S of Brest; pop. (1962c) 3655.

Camargue, La. See LA CAMARGUE.

Cam·a·ril·lo \ˌkam-ə-ˈril-(ˌ)ō\. City, Ventura co., SW California, 37 m. ESE of Santa Barbara; pop. (1970c) 19,219; diversified agriculture.

Ca·ma·ri·nal, Cape \-ˌkäm-ə-ri-ˈnyäl\. Cape on SW coast of Spain, S of Cape Trafalgar.

Ca·ma·ri·nes Nor·te \ˌkäm-ə-ˌrē-nəs-ˈnȯrt-ē\. Province, SE Luzon, Phil., on Pacific coast; 816 sq. m.; pop. (1970p) 263,226; ✱ Daet. Mountains are volcanic and a continuation of ranges in Quezon and Camarines Sur; highest peak Labo 5066 ft. on S border; soil very fertile, produces esp. rice, corn, coconuts, and tobacco; gold. Chief towns Daet, Jose Pañganiban, Paracale.

History: Was united with Camarines Sur for more than two centuries as one political unit under Spanish rule, known at first as **Camarines** 1573–1829 and later 1854–57, 1893–1919, as Ambos Camarines; in other years a separate province; region explored by Juan de Salcedo 1571; Franciscan mission established early in 17th cent.; civil government set up Apr. 1901.

Camarines Sur \-ˈsu̇(ə)r\. Province, comprising cen. part of long peninsula of SE Luzon, Phil., with coasts on both the Pacific Ocean and inland waters of the archipelago; 2034 sq. m.; pop. (1970p) 978,573; ✱ Naga. Mountain ranges extend along W coast and through Caramoan Penin.; volcanic peaks of Isarog and Iriga in cen. and S parts; the Bicol flows generally NW from Lake Bato to San Miguel Bay; on extreme E separated by narrow channel from Catanduanes I. (part of Albay). Chief exports hemp, copra, forest products, and fish. Chief towns Naga, Iriga, Nabua, Libmanan, and Caramoan.

History: See CAMARINES NORTE. From early times a well-settled region; suffered from revolt ab. 1650; civil government established Apr. 1901; set up as separate province 1919.

Camarões. See CAMEROONS.

Ca·ma·rón, Cape \-ˌkäm-ə-ˈrōn\. Cape on N coast of Honduras, projecting into the Caribbean Sea.

Cam·as \ˈkam-əs\. 1 County in Idaho. See table at IDAHO. 2 Industrial city, Clark co., SW Washington, on Columbia river 12 m. E of Vancouver; pop. (1970c) 5790; in farming region; paper and pulp industry; fruit packing.

Camau. See QUAN LONG.

Camau, Point. See BAIBUNG, POINT.

Cam·ba·luc \ˈkam-bə-ˌlək\ *or* **Cam·ba·lu** \ˈkam-bə-ˌlü\. Marco Polo's name for Khanbalik (*q.v.*), the Mongol capital of China.

Cam·bay \kam-ˈbā\. 1 Former Indian state, now part of Gujarat, W India, at head of Gulf of Cambay; 392 sq. m.; f. ab. 1730.

2 Town, its ✱, at N end of Gulf of Cambay and at mouth of Mahi river 240 m. N of Bombay; pop. (1961c) 51,291. Mentioned by Marco Polo in 1293 as one of India's two most important seaports; silting up of harbor in recent times has diverted former trade; has interesting Jain ruins and remains of encircling wall. Captured by British 1780, restored to Marathas 1783, and ceded to British by treaty 1803.

Cambay, Gulf of. Inlet of Arabian Sea on W coast of India, SE of Kathiawar Penin.; gradually being filled with silt; receives Nambada, Tapti, and Mahi rivers.

Camberiacum. See CHAMBÉRY.

Cam·ber·well \ˈkam-bər-ˌwel, -wəl\. Municipality, S Victoria, SE Australia, E suburb of Melbourne; pop. (1966c) 99,908.

Cam·bo·dia \kam-ˈbōd-ē-ə\ *or officially* **Khmer Republic** \kə-ˈme(ə)r-\ *or Fr.* **Cam·bodge** \käⁿ-bȯj\ *or formerly* **Cam·bo·ja** \kam-ˈbō-jə\. Republic, SE Asia, in S part of Indochina, bounded on N by Thailand and Laos, on E and SE by South Vietnam, on SW by Gulf of Siam, and on W and NW by Thailand; 69,898 sq. m.; pop. (1970e) 6,818,-200; ✱ Pnompenh. *Physical features:* Generally level with mountain range (Phanom Dong Rak) along N border and peaks along the coast 2300 to 5700 ft. Most of the republic lies in basin of lower Mekong with the large lake, Tonle Sap, in its W part; has large jungle areas. *Chief products:* Rice, corn, rubber, sugar, tobacco; manufacturing: cement, paper, textiles. *Chief towns:* Pnompenh, Battambang, Kampong Cham, Kampong Chhnang, Pouthisat.

History: In early times under Hindu influence; Khmer kingdom flourished around city of Kambodja founded c. 435 A.D.; at its height 9th–12th cents. when it ruled entire Mekong valley and tributary Shan States and built Angkor Thom as capital (see ANGKOR); from 13th cent. attacked by Annamese, and Siamese city-states; became province alternately of Annam or Siam; Battambang ceded to Siam 1809; became vassal of Siam 1844; a French protectorate 1863, recognized by Siam 1867; had border dispute with Siam, settled in favor of Cambodia 1907; lost Battambang and surrounding area to Thailand again 1941–46; became fully independent 1954; member of UN 1955; border areas scene of fighting in Vietnam War from 1961; civilian government overthrown by military March 1970, NE and E areas subsequently occupied by North Vietnamese and penetrated (Apr.–June) by U.S. and South Vietnamese forces; abolished monarchy Oct. 1970.

Cambodia Point. See BAIBUNG, POINT.

ə abut; ᵊ kitten, Fr. table; ər further; a back; ā bake; ä cot, cart; à Fr. bac; au̇ out; ch chin; e less; ē easy; g gift
i trip; ī life; j joke; k̲ Ger. ich, Buch; ⁿ Fr. vin; ŋ sing; ō flow; ȯ flaw; œ Fr. bœuf; œ̄ Fr. feu; ȯi coin; th thin
th̲ this; ü loot; u̇ foot; ue Ger. füllen; ue̅ Fr. rue; y yet; ʸ Fr. digne \dēnʸ\, nuit \nwʸē\; yü few; yu̇ furious; zh vision

Cam·borne–Red·ruth \ˌkam-ˌbō(ə)rn-ˈred-ˌrüth\. Urban district, Cornwall, SW England, 53 m. WSW of Plymouth; pop. (1971p) 42,029; mining machinery, textiles.

Cam·brai \kam-ˈbrā, käⁿ-\ *or older* **Cam·bray** \kam-\ *or Flem.* **Kam·bryk** \ˈkäm-brīk\ *or anc.* **Cam·e·ra·cum** \ˌkam-ər-ˈā-kəm\. Industrial city, Nord dept., N France, on Schelde river 34 m. SSE of Lille; pop. (1968c) 37,532; manufactures linen goods (esp. cambric and cambresine—both named for the city), sugar, soap; foundry, brewery; archiepiscopal see.

History: A Frankish capital 445 A.D.; made commune 1076; league against Venice formed here 1508; Peace of Cambrai signed 1529; to France 1678. Occupied by Germans 1914–18; important battles of World War I fought in villages to SW: (1) a surprise British attack with tanks on German lines and German counterattack Nov. 20–Dec. 7, 1917; in closing phase of war of attrition, a partial British success; (2) complete victory of British and Canadians Sept. 27–Oct. 5, 1918.

Cam·bria \ˈkam-brē-ə\. **1** County in Pennsylvania. See table at PENNSYLVANIA.

2 Latin name of Wales, used by modern poets.

Cam·bri·an Mountains \ˌkam-brē-ən-\. Range extending N to S through cen. Wales; highest peak Aran Mawddwy 2970 ft.

Cam·bridge \ˈkām-brij\. **1** Village, ⊗ of Henry co., NW Illinois; pop. (1970c) 2095; in agricultural region.

2 City, ⊗ of Dorchester co., SE Maryland, on E shore of Chesapeake Bay 38 m. SE of Annapolis; pop. (1970c) 11,-595; lumber, flour, fertilizer; fisheries; shipbuilding yards.

3 City, a ⊗ of Middlesex co., NE Massachusetts, 3 m. W of Boston; pop. (1970c) 100,361; educational center; also manufacturing and commercial center; electrical machinery, scientific instruments, inks, glass, rubber goods, wire cables, paper boxes; printing and publishing; Harvard Univ. (1636), Radcliffe Coll. (1879, affiliated with Harvard Univ.), Massachusetts Institute of Technology (founded in Boston 1859; removed to Cambridge 1915), Lesley Coll. (1909), Cambridge Junior Coll. (1934).

History: Founded 1630 as one of the Massachusetts Bay settlements and known as **New Towne** \-ˌtau̇n\ until 1638; Harvard College (first institution of learning in U.S.) founded 1636 and first printing press in U.S. set up 1640 by Stephen Day; Gen. Washington took command of American Army July 3, 1775; at Craigie House (built 1759), his headquarters 1775–76, Cambridge flag first used Jan. 2, 1776; in 19th cent. home of many American literary leaders; incorporated as city 1846; adopted council-manager form of government 1940.

4 Village, ⊗ of Isanti co., E Minnesota, 41 m. N of Minneapolis; pop. (1970c) 2720.

5 City, Furnas co., S Nebraska, on Republican river; pop. (1970c) 1145; fossilized bones of saber-toothed tiger discovered 1947.

6 Village, Washington co., E New York, 26 m. NNE of Troy; pop. (1970c) 1769; agriculture, stockbreeding.

7 City, ⊗ of Guernsey co., E Ohio, 21 m. ENE of Zanesville; pop. (1970c) 13,656; coal, pottery clay, oil, and natural-gas deposits nearby; settled 1806.

8 County in England. See CAMBRIDGESHIRE.

9 *or Lat.* **Can·ta·brig·ia** \ˌkant-ə-ˈbrij-(ē-)ə\. Municipal borough, ⊗ of Cambridgeshire and Isle of Ely co., E England, on the Cam 48 m. NNE of London; pop. (1971p) 98,519; electronic equipment, cement; printing and publishing; many churches, esp. the Holy Sepulchre (round church, c. 1130) and Saint Benedict. Dates from early times, its site probably occupied by Romans. Chiefly important because of Cambridge University (dating from the 12th cent., probably c. 1110).

Cambridge City. Town, Wayne co., E Indiana, 15 m. W of Richmond; pop. (1970c) 2481; malleable castings; wheat; hogs.

Cam·bridge·shire \ˈkām-brij-ˌshi(ə)r, -shər\ *or* **Cambridge.** Former county in E England; 492 sq. m.; joined with Isle of Ely 1965 forming county of Cambridgeshire and Isle of Ely.

Cambridgeshire and Isle of Ely \ˈē-lē\. Administrative county in E England; 831 sq. m.; pop. (1971p) 302,507; ⊗ Cambridge; chief rivers Ouse, Cam, Lark, Nene; mainly agricultural; wheat, barley, potatoes; market gardening.

Cambridge Springs. Borough and resort, Crawford co., NW Pennsylvania; pop. (1970c) 1998; evaporated milk; mineral spring; Alliance Coll. (1912).

Cam·bu·ni·an Mountains \kam-ˌbyü-nē-ən-\. Mountain range on N border of Thessaly, NE Greece, and separating it from SW Macedonia; terminates in Mt. Olympus on the E.

Cam·den \ˈkam-dən\. **1** Name of counties in four states of the U.S. See tables at GEORGIA, MISSOURI, NEW JERSEY, NORTH CAROLINA.

2 Town, ⊗ of Wilcox co., SW cen. Alabama; pop. (1970c) 1742; corn.

3 City, ⊗ of Ouachita co., S Arkansas, on Ouachita river 29 m. N of El Dorado; pop. (1970c) 15,147; fertilizer, furniture; timber; made ⊗ 1843, incorp. 1844.

4 Town, Knox co., S Maine, on W shore of Penobscot Bay 37 m. E of Augusta; pop. (1970c) 4115; resort.

5 City and port of entry, ⊗ of Camden co., SW New Jersey, on Delaware river across from Philadelphia, with which it is connected by bridge; pop. (1970c) 102,551; electrical appliances, chemicals, leather, automobile accessories; shipyards; settled c. 1681; originally part of Newton township; incorporated as city 1828; railroad terminus 1834; made ⊗ of Camden co. 1844; grew rapidly in industrial expansion following Civil War; home of Walt Whitman 1873–92.

6 Village, Oneida co., cen. New York, 16 m. WNW of Rome; pop. (1970c) 2936; furniture; poultry farms.

7 Village, ⊗ of Camden co., NE North Carolina, 4 m. E of Elizabeth City.

8 City, ⊗ of Kershaw co., N cen. South Carolina, near Wateree river 31 m. ENE of Columbia; pop. (1970c) 8532; winter resort; textiles, veneer, lumber. First settled 1733–34 near scene of American defeat (under Gen. Gates) and mortal wounding of Gen. De Kalb in battle of Camden Aug. 16, 1780, and of Rawdon-Hastings' victory over Americans under Gen. Nathanael Greene at Hobkirk's Hill Apr. 25, 1781; became Confederate storehouse, hospital, and haven of refuge until burned by Sherman in 1865.

9 Town, ⊗ of Benton co., W Tennessee; pop. (1970c) 3052; sand and gravel pits; sawmills.

10 A borough of Greater London, SE England. See table at LONDON 4.

Cam·den·ton \ˈkam-dən-tən\. Town, ⊗ of Camden co., S cen. Missouri; pop. (1970c) 1636.

Cam·el \ˈkam-əl\. River in Cornwall, SW England; ab. 30 m. long; flows NW into Atlantic Ocean.

Cam·el·ford \ˈkam-əl-fərd\. Rural district, Cornwall, SW England, on the Camel river; pop. (1971p) 7297.

Cam·e·lot \ˈkam-ə-ˌlät\. In the Arthurian legends, the place where King Arthur had his palace and court and where the Round Table was; has been variously located in Somersetshire, at or near Winchester, and in Wales.

Cam·els Hump \ˈkam-əlz-\. Peak of the Green Mts., Vermont, 20 m. SE of Burlington; 4083 ft.

Cam·em·bert \ˈkam-əm-ˌbe(ə)r\. Village, Orne dept., NW France, E of Falaise; pop. (1962c) 234; Camembert cheese first made here ab. 1761, chief center for the cheese now in nearby Vimoutiers (*q.v.*).

Cameracum. See CAMBRAI.

Ca·me·ri·no \ˌkäm-ə-ˈrē-nō\ *or anc.* **Cam·e·ri·num** \ˌkam-ə-ˈrī-nəm\. Commune, Macerata prov., Marches, cen. Italy, 23 m. SW of Macerata; pop. (1968e) 9180; univ. (1336, univ. status 1727).

Cam·er·on \ˈkam-(ə-)rən\. **1** Name of a parish in Louisiana and of counties in two states of the U.S. See tables at LOUISIANA, PENNSYLVANIA, and TEXAS.

2 Town, ⊗ of Cameron parish, SW corner of Louisiana; pop. (1970c) 3205; shrimp packing.
3 City, Clinton and De Kalb cos., NW Missouri, 47 m. NNE of Kansas City; pop. (1970c) 3960; corn, oats.
4 City, ⊗ of Milam co., cen. Texas, 27 m. SE of Temple; pop. (1970c) 5546; fertilizer plants; cattle.
5 City, Marshall co., N West Virginia, 12 m. SE of Moundsville; pop. (1970c) 1537; in farming region.

Cameron, Mount. Peak, Park co., cen. Colorado; 14,238 ft.

Cameron Pass. Mountain pass, Larimer and Jackson cos., N Colorado, in Medicine Bow Mountains; alt. 10,285 ft.

Cam·er·oon \ˌkam-ə-ˈrün\ *or Fr.* **Ca·me·roun** \kȧm-rün\ *or in full* **Federal Republic of Cameroon.** Republic, W Africa, bounded on N and NE by Chad, on E by Central African Republic, on S by Congo, Gabon, and Equatorial Guinea, on SW by the Bight of Biafra, and on W and NW by Nigeria; 183,591 sq. m.; pop. (1970e) 5,840,000; ✱ Yaoundé. *Physical features:* Plateau region inland, marshes along coast and lower courses of rivers; chief rivers Nyong and Sanaga. *Chief products:* Cocoa, coffee, timber, bananas, peanuts, bauxite; livestock. *Chief towns:* Yaoundé, Edéa, Douala, Kribi.

History: For history prior to 1922, see CAMEROONS. French mandate 1922–46; became a UN trust territory under French administration 1946; achieved independence 1960; united with former British trust territory of Southern Cameroons 1961.

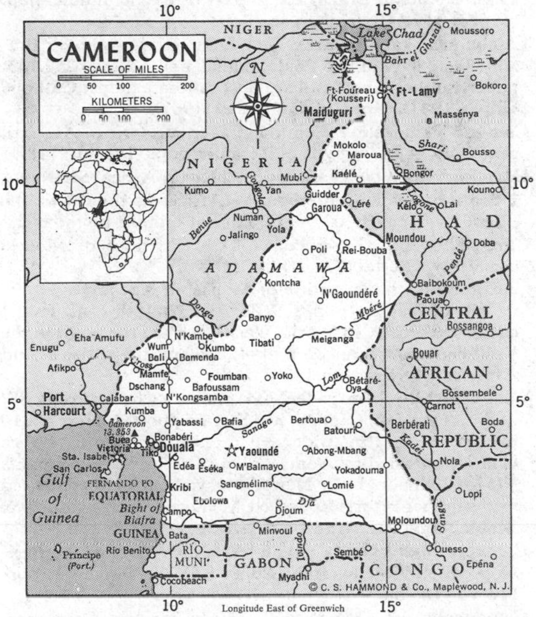

Cameroon, Mount. Highest mountain in the W African republic of Cameroon, ab. 40 m. NW of Douala; 13,353 ft.

Cam·er·oons \ˌkam-ə-ˈrünz\ *or Port.* **Ca·ma·rões** \ˌkam-ə-ˈrȯi^{n}sh\ *or Ger.* **Ka·me·run** \ˌkäm-ə-ˈrün\ *or Fr.* **Ca·me·roun** \kȧm-rün\. Former German protectorate, W Africa.

History: Factory estab. on coast by German company 1868; German protectorate proclaimed 1884; boundary agreements with Great Britain 1893 and France 1894; invaded by Anglo-French forces 1914; formally divided into British and French administrative zones 1919, which in 1922 became League of Nations mandates and in 1946 UN trust territories; French trust territory became independent republic 1960 (see CAMEROON); in 1961 S part of British trust territory voted for union with Cameroon, N part for union with Nigeria.

Ca·me·tá \ˌkam-ə-ˈtä\. Municipality, Pará state, N Brazil; pop. (1968e) 59,839.

Ca·mi·guin \ˌkam-ə-ˈgwēn\. 1 Island in Babuyan group, N of Luzon, Phil.; 63 sq. m.; mountainous.
2 Volcano, N part of Camiguin I., Babuyan Is., Phil.; 2602 ft.
3 Island in Mindanao Sea ab. 6 m. off N coast of Mindanao, Phil., constituting a province of Phil.; 98 sq. m.; pop. (1970p) 56,976; mountainous; highest peak 5620 ft.; produces much sugar, tobacco, rice, cacao; volcanic in formation; eruptions in 1871 and 1948; chief towns Mambajao, Catarman, and Sagay.

Ca·mi·ling \ˌkä-mi-ˈlēŋ\. Municipality, NW Tarlac prov., Luzon, Phil., on a tributary of the Agno 19 m. NW of Tarlac; pop. (1969e) 55,600; important market town.

Ca·mil·la \kə-ˈmil-ə\. City, ⊗ of Mitchell co., SW Georgia, 25 m. S of Albany; pop. (1970c) 4987; cotton, corn, timber; livestock.

Ca·mil·lus \kə-ˈmil-əs\. Village, Onondaga co., cen. New York, 9 m. W of Syracuse; pop. (1970c) 1534; farming, dairying; claims title of "birthplace of the Republican party" (1852).

Ca·mi·ri \kə-ˈmir-ē\. Town, Santa Cruz dept., S Bolivia, 140 m. SE of Sucre; oil refineries.

Ca·mi·rus \kə-ˈmī-rəs\. Ancient town on W coast of island of Rhodes; chief town of the island before Rhodes was founded. See PENTAPOLIS.

Cam·lan \ˈkam-lən\. Locality, SW England, where King Arthur is said to have died in battle 537; site unidentified but possibly near Camelford in Cornwall.

Ca·mo·cim \ˌka-mü-ˈsē(^{n})m\. City and port, Ceará state, NE Brazil; munic. pop. (1969e) 30,699.

Ca·mo·ghe \ˌkäm-ə-ˈgā\. Peak, Ticino canton, SE cen. Switzerland; 7310 ft.

Ca·mo·ni·ca \kə-ˈmȯ-ni-kə\. Valley in the Alps, in Brescia prov., Lombardy, N Italy; 50 m. long.

Ca·mor·ta \kə-ˈmȯrt-ə\. Island, cen. Nicobar Is., India, just N of Nancowry I.; 58 sq. m.

Ca·mo·tes Islands \kə-ˈmō-ˌtās-\. Group of three islands, Poro, Pacijan, and Ponson, N of Camotes Sea near W coast of Leyte and ab. 20 m. E of the N end of Cebu I., Visayan Is., E cen. Phil.; 86 sq. m.; largest town San Francisco on Pacijan I. Belong to Cebu prov.; mountainous; formerly part of Leyte prov.

Camotes Sea. Body of water in Visayan Is., E cen. Phil., E of N end of Cebu I., N of Bohol, W of Leyte, and S of Camotes Is. Scene of several naval and air battles during Leyte campaign 1944.

Camp \ˈkamp\. County in Texas. See table at TEXAS.

Camp. See CAMPERDOWN.

Cam·pa·gna \kam-ˈpän-yə\. 1 Region, Italy. See CAMPAGNA DI ROMA.
2 Commune, Salerno prov., Campania, S Italy, 18 m. E by S of Salerno; pop. (1968e) 11,889; cathedral.

Campagna di Ro·ma \-dē-ˈrō-mə\ *or Eng. often* **Roman Campagna.** Region surrounding Rome, Italy; ab. 800 sq. m.; almost coextensive with Rome commune; in recent years largely reclaimed and repopulated.

Cam·pal·di·no \ˌkam-pəl-ˈdē-nō\. Village, Tuscany, Italy, on the upper Arno ESE of Florence; scene of battle June 11, 1289 in which the Ghibelline supporters of Arezzo were severely defeated by the Guelphs of Florence.

Cam·pa·na \käm-ˈpän-ə\. 1 Town, Buenos Aires prov., E Argentina, on the Paraná river 45 m. NW of Buenos Aires; pop. (1960c) 24,781; commercial center with meat-freezing, oil-refining, and grain-storage industries.
2 Island in Pacific Ocean off SW coast of Chile, NW of Wellington I.; ab. 55 m. long, 10 m. wide.

Cam·pa·na·rio \ˌkäm-pə-ˈnär-ē-ˌō\. Peak on Argentina-Chile boundary, bet. SW Mendoza prov., W Argentina, and E Talca prov., cen. Chile; 13,284 ft.

Cam·pa·nel·la, Point \-ˌkäm-pə-ˈnel-ə, -ˌkam-\. Cape at S end of the Bay of Naples, Italy, opp. island of Capri.

Cam·pa·nia \kam-ˈpā-nyə, -nē-ə\. 1 Region, France. See CHAMPAGNE.

2 Autonomous region, S Italy; lies on Tyrrhenian Sea bet. Latium and Basilicata; 5250 sq. m.; pop. (1968e) 5,132,-860; ✱ Naples; exceedingly fertile and generally mountainous region; produces principally wine, olives, citrus fruits, and grain; fishing; chemical and metallurgical industries; tourism.

History: Noted in ancient times as a favorite resort of distinguished Romans; noted for its natural beauty and famous old towns (Cumae, Stabiae, Pompeii, Capua, Salernum, Neapolis, etc.). Occupied successively by Oscans, Greeks, Etruscans, Samnites, and from 350 B.C. by Romans; region became part of kingdom of Italy 1860; held elections for regional parliament 1970.

Camp·bell \ˈkam-(b)əl\. 1 Name of counties in five states of the U.S. See tables at KENTUCKY, SOUTH DAKOTA, TENNESSEE, VIRGINIA, WYOMING.

2 Former county in Georgia; part annexed to Fulton co. 1926, the rest 1932.

3 City, Santa Clara co., W California, SW of San Jose; pop. (1970c) 24,770; electronic equipment; fruit packing; West Valley Junior Coll. (1963).

4 City, Dunklin co., SE Missouri; pop. (1970c) 1979; cotton, wheat, timber.

5 Industrial city, Mahoning co., NE Ohio, 4 m. SE of Youngstown; pop. (1970c) 12,577; iron and steel works.

Campbell, Cape. Cape on NE coast of South I., New Zealand, at W side of S Cook Strait.

Campbell, Mount. Peak, Antarctica, 84°55′S, 174°00′W; 12,434 ft.

Camp·bell·ford \ˈkam-(b)əl-fərd\. Town, Northumberland co., SE Ontario, Canada, on Trent river 28 m. E of Peterborough; pop. (1968e) 3505; woolens; resort.

Campbell Hill. Elevation near Bellefontaine, Logan co., W Ohio; 1550 ft.; highest point in the state.

Campbell Island. Island in S Pacific Ocean, lat. 52°33′S and long. 169°9′E; 44 sq. m.; discovered 1810; has good harbours; annexed to New Zealand.

Campbell Mountain. Peak in Glacier National Park, NW Montana; 8207 ft.

Camp·bell·pore \ˈkam-bəl-ˌpō(ə)r\ *also* **Camp·bell·pur** \-ˌpu̇(ə)r\ *or formerly* **At·tock** \ə-ˈtäk\. 1 District, Rawalpindi div., Pakistan; pop. (1961c) 766,813; ✱ Campbellpore.

2 Town, its ✱, Punjab, Pakistan, ab. 50 m. SE of Peshawar; pop. (1961c) 19,041; has fortress built by Akbar 1581.

Camp·bell's Bay \ˈkam-(b)əlz-\. Village, ⊗ of Pontiac co., SW Quebec, Canada, on Ottawa river opp. Calumet I. 50 m. NW of Ottawa; pop. (1966c) 1084.

Camp·bells·ville \ˈkam-(b)əlz-ˌvil\. City, ⊗ of Taylor co., cen. Kentucky, SW of Danville; pop. (1970c) 7598; tobacco growing.

Camp·bell·ton \ˈkam-(b)əl-tən\. City, Restigouche co., N New Brunswick, Canada, on Restigouche river 15 m. from its mouth; pop. (1971p) 10,232; at head of deep-water navigation; exports fish and lumber; resort; founded 1776; almost completely destroyed by fire 1910.

Camp·bell·town \ˈkam-(b)əl-ˌtau̇n\. 1 *or* **Campbell Town.** Town and municipality, E Tasmania, Australia, 40 m. SSE of Launceston; munic. pop. (1970e) 1590.

2 Borough, New Zealand. See BLUFF.

Camp·bel·town \ˈkam-bəl-ˌtau̇n\. Seaport burgh, Argyll co., W Scotland, on the E side of S end of Kintyre Penin.; pop. (1971p) 5961; fisheries, distilleries.

Cam·pe·che \kam-ˈpē-chē\. 1 State, SE Mexico. See table at MEXICO.

2 City, its ✱, on W coast of Yucatán penin.; pop. (1969e) 59,627; exports logwood and mahogany, cigars, cotton; univ. (1756, univ. status 1965); founded 1540.

Campeche, Bank of *or Span.* **Ban·co Campeche** \ˌbäŋ-(ˌ)kō-käm-ˈpā-chē\. Shoal, N of Yucatán penin., state of Yucatán, SE Mexico.

Campeche, Bay of *or Span.* **Ba·hía de Campeche** \bä-ˈē-ə-də-käm-ˈpā-chē\. SW section of the Gulf of Mexico, forming a wide shallow bay extending into SE Mexico.

Cam·pe·chue·la \ˌkäm-pə-chə-ˈwā-lə\. Town, Oriente prov., E Cuba, on coast of Gulf of Guacanayabo 15 m. SW of Manzanillo; munic. pop. (1967e) 41,820.

Cam·per·down \ˈkam-pər-ˌdau̇n\ *or mod. Dutch* **Camp** \ˈkämp\. Village, North Holland prov., W Netherlands, on North Sea coast 8 m. NW of Alkmaar; nearby occurred naval battle Oct. 11, 1797 in which British under Duncan defeated Dutch under De Winter.

Camp Hill \ˈkamp-\. Residential borough, Cumberland co., S Pennsylvania, 5 m. WSW of Harrisburg; pop. (1970c) 9931; suburb of Harrisburg.

Cam·pi Bi·sen·zio \ˈkäm-pē-bi-ˈzen(t)-sē-ˌō\. Commune, Firenze prov., Tuscany, cen. Italy, 7 m. WNW of Florence; pop. (1968e) 23,146.

Campi Flegrei. See PHLEGRAEAN FIELDS.

Cam·pi·glia Ma·rit·ti·ma \kam-ˌpēl-yə-mə-ˈrēt-ə-mə\. Commune, Livorno prov., Tuscany, cen. Italy, 35 m. S by E of Leghorn; pop. (1968e) 10,636.

Câmpina. See CÎMPINA.

Cam·pi·na Gran·de \kam-ˌpē-nə-ˈgran-də, -dē\. City, E Paraíba state, E Brazil, 100 m. NW of Recife; munic. pop. (1968e) 157,149; leather, textiles.

Cam·pi·nas \kam-ˈpē-nəs\. City, E São Paulo state, SE Brazil, 68 m. NNW of São Paulo; munic. pop. (1968e) 252,145; paper, rubber, and textile goods; railroad shops; Catholic Univ. (1944), Univ. of Campinas (1962).

Cam·pli \ˈkäm-plē\. Commune, Teramo prov., Abruzzi, cen. Italy, 4 m. N by E of Teramo; pop. (1968e) 9718.

Cam·po *or* **Kam·po** \ˈkäm-(ˌ)pō\. 1 River, Africa. See NTEM.

2 Seaport town, Cameroon, W Africa, at mouth of the Ntem river just N of the Equatorial Guinea boundary.

Cam·po·bas·so \ˌkäm-pō-ˈbäs-(ˌ)ō\. 1 Province of Molise, cen. Italy. See table at ITALY.

2 Commune, its ✱, and ✱ of Molise, in Apennines ab. 95 m. NE of Naples; pop. (1968e) 39,637; 15th cent. feudal castle; cathedral. In World War II marked the point in the Volturno campaign Oct. 1943 where the British and American forces joined.

Cam·po·bel·lo \ˌkam-pə-ˈbel-(ˌ)ō\. Island, Charlotte co., SW New Brunswick, Canada, just E of Eastport, Maine; ab. 10 m. long, 2 to 3 m. wide; separated from U.S. by Lubec Channel. Owned by Adm. William Owen and descendants 1767–1880; bought by New York syndicate and converted into summer resort; Roosevelt Memorial Bridge to Lubec, Maine, completed 1962.

Campobello di Li·ca·ta \-dē-li-ˈkä-tə\. Commune, Agrigento prov., SW Sicily, Italy, 20 m. ESE of Agrigento; pop. (1968e) 12,108.

Campobello di Ma·za·ra \-dē-mät-ˈsär-ə\. Commune, Trapani prov., NW Sicily, Italy; pop. (1968e) 12,491.

Campo de Crip·ta·na \ˌkäm-pō-də-krēp-ˈtän-ə\. Commune, Ciudad Real prov., S cen. Spain, 52 m. NE of Ciudad Real; pop. (1970p) 13,405; agricultural products.

Campo de la Cruz \-ˌdel-ə-ˈkrüs\. Town, Atlántico dept., N Colombia; munic. pop. (1968e) 20,835.

Cam·po·for·mi·do \ˌkam-pō-ˈfȯr-mə-ˌdō\ *or formerly* **Campo For·mio** \-mē-ˌō\. Village, Udine prov., E Friuli-Venezia Giulia, NE Italy, SW of Udine; pop. (1968e) 4495; treaty Oct. 17, 1797 bet. France and Austria ending first phase of Napoleonic Wars.

Campo Gran·de \ˌkam-pü-ˈgran-dē\. City, Mato Grosso state, SW Brazil; munic. pop. (1968e) 111,205; on railroad in center of S part of the state.

Campo Mai·or \ˌkam-pō-mī-ˈyȯr\. Municipality, Piauí state, NE Brazil, ab. 50 m. NE of Teresina; pop. (1968e) 62,325.

Cam·pos \'kam-pəs\. City, Rio de Janeiro state, SE Brazil, 35 m. from mouth of the Paraíba river; munic. pop. (1968e) 389,045; aluminum, cement; in rich agricultural area.

Camp·ton \'kam(p)-tən\. 1 City, ⊗ of Wolfe co., E Kentucky; pop. (1970c) 419.

2 Town, in Grafton co., cen. New Hampshire, 25 m. NNW of Laconia; pop. (1970c) 1171; resort; settled 1765.

Câmpulung. See CÎMPULUNG.

Camp Upton. See UPTON 3.

Cam·ranh Bay *or* **Cam–ranh Bay** *also* **Kam·ranh Bay** \ˌkam-ˌran-\. Inlet of South China Sea on E coast of South Vietnam, ab 12°N, bet. Phan Rang and Nha Trang. Former French naval base with large protected anchorage; used by Japanese 1940–45; Japanese vessels bombed by Allied planes Jan. 11, 1945; major U.S. base (from 1965) during Vietnam War.

Cam·rose \'kam-ˌrōz\. Town, S cen. Alberta, Canada, 44 m. SSE of Edmonton; pop. (1966c) 8362; grain elevators; Camrose Junior Coll. (1911).

Camulodunum. See COLCHESTER 4.

Ca·muy \käm-'wē\. Town and municipality, NW Puerto Rico, W of Arecibo; pop. (1970p) 3882 (town), 19,796 (munic.).

Ca·na \'kā-nə\ *or often* **Cana of Gal·i·lee** \-'gal-ə-ˌlē, -ˌgal-ə-'\. Village, Israel, ab. 4 m. NE of Nazareth; where Christ performed his first miracle.

Ca·naan \'kā-nən\. 1 Village, N Litchfield co., NW corner of Connecticut; pop. (1970c) 931; incorp. 1739.

2 Town, Grafton co., W New Hampshire, on Indian river 11 m. E of Lebanon; pop. (1970c) 1923; resort; Canaan Coll. (1955).

3 The ancient name of that part of Palestine (*q.v.*) bet. the Jordan and the Mediterranean, but sometimes vaguely used as the equivalent of all of Palestine; had settlements in Early Bronze Age (3200–2100 B.C.), probably Amorites and Hittites; later, its inhabitants, a pre-Israelite race (Canaanites), overcome by Hebrews c. 1200 B.C. returning from Egypt; the Promised Land (Land of Promise) of the Israelites (*Exod.* iii. 8).

Canaan Mountain. Peak, Preston co., N West Virginia; 3702 ft.

Ca·ña·cao Bay \ˌkän-yə-ˌkaů-\. Inlet of Manila Bay at end of Cavite Penin., Cavite prov., Luzon, Phil.; good anchorage; the N harbor of Cavite naval base.

Can·a·da \'kan-əd-ə\ *or formerly, esp. before 1867, called* **British North America.** Independent country in northern North America, bounded on N by Arctic Ocean, on E by Atlantic Ocean (incl. Davis Strait and Baffin Bay), on S by U.S., and on W by U.S. (Alaska) and Pacific Ocean; 3,851,-809 sq. m. (incl. 291,571 sq. m. of water); pop. (1970e) 21,377,000; ✱ Ottawa. *Physical features:* Northernmost point (83°07′N) is Cape Columbia on Ellesmere I.; length of U.S.-Canada border 3987 m.; incl. many islands: Baffin, Ellesmere, Victoria, Newfoundland, Melville. *Rivers:* St. Lawrence (draining Great Lakes and in part forming boundary with U.S.), Columbia (upper course, flows into Washington state, U.S.), Mackenzie (with great tributaries Liard, Slave, Peace, Athabaska, etc.), Yukon (upper course, flows into Alaska), Nelson (with upper tributaries of North and South Saskatchewan), Red River of the North (lower course), Dubawnt, Fraser, Severn, Albany, Ottawa, and Saguenay. *Lakes:* Parts of lakes Ontario, Erie, Huron, Superior, and Lake of the Woods; Great Bear, Great Slave, Athabaska, Winnipeg, Winnipegosis, and many smaller ones such as Nipigon, Mistassini, and Louise (Banff National Park). *Mountains:* Rocky Mts. in W with many high peaks extending from Alaska to U.S. border (including Selkirk, Cariboo, and other ranges), Coast Mts. along British Columbia coast, Laurentian Hills in Quebec; highest point Mt. Logan 19,850 ft. in Yukon Terr., second in height in North America. *Chief products:* Wheat, oats, barley, potatoes, dairy products; livestock raising, fishing; petroleum, natural gas, copper, iron ore, nickel, zinc, asbestos, potash; manufacturing: iron and steel, textiles, pulp and paper, chemicals; food processing. *Chief cities:* Montreal, Toronto, Vancouver, Edmonton, Calgary, Hamilton, Ottawa, Winnipeg, London, Windsor. Divided into 10 provinces and 2 territories—see table below (see also their individual entries):

NAME	AREA (sq. m.)	POP. (1970e)	CAPITAL
Provinces			
Alberta	255,285	1,600,000	Edmonton
British Columbia	366,255	2,137,000	Victoria
Manitoba	251,000	981,000	Winnipeg
New Brunswick	28,354	624,000	Fredericton
Newfoundland	156,185	518,000	St. John's
Nova Scotia	21,425	766,000	Halifax
Ontario	414,582	7,637,000	Toronto
Prince Edward I.	2,184	110,000	Charlottetown
Quebec	594,861	6,013,000	Quebec
Saskatchewan	251,700	942,000	Regina
Territories			
Northwest Territories	1,304,903	33,000	Yellowknife
Yukon Territory	207,076	16,000	Whitehorse

History: Early (c. 1000 A.D.) discovered by Norsemen: Atlantic coast frequented by European fishermen from 15th cent. (see NEWFOUNDLAND); mainland discovered by explorers in search of Northwest Passage to Asia (see HUDSON BAY and ARCTIC, THE); Gulf of St. Lawrence and river to sites of Quebec and Montreal discovered by Cartier 1534–41 under whom French attempted their first colony; Quebec (city) founded 1608 by Champlain, who explored St. Lawrence, discovered Lake Champlain, and penetrated interior to Georgian Bay 1603–15; Hudson Bay entered by Henry Hudson 1610; under influence of French missionaries after 1615; part of New France granted to Company of the Hundred Associates 1627 (returned to French crown 1664); Montreal founded by Maisonneuve 1642; expeditions of Nicolet, Marquette and Jolliet, and La Salle; object of Anglo-French rivalry from 17th cent.; Acadia (see ACADIA 2), Newfoundland, and Hudson Bay region relinquished to England 1713; rest of country ceded by Treaty of Paris 1763; region of Ottawa and St. Lawrence rivers organized 1774 as Quebec prov. (*q.v.*). Boundaries with U.S. settled 1783 (see NORTHWEST TERRITORY), 1846 (see OREGON COUNTRY), and 1903 (see ALASKA). Dominion of Canada established 1867 by union of New Brunswick and Nova Scotia with Quebec, whose two parts (formerly known as Upper and Lower Canada) became present Ontario and Quebec provs.; purchased 1869 the western regions explored by Hudson's Bay Company (chartered 1670 by Charles II) and North West Company (consolidated with Hudson's Bay Company 1821); put down Riel's Rebellion 1869; admitted as provinces Manitoba 1870, British Columbia 1871, Prince Edward Island 1873, Alberta and Saskatchewan 1905, Newfoundland 1949; see NORTHWEST TERRITORIES, YUKON; entered World War I 1914, World War II 1939; through Statute of Westminster recognized as equal partner of Great Britain 1931; joined UN 1945, NATO 1949; reached agreement with U.S. on joint air defense of North America 1958.

Ca·ña·da de Gó·mez \kən ˌyü-də-də-'gō-məs\. Town, Santa Fe prov., E cen. Argentina, 40 m. NNW of Rosario; pop. (1960c) 20,462.

Canada East \ˌkan-əd-ə-\. Quebec province, Canada—a name used from 1841 to 1867.

Canada West. Ontario prov., Canada, and unsettled regions to the W—a name used from 1841 to 1867.

Ca·na·di·an \kə-'nād-ē-ən\. 1 River, SW United States; 906 m. long; flows from Las Animas co., S Colorado, S and E across NE New Mexico and NW Texas and through cen. Oklahoma to Arkansas river in SE Muskogee co., E Oklahoma.

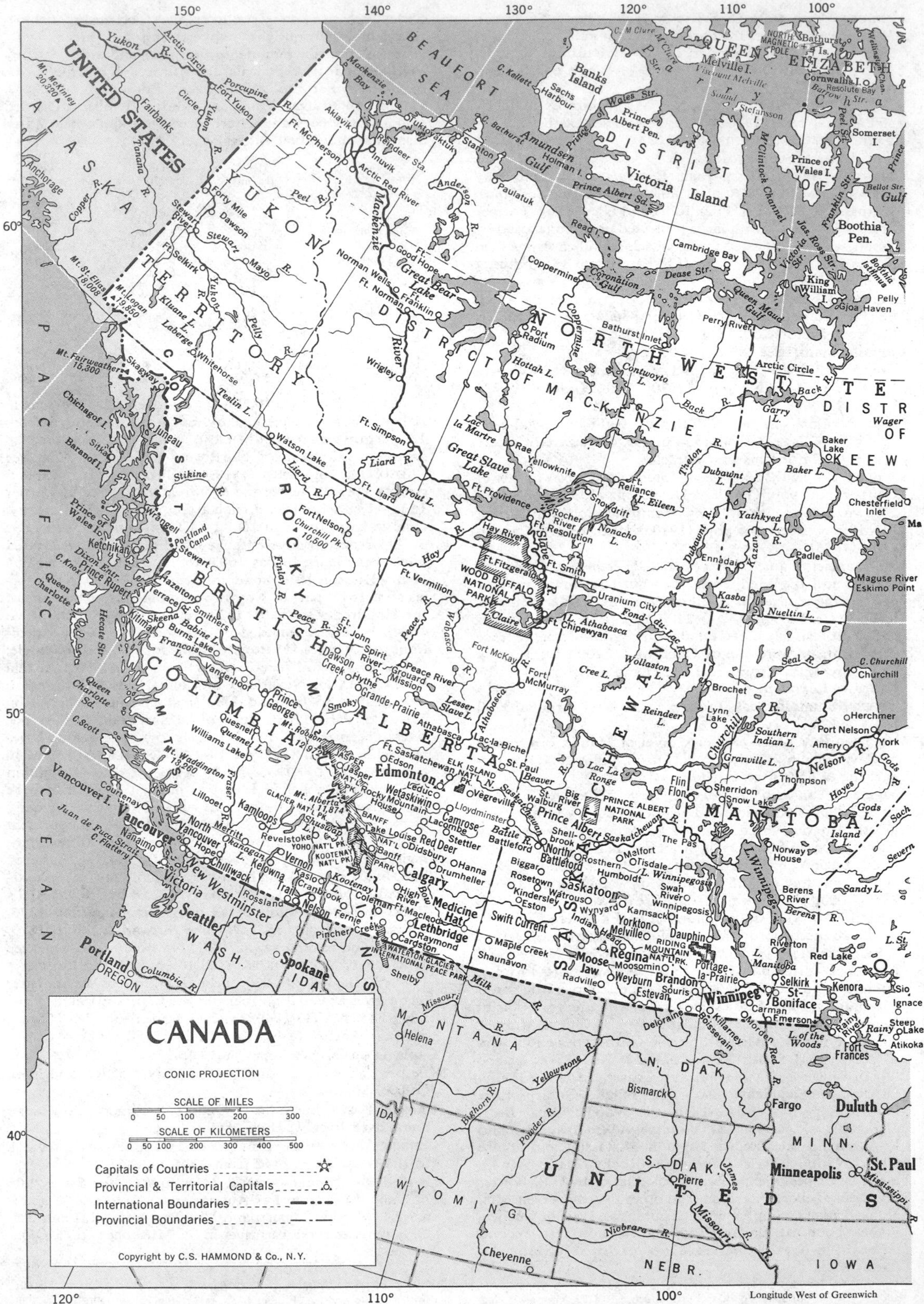
CANADA
CONIC PROJECTION
SCALE OF MILES
0 50 100 200 300
SCALE OF KILOMETERS
0 50 100 200 300 400 500
Capitals of Countries
Provincial & Territorial Capitals
International Boundaries
Provincial Boundaries
Copyright by C.S. HAMMOND & Co., N.Y.
Longitude West of Greenwich
150° 140° 130° 120° 110° 100°
60° 50° 40°
120° 110° 100°
BEAUFORT SEA
UNITED STATES
ALASKA
PACIFIC OCEAN
YUKON TERRITORY
DISTRICT OF MACKENZIE
NORTHWEST TERRITORIES
DISTRICT OF KEEWATIN
BRITISH COLUMBIA
ALBERTA
SASKATCHEWAN
MANITOBA
ROCKY MOUNTAINS
COAST MTS.
QUEEN ELIZABETH
Victoria Island
Banks Island
Great Bear Lake
Great Slave Lake
L. Athabasca
L. Winnipeg
WOOD BUFFALO NATIONAL PARK
PRINCE ALBERT NATIONAL PARK
ELK ISLAND NAT'L PK.
JASPER NAT'L PK.
BANFF NAT'L PARK
YOHO NAT'L PK.
KOOTENAY NAT'L PK.
GLACIER NAT'L PK.
RIDING MOUNTAIN NAT'L PK.
WATERTON-GLACIER INTERNATIONAL PEACE PARK
Whitehorse
Yellowknife
Edmonton
Calgary
Regina
Saskatoon
Winnipeg
Victoria
Vancouver
Seattle
Portland
Spokane
MONTANA
N. DAK.
S. DAK.
WYOMING
NEBR.
IOWA
MINN.
UNITED STATES
Mt. McKinley 20,320
Mt. St. Elias 18,008
Mt. Logan 19,850
Mt. Fairweather 15,300
Mt. Robson 12,972
Mt. Waddington 13,260
Mt. Alberta 11,874
Churchill Pk. 10,500

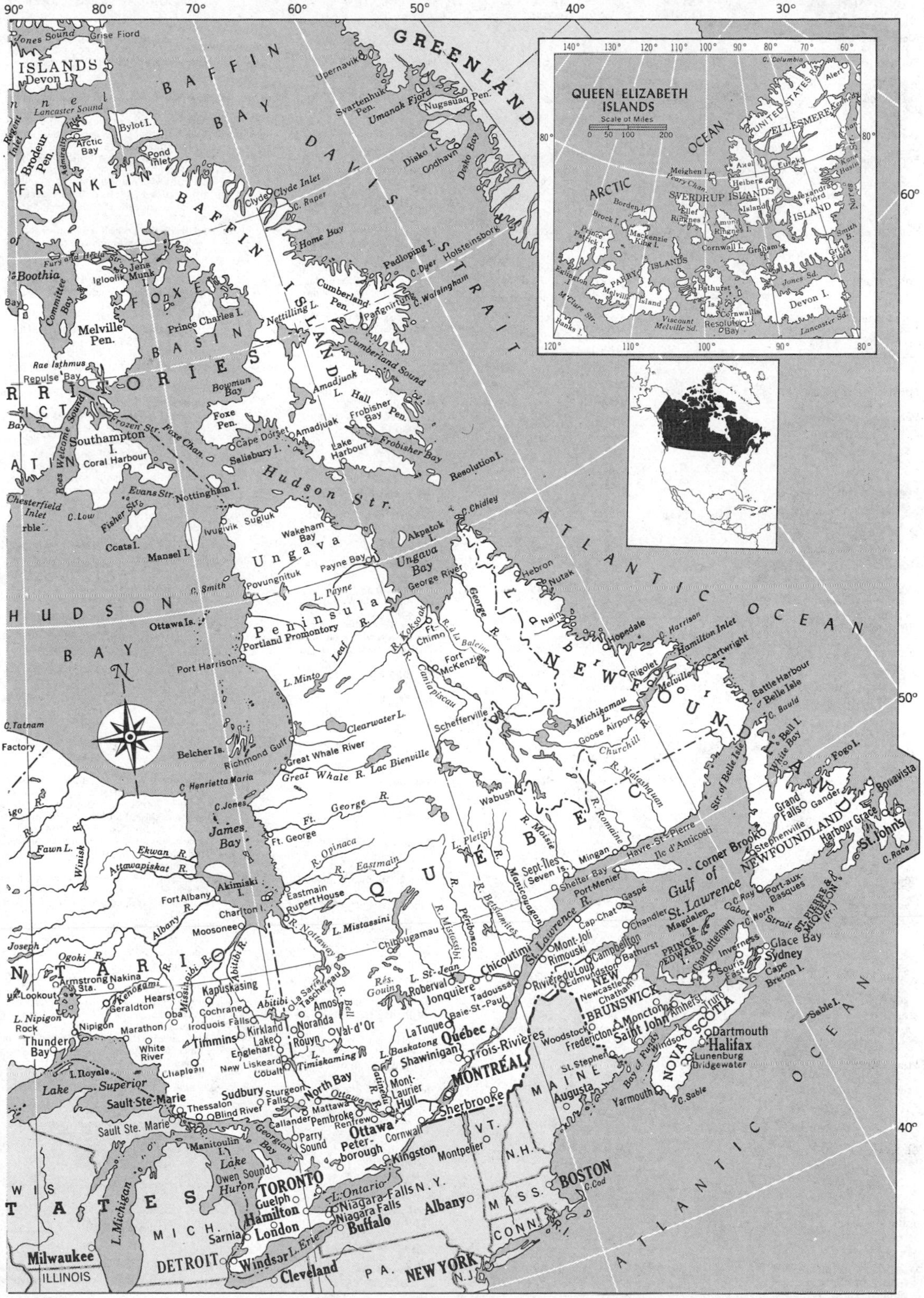
GREENLAND
BAFFIN BAY
DAVIS STRAIT
BAFFIN ISLAND
FOXE BASIN
FRANKLIN
HUDSON BAY
Hudson Str.
Ungava Peninsula
Ungava Bay
ATLANTIC OCEAN
QUEBEC
NEWFOUNDLAND
ONTARIO
NEW BRUNSWICK
NOVA SCOTIA
PRINCE EDWARD I.
Gulf of St. Lawrence
MAINE
VT.
N.H.
MASS.
CONN.
R.I.
N.Y.
PA.
MICH.
ILLINOIS
QUEEN ELIZABETH ISLANDS
Scale of Miles
ARCTIC OCEAN
SVERDRUP ISLANDS
PARRY ISLANDS
ELLESMERE ISLAND
Devon I.
Melville Island
Cornwallis I.
Resolute Bay
Alert
Eureka
Grise Fiord
Pond Inlet
Arctic Bay
Clyde
Igloolik
Melville Pen.
Southampton I.
Coral Harbour
Cape Dorset
Frobisher Bay
Lake Harbour
Resolution I.
Port Harrison
Great Whale River
Lac Bienville
Fort Chimo
Fort McKenzie
Schefferville
Wabush
Hopedale
Nain
Hebron
Cartwright
Goose Airport
Churchill R.
Hamilton Inlet
James Bay
Akimiski I.
Moosonee
Fort Albany
Eastmain
Rupert House
L. Mistassini
Chibougamau
Sept-Îles
Mingan
Gaspé
Rimouski
Chicoutimi
Jonquière
Roberval
Québec
Trois-Rivières
MONTRÉAL
Sherbrooke
Ottawa
Hull
Kingston
Peterborough
TORONTO
Hamilton
Guelph
London
Windsor
Sarnia
DETROIT
Milwaukee
Cleveland
Buffalo
Niagara Falls
Albany
NEW YORK
BOSTON
Augusta
Montpelier
Fredericton
Moncton
Saint John
Halifax
Dartmouth
Yarmouth
Sydney
Glace Bay
Charlottetown
Corner Brook
Gander
Grand Falls
St. John's
Harbour Grace
Bonavista
Sault Ste. Marie
Sudbury
North Bay
Timmins
Kapuskasing
Thunder Bay
Lake Superior
Lake Huron
L. Michigan
L. Ontario
L. Erie
Georgian Bay
Manitoulin I.
Owen Sound
90°
80°
70°
60°
50°
40°
30°

NAME	ESTABLISHED	AREA (acres)	LOCATION	HISTORICAL SIGNIFICANCE
Alexander Graham Bell	*	21	Baddeck, N.S.	Museum commemorating the work of Alexander Graham Bell
Fort Amherst	*	222	Prince Edward Island, ab. 5 m. S of Charlottetown	Earthworks of British fort constructed after 1758
Fort Anne	1917	31	Annapolis Royal, W Nova Scotia	Site of early Acadian settlement at Port Royal; first fort built c. 1635; named 1710 in honor of Queen Anne of England; several times rebuilt and added to by English
Fort Battleford	1951	36.7	S of North Battleford, Saskatchewan	North West Mounted Police post built 1876
Fort Beauséjour	1926	93	Near Sackville, SE New Brunswick	Fort built by French 1751–55; captured by English 1755; its defenses strengthened in Amer. Revolution, War of 1812
Fort Chambly	1940	2.5	Chambly Canton on Richelieu river, 20 m. E of Montreal	Fort built by French 1665; burned by Indians 1702; rebuilt of stone 1709–11; captured by U.S. forces 1775; contains museum
Fort Langley	*	11	SW British Columbia, ab. 26 m. SE of Vancouver	Trading post established 1827; site of proclamation of colony of British Columbia 1858
Fort Lennox	1940	210	On Ile-aux-Noix in Richelieu river, 12 m. S of St. Johns, Quebec	Advance post against Indians in 18th cent.; present fortifications built by English 1812-27
Fort Malden	1940	10	Amherstburg, Ontario	Built by English 1797–99 on Detroit river; important frontier defense post in War of 1812
Fort Prince of Wales	1940	50	Churchill, NE Manitoba, on Hudson Bay	Built by English 1733–71 to control Hudson Bay; now in ruins
Fortress of Louisbourg	1940	13,000	Near Louisburg, E Cape Breton I., Nova Scotia	Built by French 1720–40 as strategic military and naval base; captured by New England volunteers 1745; restored to France but captured by British 1758 in Seven Years' War; now group of picturesque ruins
Fort Rodd Hill	1962	44.4	Esquimalt, Vancouver I., British Columbia	19th cent. stone coastal fortifications
Fort Wellington	1940	12	Prescott, Ontario, on St. Lawrence	Defense post built 1812–13; strengthened during rebellion of 1837–38; blockhouse within earthworks and palisade
Grand Pré	1957	20	Grand Pré, Nova Scotia	Museum illustrating history of the Acadians
Halifax Citadel	1951	20	Halifax, Nova Scotia	Defense post constructed 1828–42
Lower Fort Garry	1951	13	20 m. N of Winnipeg, Manitoba	Hudson's Bay Company fort built between 1831 and 1839
Port Royal	1940	20.5	Lower Granville village, 8 m. SW of Annapolis Royal; Nova Scotia	Replica on Annapolis Basin of "Habitation" built 1605 by Champlain and De Monts; site of first permanent settlement in Canada
Signal Hill	1958	243.4	St. John's, Nfld.	Location of fortifications and site of battles in 1700's
Woodside	1954	12	Kitchener, Ontario	Boyhood home of W. L. Mackenzie King

NATIONAL PARKS

NAME	ESTABLISHED	AREA (sq. m.)	LOCATION	FEATURES
Banff	1885	2,564	SW Alberta	Mountains, glaciers; game sanctuary; summer and winter sports center; resorts of Banff and Lake Louise
Cape Breton Highlands	1936	367	N Cape Breton Island, N.S.	Rugged highland and coastal scenery
Elk Island	1913	75	E cen. Alberta ab. 30 m. E of Edmonton	Fenced enclosure containing buffalo, moose, deer, wapiti; recreational and camping resort
Fundy	1948	79.5	On Bay of Fundy, Nova Scotia	Interesting rock formations; recreational areas
Georgian Bay Islands	1929	5.37	Thirty islands in Georgian Bay	Limestone caves and formations; resort
Glacier	1886	521	SE British Columbia	Peaks, glaciers, valleys in heart of Selkirk Mts.
Jasper	1907	4,200	W Alberta	Mountains, lakes; big-game sanctuary; resorts
Kejimkujik	*	150	SW cen. Nova Scotia	Varied fauna and flora; numerous lakes and streams
Kootenay	1920	543	SE British Columbia	Mountains, canyons, hot mineral springs
Mount Revelstoke	1914	100	SE British Columbia	Plateau region on Mt. Revelstoke, W slope of Selkirk Mts.
Point Pelee	1918	6	Ontario, on Lake Erie	Most southerly mainland point in Canada; resort
Prince Albert	1927	1,496	Central Saskatchewan	Forested region with many lakes and waterways; resort
Prince Edward Island	1937	7	Strip 25 m. long on N coast of Prince Edward Island	Bathing beaches and recreational area
Riding Mountain	1929	1,148	SW Manitoba	Forested highland area, with many lakes; game preserve
St. Lawrence Islands	1914	260 (acres)	Mainland area and 13 islands of the Thousand Islands	Recreational areas
Terra Nova	1957	153	On Bonavista Bay, Newfoundland, 205 m. N of St. John's	Varied scenery; fishing; camping facilities
Waterton Lakes	1895	203	S Alberta; Canadian part of Waterton-Glacier International Peace Park (*q.v.*)	Mountain recreational area
Wood Buffalo (includes former Buffalo National Park, established 1908, 197.5 sq. m., in Alberta)	1922	17,300	N Alberta and S Northwest Territories, W of Slave river and bet. Athabaska and Great Slave Lakes	Immense forested and plains region; large herd of buffalo and other game
Yoho	1886	507	SE British Columbia	Peaks, waterfalls, lakes, valleys, on W slopes of Rocky Mts.

*Not yet established.

2 County in Oklahoma. See table at OKLAHOMA.

3 Town, ⊗ of Hemphill co., NW Texas, 38 m. NE of Pampa; pop. (1970c) 2292; in farming area.

Canadian Arctic Islands. See ARCTIC ARCHIPELAGO.

Canadian Fall *or* **Canadian Falls.** See NIAGARA FALLS.

Canadian Shield. See LAURENTIAN HIGHLANDS.

Can·a·jo·har·ie \ˌkan-ə-jō-ˈhar-ē\. Village, Montgomery co., E New York, on Mohawk river 21 m. W of Amsterdam; pop. (1970c) 2686; settled c. 1730; figured in American Revolution as meeting place (Fort Rensselaer); food-packing plants.

Ça·nak·ka·le \ˌchän-ə-kə-ˈlā\. 1 Province, NW Turkey, extending on both sides of the Dardanelles. See table at TURKEY.

2 *or formerly* **Cha·nak** \chə-ˈnäk\ *also* **Ka·le Sul·ta·nie** \kə-ˌlā-su̇l-ˌtän-ē-ˈä\. Commercial town and fort, its ✱, on the Asiatic shore of the Dardanelles; pop. (1965c) 22,789; unsuccessfully bombarded Mar. 1915 by Allied fleet in World War I.

Çanakkale Boğazi. See DARDANELLES.

Ca·nal Zone \kə-ˈnal-\. Strip of territory in Panama; 10 m. wide; 647 sq. m. (including 275 sq. m. of water); pop. (1970p) 44,650; administrative center Balboa Heights; under perpetual lease to United States for Panama Canal; includes Gatun Lake and district above Alhajuela for a reservoir (Madden Lake), but not cities of Panama and Colón; chief cities Balboa, Rainbow City, Gamboa.

History: Acquisition of zone by U.S. provided for in Hay-Herrán Treaty with Colombia (not ratified by Colombia); rights over it granted to U.S. by treaty with Panama 1903; governed and operated according to act of Congress of 1912; boundaries determined 1914; sovereignty disputed by U.S. and Panama 1926; U.S.-Panama treaty of 1967 regarding future status of zone rejected by Panama 1970.

Can·an·dai·gua \ˌkan-ən-ˈdā-gwə\. City, ⊗ of Ontario co., W New York, at N end of Canandaigua Lake 26 m. SE of Rochester; pop. (1970c) 10,488; Community Coll. of the Finger Lakes (1965); resort.

Canandaigua Lake. Lake in Ontario and Yates cos., W New York; one of the Finger Lakes (*q.v.*); ab. 15 m. long and 2 m. wide at its greatest extent. The **Canandaigua Outlet** flows from N end of the lake into Seneca river N of Cayuga Lake; from Lyons, Wayne co., also called the Clyde river.

Ca·na·nea \ˌkän-ə-ˈnā-ə\. Municipality, Sonora state, NW Mexico, 135 m. NNE of Hermosillo; pop. (1970p) 21,824; alt. 5150 ft.; cattle; mining (copper, silver, lead, zinc).

Cana of Galilee. See CANA.

Ca·ñar \kən-ˈyär\. 1 Province of W cen. Ecuador. See table at ECUADOR.

2 Town, Cañar prov., W cen. Ecuador, in the Andes 70 m. ESE of Guayaquil; pop. (1962c) 4935.

Canarias, Islas. See CANARY ISLANDS.

Canaries. See CANARY ISLANDS.

Canaries Mountain. Peak on Saint Lucia I., West Indies; 3145 ft.

Ca·na·rio \kə-ˈnar-ē-ˌü\. Mountain peak on the island of Madeira; 5449 ft.

Ca·nar·sie \kə-ˈnär-sē\. Section of Brooklyn, New York City, N.Y., in S part on Jamaica Bay.

Ca·nary Islands \kə-ˌne(ə)r-ē-\ *or* **Ca·nar·ies** \-ˈne(ə)r-ēz\ *or Span.* **Is·las Ca·na·rias** \ˈēz-ˌläs-kə-ˈnär-ē-ˌäs\. Island group in Atlantic Ocean off NW coast of Africa, 823 m. SW of Spain; 2808 sq. m.; pop. (1970p) 1,170,224; forms two provinces of Spain: (1) Santa Cruz de Tenerife prov. which comprises Tenerife, La Palma, Gomera, and Hierro (*qq.v.*) Is., and (2) Las Palmas prov. which comprises Grand Canary, Fuerteventura, Lanzarote (*qq.v.*), Alegranza, Graciosa, and Isla de Lobos Is., the last three of which are barren and uninhabited; volcanic in origin; mountainous, generally rugged in contour; has some fertile valleys; mild, pleasant climate; subject to severe droughts and tornadoes; irrigated farming; has both Mediterranean and African flora; produces grain, fruits, esp. bananas, oranges, and lemons, vegetables, wines; fishing; tourism.

History: Known in ancient times as the "Fortunate Isles"; rediscovered and claimed by Portuguese 1341 but awarded to Castile by papal bull 1344; taken possession of by Castile 1402; their conquest the object of expedition sent by Prince Henry the Navigator 1425 who tried to secure them to cut off Castilian trade to West Africa; later acquired by Aragon; thought to be W limit of world (see HIERRO); on usual route of Spanish vessels in trade with New World; supplied wine in exchange for fish brought by New England traders 17th to early 19th cents.; divided 1927 into two provinces.

Can·a·sto·ta \ˌkan-ə-ˈstō-tə\. Village, Madison co., cen. New York, on N.Y. State Barge Canal 22 m. E of Syracuse; pop. (1970c) 5033; settled c. 1806.

Canati. See FELANITX.

Ca·na·tlán \ˌkä-nə-ˈtlän\. Municipality, Durango state, Mexico, 30 m. NNW of Durango; pop. (1970p) 63,871; timber; diversified agriculture.

Canaveral, Cape. See KENNEDY, CAPE.

Ca·nav·er·al Peninsula \kə-ˈnav-(ə-)rəl-\. Narrow strip of land extending S from SE Volusia co., off E coast of Florida; ab. 100 m. long; encloses Indian River; near central part is separated from Merritt I. by Banana river.

Can·ber·ra \ˈkan-ˌber-ə, -b(ə-)rə\. City, ✱ of Australia, in Australian Capital Territory, SE New South Wales, on Molonglo river, branch of Murrumbidgee river, ab. 155 m. SW of Sydney; pop. (Capital Territory [1970e]) 133,100; chosen 1908 to be site of Australian capital; construction of city begun 1913; first meeting of Commonwealth's Parliament held 1927; government offices, Australian National Univ. (1946), military coll., numerous research institutes.

Can·by \ˈkan-bē\. 1 City, Yellow Medicine co., SW Minnesota, 31 m. WSW of Montevideo; pop. (1970c) 2147; dairying; poultry.

2 City, Clackamas co., NW Oregon, 22 m. S of Portland; pop. (1970c) 3813; diversified agriculture.

Can·cale \kän-ˈkäl\. Town, Ille-et-Vilaine dept., NW France, on coast E of Saint-Malo; pop. (1962c) 5236.

Can·da·ba \kän-ˈdä-bə\. Municipality, E Pampanga prov., Luzon, Phil., on left bank of Pampanga river 10 m. ENE of San Fernando; pop. (1969e) 39,700; on W margin of large lagoon and swamp area E of the Pampanga, known as **Candaba Swamp** (*or Span.* **Pi·nag de Candaba** \pi-ˌnäg-dä-\); melon-producing region.

Can·de·la·ria \ˌkan-də-ˈlär-ē-ə\. 1 Municipality, Pinar del Río prov., W Cuba; pop. (1967e) 18,790.

2 River in S Campeche state, Mexico; flows W and N into Laguna de Términos.

Can·dia \ˈkan-dē-ə\. 1 Island. See CRETE 3.

2 *or* **He·rak·li·on** \hi-ˈrak-lē-ən\ *or Gk.* **Irá·kli·on** \i-ˈrä-klē-ˌȯn\ *or anc.* **Her·a·cle·um** \ˌher-ə-ˈklē-əm\. Seaport city, ✱ of Hērákleion dept., E cen. Crete, Greece, on N shore of island; pop. (1971p) 77,783; exports incl. grapes, olives, wine, leather; episcopal see. Founded by Saracens near site of ancient Knossos; occupied by Venetians (whence its Italian name Candia) 13th–17th cents.; captured by Turks 1669; in modern times largest city in Crete; before 1841 capital of the island; devastated in German invasion May 1941.

Candia, Sea of. See CRETE, SEA OF.

Can·di·ac \ˈkan-dē-ˌak\. Town, Laprairie co., S Quebec, Canada, 5 m. S of Montreal; pop. (1971p) 5189.

Can·dler \ˈkan-(d)lər\. County in Georgia. See table at GEORGIA.

Can·dle·wood, Lake \-ˈkan-dᵊl-ˌwu̇d\. Lake, W Connecticut, near New York border bet. Litchfield and Fairfield cos.; 15 m. long; drains N into Housatonic river.

Can·do \ˈkan-(ˌ)dü\. City, ⊗ of Towner co., N North Dakota; pop. (1970c) 1512; grain elevator.

Can·don \kän-ˈdȯn\. Municipality, S Ilocos Sur prov., Luzon, Phil., near coast and on main highway 25 m. S of Vigan; pop. (1969e) 37,700; coastwise trade.

Ca·nea *also* **Ka·nea** \kə-ˈnē-ə\ *or Gk.* **Kha·niá** *also* **Cha·nia** \kän-ˈyä\. 1 Department of Greece. See table at GREECE.

2 *or anc.* **Cy·do·nia** \sī-ˈdō-nē-ə, -nyə\. Commercial seaport city, its ✱ and ✱ of Crete since 1841, on N coast of island at base of Akroteri Penin. on Bay of Canea; pop. (1971p) 40,452; exports citrus fruit, wine; Orthodox and Catholic bishoprics. Prospered under Venetian rule; taken by Turks 1646; suffered heavily during German invasion May 1941.

Canea, Bay of. Inlet of Sea of Crete on N coast of Crete, Greece, at its W end; enclosed on E by Akroteri Penin.

Ca·ne·lo·nes \ˌkä-nə-ˈlō-nəs\. 1 Department of S Uruguay. See table at URUGUAY.

2 *or* **Gua·da·lu·pe** \ˌgwäd-ᵊl-ˈüp-ē\. Town, its ✱, 27 m. N of Montevideo; pop. (1963c) 14,180; flour mills.

Ca·ñe·te \kän-ˈyāt-ē\. 1 River, W cen. Peru; 120 m. long; flows SW into Pacific Ocean 80 m. S of Lima.

2 Town at mouth of the Cañete, Peru; pop. (1961c) 7200.

Ca·ney \ˈkā-nē\. City, Montgomery co., SE Kansas, 20 m. SW of Independence; pop. (1970c) 2192; oil and gas wells; corn, wheat.

Caney. See EL CANEY.

Caney, Point \-kä-ˈnā\. Cape on SE coast of Las Villas prov., W cen. Cuba.

Caney Fork \ˌkā-nē-\. River, cen. Tennessee; formed by confluence of branches in SE White co., flows W and NW into Cumberland river near Carthage, Smith co.; traverses Great Falls Lake (bet. White, Van Buren, and Warren cos.), formed by Great Falls Dam, one of the dams of the Tennessee Valley Authority (*q.v.*).

Can·field \ˈkan-ˌfēld\. Village, Mahoning co., NE Ohio, 10 m. SW of Youngstown; pop. (1970c) 4997; metal fabricating; fruit growing.

Can·gas \ˈkaŋ-gəs\. Commune, Pontevedra prov., NW Spain, on Bay of Vigo 14 m. SW of Pontevedra; pop. (1970p) 19,026; cloth manufactures, sardine canning; cattle.

Cangas de Nar·cea \-ˌdā-när-ˈsā-ə\ *also* **Cangas de Ti·neo** \-ti-ˈnā-(ˌ)ō\. Commune, Oviedo prov., NW Spain, 37 m. WSW of Oviedo; pop. (1970p) 19,713; coal mining, farming.

Cangas de Onís \-dā-ō-ˈnēs\. Commune, Oviedo prov., NW Spain, 35 m. E of Oviedo; pop. (1970p) 6922; agriculture; copper and coal mining; tanneries. Ancient seat of Asturian kings. See COVADONGA.

Can·go Caves \ˌkäŋ-(ˌ)gō-\. Stalactite caves in the Swartberg Mts., S Cape Province, Rep. of South Africa, N of Oudtshoorn.

Can·i·a·pis·cau *also* **Kan·i·a·pis·kau** \ˌkan-ē-ə-ˈpis-(ˌ)kō\. River, N Quebec, Canada; 575 m. long; flows from **Lake Caniapiscau** *or* **Lake Kaniapiskau** (210 sq. m., 54°N, 69°W) in cen. Quebec, N to unite with the Larch river and form Koksoak river.

Ca·ni·cat·tì \ˌkän-i-kä-ˈtē\. Commune, Agrigento prov., SW Sicily, Italy, 16 m. E by N of Agrigento; pop. (1968e) 31,501; sulfur mines.

Ca·ni·gao Channel \ˌkän-i-ˌgau̇-\. Passage bet. SW Leyte and E Bohol, S cen. Phil.; 18 to 28 m. wide; connects NE Mindanao Sea with Camotes Sea.

Ca·ni·gou \ˌkan-i-ˈgü\. Peak, S Pyrénées-Orientales dept., S France, in the E Pyrenees ab. 20 m. SW of Perpignan; 9135 ft.

Ca·ni·llas \kə-ˈnē-yəs\. Commune, Madrid prov., cen. Spain, NE suburb of Madrid.

Ca·ni·no \kä-ˈnē-nō\. Village, Viterbo prov., W Latium, cen. Italy, WNW of Viterbo; pop. (1968e) 5094; in 1814 made a principality for Lucien Bonaparte.

Can·is·teo \ˌkan-ə-ˈstē-(ˌ)ō\. 1 River, SW New York; ab. 60 m. long; rises in Allegany co., flows SE into Tioga river ab. 5 m. SW of Corning in SE Steuben co.

2 Residential village, Steuben co., S New York, on Canisteo river 6 m. SSE of Hornell; pop. (1970c) 2772. Former Indian village; settled by whites 1788.

Can·ji·lon, Mount \-ˈkan-(h)i-ˌlōn\. Mountain, Rio Arriba co., N New Mexico; 10,700 ft.

Çan·kırı \ˌchän-kə-ˈrə\ *or* **Chan·ki·ri** \ˌchäŋ-\. 1 Province of N cen. Turkey, Asia. See table at TURKEY.

2 *anc.* **Gan·gra** \ˈgaŋ-grə\ *or later* **Ger·man·i·cop·o·lis** \gər-ˌman-ə-ˈkäp-ə-ləs\. Town, its ✱, on tributary of Kızıl Irmak ab. 60 m. NE of Ankara; pop. (1965c) 21,450; salt deposits nearby; scene of Synod of Gangra c. 350 A.D.

Can·la·on \ˌkän-lə-ˈōn\. Chartered city, N Negros Oriental prov., Negros I., Phil.; pop. (1970e) 32,300.

Canlaon, Mount *or* **Ma·la·spi·na** \ˌmäl-ə-ˈspē-nə\. Active volcano, N cen. Negros I., cen. Phil.; 8070 ft.; in eruption 1866 and 1893.

Can·na \ˈkan-ə\. Island of the Inner Hebrides, off W coast of Scotland; part of Inverness co.; 4½ m. long.

Can·nae \ˈkan-(ˌ)ē\. Battlefield near modern Barletta, Bari prov., Apulia, SE Italy, where, in 216 B.C., during Second Punic War, Hannibal inflicted on Roman army the severest defeat ever sustained by Rome.

Can·na·nore \ˈkan-ə-ˌnō(ə)r, -ˌnȯ(ə)r\ *or* **Ka·na·nur** \ˌkən-ə-ˈnu̇(ə)r\. Town, N Kerala, SW India, on the Malabar Coast 50 m. NNW of Calicut; pop. (1961c) 48,960; has some export trade. Visited by Vasco da Gama 1498; Portuguese settlement made 1501, fort built 1505; present fort built by Dutch 1656; captured by British 1783.

Can·nel·ton \ˈkan-əlt-ᵊn\. City, ⊗ of Perry co., S Indiana, on Ohio river 43 m. E of Evansville; pop. (1970c) 2280; sewer pipes; timber.

Cannes \ˈkan\. Seaport and commune, Alpes-Maritimes dept., SE France, on Mediterranean 18 m. SW of Nice; pop. (commune [1968c]) 67,152; international resort; perfumes, soap; exports fruit, oils, anchovies. Twice destroyed by Moors; Napoleon landed nearby on his escape from Elba Mar. 1815; in World War II marked E limit of landing of Americans Aug. 15, 1944.

Cannet, Le. See LE CANNET.

Can·ning Basin \ˌkan-iŋ-\ *or* **Desert Basin.** Arid region of Western Australia, ab. 90 m. NNE of Perth; ab. 200,000 sq. m.; approx. coextensive with the Great Sandy Desert.

Can·nock \ˈkan-ək\. Urban district, Staffordshire, W cen. England, 16 m. NNW of Birmingham; pop. (1971p) 55,873; metalworking, coal mining.

Can·non \ˈkan-ən\. 1 River, SE Minnesota; ab. 95 m. long; rises in S Le Sueur co., flows NE to the Mississippi.

2 County in Tennessee. See table at TENNESSEE.

Can·non·ball \ˈkan-ən-ˌbȯl\. River, SW North Dakota; ab. 140 m. long; rises in Slope co., flows E into Missouri river on NW boundary of Sioux co.

Cannon Falls. City, Goodhue co., SE Minnesota, 24 m. NE of Faribault; pop. (1970c) 2072; farm products.

Cannon Mountain. 1 Peak in Glacier National Park, NW Montana; 8460 ft.

2 *or* **Pro·file Mountain** \ˌprō-ˌfīl-\. Peak, N Grafton co., W New Hampshire, in White Mts. on W side of Franconia Notch; 4077 ft.; on a SE shoulder is a natural formation (the Profile, or Old Man of the Mountain) which resembles a human face seen in profile; on NE is a formation resembling a cannon; aerial tramway.

Cann·statt *or* **Kann·statt** \ˈkän-ˌs(h)tät\. Northern suburb of Stuttgart, Baden-Württemberg, West Germany; formerly an independent town, became part of Stuttgart 1905; mineral springs; received municipal charter 1330; site of discovery 1700 of human skull (the Cannstatt skull) thought to be representative of a Neolithic race.

Ca·no·as \kə-'nō-əs\. City, Rio Grande do Sul state, S Brazil, a N suburb of Pôrto Alegre; munic. pop. (1968e) 122,-040.

Can·on City \ˌkan-yən-\. City, ⊗ of Fremont co., S cen. Colorado, on Arkansas river 35 m. SW of Colorado Springs; pop. (1970c) 9206; resort in mining district; marble, limestone quarries; state penitentiary; settled 1859.

Can·ons·burg \'kan-ənz-ˌbərg\. Borough, Washington co., SW Pennsylvania, 18 m. SSW of Pittsburgh; pop. (1970c) 11,439; platted 1787; active center of Whisky Insurrection 1794; coal-mining center; gas and oil wells.

Ca·no·pus \kə-'nō-pəs\. City of anc. Egypt, 15 m. E of Alexandria at Abukir; in early times of much importance because of its great temple of Serapis; the most westerly branch of the Nile delta then had its mouth here, **Ca·no·pic Mouth** \kə-'nō-pik-\.

Ca·nora \kə-'nōr-ə, -'nȯr-\. Town, Saskatchewan, Canada, 130 m. NE of Regina; pop. (1971p) 2612; diversified agriculture.

Ca·no·sa di Pu·glia \kə-ˌnō-sə-di-'pül-yə\ *or anc.* **Ca·nu·si·um** \kə-'n(y)ü-z(h)ē-əm\. Commune, Bari prov., Apulia, SE Italy, 43 m. W by N of Bari; pop. (1968e) 33,080; Romanesque cathedral built 1101; ruined castle; ancient Roman remains.

Canossa. See CIANO D'ENZA.

Ca·nou·an \ˌkan-ə-'wän\. Small island, Windward Is., West Indies; a dependency of St. Vincent.

Canóvanas. See LOÍZA.

Can·so \'kan(t)-(ˌ)sō\. Fishing town, Guysborough co., E Nova Scotia, Canada, on Atlantic Ocean at mouth of Chedabucto Bay near Cape Canso; pop. (1971p) 1202; reputed to have been inhabited by European fishermen and fur traders shortly after Columbus' discovery of America; became English post 1718; recaptured by French 1744 but left unoccupied; held by British 1745–49; had repeated Indian trouble; ravaged and largely destroyed by privateers 1812. American terminus of several Atlantic cables and port of call for Gloucester fishing fleet.

Canso, Cape. Cape at NE end of Nova Scotia mainland, Canada, at S entrance to Chedabucto Bay.

Canso, Strait of *or* **Gut of Canso.** Deep, narrow channel bet. NE Nova Scotia mainland and S Cape Breton I., Canada; ab. 14½ m. long and 1 m. wide.

Cantaber Oceanus. See BISCAY, BAY OF.

Can·ta·bri·an Mountains \kan-'tā-brē-ən-\ *or Span.* **Cor·dil·le·ra Can·tá·bri·ca** \ˌkȯrd-ᵊl-'(y)er-ə-kən-'täb-ri-kə\. Range in N and NW Spain; highest peak Torre de Cerredo 8787 ft.

Cantabrigia. See CAMBRIDGE 9.

Can·tal \käⁿ-'täl\. Department of S cen. France. See table at FRANCE.

Can·ter·bury \'kant-ə(r)-ˌber-ē\. **1** Town, Windham co., NE Connecticut; pop. (1970c) 2673.

2 Municipality, E New South Wales, SE Australia, SW suburb of Sydney; pop. (1966c) 115,802.

3 *or anc.* **Du·ro·ver·num** \ˌd(y)u̇r-ə-'vər-nəm\ *or ecclesiastical Lat.* **Can·tu·ar·ia** \ˌkan-chə-'war-ē-ə, -'wer-\ *or O.E.* **Cant·wa·ra·burh** \'kant-(ˌ)-war-ə-bu̇rk\. City and county borough, Kent, SE England, on the Stour 53 m. ESE of London; pop. (1971p) 33,157; tourism; Univ. of Kent at Canterbury (1964); ecclesiastical metropolis of England since the founding 602 of a monastery by Saint Augustine. Church, later the cathedral, destroyed by fire 1067, E part rebuilt, destroyed again by fire 1174, rebuilt 1175–80; improved by changes and additions 1379–1503; scene of murder of Thomas à Becket 1170 and after his canonization 1172 made a place of pilgrimage (shrine, built after 1175, destroyed by Henry VIII 1538); damaged by German bombing May 31, 1942.

Canterbury Bight. Wide inlet of Pacific Ocean, E cen. coast of South I., New Zealand, S of Banks Penin.

Can Tho \ˌkən-'tō\. Town, South Vietnam, on right bank of the Mekong in its delta 90 m. SW of Saigon; pop. (1968e) 87,675; trades in rice and fish; a port of call for river and coastal steamers; univ. (1966).

Can·ti·gny \ˌkäⁿ-ˌtēn-'yē\. Village, Somme dept., N France, ab. 18 m. S of Amiens; pop. (1962c) 110; battle May 28, 1918, first offensive by U.S. forces in World War I.

Can·ti·les Cay \kän-ˌtē-ləs-\. Island in N Caribbean Sea, E of Isle of Pines and S of W Cuba.

Can·ton \'kant-ᵊn\. **1** Manufacturing town, W Hartford co., N Connecticut; pop. (1970c) 6868; incorp. 1806; includes Collinsville (*q.v.*).

2 City, ⊗ of Cherokee co., NW Georgia, 33 m. NNW of Atlanta; pop. (1970c) 3654; poultry; timber; cotton mills.

3 City, Fulton co., W cen. Illinois, 25 m. WSW of Peoria; pop. (1970c) 14,217; farm implements; lumber; Spoon River Coll. (1959); settled 1825; incorp. 1854.

4 Industrial town, Norfolk co., E Massachusetts, 14 m. SSW of Boston; pop. (1970c) 17,100; rubber goods, electrical equipment; site of Paul Revere's brass and bell foundry.

5 City, ⊗ of Madison co., cen. Mississippi, 25 m. NNE of Jackson; pop. (1970c) 10,503; cotton, timber.

6 City, Lewis co., NE Missouri, on Mississippi river 33 m. N of Hannibal; pop. (1970c) 2680; fisheries, poultry farms; Culver-Stockton Coll. (1853).

7 Village, ⊗ of St. Lawrence co., N New York, 18 m. ESE of Ogdensburg; pop. (1970c) 6398; St. Lawrence Univ. (1856), State Univ. of New York Agricultural and Technical Coll. (1907).

8 Town, Haywood co., W North Carolina, 15 m. W of Asheville; pop. (1970c) 5158; pulp, paper, tannic extract; wheat, tobacco.

9 Industrial city, ⊗ of Stark co., NE Ohio, 20 m. SSE of Akron; pop. (1970c) 110,053; steel, office equipment, water softeners, forgings; Malone Coll. (1892), Walsh Coll. (1960); settled c. 1805; became ⊗ 1809; incorporated as village 1822, as city 1854. Home of President McKinley, who is buried here in National McKinley Memorial (erected 1907).

10 Borough, Bradford co., N Pennsylvania, 30 m. NNE of Williamsport; pop. (1970c) 2037; leather goods, plastics.

11 City, ⊗ of Lincoln co., SE South Dakota, on Big Sioux river 20 m. S of Sioux Falls; pop. (1970c) 2665; shipping point for corn and poultry; road machinery.

12 Town, ⊗ of Van Zandt co., NE Texas; pop. (1970c) 2283; peas, peaches; poultry.

Canton \'kan-ˌtän, kan-'\ *also* **Kuang–chou** \'kwäŋ-'jō\. Commercial city and port, ✱ of Kwangtung prov., SE China, on Pearl river in Hsi delta ab. 80 m. from the sea; pop. (1970e) 2,300,000; chief port and city of S China; city proper (Old City) enclosed by walls with twelve gates; has very large floating population on riverboats; chemicals, paper, sugar, jute; light engineering; univ. (1958), medical college (1953).

History: In early history of China an outpost of minor importance; incorporated in empire 3d cent. B.C.; made capital of Kwangtung under the Mings; first seaport of China opened to foreigners; regularly visited for centuries by Arab, Hindu, and Parsi traders, in 16th cent. by Portuguese; in 1684 granted right to English East India Company to establish factory; later opened to French and Dutch and (except for Macao) remained the only Chinese trading port down to 1842; its resistance to English opium trade led to war with Great Britain 1839–42; became one of the first treaty ports by Treaty of Nanking 1842. Scene of incident 1856 that led to second war with Great Britain; occupied by British and French 1856–61; granted 1859 new concession area (Shamien) to foreigners; its commercial prosperity affected by growth of Hong Kong; in 19th cent. seat of nationalist ideas and Kuomintang (see KWANGTUNG); occupied by Japanese Oct. 21, 1938; base for later Japanese offensives, esp. in 1944; fell to Communist forces 1949.

Canton Island \'kant-ᵊn-\ *or formerly* **Mary Island** \ˌme(ə)rē-, ˌma(ə)r-ē-, ˌmā-rē-\. One of the more important of the Phoenix Is. (*q.v.*), cen. Pacific Ocean, 2°48'S lat., 171°43'W long., an atoll 8 m. long by 4 m. wide, enclosing large lagoon; has stunted vegetation, with coconut groves at S end; affords excellent base for seaplanes and airplanes. Visited by expedition to observe total eclipse of sun June 8, 1937; since 1939 has become important aviation station under Anglo-American condominium on S route from Honolulu to New Caledonia.

Can·tù \kän-'tü\. Commune, Como prov., Lombardy, N Italy, 5 m. SSE of Como; pop. (1968e) 31,181.

Cantuaria *or* **Cantwaraburh.** See CANTERBURY 3.

Cantyre. See KINTYRE.

Cantyre, Mull of. See KINTYRE, MULL OF.

Ca·ñue·las \ˌkä-nyə-'wā-ləs\. Town, E Argentina, ab. 37 m. SW of Buenos Aires; pop. (1960c) 8842.

Canusium. See CANOSA DI PUGLIA.

Can·vey Island \'kan-vē-\. Urban district, Essex, SE England, ab. 30 m. E of London; pop. (1971p) 26,462.

Can·yon \'kan-yən\. 1 County in Idaho. See table at IDAHO.
2 City, ⊗ of Randall co., NW Texas, in the Panhandle 18 m. S of Amarillo; pop. (1970c) 8333; farming, stock raising; West Texas State Univ. (1909).

Canyon City. Town, ⊗ of Grant co., E cen. Oregon; pop. (1970c) 600.

Canyon de Chel·ly National Monument \-də-'shā-\. See UNITED STATES, *National Monuments.*

Canyon Di·ab·lo \-dī-'ab-(ˌ)lō\. Gorge, SE Coconino co., N Arizona, in **Canyon Diablo River;** ab. 225 ft. deep and 500 ft. wide; a tributary of the Little Colorado river; Crater Mound is nearby.

Canyon Lake. See MORMON FLAT DAM.

Can·yon·lands National Park \'kan-yən-ˌlan(d)z-\. See UNITED STATES, *National Parks.*

Cao·bang \'kaů-(ˌ)bäŋ\. Town, North Vietnam, near China border ab. 115 m. NE of Hanoi.

Ca·or·le \kä-'ȯr-lē\. Commune, Venezia prov., Veneto, NE Italy, on Gulf of Venice at mouth of Livenza river; pop. (1968e) 11,220; fishing; resort; cathedral.

Cap, Le. See CAP HAITIEN.

Capac–Urcu. See ALTAR.

Ca·pan·no·ri \kə-'pän-ə-rē\. Commune, Lucca prov., Tuscany, cen. Italy, 4 m. E of Lucca; pop. (1968e) 40,772; consists of a group of villages.

Ca·pa·rra \kə-'pär-ə\. Settlement on Puerto Rico near San Juan, founded 1509 by Ponce de León, abandoned 1511.

Ca·pas \'kä-pəs\. Municipality, S Tarlac prov., Luzon, Phil.; pop. (1969e) 36,600.

Cap–Chat \ˌkäp-'shä\. Village, West Gaspé co., Gaspé Penin., SE Quebec, Canada, on St. Lawrence river 46 m. ENE of Matane; pop. (1966c) 2026; summer resort.

Cap de la Ma·de·leine \ˌkap-də-ˌlä-ˌmad-ᵊl-'ān\. City, Champlain co., S Quebec, Canada, on N bank of St. Lawrence river 4 m. ENE of Three Rivers; pop. (1966c) 29,433; aluminum products, chemicals; foundry.

Cape Bar·ren Island \-ˌbar-ən-\. Second largest island in the Furneaux Group, NE of Tasmania, Australia.

Cape Bret·on \kāp-'bret-ᵊn, kə-'bret-, -'brit-\. County, Nova Scotia, Canada. See table at NOVA SCOTIA.

Cape Breton Highlands National Park. See CANADA, *National Parks.*

Cape Breton Island. Island, E part of Nova Scotia, E Canada; 3970 sq. m.; pop. (1966c) 166,943; comprises four counties: Cape Breton, Inverness, Richmond, and Victoria; separated from mainland by narrow Strait of Canso; in central part are Bras d'Or salt lakes; its highest peak, North Barren 1747 ft., is highest peak in Nova Scotia; has many summer resorts and one national park; its extensive Sydney coalfields are of economic value. Assigned to France 1632 and retained by Treaty of Utrecht 1713; ceded to England 1763; independent of Nova Scotia 1784–1820 (✱ Sydney); linked with mainland by causeway since 1955.

Cape Ca·nav·er·al \-kə-'nav-(ə-)rəl\. 1 Cape. See KENNEDY, CAPE.
2 City, Brevard co., E Florida, 40 m. ESE of Orlando; pop. (1970c) 4258.

Cape Charles \-'chär(-ə)lz\. 1 Cape, Virginia. See CHARLES, CAPE.
2 Town, Northampton co., S Virginia penin., on Chesapeake Bay 33 m. NNE of Norfolk; pop. (1970c) 1689; sea-food industries.

Cape Coast *or formerly* **Cape Coast Castle.** Seaport town, ✱ of Central Region, S Ghana, W Africa, 75 m. WSW of Accra; pop. (1970p) 51,764; univ. coll. (1962); first settlement by Portuguese 1610; site of castle (hence the early name) built by Swedes 1652; seized by English 1664 and held against various attacks; capital of colony to 1877.

Cape Cod \-'käd\. 1 Sandy peninsula, SE Massachusetts, nearly coextensive with Barnstable co.; 1 to 20 m. wide, ab. 65 m. long, extends E from the mainland and forms a wide curve toward the N enclosing Cape Cod Bay; has open ocean (Atlantic) on the E, Nantucket Sound on the S (separating it from Martha's Vineyard and Nantucket I.), Buzzards Bay on the SW; its base on the W is crossed by the Cape Cod Canal (8 m. long); extending from its SE corner is Monomoy Point, a long narrow sand spit, and extending from its SW corner are the Elizabeth Is. Its N tip, N of Provincetown, discovered by Gosnold 1602; Pilgrims from *Mayflower* landed near Provincetown Nov. 1620.
2 The N tip of the peninsula.

Cape Cod Bay. South end of Massachusetts Bay off E coast of Massachusetts; formed within the northward sweep of Cape Cod; see CAPE COD CANAL.

Cape Cod Canal. Ship canal in Barnstable co., Massachusetts, crossing Cape Cod at its base; 17½ m. long (with dredged approaches), 500 ft. wide, 32 ft. deep; connects Buzzards Bay with Cape Cod Bay; completed 1914, owned by U.S. government.

Cape Colony. See CAPE PROVINCE.

Cape Eliz·a·beth \-i-'liz-ə-bəth\. Town, Cumberland co., SW Maine, on Atlantic Ocean 7 m. S of Portland; pop. (1970c) 7873; summer resort.

Cape Fear \-'fi(ə)r\. River, cen. and SE North Carolina; 202 m. long; navigable to Fayetteville; formed by confluence of Deep and Haw rivers in Chatham co., flows SE into Atlantic Ocean in E Brunswick co.

Cape Gi·rar·deau \-jə-'rä(r)d-(ˌ)ō\. 1 County in Missouri. See table at MISSOURI.
2 City, Cape Girardeau co., SE Missouri, on Mississippi river 30 m. NNW of its confluence with Ohio river; pop. (1970c) 31,282; shoe factories, cement plants, sawmills; furniture, electrical equipment; timber; Southeast Missouri State Coll. (1873).

Cape Hat·ter·as National Seashore Park \-'hat-ə-rəs-, -'ha-trəs-\. See table, note 5, at NORTH CAROLINA.

Cape Horn Mountain \-ˌhȯ(ə)rn-\. Peak in Salmon River Mts., W Custer co., cen. Idaho; 9500 ft.

Cape Le Grand National Park \-lə-'grand-\. National park, S Western Australia; 62 sq. m.; ocean beach; established 1966.

Ca·pel·le aan de IJs·sel \kə-'pel-ə-ˌän-də-'ī-səl\. Commune, South Holland prov., Netherlands, ab. 5 m. E of Rotterdam; pop. (1970e) 25,766.

Cape May \-'mā\. 1 Cape, S New Jersey. See MAY, CAPE 1.
2 County in New Jersey. See table at NEW JERSEY.
3 City, Cape May co., S New Jersey, ab. 40 m. SW of Atlantic City on Atlantic Ocean; pop. (1970c) 4392; early settlement (from ab. 1664) known as Cape Island; one of oldest Atlantic coast resorts.

Cape May Court House. Village, ⊗ of Cape May co., S New Jersey, 28 m. SW of Atlantic City; pop. (1970c) 2062; poultry and dairy farms.

Cape of Good Hope. 1 Cape, Rep. of South Africa. See GOOD HOPE, CAPE OF.

2 Province, Rep. of South Africa. See CAPE PROVINCE.

Cape Province *or officially* **Cape of Good Hope** *or Afrikaans* **Kaap·pro·vin·sie** \ˌkäp-ˌprō-ˈvin(t)-sē\ *or before 1910* **Cape Colony.** Province, Rep. of South Africa; 278,380 sq. m.; pop. (1967e) 6,199,634; ✻ Cape Town; part of its N boundary formed by Orange river, its principal stream, which separates it from Orange Free State on NE and from South-West Africa on NW; bounded in extreme NE by Lesotho and Natal; rivers include the Olifants and Great Berg in SW and streams flowing S or SE to South Atlantic and Indian oceans, as the Bree, Fish, Gourits, Great Kei, and Umzimvubu; has inner plateau bordered by an escarpment roughly parallel with the coast; many short ranges 6000 to 8500 ft. in height; S of the escarpment in central part is the Great Karroo, a dry tableland 2000 to 3000 ft. above sea level; its most southerly point—also most southerly point of continent of Africa—is Cape Agulhas 34°52′S (most southerly point of Cape of Good Hope, 92 m. WNW of Cape Agulhas, is 34°21′S). *Chief products:* Wheat, corn, fruit (esp. grapes, apples, peaches); livestock; diamonds, asbestos, manganese, copper; fishing; manufacturing: engineering, food processing; foundries, sawmills. *Chief cities:* Cape Town, Port Elizabeth, East London, Kimberley, Uitenhage, Paarl.

History: Cape of Good Hope discovered 1488 by Bartholomeu Dias while en route to India 1487–88; colony founded by Dutch who began settlement at Table Bay 1652; occupied by British 1795–1803 and 1806–14; ceded to British by Dutch 1814; Natal united with Cape Colony for administrative purposes 1843–56; annexed British Kaffraria 1865 and British Bechuanaland 1895; administered Lesotho (formerly Basutoland) 1871–84; received responsible government 1872; joined Union (now Republic) of South Africa 1910.

Cape Range National Park. National park, Western Australia; 52 sq. m.; mountainous region; established 1965.

Ca·per·na·um \kə-ˈpər-nē-əm\. Ruined city of ancient Palestine, on the NW shore of the Sea of Galilee; home of Jesus during most of the period of his ministry.

Cape Sa·ble Island \-ˈsā-bəl-\. Small island off the SW tip of Nova Scotia, Canada; **Cape Sable** is its S point.

Ca·pes·terre \ˌkap-ˌes-ˈte(ə)r\. Commune, SE Marie-Galante I., Guadeloupe, West Indies.

Capesterre–le–Ma·ri·got \-lə-ˌmar-i-ˈgō\. Commune, SE Basse-Terre, Guadeloupe, West Indies.

Cape Town *or* **Cape·town** \ˈkāp-ˌtau̇n\ *or Afrikaans* **Kaap·stad** \ˈkäp-ˌstät\. Seaport city, ✻ of Cape Province and legislative ✻ of Rep. of South Africa, in SW part on Table Bay; pop. (1970p) 691,296, met. area pop. 1,096,597; resort; harbor sheltered by artificial breakwater; the republic's chief port; observatory (1827–28), South African Museum (1825), botanical gardens (1913), South African Public Library (1818), Univ. of Cape Town (at Rondebosch, 1918); exports gold and diamonds, fruits, wines, skins, wool, mohair, corn.

History: First settlement at Table Bay founded 1652 by Dutch navigator, Jan van Riebeeck, for the Dutch East India Company; served as a stopover for ships plying the Europe-to-India route; under Dutch rule until 1795, when it was captured by a British force; returned to the Dutch by the Treaty of Amiens 1803, retaken by the British 1806.

Cape Verde Islands \-ˈvərd-\ *or Port.* **Ilhas do Ca·bo Ver·de** \ˈēl-yəz-du̇-ˌkab-ü-ˈve(ə)rd-ə\. Group of volcanic islands in the Atlantic Ocean, bet. 14°47′ and 17°13′N lat.; 1557 sq. m.; pop. (1970e) 246,000; ✻ Praia on São Tiago; constitutes a Portuguese overseas province; main islands: São Tiago, Santo Antão, São Vicente, São Nicolau, Sal Rei, Boa Vista, Fogo, Maio, Brava, Santa Luzia. Generally mountainous, highest peak 9281 ft. on Fogo; produces sugar, tobacco, oranges and other fruits, coffee, peanuts, hides; fishing; chief towns are Praia, the capital, and Mindelo on São Vicente, an important coaling station. Discovered 1456 by Ca Da Mosto, Venetian navigator in service of Prince Henry of Portugal; ruled privately 1456–95; became part of royal domain 1495.

Cape York Peninsula \-ˈyȯ(ə)rk-\. Peninsula forming NE part of Queensland, Australia; ab. 450 m. long; terminates in Cape York on Torres Strait.

Cap Hai·tien \kāp-ˈhā-shən\ *or Fr.* **Cap–Ha·ï·tien** \ka̅-pä-is-yäⁿ\ *or locally* **Le Cap** \lə-ˈkap\. Seaport, N Haiti; pop. (1971e) 44,123; exports incl. coffee and sugar; earthquake 1842.

Ca·pha·reus \kə-ˈfa(ə)r-ˌyüs, -ˈfar-ē-əs\ *or Gk.* **Ka·fi·révs** \ˌkäf-ē-ˈrefs\ *also* **Do·ro** \ˈdȯr-(ˌ)ō\. Cape, SE coast of Euboea I., Greece; extends into Aegean Sea as rocky and dangerous promontory; in legend, scene of wreck of Greek fleet returning from Troy.

Ca·pia·tá \ˌkäp-yə-ˈtä\. City, Central dept., S cen. Paraguay; munic. pop. (1970e) 23,994.

Ca·pi·ba·ri·be \ˌkap-i-bə-ˈrē-bə\. River, Pernambuco state, NE Brazil; 140 m. long; flows E into Atlantic Ocean at Recife.

Ca·pi·lla del Mon·te \kə-ˈpē-zhə-del-ˈmänt-ē\. Mountain resort, W Córdoba prov., N cen. Argentina; altitude ab. 3000 ft.

Capital Federal. See FEDERAL DISTRICT 1.

Capitan, El. See EL CAPITAN.

Cap·i·tan Peak \ˌkap-ə-ˌtan-\. Mountain, Lincoln co., cen. New Mexico; 10,083 ft.

Cap·i·to·la \ˌkap-ə-ˈtō-lə\. City, Santa Cruz co., W California, 5 m. E of Santa Cruz; pop. (1970c) 5080.

Cap·i·tol Heights \ˌkap-ət-ᵊl-, ˌkap-tᵊl-\. Town, Prince Georges co., S cen. Maryland, 6 m. E of Washington; pop. (1970c) 2852.

Cap·i·to·line \ˈkap-ət-ᵊl-ˌīn, *Brit. often* kə-ˈpit-ᵊl-\. One of the seven hills of Rome; once had 2 peaks, the Arx and the **Cap·i·to·li·um** \ˌkap-ə-ˈtō-lē-əm\. See SEVEN HILLS.

Capitol Peak. Mountain, Pitkin co., W cen. Colorado; 14,-130 ft.

Capitol Reef National Park. See UNITED STATES, *National Parks.*

Ca·piz \ˈkäp-(ˌ)ēs\. **1** Province, N Panay, Phil.; borders Sibuyan Sea on the N with Jintotolo Channel on NE; 1017 sq. m.; pop. (1970p) 395,774; ✻ Roxas; good harbors at Roxas and in Pilar Bay; mountainous in W and SW; fertile plain in the E in the Panay valley. Produces sugar and rice; timber; fishing. Chief towns Roxas, Pontevedra, Ibajay, Pilar, and Libacao.

History: Town of Panay second Spanish settlement in the Philippines, built 1569; native settlements increased in 17th cent.; region organized 1716 as a politico-military province; seized by Revolutionists 1898; civil government established Apr. 1901; Aklan prov. created from part of its territory 1957.

2 Chartered city, its ✻. See ROXAS.

Capodistria. See KOPER.

Caporetto. See KOBARID.

Cap·pa·do·cia \ˌkap-ə-ˈdō-sh(ē-)ə\. Mountainous district of E Asia Minor (cen. modern Turkey) of varying boundaries; watered by the Halys river; a satrapy of the Persian Empire, it became a semi-independent kingdom under Ariarathes I, a contemporary of Alexander of Macedon; established as a separate dynasty c. 255 B.C.; aided Rome in her wars in Asia Minor; Roman province 17 A.D.; Caesarea Mazaca was its chief city.

Ca·pra·ia \kə-ˈprī-ə\. Island in Mediterranean Sea NNW of Elba and E of N tip of Corsica; ab. 7 sq. m.; part of Genova prov., Italy; penal colony.

Ca·pra·ra, Point \-kə-ˈprär-ə\. Northern point of Asinara I. off NW coast of Sardinia, Italy.

Capraria. See CABRERA.

Ca·pra·ro·la \ˌkä-prə-ˈrȯl-ə\. Commune, Viterbo prov., N Latium, cen. Italy, 9 m. SE of Viterbo; pop. (1968e) 4892; castle built 1547–59 for Alessandro Farnese.

Capreae. See CAPRI.

Ca·pre·ol \ˈkā-pri-(ˌ)ōl, ˈkap-ri-\. Town, Sudbury dist., SE Ontario, Canada, 15 m. N of Sudbury; pop. (1971p) 3471.

Ca·pre·ra \kə-ˈprer-ə\. Island in Tyrrhenian Sea off NE coast of Sardinia; 6 sq. m.; a part of Sassari prov., Sardinia, Italy; Garibaldi's home 1856–82.

Ca·pre·se \kä-ˈprā-sē\ *or* **Caprese Mi·chel·an·ge·lo** \-ˌmē-kə-ˈlän-jə-ˌlō\. Commune, Arezzo prov., E Tuscany, Italy; pop. (1968e) 2220; birthplace of Michelangelo.

Ca·pri \ka-ˈprē, kə-; ˈkäp-(ˌ)rē, ˈkap-\ *or anc.* **Cap·re·ae** \ˈkap-rē-ˌē\. Island in the Bay of Naples, Italy, part of Napoli prov.; 4 sq. m.; cliffs on E side rise 900 ft.; highest point 1923 ft. is on W side; on N shore is the Blue Grotto (*q.v.*); chief town Capri; tourist resort. During Napoleonic Wars captured by British 1806, French 1808; returned to Ferdinand I of the Two Sicilies 1813.

Cap·ri·corn Channel \ˌkap-rə-ˌkȯ(ə)rn-\. Passage in Pacific Ocean off E coast of Queensland, Australia; entrance to waters inside Great Barrier Reef at its S end.

Ca·pri·vi Strip \kə-ˌprē-vē-\ *or formerly* **Caprivi Concession** *or Ger.* **Ca·pri·vi·zip·fel** \-ˈtsip-fəl\. Strip of land, NE South-West Africa; 40 m. wide, runs E ab. 300 m. bet. Angola and Zambia on N and Botswana on S; ab. 7000 sq. m.; known also as "Caprivi's Finger"; obtained 1890 by the German chancellor Count Georg Leo von Caprivi in negotiations with the British.

Capsa. See GAFSA.

Cap San·té \ˌkap-säⁿ-ˈtā\. Village (unincorporated), ⊗ of Portneuf co., S Quebec, Canada, on N bank of St. Lawrence river 28 m. WSW of Quebec; pop. (1966c) 1803; an old parish dating back to 17th cent.; noted as a resort.

Cap·ua \ˈkap-yə-wə\. Commune, Caserta prov., Campania, S Italy, on Volturno river 19 m. N of Naples; pop. (1968e) 19,176; 9th cent. cathedral (modernized).

History: Founded 856 A.D. on site of ancient **Cas·i·li·num** \ˌkas-ə-ˈlī-nəm\ 2½ m. NW of the original ancient city of Capua (devastated by Genseric 456 A.D., completely destroyed 840 by the Saracens); captured 1501 by Caesar Borgia; as fortified city, one of defenses of kingdom of Naples; fell to kingdom of Italy 1860; scene of heavy fighting Oct. 1943 in World War II.

Ca·pu·lin Mountain National Monument \ˌkap-(y)ə-lən-\. See UNITED STATES, *National Monuments.*

Ca·que·tá \ˌkä-kə-ˈtä\. 1 Name given in Colombia to the upper course of the Japurá river. See JAPURÁ.

2 Intendancy of S Colombia. See table at COLOMBIA.

Car, Slieve. See SLIEVE CAR.

Ca·ra·ba·llo Mountains \ˌkar-ə-ˌbī-ō-\ *also* **Ca·ra·bal·los** \-ˈbī-(ˌ)ōs\. 1 The mountain group in cen. and S Nueva Vizcaya prov., cen. Luzon, Phil., with general elevation of 2000 to 5000 ft.; joined from the N by the Cordillera Central and on the E by the Sierra Madre; the range extending to the S into Quezon prov. is sometimes called the **Caraballo Sur** \-ˈsu̇(ə)r\.

2 The Cordillera Central, Phil.—formerly so called.

Ca·ra·ban·chel Al·to \ˌkär-ə-bän-chel-ˈäl-(ˌ)tō\. Commune, Madrid prov., cen. Spain, SW suburb of Madrid.

Carabanchel Ba·jo \-ˈbä-(ˌ)hō\. Commune, Madrid prov., cen. Spain, SW suburb of Madrid.

Ca·ra·bao \ˌkar-ə-ˈbau̇, ˌkär-\. Islet off W shore of Cavite prov. on S side of entrance to Manila Bay, Phil.; has American fortification, Fort Frank. See CORREGIDOR.

Carabaya, Cordillera de. See CORDILLERA DE CARABAYA.

Ca·ra·bo·bo \ˌkär-ə-ˈbō-(ˌ)bō\. 1 State of N Venezuela. See table at VENEZUELA.

2 Village in Carabobo state, ab. 20 m. SW of Valencia; battle June 24, 1821 in which Sucre defeated royalists thereby winning independence for Venezuela.

Ca·ra·cal \ˌkär-ə-ˈkäl\. City, Olt co., S Romania, 30 m. ESE of Craiova; pop. (1966c) 22,714.

Ca·rac·as \kə-ˈrak-əs, -ˈräk-\. City, ✱ of Venezuela and of the Federal District, N Venezuela; met. area pop. (1970e) 2,175,438; alt. ab. 3000 ft.; connected with its seaport La Guaira, 8 m. directly N, by a railroad ab. 23 m. long; rubber goods, textiles, glassware, chemicals, pharmaceuticals, cement, paper; food processing; several universities and colleges including Central Univ. of Venezuela (1696, univ. status 1725) and Simón Bolívar Univ. (1970); cathedral (1614).

History: Founded 1567 by Diego de Losada; sacked by Drake 1595; capital of captaincy-general of Caracas erected 1731; birthplace of Simón Bolívar 1783; under Bolívar's leadership, first colony to revolt from Spain 1810; visited by earthquake which helped those loyal to Spain to recover city 1812; reentered by Bolívar 1813 and occupied by him again June 29, 1821 (after Carabobo); became capital of independent Venezuela.

Ca·ra·gua·tay \ˌkär-ə-gwə-ˈtī\. Town, E cen. Cordillera dept., cen. Paraguay, 50 m. E of Asunción; pop. (1962c) 18,503.

Caralis. See CAGLIARI 2.

Caraman *or* **Caramania.** See KARAMAN.

Ca·ra·mo·an \ˌkär-ə-ˈmō-ˌän\. Municipality at E end of Caramoan Penin., NE Camarines Sur prov., Luzon, Phil., near shore of Lagonoy Gulf; pop. (1969e) 37,400.

Caramoan Peninsula. Peninsula extending into Pacific Ocean and forming NE part of Camarines Sur prov., SE Luzon, Phil.; on W is San Miguel Bay and on SE Lagonoy Gulf; ab. 53 m. long, 13 m. wide.

Ca·ran·go·la \ˌkar-aŋ-ˈgō-lə\. City, SE Minas Gerais state, E Brazil; munic. pop. (1968e) 40,036.

Carapacheta. See KARAPACHETA.

Ca·ra·pe·guá \ˌkär-ə-pə-ˈgwä\. Town, Paraguarí dept., S cen. Paraguay, ab. 40 m. SE of Asunción; pop. (1970e) 27,991; founded 1725.

Car·a·quet \ˈkar-ə-(ˌ)ket\. Village, NE New Brunswick, Canada, on S shore of Chaleur Bay; pop. (1966c) 3047; in 19th cent. an important cod-fishing village, with 22 m. of beach.

Ca·raş–Se·ve·rin \ˈkär-ˌäsh-ˌsev-ə-ˈrēn\. County of SW Romania. See table at ROMANIA.

Ca·ra·tas·ca Lagoon \ˌkär-ə-ˈtäs-kə-\. Large lagoon on E coast of Honduras, an inlet of the Caribbean Sea.

Ca·ra·tin·ga \ˌkär-ə-ˈtēŋ-gə\. Municipality, Minas Gerais state, E Brazil, 120 m. E of Belo Horizonte; pop. (1968e) 123,344.

Ca·ra·va·ca \ˌkär-ə-ˈväk-ə\. Commune, Murcia prov., SE Spain, 38 m. WNW of Murcia; pop. (1970p) 18,415; paper, textiles, leather, brandy, chocolate.

Ca·ra·vag·gio \ˌkär-ə-ˈvä-(ˌ)jō\. Commune, Bergamo prov., Lombardy, N Italy, 13 m. S of Bergamo; pop. (1968e) 13,210; formerly defended by walls, castle, and moat; birthplace of Michelangelo da Caravaggio.

Car·a·van·ca Mons \ˌkar-ə-ˌvaŋ-kə-mänz\ *or Ital.* **Ca·ra·van·che** \ˌkär-ə-ˈväŋ-(ˌ)kā\. See table at ALPS.

Ca·ra·vé·la \ˌkär-ə-ˈvā-lə\. See BIJAGÓS, ARQUIPÉLAGO DOS.

Ca·ra·zo \kə-ˈrä-(ˌ)sō\. Department of SW Nicaragua. See table at NICARAGUA.

Car·bal·lo \kär-ˈbäl-(ˌ)yō, -ˈbī-(ˌ)ō\. Commune, La Coruña prov., NW Spain, 19 m. SW of La Coruña; pop. (1970p) 23,508; thermal mineral springs and baths.

Car·ber·ry Hill \ˌkär-b(ə-)rē-\. Hill, East Lothian, Scotland, E of Edinburgh; 500 ft.; Mary, Queen of Scots, surrendered to barons here June 15, 1567.

Carbilo. See SAINT-NAZAIRE.

Car·bon \ˈkär-bən\. Counties in four states of U.S. See tables at MONTANA, PENNSYLVANIA, UTAH, WYOMING.

Car·bo·na·ra, Cape \-ˌkär-bə-ˈnär-ə\. Cape on SE extremity of Sardinia, Italy, E of the Gulf of Cagliar.

Car·bon·ate Mountain \ˌkär-bə-ˌnāt-, -nət-\. Peak, Chaffee co., cen. Colorado; 13,900 ft.

Car·bon·dale \ˈkär-bən-ˌdāl\. 1 City, Jackson co., SW Illinois, 17 m. W of Marion; pop. (1970c) 22,816; Southern Illinois Univ. (opened 1874).

2 City, Lackawanna co., NE Pennsylvania, 14 m. NE of Scranton; pop. (1970c) 12,808; chemicals; coal mining.

Car·bo·near \ˌkär-bə-ˈni(ə)r\. Seaport, SE Newfoundland, Canada, on W shore of Conception Bay 27 m. WNW of St. John's; pop. (1971p) 4673; fish trade.

Car·bon Hill \ˌkär-bən-\. Mining city, Walker co., NW cen. Alabama, 50 m. NW of Birmingham; pop. (1970c) 1929.

Car·bo·nia \kär-ˈbō-nyə\. Town, Cagliari prov., SW Sardinia, Italy, near coast; pop. (1968e) 32,661; near coal mines.

Car·ca·gen·te \kär-kə-ˈhān-tə\. Commune, Valencia prov., E Spain, on Júcar river 29 m. SSW of Valencia; pop. (1970p) 18,971; textiles; Roman and Moorish ruins.

Car·car \ˈkär-ˌkär\. Municipality on E coast of Cebu I., Phil., 22 m. SW of City of Cebu; pop. (1969e) 49,000.

Car·ca·ra·ñá \ˌkär-kə-rən-ˈyä\. River in cen. Argentina; formed by Saladillo and Tercero rivers, flows E into Paraná river above Rosario.

Car·cas·sonne \ˌkär-kə-ˈsȯn, -ˈsän\ *or anc.* **Car·ca·so** \ˈkär-kə-ˌsō\. Manufacturing city, ✱ of Aude dept., S France, on Aude river 57 m. SE of Toulouse; pop. (1968c) 43,616; agricultural implements; tourism; twelve-arch bridge; partly surrounded by walls attributed in part to Visigoths; castle; 13th cent. Gothic cathedral. Taken by Saracens 728 A.D.; viscountship 11th–13th cents.; taken by Simon de Montfort 1209; joined to French crown 1247; pillaged and destroyed by Black Prince 1355; Huguenots massacred here 1566.

Car·che·mish \ˈkär-kə-ˌmish, kär-ˈkē-mish\. Ruined city on the W bank of the Euphrates river at Syrian border, S Turkey, 35 m. SE of Gaziantep; ancient city of Mitanni kingdom in 2d millennium B.C.; later a chief city of the Hittites; captured by Egyptians under Thutmose III in 15th cent. B.C., came under Assyria after 717 B.C.; scene of great battle 605 B.C. in which Nebuchadnezzar II of Babylon defeated Necho II and destroyed Egyptian power in Asia (*2 Chron.* xxxv. 20; *Jer.* xlvi. 2).

Car·chi \ˈkär-chē\. Province of N Ecuador. See table at ECUADOR.

Car·cross \ˈkär-ˌkrȯs\. Village and station, on N shore of Lake Bennett, S Yukon, Canada; pop. (1966c) 199; on railroad; terminus of a short branch of the Alaska Highway.

Car·da·mom Hills \ˌkärd-ə-məm-\. Range, S India, on E border of Kerala state; averages 2000 to 4000 ft.

Cár·de·nas \ˈkärd-ᵊn-ˌäs, ˈkär-t͟hā-ˌnäs\. 1 Seaport city on **Cárdenas Bay,** N Matanzas prov., W cen. Cuba, 23 m. E of Matanzas; pop. (1967e) 73,460; exports sugar and sisal fiber.

2 Municipality, Tabasco state, Mexico, 30 m. W of Villahermosa; pop. (1970p) 78,477; chocolate factory; cacao, sugarcane, bananas; founded late 18th cent.

Car·diff \ˈkärd-əf\. 1 Town, Onondaga co., New York, S of Syracuse; the "Cardiff giant" reported found nearby 1869 was a rude figure of a man 10½ ft. high, carved out of gypsum obtained at Fort Dodge, Iowa, exhibited for a time as a "petrified man."

2 County borough and seaport city, ✱ of Wales and ⊗ of Glamorganshire, SE Wales; pop. (1971p) 278,221; shipbuilding, steel manufacturing; paper mills, chemical works, engineering works, breweries; extensive cold-storage facilities; Cardiff Castle (dating from 1090), Univ. of Wales (1893), National Museum of Wales (1927); officially recognized as ✱ of Wales 1955.

Car·di·gan \ˈkärd-i-gən\. 1 Mountain, S Grafton co., W New Hampshire; 3121 ft.

2 County, W Wales. See CARDIGANSHIRE.

3 Municipal borough, ⊗ of Cardiganshire, W Wales; pop. (1971p) 3800; site of ancient Celtic castle, rebuilt by Normans and demolished by Cromwell's Parliamentarians.

Cardigan Bay. Widemouthed inlet of St. George's Channel on W coast of Wales.

Car·di·gan·shire \ˈkärd-i-gən-ˌshi(ə)r, -shər\ *or* **Cardigan.** County, W Wales; area 693 sq. m.; pop. (1971p) 54,844; ⊗ Cardigan; livestock raising; predominantly Welsh-speaking.

Car·di·nal \ˈkärd-nəl, -ᵊn-əl\. Village, Grenville co., SE Ontario, Canada, 46 m. S of Ottawa; pop. (1968e) 1907.

Cardinal Mountain. Peak, E Fresno co., S cen. California, in Sierra Nevada; 13,388 ft.

Car·do·na \kär-ˈdō-nə, -t͟hō-\. Commune, Barcelona prov., Spain, 45 m. NW of Barcelona; pop. (1970p) 7006; nearby is a hill 260 ft. formed of rock salt.

Car·dross \kär-ˈdrȯs\. Parish and village, Dunbarton co., Scotland, on the Firth of Clyde ab. 4 m. NW of Dumbarton; nearby is the castle where Robert Bruce died 1329.

Card·ston \ˈkärdz-tən\. Town, S Alberta, Canada, on St. Mary river 40 m. SSW of Lethbridge; pop. (1971p) 2744.

Ca·rei \kä-ˈrā\ *also* **Ca·reŭ Ma·re** \kä-ˌrā-u̇-ˈmär-ə\ *or Hung.* **Nagy·ká·roly** \näj-ˈkär-ōlʸ\. Commune, Satu-Mare co., Romania, SW of Satu-Mare; pop. (1966c) 19,686; formerly belonged to Hungary; once seat of Károlyi family; Piarist monastery.

Ca·ren·tan \ˌkar-äⁿ-ˈtäⁿ\. Town, Manche dept., NW France, at base of Cotentin Penin. 23 m. W of Bayeux; pop. (1962c) 5534; has small port; strong fortress in Middle Ages; suffered much during religious wars of 16th cent.; during World War II captured by U.S. troops after severe battle June 8–12, 1944.

Car·ew \ˈka(ə)r-ē, ˈke(ə)r-, -ü\. Village, Pembrokeshire, SW Wales, on Milford Haven 5 m. E of Pembroke; ½ m. N are ruins of a castle of ab. 13th cent.; 14-ft. Celtic cross near the castle entrance.

Car·ey \ˈka(ə)r-ē, ˈke(ə)r-\. Village, Wyandot co., NW cen. Ohio, 14 m. ESE of Findlay; pop. (1970c) 3523; limestone quarries; corn, oats; livestock.

Carey, Lake. Dry salt lake, S cen. Western Australia.

Car·fin \ˈkär-(ˌ)fin\. Mining village, N Lanark co., S Scotland; pop. (1961c) 2220; shrine dedicated to Our Lady of Lourdes.

Car·ia \ˈkar-ē-ə, ˈker-\. Ancient division of SW Asia Minor bordering on the S and SW on the Aegean Sea, on the N on Lydia, and on the E on Phrygia and Lycia; coextensive with modern S Aydın and W Muğla, Turkey; coastline marked by several long peninsulas (esp. Bodrum) and gulfs and numerous Aegean Is. (now parts of the Dodecanese); covered with fairly high mountains; traversed in the N by the Menderes. In early times settled by Doric and Ionic colonies; absorbed by Lydia but for a time under independent king, Mausolus, c. 377–353 B.C.; taken from Persia 334 B.C. by Alexander; came under Syria and Pergamum and in 129 B.C. incorporated in the Roman province of Asia. Chief cities Halicarnassus (the capital), Miletus, Cnidus, Magnesia, and Tralles.

Ca·ri·a·ci·ca \ˌkär-ē-ə-ˈsē-kə\. Municipality, Espírito Santo state, E Brazil, just W of Vitoria; pop. (1968e) 53,997.

Ca·ria·co, Gulf of \-ˌkar-ē-ˈäk-(ˌ)ō\. Inlet of Caribbean Sea on NE coast of Venezuela, S of Araya Penin.

Ca·ria·man·ga \ˌkär-yə-ˈmäŋ-gə\. Town, Loja prov., SW Ecuador.

Ca·ri·ba·na, Point \-ˌkar-ə-ˈbän-ə\. Cape on NW coast of Colombia, at E side of Gulf of Urabá.

Car·ib·be·an Free Trade Association \ˌkar-ə-ˈbē-ən-, kə-ˈrib-ē-ən-\. Economic community, consisting of Antigua, Barbados, Dominica, Grenada, Guyana, Jamaica, Montserrat, Saint Christopher-Nevis; purpose is to reduce customs barriers and promote free flow of labor within the region. Formed 1967; founding members Antigua, Barbados, Grenada; established Caribbean Development Bank (1970) with headquarters at Nassau, Bahamas.

Caribbean Sea. Arm of the Atlantic Ocean, bounded by the West Indies on the N and E, N South America on the S, and Central America on the W; connects with Gulf of Mexico on the NW through Yucatán Channel; ab. 1,049,500 sq. m.; max. depth 24,720 ft. in Cayman Trench (*q.v.*).

Caribbees. See WEST INDIES.

Car·i·boo Mountains \ˌkar-ə-ˌbü-\. Range of the Rocky Mts., E cen. British Columbia, Canada, in the great bend of the Fraser River; ab. 200 m. long; separated from main range of Rocky Mts. by upper Fraser river; highest point Mt. Sir Wilfrid Laurier 11,750 ft.; district in W foothills scene of famous gold rush of 1860.

Cariboo Road *or* **Car·i·bou Road** \ˌkar-ə-ˌbü-\. Highway, British Columbia, W Canada; follows Fraser river, turns NW at N end of Cariboo Mts. and ends at Hazelton (*q.v.*); modern highway is ab. 500 m. long; original road (begun 1862, opened 1865) was ab. 400 m. long and passable for stagecoaches.

Car·i·bou \ˈkar-ə-ˌbü\. **1** County in Idaho. See table at IDAHO.

2 Town, Aroostook co., N Maine, on Aroostook river 13 m. N of Presque Isle; pop. (1970c) 10,419; potatoes, sugar beets.

Caribou Mountain. Peak, SE Bonneville co., SE Idaho; 9816 ft.

Caribou Mountains. Range, N Alberta, Canada, N of Peace river; average height ab. 2000 ft.; N part in Wood Buffalo National Park.

Caribou Road. See CARIBOO ROAD.

Ca·ri·ga·ra \ˌkär-i-ˈgär-ə\. Municipality on Carigara Bay, N Leyte I., Phil., 22 m. W of Tacloban; pop. (1969e) 36,300; taken by Americans Nov. 2, 1944.

Carigara Bay. Southern part of Samar Sea at N end of Leyte I., Phil.; enclosed on NW by Biliran I.

Ca·rig·nan \ˌkär-i-ˈnyäⁿ\. Town, Chambly co., S Quebec, Canada; pop. (1966c) 2975.

Ca·ri·huai·ra·zo \ˌkar-ē-wī-ˈräz-(ˌ)ō\. Peak, cen. Ecuador, NNE of Riobamba, in the Andes Mts.; 16,515 ft.

Ca·ri·ni \kə-ˈrē-nē\. Commune, Palermo prov., NW cen. Sicily, Italy, 10 m. W of Palermo; pop. (1968e) 16,761; 14th cent. Gothic castle; scene of defeat of Sicilian revolutionists by Bourbon forces 1860.

Ca·ri·no·la \kä-ˈrē-nə-lə\. Commune, Caserta prov., Campania, S Italy; pop. (1968e) 9558.

Ca·rin·thia \kə-ˈrin(t)-thē-ə\ *or Ger.* **Kärn·ten** \ˈkernt-ᵊn\. State of S Austria, bordering on Italy and Yugoslavia; 3681 sq. m.; pop. (1971p) 526,000; ✱ Klagenfurt; forms basin watered by the Drava with several lakes (Wörther See, Millstätter See, etc.); rye, oats, wheat; livestock; magnesite, iron ore, lead, zinc; center of a summer resort area; bordered on S by Karawanken and Carnic Alps and separated from Salzburg state on NW by the Hohe Tauern.

History: Inhabited originally by Celtic stock; part of Roman province of Noricum; invaded by Germans, then by Slovenes in period of migrations; in 8th cent. A.D. belonged to Carolingian empire (part of Bavaria); made a separate duchy 976 which, for a time, included Verona and Styria and finally came to Hapsburgs in 1335; parts of Carinthia belonged to Illyrian Provinces (*q.v.*) 1809–13; became Austrian crownland 1849; after 1918 southern part taken by Yugoslavia; in 1920, possession of S part by Yugoslavia confirmed by a plebiscite, but Klagenfurt region retained by Austria.

Ca·ri·pi·to \ˌkär-i-ˈpē-tō\. Town, Monagas state, NE Venezuela, 30 m. NNE of Maturín; pop. (1970e) 27,475.

Car·is·brooke \ˈkar-əz-ˌbru̇k, -əs-\. Village and parish, Isle of Wight, S England; castle in which Charles I was imprisoned 1647–48.

Car·len·ti·ni \ˌkär-lən-ˈtē-nē\. Commune, Siracusa prov., SE Sicily, Italy, 22 m. NW of Syracuse; pop. (1968e) 12,092.

Carle·ton \ˈkär(ə)l-tən, ˈkärlt-ᵊn\. **1** County, New Brunswick, Canada. See table at NEW BRUNSWICK.

2 Former county, Ontario, Canada; now part of Ottawa-Carleton. See table at ONTARIO.

Carleton, Mount. Mountain, N New Brunswick, Canada; 2690 ft.; highest peak in the province.

Carleton Place. Industrial town, Lanark co., SE Ontario, Canada, on Mississippi river at foot of Mississippi Lake, 28 m. SW of Ottawa; pop. (1968e) 4938; resort.

Car·ling·ford Lough \ˌkär-liŋ-fərd-ˈläk\. Inlet of Irish Sea on E coast of Ireland, on boundary bet. SE Northern Ireland and NE Eire.

Car·lin·ville \ˈkär-lən-ˌvil\. City, ⊗ of Macoupin co., SW cen. Illinois, 38 m. SSW of Springfield; pop. (1970c) 5675; Blackburn Coll. (1835).

Car·lisle \kär-ˈlī(ə)l, kər-, ˈkär-ˌ\. **1** County in Kentucky. See table at KENTUCKY.

2 City, ⊗ of Nicholas co., NE Kentucky; pop. (1970c) 1579.

3 Town, Middlesex co., NE Massachusetts, 18 m. NW of Boston; pop. (1970c) 2871.

4 Village, Montgomery and Warren cos., SW Ohio, 15 m. SW of Dayton; pop. (1970c) 3821.

5 Borough, ⊗ of Cumberland co., S Pennsylvania, 19 m. W of Harrisburg; pop. (1970c) 18,079; steel products, office furniture, radio crystals, radio switches; settled 1720; scene of treaty bet. Ohio Indians and Benjamin Franklin 1753; headquarters of Washington during Whisky Insurrection 1794; station on Underground Railroad before Civil War; occupied by Confederates June 27–30, 1863. Site of Carlisle Indian School 1879–1918; Dickinson Coll. (1773). Home and grave of Molly Pitcher.

6 *anc.* **Lu·gu·val·li·um** \ˌlüg-yu̇-ˈval-ē-əm\ *or* **Lu·gu·val·lum** \-ˈval-əm\ *or later* **Caer Lu·el** \kär-ˈlü-əl\. City and county borough, ⊗ of Cumberland, NW England, on Eden river 8 m. from Solway Firth and 108 m. N of Liverpool; pop. (1971p) 71,497; textiles, coal mining machinery; railroad center; cathedral (begun in 12th cent.). Important Roman station; refounded by William Rufus; as a border fortress often attacked by Scots; place of imprisonment of Mary, Queen of Scots, May–July 1568.

Car·lo·for·te \ˌkär-lə-ˈfȯr-(ˌ)tā\. See SAN PIETRO.

Car·los Ro·jas \ˌkär-ləs-ˈrō-(h)äs\. Municipality, Matanzas prov., W cen. Cuba; pop. (1967e) 7370.

Carlota, La. See LA CARLOTA.

Car·low \ˈkär-(ˌ)lō\. **1** County, Leinster prov., SE Eire; 346 sq. m.; pop. (1971p) 34,025; ✱ Carlow; dairy farming, flour milling, malting.

2 Urban district, its ⊗; pop. (1971p) 9384; ruins of great Norman castle; St. Patrick's Coll. (1793); burned by Rory Oge O'More late 16th cent.; taken by Cromwell's forces 1650.

Carlowitz. See SREMSKI KARLOVCI.

Carls·bad \ˈkär(ə)lz-ˌbad\. **1** City, San Diego co., SW California, NW of San Diego; pop. (1970c) 14,944; electronic equipment; vegetables.

2 City, ⊗ of Eddy co., SE New Mexico, on Pecos river 70 m. S of Roswell; pop. (1970c) 21,297; potash mines; to the SW are Carlsbad Caverns (*q.v.*), and to the N is the Carlsbad Reclamation Project (developed by U.S. government 1906 ff.) consisting of **Ava·lon Dam** \ˌav-ə-ˌlän-\ and **Mc·Mil·lan Dam** \mək-ˌmil-ən-\ across the Pecos river, with the lakes thus formed and miles of canals and ditches; founded 1887.

Carlsbad. See KARLOVY VARY.

Carlsbad Caverns. Series of limestone caves near Carlsbad, SE New Mexico; Big Room over ½ m. long, 650 ft. wide at its widest part, and 285 ft. high; now included in **Carlsbad Caverns National Park** (see UNITED STATES, *National Parks).*

Carlsruhe. See KARLSRUHE.

Carl·stadt \ˈkärl-ˌstat\. Borough, Bergen co., NE corner of New Jersey, 8 m. SE of Paterson; pop. (1970c) 6724; chemicals, surgical dressings; cheese. Bought cooperatively from original American owners by German exiles and liberals seeking political freedom.

Carl·ton \ˈkär(ə)lt-ᵊn\. **1** County in E Minnesota. See table at MINNESOTA.

2 Village, its ⊗; pop. (1970c) 884.
3 Urban district, Nottinghamshire, N cen. England, 4 m. NE of Nottingham; pop. (1971p) 45,211; furniture; printing.

Car·lyle \kär-ˈlī(ə)l, ˈkär-ˌ\. City, ⊗ of Clinton co., SW cen. Illinois, 40 m. E of East St. Louis; pop. (1970c) 3139; flour and grain trading center; paper factories.

Car·ma·gno·la \ˌkär-mən-ˈyōl-ə\. Commune, Torino prov., Piedmont, NW Italy, on Po river 17 m. S of Turin; pop. (1968e) 20,178; textiles; ruins of ancient castle; gave its name to the *carmagnole,* costume worn in S France by Piedmontese workmen and adopted, after 1792, by the French Revolutionists, whose revolutionary song was *La Carmagnole.*

Car·man \ˈkär-mən\. Town, S Manitoba, Canada, 48 m. SW of Winnipeg; pop. (1966c) 1922; railroad junction.

Carmana *or* **Carmania.** See KERMĀN.

Car·mar·then \kər-ˈmär-t͟hən, kär-\. 1 County, Wales. See CARMARTHENSHIRE.
2 Municipal borough and commercial seaport, ⊗ of Carmarthenshire, S Wales; pop. (1971p) 13,072; milk processing; ruins of Norman castle on site of ancient Roman station; received first town charter 1227; residence of Sir Richard Steele at time of his death 1729.

Carmarthen Bay. Inlet of Bristol Channel on S coast of Wales; Caldy I. is at its W entrance.

Car·mar·then·shire \kər-ˈmär-t͟hən-ˌshi(ə)r, -shər; kär-\ *or* **Carmarthen.** County, S Wales; area 920 sq. m.; pop. (1971p) 162,313; ⊗ Carmarthen; hilly area; chief river the Towy; dairy farming, coal mining, quarrying; textiles.

Car·maux \kär-ˈmō\. Commune, Tarn dept., S France, 48 m. NE of Toulouse; pop. (1968c) 14,755; coal mining.

Car·mel \ˈkär-məl\. 1 Town, Hamilton co., cen. Indiana, 15 m. N of Indianapolis; pop. (1970c) 6568; bottling plant; corn, wheat.
2 Residential village and resort in Carmel town, ⊗ of Putnam co., SE New York, 20 m. ESE of Newburgh; pop. (1970c) 3395.

Carmel \kär-ˈmel\ *or* **Carmel–by–the–Sea.** City, Monterey co., W California, on Pacific Ocean S of Monterey Bay; pop. (1970c) 4525; founded c. 1904 by several artists as rustic refuge; art and recreation center.

Carmel, Mount \-ˈkär-məl\. Mountain, N Israel, near Mediterranean coast; 1789 ft.; extends southeasterly ab. 15 m. along S bank of the Qishon river; early became sacred to both Yahweh and Baal (cf. *1 Kings* xviii. 19 ff.); after 6th cent. A.D. a favored site for monasteries, esp. that of the Order of Carmelites founded 1156 A.D.

Car·me·lo \kär-ˈmā-lō\. Town, Colonia dept., SW Uruguay, 140 m. NW of Montevideo; at mouth of the Uruguay river; pop. (1963c) 12,707; historic ruins in vicinity.

Car·men \ˈkär-mən\. 1 Island enclosing Laguna de Términos, SE Bay of Campeche, Campeche state, SE Mexico.
2 Small island off SE coast of Baja California, NW Mexico, in the Gulf of California; salt deposits.
3 *or* **Ciu·dad del Carmen** \ˌsē-ü-ˈt͟hä-del-, -ü-ˈdad-del-\. Town on W end of Carmen I., Campeche state, SE Mexico; pop. (1969e) 36,511; has a good port.

Carmen del Pa·ra·ná \-del-ˌpar-ə-ˈnä\. Town, Itapúa dept., SE Paraguay, on Paraná river W of Encarnación; pop. (1970e) 5933.

Car·mi \ˈkär-ˌmī\. City, ⊗ of White co., SE Illinois, 45 m. ESE of Mt. Vernon; pop. (1970c) 6033; bottling plant, grain elevator.

Car·mi·chael \ˈkär-ˌmī-kəl\. Urban community (unincorporated), Sacramento co., N cen. California, NE of Sacramento; pop. (1970c) 37,625.

Car·mi·gna·no \ˌkar-min-ˈyä-nō\. Commune, Firenze prov., Tuscany, cen. Italy; pop. (1968e) 7881.

Car·mo·na \kär-ˈmō-nə\ *or anc.* **Car·mo** \ˈkär-(ˌ)mō\. Industrial and commercial commune, Sevilla prov., SW Spain, 18 m. ENE of Seville; pop. (1970p) 24,378; ancient Roman necropolis, city gates, Moorish wall and alcazar; captured from Moors 1247 by Ferdinand III.

Car·nac \ˈkär-(ˌ)nak\. Commune, Morbihan dept., NW France, on Quiberon Bay ab. 17 m. SE of Lorient; pop. (1962c) 3641; region noted for many stone monuments including dolmens and long rows of menhirs; mounds; remains of a Gallo-Roman town.

Car·na·ro \kär-ˈnär-(ˌ)ō\ *also* **Fiu·me** \ˈfyü-(ˌ)mā\. Former province of Italy, including the islands of the Gulf of Quarnero (Cherso, Lussino, Unie)—name used by D'Annunzio. Now (by treaty of 1947) part of Croatia, NW Yugoslavia.

Car·nar·von \kär-ˈnär-vən, kər-\. 1 Town, W Western Australia, on Shark Bay; pop. (1966c) 2956.
2 Town, cen. Cape Province, S Rep. of South Africa, 290 m. NE of Cape Town; pop. (1967e) 4800; sheep.
3 Municipal borough, Wales. See CAERNARVON.

Carnarvon Bay. See CAERNARVON BAY.

Carnarvonshire. See CAERNARVONSHIRE.

Car·nat·ic \kär-ˈnat-ik\ *or* **Kar·na·tik** \kər-ˈnät-ik\. A region and former administrative unit bet. Eastern Ghats and Coromandel Coast, S India, S of 16°N; now a part of Tamil Nadu and Andhra Pradesh, India; orig. the country of the Kanarese, an irregular area in S cen. India including Mysore and parts of Andhra Pradesh. Historically of great importance; divided for centuries bet. Pandya and Chola kingdoms; from 1310 to 1710 under Muslims and the Delhi kings; for a time independent, with capital at Arcot; during 18th cent. the scene of Anglo-French rivalry, British gaining ascendancy after seizure of Arcot 1751 and defeat of Haidar Ali in Second Mysore War (1780–84); annexed by British 1801.

Car·nedd Da·fydd \ˌkär-ˌnet͟h-ˈdäv-ət͟h\. Mountain, E Caernarvonshire, NW Wales, NE of Snowdon; 3426 ft.

Carnedd Llew·el·yn \-lü-ˈel-ən\. Mountain, E Caernarvonshire, NW Wales; 3484 ft.

Car·ne·gie \ˈkär-nə-gē, kär-ˈneg-ē\. 1 Town, Caddo co., W cen. Oklahoma, on Washita river 37 m. NNW of Lawton; pop. (1970c) 1723; cotton gin, elevators; farming.
2 Borough, Allegheny co., SW Pennsylvania, 6 m. WSW of Pittsburgh; pop. (1970c) 10,864; steel, iron, chemicals, electrical equipment; coal mines.

Carnegie, Lake. Lake (dry) on W edge of Gibson Desert, cen. Western Australia.

Carn Eige. See CAIRN EIGE.

Car·ne·ro, Point \-kär-ˈne(ə)r-(ˌ)ō\. Point on S coast of Spain extending into the Strait of Gibraltar at W entrance to the Bay of Gibraltar.

Carnes·ville \ˈkärnz-ˌvil\. City, ⊗ of Franklin co., NE Georgia; pop. (1970c) 510.

Carnic Alps. See table at ALPS.

Car Nic·o·bar *or* **Kar Nicobar** \ˈkär-ˈnik-ə-ˌbär\. Most northerly island of Nicobar group, Andaman and Nicobar Is., India; 49 sq. m.

Car·nio·la \ˌkär-nē-ˈō-lə, kärn-ˈyō-\ *or Ger.* **Krain** \ˈkrīn\. 1 Region of S Europe, NE of head of Adriatic Sea; mountainous, having E end of Carnic Alps in NW and traversed on W by the Julian Alps; chief town Ljubljana, Yugoslavia.
History: Belonged to Roman province of Pannonia; received influx of Slovenes c. 590 A.D.; with Carinthia, ruled by Carolingian mark of Bavaria; twice founded as independent mark; in 13th cent. a part of the Holy Roman Empire **(March of Carniola)** in SE bordering on kingdom of Hungary; came under the Hapsburgs 1335 who took title of duke of Carinthia; ceded to Napoleon by Austria 1809–13 (see ILLYRIAN PROVINCES), remained duchy of Austria until 1849.
2 Austrian crownland 1849–1918, bounded on N by Carinthia, on NE by Styria, on E, SE, and S by Croatia, and on W by Italy (Istria and Gorizia); divided after World

War I bet. Italy (782 sq. m.) and Yugoslavia (3060 sq. m.); by 1947 treaty entirely in Yugoslavia.

Carn Mairg. See MONADHLIATH MOUNTAINS.

Car·not \kär-ˈnō\. Town, SW Central African Republic, ab. 190 m. WNW of Bangui; pop. (1968c) 40,259.

Car·nous·tie \ˈkär-ˈnü-stē\. Seaport burgh, SE Angus co., E Scotland, on North Sea ab. 11 m. ENE of Dundee; pop. (1971p) 6234; resort with fine beach and golf course.

Carn·sore Point \ˌkärn-ˌsō(ə)r-, -ˌsȯ(ə)r-\. Cape on SE extremity of Ireland, projecting into St. George's Channel.

Carntoul. See CAIRNTOUL.

Car·nun·tum \kär-ˈnən-təm\. Ancient town, N Pannonia, on S bank of the Danube; ruins near Hainburg, Austria; originally Celtic, became important Roman post from the time of Augustus; used as base 171–173 A.D. by Marcus Aurelius in his campaign against the Marcomanni; destroyed by Germans 4th cent.

Caro \ˈkar-(ˌ)ō\. Village, ⊗ of Tuscola co., E Michigan, 28 m. E of Saginaw; pop. (1970c) 3701; beet-sugar refinery; diversified farming.

Carola Hafen. See QUEEN CAROLA HARBOUR.

Car·ol City \ˌkar-əl-\. Urban community (unincorporated), Dade co., SE Florida, NW of Miami Beach; pop. (1970c) 27,361.

Car·o·li·na \ˌkar-ə-ˈlī-nə\. Early American colony; as granted by Charles II to eight Lords Proprietors 1663 included land from ocean to ocean bet. 31st and 36th parallels; in 1665 boundaries extended to include area around Albemarle Sound where settlers from Virginia had located since ab. 1650. Fundamental Constitutions by John Locke adopted by proprietors in 1669 and later abandoned; first permanent settlement by English 1670 (in South Carolina); Spanish ceded claim to territory 1670; because of neglect of proprietors to defend colony in Tuscarora War (1711–12) and Yamassee War (1715–16) and other reasons, charter abrogated and separate royal governments established in North and South Carolina (*qq.v.*) 1729—hence, **the Carolinas.**

Ca·ro·li·na \ˌkar-ə-ˈlē-nə, ˌkär-\. Municipality, NE Puerto Rico, 11 m. ESE of San Juan; pop. (1970p) 94,635.

Carolina, La. See LA CAROLINA.

Car·o·line \ˈkar-ə-ˌlīn\. Name of counties in two states of the U.S. See tables at MARYLAND and VIRGINIA.

Caroline Island. Small atoll of the Line Is. in cen. Pacific Ocean, ab. 400 m. E of Penrhyn I., 9°58'S, 150°13'W; 6 m. long by 1 m. wide; shallow lagoon.

Caroline Islands *or* **Car·o·lines** \ˈkar-ə-ˌlīnz, -lənz\ *or Ger.* **Ka·ro·lin·en** \ˌkär-ə-ˈlēn-ən\. Extensive archipelago in W Pacific Ocean, E of S Phil., part of the U.S. Trust Territory of the Pacific Islands; lat. ab. 5° to 10°N and long. 130° to 166°E; includes 550 to 680 islands (depending on definition of "island"); has many coral islets and reefs; 457 sq. m., including lagoons 3740 sq. m.; pop. (1969e) 66,900; most important islands Yap, Ponape, Truk, Kusaie, and Palau. Some islands are fertile and populous; the larger are volcanic, the smaller are atolls, generally uninhabited; natives are Micronesians; on some islands are massive ruins, still unexplained, indicating presence of people centuries ago (see EASTER ISLAND).

History: Annexed by Spain 1686; rarely visited down to latter part of 19th cent.; German seizure of Yap 1885 aroused protest (dispute settled 1887 by decision of Pope Leo XIII); islands purchased by Germany 1899; seized by Japan 1914 and granted as mandate to Japan 1919; after 1935 prohibited territory to all foreigners; fortified by Japan; Ulithi and southern islands (Peleliu and Angaur) of the Palau group occupied by Americans Sept.–Oct. 1944; placed under U.S. trusteeship 1947.

Carolopolis. See CHARLEVILLE-MÉZIÈRES.

Car·ol Stream \ˈkar-əl-\. Village, Du Page co., NE Illinois, 27 m. W of Chicago; pop. (1970c) 4434.

Ca·ro·ní \ˌkär-ə-ˈnē, ˌkar-\. River, E Venezuela; 550 m. long; rises in Serra Pacaraima in SE Venezuela; flows N into Orinoco river near its mouth.

Caronium. See LA CORUÑA 2.

Ca·ro·ra \kə-ˈrōr-ə, -ˈrȯr-\. Town, Lara state, NW Venezuela, ab. 53 m. W of Barquisimeto; pop. (1970e) 37,118.

Ca·rouge \kə-ˈrüzh\. Commune, Geneva canton, SW Switzerland; pop. (1970c) 14,055; suburb of Geneva.

Car·pa·thi·an Mountains \kär-ˈpā-thē-ən-\ *or* **Car·pa·thi·ans** \-ənz\ *or anc.* **Car·pa·tes** \ˈkär-pə-ˌtēz\. Mountain system of E Europe, along boundary bet. Czechoslovakia and Poland and extending southward through the Ukrainian S.S.R., U.S.S.R., and E Romania; max. width 180 m.; highest peak Gerlachovka 8711 ft.; subdivided into East and West Beskids (*q.v.*) and the Tatra Mts. (or High Tatra) in cen. part; extensions to SW are Little Carpathian Mts. and White Carpathian Mts. (*qq.v.*); Transylvanian Alps are sometimes called the South Carpathians. Source of Vistula, Dniester, and Tisza rivers; many battles fought on or near its slopes, esp. in World Wars I and II; among best-known passes are Yablonitski Pass and Lupków Pass.

Carpathian Ruthenia. See TRANSCARPATHIAN OBLAST.

Carpathus *or* **Carpathos.** See KARPATHOS.

Carpenisi. See KARPENISION.

Car·pen·tar·ia, Gulf of \-ˌkär-pən-ˈter-ē-ə, -ˌkärp-ᵊm-, -ˈtar-\. Large gulf, NE Australia, inlet of Arafura Sea; ab. 480 m. N to S and 400 m. E to W; bordered on W by Northern Territory, and on E by Cape York Penin. of Queensland; for the most part shallow (average 30 to 40 fathoms).

Carpenter Dam. See HAMILTON, LAKE 1.

Car·pen·ters·ville \ˈkär-pən-tərz-ˌvil, ˈkärp-ᵊm-\. Village, Kane co., NE Illinois, N of Elgin; pop. (1970c) 24,059.

Car·pen·tras \ˌkär-päⁿ-ˈträs\ *or anc.* **Car·pen·to·rac·te** \kär-ˌpen-tə-ˈrak-tē\. Manufacturing city, Vaucluse dept., SE France, 12 m. NE of Avignon; pop. (1968c) 21,388; Gothic cathedral; Roman remains, including triumphal arch, aqueduct. A former episcopal see; scene of council 527; residence of Pope Clement V 1313; former capital of papal countship of Venaissin.

Car·pi \ˈkär-pē\. Commune, Modena prov., Emilia-Romagna, N Italy, 10 m. NNW of Modena; pop. (1968e) 52,186; episcopal see; 16th cent. castle; citadel.

Car·pin·te·ria \ˌkär-pən-tə-ˈrē-ə\. Urban community (unincorporated), Santa Barbara co., SW California, SE of Santa Barbara; pop. (1970c) 6982.

Car·qui·nez Strait \kär-ˌkē-nəs-\. Strait joining San Pablo and Suisun bays, California; 8 m. long.

Car·ra·belle \ˌkar-ə-ˈbel\. City, Franklin co., NW Florida, on Gulf of Mexico E of Apalachicola river; pop. (1970c) 1044.

Carrae. See HARAN.

Car·ran·tuo·hill *also* **Car·ran·tu·al** \ˌkar-ən-ˈtü-əl\. Highest peak in Ireland, in Macgillicuddy's Reeks, co. Kerry; 3414 ft.

Car·ra·ra \kə-ˈrär-ə\ *or formerly* **Apua·nia** \ä-ˈpwän-yə\. Commune, Massa-Carrara prov., Tuscany, cen. Italy; pop. (1968e) 66,821; quarries nearby produce Carrara marble; 13th cent. castle, 15th cent. cathedral, 16th cent. Baroque palace.

Carr·bo·ro \ˈkär-ˌbər-ə, -ˌbə-rə\. Town, Orange co., N North Carolina, 10 m. SW of Durham; pop. (1970c) 5058.

Car·re·ño \kä-ˈren-(ˌ)yō\. Commune, Oviedo prov., NW Spain, on Bay of Biscay; pop. (1970p) 11,529.

Carreta, Point. See MANSO, POINT.

Carrhae. See HARAN.

Car·ri·a·cou \ˌkar-ē-ə-ˈkü\. Largest island of the Grenadines (*q.v.*); 13 sq. m.; pop. (1968e) 8179; chief town Hillsborough; administered as part of Grenada.

Car·rick·fer·gus \ˌkar-ik-ˈfər-gəs\. Municipal borough, co. Antrim, NE Northern Ireland, on N shore of Belfast Lough 9½ m. NE of Belfast; pop. (1971p) 15,034; seaport; historic settlement of Scottish Protestants.

Car·rick·ma·cross \ˌkar-ik-mə-ˈkräs\. Town, co. Monaghan, NE Eire; pop. (1971p) 2099.

Car·rick on Shan·non \ˈkar-ik . . . ˈshan-ən\. Town, ⊗ of co. Leitrim, N Eire, 28 m. SE of Sligo; pop. (1966c) 1394.

Carrick on Suir \-'shu̇(ə)r\. Urban district, SE co. Tipperary, S Eire, 18 m. WNW of Waterford; pop. (1971p) 5008; slate quarrying; 14th cent. castle; at nearby Carrickbeg are ruins of a 14th cent. abbey.

Car·ri·er Mills \ˌkar-ē-ər-'milz\ *also* **Car·ri·ers Mills** \-ərz-\. Village, Saline co., SE Illinois, 17 m. E of Marion; pop. (1970c) 2013.

Car·ring·ton \'kar-iŋ-ˌtən\. City, ⊗ of Foster co., E cen. North Dakota, NNW of Jamestown; pop. (1970c) 2491; dairy products.

Carr Inlet \'kär-\. Inlet, S end of Puget Sound, W of Tacoma, Washington.

Car·ri·zal \ˌkär-ə-'säl\. Village, Chihuahua state, Mexico, ab. 85 m. S of Ciudad Juárez; scene of skirmish June 21, 1916 in which Mexican government troops defeated Pershing's forces who were in pursuit of Villa.

Car·ri·zo Springs \kə-ˌrē-zō-\. City, ⊗ of Dimmit co., S Texas, 47 m. S of Uvalde; pop. (1970c) 5374; fruit packing, oil refining.

Car·ri·zo·zo \ˌkär-ə-'zō-(ˌ)zō\. Town, ⊗ of Lincoln co., cen. New Mexico, 75 m. W of Roswell; pop. (1970c) 1123.

Car·roll \'kar-əl\. **1** Name of counties in thirteen states of the U.S. See tables at ARKANSAS, GEORGIA, ILLINOIS, INDIANA, IOWA, KENTUCKY, MARYLAND, MISSISSIPPI, MISSOURI, NEW HAMPSHIRE, OHIO, TENNESSEE, VIRGINIA. For parishes of Louisiana, see *East Carroll* and *West Carroll* in table at LOUISIANA.

2 City, ⊗ of Carroll co., W cen. Iowa, 47 m. SW of Fort Dodge; pop. (1970c) 8716; poultry processing; beans, oats.

Car·roll·ton \'kar-əl-tən\. **1** Town, ⊗ of Pickens co., W Alabama; pop. (1970c) 923; cotton gin; lumber.

2 City, ⊗ of Carroll co., W Georgia, 40 m. WSW of Atlanta; pop. (1970c) 13,520; wire cable; cotton; West Georgia Coll. (1933); incorp. 1856.

3 City, ⊗ of Greene co., W Illinois, 33 m. NNW of Alton; pop. (1970c) 2866; settled 1818, incorp. as city 1853.

4 City, ⊗ of Carroll co., N Kentucky, on Ohio river 37 m. N of Frankfort; pop. (1970c) 3884; livestock, tobacco.

5 Town, a ⊗ of Carroll co., cen. Mississippi; pop. (1970c) 295.

6 City, ⊗ of Carroll co., NW cen. Missouri, 30 m. S of Chillicothe; pop. (1970c) 4847; dairy products.

7 Village, ⊗ of Carroll co., E Ohio, 21 m. SE of Canton; pop. (1970c) 2817; coal mines nearby.

8 City, Dallas and Denton cos., N Texas, 15 m. NNW of Dallas; pop. (1970c) 13,855; wheat farming.

Car·ron \'kar-ən\. **1** River, Stirling co., S cen. Scotland; 20 m. long; flows E into the Firth of Forth.

2 Village, Stirling co., Scotland, on Carron river ab. 2 m. NW of Falkirk; noted for ironworks, established 1760.

Car·rot \'kar-ət\. River, cen. Saskatchewan, Canada; 250 m. long; flows ENE across Manitoba border into Saskatchewan river.

Car·rum \'kar-əm\. Town, Victoria, SE Australia, on E shore of Port Phillip Bay.

Carso. See KRAS.

Car·son \'kärs-ᵊn\. **1** River, rising in Alpine co., E California, and flowing N and E into Carson Sink, N Churchill co., W Nevada; ab. 170 m. long.

2 County in Texas. See table at TEXAS.

3 Urban community (unincorporated), Los Angeles co., California, SE of Los Angeles; pop. (1970c) 71,150.

4 Village, ⊗ of Grant co., S North Dakota; pop. (1970c) 466.

Carson City. City, ✱ of Nevada, near Lake Tahoe and Carson river 30 m. S of Reno; pop. (1970c) 15,468; alt. 4678 ft.; in agricultural region; tourism; surrounding region formerly important for silver production; site of branch of U.S. mint 1870–93; settled 1858 and named for Kit Carson; became ✱ 1861; made an independent city 1969.

Carson Lake. Lake, SW Churchill co., W Nevada, in S part of Carson Sink; ab. 12 m. long; no outlet.

Carson Pass. Mountain pass, Alpine co., E California, in main range of the Sierra Nevada Mts.; elev. 8634 ft.; discovered during winter 1834–44 by Capt. John Frémont and Kit Carson; used by the forty-niners.

Carson Peak. Mountain, Hinsdale co., SW Colorado; 13,600 ft.

Carson Sink. Shallow marshy region in N Churchill co., W Nevada. See CARSON LAKE.

Carstensz, Mount. See DJAJA, MOUNT.

Car·ta·ge·na \ˌkärt-ə-'gā-nə, -'jē-, -'hā-\. **1** Seaport, ✱ of Bolívar dept., on NW coast of Colombia, 60 m. SW of Barranquilla; pop. (1968e) 256,598; textiles, leather goods; has good harbor with narrow entrance; Colombia's principal oil port; univ. (1824); founded 1533, became one of the most important cities of Spanish America; in 17th cent. second only to Mexico City in W hemisphere; strongly fortified in Spanish times; often attacked by the French and English (Drake in 1585 and Vernon in 1741); Spanish until 1815 when it was taken by Bolívar but soon lost, retaken 1821.

2 *or anc.* **Car·tha·go No·va** \kär-ˌtäg-ō-'nō-və\. Seaport city, Murcia prov., SE Spain, on Mediterranean 28 m. ESE of Murcia; pop. (1970p) 146,904; naval arsenal; lead, iron, zinc, copper mines; medieval Gothic cathedral; ancient castle.

History: Founded by Carthaginians under Hasdrubal 227 B.C.; captured by Scipio Africanus 209 B.C. and made a Roman colony; sacked by Goths 425 A.D.; taken by Byzantines 534 and Visigoths 624; held by Moors from 711 until freed by James I of Aragon 1269; sacked by Sir Francis Drake 1585; occupied by duke of Berwick 1707; site of communistic revolt 1873–74.

Car·ta·go \kar-'täg-(ˌ)ō\. **1** Town, Valle dept., W Colombia, 125 m. W of Bogotá; pop. (1968e) 60,554.

2 Province of cen. Costa Rica. See table at COSTA RICA.

3 City, ✱ of Cartago prov., Costa Rica, at foot of Mt. Irazú 14 m. SE of San José; pop. (1968e) 21,596; alt. 4765 ft.; in agricultural region; former capital of Costa Rica; founded 1563; destroyed by earthquakes 1841 and 1910.

Car·te·ia \kär-'tē-(y)ə\. Ancient town and port on S coast of Spain (Hispania), at head of bay bordered on E by Mt. Calpe (*or mod.* Gibraltar); founded by Phoenicians; colonized 170 B.C. by Roman soldiers.

Car·ter \'kärt-ər\. Name of counties in five states of the U.S. See tables at KENTUCKY, MISSOURI, MONTANA, OKLAHOMA, TENNESSEE.

Carter, Mount. Peak in Glacier National Park, NW Montana; 9834 ft.

Carter Dome \-'dōm\. Peak, SE Coos co., N New Hampshire, E of **Carter Notch;** 4860 ft.

Car·ter·et \ˌkärt-ə-'ret\. **1** County in North Carolina. See table at NORTH CAROLINA.

2 Borough, Middlesex co., cen. New Jersey, 6 m. NNE of Perth Amboy near Staten I.; pop. (1970c) 23,137; metal and oil refining; manufactures steel, tobacco, chemicals.

Car·te·ret \ˌkärt-ə-'rā\. Village, W coast of Manche dept., NW France, 20 m. SW of Cherbourg; pop. (1962c) 754; small port. When reached by Allied forces June 18, 1944, N part of Cotentin Penin. (*q.v.*) was cut off; important point in battle of Normandy.

Cart·ers Dam *and* **Carters Reservoir** \'kärt-ərz-\. See UNITED STATES, *Dams and Reservoirs.*

Car·ters·ville \'kärt-ərz-ˌvil\. City, ⊗ of Bartow co., NW Georgia, 35 m. NW of Atlanta; pop. (1970c) 9929; cotton; iron ore deposits nearby.

Car·ter·ville \'kärt-ər-ˌvil\. **1** City, Williamson co., S Illinois, 10 m. W of Marion; pop. (1970c) 3061; coal mining; John A. Logan Coll. (1967).

2 City, Jasper co., SW Missouri, 7 m. NNE of Joplin; pop. (1970c) 1716; lead and zinc deposits nearby.

Car·thage \'kär-thij\. 1 City, ⊗ of Hancock co., W Illinois, 38 m. NNE of Quincy; pop. (1970c) 3550; Robert Morris Coll. (1965); place where Joseph Smith was imprisoned and killed 1844.

2 Town, ⊗ of Leake co., cen. Mississippi, 48 m. NE of Jackson; pop. (1970c) 3031; lumber.

3 City, ⊗ of Jasper co., SW Missouri, 14 m. NE of Joplin; pop. (1970c) 11,035; livestock; lead and zinc deposits.

4 Village, Jefferson co., N New York, 16 m. E of Watertown; pop. (1970c) 3889; concrete, machinery.

5 Town, ⊗ of Moore co., cen. North Carolina; pop. (1970c) 1034.

6 Town, ⊗ of Smith co., N cen. Tennessee, on Cumberland river 21 m. E of Lebanon; pop. (1970c) 2491.

7 City, ⊗ of Panola co., E Texas, 28 m. S of Marshall; pop. (1970c) 5392; lumber; Panola Coll. (1947).

8 *or anc.* **Car·tha·go** \kär-'thä-gō, -'tä-\. Ancient city and state, N Africa, on coast NE of modern Tunis; built on tip of a peninsula, originally around a citadel known as the Byrsa; comprised inner and outer harbor, extensive walls, old and new city (suburb of Megara).

History: Founded by colonists from Phoenician kingdom of Tyre late 8th cent. B.C.; from 6th cent. B.C. began conquests in W Africa, Sicily, and Sardinia; after defeat at Himera (*q.v.*) 480 B.C., developed sea power and, under descendants of Hamilcar, came to dominate W Mediterranean; fought Sicily 4th cent. B.C.; engaged in series of bitter wars with Rome, known as Punic Wars: in First Punic War 264–241 B.C. lost Sicily to Rome; conquered Spain to Ebro 237–228 B.C.; in Second (led by Hannibal) 218–201 B.C. fought battles of Cannae and Zama (*qq.v.*); at end of Third 149–146 B.C. city utterly destroyed by the younger Scipio; site of colony founded by Caesar 44 B.C.; captured by Vandals 439 A.D.; won for Byzantine Empire by Belisarius 533–34; lost to Arabs 697.

Carthago Nova. See CARTAGENA 2.

Cartier Island. See ASHMORE AND CARTIER ISLANDS.

Cart·wright \'kärt-ˌrīt\. Coastal village and harbor on inlet of SE Labrador, Newfoundland, Canada.

Ca·rua·ru \ˌkär-wə-'rü\. City, E Pernambuco state, E Brazil; munic. pop. (1968e) 115,414.

Ca·rú·pa·no \kə-'rü-pə-ˌnō\. Seaport, N Sucre state, N Venezuela, on Paria Penin. 100 m. ENE of Barcelona; pop. (1970e) 46,155; oil fields nearby.

Ca·ruth·ers·ville \kə-'rəth-ərz-ˌvil\. City, ⊗ of Pemiscot co., SE corner of Missouri, on Mississippi river 60 m. SW of its conjunction with Ohio river; pop. (1970c) 7350; bottling plant; cotton, wheat.

Car·ver \'kär-vər\. County in Minnesota. See table at MINNESOTA.

Car·vin \kär-'vaⁿ\. Commune, Pas-de-Calais dept., N France, 18 m. NNE of Arras; pop. (1968c) 17,097; coal.

Car·vo·ei·ro, Cape \-kərv-'we(ə)r-(ˌ)ü\. Cape on W coast of Portugal, 39°21′N, 9°24′W.

Cary \'ka(ə)r-ē, 'ke(ə)r-\. 1 Village, McHenry co., N Illinois, 34 m. W of Chicago; pop. (1970c) 4358; tools and dies, septic tanks; agriculture.

2 Town, Wake co., E cen. North Carolina, 7 m. W of Raleigh; pop. (1970c) 7430; chemicals; tobacco.

Ca·rys·tus \kə-'ris-təs\ *or Gk.* **Ká·ris·tos** \'kär-əs-ˌtȯs\. Ancient town at S end of island of Euboea, Greece; noted for marble and asbestos.

Cas·a·blan·ca \ˌkas-ə-'blaŋ-kə, ˌkaz-; ˌkäs-ə-'bläŋ-, ˌkäz-\; *Arab.* **Dar el Bei·da** *or* **Dar–al–Bai·da** \ˌdä-ˌrel-bī-'dä, -bā-'dä\. Seaport city, W coast of Morocco, NW Africa; pop. (1970e) 1,395,000; largest city in Morocco; large harbor; cement, chemicals, textiles, tobacco; food processing.

History: Founded by Portuguese on site of ancient city of Anfa, destroyed in 1468; occupied 1757 by Moroccan sultan and in 1907 by French as result of murder of some French workers; large-scale construction of new housing initiated 1923; in World War II surrendered to Allies Nov. 11, 1942; scene of conference bet. Prime Minister Churchill and President Roosevelt Jan. 14–26, 1943, at which the "unconditional surrender" of Axis countries was determined upon.

Casa Gran·de \ˌkas-ə-'gran-dē\. City, Pinal co., S Arizona, 43 m. SSE of Phoenix; pop. (1970c) 10,536; copper mining; alfalfa, cotton; to NE is **Casa Grande National Monument:** see UNITED STATES, *National Monuments.*

Ca·sa·lec·chio di Re·no Bo·lo·gna \ˌkä-zə-'lek-yō-dē-ˌrā-nō-bə-'lōn-(y)ə\. Commune, Bologna prov., Emilia-Romagna, N Italy, 4 m. WSW of Bologna; pop. (1968e) 34,492; a suburb of Bologna.

Ca·sa·le Mon·fer·ra·to \kə-'säl-ē-ˌmän-fə-'rät-(ˌ)ō\. Commune, Alessandria prov., Piedmont, NW Italy, on Po river 18 m. NNW of Alessandria; pop. (1968e) 43,896; cement; 12th cent. cathedral; citadel (founded 1590 by Duke Vicenzo) one of strongest in Italy. Founded 730 on site of ancient **Bo·din·com·a·gus** \ˌbō-diŋ-'käm-ə-gəs\; fell to marquises of Montferrat 1246, becoming capital of the duchy of Montferrat; later fell to Mantua 1559, Savoy, France 1681, Piedmont 1703, Italy 1860.

Ca·sal·mag·gio·re \kə-ˌsäl-mə-'jōr-ē, -jȯr-\. Commune, Cremona prov., Lombardy, N Italy, on Po river; pop. (1968e) 13,390; cathedral; Venetians defeated by Francesco Sforza in battle 1448.

Ca·sa·mance \ˌkaz-ə-'mäⁿs\ *also* **Ka·sa·man·sa** \ˌkäs-ə-'män-sə\. 1 River, Senegal, W Africa, S of Gambia; 200 m. long.

2 Region bet. Gambia and Portuguese Guinea, W Africa, a part of Senegal; pop. (1969e) 661,000; ✱ Ziguinchor.

Ca·sa·ra·no \ˌkäs-ə-'rä-(ˌ)nō\. Commune, Lecce prov., Apulia, SE Italy, 22 m. S of Lecce; pop. (1968e) 15,760.

Ca·sas Gran·des \ˌkäs-əs-'grän-dəs\. Town, NW Chihuahua state, N Mexico, on Casas Grandes river; munic. pop. (1970p) 11,207; nearby to the S are ruins of ancient city, perhaps built by Aztecs 1000 years ago.

Cascadas, Las. See LAS CASCADAS.

Cas·cade \(ˌ)ka-'skād\. 1 County in Montana. See table at MONTANA.

2 City, ⊗ of Valley co., W cen. Idaho; pop. (1970c) 833.

Cascade Point. Cape on S cen. part of W coast of South I., New Zealand, 44°S, 168°22′E.

Cascade Range. Mountain range, W United States; N continuation of Sierra Nevada Mts., extending N from Lassen Peak, NE California, across Oregon and Washington; highest peak Mt. Rainier 14,410 ft., in Washington; its continuation N in British Columbia, Canada, is known as the Coast Mts.

Cascade Tunnel. Railroad tunnel, Chelan and King cos., cen. Washington, ab. 55 m. ENE of Seattle, through Cascade Range; 7.79 m. long.

Ca·sci·na \'kash-i-nə, -ˌnä\. Commune, Pisa prov., Tuscany, cen. Italy, on Arno river 8 m. ESE of Pisa; pop. (1968e) 32,497; Florentine victory over Pisans 1364.

Cas·co Bay \ˌkas-(ˌ)kō-\. Inlet of Atlantic Ocean on SE coast of Cumberland co., SW Maine, containing many islands including Orrs I. and Chebeague I.; the city of Portland is situated on its W shore.

Case Inlet \ˌkās-\. Inlet, bet. Mason and Pierce cos., Washington, at S end of Puget Sound.

Ca·se·ros \kə-'se(ə)r-ōz\. Town, W suburb of Buenos Aires, Argentina; pop. (1960c) 263,391.

Ca·ser·ta \kə-'zert-ə, -'zərt-\. 1 Province of Campania, Italy. See table at ITALY.

2 Commune, ✱ of Caserta prov., Campania, S Italy, 16 m. NNE of Naples; pop. (1968e) 59,223; 12th cent. cathedral; palace (begun 1752; designed by Vanvitelli) built by Charles III of Spain; often called the "Versailles of Naples." Headquarters of Garibaldian campaigns 1860. Field Marshal Alexander's headquarters during latter part of Italian campaign in World War II; here "Act of Surrender" of German Army Group in Italy and Yugoslavia signed Apr. 29, 1945.

Ca·sey. 1 \ˈkā-sē\. County in Kentucky. See table at KENTUCKY.
2 \ˈkā-zē, -sē\. City, Clark co., E Illinois, 67 m. SE of Decatur; pop. (1970c) 2994; auto parts; grain farms.

Ca·sey·ville \ˈkā-sē-ˌvil\. Village, Saint Clair co., SW Illinois, 6 m. E of East St. Louis; pop. (1970c) 3411; leather products; diversified agriculture.

Cash·el \ˈkash-əl\. Town, S cen. co. Tipperary, S Eire; pop. (1971p) 2693; at the base of **Rock of Cashel** 306 ft. high, on which are the ruins of a cathedral, a chapel, and a round tower. Irish chieftains of Munster here submitted to Henry II of England 1171.

Ca·si·gu·ran \ˌkäs-i-ˈgu̇(ə)r-ˌän\. Port, cen. Sorsogon prov., SE Luzon, Phil., on Sorsogon Bay; pop. (1969e) 20,500.

Casiguran Sound. Long narrow inlet of Pacific Ocean on E coast of Luzon, Quezon prov., Phil., with Cape San Ildefonso marking its SE point of entrance.

Ca·sil·da \kə-ˈsil-də\. Town, Santa Fe prov., N cen. Argentina, 210 m. NW of Buenos Aires and 34 m. W of Rosario; pop. (1960c) 17,216.

Casilinum. See CAPUA.

Ca·si·no \kə-ˈsē-(ˌ)nō\. Town, NE New South Wales, SE Australia, 110 m. S of Brisbane; pop. (1965e) 8160.

Casinum. See CASSINO.

Ca·si·quia·re *or* **Cas·si·qui·are** \ˌkäs-i-ˈkyär-ē\. River, S Venezuela; 222 m. long; connects the upper course (Guainía) of Rio Negro with the Orinoco river; a unique stream, not having a reversible current but flowing in a channel over marshy land of slight relief; strictly an arm of the Orinoco.

Cas·ket Mountain \ˌkas-kət-\. Peak, Jeff Davis co., W Texas; 6180 ft.

Čás·lav \ˈchäs-läf\ *or Ger.* **Tschas·lau** \ˈchäs-(ˌ)lau̇\. City, Czech S.R., W Czechoslovakia, 45 m. ESE of Prague; pop. (1968e) 10,314.

Caso. See KASOS.

Ca·so·ria \kə-ˈsōr-ē-ə, -ˈsȯr-\. Commune, Napoli prov., Campania, S Italy, 3 m. N of Naples; pop. (1968e) 40,352.

Cas·per \ˈkas-pər\. City, ⊗ of Natrona co., cen. Wyoming, on North Platte river; pop. (1970c) 39,361; meat packing; bottling works; oil refineries; Casper Coll. (1945).

Cas·pi·an \ˈkas-pē-ən\. City, Iron co., SW Michigan penin., 32 m. WNW of Iron Mountain; pop. (1970c) 1165.

Caspian Gates; *anc.* **Cas·pi·ae Py·lae** \ˌkas-pē-ˌē-ˈpī-(ˌ)lē\ *or* **Al·ba·ni·ae Pylae** \al-ˈbā-nē-ˌē-\. Narrow pass, Russian S.F.S.R., U.S.S.R., on W shore of Caspian Sea, near Derbent (*q.v.*) at 42°N; trade route for centuries.

Caspian Sea *or anc.* **Cas·pi·um Ma·re** \ˌkas-pē-əm-ˈmā-(ˌ)rē, -ˈmär-(ˌ)ā\ *or* **Hyr·ca·num Mare** \(ˌ)hər-ˌkā-nəm-\. Inland salt lake bet. Europe and Asia; 746 m. long and 270 m. wide; 143,550 sq. m.; the largest inland body of water in the world; about 92 ft. below sea level. Receives the Volga, Ural, and Emba rivers at the N, and the Terek and Kura (with Araks) on the W. Has no outlet; loses more by evaporation than it receives from streams. Except for S shore, which belongs to Iran, its borders are entirely within the U.S.S.R. Chief ports Baku in U.S.S.R. and Bandar-e Pahlavī and Bandar-e Shāh in Iran. Important as commercial route during Middle Ages when it formed a part of Mongol-Baltic trade route for goods from Asia.

Cass \ˈkas\. 1 River, E Michigan; ab. 100 m. long; formed by union of headstreams in Tuscola co., flows W into the Saginaw river, Saginaw co., cen. Michigan.
2 Name of counties in nine states of the U.S. See tables at ILLINOIS, INDIANA, IOWA, MICHIGAN, MINNESOTA, MISSOURI, NEBRASKA, NORTH DAKOTA, TEXAS.

Cassai. See KASAI.

Cassandreia. See POTIDAEA.

Cas·sa·no al·l'Io·nio \kə-ˈsän-(ˌ)ō-ˌäl-ē-ˈō-(ˌ)nyō\. Commune, Cosenza prov., Calabria, S Italy, 33 m. N of Cosenza; pop. (1968e) 16,824; episcopal see; castle.

Cassano d'Ad·da \-ˈdä-də\. Commune, Milano prov., Lombardy, N Italy, on the Adda 16 m. E of Milan; pop. (1968e) 12,997; scene of defeat of Ghibellines by Guelphs 1259, victory of duke of Vendôme over Eugene of Savoy Aug. 16, 1705 in War of Spanish Succession, and in Napoleonic Wars the victory of Suvorov over French forces of Moreau Apr. 27, 1799.

Cassel. See KASSEL.

Cas·sel·berry \ˈkas-əl-ˌber-ē\. City, Seminole co., cen. Florida, 9 m. NNE of Orlando; pop. (1970c) 9438.

Cas·sel·ton \ˈkas-əl-tən\. City, Cass co., E North Dakota, 21 m. W of Fargo; pop. (1970c) 1485; wheat.

Cas·sia \ˈkash-(ē-)ə\. County in Idaho. See table at IDAHO.

Cas·sian Way \ˌkash-ən-\ *or Lat.* **Via Cas·sia** \ˌvī-ə-ˈkash-(ē-)ə\. Ancient Roman road from Rome to Florence, through Bolsena, Chiusi, and Arezzo; extension ran NW to the Aurelian Way near Luna.

Cas·si·no \kə-ˈsē-(ˌ)nō\ *or before 1871* **San Ger·ma·no** \ˌsän-jər-ˈmän-(ˌ)ō\ *or anc.* **Ca·si·num** \kə-ˈsī-nəm\. Commune, Frosinone prov., Latium, cen. Italy, near Rapido river 28 m. ESE of Frosinone; pop. (1968e) 25,088; ancient ruins; Benedictine monastery of Monte Cassino (*q.v.*) nearby; peace signed here by Emperor Frederick II and Pope Gregory IX 1230; defeat of Murat by Austrians Mar. 16, 1815. In World War II a key position in the German Gustav Line, barring entrance to Allies into valley of Liri river and road to Rome; battle for it began Feb. 1, 1944, but through Feb. and Mar. infantry, artillery, and air assaults were unsuccessful; second battle begun May 11 and town captured May 17; monastery completely destroyed.

Cassiquiare. See CASIQUIARE.

Cas·si·ter·i·des \ˌkas-ə-ˈter-ə-ˌdēz\. Ancient name of tin-producing (Gk. *kassiteros* tin) islands of W Europe; originally applied to Scilly Isles off Great Britain, but location unknown.

Cass Lake \ˈkas-\. 1 Lake on NW boundary of Cass co., N cen. Minnesota, extending into Beltrami co.; ab. 10 m. long.
2 Village, Cass co., N cen. Minnesota, on Cass Lake 15 m. ESE of Bemidji; pop. (1970c) 1317; nurseries.

Cas·sop·o·lis \kə-ˈsäp-(ə-)ləs\. Village, ⊗ of Cass co., SW Michigan; pop. (1970c) 2108; summer resort.

Cass·ville \ˈkas-ˌvil\. City, ⊗ of Barry co., SW Missouri; pop. (1970c) 1910; trout fisheries.

Castalian Spring. See PARNASSUS 2.

Cas·teau \kas-ˈtō\. Commune, Hainaut prov., Belgium, 28 m. SSE of Brussels; pop. (1969e) 2750; since 1967 site of headquarters of NATO.

Ca·stel·buo·no \kä-stel-ˈbwō-(ˌ)nō\. Commune, Palermo prov., NW cen. Sicily, Italy, ESE of Palermo; pop. (1968e) 10,822.

Ca·stel·fi·dar·do \kä-stel-fi-ˈdär-(ˌ)dō\. Commune, Ancona prov., Marches, cen. Italy, S of Ancona; pop. (1968e) 12,415; scene of battle Sept. 18, 1860 in which Italians (Piedmontese) decisively defeated papal forces.

Ca·stel·fio·ren·ti·no \käs-ˌtel-fē-ˌōr-ən-ˈtē-(ˌ)nō, -ˌȯr-\. Commune, Firenze prov., Tuscany, cen. Italy, 19 m. SW of Florence; pop. (1968e) 16,904.

Ca·stel·fran·co Emi·lia \käs-tel-ˌfräŋ-(ˌ)kō-ā-ˈmēl-yə\. Commune, Modena prov., Emilia-Romagna, N Italy, 7 m. SE of Modena; pop. (1968e) 19,276.

Castelfranco Ve·ne·to \-ˈven-ə-ˌtō\. Commune, Treviso prov., Veneto, NE Italy, 15 m. W of Treviso; pop. (1968e) 24,859; birthplace of Il Giorgione.

Ca·stel Gan·dol·fo \käs-ˌtel-gän-ˈdȯl-(ˌ)fō\. Commune, Roma prov., Latium, cen. Italy, on W shore of Lake Albano 13 m. SE of Rome; pop. (1968e) 4623; includes a group of papal estates; papal palace begun by Urban VIII; summer residence of the popes. See VATICAN CITY.

Ca·stel·lam·ma·re, Gulf of \-käs-ˌtel-ə-ˈmär-(ˌ)ā\. Inlet of Tyrrhenian Sea on NW coast of the island of Sicily, Italy.

Castellammare del Gol·fo \-del-ˈgōl-(ˌ)fō\. Seaport, Trapani prov., NW Sicily, Italy, on Gulf of Castellammare E of Trapani; pop. (1968e) 15,498; tuna fisheries; watering place.

Castellammare di Sta·bia \-di-ˈstäb-yə\ *or anc.* **Sta·bi·ae** \ˈstā-bē-ē\. Fortified seaport, Napoli prov., Campania, S Italy, on Bay of Naples 16 m. SE of Naples; pop. (1968e) 70,287; episcopal see; ruins of 13th cent. castle of Frederick II; dockyards; summer resort. Built on site of, and from ruins of, ancient Stabiae, destroyed by the eruption of Vesuvius 79 A.D. in which Pliny the Elder perished; English and Neapolitans defeated by French under Macdonald 1799.

Castellana, La. See LA CASTELLANA.

Ca·stel·la·na Grot·te \ˌkäs-tə-ˌlä-nə-ˈgrò-tā\. Commune, Bari prov., Apulia, SE Italy, 16 m. SE of Bari; pop. (1968e) 15,007.

Ca·stel·la·ne·ta \käs-ˌtel-ə-ˈnāt-ə\. Commune, Taranto prov., Apulia, SE Italy, 19 m. NW of Taranto; pop. (1968e) 14,852; 12th cent. cathedral; trade center.

Cas·te·llón de la Pla·na \ˌkas-təl-ˈyōn-də-lä-ˈplän-ə\. 1 Province of E Spain. See table at SPAIN.
2 Manufacturing city and Mediterranean seaport, its ✱, 40 m. NNE of Valencia; pop. (1970p) 93,968; paper, porcelain, wool; captured from Moors by James I of Aragon 1233.

Castellorizo. See KASTELLORIZON.

Ca·stel·mas·sa \käs-tel-ˈmä-sə\. Commune, Rovigo prov., Veneto, NE Italy; pop. (1968e) 5036.

Cas·tel·nau·da·ry \ka-ˈstel-ˌnōd-ə-ˈrē\. Commune, Aude dept., S France, ab. 22 m. WNW of Carcassonne; pop. (1962c) 9343; important in ancient Languedoc and in the wars against the Albigenses in 13th cent.; battle Sept. 1, 1632 in which Louis XIII defeated duke of Montmorency and Gaston d'Orléans.

Castelnuovo. See HERCEGNOVI.

Ca·stel·nuo·vo Be·rar·den·ga \käs-ˌtel-nə-ˈwō-(ˌ)vō-ˌbar-är-ˈdeŋ-gə\. Commune, Siena prov., Tuscany, cen. Italy, 8 m. E by N of Siena; pop. (1968e) 5823.

Cas·te·lo Bran·co \kə-ˌstel-ə-ˈbraŋ-(ˌ)kü\. 1 District of E cen. Portugal. See table at PORTUGAL.
2 Commune, its ✱, 114 m. NE of Lisbon; pop. (1970p) 21,730; cork, wool; cathedral.

Castelrosso. See KASTELLORIZON.

Ca·stel San Gio·van·ni \käs-ˈtel-sän-jō-ˈvä-nē\. Commune, Piacenza prov., Emilia-Romagna, N Italy, 15 m. W of Piacenza; pop. (1968e) 10,603; French defeated here by Austrians and Russians 1799.

Ca·stel·ter·mi·ni \käs-tel-ˈter-mi-nē\. Commune, Agrigento prov., SW Sicily, Italy, near Agrigento; pop. (1968e) 12,720.

Castelvetere. See CAULONIA.

Ca·stel·ve·tra·no \(ˌ)käs-ˌtel-və-ˈträn-(ˌ)ō\. Commune, Trapani prov., NW Sicily, Italy, 29 m. SSE of Trapani; pop. (1968e) 31,123; ruins of ancient Selinus (*q.v.*) nearby.

Ca·sti·glio·ne del La·go \ˌkäs-tēl-ˈyō-nē-de-ˈläg-(ˌ)ō\. Commune, Perugia prov., Umbria, cen. Italy, on Lake Trasimene 18 m. W by N of Perugia; pop. (1968e) 14,201; castle.

Castiglione del·le Sti·vie·re \-del-ə-stē-ˈvye(ə)r-ə\. Commune, Mantova prov., Lombardy, N Italy, 22 m. NW of Mantua; pop. (1968e) 11,676; Austrians under Wurmser defeated by French under Napoleon Aug. 5, 1796.

Ca·sti·glion Fio·ren·ti·no \ˌkäs-tēl-ˈyōn-ˌfyȯr-ən-ˈtē-nō\. Commune, Arezzo prov., Tuscany, cen. Italy, 10 m. S by E of Arezzo; pop. (1968e) 10,918.

Cas·tile \ka-ˈstē(ə)l\ *or Span.* **Cas·til·la** \kȧ-ˈstē-lʸȧ, -ˈstē-yȧ\. Region and ancient kingdom, cen. and N cen. Spain; 53,463 sq. m.; comprises the modern provinces of Ávila, Burgos, Ciudad Real, Cuenca, Guadalajara, Logroño, Madrid, Palencia, Santander, Segovia, Soria, Toledo, and Valladolid; divided into two historical regions: in the N, Old Castile (*q.v.*), and in the S, New Castile (*q.v.*); extensive plains, forming tablelands hemmed in on all sides by mountains; some fertile regions, esp. in the S, but in general arid; watered chiefly by the Duero, Guadiana, Tagus, and Júcar rivers.

History: Originally an extension of kingdom of León (see LEÓN 5); in 10th cent. A.D. countship of Castile made hereditary and practically autonomous by Count González of Burgos; united with Navarre 1029 which began conquest of León; León united with Castile by Ferdinand I 1037; expanded by series of conquests of Moorish kingdoms: Toledo (New Castile) 1085, Córdoba 1236, Murcia 1243, and Seville 1248; took Canary Is. 1402 and Gibraltar 1462; union with Aragon (*q.v.*) 1479 (after marriage of Isabella of Castile to Ferdinand of Aragon 1469) completed with accession of their grandson, Charles I of Spain, 1516. See SPAIN.

Castilla la Nueva. See NEW CASTILE.

Castilla la Vieja. See OLD CASTILE.

Cas·til·lo de San Mar·cos National Monument \kas-ˈtē-yō-də-san-ˈmärk-əs-\. See UNITED STATES, *National Monuments.*

Cas·til·lon \ˌkas-tē-ˈyōⁿ\ *or* **Castillon–la–Ba·taille** \-lä-ba-ˈtäʸ\. Commune, Gironde dept., SW France, on the Dordogne river 26 m. E of Bordeaux; pop. (1962c) 3108; scene of English defeat July 17, 1453 in last battle of Hundred Years' War.

Cas·tine \kas-ˈtēn\. Town, Hancock co., SE Maine, on E side of Penobscot Bay, 35 m. S of Bangor; pop. (1970c) 1080; fishing and resort center; Maine Maritime Academy; one of Maine's oldest towns.

Cas·tle·bar \ˌkas-əl-ˈbär\. Town, ⊗ of co. Mayo, NW Eire; pop. (1971p) 5970; site of Norman castle, home of the de Burghs; nearby is site of runaway victory ("Castlebar Races") of French auxiliaries and Irish insurrectionists over militia and yeomanry 1798.

Cas·tle Clin·ton National Monument \ˌkas-əl-ˈklint-ᵊn-\. See UNITED STATES, *National Monuments.*

Castle Dale \ˈkas-əl-ˌdāl\. City, ⊗ of Emery co., E cen. Utah; pop. (1970c) 541.

Cas·tle·ford \ˈkas-əl-fərd\. Municipal borough, West Riding, Yorkshire, N England, 11 m. ESE of Leeds; pop. (1971p) 38,220; glass, earthenware, chemicals.

Cas·tle·gar \ˌkas-əl-ˈgär\. Town, British Columbia, Canada, 90 m. E of Penticton; pop. (1966c) 3440; diversified agriculture.

Castle Gate \ˈkas-əl-ˌgāt\. Town, Carbon co., Utah, near Price river; pop. (1970c) 205; huge sandstone formations at the entrance to Price river canyon.

Castle Harbour. Gulf off NE end of Bermuda I. in the Bermuda Is., formed by St. George's I. and St. David I. on N and small islands on E.

Castle Hill. Elevation (Hill 193) near the Benedictine monastery, Cassino, Italy; after bitter fighting captured by Indian troops Mar. 15–20, 1944.

Castle Hills. City, Bexar co., S cen. Texas, entirely within city limits of San Antonio; pop. (1970c) 5311.

Castle Island. One of the Bahama Is., at SE entrance to Crooked Island Passage; lighthouse (estab. 1868).

Cas·tle·maine \ˌkas-əl-ˈmān\. Town, cen. Victoria, SE Australia, 65 m. NW of Melbourne; pop. (1966c) 7103; its gold mines among the first to be opened in Australia.

Castle Mountain. See EISENHOWER, MOUNT.

Castle Peak. 1 Mountain in Sierra Nevada Mts., E Fresno co., S cen. California; 10,668 ft.
2 Mountain, Gunnison and Pitkin cos., W cen. Colorado; 14,265 ft.
3 Mountain, SW Custer co., cen. Idaho; 11,820 ft.

Castle Point. Peak, W Klamath co., S Oregon, SW of Crater Lake; 6300 ft.

Castle Rock. Town, ⊗ of Douglas co., cen. Colorado; pop. (1970c) 1531; diversified farming.

Castle Shan·non \-ˈshan-ən\. Borough, Allegheny co., SW Pennsylvania, 6 m. S of Pittsburgh; pop. (1970c) 11,899.

Cas·tle·ton \ˈkas-əl-tən\. Town and summer resort, Rutland co., W Vermont, ab. 10 m. W of Rutland; pop. (1970c)

2837; Castleton State Coll. (1787); mobilization center of Ethan Allen and Green Mountain boys before attack on Ticonderoga 1775.

Castleton on Hud·son *or* **Castleton–on–Hudson** \-ˈhəd-sən\. Village, Rensselaer co., E New York, on Hudson river 9 m. S of Albany; pop. (1970c) 1730; high-level bridge, railroad cutoff, with channel span of 1008 ft.

Cas·tle·town \ˈkas-əl-ˌtau̇n\. Town, former ✱ of Isle of Man (*q.v.*), on S coast of the island; pop. (1971p) 2820.

Castletown Bearhaven *or* **Castletownbere.** See BEREHAVEN.

Ca·stor \ˈkas-tər\. Peak in the Pennine Alps on Swiss-Italian border, the E peak of the **Zwil·linge** \ˈtsvil-iŋ-ə\ (Twins), just W of Monte Rosa; 13,865 ft.; the W peak is **Pol·lux** \ˈpäl-əks\, 13,422 ft.

Cas·tor Peak \ˌkas-tər-\. Mountain in Yellowstone National Park, NW Wyoming; 10,854 ft.

Castra Regina. See REGENSBURG.

Cas·tres \kȧstrᵊ\ *or anc.* **Cas·tra Al·bi·en·si·um** \ˈkas-trə-ˌal-bē-ˈen(t)-sē-əm\. Commercial and manufacturing city, Tarn dept., S France, on Agout river 24 m. S of Albi; pop. (1968c) 40,457; furniture, paper; fine town hall (former episcopal palace) with gardens on plan of Tuileries; 17th cent. church. Founded on site of Roman camp around Benedictine monastery 647; to Crown 1225; episcopal see 1317–1801; made countship 1356; conquered by Louis XIII 1629.

Cas·tries \ka-ˈstrē, ˈkäs-ˌtrēs\ *or* **Port Castries.** Seaport, ✱ of Saint Lucia, on NW coast of Saint Lucia I., Windward Is., West Indies; pop. (1964c) 5100.

Cas·tro. 1 \ˈkas-(ˌ)trō\. County in Texas. See table at TEXAS.
2 \ˈkash-(ˌ)trü\. Municipality, Paraná state, S Brazil, ab. 60 m. NW of Curitiba; pop. (1968e) 54,936.
3 \ˈkäs-(ˌ)trō\. Small port, Chiloé prov., S cen. Chile; on E shore of Chiloé I.; pop. (1960c) 7001.
4 Seaport, Greece. See KASTRON.

Castro Al·ves \ˌkash-trü-ˈal-vēs\. City, Bahia state, E Brazil, on railroad ab. 68 m. W of Salvador; munic. pop. (1968e) 46,058.

Castro del Río \ˌkäs-(ˌ)trō-del-ˈrē-ō\. Commune, Córdoba prov., S Spain, 22 m. SE of Córdoba; pop. (1970p) 11,089.

Castrogiovanni. See ENNA 2.

Castron. See KASTRON.

Ca·strop–Rau·xel *also* **Ka·strop–Rauxel** \ˌkäs-ˌtrōp-ˈrau̇k-səl\. Industrial city, North Rhine-Westphalia, West Germany, 32 m. SSW of Münster; pop. (1969e) 83,892; coal mining; manufactures cement, chemicals, tile; Castrop first mentioned 834.

Ca·stro·re·a·le \ˌkäs-trō-rā-ˈäl-ē\. Commune, Messina prov., NE Sicily, Italy; pop. (1968e) 4098; warm sulfur springs.

Ca·stro–Ur·dia·les \ˌkäs-trō-u̇r-ˈdyäl-ās, -ˈt͟häl-\. Seaport, Santander prov., N Spain, on Bay of Biscay 30 m. ESE of Santander; pop. (1970p) 12,401; iron mining; ancient Roman colony; destroyed by French 1813; later rebuilt.

Cas·tro Valley \ˌkas-(ˌ)trō-\. Urban community (unincorporated), Alameda co., W California, N of Hayward; pop. (1970c) 44,760.

Ca·stro·vil·la·ri \ˌkäs-trō-ˈvēl-ə-rē\. Commune, Cosenza prov., Calabria, S Italy; pop. (1968e) 16,573.

Castrum. See AL-QASR.

Castua. See KASTAV.

Cas·tu·lo \ˈkas-tə-ˌlō\. Ancient Iberian town of Hispania Tarraconensis (in modern S Spain) on the Baetis (Guadalquivir) river; important Roman town near silver and lead mines. Scipio Africanus defeated Carthaginians here 208 B.C. Site of modern **Caz·lo·na** \käz-ˈlō-nə\, Jaén prov., 2 m. N of Linares.

Casus. See KASOS.

Cas·well \ˈkaz-ˌwel, -wəl\. County in North Carolina. See table at NORTH CAROLINA.

Catabathmus Magna. See SALŪM.

Ca·ta·ca·os \ˌkät-ə-ˈkau̇s\. Town, Piura dept., NW Peru, SW of Piura; pop. (1961c) 12,100.

Catacium. See CATANZARO.

Ca·ta·co·cha \ˌkät-ə-ˈkō-chə\. Town, Loja prov., SW Ecuador.

Ca·ta·gua·ses \ˌkat-ə-ˈgwä-zəs\. Town, SE Minas Gerais state, E Brazil, 120 m. NNE of Rio de Janeiro; munic. pop. (1968e) 39,975.

Cat·a·hou·la \ˌkat-ə-ˈhü-lə\. Parish in Louisiana. See table at LOUISIANA.

Catahoula Lake. Lake in S La Salle parish, Louisiana.

Ca·ta·ing·an \ˌkät-ə-ˈiŋ-ən\. Municipality, SE coast of Masbate I., Phil., on Samar Sea; pop. (1969e) 35,700.

Ça·tal·ca *or angl.* **Cha·tal·ja** \ˌchä-təl-ˈjä\. Town, İstanbul prov., Turkey in Europe, ab. 20 m. W of İstanbul; center of heavily fortified line across peninsula from Black Sea to Sea of Marmara, where Turks made final stand Nov. 1912 in First Balkan War; temporary W boundary of Turkey in Europe 1912–13.

Catalina. See SANTA CATALINA 1.

Cat·a·lo·nia \ˌkat-ᵊl-ˈō-nyə, -nē-ə\ *or Span.* **Ca·ta·lu·ña** \ˌkät-ᵊl-ˈü-nyə\ *or Catalan* **Ca·ta·lu·nya** \ˌkät-ə-ˈlün-yə\. Historical region in northeast corner of Spain, bounded N by France and the Pyrenees, E and S by the Mediterranean, SW by Valencia, W by Aragon; 12,329 sq. m.; pop. (1970p) 5,122,567; comprises the modern provinces of Barcelona, Gerona, Lérida, and Tarragona; traversed by spur of Pyrenees; watered principally by the Ebro; generally rugged land, but containing fertile valleys and coastlands; rich in minerals and agricultural products; its people retain own language (Catalan) and strong sense of regional unity.

History: Originally settled by numerous independent tribes, and subsequently by Phoenicians and Greeks; invaded by Carthaginians under Hamilcar Barca and Hannibal; conquered by Romans under whom it became a wealthy province with its capital at Tarragona; invaded by Visigoths early 5th cent. A.D.; S portion taken by Arabs 712 but reconquered by Charlemagne who set up Spanish March 795 with its capital later (801) at Barcelona; became independent Frankish county of Barcelona (or Catalonia) 9th cent.; united with Aragon (*q.v.*) 1137; by 13th cent. had extensive territory N of Pyrenees (including Cerdagne, Roussillon, part of Provence); Barcelona became a European trade center and point of departure for Aragonese expansion in Mediterranean (see MAJORCA; SICILY); engaged in long struggle to maintain political and cultural autonomy against frequent attempts at centralization and unification by Castile; revolted 1640–59 as result of policy of Olivares; Cerdagne and Roussillon lost to France 1659; during War of the Spanish Succession (1701–14) sided with Archduke Charles of Austria; entered most recent movement for autonomy 1917–19; autonomous 1932–34; again autonomous after joining Loyalists in Spanish Civil War 1936; lost autonomy 1939 after fall of Barcelona (Loyalist capital from 1937) and forbidden use of Catalan by Franco government.

Cat·a·mar·ca \ˌkät-ə-ˈmär-kə\. **1** Province of NW Argentina. See table at ARGENTINA.
2 Town, its ✱, 115 m. SSW of San Miguel de Tucumán; pop. (1960c) 45,929; at altitude of 1600 ft. in foothills of E Andes; agricultural and mining center.

Catana. See CATANIA 2.

Ca·tan·dua·nes \ˌkät-ən-ˈdwän-əs\. Island of SE Luzon, E Phil., constituting a prov. of Phil.; 584 sq. m.; pop. (1970p) 162,679; ✱ Virac; with Luzon coast forms Lagonoy Gulf; covered with hills and low mountain ranges, highest peak ab. 3000 ft.; soil fertile producing rice, corn, cotton, hemp, and coconuts; formerly a subprovince of Albay prov., made separate province 1945.

Ca·tan·du·va \ˌkat-ən-ˈdü-və\. City, São Paulo state, SE Brazil, 230 m. NW of São Paulo; munic. pop. (1968e) 58,459.

Ca·ta·nia \kə-ˈtān-yə, -ˈtän-\. 1 Province of E Sicily, Italy. See table at ITALY.

2 *or anc.* **Cat·a·na** \ˈkat-ə-nə\. Manufacturing and commercial commune, its ✱, at foot of Mt. Etna on Gulf of Catania; pop. (1968e) 409,088; important port; chemicals, sulfur, cement, textiles, leather; fishing; episcopal see; ancient Roman ruins; Norman cathedral (1091); university (1434).

History: Founded by Greeks 729 B.C.; Athenian base of operations against Syracuse 432 B.C.; taken by Romans 263 B.C. (First Punic War); taken by Saracens A.D. 902 and by Normans c. 1090; devastated by earthquakes, esp. in 1169 and 1693, and by volcanic eruptions, esp. in 1669; off nearby coast scene of naval victory of French under Duquesne over the Spanish and Dutch fleet under de Ruyter 1676. In World War II a German defense point; under attack by British from July 12, 1943; outflanked and abandoned Aug. 5.

Catania, Gulf of. Inlet of Mediterranean Sea on E coast of the island of Sicily, Italy; ab. 20 m. long.

Ca·ta·ño \kə-ˈtä-(ˌ)nyō\. Town and municipality, San Juan dist., NE Puerto Rico; munic. pop. (1970p) 26,056; town is on S shore of San Juan harbor S of San Juan.

Ca·tan·za·ro \ˌkä-tän-ˈzär-(ˌ)ō\. 1 Province of Calabria, S Italy. See table at ITALY.

2 *or anc.* **Ca·ta·ci·um** \kə-ˈtā-sh(ē-)əm\. City, its ✱ and ✱ of Calabria, near Gulf of Squillace 183 m. SE of Naples; pop. (1968e) 81,548; cathedral; academy of sciences; summer resort; devastated by earthquake 1783 and 1908; founded 10th cent.

Cat·a·o·nia \ˌkat-ə-ˈōn-yə\. Ancient region of Asia Minor bet. Cappadocia and Cilicia, including NE part of Taurus Mts.

Ca·ta·ra·ma \ˌkät-ə-ˈrä-mə\. Town, Los Ríos prov., W cen. Ecuador.

Ca·tar·man \ˌkät-är-ˈmän\. Municipality, ✱ of Samar del Norte prov., N coast of Samar I., Phil., 55 m. NNE of Catbalogan; pop. (1969e) 54,200.

Cat·a·sau·qua \ˌkat-ə-ˈsȯ-kwə\. Borough, Lehigh co., E Pennsylvania, on Lehigh river 4 m. N of Allentown; pop. (1970c) 5702; textiles, cement, flour.

Ca·tas·tro·phe, Cape \-kə-ˈtas-trə-(ˌ)fē\. Cape at W entrance to Spencer Gulf, S South Australia.

Ca·ta·tum·bo \ˌkät-ə-ˈtüm-(ˌ)bō\. River in N South America; ab. 210 m. long; rises in N Colombia, flows NE across Venezuelan border and into Lake Maracaibo.

Ca·taw·ba \kə-ˈtȯ-bə\. 1 River, North Carolina and South Carolina; flowing from Blue Ridge Mts., W North Carolina, S into South Carolina, where it is known as the Wateree. See WATEREE.

2 County in North Carolina. See table at NORTH CAROLINA.

Cat·a·wis·sa \ˌkat-ə-ˈwis-ə\. Borough, Columbia co., E cen. Pennsylvania, NNW of Pottsville; pop. (1970c) 1701.

Cat·ba·lo·gan \ˌkät-bə-ˈlō-gən\. Municipality, ✱ of Samar Occidental prov., Phil., on W coast of Samar I. in central part; pop. (1969e) 47,800; has fair harbor on Samar Sea.

Cateau, Le. See LE CATEAU.

Catelet, Le. See LE CATELET.

Ca·te·ma·co \ˌkät-ə-ˈmä-(ˌ)kō\. Town, Veracruz state, E Mexico, just E of San Andrés Tuxtla; munic. pop. (1970p) 23,671.

Ca·ter·ham and War·ling·ham \ˈkā-tər-əm . . . ˈwȯr-liŋ-əm\. Urban district, Surrey, S England, 18 m. S of London; pop. (1971p) 35,781; chemicals; printing.

Ca·thay \kə-ˈthā, ka-\. An old name for China, esp. during Middle Ages; introduced by Marco Polo. It comes from the Persian *Khitai,* after the Khitans, a Tatar race occupying the Sungari basin in the 10th cent. A.D. Used in cen. Asia and in countries to the W, but never by the Chinese themselves. The modern Russian form is *Kitai.*

Cat·head Point \ˌkat-ˌhed-\. Point at N extremity of Leelanau co., NW Michigan, on Lake Michigan.

Ca·the·dral Mountain \kə-ˌthē-drəl-\. Peak, Brewster co., W Texas; 6860 ft.

Cathedral Peak. Mountain in Yellowstone National Park, NW Wyoming; 10,760 ft.

Cathedral Range. Mountain range, NE Mariposa co., California, in Sierra Nevada Mts. in Yosemite National Park; highest point 11,516 ft.

Cathedral Rocks. Mountain, Mariposa co., California; 7503 ft.

Catherine, Mount. See KATHERINA, GEBEL.

Catherine Archipelago. See ALEUTIAN ISLANDS.

Cathkin Peak. See CHAMPAGNE CASTLE.

Cath·lam·et \kath-ˈlam-it\. Town, ⊗ of Wahkiakum co., SW Washington; pop. (1970c) 647.

Cat Island \ˈkat-\. 1 Island in Gulf of Mexico, off S coast of Harrison co., SE Mississippi.

2 One of the Bahama Is., in Atlantic Ocean SE of Eleuthera I. and WNW of San Salvador; 150 sq. m.; pop. (1963c) 3131; formerly identified with the San Salvador of Columbus (see SAN SALVADOR 1).

Cat·letts·burg \ˈkat-lits-ˌbərg\. City, ⊗ of Boyd co., NE Kentucky, 5 m. S of Ashland; pop. (1970c) 3420.

Ca·to·che, Cape \-kə-ˈtō-chē\. NE extremity of Yucatán penin., SE Mexico, projecting into Yucatán Channel.

Ca·tons·ville \ˈkāt-ᵊnz-ˌvil, -vəl\. Urban community (unincorporated), Baltimore co., Maryland, SW of Baltimore; pop. (1970c) 54,812; Catonsville Community Coll. (1957).

Ca·too·sa \kə-ˈtü-sə\. 1 County in Georgia. See table at GEORGIA.

2 Town, Rogers co., Oklahoma, a suburb of Tulsa; pop. (1970c) 970; port terminal on Arkansas River Navigation System.

Ca·tron \kə-ˈträn\. County in New Mexico. See table at NEW MEXICO.

Cats·kill \ˈkat-ˌskil\. Village, ⊗ of Greene co., SE New York, on W side of Hudson river 30 m. S of Albany; pop. (1970c) 5317; summer resort, gateway to Catskill Mts.; settled by Dutch c. 1680; incorp. 1806.

Catskill Mountains. Group of the Appalachian system, SE New York, along W bank of Hudson chiefly in Greene, Ulster, and Delaware cos.; highest peak Slide Mt. 4204 ft.; heavily wooded; many resorts.

Cat·tail Peak \ˌkat-ˌtāl-\. Mountain, Yancey co., W North Carolina, near Mt. Mitchell; 6600 ft.

Cat·ta·rau·gus \ˌkat-ə-ˈrȯ-gəs\. County in New York. See table at NEW YORK.

Cattaraugus Creek. River, W New York; ab. 70 m. long; forms boundary bet. Erie and Cattaraugus cos. and flows W into Lake Erie.

Cattaro. See KOTOR.

Cattegat. See KATTEGAT.

Cau·a·bu·ri \ˌkau̇-ə-bə-ˈrē\. River, NW Brazil; ab. 100 m. long; flows from S tip of Venezuela S into Rio Negro.

Ca·ua·yan \kä-ˈwä-yän\. Municipality, Negros, Phil., on Panay Gulf; pop. (1969e) 59,800.

Cau·ca \ˈkau̇-kə\. 1 River, W Colombia; 838 m. long; rises in Andes Mts., flows N into Magdalena river.

2 Department of SW Colombia. See table at COLOMBIA.

Cau·ca·sia \kȯ-ˈkā-zhə, -shə\ *or* **Cau·ca·sus** \ˈkȯ-kə-səs\. Region bet. the Black and Caspian seas, U.S.S.R.; ab. 154,250 sq. m.; extends SE and NW ab. 750 m. from Apsheron Penin. to mouth of Kuban river on Black Sea; contains the Caucasus Mts. (*q.v.*) which divide it into **Cis·cau·ca·sia** \ˌsis-\, N of the range, and **Trans·cau·ca·sia** \ˌtranz-\, on the S.

History: Inhabited from ancient times by peoples of Caucasian race to which successive invaders added numerous other elements; known to ancient Greeks (see COLCHIS); penetrated, during Middle Ages, by Greek Christianity; East Caucasus later converted to Islam; under nominal Persian and Turkish suzerainty until gradually forced into connection with Russia whose acquisition of Astrakhan (*q.v.*) had brought her to the Caspian; conquered by Russia, to the Kuban and Terek 1774, Derbent 1796 and Baku 1806, Georgia 1801, Shirvan and Karabakh 1813, Persian Armenia 1828, Akhaltsikhe 1829; mountain tribes of Caucasus became Russian subjects after arrest of their leader Shamyl 1859; Circassians surrendered 1864; Kars, Ardahan, and Batum ceded by Turkey to Russia 1878. For later history of southern part, see TRANSCAUCASIAN FEDERATION. In World War II its oil fields goal of German advance July–Nov. 1942; Ordzhonikidze farthest point reached Nov. 10–19; German armies driven out by Jan. 1943.

Caucasus Indicus. See HINDU KUSH.

Cau·ca·sus Mountains \ˌkȯ-kə-səs-\ *or Russ.* **Kav·kaz·ski Khre·bet** \kəf-ˌkä-skē-kr(y)i-ˈb(y)et\. Mountain range, S U.S.S.R., bet. the Black and Caspian seas; ab. 700 m. long; often considered the boundary bet. Europe and Asia; separates Ciscaucasia from Transcaucasia. Of volcanic origin; has many peaks above 15,000 ft., highest Mt. Elbrus 18,481 ft.; following the decision of Soviet geographers 1958, region considered to be in Asia; crossed by high passes, the two best known being Daryal and Mamison (*qq.v.*).

Cauda. See GAVDOS.

Cau·dé·ran \ˌkōd-ā-ˈräⁿ\. Former commune, Gironde dept., SW France; now part of Bordeaux.

Caudine Forks \ˌkȯ-ˌdīn-, -ˌdēn-\. Mountain passes on the road bet. Capua and Benevento, Campania, S Italy, near Caudium; defeat of Romans by the Samnites 321 B.C.

Cau·di·um \ˈkȯ-dē-əm\. Ancient town, Samnium, S Italy, E of Benevento.

Cau·dry \kō-ˈdrē\. Commune, Nord dept., N France, 40 m. SSE of Lille; pop. (1968c) 13,328; textiles.

Caugh·ley \ˈkäf-lē\. Village, E Shropshire, England; site of pottery factories (abandoned ab. 1815) where willow pattern was first made ab. 1780.

Caugh·na·wa·ga \ˌkä(g)-nə-ˈwäg-ə\. Indian village, S Quebec, Canada, on the St. Lawrence S of Montreal.

Ca·uit Point \ˌkä-wət-\. Point of land, E Surigao del Sur prov., Mindanao, Phil., SE of entrance to Lanuza Bay.

Caul·field \ˈkȯl-ˌfēld\. Municipality, S Victoria, SE Australia, SE suburb of Melbourne; pop. (1966c) 76,119.

Cau·lo·nia \kau̇-ˈlȯn-yə\ *or formerly* **Ca·stel·ve·te·re** \käs-tel-ˈvā-tə-rə\. Commune, Reggio di Calabria prov., Calabria, S Italy; pop. (1968e) 10,282.

Cau·que·nes \kau̇-ˈkā-nəs\. City, ✻ of Maule prov., S cen. Chile, ab. 198 m. S of Santiago; pop. (1960c) 17,836; in region severely damaged by earthquake Jan. 24, 1939.

Cau·ra \ˈkau̇-rə\. River, cen. Venezuela; ab. 450 m. long; rises in the Serra Pacaraima, flows N into the Orinoco.

Cau·sap·scal \ˌkō-zäp-ˈskäl\. Town, Matane co., Gaspé Penin., SE Quebec, Canada, 37 m. SSE of Matane; pop. (1971p) 2974; resort for fishermen.

Causses \ˈkōs\. District, S cen. France, on S border of the Massif Central; a limestone region, noted for gorges and subterranean rivers.

Cau·te·rets \kō-ˈtrā\. Commune, SW Hautes-Pyrénées dept., SW France; pop. (1962c) 1037; hot sulfur springs.

Cau·tín \kau̇-ˈtēn\. Province of S cen. Chile. See table at CHILE.

Cau·to \ˈkau̇-(ˌ)tō\. River, E Cuba; 155 m. long; rises in cen. Oriente prov., flows W into Guacanayabo Bay; navigable for ab. 70 m.; longest river in Cuba.

Cau·ve·ry \ˈkȯ-və-rē\ *or* **Ka·ve·ri** \ˈkäv-ə-rē\. River, S Mysore, S India; 475 m. long; rises in N Kerala, flows E and SE, and enters Bay of Bengal in a wide delta. On the border of Mysore it forms island of Sivasamudram on either side of which are the **Cauvery Falls,** descending ab. 320 ft. and supplying waterpower. Navigable in short sections for small vessels only; source of extensive irrigation system; noted for its scenery; entire course, but esp. the sections at Seringapatam and Tiruchchirappalli, regarded as sacred.

Ca·va de' Tir·re·ni \ˈkäv-ə-ˌdā-tə-ˈrā-nē\. Commune, Salerno prov., Campania, S Italy, 3 m. WNW of Salerno; pop. (1968e) 46,657; cathedral; summer resort; textiles; famous Benedictine monastery (founded 1025 by Saint Alferius over a cave he occupied) nearby.

Ca·vail·lon \ˌkä-va-ˈyōⁿ\ *or anc.* **Ca·bel·lio** \kə-ˈbel-ē-ˌō\. Commune, Vaucluse dept., SE France, on Durance river 13 m. SE of Avignon; pop. (1968c) 18,544; 12th cent. cathedral.

Cav·a·lier \ˌkav-ə-ˈli(ə)r\. 1 County, North Dakota. See table at NORTH DAKOTA.

2 City, ⊗ of Pembina co., NE corner of North Dakota; pop. (1970c) 1381; wheat; cattle.

Cavalla. See KAVALLA.

Ca·val·ly \kə-ˈval-ē\ *or* **Ca·val·la** \-ˈval-ə\ *also* **Ka·val·li** \kə-ˈval-ē\. River, W Africa, forming part of boundary bet. Ivory Coast and Liberia; 320 m. long.

Cav·an \ˈkav-ən\. 1 County, Ulster prov., N Eire; 730 sq. m.; pop. (1971p) 52,674; chief industry agriculture.

2 Urban district, its ⊗; pop. (1971p) 3268; burned 1690 by Enniskillen partisans of William of Orange after their defeat of Jacobite forces.

Ca·va·ra·ya \ˌkäv-ə-ˈrī-ə\. Peak, N Chile, W of Lake Poopó; 19,193 ft.

Ca·var·ze·re \kə-ˈvärd-zə-ˌrā\. Commune, Venezia prov., Veneto, NE Italy, on Adige river 25 m. SSW of Venice; pop. (1968e) 18,399.

Cave of the Winds. See NIAGARA FALLS.

Ca·via·na \ˌkav-ē-ˈan-ə\. Island in N branch of the mouth of the Amazon river, NE Brazil, belongs to Pará state.

Ca·vi·te \kə-ˈvēt-ē\. 1 Province, SW Luzon, Phil.; 497 sq. m.; pop. (1970p) 518,483; ✻ Trece Martires; on S side of Manila Bay; western end of NW shore is on South Channel (see CORREGIDOR). A plain except for the low mountain range in S on Batangas border; its many streams flow N or NW to Manila Bay. Fertile volcanic soil produces bananas, pineapples, papayas; fishing. Chief towns Cavite, Imus, General Trias.

History: Not populous in early Spanish times, but increased in importance with establishment of navy yard at Cavite; attacked by Dutch 1647; became stronghold of religious orders; in 19th cent. the center of revolutionary activity against Spanish government, esp. 1872 and 1896; civil government established June 11, 1901.

2 *or officially* **City of Cavite.** Chartered city, in NE part of prov., on narrow point of land **(Cavite Peninsula)** 8 m. across Manila Bay, SW of Manila; pop. (1970e) 77,100. A walled town with old forts and arsenals; its harbor part of Bacoor Bay (bet. the peninsula and the mainland); in early times made a naval base by the Spanish government.

History: Scene of defeat of Spanish fleet by Admiral Dewey May 1, 1898, known as the battle of Manila Bay (*q.v.*). Chief naval base and coaling station of U.S. fleet in Asiatic waters 1898–1941. Created a chartered city May 26, 1940. Partly destroyed by Japanese air attacks Dec. 8–10, 1941; captured by Japanese Jan. 2, 1942; retaken by Americans Feb. 13, 1945.

Caw·dor \ˈkȯd-ər\. Parish, Nairn co., N Scotland, 5 m. SW of Nairn; pop. (1961c) 849; famous castle where the murder of King Duncan in Shakespeare's *Macbeth* takes place.

Cawnpore. See KANPUR.

Caxamarca. See CAJAMARCA.

Ca·xam·bú \ˌkä-sha(ⁿ)m-ˈbü\. Municipality, S Minas Gerais state, E Brazil, 130 m. NW of Rio de Janeiro; pop. (1968e) 13,569; mineral springs.

Ca·xi·as \kə-ˈshē-əs\. City, NE Maranhão state, NE Brazil, 182 m. SE of São Luís; munic. pop. (1968e) 124,403.

Caxias do Sul \-də-'sül\. City, Rio Grande do Sul state, S Brazil, 60 m. N of Pôrto Alegre; munic. pop. (1968e) 110,-241.

Cay \'kē, 'kā\. For **Cay Lobos,** etc., see LOBOS, etc.

Ca·yam·be \kə-'yäm-bē\. 1 Dormant volcano in the Andes Mountains, N Ecuador; 18,996 ft.

2 Town, Pichincha prov., N cen. Ecuador, 33 m. NE of Quito; pop. (1962c) 8101.

Cay·ce \'kā-sē\. City, Lexington co., W cen. South Carolina, SW of Columbia; pop. (1970c) 9967; cotton, corn.

Cay·enne \kī-'en, kā-\. 1 French overseas department. See FRENCH GUIANA.

2 City, ✱ of French Guiana, on NW coast of **Cayenne Island** (ab. 30 m. in circumference); pop. (1967c) 19,668; shrimp processing; island is formed by the **Cayenne River,** a small stream that divides into two channels before emptying into the Atlantic. Founded by French 1643; held twice by Dutch in 17th cent.; received little attention until 19th cent. when penal colonies established there.

Cayes *or* **Aux Cayes** \ō-'kā(y)\. Seaport on S Tiburon Penin., SW Haiti; pop. (1961e) 15,213.

Ca·yey \kä-'yā\. Town and municipality, SE Puerto Rico, 9 m. NNW of Guayama; pop. (1970p) 21,372 (town), 38,-161 (munic.); tobacco; founded 1774.

Cay·man Islands \kā-'man-, 'kā-mən-\. Island group in NW Caribbean Sea ab. 200 m. NW of Jamaica; 118 sq. m.; pop. (1970c) 10,652; a British dependency. Group comprises three islands: **Grand Cayman,** the largest, 76 sq. m., pop. (1966c) 7323, with Georgetown, ✱ of the group, on its W end; NE of Grand Cayman **Little Cayman,** 20 sq. m., pop. (1966c) 27; and **Cayman Brac** \-'brak\, 22 sq. m., pop. (1970c) 1297. Discovered by Columbus 1503 but never occupied by Spaniards; colonized from ab. 1734 by English from Jamaica; administratively independent of Jamaica 1962.

Cayman Trench. Trench, NW Caribbean Sea, extending from ab. 75°W to ab. 85°W; contains deepest point in Caribbean Sea, 24,720 ft., 19°12′N, 80°W.

Cayo. For **Cayo Coco, Cayo Largo,** etc., see COCO CAY, LARGO CAY, etc.

Ca·yo \'kä-yō\. 1 District, W British Honduras; 2061 sq. m.; pop. (1967e) 15,139; ✱ San Ignacio.

2 Town, British Honduras. See SAN IGNACIO 1.

Cay Sal Bank \ˌkē-ˌsal-, ˌkā-\. Bank in W Bahama Is., bet. Straits of Florida and N cen. Cuba; separated from Great Bahama Bank on E by Santaren Channel; Cay Sal lighthouse (established 1839) in NW corner.

Ca·ÿs·ter \kā-'is-tər\ *or mod.* **Ba·yın·dır** \bī-ən-'di(ə)r\. River, SW Asia Minor, N of the Menderes; ab. 85 m. long; flows W to Aegean Sea near Ephesus; celebrated in Homer.

Cay·u·ga \kē-'ü-gə, 'kyü-, kā-'(y)ü-\. 1 County in New York. See table at NEW YORK.

2 Village, ⊗ of Haldimand co., SE Ontario, Canada, 22 m. S of Hamilton; pop. (1971p) 1083.

Cayuga Lake. Lake chiefly in Cayuga and Seneca cos., W cen. New York; one of the Finger Lakes (*q.v.*); 66½ m. long, av. width 2 m.; deepest point ab. 435 ft.; connected at N end with Seneca Lake by the **Cayuga and Seneca Canal** \-'sen-i-kə-\, part of N.Y. State Barge Canal system.

Ca·zal·la de la Sier·ra \kə-'säl-ə-də-lä-sē-'er-ə\. Commune, Sevilla prov., SW Spain, on S slope of the Sierra Morena 40 m. NNE of Seville; pop. (1970p) 6567; iron and lead mining.

Caz·e·no·via \ˌkaz-ə-'nō-vē-ə\. Village and resort, Madison co., cen. New York, 18 m. ESE of Syracuse; pop. (1970c) 3031; Cazenovia Coll. (1824); traditional birthplace of Hiawatha.

Cazlona. See CASTULO.

Ca·zor·la \kə-'sôr-lə\. Commune, Jaén prov., S Spain, 42 m. ENE of Jaén; pop. (1970p) 9367; reached peak of importance under Moors.

Ceanannus. See KELLS.

Ce·a·rá \ˌsā-ə-'rä\. 1 State of NE Brazil; 57,147 sq. m.; pop. (1970p) 4,440,286; ✱ Fortaleza; cotton, sugarcane, tobacco.

2 City, its ✱. See FORTALEZA.

Ce·ba·co *or* **Cé·ba·co** \'seb-ə-ˌkō\. Island at the entrance to the Gulf of Montijo, S of SW Panama.

Cebenna. See CÉVENNES.

Ce·bo·ru·co \ˌseb-ə-'rü-(ˌ)kō\. Active volcano, Nayarit state, W Mexico, SE of city of Tepic; 7098 ft.

Ce·bu \sā-'bü\ *or Visayan* **Sug·bu** \süg-'bü\. 1 Island, one of the Visayan Is., E cen. Phil., constituting with adjacent islets a province (1965 sq. m.; pop. [1970p] 1,632,642; ✱ City of Cebu); 1707 sq. m.; 139 m. long by ab. 20 m. wide, with mountain chain extending its entire length (highest 3324 ft.), crossed by only six passes. Touches Visayan Sea on N and Camotes Sea on E, separated from Bohol on SE by Bohol Strait, and from Negros on W by Tanon Strait. Its more important adjacent islands are Bantayan W of N end and Camotes group and Mactan on the E. Produces sugar, corn, coconuts, rice, tobacco, and coal. Its inhabitants are Visayans. Chief towns Cebu, Toledo, Lapu-Lapu, Balamban.

History: Before coming of Spaniards one of the more populous and prosperous islands; discovered Apr. 7, 1521 by Magellan (see MACTAN); occupied by Legaspi 1565; often raided by Moro pirates 16th and 17th cents.; opened to foreign trade 1860; evacuated by Spanish 1898; civil government created by U.S. 1901. Occupied by Japanese Apr. 1942; retaken by U.S. forces Mar. 1945.

2 *or officially* **City of Cebu.** Chartered city, ✱ of Cebu prov., in cen. part of E coast of Cebu I.; pop. (1970p) 342,116; exports incl. copra, hemp, tobacco. Oldest Spanish town in the Philippines; has excellent harbor, sheltered on E by Mactan I.; contains Santo Niño Church in front of which is the cross Magellan set up at the first Mass on the island; several universities incl. Southwestern Univ. (1950); cathedral, old Spanish stone fort. Occupied by Legaspi 1565 and until 1571 capital of Spanish possessions in the Philippines. Seized by Japanese Apr. 18, 1942, practically destroyed May 22; recaptured by U.S. forces Mar. 27, 1945.

Cec·ca·no \chə-'kän-(ˌ)ō\. Commune, Frosinone prov., Latium, cen. Italy, on Sacco river 5 m. S of Frosinone; pop. (1968e) 18,593; taken by American forces May 1944.

Čechy. See BOHEMIA.

Ce·cil \'sē-səl\. County in Maryland. See table at MARYLAND.

Ce·ci·na \'chech-i-ˌnä, 'chāch-\. Coastal commune, Livorno prov., Tuscany, cen. Italy, near mouth of **Cecina River,** 20 m. S by E of Leghorn; pop. (1968e) 19,932.

Ce·dar \'sēd-ər\. 1 River, Minnesota and Iowa; flows from SE Minnesota SE to Iowa river in Louisa co., SE Iowa; 329 m. long.

2 River, E cen. Nebraska; 120 m. long; rises in Garfield co., flows SE into Loup river in Nance co.

3 Name of counties in three states of the U.S. See tables at IOWA, MISSOURI, NEBRASKA.

Cedar Bergen. See CEDAR MOUNTAINS.

Cedar Breaks National Monument. See UNITED STATES, *National Monuments.*

Ce·dar·burg \'sēd-ər-ˌbərg\. City, Ozaukee co., E Wisconsin, 17 m. N of Milwaukee; pop. (1970c) 7697; aluminum castings, plastics.

Cedar City. Town, Iron co., SW Utah; pop. (1970c) 8946; dairy products, lumber; iron ore and coal deposits; livestock; Southern Utah State Coll. (1897); settled 1851; Zion National Park to the S, Cedar Breaks National Monument to the E.

Cedar Creek. 1 River, SW North Dakota; 200 m. long; flows E into Cannonball river.

2 Small stream in Shenandoah co., N Virginia, flowing into the N fork of the Shenandoah river; battle Oct. 19, 1864 in which Union forces under Gen. Sheridan defeated the Confederates under Gen. Early.

Cedar Creek Dam. Dam and reservoir in Cedar Creek (branch of Salmon Falls Creek), SW Twin Falls co., SW Idaho. See SALMON FALLS DAM.

Cedar Creek Peak. Mountain, E Cassia co., S Idaho; 7586 ft.

Cedar Falls. City, Black Hawk co., NE cen. Iowa, 6 m. W of Waterloo; pop. (1970c) 29,597; rotary pumps, elevator equipment, tools and dies; Univ. of Northern Iowa (1876).

Cedar Grove. Township, Essex co., NE New Jersey, 6 m. SSW of Paterson; pop. (1970c) 15,582.

Cedar Hill. Town, Dallas co., NE Texas, 18 m. SW of Dallas; pop. (1970c) 2610; furniture; agriculture.

Ce·dar·hurst \'sēd-ər-ˌhərst\. Residential village, Nassau co., SE New York, on Long Island 17 m. ESE of New York; pop. (1970c) 6941.

Cedar Keys \-'kēz\. Small group of islands in Gulf of Mexico, off SW coast of Levy co., NW Florida penin.

Cedar Lake. 1 Urban community (unincorporated), Lake co., NW corner of Indiana, SW of Valparaiso; pop. (1970c) 7589.

2 Lake, NW of Lake Winnipeg, W Manitoba, Canada; 517 sq. m.; Saskatchewan river flows through it to Lake Winnipeg.

Cedar Mountain. Locality in Culpeper co., Virginia, 10 m. S of Culpeper; battle Aug. 9,1862 in which Union forces under Gen. Banks were defeated by Gen. Ewell's Confederate troops.

Cedar Mountains *or Afrikaans* **Ce·der Ber·gen** \'sād-ər-ˌbergə\ *or* **Cedar Bergen.** Range in W Cape Province, Rep. of South Africa; highest peak 6339 ft.

Cedar Point. 1 Point, SE Mobile co., Alabama, at W entrance to Mobile Bay.

2 Point, E St. Marys co., S Maryland, on S side of mouth of Patuxent river.

3 Tip of long narrow peninsula on Lake Erie at entrance to Sandusky Bay, Erie co., Ohio; resort.

Cedar Rapids. City, ⊗ of Linn co., E Iowa, 105 m. ENE of Des Moines; pop. (1970c) 110,642; electronic equipment, mining machinery, cereals, meat products; Coe Coll. (1851), Mount Mercy Coll. (1875), Area Ten Community Coll. (1965); settled 1838, incorp. 1856.

Cedar River. See CEDAR 1.

Ce·dar·town \'sēd-ər-ˌtau̇n\. City, ⊗ of Polk co., NW Georgia, 17 m. S of Rome; pop. (1970c) 9253; chemicals, cotton goods, farm implements.

Ce·dar·ville \'sēd-ər-ˌvil\. Village, Greene co., SW cen. Ohio, NE of Xenia; pop. (1970c) 2342.

Ceder Bergen. See CEDAR MOUNTAINS.

Ce·dros \'sā-drəs\. Island in the Pacific Ocean, off the coast of Baja California, Mexico; ab. 30 m. long.

Ce·fa·lù \ˌchā-fə-'lü\ *or anc.* **Ceph·a·loe·di·um** \ˌsef-ə-'lē-dē-əm\. Seaport, Palermo prov., NW cen. Sicily, Italy, on Tyrrhenian Sea 37 m. E by S of Palermo; pop. (1968e) 13,020; cathedral (1131–48); marble quarrying. Ancient city an ally of Carthage 396 B.C.; conquered by Dionysius the Elder and later by Agathocles; taken by Moors 858 A.D.

Ceg·léd *also* **Czeg·léd** \'(t)seg-ˌlād\. City, cen. Hungary, 42 m. SE of Budapest; pop. (1970p) 38,082; trades in agricultural products.

Ce·glie Mes·sa·pi·co \'chel-yē-mə-'säp-i-ˌkō\. Commune, Brindisi prov., Apulia, SE Italy, 22 m. W of Brindisi; pop. (1968e) 22,481; castle.

Ce·he·gín \ˌsā-ə-'hēn\. Commercial commune, Murcia prov., SE Spain, 34 m. WNW of Murcia; pop. (1970p) 12,489.

Cei·ba \'sā-ə-bə, 'sā-bə, -və\. Town, E Puerto Rico, SE of San Juan; pop. (1970p) 2146.

Ceiba, La. Seaport in Honduras. See LA CEIBA.

Celaenae. See DINAR.

Ce·la·no \chā-'lä-(ˌ)nō\. Commune, Aquila prov., Abruzzi, cen. Italy, on N shore of the former Lake Fucino 22 m. SSE of Aquila; pop. (1968c) 10,127; castle.

Celano, Lake. See FUCINO.

Ce·la·ya \sə-'lī-ə\. City, Guanajuato state, cen. Mexico, 45 m. SE of Guanajuato; munic. pop. (1970p) 143,703; altitude 5750 ft.; railroad junction.

Cel·e·bes \'sel-ə-ˌbēz, sə-'lē-bēz\ *or Indonesian* **Su·la·we·si** \ˌsü-lə-'wā-sē\. Island, Indonesia, in Malay Archipelago E of Borneo, lat. 1°45′N to 5°37′S, and long. 118°49′ to 125°05′E; 69,255 sq. m.; including adjacent dependent islands, 72,986 sq. m., pop. (1970e) 8,925,000; for administrative divisions see table at INDONESIA. *Chief products:* Corn, cassava, yam, rice, tobacco, salt, sulfur.

History: Probably first visited by Portuguese 1512 while developing spice trade of the Moluccas; first foreign settlement on island was by Dutch 1607 at Makasar; Manado established 1657; scene in 17th cent. of various wars bet. Dutch and native sultans; ruler of Makasar overcome 1667; wars with Buginese pirates (of S Celebes) 17th and 18th cents.; direct Dutch rule over both N and S parts gradually established, but sultanate in SE not completely conquered until 1905. Overrun by Japanese Jan.–Feb. 1942; Manado, Kendari, and Makasar occupied; often bombed by Americans 1944–45; surrendered to Australians Sept. 1945; Communist rebellion against central government suppressed 1965.

Celebes Sea. Part of the Pacific Ocean, enclosed on N by Sulu Archipelago and Mindanao of the Phil., on E by Sangihe Is., on S by Celebes, and on W by Borneo; connected with Java Sea by Makasar Strait on SW; ab. 420 m. from N to S and 520 m. E to W at widest parts; ab. 165,000 sq. m.

Celestial Empire. See CHINA.

Ce·li·ca \'sā-li-kə\. Town, Loja prov., SW Ecuador, ab. 58 m. S of Machala; pop. (1962c) 3467.

Ce·li·na \sə-'lī-nə\. 1 City and summer resort, ⊗ of Mercer co., W Ohio, on W end of Lake St. Marys; pop. (1970c) 8072; sheet metal products; furniture.

2 Town, ⊗ of Clay co., N Tennessee; pop. (1970c) 1370.

Ce·lje \'(t)sel-(ˌ)yä\ *or Ger.* **Cil·li** \'tsil-ə\. Town, Slovenia, NW Yugoslavia, 37 m. NE of Ljubljana; pop. (1965e) 30,000; thermal springs.

Cel·le *also* **Zel·le** \'tsel-ə\. Industrial city, Lower Saxony, West Germany, on Aller river 22 m. NE of Hannover; pop. (1969e) 156,505; mining equipment, dyes; gravel, potash; 13th cent. ducal palace; 16th cent. town hall; founded 1292; residence of dukes of Brunswick and Lüneburg 1378–1705.

Celles \'sel\. Village, Namur prov., SE Belgium, ab. 8 m. E of Dinant; pop. (1969e) 538; farthest point W reached Dec. 24–25, 1944 by German counteroffensive (Battle of the Bulge); retaken by Allies Dec. 26.

Ce·lo, Mount \-'sē-(ˌ)lō\. Peak, Yancey co., W North Carolina; 6351 ft.

Celt·i·be·ria \ˌsel-tə-'bir-ē-ə, ˌsel-tī-, ˌkel-\. Mountainous district of ancient Spain, in NE bet. the Ebro and Tagus rivers.

Cemenelum. See CIMIEZ.

Cem·e·tery Ridge \ˌsem-ə-ter-ē-\. Low ridge in Adams co., Pennsylvania, extending in N and S direction S of Gettysburg; at its N end just to the E and ab. ½ m. S of the town are **Cemetery Hill** and **Culp's Hill** \'kəlps-\ where much of the fighting of the first two days of the battle of Gettysburg July 1–2, 1863 took place, partly a Confederate success; meanwhile the ridge as far S as Round Top (*q.v.*) was occupied by the center of the Union defense and received on July 3 the Confederate assault led by Gen. Pickett, who was repulsed with loss of three fourths of his division.

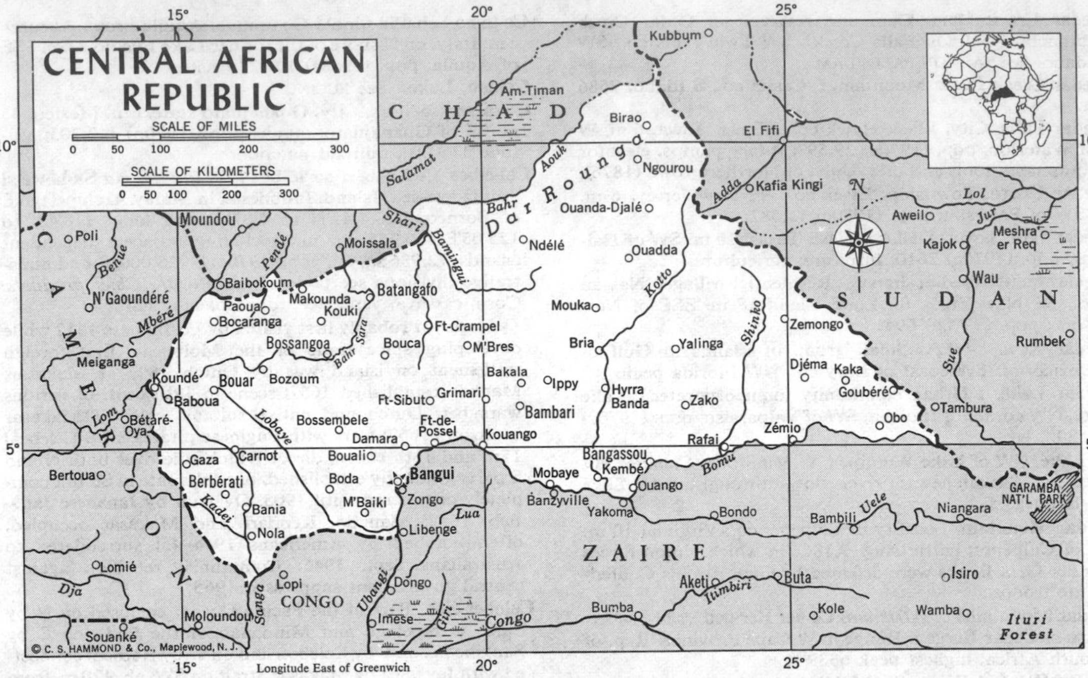

Cen·chre·ae \seŋ-ˈkrē-ē\. Ancient town, NE coast of Peloponnesus, S Greece, on Saronic Gulf SE of Corinth; visited by Paul on second missionary journey (*Acts* xviii. 18).

Ce·nis, Mont \ˌmōⁿ-sə-ˈnē, mōⁿ-ˈsnē\ *or Ital.* **Mon·te Ce·ni·sio** \ˌmōnt-ē-chə-ˈnēz-(ˌ)yō\. Alpine pass and tunnel. See ALPS.

Cen·ter \ˈsent-ər\. **1** Town, Rio Grande and Saguache cos., S Colorado, 25 m. NW of Alamosa; pop. (1970c) 1470; potatoes; livestock.
2 Village, ⊗ of Knox co., NE Nebraska; pop. (1970c) 111.
3 Village, ⊗ of Oliver co., North Dakota; pop. (1970c) 619; wheat; coal mines.
4 City, ⊗ of Shelby co., E Texas, 45 m. NE of Lufkin; pop. (1970c) 4989; lumber, brooms; cotton gins.

Center. See also CENTRE.

Center City. Village, ⊗ of Chisago co., E Minnesota; pop. (1970c) 324.

Center Line *or* **Cen·ter·line** \ˌsent-ər-ˈlīn\. Residential city, Macomb co., SE Michigan, 11 m. N of Detroit; pop. (1970c) 10,379.

Cen·ter·ville \ˈsent-ər-ˌvil\. **1** City, ⊗ of Bibb co., cen. Alabama; pop. (1970c) 2233; lumber.
2 Village, N New Castle co., Delaware, NW of Wilmington; elevation 442 ft.; highest point in state.
3 City, ⊗ of Appanoose co., S Iowa, 30 m. SW of Ottumwa; pop. (1970c) 6531; Centerville Community Coll. (1930).
4 Village, ⊗ of St. Joseph co., S Michigan; pop. (1970c) 1044.
5 Village, ⊗ of Reynolds co., SE Missouri; pop. (1970c) 209.
6 City, Montgomery co., SW Ohio, 10 m. S of Dayton; pop. (1970c) 10,333.
7 Borough, Washington co., SW Pennsylvania, on Monongahela river 17 m. WNW of Uniontown; pop. (1970c) 4175.
8 City, Turner co., SE South Dakota, 35 m. SSW of Sioux Falls; pop. (1970c) 910; farm trade center.
9 Town, ⊗ of Hickman co., Tennessee; pop. (1970c) 2592; phosphate mining.
10 City, ⊗ of Leon co., E cen. Texas; pop. (1970c) 831.
11 City, Davis co., N Utah, 12 m. N of Salt Lake City; pop. (1970c) 3268.
12 *or* **Cen·tre·ville** \ˈsent-ər-ˌvil\. Village, Fairfax co., Virginia, near field of first battle of Bull Run.

Centerville. See CENTREVILLE.

Cen·to \ˈchen-(ˌ)tō\. Commune, Ferrara prov., Emilia-Romagna, N Italy; pop. (1968e) 26,381.

Centorbi. See CENTURIPE.

Cen·tral \sen-ˈträl\. Department of S Paraguay. See table at PARAGUAY.

Central African Republic *or Fr.* **Ré·pu·blique Cen·traf·ri·caine** \rā-püē-blēk-säⁿ-trȧ-fri-kan\; *formerly* **Uban·gi–Sha·ri** \(y)ü-ˌbaŋ-(g)ē-ˈshär-ē\ *or Fr.* **Ou·ban·gui–Cha·ri** \ü-bäⁿ-gē-shȧ-rē\. Republic, cen. Africa, bounded on N by Chad, on E by Sudan, on S by Zaire and Congo, and on W by Cameroon; 240,376 sq. m.; pop. (1970e) 1,520,000; ✱ Bangui. *Physical features:* Landlocked republic, consisting of a plateau region having an av. alt. of ab. 2200 ft.; N half is characterized by savanna and is drained by tributaries of Chari; S half is densely forested and forms N extent of Congo basin. *Chief products:* Cotton, coffee, rice, rubber, peanuts; livestock raising; diamonds. *Chief towns:* Bangui, Bouar, Carnot, Berbérati.

History: Bangui established by French 1889; S boundary demarcated 1894, E boundary 1899; united with Chad 1906 to form French colony of **Ubangi–Shari–Chad** \-ˈchad\ *or Fr.* **Oubangui–Chari–Tchad** \-chȧd\; became part of French Equatorial Africa 1910; separated from Chad 1920; status changed to that of overseas territory 1946; became an autonomous republic within French Community 1958; achieved independence 1960; civilian government overthown in *coup d'état* 1966.

Central America. The S portion of North America from S boundary of Mexico to NW Colombia, South America; 228,578 sq. m.; pop. (1970e) 16,630,000; includes the 6 republics of Guatemala, Honduras, El Salvador, Nicaragua, Costa Rica, and Panama, and the colony of British Honduras (*qq.v.*); bordered on SW by Pacific Ocean and on NE by Caribbean Sea. By some geographers regarded as beginning at Isthmus of Tehuantepec and thus including also Quintana Roo territory and 4 states of Mexico: Yucatán, Campeche, Tabasco, and Chiapas. Its many mountains a connecting link between western North American system and the Andes; numerous volcanoes, many of them active; highest point Tajumulco volcano, W Guatemala, 13,845 ft. See MIDDLE AMERICA.

History: Atlantic coast from Honduras to Gulf of Darien skirted by Columbus 1501; first settlement 1510 on Gulf of Darien; explored by agents of Pedrarias from Panama; coast of Nicaragua explored and Lake Nicaragua discovered by Gil González de Ávila 1522; Granada and León founded by Córdoba 1523; Gulf of Honduras explored 1524 by Olid and Las Casas sent by Cortes from Mexico; Guatemala and El Salvador conquered by Alvarado 1524; organized (except for Chiapas and Panama) into Spanish captaincy general of Guatemala; independent in 1821; joined Mexico under Iturbide for brief period during 1822–23; loosely united as United Provinces of Central America 1823–39; separated into independent republics 1838–39; from 1848 control of Isthmian transit an issue bet. U.S. and Great Britain (see NICARAGUA and PANAMA); organized briefly as Greater Republic of Central America 1895–98; treaties of amity drawn up by Washington conference of Central American states 1923. See CENTRAL AMERICAN COMMON MARKET.

Central American Common Market. Economic community, consisting of Costa Rica, El Salvador, Guatemala, Honduras, Nicaragua; headquarters Guatemala City, Guatemala; purpose is creation of customs union and establishment of common external tariffs. Formed 1960; its activities disrupted by Honduras-El Salvador border conflict 1969.

Central Asia, Soviet. Region of U.S.S.R., W cen. Asia; 1,542,238 sq. m.; pop. (1970p) 32,804,000.

History: Before 19th cent., part ruled by Muslim khanates of Bukhara, Khiva, and Kokand, and rest inhabited by uncontrolled and warlike nomad Turkmen tribes who were subdued by Russians under Alexander II 1865 when Russian province of Turkistan was constituted, khanates being subdued later (Bukhara 1868, Khiva 1873, and Kokand 1875); Turkmen tribes broken by battle of Geok-Tepe 1881; after Russian Revolution, reorganized as Uzbek, Turkmen, Tadzhik, Kazakh, and Kirgiz Soviet Socialist Republics.

Central Australia. A territory of Australia 1927–31, 20th to 26th parallels of S lat., in cen. part of continent; ✻ Stuart (now known as Alice Springs, *q.v.*); formerly S part of Northern Territory.

Central Black Earth Region *or Russ.* **Tsen·tral·no–Cher·no·zem·ny Ray·on** \tsen-ˈträl-nə-ˌchir-nə-ˌzhòm-nē-rī-ˈòn\. Subdivision of the Russian S.F.S.R., U.S.S.R.; 64,749 sq. m.; pop. (1970p) 7,997,000; ✻ Voronezh; divided into five oblasts.

Central City. 1 Town, ⊗ of Gilpin co., N cen. Colorado; pop. (1970c) 228; center of gold-mining region.

2 Village, Marion co., S cen. Illinois, suburb of Centralia; pop. (1970c) 1377; nurseries.

3 City, Muhlenberg co., W Kentucky, 32 m. S of Owensboro; pop. (1970c) 5450; timber, corn; oil wells.

4 City, ⊗ of Merrick co., E cen. Nebraska, on Platte river 23 m. ENE of Grand Island; pop. (1970c) 2803; creamery; railroad junction.

5 Borough, Somerset co., S Pennsylvania, 18 m. SSE of Johnstown; pop. (1970c) 1547.

Central District. Administrative division of cen. Israel. See table at ISRAEL.

Central Division. Former division, cen. Bombay prov., W India; 37,296 sq. m.; now part of Maharashtra state.

Central Europe. Indefinite and occasional term applied to the countries of the central part of Europe, approximately those bet. the Baltic Sea on N and Alps on S and bet. the U.S.S.R. on E and North Sea and France on W. Apparently first used in political sense (**Mit·tel·eu·ro·pa** \ˌmit-ᵊl-òi-ˈrō-pə\, that is, **Middle Europe**) by Georg Friedrich List mid 19th cent. to denote Germany, Austria-Hungary, Switzerland, and the Low Countries; in recent use extended to include also Poland and Romania, but usually not the Baltic and Balkan States; by some in period following World War I made equivalent to the Little Entente (Czechoslovakia, Romania and Yugoslavia).

Central Falls. Industrial city, Providence co., N Rhode Island, on Blackstone river just N of Pawtucket; pop. (1970c) 18,716; glass (electric-light bulbs).

Central Greece and Euboea \-yü-ˈbē-ə\. Administrative region of Greece; 9450 sq. m.; pop. (exclusive of Greater Athens; 1971p) 991,587; includes island of Euboea, the Northern Sporades, and cen. part of Greek mainland; comprises departments of Aetolia and Acarnania, Attica, Boeotia, Euboea, Eurytania, Phocis, Phthiotis, and Piraeus (see table at GREECE).

Cen·tra·lia \sen-ˈtrāl-yə\. 1 City, Clinton and Marion cos., SW cen. Illinois, 58 m. E of East St. Louis; pop. (1970c) 15,217; Kaskaskia Coll. (1940); coal mines, oil wells; founded 1853, incorp. 1859.

2 City, Boone co., cen. Missouri, 22 m. NNE of Columbia; pop. (1970c) 3618; coal deposits nearby.

3 Borough, Columbia co., E cen. Pennsylvania, 12 m. NNW of Pottsville; pop. (1970c) 1165; iron and coal mining.

4 City, Lewis co., SW Washington, 23 m. S of Olympia; pop. (1970c) 10,054; plywood; dairy products; coal mines; Centralia Coll. (1925); one community with its sister city, Chehalis.

Central India Agency *or* **Central India.** Formerly, a group of Indian states under supervision of a British political agent, bet. 21° and 26°N and 74° and 83°E; 52,047 sq. m.; ✻ Indore; comprised 89 states, most important: Indore, Bhopal, and Rewa; bulk of population Hindu. Since Aug. 15, 1947 all have become part of India.

Central Java. Province of Java, Indonesia. See JAVA and table at INDONESIA.

Central Kalimantan. See KALIMANTAN, CENTRAL.

Central Karroo. See KARROO.

Central Ma·lu·ku \-mə-ˈlü-(ˌ)kü\ *also* **Am·boi·na** \am-ˈbòi-nə\ *or Malay* **Am·bon** \ˈam-ˌbän\. District of Maluku prov., Indonesia; area 11,348 sq. m.; chief island Ambon; chief town Ambon. Comprises islands and island groups around the Banda Sea, esp. Ambon, Ceram, Buru, Aru Is., Kai Is., Tanimbar Is., Babar Is., Wetar, and many small islands, and also the S and SE portion of mainland of Irian Barat.

Central Point. City, Jackson co., SW Oregon, 7 m. NW of Medford; pop. (1970c) 4004.

Central Province. 1 Province, S cen. Ceylon; 2159 sq. m.; pop. (1968e) 1,914,000; ✻ Kandy; mountainous terrain with highest peak on the island Pidurutalagala 8281 ft.; source of the Mahaweli; rice, tea.

2 Province, cen. Kenya. See table at KENYA.

Central Provinces and Berar. See MADHYA PRADESH.

Central Range *or Russ.* **Sre·din·ny Khre·bet** \srə-ˌdē-nē krə-ˈbet\. Mountain range extending the length of Kamchatka Penin., Khabarovsk Krai, Russian S.F.S.R., U.S.S.R.; average height 3000 ft.; highest Ichinskaya Sopka 11,880 ft.

Central Region. Administrative division of S Ghana. See table at GHANA.

Central Sulawesi. Province of Celebes, Indonesia. See CELEBES and table at INDONESIA.

Central Valley. Valley of Sacramento and San Joaquin rivers (*qq.v.*) in California, bet. Sierra Nevada and Coast Ranges; over 400 m. long, 20–50 m. wide.

Cen·tre \ˈsent-ər\. 1 County in Pennsylvania. See table at PENNSYLVANIA.

2 Town, ⊗ of Cherokee co., NE Alabama; pop. (1970c) 2418; lumber; cotton gins.

Centre. See also CENTER.

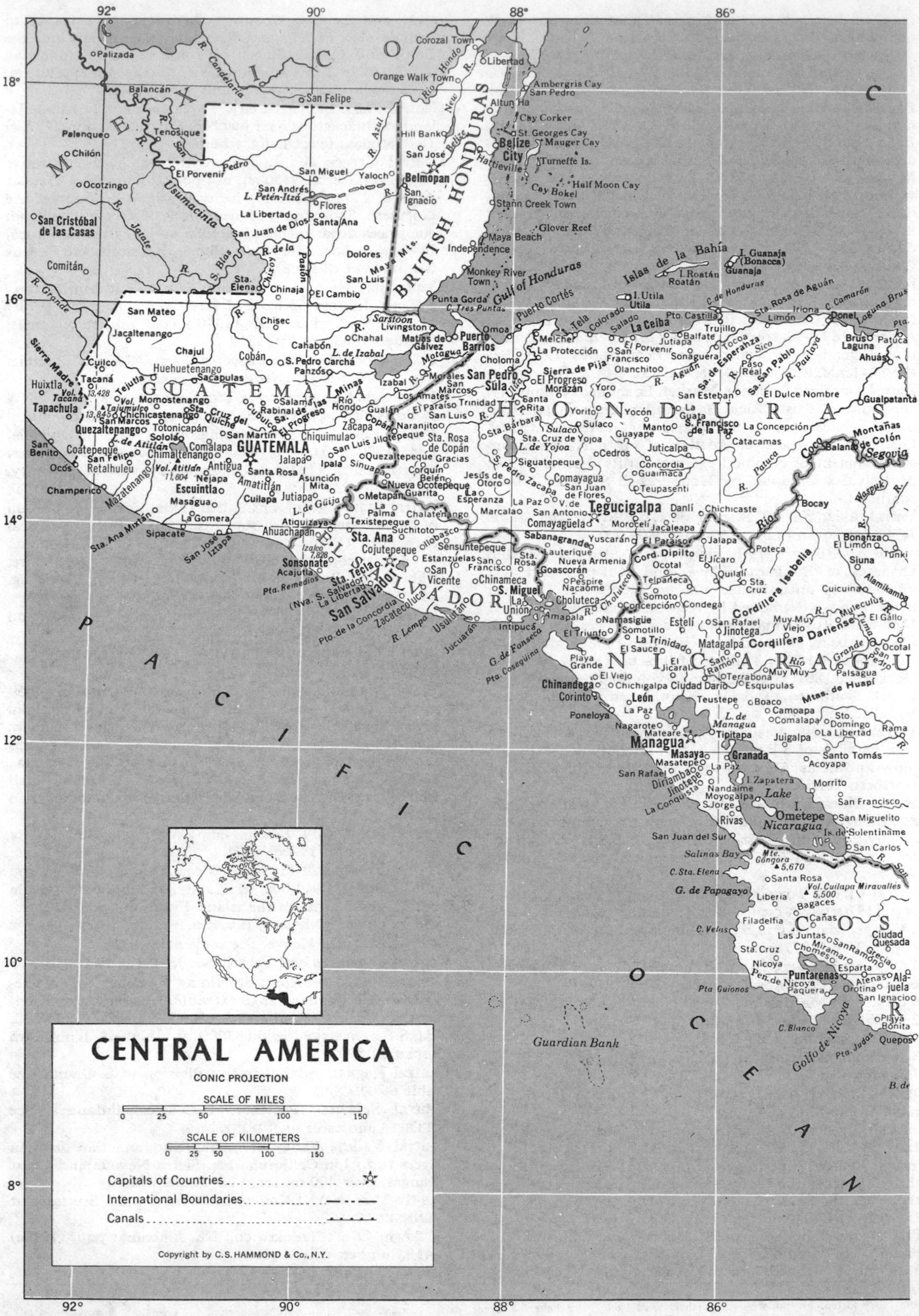
CENTRAL AMERICA
CONIC PROJECTION
SCALE OF MILES
0 25 50 100 150
SCALE OF KILOMETERS
0 25 50 100 150
Capitals of Countries
International Boundaries
Canals
Copyright by C.S. HAMMOND & Co., N.Y.
92° 90° 88° 86°
18° 16° 14° 12° 10° 8°
MEXICO
BRITISH HONDURAS
GUATEMALA
HONDURAS
EL SALVADOR
NICARAGUA
COS
PACIFIC OCEAN
Gulf of Honduras
Islas de la Bahía
G. de Fonseca
G. de Papagayo
Golfo de Nicoya
Guardian Bank
Salinas Bay
Lake Nicaragua
L. de Managua
L. de Izabal
L. Petén-Itzá
L. de Atitlán
L. de Yojoa
L. de Güija
Belize City
Belmopan
GUATEMALA
Tegucigalpa
San Salvador
Managua
Corozal Town
Orange Walk Town
Stann Creek Town
Punta Gorda
Puerto Barrios
Puerto Cortés
San Pedro Sula
La Ceiba
Trujillo
Sta. Ana
San Miguel
León
Chinandega
Corinto
Granada
Masaya
Rivas
Puntarenas
Liberia
Quetzaltenango
Tapachula
San Cristóbal de las Casas
Comitán
Cobán
Flores
Escuintla
Comayagua
Choluteca
Estelí
Jinotega
Matagalpa
Ciudad Darío
Bluefields
Cordillera Isabelia
Cordillera Dariense
Sierra Madre
Maya Mts.
Río Coco
Segovia
R. Usumacinta
R. Motagua
R. Ulúa
R. Lempa
R. Patuca
R. San Juan
Vol. Tajumulco 13,845
Vol. Tacaná 13,428
Vol. Atitlán 11,604
Izalco 7,828
Mte. Góngora 5,670
Vol. Cuilapa Miravalles 5,500

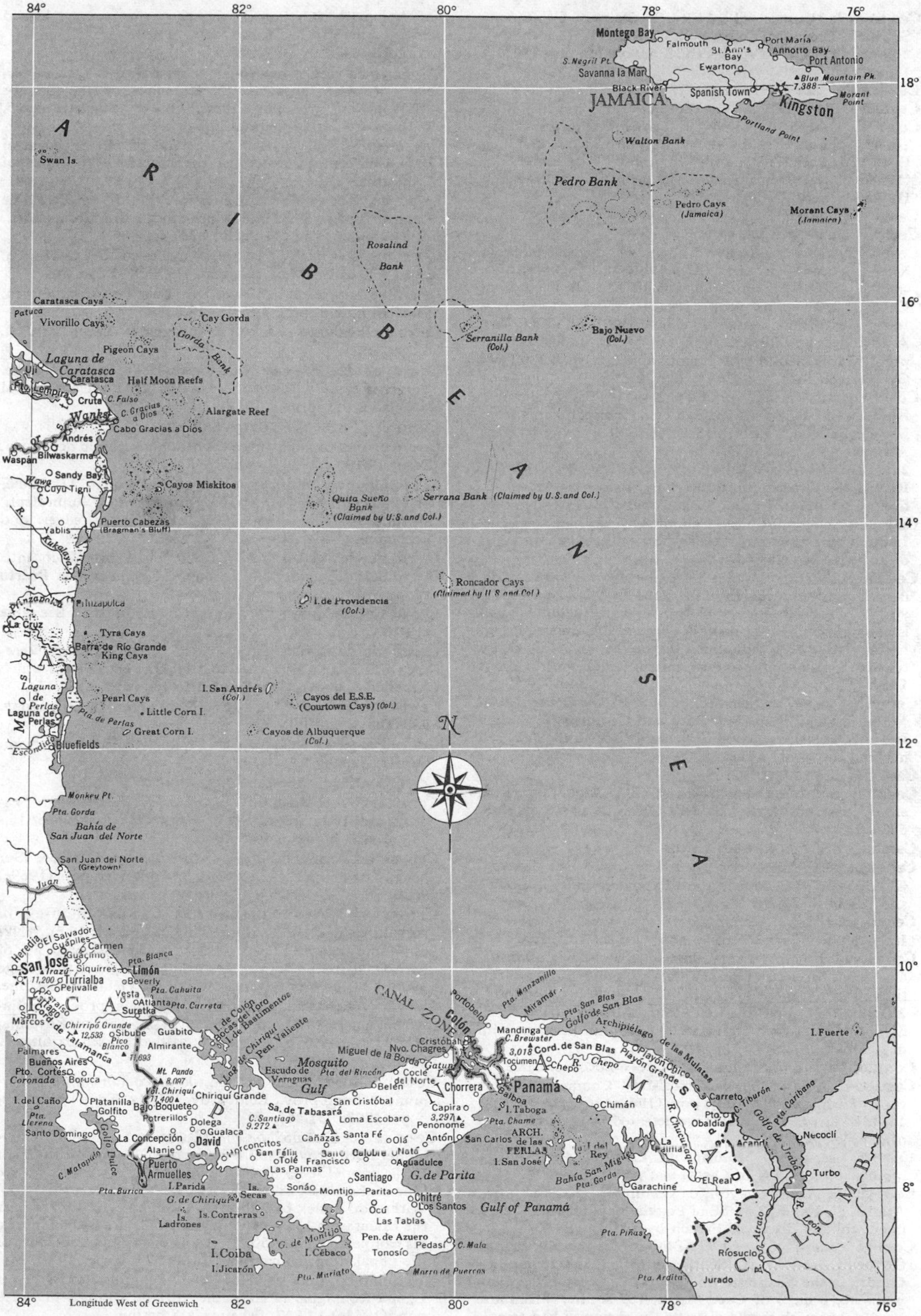
84°
82°
80°
78°
76°
18°
16°
14°
12°
10°
8°
Montego Bay
Falmouth
St. Ann's Bay
Port María
Annotto Bay
Port Antonio
S. Negril Pt.
Savanna la Mar
Ewarton
Blue Mountain Pk. 7,388
Black River
Spanish Town
Kingston
Morant Point
JAMAICA
Portland Point
Walton Bank
Pedro Bank
Pedro Cays (Jamaica)
Morant Cays (Jamaica)
C A R I B B E A N   S E A
Swan Is.
Rosalind Bank
Caratasca Cays
Patuca
Vivorillo Cays
Cay Gorda
Gorda Bank
Serranilla Bank (Col.)
Bajo Nuevo (Col.)
Pigeon Cays
Laguna de Caratasca
Uji
Caratasca
Half Moon Reefs
Pta. Lempira
Cruta
C. Falso
C. Gracias a Dios
Alargate Reef
Wanks
Cabo Gracias a Dios
Andrés
Waspan
Bilwaskarma
Sandy Bay
Wawa
Cayo Tigni
Cayos Miskitos
Quita Sueño Bank (Claimed by U.S. and Col.)
Serrana Bank (Claimed by U.S. and Col.)
Puerto Cabezas (Bragman's Bluff)
Yablis
Kukalaya
Roncador Cays (Claimed by U.S. and Col.)
Prinzapolca
I. de Providencia (Col.)
La Cruz
Tyra Cays
Barra de Río Grande
King Cays
Mosquitia
Laguna de Perlas
I. San Andrés (Col.)
Cayos del E.S.E. (Courtown Cays) (Col.)
Pearl Cays
Little Corn I.
Pta. de Perlas
Great Corn I.
Cayos de Albuquerque (Col.)
Escondido
Bluefields
Monkey Pt.
Pta. Gorda
Bahía de San Juan del Norte
San Juan del Norte (Greytown)
Juan
COSTA RICA
Heredia
El Salvador
Guápiles
Carmen
Guácimo
San José
Pta. Blanca
Irazú 11,200
Siquirres
Limón
Turrialba
Beverly
Pejivalle
Pta. Cahuita
Vesta
Atlanta
Pta. Carreta
Suretka
San Marcos
Chirripó Grande 12,533
Sibube
Guabito
Cord. de Talamanca
Pico Blanco 11,693
Almirante
I. de Colón
Bocas del Toro
I. de Bastimentos
Lag. de Chiriquí
Pen. Valiente
CANAL ZONE
Portobelo
Pta. Manzanillo
Miramar
Pta. San Blas
Golfo de San Blas
Archipiélago de las Mulatas
Colón
Cristóbal
Mandinga
C. Brewster
Nvo. Chagres
Miguel de la Borda
Mosquito Gulf
Escudo de Veraguas
Pta. del Rincón
Gatun
Cocle del Norte
3,018
Cord. de San Blas
Playón Chico
Playón Grande
Tocumen
Chepo
R. Chepo
Palmares
Buenos Aires
Pto. Cortés
Coronada
Boruca
Mt. Pando 8,097
Vol. Chiriquí 11,400
Chiriquí Grande
Belén
Chorrera
Panamá
Balboa
I. Taboga
PANAMÁ
Chimán
Carreto
C. Tiburón
Pta. Caribana
Golfo de Urabá
Pto. Obaldía
I. Fuerte
I. del Caño
Platanilla
Golfito
Bajo Boquete
Sa. de Tabasará
San Cristóbal
Capira 3,297
Pta. Llerena
Potrerillos
C. Santiago 9,272
Loma Escobaro
Penonomé
Pta. Chame
Santo Domingo
Dolega
Gualaca
Cañazas
Santa Fé
Olá
Antón
San Carlos
ARCH. de las PERLAS
I. del Rey
La Palma
R. Chucunaque
Acandí
Necoclí
Golfo Dulce
La Concepción
Alanje
David
Horconcitos
San Félix
Tolé
Calobre
Natá
I. San José
Bahía San Miguel
Pta. Gorda
El Real
Darién
Turbo
C. Matapalo
Puerto Armuelles
Francisco
Las Palmas
Aguadulce
G. de Parita
Santiago
Pta. Burica
I. Parida
G. de Chiriquí
Is. Secas
Soná
Montijo
Parita
Chitré
Los Santos
Gulf of Panamá
Garachiné
Is. Ladrones
Is. Contreras
Las Tablas
Pen. de Azuero
G. de Montijo
Pta. Piñas
I. Coiba
I. Cébaco
Pedasí
C. Mala
Tonosí
Ríosucio
Atrato
R. León
COLOMBIA
I. Jicarón
Pta. Mariato
Morro de Puercos
Pta. Ardita
Jurado
Longitude West of Greenwich

Cen·tre·ville \'sent-ər-ˌvil\. 1 City, St. Clair co., SW Illinois, SE of St. Louis, Missouri; pop. (1970c) 11,378.

2 Town, ⊗ of Queen Annes co., E Maryland; pop. (1970c) 1853.

Centreville. See CENTERVILLE 12.

Centum Cellae. See CIVITAVECCHIA.

Cen·tu·ri·pe \chän-'tu̇r-i-pə\ *or earlier* **Cen·tor·bi** \chän-'tȯr-bē\ *or anc.* **Cen·tu·ri·pa** \sen-'t(y)u̇r-i-pə\. Commune, Enna prov., cen. Sicily, Italy, 28 m. E by N of Enna; pop. (1968e) 8807; sulfur; marble; soda; destroyed by Frederick II 1232; rebuilt 1548.

Ceos. See KEOS.

Cephaloedium. See CEFALÙ.

Ceph·a·lo·nia \ˌsef-ə-'lō-nyə, -nē-ə\ *or Gk.* **Ke·fal·lin·ía** \ˌkef-ə-lə-'nē-ə\ *or anc.* **Ceph·al·le·nia** \ˌsef-ə-'lē-nē-ə, -nyə\. One of Ionian Is. in Ionian Sea off W coast of Greece; 302 sq. m.; pop (1961c) 39,790; with Ithaca forms Cephalonia dept. (see table at GREECE). Chief town Argostolion on inlet on SW coast. Mountainous, highest point 5341 ft. Seized by Romans 189 B.C.; British 1809–64, Greek since 1864.

Ce·phi·sus \sə-'fī-səs\ *or* **Ce·phis·sus** \-'fis-əs\ *or Gk.* **Ki·fi·sós** \ˌkē-fi-'sȯs\. 1 River, E cen. Greece, flowing from Mt. Pendelikon S into the Saronic Gulf, passing to W of Athens.

2 *or Gk.* **Ki·fis·sós Voio·ti·kós** \ˌkē-fi-'sȯs-ˌvyȯ-ti-'kȯs\. River, cen. Greece; ab. 60 m. long; rises near Mt. Oeta, flows E to site of former Lake Copais (*q.v.*).

Ce·pra·no \chā-'prä-(ˌ)nō\. Commune, Frosinone prov., SE Latium, cen. Italy; pop. (1968e) 7824; nearby are the ruins of ancient Fregellae (*q.v.*).

Ce·ram *or* **Se·ram** \'sā-ˌräm\ *also* **Se·rang** \'sā-ˌraŋ\. Large island, cen. Moluccas, Indonesia; 6621 sq. m.; pop. (1957e) 96,797; chief settlements Bula and Piru. Includes small islands in Manipa Strait off W end and the Gorong group to SE; has many mountains (highest 10,023 ft.), dense tropical forests. Came under nominal Dutch control about 1650.

Ceram Sea *or* **Seram Sea**. Section of W Pacific Ocean in cen. Moluccas, Indonesia; bet. Buru and Ceram Is. to S, Sula Is. to W, Obi island group to N, and Misool I. to E; ab. 250 m. long by 80 m. wide.

Cerasus. See GİRESUN 2.

Ce·rau·ni·an Mountains \sə-ˌrȯ-nē-ən-\. Mountain range along coast of NW Epirus, NW Greece; highest peak ab. 6300 ft.

Cercina. See KERKENNA ISLANDS.

Cer·dagne \ser-'dänʸ\ *or Span.* **Cer·da·ña** \ser-'dän-yə\. Old division of Europe in the E Pyrenees, partly in France and partly in Spain.

Ce·rea \che-'rā-ə\. Commune, Verona prov., Veneto, NE Italy, 19 m. SSE of Verona; pop. (1968e) 13,555.

Ce·res \'si(ə)r-(ˌ)ēz\. 1 City, Stanislaus co., cen. California, 6 m. SE of Modesto; pop. (1970c) 6029; diversified agriculture.

2 Town, SW Cape Province, S Rep. of South Africa, 63 m. ENE of Cape Town; pop. (1967e) 6200; health resort with dry climate.

Ceresio, Lago *or* **Ceresius, Lacus.** See LUGANO, LAKE.

Ce·re·so·le Al·ba \ˌcher-ə-ˌzō-lə-'äl-bə\. Commune, Cuneo prov., Piedmont, NW Italy; pop. (1968e) 1642; battle Apr. 14, 1544 in which French were defeated by imperial forces of Charles V.

Ce·re·té \ˌser-ə-'tā\. Municipality, Córdoba dept., N Colombia, 60 m. SSW of Cartagena; pop. (1968e) 38,936.

Ce·ri·gno·la \ˌcher-ən-'yō-lə\. Commune, Foggia prov., Apulia, SE Italy, 22 m. SE of Foggia; pop. (1968e) 47,940; linen; college; defeat of French by Spanish 1503.

Ce·ri·go \'cher-i-ˌgō\ *or Gk.* **Kí·thi·ra** \'kē-thə-ˌrä\ *or Lat.* **Cy·the·ra** \sə-'thir-ə\. Southernmost of the Ionian Is., Greece, in the Mediterranean Sea off SE coast of Peloponnesus ab. 8 m. S of Cape Malea; 107 sq. m.; ✱ Kíthira. Rocky, but with fertile districts. In antiquity had temple of Aphrodite (Cytherea) who according to one legend emerged here from the sea. See PAPHOS.

Cernăuţi. See CHERNOVTSY.

Cer·na·vo·dă *or* **Cer·na–Vo·dă** \ˌcher-nə-'vȯ-də\. Commercial port, Constanţa co., SE Romania, on the Danube WNW of Constanţa; pop. (1966c) 11,259; occupied Oct. 25, 1916 by Bulgarian-German forces.

Ce·rral·vo \sə-'räl-(ˌ)vō\. Small island off the SE coast of Baja California, Mexico, at the mouth of the Gulf of California.

Ce·rre·do, Tor·re de \'tȯr-ē-də-sə-'rād-(ˌ)ō\ *or* **Pe·ña de Cerredo** \'pān-yə-\. Highest peak in the Cantabrian Mts., W Santander prov., N Spain; 8787 ft.

Cer·ri·tos \sə-'rē-təs\. City, Los Angeles co., SW California, 28 m. SE of Los Angeles; pop. (1970c) 15,856.

Ce·rri·tos \sə-'rē-təs\. Town, San Luis Potosí state; cen. Mexico; munic. pop. (1970p) 18,868.

Cerro de Incahuasi *or* **Cerro de Incaguassi.** See INCAHUASI, CERRO DE.

Ce·rro de las Me·sas \ˌser-(ˌ)ō-də-läs-'mā-səs\. Village, Veracruz state, E Mexico, SE of Veracruz; archaeological site, jades found here 1941.

Cerro del Toro. See TORO, CERRO DEL.

Ce·rro de Pas·co \-'pas-(ˌ)kō\. 1 Mountain, Junín dept., cen. Peru; 15,100 ft.

2 Mining town, ✱ of Pasco dept., cen. Peru, ab. 112 m. NE of Lima; pop. (1961c) 21,363; formerly ✱ of Junín dept.; altitude 14,436 ft.; univ. (1965); in copper, silver, and gold-mining districts.

Ce·rro de Pun·ta \-'pünt-ə\. Peak, cen. Puerto Rico, in E Cordillera Central; 4389 ft.; highest mountain in Puerto Rico.

Cer·ro Gor·do \ˌser-ə-'gȯrd-(ˌ)ō\. County in Iowa. See table at IOWA.

Ce·rro Gordo \ˌser-ə-'gȯrd-(ˌ)ō\. Mountain pass bet. Veracruz and Jalapa, E Mexico; battle Apr. 18, 1847 in which Americans under Gen. Scott defeated Mexicans.

Ce·rro Lar·go \ˌser-ō-'lär-(ˌ)gō\. Department of E Uruguay. See table at URUGUAY.

Ce·rro Pal·pa·na \-pal-'pän-ə\. Peak, N Chile, near Bolivian border; 19,833 ft.

Cerro Santiago. See SANTIAGO, MOUNT.

Cer·tal·do \cher-'täl-(ˌ)dō\. Commune, Firenze prov., Tuscany, cen. Italy, 18 m. SW of Florence; pop. (1968e) 15,-343; castle; home of Boccaccio.

Cer·van·tes \ser-'vän-(ˌ)tās\. Municipality, E Ilocos Sur prov., Luzon, Phil., on left bank of Abra river; pop. (1969e) 9600.

Cer·ve·te·ri \cher-'vā-tə-rē\; *anc.* **Cae·re** \'si(ə)r-ē\ *or* **Agyl·la** \ə-'jil-ə\. Commune, Italy, near coast 18 m. WNW of Rome; pop. (1968e) 14,185; ancient stronghold of Etruria; Etruscan tombs; according to legend, the refuge 390 B.C. of the Vestal Virgins when the Gauls took Rome.

Cer·via \'cher-vyə\. Commune, Ravenna prov., Emilia-Romagna, N Italy, on Adriatic 14 m. SSE of Ravenna; pop. (1968e) 22,367; cathedral; saltworks; sea bathing.

Cervin, Mont. See MATTERHORN.

Ce·sa·no Ma·der·no \chā-ˌzän-(ˌ)ō-mə-'de(ə)r-(ˌ)nō\. Commune, Milano prov., Lombardy, N Italy, 9 m. N of Milan; pop. (1968e) 31,465.

Ce·se·na \chə-'zā-nə\ *or anc.* **Cae·se·na** \sə-'zē-nə\. Commune, Forlì prov., Emilia-Romagna, N Italy, 12 m. SE of Forlì; pop. (1968e) 85,140; food processing; episcopal see (one of the oldest in Italy); citadel; library (founded 1452). Withstood attack by Albornoz 1357; pillaged 1377; under the Malatestas 1385–1465; taken by Cesare Borgia during his campaign 1499–1501 in Romagna and became part of the papal domain; captured by British forces Oct. 1944.

Ce·se·na·ti·co \ˌchā-zə-'nät-i-ˌkō\. Commune, Forlì prov., Emilia-Romagna, N Italy, on Adriatic 18 m. E of Forlì; pop. (1968e) 17,917; fisheries, sea bathing.

Cēsis \'tsā-səs\ *or* **Tse·sis** \'tsā-səs\ *or Ger.* **Wen·den** \'ven-dən\. Town, N Latvian S.S.R., U.S.S.R., in the Gauja river valley 45 m. NE of Riga; pop. (1967c) 17,000. *History:* Formerly seat of the Livonian Knights; alternated bet. Swedish and Polish rule from 1600 until it was taken over by Russia 1721; battlefield June 1919 where the Latvian army with Estonian aid defeated the Germans; held by Germans in World War II 1941–44.

Čes·ká Lí·pa \ˌches-kə-'lē-pə\ *or Ger.* **Böh·misch–Lei·pa** \ˌbœ̄-mish-'lī-pə\. Town, Czech. S. R., W Czechoslovakia, 40 m. N of Prague; pop. (1968e) 16,291; textiles; castle (1583).

Česká Socialistická Republika. See CZECH SOCIALIST REPUBLIC.

Čes·ké Bu·dě·jo·vi·ce \'ches-kē-'bu̇d-ə-ˌyȯ-vət-ˌsā\ *or Ger.* **Bud·weis** \'bu̇t-ˌvīs\. City, Czech. S.R., W Czechoslovakia, on Vltava river 75 m. S of Prague; pop. (1968e) 75,684; furniture, metal products; food processing; breweries; cathedral; founded c. 1265.

Českomoravská Vrchovina. See BOHEMIAN-MORAVIAN HIGHLANDS.

Československá Socialistická Republika *or* **Československo.** See CZECHOSLOVAKIA.

Čes·ký–Brod \ˌches-kē-'brȯt\ *or Ger.* **Böh·misch–Brod** \ˌbœ̄-mish-'brōt\. Commune, Czech S.R., Czechoslovakia, 19 m. E of Prague; battle May 30, 1434 in which Hussite leader, Andrew Procop, was killed.

Český Les. See BOHEMIAN FOREST.

Čes·ký Tě·šín \ˌches-kē-tē-'esh-ˌēn\ *or formerly* **Tě·šín Čes·ký** \tē-ˌesh-ēn-'ches-kē\. Town, Czech S.R., Czechoslovakia, ab. 15 m. ESE of Ostrava on Polish border opp. Cieszyn (*q.v.*); pop. (1968e) 15,163.

Cess. See CESTOS.

Cess·nock \'ses-ˌnäk\. Town, E New South Wales, SE Australia, 25 m. W of Newcastle; pop. (1968e) 34,500; coal mining.

Ces·tos \'ses-təs\ *or formerly* **Cess** \'ses\. River, Liberia; ab. 200 m. long; flows into Atlantic Ocean ab. 100 m. SE of Monrovia.

Ce·ta·tea Al·bă \che-ˌtät-yə-'äl-bə\. **1** Former department, S Bessarabia, Romania; 2932 sq. m.; now a part of Ukrainian S.S.R., U.S.S.R.

2 City, its ✻, now in Odessa Oblast, Ukrainian S.S.R., U.S.S.R.. See BELGOROD-DNESTROVSKI.

Ce·ti·nje \'tset-ᵊn-ˌyā\. Town, Montenegro, Yugoslavia, in mountainous region 19 m. SE of Kotor; pop. (1965e) 12,-500; the former ✻ of Montenegro. Founded in latter part of 15th cent. by Montenegrin king, Ivan the Black; several times sacked and burned by Turkish invaders; contains tombs of Montenegrin rulers.

Cette. See SÈTE.

Ceu·ta \'sā-ˌüt-ə\. Spanish military station and seaport, N Morocco, at E end of Strait of Gibraltar opp. Gibraltar; pop. (1970p) 67,187; administratively part of Spanish province of Cádiz. Long a flourishing trading town under the Arabs; taken by Portuguese 1415; became Spanish 1580. See PILLARS OF HERCULES.

Cé·vennes \sā-'ven\ *or anc.* **Ce·ben·na** \sə-'ben-ə\. **1** Mountain range in S France extending NE and SW, W of the Rhone, from N Ardèche dept. to SW Hérault dept.; highest peak Mt. Mézenc 5755 ft.

2 Old district, France, NE part of Languedoc, comprising the region of the Cévennes Mts.; ✻ Mende. Inhabitants known as Cevenoles; refuge of Protestants in time of crusade against the Albigenses 13th cent.; also scene 1702 of uprising of Camisards in religious wars following the Edict of Nantes (1685).

Cey·han \jā-'hän\. **1** *or formerly* **Ji·hun** \jī-'hün\ *or anc.* **Pyr·a·mus** \'pir-ə-məs\. River, Turkey; 316 m. long; flows from the Anti-Taurus Mts. S and SSW through Cilicia into Gulf of İskenderun.

2 Town, Adana prov., S Turkey in Asia, on Ceyhan river and on railroad 25 m. E of Adana; pop. (1965c) 41,124.

Cey·lon \sə-'län, sē-, sā-\; *Sinhalese* **Lan·ka** \'läŋ-kə\ *or in full* **Sri Lanka** \srē-\; *Arab.* **Ser·en·dib** \'ser-ən-ˌdib, -ˌdip\ *or Lat. and Gk.* **Ta·prob·a·ne** \tə-'präb-ə-(ˌ)nē\. Independent state, consisting of an island in the Indian Ocean, S of India, with which it is connected by Adam's Bridge, a chain of shoals which divides Palk Strait on N from Gulf of Mannar on S; 25,332 sq. m.; pop. (1970p) 12,514,000; ✻ Colombo; highest point Pidurutalagala 8281 ft. Rich in tropical vegetation. *Chief products:* Tea, rubber, coconuts; fishing; manufacturing: cement, textiles, fertilizer. *Chief cities:* Colombo, Kandy, Kurunegala, Galle, Kulutara, Jaffna.

History: Original inhabitants were Veddas and Sinhalese; became center of Buddhist civilization 3d cent. B.C. with capital at Anuradhapura (now ruins); first settled by Portuguese 1505, Dutch 1658, British 1796; made British colony 1833; in World War II bombed by Japanese airplanes Apr. 4 and 9, 1942; achieved independence 1948; member of UN 1955; suppressed terrorist attempt to overthrow government 1971.

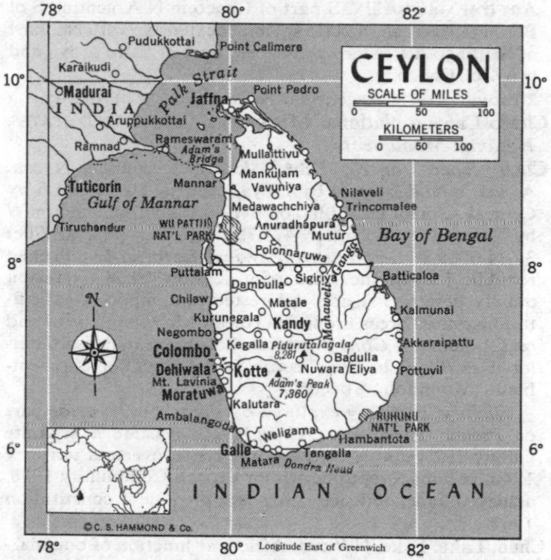

Cha·blais \sha-'blā\. Ancient region of Savoy; ✻ Thonon; now part of Haute-Savoie dept., E France, S of Lake Geneva; gained by counts of Savoy 11th cent.; became Calvinist 1535; won back 1594–98 to Catholicism by Saint Francis of Sales; part of France 1860.

Cha·blis \'sha-ˌblē, sha-'blē\. Commune, Yonne dept., NE cen. France, ab. 11 m. E of Auxerre; pop. (1962c) 1687; region produces white Burgundy wines.

Cha·ca·bu·co \ˌchä-kə-'bü-(ˌ)kō\. **1** Town, Buenos Aires prov., E Argentina, ab. 120 m. W of Buenos Aires; pop. (1966c) 22,544; in important agricultural district.

2 Village just N of Santiago, cen. Chile; scene of battle Feb. 12, 1817 in which San Martín with O'Higgins defeated the Spanish royalists.

Cha·cao Channel \chə-'kau̇-\. Strait bet. N Chiloé I. and the mainland of S cen. Chile, connecting the Gulf of Ancud with the Pacific Ocean.

Chachak. See ČAČAK.

Cha·cha·ni \chä-'chä-nē\. Peak, Arequipa dept., S Peru; 19,931 ft.; meteorological station.

Cha·cha·po·yas \ˌchä-chə-'pō-yəs\. Town, ✻ of Amazonas dept., N Peru, ab. 160 m. NE of Trujillo; pop. (1961c) 6860; altitude 7600 ft.; industrial center.

Cha·choeng·sao *or* **Cha·xerng·sao** \ˈchä-ˌchəŋ-ˈsau̇\. **1** Province, S Thailand; 2093 sq. m.; pop. (1960c) 322,660; ✱ Chachoengsao.

2 Town, its ✱, on railroad 40 m. E of Bangkok; pop. (1960c) 19,719.

Cha·co \ˈchäk-(ˌ)ō\; *Span.* **Chaco** *or* **El Chaco** \el-\ *or* **Gran Chaco** \ˈgrän-\. **1** Region, S cen. South America; ab. 300,000 sq. m.; thinly populated, swampy, drained by Paraguay river and its chief W tributaries the Pilcomayo and Bermejo; principal divisions: (1) **Chaco Bo·re·al** \-ˌbōr-ē-ˈäl, -ˌbȯr-\. Main part of region, in fork of the Paraguay and Pilcomayo; its ownership a matter of dispute bet. Bolivia and Paraguay for 86 years, and a cause of war bet. them 1932–35; by peace treaty (signed at Buenos Aires July 21, 1938, effective Aug. 29) larger central and E part (95,313 sq. m.) to Paraguay, smaller W part (ab. 46,561 sq. m.) to Bolivia. Paraguayan region divided administratively into 3 departments; Bolivian region attached to Tarija dept. (2) **Chaco Cen·tral** \-sen-ˈträl\. Part of the Chaco in N Argentina bet. the Pilcomayo and Bermejo rivers; ab. 40,000 sq. m.; comprises Formosa prov. (27,825 sq. m.) and N part of Salta prov. (ab. 12,000 sq. m.). (3) **Chaco Aus·tral** \-au̇-ˈsträl\. S part of Chaco in N Argentina S of Bermejo river; ab. 66,000 sq. m.; coextensive with NE part of Santiago del Estero prov., cen. part of Salta prov., and prov. of Chaco.

2 Province of N Argentina. See table at ARGENTINA.

Chaco Canyon National Monument. See UNITED STATES, *National Monuments.*

Chad \ˈchad\ *or Fr.* **Tchad** \ˈchad\. Republic, N cen. Africa, bounded on N by Libya, on E by Sudan, on S by Central African Republic, on SW by Cameroon, and on W by Nigeria and Niger; 495,752 sq. m.; pop. (1970e) 3,634,000; ✱ Fort-Lamy. *Physical features:* Landlocked republic having the form of a shallow basin; N region mainly desert, S region is forested and supports agriculture; elevated areas are in N (Tibesti Mountains, *q.v.*) and on E boundary. *Chief products:* Cotton, peanuts, salt, millet; livestock, fish. *Chief towns:* Fort-Lamy, Fort-Archambault, Moundou, Abéché.

History: Territory explored by French 1891; made part of French Equatorial Africa 1910; became a separate colony 1920; status changed to French overseas territory 1946; became a republic within French Community 1958; achieved independence 1960; adopted new constitution 1962.

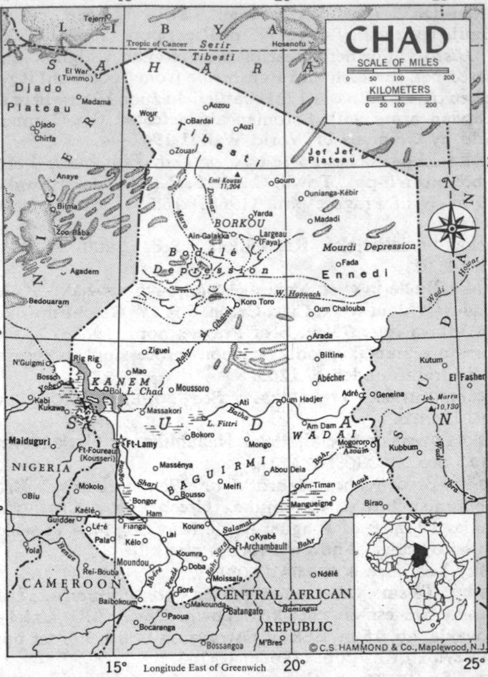

B.C. over a confederation of Greek states and of the defeat of Mithridates VI by Sulla 86 B.C.

Chad, Lake. Lake, NW cen. Africa, at junction of boundaries of Nigeria, Niger, and Chad; its S part forms N extent of Cameroon; its area ranges from ab. 3800 to ab. 9900 sq. m.; fed by Chari river from S and by numerous other streams, has no outlet but remains fresh; ab. 13 ft. deep in NW, 13 to 23 ft. in S where it is navigable. First explored by Denham, Oudney, and Clapperton 1823. See FRENCH EQUATORIAL AFRICA.

Chad·bourn \ˈchad-bərn\. Town, Columbus co., S North Carolina, 52 m. W of Wilmington; pop. (1970c) 2213.

Chad·der·ton \ˈchad-ərt-ᵊn\. Urban district, Lancashire, NW England, suburb of Oldham, on the Irk 8 m. NE of Manchester; pop. (1971p) 32,406; cotton mills.

Chadds Ford \ˈchadz-\. Village, Delaware co., Pennsylvania, on Brandywine creek; originally Chad's Ford, a crossing of the Brandywine, where the main action of the battle of Sept. 11, 1777 was fought.

Cha·di·leo \ˌchad-ᵊl-ˈā-(ˌ)ō\. Name given to lower course of Río Salado (*q.v.*), La Pampa prov., S cen. Argentina.

Chad·ron \ˈshad-rən\. City, ⊗ of Dawes co., NW Nebraska, 50 m. N of Alliance; pop. (1970c) 5921; livestock raising; Chadron State Coll. (1911).

Chad·wicks \ˈchad-wiks\. Village, Oneida co., cen. New York, ab. 9 m. SW of Utica.

Chaer·o·nea \ˌker-ə-ˈnē-ə, ˌkir-\. Ancient city, now in ruins, of W Boeotia, E cen. Greece, SE of Mt. Parnassus and near Orchomenus; scene of victory of Philip of Macedon 338 B.C. over a confederation of Greek states and of the defeat of Mithridates VI by Sulla 86 B.C.

Cha·fa·ri·nas Islands \ˌchäf-ə-ˈrē-nəs-\ *or* **Zaf·a·rin Islands** \ˈzaf-ə-rən-\. Spanish island group in the Mediterranean Sea off N end of Morocco, near Melilla.

Chaf·fee. **1** \ˈchā-fē, ˈchaf-ē\. County in Colorado. See table at COLORADO.

2 \ˈchaf-ə\. City, Scott co., SE Missouri, 12 m. SW of Cape Girardeau; pop. (1970c) 2793; timber; farming.

Cha·gai \ˈchäg-ˌī\. District, NW Baluchistan, Pakistan; 19,429 sq. m.; pop. (1961c) 41,263; mountainous; desert region; annexed in 1896.

Chagai Hills. Range, Pakistan, extending E and W along Afghan boundary of Chagai dist.; highest point 8061 ft.

Cha·gang \chä-ˈgäŋ\. Province of North Korea. See table at KOREA, NORTH.

Cha·ghā Kūr \chä-ˈgä-ˈku̇(ə)r\ *also* **Chi·gha Khur** \chi-\. Town, W Iran, in mountainous region.

Cha·gos Archipelago \ˌchäg-əs-\. Group of islands in Indian Ocean S of Maldives; 76 sq. m.; since 1965 part of British Indian Ocean Territory; chief island Diego Garcia.

Cha·gres \ˈchäg-rəs, ˈchag-\. River in Panama and the Canal Zone; rises in cen. Panama E of the Canal Zone, flows SW into Gatun Lake, and drains NW out of Gatun Lake into the Caribbean Sea.

Cha·grin Falls \shə-ˈgrin-, ˌshüg-rin-, ˌshag-rin-\. Residential village, Cuyahoga co., N Ohio, 15 m. ESE of Cleveland; pop. (1970c) 4848.

Cha·gua·ra·mas \ˌchäg-wə-ˈräm-əs\. Tract of land, NW Trinidad, West Indies, on **Chaguaramas Bay,** inlet of the Gulf of Paria, WNW of Port of Spain; site of U.S. naval base during World War II.

Cha·har \ˈchä-ˈhär\. Former province, E Inner Mongolia, N China, bounded on NW and N by the Mongolian People's Republic, on E by Jehol and Manchuria, on S by Hopeh and Shansi provs. of China, and on SW and W by Suiyuan; ✱ Kalgan. Taken over by Japanese 1935; after end of World War II came under control of Chinese Communists. Partitioned 1952 among other provinces.

Chāh Ba·hār \ˌchä-bə-ˈhär\ *also* **Chah·bar** *or* **Char·bar** \chä-ˈbär\. Seaport, on coast of Gulf of Oman, SE Iran, at S end of E Iranian highway from Mashhad.

Chai·ba·sa \chi-ˈbäs-ə\. Town, ✱ of Singhbhum district, Bihar, India; pop. (1961c) 22,019.

Chai·nat *or* **Jai·nat** *also* **Jay·a·nath** \ˈchī-ˈnät\. 1 Province, SW cen. Thailand; 1018 sq. m.; pop. (1960c) 245,317; ✱ Chainat.

2 Town, its ✱; pop. (1960c) 4652.

Chain Island. See ANAA ISLAND.

Chai·ya·phum *or* **Ja·ya·bum** \ˌchī-(y)ə-ˈpüm\. 1 Province, N Thailand; 4165 sq. m.; pop. (1960c) 486,472; ✱ Chaiyaphum.

2 Town, its ✱; pop. (1960c) 9633.

Cha·kra·ta \chə-ˈkrät-ə\. Town and hill station, N Uttar Pradesh, N India; pop. (1961c) 3194; alt. ab. 7000 ft.

Cha·la·te·nan·go \ˌchä-lə-tə-ˈnäŋ-gō\. 1 Department of NW El Salvador. See table at EL SALVADOR.

2 Town, its ✱; pop. (1968e) 9948.

Chalcedon. See KADIKÖY.

Chal·chi·co·mu·la \ˌchäl-chi-kə-ˈmü-lə\. Village, Puebla state, SE cen. Mexico, at foot of Mt. Citlaltépetl.

Chal·chua·pa \ˌchäl-chə-ˈwä-pə\. City, Santa Ana dept., W El Salvador, near Santa Ana; pop. (1961c) 13,339.

Chal·cid·i·ce \kal-ˈsid-ə-(ˌ)sē\ *or Gk.* **Khal·ki·dhi·kí** \ˌkälk-yə-t͟hi-ˈkē\. 1 Peninsula of E Macedonia, NE Greece, projecting SE into N Aegean Sea bet. Strymonic Gulf on E and Gulf of Salonika on W ; terminates in three long peninsulas: (from E to W) Acte, Sithonia, and Kassándra (*qq.v.*). In N part at its base are Lakes Bolbē and Korónia and the city of Salonika. See ATHOS.

2 Department of Greece. See table at GREECE.

Chal·cis \ˈkal-səs\ *or* **Chal·kis** \-kəs\ *also* **Ev·ri·pos** \ˈev-rə-ˌpȯs\ *or* **Neg·ro·pont** \ˈneg-rə-ˌpänt\ *or Gk.* **Khal·kís** \käl-ˈkēs\. City, ✱ of Euboea dept., Greece, on Euboea I. on Evripos strait; pop. (1971p) 36,381; important as early as 7th cent. B.C.; founded many cities in Macedonia, Italy, Sicily; invasion point for campaigns against Greece. Aristotle died here 322 B.C. See ERETRIA.

Chal·co \ˈchäl-(ˌ)kō\. 1 Dry lake in cen. Mexico, ab. 25 m. SE of Mexico City; alt. 7480 ft.

2 Municipality, México state, Mexico, 25 m. SE of Mexico City; pop. (1970p) 41,125.

Chal·dea *also* **Chal·daea** \kal-ˈdē-ə\. Ancient region on the Euphrates river and the Persian Gulf, Asia; originally the S part of Babylonia. Frequently, and esp. in Biblical use (*Gen.* xi. 28; *Dan.* ix. 1), equivalent to Babylonia (*q.v.*) after it was occupied by the Chaldeans, a Semitic people from the S who had attacked it since 11th cent. B.C. and finally secured throne under Nabopolassar 626 B.C.; with Medes, brought about fall of Assyrian Empire 612 B.C.; while ruled by Nebuchadnezzar II, subdued Judaea, and captured Jerusalem 597 and 586 B.C.; Chaldean (or Neo-Babylonian) Empire fell when Persians captured Babylon 539 B.C.

Chaldiran. See ÇALDIRAN.

Chaldran. See ÇALDIRAN.

Cha·leur Bay \shə-ˌlu̇(ə)r-, -ˌlər-\ *or Fr.* **Baie de Chaleur** \bā-də-shə-lər\. Inlet of W Gulf of St. Lawrence, SE Canada, extending bet. N New Brunswick and the Gaspé Penin. in SE Quebec; ab. 85 m. long; its S extension is Nepisiguit Bay; receives the Restigouche river; famous as a fishing ground, esp. for salmon. Discovered 1535 by Cartier.

Cha–lin \ˈchä-ˈlin\ *or* **Kya·ring Tso** \ˈkyä-riŋ-ˈtsō\. Lake, E cen. Tibet, China, 31°10′N, 88°15′E; ab. 40 m. long.

Chalkar–Tengis. See CHELKAR-TENGIZ.

Chalkis. See CHALCIS.

Chalk River \ˈchȯk-\. Village near Ottawa river, SE Ontario, Canada, 20 m. NW of Pembroke; pop. (1971p) 1095; atomic pile set up by Canadian government here during World War II.

Chal·lis \ˈchal-əs\. City, ⊗ of Custer co., cen. Idaho; pop. (1970c) 784.

Chal·mette National Historical Park \shal-ˈmet-\. See UNITED STATES, *National Historical Parks.*

Châ·lons–sur–Marne \shä-ˈlōⁿ-ˌsu̇(ə)r-ˈmärn\. Commune, ✱ of Marne dept., NE France, on Marne river 95 m. E of Paris; pop. (1968c) 50,764; automobile parts, electrodes; breweries; cathedral, restored under Louis XIV; 12th cent. Romanesque church. Chief town of the ancient Catalauni; fortified by Romans; early center of Christianity 250; on plains to the S (Catalaunian Plains) Attila defeated by Aëtius 451; united to France 1360; captured by Germans 1870; occupied by Germans 1940–44.

Cha·lon–sur–Saône \sha-ˈlōⁿ-ˌsu̇(ə)r-ˈsōn\ *or anc.* **Cab·il·lo·num** \kab-ə-ˈlō-nəm\. Manufacturing city, Saône-et-Loire dept., E cen. France, on Saône river 35 m. N of Mâcon; pop. (1968c) 50,589; iron and steel works; 12th–15th cent. cathedral; 14th cent. church; 15th cent. episcopal palace; received communal charter 1256.

Chaltel. See FITZROY 4.

Chama. See RIO CHAMA.

Chamalhari. See CHOMO LHARI.

Cha·man \ˈchä-mən\. Town, W Baluchistan, Pakistan, 60 m. NW of Quetta on Afghanistan border; pop. (1961c) 12,208; railroad terminus; on highway over **Chaman Pass.**

Cha·mar·tín de la Ro·sa \ˌchä-mär-ˈtēn-ˌdəl-ə-ˈrō-sə\. Commune, cen. Spain, NNE suburb of Madrid.

Cham·ba \ˈchəm-bə\. 1 District, Himachal Pradesh, N India; 3131 sq. m.; pop. (1961c) 210,579; a former state founded in 6th cent.; came under British influence 1846; made part of Himachal Pradesh 1948.

2 Town, its ✱, on gorge of upper Ravi river; pop. (1961c) 8609.

Cham·bal \ˈchəm-bəl\. Unnavigable river, cen. India; rises in W Vindhya Mts. near Indore and flows NE, E, and SE into the Yamuna W of Kanpur.

Cham·ber·lain \ˈchām-bər-ˌlən\. City, ⊗ of Brule co., S South Dakota, on Missouri river 10 m. N of its confluence with White river; pop. (1970c) 2626; stock raising.

Chamberlain Lake. Lake in N Piscataquis co., N cen. Maine.

Cham·bers \ˈchām-bərz\. 1 Island in Green Bay, NE Wisconsin, in Door co.

2 Name of counties in two states of the U.S. See tables at ALABAMA and TEXAS.

Cham·bers·burg \ˈchām-bərz-ˌbərg\. Industrial borough, ⊗ of Franklin co., S Pennsylvania, 50 m. WSW of Harrisburg; pop. (1970c) 17,315; limestone, freestone, marble quarries. Wilson Coll. (1869), Penn Hall Junior Coll. (1906); settled 1730; burned by Confederates 1864.

Cham·bé·ry \ˌshäⁿ-(ˌ)bā-ˈrē\ *or Lat.* **Cam·be·ri·a·cum** \ˌkam-bə-ˈrī-ə-kəm\. Commercial and manufacturing city, ✱ of Savoie dept., E France, 54 m. E of Lyons; pop. (1968c) 51,066; aluminum, cement; cathedral (14th–15th cents.), château of dukes of Savoy (1232).

Cham·bey·ron, Ai·guille de \ā-ˌgwēd-ə-ˌshäⁿ-bā-ˈrōⁿ\. Mountain in the Cottian Alps, Alpes-de-Haute Provence dept., SE France; 11,155 ft.

Cham·be·zi \cham-ˈbē-zē\. A headstream of the Congo river, Africa; ab. 300 m. long; rises in N Zambia, flows SW, forms multiple channel in swamp S of Lake Bangweulu from which it emerges as the Luapula.

Cham·blee \ˈsham-blē\. City, De Kalb co., NW cen. Georgia, N of Atlanta; pop. (1970c) 9127.

Cham·bly \ˈsham-blē, shäⁿ-ˈblē\. 1 County, Quebec, Canada. See table at QUEBEC.

2 City, Chambly co., S Quebec, Canada, on Richelieu river 14 m. ESE of Montreal; pop. (1971p) 11,446; site of fort built 1665: see CANADA, *National Historic Parks* (Fort Chambly); served as a main base of operations for Carleton and Burgoyne 1776–77.

Chambly Canal. Canal, part of Richelieu river system, Quebec, Canada, from Chambly to St. Johns; 11.78 m. long, with 9 locks.

Cham·bolle–Mu·si·gny \shäⁿ-ˌbōl-mü-zē-ˈnyē\. Commune, Côte-d'Or dept., E France, near Dijon; pop. (1962c) 444; celebrated wines (red Burgundy) from vineyard of Musigny.

Chambon–Feugerolles, Le. See LE CHAMBON-FEUGEROLLES.

Cham·bord \shäⁿ-ˈbȯr\. 1 Village, Lake St. John co., S Quebec, Canada, on Lake St. John; pop. (1971p) 1103.
2 Village, Loir-et-Cher dept., N cen. France, ab. 10 m. NE of Blois; pop. (1962c) 260; château built by Francis I.

Cha·me·le·cón \ˌchäm-ə-lə-ˈkȯn\. River in NW Honduras; ab. 125 m. long; flows NE into the Gulf of Honduras.

Cha·me Point \ˌchäm-ē-\. Cape on S coast of Panama, at W side of entrance to the Bay of Panama.

Cha·mi·zal \ˈsham-ə-ˌzal, ˌchäm-i-ˈsäl\. Tract of 437 acres N of the Rio Grande adjoining El Paso, Texas; originally in Mexico, later in U.S. because of change of course of Rio Grande; after long controversy ceded to Mexico by U.S. in 1963.

Cham·lang \ˈchäm-ˈläŋ\. Mountain in the Himalayas, Nepal; 24,014 ft.

Chamo, Lake. See SHAMO, LAKE.

Cha·mo·nix *or* **Cha·mou·ni** \ˌsham-ə-ˈnē\. Noted valley in Haute-Savoie dept., E France, near NW entrance to new Mont Blanc tunnel; ab. 14 m. long and bet. 1 and 2½ m. wide; winter sports; mountain climbing; site of Winter Olympics 1924; best starting point for ascent of Mont Blanc to the SE, at the town of **Chamonix–Mont–Blanc** \-mōⁿ-ˈbläⁿ\.

Chamouchouane. See ASHUAPMUCHUAN.

Cham·pa \ˈcham-pə\. Ancient coastal kingdom of Indochina, occupying a region now part of South Vietnam; flourished 2nd cent. A.D. to end of 14th cent. Its inhabitants were Chams, related to the Cambodians.

Cham·pagne \sham-ˈpān\ *or Lat.* **Cam·pa·nia** \kam-ˈpā-nyə, -nē-ə\. Region of NE France, bounded on N by Low Countries; ✱ Troyes; watered by Marne, Aube, Aisne, Meuse, Yonne rivers; famous for its wines. An important medieval French county, held by houses of Vermandois, Blois, and Navarre; by marriage 1284 of heiress, Jeanne de Navarre, to Prince Philip (later Philip IV) of France, came to French crown; province before 1789; scene of battles of World War I 1915,1917, 1918, esp. in hilly region ENE of Reims.

Champagne Castle *or formerly* **Cath·kin Peak** \ˌkath-kin-\. Peak in Drakensberg Mountains, Rep. of South Africa; 11,073 ft.

Cham·paign \sham-ˈpān\. 1 Name of counties in two states of the U.S. See tables at ILLINOIS and OHIO.
2 City, Champaign co., E cen. Illinois, 45 m. ENE of Decatur; pop. (1970c) 56,532; adjoins Urbana; alloy castings, air-conditioning equipment; settled ab. 1855, incorp. as city 1860.

Champaign–Urbana. See URBANA 1.

Cham·pa·quí \ˌchäm-pə-ˈkē\. Peak, W Córdoba prov., N cen. Argentina; 9350 ft; highest of the Sierras de Córdoba.

Champ·au·bert \ˌshäⁿ-pō-ˈba(ə)r, -ˈbe(ə)r\. Village, Marne dept., NE France, ab. 17 m. SSE of Épernay; scene of battle Feb. 10, 1814 in which Napoleon defeated the Allies.

Cham·pe·ri·co \ˌchäm-pə-ˈrē-(ˌ)kō\. Seaport, Retalhuleu dept., SW Guatemala; pop. (1964p) 11,473; port for Retalhuleu and Quezaltenango; chief export coffee.

Cham·pi·gny–sur–Marne \ˌshäⁿ-(ˌ)pēn-ˈyē-ˌsu̇(ə)r-ˈmärn\. Residential commune, Val-de-Marne dept., N France, SSE suburb of Paris on Marne river; pop. (1968e) 70,419; battles Nov. 30 and Dec. 2, 1870 in which the French attempted unsuccessful sorties from Paris.

Cham·pi·on's Hill \ˈcham-pē-ənz-\. Hill, Hinds co., SW cen. Mississippi, 20 m. E of Vicksburg; battle May 16, 1863 in which Union forces under Gen. Grant drove Confederates back toward Vicksburg.

Cham·plain \sham-ˈplān\. County, Quebec, Canada. See table at QUEBEC.

Champlain, Lake. Lake bet. Vermont and New York on N part of boundary, extending ab. 6 m. into Canada; ab. 125 m. long; 430 sq. m.; max. depth 399 ft. Discovered 1609 by French explorer Samuel de Champlain; scene of American naval victory over British Sept. 11, 1814.

Champlain Canal. Canal connecting Lake Champlain at Whitehall, New York with the Erie canal at Waterford, New York; 60 m. long, with 11 locks; part of the N.Y. State Barge Canal system.

Cham·po·eg \cham-ˈpō-eg\. Settlement in Willamette valley, Oregon, S of Portland, where "Champoeg meeting" was held May 2, 1843 which organized a provisional government, the only government in the Pacific Northwest until Oregon Territory organized Mar. 1848; site commemorated by Champoeg Memorial State Park.

Cham·po·tón \ˌchäm-pə-ˈtōn\. Seaport, Campeche state, Mexico, on Campeche Bay 48 m. SW of Campeche; munic. pop. (1970p) 27,581; fishing; founded 1537.

Chanak. See ÇANAKKALE 2.

Chanar. See CHUNAR.

Cha·ña·ral \ˌchän-yə-ˈräl\. Port, Atacama prov., N cen. Chile; pop. (1960c) 5210; exports nitrates and copper.

Chança. See CHANZA.

Chan·ce·lade \shäⁿ-ˈsläd\. Commune, Dordogne dept., SW cen. France; pop. (1962c) 1780; skeleton unearthed near here in 1888 considered to be representative of a late Paleolithic race (Chancelade).

Chan·cel·lor \ˈchan(t)-s(ə-)lər\ *or formerly* **Chan·cel·lors·ville** \-s(ə-)lərz-ˌvil\. Locality in Spotsylvania co., Virginia, just W of Fredericksburg; scene of battle May 2–3, 1863 which resulted in defeat of Union forces under Hooker by Confederates under Lee and Jackson and death of Jackson May 10.

Chan–chiang \ˈchän-jē-ˈäŋ\ *or* **Tsam·kong** \ˈjäm-ˈgȯŋ\. Town, Kwangtung prov., China, ab. 210 m. SW of Canton; pop. (1970e) 220,000.

Chan·da \ˈchän-də\. Town, E Maharashtra, cen. India, on affluent of Wardha river 85 m. S of Nagpur; pop. (1961c) 51,484; silk fabrics; old capital of ancient Gond dynasty.

Chan·da·lar \ˌshan-də-ˈlär\. River, NE Alaska; flows SE from Endicott Mts. to upper Yukon; 280 m. long.

Chan·dan·na·gar \ˌchən-də-ˈnəg-ər\ *or* **Chan·der·na·gor** \ˌchən-dər-nə-ˈgō(ə)r, -ˈgȯ(ə)r\ *or* **Chan·dar·na·gar** \-ˈnəg-ər\. Settlement and adjoining territory, SE India, on the Hooghly river 21 m. N of Calcutta; ab. 4 sq. m.; pop. (1961c) 67,105.

History: At first a trading post (factory) founded by Colbert's French East India Company and granted to French by Emperor Aurangzeb 1688; in 18th cent. a thriving center for maritime trade; captured by English 1757, restored to French 1763; recaptured 1794, and restored permanently 1816; under jurisdiction of governor at Pondicherry (*q.v.*). Voted 1949 to join India; became part of Republic of India 1950.

Chan·dau·si \ˌchən-ˈdau̇-sē\. Town, W Uttar Pradesh, N India, on affluent of Ganges river 95 m. E of Delhi; pop. (1961c) 48,557; rail and trade center.

Chan·de·leur Islands \ˌshan-də-ˌlu̇(ə)r-\. Chain of small islands in St. Bernard parish, off E coast of SE Louisiana, lying bet. **Chandeleur Sound** and the Gulf of Mexico.

Chandernagor. See CHANDANNAGAR.

Chan·di·garh \ˈchən-dē-gər\. City, joint ✱ of Punjab and Haryana states, N India; pop. (1971p) 256,979; a federally administered territory; following an interim period will be ✱ of Punjab only; univ. (1947).

Chan·dler \ˈchan-dlər\. 1 City, Maricopa co., SW cen. Arizona, 17 m. SE of Phoenix; pop. (1970c) 13,763; citrus fruits; fertilizers; winter resort.
2 City, ⊗ of Lincoln co., cen. Oklahoma, 26 m. N of Shawnee; pop. (1970c) 2529; pecans.
3 Town, East Gaspé co., SE Quebec, Canada, on SE Gaspé Penin. 23 m. SW of Percé; pop. (1971p) 3842.

Changan. See SIAN.

Chan·ga·na·che·ri \ˌchəŋ-gə-ˈnäch-ə-rē\. Town, cen. Kerala, S India, SE of Alleppey; pop. (1961c) 42,376.

Chang·bha·kar \ˌchäŋ-bə-ˈkär\. Former princely state, NE Central Provinces, India; 899 sq. m.; now part of Madhya Pradesh.

Chang–chêng. See GREAT WALL.

Ch'ang–chia–k'ou. See KALGAN.

Chang–chiang \ˈchäŋ-jē-ˈäŋ\. Name of Kwangchowan, after its restoration 1946 to China by France.

Ch'ang–chih \ˈchäŋ-ˈchi(ə)r\ *or* **Lu·an** \lü-ˈän\. Town, S Shansi prov., E China, ab. 100 m. NW of K'ai-feng; pop. (1970e) 300,000; communications center and Chinese military base in Chinese-Japanese War 1937–45.

Ch'ang–chou \ˈjäŋ-ˈjō, ˈchaŋ-ˈchaù\. 1 *or formerly* **Lung·ki** \ˈlùŋ-ˈkē\. City, S Fukien prov., SE China, 30 m. W of Amoy; pop. (1953c) 81,200; partially destroyed by Taiping rebels; residence of Chu Hsi (1130–1200), philosopher and expounder of Confucianism, under the Southern Sung dynasty.

2 *or* **Wu·tsin** \ˈwü-ˈjin\. City, S Kiangsu prov., E China, ab. 70 m. ESE of Nanking on the Grand Canal; known in ancient times, received name of Ch'ang-chou under Sui dynasty; has extensive trade by junk.

Changchuen. See SHANG-CH'UAN.

Ch'ang–ch'un \ˈchäŋ-ˈchùn\ *or Jap.* **Hsin·king** \ˈshin-ˈjiŋ\. City, ✱ of Kirin prov., NE China, on railroad 165 m. NNE of Mukden; pop. (1970e) 1,500,000; on edge of fertile Sungari river plain; rail junction point; trucks, light engineering; univ. (1958), technical coll. (1958).

History: Small village until end of 18th cent. when small farmers were brought into district from Shantung; gained in importance after 1900; made capital of new Japanese state of Manchukuo 1932; became special municipality 1933. In World War II captured by Russian paratroopers Aug. 22, 1945; scene of conflicts in Chinese civil war 1946–47.

Chang–kuang–tsai Ling \ˌjäŋ-ˌkwäŋ-ˌ(t)sī-ˈliŋ\. Mountain range extending NE and SW in cen. Kirin prov., NE China, E of Harbin; highest peak ab. 4400 ft.

Chang–ku Feng \ˈjäŋ-ˈgaù-ˈfəŋ\ *or Russ.* **Go·ra Za·o·zer·na·ya** \ˌgər-ə-ˌzä-əz-ˈyòr-nə-yə\. Hill on left bank of Tumen river near its mouth in disputed area on frontier of U.S.S.R., North Korea, and China; controls Russian Posyeta Bay to the NE; claimed by Japan 1938; scene of fighting bet. Russians and Japanese July–Aug. 1938.

Ch'ang–pai Shan \ˌchäŋ-ˌbī-ˈshän\. Mountain range, Kirin prov., NE China, along N North Korean border; highest point 9003 ft.; source of rivers Sungari, Yalu, and Tumen. Many Manchu legends connected with it.

Ch'ang–sha \ˈchäŋ-ˈshä\. City, ✱ of Hunan prov., SE cen. China, on right bank of the Hsiang ab. 45 m. S of Tung-t'ing Hu (lake); pop. (1970e) 850,000; machine tools, farm equipment, pharmaceuticals; univ. (1959). Formerly enclosed by wall with 12 gates, first wall built according to tradition ab. 202 B.C.; once famed as a literary center. First opened to foreign missionaries 1901; made a treaty port 1904; successfully withstood a siege of 90 days by Taiping rebels 1852. In World War II captured by Japanese Sept. 1941 but soon given up; in three other battles 1941–42 Japanese severely defeated; finally taken by Japanese June 21, 1944 and held until end of war.

Ch'ang–shu \ˈchäŋ-ˈshü\. Town, Kiangsu prov., China, 119 m. ESE of Nanking; pop. (1970e) 150,000.

Chang Tang. See CH'IANG-T'ANG.

Ch'ang–te \ˈchäŋ-ˈdə\. City, N Hunan prov., SE cen. China, on left bank of Yüan river near its mouth; pop. (1970e) 225,000; a former treaty port; center of China's "Rice Bowl." Has high mountains to the W. In World War II severely damaged in four unsuccessful attacks 1939–43 by Japanese in their campaigns against Ch'ang-sha; finally fell 1944.

Ch'ang–t'ing \ˈchäŋ-ˈtiŋ\ *or* **Ting·chow** \ˈtiŋ-ˈjō\. City, SW Fukien prov., China, on upper Han Shui near Kiangsi border 165 m. W of Swatow.

Chang–tzu \ˈchäŋ-ˈdzə\. North peak of Mt. Everest group, Himalayas, S Tibet, on Nepal border; 24,780 ft.

Ch'ang–yang \ˈchäŋ-ˈyäŋ\. Town, S Hupeh prov., E cen. China, on tributary of the Yangtze 12 m. S of I-ch'ang.

Chan·has·sen \chan-ˈhas-ən\. Village, Carver and Hennepin cos., SE cen. Minnesota, 7 m. W of Minneapolis; pop. (1970c) 4879.

Chania. See CANEA.

Chan–ka–erh–a–la–t'ao Shan. See DZUNGARIAN ALA TAU.

Chankiri. See ÇANKIRI.

Channel, The. See ENGLISH CHANNEL.

Chan·nel Islands \ˌchan-əl-\. 1 British group of islands in the English Channel 10 to 30 m. off W coast of Manche dept., France; 75 sq. m.; pop. (1971p) 125,240; comprise Jersey, Guernsey, Alderney, and Sark, and several islets. Originated noted breeds of cattle, esp. Jersey and Guernsey breeds. Fertile islands, exporting fruit, vegetables, and flowers; tourism. Inhabitants are part of Norman descent, part English.

History: Cromlechs, menhirs, etc., indicate occupation by prehistoric race; became part of Normandy 933; united to British crown at time of Norman Conquest 1066; annexed to British crown 1254; British claims recognized by Philip II of France in Treaty of Bretigny 1360; domestically independent, not controlled by British government; occupied by Germans June 30, 1940–May 9, 1945.

2 The Santa Barbara Islands, California.

Channel Islands National Monument. See UNITED STATES, *National Monuments.*

Channel–Port aux Basques \-ˌpōr-tō-ˈbask\. Town, SW Newfoundland, Canada; pop. (1971p) 5870.

Chan·ning \ˈchan-iŋ\. Town, ⊗ of Hartley co., NW Texas; pop. (1970c) 336.

Chantabun. See CHANTHABURI.

Chan·ta·da \chän-ˈtä-də\. Commune, Lugo prov., NW Spain, 32 m. SSW of Lugo; pop. (1970p) 10,666; stock raising; manufactures leather, soap, bricks and tile, linens.

Chan·tha·bu·ri \chän-ˌtä-bù-ˈrē\ *also* **Chan·ta·bun** \chän-tä-ˈbün\ *or* **Chan·ta·bu·ri** \chän-ˌtä-bù-ˈrē\. 1 Province, S Thailand; 2337 sq. m.; pop. (1960c) 157,803; ✱ Chanthaburi. 2 Commercial town, its ✱, near NE coast of Gulf of Siam 140 m. SE of Bangkok; pop. (1960c) 10,795; has good port.

Chan·til·ly \shan-ˈtil-ē\. Village, Fairfax co., Virginia, 20 m. W of Washington; battle Sept. 1, 1862 in which Jackson attempted unsuccessfully to prevent withdrawal of Pope's Union troops after 2d battle of Bull Run; Dulles International Airport.

Chantilly \ˌshäⁿ-tē-ˈyē\. Commune, Oise dept., N France; pop. (1968c) 10,246; château and park; horse racing; formerly manufactured the delicate Chantilly lace.

Chan·trey Inlet \ˌchan-trē-\. Inlet on N coast of Keewatin dist., Northwest Territories, Canada.

Cha·nute \shə-ˈnüt\. City, Neosho co., SE Kansas, 44 m. WSW of Fort Scott; pop. (1970c) 10,341; Neosho County Community Coll. (1936); near oil, gas, and clay deposits; oil refineries; cement works.

Chanute Field. U.S. Air Force base in Rantoul, Illinois, location of an Air Force Technical School.

Cha·ny, Lake \-ˈchän-ē\. Lake, SW Novosibirsk Oblast, Russian S.F.S.R., U.S.S.R., E of Omsk; ab. 1000 sq. m.

Chan·za \ˈchän(t)-sə\ *or Port.* **Chan·ça** \ˈchan(t)-sə\. River in SW Spain; flows SSW, forming a section of the Spanish-Portuguese boundary, and empties into Guadiana river ab. 20 m. from its mouth.

Ch'ao–an \ˈchaù-ˈän\ *or* **Chao·chow** \ˈchaù-ˈjō\. City, E Kwangtung prov., SE China, on Han river ab. 20 m. above Swatow; made treaty port 1858 but river too shallow for large vessels; large river trade by junk. Scene of banishment of the great poet, philosopher, and opponent of Buddhism, Han Yü (768–824 A.D.), under the T'ang dynasty.

Ch'ao–Hu \'chau̇-'hü\. Lake (*hu*), cen. Anhwei, E China, S of Ho-fei; outlet on SE to the Yangtze.

Cha·o·nia \kā-'ō-nē-ə\. District of ancient Epirus, NW Greece, extending along the coast N of the Kalamas river; its Pelasgian inhabitants were among the earliest peoples to enter Greece.

Chao Phra·ya \chau̇-'prī-ə\; *often in English sources* **Me Nam** *or* **Me·nam** \mā-'näm\. River, Thailand; 227 m. long; flows S from highlands on N border to head of Gulf of Siam near Bangkok; strictly, name applies only to lower course, 160 m., from junction of Nan and Ping rivers in 15°42'N; lower course has many branches, the W branch being the Tha Chin (*q.v.*). See NAN, PING, WANG, YOM.

Chao–t'ung \'jau̇-'tu̇ŋ\. City, NE Yunnan, S China, near the Yangtze ab. 175 m. NNE of K'un-ming; stock-farming and mining center.

Cha·pa·la, Lake \-chə-'päl-ə\. Lake, Jalisco state, Mexico; 50 m. long; 651 sq. m.; largest lake in Mexico; traversed by the Santiago river (see SANTIAGO 10).

Cha·pa·ré \ˌchäp-ə-'rā\. River, cen. Bolivia, ab. 180 m. long; flows N into the upper Mamoré river.

Cha·pa·rral \ˌchäp-ə-'räl\. Town, Tolima dept., W cen. Colombia, on the Magdalena 80 m. SW of Bogotá; munic. pop. (1968e) 40,238.

Cha·pa·yevsk \chə-'pä-yefsk\. Town, S Kuibyshev Oblast, Russian S.F.S.R., U.S.S.R., on Kuibyshev-Syzran R.R. 30 m. W of Kuibyshev; pop. (1969e) 87,000.

Chap·el Hill \'chap-əl-\. Town, Durham and Orange cos., N North Carolina, 11 m. WSW of Durham; pop. (1970c) 25,537; residential; Univ. of North Carolina at Chapel Hill (1789).

Chap·man, Mount \-'chap-mən\. Peak in Great Smoky Mts., Sevier co., E Tennessee; 6425 ft.

Chapman Peak. Mountain in Glacier National Park near N boundary, NW Montana; 9375 ft.

Chap·pa·quid·dick Island \ˌchap-ə-ˌkwid-ik-\. Island in Nantucket Sound, Massachusetts, off SE coast of Martha's Vineyard.

Chap·pell \'chap-əl\. Village, ⊗ of Deuel co., W Nebraska; pop. (1970c) 1204.

Cha·pra \'chəp-rə\. Commercial town, W Bihar, NE India, on Ganges river just below junction with the Ghāghara; pop. (incl. adjoining communities, 1961c) 88,264.

Cha·pul·te·pec \chə-'pül-tə-ˌpek\. Mexican fortress on isolated rocky hill 3 m. SW of Mexico City, captured by American assault Sept. 12–13, 1847 during the Mexican War; scene of meeting of Inter-American Conference Feb. 21–Mar. 8, 1945 that drafted Act of Chapultepec (approved Mar. 6, 1945) pledging for duration of World War II use of combined force in preserving American boundaries (act extended and implemented by conference at Petrópolis, Brazil, Aug. 15–Sept. 2, 1947).

Cha·ram·bi·rá Point \chə-ˌräm-bə-ˌrä-\. Cape on Pacific coast of Colombia, 4°N lat.

Cha·ran–Ka·noa \ˌchär-än-kə-'nō-ə\. Village on SW coast of Saipan, Mariana Is.; beachheads 2 m. S and 2 m. N secured by U.S. Marines June 15, 1944; base for advance N to Garapan and S to Aslito airfield.

Charbar. See CHĀH BAHĀR.

Char·cas \'char-kəs\. **1** Town, San Luis Potosí state, cen. Mexico, 62 m. N of San Luis Potosí; munic. pop. (1970p) 22,388.

2 *or* **Las Charcas** \läs-\. Early name for the Spanish audiencia of Upper Peru (*q.v.*).

Char·co Azul Bay \ˌchär-(ˌ)kō-ə-ˌzül-\. Inlet of Gulf of Chiriquí on the N, in extreme SW Panama.

Char·cot Island \ˌshär-ˌkō-\. Island in Palmer Archipelago, Antarctica, 69°45'S, 75°15'W.

Chard \'chärd\. Municipal borough, Somersetshire, SW England, N of Lyme Regis; pop. (1971p) 7905; market center; lace, textiles; 15th cent. church; two Roman villas.

Char·don \'shärd-^{ə}n\. Village, ⊗ of Geauga co., NE Ohio, 24 m. ENE of Cleveland; pop. (1970c) 3991; maple-syrup and maple-sugar center.

Char·dzhou \chär-'jō\ *also* **Char·jui** \chär-'jü-ē\ *or 1926–27 called* **Len·insk** \'le-(ˌ)ninsk, 'l(y)ā-n(y)insk\. Town, E Turkmen S.S.R., U.S.S.R., on left bank of Amu Darya ab. 60 m. SW of Bukhara; pop. (1969e) 93,000; chemicals; shipyards; important center in cotton trade.

Chardzhou Oblast \-'ö-bləst, -ˌblast\. Subdivision of the Turkmen S.S.R., U.S.S.R.; 36,178 sq. m.; pop. (1970p) 456,000; ✱ Chardzhou; cotton, sulfur.

Cha·rente \shə-'ränt\. **1** Navigable river, W France; 224 m. long; rises in Haute-Vienne dept., flows W into the Bay of Biscay opp. Oléron I.

2 Department of W France. See table at FRANCE.

Charente–Ma·ri·time \-mar-ə-'tēm\ *or formerly* **Charente–In·fé·rieure** \-a^{n}-fer-'yər\. Department of W France. See table at FRANCE.

Cha·ren·ton–le–Pont \ˌshar-ən-ˌtō^{n}-lə-'pō^{n}\. Commune, Val-de-Marne dept., N France, SE suburb of Paris, at confluence of Marne and Seine rivers; pop. (1968c) 22,300; porcelain, rubber goods; stone bridge across Marne river formerly important in defenses of Paris. Includes **Con·flans** \kō^{n}-'flä^{n}\ *or* **Conflans–l'Ar·che·vêque** \-ˌlär-shə-'vek\ where treaty bet. Louis XI and the League of Public Weal was signed 1465.

Chargoggagoggmanchaugagoggchaubunagungamaug, Lake. See CHAUBUNAGUNGAMAUG, LAKE.

Cha·ri *or* **Sha·ri** \'shär-ē\. River, flowing from Central African Republic NW into Lake Chad, Chad; ab. 590 m. long; many tributaries in N Central African Republic. Fort-Lamy is at head of delta.

Chā·ri·kār \'chär-i-ˌkär\. Town, ✱ of Parwān prov., E Afghanistan; pop. (1969e) 91,126; alt. 5300 ft.; pottery.

Char·ing Cross \ˌchar-iŋ-'krȯs\. District in London, England, S of Trafalgar Square, on site of old village of Cherringe; formerly site of an Eleanor Cross, destroyed 1647, now has a modern memorial cross, erected 1865.

Char·i·ton \'shar-ət-^{ə}n\. **1** River, S Iowa and N cen. Missouri; 280 m. long; rises in Clarke co., S Iowa, flows E then S across Missouri border and into the Missouri river.

2 County in Missouri. See table at MISSOURI.

3 City, ⊗ of Lucas co., S Iowa, 42 m. SSE of Des Moines; pop. (1970c) 5009; foundry, machine shops; corn, hogs; coal.

Charjui. See CHARDZHOU.

Char·kha·ri \chər-'kär-ē\. Former Indian state, NE Central India Agency, India, ab. 100 m. W of Allahabad; 785 sq. m.; now part of Uttar Pradesh.

Char·khlik \chä-kə-'lik\. Town, S cen. Sinkiang Uighur, W China, on highway S of the Takla Makan Desert 155 m. NE of Cherchen.

Char·le·magne \'shär-lə-ˌmän\. Village, L'Assomption co., S Quebec, Canada, 9 m. N of Montreal; pop. (1966c) 3569.

Charle·mont \'chärl-ˌmänt\. Village, co. Armagh, S Northern Ireland, on the Blackwater 6 m. N of Armagh; terminus of Ulster Canal.

Char·le·roi \'shär-lə-ˌrȯi\. Borough, Washington co., SW Pennsylvania, on Monongahela river 22 m. S of Pittsburgh; pop. (1970c) 6723; coal mining; glass, steel industries.

Charleroi \'shär-lə-ˌrȯi, ˌshärl-rə-'wä\. Commune, Hainaut prov., SW Belgium; pop. (1969e) 23,911; industrial center in a coal and iron mining region; captured by Germans after fierce fighting Aug. 23, 1914.

Charles \'chärlz\. **1** River, E Massachusetts; flows into Boston Bay; its estuary separates Boston from Cambridge; 47 m. long; navigable for 7 m.

2 County in Maryland. See table at MARYLAND.

Charles, Cape. Cape at S tip of Northampton co., Virginia, N of entrance to Chesapeake Bay.

Charles·bourg \shärl-ˈbu̇(ə)r\. City, Quebec co., S Quebec, Canada, 3 m. N of Quebec; pop. (1971p) 33,484; furniture.

Charles City. 1 County in Virginia. See table at VIRGINIA.
2 City, ⊗ of Floyd co., N Iowa, 30 m. ESE of Mason City; pop. (1970c) 9268; farm equipment, fertilizer.
3 Village, ⊗ of Charles City co., E Virginia; birthplaces of William Henry Harrison and John Tyler, 9th and 10th presidents of the U.S., nearby.

Charles Island. See SANTA MARÍA 3.

Charles Mix \-ˈmiks\. County in South Dakota. See table at SOUTH DAKOTA.

Charles Mound. Elevation, Jo Daviess co., NW Illinois; 1235 ft.; highest point in the state.

Charles River. See CHARLES 1.

Charles·ton \ˈchärl-stən\. 1 County in South Carolina. See table at SOUTH CAROLINA.
2 Town, a ⊗ of Franklin co., NW Arkansas; pop. (1970c) 1497.
3 City, ⊗ of Coles co., E cen. Illinois, 50 m. ESE of Decatur; pop. (1970c) 16,421; flour, shoes, dairy products. Eastern Illinois Univ. (1895).
4 City, a ⊗ of Tallahatchie co., NW Mississippi, 31 m. ESE of Clarksdale; pop. (1970c) 2821.
5 City, ⊗ of Mississippi co., SE Missouri, 28 m. SSE of Cape Girardeau; pop. (1970c) 5131; cotton; shoe factories.
6 Seaport city, ⊗ of Charleston co., SE South Carolina; on Atlantic Ocean; pop. (1970c) 66,945; paper and pulp mills, oil refineries, metallurgical works; ships coal, phosphates, petroleum products, cotton, cotton goods, tobacco, fertilizer; formerly protected by Forts Sumter and Moultrie; Coll. of Charleston (1770), The Citadel (1842), Palmer Coll. (1903), Baptist Coll. of Charleston (1960). Charleston Navy Yard is just above the city.
History: Founded 1670 on Albemarle Point on W bank of Ashley river by an English colony under William Sayle; removed across Ashley river to present location 1680; became center of wealth and culture in the South; first American fire insurance company established here 1736; successfully opposed attacks by British fleet 1776 and 1779, but was captured May 12, 1780 by Sir Henry Clinton, and held by British until Dec. 14, 1782; became center of movement for nullification 1832 and of other movements to resist federal authority; site of the convention which proclaimed secession of South Carolina from the Union Dec. 1860; scene of outbreak of hostilities in the Civil War 1861 (see FORT SUMTER); evacuated by Confederate forces Feb. 17, 1865 after two years of siege; seriously damaged by earthquake Aug. 31, 1886.
7 Industrial city, ✱ of West Virginia and ⊗ of Kanawha co., W cen. West Virginia, at confluence of Elk and Kanawha rivers; pop. (1970c) 71,505; distributing point for region producing coal, oil and gas, salt, hardwood timber; manufactures chemicals, glass, foundry products. Morris Harvey Coll. (1888; removed from Barboursville 1935). Settled around Fort Lee shortly after the Revolution; incorporated as town 1794, as city 1870; ✱ of West Virginia 1870–75, and from 1885.

Charleston Peak. Mountain, W Clark co., SE Nevada; 11,-919 ft.

Charles·town \ˈchärl-ˌstau̇n\. 1 City, Clark co., S Indiana, NE of Jeffersonville; pop. (1970c) 5933; chemicals.
2 Former city, Middlesex co., Massachusetts, since 1874 part of Boston; on Boston Harbor bet. mouths of Charles and Mystic rivers; U.S. Navy Yard; state prison (until 1956). Founded ab. 1628, oldest part of Boston; almost destroyed June 17, 1775 in battle of Bunker Hill (*q.v.*); chartered as city 1847.
3 Town, Sullivan co., SW New Hampshire, on Connecticut river 10 m. S of Claremont; pop. (1970c) 3274; military base for Colonial troops during last years of French and Indian War; rendezvous for Gen. Stark and New Hampshire troops en route to battle of Bennington.
4 Town and summer resort, Washington co., S Rhode Island, on inlet of Block Island Sound SW of Newport; pop. (1970c) 2863; taken from Westerly and incorp. 1738. Site of Indian burial ground and of Coronation Rock, where until 1770 Indians crowned their chieftains.
5 Chief town on Nevis I., Leeward Is., West Indies; pop. (1970e) 2789.

Charles Town. City, ⊗ of Jefferson co., NE West Virginia, 14 m. S of Martinsburg; pop. (1970c) 3023; scene of trial and execution of John Brown 1859.

Char·le·ville \ˈchär-lə-ˌvil, ˈchärl-ˌvil\. Town, S Queensland, Australia, on Warrego river 423 m. WNW of Brisbane; pop. (1966c) 4871.

Charleville–Mé·zières \ˌshär-lə-ˌvēl-mā-ˈzhe(ə)r\; *medieval* **Ar·cae Re·mo·rum** \ˈär-(ˌ)sē-ri-ˈmōr-əm, -ˈmȯr-\ *also* **Car·o·lop·o·lis** \ˌkar-ə-ˈläp-ə-ləs\. Commune, Ardennes dept., NE France, on Meuse river; pop. (1968c) 55,543; textiles; Charleville founded 1606.

Char·le·voix \ˈshär-lə-ˌvȯi\. 1 County in NW Michigan. See table at MICHIGAN.
2 City, its ⊗, on Lake Michigan 41 m. NNE of Traverse City; pop. (1970c) 3519; resort; fishing.

Charlevoix–Est \ˌshär-lə-ˈvwä-ˈest\ *or* **East Charlevoix** \-ˈshär-lə-ˌvȯi\. County in Quebec, Canada. See table at QUEBEC.

Charlevoix–Ouest \-ˈwest\ *or* **West Charlevoix.** County in Quebec, Canada. See table at QUEBEC.

Char·lotte \ˈshär-lət\. 1 Name of counties in two states of the U.S. See tables at FLORIDA and VIRGINIA.
2 City, ⊗ of Eaton co., S Michigan, SW of Lansing; pop. (1970c) 8244; furniture, automobile accessories.
3 Commercial and industrial city, ⊗ of Mecklenburg co., S North Carolina, in Piedmont Region 15 m. N of South Carolina border; pop. (1970c) 241,178; largest city in the state; important distribution point for cotton, tobacco, and peanut-growing region; cotton yarn and cotton goods, farm implements, electrical equipment, chemicals; oil refining. Johnson C. Smith Univ. (1867), Queens Coll. (1857), King's Coll. (1901), Univ. of North Carolina at Charlotte (1946), Central Piedmont Community Coll. (1963). Settled c. 1748, incorporated 1768, made ⊗ 1774; occupied by British under Cornwallis 1780; headquarters of Gen. Gates 1780; center of gold rush at end of 18th cent.; branch of United States mint estab. c. 1836 (closed 1913); last meeting place of Confederate Cabinet 1865.
4 Town, ⊗ of Dickson co., NW cen. Tennessee; pop. (1970c) 610.
5 County, New Brunswick, Canada. See table at NEW BRUNSWICK.

Charlotte Ama·lie \-ə-ˈmäl-yə\ *or formerly* (*1921–37*) **St. Thom·as** \-ˈtäm-əs\. Seaport, ✱ of St. Thomas I. and of the Virgin Islands of the United States, West Indies; at head of St. Thomas Harbor on S shore of St. Thomas I.; pop. (1970p) 12,372.

Charlotte Courthouse. Town, ⊗ of Charlotte co., S Virginia; pop. (1970c) 539.

Charlotte Harbor. Inlet of Gulf of Mexico, in Charlotte and Lee cos., on W coast of SW Florida; receives Peace river in NE; Pine I. extends S of it.

Char·lot·ten·burg \shär-ˈlat-ᵊn-ˌbərg, -ˌbu̇(ə)rg\. 1 A former city of Germany, since 1920 a residential section of Berlin (now part of West Berlin); pop. (1965e) 226,000; site of 17th cent. palace (damaged in World War II, now restored) of Queen Sophia Charlotte, wife of Frederick I of Prussia.
2 Coastal town, on Cottica river, NE Surinam.

Char·lottes·ville \ˈshär-ləts-ˌvil, -vəl\. City, ⊗ of Albemarle co., cen. Virginia, but politically independent, 70 m. WNW of Richmond; 6 sq. m.; pop. (1970c) 38,880; textiles, precision instruments; Univ. of Virginia (1819). Monticello (home of Jefferson; now national memorial) and Ash Lawn (home of James Monroe) nearby; settled c. 1737, chartered as city 1880.

Char·lotte·town \'shär-lət-,taun\. City, ✱ of Prince Edward I., and ⊗ of Queens co., Canada, in cen. part of island, on Hillsborough Bay; pop. (1971p) 18,631; commercial center of the province; exports potatoes; produces dairy products, woolen goods, canned products, lumber; fishing; tourism; Univ. of Prince Edward I. (1969); founded by French ab. 1720; became ✱ 1765.

Charlotte Town. See GOUYAVE.

Charl·ton \'chärlt-ᵊn\. 1 County in Georgia. See table at GEORGIA.

2 Town, Worcester co., cen. Massachusetts, 12 m. SW of Worcester; pop. (1970c) 4654; agricultural trade center.

Charlton Kings \,chärlt-ᵊn-'kiŋz\. Urban district, Gloucestershire, SW cen. England; pop. (1971p) 10,088.

Char·ny \shär-'nē\. Town, Levis co., S Quebec, Canada, on Chaudière river 8 m. SSW of Quebec; pop. (1966c) 4762.

Charran. See HARAN.

Char·ters Tow·ers \,chärt-ərz-'tau̇(-ə)rz\. Town, E Queensland, Australia, near Burdekin river 75 m. SW of Townsville; pop. (1966c) 7602; gold-mining region.

Char·tres \'shärt, 'shärtrᵊ\; *anc.* **Au·tri·cum** \'ȯ-tri-kəm\ *also* **Civ·i·tas Car·nu·tum** \,siv-ə-,tas-kär-'n(y)üt-əm\. Commercial city, ✱ of Eure-et-Loir dept., N cen. France, on Eure river 48 m. SW of Paris; pop. (1968c) 34,469; breweries, foundries; agricultural machinery, electronic equipment; flour milling; 13th cent. Gothic cathedral, noted particularly for its two spires; enclosed by ramparts. Was capital of ancient Beauce; second crusade preached here by St. Bernard 1145; taken by English 1417; recovered 1432; Henry IV crowned in cathedral here 1594; occupied by Germans 1870.

Char·treuse, La Grande \lä-,gränd-shär-'trərz\. Chief house, until 1903, of Carthusian order, near the village of **Saint–Pierre–de–Chartreuse** \saⁿ-,pye(ə)rd-ə-\, Isère dept., SE France, ab. 12½ m. N of Grenoble; religious settlement founded by St. Bruno of Cologne 1084; present buildings date from 1676; monks expelled 1903 as result of Associations Law (1901) dissolving monastic associations, restored 1940; noted for liqueur.

Cha·ryb·dis \kə-'rib-dəs\. Whirlpool near Messina, Sicily, now called Galofalo (*q.v.*). See SCILLA.

Chas·co·mús \chäs-kə-'müs\. Town, Buenos Aires prov., E Argentina, 50 m. S of La Plata; pop. (1960c) 10,521.

Chase \'chās\. Name of counties in two states of the U.S. See tables at KANSAS and NEBRASKA.

Chase City. Town, Mecklenburg co., S Virginia, 28 m. ENE of South Boston; pop. (1970c) 2909; tobacco market.

Chas·ka \'chas-kə\. City, ⊗ of Carver co., SE cen. Minnesota, on Minnesota river 20 m. SW of Minneapolis; pop. (1970c) 4352; beet-sugar refinery, dairy farms.

Chatalja. See ÇATALCA.

Cha·teau·bri·ant \,sha-,tō-brē-'äⁿ\. Commune, Loire-Atlantique dept., NW France, 40 m. NNE of Nantes; pop. (1968c) 11,986; castle.

Châ·teau·dun \,sha-,tō-'dəⁿ\. Commune, Eure-et-Loir dept., N cen. France, 28 m. SSW of Chartres; pop. (1968c) 14,-450; dates from Gallo-Roman period; château.

Cha·teau·gay \'shat-ə-gē, -,gā\ *or in Canada* **Châ·teau·guay** \,shat-ə-'gā\. River, United States and Canada; ab. 60 m. long; rises in N N.Y. in Chateaugay Lakes on border bet. Clinton and Franklin cos. and flows N through Châteauguay co. in S Quebec to the St. Lawrence ab. 14 m. above Montreal. On its banks in Canada about 15 m. from its mouth a battle was fought Oct. 26, 1813 in which the American forces under Gen. Wade Hampton were repulsed.

Chateaugay Lakes. Two lakes in NE New York, **Upper Chateaugay** in W Clinton co. and **Lower Chateaugay** in E Franklin co.; outlet, Chateaugay river flowing out of N end of Lower Chateaugay; resort.

Châ·teau·guay \'shat-ə-gē, -,gā; ,shat-ə-'gā\. 1 River, New York and Canada. See CHATEAUGAY.

2 County, Quebec, Canada. See table at QUEBEC.

3 Town, Châteauguay co., S Quebec, Canada, on St. Lawrence river 14 m. SW of Montreal; pop. (1971p) 15,759; near mouth of Châteauguay river and opp. the Ottawa.

Châteauguay Centre. Town, Châteauguay co., S Quebec, Canada, 7 m. SW of Montreal; pop. (1971p) 17,897; residential suburb of Montreal.

Châ·teau·neuf–de–Ran·don \,shä-tō-'nə(r)f-də-,raⁿ-'dōⁿ\. Village, Lozère dept., S France, NE of Mende; pop. (1962c) 439; besieged 1380 by Du Guesclin who died here.

Châ·teau Ri·cher \,shä-,tō-ri-'shā\. Town, ⊗ of Montmorency No. 1 co., S Quebec, Canada, on N bank of St. Lawrence river 25 m. NE of Quebec; pop. (1971p) 3099; dairying and market gardening.

Châ·teau·roux \,shä-tō-'rü\ *or during Revolution called* **In·dre·ville** \,aⁿ-drə-'vēl\. Commercial commune, ✱ of Indre dept., cen. France, on Indre river 80 m. S of Orléans; pop. (1968c) 49,138; textiles; metalworking; 10th cent. castle.

Château–Thier·ry \,sha-,tō-,tye-'rē, ,shä-\. Commune, Aisne dept., N France, on right bank of Marne river 37 m. SSW of Laon; pop. (1968c) 11,049; musical instruments, furniture; trades in wine; stone quarries nearby; Thierry castle said to have been built by Charles Martel 730; birthplace of La Fontaine. Battles 1814; occupied by Germans 1870; initial successes against Germans won by American troops in nearby Belleau Wood June 6, 1918, and town retaken July 21; American Military Cemetery. See MARNE.

Châtelard, Le. See LE CHÂTELARD.

Châ·te·let \,shät-ᵊl-'ā\. Industrial commune, Hainaut prov., SW Belgium, on Sambre river; pop. (1969e) 14,949; food processing.

Châ·te·li·neau \,shät-ᵊl-i-'nō\. Commune, Hainaut prov., SW Belgium, opp. Châtelet; pop. (1969e) 19,238; steel.

Châ·tel·le·rault *or in Eng. usage* **Châ·tel·he·rault** \,shä-,tel-'rō\. Commune, Vienne dept., W cen. France, on Vienne river 21 m. NNE of Poitiers; pop. (1968c) 35,337; manufactures small arms, cutlery. Built around 11th cent. castle; capital of a 16th cent. duchy.

Cha·te·nay–Ma·la·bry \,shä-tə-'nā-,mäl-ə-'brē\. Commune, Hauts-de-Seine dept., N France, 7 m. SSW of Paris; pop. (1968c) 27,484.

Chat·ham \'chat-əm\. 1 Name of counties in two states of the U.S. See tables at GEORGIA and NORTH CAROLINA.

2 Village, Sangamon co., cen. Illinois, 10 m. SSW of Springfield; pop. (1970c) 2788; agriculture.

3 Town, Barnstable co., SE Massachusetts, on Atlantic Ocean 18 m. E of Barnstable; pop. (1970c) 4554; resort.

4 Residential borough, Morris co., N New Jersey, on Passaic river 6 m. SE of Morristown; pop. (1970c) 9566.

5 Town, ⊗ of Pittsylvania co., S Virginia; pop. (1970c) 1801.

6 Seaport town, Northumberland co., E New Brunswick, Canada, on estuary of Miramichi river; pop. (1971p) 7812; good harbor; lumber trade; shipyards, foundries, pulp mills; center for fishing and hunting; founded 1800.

7 City, ⊗ of Kent co., SE Ontario, Canada, on Thames river 16 m. E of Lake St. Clair; pop. (1971p) 34,601; agricultural center, esp. for fruit and livestock; canneries, machine shops, mills, and an automobile factory; tobacco processing; settled 1835.

8 Municipal borough, Kent, SE England, on the Medway 30 m. ESE of London; pop. (1969e) 55,460; one of the chief naval and military stations of Great Britain; flour mills; timberworks; first used for naval purposes by Henry VIII; Royal Dockyard founded ab. 1700 and greatly developed since 1867.

Chatham Island. 1 Island, Galapagos Islands. See SAN CRISTÓBAL 4.

2 Island, New Zealand. See CHATHAM ISLANDS.

Chatham Islands. Island group in S Pacific Ocean 536 m. E of New Zealand; 44°S lat. and 176°W long.; 372 sq. m.;

pop. (1968e) 500; belong to New Zealand; comprise two islands: Chatham (347 sq. m.) and Pitt (25 sq. m.); discovered 1791.

Chatham Strait. Narrow passage bet. Admiralty and Kuiu Is. on E and Baranof and Chichagof Is. on W, SE Alaska.

Châ·til·lon \ˌshä-tē-ˈ(y)ō^{n}\. Commune, Hauts-de-Seine dept., N France, S suburb of Paris; pop. (1968c) 24,640; Fort de Châtillon site since 1949 of France's first atomic pile.

Châtillon–sur–Seine \-sü(ə)r-ˈsän, -ˈsen\. Commune, Côte-d'Or dept., E France, 43 m. NW of Dijon; pop. (1962c) 5913; ruined 13th cent. castle of dukes of Burgundy; unsuccessful conference Feb. 5–Mar. 19, 1814 bet. Napoleon and the Allies. In World War II junction point Sept. 12, 1944 of two American armies.

Chat·om \ˈchat-əm\. Town, ⊗ of Washington co., SW Alabama; pop. (1970c) 1059.

Châ·tou \shä-ˈtü\. Commune, Yvelines dept., N France, NNW suburb of Paris on Seine river; pop. (1968c) 22,619; summer resort; 13th cent. church.

Chats·worth \ˈchats-ˌwərth\. **1** City, ⊗ of Murray co., N Georgia; pop. (1970c) 2706; talc; corn, cotton.
2 Seat of the dukes of Devonshire, Derbyshire, N cen. England, ab. 20 m. N of Derby; one of the most splendid residences in England.

Chat·ta·hoo·chee \ˌchat-ə-ˈhü-chē\. **1** Navigable river, rising in Towns co., NE Georgia, and flowing SW to Alabama border at West Point, W cen. Georgia, then S forming a section of Alabama-Georgia boundary and a section of Georgia-Florida boundary; 436 m. long; dammed, forming Lake Seminole; section below Lake Seminole known as Apalachicola (*q.v.*).
2 County in Georgia. See table at GEORGIA.
3 Town, Gadsden co., NW Florida, NW of Tallahassee; pop. (1970c) 7944; cellulose products.

Chat·ta·noo·ga \ˌchat-ə-ˈnü-gə, ˌchat-^{ə}n-ˈü-\. Industrial city and port of entry, ⊗ of Hamilton co., SE Tennessee, on Tennessee river just N of Georgia border; pop. (1970c) 119,082; in scenic region, with Missionary Ridge to the E and Lookout Mt. to the SW; manufactures iron and steel products, farm implements, textiles, chemicals, nuclear reactors; railroad center; main headquarters of TVA since 1935; iron and coal mines; Univ. of Tennessee at Chattanooga (1886), Tennessee Temple Coll. (1946), Chattanooga State Technical Inst. (1963). Chickamauga and Chattanooga National Military Park nearby (see UNITED STATES, *National Historical Parks*).
History: First permanent white settlement c. 1835; became salt-trading center; chartered 1839, as city 1851; developed river trade (cotton, etc.) and became transportation center; served as Union base during Civil War 1863 ff.; scene of engagements including battle of Chickamauga 1863 and battle of Chattanooga Nov. 23–25, 1863 (battle of Lookout Mt., called "Battle above the Clouds," and battle of Missionary Ridge).

Chat·ter·is \ˈchat-ər-is\. Urban district, Cambridgeshire and Isle of Ely co., E England, 67 m. N of London; pop. (1971p) 5566.

Chat·too·ga \chə-ˈtü-gə\. **1** River, Georgia. See TUGALOO.
2 County in Georgia. See table at GEORGIA.

Cha·tu·ge Dam \chə-ˈtü-gə-\. See table at TENNESSEE VALLEY AUTHORITY.

Chau·bun·a·gun·ga·maug, Lake \-chȯ-ˌbən-ə-ˈgəŋ-gə-ˌmȯg\ *or* **Lake Web·ster** \-ˈweb-stər\ *or the long Indian form* **Lake Char·gog·ga·gogg·man·chau·ga·gogg·chau·bun·a·gun·ga·maug** \-chär-ˈgäg-ə-ˌgäg-man-ˈchȯ-gə-ˈgäg-chȯ-ˌbən-ə-ˈgəŋ-gə-ˌmȯg\. Lake in S Worcester co., cen. Massachusetts, near Webster.

Chau·dière \shō-ˈdye(ə)r\. River, S Quebec, Canada; ab. 120 m. long; rises in Lake Megantic and flows N to the St. Lawrence just above Quebec.

Chaudière Falls. Falls in Ottawa river at Ottawa city, Ontario, Canada; river narrows to 200 ft., descends 50 ft.; site of extensive water power development.

Chauk \ˈchau̇k\. Town, Magwe div., Burma, on Irrawaddy ab. 60 m. N of Magwe.

Chau·kan Pass \ˌchau̇-ˌkän-\. Pass over mountains, on NW boundary of Burma, NE of Patkai Range; alt. 7979 ft.

Chaulnes \ˈshōn\. Commune, Somme dept., N France, 11 m. SW of Pèronne; pop. (1962c) 1500; scene of much fighting in World War I, 1914–17 and 1918.

Chau·mont \shō-ˈmō^{n}\ *or formerly* **Chaumont–en–Bas·si·gny** \-ä^{n}-ˌbas-ē-ˈnyē\. Commune, ✻ of Haute-Marne dept., NE France, at confluence of Marne and Suize rivers 140 m. ESE of Paris; pop. (1968c) 25,779; manufactures gloves, hosiery, textiles; iron ore mined nearby; 13th cent. Gothic church, 17th cent. town hall. Received charter 1190. Treaty 1814 bet. Great Britain, Russia, Austria, and Prussia renewing and strengthening alliance against Napoleon; headquarters of American Expeditionary Force under Pershing in World War I. In World War II taken by Germans June 15, 1940; retaken by American armies Sept. 1944.

Cha·un Bay \ˌchə-ˈün-\. Inlet of the Arctic Ocean, NW Chukot National Okrug, NE Russian S.F.S.R., U.S.S.R., 69°N lat. and 170°E long.

Chau·ny \shō-ˈnē\. Commune, Aisne dept., N France, on Oise river S of St-Quentin; pop. (1968c) 13,920; destroyed in World War I.

Chau·phu \ˈchau̇-ˈpü\. Town, South Vietnam, on Cambodia border 105 m. W of Saigon; pop. (1967e) 37,175.

Chau·tau·qua \shə-ˈtȯ-kwə\. **1** Name of counties in two states of the U.S. See tables at KANSAS and NEW YORK.
2 Former town, Chautauqua co., SW corner of New York, on Chautauqua Lake; Chautauqua system of popular education inaugurated 1874.

Chautauqua Lake. Lake, Chautauqua co., SW corner of New York; ab. 18 m. long and from 1 to 2½ m. wide; outlet from SE end flows into Allegheny river.

Chaux–de–Fonds, La. See LA CHAUX-DE-FONDS.

Chav·es \ˈchav-əs, ˈshav-\. County in New Mexico. See table at NEW MEXICO.

Cha·ves \ˈshav-ēsh\ *or anc.* **Aq·uae Fla·vi·ae** \ˌak-wē-ˈflā-vē-ē, ˌäk-\. Commune, Vila Real dist., N Portugal, near Spanish border 22 m. NNE of Vila Real; pop. (1970p) 11,465; thermal salt baths and springs; cathedral; tomb of Alfonso I, Duke of Braganza; manufactures linens and silks; Convention of Chaves Sept. 18, 1837 signed here.

Cha·ville \sha-ˈvē(ə)l\. Commune, Hauts-de-Seine dept., N France, SW suburb of Paris; pop. (1968c) 17,476.

Cha·vin·da \chä-ˈvēn-də\. Town, Michoacán state, SW Mexico; pop. (1970p) 12,228.

Chaxerngsao. See CHACHOENGSAO.

Cha·zy \shā-ˈzē\. Village, Clinton co., NE New York, near Lake Champlain ab. 13 m. N of Plattsburg; nearby are limestone formations of geological interest.

Chazy Lake. Lake, Clinton co., NE corner of New York, source of Great Chazy river; ab. 4 m. long.

Chea·dle and Gat·ley \ˈchēd-^{ə}l . . . ˈgat-lē\. Urban district, Cheshire, NW England, S of Manchester; pop. (1971p) 60,648; bricks, pharmaceuticals.

Chea·ha \ˈchē-ˌhȯ\. Mountain, Cleburne co., E Alabama; 2407 ft.; highest point in state.

Cheat \ˈchēt\. River, N West Virginia; ab. 150 m. long; formed by confluence of forks in S Tucker co., flows N across Pennsylvania border and into Monongahela river in SW Fayette co., SW Pa.; E of Morgantown are lake, dam, and gorge; hydroelectric power development.

Cheat·ham \ˈchēt-əm\. County in Tennessee. See table at TENNESSEE.

Cheat Mountain \ˈchēt-\. Mountain, Randolph co., NE cen. West Virginia; 3478 ft.

Cheb \ˈkep, ˈhep\ *or Ger.* **Eger** \ˈā-gər\. City, W Czechoslovakia, in the valley of the Ohře ab. 50 m. NW of Plzeň; pop. (1968e) 25,733; industrial community; scene of assassination of Wallenstein 1634.

Che·beague \shə-ˈbēg\. Island in Casco Bay, Cumberland co., off coast of SW Maine.

Che·bo·ksa·ry \ˌcheb-äk-ˈsär-ē\. Town, ✻ of Chuvash A.S.S.R., Russian S.F.S.R., U.S.S.R., on the Volga 80 m. W of Kazan; pop. (1970p) 216,000; commercial and cultural center of the republic; alcohol, textiles; thermal power station; univ. (1967).

Che·boy·gan \shi-ˈbȯi-gən\. **1** River, N Michigan; ab. 40 m. long; flows N into Lake Huron at Cheboygan.

2 County in N Michigan. See table at MICHIGAN.

3 City, its ⊗, on Lake Huron at mouth of the Cheboygan river; pop. (1970c) 5553; summer resort and fishing center; formerly a lumbering center.

Chech, Erg. See EL ERG.

Che·chaou·èn \ˌshā-shə-ˈwen\ *or* **Xau·en** \ˈhau̇-ˌän\. Town, N Morocco, NW Africa, S of Tétouan; pop. (1960c) 13,712.

Che·cheno–In·gush Autonomous Soviet Socialist Republic \chə-ˌchen-ō-in-ˌgüsh-\. Autonomous republic, a subdivision of the Russian S.F.S.R., U.S.S.R., on N slopes of Caucasus Mts.; 7452 sq. m.; pop. (1970p) 1,065,000; ✻ Grozny; oil and natural gas, timber; chemicals; fruit canning; formed 1936 by combining the Chechen and Ingush autonomous areas; dissolved 1943–44 for collaboration with Germans during World War II; reconstituted 1957.

Che·co·tah \chi-ˈkōt-ə\. City, McIntosh co., E Oklahoma, 22 m. SSW of Muskogee; pop. (1970c) 3074; dairy and poultry farms.

Ched·a·buc·to Bay \ˌshed-ə-ˈbək-(ˌ)tō-\. Inlet of Atlantic Ocean, NE tip of the mainland of Nova Scotia, Canada, SE of Strait of Canso.

Ched·dar \ˈched-ər\. Village, Somersetshire, SW England, 22 m. SW of Bristol; pop. (1961c) 2845; cliffs and stalactite caverns; known also for its cheese (Cheddar cheese) originally made here.

Che·du·ba \chə-ˈdü-bə\. Island, Arakan, W Burma, in Bay of Bengal S of Ramree I.; 202 sq. m.; held by Japanese May 1942–Jan. 1945.

Cheek·to·wa·ga \ˌchēk-tə-ˈwäg-ə\. Urban community (unincorporated), Erie co., W New York, E of Buffalo; pop. (1970c) 113,844.

Ch'e–erh–ch'en \ˈjē-ˈər-ˈchəŋ\. River, W China; ab. 420 m. long; flows from N slopes of cen. Kunlun Mts. N and NE along SE border of Takla Makan Desert to Lop Nor.

Cheese·man Dam \ˌchēz-mən-\. Dam across South Platte river, SW Douglas co., cen. Colorado; height 236 ft.; completed 1904; forms **Cheeseman Lake.**

Che–fang \ˈche-ˈfäŋ\. Town, SW Yunnan prov., S China, near Wan-t'ing; alt. ab. 3200 ft.; held by Japanese May 1942–Nov. 26, 1944.

Che·foo \ˈjə-ˈfü\ *or formerly* **Yen–t'ai** \ˈyen-ˈtī\. Commercial city, Shantung prov., NE China, on N coast of E end of Shantung Penin., 112 m. NE of Tsingtao, at E end of Strait of Pohai; pop. (1970e) 180,000. Made open port 1863; Chefoo Convention, signed 1876, forced China to open additional ports and to improve status of foreigners in China.

Che·ha·lis \chi-ˈhā-ləs\. **1** River, W Washington; ab. 125 m. long; rises in Lewis co., flows NW into Grays Harbor at Aberdeen.

2 City, ⊗ of Lewis co., SW Washington, 5 m. S of its sister city Centralia (*q.v.*); pop. (1970c) 5727; dairy, poultry, fruit farms; lumber, milk-condensing plants.

Chehalis, Point. Point on SW coast of Grays Harbor co., W Washington, at S entrance to Grays Harbor.

Cheik–Sa·ïd \ˌshāk-sä-ˈēd\ *or Arab.* **Shaykh Sa'īd** \ˈshīk-sä-ˈēd\. Former French territory, SW tip of Arabian Penin. on Bab al-Mandab opp. Perim I.; ab. 1 sq. m.; first acquired 1868 by French commercial company; ceded to French government 1886.

Che·ju \ˈchā-ˈjü\. **1** *or Jap.* **Sai·shu To** \ˈsī-ˈshü-ˈtō\ *or formerly* **Quel·part** \ˈkwel-ˌpärt\. Island, a province of South Korea, N East China Sea; 706 sq. m.; pop. (1970e) 365,522; ✻ Cheju; cattle raising; fishing.

2 *or Jap.* **Saishu.** Town, its ✻; pop. (1970e) 106,456.

Che·ka·lin \ˌchə-kəl-ˈyēn\ *or* **Likh·vin** \ˈlik-vin, ˈlyik-vyin\. Town, W Tula Oblast, Russian S.F.S.R., U.S.S.R., 56 m. W of Tula; head of navigation of Oka river. In World War II held a few months by Germans in Moscow offensive 1941–42.

Che·kiang \ˈjəj-ē-ˈäŋ\. Coast province, E China, bounded on N by Kiangsu prov., on E by East China Sea, on S by Fukien prov., and on W by Kiangsi and Anhwei provs.; 39,305 sq. m.; pop. (1968e) 31,000,000; ✻ Hangchow. The smallest province of China but one of the most densely populated; N part lies just S of the delta of the Yangtze; cen. part drained by the Fu-ch'un, flowing into Hangchow Bay; the S part drained by the Ou; many hills and low mountain ranges. The Chou-shan Archipelago is off NE coast. *Chief products:* Wheat, beans, rice, cotton, tea, and silk; salt, fluorite; fishing. *Chief cities:* Hangchow, Wenchou, Ning-po, and Shao-hsing. A cultural center of early China; during 12th and 13th cents. A.D. its chief city, Hangchow, was capital of China under Sung dynasty; after Mongol conquest 1280 became center of Mangi (the empire of S China).

Che·lan \shə-ˈlan\. **1** County in Washington. See table at WASHINGTON.

2 Town, Chelan co., cen. Washington, at S end of Lake Chelan; pop. (1970c) 2684; summer resort.

Chelan, Lake. Lake, Chelan co., cen. Washington; from 1 to 2 m. wide; ab. 55 m. long; outlet from S end flows into Columbia river.

Chelan Range. Range in Chelan co., cen. Washington, extending along the W shore of Lake Chelan.

Ché·lia, Dje·bel \ˌjā-bəl-ˈshāl-ˌyä\ *or Arab.* **Je·bel She·lia** \ˌjeb-əl-shə-ˈlē-ə\. Peak in Aurès Mts., NE Algeria; 7648 ft.; highest peak in Algeria.

Cheliabinsk. See CHELYABINSK.

Ché·liff \shā-ˈlēf\ *also* **She·liff** \shə-ˈlēf\. River, Algeria; 422 m. long; rises in Atlas Mts., flows N and W into Mediterranean Sea E of Oran; longest river in Algeria.

Cheliuskin, Cape. See CHELYUSKIN, CAPE.

Chel·kar–Teng·iz \chel-ˌkär-teŋ-ˈēz\ **Chal·kar–Ten·gis** \ˌchäl-ˌkär-teŋ-ˈēs\. Lake, cen. Kazakh S.S.R., U.S.S.R., ab. 110 m. NE of the Aral Sea.

Chelles \ˈshel\ *or anc.* **Ca·lae** \ˈkā-(ˌ)lē\. Commune, Seine-et-Marne dept., N France, near N bank of the Marne 7 m. E of Paris; pop. (1968c) 33,281; prehistoric remains found nearby, whence the name "Chellean epoch"; site of famous convent 650–1790.

Chelly Canyon \ˈshā-\. See *Canyon de Chelly National Monument* at UNITED STATES, *National Monuments.*

Chełm \ˈkelm, ˈhelm\ *or Russ.* **Kholm** \ˈkȯlm, ˈhȯlm\. Commune, Lublin prov., E Poland, 42 m. ESE of Lublin, just W of the Bug; pop. (1970p) 38,800; cathedral; trade center for fertile agricultural region. Founded 1237; to Poland 1377; to Austria 1795; part of Polish kingdom 1815; battle Aug. 1–3, 1915 resulting in German victory.

Chełm·no \ˈkelm-(ˌ)nō, ˈhelm-\; *Ger.* **Culm** *or* **Kulm** \ˈkülm\. Commercial and industrial commune, Bydgoszcz prov., N cen. Poland, on Vistula river 24 m. NNW of Toruń; pop. (1968e) 18,400; iron goods, beer. Founded 1231 by Teutonic Knights, made city 1233; member of the Hanse; belonged to Prussia 1773–1807, 1815–1919.

Chelms·ford \ˈchelm(p)s-fərd\. **1** Town, Middlesex co., NE Massachusetts, 4 m. SSW of Lowell; pop. (1970c) 31,432; beverages; truck farms.

2 Municipal borough, ⊗ of Essex, SE England, on the Chelmer 30 m. NE of London; pop. (1971p) 58,125; electrical equipment, roller bearings; grammar school (1551).

Chełm·ża \ˈkelm-(ˌ)zhä, ˈhelm-\; *Ger.* **Culm·see** *or* **Kulm·see** \ˈku̇lm-ˌzā\. Town, Bydgoszcz prov., N cen. Poland, 12 m.

N of Toruń; pop. (1968e) 14,600; 13th cent. cathedral; manufactures beet sugar, bricks; became town 1251.

Chel·sea \'chel-sē\. 1 Town, Kennebec co., SW Maine, 6 m. SE of Augusta; pop. (1970c) 2095.

2 Industrial city, Suffolk co., E Massachusetts, 3 m. NNE of Boston; pop. (1970c) 30,625; optical instruments, rubber and rubber goods, boots and shoes, chemicals; meat-packing; Mass. Soldiers' Home and U.S. Naval Hospital. Settled 1624, set off from Boston 1739; suffered great fire Apr. 12, 1908.

3 Village, Washtenaw co., SE Michigan, 15 m. W of Ann Arbor; pop. (1970c) 3858.

4 City, Rogers co., NE Oklahoma; pop. (1970c) 1622.

5 Village in Chelsea town (township), ⊗ of Orange co., E Vermont, 14 m. S of Barre; pop. (town, 1970c) 983.

6 Former metropolitan borough of London, SE England; now part of Kensington and Chelsea.

Chel·ten·ham \'chelt-^{ə}n-ˌham, 'chelt-nəm, -^{ə}n-əm\. 1 Township, Montgomery co., SE Pennsylvania, NNE of Philadelphia; pop. (1970c) 40,238.

2 Municipal borough, Gloucestershire, SW cen. England, on the river Chelt 42 m. S of Birmingham; pop. (1971p) 69,734; light industries; tourism; mineral springs; town first mentioned 1223.

Che·lya·binsk *also* **Che·lia·binsk** \chel-'yä-bən(t)sk\. City, ✱ of Chelyabinsk Oblast, Russian S.F.S.R., U.S.S.R., 125 m. S of Sverdlovsk; pop. (1970p) 874,000; industrial center; iron and steel, agricultural implements, leather goods; on the Trans-Siberian R.R. Founded 1658. Headquarters of Czechoslovak legion in fighting after Revolution of 1917.

Chelyabinsk Oblast \-'ó-bləst, -ˌblast\. Subdivision of the Russian S.F.S.R., U.S.S.R., E of southern Urals; 33,938 sq. m.; pop. (1970p) 3,289,000; ✱ Chelyabinsk. Has much fertile and forested land; chief crops wheat, rye, millet, oats; coal, magnesite, copper, zinc, chromite. In former Ural Area and since discovery after World War I of great deposits of iron (see MAGNITOGORSK) has formed the S part of the Ural Industrial Region (*q.v.*); heavy engineering; vehicles, chemicals, steel tubing. Chief cities Chelyabinsk, Magnitogorsk, Zlatoust, Kopeysk. Organized as an administrative subdivision 1934; in World War II greatly reduced by organization of Kurgan Oblast from its E part.

Che·lyus·kin, Cape *also* **Cape Che·lius·kin** \-chel-'yüs-kən\. Cape on Taimyr Penin., NW Russian S.F.S.R., U.S.S.R.; northernmost point of Asia, 77°45′N, 104°20′E.

Che·min des Dames \shə-ma^{n}-dā-'däm\. Highway ab. 4 m. N of and parallel with the Aisne river, N France, with its E end near Craonne; literally, "Ladies Road," so-called because constructed for the journeys of the daughters of Louis XV. Scene of severe fighting in World War I, esp. as phases of several important battles, Sept. 1914, Apr., May, and Oct. 1917, and May 1918. In World War II taken by Germans June 1940.

Chemmis. See AKHMĪM.

Chemnitz. See KARL-MARX-STADT.

Chemulpo. See INCH'ŎN.

Che·mung \shi-'məŋ\. 1 River, S New York; formed by confluence of Cohocton and Tioga rivers in Steuben co.; flows SE across Pennsylvania border and into Susquehanna river. See ELMIRA.

2 County in New York. See table at NEW YORK.

Che·na \'chē-nə\. River, cen. Alaska, flowing to the Tanana river ab. 6 m. WSW of Fairbanks; ab. 160 m. long.

Che·nab \chə-'näb\ *or anc.* **Aces·i·nes** \ə-'ses-^{ə}n-ˌēz\. River, one of the "Five Rivers" of the Punjab; rises in Himachal Pradesh in the Himalayas, India, flows NW, then W and SW through Jammu and Kashmir and W cen. Punjab, Pakistan, to unite with the Sutlej to form the Panjnad; joined by the Jhelum in W Punjab; 599 m. long; source of extensive canal and irrigation system.

Che·nan·go \shə-'naŋ-(ˌ)gō\. 1 River, rises near Madison-Oneida co. boundary, S cen. New York; flows S into Susquehanna river at Binghamton; ab. 100 m. long.

2 County in New York. See table at NEW YORK.

Chen–chiang \'jən-jē-'äŋ\ *also* **Chin·kiang** \'jin-jē-'äŋ, 'chin-kē-'aŋ\. City, Kiangsu prov., E China, on S bank of Yangtze 43 m. below Nanking at the junction of the Grand Canal with the river; pop. (1970e) 250,000. About 2000 years old; important in time of Marco Polo and under Ming and Manchu dynasties.

Chê·née \she-'nā\. Commune, Liège prov., Belgium, SE suburb of Liège; pop. (1969e) 12,126; aluminum; meat processing.

Che·ney \'chē-nē\. City, Spokane co., E Washington, 14 m. SSW of Spokane; pop. (1970c) 6358; Eastern Washington State Coll. (1890).

Cheney Cob·ble \-'käb-əl\. Peak in the Adirondack Mts., Essex co., NE New York; 3673 ft.

Chengchiatun. See SHUANGLIAO.

Cheng–chou *or* **Cheng·chow** \'jəŋ-'jō\ *or* **Cheng·hsien** \'jeŋ-shē-'en\. City, ✱ of Honan prov., on right bank of Yellow river, E cen. China, 40 m. W of K'ai-feng; pop. (1970e) 1,500,000; textile mills, thermal power plant; heavy machinery; important railroad junction of the north-south line (Peking to Hankow) and the west-east line (Sian to Tung-hai). Considerable fighting in 1944 for adjacent sections of the railroad.

Ch'eng–te \'chəŋ-'də\ *or* **Je·hol** \jə-'hōl, 'rō-'hō\. City, ✱ of former Jehol prov., now in Hopeh prov., NE China, on Luan river ab. 110 m. NE of Peking; pop. (1970e) 200,000; historically famous as the summer residence of the Manchu emperors of China. The imperial estates, begun 1703 by Emperor K'ang-hsi, covered a great park; here Emperor Ch'ien Lung received in 1793 the historic British trade mission under Lord Macartney.

Ch'eng–tu \'chəŋ-'dü\. City, ✱ of Szechwan prov., S cen. China; pop. (1970e) 2,000,000; bricks and tiles, machine tools; railroad repair shops; located on remarkable irrigation system of the Min and other streams devised more than 2000 years ago, the center of an exceptionally fertile region; univ. (1931), technical coll. (1954). One of the oldest cities of China; in early times for certain periods an imperial capital; walls and broad streets; tombs and other remains of early eras; World War II American air base for B-29 bombers 1944–45.

Chen–hai *or* **Chin·hai** \'jən-'hī\. City and port, NE Chekiang prov., E China, ab. 12 m. ENE of Ning-po on SE shore of Hangchow Bay.

Chenstokhov. See CZĘSTOCHOWA.

Chen–yüan \'jən-yü-'wän\. Town, E Kweichow, S China, 110 m. ENE of Kuei-yang.

Che·pach·et \chi-'pach-it\. Village, Providence co., N Rhode Island, ab. 15 m. NNW of Central Falls; governmental center of Glocester; dairy farms.

Che·po \'chā-(ˌ)pō\. River in E cen. Panama; flows W and SW into the Bay of Panama E of the city of Panama.

Chepping Wycombe. See HIGH WYCOMBE.

Chep·stow \'chep-(ˌ)stō\. Urban district, Monmouthshire, SE Wales, on Wye river; pop. (1971p) 16,096; high tides.

Cheq·uers \'chek-ərz\. A historic Tudor mansion in Buckinghamshire, 35 m. NW of London, England; presented to the government by Lord and Lady Lee of Fareham 1917; the official country seat of the prime minister of Great Britain.

Cher \'she(ə)r\. 1 River, cen. France; 217 m. long; rises in Creuse dept., flows NW into Loire river.

2 Department of cen. France. See table at FRANCE.

Che·ra·sco \ker-'äs-(ˌ)kō\. Commune, Cuneo prov., Piedmont, Italy, on Tanaro river ab. 22 m. NE of Cuneo; pop. (1968e) 6241; treaty Apr. 26, 1631 bet. France and Spain;

ə abut; ^{ə} kitten, Fr. table; ər further; a back; ā bake; ä cot, cart; à Fr. bac; aù out; ch chin; e less; ē easy; g gift
i trip; ī life; j joke; k̲ Ger. ich, Buch; ^{n} Fr. vin; ŋ sing; ō flow; ó flaw; œ Fr. bœuf; œ̄ Fr. feu; ói coin; th thin
t̲h̲ this; ü loot; ú foot; ue Ger. füllen; ue̅ Fr. rue; y yet; ^{y} Fr. digne \dēn^{y}\, nuit \nw^{y}ē\; yü few; yú furious; zh vision

armistice Apr. 28, 1796 bet. France and Sardinia that ended Sardinian support of Austria.

Che·raw \chi-'rȯ, 'chē-(ˌ)rȯ\. Town, Chesterfield co., NE South Carolina, on Pee Dee river 14 m. WNW of Bennettsville; pop. (1970c) 5627; textiles, brick; diversified farming; settled c. 1752; site of Confederate supply depot until captured by Sherman 1865.

Cher·bourg \'she(ə)r-ˌbu̇(ə)r(g), 'shər-, sher-'bu̇(ə)r\. Manufacturing seaport and naval arsenal, Manche dept., NW France, on N coast of Cotentin Penin. on English Channel; pop. (1968c) 38,243; strongly fortified; a major French naval station; consists of old or civil town and Port Militaire, the new or military town; transatlantic port of embarkation and debarkation; shipbuilding. Occupies site of ancient Roman station; under English rule to 1200; pillaged by English 1295; sustained sieges 1378, 1418, 1450; taken by English 1758 and held for ransom. In World War II held from June 1940 by Germans; attacked from S by Allies June 21–22, 1944, taken June 27; harbor practically destroyed by Germans.

Cher·chell *or* **Sher·shell** \sher-'shel\ *or anc.* **Cae·sa·rea** \ˌsē-zə-'rē-ə, ˌses-ə-, ˌsez-\. Seaport, N Al-Asnam dept., N Algeria; pop. (1966c) 11,667.

Cher·chen \jē-'ər-'cheŋ\. Town and oasis, S Sinkiang Uighur, W China, on Ch'e-erh-ch'en river; on caravan and motor highway.

Che·rem·kho·vo \chə-'rem-kə-ˌvō\. Town, S Irkutsk Oblast, Russian S.F.S.R., U.S.S.R., on Trans-Siberian R.R. 80 m. NW of Irkutsk; pop. (1969e) 104,000; heavy engineering; large coalfields nearby.

Che·ren \'kar-ān\ *or* **Ke·ren** \'kar-ən \. Town, E cen. Eritrea, Ethiopia, NE Africa; connected by rail with Asmara. Captured by British Mar. 28, 1941.

Che·re·po·vets \ˌcher-ə-pə-'vets\. City, SW Vologda Oblast, Russian S.F.S.R., U.S.S.R., 70 m. W of Vologda, near junction of Suda and Sheksna rivers just before they enter Rybinsk Reservoir (*q.v.*); pop. (1970p) 189,000; iron and steel works; shipbuilding, timberworking; originally a settlement (in Novgorod principality) which grew up near a monastery founded before 15th cent.; became a town 1780.

Cher·gui, Chott ech \ˌshät-ˌesh-'shər-gē\ *or Arab.* **Shatt al–Sher·gui** \-al-\. Marshy saline lake, NW Algeria.

Cher·i·bon \ˌcher-i-'bän\. 1 Former residency of Neth. Indies, now part of the Indonesian prov. of West Java, on coast of Java Sea; 2097 sq. m.; fertile coastal plain, with one high mountain Tjiremaj in the SE; chief products sugar and rice. A center of Islam in Java since 1526 but the sultanate became subject to the Dutch in 17th cent.
2 City, Indonesia. See TJIREBON.

Cher·kas·sy *or* **Cher·ka·si** \chər-'kas-ē, -'käs-\. City, ✱ of Cherkassy Oblast, Ukrainian S.S.R., U.S.S.R., on the Dnieper 100 m. SE of Kiev; pop. (1970p) 159,000; center of region raising sugar beets and tobacco; textiles; timber mills. In 15th cent. an important Cossack town, esp. for trading; under Polish rule until Chmielnicki's revolt 1648; became Russian 1795; held by Germans 1941–43.

Cherkassy Oblast \-'ȯ-bləst, -ˌblast\. Subdivision of the Ukrainian S.S.R., U.S.S.R.; 8069 sq. m.; pop. (1970p) 1,536,000; ✱ Cherkassy; important sugar-beet producing region; formed 1954.

Cher·kess Autonomous Oblast \cher-'kes . . . 'ȯ-bləst, -ˌblast\. Former autonomous region, Russian S.F.S.R., U.S.S.R., in valley of upper Kuban river; 1273 sq. m.; mountainous. United with the Karachayev Autonomous Oblast 1922–26 to form an autonomous unit; made a national district 1926 and raised to rank of autonomous region 1928; reunited with the Karachayev Autonomous Oblast 1936; reconstituted as a separate oblast 1944; reunited with Karachayev areas 1957. See KARACHAYEVO-CHERKESS AUTONOMOUS OBLAST.

Cher·kessk \cher-'kesk\; *formerly* **Ba·tal·pa·shinsk** \ˌbət-əl-pə-'shinsk\ *also* **Su·li·mov** \su̇-'lē-mȯf, su̇l-'yē-məf\. Town, ✱ of Karachayevo-Cherkess Autonomous Oblast, Russian S.F.S.R., U.S.S.R., on Kuban river 160 m. SE of Krasnodar; pop. (1970p) 67,000; railroad terminus; sawmills, oil presses, factories. For a time before World War II known as **Ye·zho·vo–Cherkessk** \'yā-zhə-və-\ but name restored to Cherkessk in 1938.

Cherna. See CRNA.

Cher·na·ya \'chōr-nə-yə\. Small river in the Crimean Oblast, Ukrainian S.S.R., U.S.S.R., E of Sevastopol; flows W into the Black Sea; scene of victory of Allies over Russians Aug. 16, 1855 during Crimean War.

Cherniakovsk. See CHERNYAKHOVSK.

Cher·ni·gov \cher-'nē-gəf\. 1 Medieval principality, cen. Russia, extending NE from Kiev to borders of Ryazan; ✱ Chernigov; at height of power in 11th and 12th cents.
2 City, ✱ of Chernigov Oblast, Ukrainian S.S.R., U.S.S.R., on right bank of Desna river 77 m. NNE of Kiev; pop. (1970p) 159,000; manufactures footwear, flour, textiles, musical instruments.

History: A very old town, mentioned as early as 907; in 11th cent. capital of Chernigov principality, at which time its cathedral (still preserved) was built; partly destroyed by Mongols 1240; annexed by Lithuania in 14th cent. but lost to Poland; occupied by Russia 1686; captured by Germans Sept. 13, 1941; retaken late in 1943.

Chernigov Oblast \-'ȯ-bləst, -ˌblast\. Subdivision of the Ukrainian S.S.R., U.S.S.R.; most of W boundary formed by the Dnieper; 12,317 sq. m.; pop. (1970p) 1,560,000; ✱ Chernigov; corn, tobacco, potatoes; livestock.

Cher·no·gorsk \ˌcher-nə-'gȯ(ə)rsk\. Town, Krasnoyarsk Krai, Russian S.F.S.R., U.S.S.R., ab. 160 m. SW of Krasnoyarsk; pop. (1969e) 63,000.

Cher·nov·tsy \cher-'nȯft-sē\ *or Rom.* **Cer·nă·u·ţi** \ˌcher-nə-'üts(-ē)\ *or Ger.* **Czer·no·witz** \'cher-nə-ˌvits\. Industrial and commercial city, ✱ of Chernovtsy Oblast and former ✱ of Bukovina, on right bank of Prut river; pop. (1970p) 187,000; chemicals, textiles; university, opened by Germans 1875. Grew from small village after Austrian occupation in 1775; battlefield 1915–17 in World War I; became Romanian 1918; ceded to U.S.S.R. 1940.

Chernovtsy Oblast \-'ȯ-bləst, -ˌblast\. Subdivision of the Ukrainian S.S.R., U.S.S.R.; 3217 sq. m.; pop. (1970p) 845,000; ✱ Chernovtsy; timber; formerly a department of Bukovina in N Romania; to U.S.S.R. 1940.

Chernoye More. See BLACK SEA.

Cher·nya·khovsk *also* **Cher·nia·kovsk** \chir-'nyäk-əfsk\ *or Ger.* **In·ster·burg** \'in-stər-ˌbərg, -ˌbu̇rg\. City, Kaliningrad Oblast, Russian S.F.S.R., U.S.S.R., on Angrapa river; pop. (1967e) 29,000; chemicals, tiles; railroad junction; formerly in East Prussia, Germany; 14th cent. castle. Founded c. 1336; became city 1583; taken by U.S.S.R. Jan. 1945; assigned to U.S.S.R. by Potsdam Conference 1945.

Cher·o·kee \'cher-ə-ˌkē, 'cher-ə-'\. 1 Name of counties in eight states of the U.S. See tables at ALABAMA, GEORGIA, IOWA, KANSAS, NORTH CAROLINA, OKLAHOMA, SOUTH CAROLINA, TEXAS.
2 City, ⊗ of Cherokee co., NW Iowa, 48 m. ENE of Sioux City; pop. (1970c) 7272; farm implements.
3 City, ⊗ of Alfalfa co., N Oklahoma, 38 m. NW of Enid; pop. (1970c) 2119; feed crops, livestock; milling.

Cherokee Dam. See table at TENNESSEE VALLEY AUTHORITY.

Cherokee Outlet. Strip of land along S border of Kansas; ab. 12,000 sq. m.; guaranteed to Cherokee Indians by treaties of 1828 and 1833; held by Cherokee Nation until 1891 when it was purchased by United States for ab. $8,596,000; opened to settlers Sept. 16, 1893; became part of Territory of Oklahoma; an adjoining region, **Cherokee Strip,** became part of Kansas.

Cher·ra·pun·ji *or earlier* **Cher·ra Poon·jee** \ˌcher-ə-'pu̇n-jē\. Village and former British military station, S Meghalaya, NE India; pop. (1961c) 4122; alt. ab. 4590 ft.; has record for world's heaviest rainfall (annual average 457 inches).

Cher·ry \'cher-ē\. County in Nebraska. See table at NEBRASKA.

Cherry Hill *or formerly* **Del·a·ware** \'del-ə-ˌwa(ə)r, -ˌwe(ə)r\. Urban township, Camden co., W cen. New Jersey, E of Camden; pop. (1970c) 14,395.

Cherry Hills Village. Town, Arapahoe co., NE cen. Colorado, 4 m. SE of Denver; pop. (1970c) 4605.

Cherry Island. See ANUDA ISLAND.

Cher·ry·vale \'cher-ē-ˌvāl\. City, Montgomery co., SE Kansas, 10 m. ENE of Independence; pop. (1970c) 2609; livestock; oil and gas wells.

Cherry Valley. Village, Otsego co., New York, 50 m. W of Albany; pop. (1970c) 661; medicinal springs; Cherry Valley Massacre by Butler's Rangers and Indians Nov. 11, 1778.

Cher·ry·ville \'cher-ē-ˌvil\. Town, Gaston co., SW North Carolina, 10 m. ENE of Shelby; pop. (1970c) 5258; cotton, machinery.

Cher·skó·go Range \cher-ˈskȯ-və-\ *also* **Cher·ski Range** \ˌcher-skē-\. Mountain range, NE Yakutsk A.S.S.R., Russian S.F.S.R., U.S.S.R., N of the Sea of Okhotsk; runs NW and SE; highest point 10,217 ft.

Cherso. See CRES.

Cher·so·nese, The \-'kər-sə-ˌnēz, -ˌnēs\ *or anc.* **Cher·so·ne·sus** \ˌkər-sə-'nē-səs\. Literally "peninsula"; in ancient geography applied to several peninsulas in Europe and Asia. See CRIMEAN OBLAST, GALLIPOLI PENINSULA, JUTLAND, KHERSON, MALAY PENINSULA.

Chert·sey \'chərt-sē\. Urban district, Surrey, S England, on S bank of the Thames; pop. (1971p) 44,886; market gardens.

Cher·well \'chär-wəl\. River, cen. England; 30 m. long; rises in Northamptonshire, flows S through Oxfordshire into the Thames (Isis) at Oxford.

Ches·a·ning \'ches-ə-ˌniŋ\. Village, Saginaw co., cen. Michigan, 20 m. SW of Saginaw; pop. (1970c) 2876.

Ches·a·peake \ˌches-(ə-)ˌpēk\. Independent city, SE Virginia, S of Norfolk; pop. (1970c) 89,580; cement, fertilizer; meat-packing; traversed by inland waterways; formed 1963 by merger of former city of South Norfolk and former county of Norfolk.

Chesapeake and Del·a·ware Canal \-'del-ə-wa(ər)-, -we(ə)r-\. Canal from Delaware City, Delaware, to Chesapeake City, Maryland, connecting Chesapeake and Delaware bays; ab. 14 m. long, 90 ft. wide, and 12 ft. deep at medium low water.

Chesapeake and Ohio Canal National Monument \-ō-'hī-(ˌ)ō-\. See UNITED STATES, *National Monuments.*

Chesapeake Bay. Inlet of Atlantic Ocean, its lower section in Virginia and its upper section in Maryland; 193 m. long, from 3 to 25 m. wide; ab. 3230 sq. m.; receives the Susquehanna river in the N, the Patuxent and Potomac on the W, the Chester, Choptank, and Nanticoke on the E, and the Rappahannock, York, and James rivers on the SW.

Chesapeake City. Town, Cecil co., NE Maryland; pop. (1970c) 1031; terminus of Chesapeake and Delaware Canal.

Chesh·am \'ches(h)-əm\. Urban district, Buckinghamshire, SE cen. England, 25 m. WNW of London; pop. (1971p) 20,416.

Chesh·ire \'chesh-ər, 'chesh-ˌi(ə)r\. **1** County in New Hampshire. See table at NEW HAMPSHIRE.

2 Residential town, N cen. New Haven co., S Connecticut, 5 m. WNW of Wallingford; pop. (1970c) 19,051; machine tool accessories; incorp. 1780.

3 Town, Berkshire co., W Massachusetts, 9 m. NNE of Pittsfield; pop. (1970c) 3006; dairy products, esp. cheese.

Cheshire *or* **Ches·ter** \'ches-tər\. County, NW England; 1015 sq. m.; pop. (1971p) 1,542,624; ⊗ Chester; rivers Dee, Weaver, and Mersey; farming, dairying (Cheshire cheese), coal and salt mining, shipbuilding; chemical, engineering, and textile plants; towns incl. Birkenhead, Stockport, Wallasey, Crewe, Macclesfield.

Chesh·ska·ya Bay \'chesh-(s)kə-yə, 'ches-kə-\. Inlet of the Arctic Ocean (Barents Sea), Arkhangelsk Oblast, N coast of Russian S.F.S.R., U.S.S.R., E Kanin Penin.

Ches·hunt \'ches-ənt\. Urban district, Hertfordshire, SE England, 15 m. N of London; pop. (1971p) 44,947.

Ches·ley \'ches-lē\. Town, Bruce co., SE Ontario, Canada, 22 m. S of Owen Sound; pop. (1971p) 1700.

Chesnokovka. See NOVOALTAISK.

Ches·ter \'ches-tər\. **1** River, E Maryland; ab. 40 m. long; flows W along boundary of Kent and Queen Annes cos. into Chesapeake Bay.

2 Name of counties in three states of the U.S. See tables at PENNSYLVANIA, SOUTH CAROLINA, TENNESSEE.

3 Town, S cen. Middlesex co., S Connecticut, on Connecticut river; pop. (1970c) 2982; settled as part of Saybrook (Deep River) c. 1690, incorp. 1836.

4 City, ⊗ of Randolph co., SW Illinois, on Mississippi river 58 m. SSE of East St. Louis; pop. (1970c) 5310; shipping center for iron, lead, sand, and coal.

5 Town, ⊗ of Liberty co., N Montana; pop. (1970c) 936; oil and gas wells.

6 City and port of entry, Delaware co., SE Pennsylvania, on Delaware river 14 m. WSW of Philadelphia; pop. (1970c) 56,331; shipbuilding yards, steel mills, automobile assembly plants, oil refineries; aircraft parts, chemicals, pharmaceuticals, electrical equipment; Crozer Theological Seminary (1867); Pennsylvania Military Coll. (1821; incorp. 1862). Settled by Swedes 1644 (second oldest settlement in Pa.); under Dutch control 1655, English control 1664; became borough 1701, ⊗ 1789–1851, city c. 1866.

7 City, ⊗ of Chester co., N South Carolina, 18 m. SSW of Rock Hill; pop. (1970c) 7045; cotton textiles, yarn, flour; bottling works.

8 Residential city, Hancock co., N tip of West Virginia panhandle, on Ohio river; pop. (1970c) 3614; potteries.

9 County in England. See CHESHIRE.

10 *anc.* **De·va** \'dē-və\ *or* **De·va·na Cas·tra** \di-ˌvän-ə-'kas-trə\. City and county borough, ⊗ of Cheshire, NW England, on the Dee 15 m. S of Liverpool; pop. (1971p) 62,696; manufactures leather goods and paint; window frames; active port and railroad center; tourism. Noted for its well-preserved walls, famous "Rows" of houses, and cathedral. For several centuries after 60 A.D. Roman "camp on the Dee"; after Romans left held in turn by British, Saxons, and Danes; rebuilt 907; last place in England to surrender (1070) to William the Conqueror; during 13th to 16th cents. scene of presentation of mystery plays of the Chester Cycle.

Ches·ter·field \'ches-tər-ˌfēld\. **1** Name of counties in two states of the U.S. See tables at SOUTH CAROLINA and VIRGINIA.

2 Town, Madison co., cen. Indiana, 12 m. SW of Muncie; pop. (1970c) 3001.

3 Town, ⊗ of Chesterfield co., NE South Carolina; pop. (1970c) 1667; cotton gins.

4 Village, ⊗ of Chesterfield co., Virginia.

5 Municipal borough, Derbyshire, N cen. England, 11 m. S of Sheffield; pop. (1971p) 70,153; furniture, surgical dressings; coal and iron mines, sandstone quarries; steelworks, textile mills, potteries; incorporated 1598.

Chesterfield Inlet. **1** Inlet of Hudson Bay, E Keewatin dist., Northwest Territories, N Canada; 140 m. long, 1 to 10 m. wide; inland expands into Baker Lake (*q.v.*).

2 Station on NW coast of Hudson Bay, Canada, on S side of mouth of Chesterfield Inlet.

Chesterfield Islands. Group of eleven coral islets in cen. Coral Sea, Australia, bet. N New Caledonia I. and E coast of Queensland; total area ab. 4 sq. m. Owned by France; uninhabited; guano deposits.

Ches·ter–le–Street \ˌches-tər-lə-ˈstrēt\. Urban district, Durham, N England, 10 m. S of Newcastle upon Tyne; pop. (1971p) 20,531; coal and iron mines nearby.

Ches·ter·ton \ˈches-tərt-ᵊn\. Town, Porter co., NW Indiana, 5 m. S of Lake Michigan; pop. (1970c) 6177; bronze die castings.

Ches·ter·town \ˈches-tər-ˌtau̇n\. Town, ⊗ of Kent co., NE Maryland, 32 m. ESE of Baltimore; pop. (1970c) 3476; chemicals; fisheries; seat of Washington Coll. (1706), of whose first board of governors George Washington was a member.

Chestnut, Mount \-ˈches-(ˌ)nət\. Peak, Rabun co., NE Georgia; 4600 ft.

Chestnut Hill. 1 Suburb of Boston, Massachusetts; Boston Coll. (1863), Pine Manor Junior Coll. (1911).
2 Residential district, NW Philadelphia (city), Pennsylvania; Chestnut Hill Coll. (1871).

Chestnut Ridge. Ridge extending from Preston co., West Virginia, NE to cen. Indiana co., W cen. Pennsylvania; ab. 130 m. long; highest point 2293 ft.

Che·sun·cook Lake \chə-ˈsən-ˌku̇k-\. Lake, cen. Piscataquis co., N cen. Maine; ab. 20 m. long; traversed by West Branch of the Penobscot river.

Ches·wick \ˈchez-wik\. Borough, Allegheny co., SW Pennsylvania, on Allegheny river 12 m. NE of Pittsburgh; pop. (1970c) 2580.

Che·to·pa \shə-ˈtō-pə\. City, Labette co., SE Kansas, 34 m. SW of Pittsburg; pop. (1970c) 1596.

Che·tu·mal \ˌchā-tü-ˈmäl\. Town, ✱ of Quintana Roo territory, E Yucatán penin., Mexico; pop. (1969e) 21,529.

Chetumal Bay. Inlet of NW Caribbean Sea, SE coast of Quintana Roo territory, Mexico, and NE coast of British Honduras; ab. 70 m. long.

Che·val Blanc, Pointe du \ˌpwaⁿt-dü-shə-ˌväl-ˈbläⁿk\ *or* **Cap à Foux** \ˌkap-ə-ˈfü\. Cape at NW tip of Hispaniola, on SE side of Windward Passage.

Chev·er·ly \ˈshev-ər-lē\. Town, Prince Georges co., S cen. Maryland, E of Washington, D.C.; pop. (1970c) 6808.

Chev·i·ot \ˈshiv-ē-ət, ˈshev-\. City, Hamilton co., SW corner of Ohio, 8 m. NW of Cincinnati; pop. (1970c) 11,135.

Cheviot Hills \ˈchev-ē-ət-, ˈshev-, ˈchiv-\. Range of hills extending NE to SW along the English-Scottish border; highest peak **Cheviot** 2676 ft.

Chew Bahir. See STEFANIE, LAKE.

Chey·enne \shī-ˈan, -ˈen\. 1 River, Wyoming and South Dakota; ab. 527 m. long; rises in E Wyoming; enters South Dakota in Fall River co., and flows generally NE, joining Missouri river in cen. South Dakota.
2 Name of counties in three states of the U.S. See tables at COLORADO, KANSAS, NEBRASKA.
3 Town, ⊗ of Roger Mills co., W Oklahoma; pop. (1970c) 892; Battle of Washita (Nov. 23, 1868) nearby.
4 City, ✱ of Wyoming and ⊗ of Laramie co., SE Wyoming, 10 m. N of Colorado border; pop. (1970c) 40,914; alt. 6100 ft.; railroad center; ships cattle and sheep; packing houses, oil refineries, creameries; launching pads for intercontinental ballistic missiles nearby; founded 1867, incorp. and made state capital 1869. See FORT FRANCIS E. WARREN.

Cheyenne Wells. Town, ⊗ of Cheyenne co., E Colorado; pop. (1970c) 982.

Chey·ney \ˈchā-nē\. Village, Delaware co., SE Pennsylvania, W of Media; Cheyney State Coll. (1837).

Chha·tar·pur \ˈchət-ər-ˌpu̇(ə)r\. Former Indian state, now part of Uttar Pradesh, N India; 1170 sq. m.; ✱ Chhatarpur.

Chhat·tis·garh \ˈchət-is-ˌgär\. 1 Former division, E Central Provinces, now part of Madhya Pradesh, India; 27,742 sq. m.; ✱ Raipur.
2 Former agency, forming a group of 16 Indian states, N, W, and S of Chhattisgarh division, geographically in E Central Provinces, India; 37,688 sq. m.; chief states Bastar, Surguja, Kalahandi, Patna.

Chhin·dwa·ra \chind-ˈwär-ə\. Town, S Madhya Pradesh, India, 64 m. NNW of Nagpur; pop. (1961c) 37,244.

Chhota Udepur. See CHOTA UDEPUR.

Chi \ˈchē\ *also* **Si** \ˈsē\. River, E Thailand; ab. 300 m. long; N, and chief tributary, of the Mun river, joining it at 50 m. above its mouth.

Chia·hsing \jē-ˈä-ˈshiŋ\ *or* **Ka·shing** \kä-ˈshiŋ\. City, Chekiang prov., E China, ab. 53 m. SW of Shanghai.

Chia–ling *also* **Kia·ling** \jē-ˈä-ˈliŋ\. River, cen. China; ab. 600 m. long; rises in the Min Shan in Kansu and Szechwan provs., and flows S into Yangtze river at Chungking; has important headstream tributary in Shensi prov.

Chiambone, Ras. See DICKS HEAD.

Chiamis. See TJIAMIS.

Chia–mu–ssu *or* **Kia·mu·sze** \jē-ˈä-mü-ˈsü\. City, Heilungkiang prov., China, on lower Sungari river 185 m. NE of Harbin; pop. (1970e) 275,000.

Chi–an *or* **Ki·an** \ˈjē-ˈän\ *also* **Lu·ling** \ˈlü-ˈliŋ\. Town, S cen. Kiangsi prov., SE China, on Kan river ab. 125 m. SSW of Nan-ch'ang; pop. (1970e) 100,000; on great trade highway from Canton N to Yangtze valley.

Chiana. See CHIANI.

Chiang–ling *or* **Kiang·ling** \jē-ˈäŋ-ˈliŋ\ *or formerly* **King–Chow** \ˈjiŋ-ˈjō\. Walled city on N bank of Yangtze, S Hupeh prov., E cen. China, 2 m. W of Sha-shih (*q.v.*); one of the oldest of Chinese cities, called by various names in different periods; once the capital of kingdom of Chu (8th–5th cent. B.C.); under the Manchus was a great garrison town; has many temples; enclosed by a wall 30 ft. high.

Chiang Mai \jē-ˈäŋ-ˈmī\ *or* **Chieng·mai** \jē-ˈeŋ-ˈmī\ *or* **Kiang·mai** \jē-ˈäŋ-ˈmī, kē-\. 1 Province, NW Thailand; 8878 sq. m.; pop. (1960c) 798,483; ✱ Chiang Mai.
2 City, its ✱, on upper course of Ping river ab. 80 m. E of Burma border; pop. (1970p) 89,272; important trade center, esp. in teak; railroad terminus; univ. (1964); formerly capital of united Lao kingdom, later subject to Burma.

Chiang–men \jē-ˈäŋ-ˈmən\ *or* **Kong·moon** \ˈkäŋ-ˈmün\ *or* **Kong·moon·fow** \-ˈfō\. Town, cen. Kwangtung prov., SE China, in W part of Hsi delta, ab. 45 m. above Macao; pop. (1970e) 150,000; made a treaty port 1904.

Chiang Rai \chē-ˈäŋ-ˈrī\ *or* **Chieng·rai** \chē-ˈeŋ-ˈrī\. 1 Province, N Thailand; 7260 sq. m.; pop. (1960c) 811,771; ✱ Chiang Rai.
2 Town, its ✱, on tributary of the Mekong 90 m. NE of Chiang Mai; pop. (1960c) 11,659; trading town on junction of highways N to Burma and NW Indochina and S to Lampang.

Ch'iang–t'ang *or* **Chang Tang** \ˈjäŋ-ˈdäŋ\. Northern region of Tibet (*q.v.*), China; a desert plateau at average altitude of 17,000 ft.; has many lakes, including Na-mu Hu.

Chiang–yin *or* **Kiang·yin** \jē-ˈäŋ-ˈyin\. Town, S Kiangsu prov., E China, on the Yangtze 80 m. NW of Shanghai; center of large junk traffic on the river.

Chia·ni \kē-ˈän-ē\ *or* **Chia·na** \-ə\. River, cen. Italy, flowing N from near Chiusi to the Arno at Arezzo; ab. 25 m. long; its valley **Val·le di Chiana** \ˌväl-ā-dē-\, formerly marshy and malarial, has been drained and canalized.

Chian–ning. See NANKING.

Chi·an·ti Mountains \kē-ˌänt-ē-, -ˌant-\ *or Ital.* **Mon·ti Chianti** \ˌmȯnt-ē-kē-ˈänt-ē\. Mountain range of the Apennines in Tuscany, cen. Italy. The region is noted for its wines, esp. a dry red variety.

Chiao–hsien *or* **Kiao·hsien** \je-ˈau̇-ˈshen\ *or formerly* **Kiao-chow** \jē-ˈau̇-ˈjō\. Town, NW of Chiao-chou Bay and ab. 25 m. NW of Tsingtao (45 m. by rail), Shantung prov., NE China; once prosperous but has now lost much of its trade.

Chiao Hsien \jē-ˈau̇-ˈshen\ *or* **Kiao·chow** \jē-ˈau̇-ˈjō\. Former German territory, SE Shantung prov., NE China, surrounding **Chiao–chou Bay** \ˈjē-ˈau̇-ˈjō-\ (area 200 sq. m.); under German control 1898–1914; chief town Tsingtao (*q.v.*).

Chiao–tso *or* **Tsiao·tso** \ˈjau̇-tsō, ˈchau̇-\. Town, Honan prov., China, ab. 40 m. NW of Cheng-chou; pop. (1970e) 300,000.

Chiapas. State of SE Mexico. See table at MEXICO.

Chia·ra·mon·te Gul·fi \kē-ˌär-ə-ˌmōn-tē-ˈgül-fē\. Commune, Ragusa prov., SE Sicily, Italy; pop. (1968e) 9230.

Chia·ri \kē-ˈär-ē\ *or anc.* **Clar·i·um** \ˈklar-ē-əm, ˈkler-\. Commune, Brescia prov., Lombardy, N Italy, 16 m. W of Brescia; pop. (1968e) 16,149; textiles; old fortifications; scene of defeat of French and Spanish army by Prince Eugene Sept. 1, 1701.

Chias·so \ˈkyäs-ˌō\. Commune, Ticino canton, Switzerland, on Italian frontier W of SW end of Lake Como; pop. (1970c) 8868; tobacco; customs station on St. Gotthard railroad.

Chi·a·tu·ra \chē-ˈät-ủr-ə\ *or* **Chi·a·tu·ri** \-rē\. Town, cen. Georgian S.S.R., U.S.S.R., in S foothills of Caucasus Mts. ab. 85 m. NW of Tbilisi; pop. (1967e) 27,000; rich manganese mines.

Chia·va·ri \kē-ˈäv-ə-rē\. Commune, Genova prov., Liguria, NW Italy, on Gulf of Rapallo 22 m. ESE of Genoa; pop. (1968e) 28,036; manufactures silk, lace; fisheries.

Chia·ven·na \kyä-ˈven-ə\. Town, Sondrio prov., N Lombardy, Italy, at N end of Lake Como; pop. (1968e) 7052; S terminal of Splügen Pass.

Chia–yü–kuan \jē-ˈä-yü-ˈgwän\. See GREAT WALL.

Chiazza. See PIAZZA ARMERINA.

Chi·ba \ˈchē-bə\. 1 Prefecture, Honshū, Japan; 1950 sq. m.; pop. (1970c) 3,366,624; ✱ Chiba; rice; fisheries.
2 City, its ✱, on E shore of Tokyo Bay; pop. (1970c) 482,133; steel mill; univ. (1949); capital of a powerful daimio family 12th–16th cents.; reduced to a poor fishing village at end of 16th cent., but now prosperous commercial city.

Chi·bou·ga·mau \shə-ˈbü-gə-ˌmü\. Town, Abitibi co., SW Quebec, Canada, 150 m. NW of Roberval; pop. (1966c) 8902; gold mines, sawmill.

Chibyu. See UKHTA.

Chi·ca·go \shə-ˈkäg-(ˌ)ō, -ˈkȯg-\. 1 Small river in Chicago, Illinois, consisting of North Branch and South Branch; South Branch connected with the Des Plaines river at Lockport by the **Chicago Drainage Canal**, since 1930 called the **Sanitary and Ship Canal** (see ILLINOIS WATERWAY).
2 City, ⊗ of Cook co., NE Illinois, on Lake Michigan; pop. (1970c) 3,369,359; important port and 2d largest city in United States; a major industrial, commercial, and transportation center; steel, chemicals, diesel engines, electrical and agricultural machinery, plastics, telephone equipment, furniture, primary metals; food processing, metalworking; Chicago Board of Trade, Chicago Mercantile Exchange; Chicago Public Library, John Crerar Library, Shedd Aquarium, Planetarium, Field Museum of Natural History, Chicago Art Institute; its educational institutions include: St. Xavier Coll. (1846), Chicago State Coll. (1869), Loyola Univ. (1869), American Conservatory of Music (1886), Univ. of Chicago (1891), Illinois Inst. of Technology (1892), De Paul Univ. (1898), Chicago Technical Coll. (1904), Northwestern Univ. (branch; 1926), Mundelein Coll. (1930), Chicago City Coll. (1931), Roosevelt Univ. (1945), Univ. of Illinois (branch; 1946), Central Y.M.C.A. Community Coll. (1960), Northeastern Illinois Coll. (1961).
History: In 17th cent. name associated with portage (bet. Des Plaines and Chicago rivers) which connected St. Lawrence-Great Lakes system with Mississippi; strategic position on route for travel to Mississippi important to French, British, and Americans; tract, 6 miles square, at river mouth, acquired by U.S. from Indians 1795; Fort Dearborn built 1803, abandoned during War of 1812; gradually settled from 1830 and received city charter 1837; expanded rapidly after completion of Illinois and Michigan Canal 1848, connecting Chicago and Mississippi rivers, and its connection with railroads from east 1853; more than half destroyed by great fire of 1871; scene of Haymarket riot 1886, Pullman strike 1894.

Chicago Heights. Industrial city, Cook co., NE Illinois, 27 m. S of Chicago; pop. (1970c) 40,900; chemicals, steel, glass containers; Bloom Community Coll. (1958), Prairie State Coll. (1958).

Chicago Ridge. Village, Cook co., NE Illinois, SW of Chicago; pop. (1970c) 9187.

Chi·ca·pa \shi-ˈkap-ə\. River in the Congo basin, S Africa; 310 m. long; rises in E cen. Angola, flows N into Kasai river.

Chich·a·gof \ˈchich-ə-ˌgȯf, -ˌgäf\. Island, NW Alexander Archipelago, SE Alaska, N of Baranof I.

Chichagof Harbor. Inlet on NE coast of Attu I. at W end of Aleutian Is.; Japanese force wiped out here May–June 1943.

Chi·chén It·zá \chə-ˌchen-ət-ˈsä\. Village in Yucatán state, Mexico, ab. 20 m. W of Valladolid; once one of the principal centers of the Mayas; extensive ruins, but some of the temples, pyramids, towers, etc., of brick, marble, or stone, rich with sculptures, are still well preserved; numerous artifacts recovered through research project initiated 1961.

Chich·es·ter \ˈchich-ə-stər\. Municipal borough, ⊗ of West Sussex, S England, 16 m. ENE of Portsmouth; pop. (1971p) 20,547; early Norman cathedral (begun c. 1090); remains of city walls, constructed c. 200 A.D.

Chi·chi·bu \ˈchē-chē-ˌbü\. City, Saitama prefecture, Honshū, Japan, 45 m. NW of Tokyo; pop. (1970c) 60,867.

Ch'i–ch'i–ha–erh \ˈchi-ˈchi-ˈhä-ˈe(ə)r\ *or formerly* **Lung-kiang** \ˈlụŋ-jē-ˈäŋ\ *or Jap.* **Tsi·tsi·har** \ˈ(t)sēt-sē-ˌhär, ˈchē-chē-\. City and port, China, on left bank of Nen river 170 m. NW of Harbin; pop. (1970e) 1,500,000.

Chi·chi–shi·ma \ˌchē-chē-ˈshē-mə\ *also* **Chi·chi Ji·ma** \-ˈjē-mə\. 1 Group of islands in the Bonin Is., Japan.
2 Largest island in the group and in the Bonin Is.

Chick·a·hom·i·ny \ˌchik-ə-ˈhäm-ə-nē\. River, E Virginia; ab. 90 m. long; rises 16 m. NW of Richmond, flows SE into James river.

Chick·a·mau·ga \ˌchik-ə-ˈmȯ-gə\. City, Walker co., NW Georgia, 18 m. WNW of Dalton; pop. (1970c) 1842; near **Chickamauga Creek** (tributary of the Tennessee river) where a battle was fought Sept. 19–20, 1863 in which Confederates under Bragg defeated Unionists under Rosecrans; part of the campaign for Chattanooga.

Chickamauga and Chat·ta·noo·ga National Military Park \-ˌchat-ə-ˈnü-gə-, -ˌchat-ᵊn-ˈü-\. See UNITED STATES, *National Historical Parks.*

Chickamauga Dam. See table at TENNESSEE VALLEY AUTHORITY.

Chick·a·saw \ˈchik-ə-ˌsȯ\. 1 Name of counties in two states of the U.S. See tables at IOWA and MISSISSIPPI.
2 City, Mobile co., SW Alabama, NW of Prichard; pop. (1970c) 8447; sheet metal.

Chickasaw Bayou. An arm of the Mississippi river, W Mississippi, just N of Vicksburg and near the lower Yazoo; attack Dec. 29, 1862 by Union forces on heights (**Chickasaw Bluffs**) along its bank unsuccessful in attempt to capture Vicksburg.

Chick·a·sa·whay \ˌchik-ə-ˈsȯ-(ˌ)wā\ *or* **Chick·a·sa·wha** \-wə\. River, SE Mississippi; 210 m. long; rises in E cen. Mississippi, flows S to unite with Leaf river in N George co. and form Pascagoula river.

Chick·a·sha \ˈchik-ə-ˌshā\. City, ⊗ of Grady co., cen. Oklahoma, on Washita river 40 m. SW of Oklahoma City; pop. (1970c) 14,190; cottonseed oil, flour, machinery; dairy products; cattle raising; oil and gas wells; Oklahoma Coll. of Liberal Arts (1908).

Chi·cla·na de la Fron·te·ra \chē-ˈklän-ə-ˌdel-ə-ˌfrən-ˈter-ə\. Commune, Cádiz prov., SW Spain, 12 m. SE of Cádiz; pop. (1970p) 27,337; thermal sulfur baths.

Chi·cla·yo \chə-'klī-(,)ō\. Coastal city, ✱ of Lambayeque dept., NW Peru; pop. (1969e) 134,709; in rice and sugar district; univ. (1962), agricultural coll. (1963); its ports are Eten and Pimentel.

Chi·co \'chē-(,)kō\. 1 City, Butte co., N California, 80 m. N of Sacramento; pop. (1970c) 19,580; food processing and packing; beet sugar, lumber, cement; settled 1847, incorporated as city 1923; Chico State Coll. (1887).

2 Either of two rivers in S Argentina, one flowing NE out of Lake Musters in S Chubut prov. and emptying into Chubut river, the other in Santa Cruz prov. flowing SE into Atlantic Ocean at Santa Cruz.

3 River, NE Luzon, Phil.; 140 m. long; a W tributary of the Cagayan.

4 *or* **Pam·pan·ga Chico** \päm-,päŋ-gə-\. River, cen. Luzon, Phil.; ab. 60 m. long; a W tributary of the Pampanga river; flows S.

Chi·con·te·pec \chē-'cȯnt-ə-,pek\. Municipality, Veracruz state, Mexico, 95 m. SSW of Tampico; pop. (1970p) 46,633.

Chic·o·pee \'chik-ə-(,)pē\. 1 River, SW cen. Massachusetts; formed by junction of Quaboag and Swift rivers in N Hampden co., flows W into Connecticut river.

2 City, Hampden co., SW Massachusetts, on Connecticut river 3 m. N of Springfield; pop. (1970c) 66,676; includes **Chicopee Falls, Chicopee Center, Wil·li·man·sett** \,wil-ə-'man(t)-sət\, **Fair·view** \'fa(ə)r-,vyü, 'fe(ə)r-\, and **Al·den·ville** \'ȯl-dən-,vil\; manufactures rubber and rubber goods, sporting goods, meat products; Coll. of Our Lady of the Elms (1928); Westover Field, U.S. Air Force base, is nearby.

Chi·cot \'shē-(,)kō\. County in Arkansas. See table at ARKANSAS.

Chicot, Point. Point on E coast of St. Bernard parish, SE Louisiana, on Breton Sound.

Chi·cou·ti·mi \shə-'küt-ə-mē\. 1 River, S Quebec, Canada; ab. 100 m. long; rises in Laurentides Provincial Park, flows N to Lake Kenogami and then E to the Saguenay at Chicoutimi; in its lower course drops nearly 500 ft.; noted for its scenery.

2 County, Quebec, Canada. See table at QUEBEC.

3 City, its ⊗, on Saguenay river at head of navigation at mouth of Chicoutimi river; pop. (1971p) 32,990; lumber, pulp, paper, aluminum; diversified farming; Univ. of Quebec (branch; 1969); center of great waterpower developments; founded 1676.

Chicoutimi–nord. See NORTH CHICOUTIMI.

Chi·dam·ba·ram \chi-'dəm-bə-rəm\. Town, N cen. Tamil Nadu, S India, 125 m. SSW of Madras; pop. (1961c) 40,694; has numerous pagodas and temples, the principal temple sacred to Siva, much visited by pilgrims.

Chid·ley, Cape \-'chid-lē\. Cape at N tip of Labrador, Canada, on Killinek I. on S side of entrance to Hudson Strait.

Chief Mountain \'chēf-\. Peak in Glacier National Park, NW Montana; 9066 ft.

Chief's Head \'chēfs-\. Peak, Boulder co., N cen. Colorado; 13,579 ft.

Chiem, Lake \-'kēm\ *or Ger.* **Chiem·see** \'kēm-,zā\. Largest lake in Bavaria, West Germany, ab. 40 m. ESE of Munich; 31 sq. m.; 1699 ft. above sea level; has three islands; outlet is the Alz with course of 30 m. to the Inn.

Chiengmai. See CHIANG MAI.

Chiengrai. See CHIANG RAI.

Chien–ou *or* **Kien·ow** \jē-'en-'ō\ *or* **Kien·ning** \jē-'en-'niŋ\. Town, N cen. Fukien prov., SE China, on tributary of Min river 95 m. NW of Foochow; in World War II had American air base; captured by Japanese 1944.

Chie·ri \kē-'e(ə)r-ē\. Commune, Torino prov., Piedmont, NW Italy, 8 m. SE of Turin; pop. (1968e) 26,718; textiles; walled city; large Gothic church.

Chie·ti \kē-'et-ē\. 1 Province of Abruzzi, cen. Italy. See table at ITALY.

2 *or anc.* **Te·a·te** \tē-'āt-ē\. Commune, its ✱, near right bank of Pescara river 93 m. ENE of Rome; pop. (1968e) 52,718; archiepiscopal see; textiles; univ. (1961); Gothic church. Ruled successively by Greeks, Romans, Lombards, Franks, and Normans; under Normans was capital of the Abruzzi; taken by French 1802; Theatine Order named for ancient city.

Chi·et·la \chē-'āt-lə\. Municipality, Puebla state, Mexico, 80 m. SSE of Mexico City; pop. (1970p) 26,921; sugarcane, fruit growing.

Chi·ga·sa·ki \,chē-gə-'sä-kē\. City, Kanagawa prefecture, Honshū, Japan, ab. 16 m. SW of Yokohama; pop. (1970c) 129,621.

Chigha Khur. See CHAGHĀ KŪR.

Chi·gha Sa·rāi \chi-,gä-sə-'rī\. Town, ✱ of Konarhā prov., NE Afghanistan; pop. (1969e) 28,041.

Chig·nec·to \shig-'nek-(,)tō\. Isthmus joining Nova Scotia, Canada, to the mainland, comprising Cumberland co. and part of Colchester co.; in its narrowest part, at Amherst, ab. 12 m. wide; on N borders on Northumberland Strait and on S on Chignecto Bay and Minas Basin.

Chignecto Bay. N extremity of Bay of Fundy, Canada, bet. SE New Brunswick and NW Nova Scotia mainland; 50 m. long; extremely high tides.

Chig·nik \'chig-nik\. Bay, inlet on SE coast of Alaska Penin., S Alaska.

Chig·well \'chig-,wel, -wəl\. Urban district, Essex, SE England; pop. (1971p) 53,620.

Chih–chiang *or* **Chih·kiang** \'jə-'jäŋ, 'ji(ə)r-\ *or formerly* **Yuan·chow** \yü-'än-'jō\. City, W Hunan prov., SE cen. China, on railroad 210 m. WSW of Ch'ang-sha near border of Kweichow prov. In World War II important American air base unsuccessfully attacked by Japanese Apr.–May 1945.

Chih·li \'chē-'lē, 'ji(ə)r-\. 1 Former province in NE China; 115,830 sq. m.; ✱ Peking; divided 1928 largely into Hopeh, Jehol, and Chahar.

2 Province, China. See HOPEH.

Chihli, Gulf of *or* **Po Hai** \'bō-'hī\. The NW arm of the Yellow Sea enclosed by S Manchuria and Hopei and Shantung provs. of China; its NE extension is the Gulf of Liaotung.

Chih–lieh–p'u. See JELEP–LA.

Chi–hsi \'chē-'shē\. Town, Heilungkiang prov., China, ab. 210 m. ESE of Harbin; pop. (1970e) 350,000.

Chi·hua·hua \chə-'wä-(,)wä, shə-, -wə\. 1 State of N Mexico. See table at MEXICO.

2 City, its ✱; munic. pop. (1970p) 363,850; alt. 4600 ft.; univ. (1954); center of rich silver-mining district.

Chi·jol Canal \chē-'hōl-\. Canal, E Veracruz state, Mexico, connecting Tampico (Pánuco river) with Tuxpan; 6 ft. deep, 25 ft. wide.

Chi·ku·ho \'chē-kü-'hō\. Town, Fukuoka prefecture, N Kyūshū, Japan; pop. (1970c) 10,573; largest coal mines in Japan.

Chikuraj. See TJIKURAJ.

Chilachap. See TJILATJAP.

Chi·la·pa \chi-'läp-ə-\ *or in full* **Chilapa de Al·va·rez** \-dā-'äl-və-,rez\. Town, Guerrero, S Mexico; munic. pop. (1970p) 53,263; fruit growing.

Chil·co·tin \chil-'kōt-ᵊn\. River, S cen. British Columbia, Canada; 145 m. long; flows SE into Fraser river.

Chil·ders·burg \'chil-dərz-,bərg\. City, Talladega co., E cen. Alabama, 38 m. SE of Birmingham; pop. (1970c) 4831; lumber, chemicals; diversified agriculture.

Chil·dress \'chil-drəs\. 1 County in NW Texas. See table at TEXAS.

2 City, its ⊗, 80 m. E of Plainview; pop. (1970c) 5408; flour mills; railroad division point.

Chile \'chil-ē\. Republic, SW South America, bounded on N by Peru and Bolivia, on E by Argentina, on S by Drake Passage, and on W by the Pacific Ocean; 292,256 sq. m.; pop. (1970p) 8,834,820; ✱ Santiago.

Physical features: Long, narrow country bet. Andes Mts. and the Pacific Ocean; approx. 2650 m. long (from ab. 17°30'S to Cape Horn at 55°59'S) and nowhere above 221

m. wide. Has low coastal ranges; N part is high plateau (desert of Atacama). In N includes several peaks above 19,000 ft. (Copiapó, Palpana, Llullaillaco), but most of highest Andean peaks are on the boundaries with Bolivia and Argentina. Has no rivers of any size; largest Loa, Bío-Bío, Maipo, Itata, Maule, Copiapó; many lakes in S cen. part in resort region (Llanquihue, Ranco); S of 42° coast marked by many inlets, islands, and archipelagoes; owns W half of Tierra del Fuego and island on which is Cape Horn; also possesses small islets of Juan Fernández, Easter I., and others far out in the Pacific. *Chief export:* Copper; other products: nitrates, iodine, coal, iron ore, lead, oil; wheat, barley, fruit, sugar, tobacco. *Chief cities:* Santiago, Valparaíso, Concepción, Viña del Mar, Antofagasta, Talcahuano, Temuco, Talca. Divided into the following 25 provinces (for pronunciation of their names, see their individual entries):

NAME	AREA (sq. m.)	POP. (1970p)	CAPITAL
Aconcagua	3,812	160,821	San Felipe
Antofagasta	48,380	250,665	Antofagasta
Arauco	2,023	98,810	Lebu
Atacama	30,219	152,326	Copiapó
Aysén	39,993	51,022	Puerto Aysén
Bío-Bío	4,299	193,002	Los Ángeles
Cautín	7,095	420,682	Temuco
Chiloé	10,429	110,728	Ancud
Colchagua	3,215	167,899	San Fernando
Concepción	2,193	638,118	Concepción
Coquimbo	15,307	336,821	La Serena
Curicó	2,033	113,710	Curicó
Linares	3,634	189,010	Linares
Llanquihue	7,029	197,986	Puerto Montt
Magallanes[1]	50,978	88,706	Punta Arenas
Malleco	5,442	176,060	Angol
Maule	2,199	82,339	Cauquenes
Ñuble	5,386	314,738	Chillán
O'Higgins	2,743	306,739	Rancagua
Osorno	3,566	158,673	Osorno
Santiago	6,828	3,217,870	Santiago
Talca	3,915	231,008	Talca
Tarapacá	22,421	174,730	Iquique
Valdivia	7,132	275,404	Valdivia
Valparaíso	1,976	726,953	Valparaíso

[1]Includes Strait of Magellan and all Chilean islands of the Tierra del Fuego archipelago (*q.v.*).

History: In 15th cent. northern part conquered by Incas; first invaded by Spanish under Almagro 1536–37; settlement begun at Santiago by Pedro de Valdivia 1541; governed under viceroyalty of Peru, becoming a separate captaincy general 1778; revolted against Spain 1810, but not finally independent until Feb. 12, 1818, after battle of Chacabuco (1817); independence assured by victory of San Martín at Maipo Apr. 5, 1818; governed by O'Higgins to 1823; under presidency of Prieto (1831–41), received centralized constitution 1833 and orderly conservative government; fought confederation of Peru and Bolivia (see YUNGAY) 1836–39; took part in war with Spain 1866; in War of the Pacific against Peru and Bolivia 1879–84, won the rich nitrate fields on coast of Bolivia (see ANTOFAGASTA and IQUIQUE) and occupied Tacna and Arica (*qq. v.*) which, until 1929, were subject of dispute with Peru; boundary disputes with Argentina 1899 and 1902 settled by arbitration; neutral in World War I; adopted new constitution 1925; member of League of Nations 1919–38; neutral in World War II; initiated reform program 1964; following national election, Marxist candidate appointed president by Congress 1970.

Chiledug. See TJILEDUG.

Chilia. See KILIYA 1.

Chilia–Nouă. See KILIYA 2.

Chi·li·an·wa·la *or* **Chil·li·an·wa·la** \ˌchil-ē-än-ˈwäl-ə\. Village, Punjab, Pakistan, 5 m. E of the Jhelum; battle Jan. 13, 1849 in Sikh Wars in which English under Sir Hugh Gough defeated Sikhs.

Chi–lin. See KIRIN 4.

Chil·ka Lake \ˌchil-kə-\. Shallow inland gulf on the NE coast of India, in E Orissa state.

Chil·kat \ˈchil-ˌkat\. River, SE Alaska; flows SE to **Chilkat Inlet** at head of Lynn Canal (*q.v.*).

Chil·ko Lake \ˌchil-ˌkō-\. Lake, S cen. British Columbia, Canada; 75 sq. m.; outlet is the **Chilko River** flowing N into Chilcotin river.

Chil·koot Inlet \ˈchil-ˌküt-\. E arm of Lynn Canal (*q.v.*), SE Alaska.

Chilkoot Pass. Pass in coast range, N Rocky Mts.; highest point 3502 ft.; extends 29 m. from former village of Dyea at head of Taiya Inlet, Lynn Canal, SE Alaska, to Lake Bennett in Yukon Territory, Canada; used 1896–98 by gold seekers until opening of White Pass farther E.

Chil·la·lo \chə-ˈläl-ˌō\. Peak, cen. Ethiopia; 13,241 ft.

Chi·llán \chē-ˌ(y)än\. Commercial city, ✱ of Ñuble prov., S cen. Chile, 56 m. NE of Concepción; pop. (1966e) 77,654; birthplace of the liberator Bernardo O'Higgins; orig. town, known as **Chillán Vie·jo** \-ˈvyā-hō\, now a subdivision of the city (pop. 6058), founded 1579; destroyed by earthquake 1835 and rebuilt on present site 1836; again suffered severe earthquake destruction 1939. About 45 m. SE are the hot sulfur springs of Chillán, discovered 1795.

Chillán, Ne·va·dos de \nə-ˌväd-(ˌ)ōs-ˌdā-\. Mountain range, S cen. Chile; highest peak **Vol·cán Chillán** \vōl-ˌkän-\ 10,370 ft., volcano active 1861, 1864.

Chil·li·cothe \ˌchil-ə-ˈkäth-ē, -ˈkȯ-thē\. **1** City, Peoria co., NW cen. Illinois, on Illinois river N of Peoria; pop. (1970c) 6052.

2 City, ⊗ of Livingston co., N Missouri, 75 m. NE of Kansas City; pop. (1970c) 9519; in dairy-farming and livestock-raising region; coal and limestone deposits nearby.

3 Industrial city, ⊗ of Ross co., S Ohio, on Scioto river 44 m. S of Columbus; pop. (1970c) 24,842; shoes, paper, aluminum products; in agricultural and coal-mining region. Camp Sherman is N of city. Settled 1796; became capital of Northwest Territory 1800, capital of new state of Ohio 1803–10, 1812–16.

Chil·li·wack \ˈchil-ə-ˌwak\. City, S British Columbia, Canada, on left bank of Fraser river 55 m. E of Vancouver; pop. (1971p) 8848; fruit canneries, sawmills.

Chil·lon \shē-ˈ(y)ōⁿ, shil-ˈän, ˈshil-ˌän, ˈshil-ən\. Castle in Vaud, W Switzerland, at E end of Lake Geneva; place of imprisonment 1530–36 of François de Bonnivard, hero of Lord Byron's poem *The Prisoner of Chillon.*

Chi·loé \ˌchē-lə-ˈwā\. **1** Island in Pacific Ocean off SW coast of Chile; ab. 4700 sq. m.; forms with several smaller islands a province of Chile; coal deposits.

2 Province of S Chile. See table at CHILE.

Chi·lón \chē-ˈlōn\. Municipality, Chiapas state, Mexico, 60 m. NE of Tuxtla Gutierrez; pop. (1970p) 27,620; timber, agriculture.

Chil·pan·cin·go *or in full* **Chilpancingo de los Bra·vos** \ˌchil-pən-ˈsiŋ-(ˌ)gō-da-los-ˈbrä-vos\. Town, ✱ of Guerrero state, S Mexico; munic. pop. (1970p) 56,904; univ. (1869).

Chil·tern Hills \ˈchil-tərn-\ *or* **Chil·terns** \-tərnz\. Range of chalk hills, Oxfordshire and Buckinghamshire, S cen. England; 55 m. long; highest point Coombe Hill ab. 850 ft.

Chiltern Hundreds. Three *hundreds* (early divisions of a county)—Stoke, Burnham, and Desborough—in the Chiltern Hills, Buckinghamshire, England, the stewardship of which has long been a nominal office under the Chancellor of the Exchequer.

Chil·ton \ˈchilt-ᵊn\. **1** County in Alabama. See table at ALABAMA.

2 City, ⊗ of Calumet co., E Wisconsin, 18 m. E of Oshkosh; pop. (1970c) 3030; cheese, flour; aluminum, laminated wood products.

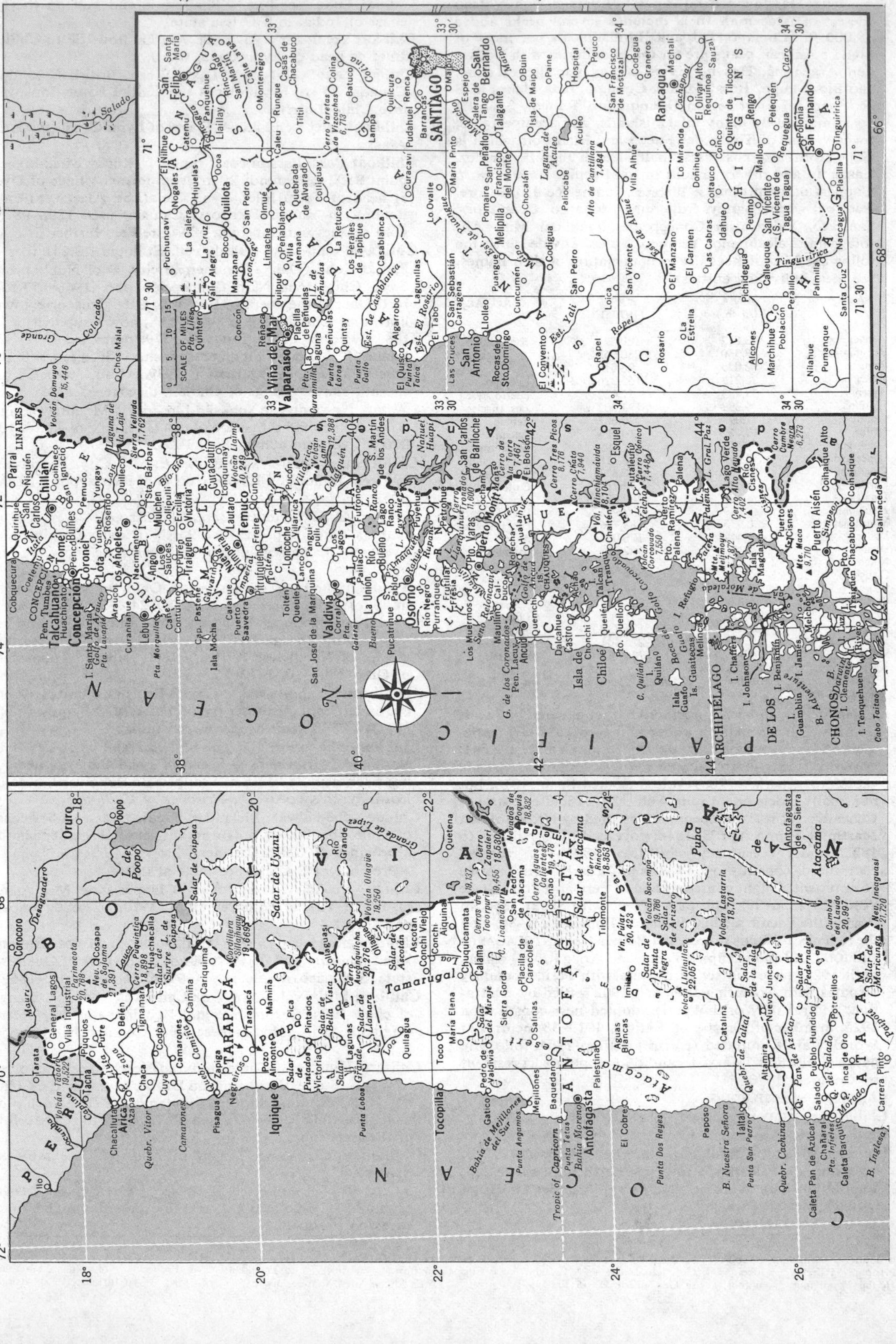
SANTIAGO
Valparaiso
Viña del Mar
San Felipe
Quillota
San Antonio
Rancagua
San Fernando
Melipilla
Talagante
San Bernardo
Puente Alto
ACONCAGUA
O'HIGGINS
SCALE OF MILES
0 5 10 15
Concepcion
Talcahuano
Chillán
Los Angeles
Temuco
Valdivia
Osorno
Puerto Montt
Ancud
Castro
Isla de Chiloé
Puerto Aisén
ARCHIPIÉLAGO DE LOS CHONOS
OCEANO PACIFICO
Tropic of Capricorn
Antofagasta
Iquique
Arica
Tocopilla
Calama
Chuquicamata
Taltal
Tacna
Oruro
PERU
BOLIVIA
TARAPACÁ
ANTOFAGASTA
ATACAMA
Salar de Uyuni
Salar de Atacama
Pampa del Tamarugal
Desierto de Atacama
Puna de Atacama
L. de Poopó
Salar de Coipasa
72°
70°
68°
66°
18°
20°
22°
24°
26°
38°
40°
42°
44°

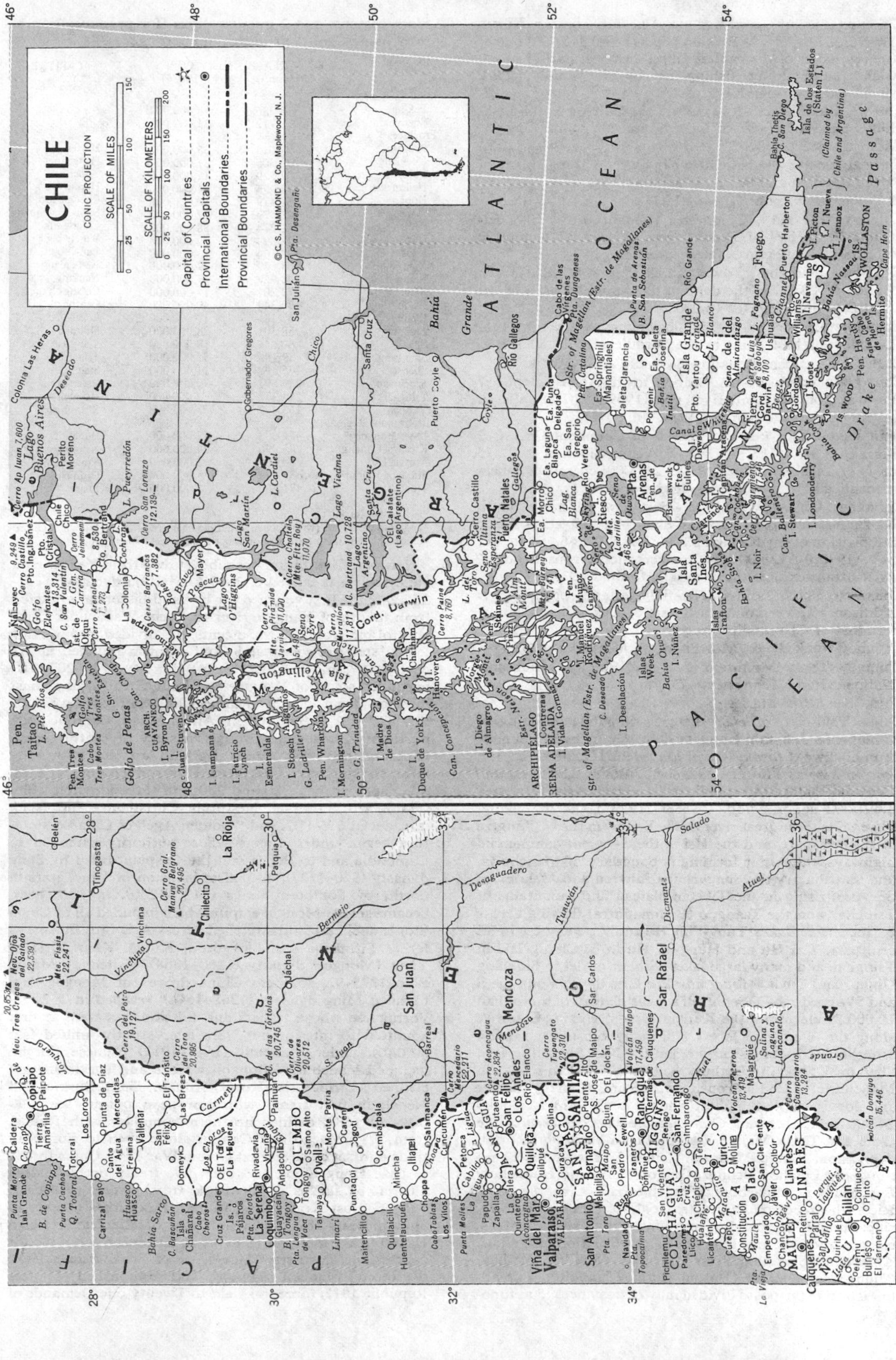
CHILE
CONIC PROJECTION
SCALE OF MILES
SCALE OF KILOMETERS
Capital of Countries
Provincial Capitals
International Boundaries
Provincial Boundaries
©C. S. HAMMOND & Co., Maplewood, N. J.
ATLANTIC OCEAN
PACIFIC OCEAN
Drake Passage
Longitude West 72° of Greenwich
SANTIAGO
VALPARAISO
COQUIMBO
ACONCAGUA
O'HIGGINS
COLCHAGUA
CURICO
TALCA
MAULE
LINARES
Isla Grande de Tierra del Fuego
Str. of Magellan (Estr. de Magallanes)
Punta Arenas
Cape Horn

Chi–lung \ˈjē-ˈlu̇ŋ\ *also* **Kee·lung** \ˈkē-ˈlu̇ŋ\ *or Jap.* **Ki·run** \ki-ˈru̇n\. Seaport, N Taiwan; pop. (1969e) 313,721; one of the two ports of the capital Taipei; has best harbor in the island; shipbuilding, fishing; nearby are valuable gold, silver, and copper mines.

Chil·wa, Lake \-ˈchil-(ˌ)wä\ *also* **Lake Shir·wa** \-ˈshī(ə)r-\. Lake, SE Malawi, SE of Lake Nyasa; ab. 40 m. long.

Chimahi. See TJIMAHI.

Chi·mal·te·nan·go \chi-ˌmält-ə-näŋ-(ˌ)gō\. 1 Department of S cen. Guatemala. See table at GUATEMALA.
2 Town, its ✱; pop. (1964p) 15,372.

Chi·may \shē-ˈmā\. Commune, Hainaut prov., SW Belgium, 30 m. SW of Dinant; pop. (1969e) 3276; marble quarries; manufactures faïence; castle.

Chim·bai \chim-ˈbī\. Town, Karakalpak A.S.S.R., Uzbek S.S.R., U.S.S.R., in the delta of the Amu Darya, S of the Aral Sea; pop. (1967e) 18,000.

Chim·bo·ra·zo \ˌchim-bə-ˈräz-(ˌ)ō, ˌshim-\. 1 Peak, W cen. Ecuador; highest point in the Cordillera Real, 20,561 ft.
2 Province of cen. Ecuador. See table at ECUADOR.

Chim·bo·te \chim-ˈbō-tē\. Seaport town, Ancash dept., W Peru, at mouth of Santa river; pop. (1969e) 97,100; suffered severe earthquake damage 1970.

Chim·kent \chim-ˈkent\. Town, ✱ of Chimkent Oblast, S Kazakh S.S.R., U.S.S.R., on Turkistan-Siberian R.R. 75 m. N of Tashkent; pop. (1970p) 247,000; chemicals, pharmaceuticals, fruit canneries, lead works.

Chimkent Oblast \-ˈō-bləst, -ˌblast\ *or formerly* **South Ka·zakh·stan Oblast** \-kə-ˈzak-ˌstan-, -kə-ˌzäk-ˈstän-, ˌkä-\. Subdivision of the Kazakh S.S.R., U.S.S.R.; 46,564 sq. m.; pop. (1970p) 1,128,000; ✱ Chimkent; nonferrous metallurgy, cotton, textiles; sheep raising; formed 1932.

Chim·ney Point \ˌchim-nē-\. Village and promontory, Addison co., Vermont, on S part of Lake Champlain; E terminal of Champlain bridge.

Chimney Rock. Peak, Morrill co., W Nebraska; 4242 ft.

Chimney Tops. Mountain in Great Smoky Mountains National Park, Tennessee; 4755 ft.

Chin. See CHIN HILLS 2.

Chi·na \ˈchī-nə\; *officially* **People's Republic of China** *or* **Chung–hua Jen–min Kung–ho–kuo** \ˈchu̇ŋ-ˈhwä-ˈjən-ˈmin-ˈku̇ŋ-hō-ˈkwȯ\; *formerly (until Jan. 1912)* **Chinese Empire;** *known also as* **Flowery Kingdom, Middle Kingdom,** *and* **Celestial Empire.** A republic of E and cen. Asia; total area 3,691,502 sq. m.; pop. (1968e) 713,400,000; ✱ Peking. *Rivers:* Its three great rivers—the Yellow in the N, Yangtze in the cen. part, and the Hsi in the S—great commercial highways; the Amur forming N boundary of Manchuria, and its tributary the Sungari; the Salween and Mekong of SE Asia, rising in the Tibetan plateau and mountains of Tsinghai; and the Tsangpo (Brahmaputra) flowing across S Tibet. *Chief lakes:* Tung-t'ing Hu and P'o-yang Hu in SE cen. part, T'ai Hu and Hung-tse Hu in E, Ch'ing Hai in Tsinghai, and many large lakes without outlet in Sinkiang Uighur and Tibet. *Mountains:* The Himalayas along the S and SW border of Tibet, itself a great plateau of more than 10,000 ft. elevation; the Kunlun Mts. stretching E and W along the N edge of Tibet, with many subsidiary ranges, esp. the A-erh-chin Shan-mo and the Nan Shan; the Tien Shan in W Sinkiang Uighur; the Great Khingan Range in Manchuria; in China Proper, esp. in S and W, many shorter and lower ranges; highest known peak Minya Konka 24,900 ft. in Szechwan. *Other notable physical features:* the Gobi and Takla Makan deserts, Tarim basin and Turfan depression, Yangtze Gorges, Hainan I., Liao-tung, Shantung, and Luichow penins., Gulf of Chihli and Hangchow Bay. Many good harbors on its long coast. *Chief products:* Rice, wheat, cotton, millet, tea, coal, iron ore, manganese, zinc; animal husbandry; manufacturing: steel, textiles, electric motors, machine tools, construction materials. *Chief cities:* Shanghai, Peking, Tientsin, Mukden, Wu-han, Chungking, Dairen, Canton, Harbin, Nanking. For administrative purposes divided into 21 provinces, 5 autonomous regions, and 2 municipalities (for pronunciation of their names, see their individual entries):

NAME	AREA (sq.m.)	POP. (1968e)	CAPITAL
Municipalities			
Peking	3,386	8,000,000[1]	
Shanghai	772	11,000,000[1]	
Provinces			
Anhwei	54,015	35,000,000	Ho-fei
Chekiang	39,305	31,000,000	Hangchow
Fukien	47,529	17,000,000	Foochow
Heilungkiang[2]	178,996	21,000,000[1]	Harbin
Honan	64,479	50,000,000	Cheng-chou
Hopeh	81,479	47,000,000	Shih-chia-chuang
Hunan	81,274	38,000,000	Ch'ang-sha
Hupeh	72,394	32,000,000	Wu-ch'ang
Kansu	137,104	13,000,000	Lan-chou
Kiangsi	63,629	22,000,000	Nan-ch'ang
Kiangsu	40,927	47,000,000	Nanking
Kirin[2]	72,201	17,000,000	Ch'ang-ch'un
Kwangtung	89,344	40,000,000	Canton
Kweichow	67,181	17,000,000[1]	Kuei-yang
Liaoning[2]	58,301	28,000,000	Mukden
Shansi	60,656	18,000,000[1]	T'ai-yüan
Shantung	59,189	57,000,000[1]	Tsinan
Shensi	75,598	21,000,000	Sian
Szechwan	219,691	70,000,000	Ch'eng-tu
Tsinghai	278,378	2,000,000[1]	Hsi-ning
Yunnan	168,417	23,000,000	K'un-ming
Autonomous Regions			
Inner Mongolia[2]	454,633	13,000,000[1]	Huhehot
Kwangsi Chuang	85,096	24,000,000	Nan-ning
Ningsia Hui	30,039	2,000,000	Yin-ch'uan
Sinkiang Uighur[2]	635,829	8,000,000	Urumchi
Tibet[2]	471,660	1,400,000	Lhasa

[1] 1967 estimate.
[2] Together constitute (with Taiwan) what has been traditionally known as **Outer China**, the remaining territory forming the historical **China Proper**.

History: Civilization probably spread from Yellow river valley where it existed c. 3000 B.C.; Chou dynasty (1122–255 B.C.) the first vouched for by valid historical evidence; from mouth of Yangtze river to Great Wall under Chou control but from 8th to 3d cents. B.C. divided into warring feudal states; Taoism and Confucianism founded in 6th cent. B.C.; under Ch'in (Ts'in) dynasty (221–207 B.C.) expanded south of Yangtze and built Great Wall against invasion from north; members of Han dynasty (202 B.C.–220 A.D.) reconquered Annam and Canton, took northern Korea and, through mastery of central Asian tribes, gained first direct overland contact with west (Rome); Buddhism (see INDIA 1) introduced by 1st cent. A.D.; split up bet. 220 and 280 into three kingdoms Shu (Han), Wu, and Wei; Nestorian Christianity and Islam introduced 618–907, and "Golden Age" of Chinese literature began under T'angs whose authority extended to Cambodia and to Persia and the Caspian; ruled by Sung dynasty (960–1127), and, after invasion of Kin Tatars in north, by Southern Sungs (1127–1280); in 13th cent. became seat of Mongol empire which included all of China (not Indochina), and stretched across Asia into Europe as far as Lithuania and Novgorod; Kublai Khan, first of Yüan (Mongol) dynasty (1260–1368), visited by Marco Polo 1275–92; southern China drove out Mongols and founded Ming dynasty (1368–1644); reached in 1521 by Portuguese whose traders and missionaries were at first admitted to interior but were later strictly limited (see MACAO); under Manchus (1644–1912) Chinese Empire included Manchuria, Mongolia, Tibet, and Turkistan, and claimed as tributaries Korea, Annam, Siam, Burma, and Nepal; in first treaty with European power (see NERCHINSK) 1689, defined northern boundary with Russia; from 1717 Macao and Canton alone open to European trade until, at close of First Opium War 1842, China forced to cede Hong Kong and open five treaty ports; eastern Siberia, as far as Vladivostok (*q.v.*) ceded to Russia 1858–60; lost Korea, Taiwan, and Pescadores (Treaty of Shimonoseki) 1895 to Japan; lease of Kiaochow (Chiao Hsien) to Germany in 1898 began European scramble for concessions; northern China scene of Boxer risings 1900; overthrew Manchu dynasty and established Chinese Republic 1912; forced to yield to Twenty-one Demands of

Japan 1915; entered World War I 1917; subject of Nine-Power Treaty after Washington Conference 1922; after civil war 1920–26 nationalist government formed at Nanking by Chiang Kai-shek 1928, 1931; Manchuria (*q.v.*) occupied by Japan 1931–32; engaged in war with Japan 1937–45; one of the four Great Powers in World War II 1939–45; civil war 1945–50, during which Communist regime established control over mainland China; suppressed Tibetan uprising 1959–60; fought border war with India 1962; exploded its first nuclear bomb 1964; deteriorating relations with U.S.S.R. accompanied by a number of border clashes through the 1960's; serious internal crises during "Great Leap Forward" (1957–61, massive communalization of agriculture and local industry) and "Great Cultural Revolution" (1966–67); became a member of the UN 1971. See also HONG KONG, MACAO, MANCHUKUO, MANCHURIA, and TAIWAN.

China Grove. Town, Rowan co., cen. North Carolina, 10 m. SW of Salisbury; pop. (1970c) 1788; cotton, wheat, tobacco.

Chi·na·me·ca \ˌchē-nə-ˈmā-kə\. Town, San Miguel dept., E El Salvador; pop. (1961c) 592.

Chinan. See TSINAN.

Chi·nan·de·ga \ˌchin-ən-ˈdā-gə\. 1 Department of NW Nicaragua. See table at NICARAGUA.
2 Town, its ✻; pop. (1970e) 35,395; sugar.

China Proper. See CHINA.

China Sea. Part of Pacific Ocean reaching from Japan to S end of Malay Penin.; divided by Taiwan into **East China Sea** or **Eastern Sea** (482,300 sq. m., max. depth 9126 ft., enclosed by E China, South Korea, Kyūshū and Ryukyu Is., and Taiwan) and **South China Sea,** often called simply **China Sea** (895,400 sq. m., max. depth ab. 15,000 ft., enclosed by SE China, Indochina, Malay Penin., Borneo, Philippines, and Taiwan).

Chi·na·ti Peak \chə-ˌnät-ē-\. Mountain, Presidio co., W Texas; 7730 ft.

Chin·cha Al·ta \ˈchin-chə-ˈäl-tə\. Town, Ica dept., SW Peru; pop. (1961c) 20,817.

Chincha Islands. Group of small islands in Pacific Ocean off coast of W cen. Peru, Ica dept.; guano.

Chinchaycocha. See JUNÍN 2.

Chin–chou *or* **Chin·chow** \ˈjin-ˈjō\. 1 *or formerly* **Kin·chow** \ˈjin-ˈjō\. Town, Liaoning prov., NE China, on NW coast of Liaotung Penin. and on railroad.
2 *or formerly* **Chin·hsien** \ˈjin-ˈshen\. Town, S Liaoning prov., NE China, at head of Gulf of Chihli on W side; pop. (1970e) 750,000; commercial center, esp. for cattle trade, on Tientsin-Mukden railroad. Fighting here 1945 in Chinese civil war.

Chin·co·teague \ˌshiŋ-kə-ˈtēg, ˌchiŋ-\. Town, NE Accomac co. E Virginia, on Chincoteague I., bet. S end of Assateague I. and the mainland; pop. (1970c) 1867.

Chincoteague Bay. Long narrow bay bet. Assateague I. and the mainland (Maryland and Virginia).

Chin·de \ˈchin-də\. Seaport town on only navigable mouth of the Zambezi, SE cen. Mozambique; pop. (1960c) 25,617; exports sugar; formerly chief port for Malawi and Zambia.

Chin·dwin \ˈchin-ˈdwin\. River, W Burma; ab. 720 m. long; chief tributary of the Irrawaddy; rises in Kumon Range in N Burma, flows NW through Hukawng Valley, then S along India border and SE to the Irrawaddy at Myingyan; generally navigable below its confluence with the Uyu, its chief tributary. Scene of much fighting 1942–44.

Chi·nen Peninsula \chi-ˌnen-\. Peninsula on E coast of Okinawa, at S end of island S of Nakagusuku Bay; Japanese on it cut off by U.S. Marines June 5–6, 1945.

Chinese Tur·ki·stan \-ˌtər-ki-ˈstan\ *or* **Kash·gar·ia** \kash-ˈgar-ē-ə, -ˈger-\ *or* **East Turkistan.** The part of Turkistan (*q.v.*) under Chinese control, now comprising the W and cen. parts of Sinkiang Uighur, W China; chief town was Kashgar, now K'o-shih. Since earliest times occupied successively by the Hiung-Nu, Yuechi, Chinese, Ephthalites, Uigurs, Muslims, and Mongols. Khotan was long the most important city. In 14th and 15th cents. visited by many Muslim scholars, but tolerance then established abolished by Chinese conquest in 18th cent.; under leadership of Uzbeks rebelled against China 1866; reconquered 1877–78.

Chinese Wall. See GREAT WALL.

Ching *or* **King** \ˈjiŋ\. River, rising in NE Kansu prov., N cen. China, and flowing SE to the Wei in cen. Shensi; ab. 200 m. long.

Ch'ing–chiang \ˈjiŋ-jē-ˈäŋ\ *or formerly* **Hwai·yin** \ˈhwī-ˈyin\. City, cen. Kiangsu prov., E China.

Ch'ing Hai. 1 Lake, China. See TSING HAI.
2 Province, China. See TSINGHAI.

Chin·gle·put \ˈchiŋ-gəl-ˌpu̇t\. Town, Tamil Nadu, S India, 14 m. SW of Madras; pop. (1961c) 25,977; important as a capital of Vijayanagar kings in 16th cent.; a strategic fort during wars bet. French and English in 18th cent.

Chin·go·la \chiŋ-ˈgō-lə\. Town, Zambia, 30 m. NW of Kitwe; pop. (1967e) 82,000.

Ching–shih *or* **Tsing·shih** \ˈchiŋ-ˈshē\. Town, Hunan prov., China, ab. 120 m. NW of Ch'ang-sha; pop. (1970e) 100,000.

Ching–te–chen *also* **King·teh·chen** \ˈjiŋ-ˈdə-ˈjən\ *or formerly* **Fow·liang** \ˈfü-lē-ˈäŋ, ˈfō-\. Town, NE Kiangsi prov., SE China, near Anhwei border, 200 m. ESE of Wu-han; pop. (1970e) 300,000; porcelain industry, established in Ch'ên dynasty (557–589 A.D.), became famous under the Sungs.

Chin·hae \ˈchin-ˈhī\ *or formerly* **Chin·kai** \-ˈkī\. Seaport town, South Kyŏngsang prov., South Korea, on inlet of Western Channel 22 m. W of Pusan; pop. (1970e) 91,947; former Japanese naval base.

Chinhai. See CHEN-HAI.

Chin Hills \ˈchin-\. 1 Range of hills along W border of Magwe div., Burma, part of Arakan Yoma system; from 7000 to 10,000 ft.; inhabited by Chin tribes.
2 *or* **Chin Special Division** *also* **Chin.** Hill district NW of Magwe div., Burma; 13,903 sq. m.; pop. (1969e) 354,000; ✻ Falam; scene of much fighting in Japanese campaign against Manipur 1942–44.

Chinhsien. See CHIN-CHOU 2.

Chin–hua *or* **Kin·hwa** \ˈjin-ˈhwä\. City, cen. Chekiang prov., E China, ab. 80 m. S of Hangchow; railroad junction; airfield, used by Americans in World War II; captured after severe fighting by Japanese 1942.

Ch'in–huang–tao *or* **Chin·wang·tao** \ˈchin-ˈhwäŋ-ˈdau̇\. Seaport town on Gulf of Chihli, NE Hopeh prov., NE China; former treaty port.

Chin·i·ot \ˈchin-ē-ət\. Town, Pakistan, on E bank of Chenab river 80 m. W of Lahore; pop. (1961c) 47,099.

Chin·ju \ˈjin-ˈjü\ *or* **Shin·shu** \ˈshin-ˈshü\. Town, South Kyŏngsang prov., South Korea, 55 m. W of Pusan; pop. (1970e) 121,622; center of cotton district.

Chinkai. See CHINHAE.

Chinkiang. See CHEN-CHIANG.

Ch'in Ling Shan *or formerly* **Tsin·ling Shan** \ˌchin-ˌliŋ-ˈshän\. Mountain range in N China, running E–W from SE Kansu across cen. Shensi into W Honan; watershed bet. Wei and Han rivers; highest peak 13,474 ft.

Chinnampo. See NAMP'O.

Chinnereth, Sea of. See GALILEE, SEA OF.

Chi·no \ˈchē-(ˌ)nō\. City, San Bernardino co., SE California, 30 m. E of Los Angeles; pop. (1970c) 20,411; bricks, mobile homes; trade center for citrus fruits and sugar beets; founded 1887.

Chi·non \shē-ˈnōⁿ\. Commune, Indre-et-Loire dept., NW cen. France, on the Vienne river; pop. (1962c) 7873; nuclear power plant; birthplace of Rabelais.

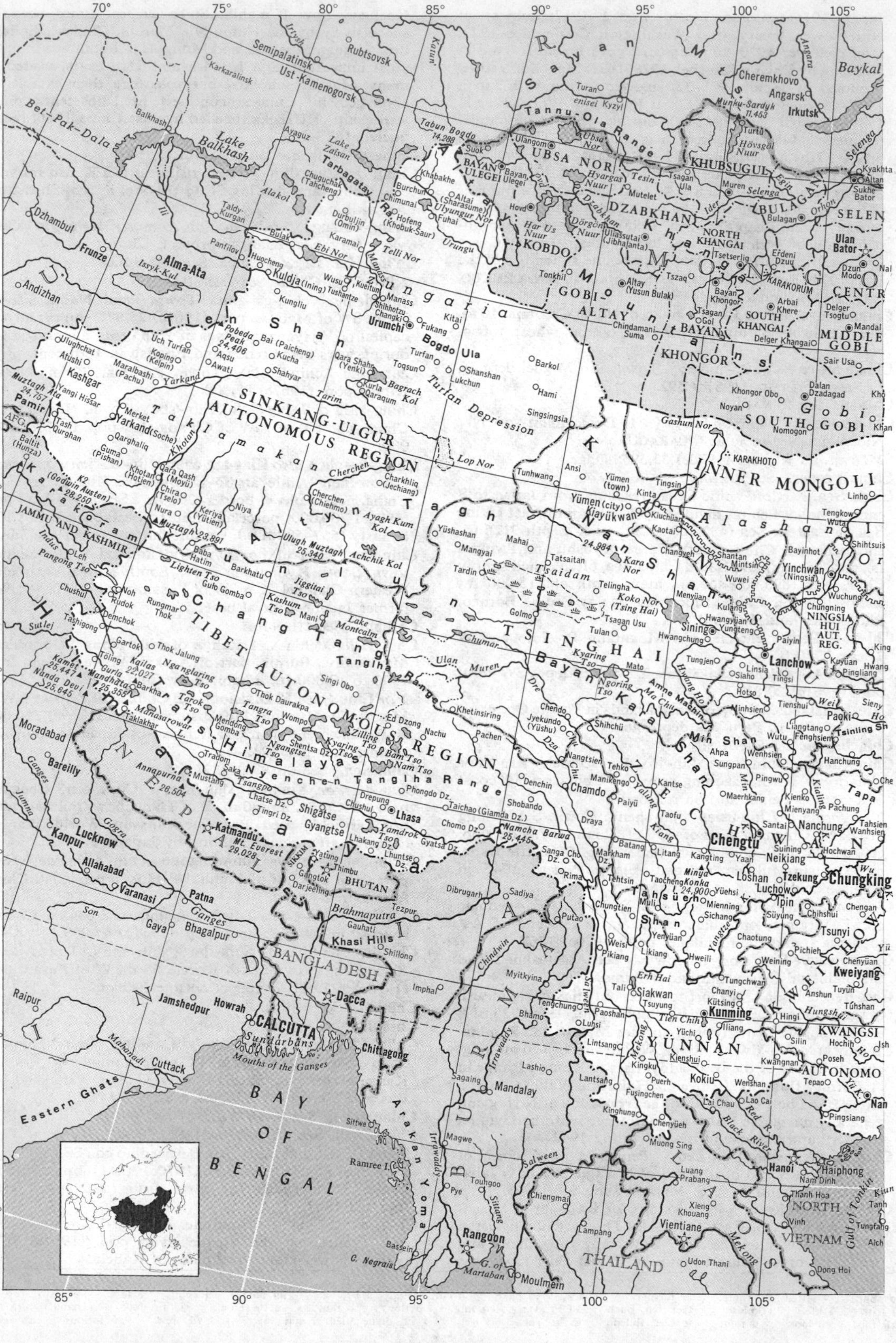

70°
75°
80°
85°
90°
95°
100°
105°
45°
40°
35°
30°
25°
20°
15°
Semipalatinsk
Rubtsovsk
Ust-Kamenogorsk
Karkaralinsk
Irtysh
Katun
Sayan Mts.
Turan
Kyzyl
enisei
Cheremkhovo
Angarsk
Irkutsk
Baykal
Angara
Munku-Sardyk 11,453
Bet-Pak-Dala
Balkhash
Lake Balkhash
Ayaguz
Lake Zaisan
Tabun Bogdo 14,288
Tannu-Ola Range
Ulangom
Ubsa Nor
UBSA NOR
Turtü
Hövsgöl Nuur
KHUBSUGUL
Selenga
Kyakhta
Altan
Sukhe Bator
Chuguchak (Tahcheng)
Tarbagatay Ra.
Alakol
Suok
BAYAN ULEGEI
Bayan Ulegei
Khabakhe
Burchun
Altai (Sharasume)
Chimunai
Ulyungur Nor
Fuhai
Hofeng (Khobuk-Saur)
Durbuljin (Omin)
Hyargas Nuur
Tesin
Tsagan Ula
Mutelet
Muren
Selenga
BULAGAN
Orhon
Bulagan
SELEN
Egin
Ider
Dzhambul
Ili
Taldy-Kurgan
Alakol
Hovd
Har Us Nuur
Dörgön Nuur
Dzabkhan
DZABKHAN
Uliassutai (Jibhalanta)
NORTH KHANGAI
Tsetserlig
Erdeni Dzuu
Ulan Bator
Nal
Dzun Modo
Bulak
Panfilov
Karamai
Telli Nor
Ebi Nor
Urungu
KOBDO
Frunze
Alma-Ata
Issyk-Kul
Hucheng
Kuldja (Ining)
Wusu
Manass
Kuetun
Tushantze
Dzungaria
Tonkhil
Altay (Yusun Bulak)
Tszaq
Khangai Mountains
KARAKORUM
Bayan Khongor
Arbai Khere
MONGOLIA
CENTR
Andizhan
Kungliu
Shihhotzu
Manass
Changki
Urumchi
Kitai
Fukang
GOBI-ALTAY
Chindamani Suma
Tsagan Gol
SOUTH KHANGAI
Delger Tsogtu
Mandal
MIDDLE GOBI
Delger Khangai
Tien Shan
Pobeda Peak 24,406
Bai (Paicheng)
Kucha
Aqsu
Awati
Ulughchat
Uch Turfan
Koping (Kelpin)
Atushi
Kashgar
Maralbashi (Pachu)
Bogdo Ula
Turfan
Toqsun
Shanshan
Lukchun
Barkol
Hami
BAYAN KHONGOR
Sair Usa
Muztagh Ata 24,757
Yangi Hissar
Pamir
Yarkand
Shahyar
Qara Shahr (Yenki)
Kurla
Qaraqum
Bagrach Kol
Tarim
Turfan Depression
Khongor Obo
Noyan
Dalan Dzadagad
Gobi
SOUTH GOBI
Nomogon
Gashun Nor
Khan
Singsingsia
AFG.
Tash Qurghan
Merket
Yarkand (Soche)
Taklamakan
Qarghaliq
Guma (Pishan)
SINKIANG-UIGUR AUTONOMOUS REGION
Baltit (Hunza)
Khotan
Khotan (Hotien)
Qara Qash (Moyü)
Cherchen
Charkhliq (Jechiang)
Lop Nor
KARAKHOTO
INNER MONGOLIA
K2 (Godwin Austen) 28,250
Karakoram
Chira (Tselo)
Nura
Keriya (Yütien)
Niya
Cherchen (Chiehmo)
Altyn Tagh
Ayagh Kum Kol
Tunhwang
Ansi
Yümen (town)
Yümen (city)
Tingsin
Kinta
Kiayükwan
Kiuchüan
Alashan
Linho
Tengkow
Wuta
Shihtsuis
JAMMU AND KASHMIR
Muztagh 23,891
Ulugh Muztagh 25,340
Yüshashan
Mangyai
Kaotai
Nan Shan
24,984
Changyeh
Shantan
Mintsin
Bayinhot
Yinchwan (Ningsia)
Indus
Leh
Pangong Tso
Baba Hatim
Lighten Tso
Achchik Kol
Mahai
Tatsaitan
Tsaidam
Kara Nor
Tardin
Wuwei
Wuchung
Chushul
Noh
Rudok
Gulo Gomba
Barkhatu
Jiggitai Tso
Kunlun
Telingha
Koko Nor (Tsing Hai)
Menyüan
Kulang
Hwangyüan
Sining
Yungteng
Chungning
NINGSIA HUI AUT. REG.
Chang Tang
Kashum Tso
Mani
Rungmar Thok
Demchok
Golmo
Tsagan Usu
Sutlej
Tashigong
Lake Montcalm
Tulan
Hwangchung
Paiyin
Lanchow
King
TIBET AUTONOMOUS REGION
Chumar
TSINGHAI
Tungjen
Linsia
Siaho
Tingsi
Kuyüan
Pingliang
Hwang
Gartok
Thok Jalung
Tanglha Range
Ulan Muren
Kyaring Tso
Mato
Bayan Kara Shan
Amne Machin
Hotso
Tienshui
Sieny
Wei
Kamet 25,447
Töling
Kailas 22,027
Ngangläring Tso
Singi Obo
Ngoring Tso
Ma Chu
Hwang Ho
Minhsien
Paoki
Ho
Nanda Devi 25,645
Mandhata 25,355
Barkha
Tarok Tso
Thok Daurakpa
Dre
Chendo
Shihchü
Liangtang
Fenghsien
Tsinling Sh
Moradabad
Trans Himalayas
Tangra Tso
Wompo
Ed Dzong
Nachu
Khetinsiring
Jyekundo (Yüshu)
Min Shan
Wutu
Taklakhar
Manasarowar L.
Mendong Gomba
Zilling Tso
Kyaring Tso
Bam Tso
Pachen
Dza
Chu
Ahpa
Sungpan
Wenhsien
Hanchung
Bareilly
Ganges
Tradom
Shentsa Dz.
Ngangtse Tso
Nam Tso
Nyenchen Tanglha Range
Nangtsien
Manikengo
Tehko
Denchin
Kantse
Pingwu
SZECHWAN
Che
Tapa
NEPAL
Annapurna 26,504
Mustang
Saka
Tsangpo
Lhatse Dz.
Tingri Dz.
Shigatse
Gyangtse
Chushul
Lhasa
Drepung
Phongdo Dz.
Chamdo
Shobando
Yalung
Paiyü
Taofu
Maerhkang
Kienko
Mienyang
Kialing
Pachung
Jumna
Gogra
Lucknow
Kanpur
Katmandu
Mt. Everest 29,028
SIKKIM
Yatung
Yamdrok Tso
Lhakang Dz.
Lhuntse Dz.
Taichao (Giamda Dz.)
Chomo Dz.
Namcha Barwa 25,445
Gyatsa Dz.
Draya
Kiang
Nanchung
Santai
Tahsien
Wanhsien
Chengtu
Batang
Litang
Kangting
Yaan
Suining
Neikiang
Hochwan
Allahabad
Thimbu
BHUTAN
Gangtok
Darjeeling
Sanga Cho Dz.
Markham Dz.
Rima
Tehtsin
Taocheng
Minya Konka 24,900
Loshan
Tzekung
Chungking
Wu
Varanasi
Patna
Ganges
Son
Brahmaputra
Tezpur
Dibrugarh
Sadiya
Putao
Chungtien
Tahsüeh Shan
Muli
Yüehsi
Mienning
Sichang
Luchow
Ipin
Chihshui
Chengan
Gaya
Bhagalpur
Gauhati
Khasi Hills
Shillong
Chindwin
Weisi
Yangtze
Yenyüan
Süyung
Tsunyi
KWEICHOW
Yü
BANGLA DESH
Pikiang
Likiang
Hweili
Chaotung
Pichieh
Chenyüan
Weining
Kweiyang
INDIA
Raipur
Jamshedpur
Howrah
Dacca
Imphal
Myitkyina
Salween
Erh Hai
Tali
Siakwan
Tsuyung
Chanyi
Kütsing
Tungchwan
Anshun
Tuyün
Tengchung
Bhamo
Paoshan
Kunming
Hungshui
Tuhshan
CALCUTTA
Sundarbans
Mouths of the Ganges
Chittagong
Luhsi
Tien Chih
Yüchi
Iliang
Hingi
KWANGSI
Mahanadi
Cuttack
Irrawaddy
BURMA
Lintsang
Mekong
YUNNAN
Silin
Hochih
Ish
Lashio
Kingku
Kienshui
Kwangnan
Poseh
AUTONOMO
Eastern Ghats
BAY OF BENGAL
Sagaing
Mandalay
Lantsang
Puerh
Kokiu
Wenshan
Tepao
Yu K.
Nan
Arakan Yoma
Fusingchen
Lai Chau
Lao Cai
Red R.
Pingsiang
Kinghung
Chenyüeh
Black River
Sittwe
Magwe
Muong Sing
Ramree I.
Irrawaddy
Hanoi
Haiphong
Luang Prabang
Kiun
Pye
Toungoo
Chiengmai
Thanh Hoa
NORTH
Tanh
Sittang
Nam Dinh
Xieng Khouang
Gulf of Tonkin
Vinh
Tungfang
Lampang
Vientiane
VIETNAM
Aich
Rangoon
Bassein
LAOS
C. Negrais
G. of Martaban
Moulmein
THAILAND
Udon Thani
Dong Hoi
85°
90°
95°
100°
105°

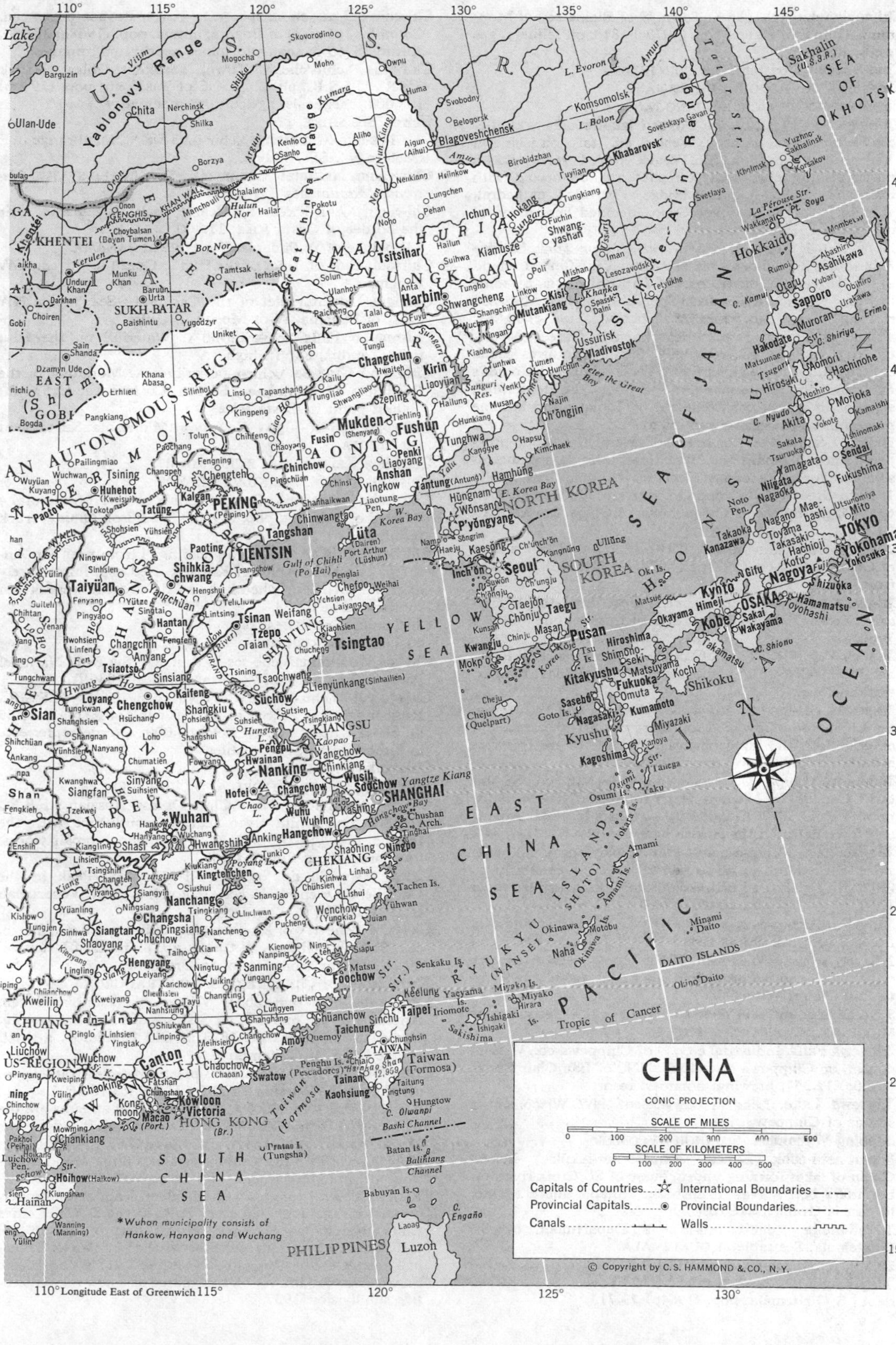
CHINA
CONIC PROJECTION
SCALE OF MILES
0 100 200 300 400 500
SCALE OF KILOMETERS
0 100 200 300 400 500
Capitals of Countries
International Boundaries
Provincial Capitals
Provincial Boundaries
Canals
Walls
© Copyright by C. S. HAMMOND & CO., N. Y.
*Wuhan municipality consists of Hankow, Hanyang and Wuchang
110° Longitude East of Greenwich 115°
120°
125°
130°
U. S. S. R.
Yablonovy Range
SEA OF OKHOTSK
MANCHURIA
HEILUNGKIANG
KIRIN
LIAONING
INNER MONGOLIAN AUTONOMOUS REGION
SEA OF JAPAN
NORTH KOREA
SOUTH KOREA
YELLOW SEA
EAST CHINA SEA
PACIFIC OCEAN
SOUTH CHINA SEA
PEKING
TIENTSIN
SHANGHAI
TOKYO
Yokohama
Seoul
P'yongyang
Harbin
Mukden
Nanking
Wuhan
Canton
Hong Kong
Kowloon
Victoria
Macao
Taipei
Taiwan (Formosa)
Hokkaido
Honshu
Kyushu
Shikoku
Sakhalin (U.S.S.R.)
Khabarovsk
Vladivostok
Blagoveshchensk
Ryukyu Islands (Nansei Shoto)
Daito Islands
Tropic of Cancer
Bashi Channel
Balintang Channel
Luzon
PHILIPPINES
Hainan

Chi·nook \shə-'nu̇k, chə-\. Town, ⊗ of Blaine co., N Montana, 22 m. E of Havre; pop. (1970c) 1813; oil refinery, gas wells; livestock.

Chin Special Division. See CHIN HILLS 2.

Chinsura. See HOOGHLY-CHINSURA.

Chinwangtao. See CH'IN-HUANG-TAO.

Chiog·gia \kē-'ò-jə\ *or anc.* **Fos·sa Clau·dia** \ˌfäs-ə-'klȯd-ē-ə\. Seaport, Venezia prov., Veneto, NE Italy, on island in Venetian lagoon 15 m. S of Venice; pop. (1968e) 48,347; major fishing port; built on piles and connected with mainland by 800-ft. stone bridge; 17th cent. cathedral; supremacy of Venice over Genoa decided here in naval campaign 1379–80.

Chi·os \'kī-äs\ *or Gk.* **Khí·os** \'kē-ˌȯs\ *or Turk.* **Sa·kis–Ada·si** \sä-'kiz-ˌäd-ə-'sē\ *or Ital.* **Scio** \'shē-(ˌ)ō\. 1 Island in the Aegean Sea off W coast of Turkey in Asia, by some included among the Southern Sporades (see SPORADES); 30 m. long by 8 to 15 m. wide; 325 sq. m.; pop. (1961c) 60,061; with adjacent islets forms a department of Greece (349 sq. m.; pop. [1971p] 53,942); hilly, fertile; produces much fruit, esp. figs. Noted in antiquity for its claims as Homer's birthplace and for its school of epic poets, the Homeridae; also for its sculptors. Colonized by Ionians and became powerful state; became subject to Persia 494 B.C.; joined Delian League 478 B.C.; revolted several times but prospered under Romans and Byzantines; later passed successively to Turks, Venetians, Genoese, Ottomans, and finally 1912 to Greece. British and Greek troops landed here Oct. 6, 1944. Birthplace of Theopompus of Chios. See AEGEAN ISLANDS.

2 *or* **Kas·tron** \'käs-(ˌ)trȯn\. City on E coast of Chios I., ✻ of Chios dept.; pop. (1971p) 24,074; exports incl. wine and fruit.

Chi·pa·ta \chə-'pät-ə\ *or formerly* **Fort James·son** \-'jām-sən\. Town, Zambia, 290 m. ENE of Lusaka; pop. (1963c) 7602.

Chip·ley \'chip-lē\. Town, ⊗ of Washington co., NW Florida, 105 m. ENE of Pensacola; pop. (1970c) 3347; lumber; watermelons.

Chi·po·la \chə-'pō-lə\. River, SE Alabama and W Florida; ab. 130 m. long; flows S from Henry co., SE Alabama, and empties into the Apalachicola river ab. 10 m. from its mouth; navigable for a short distance.

Chip·pa·wa \'chip-ə-ˌwȯ, -ˌwä\. Village, Welland co., SE Ontario, Canada, on Niagara river 2 m. above Niagara Falls; pop. (1966c) 3877; founded by Loyalists in 1783. American force defeated the British here on July 5, 1814.

Chip·pen·ham \'chip-ə-nəm\. Municipal borough, Wiltshire, S England, on the Avon 20 m. E of Bristol; pop. (1971p) 18,622; food processing, tanning; incorp. as town 1554.

Chip·pe·wa \'chip-ə-ˌwȯ, -ˌwä\. 1 River, W cen. Minnesota; flows S into Minnesota river.

2 River, W cen. Wisconsin; 183 m. long; rises in Sawyer co., flows S and SW into Mississippi river; navigable 50 m. to Eau Claire, Wisconsin.

3 Name of counties in three states of the U.S. See tables at MICHIGAN, MINNESOTA, WISCONSIN.

Chippewa Falls. Industrial city, ⊗ of Chippewa co., W Wisconsin, on Chippewa river 10 m. NNE of Eau Claire; pop. (1970c) 12,357; brewing; potatoes; resort.

Chippewa Lake. Lake in Sawyer co., NW Wisconsin; a source of Chippewa river.

Chipping Wycombe. See HIGH WYCOMBE.

Chip·ut·net·i·cook Lakes \ˌship-ət-'net-i-ˌku̇k-, -kək-\. Chain of lakes forming upper course of St. Croix river, on boundary bet. W New Brunswick, Canada, and E Maine; largest is Grand Lake (*q.v.*).

Chi·qui·mu·la \ˌchē-ki-'mü-lə\. 1 Department of SE Guatemala. See table at GUATEMALA.

2 City, its ✻; munic. pop. (1964p) 35,848.

Chi·qui·mu·li·lla \ˌchē-ki-mü-'lē-yə\. Town, Santa Rosa dept., S Guatemala; pop. (1964p) 23,713.

Chi·quin·qui·rá \chi-ˌkēŋ-ki-'rä\. Town, Boyacá dept., cen. Colombia, 65 m. N of Bogotá; munic. pop. (1968e) 28,059; altitude 8365 ft.; emerald mines nearby; pilgrimages.

Chir·chik \chir-'chēk\. Town, Tashkent Oblast, Uzbek S.S.R., U.S.S.R., ab. 20 m. NE of Tashkent; pop. (1970p) 108,000; chemicals, agricultural machinery.

Chire. See SHIRE.

Chir·i·ca·hua Mountains \ˌchir-i-ˌkä-wə-\. Small range in E Cochise co., SE Arizona.

Chiricahua National Monument. See UNITED STATES, *National Monuments.*

Chi·ri·quí \ˌchir-i-'kē\. 1 Volcanic peak, W Panama, near the border of Costa Rica; 11,400 ft.

2 Province of W Panama. See table at PANAMA.

Chiriquí, Gulf of. Inlet of the Pacific Ocean in extreme SW Panama.

Chiriquí Lagoon. Inlet of the Caribbean Sea on the NW coast of Panama, W of Mosquito Gulf.

Chi·rom·bo Falls \chi-ˌräm-bō-\. Waterfall on the Ieisa river, Zambia; 880 ft. high.

Chi·rri·pó Gran·de \ˌchir-i-ˌpō-'grän-dē\. Mountain in the Cordillera de Talamanca, SE cen. Costa Rica; 12,533 ft.; highest point in Costa Rica.

Chi·sa·go \shi-'sȯ-(ˌ)gō\. County in Minnesota. See table at MINNESOTA.

Chishima Kaikyo. See KURIL STRAIT.

Chishima Rettō. See KURIL ISLANDS.

Chis·holm \'chiz-əm\. City, St. Louis co., NE Minnesota, 4 m. ENE of Hibbing; pop. (1970c) 5913; iron mining, truck farming.

Chisholm Trail. A cattle trail leading N from near San Antonio, Texas, to Abilene, Kansas; used esp. immediately after the Civil War when large herds of cattle were driven to markets in the N.

Chisimaio. See KISMAYU.

Chişinău. See KISHINEV.

Chi·sos Mountains \ˌchē-səs-\. Range in Big Bend National Park, S Brewster co., W Texas; highest 7835 ft.

Chi·sto·pol \ˌchis-'tȯ-pəl\. Town, cen. Tatar A.S.S.R., Russian S.F.S.R., U.S.S.R., on left bank of Kama river 65 m. SE of Kazan; pop. (1969e) 63,000; a trade center esp. in lumber, grain, and textiles.

Chistyakovo. See TOREZ.

Chiswick. See BRENTFORD AND CHISWICK.

Chi·ta \chi-'tä\. City, ✻ of Chita Oblast, Russian S.F.S.R., U.S.S.R., on Chita river near its confluence with the Ingoda; pop. (1970p) 242,000; rolling stock repair works; food processing; founded 1653.

Chita, Ne·va·do de \ne-ˌväd-ōd-ə-'chēt-ə\. Peak in the Cordillera Oriental, N cen. Colombia, near Venezuelan border; 18,022 ft.

Ch'i–t'ai \'chē-'tī\ *or* **Ku·cheng·tze** \'kü-'chəŋ-'dzü\. Town, cen. Sinkiang Uighur, W China, ab. 85 m. E of Urumchi, on N highway from Ha-mi to Urumchi.

Chitaldroog *or* **Chitaldrug.** See CHITRADURGA.

Chi·tam·bo \chi-'tam-(ˌ)bō\. Village, NE Zambia, S cen. Africa, S of the marshes on S shore of Lake Bangweulu; David Livingstone died 1873 at Old Chitambo, a small village NNW of Chitambo.

Chita Oblast \chi-'tä-'ō-bləst, -ˌblast\. Administrative subdivision of the Russian S.F.S.R., U.S.S.R.; 166,602 sq. m.; pop. (1970p) 1,145,000; ✻ Chita. Its chief streams are the Amur on its SE border, the Shilka and Argun (headstreams of the Amur), and the Olekma and Zeya. Region is a plateau area, with the Yablonovy Mts. on the W and extensions of mountain ranges of Khabarovsk Krai in the E. Rich in mineral resources (gold, silver, lead, zinc); timber; crossed by the Trans-Siberian R.R. in the S. Chief cities Chita, Nerchinsk, Sretensk. Forms part of one of the earliest settled regions of E Siberia, then known as Transbaikalia; after the Russian Revolution 1917 a part of the Far Eastern Region (*q.v.*); designated as a new administrative subdivision 1937.

Chit·i·na \'chit-ə-ˌnō\. Village on Copper river, SE Alaska, 75 m. NNE of Cordova; pop. (1970c) 38.

Chi·to·se \chē-'tō-sā\. City, Hokkaidō, Japan, 8 m. SW of Sapporo; pop. (1970c) 56,118.

Chit·ra·dur·ga \ˌchit-rə-'dər-gə\ *or formerly* **Chit·al·droog** *or* **Chit·al·drug** \'chit-əl-ˌdrüg\. Town, N Mysore, S India, 137 m. N of Mysore; pop. (1961c) 33,336.

Chi·tral \chi-'träl\. 1 River, Pakistan and NE Afghanistan; ab. 300 m. long; flows S through Chitral and into Afghanistan, where it is called the Kunar, and empties into Kabul river near Jalālābād.
2 District, Malakand div., N North-West Frontier Province, Pakistan; 5727 sq. m.; pop. (1961c) 113,057; on Afghan border on S slope of the Hindu Kush; former princely state; occupied by British when dynastic succession disputed 1895; on Aug. 15, 1947 became part of Pakistan; retained limited autonomy until its incorporation into Malakand div. 1969.
3 Town, its ❋, on Chitral river at over 5000 ft. Small British force withstood siege Mar.–Apr. 1895.

Chi·tré \chi-'trā\. Town, ❋ of Herrera prov., S Panama; pop. (1970p) 20,143.

Chit·ta·gong \'chit-ə-ˌgäŋ, -ˌgȯŋ\. 1 Division, Bangla Desh; 17,032 sq. m.; pop. (1961c) 13,629,650.
2 District, Chittagong div.; 2705 sq. m.; pop. (1961c) 2,982,931; rice, tea; fishing.
3 Town, ❋ of the division, and principal port of Bangla Desh, on Karnaphuli river 12 m. from its mouth; pop. (1969e) 437,200; exports jute, tea; oil refinery, engineering works, jute mills; univ. (1966); in one of the regions of heaviest annual rainfall in the world. Known to early Portuguese mariners; conquered by nawab of Bengal 1666; ceded to British East India Company 1760; port facilities damaged in Indo-Pakistani war 1971.

Chittagong Hill Tracts. District of Chittagong division, Bangla Desh; 5093 sq. m.; pop. (1961c) 385,079; ❋ Rangamati. Hilly region along Burmese border, inhabited by descendants of Arakanese and aboriginal tribes.

Chit·te·nan·go \ˌchit-ᵊn-'aŋ-(ˌ)gō\. Village, Madison co., cen. New York, 16 m. E of Syracuse; pop. (1970c) 3605; truck farming.

Chit·ten·den \'chit-ᵊn-dən\. County in Vermont. See table at VERMONT.

Chittenden, Mount \-'chit-ᵊn-dən\. Peak in Yellowstone National Park, NW Wyoming; 10,189 ft.

Chittenden Reservoir. Reservoir at upper end of East Creek tributary of Otter Creek, W cen. Vermont.

Chit·toor \chi-'tu̇(ə)r\. Town, S Andhra Pradesh, SE India, ab. 90 m. W of Madras; pop. (1961c) 47,876.

Chiu–chiang *or* **Kiu·kiang** \jē-'ō-jē-'äŋ\. City, N Kiangsi prov., SE China, N of P'o-yang lake and on S bank of Yangtze; pop. (1970e) 120,000; rivals Hankow and Foochow in shipments of tea and is principal market for Kingtehchen (Fowliang) pottery; also exports rice, paper, and grass cloth. Opened as a treaty port 1862.

Chiu–ch'üan \jē-'ō-chü-'än\ *also* **Kiu·chuan** \-jü-'än\ *or formerly* **Su·chow** \'sü-'jō\. Town, NW Kansu prov., N cen. China, on highway to U.S.S.R. ab. 375 m. NW of Lan-chou; partially destroyed in Muslim uprising 1865–72; center of fertile agricultural region.

Ch'iung–shan \chē-'üŋ-'shän\ *also* **Kiung·shan** \jē-'üŋ-\ *or formerly* **Kiung·chow** \jē-'üŋ-'jō\. City, ❋ of Hainan I., on NE coast, SW Kwangtung prov., SE China; most important town on island; opened to foreign trade 1858 by Treaty of Tientsin but not actually used until 1876; its outport is Hai-k'ou.

Chiu–san–shui \jē-'ō-'säm-'shwā\ *or formerly* **Sam·shui** \'-säm-'shwā\. Walled town and port, cen. Kwangtung prov., SE China, on N bank of Hsi river at its junction with the Pei ab. 27 m. W of Canton; has distribution trade by river junks and steamers; opened as treaty port 1897.

Chiu·si \'kyü-sē\ *or anc.* **Clu·si·um** \'klü-zhē-əm, -zē-\. Commune, Siena prov., SE Tuscany, cen. Italy, ab. 40 m. SE of Siena; pop. (1968e) 8715; one of the 12 cities of ancient Etruria, flourished 7th–6th cents. B.C.; became subject to Rome 295 B.C.; declined in Middle Ages because of proximity to swamps of Chiani river.

Chi·u·ta, Lake \-shē-'üt-ə\. Lake in NW Mozambique, SE Africa; the Lugenda river issues from its N end.

Chi·vas·so \ki-'väs-(ˌ)ō\. Commune, Torino prov., Piedmont, NW Italy, on Po river NE of Turin; pop. (1968e) 24,689; sulfur baths; fortifications destroyed by French 1804.

Chi·vil·coy \ˌchē-vəl-'kȯi\. City, Buenos Aires prov., E Argentina, 90 m. W of Buenos Aires; pop. (1960c) 32,660.

Chixoy. See USUMACINTA.

Ch'i–yang \'chē-'yäŋ\ *also* **Ki·yang** \'kē-\. Town, Hunan prov., SE cen. China; in World War II an American outpost captured by Japanese Sept. 1944.

Chi–yün River. See PEI-T'ANG.

Chkalov. See ORENBURG.

Chkalov Oblast. See ORENBURG OBLAST.

Cho·a·pan \ˌchō-ə-'pän\. Municipality, Oaxaca state, Mexico, 55 m. NE of Oaxaca; pop. (1970p) 25,360; coffee, lumber.

Choaspes. See KARKHEH.

Cho·be \'chō-bē\. Swamp and lower course of Kwando river in Caprivi Strip, South-West Africa.

Chobe National Park. Park, N Botswana; 4500 sq. m.; noted for its wildlife; estab. ab. 1959.

Chocim. See KHOTIN.

Cho·có \chə-'kō\. Department of W Colombia. See table at COLOMBIA.

Cho·cor·ua, Mount \-shə-'kȯr-ə-wə, -'kär-\. Peak, W cen. Carroll co., E New Hampshire, in Sandwich Range of the White Mts.; 3475 ft.

Choc·taw \'chäk-(ˌ)tȯ\. 1 Counties in three states of the U.S. See tables at ALABAMA, MISSISSIPPI, OKLAHOMA.
2 Town, Oklahoma co., cen. Oklahoma, 17 m. E of Oklahoma City; pop. (1970c) 4750.

Choc·taw·hatch·ee \ˌchäk-tə-'hach-ē\. River, NW Florida; 140 m. long; rises in S Alabama; flows S, forming boundary bet. Walton and Washington cos., into **Choctawhatchee Bay,** inlet of Gulf of Mexico.

Chō·fu \'chō-ˌfü\. Town, Tokyo prefecture, Honshū, Japan; pop. (1970c) 157,488; suburb of Tokyo.

Choi·seul \shwä-'zə(r)l\. One of the Solomon Is., W Pacific Ocean, ab. 32 m. E of SE Bougainville I.; 85 m. long and bet. 4 and 20 m. wide; 1170 sq. m.; pop. (1970p) 8021; was under German control 1886–99; became part of British Solomon Is. protectorate; chief settlement Bambatana on W coast; highest point 2470 ft.; nearly surrounded by barrier reef.

Choi·sy–le–Roi \shwä-ˌzē-lər-'wä, -lə-rə-'wä\. Commune, Val-de-Marne dept., N France, SSE suburb of Paris on left bank of Seine river; pop. (1968c) 41,440. Rouget de Lisle buried here.

Choix \'chȯish\. Municipality, Sinaloa state, Mexico, 150 m. NNW of Culiacán; pop. (1970p) 27,515; agriculture.

Choj·ni·ce \kȯi-'nēt-sə\ *or Ger.* **Ko·nitz** \'kō-nits\. Commune, Bydgoszcz prov., N cen. Poland, 45 m. NW of Bydgoszcz; pop. (1970p) 23,500; scene of last great victory of Teutonic Knights over Poles 1454; recovered from Prussia after World War I.

Choj·nów \'kȯi-(ˌ)nüf\ *or Ger.* **Hay·nau** *also* **Hai·nau** \'hī-(ˌ)nau̇\. Manufacturing city, cen. Wrocław prov., SW Poland, 11 m. N of Legnica; pop. (1968e) 10,500; formerly in Silesia, Germany; assigned to Poland 1945. Battle bet. French and Prussians May 26, 1813.

Chō·kai \'chō-ˌkī\. Volcano, N Yamagata prefecture, N Honshū, Japan, near coast; 7314 ft.; last eruption 1861.

Cho–k'ou–tien *also* **Chou·kou·tien** *or* **Chow Kow Tien** \'jō-'kō-'tyen\. Village, Hopeh prov., NE China, 37 m. SW of Peking; site of discovery 1929 of skull, jaws, and teeth of extinct Peking Man (*Sinanthropus pekinensis*).

Cho·la \'chō-lə\. Early kingdom encompassing much of SE India, Kerala, Mysore, Ceylon; known from 4th cent. B.C. but especially powerful under Chola dynasty of Tamil kings (c. 850–1279 A.D.); extended from Pudukkottai N to Nellore, with capitals at Tiruchirapalli, Kumbakonam, and Thanjavur.

Cho·let \shō-'lā\. Commune, Maine-et-Loire dept., W France, on Maine river 32 m. SSW of Angers; pop. (1968c) 41,766; textiles, paper; 15th cent. bridge; completely destroyed in wars of the Vendée 1793–94.

Cho·lu·la \chə-'lü-lə\ *or in full* **Cholula de Ri·va·da·bia** \-dä-,rē-və-'däb-ē-ə\. Town, Puebla state, SE cen. Mexico, 8 m. W of Puebla; pop. (1960c) 12,833; site of the truncated Pyramid of Quetzalcoatl (base covers 42 acres), used by the Aztecs for their human sacrifices. See TEOTIHUACÁN.

Cho·lu·te·ca \,chō-lə-'tā-kə\. 1 River, S Honduras; ab. 150 m. long; flows E, S, and SW to Gulf of Fonseca.

2 Department of S Honduras. See table at HONDURAS.

3 Town, its ✱; pop. (1961c) 11,483; cattle center.

Cho·mo Lha·ri \,chō-mō-'lär-ē\ *or* **Cha·ma·lha·ri** \,chäm-ə-'lär-ē\ *or* **Chu·ma·lha·ri** \,chü-mə-'lär-ē\. Mountain peak in the Himalayas bet. Tibet, China, and NW Bhutan; 23,997 ft.

Chomo Lonzo. See MAKALU.

Chomolungma. See EVEREST, MOUNT.

Cho·mu·tov \'kō-mə-,tōf, 'hō-\ *or Ger.* **Ko·mo·tau** \'kō-mə-,taù\. Manufacturing city, Czech S.R., W Czechoslovakia, 52 m. NW of Prague; pop. (1968e) 39,425; iron and steel; coal mining.

Ch'ŏn·an \'chən-'än\. Town, South Ch'ungch'ŏng prov., South Korea, ab. 39 m. NNW of Taejŏn; pop. (1970e) 78,316.

Chon Bu·ri \'chən-bù-'rē\. 1 *or formerly* **Bang Pla Soi** \'bäŋ-'plä-'sòi\. Province, S Thailand; 1732 sq. m.; pop. (1960c) 392,025; ✱ Chon Buri.

2 Town, its ✱; pop. (1965e) 40,515.

Cho·ne \'chō-(,)nā\. 1 River, W Ecuador; ab. 60 m. long; flows from Andes Mts. W into Pacific Ocean.

2 City, Manabí prov., W Ecuador, 110 m. WSW of Quito; pop. (1962c) 12,832; cacao, coffee, and sugar.

Ch'ŏng·jin \'chəŋ-'jēn\ *or formerly* **Sei·shin** \'sā-'shēn\. Town, ✱ of North Hamgyŏng prov., North Korea.

Ch'ŏng·ju \'chəŋ-'jü\. Town, ✱ of North Ch'ungch'ŏng prov., South Korea; pop. (1966c) 123,666.

Chŏn·ju \'jən-,jü\ *or formerly* **Zen·shu** \'zen-,shü\. Town, ✱ of North Chŏlla prov., South Korea, 120 m. S of Seoul; pop. (1970e) 262,816; in rice-growing region.

Cho·nos Archipelago \,chō-nəs-\ *or Span.* **Ar·chi·pié·la·go de los Chonos** \,är-chi-'pyel-ə-,gō-,dā-ləs-'chō-,nōs\. Group of islands in S Pacific Ocean off SW coast of Chile, N of Madre de Dios Archipelago.

Chon·ta·les \chän-'täl-äs\. Department of S cen. Nicaragua. See table at NICARAGUA.

Cho Oyu \'chō-ō-'yü\. Mountain peak in the Himalayas bet. Tibet, China and Nepal, NW of Mt. Everest; 26,750 ft.; first scaled 1954.

Cho·pi·col·qui \,chō-pi-'kòl-kē\. Peak in the Cordillera Occidental, Peru; ab. 22,000 ft.

Chop·tank \'chäp-,taŋk\. River, cen. Delaware and E Maryland; ab. 65 m. long; rises in W cen. Delaware, flows SW across Maryland border to Chesapeake Bay in SE Talbot co.

Cho·ras·mia \kə-'raz-mē-ə\. Province of ancient Persia on the Oxus, W Asia, extending W to the Caspian Sea; in 12th cent. ab. equivalent to empire of Khwarizm (*q.v.*) which became the khanate of Khiva (*q.v.*). The Chorasmians, who were Aryans, formed a contingent under Xerxes.

Chor·ley \'chòr-lē\. Municipal borough, Lancashire, NW England, 19 m. WNW of Manchester; pop. (1971p) 31,609; cosmetics, rope, footwear; cotton weaving and calico printing.

Chorlu. See ÇORLU.

Cho·rol·que \chə-'ròl-(,)kā\. Peak, Potosí dept., SW Bolivia; 18,414 ft.

Chorrera, La. See LA CHORRERA.

Cho·rri·llos \chò-'rē-(,)(y)ōs\. Residential town, ab. 9 m. S of Lima, Peru; pop. (1961c) 31,703; resort; scene of Chilean victory over Peruvians Jan. 13, 1881.

Chorum. See ÇORUM.

Cho·rzów \'kò-,zhüf, 'hò-\. Manufacturing and mining city, Katowice prov., SW Poland, 5 m. NNW of Katowice; pop. (1970p) 151,000; steelworks, foundries, nitrate plant; coal mining.

Chosen. See KOREA.

Chosen Strait. See WESTERN CHANNEL.

Chō·shi \'chō-(,)shē\. Seaport town, Chiba prefecture, on SE coast of Honshū, Japan, at mouth of Tone river 60 m. E of Tokyo; pop. (1970c) 90,415; fishing.

Cho·shu \'chō-(,)shü\. Strictly, a Japanese clan, uniting in latter part of 19th cent. with three others in opposition to foreigners and in rebellion against the emperor; often applied to the old province of Nagato, their feudal territory, in SW extremity of Honshū, now part of Yamaguchi prefecture.

Cho·si·ca \chō-'sē-kə\. Town, 35 m. NE of Lima, Peru; pop. (1961c) 31,703; altitude 2800 ft.; winter resort.

Chosŏn. See KOREA.

Chosŏn Minjujuŭi In'min Konghwaguk. See KOREA, NORTH.

Choszcz·no \'kòsh(ch)-,nò, 'hòsh(ch)-\ *or formerly* **Arns·wal·de** \'arn(t)s-väl-də\. Town, S Szczecin prov., NW Poland, 40 m. SE of Szczecin; pop. (1966e) 8883; before 1945 in Prussia, Germany; coal mines, iron foundries.

Cho·ta Nag·pur \,chōt-ə-'näg-,pù(ə)r\ *or* **Chu·tia Nagpur** \,chüt-ē-ə-\. Division, SW Bihar, NE India; 25,293 sq. m.; pop. (1961c) 8,931,286; a plateau region, rich in mineral resources (coal, mica, iron ore, manganese).

Chota Nagpur States. A group of nine former Indian states, earlier in Eastern States Agency in Chota Nagpur, NE India.

Chota Ude·pur *or* **Chho·ta Udepur** \,chōt-ə-ù-'dā-,pù(ə)r, -,ü-də-'pù(ə)r\ *also* **Chota Udai·pur** \-ü-'dī-,pù(ə)r, -,ü-dī-'\. 1 Former Indian state, Gujarat States, W India; 894 sq. m.; ✱ Chota Udepur; founded ab. 1484.

2 Town, its ✱, ab. 50 m. E of Baroda; pop. (1961c) 10,829.

Cho·teau \'shō-(,)tō\. City, ⊗ of Teton co., NW cen. Montana; pop. (1970c) 1586; creamery.

Chotin. See KHOTIN.

Chott \'shät\. French form of Arabic *shatt* (saline lake), For names beginning **Chott** see the second element, as **Chott Djerid,** see DJERID, **Chott ech Chergui,** see CHERGUI.

Cho·tu·si·ce \'kòt-ə-,sit-sə, 'hòt-\ *or Ger.* **Cho·tu·sitz** \'kòt-ə-,zits, 'hòt-\. Village, Czech S.R., W Czechoslovakia, near Čáslav; scene of victory of Frederick the Great over Austrians May 17, 1742 as result of which Prussia acquired most of Silesia from Maria Theresa.

Choukoutien. See CHO-K'OU-TIEN.

Chou–shan *or* **Chu Shan** \'chü-'shän, 'jō-'shän\ *or* **Chu·san** \'chü-'sän, 'jō-'shän\. 1 Archipelago in East China Sea off NE coast of Chekiang prov., E China, at entrance to Hangchow Bay, consisting of ab. 100 islands; ✱ Ting-hai, on Chou-shan I.; for several centuries a base for trade with foreign governments, esp. Japan and Great Britain. See P'U-T'O SHAN.

2 Island, largest of the Chou-shan archipelago, East China Sea, ab. 50 m. E of Ning-po; 20 m. long, 10 m. wide; on its S shore is Ting-hai.

Chou·teau \'shō-(,)tō\. County in Montana. See table at MONTANA.

Cho·wan \chə-'wän\. 1 River, NE North Carolina; ab. 50 m. long; formed by confluence of Blackwater and Nottoway rivers, flows SE into Albemarle Sound.

2 County in North Carolina. See table at NORTH CAROLINA.

Chow·chil·la \chau̇-'chil-ə\. City, Madera co., cen. California, 35 m. NW of Fresno; pop. (1970c) 4349; creamery products, fertilizer.

Chow Kow Tien. See CHO-K'OU-TIEN.

Choy·bal·san \ˌchȯi-bäl-'sän\ *or formerly* **Ker·u·len** \'ker-ü-ˌlen\. Town, E Mongolian People's Republic, on Kerulen river, ab. 360 m. E of Ulan Bator.

Christ·church \'krīs(t)-ˌchərch\. 1 Municipal borough, Hampshire, S England, at confluence of Avon and Stour rivers 23 m. WSW of Southampton; pop. (1971p) 31,373; aircraft construction; seaside resort; received first charter c. 1150.

2 City, near E coast of South I., New Zealand, on small Avon river 8 m. NW of its port, Lyttelton; pop. (1971p) 165,086, met. area pop. 262,400; one of New Zealand's principal industrial centers; furniture, transportation equipment, carpets; food processing; center of New Zealand's most productive wheat and grain region; founded 1850 by English Anglicans.

Chris·tian \'kris(h)-chən\. Counties in three states of the U.S. See tables at ILLINOIS, KENTUCKY, MISSOURI.

Christiana. See CHRISTINA.

Chris·ti·a·na \ˌkris-tē-'än-ə\. Town, SW Transvaal, NE Rep. of South Africa, on Vaal river 65 m. NNE of Kimberley; pop. (1967e) 6800; diamonds.

Christiania. See OSLO.

Christiansand. See KRISTIANSAND.

Chris·tians·burg \'kris(h)-chənz-ˌbərg\. Town, ⊗ of Montgomery co., Virginia, 27 m. WSW of Roanoke; pop. (1970c) 7857; lumber, textiles; diversified farming; founded 1792.

Chris·tian Sound \ˌkris(h)-chən-\. Inlet of Pacific Ocean at S end of Chatham Strait, S of Baranof I., SE Alaska.

Chris·tian·sted \'kris(h)-chən-ˌsted\. Town on NE coast of St. Croix I., Virgin Is. of the United States, West Indies; pop. (1970p) 2966; ✱ of the former Danish West Indies.

Christiansund. See KRISTIANSUND.

Chris·ti·na \kris-'tē-nə\ *or formerly* **Chris·ti·ana** \ˌkris-tē-'an-ə\. A river in N Delaware uniting with Brandywine creek and flowing into Delaware river at Wilmington.

Christ·mas Island \'kris-məs-\. 1 Island in Indian Ocean, an external territory of Australia, ab. 225 m. S of W end of Java, at 10°30′S lat. and 105°34′E long.; 11 m. long, 4½ m. wide; 52 sq. m.; pop. (1970e) 3361; deposits of phosphate of lime. Known to navigators since ab. 1650; formally annexed by Great Britain June 1888, placed under Straits Settlements 1889, and incorporated with Singapore settlement 1900; under Japanese occupation 1942–45; ceded to Australia 1958.

2 One of the Line Islands (*q.v.*) in cen. Pacific Ocean S of Hawaii and 160 m. SE of Fanning I., ab 1°57′N lat. and 157°27′W long.; pop. (1963c) 477; largest atoll in the Pacific, 234 sq. m., of which 94 sq. m. is land. Discovered by Capt. Cook 1777; annexed by Great Britain 1888; included in colony of Gilbert and Ellice Is. 1919; British control disputed by United States 1936–38 but island remained British; important as air base. See AMERICA ISLANDS.

Chris·to·pher \'kris-tə-fər\. City, Franklin co., S Illinois, 28 m. SSW of Mount Vernon; pop. (1970c) 2910.

Chru·dim \'krüd-əm, 'hrüd-\. Industrial town, Czech S.R., W Czechoslovakia, 35 m. N of Brno; pop. (1968e) 17,062; textiles; founded c. 1260.

Chrysopolis. See ÜSKÜDAR.

Chrysorrhoas. See BARADA.

Chrza·nów \kə-'shän-üf, hə-\. Commune, W Kraków prov., S Poland, 27 m. WNW of Kraków; pop. (1970) 28,500; lead and coal mining.

Chu \'chü\. River, SE Kazakh S.S.R., U.S.S.R.; 700 m. long; flows from the Tien Shan W to small lake in desert.

Chu. See PEARL 2.

Ch'üan–chou *or* **Chuan–chow** \chə-'wän-'jō\ *or formerly* **Tsin·kiang** \'jin-jē-'äŋ\. Town, Fukien prov., SE China, ab. 90 m. SW of Foochow; pop. (1970e) 130,000; univ. (1960); has been identified with Zayton (or Zaitun) described by Marco Polo as one of the great ports of the East in the time of Kublai Khan (1260–94).

Chuapa. See TSHUAPA.

Chubb Crater. See NEW QUEBEC CRATER.

Chub·buck \'chəb-ək\. City, Bannock co., SE Idaho; pop. (1970c) 2924.

Chu·but \chə-'büt, -'vüt\. 1 River in S Argentina; rises in Andes Mts., flows E across Chubut prov., and empties into Atlantic Ocean near Rawson.

2 Province of S cen. Argentina. See table at ARGENTINA.

Chu–chou *or* **Chu·chow** \'chü-'jō\. Town, Hunan prov., China, ab. 25 m. SSE of Ch'ang-sha; pop. (1970e) 350,000.

Chuchow. See LI-SHUI.

Chuckchee Sea. See CHUKCHI SEA.

Chudskoye Ozero. See PEIPUS.

Ch'ü–fou *or* **Ku·fow** \'chü-'fü\. Town, W Shantung prov., NE China, ab. 65 m. S of Tsinan. Residence of Confucius during most of his life and of his descendants (K'ung family) to the present day; 1 m. N is cemetery (600 acres) containing tomb of Confucius and graves of thousands of his descendants. Town has great Confucian temple; original small structure built 478 B.C., but was rebuilt or renovated by successive emperors.

Chu·gach Mountains \'chü-ˌgach-, -ˌgash\. Mountain range along coast of S Alaska, extending from head of Cook inlet ab. 280 m. eastward to W end of St. Elias Mts.

Chuguchak. See T'A-CH'ENG.

Ch'ü–hsien \'chü-'shen\. City, W Chekiang prov., E China, on railroad 120 m. SW of Hangchow. In World War II American air base; severe fighting 1942.

Chuk·chi Sea *or* **Chuck·chee Sea** \'chək-chē-, 'chu̇k-\ *or Russ.* **Chu·kot·skoye Mo·re** \chu̇-ˌkät-skə-yə-'mȯr-yə\. Sea, part of Arctic Ocean N of Bering Strait bet. Asia and North America.

Chu·kot National Okrug \chə-'kät . . . 'ō-ˌkrük\. District, Magadan Oblast, Russian S.F.S.R., U.S.S.R.; 284,826 sq. m.; pop. (1970p) 101,000; ✱ Anadyr; comprises Chukotski Penin. and territory occupied by Anadyr river system and Chukot Range E of Yakutsk A.S.S.R. and N of Koryak National Okrug; inhabited by the Chukchi of Paleo-Asiatic origin; chief occupations reindeer breeding, hunting, and fishing; tin mines; formed 1930 and formerly a part of Khabarovsk Krai.

Chukot Range; *formerly* **Ana·dyr Range** *or* **Ana·dir Range** \ˌän-ə-'di(ə)r-, ˌan-\ *or Russ.* **Ana·dyr·ski Khre·bet** \ˌən-ə-ˌdir-skē-krə-'b(y)et\. Mountain range, NW Chukot National Okrug, U.S.S.R.; an extension of the Kolyma Mountains; runs NW and SE across Arctic Circle to Chukotski Penin.

Chu·kot·ski Peninsula \chə-'kät-skē-\ *or* **Chu·kot Peninsula** \-'kät-\. Peninsula, E Chukot National Okrug, NE U.S.S.R., bet. Bering Sea on the S and Chukchi Sea on the N; its E point is Dezhneva Cape (*q.v.*).

Chukotskoye More. See CHUKCHI SEA.

Chu·la Vis·ta \ˌchü-lə-'vis-tə\. City, San Diego co., SW California, S of San Diego; pop. (1970c) 67,901; chemicals, electric motors, aircraft parts.

Chu·lu·ca·nas \ˌchü-lə-'kän-əs\. Town, Piura dept., NW Peru, 32 m. NE of Piura; pop. (1961c) 19,700.

Chu·lym *or* **Chu·lim** \chə-'lim\. Navigable river, Russian S.F.S.R., U.S.S.R.; 1177 m. long; rises in mountains of SW Krasnoyarsk Krai and flows N and W into Ob river below Tomsk.

Chumalhari. See CHOMO LHARI.

Chumbi. See CH'U-MU-PI SHAN-KU.

Chum·phon *or* **Jum·porn** \'chu̇m-'pōn\. 1 Province, S Thailand; 2219 sq. m.; pop. (1960c) 175,284; ✱ Chumphon.

2 Town, its ✱; port on Malay Penin. on W shore of Gulf of Siam 245 m. S of Bangkok; pop. (1960c) 9314.

Ch'u–mu–pi Shan–ku \ˈchü-ˌmü-ˈpē-ˌshän-ˈkü\ *also* **Chum·bi** \ˈchu̇m-bē\. Fertile valley in the Himalayas, in S Tibet, China, bet. Sikkim and Bhutan; alt. 9500 ft.

Chu·na \chu̇-ˈnä\ *or* **Uda** \u̇-ˈdä\. River, Irkutsk Oblast and Krasnoyarsk Krai, Russian S.F.S.R., U.S.S.R.; 748 m. long; flows N and W to Upper Tunguska just above its junction with the Yenisei.

Chu·nar *also* **Cha·nar** \chə-ˈnär\. Fortified and ancient town on S bank of Ganges, SE Uttar Pradesh, N India; 20 m. SSW of Varanasi; pop. (1961c) 8904; captured by Akbar 1575; came under control of British 1763; treaty signed here 1781 bet. Warren Hastings and nawab of Oudh.

Ch'un·ch'ŏn \ˈchün-ˈchən\. Town, ✱ of Kangwŏn prov., South Korea; pop. (1970e) 122,672.

Ch'ung–ch'ing. See CHUNGKING.

Chung–hsien \ˈju̇ŋ-shē-ˈen\ *or formerly* **Chung·chow** \-ˈjō\. City, E cen. Szechwan prov., S cen. China, on Yangtze ab. 100 m. below Chungking.

Chung–hua Jen–min Kung–ho–kuo. See CHINA.

Ch'ung·ju \ˈchu̇ŋ-ˈjü\. Town, North Ch'ungch'ŏng prov., South Korea, 65 m. SE of Seoul; pop. (1970e) 87,727.

Chung·king *or* **Ch'ung–ch'ing** \ˈchu̇ŋ-ˈkiŋ\ *also* **Tchong·king** \ˈchäŋ-, ˈchəŋ-\ *or officially* **Pa·hsien** \ˈbä-shē-ˈen\. City, S Szechwan prov., S China, on N bank of Yangtze at its junction with Chia-ling; pop. (1970e) 3,500,000; 1937–45 ✱ of China; chemicals, cement, textiles; trade center for much of W China. Declared open port 1890; scene of serious rebellion 1896–98; made headquarters of Chinese Nationalist Armies 1938 and political capital of China (from Oct. 1938) by Kuomintang; bombed severely by Japanese after 1938; American air base 1944–45.

Chungshankong. See T'ANG-CHIA-HUAN.

Chung–t'iao Shan \ˌjüŋ-ˌtyau̇-ˈshän\. Mountain range along border bet. Honan and Shansi provs., NE cen. China; in bend of the Yellow river.

Chupriya. See ĆUPRIJA.

Chu·qui·ca·ma·ta \ˌchü-kē-kə-ˈmät-ə\. Subdivision of Calama commune, N Chile; pop. (1966e) 28,786; largest known single copper-mining property in the world.

Chu·qui·sa·ca \ˌchü-kē-ˈsäk-ə\. 1 Department of S Bolivia. See table at BOLIVIA.

2 City, Bolivia. See SUCRE 1.

Chur \ˈku̇(ə)r\ *or Romansh* **Cue·ra** \ˈkwer-ə\ *or Ital.* **Co·i·ra** \ˈkȯi-rə\ *or Fr.* **Coire** \ˈkwär\ *or anc.* **Cu·ria Rhae·to·rum** \ˌkyu̇r-ē-ə-rē-ˈtōr-əm\. Commune, ✱ of Graubünden canton, E Switzerland, 43 m. E of Altdorf; pop. (1968e) 30,200; ancient cathedral (oldest part dating from 4th cent.); important tourist resort. Mentioned as city and episcopal see in 5th cent. A.D.; imperial city in 15th cent.; became capital of Graubünden canton 1820.

Church \ˈchərch\. Urban district, Lancashire, NW England, on Leeds and Liverpool Canal 20 m. N of Manchester; pop. (1969e) 5870.

Church Hill. Town, Hawkins co., NE Tennessee, 23 m. NW of Johnson City; pop. (1970c) 2822.

Church·ill \ˈchər-ˌchil, ˈchərch-ˌhil\. 1 County in Nevada. See table at NEVADA.

2 Borough, Allegheny co., SW Pennsylvania, 9 m. E of Pittsburgh; pop. (1970c) 4690.

3 River, cen. Canada; 1000 m. long; rises in Lake la Loche in NW Saskatchewan, flows E across Saskatchewan and N Manitoba and turns NE into Hudson Bay at Churchill; many rapids; passes through many large lakes, esp. **Churchill Lake** (213 sq. m.) and Snake in Saskatchewan and Granville and Southern Indian in Manitoba; chief tributaries the Reindeer and Beaver.

4 *or formerly* **Hamilton** \ˈham-əl-tən, -əlt-ᵊn\. River, S cen. Labrador, Newfoundland, Canada; 208 m. long; in its upper course called Ashuanipi; rises in Ashuanipi Lake, flows N to Dyke Lake, then SE through Dyke Lake and Lobstick Lake and finally NE into Lake Melville (*q.v.*); just below outlet from Lobstick Lake is Churchill Falls.

5 Seaport, NE Manitoba, Canada, on Hudson Bay at mouth of Churchill river; pop. (1966c) 1878; terminus of branch railroad from the Pas; best harbor on W coast of Hudson Bay; construction of port for direct shipment of wheat to Europe finished 1931. Settled as Fort Churchill 1688 by Hudson's Bay Company.

Churchill, Cape. Headland on W shore of Hudson Bay, E of Churchill, NE Manitoba, Canada.

Churchill, Mount. 1 Peak in the Wrangell Mts., SE Alaska; 15,638 ft.

2 Mountain, SW British Columbia, Canada, ab. 60 m. NW of Vancouver; 10,500 ft.

Churchill Downs \-ˈdau̇nz\. Race track, Louisville, Kentucky; scene of annual Kentucky Derby, foremost American horse-racing event, held since 1875.

Churchill Falls *or formerly* **Grand Falls**. Falls in Churchill river, W Labrador, Newfoundland, Canada; ab. 225 m. from Lake Melville; ab. 300 ft. high, 200 ft. wide; hydroelectric power installations; discovered 1839, forgotten, and rediscovered 1891.

Churchill Lake. See CHURCHILL 3.

Churchill Peaks. Two principal peaks of Mt. McKinley, S cen. Alaska; N peak 19,470 ft., S peak 20,320 ft.

Church Mountain. Peak, W cen. Whatcom co., NW Washington; 6245 ft.

Church Point. Town, Acadia parish, S Louisiana, 18 m. NW of Lafayette; pop. (1970c) 3865; rice mills.

Chu·ren Hi·mal \ˈchü-ˈren-hi-ˈmäl\. Mountain in the Himalayas, Nepal; 24,158 ft.

Chu·ru \ˈchu̇r-(ˌ)ü\. Town, Rajasthan, NW India, 110 m. NNW of Jaipur; pop. (1961c) 41,727.

Chu·ru·bus·co \ˌchu̇r-ə-ˈbü-(ˌ)skō\. Locality near Mexico City, Mexico; battle Aug. 20, 1847 in which Gen. Winfield Scott defeated Mexican forces of Santa Anna.

Chusan. See CHOU-SHAN.

Chu Shan. See CHOU-SHAN.

Chu·so·va·ya \ˌchü-sə-ˈvī-ə\. River, Sverdlovsk and Perm oblasts, Russian S.F.S.R., U.S.S.R.; ab. 430 m. long; rises near Sverdlovsk and flows NW to Kama river.

Chu·so·voi \ˌchü-sə-ˈvȯi\. Town, Perm Oblast, Russian S.F.S.R., U.S.S.R., ab. 60 m. ENE of Perm; pop. (1969e) 62,000.

Chust. See KHUST.

Chutia Nagpur. See CHOTA NAGPUR.

Chu·vash Autonomous Soviet Socialist Republic \chü-ˌväsh-\ *also* **Chu·vash·ia** \-ˈväsh-ē-ə\. Autonomous republic, E cen. Russian S.F.S.R., U.S.S.R., S of the Volga; 7066 sq. m.; pop. (1970p) 1,224,000; ✱ Cheboksary. In level country of Volga basin, crossed by lower Sura river, which also forms part of W boundary; spring wheat, corn, potatoes, peas, flax; livestock; lumbering; fruit-growing; textiles; peasant industries in woodworking. Predominant ethnic strain Turko-Tatar; Chuvashes, originally a Bulgarian people allied to the Mordvinians and nominally Christian, have been affected by Tatar elements. Chief towns Cheboksary and Alatyr. Suffered much during civil war 1918–20 and in the famine that followed; created an autonomous area June 1920 and an autonomous republic Apr. 1925.

Chu·zen·ji \chü-ˈzen-jē\. Lake in Tochigi prefecture, cen. Honshū, Japan, 7 m. W of Nikkō; 15 m. in circumference; alt. 4375 ft.; resort; noted for its mountain scenery; shrines.

Cia·les \sē-ˈäl-əs\. Town and municipality, cen. Puerto Rico, 17 m. SE of Arecibo; pop. (1970p) 3994 (town), 15,422 (munic.).

Ciam·pi·no \chäm-ˈpē-nō\. Village, cen. Italy, in Latium 10 m. SE of Rome; international airport.

Cia·no d'En·za \ˌchän-ō-ˈdent-sə\. Commune, Reggio nell'Emilia prov., Emilia-Romagna; N Italy, 12 m. SW of Reggio nell'Emilia; pop. (1968e) 3488; includes village of **Ca·nos·sa** \kə-ˈnäs-ə\ containing ruins of castle in which Emperor Henry IV submitted 1077 to Pope Gregory VII and did public penance, this humiliation of Henry giving rise to the phrase (reputedly first used by Bismarck 1871) "going to Canossa" meaning "humble submission."

Ci·a·nor·te \ˌsē-ə-ˈnȯrt-ə\. Municipality, Paraná state, S Brazil; pop. (1968e) 61,065.

Ci·bao \sē-ˈbau̇\. Fertile valley, cen. Dominican Republic, running E and W parallel with and N of the Cordillera Central; chief towns Santiago de los Caballeros and La Vega.

Cí·bo·la \ˈsē-bə-lə\. Vague historical region in present N New Mexico including seven pueblos (the "Seven Cities of Cíbola") believed by earliest Spanish explorers of the region to contain vast treasures.

Ci·bo·lo \ˈsib-ə-ˌlō\. River, Texas; ab. 150 m. long; rises on Edwards Plateau, flows SE and enters San Antonio river in cen. Karnes co.

Cib·y·ra \ˈsib-ə-rə\. Important ancient city of Greater Phrygia, on the border of Caria; became part of Roman Empire 83 B.C.

Cic·ero \ˈsis-ə-ˌrō\. Industrial town, Cook co., NE Illinois, W suburb of Chicago; pop. (1970c) 67,058; copper products, rubber, electrical equipment, malleable iron castings; Morton Junior Coll. (1924).

Ci·dra \ˈsēd-rə\. Town and municipality, E cen. Puerto Rico; pop. (1970p) 6348 (town), 24,039 (munic.).

Cie·cha·nów \chə-ˈkä-nüf, -ˈhä-\. Commune, Warszawa prov., NE cen. Poland, 49 m. NNW of Warsaw; pop. (1970p) 23,200; agricultural industries.

Cie·go de Avi·la \sē-ˌā-gō-dē-ˈäv-ə-lə\. Town and municipality, W Camagüey prov., E cen. Cuba; pop. (1967e) 54,700 (town); railroad junction in sugar-producing region.

Cie·na·ga \sē-ˈān-ə-gə\. Coastal town, N Magdalena dept., N Colombia, 40 m. E of Barranquilla; munic. pop. (1968e) 135,626; exports cotton, tobacco, bananas, cocoa.

Cien·fue·gos \sē-ˌen-ˈfwā-gōs\. Town and municipality on **Cienfuegos Bay**, SW Las Villas prov., W cen. Cuba; pop. (1967e) 91,800 (town), 125,760 (munic.); exports sugar. First visited by Columbus on first voyage; surveyed by Ocampo 1508; settled 1738.

Cie·szyn \ˈchesh-ən\ *or Ger.* **Te·schen** \ˈtesh-ən\ *or Czech* **Tě·šín** \ˈtyesh-ēn\. Industrial city, Katowice prov., S Poland, 40 m. SSW of Katowice; pop. (1970p) 25,200; metal products, chemicals; divided 1920 bet. Poland (Cieszyn, on E bank of Olsa river) and Czechoslovakia (Český Těšín, on W bank of Olsa); reunited under Polish rule 1938 but W town returned to Czechoslovakia at end of World War II. Railroad junction; first mentioned 1155; seat of duchy 1290–1653; treaty ending War of the Bavarian Succession signed 1779; in World War I Austrian headquarters till 1917. See TESCHEN.

Cie·za \sē-ˈā-sə\. Manufacturing commune, Murcia prov., SE Spain, on Segura river 25 m. NNW of Murcia; pop. (1970p) 25,359; linen and hempen fabrics, flour, brown paper, lumber; remains of Roman fort, Arab ruins, medieval church.

Ci·fuen·tes \sē-ˈfwān-təs\. Municipality, Las Villas prov., W cen. Cuba; pop. (1967c) 10,500; railroad junction point 10 m. S of Sagua la Grande.

Ci·li·cia \sə-ˈlish-(ē-)ə\. Ancient country and region in SE Asia Minor, extending along Mediterranean coast S of Taurus Mts. from the Nur Mts. to Pamphylia; conquered by Cyrus and made satrapy of Persian Empire; subdued by Alexander the Great who entered it through Cilician Gates; conquered by Pompey and made a Roman province, which at first included Pamphylia and Isauria, 62 B.C.; invaded by Arabs 710–711 A.D.; theme of Byzantine Empire; an independent Armenian principality (also called Little Armenia) founded 1080, which usually joined Crusaders against Greeks; became kingdom 1198; conquered by Turks 15th cent.; a scene of Armenian massacres 1909. As a modern region in Turkey, called also **Lesser Armenia,** it includes İçel prov. and part of Maraş prov.

Ci·li·cian Gates \sə-ˌlish-ən-\ *or anc.* **Ci·li·ci·ae Py·lae** \sə-ˈlish-ē-ˌē-ˈpī-ˌlē\; *Turk.* **Kü·lek Bo·ğa·zi** \kyü-ˌlek-bō-(g)ä-ˈzē\ *or* **Gü·lek Bo·gaz** \gyü-ˌlek-bō-ˈ(g)äz\. Pass through Bulgar Dağlari, a range in the Taurus Mts., S Turkey in Asia, 38 m. NW of Adana; has been used for centuries by armies and traders.

Cilli. See CELJE.

Cim·ar·ron \ˈsim-ə-ˌrōn, -ˌrän, -rən\. 1 River, cen. and SW United States; rises in Colfax co., NE New Mexico, and flows across SW Kansas and cen. Oklahoma into Arkansas river in SE Pawnee co., N Oklahoma; ab. 500 m. long; upper reaches known as **Dry Cimarron,** 78 m. long.

2 County in Oklahoma. See table at OKLAHOMA.

3 City, ⊗ of Gray co., SW Kansas; pop. (1970c) 1737; dairy farming.

Cimbrian Chersonese *or* **Cimbric Chersonese.** See JUTLAND.

Ci·miez \sē-ˈmyāz\ *or anc.* **Cem·e·ne·lum** \ˌsem-ə-ˈnē-ləm\. Fashionable and hotel section of Nice, France; ancient town a Gallo-Roman provincial capital, destroyed during Lombard invasions; a few ruins.

Ci·mi·ni, Mon·ti \ˌmōn-tē-ˈchē-mə-nē\ *or Eng.* **Ci·min·i·an Hills** \sə-ˌmin-ē-ən-\. Small mountain range, Latium, cen. Italy, just SE of Viterbo; highest point **Mon·te Ci·mi·no** \ˌmōn-tē-ˈchē-mə-ˌnō\ 3454 ft.

Ci·mi·te·ro \ˌchē-mi-ˈte(ə)r-(ˌ)ō\. Island in the Lagoon of Venice, NE Italy.

Cim·me·ri·an Bos·po·rus \sə-ˌmir-ē-ən-ˈbäs-p(ə-)rəs\. 1 Strait, U.S.S.R. See KERCH STRAIT.

2 An ancient kingdom on and around the Cimmerian Bosporus (*or mod.* Kerch Strait); first settlement was by Milesians (5th cent. B.C.) at town of Panticapaeum, later capital of the kingdom; gradually included all of the Crimea; came under Mithridates of Pontus c. 100 B.C.; conquered by Rome 66 B.C.

Ci·mo·lus \sə-ˈmō-ləs\ *or Gk.* **Kí·mo·los** \ˈkē-mə-ˌlȯs\ *or Ital.* **Ar·gen·tie·ra** \ˌär-jən-tē-ˈer-ə\. Island, SW Cyclades, S Aegean Sea, just NE of Melos, in Cyclades dept., Greece; 16 sq. m.; has produced much cimolite, an aluminum silicate in the form of a fine white earth, used by fullers.

Ci·mo·ne, Mon·te \ˌmōn-tē-chi-ˈmō-nē\. Peak in the Tuscan Apennines, Modena prov., N Italy; 7103 ft.

Cîm·pi·na *or* **Câm·pi·na** \kim-ˈpē-nə\. Town, Prahova co., S cen. Romania; pop. (1970e) 24,767.

Cîm·pu·lung *or* **Câm·pu·lung** *or formerly* **Kim·po·lung** \ˌkim-pu̇-ˈlu̇ŋ\. Town, Argeş co., S cen. Romania; pop. (1970e) 26,675; founded by German colonists in 12th cent.

Ci·na·ru·co \ˌsē-nə-ˈrü-(ˌ)kō\. River, NE Colombia and W Venezuela; flows E to the Orinoco; ab. 280 m. long; joined on S by the **Ci·na·ru·qui·to** \ˌsē-nə-rü-ˈkē-tō\, ab. 250 m. long, its main tributary.

Cin·ca \ˈsēŋ-kə\. River, NE Spain; 110 m. long; rises in the Pyrenees on the French frontier, flows S into Segre river above its junction with the Ebro.

Cin·cin·nati \ˌsin(t)-sə-ˈnat-ē, -ˈnat-ə\. Commercial and manufacturing city, ⊗ of Hamilton co., SW corner of Ohio, on Ohio river; pop. (1970c) 452,524; railroad center and distributing port (esp. coal, iron, lumber, salt); electric motors, machine-shop products, jet engines; brewing, meat-packing; Univ. of Cincinnati (1819), Ohio Coll. of Applied Science (1828), Xavier Univ. (1831), Hebrew Union Coll. (1875), Our Lady of Cincinnati Coll. (1935).

History: Laid out 1788 (Fort Washington built 1789); became ⊗ 1790; incorp. as town 1802, as city 1819; developed esp. with opening of Miami and Erie Canal 1832; became grape culture center and wine market following influx of Germans 1840. Known as "Queen City" or "Queen of the West." Birthplace of William Howard Taft.

Cin·go·li \ˈchēŋ-gə-lē\. Commune, Macerata prov., Marches, cen. Italy, NW of Macerata; pop. (1968e) 11,628.

Ci·ni·sel·lo Bal·sa·mo \ˌchē-nə-ˈzel-ō-ˈbȯl-sə-ˌmō\. Commune, Milan prov., Lombardy, N Italy, 4 m. N of Milan; pop. (1968e) 69,485.

Cin·na·min·son \ˌsin-ə-ˈmin(t)-sən\. Township, Burlington co., S cen. New Jersey, near Riverton; pop. (1970c) 16,962; known as initial port of entry of Japanese beetle in 1916.

Cinque Ports \ˈsiŋk-\. A number of seaport towns on the coast of Kent and Sussex in England, originally five—Dover, Sandwich, Romney (now New Romney), Hastings, and Hythe–to which were later added Winchelsea, Rye, and other minor places; enfranchised by Edward the Confessor; in return for special sea service in defense of the coast, granted many special privileges, as of civil and criminal jurisdiction, most of which have been annulled.

Cin·ta·la·pa \ˌsēn-tə-ˈläp-ə\. Town and municipality, Chiapas state, SE Mexico, 40 m. W of San Andrés Tuxtla; munic. pop. (1970p) 31,252.

Cin·to, Mont \mȯnt-ˈchēn-(ˌ)tō\. Mountain, NW Corsica, France; 8891 ft.

Cintra. See SINTRA.

Çiotat, La. See LA CIOTAT.

Či·o·vo \ˈchē-ə-ˌvō\ *or Ital.* **Bua** \ˌbü-ə\. Yugoslav island in the Adriatic Sea off the Dalmatian coast opp. Trogir.

Ci·pan·go \sə-ˈpaŋ-(ˌ)gō\ *also* **Ci·pan·gu** \-(ˌ)gü\. In medieval legend an island, or islands, east of Asia; described by Marco Polo by the name Zipangu. It was sought by Columbus and is generally identified with the modern Japan.

Circars. See NORTHERN CIRCARS.

Cir·cas·sia \(ˌ)sər-ˈkash-(ē-)ə\. Region in S Russian S.F.S.R., U.S.S.R., N of the W end of the Caucasus Mts. and on the NE coast of the Black Sea; has no political significance. Inhabited from ab. 13th cent. by races subject to Georgia, who became independent in first half of 15th cent. They occupied the basins of tributaries of the Terek and Kuban rivers, a warlike people noted for their beautiful women; their two leading branches are today the Adygei and Cherkess, now forming two autonomous regions of the Russian S.F.S.R. (see ADYGEI AUTONOMOUS OBLAST and KARACHAYEVO-CHERKESS AUTONOMOUS OBLAST). Taken over by Russians by 1829; after long war of resistance to Russia 1830–59, large numbers deported 1864 to Turkey. After Revolution 1917 autonomous areas established for remaining members of race.

Cir·ceo, Mon·te \ˌmänt-ē-chir-ˈchā-(ˌ)ō\ *or anc.* **Cir·cae·um Prom·on·to·ri·um** \(ˌ)sər-ˈsē-əm-ˌpräm-ən-ˈtōr-ē-əm, -tȯr-\. Mountain and promontory on N side of the Gulf of Gaeta, W Italy, W of Terracina; 1775 ft.; in very early times an island called **Ae·aea** \ē-ˈē-ə\, legendary home of Circe.

Cir·cle \ˈsər-kəl\. 1 Village, E Alaska, on upper Yukon river ab. 85 m. above Ft. Yukon; pop. (1970c) 54; mining village settled ab. 1890, deserted during Klondike rush.
2 Town, ⊗ of McCone co., E Montana; pop. (1970c) 964; wheat; livestock.

Circle Pines. Village, Anoka co., E Minnesota, 10 m. N of St. Paul; pop. (1970c) 3918.

Cir·cle·ville \ˈsər-kəl-ˌvil\. City, ⊗ of Pickaway co., S cen. Ohio, on Scioto river 25 m. S of Columbus; pop. (1970c) 11,687; in agricultural region; settled 1806 on site once occupied by mound builders; incorp. as village 1814, as city 1853.

Cir·cu·lar Head \ˈsər-kyə-lər-\. 1 A promontory at tip of a peninsula on N coast of Tasmania, Australia, ab. 40 m. NW of Burnie; 478 ft. high; a steep mass of greenstone; at its foot on mainland side is the town of Stanley.
2 Town, Australia. See STANLEY 4.

Cirenaica. See CYRENAICA.

Ci·ren·ces·ter \ˈsi(ə)r-ən-ˌses-tər, ˈsis-ə-tər\ *or anc.* **Co·rin·i·um** \kōr-ˈin-ē-əm, kȯr-\. Urban district, Gloucestershire, SW cen. England, 14 m. SE of Gloucester; pop. (1971p) 13,022; remains of an abbey dating from 1117.

Cirene. See CYRENE.

Ci·rey *or in full* **Cirey–sur–Blaise** \si-ˌrā-sü(ə)r-ˈblaz\. Village, Haute-Marne dept., NE France, NW of Chaumont; on Blaise river, tributary of Marne; château of Mme du Châtelet; residence of Voltaire 1734–49.

Ci·riè \chir-ē-ˈā\. Commune, Torino prov., Piedmont, NW Italy, 12 m. NNW of Turin; pop. (1968e) 13,924.

Cirque de Gavarnie. See GAVARNIE.

Cirque Mountain \ˈsərk-\. Highest point in Torngat Mts., Labrador, Newfoundland, Canada, at S end of the range; 5160 ft.

Cirta. See CONSTANTINE 2.

Cisalpine Gaul. See GAUL.

Cis·al·pine Republic \sis-ˌal-pīn-\. Republic in N Italy created by Napoleon 1797 by combining the Cispadane and Transpadane Republics; ✱ Milan; embraced lands around Milan N of the Po and around Ferrara and Bologna S of Po; incorporated into kingdom of Italy 1805.

Cisa Pass *or* **La Cisa.** See table at APENNINES.

Cis·cau·ca·sia \ˌsis-kȯ-ˈkā-zhə, -shə\ *also* **Northern Caucasia** *or Russ.* **Pred·kav·kazye** \ˌprid-kəf-ˈkäs-yə\. Region N of the Caucasus Mts. in the Russian S.F.S.R., U.S.S.R.; 82,600 sq. m. (see CAUCASIA); comprises Checheno-Ingush A.S.S.R., S half of Krasnodar Krai, and the Dagestan, Kabardino-Balkarian and North Ossetian A.S.S.Rs.

Cis·co \ˈsis-(ˌ)kō\. City, Eastland co., N cen. Texas, 40 m. E of Abilene; pop. (1970c) 4160; bricks; peanuts; gas and oil wells.

Cis·lei·tha·nia \ˌsis-lī-ˈthān-yə, -ˈthā-nē-ə\. Formerly, that part of Austria-Hungary W of Leitha river.

Cis·ne·ros \sis-ˈner-əs\. Town, Antioquia dept., NW Colombia, 40 m. NE of Medellín; pop. (1968e) 10,360.

Cispadane Gaul. See GAUL.

Cis·pa·dane Republic \ˌsis-pə-ˌdān-, sis-ˈpā-ˌdān-\. Republic in N Italy created by Napoleon 1796 from lands S of Po around Modena, Reggio nell'Emilia, Ferrara, and Bologna; ✱ Bologna; incorporated 1797 into Cisalpine Republic (*q.v.*).

Cis·pla·tine Province \sis-ˈplā-ˌtīn-\. See URUGUAY 1, *History.*

Cistercium. See CÎTEAUX.

Cis·ter·na di La·ti·na \chēs-ˌter-nə-dē-lä-ˈtēn-ə\. Commune, Latina prov., Latium, W cen. Italy, 8 m. NNW of Latina; pop. (1968e) 20,718.

Ci·ster·ni·no \ˌchēs-tər-ˈnē-nō\. Commune, Brindisi prov., Apulia, SE Italy, 28 m. WNW of Brindisi; pop. (1968e) 11,562.

Cit·a·del, Mount \-ˈsit-əd-ᵊl, -ə-ˌdel\. Peak in Glacier National Park, NW Montana; 9024 ft.

Cî·teaux \si-ˈtō\ *or Lat.* **Cis·ter·ci·um** \sis-ˈtər-sh(ē-)əm\. Village in the commune **Saint–Ni·co·las–lès–Cîteaux** \ˌsaⁿ-ˌnē-kə-ˈlä-lā-\, Côte-d'Or dept., E France, ab. 16 m. SSE of Dijon; abbey of Cistercian Order, founded 1098 by Robert de Molesmes.

Ci·thae·ron \sə-ˈthē-rən\ *or* **Ki·thai·rón** \ˌkē-thə-ˈrȯn\ *also* **El·a·tea** \ˌel-ə-ˈtē-ə\. Mountain, Greece, on Attica-Boeotia boundary; 4623 ft; sacred to Dionysus and the Muses.

Citharista. See LA CIOTAT.

Ci·ti·um \ˈsish(-ē)-əm\. Ancient city on SE coast of Cyprus, center of Phoenician influence in the island; part of its site is now port of Larnaca. Founded before Phoenician era; under control of Assyria in 7th cent. B.C. In the Bible known as **Kit·tim** \ˈkit-əm\ (*Gen.* x. 4; *Isa.* xxiii. 12). During period of Greek revolts was loyal to Persia. Birthplace of Zeno, Greek Stoic philosopher.

Ci·tlal·té·petl \sē-ˌtläl-ˈtā-ˌpet-ᵊl\ *or* **Ori·za·ba** \ˌōr-ə-ˈzäb-ə, ȯr-\. Volcanic peak in cen. Veracruz state, Mexico; 18,700 ft.; highest point in Mexico.

Cit·ro·nelle \ˌsit-rə-ˈnel\. Town, Mobile co., SW Alabama, 30 m. NW of Mobile; pop. (1970c) 1935; surrender of last Confederate army E of Mississippi river May 4, 1865.

Cit·rus \ˈsit-rəs\. County in Florida. See table at FLORIDA.

Cit·ta·del·la \ˌchē-tə-ˈdel-ə\. Manufacturing commune, Padova prov., Veneto, NE Italy, 16 m. N by W of Padua; pop. (1968e) 15,221; textiles; founded 1220; ancient city walls and tower.

Cit·ta della Pie·ve \chi-'tä-del-ə-'pyā-vē\. Commune, Perugia prov., Umbria, cen. Italy; pop. (1968e) 6893; cathedral. Birthplace of Il Perugino.

Città del Vaticano. See VATICAN CITY.

Cit·tà di Cas·tel·lo \chē-ˌtä-dē-kä-'stel-(ˌ)ō\. Commune, Perugia prov., Umbria, cen. Italy, on Tiber river 27 m. NNW of Perugia; pop. (1968e) 36,274; Renaissance cathedral; mineral springs; ironworks.

Cit·ta·no·va \ˌchē-tə-'nō-və\. Commune, Reggio di Calabria prov., Calabria, S Italy; pop. (1968e) 13,023.

Cittavecchia. See STARI GRAD.

Città Vec·chia \chi-'tä-'vek-(ˌ)yä\ *or* **No·ta·bi·le** \nō-'täb-i-lē\. Fortified city, cen. Malta I., 6 m. W of Valletta; capital of the island until 1570; cathedral, catacombs.

City Island \'sit-ē-\. Island in Long Island Sound off E coast of the Bronx, New York City.

City of Refuge National Historical Park \-'ref-(ˌ)yüj-\. See UNITED STATES, *National Historical Parks.*

City Point. Formerly a village, now part of Hopewell, Prince George co., Virginia, on James river; base of operations in Civil War.

Ci·u·dad Acu·ña \ˌsē-ü-ˌthä(th)-ə-'kün-yə, -ü-ˌdad-\ *or formerly* **Vil·la Acuña** \ˌvē-(y)ə-\. Town, NE Coahuila state, NE Mexico, on the Rio Grande opp. Del Rio, Texas; munic. pop. (1970p) 32,760.

Ciudad Bo·lí·var \-bə-'lē-ˌvär\. River port, ✻ of Bolívar state, NE Venezuela, on the narrows (Span. *angosturas*) of the Orinoco river, whence its former popular name **An·gos·tu·ra** \ˌaŋ-gəs-'tů(ə)r-ə\; pop. (1970e) 109,605; exports include cattle, hides, timber; gold; founded 1764.

Ciudad Ca·mar·go \-kə-'mär-(ˌ)gō\. Town, SE Chihuahua state, N Mexico, 85 m. SE of Chihuahua; part of munic. of **Camargo,** pop. (1970p) 35,211.

Ciudad de las Casas. See SAN CRISTÓBAL 6.

Ciudad del Carmen. See CARMEN 3.

Ciudad del Ma·íz \-ˌdel-mä-'ēs\. Municipality, San Luis Potosí state, Mexico, 95 m. ENE of San Luis Potosí; pop. (1970p) 35,502; agriculture; cattle raising.

Ciudad de Mexico, D.F. See MEXICO CITY.

Ciudad de Valles. See VALLES 2.

Ciu·da·de·la \ˌsē-ü-thä-'thā-lə, -dä-'dā-lə\. Manufacturing seaport, Baleares prov., Spain, on W coast of Minorca I. 70 m. NE of Palma; pop. (1970p) 15,140.

Ciudad Guayana. See SANTO TOMÉ DE GUAYANA.

Ciudad Guz·mán \-güz-'män\. City, Jalisco state, W cen. Mexico; 35 m. S of Lake Chapala; munic. pop. (1970p) 48,142.

Ciudad Hi·dal·go \-hid-'al-(ˌ)gō, -ē-'thäl-\. Town, Michoacán state, SW Mexico; munic. pop. (1970p) 59,159.

Ciudad Ix·te·pec \-ˌēs-tə-'pek\ *or formerly* **San Je·ró·ni·mo Ixtepec** \ˌsan-her-'ōn-ə-ˌmō-\. Town, Oaxaca state, SE Mexico, ab. 115 m. ESE of Oaxaca; pop. (1960c) 12,087.

Ciudad Juá·rez \-'(h)wär-ˌez, -es; -'wär-əs\. City, Chihuahua state, N Mexico, opp. El Paso, Texas; munic. pop. (1970p) 436,054; alt. 3117 ft.; connected with El Paso by bridge over the Rio Grande; founded in latter part of 17th cent.; important as early transportation center; headquarters of Benito Juárez 1865.

Ciudad Ma·de·ro \-mə-'de(ə)r-(ˌ)ō\ *also* **Vil·la Ce·ci·lia** \ˌvē-(y)ə-sə-'sēl-yə\. City, Tamaulipas state, E Mexico, S suburb of Tampico; munic. pop. (1970p) 89,994.

Ciudad Man·te \-'män-tā\. Town, Tamaulipas state, E Mexico; munic. pop. (1970p) 79,130.

Ciudad Man·u·el Do·bla·do \-män-ˌwel-dō-'blä-thō, -'blä-dō\. Municipality, Guanajuato state, Mexico, 50 m. SW of Guanajuato; pop. (1970p) 30,177; tanneries, spinning mills, diversified agriculture.

Ciudad Men·do·za \-men-'dō-zə\. Town, Veracruz state, E Mexico, just SW of Orizaba; pop. (1960c) 16,051.

Ciudad Obre·gón \-ˌō-brā-'gōn\. Town, Sonora state, NW Mexico, 65 m. SE of Guaymas; pop. (1969e) 138,506.

Ciudad Oje·da \-ō-'hā-də\. Municipality, Zulia state, NW Venezuela, 40 m. SE of Maracaibo, on shore of Lake Maracaibo; pop. (1970e) 80,480.

Ciudad Porfirio Díaz. See PIEDRAS NEGRAS 2.

Ciudad Re·al \-rā-'äl\. 1 Province of S cen. Spain. See table at SPAIN.

2 Commune, its ✻, near Guadiana river 99 m. S of Madrid; pop. (1970p) 41,708; woolen and linen goods, brandies; Gothic cathedral; founded by Alfonso el Sabio; Spaniards defeated by French nearby 1809.

Ciudad Ro·dri·go \-rō-'drē-(ˌ)gō\. Manufacturing commune, Salamanca prov., W Spain, 53 m. WSW of Salamanca; pop. (1970p) 13,320; cathedral (begun 1190); taken by English 1706 but recovered 1707; in Peninsular War twice captured: by the French under Ney July 10, 1810 and by the British under Wellington Jan. 19, 1812.

Ciudad Trujillo. See SANTO DOMINGO 3.

Ciudad Va·lles \-'väl-ās\. Municipality, San Luis Potosí state, Mexico, 80 m. W of Tampico; pop. (1970p) 71,098; cotton gins, alcohol and plywood factories; diversified agriculture.

Ciudad Vic·to·ria \-ˌvik-tōr-ē-ə, -'tòr-\. Town, ✻ of Tamaulipas state, E cen. Mexico; in center of sugar-growing region 150 m. SE of Monterrey; munic. pop. (1970p) 94,304; univ. (1956); founded 1750.

Ciudad Vie·ja \-vē-'ā-hə\. Town and municipality, Sacatepéquez dept., S cen. Guatemala; munic. pop. (1964p) 7190.

Ci·vi·ta Ca·stel·la·na \ˌchē-və-ˌtä-ˌkäs-tə-'län-ə\ *or anc.* **Fa·le·rii** \fə-'ler-ē-ˌī\. Commune, Viterbo, N Latium, cen. Italy, N of Rome; pop. (1968e) 14,053; 13th cent. cathedral of Santa Maria; ancient Falerii one of 12 cities of Etruria; built on a plateau surrounded except on W side by gorges 200 ft. deep; conquered by Romans 241 B.C.

Civita Lavinia. See LANUVIUM.

Ci·vi·ta·no·va Mar·che \ˌchē-vē-tä-ˌnò-və-'mär-(ˌ)kā\. Commune, Macerata prov., Marches, E Italy, on coast, ab. 15 m. E of Macerata; pop. (1968e) 31,068.

Civitas Altae Ripae. See BRZEG.

Civitas Carnutum. See CHARTRES.

Civitas Eburovicum. See ÉVREUX.

Civitas Nemetum. See SPEYER.

Ci·vi·ta·vec·chia \ˌchē-vē-tä-'vek-(ˌ)yä\ *or anc.* **Cen·tum Cel·lae** \ˌsent-əm-'sel-(ˌ)ē\ *also* **Tra·ja·ni Por·tus** \trə-ˌjā-nī-'pōrt-əs, -'pòrt-\. Fortified seaport, Roma prov., Latium, cen. Italy, on Tyrrhenian Sea 39 m. WNW of Rome; pop. (1968e) 42,570; cement; maritime traffic; episcopal see; chief port of Rome; citadel (designed by Michelangelo; erected by Pope Urban VIII), arsenal (designed by Bernini and Bramante), aqueduct; Etruscan and ancient Roman antiquities; occupied by French 1849–70.

Ci·vi·tel·la del Tron·to \ˌchē-və-ˌtel-ə-del-'trōn-tō\. Commune, Teramo prov., Abruzzi, cen. Italy, 8 m. N of Teramo; pop. (1968e) 7426.

Ciz·re \jēz-'rē\ *or formerly* **Je·zi·ret ibn Omar** \jə-ˌzir-ət-ˌeb-ən-'ō-(ˌ)mär\. Town, SE Mardin prov., SE Turkey, on the Tigris on Syrian border.

Clack·a·mas \'klak-ə-məs\. 1 River, NW Oregon; ab. 80 m. long; flows NW into Willamette river.

2 County in Oregon. See table at OREGON.

Clack·man·nan \klak-'man-ən\. 1 *or* **Clack·man·nan·shire** \-ˌshi(ə)r, -shər\. County, cen. Scotland; 55 sq. m.; pop. (1971p) 45,553; ⊗ Alloa; coal mining, sheep raising; engineering, brewing; Scotland's smallest county.

2 Parish and town, ab. 7 m. E of Stirling; its former ⊗; associated with Robert Bruce and Robert Burns.

Clac·ton \'klak-tən\. Urban district, Essex, SE England, on North Sea 59 m. ENE of London; pop. (1971p) 37,942; seaside resort.

Clai·borne \'klā-bərn\. Name of a parish in Louisiana and of counties in two states of the U.S. See tables at LOUISIANA, MISSISSIPPI, TENNESSEE.

Claire, Lake \-ˈkla(ə)r, -ˈkle(ə)r\. Lake, NE Alberta, Canada, W of Lake Athabaska; 545 sq. m.

Claire·mont \ˈkla(ə)r-ˌmänt, ˈkle(ə)r-\. Town, ⊗ of Kent co., NW Texas.

Clair·ton \ˌkla(ə)rt-ᵊn, ˈkle(ə)rt-\. Industrial city, Allegheny co., SW Pennsylvania, on Monongahela river 12 m. SSE of Pittsburgh; pop. (1970c) 15,051; manufactures coke and its by-products, also steel, chemicals; settled 1770.

Clair·vaux \kler-ˈvō\. Hamlet, Aube dept., NE France, 40 m. ESE of Troyes; contains Cistercian abbey, since 1808 a prison, founded 1115 by St. Bernard of Clairvaux.

Clal·lam \ˈklal-əm\. County in Washington. See table at WASHINGTON.

Cla·mart \kla-ˈmär\. Commune, Hauts-de-Seine dept., N France, suburb of Paris near Forest of Meudon; pop. (1968c) 54,906.

Cla·me·cy \klam-ˈsē\. Commune, Nièvre dept., cen. France, 36 m. NNE of Nevers on the Canal of Nivernais; pop. (1962c) 5760; seat of bishops of Bethlehem after Saladin's capture of Jerusalem 1188 and until 1789.

Clan·ton \ˈklant-ᵊn\. City, ⊗ of Chilton co., cen. Alabama, 41 m. NW of Montgomery; pop. (1970c) 5868; timber; fruit.

Clare \ˈkla(ə)r, ˈkle(ə)r\. 1 County, Michigan. See table at MICHIGAN.

2 City, Clare co., cen. Michigan, 15 m. N of Mt. Pleasant; pop. (1970c) 2639; electronic equipment; meat packing; oil and gas wells.

3 River, co. Galway, Eire; flows S through center of county then W and into Lough Corrib near its S end.

4 County, Munster prov., W Eire; 1231 sq. m.; pop. (1971p) 74,844; ⊗ Ennis; oats, potatoes; livestock raising, quarrying (marble, slate), fishing.

5 Island off W coast of Ireland at entrance to Clew Bay and S of Achill I.; 6.3 sq. m.; administratively in co. Mayo, Eire.

Clare·mont \ˈkla(ə)r-ˌmänt, ˈkle(ə)r-\. 1 City, Los Angeles co., SW California, 28 m. E of Los Angeles; pop. (1970c) 23,464; scientific instruments; citrus fruits; Pomona Coll. (1887), Scripps Coll. (1926), Claremont Men's Coll. (1946), Harvey Mudd Coll. (1955), Pitzer Coll. (1964).

2 City, Sullivan co., SW New Hampshire, 30 m. N of Keene; pop. (1970c) 14,221; mining machinery, footwear; summer resort.

3 Town, W Western Australia, W suburb of Perth on Melville Water, the estuary of Swan river; pop. (1966c) 8938.

Clare·more \ˈkla(ə)r-ˌmō(ə)r, ˈkle(ə)r-, -mȯ(ə)r\. City and health resort, ⊗ of Rogers co., NE Oklahoma, 25 m. ENE of Tulsa; pop. (1970c) 9084; castings; mineral springs; gas, oil, coal deposits; Oklahoma Military Acad. (1920); birthplace of Will Rogers nearby bet. Claremore and Oologah (to NW).

Clar·ence \ˈklar-ən(t)s\. 1 River, NE New South Wales, SE Australia; 245 m. long; flows SE to Pacific Ocean.

2 River, NE South I., New Zealand; 130 m. long; flows NE, E, and SE to Pacific S of Waipapa Point.

Clarence Island. 1 Small island in Scotia Sea, in NE part of South Shetlands, 54°05′W, 61°12′S; part of British Antarctic Territory.

2 Chilean island in Tierra del Fuego Archipelago (*q.v.*), SW of Brunswick Penin.

Clarence Strait. 1 Narrow passage, SE Alaska, bet. Prince of Wales I. on W and Wrangell and Revillagigedo Is. and mainland on E; ab. 135 m. long.

2 Channel bet. Bathurst and Melville Is. on N and mainland of Northern Territory, Australia, on S; connects Van Diemen Gulf with Timor Sea; ab. 90 m. long.

3 *or* **Khū·rān Strait** \kü-ˈrän-\. Strait in E Persian Gulf, extending bet. Qeshm I. and the mainland of Iran.

Clar·en·don \ˈklar-ən-dən\. 1 County in South Carolina. See table at SOUTH CAROLINA.

2 City, ⊗ of Monroe co., E Arkansas; pop. (1970c) 2563; lumber mills.

3 City, ⊗ of Donley co., NW Texas, in the Panhandle 52 m. ESE of Amarillo; pop. (1970c) 1974; cattle, cotton.

4 Parish, England. See CLARENDON PARK.

Clarendon Hills. Village, Du Page co., NE Illinois, SW of Chicago; pop. (1970c) 6750.

Clarendon Park *or* **Clarendon.** Parish, S Wiltshire, England, 2 m. SE of Salisbury; scene 1164 of council of bishops and barons who issued the *Constitutions of Clarendon* defining and limiting the rights of the clergy.

Cla·rens \kla-ˈräⁿ(s)\. Village, one of the Montreux group, Vaud canton, Switzerland, at E end of Lake Geneva; pop. (1965e) 3600; winter resort; chief scene of Rousseau's *Nouvelle Héloïse.*

Clares·holm \ˈkla(ə)rz-ˌhōm\. Town, Alberta, Canada, 75 m. SSE of Calgary; pop. (1971p) 2957; diversified agriculture; flour mills, creamery.

Cla·ri·den·stock \klä-ˈrēd-ᵊn-ˌshtȯk\. Peak in the Alps, Uri canton, cen. Switzerland; 10,730 ft.

Cla·rin·da \klə-ˈrin-də\. City, ⊗ of Page co., SW Iowa; pop. (1970c) 5420; meat products; Iowa Western Community Coll. (1923).

Clar·i·on \ˈklar-ē-ən\. 1 River, NW cen. Pennsylvania; rises in McKean co., flows SW into Allegheny river.

2 County in Pennsylvania. See table at PENNSYLVANIA.

3 City, ⊗ of Wright co., N cen. Iowa; pop. (1970c) 2972; hatcheries; corn.

4 Borough, ⊗ of Clarion co., W Pennsylvania, on Clarion river; pop. (1970c) 6095; Clarion State Coll. (1866).

Clarium. See CHIARI.

Clark \ˈklärk\. 1 Name of counties in twelve states of the U.S. See tables at ARKANSAS, IDAHO, ILLINOIS, INDIANA, KANSAS, KENTUCKY, MISSOURI, NEVADA, OHIO, SOUTH DAKOTA, WASHINGTON, WISCONSIN.

2 Township, Union co., NE New Jersey, SW of Elizabeth; pop. (1970c) 18,829.

3 City, ⊗ of Clark co., NE South Dakota; pop. (1970c) 1356.

Clark, Mount. 1 Peak in Sierra Nevada, E Mariposa co., cen. California; 11,522 ft.

2 Peak in Franklin Mts., Mackenzie dist., Northwest Territories, Canada; 4798 ft.

3 Peak, N South I., New Zealand; 7085 ft.

Clark·dale \ˈklärk-ˌdāl\. Town, Yavapai co., cen. Arizona; pop. (1970c) 892; copper smelting.

Clarke \ˈklärk\. Name of counties in five states of the U.S. See tables at ALABAMA, GEORGIA, IOWA, MISSISSIPPI, VIRGINIA.

Clarkes·ville \ˈklärks-ˌvil\. City, ⊗ of Habersham co., NE Georgia; pop. (1970c) 1294; truck farming.

Clark Fork. River, Montana and Idaho; ab. 300 m. long; rises near Butte, Silver Bow co., SW Montana, and flows NW across Idaho border to Pend Oreille Lake in N Idaho.

Clark Hill Reservoir. Reservoir on Georgia-South Carolina boundary; formed by damming of Savannah river; ab. 35 m. long.

Clarks·burg \ˈklärks-ˌbərg\. Industrial city, ⊗ of Harrison co., N West Virginia, on West Fork, headstream of the Monongahela river; pop. (1970c) 24,684; cement, glass; coal mines, oil and gas.

Clarks·dale \ˈklärks-ˌdāl\. City, ⊗ of Coahoma co., NW Mississippi, 53 m. NNW of Greenwood; pop. (1970c) 21,673; farm machinery, fertilizer; Coahoma Junior Coll. (1926).

Clarks Fork \ˈklärks-\. River, NW Wyoming and S Montana; ab. 120 m. long; rises in Absaroka Range in S Montana, flows E through NW Wyoming, then N into Yellowstone river in S cen. Montana.

Clarks Summit. Borough, Lackawanna co., NE Pennsylvania, 7 m. N of Scranton; pop. (1970c) 5376.

Clarks·ton \ˈklärk-stən\. 1 Town, De Kalb co., NW cen. Georgia; pop. (1970c) 3127; residential suburb of Atlanta.

2 City, Asotin co., SE Washington, on Snake river opp. Lewiston, Idaho; pop. (1970c) 6312.

Clarks·ville \ˈklärks-ˌvil, -vəl\. 1 City, ⊗ of Johnson co., NW Arkansas, near Arkansas river 56 m. E of Fort Smith; pop. (1970c) 4616; settled 1837. College of the Ozarks (1891).

2 Town, Clark co., S Indiana; pop. (1970c) 13,806.

3 City, ⊗ of Montgomery co., N Tennessee, on peninsula at confluence of Cumberland and Red rivers 40 m. WNW of Nashville; pop. (1970c) 31,719; tobacco processing; limestone quarries; settled 1784.

4 City, ⊗ of Red River co., NE Texas, 29 m. E of Paris; pop. (1970c) 3346; cotton, lumber, corn, oats; livestock.

Clat·sop \ˈklat-səp\. County in Oregon. See table at OREGON.

Clauda. See GAVDOS.

Claude \ˈklȯd\. City, ⊗ of Armstrong co., NW Texas, in the Panhandle; pop. (1970c) 992.

Clau·di·op·o·lis \ˌklȯd-ē-ˈäp-ə-ləs\ *or earlier* **Bi·thyn·i·um** \bə-ˈthin-ē-əm\. Ancient city in Bithynia, Asia Minor, near modern Bolu; destroyed by earthquake.

Claus·thal–Zel·ler·feld *also* **Klaus·thal–Zellerfeld** \ˌklau̇s-täl-ˈtsel-ər-ˌfelt\. City, Lower Saxony, West Germany, in NW Harz Mts. 32 m. SSW of Brunswick; pop. (1968e) 15,817; technical univ. (1775, univ. status 1912); formerly an important mining center: iron, lead, copper, silver, zinc; winter resort; city charter received by Clausthal 1554, by Zellerfeld 1532.

Claw·son \ˈklȯs-ᵊn\. City, Oakland co., SE Michigan, 11 m. SE of Pontiac; pop. (1970c) 17,617; tools and dies.

Clax·ton \ˈklak-stən\. City, ⊗ of Evans co., SE cen. Georgia, 48 m. W of Savannah; pop. (1970c) 2669.

Clay \ˈklā\. 1 Name of counties in eighteen states of the U.S. See tables at ALABAMA, ARKANSAS, FLORIDA, GEORGIA, ILLINOIS, INDIANA, IOWA, KANSAS, KENTUCKY, MINNESOTA, MISSISSIPPI, MISSOURI, NEBRASKA, NORTH CAROLINA, SOUTH DAKOTA, TENNESSEE, TEXAS, WEST VIRGINIA.

2 Town, ⊗ of Clay co., cen. West Virginia; pop. (1970c) 479.

Clay, Mount. Peak of the White Mts. in S Coos co., N New Hampshire, just N of Mt. Washington; 5532 ft.

Clay Center. 1 City, ⊗ of Clay co., NE cen. Kansas, NW of Manhattan; pop. (1970c) 4963; flour mills.

2 City, ⊗ of Clay co., S Nebraska; pop. (1970c) 952.

Clay Cross \ˈklā-ˈkrȯs\. Urban district, Derbyshire, N cen. England, 15 m. S of Sheffield; pop. (1971p) 9726.

Clay·pool \ˈklā-(ˌ)pül\. Town (unincorp.), Gila co., E cen. Arizona, NW of Globe; pop. (1970c) 2245; copper region.

Clay·ton \ˈklāt-ᵊn\. 1 Name of counties in two states of the U.S. See tables at GEORGIA and IOWA.

2 Town, a ⊗ of Barbour co., SE Alabama; pop. (1970c) 1626.

3 City, ⊗ of Rabun co., NE corner of Georgia; pop. (1970c) 1569.

4 City, ⊗ of St. Louis co., E Missouri, 8 m. W of St. Louis; pop. (1970c) 16,222; residential suburb of St. Louis.

5 Borough, Gloucester co., SW New Jersey, 21 m. S of Camden; pop. (1970c) 5193; in farming region.

6 Town, ⊗ of Union co., NE corner of New Mexico, on high plateau; pop. (1970c) 2931.

7 Village, Jefferson co., N New York, on St. Lawrence river in Thousand Is. region, 20 m. NNW of Watertown; pop. (1970c) 1970; summer resort, fishing center; port of entry.

8 Town, Johnston co., E North Carolina, 13 m. SE of Raleigh; pop. (1970c) 3103; lumber, cotton.

Clayton–le–Moors \-lə-ˈmu̇(ə)rz, -ˈmō(ə)rz\. Urban district, Lancashire, NW England, 21 m. N of Manchester; pop. (1971p) 6760; coal mining.

Cla·zom·e·nae \klə-ˈzäm-ə-ˌnē\. Ancient city in Asia Minor, 20 m. W of İzmir (Turkey), on the Gulf of İzmir; one of the 12 Ionian Cities, celebrated for its temples. Birthplace of the philosopher Anaxagoras.

Clear, Cape \-ˈkli(ə)r\. Headland, S Clear I., off SW Eire.

Clear Creek. 1 River, cen. Colorado; ab. 80 m. long; rises SW Clear Creek co., flows E into South Platte river.

2 County in Colorado. See table at COLORADO.

Clear·field \ˈkli(ə)r-ˌfēld\. 1 County in W cen. Pennsylvania. See table at PENNSYLVANIA.

2 Borough, its ⊗, 20 m. ESE of Du Bois; pop. (1970c) 8176; settled 1805.

3 City, Davis co., N Utah, S of Ogden; pop. (1970c) 13,316.

Clear Fork. River, N cen. Texas; 220 m. long; flows E across Jones co., follows winding course through Shackelford, Throckmorton, and Stephens cos.; enters Brazos river in S Young co.

Clear Island. Island off S coast of co. Cork, Eire; 3 m. long; its S point is Cape Clear; 4 m. to the SW is Fastnet lighthouse.

Clear Lake. 1 Lake, Lake co., W California; 25 m. long, 2 to 10 m. wide.

2 Reservoir in California. See CLEAR LAKE RESERVOIR.

3 *or in full* **Clear Lake City.** City on Clear Lake, Cerro Gordo co., N Iowa, 14 m. W of Mason City; pop. (1970c) 6430.

4 City, ⊗ of Deuel co., E South Dakota; pop. (1970c) 1157.

Clear Lake Reservoir *or* **Clear Lake.** Large reservoir in NW Modoc co., NE California, ab. 10 m. below Oregon border; its outlet, an upper tributary (Lost River) of the Klamath, flows NW into Oregon.

Clear·wa·ter \ˈkli(ə)r-ˌwȯt-ər, -ˌwät-\. 1 River, NW Idaho; formed by forks uniting in N Idaho co., flows N and W into Snake river at Lewiston, NW Nez Perce co.

2 Name of counties in two states of the U.S. See tables at IDAHO and MINNESOTA.

3 City, ⊗ of Pinellas co., W Florida penin., on Gulf of Mexico 18 m. NW of St. Petersburg; pop. (1970c) 52,074; citrus fruit, flowers, electronic equipment; fishing; connected by two-mile causeway with **Clearwater Beach Island,** a beach resort; incorp. 1891.

4 Lake, Quebec, Canada; 478 sq. m.; outlet on W connects it with Richmond Gulf (*q.v.*).

5 River, SW Alberta, Canada; 100 m. long; flows from N Banff National Park to North Saskatchewan river.

6 River, cen. Canada; ab. 130 m. long; rises in lakes in NW Saskatchewan and flows W to the Athabasca in NE Alberta; midway in its course is accessible from Lake la Loche (source of Churchill river) by La Loche Portage.

Clearwater Mountains. Mountain group in Idaho co., N cen. Idaho; highest point ab. 8000 ft.

Cle·burne \ˈklē-bərn\. 1 Name of counties in two states in the U.S. See tables at ALABAMA and ARKANSAS.

2 City, ⊗ of Johnson co., N cen. Texas, 27 m. S of Fort Worth; pop. (1970c) 16,015; trading center for agricultural area (esp. cotton, livestock, dairy products).

Clee Hills \ˈklē-\. Range of hills, S Shropshire, W England; 14 m. long; highest peaks **Brown Clee Hill** 1792 ft. and **Tit·ter·stone Clee Hill** \ˈtit-ər-stən-\ 1750 ft.

Cle El·um \klē-ˈel-əm\. City, Kittitas co., cen. Washington, at junction of Cle Elum and Yakima rivers 35 m. WSW of Wenatchee; pop. (1970c) 1725; coal mining.

Cle Elum Lake. Lake, NW Kittitas co., cen. Washington; 8 m. NE of Cle Elum; a widening of **Cle Elum River,** which flows into Yakima river at Cle Elum; **Cle Elum Dam** (135 ft.; completed 1933) at S end of lake aids in water conservation for irrigation.

Clee·thorpes \ˈklē-ˌthȯrps\. Municipal borough, Parts of Lindsey, Lincolnshire, E England, at mouth of the Humber 18 m. SE of Hull; pop. (1971p) 35,785; seaside resort.

Cleeve Cloud \ˈklēv-ˈklau̇d\. Highest point in the Cotswold Hills, in NE Gloucestershire, SW cen. England, 3¼ m. NE of Cheltenham; 1031 ft.

Clem·en·ton \ˈklem-ən-tən\. Borough, Camden co., SW New Jersey, SSE of Camden; pop. (1970c) 4492.

Clem·son \ˈklem(p)-sən\ *or formerly* **Clemson College.** Village, Anderson and Pickens cos., NW South Carolina, SE of Walhalla; pop. (1970c) 5578; fruit, poultry; Clemson Univ. (1889).

Cleofás. See MARÍA CLEOFÁS.

Cler·mont \ˈkle(ə)r-ˌmänt\. 1 County in Ohio. See table at OHIO.

2 City, Lake co., cen. Florida penin., 24 m. W of Orlando; near Lake Apopka; pop. (1970c) 3361.

3 Village, Charlevoix-Est co., S Quebec, Canada, on St. Lawrence river 75 m. NE of Quebec; pop. (1971p) 3386.

Clermont \kler-ˈmō^{n}\. Commune, Oise dept., N France, 41 m. N of Paris; pop. (1962c) 7689; once seat of countship, united to crown by St. Louis who gave it 1269 to his son Robert de France, first of the House of Bourbon; pillaged 1359 and 1415 by English.

Clermont–Fer·rand \ˌkler-ˌmō^{n}-fə-ˈrä^{n}\. Commercial and manufacturing city, ❋ of Puy-de-Dôme dept., S cen. France, 88 m. E of Limoges; pop. (1968c) 148,896; rubber goods, chemicals, linen, machinery; univ. (1854, univ. status 1896); 13th cent. Gothic cathedral; 6th cent. church; observatory.

History: **Clermont** *or anc.* **Au·gus·to·nem·e·tum** \ȯ-ˌgəs-tə-ˈnem-ət-əm, ə-ˌgəs-\, founded by Romans; capital of the Arverni; made episcopal see 4th cent.; scene of several councils, esp. the council 1095 giving rise to the Crusades; became capital of duchy of Auvergne 1556; officially united 1731 with **Mont·fer·rand** \ˌmō^{n}-fə-ˈrä^{n}\, nearby town founded 11th cent. by lords of Auvergne.

Clermont–l'Hé·rault \-lā-ˈrō\. Commune, Hérault dept., S France; pop. (1962c) 5767; dates from Roman times; occupied by Saracens; scene of much conflict during 16th cent. religious wars in Languedoc.

Clermont–Tonnerre. See REAO.

Clé·ry–sur–Somme \klā-ˌrē-su̇(ə)r-ˈsäm, -ˈsəm\. Commune, Somme dept., N France, on the Somme near Péronne; pop. (1962c) 505; destroyed by Germans in World War I.

Cleuch, Ben. See OCHIL HILLS.

Cleve. See KLEVE.

Cleve·don \ˈklēv-dən\. Urban district, Somersetshire, SW England, on Bristol Channel 11 m. W of Bristol; pop. (1971p) 14,285; seaside resort.

Cleve·land \ˈklēv-lənd\. 1 Name of counties in three states of the U.S. See tables at ARKANSAS, NORTH CAROLINA, OKLAHOMA.

2 City, ⊗ of White co., NE Georgia; pop. (1970c) 1353; Truett McConnell Junior Coll. (1947).

3 City, a ⊗ of Bolivar co., NW Mississippi, 30 m. NNE of Greenville; pop. (1970c) 13,327; in cotton-growing region; Delta State Coll. (1924).

4 Commercial and industrial city and port of entry, ⊗ of Cuyahoga co., N Ohio, at mouth of Cuyahoga river on Lake Erie; pop. (1970c) 750,879; largest city in the state; iron and steel, chemicals, electrical equipment, automobile parts, machinery; oil refining, food processing. Case Western Reserve Univ. (1826), John Carroll Univ. (1886), Cleveland State Univ. (1923), Cuyahoga Community Coll. (1963). Surveyed by Moses Cleaveland for Conn. Land Company 1796; incorp. as village 1814, as city 1836; expanded following opening of first section of Ohio and Erie Canal 1827; annexed rival Ohio City 1854.

5 City, Pawnee co., N Oklahoma, on Arkansas river 30 m. WNW of Tulsa; pop. (1970c) 2573; oil center.

6 Industrial city, ⊗ of Bradley co., SE Tennessee, 26 m. ENE of Chattanooga; pop. (1970c) 20,651; Tomlinson Coll. (1966), Cleveland State Community Coll. (1967); settled 1820; manganese and silica mines.

7 City, Liberty co., E Texas, 42 m. NNE of Houston; pop. (1970c) 5627; manufactures lumber; oil wells.

8 District, North Riding, Yorkshire, England; bounded on N by Tees estuary and North Sea, on S by **Cleveland Hills** (highest ab. 1400 ft.); ab. 420 sq. m.; yields iron, manufactured chiefly at Middlesbrough on W border; Cleveland bay horses first bred in this region.

Cleveland, Mount. Peak, highest point in Glacier National Park, NW Montana; 10,448 ft.

Cleveland Heights. City, Cuyahoga co., N Ohio, 7 m. E of Cleveland; pop. (1970c) 60,767; residential suburb.

Cleveland Hills. See CLEVELAND 8.

Cleves \ˈklēvz\. Village, Hamilton co., SW corner of Ohio, on Ohio river 13 m. W of Cincinnati; pop. (1970c) 2044.

Cleves *or* **Clèves.** See KLEVE.

Clew Bay \ˌklü-\. Inlet of Atlantic Ocean in co. Mayo, NW Eire; ab. 8 m. wide, extends inland 15 m.

Clew·is·ton \ˈklü-əs-tən\. City, Hendry co., S Florida, on Lake Okeechobee 55 m. W of West Palm Beach; pop. (1970c) 3896; diversified agriculture.

Cli·chy *or* **Clichy–la–Ga·renne** \kli-ˌshē-ˌläg-ə-ˈren\ *or anc.* **Clip·pi·a·cum** \klip-ˈī-ə-kəm\. Manufacturing commune, Hauts-de-Seine dept., N France, NW suburb of Paris; pop. (1968c) 52,477; manufactures rubber, chemical goods; a residence of the Merovingian court in 7th cent.

Clif·den \ˈklif-dən\. Town and seaport, W co. Galway, W Eire; pop. (1966c) 989; lobster fishing.

Cliffside Park \ˈklif-(ˌ)sīd-\. Borough, Bergen co., NE corner of New Jersey, on Hudson river 8 m. NNE of Jersey City and opp. New York City; pop. (1970c) 18,891; residential suburb.

Clif·ton \ˈklif-tən\. 1 Town, ⊗ of Greenlee co., SE Arizona, on San Francisco river 110 m. NE of Tucson near New Mexico border; pop. (1970c) 5087; settled 1872.

2 City, Passaic co., N New Jersey, NNW of Passaic; pop. (1970c) 82,437; formerly part of Passaic, made separate city 1917; manufactures steel, textiles, chemicals.

3 City, Bosque co., cen. Texas, NW of Waco; pop. (1970c) 2578.

4 City, Canada. See NIAGARA FALLS 3.

5 Residential suburb of Bristol, Gloucestershire, England, on the Avon where it forms a gorge 245 ft. deep which is crossed by a suspension bridge, 702-ft. span, built 1832–64 by I. K. Brunel; hot springs.

Clifton Forge \ˌklif-tən-\. City in Alleghany co. but politically independent, W Virginia, 10 m. E of Covington; 1 sq. m.; pop. (1970c) 5501; Dabney S. Lancaster Community Coll. (1964).

Clifton Heights. Manufacturing borough, Delaware co., SE Pennsylvania, 7 m. W of Philadelphia; pop. (1970c) 8348; machine parts.

Clifton Springs. Village, Ontario co., W New York, 29 m. ESE of Rochester; pop. (1970c) 2058; sulfur springs.

Cli·max \ˈklī-ˌmaks\. Village, Lake co., cen. Colorado, NE of Leadville on Fremont Pass; site of Harvard Observatory high-altitude station for solar research; world's largest molybdenum mine.

Clinch \ˈklinch\. 1 River, Virginia and E Tennessee; ab. 300 m. long; rises in Tazewell co., SW Virginia, flows SW across Tennessee border and joins the Tennessee river in Roane co.; passes through Norris Lake, earlier named **Clinch–Pow·ell Reservoir** \-ˈpau̇(-ə)l-\, formed by Norris Dam near junction of Powell and Clinch rivers, one of the dams of the Tennessee Valley Authority (*q.v.*).

2 County in Georgia. See table at GEORGIA.

Clinch Mountain. Ridge, extending from SW Virginia SW across border into NE Tennessee, bet. the Clinch and Holston rivers; 4724 ft.

Cling·mans Dome \ˌkliŋ-mənz-\. Mountain in the Great Smoky Mts., on Tennessee-North Carolina boundary; highest peak 6643 ft., highest point in Tennessee.

Clin·ton \ˈklint-^{ə}n\. 1 Name of counties in nine states of the U.S. See tables at ILLINOIS, INDIANA, IOWA, KENTUCKY, MICHIGAN, MISSOURI, NEW YORK, OHIO, PENNSYLVANIA.

2 City, ⊗ of Van Buren co., N cen. Arkansas; pop. (1970c) 1029.

3 Town, SW Middlesex co., S Connecticut, on Long Island Sound and on Hammonasset river; pop. (1970c) 10,267; cosmetics.
4 City, ⊗ of De Witt co., cen. Illinois, 22 m. N of Decatur; pop. (1970c) 7570; in agricultural region.
5 City, Vermillion co., W Indiana, 12 m. N of Terre Haute; pop. (1970c) 5340; agriculture; coal mining.
6 City, ⊗ of Clinton co., E Iowa, on Mississippi river 30 m. NE of Davenport; pop. (1970c) 34,719; Mount St. Clare Coll. (1895), Eastern Iowa Community Coll. (1929); trade and industrial center; ironworks, machine shops.
7 City, ⊗ of Hickman co., SW Kentucky, 24 m. WSW of Mayfield; pop. (1970c) 1618; in agricultural region.
8 Town, ⊗ of East Feliciana parish, E Louisiana; pop. (1970c) 1884; cotton gins; dairy farms.
9 Town, Worcester co., cen. Massachusetts, 12 m. NNE of Worcester; pop. (1970c) 13,383; chemicals, metal goods.
10 Town, Hinds co., SW cen. Mississippi; pop. (1970c) 7289; sawmill; Mississippi Coll. (1826).
11 City, ⊗ of Henry co., W Missouri, 40 m. SW of Sedalia; pop. (1970c) 7504; hatcheries, coal mines.
12 Village, Oneida co., cen. New York, 9 m. WSW of Utica; pop. (1970c) 2271; Hamilton Coll. (1793), Kirkland Coll. (1965).
13 Town, ⊗ of Sampson co., SE North Carolina; pop. (1970c) 7157; lumbering; cotton; fertilizer; poultry farms.
14 City, Custer co., W Oklahoma, on Washita river 86 m. W of Oklahoma City; pop. (1970c) 8513; shipping center for cattle and wheat country; founded 1903.
15 Town, Laurens co., NW South Carolina, 27 m. NE of Greenwood; pop. (1970c) 8138; cotton cloth, hosiery, lumber. Presbyterian Coll. (1880).
16 Town, ⊗ of Anderson co., E Tennessee, 15 m. NW of Knoxville; pop. (1970c) 4794, site of Clinton Engineer Works covering 59,000 acres, built 1943 to produce plutonium and originally operated by University of Chicago. See OAK RIDGE.
17 Town, Huron co., SE Ontario, Canada, 12 m. SE of Goderich; pop. (1971p) 3113; piano factory; flour mills.

Clinton, Mount. Peak of the White Mts., in S Coos co., N New Hampshire, SW of Mt. Washington; 4275 ft.

Clinton–Col·den Lake \-ˈkōl-dən-\. Lake, E cen. Mackenzie dist., Northwest Territories, Canada, NE of Great Slave Lake; 253 sq. m.

Clin·ton·ville \ˈklint-ᵊn-ˌvil\. City, Waupaca co., E cen. Wisconsin, 30 m. NNW of Appleton; pop. (1970c) 4600; trucks, conveyors, dairy products.

Clint·wood \ˈklint-ˌwu̇d\. Town, ⊗ of Dickenson co., SW Virginia; pop. (1970c) 1320.

Clio \ˈklī-(ˌ)ō\. City, Genesee co., SE cen. Michigan, 12 m. N of Flint; pop. (1970c) 2357.

Clip·per·ton \ˈklip-ərt-ᵊn\. Uninhabited island, E Pacific Ocean, 670 m. SW of Mexico, 10°17′N lat. and 109°13′W long.; 2 sq. m.; a low atoll bet. 2 and 3 m. in diameter, enclosing a rock 82 ft. high. Discovered and used as a base by John Clipperton, English pirate, in early 18th cent.; claimed by France 1858; forcibly occupied by Mexico 1897; awarded to France 1930 by King of Italy as arbitrator, turned over 1932.

Clippiacum. See CLICHY.

Clith·er·oe \ˈklit͟h-ə-(ˌ)rō\. Municipal borough, Lancashire, NW England, on the Ribble 28 m. N of Manchester; pop. (1971p) 13,191; ancient castle; textiles.

Cli·tun·no \klē-ˈtün-(ˌ)ō\ *or formerly* **Cli·tum·nus** \klī-ˈtəm-nəs\. River, Umbria, cen. Italy; rises W of Spoleto in a beautiful spring (described by Pliny the Younger: *Epistles,* viii. 8) and flows N into the Topino.

Cloates, Point \-ˈklōts\. Cape on Indian Ocean, W Western Australia, S of North West Cape.

Clon·a·kil·ty \ˌklän-ə-ˈkil-tē\. Urban district, S coast of co. Cork, SW Eire, at head of **Clonakilty Bay,** an inlet of Atlantic Ocean; pop. (1971p) 2431; fisheries, breweries; trade in farm produce. Birthplace of Michael Collins.

Clon·ard \ˈklän-ərd\. Village, co. Meath, E Eire, on the Boyne 30 m. WNW of Dublin; ruins of famous college, founded c. 520 by St. Finnian, at which St. Columba was a pupil.

Clon·cur·ry \klän-ˈkər-ē\. Town in rich mining district, W Queensland, Australia; pop. (1966c) 1649.

Clon·fert \ˈklän-fərt\. Village, SE co. Galway, W Eire; has ruined cathedral founded by St. Brendan, who established monastery here ab. 553.

Clon·mac·noise \ˌklän-mək-ˈnȯiz\. Parish, NW co. Offaly, cen. Eire, on Shannon river ab. 9 m. S of Athlone; pop. (1961c) 1899; early center of Christianity, site of an abbey founded 541; laid waste by English 1552.

Clon·mel \klän-ˈmel\. Municipal borough, ⊗ of co. Tipperary, S Eire; pop. (1971p) 11,630.

Clon·tarf \klän-ˈtärf\. Residential suburb of Dublin, Eire, on N shore of Dublin Bay; pop. (1961c) 4613; scene Apr. 23, 1014 of defeat of Danes by Brian Boru, who was killed here.

Clo·quet \klō-ˈkā\. 1 River, NE Minnesota; rises in Lake co., flows SW into St. Louis river in S St. Louis co.
2 City, Carlton co., E Minnesota, 17 m. WSW of Duluth; pop. (1970c) 8699; paper and wood products.

Clos·ter \ˈkläs-ter\. Borough, Bergen co., NE corner of New Jersey, 11 m. ENE of Paterson; pop. (1970c) 8604; residential.

Cloud \ˈklau̇d\. County in Kansas. See table at KANSAS.

Cloud·cap \ˈklau̇d-ˌkap\. Mountain, W Klamath co., SW Oregon, near E shore of Crater Lake; 8070 ft.

Cloud Peak. Mountain on boundary bet. Big Horn and Johnson cos., N Wyoming; 13,175 ft.; highest point in Big Horn Mts.

Clouds Rest \ˈklau̇dz-ˈrest\. Mountain, Mariposa co., cen. California; 9930 ft.; rises 5964 ft. above Yosemite Valley, in Yosemite National Park.

Cloud·veil Dome \ˌklau̇d-ˌvāl-\. Peak in cen. Grand Teton National Park, NW Wyoming; 12,026 ft.

Cloudy Bay \ˌklau̇d-ē-\. Inlet of Cook Strait on NE coast of South I., New Zealand; Blenheim is on its S shore.

Clo·vel·ly \klō-ˈvel-ē\. Village, Devonshire, SW England, on SW shore of Barnstaple Bay ab. 11 m. WSW of Bideford; on a cliff, its main street is like a staircase and is too steep for wheeled vehicles; resort.

Clo·ver \ˈklō-vər\. Town, York co., N South Carolina, 17 m. NW of Rock Hill; pop. (1970c) 3506; cotton; lumber.

Clo·ver·dale \ˈklō-vər-ˌdāl\. City, Sonoma co., W California, 27 m. NW of Santa Rosa; pop. (1970c) 3251; wineries, diversified agriculture.

Clo·vis \ˈklō-vəs\. 1 City, Fresno co., S cen. California, 10 m. NE of Fresno; pop. (1970c) 13,856; fruit packing; granite quarries.
2 City, ⊗ of Curry co., E New Mexico, near Texas boundary; pop. (1970c) 28,945; four-way railroad division point; trade center for wheat and cattle region.

Cloyne \ˈklȯin\. Village, co. Cork, SW Eire, 15 m. ESE of Cork; pop. (1961c) 756; ancient bishopric of which Berkeley was bishop 1734–53; 14th cent. cathedral.

Cluj \ˈklüzh\. 1 County of NW cen. Romania. See table at ROMANIA.
2 *or Ger.* **Klau·sen·burg** \ˈklau̇z-ᵊn-ˌbu̇(ə)rg\ *or Hung.* **Ko·lozs·vár** \ˈkō-lōzh-ˌvär\. City, its ⊗, in Transylvania in hills on right bank of the Someşul Mic; pop. (1970e) 202,715; chemicals, textiles, ceramics; metalworking; univ. (1959); begun 12th cent. as German settlement on site of older town; declared a free town 1405.

Clunia. See FELDKIRCH.

Clu·ny \ˈklü-nē, klü-ˈnē\. Commune, Saône-et-Loire dept., E cen. France; pop. (1962c) 4412; remains of Benedictine abbey of Cluny, founded c. 910 by William I, Duke of

Aquitaine; Cluny lace, formerly made in Auvergne, named from its use by monks of the abbey.

Clusium. See CHIUSI.

Clute \'klüt\. Town, Brazoria co., SE Texas, 53 m. S of Houston; pop. (1970c) 6023.

Clu·tha \'klü-thə\. River in SE South I., New Zealand; 200 m. long; flows SE into the Pacific Ocean; headstreams rise in lakes Wanaka and Wakatipu.

Clw·yd \'klü-əd\. River in N Wales; 35 m. long; flows N into Irish Sea at Rhyl; vale of Clwyd noted for scenery.

Clyde \'klīd\. 1 River, W New York, from Lyons in Wayne co. to Seneca river; part of Canandaigua Outlet.

2 Town, former ⊗ of Bryan co., SE Georgia.

3 Village, Wayne co., W New York, on N.Y. State Barge Canal 18 m. NW of Auburn; pop. (1970c) 2828; steam engines, farm implements, glass.

4 Village, Sandusky co., N Ohio, 17 m. SW of Sandusky; pop. (1970c) 5503; settled c. 1820; farming; canneries.

5 River, S Scotland; 106 m. long; catchment area ab. 1481 sq. m.; rises in N Dumfries, flows N, near Lanark descends by four waterfalls a distance of 320 ft. in less than four miles; flows NW, near Hamilton, past Glasgow (head of navigation for oceangoing vessels), and Renfrew; at Dumbarton expands into the **Firth of Clyde,** an estuary extending 64 m. to the island of Ailsa Craig where it is ab. 37 m. wide. **Clydes·dale** \'klīdz-ˌdāl\, the valley of the upper Clyde, ab. 50 m. long, has coal and iron; noted also for agriculture and for a breed of heavy draft horses (*Clydesdale*).

Clyde·bank \'klīd-ˌbaŋk\. Burgh, Dunbarton co., W cen. Scotland, on the Clyde; pop. (1971p) 48,296; has shipbuilding yards, engineering works.

Clyde Hill. Town, King co., W cen. Washington; pop. (1970c) 2987.

Clyth Ness \'klīth-'nes\. Headland projecting into North Sea, E cen. Caithness co., on NE coast of Scotland, S of Wick; lighthouse.

Cni·dus \'nīd-əs\. Ruins of ancient town at Cape Krio, end of long promontory of Caria, SW Asia Minor; a Dorian city noted for its wealth, temples, statues, and fine buildings; belonged to the Pentapolis of Asia Minor. Nearby was fought naval battle 394 B.C. in which Athenian leader Conon defeated Spartans under Pisander.

Cnossus. See KNOSSOS.

Co·a·chel·la Valley \kō-'chel-ə-\. Valley in SE California bet. Salton Sea and the San Bernardino Mts.

Coa·ho·ma \kō-'hō-mə\. County in Mississippi. See table at MISSISSIPPI.

Co·a·hui·la \ˌkō-ə-'wē-lə\. State, NE Mexico. See table at MEXICO.

Coal \'kōl\. County in Oklahoma. See table at OKLAHOMA.

Coal City. City, Grundy co., NE Illinois, 20 m. SSW of Joliet; pop. (1970c) 3040; in coal-mining region; clay products.

Coal·dale \'kōl-ˌdāl\. 1 Borough, Schuylkill co., E cen. Pennsylvania, 20 m. ENE of Pottsville; pop. (1970c) 3023; coal.

2 Town, Alberta, Canada, 10 m. E of Lethbridge; pop. (1966e) 2541; diversified agriculture.

Coal·gate \'kōl-(ˌ)gāt\. City, ⊗ of Coal co., S Oklahoma, 33 m. SE of Ada; pop. (1970c) 1859; oil and gas wells nearby.

Coal Grove. Village, Lawrence co., S Ohio, on Ohio river 3 m. SE of Ironton; pop. (1970c) 2759.

Coal·in·ga \kō-'liŋ-gə\. City, Fresno co., S cen. California, 50 m. SW of Fresno; pop. (1970c) 6161; Coalinga Coll. (1932); oil fields.

Coal·ville \'kōl-ˌvil\. 1 City, ⊗ of Summit co., NE Utah; pop. (1970c) 864.

2 Urban district, Leicestershire, cen. England, 14 m. WNW of Leicester; pop. (1971p) 28,334; coal mining.

Co·a·mo \kō-'äm-(ˌ)ō\. Town and municipality, S cen. Puerto Rico, ENE of Ponce; pop. (1970p) 11,957 (town), 26,179 (munic.).

Coast \'kōst\. 1 Province of SE Kenya. See table at KENYA. 2 Administrative region of E Tanzania. See table at TANZANIA.

Coastland. See KÜSTENLAND.

Coast Ranges. Mountains along the Pacific coast of North America from the southern part of California, where they meet the Sierra Nevada Mts. (see SAN BERNARDINO MOUNTAINS), through Oregon and Washington, into British Columbia and Alaska (Vancouver I., Queen Charlotte Is., Alexander Archipelago, St. Elias and Chugach mountains, Kenai Peninsula, and Kodiak I.); in California peaks are from 3800 ft. to 8831 ft. (Mt. Pinos); in Oregon from 2500 ft. to 7000 ft.; in Washington to 8150 ft. (highest point in the Olympic Mts.). The **Coast Mountains** of British Columbia, including Mt. Waddington 13,260 ft., are not a continuation of the U.S. Coast Ranges but of the Cascade Range (*q.v.*).

Coat·bridge \'kōt-(ˌ)brij\. Manufacturing burgh, Lanark co., S cen. Scotland, 9 m. E of Glasgow; pop. (1971p) 52,131; coal and iron mining; iron founding; manufactures steam boilers, firebrick, railroad rolling stock.

Co·a·te·pec \kō-ˌät-ə-'pek\. Town, Veracruz state, E Mexico, just S of Jalapa; munic. pop. (1970p) 34,161.

Co·a·te·pe·que \kō-ˌät-ə-'pā-kē\. Town, Quezaltenango dept., SW Guatemala; munic. pop. (1964p) 40,913; in coffee-growing region.

Coates·ville \'kōts-ˌvil\. City, Chester co., SE Pennsylvania, 28 m. E of Lancaster; pop. (1970c) 12,331; steel, brass, and iron products, textiles.

Co·at·i·cook \kō-'at-i-ˌku̇k\. Industrial town, Stanstead co., S Quebec, Canada, 20 m. S of Sherbrooke; pop. (1971p) 6566; wood products, woolens, bricks, milk products.

Coats Island \'kōts-\. Island in N Hudson Bay, Keewatin dist., Northwest Territories, Canada; 2206 sq. m.

Coats Land. Largely ice-covered section of Antarctica on SE coast of Weddell Sea from 18°W to 40°W; includes Caird Coast and Luitpold Coast.

Co·at·za·co·al·cos \kō-ˌät-sə-kō-'äl-kəs\ *or* **Quet·zal·co·al·co** \ket-ˌsäl-kō-'äl-(ˌ)kō\. 1 River in the Isthmus of Tehuantepec, Mexico; ab. 175 m. long; rises in the Sierra Madre, flows NE into the Bay of Campeche.

2 *or formerly* **Puer·to Mé·xi·co** \ˌpwert-ō-'me-hē-ˌkō\. Town, Veracruz state, E Mexico; located on Coatzacoalcos river 1 m. from its mouth; munic. pop. (1970p) 108,818; port of entry.

Co·bá \kō-'bä\. Ancient Maya city, NE Yucatán penin., Mexico; ruins now in Quintana Roo Territory.

Co·balt \'kō-ˌbȯlt\. Mining town, Timiskaming dist., SE Ontario, Canada, 70 m. N of North Bay and just W of Lake Timiskaming; pop. (1971p) 2191; extensive ore bodies containing silver and cobalt, discovered 1903; mining for silver has much declined but in World War II mining for cobalt resumed.

Co·bán \kō-'bän\. City, ✱ of Alta Verapaz dept., cen. Guatemala; munic. pop. (1964p) 38,426; in rich coffee-growing area.

Co·bar \'kō-(ˌ)bär\. Town, cen. New South Wales, SE Australia, 360 m. WNW of Sydney; pop. (1966c) 4896; formerly had rich copper and gold mines.

Cobb \'käb\. County in Georgia. See table at GEORGIA.

Cob·ble Mountain Dam \ˌkäb-əl-\. Dam across Little river, W Hampden co., W Massachusetts; height 253 ft.; completed 1932; impounds water, **Cobble Mountain Reservoir,** for water supply and power.

Cob·e·quid Bay \ˌkäb-ə-ˌkwid-\. Eastern arm of Minas Basin, cen. Nova Scotia, Canada; Truro at its head.

Cobh \'kōv\ *or formerly* **Queens·town** \'kwēnz-ˌtau̇n\. Urban district and seaport on Great I. in Cork Harbour, SE co. Cork, SW Eire; pop. (1971p) 6049; port of call for ocean liners. Adjacent Haulbowline I. was formerly an important British naval base.

Co·bi·ja \kō-'bē-hə\. City, ✱ of Pando dept., NW Bolivia, on Acre river; pop. (1962e) 2780; rubber.

Coblenz. See KOBLENZ.

Co·bles·kill \ˈkōb-əlz-ˌkil\. Village, Schoharie co., E New York, SW of Amsterdam; pop. (1970c) 4368; State Univ. of New York Agricultural and Technical Coll. (1911); battle May 30, 1778 bet. patriots and Indians led by Tories.

Co·bourg \ˈkō-ˌbərg\. Manufacturing town, ⊗ of Northumberland and Durham cos., SE Ontario, Canada, on Lake Ontario 70 m. ENE of Toronto; pop. (1971p) 11,214; chemicals; lumbering; good harbor; summer resort.

Cobourg Peninsula *or* **Co·burg Peninsula** \ˈkō-ˌbərg-\. Peninsula, N Australia; on N side of Van Diemen Gulf; 50 m. long, 20 m. broad.

Co·bre \ˈkō-(ˌ)brā\ *or* **El Cobre** \el-\. Municipality, Oriente prov., E Cuba, 8 m. W of Santiago de Cuba; pop. (1967e) 41,150; copper mines, worked since 1547.

Co·burg \ˈkō-ˌbərg\. 1 Municipality, S Victoria, SE Australia, N suburb of Melbourne; pop. (1966c) 68,568.
2 Manufacturing and commercial city, Bavaria, West Germany, 36 m. NW of Bayreuth; pop. (1969e) 41,456; machinery, toys; 13th cent. church; 16th cent. castle (Ehrenberg). First mentioned 1056; passed to Ernestine line of dukes of Saxony 1485; seat of dukes of Coburg; residence of dukes of Saxe-Coburg-Gotha; capital of Saxe-Coburg 1735; to Bavaria 1920.

Coburg Peninsula. See COBOURG PENINSULA.

Cocanada. See KAKINADA.

Co·cha·bam·ba \ˌkō-chə-ˈbäm-bə\. 1 Department of W cen. Bolivia. See table at BOLIVIA.
2 City, its ✱, ab. 80 m. NE of Oruro; pop. (1971e) 180,000; 8392 ft. above the sea; second largest city of the republic, originally known as **Oro·pe·za** \ˌōr-ə-ˈpā-sə\; oil refining; cathedral, univ. (1832); chief distributing point for E Bolivia; founded 1574.

Co·chel·la \kō-ˈchel-ə\. City, Riverside co., SE California, 80 m. NE of San Diego; pop. (1970c) 8353; diversified agriculture.

Co·chin \ˈkō-chən, ˈkäch-ən\. 1 Region, former state, SW India, on Malabar Coast; merged 1949 with Travancore forming state of **Trav·an·core and Cochin** \ˈtrav-ən-ˌkō(ə)r-, -kȯ(ə)r-\ which became in 1956 part of new state of Kerala; area 1493 sq. m.; ✱ Ernakulam; has forested regions and is center of trade in coconut products. Its history is practically that of the town Cochin (see below).
2 Town, N Kerala state, SW India; situated on a long strip of land of Malabar Coast 125 m. W of Madurai; pop. (1961c) 35,076; maintains harbor facilities with difficulty, esp. from May to August; exports mainly coconut products, tea, and nuts.
History: Portuguese factory founded by Vasco da Gama 1502; fort built by Albuquerque 1503, first European fort in India; British settled 1635 but forced out by Dutch 1663, under whom town became important trade center; came under sovereignty of Haidar Ali 1776 but was surrendered by his son Tipu Sahib to the British 1791; occupied by British 1795 and fortifications destroyed; formally ceded by Dutch 1814. Burial place of Albuquerque.

Cochin China *or Fr.* **Co·chin·chine** \kȯ-shaⁿ-shēn\. A former French possession, now that part of South Vietnam lying S of 10°50′N; 29,974 sq. m.; ✱ Saigon; with exception of few hills (c. 3000 ft.) in N part, flat alluvial plain of Mekong delta and several short streams; river channels and irrigation canals form one of the greatest rice-producing areas in Asia; fishing an important industry. Inhabitants are mainly Annamese, with some Cambodians, Chams, Chinese.
History: Vassal of Chinese Empire; later part of Khmer kingdom of Cambodia (*q.v.*) and of empire of Annam; in French war with Annam, Saigon was occupied 1859; by Treaty of Saigon 1862, its three eastern provinces were ceded to French who occupied its western provinces in 1867 and made it a colony; united administratively with French protectorates of Annam, Tonkin, and Cambodia to form French Indochina 1887; made an autonomous republic within the French Union 1946; incorporated in Vietnam 1949; became part of South Vietnam 1954.

Co·chi·nos Bay \kə-ˌchē-nəs-\ *or* **Bay of Pigs.** Bay on SW coast of Las Villas prov., W cen. Cuba; scene of attempted invasion of Cuba by anti-Castro force April 17, 1961.

Cochinos Point. Point at S end of Bataan Penin., Luzon, Phil., near Mariveles; actually formed by group of islets, Los Cochinos.

Co·chise \kə-ˈchēs\. County in Arizona. See table at ARIZONA.

Coch·ran \ˈkäk-rən\. 1 County in Texas. See table at TEXAS.
2 City, ⊗ of Bleckley co., cen. Georgia; pop. (1970c) 5161; cotton gins; peaches.

Coch·rane \ˈkäk-rən\. 1 District, E Ontario, Canada. See table at ONTARIO.
2 Town, its ⊗, 48 m. NNE of Timmins; pop. (1971p) 4926; pulp; poultry.

Cock·burn Channel \ˌkō-(ˌ)bərn-, ˌkäk-\. Passage off S Chile extending S and W from Strait of Magellan to the Pacific bet. Clarence I. on W and SW Tierra del Fuego.

Cockburn Island. Island in N Lake Huron, off W tip of Manitoulin I., administratively a part of Manitoulin dist., S Ontario, Canada.

Cocke \ˈkäk\. County in Tennessee. See table at TENNESSEE.

Cock·er \ˈkäk-ər\. River in Cumberland, NW England; 15 m. long; flows out of Lake Buttermere N into the Derwent at **Cock·er·mouth** \ˈkäk-ər-məth, -ˌmau̇th\, urban district, Cumberland, pop. (1971p) 6365; birthplace of William Wordsworth.

Cock·rell Hill \ˌkäk-rəl-\. City, Dallas co., NE Texas, 8 m. SW of Dallas; pop. (1970c) 3515.

Co·clé \kō-ˈklā\. Province of cen. Panama. See table at PANAMA.

Co·co \ˈkō-(ˌ)kō\ *or formerly* **Se·go·via** \si-ˈgō-vē-ə\. River, N Nicaragua; ab. 300 m. long; flows NE into the Caribbean Sea; greater part of its course forms boundary bet. Nicaragua and Honduras.

Co·coa \ˈkō-(ˌ)kō\. City, Brevard co., E Florida, on Indian river 42 m. SE of Orlando; pop. (1970c) 16,110; citrus-shipping center; fishing resort; Brevard Junior Coll. (1960); incorp. 1895.

Cocoa Beach. City, Brevard co., E Florida, 45 m. ESE of Orlando; pop. (1970c) 9952; missile equipment; resort.

Co·co Cay \ˌkō-(ˌ)kō-ˈkē, -ˈkā\ *or Span.* **Ca·yo Coco** \ˌkī-ə-ˈkō-(ˌ)kō\. Island off NW coast of Camagüey prov., E cen. Cuba.

Coco Channel. Strait off N point of North Andaman I., Andaman Is., Bay of Bengal.

Co·co·ni·no \ˌkō-kə-ˈnē-nō\. County in Arizona. See table at ARIZONA.

Coconino Plateau. Tableland in cen. Coconino co., N cen. Arizona, S of Grand Canyon National Park.

Co·co·nut Grove \ˌkō-kə-(ˌ)nət-\. South suburban section of Miami, Florida.

Co·cos Island \ˌkō-kəs-\. Uninhabited island, Pacific Ocean, SW of Costa Rica, 5°32′N, 87°04′W; 18 sq. m.

Cocos Islands *or* **Kee·ling Islands** \ˈkē-liŋ-\. Australian external territory, consisting of a group of 27 small coral islands in the Indian Ocean, ab. 580 m. SW of Java; lat. 12°5′S and long. 96°53′E; ab. 5 sq. m.; pop. (1970e) 611; chief product coconuts.
History: Discovered 1609; acquired by Great Britain 1857, placed under Ceylon governor 1878, under Straits Settlements 1886; incorporated with Singapore settlement 1903; placed under Australian authority 1955; scene of sinking of German cruiser *Emden* by Australian cruiser *Sydney* Nov. 9, 1914.

Coco So·lo \ˌkō-kə-ˈsō-(ˌ)lō\. Village on inlet just E of Colón, N end of Canal Zone, N of France Field; pop. (1970p) 1069; U.S. Naval Reservation and Fleet Air Base.

Co·cu·la \kə-ˈkü-lə\. Town, Jalisco state, W cen. Mexico, 32 m. SW of Guadalajara; munic. pop. (1970p) 20,273.

Cocuy, Sierra Nevada de. See SIERRA NEVADA DE COCUY.

Cod, Cape. See CAPE COD.

Co·de·ra, Cape \-kə-ˈder-ə\. Cape extending into Caribbean Sea on N cen. coast of Venezuela, E of Caracas.

Co·di·go·ro \ˌkō-di-ˈgōr-(ˌ)ō, -ˈgȯr-\. Commune, Ferrara prov., Emilia-Romagna, N Italy, 25 m. E of Ferrara; pop. (1968e) 14,815.

Cod·ing·ton \ˈkäd-iŋ-tən\. County in South Dakota. See table at SOUTH DAKOTA.

Co·dó \kə-ˈdō\. Municipality, Maranhão state, NE Brazil, ab. 110 m. SSE of São Luis; pop. (1968e) 100,933.

Co·do·gno \kə-ˈdōn-(ˌ)yō\. Commune, Milano prov., Lombardy, N Italy, 34 m. SE of Milan; pop. (1968e) 14,700; scene of defeat of Austrians by French 1796.

Cod·ring·ton \ˈkäd-riŋ-tən\. Village on Barbuda I., dependency of Antigua, West Indies.

Co·dro·i·po \kə-ˈdrō-i-ˌpō\. Commune, Udine prov., Veneto, NE Italy, SW of Udine; pop. (1968e) 11,540.

Co·dy \ˈkōd-ē\. City, ⊗ of Park co., NW Wyoming, on Shoshone river E of Buffalo Bill Reservoir; pop. (1970c) 5161; tourist resort at E entrance to Yellowstone Park.

Cody Peak. Mountain on E boundary of Yellowstone National Park, NW Wyoming; 10,246 ft.

Coele–Syria *or* **Coelesyria.** See BIKA.

Coe·neo \kwä-ˈnā-ō\ *also* **Coeneo de la Li·ber·tad** \-del-ə-ˌlē-bər-ˈtäth, -ˈtäd\. Municipality, Michoacán state, Mexico, 45 m. NE of Uruapan; pop. (1970p) 25,325; agriculture; founded 1550.

Coes·feld \ˈkōs-ˌfelt\ *also* **Koes·feld** \ˈkōs-\. City, North Rhine-Westphalia, West Germany, 21 m. W of Münster; pop. (1969e) 21,924; 13th cent. town hall; manufactures textiles, agricultural machinery, furniture. Became city 1197; under bishop of Münster 1246; member of Hanseatic League; to Prussia 1815.

Coët·qui·dan \ˌkwet-kē-ˈdäⁿ\. Military camp, Morbihan dept., NW France; site of St-Cyr after 1945.

Coeur d'Alene \ˌkȯrd-ᵊl-ˈān\. 1 River, N Idaho; ab. 100 m. long; flows W from Shoshone co. into Coeur d'Alene Lake. 2 City, ⊗ of Kootenai co., N Idaho, 32 m. E of Spokane, Washington; pop. (1970c) 16,228; discovery of silver and lead deposits 1882; mining, lumbering, farming; North Idaho Junior Coll. (1939); on site of military post established 1879.

Coeur d'Alene Lake. Lake in Kootenai co., N Idaho; ab. 30 m. long; ab. 60 sq. m.; center of large resort area.

Cof·fee \ˈkȯ-fē, ˈkäf-ē\. Name of counties in three states of the U.S. See tables at ALABAMA, GEORGIA, TENNESSEE.

Cof·fee·ville \ˈkȯ-fē-ˌvil, ˈkäf-ē-\. Town, a ⊗ of Yalobusha co., N Mississippi; pop. (1970c) 1024.

Cof·fey \ˈkȯ-fē, ˈkäf-ē\. County in Kansas. See table at KANSAS.

Cof·fey·ville \ˈkȯ-fē-ˌvil, ˈkäf-ē-\. City, Montgomery co., SE Kansas, 15 m. S of Independence; pop. (1970c) 15,116; former frontier town and cattle-shipping point; near oil and gas fields; manufactures structural steel, chemicals; Coffeyville Coll. (1923).

Cof·fin Island \ˌkȯ-fən-\. See MAGDALEN ISLANDS.

Co·fre de Pe·ro·te \ˌkō-frē-də-pə-ˈrōt-ē\ *or Indian name* **Nau·cham·pa·te·petl** \ˌnaů-ˌchäm-pä-ˈtā-ˌpet-ᵊl\. Mountain, Veracruz state, Mexico; 15,816 ft.

Co·ghi·nas \kə-ˈgē-nəs\. River in N Sardinia, Italy; ab. 60 m. long; flows N into Gulf of Asinara.

Coglians, Monte. See KELLERWAND.

Co·gnac \ˈkōn-ˌyak, ˈkän-, ˈkȯn-\ *or anc.* **Comp·ni·a·cum** \kämp-ˈnī-ə-kəm\. Commune, Charente dept., W France, on Charente river 24 m. W of Angoulême; pop. (1968c) 22,062; famous for its distilleries producing cognac (named for it). Belonged to Richard Cœur de Lion; made commune 1352; Protestant stronghold in latter part of 16th cent.; a center for ceramic manufactures in 18th cent.

Co·has·set \kō-ˈhas-ət\. Town, Norfolk co., E Massachusetts, on Atlantic Ocean 15 m. SE of Boston; pop. (1970c) 6954; summer resort.

Cohasset Rocks. See MINOTS LEDGE.

Co·hoc·ton *or* **Con·hoc·ton** \kə-ˈhäk-tən\. River, S New York; ab. 60 m. long; flows SE and unites with Tioga river near Corning to form Chemung river.

Co·hoes \kə-ˈhōz\. City, Albany co., E New York, at confluence of Mohawk and Hudson rivers near E terminus of N.Y. State Barge Canal, 10 m. N of Albany; pop. (1970c) 18,613; textile machinery; manufacturing center, with power from 70-foot falls of Mohawk river. First settled by Dutch 1665; chartered as city 1870; headquarters of Gen. Gates in Revolutionary War.

Coi. See RED 4.

Coi·ba \ˈkȯi-bə\. Island in Pacific Ocean off SW coast of Panama; 20 m. long.

Co·ig \ˈkȯig\; *formerly* **Coy·le** *or* **Coi·le** \ˈkȯi-(ˌ)lā\. River, Santa Cruz prov., S Argentina; ab. 180 m. long; rises near Chilean border, flows E and NE into Atlantic Ocean.

Coim·ba·tore \ˌkȯim-bə-ˌtō(ə)r, -ˈtȯ(ə)r\. City, W Tamil Nadu, S India, 280 m. SW of Madras; on S slope of Nilgiri Hills; pop. (1970e) 405,952; has cotton mills, tanneries, coffee and sugar factories; agricultural college; 3 m. to the E is the pagoda of **Pe·rur** \pə-ˈrü(ə)r\, of archaeological interest.

Co·im·bra \kü-ˈim-brə\. 1 District of W cen. Portugal. See table at PORTUGAL.

2 *anc.* **Co·nim·bria** \kə-ˈnim-brē-ə\ *or* **Co·nim·bri·ga** \-bri-gə\. City, its ✱, on Mondego river 108 m. NNE of Lisbon; munic. pop. (1970p) 108,046; pottery, fabrics, paper; tanning, food processing; former ✱ of Portugal (1139–c. 1260); 12th cent. cathedral; Univ. of Coimbra (founded 1290 at Lisbon; transferred to Coimbra 1537). Major city under Romans; conquered by Visigoths and later by Moors; finally recaptured 1064 by Ferdinand I (the Great) and the Cid; Inés de Castro murdered here 1355.

Co·ín \kō-ˈēn\. Commune, Málaga prov., S Spain, 19 m. W of Málaga; pop. (1970p) 20,283; soap, paper, textiles, oil, wine, esparto mats; marble quarries nearby.

Coira *or* **Coire.** See CHUR.

Co·je·des \kȯ-ˈhā-dəs\. State of NW cen. Venezuela. See table at VENEZUELA.

Co·ju·te·pe·que \kō-ˌhüt-ə-ˈpā-kē\. City, ✱ of Cuscatlán dept., cen. El Salvador, 16 m. E of San Salvador; pop. (1968e) 12,628; produces rice, coffee, sugar, indigo.

Coke \ˈkōk\. County in Texas. See table at TEXAS.

Co·lac \kō-ˈlak\. Town, S Victoria, SE Australia, 40 m. WSW of Geelong; pop. (1966c) 9498.

Co·la·ti·na \ˌkō-lə-ˈtē-nə\. Municipality, Espírito Santo state, E Brazil, ab. 60 m. NNW of Vitória; pop. (1968e) 140,729.

Col·bert \ˈkäl-bərt\. County in Alabama. See table at ALABAMA.

Col·by \ˈkōl-bē\. City, ⊗ of Thomas co., NW Kansas, 38 m. E of Goodland; pop. (1970c) 4658; Colby Community Junior Coll. (1964).

Colby Mountain. Peak in Sierra Nevada, in SE Tuolumne co., cen. California; 9631 ft.

Col·cha·gua \kōl-ˈchä-gwə\. Province of cen. Chile. See table at CHILE.

Col·ches·ter \ˈkōl-ˌches-tər, -chəs-\. 1 Town, NW New London co., SE Connecticut; pop. (1970c) 6603; settled 1699; includes borough of Colchester (pop. 3529).

2 Town, Chittenden co., NW Vermont, 6 m. NE of Burlington; pop. (1970c) 8776.

3 County, Nova Scotia, Canada. See table at NOVA SCOTIA.

4 *or anc.* **Cam·u·lo·du·num** \ˌkam-yə-lō-ˈd(y)ü-nəm\. Municipal borough, Essex, SE England, on the Colne 53 m. NE of London; pop. (1971p) 76,145; agricultural machinery; oyster fisheries; in agricultural region; Univ. of Essex (1961); site of ancient Roman settlement, the first Roman colony in Britain, founded by Claudius 43 A.D.; burned by Boadicea's warriors; received first charter 1189.

Col·chis \ˈkäl-kəs\. Ancient country on the Black Sea S of Caucasus Mts. corresponding to W part of the Georgian S.S.R., U.S.S.R.; watered by the Phasis (*or mod.* Rioni); ✱ Aea; in Greek legend the home of Medea and magic, where in a sacred grove was the Golden Fleece sought by the Argonauts; in 1st cent. B.C. Colchians were overcome by Mithridates VI, King of Pontus.

Col·den Mountain \ˌkōl-dən-\. Peak in the Adirondack Mts., in Essex co., NE New York; 4713 ft.

Cold Harbor \ˌkōld-\. Locality, Hanover co., E cen. Virginia, N of the Chickahominy river ab. 10 m. ENE of Richmond; site of two battles of the Civil War: (1) in 1862, better known as Gaines' Mill (*q.v.*); (2) June 1 and 3, 1864, in which Gen. Lee forced Union troops to retire with heavy losses.

Cold·spring \ˈkōld-ˌspriŋ\. Village, ⊗ of San Jacinto co., E Texas.

Cold Spring. 1 City, Campbell co., N Kentucky; pop. (1970c) 1406.

2 Village, Putnam co., SE New York, on Hudson river 20 m. S of Poughkeepsie; pop. (1970c) 2083; in farming country; made Parrott guns used in Civil War.

Cold·stream \ˈkōl(d)-ˌstrēm\. Burgh, Berwick co., SE Scotland, on English border; pop. (1971p) 1270; the Coldstream Guards originally organized here by Gen. Monck 1659–60; once a popular runaway-marriage resort.

Cold·water \ˈkōl-ˌdwȯt-ər, -ˌdwät-\. 1 River, NW Mississippi; 220 m. long; rises in NE Marshall co., flows SW and S into Tallahatchie river in Quitman co.

2 City, ⊗ of Comanche co., S Kansas; pop. (1970c) 1016.

3 City, ⊗ of Branch co., S Michigan, 28 m. S of Battle Creek; pop. (1970c) 9155; manufactures furnaces, marine engines; lake resort.

4 Village, Mercer co., W Ohio, 33 m. SW of Lima; pop. (1970c) 3533; farm implements.

Cole \ˈkōl\. County in Missouri. See table at MISSOURI.

Cole·brook \ˈkōl-(ˌ)brůk\. Town, Coos co., N New Hampshire, on Connecticut river 33 m. NNW of Berlin; pop. (1970c) 2094; tourist center; potato growing, lumbering.

Cole·man \ˈkōl-mən\. 1 County in cen. Texas. See table at TEXAS.

2 City, its ⊗, 28 m. WNW of Brownwood; pop. (1970c) 5608; manufactures cottonseed oil, bricks.

3 Coal-mining town, S Alberta, Canada, ab. 74 m. W of Lethbridge; pop. (1971p) 1526.

Cö·le·me·rik \ˈchə(r)l-ə-mə-ˌrēk\ *or formerly* **Ha·kkâ·ri** *also* **Ha·kâ·ri** \hä-ˈkär-ē\. Town, ✱ of Hakkâri prov., SE Turkey; pop. (1965c) 6129.

Co·len·so \kə-ˈlen-(ˌ)zō\. Village on Tugela river, W Natal, Rep. of South Africa, 65 m. NW of Pietermaritzburg; pop. (1960c) 2063; scene of battle Dec. 1899 in Boer War which halted Gen. Butler's advance to relief of Ladysmith 14 m. N; occupied by British Feb. 20, 1900.

Cole·raine \kōl-ˈrān, ˈkōl-ˌrān\. Municipal borough and shipping port, co. Londonderry, NW Northern Ireland, on Bann river; pop. (1971p) 14,851; fisheries, distilleries; milk products; linen manufacture, ham curing; New Univ. of Ulster (1965).

Cole·roon \ˈkōl-(ə-)ˌrün\. The northern and largest branch of the Cauvery river (*q.v.*), India, in its delta; empties into Bay of Bengal ab. 25 m. S of Cuddalore.

Coles \ˈkōlz\. County in Illinois. See table at ILLINOIS.

Coles·berg \ˈkōlz-ˌbərg\. Town, N Cape Province, S Rep. of South Africa, 130 m. SW of Bloemfontein; pop. (1967e) 6800; occupied by Boers during Boer War and scene of repeated clashes 1899–1900.

Col·fax \ˈkōl-ˌfaks\. 1 Name of counties in two states of the U.S. See tables at NEBRASKA and NEW MEXICO.

2 City, Jasper co., S cen. Iowa, 18 m. E of Des Moines; pop. (1970c) 2293; near coalfields.

3 Town, ⊗ of Grant parish, cen. Louisiana; pop. (1970c) 1892.

4 City, ⊗ of Whitman co., SE Washington, 15 m. NNW of Pullman; pop. (1970c) 2664; wheat and livestock.

Col·hué \kȯl-ˈwā\ *or* **Colhué Hua·pí** \-wä-ˈpē\. Lake in S Chubut prov., S Argentina, E of Lake Musters.

Co·li·ma \kə-ˈlē-mə\. 1 Volcano, Jalisco state, W cen. Mexico; 13,993 ft.

2 State of SW Mexico. See table at MEXICO.

3 City, its ✱; munic. pop. (1970p) 72,074; altitude 1600 ft.; leather goods; in region producing cotton, sugarcane, rice, tobacco; univ. (1850); founded 1522.

Coll \ˈkȯl\. Island of the Inner Hebrides, W of N Mull I., off W coast of Scotland; ab. 12 m. long; administratively a part of Argyll co.

Co·lla·dor \ˌkō-yə-ˈdȯ(ə)r, ˌkȯi-ə-\. Peak, Cajamarca dept., N Peru; 12,835 ft.

Col·la·tia \kə-ˈlā-sh(ē-)ə\. Ancient Sabine town, Latium, Italy, ab. 10 m. NE of Rome; scene, in Roman legend, of the rape of Lucrece, wife of Tarquinius Collatinus; referred to as **Col·la·ti·um** \-sh(ē-)əm\ in Shakespeare's poem *The Rape of Lucrece.*

Col·le di Val d'El·sa \ˌkȯ-lə-dē-ˌväl-ˈdel-sə\. Industrial commune, Siena prov., Tuscany, cen. Italy, 14 m. NW of Siena; pop. (1968e) 14,156; 13th cent. cathedral; ironworks.

Col·lege \ˈkäl-ij\. Village (unincorp.), W suburb of Fairbanks, Alaska; pop. (1970c) 3434; seat of Univ. of Alaska (authorized 1915, opened 1922).

Col·lege·dale \ˈkäl-ij-ˌdāl\. Village, Hamilton co., SE Tennessee, E of Chattanooga; pop. (1970c) 3031; Southern Missionary Coll. (1893).

College Park. 1 City, Clayton and Fulton cos., NW cen. Georgia, 8 m. SSW of Atlanta; pop. (1970c) 18,203.

2 City, Prince Georges co., Maryland, 8 m. NE of Washington; pop. (1970c) 26,156; Univ. of Maryland (1807).

College Place. City, Walla Walla co., SE Washington, 8 m. SW of Walla Walla; pop. (1970c) 4150; diversified agriculture.

College Station. City, Brazos co., E cen. Texas, 4 m. S of Bryan; pop. (1970c) 17,676; Texas Agricultural and Mechanical Univ. (1876).

Col·lege·ville \ˈkäl-ij-ˌvil\. 1 Township, Stearns co., cen. Minnesota, 10 m. W of St. Cloud; pop. (1970c) 2371; St. John's Univ. (1857).

2 Borough, Montgomery co., SE Pennsylvania, ab. 8 m. NW of Norristown; pop. (1970c) 3191; Ursinus Coll. (1869).

Col·le·gno \kə-ˈlān-(ˌ)yō\. Commune, Torino prov., Piedmont, NW Italy, NW of Turin; pop. (1968e) 36,069.

Col·le Sal·vet·ti \ˌcȯ-lə-säl-ˈvet-ē\. Commune, Livorno prov., Tuscany, Italy, NE of Leghorn; pop. (1968e) 10,181.

Col·le·ton \ˈkäl-ət-ᵊn\. County in South Carolina. See table at SOUTH CAROLINA.

Col·ley·ville \ˈkäl-ē-ˌvil\. Village, Tarrant co., N Texas; pop. (1970c) 3368.

Col·lie \ˈkäl-ē\. Town, SW Western Australia, 110 m. S of Perth; pop. (1966c) 7628.

Col·lier \ˈkäl-yər\. County in Florida. See table at FLORIDA.

Collier Bay. Large inlet of Indian Ocean, N coast of Western Australia.

Col·lier·ville \ˈkäl-yər-ˌvil\. Town, Shelby co., SW Tennessee, 22 m. SE of Memphis; pop. (1970c) 3625; furniture; diversified agriculture.

Colli Euganei. See EUGANEAN HILLS.

Col·lin \ˈkäl-ən\. County in Texas. See table at TEXAS.

Col·ling·dale \ˈkäl-iŋ-ˌdāl\. Borough, Delaware co., SE Pennsylvania, 7 m. WSW of Philadelphia; pop. (1970c) 10,605.

Col·lings·wood \ˈkäl-iŋz-ˌwu̇d\. Borough, Camden co., SW New Jersey, 3 m. SE of Camden; pop. (1970c) 17,422; settled by Quakers 1682; incorp. 1888; residential.

Col·lings·worth \ˈkäl-iŋz-ˌwərth\. County in Texas. See table at TEXAS.

Col·ling·wood \ˈkäl-iŋ-ˌwu̇d\. 1 City, S Victoria, SE Australia; NE suburb of Melbourne; pop. (1966c) 22,459.
2 Town, Simcoe co., SE Ontario, Canada, on Nottawasaga Bay 29 m. WNW of Barrie; pop. (1971p) 9719; shipbuilding; aircraft parts; steelworks, foundries, machine shops; fisheries.

Collingwood Bay. Inlet of Solomon Sea on SE coast of island of New Guinea, Papua New Guinea.

Col·lins \ˈkäl-ənz\. 1 Short stream, cen. Tennessee; rises near W boundary of Sequatchie co., flows N into Caney Fork at Great Falls Lake; forms part of system of Tennessee Valley Authority (*q.v.*).
2 Town, ⊗ of Covington co., S Mississippi; pop. (1970c) 1934.

Collins, Mount. Peak in Great Smoky Mts., on boundary bet. Tennessee and North Carolina 2½ m. NE of Clingmans Dome; 6188 ft.

Collins Landing. See THOUSAND ISLANDS 1.

Col·lins·ville \ˈkäl-ənz-ˌvil\. 1 Subdivision of the town of Canton, Connecticut; pop. (1970c) 2897; manufactures axes and other edged tools.
2 City, Madison and St. Clair cos., SW Illinois, 10 m. E of East St. Louis; pop. (1970c) 18,015; in coal-mining section; has zinc smelter, cannery; manufactures women's clothing.
3 City, Tulsa co., NE Oklahoma, 17 m. NNE of Tulsa; pop. (1970c) 3009; near oil and gas wells.

Col·lo \ˈkȯ-lō\. Coastal town, Constantine dept., NE Algeria, 37 m. NNE of the city of Constantine; pop. (1966c) 10,803; lead and mercury mines.

Col·mar \ˈkōl-ˌmär, kōl-ˈ\ *or Ger.* **Kol·mar** \ˈkōl-mär\. Manufacturing commune, ✱ of Haut-Rhin dept., NE France, 105 m. E of Chaumont; pop. (1968c) 59,550; manufactures printed goods, calicoes, silks, cotton goods; tourism. Became free imperial city 1226; under Swedes 1632–34; to France 1697, Germany 1871, France 1919; in World War II taken by Germans June 17, 1940, retaken by French Feb. 2, 1945.

Cöln. See COLOGNE.

Colne \ˈkō(l)n\. 1 River, Essex, SE England; 35 m. long; flows SE into North Sea.
2 River, Hertfordshire and Buckinghamshire, SE cen. England; 35 m. long; flows into the Thames.
3 Municipal borough, Lancashire, NW England, 27 m. N of Manchester; pop. (1971p) 18,873; cotton mills, quarries.

Col·nett \ˈkäl-nət\. Peak, NE coast of New Caledonia I., SW Pacific Ocean; 4954 ft.

Colne Valley. Urban district, West Riding, Yorkshire, N England; pop. (1971p) 21,188.

Co·lô·a·ne \ku̇-ˈlō-ə-nə\. See MACAO 1.

Co·lo·gna Ve·ne·ta \kə-ˌlōn-yə-ˈven-ə-tə, -ˈvā-nə-tə\. Commune, Verona prov., Veneto, NE Italy; pop. (1968e) 8688.

Co·logne \kə-ˈlōn\; *Ger.* **Köln** *or less often* **Cöln** \ˈkœln\; *anc.* **Op·pi·dum Ubi·o·rum** \ˈäp-əd-əm-ˌ(y)ü-bē-ˈōr-əm, -ˈȯr-\ *later, because birthplace of Nero's mother, Agrippina,* **Co·lo·nia Ag·rip·pi·na** \kə-ˈlō-nyə-ˌag-rə-ˈpī-nə\. Manufacturing and commercial city, North Rhine-Westphalia, West Germany, on W bank of Rhine river 20 m. SSE of Düsseldorf; pop. (1969e) 860,818; chemicals, textiles, electrical equipment, eau de cologne, brown coal; important river port; banking center; has a number of Roman remains, incl. 3d cent. tower; 11th cent. church, famous 13th cent. cathedral (completed 19th cent.), univ. (1388, dissolved 1798, refounded 1919), opera house (1957); botanical and zoological gardens.
History: Roman name, Colonia Agrippina, given in 50 A.D. to colony of veterans and of German Ubii; captured by Franks; became an episcopal see 4th cent. and archiepiscopal see 785; its archbishop increased holdings (acquired duchy of Westphalia 1180) until he became one of most powerful princes of Germany; one of most important centers of Hanseatic League; after battle of Worringen 1288, citizenry established their independence of archbishop; a center of medieval German art and learning; archbishop confirmed as elector of the empire 1356; city's prosperity declined, esp. after Thirty Years' War; occupied by French 1794; territories of archbishop secularized 1803; given to kingdom of Prussia by Congress of Vienna 1815; after World War I occupied by British troops 1918–26. In World War II object of first great air raid of the war May 30, 1942; frequently bombed 1943–45 by British and American air forces; entered by American troops Mar. 5–6, 1945; extensively damaged in World War II, but since rebuilt.

Co·lo·gno Mon·ze·se \kə-ˌlōn-yō-mänt-ˈsā-zə\. Commune, Milano prov., Lombardy, N Italy, ab. 6 m. NE of Milan; pop. (1968e) 40,889.

Co·lo·ma \kə-ˈlō-mə\. Village, El Dorado co., California, near Placerville 36 m. NE of Sacramento; site of Sutter's Mill where gold was discovered Jan. 24, 1848.

Colomb *or* **Colomb–Béchar.** See BÉCHAR.

Co·lombes \kə-ˈlōm, -ˈlōⁿb\. Manufacturing commune, Hauts-de-Seine dept., N France, NW suburb of Paris; pop. (1968c) 80,357.

Co·lom·bey *or* **Colombey–Nouil·ly** \kȯ-lōⁿ(m)-ˈbā-nü-ˈyē\. Village, Moselle dept., NE France, ab. 4 m. E of Metz; scene of battle (called also battle of Borny and of Courcelles from towns nearby) Aug. 14, 1870 in which Steinmetz failed to check Bazaine's retreat.

Colombey–les–Deux–Églises \-lā-ˈdə(r)z-ā-ˈglēz\. Commune, Haute-Marne dept., NE France; pop. (1962c) 399; home and burial place of Charles de Gaulle, president of France 1958–69.

Co·lom·bia \kə-ˈləm-bē-ə, -ˈlōm-\. Republic, NW South America, bounded on N by the Caribbean Sea, on E by Venezuela and Brazil, on S by Peru and Ecuador, on W by the Pacific Ocean and Panama; 439,735 sq. m.; pop. (1968e) 19,829,185; ✱ Bogotá. *Physical features:* Covered in W and cen. parts by N end of great Andes system, here separating into 3 parallel ranges: Cordillera Oriental (E), extending into NW Venezuela; Cordillera Central (cen.); and Cordillera Occidental (W); highest peak Cristóbal Colón 19,020 ft.; other peaks, above 16,000 ft., are Tolima, Chita, Puracé; has many volcanoes. *Rivers:* In cen. part the Magdalena and the Cauca (W tributary of the Magdalena), both flowing N bet. main ranges of the Andes; in W the Atrato flowing N to Gulf of Urabá and many short rapid streams on the coast flowing W to the Pacific; in E tributaries of the Orinoco (Meta, Vichada, Guaviare), the Vaupés (tributary of the Rio Negro), and in SE the Apaporis and Caquetá; in S the Putumayo forming most of boundary with Peru. *Chief products:* Coffee, bananas, sugar, cotton, tobacco, rice; oil, iron ore, platinum, emeralds; manufacturing: textiles, building materials; food processing. *Chief cities:* Bogotá, Barranquilla, Cartagena, Bucaramanga, Manizales, Pereira, Cúcuta, Ibagué. Divided into 22 departments, 3 intendancies, 5 commissaries, and one special district (for pronunciation of their names, see their individual entries):

NAME	AREA (sq. m.)	POP. (1968e)	CAPITAL
Special District	613	2,148,387	Bogotá
Departments			
Antioquia	24,274	2,828,008	Medellín
Atlántico	1,263	833,913	Barranquilla
Bolívar	10,190	791,851	Cartagena
Boyacá	26,158	1,144,415	Tunja
Caldas	2,812	775,423	Manizales
Cauca	11,774	664,003	Popayán
Chocó	18,226	199,665	Quibdó
Córdoba	9,720	695,351	Montería
Cundinamarca	8,638	1,165,095	Bogotá
El Cesar	9,186	334,641	Valledupar
Huila	7,718	460,021	Neiva
La Guajira	7,791	201,334	Riohacha
Magdalena	8,843	626,989	Santa Marta
Meta	33,116	216,030	Villavicencio

NAME	AREA (sq. m.)	POP. (1968e)	CAPITAL
Nariño	11,986	757,618	Pasto
Norte de Santander	8,037	585,794	Cúcuta
Quindío	705	331,164	Armenia
Risaralda	1,530	483,461	Pereira
Santander	11,950	1,087,462	Bucaramanga
Sucre	4,063	343,223	Sincelejo
Tolima	9,006	879,751	Ibagué
Valle	8,203	1,973,816	Cali
Intendancies			
Arauca	9,069	28,867	Arauca
Caquetá	34,820	136,913	Florencia
San Andrés y Providencia*	17	23,128	San Andrés
Commissaries			
Amazonas	46,811	14,875	Leticia
Guinía	30,141	4,083	San Felipe
Putumayo	9,873	67,865	Mocoa
Vaupés	34,990	15,789	Mitú
Vichada	38,212	10,250	Puerto Carreño

*Islands in Caribbean Sea E of Nicaragua.

History: Coasts visited by Spanish adventurer, Ojeda, 1500; first successfully colonized after Jiménez de Quesada had defeated Chibchas, a nation of highly civilized Indians, on Colombian plateau 1536–38; Santa Fé de Bogotá founded 1538; in 1718 and 1740 made separate viceroyalty of New Granada (*q.v.*) which included modern Colombia, Panama, Ecuador, and Venezuela; after unsuccessful attempt in 1811, achieved independence from Spain under leadership of Bolívar 1819 (see BOYACÁ); lost Venezuela and Ecuador by secession 1830; reorganized into: Grenadine Confederation 1858, United States of New Granada 1861, United States of Colombia 1863, and republic of Colombia (including Panama) 1886; fought civil war 1899–1902; lost Panama (*q.v.*) by revolt after failure to ratify Hay-Herrán Treaty 1903; neutral in World War I; settled Panama controversy with U.S. 1921; settled border disputes with Ecuador 1919, Venezuela 1922, Brazil 1929, settled Leticia dispute with Peru 1934, after it had threatened war 1932; in World War II broke off relations 1941 with Axis countries but did not declare war; declared state of siege 1949; under military dictatorship 1953–57; ended state of siege 1958; joined Andean Group (*q.v.*) 1969. See also GREAT COLOMBIA.

Co·lom·bo \kə-ˈləm-(ˌ)bō\. Seaport and commercial city, ✱ of Ceylon, near mouth of Kelani river on Indian Ocean; pop. (1970e) 582,767; Ceylon's largest city and port; has artificial harbor; iron and steel; oil refinery; transportation center; exports include tea, rubber, cocoa; three universities. Occupied 1517 by Portuguese, captured by Dutch 1658, and taken over by English 1796 (see CEYLON); a British defense base in Indian Ocean 1942–45; site of conference 1950 leading to formation of Colombo Plan (economic assistance program for Asian countries).

Co·lón \kə-ˈlōn\. 1 Town, Entre Ríos prov., E Argentina; pop. (1960c) 10,209.

2 Town and municipality, Matanzas prov., W cen. Cuba, 27 m. SE of Cárdenas; munic. pop. (1967e) 84,100.

3 Department of N Honduras. See table at HONDURAS.

4 Province of N cen. Panama. See table at PANAMA.

5 *or formerly* **As·pin·wall** \ˈas-pən-ˌwȯl\. City, ✱ of Colón prov., N cen. Panama, on Limon Bay at N entrance to Panama Canal; pop. (1970p) 95,308; N terminus of Panama R.R. (built 1850–55); founded 1850 and named for William H. Aspinwall, one of builders of railroad; with its suburb Cristobal (*q.v.*) an important port.

Colón, Archipiélago de. See GALÁPAGOS ISLANDS.

Co·lo·nia \kə-ˈlōn-yə\. 1 Department of SW Uruguay. See table at URUGUAY.

2 *or* **Colonia del Sa·cra·men·to** \-del-ˌsak-rə-ˈment-(ˌ)ō\. Seaport and resort, its ✱, on La Plata river opp. Buenos Aires; pop. (1963c) 12,839; founded by Portuguese from Brazil 1680; fought over by Spanish and Portuguese; acquired by Spain in treaties of 1777 and 1778; center of rich agricultural and dairying district.

Colonia Agrippina. See COLOGNE.

Colonia Julia Fanestris. See FANO.

Co·lo·ni·al Beach \kə-ˌlō-nyəl-, -nē-əl-\. Town and resort, Westmoreland co., E Virginia, on Potomac river 30 m. E of Fredericksburg; pop. (1970c) 2058; fisheries.

Colonial Heights. Independent city, SE cen. Virginia, on Appomattox river opp. Petersburg; pop. (1970c) 15,097.

Colonial National Historical Park. See UNITED STATES, *National Historical Parks.*

Colonial Territories *or* **Colonias.** See PANDO 1.

Col·o·nie \ˌkäl-ə-ˈnē\. Village, Albany co., New York, NW of Albany; pop. (1970c) 8701.

Co·lon·na, Cape \-kə-ˈlo-nə\ *also* **Cape Sou·ni·on** \-ˈsü-nē-ən\ *or anc.* **Su·ni·um Prom·on·to·ri·um** \ˈsü-nē-əm-ˌpräm-ən-ˈtōr-ē-əm, -ˈtȯr-\. Cape, E cen. Greece; summit contains ruins of ancient temple.

Co·lon·ne, Cape \-kə-ˈlō-(ˌ)nā\ *or anc.* **La·cin·i·um Prom·on·to·ri·um** \lə-ˈsin-ē-əm-ˌpräm-ən-ˈtōr-ē-əm, -ˈtȯr-\. Cape on E coast of Calabria, S Italy, projecting into Ionian Sea S of Gulf of Taranto.

Col·on·say \ˈkäl-ən-ˌzā, -ˌsā\. Island of the Inner Hebrides, W Scotland; ab. 16 sq. m.; part of Argyll co.

Co·lo·nus \kə-ˈlō-nəs\. Ancient village, Attica, Greece, ab. 1½ m. N of Athens; birthplace of Sophocles.

Col·o·phon \ˈkäl-ə-fən, -ˌfän\. Ancient city, one of the 12 Ionian Cities, 15 m. NW of Ephesus, in Lydia, Asia Minor; famous for its troop of cavalry; destroyed by Lysimachus 287 B.C.

Col·o·ra·do \ˌkäl-ə-ˈrad-(ˌ)ō, -ˈräd-\. 1 River, SW United States; 1450 m. long; rises in NE Grand co., N Colorado; flows SW across Colorado receiving the Gunnison from SE, across SE corner of Utah receiving Green river from N and the San Juan from E, across NW corner of Arizona receiving the Little Colorado from SE; turns S and becomes lower section of Arizona-Nevada boundary and entire California-Arizona boundary; joined in SW Arizona by Gila river from E; flows through Mexico ab. 90 m., empties into Gulf of California. Passes through two notable canyons, Grand Canyon and Black Canyon (*qq.v.*). See SALTON SEA.

2 River, cen. Texas; rises in Dawson co., flows SE into Matagorda Bay; navigable to Austin; 840 m. long.

3 A west central state of U.S.A., bounded on N by Wyoming and Nebraska, on E by Nebraska and Kansas, on S by Oklahoma and New Mexico, on W by Utah; 8th state in area, 104,247 sq. m. (land area 103,797 sq. m.); 30th state in population, (1970c) 2,207,259; ✱ Denver; 38th state admitted to Union (1876).

Nickname: Centennial State, also Silver State. *State flower:* Columbine. *Motto:* Nil Sine Numine (Nothing Without the Deity). *Rivers:* Colorado (see 1, above); Arkansas, from cen. region E into Kansas; South Platte, from cen. region NE into Nebraska; Rio Grande, rising in SW, flowing SE into New Mexico. *Highest point:* Mount Elbert 14,433 ft., in Lake co.; has 55 peaks above 14,000 ft. and 1090 above 10,000 ft. *Chief products:* Wheat, sugar beets, corn; livestock; oil, molybdenum, coal, vanadium; manufacturing: food processing, chemicals, printing and publishing, primary metals. *Chief cities:* Denver, Colorado Springs, Pueblo, Lakewood, Aurora. See *Table of States* at UNITED STATES. Divided into the following 63 counties (for pronunciations, see their individual entries):

NAME	LOCATION	AREA[1] (sq. m.)	POP. (1970c)	CO. SEAT
Adams	NE cen.	1,245	185,789	Brighton
Alamosa	S	719	11,422	Alamosa
Arapahoe	NE cen.	815	162,142	Littleton
Archuleta	S	1,364	2,733	Pagosa Springs
Baca	SE corner	2,563	5,674	Springfield
Bent	SE	1,519	6,493	Las Animas
Boulder[2]	N cen.	748	131,889	Boulder
Chaffee	cen.	1,038	10,162	Salida
Cheyenne	E	1,772	2,396	Cheyenne Wells

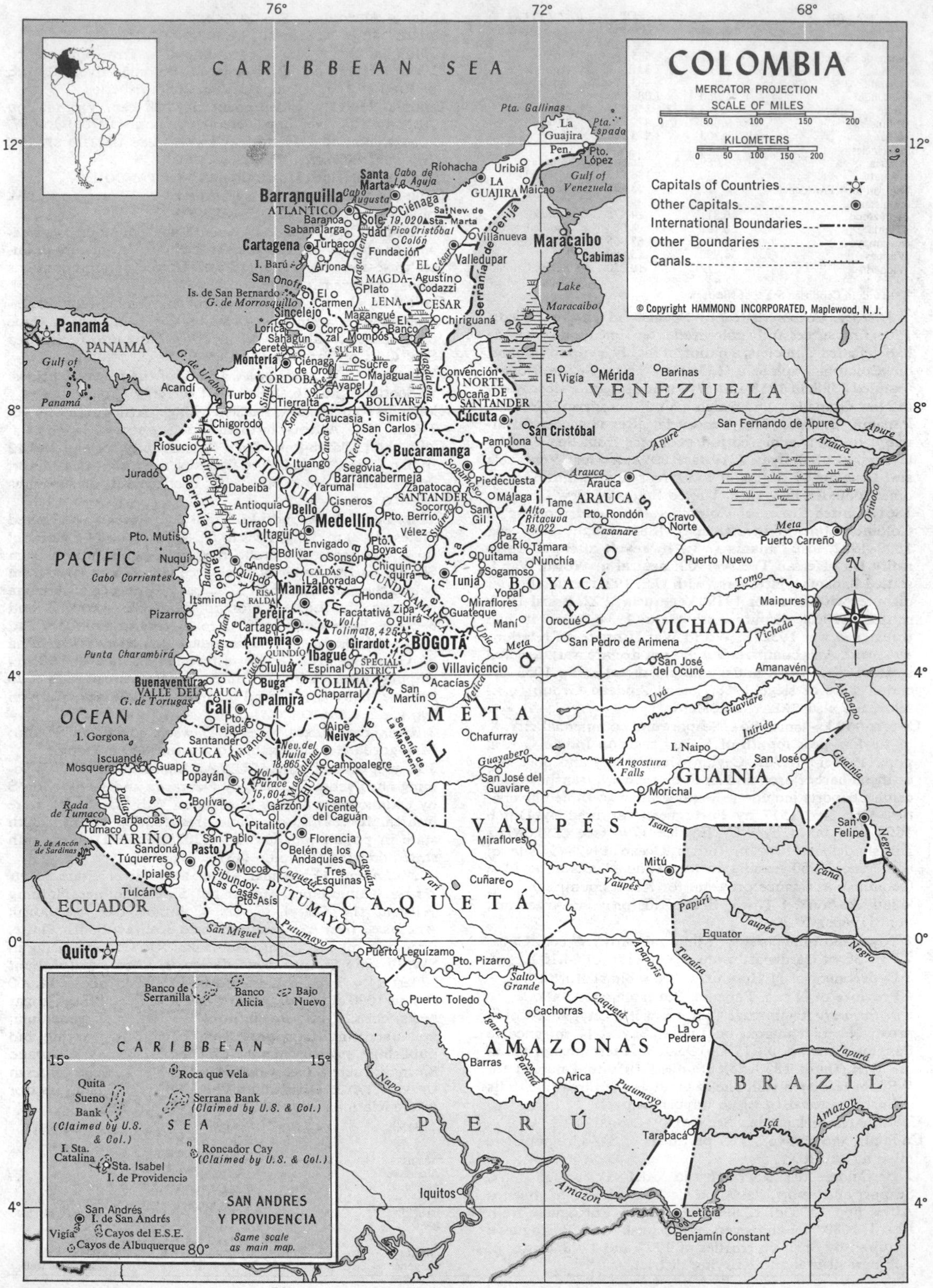
COLOMBIA
MERCATOR PROJECTION
SCALE OF MILES
0 50 100 150 200
KILOMETERS
0 50 100 150 200
Capitals of Countries
Other Capitals
International Boundaries
Other Boundaries
Canals
© Copyright HAMMOND INCORPORATED, Maplewood, N. J.
76°
72°
68°
12°
8°
4°
0°
CARIBBEAN SEA
PACIFIC
OCEAN
VENEZUELA
BRAZIL
PERÚ
ECUADOR
PANAMÁ
Panamá
Quito
Gulf of Panamá
Pta. Gallinas
La Guajira Pen.
Pta. Espada
Pto. López
Gulf of Venezuela
Uribia
LA GUAJIRA
Maicao
Ríohacha
Santa Marta
Cabo de la Aguja
Barranquilla
Cabo Augusta
ATLANTICO
Ciénaga
Baranoa
Soledad
Sabanalarga
Sa. Nev. de Sta. Marta
Pico Cristóbal Colón
Villanueva
Cartagena
Turbaco
Fundación
I. Barú
Arjona
Valledupar
San Onofre
EL CESAR
MAGDALENA
Agustín Codazzi
Plato
Is. de San Bernardo
G. de Morrosquillo
El Carmen
Sincelejo
Chiriguaná
Maracaibo
Cabimas
Lake Maracaibo
Serranía de Perijá
Lorica
Corozal
Magangué
El Banco
Mompós
Sahagún
Cereté
SUCRE
Montería
Ciénaga de Oro
Sucre
Majagual
CÓRDOBA
Ayapel
Convención
NORTE DE SANTANDER
Ocaña
El Vigía
Mérida
Barinas
Acandí
G. de Urabá
Turbo
Tierralta
BOLÍVAR
Cúcuta
San Cristóbal
Chigorodó
Caucasia
Simití
San Carlos
Pamplona
Ríosucio
ANTIOQUIA
Ituango
Bucaramanga
Jurado
Segovia
Barrancabermeja
Piedecuesta
Dabeiba
Yarumal
Zapatoca
SANTANDER
Málaga
Antioquia
Cisneros
Socorro
San Gil
Alto Ritacuva 18,022
Tame
ARAUCA
Arauca
Medellín
Bello
Pto. Berrío
Urrao
Itagüí
Vélez
Pto. Rondón
Cravo Norte
Pto. Mutis
Envigado
Bolívar
Sonsón
Pto. Boyacá
Paz de Río
Támara
Nuquí
CHOCÓ
Serranía de Baudó
Quibdó
Andes
Chiquinquirá
Duitama
Nunchía
Cabo Corrientes
CALDAS
La Dorada
Manizales
Tunja
Sogamoso
BOYACÁ
RISARALDA
Honda
Yopal
Itsmina
Pereira
CUNDINAMARCA
Miraflores
Pizarro
Cartago
Facatativá
Zipaquirá
Guateque
Maní
Orocué
Armenia
QUINDÍO
Vol. Tolima 18,425
Girardot
BOGOTÁ
SPECIAL DISTRICT
Punta Charambirá
Ibagué
Tuluá
Espinal
Villavicencio
Buenaventura
VALLE DEL CAUCA
Buga
TOLIMA
Acacías
G. de Tortugas
Palmira
Chaparral
San Martín
Cali
Pto. Tejada
Santander
META
LLANOS
I. Gorgona
Aipe
Neiva
Serranía de La Macarena
Chafurray
Iscuandé
Mosquera
Guapí
CAUCA
Neu. del Huila 18,865
Campoalegre
Popayán
Vol. Puracé 15,604
HUILA
San José del Guaviare
Rada de Tumaco
Bolívar
San Vicente del Caguán
Garzón
Barbacoas
Tumaco
NARIÑO
Pitalito
San Pablo
Florencia
B. de Ancón de Sardinas
Sandoná
Pasto
Túquerres
Belén de los Andaquíes
Ipiales
Sibundoy
Las Casas
Mocoa
Tres Esquinas
Tulcán
PUTUMAYO
Pto. Asís
CAQUETÁ
VAUPÉS
Miraflores
Cuñare
San Miguel
Putumayo
Puerto Leguízamo
Pto. Pizarro
Salto Grande
Puerto Toledo
Cachorras
AMAZONAS
Barras
Arica
Tarapacá
Iquitos
Leticia
Benjamín Constant
Amazon
Napo
Caquetá
Apaporis
Taraira
La Pedrera
Japurá
Içá
Yari
Igará-Paraná
Equator
Mitú
Papurí
Vaupés
Isana
Negro
Içana
San Felipe
GUAINÍA
Morichal
Angostura Falls
Guayabero
Guaviare
Inírida
I. Naipo
San José
Guainía
Atabapo
Amanavén
San José del Ocuné
Uvá
VICHADA
Vichada
San Pedro de Arimena
Meta
Maipures
Tomo
Puerto Nuevo
Puerto Carreño
Orinoco
Casanare
Arauca
Apure
San Fernando de Apure
N
Banco de Serranilla
Banco Alicia
Bajo Nuevo
CARIBBEAN SEA
15°
Roca que Vela
Quita Sueno Bank (Claimed by U.S. & Col.)
Serrana Bank (Claimed by U.S. & Col.)
Roncador Cay (Claimed by U.S. & Col.)
I. Sta. Catalina
Sta. Isabel
I. de Providencia
San Andrés
I. de San Andrés
Vigía
Cayos del E.S.E.
Cayos de Albuquerque
80°
SAN ANDRES Y PROVIDENCIA
Same scale as main map.
Longitude West 72° of Greenwich

NAME	LOCATION	AREA[1] (sq. m.)	POP. (1970c)	CO. SEAT
Clear Creek	N cen.	394	4,819	Georgetown
Conejos	S	1,268	7,846	Conejos
Costilla	S	1,213	3,091	San Luis
Crowley	E	802	3,086	Ordway
Custer	S cen.	737	1,120	Westcliffe
Delta	W	1,154	15,286	Delta
Denver[3]	NE cen.	68	514,678	Denver
Dolores	SW	1,026	1,641	Dove Creek
Douglas	cen.	843	8,407	Castle Rock
Eagle	NW cen.	1,682	7,498	Eagle
Elbert	E cen.	1,864	3,903	Kiowa
El Paso[4]	E cen.	2,157	235,972	Colorado Springs
Fremont	S cen.	1,561	21,942	Canon City
Garfield	W	2,997	14,821	Glenwood Springs
Gilpin	N cen.	148	1,272	Central City
Grand[2]	N	1,854	4,107	Hot Sulphur Springs
Gunnison	W cen.	3,236	7,578	Gunnison
Hinsdale	SW	1,054	202	Lake City
Huerfano	S	1,574	6,590	Walsenburg
Jackson	N	1,622	1,811	Walden
Jefferson	cen.	785	233,031	Golden
Kiowa	E	1,767	2,029	Eads
Kit Carson	E	2,171	7,530	Burlington
Lake	cen.	379	8,282	Leadville
La Plata	SW	1,684	19,199	Durango
Larimer[2]	N	2,611	89,900	Fort Collins
Las Animas	SE	4,794	15,744	Trinidad
Lincoln	E	2,593	4,836	Hugo
Logan	NE	1,822	18,852	Sterling
Mesa	W	3,303	54,374	Grand Junction
Mineral	S	921	786	Creede
Moffat	NW corner	4,743	6,525	Craig
Montezuma[5]	SW corner	2,094	12,952	Cortez
Montrose	W	2,238	18,366	Montrose
Morgan	NE	1,278	20,105	Fort Morgan
Otero	SE	1,254	23,523	La Junta
Ouray	SW	540	1,546	Ouray
Park	cen.	2,002	2,185	Fairplay
Phillips	NE	680	4,131	Holyoke
Pitkin	W cen.	973	6,185	Aspen
Prowers	SE	1,621	13,258	Lamar
Pueblo	SE cen.	2,405	118,238	Pueblo
Rio Blanco	NW	3,263	4,842	Meeker
Rio Grande	S	915	10,494	Del Norte
Routt	NW	2,330	6,592	Steamboat Springs
Saguache	S	3,144	3,827	Saguache
San Juan	SW	391	831	Silverton
San Miguel	SW	1,283	1,949	Telluride
Sedgwick	NE corner	544	3,405	Julesburg
Summit	cen.	611	2,665	Breckenridge
Teller	cen.	553	3,316	Cripple Creek
Washington	NE	2,526	5,550	Akron
Weld	N	4,002	89,297	Greeley
Yuma	NE	2,379	8,544	Wray

[1] Area = land area.
[2] Rocky Mountain National Park occupies SW corner of Larimer co., NE corner of Grand co., and NW corner of Boulder co.
[3] Coextensive with city of Denver.
[4] Pikes Peak within county, near W boundary.
[5] Its SW point the only point in U.S. common to four states (Colo., Utah, Ariz., and N. Mex.). Mesa Verde National Park in SE cen. part.

History: Explored (chiefly during 18th cent.) and claimed by Spanish; E part included in Louisiana Purchase (*q.v.*) 1803, rest in territory yielded by Mexico 1848; explored by Pike 1806, Long 1820, Frémont 1842–53, and by a host of fur trappers; gold, discovered at Cherry Creek near Pikes Peak in 1858, attracted American settlers; first settlement at Auraria 1858; organized as territory 1861; held first constitutional convention 1864; admitted as state Aug. 1, 1876.

4 County in Texas. See table at TEXAS.

5 *or* **Colorado City.** City, ⊗ of Mitchell co., NW cen. Texas, on Colorado river 25 m. W of Sweetwater; pop. (1970c) 5227; oil; livestock.

Co·lo·ra·do \ˌkäl-ə-ˈräd-(ˌ)ō\. River in cen. Argentina; 530 m. long; formed by confluence of Río Grande and Barrancas river near Chilean border, flows SE into Atlantic Ocean below Bahía Blanca.

Col·o·ra·do Desert \-ˌrad-ō-, -ˌräd-\. Arid region in SE California, W of the Colorado river; includes Salton Sea; ab. 2000 sq. m. See IMPERIAL VALLEY.

Colorado National Monument. See UNITED STATES, *National Monuments.*

Co·lo·ra·dos, Cerro \ˌser-(ˌ)ō-ˌkäl-ə-ˈräd-əs, -(ˌ)ōs\. Volcano on border bet. NW Argentina and Chile; 19,846 ft.

Col·o·ra·do Springs \-ˌrad-ō-, -ˌräd-\. Residential and resort city, ⊗ of El Paso co., E cen. Colorado, at foot of Pikes Peak; pop. (1970c) 135,060; alt. 5980; tourism; founded 1871, incorp. as city 1878; trade center for Cripple Creek goldfield. Colorado Coll. (1874); U.S. Air Force Academy (1954; transferred 1958 from Lowry Air Force Base, Denver, Colorado, to site NNW of city).

Co·los·sae \kə-ˈläs-ē\. An ancient city in SW Phrygia; a flourishing commercial town in time of Herodotus but declined on founding of Laodicea nearby; seat of an early Christian church to which Saint Paul wrote the *Epistle to the Colossians.*

Col·quitt \ˈkäl-(ˌ)kwit\. **1** County in Georgia. See table at GEORGIA.

2 City, ⊗ of Miller co., SW Georgia; pop. (1970c) 2026.

Col·ter Peak \ˌkōl-tər-\. Mountain in Yellowstone National Park, NW Wyoming; 10,683 ft.

Col·ton \ˈkōlt-ᵊn\. City, San Bernardino co., SE California, 3 m. S of San Bernardino; pop. (1970c) 20,016; ships fruit.

Co·lum·bia \kə-ˈləm-bē-ə\. **1** River, SW Canada and NW United States; 1214 m. long; drainage area 258,000 sq. m.; rises in Columbia Lake, SE British Columbia, flows NW, around N end of Selkirk Mts., turns S; widens into Arrow Lake (*q.v.*); crosses Washington boundary, forms large curve to W, called Big Bend; near Oregon border receives its largest tributary, Snake river, from E; turns W and becomes W part of Washington-Oregon boundary; turns N below Portland and empties into Pacific; its mouth the only deepwater harbor bet. San Francisco and Cape Flattery; navigable 95 m. for seagoing boats; upper course source of hydroelectric power (see UNITED STATES, *Dams and Reservoirs* [Grand Coulee Dam]). Discovered 1792 by Capt. Robert Gray of Boston; a U.S.-Canada treaty (1961, revised 1964) provides for cooperative development of the river.

2 Name of counties in eight states of the U.S. See tables at ARKANSAS, FLORIDA, GEORGIA, NEW YORK, OREGON, PENNSYLVANIA, WASHINGTON, WISCONSIN.

3 Town, Tolland co., N Connecticut, 20 m. ESE of Hartford; pop. (1970c) 3129.

4 City, Monroe co., SW Illinois; pop. (1970c) 4188.

5 City, ⊗ of Adair co., S cen. Kentucky; pop. (1970c) 3234; Lindsey Wilson Coll. (1903).

6 City, ⊗ of Caldwell parish, Louisiana; pop. (1970c) 1000.

7 City, ⊗ of Marion co., S Mississippi, 32 m. W of Hattiesburg; pop. (1970c) 7587; agriculture, dairying.

8 City, ⊗ of Boone co., cen. Missouri, 27 m. N of Jefferson City; pop. (1970c) 58,804; in agricultural section; Stephens Coll. (1833), Univ. of Missouri (1839), Christian Coll. (1851), Columbia Coll. (1851).

9 Town, ⊗ of Tyrrell co., E North Carolina; pop. (1970c) 902.

10 Industrial borough, Lancaster co., SE Pennsylvania, on Susquehanna river 11 m. W of Lancaster; pop. (1970c) 11,237; steel, foundry products; settled by Quakers 1726; proposed as site for national capital 1789.

11 City, ✱ of South Carolina and ⊗ of Richland co., in W cen. part of the state on Congaree river, 12 m. E of Lake Murray; pop. (1970c) 113,542; electronic equipment, glass, textiles, office machinery, plastics; Univ. of South Carolina (1801), Columbia Coll. (1854), Columbia Bible Coll. (1923), Allen Univ. (1870), Benedict Coll. (1870); settled c. 1700; founded as capital of the state 1786; incorp. as village 1805, as city 1854; figured as city of refuge in American Revolution; shelled, entered, and burned by Sherman 1865.

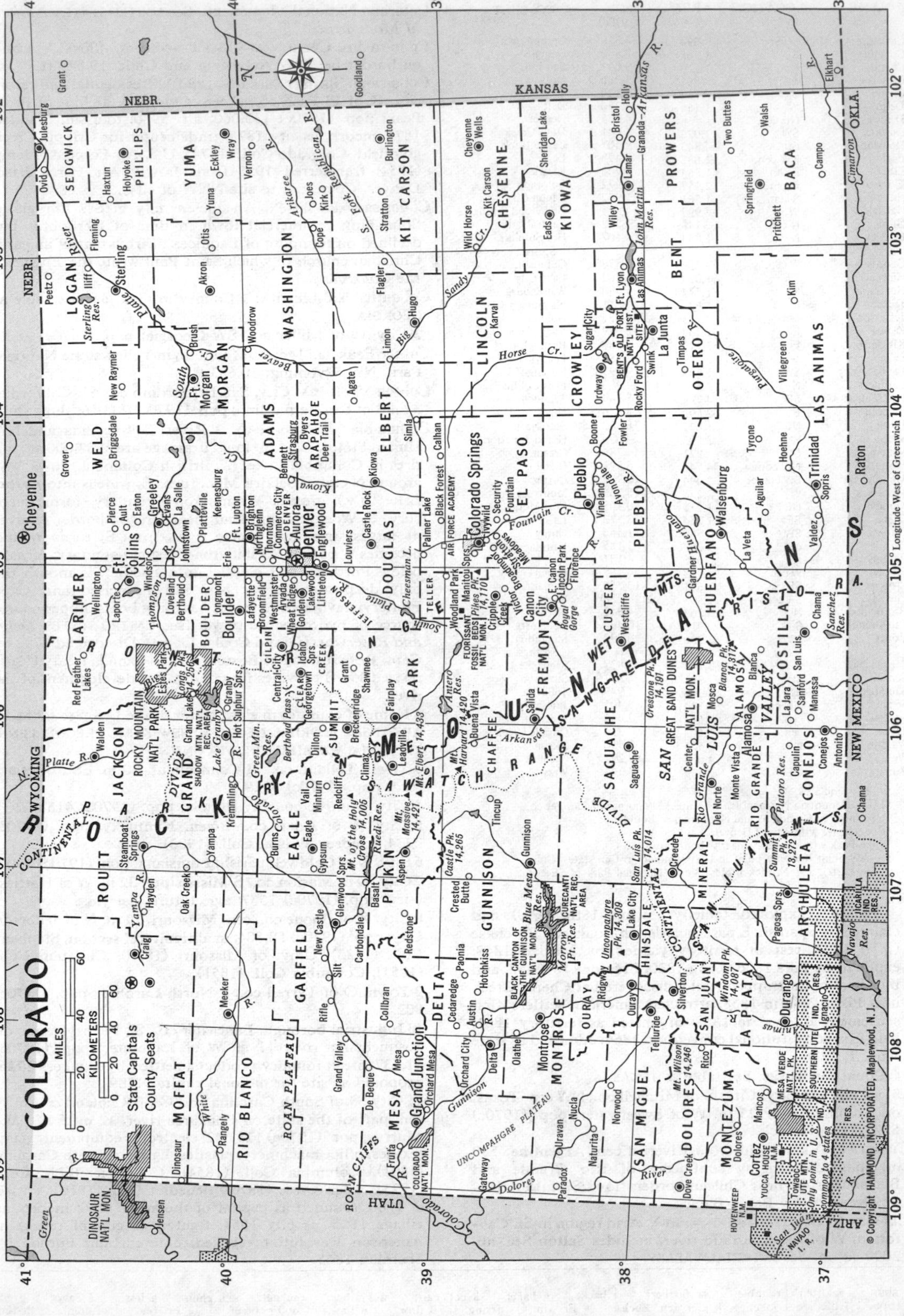
COLORADO
MILES
0 20 40 60
KILOMETERS
0 20 40 60
State Capitals
County Seats
WYOMING
NEBR.
KANSAS
OKLA.
NEW MEXICO
ARIZ.
UTAH
ROCKY MOUNTAINS
SANGRE DE CRISTO MTS.
SAN JUAN MTS.
SAWATCH RANGE
WET MTS.
PARK RANGE
FRONT RANGE
CONTINENTAL DIVIDE
SEDGWICK
LOGAN
PHILLIPS
YUMA
WASHINGTON
KIT CARSON
CHEYENNE
KIOWA
PROWERS
BACA
BENT
LAS ANIMAS
OTERO
CROWLEY
LINCOLN
ELBERT
ADAMS
ARAPAHOE
MORGAN
WELD
LARIMER
BOULDER
JEFFERSON
DOUGLAS
EL PASO
PUEBLO
HUERFANO
COSTILLA
ALAMOSA
CONEJOS
RIO GRANDE
SAGUACHE
CUSTER
FREMONT
TELLER
PARK
CHAFFEE
LAKE
SUMMIT
CLEAR CREEK
GILPIN
GRAND
JACKSON
ROUTT
MOFFAT
RIO BLANCO
GARFIELD
EAGLE
PITKIN
GUNNISON
DELTA
MESA
MONTROSE
OURAY
HINSDALE
MINERAL
SAN JUAN
SAN MIGUEL
DOLORES
MONTEZUMA
LA PLATA
ARCHULETA
Denver
Cheyenne
Colorado Springs
Pueblo
Grand Junction
Boulder
Ft. Collins
Greeley
Durango
Trinidad
Sterling
La Junta
DINOSAUR NAT'L MON.
ROCKY MOUNTAIN NAT'L PARK
BLACK CANYON OF THE GUNNISON NAT'L MON.
GREAT SAND DUNES NAT'L MON.
MESA VERDE NAT'L PK.
COLORADO NAT'L MON.
FLORISSANT FOSSIL BEDS NAT'L MON.
BENT'S OLD FORT NAT'L HIST. SITE
HOVENWEEP N.M.
YUCCA HOUSE N.M.
SOUTHERN UTE IND. RES.
UTE MTN. IND. RES.
JICARILLA IND. RES.
NAVAJO I.R.
Pikes Pk. 14,110
Mt. Elbert 14,433
Mt. Massive 14,421
Mt. Harvard 14,420
Longs Pk. 14,256
Blanca Pk. 14,317
Castle Pk. 14,265
Mt. of the Holy Cross 14,005
Uncompahgre Pk. 14,309
Mt. Wilson 14,246
Windom Pk. 14,087
San Luis Pk. 14,014
Crestone Pk. 14,191
Summit Pk. 13,272
Four Corners: Only point in U.S. common to 4 states
105° Longitude West of Greenwich
© Copyright HAMMOND INCORPORATED, Maplewood, N.J.

12 City, ⊗ of Maury co., W cen. Tennessee, on Duck river 43 m. SSW of Nashville; pop. (1970c) 21,471; flour, fertilizer; Columbia State Community Coll. (1966); first settled 1807.

Columbia, Cape. Northernmost point of Canada, on N coast of Ellesmere I., NE Arctic Archipelago, 83°07′N.

Columbia, District of. See DISTRICT OF COLUMBIA.

Columbia, Mount. Peak bet. SW Alberta and SE British Columbia, Canada, on S border of Jasper National Park; 12,294 ft.

Columbia City. City, ⊗ of Whitley co., NE Indiana, 18 m. WNW of Fort Wayne; pop. (1970c) 4911.

Columbia Falls. Town, Flathead co., NW Montana, 14 m. NE of Kalispell; pop. (1970c) 2652; agriculture; resort area.

Columbia Glacier. Glacier, Chugach Mts., S Alaska; 41 m. long; ab. 4 m. wide near its terminus.

Columbia Heights. Residential city, Anoka co., E Minnesota, on Mississippi river 5 m. N of Minneapolis; pop. (1970c) 23,837.

Columbia Lake. Lake, SE British Columbia, W Canada; ab. 14 m. long; elev. 2700 ft.; source of the Columbia river.

Co·lum·bi·ana \kə-ˌləm-bē-ˈan-ə\. **1** County in Ohio. See table at OHIO.

2 Town, ⊗ of Shelby co., cen. Alabama; pop. (1970c) 2248; cotton, timber.

3 Village, Columbiana co., E Ohio, 15 m. S of Youngstown; pop. (1970c) 4959; foundries, machine shops.

Columbia Peak. Peak in Chaffee co., Colorado; 14,073 ft.

Co·lum·bre·tes \ˌkō-ləm-ˈbrā-(ˌ)tās\. Group of small islands in Mediterranean Sea off E Spain.

Co·lum·bus \kə-ˈləm-bəs\. **1** County in North Carolina. See table at NORTH CAROLINA.

2 City, ⊗ of Muscogee co., W Georgia, on Chattahoochee river 80 m. WSW of Macon; pop. (1970c) 155,028; brick and tile, fertilizer, textiles, agricultural implements; Columbus Coll. (1958); established 1828 as frontier post; Fort Benning (*q.v.*) 8 m. S.

3 City, ⊗ of Bartholomew co., cen. Indiana, 34 m. E of Bloomington; pop. (1970c) 26,457; diesel engines, automobile accessories, leather.

4 City, ⊗ of Cherokee co., SE corner of Kansas, 18 m. SW of Pittsburg; pop. (1970c) 3356; fertilizer; lead and zinc works; coal.

5 City, NW Hickman co., SW Kentucky, on Mississippi river just below confluence with the Ohio; pop. (1970c) 351; fortified 1861 by Confederates but evacuated 1862.

6 City, ⊗ of Lowndes co., E Mississippi, 7 m. W of Alabama border; pop. (1970c) 25,795; automobile parts, lumber; temporary capital of Mississippi 1863 when Jackson was occupied by Union troops. Mississippi State Coll. for Women (1884).

7 Town, ⊗ of Stillwater co., S cen. Montana; pop. (1970c) 1281.

8 City, ⊗ of Platte co., E Nebraska, at confluence of Loup and Platte rivers; pop. (1970c) 15,741; headquarters of Loup River Public Power District Project.

9 Village, Luna co., SW New Mexico; pop. (1970c) 241; raided by Pancho Villa 1916.

10 Town, ⊗ of Polk co., SW North Carolina; pop. (1970c) 731.

11 Commercial and manufacturing city, ✱ of Ohio and ⊗ of Franklin co., cen. Ohio, on the Scioto 97 m. NE of Cincinnati; pop. (1970c) 540,025; in agricultural region, near supplies of coal, iron, natural gas, limestone, clay; automobile parts, electrical equipment, glass, food products; railroad shops; Ohio State Capitol, Gallery of Fine Arts, Battelle Memorial Institute (1929), Ohio State Penitentiary; Lockbourne Air Force Base; Ohio State Univ. (1870), Capital Univ. (1850), Bliss Coll. (1899), Franklin Univ. (1902), Ohio Dominican Coll. (1911), Ohio Technical Coll. (1952); first settlement at Franklinton 1797 on W bank of Scioto; site opposite laid out 1812 as new capital and named Columbus; made ⊗ 1824; became city 1834; absorbed Franklinton 1871.

12 Town, ⊗ of Colorado co., SE cen. Texas, on Colorado river 33 m. S of Brenham; pop. (1970c) 3342; rice, cotton; oil and gas wells.

13 City, Columbia co., S cen. Wisconsin, 25 m. NE of Madison; pop. (1970c) 3789; dairying; Columbia County Teachers Coll. (1908); settled 1839.

Columbus Grove. Village, Putnam co., NW Ohio, 12 m. N of Lima; pop. (1970c) 2690; timber; livestock.

Co·lu·sa \kə-ˈlü-sə\. **1** County in N cen. California. See table at CALIFORNIA.

2 City, its ⊗, on Sacramento river 53 m. NW of Sacramento; pop. (1970c) 3842; sugar beets.

Col·ville \ˈkōl-ˌvil, ˈkäl-\. **1** River, N Alaska; 375 m. long; flows E along N slope of Brooks Range, then N to Beaufort Sea.

2 City, ⊗ of Stevens co., NE Washington, ab. 68 m. N of Spokane; pop. (1970c) 3742; silver and lead mining.

Colville, Cape. Cape on N coast of North I., New Zealand, on E side of Hauraki Gulf.

Col·vin, Mount \-ˈkäl-vən\. Peak in the Adirondack Mts., Essex co., NE New York; 4074 ft.

Col·vos Passage \ˌkäl-vəs-\. Strait at S end of Puget Sound, Washington, W of Vashon I.

Col·wyn \ˈkäl-wən\. Borough, Delaware co., SE Pennsylvania, 6 m. WSW of Philadelphia; pop. (1970c) 3169.

Colwyn Bay. Municipal borough, Denbighshire, N Wales; pop. (1971p) 25,535; popular seaside resort.

Co·mac·chio \kə-ˈmäk-ē-ˌō\ *or anc.* **Co·mac·ti·um** \kə-ˈmak-shē-əm, -tē-əm\. Fortified commune, Ferrara prov., Emilia-Romagna, N Italy, 30 m. ESE of Ferrara; pop. (1968e) 18,491; built on 13 islands connected by bridges; fisheries.

Comagene. See COMMAGENE.

Co·mal \kə-ˈmäl\. County in Texas. See table at TEXAS.

Co·ma·la·pa \ˌkō-mə-ˈläp-ə\. Town, Chimaltenango dept., S cen. Guatemala.

Co·mal·cal·co \ˌkō-mäl-ˈkäl-(ˌ)kō\. Municipality, Tabasco state, Mexico, 26 m. NW of Villahermosa; pop. (1970p) 71,651; lumber; cacao, bananas; major 6th cent. Mayan ruins.

Co·man, Mount \-ˈkō-mən\. Mountain, Antarctica, 73°49′S, 64°18′W; 12,000 ft.

Co·ma·na \kə-ˈmā-nə\. Ancient city of S Cappadocia, Asia Minor, in Taurus Mts. on upper Seyhan river; exact site uncertain; important religious center 1st cent. B.C.

Co·man·che \kə-ˈman-chē\. **1** Counties in three states of the U.S. See tables at KANSAS, OKLAHOMA, TEXAS.

2 City, Stephens co., S Oklahoma; pop. (1970c) 1862; corn, cotton.

3 City, ⊗ of Comanche co., cen. Texas, 24 m. ENE of Brownwood; pop. (1970c) 3933; fertilizer; peanuts; poultry.

Co·ma·ya·gua \ˌkō-mə-ˈyä-gwə\. **1** Department of S cen. Honduras. See table at HONDURAS.

2 Town, its ✱, 35 m. W of Tegucigalpa; pop. (1961c) 8473; former ✱ of Honduras.

Combaconum. See KUMBAKONAM.

Com·ba·hee \ˌkəm-ˈbē, ˈkəm-ˌbē\. River, S South Carolina; ab. 140 m. long; formed by confluence of Salkehatchie and Little Salkehatchie rivers; flows SE to Atlantic Ocean.

Combarelles. See EYZIES, LES.

Combe Ca·pelle \ˌkōm-ka-ˈpel\. Rock shelter, near Bergerac, Dordogne dept., SW cen. France; noted for discovery 1909 of a skeleton, the type specimen of the Combe-Capelle race of the Aurignacian period.

Com·ber·mere Bay \ˌkəm-bər-ˌmi(ə)r-\. Inlet of Bay of Bengal on W coast of Burma, SE of Sittwe.

Combin, Grand. See GRAND COMBIN.

Com·bined Locks \kam-ˌbīnd-ˈläks\. Village, Outagamie co., E Wisconsin, 7 m. E of Appleton; pop. (1970c) 2734.

Com·bles \ˈkōⁿblᵊ\. Commune, Somme dept., NW France, 6 m. NNW of Péronne; pop. (1962c) 707; scene of much fighting during World War I; left in ruins.

Come·ragh Mountains \ˌkyüm-rə-\. Mountain range in S Ireland, in co. Waterford; highest peak **Knock·a·naf·frin** \ˌnäk-ə-ˈnaf-rən\ 2597 ft.

Co·me·río \ˌkō-mə-ˈrē-(ˌ)ō\. Town and municipality, E cen. Puerto Rico; pop. (1970p) 6267 (town), 18,738 (munic.).

Co·mil·la \kə-ˈmil-ə\ *or* **Ku·mil·la** \kü-\. Town, Bangla Desh, on affluent of Meghna river 50 m. SE of Dacca; pop. (1961c) 54,504.

Co·mi·no \kə-ˈmē-(ˌ)nō\. 1 Cape on E coast of Sardinia, Italy, N of Gulf of Orosei.
2 Island of the Malta group in the Mediterranean Sea, bet. Malta and Gozo; 1 sq. m.

Co·mi·so \ˈkō-mi-ˌzō\. Commune, Ragusa prov., SE Sicily, Italy, 7 m. W of Ragusa; pop. (1968e) 26,873; castle.

Co·mi·tán *or in full* **Comitán de Do·mín·guez** \ˌkō-mi-ˈtän-ˈdād-ə-ˈmiŋ-ˌgez\. Town, Chiapas state, SE Mexico, ab. 70 m. ESE of San Andrés Tuxtla; munic. pop. (1970p) 38,137.

Com·mack \ˈkäm-ˌak\. Urban community (unincorporated), Suffolk co., New York, in cen. Long I. ESE of Huntington; pop. (1970c) 22,507.

Com·ma·ge·ne *or* **Com·a·ge·ne** \ˌkäm-ə-ˈjē-nē\. District of ancient Syria, bet. Taurus Mts. and Euphrates river SE of Cappadocia; independent under a branch of the Seleucids; came under Romans in Vespasian's reign; ✱ Samosata.

Commander Islands. See KOMANDORSKIYE ISLANDS.

Commedagh, Slieve. See SLIEVE COMMEDAGH.

Com·merce \ˈkäm-(ˌ)ers\. 1 City, Los Angeles co., SW California, NW of Downey; pop. (1970c) 10,536.
2 City, Jackson co., NE Georgia; pop. (1970c) 3702; lumber, cotton, peaches.
3 City, Ottawa co., NE corner of Oklahoma, 65 m. ENE of Bartlesville; pop. (1970c) 2593; zinc and lead mines.
4 City, Hunt co., NE Texas, 15 m. ENE of Greenville; pop. (1970c) 9534; flour; cotton, oats; East Texas State Univ. (1889).

Commerce Town. City, Adams co., NE cen. Colorado, NE of Denver; pop. (1970c) 17,407.

Com·mer·cy \ˌkō-mer-ˈsē\. Commune, Meuse dept., NE France, on Meuse river; pop. (1962c) 7918.

Com·me·wij·ne \ˌkōm-ə-ˈwī-nə\. 1 *or* **Com·me·wy·ne** \-ˈwī-\. River, NE Surinam; ab. 100 m. long; flows NNW into the Suriname estuary near Paramaribo.
2 District of Surinam.

Commonwealth of Australia. See AUSTRALIA.

Commonwealth of Nations *or formerly* **British Commonwealth of Nations.** An association of sovereign states, consisting of Great Britain and a number of its former dependencies; formerly constituted, with several other British-controlled territories, the **British Empire;** formally established by Statute of Westminster (1931) and consisting at the time of its formation of United Kingdom, Australia, Canada, Irish Free State (withdrew 1949), Newfoundland (became a province of Canada 1949), New Zealand, and the Union (now Republic) of South Africa (withdrew 1961). After World War II the following countries (with year of independence) became members: India and Pakistan (1947; Pakistan withdrew 1972), Ceylon (1948), Ghana (1957), Nigeria (1960), Cyprus and Sierra Leone (1961), Jamaica, Trinidad and Tobago, Uganda, and Western Samoa (1962), Kenya and Malaysia (1963), Malawi, Malta, Tanzania, and Zambia (1964), Gambia and Singapore (1965), Barbados, Botswana, Guyana, Lesotho (1966), Mauritius, Nauru (special status), and Swaziland (1968), Tonga and Fiji (1970).
History: (1) *Territorial development:* Territorial acquisition began in early 17th cent. with group of settlements in North America and Caribbean and East Indian trading posts founded by private individuals and trading companies; captured Gibraltar 1704; by 18th cent., held 13 Atlantic seaboard colonies (see UNITED STATES) and began to add territory in India (see INDIA 1); as result of French defeat (completed by 1763) secured Acadia, Canada, eastern Mississippi valley, and supremacy in India; began to build power in Malaya 1786 (see PENANG); acquired Cape of Good Hope, Ceylon, and Malta as result of Napoleonic Wars; secured Aden 1839, Hong Kong 1841, and controlled Suez Canal from 1875; in 19th cent. European partition of Africa, acquired Nigeria, Egypt, and territories later comprising British East Africa and Union (now Republic) of South Africa; after World War I, secured mandates to German East Africa, Cameroons, part of Togo, German South-West Africa, Mesopotamia, Palestine, and part of German Pacific islands. (2) *Political development:* Prior to 1783, Crown and Parliament claimed full authority over colonial legislatures; after 1783 evolved system of self-government for advanced colonies; gave dominion status to Canada 1867, then to Australia 1901, New Zealand 1907, Union of South Africa 1910, and Irish Free State 1921; by Statute of Westminster 1931 gave legal expression to the Commonwealth of Nations (for other territories with year of independence see above).

Commonwealth of the Bahama Islands. See BAHAMA ISLANDS.

Communauté Française. See FRENCH COMMUNITY.

Com·mun·ism Peak \ˈkäm-yə-ˌniz-əm-\ *or* **Mount Communism** *or Russ.* **Pik Kom·mun·iz·ma** \ˈpēk-ˌkäm-ü-ˈnēz-mə\; *formerly* **Sta·lin Peak** \ˌstäl-ən-, ˌstal-, -ˌēn-\ *or* **Gar·mo Peak** \ˌgär-(ˌ)mō-\. Highest peak in the Russian Pamirs, SE Tadzhik S.S.R., U.S.S.R.; 24,590 ft.; highest peak in the U.S.S.R.

Co·mo \ˈkō-(ˌ)mō\. 1 Province of Lombardy, N Italy. See table at ITALY.
2 *or anc.* **Co·mum** \ˈkō-məm\. Commune, its ✱, at SW end of Lake Como 24 m. N of Milan; pop. (1968e) 93,199; tourism; 14th cent. cathedral. Headquarters of Ghibelline party in 11th and 12th cents.; destroyed 1127 by Milanese and rebuilt 1159 by Frederick I; from 1335 under the Visconti family; center of Garibaldian agitation 1859. Mussolini arrested here Apr. 28, 1945 and shot.

Como, Lake *or anc.* **La·cus Lar·i·us** \ˌlā-kə-ˈslar-ē-əs, -ˈsler-\. Lake in Lombardy, N Italy, expansion of Adda river; 37 m. by ab. 3 m.; 56 sq. m.; surrounded by mountains 3000 to 7000 ft. high; many resorts.

Co·mo·do·ro Ri·va·da·via \ˌkäm-ə-ˈdōr-(ˌ)ō-ˌrē-və-ˈdäv-ē-ə, -ˈdȯr-\. Seaport on SE coast, Chubut prov., S Argentina, on Gulf of San Jorge; pop. (1960c) 35,966; univ. (1961); oil.

Co·mon·dú \ˌkō-mən-ˈdü\. Municipality, Baja California Sur terr., Mexico, 525 m. SE of Ensenada; pop. (1970p) 30,872; dates.

Co·mon·fort \ˌkō-mōn-ˈfō(ə)rt, -ˈfȯ(ə)rt\. Town, Guanajuato state, cen. Mexico, 38 m. SE of Guanajuato; munic. pop. (1970p) 34,462.

Com·o·rin, Cape \-ˈkam-ə-rən\. Cape on S extremity of India, in Tamil Nadu.

Com·o·ro Islands \ˈkäm-ə-ˌrō-\ *or Fr.* **Îles Co·mores** \ē(ə)l-kə-mȯ(ə)r\. Group of volcanic islands in N Mozambique Channel, bet. NE Mozambique and NW Malagasy Republic; 863 sq. m.; pop. (1970e) 267,000; ✱ Moroni; an overseas territory of France; includes islands of Great Comoro, Anjouan, Mayotte, and Mohéli; exports vanilla, sugar, copra, sisal. Mayotte occupied by French 1843, other islands secured by treaty 1886; became 1914 a colony attached administratively to Madagascar (Malagasy Republic); made a French overseas territory 1947; internal autonomy 1960.

Co·mox \ˈkō-ˌmäks\. Village, British Columbia, Canada, on the Strait of Georgia 5 m. E of Courtenay; pop. (1971p) 3884.

Com·piègne \kōmp-ˈyān\. Commune, Oise dept., N France, on left bank of Oise river 34 m. E of Beauvais; pop. (1968c) 29,700; 16th cent. Gothic town hall; fine château.
History: Taken from duke of Burgundy by Charles VI 1415; scene of capture of Joan of Arc by English 1430;

German headquarters 1870–71; armistice ending World War I signed in forest nearby Nov. 11, 1918; armistice bet. France and Germany signed on same spot June 22, 1940; retaken by Allies Aug. 1944.

Complutum. See ALCALÁ DE HENARES.

Compniacum. See COGNAC.

Com·po·ste·la \ˌkäm-pə-ˈstel-ə\. Municipality, Nayarit state, Mexico, 25 m. S of Tepic; pop. (1970p) 59,422; sugar processing; cigars; diversified agriculture; founded 1535.

Compostela, Santiago de. See SANTIAGO 15.

Comp·ton \ˈkäm(p)-tən\. 1 Industrial city, Los Angeles co., SW California, 13 m. S of Los Angeles; pop. (1970c) 78,611; aircraft parts, chemicals, steel castings; Compton Coll. (1927).

2 County in Quebec, Canada. See table at QUEBEC.

Com·stock Lode \ˌkäm-ˌstäk-ˈlōd\. See VIRGINIA CITY 2.

Com·tat Ve·nais·sin \kōⁿ-ˌtäv-ə-ne-ˈsaⁿ\ *or* **Comtat** *or* **Venaissin.** Historical region of SE France, bounded on N by Dauphiné, E and S by Provence, W by Languedoc; ✱ Carpentras; under papal rule 1274–1791.

Comum. See COMO 2.

Con·a·kry *or* **Kon·a·kri** \ˈkän-ə-krē\. Seaport town, ✱ of Guinea, W Africa, on Tombo I. (*q.v.*); pop. (1967e) 197,267; port facilities, textile mill; bauxite deposits nearby; technical coll. (1963).

Co·nan·i·cut Island \kə-ˈnan-i-kət-\. Island in Narragansett Bay W of Rhode Island (island); a part of Newport co., Rhode Island; coextensive with Jamestown.

Con·a·sau·ga \ˌkän-ə-ˈsȯ-gə\. River, NW Georgia; rises in SE Tennessee, flows S into Georgia, unites with Coosawattee river to form Oostanaula river.

Conca. See CUENCA.

Con·car·neau \ˌkōⁿ-kär-ˈnō\. Commune, Finistère dept., NW France, on Atlantic coast NW of Lorient; pop. (1962c) 16,271; old part of town walled, on an island, new part on mainland a seaside resort; sardine fishing.

Con·cep·cion *or Span.* **Con·cep·ción** \kən-ˌsep-sē-ˈōn, -ˈsep-shən\. Municipality, SE Tarlac prov., Luzon, Phil., 13 m. SSE of Tarlac; pop. (1968e) 61,800.

Con·cep·ción \kən-ˌsep-sē-ˈōn, -ˈsep-shən\. 1 Town, Santa Cruz dept., E Bolivia, 165 m. NE of Santa Cruz.

2 Province of S cen. Chile. See table at CHILE.

3 Commercial city, ✱ of Concepción prov., S cen. Chile, on the Bío-Bío river 6 m. from its mouth and 260 m. SW of Santiago; pop. (1970p) 185,227; distributing center for S Chile; its ports are Tomé and Talcahuano; textiles; food processing; coal mines nearby; univ. (1920).

History: Founded by Pedro de Valdivia ab. 6 m. from its present site 1550; laid waste by Araucanian Indians 1555; refounded 1557; destroyed by earthquakes 1570, 1730, 1751; rebuilt on present location 1755; again ruined by earthquake 1835; severely damaged by earthquake of Jan. 24, 1939.

4 Active volcano, Nicaragua; 5105 ft.; one of two peaks (see MADERA 4) on the island of Ometepe in Lake Nicaragua.

5 Department of E Paraguay. See table at PARAGUAY.

6 *or* **Vi·lla Concepción** \ˌvē-(y)ə-\. Town and river port, ✱ of Concepción dept., E Paraguay, on E bank of Paraguay river 125 m. N of Asunción; pop. (1968e) 17,200.

7 Island, West Indies. See GRENADA 3.

Concepción, La. See LA CONCEPCIÓN.

Concepción Bay. Inlet of Pacific Ocean in coast of S cen. Chile, near city of Concepción.

Concepción de la Vega. See LA VEGA 2.

Concepción del Uru·guay \-del-ˌu̇r-ə-ˈgwī\. River port, Entre Ríos prov., E Argentina, on the border of Uruguay; pop. (1960c) 36,486; National Univ. (1778).

Concepción Strait *or* **Concepción Channel.** Strait, S of Duke of York I. (Madre de Dios Archipelago), off SW Chile, leading from Pacific Ocean NE into Trinidad Gulf.

Con·cep·tion, Point \-kən-ˈsep-shən\. Point on SW extremity of Santa Barbara co., SW California.

Conception Bay. Inlet of Atlantic Ocean in SE Newfoundland, Canada, W of city of St. John's; ab. 40 m. long.

Con·cha·gua \kən-ˈchäg-wə\. Volcano, El Salvador, 95 m. ESE of the city of San Salvador; 4101 ft.

Conchas, Las. See TIGRE 1.

Con·chas Dam \ˌkän-chəs-\. Dam across S Canadian river, E San Miguel co., New Mexico; height 188 ft.; completed 1939; impounds water for flood control and irrigation, forming **Conchas Reservoir** (ab. 25 sq. m.).

Con·cho \ˈkän-(ˌ)chō\. 1 River, Texas; 53 m. long; rises in Tom Green co., flows E to join Colorado river. See MIDDLE CONCHO, NORTH CONCHO, and SOUTH CONCHO.

2 County in Texas. See table at TEXAS.

Con·chos \ˈkän-chəs\. River, Chihuahua state, N Mexico; ab. 300 m. long; flows N into the Rio Grande.

Con·cord \ˈkäŋ-kərd, ˈkän-, -ˌkȯ(ə)rd\. 1 River, NE Massachusetts; formed by junction of Sudbury and Assabet rivers, flows N into the Merrimack river at Lowell.

2 City, Contra Costa co., W California, NNE of Berkeley; pop. (1970c) 85,164; electronic equipment, cement; oil refining.

3 Residential town, Middlesex co., NE Massachusetts, 12 m. S of Lowell; pop. (1970c) 16,148; fruit, poultry; settled 1635; in 1775 had storehouse of munitions and military supplies which the British were marching to seize when they were checked by minutemen in battles at Lexington and Concord April 19, 1775; statue of the *Minute Man of Concord* by D. C. French at the bridge over Concord river where battle was fought; residence of A. Bronson Alcott, Louisa May Alcott, Ralph Waldo Emerson, Margaret Fuller, Nathaniel Hawthorne, Henry David Thoreau.

4 City, ✱ of New Hampshire and ⊗ of Merrimack co., S cen. New Hampshire, on Merrimack river 15 m. N of Manchester; pop. (1970c) 30,022; electrical equipment, leather goods; granite quarries; St. Paul's School (preparatory school; 1856); New Hampshire Technical Inst. (1961); home of Mary Baker Eddy. Original grant 1659; settled 1727; incorp. by Massachusetts as Rumford 1733, by New Hampshire as "parish of Concord" 1765, town 1784, city 1853; became capital 1808; figured in Indian wars, esp. in massacre of 1746.

5 City, ⊗ of Cabarrus co., S cen. North Carolina, 18 m. NE of Charlotte; pop. (1970c) 18,464; former gold-mining center (gold discovered 1799); manufactures cotton goods, cottonseed oil, lumber, flour; Barber-Scotia Coll. (1867).

6 Municipality, E New South Wales, SE Australia, W suburb of Sydney on S bank of lower Parramatta river; pop. (1966c) 27,037.

Con·cor·dia. 1 \kən-ˈkȯrd-ē-ə\. Parish in Louisiana. See table at LOUISIANA.

2 \kän-ˈkȯrd-ē-ə\. City, ⊗ of Cloud co., N Kansas, 50 m. N of Salina; pop. (1970c) 7221; in agricultural region; brick kilns.

Concordia \kən-ˈkȯrd-ē-ə\. City, Entre Ríos prov., E Argentina, on right bank of Uruguay river opp. Salto in Uruguay; pop. (1960c) 56,654.

Concordia sul·la Sec·chia \kən-ˈkȯr-dyə-ˌsül-ə-ˈsāk-yə\. Commune, Modena prov., Emilia-Romagna, N Italy, on Secchia river 20 m. N of Modena; pop. (1968e) 8870.

Con·da·mine \ˈkän-də-ˌmīn\. River, SE Queensland, Australia; 430 m. long; flows W through Darling Downs; joins Maranoa to form Culgoa.

Condamine. See LA CONDAMINE.

Con·da·te \kən-ˈdāt-ē\. Name, meaning "at the confluence of two rivers," given to many towns in ancient Gaul, esp. modern Cosne-sur-Loire, Montereau-faut-Yonne, Rennes, and Saint-Claude (*qq.v.*), and retained in its modern French form **Con·dé** \kōⁿ-dā\ in many such names.

Condé–Smendou. See ZIGHOUT YOUCEF.

Con·dé–sur–l'Es·caut \kōⁿ-ˌdā-sü(ə)r-les-ˈkō\. Commune, Nord dept., N France, 7 m. NE of Valenciennes and 2 m. from Belgian border; pop. (1968c) 13,607; principality from which the Condé branch of house of Bourbon held their title.

Condé–sur–Noi·reau \kōⁿ-ˌdā-sü(ə)r-nwä-ˈrō\. Commune, Calvados dept., NW France, 33 m. SSW of Caen; pop. (1962c) 6324; important during Middle Ages; held by English 1417–49; noted for cotton spinning and weaving.

Con·de·u·ba \ˌkō(ⁿ)n-dā-ˈü-və\. City, S Bahia state, E Brazil, 270 m. SW of Salvador; munic. pop. (1968e) 21,272.

Condivincum. See NANTES.

Con·dom \kōⁿ-ˈdōⁿ\. Commune, Gers dept., SW France, 20 m. SW of Agen; pop. (1962c) 7116; founded 8th cent.; episcopal see 1317–1790; sacked 1569 by Huguenots; trades in armagnac, the brandy made in this region.

Con·don \ˈkän-dən\. City, ⊗ of Gilliam co., N Oregon; pop. (1970c) 973.

Co·ne·cuh \kə-ˈnā-kə\. **1** River, S Alabama; 145 m. long; flows SW into the Escambia river.

2 County in Alabama. See table at ALABAMA.

Co·ne·glia·no \ˌkōn-ᵊl-ˈyän-(ˌ)ō\. Manufacturing commune, Treviso prov., Veneto, NE Italy, 15 m. N of Treviso; pop. (1968e) 28,504; wine, textiles (esp. silks).

Co·ne·jos \kə-ˈnā-əs, -həs\. **1** County in Colorado. See table at COLORADO.

2 Village, its ⊗, S Colorado.

Con·e·maugh \ˈkän-ə-ˌmȯ\. River, SW Pennsylvania; ab. 45 m. long; formed by confluence of **Little Conemaugh River** and Stony Creek at Johnstown, in Cambria co., flows W to unite with Loyalhanna Creek and form Kiskiminetas river. See JOHNSTOWN 3.

Con·es·to·ga \ˌkän-ə-ˈstō-gə\. Township, Lancaster co., Pennsylvania, SSW of Lancaster; pop. (1970c) 2447; place of manufacture of Conestoga wagon, developed ab. 1750.

Co·ney Island \ˌkō-nē-\. Pleasure resort, Brooklyn borough, New York City; formerly an island 5 m. long, now part of Long Island (since silting up of Coney Island Creek); first pavilion and bathhouse erected 1844.

Confederation of Arab Republics. See ARAB REPUBLICS, CONFEDERATION OF.

Conflans *or* **Conflans–l'Archevêque.** See CHARENTON-LE-PONT.

Con·flans–Sainte–Ho·no·rine \kōⁿ-ˌfläⁿ-saⁿ-tȯ-nȯ-ˈrēn\. Commune, Yvelines dept., N France, at confluence of Oise and Seine rivers; pop. (1968c) 26,304.

Confluentes. See KOBLENZ.

Con·fu·so \kən-ˈfü-(ˌ)sō\. River, S Chaco Boreal, W Paraguay; rises in swamp of the Pilcomayo, flows E, parallel to Pilcomayo for ab. 200 m., into the Paraguay.

Cong \ˈkäŋ\. Village, co. Galway, Eire, bet. Lough Mask and Lough Corrib; pop. (1961c) 145; abbey and stone cross; caves; region noted for archaeological remains and for connection with legends of the Firbolg. See MOYTURA.

Con·ga·mond, Lake \-ˈkäŋ-gə-mənd\. Series of ponds in S Hampden co., SW Massachusetts, on Mass.-Conn. boundary line; 3 m. long.

Con·ga·ree \ˈkäŋ-gə-ˌrē\. River, cen. South Carolina; ab. 60 m. long; formed by confluence of Broad and Saluda rivers near Columbia; forms S boundary of Richland co.; unites with Wateree river to form Santee river.

Con·gle·ton \ˈkäŋ-gəl-tən\. Municipal borough, Cheshire, NW England, 22 m. S of Manchester; pop. (1971p) 20,324; textiles, electrical equipment.

Con·go \ˈkäŋ-(ˌ)gō\. **1** Indefinite term used for territory in central Africa on both sides of the Congo river.

2 Republic, Africa. See ZAIRE 1.

3 *officially* **People's Republic of the Congo** *or formerly* **Middle Congo.** Republic, equatorial Africa, bounded on N by Cameroon and Central African Republic, on E and S by Zaire, on SW by Cabinda (Angola) and the Atlantic Ocean, and on W by Gabon; 132,047 sq. m.; pop. (1970p) 1,089,300; ✱ Brazzaville. *Chief products:* Peanuts, palm kernels, coffee, timber; potash, gold. *Chief towns:* Brazzaville, Pointe Noire, Dolisie, Jacob.

History: Became a territory of French Equatorial Africa (*q.v.*) 1910; status changed to that of French overseas territory 1946; became an autonomous republic within the French Community 1958; achieved independence 1960.

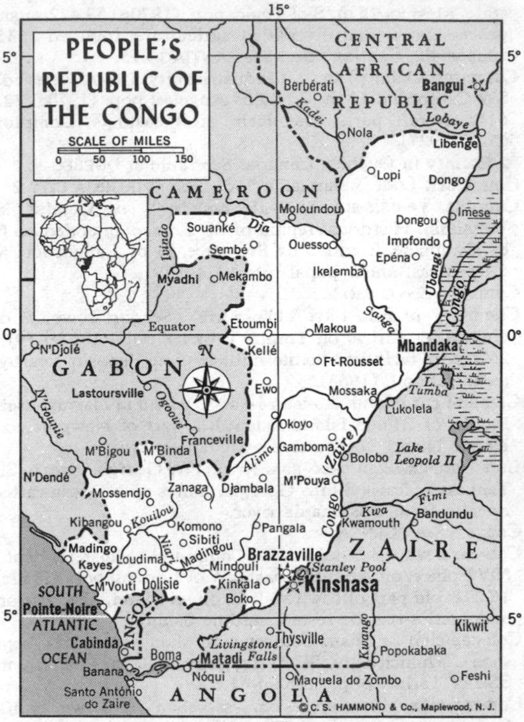

Longitude East of Greenwich 15°

4 *also* **Kongo** \ˈkäŋ-(ˌ)gō\; *called* **Rio Za·i·re** (*Angola* \ˌrē-ō-zä-ˈir-ē\) *or* **Za·ïre** (*Zaire* \zä-ˈi(ə)r\). River, W cen. Africa; 2716 m. long; drainage area 1,425,000 sq. m.; one of largest rivers in the world; formed by confluence of Luapula and Lualaba rivers: the Luapula, a continuation of the Chambezi (*q.v.*), after it flows through the swamp S of Lake Bangweulu, flows N through Lake Mweru forming the boundary bet. Zambia and Zaire; the Lualaba rises in SE Zaire and flows N to join the Luapula at ab. 6°45′S, 26°50′E. From this junction to Stanley Falls (*q.v.*), the Congo is sometimes known as the Lualaba; below Stanley Falls, turns NW and W in a big curve, receiving the Lindi and Aruwimi rivers from the N and the Lomami from the S; begins to turn SW, receives Mongala from N, turns more sharply S and is joined by the Ubangi; from this point to ab. 200 m. from mouth on Atlantic Ocean forms boundary bet. Congo and Zaire; receives the Kasai from the E; at Stanley Pool (*q.v.*) ab. 330 m. from its mouth are located Brazzaville and Kinshasa; navigable for 83 m. from mouth to Matadi and for 1050 m. bet. Stanley Pool and Stanley Falls, and for 585 m. above the falls. Estuary ab. 7 m. wide from Banana Point on N to Sharks Point on S; its mouth discovered 1484 by Diogo Cam, Portuguese navigator; lower course ascended by British expedition 1816; headstreams traced by David Livingstone 1867–73; entire river system explored by Henry M. Stanley 1874–84.

5 District, Angola. See ZAIRE 2.

Congo Belge. See ZAIRE 1.

Congo Free State. See ZAIRE 1.

Congress Poland. See POLAND 1.

Conhocton. See COHOCTON.

Coni. See CUNEO.

Conimbria *or* **Conimbriga.** See COIMBRA 2.

Con·is·brough \'kän-əs-brə\. Urban district, West Riding, Yorkshire, N England, on the Don near Doncaster; pop. (1971p) 16,800; has Norman castle of 12th cent., home (Coningsburgh) of Athelstane in *Ivanhoe.*

Con·is·ton \'kän-ə-stan\. 1 Industrial town, Sudbury dist., SE Ontario, Canada, suburb of Sudbury; pop. (1971p) 2917.

2 Village, N Lancashire, England, at N end of Coniston Water; burial place of John Ruskin.

Coniston Fells. Mountain range in N Lancashire, NW England; highest peak **Coniston Old Man** *or* **Old Man of Coniston** 2633 ft.; on W side of **Coniston Water** *or* **Coniston Lake,** ab. 5 m. long, maximum depth 184 ft.

Conjeeveram. See KANCHIPURAM.

Conn, Lough \ˌläk-'kän, ˌläk-\. Lake, co. Mayo, NW Eire; 8 m. long, 4 m. wide.

Con·nacht \'kän-ˌȯt\ *also* **Con·naught** \'kän-ˌȯt, kə-'nȯt\. Province, NW Eire; 6611 sq. m.; pop. (1971p) 389,763; counties: Galway, Leitrim, Mayo, Roscommon, Sligo.

History: An ancient native kingdom in W Ireland; converted to Christianity by St. Patrick c. 432; from 11th cent. dominated by the O'Connors of Roscommon whose feuds with other kingdoms led to English invasion in 12th cent. (see IRELAND); led by Bourkes, rose against English 16th cent.; divided into counties 1590.

Con·nah's Quay \ˌkän-əz-'kē\. Urban district, Flintshire, NE Wales; pop. (1971p) 12,296.

Connaught. See CONNACHT.

Con·naught Tunnel \ˌkän-ˌȯt-\. Railroad tunnel through Selkirk Mts. at Rogers Pass, British Columbia, Canada; 5 m. long; alt. 3790 ft.; constructed 1913–16.

Con·ne·aut \'kän-ē-ˌät\. City, Ashtabula co., NE corner of Ohio, on Lake Erie; pop. (1970c) 14,552; ore and coal port.

Con·nect·i·cut \kə-'net-i-kət\. 1 River, NE United States; 407 m. long; rises in Connecticut Lakes, N New Hampshire, near Canadian border, flows S, its W bank forming New Hampshire-Vermont boundary, crosses W cen. Massachusetts and cen. Connecticut, empties into Long Island Sound near Saybrook; chief tributaries are White river in Vt., Ashuelot in N.H., Deerfield, Millers, Westfield, and Chicopee in Mass., and Farmington in Conn.; navigable to Windsor; provides waterpower for industries. See history of state, below.

2 An eastern state of U.S.A., southernmost of the New England states, bounded on N by Massachusetts, on E by Rhode Island, on S by Long Island Sound, and on W by New York; 48th state in area, 5009 sq. m. (land area 4870 sq. m.); 24th state in population, (1970c) 3,032,217; ✻ Hartford; original state of the Union, the 5th to ratify the Federal Constitution (Jan. 9, 1788).

Nicknames: Constitution State; Nutmeg State; Land of Steady Habits; Blue Law State. *State flower:* Mountain laurel. *Motto:* Qui Transtulit Sustinet (He Who Transplanted Sustains). *Chief rivers:* Connecticut (see 1, above); Housatonic in W and Thames in E, flowing S into Long Island Sound. Highest point Mt. Frissell 2380 ft. in Litchfield co. *Chief products:* Dairy products, tobacco; poultry; manufacturing: jet engines, helicopters, office machines, felt hats; insurance. *Chief cities:* Hartford, Bridgeport, New Haven, Waterbury, Stamford, New Britain. See Table of States at UNITED STATES. Divided into the following 8 counties (for pronunciation of their names, see their individual entries):

NAME	LOCATION	AREA[1] (sq. m.)	POP. (1970c)	FORMER CO. SEAT[2]
Fairfield	SW corner; coastal	627	792,814	Bridgeport
Hartford	N	739	816,737	Hartford
Litchfield	NW corner	930	144,091	Litchfield
Middlesex	S; coastal	372	115,018	Middletown
New Haven	S; coastal	605	744,948	New Haven and Waterbury
New London	SE corner; coastal	667	230,654	New London and Norwich
Tolland	N	416	103,440	Tolland
Windham	NE corner	516	84,515	Putnam and Willimantic

[1]Area = land area.
[2]County governments abolished 1960.

History: Coast explored and Connecticut river discovered by Adrian Block, a Dutch trader, 1614; lower course of river explored by men from Plymouth 1632; fort built by Dutch on present site of Hartford 1633; first permanent settlements made by colonists from Massachusetts Bay who founded the three river towns Hartford, Windsor, and Wethersfield 1635–36; New Haven colony the settlement of third (Puritan) group 1638; river towns adopted Fundamental Orders 1639, the first American constitution based on the consent of the governed; in New England Confederation 1643–84; received charter 1662 which united Connecticut and New Haven colonies and granted strip of land extending to Pacific; included in Dominion of New England, the government of Connecticut was taken over by Andros 1687; relinquished claims to western lands 1786 except for Western Reserve to which it abandoned jurisdiction 1800; participated in Hartford Convention 1814–15; adopted new constitution 1818, in force until 1965, when it was replaced by another.

Connecticut Farms. See UNION 4.

Connecticut Lakes. Four small lakes in N Coos co., N New Hampshire; the fourth lake, within half a mile of the Canadian border, and the third lake are the ultimate sources of the Connecticut river.

Connecticut Reserve. See WESTERN RESERVE.

Con·nells·ville \'kän-ᵊlz-ˌvil\. Industrial city, Fayette co., SW Pennsylvania, on Youghiogheny river 12 m. NNE of Uniontown; pop. (1970c) 11,643; metal castings, plastics; settled 1770.

Con·ne·ma·ra \ˌkän-ə-'mär-ə, -'mar-\. Barren, mountainous coastal district in W co. Galway, W Eire; bounded on N by Clew Bay, on E by Lough Mask and Lough Corrib, on S by Galway Bay, on W by Atlantic Ocean; Twelve Bens of Bennebeola in W (highest point 2395 ft.).

Con·ners·ville \'kän-ərz-ˌvil\. City, ⊗ of Fayette co., E Indiana, 18 m. SW of Richmond; pop. (1970c) 17,604; automobile accessories, furniture, refrigerators.

Con·ness, Mount \-kə-'nes\. Peak in the Sierra Nevada, in E Tuolumne co., cen. California; 12,595 ft.

Con·o·ver \'kän-ˌō-vər\. Town, Catawba co., W cen. North Carolina, 40 m. NW of Charlotte; pop. (1970c) 3355.

Con·rad \'kän-ˌrad\. City, ⊗ of Pondera co., NW Montana; pop. (1970c) 2770.

Con·roe \'kän-(ˌ)rō\. City, ⊗ of Montgomery co., E Texas, 38 m. N of Houston; pop. (1970c) 11,969; oil wells; timber.

Con·se·lhei·ro La·fa·ie·te \ˌkän(t)-səl-'ye(ə)r-(ˌ)ü-ˌlaf-ə-'yät-ə\. City, Minas Gerais state, E Brazil; munic. pop. (1968e) 40,316.

Consentia. See COSENZA 2.

Con·sett \'kän(t)-sət\. Urban district, Durham, N England, on the Derwent river; pop. (1969e) 37,010.

Con·sho·hock·en \ˌkän-chə-'häk-ən\. Industrial borough, Montgomery co., SE Pennsylvania, on Schuylkill river 13 m. NW of Philadelphia; pop. (1970c) 10,195; tires, steel and iron products; Montgomery County Community Coll. (1964).

Con·so·la·ción del Nor·te \ˌkōn-sə-ˌläs-ē-ˌōn-del-'nȯrt-ē\. Municipality, Pinar del Río prov., W Cuba, near N coast; pop. (1967e) 24,050.

Consolación del Sur \-'sü(ə)r\. Town and municipality, Pinar del Río prov., W Cuba, 13 m. NE of Pinar del Río; pop. (1967c) 7300 (town), 69,460 (munic.).

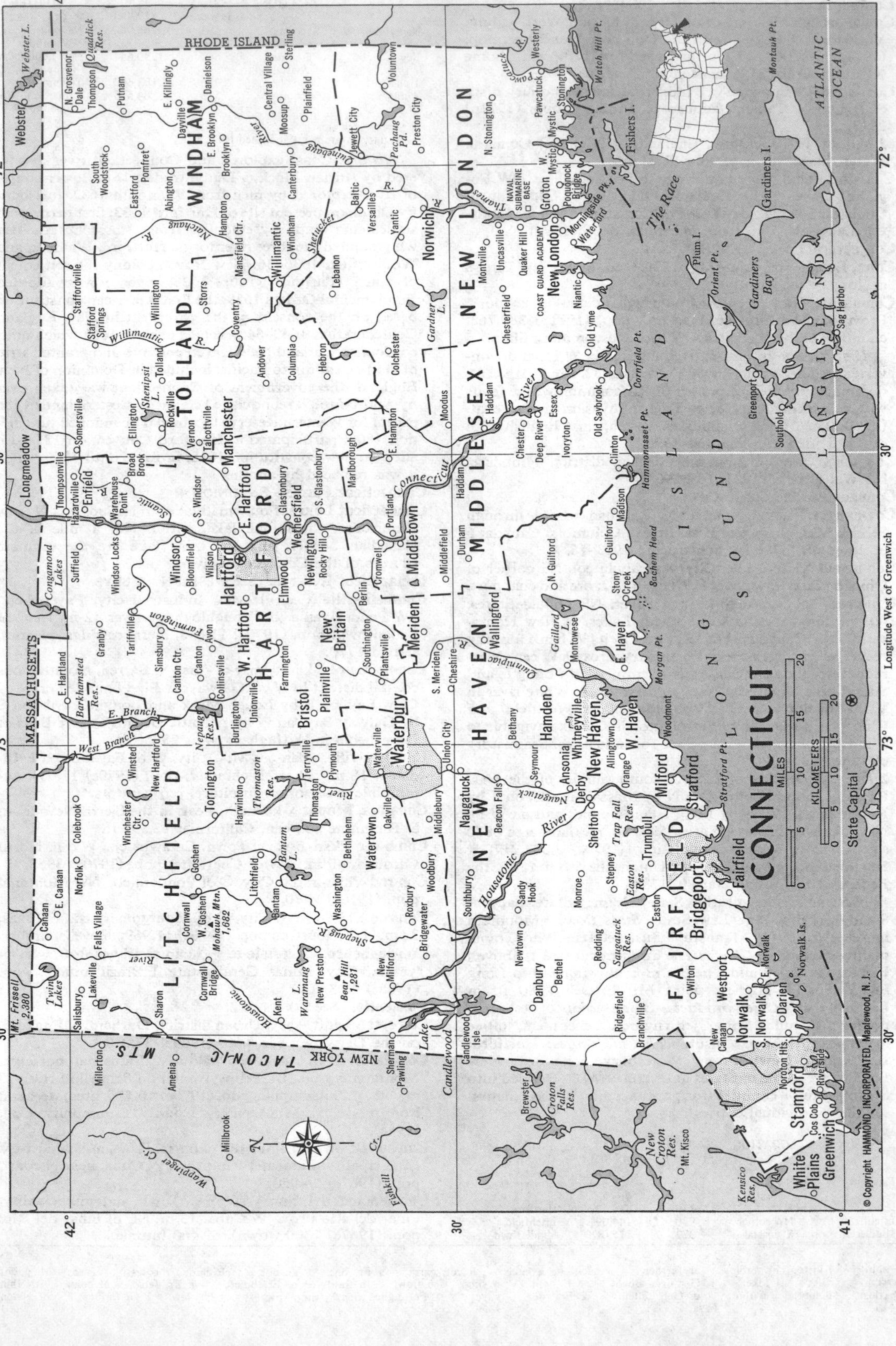
CONNECTICUT
MASSACHUSETTS
RHODE ISLAND
NEW YORK
LITCHFIELD
HARTFORD
TOLLAND
WINDHAM
NEW HAVEN
MIDDLESEX
NEW LONDON
FAIRFIELD
LONG ISLAND SOUND
LONG ISLAND
ATLANTIC OCEAN
TACONIC MTS.
Mt. Frissell 2,380
Mohawk Mtn. 1,682
Bear Hill 1,281
Hartford
New Haven
Bridgeport
Waterbury
Stamford
Norwalk
Danbury
New Britain
Meriden
Middletown
Norwich
New London
Groton
Bristol
Torrington
Manchester
Willimantic
Greenwich
White Plains
Webster
Longmeadow
Enfield
Windsor
W. Hartford
E. Hartford
Wethersfield
Milford
Stratford
Fairfield
Westport
Hamden
Ansonia
Derby
Shelton
Naugatuck
Wallingford
Rockville
Danielson
Putnam
Mystic
Stonington
Westerly
Fishers I.
Gardiners Bay
Gardiners I.
Montauk Pt.
The Race
Housatonic River
Naugatuck River
Connecticut River
Thames R.
Shetucket R.
Quinebaug River
Farmington R.
Candlewood Lake
Barkhamsted Res.
MILES
0 5 10 15 20
KILOMETERS
0 5 10 15 20
State Capital
Longitude West of Greenwich
42°
41°
73°
72°
30'
© Copyright HAMMOND INCORPORATED, Maplewood, N. J.

Con Son \'kōn-'sōn\. Island in the South China Sea, off S coast of South Vietnam; occupied by French 1861–1954.

Constance. See KONSTANZ.

Con·stance, Lake \-'kän(t)-stən(t)s\ *or Ger.* **Bo·den·see** \'bōd-ᵊn-ˌzā\ *or anc.* **Brig·an·ti·nus La·cus** \ˌbrig-ən-ˌtī-nəs-'lā-kəs\. Lake on the border bet. West Germany, Austria, and Switzerland; 46 m. long; 210 sq. m.; max. depth 827 ft.

Constance, Mount. Peak in Olympic Mts., in E Jefferson co., W Washington; 7743 ft.

Con·stan·ţa *or* **Con·stan·tsa** \kən-'stän(t)-sə\. 1 County of SE Romania. See table at ROMANIA.

2 *or Turk.* **Küs·ten·ja** \ˌkue-stən-'yä, ˌkyü-\; *anc.* **Con·stan·ti·a·na** \kən-ˌstan(t)-shē-'ā-nə\ *or* **To·mi** \'tō-ˌmī\ *or* **To·mis** \-məs\. Seaport city, its ⊗, on the Black Sea; pop. (1970e) 172,464; chief seaport of Romania, exporting esp. petroleum; flour mills, textile mills, railroad shops; seaside resort. Under the Turks from 1413 to 1878; captured by U.S.S.R. Aug. 29, 1944.

Constantia. 1 City, Cyprus. See SALAMIS 1.

2 Commune, France. See COUTANCES.

3 Lake port, West Germany. See KONSTANZ.

Cons·tan·ti·na \ˌkän(t)-stən-'tē-nə\. Commune, Sevilla prov., SW Spain, 40 m. NNE of Seville; pop. (1970p) 10,914; lead mining; founded by the Roman Emperor Constantine; Roman ruins.

Cons·tan·tine \'kän(t)-stən-ˌtēn\. 1 Department of NE Algeria. See table at ALGERIA.

2 *or anc.* **Cir·ta** \'sərt-ə\. Fortified city, its ✱, 200 m. ESE of Algiers; pop. (1966c) 240,672; leather goods, cement; its port is Skikda; built by Arabs on rocky height over 800 ft. above river valley; has medieval walls and gates; Roman ruins nearby. Capital of Numidian kings at height of influence under Micipsa 2d cent. B.C.; ruined in wars, restored by Constantine 313 A.D.; taken by French 1837 after long siege; occupied by U.S. troops Nov. 1942.

Con·stan·tine Harbor \ˌkän(t)-stən-ˌtēn-\. Inlet at E end of Amchitka I. on N coast, Aleutian Is.; airport.

Constantinople. See İSTANBUL.

Constantiola. See OLTENIŢA.

Constantsa. See CONSTANŢA.

Constanz. See KONSTANZ.

Cons·ti·tu·ción \ˌkōn(t)s-tə-ˌtü-sē-'ōn\. 1 Port, Argentina. See VILLA CONSTITUCIÓN.

2 Port and summer resort, Maule prov., S cen. Chile, near mouth of the Maule river 163 m. SSW of Valparaíso; pop. (1960c) 9536; exports grain and lumber.

Con·sti·tu·tion Island \ˌkän(t)-stə-ˌt(y)ü-shən-\. Small island in Hudson river opp. West Point, New York.

Con·tal·mai·son \kōⁿ-ˌtȧl-mā-'zōⁿ\. Village, Somme dept., N France, 3 m. ENE of Albert; pop. (1962c) 92; taken by British from Germans July 11, 1916, one of the first of the battles of the Somme; completely destroyed.

Continental Divide *or* **Great Divide.** The watershed of the North American continent; the line of highest points of land separating the waters flowing W from those flowing N or E and extending SSE from NW Canada across W United States through Mexico and Central America to South America where it joins the Andes Mts.; in Canada and U.S. generally coincides with various ranges of the Rocky Mts.; in Mexico comprises the great plateau bet. the Sierra Madre ranges (Occidental and Oriental); in Central America lies generally much nearer the Pacific Ocean than the Caribbean Sea. Its central point is the state of Colorado where it comprises many peaks above 13,000 ft.

Con·tooc·ook \kən-'tu̇k-ək\. River, S New Hampshire; ab. 80 m. long; rises in Hillsborough co., flows N and NE into the Merrimack above Concord.

Con·tra Cos·ta \ˌkänt-rə-'käs-tə, -'kȯs-\. County in California. See table at CALIFORNIA.

Con·tra·ta·ción \ˌkän-trə-ˌtäs-ē-'ōn\. Municipality, Santander dept., N cen. Colombia; pop. (1968e) 4716.

Con·tre·ras \kōn-'trär-əs\. Town, Federal District, cen. Mexico, 14 m. SSW of Mexico City; pop. (1960c) 12,156; scene of battle Aug. 19–20, 1847 in which the Americans under Gen. Winfield Scott defeated the Mexican forces.

Con·vent \'kän-(ˌ)vent\. Village, ⊗ of St. James parish, SE Louisiana.

Convent Station. Village, Morris co., New Jersey, SE of Morristown; College of St. Elizabeth (1899).

Con·ver·sa·no \ˌkän-vər-'sän-(ˌ)ō\. Commune, Bari prov., Apulia, SE Italy, near Adriatic coast 17 m. ESE of Bari; pop. (1968e) 18,441; Norman castle, 11th cent. cathedral.

Con·verse \'kän-(ˌ)vərs\. County in Wyoming. See table at WYOMING.

Con·way \'kän-(ˌ)wā\. 1 County in Arkansas. See table at ARKANSAS.

2 City, ⊗ of Faulkner co., cen. Arkansas, 25 m. NNW of Little Rock; pop. (1970c) 15,510; timber; poultry farms; Hendrix Coll. (1876), Central Baptist Coll. (1950); founded 1871, incorp. 1874.

3 Town, Carroll co., E New Hampshire, 36 m. NNE of Laconia in S region of the White Mts.; pop. (1970c) 4865; summer and winter resort.

4 Borough, Beaver co., W Pennsylvania, on Ohio river 20 m. NW of Pittsburgh; pop. (1970c) 2822.

5 Town, ⊗ of Horry co., E South Carolina, on Waccamaw river 35 m. NNE of Georgetown; pop. (1970c) 8151; river port; manufactures lumber, cotton, tobacco.

6 River, N Wales; 30 m. long; flows N, forming boundary bet. Denbighshire and Caernarvonshire, into Beaumaris Bay at Conway.

7 Municipal borough, Caernarvonshire, NW Wales, at mouth of the Conway river; pop. (1971p) 12,158; castle dating from 13th cent.; remains of ancient Roman fort.

Con·yers \'kän-yərz\. City, ⊗ of Rockdale co., N cen. Georgia; pop. (1970c) 4890; fabricated steel.

Coo. See KOS.

Cooch Be·har \ˌküch-bə-'här\. 1 Former Indian state, NE India; 1321 sq. m.; ✱ Cooch Behar; once under the government of Bengal, later one of the states of the Eastern States Agency; since 1947 part of West Bengal state, India; in earlier times a powerful state in Assam; came under British control 1772.

2 Town, its ✱, 265 m. NNE of Calcutta; pop. (1961c) 41,922.

Cook \'ku̇k\. Name of counties in three states of the U.S. See tables at GEORGIA, ILLINOIS, MINNESOTA.

Cook, Mount. 1 Mountain, Yukon, Canada, SE of Mount Logan; 13,760 ft.

2 *or formerly* **Ao·ran·gi** \au̇-'räŋ-ē\. Peak in Southern Alps, W cen. South I., New Zealand; 12,349 ft.; highest peak in New Zealand.

Cook and Northern Islands. A name sometimes given to the Cook Is. and Northern Cook (Manihiki) Is., S Pacific Ocean.

Cooke \'ku̇k\. County in Texas. See table at TEXAS.

Cooke·ville \'ku̇k-ˌvil, -vəl\. Town, ⊗ of Putnam co., N cen. Tennessee, 79 m. N of Chattanooga; pop. (1970c) 14,270; poultry shipping center; Tennessee Technological Univ. (1915).

Cook Inlet. Arm of Pacific Ocean, S Alaska, W of Kenai Penin.; ab. 150 m. long; 80 m. at its widest point; Anchorage is at its head; has largest tidal bore in U.S. with 45-foot range in one arm of it. First explored by Capt. Cook 1778.

Cook Islands *or* **Southern Cook Islands.** Group of fifteen islands in S Pacific Ocean, W of French Polynesia; lat. 8° to 23°S and long. 156° to 167°W; 92 sq. m.; pop. (1970e) 22,000; includes Rarotonga (seat of the government), Aitutaki, Atiu, Mangaia, Mauke, Mitiaro, Manahiki, and

Nassau; citrus fruit, copra; some of smaller islands discovered by Capt. Cook 1773; British protectorate proclaimed 1888; part of New Zealand 1901; achieved self-government in free association with New Zealand 1965.

Cook·shire \'ku̇k-ˌshi(ə)r, -shər\. Town, ⊗ of Compton co., S Quebec, Canada, 14 m. E of Sherbrooke; pop. (1971p) 1490.

Cook Strait *also* **Rau·ka·wa** \'rau̇-kə-wə\. Channel bet. North I. and South I., New Zealand; 16 to 90 m. wide; discovered by Capt. Cook 1770.

Cook·town \'ku̇k-ˌtau̇n\. Town, NE Queensland, Australia, on Coral Sea within Great Barrier Reef 295 m. N of Townsville; trades with Papua New Guinea; place where Capt. James Cook beached the *Endeavor* for repairs 1770.

Cool·gar·die \kül-'gärd-ē\. Municipality and district (pop. [1962c] 1762), SW Western Australia, 351 m. E of Perth; in gold-mining region.

Coo·lidge \'kü-lij\. City, Pinal co., S Arizona; pop. (1970c) 5314; cotton; diversified farming; Central Arizona Coll. (1969).

Coolidge, Mount. Peak in Custer co., SW South Dakota; 6400 ft.

Coolin Hills. See CUILLIN HILLS.

Coomassie. See KUMASI.

Coombe Hill \'küm-\. See CHILTERN HILLS.

Coon Butte. See CRATER MOUND.

Coo·noor \ku̇-'nu̇(ə)r\. Town in Nilgiri Hills, Tamil Nadu, S India; pop. (1961c) 30,690.

Coon Rapids \'kün-\. 1 Town, Carroll co., W cen. Iowa, 60 m. WNW of Des Moines; pop. (1970c) 1381.

2 City, Anoka co., E Minnesota; pop. (1970c) 30,505; Anoka-Ramsey State Junior Coll. (1965).

Coo·per \'kü-pər, 'ku̇p-ər\. 1 County in Missouri. See table at MISSOURI.

2 City, ⊗ of Delta co., NE Texas, 21 m. SSW of Paris; pop. (1970c) 2258; in cotton-raising region.

Cooper Mountain. See KENAI MOUNTAINS.

Coo·per's Creek \'kü-pərz-, 'ku̇p-ərz-\ *or formerly* **Bar·coo** \bär-'kü\. Intermittent river, Australia; ab. 600 m. long; flows from SW Queensland to Lake Eyre in South Australia; discovered 1845.

Coo·pers·town \'kü-pərz-ˌtau̇n, 'ku̇p-ərz-\. 1 Residential village, ⊗ of Otsego co., cen. New York, at S end of Otsego Lake near Susquehanna river, 31 m. SSE of Utica; pop. (1970c) 2403; site bought 1785 by William Cooper, father of James Fenimore Cooper, who made it the setting of his *Leatherstocking Tales;* scene 1939 of the official celebration of the centenary of the origin of baseball; National Baseball Museum.

2 City, ⊗ of Griggs co., E North Dakota; pop. (1970c) 1485.

Coorg *or* **Kurg** \'ku̇(ə)rg\. District, Mysore, India; 1587 sq. m.; pop. (1961c) 322,829; ✱ Mercara; mountainous region on top of Western Ghats. Inhabited by Kodagu and Yerava. In earlier times a kingdom comprising more territory; occupied by Haidar Ali 1780–82 and later by Tipu Sahib; came under British 1834; administered by chief commissioner of Mysore 1881–1947.

Coo·rong, The \-kü-ˌräŋ\. Southern arm of Lake Alexandrina, SE South Australia; 80 m. long; extends SE parallel with the coast.

Co·os \kō-'äs, 'kō-(ˌ)äs\. County in New Hampshire. See table at NEW HAMPSHIRE.

Coos \'küs\. County in Oregon. See table at OREGON.

Coo·sa \'kü-sə\. 1 Navigable river, Alabama; 286 m. long; formed by confluence of Etowah and Oostanaula rivers near Rome, Floyd co., NW Georgia; flows W across border into Alabama and SW to join Tallapoosa river S of Wetumpka, Elmore co., to form Alabama river; has great locks and waterpower developments.

2 County in Alabama. See table at ALABAMA.

Coosa Bald. Peak, Union co., N Georgia; 4287 ft.

Coo·sa·wat·tee \ˌkü-sə-'wät-ē\. River, NW Georgia; rises in Gilmer co., flows SW to unite with the Conasauga river and form the Oostanaula river.

Coos Bay \'küs-\. 1 Inlet on coast of Coos co., SW Oregon, at mouth of the **Coos River.**

2 *or until 1944* **Marsh·field** \'märsh-ˌfēld\. City, Coos co., SW Oregon, on inlet of Pacific Ocean; pop. (1970c) 13,466; port of entry; ships lumber; fisheries; Southwestern Oregon Community Coll. (1961).

Coo·ta·mun·dra \ˌküt-ə-'mənd-rə\. Town, SE New South Wales, SE Australia, ab. 80 m. NW of Canberra; pop. (1966c) 6219.

Co·pa·ca·bana Beach \ˌkō-pə-kə-ˌban-ə-\ *or Port.* **Praia de Copacabana** \'prī-əd-ə-\. Beach on Atlantic Ocean, SE part of city of Rio de Janeiro, Brazil, at W side of entrance to Guanabara Bay; resort.

Co·pa·hué \ˌkō-pə-'wā\. Volcanic peak, W Neuquén prov., W Argentina, on Chile border; 9875 ft.

Co·pa·is \kō-'pā-əs\; *Gk.* **Ko·pa·ïs** \ˌkȯ-pə-'ēs\ *or* **To·po·lia** \tə-'pȯl-yə\. Former lake in N Boeotia, Greece; received the Cephisus; formed extensive marshland, at several periods drained by underground channels to Euboean Sea; in 1886 properly drained and much ground reclaimed for agriculture.

Co·pán \kō-'pän\. 1 Department of W Honduras. See table at HONDURAS.

2 Ruined city near Santa Rosa. See SANTA ROSA 8.

Cop·co No. 1 \'käp-kō-\. Dam across Klamath river, N Siskiyou co., N California; height 239 ft.; completed 1922; impounds water for water power.

Co·pen·ha·gen \ˌkō-pən-'hā-gən, -'häg-ən, 'kō-pən-ˌ\ *or Danish* **Kø·ben·havn** \ˌkœ-bən-'hau̇n\. 1 County of Denmark, Sjælland I. See table at DENMARK.

2 Seaport city, ✱ of Denmark, on E coast of Sjælland I., and N part of Amager I., Denmark; pop. (1971c) 625,678, with suburbs, **Greater Copenhagen,** 1,384,411; Denmark's leading commercial and industrial center; shipping center; shipbuilding, brewing and distilling, sugar refining; manufactures porcelain, marine engines; exports incl. dressed meat and dairy products, chemicals, iron and steel products; Univ. of Copenhagen (1479), Technical Univ. of Denmark (1829), Amalienborg Palace (residence of the Danish monarch since 1794), Christiansborg Palace (rebuilt after 1907), botanical gardens (1874), town hall (1894–1905), national (Thorwaldsen) museum, cathedral (rebuilt after 1807); cultural center of northern literature and art.

History: A fishing village fortified by Absalon in 12th cent.; given municipal privileges 1254; frequently attacked and taken by Hanseatic League; made capital of kingdom of Denmark 1443; besieged unsuccessfully by Charles X of Sweden 1658–60; scene of treaty 1660 by which Denmark ceded to Sweden the southern part of Scandinavian penin.; harbor scene of destruction of Danish fleet by British under Nelson 1801; bombarded 1807; occupied by Germans Apr. 1940 to May 5, 1945.

Cö·pe·nick *or* **Kö·pe·nick** \'kə(r)p-ə-ˌnik\. Former commune, now part of East Berlin, East Germany; scene of trial of Crown Prince Frederick (Frederick the Great) 1730 after his attempt to escape to England.

Co·per·ti·no \ˌkō-pər-'tē-(ˌ)nō\. Commune, Lecce prov., Apulia, SE Italy; pop. (1968e) 19,369; Angevin château.

Co·piague \'kō-ˌpāg, -ˌpeg\. Urban community (unincorporated), Suffolk co., SE New York, on Long I. W of Lindenhurst; pop. (1970c) 19,578.

Co·pi·ah \kə-'pī-ə\. County in Mississippi. See table at MISSISSIPPI.

Co·pia·pó \ˌkō-pē-ə-'pō\ *also* **San Fran·cis·co de la Sel·va** \ˌsan-frən-'sis-(ˌ)kō-ˌdā-lə-'sel-və\. 1 River, Atacama prov., N cen. Chile; flows NW and W into the Pacific Ocean.

2 Town, ✱ of Atacama prov., N cen. Chile, on the Copiapó river ab. 42 m. N of Santiago; pop. (1966e) 36,767; important as a silver and copper-mining center; settled 1540; ruined by earthquakes 1819, 1822, 1851, and 1939.

Cop·lay \ˈkäp-lē\. Borough, Lehigh co., E Pennsylvania, on Lehigh river 5 m. N of Allentown; pop. (1970c) 3642.

Cop·pa·ro \kə-ˈpär-(ˌ)ō\. Commune, Ferrara prov., Emilia-Romagna, N Italy, 13 m. ENE of Ferrara; pop. (1968e) 21,010; in Po delta, formerly undrained marshland.

Cop·pe·na·me \ˌkäp-ə-ˈnäm-ə\. River, N Surinam; 250 m. long; flows N into Atlantic Ocean.

Cop·per \ˈkäp-ər\. River, S Alaska; ab. 300 m. long; flows S around W end of Wrangell Mts. and through Chugach Mountains to Gulf of Alaska.

Cop·per·as Cove \ˌkäp-(ə-)rəs-\. Town, Coryell co., cen. Texas, 53 m. SW of Waco; pop. (1970c) 10,818; diversified agriculture.

Copper Center. Village, SE Alaska, on Copper river, 90 m. N of Cordova; pop. (1970c) 206.

Copper Cliff. Mining town, Sudbury dist., SE Ontario, Canada, 5 m. WSW of Sudbury; pop. (1971p) 3344; mining center with large nickel-copper smelter.

Cop·per·mine \ˈkäp-ər-ˌmīn\. River, Mackenzie dist., Northwest Territories, Canada; 525 m. long; rises in lakes of cen. part, flows NW and N to Coronation Gulf.

Coptos. See QIFT.

Co·pul·hué, Pa·so \ˈpäs-(ˌ)ō-ˌkō-pəl-ˈwā\. Andean mountain pass on boundary bet. Neuquén prov., W Argentina, and Bío-Bío prov., S cen. Chile; alt. 6891 ft.

Co·quei·ros, Point \-kō-ˈkā-ə-rüs\ *or Braz.* **Pon·ta de Coqueiros** \ˈpō(ⁿ)n-tə-də-\ *or formerly* **Point Pe·dras** \-ˈpād-rəs\. Cape extending into Atlantic Ocean on SE coast of Paraíba state, E Brazil; most easterly point of South America, 7°38′S, 34°47′W.

Co·quet \ˈkō-kət\. 1 Island in the North Sea off NE coast of Northumberland, N England.
2 River, N Northumberland, N England; ab. 40 m. long; rises in the Cheviot Hills, flows E into the North Sea.

Co·qui·lhat·ville \ˌkō-kē-ˈat-ˌvil, kō-ˈkē-ə-ˌvil\. 1 Province, Zaire. See ÉQUATEUR.
2 Town, Zaire. See MBANDAKA.

Co·quille \kō-ˈkēl\. 1 River, SW Oregon; formed by confluence of branches in Coos co., flows N and W into Pacific Ocean; with longest branch ab. 70 m. long; navigable to Coquille.
2 City, ⊗ of Coos co., SW Oregon, on Coquille river 13 m. S of Coos Bay city; pop. (1970c) 4437; timber; livestock, poultry.

Co·quim·bo \kō-ˈkim-(ˌ)bō, -ˈkēm-\. 1 Province of cen. Chile. See table at CHILE.
2 Port, Coquimbo prov., cen. Chile, 215 m. N of Valparaíso; pop. (1966e) 39,610; the port for La Serena.

Co·ra·co·ra \ˌkōr-ə-ˈkōr-ə\. Mining town, S Ayacucho dept., S Peru; pop. (1961c) 4100.

Cor·al Bay \ˌkȯr-əl-, ˌkär-\. Bay on E end of St. John I., Virgin Is. of the United States, West Indies.

Coral Ga·bles \-ˈgā-bəlz\. City, Dade co., SE Florida, on Biscayne Bay 5 m. SW of Miami; pop. (1970c) 42,494; cosmetics, fiberglass boats; resort; Univ. of Miami (1925); incorporated 1925.

Coral Harbour. Port and station on inlet on S coast of Southampton I., Keewatin dist., Northwest Territories, Canada; airport.

Coral Sea. Part of the Pacific Ocean bet. Queensland, Australia, on the W, and the New Hebrides and New Caledonia on the E; bordered on N by Terr. of Papua and Solomon Is.; N part known as the Solomon Sea (*q.v.*). Scene of U.S. victory over Japanese May 7–8, 1942.

Coral Sea Islands Territory. Australian external territory, consisting of several uninhabited islets bet. 10°S and 23°30′S and bet. 154°E and 158°E; Australian sovereignty formally acknowledged by Great Britain 1968.

Co·rang·a·mite, Lake \-kə-ˈraŋ-gə-ˌmīt\. Lake, Victoria, Australia, 50 m. W of Port Philip Bay; ab. 100 sq. m.

Corantijn. See COURANTYNE.

Co·ra·op·o·lis \ˌkōr-ē-ˈäp-(ə-)ləs\. Borough, Allegheny co., SW Pennsylvania, on Ohio river 11 m. WNW of Pittsburgh; pop. (1970c) 8435; iron, steel, glass; settled c. 1760.

Co·rato \kə-ˈrät-(ˌ)ō\. Commune, Bari prov., Apulia, SE Italy, 25 m. W by N of Bari; pop. (1968e) 39,311.

Cor·beil–Es·sonnes \kȯr-ˌbā-e-ˈsȯn\. Commune, Essonne dept., N France, at confluence of Seine and Essonne rivers 16 m. SSE of Paris; pop. (1968c) 32,192; flour mills (noted since 12th cent.). Under Carolingian kings **Corbeil** (*or anc.* **Cor·bo·li·um** \kȯr-ˈbō-lē-əm\) capital of a countship; annexed to France 1108; royal residence; treaty bet. St. Louis and King of Aragon signed here 1258.

Cor·bie \kȯr-ˈbē\. Commune, Somme dept., N France, 10 m. NE of Amiens; pop. (1962c) 4762; ruins of Benedictine abbey, founded 7th cent. by Bathilde, Queen of Clovis II; ruined 1918.

Cor·bin \ˈkȯr-bən\. City, Knox and Whitley cos., SE Kentucky; pop. (1970c) 7317; auto parts, bricks; corn; coal mining.

Corbolium. See CORBEIL-ESSONNES.

Cor·bridge \ˈkō(ə)r-brij, ˈkȯ(ə)r-\. Market town, Northumberland, N England, on N bank of Tyne river just E of Hexham; pop. (1961c) 2415; nearby is site of Corstopitum, Roman military post; capital of Northumbria in 8th cent.

Cor·by \ˈkȯr-bē\. Urban district, Northamptonshire, cen. England; pop. (1971p) 47,716; steel tubes; technical coll.

Cor·co·ran \ˈkȯr-kə-rən\. City, Kings co., SW cen. California, 45 m. SE of Fresno; pop. (1970c) 5249; cotton gins.

Cor·co·va·do \ˌkȯr-kə-ˈväd-(ˌ)ō\. 1 Peak on S side of city of Rio de Janeiro, SE Brazil; 2310 ft.; has gigantic concrete figure of Christ the Redeemer on its top; funicular railway.
2 Volcanic peak in the Andes Mts., S Chile, opp. Chiloé I.; 7550 ft.

Corcovado Gulf. Inlet of Pacific Ocean lying bet. Chiloé I. and the mainland of SW Chile.

Corcyra. See CORFU.

Corcyra Nigra. See KORČULA 1.

Cor·dele \kȯr-ˈdē(ə)l, ˈkȯr-ˌ\. City, ⊗ of Crisp co., SW cen. Georgia, 35 m. NE of Albany; pop. (1970c) 10,733; cotton mills, sawmills; peanuts.

Cor·di·lle·ra \ˌkȯrd-ᵊl-ˈ(y)er-ə, kȯrd-ē-ˈer-ə\. Department of cen. Paraguay. See table at PARAGUAY.

Cordillera Cantábrica. See CANTABRIAN MOUNTAINS.

Cordillera Cen·tral \-ˌsen-ˈträl\. 1 Range of the Andes (*q.v.*) in Colombia.
2 Chief range of the Dominican Republic; includes Pico Duarte, 10,414 ft. high.
3 Range of the Andes extending NW and SE in N cen. Peru, E of the Marañón.
4 The main mountain range of N Luzon, Phil., extending from N edge of its central plain to N coast of the island; highest point Mt. Pulog 9606 ft.; unites with the Caraballo Mts. (*q.v.*) in cen. Luzon.
5 Mountain range in SW cen. Puerto Rico; highest peak Cerro de Punta 4389 ft.

Cordillera de Agostini. See ANDES.

Cordillera de Amambay. See SERRA DE AMAMBAHY.

Cordillera de Ca·ra·ba·ya \-ˌdā-ˌkär-ə-ˈbī-ə\. A range of the Andes (*q.v.*), E of Cuzco, SE Peru; highest point Nevado Ausangate 20,945 ft.

Cordillera de Los Andes. See ANDES.

Cordillera de Ta·la·man·ca \-ˌdā-ˌtäl-ə-ˈmäŋ-kə\. Range in S Costa Rica, extending SE into W Panama; highest point Chirripó Grande 12,533 ft.

Cordillera de Ve·ne·zue·la \-ˌdā-ˌven-əz-(ə-)ˈwā-lə\. Mountain range in N Venezuela; highest point ab. 8530 ft.

Cordillera Domeyko. See ANDES.

Cordillera Huayhuash. See ANDES.

Cordillera Ma·rí·ti·ma \-mə-ˈrēt-ə-mə\. The Cordillera Occidental in Peru. See ANDES.

Cordillera Mé·ri·da \-'mer-əd-ə\ *also* **Sier·ra Ne·va·da de Mérida** \sē-ˌer-ə-nə-'väd-əd-ə-, -'vad-\. Range of mountains extending NE and SW in W Venezuela; highest point Pico Bolivar, 16,427 ft.; a NE extension of the Andes.

Cordillera Occidental. See ANDES.

Cordillera Orien·tal \-ˌōr-ē-ˌen-'täl, -ˌȯr-\. 1 Eastern range of the Andes in cen. Bolivia.

2 Eastern range of the Andes in Colombia. See ANDES.

3 Eastern range of the Andes in N Peru.

4 Eastern range of the Andes in SE Peru; highest point Salcantay 20,574 ft.

Cordillera Re·al \-rā-'äl\. 1 Range of the Andes, W Bolivia. See ANDES.

2 Range of the Andes in Ecuador. See ANDES.

Cór·do·ba \'kȯrd-ə-bə, -ə-və\. 1 Province of N cen. Argentina. See table at ARGENTINA.

2 City, its ✱, on the Primero river 387 m. NW of Buenos Aires; pop. (1960c) 586,015; cement, glass, leather, textiles; transportation center; National Univ. of Córdoba (1613), Catholic Univ. (1956), astronomical observatory; founded 1573.

3 Department of N Colombia. See table at COLOMBIA.

4 Town, Veracruz state, E Mexico, 55 m. WSW of Veracruz; munic. pop. (1970p) 92,870; alt. 2700 ft.; chief product coffee.

5 *or Eng.* **Cor·do·va** \'kȯrd-ə-və\. Province of S Spain. See table at SPAIN.

6 *or Eng.* **Cor·do·va** \'kȯrd-ə-və\ *or anc.* **Cor·du·ba** \'kȯrd-yə-bə, 'kȯrd-ü-bə\. City, ✱ of Córdoba prov., S Spain, on Guadalquivir river 73 m. ENE of Seville; pop. (1970p) 235,632; textiles; brewing and distilling; gold and silver filigree ornaments; copper mines nearby. Roman and Moorish remains, including an 8th cent. mosque (now a cathedral) built by Abd-er-Rahman I, an alcazar, and a Moorish bridge over the Guadalquivir.

History: Probably founded by Carthaginians; ruled by Romans, Visigoths, and 711–1236 by the Arabs; in 756 A.D. became independent of Damascus caliphate and under Abd-er-Rahman I and successors, became seat of emirate, later the Western Caliphate of Córdoba; flourishing capital of the most powerful state in Spain (at height in 10th cent.); under Arabic rule became renowned throughout Europe as home of most brilliant intellectual achievements of its time—whence the epithet "Athens of the West"; declined gradually after overthrow of caliphate 1031; captured by Ferdinand III of Castile 1236; pillaged by French 1808 and 1811.

Cor·do·va \kȯr-'dō-və\. 1 Town, Walker co., NW cen. Alabama, 28 m. NW of Birmingham; pop. (1970c) 2750.

2 Coast town, SE Alaska, on inlet at SE corner of Prince William Sound; pop. (1970c) 1164; cans clams and salmon; timber; cold storage facilities.

Cór·do·va Island \ˌkȯrd-ə-və-\. Tract of land on N bank of the Rio Grande forming an enclave of Mexico within the city of El Paso, Texas; 385 acres; northern 193 acres ceded to U.S. in return for Chamizal (*q.v.*) 1963.

Corduba. See CÓRDOBA 6.

Corduene. See GORDYENE.

Core Sound \'kō(ə)r-, 'kȯ(ə)r-\. Sound bet. mainland of Carteret co., SE North Carolina, and **Core Bank,** one of chain of islands or reefs, having Cape Lookout at S tip.

Cor·fin·i·um \kȯr-'fin-ē-əm\. Ancient town, Samnium, Italy, ab. 7 m. N of Sulmo, on the Valerian Way; capital of short-lived republic of Italia, formed by Allies during Social War (90–88 B.C.).

Cor·fu \kȯr-'fü, 'kȯr-(ˌ)f(y)ü\ *or Gk.* **Kér·ky·ra** \'ker-ki-rə\ *or anc.* **Cor·cy·ra** \kȯr-'sī-rə\. 1 One of the Ionian Is. in the Ionian Sea off the coast of SW Albania and NW Greece; 40 m. long by 7 to 17 m. wide; 229 sq. m.; pop. (1961c) 97,412; with Paxos forms a department of Greece (see table at GREECE); fertile, produces olives, olive oil, and fruits.

History: Settled by Corinthians c. 700 B.C.; probably the **Sche·ria** \'skir-ē-ə\ of Homer; off its coasts first naval battle of Greek history fought c. 664 B.C.; 435 B.C. sought help of Athens against Corinth, one of the causes of Peloponnesian War; became Roman possession 229 B.C.; Venetian from 1386 to 1797, when it took the name Corfu; under British 1809–64; since 1864 part of Greece. In World War I refuge of Serbs 1916–19 and scene of signing July 20, 1917 of "Pact of Corfu" which established new Serb, Croat, and Slovene state; in World War II fell to Germans Apr. 1941, retaken by Greek and British forces Oct. 6, 1944.

2 Seaport city, ✱ of Corfu dept., Ionian Is., W Greece, on E coast of the island; pop. (1971p) 29,374; palace.

Corfu Straits *or* **Corfu Channel.** Narrow channel bet. NE Corfu I. and SW coast of Albania.

Co·ria del Río \ˌkōr-ē-ə-del-'rē-(ˌ)ō\. Commune, Sevilla prov., SW Spain, on Guadalquivir river 9 m. SSW of Seville; pop. (1970p) 18,910.

Co·ri·glia·no \ˌkōr-ēl-'yän-(ˌ)ō, ˌkȯr-\ *or in full* **Corigliano Ca·la·bro** \-'käl-ə-ˌbrō\. Commune, Cosenza prov., Calabria, S Italy, near W shore of Gulf of Taranto 25 m. NNE of Cosenza; pop. (1968e) 28,580; olive groves; castle, aqueduct.

Corinium. See CIRENCESTER.

Co·rin·na \kə-'rin-ə\. Town, Penobscot co., E cen. Maine, 26 m. WNW of Bangor; pop. (1970c) 1700.

Cor·inth \'kȯr-ən(t)th, 'kär-\. 1 City, ⊗ of Alcorn co., NE Mississippi; pop. (1970c) 11,581; telephone equipment, textiles, dairy products; severe fighting Oct. 3–4, 1862, when Union forces under Rosecrans repulsed Confederates under Van Dorn.

2 Village, Saratoga co., E New York, on Hudson river 28 m. NE of Amsterdam; pop. (1970c) 5442; paper mills.

3 *or Gk.* **Kó·rin·thos** \'kȯr-in-'thȯs\ *or Lat.* **Co·rin·thia** \kə-'rin(t)-thē-ə\. Division of ancient Greece, occupying greater part of Isthmus of Corinth and part of NE Peloponnesus; bounded on N and W by Gulf of Corinth, on NE by Megaris, on E by Saronic Gulf, on S by Argolis, and on W by Sicyonia.

4 Department of Peloponnesus, Greece. See table at GREECE.

5 City, Argolis and Corinth dept., NE Peloponnesus, Greece, on Gulf of Corinth; pop. (1961c) 15,892; 3 m. NE by E of site of ancient city of Corinth. See ACROCORINTHUS.

History: Ancient Corinth appears to have been founded in 9th cent. B.C. by Dorian invaders of Greece; by position on Isthmus of Corinth became leading commercial city and founded Syracuse, Corcyra (see CORFU) c. 700 B.C. and numerous other colonies, including Potidaea 609 B.C.; member of Peloponnesian League in Peloponnesian War (see SPARTA 7); in Corinthian War 395–387 B.C., joined Athens, Thebes, and Argos against Sparta; joined Achaean League 243 B.C.; destroyed by Roman general, Mummius, 146 B.C.; refounded by Roman colony sent out by Caesar 44 B.C.; scene of early mission of St. Paul 52–54 A.D.; taken from Byzantine Empire by Latin Crusaders 1205; after a period of Venetian rule, conquered by Ottoman Turks 1458; controlled by Venice 1682–1715, Turks 1715–1822, and Greece from 1822; old city destroyed by earthquake and new city founded 1858. In World War II occupied by Germans Apr. 1941; liberated by British Oct. 10, 1944.

Corinth, Gulf of *or* **Gulf of Le·pan·to** \-'lep-ən-ˌtō, -li-'pan-(ˌ)tō\ *or Gk.* **Ko·rin·thi·a·kós Kól·pos** \kȯ-ˌrēn-thē-ä-'kȯs-'kȯl-(ˌ)pȯs\ *or anc.* **Si·nus Cor·in·thi·a·cus** \ˌsī-nəs-ˌkȯr-ən-'thī-ə-kəs\. Inlet of Mediterranean Sea, cen. Greece, NE of the Peloponnesus, extending E from Lepanto Strait to Isthmus of Corinth (*q.v.*).

Corinth, Isthmus of *or Gk.* **Isth·mos Ko·rin·thou** \ēsth-'mȯs-kȯ-'rēn-thü\. Isthmus connecting Peloponnesus with E cen. Greece; 4 to 8 m. wide, 20 m. long; crossed by a ship canal (4 m. long; constructed 1881–93) connecting the Gulf of Corinth with the Saronic Gulf.

Co·rin·to \kə-'rin-(ˌ)tō, -'rēn-\. Seaport, Chinandega dept., NW Nicaragua; pop. (1970e) 12,985; most important port in Nicaragua; exports coffee, sugar, hides.

Co·ri·o·li \kə-'rī-ə-ˌlī\. Ancient Volscian town, Latium, Italy; legendary scene of siege 493 B.C. by Romans under Gaius Marcius Coriolanus.

Co·ris·co \kə-'ris-(ˌ)kō\. Island in Bight of Biafra, W Africa, off SW coast of mainland of Equatorial Guinea; 5½ sq. m.; originally a slave-trading station; later a trading and shipbuilding post.

Corizza. See KORÇË.

Cork \'kȯ(ə)rk, 'kärk\. **1** County, Munster prov., SW Eire; 2880 sq. m.; pop. (1971p) 351,735; ⊗ Cork; oats, potatoes, sugar beets; livestock.

2 County borough, its ⊗, at mouth of Lee river at head of Cork Harbour 15 m. from the Atlantic Ocean; pop. (1971p) 128,235; seaport; chemicals, carpets, leather goods; bacon curing; breweries, distilleries, oil storage depots; its ocean steamer port is Cobh (*q.v.*); seat of University College (1845), a constituent college of the National Univ. of Ireland (1908). Frequently ravaged by the Danes (9th–11th cents.); taken by Henry II 1172 and by Oliver Cromwell 1649.

Cork Harbour. Harbor on S coast of Ireland; 1 m. wide at the entrance, expands to width of 4 m. inland.

Cor·le·o·ne \ˌkōr-lē-'ō-nē, ˌkȯr-\. Commune, Palermo prov., NW cen. Sicily, Italy; pop. (1968e) 12,962; Saracenic origin.

Çor·lu *or* **Chor·lu** \chȯr-'lü\. Town, Tekirdağ prov., Turkey in Europe, NE of Tekirdağ; pop. (1965c) 27,187.

Cormantyne. See KORMANTINE.

Cor·ne·lia \kȯr-'nēl-yə\. City, Habersham co., NE Georgia, 39 m. NNW of Athens; pop. (1970c) 3104; furniture; fruit.

Cor·ne·lio Pro·có·pio \kȯr-ˌnel-yü-prü-'kȯp-yü\. Municipality, Paraná state, S Brazil, ab. 250 m. W of São Paulo.

Cor·nell \kȯr-'nel\. City, Chippewa co., W Wisconsin, 20 m. NNE of Chippewa Falls; pop. (1970c) 1616.

Cornell, Mount. Peak in the Catskill Mts., Ulster co., SE New York; 3906 ft.

Cor·ne·llá \ˌkȯr-nᵊl-'yä, -nə-'yä\. Commune, Barcelona prov., E Spain, ab. 5 m. WSW of Barcelona; pop. (1970p) 77,314; a suburb of Barcelona.

Cor·ner Brook \'kȯ(ə)r-nər-\. City at head of estuary of Humber river, W Newfoundland, Canada; pop. (1971p) 25,929; cement; paper mills, gypsum plants, fisheries.

Corneto. See TARQUINIA.

Cor·niche \kȯr-'nēsh\. Road, actually three more or less parallel highways along the Riviera, France, from Nice to Menton; ab. 19 m. long; cuts across the precipitous cliffs (Fr. *corniche,* "shelf, cornice") of the Maritime Alps: (1) Grande Corniche, the upper road, part of great military road built by Napoleon 1806; for through and heavy traffic; (2) Petite Corniche, the lower road, along the coast; and (3) Moyenne Corniche, the middle road, affording better access to the towns.

Cor·ning \'kȯr-niŋ\. **1** City, a ⊗ of Clay co., NE corner of Arkansas; pop. (1970c) 2705; lumber.

2 City, Tehama co., N California, 5 m. W of Sacramento river and 21 m. NW of Chico; pop. (1970c) 3573; furniture, olive oil.

3 City, ⊗ of Adams co., SW Iowa; pop. (1970c) 2095; corn, wheat.

4 Manufacturing city, Steuben co., S New York, on Chemung river 14 m. W of Elmira; pop. (1970c) 15,792; manufactures many kinds of glassware, radio tubes, lenses (including the 200-in. lens for the telescope of Mount Palomar observatory in Calif. 1934), also aircraft parts, precision instruments; Corning Community Coll. (1956); settled 1789.

Cor·nish \'kȯr-nish\. Town, Sullivan co., SW New Hampshire, ab. 8 m. NW of Claremont; pop. (1970c) 1268.

Corn Islands \'kȯ(ə)rn-\. Two small islands, **Great Corn Island** and **Little Corn Island,** in Caribbean Sea ab. 40 m. off E coast of Nicaragua; 4 sq. m.; pop. (1967e) 2116; leased by Nicaragua to U.S. 1916–71.

Cor·no, Mon·te \ˌmänt-ē-'kȯr-(ˌ)nō\. Peak, Teramo prov., cen. Italy, in the Gran Sasso d'Italia, Abruzzi Apennines; 9560 ft.; highest peak in the Apennines.

Corn·wall \'kȯrn-ˌwȯl, -wəl\. **1** Village, Orange co., SE New York, on Hudson river S of Newburgh; pop. (1970c) 2032; summer resort on Hudson river at foot of Storm King Mt.

2 Borough, Lebanon co., SE cen. Pennsylvania, 17 m. N of Lancaster; pop. (1970c) 2111; iron ore deposits.

3 City, ⊗ of Stormont, Dundas, and Glengarry cos., SE Ontario, Canada, on St. Lawrence river 53 m. SE of Ottawa; pop. (1968e) 45,146; chemicals, lumber; foundries; dairy farms; founded 1776.

4 Maritime county, extreme SW part of England; 1357 sq. m.; pop. (1971p) 379,892; ⊗ Bodmin; forms a peninsula ab. 75 m. long (45 m. wide at base), terminating in Lands End; has rocky coast, much indented. Highest point Brown Willy 1375 ft. *Rivers:* Tamar, Camel. *Chief towns:* St. Austell with Fowey, Penzance, Falmouth, Truro. *Chief industries:* Agriculture (cattle, oats, turnips), fishing, ship repairing; tourism; tin mining formerly important (region famous as source of tin for Phoenicians in ancient times). Many remains (cromlechs, dolmens, etc.) of early inhabitants. Given by William the Conqueror to his brother Robert as an earldom; created a duchy 1337 by Edward III for Prince of Wales and still is appanage of male member of highest rank in reigning family, next to sovereign.

Corn·wal·lis Island \kȯrn-ˌwäl-əs-\. One of the Parry Is., cen. Franklin dist., Northwest Territories, Canada, bet. Bathurst I. and Devon I., N of Barrow Strait.

Co·ro \'kōr-(ˌ)ō, 'kȯr-\ *or formerly* **San·ta Ana de Coro** \ˌsänt-ə-'än-ə-di-\. Town, ✻ of Falcón state, NW Venezuela, SE of Gulf of Coro at base of Paraguaná Penin.; pop. (1970e) 55,955; La Vela (La Vela de Coro), its port, 14 m. ENE; founded 1527; for a few years before 1578 capital of Venezuela; site of Miranda's unsuccessful attempt 1806 to free Venezuela from Spain.

Co·ro·a·tá \ˌkȯr-ə-ə-'tä\. Municipality, Maranhão state, NE Brazil, ab. 100 m. WSW of São Luís; pop. (1968e) 84,902.

Coroch. See ÇORUH.

Co·ro·co·ro \ˌkȯr-ə-'kȯr-(ˌ)ō\. Town, La Paz dept., W Bolivia, ab. 55 m. SSW of La Paz near Desaguadero river; copper mining.

Cor·o·man·del Channel \ˌkȯr-ə-'man-dᵊl-, ˌkär-\. Strait bet. S end of Great Barrier I. and mainland of North I., New Zealand; ab. 10 m. wide.

Coromandel Coast. Coast of SE India from Point Calimere N to mouths of Krishna river; has low shoreline with no good harbors; beaten by heavy seas throughout the year, especially during northeast monsoon (Oct. to Apr.); chief ports Nellore, Madras, Pondicherry, Cuddalore, Tranquebar, and Nagappattinam.

Co·ron \kə-'rȯn\. **1** Island, Calamian Is., W Phil., off SE coast of Busuanga I.; 27 sq. m.; high, rocky, and thinly inhabited.

2 Municipality, N Palawan prov., Phil., on SE coast; pop. (1969e) 6000; chief town of Busuanga I.

Co·ro·na \kə-'rō-nə\. City, Riverside co., SE California, 12 m. SW of San Bernardino; pop. (1970c) 27,519; die castings; shipping center for citrus fruits; settled 1898, incorp. 1906.

Cor·o·na·do \ˌkȯr-ə-'näd-(ˌ)ō, ˌkär-\. Residential city, San Diego co., SW California, on bay opp. San Diego; pop. (1970c) 20,910.

Coronado Bay. Widemouthed inlet of Pacific Ocean on W coast of Costa Rica.

Cor·o·na·tion Gulf \ˌkȯr-ə-ˌnā-shən-, ˌkär-\. Gulf, N Mackenzie dist., Northwest Territories, Canada, bet. the mainland and S Victoria I., ab. 109°–115°W.

Coronation Island. Largest island of the South Orkney group, South Atlantic Ocean, 60°37'S, 45°35'W; 193 sq. m.

Cor·o·nea \ˌkȯr-ə-ˈnē-ə\. Town in W part of ancient Boeotia, E cen. Greece, SW of Lake Copais; scene of battles: (1) 447 B.C. Boeotians defeated the Athenians, and (2) 394 B.C. Spartans under Agesilaus in the Corinthian War defeated the coalition led by Thebes.

Co·ro·nel \ˌkȯr-ə-ˈnel, ˌkär-\. Seaport, Concepción prov., S cen. Chile, 17 m. S of Concepción; pop. (1966e) 43,324; important coal-mining center; founded 1851, was granted city status 1875; scene of a naval battle Nov. 1, 1914 bet. British squadron under Rear Admiral Sir Christopher Cradock and German squadron under Vice-Admiral von Spee in which British were defeated, Cradock himself going down with his flagship the "Good Hope." See history at FALKLAND ISLANDS.

Coronel Bo·ga·do \-bō-ˈgä-t͟hō\. Town, Itapúa dept., SE Paraguay; munic. pop. (1962c) 12,235.

Coronel Ovie·do \-ˌō-vē-ˈā-(ˌ)t͟hō\. City, ✻ of Caaguazú dept., E Paraguay; munic. pop. (1970e) 59,307.

Co·ro·pu·na, Ne·va·do \nə-ˈväd-ō-ˌkȯr-ə-ˈpü-nə, -ˌkär-\. Peak in Andes (Cordillera Occidental), S Peru, NW of Arequipa; 21,079 ft.

Co·ro·vo·dë \ˌchȯr-ə-ˈvō-də\. Town, ✻ of Skrapar prov., S cen. Albania; pop. (1967e) 2178.

Co·ro·zal \ˌkȯr-ə-ˈzäl, ˌkär-\. 1 District, NE British Honduras; 718 sq. m.; pop. (1967e) 12,577; ✻ Corozal.

2 Seaport, its ✻; pop. (1970p) 4640; produces sugar, rum, corn.

3 Town, Canal Zone, on the Panama Canal ab. 2 m. NNW of Balboa; military reservation.

4 Municipality, Sucre dept., N Colombia, ab. 80 m. SSE of Cartagena; pop. (1968e) 45,858.

5 Town and municipality, N cen. Puerto Rico; town 16 m. SW of San Juan; pop. (1970p) 5085 (town), 24,194 (munic.).

Cor·pus Chris·ti \ˌkȯr-pə-ˈskris-tē\. City and port of entry, ⊗ of Nueces co., S Texas, on SW shore of Corpus Christi Bay at mouth of Nueces river; pop. (1970c) 204,525; chemicals, aluminum, refined zinc, cement; railroad and shipping center; seaside and fishing resort; oil and gas fields; oil refineries; fisheries; naval air training station; Del Mar Coll. (1935), Univ. of Corpus Christi (1947); settled 1839, incorp. 1852; figured in Mexican and U.S. Civil Wars. See GULF INTRACOASTAL WATERWAY.

Corpus Christi Bay. Inlet of Gulf of Mexico in NE Nueces co., S Texas; sheltered from the gulf by Mustang I., its connection with the gulf being the strait **Corpus Christi Pass** (S of the island).

Co·rral \kə-ˈral, kȯ-ˈräl\. Port and commune, Valdivia prov., S cen. Chile, near mouth of Valdivia river; pop. (1960c) 3740; scene of Chilean victory 1819 in War of Independence.

Co·rra·li·llo \ˌkȯr-ə-ˈlē-(ˌ)yō\. Municipality, Las Villas prov., W cen. Cuba, 40 m. E of Cárdenas; pop. (1967e) 13,710.

Cor·reg·gio \kə-ˈrej-(ˌ)ō, -ˈrej-ē-ˌō\. Commune, Reggio nell'-Emilia prov., Emilia-Romagna, N Italy, 8 m. NE of Reggio; pop. (1968e) 20,062; birthplace of Correggio.

Cor·reg·i·dor \kə-ˈreg-ə-ˌdȯ(ə)r\. Island in entrance to Manila Bay, Phil., 3½ m. off S point of Bataan Peninsula, ab. 6 m. SE of Mariveles and 28 m. WSW of Manila; belongs to Cavite prov.; rocky; area about 2 sq. m.; highest point 649 ft.; divides entrance to Manila Bay into two channels: North Channel (also Boca Chica), 2 m. wide, and South Channel (also Boca Grande), 6½ m. wide; nearby are two small islands La Monja and Caballo I., site of Fort Hughes; associated with it before the war as an American military defense unit were the small islands of El Fraile, site of Fort Drum, and Carabao I., site of Fort Frank. Semaphore station, four lighthouses, and American-built fortification, Fort Mills; extensive tunnels in the rock. First fortified by Spanish 18th cent.; passed successfully by Admiral Dewey's fleet May 1, 1898; made a U.S. military station 1900 and later strengthened by other fortifications; after Japanese invasion of the Philippines Dec. 1941 chosen with Bataan (*q.v.*) by Gen. MacArthur as major defense position; after long resistance, Jan.–Apr. 1942, surrendered May 6, 1942; invaded by Americans Feb. 16, 1945, all Japanese overcome by Feb. 22.

Cor·rèze \kȯr-ˈez\. Department of S cen. France. See table at FRANCE.

Cor·rib, Lough \ˌläk-ˈkȯr-əb, -ˈkär-\. Lake in W co. Galway, W Eire, S of Lough Mask; 27 m. long; 65 sq. m.; has outlet, **Corrib River,** on SE flowing into Galway Bay.

Corridor, Polish. See POLISH CORRIDOR.

Cor·rien·tes \ˌkȯr-ē-ˈen-ˌtās, ˌkär-\. 1 Province of NE Argentina. See table at ARGENTINA.

2 Commercial city, its ✻, on the Paraná river opp. Resistencia; pop. (1960c) 97,507; commercial center; museum (1854), univ. (1957); founded by Spanish 1588.

Corrientes, Cape. 1 Cape, SE Buenos Aires prov., extending into Atlantic Ocean from E Argentina.

2 Cape extending into Pacific Ocean from cen. part of W coast of Colombia.

3 Cape on SW coast of Pinar del Río prov., W Cuba.

4 West extremity of state of Jalisco, W cen. Mexico, projecting into the Pacific Ocean, 20°25′N.

Corrientes Bay. Bay in SW coast of Pinar del Río prov., W Cuba, W of Cape Corrientes.

Corrigain, Mount \-ˈkȯr-ə-gən\. Mountain, Grafton co., New Hampshire, in White Mts.

Cor·ry \ˈkȯr-ē, ˈkär-\. City, Erie co., NW corner of Pennsylvania, 28 m. ESE of Erie; pop. (1970c) 7435; precision tools, aircraft parts, metal products, furniture.

Cor·ry·vreck·an *or* **Cor·rie·vrech·an** *or* **Cor·rie·vrek·in** \ˌkȯr-i-ˈvrek-ən, ˌkär-\. Whirlpool and strait off W coast of Scotland, N of Jura I.

Corse. See CORSICA 1.

Corse, Cape \-ˈkȯ(ə)rs\ *or anc.* **Sa·crum Pro·mon·to·ri·um** \ˈsak-rəm-ˌpräm-ən-ˈtōr-ē-əm, ˈsā-krəm-, -ˈtȯr-\. Northern point of Corsica, France.

Corse·wall Point \ˌkȯrs-ˌwȯl-\. Cape on the N coast of the Rinns, Wigtown co., SW Scotland; lighthouse.

Cor·si·ca \ˈkȯr-si-kə\. 1 *or Fr.* **Corse** \kȯ(ə)rs\. French island in the Mediterranean Sea W of N Italy and ab. 100 m. SE of SE coast of France; 3352 sq. m.; pop. (1968c) 269,831; ✻ Ajaccio; since 1815 a department (Corse) of France; ab. 114 m. long from Cape Corse in the N to the Strait of Bonifacio on the S separating it from Sardinia; mountainous with highest point Mont Cinto 8891 ft.; has numerous short streams; E coastline is unbroken by harbors or bays but W coast is quite irregular with Gulf of Ajaccio its largest inlet. Chief products wine, olive oil, citrus fruits, chestnuts, silk; chief towns Ajaccio, Bastia, Calvi, Corte, Bonifacio.

History: Settled in ancient times by Etruscan, Phoenician, Phocaean, and Carthaginian traders; conquered by Romans in 3d cent. B.C., by Vandals in 5th cent. A.D., and by Belisarius (for Byzantine Empire) 534; overrun by Goths, Franks, Saracens; came under rule of Pisa which was finally ousted after a bitter struggle with republic of Genoa; most of the time from 1347 to 1768 ruled by Genoa; in revolt 1729–68; sold by Genoa to France 1768; occupied by British 1794–96 and 1814–15. In World War II occupied by Axis forces Nov. 1942–Sept. 1943.

2 Village, Ohio. See BLOOMING GROVE.

Cor·si·cana \ˌkȯr-sə-ˈkan-ə\. City, ⊗ of Navarro co., NE cen. Texas, S of Dallas; pop. (1970c) 19,972; oil and gas wells; oil refineries, flour mills; Navarro Junior Coll. (1946).

Cor·si·co \ˈkȯr-sə-ˌkō\. Commune, Milano prov., Lombardy, N Italy, 4 m. SW of Milan; pop. (1968e) 30,175.

Cor·son \ˈkȯr-sən\. County in South Dakota. See table at SOUTH DAKOTA.

Corson Inlet. Narrow strait leading from Atlantic Ocean through barrier reefs off NE coast of Cape May co., S New Jersey.

Cor·stop·i·tum \kȯr-ˈstäp-ē-əm\. See CORBRIDGE.

Cor·ta·zar \ˌkȯrt-ə-ˈzär\. Municipality, Guanajuato state, cen. Mexico, just W of Querétaro; pop. (1970p) 45,744.

Cor·te \ˈkȯr-tā\. Commune, cen. Corsica, France; pop. (1962c) 5491; partly built on steep, high rock; home 1755–69 of Pasquale di Paoli; marble quarries nearby; wine trade.

Corte Ma·dera \ˌkȯrt-ə-mə-ˈder-ə\. Town, Marin co., W coastal California, N of San Francisco; pop. (1970c) 8464; chemicals, fiber glass.

Cor·te·nuo·va \ˌkȯr-tā-nü-ˈwō-və\. Commune, Bergamo prov., Lombardy, Italy, bet. Bergamo and Brescia; pop. (1968e) 1158; scene of victory Nov. 27, 1237 of Emperor Frederick II over the Lombards.

Cor·tés \kȯr-ˈtās\. Department of NW Honduras. See table at HONDURAS.

Cortés, Sea of. See CALIFORNIA, GULF OF.

Cor·tez \kȯr-ˈtez\. City, ⊗ of Montezuma co., SW corner of Colorado; pop. (1970c) 6032; sheep, cattle.

Cor·ti·na \kȯr-ˈtē-nə\ *or in full* **Cortina d'Am·pez·zo** \-däm-ˈpet-ˌsō\. Village in Belluno prov., N Italy, N of Belluno; noted ski resort, in the Dolomites; site of winter Olympic Games 1956.

Cort·land \ˈkȯrt-lənd\. **1** County in New York. See table at NEW YORK.

2 City, its ⊗, 30 m. S of Syracuse; pop. (1970c) 19,621; canneries; motortrucks, motorboats, airplane equipment; State Univ. of New York Coll. at Cortland (1863); settled 1792.

3 Village, Trumbull co., NE Ohio, 9 m. E of Warren; pop. (1970c) 2525.

Cor·to·na \kȯr-ˈtō-nə\. Commune, Arezzo prov., Tuscany, cen. Italy, 14 m. SSE of Arezzo; pop. (1968e) 23,564; cathedral (15th and 18th cents.), remains of cyclopean walls, Roman baths, temple; museum of Etruscan antiquities, tomb of St. Margaret. Ancient Etruscan city; confederated with Rome 310 B.C.; under Casale family 14th cent.; passed to Naples 1409, to Florence 1412.

Corubal. See GRANDE, RIO 1.

Ço·ruh \chō-ˈrüḱ\ *or* **Co·roch** \chȯ-ˈrȯk\. **1** River in NE Turkey; 234 m. long; flows ENE, then N across Russian border into Black Sea S of Batumi.

2 Seaport, Turkey. See RİZE.

Ço·rum *or* **Cho·rum** \chō-ˈrüm\. **1** Province of N cen. Turkey, Asia. See table at TURKEY.

2 Town, its ✱, E of the Kızıl Irmak 116 m. ENE of Ankara; pop. (1965c) 41,574.

Co·rum·bá \ˌkȯr-əm-ˈbä, ˌkōr-\. Commercial city on the Paraguay river, Mato Grosso state, SW Brazil, ab. 11 m. from the border of SE Bolivia; munic. pop. (1968e) 89,199.

Coruña, La *or* **Corunna**. See LA CORUÑA.

Co·run·na \kə-ˈrən-ə\. City, ⊗ of Shiawassee co., S cen. Michigan, 23 m. W of Flint; pop. (1970c) 2829; furniture.

Cor·u·pe·di·on \ˌkȯr-(y)ə-ˈpē-dē-ən\ *or* **Cor·u·pe·di·um** \-əm\. Battlefield in ancient Lydia, Asia Minor, ENE of Magnesia, where Seleucus Nicator defeated Lysimachus 281 B.C.

Cor·val·lis \kȯr-ˈval-əs\. City, ⊗ of Benton co., W Oregon, on Willamette river 30 m. SSW of Salem; pop. (1970c) 35,056; lumber products, tile; dairy products; Oregon State Univ. (1858); settled 1845.

Cor·vo \ˈkȯ(ə)r-(ˌ)vü\. Island in the district of Horta, NW Azores; 7 sq. m.; smallest island of the group.

Corycian Cave. See PARNASSUS 2.

Cor·y·don \ˈkȯr-ə-dən, ˈkär-\. **1** Town, ⊗ of Harrison co., S Indiana, 18 m. WSW of New Albany; pop. (1970c) 2719; lumber; poultry; capital of Indiana Territory 1813–16 and of the state of Indiana until 1825; captured and held for a short time 1863 by Confederate raiding party under Gen. J. H. Morgan.

2 Town, ⊗ of Wayne co., S Iowa; pop. (1970c) 1745; dairy farming.

Cor·yell \kȯr-ˈyel, kōr-\. County in Texas. See table at TEXAS.

Cos. See KOS.

Co·sa·ma·lo·a·pan \ˌkō-sə-mäl-ˈwä-(ˌ)pän\. Municipality, Veracruz state, Mexico, 63 m. S of Veracruz; pop. (1970p) 75,412; sugar processing; diversified agriculture.

Cos Cob \ˈkäs-ˈkäb\. Subdivision of town of Greenwich, Connecticut.

Cos·co·ma·te·pec \kōs-ˌkō-mə-tə-ˈpek\ *or in full* **Coscomatepec de Bra·vo** \-də-ˈbräv-(ˌ)ō\. Town, Veracruz state, E Mexico; munic. pop. (1970p) 19,890.

Cosel. See KOŹLE.

Co·sen·za \kō-ˈzen(t)-sə\. **1** Province of Calabria, S Italy. See table at ITALY.

2 *or anc.* **Con·sen·tia** \kən-ˈsen-ch(ē-)ə\. Commune, its ✱, at confluence of Busento and Crati rivers 150 m. SE of Naples; pop. (1968e) 94,800; furniture, wool, tannic acid; 13th cent. cathedral containing tombs of Louis III of Anjou and Isabella of Aragon; college. Ancient capital of the Brutii; important in Second Punic War; devastated by earthquakes 1181, 1638, 1783, 1854, 1870, 1908.

Co·shoc·ton \kə-ˈshäk-tən\. **1** County in E cen. Ohio. See table at OHIO.

2 City, its ⊗, on Muskingum river; pop. (1970c) 13,747; enamelware, iron pipes; on site of Indian village destroyed 1781.

Co·si·güi·na Vol·cán \ˌkō-sə-ˈgwē-nə-vȯl-ˈkän\. Volcano, Nicaragua, on the Gulf of Fonseca; 2818 ft.; eruption Jan. 20, 1835.

Cos·mo·le·do Islands \ˌkäz-mə-ˌläd-ō-\. Group of small islands in the Aldabra Is. (*q.v.*).

Cosne–sur–Loire \ˈkōn-s(y)u̇r-lə-ˈwär\ *or anc.* **Con·da·te** \kən-ˈdā-tē\. Commune, Nièvre dept., cen. France, on the Loire 37 m. NNW of Nevers; pop. (1962c) 9010; important military post in Middle Ages, taken by English 1420; 12th cent. church.

Co·spi·cua \kə-ˈspēk-wə\. Urban district, SE Malta, across the harbor from Valletta; pop. (1968e) 9191; with adjacent towns of **Sen·glea** \seŋ-ˈglā-ə\ and **Vit·to·rio·sa** \vi-ˌtōr-ē-ˈō-sə, -ˌtȯr-\ often called the "Three Cities."

Cossimbazar. See BERHAMPORE.

Cossyra. See PANTELLERIA.

Cos·ta Bra·va \ˌkäs-tə-ˈbräv-ə, kȯs-, ˌkōs-\. The coast of Catalonia, Spain, NE of Barcelona.

Costa del Sol \-t͟hel-ˈsȯl, -ˈsōl\. The southern coast of Spain from Estepona to Motril.

Costa Me·sa \ˌkōs-tə-ˈmā-sə\. City, Orange co., SW coastal California, SSW of Santa Ana; pop. (1970c) 72,660; electronic equipment, aircraft parts, plastics; Southern California Coll. (1920), Orange Coast Coll. (1947).

Costa Ri·ca \ˌkäs-tə-ˈrē-kə, ˌkȯs-, ˌkōs-\. Republic, S Central America, bounded on N by Nicaragua, on E by the Caribbean Sea and Panama, and on S and W by the Pacific Ocean; 19,652 sq. m.; pop. (1970p) 1,710,083; ✱ San José. *Physical features:* Traversed from NW to SE by the mountains of the Continental Divide, its SE section known as the Cordillera de Talamanca; highest point Chirripó Grande 12,533 ft.; chief volcanoes Irazú, Turrialba, and Barba. Only large river is the San Juan on NE boundary; its main tributaries are San Carlos and Sarapiquí. Its Caribbean coastline has only one good harbor, Puerto Limón; on Pacific coast has large peninsula of Nicoya in NW and smaller peninsula of Osa in S, the Gulfs of Nicoya and Dulce, and the wide Coronado Bay. *Chief products:* Coffee, bananas, cocoa, timber, sugar; livestock; salt, sulfur. *Chief towns:* San José, Alajuela, Guadalupe, Puntarenas, Heredia, Puerto Limón. Divided into seven provinces (for pronunciation of their names, see their individual entries):

NAME	AREA (sq. m.)	POP. (1970p)	CAPITAL
Alajuela	3,669	308,907	Alajuela
Cartago	1,004	198,049	Cartago
Guanacaste	4,015	188,972	Liberia
Heredia	1,120	105,310	Heredia
Limón	3,591	87,074	Puerto Limón
Puntarenas*	4,358	209,937	Puntarenas
San José	1,896	611,834	San José

*Includes islands of Chira and Coco.

History: Discovered by Columbus on last voyage 1502; Gulf of Nicoya object of expedition sent by Pedrarias, governor of Isthmus of Panama; region conquered by Spanish by 1530; became a Spanish province 1540; with other countries of Central America (*q.v.*), revolted against Spain 1821; in Iturbide's Mexican empire 1822–23; nominally part of United Provinces of Central America 1823–38; declared itself independent republic 1848; boundary with Panama arbitrated 1900 but not finally settled until 1941; bloodless revolution 1917 brought trouble with U.S.; entered World War I 1918; joined League of Nations 1920; in World War II declared war on Axis countries Dec. 8, 1941; adopted new constitution 1949; joined Central American Common Market 1962.

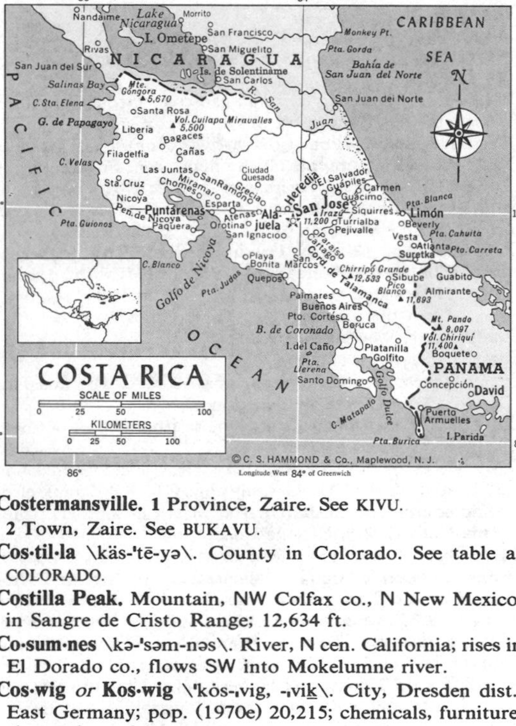

Costermansville. 1 Province, Zaire. See KIVU.
2 Town, Zaire. See BUKAVU.

Cos·til·la \käs-ˈtē-yə\. County in Colorado. See table at COLORADO.

Costilla Peak. Mountain, NW Colfax co., N New Mexico, in Sangre de Cristo Range; 12,634 ft.

Co·sum·nes \kə-ˈsəm-nəs\. River, N cen. California; rises in El Dorado co., flows SW into Mokelumne river.

Cos·wig *or* **Kos·wig** \ˈkȯs-ˌvig, -ˌvik\. City, Dresden dist., East Germany; pop. (1970e) 20,215; chemicals, furniture, electronic equipment.

Cosyra. See PANTELLERIA.

Co·ta·ba·to \ˌkōt-ə-ˈbät-(ˌ)ō\. 1 River, Mindanao, Phil. See MINDANAO 2.
2 Province, SW Mindanao, Phil.; 6348 sq. m.; pop. (1970p) 1,153,640; ✱ Pagalungan; mountainous in S and on E and N borders; Mt. Apo (*q.v.*) on E boundary the highest mountain 9690 ft. in the Phil.; mountains densely wooded with much fine, hard timber. Central and W part occupied with basin of the Mindanao river and lower course of its tributary, the Pulangi. Chief product rice, but forest products and fish important; inhabitants chiefly the Moro people, known as the Magindanao, also several pagan tribes. Became Muslim stronghold, probably toward end of 15th cent.; practically an independent Moro sultanate until ab. 1850; in almost constant conflict with Spaniards 1850–99.
3 Chartered city in NW part, in the delta of the Mindanao, Mindanao I., Phil.; pop. (1970e) 51,900; founded as a fort by the Spanish ab. 1862; has good harbor 7 m. from town.

Cotabato del Sur \-del-ˈsu̇(ə)r\. Province, S Mindanao, Phil.; 2840 sq. m.; pop. (1970p) 470,527; ✱ Koronadal; formed 1967.

Co·ta·ca·chi \ˌkō-tə-ˈkäch-ē\. Town, Imbabura prov., N Ecuador, 50 m. NNE of Quito; pop. (1962c) 4314.

Co·teau Landing \kō-ˈtō-\. Village, ⊗ of Soulanges co., S Quebec, Canada, on St. Lawrence river; pop. (1971p) 850.

Cote Blanche Bay \ˌkōt-ˌblä^{n}sh-\. Inlet of Gulf of Mexico on SW coast of St. Mary parish, S Louisiana; divided into **East Cote Blanche Bay** and **West Cote Blanche Bay.**

Côte d'Azur \ˌkōt-də-ˈzu̇(ə)r\. The Mediterranean coast of France, esp. its E end; part of the Riviera (*q.v.*).

Côte des Allemands. See GERMAN COAST.

Côte d'Ivoire. See IVORY COAST.

Côte d'Or \kōt-ˈdȯ(ə)r\. Range of hills, Côte-d'Or dept., E France, SW of Dijon; noted for rich vineyards.

Côte–d'Or. Department of E France. See table at FRANCE.

Côte française des Somalis. See AFARS AND ISSAS.

Co·ten·tin Peninsula \ˌkō-tä^{n}-ˌta^{n}-\. Peninsula formed by N end of Manche dept., NW France, bet. Channel Is. and Bay of the Seine. In World War II scene of fighting from beginning of Allied invasion June 6, 1944 to capture of Cherbourg June 27.

Côte Saint Luc \ˌkōt-sānt-ˈlük, -sənt-, -sa^{n}-\. City, Montreal and Jesus Islands co., S Quebec, Canada; pop. (1971p) 24,358; residential suburb of Montreal.

Côtes–du–Nord \ˌkōt-dü-ˈnȯr\. Department of NW France. See table at FRANCE.

Cöthen. See KÖTHEN.

Co·tin·go \kō-ˈtē(ⁿ)ŋ-(ˌ)gō\. River, N Brazil; 180 m. long; rises near border, flows S into the Tacutu.

Co·to \ˈkōt-(ˌ)ō\. Small stream in SE Costa Rica, flowing into the Gulf of Dulce; 25 m. long; ownership of region disputed with Panama.

Co·to·nou *or* **Ko·to·nu** \ˌkōt-^{ə}n-ˈü\. Seaport, Dahomey, W Africa; pop. (1970e) 208,000; commercial center; former ✱ of Dahomey.

Co·to·paxi \ˌkōt-ə-ˈpak-sē, -ˈpä-(ˌ)hē\. 1 Active volcano, N cen. Ecuador; 19,347 ft.
2 *or formerly* **Le·ón** \lā-ˈōn\. Province of cen. Ecuador. See table at ECUADOR.

Cotrone. See CROTONE.

Cots·wold Hills \ˈkät-ˌswōld-, -swəld-\ *or* **Cots·wolds** \-ˌswōl(d)z, -swəl(d)z\. Range of hills in Gloucestershire, SW cen. England; highest point Cleeve Cloud 1031 ft.

Cot·tage Grove \ˌkät-ij-ˈgrōv\. 1 Village, Washington co., E Minnesota, 11 m. SE of St. Paul; pop. (1970c) 13,419; residential suburb of St. Paul.
2 City, Lane co., W Oregon, S of Eugene; pop. (1970c) 6004; livestock; lumbering.

Cott·bus *or* **Kott·bus** \ˈkät-bəs, -ˌbu̇s\. 1 District, East Germany. See table at GERMANY, EAST.
2 City, its ✱, on Spree river 64 m. SE of Berlin; pop. (1970e) 82,897; textiles, electrical machinery, transportation equipment; metallurgical industries; railroad center. First mentioned 1156; passed 1445 to elector of Brandenburg, 1807 to Saxony, 1813 to Prussia; in World War II captured by Soviet troops Apr. 24, 1945.

Cot·tes·loe \ˈkät-(ə-)ˌslō\. Town, W Western Australia, 7 m. SW of Perth on Indian Ocean; pop. (1966c) 8122.

Cottian Alps. See table at ALPS.

Cot·ti·ca \ˈkät-i-kə\. Navigable river, N Surinam; ab. 80 m. long; flows W into the Commewijne near its mouth; large bauxite deposits along its course.

Cot·tle \ˈkät-^{ə}l\. County in Texas. See table at TEXAS.

Cot·ton \ˈkät-^{ə}n\. County in Oklahoma. See table at OKLAHOMA.

Cotton Plant \-ˌplant\. City, S Woodruff co., NE cen. Arkansas; pop. (1970c) 1657; battle 1862.

Cot·ton·wood \'kät-^{ə}n-ˌwu̇d\. 1 River, S Minnesota; ab. 140 m. long; rises in Lyon co., flows E into Minnesota river below New Ulm in Brown co.
2 County in Minnesota. See table at MINNESOTA.
3 Town, Yavapai co., cen. Arizona, 15 m. SW of Flagstaff; pop. (1970c) 2815; livestock and fodder crops; cement works.

Cottonwood Creek. Creek in S San Diego co., SW California; contains Barrett Dam and Morena Dam (*qq.v.*).

Cottonwood Falls. City, ⊗ of Chase co., E cen. Kansas; pop. (1970c) 987.

Cottonwood Mountain. Peak, S Idaho co., N cen. Idaho; 9321 ft.

Co·tuí \kō-'twē\. Town, ✱ of Sánchez Ramírez dept., cen. Dominican Republic; pop. (1970e) 6296.

Co·tu·it \kə-'t(y)ü-ət\. Town, Barnstable co., SE Massachusetts, on Nantucket Sound; summer resort; noted oyster beds.

Co·tul·la \kə-'tü-lə\. City, ⊗ of La Salle co., S Texas, 70 m. N of Laredo; pop. (1970c) 3415; in farming region.

Cotyora. See ORDU 2.

Cou·cy–le–Châ·teau \ku̇-ˌsēl-shä-'tō\ *or in full* **Coucy–le–Château–Auf·frique** \-ō-'frēk\. Commune, Aisne dept., N France, 18 m. WSW of Laon; pop. (1962c) 1151; ruins of feudal castle, destroyed by Germans during World War I.

Cou·de·kerque–Branche \ˌküd-ə-ˌke(ə)rk-'brä^{n}sh\. Commune, Nord dept., N France, SE suburb of Dunkerque; pop. (1968c) 23,039.

Cou·ders·port \'kau̇-dərz-ˌpō(ə)rt, -ˌpȯ(ə)rt\. Borough and mountain resort, ⊗ of Potter co., N Pennsylvania, on Allegheny river 36 m. ESE of Bradford; pop. (1970c) 2831; dairy products.

Cou·gar Dam *and* **Cougar Reservoir** \'kü-gər-\. See UNITED STATES, *Dams and Reservoirs.*

Couil·let \kü-'yā\. Commune, Hainaut prov., SW Belgium, just SE of Charleroi; pop. (1969e) 14,631; steel; brewery.

Cou·lee Dam \ˌkü-lē-\. Town, Grant, Douglas, and Okanogan cos., NE cen. Washington, on Columbia river; includes former town of Mason City; pop. (1970c) 1425.

Coul·man Island \'kōl-mən-\. Island in Ross Dependency off coast of Victoria Land, Antarctica, lat. 73°28′S and long. 169°45′E.

Coul·miers \kül-'myā\. Commune, Loiret dept., N cen. France, W of Orléans; pop. (1962c) 326; scene of battle Nov. 9, 1870 in which Bavarians were defeated by the French under Aurelle de Paladines.

Cou·lom·miers \ˌkü-lȯ-'myā\. Commune, N Seine-et-Marne dept., N France; pop. (1968c) 11,263; 13th–16th cent. church of St. Denis; suffered during World War I.

Coun·cil \'kau̇n(t)-səl\. Village, ⊗ of Adams co., W Idaho; pop. (1970c) 899; in apple-growing area.

Council Bluffs. City, ⊗ of Pottawattamie co., SW Iowa, on Missouri river opp. Omaha, Nebraska; pop. (1970c) 60,348; farm machinery, plastics; grain elevators; site of Mormon settlement 1846–52; outfitting point for emigrants to California during gold rush 1849–50; selected as eastern terminus of Union Pacific R.R. 1863.

Council For Mutual Economic Assistance; *abbr.* **COMECON** \ˌkäm-ē-'kän, -e-\. Economic organization, consisting of Bulgaria, Czechoslovakia, East Germany, Hungary, Mongolian People's Republic, Poland, Romania, U.S.S.R.; headquarters Moscow, U.S.S.R. Formed 1949; represents Soviet counterpart to EEC; Albania not active since 1961; Yugoslavia given limited membership 1964.

Council Grove. City, ⊗ of Morris co., E cen. Kansas, 25 m. NW of Emporia; pop. (1970c) 2403.

Council of Europe. Political organization, consisting of Austria, Belgium, Cyprus, Denmark, Eire, France, West Germany, Iceland, Italy, Luxembourg, Malta, Netherlands, Norway, Sweden, Switzerland, Turkey, and the United Kingdom; headquarters Strasbourg, France; purpose is to promote cooperation among the members in safeguarding democratic political principles; established 1949; Greece withdrew from the Council 1969.

Coun·try Club Hills \ˌkən-trē-ˌkləb-\. City, Cook co., NE Illinois, 25 m. S of Chicago; pop. (1970c) 6920.

Coun·try·side \'kən-trē-ˌsīd\. City, Cook co., NE Illinois, 14 m. SW of Chicago; pop. (1970c) 2864.

Coupe·ville \'küp-ˌvil\. Town and resort, ⊗ of Island co., NW Washington, on Whidbey I.; pop. (1970c) 678.

Cour·an·tyne *or Du.* **Co·ran·tijn** \'kōr-ən-ˌtīn, 'kȯr-\. River, N South America; 475 m. long; rises in the Serra Acaraí, flows N to Atlantic Ocean forming boundary bet. Guyana and Surinam.

Cour·be·voie \ˌku̇r-bəv-'wä\. Manufacturing commune, Hauts-de-Seine dept., N France, on the Seine, a NW suburb of Paris; pop. (1968c) 58,118; textiles; foundries.

Cour·ce·lette \ˌku̇r-sə-'let\. Village, Somme dept., N France, 5 m. NE of Albert; pop. (1962c) 202; in World War I captured by Canadians 1916 during battle of the Somme; taken and retaken in 1918.

Cour·celles \ku̇r-'sel\. 1 Commune, Hainaut prov., SW Belgium, just NNW of Charleroi; pop. (1969e) 16,942.
2 *or* **Courcelles–sur–Nied** \-su̇(ə)r-'nyā\. Village, Moselle dept., NE France, 7 m. SE of Metz; pop. (1962c) 340; battle fought nearby at Colombey (*q.v.*) Aug. 14, 1870.

Courland. See KURLAND.

Cour·ma·yeur \ˌku̇r-mə-'yər\. Village, Aosta prov., NW Italy, SE of Mont Blanc; pop. (1968e) 2118; resort.

Courneuve, La. See LA COURNEUVE.

Cour·rières \ku̇r-'ye(ə)r\. Commune, Pas-de-Calais dept., N France, SSW of Lille; pop. (1962c) 7738; coal.

Courte·nay \'kȯrt-nē\. City, E Vancouver I., British Columbia, Canada, on Strait of Georgia 90 m. WNW of Vancouver; pop. (1971p) 6968; resort.

Court·house Rock \ˌkōrt-ˌhau̇s-, ˌkȯrt-\. Elevation in Cheyenne co., W Nebraska; 4100 ft.; ab. 500 ft. above surrounding country; historic landmark.

Court·land \'kō(ə)rt-lənd, 'kȯ(ə)rt-\. Town, ⊗ of Southampton co., SE Virginia; pop. (1970c) 899; nearby was scene of Nat Turner's Insurrection Aug. 1831.

Courtrai. See KORTRIJK.

Cour·ville \'ku̇(ə)r-ˌvil, ku̇r-'vil\. Town, Quebec co., S Quebec, Canada, on St. Lawrence river 6 m. NE of Quebec; pop. (1971p) 6217.

Cou·shat·ta \ku̇-'shat-ə\. Town, ⊗ of Red River parish, NW Louisiana; pop. (1970c) 1492.

Cou·tances \ku̇-'tä^{n}s\ *or anc.* **Con·stan·tia** \kən-'stan-shə, -shē-ə\. Commune, Manche dept., NW France, 17 m. WSW of Saint-Lô; pop. (1968c) 9061; ancient Celtic town, in 3d cent. fortified by Constantius Chlorus and named in his honor; often besieged in Middle Ages; in World War II captured by Allies July 28, 1944.

Cou·tras \ku̇-'trä\. Commune, Gironde dept., SW France, 56 m. NE of Bordeaux; pop. (1962c) 6038; wine-producing region; scene Oct. 20, 1587 of battle in which Henry of Navarre defeated the Catholics.

Co·va·don·ga \ˌkō-və-'dȯŋ-gə, -t͟hȯŋ-\. Village, Oviedo prov., NW Spain, 5 m. from Cangas de Onís; scene of victory of Pelayo over the Moors 718.

Co·vas·na \kə-'väs-nə\. County of cen. Romania. See table at ROMANIA.

Cove Neck. See OYSTER BAY 2.

Cov·en·try *usu. Brit.* 'käv-ən-trē; 'kəv-\. 1 Manufacturing town, S cen. Tolland co., N Connecticut; pop. (1970c) 8140; incorp. 1712.
2 Town, Kent co., cen. Rhode Island, 15 m. SW of Providence; pop. (1970c) 22,947; governmental seat Washington village; taken from Warwick and incorporated 1741.
3 City and county borough, Warwickshire, cen. England, near the Avon 18 m. ESE of Birmingham; pop. (1971p) 334,839; automobiles and bicycles, motorcycles, airplanes,

machinery, telecommunication equipment; Univ. of Warwick (1965). Home of Lady Godiva, who, with her husband, founded a Benedictine abbey here c. 1043; meeting place of parliaments under Henry IV and Henry VI; probably center of the presentation of the Coventry Mysteries 15th–16th cents. Severely damaged by German Luftwaffe Nov. 14–15, 1940.

Co·vi·lhã \ˌkü-vəl-ˈyaⁿ\. Commune, Castelo Branco dist., E cen. Portugal, N of Castelo Branco; munic. pop. (1970p) 60,768; woolen and cotton cloth; dyeworks.

Coville, Lake. See NAKNEK LAKE.

Co·vi·na \kō-ˈvē-nə\. City, Los Angeles co., SW California, 20 m. E of Los Angeles; pop. (1970c) 30,380; citrus-fruit packing.

Cov·ing·ton \ˈkəv-iŋ-tən\. 1 Counties in two states of the U.S. See tables at ALABAMA and MISSISSIPPI.

2 City, ⊗ of Newton co., N cen. Georgia, 32 m. ESE of Atlanta; pop. (1970c) 10,267; concrete pipes, lumber; incorporated 1822.

3 City, ⊗ of Fountain co., W Indiana, on Wabash river 27 m. WNW of Crawfordsville; pop. (1970c) 2641; diversified agriculture.

4 City, a ⊗ of Kenton co., N Kentucky, at confluence of Ohio and Licking rivers opp. Cincinnati; pop. (1970c) 52,535; precision instruments, electrical equipment, iron and steel products; founded 1815.

5 City, ⊗ of St. Tammany parish, SE Louisiana, 37 m. N of New Orleans; pop. (1970c) 7170; lumber; fishing and hunting.

6 Village, Miami co., W Ohio; pop. (1970c) 2575.

7 Town, ⊗ of Tipton co., W Tennessee, 39 m. NE of Memphis; pop. (1970c) 5801; in cotton-growing area.

8 City, ⊗ of Alleghany co., western Virginia; pop. (1970c) 10,060; politically independent; paper, rayon textiles.

Cow·an, Lake \-ˈkau̇-ən\. Dry lake, S Western Australia, in E Swanland S of Kalgoorlie.

Cow·ans·ville \ˈkau̇-ənz-ˌvil\. Town, Missisquoi co., S Quebec, Canada, 48 m. ESE of Montreal; pop. (1971p) 11,906; furniture, truck bodies.

Cow·den·beath \ˌkau̇d-ᵊn-ˈbēth\. Burgh, Fife co., E Scotland; pop. (1971p) 10,460; coal mining; place where much of the drafting of the Solemn League and Covenant was done (c. 1642).

Cow·en, Mount \-ˈkau̇-ən\. Mountain, Park co., S Montana; 11,190 ft.

Cowes \ˈkau̇z\. Urban district, N Isle of Wight, England, 9 m. WSW of Portsmouth; pop. (1971p) 18,895; seaport and shipbuilding center; yachting resort.

Co·we·ta \kə-ˈwē-tə\. County in Georgia. See table at GEORGIA.

Cow·ley \ˈkau̇-lē\. County in Kansas. See table at KANSAS.

Cow·litz \ˈkau̇-ləts\. 1 River, SW Washington; 130 m. long; formed by confluence of forks in E Lewis co., flows W, then S into Columbia river in Cowlitz co.

2 County in Washington. See table at WASHINGTON.

Cow·pas·ture \ˈkau̇-ˌpas-chər\. River, western Virginia; ab. 60 m. long; rises in Highland co., flows SW, unites with Jackson river to form the James.

Cow·pens \ˈkau̇-ˌpenz\. Town, Spartanburg co., NW South Carolina, in the Piedmont 8 m. ENE of Spartanburg; pop. (1970c) 2109; just N of town is scene of battle Jan. 17, 1781 in which Gen. Daniel Morgan defeated British under Col. Tarleton, commemorated by **Cowpens National Battlefield Site** (see UNITED STATES, *National Historical Parks*).

Cow·ra \ˈkau̇-rə\. Mining town, SE cen. New South Wales, SE Australia, 100 m. N of Canberra; pop. (1966c) 5502.

Cox·comb Mountain \ˌkäks-ˌkōm-\. Peak, cen. Park co., NW Wyoming; 11,000 ft.

Coxcomb Peak. Mountain, Hinsdale and Ouray cos., SW Colorado; 13,663 ft.

Coxin's Hole. See ROATÁN 2.

Cox·sack·ie \ku̇k-ˈsäk-e\. Village, Greene co., SE New York, on Hudson river 22 m. S of Albany; pop. (1970c) 2399.

Coyle. See COIG.

Co·yo·a·cán \ˌkȯi-ō-ə-ˈkän\. City, Federal District, cen. Mexico, suburb of Mexico City; munic. pop. (1970p) 338,850; contains the old Cortes palace, first seat of the Spanish government, now used as a municipal building.

Coy·o·te Peaks \kī-ˌōt-ē-, ˌkī-ˌōt-\. Mountain in Sierra Nevada, E Tulare co., S cen. California; 10,919 ft.

Co·yu·ca de Be·ní·tez \kȯi-ˈyü-kə-dā-be-ˈnē-(ˌ)tez, -tās\. Municipality, Guerrero state, Mexico, 18 m. WNW of Acapulco; pop. (1970p) 36,032; fishing; textiles; cattle raising.

Coyuca de Ca·ta·lán \-ˌkat-ᵊl-ˈän\. Municipality, Guerrero state, Mexico, 120 m. NW of Acapulco; pop. (1970p) 25,128; mining, cattle raising.

Co·zad \kō-ˈzad\. City, Dawson co., S cen. Nebraska, on Platte river; pop. (1970c) 4219; livestock; shipping point for alfalfa.

Co·zu·mel \ˌkō-zə-ˈmel\. Island off NE coast of Quintana Roo territory, SE Mexico; 24 m. long, 7 m. wide.

Crab Island. See VIEQUES.

Cracow. See KRAKÓW.

Cra·dle Mountain \ˌkrād-ᵊl-\. Mountain, NW cen. Tasmania, Australia, on W edge of cen. highlands; 5069 ft.

Crad·ock \ˈkrad-ək\. Town, SE cen. Cape Province, S Rep. of South Africa, 125 m. N of Port Elizabeth; pop. (1967e) 21,300; at ab. 3000 ft. surrounded by mountains; cattle, sheep, and Angora goats; health resort, warm sulfur baths.

Craf·ton \ˈkraf-tən\. Borough, Allegheny co., SW Pennsylvania, 4 m. W of Pittsburgh; pop. (1970c) 8233; coal mines.

Craggy Dome, Craggy Gardens, Craggy Pinnacle. See GREAT CRAGGY MOUNTAINS.

Craig \ˈkrāg\. 1 Name of counties in two states of the United States. See tables at OKLAHOMA and VIRGINIA.

2 Town on W coast of Prince of Wales I., SE Alaska; pop. (1970c) 272; government telegraph station.

3 City, ⊗ of Moffat co., NW corner of Colorado, on Yampa river; pop. (1970c) 4205; center of oil-producing region.

Craig·a·vad \ˌkrāg-ə-ˈvad\. Suburb of Belfast, Northern Ireland, on Belfast Lough 5½ m. NE of Belfast; scene of meeting July 12, 1913 of 150,000 Ulstermen to protest against the Home Rule Bill.

Crai·gen·put·tock \ˌkrāg-ən-ˈpət-ək\. Farm near Dumfries, S Scotland; home of Thomas Carlyle 1828–34.

Craig·head \ˈkrāg-ˌhed\. County in Arkansas. See table at ARKANSAS.

Craig Head. Cape on N coast of Moray co., NE Scotland; lighthouse.

Cra·io·va \krə-ˈyō-və\. City, ⊗ of Dolj co., S Romania, on the Jiul river 112 m. W of Bucharest; pop. (1970e) 175,454; chemicals, agricultural machinery, fertilizer; cathedral, univ. (1966).

Cra·mer·ton \ˈkrām-ərt-ᵊn\. Town, Gaston co., SW North Carolina; pop. (1970c) 2142; textile mills.

Cran·ber·ry Lake \ˌkran-ˌber-ē-\. Lake, in S St. Lawrence co., N New York; 6 m. long.

Cran·brook \ˈkran-ˌbru̇k\. City, SE British Columbia, Canada, in Kootenay Valley 70 m. E of Nelson; pop. (1971p) 11,710; active trade center, esp. in lumber; lead and silver mines.

Cran·don \ˈkran-dən\. City, ⊗ of Forest co., NE Wisconsin, 25 m. E of Rhinelander; pop. (1970c) 1582; lakeside resort, built around and bet. four lakes.

Crane \ˈkrān\. 1 County in W Texas. See table at TEXAS.

2 City, its ⊗, 128 m. W of San Angelo; pop. (1970c) 3427; dairy farms, oil wells.

Cran·ford \ˈkran-fərd\. Township, Union co., NE New Jersey, 5 m. W of Elizabeth; pop. (1970c) 27,391; electrical equipment, fabricated metal goods; Union Junior Coll. (1933).

Cran·non \ˈkran-(ˌ)än\ *or* **Cra·non** \ˈkrā-(ˌ)nän\. Ancient town in cen. Thessaly, NE Greece, ab. 13 m. SW of Larisa; scene of battle 322 B.C. in which Antipater defeated the league of cities of cen. Greece.

Cran·ston \ˈkran(t)-stən\. City, Providence co., N Rhode Island, on Pawtuxet river 5 m. S of and adjoining Providence; pop. (1970c) 74,287; wire, rubber; breweries; settled 1636.

Craonne \ˈkrän\. Village, Aisne dept., N France, ab. 15 m. SE of Laon; pop. (1962c) 150; battle Mar. 7, 1814 in which Napoleon repulsed the Allies; in struggle for Chemin des Dames in World War I taken and retaken three times 1917 and 1918.

Cratère du Nouveau–Québec. See NEW QUEBEC CRATER.

Cra·ter Lake \ˈkrāt-ər-\. Lake in Cascade Mts., W Klamath co., S Oregon; ab. 6 m. long, 5 m. wide, and 1932 ft. deep; occupies caldera of Mt. Mazama, an extinct volcano; remarkable esp. for the intensity of color of the water; region has been set aside as **Crater Lake National Park** (see UNITED STATES, *National Parks*).

Crater Mound *or* **Me·te·or Crater** \ˌmēt-ē-ər-\ *also* **Coon Butte** \ˌkün-ˈbyüt\. Depression, SE Coconino co., Arizona, 20 m. W of Winslow; 4000 ft. in diameter, 600 ft. deep; encircled by a ridge 100–150 ft. high, containing loose pieces of rock and sand; many fragments of meteoric iron are found in the region; believed to be of meteoric origin; estimated age 50,000 years.

Crater Peak. Mountain, W Klamath co., S Oregon, S of Crater Lake; 7265 ft.

Cra·ters of the Moon National Monument \ˌkrāt-ərz-\. See UNITED STATES, *National Monuments.*

Cra·ti \ˈkrät-ē\ *or anc.* **Cra·this** \ˈkrā-thəs\. River, Calabria, S Italy; 58 m. long; rises S of Cosenza, flows to Gulf of Taranto; ancient Sybaris at its mouth.

Cra·to \ˈkra-(ˌ)tü\. City, S Ceará state, NE Brazil; munic. pop. (1968e) 63,029; a railroad terminus.

Cra·ven \ˈkrā-vən\. County in North Carolina. See table at NORTH CAROLINA.

Craw·ford \ˈkrȯ-fərd\. 1 Name of counties in eleven states of the U.S. See tables at ARKANSAS, GEORGIA, ILLINOIS, INDIANA, IOWA, KANSAS, MICHIGAN, MISSOURI, OHIO, PENNSYLVANIA, WISCONSIN.

2 City, Dawes co., NW Nebraska, 50 m. NW of Alliance; pop. (1970c) 1291; trade center in irrigated agricultural region.

Crawford Notch. Defile in White Mts. (*q.v.*) in NW Carroll co., New Hampshire, traversed by Saco river.

Craw·fords·ville \ˈkrȯ-fərdz-ˌvil\. Commercial city, ⊗ of Montgomery co., W cen. Indiana, 43 m. WNW of Indianapolis; pop. (1970c) 13,842; steel, foundry products, plastics; meat packing; Wabash Coll. (1832).

Craw·ford·ville \ˈkrȯ-fərd-ˌvil\. 1 Village, ⊗ of Wakulla co., NW Florida.

2 City, ⊗ of Taliaferro co., NE cen. Georgia; pop. (1970c) 735.

Craw·ley \ˈkrȯ-lē\. Urban district, West Sussex, S England; pop. (1971p) 67,517.

Cra·zy Mountains \ˌkrā-zē-\. Mountain group, Meager, Park, and Sweet Grass cos., S Montana; highest point, **Crazy Peak** 11,214 ft., is in N Sweet Grass co.

Cré·cy \krā-ˈsē, ˈkres-ē\ *or in full* **Crécy–en–Pon·thieu** \krā-ˈsē-äⁿ-pōⁿ-ˈtyə(r)\ *or Eng.* **Cres·sy** \ˈkres-ē\. Commune, Somme dept., N France, ab. 12 m. N of Abbeville; pop. (1962c) 1419; scene Aug. 26, 1346 of first decisive battle of Hundred Years' War, a victory for Edward III of England over Philip VI of Valois; noted for weapons and tactics of the English, who used longbows, small bombards, one of earliest forms of artillery, and dismounted men-at-arms; established England as a military power.

Cred·i·ton \ˈkred-i-tən\. Urban district, Devonshire, SW England, ab. 8 m. NW of Exeter; pop. (1971p) 5144; episcopal see 909–1049; important wool industries 13th–17th cents.

Cree \ˈkrē\. Lake, N Saskatchewan, Canada; 446 sq. m.; discharges through **Cree River** (ab. 90 m. long) to the Fond du Lac river.

Creede \ˈkrēd\. Town, ⊗ of Mineral co., S Colorado, in gorge of Rio Grande; pop. (1970c) 653; founded 1890 as mining camp (silver, gold, zinc).

Creek \ˈkrēk\. County in Oklahoma. See table at OKLAHOMA.

Creil \ˈkrā\. Commune, Oise dept., N France, on Oise river 28 m. N of Paris; pop. (1968c) 32,544; stone quarries.

Cre·ma \ˈkrā-mə, ˈkrem-ə\. Commune, Cremona prov., Lombardy, N Italy, on Serio river 23 m. NW of Cremona; pop. (1968e) 32,070; produces wine, silk, linen, lace; cathedral. Taken 1160 by Frederick Barbarossa; under Milan 1338–1453, Venice 1453–1797, and Austria 1815 until becoming part of the kingdom of Italy.

Cre·mo·na \krə-ˈmō-nə\. 1 Province of Lombardy, N Italy. See table at ITALY.

2 Fortified commune, its ✱, on Po river 49 m. ESE of Milan; pop. (1968e) 80,798; agricultural machinery, bricks; 12th cent. cathedral, 13th cent. palace; in 16th–18th cents. violins manufactured by the Amati and Guarnieri families and by Antonio Stradivari. Colonized by Romans 218 B.C. as fort against Gallic tribes; destroyed 69 A.D. by Vespasian, who helped rebuild it; medieval town incorporated by Milan 1334.

Cren·shaw \ˈkren-ˌshȯ\. County in Alabama. See table at ALABAMA.

Cré·py \krā-ˈpē\ *or in full* **Cré·py–en–Laon·nois** \-ˌäⁿ-läⁿ-ˈnwä\. Commune, Aisne dept., N France, ab. 6 m. NW of Laon; pop. (1962c) 1641; treaty of Crépy signed Sept. 18, 1544 bet. Francis I of France and Emperor Charles V.

Crépy–en–Va·lois \-äⁿ-val-ˈwä\. Commune, Oise dept., N France, ab. 16 m. S of Compiègne; pop. (1962c) 7417; ancient capital of Valois; remains of castle; church of Saint Denis.

Cres \ˈ(t)sres\ *or Ital.* **Cher·so** \ˈke(ə)r-(ˌ)sō\. Island in the Kvarner Gulf (Gulf of Quarnero), at the head of the Adriatic Sea; 158 sq. m.; pop. (1961c) 4113; belonged to Austria before World War I, to Italy 1919–47, since 1947 part of Croatia, NW Yugoslavia.

Cres·cent, Lake \-ˈkres-ᵊnt\. Lake, Clallam co., NW Washington, N of Olympic Mts.; source of the blueback trout (*Salmo beardsleei*).

Crescent City. City, ⊗ of Del Norte co., NW corner of California, on coast; pop. (1970c) 2586; lumber; dairy farms, fisheries.

Cres·co \ˈkres-(ˌ)kō\. City, ⊗ of Howard co., N Iowa, 18 m. WNW of Decorah; pop. (1970c) 3297; automobile parts; livestock.

Cress·kill \ˈkres-ˌkil\. Borough, Bergen co., NE corner of New Jersey, 11 m. E of Paterson; pop. (1970c) 8298.

Cressy. See CRÉCY.

Crest \ˈkrest\. Commune, Drôme dept., SE France; pop. (1962c) 6793; the keep of a 12th cent. castle (destroyed 17th cent.) used as a prison; makes silk, woolens, paper.

Crest Hill. City, Will co., NE Illinois, W of Hammond, Indiana; pop. (1970c) 7460.

Crest·line \ˈkrest-ˌlīn\. City, Crawford co., N cen. Ohio, 12 m. W of Mansfield; pop. (1970c) 5947; sporting equipment; dairy products.

Cres·ton \ˈkres-tən\. 1 City, ⊗ of Union co., S Iowa, 57 m. SW of Des Moines; pop. (1970c) 8234; corn; livestock; Southwestern Community Coll. (1926).

2 Town, British Columbia, Canada, 45 m. SE of Nelson; pop. (1971p) 3175; timber; agriculture.

Cres·tone Needle \ˈkres-tōn-\. Peak, Custer and Saguache cos., S cen. Colorado; 14,130 ft.

Crestone Peak. Peak, Custer and Saguache cos., S cen. Colorado; 14,294 ft.

Crest·view \ˈkrest-ˌvyü\. City, ⊗ of Okaloosa co., NW Florida, 47 m. ENE of Pensacola; pop. (1970c) 7952; sawmills; pecans.

Crest·wood \'krest-ˌwu̇d\. 1 Village, Cook co., NE Illinois, 17 m. SSW of Chicago; pop. (1970c) 5770.
2 City, St. Louis co., E Missouri; pop. (1970c) 15,398.

Crete \'krēt\. 1 Village, Will co., NE Illinois, 30 m. S of Chicago; pop. (1970c) 4656; diversified farming.
2 City, Saline co., SE Nebraska, 19 m. SW of Lincoln; pop. (1970c) 4444; flour mills; Doane Coll. (1872).
3 *or Gk.* **Krí·ti** \'krē-tē\; *anc.* **Cre·ta** \'krēt-ə\ *also* **Can·dia** \'kan-dē-ə\. Greek island in E Mediterranean Sea, SSE of Greece; ab. 160 m. long and from 6 to 35 m. wide; 3189 sq. m.; pop. (1961c) 483,075; ✻ Canea; with several smaller islands forms an administrative division of Greece, comprising the departments of Canea, Hērákleion, Lasithion, and Rethýmnē. Has high central range of mountains, highest Ida 8058 ft.; many short streams, watering districts that produce various fruits; olives, barley, oats; has several prominent capes (as Busa, Krio, Sidero) and is indented by many bays, esp. Suda, Canea, Messara; chief towns Canea, Candia, Rethymnon.
History: Developed an advanced civilization which was based upon copper and bronze (Early Minoan or Aegean) c. 3000–2100 B.C.; c. 2000 B.C. its cities Knossos and Phaistos centers of Cretan dynasties; its culture expanded to islands and to mainland (Middle Minoan) c. 2100–1600 B.C.; ab. 16th cent. B.C., the cultural center of Aegean and eastern Mediterranean (see MYCENAE and TIRYNS); decline hastened by invasion from mainland c. 1400 B.C. and later under pressure of Greeks; 67 B.C. annexed to Rome for having given aid to pirates of Cilicia; part of Byzantine Empire; became headquarters of Saracen pirates in 9th cent. A.D.; reconquered for Byzantines by Nicephorus Phocas 960–961; sold to Venice by Boniface III, Count of Montferrat, a leader of 4th Crusade (1202–04); conquered 1669 by Ottoman Turks who completed Venetian expulsion 1715. In late 19th cent., sought independence and annexation to Greece; by Pact of Halepa 1878 received practical self-government (see HALEPA); after three unsuccessful revolts, obtained assistance of Greece 1896 (cause of Greco-Turkish War 1897); occupied by forces of powers 1898; semi-independent state, preliminary union with Greece 1908, and final annexation 1913. In World War II captured by German airborne forces May 20–30, 1941, first successful use of airborne forces in a major campaign.

Crete, Sea of *or formerly* **Sea of Can·dia** \-'kan-dē-ə\ *or Gk.* **Krē·ti·kòn Pé·la·gos** \ˌkrēt-i-ˌkȯn-'pal-ə-ˌgȯs\. Part of the E Mediterranean Sea N of Crete and S of the Cyclades Is.

Crête de la Neige. See NEIGE, CRÊTE DE LA.

Cré·teil \krā-'tā\. Commune, ✻ of Val-de-Marne dept., N France, SE suburb of Paris on Marne river; pop. (1968c) 49,197; battle during siege of Paris 1870.

Creus, Cape \-'krā-əs\. Cape on extreme NE coast of Spain; W limit of Gulf of Lions.

Creuse \'krə(r)z, 'krüz\. 1 River, France; 160 m. long; rises in Creuse dept., flows NW into Vienne river.
2 Department of cen. France. See table at FRANCE.

Creusot, Le. See LE CREUSOT.

Creutz·wald *or formerly* **Creutzwald–la–Croix** \'krə(r)ts-ˌväld-lä-krə-'wä\. Commune, Moselle dept., NE France; pop. (1968c) 14,471.

Creux \'krər\. Chief landing place on the island of Sark, Channel Is.

Cre·val·co·re \ˌkrā-väl-'kō-rā\. Commune, Bologna prov., Emilia-Romagna, N Italy; pop. (1968e) 12,355.

Creve Coeur. 1 \'krēv-'ku̇(ə)r\. Village, Tazewell co., cen. Illinois; pop. (1970c) 6440.
2 \'krēv-ˌkō(ə)r, -ˌkär\. City, St. Louis co., E Missouri, W of St. Louis; pop. (1970c) 8897.

Cre·vil·len·te \ˌkrā-vē(l)-'yän-tē\. Commune, Alicante prov., SE Spain, 20 m. SW of Alicante; pop. (1970p) 16,901.

Crewe \'krü\. 1 Town, Nottoway co., S cen. Virginia, 42 m. W of Petersburg; pop. (1970c) 1767; hosiery manufactures.
2 Municipal borough, Cheshire, NW England, 30 m. SE of Liverpool; pop. (1971p) 51,302; important railroad center; manufactures locomotives and railroad cars. A hamlet in 1840; incorporated 1877.

Crick·lade \'krik-(ˌ)lād\. Market town, Wiltshire, England, on the Thames 9 m. NW of Swindon; pop. (1961c) 1425; very old, mentioned in *Anglo-Saxon Chronicle.*

Crieff \'krēf\. Burgh, Perth co., cen. Scotland; pop. (1971p) 5604; health resort; before 1770 scene of famous cattle fair.

Cril·lon, Mount \-'kril-ən\. Peak, S Alaska, on Fairweather Penin. S of Mt. Fairweather; 12,736 ft.; summit reached for first time July 19, 1934.

Cri·me·an Oblast \krī-'mē-ən-'ō-bləst, krə-, -ˌblast\ *also* **Cri·mea** \krī-'mē-ə, krə-\ *or Russ.* **Krym** \'krim\. Subdivision of the Ukrainian S.S.R., U.S.S.R.; 10,425 sq. m.; pop. (1970p) 1,814,000; ✻ Simferopol; a peninsula extending into the Black Sea and having the Sea of Azov to the NE; joined to mainland by isthmus of Perekop which has Karkinit Bay on W and Sivash or Putrid Sea on E; its E extension is the Kerch Penin., separated from Soviet mainland (Krasnodar Krai) by Kerch Strait, the entrance to the Sea of Azov; from W end of Kerch Penin. a long narrow spit of land, the Arabat, extends NW bet. Sea of Azov and the Sivash; N two thirds is steppe country, with good soil for agriculture; along SE shore extends the Yaila Range reaching a height of 5000 ft.; its rivers are short unnavigable streams. Chief products: Wheat, corn, tobacco, flowers; livestock raising, fishing; vineyards; iron ore; tourism. Chief towns: Simferopol, Sevastopol, Kerch, Yevpatoriya.
History: Inhabitants in very early times (8th cent. B.C.) were Cimmerians, who were expelled by Scythians 7th cent.; settled on the southern coast 6th cent. B.C. (see KERCH and FEODOSIYA) by Greek traders; in early 5th cent. B.C., seat of Greek kingdom of the Cimmerian Bosporus with which Athens had extensive commercial relations; invaded by Goths, Huns, and by Khazars, who held Crimean part of their kingdom in southern Russia from ab. 7th cent. A.D. to 10th cent.; Greek coastal towns (theme of Cherson) in Byzantine Empire until c. 1000; after Tatar invasion 13th cent. belonged to Khanate of Golden Horde (see RUSSIA); 15th cent. became independent Khanate of Crimea which at first extended beyond the peninsula; southeast coastal strip held by Genoese; Tatar khanate overthrown by Ottoman Turks 1475; recognized as Russian dependency in Treaty of Kuchuk Kainarji 1774; incorporated by Russia 1783. Scene of Crimean War (England, France, Sardinia against Russia) 1854–56; proclaimed independent Crimean Republic 1918; became an autonomous republic of the Russian S.F.S.R. 1921; in World War II overrun by Nazi armies in fall of 1941 (see SEVASTOPOL); isolated by Soviet troops Oct. 1943 and retaken Mar.–May 1944; republic liquidated 1945 for collaboration with Nazis, and status changed to oblast; reconstituted as a Ukrainian oblast 1954. See YALTA.

Cri·mi·sus \krə-'mī-səs\ *or* **Cri·mis·sus** \-'mis-əs\. River, W Sicily, Italy; scene of battle in which Timoleon defeated the Carthaginians 341 B.C.

Crim·mit·schau *or* **Krim·mit·schau** \'krim-ət-ˌshau̇\. Manufacturing city in Karl-Marx-Stadt dist., East Germany, 36 m. S of Leipzig; pop. (1970e) 29,932; textiles; church (14th cent., rebuilt 16th cent.).

Crip·ple Creek \'krip-əl-\. City, ⊗ of Teller co., cen. Colorado, SW of Colorado Springs; pop. (1970c) 425; in a major gold-producing district.

Cri·sa \'krī-sə\. Ancient city of Phocis, cen. Greece, near Delphi and bet. it and its port on the Gulf of Corinth; destroyed by Amphictyonic Council in First Sacred War c. 590 B.C.; its rebuilding by Amphissa brought on Fourth Sacred War 339 B.C. See DELPHI 2.

Cris·field \'kris-ˌfēld\. City, Somerset co., SE Maryland, on Chesapeake Bay 32 m. SW of Salisbury; pop. (1970c) 3078; shipping point for oysters, crabs, and fish.

Crisp \'krisp\. County in Georgia. See table at GEORGIA.

Cris·to·bal *or Span.* **Cris·tó·bal** \kris-'tō-bəl\. 1 District in NW Canal Zone; pop. (1970p) 11,600.

2 Town in the district, at Atlantic entrance to Panama Canal; a suburb of Colón and Rainbow City.

Cristóbal Co·lón, Pi·co \ˈpē-(ˌ)kō-kris-ˌtō-bəl-kə-ˈlōn\. Peak in Sierra Nevada de Santa Marta, N Colombia; 19,020 ft.; highest peak in Colombia.

Crit·ten·den \ˈkrit-ən-dən\. Counties in two states of the U.S. See tables at ARKANSAS and KENTUCKY.

Cr·na \ˈ(t)sər-nə\ *or* **Cher·na** \ˈcher-nə\. River, S Yugoslavia; 125 m. long; flows SE and N into Vardar river.

Crna Gora. See MONTENEGRO 1.

Croagh Pat·rick \krō-ˈpa-trik\. Mountain in S co. Mayo, W Eire; 2510 ft.; according to tradition, place where Saint Patrick began his missionary work in Ireland.

Cro·atan Sound \ˌkrō-ə-ˈtan-\. Strait bet. Roanoke I. and the mainland of Dare co., E North Carolina.

Cro·a·tia \krō-ˈā-sh(ē-)ə\ *or Serb.* **Hr·vat·ska** \hər-ˈvät-skä\. A constituent republic of Yugoslavia; 21,829 sq. m.; pop. (1971p) 4,422,564; ✱ Zagreb; fruit, livestock; bauxite, coal, oil; tourism. Chief towns: Zagreb, Rijeka, Split, Osijek. Boundaries have varied greatly at different periods: as medieval kingdom extended at times NE to the Drava and S to Montenegro; as separate county 1939 included coastal region as far S as Mostar, and in World War II under German rule included territory around Banja Luka.

History: For earlier history of region, see PANNONIA. From 7th cent. AD., inhabited by Croats, a south Slavic people, whom Charlemagne made tributary to Franks; formed into kingdom under Tomislav 924; joined with Hungary in dynastic union (1102), whence the Croats became westernized and separated from Slavs under Serbian influence; retained autonomy under Hungarian crown; with Slavonia taken by Turks in 16th cent., N part restored by Treaty of Karlowitz 1699; parts of Croatia included in Napoleon's Illyrian Provinces (*q.v.*) 1809–13; helped Austria to put down Hungarian revolution 1848–49 and as a result set up with Slavonia as separate Austrian crownland **Croatia and Sla·vo·nia** \-slə-ˈvō-nē-ə, -nyə\ which was reunited to Hungary as part of *Ausgleich* 1867 (see AUSTRIA-HUNGARY) and set up as a Hungarian crownland; became a leader in prewar agitation 1912–14 of South Slavs for independence from Austria-Hungary, and united with other Yugoslav areas to proclaim kingdom of Serbs, Croats, and Slovenes 1918 (see YUGOSLAVIA); at reorganization of Yugoslavia 1929 Croatia and Slavonia became Savska co., which in 1939 was united with Primorje co. to form county of Croatia; nominally independent state 1941–45; became a constituent republic in 1946 constitution.

Crock·ett \ˈkräk-ət\. 1 Name of counties in two states of the U.S. See tables at TENNESSEE and TEXAS.

2 City, ⊗ of Houston co., E Texas, 32 m. S of Palestine; pop. (1970c) 6616; cottonseed-oil mills, lumber mills; pecans.

Croc·o·dile \ˈkräk-ə-ˌdīl\. 1 River, Africa. See LIMPOPO

2 A headstream of the Komati river, Transvaal, Rep. of South Africa.

Crocodilopolis. See ARSINOË 2.

Croia. See KRUJË.

Croi·silles \krwä-ˈzē\. Village, Pas-de-Calais dept., N France, 8 m. SE of Arras; pop. (1962c) 715; destroyed during World War I in battles of 1917–18.

Croix \ˈkrwä\. Industrial commune, Nord dept., N France, NE suburb of Lille; pop. (1968c) 21,424; metalworks, dyeworks, breweries.

Cro·ker Island \ˌkrō-kər-\. Island off N coast of Cobourg Penin., Northern Territory, Australia; 30 m. long.

Cro–Magnon. See EYZIES, LES.

Crom·ar·ty Firth \ˌkräm-ərt-ē-\. Inlet of Moray Firth, Ross and Cromarty co., N Scotland.

Cro·mer \ˈkrō-mər\. Urban district, Norfolk, England, on North Sea coast 24 m. N of Norwich; pop. (1971p) 5336; coast guard and lifeboat station.

Cromp·ton \ˈkrəm(p)-tən\. Urban district, Lancashire, NW England, NE of Manchester; pop. (1971p) 17,027.

Crom·well \ˈkräm-ˌwel, -wəl\. 1 Town, NW Middlesex co., S Connecticut, on Connecticut river; pop. (1970c) 7400; Holy Apostles Seminary (1956); incorporated 1851.

2 Borough, S South I., New Zealand, on upper Clutha river in lake region; pop. (1968e) 1100.

Cronstadt. See KRONSHLOT.

Cro·nul·la \krō-ˈnəl-ə\. Coastal village, New South Wales, Australia, 13 m. S of Sydney.

Crook \ˈkru̇k\. Name of counties in two states of the U.S. See tables at OREGON and WYOMING.

Crook and Wil·ling·ton \-ˈwil-iŋ-tən\. Urban district, Durham, N England, 20 m. SSW of Newcastle upon Tyne; pop. (1971p) 21,485.

Crook·ed \ˈkru̇k-əd\. River, cen. Oregon; 105 m. long; flows W and NW into Deschutes river.

Crooked Creek. River, SW Illinois; ab. 50 m. long; flows into Kaskaskia river.

Crooked Island. One of the Bahama Is., in cen. part of group S of San Salvador (Watlings I.); 76 sq. m.; pop. (1963c) 766.

Crooked Island Passage. Deep-water channel in the Bahama Is., S and SE of Long I. and NW of Crooked I. and Acklins I.; ab. 40 m. wide.

Crooked Lake. See KEUKA LAKE.

Crooks·ton \ˈkru̇k-stən\. City, ⊗ of Polk co., NW Minnesota, 32 m. SW of Thief River Falls; pop. (1970c) 8312; livestock; wheat, sugar beets; Corbett Coll. (1957).

Crooks·ville \ˈkru̇ks-ˌvil\. Village, Perry co., SE cen. Ohio, 13 m. S of Zanesville; pop. (1970c) 2828; chinaware, tile; coal mines, clay deposits.

Crop·redy \ˈkräp-ˌred-ē\. Village, N Oxfordshire, cen. England, ab. 3½ m. N of Banbury; pop. (1961c) 409; scene of battle (Cropredy Bridge) June 29, 1644 in which the Royalists defeated the Parliamentarians under Sir William Waller.

Cros·by \ˈkrȯz-bē\. 1 County, Texas. See table at TEXAS.

2 Village, Crow Wing co., cen. Minnesota, 16 m. NE of Brainerd; pop. (1970c) 2241; iron and manganese mining.

3 City, ⊗ of Divide co., NW North Dakota; pop. (1970c) 1545.

4 *or* **Great Crosby.** Municipal borough, Lancashire, NW England, on Irish Sea at mouth of the Mersey 6 m. NNW of Liverpool; pop. (1971p) 57,405.

Crosby, Mount. Peak, S Park co., NW Wyoming; 12,435 ft.

Cros·by·ton \ˈkrȯz-bēt-ᵊn\. City, ⊗ of Crosby co., NW Texas, E of Lubbock; pop. (1970c) 2251; grain.

Cross \ˈkrȯs\. 1 County in Arkansas. See table at ARKANSAS.

2 River, Cameroon and Nigeria, W Africa; ab. 300 m. long; flows W and S to Bight of Biafra.

Cross, Cape. Cape on NW coast of South-West Africa; point farthest S (22°S) reached by Diogo Cam 1484; stone cross erected here by him.

Cross Bay. Bay on NW coast of Spitsbergen I., Norway.

Cross City. Town, ⊗ of Dixie co., NW Florida penin., 50 m. W of Gainesville; pop. (1970c) 2268; lumber center.

Cros·sett \ˈkrȯs-ət\. City, Ashley co., SE Arkansas, 42 m. E of El Dorado; pop. (1970c) 6191; lumber.

Cross Fell. See PENNINE CHAIN.

Cross–Florida Waterway *or officially* **Okee·cho·bee Water·way** \ˌō-kə-ˌchō-bē-\. Waterways linking the Atlantic coast at Stuart, Florida, with the Gulf of Mexico at the mouth of the Caloosahatchee river by way of St. Lucie Canal, Lake Okeechobee, and Lake Hicpochee.

Cross Keys \-ˌkēz\. Formerly a post village, S Rockingham co., Virginia, 20 m. NE of Staunton; battle June 8, 1862 in which Confederates under Gen. Ewell defeated Union troops under General Frémont.

Cross Mountain. Peak in Sierra Nevada, in N Tulare co., S cen. California; 12,140 ft.

Cross River. See CROSS 2.

Cross Sound. Inlet of Pacific Ocean bet. SE Alaska and N Chichagof I.; joins S end of Glacier Bay.

Cross·ville \ˈkrȯs-ˌvil\. Town, ⊗ of Cumberland co., E cen. Tennessee, 28 m. W of Harriman; pop. (1970c) 5381; rubber products, appliances, knit goods.

Cro·ton \ˈkrōt-ᵊn\. River, SE New York; ab. 60 m. long; flows from Dutchess co. S and SW through Putnam and Westchester cos. into Hudson river; important source of water supply for New York City since 1842, when **Croton Aqueduct** (tunnel 31 m. long when completed) first brought in water from original reservoir near its mouth; now contains a system of dams and reservoirs including Croton Falls and New Croton.

Cro·to·ne \krə-ˈtō-nē\ *or sometimes* **Co·tro·ne** \kə-ˈtrō-nē\; *anc.* **Cro·to·na** \krə-ˈtō-nə\ *or* **Cro·ton** \ˈkrō-ˌtän, ˈkrōt-ᵊn\. Commune, Catanzaro prov., Calabria, S Italy, on Gulf of Taranto; pop. (1968e) 49,732; cathedral; old castle. Ancient Greek republic, founded by Achaeans c. 700 B.C.; home of Milo and, 540–530 B.C., of Pythagoras; scene of battles before and during Second Punic War; scene of defeat of Otto II by Byzantines and Saracens 982 A.D.

Croton Falls Dam \ˌkrōt-ᵊn-\. Dam across west branch of Croton river, Putnam co., SE New York, height 167 ft.; completed 1911; forms **Croton Falls Reservoir,** part of Croton system of water supply for New York City.

Croton–on–Hud·son \-ˈhəd-sən\. Village, Westchester co., SE New York, on Hudson river, 34 m. N of New York; pop. (1970c) 7523.

Crow \ˈkrō\. River, S Minnesota; ab. 50 m. long; flows NE into Mississippi river above Anoka; formed by junction of North Fork and South Fork on boundary bet. Hennepin and Wright cos.

Crow·ell \ˈkrō-əl\. City, ⊗ of Foard co., N Texas, 30 m. SW of Vernon; pop. (1970c) 1399; grain, stock, poultry.

Crow·ley \ˈkrau̇-lē\. 1 County in Colorado. See table at COLORADO.

2 City, ⊗ of Acadia parish, S Louisiana, 24 m. W of Lafayette; pop. (1970c) 16,104; rice mills.

3 City, Tarrant co., N Texas, 10 m. S of Fort Worth; pop. (1970c) 2662.

Crown Mountain \ˈkrau̇n-\. 1 Peak, Hinsdale and San Juan cos., SW Colorado; 13,600 ft.

2 Peak, S Brewster co., W Texas; 7186 ft.

3 *or* **Crown Hill.** Peak, W cen. St. Thomas I., in the Virgin Is. of the United States, West Indies; 1556 ft.; highest point in the Virgin Is.; Marine air base nearby.

Crown Point. 1 City, ⊗ of Lake co., NW corner of Indiana, 13 m. S of Lake Michigan; pop. (1970c) 10,931; wheat, oats.

2 Town, Essex co., NE New York, on W shore of S part of Lake Champlain ab. 7 m. S of Ticonderoga; pop. (1970c) 1789; became an English trading post 1714 and strategic point on route from New York to Canada; called **Pointe à la Che·ve·lure** \pwaⁿ-tä-lä-shev-(ə-)lu̅e̅r\ (Scalp Point) by the French who built Fort St. Frédéric here 1731 as proposed capital of territory; goal of expedition led by Sir Wm. Johnson 1755 ending in battle of Lake George; taken by Gen. Jeffrey Amherst 1759 who began Fort Amherst (renamed Fort Crown Point); captured by Seth Warner and Green Mountain Boys 1775; again held by British 1777 until after defeat at Saratoga; seat of Crown Point Reservation (includes ruins of forts, etc.).

Crown Prince Range. Mountain range in S part of Bougainville I., NW Solomon Is.; highest peak 7383 ft.

Crown Prince Rudolf Island \-ˈrü-ˌdȯlf-\. Northernmost island of Franz Josef Land, Arctic Ocean.

Crown Princess Martha Land. See PRINCESS MARTHA COAST.

Crow Peak \ˈkrō-\. Mountain, Lawrence co., W South Dakota; 5772 ft.

Crow's Nest \ˈkrōz-ˌnest\. Mountain, Orange co., New York, on W bank of Hudson above West Point; 1396 ft.

Crows·nest Pass \ˌkrōz-ˌnest-\. Pass through the Rocky Mts., in SE British Columbia, Canada, on Alberta border; lat. 49°35′N; alt. 5500 ft.

Crows Nest Peak. Mountain, Pennington co., SW South Dakota; 7048 ft.

Crow Wing \ˈkrō-ˌwiŋ\. 1 River, Minnesota; formed by branches in N Wadena co., cen. Minnesota; flows SE and E into the Mississippi on SW boundary of Crow Wing co.

2 County in Minnesota. See table at MINNESOTA.

Croy·don \ˈkrȯid-ᵊn\. A borough of Greater London, SE England. See table at LONDON 4.

Cro·zet Islands \krō-ˈzā-\. Five small French islands in S Indian Ocean, lat. 46°S and long. 52°E; 195 sq. m.; discovered 1772 by Marion-Dufresne.

Cruachan, Ben. See BEN CRUACHAN.

Cru·ces \ˈkrü-səs\. Town and municipality, Las Villas prov., W cen. Cuba; munic. pop. (1967e) 26,790.

Crum El·bow \ˌkrəm-ˈel-(ˌ)bō\. Double bend in Hudson river ab. 4 m. above Poughkeepsie, New York.

Crum·mock Water \ˈkrəm-ək-\. Lake in Cumberland co., NW England; 2½ m. long, maximum depth 144 ft.

Cruz, Cape \-ˈkrüz\. Cape at SW point of Oriente prov., E Cuba, projecting into Caribbean Sea.

Cruz, Point. Small coral promontory just W of mouth of Mataniko river, NW coast of Guadalcanal I., SE Solomon Is.; in World War II scene of considerable fighting, esp. in Oct. and Nov. 1942.

Cruz Al·ta \krü-ˈzäl-tə\. City, Rio Grande do Sul state, S Brazil; munic. pop. (1968e) 54,447.

Cruz Bay. Town at W end of St. John I., Virgin Is. of the United States, West Indies.

Cruz del Eje \-del-ˈā-hē\. Town, Córdoba prov., N cen. Argentina; pop. (1960c) 22,026.

Cruzeiro. See JOACABA.

Cruz Gran·de \-ˈgränd-ē\. Seaport, Coquimbo prov., cen. Chile, 32 m. N of Coquimbo; pop. (1960c) 478; subdivision of **La Hi·gue·ra** \ˌlä-ē-ˈger-ə\ commune (pop. 7052); shipping point for iron ore from the nearby mines of El Tofo.

Crys·tal \ˈkrist-ᵊl\. Village, Hennepin co., SE cen. Minnesota, 15 m. W of Minneapolis; pop. (1970c) 30,295.

Crystal Beach. Village, Welland co., Ontario, Canada, on shore of Lake Erie; pop. (1968e) 2037; bathing, amusement park.

Crystal City. 1 City, Jefferson co., E Missouri, on Mississippi river 30 m. S of St. Louis; pop. (1970c) 3898.

2 City, ⊗ of Zavala co., S Texas, 35 m. S of Uvalde; pop. (1970c) 8104; shipping center for winter garden area growing esp. spinach.

Crystal Falls. City, ⊗ of Iron co., SW Michigan penin., 23 m. NNW of Iron Mountain (city); pop. (1970c) 2000; iron mines of the Menominee Range area.

Crystal Lake. City, McHenry co., N Illinois, 28 m. WSW of Waukegan; pop. (1970c) 14,541; McHenry County Coll. (1967); summer resort.

Crystal Springs. City, Copiah co., SW Mississippi, 23 m. SSW of Jackson; pop. (1970c) 4195; ships tomatoes.

Csallóköz. See GREAT SCHÜTT.

Cse·pel \ˈchep-ˌel\. 1 Island in Danube river S of Budapest, cen. Hungary; 30 m. long.

2 Industrial commune on N tip of Csepel island; incorporated with Budapest 1950.

Cson·grád \ˈchōn-ˌgräd\. 1 County of S Hungary. See table at HUNGARY.

2 City, Csongrád co., S Hungary, at the confluence of the Körös and Tisza rivers; pop. (1970p) 20,331; market center for farm products, cattle, and wine.

Ctes·i·phon \ˈtes-ə-ˌfän, ˈtē-sə-\. Ancient ruined city in cen. Iraq, on E bank of the Tigris opp. Seleucia and 20 m. SSE of Baghdad; capital of the ancient kingdom of Parthia (*q.v.*) and of later Sassanid empire (see IRAN); part of the great vaulted hall of this later period still standing. Captured by Arabs 637 A.D.; declined after building of Arab capital at Baghdad (*q.v.*); scene of battle won by Turks over the British Nov. 21, 1915.

Cua·ji·mal·pa \ˌkwä-hē-ˈmäl-pə\. Municipality, Federal Dist., Mexico, 11 m. SW of Mexico City; pop. (1970p) 35,202; lumber, agriculture.

Cuando. See KWANDO.

Cuango. See KWANGO.

Cuan·za *or* **Kwan·za** \ˈkwän-zə\. River, cen. Angola, SW Africa; 600 m. long; rises in S cen. Angola, flows NW into Atlantic Ocean near Luanda.

Cuauh·té·moc \kwau̇-ˈtā-(ˌ)mäk\. Municipality, Chihuahua state, Mexico, 55 m. W of Chihuahua; pop. (1970p) 65,160.

Cuau·ti·tlán \ˌkwau̇-tē-ˈtlän\. Municipality, México state, Mexico, 23 m. N of Mexico City; pop. (1970p) 40,622; textiles, fertilizers; dairy farming; ruins of Franciscan convent (1527); ancient Chichimec city.

Cuau·tla \ˈkwau̇-tlə\. Town, Morelos state, S cen. Mexico, ab. 18 m. SE of Cuernavaca; munic. pop. (1970p) 67,869; alt. 4350 ft.; sulfur springs; resort.

Cu·ba \ˈkyü-bə\. 1 Island in the Greater Antilles, West Indies, S of Florida and N of W Caribbean Sea; with adjacent islands forms **Republic of Cuba** (44,218 sq. m.; pop. [1970p] 8,523,292; ✱ Havana); island 746 m. long from Cape Maisí on E to Cape San Antonio on W; varies in width from 25 to 125 m.; has coastline of ab. 2000 m. with many cays and islands (largest Isle of Pines off SW); largely flat or rolling country; highest point in Oriente prov. (Pico Turquino 6560 ft.); rivers mostly short and rapid. *Chief export:* Sugar; other products: tobacco, nickel, manganese; livestock raising, fishing; manufacturing: food processing (esp. sugar refining), tobacco products, textiles. *Chief cities:* Havana, Santiago de Cuba, Camagüey, Santa Clara, Guantánamo. Divided into the following six provinces (for pronunciation of their names, see their individual entries):

NAME	AREA (sq. m.)	POP. (1970p)	CAPITAL
Camagüey	10,172	813,204	Camagüey
La Habana	3,174	2,305,241	Havana
Las Villas	8,267	1,362,179	Santa Clara
Matanzas	3,260	501,273	Matanzas
Oriente	14,132	2,998,972	Santiago de Cuba
Pinar del Río	5,212	542,423	Pinar del Río

History: Discovered by Columbus on his first voyage 1492; conquered by Spanish under Velásquez 1511, present site of Havana settled 1519; part of viceroyalty of New Spain; Havana captured by British 1762, but restored to Spain 1763; became captaincy general 1777 and entered prosperous period under Las Casas from 1790; revolted unsuccessfully 1868–78; rose again in 1895, as result of which United States entered Spanish-American War 1898; in 1901 adopted constitution including Platt Amendment which made Cuba virtually a protectorate of U.S.; took over government May 20, 1902 from American military authorities; occupied by U.S. marines 1906–09 and on other occasions; entered World War I 1917; joined League of Nations 1920; given full claim to Isle of Pines 1925; under President Machado 1925–33; Cuban sovereignty unrestricted after U.S. abrogation of Platt Amendment and certain treaty rights 1934; began operation of new constitution 1940 (suspended 1959); declared war on Axis powers Dec. 9 and 11, 1941. Regime of President Fulgencio Batista y Zaldívar fell Jan. 1959 to forces of Fidel Castro, who proclaimed Cuba a Communist state 1961; following sharp U.S. reaction U.S.S.R. forced to remove its missiles from Cuban soil 1962; inability to meet stated production goal of ten million tons of sugar (exported chiefly to U.S.S.R. in return for economic support) conceded by regime 1970.

2 City, Fulton co., W cen. Illinois, 35 m. WSW of Peoria; pop. (1970c) 1581.

3 Village, Allegany co., SW New York, 13 m. NE of Olean; pop. (1970c) 1735.

Cubango. See OKOVANGO.

Cu·buk \chə-ˈbu̇k\. 1 River, tributary of the Ankara, N Turkey; 52 m. long; dam and reservoir (completed 1935) furnish water for irrigation in region around Ankara.

2 Town on river 8 m. N of Ankara.

Cuck·field \ˈkək-ˌfēld\. Urban district, East Sussex co., S England; pop. (1971p) 25,888.

Cú·cu·ta \ˈkü-kət-ə\ *also* **San Jo·sé de Cúcuta** \ˌsən-ə-ˈzā-də-\. City, ✱ of Norte de Santander dept., N Colombia, near the Venezuelan border, on Colombia-Venezuela highway; pop. (1968e) 167,404; destroyed by earthquake 1875, rebuilt.

Cud·a·hy \ˈkəd-ə-(ˌ)hē\. 1 City, Los Angeles co., SW California, 20 m. SE of Los Angeles; pop. (1970c) 16,998.

2 City, Milwaukee co., SE Wisconsin, on Lake Michigan 7 m. S of Milwaukee; pop. (1970c) 22,078; meat packing, tanning; foundry products.

Cud·da·lore \ˈkəd-ᵊl-ˌō(ə)r, -ˌȯ(ə)r\. Town, E Tamil Nadu, S India, on Coromandel Coast 18 m. S of Pondicherry; pop. (1961c) 79,168; seaport with mostly coastal trade; exports sugar, oilseeds and oil cake; health resort. Just to the N are ruins of Fort St. David (*q.v.*).

Cud·da·pah \ˈkəd-ə-pə\. Town, SW Andhra Pradesh, S India, near Penner river 140 m. NW of Madras; pop. (1961c) 49,027; former capital of nawabs of Cuddapah.

Cu·di·lle·ro \ˌkü-di-ˈyer-(ˌ)ō, -t͟hi-\. Commune, Oviedo prov., NW Spain, on Bay of Biscay 22 m. NW of Oviedo; pop. (1970p) 10,568; manganese mines nearby.

Cud·worth \ˈkəd-(ˌ)wərth\. Urban district, West Riding, Yorkshire, N England; pop. (1971p) 8838.

Cuen·ca \ˈkweŋ-kə\. 1 City, ✱ of Azuay prov., S Ecuador, ab. 68 m. SE of Guayaquil; pop. (1970e) 77,300; alt. 8468 ft.; Panama hats, leather, textiles; univ. (1867), cathedral; founded by Spanish 1557 on site of native town called Tumibamba; made episcopal see 1786.

2 Province of cen. Spain. See table at SPAIN.

3 *or anc.* **Con·ca** \ˈkȯŋ-kə\. Commune, ✱ of Cuenca prov., E cen. Spain, on Júcar river 89 m. ESE of Madrid; pop. (1970p) 34,485; castle; 13th cent. Gothic cathedral; built by Moors; captured by Alfonso VIII of Castile 1177; made municipality 1257; under attack by English 1706, by French 1808 and 1810, and by Carlists 1874.

Cuenca, Serranía de. See SERRANÍA DE CUENCA.

Cuen·ca·mé \ˌkweŋ-kə-ˈmā\. Municipality, Durango state, Mexico, 90 m. NE of Durango; pop. (1970p) 31,170.

Cuera. See CHUR.

Cuer·na·va·ca \ˌkwer-nə-ˈväk-ə, -ˈvak-\. Town, ✱ of Morelos state, S cen. Mexico; pop. (1969e) 44,278; alt. 5058 ft.; univ. (1938); Cacahuamilpa Caverns, among largest in North America, are nearby; resort.

Cuer·nos of Ne·gros \ˈkwer-nəs . . . ˈnā-grəs\. Highest peak in Negros Oriental prov., Negros, Phil., in SE part W of Dumaguete; 6101 ft.

Cue·ro \ˈkwe(ə)r-(ˌ)ō\. City, ⊗ of De Witt co., S Texas, on Guadalupe river 27 m. NNW of Victoria; pop. (1970c) 6956; center for cotton-growing and turkey-raising area.

Cuers \ku̇-ˈwe(ə)r\. Commune, Var dept., SE France, N of Hyères; pop. (1962c) 4697; **Cuers–Pierre·feu** \-pyer-ˈfə(r)\ airdrome bet. Cuers and commune of Pierrefeu to the E.

Cuesmes \ˈkwem\. Commune, Hainaut prov., SW Belgium; pop. (1969e) 11,450; coal mines.

Cuet·za·lán \ˌkwet-sə-ˈlän\ *or in full* **Cuetzalán del Pro·gre·so** \-del-prə-ˈgres-(ˌ)ō\. Municipality, Puebla state, SE cen. Mexico; pop. (1970p) 24,644.

Cue·vas del Al·man·zo·ra \ˈkwā-vəs-del-ˌäl-mən-ˈzo(ə)r-ə\ *or formerly* **Cuevas de Ve·ra** \-də-ˈver-ə\. Commune,

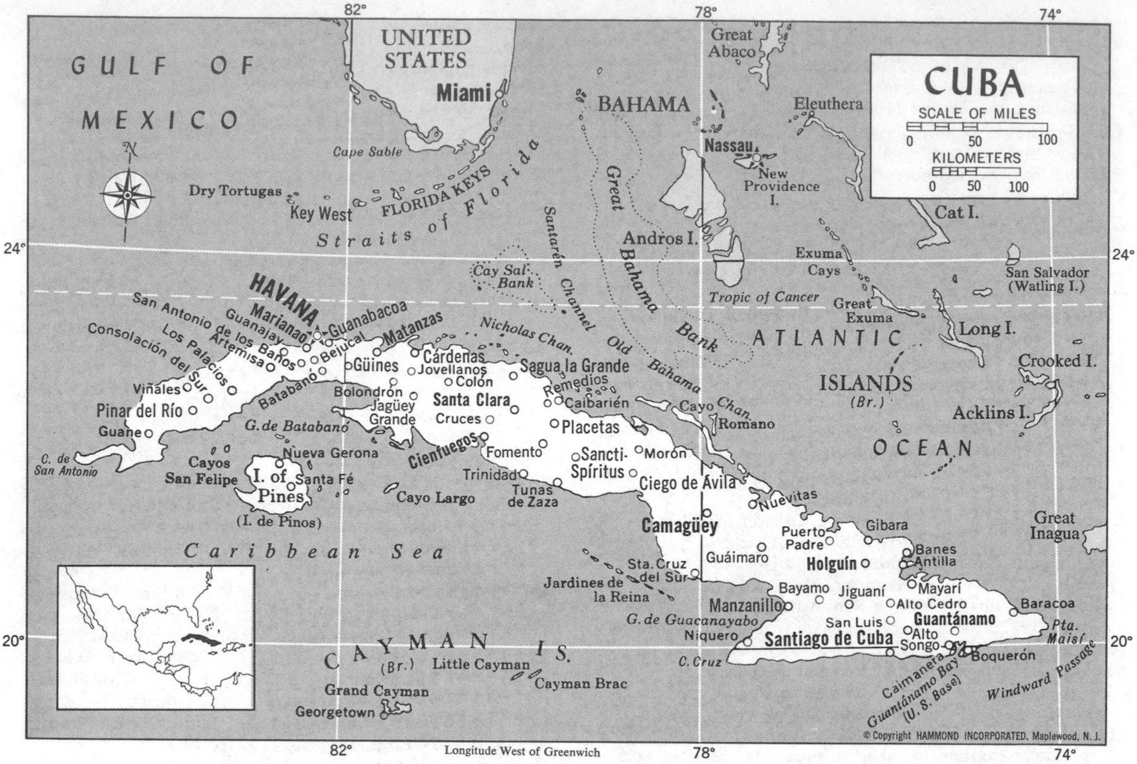

Almería prov., SE Spain, 42 m. NE of Almería; pop. (1970p) 7665; silver, lead, and iron mining.

Cufra, Oases of. See AL-KUFRAH.

Cu·ia·bá *or formerly* **Cu·ya·bá** \ˌkü-yə-ˈbä\. 1 River, Mato Grosso state, SW Brazil; ab. 300 m. long; rises near Diamantino, flows S into São Lourenço river.

2 City, ✻ of Mato Grosso state, SW Brazil, on Cuiabá river; munic. pop. (1970p) 103,262; active river trade; on highway at W edge of plateau; founded in 18th cent.

Cui·ca·tlán \ˌkwē-kə-ˈtlän\. Municipality, Oaxaca state, Mexico, 50 m. NW of Oaxaca; pop. (1970p) 45,013; porcelain; agriculture.

Cuicuilco. See SAN CUICUILCO.

Cui·la·pa \kwē-ˈläp-ə\. Town, ✻ of Santa Rosa dept., S Guatemala, SE of Guatemala City; munic. pop. (1964p) 12,621.

Cuil·lin Hills *or* **Coo·lin Hills** \ˌkü-lən-\. Hills on Skye I., NW Scotland; highest peak 3309 ft.

Cuillin Sound. Body of water off NW coast of Scotland, bet. Skye and Rum Is., Inner Hebrides.

Cuin·chy \kü-aⁿ-ˈshē\. Commune, Pas-de-Calais dept., N France, 8 m. ESE of Béthune; pop. (1962c) 1500; severe fighting, esp. 1915, in World War I.

Cuí·to \ˈkwē-(ˌ)tō\. River, SW Africa; ab. 400 m. long; rises in cen. Angola, flows through marshland, S and SE into Okavango river on Angola border.

Cuit·zeo, Lake \-kwit-ˈsā-(ˌ)ō\. Lake, Michoacán state, SW Mexico; 31 m. long.

Cularo. See GRENOBLE.

Cul·ber·son \ˈkəl-bər-sən\. County in Texas. See table at TEXAS.

Cu·le·bra \k(y)ü-ˈlā-brə, -ˈleb-rə\. Island off E coast of Puerto Rico; pop. (1970p) 726; belongs to Puerto Rico; site of U.S. naval base.

Culebra Gulf. See MURCIÉLAGOS, GULF OF.

Culebra Mountain. Hill, SE Canal Zone, through which **Culebra Cut** (see GAILLARD CUT) was made.

Culebra Peak. Mountain, Costilla and Las Animas cos., S Colorado; in cen. part, called the **Culebra Range,** of the Sangre de Cristo Range; 14,069 ft.

Cul·goa \ˈkəl-ˌgō-ə\. River, SE Queensland and NE New South Wales, Australia; ab. 200 m. long; formed by junction of Maranoa and Condamine rivers, flows SW; with these streams the longest tributary of the Darling.

Cu·lia·cán \ˌkül-yə-ˈkän\ *or officially* **Culiacán–Ro·sa·les** \-rō-ˈzäl-əs, -ˈsäl-\. Commercial city, ✻ of Sinaloa state, W Mexico, on **Culiacán River** (ab. 175 m. long) 40 m. from its mouth; munic. pop. (1970p) 358,812; univ. (1873, univ. status 1922); founded 1599.

Cu·lion \kül-ˈyōn\. 1 Island, S part of Calamian Is., N Palawan prov., Phil.; 150 sq. m.; has fertile soil.

2 Town on NE coast of island; pop. (1969e) 6500.

Cul·le·ra \kül-ˈ(y)er-ə\. Commune, Valencia prov., E Spain, on Júcar river near its mouth on the Mediterranean 24 m. SSE of Valencia; pop. (1970p) 15,738; fishing; captured from Moors by James I of Aragon.

Cul·li·nan \ˈkəl-ə-nən, -(ˌ)nan\. Town, S cen. Transvaal, NE Rep. of South Africa, 20 m. E of Pretoria; site of the Premier diamond mine (opened 1902, closed 1932) in which was discovered 1905 the Cullinan diamond.

Cull·man \ˈkəl-mən\. 1 County in N Alabama. See table at ALABAMA.

2 City, its ⊗, 45 m. N of Birmingham; pop. (1970c) 12,601; cigars, fertilizer; cotton; Sacred Heart Coll. (1940).

Cul·lod·en Moor \kə-ˈläd-ᵊn-, -ˈlōd-\ *also* **Drum·mos·sie Moor** \ˌdrəm-ˈmò-sē-\. Moor, Inverness co., NW Scotland; battle Apr. 16, 1746 in which British force under duke of Cumberland defeated Highland Jacobite force under Prince Charles Edward, thus ending last armed outbreak of the Stuart cause; notorious for slaughter of Highland wounded after battle.

Cul·lo·whee \ˈkəl-ə-ˌwē\. Town in Cullowhee township (pop. [1970c] 4885), Jackson co., SW North Carolina, ab. 16 m. SW of Waynesville; Western Carolina Univ. (1889).

Culm. See CHEŁMNO.

Culmsee. See CHEŁMŻA.

Cul·pep·er \'kəl-(ˌ)pep-ər\. 1 County in N Virginia. See table at VIRGINIA.
2 Town, its ⊗, W of Fredericksburg; pop. (1970c) 6056; muster place in 1775 for Culpeper minutemen.
Culp's Hill. See CEMETERY RIDGE.
Cul·ver \ˌkəl-vər\. Town, Marshall co., N Indiana, 33 m. SSW of South Bend; pop. (1970c) 1783.
Culver City. City, Los Angeles co., SW California, SW of Los Angeles; pop. (1970c) 34,526; aircraft production; motion-picture studios.
Cu·mae \'kyü-(ˌ)mē\. Ancient town, Campania, Italy, on coast W of Neapolis (Naples); oldest Greek colony in Italy or Sicily, founded c. 750 B.C.; defeated the Etruscans 524 B.C.; allied with Hiero of Syracuse in his defeat of Etruscans in naval battle 474 B.C.; came under supremacy of Rome 338 B.C.; destroyed by Neapolitans 1205 A.D. On the site near the shore is the acropolis containing caves said to have been seat of the oracle of the Cumaean Sibyl.
Cu·ma·ná \ˌkü-mə-'nä\. Seaport city, ✱ of Sucre state, N Venezuela, 185 m. E of Caracas; pop. (1970e) 100,498; exports tobacco, cacao, fish, cotton textiles, coffee; univ. (1958).
History: Settled 1520 by Las Casas who established a model Indian colony; destroyed by natives 1522; settled again 1523 by Diego Castellón under the name Nueva Toledo; oldest existing European settlement in South America; has often suffered from earthquakes, esp. 1766, when it was almost completely destroyed, and Jan. 1929.
Cum·bal \küm-'bäl\. Volcano in the Andes, Nariño dept., SW Colombia, on border of Ecuador; 16,039 ft.
Cum·ber·land \'kəm-bər-lənd\. 1 Navigable river, S Kentucky and N Tennessee; 687 m. long; formed by confluence of forks in Harlan co., SE Kentucky, flows W through S Kentucky, turns S in Monroe co. and makes great loop in N Tennessee, reenters Kentucky running N into Ohio river in W Livingston co., W Kentucky. The **Cumberland Falls** *or* **Great Falls** (92 ft. high, over 100 ft. wide) are in cen. Whitley co., Ky. See *Great Falls Dam* at table at TENNESSEE VALLEY AUTHORITY.
2 Name of counties in eight states of the U.S. See tables at ILLINOIS, KENTUCKY, MAINE, NEW JERSEY, NORTH CAROLINA, PENNSYLVANIA, TENNESSEE, VIRGINIA.
3 City, Harlan co., SE Kentucky, 21 m. SSE of Hazard; pop. (1970c) 3624; mining center.
4 Town, Cumberland co., SW Maine, 14 m. NNW of Portland; pop. (1970c) 4096.
5 City, ⊗ of Allegany co., NW Maryland, on Potomac river; pop. (1970c) 29,724; railroad and industrial center; coal mines; iron and steel products; Allegany Community Coll. (1961).
6 Town, Providence co., N Rhode Island, 4 m. SE of Woonsocket; pop. (1970c) 26,605; Mercy Coll. (1957); governmental center Valley Falls. Originally part of Massachusetts; annexed to Rhode Island 1746, incorp. 1747.
7 Village, ⊗ of Cumberland co., cen. Virginia.
8 County, Nova Scotia, Canada. See table at NOVA SCOTIA.
9 County, NW England; 1520 sq. m.; pop. (1971p) 292,009; ⊗ Carlisle; lakes include Derwent Water, Ullswater, Thirlmere; rivers include Derwent, Ehen, Esk; potatoes, beets, oats; coal, iron ore, gypsum; sheep raising; tourism; towns incl. Whitehaven, Workington, Penrith.
Cumberland Caverns. Large cave, Warren co., cen. Tennessee 10 m. SE of McMinnville.
Cumberland Gap. Pass through Cumberland Plateau in Claiborne co., NE Tennessee; alt. 1640 ft.; discovered 1750, became an early emigrant route; used by Daniel Boone in his pioneer trips into Kentucky 1767–71 and when he led settlers to site of Boonesborough 1775 blazing and clearing the Wilderness Road; first mail route through Gap to Danville, Ky., 1792; strategic point in Civil War; established as **Cumberland Gap National Historical Park.** See UNITED STATES, *National Historical Parks.*
Cumberland Island. Island in Atlantic Ocean, off mainland of Camden co., SE Georgia; 34 sq. m.
Cumberland Islands. Group of small islands off E coast of Queensland, Australia, SE of Townsville.
Cumberland Lake. Lake, NE Saskatchewan, Canada; 166 sq. m.; drains S into Saskatchewan river.
Cumberland Peninsula. Peninsula, E Baffin I., E Franklin dist., Northwest Territories, Canada; its easternmost point, Cape Dyer, on Davis Strait.
Cumberland Plateau *or* **Cumberland Mountains.** Tableland extending NE to SW from S West Virginia to NE Alabama N of Birmingham; extends along border bet. Kentucky and Virginia and in E Tennessee W of the Tennessee river; average height ab. 2000 ft., average width ab. 50 m.; structurally the W section of the Appalachian Mts. and a part of the Allegheny highlands. Rich deposits of bituminous coal in the Tennessee area.
Cumberland Road. First national road in the United States; originally started at Cumberland, Maryland; construction began 1811; extended to Vandalia, Illinois.
Cumberland Sound. 1 Inlet of Atlantic Ocean, on Georgia-Florida boundary; receives the St. Marys river.
2 Inlet of Davis Strait, SE Baffin I., Northwest Territories, N Canada, SW of Cumberland Penin.
Cum·braes, The \-ˌkəm-'brāz, -'kəm-ˌ\. Two islands in the Firth of Clyde, forming a civil parish of Bute co., SW Scotland: **Great Cumbrae Island,** WSW of Largs; 5 sq. m.; summer resort; **Little Cumbrae Island,** S of Great Cumbrae; 1 sq. m.; lighthouse.
Cumbre, La. See USPALLATA PASS.
Cum·bre Ne·gra \ˌküm-brē-'neg-rə\. Peak, W Chubut prov., S Argentina, on Chile border; 6273 ft.
Cum·bres Pass \ˌkəm-brəs-\. Mountain pass, Conejos co., S Colorado, in San Juan Mts.; alt. 10,022 ft.; used by Indians and early Spanish explorers; highway.
Cum·bria \'kəm-brē-ə\. Ancient Celtic kingdom, NW Britain; S part (Cumberland, Westmorland and Lancashire [in part]) under Anglo-Saxon control c. 944, N part (Ayr, Dumfries, Lanark, Kirkcudbright, Renfrew, and Wigton) to Scotland 1018. Name survives in *Cumberland.*
Cum·bri·an Mountains \'kəm-brē-ən-\. Range of hills in Cumberland, Westmorland, and Lancashire, NW England; highest peak Scafell Pike 3210 ft., highest mountain in England.
Cu·mières *or in full* **Cumières–le–Mort–Homme** \kü-ˌmyer-lə-ˌmȯr-'tȯm\. Former village, Meuse dept., NE France, ab. 6 m. NW of Verdun just E of Le Mort Homme, on the Meuse; destroyed in fighting around Verdun during World War I.
Cu·mi·na·pa·ne·ma \'kü-mə-ˌnä-ˌpan-ə-'mä\. River, N Brazil; ab. 150 m. long; flows S and unites with Curuapanema to form Curuá river emptying into the Amazon.
Cum·ing \'kəm-iŋ\. County in Nebraska. See table at NEBRASKA.
Cum·ming \'kəm-iŋ\. Town, ⊗ of Forsyth co., N Georgia; pop. (1970c) 2031; cattle; cotton.
Cu·naxa \kyü-'nak-sə\. Town, ancient Babylonia, E of the Euphrates river ab. 87 m. NW of Babylon, scene of battle 401 B.C. bet. Artaxerxes II of Persia and his brother Cyrus the Younger in which the latter was killed; as a result of the demoralization of Cyrus' army, the Greek mercenary force, originally led by Clearchus, made (401–399 B.C.) their famous Retreat of the Ten Thousand (the *Anabasis*) under Xenophon to Cotyora on the Black Sea.
Cun·di·na·mar·ca \ˌkün-di-nə-'mär-kə\. Department of cen. Colombia. See table at COLOMBIA.
Cu·ne·ne *or* **Ku·ne·ne** \kü-'nā-nə\. River, SW Angola, SW Africa; 700 m. long; flows S and W to Atlantic Ocean; in its lower course forms a section of the boundary bet.

Angola and South-West Africa; in its westward descent to coast are several cataracts, esp. the **Ru·a·ca·na Falls** \ˌrü-ə-ˌkän-ə-\ (17°22′S, 14°12′E), which fall 406 ft.

Cu·neo \ˈkü-nē-ˌō\. 1 Province of Piedmont, NW Italy. See table at ITALY.
2 *or Fr.* **Co·ni** \kȯ-ˈnē\. Commune, its ✱, 69 m. W of Genoa; pop. (1968e) 52,574; episcopal see.

Cuor·gnè \kwȯr-ˈnyā\. Commune, Torino prov., Piedmont, NW Italy, 28 m. SE of Aosta; pop. (1968e) 8971.

Cu·par \ˈkü-pər, -pär\. Burgh, ⊗ of Fife co., E Scotland; pop. (1971p) 5604; site of a 12th cent. castle of the MacDuffs, earls of Fife.

Cu·per·ti·no \ˌk(y)ü-pə(r)-ˈtē-(ˌ)nō\. City, Santa Clara co., W California, 8 m. W of San Jose; pop. (1970c) 18,216; electronic products; fruit growing.

Ću·pri·ja *or* **Chu·pri·ya** \ˈchü-prē-(y)ə\. Town, Serbia, E Yugoslavia, ab. 70 m. SE of Belgrade; pop. (1965e) 12,000; during World War I central ammunition depot of Serbian army; occupied by Germans in World War II.

Cura. See VILLA DE CURA.

Cu·ra·çao \ˌk(y)u̇r-ə-ˈsō, -ˈsau̇\. 1 Territory, West Indies. See NETHERLANDS ANTILLES.
2 Largest island of the Netherlands Antilles (*q.v.*), in the Caribbean Sea, 60 m. N of NW Venezuela; 36 m. long by 8 m. wide; 182 sq. m.; pop. (1969e) 143,778; chief town Willemstad (✱ of the Netherlands Antilles); surface generally flat, highest point 1220 ft.; chief products cereals, cattle, fruits; chief industry oil refining (oil from Venezuela); tourism.
History: Discovered by Spaniards 1499, first settled by them 1527; captured by Dutch West India Company 1634; held by British 1807–15; with Aruba awarded to Netherlands by Treaty of Paris 1815; capital temporarily seized by Venezuelan revolutionaries 1929; in World War II oil refineries on Aruba and Curaçao damaged by shells from German submarines Feb. and Apr. 1942.

Cu·ra·cau·tín \ˌku̇r-ə-kau̇-ˈtēn\. City, Malleco prov., S cen. Chile, 45 m. NE of Temuco; pop. (1960c) 9601.

Cu·ra·ni·la·hue \ku̇-ˌrän-i-ˈlä-wā\. Town, Arauco prov., S cen. Chile; pop. (1960c) 12,117; coal mines.

Cu·ra·ray \ˌku̇r-ə-ˈrī\. River, rising in E cen. Ecuador and flowing E into Napo river in N Loreto dept., NE Peru; ab. 500 m. long.

Cu·re·pipe \ku̇(ə)r-ˈpēp\. Town and health resort, cen. Mauritius; pop. (1969e) 51,460.

Cu·res \ˈkyu̇r-(ˌ)ēz\. Ancient town, Latium, Italy, NE of Rome; famous in legend as original home of Sabines who settled the Quirinal and as birthplace of Numa Pompilius, second king 715–673 B.C. of Rome; site is a hill with two summits and a ditch around the base.

Curia Rhaetorum. See CHUR.

Cu·ri·có \ˌku̇-ri-ˈkō\. 1 Province of cen. Chile. See table at CHILE.
2 City, its ✱, 110 m. S of Santiago; pop. (1966e) 39,392; founded 1743.

Cu·ri·ti·ba *or formerly* **Cu·ry·ti·ba** \ˌku̇r-ə-ˈtē-bə\. City, ✱ of Paraná state, S Brazil, ab. 70 m. from the coast; met. area pop. (1970p) 603,227; cement, furniture; Federal Univ. (1912), Catholic Univ. (1959); founded 1654.

Cu·ri·ti·ba·nos \ˌku̇r-ət-ē-ˈban-əs\. Municipality, cen. Santa Catarina state, S Brazil; pop. (1968e) 28,402.

Cur·ragh \ˈkər-ə, ˈkə-rə\. Plain, co. Kildare, E Eire, on W bank of the Liffey; site of a racecourse.

Cu·rral das Frei·ras \ku̇-ˌräl-dəs-ˈfrer-əs\. Vast natural amphitheater in cen. Madeira I.

Cur·rent \ˈkər-ənt, ˈkə-rənt\. River, Missouri and Arkansas; ab. 250 m. long; flows from Texas co., S Missouri, E and SE into Black river in Randolph co., NE Arkansas.

Cur·ri·tuck \ˈkər-ə-ˌtək\. 1 County in NE North Carolina. See table at NORTH CAROLINA.
2 Village, its ⊗.

Currituck Sound. Sound, W of barrier reef in E Currituck co., NE North Carolina, extends N ab. 35 m. from mouth of Albemarle Sound.

Cur·ry \ˈkər-ē\. Name of counties in two states of the U.S. See tables at NEW MEXICO and OREGON.

Cur·tea–de–Ar·geş \ˌku̇r-tyä-dā-ˈär-jesh\. Commune, S cen. Romania, on the Argeş, SW of Cîmpulung; pop. (1966c) 16,424; Byzantine cathedral in monastery grounds to the N.

Cu·ruá \ku̇r-ˈwä\. River, N Brazil; 65 m. long; flows S into the Amazon.

Cu·ru·a·pa·ne·ma \ku̇r-ˌwä-ˌpan-ə-ˈmä\. River, N Brazil; ab. 170 m. long; flows S and unites with Cuminapanema river to form Curuá river emptying into the Amazon.

Curupira, Serra. See SERRA CURUPIRA.

Cu·ru·zú Cua·tiá \ˌku̇r-ə-ˌzü-kwät-ˈyä\. Town, Corrientes prov., NE Argentina, 160 m. SSE of Corrientes; pop. (1960c) 16,567.

Cur·wens·ville \ˈkər-wənz-ˌvil\. Borough, Clearfield co., W cen. Pennsylvania, on West Branch of Susquehanna river 16 m. ESE of Du Bois; pop. (1970c) 3189; produces firebrick, leather, clay, stone; settled 1812.

Cur·wood, Mount \-ˈkər-(ˌ)wu̇d\. Peak, Baraga co., NW Michigan penin.; 1980 ft.; highest peak in the state.

Curytiba. See CURITIBA.

Curzola. See KORČULA.

Cur·zon Line \ˌkərz-ᵊn-\. A line suggested by Lord Curzon to the Supreme Council in Dec. 1919 as a practical line of demarcation bet. Soviet Russia and the then new state of Poland; began at the S tip of Lithuania just N of Grodno, extended S to the right bank of the Bug river near Brest, then followed the Bug for ab. 200 m., turned W near Sokal and SSW across E Galicia to the N boundary of Czechoslovakia at a point ab. 50 m. S of Przemyśl; primarily an ethnic boundary with areas to W inhabited chiefly by Poles and those to E by Russians. Again used 1920 as basis for armistice bet. Russians and Poles, but final E boundary of Poland, fixed by Treaty of Riga 1920, was approximately parallel but 120 to 160 m. farther E. Used in part by Germany and U.S.S.R. for partition of Poland Sept. 1939 but with W extensions at N and S ends; by Yalta Conference and later action claimed by U.S.S.R. as basis for new boundary bet. U.S.S.R. and Poland.

Cus·ca·tlán \ˌküs-kə-ˈtlän\. Department, cen. El Salvador. See table at EL SALVADOR.

Cusco. See CUZCO.

Cush *or* **Kush** \ˈkəsh, ˈku̇sh\. Ancient country in the Nile valley, adjoining Egypt, S of ab. lat. 24°N.

Cush·ing \ˈku̇sh-iŋ\. City, Payne co., N cen. Oklahoma, 40 m. W of Sapulpa; pop. (1970c) 7529; oil and gas wells and refineries; founded 1892.

Cushing, Mount. Mountain, N British Columbia, Canada; 8676 ft.; highest peak in Stikine Mts.

Cush·man, Lake \-ˈku̇sh-mən\. Reservoir across N fork of Skokomish river, Mason co., W Washington; created by dams (275 and 240 ft. high) completed 1926; supplies waterpower for Tacoma.

Cus·set \kü-ˈsā\. Commune, Allier dept., cen. France, ab. 2 m. E of Vichy; pop. (1968c) 13,117; mineral springs.

Cus·se·ta \kə-ˈsē-tə\. Town, ⊗ of Chattahoochee co., W Georgia; pop. (1970c) 1251.

Cus·ter \ˈkəs-tər\. 1 Name of counties in six states of the U.S. See tables at COLORADO, IDAHO, MONTANA, NEBRASKA, OKLAHOMA, SOUTH DAKOTA.
2 City and summer resort, ⊗ of Custer co., SW South Dakota, 30 m. SW of Rapid City; pop. (1970c) 1597; tourist center (near Wind Cave National Park and other scenic spots); gold, silver, lead mines nearby.

Custer, Mount. Peak, NW Montana, in Glacier National Park on Continental Divide; 8700 ft.

Custer Battlefield National Monument. See UNITED STATES, *National Monuments.*

Custer Peak. Mountain, Lawrence co., W South Dakota; 6804 ft.

Cu·sto·za \ku̇-ˈstōt-sə\ *or* **Cu·stoz·za** \-ˈstȯt-\. Village, Verona prov., Veneto, NE Italy, 11 m. SW of Verona; scene of two Italian defeats in wars for unity and independence:

(1) July 24, 1848 by Austrians under Count Radetzky; (2) June 24, 1866 by forces of Archduke Albert.

Cüstrin. See KOSTRZYN.

Cut Bank \ˈkət-ˌbaŋk\. Town, ⊗ of Glacier co., NW Montana, 95 m. NNW of Great Falls; pop. (1970c) 4004; oil wells; livestock.

Cutch. See KUTCH.

Cutch, Gulf of. See KUTCH, GULF OF.

Cutch, Rann of. See KUTCH, RANN OF.

Cu·thah \ˈkyü-thə\. Ancient city, Babylonia; devoted to worship of Nergal, ruler of Aralu, the abode of the dead; one of cities from which people were taken by the king of Assyria to colonize Samaria (2 *Kings* xvii. 24).

Cuth·bert \ˈkəth-bərt\. City, Randolph co., SW Georgia, 38 m. WNW of Albany; pop. (1970c) 3972; lumber mills, cotton mills; Andrew Coll. (1854); incorp. 1834.

Cut·off Peak \ˌkət-ˌȯf-\. Mountain, S Montana, in Yellowstone National Park; 10,300 ft.

Cut·tack \ˈkət-ək\. City, Orissa, E India, on Mahanadi river 220 m. SW of Calcutta; pop. (1970e) 204,356; noted for its excellent silver filigree work; seat of Orissa high court; several colleges. Successively capital of Orissa for Hindu kings, the Moguls, and Maratha governors; captured by British in Second Maratha War 1803.

Cutts Peak \ˈkəts-\. Mountain, Washington co., N cen. Vermont; 4080 ft.

Cut·ty·hunk Island \ˌkət-ē-ˌhəŋk-\. Island, SW Elizabeth Is., Buzzards Bay, SE Massachusetts.

Cux·ha·ven \ku̇ks-ˈhäf-ən\. Seaport, Lower Saxony, West Germany, on North Sea at mouth of Elbe river; pop. (1969e) 45,383; important fisheries; bathing resort; shipbuilding; church (13th cent.); frequently bombed by Allied air forces in World War II.

Cuyabá. See CUIABÁ.

Cuy·a·hoga \ˌkī-(ə-)ˈhō-gə, kə-ˈhō-, -ˈhä-, -ˈhȯ-\. **1** River, NE Ohio; ab. 100 m. long; rises in Geauga co., flows SW through Portage co. into Summit co., turns abruptly N and flows into Lake Erie at Cleveland; near Akron receives the **Little Cuyahoga River.**

2 County in Ohio. See table at OHIO.

Cuyahoga Falls. City, Summit co., NE Ohio, on Cuyahoga river 5 m. N of Akron; pop. (1970c) 49,678; chemicals, lumber, tires, tools, dies.

Cu·ya·po \ˌkü-yə-ˈpō\. Municipality, NW Nueva Ecija prov., Luzon, Phil.; pop. (1969e) 41,700.

Cu·yo \ˈkü-(ˌ)yō\. **1** Island group, cen. Phil., N of Sulu Sea and ab. 65 m. E of N end of Palawan I.; ab. 50 sq. m.; pop. (1969e) 33,900; comprises Cuyo and Agutaya Is., and ab. 45 islets; forms part of Palawan prov.

2 Largest island in group, volcanic in origin; 22 sq. m.; highest point ab. 600 ft.

3 Municipality, coextensive with Cuyo I. and nearby islets; pop. (1969e) 27,900.

Cuy·u·na Range \kī-ˌyü-nə-\. Iron-ore belt, in Crow Wing and Aitkin cos., cen. Minnesota, NW of Mille Lacs.

Cu·yu·ni \ku̇-ˈyü-nē\. River, N South America; 350 m. long; rises in E Venezuela, flows N, then E forming section of Venezuela-Guyana boundary, continues E across N Guyana to the Essequibo river near its mouth; just before entering the Essequibo, is joined by the Mazaruni river.

Cuz·co *also* **Cus·co** \ˈkü-(ˌ)skō\. **1** Peak, Potosí dept., SW Bolivia; 17,830 ft.

2 Department of SE Peru. See table at PERU.

3 City, its ✱, ab. 350 m. SE of Lima; pop. (1969e) 105,400; alt. 11,024 ft.; univ. (1597), Renaissance cathedral. Sometimes called the "Archaeological Capital of South America," was once capital of vast Inca empire and known as the "City of the Sun;" supposedly founded in 11th cent. by Manco Capac; taken by the Spanish under Pizarro 1533; famous for its ruins of Inca temples, fortresses, walls, and palaces, esp. of the fortress of Sacsahuaman and of the nearby city of Machu Picchu (*qq.v.*) and of the Temple of the Sun; suffered earthquake damage 1950.

Cwm·am·man \ku̇m-ˈam-ən\. Urban district, Carmarthenshire, S Wales; pop. (1969e) 4050.

Cwm·bran \ku̇m-ˈbrän\. Urban district, Monmouthshire, SE Wales, 15 m. NNE of Cardiff; pop. (1970p) 31,614.

Cyc·la·des \ˈsik-lə-ˌdēz\ *or Gk.* **Ki·klá·dhes** \kē-ˈklät͟h-(ˌ)es\. Group of ab. 220 islands in S Aegean Sea, bet. the Peloponnesus and the Dodecanese; 993 sq. m.; pop. (1971p) 86,084; administratively a department of Greece; ✱ Hermoupolis; chief islands: Andros, Tenos, Naxos, Amorgos, Melos, Paros, Syros, Keos, Kythnos, Seriphos, Ios, and Thira. So called by the ancients because they formed a circle or cluster (*Gk. kyklos*) around the small island of Delos, then the seat of Delian League (see ATHENS 10).

History: Under Mycenaean culture 2d millennium B.C.; held successively by Persians, Athenians (after Mycale 479 B.C.), Carians, Ptolemaic Egypt, and Macedonia; ruled by Venetians as duchy of Naxos after 1207; for rest of history, see as part of AEGEAN ISLANDS.

Cy·clone Mountain \ˌsī-ˌklōn-\. Peak, Chaffee co., cen. Colorado; 13,800 ft.

Cyd·nus \ˈsid-nəs\. Historic river in Cilicia, in modern İçel prov., Turkey in Asia; flows SE from Taurus Mts. past Tarsus to the Mediterranean.

Cy·do·nia \sī-ˈdō-nē-ə, -nyə\. Ancient city on NW coast of Crete, on whose site is modern Canea (*q.v.*).

Cyl·le·ne \sə-ˈlē-nē\ *or Gk.* **Kil·lí·ni** \kə-\ *or* **Zir·ia** *also* **Ze·ria** \ˈzir-ē-ə\. Mountain, NE Peloponnesus, S Greece; 7789 ft.; in ancient times was on border bet. Achaea and Arcadia; in Greek legend sacred to Hermes as his birthplace.

Cy·me \ˈsī-mē\. City of ancient Aeolis, in Asia Minor, on the W coast N of the mouth of the Gediz.

Cyn·os·ceph·a·lae \ˌsin-ə-ˈsef-ə-(ˌ)lē, ˌsī-nə-\. Two hills in a low range ab. 18 m. SSE of Larissa, SE Thessaly, NE Greece; scene of battles: (1) 364 B.C. in which the Thebans under Pelopidas defeated the tyrant of Pherae; and (2) 197 B.C., the decisive battle of the Second Macedonian War, in which the Roman general T. Quinctius Flamininus defeated King Philip V of Macedon.

Cy·nos·se·ma \ˌsin-ə-ˈsē-mə, ˌsī-nə-\. Promontory on E side of Chersonesus Thracica (Gallipoli Penin.); naval battle in which Athenians under Alcibiades and Thrasybulus defeated Spartans occurred off promontory 411 B.C.

Cyn·o·su·ra \ˌsin-ə-ˈsu̇r-ə, ˌsī-nə-\ *or* **Kyn·o·su·ra** \ˌkin-ə-ˈsu̇r-ə, ˌkī-nə-\. Promontory, E Salamis I., Greece, just SE of Salamis town and opp. Mt. Aegaleos on coast of Attica; battle of Salamis occurred off promontory 480 B.C.

Cyn·thi·ana \ˌsin(t)-thē-ˈan-ə\. City, ⊗ of Harrison co., N Kentucky, 27 m. NNE of Lexington; pop. (1970c) 6356; dairy products, tobacco, fertilizer.

Cyn·thus \ˈsin(t)-thəs\. Mountain, Delos I., Cyclades Is., Aegean Sea; legendary birthplace of Apollo and Artemis.

Cy·press \ˈsī-prəs\. City, Orange co., SW California, 9 m. NE of Long Beach; pop. (1970c) 31,894.

Cypress Hills. Hilly region, SE Alberta and SW Saskatchewan, Canada; extends ab. 100 m. E–W; contains two provincial parks; has highest peak in Saskatchewan, 4546 ft.

Cypress Hills Provincial Park. **1** Provincial park, SE Alberta, Canada; 78 sq. m.; largest provincial park in Alberta.

2 Provincial park, S of Maple Creek, SW Saskatchewan, Canada.

Cy·prus \ˈsī-prəs\ *or Gk.* **Ky·pros** \ˈkē-prȯs\ *or Turk.* **Ki·bris** \ˈkē-bris\. Island, a republic, E Mediterranean Sea, 60 m. W of coast of Syria and 40 m. S of coast of Turkey; area 3572 sq. m.; pop. (1971e) 634,000; ✱ Nicosia; of irregular shape with a number of wide bays and prominent capes, esp. Cape Andreas which terminates a long narrow peninsula on the NE; in cen. part has a plain, enclosed on N by mountain range which reaches 3357 ft. and on S by range culminating in Mt. Olympus 6403 ft.; no rivers or lakes of any size. *Chief products:* Cereals, grapes, pulses, cotton, citrus fruits, tobacco; copper, asbestos; in early times famous for its copper (the English word derived from Greek name of island, *Kypros,* through the Latin *cuprum*). *Chief towns:* Nicosia, Limassol, Famagusta, Larnaca; has ruins of several famous towns of ancient times, esp. Citium and Paphos.

History: Colonized by Phoenicians and ancient Greeks; ruled by Assyrian, Persian (after 525 B.C.), Ptolemaic, and Roman Empires (see PAPHOS); as part of Byzantine Empire, frequently raided or captured by Saracens 7th–10th cents. A.D.; captured by Richard I of England during Third Crusade 1191; sold to Lusignan dynasty which ruled 1192–1474; Famagusta, leading port, held by Genoese 1376–1464; 1489 acquired by Venetians whom Turks expelled 1571; according to convention with Turkey, administered by Great Britain 1878–1914; annexed by British at outbreak of war with Turkey 1914; made a crown colony 1925; became an independent republic 1960; establishment of UN peace-keeping mission 1964 following period of armed strife between Greek and Turkish sectors of population.

Cyr·e·na·i·ca *also* **Ci·re·na·i·ca** \ˌsir-ə-ˈnā-ə-kə, ˌsī-rə-\. Easternmost part of Libya.

History: Ancient Cyrenaica settled by Greeks who founded Cyrene (Cirene) c. 630 B.C.; under Greek dynasty established by Battus of Thera, kingdom of Cyrene or Cyrenaica took form, and other cities were founded; after death of Alexander the Great, ruled by Ptolemies who called it Pentapolis because it included 5 cities (Cyrene, Arsinoë, Berenice, Ptolemaïs, Apollonia); bequeathed to Romans 96 B.C. and in 67 B.C. made Roman province which included Crete; overrun by Arabs in 7th cent. A.D.; nominally under Ottoman Empire after conquest of Egypt (*q.v.*); part of Tripoli (*q.v.*) which was annexed to Italy 1911 (see LIBYA). Scene of many battles in World War II 1940–42: see BARDĪYAH, DERNA, TOBRUK, BENGHAZI, BIR HACHEIM; a province of Libya 1951–63 (330,258 sq. m.; pop. [1963e] 350,024; ✻ Benghazi).

Cy·re·ne \sī-ˈrē-(ˌ)nē\ *or Ital.* **Ci·re·ne** \chē-ˈren-ē, -ˈrā-nē\. Ancient city in North Africa, founded by Greeks c. 630 B.C.; original capital of Cyrenaica and a city of the Pentapolis; taken by Alexander the Great 331 B.C. and soon after came under the Ptolemies; belonged to Romans after 96 B.C.; has interesting ruins.

Cyrus. See KURA.

Cythera. See CERIGO.

Cythnos. See KYTHNOS.

Cyz·i·cus \ˈsiz-i-kəs\. 1 Peninsula, Turkey. See KAPIDAĞI. 2 Ancient city, Mysia, Asia Minor, on isthmus leading to Kapıdağı Penin. on Sea of Marmara; founded by Greeks from Miletus 756 B.C.; in naval battle off its shore 410 B.C. Alcibiades destroyed Spartan fleet.

Czech·o·slo·va·kia \ˌchek-ə-slō-ˈväk-ē-ə, -ˈvak-\ *or Czech* **Čes·ko·slo·ven·sko** \ˌches-kə-ˈslȯ-vən-ˌskȯ\; *officially* **Czech·o·slo·vak Socialist Republic** \ˌchek-ə-ˈslō-ˌväk-, -ˌvak-\ *or Czech* **Čes·ko·slo·ven·ská So·ci·a·lis·tická Re·pu·bli·ka** \ˌches-kə-ˈslȯ-vən-skä-ˌsō-tsē-ə-ˈlēs-ti-kä-rā-ˈpüb-li-kə\; *formerly* **Czecho–Slo·va·kia.** Republic, cen. Europe, bounded on NW by East Germany, on N by Poland, on E by U.S.S.R., on S by Hungary and Austria, and on W by West Germany; 49,371 sq. m.; pop. (1970e) 14,484,620; ✻ Prague. *Physical features:* Mountainous country, Bohemia shut in on SW by the Bohemian Forest (Böhmer Wald), on the NW by Erzgebirge, and on NE by the Sudetic Mts. which also extend into N Moravia; Moravia crossed by several ranges NE to SW, esp. the Bohemian-Moravian Highlands on W border; Slovakia separated from Poland on N by Carpathian Mts. (containing highest point in country Gerlachovka 8711 ft.) and on NW by White Carpathian Mts. *Rivers:* Labe (upper Elbe) in Bohemia and its important branches, the Ohře, Berounka, and Vltava; in Moravia the upper courses of the Oder (*Czech* Odra) and March (*Czech* Morava); in Slovakia numerous tributaries of the Danube and Tisza (Váh, Nitra, Hron). *Chief products:* Wheat, barley, sugar beets; brown coal, iron ore, lead; manufacturing: iron and steel, chemicals, textiles, glassware, machine tools. *Chief cities:* Prague, Brno, Bratislava, Ostrava, Plzeň, Košice. Divided into two constituent republics, the Czech Socialist Republic and the Slovak Socialist Republic.

History: See BOHEMIA, MORAVIA, SLOVAK SOCIALIST REPUBLIC, SILESIA, and TRANSCARPATHIAN OBLAST; republic formed in 1918 by Czechs and Slovaks from territories formerly part of the Austro-Hungarian Empire; Tomáš G. Masaryk first president 1918–35; received Teschen after dispute with Poland 1919–20; ratified constitution and began its operation 1920; entered treaty with Yugoslavia 1920, with Romania 1921 (basis of Little Entente); allied with France 1924; political life disturbed by minority demands for autonomy, including those of Sudeten Germans who were supported by Hitler's Germany; after Munich agreement which settled German-Czech crisis of 1938, Sudetenland annexed to Germany, Teschen (now Český Těšín) to Poland, and a strip of Slovakia and of Ruthenia to Hungary; Slovakia and Ruthenia, given autonomy 1938, declared independence 1939; remainder of Czech state became German protectorate of Bohemia and Moravia 1939–45; after World War II lost Carpathian Ruthenia (Carpatho-Ukraine) to the U.S.S.R.; formed close political and economic union with U.S.S.R., and by Communist coup Feb. 1948 came under Soviet domination; member of Warsaw Pact 1955; its political liberalization (1967–68) suppressed by Soviet invasion Aug. 1968; federal constitution adopted Oct. 1968, put into effect Jan. 1969.

Czechoslovak Socialist Republic. See CZECHOSLOVAKIA.

Czech·o·wi·ce–Dzie·dzi·ce \ˌchek-ə-ˈvēt-sə-je-ˈjēt-sə\. Town, Katowice prov., S Poland, ab. 25 m. S of Katowice; pop. (1970p) 25,400.

Czech Socialist Republic \ˈchek-\ *or Czech* **Čes·ká So·ci·a·lis·tická Re·pu·bli·ka** \ˈches-kä-ˌsō-tsē-ə-ˈlēs-ti-kä-rā-ˈpüb-li-kə\. Constituent republic of Czechoslovakia; 30,448 sq. m.; pop. (1970e) 9,921,160; ✻ Prague; includes Bohemia and Moravia (*qq.v.*); formally established 1968.

Czegléd. see CEGLÉD.

Cze·ladź \ˈ(t)seg-ˌläd\ *or Ger.* **Tsche·li·ads** \ˈchā-lē-ˌäts\. Commune, Katowice prov., S Poland, 5 m. N of Katowice; pop. (1970p) 31,800; coal mining.

Czenstochau. See CZĘSTOCHOWA.

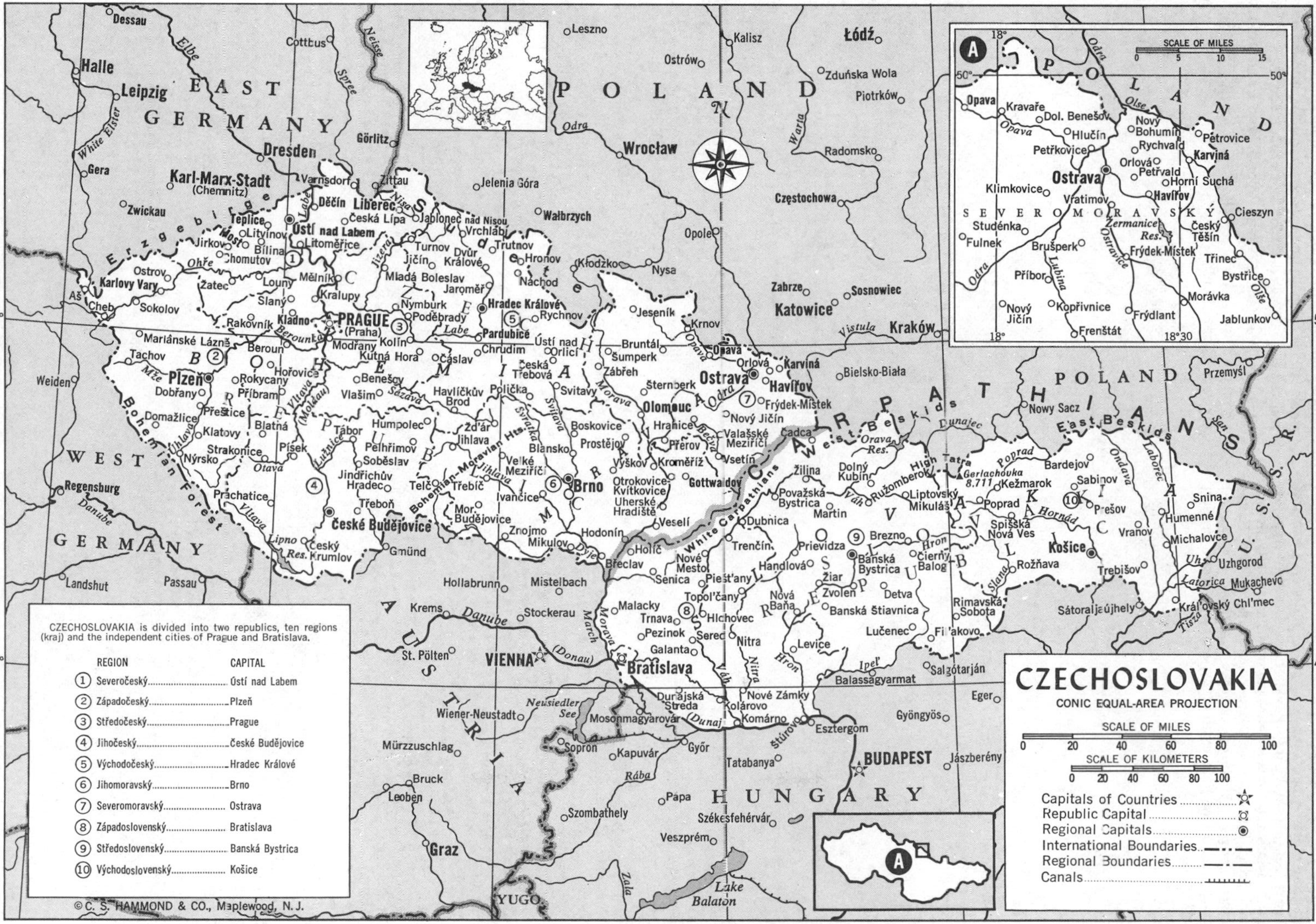
CZECHOSLOVAKIA
CONIC EQUAL-AREA PROJECTION
SCALE OF MILES
0 20 40 60 80 100
SCALE OF KILOMETERS
0 20 40 60 80 100
Capitals of Countries
Republic Capital
Regional Capitals
International Boundaries
Regional Boundaries
Canals
CZECHOSLOVAKIA is divided into two republics, ten regions (kraj) and the independent cities of Prague and Bratislava.
REGION CAPITAL
1 Severočeský Ústí nad Labem
2 Západočeský Plzeň
3 Středočeský Prague
4 Jihočeský České Budějovice
5 Východočeský Hradec Králové
6 Jihomoravský Brno
7 Severomoravský Ostrava
8 Západoslovenský Bratislava
9 Středoslovenský Banská Bystrica
10 Východoslovenský Košice
© C. S. HAMMOND & CO., Maplewood, N. J.
Longitude East of Greenwich
12° 14° 16° 18° 20° 22°
50° 48°
EAST GERMANY
WEST GERMANY
POLAND
AUSTRIA
HUNGARY
YUGO.
BOHEMIA
MORAVIA
SLOVAKIA
CARPATHIANS
Erzgebirge
Sudeten
Bohemian Forest
Bohemian-Moravian Hts.
White Carpathians
West Beskids
East Beskids
High Tatra
Gerlachovka 8,711
PRAGUE (Praha)
Plzeň
Karlovy Vary
Cheb
Ústí nad Labem
Liberec
Hradec Králové
Pardubice
České Budějovice
Brno
Olomouc
Ostrava
Gottwaldov
Bratislava
Žilina
Banská Bystrica
Prešov
Košice
Dresden
Karl-Marx-Stadt (Chemnitz)
Leipzig
Halle
Wrocław
Kraków
Katowice
Łódź
VIENNA
BUDAPEST
Lake Balaton
Danube
Elbe
Vltava (Moldau)
Morava
Váh
Odra
A
SCALE OF MILES
0 5 10 15
Opava
Ostrava
Karviná
Havířov
Frýdek-Místek
Český Těšín
Cieszyn
Třinec
Jablunkov
Nový Jičín
Kopřivnice
Frenštát
Příbor
Fulnek
Studénka
SEVEROMORAVSKÝ
Žermanice Res.
POLAND
18° 18°30 50°

Czernowitz. See CHERNOVTSY.

Czę·sto·cho·wa \ˌchen(t)-stə-ˈkō-və\ *or Russian* **Chen·sto·khov** \ˌchen(t)-stə-ˈkȯf, -ˈkȯv\; *Ger.* **Czen·sto·chau** *or* **Tschen·sto·chau** \ˈchen(t)-stə-ˌkau̇\. Industrial city, Katowice prov., S Poland, on Warta river ab. 40 m. N of Katowice; pop. (1970p) 187,600; railroad junction; manufactures include textiles, paper, steel, iron, leather; famous shrine of Virgin in ancient monastery; technical univ. (1955). A historic town, very wealthy in 15th cent.; resisted siege by Swedes 1655 and 1705; taken by Russians 1772, by Prussians 1793; in World War I captured by Germans Nov. 1914, in World War II again captured by Germans Sept. 1939.

Da·an·ban·ta·yan \dä-ˌän-bän-tä-ˈyän\. Municipality on coast at N tip of Cebu I., Phil., 69 m. N of City of Cebu; pop. (1969e) 47,000.

Daba, Al–. See AD DABAH.

Da·bhoi \də-ˈbȯi\. Town, SE Gujarat state, W India, 20 m. SE of Baroda; pop. (1961c) 30,841; has fine architectural remains of Hindu temples, gates, etc.

Da·bob Bay \ˌdā-ˌbäb-\. Inlet of Hood Canal, Jefferson co., W Washington.

Dą·bro·mierz \dȯm-ˈbrȯ-myesh\ *or Ger.* **Ho·hen·frie·de·berg** \hō-ən-ˈfrēd-ə-ˌbe(ə)rg, -ˌbe(ə)rk\. Village, SW Poland, near Strzegom; pop. (1966e) 950; formerly in Silesia, Prussia, Germany; in Second Silesian War scene of victory of Prussians under Frederick the Great over Austrians and Saxons under Charles of Lorraine June 4, 1745.

Dą·bro·wa Gór·ni·cza \dȯm-ˈbrȯ-və-gu̇r-ˈnē-chə\ *or Ger.* **Dom·brau** \ˈdȯm-ˌbrau̇\. Coal-mining commune, Katowice prov., S Poland, 8 m. ENE of Katowice; pop. (1970p) 61,700.

Dac·ca \ˈdak-ə, ˈdäk-ə\. City, ✻ of Bangla Desh, just W of Meghna river, 80 m. NE of Khulna; met. area pop. (1971e) 915,100; river port; textiles, soap, rubber goods, jewelry, jute carpets; boatbuilding; Univ. of Dacca (1921), Univ. of Engineering and Technology (1961). Site of French, Dutch, and English trading posts at various times; capital of Mogul province of East Bengal 1608–1704 and of former British province of Eastern Bengal and Assam 1905–12; scene of surrender of Pakistani forces to Indian troops 1971.

Da·chau \ˈdäk-ˌau̇\. Town, Bavaria, West Germany, 10 m. NNW of Munich on the Ammer river; pop. (1969e) 32,713; electrical equipment; site, prior to and during World War II, of large concentration camp, captured by Allies Apr. 29, 1945 (32,000 prisoners liberated).

Dach·stein \ˈdäk-ˌs(h)tīn\. Highest peak in the **Dachstein Mountains** in W cen. Austria, ab. 35 m. SE of Salzburg; 9829 ft.; mountains form part of boundary where the three states—Salzburg, Styria, and Upper Austria—meet.

Da·cia \ˈdā-sh(ē-)ə\. Ancient country, cen. Europe; bounded on N by Carpathians, NE by the Tyras (Dniester), E and S by Danubius (Danube), and W by the Tissus (Tisza); roughly equivalent to modern Romania; ✻ Sarmizegetusa.

History: Inhabited before Roman conquest by Getae and Dacians, peoples of Thracian stock, who invaded Roman Empire in Domitian's reign; conquered by Trajan, and made Roman province at death of Dacian king, Decebalus, 107 A.D.; fortified and colonized by Rome as its trans-Danube frontier; abandoned to Goths when Aurelian withdrew Roman colonists to a new Dacia carved out of Moesia (*q.v.*) 270; region of older Dacia invaded by Goths, Huns, Avars, Bulgars, Magyars, Pechenegs, and Cumans before founding of principalities, Walachia and Moldavia (*qq.v.*).

Dade \ˈdād\. Name of counties in three states of the U.S. See tables at FLORIDA, GEORGIA, MISSOURI.

Dade City. City, ⊗ of Pasco co., W Florida penin., 35 m. NE of Tampa; pop. (1970c) 4241; center of truck-farming and citrus-growing region; kaolin deposits nearby.

Dade·ville \ˈdād-ˌvil\. Town, ⊗ of Tallapoosa co., E Alabama; pop. (1970c) 2847; lumber; asbestos.

Da·dra and Na·gar Ha·ve·li \də-ˈdrä . . . ˌnəg-ər-ə-ˈvel-ē\. Centrally administered territory of India, bordering on Gujarat and Maharashtra; 189 sq. m.; pop. (1971p) 74,165; ✻ Silvassa.

Da·et \ˈdä-ˌet\. Municipality, ✻ of Camarines Norte, near coast, Luzon, Phil.; pop. (1969e) 48,600; chief commercial town of province; rice mills.

Da·ga·mi \də-ˈgäm-ē\. Municipality, Leyte prov., N cen. Leyte I., Phil., 16 m. SSW of Tacloban; on E slope of mountains; pop. (1969c) 25,300. Taken by Americans Oct. 29, 1944.

Dag·es·tan Autonomous Soviet Socialist Republic \ˌdag-ə-ˈstan-, ˌdäg-ə-ˈstän-\; *frequently shortened to* **Dagestan** *or* **Dagh·es·tan.** Autonomous republic on W shore of Caspian Sea, a subdivision of the Russian S.F.S.R., U.S.S.R.; bounded on NW and N by Checheno-Ingush A.S.S.R., on E by Caspian Sea, on S by Azerbaijan S.S.R., and on W by Georgian S.S.R.; 19,421 sq. m.; pop. (1970p) 1,429,000; ✻ Makhachkala. Along its S and SW border stretch the Caucasus Mts.; the S two thirds a mountainous region, the N part and along the Caspian mostly sandy plain and salt marsh; the rivers are comparatively short mountain streams; forests small, little good agricultural land; main occupation raising cattle and sheep; large but undeveloped mineral resources, esp. iron, sulfur, mercury; oil, natural gas; glassworks, hydroelectric power plants. Chief towns Makhachkala, Derbent.

History: From early times inhabited by warlike tribes; ceded by Persia to Russia 1813; not subjugated until 1859 (see GUNIB); rose again during Russo-Turkish War 1877; formed separate republic 1917; scene of severe fighting until 1921 and of subsequent famine; became autonomous republic 1921 in North Caucasus Region of U.S.S.R.; reorganized 1936 with change of boundaries; N part to Checheno-Ingush A.S.S.R. 1943–57.

Dag·gett \ˈdag-ət\. County in Utah. See table at UTAH.

Dagö. See HIIUAMA.

Da·go Peak \ˌdā-ˌgō-\. Mountain, in Shoshone co., NE Idaho; 4999 ft.

Da·gu·pan \də-ˈgü-ˌpän\. Municipality, N Pangasinan prov., Luzon, Phil., on S shore of Lingayen Gulf 6 m. E of Lingayen; pop. (1970e) 89,000; most important commercial port of the province.

Da·ha·na \ˈda-hə-nə\. See RUBʻ AL-KHALI.

Dah·lak Archipelago \ˈdäl-ˌak-\ *or Ital.* **Iso·le Da·ha·lach** \ˈē-zə-lā-ˌdä-hə-ˈläk\. Island group, S Red Sea, off Mesewa Channel on coast of Ethiopia, part of Eritrea province; **Dahlak Ke·bir** \-kə-ˈbi(ə)r\, chief island, 290 sq. m.

Dah·lon·e·ga \də-ˈlän-ə-gə\. City, ⊗ of Lumpkin co., N Georgia; pop. (1970c) 2658; gold-mining town; trading center; site of a branch of United States mint 1838–61. North Georgia Coll. (1873); settled 1833.

Dah·na \ˈda-hə-nə\. See RUBʻ AL-KHALI.

Da·ho·mey \də-ˈhō-mē\. Republic, W Africa, bounded on N by Niger, on E by Nigeria, on S by the Gulf of Guinea, on W by Togo, and on NW by Upper Volta; 43,483 sq. m.; pop. (1970e) 2,718,000; ✻ Porto-Novo. *Physical features:* Extending ab. 420 m. inland from the Gulf of Guinea, the republic consists of a hilly region in the NW (max. elev. 2146 ft.), plains in the E and N, and a marshy coastal region in the S. *Chief exports:* Palm kernels, copra, cotton; other products: peanuts, corn, cassava. *Chief towns:* Porto-Novo, Cotonou, Abomey, Parakou.

History: Negro kingdom which, in 17th cent., rose around Abomey; expanded north and to Slave Coast on south; coastal footholds, Cotonou (1851) and Porto-Novo (1863), established by French who finally captured Abomey and deposed ruler in 1892; made a French colony 1894 and part of French West Africa 1895; boundaries with Togo and Lagos determined in treaties with Germany 1897 and Great Britain 1898; made an overseas territory of France 1946; became an autonomous republic of the French Community; achieved independence 1960.

Dah·shûr *or* **Da·shur** \də-ˈshu̇(ə)r\. Site near Memphis, Egypt, of pyramid built by Sesostris III (c. 1887–1849 B.C.).

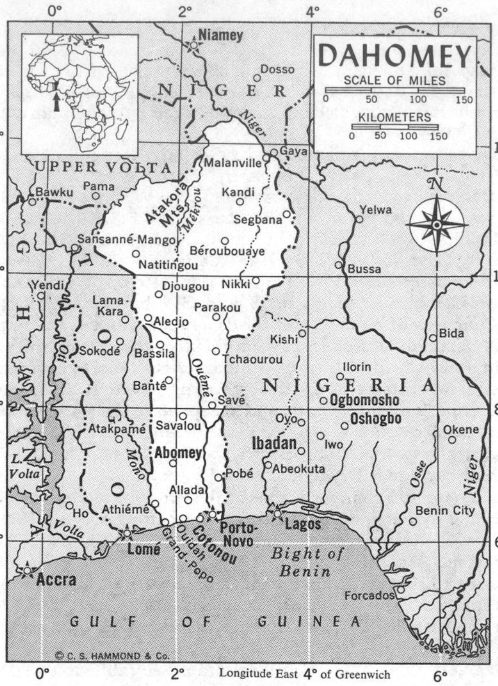

Daido. See TAEDONG.

Daihoku. See TAIPEI.

Dai·miel \dīm-'yel\. Manufacturing commune, Ciudad Real prov., S cen. Spain, 19 m. ENE of Ciudad Real; pop. (1970p) 17,710; manufactures linens, woolens, liquors, soap, lace; Gothic and Doric parish churches.

Dainan. See T'AI-NAN.

Dain·ger·field \'dān-jər-ˌfēld\. Town, ⊗ of Morris co., NE Texas; pop. (1970c) 2630.

Dai·qui·rí \ˌdī-kə-'rē\. Commune, El Caney municipality, Oriente prov., E Cuba, on coast 14 m. E of Santiago Bay; American troops landed June 22, 1898.

Dai·ren \'dī-'ren\; *Chin.* **Ta–lien** \'dä-lē-'en\ *or when grouped with Port Arthur* **Lü–ta** \'lü-'dä\; *Russ.* **Dal·ny** \'dal-nē\. City on S coast of Liao-tung Penin., Liaoning prov., China, 20 m. E of Port Arthur; pop. (1970e, including Port Arthur) 4,000,000; has one of finest harbors on East Asia coast and is NE China's leading port; sheltered on N, W, and S by hills; connects by rail with Mukden and railroad system of E China; shipbuilding; manufactures mining equipment, electrical machinery, machine tools; medical coll. (1949), technical coll. (1950).

History: Seaport and terminus of Siberian railroad by edict of Russian tsar July 30, 1899; opened to commerce 1901; in Russo-Japanese War occupied by Japanese May 1904; part of Kwantung (*q.v.*) leased to Japan by Treaty of Portsmouth Sept. 1905; again a free port 1906. In World War II bombed by American planes Sept.–Dec. 1944; taken by Soviet troops Aug. 1945; by Chinese-Soviet treaty of Aug. 1945 remained under Chinese sovereignty but a port with preferential rights for U.S.S.R.; Soviet troops withdrawn from area 1955.

Dai–sen \'dī-'sen\ *or* **Oya·ma** \ō-'yäm-ə\. Peak in Tottori prefecture, W Honshū, Japan, SE of Matsue; 5620 ft.; a beautiful cone-shaped peak, the highest of the volcanic peaks of SW Honshū.

Dai·tō \'dī-'tō\. City, Ōsaka prefecture, Honshū, Japan, 8 m. E of Ōsaka; pop. (1970c) 93,136.

Da·ja·bón \ˌdä-hə-'bōn\. **1** Province of N Dominican Republic. See table at DOMINICAN REPUBLIC.
2 Commune, its ✱; pop. (1970p) 5507.

Dakahliya. See DAQAHLIYA.

Da·kar \də-'kär, 'dak-ˌär\. Seaport, ✱ of Senegal and of former French West Africa, on S side of Cape Vert Penin.; pop. (1970e) 580,000; with Gorée, Rufisque, and adjacent area formed from 1924 to 1946 an autonomous circumscription, **Dakar and Dependencies** (60 sq. m.); naval yards, railroad workshops; footwear, textiles, soap; zoological garden (1903), univ. (1957); has one of best harbors on Atlantic coast of Africa; of strategic importance as dominating W tip of Africa equidistant (1860 m.) from Brazil and Europe.

History: Founded 1857 opp. settlement of Gorée (*q.v.*) which had been French since 17th cent.; railroad built from Dakar to Saint-Louis 1882–85; became naval base and, in 1902, capital of French West Africa (*q.v.*); after defeat of France, attacked unsuccessfully by forces of Free French and British Sept. 23–25, 1940; by decree of May 17, 1946 reunited with Senegal; became capital of Senegal 1958.

Da·khin Shah·baz·pur \də-ˌkin-shə-'baz-pu̇(ə)r, -'bäz-\ *or formerly* **Dak·shin** \'dək-shin\. Island in Meghna river, Bangla Desh; 615 sq. m.

Dakh·la \'däk-lə\. Oasis, Egypt, lat. 25°30′N and long. 29°E; chief town Al-Qasr.

Da·ko·ta \də-'kōt-ə\. **1** *or often called* **James** \'jāmz\. Name, by act of Territorial legislature, of river in North Dakota and South Dakota; 710 m. long; rises in Wells co., cen. North Dakota, flows S across E cen. South Dakota and empties into Missouri river at Yankton, Yankton co., SE South Dakota.
2 Name of counties in two states of the U.S. See tables at MINNESOTA and NEBRASKA.

Dakota City. 1 Town, ⊗ of Humboldt co., NW cen. Iowa; pop. (1970c) 746.
2 Village, ⊗ of Dakota co., NE Nebraska; pop. (1970c) 1057.

Dakota Territory. Former territory, U.S.A., named from important group of Siouan tribes; comprised the region on both sides of the middle course of Missouri river and W of the Red River of the North. First visited by La Vérendrye brothers 1742–43; greater part included in Louisiana Purchase 1803; N limit of NE section determined by treaty with Great Britain 1818; parts included in various territories of the U.S. bet. 1805 and 1861; organized as Dakota Territory (capital Yankton 1861–83, Bismarck 1883–89) Mar. 2, 1861 including much of Wyoming and Montana; reduced to area of present two states 1868; settlement hastened by discovery of gold 1874 in the Black Hills; admitted to the Union Nov. 2, 1889, by division into two states, "the Dakotas"—North Dakota and South Dakota (*qq.v.*).

Da·ko·vi·ca \dä-'kō-vət-sə\ *or* **Dja·ko·vi·ca** \dyä-\. Town, Serbia, S Yugoslavia, near Albanian border; pop. (1965e) 23,000.

Đa·ko·vo *or* **Dja·ko·vo** \'jä-kə-ˌvō\. Town, N Yugoslavia, 22 m. SW of Osijek; pop. (1965e) 13,000; episcopal see, one of whose bishops was Joseph G. Strossmayer, leader of Croatian National Party.

Dakshin. See DAKHIN SHAHBAZPUR.

Dal \'dəl\. Lake near Srinagar (*q.v.*), Jammu and Kashmir, N India.

Dal \'däl\ *also* **Dal·elf** \'däl-ˌelf\ *or* **Dal·älv** \-ˌelv\. River, S cen. Sweden; 250 m. long; formed by two forks, the **Ös·ter Dal** \'əs-tər-\ and **Väs·ter Dal** \'ves-tər-\; flows SE into Gulf of Bothnia.

Da·la·gue·te \ˌdäl-ə-'gā-tə\. Municipality on E coast of Cebu I., Phil., near S end on Bohol Strait 46 m. SSW of City of Cebu; pop. (1969e) 38,700.

Dalai. See HU-LUN.

Dalälv. See DAL.

Da·la·man \ˌdäl-ə-'män\. River, SW Turkey in Asia; 116 m. long; flows S to the Mediterranean.

Dalarna *or* **Dalarne.** See DALECARLIA.

Da Lat \'dä-'lät\. Town, South Vietnam, 48 m. NE of Saigon; pop. (1968e) 83,651.

Dalbo. See VÄNERN.

Dal·by \'dòl-bē\. Town, SE Queensland, Australia, in Darling Downs region on Condamine river 115 m. WNW of Brisbane; pop. (1966c) 8860.

Dale \'dāl\. 1 County in Alabama. See table at ALABAMA.

2 Borough, Cambria co., SW cen. Pennsylvania, near Johnstown; pop. (1970c) 2274.

Dal·e·car·lia \ˌdal-ə-'kär-lē-ə\; *Swed.* **Da·lar·na** \'däl-ər-ˌnä\ *or* **Da·lar·ne** \-nə\. Region in W cen. Sweden, approx. coextensive with Kopparberg co. (see table at SWEDEN); region of many historical associations; its people noted for their dialect, colorful costumes, and patriotism, esp. in 15th and 16th cents. (revolted against Eric XIII 1434–36, were strong supporters of Gustavus Vasa 1519–23). Rich in forests; iron and copper mines.

Dale·garth Force \ˌdāl-ˌgärth-'fō(ə)rs, -ˌfȯ(ə)rs\. Waterfall in W Cumberland, NW England, in the Lake District.

Dalelf. See DAL.

Dale·ville \'dāl-ˌvil\. Town, Dale co., SE Alabama, 22 m. WNW of Dothan; pop. (1970c) 5182.

Dal·ga \'dal-gə\. Town, Egypt, on left bank of Nile ab. 45 m. below Asyūt; pop. (1966c) 25,000.

Dal·hart \'dal-ˌhärt\. City, Dallam and Hartley cos., ⊗ of Dallam co., NW corner of Texas, in the Panhandle; 70 m. NNW of Amarillo; pop. (1970c) 5705; ships cattle and grain.

Dal·hou·sie \dal-'hau̇-zē\. 1 Seaport town, ⊗ of Restigouche co., N New Brunswick, Canada, on Chaleur Bay at mouth of Restigouche river; pop. (1971p) 6247; extensive lumber, lobster, and salmon trade; potatoes; resort; f. 1810.

2 *or locally* dəl-'hau̇-zē\. Town and hill station, Himachal Pradesh, N India, in Himalayas just E of upper Ravi river; elevation 7700 ft.; pop. (1961c) 2700.

Dali. See IDALIUM.

Da·lí·as \dä-'lē-əs\. Commune, Almería prov., SE Spain, 18 m. WSW of Almería; pop. (1970p) 21,230; lead mines; mineral baths nearby.

Dal·keith \dal-'kēth\. Burgh, Midlothian co., SE Scotland; pop. (1971p) 9529; trading center for grain; coal mining, brass founding; Dalkeith palace, residence of several British monarchs, has a noted picture gallery.

Dall \'dȯl\. Narrow island, S Alexander Archipelago, SE Alaska, SW of Prince of Wales I.; 43 m. long.

Dal·lam \'dal-əm\. County in Texas. See table at TEXAS.

Dal·las \'dal-əs, -is\. 1 Name of counties in five states of the U.S. See tables at ALABAMA, ARKANSAS, IOWA, MISSOURI, TEXAS.

2 City, ⊗ of Paulding co., NW Georgia, 30 m. WNW of Atlanta; pop. (1970c) 2133; lumber and cotton mills; scene of indecisive battle bet. the armies of Grant and Lee May 25–28, 1864 (battle of New Hope Church).

3 Town, Gaston co., SW North Carolina, 5 m. N of Gastonia; pop. (1970c) 4059; was ⊗ 1846–1911.

4 City, ⊗ of Polk co., NW Oregon, 15 m. W of Salem; pop. (1970c) 6361; lumber, leather, prunes; settled 1845.

5 Residential borough, Luzerne co., E Pennsylvania, 9 m. NNW of Wilkes-Barre; pop. (1970c) 2913; College Misericordia (1923).

6 Industrial and commercial city, ⊗ of Dallas co., NE Texas, on Trinity river ab. 33 m. E of Fort Worth; pop. (1970c) 844,401; commercial, financial, and transportation center; cotton market; manufactures cotton gins and other machinery, petroleum products, cotton textiles, airplanes and parts, electronic equipment; meat packing, motorcar assembling, printing and publishing; Dallas Baptist Coll. (1891), Southern Methodist Univ. (1910), Dallas Bible Coll. (1940), Univ. of Dallas (1956). Scene of Texas Centennial Exposition (1936), Pan American Exposition (1937); site first settled 1841; platted 1846 and became ⊗; incorp. as town 1856, as city 1871. President John F. Kennedy assassinated in city Nov. 1963.

Dallas, Lake. See GARZA DAM.

Dallas Peak. Mountain in Ouray and San Miguel cos., SW Colorado; 13,800 ft.

Dal·las·town \'dal-əs-ˌtau̇n\. Borough, York co., S Pennsylvania, 6 m. SE of York; pop. (1970c) 3560.

Dalles, The \-'dalz\. 1 *also* **City of the Dalles.** City, ⊗ of Wasco co., N Oregon, on Columbia river 13 m. W of its confluence with Deschutes river ab. 72 m. E of Portland; pop. (1970c) 10,423; E terminus of 200-mile waterway from the sea, opened by completion of Bonneville Dam and lock; salmon-packing plants, flour and lumber mills, canneries; ships fruit, grain, meat, wool. Indian mart found here by Lewis and Clark 1805; first settled by whites 1838; chartered 1857.

2 River, Wisconsin and Minnesota. See SAINT CROIX 2.

Dal·ma·tia \dal-'mā-sh(ē-)ə\ *or Serbo-Croat.* **Dal·ma·ci·ja** \'däl-ˌmät-sē-'(y)ä\. A region on the Adriatic coast of Yugoslavia; ab. 4916 sq. m.; former Austrian crownland; extends from near Albanian border on the S to Zadar on the N and includes many islands; name sometimes applied to most of the Yugoslav coast; mountainous (Dinaric Alps), many good harbors.

History: Conquered by Rome 34 B.C.; province of prefecture of Illyricum (*q.v.*) under Diocletian (d. 313 A.D.); in western part of Roman Empire after division of 395; part of Gothic kingdom of Odoacer; reconquered by Eastern Roman Empire under Justinian; invaded and settled by Slavonic peoples in 7th cent.; possession of coastal towns the goal of successive rulers of Croatia, Hungary, and Serbia, with Venetians endeavoring to gain foothold from 10th cent.; coast came under rule of Venice, 1420–1699; province, including interior, finally ceded to Venice by Turkey 1718; with suppression of Venetian Republic, held by Austria 1797–1805, 1815–1918 (part of Illyrian Provinces 1809–15); partly occupied by Italy 1918–19; joined Kingdom of Serbs, Croats, and Slovenes 1918 (see YUGOSLAVIA); Zara (Zadar) held by Italy which was forced to give up her other Dalmatian claims in Treaty of Rapallo 1920. In World War II seizure attempted by Germans but for the most part held under control of Yugoslav partisans; since 1945 included in federated republic of Croatia.

Dal·meny \dal-'men-ē\. Village, West Lothian co., Scotland, on Firth of Forth; pop. (1961c) 3429; cathedral.

Dal·ness \dal-'nes\. Deer forest, N Argyll co., W Scotland, NE of Loch Etive; 7520 acres.

Dalnevostochny Rayon. See FAR EASTERN REGION.

Dalny. See DAIREN.

Dal·ri·a·da \ˌdal-rē-'ad-ə\. 1 Ancient kingdom, N Ireland; now N part of co. Antrim, Northern Ireland.

2 Ancient kingdom, Argyll co., W Scotland; founded ab. 500 A.D. by emigrants from the Irish kingdom.

Dal·ton \'dȯlt-ᵊn\. 1 Industrial city, ⊗ of Whitfield co., NW Georgia, 38 m. N of Rome; pop. (1970c) 18,872; incorp. 1847, ⊗ 1851; headquarters of Gen. Joseph E. Johnston 1863–64; cotton and lumber mills; center of candlewick bedspread industry.

2 Town, Berkshire co., W Massachusetts, 5 m. ENE of Pittsfield; pop. (1970c) 7505; paper manufacturing.

Dal·ton·ganj \'dȯlt-ᵊn-ˌgənj\. Town, W Bihar state, NE India; pop. (1961c) 25,270; coal-mining region.

Dalton-in-Fur·ness \-'fər-nəs\. Urban district, Lancashire, NW England, near Irish Sea 52 m. N of Liverpool; pop. (1971e) 11,217.

Da·lu·pi·ri \ˌdäl-ü-'pi(ə)r-ē\. 1 Island in Babuyan group, Phil., N of Luzon; 24 sq. m.

2 Island off NW coast of Samar, Phil., on S side of San Bernardino Strait bet. Capul I. and Samar coast; 11 sq. m.; pop. (San Antonio municipality, 1969e) 7900.

Da·ly \'dā-lē\. River, N Northern Territory, Australia, flows W to Anson Bay; 225 m. long; navigable for 70 m.

Daly City. Residential city, San Mateo co., W California, S suburb of San Francisco; pop. (1970c) 66,922; absorbed town of Colma 1936.

Daly Waters. Village and post station on upper Roper river, N cen. Northern Territory, Australia.

Dam \'däm\. Town on Suriname river, E Surinam, 107 m. S from Paramaribo; terminus of only railroad in Surinam.

Da·man \də-'män\ *or Port.* **Da·mão** \də-'maůn\. 1 A constituent part of the centrally administered territory of Goa, Daman, and Diu, India; 22 sq. m.; captured by Portuguese 1559; annexed by India 1962.

2 Its chief town, a seaport, on Gulf of Cambay, W India, at mouth of Damanganga river 100 m. N of Bombay; pop. (1960c) 9194; once an active harbor, but now of decreasing importance; carries on fishing, shipbuilding, salt extracting, and cotton weaving.

Da·man·hūr \ˌdam-ən-'hů(ə)r\ *or anc.* **Her·mop·o·lis Par·va** \(ˌ)hər-ˌmäp-ə-lə-'spär-və\. City, ✱ of Beheira gov., Egypt, on railroad E of Alexandria and W of Rosetta branch of the Nile; pop. (1970e) 161,400; cotton.

Da·man·sky Island \də-'män(t)-skē-\. Island in Ussuri river on Sino-Soviet border; claimed by China and U.S.S.R.; scene of clashes between Soviet and Chinese forces 1969.

Damar. See DHAMAR.

Da·mar \'däm-ˌär\. Group of small islands in S Banda Sea, S Moluccas, Indonesia, NW of Babar Is.; part of the Serawatti Is. Chief island Damar, ab. 11 m. in diameter, has active volcano.

Da·ma·ra·land \də-'mär-ə-ˌland, 'dam-ə-rə-\. Region, cen. South-West Africa; a plateau region inhabited chiefly by the Damara, a race including two different peoples: the warlike Herero of Bantu stock (hence **Her·re·ro·land** \hə-'re(ə)r-ō-ˌland\ as an alternative name) and the Hill Damara of Hottentot and mixed breeds. Chief occupation cattle raising.

Dam·a·ri·scot·ta \ˌdam-ə-(ri-)ˌskät-ə\. Narrow inlet of the Atlantic Ocean, on the coast of Lincoln co., S Maine; 22 m. long.

Da·mas·cus \də-'mas-kəs\ *or French* **Da·mas** \da-mä\; *Arab.* **Ash Shām** \esh-'sham\ *or* **Di·mash** \di-'mäshk\. City, ✱ of Syria, on the Barada river, with Anti-Lebanon Mts. to the W and desert to the E; munic. pop. (1970e) 835,000; cement, glass, textiles, furniture; sugar refineries; univ. (1923), technical coll. (1963); believed to be the oldest city in the world having continuous existence; for centuries a great trade mart with many shops and bazaars; situated on edge of an oasis near beautiful gardens and groves; has Great Mosque (partly ruined), many small mosques.

History: Ancient city ruled by Egyptians and Hittites before it became an independent Aramaean kingdom c. 1000 B.C.; prominent in Hebrew history; fell before Assyrians 732 B.C.; later included in kingdoms of Babylonians, Persians, Alexander the Great, Ptolemies, and Seleucids; 661 A.D. became residence of caliph until overthrow of Ommiad line 750; frequently attacked during Crusades; occupied 1918 by British and Arabs as part of campaign in Syria; center of Syrian independence movement until seized by French 1920 and made a state in French mandate of Syria; united with Alep to form state of Syria 1925; forced by bombardment to submit to French after its occupation 1925 by Druses; captured by Free French and British June 1941.

Da·mā·vand \'dam-ə-ˌvand\ *or* **Dem·a·vend** \'dem-ə-ˌvend\. Peak, N Iran, NE of Tehran; 18,934 ft.; highest point in the Elburz Mts.

Damer, Ed. See ED DAMER.

Dām·ghān \däm-'gän\. Town, NW Khorāsān prov., NE Iran; pop. (1966c) 13,197; on main highway from Tehran to Khorāsān and terminus of railroad E from Tehran; was of greater importance in the Middle Ages; has interesting ruins dating from the 11th cent. See HECATOMPYLOS.

Dam·i·et·ta \ˌdam-ē-'et-ə\ *or Arab.* **Dum·yāṭ** \dům-'yät\. 1 *or anc.* **Phat·nit·ic** \fat-'nit-ik\. Eastern mouth of the Nile, W of Port Said, Egypt; partly silted up and not navigable to large vessels.

2 Governorate of N Egypt. See table at EGYPT.

3 Commercial city, N Egypt, port at mouth of the Damietta branch of the Nile, on E bank in the Nile delta 8 m. from the sea; pop. (1970e) 98,000; market center; cotton, silk, glassware; rice, fish; conquered by Crusaders 1219; taken by French Crusaders 1249.

Dam·loup \däⁿ-'lü\. Village, Meuse dept., NE France, 5 m. NE of Verdun; pop. (1962c) 116; severe fighting 1916 during World War I.

Dam·mam \dam-'mam\. Oil center, Saudi Arabia, near coast of Persian Gulf opp. Bahrain; cement plant.

Dam·ma·rie, Cape \-ˌdam-ə-'rē\. Cape at NW point of Tiburon Penin., SW Haiti, on S side of entrance to Gulf of Gonave.

Dammarie–les–Lys \-lā-'lē\. Commune, Seine-et-Marne dept., N France, near Melun; pop. (1968c) 12,057; ruins of 13th cent. abbey founded by Blanche of Castile.

Da·mo·dar \'däm-ə-ˌdär\. Navigable river, cen. Bihar and West Bengal states, NE India; 368 m. long; flows ESE into Hooghly river just below Nabadwip; several dams provide power for industrial projects in the region.

Da·moh \'dəm-(ˌ)ō\. Town, N Madhya Pradesh, India, 190 m. N of Nagpur; pop. (1961c) 46,656; market place for cattle and farm produce of district; pillaged by mutineers in Sepoy Mutiny 1857.

Dam·pier Archipelago \ˌdam-ˌpi(ə)r-\. Group of ab. 20 small rocky islands off NW coast of Western Australia, lat. 20°40′S.

Dampier Land. Peninsula, N Western Australia, bet. Indian Ocean and King Sound; Cape Leveque at tip.

Dampier Strait. 1 Passage off W end of New Britain I., Bismarck Archipelago, W Pacific Ocean; separates New Britain from Umboi I.; ab. 15 m. wide.

2 Channel bet. Waigeo I. and W end of the island of New Guinea; ab. 100 m. long and 35 m. wide.

Damp·re·my \däⁿ-rə-'mē\. Commune, Hainaut prov., SW Belgium; pop. (1969e) 9363; coal mines.

Dan \'dan\. 1 River, S Virginia; 180 m. long; rises in Patrick co., flows S into North Carolina, then E crossing state border several times before joining Roanoke river in S Virginia.

2 Ancient village at N extremity of Palestine (*Judges* xx. 1) on Lebanon border N of the Waters of Merom; now a mound 2 m. W of Baniyas, Syria. See BEERSHEBA.

Da·na, Mount \-'dā-nə\. Peak in Sierra Nevada, in E Tuolumne co., cen. California; 13,050 ft.

Dan·a·kil \'dan-ə-ˌkil\ *or Ital.* **Dan·ca·lia** \däŋ-'käl-yə\. Desert region, E Africa, in NE Ethiopia and N Afars and Issas; mostly in Great Rift Valley; inhabited by the Danakil, or Afar, people.

Da Nang \'dän-'äŋ\ *or formerly* **Tou·rane** \tü-'rän\. Seaport city, South Vietnam, 55 m. SE of Hue; pop. (1968e) 334,229; site of U.S. military base during Vietnam War 1965 *ff.*

Da·nao \də-'naů\. Chartered city on E coast of Cebu I., Phil., 17 m. NNE of City of Cebu; pop. (1970e) 45,500; port for nearby coal mines.

Danastris. See DNIESTER.

Dan·bury \'dan-ˌber-ē, -b(ə-)rē\. 1 City, Fairfield co., SW Connecticut, 20 m. NW of Bridgeport; pop. (1970c) 50,781; electronic equipment, aircraft parts, plastics, surgical instruments; Western Connecticut State Coll. (1903). Settled 1685; burned by British 1777 during Revolutionary War; became borough 1822, incorp. as city 1889; point of origin of Danbury's Hatters' Case 1902 (Supreme Court decision 1908 against boycott by labor organizations).

2 Town, ⊗ of Stokes co., N North Carolina; pop. (1970c) 152.

Dancalia. See DANAKIL.

Dandarah. See DENDERA.

Dan·dridge \'dan-drij\. Town, ⊗ of Jefferson co., E Tennessee; pop. (1970c) 1270.

Dane \'dān\. County in Wisconsin. See table at WISCONSIN.

Dane·law *also* **Dane·lagh** \'dān-ˌlo\. The NE part of England where Danish law was in force 9th and 10th cents.; covered East Anglia, Essex, a large part of Mercia, and most of Northumbria. See WEDMORE.

Dan·ger, Point \-'dān-jər\. Cape on E coast of Australia, most northerly point of New South Wales, at 28°09'S, 153°34'E.

Danger Islands. Island group in W Northern Cook Is., cen. Pacific Ocean, N of Cook Is.; chief island Pukapuka; administratively part of Cook Is.

Dangerous Islands. See TUAMOTU ARCHIPELAGO.

Dangla *or* **Dang–la.** **1** Mountain pass, Tibet. See T'ANG-LA. **2** Mountain range, Tibet. See T'ANG-KU-LA.

Dangra Yum. See T'ANG-KU-LA-YU-MU HU.

Dangrek Mountains. See PHANOM DONG RAK.

Dangs, The \-'daŋz\. Former group of 14 petty Indian states (once included in the Rewa Kantha Agency), subordinate to Gujarat States Agency, W India; 689 sq. m.; since 1960 part of Gujarat.

Da·nia \'dā-nē-ə\. City, Broward co., SE Florida, on Atlantic Ocean 20 m. N of Miami; pop. (1970c) 9013; resort; citrus fruit; incorporated 1927.

Dan·iels \'dan-yəlz\. County in Montana. See table at MONTANA.

Dan·iel·son \'dan-yəl-sən\. Borough in town of Killingly, Connecticut; pop. (1970c) 4580; paper products; incorporated 1854.

Dan·iels·ville \'dan-yəlz-ˌvil\. City, ⊗ of Madison co., NE Georgia; pop. (1970c) 378.

Danish West Indies. See VIRGIN ISLANDS.

Dan·lí \dän-'lē\. Town, El Paraíso dept., S Honduras, 45 m. E of Tegucigalpa; pop. (1961c) 6300; produces coffee, tobacco, sugar; gold mine nearby.

Danmark. See DENMARK.

Dan·ne·mo·ra \ˌdan-ə-'mō(ə)r-ə, -'mȯ(ə)r-\. **1** Village, Clinton co., NE corner of New York, 13 m. W of Plattsburg; pop. (1970c) 3755; iron deposits; manufactures toweling, ticking, yarn; Clinton State Prison (1845).
2 Commune, Uppsala co., SE Sweden, 22 m. N of Uppsala; pop. (1970e) 4147; iron mines.

Dan·ne·virke \'dan-ə-ˌvərk\. Borough, SE North I., New Zealand, 110 m. NE of Wellington; pop. (1970e) 5830; founded by Scandinavians.

Dan·no–ura *or* **Dan·no·u·ra** \ˌdän-ˌnō-ü-'rä\. Locality, E end of Shimonoseki (*q.v.*), Japan; naval battle 1185 in which the Taira clan was totally defeated by the Minamoto.

Dan River. See DAN.

Dansalan. See MARAWI.

Dans·ville \'danz-ˌvil\. Village, Livingston co., W New York, 21 m. NW of Hornell; pop. (1970c) 5436; fruit tree nurseries, canneries; health resort, sanitarium; birthplace of American Red Cross (founded by Clara Barton 1881).

Dan·ta \'dän-tə\. Former Indian state, Rajputana, NW India, NW of Jaipur; 347 sq. m.

Dantzig. See GDAŃSK.

Dan·ube \'dan-(ˌ)yüb\ *or Bulg.* **Du·nav** \'dü-'näv\ *or Ger.* **Do·nau** \'dō-ˌnaů\ *or Hung.* **Du·na** \'dün-(ˌ)ȯ\ *or Rom.* **Du·nă·rea** \'dü-nər-ˌyä\ *or Russ.* **Du·nai** \'dü-nī\; *anc.* **Da·nu·bi·us** \də-'n(y)ü-bē-əs, da-\ *or in lower course* **Is·ter** \'is-tər\. River in cen. Europe; 1776 m. long; drainage area 315,444 sq. m.; second longest river in Europe (Volga is longest); formed by confluence of Breg and Brigach rivers in the Black Forest, Baden-Württemberg, West Germany, 37 m. WNW of Lake Constance; flows E across S West Germany, across N Austria and Hungary; ab. 20 m. N of Budapest turns S and traverses cen. Hungary before entering Yugoslavia where it turns SE; flows E as it forms section of the Romanian-Bulgarian boundary; finally turns N across SE Romania and E into the Black Sea through several mouths (delta ab. 1000 sq. m. in area), the northernmost channel, the Kiliya mouth, now forming boundary bet. Romania and the Ukrainian S.S.R., U.S.S.R. Has many tributaries (approximately 300) draining the various ranges of the Alps and the Carpathians; chief tributaries on the left (N): Altmühl, Naab (West Germany), Morava (Austria and Czechoslovakia), Váh, Nitra, Hron (Czechoslovakia), Tisza (Yugoslavia and Hungary), Olt, Argeş, Siretul (Romania), and Prut (Romania and Moldavian S.S.R., U.S.S.R.); on the right (S): Iller, Lech, Isar, Inn (West Germany), Enns, Leitha (Austria), Rába (Hungary), Drava (Hungary and Yugoslavia), Sava, Morava (Yugoslavia), and Iskŭr (Bulgaria). Navigable as far as Ulm by boats of limited draft; in Austria bet. Linz and Vienna passes through defiles with picturesque scenery; just W of Turnu-Severin in Romania passes through the famous defile of the Iron Gate (*q.v.*).
History: Long an important highway for trade bet. central and E Europe, its significance increased with development of steam navigation in 19th cent.; free navigation of Danube established in 1856 (Declaration of Paris) and placed under supervision of a European Commission which was renewed several times; closed to ships of war 1878; internationalized 1919 by Treaty of Versailles; regulated by postwar commission operating under Danube Convention of 1921; part of regulation passed to Romania 1938; dominated by Germany who was admitted to membership of commission 1939; following World War II, new (Soviet dominated) regulatory body established with headquarters in Budapest, Hungary.

Da·nu·bia \da-'nyü-bē-ə\. Occasional name for countries and regions of the Danube basin.

Da·nu·bi·an Principalities \da-ˌnyü-bē-ən-\. Former name for Moldavia and Walachia (*qq.v.* for earlier history); ruled by Turkish governors although by treaty of Kuchuk Kainarji 1774, Russian intervention permitted; occupied by Russia 1810 and made subject to further Russian control 1812; guaranteed withdrawal of Turkish troops and greater autonomy 1829; occupied by Russia 1829–34, 1849–51, and 1853–56; as United Principalities of Moldavia and Walachia, had separate identical administrations 1858–61; completely united and named Romania 1861; union recognized by Sultan 1862; for later history, see ROMANIA.

Danubius. See DANUBE.

Danum. See DONCASTER.

Dan·vers \'dan-vərz\. Town, Essex co., NE corner of Massachusetts, 16 m. NNE of Boston; pop. (1970c) 26,151; leather and leather goods and chemicals; birthplace of Israel Putnam, Revolutionary commander.

Dan·ville \'dan-ˌvil\. **1** City, a ⊗ of Yell co., W cen. Arkansas; pop. (1970c) 1362.
2 City, ⊗ of Vermilion co., E Illinois, 33 m. E of Champaign; pop. (1970c) 42,570; commercial center of farming, dairy, and coal-mining region; flour and lumber mills; made ⊗ 1827, incorp. 1869.
3 Town, ⊗ of Hendricks co., cen. Indiana, 20 m. W of Indianapolis; pop. (1970c) 3771; Canterbury Coll. (1946; coed.).
4 City, ⊗ of Boyle co., cen. Kentucky, 32 m. SSW of Lexington; pop. (1970c) 11,542; market center for tobacco, hemp, and livestock, esp. horses. Centre College of Kentucky (1819); founded 1775; seat of government for the area 1785–92.
5 Borough, ⊗ of Montour co., E cen. Pennsylvania, 30 m. SE of Williamsport; pop. (1970c) 6176; iron ore, coal, limestone deposits; manufactures iron and steel; settled 1792.
6 Industrial city, Pittsylvania co., S Virginia, on Dan river 3 m. N of North Carolina border; 14 sq. m.; pop. (1970c) 46,391; politically independent; tobacco market; shipping

and trading center; manufactures textiles, brick, flour, paint; Stratford Coll. (1852), Averett Coll. (1859); Confederate Memorial Mansion. Founded 1793; seat of government briefly during last days of Southern Confederacy 1865.

7 Town, Richmond co., S Quebec, Canada, 27 m. N of Sherbrooke; pop. (1971p) 2589.

Danzig. See GDAŃSK.

Danzig, Gulf of *or* **Bay of Danzig.** Wide inlet of S Baltic Sea, N Poland.

Dao \ˈdaů, ˈdä-ō\. 1 Municipality, S Antique prov., Panay, Phil., on coastal highway 16 m. S of San Jose de Buenavista; pop. (1969e) 21,000.

2 Municipality, E cen. Capiz prov., Panay, Phil., on the Panay river and on railroad 15 m. SSW of Roxas; pop. (1969e) 22,600; trades in forest products.

Daph·nae \ˈdaf-nē\ *or Bib.* **Tah·pan·hes** \ˈtäp-ən-ˌhēz\ *or mod.* **Tall al–Da·fa·na** \ˌtal-al-ˈdäf-ə-nə\. Ancient fortress, NE Egypt, W of Suez Canal near Al-Qantara; archaeological site.

Daph·nē \ˈdaf-nē\. Town on coast near tip of Acte Penin., Chalcidice, Greece; has famous monastery.

Da·piak, Mount \-ˈdäp-ˌyäk\. Mountain, Zamboanga del Sur prov., Mindanao, Phil., 25 m. SSE of Dipolog; 8416 ft.; highest peak in province.

Da·pi·tan \də-ˈpē-ˌtän\. Chartered city, N Zamboanga del Norte prov., Mindanao, Phil., on **Dapitan Bay** (inlet of S side of passage bet. Sulu Sea and Mindanao Sea); pop. (1970e) 38,600; important trade center with good harbor; one of the oldest towns in the Philippines; place where Dr. José Rizal spent four years of exile 1893–96.

Dapsang. See GODWIN AUSTEN.

Da·qah·li·ya *also* **Da·kah·li·ya** \ˌdäk-ə-ˈlē-(y)ə\. Governorate of N Egypt. See table at EGYPT.

Da·ra \ˈdar-ə, ˈder-ə\. Ancient fortress in N Mesopotamia; captured by Persians 573 A.D. during war of Khosrau I against Justin II, ruler of Byzantine Empire.

Da·rab \də-ˈräb\. Town, Fārs prov., SW Iran, 130 m. SE of Shīrāz; pop. (1966c) 13,419; noted for its groves of oranges and lemons and for the large sculptured bas-relief nearby commemorating the victory 260 A.D. of Shapur I over the Roman emperor Valerian.

Dar–al–Baida. See CASABLANCA.

Da·ram \də-ˈräm\. Largest of coastal islands of Samar, Phil., off W coast in Samar Sea, W of Buad I.; 39 sq. m.

Dar·bhan·ga \dər-ˈbəŋ-gə\. City, N Bihar, NE India, 70 m. NE of Patna; pop. (1970e) 123,650; chief distribution and trade point for district's agricultural products; univ. (1961).

Dar·by \ˈdär-bē\. Borough, Delaware co., SE Pennsylvania, 5 m. W of Philadelphia; pop. (1970c) 13,729; industrial cranes, plastics; settled 1660.

Darchan. See DARHAN.

Dar·da·nelle \ˌdärd-ᵊn-ˈel\. City, a ⊗ of Yell co., W cen. Arkansas, on Arkansas river; pop. (1970c) 3297.

Dar·da·nelles \ˌdärd-ᵊn-ˈelz\ *or Turk.* **Ça·nak·ka·le Bo·ğa·zı** \ˌchän-ə-kə-ˈlā-ˌbō-(g)ä-ˈzē\; *anc.* **Hel·les·pon·tus** \ˌhel-ə-ˈspänt-əs\ *or angl.* **Hel·les·pont** \ˈhel-ə-ˌspänt\. Narrow strait, bet. Europe (Gallipoli Penin.) and Turkey in Asia; 38 m. long, 3/4 to 4 m. wide; connects Sea of Marmara with Aegean Sea.

History: Ancient Hellespont the scene of Xerxes' crossing to Europe in invasion of Greece 480 B.C. (see IRAN); crossed by Alexander the Great 334 B.C.; part of Eastern Roman (Byzantine) Empire until 14th cent.; crossed 1356 by Ottoman Turks who had settled at Gelibolu (*q.v.*) and fortified by Sultan Mohammed II 1462; with expansion of Russia to Black Sea, increased in strategic importance as only outlet for Russian fleet to Mediterranean; for history of control as an issue of European politics, part of Near Eastern Question, see the STRAITS; scene of Allied campaign during World War I 1915 (for land attack see GALLIPOLI PENINSULA).

Dar·di·stan \ˌdärd-ə-ˈstän\. Region, NW Jammu and Kashmir, N India, and N North-West Frontier Province, Pakistan; inhabited by the Dard, an Indo-Aryan people of the upper Indus valley, an important linguistic group.

Dare \ˈda(ə)r, ˈde(ə)r\. County in North Carolina. See table at NORTH CAROLINA.

Dar el Beida. See CASABLANCA.

Dar·ent \ˈdar-ənt\. River, W Kent, SE England; 20 m. long; flows NE to the Thames; navigable to Dartford.

Dar es Sa·laam *or* **Dar·es·sa·lam** \ˌdär-ˌes-sə-ˈläm\. Seaport city, ✱ of Tanzania, also ✱ of Coast region; pop. (1967c) 272,515; cement, glass, textiles, enamelware, footwear; food processing; univ. (1961); founded 1862 by sultan of Zanzibar; taken by Carl Peters for German East Africa Company, 1887; made capital of German East Africa 1891; captured by British 1916; became ✱ of Tanzania 1964.

Dar·field \ˈdär-ˌfēld\. Urban district, West Riding, Yorkshire, N England; pop. (1971p) 7739.

Dar·fur \där-ˈfů(ə)r\. Province, W Sudan, NE Africa; 199,650 sq. m.; pop. (1969e) 1,683,000; ✱ Al-Fashir; pastorialism; an independent kingdom until annexed by Egypt 1874; made part of Sudan (formerly Anglo-Egyptian Sudan) 1898.

Dar·ga·ville \ˈdär-gə-ˌvil\. Borough, North I., New Zealand, on Wairoa river near W coast 80 m. NNW of Auckland; pop. (1970e) 4060.

Darg Plateau \ˈdärg-\. Highland region, S end of Great Dividing Range, E Victoria, SE Australia; highest Mt. Bogong 6508 ft.

Dar Ha·mid \ˌdär-ha-ˈmēd\. Desert region, cen. Kordofan prov., Sudan.

Dar·han \ˈdär-ˌkän\ *also* **Dar·chan** \ˈdär-ˌkän\. Town, N Mongolian People's Republic, ab. 117 m. NNW of Ulan Bator; pop. (1969e) 22,800.

Darial Pass *or* **Dariel Pass.** See DARYAL PASS.

Dar·i·en \ˌdar-ē-ˈen, ˌder-\. 1 Residential town, SW Fairfield co., SW Connecticut, on Long Island Sound; pop. (1970c) 20,411; incorporated 1820; floral gardening.

2 City, ⊗ of McIntosh co., SE Georgia; pop. (1970c) 1826.

3 Village, Du Page co., NE Illinois, W of Chicago, pop. (1970c) 8077.

Da·rién \där-ˈyen\. 1 *or originally* **San·ta Ma·ría la An·ti·gua del Darién** \ˌsänt-ə-mə-ˈrē-ə-län-ˈtē-gwə-ˌdel-där-ˈyen\. Settlement and colony established by Spaniards on W shore of Gulf of Urabá on N coast (Pearl Coast) of Isthmus of Darien (later Isthmus of Panama, discovered early in 16th cent.); colony founded 1510 by Balboa, Pizarro, and others, by removing unsuccessful settlement (1509) of San Sebastián from E side of gulf; from here Balboa crossed the isthmus 1513 to discover the South Sea (Pacific); center of early Spanish exploration until replaced 1519 by Panama (Panamá); part of province of New Granada; in 1698 site of New Caledonia, founded by Darien company, a Scottish undertaking under William Paterson which sought to cut off Spanish colonies but was not maintained. For later history, see PANAMA.

2 Province of E Panama. See table at PANAMA.

3 Village, Canal Zone, on SE shore of Gatun Lake.

Darien, Gulf of. Inlet of the Caribbean Sea extending bet. E Panama and NW Colombia; receives the Atrato river; its inner section is the Gulf of Urabá.

Darien, Isthmus of. See PANAMA, ISTHMUS OF.

Da·rién, Ser·ra·nía del \ˌser-ə-ˈnē-ə-ˌdel-där-ˈyen\. Range in E Panama, extending in part along the Panama-Colombia boundary; average height ab. 3000 ft.

Dariorigum. See VANNES.

Dar·jee·ling *or* **Dar·ji·ling** \där-ˈjē-liŋ\. 1 District, West Bengal, NE India; 1160 sq. m.; pop. (1961c) 624,640; tea, rice, cardamom.

2 Town and hill station, Darjeeling dist., West Bengal, India; pop. (1961c) 40,651, including cantonments of Jalapahar and Lebong; on Sikkim border at av. elevation of 7500 ft.; commands one of finest views in the world

including Mt. Kanchenjunga, 40 m. directly N, and Mt. Everest (visible on clear days from nearby **Ti·ger Hill** \ˌtī-gər-\ 8515 ft.) 110 m. to the NW. Inhabitants chiefly Nepalese and Bhutanese; British connection began 1816. Summer headquarters of Bengal government. See SILIGURI.

Darke \'därk\. County in Ohio. See table at OHIO.

Dar·kot Pass \ˌdär-ˌkät-\. Mountain pass in a range of the E Hindu Kush, from Gilgit, in Jammu and Kashmir, to Chitral, in North-West Frontier Province, Pakistan; elev. 15,380 ft.

Dar·ling \'där-liŋ\. River, S Queensland and N and W New South Wales, SE Australia; 1702 m. long; navigable in part and at certain seasons; volume is very irregular; has headstreams in Great Dividing Range and Darling Downs; flows SW into Murray river near South Australia border.

Darling Downs \-'daůnz\. Pastoral district, SE Queensland, Australia, W of Brisbane; ab. 25,000 sq. m.; drained by upper tributaries of Darling river.

Darling Range. Mountain range, SW Western Australia, parallel with the coast; ab. 250 m. long; highest point 1910 ft.

Dar·ling·ton \'där-liŋ-tən\. **1** County in NE South Carolina. See table at SOUTH CAROLINA.

2 Town, its ⊗, 10 m. NW of Florence; pop. (1970c) 6990; trade center for agricultural region; manufactures cotton goods, tobacco, veneers; settled 1798.

3 City, ⊗ of Lafayette co., S Wisconsin, 18 m. E of Platteville; pop. (1970c) 2351.

4 County borough, Durham, N England, on the Skerne 50 m. N of Leeds; pop. (1971p) 85,889; railroad center; locomotive works, iron foundries, steel plants, woolen mills.

Darm·stadt \'därm-ˌstat, -ˌs(h)tät\. City, S Hesse state, West Germany, 17 m. S of Frankfurt-am-Main; pop. (1969e) 140,214; former ✱ of Hesse; chemicals, machinery, electrical equipment; printing; museum; 16th cent. town hall; technical univ. (1836, univ. status 1895). Made city 1330; to Hesse 1479; became capital of Hesse-Darmstadt 1567; burned by French 1688 and 1693; in World War II taken by Americans Mar. 26, 1945.

Darnah. See DERNA.

Dar·rell's Island \ˌdar-əlz-\ *or* **Dar·rell Island** \-əl-\. Small island in Great Sound, Bermuda, SW of Hamilton; transatlantic air base.

Dart \'därt\. River, S Devonshire, SW England; 46 m. long (incl. estuary); flows SE to English Channel at Dartmouth.

Dart, Cape. Cape at foot of Mt. Siple promontory, Marie Byrd Land, Antarctica, 123°W.

Dart·ford \'därt-fərd\. Municipal borough, Kent, SE England, on the Darent 15 m. ESE of London; pop. (1971p) 45,670; site of the first paper mill in England; scene of the outbreak of Peasants' Revolt (Wat Tyler's Rebellion) June 1381.

Dart·moor \'därt-ˌmů(ə)r, -ˌmō(ə)r, -mȯ(ə)r\. Tableland, S Devonshire, SW England; 365 sq. m.; mean elevation 1700 ft.; has wild open places, many tors (highest High Willhays 2039 ft.), and morasses; source of all principal Devonshire rivers; its forests, in cen. part, are only small tracts of dwarf oaks; prehistoric remains; established as a national park 1951; prison at Princetown built 1806 for French captives, convict station since 1850.

Dart·mouth \'därt-məth\. **1** Town, Bristol co., SE Massachusetts, 6 m. SW of New Bedford; pop. (1970c) 18,800; formerly a shipbuilding center; fishing.

2 Coastal town, Halifax co., S Nova Scotia, Canada, on Halifax harbor across from Halifax; pop. (1971p) 64,002; electronic equipment, wire and cable; breweries, oil refineries; founded by the English 1750; destroyed by Indians 1751 and rebuilt. Fort Clarence below the town overlooks narrow E passage of Halifax harbor.

3 Municipal borough, Devonshire, SW England, on English Channel at mouth of the Dart 25 m. E of Plymouth; pop. (1971p) 5696; shipbuilding yards; Royal Naval Cadet Training Coll.

Dar·ton \'därt-ᵊn\. Urban district, West Riding, Yorkshire, N England; pop. (1971p) 15,145.

Da·ru \'där-ü\. Town and port of entry on a small island, Papua New Guinea, lat. 9°04'S and long. 143°12'E, on N side of Torres Strait; pop. (1966p) 3663.

Dar–ul–Aman \ˌdär-ůl-ə-'män\. Suburb of Kabul, Afghanistan; planned by Amanullah Khan before his downfall 1929 as new modern capital; contains unfinished parliament buildings.

Da·ru·var \'där-ů-ˌvär\. Commune, Croatia, N Yugoslavia, 64 m. ESE of Zagreb; thermal springs.

Dar·vel Bay \ˌdär-vəl-\. Inlet of Celebes Sea, on SE coast of Sabah, East Malaysia, opp. W end of Sulu Archipelago of the Philippines.

Dar·wen \'där-wən, 'dar-ən\. Municipal borough, Lancashire, NW England, 17 m. NNW of Manchester; pop. (1969c) 28,500; coal mines, stone quarries; manufactures paper and cotton.

Dar·win \'där-wən\; *orig.* **Palm·er·ston** \'päm-ər-stən, 'päl-mər-\ *or later* **Port Darwin.** Seaport, ✱ of Northern Territory, Australia, on **Port Darwin** (an inlet of Clarence Strait); pop. (1968e) 21,617; one of the best harbors in Australia; supply and shipping point for N Australia; terminus of overland telegraph and highway from Adelaide; center of sparsely populated and largely undeveloped region. Founded 1869; headquarters of Allied armies in N Australia 1941–45; bombed by Japanese 1942.

Darwin, Mount. Peak in Sierra Nevada, on boundary bet. Fresno and Inyo cos., SE cen. California; 13,841 ft.

Daryācheh–ye Namak. See NAMAK, DARYĀCHEH-YE.

Daryācheh–ye Sīstān. See HELMAND 1.

Dar·yal Pass *or* **Dar·i·al Pass** \där-'yal-\ *or* **Dar·i·el Pass** \där-'yel-\. Gorge in the Caucasus Mts., Russian S.F.S.R., U.S.S.R., E of Mt. Kazbek; traversed by Terek river; has vertical rock walls 5900 ft. high. Probably the only early passage across the Caucasus Mts.; fortified as early as 150 B.C.; through it was constructed 1811–64 the Georgian Military Road from Tbilisi to Ordzhonikidze.

Dasht \'dasht\. River, SW Baluchistan, Pakistan; 265 m. long; flows SW into Arabian Sea.

Dasht–e–Ka·vir \-ˌē-kə-'vi(ə)r\ *or* **Great Salt Desert.** Salt desert, a plateau, in N cen. Iran; alt. 2500 ft.

Dasht–e–Lūt \-ē-'lüt\. Tableland, cen. and E cen. Iran; alt. 1000 ft.; largely desert.

Dashur. See DAHSHÛR.

Da·sol Bay \dä-ˌsȯl-\. Inlet of South China Sea on SW coast of Pangasinan prov., Luzon, Phil.

Das·pal·la \dəs-'pəl-ə\. Former Indian state, SE Eastern States, NE India, W of Cuttack; region now in Orissa state; 556 sq. m.

Da·ta \'dät-ə\. Mountain in S part of Cordillera Central, N Luzon, Phil.; 7577 ft.

Date Line *or* **International Date Line.** A hypothetical line coinciding approximately with the meridian 180° from Greenwich, fixed by international or general agreement as the place where each calendar day first begins. The day for any given locality commences when it is midnight at that place; hence, any given day, say Monday, first begins at midnight on the date line, and following the midnight line begins continuously farther westward, in New Zealand, Australia, etc. It is thus Monday from the date line westward to the midnight line and Sunday from the date line eastward to the midnight line. Finally, as the midnight line reaches the date line again, it is for the instant Monday over practically the whole world; then Tuesday begins, and so on. Thus for the greater part of the twenty-four hours Hawaii has the same day name as San Francisco, and

Manila the same day name (one day later than the day of Hawaii) as Australia. Thus, when it is Monday noon, May 1, at San Francisco, it is 4 o'clock (standard time) or 14 minutes past 4 (local mean time) Tuesday morning, May 2, at Manila. A vessel crossing the date line to the westward sets the date forward by one day, as from Sunday to Monday; if the line is crossed in going eastward, the date is set back. To avoid dividing places in close intercourse, the line is deflected bet. 45°N lat. and 80°N lat., so that all Asia lies to the W of it, all North America, including the Aleutian Is., to the E; and bet. 12°S lat. and 56°S lat. the line is deflected so that Chatham Is. and the Tonga group lie to the W.

Da·tia *also* **Dut·tia** \'dət-ē-ə\. 1 Former Indian state, now part of Madhya Pradesh, N cen. India; 846 sq. m.; ✱ Datia; came under British government by treaty 1802.

2 Town, its ✱, 45 m. SSE of Gwalior; pop. (1961c) 29,420; has Hindu palace.

Dat·il Range \ˌdat-ᵊl-\. Range in W cen. New Mexico, extending across N part of boundary bet. Catron and Socorro cos.

Dat·teln \'dät-ᵊln\. Commune, North Rhine-Westphalia, West Germany, in the valley of the Lippe 24 m. SSW of Münster; pop. (1969e) 34,659; coal mining; manufactures leather, chemicals, wire.

Da·tu, Cape \-dä-'tü\ *or Du.* **Tan·djoeng Da·toek** \ˌtän-ˌju̇ŋ-dä-'tu̇k\. Cape, W Borneo, projecting into South China Sea at ab. 109°30′E, marking the boundary bet. W Sarawak, East Malaysia and the NW part of the Indonesian prov. of West Kalimantan.

Datu Bay. Inlet of South China Sea in SW Sarawak, bet. delta of Rajang river and mouth of Sarawak river, N of Kuching; receives the Batang Lupar.

Daugava. See DVINA, WESTERN.

Dau·gav·grī·va \'dau̇-gəv-ˌgrē-və\ *or Russ.* **Dau·ga·va** \'dau̇-gə-və\ *or Ger.* **Dü·na·mün·de** \ˌd(y)ün-ə-'m(y)ün-də\ *or formerly* **Ust Dvinsk** \'üst-də-'vin(t)sk\. Harbor and fortress on island at mouth of the Western Dvina on the Gulf of Riga, cen. Latvian S.S.R., U.S.S.R., 8 m. N of Riga; serves as Riga's port in winter; held by Germans 1917–18 in World War I and 1941–44 in World War II.

Dau·gav·pils \'dau̇-gəf-ˌpilz\ *or Russ.* **Dvinsk** \də-'vin(t)sk\ *or Ger.* **Dü·na·burg** \'d(y)ü-nə-ˌbu̇(ə)rg\. City, E Latvian S.S.R., U.S.S.R., on Western Dvina river; pop. (1970p) 101,000; railroad junction 136 m. SE of Riga; trade center for lumber and agricultural products (esp. grain, flax). Founded 1274 by Teutonic Knights; under Polish rule 1559–1772, Russian rule 1772–1915; resisted repeated attacks by Germans 1915–18; occupied 1918 by Bolshevik army, which was expelled Jan. 1920 by Latvian-Estonian-Polish force; held 1941–44 by Germans in World War II.

Dau·lat·a·bad \ˌdau̇-lət-ə-'bäd\. Town, NW cen. Maharashtra state, S cen. India, ab. 10 m. NW of Aurangabad; has remarkable fortress on rock ab. 600 ft. high within which are ruins of tower, palace, temple, and other structures. As **De·o·gi·ri** \ˌdā-ə-'jir-ē\ founded c. 1187; captured 1296 by Ala-ud-din of the Khilji dynasty; made capital of India by Mohammed Tughlak in 1339 who gave it its present name; later, held by various Muslim rulers; after 1707 came into possession of nizam of Hyderabad.

Dau·le \'dau̇-(ˌ)lā\. 1 River, NW Ecuador; 55 m. long; flows N into Esmeraldas river.

2 Town, Guayas prov., W Ecuador, on E bank of Daule river 22 m. N of Guayaquil; pop. (1962c) 7428.

Dau·lis \'dȯ-ləs\. Ancient city of Phocis, cen. Greece, 12 m. E of Delphi; scene of legend of Philomela.

Daung Island \'dau̇ŋ-\ *or formerly* **Ross Island** \'rȯs-\. Island, N Mergui Archipelago (*q.v.*), Burma.

Dau·phin \'dȯ-fən\. 1 County in Pennsylvania. See table at PENNSYLVANIA.

2 River, S cen. Manitoba, Canada, connecting Lake Manitoba with Lake Winnipeg; ab. 70 m. long; passes through Lake St. Martin.

3 Town, SW cen. Manitoba, Canada, 10 m. W of S end of Lake Dauphin; pop. (1971p) 8860; barley, timber; fisheries.

Dauphin, Lake. Lake, SW Manitoba, Canada, W of N Lake Manitoba; 200 sq. m.

Dau·phi·né \ˌdō-fi-'nā\. Historical region and former province of SE France; bounded anciently on N by Burgundy, E by Savoy (kingdom of Sardinia), S by Provence, SW by Comtat Venaissin, W by Languedoc, NW by Lyonnais; equivalent to modern departments of Drôme, Hautes-Alpes, Isère; ✱ Grenoble; watered by Drôme, Isère, and Durance rivers; mountainous in E.

History: Region occupied by Burgundians, later by Franks; formed part of Lothair's kingdom (see LORRAINE) and of kingdom of Arles (*q.v.*); from 10th to 13th cents. consolidated and expanded by counts of Vienne who were vassals of Holy Roman Empire; acquired by Philip VI of France 1349; became appanage of eldest son of French king who assumed title (*dauphin*) attached to the land.

Dauphiné Alps. See table at ALPS.

Dauphin Island \'dȯ-fən-\. Island at entrance to Mobile Bay, off SW coast of Alabama; included in Mobile co.; discovered by Iberville 1699.

Da·van·ge·re \də-'vəŋ-gə-ˌrā\. Town, E Mysore state, S India, 155 m. NW of Bangalore; pop. (1961c) 78,124.

Da·vao \'dä-ˌvau̇\. 1 Former province, SE Mindanao, Phil., now consisting of the provinces of Davao del Sur, Davao del Norte, and Davao Oriental; region very mountainous with high peaks in E and Mt. Apo 9690 ft., highest in the Philippines, on W border. Agusan river rises in SE and flows N, other short streams flow E to Pacific or S or E to Davao Gulf; at N end of Davao Gulf is large Samal I. and off Tinaca Point in SW are Sarangani Is.

History: Visited by Spaniards in 16th cent. but region under jurisdiction of sultanate of Mindanao until middle of 19th cent.; organized as a Spanish province 1849 and changed to a military district 1860; under Americans became part of Moro Province 1903; granted civil government 1914; from ab. 1902 when Japanese colonies were formed to raise hemp, received increasing numbers of Japanese, until in 1940 there were ab. 20,000 of them; seized by Japanese navy Dec. 20, 1941; partitioned into the provinces Davao del Norte, Davao del Sur, and Davao Oriental 1969.

2 *or officially* **City of Davao.** Chartered city, ✱ of former Davao prov., Mindanao, Phil., on NW shore of Davao Gulf opp. Samal I.; pop. (1970p) 392,473; shipping point for copra, corn, rice; univ. (1965). Founded 1849; in 20th cent. developed as part of Japanese colony; seized by Japanese navy Dec. 20, 1941 and made a naval base; bombed by U.S. planes Sept. 1944; retaken by Allied forces May 1945.

Davao del Nor·te \-del-'nȯrt-ē\. Province, Mindanao, Phil.; 3138 sq. m.; pop. (1970p) 438,795; ✱ Tagum; abacá, copra, corn, rice. See DAVAO 1.

Davao del Sur \-del-'su̇(ə)r\. Province, Mindanao, Phil.; 2462 sq. m.; pop. (1970p) 733,873; ✱ Digos; abacá, copra, rice. See DAVAO 1.

Davao Gulf. Large inlet of Pacific Ocean, Mindanao, Phil.; ab. 80 m. long by 45 m. wide; marked on SE side of entrance by Cape San Agustin and on SW by Calian Point; Samal I. is at its N end.

Davao Ori·en·tal \-ȯr-ē-en-'täl\. Province, Mindanao, Phil.; 1994 sq. m.; pop. (1970p) 247,388; ✱ Mati; abacá, copra, corn. See DAVAO 1.

Dav·en·port \'dav-ən-ˌpō(ə)rt, -ˌpȯ(ə)rt\. 1 City, ⊗ of Scott co., E Iowa, on Mississippi river across from Rock Island, Ill.; pop. (1970c) 98,469; railroad, commercial, and industrial center; shipping point for grain; manufactures railroad equipment, aluminum sheets and plates, cereal products, cement, farm implements; St. Ambrose Coll. (1882), Marycrest Coll. (1939). Founded 1835 on the site of an Indian village; made ⊗ 1838; site of the first railroad bridge across the Mississippi river, completed 1856.

2 Town, ⊗ of Lincoln co., E Washington; pop. (1970c) 1363.

Dav·en·try \'dav-ən-trē\. Municipal borough, Northamptonshire, cen. England; pop. (1971p) 11,813.

Da·vid \dä-'vēd\. Town, ✻ of Chiriquí prov., W Panama; pop. (1970p) 58,827; its port, Pedregal, is 5 m. to the S.

David City \'dā-vəd-\. City, ⊗ of Butler co., E Nebraska, 39 m. NNW of Lincoln; pop. (1970c) 2380; trade center.

David–Go·ro·dok \də-'vēd-ˌgȯr-ə-'däk\ *or Pol.* **Da·wid·gró·dek** \ˌdäv-əd-'grü-ˌdek\. Town, Belorussian S.S.R., U.S.S.R., on Goryn river 49 m. E of Pinsk; pop. (1959c) 9000; formerly in Poland.

David Point \ˌdā-vəd-\. Cape on S side of W St. Thomas I., Virgin Is., West Indies, W of Fortuna Bay.

Da·vids Island \ˌdā-vədz-\. Island in Long Island Sound, New York, near New Rochelle; Fort Slocum.

Da·vid·son \'dā-vəd-sən\. **1** Name of counties in two states of the United States. See tables at NORTH CAROLINA and TENNESSEE.

2 Town, Mecklenburg co., S North Carolina, 18 m. N of Charlotte; pop. (1970c) 2931; Davidson Coll. (1837).

Davidson, Mount. Peak, site of Virginia City, Storey co., W Nevada; 7870 ft.

Da·vie \'dāv-ē\. **1** County in North Carolina. See table at NORTH CAROLINA.

2 Town, Broward co., SE Florida; pop. (1970c) 4977.

Da·viess \'dā-vəs\. Name of counties in three states of the U.S. See tables at INDIANA, KENTUCKY, MISSOURI.

Da·vis \'dā-vəs\. **1** Name of counties in two states of the U.S. See tables at IOWA and UTAH.

2 City, Yolo co., N cen. California, 15 m. W of Sacramento; pop. (1970c) 23,488; agricultural implements; University of California at Davis (1908); experimental farm.

3 Town, Murray co., S Oklahoma, on Washita river 23 m. N of Ardmore; pop. (1970c) 2223; oil wells.

Davis, Mount *also* **Davis Mountain** *or formerly* **Ne·gro Mountain** \ˌnē-grō-\. Peak, Somerset co., S Pennsylvania; 3213 ft.; highest peak in the state.

Davis Bridge Dam. See HARRIMAN DAM.

Davis Islands. Three man-made islands, Tampa, Florida, at mouth of Hillsborough river; municipal hospital and several recreational centers.

Davis Mountain. See DAVIS, MOUNT.

Davis Mountains. Small range in Jeff Davis co., W Texas; includes Mt. Livermore 8382 ft.

Da·vi·son \'dā-və-sən\. **1** County in South Dakota. See table at SOUTH DAKOTA.

2 City, Genesee co., SE cen. Michigan, 10 m. E of Flint; pop. (1970c) 5259; diversified agriculture.

Davis Peak. Mountain, N Cascade Range, NW Washington; 7150 ft.

Davis Strait. Strait bet. SW Greenland and E Baffin I., connecting Baffin Bay with the Atlantic Ocean; width at its narrowest point 200 m. Discovered by John Davis during voyage in search of Northwest Passage (*q.v.*) 1585; Greenland side of strait explored by Davis in 1587 when he sailed through it into Baffin Bay.

Da·vos \dä-'vōs\. Commune, Graubünden canton, E Switzerland, in Davos valley 13 m. ESE of Chur; pop. (1970c) 10,238; site of Federal Institute for Snow and Avalanche Research; consists of villages of **Davos–Platz** \-'pläts\ and **Davos–Dorf** \-'dȯ(ə)rf\; famous as a center for winter sports and, owing to its dry and sunny climate, as a winter and summer health resort, esp. for tuberculars.

Da·wa \də-'wä\. River, S Ethiopia; flows SE to join the Genale and Weyib rivers and form the Juba; also forms part of the boundary bet. Ethiopia and Kenya.

Da·wa·sir \də-'wäs-ər\. Watercourse in SW cen. Saudi Arabia; flows NE, then NW; dry at some seasons.

Dawes \'dȯz\. County in Nebraska. See table at NEBRASKA.

Dawidgródek. See DAVID-GORODOK.

Daw·ley \'dȯ-lē\. Urban district, Shropshire, W England, on Shrewsbury Canal 28 m. WNW of Birmingham; pop. (1971p) 25,935.

Daw·lish \'dȯ-lish\. Coast town, Devonshire, SW England, on the English Channel 12 m. S of Exeter; pop. (1971p) 9505; seaside resort.

Daw·na Range \ˌdȯ-nə-\. Mountain range extending NW and SE along boundary bet. E cen. Burma and W Thailand, W of Thaungyin river; highest point 6819 ft.

Daw·ros Head \ˌdȯ-ˌräs-\. Cape on W coast of co. Donegal, N Eire, N of Donegal Bay.

Daw·son \ˌdȯs-ᵊn\. **1** Name of counties in four states of the U.S. See tables at GEORGIA, MONTANA, NEBRASKA, TEXAS.

2 City, ⊗ of Terrell co., SW Georgia, 22 m. NW of Albany; pop. (1970c) 5383; lumber, peanuts.

3 River, E Queensland, Australia, S tributary of Fitzroy river; 312 m. long; flows N.

4 City, Yukon Territory, N Canada, on right bank of the Yukon near where it is joined by the Klondike, ab. 50 m. E of Alaska boundary; pop. (1971p) 745; elevation 1400 ft.; a receiving and distributing center of the Klondike mining region; has steamer connections both up and down the Yukon; temperature frequently averages 40° below zero for several days. Had its beginnings in 1896 in the Klondike gold rush, when for several years it was much larger than now; capital of Yukon Terr. 1898–1951.

5 Chilean island in Tierra del Fuego archipelago (*q.v.*) off W coast of Tierra del Fuego I.; separated from Brunswick Penin. on W by Strait of Magellan.

Dawson, Mount. Mountain, SE British Columbia, Canada; 11,023 ft.; in Selkirk Mts., in Glacier National Park.

Dawson Creek. City, NE British Columbia, Canada, 315 m. NW of Edmonton near Alberta border; pop. (1971p) 11,488; wheat, livestock; timber; starting point of the Alaska Highway (*q.v.*).

Dawson Springs. Resort city, Hopkins co., W Kentucky, 53 m. E of Paducah; pop. (1970c) 2830; chemicals; mineral springs.

Daw·son·ville \'dȯs-ᵊn-ˌvil\. Town, ⊗ of Dawson co., N Georgia; pop. (1970c) 288.

Dax \'daks\ *or* **Ax** \'aks\; *anc.* **Aq·uae Tar·bel·li·cae** \'ak-(ˌ)wē-tär-'bel-ə-ˌsē, 'ak-\ *or later* **Aquae Au·gus·tae** \-ȯ-'gəs-(ˌ)tē\. Commune, Landes dept., SW France, on Adour river 30 m. SW of Mont-de-Marsan; pop. (1968c) 19,348; hot saline springs; mineral baths; 14th cent. castle; 18th cent. cathedral; terminus of French-Spanish tunnel. Ancient Gallic town; made episcopal see early in Christian era; capital of viscountship in Béarn during Middle Ages.

Day \'dā\. County in South Dakota. See table at SOUTH DAKOTA.

Dayr–az–Zawr. See DEIR-EZ-ZOR.

Day·ton \'dāt-ᵊn\. **1** City, Campbell co., N Kentucky, on Ohio river 3 m. above Newport; pop. (1970c) 8751; corn, tobacco.

2 Village, Lyon co., W Nevada, ab. 11 m. NE of Carson City; gold discovered here 1849.

3 Manufacturing city, ⊗ of Montgomery co., SW Ohio, on Miami river 47 m. N of Cincinnati; pop. (1970c) 243,601; aviation and aeronautical research center, site of government-owned Wright-Patterson Air Force Base and Fairfield Air Depot; cash registers, electric refrigerators, air-conditioning equipment, paper, computing scales, machinery and tools, automotive parts and accessories, rubber products, U.S. stamped envelopes, household appliances. Sinclair Community Coll. (1887), Univ. of Dayton (1850), Wright State Univ. (1964). Settled 1796, became ⊗ 1803, incorp. 1805; suffered from disastrous flood Mar. 1913; first large city to adopt commission-manager form of government (1913). Home of Wilbur and Orville Wright.

4 City, ⊗ of Rhea co., E cen. Tennessee; pop. (1970c) 4361; hosiery, lumber, flour; coal mining. William Jennings Bryan Coll. (1930); scene of Scopes test case evolution trial July 1925.

5 Town, Liberty co., E Texas, 43 m. NE of Houston; pop. (1970c) 3804; diversified agriculture.

6 City, ⊗ of Columbia co., SE Washington, 27 m. NE of Walla Walla; pop. (1970c) 2596; fruit and vegetable canneries and packing plants, sawmills, creamery.

Day·to·na Beach \dā-ˌtō-nə-\. Winter resort city, Volusia co., E Florida, on Atlantic Ocean 92 m. SSE of Jacksonville; pop. (1970c) 45,327; noted esp. for its hard, white beach; Daytona International Speedway; Bethune-Cookman Coll. (1872), Daytona Beach Junior Coll. (1958); settled c. 1870; formed 1926 by consolidation of municipalities of Seabreeze, Daytona Beach, and Daytona.

De Aar \dē-'är\. Town, cen. Cape Province, S Rep. of South Africa, 240 m. NNW of Port Elizabeth; pop. (1967e) 16,600; important railroad junction of main lines from Cape Town and Port Elizabeth; in grazing region.

Dead Indian Peak. Mountain, W Park co., NW Wyoming, in the Absaroka Range, 28 m. WNW of Cody; 12,216 ft.

Dead·man Mountain \ˌded-ˌman-\. Peak, N Lincoln co., W Wyoming; 10,365 ft.

Dead·mans Bay \ˌded-ˌmanz-\. Inlet of Gulf of Mexico on coast of upper Dixie and lower Taylor cos., NW Florida penin.

Dead Man's Hill. See LE MORT HOMME.

Dead Sea *or anc.* **La·cus As·phal·ti·tes** \'lā-kə-ˌsas-ˌfȯl-'tīt-ēz\ *or Arab.* **Bah·ret Lut** \ˌbä-ret-'lüt\. Salt lake on the boundary between Israel and Jordan; 51 m. long, 11 m. wide at its greatest breadth; 394 sq. m.; surface 1302 ft. below the level of the Mediterranean Sea; lowest point on earth's surface; receives the Jordan at N end; has had many names and has figured in many events of Biblical history.

Dead·wood \'ded-ˌwu̇d\. 1 River in Valley and Boise cos., W cen. Idaho; tributary of S fork of Payette river; **Deadwood Dam** (height 165 ft.; completed 1931) and **Deadwood Reservoir** in S Valley co. impound its waters for irrigation purposes.

2 City, ⊗ of Lawrence co., W South Dakota, in **Deadwood Gulch** in N Black Hills, 4 m. N of Lead; pop. (1970c) 2409; trade center for surrounding mining camps and cattle ranches; mining, ore smelting and refining, lumbering, livestock raising; tourist center; laid out in 1876 following discovery of gold in Deadwood Gulch (1875).

Deaf Smith \'def-'smith, 'dēf-\. County in Texas. See table at TEXAS.

Deal \'dē(ə)l\. 1 Borough and summer resort, Monmouth co., E cen. New Jersey, on Atlantic Ocean ab. 4 m. S of Long Branch; pop. (1970c) 2401.

2 Municipal borough, Kent, SE England, on Strait of Dover 8 m. NNE of Dover; pop. (1971p) 25,413; large safe anchorage; boatbuilding center; reputed landing place of Julius Caesar 55 B.C.

Deal Island. Small island, partly marshland, in Tangier Sound, Chesapeake Bay, NW Somerset co., Maryland.

Dean, Forest of \-'dēn\. Ancient royal forest, since 1938 a national park, W Gloucestershire, SW cen. England, bet. the Severn and the Wye; ab. 20 m. long, 10 m. wide; contains iron and coal mines.

Dean Channel. Inlet of Pacific Ocean (Queen Charlotte Sound), W British Columbia, Canada; ab. 75 m. long; receives **Dean River** (ab. 150 m. long) from the E; connects with Burke Channel on S.

De·án Fu·nes \dā-'än-'fü-nəs\. Town, Córdoba prov., N cen. Argentina, on railroad 75 m. NNW of Córdoba; pop. (1960c) 16,280.

Dear·born \'di(ə)r-ˌbȯ(ə)rn, -bərn\. 1 County in Indiana. See table at INDIANA.

2 City, Wayne co., SE Michigan, 10 m. W of Detroit; pop. (1970c) 104,199; Henry Ford Community Coll. (1938); site of the Ford automobile-manufacturing plant; aircraft parts, tools and dies; incorporated as city 1925.

Dearborn Heights. City, Wayne co., SE Michigan, 8 m. E of Detroit; pop. (1970c) 80,069.

Dearg, Ben. See BEN DEARG.

Dearne \'dərn\. 1 River, West Riding, Yorkshire, N England; 25 m. long; tributary of the Don.

2 Urban district, West Riding, Yorkshire, N England; pop. (1971p) 25,029.

Dease \'dēs\. River, British Columbia, Canada; ab. 120 m. long; flows N from small Dease Lake to the Liard at Lower Post on the Alaska Highway.

Dease Strait. Channel bet. S Victoria I. and N Canada mainland, E of Coronation Gulf.

Death Valley \ˌdeth-\. 1 Valley in Inyo co., E California, bet. Panamint Mts. on W and Amargosa Range on E; ab. 140 m. long; Amargosa river flows into it from S; contains small pool, Badwater, lowest point in U.S., 282 ft. below sea level, less than 80 m. from Mt. Whitney (14,494 ft., highest point in U.S. outside of Alaska); has been set aside as **Death Valley National Monument:** see UNITED STATES, *National Monuments.*

2 Post office, Inyo co., E California, E of Death Valley National Monument.

Deau·ville \'dō-ˌvil, dō-'vē(ə)l\. Commune, Calvados dept., NW France, on the Bay of the Seine ab. 20 m. NE of Caen; pop. (1962c) 5239; resort, racecourse; just E of Normandy invasion coast 1944.

De·ba \'dā-bə\. Town, North-Eastern State, Nigeria; pop. (1969e) 70,369.

De Ba·ca \dē-'bä-kə\. County in New Mexico. See table at NEW MEXICO.

De·bar \'deb-är\. Fortified town, W Macedonia, Yugoslavia, near the Drin river and Albanian border; pop. (1961c) 6341; commercial center; cattle breeding; nearby sulfurous springs. Assigned to Serbia 1913; belonged to Vardarska co. 1929–45.

Debba, Ed. See ED DEBBA.

Deb·dou \deb-'dü\. Town, NE Morocco, NW Africa, ab. 80 m. SW of Oujda.

Dę·bi·ca \də-'bēt-sə\. Town, Rzeszów prov., SE Poland; pop. (1970p) 22,900.

De Bildt \də-'bilt\. Commune, Utrecht prov., cen. Netherlands, a suburb of Utrecht; pop. (1970e) 29,153.

Dę·blin \'dem-blən\; *Russ.* **Ivan·go·rod** \i-'van-gə-(ˌ)rət\. Town, Lublin prov., E Poland, at junction of Wieprz and Vistula rivers; pop. (1966e) 11,700; taken by Germans Aug. 4, 1915.

De·bo, Lake \-'dā-(ˌ)bō\. Lake, cen. Mali, W Africa, ab. 150 m. SW of Tombouctou; traversed from SW to N by the Niger river.

De·bre·cen \'deb-rət-ˌsen\. City, ⊗ of Hajdú-Bihar co., E Hungary, 120 m. E of Budapest; 172 sq. m.; pop. (1970p) 155,122; has county rank; commercial center in agricultural and livestock-raising region; furniture, chemicals, ball bearings; univ. (1912); founded in 14th cent.; scene of Kossuth's proclamation 1849 decreeing deposition of the Hapsburgs; in World War II taken by Soviet troops Sept. 1944; meeting place of provisional Hungarian National Assembly Dec. 21, 1944.

De·bre Mar·kos \ˌdeb-rə-'mär-kōs\. Town, ✱ of Gojam prov., W Ethiopia, 110 m. NW of Addis Ababa; pop. (1970e) 27,170.

Debre Zeit \ˌdeb-rə-'zāt\. Town, Shewa prov., Ethiopia, 25 m. SE of Addis Ababa; pop. (1970e) 27,627.

De·cap·o·lis \di-'kap-ə-ləs\. Region in N of ancient Palestine, beginning W of Jordan river at E end of Plain of Esdraelon and stretching to the E and NE of the Sea of Galilee; settled by many Greeks following Alexander's conquests, but got its name (Greek, literally, "ten cities") from the league of 10 (originally) Greek cities formed after Pompey's campaign 64–63 B.C.; generally under Roman control. Damascus was only important city; Scythopolis (Beisan) the only one W of the Jordan.

De·ca·tur \di-ˈkāt-ər\. 1 Name of counties in five state of the U.S. See tables at GEORGIA, INDIANA, IOWA, KANSAS, TENNESSEE.

2 Industrial city, ⊗ of Morgan co., N Alabama, on Tennessee river 75 m. N of Birmingham; pop. (1970c) 38,044; chemicals, automobile parts; shipyard; John C. Calhoun State Technical Junior Coll. (1965); chartered as city 1826; devastated by Civil War; consolidated 1927 with city of Albany.

3 City, ⊗ of De Kalb co., NW cen. Georgia, 5 m. E of Atlanta; pop. (1970c) 21,943; residential suburb of Atlanta; Agnes Scott Coll. (1889); incorporated 1823.

4 City, ⊗ of Macon co., cen. Illinois, on Sangamon river 35 m. E of Springfield; pop. (1970c) 90,397; incorporated as city 1839; in corn-growing and coal-mining section; manufactures starch, corn meal, corn syrup, livestock feed, and metal products; railroad center; Millikin Univ. (1901); in May 1860, Abraham Lincoln here received his first endorsement by a party convention for the presidential nomination.

5 City, ⊗ of Adams co., E Indiana, 20 m. SSE of Fort Wayne; pop. (1970c) 8445; in agricultural, dairy, and lumbering region.

6 Village, Van Buren co., SW Michigan, 24 m. WSW of Kalamazoo; pop. (1970c) 1764.

7 Town, ⊗ of Newton co., E cen. Mississippi; pop. (1970c) 1311.

8 Town, ⊗ of Meigs co., SE Tennessee; pop. (1970c) 698.

9 City, ⊗ of Wise co., N Texas, 25 m. W of Denton; pop. (1970c) 3240; East Central Junior Coll. (1914); trade center and shipping point for agricultural and dairy region.

Decatur, Lake. Lake, Macon co., cen. Illinois; 13 m. long, ½ m. wide; made by damming Sangamon river E of Decatur.

Decatur City. Town, Decatur co., S Iowa, 5 m. W of Leon; pop. (1970c) 7458.

De·ca·tur·ville \di-kāt-ər-ˌvil\. Town, ⊗ of Decatur co., W Tennessee; pop. (1970c) 958.

De·caze·ville \də-käz-ˈvēl\. Mining and manufacturing commune, Aveyron dept., S France, on Lot river 20 m. NW of Rodez; pop. (1968c) 10,532; coal mines; foundries, steel mills.

Dec·can *also* **Dek·kan** \ˈdek-ən, -ˌan\. The peninsula of India S of the Narmada river; in a more restricted sense the tableland bet. the Narmada and Krishna, comprising Maharashtra and parts of Madhya Pradesh, Andhra Pradesh, Mysore, and Orissa. See SOUTHERN DECCAN, UNITED DECCAN STATE. Region of predominantly Dravidian population not reached by Aryan invasion (see INDIA 1); states of Deccan vassals of Maurya rulers c. 3d cent. B.C.; gradually passed under rule of kings of Andhra, a state which expanded from original location on E coast of Deccan to become paramount in cen. and N India 1st cent. B.C.–3d cent. A.D.; invaded by Muslims in 13th cent. and conquered in 14th cent.; ruled by independent Muslim Bahmani sultanate which later split up into five Muslim kingdoms of Deccan (Ahmadnagar, Berar, Bidar, Bijapur, and Golconda); in 18th cent. became scene of rivalry of British and French and subsequently of British struggle against Marathas.

Deccan and Kol·ha·pur States \-ˈkō-lə-ˌpu̇(ə)r-\. Former agency division, W India, comprising 18 Indian states (6 salute and 12 nonsalute), now part of Maharashtra; 10,870 sq. m.; chief state Kolhapur, with former agency headquarters at city of Kolhapur; area of 6 salute states (Bhor, Janjira, Kolhapur, Mudhol, Sangli, and Savantvadi) 6888 sq. m. On Aug. 26, 1947, seven of the states (Aundh, Bhor, Kurundwad [Sr.], Miraj [Jr.], Phaltan, Ramdurg, and Sangli) formed a new state, the United Deccan State.

Deccan Proper. See SOUTHERN DECCAN.

De·cep·tion Island \di-ˈsep-shən-\. See SOUTH SHETLAND ISLANDS.

Dě·čín \ˈd(y)ech-ˌēn\ *or Ger.* **Tet·schen** \ˈtā-chən\. City, Czech S.R., W Czechoslovakia, on the Labe (Elbe) opp. Podmokly, near border of East Germany; pop. (1968e) 43,340; manufactures chemicals, confectionery, cotton goods; 17th cent. castle.

De·cize \də-ˈsēz\. Commune, S Nièvre dept., cen. France; pop. (1962c) 6796; S terminus of the Canal du Nivernais.

De·co·rah \di-ˈkōr-ə, -ˈkȯr-\. City, ⊗ of Winneshiek co., NE Iowa, 62 m. NE of Waterloo; pop. (1970c) 7458; Luther Coll. (1861).

Dede Agach. See ALEXANDROÚPOLIS.

Ded·ham \ˈded-əm\. Town, ⊗ of Norfolk co., E Massachusetts, on Charles river 9 m. SW of Boston; pop. (1970c) 26,938; primarily residential; one of oldest towns in state, settled 1635; first free school in America supported by general tax, built 1649.

Dee \ˈdē\. 1 River, NE Scotland; 87 m. long; rises on the slopes of the Cairngorm Mts., flows E into North Sea at Aberdeen; noted for its scenery and its salmon fishing.

2 River, S Scotland; 50 m. long; flows S in Kirkcudbright co. into Solway Firth.

3 River, N Wales and W England; 70 m. long; rises in Bala Lake, N Wales; flows E, NE, and N, forming a section of the English-Welsh boundary; crosses into W England, passes through Chester, and empties into Irish Sea through a broad estuary.

Deel \ˈdē(ə)l\. River, co. Limerick, SW Eire; 26 m. long; flows into Shannon river.

Deep \ˈdēp\. River, N cen. North Carolina; ab. 125 m. long; rises in Guilford co., flows SE and E to unite with Haw river in Chatham co. and form Cape Fear river.

Deep Bay. 1 Bay, NW of Kowloon Penin., Hong Kong, SE China; controlled by Great Britain.

2 Inlet on SE cen. coast of Malaita I., SE Solomon Is.

Deep Bot·tom \-ˈbät-əm\. Hamlet, Henrico co., E cen. Virginia; scene of fighting during Civil War 1864.

Deep Creek Lake. Artificial lake, Garrett co., NW corner of Maryland; 4000 acres; formed by dam of the Youghiogheny Hydro-Electric Power Company in **Deep Creek** near its confluence with the Youghiogheny river.

Deep·ha·ven \ˈdep-(ˌ)hā-vən\. Village, Hennepin co., SE cen. Minnesota, W of Minneapolis; pop. (1970c) 3853.

Deep Hole Harbor. Inlet of Nantucket Sound on S coast of W Barnstable co., SE Massachusetts.

Deep River. 1 River, North Carolina. See DEEP.

2 *or formerly* **Say·brook** \ˈsā-(ˌ)bru̇k\. Town, S cen. Middlesex co., S Connecticut, on Connecticut river; pop. (1970c) 3690; settled 1635; united with Connecticut 1644.

3 Village, Middlesex co., Connecticut, in town of Deep River; pop. (1970c) 2333; truck farming.

4 Town, Renfrew co., SE Ontario, Canada, on Ottawa river, 25 m. NW of Pembroke; pop. (1971p) 5661.

Deer, Old \ōl-ˈdi(ə)r\. Parish, Aberdeen co., NE Scotland, 9 m. W of Peterhead; pop. (1961c) 3717; site of ancient abbey the founding of which is related in the *Book of Deer*, a MS. copy of portions of the Gospels in Latin Vulgate version containing marginal notes in Gaelic; the oldest Scottish document containing Gaelic, it was discovered 1857 at Cambridge University by Henry Bradshaw; no part of the original abbey remains.

Deer Creek. River, cen. Ohio; 80 m. long; rises in Madison co., flows SE through Pickaway co., enters Scioto river in N Ross co.

Deer Creek Dam. Dam across Provo river, N cen. Utah; height 235 ft.; completed 1941; impounds water, **Deer Creek Reservoir,** for irrigation.

Deer·field \ˈdi(ə)r-ˌfēld\. 1 River, NW Massachusetts; ab. 100 m. long; rises in Windham co., SE Vermont, flows S

across Mass. border and E into Connecticut river in cen. Franklin co., NW Mass.
2 Village, Cook and Lake cos., NE corner of Illinois, 18 m. S of Waukegan; pop. (1970c) 18,876; Trinity Coll. (1897).
3 Town, Franklin co., NW Massachusetts, 4 m. S of Greenfield; pop. (1970c) 3850; one of oldest towns in Connecticut valley, founded 1669–72; suffered from two serious Indian attacks, the Bloody Brook massacre 1675, and the raid of 1704 when a band of Indians and French burned the town, killed 49 and carried ab. 100 captive to Canada. Seat of Deerfield Academy (estab. 1797), now a boys' preparatory school.

Deerfield Beach. Town, Broward co., SE Florida, on Atlantic Ocean 38 m. N of Miami; pop. (1970c) 17,130; agricultural center; incorporated 1925.

Deer Flat Dam. Earth-embankment dam in Canyon co., SW Idaho; forms **Lake Low·ell** \-'lō-əl\ *or* **Deer Flat Reservoir;** reservoir filled by water diverted through canal from Boise river.

Deer Island. 1 Island on E side of entrance to Penobscot Bay, SE Maine; part of Hancock co.; chief village Deer Isle.
2 Island bet. Boston Bay and Boston Harbor, Massachusetts.
3 Island, Charlotte co., SW New Brunswick, Canada, in S part of Passamaquoddy Bay near coast of Maine.

Deer Isle. 1 Island adjacent to Deer I., in Penobscot Bay, SE Maine; 9 m. long; noted for its pink granite.
2 Town, Hancock co., SE Maine, on Deer I. in Penobscot Bay; pop. (1970c) 1211; fishing and summer resort.

Deer Lake. Town, Newfoundland, Canada, 30 m. N of Corner Brook; pop. (1971p) 4403.

Deer Lodge. 1 County in Montana. See table at MONTANA.
2 City, ⊗ of Powell co., W Montana, 37 m. WSW of Helena; pop. (1970c) 4306.

Deer Mountain. 1 Peak, W North Carolina; 6233 ft.
2 Peak, Pennington co., SW South Dakota; 5500 ft.

Deer Park. 1 Unincorporated community, Suffolk co., New York, in cen. Long I. N of Babylon; pop. (1970c) 31,120.
2 City, Hamilton co., SW corner of Ohio, 9 m. NNE of Cincinnati; pop. (1970c) 7415.
3 City, Harris co., SE Texas, 15 m. E of Houston; pop. (1970c) 12,773; plastics, refrigerators; truck farming.

De·fi·ance \di-'fī-ən(t)s\. 1 County in NW Ohio. See table at OHIO.
2 City, its ⊗, at confluence of Auglaize and Maumee rivers 40 m. NNW of Lima; pop. (1970c) 16,281; on site of Fort Defiance built by Gen. Anthony Wayne 1794; iron castings, automobile parts, dairy products; Defiance College (founded 1850, as college 1885); incorp. as village 1836, as city 1881.

De Fu·ni·ak Springs \də-ˌfyü-nē-ˌak-\. Town, ⊗ of Walton co., NW Florida, 70 m. ENE of Pensacola; pop. (1970c) 4966; in region producing cotton, rice, sugarcane, grapes, peaches; manufactures turpentine; large freshwater spring; site of Florida Chautauqua (second in U.S.).

Degh \'dāg\. River, India and Pakistan; ab. 200 m. long; flows SW out of S Jammu and Kashmir, India, through Punjab, Pakistan, to the Ravi river SW of Lahore.

De·go \'dā-gō\. Commune, Savona prov., W cen. Liguria, NW Italy; pop. (1968e) 2425; scene Apr. 14, 1796 of defeat of Austrians by Napoleon's forces.

De Grey \də-'grā\. River, NW Western Australia; ab. 190 m. long; flows N and NW to Indian Ocean near Point Larrey.

De·hi·bat \da-hi-'bat\. Town, SE Tunisia, on boundary with Libya 95 m. S of Médenine.

De·hi·wa·la–Mount La·vin·ia \ˌdā-hē-'wäl-ə . . . lə-'vin-ē-ə\. Urban district, W Western Province, Ceylon, on Indian Ocean 8 m. S of Colombo; pop. (1968e) 122,000; health and pleasure resort located on rock ledge.

Dehli. See DELHI.

Deh·ra Dun \ˌder-ə-'dün\. Town, NW Uttar Pradesh, N India, 140 m. NNE of Delhi; pop. (1970e) 137,604; headquarters of Government Forest Department and Survey of India; also seat of Indian Forest College and its associated Research Institute and India Military College (1934); has large military cantonment; fine temple in Muslim style erected 1699 by the Sikh guru, Ram Rai.

De·i·ra \dā-rə\. Anglian kingdom which emerged in second half of 6th cent. A.D. and extended from Tees river to the Humber (E part of modern Yorkshire); after long conflict with its N neighbor, Bernicia, both were united in 7th cent. to form kingdom of Northumbria (*q.v.*); partitioned by Danes in 9th cent.; before Norman Conquest a separate earldom, occasionally united with Bernicia.

Deir al–Bah·ri \'de(ə)r-el-'bär-ē\. Temple site, Egypt, on W bank of Nile near Thebes and opp. Karnak; important archaeological site; tombs opened by Maspero 1881; temple, excavated 1906 and later, built by Queen Hatshepsut; situated at base of a cliff 400 ft. high; contains pictorial representations on its walls of expedition to land of Punt on the Somali coast.

Dier–ez–Zor \'de(ə)r-ez-'zȯ(ə)r\ *or* **Dayr–az–Zawr** \-az-\. Town, E Syria, on the right bank of Euphrates river; pop. (1960c) 42,036; most important town of a large area; lies at junction of river route from Aleppo to Baghdad and from Damascus NE to Mosul.

Dej \'dezh\ *or Hung.* **Dés** \'dāsh\. City, Cluj co., NW Romania, on the Someşul river; pop. (1970e) 30,869.

Dej·vi·ce \'dā-vət-ˌsā\ *or Ger.* **Dej·witz** \'dā-vəts\. Part of Prague, Czech S.R., Czechoslovakia.

De Kaap \də-'käp\. Mountain, N Drakensberg Mts., Transvaal, NE Rep. of South Africa; goldfields in **De Kaap Valley** where town of Barberton was founded during the gold rush of 1884.

De Kalb \di-'kalb\. 1 Name of counties in six states of the U.S. See tables at ALABAMA, GEORGIA, ILLINOIS, INDIANA, MISSOURI, TENNESSEE.
2 City, De Kalb co., N Illinois, 28 m. SSE of Rockford; pop. (1970c) 32,949; manufactures farm equipment, wire products, esp. barbed wire; Northern Illinois Univ. (1895); incorporated 1877.
3 Town, ⊗ of Kemper co., E Mississippi; pop. (1970c) 1072.

Dekkan. See DECCAN.

De la Beche \ˌdel-ə-'bāsh\. Mountain, Southern Alps, South I., New Zealand, 9 m. NE of Mt. Cook; 9817 ft.

Del·a·goa Bay \ˌdel-ə-ˌgō-ə-\. Inlet of the Indian Ocean on extreme SE coast of Mozambique, SE Africa; 55 m. long; the city of Lourenço Marques lies at its head.
History: Discovered by Portuguese 1502; neighboring territory explored 1544 by Lourenço Marques; site of trading settlement of Dutch 1721–30; islands in bay occupied by British 1861; claimed by Portuguese and British until attempt of Transvaal to occupy it 1868 brought dispute to a head; awarded to Portugal by arbitration 1875; after building of Delagoa Bay R.R. connecting Lourenço Marques (*q.v.*) with Pretoria 1895, as economic outlet for Transvaal, it became subject of British agreements with Germany (1898) and Portugal (1899); by Delagoa Bay R.R. arbitral award 1900, Portugal forced to pay indemnity for seizure of road.

De Lan·cey \di-'lan(t)-sē\. Locality, Jefferson co., W cen. Pennsylvania, ab. 14 m. SW of Du Bois.

De Land \di-'land\. City, ⊗ of Volusia co., E Florida, 22 m. WSW of Daytona Beach; pop. (1970c) 11,641; center of citrus-growing region; winter resort; Ponce de Leon springs nearby; Stetson Univ. (1883); founded 1876.

De·la·no \də-'lā-(ˌ)nō\. City, Kern co., S California, 30 m. NNW of Bakersfield; pop. (1970c) 14,559; ships grain and fruit.

Del·a·no, Mount \-'del-ə-ˌnō\. Peak of Rocky Mts., in Beaverhead co., SW Montana; 10,200 ft.

Delano Peak \ˌdel-ə-ˌnō-\. Mountain on boundary bet. Piute and Beaver cos., SW cen. Utah; 12,173 ft.

Delatyn. See DELYATIN.

Delatyn Pass. See JABLONICA PASS.

Del·a·van \'del-ə-(ˌ)van\. City and summer resort, Walworth co., S Wisconsin, 19 m. E of Janesville; pop. (1970c) 5526; manufactures knit goods, electric pumps, cigars.

Del·a·ware \'del-ə-ˌwa(ə)r, -ˌwe(ə)r, -wər\. 1 River, Pennsylvania and Delaware; 280 m. long; formed by junction of east and west branches in Delaware co., S New York, flows SE to form Pennsylvania-New York, Pennsylvania-New Jersey, and Delaware-New Jersey boundaries, and empties into Delaware Bay; navigable to Trenton, New Jersey. See WASHINGTON CROSSING.

2 Middle Atlantic state of U.S.A., bounded on N and NW by Pennsylvania, on E by Delaware river and Delaware Bay and the Atlantic Ocean, and on S and W by Maryland; 49th state in area, 2057 sq. m. (land area 1983 sq. m.); 46th state in population (1970c) 548,104; ✱ Dover; an original state of the Union, the first state to ratify the Federal Constitution (Dec. 7, 1787).

Nicknames: First State; Diamond State; Blue Hen State. *State flower:* Peach blossom. *Motto:* Liberty and Independence. *River:* Delaware (see 1, above). *Highest point:* Centerville (442 ft.), in New Castle co. *Chief industries:* Chemicals, textiles, primary metals; food processing; poultry raising. *Chief cities:* Wilmington, Newark, Dover, Elsmere. See *Table of States* at UNITED STATES. Divided into the following 3 counties (for pronunciations, see their individual entries):

NAME	LOCATION	AREA[1] (sq. m.)	POP. (1970c)	CO. SEAT
Kent	cen.	594	81,892	Dover
New Castle	N	439	385,856	Wilmington
Sussex	S; coastal	950	80,356	Georgetown

[1]Area = land area.

History: Earliest settlements made by Dutch 1631, first permanent settlements made by Swedes 1638 (see NEW SWEDEN; WILMINGTON 1); New Sweden captured by Dutch 1655 and, as part of New Netherland, by English 1664; became part of a grant made to Penn (see PENNSYLVANIA) 1682; in 1704 lower counties received right to separate legislative assembly, but remained under governor of Pennsylvania until 1776; active in American Revolution; formulated first constitution 1776, adopted present constitution 1897.

3 Name of counties in six states of the U.S. See tables at INDIANA, IOWA, NEW YORK, OHIO, OKLAHOMA, PENNSYLVANIA.

4 Township, New Jersey. See CHERRY HILL.

5 City, ⊗ of Delaware co., cen. Ohio, 23 m. N of Columbus; pop. (1970c) 15,008; machine screws, tiles, rubber goods; mineral springs; Ohio Wesleyan Univ. (1841); birthplace of Rutherford B. Hayes, 19th president of U.S.; founded 1808.

Delaware Bay. Arm of Atlantic Ocean, bet. SW coast of New Jersey and E coast of Delaware.

Delaware City. Town, New Castle co., N Delaware; pop. (1970c) 2024; terminus of Chesapeake and Delaware Canal.

Delaware Water Gap. 1 Borough, Monroe co., E Pennsylvania, E of Stroudsburg; pop. (1970c) 533; summer resort on Delaware river at Delaware Water Gap. See 2 below.
2 Gorge, ab. 2 m. long through the Kittatinny Mts., having on W Mount Minsi, Pa. (ab. 1500 ft.) and on E Mount Tammany, N.J. (1480 ft.).

Del Car·men Mountains \del-ˌkär-mən-\. Range in N Coahuila state, N Mexico; max. height ab. 10,000 ft.; a subsidiary range of the Sierra Madre Oriental. See SANTIAGO MOUNTAINS.

Del City \'del-\. City, Oklahoma co., cen. Oklahoma, 4 m. E of Oklahoma City; pop. (1970c) 27,133; residential suburb of Oklahoma City.

De·lé·mont \də-lā-'mōⁿ\ *or Ger.* **Dels·berg** \'dels-ˌbərg, -ˌbu̇(ə)rk\. Commune, N Bern canton, Switzerland, in the Jura Mts.; pop. (1970c) 11,797; watchmaking.

De Le·on \ˌdā-lē-'än\. City, Comanche co., cen. Texas, 35 m. NNE of Brownwood; pop. (1970c) 2170.

Delft \'delft\. Commune, South Holland prov., SW Netherlands; pop. (1970e) 83,698; cables, penicillin, spirits; technical univ. (1905); during 17th–18th cents. noted for its pottery manufacture (delftware); received charter 1246; scene of the assassination of William the Silent 1584; birthplace of Grotius.

Delft Island. Island in waters bet. Palk Strait and Palk Bay, off NW coast of Ceylon.

Delf·zijl \delf-'zī(ə)l\. Commune, Groningen prov., NE Netherlands, on Ems estuary; pop. (1970e) 21,990; port; aluminum, chemicals.

Del·ga·da Point \del-ˌgäd-ə-\. Cape extending into Atlantic Ocean from S end of Valdés Penin., off E cen. coast of Argentina, S of the Gulf of San Matías.

Del·ga·do, Cape \-del-'gäd-(ˌ)ō\. Cape extending into Indian Ocean on extreme NE coast of Mozambique, SE Africa.

Del·hi \'del-(ˌ)hī\. 1 Town, Richland parish, NE Louisiana, 38 m. E of Monroe; pop. (1970c) 2887; aluminum boats; agriculture.
2 Village, ⊗ of Delaware co., S New York, 50 m. S of Utica; pop. (1970c) 3017; State Univ. of New York Agricultural and Technical Coll. (1913).
3 Town, Norfolk co., SE Ontario, Canada, 25 m. SSW of Brantford; pop. (1968e) 3696; gas wells; tobacco.

Delhi \'del-ē\ *also* **Dil·li** \'dil-ē\ *or* **Deh·li** \'del-ē\. 1 Territory, N India, bordering on Haryana and Uttar Pradesh; 573 sq. m.; pop. (1971p) 4,044,338; ✱ New Delhi; created 1912 for administrative purposes when city of Delhi was made capital of India; became a territory 1956.
2 *or* **Old Delhi.** City, its new section (*officially* **New Delhi**) ✱ of India and ✱ of the territory, on W bank of Yamuna river; pop. (1970e) 3,772,457; textiles, chemicals, rubber goods; metalworking; important rail and trade center; has examples of Muslim and Hindu architecture, among the finest being the Red Fort (which contains the Diwan-î-Am or Hall of Public Audience, where was formerly placed the famous Peacock Throne, and the Diwan-i-Khas or Hall of Private Audience), the Jama Masjid or Great Mosque (one of largest mosques in the world), the tomb of Humayun, and the Kutb Minar (one of world's most perfect towers). South of the old walled city (Old Delhi, or **Shah·ja·han·a·bad** \ˌshäj-ə-'hän-ə-ˌbäd\, as it is still called locally) is located the modern seat of the Indian government (New Delhi) with symmetrically planned streets, attractive buildings, and an imposing capitol. The present city, seventh on this site (the most ancient known as **In·dra·pras·tha** \ˌin-drə-'prəs-tə\), was reconstructed by Shah Jahan (see below). Seat of the Univ. of Delhi (1922), Indian Institute of Technology (1961), and of several other colleges. See FIROZABAD; TUGHLAKABAD.

History: Chosen as capital by founder of Muslim Slave dynasty 1206; at height in 13th cent. when Sultanate of Delhi controlled northern India; laid waste by invasion of Tamerlane 1398; conquered by Babur, founder of Mogul dynasty in India, 1526; although Mogul capital mostly at Agra (*q.v.*), city beautified, beginning in 1631 with building under Shah Jahan; pillaged by Nadir Shah 1739; with its surrender to Marathas 1772, Mogul emperor came under Maratha control; taken by British under Lake 1803; a center of Sepoy Mutiny 1857, held by mutineers for several weeks; scene of coronation durbars 1903, 1911; replaced Calcutta as capital of British India 1912, became capital of independent India 1947 (see NEW DELHI).

De·li \'dā-lē\. Short but important stream of NE Sumatra, Indonesia; flowing NE to Strait of Malacca at Belawan, the port of Medan.

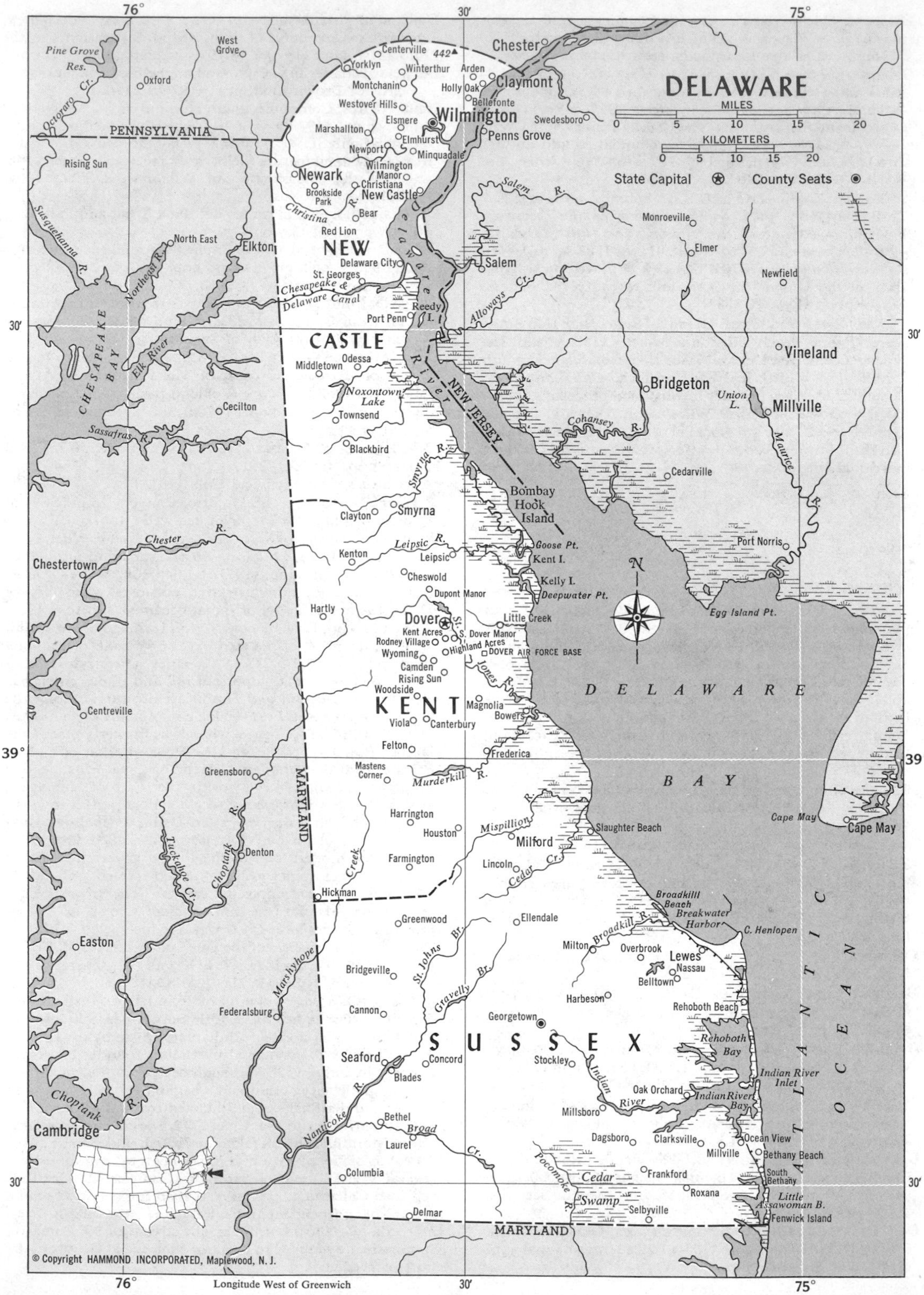

DELAWARE
MILES
0 5 10 15 20
KILOMETERS
0 5 10 15 20
State Capital
County Seats
76°
30′
75°
39°
Longitude West of Greenwich
NEW CASTLE
KENT
SUSSEX
PENNSYLVANIA
MARYLAND
NEW JERSEY
DELAWARE BAY
ATLANTIC OCEAN
CHESAPEAKE BAY
N
Pine Grove Res.
Octoraro Cr.
West Grove
Oxford
Rising Sun
Centerville
442
Yorklyn
Winterthur
Arden
Chester
Claymont
Montchanin
Holly Oak
Bellefonte
Westover Hills
Elsmere
Wilmington
Swedesboro
Marshallton
Elmhurst
Penns Grove
Newport
Minquadale
Newark
Wilmington Manor
Christiana
Brookside Park
New Castle
Christina R.
Bear
Red Lion
Delaware City
St. Georges
Chesapeake & Delaware Canal
Port Penn
Reedy I.
Delaware River
Salem
Salem R.
Alloways Cr.
Monroeville
Elmer
Newfield
Vineland
Bridgeton
Union L.
Millville
Cohansey R.
Maurice R.
Cedarville
Port Norris
Egg Island Pt.
Susquehanna R.
North East
Northeast R.
Elkton
Elk River
Cecilton
Sassafras R.
Odessa
Middletown
Noxontown Lake
Townsend
Blackbird
Smyrna R.
Clayton
Smyrna
Bombay Hook Island
Goose Pt.
Kent I.
Kelly I.
Deepwater Pt.
Chester R.
Chestertown
Kenton
Leipsic R.
Leipsic
Cheswold
Dupont Manor
Hartly
Dover
St. Jones R.
Little Creek
Kent Acres
S. Dover Manor
Rodney Village
Highland Acres
Wyoming
DOVER AIR FORCE BASE
Camden
Rising Sun
Woodside
Magnolia
Bowers
Viola
Canterbury
Centreville
Felton
Frederica
Greensboro
Mastens Corner
Murderkill R.
Harrington
Houston
Mispillion R.
Milford
Slaughter Beach
Cape May
Tuckahoe Cr.
Choptank R.
Denton
Farmington
Lincoln
Cedar Cr.
Creek
Hickman
Broadkill Beach
Breakwater Harbor
C. Henlopen
Greenwood
Ellendale
Broadkill R.
Easton
Milton
Overbrook
Lewes
Nassau
St. Johns Br.
Bridgeville
Belltown
Gravelly Br.
Harbeson
Rehoboth Beach
Marshyhope
Federalsburg
Cannon
Georgetown
Rehoboth Bay
Seaford
Concord
Stockley
Blades
Indian River
Indian River Inlet
Oak Orchard
Indian River Bay
Choptank R.
Cambridge
Nanticoke R.
Bethel
Broad Cr.
Millsboro
Laurel
Dagsboro
Clarksville
Ocean View
Millville
Bethany Beach
Columbia
Pocomoke R.
Cedar Swamp
Frankford
South Bethany
Roxana
Little Assawoman B.
Selbyville
Delmar
Fenwick Island
© Copyright HAMMOND INCORPORATED, Maplewood, N. J.

De·li·ce \də-ˈlē-jə\. River, cen. Turkey in Asia; 265 m. long; flows NW and N into the Kızıl Irmak.

De·li·cias \də-ˈlēs-ˌyäs\. Municipality, Chihuahua state, N Mexico; pop. (1970p) 64,385; dairying.

De·litzsch \ˈdā-lich\. Manufacturing city, Leipzig dist., East Germany, 22 m. SSE of Dessau; pop. (1970e) 24,270; manufactures chocolates, sugar, chemicals; rolling mills; made city 1306.

De·li·um \ˈdēl-ē-əm\. Ancient seaport in Boeotia, E cen. Greece, on the E coast; battle 424 B.C. in which Boeotians defeated the Athenians.

Del·len·baugh, Mount \-ˈdel-ən-ˌbȯ\. Peak in N Mohave co., NW Arizona; 6750 ft.

Dell Rapids \ˈdel-\. City and resort, Minnehaha co., SE South Dakota, on Big Sioux river 20 m. N of Sioux Falls; pop. (1970c) 1991; rock quarries.

Dell·wood \ˈdel-ˌwu̇d\. City, St. Louis co., E Missouri; pop. (1970c) 7137; residential suburb of St. Louis.

Del·lys \de-ˈlēs\. Seaport, N Tizi-Ouzou dept., N Algeria, 45 m. E of Algiers; pop. (1966c) 10,268.

Del Mar \ˈdel-ˌmär\. City, San Diego co., SW California, on Pacific Ocean 20 m. N of San Diego; pop. (1970c) 3956; residential.

Del·mar·va Peninsula \del-ˈmär-və-\. Peninsula, E United States, bet. Chesapeake and Delaware Bays; includes Eastern Shore (*q.v.*) and all of Delaware;— so called from *Del*aware, *Mar*yland, *Va.* (Virginia).

Del·men·horst \ˈdel-mən-ˌhȯrst\. Commercial and manufacturing commune, Lower Saxony, West Germany, 9 m. WSW of Bremen; pop. (1969e) 63,068; linoleum, textiles.

Del Mon·te \del-ˈmänt-ē\. 1 Seaside resort, Monterey co., W California, on S shore of Monterey Bay.

2 Town, N Bukidnon prov., N Mindanao, Phil., 15 m. SE of Cagayan de Oro; pineapple plantation.

Del Norte \del-ˈnō(ə)rt, -ˈnȯ(ə)rt\. 1 County in California. See table at CALIFORNIA.

2 Town, ⊗ of Rio Grande co., S Colorado, on the Rio Grande 30 m. WNW of Alamosa; pop. (1970c) 1516.

De Long Islands \di-ˌlȯŋ-\. Group of three small islands (Bennet, Henrietta, and Zhokova) in Arctic Ocean NE of New Siberian Is.; belong to Yakutsk A.S.S.R., U.S.S.R.

De Long Mountains. Range, W end of Brooks Range, NW Alaska, N of Noatak river; highest peak 4800 ft.

Del·o·raine \ˌdel-ə-ˈran\. Town, N Tasmania, Australia, 25 m. W of Launceston; pop. (1970e) 5110; farming.

De·los \ˈdē-ˌläs\ *or Gk.* **Dhí·los** \ˈthē-ˌlȯs\. Smallest island of the Cyclades, S Aegean Sea, in the narrow passage bet. Mykonos and Rhenea islands; 2 sq. m. By ancient Greeks considered the center of the archipelago (whence the name: see CYCLADES), sacred as the legendary birthplace of Apollo and Artemis; guarded treasure of Delian League 478–454 B.C. (see ATHENS 10); became flourishing commercial center and important slave market, especially after Rome made it a free port 166 B.C.; sacked during Mithridatic Wars; gradually declined and became deserted; excavations by the French since 1877 have uncovered many remains of interest.

Del·phi \ˈdel-ˌfī\. 1 City, ⊗ of Carroll co., NW cen. Indiana, on Wabash river 30 m. WNW of Kokomo; pop. (1970c) 2582; furniture; livestock farms.

2 *or modern* **Dhel·foí** \thel-ˈfē\ *or in early times* **Py·tho** \ˈpī-(ˌ)thō\. Town, Greece, situated nearly equidistant (ab. 6 m.) from N shore of Gulf of Corinth and from Mt. Parnassus.

History: From at least 7th cent. B.C., visited by ancient Greeks as the seat of Delphic oracle and of worship of Apollo, Pythius and Dionysus; scene of Pythian games, held every fourth year; c. 590 B.C. Crisa punished by Thessaly and allies for levying tolls upon pilgrims to the oracle (First Sacred War); enriched by gifts from all Greece, it became coveted booty, as when Phocians used its wealth to finance Third Sacred War (355–346 B.C.), and its temples were plundered by Sulla and other Romans.

Del·phos \ˈdel-fəs\. City, Allen and Van Wert cos., NW Ohio, 13 m. WNW of Lima; pop. (1970c) 7608; motor trucks, trailers, bank furniture; settled 1834.

Del·ray Beach \ˌdel-ˌrā-\. City, Palm Beach co., SE Florida, on Atlantic Ocean 18 m. S of West Palm Beach; pop. (1970c) 19,366; tourist resort; settled 1901, incorp. 1927.

Del Rio \del-ˈrē-(ˌ)ō\. City and port of entry, ⊗ of Val Verde co., SW Texas, on Rio Grande 37 m. SE of its confluence with Pecos river; pop. (1970c) 21,330; market and distributing center for agricultural area; goats, sheep; grape culture; international flood control dam dedicated 1969.

Delsberg. See DELÉMONT.

Del·son \ˈdel-sən\. Town, Laprairie co., S Quebec, Canada, 5 m. S of Montreal; pop. (1971p) 2930.

Del·ta \ˈdel-tə\. 1 Name of counties in three states of the U.S. See tables at COLORADO, MICHIGAN, TEXAS.

2 City, ⊗ of Delta co., W Colorado, on Gunnison river 35 m. SE of Grand Junction; pop. (1970c) 3694; ships fruit.

3 Village, Fulton co., NW Ohio, 24 m. W of Toledo; pop. (1970c) 2544; dairy farms.

Delta Ama·cu·ro \ˈdel-tə-ˌäm-ə-ˈku̇(ə)r-ˌō\. Territory of NE Venezuela. See table at VENEZUELA.

Del·ville Wood \ˌdel-ˌvil-, del-ˌvēl-\. Forested area near Longueval, Somme dept., N France; taken by Allies as part of the battle of the Somme 1916.

Del·vi·në \del-ˈvē-nə\ *or Ital.* **Del·vi·no** \-ˈvē-(ˌ)nō\. Town, S Albania, 10 m. S of Gjirokastër; pop. (1967e) 6092.

De·lya·tin \dəl-ˈyät-ᵊn\ *or* **De·la·tyn** \də-ˈlät-\. Town, SW Ukrainian S.S.R., U.S.S.R., at E end of Yablonitski Pass on Prut river, 28 m. SSW of Ivano-Frankovsk; salt deposits, mineral baths; formerly in Poland; occupied by Russians 1916; reoccupied 1917 by Germany.

De·mar·ca·tion Point \ˌdē-ˌmär-ˈkā-shən-\. Cape extending N into Beaufort Sea, marking boundary bet. Alaska and Yukon Territory, Canada, 69°40′N, 141°15′W.

Dem·a·rest \ˈdem-ə-ˌrest\. Borough, Bergen co., NE New Jersey, 13 m. ENE of Paterson; pop. (1970c) 5133.

Demavand. See DAMĀVAND.

De·mer \ˈdā-mər\. River, E cen. Belgium; 47 m. long; flows W in Limburg and Brabant provs., empties into Dijle river 6 m. N of Louvain.

Dem·e·rara \ˌdem-ə-ˈrar-ə, -ˈrär-\. 1 River, Guyana; ab. 200 m. long; flows N parallel with and E of the Essequibo river, empties into Atlantic Ocean at Georgetown; navigable for ab. 65 m.

2 County, N Guyana, divided into two districts, **East Demerara** (pop. [1970p] 175,994) and **West Demerara** (pop. 87,337).

De·me·tri·as \di-ˈmē-trē-əs\. Ruined city, SE Thessaly, NE Greece, near modern Volos; founded c. 290 B.C. by Demetrius Poliorcetes and a favorite residence of Macedonian kings.

Dem·ing \ˈdem-iŋ\. Village, ⊗ of Luna co., SW New Mexico, W of Las Cruces; pop. (1970c) 8343; copper mines; livestock; health resort.

Demir Hissár *or* **Demir Hisar.** See SIDEROKASTRON.

Dem·min \de-ˈmēn\. Manufacturing city, Neubrandenburg dist., East Germany, on Peene river ab. 40 m. ESE of Rostock; pop. (1970e) 17,062; sugar, brewery products. One of the oldest Slavic settlements in Pomerania; unsuccessfully besieged by Germans 1148; conquered by Henry the Lion 1164; became member of Hanseatic League 1283; to Sweden 1648, to Prussia 1720, to Mecklenburg 1946–52.

Dem·nate \dəm-ˈnät\. Town, S cen. Morocco, NW Africa, 60 m. E of Marrakech; pop. (1960c) 6223.

Dem·o·crat, Mount \-ˈdem-ə-ˌkrat\. Peak, Park and Lake cos., cen. Colorado; 14,148 ft.

Democratic and Popular Republic of Algeria. See ALGERIA.

Democratic People's Republic of Korea. See KOREA, NORTH.

Democratic Republic of the Congo. See ZAIRE 1.

Democratic Republic of the Sudan. See SUDAN 2.

Democratic Republic of Vietnam. See VIETNAM, NORTH.

Demonesi Insulae. See KIZIL ISLANDS.

De·mop·o·lis \di-ˈmäp-(ə-)ləs\. City, Marengo co., W Alabama, on Tombigbee river 48 m. W of Selma; pop. (1970c) 7651; cotton and allied products.

Dem·o·rest \ˈdem-ə-ˌrest\. Town, Habersham co., NE Georgia, 7 m. from Clarkesville; pop. (1970c) 1070; Piedmont Coll. (1897).

Dem·po \ˈdem-(ˌ)pō\. Volcanic peak, S Sumatra, Indonesia, in the Barisan Mts. E of Bengkulu; 10,361 ft.

De·nain \də-ˈnaⁿ\. Commune, Nord dept., N France, 26 m. SE of Lille; pop. (1968c) 27,973; coal mining; metalworks. Fortified at early date; scene of battle July 24, 1712 (during War of Spanish Succession) in which Marshal Villars defeated Prince Eugene of Savoy.

Denali. See MCKINLEY, MOUNT.

Den·bigh \ˈden-bē\. 1 Former village, ⊗ of former Warwick co., SE Virginia; now part of city of Newport News.

2 County in Wales. See DENBIGHSHIRE.

3 Municipal borough, Denbighshire, N Wales; pop. (1971p) 8100; agriculture, stone quarrying; ruined Norman castle besieged for eleven months by Cromwell's Parliamentarians before it capitulated 1646.

Den·bigh·shire \ˈden-bē-ˌshi(ə)r, -shər\ *or* **Denbigh.** County, N Wales; area 669 sq. m.; pop. (1971p) 184,824; ⊗ Ruthin; hilly area; rivers Dee, Conway, Clwyd; agriculture; stock raising (esp. sheep), coal mining, quarrying (limestone, slate); light engineering; tourism; chief towns: Wrexham, Colwyn Bay.

Den·by Dale \ˌden-bē-ˈdāl\. Urban district, West Riding, Yorkshire, N England; pop. (1971p) 11,093.

Den·der \ˈden-dər\ *or* **Din·dar** \ˈdin-dər\. 1 Navigable river, W cen. Belgium; 42 m. long; flows N out of Hainaut prov. into the Schelde river at Dendermonde.

2 River, E Sudan; 300 m. long; rises in Ethiopia; flows NW into Blue Nile N of Sennar.

Den·de·ra \ˈden-də-ˌrä\ *or* **Dan·da·rah** \ˈdan-\ *or anc.* **Ten·ty·ra** \ˈtent-ə-rə\. Village, Upper Egypt, on left side of Nile opp. Qena; ancient city dedicated to worship of goddess Hathor; temple was begun 1st cent. B.C. and added to by the Romans, esp. Augustus and Domitian; among temple decorations was a celebrated zodiac now in Bibliothèque Nationale in Paris.

Den·der·mon·de \ˌden-dər-ˈmòn-də\ *or Fr.* **Ter·monde** \ter-mòⁿd\. Commune, East Flanders prov., NW cen. Belgium, at the confluence of the Schelde and Dender rivers; pop. (1969e) 9300; pillaged by Germans Sept. 1914.

Den·ham Springs \ˌden-əm-\. Town, Livingston parish, SE Louisiana, E of Baton Rouge; pop. (1970c) 6752; wood products; livestock.

Den Hel·der \də(n)-ˈhel-dər\. Commune, North Holland prov., W Netherlands; pop. (1970e) 60,612; fortified port on the Mars Diep, an outlet from Wadden Zee into North Sea; fortified by Napoleon 1811; Dutch naval station.

De·nia \ˈdā-(ˌ)nyä\ *or anc.* **Di·a·ni·um** \dī-ˈā-nē-əm, -ˈan-ē-\. Seaport commune, Alicante prov., SE Spain, on Mediterranean Sea 45 m. NE of Alicante; pop. (1970p) 16,484.

De·nil·i·quin \də-ˈnil-ə-kwən\. Town, S New South Wales, SE Australia, 250 m. W of Canberra; pop. (1965e) 6080; in the Riverina, a pastoral and agricultural region.

Den·i·son \ˈden-ə-sən\. 1 City, ⊗ of Crawford co., W Iowa, 58 m. NNE of Council Bluffs; pop. (1970c) 6300; in region producing grain, cattle, hogs, dairy products; Midwestern Coll. (1965).

2 City, Grayson co., NE Texas, in valley of Red river 10 m. N of Sherman; pop. (1970c) 24,923; railroad center; shipping point for agricultural region (esp. cheese, cotton, processed pecans and peanuts); grape culture; Grayson County Coll. (1963); birthplace of Dwight D. Eisenhower, 34th president of the U.S.

De·niz·li \ˌden-əz-ˈlē\. 1 Province of SW Turkey, Asia. See table at TURKEY.

2 Town, its ✱, on a tributary of the Menderes ab. 112 m. SE of İzmir, with which it has rail connections; pop. (1965c) 64,331; during wars bet. Seljuks and Byzantines in 12th cent. replaced ancient **La·od·i·cea** \(ˌ)lā-ˌäd-ə-ˈsē-ə\ *or* **Laodicea ad Ly·cum** \-ˌad-ˈlī-kəm\, now in ruins nearby, founded by Antiochus II and several times destroyed by earthquake or conquest, but recovered; one of the Seven Churches of Asia Minor (*Rev.* i–iii).

Den·mark \ˈden-ˌmärk\. 1 *or Dan.* **Dan·mark** \ˈdän-ˌmärk\. Kingdom, NW Europe, bounded on the N by the Skagerrak, on the E by the Kattegat, Øresund and the Baltic Sea, on the S by West Germany, and on the W by the North Sea; 16,629 sq. m.; pop. (1971c) 4,950,597; ✱ Copenhagen; comprises most of Jutland (*Dan.* Jylland) Penin. and a group of islands in Baltic Sea, the most prominent of which are Sjælland, Fyn, Falster, Lolland, Langeland, and Bornholm (90 m. E of Sjælland); included in the Danish realm are Greenland (839,999 sq. m.) and the Faeroe Is. (540 sq. m.).

Physical features: Low, flat land with highest point (on E coast of Jutland) not above 550 ft.; has no large rivers and few lakes, but its shoreline, esp. in N and W of Jutland, is indented by many lagoons and fjords; most important is Lim Fjord extending across N Jutland from North Sea to Kattegat. Great Belt is passage bet. Sjælland and Fyn, and Little Belt a narrower channel bet. Fyn and mainland. *Chief products:* Wheat, rye, barley, dairy products; livestock raising; salt, limestone; manufacturing: chemicals, textiles, agricultural machinery, electrical equipment; food processing. *Chief cities:* Copenhagen, Århus, Frederiksberg, Odense, Ålborg, Gentofte, Esbjerg. Divided into the following 14 counties and 2 communes (for pronunciation of their names, see their individual entries):

NAME	AREA (sq. m.)	POP. (1971c)	CAPITAL
Århus	1,764	534,333	Århus
Bornholm[1]	227	47,241	Rønne
Copenhagen (commune)	33	625,678	
Copenhagen	201	616,570	Copenhagen
Frederiksberg (commune)	3	101,970	
Frederiksberg	520	260,825	Hillerød
Fyn	1,346	433,765	Odense
Nordjylland	2,383	457,165	Ålborg
Ribe	1,210	198,153	Ribe
Ringkøbing	1,872	242,006	Ringkøbing
Roskilde	344	154,314	Roskilde
Sønderjylland	1,517	238,502	Åbenrå
Storstrøm	1,311	252,780	Nykøbing Falster
Vejle	1,155	306,809	Vejle
Vestsjælland	1,152	259,484	Sorø
Viborg	1,591	221,002	Viborg

[1]Coextensive with Bornholm I.

History: Settled by Danes, a Scandinavian branch of Teutons, c. 6th cent. A.D.; participated in Viking raids on England, France, and Low Countries 8th–10th cents.; by 1014 the united Danish kingdom occupied Schleswig (*q.v.*), southern Sweden, and England; under Canute the Great 1018–35, converted to Christianity and ruled a short-lived "northern empire" which included Norway; Copenhagen (*q.v.*) made the capital and expansion begun along S shore of Baltic by dynasty founded by Waldemar the Great (1157–82); by 14th cent., despite opposition of Waldemar IV, came increasingly under German influence, and, especially after Peace of Stralsund 1370, was dominated by Hanseatic League (see HANSE TOWNS); Scandinavia united under Margaret of Denmark 1387 (Union of Kalmar 1397); Danish monarchy of the Oldenburg line 1448–1863; Sweden (*q.v.*) became independent and began to threaten Danish supremacy; accepted Protestant Reformation 1536; lost power and territory in wars with Sweden in 17th cent.; abolished serfdom under Bernstorff; in Leagues of Armed Neutrality 1780 and 1800; after bombardment of Copenhagen 1807, joined Napoleon; forced to cede Norway and Helgoland 1814; duchies of Schleswig and Holstein (*qq. v.*) lost in war with Austria and Prussia 1864; neutral in World War I; sold Danish West Indies (see VIRGIN ISLANDS) to U.S. 1917; recognized Iceland (*q. v.*) as sovereign state in personal union with Denmark 1918 (union terminated 1944); received Northern Schleswig (*Dan.* Nord Slesvig) by plebiscite 1920; in 1933 was awarded E Greenland (occupied by Norway 1931); occupied by Germany Apr. 1940–May 1945; member of NATO 1949; adopted new constitution 1953; signed treaty of accession to European Economic Community 1972.

2 Town, Bamburg co., SW South Carolina, 21 m. SW of Orangeburg; pop. (1970c) 1897; lumber; Voorhees Coll. (1897).

Denmark Strait. Channel bet. SE Greenland and Iceland; 130 m. wide; connects Arctic Ocean with the North Atlantic; here in World War II on May 24, 1941 the German battleship *Bismarck* sank the British *Hood.*

Den·ne·witz \'den-ə-ˌvits\. Village, Potsdam dist., East Germany, 42 m. SSW of East Berlin; formerly in Brandenburg; scene of victory Sept. 6, 1813 of Prussians under von Bülow over the forces of Marshal Ney.

Den·nis \'den-əs\. Town, Barnstable co., SE Massachusetts, on Cape Cod 7 m. ENE of Barnstable; pop. (1970c) 6454; summer and fishing resort; site of the Cape Playhouse and Cape Cinema.

Dennis Ness \-'nes\. Headland on N coast of North Ronaldsay I., Orkney Is., off N Scotland; lighthouse.

Den·ni·son \'den-ə-sən\. Village, Tuscarawas co., E Ohio, 27 m. S of Canton; pop. (1970c) 3506; meat-packing; manufactures sewer pipe, clay products, batteries, sheet iron. See UHRICHSVILLE.

Den·ny and Dun·i·pace \'den-ē . . . 'dən-ə-ˌpās\. Burgh, Stirling co., cen. Scotland; pop. (1971p) 9841.

De·nou·sa \də-'nü-sə\. Small island, E Cyclades, S Aegean Sea, 12 m. E of Naxos; in Cyclades dept., Greece.

Den·pa·sar *also* **Den Pa·sar** \dən-'päs-ˌär\. Town, ✱ of Bali prov., S Bali, Lesser Sunda Is., Indonesia; pop. (1961c) 56,780; administrative and commercial center; has seaport and airport.

Dent \'dent\. County in Missouri. See table at MISSOURI.

Dent Blanche \'dän-'blänsh\. Peak in the Pennine Alps, S Switzerland; 14,293 ft.

Dent d' Hérens. See HÉRENS, DENT D'.

Dent du Mi·di \'dän-dü-mē-'dē\. Mountain, SW Switzerland, near French border SSW of Bex; 10,686 ft.

Den·ton \'dent-ᵊn\. 1 County in Texas. See table at TEXAS.

2 Town, ⊗ of Caroline co., E Maryland, 40 m. E of Annapolis; pop. (1970c) 1561; canneries.

3 City, ⊗ of Denton co., N Texas, 35 m. NNW of Dallas; pop. (1970c) 39,874; trade and agricultural center; brick, machine tools; North Texas State Univ. (1890), Texas Women's Univ. (1901).

4 Urban district, Lancashire, NW England, 6 m. ESE of Manchester; pop. (1971p) 38,107; felt hats, plastics; rubber goods.

D'En·tre·cas·teaux Channel \ˌdän-trə-'kas-(ˌ)tō-\. Strait separating S end of Bruny I. from Tasmania mainland, Australia.

D'Entrecasteaux Islands. Island group in the W Pacific Ocean, off SE coast of New Guinea I.; 1200 sq. m.; pop. (1969e) 32,336; administratively part of Papua New Guinea; chief settlement Dobu; include Goodenough, Fergusson, and Normanby Is. and many islets, small coral atolls, and reefs; separated from the mainland by Ward Hunt and Goschen Straits; copra; mountainous, with many extinct volcanoes; discovered 1793.

D'Entrecasteaux Point. Cape, SW point of Australia, in Western Australia.

Den·ver \'den-vər\. 1 County in Colorado. See table at COLORADO.

2 City, its ⊗ and ✱ of Colorado, in NE cen. part of the state on South Platte river; pop. (1970c) 514,678; alt. 5280 ft.; largest city in the state; commercial, industrial, and transportation center; headquarters for mining (gold, silver, coal) and beet-sugar industries in the surrounding area; manufactures include mining machinery, rubber products, scientific apparatus; publishing; aerospace industry; stockyard; tourism; Lowry Air Force Base with U.S. Air Force Technical School. Botanical Gardens, Colorado State Historical Museum, Denver Art Museum, Univ. of Denver (1864), Iliff School of Theology (1892), Regis College (1877), Loretto Heights Coll. (1891), Temple Buell Coll. (1909), Rockmont Coll. (1914). Settlement called Auraria (*q. v.*) made 1858 by gold prospectors and miners and united with two other villages to form Denver 1860; incorp. as city 1861; made state capital 1867.

3 Borough, Lancaster co., Pennsylvania, NE of Ephrata; pop. (1970c) 2248.

Denver City. Town, Yoakum co., NW Texas, 72 m. SW of Lubbock; pop. (1970c) 4133; oil wells; diversified agriculture.

De·o·band \'dē-ə-ˌbənd, 'dā-\. Town, NE Uttar Pradesh, N India, 75 m. NNE of Delhi; pop. (1961c) 29,080; an ancient town, with numerous temples, ghats, etc., a resort of pilgrims.

De·o·ghar *or* **De·o·garh** \'dē-ə-ˌgär, 'dā-\. Town, E Bihar, NE India, 170 m. NW of Calcutta; pop. (1961c) 30,800; has temple dedicated to Hindu god Siva; visited by many pilgrims; health resort.

Deogiri. See DAULATABAD.

De Pere \di-'pi(ə)r\. City, Brown co., E Wisconsin, on Fox river 5 m. S of Green Bay (city); pop. (1970c) 13,309; agricultural and industrial center; manufactures paper, boats, medicines, feeds, brick; site of St. Francis Xavier Mission, first permanent Jesuit mission in Wisconsin (estab. 1671); St. Norbert Coll. (1898) at West De Pere.

De·pew \di-'pyü\. Village, Erie co., W New York, 9 m. E of Buffalo; pop. (1970c) 22,158; industrial suburb of Buffalo; manufactures storage batteries, food products, steel castings.

De·pos·it \di-'päz-ət\. Village and summer resort, Broome and Delaware cos., S New York, 25 m. E of Binghamton; pop. (1970c) 2061.

De Queen \də-'kwēn\. City, ⊗ of Sevier co., SW Arkansas; pop. (1970c) 3863; dairy farms; timber, fruit; incorporated 1897; made ⊗ 1905.

De Quin·cy \də-'kwin(t)-sē\. Town, Calcasieu parish, SW Louisiana, 20 m. NW of Lake Charles (city); pop. (1970c) 3448; in region producing rice, sugar, lumber; oil and natural-gas deposits nearby.

De·ra Gha·zi Khan \ˌder-ə-ˌgäz-ē-'kän\. Town, Punjab, Pakistan, on Indus river 45 m. W of Multan; pop. (1961c) 47,105; founded at close of 15th cent. by Ghazi Khan, son of a Baluch chieftain.

Dera Is·mail Khan \-ˌis-mīl-'kän\. Town, North-West Frontier Province, Pakistan, on the right bank of the Indus river 155 m. S of Peshawar; pop. (1961c) 44,319; founded at close of the 15th cent. by Ismail Khan, a Baluch chieftain; active bazaar; conducts trade with Afghanistan through the Gumal Pass (*q. v.*).

De·ra·i·yeh *or* **Der·a·yah** \də-'rī-ə\ *also* **Ad Dir'īyah** \ad-\. Town, cen. Saudi Arabia, just W of Riyadh; formerly capital of the Wahabis; sacked by Ibrahim Pasha 1819.

Der·be \'dər-(ˌ)bē\. Ancient town, S Lycaonia, Asia Minor, on border of Cilicia; visited by St. Paul on first and second journeys; exact site not known.

Der·bent \dər-'bent\ *or* **Der·bend** \-'bend\ *or anc.* **Al·ba·na** \al-'bā-nə\. Town, SE Dagestan A.S.S.R., Russian S.F.S.R., U.S.S.R., on Caspian Sea 70 m. SE of Makhach-

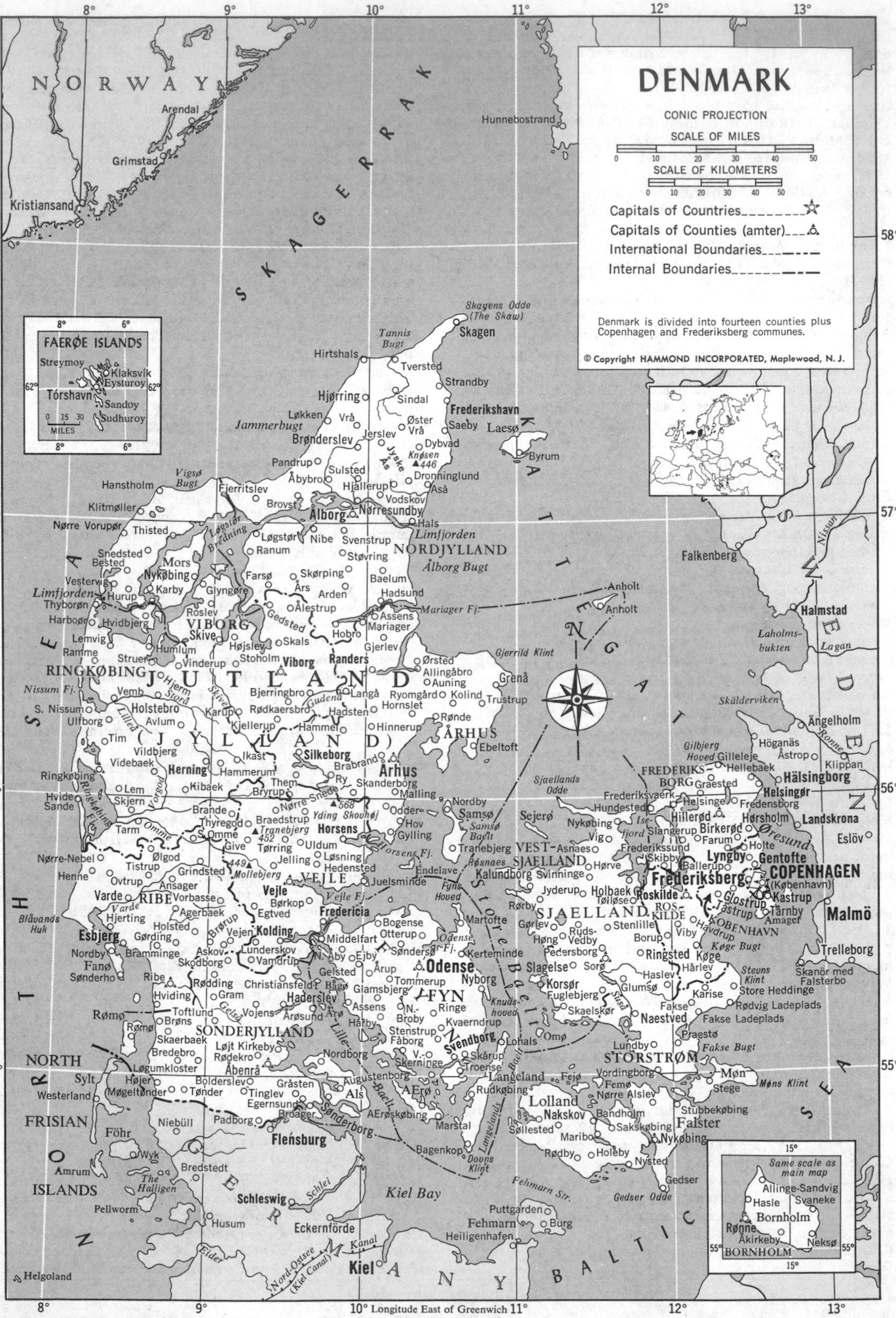
DENMARK
CONIC PROJECTION
SCALE OF MILES
0 10 20 30 40 50
SCALE OF KILOMETERS
0 10 20 30 40 50
Capitals of Countries
Capitals of Counties (amter)
International Boundaries
Internal Boundaries
Denmark is divided into fourteen counties plus Copenhagen and Frederiksberg communes.
© Copyright HAMMOND INCORPORATED, Maplewood, N. J.
FAERØE ISLANDS
Streymoy
Klaksvík
Eysturoy
Tórshavn
Sandoy
Sudhuroy
MILES
8° 9° 10° 11° 12° 13°
58° 57° 56° 55°
NORWAY
Arendal
Grimstad
Kristiansand
SKAGERRAK
Hunnebostrand
Skagens Odde (The Skaw)
Skagen
Tannis Bugt
Hirtshals
Tversted
Strandby
Hjørring
Sindal
Frederikshavn
Løkken
Vrå
Øster Vrå
Saeby
Laesø
Byrum
Jammerbugt
Brønderslev
Jerslev
Dybvad
Jyske Ås
Knøsen 446
Pandrup
Sulsted
Åbybro
Dronninglund
Hjallerup
Aså
Vodskov
Vigsø Bugt
Hanstholm
Fjerritslev
Brovst
Ålborg
Nørresundby
Klitmøller
Nørre Vorupør
Thisted
Hals
Limfjorden
Løgstør Bredning
Løgstør
Nibe
Svenstrup
Ranum
Støvring
NORDJYLLAND
Ålborg Bugt
Snedsted
Bested
Mors
Nykøbing
Farsø
Skørping
Års
Baelum
Vestervig
Karby
Glyngøre
Arden
Hadsund
Limfjorden
Hurup
Thyborøn
Roslev
Ålestrup
Mariager Fj.
Harboør
Hvidbjerg
VIBORG
Gedsted
Assens
Mariager
Anholt
Lemvig
Skive
Skals
Hobro
Ramme
Humlum
Højslev
Gjerlev
Struer
Vinderup
Stoholm
Viborg
Randers
Ørsted
Gjerrild Klint
RINGKØBING
JUTLAND (JYLLAND)
Allingåbro
Auning
Grenå
Nissum Fj.
Vemb
Hjerm
Storå
Skive
Bjerringbro
Gudenå
Langå
Ryomgård
Kolind
Trustrup
S. Nissum
Holstebro
Karup
Rødkaersbro
Hadsten
Hornslet
Ulfborg
Avlum
Kjellerup
Hammel
Hinnerup
Rønde
ÅRHUS
Tim
Vildbjerg
Ikast
Silkeborg
Ebeltoft
Videbaek
Herning
Brabrand
Århus
Ringkøbing
Hammerum
Them
Ry
Skanderborg
Lem
Kibaek
Skjern
Vorgod
Bryrup
Nørre Snede
568 Yding Skovhøj
Malling
Hvide Sande
Ringkøbing Fj.
Brande
Odder
Nordby
Samsø
Samsø Baelt
Thyregod
Braedstrup
Hov
Tarm
Omme
Tranebjerg 452
Horsens
Gylling
Tranebjerg
Give
Tørring
Uldum
Horsens Fj.
Nørre-Nebel
Ølgod
Jelling
Løsning
Hedensted
Henne
Tistrup
Grindsted
449 Møllebjerg
VEJLE
Juelsminde
Endelave
Ovtrup
Ansager
Vejle
Vejle Fj.
Fyns Hoved
Varde
RIBE
Vorbasse
Børkop
Fredericia
Varde
Agerbaek
Egtved
Bogense
Martofte
Blåvands Huk
Hjerting
Holsted
Brørup
Vejen
Kolding
Otterup
Odense Fj.
Esbjerg
Gørding
Middelfart
Kerteminde
Nordby
Bramminge
Askov
Lunderskov
Ejby
Søndersø
Fanø
Skodborg
Vamdrup
Gelsted
Årup
Odense
Sønderho
Ribe
Rødding
Christiansfeld
Bågø
Tommerup
Nyborg
Hviding
Gram
Glamsbjerg
FYN
Rømø
Toftlund
Haderslev
Assens
Ringe
Brøns
Gelså
Vojens
Årø
N. Broby
Kvaerndrup
Skaerbaek
SØNDERJYLLAND
Årøsund
Hårby
Stenstrup
Bredebro
Løjt Kirkeby
Lille Baelt
Fåborg
Svendborg
Lohals
Løgumkloster
Rødekro
Nordborg
V. Skerninge
Skårup
Troense
NORTH FRISIAN ISLANDS
Åbenrå
Augustenborg
Langeland
Sylt
Højer
Bolderslev
Gråsten
Als
Ærø
Rudkøbing
Westerland
Møgeltønder
Tønder
Tinglev
Egernsund
Broager
Ærøskøbing
Marstal
Langelands Baelt
Sønderborg
Niebüll
Padborg
Flensburg
Bagenkop
Dovns Klint
Föhr
Wyk
Amrum
Bredstedt
The Halligen
Schlei
Kiel Bay
Schleswig
Pellworm
Husum
Eckernförde
Eider
Nord-Ostsee (Kiel Canal) Kanal
Kiel
GERMANY
Helgoland
BALTIC SEA
NORTH SEA
KATTEGAT
Sjaellands Odde
Sejerø
Nykøbing
Isefjord
Vig
Asnaes
VEST-SJAELLAND
Røsnaes
Kalundborg
Svinninge
Hørve
Store Baelt
Jyderup
Holbaek
Roskilde
Rørby
SJAELLAND
ROSKILDE
Gørlev
Ruds-Vedby
Stenlille
Høng
Pedersborg
Borup
Ringsted
Køge
Slagelse
Sorø
Haslev
Hårlev
Korsør
Glumsø
Fuglebjerg
Suså
Karise
Knudshoved
Skaelskør
Fakse
Omø
Naestved
Fakse Ladeplads
Praestø
Fakse Bugt
Lundby
STORSTRØM
Vordingborg
Møn
Fejø
Femø
Stege
Møns Klint
Nørre Alslev
Lolland
Nakskov
Bandholm
Stubbekøbing
Falster
Søllested
Maribo
Sakskøbing
Nykøbing
Rødby
Holeby
Nysted
Gedser
Gedser Odde
Fehmarn Str.
Puttgarden
Fehmarn
Burg
Heiligenhafen
Gilbjerg Hoved
Gilleleje
FREDERIKSBORG
Hellebaek
Graested
Frederiksvaerk
Helsinge
Helsingør
Fredensborg
Hundested
Hillerød
Hørsholm
Slangerup
Birkerød
Øresund
Frederikssund
Farum
Holte
Skibby
Lyngby
Gentofte
Ballerup
Frederiksberg
COPENHAGEN (København)
Tølløse
Glostrup
Kastrup
Taastrup
Tårnby
Amager
KØBENHAVN
Havdrup
Viby
Køge Bugt
Stevns Klint
Store Heddinge
Rødvig Ladeplads
SWEDEN
Falkenberg
Nissan
Halmstad
Laholmsbukten
Lagan
Skälderviken
Ängelholm
Rönne å
Höganäs
Åstrop
Klippan
Hälsingborg
Landskrona
Eslöv
Malmö
Trelleborg
Skanör med Falsterbo
Same scale as main map
Allinge-Sandvig
Hasle
Svaneke
Bornholm
Rønne
Åkirkeby
Neksø
BORNHOLM
15°
10° Longitude East of Greenwich 11°

kala; pop. (1969e) 61,000; in narrow strip of land with high hills immediately behind, actually forming a pass, **Derbent Gateway;** hills covered with orchards and vineyards; chief industries making of wine, fishing, wool spinning.

History: At S end of pass are remains of wall anciently known as Caspian Gates (Caspiae Pylae), a Persian defense against inroads of nomadic tribes of the N; wall and citadel supposed to have been built (6th cent.) by Khosrau I; seized by Arabs 728; noted as a residence of Harun al-Rashid, who made it a cultural center; captured by Mongols 1220; seized by Peter the Great 1722 but lost to Russians by 1736; again conquered from Persia 1796 and finally annexed 1813; largely destroyed in civil war of 1917–21.

Der·by *U.S.* 'dər-bē, *Brit. usu.* 'där-bē\\. **1** Manufacturing city, New Haven co., S Connecticut, at confluence of Naugatuck and Housatonic rivers opp. Shelton, 8 m. W of New Haven; pop. (1970c) 12,599; manufactures sponge rubber, metal (brass, copper, bronze) specialties, pins, hardware; the town (incorp.) is coextensive with the city; settled 1642, incorp. 1893.

2 City, Sedgwick co., S cen. Kansas, ab. 13 m. SE of Wichita; pop. (1970c) 7947.

3 Town in Vermont. See DERBY LINE.

4 County in England. See DERBYSHIRE.

5 County borough, ⊗ of Derbyshire, N cen. England, on the Derwent 37 m. NNE of Birmingham; pop. (1971p) 219,348; railroad and manufacturing center; manufactures aircraft engines, chemicals, textiles, paper, silk, pottery (Chelsea-Derby ware); birthplace of Herbert Spencer; home of George Eliot.

Derby Line \\ˌdər-bē-'līn\\. Village in Derby town (pop. [1970c] 3252), Orleans co., N Vermont, on Canadian border ab. 7 m. NE of Newport; pop. (1970c) 834; forms single community with Canadian villages of Stanstead and Rock Island in Quebec.

Der·by·shire \\'där-bē-ˌshi(ə)r, -shər, *U.S. also* 'der-\\. Mining and manufacturing county, N cen. England; area 997 sq. m.; pop. (1971p) 884,339; ⊗ Derby; rivers include the Derwent and the Trent; wheat, oats; sheep raising; dairying, textile manufacture, porcelain and paper making, chemicals; engineering; major towns: Derby, Chesterfield, Ilkeston, Glossop.

Derg, Ben. See BEN DEARG.

Derg, Lough \\-'dərg\\. **1** Lake in SE co. Donegal, Eire; according to legend, the entrance to Saint Patrick's Purgatory was on a small island in this lake.

2 Lake in Galway, Clare, and Tipperary cos., SW cen. Eire; traversed N to S by the Shannon river; ab. 24 m. long, bet. 2 and 6 m. wide.

De Rid·der \\də-'rid-ər\\. City, ⊗ of Beauregard parish, SW Louisiana, 42 m. N of Lake Charles (city); pop. (1970c) 8030; in region producing soybeans, corn, rye, oats, and oranges, also turpentine and lumber.

Der·mott \\'dər-mət\\. City, Chicot co., SE corner of Arkansas, 12 m. W of Mississippi river; pop. (1970c) 4250; lumber mills; settled 1832.

Der·na \\'de(ə)r-nə\\ *or* **Dar·nah** \\'där-nə\\. Coastal city, Libya, ab. 165 m. ENE of Benghazi; pop. (1970e) 26,000; exports wool, corn, wax, honey, bananas. Captured by American navy Apr. 1805 in war with Barbary pirates; in World War II changed hands several times 1941–42.

Dern·berg, Cape \\-'dərn-ˌbərg, -'de(ə)rn-ˌbe(ə)rg\\. Cape extending into Atlantic Ocean on SW coast of South-West Africa.

Der·ry \\'der-ē\\. **1** Manufacturing town, Rockingham co., SE New Hampshire, 10 m. SE of Manchester; pop. (1970c) 11,712; manufactures boots and shoes.

2 Borough, Westmoreland co., SW Pennsylvania, 21 m. W of Johnstown; pop. (1970c) 3338.

3 County and county borough in Northern Ireland. See LONDONDERRY.

Derryfield. See MANCHESTER 7.

Dertona. See TORTONA.

Dertosa. See TORTOSA 1.

Der·went \\'dər-wənt\\. **1** River, S cen. Tasmania, Australia; 107 m. long; rises in Lake St. Clair and flows SE to Storm Bay; has many affluents on its left bank, outlets of the lakes of the central highlands, esp. the Dee, Ouse, Clyde, and Jordan; navigable to Hobart on its right bank on the estuary (4 m. wide).

2 River, Cumberland, NW England; 33 m. long; flows N through lakes Derwent Water and Bassenthwaite, turns WSW to Solway Firth at Workington.

3 River, N Derbyshire, N cen. England; 60 m. long; flows SE into the Trent on border of Leicestershire.

4 River, Durham and Northumberland, N England; 30 m. long; flows NE to the Tyne 3 m. W of Gateshead.

5 River, Yorkshire, N England; 57 m. long; flows N into the Ouse.

Derwent Water. Lake in the Lake District, Cumberland, NW England; 3 m. long; max. depth 72 ft.; has several islands on one of which, Lord Island, was the residence of the earls of Derwentwater; traversed from S to N by the Derwent river; in S receives also the brook which contains Lodore waterfall.

Dés. See DEJ.

Des·a·gua·de·ro \\ˌdā-ˌsäg-wə-'the(ə)r-(ˌ)ō\\. **1** Name given to upper course of Río Salado (see SALADO, RÍO 1) in W Argentina.

2 River, W Bolivia; 200 m. long; flows from Lake Titicaca on the Peruvian border to Lake Poopó.

Des·a·güe, Ca·nal del \\kə-'nal-ˌdel-də-'säg-(ˌ)wā\\. Canal, cen. Mexico, ab. 30 m. long; built bet. 1879 and 1900 to drain the Valley of Mexico; removed danger of floods from the city of Mexico.

Des Al·le·mands, Lake \\-des-'al-ˌman\\. Lake in S Saint John the Baptist parish, SE Louisiana.

Des Arc \\dez-'ärk\\. Town, a ⊗ of Prairie co., E cen. Arkansas, on White river; pop. (1970c) 1714; river port.

Des·ca·be·za·do \\ˌdes-ˌkäb-ə-'zäd-(ˌ)ō\\. Two mountains in E cen. Chile, near Argentine border: **Descabezado Gran·de** \\-'grän-(ˌ)dā\\ 12,565 ft. and **Descabezado Chi·co** \\-'chē-(ˌ)kō\\ 10,660 ft.

Des·chail·lons \\ˌdā-shī-'yōⁿ\\ *or in full* **Deschaillons sur St–Lau·rent** \\-ˌsü(ə)r-ˌsaⁿ-le-'räⁿ\\. Village, Lotbinière co., S Quebec, Canada, on St. Lawrence river 27 m. ENE of Three Rivers; pop. (1971p) 1174.

Des·chutes \\dā-'shüt\\. **1** River, cen. and N Oregon; 250 m. long; rises in SW Deschutes co., flows N into Columbia river forming part of boundary bet. Wasco and Sherman cos.

2 County in Oregon. See table at OREGON.

De·se \\'dā-sā\\ *or* **Des·se** \\'des-\\. Town, ✱ of Welo prov., N cen. Ethiopia; pop. (1970e) 45,731.

De·se·a·do \\ˌdes-ē-'äd-(ˌ)ō\\. River, S Argentina; 380 m. long; flows E from Andes Mts. in NW Santa Cruz territory on the Chilean border and empties into Atlantic Ocean at Puerto Deseado.

De·se·cheo Island \\ˌdes-ə-ˌchā-ō-\\. Small island off NW corner of Puerto Rico.

De·sen·ga·ño, Cape \\-ˌdes-ᵊn-'gän-(ˌ)yō\\. Cape on E coast of Santa Cruz prov., S Argentina, extending into Atlantic Ocean.

De·sen·za·no del Gar·da \\ˌdaz-ᵊn(t)-'sän-ō-del-'gärd-ə\\. Commune, Brescia prov., Lombardy, N Italy, on S shore of Lake Garda 16 m. ESE of Brescia; pop. (1968e) 17,201; important harbor.

Des·er·et \\ˌdez-ə-'ret\\. The provisional state comprising the greater part of the SW United States S of the 42d parallel and W of the Rocky Mts.; organized 1849 by a convention of Mormons; ✱ Salt Lake City; refused recognition by the U.S. Congress and Territory of Utah created in its stead 1850.

De·ser·tas \də-ˈzert-əs(h)\. Small group of rocky islets in the Madeira Is. (*q.v.*), 30 m. SE of Madeira; lat. 32°31′N and long. 16°30′W.

Desert Basin. See CANNING BASIN.

Des·ert Hot Springs \ˈdez-ərt-\. City, Riverside co., SE California, 8 m. N of Palm Springs; pop. (1970c) 2738; health resort; diversified agriculture.

De·sha \də-ˈshā\. County in Arkansas. See table at ARKANSAS.

De·shi·ma \dā-ˈshē-mə, ˈdā-shi-ˌmä\. Former island, at the head of Nagasaki harbor, Kyūshū, Japan; now a reclaimed part of mainland; the residence of representatives of the Dutch East India Company 1641–1859; during these two centuries, when Japan was closed to all foreigners, the only point of contact bet. the Japanese and the outside world; usually six or eight Dutch agents in residence to carry on a restricted trade, they were allowed to leave the island only once a year, when they made a journey to Yedo to report to the shogun.

Desiderii Fanum. See SAINT-DIZIER.

De·sio \ˈdez-(ˌ)yō, ˈdāz-\. Commune, Milano prov., Lombardy, N Italy, 11 m. NNW of Milan; pop. (1968e) 28,199.

Dé·si·rade \ˌdā-zə-ˈräd\. Island in West Indies, a dependency of Guadeloupe (*q.v.*); 11 sq. m.

De Smet \də-ˈsmet\. City, ⊗ of Kingsbury co., E South Dakota; pop. (1970c) 1336.

Des Moines \di-ˈmȯin\. **1** River, formed by junction of E and W forks in Humboldt co., NW cen. Iowa; 327 m. long; flows SE diagonally across Iowa to empty into the Mississippi at Keokuk, SE extremity of Iowa; including W fork which rises in Murray co., SW Minnesota, it is 535 m. long; forms extreme E section of Iowa-Missouri boundary.

2 County in Iowa. See table at IOWA.

3 City, ✱ of Iowa, and ⊗ of Polk co., S cen. Iowa, at confluence of Des Moines and Raccoon rivers; pop. (1970c) 201,404; largest city in the state; in the Iowa corn belt and coal-mining region; packing houses, chemical works, dairies, flour mills; aircraft parts, farm machinery, brick, leather goods, cement; publishing; Drake Univ. (1881), Grand Valley Coll. (1896), Open Bible Coll. (1931); Fort Des Moines built on this site 1843; settlement incorporated as Fort Des Moines 1851; made capital of Iowa and chartered as city of Des Moines 1857. Army post (cavalry), Fort Des Moines, estab. 1900, adjoins the city on the S; in World War II location of first WAC training center (opened July 20, 1942).

4 City, King co., W cen. Washington, on Puget Sound 15 m. S of Seattle; pop. (1970c) 4099.

Des·mond \ˈdez-mənd\. Ancient kingdom, S Munster, S Ireland; comprised present cos. Cork and Kerry (Eire).

Des·na \də-ˈsnä\. River, Russian S.F.S.R. and Ukrainian S.S.R., U.S.S.R.; ab. 550 m. long; rises E of Smolensk and flows generally S to join the Dnieper near Kiev; navigable to Bryansk and is an important channel for the lumber trade; chief tributary the Seim; much fighting on its banks 1943.

De·so·la·ción \ˌdes-ə-ˌläs-ē-ˈōn\ *also Eng.* **Des·o·la·tion** \ˌdes-ə-ˈlā-shən\. Uninhabited Chilean island, northernmost of the Tierra del Fuego archipelago; 70 m. long.

Desolation Islands. See KERGUELEN ISLANDS.

Des·o·la·tion Point \ˌdes-ə-ˌlā-shən-\. Point at N end of Dinagat I., Surigao del Norte prov., Mindanao, Phil., on E side of Surigao Strait.

De So·to \di-ˈsōt-(ˌ)ō\. **1** Name of a parish in Louisiana and of counties in two states of the U.S. See tables at FLORIDA, LOUISIANA, MISSISSIPPI.

2 City, Jefferson co., E Missouri, 38 m. SSW of St. Louis; pop. (1970c) 5984; diversified farming; lead and zinc deposits nearby.

3 City, Dallas co., NE Texas, 14 m. S of Dallas; pop. (1970c) 6617.

De·spair, Mount \-di-ˈspa(ə)r, -ˈspe(ə)r\. Peak in Glacier National Park, NW Montana; 8585 ft.

Des·patch \dis-ˈpach\. Town, Cape Province, Rep. of South Africa, ab. 18 m. NW of Port Elizabeth; pop. (1967e) 9700.

Des Peres \də-ˈpe(ə)r\. City, St. Louis co., E Missouri, 8 m. W of St. Louis; pop. (1970c) 5333.

Des Plaines \de-ˈsplānz\. **1** River, NE Illinois; 150 m. long; rises in SE Wisconsin, flows S to unite with the Kankakee river and form the Illinois river. See ILLINOIS WATERWAY.

2 City, Cook co., NE Illinois, 20 m. NW of Chicago; pop. (1970c) 57,239; electronic equipment, chemicals; De Lourdes Coll. (1951).

Despoto Planina. See RHODOPE.

Des·sau \ˈdes-ˌau̇\. Manufacturing city, Halle dist., East Germany, on Mulde river 71 m. SW of Berlin; pop. (1970e) 98,261; machinery, electrical equipment, chemicals, precision instruments, paper, sugar; 16th cent. palace, municipal theater, old and new town halls, 16th cent. church. First mentioned 1213; capital of Anhalt-Dessau 1603; scene of victory of Wallenstein over Count Mansfeld Apr. 15–25, 1626 (Thirty Years' War); made capital of Anhalt 1863; in World War II frequently bombed 1942–45, ab. 80 percent of city destroyed, but since rebuilt.

Desse. See DESE.

Destêrro. See FLORIANÓPOLIS.

De·struc·tion Island \di-ˌstrək-shən-\. Island in Pacific Ocean, Jefferson co., W Washington.

Det·mold \ˈdet-ˌmōld, -ˌmȯlt\. City, North Rhine-Westphalia, West Germany, 54 m. E of Münster; pop. (1969e) 28,347; furniture, electrical apparatus; summer resort; formerly ✱ of Lippe; large statue to Arminius, conqueror of Varus (9 A.D.), nearby; Charlemagne defeated Saxons nearby (at ancient Theotmalli) 783 A.D.; founded c. 1300; became city 1305.

De·tour \ˈdē-ˌtu̇(ə)r, ˈdi-ˈtu̇(ə)r\. Village, SE tip of Chippewa co., E and NE Michigan penin.; pop. (1970c) 494; at mouth of St. Marys river which enters Lake Huron through **Detour Passage,** a strait bet. the mainland and Drummond I.

Detour, Point. Point at SE extremity of Delta co., S Michigan penin., extending into Lake Michigan.

Détour des Anglais. See ENGLISH TURN.

De·troit \di-ˈtrȯit\. **1** River, SE Michigan; ab. 31 m. long; connects Lake St. Clair with Lake Erie and forms part of U.S.-Canada boundary; crossed by railroad tunnel (2668 ft. long) and vehicular tunnel (2200 ft. long), connecting Detroit, Mich. with Windsor, Canada.

2 City, ⊗ of Wayne co., SE Michigan, on Detroit river just W of Lake St. Clair; pop. (1970c) 1,512,893; largest city in the state; automobile-manufacturing center; also manufactures airplanes, electrical machinery, aluminum products, foundry products, pharmaceuticals, ball bearings, chemicals, adding machines and calculators; Univ. of Detroit (1877), Detroit Institute of Technology (1891), Marygrove Coll. (1910), Wayne State Univ. (1933), Mercy Coll. of Detroit (1941), Detroit Bible Coll. (1945), Michigan Lutheran Coll. (1962).

History: Fort Pontchartrain du Détroit (Ft. Pontchartrain of the Straits) founded by French 1701 as part of chain of posts intended to control Illinois country; from foundation, it was trading and political center for Great Lakes region; surrendered to English during Seven Years' War 1760; besieged by Pontiac 1763–64; chief center of British control of western country during War of Independence; finally turned over to U.S. 1796; almost destroyed by fire 1805; surrendered by Hull to British 1812 but reoccupied by Americans 1813; capital of Michigan Territory 1805–37 and of state 1837–47; incorporated as village 1815, as city 1824; auto manufacturing begun in the city 1899; scene of major race riots 1943 and 1967.

Detroit Dam *and* **Detroit Reservoir.** See UNITED STATES, *Dams and Reservoirs.*

Detroit Lakes. City, ⊗ of Becker co., NW cen. Minnesota, 42 m. E of Fargo, North Dakota; pop. (1970c) 5797; trade center and summer resort in a lake region.

Detskoye Selo. See PUSHKIN.

Det·ti·foss \'det-ē-ˌfȯs\. Waterfall in Jökulsá á Fjöllum river, NE Iceland; 144 ft. high.

Det·ting·en \'det-iŋ-ən\. Village, Bavaria, West Germany; pop. (1967e) 3600; scene in War of the Austrian Succession of victory of George II of England, commanding an army of English, Hanoverian, and Hessian troops, over the French June 27, 1743.

Deu·el \'d(y)ü-əl\. Name of counties in two states of the U.S. See tables at NEBRASKA and SOUTH DAKOTA.

Deur·ne \'dər-nə\. 1 Commune, Antwerp prov., N Belgium; pop. (1969e) 79,106; E suburb of Antwerp; electrical equipment, plastics.

2 Commune, North Brabant prov., S Netherlands, just E of Eindhoven; pop. (1970e) 23,949.

Deutsch–Brod. See HAVLÍČKŮV BROD.

Deutsche Demokratische Republik. See GERMANY, EAST.

Deutsches Reich. See GERMANY.

Deutsch–Eylau. See IŁAWA.

Deutschland. See GERMANY.

Deutsch–Südwestafrika. See SOUTH-WEST AFRICA.

Deutz \'dȯits\. Part of Cologne, West Germany, on right bank of Rhine; independent town until 1888; castle, made Benedictine monastery 1002.

Deux–Montagnes. See TWO MOUNTAINS.

Deux–Montagnes, Lac des. See TWO MOUNTAINS, LAKE OF.

Deuxponts. See ZWEIBRÜCKEN.

Deux–Sè·vres \'dər-'sevrᵊ\. Department of W France. See table at FRANCE.

Deva. See CHESTER 10.

De·va \'dev-(ˌ)ä\ *or Ger.* **Diem·rich** \'dēm-rik\. City, ⊗ of Hunedoara co., W cen. Romania, on the Mureşul river 78 m. ESE of Arad; pop. (1970e) 38,579.

De Valls Bluff \di-'valz-\. Town, a ⊗ of Prairie co., E cen. Arkansas, on White river; pop. (1970c) 622.

Devana. See ABERDEEN 2.

Devana Castra. See CHESTER 10.

Dé·va·vá·nya \ˌdā-ˌvȯ-'vän-(ˌ)yō\. Commune, Békés co., SE Hungary, 47 m. SW of Debrecen; pop. (1970p) 11,207.

De·ve·li \ˌdev-ə-'lē\. Town, Kayseri prov., cen. Turkey, ab. 33 m. SW of Kayseri; pop. (1965c) 13,411.

De·ven·ter \'dā-vən-tər\. Commercial commune, Overijssel prov., E Netherlands, on IJssel river; pop. (1970e) 65,319; textiles, brick; carpet factories; founded 8th cent.; belonged to Hanseatic League.

Dev·er·on \'dev-(ə-)rən\. River in NE Scotland; 61 m. long; flows into North Sea at Banff.

Dev·gad Ba·ria \ˌdāv-gəd-'bär-ē-ə\. Town, E Gujarat, W India, 52 m. NE of Baroda; pop. (1961c) 11,500.

De·vies Mountain \də-ˌvēs-\. Peak, Fayette co., SW Pennsylvania; 2760 ft.

Dé·ville–lès–Rou·en \dā-'vē(ə)l-ˌler-ü-'äⁿ, -'än\. Commune, Seine-Maritime dept., N France, ab. 2 m. W of Rouen of which it is an industrial suburb; pop. (1968c) 10,377.

Dev·ils \'dev-əlz\. River, SW Texas; 100 m. long; rises in NW Sutton co., flows S.

Dev·il's Bit Mountains \ˌdev-əlz-ˌbit-\. Range in N co. Tipperary, S Eire; highest peak 1583 ft.

Devil's Bridge. Locality, Cardiganshire, W Wales, on Rheidol river; noted for scenery, stone bridges, chasm 114 ft. deep.

Devil's Ear Mountain. Peak in the Adirondack Mts., NE New York; 3903 ft.

Devil's Island *or Fr.* **Île du Dia·ble** \ēl-dūē-dyäblᵊ\. One of the Safety Is. (*q.v.*) off the N coast of French Guiana; became a penal colony of the French government in latter part of 19th cent.; here Captain Alfred Dreyfus was a prisoner 1895–99; penal colonies abolished 1938.

Devils Lake. 1 Saline lake bet. Ramsey and Benson cos., NE cen. North Dakota.

2 City, ⊗ of Ramsey co., NE North Dakota, on former N shore of Devils Lake; pop. (1970c) 7078; railroad and trading center in agricultural region; Lake Region Junior Coll. (1941).

Devils Post·pile National Monument \ˌdev-əlz-'pōst-ˌpīl-\. See UNITED STATES, *National Monuments.*

Devils River. See DEVILS.

Devils Tower National Monument. See UNITED STATES, *National Monuments.*

De·vine \də-'vīn\. City, Medina co., S cen. Texas, 33 m. SW of San Antonio; pop. (1970c) 3311; truck farming, peanuts.

De·vi·zes \di-'vī-zəz\. Municipal borough, Wiltshire, S England, on the Kennet 28 m. ESE of Bristol; pop. (1971p) 10,170; market center; agricultural implements.

Dev·on \'dev-ən\. 1 County in England. See DEVONSHIRE.

2 River, E Scotland; ab. 34 m. long; rises in Ochil Hills, Perth co., flows into Forth river in Clackmannan co. ab. 3 m. NW of Alloa.

Devon Island *also* **North Devon Island.** Island, NE Franklin dist., Northwest Territories, Canada, N of Baffin I. and at the head of Baffin Bay; 20,861 sq. m.

Dev·on·port \'dev-ən-ˌpō(ə)rt, -ˌpȯ(ə)rt\. 1 Town, on N coast of Tasmania, Australia, at mouth of Mersey river 50 m. WNW of Launceston; munic. pop. (1970e) 19,240; active port; recreational resort.

2 Seaport, Devonshire, SW England; on E side of Tamar estuary NW of Plymouth, of which it is a part; dockyard, military and naval station.

3 Borough, North I., New Zealand, suburb of Auckland on N side of Waitemata Harbor; pop. (1968e) 11,100; important naval station.

Dev·on·shire \'dev-ən-ˌshi(ə)r, -shər\ *or* **Devon.** County, SW England; area 2591 sq. m.; pop. (1971p) 896,245; ⊗ Exeter; rivers Exe and Dart; agriculture, livestock raising (Devon cattle), quarrying (limestone, clay), fisheries, manufacturing (textiles, paper, pottery); tourism; towns incl. Plymouth, Torbay, Paignton, Newton Abbot, Barnstaple, Brixham, Dartmouth, Exmouth.

De·vrez \dəv-'rez\. River, N cen. Turkey in Asia; 115 m. long; flows E into the Kızıl Irmak.

De·was \dā-'wäs\. 1 Two former Indian states, now part of Madhya Pradesh, cen. India: Senior Branch, 449 sq. m.; Junior Branch, 419 sq. m. Founded in first half of 18th cent. by two brothers, Maratha chieftains.

2 Town, their ✱, 23 m. NE of Indore; pop. (1961c) 34,577.

Dew·ey \'d(y)ü-ē\. 1 Name of counties in two states of the U.S. See tables at OKLAHOMA and SOUTH DAKOTA.

2 City, Washington co., NE Oklahoma, 6 m. NE of Bartlesville; pop. (1970c) 3958; manufactures cement, gasoline.

De Witt \di-'wit\. 1 Name of counties in two states of the U.S. See tables at ILLINOIS and TEXAS.

2 City, a ⊗ of Arkansas co., E Arkansas, 40 m. E of Pine Bluff; pop. (1970c) 3728; rice mills, cotton gins; shipping point for lumber and livestock.

3 City, Clinton co., E Iowa, 18 m. W of Clinton; pop. (1970c) 3647; ships livestock.

Dews·bury \'d(y)üz-ˌber-ē, -b(ə-)rē\. County borough, West Riding, Yorkshire, N England, on the Calder 9 m. S of Leeds; pop. (1971p) 51,310; ironworks; woolen goods; became a county borough 1913.

Dex·ter \'dek-stər\. 1 Industrial town, Penobscot co., E cen. Maine, 30 m. WNW of Bangor; pop. (1970c) 3725; dairy and fruit farms.

2 City, Stoddard co., SE Missouri, 26 m. E of Poplar Bluff; pop. (1970c) 6024; trade and industrial center; cotton gin, flour mill, shirt factory, poultry packing house.

Dez, Ab–i– \ˌäb-i-'dez\ *or* **Ab–i–Diz** \-'dēz\. River, W Iran; 250 m. long; tributary of Kārūn river. See DEZFŪL.

Dez·fūl \dez-'fül\ *or* **Diz·ful** \diz-'fül\. Town, Khūzestān prov., SW Iran, ab. 130 m. N of Khorramshahr; pop. (1971e) 88,000; on Ab-i-Dez river, a dam 20 m. upstream providing power and water for irrigation; its chief local industries are dyeing and manufacture of felts. The ruins of ancient Susa are ab. 15 m. S.

Dezh·ne·va Cape \ˌdezh-nē-ˌō-və-, ˌdesh-\ *also* **East Cape** *or* **Cape Dezh·nev** \-ˌdezh-nē-'ōf, -ˌdesh-\. Cape at E end of Chukotski Penin., Chukot National Okrug, Russian S.F.S.R., U.S.S.R., projecting into Bering Strait; most easterly point in Asia, 169°40'W.

Dhah·ran \dä-'rän, ˌdä-hə-'rän\ *or Arab.* **Aẓ Ẓah·rān** \ˌäz-zə-'rän\. Town, E Saudi Arabia, near W coast of Persian Gulf near Bahrain; adjacent to Dammam in extensive oil regions; engineering coll. (1964); pipeline connection with Abqaiq oil field 40 m. to the SW.

Dha·mar *or* **Da·mar** \də-'mär\. Town, S cen. Yemen, SSE of San'a.

Dha·nush·ko·di \ˌdən-əsh-'kōd-ē\. Seaport at E tip of Rameswaram I., Tamil Nadu, SE India, bet. Palk Strait and Gulf of Mannar; created 1913.

Dhar \'där\. 1 Former Indian state, now part of Madhya Pradesh, cen. India; 1798 sq. m.; founded by Rajputs 9th cent. A.D.; conquered by Muslims 13th cent.; made a fief of the Marathas 1730; came under British control 1819.
2 Town, its ✻, 33 m. SW of Indore; pop. (1961c) 28,325; of great antiquity; famous in medieval India as capital of Rajput dynasty of Malwa; long a center of culture and learning; has fine Pillar Mosque and other structures of interest.

Dha·ram·pur \'dər-əm-ˌpu̇(ə)r, 'də-rəm-\. 1 Former Indian state, now part of Gujarat state, W India; 719 sq. m.
2 Town, its ✻, 115 m. N of Bombay; pop. (1961c) 9800.

Dhar·ma \'dər-mə, 'th̲ər-\ *or Arab.* **Ḍur·mā** \'dər-mə\. Town, cen. Saudi Arabia, ab. 45 m. W of Riyadh.

Dharwar. See HUBLI-DHARWAR.

Dhau·la·gi·ri, Mount \-ˌdau̇-lə-'gi(ə)r-ē\. Peak in the Himalayas, W cen. Nepal, 28°42'N, 83°31'E; 26,810 ft.; first scaled 1960.

Dhe·ké·lia \de-'kāl-yä\ *also* **Ta·toi** *or* **Ta·tóï** \tä-'tōi\. Town, Greece, ab. 16 m. N of Athens; royal palace.

Dhelfoí. See DELPHI 2.

Dhen·ka·nal \den-'kan-^{ə}l\. 1 District, Orissa, E India; 4177 sq. m.; pop. (1961c) 1,028,935; ✻ Dhenkanal.
2 Town, its ✻, 25 m. NW of Cuttack; pop. (1961c) 13,727.

Dhi·ban \di-'ban\ *or anc.* **Di·bon** \'dī-ˌbän\. Ruins of an ancient city of Palestine, 32 m. SSW of Amman, Jordan; place where the Moabite stone was found 1868, a block of black basalt bearing an inscription of 34 lines, dating from the 9th cent. B.C. and written in the Moabite alphabet, an important representative of the Phoenician script. See MOAB.

Dhík·ti \'th̲ēk-tē\ *or Eng.* **Dic·te** \'dik-tē\. Mountain peak in Dhíkti Mts., E Crete, Greece, SE of Candia; 7045 ft.; in Greek mythology the place where Zeus was reared.

Dhíkti Mountains. Mountains, E Crete, Greece; highest point Dhíkti (*q.v.*) 7045 ft.

Dhílos. See DELOS.

Dhodhekánisos. See DODECANESE.

Dho·far \dō-'fär\ *or Arab.* **Ẓu·fār** \zu̇-'fär\. Province, S Oman; ✻ Salalah; scene of revolt (c. 1960 ff.) against rule of sultans of Oman.

Dhol·pur \'dōl-ˌpu̇(ə)r\. 1 Former Indian state, now part of Rajasthan state, NW India; 1173 sq. m.; from 1805 under Jat rulers; under Mogul emperors 1527–1707.
2 Town, its ✻, 34 m. S of Agra; pop. (1961c) 27,412.

Dhonburi. See THON BURI.

Dho·ra·ji \dō-'räj-ē\. Town, Gujarat, W India, near Bhadar river 250 m. NW of Bombay; pop. (1961c) 48,951.

Dhran·ga·dhra \'dräŋ-gə-ˌdrä\. 1 Former Indian state, now part of Gujarat state, W India; 1167 sq. m.
2 Town, its ✻, 75 m. W of Ahmadabad; pop. (1961c) 32,197.

Dhrol \'drōl\. Former Indian state, now part of Gujarat state, W India; 283 sq. m.

Dhu·bri \'du̇b-rē\. Town, NW Assam, NE India, on right bank of Brahmaputra river ab. 260 m. NNE of Calcutta; pop. (1961c) 28,355.

Dhu·lia \'dü-lē-ə\. Town, N Maharashtra, W India, on Panjhra river 200 m. NE of Bombay; pop. (1961c) 98,893; important cotton market.

Día \'dē-ə\. Small island off N coast of Crete, Greece, E Mediterranean Sea, ab. 10 m. NNE of Candia.

Diable, Île du. See DEVIL'S ISLAND.

Dia·ble·rets \dē-ˌab-lə-'rā\. Peak in the Bernese Alps, Valais canton, SW cen. Switzerland; 10,531 ft.

Diablo, Canyon. See CANYON DIABLO.

Di·ab·lo, Mount \-dī-ˌab-lō\. Isolated peak, Contra Costa co., W California, 32 m. E of Oakland; 3848 ft.

Diablo Dam *and* **Diablo Reservoir.** See UNITED STATES, *Dams and Reservoirs.*

Dia·blo·tin, Morne \'mȯ(ə)rn-dē-ˌab-lə-'ta^{n}\. Peak on the island of Dominica, West Indies; 4747 ft.

Diala. See DIYALA.

Di·a·lao Point \ˌdē-ə-ˌlau̇-\. Point on N coast of Ilocos Norte prov., Luzon, Phil., W of Mayraira Point; marks NE point of Bangui Bay.

Di·al Mountain \'dī(-ə)l-\. Peak in the Adirondack Mts., Essex co., NE New York; 4023 ft.

Dia·man·te \ˌdē-ə-'mänt-ē\. River in Mendoza prov., W Argentina; rises in Andes Mts. near Chile-Argentina border, flows E to the Río Salado.

Di·a·man·ti·na \ˌdī-ə-ˌman-'tē-nə\. River, SW Queensland, Australia; 560 m. long; upper tributary of the Warburton river.

Diamantina \ˌdē-ə-ˌman-'tē-nə\. City, cen. Minas Gerais state, E Brazil; munic. pop. (1968e) 34,267; center of the diamond industry.

Di·a·man·ti·no \ˌdē-ə-ˌman-'tē-(ˌ)nü\. Town, Mato Grosso state, SW Brazil, near source of Paraguay river 80 m. NNW of Cuiabá.

Diamant Punt. See DJAMBUAIR POINT.

Di·a·mond, Cape \-'dī-(ə-)mənd\. Promontory, E end of city of Quebec, Canada; alt. 333 ft.; site of citadel.

Diamond Harbour. Port, West Bengal, NE India, at the head of the estuary of the Hooghly, 30 m. SSW of Calcutta with which it is connected by rail; pop. (1961c) 10,100.

Diamond Head. Cape and landmark, SE Oahu I., Hawaii, SE of Honolulu; 761 ft. high.

Diamond Mountains. 1 Range in E cen. Nevada, extending from SW Elko co. S along boundary bet. Eureka and White Pine cos.
2 Mountain peaks, North Korea. See KŬMGANG MOUNTAINS.

Diamond Peak. 1 Mountain in Sierra Nevada, in E Fresno co., S cen. California; 13,105 ft.
2 Mountain, SE tip of Lane co., W Oregon; 8744 ft.

Diamond Point. See DJAMBUAIR POINT.

Dianium. See DENIA.

Diarbekr. See DİYARBAKİR.

Di·bang *or* **Di·bong** \'dē-'bäŋ\. Tributary of the Brahmaputra river, in NE India and SW Tibet, China; flows into the Brahmaputra at the great bend in NE Assam.

Di·bër \'dē-bər\ *or Ital.* **Di·bra** \'dē-brə\. Province of NE Albania. See table at ALBANIA.

Dibio. See DIJON.

Di·boll \'dī-ˌbȯl\. City, Angelina co., E Texas, 15 m. SSW of Lufkin; pop. (1970c) 3557; furniture; diversified agriculture.

Dibon. See DHIBAN.

Dibong. See DIBANG.

Dibra. See DIBËR.

Di·bru·garh \'dib-rə-ˌgär\. Town, NE Assam, NE India, head of navigation on left bank of Brahmaputra river; pop. (1961c) 58,480; univ. (1965); center of tea-raising region; in World War II an Allied air base.

Dibse. See THAPSACUS.

Dick·ens \'dik-ənz\. 1 County in NW Texas. See table at TEXAS.

2 City, its ⊗; pop. (1970c) 295.

Dick·en·son \'dik-ən-sən\. County in Virginia. See table at VIRGINIA.

Dick·er·son, Mount \-'dik-ər-sən\. Mountain, Antarctica, 84°20′S, 167°09′E; 13,517 ft.

Dick·ey \'dik-ē\. County in North Dakota. See table at NORTH DAKOTA.

Dick·in·son \'dik-ən-sən\. 1 Counties in three states of the U.S. See tables at IOWA, KANSAS, MICHIGAN.

2 City, ⊗ of Stark co., SW North Dakota, 100 m. W of Bismarck; pop. (1970c) 12,405; livestock and wheat shipping point; manufactures brick, pottery; lignite coal mines, clay deposits; Dickinson State Coll. (1918); founded c. 1880; became ⊗ 1884.

Dicks Head \'diks-\ *or Arab.* **Ras Chiam·bo·ne** *also* **Ras Kiam·bo·ne** \ˌräs-kyäm-'bō-nē\. Promontory extending into Indian Ocean at boundary bet. SE Somalia and NE Kenya.

Dick·son \'dik-sən\. 1 County in Tennessee. See table at TENNESSEE.

2 Town, Dickson co., NW cen. Tennessee, 35 m. WSW of Nashville; pop. (1970c) 5665; cigars, raincoats, shuttles.

Dickson City. Borough, Lackawanna co., NE Pennsylvania, 5 m. NE of Scranton; pop. (1970c) 7698; coal-mining center; foundry and machine-shop products, silks.

Dickson Island *or Russ.* **Os·trov Dik·son** \ˌòs-trəf-'dēk-sən\. Small island off NW coast of Siberia, Russian S.F.S.R., U.S.S.R., at mouth of Yenisei river, ab. 73°30′N lat., 80°20′E long.; has settlement and harbor.

Dic·le Ne·hri \dij-ˌlā-nə-'(h)rē\. Turkish name of upper Tigris river.

Dicte. See DHÍKTI.

Did·y·ma \'did-ə-mə\. Ruins of town on W coast of Asia Minor, S of Miletus; in ancient times was in Caria; oracle of Apollo; famous temple.

Didyme. See SALINA.

Diedenhofen. See THIONVILLE.

Die·go Gar·cia \dē-ˌā-gō-gär-'sē-ə\. Chief island of the Chagos Archipelago (*q.v.*), British Indian Ocean Territory, 7°20′S, 72°25′E; site of Anglo-American naval communication facilities.

Diego Ra·mí·rez \-rə-'mir-əs\. Chilean island group, southernmost of the Tierra del Fuego archipelago (*q.v.*), 60 m. SW of Cape Horn.

Dié·go–Sua·rez \dē-ˌā-gō-'swär-əs\ *or* **An·tsi·ra·ne** \ˌänt-sə-'rän-ē\. Harbor and town near N end of Malagasy Republic; pop. (1968e) 40,237; exports coffee and peanuts; has served as French naval base.

Die·kirch \'dē-ˌki(ə)rk\. Town, Grand Duchy of Luxembourg; pop. (1967e) 4874; brewery; became town 1260.

Diemrich. See DEVA.

Dien Bien Phu \ˌdyen-ˌbyen-'fü\. Village, North Vietnam; French military post in Indochina war; in 1954 besieged 55 days, fell to Vietminh May 7.

Dien Khanh \'dyen-'kän\ *or* **Khanh·hoa** \'kän-'hwä\. Coastal town, South Vietnam, 45 m. N of Phan Rang.

Di·eppe \dē-'ep\. 1 Town, New Brunswick, Canada; pop. (1971p) 4261.

2 Seaport, Seine-Maritime dept., N France, on English Channel 34 m. N of Rouen; pop. (1968c) 29,970; shipbuilding, oil refining; known esp. for manufacture of ivory and bone goods, which dates from 15th cent.; trades in fish, silk, wine, brandy, fruit; textiles. Important naval base in 17th cent.; suffered from plague 1668, 1670; destroyed by English and Dutch 1694; occupied by Germans 1870–71 in Franco-Prussian War and 1940–44 in World War II; site of commando raid by Canadians and British Aug. 19, 1942; captured by Canadians Aug. 31, 1944.

Diest \'dēst\. Manufacturing commune, Brabant prov., cen. Belgium; pop. (1969e) 9458; breweries.

Die·ti·kon \'dēt-i-ˌkōn\. Commune, Zurich canton, Switzerland, NE of Zurich; pop. (1970c) 22,705.

Dif·fer·dange \dē-fer-dänzh\ *or Ger.* **Dif·fer·ding·en** \'dif-ər-ˌdiŋ-ən\. Town, SW Grand Duchy of Luxembourg, 12 m. SW of Luxembourg; pop. (1970e) 17,963; iron and steel.

Dig \'dēg\. Town, NE Rajasthan, NW India; has palace ruins and fort, built 1730; scene of battle 1803 in which Gen. Lake defeated Marathas.

Dig·by \'dig-bē\. 1 County, W Nova Scotia, Canada. See table at NOVA SCOTIA.

2 Resort town, its ⊗, on Annapolis Basin 57 m. NNE of Yarmouth; pop. (1971p) 2324; founded 1783 by body of Loyalists from New England; exports "Digby chickens," a variety of small herring.

Digby Gut. Passage in W Nova Scotia, Canada; 2 m. long and ½ m. wide; forms outlet of Annapolis Basin into Bay of Fundy; actually a gap or cleft in elevated ridge along SW coast of Nova Scotia, its steep sides 400 to 600 ft. high; strong tides and winds.

Digh·ton \'dīt-ᵊn\. 1 City, ⊗ of Lane co., W Kansas; pop. (1970c) 1540.

2 Town, Bristol co., SE Massachusetts, 7 m. N of Fall River; pop. (1970c) 4667; market gardening. On E bank of Taunton river opp. the town is **Dighton Rock,** a boulder of green stone curiously marked; many theories of its origin have been given but now generally believed to be American Indian; first observed c. 1680.

Dignano d'Istria. See VODNJAN.

Digne \'dēnʸ\. Commune, ✱ of Alpes-de-Haute Provence dept., SE France, 71 m. NE of Marseilles; pop. (1968c) 14,661; 13th cent. cathedral; mineral springs nearby.

Di·goin \dē-'gwaⁿ\. Commune, W Saône-et-Loire dept., E cen. France, on the Loire; pop. (1968c) 14,661; manufactures pottery and porcelain.

Di·gos \'dē-gəs\. Municipality, ✱ of Davao del Sur prov., Mindanao, Phil.; pop. (1969e) 42,000.

Di·gul *or Du.* **Di·goel** \'dē-ˌgül\. Navigable river, SE Irian Barat, Indonesia; ab. 400 m. long; rises in E end of Maoke Mts. and flows S and W to Arafura Sea, N of Dolak I.; its basin largely swampy jungle.

Di·hang *or* **Di·hong** \'dē-'häŋ\. Name applied to the Brahmaputra river (*q.v.*) in its middle course, where it turns and breaks through the Himalayas in Tibet, China, and Assam, India.

Dijeng Plateau \ˌdēŋ-\. Small plateau region, on Mt. Perahu, cen. Java, Indonesia, SW of Semarang; once a crater; on it are ruins of Hindu (Brahmanic) temples, built c. 9th cent. A.D.

Dij·le \'dī-lə\ *or* **Dy·le** \'dī-lə, 'dē(ə)l\. River, Belgium; ab. 50 m. long; flows N and W in Brabant and Antwerp provs. and unites with the Nethe river 4 m. NW of Mechelen to form the Rupel river; Belgian and British line of defense May 1940.

Di·jon \dē-'zhōⁿ\ *or anc.* **Dib·io** \'dib-ē-ˌō\. Commercial and manufacturing city, ✱ of Côte-d'Or dept., E France, on Ouche river 168 m. SE of Paris; pop. (1968c) 145,357; electrical and optical equipment, pharmaceuticals; railroad shops; tourism; surrounded by eight forts; 13th cent. church; 14th cent. town hall (former palace of dukes of Burgundy); univ. (1722); birthplace of Bossuet. Site occupied from pre-Roman times; ✱ of Burgundy from 10th cent.; great prosperity under Valois dynasty 1364–1477; to France 1678.

Dikh Tau. See DYKH TAU.

Diks·mui·de *or* **Dix·mui·de** \dik-'smīd-ə\ *or Fr.* **Dix·mude** \dē(k)-smu̅e̅d\. Commune, W Flanders prov., Belgium, 13 m. N of Ieper (Ypres); pop. (1969e) 6786; in World War I destroyed during heavy fighting Oct. 22–Nov. 10, 1914 when Germans were prevented from reaching the sea by flooding of the region.

Dikson, Ostrov. See DICKSON ISLAND.

Dik·wa \'dik-(ˌ)wä\. 1 District, North-Eastern State, NE Nigeria; 5149 sq. m.; the N part of former British Cameroons trust territory.

2 Town, its ✱, near SW shore of Lake Chad; pop. (1963c) 6751.

Di·lam \'dil-ˌam\. Town, Saudi Arabia, ab. 60 m. SE of Riyadh.

Di·la Point \ˌdē-lə-\. Most westerly point of Ilocos Sur prov., Luzon, Phil., ab. 4 m. W of Vigan.

Dil·ā·rām \ˌdil-ə-'räm\. Town, SW cen. Afghanistan, on main highway 140 m. WNW of Kandahār.

Di·li *or* **Dil·li** \'dil-ē\. Town, ✱ of Portuguese Timor, on N coast, E section of the island of Timor; pop. (1970p) 29,-312; good harbor for small craft; held by Japanese from Feb. 1942 to end of World War II.

Dil·len·burg \'dil-ən-ˌbu̇(ə)rg\. Town, Hesse, West Germany, ab. 25 m. WSW of Marburg; pop. (1968e) 10,310; ruins of castle where William the Silent was born; received town charter 1344.

Dil·li \'dil-ē\. 1 Territory and city, India. See DELHI.

2 Town, Portuguese Timor. See DILI.

Dil·ling·en \'dil-iŋ-ən\. 1 *or in full* **Dillingen an der Do·nau** \-ˌän-dər-'dō-ˌnau̇\. Town, Bavaria, West Germany, on the N bank of the Danube 19 m. NE of Ulm; pop. (1967e) 11,600; became town in 13th cent.; taken by Allies Apr. 27, 1945 after several days' fighting.

2 *or in full* **Dillingen an der Saar** \-ˌän-dər-'zär, -'sär\. Town, Saarland, West Germany, on the Saar 28 m. S of Trier; pop. (1967e) 18,100; machinery; became town 1949.

Dil·lon \'dil-ən\. 1 County in South Carolina. See table at SOUTH CAROLINA.

2 City, ⊗ of Beaverhead co., SW Montana, 53 m. S of Butte; pop. (1970c) 4548; shipping point for wool; Western Montana Coll. (1893).

3 Town, ⊗ of Dillon co., NE South Carolina, 29 m. ENE of Florence; pop. (1970c) 5286; textiles, flour, lumber.

Dillon Bay \ˌdil-ən-\. Bay with good anchorage on W coast of Eromanga I., New Hebrides, SW Pacific; site of Martyrs' Memorial Church, in memory of several missionaries killed on the island by natives 1839–72.

Di·lo·lo \di-'lō-(ˌ)lō\. Lake in E Angola, SW Africa, near Zaire border, lat. 11°31'S and long. 22°20'E.

Di·ma·pur \'dē-mə-ˌpu̇(ə)r\. Town, Nagaland, NE India, at foot of W slope of Naga Hills and key point on Bengal-Assam R.R.; pop. (1961c) 5800; goal of Japanese advance 1944 but not taken.

Di·ma·sa·lang \dē-ˌmäs-ə-'läŋ\. Municipality, E coast of Masbate I., Phil., 20 m. SE of Masbate; pop. (1969e) 20,-500.

Dimashq. See DAMASCUS.

Dîm·bo·vi·ta \'dim-bə-ˌvēt-sə\. 1 River, S cen. Romania; 155 m. long; flows out of the Transylvanian Alps SSE past Bucharest into the Argeş river.

2 County of S cen. Romania. See table at ROMANIA.

Di·mi·trov·grad \də-'mē-trəf-ˌgrad\. Town, Khaskovo prov., S Bulgaria; pop. (1968e) 44,302; chemicals; lime kilns; founded 1947.

Dim·mit \'dim-ət\. County in Texas. See table at TEXAS.

Dim·mitt \'dim-ət\. Town, ⊗ of Castro co., NW Texas; pop. (1970c) 4327; diversified farming.

Di·na·gat \dē-'näg-ət\. 1 Island, N of extreme NE point of Mindanao, SE Phil., a part of Surigao del Norte prov.; 309 sq. m.; separated from Mindanao by channel ab. 5 m. wide, from Siargao I. on E by **Dinagat Sound,** and from S Leyte and Panaon Is. on W by Surigao Strait (*q.v.*); has chain of mountains from N to S with several peaks above 1700 ft. and highest 3300 ft.; chief towns Dinagat and Loreto.

2 Municipality and chief town of Dinagat I., on SW coast; pop. (1969e) 13,700.

Di·naj·pur \di-'näj-ˌpu̇(ə)r\. 1 District, Bangla Desh; 2609 sq. m.; pop. (1961c) 1,709,917; ✱ Dinajpur; formerly a prov. of British India; partitioned between India and Pakistan 1947 (Indian sector constitutes the district **West Dinajpur** 1418 sq. m.); rice, sugarcane.

2 Town, its ✱; pop. (1961c) 37,711.

Di·na·lu·pi·han \ˌdē-nə-lu̇-'pē-ˌhän\. Municipality, N Bataan prov., Luzon, Phil., near Pampanga border and ab. 14 m. NNW of Balanga; pop. (1969e) 29,200; scene of fierce fighting with Japanese Jan. 1942.

Di·nan \dē-'nä^{n}\. City, Côtes-du-Nord dept., NW France, on Rance river 35 m. E of Saint-Brieuc; pop. (1968c) 13,-137; remains of 13th cent. ramparts; 15th cent. cloister; 12th cent. churches; tourism.

Di·nant \dē-'nä^{n}\. Commune, Namur prov., S Belgium, on the Meuse; pop. (1969e) 9815; in the Ardennes forest region; sacked by the Germans Aug. 15, 1914.

Di·na·pur \'din-ə-ˌpu̇(ə)r\ *or* **Di·na·pore** \-ˌpō(ə)r, -ˌpȯ(ə)r\. Town, NW Bihar, NE India, on right bank of Ganges river 12 m. W of Patna; pop. (1961c) 35,200; iron foundries; includes military cantonment; Sepoy troops stationed here joined mutiny in 1857.

Di·nar \di-'när\ *or anc.* **Ce·lae·nae** \sə-'lē-(ˌ)nē\. Town, Afyonkarahisar prov., W cen. Turkey in Asia, on railroad 50 m. SSW of Afyonkarahisar; pop. (1965c) 11,298; ancient Celaenae a great city of Phrygia at the source of the Maeander (Menderes); setting of legend of Apollo and Marsyas.

Di·nard \dē-'när\. Commune, Ille-et-Vilaine dept., NW France, on the Gulf of Saint-Malo at the mouth of the Rance, opp. Saint-Malo; pop. (1962c) 9432; resort.

Di·nar·ic Alps \də-ˌnar-ik-\ *or Serbo-Croat.* **Di·na·ra Pla·ni·na** \ˌdē-nə-ˌrä-'plän-i-ˌnä\. See table at ALPS.

Dindar. See DENDER.

Din·di·gul \'din-di-ˌgəl\. Town, S Tamil Nadu, S India, 35 m. NNW of Madurai; pop. (1961c) 92,947; trade center, especially for tobacco and cigars; includes overlooking fort formerly of great strategic importance during the wars with the Marathas and in the time of Haidar Ali.

Din·dy·mus, Mount \-'din-də-məs\. See PESSINUS.

Ding·a·lan Bay \diŋ-ˌäl-ən-\. Inlet of Pacific Ocean on E coast of Luzon, Quezon prov., Phil., S of Baler Bay; its coast subleased to and exploited by Japanese before World War II.

Din·gle \'diŋ-gəl\. Seaport, W co. Kerry, SW Eire; on a small harbor on NW shore of **Dingle Bay** (an inlet of Atlantic Ocean extending ab. 30 m. inland); pop. (1961c) 1801; as a port of Desmond important in 16th cent.

Din·gras \diŋ-'gräs\. Municipality, S cen. Ilocos Norte prov., Luzon, Phil., on a tributary of the Laoag river 8 m. ESE of Laoag; pop. (1969e) 38,400.

Ding·wall \diŋ-(ˌ)wȯl, -wəl\. Burgh, ⊗ of Ross and Cromarty co., N Scotland, near the head of Cromarty Firth; pop. (1971p) 4109; whiskey distilling.

Din·kels·bühl \'diŋ-kəls-ˌbyü(ə)l\. Town, W Bavaria, West Germany, ab. 45 m. SW of Nürnberg; pop. (1967e) 8100; brushes; first mentioned 1188; free imperial city 1351–1802.

Di·no·saur National Monument \'dī-nə-ˌsȯ(ə)r-\. See UNITED STATES, *National Monuments.*

Dins·la·ken \'din(t)s-ˌläk-ən\. Industrial city, North Rhine-Westphalia, West Germany, near Rhine river 10 m. N of Duisburg; pop. (1969e) 53,991; coal mining; manufactures steel, wire, nails, tile, lumber; received city charter 1273.

Di·nu·ba \dī-'n(y)ü-bə\. City, Tulare co., S cen. California, 25 m. SE of Fresno; pop. (1970c) 7917; in irrigated region.

Din·wid·die \'din-ˌwid-ē, ˌdin-'wid-\. 1 County in SE Virginia. See table at VIRGINIA.

2 Village, its ⊗, 15 m. SW of Petersburg; scene of Sheridan's defeat of Pickett near Dinwiddie Courthouse before fall of Petersburg Mar. 31, 1865, a part of the battle of Five Forks.

Di·oc·lea \dī-'äk-lē-ə\. See SALONA.

Di·o·mede Islands \'dī-ə-ˌmēd-\. Two islands **Big Diomede** (Russian) and **Little Diomede** (American) in middle of Bering Strait, ab. 2 m. apart; separated by date line.

Discovered and named by Vitus Bering, Danish explorer in the employ of Russia, on Aug. 16, 1728 (St. Diomedes' Day); Big Diomede has important Soviet weather station.

Dio·ny·si·a·des \ˌdī-ə-nə-ˈsī-ə-ˌdēz\. Group of small islands in Mediterranean Sea just W of Cape Sidero, NE point of Crete; belong to Greece.

Dioscurias. See SUKHUMI.

Diospolis *or* **Diospolis Magna.** See THEBES 1.

Diour·bel \dyu̇r-ˈbel\. Town, Senegal, W Africa, E of Dakar; pop. (1967e) 36,326.

Di·po·log \dē-ˈpō-ˌlȯg\. Municipality, ✱ of Zamboanga del Norte prov., Mindanao, Phil., on S coast of passage bet. Sulu Sea and Mindanao Sea; pop. (1969e) 43,900.

Dir \ˈdi(ə)r\. 1 District, Malakand div., N cen. North-West Frontier Province, Pakistan; 2040 sq. m.; pop. (1961c) 385,183; former independent state, retaining limited autonomy until its total integration with Pakistan 1969.
2 Its chief town, 85 m. NNE of Peshawar.

Di·rec·tion, Cape \-də-ˈrek-shən\. Cape, cen. E coast of Cape York Penin., Queensland, NE Australia.

Di·re Da·wa *or* **Di·re·da·wa** \ˌdir-id-ə-ˈwä\. City, E Ethiopia, on the Addis Ababa-Djibouti railroad; pop. (1970e) 60,925; exports incl. hides and coffee; taken by British Mar. 30, 1941.

Di·ri·am·ba \ˌdir-ē-ˈäm-bə\. Town, Carazo dept., SW Nicaragua, 20 m. S of Managua; munic. pop. (1970e) 30,431.

Dirk Har·tog Island \ˈdərk-ˈhär-ˌtȯg-, -ˌtäg-\. Island off W coast of Western Australia; 25°48′S, 113°E; 239 sq. m.

Dirschau. See TCZEW.

Dis·ap·point·ment, Cape \-ˌdis-ə-ˈpȯint-mənt\. Cape on SW extremity of Pacific co., SW Washington, on N side of entrance to Columbia river.

Disappointment, Lake. Dry salt lake, N cen. Western Australia, crossed by Tropic of Capricorn.

Disappointment Islands. Small island group, N Tuamotu Archipelago, S Pacific Ocean.

Dis·cov·ery Bay \dis-ˈkəv-(ə-)rē-\. Inlet of Indian Ocean, S coast of Australia, at boundary bet. Victoria and South Australia.

Dis·gra·zia, Mon·te \ˌmōn-tā-dis-ˈgräts-yä\. Peak in the Bernina Alps, N Italy, NNW of Sondrio; 12,067 ft.

Dis·ko \ˈdis-(ˌ)kō\. Island in Davis Strait, on W coast of Greenland, 70°N lat.; 3200 sq. m.; has extensive coal deposits; Godhavn is on S shore.

Disko Bay. Bay on the W coast of Greenland, S of Disko I.

Dis·mal Swamp \ˌdiz-məl-\. Swamp area, SE Virginia and NE North Carolina; ab. 30 m. long, 10 m. wide; traversed by **Dismal Swamp Canal** (22 m. long) connecting Chesapeake Bay with Albemarle Sound.

Dis·na \dis-ˈnä\ *or Pol.* **Dzis·na** \ˈjēs-(ˌ)nä\. 1 River, Belorussian S.S.R., U.S.S.R., flows E into Western Dvina river at Disna, formerly on Russian border.
2 Town, N Belorussian S.S.R., U.S.S.R., 128 m. NE of Vilnius; formerly in Poland.

Di·son \dē-ˈzōⁿ\. Manufacturing commune, Liège prov., E Belgium; pop. (1969e) 8411; artificial fibers.

Dis·raë·li \diz-ˈrā-lē\. Village, Wolfe co., S Quebec, Canada, 43 m. NNE of Sherbrooke; pop. (1971p) 3394; wood products, butter; dairy farming.

Dis·te·ghil \ˌdēs-tə-ˈgēl\. Peak in the Himalayas, in region controlled by Pakistan, 36°22′N, 75°12′E; 25,871 ft.

District Heights. Town, Prince Georges co., S cen. Maryland, SE of Washington, D.C.; pop. (1970c) 8424.

District of Co·lum·bia \-kə-ˈləm-bē-ə\. Federal district of U.S.A., coextensive with the city of Washington (see WASHINGTON 5), bounded on N, E, and S by Maryland, and on W by Virginia; 69 sq. m. (land area 61 sq. m.); pop. (1970c) 756,510; estimated pop. during World War II 1,250,000. *Official flower:* American Beauty rose. *Motto:* Justitia Omnibus (Justice to All).
History: Territory for seat of Federal government originally 100 square miles; authorized by Congressional act 1790 and granted by Maryland and Virginia 1790–91; site of Washington chosen by President Washington, occupied by government 1800; part (see ALEXANDRIA 6) retroceded to Virginia 1846; slave trade forbidden in District 1850 and slavery abolished with compensation 1862; governed by Commission appointed by President (1874; formalization 1878), by mayor-council since 1967; by consolidation of Georgetown (*q.v.*) with city of Washington, Federal district became coterminous with city of Washington. Granted national suffrage 1961 by 23d amendment to U.S. Constitution; administrative structure reorganized 1967.

Dis·tri·to Fe·de·ral \di-ˈstrē-tō-ˌfeth-ə-ˈräl\. Spanish and Portuguese for FEDERAL DISTRICT.

Di·sūq \di-ˈsük\. Town, Kafr al-Sheikh gov., Lower Egypt, on Rosetta branch of the Nile E of Damanhūr; pop. (1966c) 45,000.

Dith·mar·schen \ˈdit-ˌmär-shən\ *or Eng.* **Dit·marsh** \-ˌmärsh\. Region, SW Schleswig-Holstein, West Germany, bet. the Elbe and Eider rivers; partly marsh, partly sandy; in Charlemagne's time known as **Nord·al·bin·gia** \ˌnȯr-dal-ˈbin-j(ē-)ə\; peasant independent self-government formed in 13th cent., finally overcome in 1559 and divided; annexed to Schleswig-Holstein 1866.

Diu \ˈdē-(ˌ)ü\. District of former Portuguese India, W India, 170 m. NW of Bombay; 14 sq. m.; comprises island and seaport town, now part of the Indian terr. of Goa, Daman, and Diu; includes also two small towns on the mainland; came into Portuguese possession in 1535; invaded by India 1961, annexed 1962.

Di·ua·ta Mountains \dē-ˌwät-ə-\. Mountain range, NE Mindanao, Phil., running N and S along boundary of Agusan del Norte prov.; highest peak Mt. Hilonghilong 6599 ft.

Diuata Point. Point on NE coast of Mindanao, Phil., marking boundary bet. Agusan del Norte and Misamis Oriental provs. and also W side of entrance to Butuan Bay.

Dives \ˈdēv\ *or in full* **Dives–sur–Mer** \-su̇(ə)r-ˈme(ə)r\. Town, Calvados dept., NW France; pop. (1962c) 6521; on the Bay of the Seine ab. a mile inland from the harbor from which William the Conqueror set sail on his first attempt to reach England 1066 (see SAINT-VALÉRY-SUR-SOMME).

Di·vide \də-ˈvīd\. County in North Dakota. See table at NORTH DAKOTA.

Divide Mountain. Peak, E border of Glacier National Park, NW Montana; 8647 ft.

Di·vid·ing Ridge \də-ˈvīd-iŋ-\. Ridge extending along W section of boundary between Virginia and West Virginia.

Di·vion \dē-ˈvyōⁿ\. Commune, Pas-de-Calais dept., N France, 17 m. NW of Arras; pop. (1968c) 10,407; coal mining.

Di·vi·sion Peak \də-ˌvizh-ən-\. Mountain, W Humboldt co., NW Nevada; 8585 ft.

Divisões, Serra das. See SERRA DAS DIVISÕES.

Divodurum *or* **Divodurum Mediomatricum.** See METZ.

Divona. See CAHORS.

Di·wa·ni·yah \ˌdē-wə-ˈnē-(y)ə\ *or Arab.* **Ad Di·wa·ni·ya** \ˌad-\. Town, S cen. Iraq, on the Euphrates river 40 m. SE of Hilla; on the Baghdad-Basra railroad; pop. (1965c) 60,553; in region producing rice, barley, and wheat.

Dix \ˈdiks\. River, cen. Kentucky; flows N into Kentucky river. See DIX RIVER DAM.

Dix·ie \ˈdik-sē\. 1 The southern states of the U.S.
2 County in Florida. See table at FLORIDA.

Dix·moor \ˈdiks-ˌmu̇(ə)r\. Village, Cook co., NE Illinois, 17 m. S of Chicago; pop. (1970c) 4735.

Dix Mountain. Peak in the Adirondack Mts., Essex co., NE New York; 4857 ft.

Dixmuide *or* **Dixmude.** See DIKSMUIDE.

Dix·on \'dik-sən\. 1 County in Nebraska. See table at NEBRASKA.
2 City, Solano co., cen. California, 20 m. SW of Sacramento; pop. (1970c) 4432; meat packing; feed mill; diversified agriculture.
3 City, ⊗ of Lee co., N Illinois, 40 m. SSW of Rockford; pop. (1970c) 18,147; cement, electronic equipment; Sauk Valley Coll. (1965); founded 1830.
4 City, ⊗ of Webster co., W Kentucky; pop. (1970c) 572; coal mining.

Dixon Entrance. Strait bet. N Queen Charlotte Is., Canada, and S Prince of Wales I., SE Alaska, and W British Columbia; ab. 40 m. wide; connects Hecate Strait with the Pacific Ocean.

Dix River Dam. Dam across Dix river in Kentucky; height 270 ft.; completed 1924; water power.

Di·ya·la \dē-'yal-ə\ *or* **Di·a·la** \dē-'al-ə\. River, cen. Iraq; ab. 275 m. long; rises in mountains of N Iraq, flows SW into the Tigris river at Baghdad; navigable for 50 m.; traverses a fertile region.

Di·yar·ba·kır \di-ˌ(y)är-bə-'ki(ə)r\ *or* **Di·ar·bekr** \-'bek-ər\. 1 Province of SE Turkey, Asia. See table at TURKEY.
2 *or anc.* **Am·i·da** \'am-əd-ə\. Commercial city, its ✱, on right bank of the Tigris; pop. (1965c) 102,653; trades in wool, mohair, and copper; esp. flourishing in 19th cent. As Amida became Roman colony 230 A.D.; captured after long siege 363 A.D. by Shapur II of Persia; several times taken by Persians and Arabs before finally being taken by the Turks 1515.

Dizful. See DEZFŪL.

Dj-. For some words beginning thus, see J-.

Djailolo. See HALMAHERA.

Djai·lo·lo Passage \jī-ˌlō-lō-\. Strait bet. SE Halmahera I. on the W and the small islands off W Waigeo I. on the E, in the Moluccas, E Malay Archipelago; connects Ceram Sea with the Pacific Ocean; extreme width is ab. 100 m.

Dja·ja, Mount \-'jä-yə\; *formerly* **Mount Su·kar·no** \-sü-'kär-nō\ *also* **Mount Car·stensz** \-'kär-stənz\. Peak in W cen. Irian Barat, Indonesia, in the Sudirman Range; 16,535 ft., highest mountain on New Guinea I.

Dja·ja·pu·ra \ˌjä-yə-'pu̇r-ə\; *formerly* **Hol·lan·dia** \hä-'lan-dē-ə\ *or* **Ko·ta·ba·ru** \ˌkōt-ə-'bär(ˌ)ü\ *or* **Su·kar·na·pu·ra** \sü-ˌkär-nə-'pu̇r-ə\. Town, ✱ of Irian Barat, Indonesia, on NE coast; good harbor; seized from Japanese by U.S. forces Apr. 22, 1944; became headquarters of Gen. MacArthur Sept. 8, 1944.

Dja·ja·wi·dja·ja Range \ˌjä-yə-wi-'jä-yə-\; *formerly* **Or·ange Range** \'ör-inj-, 'är-, -ənj-\ *or Du.* **Oran·je Ge·berg·te** \ō-ˌrän-yə-gə-'be(ə)rk-tə\. Mountain range, E cen. Irian Barat, Indonesia, E of Sudirman Range and forming E end of Maoke Mts.; highest peak Trikora 15,585 ft.; source of the Digul and many other streams.

Dja·kar·ta *or* **Ja·kar·ta** \jə-'kärt-ə\ *or formerly* **Ba·ta·via** \bə-'tā-vē-ə\. Seaport city, ✱ of Indonesia, on NW coast of Java, on Djakarta Bay at mouth of Liwung river; forms capital territory (228 sq. m.; pop. [1971e] 4,542,146); largest city and principal port of Indonesia; iron foundries, sawmills, textile mills, tanneries; exports incl. rubber, tea, quinine; several universities incl. the Univ. of Indonesia (1950).
History: Founded 1619 on site of Jacatra (*q.v.*) by Jan P. Coen; became headquarters of Dutch East India Company; gradually extended control over neighboring sultanates and principalities; suffered severe earthquake 1699; defended by Allies 1942 but captured by Japanese Mar. 5; proclaimed ✱ of Indonesia 1949.

Djakarta Bay *or formerly* **Batavia Bay.** Inlet of Java Sea on NW coast of Java, Indonesia.

Djakovica. See DAKOVICA.

Djakovo. See ĐAKOVO.

Djam·bi *or* **Jam·bi** \'jäm-bē\. 1 River, Sumatra, Indonesia. See HARI.
2 Province, S cen. Sumatra, Indonesia, extending nearly across the island from Barisan Mts. to South China Sea; 17,345 sq. m.; pop. (1970e) 939,000; ✱ Djambi; its low marshy area drained by Hari river; rubber, cotton, rice; fishing; oil.
3 Town, its ✱, a river port on the Hari river ab. 60 m. from its mouth; pop. (1961c) 113,000; univ. (1963); an important oil center and trading town; exports incl. indigo, timber; in 17th and 18th cents. capital of an influential sultanate.

Djam·bu·air Point \ˌjäm-bü-'ī(ə)r-\ *or Du.* **Di·a·mant Punt** \ˌdē-ə-ˌmänt-'pənt\ *or Eng.* **Di·a·mond Point** \ˌdī-(ə-)mənd-\. Cape on NE tip of Sumatra, Indonesia, at NW end of Strait of Malacca.

Djapara. See DJEPARA.

Dja·pa·ra–Rem·bang *or* **Ja·pa·ra–Rembang** \jə-ˌpär-ə-'rem-ˌbäŋ\. Former residency, Neth. Indies, now part of the Indonesian prov. of Central Java; 2339 sq. m.; ✱ Kudus; long coastline on Java Sea; lowland around Kudus but volcanic mountains in NW and S; oil; sugar, rice.

Dja·ti·wangi *or* **Ja·ti·wangi** \ˌjät-ē-'wäŋ-ē\. Town, West Java prov., Indonesia, ab. 20 m. W of Tjirebon.

Djawa. See JAVA.

Djebeïl. See JUBAYL.

Djebel. See JEBEL.

Dje·bel Bou Hed·ma State Park \ˌjeb-əl-bü-'hed-mə-\. National park, S Tunisia; 508 sq. m.; plateau region; established 1936.

Djebel Druze. See JEBEL ED DRUZ.

Djeddah. See JIDDA.

Dje·dei·da \jə-'dād-ə\. Railroad junction town on the Medjerda river, N Tunisia, ab. 17 m. W of the city of Tunis; in World War II held by British for a few days in Nov. 1942; German base in Tunisian campaign, taken by Allied armies May 1943.

Djel·fa \'jel-fə\. Town, Médéa dept., Algeria, ab. 140 m. S of Algiers; pop. (1966c) 25,472; railroad terminal.

Djem, El. See AL-JEM.

Dje·ma·dja \jə-'mäj-ə\. Largest island of Anambas Is., Indonesia, in W part of group; 15 m. long, 10 m. wide.

Djem·ber *or* **Jem·ber** \'jem-bər\. Town, East Java prov., Indonesia, SSW of Bondowosa; pop. (1961c) 94,089; univ. (1964).

Djen·né *or* **Jen·né** \je-'nā\. Commercial town, S cen. Mali, W Africa, 250 m. NW of Bamako; founded probably 8th cent. by the Songhai; for a time their capital; flourished 12th–16th cents.; name thought by some to be origin of name, Guinea; taken by the French 1893.

Dje·pa·ra *or* **Dja·pa·ra** *or* **Ja·pa·ra** \jə-'pär-ə\. Town, on coast of N cen. Java, Indonesia; pop. (1961c) 18,921.

Djerablous. See JERABLUS.

Djerba. See JERBA.

Dje·rid, Chott \ˌshät-jə-'rēd\ *or Arab.* **Shatt al–Je·rid** *also* **Shott al–Jerid** \ˌshät-ˌal-jə-'rēd\ *or anc.* **Pa·lus Tri·to·nis** \ˌpā-lə-strī-tō-nəs\. Large saline lake in SW cen. Tunisia, N Africa; ab. 1900 sq. m.; in Greek mythology believed by some to have been the scene of the birth of Athena, whence her name *Athena Tritogeneia.*

Djev·dje·li·ja \'jev-jə-ˌlē-(y)ə\. Town, Macedonia, SE Yugoslavia, on Vardar river at Greek border.

Dji·bou·ti *or* **Ji·bu·ti** \jə-'büt-ē\. City, ✱ of Afars and Issas, E Africa, on S shore of Gulf of Tadjoura; pop. (1964c) 41,536; terminus of railroad from Addis Ababa, Ethiopia; has large landlocked harbor; salt production; founded as port by French 1888; made capital 1892, free port 1949.

Dji·djel·li *or* **Ji·jel·li** \jə-'jel-ē\ *or anc.* **Igil·gi·li** \ī-'jil-jə-lē\. Commune, NW Constantine dept., NE Algeria, on coast 50 m. NW of Constantine; pop. (1966c) 25,007.

Djoc·ja *or* **Djok·ja** \'jäk-yə\. Common short form of *Djokjakarta:* see JOGJAKARTA.

Djokjakarta. See JOGJAKARTA.

Djom·bang \'jȯm-ˌbäŋ\. Town, East Java prov., Indonesia, in wide plain ab. 40 m. SW of Surabaja; pop. (1961c) 68,963.

Djouf, El. See AL-JUF.

Djulfa. See DZHULFA.

Djur·dju·ra *also* **Jur·jura** \jůr-'jůr-ə\. Mountain range of the Little Atlas Mts., N Algeria; highest point 7572 ft.

Dmi·tri Lap·tev Strait \də-ˌmēt-rē-'läp-t(y)ef-\ *or* **Lap·te·va Strait** \'läp-t(y)ə-və-\ *or Russ.* **Pro·liv Dmi·trya Lapteva** \ˌpräl-əf-də-ˌmēt-rē-ə-\. Passage bet. mainland of N Yakutsk A.S.S.R., Russian S.F.S.R., U.S.S.R., and Bolshoi I. of the Lyakhov Is.; connects East Siberian Sea and Laptev Sea; ab. 27 m. wide.

Dmi·trov \də-'mē-ˌtröf, -trəf\. Town, Moscow Oblast, Russian S.F.S.R., U.S.S.R., on railroad ab. 40 m. N of Moscow; pop. (1967e) 38,000; has iron, metal, and cellulose factories; dates from 12th cent.; suffered damage from the Tatars; reached by Germans Dec. 1941.

Dnepr. See DNIEPER.

Dne·pro·dzer·zhinsk \ˌnep-rōd-ər-'zhin(t)sk\; *formerly* **Ka·men·sko·ye** \'käm-ən-skə-yə\. City, cen. Dnepropetrovsk Oblast, E cen. Ukrainian S.S.R., U.S.S.R., on right bank of the Dnieper ab. 20 m. W of Dnepropetrovsk; pop. (1970p) 227,000; cement, chemicals; founded c. 1750.

Dne·pro·pe·trovsk \ˌnep-rō-pə-'tröfsk\ *or formerly* **Eka·te·ri·no·slav** \i-ˌkat-ə-'rē-nə-ˌsläf, -ˌsläv\. City, ✱ of Dnepropetrovsk Oblast, on right bank of the Dnieper at its big bend, 120 m. SW of Kharkov; pop. (1970p) 863,000; an industrial city and railroad junction, a center of the wheat trade of cen. Ukrainian S.S.R., also handles coal, iron, timber; cement, chemicals, footwear; metallurgical industries; has railroad bridge across the Dnieper; cathedral, museum, library, univ. (1919). Founded by Potëmkin 1787 and named Ekaterinoslav after Empress Catherine II; occupied by Germans Aug. 23, 1941; retaken Oct. 25, 1943.

Dnepropetrovsk Oblast \-'ö-bləst, -ˌblast\. Subdivision of the Ukrainian S.S.R., U.S.S.R.; crossed by the Dnieper river; 12,317 sq. m.; pop. (1970p) 3,344,000; ✱ Dnepropetrovsk; manganese, iron ore; winter wheat, corn; formed 1932.

Dnestr. See DNIESTER.

Dnie·per \'nē-pər\ *or Russ.* **Dne·pr** \də-'nyeprᵊ\ *or anc.* **Bo·rys·the·nes** \bə-'ris-thə-ˌnēz\. River, W and SW Russian S.F.S.R., U.S.S.R.; 1420 m. long; second longest river in U.S.S.R.; rises in Smolensk Oblast in S Valdai Hills near the source of the Volga, flows SW, then S through E Belorussian S.S.R., SE and SW through the Ukrainian S.S.R., with a big bend at Dnepropetrovsk, into the Black Sea near Kherson; third longest river of Europe (after the Volga and the Danube), has drainage basin of 194,208 sq. m.; navigable for most of its course to a point above Smolensk. Chief tributaries the Berezina, Sozh, Pripyat, Desna, Sula, Psel, and Vorskla rivers. Chief cities on its course Smolensk, Orsha, Mogilev, Kiev, Cherkassy, Kremenchug, Dnepropetrovsk, Zaporozhye, Nikopol, and Kherson; important for hydroelectric power production. In 1667 became frontier bet. Russia and Poland; large territories on upper Dnieper acquired by Russia in first partition of Poland 1772.

Dnies·ter \'nēs-tər\ *or Russ.* **Dnes·tr** \də-'nyestrᵊ\ *or Rom.* **Ni·stru** \'nē-(ˌ)strü\; *anc.* **Ty·ras** \'tī-rəs\ *or* **Da·nas·tris** \də-'nas-trəs\. River, U.S.S.R.; 877 m. long; rises in SW Ukrainian S.S.R., on N slope of Carpathian Mts. and flows SE in winding course to the Black Sea SW of Odessa; ab. 360 m. of its course formerly in Poland above Khotin where it crosses the old Russian border; recent improvements at rapids of Yampol have rendered it navigable to Khotin; has considerable traffic. Chief tributaries the Seret and Stry; chief towns on its course Khotin, Mogilev Podolski, Bendery, and Belgorod-Dnestrovski. Has long been the E boundary of Bessarabia; since 1940 its entire course in U.S.S.R.

Do·ab \dō-'äb\. Tract of land in India and Pakistan, bet. two rivers whose courses are approximately parallel; specifically, the region in Uttar Pradesh bet. the Ganges and the Yamuna rivers from the Siwalik Hills to their junction.

Doane, Mount \-'dōn\. Peak in Yellowstone National Park, NW Wyoming; 10,656 ft.

Doane Mountain. Peak, Pennington co., SW South Dakota; 5500 ft.

Dobbs Ferry \'däbz-\. Village, Westchester co., SE New York, on Hudson river 20 m. N of New York; pop. (1970c) 10,353; residential suburb of New York City; seat of Children's Village, home and training school for emotionally disturbed children (estab. in New York 1851; moved here 1901); place where General Washington and General Rochambeau planned the Yorktown campaign and where Washington met with Clinton and Sir Guy Carleton May 6, 1783.

Dö·beln \'dər-bəln\. Industrial city, Leipzig dist., East Germany, on the Mulde river 36 m. ESE of Leipzig; pop. (1970e) 27,754; railroad junction; manufactures machinery, metal and wooden goods; 15th cent. church; monument to Luther.

Do·be·rai \'dō-bə-ˌrī\; *formerly* **Vo·gel·kop** \'vō-gəl-ˌkäp\ *or* **Be·rau** \bə-'raů\. Peninsula, NW extension of Irian Barat, Indonesia, N of Berau Bay; Arfak Mts. extend along N coast; highest point Kwoka 8042 ft.; Sorong and Manokwari are chief towns. In World War II secured by Allies July 30, 1944, by landing at Sansapor.

Do·bo \'dō-(ˌ)bō\. Village and only port of Aru Is., Indonesia, on small island off W coast of Wokam I.

Dobrich. See TOLBUKHIN 2.

Do·bru·ja *or* **Do·bru·dja** \'dö-brə-ˌjä\ *or Rom.* **Do·bro·gea** \'dö-brə-ˌjä\. Region, SE Romania and NE Bulgaria, comprising Black Sea coastal strip S of Danube river; area 8979 sq. m.; a province of Romania 1913–40, S half to Bulgaria 1940; Romanian sector now part of Constanţa and Galaţi cos.

Dob·son \'däb-sən\. Town, ⊗ of Surry co., N North Carolina; pop. (1970c) 933; Surry Community Coll. (1965).

Do·bu \'dō-bü\. Chief settlement of D'Entrecasteaux Is. (*q.v.*), on small island bet. Fergusson and Normanby Is.

Do·ce \'dō-sə\. River, E Brazil; ab. 360 m. long; rises in S cen. Minas Gerais state, flows E across border of Espírito Santo state and into Atlantic Ocean N of Vitória; in a region of many rich iron ore deposits.

Doch·art, Loch \-'däk-ərt, -'däk-\. Lake, Perth co., cen. Scotland; 3 m. long.

Doc·tor Ar·ro·yo \dōk-ˌtör-ä-'rō-(ˌ)yō\. Municipality, Nuevo León state, Mexico, 70 m. W of Ciudad Victoria; pop. (1970p) 45,889; diversified agriculture.

Doda Betta, Mount. See NILGIRI HILLS.

Dod·dridge \'däd-rij\. County in West Virginia. See table at WEST VIRGINIA.

Do·dec·a·nese \dō-'dek-ə-ˌnēz, -ˌnēs\ *or* **Do·dec·a·ne·sus** \(ˌ)dō-ˌdek-ə-'nē-səs\ *or Gk.* **Dho·dhe·ká·ni·sos** \ˌthö-thə-'kän-i-ˌsös\. Group of islands in SE Aegean Sea, forming a department of Greece (see table at GREECE); included in the Southern Sporades (see SPORADES); formerly part of Italian Aegean Is. (Isole Italiane dell 'Egeo); includes 12 main islands (Greek and Italian names): Astypalaia (Stampalia), Kalymnos (Calino), Karpathos (Scarpanto), Kasos (Caso), Khalkē (Calchi), Kos (Coo), Leros (Lero), Lipsos (Lisso or Lipso), Nisyros (Nisiro), Patmos (Patmo), Symē (Simi), Telos (Piscopi), and numerous small islands; administrative center Rhodes. Held as part of Ottoman Empire from 16th cent. until 1912; seized (with Rhodes) by Italy in war with Turkey over Tripoli 1912; promised by Italians to Greece 1913 but not surrendered; turned over to Greece after Turkey had ceded them to Italy by Treaty of Sèvres 1920; Rhodes, Dodecanese, and Kastellorizon (*q.v.*) given to Italy in Treaty of Lausanne 1923, restored to Greece by treaty of March 31, 1947. See AEGEAN ISLANDS, RHODES.

Dodge \'däj\. Counties in four states of the U.S. See tables at GEORGIA, MINNESOTA, NEBRASKA, WISCONSIN.

Dodge City. City, ⊗ of Ford co., S Kansas, on Arkansas river 120 m. E of Colo. border; pop. (1970c) 14,127; alt. 2480 ft.; agricultural implements; wheat, livestock; Dodge City Community Junior Coll. (1935); formerly frontier town and cattle-shipping point on the old Santa Fe Trail.

Dodge·ville \'däj-vil\. City, ⊗ of Iowa co., SW Wisconsin, 24 m. NE of Platteville; pop. (1970c) 3255; retail and shipping center for dairy and corn-hog district and pea-growing region; lead and zinc mines nearby.

Dod·man Point \ˌdäd-mən-\. Cape on SE coast of Cornwall, SW England.

Do·do·ma \'dōd-ə-ˌmä\. 1 Administrative region of NE cen. Tanzania. See table at TANZANIA.
2 Town, its ✱; pop. (1967c) 23,559.

Do·do·na \də-'dō-nə\. Town and oracle on Mt. Tomarus, Epirus, NW Greece, in E part of Thesprotia; a center of Pelasgic worship; dedicated to Zeus and consulted from very early times; temple destroyed by Aetolians 219 B.C. but oracle survived several centuries.

Doe·tin·chem \'düt-ē-kəm, -həm\. Commune Gelderland prov., E Netherlands, E of Arnhem; pop. (1970e) 31,097; artificial fibers.

Dog·ger Bank \ˌdȯg-ər-, ˌdäg-\. Submerged sand bank in cen. North Sea, ab. 60 m. E of England; fishing; naval battle nearby Jan. 24, 1915 bet. battle cruiser squadrons of Vice-Admiral Beatty and Rear-Admiral Hipper in which the Germans escaped with one cruiser, the *Blücher,* lost.

Dog Island \'dȯg-\. Island off S Franklin co., NW Florida, separated from mainland by St. George Sound.

Dō·go \'dō-(ˌ)gō\. See OKI ARCHIPELAGO.

Do·ha \'dō-hə\ *or* **Bi·da** \'bī-də\ *or* **Ad–Daw·hah** \ad-'dä-wə\. Town, ✱ of Qatar, Arabian Penin., on the Persian Gulf; pop. (1971e) 95,000; residence of the sultan.

Do·had \'dō-ˌhəd\. Town, E Gujarat, W India, 105 m. ESE of Ahmadabad; pop. (1961c) 35,483.

Doi In·tha·non \'dȯi-'in-tə-ˌnən\. Mountain, NW Thailand, near the upper course of the Ping river 35 m. WSW of Chiang Mai; 8512 ft.; highest mountain in Thailand.

Doj·ran, Lake *or* **Lake Doi·ran** \-'dȯi-ˌrän\. Small lake on boundary line bet. N Macedonia, Greece, and SE Yugoslavia, E of the Vardar; 18 sq. m.; divided bet. the two countries; scene 1916–17 of conflict bet. Allies (British and French armies) and Central Powers (Germans and Bulgarians). On W shore is the Yugoslav commune **Dojran.**

Dok·kum \'dȯk-əm\. Town, Friesland prov., N Netherlands, ab. 12 m. NE of Leeuwarden; pop. (1970e) 3886; textiles, wire; scene of death of Saint Boniface 755.

Dol \'dȯl\ *or in full* **Dol–de–Bre·tagne** \-də-brə-'tan(-yə)\. Commune, Ille-et-Vilaine dept., NW France, SE of Saint-Malo; pop. (1962c) 5077; menhir ab. 30 ft. high nearby; 13th cent. cathedral. On frontier bet. Normandy and Brittany, formerly an important fortress; captured by Henry II of England 1164.

Do·lak Island \də-'läk-\; *formerly* **Fre·de·rik Hen·drik** \ˌfrād-ə-rik-'hen-drik\ *also* **Fred·e·rick Hen·ry** \ˌfred-(ə-)rik-'hen-rē\. Island in Arafura Sea, off S coast of island of New Guinea; ab. 110 m. by 55 m.; 3000 sq. m.; administratively a part of Irian Barat, Indonesia; low, covered with swamps and jungles.

Dol·beau \dȯl-'bō\. Town, East Lake St. John co., S Quebec, Canada, on Mistassini river 8 m. N of Lake St. John; pop. (1971p) 7656.

Dôle \'dōl\. 1 Commercial and manufacturing commune, Jura dept., E France, on Doubs river 30 m. N of Lons-le-Saunier; pop. (1968c) 27,188; 16th cent. church; hospital in Renaissance style; Roman ruins.
2 *or* **La Dôle** \lə-\. Peak, Vaud canton, W Switzerland, on French border ab. 16 m. N of Geneva; 5502 ft.

Dol·gel·lau \däl-'gel-ˌī\. Urban district, ⊗ of Merionethshire, W Wales; pop. (1971p) 2564.

Dolge·ville \'dälj-ˌvil\. Village, Fulton and Herkimer cos., E New York, 25 m. E of Utica; pop. (1970c) 2872.

Dol·go·prud·ny \ˌdȯl-gə-'prüd-nē\. Town, Moscow Oblast, Russian S.F.S.R., U.S.S.R., 14 m. NNW of Moscow; pop. (1969e) 52,000.

Do·linsk \dȯ-'lin(t)sk\ *or Jap.* **Ochi·ai** \ˌō-chē-'ī\. Town, Sakhalin I., Russian S.F.S.R., U.S.S.R.; on coast 50 m. N of Korsakov, with which it is connected by rail; formerly Japanese.

Do·li·sie \ˌdō-lə-'zē\. Town, S Congo; pop. (1970p) 25,000.

Dolj \'dälzh\. County of S Romania. See table at ROMANIA.

Dol·lard des Or·meaux \dō-ˌyär-dā-zȯr-'mō\. Town, Montreal and Jesus Islands co., S Quebec, Canada; pop. (1971p) 25,284; residential suburb of Montreal.

Dol·lar Law \'däl-ər-ˌlȯ\. Mountain, Peebles co., S Scotland; 2680 ft.

Dol·lart \'dȯl-ˌärt\. Basin of upper (S) end of the Ems estuary, NW West Germany and NE Netherlands; 10 m. long by 7 m. wide; Emden is on its N shore.

Dolnja Tuzla. See TUZLA.

Dol·o·mites \'dō-lə-ˌmīts, 'däl-ə-\ *or Ital.* **Do·lo·mi·ti** \ˌdōl-ə-'mēt-ē\. See table at ALPS.

Dolon. See TO-LUN.

Do·lo·res \də-'lōr-əs, -'lȯr-\. 1 River, SW Colorado and E Utah; 230 m. long; rises in NW end of San Juan Mts., Colorado, flows SW, then N and NW across Utah boundary into Colorado river in E cen. Grand co., E Utah.
2 County in Colorado. See table at COLORADO.
3 Town, Buenos Aires prov., E Argentina, 125 m. SE of Buenos Aires; pop. (1960c) 16,003.
4 Port, Soriano dept., SW Uruguay, on San Salvador river ab. 18 m. above its confluence with the Uruguay, ab. 145 m. NW of Montevideo; pop. (1963c) 12,483; shipping point for grain.

Dolores Hi·dal·go \-ē-'däl-(ˌ)gō\. Municipality, Guanajuato state, cen. Mexico, on railroad 30 m. NE of Guanajuato; pop. (1970p) 71,212.

Dolores Peak. Mountain, Dolores and San Miguel cos., SW Colorado; 13,502 ft.

Dol·phin, Cape \-'däl-fən, -'dȯl-\. Cape extending into South Atlantic Ocean from NW coast of East Falkland I., off SE South America.

Dolphin and Un·ion Strait \-yü-nyən-\. Channel bet. SW Victoria I. and N Canada mainland; connects Coronation Gulf with Amundsen Gulf.

Dolphin Head. 1 Promontory extending into Atlantic Ocean on SW cen. coast of South-West Africa.
2 Peak, W Jamaica, West Indies; 1788 ft.

Dol·ton \'dōlt-ᵊn\. Village, Cook co., NE Illinois, 17 m. S of Chicago; pop. (1970c) 25,937.

Dom \'dōm\. Highest peak in Mischabelhörner, Valais canton, SW cen. Switzerland; 14,913 ft.

Domb·ås \'dōm-ˌȯs, 'dúm-\. Village, Oppland co., S cen. Norway, on S edge of Dovrefjell; scene of fighting bet. Allies and Germans Apr. 30–May 2, 1940.

Dom·basle \dōⁿ-'bäl\. Commune, Meurthe-et-Moselle dept., NE France, ab. 10 m. SE of Nancy; pop. (1962c) 9371; soda factories.

Dombes \'dōⁿb, 'dōm\. Region, S Ain dept., E France, bet. the Ain, Rhone, and Saône rivers; has many low hills and stagnant ponds; unhealthful. Once part of kingdom of Arles, later principality with capital at Trévoux; united to crown 1762.

Dombrau. See DĄBROWA GÓRNICZA.

Dombrek. See SIMOÏS.

Dôme, Puy de \ˌpwēd-ə-'dōm\. Peak, Puy-de-Dôme dept., S cen. France, W of Clermont-Ferrand; 4806 ft.

Domel Island. See LETSÔK-AW ISLAND.

Dome Peak \'dōm-\. 1 Mountain, N Washington, on boundary bet. Chelan and Skagit cos.; 8860 ft.
2 Mountain, Yakima co., S Washington; 6586 ft.

Dome Rock. Height in Scotts Bluff co., W Nebraska; 4560 ft.

Domesnes, Cape. See KOLKASRAGS.

Domeyko, Cordillera. See ANDES.

Dom·front \dō^{n}-'frō^{n}\. Commune, W Orne dept., NW France, 30 m. E of Avranches; pop. (1962c) 3982; dates from 6th cent.; Norman stronghold of Middle Ages, scene of fighting in many wars 14th–16th cents.; in World War II taken by Americans Aug. 13–15, 1944 after having been once taken and lost.

Dom·i·ni·ca \ˌdäm-ə-'nē-kə, -'nik-ə, də-'min-i-kə\. Island, West Indies, a self-governing state in association with Great Britain; in center of Lesser Antilles bet. Guadeloupe (S Leeward Is.) and Martinique (N Windward Is.); 289 sq. m.; ab. 29 m. from N to S, 16 m. wide; pop. (1970p) 70,302; ✱ Roseau; mountainous and volcanic; highest peak Morne Diablotin 4747 ft., highest point in the Lesser Antilles; bananas, cocoa, coconuts, copra.

History: Discovered by Columbus 1493; included in grant to earl of Carlisle but Caribs left in possession until 18th cent.; settled by French from whom English took it 1759; captured by French 1778 but restored to Great Britain 1783; incorporated with Leeward Is. 1833; administration transferred to Windward Is. Jan. 1, 1940; member of West Indies Federation 1958–62; achieved internal self-government 1967.

Do·min·i·can Republic \də-ˌmin-i-kən-\ *or Sp.* **Re·pú·bli·ca Do·mi·ni·ca·na** \re-'pü-bli-kə-də-ˌmin-i-'kän-ə\. Republic occupying E two thirds of Hispaniola I., West Indies; 18,657 sq. m.; pop. (1970p) 4,011,589; ✱ Santo Domingo. *Physical features:* On E terminates in Cape Engaño on Mona Passage (separates Hispaniola from Puerto Rico); capes Isabela and Francés Viejo are prominent points on N coast and Cape Beata on SW; coastline generally regular except for long peninsula of Samaná on N enclosing Bay of Samaná; N part covered by rich Vega Real valley formed by two streams flowing in opposite directions; cen. part traversed by the Cordillera Central; highest point Pico Duarte, 10,414 ft., several peaks above 5000 ft.; mountainous SW part contains Lake Enriquillo. *Chief products:* Sugar, bananas, cocoa, coffee, tobacco; bauxite, nickel. *Chief towns:* Santo Domingo, Santiago de los Caballeros, San Francisco de Macorís, La Romana, San Juan de la Maguana. Divided into the National District and 26 provinces (for pronunication of their names, see their individual entries):

NAME	AREA (sq. m.)	POP. (1970p)	CAPITAL
National District	533	817,467	Santo Domingo
Provinces			
Azua	983	91,511	Azua
Bahoruco	517	66,572	Neiba
Barahona	661	112,914	Barahona
Dajabón	343	50,780	Dajabón
Duarte	553	200,813	San Francisco de Macorís
El Seibo	1,178	132,795	El Seibo
Espaillat	337	139,579	Moca
Independencia	775	32,580	Jimaní
La Altagracia	1,124	87,180	Higüey
La Estrelleta	601	53,228	Elías Piña
La Romana	257	56,955	La Romana
La Vega	1,304	293,694	La Vega
María Trinidad Sánchez	506	97,043	Nagua
Montecristi	768	69,276	Montecristi
Pedernales	708	12,547	Pedernales
Peravia	628	127,587	Baní
Puerto Plata	671	185,800	Puerto Plata
Salcedo	168	89,773	Salcedo
Samaná	382	53,893	Samaná
Sánchez Ramírez	448	106,177	Cotuí
San Cristóbal	1,498	324,395	San Cristóbal
San Juan	1,313	191,065	San Juan de la Maguana
San Pedro de Macorís	486	105,490	San Pedro de Macorís
Santiago	1,188	386,269	Santiago
Santiago Rodríguez	487	49,598	Santiago Rodríguez
Valverde	243	76,608	Mao

History: For earlier history, see HISPANIOLA. Created 1844 after revolt against Boyer's rule of entire island of Hispaniola; except for brief period (1861–65) of annexation to Spain, has since then been independent, although its customs were controlled by United States 1905–41, and it was under U.S. military occupation 1916–24; broke off diplomatic relations with Germany 1917 in World War I; declared war on Axis powers 1941 in World War II; termination of Trujillo dictatorship 1961; civil war 1965, leading to U.S. and OAS military intervention; adoption of new constitution 1966.

Do·min·ion \də-'min-yən\. Town, Cape Breton co., E Nova Scotia, Canada, on Atlantic Ocean 7 m. ENE of Sydney; pop. (1971p) 2860; coal mines.

Dom·joch \'dōm-ˌyök\. Mountain pass over the Mischabelhörner, S of the Dom, Valais canton, SW cen. Switzerland; elev. 14,060 ft.

Dom·mel \'döm-əl\. River, S Netherlands; ab. 62 m. long; rises in Belgium, flows N across the border through cen. North Brabant prov., S Netherlands, into the Meuse.

Do·mo \'dō-(ˌ)mō\. Small village, E Ethiopia, near the border of Somalia.

Do·mo·dos·so·la \ˌdō-mō-'dó-sə-lə\ *or anc.* **Do·mus Dei** \ˌdō-məs-'dē-ˌī\. Commune, Novara prov., Piedmont, NW Italy, in river valley 47 m. N of Novara near Italian end of Simplon Tunnel; pop. (1968e) 18,684; made countship under bishop of Novara by Charlemagne; captured by Swiss 1416; laid waste by Valaisans 1487; to Austria 1714, Savoy 1735.

Dom Pe·dri·to \ˌdō(^{n})m-pə-'drēt-(ˌ)ü\. City, Rio Grande do Sul state, S Brazil; munic. pop. (1968e) 33,087.

Dom·ré·my–la–Pu·celle \ˌdō^{n}-(ˌ)rā-ˌmē-(ˌ)läp-(y)ü-'sel\. Village, Vosges dept., NE France, on the Meuse; pop. (1962c) 171; birthplace of Joan of Arc.

Domus Dei. See DOMODOSSOLA.

Do·mu·yo \dō-'mü-(ˌ)yō\. Volcanic peak in the Andes Mt., N Neuquén prov., Argentina, near Chilean boundary; 15,446 ft.

Don \'dän\. 1 River, Yorkshire, N cen. England; 70 m. long; flows NE into the Ouse at Goole.

2 River, Aberdeen co., NE Scotland; 82 m. long; flows E into North Sea 1½ m. N of Aberdeen.

3 *or Tatar* **Du·na** \'dü-nə\ *or anc.* **Tan·a·is** \'tan-ē-əs\. River, U.S.S.R.; 1224 m. long; rises just SE of Tula, flows SE in a big bend to within 48 m. of the Volga, then turns SW to the Sea of Azov (Gulf of Taganrog) at Rostov-na-Donu; its drainage basin of 170,849 sq. m. covers E part of rich black earth region; has abundant fish (salmon and herring) and along its banks are many fishing villages; the only cities of size along its course are Rostov-na-Donu and Voronezh; chief tributaries the Manych, Donets, Chir, Medveditsa, Khoper, Voronezh, and Sosna rivers. Although shallow it is navigable for larger vessels as far as the bend, where the Volga-Don canal enters it. See DON COSSACKS, TERRITORY OF THE.

Do·na Ana \ˌdōn-yə-'an-ə\. County in New Mexico. See table at NEW MEXICO.

Don·ald·son, Mount \-'dän-ᵊl(d)-sən\. Mountain, Antarctica, 84°37′S, 172°12′E; 12,894 ft.

Don·ald·son·ville \'dän-ᵊl(d)-sən-ˌvil\. City, ⊗ of Ascension parish, SE Louisiana, on Mississippi river 28 m. SSE of Baton Rouge; pop. (1970c) 7367; state capital 1830–31.

Don·al·son·ville \'dän-ᵊl-sən-ˌvil\. City, ⊗ of Seminole co., SW Georgia; pop. (1970c) 2907; peanuts; naval stores.

Donard, Slieve. See SLIEVE DONARD.

Donau. See DANUBE.

Do·nau·wörth \'dō-nou-ˌvərt\. Town, Bavaria, West Germany, on the Danube 25 m. N of Augsburg; pop. (1968e) 11,130; an old town with fort and castle; in 13th cent. seat of duke of Upper Bavaria; became imperial city 1348; important in Thirty Years' War; site of two battles: (1)

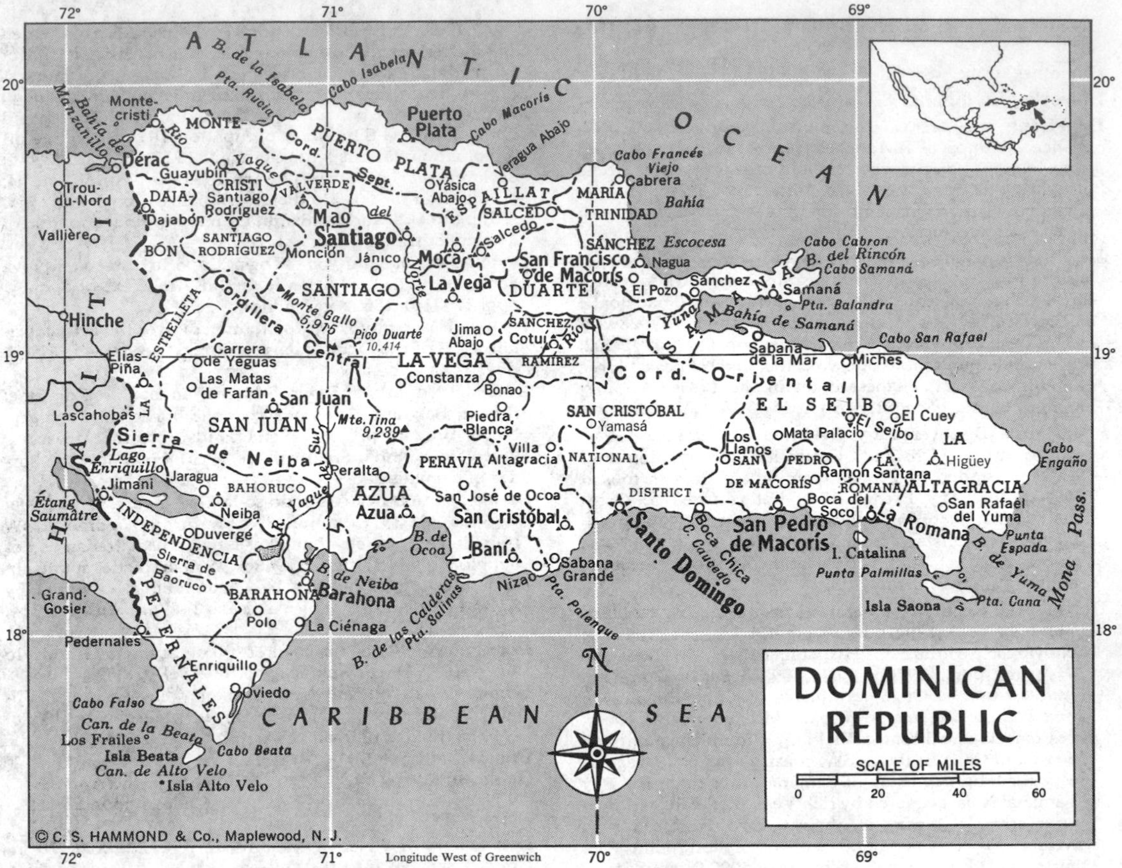

1704 in which it was captured by duke of Marlborough and Louis of Baden; (2) 1805 in which Austrians were defeated by Marshal Soult.

Donbas *or* **Donbass.** See DONETS BASIN.

Don Be·ni·to \ˌdän-bə-ˈnēt-(ˌ)ō\. Commune, Badajoz prov., SW Spain, 57 m. ENE of Badajoz; pop. (1970p) 26,295.

Don·cas·ter \ˈdäŋ-kə-stər\ *or anc.* **Da·num** \ˈdā-nəm\. County borough, West Riding, Yorkshire, N England, on the Don river 45 m. E of Manchester; pop. (1971p) 82,505; coal; railroad cars, farm machines; horse racing center (scene of the annual St. Leger).

Don Cos·sacks, Territory of the \-ˈdän-ˈkäs-ˌaks\. Region in the basin of the lower Don river, SE Russian S.F.S.R., U.S.S.R., now approx. coextensive with Rostov Oblast; once held by Khan of the Crimea (see CRIMEAN OBLAST); settled by Cossacks by 16th cent.; lower Don basin, although controlled by Russia in early 17th cent., not formally acquired until Turkey ceded to Russia her claim to Azov 1739; Cossack communities had special political status in return for military service; in 1918, erected Republic of the Don, soon defeated by Bolsheviki; part of North Caucasus Region 1923–36.

Don·do \ˈdän-(ˌ)dō\. **1** Town, NW Angola, SW Africa, on Cuanza river at head of navigation; pop. (1960c) 12,089. **2** Town, SE cen. Mozambique, SE Africa, ab. 30 m. NNW of Beira; railroad junction.

Don·dra Head \ˌdän-drə-\. Cape on S extremity of the island of Ceylon, 6°N, projecting into the Indian Ocean.

Don·e·gal \ˌdän-i-ˈgȯl, ˌdən-\. **1** County, Ulster prov., N Eire; 1865 sq. m.; pop. (1971p) 108,000; ⊗ Lifford; rivers Foyle, Derg, Finn; oats, potatoes; livestock grazing, fishing, quarrying (granite, sandstone); linen and woolen goods; tourism. **2** Town, S co. Donegal, N Eire, at head (25 m. inland) of **Donegal Bay** and at mouth of Eask river; pop. (1966c) 1507; ancient seat of the O'Donnell clan; ruins of a Franciscan monastery (founded 1474) and of a 17th cent. castle.

Do·nets \də-ˈnets\ *also* **Northern Donets.** River, E Ukrainian S.S.R. and S Russian S.F.S.R., U.S.S.R.; 631 m. long; rises in E Kursk Oblast N of Belgorod and flows SE into the Don river ENE of Rostov-na-Donu; drainage area 38,439 sq. m.; chief tributary the Oskol; navigable for ab. three quarters of its course and flows through the Donets Basin, affording means of transportation of heavy products. See DONETS BASIN.

Donets Basin *or Russ.* **Do·net·ski Bas·sein** \dən-ˌyet-skē-bäs-ˈyān\; *Russ. short form* **Don·bas** *or* **Don·bass** \ˈdän-ˌbas\. Region in plain of Donets river and lower Dnieper, E Ukrainian S.S.R. and Russian S.F.S.R., U.S.S.R., producing ab. 35 percent of the U.S.S.R.'s coal; adjoins the rich iron field of Krivoi Rog; contains many industrial cities, as Artemovsk, Donetsk, Voroshilovgrad, Makeyevka, Gorlovka, Yenakiyevo; in World War II occupied by Germans Oct. 1941 to Jan. 1943.

Do·netsk \də-ˈnetsk\; *formerly* **Stal·i·no** \ˈstäl-i-ˌnō, ˈstal-\ *or* **Sta·lin** \ˈstäl-ən, ˈstal-, -ˌēn\ *also* **Yu·zov·ka** \ˈyü-zəf-kə\. City, ✱ of Donetsk Oblast, Ukrainian S.S.R., U.S.S.R., on Kalmius river 100 m. NW of Rostov-na-Donu; pop. (1970p) 879,000; one of the leading industrial centers of the Donets Basin; has foundries, chemical works, metallurgical plants, mills, and factories; several technical colleges, also univ. (1965). Founded 1870 by a British subject named Hughes (hence **Hughes·ov·ka** \ˈhyü-zəf-kə\, or in the U.S.S.R. Yuzovka); developed rapidly up to World War I and then again after 1924. In World War II held by Germans Oct. 22, 1941–Sept. 9, 1943.

Donetsk Oblast *or formerly* **Stalino Oblast** \-'ó-bləst, -ˌblast\. Subdivision of the E Ukrainian S.S.R., U.S.S.R., cen. part of Donets Basin, touches on N shore of Sea of Azov; 10,232 sq. m.; pop. (1970p) 4,894,000; ✱ Donetsk; important industrial area; iron and steel, chemicals; coal mining, heavy engineering; winter wheat, corn; formed 1938.

Donetski Bassein. See DONETS BASIN.

Don Fernando de Taos. See TAOS 2.

Dong·ga·la \dȯŋ-'gäl-ə, däŋ-\. Town and port, Celebes I., Indonesia, on W coast on Makasar Strait 310 m. N of Makasar.

Dong–nai \'däŋ-'nī\ *or* **Don·nai** \də-'nā, dȯ-\. River, South Vietnam; ab. 300 m. long; flows W and S to unite with other streams (on one of which is Saigon) and form an extensive delta just N of the Mekong delta.

Don·go·la \'däŋ-gə-lə, dän-'gō-lə, däŋ-\. 1 Subdistrict, Northern Province, Sudan; 27,520 sq. m.
2 Town. See DUNQULAH.

Don·i·phan \'dän-ə-fən\. 1 County in Kansas. See table at KANSAS.
2 City, ⊗ of Ripley co., S Missouri, 28 m. WSW of Poplar Bluff; pop. (1970c) 1850.

Don·jek \'dän-ˌjek\. River, SW Yukon Territory, NW Canada; flows into White river; crossed by Alaska Highway NW of Burwash Landing.

Don·ley \'dän-lē\. County in Texas. See table at TEXAS.

Don·na \'dän-ə\. City, Hidalgo co., S Texas, 12 m. E of McAllen; pop. (1970c) 7365; ships citrus fruits, vegetables, canned goods; sugar refining.

Døn·na \'dər-nə\ *also* **Døn·naesø** \-nəs-ˌər\. Island in Nordland co., in Norwegian Sea off W coast of Norway.

Don·na·co·na \ˌdän-ə-'kō-nə\. Town, Portneuf co., S Quebec, Canada, on St. Lawrence river 27 m. W of Quebec; pop. (1971p) 5846.

Donnai. See DONGNAI.

Don·nells Dam \'dän-ᵊlz-\ *and* **Donnells Reservoir.** See UNITED STATES, *Dams and Reservoirs.*

Don·ner Lake \ˌdän-ər-\. Small lake, Nevada co., E California, in Sierra Nevada Mts. ab. 13 m. NW of Lake Tahoe; W of the lake are **Donner Peak** 8315 ft. and **Donner Pass** 7089 ft., traversed by highway and site of U.S. Weather Bureau observatory.

Don·ners·berg \'dȯn-ərz-ˌbe(ə)rg, -ərs-\. Mountain, N Rhineland-Palatinate, West Germany, at N end of Vosges Mts.; 2254 ft.; the surrounding district was a department of France 1801–14 with capital at Kaiserslautern.

Don·ny·brook \'dän-ē-ˌbru̇k\. Suburb of city of Dublin, E Eire; scene of an annual fair, founded 1204 by King John and suppressed 1855, notorious for debauchery and fighting.

Do·no·ra \də-'nōr-ə, -'nȯr-\. Industrial borough, Washington co., SW Pennsylvania, on Monongahela river 20 m. SSE of Pittsburgh; pop. (1970c) 8825; wire, steel, household appliances.

Don Ped·ro Chris·to·pher·sen, Mount \-dōn-ˌpā-drō-kri-'stäf-ər-sən\. Peak, Antarctica, 85°31′S, 165°43′W; 12,355 ft.

Don Pedro Dam \dän-'pē-drō-\. Irrigation dam, SW Tuolumne co., cen. California, across Tuolumne river (*q.v.*); height 288 ft.; completed 1923.

Donrek Mountains. See PHANOM DONG RAK.

Don·sol \dȯn-'sȯl\. Municipality, NW Sorsogon prov., Luzon, Phil., on W coast at N end of Ticao Pass 28 m. W of Sorsogon; pop. (1968e) 32,300.

Doobaunt. See DUBAWNT.

Doo·ly \'dü-lē\. County in Georgia. See table at GEORGIA.

Doon \'dün\. River, Ayrshire, SW Scotland; ab. 25 m. long; flows through Loch Doon and empties into Firth of Clyde 3 m. S of Ayr; immortalized by Burns.

Doon, Loch \'läk-\. Lake, Ayrshire, SW Scotland, 22 m. SSE of Ayr; ab. 5 m. long.

Doone Valley \'dün-\. Valley, N Devonshire, SW England, just N of Exmoor, Somersetshire; scene of legend of the Doones, a band of outlaws of 17th cent. who figured in Blackmore's novel *Lorna Doone.*

Door \'dō(ə)r, 'dȯ(ə)r\. County in Wisconsin. See table at WISCONSIN.

Doorman *or* **Doorman Top.** See SIMANGGELA.

Doorn \'dō(ə)rn\. Commune, Utrecht prov., cen. Netherlands, ab. 10 m. SE of Utrecht; pop. (1970e) 10,084; residence of Emperor William II of Germany 1920–41.

Doornik. See TOURNAI.

Doorn·kop \'du̇(ə)rn-ˌkäp\. Village, Transvaal, NE Rep. of Africa, 15 m. SW of Johannesburg; scene Jan. 2, 1896 of Jameson's surrender to Cronjé after the raid on Johannesburg.

Door Peninsula. Peninsula, E Wisconsin, bet. Green Bay and Lake Michigan; includes Door co. and parts of Kewaunee and Brown cos.

Dor \'dȯr\ *or Arab.* **Tan·tu·ra** \tän-'tu̇(ə)r-ə\ *or anc.* **Do·ra** \'dōr-ə, 'dȯr-\. Settlement on Mediterranean coast, Israel, 15 m. S of Haifa; marked S limit of Phoenician rule at height of its power. A kingdom in the time of the judges of Israel c. 1200–1000 B.C. (*Josh.* xi. 2; *Judges* i. 27), but excavations show that it was a very old settlement; of importance during the Crusades.

Do·ra Bal·tea \ˌdȯr-ə-'bȯl-tē-ə, ˌdōr-\. River, NW Italy; ab. 110 m. long; rises at foot of Little Saint Bernard Pass and flows E and SE into Po river ab. 20 m. below Turin.

Dorada, La. See LA DORADA.

Do·ra·do \ˌdə-'räd-(ˌ)ō\. Town and municipality, N Puerto Rico; town near coast 10 m. W of San Juan; pop. (1970p) 4361 (town), 17,264 (munic.).

Do·rah Pass \ˌdōr-ə-, ˌdȯr-ə-\ *or* **Du·rah Pass** \ˌdu̇r-ə-\. Mountain pass in Hindu Kush Mts., from Afghanistan to Chitral in Pakistan; alt. 14,711 ft.

Doran, Ben. See BEN DOURAN.

Dora Ri·pa·ria \'dȯr-ə-ri-'pär-ē-ə, 'dōr-\. River, Piedmont, NW Italy; ab. 60 m. long; rises in Cottian Alps, flows E into Po river near Turin.

Do·ra·ville \'dōr-ə-ˌvil, 'dȯr-\. City, De Kalb co., NW cen. Georgia; pop. (1970c) 9157.

Dor·cheat \'dȯr-ˌchēt\. Bayou, S United States; ab. 100 m. long; rises in S Nevada co., SW Arkansas, flows S into N end of Bistineau Lake, Webster parish, NW Louisiana.

Dor·ches·ter \'dȯr-chə-stər, -ˌches-tər\. 1 Name of counties in two states of the United States. See tables at MARYLAND and SOUTH CAROLINA.
2 Former town, since 1868 a ward of the city of Boston, E Massachusetts; settled 1630; extended nearly to Rhode Island boundary; included **Dorchester Heights** (a hill SE of Boston) the fortification of which resulted in the evacuation of Boston by the British Mar. 17, 1776.
3 County, Quebec, Canada. See table at QUEBEC.
4 Town (unincorporated), ⊗ of Westmoreland co., SE New Brunswick, Canada, near mouth of Petitcodiac estuary 6 m. W of Sackville; pop. (1966c) 1595.
5 *or anc.* **Dur·no·var·ia** \ˌdər-nə-'var-ē-ə, -'ver-\. Municipal borough, ⊗ of Dorsetshire, S England, on the Frome; pop. (1971p) 13,737; the Casterbridge of Thomas Hardy's Wessex novels.

Dor·dogne \dȯr-'dōn\. 1 *or anc.* **Du·ra·ni·us** \d(y)u̇-'rā-nē-əs\. River, SW France; 293 m. long; formed by confluence of Dor and Dogne rivers in Puy-de-Dôme dept., S cen. France, flows SW and W to unite with Garonne river 13 m. N of Bordeaux and form the Gironde estuary; navigable for ab. 190 m.

2 Department of SW cen. France. See table at FRANCE.

Dor·drecht \'dȯr-ˌdrekt\. **1** *also* **Dordt** *or* **Dort** \'dȯ(ə)rt\. Commune, South Holland prov., SW Netherlands, on Meuse river ab. 12 m. ESE of Rotterdam; pop. (1970e) 88,699; commercial and shipping center; chemical and metallurgical works; founded 1008, received town charter c. 1200; scene of meeting of first congress of Protestant provinces of the Netherlands July 15, 1572; scene of religious congress known as Synod of Dort 1618–19.

2 Town, E Cape Province, S Rep. of South Africa, 120 m. NNW of East London; pop. (1967e) 4600; alt. 5389 ft.; health and pleasure resort.

Dore, Monts \mōⁿ-'dō(ə)r, -'dȯ(ə)r\. Mountain group in Auvergne Mts., Puy-de-Dôme dept., S cen. France; highest peak Puy de Sancy 6186 ft.

Dör·gön Nuur \ˌdər-ˌgən-'nu̇(ə)r\ *also* **Dur·ge Nur** \ˌdu̇r-gə-'nu̇(ə)r\. Salt lake, W Mongolian People's Republic, 47°40'N, 93°30'E.

Do·ri·on \'dȯr-ē-ˌōⁿ, 'dōr-\. Town, Vaudreuil co., S Quebec, Canada, 25 m. SW of Montreal; pop. (1971p) 6195; furniture, cotton goods, bricks.

Do·ris \'dōr-əs, 'dȯr-, 'där-\. **1** Small country in cen. part of ancient Greece, bet. Oeta and Parnassus mountains and containing sources of Cephisus river; important in Greek history only as alleged home of the Hellenic people that entered and conquered Greece 12th cent. B.C.; Corinth and Sparta were Dorian cities.

2 District or region on coast of Caria, Asia Minor, and adjacent islands, made up of Dorian settlements.

Dor·king \'dȯr-kiŋ\. Urban district, Surrey, S England, 22 m. SSW of London; pop. (1971p) 22,354; market and residential community; home of George Meredith (at Box Hill, just N).

Dor·ma·gen \'dō(ə)r-ˌmäg-ən\. City, North Rhine-Westphalia, West Germany, 10 m. S of Düsseldorf; pop. (1969e) 24,769; chemicals; sugar refining; rayon mills.

Dor·mont \'dȯ(ə)r-ˌmänt\. Residential borough, Allegheny co., SW Pennsylvania, 4 m. S of Pittsburgh; pop. (1970c) 12,856.

Dorn·birn \'dȯ(ə)rn-ˌbi(ə)rn\. Manufacturing commune, Vorarlberg, Austria, 6 m. S of Bregenz; pop. (1966e) 32,-200; textiles, machinery, electrical equipment; brewing.

Dor·noch \'dȯr-ˌnäk, -nək\. Burgh on Dornoch Firth, ⊗ of Sutherland co., N Scotland; pop. (1971p) 896; health resort; scene 1722 of last execution in Scotland for witchcraft.

Dornoch Firth. Inlet of North Sea bet. Sutherland and Ross and Cromarty cos. on NE coast of Scotland.

Doro. See CAPHAREUS.

Do·ro·hoi \ˌdȯr-ə-'hȯi\. Commercial city, Botoşani co., NE Romania, 75 m. NW of Iaşi; pop. (1966c) 16,699.

Dorozsma. See KISKUNDOROZSMA.

Dorpat. See TARTU.

Dorris Bridge. See ALTURAS.

Dor·set, Cape \-'dȯr-sət\. Cape, SW Baffin I. (*q.v.*), S tip of Foxe penin.

Dor·set·shire \'dȯr-sət-'shi(ə)r, -sher\ *or* **Dorset.** County, S England; area 978 sq. m.; pop. (1971p) 361,213; ⊗ Dorchester; rivers Stour and Frome; barley, wheat, oats, beans; dairy farming, sheep grazing; quarrying; shipbuilding, tourism; major towns Poole, Weymouth and Melcombe Regis, Dorchester, Portland, Sherborne, Swanage. See WESSEX.

Dor·sten \'dōr-stən, 'dȯr-\. City, North Rhine-Westphalia, West Germany, 14 m. N of Essen; pop. (1969e) 39,354; coal mines; textiles, chemicals, building materials. Founded 11th cent., city 1251; heavily bombed in World War II but since rebuilt.

Dort. See DORDRECHT.

Dort·mund \'dȯ(ə)rt-ˌmu̇nt, -mənd\. Industrial, mining, and commercial city, North Rhine-Westphalia, West Germany, on the Ems river in the Ruhr valley 31 m. S of Münster; pop. (1969e) 647,047; connected with North Sea by Dortmund-Ems canal; well-developed harbor; important railroad center; manufactures machinery, steel rails, wire rope, metal plate; breweries, coal mines; univ. (1966).

History: Ancient walled city; first mentioned c. 885 A.D. as **Throt·man·nia** \thrät-'man-ē-ə\; in 12th cent. called **Tre·mo·nia** \trē-'mō-nē-ə\; member of Hanseatic League; to Prussia 1815; occupied by French troops 1923–24; phenomenal growth after World War I; bombed many times by Allies 1943–45; ab. 60 percent of city destroyed in World War II, but since rebuilt.

Dor·val \dȯr-'val\. Residential town, Montreal I., S Quebec, Canada, 10 m. WSW of Montreal; pop. (1971p) 20,-471.

Dorylaeum. See ESKİŞEHİR 2.

Dos Ba·hí·as, Cape \-ˌdōz-bə-'(h)ē-əs\. Cape extending into Atlantic Ocean on E coast of Chubut prov., S Argentina, at N side of entrance to Gulf of San Jorge.

Dos Her·ma·nas \ˌdōs-er-'män-əs\. Commune, Sevilla prov., SW Spain, 10 m. SSE of Seville; pop. (1970p) 39,387.

Dospad Dagh. See RHODOPE.

Do·than \'dō-thən\. **1** City, ⊗ of Houston co., SE Alabama, 15 m. N of Florida border and 15 m. W of Chattahoochee river; pop. (1970c) 36,733; trading center for large agricultural region; manufactures hosiery, cotton compresses, fertilizers, cigars, peanut oil; George C. Wallace State Junior Coll. (1965); settled 1885.

2 Ancient town of Samaria, Palestine, on the highway N of Samaria at a pass leading to the Plain of Esdraelon; here Joseph was sold into slavery (*Gen.* xxxvii. 17).

Dou·ai \du̇-'ā\ *or formerly* **Dou·ay** \du̇-'ā\ *or anc.* **Du·a·cum** \d(y)u̇-'ā-kəm\. Commercial and manufacturing city, Nord dept., N France, on Scarpe river 19 m. S of Lille; pop. (1968c) 49,187; steel, chemicals; printing; important educational center to 1887; gives its name to the Douay Bible or Version, an English version from the Latin Vulgate for Roman Catholics (New Testament published at Rheims 1582, Old Testament at Douai 1609–10).

Dou·a·la *or* **Du·a·la** \du̇-'äl-ə\. Seaport, Cameroon, W equatorial Africa, on Bight of Biafra; pop. (1970e) 250,000; beer, textiles; metalworking; most important port of country; terminus of railroad inland; taken from Germans Sept. 1914 in World War I.

Dou·ar·ne·nez \ˌdwär-nə-'nez, -'nā\. Commune, Finistère dept., NW France, 12 m. NW of Quimper; pop. (1968c) 19,705; fisheries.

Dou·au·mont \dwō-'mōⁿ\. Fort in Meuse dept., NE France, just N of Verdun; fighting June to Oct. 1916.

Douay. See DOUAI.

Dou·ble Mountain Fork \ˌdəb-əl-\. River, rising in E New Mexico, uniting with Salt Fork in Stonewall co., NW Texas to form Brazos river; ab. 200 m. long.

Double Springs. Town, ⊗ of Winston co., NW Alabama; pop. (1970c) 957.

Dou·ble·top Peak \ˌdəb-əl-ˌtäp-\. Mountain, N Sublette co., W Wyoming; 11,713 ft.

Doubs \'dü\. **1** *or anc.* **Du·bis** \'d(y)ü-bəs\. River, E France; ab. 270 m. long; rises in Jura Mts., flows NE; becomes French-Swiss border; flows into Switzerland, turns W then, in France, N and finally SW to enter the Saône.

2 Department of E France. See table at FRANCE.

Doubt, River of. See ROOSEVELT, RIO.

Dougga. See THUGGA.

Dou·gher·ty \'dä-ər-tē\. County in Georgia. See table at GEORGIA.

Doug·las \'dəg-ləs\. **1** Island on Gastineau Channel, SE Alaska, opp. Juneau.

2 Name of counties in twelve states of the U.S. See tables at COLORADO, GEORGIA, ILLINOIS, KANSAS, MINNESOTA, MISSOURI, NEBRASKA, NEVADA, OREGON, SOUTH DAKOTA, WASHINGTON, WISCONSIN.

3 Former town on Douglas I., SE Alaska; merged with Juneau 1970.

4 City, Cochise co., SE corner of Arizona, on Mexican border; pop. (1970c) 12,462; stock raising; copper and lead smelters; Cochise Coll. (1962).

5 City, ⊗ of Coffee co., S Georgia, 35 m. WNW of Waycross; pop. (1970c) 10,195; agricultural trading center; South Georgia Coll. (1907).

6 Town, Worcester co., cen. Massachusetts, 14 m. S of Worcester; pop. (1970c) 2947.

7 Town, ⊗ of Converse co., E Wyoming, on North Platte river 50 m. E of Casper; pop. (1970c) 2677; livestock; uranium mining.

8 Town, ✱ of Isle of Man, England, in SE part of island; pop. (1970p) 20,385; seaside resort.

Douglas, Mount. Peak, S Sweet Grass co., S cen. Montana; 11,300 ft.

Douglas Channel. Inlet of Pacific Ocean, W British Columbia, Canada, joining Gardner Canal at its mouth, N of Princess Royal Island; ab. 60 m. long.

Douglas Dam. See table at TENNESSEE VALLEY AUTHORITY.

Doug·las·ville \ˈdəg-ləs-ˌvil\. City, ⊗ of Douglas co., W Georgia, 20 m. W of Atlanta; pop. (1970c) 5472; corn; lumber mills.

Douglas Water. River in S cen. Scotland, flowing NE in Lanark co. to empty into Clyde river.

Dou·ka·to, Cape *or* **Cape Du·ca·to** \-dü-ˈkät-(ˌ)ō\ *or Gk.* **Ák·ra Dou·ká·ton** \ˈäk-rə-dü-ˈkä-(ˌ)tȯn\ *or anc.* **Leu·ca·tes** \lu̇-ˈkāt-ēz\. Promontory and S point of island of Leukas, Ionian Is., Greece; traditional scene of Sappho's leap into the sea.

Doul·lens \dü-ˈlä^{n}\. Commune, Somme dept., N France, N of Amiens; pop. (1962c) 7008; medieval stronghold; scene of inter-Allied conference Mar. 1918.

Dour \ˈdu̇(ə)r\. Commune, Hainaut prov., SW Belgium, 9 m. WSW of Mons; pop. (1969e) 10,242.

Dou·ra·dos \du̇-ˈrä-düs\. Municipality, Mato Grosso state, cen. Brazil, 120 m. SW of Campo Grande; pop. (1968e) 63,318.

Douran, Ben. See BEN DOURAN.

Dou·ro \ˈdōr-(ˌ)ü, ˈdȯr-\ *or Span.* **Due·ro** \ˈdwe(ə)r-(ˌ)ō\ *or anc.* **Du·ri·us** \ˈd(y)u̇r-ē-əs\. River in Spain and Portugal; 556 m. long; rises in Soria prov., N cen. Spain; flows W to NE Portugal, then turns S, forming section of Portuguese-Spanish boundary, then W into Atlantic Ocean 2 m. S of Pôrto; in Portugal goes through deep gorges; Portuguese section developed for hydroelectric power production.

Douro Li·to·ral \-ˌlēt-ə-ˈräl\. Former province of Portugal; abolished 1959.

Douve \ˈdüv\. River in Manche dept., Normandy, NW France; ab. 40 m. long; flows S and E into Bay of the Seine NE of Carentan, which is near it on a tributary.

Dou·vres \ˈdüvr^{ə}\. 1 Commune, Calvados dept., NW France, N of Caen; pop. (1962c) 2027; held by Germans against Allied advance June 7–11, 1944.

2 City, England. See DOVER 7.

Dove \ˈdəv, ˈdōv\. River, Derbyshire and Staffordshire, cen. England; ab. 39 m. long; flows S from near Buxton and empties into the Trent below Burton; favorite stream of Izaak Walton.

Dove Creek \ˈdəv-\. Town, ⊗ of Dolores co., SW Colorado; pop. (1970c) 619.

Do·ver \ˈdō-vər\. 1 Commercial city, ✱ of Delaware and ⊗ of Kent co., cen. Del., 40 m. S of Wilmington; pop. (1970c) 17,488; shipping point for fruits and vegetables; bottling works, foundry; Wesley Coll. (1873), Delaware State Coll. (1891), Delaware Technical and Community Coll. (1967); laid out 1717, made state capital 1777; incorp. as town 1829, as city 1929.

2 City, ⊗ of Stafford co., SE New Hampshire, 11 m. NNW of Portsmouth; pop. (1970c) 20,850; shoes, lumber; settled c. 1622; attacked by Indians June 28, 1689; incorporated as city 1855.

3 Town, Morris co., N New Jersey, 8 m. NNW of Morristown; pop. (1970c) 15,309; center of iron-ore area; government munition depot; manufactures explosives; County Coll. of Morris (1968); settled 1722, chartered 1875.

4 Village, Ohio. See WESTLAKE.

5 City, Tuscarawas co., E Ohio; pop. (1970c) 11,516; chemicals, sheet steel; oil refining; coal.

6 Town, ⊗ of Stewart co., NW Tennessee; pop. (1970c) 1179; burned by Union forces 1862.

7 *or Fr.* **Dou·vres** \ˈdüvr^{ə}\ *or anc.* **Du·bris Por·tus** \ˌd(y)ü-brə-ˈspōrt-əs, -ˈspȯrt-\. Municipal borough, Kent, SE England, on the Strait of Dover 67 m. ESE of London; pop. (1971p) 34,322; metal foundries, flour mills; chief of the Cinque Ports; port, naval base, resort and the leading passenger port in Great Britain.

History: In Roman times an important landing place; Dover castle, a stronghold of medieval England, besieged by Dauphin Louis (later Louis VIII of France) and rebellious barons 1216; held by Parliamentarians during Civil War; scene of secret treaty bet. Charles II and Louis XIV 1670; headquarters of Dover patrol which protected shipping during World War I; in World War II under fire from German heavy guns Aug. 10, 1940 to Sept. 30, 1944.

Dover, Strait of *also* **Straits of Dover** *or Fr.* **Pas de Ca·lais** \päd-kȧ-lā\ *or anc.* **Fre·tum Gal·li·cum** \ˌfrēt-əm-ˈgal-i-kəm\. Channel bet. SE England and N France; 20 m. wide at narrowest point; the easternmost and narrowest section of the English Channel.

Dover–Fox·croft \ˌdōv-ər-ˈfäks-ˌkrȯft\. Town, ⊗ of Piscataquis co., N cen. Maine, 34 m. NW of Bangor; pop. (1970c) 4178; lumber; woolen mills.

Dovey. See DYFI.

Dov·re·fjell \ˈdȯv-rə-ˌfyel\. Plateau in cen. Norway; highest point ab. 7565 ft.

Do·wa·giac \də-ˈwäj-ˌak\. City, Cass co., SW Michigan, 35 m. SW of Kalamazoo; pop. (1970c) 6583; auto parts, condensers, household appliances; Southwestern Michigan Coll. (1964).

Down \ˈdau̇n\. County, SE Northern Ireland; 952 sq. m.; pop. (1971p) 311,266; ⊗ Downpatrick; rivers Bann, Newry, Lagan; flax, potatoes; stock raising (esp. race horses and hogs), quarrying (granite), linen weaving; chief towns Bangor, Newtownards, Newry, Downpatrick.

Dow·ners Grove \ˌdau̇-nərz-\. Village, Du Page co., NE Illinois, 20 m. W of Chicago; pop. (1970c) 32,751; furniture and tools; George Williams Coll. (1884).

Dow·ney \ˈdau̇-nē\. City, Los Angeles co., SW California, SE of Los Angeles; pop. (1970c) 88,445; textiles, agricultural machinery, asbestos, aircraft, chemicals, brass fittings, rubber goods.

Dow·nie·ville \ˈdau̇-nē-ˌvil\. Village, ⊗ of Sierra co., NE California, 78 m. NNE of Sacramento; pop. (1971e) 400.

Dow·ning·town \ˈdau̇-niŋ-ˌtau̇n\. Industrial borough, Chester co., SE Pennsylvania, on E branch of Brandywine Creek 32 m. W of Philadelphia; pop. (1970c) 7437; paper, paper-mill machinery.

Down·pat·rick \dau̇n-ˈpat-rik\. Urban district, ⊗ of co. Down, SE Northern Ireland, at SW end of Strangford Lough; pop. (1971p) 8401; cathedral; linen weaving; burial place of St. Patrick, St. Columba, and St. Brigid.

Downs, The \-ˈdau̇nz\. 1 Range of hills in S England. See NORTH DOWNS, SOUTH DOWNS.

2 Roadstead in English Channel, along E coast of Kent bet. North and South Foreland; ab. 9 m. long and 6 m. wide; affords excellent anchorage, protected by a natural breakwater, the Goodwin Sands; scene of battle of Goodwin Sands 1652, English naval victory over Dutch, and of drawn battle bet. English and Dutch 1666.

Doyles·town \ˈdȯi(ə)lz-ˌtau̇n\. Borough, ⊗ of Bucks co., SE Pennsylvania, 25 m. N of Philadelphia; pop. (1970c) 8270;

electronic components; dairying; Delaware Valley Coll. of Science and Agriculture (1896); settled 1735.

Dra, Wad \wad-'drä\. River (often dry), SW Morocco, NW Africa; empties into Atlantic Ocean at **Cape Dra.**

Drabescus. See DRAMA 2.

Dra·chen·fels \'drak-ən-ˌfelz\. Peak in the Siebengebirge, West Germany, on E bank of Rhine S of Bonn; 1053 ft. high; resort; in German legend said to be scene of the slaying of the dragon by Siegfried.

Dra·cut \'drā-kət\. Town, Middlesex co., NE Massachusetts, 2 m. N of Lowell; pop. (1970c) 18,214.

Dra·go·ne·ra \ˌdrag-ə-'ner-ə, ˌdräg-\. Spanish island in Mediterranean Sea off W coast of Majorca; 1⅔ sq. m.

Drag·on's Mouth \'drag-ənz-\. Strait bet. Paria Penin., NE Venezuela, and NW coast of Trinidad; ab. 10 m. wide; so called because of the many small rocky islands in its several channels.

Dra·gui·gnan \ˌdrag-ē-'nyäⁿ\. Commune, ✱ of Var dept., SE France, 40 m. NE of Toulon; pop. (1968c) 18,376; tanneries; textiles; resort.

Dra·kens·berg Mountains \'dräk-ənz-ˌberg-\ *or* **Quath·lam·ba** *or* **Kwath·lam·ba** \kwat-'lam-bə\ *also* **Kah·lam·ba** \kä-'läm-bə\. Mountain range extending from SW to NE in Cape Province and Natal, Rep. of South Africa and Lesotho; highest peak Thabana Ntlenyana 11,425 ft.

Drake Passage *or* **Drake Strait** \'drāk-\. Strait bet. Cape Horn on N and South Shetland Is., connecting South Atlantic Ocean (Scotia Sea) and South Pacific Ocean.

Drake's Bay \'drāks-\. Inlet of Pacific E of Point Reyes, Marin co., W California; U.S. Coast Guard Station; landing of Sir Francis Drake from *Golden Hind* June 15, 1579.

Drakhmani. See ELATEIA.

Dra·ma *or Gk.* **Drá·ma** \'dräm-ə\. 1 Department of Macedonia, Greece. See table at GREECE.
2 *or anc.* **Dra·bes·cus** \drə-'bes-kəs\. City, its ✱, in fertile valley bet. Strymon and Nestos rivers; pop. (1971p) 30,592; raises tobacco.

Dram·men \'dräm-ən\. Seaport, ⊗ of Buskerud co., S Norway, at mouth of the **Drams·el·va** \'dräms-ˌel-və\ on a branch of the Oslo Fjord; pop. (1970e) 49,271; sawmills, paper mills, cellulose factories; electronic equipment.

Dran·cy \dräⁿ-'sē\. Commune, Seine-St-Denis dept., N France, NE suburb of Paris; pop. (1968c) 69,444; scene of battles bet. French and Prussians Nov. 29 and Dec. 21, 1870.

Dran·gi·a·na \ˌdran-jē-'ā-nə, -'an-ə\. Ancient region of Asia, a part of Ariana and a province of ancient Persian Empire and of the Grecian empire of Alexander; now included in W Afghanistan and E Iran. See SEISTAN.

Dra·no·va Island \ˌdrän-ə-və-\. Island, E Romania, in S part of Danube delta.

Dra·va *or* **Dra·ve** \'dräv-ə\ *or Ger.* **Drau** \'drau̇\ *or anc.* **Dra·vus** \'drā-vəs\. River in Austria and Yugoslavia; 447 m. long; rises in the Carnic Alps, S Austria, flows E into and across N Yugoslavia, then SE forming section of Yugoslav-Hungarian boundary, empties into Danube river 14 m. E of Osijek, Yugoslavia; navigable for small boats for ab. 350 m.

Dra·vos·burg \drə-'vōs-ˌbərg\. Borough, Allegheny co., SW Pennsylvania, on Monongahela river 9 m. SE of Pittsburgh; pop. (1970c) 2916.

Drav·ska \'dräv-skə\. Former county (1929–45), NW Yugoslavia; 6151 sq. m.; ⊗ Ljubljana; since 1945 approx. coextensive with Slovenia.

Dray·ton Valley \ˌdrāt-ᵊn-\. Town, Alberta, Canada, 63 m. SW of Edmonton; pop. (1971p) 3916; agriculture.

Dreketi. See NDREKETI.

Dren·the \'drent-ə\. Province, NE Netherlands; 1037 sq. m.; pop. (1970e) 366,590; ✱ Assen; oats, potatoes, rye; livestock raising, truck farming; cottage industries; oil; under French rule 1795–1813.

Drepanum. See TRAPANI.

Dres·den \'drez-dən\. 1 Town, ⊗ of Weakley co., NW Tennessee; pop. (1970c) 1939.
2 Town, Kent co., SE Ontario, Canada, 13 m. N of Chatham; pop. (1971p) 2364; gas wells.
3 District of East Germany. See table at GERMANY, EAST.
4 Industrial city, ✱ of Dresden dist., East Germany, on Elbe river 63 m. ESE of Leipzig; pop. (1970e) 501,508; electrical equipment, precision tools, optical instruments, adding machines; Dresden china manufactured at Meissen (*q.v.*); technical univ. (1828, univ. status 1961), conservatory of music, academy of fine arts, opera house (completed 1878), world-famous art galleries, and museums containing collections of porcelain, medieval artifacts, zoological specimens, etc.

History: Original Slavonic settlers subjugated c. 922 A.D.; residence of margraves of Meissen at beginning of 13th cent.; residence of Albertine dukes of Saxony 1485–1918; bombarded by Frederick the Great 1760; occupied by Austrians 1809; scene of famous battle Aug. 26–27, 1813, in which Allies under Schwarzenberg unsuccessfully attempted to wrest it from Napoleonic troops in occupation; occupied by Prussians 1866; severely damaged in World War II, now largely rebuilt; captured by U.S.S.R. May 8, 1945.

Dreux \'drər\; *anc.* **Du·ro·cas·ses** \ˌd(y)u̇r-ə-'kas-ēz\ *or later* **Dro·cae** \'drō-(ˌ)sē\. Commune, Eure-et-Loir dept., N cen. France, 20 m. NNW of Chartres; pop. (1968c) 29,408; paper goods, electrical equipment.

Drew \'drü\. 1 County in Arkansas. See table at ARKANSAS.
2 Town, Sunflower co., W Mississippi, 27 m. S of Clarksdale; pop. (1970c) 2547; cotton.

Drew·ry's Bluff *or formerly* **Dru·ry's Bluff** \ˌdru̇(ə)r-ēz-\. Height on right bank of James river 5 m. S of Richmond, Virginia, near Bermuda Hundred; in campaign for Richmond 1864 Union advance under Gen. Butler stopped here May 12–16 by Gen. Beauregard.

Drif·field \'dri-ˌfēld\ *or formerly* **Great Driffield.** Urban district, East Riding, Yorkshire, N England; pop. (1971p) 7899.

Driggs \'drigz\. Village, ⊗ of Teton co., E Idaho; pop. (1970c) 727.

Drin \'drēn, 'drin\ *or* **Dri·ni** \'drē-nē\ *or anc.* **Dri·lo** \'drī-(ˌ)lō\. River, Albania; 175 m. long; flows N out of Lake Ohrid into E Albania, turns W in N Albania and empties into Adriatic Sea; its N mouth is the Buenë river.

Dri·na \'drē-nə\ *or anc.* **Dri·nus** \'drī-nəs\. River, cen. Yugoslavia; 285 m. long; flows N into Sava river ab. 60 m. W of Belgrade; constitutes a large section of the boundary bet. Serbia and Bosnia and Herzegovina.

Drin·ska \'drēn(t)s-kə, 'drin(t)s-\. Former county (1929–45), cen. Yugoslavia; 11,417 sq. m.; ⊗ Sarajevo; since 1945 divided bet. the two federated republics of Serbia and of Bosnia and Herzegovina.

Dris·kill Mountain \ˌdris-kəl-\. Elevation, Bienville parish, Louisiana; 535 ft.; highest peak in the state.

Drø·bak \'drər-ˌbäk\. Seaport town, Akershus co., SE Norway; used as a winter port for Oslo; summer resort.

Drobeta. See TURNU-SEVERIN.

Drocae. See DREUX.

Dro·court \drō-'ku̇(ə)r\. Commune, Pas-de-Calais dept., N France, 9 m. NE of Arras; pop. (1962c) 2475; N end of Drocourt-Quéant Line, strong German defense line 1917, extending N from Quéant in the Hindenburg Line; taken by Allies Sept. 1918.

Dro·ghe·da \'drȯ(i)-əd-ə, 'drȯid-ə\. Municipal borough and port, S co. Louth, NE Eire, on Boyne river; pop. (1971p) 19,744; salmon fisheries, cotton mills, tanneries, brewery. Site of noted synod 1152; besieged 1649 by Cromwell who stormed it and put most of the Royalist garrison to the sword; surrendered to William of Orange immediately after battle of the Boyne.

Dro·go·bych \ˌdrəg-ə-'bich\ *or Pol.* **Dro·ho·bycz** \drə-'hȯ-bich\. City, SW Ukrainian S.S.R., U.S.S.R., 39 m. SW of Lvov (formerly in Poland); pop. (1969e) 58,000; metalworking, oil refining; oil and natural gas deposits nearby;

scene of battle 1915 bet. Austrians and Russians; taken by U.S.S.R. Sept. 1939 and by Germany June 1941.

Droit·wich \'drȯit-(ˌ)wich\. Municipal borough, Worcestershire, W cen. England; pop. (1971p) 12,766; brine springs; health resort.

Drôme \'drōm\. 1 River, SE France; ab. 60 m. long; rises in Hautes-Alpes dept., flows NW and W into Rhone river 12 m. SSW of Valence.

2 Department of SE France. See table at FRANCE.

Dro·more \drō-'mō(ə)r, -'mȯ(ə)r\. Urban district, co. Down, SE Northern Ireland, on Lagan river 17 m. SW of Belfast; pop. (1971p) 2304; linen weaving.

Dron·field \'drän-ˌfēld\. Urban district, Derbyshire, N cen. England; pop. (1971p) 17,826.

Droyls·den \'drȯi(ə)lz-dən\. Urban district, Lancashire, NW England, E suburb of Manchester; pop. (1971p) 24,-134; chemicals, textile machinery.

Drug. See DURG.

Druk–yul. See BHUTAN.

Drum·clog \ˌdrəm-'kläg\. Moorland in Lanark co., S cen. Scotland, 16 m. SE of Glasgow; scene of defeat of Royalists under John Graham of Claverhouse by the Covenanters June 11, 1679.

Drum·hel·ler \'drəm-ˌhel-ər\. Mining city, S Alberta, Canada, on Red Deer river 62 m. ENE of Calgary; pop. (1971p) 5428; produces lignite.

Drum·mond \'drəm-ənd\. County, Quebec, Canada. See table at QUEBEC.

Drummond, Lake. Lake in Dismal Swamp, SE Virginia, near North Carolina border; ab. 7 m. long by 5 m. wide; ab. 20 ft. above sea level.

Drummond Island. Island in N Lake Huron, a part of Chippewa co., NE Michigan, off SE extremity of mainland; site of fort built by the British 1815 and held by them until 1822.

Drum·mond·ville \'drəm-ən-ˌ(d)vil\. Industrial city, ⊗ of Drummond co., S Quebec, Canada, on St. Francis river 32 m. S of Three Rivers; pop. (1966c) 29,216; Coll. Marie-de-la-Présentation (1955).

Drummondville–Sud. See SOUTH DRUMMONDVILLE.

Drummondville West. Village, Drummond co., S Quebec, Canada; pop. (1966c) 2682.

Drummossie Moor. See CULLODEN MOOR.

Drum·moyne \(ˌ)drə-'mȯin\. Municipality, E New South Wales, SE Australia, W suburb of Sydney on S bank of Parramatta river; pop. (1966c) 30,630.

Drum·right \'drəm-(ˌ)rīt\. City, Creek and Payne cos., E cen. Oklahoma, 30 m. W of Sapulpa; pop. (1970c) 2931; oil refining.

Drury's Bluff. See DREWRY'S BLUFF.

Druze, Jeb·el \ˌjeb-əl-'drüz\ *or* **Ja·bal ad Du·rūz** \ˌjab-əl-ˌad-də-'rüz\ *or* **Jebel ed Druz** \-ed-'drüz\. 1 Mountain, SW Syria; 5907 ft.

2 Region, Syria. See JEBEL ED DRUZ 1.

Druzh·kov·ka \drüsh-'kȯf-kə, -'kəf-\. Town, Donetsk Oblast, Ukrainian S.S.R., U.S.S.R., 43 m. NNW of Donetsk; pop. (1969e) 51,000.

Drwę·ca \dər-'ven(t)-sə\. River, N Poland; ab. 75 m. long; flows SW into the Vistula at Toruń.

Dry·burgh Abbey \ˌdrī-b(ə-)rə-\. Ruin on the Tweed, Berwick co., SE Scotland; Walter Scott's tomb.

Dry Cimarron. See CIMARRON 1.

Dry·den \'drīd-ᵊn\. Town, Kenora dist., W Ontario, Canada, 76 m. E of Kenora; pop. (1971p) 6935; pulp and paper mill; provincial experimental farm.

Dry·gal·ski Island \drə-ˌgal-skē-\. Island off Queen Mary Coast, Antarctica, 66°45′S, 92°30′E; discovered by Rawson 1912 but named after German explorer Erich von Drygalski who first observed it from balloon 1902.

Dry Tor·tu·gas \-(ˌ)tȯr-'tü-gəz\. Small group of islands at entrance to Gulf of Mexico, a part of Monroe co., SW Florida, W of Marquesas Keys; site of Fort Jefferson National Monument (see UNITED STATES, *National Monuments*).

Duacum. See DOUAI.

Duala. See DOUALA.

Duar·te \'dwärt-ē, dü-'ärt-\. City, Los Angeles co., SW California, E of Pasadena; pop. (1970c) 14,981.

Duarte \'dwärt-ē, dü-'art-\. Province, N cen. Dominican Republic. See table at DOMINICAN REPUBLIC.

Duarte, Pi·co \ˌpe-kō-'dwärt-ē, -dü-'ärt-\ *formerly* **Monte Tru·jil·lo** \ˌmȯnt-ē-trü-'hē-(ˌ)(y)ō\. Mountain in Cordillera Central, Dominican Republic; 10,414 ft.

Du·bai \də-'bī\. 1 Emirate. See UNITED ARAB EMIRATES.

2 Coastal town, its ✱; pop. (1968c) 13,092; deepwater port.

Du·bawnt *also* **Doo·baunt** \dü-'bȯnt\. River, N cen. Canada; 580 m. long; rises in lakes in SE Mackenzie dist., Northwest Territories, flows N through **Dubawnt Lake** (1600 sq. m.) and E through Aberdeen Lake into Baker Lake, cen. Keewatin dist.

Dub·bo \'dəb-(ˌ)ō\. Town, E cen. New South Wales, SE Australia, on Macquarie river 165 m. NW of Sydney; pop. (1968e) 15,970; center of coal and copper mining region.

Dü·ben·dorf \'d(y)ü-bən-ˌdȯrf\. Commune, Zurich canton, NE cen. Switzerland, NE of Zurich; pop. (1970c) 19,639; chemicals; airport, scene of start of Piccard-Cosyns stratosphere balloon flight Aug. 18, 1932 that attained alt. of 55,577 ft.

Du·ber·ger \dü-ber-'zhā\. Town, Quebec co., S Quebec prov., Canada; pop. (1966c) 8489.

Dubis. See DOUBS 1.

Dub·lin \'dəb-lin\. 1 City, ⊗ of Laurens co., cen. Georgia, 47 m. ESE of Macon; pop. (1970c) 15,143; lumber industry; incorp. and made ⊗ 1812.

2 Town, Cheshire co., SW corner of New Hampshire, ab. 12 m. SSE of Keene; pop. (1970c) 837; summer resort.

3 City, Erath co., N cen. Texas, 43 m. NE of Brownwood; pop. (1970c) 2810; agricultural market.

4 County in Leinster prov., E Eire. See table at EIRE.

5 *or Gaelic* **Bai·le Atha Cli·ath** \blä-'klē-ə\ *or anc.* **Eb·la·na** \'eb-lə-nə\. Seaport and county borough, ✱ of Eire and ⊗ of co. Dublin, E Eire, at mouth of Liffey river on **Dublin Bay;** pop. (1971p) 566,034; iron founding, shipbuilding, glass manufacture, stout brewing; noted castle, founded c. 1200; Christ Church cathedral (Anglican), started 1053, the only one of Danish foundation in British Isles; St. Patrick's cathedral (Anglican), which had Jonathan Swift as dean 1713–45; seat of Trinity College (called also Univ. of Dublin), founded 1591, and of University College of the National Univ. of Ireland (1908).

History: Stronghold of Norse power in Ireland from 9th cent.; in battle of Clontarf (suburb of Dublin) occurred the Danish defeat at hands of Irish led by Brian Boru 1014; given charter and made center of English Pale by Henry II in expedition of 1171–72; besieged 1646 and surrendered to Parliamentarians 1647; scene of Phoenix Park murders May 6, 1882 and of Easter Rebellion Apr. 24, 1916 (see IRELAND).

Du·blon \'dü-ˌblän\. Main island of Truk (*q.v.*), in E part.

Dub·no \'düb-(ˌ)nō\. Town, Rovno Oblast, Ukrainian S.S.R., U.S.S.R., 30 m. SE of Lutsk; pop. (1967e) 22,000; formerly in Poland; in World War I scene of battles 1915, 1916, 1918; occupied by Austrians Sept. 1915–June 1916, by Germans Feb. 1918 ff.; in World War II held by Russians until July 1941 when it was taken in German advance.

Du·bois \dü-'bȯis, 'dü-ˌ\. 1 County in Indiana. See table at INDIANA.

2 Village, ⊗ of Clark co., E Idaho; pop. (1970c) 400.

Du Bois \dü-'bȯis, 'dü-ˌ\. Industrial city, Clearfield co., W cen. Pennsylvania, 46 m. NNW of Altoona; pop. (1970c) 10,112; in coal-mining and agricultural region.

Du·bov·ka \dù-'bȯf-kə\. Town, cen. Volgograd Oblast, Russian S.F.S.R., U.S.S.R., on the Volga 33 m. N of Volgograd; formerly an important Cossack center.

Du·bré·ka \dù-'brā-kə\. Town near coast, W Guinea, W Africa, just N of Conakry.

Dubris Portus. See DOVER 7.

Du·brov·nik \'dü-ˌbrȯv-nik\ *or Ital.* **Ra·gu·sa** \rə-'gü-zə\. Seaport, Croatia, Yugoslavia, on the coast ab. 90 m. SSW of Sarajevo; pop. (1965e) 26,000; tourism; oil refining, slate mining. Founded 7th cent. by Greeks; independent republic until conquered by Napoleon 1808; in Illyrian Provinces 1809–13; center of art and literature in Middle Ages; passed to Austria 1814; 17th cent. cathedral, 15th cent. palace.

Du·buque \də-'byük\. 1 County in E Iowa. See table at IOWA.
2 City, its ⊗, on Mississippi river; pop. (1970c) 62,309; important river port, has shipbuilding yard, packinghouses, lumber mills; Univ. of Dubuque (1852), Clarke Coll. (1843), Loras Coll. of Dubuque (1839); first settled permanently 1833 (oldest city in Iowa); incorporated 1841.

Ducato, Cape. See DOUKATO, CAPE.

Ducatus Romae. See ROME, DUCHY OF.

Duch·cov \'dùk-ˌtsȯf\ *or Ger.* **Dux** \'dùks\. City, Czech S.R., Czechoslovakia, in foothills of Erzgebirge 48 m. NW of Prague; pop. (1968e) 10,639; chemicals, glass; coal.

Du·chesne \dù-'shān\. 1 River, NE Utah; ab. 120 m. long; rises in Uinta Mts., flows S and E into Green river.
2 County in Utah. See table at UTAH.
3 City, ⊗ of Duchesne co., NE cen. Utah; pop. (1970c) 1094.

Du·cie Island \ˌd(y)ü-sē-\. Uninhabited coral island 325 m. E of Pitcairn I., in S Pacific Ocean, lat. 24°40'S and long. 124°48'W; 2½ sq. m.; annexed by Great Britain 1902 and attached to Pitcairn I. colony.

Duck \'dək\. River, W cen. Tennessee; 250 m. long; rises in Coffee co., flows W and NW into Tennessee river.

Duck Mountain Park. Canadian provincial park, SE Saskatchewan, on Manitoba boundary, 15 m. NE of Kamsack; 133 sq. m.; forests, lake; estab. 1931.

Duckwater Peak. See WHITE PINE MOUNTAINS.

Dud·don \'dəd-ᵊn\. River bet. Lancashire (Furness) and Cumberland, NW England; ab. 20 m. long; flows into the Irish Sea by an estuary 7 m. long.

Du·de·lange \d(y)üd-'läⁿzh\ *or Ger.* **Dü·de·ling·en** \'d(y)üd-ᵊl-ˌiŋ-ən\. Industrial commune, S Luxembourg, on French border 10 m. S of Luxembourg city; pop. (1970e) 14,612; iron and steel, aluminum.

Du·din·ka \dù-'diŋ-kə\. Town, ✱ of Taimyr National Okrug, Russian S.F.S.R., U.S.S.R., on Yenisei river near its mouth; pop. (1965e) 16,000; port; coal mines.

Dud·ley \'dəd-lē\. 1 Industrial town, Worcester co., cen. Massachusetts, 16 m. SSW of Worcester; pop. (1970c) 8087; chemicals, paperboard; Nichols Coll. of Business Administration (1815).
2 County borough, Worcestershire, W cen. England, 10 m. WNW of Birmingham; pop. (1971p) 185,535; coal mines, brick kilns, iron and brass foundries.

Dud·na \'düd-nə\. River, E Maharashtra, S cen. India; flows SE into Godavari river W of Nander.

Dud·wei·ler \'düt-ˌvī-lər\. Industrial town, Saarland, West Germany, just N of Saarbrücken; pop. (1969e) 30,008; iron and steel; coal; became town 1962.

Dueim, Ed. See ED DUEIM.

Due·ñas \dù-'ā-nyəs\. Municipality, N cen. Iloilo prov., Panay, Phil., near Jalaud river 25 m. N of City of Iloilo; pop. (1969e) 26,000.

Duero. See DOURO.

Due West \'d(y)ü-'west\. Town in Due West township, Abbeville co., W South Carolina, ab. 17 m. NW of Greenwood; pop. (1970c) 1380; Erskine Coll. (1839).

Duf·fel \d(y)ü-fəl, 'dəf-\. Commune, Antwerp prov., N Belgium, 10 m. SSE of Antwerp; pop. (1969e) 13,755; foundries, distilleries, paper factory; a coarse woolen cloth (*duffel*) originally made here.

Duf·fer·in \'dəf-(ə-)rin\. County, Ontario, Canada. See table at ONTARIO.

Duff Islands \'dəf-\. Small island group in N part of Santa Cruz Is., SW Pacific Ocean; lat. 9°50'S and long. 167°10'E.

Du·four·spit·ze \dù-'fù(ə)r-ˌs(h)pit-sə\. Highest peak of Monte Rosa, in the Pennine Alps, on the Swiss-Italian border; 15,203 ft.

Du·gi Otok \ˌdü-gē-'ō-ˌtäk\ *or Ital.* **Iso·la Lun·ga** \ˌē-zə-lə-'lüŋ-gə, -'lùŋ-\. Yugoslav island in the Adriatic Sea off the Dalmatian coast; 27 m. long; 46 sq. m.

Dui·da \dù-'ēd-ə\. Mountain, cen. Amazonas territory, S Venezuela; 7952 ft.

Duis·burg \'d(y)üs-ˌbù(ə)rg, 'd(y)üz-, -ˌbərg\ *or from 1929 to 1934* **Duisburg–Ham·born** \-häm-'bȯ(ə)rn\. Industrial city and river port, North Rhine-Westphalia, West Germany, on the Rhine river at confluence of the Ruhr 12 m. NNW of Düsseldorf; pop. (1969e) 460,517; Europe's largest inland river port (above tidewater); on W border of Ruhr industrial district; manufactures steel, machinery, chemicals; shipbuilding; coal. Ancient town; became member of Hanseatic League; site of a university 1655–1802; formed 1929 by consolidation of former cities of Duisburg (residence of Gerhardus Mercator 1552 to his death 1594) and Hamborn; in World War II frequently bombed by Allied air forces 1943–45.

Dui·ve·land \'dȯi-və-ˌlänt\. East part of Schouwen I., Zeeland prov., SW Netherlands; pop. (1969e) 4046.

Duke of Clarence. Island in Tokelau Is., cen. Pacific Ocean. See NUKUNONO.

Duke of Glouces·ter Islands \-ˌgläs-tər-, -ˌglȯs-\. Group of 3 small uninhabited islands in S Pacific Ocean, 470 m. SE of Tahiti and 360 m. NE of Raevavae in the Tubuai Is.; generally considered a part of the Tuamotu Archipelago, French Polynesia.

Duke of York Island \-ˌyȯrk-\. 1 Island in Madre de Dios Archipelago, in S Pacific Ocean off SW coast of Chile, at entrance to Concepción Strait.
2 Island in Tokelau Is., cen. Pacific Ocean. See ATAFU.

Duke of York Islands. Group of 13 small islands in Bismarck Archipelago, W Pacific Ocean, at N end of St. George's Channel bet. NE New Britain I. and SW New Ireland I.; total area 23 sq. m.; pop. (1969e) 5870.

Dukes \'d(y)üks\. County in Massachusetts. See table at MASSACHUSETTS.

Duk·in·field \'dək-ən-ˌfēld\. Municipal borough, Cheshire, NW England, 6 m. E of Manchester; pop. (1971p) 17,294; cotton textiles, firebricks.

Du·kla \'dü-klə\. Town, Rzeszów prov., SE Poland, 43 m. SE of Tarnów; pop. (1966e) 1087; just N of **Dukla Pass** in Carpathian Mts., through which Russian army entered Hungary 1849 and which was used again by Russians 1915 and Jan. 1945.

Du·lag \'dü-(ˌ)läg\. Municipality on E coast of Leyte I. on Leyte Gulf, Phil., 19 m. S of Tacloban; pop. (1969e) 32,600; marked S limit of beachhead in invasion by U.S. forces on Oct. 20, 1944: town and airfield seized.

Dul·ce \'dül-(ˌ)sā\. 1 River, N cen. Argentina; 400 m. long; rises in Tucumán prov., flows SE through several channels into the marsh region N of Mar Chiquita in N Córdoba prov.; in upper course called the **Sa·la·dil·lo** \ˌsäl-ə-'dē-(ˌ)(y)ō\.
2 River in SE Guatemala; flows from Lake Izabal (or Dulce Gulf) into Honduras Bay; link in commercial waterway from Panzós on the Polochic river to the Caribbean Sea.

Dulce, Gulf of. Inlet of Pacific Ocean in S Costa Rica, E of Osa Penin.

Dulce Gulf. See IZABAL, LAKE.

Dulcigno. See ULCINJ.

Dül·ken \'d(y)ül-kən\. Industrial city, North Rhine-Westphalia, West Germany, 20 m. WNW of Düsseldorf; pop. (1969e) 21,668; chemicals, footwear, textiles; received city charter 14th cent.; in World War II taken by Allies Mar. 1945.

Dül·men \ˈd(y)ül-mən\. City, North Rhine-Westphalia, West Germany, 16 m. SW of Münster; pop. (1969e) 20,890; textiles, furniture; 14th cent. church. Founded 9th cent., became city 1311.

Du·luth \də-ˈlüth\. City, ⊗ of St. Louis co., NE Minnesota, at W end of Lake Superior; pop. (1970c) 100,578; third largest city in the state; commercial and industrial center; excellent harbor; ships iron ore, grain, crude oil; steel mill. Univ. of Minnesota, Duluth Branch (1905); Coll. of Saint Scholastica (1912). Region probably explored by Radisson and Groseilliers 1654–60; site of city visited by Daniel Greysolon, Sieur Duluth, in 1679; first permanent settlement 1852; incorporated 1870.

Dul·wich \ˈdəl-ij, -ich\. District of Southwark borough, S London, England; residential; Dulwich College, founded and endowed 1619 by English actor Edward Alleyn, contains notable picture gallery of works esp. of Dutch and Flemish masters.

Du·ma·gue·te \ˌdü-mə-ˈgāt-ē\. Chartered city, ✱ of Negros Oriental, Negros, Phil., in SE part on coast at S end of Tanon Strait; pop. (1970e) 49,600; oldest town in the province; univ. (1901, univ. status 1938).

Du·ma·lag \dü-ˈmäl-əg\. Municipality, S Capiz prov., Panay, Phil., on upper Panay river 21 m. SSW of Roxas; pop. (1969e) 20,200; noted for its natural bridge and caves.

Du·man·gas \dü-ˈmäŋ-gəs\. Municipality, SE Iloilo prov., Panay, Phil., near coast E of Jalaud river 13 m. ENE of City of Iloilo; pop. (1969e) 41,200.

Du·man·jug \ˌdü-mən-ˈhüg\. Municipality, Cebu prov., W coast of Cebu I., Phil., on Tanon Strait 37 m. SW of City of Cebu; pop. (1969e) 27,400.

Du·ma·ran \ˌdü-mə-ˈrän\. Island in Sulu Sea off NE coast of Palawan I., Palawan prov., W Phil.; 120 sq. m.; chief town Araceli (munic. pop. [1969e] 6800) on E coast; thickly wooded.

Du·mas \ˈd(y)ü-məs\. 1 City, Desha co., SE Arkansas, 39 m. SE of Pine Bluff; pop. (1970c) 4600; cotton gins; timber; livestock.

2 City, ⊗ of Moore co., NW Texas, 30 m. WNW of Borger; pop. (1970c) 9771; zinc smelter; fertilizer; cattle; oil wells.

Dum·bar·ton \ˌdəm-ˈbärt-ᵊn\. 1 *or* **Dum·bar·ton·shire** \-ˌshi(ə)r, -shər\. County, W cen. Scotland. See DUNBARTON.

2 Burgh, its ⊗, on Leven river near its junction with the Clyde; pop. (1971p) 25,640; shipbuilding; engineering works; in S part rising abruptly from the bank of the Clyde is Dumbarton Rock, a twin-peaked hill, site of Pictish and Norse fortresses and of a Scottish castle, which was prison of William Wallace before his removal to London for trial and execution (1305) and residence from which infant Mary, Queen of Scots, was spirited away to France 1548. Capital of medieval Celtic kingdom of Strathclyde.

Dumbarton Oaks \ˌdəm-ˌbärt-ᵊn-ˈōks, -ˈbärt-\. Mansion, Georgetown, Washington, D.C., where representatives of China, U.S.S.R., United Kingdom, and U.S. met Aug. 21 to Oct. 7, 1944 and formulated proposals for a world organization which were the basis of the organization of the United Nations as created at San Francisco Apr. 1945.

Dum Dum \ˈdəm-ˌdəm\. Town, West Bengal, NE India, near Calcutta; pop. (3 municipalities [1961c]) 173,100; military station (headquarters of Bengal artillery 1783–1853) and ammunition factory where dumdum bullets were first made; treaty bet. Siraj-ud-daula and Clive signed here 1757.

Du·mei·ra \dü-ˈmi(ə)r-ə, -ˈme(ə)r-\. Small island off coast of Ethiopia, NE Africa, in Bab al-Mandab strait.

Dum·fries \ˌdəm-ˈfrēs\. 1 *or* **Dum·fries·shire** \-ˈfrēs(h)-ˌshi(ə)r, -shər\. County, S Scotland; 1075 sq. m.; pop. (1971p) 88,215; ⊗ Dumfries; the rivers Nith, Annan, Esk; oats, turnips, barley, potatoes; livestock grazing, quarrying (limestone, sandstone); salmon fisheries.

2 Burgh, its ⊗; pop. (1971p) 29,384; trade and industrial center; manufactures esp. hosiery and tweeds; residence (1791–96) and burial place of Robert Burns; chartered 1395.

Dum·ka \ˈdu̇m-kə\. See SANTAL PARGANAS.

Du·mont \ˈd(y)ü-ˌmänt\. Borough, Bergen co., NE corner of New Jersey, 9 m. E of Paterson; pop. (1970c) 20,155.

Dumyaṭ. See DAMIETTA.

Du·na \ˈdu̇n-(ˌ)ȯ, ˈdü-nə\. 1 River, Hungary. See DANUBE. 2 River, U.S.S.R. See DON 3.

Düna. See DVINA, WESTERN.

Dünaburg. See DAUGAVPILS.

Du·na·föld·vár \ˈdu̇-nə-ˌfəld-vär\. Commune, S Hungary, 50 m. S of Budapest on right bank of the Danube; pop. (1970p) 10,343.

Du·na·gi·ri \ˌdü-nə-ˈgi(ə)r-ē\. Mountain in the Himalayas, Uttar Pradesh, N India; 23,184 ft.

Dunai. See DANUBE.

Du·na·jec \du̇-ˈnä-yəts, -ˈnī-əts\. River, S Poland; 128 m. long; flows N from Carpathian Mts. into Vistula river; in World War I scene of battles in the two stages of Austro-German offensive under Gen. Mackensen against Russia May 1–14, 1915 and May 24–June 15, 1915; in World War II overrun by German armies by Sept. 14, 1939.

Dünamünde. See DAUGAVGRIVA.

Dunărea. See DANUBE.

Du·na·új·vá·ros \ˈdu̇n-ˌȯ-ˈüē-ˌvär-ōsh\. Town, W cen. Hungary, ab. 35 m. SSW of Budapest, on the Danube; pop. (1970p) 44,200; iron and steel, textiles.

Dunav. See DANUBE.

Du·nav·ska \ˈdü-nəv-skə, -nəf-\. Former county (1929–45), NE Yugoslavia; ⊗ Novi Sad; 11,461 sq. m.; since 1945 divided bet. federated republic of Serbia and autonomous province of Vojvodina.

Dun·bar \ˈdən-ˌbär\. City, Kanawha co., W cen. West Virginia, on Kanawha river W of Charleston; pop. (1970c) 9151.

Dunbar \ˌdən-ˈbär\. Burgh, East Lothian co., SE Scotland, at mouth of the Firth of Forth E of Edinburgh; pop. (1971p) 4586; fishing port and summer resort; scene of Cromwell's victory Sept. 3, 1650 over Leslie's Covenanters.

Dun·bar·ton \dən-ˈbärt-ᵊn\ *or* **Dun·bar·ton·shire** \-ˌshi(ə)r, -shər\ *or also* **Dum·bar·ton** \dəm-\ *or* **Dum·bar·ton·shire.** County, W cen. Scotland; 242 sq. m.; pop. (1971p) 237,518; ⊗ Dumbarton; its only important river the Clyde; oats, potatoes, turnips; stock raising, dairying, shipbuilding, coal mining, quarrying, fishing.

Dun·can \ˈdəŋ-kən\. 1 City, ⊗ of Stephens co., S Oklahoma, 27 m. E of Lawton; pop. (1970c) 19,718; oil wells; manufactures cottonseed oil, asphalt, gasoline, oil-well machinery; founded 1891.

2 City, SE Vancouver I., British Columbia, Canada, 28 m. NNW of Victoria; pop. (1971p) 4391; lake resort.

Duncan Passage. Channel separating Rutland and Great Andaman Is. on the N from Little Andaman I. on the S, E Bay of Bengal; ab. 32 m. wide.

Dun·cans·by Head \ˌdəŋ-kənz-bē-\. Extreme NE point of the mainland in Caithness co., Scotland; alt. 210 ft.

Dun·can·ville \ˈdəŋ-kən-ˌvil\. Town, Dallas co., NE Texas, 12 m. SW of Dallas; pop. (1970c) 14,105; dairy farming; cotton.

Dun·dalk \ˈdən-ˌdȯk\. Urban community (unincorporated), Baltimore co., N Maryland; pop. (1970c) 85,577.

Dundalk \dən-ˈdȯ(l)k\. Urban district and seaport, ⊗ of co. Louth, NE Eire, on Dundalk Bay near mouth of Castletown river; pop. (1971p) 21,718; fisheries; trades in livestock and farm products. Captured 1315 by Edward

Bruce who proclaimed himself king here; nearby was scene of Bruce's defeat and death in battle against forces of Edward II 1318.

Dundalk Bay. Inlet of Irish Sea on extreme NE coast of Eire.

Dun·das \ˌdən-ˈdas\. 1 County, Ontario, Canada. See table at ONTARIO.

2 Manufacturing town, Wentworth co., SE Ontario, Canada, 5 m. W of Hamilton; pop. (1971p) 17,211; diversified farming.

Dundas Strait \ˌdən-dəs-\. Passage from Van Diemen Gulf to Arafura Sea, separating Cobourg Penin. from Melville I.; ab. 18 m. wide.

Dun·dee \ˌdən-ˈdē\. 1 Village, Monroe co., SE corner of Michigan, 23 m. S of Ann Arbor; pop. (1970c) 2472; cement plants, hatcheries.

2 Seaport and manufacturing burgh, Angus co., E Scotland; pop. (1971p) 182,084; the third largest burgh in Scotland; jute fabrics, linen, canvas; breweries, foundries; shipbuilding; Univ. of Dundee (1967); ravaged many times in Scottish-English wars.

3 Town, W Natal, E Rep. of South Africa, 120 m. NNW of Durban; pop. (1967e) 16,600; center of rich iron and coal district; battle of Talana Hill, which opened Boer War, fought nearby Oct. 20, 1899.

Dun·drum Bay \ˌdən-ˌdrəm-, -ˈdrəm-\. Inlet of Irish Sea in co. Down, on SE coast of Northern Ireland, S of Strangford Lough.

Dun·dy \ˈdən-dē\. County in Nebraska. See table at NEBRASKA.

Dun·e·din \ˌdə-ˈnēd-ᵊn\. 1 City, Pinellas co., W Florida penin., on Gulf of Mexico 20 m. NW of St. Petersburg; pop. (1970c) 17,199; citrus fruit; winter resort; settled c. 1855, incorp. 1927.

2 City, SE South I., New Zealand, at head of Otago Harbor 190 m. SW of Christchurch; pop. (1971p) 82,216; port; chemicals, fertilizer, soap, paper, furniture; exports incl. frozen meat, wool, dairy products; ship repairing, brewing; Univ. of Otago (1869); founded by Scottish Presbyterians 1848; gold discovered nearby 1861; base for ships of Byrd's Antarctic explorations (1928–30, 1933–35).

Dun·el·len \də-ˈnel-ən\. Borough, Middlesex co., cen. New Jersey, 7 m. N of New Brunswick; pop. (1970c) 7072.

Dun·ferm·line \dən-ˈfərm-lən, dəm-\. Burgh, Fife co., E Scotland; pop. (1971p) 49,882; manufactures linen and metal products, cordage, soap; coal mining; Dunfermline Abbey, burial place of Robert Bruce and of many Scottish kings (11th–17th cents.); birthplace of Andrew Carnegie.

Dun·gan·non \dən-ˈgan-ən\. Rural district, co. Tyrone, W cen. Northern Ireland, 8 m. W of Lough Neagh; pop. (1971p) 25,701; in coal-mining section; linen, pottery.

Dun·gar·pur \ˈdůŋ-gər-ˌpů(ə)r\. 1 District, Rajasthan, NW India; 1460 sq m.; pop. (1961c) 407,382; former state; under British protection 1818; became part of Rajasthan 1948.

2 Town, its ✻, 90 m. NE of Ahmadabad; pop. (1961c) 12,800.

Dun·gar·van \dən-ˈgär-vən\. Urban district and seaport, S co. Waterford, S Eire, on **Dungarvan Harbour** at mouth of Colligan river; pop. (1971p) 5584; remnants of a castle built by King John and of 14th cent. priory.

Dunge Ness *or* **Dunge·ness** \ˈdənj-(ə-)ˈnes\. Headland on SE coast of England, projecting into Strait of Dover; lighthouse.

Dunge·ness Point \ˌdənj-(ə-)ˌnes-\. Cape in S Argentina, at N side of entrance to Strait of Magellan.

Dun·geon Gill Force \ˌdən-jən-gil-ˈfō(ə)rs, -ˈfȯ(ə)rs\. Waterfall, Westmorland, NW England, near Grasmere in Lake District; 90 ft. high.

Dunheved. See LAUNCESTON.

Dunholme. See DURHAM 8.

Dun·keld \dən-ˈkeld\. Town, Perth co., cen. Scotland, on Tay river NW of Perth; ruins of early 9th cent. Culdee abbey and of 12th cent. cathedral.

Dun·kerque *or Eng.* **Dun·kirk** \ˈdən-ˌkərk, dən-ˈ\ *or earlier French* **Dun·querque** \dəⁿ-kerk\. Fortified seaport and industrial city, Nord dept., N France, on Strait of Dover 44 m. NW of Lille; pop. (1968c) 27,504; shipbuilding yard; oil refining; fertilizer, foodstuffs; 16th cent. church, 15th cent. chapel.

History: Founded before 9th cent. A.D.; as part of Flanders, ruled by Burgundians and Spanish; besieged by English and French who defeated Spanish in "Battle of the Dunes" June 4, 1658; awarded to England 1659 and sold to France by Charles II 1662; center for piracy 17th cent.; in 1713 (Treaty of Utrecht) and in succeeding treaties, France promised to demolish its fortifications; in World War I object of German drives. In World War II scene of evacuation of 225,000 British and ab. 112,000 French and Belgian soldiers from Flanders after fall of France May 29–June 2, 1940; at end of war surrendered by Germans May 9, 1945.

Dun·kirk \ˈdən-ˌkərk\. 1 City, Blackford and Jay cos., E Indiana, 11 m. NE of Muncie; pop. (1970c) 3465; poultry farms.

2 City and port of entry, Chautauqua co., SW corner of New York, on Lake Erie 35 m. SW of Buffalo; pop. (1970c) 16,855; in grape-growing region; agricultural implements, oil-refining machinery.

3 City, France. See DUNKERQUE.

Dunk Island \ˈdəŋk-\. Island, 2½ m. off E coast of Queensland, NE Australia, ab. 60 m. S of Cairns; home for 25 years of the Australian naturalist and journalist Edmund James Banfield, author of *The Confessions of a Beachcomber.*

Dunk·lin \ˈdənk-lən\. County in Missouri. See table at MISSOURI.

Dun Laoghai·re \dən-ˈle(ə)r-ə\ *or* **Dun·lea·ry** \dən-ˈlē(ə)r-ē\ *or formerly* **Kings·town** \ˈkiŋ-ˌstaůn\. Borough, SE co. Dublin, E Eire, on S shore of Dublin Bay; pop. (1971p) 52,990; seaport noted for export of live cattle; fisheries; noted yachting center.

Dun·lap \ˈdən-(ˌ)lap\. City, ⊗ of Sequatchie co., SE Tennessee; pop. (1970c) 1672.

Dun·man·us Bay \dən-ˈman-əs-\. Inlet of Atlantic Ocean on SW coast of Ireland, S of Bantry Bay.

Dun·more \ˈdən-ˌmō(ə)r, -ˌmȯ(ə)r\. Manufacturing borough, Lackawanna co., NE Pennsylvania, 3 m. E of Scranton; pop. (1970c) 17,300; center of anthracite mining region.

Dunmore Head. Promontory, co. Kerry, Munster prov., SW Eire, N of Dingle Bay; most W point of mainland of Ireland, 10°30′W.

Dun·mow \ˈdən-(ˌ)mō\ *or* **Little Dunmow.** Village, Essex, SE England, ab. 35 m. NE of London; known for the custom (originated 13th cent., revived 1855) of awarding a flitch of bacon to any couple who will swear that they have not quarreled or repented of their marriage within a year and a day of its celebration.

Dunn \ˈdən\. 1 Name of counties in two states of the U.S. See tables at NORTH DAKOTA and WISCONSIN.

2 Town, Harnett co., cen. North Carolina, 24 m. NE of Fayetteville; pop. (1970c) 8302; fertilizer, lumber.

Dun·net Head \ˌdən-ət-\. Cape on NE coast of Scotland; the northernmost point of the Scottish mainland, 58°39′N; lighthouse.

Dunn·ville \ˈdən-ˌvil\. Town, Haldimand co., SE Ontario, Canada, on Grand river 29 m. SSE of Hamilton; pop. (1971p) 5509; canned goods; summer resort.

Dun·oon \də-ˈnün\. Coastal burgh, Argyll co., W Scotland; pop. (1971p) 9824; resort; ruins of ancient castle; statue of Burns's "Highland Mary," who was born nearby.

Dunquerque. See DUNKERQUE.

Dun·qu·lah \ˈdůŋk-ə-lə\ *also* **Don·go·la** \ˈdäŋ-gə-lə; dän-ˈgō-lə, däŋ-\. Town, Northern Province, Sudan, on Nile ab. 47 m. above the Third Cataract; pop. (1965e) 4970; an old town, capital of the Nubian Kingdom 6th to 14th cents.

Dun·ra·ven, Mount \-dən-ˈrā-vən\. Mountain, Larimer co., N cen. Colorado, in Rocky Mountain National Park; 12,548 ft.

Duns \ˈdənz\. Burgh, ⊗ of Berwick co., SE Scotland; pop. (1971p) 1767; castle.

Dun·score \dən-ˈskō(ə)r, -ˈskȯ(ə)r\. Civil parish, Dumfries co., S Scotland; pop. (1961c) 1036; site of Craigenputtock, farm home of Thomas Carlyle.

Dun·si·nane \dən-ˈsin-ən; *in "Macbeth",* ˈdən(t)-sə-ˌnān\. Hill in Sidlaw Hills, Perth co., cen. Scotland; 1012 ft.; scene of defeat of Macbeth by Siward 1054.

Duns·muir \ˈdənz-(ˌ)myu̇(ə)r\. City, Siskiyou co., N California, near Mt. Shasta ab 100 m. ENE of Eureka; pop. (1970c) 2214; summer resort (hunting and fishing).

Dun·sta·ble \ˈdən-stə-bəl\. Municipal borough, Bedfordshire, SE cen. England, 32 m. NNW of London; pop. (1971p) 31,790; motor vehicles; ancient Roman walled camp; venue of court at which Cranmer ruled Catherine of Aragon's marriage to Henry VIII invalid (1533).

Dun·veg·an, Loch \läk-dən-ˈveg-ən, läk-\. Sea inlet on W coast of Skye I. in the Inner Hebrides, off NW coast of Scotland; enclosed on W by peninsula ending in **Dunvegan Head,** 100 ft. high.

Du Page \dü-ˈpāj\. County in Illinois. See table at ILLINOIS.

Du·plin \ˈd(y)ü-plən\. County in North Carolina. See table at NORTH CAROLINA.

Du·po \ˈd(y)ü-(ˌ)pō\. Village, St. Clair co., SW Illinois, 10 m. S of East St. Louis; pop. (1970c) 2842; limestone quarries.

Du·pont \d(y)ü-ˈpänt, ˈd(y)ü-ˌ\. Borough, Luzerne co., E Pennsylvania, 9 m. NE of Wilkes-Barre; pop. (1970c) 3431; coal.

Düppel. See DYBBØL.

Du·pree \dü-ˈprē\. Town, ⊗ of Ziebach co., NW cen. South Dakota; pop. (1970c) 523.

Du·que de Bra·gan·ça Falls \ˌdü-kē-də-brə-ˈgan(t)-sə-\. Falls in the Lucala river, NW Angola, 188 m. E of Luanda; 344 ft. high.

Duque de Ca·xi·as \-kə-ˈshē-əs\. City, Rio de Janeiro state, SE Brazil; munic. pop. (1968e) 324,261.

Du·quesne \du̇-ˈkān\. City, Allegheny co., SW Pennsylvania, on Monongahela river 10 m. ESE of Pittsburgh; pop. (1970c) 11,410; iron and steel.

Du Quoin \dü-ˈkȯin\. City, Perry co., SW Illinois, 30 m. SW of Mount Vernon; pop. (1970c) 6691; electronic equipment; meat-packing plants, bottling works.

Du·ra–Eu·ro·pos \ˌd(y)u̇r-ə-yu̇-ˈrō-pəs\. Ancient town of Mesopotamia on right bank of the Euphrates; now village of **Sa·la·hi·yeh** \ˌsäl-ə-ˈhē-(y)ə\ in SE Syria near Iraqi border; important archaeological site.

Durah Pass. See DORAH PASS.

Durán. See ALFARO.

Du·rance \d(y)u̇-ˈräⁿs\. River, SE France; ab. 180 m. long; rises in Hautes-Alpes dept., flows SW into Rhone river 3 m. SW of Avignon.

Du·rand \d(y)u̇-ˈrand\. **1** City, Shiawassee co., S cen. Michigan, 17 m. WSW of Flint; pop. (1970c) 3678; machinery parts; grain elevators.

2 City, ⊗ of Pepin co., W Wisconsin, 16 m. S of Menomonie; pop. (1970c) 2103; dairy products.

Du·ran·go \d(y)u̇-ˈraŋ-(ˌ)gō\. **1** City, ⊗ of La Plata co., SW Colorado, 18 m. N of New Mexico border and 70 m. ENE of SW corner of Colo.; pop. (1970c) 10,333; oil and natural gas wells; Fort Lewis Coll. (1911); settled 1880.

2 State of NW cen. Mexico. See table at MEXICO.

3 *or officially* **Vic·to·ria de Durango** \vik-ˈtōr-ē-ə-ˈdā-, -ˈtȯr-\. City, its ✱, NW cen. Mexico; munic. pop. (1970p) 192,934; alt. 6314 ft.; center of lumbering, mining, and farming district; univ. (1856, univ. status 1957). Founded 1556; important political and religious center in early history of N Mexico.

Duranius. See DORDOGNE.

Du·rant \d(y)u̇-ˈrant\. **1** Town, Holmes co., W cen. Mississippi, 36 m. SE of Greenwood; pop. (1970c) 2752; in agricultural region.

2 City, ⊗ of Bryan co., S Oklahoma, 46 m. ESE of Ardmore; pop. (1970c) 11,118; cotton gins and compresses, cottonseed oil; Southeastern State Coll. (1909); settled 1870.

Du·raz·no \du̇-ˈräz-(ˌ)nō\. **1** Department of cen. Uruguay. See table at URUGUAY.

2 *or* **San Pe·dro del Durazno** \san-ˌpā-drō-ˌdel-\. Town, its ✱, near Yi river 105 m. N of Montevideo; pop. (1963c) 22,495.

Durazzo. See DURRËS.

Dur·ban \ˈdər-bən\. Seaport, E Natal, Rep. of South Africa, on landlocked lagoon, inlet of Indian Ocean; pop. (1970p) 729,857; the republic's leading port; shipbuilding, oil refining; chemicals, fertilizers, food products, footwear, textiles; resort; Univ. of Natal (1949); Univ. College (1960); large Indian and Malayan population. Founded 1824, oldest settlement in Natal; township laid out 1835 and named after Sir Benjamin D'Urban, then governor of Cape Colony; British garrison, besieged by Boers 1842, saved by famous 600-mile ride of Dick King to Grahamstown. See NATAL.

Dü·ren \ˈd(y)u̇r-ən\ *or anc.* **Mar·co·du·rum** \ˌmär-kō-ˈd(y)u̇r-əm\. Industrial city, North Rhine-Westphalia, West Germany, on Rur river 18 m. E of Aachen; pop. (1969e) 54,745; paper, sugar; botanical garden, astronomical observatory. Probably of Roman origin; scene of diets held by Charlemagne 775 and 779; burned by Emperor Charles V 1543; to France 1801, Prussia 1814; severely damaged in World War II, since rebuilt.

Dur·fee Hill \ˌdər-fē-\. Elevation, Providence co., Rhode Island, NW of Providence; 805 ft.

Durg \ˈdu̇(ə)rg\ *or formerly* **Drug** \ˈdru̇g\. Town, SE Madhya Pradesh, E cen. India, 150 m. E of Nagpur; pop. (1961c) 47,100.

Dur·ga·pur \ˈdu̇r-gə-ˌpu̇(ə)r\. Town, West Bengal, NE India; pop. (1961c) 41,700; steel plant.

Durge Nur. See DÖRGÖN NUUR.

Dur·ham \ˈdər-əm, ˈdə-rəm, ˈdu̇r-əm\. **1** County in North Carolina. See table at NORTH CAROLINA.

2 Town, Middlesex co., S Connecticut, 6 m. S of Middletown; pop. (1970c) 4489; settled 1699.

3 Town, Strafford co., SE New Hampshire, 5 m. SSW of Dover; pop. (1970c) 8869; Univ. of New Hampshire (founded at Hanover as part of Dartmouth Coll. 1866, removed to Durham 1893); settled 1635; scene of Indian massacres, notably 1675, 1694, 1704.

4 Industrial city, ⊗ of Durham co., NE cen. North Carolina, 20 m. NW of Raleigh; pop. (1970c) 95,438; cigarettes, textiles, lumber, precision instruments; Duke Univ. (1838), North Carolina Central Univ. (1909); region settled c. 1750, town founded 1853, incorp. 1869, made ⊗ 1881.

5 County, Ontario, Canada. See table at ONTARIO.

6 Town, Grey co., SE Ontario, Canada, 28 m. S of Owen Sound; pop. (1971p) 2439; dairy farms.

7 County, N England; 991 sq. m.; pop. (1971p) 1,408,103; ⊗ Durham; rivers include Tees and Wear; shipbuilding, coal and iron mining, iron and steel manufacturing, grazing and farming; chief towns Sunderland, South Shields, Gateshead, Hartlepool.

8 *or Saxon* **Dun·holme** \ˈdən-əm\. Municipal borough, ⊗ of Durham co., N England, on the Wear 15 m. S of Newcastle upon Tyne; pop. (1971p) 24,744; cathedral, castle, Univ. of Durham (1832).

Durius. See DOURO.

Dürkheim. See BAD DÜRKHEIM.

Durle·ston Head \ˌdərl-stən-\. Headland on S coast of Dorsetshire, S of Bournemouth, S England; lighthouse.

Durmā. See DHARMA.
Dur·mi·tor \'du̇(ə)r-mə-ˌtȯ(ə)r\. Mountain, cen. Montenegro, Yugoslavia, ESE of Mostar; 8274 ft.; highest point of inland mountain ranges of Yugoslavia.
Durnovaria. See DORCHESTER 5.
Durobrivae. See ROCHESTER 7.
Durocasses. See DREUX.
Durocortorum. See REIMS.
Durostorum. See SILISTRA 2.
Durovernum. See CANTERBURY 3.
Dur·rës \'du̇r-əs\ *or Ital.* **Du·raz·zo** \du̇-'rät-(ˌ)sō\. 1 Province of W Albania. See table at ALBANIA.
2 *or anc.* **Ep·i·dam·nus** \ˌep-ə-'dam-nəs\; later **Dyr·ra·chi·um** *or* **Dyr·rha·chi·um** \də-'rā-kē-əm\. Seaport, its ✻, on Adriatic Sea; pop. (1967e) 53,160; Albania's major port; outlet for Tiranë and shipping point esp. for grain, olive oil, and tobacco; oil storage plants; rubber products; has large Muslim population; Grand Mosque.
History: Ancient Epidamnus a colony founded by Corcyra and Corinth c. 625 B.C.; dispute over it a cause of Peloponnesian War; under Romans (after 229 B.C.) an important port at start of overland route across Greece; by Emperor Augustus made over to his veterans after Actium 31 B.C.; theme of Dyrrachium a division of Byzantine Empire; taken by Robert Guiscard (see SICILY) 1081–82 and by Normans 1185; after its capture by Angevins 1272, changed hands frequently bet. Albanians, Serbians, and Angevins; ruled by Venice 1392–1501, and by Turks 1501–1913; after occupation by Serbs 1913, made part of principality of Albania (*q.v.*). In World War I occupied by Italians 1915 and by Austrians 1916; as Austrian naval base destroyed 1918 by Allied naval force; in World War II during Italian-Greek conflict 1940 repeatedly bombed by Greeks and British.
Dur Shar·ru·kin \ˌdu̇(ə)r-shä-'rü-kən\. See KHORSABAD.
d'Urville, Cape. See PERKAM, CAPE.
D'Ur·ville Island \'dər-ˌvil-\. Island, lying bet. Tasman Bay and Cook Strait off N coast of South I., New Zealand.
Dur·yea \'du̇(ə)r-(ˌ)yā, 'du̇r-ē-ˌā\. Borough, Luzerne co., E Pennsylvania, 7 m. SW of Scranton; pop. (1970c) 5264; coal mines.
Dushambe. See DUSHANBE.
Du·shan·be \d(y)ü-'shan-bə, -'shän-\; *until 1929* **Du·sham·be** \-'sham-, -shäm-\ *or* **Dyu·sham·be** \dyü-\; *from 1929 to 1961* **Sta·lin·a·bad** \ˌstäl-i-nə-'bäd ˌstal-i-nə-'bad\. City, ✻ of Tadzhik S.S.R., U.S.S.R.; pop. (1970p) 374,000; textiles; railroad terminus, connecting via Termez with Bukhara; Academy of Sciences (1951).
Düs·sel \'d(y)ü-səl\. River, North Rhine-Westphalia, West Germany; ab. 20 m. long; flows SW into the Rhine at Düsseldorf.
Düs·sel·dorf \'d(y)ü-səl-ˌdȯrf\. Industrial city and river-port, ✻ of North Rhine-Westphalia, West Germany, on Rhine river 21 m. NNW of Cologne; pop. (1970c) 663,586; iron and steel, automobiles, paper, clothing, chemicals, precision instruments; 14th cent. Gothic church, Academy of Art (1767), univ. (1965). Birthplace of Heinrich Heine. Founded before 11th cent.; became city 1288; residence of dukes of Berg, electors of the Palatinate; 1805 became center of grand duchy of Berg created by Napoleon; transferred to Prussia 1815; occupied by Allies 1921–25; in World War II bombed by Allies May 1943 to 1945, partly occupied by Allies Mar. 1945, final surrender Apr. 17, 1945.
Dutch Borneo. See BORNEO.
Dutch East Indies. See INDONESIA 2.
Dutch·ess \'dəch-əs\. County in New York. See table at NEW YORK.
Dutch Guiana. See SURINAM 1.
Dutch Harbor \'dəch-\. Port, village, and U.S. Naval Station on E Amaknak I. in Unalaska Bay, on N side of E end of Unalaska I., E Aleutian Is., SW Alaska; has harbor 1¾ m. long by ¾ m. wide; the port, ab 1½ m. N of Unalaska village, is used as port of call for steamers; in early days the capital of the fur-sealing industry; deteriorated until taken over by Navy; attacked by the Japanese June 1942.
Dutch New Guinea. See IRIAN BARAT.
Dutch Timor. See TIMOR.
Duttia. See DATIA.
Dut·ton, Mount \-'dət-ᵊn\. Peak, NW Garfield co., S Utah; 10,800 ft.
Du·val \dü-'vȯl, də-, -'val\. Name of counties in two states of the U.S. See tables at FLORIDA and TEXAS.
Dúvida, Rio da. See ROOSEVELT, RIO.
Du·wa·mish \də-'wäm-ish\ *or* **Dwa·mish** \'dwäm-\. Navigable river, W cen. Washington; formed by confluence of Green and White rivers in SW King co., flows N into Puget Sound at Seattle.
Dux. See DUCHCOV.
Dux·bury \'dəks-ˌber-ē, -bə-rē\. Residential town, Plymouth co., SE Massachusetts, on Plymouth Bay 17 m. ESE of Brockton; pop. (1970c) 7636; summer resort.
Du·zakh Tagh \du̇-'zäk-'tä(g)\. Peak in the Kunlun Shan, Sinkiang Uighur, China; 23,922 ft.
Duzdab. See ZĀHEDĀN.
Dvi·na, Northern \-də-vē-'nä\ *or Russ.* **Se·ver·na·ya Dvina** \'sev-ər-nə-yə-\. River, N Russian S.F.S.R., U.S.S.R.; 466 m. long; drainage basin 140,000 sq. m.; navigable length 342 m.; chief river of White Sea basin; major tributaries: Pinegskaya Yentala, Vaga, Vychegda; annual av. discharge 124,661 cu. ft.
Dvina, Western *or Russ.* **Za·pad·na·ya Dvina** \'zäp-əd-nə-yə-\ *or Lettish* **Dau·ga·va** \'dau̇-gə-və\ *or Ger.* **Dü·na** \'d(y)ü-nə\. River, U.S.S.R.; 634 m. long; drainage basin 32,900 sq. m.; rises in Valdai Hills, near sources of the Volga and the Dnieper, flows SW and W across N Belorussian S.S.R. and SE and S Latvian S.S.R. to Gulf of Riga near Riga; generally navigable to Vitebsk; has many short tributaries; connected by canal systems with the Neva, Volga, and Dnieper rivers; annual av. discharge 24,014 cu. ft.
Dvina Gulf *or* **Dvina Bay** *also* **Gulf of Dvinsk** \-'də-'vin(t)sk\ *or Russ.* **Dvin·ska·ya Gu·ba** \də-'vin-skə-yə-gə-'bä\ *or formerly* **Gulf of Arch·an·gel** \-'är-ˌkān-jəl\. Southeast arm of White Sea, Arkhangelsk Oblast, N Russian S.F.S.R., U.S.S.R.; receives Northern Dvina river; port of Arkhangelsk at its head.
Dvinsk. See DAUGAVPILS.
Dvůr Krá·lo·vé nad La·bem \də-ˌvu̇(ə)r-'krä-lə-ˌvā-nät-'läb-ˌem\ *or Ger.* **Kö·ni·gin·hof** \ˌkər-ni-gən-'hōf\. Town, Czech S.R., W Czechoslovakia, 65 m. ENE of Prague on Elbe river; pop. (1968e) 16,160.
Dwamish. See DUWAMISH.
Dwar·ka \'dwär-kə\. Seaport, Gujarat, W India, at W end of Kathiawar Penin.; pop. (1961c) 14,300; temple of Krishna; one of the seven sacred cities of India.
Dwight \'dwīt\. Village, Livingston co., NE cen. Illinois, 35 m. SW of Joliet; pop. (1970c) 3841.
Dwin \də-'vēn\ *or* **Tvin** \tə-'vēn\. Ancient Armenian town, SW of Lake Sevan (in modern Turkey); medieval capital of Armenia.
Dwor·shak Dam *and* **Dworshak Reservoir** \'dwȯr-ˌshäk-\. See UNITED STATES, *Dams and Reservoirs.*
Dwy·ka \'dwī-ka\. River in Great Karroo region of Cape Province, Rep. of South Africa; ab. 90 m. long; flows into the Gamka NW of Oudtshoorn; has given its name to a geological division of South Africa.
Dyardanes. See BRAHMAPUTRA.
Dyaul \'dyau̇(ə)l, 'jau̇l\. Island, 30 m. off the NW coast of New Ireland, Bismarck Archipelago, W Pacific Ocean; ab. 14 m. long.
Dyb·bøl \'dib-ˌər(-ə)l, -ˌəl\ *or Ger.* **Düp·pel** \'d(y)ü-pəl\. Town, Sønderjylland co., Denmark, on coast 6 m. SW of Sønderborg; pop. (1965c) 1544; scene of several struggles bet. Danes and Germans 1848 and 1849; held by Denmark 1860 until recaptured by Prussians 1864; held by Germany until returned to Denmark under plebiscite 1920.

Dy·ea \'dī-ˌā\. Former village at head of Taiya Inlet, N end of Lynn Canal, SE Alaska; after discovery of gold (1896–97) in Klondike region, became supply center and starting point for trail over Chilkoot Pass to Dawson and northern mining fields; just NW of Skagway, which superseded it on opening of White Pass.

Dy·er \'dī(-ə)r\. 1 County in Tennessee. See table at TENNESSEE.
2 Town, Lake co., NW Indiana; pop. (1970c) 4906.
3 Town, Gibson co., NW Tennessee, 33 m. NNW of Jackson; pop. (1970c) 2501; diversified agriculture; cotton gins, sawmill.

Dyer, Cape. Easternmost point of Cumberland Penin., Baffin I., Canada, on Davis Strait, 61°18′W.

Dy·ers·burg \'dī(-ə)rz-ˌbərg\. City, ⊗ of Dyer co., NW Tennessee, 45 m. NW of Jackson; pop. (1970c) 14,523; cotton, wheat; manufactures textiles, cottonseed oil, flour.

Dy·ers·ville \'dī(-ə)rz-ˌvil\. City, Delaware and Dubuque cos., E Iowa, 25 m. W of Dubuque; pop. (1970c) 3437.

D'Yeu, Île. See YEU, ÎLE D'.

Dy·fed \'div-əd\. Ancient region in SW Wales, now Pembrokeshire.

Dy·fi \'div-ē\ *or* **Dov·ey** \'dəv-ē\. River, W Wales; 30 m. long; flows S and SW into Cardigan Bay.

Dyke Ack·land Bay \(ˌ)dī-ˌkak-lən(d)-\ *or* **Dyke Ac·land Bay.** Inlet of Solomon Sea on SE coast of island of New Guinea, SE of Holnicote Bay. See ORO BAY.

Dyke Lake \'dīk-\. Large lake in W Labrador, Canada; forms part of course of Churchill river.

Dykh Tau *or* **Dykh·tau** *or* **Dikh Tau** \'dik-ˌtau̇\. Mountain (*tau*) in a N spur of the Caucasus Mts., S Kabardino-Balkarian A.S.S.R., U.S.S.R., 43°03′N, 43°08′E; 17,070 ft.

Dyle. See DIJLE.

Dyrrachium *or* **Dyrrhachium.** See DURRËS 2.

Dy·sart \'dī-zərt\. Former burgh and seaport, Fife co., Scotland, on the Firth of Forth; since 1930 part of Kirkcaldy; ruins of chapels of St. Dennis and St. Serf; in 15th and 16th cents. manufactured salt.

Dytikē Thrakē. See THRACE.

Dyushambe. See DUSHANBE.

Dza–chu. See MEKONG.

Dzaudzhikau. See ORDZHONIKIDZE.

Dzer·zhinsk \dər-'zhin(t)sk, (d)zər-\. 1 City, W Gorki Oblast, Russian S.F.S.R., U.S.S.R., just W of Gorki on Oka river; pop. (1970p) 221,000; chemicals, artificial fibers; engineering.
2 Town, Donetsk Oblast, Ukrainian S.S.R., U.S.S.R., ab. 25 m. N of Donetsk; pop. (1967e) 47,000.

Dzha·lal Abad \jə-'läl-ə-ˌbäd\. Town, SW Kirgiz S.S.R., U.S.S.R., in upper Syr Darya valley on the Uzbek border, NE of Andizhan; pop. (1967c) 42,000.

Dzham·bul \jäm-'bül\ *or formerly* **Au·lie Ata** \ˌau̇-lē-ˌā-ə-'tä\. Town, ❋ of Dzhambul Oblast, SE Kazakh S.S.R., U.S.S.R., on Turkistan-Siberian R.R. 130 m. NE of Tashkent; pop. (1970p) 188,000; sugar refineries; fruit canning.

Dzhambul Oblast \-'ō-bləst, -ˌblast\. Subdivision of Kazakh S.S.R., U.S.S.R.; 55,830 sq. m.; pop. (1970p) 795,000; ❋ Dzhambul; mostly steppe and desert; traversed by Chu river; cotton, rice, wheat, tobacco; livestock raising; formed 1939.

Dzhan·koi \jəŋ-'kȯi\. Town, Crimean Oblast, Ukrainian S.S.R., U.S.S.R., 55 m. N of Simferopol; pop. (1967e) 39,000; railroad junction; several industrial plants; center for grain export; held by Germans 1941–44.

Dzhez·kaz·gan \ˌjes-kəz-'gän\. Town, Karaganda Oblast, Kazakh S.S.R., U.S.S.R., ab. 280 m. SW of Karaganda; pop. (1969e) 61,000; copper mining.

Dzhibkhalantu. See ULIASTAY.

Dzhirgalantu. See HOVD.

Dzhul·fa *or* **Djul·fa** *or formerly* **Jul·fa** \jül-'fä\. Town, Nakhichevan A.S.S.R., Azerbaijan S.S.R., U.S.S.R., on Araks river 25 m. SE of Nakhichevan; junction point of Soviet railroad lines for Tabrīz in Iran; important town in Armenian history; has ruins of churches and monasteries.

Dzier·żo·niów \jer-'zhō-ˌnyüf\ *or Ger.* **Rei·chen·bach** \'rī-kən-ˌbäk\. Town, S cen. Wrocław prov., SW Poland, ab. 30 m. SW of Wrocław; pop. (1970p) 32,900; machinery, textiles; grain and cattle market. Founded in 12th cent.; scene of battle of Reichenbach Aug. 16, 1762 in which Frederick the Great defeated the Austrians; scene of diplomatic congress 1790 and of conference bet. Prussia and Russia 1813; assigned to Poland by Potsdam Conference 1945.

Dzisna. See DISNA.

Dzun·gar·ia \ˌ(d)zəŋ-'gar-ē-ə, (d)zu̇ŋ-, -'ger-\ *or* **Zun·gar·ia** \ˌzəŋ-, zu̇ŋ-\ *also* **Sun·gar·ia** \ˌsəŋ-, su̇ŋ-\. Region, N Sinkiang Uighur, W China, N of the Tien Shan; its chief centers in rich valley of the I-li river. From 11th to 14th cents. a Mongol kingdom; devastated by Tamerlane 1389; ruled by a Kalmuck confederation until 1758–59 when it was conquered by Chinese.

Dzun·gar·ian Ala Tau \(d)zəŋ-'gar-ē-ən-ˌal-ə-'tau̇, (d)zu̇ŋ-, -'ger-, -ˌäl-\ *or* **Chan–ka–erh–a–la–t'ao Shan** \'chän-'kä-'er-ä-'la-'tau̇-'shän\. Mountain range bet. E Kazakh S.S.R., U.S.S.R., and NW Sinkiang Uighur, W China; highest peak 16,550 ft.

Eads \'ēdz\. Town, ⊗ of Kiowa co., E Colorado; pop. (1970c) 795; natural gas.

Ea·gle \'ē-gəl\. 1 County in Colorado. See table at COLORADO.

2 Town, its ⊗, NW cen. Colorado; pop. (1970c) 790; timber.

Eagle Grove. City, Wright co., N cen. Iowa, 20 m. NE of Fort Dodge; pop. (1970c) 4489; fertilizer.

Eagle Lake. 1 Lake in cen. Lassen co., NE California.

2 Lake in N Aroostook co., N Maine; drains into a tributary of Aroostook river.

3 Lake in N Piscataquis co., N cen. Maine.

4 City, Colorado co., SE cen. Texas, 40 m. S of Brenham; pop. (1970c) 3587; rice-milling center.

5 Lake, Kenora dist., SW Ontario, Canada; 140 sq. m.; chief outlet through Rainy Lake.

Eagle Mountain. 1 Peak, Cook co., NE Minnesota; 2301 ft.; highest peak in the state.

2 Peak, Hudspeth co., W Texas; 7516 ft.

Eagle Pass. City and port of entry, ⊗ of Maverick co., SW Texas, on the Rio Grande 52 m. SSE of Del Rio; pop. (1970c) 15,364; site of U.S. Army encampment (Camp Eagle Pass) during war with Mexico; on one of favorite routes to California during gold rush of 1849; resort.

Eagle Peak. Mountain in SE Yellowstone National Park, NW Wyoming; 11,358 ft.

Eagle River. 1 Village, ⊗ of Keweenaw co., N Michigan penin., on Lake Superior.

2 City, ⊗ of Vilas co., N Wisconsin; pop. (1970c) 1326; summer resort.

Eagles Rest \'ē-gəlz-\. Peak in N Grand Teton National Park, NW Wyoming; 11,257 ft.

Ea·gle·ton Village \ˌē-gəlt-ᵊn-\. Urban community (unincorporated), Blount co., E Tennessee, S of Knoxville; pop. (1970c) 5345.

Ea·ling \'ē-liŋ\. A borough of Greater London, SE England; birthplace of Thomas Huxley. See table at LONDON 4.

Ear·by \i(ə)r-bē\. Urban district, West Riding, Yorkshire, N England; pop. (1971p) 4816.

Earle \'ərl\. City, Crittenden co., E Arkansas, 27 m. WNW of Memphis, Tenn.; pop. (1970c) 3146; cotton.

Ear·ling·ton \'ərl-iŋ-tən\. City, Hopkins co., W Kentucky, 28 m. N of Hopkinsville; pop. (1970c) 2321; coal mining.

Earl's Seat. See LENNOX HILLS.

Earls·ton \'ərl-stən\; *orig.* **Er·cel·doune** *also* **Er·cil·doune** \'ər-səl-ˌdün\. Parish and market town, S Berwick co., SE Scotland, near Melrose; pop. (1961c) 1643; ruin of ancient tower, the "Rhymer's Castle," residence of Thomas Learmont or Thomas of Erceldoune, seer and poet; manufactures tweed and gingham.

Ear·ly \'ər-lē\. County in Georgia. See table at GEORGIA.

Earn \'ərn\. River, Perth co., cen. Scotland; 46 m. long; flows out of Loch Earn and into the Tay river.

Earn, Loch. Lake, Perth co., cen. Scotland; 6½ m. long.

Earns·law, Mount \-'ərnz-(ˌ)lȯ\. Peak in Southern Alps, SW cen. South I., New Zealand; 9261 ft.

Ear of Di·o·ny·si·us \-ˌdī-ə-'nis(h)-ē-əs, -'nish-əs, -'nī-sē-əs\. A narrow cavern in one of the ancient quarries of Syracuse, Sicily, Italy, tapering to an orifice above, where the tyrant Dionysius the Elder is said to have listened, as one still may, to conversation below.

Eas·ley \'ēz-lē\. City, Pickens co., NW South Carolina, 13 m. W of Greenville; pop. (1970c) 11,175; cotton, flour; diversified farming.

East, The. 1 The countries of Asia and of the Asiatic archipelagoes; the countries E of Europe; the Orient. See FAR EAST, MIDDLE EAST, NEAR EAST.

2 In United States history and geography, formerly the part E of the Allegheny Mts., esp. the New England states; now, often, the region E of the Mississippi river.

East Africa Community. Economic organization, consisting of Kenya, Tanzania, Uganda; headquarters Arusha, Tanzania; purpose is to strengthen economic cooperation among the members; members maintain a common external tariff and share a number of services; formed 1967.

East Africa Protectorate. See KENYA.

East Al·ton \-'ȯlt-ᵊn\. Village, Madison co., SW Illinois, on Mississippi river 5 m. E of Alton; pop. (1970c) 7309.

East An·glia \-'aŋ-glē-ə\. 1 Ancient division, including modern Norfolk and Suffolk, England; probably settled by Angles (see ANGELN), it emerged as one of kingdoms in Anglo-Saxon Heptarchy (*q.v.*); converted to Christianity and subjugated by Mercia 7th cent.; practically absorbed in Mercia by 8th cent.; Danish territory according to the Peace of Wedmore 878; conquered by Wessex 10th cent.; Danish earldom under Canute.

2 Geographical region of modern England; the counties of Norfolk and Suffolk.

East An·gus \-'aŋ-gəs\. Mill town, Compton co., S Quebec, Canada, on St. Francis river; pop. (1971p) 4747.

East Antarctica. See ANTARCTICA.

East Aurora. Village, Erie co., W New York, 15 m. ESE of Buffalo; pop. (1970c) 7033; seat of former Roycroft colony (handicrafts) and Roycroft Press, estab. by Elbert Hubbard 1895; settled 1804.

East Australian Current. Warm ocean current flowing S off E coast of Australia.

East Avon. See AVON 6.

East Azerbaijan. Province of NW Iran. See AZERBAIJAN 1.

East Bat·on Rouge \-ˌbat-ᵊn-'rüzh\. Parish in Louisiana. See table at LOUISIANA.

East Bengal. Region, approx. coextensive with Bangla Desh; formerly part of Bengal prov., British India; to Pakistan 1947; merged with other smaller areas 1955 forming East Pakistan prov.; part of Bangla Desh 1971.

East Berbice. See BERBICE 2.

East Berlin. See BERLIN, EAST.

East Beskids. See BESKIDS.

East Beth·el \-'beth-əl\. Village, Anoka co., E Minnesota, 27 m. N of Minneapolis; pop. (1970c) 2586.

East Boston. Section of Boston, Massachusetts, on E side of Charles river estuary; Boston airport.

East·bourne \'ēs(t)-ˌbō(ə)rn, -ˌbȯ(ə)rn\. County borough, East Sussex, S England, on English Channel 57 m. S of London; pop. (1971p) 70,495; resort.

East Bridgewater. Town, Plymouth co., SE Massachusetts, 5 m. SSE of Brockton; pop. (1970c) 8347.

East Cape. 1 Most easterly point of the island of New Guinea, 151°E lat.; marks NE corner of Milne Bay.

2 Cape on E coast of North I., New Zealand, easternmost point of North I., 178°33'E.

3 Cape, U.S.S.R. See DEZHNEVA CAPE.

East Car·roll \-'kar-əl\. Parish, Louisiana. See table at LOUISIANA.

East–Central State. State of S Nigeria. See table at NIGERIA.

East Charlevoix. See CHARLEVOIX-EST.

East Chicago. City, Lake co., NW corner of Indiana, on Lake Michigan 18 m. SE of Chicago; pop. (1970c) 46,982; manufactures steel, chemicals, railroad equipment, tinplate; refines oil.

East Chicago Heights. Village, Cook co., NE Illinois, 25 m. S of Chicago; pop. (1970c) 5000.

East China Sea. See CHINA SEA.

East Chosen Bay. See TONGJOSŎN.

East Cleveland. City, Cuyahoga co., N Ohio, 5 m. ENE of Cleveland; pop. (1970c) 34,600; residential suburb; manufactures electrical appliances; electrical research laboratories.

East Coast Bays. Borough, North I., New Zealand; pop. (1968e) 13,150.

East Con·e·maugh \-ˈkän-ə-ˌmȯ\. Borough, Cambria co., SW cen. Pennsylvania, 3 m. NE of Johnstown; pop. (1970c) 2710.

East Demerara. See DEMERARA 2.

East Dere·ham \-ˈdi(ə)r-əm\. Urban district, Norfolk, E England, 14 m. W of Norwich; pop. (1971p) 9391; home of Cowper 1796–1800.

East Detroit. Residential city, Macomb co., SE Michigan, 10 m. NE of Detroit; pop. (1970c) 45,920; structural steel, tools.

East Dun·dee \-dən-ˈdē\. Village, Kane co., NE Illinois, 35 m. WNW of Chicago; pop. (1970c) 2920.

Eas·ter Island \ˈē-stər-\ *or Span.* **Is·la de Pas·cua** \ˌēz-lä-t͟hā-ˈpäs-kwä\ *or native* **Ra·pa Nui** \ˌräp-ə-ˈnü-ē\. Island in S Pacific Ocean, lat. 27°08′S and long. 109°23′W, ab. 2000 m. W of the Chilean coast; 46 sq. m.; pop. (1960c) 1135; highest point 1765 ft.; has gigantic statues and other archaeological remains of unknown origin. Discovered on Easter Sunday 1722 by Dutch admiral, Roggeveen; annexed by Chile 1888.

Eastern Bay. Inlet of Chesapeake Bay on SW coast of Queen Annes co., E Maryland.

Eastern Bengal. Former province of India. See ASSAM, BENGAL.

Eastern Desert. See ARABIAN DESERT.

Eastern Empire. See BYZANTINE EMPIRE.

Eastern Euphrates. See MURAT NEHRI.

Eastern Fle·vo·land \-ˈflā-və-ˌland\. See ZUIDER ZEE.

Eastern Ghats. See GHATS.

Eastern Group. See LAU GROUP.

Eastern Highlands. See GREAT DIVIDING RANGE.

Eastern Island. See MIDWAY.

Eastern Ka·thi·a·war \-ˌkät-ē-ə-ˈwär\. Former agency, subdivision of Western India States Agency, W India, now part of Gujarat state.

Eastern Locris. See LOCRIS.

Eastern Manych. See MANYCH.

Eastern Province. 1 Province, E Ceylon, on Bay of Bengal; 3840 sq. m.; pop. (1963e) 547,000; ✱ Trincomalee.
2 Province, E Kenya. See table at KENYA.

Eastern Rajputana States Agency. Eastern part of former Rajputana Agency, NW India, comprising states of Bharatpur, Bundi, Dholpur, Jhalawar, Karauli and Kotah (*qq.v.*). See RAJPUTANA AGENCY.

Eastern Range. Mountain range, Kamchatka (*q.v.*), Russian S.F.S.R., U.S.S.R.; has several high volcanic peaks, including Klyuchevskaya Sopka 15,580 ft., highest peak in Siberia.

Eastern Region *or Span.* **El Ori·en·te** \el-ˌōr-ē-ˈen-tē, -ˌȯr-\. 1 The part of Ecuador beyond (E of) the Andes Mts.; boundaries of region have been in dispute bet. Ecuador, Colombia, and Peru since 1860; by settlement of 1942 at Rio de Janeiro Conference now comprises the provinces of Morona-Santiago, Napo, Pastaza, and Zamora-Chinchipe.
2 Administrative region of SE Ghana. See table at GHANA.

Eastern Roman Empire. See BYZANTINE EMPIRE.

Eastern Ru·me·lia \-rü-ˈmēl-yə, -ˈmē-lē-ə\. Balkan region, now S part of Bulgaria, including Rhodope Mts. and Maritsa river valley; 12,585 sq. m.; chief town Plovdiv (Philippopolis); established as autonomous province of Turkey 1878; annexed to Bulgaria 1885; Bulgarian annexation caused Serbian war against Bulgaria 1885–86 and a crisis in European diplomacy (1885–88) in which Russia failed to achieve separation of region from Bulgaria.

Eastern Samoa. See AMERICAN SAMOA.

Eastern Sea. See CHINA SEA.

Eastern Shore. The part of Maryland E of Chesapeake Bay and the counties of Accomac and Northampton in Virginia; sometimes includes all of Delaware and then considered as equivalent to the Delmarva Penin.

Eastern Siberian Region. See EAST SIBERIA REGION.

Eastern Sierra Madre. See SIERRA MADRE ORIENTAL.

Eastern Silesia. Former duchy in N Austria-Hungary, bet. Prussian Silesia and Moravia; chief town Opava; in 20th cent. its W two thirds became Czech province of Slezsko (Silesia); its E section was nearly equivalent to Teschen (*q.v.*).

Eastern States. 1 The New England states: Maine, New Hampshire, Vermont, Massachusetts, Rhode Island, and Connecticut— popularly so called; in certain groupings, as in the Federal Land Bank system, New York and New Jersey are included.
2 The states of the U.S. along the Atlantic seaboard E of the Allegheny Mts.— a term occasionally used in the Mississippi valley and in states W of it. See EAST, THE 2.
3 Former group of Indian states, NE India; area 66,989 sq. m.; comprised 42 states, two of which, Cooch Behar and Tripura (*qq.v.*), were on E border of Bengal prov.; others in region bet. Bihar on NE and Central India on SW, at one time part in Central Provinces and part (Orissa Feudatory States; 18,151 sq. m.) in Orissa. Under the British government had direct relations with the Crown Representative through Resident at Calcutta, assisted by two political agents at Sambalpur and Raipur; July 15, 1947, 39 of the 42 states formed an administrative union within India for more coordinated action on matters of common interest.

Eastern Thrace. See THRACE.

Eastern Townships. Towns of S Quebec, Canada, E of Montreal and S of the St. Lawrence— popularly so called; chief center Sherbrooke.

Eastern Turkistan. See CHINESE TURKISTAN.

East Falkland. See FALKLAND ISLANDS.

East Fe·li·ci·ana \-fə-ˌlish-e-ˈan-ə\. Parish in Louisiana. See table at LOUISIANA.

East Flanders. Province, NW cen. Belgium; 1151 sq. m.; pop. (1970e) 1,314,031; ✱ Gent; formerly part of the county of Flanders (*q.v.*); rivers Schelde, Lys; potatoes, flax, hops, sugar beets; livestock; manufactures linen and laces.

East Florida. See FLORIDA, *History.*

East Fremantle. See FREMANTLE.

East Friesland. See OSTFRIESLAND.

East Frisian Islands. See FRISIAN ISLANDS.

East Gary. City, Lake co., NW corner of Indiana, 5 m. S of Lake Michigan; pop. (1970c) 9858.

East Gaspé. See GASPÉ-EST.

East Germany. See GERMANY, EAST.

East Gran·by \-ˈgran-bē\. Town, Hartford co., N Connecticut, 12 m. N of Hartford; pop. (1970c) 3538; incorporated 1858; nearby is Newgate Prison, used in Revolutionary days and one of early state prisons.

East Grand Forks. City, Polk co., NW Minnesota, on Red river opp. Grand Forks, North Dakota; pop. (1970c) 7607; beet-sugar refinery.

East Grand Lake. See GRAND LAKE 8.

East Grand Rapids. City, Kent co., W Michigan, suburb of Grand Rapids; pop. (1970c) 12,565; incorporated as a village 1891, as a city 1926.

East Green·wich \-ˈgren-ich\. Manufacturing town and summer resort, ⊗ of Kent co., cen. Rhode Island, 12 m. WSW of Providence; pop. (1970c) 9577; ships shellfish.

East Grin·stead \-ˈgrin-stəd\. Urban district, East Sussex, S England; pop. (1971p) 18,569; brick and tile.

East Had·dam \-ˈhad-əm\. Town, E Middlesex co., S Connecticut, on Connecticut river; pop. (1970c) 4676; incorp. 1734.

East·ham \ˈē-ˌstam\. Town, Barnstable co., SE Massachusetts, ab. 25 m. from Provincetown; pop. (1970c) 2043.

East Ham \ˈēst-ˈham\. Former county borough, England, now part of the Greater London borough of Newham.

East·hamp·ton \ē-'stam(p)-tən\. Town, Hampshire co., W Massachusetts, 12 m. NNW of Springfield; pop. (1970c) 13,012; Williston Academy, boys' preparatory school.

East Hamp·ton \ē-'stam(p)-tən\. 1 Residential, manufacturing, and agricultural town, NE Middlesex co., S Connecticut; pop. (1970c) 7078; incorp. as Chatham 1767.
2 Village and summer resort, Suffolk co., SE New York, on Long I., on Atlantic Ocean 20 m. W of Montauk Point; pop. (1970c) 1753; seat of Clinton Academy (1784), first academy of higher education in N.Y.; home of John Howard Payne, author of *Home, Sweet Home;* settled 1648; considered part of Connecticut until 1664.

East Hartford. Town, E cen. Hartford co., N Connecticut, on E side of Connecticut river opp. Hartford; pop. (1970c) 57,583; airplane engines, furniture; bottling works; settled c. 1650.

East Haven. Suburban residential town, S New Haven co., Connecticut, on Long Island Sound; pop. (1970c) 25,120; summer resort; includes Lake Saltonstall, site of first iron mill in Connecticut; incorporated 1785.

East Helena. Town, Lewis and Clark co., W cen. Montana, 5 m. E of Helena; pop. (1970c) 1651.

East Hills. Village, Nassau co., New York, in SW cen. Long I.; pop. (1970c) 8675.

East In·dies \-'in-(,)dēz\. 1 *also* **East In·dia** \-'in-dē-ə\. Collective name applied, loosely and vaguely, to India, Indochina, and the Malay Archipelago.
2 In better usage, politically, the Republic of Indonesia, formerly the Netherlands East Indies. See INDIES. By some writers used to include all the islands of the Malay Archipelago.

East Indonesia. State of the former United States of Indonesia (see INDONESIA 2), now part of the Republic of Indonesia; included Celebes, the Moluccas, Bali, Lombok, Flores, Timor (Dutch sector), and other smaller islands of cen. Malay Archipelago; ✱ Makasar. Established Dec. 25, 1946, first state to be set up with the approval of the Netherlands in movement to form the United States of Indonesia.

East Islip \-'ī-sləp\. Village, Suffolk co., SE New York, on S shore of Long I.; pop. (1970c) 6819.

East Jaffrey. See JAFFREY.

East Java. Province of Indonesia, Java. See JAVA and table at INDONESIA.

East Jer·sey \-'jər-zē\. Eastern and northern New Jersey constituting a proprietary colony from 1676 to 1702 when it was united with West Jersey to form the royal province of New Jersey (*q.v.*); ✱ (from 1686) Perth Amboy; held by William Penn and associates from 1682.

East Jor·dan \-'jȯrd-ᵊn\. City, Charlevoix co., NW Michigan, 35 m. NE of Traverse City; pop. (1970c) 2041.

East Kalimantan. See KALIMANTAN, EAST.

East Ka·zakh·stan Oblast \-kə-,zak-,stan-'ó-bləst, -zäk-,stän-, -kä-, -,blast\. Subdivision of the Kazakh S.S.R., U.S.S.R.; bounded on N by Altai Krai, on NE by Gorno-Altai Autonomous Oblast, on E and S by Sinkiang Uighur, China, and on W by Semipalatinsk Oblast; 37,568 sq. m.; pop. (1970p) 846,000; ✱ Ust Kamenogorsk; silver, lead, and zinc deposits.

East Kil·bride \-kil-'brīd\. Burgh, Lanark co., Scotland, ab. 9 m. SE of Glasgow; pop. (1971p) 63,505; electrical appliances, agricultural machinery; aeronautical engineering.

East Kil·do·nan \-kil-'dō-nən\. City, Manitoba, Canada, 4 m. NE of Winnipeg; pop. (1966c) 29,796; residential suburb of Winnipeg.

East Killingly. See KILLINGLY.

East·lake \'ēst-(,)lāk\. City, Lake co., NE Ohio, on Lake Erie 20 m. NE of Cleveland; pop. (1970c) 19,690; residential suburb of Cleveland.

East Lake Saint John. See LAKE SAINT JOHN, EAST.

East·land \'ēst-lənd\. 1 County in N cen. Texas. See table at TEXAS.
2 City, its ⊗, 50 m. E of Abilene; pop. (1970c) 3178; oil; trade center in farming region.

East Lans·downe \-'lanz-,daùn\. Borough, Delaware co., SE Pennsylvania, near Philadelphia; pop. (1970c) 3186.

East Lansing. City, Ingham co., S Michigan, 5 m. E of Lansing; pop. (1970c) 47,540; Michigan State Univ. (1855).

East Las Vegas. See LAS VEGAS 2.

East·leigh \'ēst-,lē\. Municipal borough, Hampshire, S England, 6 m. NNE of city of Southampton; pop. (1971p) 45,320; railroad shops.

East Liverpool. City, Columbiana co., E Ohio, on Ohio river 18 m. N of Steubenville; pop. (1970c) 20,000; center of ceramic industry; settled 1798, incorp. 1834.

East London *or Afrikaans* **Oos–Lon·den** \ōs-'lən-də(n)\ *or orig.* **Port Rex** \-'reks\. City, SE Cape Province, S Rep. of South Africa, at mouth of Buffalo river 150 m. ENE of Port Elizabeth; pop. (1968e) 36,757; wool center; furniture, glass, textiles; fishing, fruit canning; resort; founded 1847, an early settlement in British Kaffraria.

East Long·mead·ow \-'lȯŋ-,med-(,)ō\. Town, Hampden co., SW Massachusetts, 5 m. SE of Springfield; pop. (1970c) 13,029.

East Los Angeles. Urban community (unincorporated), Los Angeles co., SW California; pop. (1970c) 105,033.

East Lo·thi·an \-'lō-thē-ən\ *or* **Had·ding·ton** \'had-iŋ-tən\ *or* **Had·ding·ton·shire** \-,shi(ə)r, -shər\. County, SE Scotland; area 267 sq. m.; pop. (1971p) 55,891; ⊗ Haddington; chief river the Tyne; barley, wheat, potatoes; fishing; light engineering.

East Lyme \-'līm\. Residential town, SW New London co., SE Connecticut, on Long Island Sound; pop. (1970c) 11,-399; incorporated 1839; quarries pink granite.

East McKeesport. Residential borough, Allegheny co., SW Pennsylvania, 12 m. E of Pittsburgh; pop. (1970c) 3233.

East·main \'ēst-,mān\. River, W Quebec, Canada; 510 m. long; flows W into James Bay.

East Malaysia. See MALAYSIA.

East·man \'ēst-mən\. City, ⊗ of Dodge co., S cen. Georgia, 52 m. SE of Macon; pop. (1970c) 5416; tobacco, timber, cotton, corn.

East Mas·sa·pe·qua \-,mas-ə-'pē-kwə\. Urban community (unincorporated), Nassau co., New York, on Long I., SE of Mineola; pop. (1970c) 15,926.

East Mauch Chunk. See JIM THORPE.

East Meadow. Urban community (unincorporated), Nassau co., New York, on Long I. E of Hempstead; pop. (1970c) 46,352.

East Mil·li·nock·et \-,mil-ə-'näk-ət\. Town, Penobscot co., E cen. Maine, 50 m. SW of Houlton; pop. (1970c) 2567; paper mill.

East Moline. City, Rock Island co., NW Illinois, a suburb of Moline on Mississippi river; pop. (1970c) 20,832; manufactures farm implements.

East Montreal *or Fr.* **Mont·réal–Est** \,mōⁿ-rā-,ál-'est\. Town, Montreal and Jesus Islands co., S Quebec, Canada; pop. (1971p) 5048; residential suburb of Montreal.

East Naples. Urban community, ⊗ of Collier co., SW Florida; pop. (1970c) 6152.

East Newark. Manufacturing borough, Hudson co., NE New Jersey, on Passaic river opp. Newark; pop. (1970c) 1922.

East New Britain. See NEW BRITAIN 2.

East Nishnabotna. See NISHNABOTNA.

East North·port \-'nȯ(ə)rth-,pō(ə)rt, -,pȯ(ə)rt\. Urban community (unincorporated), Suffolk co., New York, on Long I. E of Huntington; pop. (1970c) 12,392.

East Nusa Tenggara. See NUSA TENGGARA, EAST.

East Okoboji. See OKOBOJI.

Eas·ton \'ē-stən\. 1 Town, Fairfield co., SW Connecticut, 6 m. E of Bridgeport; pop. (1970c) 4885.
2 Town, ⊗ of Talbot co., E Maryland, on E shore of Chesapeake Bay 28 m. ESE of Annapolis; pop. (1970c) 6809; Kirkland Hall Coll. (1967).
3 Manufacturing town, Bristol co., SE Massachusetts, 7 m. SW of Brockton; pop. (1970c) 12,157; foundry.

4 City, ⊗ of Northampton co., E Pennsylvania, at junction of Lehigh and Delaware rivers 15 m. ENE of Allentown; pop. (1970c) 30,256; electronic equipment, aluminum castings, diesel engines, cement; Lafayette Coll. (1826); became ⊗ 1752, incorp. as borough 1789, as city 1887.

East Orange. City, Essex co., NE New Jersey, residential suburb ab. 4 m. WNW of Newark; pop. (1970c) 75,471; aeronautical equipment, electric motors, hydrants; Upsala Coll. (1893); largest of "The Oranges" (Orange, East Orange, West Orange, South Orange); incorp. as separate township 1863, as city 1899.

East Pakistan. See BANGLA DESH.

East Palestine. City, Columbiana co., E Ohio, 18 m. S of Youngstown; pop. (1970c) 5604; pottery ware, automobile tires; clay, coal, petroleum; estab. 1828.

East Paterson. Borough, Bergen co., NE corner of New Jersey, 2 m. SE of Paterson; pop. (1970c) 20,511.

East Peak. See BOUNDARY PEAK.

East Peoria. City, Tazewell co., cen. Illinois, across Illinois river from Peoria; pop. (1970c) 18,455; Illinois Central Coll. (1966).

East Petersburg. Borough, Lancaster co., SE Pennsylvania, 3 m. NW of Lancaster; pop. (1970c) 3407.

East·pha·lia \ēst-'fāl-yə, -'fā-lē-ə\. East section of the ancient duchy of Saxony, Germany; bordered on the E by the Elbe river and on the S by the Harz Mts.

East Pittsburgh. Industrial borough, Allegheny co., SW Pennsylvania, 10 m. E of Pittsburgh; pop. (1970c) 3006; electrical equipment.

East Point. 1 City, Fulton co., NW cen. Georgia, 7 m. SSW of Atlanta; pop. (1970c) 39,315; Atlanta Christian Coll. (1937); incorporated 1887.

2 Point at E tip of Prince Edward I., Canada, extending into the Gulf of St. Lawrence.

3 Cape at E end of Anegada I. in the British Virgin Is., West Indies.

4 Cape at E end of island of St. Croix in the Virgin Is. of the U.S., West Indies.

5 Cape at E end of Vieques I., E of Puerto Rico in the West Indies.

East·port \'ēst-ˌpō(ə)rt, -ˌpȯ(ə)rt\. City, Washington co., SE corner of Maine, on island in Passamaquoddy Bay 24 m. SE of Calais; pop. (1970c) 1989; easternmost city in U.S.; fisheries, sardine canneries.

East Prairie. City, Mississippi co., SE Missouri, 38 m. S of Cape Girardeau; pop. (1970c) 3275.

East Providence. City, Providence co., N Rhode Island; pop. (1970c) 48,207; chemicals, jewelry, plastics; oil refining; suburb of Providence; originally part of Seekonk, Mass.; set off and incorporated 1862.

East Prussia *or Ger.* **Ost·preus·sen** \'ȯst-ˌprȯis-ᵊn\. Historical region and former province of Prussia, E of Pomerania, on SE Baltic shore; inhabited by Old Prussians, conquered by Teutonic Knights 1226 (see PRUSSIA); after (Second) Peace of Thorn 1466, retained by Teutonic Knights as vassal of Poland; included in duchy of Prussia secularized by Albert of Brandenburg 1525; province of kingdom of Prussia; scene of Hindenburg's successful resistance against Russians (see STĘBARK and MASURIA) in World War I; 1919 separated from rest of Germany by Polish Corridor (*q.v.*) and southern part returned to Germany by plebiscite; reunited with territory of the Reich by German conquest of Poland 1939; invaded by Soviet armies in fall of 1944 and overrun Jan.–May 1945; by decision of Potsdam Conference 1945, divided bet. U.S.S.R. and Poland, with Kaliningrad (Königsberg), Chernyakhovsk (Insterburg), and all N of a line drawn E to W just S of the Pregolya (Pregel) assigned to U.S.S.R. and S two thirds to Poland.

East Punjab. Eastern part of former Punjab prov., India; after 1947 a province (later **Punjab** state, ✱ Chandigarh) of N India; comprising all of Jullundur and Ambala divisions of the former Punjab, the entire Amritsar dist. and parts of Gurdaspur and Lahore dists. of Lahore division; 47,456 sq. m. In 1966 divided into states of Punjab and Haryana (*qq.v.*).

East Ret·ford \-'ret-fərd\. Municipal borough, Nottinghamshire, N cen. England, on the Idle 23 m. E of Sheffield; pop. (1971p) 18,402.

East Ridge. Town, Hamilton co., SE Tennessee, on Georgia border 5 m. ESE of Chattanooga; pop. (1970c) 21,799.

East Riding. See YORKSHIRE.

East River. Strait connecting Long Island Sound and Upper New York Bay, New York; separates Manhattan from Brooklyn and Queens on Long I.

East River Mountain. Mountain, Bland co., SW Virginia; 3388 ft.

East Rochester. Manufacturing village, Monroe co., W New York, 7 m. E of Rochester; pop. (1970c) 8347.

East Rock·a·way \-'räk-ə-ˌwā\. Residential village and resort, Nassau co., SE New York, on cen. Long Island 20 m. ESE of New York City; pop. (1970c) 10,323.

East Rutherford. Industrial borough, Bergen co., NE corner of New Jersey, 8 m. NNE of Newark; pop. (1970c) 8536.

East Saint Louis. Manufacturing city, St. Clair co., SW Illinois, on Mississippi river opp. St. Louis, Mo.; pop. (1970c) 69,996; railroad center; smelters; meat packing; iron and steel products, glass, aluminum, chemicals.

East Schel·de Estuary \-'skel-də-\. Inlet of the North Sea on SW coast of Netherlands, at mouth of Schelde river, N of Walcheren, North Beveland, and South Beveland Is.

East Siberian Sea. Part of Arctic Ocean, N of Yakutsk A.S.S.R. and Chukot National Okrug, Russian S.F.S.R., U.S.S.R.; extends from New Siberian Is. to Wrangel I.

East Siberia Region *or* **Eastern Siberian Region.** One of the subdivisions of the U.S.S.R. in Asia, consisting of the cen. and E parts of Siberia (see SIBERIA); 1,591,813 sq. m.; pop. (1970p) 7,464,000; chief town Irkutsk.

East Side. The E part of Manhattan borough, New York City, esp. below 14th St. (Lower East Side); site of headquarters of United Nations (42d St. to 48th St.).

East Spencer. Town, Rowan co., cen. North Carolina, 4 m. ENE of Salisbury; pop. (1970c) 2217.

East Stoke. See STOKE, EAST.

East Stroudsburg. Borough, Monroe co., E Pennsylvania, 32 m. NNE of Allentown; pop. (1970c) 7894; East Stroudsburg Coll. (1893), Pinebrook Junior Coll. (1950).

East Suffolk. See SUFFOLK 3.

East Sussex. See SUSSEX 6.

East Syracuse. Village, Onondaga co., cen. New York, 5 m. E of Syracuse; pop. (1970c) 4333; steel products.

East Ta·was \-'tȯ-wəs\. City, Iosco co., NE Michigan, at N side of mouth of Saginaw Bay; pop. (1970c) 2372.

East Tirol *or Ger.* **Ost·ti·rol** \ˌȯst-tə-'rōl\. Eastern part of the Austrian Tirol; 763 sq. m.; before World War II formed an exclave of Tirol state, SW Austria, and the political district of Lienz.

East Turkistan. See CHINESE TURKISTAN.

East Van·der·grift \-'van-dər-ˌgrift\. Borough, Westmoreland co., SW Pennsylvania, on Kiskiminetas river; pop. (1970c) 1167.

Eastview. See VANIER 1.

East·ville \'ēst-ˌvil\. Town, ⊗ of Northampton co., S part of E Virginia penin.; pop. (1970c) 203.

East Washington. Borough, Washington co., SW Pennsylvania, SW of Pittsburgh; pop. (1970c) 2198.

East Williston. Village, Nassau co., SE New York, 7 m. S of Glen Cove; pop. (1970c) 2808.

East Windsor. Town, N cen. Hartford co., N Connecticut, on Connecticut river; pop. (1970c) 8513.

East·wood \'ēst-wu̇d\. Urban district, Nottinghamshire, N cen. England, 8 m. NW of Nottingham; pop. (1971p) 10,-864; in coal-mining region.

Ea·ton \'ēt-ᵊn\. 1 County in Michigan. See table at MICHIGAN.

2 City, ⊗ of Preble co., SW Ohio, 22 m. W of Dayton; pop. (1970c) 6020; oil filters; founded 1806.

Eaton Rapids. City, Eaton co., S Michigan, 15 m. SSW of Lansing; pop. (1970c) 4494; dairy products; woolen mills.

Ea·ton·ton \'ēt-ᵊn-tən\. City, ⊗ of Putnam co., cen. Georgia, 38 m. NNE of Macon; pop. (1970c) 4125; lumber.

Ea·ton·town \'ēt-ᵊn-ˌtau̇n\. Borough, Monmouth co., E cen. New Jersey, 6 m. NNW of Asbury Park; pop. (1970c) 14,619; electronic equipment.

Eau·bonne \ō-'bȯn\. Commune, Val-d'Oise dept., N France; pop. (1968c) 22,278.

Eau Claire \ō-'kla(ə)r, -'kle(ə)r\. 1 River, W cen. Wisconsin; ab. 70 m. long; rises in Clark co., flows W into Chippewa river at Eau Claire.

2 County in W Wisconsin. See table at WISCONSIN.

3 Commercial and industrial city, its ⊗, on Chippewa river; pop. (1970c) 44,619; automobile parts, railroad equipment; farm center; Wisconsin State Univ. (1916); settled in 1840's; developed as outlet for Chippewa lumber district.

Eaux–Bonnes \ō-'bȯn\. Town, Pyrénées-Atlantiques dept., SW France, ab. 23 m. S of Pau; pop. (1962c) 132; thermal mineral waters famous since 14th cent.; ab. 5 m. to the SW is the watering place of **Eaux–Chaudes** \ō-'shōd\, with warm sulfur springs.

Eaux Vives \ō-'vēv\. Former commune, Geneva canton, Switzerland; now in E part of city of Geneva.

Eauze \ā-'ōz\. Commune, W Gers dept., SW France, 15 m. NW of Auch; pop. (1962c) 3807; ancient capital of Aquitania Tertia.

Eba, Mount. See MOUNT EBA.

Ebal, Mount \-'ē-bəl\ *or Arab.* **Ja·bal 'Ay·bāl** \ˌjab-əl-'ī-(ˌ)bal\. Mountain, Jordan, N of Nablus, in area occupied by Israel 1967; 3084 ft.

Eb·bw \'eb-(ˌ)ü\. River, NW Monmouthshire, SE Wales; 24 m. long; flows S into the Usk S of Newport.

Ebbw Vale. Urban district, Monmouthshire, SE Wales, on the Ebbw 35 m. NW of Bristol; pop. (1971p) 26,049; coal mines; steelworks.

Eben Emael, Fort. See FORT EBEN EMAEL.

Eb·ens·burg \'eb-ᵊnz-ˌbərg\. Borough, ⊗ of Cambria co., SW cen. Pennsylvania, 15 m. NE of Johnstown; pop. (1970c) 4318; timber.

Ebers·wal·de \ˌā-bərs-'väl-də\. City, Frankfurt dist., East Germany, 28 m. NE of Berlin; pop. (1970e) 46,090; manufactures cranes; foundries; forestry school; 14th cent. Gothic church; prehistoric (1050–850 B.C.) gold artifacts found here 1913; received charter 1257.

Ebing·en \'ā-biŋ-ən\. City, Baden-Württemberg, West Germany, 41 m. S of Stuttgart; pop. (1969e) 22,019; metalworking.

Ebi Nor. See AI-PI.

Eblana. See DUBLIN.

Eb·o·la \'eb-ə-lə\. Headstream of the Mongala river (*q.v.*), N Zaire; flows W.

Ebo·li \'eb-ə-lē\. Commune, Salerno prov., Campania, S Italy, 16 m. ESE of Salerno; pop. (1968e) 27,168; castle.

Eb·on \'eb-ən\. Atoll at S end of Ralik Chain, Marshall Is., W Pacific Ocean; 4°38'N, 168°43'E; 22 islets (largest Ebon).

Ebora. See ÉVORA 2.

Eboracum. See YORK 12.

Ebro \'ā-(ˌ)brō\ *or anc.* **Ibe·rus** \ī-'bir-əs\. River, NE Spain; 565 m. long; 2d longest river in Spain; rises in the Cantabrian Mts. in Santander prov., flows ESE into Mediterranean Sea ab. 80 m. SW of Barcelona; has drainage basin of 33,600 sq. m.; chief tributaries the Aragon, Segre, and Jalón rivers; has long been used for irrigation; navigable to seafaring vessels as far as Tortosa (ab. 22 m. from its mouth) and to small boats as far as Tudela (in Navarra prov.).

Ebudae. See HEBRIDES.

Eburacum. See YORK 12.

Eburodunum. See EMBRUN; YVERDON.

Ebusus. See IBIZA.

Eca·te·pec de Mo·re·los \ā-ˌkät-ə-'pek-də-mȯ-'rāl-əs\. City, México state, Mexico, 11 m. NE of Mexico City; munic. pop. (1970p) 220,918; commercial center for agricultural region.

Ecbatana. See HAMADAN 2.

Ec·cle·fech·an \ˌek-əl-'fek-ən\. Village near Dumfries, Dumfries co., S Scotland; birthplace of Thomas Carlyle.

Ec·cles \'ek-əlz\. Municipal borough, Lancashire, W England, on the Irwell 4 m. W of Manchester; pop. (1971p) 38,413; metalworking; 12th cent. church (restored); incorp. 1892.

Ec·cle·shall \'ek-əl-shəl, -(ˌ)shȯl\. Market town, Staffordshire, England, 7 m. NW of Stafford; pop. (1961c) 3630; walls and moat of castle which was episcopal residence 13th cent. to 1867.

Echa·gue \ā-'chä-gwā\. Municipality, S Isabela prov., Luzon, Phil., on W bank of Cagayan river 34 m. S of Ilagan; pop. (1969e) 39,900; taken by Americans June 15, 1945.

Ech·mi·a·dzin *or* **Etch·mi·a·dzin** \ˌech-mē-əd-'zēn\ *or* **Ej·mi·a·dzin** \ˌej-\. Monastery, Armenian S.S.R., U.S.S.R., 12 m. W of Yerevan; seat of the Armenian patriarch; founded by Gregory the Illuminator c. 302 A.D.; contains large and valuable library of Armenian literature.

Echmiadzin *or formerly* **Va·gar·sha·pat** \ˌvä-gär-shä-'pät\. Town, Armenian S.S.R., U.S.S.R., 12 m. W of Yerevan, in valley of the Araks; pop. (1967e) 26,000. An old town dating from 6th cent. B.C.; capital of ancient kingdom of Armenia 184 to 344 A.D.

Echo, Lake \-'ek-(ˌ)ō\. Lake, cen. Tasmania, Australia, ab. 60 m. NW of Hobart; ab. 7 m. long; source of Dee river, a tributary of the Derwent.

Echo Canyon. Ravine in Summit co., NE Utah, with walls 800 to 1200 ft. high; railroad passes through it; important in early history of the state.

Echo Dam. Dam across Weber river, Summit co., N Utah, NE of Salt Lake City; height 158 ft.; completed 1931; impounds water for irrigation, forming **Echo Reservoir.**

Echo Lake. Small lake, N Grafton co., W New Hampshire, in White Mts. near Franconia; alt. 1931 ft.; shut in by mountains (Cannon Mt. on W).

Ech·ols \'ek-əlz\. County in Georgia. See table at GEORGIA.

Echt \'ekt\. Commune, Drenthe prov., E Netherlands; pop. (1970e) 15,795.

Ech·ter·nach \'ek-tər-ˌnäk\. Town, NE Luxembourg, on the Sauer 18 m. NE of Luxembourg city; pop. (1967e) 3620; nylon; tourism; an old town famous for its festival on Whit-Tuesday; place where St. Willibrord is buried. Figured in fighting in Battle of the Bulge 1944–45.

Éci·ja \'ā-sē-ˌhä\ *or anc.* **As·ti·gi** \'as-tə-ˌjī\. Manufacturing city, Sevilla prov., SW Spain, 48 m. ENE of Seville; pop. (1970p) 36,056; leather products; episcopal see; ancient Roman colony; Roman ruins.

Eck·ern·för·de \ˌek-ərn-'fərd-ə\. Seaport, Schleswig-Holstein, West Germany, on Kiel Bay, just NW of Kiel; pop. (1969e) 21,925; fisheries; became town 1288.

Eckmühl. See EGGMÜHL.

Écluse. See SLUIS.

Ecnomus. See SOLE, MONTE.

Econ·o·my \i-'kän-ə-mē\. Borough, Beaver co., W Pennsylvania, NW of Pittsburgh; pop. (1970c) 7176. See AMBRIDGE.

Eco·po·ran·ga \ˌek-ə-pə-'raŋ-gə\. Municipality, Espírito Santo state, E Brazil; pop. (1968e) 75,455.

Ecorse \'ē-ˌkȯrs\. City, Wayne co., SE Michigan, on Detroit river 8 m. SW of Detroit; pop. (1970c) 17,515; steel manufacturing.

Écrins, Barre des. See BARRE DES ÉCRINS.

Ec·tor \ˌek-tər\. County in Texas. See table at TEXAS.

Ec·ua·dor \ˈek-wə-ˌdȯ(ə)r\. Republic, NW South America; bounded on N by Colombia, on E and S by Peru, and on W by the Pacific Ocean; 109,483 sq. m.; pop. (1970e) 6,177,100; ✱ Quito. *Physical features:* Mountains include central range of the Andes Mts. with highest volcanic peaks Chimborazo 20,561 ft., Cotopaxi 19,347 ft., Cayambe 18,996 ft., Sangay 17,159 ft.; country subject often to volcanic disturbances and earthquakes. Short streams flowing W to Pacific, including the Esmeraldas, and the Guayas flowing to wide Gulf of Guayaquil in SW; streams on E slope of Andes in Eastern Region, tributaries of the Amazon and of its headstream the Marañón, most important being the Napo and its tributary the Curaray, the Tigre, Pastaza, Morona (Macuma in Ecuador), and Santiago (Zamora in Ecuador). *Island possessions:* The Galápagos Is. (*q.v.*) ab. 600 m. off the coast, constituting Archipiélago de Colón territory. *Chief products:* Corn, coffee, rice, bananas, cotton; oil; manufacturing: food processing, textiles, leather, building materials. *Chief cities:* Guayaquil, Quito, Cuenca, Ambato, Esmeraldas, Machala, Riobamba. Divided into the following 19 provinces and one territory (for pronunciation of their names, see their individual entries):

NAME	AREA (sq. m.)	POP. (1970e)	CAPITAL
Provinces			
Azuay	3,211	316,800	Cuenca
Bolívar	1,288	179,000	Guaranda
Cañar	1,614	135,600	Azogues
Carchi	1,581	120,000	Tulcán
Chimborazo	2,322	373,300	Riobamba
Cotopaxi	2,241	237,000	Latacunga
El Oro	3,053	240,000	Machala
Esmeraldas	5,680	177,600	Esmeraldas
Guayas	7,368	1,405,000	Guayaquil
Imbabura	3,458	213,500	Ibarra
Loja	4,445	377,600	Loja
Los Ríos	3,076	356,100	Babahoyo
Manabí	7,602	821,500	Portoviejo
Morona-Santiago[1]		40,400	Macas
Napo[1]		38,500	Tena
Pastaza[1]		21,700	Puyo
Pichincha	5,976	843,000	Quito
Tungurahua	1,366	258,700	Ambato
Zamora-Chinchipe[1]		18,200	Zamora
Territory			
Galápagos Is.	3,075	3,600	

[1]The total area of the four provinces is 52,129 sq. m.

History: Quito, ancient name of Ecuador, conquered by Peru before advent of Spanish; conquered by Spanish 1534; a presidency under viceroyalty of Peru, later of New Granada; after earlier unsuccessful risings, won final independence from Spain at battle of Mt. Pichincha May 24, 1822; part of Great Colombia until 1830 when it seceded to become republic of Ecuador; in league with Chile and Peru in war against Spain 1866; its political history a turbulent one; its boundaries, especially with Peru, a long-standing cause of friction with its neighbors; boundary with Colombia settled 1916 but that with Peru, in spite of treaties of 1860, 1887, and 1890, not settled until 1942 when the larger part of the region bet. the Marañón and the Putumayo was assigned to Peru; member of UN 1945.

Edam \ˈēd-əm, ˈē-ˌdam\. Commune and seaport, North Holland prov., W Netherlands, on the IJsselmeer; pop. (1970e) 18,184; market for the cheese to which it gives its name (Edam cheese); textiles.

Ed·couch \ˈed-ˈkau̇ch\. Town, Hidalgo co., S Texas, 20 m. ENE of McAllen; pop. (1970c) 2656.

Ed Da·mer \ed-ˈdam-ər\ *or* **Ad Da·mir** \ad-\. Town, ✱ of Northern Province, N Sudan, on the Nile.

Ed Deb·ba \ed-ˈdeb-ə\ *or* **Ad Dab·bah** \ad-ˈdab-ə\. Town in Northern Province, N cen. Sudan, on the Nile WSW of Marawī.

Ed·dra·chil·lis Bay \ˌed-rə-ˌkil-əs-\. Bay, Sutherland co., on NW coast of Scotland.

Ed Du·eim \ed-du̇-ˈām\ *or* **Ad Du·waym** \ad-du̇-ˈwām, -ˈwīm\. Town, Blue Nile prov., E Sudan, on White Nile; pop. (1965e) 16,352; ✱ of former White Nile prov.

Ed·dy \ˈed-ē-\. Name of counties in two states of the U.S. See tables at NEW MEXICO and NORTH DAKOTA.

Eddy Mountain. Peak, S cen. Siskiyou co., N California; 9038 ft.

Ed·dy·stone \ˈed-ē-ˌstōn\. Borough, Delaware co., SE Pennsylvania, on Delaware river 12 m. WSW of Philadelphia; pop. (1970c) 2706; locomotive works; munitions center during World War I.

Eddystone Rocks. Rocky islet in the English Channel, 14 m. SW of Plymouth; lighthouse.

Ed·dy·ville \ˈed-ē-ˌvil\. City, ⊗ of Lyon co., W Kentucky, on Cumberland river 30 m. E of Paducah; pop. (1970c) 1981.

Ede \ˈād-ə\. Commune, Gelderland prov., E Netherlands, 13 m. NW of Arnhem; pop. (1970e) 71,952; rayon-yarn factory, metallurgical works; pianos.

Ede \ˈā-ˌdā\. City, Western State, Nigeria, 45 m. NNE of Ibadan; pop. (1969e) 156,036; cocoa, wool; a Yoruba city.

Edéa \ā-ˈdā-ə\. Town, E Cameroon, W Africa, on railroad ab. 40 m. SE of Douala; pop. (1970e) 23,000.

Eden \ˈēd-ᵊn\. **1** Town, Rockingham co., N North Carolina, 28 m. N of Greensboro; pop. (1970c) 15,871; corn, wheat, tobacco.

2 Village, Concho co., W cen. Texas, 38 m. ESE of San Angelo; pop. (1970c) 1291; sheep and goats, cotton.

3 Seaport town with large harbor on Twofold Bay, SE New South Wales, SE Australia; pop. (1966c) 1416.

4 River, Westmorland and Cumberland, NW England; 65 m. long; flows N into head of Solway Firth.

5 River, Fife co., E Scotland; 29½ m. long; flows NE into St. Andrews Bay.

Eden Prairie. Village, Hennepin co., SE cen. Minnesota; pop. (1970c) 6938; residential suburb of Minneapolis.

Eden Reservoir. Reservoir in a tributary of Green river, NW Sweetwater co., SW Wyoming.

Eden·ton \ˈēd-ᵊn-tən\. Town, ⊗ of Chowan co., NE North Carolina, on Albemarle Sound near mouth of Chowan river; pop. (1970c) 4956; formerly horse-racing center; produces peanuts, cotton; shad and herring fisheries. Settled 1658; capital of colony 1722–66; scene of "Edenton tea party" Oct. 25, 1774, a meeting of 51 ladies who signed a pact resolving not to drink tea or wear clothing made in England until the tax on tea should be repealed.

Eden·vale \ˈēd-ᵊn-ˌvāl\. Town, Transvaal, Rep. of South Africa, suburb of Johannesburg; pop. (1967e) 30,200.

Eder \ˈād-ər\. River, chiefly in Hesse, West Germany; 110 m. long; flows E to join the Fulda just S of Kassel; in its course is Eder reservoir dam, which was bombed by British May 16, 1943.

Edes·sa \i-ˈdes-ə\. **1** *or Gk.* **Édhes·sa** \ˈā-t͟hə-sä\ *also* **Vo·de·na** \ˌvȯ-t͟hə-ˈnä\. City, ✱ of Pella dept., W Macedonia, Greece, 48 m. WNW of Salonika; pop. (1971p) 16,521; textiles, tobacco; anciently a capital of Macedonian kings; scene of assassination of Philip II of Macedon 336 B.C.

2 Ancient city, Asia Minor. See URFA 2.

Edfu. See IDFU.

Ed·gar \ˈed-gər\. County in Illinois. See table at ILLINOIS.

Ed·gard \ˈed-ˌgärd\. Village, ⊗ of Saint John the Baptist parish, SE Louisiana.

Ed·gar·town \ˈed-gər-ˌtau̇n\. Town, ⊗ of Dukes co., SE Massachusetts, E Martha's Vineyard on **Edgartown Harbor,** on inlet of Nantucket Sound; pop. (1970c) 1481.

Edge·combe \ˈej-kəm\. County in North Carolina. See table at NORTH CAROLINA.

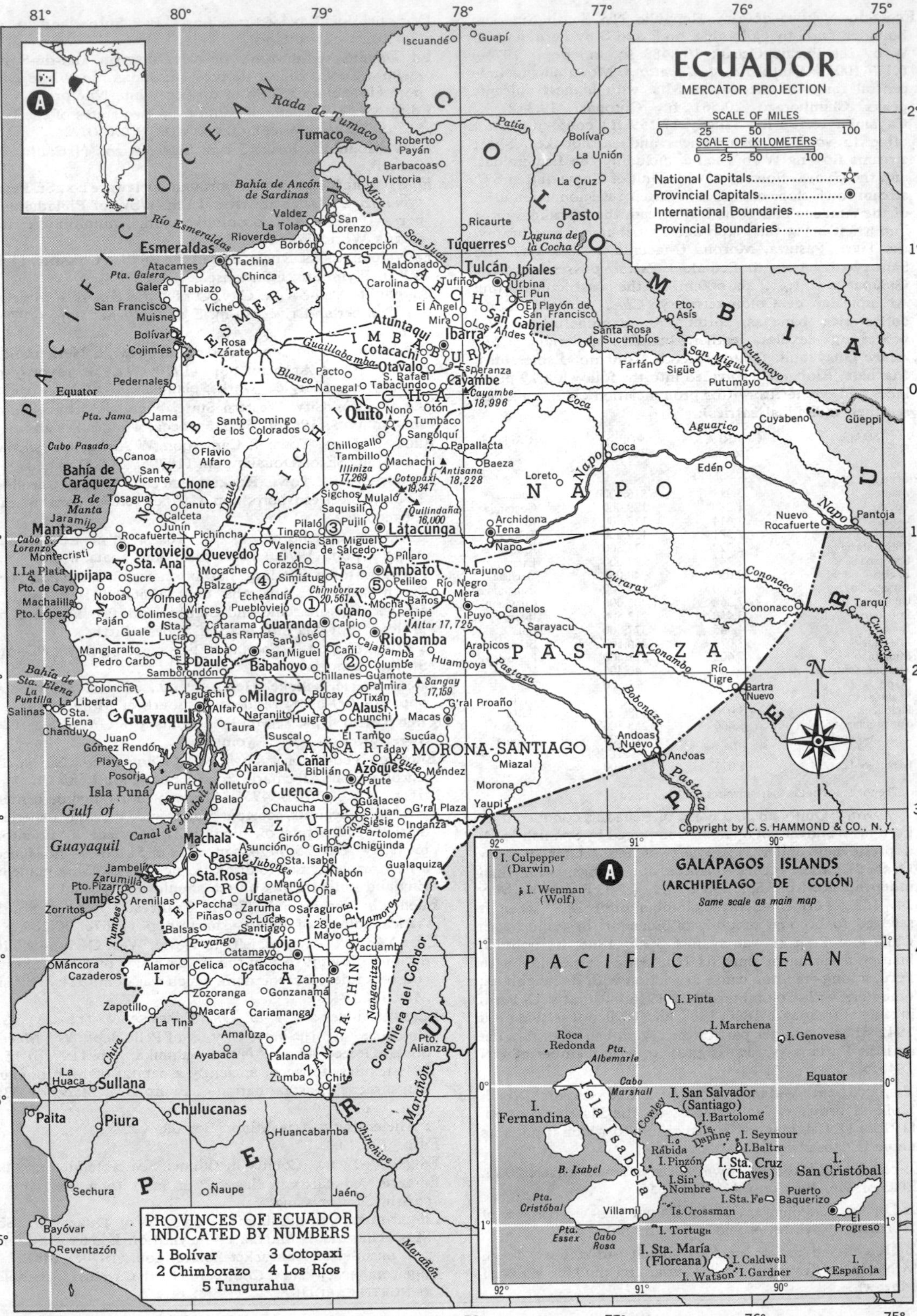
ECUADOR
MERCATOR PROJECTION
SCALE OF MILES
0 25 50 100
SCALE OF KILOMETERS
0 25 50 100
National Capitals
Provincial Capitals
International Boundaries
Provincial Boundaries
PACIFIC OCEAN
COLOMBIA
PERU
ESMERALDAS
CARCHI
IMBABURA
PICHINCHA
MANABI
NAPO
PASTAZA
MORONA-SANTIAGO
GUAYAS
CAÑAR
AZUAY
EL ORO
LOJA
ZAMORA-CHINCHIPE
Quito
Guayaquil
Cuenca
Esmeraldas
Tulcán
Ibarra
Latacunga
Ambato
Riobamba
Guaranda
Babahoyo
Portoviejo
Machala
Loja
Azogues
Tena
Puyo
Macas
Zamora
Manta
Tumaco
Pasto
Ipiales
Rada de Tumaco
Bahía de Ancón de Sardinas
Gulf of Guayaquil
Isla Puná
Canal de Jambelí
Cotopaxi 19,347
Chimborazo 20,561
Cayambe 18,996
Antisana 18,228
Illiniza 17,269
Quilindaña 16,000
Altar 17,725
Sangay 17,159
Cordillera del Cóndor
Napo
Pastaza
Marañón
Putumayo
Aguarico
Curaray
Copyright by C. S. HAMMOND & CO., N. Y.
Longitude West 78° of Greenwich
PROVINCES OF ECUADOR INDICATED BY NUMBERS
1 Bolívar
2 Chimborazo
3 Cotopaxi
4 Los Ríos
5 Tungurahua
A
GALÁPAGOS ISLANDS (ARCHIPIÉLAGO DE COLÓN)
Same scale as main map
I. Culpepper (Darwin)
I. Wenman (Wolf)
I. Pinta
I. Marchena
I. Genovesa
Roca Redonda
I. Fernandina
Isla Isabela
I. San Salvador (Santiago)
I. Bartolomé
I. Seymour
I. Baltra
I. Rábida
I. Pinzón
I. Sta. Cruz (Chaves)
I. San Cristóbal
Puerto Baquerizo
I. Sta. Fe
Villamil
I. Tortuga
I. Sta. María (Floreana)
I. Caldwell
I. Gardner
I. Watson
I. Española
Equator

Edge·cumbe, Mount \-'ej-kəm\. Extinct volcano at S end of Kruzof I. opp. Sitka, SE Alaska; 3467 ft.; known also as **Cape Edgecumbe.**

Edge·field \'ej-ˌfēld\. 1 County in W South Carolina. See table at SOUTH CAROLINA.
2 Town, its ⊗, 21 m. NW of Aiken; pop. (1970c) 2750; cotton, peaches.

Edge·hill *or* **Edge Hill** \'ej-'hil\. Ridge in S Warwickshire, cen. England, 7 m. NW of Banbury; scene of an indecisive battle Oct. 23, 1642 bet. Royalists under Charles I and forces of Parliament under earl of Essex.

Edge Island. Island, SE Spitsbergen archipelago, Norway, Arctic Ocean; 1970 sq. m.

Edge·mont \'ej-ˌmänt\. City, Fall River co., SW corner of South Dakota, near Black Hills 22 m. WSW of Hot Springs; pop. (1970c) 1174; diversified farming.

Edg·er·ton \'ej-ər-tən\. City, Rock co., S Wisconsin, 11 m. N of Janesville; pop. (1970c) 4118; tobacco.

Edge·wa·ter \'ej-ˌwȯt-ər, -ˌwät-\. 1 Town, Jefferson co., cen. Colorado, 5 m. W of Denver; pop. (1970c) 4886.
2 Town, Volusia co., E Florida; pop. (1970c) 3348.
3 Borough, Bergen co., NE corner of New Jersey, on Hudson river 7 m. NNE of Jersey City; pop. (1970c) 4987; aluminum, chemicals.

Edge·wood \'ej-ˌwu̇d\. 1 City, Kenton co., N Kentucky; pop. (1970c) 4139.
2 Village, S Harford co., NE Maryland, 18 m. NE of Baltimore; pop. (1970c) 8551; site of **Edgewood Arsenal,** with Army Chemical Center and Chemical Corps School.
3 Borough, Allegheny co., SW Pennsylvania, 7 m. E of Pittsburgh; pop. (1970c) 5138.

Edge·worth \'ej-wərth\. Borough, Allegheny co., SW Pennsylvania, on Ohio river 13 m. WNW of Pittsburgh; pop. (1970c) 3186; birthplace of Ethelbert Nevin.

Édhessa. See EDESSA 1.

Edi·na \i-'dī-nə\. 1 Village, Hennepin co., SE cen. Minnesota, 8 m. SW of Minneapolis; pop. (1970c) 44,046.
2 City, ⊗ of Knox co., NE Missouri, 22 m. E of Kirksville; pop. (1970c) 1574.

Ed·in·boro \'ed-ən-ˌbər-ə, -ˌbə-rə\. Borough, Erie co., NW corner of Pennsylvania, on a lake ab. 18 m. S of Erie; pop. (1970c) 4871; Edinboro State Coll. (1859).

Ed·in·burg \'ed-ᵊn-ˌbərg\. 1 Town, Bartholomew and Johnson cos., cen. Indiana, 30 m. SSE of Indianapolis; pop. (1970c) 4906; veneer mill, furniture factory.
2 City, ⊗ of Hidalgo co., S Texas, 10 m. NNE of McAllen; pop. (1970c) 17,163; citrus-fruit canning; Pan American Coll. (1927).

Ed·in·burgh \'ed-ᵊn-ˌbər, -ˌbə-rə, -b(ə-)rə\. 1 *or* **Edinburghshire.** See MIDLOTHIAN.
2 City and burgh, ✱ of Scotland and ⊗ of Midlothian co., SE Scotland, on S shore of Firth of Forth; pop. (1971p) 453,422; publishing, marine engineering; glassware, chemicals; tourism; built on several hills; the Old Town is on a rock, very steep on W end where castle stands and sloping toward the E where Holyrood palace is located; New Town is W of the castle rock, separated from it by a valley, now site of public gardens; Univ. of Edinburgh (1583), Heriot-Watt Univ. (1966).
History: Probably originated with castle erected by Edwin of Northumbria who defeated the Picts early in 7th cent. A.D.; royal residence of Malcolm Canmore in 11th cent.; Canongate, later annexed to Edinburgh, rose about the abbey of Holyrood (*q.v.*); granted charter and rights over town of Leith by Robert the Bruce; capital of Scottish kingdom and meeting place of Parliament after 1437; lost political importance after accession of James VI to English throne 1603 and union of Scotland (*q.v.*) with England 1707; proclaimed Charles II king 1649 and captured by Cromwell 1650; New Town built in 18th cent.; became a literary and educational center.

Ed·ing·ton \'ed-iŋ-tən\. Village and parish, Wiltshire, S England; pop. (1961c) 748; 14th cent. priory church; scene of Alfred's victory over the Danes 878.

Edir·ne \ā-'dir-nə\ *or formerly* **Adri·an·o·ple** \'ā-drē-ə-'nō-pəl\. 1 Province of W Turkey, Europe, a part of E Thrace. See table at TURKEY.
2 *anc.* **Adri·an·op·o·lis** \ˌā-drē-ə-'näp-ə-ləs\ *or* **Ha·dri·an·op·o·lis** \ˌhā-\. City, its ✱, on both banks of the Tundzha river at its confluence with the Maritsa (Meriç), NW Turkey, 130 m. NW of İstanbul; pop. (1965c) 46,091; cheese, leather, soap, cotton; a number of mosques, incl. one built by Sinan.
History: Early Thracian town rebuilt and renamed by Roman emperor Hadrian c. 125 A.D.; scene of the important battle in which the Roman emperor Valens fell before the Visigoths who had crossed the Danube 378; scene of defeat of the Bulgarian dynasty of Asen by the Greek emperor Theodore II 1254; conquered by the Avars, Bulgarians, and Crusaders, became Turkish 1361; residence of sultans until 1453; captured by the Russians 1829, 1879; by Treaty of Adrianople 1829 Russia secured control of Danube mouths; taken by Bulgaria 1913, restored to Turks 1922.

Ed·i·son \'ed-ə-sən\. Urban township, Middlesex co., cen. New Jersey, SW of Elizabeth; pop. (1970c) 67,120; Middlesex County Coll. (1964).

Ed·is·to \'ed-ə-ˌstō\. River, S and SW South Carolina; ab. 150 m. long; rises (**South Fork Edisto**) in E Edgefield co., flows SE into Atlantic Ocean.

Edisto Island. 1 Island at mouth of Edisto river, S extremity of Charleston co., SE South Carolina; 54 sq. m.
2 Village on the island, in Edisto Island township.

Edith Cav·ell, Mount \-ˌēd-əth-'kav-əl, -kə-'vel\. Peak, Jasper National Park, SW Alberta, Canada, near British Columbia border; 11,033 ft.

Ed·mond \'ed-mən(d)\. City, Oklahoma co., cen. Oklahoma, 13 m. N of Oklahoma City; pop. (1970c) 16,653; gas and oil wells; Central State Coll. (1891).

Ed·monds \'ed-mən(d)z\. City, Snohomish co., NW cen. Washington, N of Seattle; pop. (1970c) 23,998; oil refining; fruit; Edmonds Community Coll. (1967).

Ed·mon·son \'ed-mən-sən\. County in Kentucky. See table at KENTUCKY.

Ed·mon·ton \'ed-mən-tən\. 1 City, ⊗ of Metcalfe co., S Kentucky; pop. (1970c) 958.
2 City, ✱ of Alberta, Canada, in S cen. part of province on both banks of North Saskatchewan river; pop. (1971p) 434,116, met. area pop. 490,811; petrochemicals; oil refineries, meat-packing plants; retailing center of rich agricultural area; Univ. of Alberta (1906), Concordia Coll. (1921), Saint Joseph's Coll. (1927), Christian Training Inst. (1939); portion on S bank is former town of **Strath·co·na** \strath-'kō-nə\, annexed 1911; a leading railroad and air center of W Canada; originally established 1795 as a fort and trading post of the Hudson's Bay Company; major oil reserves discovered nearby 1947.
3 Former municipal borough, now part of the Greater London borough of Enfield, England; residence of Charles Lamb, William Cowper, and John Keats.

Ed·munds \'ed-mən(d)z\. County in South Dakota. See table at SOUTH DAKOTA.

Ed·munds·ton \'ed-mən-stən\. City, ⊗ of Madawaska co., NW New Brunswick, Canada, on upper St. John river across from NE Maine; pop. (1971p) 12,089; lumber; fishing; Coll. Saint-Louis (1946), École de Musique (1950).

Ed·na \'ed-nə\. City, ⊗ of Jackson co., SE Texas, 25 m. ENE of Victoria; pop. (1970c) 5332.

Edo. See TOKYO 2.

Edom \'ēd-əm\ *also* **Se·ir** \'sē-ər\. Ancient country S of Dead Sea, along both sides of the Wadi al-'Araba, with indefinite boundaries; mountainous and largely barren;

included summits of Hor and Seir; according to Bible (*Gen.* xxxvi) the land given to Esau (or Edom); chief town and capital Sela (Petra); with some shifting of boundaries to include S Judaea, became known in Maccabean and Roman times as Idumaea (*q.v.*).

Edre·mit \ˌed-rə-ˈmēt\ *or anc.* **Ad·ra·myt·ti·um** \ˌad-rə-ˈmit-ē-əm\. Town, Balıkesir prov., NW Turkey in Asia, near Aegean Sea at head of Gulf of Edremit; pop. (1965c) 25,003.

Edremit, Gulf of *or anc.* **Gulf of Adramyttium.** Inlet of Aegean Sea, on W coast of Turkey in Asia, opp. N coast of island of Lesbos.

Edsel Ford Ranges. See FORD RANGES.

Edsin. See O-CHI-NA.

Ed·son \ˈed-sən\. Town, Alberta, Canada, 117 m. W of Edmonton; pop. (1971p) 3817; timber; agriculture.

Edu·ni, Mount \-i-ˈd(y)ü-nē\. Peak, W Mackenzie dist., Northwest Territories, Canada, in NE part of Mackenzie Mts.; 7716 ft.

Ed·ward, Lake \-ˈed-wərd\. Lake in E cen. Africa, on the boundary bet. NE Zaire and SW Uganda, S of Lake Albert with which it is connected by the Semliki river; 830 sq. m.; discovered by Stanley 1889; formerly called **Al·bert Ed·ward Ny·an·za** \ˌal-bərt . . . nē-ˈan-zə, -nī-\.

Edward VIII Bay. Inlet of Indian Ocean on coast of Antarctica, bet. Kemp Coast and Enderby Land, at 66°50′S, 57°E; ab. 12 m. wide.

Edwardesabad. See BANNU 2.

Ed·wards \ˈed-wərdz\. Name of counties in three states of the U.S. See tables at ILLINOIS, KANSAS, TEXAS.

Edward VII Peninsula *or formerly* **King Edward VII Land.** Peninsula, Marie Byrd Land, on E shore of Ross Sea, Antarctica, lat. 77°44′S, long. 155°W; claimed for Great Britain by Capt. Scott 1902; included in Ross Dependency (*q.v.*).

Edwards Plateau. Highland region of W Texas; alt. bet. 2000 and 5000 ft.; source of tributaries of the Colorado, Nueces, and Rio Grande rivers and bordered on the W by the Pecos; centers in Schleicher and Sutton cos.

Ed·wards·ville \ˈed-wərdz-ˌvil\. 1 City, ⊗ of Madison co., SW Illinois, 17 m. NE of East St. Louis; pop. (1970c) 11,070; coal mining; radiators and brass products.
2 Borough, Luzerne co., E Pennsylvania, 3 m. WNW of Wilkes-Barre; pop. (1970c) 5633; coal mining.

Eek·loo \ˈāk-(ˌ)lō\. Commune, East Flanders prov., NW cen. Belgium, 11 m. NW of Gent; pop. (1969e) 19,141; steel, textiles; brewing; received town charter 1270.

Eel \ˈē(ə)l\. River, NW California, rises in N Mendocino co., flows NW into Pacific Ocean.

Ee·ragh \ˈē-rək\. See ARAN ISLANDS.

Eesti. See ESTONIAN SOVIET SOCIALIST REPUBLIC.

Eestimaa. See ESTONIAN SOVIET SOCIALIST REPUBLIC.

Efa·te \ā-ˈfät-ē\ *or* **Va·té** \vä-ˈtā\ *also* **Sand·wich Island** \ˈsan-(ˌ)(d)wich-\. Island, cen. New Hebrides Is., SW Pacific Ocean; 26 m. long by 14 m. wide; 353 sq. m.; pop. (1967c) 9452; chief town Vila, which is the administrative center of New Hebrides Is.; good harbors at Vila and Havannah.

Ef·fi·gy Mounds National Monument \ˌef-ə-jē-\. See UNITED STATES, *National Monuments.*

Ef·fing·ham \ˈef-iŋ-ˌham\. 1 Name of counties in two states of the U.S. See tables at GEORGIA and ILLINOIS.
2 City, ⊗ of Effingham co., SE cen. Illinois; pop. (1970c) 9458; electrical appliances, lumber.

Ef·fon–Alai·ye \ˌe-fōn-ə-ˈlī-(y)ə\. Town, Western State, Nigeria; pop. (1969e) 77,804.

Efo·gi \e-ˈfō-gē\. Village in Owen Stanley Range, Papua New Guinea, New Guinea I., 20 m. NE of Port Moresby; severe fighting Sept.–Oct. 1942.

Ega·di Islands \ˈeg-ə-dē-\ *or Ital.* **Iso·le Egadi** \ˌē-zə-(ˌ)lā-\ *or Eng.* **Ae·ga·di·an Isles** \ē-ˈgād-ē-ən-\ *or anc.* **Ae·ga·tes** \ē-ˈgāt-ēz\. Group of islands in Mediterranean Sea off W coast of Sicily, Italy; 15 sq. m.; pop. (1968e) 5782; politically constitute Favignana commune in Trapani prov., NW Sicily; chief islands Marettimo and Favignana. Scene of naval battle in which Romans destroyed the Carthaginian fleet thus terminating the First Punic War 241 B.C.

Ege·des·min·de \ˈā-gəd-ə-ˌsmin-(d)e\. Settlement on S Disko Bay, W Greenland; pop. (1968e) 3543.

Egeo, Isole Italiane Dell'. See AEGEAN ISLANDS 3.

Eger \ˈā-gər\. 1 River, West Germany and Czechoslovakia. See OHŘE.
2 City, Czechoslovakia. See CHEB.

Eger \ˈeg-ˌe(ə)r\ *or Ger.* **Er·lau** \ˈe(ə)r-ˌlau̇\. City, ⊗ of Heves co., N cen. Hungary, 25 m. SW of Miskolc; pop. (1970p) 45,229; machinery; exports wine; occupied by Turks 1596–1687.

Egerdir. See EĞRİDİR.

Eger·sund \ˈā-gər-ˌsu̇n\. Seaport town, Rogaland co., SW Norway, 35 m. S of Stavanger; pop. (1970e) 10,197; fisheries.

Egg Harbor \ˈeg-, ˈāg-\. Early name of Somers Point, New Jersey.

Egg Harbor City. City, Atlantic co., SE New Jersey, 17 m. NW of Atlantic City; pop. (1970c) 4304; vineyards; founded by German immigrants 1850.

Egg Island. Barren rock off Niihau, NW Hawaii. See LEHUA ISLAND.

Egg Island Point. Point on S coast of Cumberland co., SW New Jersey, extending into Delaware Bay.

Egg·mühl *or* **Eck·mühl** \ˈek-ˌmyü(ə)l\. Village, Bavaria, West Germany, S of Regensburg; pop. (1967e) 930; scene of battle Apr. 22, 1809 in which French, Bavarians, and Württembergers under Napoleon defeated Austrians under Archduke Charles.

Eg·ham \ˈeg-əm\. Urban district, Surrey, S England, on the Thames 20 m. WSW of London; pop. (1971p) 30,510; light engineering; the field of Runnymede (*q.v.*) lies along the riverside; Royal Holloway Coll. for Women (1886).

Eg·ma Plateau \ˌeg-mə-\. Highland region, cen. Sinai Penin. (*q.v.*), NE Egypt; highest point Ras al-Geneina 5334 ft.

Egmont, Cape. Cape on SW cen. coast of North I., New Zealand, at end of W bulge of North I.

Egmont Cape. 1 Cape, NE Cape Breton I., Nova Scotia, SE Canada.
2 Cape at S end of **Egmont Bay** (inlet of Northumberland Strait), W Prince Edward I., SE Canada.

Eg·mont, Mount \-ˈeg-ˌmänt\ *or Maori* **Ta·ra·na·ki** \ˌtär-ə-ˈnäk-ē\. Volcanic peak, W cen. North I., New Zealand; 8260 ft.; noted for its symmetry and beauty.

Egorevsk. See YEGORYEVSK.

Egou·me·nit·sa *or* **Igou·me·nít·sa** \ˌē-gə-mə-ˈnēt-sə\. Town, ✱ of Thesprotia dept., Epirus, Greece; pop. (1971p) 4395.

Eg·re·mont \ˈeg-rə-ˌmänt\. Parish, formerly urban district, Cumberland, NW England, on the Ehen 38 m. SW of Carlisle; pop. (1961c) 6582.

Eğ·ri·dir \ˌā-rə-ˈdi(ə)r, ˌeg-rə-\ *or* **Eger·dir** \ˌā-ər-ˈdi(ə)r, ˌā-gər-\ *also* **Ig·ri·dir** \ˌē(g)-rə-ˈdi(ə)r\. Town, İsparta prov., Turkey in Asia, at S end of Eğridir Lake.

Eğridir Lake *or Turk.* **Eğridir Gö·lü** \-gə-ˈ(y)ü\. Lake (*gölü*) in W Turkey in Asia, NEof İsparta; 30 m. long by 3 to 10 m. wide; no known outlet.

Egripos. See EVRIPOS.

Egypt \ˈē-jəpt\; *officially* **Arab Republic of Egypt** *or formerly* **United Arab Republic;** *Arab.* **Miṣr** \ˈmisrᵊ\; *anc.* **Ae·gyp·tus** \ē-ˈjip-təs\. Republic, NE Africa (with small part [Sinai Penin.] in Asia), bounded on N by the Mediterranean Sea, on E by Israel and the Red Sea, on S by Sudan, and on W by Libya; 386,900 sq. m., total habitable area ab. 13,835 sq. m.; pop. (1970e) 33,329,000; ✱ Cairo.

Physical features: Only mountains are those in Sinai Penin. in NE (bet. Gulf of Suez on W and Gulf of ʻAqaba on E) where Egma Plateau culminates in Ras al-Geneina 5328 ft. and Gebel Musa group (highest point Gebel Katherina, 8652 ft.) and in the range (3000 to 7150 ft.) extending along Red Sea coast from Suez to border of

Sudan. *Deserts:* Has 3 large deserts: (1) Arabian, in E bet. the Nile and the mountains along the Red Sea and Gulf of Suez; (2) Western, in W cen. part; (3) E part of Libyan Desert along SW border; best known oases the Khārga (S cen. part), Dakhla (cen.), Farafra (W cen.), and Siwa (NW); bet. Western Desert and Mediterranean coast is Qattara Depression. *Nile river:* Of critical importance to the life of the country is the Nile; its delta traditionally referred to as **Lower Egypt** and its valley S of 30°N lat. is known as **Upper Egypt;** in S Aswān High Dam forms Lake Nasser. *Chief products:* Cotton, wheat, barley, corn; livestock; oil, manganese, phosphates, iron ore, salt; manufactured products include: textiles, iron and steel, chemicals, leather goods, cement. *Chief cities:* Cairo, Alexandria, Giza, Suez, Port Said, Tanta. Divided into the following 25 governorates (for pronunciation of their names, see their individual entries):

NAME	AREA (sq. m.)	POP. (1970e)	CAPITAL
Alexandria	1,035	2,032,000	Alexandria
Aswān	262	651,000	Aswān
Asyūt	591	1,487,000	Asyūt
Beheira	1,772	2,215,000	Damanhūr
Beni Suef	510	979,000	Beni Suef
Cairo	83	4,961,000	Cairo
Damietta	227	472,000	Damietta
Daqahlīya	1,340	2,492,000	Al-Mansūra
Faiyūm	705	1,008,000	Al-Faiyūm
Gharbīya	750	2,080,000	Tanta
Giza	390	1,934,000	Giza
Ismailia	557	395,000	Ismailia
Kafr al-Sheikh	1,327	1,234,000	Kafr al-Sheikh
Matrūh	1,144	132,000	Matrūh
Minūfīya	662	1,529,000	Shibīn al-Kōm
Minya	873	1,813,000	Al-Minya
New Valley	145,369	63,000	Al-Kharijah
Port Said	28	313,000	Port Said
Qalyubīya	375	1,379,000	Benha
Qena	715	1,559,000	Qena
Red Sea	78,643	40,000	Ghurdaqah
Sawhaj	597	1,764,000	Sawhaj
Sharqīya	1,614	2,344,000	Zagazig
Sinai[1]	23,442	140,000	Al-'Arīsh
Suez	6,888	315,000	Suez

[1] Occupied by Israel 1967.

History: A very ancient kingdom, by about 3000 B.C. Egypt had developed one of the early civilizations of ancient world; Thinite dynasty, founded by Menes, which united Upper and Lower Egypt c. 3100 B.C., the first of 30 dynasties which ruled ancient Egypt (c. 3100–332 B.C.); pyramids built under IVth dynasty (c. 2613–2494 B.C.) of Old Kingdom which had capital at Memphis; Karnak, near Thebes, monument of XIIth dynasty (c. 2000–1788 B.C.) under which Egypt began expansion as an imperial power, conquering Ethiopia, and later, under Thutmose III 1501–1447 B.C. (XVIIIth dynasty), Palestine and Syria; in decline from c. 1100 B.C. dominated by priest-kings, Libyan, Ethiopian, Assyrian, and Persian rulers; driven from Asiatic holdings by Nebuchadnezzar (see BABYLON 2) 605 B.C.; history of ancient dynasties closed with Alexander's conquest 332 B.C.; ancient Egyptians invented calendar (traditional date 4241 B.C.), papyrus and hieroglyphic writing, earliest sea-going ships, created massive architectural monuments, pyramids, temples, sculpture (see ABU SIMBEL, ABYDOS 2, GIZA, PYRAMIDS, KARNAK, LUXOR, etc.).

Center of Hellenistic culture at Alexandria (*q.v.*) under Ptolemies 323–30 B.C.; part of Roman Empire from 30 B.C. until Arab conquest 640 A.D.; Cairo (*q.v.*) seat of Fatimid caliphate which ruled Egypt 969–1171; ruled by Mamelukes 1250–1517; nominally part of Ottoman Empire 1517–1914; invaded by Napoleon 1798, but French forced to withdraw (see ABUKIR); became virtually independent with accession of pasha, Mehemet Ali, 1805; by revolts against Sultan 1832 and 1839, obtained status of autonomous hereditary principality; under Khedive Ismail Pasha, Suez Canal (*q.v.*) completed 1869; occupied 1882 by British, who shared dual control with France 1879–82; (for problem of Sudan, see history at SUDAN 2); administered by Evelyn Baring (Lord Cromer) 1883–1907; declared British protectorate 1914. Achieved independence 1922, but issues of British military occupation and Sudan only settled by treaty of 1936; 1923 constitution reintroduced 1935. Neutral in World War II; invaded Sept. 1940 by Italians, who were driven out by British Dec. 1940; invaded by Germans Nov. 1941 and again June–July 1942 when they reached Al-Alamein, but they were driven out after battle of Al-Alamein Oct. 1942. For 1948–49 clash with Israelis, see history at ISRAEL 2; established a republic 1953, a year after overthrow of King Farouk by a military coup; intervention by British, French, and Israeli forces (Oct.–Nov.) following nationalization of Suez Canal Company July 1956; foreign troops evacuated (Dec. 1956–Jan. 1966) and replaced by a United Nations peace-keeping force (arrival of first units Nov. 15, 1956); union with Syria formed 1958, dissolved 1961; intervened in support of republican regime in Yemen (✻ San'a) 1962–67; fought war with Israel (June 1967) in which Israelis occupied Sinai Peninsula; formed confederation with Libya and Syria 1971 (see ARAB REPUBLICS, CONFEDERATION OF).

Ehen \ˈē-ən\. River in Cumberland, NW England; 12 m. long; flows out of Ennerdale Water past Egremont and on S to the Irish Sea.

Ehi·me \ā-hē-ˌmā\. Prefecture, Shikoku, Japan; 2183 sq. m.; pop. (1970c) 1,418,124; ✻ Matsuyama; interior mountainous; rice, tea; fishing; chemicals, salt, machinery.

Eh·ren·breit·stein \ˌer-ən-ˈbrīt-ˌs(h)tīn\. Former town, now part of Koblenz, Rhineland-Palatinate, West Germany, on the right bank of the Rhine river, at foot of a rocky ridge 387 ft. high which was formerly site of an ancient fortress; ridge became a possession 1018 of Emperor Henry II; fortress often besieged, later strengthened during wars of 18th cent., and finally razed by Treaty of Versailles; taken by American army Mar. 27, 1945.

Eïao \ē-ˈyau̇, -ˈyä-ˌō\. Small island, Marquesas Is., ab. 56 m. NW by N of Nuku Hiva I.; 6½ m. long; formerly a place of exile for French convicts; now uninhabited.

Ei·bar \ˈā-ˌbär\. City, Guipúzcoa prov., N Spain, 27 m. WSW of San Sebastián; pop. (1970p) 37,073; manufactures steel products.

Ei·ben·stock \ˈī-bən-ˌstäk, -shtȯk\. Town, Karl-Marx-Stadt dist., East Germany, near Mulde river ab. 16 m. SSE of Zwickau; pop. (1965e) 9100; tambour embroidery introduced 1775; manufactures lace, tin, and iron; cattle market; to Saxony 1534.

Ei·bhinn \ˈā-vən\. Mountain, S Inverness co., NW cen. Scotland, 6 m. W of Loch Ericht; 3611 ft.

Eichs·feld \ˈīks-ˌfelt\. Hilly district in W Erfurt dist., East Germany, just NW of Thuringia; contains source of Leine river.

Eich·stätt \ˈīk-ˌs(h)tet\ *or* **Eich·stadt** \-ˌs(h)tät\. Town, W Bavaria, West Germany, on the Altmühl ab. 67 m. NNW of Munich; pop. (1968e) 10,274; tourism; old town and place of pilgrimage containing tomb of St. Willibald (700?–786); has fine Gothic cathedral. Originally a Roman station; made bishopric 745 by Boniface, its bishops becoming princes of the empire; in 19th cent. a princedom granted to Eugène de Beauharnais, subject to Bavaria.

Eick·el \ˈī-kəl\. Former town; since 1927 part of Wanne-Eickel (*q.v.*), West Germany.

Ei·der \ˈīd-ər\. River, West Germany, forming boundary bet. Schleswig and Holstein; 117 m. long; rises E of Rendsburg and flows W into North Sea S of the Eiderstedt Penin.; importance decreased since completion of the Kiel Canal (Nord-Ostsee Kanal). In 19th cent. gave its name to a Danish party (the *Eider Danes*) which advocated the incorporation of Schleswig into Denmark.

Ei·der·stedt \ˈīd-ər-ˌs(h)tet\. Peninsula extending into Heligoland Bight on W coast of Schleswig-Holstein, West Germany.

Eids·vold \ˈāts-ˌvȯl\. Commune, Akershus co., SE Norway, 30 m. NE of Oslo; pop. (1970e) 13,501; paper; new constitution drawn up here May 17, 1814 providing for a unicameral national assembly and denying the king an absolute veto.

Ei·el·son Field \ˌī-əl-sən-\. U.S. airfield, E Alaska, on Tanana river on Alaska Highway, 26 m. SE of Fairbanks; formerly known as **Mile 26.**

Ei·fel \ˈī-fəl\. Hilly region in West Germany, W of the Rhine river, NW of the Moselle river and NE of Luxembourg; ab. 40 m. long, 20 m. wide; highest point 3280 ft. in E part; a barren region, chiefly of geologic interest; shows evidence of volcanic action; limestone moors, many lakes (called crater lakes).

Ei·ger \ˈī-gər\. Peak in the Bernese Alps, W cen. Switzerland, NW of the Finsteraarhorn; 13,025 ft.

Eigg \ˈeg, ˈāg\. Small island of the Inner Hebrides, off W coast of Scotland; administratively a part of Inverness co.

Ei·jer·land \ˈī-(y)ər-ˌlänt\. North section of Texel I., Netherlands.

Eil \ˈī(ə)l\. Coastal town, NE Somalia, E Africa; terminus of road from Mogadisho.

Eil, Loch \läk-ˈē(ə)l, läk-\. Sea inlet, on border bet. Argyll and Inverness cos., W Scotland, extending 8½ m. W from N end of Loch Linnhe; connects on E with Caledonian Canal system.

Eilat. See ELATH 2.

Eil·don Hills \ˌē(ə)l-dən-\. Three conical peaks, Roxburgh co., SE Scotland, S of Melrose; highest 1385 ft.; prehistoric and Roman remains; rich in legendary lore.

Ei·len·burg \ˈī-lən-ˌbu̇(ə)rg\. Manufacturing city, Leipzig dist., East Germany, on the Mulde river 13 m. NE of Leipzig; pop. (1970e) 21,888; railroad junction; textiles, machinery, furniture; castle dating at least from the 10th cent.; town hall 1544–45; town dates from early 13th cent.; passed to Prussia 1815.

Ei·len·dorf \ˈī-lən-ˌdȯrf\. Commune, North Rhine-Westphalia state, West Germany, 4 m. E of Aachen; pop. (1968e) 13,094; stone quarries; chemicals, refractory products.

Eil Malk \ˈā(ə)l-ˈmälk\. Island, S cen. Palau Is., W Pacific Ocean, S of Urukthapel; bet. it and Peleliu I. 10 m. to the SW are many islets and reefs.

Ei·meo \ī-ˈmā-ō\. One of the Windward Is., Society Is., French Polynesia. See MOORÉA.

Ein·beck \ˈīn-ˌbek\. Industrial town, S Lower Saxony, West Germany, ab. 40 m. S of Hannover; pop. (1968e) 18,684; important esp. 15th–17th cents.; manufactures Einbeck (bock) beer, carpets. Grew up around monastery founded 1080; seat of princes of Grubenhagen (branch of the ducal house of Brunswick) 14th cent. to 1596; member of Hanseatic League.

Eind·ho·ven \ˈīnt-ˌhō-vən, ˈānt-\. Commercial and industrial commune, North Brabant prov., S Netherlands, 55 m. SE of Rotterdam; pop. (1970e) 188,831; produces electrical and radio apparatus, steel, textiles; technical univ. (1956); received charter 1232; in World War II marked S point of region invaded by Allied airborne troops Sept. 1944.

Ein·sie·deln \ˈīn-ˌzēd-ᵊln\. Commune, Schwyz canton, E cen. Switzerland, 9 m. NNE of Schwyz; pop. (1970c) 10,020; furniture; 18th cent. Benedictine abbey (founded 9th or 10th cent.) containing a famous image of the Virgin which is the object of annual pilgrimages; Zwingli parish priest here 1516–18; birthplace of Paracelsus.

Eipel. See IPEL'.

Ei·re \ˈar-ə, ˈar-ē, ˈer-, ˈār-, ˈī-r-\ *or* **Ire·land** \ˈī(ə)r-lənd\; *from 1922 to 1937* **Irish Free State** \ˈī(ə)r-ish-\ *or Gaelic* **Saor·stat Eir·eann** *or* **Saor·stát Éir·eann** \ˌsa(ə)r-ˌstȯt-ˈer-ən\; *since Apr. 18, 1949 officially called* **Republic of Ireland.** Republic occupying S, cen., and NW Ireland; 26,600 sq. m.; pop. (1971p) 2,971,230; ✱ Dublin. *Physical features:* Extends bet. 51°27′N (Mizen Head in co. Cork the southernmost point of the island) and 55°23′N (Malin Head in co. Donegal the northernmost point of Ireland); comprises most of the territory of Ireland, which consists geographically of a central plain with lakes (*loughs*) in N, cen., and W parts, and with groups of hills averaging 2000 to 3000 ft. on N, W, and S. Contains the island's highest point Carrantuohill 3414 ft., in Macgillicuddy's Reeks in SW. Coastline irregular, esp. in SW and W where it is indented by Bantry Bay, Kenmare River, Dingle Bay, Galway Bay, Clew Bay, Sligo Bay, Donegal Bay, and the estuary of the Shannon; has many good harbors. *Chief lakes:* Loughs Mask, Corrib, and Conn in W, Ree and Derg in cen. part, and the beautiful lakes of Killarney in SW; shares with Northern Ireland the Erne and Foyle rivers (*qq.v.*) and Loughs Foyle and Carlingford (*qq.v.*). *Chief rivers:* Shannon (ab. 240 m. long, longest in the British Isles), in cen. part, Boyne and Liffey in E, Barrow, Nore, and Suir in SE, Blackwater and Lee in S. *Chief products:* Barley, wheat, oats, potatoes, sugar beets; livestock; manufacturing: textiles, farm machinery, fertilizers; brewing and distilling; tourism. *Chief cities:* Dublin, Cork, Limerick, Dun Laoghaire, Waterford, Galway, Dundalk. Divided into the following 26 counties (listed according to province; for pronunciation of their names, see their individual entries):

NAME[1]	AREA (sq. m.)	POP. (1971p)	CAPITAL
Connacht			
Galway	2,293	148,220	Galway
Leitrim	589	28,313	Carrick on Shannon
Mayo	2,084	109,497	Castlebar
Roscommon	951	53,497	Roscommon
Sligo	693	50,236	Sligo
Leinster			
Carlow	346	34,025	Carlow
Dublin	356	849,542	Dublin
Kildare	654	71,522	Naas
Kilkenny	796	61,811	Kilkenny
Laoighis	664	45,349	Maryborough
Longford	403	28,227	Longford
Louth	317	74,899	Dundalk
Meath	903	71,616	Trim
Offaly	771	51,834	Tullamore
Westmeath	681	53,557	Mullingar
Wexford	908	85,892	Wexford
Wicklow	782	66,270	Wicklow
Munster			
Clare	1,231	74,844	Ennis
Cork	2,880	351,735	Cork
Kerry	1,815	112,941	Tralee
Limerick	1,037	141,370	Limerick
Tipperary[2]	1,643	123,196	Clonmel
Waterford	710	76,932	Waterford
Ulster			
Cavan	730	52,674	Cavan
Donegal	1,865	108,000	Lifford
Monaghan	498	46,231	Monaghan

[1]In Irish idiom, *county* precedes the name, as in *county Cork, county Meath*.
[2]Divided for administrative purposes into Tipperary North Riding and Tipperary South Riding.

History: For history before 1922, see IRELAND. As Irish Free State, estab. 1922, a dominion in the (British) Commonwealth of Nations, Northern Ireland (*q.v.*) having been formed 1920; adopted constitution 1922; settled boundary with Northern Ireland 1925; under De Valera, gradually abandoned ties with British crown, in 1937 declaring Eire (its official new name) a sovereign, independent democratic state; remained associated for certain purposes with Commonwealth of Nations; neutral throughout World War II; refused request of Great Britain and United States Mar. 1944 to expel Axis representatives; by Republic of Ireland Act Dec. 1948 declared itself completely independent with no allegiance to British crown or membership in Commonwealth of Nations; officially proclaimed the Republic of Ireland Apr. 18 (Easter Monday), 1949; member of UN 1955; signed treaty of accession to European Economic Community 1972.

Eirinn. See ERIN.

Ei·se·nach \ˈīz-ᵊn-ˌäk, -ˌäḵ\. Manufacturing city, Erfurt dist., East Germany, 31 m. W of Erfurt; pop. (1969e) 50,777; agricultural machinery, electrical equipment, motor vehicles; 16th cent. town hall. Birthplace of Johann Sebastian Bach; place where Luther attended school 1498–1501. Originated in 12th cent.; capital of Thuringian landgraves; residence 1596 ff. of Ernestine line of princes; capital of duchy of Eisenach 1672–1741; united with Weimar 1741; part of Thuringia 1815.

Ei·sen·berg \ˈīz-ᵊn-ˌbərg, -ˌbe(ə)rg\. City, Gera dist., East Germany, 38 m. E of Erfurt; pop. (1970e) 13,671; bricks; foundry; first mentioned 1171; 16th cent. town hall, palace (1677–92).

Eisenburg. See VASVÁR.

Ei·sen·erz \ˈīz-ᵊn-ˌe(ə)rts\. Mining commune, N Styria, Austria, 16 m. NW of Leoben; pop. (1967e) 12,400; mining school; nearby is the Erzberg (*q.v.*); became city 1948.

Ei·sen·how·er, Mount \-ˈīz-ᵊn-ˌhau̇(-ə)r\ *or formerly* **Cas·tle Mountain** \ˌkas-əl-\. Mountain, S Alberta, Canada, W of Calgary, in Banff National Park; 8950 ft.; renamed 1946.

Ei·sen·hut \ˈīz-ᵊn-ˌhüt\. Mountain, SW Styria, Austria, NW of Klagenfurt; 8006 ft.; highest peak in Noric Alps.

Ei·sen·hüt·ten·stadt \ˈīz-ᵊn-ˌh(y)üt-ᵊn-ˌstat, -ˌs(h)tät\. City, Frankfurt dist., East Germany; pop. (1970e) 45,194; metallurgical works; pig iron; formed 1961.

Ei·sen·stadt \ˈīz-ᵊn-ˌstat, -ˌs(h)tät\. Town, ✱ of Burgenland, Austria, just W of Neusiedler Lake; pop. (1966e) 7700; textiles; in wine-producing region; home of Joseph Haydn 1760–90; until 1921 in Hungary.

Ei·ser·feld \ˈī-zər-ˌfelt\. City, North Rhine-Westphalia, West Germany, 56 m. NW of Frankfurt am Main; pop.

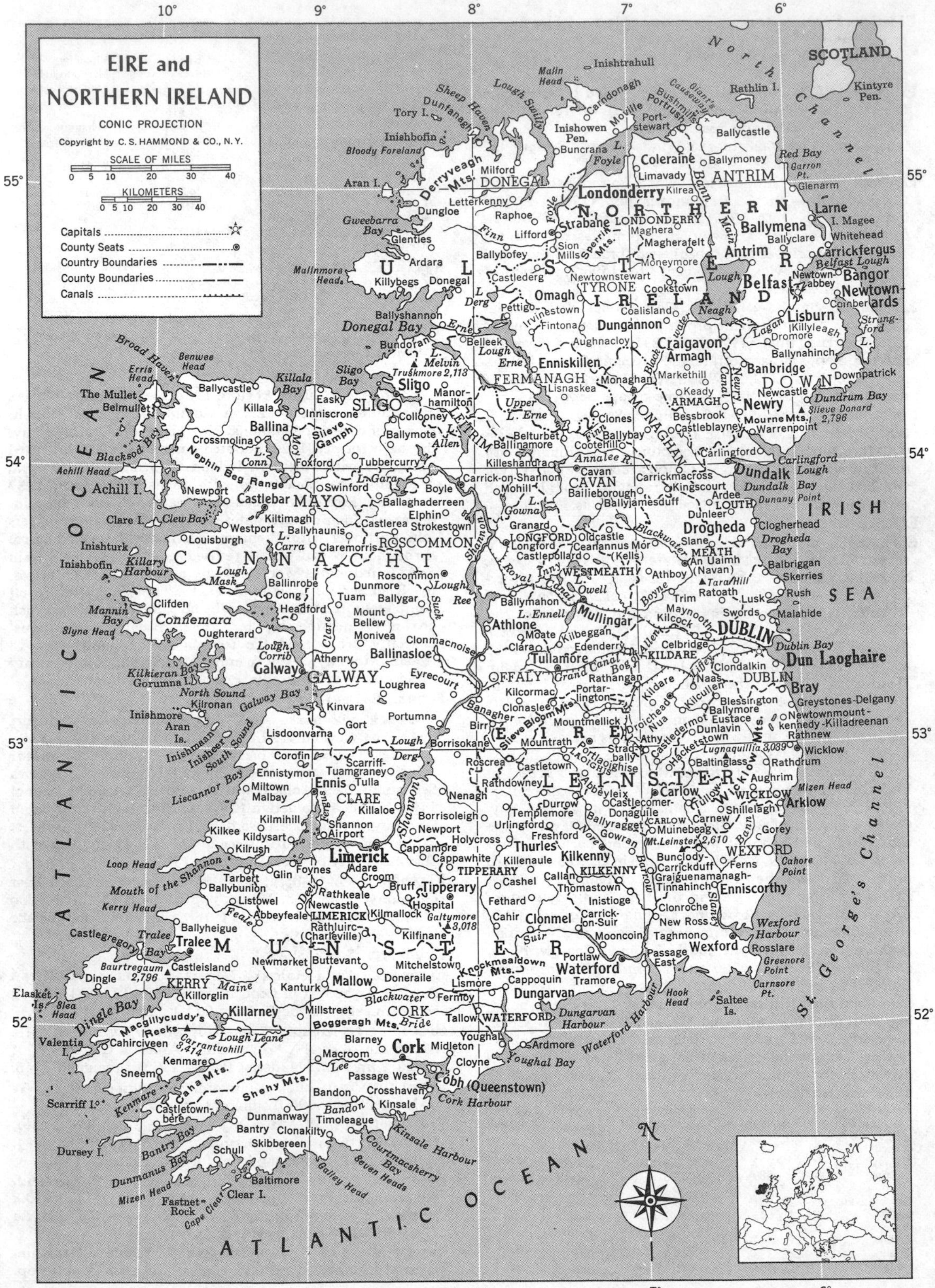

EIRE and
NORTHERN IRELAND
CONIC PROJECTION
Copyright by C. S. HAMMOND & CO., N. Y.
SCALE OF MILES
0 5 10 20 30 40
KILOMETERS
0 5 10 20 30 40
Capitals
County Seats
Country Boundaries
County Boundaries
Canals
10°
9°
8°
7°
6°
55°
54°
53°
52°
Longitude West of Greenwich
SCOTLAND
Kintyre Pen.
North Channel
Rathlin I.
Ballycastle
Red Bay
Garron Pt.
Glenarm
Larne
I. Magee
Whitehead
Carrickfergus
Belfast Lough
Bangor
Newtownards
Newtownabbey
Comber
Strangford L.
Killyleagh
Dromore
Ballynahinch
Downpatrick
Dundrum Bay
Newcastle
Slieve Donard 2,796
Mourne Mts.
Warrenpoint
Newry
Banbridge
DOWN
Lisburn
Lagan
Belfast
Antrim
Ballyclare
Ballymena
ANTRIM
Ballymoney
Coleraine
Giant's Causeway
Bushmills
Portrush
Portstewart
Limavady
Kilrea
Bann
Main
Malin Head
Inishtrahull
Carndonagh
Moville
Inishowen Pen.
Buncrana
L. Foyle
Lough Swilly
Sheep Haven
Dunfanaghy
Tory I.
Inishbofin
Bloody Foreland
Aran I.
Derryveagh Mts.
Milford
DONEGAL
Letterkenny
Raphoe
Lifford
Strabane
Sion Mills
Sperrin Mts.
Londonderry
LONDONDERRY
NORTHERN IRELAND
Maghera
Magherafelt
Moneymore
Cookstown
Newtownstewart
TYRONE
Omagh
Castlederg
Coalisland
Dungannon
Lough Neagh
Craigavon
Armagh
Markethill
Keady
ARMAGH
Bessbrook
Castleblayney
Newry Canal
Blackwater
Aughnacloy
Fintona
Irvinestown
Pettigo
L. Derg
Gweebarra Bay
Glenties
Dungloe
Ardara
Malinmore Head
Killybegs
Donegal
Ballybofey
Finn
Foyle
Ballyshannon
Donegal Bay
Erne
Bundoran
Belleek
Lough Erne
Enniskillen
FERMANAGH
Lisnaskea
Monaghan
MONAGHAN
Upper L. Erne
Clones
Ballybay
Castleblayney
Carlingford
Carlingford Lough
Dundalk
Dundalk Bay
Dunany Point
IRISH SEA
L. Melvin
Truskmore 2,113
Sligo
Sligo Bay
Manorhamilton
Collooney
LEITRIM
Ballymote
L. Allen
Belturbet
Ballinamore
Cootehill
Killeshandra
Annalee R.
Cavan
CAVAN
Carrickmacross
Kingscourt
Bailieborough
Ballyjamesduff
Ardee
LOUTH
Dunleer
Drogheda
Clogherhead
Drogheda Bay
Slane
MEATH
An Uaimh (Navan)
Balbriggan
Skerries
Rush
Lusk
Tara Hill
Ratoath
Athboy
Trim
Maynooth
Kilcock
Swords
Malahide
DUBLIN
Dublin Bay
Dun Laoghaire
Clondalkin
Bray
Greystones-Delgany
Newtownmountkennedy-Killadreenan
Rathnew
Wicklow
Rathdrum
Aughrim
WICKLOW
Arklow
Mizen Head
Wicklow Mts.
Lugnaquillia 3,039
Baltinglass
Blessington
Ballymore Eustace
Dunlavin
Hacketstown
Broad Haven
Benwee Head
Erris Head
Ballycastle
Killala Bay
Killala
The Mullet
Belmullet
Blacksod Bay
Crossmolina
L. Conn
Ballina
Moy
Inniscrone
Easky
SLIGO
Slieve Gamph
Nephin Beg Range
Achill Head
Achill I.
Newport
Castlebar
MAYO
Foxford
Swinford
Tubbercurry
L. Gara
Boyle
Carrick-on-Shannon
Mohill
L. Gowna
Granard
LONGFORD
Longford
Oldcastle
Ceanannus Mór (Kells)
Castlepollard
Blackwater
Ballaghaderreen
Elphin
Strokestown
Castlerea
Kiltimagh
Ballyhaunis
Claremorris
ROSCOMMON
Clare I.
Clew Bay
Westport
Louisburgh
L. Carra
Inishturk
Inishbofin
Killary Harbour
CONNACHT
Lough Mask
Ballinrobe
Cong
Roscommon
Lough Ree
Shannon
Royal Canal
Inny
WESTMEATH
L. Owell
Mullingar
Boyne
Ballymahon
L. Ennell
Athlone
Moate
Kilbeggan
Clara
Edenderry
KILDARE
Celbridge
Dunmore
Tuam
Ballygar
Suck
Mount Bellew
Monivea
Headford
Clifden
Mannin Bay
Connemara
Slyne Head
Oughterard
Lough Corrib
Clare
Athenry
Ballinasloe
Clonmacnoise
Tullamore
Grand Canal
Bog of Allen
Rathangan
Kildare
Naas
Kilcullen
Liffey
Galway
GALWAY
Galway Bay
Kilkieran Bay
Gorumna I.
North Sound
Kilronan
Inishmore
Aran Is.
Inishmaan
Inisheer
South Sound
Loughrea
Eyrecourt
OFFALY
Kilcormac
Portarlington
Banagher
Clonaslee
Slieve Bloom Mts.
Droichead Nua
Castledermot
Athy
Kinvara
Gort
Portumna
Birr
Mountmellick
EIRE
Lisdoonvarna
Lough Derg
Borrisokane
Mountrath
Portlaoighise
LAOIGHIS
Stradbally
Corofin
Ennistymon
Scarriff
Tuamgraney
Tulla
Roscrea
Castletown
Rathdowney
LEINSTER
Carlow
Tullow
Shillelagh
Liscannor Bay
Miltown Malbay
Ennis
Fergus
CLARE
Killaloe
Nenagh
Abbeyleix
Castlecomer-Donaguile
Durrow
Templemore
Ballyragget
CARLOW
Carnew
Muinebeag
Mt. Leinster 2,610
Gorey
Kilmihill
Kilkee
Kildysart
Shannon Airport
Borrisoleigh
Newport
Urlingford
Freshford
Nore
Gowran
Bunclody-Carrickduff
Ferns
WEXFORD
Bann
Loop Head
Kilrush
Limerick
Cappamore
Holycross
Thurles
Cappawhite
Killenaule
Kilkenny
KILKENNY
Barrow
Graiguenamanagh-Tinnahinch
Enniscorthy
Cahore Point
Mouth of the Shannon
Tarbert
Glin
Foynes
Adare
Croom
TIPPERARY
Tipperary
Cashel
Callan
Thomastown
Inistioge
Ballybunion
Listowel
Deel
Rathkeale
Newcastle
Bruff
Hospital
Kerry Head
Abbeyfeale
Feale
LIMERICK
Kilmallock
Galtymore 3,018
Fethard
Cahir
Clonmel
Carrick-on-Suir
Clonroche
Slaney
New Ross
Wexford Harbour
Castlegregory
Ballyheigue
Rathluirc (Charleville)
Kilfinane
Suir
Tralee
Tralee Bay
MUNSTER
Mooncoin
Taghmon
Wexford
Rosslare
Portlaw
Passage East
Greenore Point
Baurtregaum 2,796
Castleisland
Dingle
Newmarket
Buttevant
Mitchelstown
Knockmealdown Mts.
Waterford
Tramore
KERRY
Maine
Kanturk
Mallow
Doneraile
Lismore
Cappoquin
Dungarvan
Carnsore Pt.
Elasket Is.
Slea Head
Killorglin
Dingle Bay
Killarney
Millstreet
Blackwater
Fermoy
Hook Head
Saltee Is.
St. George's Channel
Macgillycuddy's Reeks
Carrantuohill 3,414
Lough Leane
Boggeragh Mts.
CORK
Bride
Tallow
WATERFORD
Dungarvan Harbour
Waterford Harbour
Valentia I.
Cahirciveen
Blarney
Cork
Midleton
Youghal
Ardmore
Youghal Bay
Macroom
Lee
Cloyne
Kenmare
Sneem
Caha Mts.
Passage West
Cobh (Queenstown)
Shehy Mts.
Bandon
Crosshaven
Cork Harbour
Kinsale
Scarriff I.
Kenmare
Castletown-bere
Dunmanway
Bandon
Timoleague
Bantry
Clonakilty
Kinsale Harbour
Dursey I.
Bantry Bay
Skibbereen
Courtmacsherry Bay
Schull
Seven Heads
Dunmanus Bay
Baltimore
Galley Head
Mizen Head
Fastnet Rock
Cape Clear
Clear I.
ATLANTIC OCEAN
N

(1969e) 22,531; office machines; iron foundry; founded 1966.

Eisernes Tor. See IRON GATE.

Eisk. See YEISK.

Eis·le·ben \'īs-ˌlā-bən\. Mining city, Halle dist., East Germany, in the E spurs of Harz Mts. 22 m. NW of Merseburg; pop. (1970e) 30,386; apparel, furniture; first mentioned 994; 16th cent. town hall; house in which Martin Luther was born (a museum since 1917) and the house in which he died.

Eitape. See AITAPE.

Ejmiadzin. See ECHMIADZIN.

Eju·tla de Cres·po \ā-ˌhüt-lə-dā-'kres-(ˌ)pō\. Municipality, Oaxaca state, Mexico, 35 m. S of Oaxaca; pop. (1970p) 34,890; dairy farming, diversified agriculture.

Eka·laka \ˌēk-ə-'lak-ə\. Town, ⊗ of Carter co., SE corner of Montana; pop. (1970c) 663.

Ekaterinburg. See SVERDLOVSK 1.

Ekaterinenstadt. See MARKS.

Ekaterinodar. See KRASNODAR.

Ekaterinoslav. See DNEPROPETROVSK.

Eke \'ā-(ˌ)kā\. See MAUI 1.

Eker·en \'āk-ər-ən\. Commune, Antwerp prov., Belgium; pop. (1969e) 26,694; metal goods.

Ekhmîm. See AKHMÎM.

Eki·bas·tuz \ˌek-ə-'bäs-təs\. Town, Pavlodar Oblast, Kazakh S.S.R., U.S.S.R., ab. 80 m. SW of Pavlodar; pop. (1967e) 40,000.

Ek·ron \'ek-ˌrän\. City of ancient Palestine; its site now in Israel; one of the 5 chief city-kingdoms of Philistia.

Elabuga. See YELABUGA.

El Agheila. See AL-AGHEILA.

Elah, Vale of \-'ē-lə\. Valley of middle course of northern branch of Nahr Suqreir, Israel, ab. 15 m. W of Bethlehem; probable site of the combat bet. David and Goliath (*1 Sam.* xvii. 2, 19).

El Alamein. See AL-ALAMEIN.

Elam \'ē-ləm\ *also* **Su·si·a·na** \ˌsü-zē-'an-ə, -'än-ə, -'ā-nə\. Ancient kingdom at head of Persian Gulf E of Babylonia, dating back possibly to 5th millennium B.C.; from c. 3000 B.C., there was a conflict between Elamites, non-Semitic inhabitants of Elam, and the Sumerians and Akkadians; with its capital at Susa, kingdom of Elam flourished c. 1200–c. 640 B.C. when it was absorbed by Assyria, which destroyed Susa; Susa later became one of capitals of Persian Empire of Cyrus the Great (see IRAN).

Elands·laag·te \'ē-ˌlän(t)s-ˌläk-tə\. Settlement, NW Natal, Rep. of South Africa; scene of battle Oct. 21, 1899 in which Boers under Joubert were temporarily repulsed by British.

El Aqqaqir. See AL-AQQAQIR.

El Ara·hal \el-ˌär-ə-'äl\. Commune, Sevilla prov., SW Spain, 23 m. ESE of Seville; pop. (1970p) 15,970.

El 'Arîsh. See AL-'ARĪSH.

El Ashmûnein. See AL-ASHMŪNEIN.

Elat. See ELATH 2.

Elatea. 1 Mountain. See CITHAERON.
2 Town. See ELATEIA.

Ela·teia \e-'lät-ē-ə\ *or* **Drakh·ma·ni** \dräk-'män-(y)ē\ *or anc.* **El·a·tea** \ˌel-ə-'tē-ə\. Town, NE Phthiotis and Phocis dept., Greece, NE of Mt. Parnassus.

Elath \'ē-ˌlath\. 1 Town, Jordan. See 'AQABA.
2 *or* **Elat** \'ē-ˌlat\ *or* **Ei·lat** \ā-'lät\. Seaport, S Israel, W of 'Aqaba at head of Gulf of 'Aqaba; pop. (1970e) 14,600; Israel's leading oil port; fishing; built since 1948.

Elaver. See ALLIER.

Elâ·zığ \ˌel-ə-'zə, -'zē(g)\ *or formerly* **Elâ·ziz** \-zēz\. 1 Province of E cen. Turkey, Asia. See table at TURKEY.
2 Town, its ✱; pop. (1965c) 78,605; textiles; food processing.

El·ba \'el-bə\. 1 City, a ⊗ of Coffee co., SE Alabama; pop. (1970c) 4634; lumber.
2 *anc.* **Il·va** \'il-və\ *also* **Ae·tha·lia** \i-'thā-lē-ə\. Italian island in Mediterranean Sea bet. NE coast of Corsica and mainland of Italy; 86 sq. m.; pop. (1961c) 27,602; politically a part of Italian province of Livorno, Tuscany; chief town Portoferraio; has iron-ore deposits which have been worked since ancient times. Residence of Napoleon after his first abdication May 1814 to Feb. 26, 1815 when he left secretly to begin his career of the "Hundred Days"; in World War II taken from Germans by French June 17–19, 1944.

Elba, Cape. See HADARBA, RAS.

El Ban·co \el-'bäŋ-(ˌ)kō\. Town, Magdalena dept., N Colombia, ab. 148 m. SE of Cartagena; munic. pop. (1968e) 35,732.

El·ba·san \ˌel-bə-'sän\ *or formerly* **El·ba·sa·ni** \-'sän-ē\. 1 Province of cen. Albania. See table at ALBANIA.
2 Town, its ✱, on Shkumbin river 20 m. SE of Tiranë; pop. (1967e) 38,885; market center in agricultural region producing esp. tobacco, fruit, and olive oil; cement, timber; E terminus of railroad line from Durrës; Italian base in early part of World War II.

El Bayadiya. See AL-BAYADIYA.

El·be \'el-bə, 'elb\ *or Czech* **La·be** \'lä-be\ *or anc.* **Al·bis** \'al-bəs\. River in Czechoslovakia, East Germany, and West Germany; 724 m. long; rises on S slopes of the Riesengebirge, Czechoslovakia, flows S, W, and NW in Czechoslovakia, then N across East Germany, turning NW to flow into North Sea at Cuxhaven, West Germany; navigable to beyond Czechoslovakian border; just N of Litoměřice cuts through the Erzgebirge in a narrow gorge. Chief tributaries Vltava and Ohře in Czechoslovakia, and Mulde, Saale, Schwarze Elster, Havel, and Elde in East Germany; connected by canals with Oder river and Baltic Sea. Meeting point April 27, 1945 of British and American armies with Soviet armies (see TORGAU); part of lower course established 1945 as line of demarcation bet. British and Soviet zones of administration in Germany.

El Be·ni \el-'ben-ē\ *or* **Beni.** Department of N Bolivia. See table at BOLIVIA.

El·bert \'el-bərt\. Name of counties in two states of the U.S. See tables at COLORADO and GEORGIA.

Elbert, Mount. Peak, Lake co., cen. Colorado; 14,433 ft.; highest peak in the state and in the Rocky Mts.

El·ber·ton \'el-bərt-ᵊn\. City, ⊗ of Elbert co., NE Georgia, E of Athens; pop. (1970c) 6438; corn, cotton, timber; granite quarries.

El·beuf \el-'bəf\. Commune, Seine-Maritime dept., N France, on Seine river 14 m. SSW of Rouen; pop. (1968c) 19,407; textiles, machinery; Renaissance churches.

El·bląg \'el-ˌblȯŋ\ *or Ger.* **El·bing** \'el-biŋ\. Seaport and industrial city, Gdańsk prov., N Poland, 30 m. ESE of Gdańsk; pop. (1970p) 89,800; important shipbuilding and repair yards; metallurgical industries; machinery. Founded 1237; became member of Hanseatic League; taken by Poland 1454; annexed to Prussia 1772; captured by Soviet troops Jan. 26–Feb. 7, 1945, after severe fighting; in section of East Prussia assigned to Poland by Potsdam Conference 1945.

Elborus. See ELBRUS.

El·bow Lake \ˌel (ˌ)bō-\. Village, ⊗ of Grant co., W Minnesota, 29 m. W of Alexandria; pop. (1970c) 1484.

El·brus \el-'brüz\ *also* **El·bo·rus** \ˌel-bə-'rüz\. Peak in the Caucasus Mts., Russian S.F.S.R., U.S.S.R.; 18,481 ft. (W peak; E peak slightly lower); highest peak in Europe; actually in a N subsidiary spur of the main range of the Caucasus.

El·burz Mountains \el-'bu̇(ə)rz-\. Range in N Iran, extending W to E parallel with S shore of Caspian Sea, from which it is separated by a lowland strip not at any point more than 25 m. wide; highest peak Damāvand 18,934 ft.; has many peaks above 10,000 ft.

El Ca·jon \ˌel-kə-ˈhōn\. City, San Diego co., SW coastal California, E of San Diego; pop. (1970c) 52,273; aircraft components, electronic equipment; fruit packing; Grossmont Coll. (1961).

El Cam·po \el-ˈkam-(ˌ)pō\. City, Wharton co., SE Texas, 25 m. NW of Bay City; pop. (1970c) 9332; rice; oil, sulfur.

El Ca·ney \ˌel-kə-ˈnā\ *or* **Caney.** Municipality, Oriente prov., E Cuba; pop. (1967e) 27,430; scene of battle July 1, 1898, in the Spanish-American War, in which Gen. Henry Lawton's division defeated the Spaniards; this and victory at San Juan Hill (*q.v.*) on same day led to American control of Santiago de Cuba and destruction of Cervera's fleet July 3.

El Cap·i·tan \ˌel-ˌkap-ə-ˈtan\. 1 Peak in Sierra Nevada, Yosemite Valley, cen. California; 7569 ft.; largest exposed monolith in the world, rising 3604 ft. above the valley floor.

2 Peak, Ravalli co., W Montana; 9983 ft.

3 Peak, Guadalupe Mts., NW Culberson co., W Texas; 8078 ft.

El Capitan Dam. Dam across San Diego river, California; height 270 ft.; completed 1934; impounds water for water supply.

El Cayo. See SAN IGNACIO 1.

El Cen·tro \el-ˈsen-(ˌ)trō\. City, ⊗ of Imperial co., SE corner of California, in Imperial Valley 86 m. E of San Diego, near Mexican border; pop. (1970c) 19,272; 52 ft. below sea level; shipping point for fruits and vegetables; settled 1906.

El Cer·ri·to \ˌel-sə-ˈrēt-(ˌ)ō\. Residential city, Contra Costa co., W California, on San Francisco Bay 6 m. N of Oakland; pop. (1970c) 25,190.

El Ce·sar \el-ˈsā-(ˌ)sär\. Department of N Colombia. See table at COLOMBIA.

El Chaco. See CHACO.

El·chaig \el-ˈkāg, -ˈk̲āg\. Stream, Ross and Cromarty co., Scotland; 6½ m. long. See GLOMACH, FALLS OF.

El·che \ˈel-(ˌ)chā\ *or anc.* **Il·i·ci** \ˈil-ə-ˌsī\. City, Alicante prov., SE Spain, 13 m. SW of Alicante; pop. (1970p) 122,663; dates, palm fronds; manufactures leather, and shoes and sandals of esparto grass; episcopal palace; scene of annual mystery play; ancient Roman colony; held by Moors 8th–13th cents.

El Cobre. See COBRE.

El·da \ˈel-də\. Commune, Alicante prov., SE Spain, 18 m. NW of Alicante; pop. (1970p) 41,511; agricultural produce; manufactures paper and esparto articles; remains of old Gothic castle.

El·de \ˈel-də\. River, East Germany; ab. 135 m. long; flows SW through several lakes into Elbe river ab. 65 m. NW of Magdeburg.

El·den Mountain \ˌel-dən-\. Peak, cen. Coconino co., N cen. Arizona; 9280 ft.

El Djem. See AL-JEM.

El Djouf. See AL-JUF.

El·don \ˈel-dən\. 1 City, Wapello co., SE Iowa, 12 m. SE of Ottumwa on Des Moines river; pop. (1970c) 1319.

2 City, Miller co., cen. Missouri, 23 m. SW of Jefferson City; pop. (1970c) 3520; cheese; clothing.

El·do·ra \el-ˈdōr-ə, -ˈdȯr-\. City, ⊗ of Hardin co., N cen. Iowa, 24 m. NNW of Marshalltown; pop. (1970c) 3223; creameries, hatcheries.

El·do·ra·do \ˌel-də-ˈrād-ˌō\. 1 Commercial city, Saline co., SE Illinois, 25 m. W of confluence of Ohio and Wabash rivers; pop. (1970c) 3876; coal mines.

2 Town, ⊗ of Schleicher co., W cen. Texas, 45 m. S of San Angelo; pop. (1970c) 1446; oil and gas well.

El Do·ra·do \ˌel-də-ˈräd-(ˌ)ō\. County in California. See table at CALIFORNIA.

El Dorado \ˌel-də-ˈrād-(ˌ)ō\. 1 City, ⊗ of Union co., S Arkansas, 80 m. ESE of Texarkana; pop. (1970c) 25,283; chief city of Arkansas oil industry; oil discovered 1921; settled 1843, made ⊗ 1844, incorp. 1851.

2 City, ⊗ of Butler co., S Kansas, 28 m. ENE of Wichita; pop. (1970c) 12,308; agriculture, oil refineries; Butler County Community Coll. (1927).

Eldorado Range \ˌel-də-ˌräd-ə-\. Range in extreme S tip of Nevada, running N to S along Colorado river.

Eldorado Springs \ˌel-də-rād-(ˌ)ō-\. City, Cedar co., W Missouri, 18 m. E of Nevada; pop. (1970c) 3300; mineral springs.

El·do·ret \ˌel-də-ˈret\. Town, W cen. Kenya, E Africa, on railroad ab. 50 m. NE of Kisumu; pop. (1962c) 19,605.

Elea. See VELIA.

Elec·tra \i-ˈlek-trə\. City, Wichita co., N Texas, 25 m. WNW of Wichita Falls; pop. (1970c) 3895; oil; manufactures drilling tools, oil-well equipment.

Elec·tric Peak \i-ˌlek-trik-\. Mountain, S Montana, near Wyoming border, in Yellowstone National Park; 11,155 ft.; highest point in Gallatin Range.

Ele·e·le \ˌā-lē-ˈā-lē\. Village, Koloa div., S coast of Kauai I., Hawaii, E of Hanapepe; pop. (1970c) 758.

Elek·tro·stal \el-ˌyek-trə-ˈstäl\ *or formerly* **Za·tish·ye** \zä-ˈtēsh-(y)ə\. Town, Moscow Oblast, Russian S.F.S.R., U.S.S.R., ab. 30 m. E of Moscow; pop. (1970p) 123,000; heavy machinery.

Elektrovoz. See STUPINO.

El·e·phant \ˈel-ə-fənt\. 1 Island in Scotia Sea, in NE part of South Shetland Is., British Antarctic Territory, ab. 61°10′S, 55°14′W.

2 *or* **Oli·fants** \ˈäl-ə-fən(t)s\. River, SE cen. South-West Africa; ab. 250 m. long.

El·e·phan·ta \ˌel-ə-ˈfant-ə\ *or Hind.* **Gha·ra·pu·ri** \ˌgär-ə-ˈpu̇(ə)r-ē\. Small island in Bombay Harbor, W India, ab. 6 m. E of the city of Bombay; famous for its Temple Caves, excavations cut out of solid rock probably 1000 to 1200 years ago; contains colossal carved figures of the Trimurti, Siva, Parvati, and other Hindu deities.

El·e·phan·ti·ne \ˌel-ə-ˌfan-ˈtī-nē, -ˈtē-\. Island in Nile river, in Upper Egypt, opp. Aswān just below the First Cataract; ruins of many structures—Egyptian, Roman, Saracen, and Arabic; at its upper end had ancient Nilometer; site of discovery 1903 of the *Elephantine papyri,* dating from end of 5th cent. B.C. and containing varied information about the Jewish people.

Elephant Mound. Prehistoric earthwork 4 m. S of Wyalusing, NW Grant co., SW Wisconsin, on Mississippi river; once thought to resemble an elephant; first noticed 1872.

Elephant Mountain. Peak, W Brewster co., W Texas; 6200 ft.

Elephant Tusk. See INDIANOLA PEAK.

El Es·co·ri·al \ˌel-e-ˈskōr-ē-əl, -ˌskōr-ē-ˈäl, -ˈskȯr-, -ˌskȯr-\. Commune, Madrid prov., cen. Spain, 25 m. NW of Madrid in SW Sierra de Guadarrama; pop. (1970p) 3839; site of the Escorial, a vast structure erected 1563–84 at the direction of Philip II, comprising a royal palace, a royal mausoleum, a church, a college, and a monastery, and containing many works of art.

Elets. See YELETS.

Eleu·sis \i-ˈlü-səs\ *or Gk.* **Elev·sís** \ˌel-əf-ˈsēs\. Village with ruins of an ancient city, ab. 14 m. NW of Athens, E Greece, on N shore of Bay of Eleusis opp. Salamis I.; a place of great antiquity; in early times independent of Athens; seat of the Eleusinian Mysteries, the most famous of the Greek religious mysteries, in honor of Demeter; sacred buildings destroyed 395 A.D. by Alaric.

Eleusis, Bay of *or Gk.* **Kól·pos Elev·sí·nos** \ˌkȯl-pȯs-ˌel-əf-ˈsē-ˌnȯs\. Inlet of Saronic Gulf, Attica and Boeotia dept., Greece, almost completely shut in by Salamis I.

Eleu·thera \i-ˈlü-thə-rə\. One of the Bahama Is., in the Atlantic Ocean E of New Providence I.; ab. 80 m. long; 164 sq. m.; pop. (1963c) 7247; site of U.S. missile-tracking station; one of the earliest islands in the Bahama Is. to be colonized, in mid-17th cent.

Eleu·ther·op·o·lis \i-ˌlü-thə-ˈräp-ə-ləs\; *mod.* **Bet Gu·vrin** \ˌbāt-gə-ˈvrēn\ *or* **Beit Ji·brin** \ˌbāt-jə-ˈbrēn\. Ancient city in Palestine, ab. 40 m. WNW of Hebron; site of Roman ruins; sacked or destroyed several times; rebuilt and renamed by Septimius Severus 200 A.D.; important in time of Crusades.

Eleven Thousand Virgins, Cape of the. See VIRGENES.

Elevsínos, Kólpos. See ELEUSIS, BAY OF.

Elevsís. See ELEUSIS.

El Faiyūm. See AL-FAIYŪM.

El Fasher. See AL-FASHIR.

Elfeld. See ELTVILLE.

El Fe·rrol de Cau·di·llo \ˌel-fə-ˈrōl-ˌdel-kaủ-ˈdē-(ˌ)(y)ō, -ˈdēl-(ˌ)yō\ *or shortened to* **El Ferrol.** City, La Coruña prov., NW Spain, 11 m. NE of La Coruña on a fine natural harbor; pop. (1970p) 87,736; important naval station; shipbuilding; chosen as site of naval arsenal by Charles IV 1726; shipbuilding established in mid-18th cent.; surrendered to English 1805; occupied by French Jan.–June 1809.

El Frai·le \el-ˈfrī-lē\. Rocky islet on S side of South Channel, part of entrance to Manila Bay, Phil., ab. 2 m. from Cavite shore; had American fortification, Fort Drum. See CORREGIDOR.

Elfsborg. See ÄLVSBORG.

El Fuer·te \el-fü-ˈer-tē\. Municipality, Sinaloa state, Mexico, 150 m. NE of Culiacán; pop. (1970p) 62,001.

El Fung. See AL-FUNG.

El Gazala. See AL-GAZALA.

El Geneina. See AL-GENEINA.

El·gin \ˈel-jən\. City, Cook and Kane cos., NE Illinois, 38 m. WNW of Chicago; pop. (1970c) 55,691; dairy products, esp. butter; watch manufacturing; Elgin Community Coll. (1949).

Elgin \ˈel-gən\. 1 City, Bastrop co., S cen. Texas, 23 m. E of Austin; pop. (1970c) 3832; oil wells.

2 County, Ontario, Canada. See table at ONTARIO.

3 *or* **Elginshire** \-ˌshi(ə)r, -shər\. County in Scotland. See MORAY.

4 Burgh, ⊗ of Moray co., NE Scotland; pop. (1971p) 16,401; distilleries; wool, iron; ruins of noted cathedral.

El·gon, Mount \-ˈel-ˌgän\. Volcanic peak on the Uganda-Kenya boundary, NE of Lake Victoria; 14,178 ft.

El Gru·llo \el-ˈgrü-(ˌ)yō\. Town, Jalisco state, W cen. Mexico; munic. pop. (1970p) 12,949.

El Guettar. See AL-GUETTAR.

El Hamma. See AL-HAMMA.

El Hammām. See AL-HAMMĀM.

El Hasa. See AL-HASA.

Elias, Mount. See SAINT ELIAS MOUNTAINS.

Elí·as Pi·ña \ā-ˌlē-əs-ˌpēn-yə\. Commune, ✱ of La Estrelleta prov., Dominican Republic; pop. (1970p) 3770.

Elichpur. See ACHALPUR.

Elikón. See HELICON.

Elimberrum. See AUCH.

Eliocroca. See LORCA.

El·i·ot \ˈel-ē-ət, ˈel-yət\. Town, York co., SW Maine, 28 m. SSW of Biddeford; pop. (1970c) 3497.

Elis \ˈē-ləs\. 1 Ancient country in NW Peloponnesus, Greece; bounded on N by Achaea, on E by Arcadia, on S by Messenia, and on W by Ionian Sea; extent varied in accordance with changes in its political influence; district of Triphylia in S for a time held by Arcadia. Watered by Peneus and Alpheus rivers; mountain range on E border including Mt. Erymanthus (at NE corner); chief town Elis; in S was plain of Olympia (*q.v.*). After First Peloponnesian War involved in most of the wars of Greece, usually but not always as ally of Sparta; control of Olympian games for several centuries gave Eleans considerable prestige.

2 Department of Greece. See table at GREECE.

3 City, ✱ of ancient Elis, in W cen. part on Peneus river; now only ruins.

Elis·a·beth·ville \i-ˈliz-ə-bəth-ˌvil\. 1 Province, Zaire. See SHABA.

2 City, Zaire. See LUBUMBASHI.

Elisavetgrad. See KIROVOGRAD.

Elisavetpol. See KIROVABAD.

Elis·ta \ē-ˈlis-tə, e-ˈlyē-stə\ *or formerly* **Step·noi** \st(y)ep-ˈnȯi\. Town, ✱ of Kalmyk A.S.S.R., Russian S.F.S.R., U.S.S.R., 220 m. ESE of Rostov-na-Donu; pop. (1970p) 50,000; in World War II occupied by German forces Aug. 1942 but retaken by U.S.S.R. before the end of the year.

Eliz·a·beth \i-ˈliz-ə-bəth\. 1 Navigable river, Norfolk co., SE Virginia, emptying into Hampton Roads; the cities of Norfolk and Portsmouth are on its banks.

2 City, ⊗ of Union co., NE New Jersey, on Newark Bay 5 m. S of Newark; pop. (1970c) 112,654; residential suburb of New York City; connected with Staten I. by Goethals Bridge; transships coal and iron; manufactures machinery, chemicals, beds, printing presses, clothing; has oil refineries, foundries, steelworks, shipbuilding yards.

History: Purchased by English from Indians 1664 and settled as Elizabethtown; capital of New Jersey until 1686; meeting place of colonial assembly 1668–82; important point in Washington's maneuvers during Revolution; chartered as borough of Elizabeth 1740 and 1789, as town 1796, as city 1855; original seat of Princeton Univ.; home of Alexander Hamilton and Aaron Burr.

3 Borough, Allegheny co., SW Pennsylvania, on Monongahela river 14 m. SSE of Pittsburgh; pop. (1970c) 2273; formerly important boat-building center.

4 Town, ⊗ of Wirt co., W West Virginia; pop. (1970c) 821.

Elizabeth, Cape. 1 Cape, Cumberland co., on coast of SW Maine, 8 m. S of Portland.

2 *or Russ.* **Ye·li·za·ve·ty** \yi-ˌliz-ə-ˈv(y)et-ē\. North point of Sakhalin I., Khabarovsk Krai, Russian S.F.S.R., U.S.S.R., 54°26′N.

Elizabeth, Mount. Mountain, Antarctica, 83°54′S, 168°23′E; 14,698 ft.

Elizabeth City. 1 Former county in Virginia; since 1958, comprises independent city of Hampton.

2 Town, ⊗ of Pasquotank co., NE North Carolina, on N arm of Albemarle Sound; pop. (1970c) 14,381; excellent harbor; fisheries; manufactures cotton textiles, veneer, furniture; U.S. Coast Guard air base, shipyard, and supply base; Elizabeth City State Coll. (1891), Coll. of the Albemarle (1960); became ⊗ 1799; naval victory won near here by Unionists 1862.

Elizabeth Island. See HENDERSON ISLAND.

Elizabeth Islands. Group of 16 small islands extending SW from SW point of Cape Cod, SE Massachusetts; in Dukes co., SE Mass., separated from Martha's Vineyard by Vineyard Sound and from mainland of Mass. by Buzzards Bay.

Elizabeth Point. Cape on SW coast of South-West Africa, S of Lüderitz.

Eliz·a·beth·ton \i-ˌliz-ə-ˈbeth-tən\. City, ⊗ of Carter co., NE Tennessee, on Watauga river 9 m. E of Johnson City; pop. (1970c) 12,269; manufactures rayon and rayon yarn; manganese deposits.

Eliz·a·beth·town \i-ˈliz-ə-bəth-ˌtaủn\. 1 Village, ⊗ of Hardin co., SE Illinois; pop. (1970c) 436.

2 City, ⊗ of Hardin co., cen. Kentucky, 40 m. S of Louisville; pop. (1970c) 11,748; plastics, metal products; limestone quarries.

3 Village, ⊗ of Essex co., NE New York, in Adirondack Mts. 32 m. S of Plattsburg; pop. (1970c) 607.

4 Town, ⊗ of Bladen co., S North Carolina, on Cape Fear river 35 m. SSE of Fayetteville; pop. (1970c) 1418; cotton, tobacco.

5 Borough, Lancaster co., SE Pennsylvania, 18 m. WNW of Lancaster; pop. (1970c) 8072; Elizabethtown Coll. (1899); founded 1732.

El Juf. See AL-JUF.

Elk \ˈelk\. 1 River, Pennsylvania and Maryland; ab. 40 m. long; flows S from Chester co., SE Pennsylvania, into N

Chesapeake Bay in NE corner of Maryland; has wide estuary ab. 13 m. long.
2 River, Tennessee and Alabama; ab. 200 m. long; flows SW from Grundy co., S Tennessee, into Tennessee river near upper end of Muscle Shoals, N Alabama.
3 River, cen. West Virginia; 172 m. long; rises in Pocahontas co., flows N, NW, and W into Kanawha river at Charleston in Kanawha co.
4 Name of counties in two states of the U.S. See table at KANSAS and PENNSYLVANIA.

Ełk \elk\ *or Ger.* **Lyck** \'lik\. Manufacturing city, Białystok prov., NE Poland, ab. 60 m. NW of Białystok; pop. (1970p) 27,200; railroad junction; formerly in East Prussia, Germany; assigned to Poland by Potsdam Conference 1945.

El·ka·der \el-'kād-ər\. Town, ⊗ of Clayton co., NE Iowa, 46 m. NW of Dubuque; pop. (1970c) 1592.

El Kala \el-'käl-ə\ *or formerly* **La Calle** \lə-'käl\. Seaport, NE Annaba dept., NE Algeria, 10 m. from Tunisia border; pop. (1966c) 8217; lost by French and burned 1827, rebuilt 1836.

El Kantara. See AL-KANTARA.

Elk City \'elk-\. City, Beckham co., W Oklahoma, 27 m. WSW of Clinton; pop. (1970c) 7323; beverages; livestock.

El Kerak. See AL-KARAK.

Elk Grove Village. Village, Cook and Du Page cos., NE Illinois, NW suburb of Chicago; pop. (1970c) 21,907.

El Khārga. See AL-KHARGA.

Elk·hart \'el-ˌkärt, 'elk-ˌhärt\. 1 County in Indiana. See table at INDIANA.
2 City, Elkhart co., N Indiana, 15 m. E of South Bend; pop. (1970c) 43,152; band instruments, proprietary medicines, telephone equipment, mobile homes.

Elk Hills. United States naval oil reservation in Kern co., S California; leased by Secretary of the Interior Albert B. Fall at time of Teapot Dome oil scandals but lease canceled 1924.

Elk·horn \'elk-ˌhȯ(ə)rn\. 1 River, NE Nebraska; 333 m. long; rises in Rock co., flows SE into Platte river.
2 City, ⊗ of Walworth co., S Wisconsin, 24 m. E of Janesville; pop. (1970c) 3992; musical instruments, shoes.

El Khroub *also* **El Kroub** \el-'krüb\. Commune, Constantine dept., NE Algeria, just SE of Constantine; pop. (1966e) 31,000.

El·kin \'el-kən\. Industrial town, Surry and Wilkes cos., N North Carolina, on Yadkin river; pop. (1970c) 2889; dairying; tobacco.

El·kins \'el-kənz\. City, ⊗ of Randolph co., NE cen. West Virginia, 37 m. SE of Clarksburg; pop. (1970c) 8287; foundry products; Davis and Elkins Coll. (1903).

Elk Island National Park. See CANADA, *National Parks.*

Elk·land \'elk-lənd\. Borough, Tioga co., N Pennsylvania, on New York border; pop. (1970c) 1942; leather.

Elk Mountain. 1 Peak, San Miguel co., NE cen. New Mexico; 11,661 ft.
2 Peak, one of the highest peaks in Medicine Bow Mts., S cen. Wyoming; 11,156 ft.

El·ko \'el-(ˌ)kō\. 1 County, NE corner of Nevada. See table at NEVADA.
2 City, its ⊗, on Humboldt river 32 m. NNW of Franklin Lake; pop. (1970c) 7621; stock farms.

Elk Point. City, ⊗ of Union co., SE corner of South Dakota; pop. (1970c) 1372.

Elk River. 1 Three rivers in the U.S. See ELK.
2 Village, ⊗ of Sherburne co., cen. Minnesota, on Mississippi river NW of Minneapolis; pop. (1970c) 2252.

El Kroub. See EL KHROUB.

Elk·ton \'elk-tən\. 1 City, ⊗ of Todd co., SW Kentucky; pop. (1970c) 1612; tobacco.
2 Town, ⊗ of Cecil co., NE Maryland, on Elk river; pop. (1970c) 5362; explosives, plastics. American "Gretna Green" until passage of a 48-hour marriage law 1938.

El Kuneitra. See AL-KUNEITRA.

El·land \'el-ənd\. Urban district, West Riding, Yorkshire, N England; pop. (1971p) 17,817; woolens; ironworks.

Ellás. See GREECE.

Ellasar. See LARSA.

El·la·ville \'el-ə-ˌvil\. City, ⊗ of Schley co., SW cen. Georgia; pop. (1970c) 1391.

El Ledja. See AL-LEDJA.

El·lef Ring·nes Island \ˌel-əf-'riŋ-ˌnās-\. One of the Sverdrup Is. (*q.v.*); 5139 sq. m.

El·len, Mount \-'el-ən\. 1 Peak, NE Garfield co., S Utah; 11,522 ft.
2 Peak, Washington co., N cen. Vermont; 4135 ft.

El·len·dale \'el-ən-ˌdāl\. City, ⊗ of Dickey co., S North Dakota, 64 m. S of Jamestown; pop. (1970c) 1517.

El·lens·burg \'el-ənz-ˌbərg\. City, ⊗ of Kittitas co., cen. Washington, on Yakima river 27 m. N of Yakima; pop. (1970c) 13,568; meat packing; lumber; coal mines; Central Washington State Coll. (1891).

El·len's Isle \ˌel-ənz-\. Small island in Loch Katrine, Perth co., cen. Scotland; Ellen's haunt in Sir Walter Scott's *Lady of the Lake.*

El·len·ville \'el-ən-ˌvil\. Residential village, Ulster co., SE New York, in Shawangunk Mts. 26 m. W of Poughkeepsie; pop. (1970c) 4482.

Elles·mere, Lake \-'elz-ˌmi(ə)r\. Coastal lake in E South I., New Zealand, on S side of Banks Penin.; 70 sq. m.; 14 m. long; tidal.

Ellesmere Island. Island, N Franklin dist., Northwest Territories, Canada, W of NW Greenland; 82,119 sq. m.; its N point, Cape Columbia, is the northernmost point of Canada (83°08'N).

Ellesmere Port. Municipal borough, Cheshire, NW England, on the Mersey 10 m. SSE of Liverpool; pop. (1971p) 81,556; paper; oil refineries.

El·lice Islands \'el-əs-\ *or* **La·goon Islands** \lə-'gün-\. Island group consisting of 9 coral atolls, all inhabited, in W Pacific Ocean, N of Fiji and SSE of Gilbert Is., extending from 5° to 10°30'S lat. and 176°E to 179°58'W long. (all lie W of the date line); 9 sq. m.; pop. (1968p) 5782; government headquarters and chief village on Funafuti I.; belongs to British colony of Gilbert and Ellice Islands; chief islands Funafuti, Nukufetau, Nukulailai, and Nanumea. Group has interesting ethnological history: in early centuries Ellice Islanders and Gilbertese of same race (Melanesian) but in 16th cent. Ellice Is. invaded and occupied by Samoans who established Polynesian race. Nanumea probably discovered 1781 and Funafuti 1819; in 19th cent. visited often by blackbirders who gradually decimated the population; made part of Gilbert and Ellice Islands Colony 1915.

Ellichpur. See ACHALPUR.

El·li·cott City \ˌel-i-kət-\. Town (unincorp.), ⊗ of Howard co., cen. Maryland; pop. (1970c) 9506.

El·li·jay \ˌel-ə-'jā\. City, ⊗ of Gilmer co., N Georgia; pop. (1970c) 1326.

El·ling·ton \'el-iŋ-tən\. Agricultural town, NW Tolland co., N Connecticut; pop. (1970c) 7707; incorporated 1786.

El·lin·wood \'el-ən-ˌwu̇d\. City, Barton co., cen. Kansas, 43 m. NW of Hutchinson; pop. (1970c) 2416.

El·li·ott \'el-ē-ət, 'el-yət\. County in Kentucky. See table at KENTUCKY.

Elliott Bay. Inlet of Puget Sound, waterfront of the city of Seattle, Washington.

El·lis \'el-əs\. 1 Name of counties in three states of the U.S. See tables at KANSAS, OKLAHOMA, TEXAS.
2 City, Ellis co., cen. Kansas, 60 m. NW of Great Bend; pop. (1970c) 2137.

Ellis Island. Island, Upper New York Bay, ab. 1 m. SW of S point of Manhattan I.; sold by N.Y. state to national government 1808; became immigrant station 1891 and for many years received great majority of immigrants and nonimmigrant aliens entering the U.S.; ceased as immigration station 1954.

El·lis·land \'el-əs-ˌland\. Farm, Dumfries co., S Scotland, on the Nith 6 m. NW of Dumfries; home of Robert Burns 1788–91; property of British nation since 1928.

El·lis·ville \'el-əs-ˌvil\. 1 City, a ⊗ of Jones co., SE Mississippi, 8 m. SW of Laurel; pop. (1970c) 4643; sawmills; Jones County Junior Coll. (1911).
2 City, St. Louis co., E Missouri; pop. (1970c) 4681.

El·lo·ra \e-'lōr-ə, -'lȯr-\ *also* **Elu·ra** \-'lu̇r-ə\. Village, cen. Maharashtra state, S cen. India, 15 m. NW of Aurangabad; famous for its rock temples, a series of caves carved out of the rocky hillside 1¼ m. long; in 3 sections: Buddhist, Brahmanical, and Jain; finest is Kailas of the Brahmanical group.

Ellore. See ELURU.

Ells·worth \'elz-wərth\. 1 County in Kansas. See table at KANSAS.
2 City, ⊗ of Ellsworth co., cen. Kansas, 36 m. W of Salina; pop. (1970c) 2080; winter wheat; petroleum, limestone.
3 City, ⊗ of Hancock co., SE Maine, 27 m. SE of Bangor; pop. (1970c) 4603; truck farming; summer resort.
4 Borough, Washington co., SW Pennsylvania, 23 m. S of Pittsburgh; pop. (1970c) 1268.
5 Village, ⊗ of Pierce co., W Wisconsin; pop. (1970c) 1983; livestock.

Ellsworth, Mount. Peak in Glacier National Park, NW Montana; 8595 ft.

Ellsworth Land; *formerly* **Ellsworth Highland** *or* **James W. Ellsworth Land.** High plateau, Antarctica, extending E from Marie Byrd Land to W coast of Weddell Sea S of Antarctic Penin., bet. 60° and 100°E.

Ellsworth Mountains. Mountain range, consisting of Sentinel Range and Heritage Range, Antarctica, S of Ellsworth Land; highest peak Vinson Massif 16,860 ft.

Ell·wang·en \'el-väŋ-ən\. Town, E Baden-Württemberg, West Germany, 46 m. ENE of Stuttgart; pop. (1966e) 13,-300; textiles; church 1182–1233; became town c. 1229; captured by Allies Apr. 25, 1945.

Ell·wood City \ˌel-ˌwu̇d-\. Borough, Beaver and Lawrence cos., W Pennsylvania, 11 m. S of New Castle; pop. (1970c) 10,857; metal products (pipe, tubing); coal mines.

El·ma·lı \ˌel-mə-'lē\. Town, W Antalya prov., SW Turkey in Asia, on highway in mountains 45 m. W of Antalya; pop. (1965c) 8482; inhabited by direct descendants of the ancient Lycians.

El Mansūra. See AL-MANSŪRA.

El Mar del Sur. See SOUTH SEA.

El Matarīya. See AL-MATARĪYA.

El Mechili. See AL-MECHILI.

El·men·dorf Field \'el-mən-ˌdȯrf-\. U.S. airfield just E of Anchorage, at head of Cook Inlet, S cen. Alaska.

Elm Grove \'elm-\. Village, Waukesha co., Wisconsin, 10 m. W of Milwaukee; pop. (1970c) 7201; die castings; diversified agriculture.

Elm·hurst \'elm-ˌhərst\. Residential city, Du Page co., NE Illinois, 17 m. W of Chicago; pop. (1970c) 48,887; Elmhurst Coll. (1871).

El·mi·na \el-'mē-nə\. Seaport town, S Ghana, W Africa; pop. (1970p) 11,612; founded by Portuguese traders 1482.

El Minya. See AL-MINYA.

El·mi·ra \el-'mī-rə\. 1 Industrial city, ⊗ of Chemung co., S New York, on Chemung river 48 m. W of Binghamton; pop. (1970c) 39,945; large coal shipments; dairying industry; manufactures office equipment, business machines, fire-fighting apparatus and chemicals, dental supplies, television tubes; site of Elmira Coll. (1853), one of first in U.S. to grant degrees to women; Elmira State reformatory for men (1876), pioneer in modern penological methods. Nearby at Newtown (name also of the city 1815–28) was fought Aug. 29, 1779 the battle in which forces of expedition under Gen. John Sullivan and Gen. James Clinton defeated Indians and Tories who had been harassing New York and Pennsylvania frontiers, also sometimes known as battle of Chemung river; settled c. 1788; became ⊗ 1836; chartered as city 1864; home and burial place of Mark Twain.
2 Town, Waterloo co., SE Ontario, Canada, 12 m. N of Kitchener; pop. (1971p) 4722; in agricultural region.

El Mi·rage \ˌel-mə-'räzh\. Town, Maricopa co., SW cen. Arizona, 5 m. NW of Phoenix; pop. (1970c) 3258.

Elmira Heights. Village, Chemung co., S New York, N suburb of Elmira; pop. (1970c) 4906.

El Mis·ti \el-'mēs-tē\ *also* **El Vol·cán de Are·qui·pa** \el-vȯl-'kän-ˌdā-ˌär-ə-'kē-pə\. Dormant volcano, S Peru, NE of Arequipa; 19,031 ft.

El·mont \'el-ˌmänt\. Urban community (unincorporated), Nassau co., New York, on Long I. SW of Garden City; pop. (1970c) 29,363.

El Mon·te \el-mänt-ē\. City, Los Angeles co., SW California, 12 m. E of Los Angeles; pop. (1970c) 69,852; electronic equipment, pressed steel, airplane accessories.

El·more \'el-ˌmō(ə)r, -mȯ(ə)r\. Name of counties in two states of the U.S. See tables at ALABAMA and IDAHO.

El Mor·ro National Monument \el-'mōr-(ˌ)ō-, -'mȯr-\. See UNITED STATES, *National Monuments.*

Elms·ford \'elmz-fərd\. Village, Westchester co., SE New York, 26 m. N of New York; pop. (1970c) 3911; residential suburb.

Elms·horn \'elmz-ˌhȯ(ə)rn, 'elms-\. Manufacturing city, Schleswig-Holstein, West Germany, 20 m. NW of Hamburg; pop. (1969e) 40,896; food processing; radio communication center; first mentioned c. 1141; destroyed by Swedish forces 1657.

Elm·wood \'elm-(ˌ)wu̇d\. 1 Subdivision of town of West Hartford, Connecticut. See WEST HARTFORD.
2 City, Peoria co., NW cen. Illinois, 20 m. WNW of Peoria; pop. (1970c) 2014; birthplace of the sculptor Lorado Taft.

Elmwood Park. Residential village, Cook co., NE Illinois, suburb of Chicago; pop. (1970c) 26,160.

Elmwood Place. Village, Hamilton co., SW corner of Ohio, 7 m. N of Cincinnati; pop. (1970c) 3525; manufactures steel and foundry products.

Elne \'eln\ *or anc.* **Il·lib·e·ris** \il-'ib-ə-rəs\. Commune, Pyrénées-Orientales dept., S France, 10 m. SSE of Perpignan; pop. (1962c) 5744; early 12th cent. Romanesque cathedral; scene of murder of Emperor Constans 350.

El Obeid. See AL-UBAYYID.

Elo·bey, Great \-ˌel-ə-'bā\ *and* **Little Elobey.** Two islands in Gulf of Guinea, W Africa; combined area ab. 1 sq. m.; part of Equatorial Guinea.

Elon College \ˌē-ˌlän-\. Town, Alamance co., N cen. North Carolina, ab. 3 m. NNW of Burlington; pop. (1970c) 2150; Elon Coll.

El Oriente. See EASTERN REGION.

El Oro \el-'ōr-ō\. Province of SW Ecuador. See table at ECUADOR.

El Oued. See AL OUED.

Eloy \'ē-ˌlȯi\. Town, Pinal co., S Arizona, 48 m. NW of Tucson; pop. (1970c) 5361; cotton.

El Pa·ra·í·so \el-ˌpär-ə-'ēs-ō\. Department of S Honduras. See table at HONDURAS.

El Paso \el-'pas-(ˌ)ō\. 1 Name of counties in two states of the U.S. See tables at COLORADO and TEXAS.
2 City, Woodford co., N cen. Illinois; pop. (1970c) 2291.
3 City and port of entry, ⊗ of El Paso co., W tip of Texas, on Rio Grande river opp. Ciudad Juárez, Mexico; pop. (1970c) 322,261; alt. 3695 ft.; commercial and manufacturing center in region growing fruit, vegetables, and cotton (irrigation furnished by Elephant Butte Dam); railroad center and gateway to Mexico; ore smelters, copper and oil refineries; meat packing; Univ. of Texas at El Paso (1913); Fort Bliss (*q.v.*) and Biggs Air Force Base nearby. First settled 1827; alternately occupied by Union and Confeder-

ate troops during Civil War; incorporated 1873. See CHAMIZAL.

El Paso del Nor·te \-del-ˈnȯrt-ē\. Gorge of the Rio Grande river near El Paso, Texas.

El Paso de Robles. See PASO ROBLES.

Elphinstone Island. See THAYAWTHADANGYI ISLAND.

El Pro·gre·so \ˌel-prə-ˈgres-(ˌ)ō\. 1 Department of SE cen. Guatemala. See table at GUATEMALA.

2 Town, ✱ of El Progreso dept., Guatemala, on a tributary of the Usumacinta river; pop. (1964p) 9534.

3 Town, Yoro prov., NW Honduras, on Ulúa river 48 m. WNW of Yoro; pop. (1961c) 13,800.

El Puerto. See PUERTO DE SANTA MARÍA.

El Qantara. See AL-QANTARA.

El Qasr. See AL-QASR.

El Qatrani. See AL-QATRANI.

El Quseir. See AL-QUSEIR.

El Re·no \el-ˈrē-(ˌ)nō\. Industrial city, ⊗ of Canadian co., cen. Oklahoma, 27 m. W of Oklahoma City; pop. (1970c) 14,150; cotton, wheat; Fort Reno and U.S. reformatory nearby.

El·roy \ˈel-(ˌ)rȯi\. City, Juneau co., cen. Wisconsin, 30 m. ESE of Sparta; pop. (1970c) 1513; butter.

El·sa \ˈel-sə\. City, Hidalgo co., S Texas, 40 m. NW of Brownsville; pop. (1970c) 4400.

El·sah \ˈel-sə\. Village, Jersey co., W Illinois, on Mississippi river; pop. (1970c) 142; The Principia Coll. (1898).

El Sal·to \el-ˈsäl-tō\. Town, Jalisco state, W cen. Mexico; munic. pop (1970p) 11,915.

El Sal·va·dor \el-ˈsal-və-ˌdȯ(ə)r, -ˌsal-və-ˈ\. Republic, Central America, bounded on NW by Guatemala, on N, NE, and E by Honduras, and on S and SW by the Pacific Ocean; 8098 sq. m.; pop. (1970e) 3,533,628; ✱ San Salvador. *Physical features:* Smallest and most densely populated of the Central American republics and the only one without an Atlantic seaboard. Crossed from NW to SE by two mountain ranges with many volcanic peaks, highest Santa Ana 7724 ft., San Miguel 6957 ft., San Salvador, and San Vicente; narrow coastal region is low plain, but most of country is plateau averaging 2000 ft. Only river the Lempa; several lakes in plateau region, largest Ilopango. *Chief products:* Coffee, sugar, cotton, corn; fishing. *Chief towns:* San Salvador, Santa Ana, San Miguel, Nueva San Salvador, Sonsonate, Villa Delgado. Divided into the following 14 departments (for pronunciation of their names, see their individual entries):

NAME	AREA (sq. m.)	POP. (1968e)	CAPITAL
Ahuachapán	686	167,579	Ahuachapán
Cabañas	420	125,404	Sensuntepeque
Chalatenango	622	168,281	Chalatenango
Cuscatlán	299	144,868	Cojutepeque
La Libertad	646	266,552	Nueva San Salvador
La Paz	478	175,583	Zacatecoluca
La Unión	841	204,019	La Unión
Morazán	519	155,196	San Francisco
San Miguel	773	305,439	San Miguel
San Salvador	341	616,182	San Salvador
Santa Ana	702	343,882	Santa Ana
San Vicente	477	146,496	San Vicente
Sonsonate	465	218,185	Sonsonate
Usulután	829	275,620	Usulután

History: Discovered by Alvarado 1523; in captaincy general of Guatemala; with rest of Central America (*q.v.*), became independent of Spain 1821, of Mexico 1823; member of United Provinces of Central America 1823–39; a leading advocate of various other projects for union; remained neutral in World War I but declared war on Axis powers 1941 in World War II; became a founding member of the Central American Common Market 1960; adopted new constitution 1962; fought brief border war with Honduras 1969.

Elsass. See ALSACE.

Elsass–Lothringen. See ALSACE-LORRAINE.

Els·ber·ry \ˈelz-(ˌ)ber-ē\. City, Lincoln co., E Missouri, on Mississippi river 30 m. NNW of St. Charles; pop. (1970c) 1398; limestone quarries.

El Se·gun·do \ˌel-sə-ˈgün-(ˌ)dō\. City, Los Angeles co., SW California, 14 m. SW of Los Angeles; pop. (1970c) 15,620; chemicals; oil refining; founded by Standard Oil Company, incorp. 1917.

El Sei·bo *or* **El Sey·bo** \el-ˈsā-(ˌ)bō\. 1 Province, E Dominican Republic. See table at DOMINICAN REPUBLIC.

2 *or formerly* **San·ta Cruz del Seibo** *or* **Santa Cruz del Seybo** \ˌsant-ə-ˈkrüz-del-\. Municipality, its ✱; pop. (1970p) 60,810; produces cacao, coffee, wax, sugar.

El·si·nore \ˈel-sə-ˌnō(ə)r\. 1 City, Riverside co., SE California, on **Elsinore Lake** 30 m. S of San Bernardino; pop. (1970c) 3530; mineral springs in vicinity.

2 Seaport, Denmark. See HELSINGØR.

Els·mere \ˈelz-ˌmi(ə)r\. 1 Residential town, New Castle co., N Delaware, suburb of Wilmington; pop. (1970c) 8415.

2 City, Kenton co., N Kentucky, 8 m. SW of Covington; pop. (1970c) 5161.

El·ster \ˈel-stər\. 1 Name of two rivers in East Germany: (1) **Schwar·ze Elster** \ˌshfärt-sə-\, literally "Black Elster," in cen. part, 117 m. long; flows N and NW into Elbe river 8 m. E of Wittenberg; (2) **Weis·se Elster** \ˌvī-sə-\, literally "White Elster," 153 m. long; rises in NW Czechoslovakia and flows N past Leipzig to the Saale near Halle.

2 Town, East Germany, on the Weisse Elster just W of Leipzig; pop. (1965e) 3400; mineral springs, baths.

El·stow \ˈel-(ˌ)stō\. Village, Bedfordshire, S England, ab. 1 m. S of Bedford; birthplace of John Bunyan.

Els·tree \ˈel-strē\. Parish, S Hertfordshire, England, NW of London; motion-picture industry.

El Teb. See AL-TEB.

El·te·keh \ˈel-tə-ˌkā\. Ancient village; its site now in Israel, W of Jerusalem and near Ekron; scene of battle 701 (or 700) B.C. in which Sennacherib defeated Egyptians.

El Te·ni·en·te \ˌel-ˌten-ē-ˈent-ē\. Mining town, O'Higgins prov., cen. Chile, 45 m. S of Santiago; pop. (1960c) 10,866; has large copper mines. See SEWELL.

El·tham \ˈel-thəm\. Borough, SW North I., New Zealand; pop. (1968e) 2300.

El Ti·gre \el-ˈtē-grā\. Town, Anzoátegui state, Venezuela, ab. 200 m. SE of Caracas; pop. (1970e) 54,530.

El Tih. See AL-TIH.

El To·cu·yo \ˌel-tə-ˈkü-(ˌ)yō\. Town, Lara state, NW Venezuela, in Cordillera Mérida 40 m. SW of Barquisimeto; pop. (1961c) 14,560.

El To·fo \el-'tō-(,)fō\. Mining town, Coquimbo prov., cen. Chile, ab. 250 m. N of Valparaíso; pop. (1960c) 1175; subdivision of La Higuera commune; iron mines.

El·ton, Lake \-'elt-ᵊn\ *or Russ.* **El·ton·skoye Oze·ro** \'elt-ᵊn-skə-yə-'oi-zer-ə\ *or Kalmyk* **Al·tan–Nor** \äl-tän-'nȯ(ə)r\. Salt lake, Volgograd Oblast, Russian S.F.S.R., U.S.S.R., in steppe E of Volga river; very shallow, much of it dry in the summer; yields large quantities of salt.

El Tronador. See TRONADOR, MONTE.

Elt·ville \'elt-,vil\ *or formerly* **El·feld** \'el-,felt\. Town, Hesse, West Germany, on the Rhine 5 m. SW of Wiesbaden; pop. (1966e) 7400; received town rights 1332; Gutenberg established his press here 1465.

Elura. See ELLORA.

Elu·ru \e-'lu̇(ə)r-(,)ü\ *or formerly* **El·lore** \e-'lō(ə)r, -'lȯ(ə)r\. City, NE Andhra Pradesh, E India, 225 m. NNE of Madras at junction of Godavari and Krishna canal systems; pop. (1970e) 132,791; large grain trade, important carpet manufactures; its fort was constructed of materials from nearby ruins of Pedda Vegi, supposed remains of Buddhist kingdom of Vengi; former capital of Northern Circars.

El Va·do Dam \el-,väd-ō-\. Dam across Chama river, NW cen. Rio Arriba co., NW New Mexico; height 175 ft.; completed 1955; impounds water, **El Vado Reservoir,** for irrigation.

El·vas \'el-vəs(h)\ *or Lat.* **Al·pe·sa** \al-'pē-sə\ *or Arab.* **Ba·lesh** \'bal-,esh\. Fortified city, Portalegre dist., E cen. Portugal, near Spanish frontier 30 m. SSE of Portalegre; munic. pop. (1970p) 24,510; manufactures jewelry; 16th cent. cathedral, Moorish aqueduct (1498–1622; largest in Portugal). Fortified by Moors; taken by Portugal 1226; conquered by French 1808; ceded to Portugal by Convention of Sintra 1808.

Elvend, Mount. See ALWAND, MOUNT.

El·ve·rum \'el-və-,ru̇m\. Town, Hedmark co., E Norway, SE of Lillehammer; pop. (1970e) 14,276; temporary meeting place of Norwegian government Apr. 1940.

El Vie·jo \,el-vē-'e-(,)hō\. Town, a NW suburb of Chinandega, NW Nicaragua.

El·vins \'el-vinz\. City, St. Francois co., E Missouri, 57 m. SSW of St. Louis; pop. (1970c) 1603.

El Volcán de Arequipa. See EL MISTI.

El·wood \'el-,wu̇d\. 1 City, Madison co., cen. Indiana, 25 m. WNW of Muncie; pop. (1970c) 11,196; industrial center in tomato-growing section.

2 Village, ⊗ of Gosper co., S Nebraska; pop. (1970c) 601.

Ely \'ē-lē\. 1 City, St. Louis co., NE Minnesota, 40 m. NE of Virginia; pop. (1970c) 4904; Ely State Junior Coll. (1922); in iron-mining section.

2 City, ⊗ of White Pine co., E Nevada, 63 m. SSE of Ruby Lake; pop. (1970c) 4176; copper mines; Lehman Caves National Monument nearby.

3 Urban district, Cambridgeshire and Isle of Ely co., E England, on the Ouse 18 m. NNE of Cambridge; pop. (1971p) 9969; beet-sugar refining; its cathedral, begun 1083, one of the most notable in architecture in England; stronghold of Hereward the Wake 1070–71.

Ely, Isle of. Former administrative county, E England, now part of Cambridgeshire and Isle of Ely co. (*q.v.*).

Ely, Mount. Peak, N cen. Lincoln co., E Nevada; 7310 ft.

El·y·ma·ïs \,el-ə-'mā-əs\. Greek form of Elam (*q.v.*), sometimes used to designate a district of ancient Elam, in its S part at head of Persian Gulf, inhabited by the Elymeans.

Elyr·ia \i-'lir-ē-ə\. Industrial city, ⊗ of Lorain co., N Ohio, 23 m. WSW of Cleveland; pop. (1970c) 53,427; automobile parts, electrical machinery, steel tubing; Lorain Community Coll. (1963); settled 1817.

El Yun·que \el-'yu̇ŋ-(,)kā\. 1 *also* **Ro·ca El Yunque** \'rō-kə-\. Anvil-shaped peak, on Robinson Crusoe I. in the Juan Fernández group in the Pacific Ocean, ab. 420 m. W of Valparaíso, Chile; 3002 ft. high.

2 Peak in the Luquillo Mts., E Puerto Rico; 3496 ft.

Ema \'em-ə\. River, Estonian S.S.R., U.S.S.R.; 130 m. long; outlet of Vorts-Jarv flowing E to Lake Peipus.

Eman·u·el \i-'man-yə(-wə)l\. County in Georgia. See table at GEORGIA.

Emaus. See EMMAUS.

Em·ba \em-'bä\. River, W Kazakh S.S.R., U.S.S.R.; ab. 350 m. long; flows SW into NE corner of Caspian Sea; extensive oil fields on its lower course.

Em·bar·ca·de·ros, Point \-em-,bär-kə-'der-əs\. Cape on NE coast of Puerto Rico, W of Cape San Juan.

Em·bar·ras *or* **Em·bar·rass** \'am-,brȯ\. River, E Illinois; 185 m. long; rises in Champaign co., flows S and SE into Wabash river.

Em·bos·ca·da \,em-bə-'skäd-ə\. Town, W Cordillera dept., cen. Paraguay, NE of Asunción; munic. pop. (1962c) 5902.

Em·brun \äⁿ(m)-'brən\ *or anc.* **Eb·u·ro·du·num** \,eb-yə-rō-'d(y)ü-nəm\. Commune, Hautes-Alpes dept., SE France, on the Durance ab. 100 m. NE of Marseilles; pop. (1962c) 4285; archiepiscopal see c. 800–1791; 12th cent. cathedral.

Em·bu \'em-(,)bü\. Town, ✱ of Eastern Province, Kenya; pop. (1962c) 5213.

Em·den \'em-dən\. Seaport and city, Lower Saxony, West Germany, at mouth of Ems river on N coast of the Dollart, 46 m. WNW of Oldenburg; pop. (1969e) 48,098; shipbuilding, fishing; connected with interior by means of Dortmund-Ems and other canals; protected by dikes; 12th cent. church; 16th cent. town hall.

History: Founded 9th cent.; annexed to Hamburg 1453; made free city 1595; free port 1751; passed to Holland 1806 and to Hannover 1815; to Prussia 1866; in World War II an important naval base with oil tanks and refineries; frequently heavily bombed by Allies 1943–45; ab. 75 percent of city destroyed in World War II, since rebuilt.

Emerald Isle. See IRELAND.

Emerita Augusta. See MÉRIDA 2.

Em·er·son \'em-ər-sən\. 1 Borough, Bergen co., NE New Jersey, NE of Paterson; pop. (1970c) 8428.

2 Town, SE Manitoba, Canada, on Red River of the North, at Minnesota border 63 m. S of Winnipeg; pop. (1971p) 826; frontier customs town.

Em·ery \'em-(ə-)rē\. County in Utah. See table at UTAH.

Em·er·y·ville \'em-(ə-)rē-,vil\. Town, Alameda co., W California, on San Francisco Bay; pop. (1970c) 2681; suburb of Oakland; packinghouses, stockyards, iron foundries.

Emesa. City, Syria. See HOMS.

Em·i·grant Peak \,em-ə-grənt-, -,grant-\. 1 Mountain, S Park co., S Montana; 10,921 ft.

2 Mountain, Esmeralda co., SW Nevada; 6784 ft.

Emi Kous·si \ā-mē-'kü-sə\. Peak, N Chad, highest point of Tibesti massif; 11,204 ft.

Emi·lia–Ro·ma·gna \ā-,mēl-yə-rō-'män-yə\ *or formerly* **Emilia** *or anc.* **Æmil·ia** \ē-'mil-ē-ə, -'mil-yə\. Autonomous region, N Italy, on Adriatic Sea bet. Tuscany and Lombardy; 8543 sq. m.; pop. (1968e) 3,815,254; ✱ Bologna; mountainous in S, fertile plain (**Emil·ian Plain** \ē-,mil-yən-\) in N; important agriculturally, producing wheat, corn, sugar beet, wine; pharmaceuticals, motor vehicles; formerly formed duchies of Parma and Modena and the papal Romagna; named for ancient Æmilian Way (built 187 B.C., ran from Rimini to Piacenza, 176 m.); to kingdom of Italy 1860.

Em·i·nence \'em-ə-nən(t)s\. City, ⊗ of Shannon co., S Missouri; pop. (1970c) 520.

Emin·ö·nü \,em-ə-nə-'nü\. District and suburb of İstanbul, Turkey, Europe.

Emi·rau \,ā-mə-'rau̇\. Island in S part of St. Matthias group, Bismarck Archipelago, W Pacific Ocean; occupied by U.S. Marines Mar. 19, 1944.

Emmahaven. See TELUKBAJUR.

Em·ma·stad \'em-ə-ˌstät, -ˌstad\. Town on island of Curaçao, Netherlands Antilles, near Willemstad; oil refineries.

Em·ma·us \e-'mā-əs\. 1 *or formerly* **Emaus** \'ē-ˌmaůs, -ˌmos\. Borough, Lehigh co., E Pennsylvania, 5 m. S of Allentown; pop. (1970c) 11,511; concrete blocks; diversified farming; founded by Moravians c. 1740.

2 Town of anc. Palestine, its site ab. 4 m. NW of Jerusalem, Israel; probably modern **Qa·lun·ya** \kə-'lün-yə\.

3 *or* **Emmaus Ni·cop·o·lis** \-ni-'käp-ə-ləs\. Town of anc. Palestine, 14 m. WNW of Jerusalem near the Roman road to Joppa; probably modern **'Im·was** \im-'was\ (in part of Jordan occupied by Israel 1967; pop. [1961c] 1955).

Em·me \'em-ə\. River, W cen. Switzerland; 50 m. long; flows NNW in Bern canton, joins the Aare river 1½ m. NE of Solothurn.

Em·men \'em-ən\. Commune, Drenthe prov., NE Netherlands, near West German border ab. 28 m. SE of Groningen; pop. (1970e) 79,707; textiles, pharmaceuticals.

Em·me·rich \'em-ə-rik\. City, North Rhine-Westphalia, West Germany, near the Dutch border on Rhine river 61 m. WSW of Münster; pop. (1968e) 23,882; chocolate, machinery, chemicals, pharmaceuticals; river port; 15th cent. town hall. First mentioned 697 A.D.; passed to counts of Gelder 1233; made city 1247; passed to Cleves 1402; member of Hanseatic League 1407; with Cleves, passed to Brandenburg 1614; in World War II frequently bombed; in 1945 one of the crossings of the Rhine made here by Allies.

Em·met \'em-ət\. Name of counties in two states of the U.S. See tables at IOWA and MICHIGAN.

Em·mets·burg \'em-əts-ˌbərg\. City, ⊗ of Palo Alto co., N Iowa, 48 m. NW of Fort Dodge; pop. (1970c) 4150; Emmetsburg Community Coll. (1930).

Em·mett \'em-ət\. City, ⊗ of Gem co., SW Idaho, 23 m. NW of Boise; pop. (1970c) 3945; ships fruit; lumber; estab. as trading post 1864, incorp. 1900.

Em·mits·burg \'em-əts-ˌbərg\. Town, Frederick co., N Maryland, 20 m. N of Frederick; pop. (1970c) 1532; Mount St. Mary's Coll. (1808), St. Joseph's Coll. (1809).

Em·mons \'em-ənz\. County in North Dakota. See table at NORTH DAKOTA.

Emmons Peak *or* **Mount Emmons.** Mountain, N Duchesne co., NE cen. Utah; 13,428 ft.

Emona. See LJUBLJANA.

Em·o·ry \'em-(ə-)rē\. 1 Village, ⊗ of Rains co., NE Texas; pop. (1970c) 693.

2 Town, Washington co., SW Virginia; Emory and Henry Coll. (1838).

Emory Peak. Mountain, S Brewster co., W Texas; 7835 ft; highest peak in Chisos Mts.

Em·pal·me \em-'päl-mē\. Municipality, Sonora state, Mexico, 5 m. NE of Guaymas; pop. (1970p) 32,541; wheat, cotton.

Em·pan·ge·ni \ˌem-päŋ-'gēn-ē\. Town, Natal, Rep. of South Africa, ab. 92 m. NE of Durban; pop. (1967e) 9900.

Em·pe·dra·do \em-pə-'dräd-(ˌ)ō\. Town, Corrientes prov., NE Argentina, on left bank of the Paraná ab. 30 m. S of Corrientes; pop. (1960c) 3735.

Em·per·or Range \'em-pər-ər-, -prər-\. Mountains forming N part of range that traverses Bougainville I., Solomon Is.; includes Mt. Balbi 8999 ft., highest point in entire range; S extension is Crown Prince Range.

Em·po·li \'em-pə-lē\. Commune, Firenze prov., Tuscany, cen. Italy, on Arno river 18 m. WSW of Florence; pop. (1968e) 42,768; cotton goods, leather, faïence, glass, macaroni; 11th cent. cathedral.

Em·po·ria \em-'pōr-ē-ə\. 1 City, ⊗ of Lyon co., E Kansas, 52 m. SW of Topeka; pop. (1970c) 23,327; railroad division point; flour mills, cheese factory; Kansas State Teachers Coll. (1863), Coll. of Emporia (1882); home of William Allen White, editor and proprietor of Emporia *Gazette* from 1895 to his death 1944; founded 1856.

2 Manufacturing town, ⊗ of Greensville co. but politically independent, S Virginia, 38 m. S of Petersburg; pop. (1970c) 5300; composed of **North Emporia** and **South Emporia.**

Em·po·ri·um \em-'pōr-ē-əm\. Borough, ⊗ of Cameron co., N cen. Pennsylvania, 38 m. SSE of Bradford; pop. (1970c) 3074; manufactures radio tubes, leather.

Em·press Au·gus·ta Bay \'em-prəs-ȯ-ˌgəs-tə-, -ə-ˌgəs-\. Widemouthed inlet of Solomon Sea on W coast of Bougainville I., NW Solomon Is., W Pacific Ocean; scene Nov. 1, 1943 of first landing by U.S. Marines in invasion of Bougainville (*q.v.*).

Ems \'emz, 'em(p)s\. 1 *or anc.* **Ami·sia** \ə-'mizh-(ē-)ə\. River, West Germany; 231 m. long; rises in NE North Rhine-Westphalia, flows NW and N to the North Sea; its mouth is a wide estuary bordering on NE Netherlands, the upper part forming the Dollart (*q.v.*) and the lower comprising the navigable main channel which divides, passing to the W (**West Ems**) and E (**East Ems**) of Borkum I. in the East Frisian Is.; connected with the Ruhr region by the Dortmund-Ems canal system.

2 Town, West Germany. See BAD EMS.

Ems·det·ten \'emz-ˌdet-ᵊn, 'em(p)s-\. Commune, North Rhine-Westphalia, West Germany, on Ems river 16 m. NNW of Münster; pop. (1969e) 28,417; textiles; became town 1938.

Ems·worth \'emz-wərth\. Residential borough, Allegheny co., SW Pennsylvania, on Ohio river 8 m. WNW of Pittsburgh; pop. (1970c) 3345.

Enard Bay \ˌen-ˌärd-\. Bay on NW coast of Scotland, S of Point of Stoer and N of Loch Broom.

Enare. See INARI.

Enare, Lake. See INARI, LAKE.

En·can·to, Cape \-en-'kän-(ˌ)tō\ *or* **Encanto Point.** Cape on E coast of Luzon, Phil., at SE point of Baler Bay.

En·car·na·ción \ˌen-kär-ˌnäs-ē-'ōn\. 1 *or in full* **Encarnación de Di·az** \-dā-'dē-ˌäs\. Town, Jalisco state, W cen. Mexico, 25 m. S of Aguascalientes; munic. pop. (1970p) 29,533.

2 Town, ✱ of Itapúa dept., SE Paraguay, on Paraná river opp. Posadas, Argentina, with which it is connected by ferry, 180 m. SE of Asunción; munic. pop. (1970e) 47,333; railroad terminus; in agricultural and grazing district; founded 1614.

En·con·tra·dos \ˌen-kən-'träd-əs\. Town, Zulia state, NW Venezuela, on Catatumbo river 125 m. SW of Maracaibo; center of coffee-growing region near Colombia border.

En·coun·ter Bay \in-'kaůnt-ər-\. Inlet of Indian Ocean, SE South Australia, at outlet of Murray river.

En·cru·ci·ja·da \en-ˌkrü-sē-'(h)äd-ə\. Town and municipality, Las Villas prov., W cen. Cuba, 15 m. N of Santa Clara; munic. pop. (1967e) 23,020.

En·dau \'en-ˌdaů\. River, NE Johore and SE Pahang states, West Malaysia, S Malay Penin.; flows NE into South China Sea near SE boundary of Pahang state.

En·de \'en-də\. Town and port on S coast of Flores I., Lesser Sunda Is., Indonesia; pop. (1961c) 26,843; chief administrative center of E Sunda Is.

En·der·bury \'en-dər-ˌber-ē\. One of the more important of the Phoenix Is., cen. Pacific Ocean, 3°08'S lat. and 171°05'W long; an atoll 3 m. long by ¾ m. wide; 4 sq. m.; formerly worked for guano. As an important airplane base visited and claimed 1937–39 by both Great Britain and U.S.A.; with Canton I. placed 1939 under joint control; has no good anchorage and no seaplane facilities, its lagoon being merely a shallow pool.

En·der·by Land \'en-dər-bē-\. Semicircular projection of Antarctica, extending from Prince Olav Coast (ab. 45°E) to Edward VIII Bay at ab. 57°20'E and extending S from ab. lat. 67°30'S; first sighted by John Biscoe 1831–32; claimed by Australia.

Enderby Quadrant. Formerly, the quarter section of the Antarctic Continent (see ANTARCTICA) bet. the Greenwich meridian and 90°E; now chiefly Queen Maud Land,

Enderby Land, Mac Robertson Land, and Luitpold and Astrid Coast.

En·der·lin \'en-dər-lən\. City, Ransom co., SE North Dakota, 29 m. SE of Valley City; pop. (1970c) 1343.

En·di·cott \'en-di-kət, -də-ˌkät\. Village, Broome co., S New York, on Susquehanna river, 8 m. W of Binghamton; pop. (1970c) 16,556; with Binghamton and Johnson City, one of so-called Triple Cities; manufactures shoes, business machines.

Endicott Mountains. Subsidiary mountain range, cen. part of Brooks Range, N Alaska; highest peak ab. 9000 ft.

En·dor \'en-ˌdȯ(ə)r\ *or* **'En Dor** \-'dō(ə)r, -'dȯ(ə)r\. Town of anc. Palestine, its site now in Israel near Mt. Tabor 6 m. SE of Nazareth (*1 Sam.* xxviii. 7).

En·dröd \'en-drəd\. Commune, SE Hungary, on Körös river 60 m. SW of Debrecen; pop. (1970p) 8124.

Enez \e-'nez\ *or anc.* **Ae·nos** \'ē-nəs\. Town and port, Edirne prov., SW Turkey in Europe, on Meriç (Maritsa) river in its delta.

En·fi·da \en-'fēd-ə\ *or Fr.* **En·fi·da·ville** \äⁿ-fēd-ə-vēl\. Town, NE Tunisia, near the coast ab. 30 m. SW of Hammamet; pop. (1966c) 2900; in World War II center of fighting Apr. 1943, taken by British Apr. 20.

En·field \'en-ˌfēld\. 1 Manufacturing town, NE Hartford co., N Connecticut, on E bank of Connecticut river on Mass. border; pop. (1970c) 46,189; tobacco growing; Our Lady of the Angels Junior Coll. (1945); settled 1681 as part of Massachusetts; annexed to Connecticut 1749; includes Thompsonville (*q.v.*).

2 Manufacturing town, Grafton co., W New Hampshire, 6 m. E of Lebanon; pop. (1970c) 2345; formerly site of Shaker settlements.

3 Town, Halifax co., NE North Carolina, 18 m. NNE of Rocky Mount; pop. (1970c) 3272; ⊗ of Edgecombe co. 1745–58.

4 A borough of Greater London, SE England. See table at LONDON 4.

En·ga·dine \ˌeŋ-gə-'dēn\ *or Ger.* **En·ga·din** \ˌeŋ-gä-'dēn\ *or Ital.* **En·ga·di·na** \ˌeŋ-gə-'dē-nə\. Swiss portion of valley of the Inn river, in E Graubünden canton, E Switzerland; ab. 60 m. long; SW part is called the **Upper Engadine** and NE part the **Lower Engadine**; Saint-Moritz is near SW end.

Engannim. See JENIN.

Engano. See ENGGANO.

En·ga·ño, Cape \-en-'gän-(ˌ)yō\. 1 Cape at E end of island of Hispaniola, on NW side of Mona Passage.

2 Northeast point of Cagayan prov., Luzon, Phil., formed by N tip of Palaui I., 18°35'N; lighthouse; important naval battle off this cape Oct. 25, 1944 in which American fleet defeated Japanese force.

En·ge·bi \en-'gā-bē\. Islet of Eniwetok (*q.v.*) atoll, Marshall Is.; captured by Americans Feb. 17–19, 1944.

En–ge·di \en-'gē-ˌdī, -'gēd-ē\ *or* **'En Ge·di** \-'gē-dī\. Village and spring on W shore of Dead Sea, Israel, 18 m. E of Hebron (*1 Sam.* xxiv. 1).

Eng·el·berg \'eŋ-əl-ˌbe(ə)rg\. Valley in the Alps, in Unterwalden canton, cen. Switzerland.

En·gel·mann Peak \ˌeŋ-gəl-mən-\. Mountain in Clear Creek co., N cen. Colorado; 13,500 ft.

Eng·els \'eŋ-(g)əlz\ *or formerly* **Po·krovsk** \pə-'krȯfsk\. Town, Saratov Oblast, Russian S.F.S.R., U.S.S.R., on the Volga opp. Saratov; pop. (1970p) 130,000; bricks, chemicals, machinery; food processing; ✱ of former Volga German A.S.S.R.; founded 1747; renamed 1932 in honor of Friedrich Engels.

Eng·ga·no *or* **En·ga·no** \eŋ-'gän-(ˌ)ō\. Island in the Indian Ocean off SW coast of Sumatra, Indonesia; 18 m. long by 11 m. wide; area (with nearby islets) 171 sq. m.; chief export copra.

Enghien. See MONTMORENCY 4.

En·ghien–les–Bains \äⁿ-'gaⁿ-lā-'baⁿ\. Commune, Val-d'Oise dept., N France, N suburb of Paris; pop. (1968c) 12,152; mineral springs and baths.

En·gland \'iŋ-glənd *also* 'iŋ-lənd\. 1 *or Lat.* **An·glia** \'aŋ-glē-ə\. South part of the island of Great Britain, excluding Wales; largest unit of the United Kingdom of Great Britain and Northern Ireland; 50,333 sq. m.; pop. (1971p) 45,870,062; ✱ London. *Physical features:* In N the Pennine Chain, Cumbrian Mts. (including Scafell Pike 3210 ft., highest in country), and Cheviot Hills (along Scottish border); in SW the Cotswold Hills and plateau regions of Exmoor and Dartmoor; in SE the Downs, and in S Salisbury Plain. *Chief rivers:* Thames in S, Ouse in cen. and E, Humber (with Ouse and Trent) in NE, Mersey in W, and Severn in SW. *Chief lakes:* Bassenthwaite, Derwent Water, Ullswater, Windermere, all of great scenic beauty in the Lake District in Cumberland, Westmorland, and Lancashire in NW. *Islands:* Isle of Man in Irish Sea off NW coast, Isle of Wight in English Channel off S coast, Lundy I. at entrance to Bristol Channel, and Scilly Is. off Lands End (the SW tip of England). *Chief products:* Barley, wheat, sugar beets, vegetables; livestock raising, fishing; coal, salt; manufacturing: iron and steel, chemicals, textiles, transportation and electronic equipment, rubber goods, glass, pharmaceuticals; power production, publishing; tourism. *Chief cities:* London, Birmingham, Liverpool, Manchester, Sheffield, Leeds, Bristol. For history, see GREAT BRITAIN. Divided into the following counties (for pronunciation of their names, see their individual entries):

NAME[1]	AREA (sq. m.)	POP. (1971p)	CO. SEAT
Bedfordshire	477	463,493	Bedford
Berkshire	725	633,457	Reading
Buckinghamshire	746	586,211	Aylesbury
Cambridgeshire and Isle of Ely	831	302,507	Cambridge
Cheshire	1,015	1,542,624	Chester
Cornwall	1,375	379,892	Bodmin
Cumberland	1,520	292,009	Carlisle
Derbyshire	997	884,339	Derby
Devonshire	2,591	896,245	Exeter
Dorsetshire	978	361,213	Dorchester
Durham	991	1,408,103	Durham
Essex	1,418	1,353,564	Chelmsford
Gloucestershire	1,259	1,069,454	Gloucester
Greater London	610	7,379,014	London
Hampshire	1,503	1,561,605	Winchester
Herefordshire	842	138,425	Hereford
Hertfordshire	631	922,188	Hertford
Huntingdon and Peterborough	486	202,337	Huntingdon and Godmanchester
Kent	1,443	1,396,030	Maidstone
Lancashire	1,878	5,106,123	Lancaster
Leicestershire	834	771,213	Leicester
Lincolnshire			
The Parts of Holland	418	105,643	Boston
The Parts of Kesteven	734	232,215	Sleaford
The Parts of Lindsey	1,510	470,526	Lincoln
Norfolk	2,054	616,427	Norwich
Northamptonshire	914	467,843	Northampton
Northumberland	2,019	794,975	Newcastle
Nottinghamshire	843	974,640	Nottingham
Oxfordshire	749	380,814	Oxford
Rutland	153	27,463	Oakham
Shropshire	1,348	336,934	Shrewsbury
Somersetshire	1,613	681,974	Taunton
Staffordshire	1,157	1,856,890	Stafford
Suffolk			
East Suffolk	871	380,524	Ipswich
West Suffolk	611	164,201	Bury St. Edmunds
Surrey	654	999,588	Kingston Upon Thames
Sussex			
East Sussex	824	750,312	Lewes
West Sussex	633	491,020	Chichester
Warwickshire	973	2,079,799	Warwick
Westmorland	789	72,724	Appleby
Wight, Isle of	147	109,284	Newport
Wiltshire	1,344	486,048	Salisbury
Worcestershire	704	692,605	Worcester

NAME[1]	AREA (sq. m.)	POP. (1971p)	CO. SEAT
Yorkshire			
East Riding	1,172	542,565	Beverly
North Riding	2,152	724,463	Northallerton
West Riding	2,799	3,780,539	Wakefield

[1]For county names ending in *-shire*, the *-shire* is often omitted in informal use when there is no ambiguity. In legal use, *county of Gloucester, Hereford, Stafford,* etc., not *Gloucestershire, Herefordshire,* etc., is preferred. The redundant *county of Gloucestershire, Herefordshire,* etc., is incorrect.

2 City, Lonoke co., cen. Arkansas, 22 m. SE of Little Rock; pop. (1970c) 3075; cotton, lumber; truck farms.

En·gle·wood \ˈeŋ-gəl-ˌwu̇d\. 1 Suburban residential city, Arapahoe co., NE cen. Colorado, 5 m. S of Denver; pop. (1970c) 33,695.

2 City, Bergen co., NE corner of New Jersey, W of Hudson river 10 m. E of Paterson; pop. (1970c) 24,985; incorporated as city 1895; Palisades Interstate Park nearby.

3 Village, Montgomery co., SW Ohio, 10 m. NW of Dayton; pop. (1970c) 7825.

Englewood Cliffs. Borough, Bergen co., NE New Jersey, 12 m. SSE of Paterson; pop. (1970c) 5938; residential.

En·glish \ˈiŋ-glish\. 1 Town, ⊗ of Crawford co., S Indiana, 33 m. W of New Albany; pop. (1970c) 664.

2 River, largest tributary of the Winnipeg, in SW Ontario, Canada; flows W through chain of lakes; ab. 100 m. long.

English Ba·zar \-bə-ˈzär\. Town, West Bengal, NE India, 170 m. N of Calcutta; pop. (1961c) 45,900.

English Channel *or often* **The Channel** *or Fr.* **La Manche** \lå-mä^{n}sh\ *or anc.* **Oce·a·nus Bri·tan·ni·cus** \ō-ˈsē-ə-nəs-bri-ˈtan-i-kəs\. Strait bet. S England and N France; connects with Atlantic Ocean on the W and with North Sea (through the Strait of Dover) on the NE; varies in width bet. 20 and 100 m.

En·glish·man Bay \ˈiŋ-glish-mən-, ˈiŋ-lish-\. Inlet of Atlantic Ocean on S cen. coast of Washington co., SE Maine.

English Turn \-ˈtərn\ *or Fr.* **Dé·tour des An·glais** \dā-ˈtu̇(ə)r-dā-zä^{n}-ˈglā\. Bend of Mississippi river just below New Orleans, Louisiana, also the village in the bend; here an English expedition was turned back Sept. 1699 by Bienville's story of French forces farther up the river.

En·gui·ne·gatte \ä^{n}-gēn-ˈgät\; *formerly* **Gui·ne·gate** *or* **Gui·ne·gaste** \gēn-ˈgät\. Commune, Pas-de-Calais dept., N France, S of Saint-Omer; pop. (1962c) 422; scene of two battles: (1) bet. Louis XI and Emperor Maximilian Aug. 7, 1479 and (2) bet. Henry VIII and France Aug. 16, 1513 in which the French were defeated, known as "Battle of the Spurs" from hasty flight of the French.

Engyum. See GANGI.

Enid \ˈē-nəd\. City, ⊗ of Garfield co., N Oklahoma, 68 m. NNW of Oklahoma City; pop. (1970c) 44,986; agricultural machinery; meat packing; grain elevators, oil refineries; wheat; poultry; Phillips Univ. (1907); founded 1893.

Enikale Strait. See KERCH STRAIT.

Eni·peus \i-ˈnī-ˌpyüs\ *or* **Eni·pévs** \ˌen-i-ˈpefs\. River in Thessaly, Greece, tributary of the Pinios; rises in Othrys Mts.

Enisei. See YENISEI.

Enisei Bay. See YENISEI BAY.

Eniseisk. See YENISEISK.

Eni·we·tok \ˌen-i-ˈwē-ˌtäk, e-ˈnē-wə-\. Atoll at extreme NW end of Ralik Chain, NW Marshall Is., W Pacific Ocean, 11°30′N lat. and 162°15′E long.; circular in shape with 40 islets around lagoon 23 m. in diameter; good anchorage; main islets Eniwetok in S and Engebi in N; taken by Americans from Japanese Feb. 17–22, 1944 and made into a naval base; in 1947 designated by U.S. Atomic Energy Commission as permanent mid-Pacific proving ground for atomic weapons.

Enk·hui·zen \eŋk-ˈhȯiz-ᵊn, -ˈhīz-\. Commune and seaport, North Holland prov., W Netherlands, on W shore of IJsselmeer 28 m. NE of Amsterdam; pop. (1970e) 11,502; received town rights 1355; important commercial and fishing center in early 17th cent.

En·na \en-ə\. 1 Province of cen. Sicily, Italy. See table at ITALY.

2 *or before 1927* **Ca·stro·gio·van·ni** \ˌkäs-trō-jə-ˈvän-ē\; *anc.* **En·na** \ˈen-ə\ *or* **Hen·na** \ˈhen-ə\. Commune, its ✱, 64 m. SE of Palermo; pop. (1968e) 28,653; summer resort; trades in sulfur and rock salt; cathedral (founded 1307), old feudal fortress, castle built by Frederick II of Aragon. Ancient site of principal temple of Ceres (Demeter) and, in mythology, her birthplace; headquarters of slaves in First Servile War 134–32 B.C.; nearby Lake of Pergusa site of fabled rape of Proserpine by Pluto; captured by Saracens 9th cent. and by Normans 11th cent.

En Na·hud \ˌen-na-ˈhüd\ *or* **An Nu·hūd** \ˌan-nə-\. Commercial town, W Kordofan prov., cen. Sudan, 120 m. WSW of Al-Ubayyid; trades in cattle and cotton goods.

En Na·qu·ra \ˌen-nə-ˈku̇r-ə\ *or* **An Nā·qū·rah** \ˌan-\. Village and cape (*Arab.* **Ras en Naqura** \ˈräs-\) on SW coast of Lebanon.

En Nasira. See NAZARETH 2.

En Nebk \en-ˈneb-ək\ *or* **An Nabk** \ˈan-ˈnab-ək\ *also* **Neb·ek** \ˈneb-ək\. Town, SW Syria, ab. 42 m. NE of Damascus.

En·ne·di \ˌen-ə-ˈdē\. Mountains, NE Chad, N cen. Africa; highest peak 4298 ft.

En·ne·pe·tal \ˈen-ə-pə-ˌtäl\. City, North Rhine-Westphalia, West Germany; pop. (1969e) 36,922; formed 1949.

En·ner·dale Water \ˌen-ər-ˌdāl-\. Lake in the Lake District, Cumberland, NW England; 2½ m. long; maximum depth 148 ft.

En·nis \ˈen-əs\. 1 Industrial city, Ellis co., NE cen. Texas, 20 m. N of Corsicana; pop. (1970c) 11,046; cotton compresses and gins; cottonseed oil.

2 Urban district, ⊗ of co. Clare, W Eire; pop. (1971p) 5934; limestone quarrying, brewing, whiskey distilling; ruins of two abbeys nearby. Franciscan abbey (1242; now a national monument), Clare abbey (1195).

En·nis·cor·thy \ˌen-ə-ˈskȯr-thē\. Urban district, cen. co. Wexford, SE Eire, on river Slaney; pop. (1971p) 5559; brewing, manufacture of woolens, tanning; agricultural trading center; remains of 13th cent. castle.

En·nis·kil·len \ˌen-ə-ˈskil-ən\ *or* **In·nis·kil·ling** \ˌin-ə-ˈskil-iŋ\. Urban district, ⊗ of co. Fermanagh, SW Northern Ireland, on an island in the Erne river just S of Lough Erne; pop. (1971p) 6518; trading center for agricultural region; manufactures cutlery. Scene of battle 1689 in which forces of William III defeated those of James II; famous regiment of Enniskillen Dragoons formed at the time.

En Nofilia. See NOFILIA.

Enns \ˈenz\. 1 River, cen. Austria; 158 m. long; flows E and N from Styria into Danube river 11 m. SE of Linz; forms section of boundary bet. Upper Austria and Lower Austria.

2 Town, Austria, on Enns river near its confluence with the Danube; pop. (1964e) 9300; one of the oldest towns in Austria, receiving charter 1212; on old trade route across the Danube; in medieval times a prosperous market town; nearby is famous Augustinian monastery of St. Florian, with fine manuscript library.

En·o·ree \ˈen-ə-ˌrē\. River, NW South Carolina; ab. 80 m. long; rises in Blue Ridge Mts. in Greenville co., flows SE into Broad river.

Enotah, Mount. See BRASSTOWN BALD.

En·ri·qui·llo, Lake \-ˌen-rə-ˈkē-(ˌ)(y)ō\. Salt lake, SW Dominican Republic, E Hispaniola I., West Indies; 150 ft. below sea level.

En·sche·de \ˌen(t)-skə-ˈdā\. Industrial commune, Overijssel prov., E Netherlands, near West German frontier; pop. (1970e) 139,245; beer, pharmaceuticals, textiles, rubber goods; natural history museum, technical univ. (1961); first mentioned 1118.

En·se·na·da \ˌen(t)-sən-ˈ(y)äd-ə\. 1 Town on coast of Río de la Plata, Buenos Aires prov., E Argentina, ab. 35 m. SE of Buenos Aires; pop. (1960c) 26,086; forms part of the port of La Plata.

2 Seaport, N Baja California, NW Mexico, on Pacific Ocean; munic. pop. (1970p) 113,320.

Ensham. See EYNSHAM.

En·shū Bight \ˌen-ˌshü-\ *or formerly* **To·to·mi Sea** \tō-ˌtō-me-\. Inlet of W Pacific Ocean, S coast of Honshū, Japan.

En·teb·be \en-ˈteb-ə\. Town, formerly administrative ✱ of Uganda, E Africa, 19 m. SW of Kampala, on N shore of Lake Victoria; pop. (1969c) 10,900; alt. 3760 ft.; on the equator; botanical gardens; in region producing bananas, coffee, cotton; connected by rail via Nairobi with Mombasa; founded 1893; was capital of Uganda 1894–1962.

En·ter·prise \ˈent-ər-ˌprīz\. 1 City, Coffee co., SE Alabama, 27 m. W of Dothan; pop. (1970c) 15,591; concrete products, soap; meat packing; Enterprise State Junior Coll. (1965).

2 City, ⊗ of Wallowa co., NE corner of Oregon, 54 m. NE of Baker; pop. (1970c) 1680; pine timber; ranching, agriculture.

En·tre–Dou·ro–e–Mi·nho \ˌen-trə-ˈdōr-(ˌ)ü-ē-ˈmē-(ˌ)nyü, -ˈdȯr-\ *or popularly* **Minho.** Former province, NW Portugal; 2749 sq. m.; ✱ Braga.

En·tre Rí·os \ˌen-trə-ˈrē-əs\. Province of E Argentina. See table at ARGENTINA.

Enu·gu \ā-ˈnü-(ˌ)gü\. City, ✱ of East-Central State, Nigeria; pop. (1969e) 160,567; coal mining; pottery; railway workshop; technical coll. (1955).

Enum·claw \ˈē-nəm-ˌklȯ\. Town, King co., W cen. Washington, 23 m. E of Tacoma; pop. (1970c) 4703; gateway to recreation areas of Mount Rainier.

En·yu; Enyu Channel \ˈen-(ˌ)yü\. See BIKINI.

Eolie, Isole. See LIPARI ISLANDS.

Eo·lus, Mount \-ē-ˈō-ləs\. Peak, La Plata co., SW Colorado; 14,084 ft.

Éparges, Les. See LES ÉPARGES.

Ep·au·let Mountain \ˌep-ə-ˌlet-, -lət-\. Peak, Clear Creek co., N cen. Colorado; 13,500 ft.

Epe \ˈā-pə\. Commune, Gelderland prov., E Netherlands, 9 m. N of Apeldoorn; pop. (1970e) 27,515; food processing.

Epe·cuén, Lake \-ˌep-ə-ˈkwen\. Lake, S Buenos Aires prov., E Argentina; 15 sq. m.; resort.

Epe·hy \e-ˈpē\. Village, Somme dept., N France, S of Cambrai; pop. (1962c) 1252; destroyed in World War I; taken by the British Sept. 1918.

Epeiros. See EPIRUS.

Éper·nay \ˌā-per-ˈnā\ *or anc.* **Spar·na·cum** \ˈspär-nə-kəm\. Commune, Marne dept., NE France, on the Marne 21 m. WNW of Châlons-sur-Marne; pop. (1968c) 26,583; in region famous for production of champagne wines; manufactures earthenware; railway workshops. Fortified city in Middle Ages; besieged by Henry IV 1592; scene of violent fighting and air raids 1914–18.

Eph·e·sus \ˈef-ə-səs\. Ruins of ancient Ionian city, W Asia Minor, near coast of Aegean Sea 35 m. SSE of İzmir, in fertile plain near the mouth of the Caÿster river. Traditionally founded by Carians; one of the 12 Ionian Cities; conquered by Persians; its democracy restored by Alexander the Great 334 B.C.; had famous temple, a center of cult of Diana; finally came to Romans from king of Pergamum (*q.v.*); capital of Roman province of Asia; early seat of Christianity (visited by Saint Paul on second and third missionary journeys, church to which he wrote the *Epistle to the Ephesians*); sacked by Goths 262 A.D.; seat of church council which condemned heresy of Nestorius 431.

Ephra·im \ˈē-frē-əm\. 1 City, Sanpete co., cen. Utah, 43 m. WSW of Price; pop. (1970c) 2127; timber; center of turkey and sheep-raising area; settled 1853.

2 Sometimes, the Northern Kingdom, or Kingdom of Israel (see ISRAEL 1).

3 Mountainous region or range (**Mount Ephraim**) of Jordan, originally the country allotted to the tribe of Ephraim; extended S from near Shechem to neighborhood of Bethel.

Eph·ra·ta \ˈef-rət-ə\. Borough, Lancaster co., SE Pennsylvania, 13 m. NE of Lancaster; pop. (1970c) 9662; stock raising. Founded c. 1732 as German Seventh-day Baptist monastic community (Society of the Solitary) by Johann Conrad Beissel; Ephrata Cloisters built and printing press established 1745.

Ephra·ta \i-ˈfrāt-ə\. City, ⊗ of Grant co., cen. Washington at S end of the Grand Coulee valley; pop. (1970c) 5255; diversified farming.

Epi *or* **Api** \ˈā-pē\. One of the New Hebrides Is., SW Pacific Ocean, in E part of the group, 25 m. SE of Malekula; 27 m. long by 11 m. wide; pop. (1967c) 1718; has mountain peak 2770 ft.; fertile soil; fine plantations (esp. coconut).

Epidamnus. See DURRËS 2.

Ep·i·dau·rus \ˌep-ə-ˈdȯr-əs\. Ancient seaport town in Greece, on E coast of Argolis on Saronic Gulf, 25 m. E of Argos; site of famous temple dedicated to Asclepius, Greek god of medicine and healing; also site of theater and a Greek round structure (*tholos,* rotunda); much visited for centuries; until Roman times town and vicinity were semi-independent.

Épi·nal \ˌā-pi-ˈnäl\. Commune, ✱ of Vosges dept., NE France, on Moselle river 65 m. E of Chaumont; pop. (1968c) 36,856; textiles; printing; metallurgical works; freestone and marble quarried nearby; founded 10th cent.; in World War II captured by U.S. forces Sept. 25, 1944.

Épi·nay–sur–Seine \ˌā-pə-ˌnā-sü(ə)r-ˈsān, -ˈsen\. Industrial commune, Seine-St-Denis dept., N France, N suburb of Paris on the Seine; pop. (1968c) 41,774.

Epiphania. See HAMA.

Epiphanie, L'. See L'EPIPHANIE

Epi·rus \i-ˈpī-rəs\ *or Gk.* **Epei·ros** \ˈē-pi-ˌrȯs\. 1 An ancient country in NW Greece, bounded on N by Illyria, on E by Macedonia and Thessaly, on S by Aetolia and Acarnania, and on W by Ionian Sea, extending along coast of latter from Acroceraunia promontory on N to the Ambracian Gulf on S; mountainous, traversed by main range of Pindus Mts. and parallel ranges; mountains cut by Inachus, Achelous, and Thíamis rivers; more important of its districts were Athamania, Thesprotia (*q.v.*), Molossis, and Chaonia; chief towns Phoenice, Dodona, Buthrotum.

History: United by King Pyrrhus (d. 272 B.C.); made a republic c. 200 B.C.; after Roman defeat of Macedonians 197 B.C. retained independence; punished by Rome for supporting Perseus 168 B.C.; set up as Roman province 146 B.C.; under Byzantine Empire until Michael Angelus Comnenus erected an independent state 1204; conquered by Turks 1430–40; Greece received E part 1881, captured Ioannina 1913, and was awarded 1919 the W part as far N as a point on the coast off N Corfu; N part is now in S Albania; formed battleground for Greeks and Italians 1940–41.

2 Administrative division of modern Greece, its W part N of the Peloponnesus; forms departments of Arta, Ioannina, Preveza, and Thesprotia. See table at GREECE.

Epo·meo, Mon·te \ˈmȯn-tē-ˌā-pə-ˈmā-(ˌ)ō\. Highest point on island of Ischia (*q.v.*); 2585 ft.

Eporedia. See IVREA.

Ep·per·ly, Mount \-ˈep-ər-lē\. Mountain, Antarctica, 78°26′S, 85°53′W; 15,100 ft.

Ep·ping \ˈep-iŋ\. 1 Manufacturing town, Rockingham co., SE New Hampshire, 15 m. W of Portsmouth; pop. (1970c) 2356; shoes, bricks.

2 Urban district, Essex, SE England, 17 m. NE of London; pop. (1971p) 11,681; on N edge of **Epping Forest,** a former royal forest of large extent, now a pleasure ground.

Ep·som and Ew·ell \ˈep-səm . . . ˈyü-əl\. Municipal borough, Surrey, S England, on the edge of Banstead Downs; pop. (1971p) 72,054; the seat of Epsom College;

nearby is **Epsom Downs** racecourse, where the Derby and the Oaks are run annually; magnesia springs in the vicinity from which Epsom salts formerly were made.

Ep·worth \'ep-(,)wərth\. Parish in the Parts of Lindsey, Lincolnshire, E England; pop. (1961c) 1822; birthplace of John Wesley—hence the name Epworth League for the Methodist young people's organization founded 1889 at Cleveland, Ohio.

Équa·teur \,ā-kwə-'tər\ *or formerly* **Co·quil·hat·ville** \,kō-kē-'at-,vil, kō-'kē-ə-,vil\. Province of NW Zaire. See table at ZAIRE.

Equa·to·ria \,ē-kwə-'tōr-ē-ə, ,ek-wə-, -'tȯr-\. 1 Occasional name used somewhat indefinitely for the equatorial regions of Africa.

2 Province, S Sudan; 76,495 sq. m.; pop. (1969e) 1,295,000; ✻ Juba; traversed by White Nile; timber, hides; scene of sporadic anti-government activity 1955–70.

Equatorial Africa. See FRENCH EQUATORIAL AFRICA.

Equatorial Countercurrent. The surface current moving E in a few places in the oceans near the equator.

Equatorial Current. The surface current moving W in the oceans near the equator.

Equatorial Guin·ea \-'gin-ē\; *formerly* **Spanish Guinea** *or Span.* **Te·rri·to·rios Es·pa·ño·les del Gol·fo de Gui·nea** \,ter-ə-'tōr-yōs-,es-pən-'yō-lās-del-,gȯl-fō-dā-gē-'nā-ə\. Republic, W Africa, consisting of: (1) Province of Río Muni, bounded on N by Cameroon, on E and S by Gabon, and on W by the Atlantic Ocean; includes islands of Corisco, Great Elobey, and Little Elobey. (2) Province of Fernando Póo, consisting of the islands of Fernando Póo and Annobón (1°25′S, 5°36′E). Total area 10,825 sq. m.; total pop. (1970e) 290,000; ✻ Santa Isabel, on the island of Fernando Póo. *Physical features:* (1) Río Muni has a coastal plain varying in width from 10 to 15 m.; cen. and E regions consist of a series of plateaus, reaching a max. height of ab. 4000 ft.; soils less fertile than those of Fernando Póo. (2) Fernando Póo I. has volcanic formations; soils highly fertile; av. annual rainfall ab. 100 in.; highest peak, Santa Isabel, 9865 ft. *Chief products:* Cocoa, coffee, palm oil, timber; fishing. *Chief towns:* Santa Isabel and Bata.

History: Island of Fernando Póo discovered by Portuguese 1471; ceded to Spain along with commercial rights on mainland 1778; Fernando Póo under British administration 1829, returned to Spain 1843; period 1857–77 marked by Spanish exploration of mainland territory; Franco-Spanish agreement regarding borders of mainland territory 1900; was granted limited self-government 1963; achieved independence 1968.

Equi·nox, Mount \-,ē-kwə-,näks-, -,ek-wə-\ *also* **Big Equinox.** Peak in Taconic Range, in Bennington co., SW Vermont; 3816 ft.

Erath \'ē-,rath\. County in Texas. See table at TEXAS.

Er·bil \'e(ə)r-,bil\ *or* **Ir·bīl** \'ər-(,)bēl\ *or* **Ar·bil** \'ar-bil, 'är-\ *or anc.* **Ar·be·la** \är-'bē-lə\. City, N Iraq, 50 m. E of Mosul and S of the Great Zab; pop. (1965c) 90,320; in rich agricultural region; a very old city, probably a Sumerian settlement that came to be one of chief places of Assyria; still has important trade; not scene of battle of Arbela, which was really fought at Gaugamela (*q.v.*) 331 B.C.; neighborhood overrun and conquered by Mongols 1236 A.D.

Erceldoune *or* **Ercildoune.** See EARLSTON.

Er·ci·yas Da·ği \,er-jē-,(y)äs-dä-'(g)ē\ *or anc.* **Ar·gae·us** \är-'jē-əs\. Peak, cen. Turkey, Asia, S of Kayseri; 12,848 ft.

Erdély. See TRANSYLVANIA.

Er·e·bus, Mount \-'er-ə-bəs\. Active volcano on James Ross I. in Ross Sea, Antarctica, 77°32′S, 167°09′E; 12,450 ft.

Erech \'ē-,rek\ *or Akkadian* **Uruk** \'ü-,rük\. Ancient Sumerian city (c. 2300 B.C.) in S Babylonia, on the Euphrates NW of Ur of the Chaldees; the modern **War·ka** \wər-'ka\, Iraq; in the Bible a city of Nimrod's kingdom in land of Shinar (*Gen.* x. 10); excavations on the site have

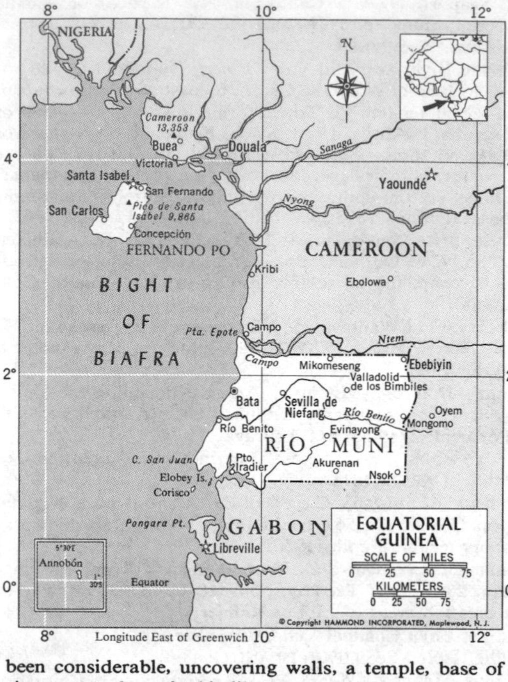

been considerable, uncovering walls, a temple, base of a ziggurat, and a valuable library.

Ereğ·li \,er-ī-'lē, ,er-ə-'glē\. 1 Town, Konya prov., SW cen. Turkey, Asia, 85 m. ESE of Konya; pop. (1965c) 38,362; textile manufacturing.

2 *or anc.* **Her·a·clea Pon·ti·ca** \,her-ə-,klē-ə-'pänt-i-kə\. Seaport on Black Sea, Zonguldak prov., NW Turkey, Asia, 40 m. ENE of mouth of the Sakarya river; pop. (1965c) 18,978.

Ere·pe·cu, Lake \-,er-ə-pə-'kü\. Lake, NW Pará state, N Brazil, N of the Amazon; traversed by Trombetas river, a tributary of the Amazon.

Erepecurú. See PARU DE OESTE.

Ere·tria \e-'rē-trē-ə\. City of ancient Greece, on S coast of Euboea I. ab. 15 m. ESE of Chalcis, its rival in the early period. Founded as an Ionian colony; destroyed by Persians 490 B.C. (before battle of Marathon) for earlier assistance to revolting Ionian Greeks; rebuilt but less significant.

Erevan. See YEREVAN.

Erft \'e(ə)rft\. River, West Germany; 71 m. long; rises in Eifel region and flows N to the Rhine near Neuss.

Er·furt \'e(ə)r-fərt, -fu̇(ə)rt\. 1 District of East Germany. See table at GERMANY, EAST.

2 Manufacturing city, its ✻, 64 m. WSW of Leipzig; pop. (1970e) 195,994; precision tools, optical instruments; food processing. Commercial flower growing, large trade in plants and seed; 12th cent. cathedral.

History: According to tradition, founded 6th cent.; episcopal see founded by Saint Boniface 742; famous university founded 1379 (closed 1812); signed protective treaty with Saxony 1483; residence of Luther as Augustinian monk 1505–08; passed to elector of Mainz 17th cent.; scene of Congress of Erfurt (Napoleon, Alexander of Russia, numerous German sovereigns) 1808; taken by Prussia 1813; Prussian rule confirmed by Congress of Vienna 1814; captured by American forces Apr. 12, 1945; scene of first meeting of heads of government of East and West Germany 1970.

Erg, Al– \al-'e(ə)rg\. Any of certain regions of sand dunes in the Sahara, N Africa, including: **Erg Igui·di** *also* **Erg Igi·di** \-,ē-gə-'dē\ in W Algeria and N Mauritania; **Erg Chech** \-'shesh\ in SW Algeria and N Republic of Mali;

Grand Erg Oc·ci·den·tal \grän-'te(ə)rg-ˌäk-sə-ˌdän-'tal\ in N cen. Algeria S of Saïda dept.; **Grand Erg Orien·tal** \-ˌōr-ē-ˌän-'tal, -ˌòr-\ in Oasis dept., E Algeria.

Er·ga·ni \'er-(g)ə-ˌnē\. Town, Diyarbakır prov., E cen. Turkey in Asia; pop. (1965c) 10,528.

Er·ge·ne \ˌer-gə-'nā\. River, NW Turkey, Europe; rises near Black Sea coast, flows W into Maritsa (Meriç) river on Greek border; 175 m. long.

Erh Hai \'e(ə)r-'hī\ *or* **Ta·li Lake** \ˌtä-ˌlē-\. Lake in W Yunnan prov., S China; 30 m. long by 10 to 15 m. wide; alt. ab. 6600 ft.; has Ta-li city on W shore; resorts, many white marble pagodas built 1000 years ago by Sung dynasty; outlet to Yang-p'i river, a tributary of the Mekong.

Eri·ce \e-'rē-chə\. Commune, Trapani prov., Sicily, S Italy; pop. (1968e) 22,570.

Er·icht, Loch \-'er-ikt\. Lake, Perth and Inverness cos., N cen. Scotland; 14 m. long.

Er·ick \'er-ik\. City, Beckham co., W Oklahoma, 50 m. NNW of Altus; pop. (1970c) 1285; cattle ranches, gas wells.

Er·ics·son, Mount \-'er-ik-sən\. Peak in Sierra Nevada, in N Tulare co., S cen. California; 13,625 ft.

Eridanus. See PO.

Eri·du \'er-ə-ˌdü\. Ancient city, the chief seaport of Sumer and Babylonia, close to shore of Persian Gulf; its site now in Iraq, 120 m. from the gulf near the lower Euphrates, S of An Nasiriya and near Ur of the Chaldees; the first royal city of Sumerian tradition; perhaps dates back to 7000 B.C.; seat of the god Ea; excavations begun 1855.

Erie \'ir-ē\. **1** Name of counties in three states of the U.S. See tables at NEW YORK, OHIO, PENNSYLVANIA.

2 City, ⊗ of Neosho co., SE Kansas; pop. (1970c) 1414.

3 City and port of entry, ⊗ of Erie co., NW corner of Pennsylvania, on Lake Erie; pop. (1970c) 129,231; large harbor, ships lumber, coal, iron ore, petroleum, grain, fish; coal and natural gas deposits; manufactures boilers and engines, stoves, machinery, electric locomotives, asbestos and paper products; Villa Maria Coll. (1882), Mercyhurst Coll. (1871). Laid out 1795 on site of old French Fort Presque Isle (1753); incorp. as borough and became ⊗ 1803; headquarters of Commodore Perry (most of whose vessels were built here) in War of 1812; chartered as city 1851.

Erie, Lake. Lake in U.S. and Canada, bounded on W and N by Ontario prov., Canada, on E by New York, on S by Pennsylvania and Ohio, and on SW by Michigan, the U.S.-Canada boundary passing through the lake; ab. 241 m. long; 9910 sq. m.; 4th in size of the five Great Lakes (*q.v.*); greatest depth 210 ft.; elevation 570 ft.; area of drainage basin 40,000 sq. m.; at W end connected through Detroit river, Lake St. Clair, and St. Clair river with Lake Huron, and at E end through Niagara river and Welland Ship Canal with Lake Ontario. Battle of Lake Erie, in which Commodore Perry defeated British naval force, fought in Put-in-Bay Sept. 10, 1813. See ERIE CANAL; NEW YORK STATE BARGE CANAL.

Erie Canal. Canal, from Buffalo, New York, on Lake Erie to Albany, New York, on Hudson river; 363 m. long; 40 ft. wide at surface and 4 ft. deep; built 1817–25; enlarged several times and finally (work begun 1909) made a barge canal and became main waterway (340 m. long, 150 ft. wide, and 12 ft. deep) of the New York State Barge Canal (*q.v.*).

Erímanthos. See ERYMANTHUS.

Eri·mo, Cape \-'er-i-ˌmō\. Cape on SE coast of Hokkaidō I., Japan.

Erin \'i(ə)r-ən\. Town, ⊗ of Houston co., NW Tennessee; pop. (1970c) 1157.

Er·in \'er-ən\ *also* **Ei·rinn** \'ā-rin, 'ar-ən\. Ireland—now a poetic name.

Er·i·trea \ˌer-ə-'trē-ə, -'trā-\. Province, N Ethiopia, NE Africa; 45,405 sq. m.; pop. (1970e) 1,836,800; ✱ Asmara. *Physical features:* Includes the many islands of the Dahlak Archipelago and Zuqar I. farther S; has low coastal plain and interior mountain range with peaks 5300 ft. to 9882 ft.; has two streams in the N, the Anseba and Barka; headstreams of the Barka flow N to Red Sea in Sudan, and cross its W part the Gash, tributary of Atbara. *Chief products:* Cotton, coffee, tobacco, salt. *Chief towns:* Asmara, Mesewa, Aseb.

History: Part of ancient Ethiopia (*q.v.*); Aseb (*q.v.*) taken over by Italian government 1882; became a colony of Italy 1890; used as base for Italian invasion of Ethiopia 1935; made part of Italian East Africa 1936; conquered by British forces 1941; became federated with Ethiopia 1952; was made a province of Ethiopia 1962.

Erivan. See YEREVAN.

Er·lang·en \'e(ə)r-ˌläŋ-ən\. City, Bavaria, West Germany, on Regnitz river 12 m. NNW of Nürnberg; pop. (1969e) 84,619; electronic equipment, textiles, machinery; brewing; 18th cent. baroque town hall; 18th cent. castle; univ. (1743). Received city rights 1398; passed to burgraves of Nürnberg 1402, margraves of Bayreuth 1541, Prussia 1791, Bavaria 1810.

Er·lang·er \'ər-laŋ-gər\. Residential city, Kenton co., N Kentucky, 7 m. SW of Covington and 4 m. SE of Greater Cincinnati airport; pop. (1970c) 12,676.

Erlau. See EGER.

Er·me·land \'er-mə-ˌlänt\ *or* **Erm·land** \'e(ə)rm-ˌlänt\ *or* *Pol.* **War·mia** \'vär-mē-ə\. Region, Olsztyn prov., N Poland; ab. 1650 sq. m.; formerly in East Prussia, Germany; extends SE from Vislinski Zaliv; became bishopric under Teutonic Knights 1250; attached to Poland by Treaty of Thorn 1466; became part of Prussia 1772; to Poland 1945.

Er·me·lo \'er-mə-ˌlō\. **1** Commune, Gelderland prov., E Netherlands, 14 m. NE of Amersfoort; pop. (1970e) 37,-198; plastics.

2 Town, SE Transvaal, NE Rep. of South Africa, 120 m. E of Johannesburg near source of Vaal river; pop. (1967e) 22,800.

Er·mine Street \'ər-mən-\. Ancient Roman road from London to York, Britain, passing through Lincoln and Doncaster; from York had an extension past Hadrian's Wall to Scotland; one of four great Roman roads of Britain (see FOSSE WAY, ICKNIELD STREET, WATLING STREET).

Er·mont \e(ə)r-'mōn\. Commune, Val-d'Oise dept., N France; pop. (1968c) 23,842.

Er·na·ku·lam \er-'näk-ə-ləm\. Town, cen. Kerala state, S India, on Malabar Coast 120 m. W of Madurai; pop. (1970e) 213,811; fishing; several colleges.

Erne \'ərn\. River, N Ireland; 72 m. long; rises in co. Cavan, N Eire, flows N across border of Northern Ireland, turns NW and widens into **Upper Lough Erne** \-ˌläk-\, 13 m. long; continues as a winding river past Enniskillen and expands into **Lough Erne** (18 m. long; 53 sq. m.), then flows W into Donegal Bay; fine waterfall bet. Lough Erne and the bay.

Erode \i-'rōd\. Town, cen. Tamil Nadu, S India, on right bank of Cauvery river 75 m. WNW of Tiruchchirappalli; pop. (1961c) 73,762; trade center.

Er·o·manga *or* **Er·ro·manga** \ˌer-ə-'maŋ-gə\. Island in S group of New Hebrides Is., SW Pacific Ocean, 62 m. SSE of Efate; 35 m. long, 25 m. wide; pop. (1967c) 10,476; has several mountain ranges, highest point 2600 ft., and several bays with good anchorages, esp. Dillon Bay on W coast.

Er Rafa. See RAFA.

Er Ramle. See RAMLA.

Er Riad. See RIYADH.

Er·ri·boll, Loch \ˌläk-'er-ə-ˌbäl, ˌläk-\. Inlet of Atlantic Ocean on extreme N coast of Scotland; ab. 10 m. long.

Er Rif \er-'rif\ *or* **Er Riff** *also* **Rif** *or* **Riff.** Hilly coastal region in N Morocco, NW Africa, constituting cen. and E parts of former Spanish Morocco, extending from a point

E of Melilla to Ceuta; inhabited by Berber tribes (Riffians), who rose in revolt 1921; at first they defeated Spanish forces and, under leadership of Abd-al-Krim from 1923, they held out until overcome by combined Spanish and French forces 1926.

Er·ri·gal, Mount \-'er-ə-ˌgȯl\. Peak, co. Donegal, N Eire; 2466 ft.

Er·ris Head \ˌer-əs-\. Cape on NW coast of co. Mayo, NW Eire, projecting into Atlantic Ocean.

Erromanga. See EROMANGA.

Erseke. See KOLONJË.

Érsekújvár. See NOVÉ ZÁMKY.

Er·win \'ər-win\. 1 Town, Harnett co., cen. North Carolina, ab. 4 m. NW of Dunn; pop. (1970c) 2852; cotton manufactures.

2 Town, ⊗ of Unicoi co., NE Tennessee, 12 m. S of Johnson City; pop. (1970c) 4715; pottery manufactures.

Er·y·man·thus \ˌer-ə-'man(t)-thəs\; *Gk.* **Erí·man·thos** \e-'rē-män-ˌthȯs\ *or* **Olo·nos** \ˌō-lə-'nȯs\. Peak in Achaea dept., NW Peloponnesus, S Greece; 7296 ft.; in ancient times was where Arcadia, Achaea, and Elis met; in Greek mythology, scene of killing of the Erymanthian boar by Hercules.

Er·y·thrae \'er-ə-ˌthrē\. Ancient city of Lydia, on coast of the peninsula opp. island of Chios; one of the 12 Ionian Cities; dwelling place of a sibyl, Herophile, regarded usually as identical with the Cumaean sibyl.

Er·y·thrae·an Sea \er-ə-ˌthrē-ən-\ *or Lat.* **Ma·re Ery·thrae·um** \'mā-rē-ˌer-ə-'thrē-əm, 'mär-ē-\. In ancient geography, the part of the Indian Ocean now known as the Arabian Sea and the Persian Gulf; also called the Red Sea, the **Mare Ru·brum** \-'rüb-rəm\.

Er·y·thrai·on, Cape \-ˌer-ə-'thrī-ˌän\. The SE point of Crete, Greece, extending into the Mediterranean Sea.

Erz·berg \'e(ə)rts-ˌbe(ə)rg\. Mountain at Eisenerz, Styria, Austria; 5032 ft.; rich in iron ore; the mines have been worked for over 1000 years.

Erzerum. See ERZURUM.

Erz·ge·bir·ge \'erts-gə-ˌbir-gə\ *or Eng.* **Ore Mountains** \'ō(ə)r-, 'ȯ(ə)r-\ *or Czech* **Kruš·né·ho·ry** \ˌkrùsh-nə-'hȯr-ē\. Mountain range bet. East Germany and Czechoslovakia; highest peak Klínovec 4080 ft.

Er·zin·can *or* **Er·zin·jan** \ˌer-zin-'jän\. 1 Province of E cen. Turkey, Asia. See table at TURKEY.

2 Town, its ✱, on N bank of Kara Su 96 m. W of Erzurum, in Turkish Armenia; pop. (1965c) 45,197; in fertile river plain in midst of orchards and gardens; chief agricultural products wheat, fruit, and cotton; cotton and silk industries; a military station with barracks and hospital; nearby in 4th cent. A.D. was home of Gregory the Illuminator. Came under control of Seljuks 1071 but they were defeated here by Mongols 1243; added to Ottoman Empire by Sultan Mohammed II 1473.

Er·zu·rum *or* **Er·ze·rum** \ˌerz-(ə-)'rüm, ərz-\. 1 Province of NE Turkey, Asia. See table at TURKEY.

2 City, its ✱, on Turkish-Russian railroad; pop. (1965c) 105,317; univ. (1958); in mountains of W Turkish Armenia, a military station of strategical importance. Of great antiquity, important in Armenian and Arabic history; seized by Seljuks 1071; came under Turks 1515; three times captured by Russians—1828, 1878, 1916; meeting of First Nationalist Congress July 23, 1919.

Esan, Cape \-ā-'sän\ *or* **Cape Ezan** \-'ā-ˌzän\. Cape on S coast of Hokkaidō, Japan, at S of entrance to Uchiura Bay.

Es·bjerg \'es-bē-ˌe(ə)rg, -ˌərg\. Seaport, Ribe co., SW Jutland Penin., Denmark, on North Sea; pop. (1970e) 76,056; Denmark's largest fishing port; exports meats and dairy products; cement works; only good harbor on W coast of Jutland; received municipal charter 1899.

Esbo. See ESPOO.

Es·ca·lan·te \ˌes-kə-'lant-ē\. River, S Utah; flows SE into Lake Powell; ab. 80 m. long.

Escalante \ˌes-kə-'länt-ē\. Municipality, NE Negros Occidental, Negros, Phil., on coast at N end of Tanon Strait; pop. (1969e) 80,900; important local trade center, founded ab. 1860.

Es·cam·bia \e-'skam-bē-ə\. 1 Navigable river, SE United States; ab. 75 m. long; flows S from SW Alabama into Florida, where it forms boundary bet. Escambia and Santa Rosa cos.; empties into Pensacola Bay.

2 Name of counties in two states of the U.S. See tables at ALABAMA and FLORIDA.

Es·ca·na·ba \ˌes-kə-'näb-ə\. 1 River, N Michigan penin.; ab. 100 m. long; rises in Marquette co., N Michigan penin., flows SE into Little Bay de Noc.

2 City, ⊗ of Delta co., S Michigan penin., on Little Bay de Noc; pop. (1970c) 15,368; port of entry; ships iron ore; manufactures paper, chemicals, iron; Bay de Noc Community Coll. (1963).

Es·car·pa·do, Point \-ˌes-kər-'päd-(ˌ)ō\. Cape on SW coast of Panama, at S side of entrance to Gulf of San Miguel.

Es·cau·dain \ˌes-kō-'daⁿ\. Commune, Nord dept., N France, 23 m. SSE of Lille; pop. (1968c) 11,770; coal.

Escaut. See SCHELDE.

Esch \'esh\ *or in full* **Esch–sur–Al·zette** \-ˌsü(ə)r-ˌal-'zet\. Industrial commune, S Luxembourg, on French border 10 m. SW of Luxembourg city; pop. (1970e) 27,575; second largest city of Luxembourg; steel; in coal-mining region.

Esch·we·ge \'esh-ˌvā-gə\. Industrial city, NE Hesse, West Germany, on Werra river 25 m. ESE of Kassel; pop. (1969e) 22,227; 14th cent. castle; 17th cent. town hall; varied manufactures, including soap, esp. a mottled type known as Eschwege, or Eschweger, soap; agricultural and textile machinery; first mentioned 974; received city charter 13th cent.

Esch·wei·ler \'esh-ˌvī-lər\. City, North Rhine-Westphalia, West Germany, 11 m. NE of Aachen; pop. (1969e) 39,756; manufactures include iron and steel, chemicals, textiles, tin plate, machinery, boilers, bricks, sugar; coal mining nearby. In World War II town and vicinity scene of severe fighting 1944.

Es·co·bal \ˌes-kə-'bäl\. Town, Colón prov., Panama, on W shore of Gatun Lake on border of Canal Zone.

Es·co·bar \ˌes-kə-'bär\. Town, Paraguarí dept., S cen. Paraguay, just SE of Asunción; munic. pop. (1970e) 8031.

Es·co·ce·sa Bay \ˌes-kə-'ses-ə-\. Bay on NE coast of Dominican Republic, NW of Cape Samaná, Hispaniola I., West Indies.

Es·con·di·do \ˌes-kən-'dēd-(ˌ)ō\. City, San Diego co., SW corner of California, 28 m. N of San Diego; pop. (1970c) 36,792; electronic equipment, chemicals, wire; vineyards; citrus fruit; founded 1885.

Escondido *or* **Blue·fields** \'blü-ˌfēl(d)z\. Navigable river, S cen. Nicaragua; 60 m. long; formed by the Siquia and other headstreams, flows E into the Caribbean Sea at Bluefields.

Escorial, El. See EL ESCORIAL.

Es·cu·dil·la Mountain \ˌes-kə-ˌdē-ə-\. Peak in E Arizona, SE extremity of Apache co.; 10,691 ft.

Es·cui·na·pa \ˌes-kwi-'näp-ə\ *or in full* **Escuinapa de Hi·dal·go** \-dā-hid-'al-(ˌ)gō, -thā-ē-'thäl-\. Municipality, Sinaloa state, W Mexico, on railroad ab. 40 m. SE of Mazatlán; pop. (1970p) 30,763.

Es·cuin·tla \es-'kwint-lə\. 1 Department of S Guatemala. See table at GUATEMALA.

2 City, its ✱, 30 m. SSW of Guatemala; munic. pop. (1964p) 54,191; medicinal baths; fruit-growing.

Es·cu·mi·nac, Point \-e-'skyü-mə-ˌnak\. Cape, E Northumberland co., E New Bruswick prov., SE Canada, on S side of entrance to Miramichi Bay.

Es·dra·e·lon, Plain of \-ˌez-drə-'ē-lən\ *also* **Valley of Jez·re·el** \-'jez-rē-ˌel, -ˌrē(ə)l\ *or Heb.* **ʽEm·eq Yiz·reʽel** \ˌem-ek-ˌyē-zā-'el\. Plain, N Israel, separating Galilee in the N from Samaria in the S; important agricultural region; formerly swampy, drained in 1920's and 1930's. See MEGIDDO.

Eş·fa·hān \ˌes-fə-'hän\ *or* **Is·fa·han** \ˌis-\ *or formerly* **Is·pa·han** \ˌis-pə-\. 1 Province of W cen. Iran. See table at IRAN.

2 *or anc.* **As·pa·da·na** \ˌas-pə-ˈdān-ə\. Industrial city, its ✱; pop. (1971e) 444,000; on main highways S to Shīrāz, N to Tehran, and E to Yazd; in center is Maidan-i-Shah, a great rectangular garden enclosing royal mosque, Masjid-i-Shah, built by Shah Abbas I at end of 16th cent.; has large bazaar; particularly noted for silver filigree and metal work, lacquered ware, brocades; univ. (1966).

History: As Aspadana, ancient Median town; captured by Arabs during their conquest of Persia 641–650 A.D.; a seat of Seljuk power in late 11th cent.; captured by Tamerlane 1388; capital of Persia 1598–1722; reached height of prosperity during 17th cent. when it was residence of Shah Abbas I; declined after capture by Afghans 1722.

Esher \ˈē-shər\ *or formerly* **Esher and The Dit·tons** \-ˈdit-ᵊnz\. Urban district, Surrey, S England, 15 m. SW of London; pop. (1971p) 64,186; residential; site of the mansion, Esher Place, occupied 1529 by Cardinal Wolsey.

Eshnunna. See TELL ASMAR.

Esh·o·we \ˈesh-ə-ˌwā\. Village, chief town of Zululand, NE Natal, Rep. of South Africa, 70 m. NNE of Durban; pop. (1967e) 4800; resort.

Esh Shām. See SYRIA 1.

Esk \ˈesk\. 1 River in NE England, flowing E into North Sea at Whitby; 24 m. long.

2 River, S Scotland; 28 m. long; rises in NE Dumfries co. and flows S into the head of Solway Firth; its lower course for a few miles lies in Cumberland, England; bet. it and the Sark (a small stream of Dumfries, Scotland) is a small tract of land (8 m. long by 4 m. wide) known for years as the "Debatable Land," a disputed border tract; the Sark established as boundary bet. Scotland and England 1552; Gretna Green is on N bank of Sark.

3 River, Midlothian co., SE Scotland; formed by confluence of **North Esk** and **South Esk** in Dalkeith, flows N to Firth of Forth at Musselburgh; 3½ m. long (see NORTH ESK 3 and SOUTH ESK 3).

Esk Hause \ˈesk-ˌhȯs\. Mountain pass, W Cumberland, NW England, in the Lake District; 2490 ft.

Es·ki·fjör·dhur \ˈes-kē-ˌfyər-t͟hər\. 1 Fjord on E coast of Iceland.

2 Village, E Iceland; pop. (1970c) 936.

Eski Foça. See FOÇA 2.

Eskije. See XANTHE 2.

Eskil·stu·na \ˈes-kəl-ˌstü-nə\. City, Södermanland co., SE Sweden, S of Lake Mälaren 45 m. W of Stockholm; pop. (1970e) 67,536; steelworks, engineering plants; manufactures esp. cutlery and swords.

Es·ki·şe·hir \ˌes-ki-shə-ˈhi(ə)r\ *or* **Es·ki·shehr** \-ˈshe(ə)r\. 1 Province of W cen. Turkey. See table at TURKEY.

2 City, its ✱, on tributary of Sakarya river, 128 m. W of Ankara; pop. (1965c) 173,882; agricultural machinery, cement and bricks; sugar refining; famous for its deposits of meerschaum; nearby are ruins of ancient Phrygian city of **Dor·y·lae·um** \ˌdȯr-ə-ˈlē-əm\, a city that was mentioned in wars of Lysimachus and Antigonus and acquired importance in Byzantine times; scene of defeat of Seljuk sultan, Kilij Arslan, 1097 by Godfrey of Bouillon; taken by Turks 1176.

Es·la \ˈāz-lə, ˈez-\. River, NW Spain; 171 m. long; rises in N León prov., flows SSW into Duero river ab. 15 m. below Zamora.

Es·me·ral·da \ˌez-mə-ˈral-də\. County in Nevada. See table at NEVADA.

Es·me·ral·das \ˌez-mə-ˈräl-dəs\. 1 River, NW Ecuador; ab. 150 m. long; flows W from Andes Mts. into Pacific Ocean.

2 Province of NW Ecuador. See table at ECUADOR.

3 Town, its ✱, 2 m. from mouth of Esmeraldas river 118 m. NW of Quito; pop. (1970e) 59,000; gold mines in vicinity.

Esna. See ISNA.

Eso·pus Creek \i-ˈsō-pəs-\. Creek in Ulster co., SE New York; rises in Catskill Mts., flows SE then N into Hudson river ab. 10 m. above Kingston. See ASHOKAN DAM.

Es·pail·lat \ˌes-pə-ˈyä\. Province, N cen. Dominican Republic. See table at DOMINICAN REPUBLIC.

España. See SPAIN.

Es·pa·no·la. 1 \ˌes-pən-ˈyō-lə\. Village, Rio Arriba and Santa Fe cos., N cen. New Mexico, 23 m. NNW of Santa Fe; pop. (1970c) 4316.

2 \ˌes-pə-ˈnō-lə\. Town, Sudbury dist., SE Ontario, Canada, 45 m. WSW of Sudbury; pop. (1971p) 6059; lumbering; diversified agriculture.

Es·pa·ño·la \ˌes-ˌpän-ˈyō-lə\. 1 *also* **Hood Island** \ˈhu̇d-\. One of the Galápagos Is. (*q.v.*).

2 Island, West Indies. See HISPANIOLA.

Es·pe·rance, Cape \-ˈes-pə-rən(t)s\. Cape on NW coast of Guadalcanal I., SE Solomon Is., W Pacific Ocean; landing place for Japanese forces 1942–43; naval battle off coast near here Oct. 11–12, 1942; last Japanese foothold on island. See SAVO.

Es·pe·ran·za \ˌes-pə-ˈran-zə, -ˈrän-\. 1 Town, Santa Fe prov., E cen. Argentina, 20 m. NW of Santa Fe; pop. (1960c) 16,606.

2 Town and municipality, Las Villas prov., W cen. Cuba, on railroad 10 m. W of Santa Clara; munic. pop. (1967e) 16,220.

Esperanza, La. See LA ESPERANZA.

Es·pi·chel, Cape \-ˌes(h)-pə-ˈshel\. Promontory on SW coast of Portugal, 21 m. S of Lisbon.

Es·pi·nal \ˌes-pə-ˈnäl\. Municipality, Tolima dept., W cen. Colombia, on the upper Magdalena 30 m. SE of Ibagué; pop. (1968e) 50,402.

Es·pí·ri·to San·to \ə-ˌspir-ə-ˌtü-ˈsan-(ˌ)tü\. 1 Island a few hundred yards off mainland of Espírito Santo state, E Brazil; site of the city of Vitória.

2 State, E Brazil; 17,605 sq. m.; pop. (1970p) 1,597,389; ✱ Vitória; in E part has swampy coastal plain; coffee, sugarcane, cotton, tobacco.

Es·pí·ri·tu Santo \ə-ˌspir-ə-ˌtü-ˈsan-(ˌ)tō\. 1 *or* **Ma·ri·na** \mə-ˈrē-nə\ *also* **Santo.** Largest island of the New Hebrides in NW part of group, SW Pacific Ocean; 76 m. long by 45 m. wide, 1420 sq. m.; pop. (1967c) 8909; has mountain range along W coast, highest point Mt. Tabwemasana 6167 ft; coastline marked on the N by two peninsulas, largest on NW, with St. Philip and St. James Bay bet. them; agriculturally well developed; principal settlement Santo on SE coast. During World War II site of military and naval bases established by Americans, who first landed Mar. 12, 1942.

2 Island off SE coast of Baja California, near mouth of Gulf of California; 13 m. long.

Espi·ri·tu San·to, Cape \-ə-ˌspir-ə-ˌtü-ˈsän-(ˌ)tō\. Northeast point of Samar I., E Phil., 12°35′N, 125°11′E.

Espíritu Santo, Cape. Cape on N coast of Tierra del Fuego I. (*q.v.*), S of entrance to Strait of Magellan.

Espíritu Santo Bay. Inlet of Caribbean Sea on E coast of Yucatán penin., Quintana Roo territory, Mexico, S of Ascensión Bay.

Es·poo \ˈes-(ˌ)pō\ *or Swed.* **Es·bo** \ˈes-(ˌ)bü\. Town, Uusimaa prov., S Finland, ab. 11 m. W of Helsinki; pop. (1967e) 84,805; est. 1963.

Es·qui·line \ˈes-kwə-ˌlīn, -lən\. One of the seven hills of Rome. See SEVEN HILLS.

Es·qui·malt \ə-ˈskwī-ˌmȯlt\. Seaport and naval station, SE Vancouver Is., British Columbia, Canada, on Juan de Fuca Strait 4 m. W of Victoria of which it is a suburb; spacious harbor; British navy station until 1905 when Canadian government took it over; its drydock (built 1888) transferred to Canada 1910; shipyard, salmon cannery.

Es·qui·pu·las \ˌes-ki-ˈpü-ləs\. Town, Chiquimula dept., SE Guatemala, 73 m. E of Guatemala; munic. pop. (1964p)

19,164; church contains a black image of Christ (the "Black Christ") worshipped by the Indians.

Es·rum \'es-rəm\. Lake in NE Sjælland I., Denmark.

Es Salt \es-'salt\. Town, NW Jordan, W of Amman.

Es·sa·oui·ra \ˌes-ə-'wir-ə\ *or formerly* **Mog·a·dor** \'mäg-ə-ˌdȯ(ə)r\. City and seaport, SW cen. coast of Morocco; munic. pop. (1960c) 26,392; fish processing, tanning; has highway connections with Agadir, Casablanca, and Marrakech. Founded 1765 as rival to Agadir and Safi; landing place of U.S. forces Nov. 1942.

Es·sen \'es-ᵊn\ *also* **Essen an der Ruhr** \-ˌän-dər-'rů(ə)r\. Industrial city, North Rhine-Westphalia, West Germany, 18 m. NNE of Düsseldorf, near right bank of the Ruhr river ab. 13 m. from where it enters the Rhine; pop. (1969e) 698,102; contains the most extensive iron and steel works in Europe; coal mining; glass, chemicals, trucks, textiles; railroad center; 11th cent. cathedral, opera house, technical colleges. Founded 9th cent.; made a city 10th cent.; passed to Prussia 1803; bombed in World War I; heavily bombed by Allies 1943–45, esp. the Krupp works; taken with other cities in fall of the Ruhr Apr.–May 1945.

Es·sen·don \'es-ᵊn-dən\. Municipality, S Victoria, SE Australia, NW suburb of Melbourne; pop. (1966c) 58,258.

Essentuki. See YESSENTUKI.

Es·se·qui·bo \ˌes-ə-'kwē-(ˌ)bō\. 1 River, Guyana; 630 m. long; the republic's longest river; rises in Serra Uaçari on Brazilian border, flows N into Atlantic Ocean; has wide estuary; navigable for some distance; main tributaries all from W: the Cuyuni and Mazaruni near its mouth, Potaro in cen. part, and Rupununi in S cen. part.

2 County, N Guyana, divided into four districts: Essequibo, **Essequibo Islands,** Mazaruni-Potaro, and North West.

Es·sex \'es-iks\. 1 Name of counties in five states of the U.S. See tables at MASSACHUSETTS, NEW JERSEY, NEW YORK, VERMONT, VIRGINIA.

2 Agricultural and manufacturing town, SE Middlesex co., S Connecticut, on W bank of Connecticut river near its mouth; pop. (1970c) 4911; settled 1690, incorp. 1852; as maritime trade center, attacked by British in War of 1812.

3 Urban community (unincorporated), Baltimore co., Maryland, E of Baltimore; pop. (1970c) 38,193; Essex Community Coll. (1957).

4 Town, Essex co., NE Massachusetts, 23 m. NE of Boston; pop. (1970c) 2670.

5 Town in Vermont. See ESSEX JUNCTION.

6 County, Ontario, Canada. See table at ONTARIO.

7 Town, Essex co., SE Ontario, Canada, 16 m. ESE of Windsor; pop. (1971p) 4034; bricks, flour; canning factory.

8 County, SE England; 1418 sq. m.; pop. (1971p) 1,408,-103; ⊗ Chelmsford; rivers Thames, Stour, Colne, Blackwater, Lea, Crouch; wheat, barley, sugar beets; manufacturing (machinery, textiles, chemicals, cement); engineering works, nuclear power stations; chief towns incl. Southend-on-Sea, Colchester, Chelmsford, Harwich.

History: Region a Roman center before invasion by East Saxons; Anglo-Saxon kingdom of Heptarchy (*q.v.*) with its center at London; received Christianity and submitted to Mercia (*q.v.*) 7th cent. A.D.; its subkings later disappeared; included in territory under the Danelaw 9th cent.; reconquered by Wessex, it became a shire and later a powerful English earldom.

Essex Fells \-'felz\. Borough, Essex co., NE New Jersey, 7 m. SW of Paterson; pop. (1970c) 2541.

Essex Junction. Industrial village in Essex town, Chittenden co., NW Vermont, on Winooski river 5 m. E of Burlington; pop. (1970c) 6511 (village), 10,951 (town); Fort Ethan Allen nearby.

Es·sex·ville \'es-iks-ˌvil\. City, Bay co., E Michigan, on Saginaw Bay 4 m. E of Bay City; pop. (1970c) 4990.

Ess·ling \'es-liŋ\. Village near Vienna, Austria. See ASPERN.

Ess·ling·en \'es-liŋ-ən\. Manufacturing city, Baden-Württemberg, West Germany, on the Neckar river 6 m. ESE of Stuttgart; pop. (1969e) 85,350; metalworking; electronic equipment, furniture; founded in 8th cent.; free imperial town; became part of Swabian League of cities.

Es·sonne \e-'sən, -'sȯn\. 1 River, N France; rises in Loiret dept., flows N to the Seine at Corbeil-Essonnes; ab. 56 m. long.

2 Department of N France. See table at FRANCE.

Es Sur. See TYRE.

Es Su·wei·da \ˌes-sə-'wād-ə\ *or* **As Su·way·dā** \as-\ *or Fr.* **Sou·ei·da** \swā-dá\. Town, ✱ of former Druse territory of Jebel ed Druz, now a part of Syria, railroad terminus ab. 56 m. S of Damascus; on site of an ancient Roman settlement.

Estado Libre Asociado Puerto Rico. See PUERTO RICO.

Es·ta·dos, Is·la de los \ˌēz-lə-ˌdā-lȯs-ā-'stäth-(ˌ)ōs, -'städ-\ *also* **Stat·en Island** \'stat-ən-\. Argentine island, S Atlantic Ocean off E tip of Tierra del Fuego; ab. 45 m. long; chief town San Juan de Salvamento, at E end. See TIERRA DEL FUEGO 2.

Estados Unidos de Venezuela. See VENEZUELA.

Estados Unidos Mexicanos. See MEXICO.

Es·tan·cia \ə-'stan-chə\. Town, ⊗ of Torrance co., cen. New Mexico; pop. (1970c) 721.

Es·tân·cia \ə-'stan-shə\. Town on coast, S Sergipe state, E Brazil; munic. pop. (1968e) 26,125.

Est·court \'est-ˌkō(ə)rt\. Town, W Natal, E Rep. of South Africa, 85 m. NW of Durban; pop. (1967e) 12,900.

Este \'es-(ˌ)tā\ *or anc.* **Ates·te** \ə-'tes-tē\. Commune, Padova prov., Veneto, NE Italy, 17 m. SW of Padua; pop. (1968e) 16,858; medieval fortress; campanile; manufactures iron products, pottery, cordage, chemicals. Ancient Roman military colony; seat of Este family until their expulsion by Paduans in 12th cent.; with Padua fell to Venetians 1405.

Es·te·ban Eche·ve·rría \e-'stā-vän-ˌā-chə-və-'rē-ə\. Town, S suburb of Buenos Aires, Argentina; pop. (1960c) 69,730.

Es·te·lí \ˌes-tə-'lē\. 1 Department of W Nicaragua. See table at NICARAGUA.

2 Town, its ✱, 65 m. N of Managua; munic. pop. (1960e) 34,972.

Es·te·po·na \ˌes-tə-'pō-nə\. Seaport commune, Málaga prov., S Spain, on Mediterranean Sea 46 m. SW of Málaga; pop. (1970p) 21,163.

Es·té·rel \ˌes-tə-'rel\. Mountainous forested region, S France, on coast of departments of Var and Alpes-Maritimes, bet. Fréjus and Cannes; highest point Mont Vinaigre 2020 ft.

Es·ter·ha·zy \'es-tər-ˌhäz-ē\. Town, Saskatchewan, Canada, 120 m. E of Regina; pop. (1971p) 2886; agriculture; grain elevators, creamery.

Es·té·rias, Cape \-e-'ster-ē-əs\. Cape extending into Gulf of Guinea on coast of Gabon, W equatorial Africa, bet. Corisco Bay on the N and Gabon river on the S; Libreville is on its S coast.

Es·tes Park \'es-tēz-, -tis-\. 1 A high-level valley of the Front Range, Rocky Mts., N Colorado; now a part of Rocky Mountain National Park (see UNITED STATES, *National Parks*).

2 Village in Larimer co., N Colorado, 28 m. SW of Fort Collins; pop. (1970c) 1616; alt. 7500 ft.; entrance to Rocky Mountain National Park.

Es·te·van \'es-tə-ˌvan\. Town, SE Saskatchewan, Canada, on Souris river 54 m. SE of Weyburn; pop. (1966c) 9062; brick works, oil wells, lumberyards, coal mines.

Es·ther, Mount \-'es-tər\. Peak in the Adirondack Mts., Essex co., NE New York; 4270 ft.

Es·ther·ville \'es-tər-ˌvil\. City, ⊗ of Emmet co., N Iowa, 58 m. NE of Cherokee; pop. (1970c) 8108.

Esthonia. See ESTONIAN SOVIET SOCIALIST REPUBLIC.

Es·till \'est-ᵊl\. County in Kentucky. See table at KENTUCKY.

Es·to·ni·an Soviet Socialist Republic \e-'stō-nē-ən-\ *also* **Es·to·nia** \e-'stō-nē-ə, -nyə\ *or less correctly* **Es·tho·nia** \e-'stō-, es-'thō-\; *Estonian* **Ees·ti** \'ā-stē\ *also* **Ees·ti·maa** \'ās-ti-ˌmä\. A constituent republic of the U.S.S.R., bounded on N by Gulf of Finland, on E by Russian S.F.S.R., on S by Latvian S.S.R., and on W by the Baltic Sea; 17,413 sq. m.; pop. (1970p) 1,357,000; ✱ Tallinn. *Physical features:* Coast is low and there are no heights of land; its SW coast is N shore of Gulf of Riga; includes four islands in Baltic Sea off W coast: Saaremaa, Hiiumaa, Muhu, and Vormsi; on E shares ab. one half of lakes Peipus (*q.v.*) and Pskov with the Russian S.F.S.R.; has many other lakes, largest of which is Vorts-Jarv, in S cen. part; many rivers, most important being the Pärnu, Kasari, and Narva. *Chief products:* Dairy produce, potatoes, rye, flax; cement, textiles; shipbuilding, electrical engineering. *Chief towns:* Tallinn, Tartu, Pärnu.

History: Estonians conquered by Danes who founded Reval (see TALLINN) 1219; after ferocious revolt of peasantry 1343–45, taken over by Teutonic Order 1346; under rule of Swedish in N from 1558 and entirely from 1629; ceded to Russia (see BALTIC PROVINCES) 1721; became independent republic Feb. 24, 1918; recognized by U.S.S.R. 1920 (peace signed at Tartu); joined League of Nations 1921; ruled as dictatorship 1934–37; joined nonaggression pact with Germany (see LATVIAN SOVIET SOCIALIST REPUBLIC) 1939; occupied by Soviet army June 1940 and annexed to U.S.S.R. as Estonian S.S.R. Aug. 3, 1940; overrun by German army 1941 and retaken by U.S.S.R. 1944; incorporation in U.S.S.R. not recognized by United States.

Es·to·ril \ˌesh-tə-ˈril\. Resort town, Portugal, on coast W of Lisbon; pop. (1970p) 15,740.

Estrada, La. See LA ESTRADA.

Estrela, Serra da. See SERRA DA ESTRELA.

Es·tre·ma·du·ra \ˌes-trə-mə-ˈdu̇r-ə\. 1 Former province, W Portugal; ✱ Lisbon; comprised S Leiría, part of Lisboa, and N Setúbal districts.

2 *or* **Ex·tre·ma·du·ra** \ˌek-strə-\. Region, W cen. Spain; 16,065 sq. m.; bounded on N by León, E by New Castile, S by Andalusia, W by Portugal; comprises modern provinces of Cáceres and Badajoz; tableland; watered by Tagus and Guadiana rivers; raises sheep and swine; large forests in N portion, agricultural land in S; noted for its ilex trees; deposits of silver, coal, copper.

Es·tre·moz \ˌes(h)-trə-ˈmȯsh\. Town, Évora dist., Portugal, ab. 25 m. NE of Évora; pop. (1970p) 18,907; ruins of ancient castle; marble quarries; pottery; Portuguese victories over Spanish nearby 1663, 1665.

Estrondo, Serra do. See SERRA DO ESTRONDO.

Esutoru. See UGLEGORSK.

Esz·ter·gom \ˈesh-tər-ˌgōm\ *or Ger.* **Gran** \ˈgrän\. City, N Hungary, on the Danube 27 m. NW of Budapest; pop. (1970p) 26,955; cathedral, ancient ecclesiastical center.

Établissements de l'Océanie *or* **Établissements français de l'Océanie.** See FRENCH POLYNESIA.

Établissements français dans l'Inde. See FRENCH INDIA.

Etah \ˈē-(ˌ)tä\. 1 Eskimo settlement in NW Greenland, on Smith Sound N of Cape York; known as point of departure for polar exploration expeditions.

2 Town, W cen. Uttar Pradesh, N India, 46 m. NE of Agra; pop. (1961c) 24,700.

Étampes \ā-ˈtäⁿ(m)p\. Commune, Essonne dept., N France, 30 m. SSW of Paris; pop. (1968c) 16,493; dates back to early 7th cent.; scene of a council which recognized Innocent II as legitimate pope 1130.

Étang de Berre. See BERRE, ÉTANG DE.

Étang de Thau. See THAU, ÉTANG DE.

Éta·ples \ā-ˈtaplᵊ\. Commune, Pas-de-Calais dept., N France, S of Boulogne; pop. (1962c) 8647; fishing; boatbuilding; treaty 1492 bet. Henry VII of England and Charles VIII of France; important British base in World War I.

Etats, Pic d' \ˌpēk-dā-ˈtä\. Highest mountain in Andorra; 10,295 ft.

Eta·wah \i-ˈtä-wə\. 1 District, Uttar Pradesh, N India; 1669 sq. m.; pop. (1961c) 1,182,202.

2 Town, SW Uttar Pradesh, N India, 67 m. ESE of Agra; pop. (1961c) 69,681; cotton mills, hornware factories; has a ruined fort and several mosques including the Jama Masjid, adapted from a Hindu temple.

Etchmiadzin. See ECHMIADZIN.

Etcho·joa \ˌech-ə-ˈhō-ə\. Municipality, Sonora state, Mexico, 120 m. SE of Guaymas; pop. (1970p) 53,767; hog raising, diversified agriculture.

Eten \ˈā-ˌten\. Seaport, Lambayeque dept., NW Peru, ab. 12 m. S of Chiclayo; open roadstead.

Eter·ni·ty, Cape \-i-ˈtər-nət-e\. Promontory, Quebec, Canada, on S shore of Saguenay river 39 m. from its mouth; 1400 ft. high; forms E portal of inlet of **Eternity Bay.** See TRINITY, CAPE.

Ethi·o·pia \ˌē-thē-ˈō-pē-ə\ *also* **Ab·ys·sin·ia** \ˌab-ə-ˈsin-ē-ə, -ˈsin-yə\. Independent state, E Africa, bounded on N by the Red Sea, on E by Afars and Issas and Somalia, on S by Somalia and Kenya, and on W and NW by Sudan; 471,775 sq. m.; pop. (1970e) 24,315,400; ✱ Addis Ababa. *Physical features:* Mountainous in N, cen., and S parts with many peaks 7000 to 13,000 ft., highest point Ras Dashan in N 15,158 ft.; lowlands on E border include Danakil Desert in NE and the Haud in SE extending into coastal Somalia. *Rivers:* Main streams in N and NW the Tekeze and the Abay (Blue Nile), the outlet of Lake Tana, both tributaries of the Nile; in SW the Omo flowing S to Lake Rudolf on Kenya border; in E the Awash, rising in cen. part SE of Addis Ababa and losing itself in Danakil Desert; in SE many streams flowing SE forming headstreams of the Juba and Shebelle rivers in Somalia. *Chief products:* Coffee, barley, corn, sorghum, sugarcane, hides, skins; potash; manufactured goods include footwear and textiles; ab. 90 percent of labor force is engaged in agriculture. *Chief towns:* Addis Ababa, Asmara, Dire Dawa, Harer, Dese, Gonder, Jima, Debre Markos. Divided into the following 14 provinces (for pronunciation of their names, see their individual entries):

NAME	AREA (sq. m.)	POP. (1970e)	CAPITAL
Arusi	9,073	818,200	Asela
Bale	48,109	190,400	Goba
Begemdir and Simen	28,649	1,294,600	Gonder
Eritrea	45,405	1,836,800	Asmara
Gemu Gefa	15,251	668,100	Arba Minch
Gojam	23,784	1,668,700	Debre Markos
Harer	100,270	3,215,600	Harer
Ilubabor	18,301	659,600	Gore
Kefa	21,081	1,224,300	Jima
Shewa	32,973	5,051,400	Addis Ababa
Sidamo	45,289	2,369,200	Yirga Alem
Tigre	25,444	1,748,700	Mekele
Welega	27,490	1,214,200	Nekemte
Welo	30,656	2,355,600	Dese

History: Ancient country W of Red Sea, NE Africa, bet. ab. lat. 24° and 10°N; included S Egypt, E Rep. of the Sudan, and N (modern) Ethiopia; sometimes name referred just to the Nile valley above Syene (Aswān), but in classical writings it referred to that part of Africa S from Egypt as far as Zanzibar; dominated by Egypt from XIth dynasty; became independent of Egypt during XXIIId dynasty; the Biblical land of Cush; part of Sabaean kingdom of Aksum ruled by dynasty descended from Menelik, traditionally son of Hebrew King Solomon and Queen of Saba (Sheba); under Jewish influence until converted to Christianity by bishop Frumentius 4th cent. A.D.; became Monophysite Christian 7th cent.; from 675 cut off from rest of Christian world by Muslim conquest of Egypt and Nubia; 1490 resumed contact when visited by Covilhão who was believed to have found kingdom of Prester John; aided by Portuguese in expelling Muslim sultan of the Somali 1541; center of missionary activity of Jesuits until their expulsion

1633; explored 1768–73 by James Bruce who reported decayed empire restricted to region N of Blue Nile. Modern Ethiopia began with reign of Theodore II, established by conquest of other chiefs 1855–56 and terminated by Napier's expedition 1868; cut off from Red Sea by Egypt 1875–79; Aseb (*q.v.*) made Italian 1882; claimed as an Italian protectorate (through Treaty of Uccialli 1889); coastal region made separate Italian colony 1890 (see ERITREA); under Menelik, defeated Italians at Aduwa (now Adwa) 1896; territorial integrity recognized by Great Britain, France, and Italy 1906; admitted to League of Nations 1923; promulgated first constitution 1931; after failure of League to settle an Italo-Ethiopian clash at Walwal 1934, invaded by Italy 1935; formally annexed to Italy and organized with Eritrea and Italian Somaliland as Italian East Africa (1936–41); regained independence after being liberated by British 1941; became federated with Eritrea 1952; adopted revised constitution 1955; Eritrea made a province 1962; founding member of Organization of African Unity 1963; border conflict with Somalia 1964.

Et·ive, Loch \läk-'et-iv, läk-\. Inlet of Atlantic Ocean extending from Firth of Lorn inland E (8½ m.) and NE (10½ m.) in Argyll co., W Scotland.

Et·na \'et-nə\. Manufacturing borough, Allegheny co., SW Pennsylvania, on Allegheny river 5 m. NNE of Pittsburgh; pop. (1970c) 5819; iron and steel products.

Etna *or Lat.* **Aet·na** \'et-nə\; *also* **Mon·gi·bel·lo** \ˌmän-jə-'bel-(ˌ)ō\. Active volcano in NE Sicily, Italy, near the coast; 10,902 ft.; ab. 140 eruptions have been recorded, notably destructive ones 1169, 1669, and 1852; highest peak in Italy S of Alps.

Etna, Mount. Peak, Chaffee co., cen. Colorado; 13,800 ft.

Eto·lin Strait \ē-ˌtō-lən-\. Passage in Bering Sea separating Nunivak I. from mainland of SW Alaska.

Eton \'ēt-ᵊn\. Urban district, Buckinghamshire, SE cen. England, on the Thames opp. Windsor; Eton College founded by Henry VI 1440.

Etorofu. See ITURUP.

Eto·sha Pan \i-ˌtō-shə-'pan\. Large salt basin in N South-West Africa.

Et·o·wah \'et-ə-ˌwȯ, 'ēt-ē-, -ˌwä\. 1 River, NW Georgia; ab. 150 m. long; rises in SE extremity of Tennessee, flows S across Georgia border, then W to unite with the Oostanaula near Rome in Floyd co. and form Coosa river.
2 County in Alabama. See table at ALABAMA.
3 Town, McMinn co., SE Tennessee, 25 m. NE of Cleveland; pop. (1970c) 3736.

Etowah Mound. Prehistoric earthwork, Bartow co., NW Georgia, 3 m. SE of Cartersville, on Etowah river; a quadrilateral, truncated pyramid, base covers ab. 3 acres, top ab. 170 by 176 ft.; 61 ft. high; copper plates with repoussé figures have been found in it.

Étre·tat \ˌā-trə-'tä\. Town, Seine-Maritime dept., N France, on coast N of Le Havre; pop. (1962c) 1543; resort.

Etru·ria \i-'trür-ē-ə\. Ancient country in cen. Italy, covering region now comprising Tuscany and part of Umbria; home of Etruscans, a people who probably migrated from Asia Minor c. 900 B.C.; their chief confederation, traditionally of 12 cities, included Veii, Florentia, Volsinii, etc.; traded extensively with Greeks and Phoenicians and built up civilization, noted for its art, at height c. 500 B.C.; at its peak Etruscan power extended into N Italy; gradually declined after defeat of its sea power off Cumae (*q.v.*) and absorption of its cities, one by one, by Rome (by 3d cent. B.C.); kingdom of Etruria erected by Napoleon in 1801 incorporated in French Empire 1808.

Etsch. See ADIGE.

Etsin. See O-CHI-NA.

Et Ta·fi·la \ˌet-tə-'fē-lə\ *or* **At Ta·fi·lah** \ˌat-\. Town, cen. Jordan, SE of Dead Sea NNW of Ma'an.

Et·ten en Leur \ˌet-ən-ən-'lər\. Commune, North Brabant prov., Netherlands, just W of Breda; pop. (1970e) 19,698; footwear; residence of van Gogh 1881.

Et·ter·beck \'et-ər-ˌbāk\. Commune, Brabant prov., cen. Belgium, a suburb of Brussels; pop. (1969e) 50,936.

Ett·ling·en \'et-liŋ-ən\. City, Baden-Württemberg, West Germany, 6 m. S of Karlsruhe; pop. (1969e) 21,140; paper, textiles, food processing. Roman foundation; city 1192; to Baden 1219.

Et·trick \'e-trik\. River, SE Scotland, flows NE through Selkirk co. into the Tweed; 32 m. long.

Ettrick Forest. Former forest and hunting ground in Selkirk co., SE Scotland; now converted into a pastoral region; James Hogg (1770–1835), Scottish poet, a native of the region, was known as "The Ettrick Shepherd."

Etymander. See HELMAND.

Et·za·tlán \ˌet-sə-'tlän\. Town, Jalisco state, W cen. Mexico, ab. 50 m. W of Guadalajara; munic. pop. (1970p) 14,276.

Etzina. See KHARA KHOTO.

Eu \'ər\. Commune, Seine-Maritime dept., N France, 17 m. NE of Dieppe; pop. (1962c) 7512; ancient countship, supposedly descended from dukes of Normandy, which passed successively to houses of Brienne, Artois, Cleves, Lorraine-Guise, and Orléans; château begun in 16th cent., largely destroyed by fire 1902; extensive forest to SE.

Eua \'ā-(ə-)ˌwä\. Island of the Tongatapu group in S Tonga, SW Pacific Ocean, 9 m. SE of Tongatapu I.; 34 sq. m.; pop. (1966c) 3391.

Eu·boea \yü-'bē-ə\ *or Gk.* **Év·voia** \'ev-(ˌ)yä\ *or Ital.* **Ne·gro·pon·te** \ˌneg-rə-'pänt-ē\ *or Eng.* **Neg·ro·pont** \'neg-rə-ˌpänt\. One of the largest islands of Greece, in the Aegean Sea; 90 m. long by 4 to 30 m. wide; 1411 sq. m.; with Northern Sporades forms a department of the Central Greece and Euboea region (see table at GREECE). Separated on N from Magnesia and Achaea Phthiotis by narrow strait, on NW from Locris by the Atalante channel, and in cen. part of W coast separated from Boeotia by narrow Evripos strait, on which Chalcis and ruins of Aulis are situated; its mountains (highest 5718 ft.) are part of the chain in Thessaly and the Cyclades; on NE coast is promontory of Artemisium and on SE Cape Caphareus. Connected with Boeotia by a bridge built by Chalcidians; dominated by Athens in 5th cent. B.C.; from 146 B.C. in Roman province of Macedon; to Venice 1204 but not subdued until 1366; conquered by Turks 1470; to Greece 1830. See CHALCIS and ERETRIA.

Eu·boe·an Sea \yü-ˌbē-ən-\ *or anc.* **Ma·re Eu·bo·i·cum** \'mä-(ˌ)rē-yü-'bō-ə-kəm, 'mär-(ˌ)ā-\. See ATALANTE.

Eu·clid \'yü-kləd\. City, Cuyahoga co., N Ohio, on Lake Erie, a NE suburb of Cleveland; pop. (1970c) 71,552; grape culture; manufactures machinery, airplane parts; settled 1798.

Eu·do·ra \yü-'dōr-ə, -'dȯr-\. City, Chicot co., SE corner of Arkansas, 85 m. E of El Dorado; pop. (1970c) 3687; cotton, soybeans, timber.

Eu·fau·la \yü-'fȯ-lə\. 1 City, Barbour co., SE Alabama, on Chattahoochee river 75 m. SE of Montgomery; pop. (1970c) 9102; shipping center; before 1843 known as Irwinton.
2 City, ⊗ of McIntosh co., E Oklahoma, on Canadian river 27 m. NNE of McAlester; pop. (1970c) 2355.

Eu·ga·ne·an Hills \yü-'gā-nē-ən-, ˌyü-gə-'nē-\ *or Ital.* **Col·li Eu·ga·nei** \'kȯ-lē-eü-'gän-ē-ˌē\. Range of hills, W Padova prov., Veneto, NE Italy; ab. 2000 ft. high.

Eu·gene \yü-'jēn\. Industrial city, ⊗ of Lane co., W Oregon, on Willamette river 62 m. S of Salem; pop. (1970c) 78,389; fruit and vegetable canning, meat packing; timber; Univ. of Oregon (1872), Lane Community Coll. (1965); settled 1851, became ⊗ 1853, incorp. as city 1864.

Eu·ge·nia, Point \-yü-'jē-nyə\ *or* **Point San·ta Eugenia** \-ˌsant-ə-\. Cape on W coast of Baja California Sur terr., Mexico, S of Sebastián Vizcaíno Bay.

Eugubium. See GUBBIO.

Eu·len·ge·bir·ge \ˌȯi-lən-gə-'bir-gə\. See SUDETIC MOUNTAINS.

Eu·less \'yü-ləs\. Village, Tarrant co., N Texas, 16 m. NE of Fort Worth; pop. (1970c) 19,316; cement; diversified agriculture.

Eumolpias. See PLOVDIV 2.

Eu·nice \'yü-nəs\. 1 Town, St. Landry and Acadia parishes, S cen. Louisiana, 32 m. NW of Lafayette; pop. (1970c) 11,390; oil and gas wells.

2 City, Lea co., SE corner of New Mexico, ab. 18 m. S of Hobbs; pop. (1970c) 2641; oil (discovered in nearby Jal 1927); founded 1909, made city 1937.

Euonymus. See PANAREA.

Eupatoria. See YEVPATORIYA.

Eu·pen \ə(r)-'pen, 'òi-pən\. Commune, E Liège prov., E Belgium, 21 m. E of Liège; pop. (1969e) 14,891; cables, soap; brewing; formerly in Germany; transferred with Malmédy and Moresnet to Belgium by Treaty of Versailles 1919; in World War II taken in Allied advance Sept. 12, 1944; with Malmédy (*q.v.*) forms **Eupen–et–Mal·mé·dy** \ə-'pen-ā-ˌmal-mā-'dē\ district, 382 sq. m.

Eu·phra·tes \yu̇-'frāt-(ˌ)ēz\ *or Turk.* **Fı·rat Neh·ri** \fə-'rät-'ner-ē\ *or Arab.* **Al–Fu·rāt** \ˌal-fə-'rät\. River, SW Asia; 2235 m. long; formed by confluence of the Murat Nehri (Eastern Euphrates) and the Kara Su (Western Euphrates, the main stream) in E Turkey; flows S and SE across NE Syria, through W and cen. Iraq to unite with the Tigris and continues, as Shatt-al-Arab, to Persian Gulf; has few important tributaries but in Syria on the N receives the Balikh and the Khabur; in middle course crosses Syrian Desert; in lower course in Iraq is used for irrigation, expands into swamps and side streams; navigable for small vessels below Hit. Has on its banks several modern cities of importance: Erzincan (on the Kara Su), Rakka, Deir-ez-Zor, An Najaf, An Nasiriya, and ruins of many ancient cities. Its valley was extensively irrigated in ancient times and gave growth to civilizations of Babylonia, Assyria, Chaldea (see MESOPOTAMIA).

Eur·a·sia \yu̇-'rā-zhə, -shə\. Name given to Europe and Asia as one continent.

Euratom. See EUROPEAN ATOMIC ENERGY COMMUNITY.

Eure \'ər\. 1 River, NW France; 140 m. long; rises in Orne dept., flows N into the Seine above Rouen; navigable for ab. 50 m.

2 Department of N France. See table at FRANCE.

Eure–et–Loir \ˌər-ā-lə-'wär\. Department of N cen. France. See table at FRANCE.

Eu·re·ka \yu̇-'rē-kə\. 1 County in Nevada. See table at NEVADA.

2 City, ⊗ of Humboldt co., NW California, on Humboldt Bay 83 m. S of Oregon border; pop. (1970c) 24,337; port of entry; glass, brick, tile; fisheries; redwood mills, chief redwood outlet for Pacific coast; Coll. of the Redwoods (1965); settled 1850, incorp. as city and made ⊗ 1856.

3 City, ⊗ of Woodford co., N cen. Illinois, 17 m. E of Peoria; pop. (1970c) 3028; stock farms; Eureka Coll. (1848).

4 City, ⊗ of Greenwood co., SE Kansas, 40 m. S of Emporia; pop. (1970c) 3576; grain and stock farms.

5 Village, ⊗ of Eureka co., cen. Nevada, 42 m. SSW of Ruby Lake; lead mines.

6 City, McPherson co., N South Dakota, 62 m. WNW of Aberdeen; pop. (1970c) 1547; wheat market.

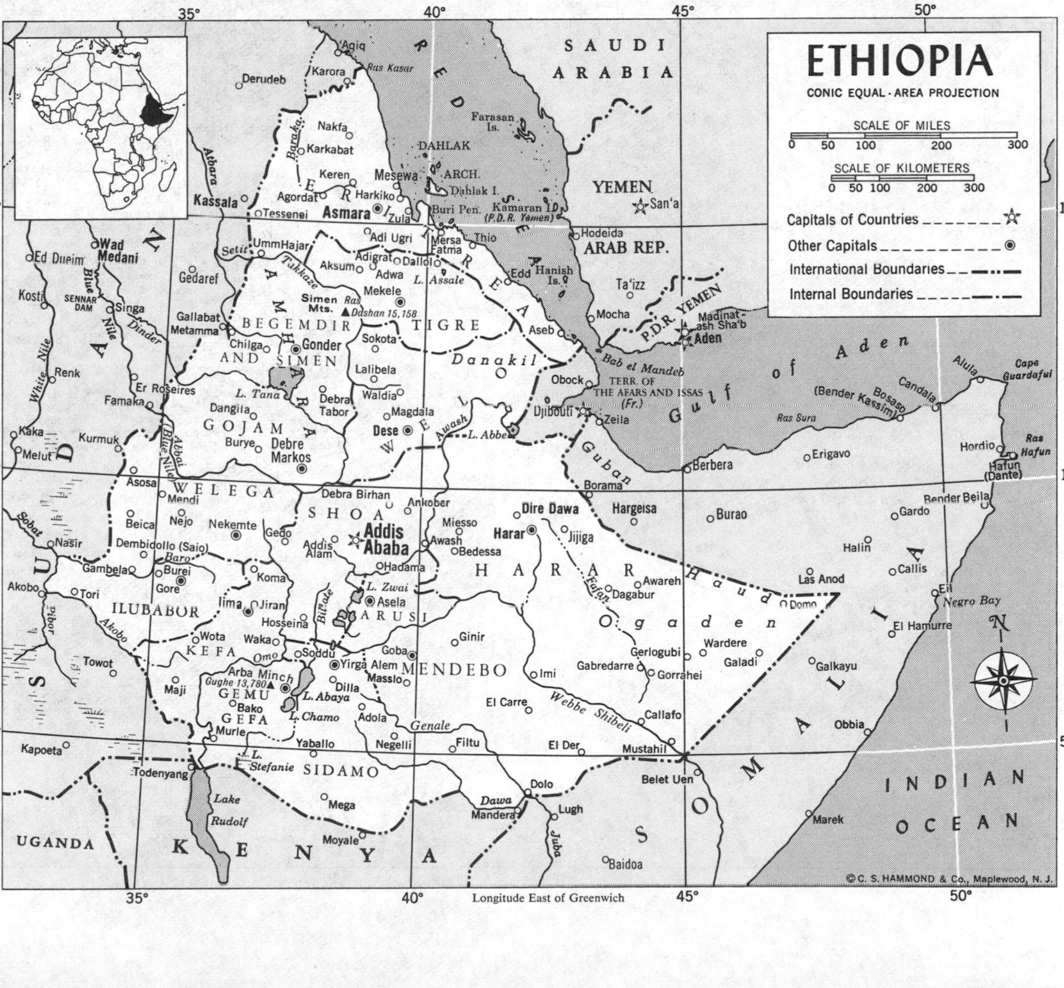

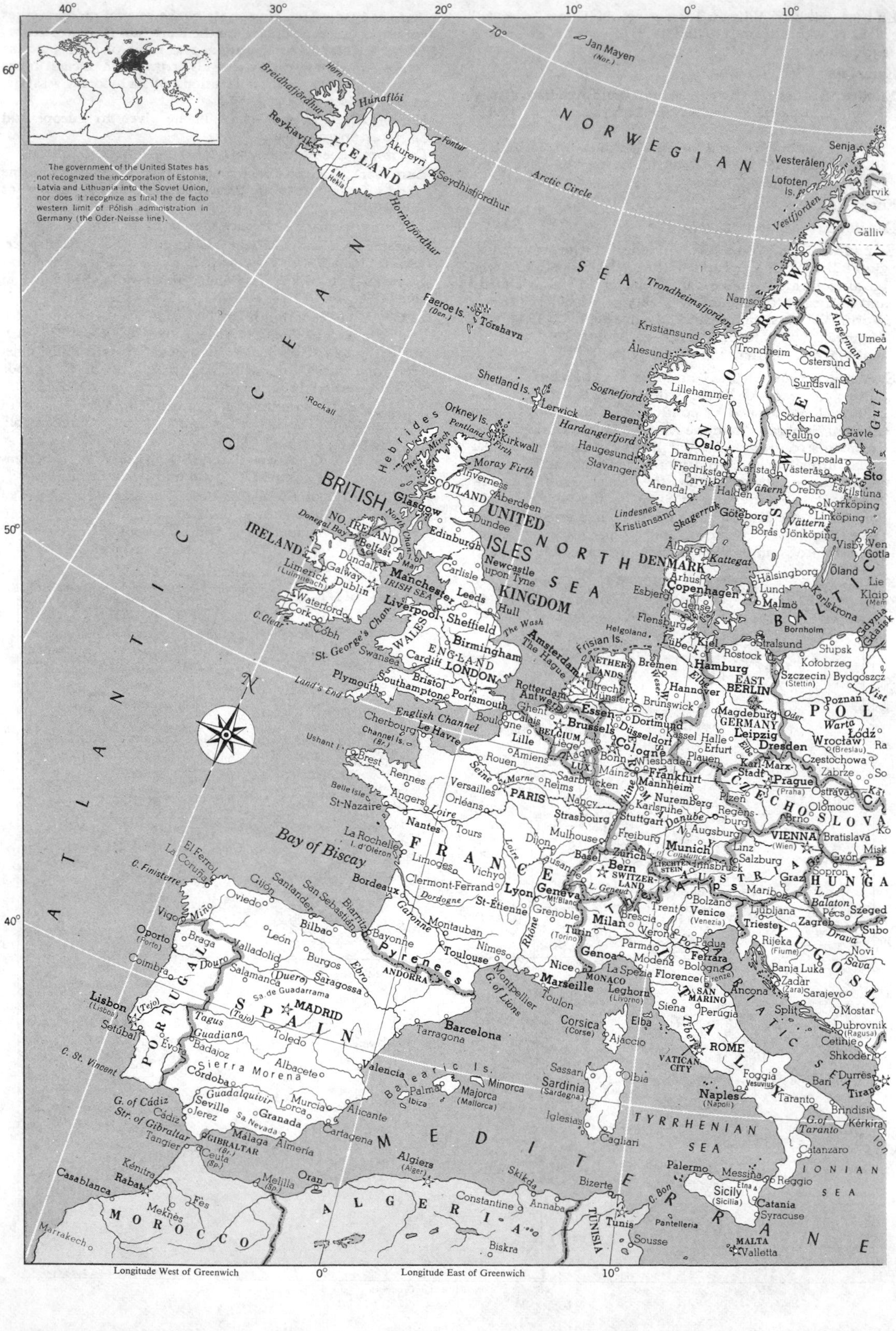
40°
30°
20°
10°
0°
10°
60°
50°
40°
70°
The government of the United States has not recognized the incorporation of Estonia, Latvia and Lithuania into the Soviet Union, nor does it recognize as final the de facto western limit of Polish administration in Germany (the Oder-Neisse line).
Jan Mayen (Nor.)
NORWEGIAN SEA
Arctic Circle
ICELAND
Reykjavik
Akureyri
Húnaflói
Breidhafjördhur
Horn
Fontur
Seydhisfjördhur
Hornafjördhur
Mt. Hekla
ATLANTIC OCEAN
Faeroe Is. (Den.)
Tórshavn
Shetland Is.
Lerwick
Rockall
Orkney Is.
Kirkwall
Pentland Firth
Hebrides
The Minch
Moray Firth
Inverness
Aberdeen
Dundee
SCOTLAND
Glasgow
Edinburgh
BRITISH ISLES
UNITED KINGDOM
NO. IRELAND
Belfast
IRELAND
Donegal Bay
North Channel
Dundalk
Galway
Dublin
Limerick (Luimneach)
Waterford
Cork
Cobh
C. Clear
Isle of Man
IRISH SEA
Carlisle
Newcastle upon Tyne
Manchester
Leeds
Liverpool
Sheffield
Hull
The Wash
WALES
St. George's Chan.
Swansea
Cardiff
Birmingham
ENGLAND
LONDON
Bristol
Southampton
Portsmouth
Plymouth
Land's End
English Channel
Channel Is. (Br.)
NORTH SEA
Senja
Vesterålen
Lofoten Is.
Narvik
Vestfjorden
Gälliv
Mo
Trondheimsfjorden
Namsos
Kristiansund
Ålesund
Trondheim
Östersund
Ångerman
Umeå
Sundsvall
Lillehammer
Sognefjord
Bergen
Hardangerfjord
Haugesund
Stavanger
Söderhamn
Falun
Gävle
Oslo
Drammen
Fredrikstad
Larvik
Karlstad
Västerås
Uppsala
Arendal
Halden
Vänern
Örebro
Eskilstuna
Norrköping
Lindesnes
Kristiansand
Skagerrak
Göteborg
Vättern
Linköping
Jönköping
Borås
Visby
Ålborg
DENMARK
Kattegat
Århus
Copenhagen
Esbjerg
Odense
Hälsingborg
Lund
Malmö
Öland
Karlskrona
Bornholm
BALTIC
Gdynia
Gdańsk
Flensburg
Kiel
Lübeck
Stralsund
Rostock
Helgoland
Frisian Is.
Amsterdam
The Hague
NETHERLANDS
Utrecht
Rotterdam
Antwerp
Bremen
Hamburg
Elbe
Weser
Hannover
Brunswick
EAST BERLIN
Szczecin (Stettin)
Kołobrzeg
Słupsk
Bydgoszcz
Poznań
Oder
Warta
POL
Münster
Essen
Dortmund
Düsseldorf
Cologne
Bonn
Brussels
BELGIUM
Ghent
Calais
Boulogne
Lille
Liège
Aachen
Kassel
Halle
Magdeburg
GERMANY
Leipzig
Dresden
Erfurt
Plauen
Wrocław (Breslau)
Łódź
Częstochowa
Zabrze
Karl-Marx-Stadt
Prague (Praha)
Ostrava
Wiesbaden
Frankfurt
Mainz
LUX.
Saarbrücken
Mannheim
Karlsruhe
Nuremberg
Regensburg
Danube
Stuttgart
Plzeň
CZECHOSLOVA
Olomouc
Brno
VIENNA (Wien)
Bratislava
Cherbourg
Le Havre
Ushant I.
Brest
Rennes
Amiens
Rouen
Seine
Marne
Reims
Versailles
PARIS
Nancy
Strasbourg
Belle Isle
St-Nazaire
Angers
Orléans
Loire
Nantes
Tours
Dijon
Mulhouse
Freiburg
Augsburg
Munich
Linz
Salzburg
Lake of Constance
Bay of Biscay
La Rochelle
I. d'Oléron
FRANCE
Limoges
Vichy
Clermont-Ferrand
Lyon
Geneva
Lausanne
Basel
Zürich
Bern
SWITZERLAND
LIECHTENSTEIN
Innsbruck
AUSTRIA
Graz
Győr
Sopron
HUNGA
Balaton
Pécs
Szeged
Bordeaux
Dordogne
Garonne
St-Étienne
Grenoble
Mt. Blanc
L. Geneva
Bolzano
Trento
Venice (Venezia)
Maribor
Ljubljana
Trieste
Zagreb
Drava
Rijeka (Fiume)
Sava
Novi
YUGOSL
Banja Luka
Zadar (Zara)
Sarajevo
Mostar
Split
Dubrovnik (Ragusa)
Cetinje
Shkodër
Durrës
Tiranë
El Ferrol
La Coruña
C. Finisterre
Gijón
Oviedo
Santander
Bilbao
San Sebastián
Biarritz
Bayonne
Montauban
Toulouse
Nîmes
Rhône
Turin (Torino)
Milan
Brescia
Verona
Padua
Po
Ferrara
Parma
Modena
Bologna
Genoa
La Spezia
Florence (Firenze)
SAN MARINO
Ancona
ADRIATIC SEA
Vigo
Miño
Oporto (Porto)
Braga
León
Burgos
Valladolid
Douro
Coimbra
Ebro
Salamanca
(Duero)
Saragossa
Sa. de Guadarrama
Pyrenees
ANDORRA
Montpellier
G. of Lions
Marseille
Nice
MONACO
Toulon
Leghorn (Livorno)
Elba
Siena
Perugia
Lisbon (Lisboa)
(Tejo)
Tagus (Tajo)
MADRID
SPAIN
PORTUGAL
Setúbal
Évora
Guadiana
Toledo
Badajoz
Barcelona
Tarragona
Corsica (Corse)
Ajaccio
Tiber
ROME
VATICAN CITY
ITALY
C. St. Vincent
Sierra Morena
Córdoba
Albacete
Valencia
Balearic Is.
Minorca
Majorca (Mallorca)
Palma
Ibiza
Sassari
Olbia
Sardinia (Sardegna)
Foggia
Vesuvius
Bari
Naples (Napoli)
Guadalquivir
Murcia
Lorca
Alicante
Seville
Granada
G. of Cádiz
Cádiz
Jerez
Sa. Nevada
Str. of Gibraltar
Málaga
Almería
Cartagena
GIBRALTAR (Br.)
Tangier
Ceuta (Sp.)
MEDITERRANEAN
Iglesias
Cagliari
TYRRHENIAN SEA
Taranto
Brindisi
G. of Taranto
Kérkira
Catanzaro
IONIAN SEA
Kénitra
Rabat
Casablanca
Melilla (Sp.)
Oran
Algiers (Alger)
Skikda
Bizerte
Palermo
Messina
Reggio
Etna
Sicily (Sicilia)
Catania
Syracuse
C. Bon
Fès
Meknès
MOROCCO
ALGERIA
Constantine
Annaba
TUNISIA
Tunis
Pantelleria
Sousse
MALTA
Valletta
Marrakech
Biskra
Longitude West of Greenwich
0°
Longitude East of Greenwich
10°

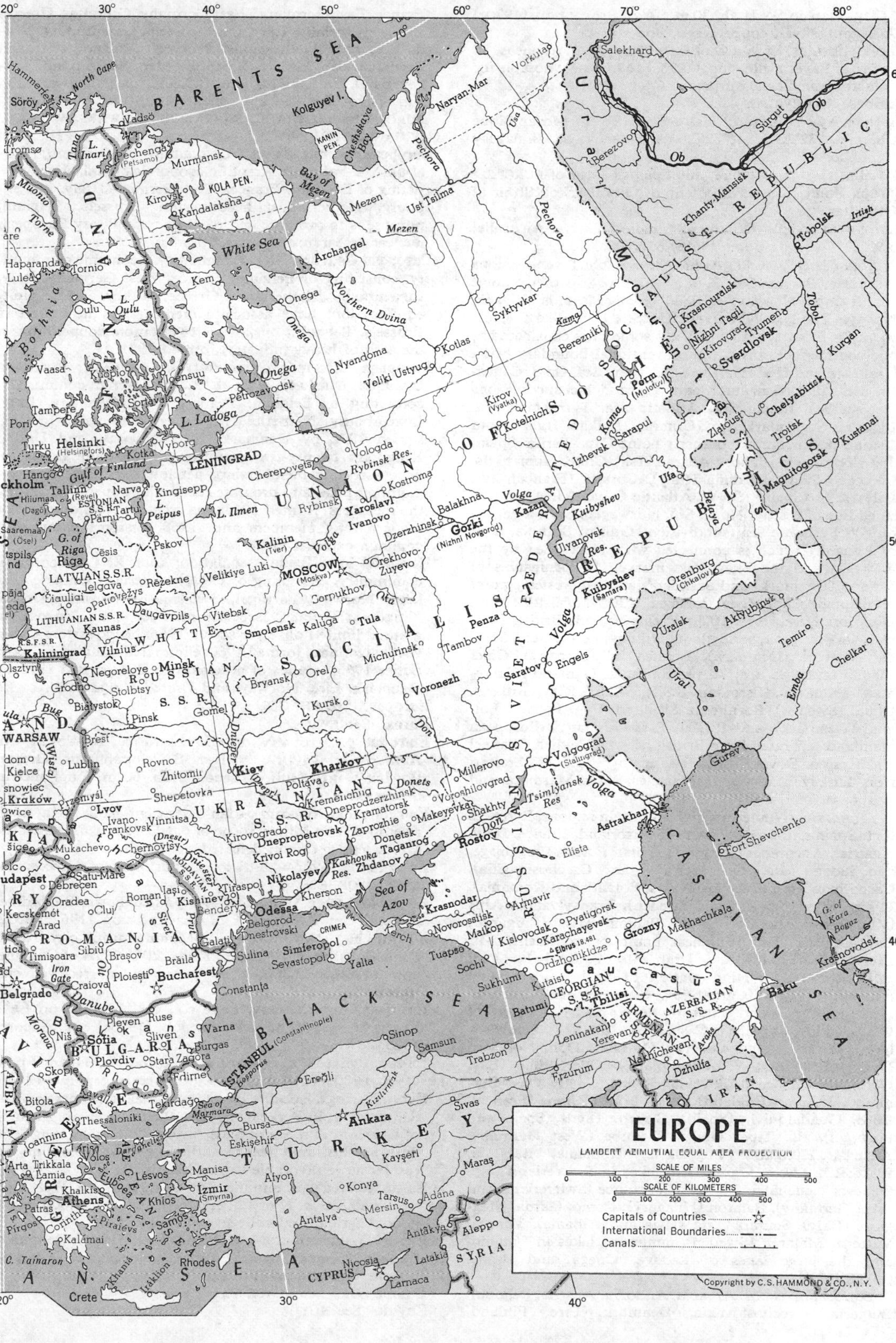
EUROPE
LAMBERT AZIMUTHAL EQUAL AREA PROJECTION
SCALE OF MILES
0 100 200 300 400 500
SCALE OF KILOMETERS
0 100 200 300 400 500
Capitals of Countries
International Boundaries
Canals
Copyright by C.S. HAMMOND & CO., N.Y.
BARENTS SEA
WHITE Sea
BLACK SEA
CASPIAN SEA
UNION OF SOVIET SOCIALIST REPUBLICS
RUSSIAN SOVIET FEDERATED SOCIALIST REPUBLIC
FINLAND
POLAND
ROMANIA
BULGARIA
GREECE
TURKEY
SYRIA
CYPRUS
IRAN
ALBANIA
WHITE RUSSIAN S.S.R.
UKRAINIAN S.S.R.
LATVIAN S.S.R.
LITHUANIAN S.S.R.
ESTONIAN S.S.R.
GEORGIAN S.S.R.
ARMENIAN S.S.R.
AZERBAIJAN S.S.R.
MOLDAVIAN S.S.R.
Caucasus
LENINGRAD
MOSCOW (Moskva)
Helsinki (Helsingfors)
WARSAW
Bucharest
Sofia
Ankara
Athens
Tbilisi
Kiev
Kharkov
Odessa
Rostov
Volgograd (Stalingrad)
Astrakhan
Gorki (Nizhni Novgorod)
Kuibyshev (Samara)
Kazan
Saratov
Sverdlovsk
Chelyabinsk
Magnitogorsk
Archangel
Murmansk
Riga
Minsk
Vilnius
Kaunas
Tallinn (Revel)
Kaliningrad
Baku
Grozny
Krasnodar
Sevastopol
Simferopol
Istanbul (Constantinople)
Izmir (Smyrna)
Belgrade
Budapest
Ob
Volga
Don
Dnieper
Danube
Kama
Ural
Pechora
Northern Dvina
Sea of Azov
L. Ladoga
L. Onega
L. Peipus
Gulf of Finland
G. of Riga
Bosporus
Sea of Marmara
Kolguyev I.
KANIN PEN.
KOLA PEN.
CRIMEA
Elbrus 18,481
20°
30°
40°
50°
60°
70°
80°

7 City, Juab co., W Utah, 30 m. SW of Provo; pop. (1970c) 753; gold, silver, copper, lead, zinc mines.

Eureka Springs. City, a ⊗ of Carroll co., NW Arkansas, 35 m. NE of Fayetteville; pop. (1970c) 1670; resort notable for numerous medicinal springs.

Euripos. See EVRIPOS.

Eu·ro·pa \yu̇-ˈrō-pə\. 1 Small island, S cen. Mozambique Channel, 22°20′S, 40°22′E; dependency of Malagasy Republic.

2 Latin, German, Italian, and Spanish form of EUROPE.

Europa Point. Southernmost tip of Gibraltar, on Strait of Gibraltar.

Eu·rope \ˈyu̇r-əp\. Continent, smallest except Australia; 3,997,929 sq. m.; pop. (1969e) 652,700,000.

Boundaries: On N, Arctic Ocean (chief subdivisions Kara Sea, Barents Sea, White Sea); most northerly point North Cape, Norway, 71°10′20″N; chief islands Vaigach, Novaya Zemlya, Kolguyev (U.S.S.R.), Svalbard (Norway). On E, Asia, with which it is sometimes considered as one continent, Eurasia, the conventional boundary being Ural Mts. and Ural river; on SE Caspian Sea. On S, Caucasus Mts., Black Sea, and Mediterranean (chief subdivisions Aegean Sea, Ionian Sea, Adriatic Sea, Tyrrhenian Sea, Ligurian Sea); marked by Crimean, Balkan, Italian, and Iberian penins.; most southerly point Cape Tarifa, Spain, 36°01′N; chief islands Aegean Is., Crete, Ionian Is. (Greece), Sicily, Sardinia (Italy), Corsica (France), and Balearic Is. (Spain). On W, Atlantic Ocean (chief subdivisions Bay of Biscay, North Sea, Norwegian Sea); indented on NW by Baltic Sea (subdivisions Gulf of Bothnia, Gulf of Finland) which is connected with North Sea by the Kattegat and the Skagerrak; marked by peninsulas of Jutland (Denmark) and Scandinavia; most westerly point of mainland Cape Roca, Portugal, 9°30′W, of British Isles, Dunmore Head, Eire, 10°30′W; chief islands British Isles, with smaller groups: Shetland, Orkney, and Outer Hebrides; Faeroes (Denmark), Lofoten Is. (Norway). Chief islands of Baltic Sea; Ahvenanmaa Is. (Finland), Saaremaa, Hiiumaa (Estonian S.S.R., U.S.S.R.), Gotland, Öland (Sweden), Bornholm, Sjælland, Fyn, Falster, Lolland (Denmark), and Rügen (East Germany). European mainland separated from British Isles by English Channel and Strait of Dover; from NE Africa by Strait of Gibraltar; from Turkey in Asia by Dardanelles, Sea of Marmara, and Bosporus.

Mountains: Numerous high mountain regions; Pyrenees (bet. Spain and France), Alps (Switzerland, France, Italy, Austria), Apennines (Italy), Bohemian Forest, Erzgebirge, and Sudetic Mts. (East Germany and Czechoslovakia), Carpathian Mts. (Czechoslovakia, Poland, and Romania), Kjølen Mts. (Norway and Sweden), Transylvanian Alps (Romania), Rhodope Mts., Balkan Mts. (Bulgaria), Caucasus (including highest point of continent, Mt. Elbrus, 18,481 ft.) and Ural Mts. (U.S.S.R.). *Other physical features:* High plateau of Spain with several mountain ranges (Cantabrian, Sierra de Guadarrama, Sierra Nevada) and extensive level plain of much of U.S.S.R.; lowest point is Caspian Sea (ab. 92 ft. below sea level). *Rivers:* Volga, Dnieper, Dniester, Don, Northern Dvina (U.S.S.R.), Vistula (Poland), Oder, Elbe (East Germany and Czechoslovakia), Rhine (chiefly West Germany), Thames (England), Seine, Loire, Rhone (France), Ebro, Guadalquivir (Spain), Douro, Tagus (Spain and Portugal), Po, Tiber (Italy), Danube (West Germany, Austria, Hungary, Yugoslavia, Romania, Bulgaria, U.S.S.R.). *Lakes:* Many small lakes in Switzerland (esp. Geneva, Neuchâtel, Zurich), Constance (Switzerland and West Germany), Balaton (Hungary), Como, Garda, Maggiore (Italy), Scutari (Yugoslavia and Albania), Vänern, Vättern, Mälaren (Sweden), numerous lakes in Finland, and the large lakes of Ladoga, Onega, and Peipus (U.S.S.R.).

Political divisions: Albania, Andorra, Austria, Belgium, Bulgaria, Czechoslovakia, Denmark, Eire, Finland, France, East Germany, West Germany, Gibraltar, Greece, Hungary, Iceland, Italy, Liechtenstein, Luxembourg, Malta, Monaco, Netherlands, Norway, Poland, Portugal, Romania, San Marino, Spain, Sweden, Switzerland, Turkey (part), United Kingdom, U.S.S.R. (part), Vatican City, and Yugoslavia. See EUROPEAN ECONOMIC COMMUNITY, EUROPEAN FREE TRADE ASSOCIATION, and WARSAW TREATY ORGANIZATION

European Atomic Energy Community *or frequently* **Eur·at·om** \yu̇-ˈrat-əm\. Scientific-economic organization, consisting of Belgium, France, West Germany, Italy, Luxembourg, Netherlands; headquarters Brussels, Belgium; purpose is to promote and regulate nonmilitary European nuclear research; formed 1958.

European Coal and Steel Community. Economic community, consisting of Belgium, France, West Germany, Italy, Luxembourg, Netherlands; Greece, Turkey, and the United Kingdom have associate membership; headquarters Brussels, Belgium; purpose is to promote cooperation in the area of heavy industry; formed 1951.

European Economic Community *or frequently* **European Common Market;** *abbr.* **EEC.** Economic community, consisting of Belgium, France, West Germany, Italy, Luxembourg, Netherlands; treaties of accession to EEC signed 1972 by Denmark, Eire, Norway, and United Kingdom; twenty-two countries of sub-Saharan Africa have associate membership; headquarters Brussels, Belgium; purpose is to promote economic cooperation among the members; formed 1958; has created free movement of labor among members and, 1968, customs union with common external tariff.

European Free Trade Association; *abbr.* **EFTA.** Economic community, consisting of (1972) Austria, Denmark, Iceland, Norway, Portugal, Sweden, Switzerland, United Kingdom; Finland associate member 1961; Yugoslavia granted limited observer status 1966; headquarters Geneva, Switzerland; formed 1960; eliminated industrial import duties 1966; treaties of accession to EEC signed 1972 by Denmark, Eire, Norway, and United Kingdom.

Europus. See RHAGES.

Euros. See EVROS.

Eu·ro·tas \yu̇-ˈrōt-əs\ *or Gk.* **Ev·ró·tas** \ev-ˈrō-täs\ *or formerly* **Iri** \ˈi(ə)r-ē\. River, S Peloponnesus, Greece, flowing S into Gulf of Laconia; ab. 60 m. long; ancient Sparta on it.

Eu·rym·e·don \yu̇-ˈrim-ə-ˌdän\. Ancient name of a small river in S Asia Minor; scene of battle 466 B.C. in which the Greek leader Cimon defeated the Persians.

Eu·ry·ta·nia \ˌyu̇r-ə-ˈtā-nē-ə\. Department of Greece. See table at GREECE.

Eu·se·bio Aya·la \ā-ü-ˈsā-bē-ˌō-ə-ˈyä-lə\. Town, S Cordillera dept., cen. Paraguay, E of Caacupé; pop. (1962c) 3532.

Eus·kir·chen \ˈȯis-ˌki(ə)r-kən\. Manufacturing city, North Rhine-Westphalia, West Germany, 20 m. SSW of Cologne; pop. (1966e) 22,300; glass, paper; sugar; received city rights 1302.

Eus·tis \ˈyü-stəs\. City, Lake co., cen. Florida, on **Lake Eustis** 30 m. NW of Orlando; pop. (1970c) 6722; incorp. 1925.

Eu·taw \ˈyü-ˌtȯ\. City, ⊗ of Greene co., W Alabama; pop. (1970c) 2805; cotton, potatoes, timber; incorporated 1838.

Eutaw Springs. Locality on **Eutaw Creek**, a tributary of the Santee river, in Berkeley co., South Carolina, ab. 45 m. N of Charleston; scene of battle in Revolutionary War Sept. 8, 1781, last important conflict in South Carolina, its results more favorable to Americans.

Eu·tin \ȯi-ˈtēn\. Commune, Schleswig-Holstein, West Germany, ab. 20 m. N of Lübeck; pop. (1967e) 17,600; metal goods; agricultural college; founded c. 1143.

Eut·suk Lake \ˈüt-ˌsək-\. Lake in W cen. British Columbia, Canada; 96 sq. m.; drains E through Nechako river; largest lake in Tweedsmuir (Provincial) Park.

Euxine Sea. See BLACK SEA.

Euyuk. See HÜYÜK.

Evan·ge·line \i-ˈvan-jə-ˌlēn\. Parish in Louisiana. See table at LOUISIANA.

Ev·ans \ˈev-ənz\. 1 County, Georgia. See table at GEORGIA. 2 Town, Weld co., N Colorado, 4 m. S of Greeley; pop. (1970c) 2570.

Evans, Mount. 1 Peak, Clear Creek co., N cen. Colorado; 14,264 ft.; on its crest is Cosmic Ray Laboratory of Univ. of Denver, built 1936; jointly sponsored 1948 with four other universities as the Inter-University High-Altitude Laboratory; automobile highway to summit.

2 Peak, Park and Lake cos., cen. Colorado; 13,580 ft.

Evans City *or* **Ev·ans·burg** \ˈev-ənz-ˌbərg\. Residential borough, Butler co., W Pennsylvania, 23 m. N of Pittsburgh; pop. (1970c) 2144.

Ev·ans·dale \ˈev-ənz-ˌdāl\. Town, Black Hawk co., NE cen. Iowa, SE of Waterloo; pop. (1970c) 5038.

Ev·ans·ton \ˈev-ən(t)-stən\. 1 Residential city, Cook co., NE Illinois, 15 m. N of Chicago; pop. (1970c) 79,808; Northwestern Univ. (1851), National Coll. of Education (1886), Kendall Coll. (1934).

2 Town, ⊗ of Uinta co., SW corner of Wyoming, on Bear river 5 m. E of Utah border; pop. (1970c) 4462; dairy farming, agriculture; coal, iron, and petroleum deposits.

Ev·ans·ville \ˈev-ənz-ˌvil\. 1 City, ⊗ of Vanderburgh co., SW Indiana, on Ohio river 29 m. ENE of confluence with Wabash river; pop. (1970c) 138,764; 4th largest city in the state; aluminum, chemicals, furniture, refrigerators, plastics; Evansville Coll. (1854).

2 City, Rock co., S Wisconsin, 15 m. WNW of Janesville; pop. (1970c) 2992; manufactures windmills, auto trailers, dairy products, farm machinery; settled 1839.

Ev·arts \ˈev-ərts\. City, Harlan co., SE Kentucky, in Cumberland Mts. 35 m. ENE of Middlesborough; pop. (1970c) 1182.

Ev·e·leth \ˈev-ə-ləth\. City, St. Louis co., NE Minnesota, 5 m. S of Virginia; pop. (1970c) 4721; iron ore mined nearby.

Eve·ning Shade \ˌēv-niŋ-ˈshād\. Town, a ⊗ of Sharp co., N Arkansas; pop. (1970c) 302.

Even·ki National Okrug *or* **Even·ky National Okrug** \e-ˈveŋ-kē-\. National okrug (district) in E part of Krasnoyarsk Krai, Russian S.F.S.R., U.S.S.R.; 296,370 sq. m.; pop. (1970p) 13,000; ✱ Tura; in N cen. Siberia, crossed by the Lower (Nizhnyaya) Tunguska river; graphite, coal; timber; formed 1930; inhabited by Evenkis, a race of Mongol origin.

Ev·er·ard, Lake \-ˈev-ə-ˌrärd\. Lake, S South Australia, W of Lake Gairdner.

Eve·re \ˈā-və-rə\. Commune, Brabant prov., cen. Belgium, NE of Brussels; pop. (1969e) 25,629; agriculture, horticulture (esp. production of witloof).

Ev·er·est, Mount \-ˈev-(ə-)rəst\ *or Tibetan* **Cho·mo·lung·ma** \ˌchō-mə-ˈlu̇ŋ-mə\. Highest mountain in the world, in the Himalayas bet. Nepal and Tibet, China, at 27°59′N, 86°56′E; 29,028 ft.; scene of numerous climbing attempts 1921–52; summit first photographed from airplane Apr. 19, 1933 and first reached May 29, 1953 by members of a British expedition led by Sir John Hunt; scaled by Swiss 1956, by Americans 1963, by Indians 1965.

Ev·er·ett \ˈev-(ə-)rət\. 1 City, Middlesex co., NE Massachusetts, 3 m. N of Boston; pop. (1970c) 42,485; coal and petroleum storage plants; manufactures paints and varnishes, chemicals, truck bodies, foundry products.

2 Borough, Bedford co., S Pennsylvania, 28 m. S of Altoona; pop. (1970c) 2243; chemicals; lumber; coal mines, stone quarries.

3 Industrial city and seaport, ⊗ of Snohomish co., NW cen. Washington, on Puget Sound at mouth of Snohomish river 28 m. N of Seattle; pop. (1970c) 53,622; aircraft, boats, sawmill machinery; lumbering center; fisheries, canneries; poultry packing; shipyards; Everett Community Coll. (1941).

Everett, Mount. Peak, Berkshire co., SW corner of Massachusetts; 2624 ft.

Ev·er·glades, The \-ev-ər-ˌglādz\. A vast tract of marshland in Palm Beach, Broward, Dade, Monroe, and Collier cos., S Florida, lying S of Lake Okeechobee; ab. 40 m. wide; large area has been reclaimed by drainage canals with locks and levees; the S part has been set aside as **Everglades National Park:** see UNITED STATES, *National Parks.*

Ev·er·green \ˈev-ər-ˌgrēn\. City, ⊗ of Conecuh co., S Alabama, 80 m. NE of Mobile Bay; pop. (1970c) 3924; mineral springs; agricultural experiment station.

Evergreen Park. Village, Cook co., NE Illinois, 10 m. SW of Chicago; pop. (1970c) 25,487.

Ev·er·man \ˈev-ər-mən\. Village, Tarrant co., N Texas, 9 m. S of Fort Worth; pop. (1970c) 4570; diversified agriculture.

Ev·ers·ley \ˈev-ərz-lē\. Village, NE Hampshire, S England, NW of Aldershot; residence of Charles Kingsley.

Ev·er·son \ˈev-ər-sən\. Borough, Fayette co., SW Pennsylvania, 16 m. NNE of Uniontown; pop. (1970c) 1143.

Eve·sham \ˈēv-shəm\. Municipal borough, Worcestershire, W cen. England, on the Avon 27 m. S of Birmingham; pop. (1971p) 13,847; trade center in section raising fruit and vegetables; scene of battle Aug. 4, 1265 in which Simon de Montfort was defeated and killed by Royalist forces.

Évian \ā-ˈvyäⁿ\ *or* **Évian–les–Bains** \-le-ˈbaⁿ\. Commune, Haute-Savoie dept., E France, on S shore of Lake Geneva; pop. (1962c) 5200; fashionable health resort.

Évo·ra \ˈev-ə-rə\. 1 District of SE cen. Portugal. See table at PORTUGAL.

2 *or anc.* **Eb·o·ra** \ˈeb-ə-rə\ *or* **Lib·er·al·i·tas Ju·li·a** \ˌlib-ə-ˈral-ə-ˌtas-ˈjül-yə\. Commune, its ✱, 68 m. E by S of Lisbon; munic. pop. (1970p) 47,806; manufactures cotton, cloth; iron founding; 13th cent. Gothic cathedral, Roman temple of Diana, Roman aqueduct, archiepiscopal library. Captured by Sertorius 80 B.C., by Moors 712 A.D., by Portuguese 1166; residence of Portuguese court 15th and 16th cents.

Evpatoria. See YEVPATORIYA.

Évreux \āv-ˈrə(r)\ *or anc.* **Civ·i·tas Ebu·ro·vi·cum** \ˈsiv-ə-ˌtas-i-ˌbyu̇r-ə-ˈvī-kəm\. Commune, ✱ of Eure dept., N France, 55 m. WNW of Paris; pop. (1968c) 42,550; metal and rubber products; one of oldest towns in France; ancient Norman church; 11th–18th cent. cathedral; Roman ruins. Taken from Romans by Clovis; pillaged by Normans 892; taken and burned by Henry I of England 1119; captured by Philip Augustus of France 1194, 1199; alternated bet. English and French control in 15th cent.

Ev·ri·pos \ˈev-ri-ˌpȯs\ *also* **Eu·ri·pos** \yu̇-ˈrī-pəs\. 1 *or* **Egripos** \ˈeg-ri-pəs\. Narrow strait bet. cen. part of W Euboea I. and the mainland of Greece, S of Atalante channel; the tide or current flows through it violently.

2 City on Euboea I., Greece. See CHALCIS.

Ev·ros \ˈev-ˌrȯs\. 1 River, SE Europe. See MARITSA.

2 *or* **Eu·ros** \ˈyu̇r-(ˌ)ȯs\. Department of Greece. See table at GREECE.

Evrótas. See EUROTAS.

Évry \ā-ˈvrē\. Town, ✱ of Essonne dept., N France, ab. 15 m. S of Paris; pop. (1968c) 7113.

Ev·ry·khou \ev-ˈrē-(ˌ)kü, -(ˌ)hü\. Village, W cen. Cyprus; terminus of railroad from Famagusta.

Evstrátios, Hagios. See HAGIOS EVSTRÁTIOS.

Évvoia. See EUBOEA.

Ewa \ˈev-ə\. 1 Division, Honolulu co., S Oahu I., Hawaii; pop. (1970c) 130,947; sugar plantations.

2 City in division at W end of Pearl Harbor; pop. (1970c) 2906.

Ewa Beach. City, Honolulu co., Hawaii, 10 m. W of Honolulu; pop. (1970c) 7765.

Ewa·so Ng'iro \ə-ˌwä-sō-nə-ˈgir-(ˌ)ō\ *also* **Va·so Nyi·ro** \ˌwä-sō-ˈnyir-(ˌ)ō\ *or* **Wa·so Nyiro** \ˌwä-sō-\ *or* **Gua·so Nyiro** \ˌwä-sō-\. River, Kenya, E Africa; flows NE 350 m.

into Lorian Swamp in E Kenya; issues from the swamp as the **Lach De·ra** \läk-ˈder-ə\ and in certain seasons empties into the Juba river in S Somalia.

Ewau·na, Lake \-i-ˈwȯ-nə\. Small lake, SW Klamath co., S Oregon, just S of Upper Klamath Lake; source of Klamath river.

Ewe, Loch \läk-ˈyü, läk-\. Inlet of the Atlantic Ocean on W coast of Ross and Cromarty co., N Scotland; 10 m. long; connected with Loch Maree by Ewe river, 3 m. long.

Ewe·land \ˈā-wā-ˌland\. Region extending ab. 80 m. along coast of W Africa, bet. mouth of Volta river and Grand Popo at mouth of the Mono; ab. 10,000 sq. m.; pop. (1965e) 1,000,000; inhabited by the Ewe tribe; part of former Slave Coast.

Ew·ing \ˈyü-iŋ\. Township, Mercer co., W cen. New Jersey, NNW of Trenton; pop. (1970c) 32,831.

Ex·cel·si·or \ik-ˈsel-sē-ər\. Village, Hennepin co., SE cen. Minnesota, 8 m. W of Minneapolis; pop. (1970c) 2563.

Excelsior Mountain. Peak in Sierra Nevada, in Mono co., E California; 12,446 ft.

Excelsior Mountains. Mountain range in Mineral co., SW Nevada; highest Pilot Peak 9187 ft.

Excelsior Springs. City, Clay co., NW Missouri, 25 m. NE of Kansas City; pop. (1970c) 9411; plastics; mineral springs; resort.

Exe \ˈeks\. River, SW England; 55 m. long; rises in NW Somersetshire, flows S past Tiverton and Exeter into English Channel at Exmouth.

Ex·e·ter \ˈek-sət-ər\. 1 City, Tulare co., S cen. California, 45 m. SE of Fresno; pop. (1970c) 4475; in agricultural region.

2 Manufacturing town, ⊗ of Rockingham co., SE New Hampshire, 12 m. WSW of Portsmouth; pop. (1970c) 8892; settled and incorporated 1638; capital of N.H. in Revolutionary days 1775 ff.; Phillips Exeter Academy (estab. 1781, opened 1783; see ANDOVER 1).

3 Borough, Luzerne co., E Pennsylvania, on Susquehanna river 9 m. W of Scranton; pop. (1970c) 4670; coal mines; timber.

4 Town, Washington co., S Rhode Island, 13 m. WNW of Newport; pop. (1970c) 3245; formerly part of North Kingstown.

5 Village, Huron co., SE Ontario, Canada, 27 m. W of Stratford; pop. (1971p) 3379; lumber mill.

6 *or anc.* **Is·ca Dam·no·ni·o·rum** \ˈis-kə-dam-ˌnō-nē-ˈōr-əm, -ˈȯr-\. City and county borough, ⊗ of Devonshire, SW England, on the Exe 37 m. NE of Plymouth; pop. (1971p) 95,598; has cathedral; railroad center; agricultural center; shipping (city connected with tidal estuary of the Exe by a ship canal); Univ. of Exeter (1955). Probably a trading center and fort existed here even before Roman times; a center of resistance of Britons to Anglo-Saxon invasion; withstood Danish attack 1001, but captured by Sweyn 1003; capitulated to William the Conqueror 1068; Royalist stronghold in Civil War 1642–46; in World War II site of largest U.S. Navy supply depot in England.

Ex·moor \ˈek-ˌsmu̇(ə)r, -ˌsmō(ə)r, -smȯ(ə)r\. Tract of moorland in Somersetshire, SW England; 32 sq. m.; highest point 1707 ft.

Ex·mouth \ˈek-ˌsmau̇th\. Urban district, Devonshire, SW England, on English Channel at mouth of the Exe, 10 m. SSE of Exeter; pop. (1971p) 25,815; summer resort, fishing and yachting.

Exmouth Gulf. Inlet of Indian Ocean, W Western Australia, bet. 21° and 23°S lat.; North West Cape is its NW point.

Exmouth Peninsula. Peninsula extending S from SW coast of Chile, E of Wellington I.

Ex·ploits \ˈek-ˌsplȯits\. River, Newfoundland, Canada; 153 m. long; flows NE through Red Indian Lake into Notre Dame Bay.

Ex·plor·ing Islands \ik-ˈsplō(ə)r-iŋ-, -ˈsplȯ(ə)r-\. Island group, N end of Lau group, E Fiji, SW Pacific Ocean, 17°15′S, 178°52′W; ab. 10 islands, largest Vanua Mbalavu.

Ex·port \ˈek-spō(ə)rt, -spȯ(ə)rt\. Borough, Westmoreland co., SW Pennsylvania, 20 m. E of Pittsburgh; pop. (1970c) 1402; coal mining.

Extremadura. See ESTREMADURA 2.

Ex·u·ma \ik-ˈsü-mə, ig-ˈzü-\. Island group of the Bahama Is., in Atlantic Ocean SE of New Providence I.; 130 sq. m.; pop. (1963c) 3440; consists of **Great Exuma, Little Exuma,** and adjacent cays.

Exuma Sound. Body of water in Bahama Is., SE of New Providence and Eleuthera Is. and W of Cat I.

Eye \ˈī\. Peninsula extending into North Minch on NE coast of island of Lewis with Harris, Outer Hebrides, off NW coast of Scotland.

Ey·ja Fjord \ˌā-(y)ə-\. Inlet of Arctic Ocean on N coast of Iceland, E of Skaga Fjord.

Eylau. See BAGRATIONOVSK.

Eyn·sham \ˈen-shəm, ˈān-\ *or* **En·sham** \ˈen-\. Parish and village, Oxfordshire, cen. England, 7½ m. NW of Oxford; few remains of ancient Benedictine abbey of which Ælfric Grammaticus was first abbot (1005).

Ey·rar·bak·ki \ˈā-ˌrär-ˌbäk-yē\. Village, SW coast of Iceland, ab. 32 m. SE of Reykjavík; pop. (1970c) 511.

Eyre, Lake \-ˈa(ə)r, -ˈe(ə)r\. Salt lake, NE South Australia; 3600 sq. m.; 90 m. long; max. depth 4 ft.; largest salt lake in Australia.

Eyre Peninsula. Large peninsula, S South Australia, W of Spencer Gulf; ab. 200 m. long.

Eysk. See YEISK.

Ey·zies, Les \ˌlā-zā-ˈzē\ *or in full* **Les Eyzies–de–Ta·yac** \-də-tī-ˈak\. Commune, Dordogne dept., SW cen. France, ab. 22 m. SE of Périgueux on the Vézère; pop. (1962c) 958; region containing many caves, notably **Cro–Ma·gnon** \ˌkrō-ma-ˈnyōⁿ\, where type specimens of the Cro-Magnon race dating from the Aurignacian period were found 1868, and **Com·ba·relles** \ˌkōⁿ(m)-bə-ˈrel\ and **Font–de–Gaume** \ˌfōⁿ-də-ˈgōm\ discovered 1901, decorated with Paleolithic paintings and engravings. See also LE MOUSTIER and LA MADELEINE.

Ezan, Cape. See ESAN, CAPE.

Ezi·on–ge·ber \ˌē-zē-ən-ˈgē-bər\. Ancient town, now an archaeological site, near ʻAqaba at head of Gulf of ʻAqaba, SW corner of Jordan; place where Solomon built a navy (*1 Kings* ix. 26); came under control of Edomites in middle of 8th cent. B.C.

Ezo. See HOKKAIDŌ.

Ez·ra Church \ˈez-rə-\. Site in SW Atlanta, Georgia, of battle July 28, 1864 in which Confederates tried unsuccessfully to check Sherman's advance.

Ez Zue·ti·na \ˌez-zwā-ˈtē-nə\ *or* **Az Zu·way·ti·nah** \ˌaz-zwā-ˈtē-nə\. Town on coastal road, N Libya, N Africa, on E shore of Gulf of Sidra ab. 40 m. S of Benghazi.

Fa·bens \ˈfāb-ənz\. Town, El Paso co., W tip of Texas, on the Rio Grande ab. 25 m. SE of El Paso; pop. (1970c) 3241; cotton; stock raising.

Fa·bri·a·no \ˌfäb-rē-ˈän-(ˌ)ō\. Commune, Ancona prov., Marches, cen. Italy, 38 m. SW of Ancona; pop. (1968e) 27,252; manufactures paper; sulfur springs.

Fa·ca·ta·ti·vá \ˌfäk-ə-ˌtät-i-ˈvä\. City, Cundinamarca dept., cen. Colombia, 25 m. NW of Bogotá; pop. (1968e) 26,327; alt. 8270 ft.

Fad·de·yev·ski \fə-ˈdā-əf-skē\. One of New Siberian Is. (*q.v.*).

Fæmund. See FEMUND.

Fa·en·za \fä-ˈen-zə, -ˈen(t)-sə\ *or anc.* **Fa·ven·tia** \fə-ˈven-ch(ē-)ə\. Commune, Ravenna prov., Emilia-Romagna, N Italy, 19 m. SW of Ravenna; pop. (1968e) 54,065; connected with Adriatic Sea by canal (opened 1782); early Renaissance cathedral; iron and salt springs; pottery center; International Museum of Ceramics. Scene of victory of Sulla over followers of Marius 82 B.C. and of Totila over the Byzantines 542 A.D.; became famous in 15th and 16th cents. for its manufacture of Faenza ware and faïence (both named for the town); during World War II in center of fighting Dec. 1944.

Faer·oes \ˈfa(ə)r-(ˌ)ōz, ˈfe(ə)r-\ *or* **Far·oe Islands** \-(ˌ)ō-\ *or* **Far·oes** *or Dan.* **Fær·ø·er·ne** \ˈfa(ə)r-ˈœ-ər-nə, ˈfe(ə)r-\. Island group in Atlantic Ocean N of British Isles, ab. 200 m. NW of Shetland Is.; 540 sq. m.; pop. (1970e) 38,681; of the 22 islands only 17 are inhabited, largest Strømø; constitute a self-governing unit within the Danish realm; ✱ Thorshavn; islands generally hilly and precipitous; highest point 2894 ft.; fishing and sheep raising. Possession of Denmark since 1380; inhabitants, of Norse descent, have control of local affairs and are represented in Danish Parliament; unsuccessfully sought independence 1946; received self-government 1947.

Faesulae. See FIESOLE.

Fa·e·te, Mon·te \ˌmōn-tē-fä-ˈet-ē, -ˈāt-\. Mountain, S of Rome, Italy; 3136 ft.; taken by American forces June 2, 1944 just before capture of Rome on June 4.

Fă·gă·raş \fə-gə-ˈräsh\. Town, Braşov co., N cen. Romania, on Olt river NW of Braşov; pop. (1970e) 24,673.

Fa·ga·to·go \ˌfäŋ-gə-ˈtōŋ-(ˌ)gō\. Village on Pago Pago Harbor, Tutuila Is., American Samoa.

Fa·ger·sta \ˈfäg-ər-ˌstä\. Town, Västmanland co., E cen. Sweden, 37 m. N of Västerås; pop. (1970e) 17,054; manufactures pig iron.

Fa·gui·bine, Lake \-ˌfag-ˈə-ˈbēn\ *or* **Lake Fa·gi·bi·ni** \-ˌfäg-ə-ˈbē-nē\. Lake, Mali, W Africa, W of Tombouctou and N of Niger river; ab. 70 m. long.

Fahlun. See FALUN.

Fa·ial *or also* **Fa·yal** \fə-ˈyäl, fī-ˈäl\. Westernmost island of cen. group of the Azores, W of Pico I.; lat. 38°34′N and long. 28°42′W; 66 sq. m.; pop. (1960c) 20,343; in district of Horta; presented by Alfonso V to his aunt, Isabella of Burgundy 1466; Horta, its chief town, on SE coast, the sailing port for shipping trade of Azores 18th and 19th cents.

Fa·ïd Pass \ˌfa-ˌēd-, ˈfīd-\. Mountain pass, N Tunisia, N Africa, E of Sbeïtla and on highway to Sfax; scene of American defeat by Germans under Rommel Feb. 14, 1943; retaken in April.

Faifo. See HOI AN.

Fails·worth \ˈfālz-ˌwərth\. Urban district, Lancashire, NW England, 5 m. NE of Manchester; pop. (1971p) 23,233.

Fair·banks \ˈfa(ə)r-ˌban(k)s, ˈfe(ə)r-\. Town, ⊗ of Fairbanks North Star borough, Alaska, at junction of Tanana and Chena rivers; pop. (1970c) 22,640; alt. 448 ft.; chief town of cen. Alaska; port of entry; terminus of railroad to Seward and of Alaska Highway; Univ. of Alaska (1922) at suburban village of College (ab. 2 m. W); gold mining, lumbering. Founded 1902 as result of a gold rush; severe flood damage 1967.

Fairbanks North Star. Borough in Alaska. See table at ALASKA.

Fair·born \ˈfa(ə)r-ˌbȯ(ə)rn, ˈfe(ə)r-\. City, Greene co., SW Ohio, NE of Dayton; pop. (1970c) 32,267; corn, wheat; formed 1950 by consolidation of former villages of Fairfield and Osborn.

Fair·burn \ˈfa(ə)r-bərn, ˈfe(ə)r-\. City, Fulton co., NW cen. Georgia, 18 m. SW of Atlanta; pop. (1970c) 3143; lumber; poultry.

Fair·bury \ˈfa(ə)r-ˌber-ē, ˈfe(ə)r-\. **1** City, Livingston co., NE cen. Illinois, 33 m. NE of Bloomington; pop. (1970c) 3359.

2 City, ⊗ of Jefferson co., SE Nebraska; pop. (1970c) 5265; packing plant; manufactures pumps; Fairbury Junior Coll. (1941).

Fair·chance \ˈfa(ə)r-ˌchans, fe(ə)r-\. Borough, Fayette co., SW Pennsylvania, 6 m. S of Uniontown; pop. (1970c) 1906.

Fair·fax \ˈfa(ə)r-ˌfaks, ˈfe(ə)r-\. **1** County in Virginia. See table at VIRGINIA.

2 Town, Marin co., W California, 15 m. NW of San Francisco; pop. (1970c) 7661.

3 Village, Hamilton co., SW Ohio; pop. (1970c) 2705.

4 Town, Osage co., N Oklahoma, 25 m. ESE of Ponca City; pop. (1970c) 1889; oil wells, refineries.

5 Town, ⊗ of Fairfax co., but politically independent, NE Virginia; 6 sq. m.; pop. (1970c) 21,970.

Fair·field \ˈfa(ə)r-ˌfēld, ˈfe(ə)r-\. **1** Name of counties in three states of the U.S. See tables at CONNECTICUT, OHIO, SOUTH CAROLINA.

2 City, Jefferson co., cen. Alabama, 5 m. W of Birmingham; pop. (1970c) 14,369; founded 1910; planned city, laid out by U.S. Steel Corp. (see also GARY, Indiana); once known as Corey.

3 City, ⊗ of Solano co., cen. California, 40 m. SW of Sacramento; pop. (1970c) 44,146; dairying; fruit; Travis Air Force Base.

4 Town, SE Fairfield co., SW Connecticut, on Long Island Sound; pop. (1970c) 56,487; chemicals, roller bearings; Fairfield Univ. (1942); port of entry; summer resort; settled 1639.

5 City, ⊗ of Camas co., S cen. Idaho; pop. (1970c) 336.

6 City, ⊗ of Wayne co., SE Illinois, 30 m. E of Mt. Vernon; pop. (1970c) 5897; auto parts.

7 City, ⊗ of Jefferson co., SE Iowa, 24 m. E of Ottumwa; pop. (1970c) 8715; aluminum castings, plastics; Parsons Coll. (1875).

8 Town, Somerset co., W Maine, on Kennebec river 4 m. N of Waterville; pop. (1970c) 5684; pulp and woolen mills.

9 Borough, Essex co., NE New Jersey, 6 m. SSW of Paterson; pop. (1970c) 6731.

10 City, Butler co., SW Ohio, 18 m. N of Cincinnati; pop. (1970c) 14,680.

11 Town, ⊗ of Freestone co., E cen. Texas; pop. (1970c) 2074.

12 Town, Franklin co., NW Vermont, 8 m. E of St. Albans; pop. (1970c) 1285; birthplace of Chester A. Arthur, 21st president of the U.S.

13 Municipality, E New South Wales, SE Australia, W suburb of Sydney; pop. (1966c) 101,226.

Fairfield Village. See BRIDGEPORT 3.

Fair·ha·ven \ˈfa(ə)r-ˌhā-vən, ˈfe(ə)r-, fa(ə)r-ˈ, fe(ə)r-ˈ\. **1** Town, Bristol co., SE Massachusetts, on Buzzards Bay across harbor from New Bedford; pop. (1970c) 16,332; former whaling center; boatyards.

2 Town, Washington. See BELLINGHAM 2.

Fair Ha·ven \-ˌhā-vən\. **1** Borough and resort, Monmouth co., E cen. New Jersey, 16 m. SE of Perth Amboy; pop. (1970c) 6142.
2 Village, Rutland co., W Vermont, on Poultney river 15 m. W of Rutland; pop. (1970c) 2777; slate; chartered 1783.

Fair Ha·vens \-ˈhā-vənz\. Sheltered harbor on S coast of Crete, Greece, E of Bay of Messara; port where Paul's ship touched on his journey to Rome (*Acts* xxvii 8).

Fair Head. Basaltic headland projecting into North Channel on extreme NE coast of Ireland; 636 ft. high.

Fair·hope \ˈfa(ə)r-ˌhōp, ˈfe(ə)r-\. City, Baldwin co., SW Alabama, on Mobile Bay SE of Mobile; pop. (1970c) 5720; sawmills; resort; settled 1893–94 on basis of single-tax doctrine promulgated by Henry George.

Fair·lawn \ˈfa(ə)r-ˌlȯn, ˈfe(ə)r-\. Village, Summit co., NE Ohio; pop. (1970c) 6102; residential suburb of Akron.

Fair Lawn. Borough, Bergen co., NE corner of New Jersey, 3 m. ENE of Paterson; pop. (1970c) 37,795; textiles, cement products.

Fair·mont \ˈfa(ə)r-ˌmänt, ˈfe(ə)r-\. **1** City, ⊗ of Martin co., S Minnesota, 41 m. SSW of Mankato; pop. (1970c) 10,751; canned goods; lake resort.
2 Town, Robeson co., S North Carolina, 41 m. SSW of Fayetteville; pop. (1970c) 2827; fertilizer; tobacco; livestock farms.
3 Manufacturing city, ⊗ of Marion co., N West Virginia, on Monongahela river 18 m. NNE of Clarksburg; pop. (1970c) 26,093; aluminum, chemicals; fruit; center of coal-mining region; Fairmont State Coll. (1867); settled 1793, became ⊗ 1842.

Fairmont City. Village, St. Clair co., SW Illinois, 5 m. E of East St. Louis; pop. (1970c) 2769.

Fairmount \ˈfa(ə)r-ˌmau̇nt, ˈfe(ə)r-\. Town, Grant co., N cen. Indiana, 9 m. S of Marion; pop. (1970c) 3247; steel products.

Fair Oaks. Locality just E of Richmond, Virginia; battlefield (called also Seven Pines), scene of engagement May 31–June 1, 1862 in which Union troops under McClellan repulsed Confederates under Johnston (Johnston wounded; on June 1 Robert E. Lee took command of Confederate forces).

Fair Plain. Urban community (unincorp.), Berrien co., SW Michigan, WSW of Kalamazoo; pop. (1970c) 3680.

Fair·play \ˈfa(ə)r-ˌplā, ˈfe(ə)r-\. Town, ⊗ of Park co., cen. Colorado; pop. (1970c) 419; alt. 9964 ft.

Fair·port \ˈfa(ə)r-ˌpō(ə)rt, ˈfe(ə)r-, -ˌpȯ(ə)rt\. **1** Industrial village, Monroe co., W New York, 10 m. E of Rochester; pop. (1970c) 6474.
2 Village (post office **Fairport Harbor**), Lake co., NE Ohio, on Lake Erie 28 m. NE of Cleveland; pop. (1970c) 3665; fisheries.

Fair·view \ˈfa(ə)r-ˌvyü, ˈfe(ə)r-\. **1** City, Nelson co., cen. Kentucky; pop. (1970c) 253; birthplace of Jefferson Davis.
2 City, Massachusetts. See CHICOPEE 2.
3 Borough, Bergen co., NE corner of New Jersey, 7 m. N of Jersey City; pop. (1970c) 10,698; chemical products, furniture.
4 Urban community (unincorporated), Dutchess co., SE New York, NE of New York City; pop. (1970c) 8517.
5 City, ⊗ of Major co., NW Oklahoma, 37 m. WSW of Enid; pop. (1970c) 2894; dairy farms.

Fairview Heights. City, Saint Clair co., SW Illinois, 10 m. E of East St. Louis; pop. (1970c) 8625.

Fairview Park. City, Cuyahoga co., N Ohio, SW suburb of Cleveland; pop. (1970c) 21,681.

Fair·way \ˈfa(ə)r-ˌwā, ˈfe(ə)r-\. City, Johnson co., E Kansas, S of Kansas City; pop. (1970c) 5133.

Fair·weath·er, Cape \-ˈfa(ə)r-ˌweth-ər, -ˈfe(ə)r-\. Cape on SE coast of Alaska, 58°55′N, 138°W, ab. 35 m. S of Mt. Fairweather.

Fairweather, Mount. Peak on boundary bet. Alaska and NW British Columbia, Canada, on NW border of Glacier Bay National Monument; 15,300 ft.

Fa·i·si \fä-ˈē-sē, -zē\. Town, E coast of Shortland I., NW Solomon Is., W Pacific Ocean; government station, chief town of Shortland Is.; became naval base under Japanese; center of copra trade.

Fai·yūm *or* **Fa·yum** \fä-ˈ(y)üm, fī-\. Governorate of N Upper Egypt. See table at EGYPT.

Faiyūm, Al–. See AL-FAIYŪM.

Faiz·ā·bād *or* **Fyz·a·bad** \ˈfī-zə-ˌbad\. **1** Town, ✱ of Badakhshān prov., NE Afghanistan; pop. (1969e) 62,853; alt. 4000 ft.; flour mills.
2 *or formerly* **Faizābād–cum–Ajodh·ya** \-ˌkəm-ə-ˈyōd-yə\. City, E cen. Uttar Pradesh, N India, on Ghagara river 75 m. E of Lucknow; pop. (1961c) 83,700; rail center; refines sugar. Founded 1730; later became residence of the begums of Oudh; station for troops. Includes nearby Ajodhya (*q.v.*).

Fa·jar·do \fə-ˈhärd-(ˌ)ō\. Town, NE Puerto Rico; pop. (1970p) 18,127.

Fa·ka·o·fo \ˌfäk-ə-ˈō-(ˌ)fō\. Atoll of Tokelau group, cen. Pacific Ocean, N of Samoa; lagoon 7 m. by 4 m.; pop. (1970c) 679; has chief settlement (**Fakaofo**) of the group.

Fa·ka·ra·va \ˌfäk-ə-ˈräv-ə\. Atoll in Tuamotu Archipelago, French Polynesia, South Pacific Ocean, lat. 16°S and long. 145°31′W; 32 m. long by 10 m. wide; chief village Rotoava.

Fak·fak \ˈfäk-ˌfäk\. Coastal settlement at W end of Irian Barat, Indonesia, just S of entrance to Berau Bay.

Fa·laise \fə-ˈlāz, fa-\. Commune, S Calvados dept., NW France, 19 m. SE of Caen; pop. (1962c) 6711; ruined castle; celebrated since 11th cent. for fair, held annually in Aug., for livestock and wool at Guibray, a suburb. Seat of dukes of Normandy, probably birthplace of William the Conqueror; held by English 1417–50; in World War II Normandy campaign captured by Canadians Aug. 16, 1944 and formed N point of Falaise pocket (see ARGENTAN).

Fa·la·lop \fə-ˈläl-əp\. See ULITHI.

Fa·lam \fə-ˈläm\. Town, ✱ of Chin Special div., W Upper Burma, on Manipur river 175 m. NW of Mandalay.

Fal·cón \fal-ˈkōn, fäl-\. State of Venezuela. See table at VENEZUELA.

Fal·co·na·ra Ma·rit·ti·ma \ˌfäl-kə-ˌnär-ə-mä-ˈrit-ə-mə\. Commune, Ancona prov., Marches, E Italy, ab. 10 m. W of Ancona; pop. (1968e) 21,272.

Fal·con·er \ˈfal-kən-ər, ˈfȯl-\. Manufacturing village, Chautauqua co., SW New York; pop. (1970c) 2983.

Fal·con Heights \ˌfal-kən-\. Village, Ramsey co., E Minnesota, N suburb of St. Paul; pop. (1970c) 5641.

Fa·lé·mé \ˌfal-ə-ˈmā\. River, Senegal, W Africa; ab. 250 m. long; tributary of Senegal river.

Falerii. See CIVITA CASTELLANA.

Fal·fur·ri·as \fal-ˈfyu̇r-ē-əs\. City, ⊗ of Brooks co., S Texas, 53 m. SW of Corpus Christi; pop. (1970c) 6355; gypsum mines, oil wells.

Falkenau. See SOKOLOV.

Fal·ken·see \ˈfäl-kən-ˌzā\. City, Potsdam dist., East Germany, 12 m. E of Berlin; pop. (1970e) 25,891; tractors, plastics.

Fal·ken·stein \ˈfäl-kən-ˌs(h)tīn\ *also* **Falkenstein in Sachsen** \-in-ˈzäk-sən\. Industrial city, Karl-Marx-Stadt dist., East Germany, 36 m. SW of Karl-Marx-Stadt; pop. (1970e) 14,951.

Fal·kirk \ˈfȯl-ˌkərk\. Burgh, Stirling co., cen. Scotland, 20 m. ENE of Glasgow; pop. (1971p) 37,587; coal and iron mines, flour mills, chemical factories, and breweries. Scene of two battles: (1) July 22, 1298, in which Edward I of England defeated Scots under Wallace; (2) Jan. 17, 1746, in which Prince Charles Edward and his Highlanders defeated Gen. Hawley.

Falk·land Islands \ˈfȯ(l)-klənd-\ *or Span.* **Is·las Mal·vi·nas** \ˈēz-ˌläs-mal-ˈvē-nəs\. British colony in South Atlantic Ocean, 300 m. E of Strait of Magellan; 4700 sq. m.; pop. (1970e) 2045; ✱ Stanley; comprises two principal islands, **East Falkland** (2550 sq. m.; with adjacent small islands 2610 sq. m.) and **West Falkland** (1750 sq. m.; with adjacent small islands 2090 sq. m.); the smaller islands include Weddell I., Pebble I., and Jason Is.; main islands of quite irregular shape with wide channel (**Falkland Sound**) bet. them; many fjords and bays; highest point Mt. Usborne 2312 ft. on East Falkland; sheep raising; claimed by Argentina.

History: Discovered 1592; not occupied until French made short-lived settlement 1764; settlement of English and their expulsion by Spanish 1770 at one time threatened to cause war bet. England and countries party to Family Compact; although claimed by Argentina after she won independence (and still claimed), occupied by British 1833; in nearby waters a British fleet destroyed German Pacific fleet Dec. 8, 1914.

Falkland Islands Dependencies. Collective name for South Georgia I., South Sandwich Is., (*qq.v.*), and several other islets; total area ab. 1570 sq. m.; whaling stations; administered from the Falkland Islands (*q.v.*).

Falk·ner Island \ˌfȯk-nər-\. Island in Long Island Sound off SE coast of New Haven co., Connecticut.

Falknov. See SOKOLOV.

Fal·kö·ping \ˈfäl-ˌchəp-iŋ\. Town, Skaraborg co., S Sweden, W of Lake Vättern; pop. (1970e) 15,968; scene of battle Feb. 24, 1389 in which Albert, Duke of Mecklenburg, was defeated and taken prisoner by forces of Margaret of Denmark.

Fal·la, Mount \-ˈfal-ə\. Mountain, Antarctica, 84°22′S, 164°55′E; 12,549 ft.

Fall·en Tim·bers \ˌfȯl-ən-ˈtim-bərz\. Locality on Maumee river SW of Toledo, NW Ohio; scene of victory Aug. 20, 1794 of Anthony Wayne over the Indians which led to enforcement of Jay's Treaty (Nov. 1794) and British evacuation of border forts.

Fal·lon \ˈfal-ən\. 1 County in Montana. See table at MONTANA.

2 City, ⊗ of Churchill co., W Nevada, near Carson Lake and Carson Sink 53 m. E of Reno; pop. (1970c) 2959; livestock.

Fall River \ˌfȯl-\. 1 County in South Dakota. See table at SOUTH DAKOTA.

2 Seaport and manufacturing city, a ⊗ of Bristol co., SE Massachusetts, on Mt. Hope Bay at mouth of Taunton river 12 m. NW of New Bedford; pop. (1970c) 96,898; plastics, rubber goods, textile machinery; Coll. of the Sacred Hearts (1934), Bristol Community Coll. (1966); in 19th cent. one of largest centers in U.S. for cotton mills and textile machinery works. Originally part of Plymouth colony; settled 1656; severe fires 1843 and 1928.

Falls \ˈfȯlz\. County in Texas. See table at TEXAS.

Falls Church. Independent city, NE Virginia, 10 m. NW of Alexandria; 2 sq. m.; pop. (1970c) 10,772.

Falls City. City, ⊗ of Richardson co., SE corner of Nebraska, 65 m. ESE of Beatrice; pop. (1970c) 5444; meat processing.

Falluja, Al–. See AL-FALLUJA.

Fal·mouth \ˈfal-məth\. 1 City, ⊗ of Pendleton co., N Kentucky, 30 m. SSE of Covington; pop. (1970c) 2593; dairying; tobacco.

2 Town, Cumberland co., SW Maine, 6 m. N of Portland; pop. (1970c) 6291.

3 Residential and resort town, Barnstable co., SE Massachusetts, 16 m. ESE of New Bedford near E shore of Buzzards Bay; pop. (1970c) 15,942; formerly whaling and boatbuilding center, Otis Air Force Base; includes **Woods Hole**, seat of Woods Hole Oceanographic Institution (founded 1930).

4 Seaport town on S coast of island of Antigua, West Indies.

5 Municipal borough, Cornwall, SW England, on English Channel at mouth of the Fal 44 m. WSW of Plymouth; pop. (1971p) 17,883; port, fishing center, seaside resort; a U.S. Naval training base 1943–45.

6 Coastal town, Jamaica, West Indies; pop. (1960c) 3727.

False Bay \ˈfȯls-\. Bay on SW coast of Cape Province, Rep. of South Africa, E of Cape of Good Hope.

False Cape. See VALS, CAPE.

False Cape Horn. Cape at SE tip of Hoste I., Chile, S of Tierra del Fuego I. and NW of Cape Horn.

False Di·vi, Point \-ˈdiv-ē\. Cape, E coast of India, E of Krishna delta and S of Machilipatnam.

False Pass. Village on E coast of Unimak I. opp. tip of Alaska Penin., Aleutian Is.

False Point. Cape on NE coast of India, in Orissa, projecting into Bay of Bengal just N of mouth of Mahanadi river.

Fal·so, Cape \-ˈfäl-(ˌ)sō, -ˈfȯl-\. Southwest extremity of Baja California, extending into Pacific Ocean.

Fal·ster \ˈfäl-stər, ˈfȯl-\. Island forming a part of Denmark, lying in Baltic Sea S of the island of Sjælland (with which it is connected by a bridge over 10,000 feet long), SW of Møn, and E of Lolland; 198 sq. m.; pop. (1965c) 45,906.

Făl·ti·ce·ni \ˌfəl-tə-ˈchen(-ē)\. City, NE Romania, 68 m. NW of Bacău; pop. (1966c) 17,839.

Fa·lun *or* **Fah·lun** \ˈfä-ˌlən\. City, ⊗ of Kopparberg co., cen. Sweden, 130 m. NW of Stockholm; pop. (1970e) 34,550; railroad car factories, iron mines and foundries, pyrite mines; former copper-mining center.

Fa·ma·gu·sta \ˌfäm-ə-ˈgüs-tə, ˌfam-\. 1 District, E part of island of Cyprus, E Mediterranean Sea; 764 sq. m.; pop. (1968e) 124,500; oranges.

2 Seaport, its ✱, on Famagusta Bay on E coast NW of Cape Greco; pop. (1970e) 42,500; footwear; 3 m. S of ruins of Salamis (*q.v.*); has fortifications, castle, and large cathedral (now a mosque); connected by rail with Nicosia. Important during Crusades, receiving many refugees after fall of Acre 1291; taken by Genoese 1373 and by Turks 1571 after siege of a year; nearby was British internment camp for Jews attempting illegally to enter Palestine 1946–48.

Famagusta Bay. Broad inlet of Mediterranean Sea on E coast of Cyprus.

Famatina, Nevado de. See SIERRA DE FAMATINA.

Famatina, Sierra de. See SIERRA DE FAMATINA.

Fa·na \ˈfän-ə\. Commune, Hordaland co., SW Norway; pop. (1970e) 43,083.

Fan·ad Head \ˌfan-əd-\. Cape on N coast of Ireland, at W of entrance to Lough Swilly; lighthouse.

Fan·nin \ˈfan-ən\. Name of counties in two states of the U.S. See tables at GEORGIA and TEXAS.

Fan·ning Island \ˈfan-iŋ-\. One of the Line Is. (*q.v.*) in cen. Pacific Ocean, S of Hawaii, lat. 3°52′N and long. 159°W; 15 sq. m.; included 1916 in British colony of Gilbert and Ellice Is.; discovered 1798 by American navigator, Capt. Edward Fanning. See AMERICA ISLANDS.

Fa·no \fä-ˈnȯ, -ˈnō\ *or anc.* **Pha·nos** \ˈfā-ˌnäs\ *or Gk.* **Otho·noí** \ˌō-thə-ˈnē\. Island of the Ionian Is., 14 m. NW of Corfu.

Fano \ˈfän-(ˌ)ō\; *anc.* **Fa·num For·tu·nae** \ˌfā-nəm-fȯr-ˈt(y)ü-(ˌ)nē\ *or later* **Co·lo·nia Ju·lia Fa·nes·tris** \kə-ˌlō-nē-ə-ˌjül-yə-fə-ˈnes-trəs\. Commune, Pesaro e Urbino prov., Marches, cen. Italy, on Adriatic Sea near mouth of Metauro river, 6 m. SE of Pesaro; pop. (1968e) 45,879; manufactures silk, oil, hemp; fisheries; cathedral; remains of triumphal arch and city walls. Under Papal States 1463–1860; first printing press with movable Arabic type set up here 1513 by Pope Julius II; seat of a university until 1828. See PENTAPOLIS.

Fanø \ˈfan-ˌər, ˈfän-\. Island of Denmark, in North Sea off SW coast of Jutland Penin.; in North Frisian Is.; 22 sq. m.; pop. (1970e) 2717.

Fan–si–pan \ˈfaⁿ-sē-ˈpaⁿ\. Mountain, North Vietnam, 155 m. NW of Hanoi; 10,306 ft.; highest mountain in North Vietnam.

Fan·wood \'fan-ˌwu̇d\. Borough, Union co., NE New Jersey, 9 m. W of Elizabeth; pop. (1970c) 8920.

Fao \'fau̇\. Port, SE Iraq, near Persian Gulf at mouth of the Shatt-al-Arab, which is 1 m. wide here but obstructed by bar across channel.

Fara. See SHURUPPAK.

Fa·ra·fan·ga·na \ˌfar-ə-fən-'gän-ə\. Town, SE coast of Malagasy Republic, S of Manakara.

Fa·raf·ra \fə-'räf-rə\ *or* **Fa·ra·fi·rah** \-'räf-ə-rə\. Oasis, Matrūh gov., Egypt, in Libyan Desert, 27°N, 28°E.

Fa·rah \fə-'rä\. 1 River, rising in mountains in W cen. Afghanistan and flowing SW into Lake Helmand; ab. 200 m. long; drainage area 12,500 sq. m.

2 Province of SW Afghanistan. See table at AFGHANISTAN.

3 Town, its ✱; pop. (1969e) 28,712.

Fa·ra·llo·nes de Ca·li National Park \ˌfär-ə-'yō-nās-də-'käl-ē-\. National park, Cauca dept., Colombia; 463 sq. m.; established 1962.

Far·al·lon Islands \'far-ə-ˌlän-\. Small group of islands in Pacific Ocean, a part of San Francisco co., W cen. California, ab. 30 m. W of Golden Gate.

Fa·ra·san Islands \ˌfär-ə-ˌsan-\. Group of islands in SE Red Sea, off SW coast of Asir, Saudi Arabia.

Far·ciennes \ˌfär-sē-'en\. Commune, Hainaut prov., SW Belgium, near Charleroi; pop. (1969e) 10,676.

Far East. 1 The countries of E and SE Asia: Burma, Cambodia, China, Indonesia, Japan, Korea (North and South), Laos, Malaysia, Philippines, Taiwan, and Vietnam (North and South); term sometimes expanded to include E Siberia (U.S.S.R.) and Mongolian People's Republic.

2 The E strip of Siberia along the coast, in 19th cent. a viceroyalty of Russian empire, later known as Maritime Province. See FAR EASTERN REGION; SIBERIA.

Far Eastern Region *or* **Far Eastern Area** *or Russ.* **Dal·ne·vos·toch·ny Ra·yon** \'däl-n(y)ə-və-'stȯch-n(y)i-rä-'yȯn\. Economic region, Russian S.F.S.R., U.S.S.R.; 2,399,958 sq. m.; pop. (1970p) 5,780,000; coextensive with Khabarovsk and Primorski krais and Amur, Kamchatka, Magadan, and Sakhalin oblasts; greater part of region first known as **Far Eastern Republic,** formed 1920 of four republics of E Siberia with capital at Chita, which was supplanted 1922 by Far Eastern Region, with capital first at Vladivostok and later at Khabarovsk; reorganized 1926 as Far Eastern Area; reorganized again 1938 when it was divided.

Fa·regh \fə-'reg\. Short river in NE Libya, N Africa; drains W into marshes S of Al-Agheila.

Fare·ham \'fa(ə)r-əm, 'fe(ə)r-\. Urban district, Hampshire, S England, on NW Portsmouth harbor 6 m. NNW of Portsmouth; pop. (1971p) 80,296; boatbuilding; light engineering; leather.

Fare·well, Cape \-'fa(ə)r-ˌwel, -'fe(ə)r-\. 1 *or Dan.* **Kap Far·vel** \ˌkap-fär-'vel\. Southern point of Greenland, 59°45′N, 44°W.

2 Northernmost point of South I., New Zealand, 40°30′S.

Far·go \'fär-(ˌ)gō\. City, ⊗ of Cass co., E North Dakota, on Red river at head of navigation; pop. (1970c) 53,365; largest city in the state; agricultural machinery, concrete; food processing; foundry products; meat-packing plants (in suburb of **West Fargo,** pop. [1970c] 5161); North Dakota State Univ. of Agriculture and Applied Science (1890); settled 1871, incorp. 1875.

Fargues \'färg\. Village, Gironde dept., SW France; pop. (1962c) 643; produces wine (see SAUTERNES).

Far·i·bault \'far-ə-ˌbō\. 1 County in Minnesota. See table at MINNESOTA.

2 City, ⊗ of Rice co., S Minnesota, 47 m. S of Minneapolis; pop. (1970c) 16,595; air conditioners, foundry products; on site of trading post established 1826 by Alexander Faribault.

Fa·ri·da·bad \fə-'rēd-ə-ˌbäd\. Town, Haryana, N India; pop. (1961c) 50,709.

Fa·rid·kot \fe-'rēd-ˌkōt\. 1 Former Indian state, now part of Punjab, N India, S of the Sutlej; 637 sq. m.; under British influence 1809–1947.

2 Town, its ✱; pop. (1961c) 26,700.

Fa·rid·pur \fə-'rēd-ˌpu̇(ə)r\. Town, Bangla Desh, on S bank of an old channel of the Ganges, 35 m. WSW of Dacca; pop. (1961c) 28,333.

Fa·ri·lhões \ˌfar-əl-'yȯi^{n}sh\. Group of Portuguese islets off W cen. coast of Portugal, just N of the Berlengas Is.

Farm·er City \ˌfär-mər-\. City, De Witt co., cen. Illinois, 34 m. NE of Decatur; pop. (1970c) 2217.

Farm·ers Branch \'fär-mərz-\. City, Dallas co., NE Texas, NNE suburb of Dallas; pop. (1970c) 27,492.

Farm·ers·ville \'fär-mərz-ˌvil\. 1 City, Tulare co., S cen. California, 45 m. SE of Fresno; pop. (1970c) 2517; fruit and vegetable packing; diversified agriculture.

2 City, Collin co., NE Texas, W of Greenville; pop. (1970c) 2311; onions.

Farm·er·ville \'fär-mər-ˌvil\. Town, ⊗ of Union parish, N Louisiana; pop. (1970c) 3416.

Farm·ing·dale \'fär-miŋ-ˌdāl\. Village, Nassau co., SE New York, on Long I. 30 m. E of New York City; pop. (1970c) 9267; manufactures airplanes; State Univ. of New York Agricultural and Technical Coll. (1912).

Farm·ing·ton \'fär-miŋ-tən\. 1 River, N Connecticut; formed by confluence in NE Litchfield co. of East Branch and West Branch (ab. 30 m. long) both of which rise in Massachusetts; flows into Connecticut river at Windsor.

2 Residential and industrial town, W cen. Hartford co., N Connecticut; pop. (1970c) 14,390; watered by Farmington river; Tunxis Community Coll. (1970); settled 1640, incorp. 1645. Includes 2 communities: (1) Farmington, former industrial center, now residential suburb; and (2) Unionville (*q.v.*).

3 City, Fulton co., W cen. Illinois; pop. (1970c) 2959.

4 Town, ⊗ of Franklin co., W Maine, 26 m. WNW of Waterville; pop. (1970c) 5657; Farmington State Coll. (1864).

5 Residential city, Oakland co., SE Michigan, 14 m. SSW of Pontiac; pop. (1970c) 10,329.

6 Village, Dakota co., SE Minnesota, 22 m. S of St. Paul; pop. (1970c) 3104.

7 City, ⊗ of St. Francois co., E Missouri, 59 m. S of St. Louis; pop. (1970c) 6509; lead deposits.

8 Town, Strafford co., SE New Hampshire, 6 m. NW of Rochester; pop. (1970c) 3588; shoe manufacturing; summer resort.

9 City, San Juan co., NW corner of New Mexico, on San Juan river near NE corner of Northern Navajo Indian Reservation; pop. (1970c) 21,979; near oil, gas, and coal fields; has oil refineries.

10 City, ⊗ of Davis co., N Utah, on Great Salt Lake 15 m. N of Salt Lake City; pop. (1970c) 2526.

Farm·ville \'färm-ˌvil, -vəl\. 1 Town, Pitt co., E North Carolina, 21 m. SSE of Wilson; pop. (1970c) 4424; fertilizer, lumber.

2 Town, ⊗ of Prince Edward co., S cen. Virginia, 45 m. E of Lynchburg; pop. (1970c) 5127; tobacco warehouses, lumber mills; Longwood Coll. (1884); settled 1754.

Farn·bor·ough \'färn-b(ə-)rə\. Urban district, Hampshire, S England, 31 m. WSW of London; pop. (1971p) 41,233; site of Royal Aircraft Establishment.

Farne Islands \'färn-\ *also* **The Sta·ples** \-'stā-pəlz\. Group of 17 small islands off NE coast of Northumberland, N England; scene of wreck of the *Forfarshire* 1838 and the rescue, from Longstone lighthouse, by Grace Darling.

Farn·ham \'fär-nəm\. 1 City, Missisquoi co., S Quebec, Canada, on Yamaska river 35 m. ESE of Montreal; pop. (1971p) 6462; important railroad junction.

2 Urban district, Surrey, S England, on Wey river 38 m. SW of London; pop. (1971p) 30,175; ruins of Waverley Abbey, founded 1128, earliest Cistercian abbey in England.

Farnham, Mount. See PURCELL MOUNTAINS.

Farn·worth \'färn-(,)wərth\. Urban district, Lancashire, NW England, 7 m. NW of Manchester; pop. (1971p) 26,-841; collieries, iron foundries; manufactures paper, cotton; engineering.

Fa·ro \'far-(,)ü, 'fär-\. 1 District of S Portugal. See table at PORTUGAL.

2 Seaport commune, its ✱, on Atlantic Ocean 137 m. SSE of Lisbon; munic. pop. (1970p) 30,269; trades in fish, wine, oil, cork, dried and fresh fruits, basketry; antimony and salt deposits; cathedral; taken from Moors 1249; sacked by English 1596; earthquakes 1722, 1755.

Faro, Cape \-'fär-(,)ō\ *or Ital.* **Pun·ta del Faro** \,pün-tə-del-\ *or anc.* **Pe·lo·rus** \pə-'lōr-əs, -'lȯr-\. Cape on NE extremity of Sicily, Italy.

Faroe Islands *or* **Faroes.** See FAEROES.

Får·ön \'fȯr-ən\. Island in Baltic Sea off NE coast of Gotland I.; a part of Gotland co., Sweden; 56 sq. m.

Far·quhar, Cape \-'fär-k(w)ər\. Point on W coast of Western Australia, near Tropic of Capricorn.

Farquhar Islands. Group of small British islands in Indian Ocean NE of Malagasy Republic; 3 sq. m.; part of British Indian Ocean Territory.

Far·rell \'far-əl\. City, Mercer co., W Pennsylvania, on Shenango river 17 m. NNW of New Castle; pop. (1970c) 11,-022; steel mills.

Far Rock·a·way \'fär-'räk-ə-,wā\. Seashore resort, Queens borough, New York City, on S shore of Long I. SE of Jamaica Bay.

Far·rukh·a·bad \fə-'rü-kə-,bad\. 1 District, Uttar Pradesh, N India; 1645 sq. m.; pop. (1961c) 1,295,071; ✱ Farrukhabad; rice, barley, wheat, cotton, tobacco.

2 City, its ✱, on right bank of Ganges river 90 m. WNW of Lucknow; pop. (1961c) 94,951; with **Fa·te·garh** \'fat-i-,gär\ forms joint municipality; sugar, tobacco. Farrukhabad founded 1714; scene of defeat of Marathas by Lord Lake 1804; in Sepoy Mutiny 1857–58 scene of a massacre of English and of several engagements.

Fārs \'färz\ *or* **Fār·si·stan** \,fär-si-'stan\ *or anc.* **Per·sis** \'pər-səs\. Province, SW Iran; 51,465 sq. m.; pop. (1966c) 1,439,804; ✱ Shīrāz; cotton, rice, tobacco; ancient Persis the original home of Persians and nucleus of later Persian Empire, in extent corresponded closely with modern Fārs; chief cities were Persepolis and Pasargadae. See IRAN.

Fars·hut \färs-'hüt\. Town, Upper Egypt, near left bank of the Nile ab. 35 m. W of Qena; pop. (1966c) 23,600.

Far·tak, Cape \-'fär-,tak\ *or Arab.* **Ras Fartak** \räs-\. Cape on coast of Hadhramaut, Yemen (✱ Aden), S Arabian Penin., SW of Al-Qamar Bay projecting into Arabian Sea.

Farther India. See INDOCHINA.

Farther Pomerania. See POMERANIA 1.

Farvel, Kap. See FAREWELL, CAPE 1.

Far·well \'fär-,wel, -wəl\. City, ⊗ of Parmer co., NW Texas; pop. (1970c) 1185.

Far West. The part of the U.S. W of the Mississippi river, or, now more generally, the part W of Great Plains.

Far·yab \fär-'yäb\. Province of N Afghanistan. See table at AFGHANISTAN.

Fas. See FÈS.

Fa·sa·no \fə-'zän-(,)ō\. Commune, Brindisi prov., Apulia, SE Italy, near Adriatic Sea 33 m. NW of Brindisi; pop. (1968e) 31,948.

Fashir, Al–. See AL-FASHIR.

Fashoda. See KODOK.

Fast·net \'fas(t)-nət\. Rocky islet in Atlantic Ocean 4 m. SW of Cape Clear, off S Ireland, 51°24′N, 9°35′W; lighthouse.

Fa·stov \fə-'stȯf\. Town, W Kiev Oblast, N cen. Ukrainian S.S.R., U.S.S.R., 35 m. SW of Kiev; pop. (1967e) 37,000.

Fategarh. See FARRUKHABAD 2.

Fa·teh·pur \'fät-ə-,pu̇(ə)r\. 1 District, Uttar Pradesh, N India; 1625 sq. m.; pop. (1961c) 1,072,940; ✱ Fatehpur; rice, wheat, sugarcane.

2 Town, its ✱, Uttar Pradesh, N India, 50 m. SE of Kanpur; pop. (1961c) 28,323.

3 Town, E Rajasthan, NW India, formerly in NW Jaipur state, Rajputana; pop. (1961c) 27,000.

Fatehpur Si·kri \-'sē-krē\. Town, SW Uttar Pradesh, N India, 23 m. W of Agra; pop. (1961c) 10,600; ancient city founded 1570 by Akbar, who made it his capital of the Mogul Empire; abandoned after his death 1605; remains include magnificent structures, partly in ruins; palaces, audience halls, tombs, great gate of victory (Boland Darwaza), etc.

Father, The *or* **Ula·wun** \ü-'lä-(,)wün\. Active volcano, Whiteman Range, on the island of New Britain, near N coast at E end, W Pacific Ocean; 7546 ft.; highest point on the island.

Fá·ti·ma \'fat-ə-mə\. Village, cen. Portugal, SE of Leiria; shrine of the Virgin (Our Lady of Fátima); visited by Pope Paul VI 1967.

Fatshan. See FO-SHAN.

Fa·tu Hi·va \,fät-ü-'hē-və\ *or formerly* **Mag·da·le·na** \,mag-də-'lē-nə\. Island, Marquesas Is., South Pacific Ocean, ab. 36 m. S of E end of Hiva Oa I., French Polynesia; 31 sq. m.; pop. (1967e) 459.

Faulk \'fȯlk\. County in South Dakota. See table at SOUTH DAKOTA.

Faulk·ner \'fȯk-nər\. County in Arkansas. See table at ARKANSAS.

Faulk·ton \'fȯk-tən\. City, ⊗ of Faulk co., N cen. South Dakota; pop. (1970c) 955.

Fau·quier \'fȯ-,ki(ə)r\. County in Virginia. See table at VIRGINIA.

Faure·smith \'fau̇(ə)r-,smith\. Town, S Orange Free State, Rep. of South Africa, just W of Jagersfontein and 70 m. SW of Bloemfontein; founded 1848, year of battle of Boomplaats (*q.v.*).

Fau·ro \'fau̇(ə)r-(,)ō\. Island, one of Shortland Is. group S of Bougainville I., British Solomon Is., W Pacific Ocean; ab. 10 m. long.

Fa·va·ra \fə-'vär-ə\. Commune, Agrigento prov., SW Sicily, Italy, 5 m. E of Agrigento; pop. (1968e) 30,820; castle; sulfur mines, marble quarries.

Faventia. See FAENZA.

Fav·er·sham \'fav-ər-shəm\. Municipal borough, Kent, SE England, on Faversham Creek 45 m. ESE of London; pop. (1971p) 14,807; oyster fisheries; brewing, light engineering; tombs of King Stephen, his queen Matilda, and his son.

Fa·vi·gna·na \,fäv-ə-'nyän-ə\. An island and commune of Egadi Is. (*q.v.*).

Faxa Bay \'fäk-sə-\ *or Icel.* **Fax·a·flói** \'fäk-sə-,flō-ē, -,flȯi\. Bay on SW coast of Iceland on SE shore of which Reykjavík is situated.

Fayal. See FAIAL.

Fay·ette \fā-'et, 'fā-ət\. 1 Name of counties in eleven states of the U.S. See tables at ALABAMA, GEORGIA, ILLINOIS, INDIANA, IOWA, KENTUCKY, OHIO, PENNSYLVANIA, TENNESSEE, TEXAS, WEST VIRGINIA.

2 City, ⊗ of Fayette co., NW Alabama, 35 m. NNW of Tuscaloosa; pop. (1970c) 4568.

3 Town, Fayette co., NE Iowa, 32 m. S of Decorah; pop. (1970c) 1947; Upper Iowa Coll. (1857).

4 Town, ⊗ of Jefferson co., SW Mississippi; pop. (1970c) 1725; lumbering.

5 City, ⊗ of Howard co., N cen. Missouri, 25 m. NW of Columbia; pop. (1970c) 3520; Central Methodist Coll. (1854).

6 Town, Seneca co., W cen. New York; pop. (1960c) 2825; scene of organization by Joseph Smith Apr. 6, 1830 of Church of Jesus Christ of Latter-day Saints.

Fayette City. Borough, Fayette co., SW Pennsylvania, on Monongahela river 25 m. SSE of Pittsburgh; pop. (1970c) 968.

Fay·ette·ville \ˈfā-ət-ˌvil, -vəl\. 1 City, ⊗ of Washington co., NW Arkansas, 50 m. N of Fort Smith; pop. (1970c) 30,729; trade center; summer mountain resort; manufactures hardwood products, farm implements, electrical components; Univ. of Arkansas (1871), Agricultural Experiment Station. Settled 1828; incorp. as city 1906; battle of Pea Ridge (Mar. 7–8, 1862) fought nearby.

2 City, ⊗ of Fayette co., W Georgia; pop. (1970c) 2160.

3 Manufacturing village, Onondaga co., cen. New York, 10 m. E of Syracuse; pop. (1970c) 4996; chemicals, die castings.

4 Manufacturing city, ⊗ of Cumberland co., S cen. North Carolina, on Cape Fear river at head of navigation, 50 m. S of Raleigh; pop. (1970c) 53,510; chemicals, furniture, textiles; formerly important turpentine and lumber center; Fayetteville State Coll. (1867), Methodist Coll. (1956), Fayetteville Technical Inst. (1961). Founded by Scottish colonists 1739; occupied by Cornwallis 1781; state capital 1789–93; occupied by Gen. Sherman 1865.

5 Commercial and manufacturing town, ⊗ of Lincoln co., S Tennessee, 44 m. SW of Columbia; pop. (1970c) 7030; lumber, flour; site of Camp Blount, where Andrew Jackson mobilized his troops 1813 for victory over Creek Indians 1814.

6 Town, ⊗ of Fayette co., S cen. West Virginia; pop. (1970c) 1712.

Fayum. See FAIYŪM.

Fa·zog·li \fə-ˈzȯg-lē\. District, E Sudan, E Africa, on Ethiopia border S of Sennar; traversed by the Blue Nile; conquered 1821 by Mehemet Ali.

Fear, Cape \-ˈfi(ə)r\. Cape on Smith I., SE coast of Brunswick co., North Carolina, at mouth of Cape Fear river.

Feath·er \ˈfeth-ər\. River, N cen. California; ab. 100 m. long; including its forks 250 m. long; rises in Plumas co. and flows SW into Sacramento river above city of Sacramento. See BIG MEADOWS DAM.

Feather Falls. Falls in middle fork of Feather river, N cen. California; 640 ft. high.

Feath·er·stone \ˈfeth-ər-stən, -ˌstōn\. Urban district, West Riding, Yorkshire, N England, E of Wakefield; pop. (1971p) 15,242; coal mining.

Feath·er·top, Mount \-ˈfeth-ər-ˌtäp\. Peak, E cen. Victoria, SE Australia; 6307 ft.

Fé·camp \fā-ˈkäⁿ\ *or anc.* **Fis·cam·num** \fis-ˈkam-nəm\. Seaport, Seine-Maritime dept., N France, on English Channel 40 m. NW of Rouen; pop. (1968c) 21,406; fisheries; Benedictine liqueurs, still made (now by secular corporation) in same place where formula was discovered in early 16th cent. by monks of Benedictine monastery.

Fedala. See MOHAMMEDIA.

Fe·dchen·ko Glacier \fed-ˌcheŋ-(ˌ)kō-\. Glacier in the Pamirs, Tadzhik S.S.R., U.S.S.R.; 44 m. long; ab. 1½ m. wide at its terminus.

Federal Capital Territory. See AUSTRALIAN CAPITAL TERRITORY.

Federal District *or Span.* **Dis·tri·to Fe·de·ral** \di-ˌstrē-tō-ˌfā-də-ˈräl\ *or Port.* **Distrito Federal** \dis(h)-ˈtrē-tü-ˌfā-də-ˈräl\. 1 *also* **Federal Capital** *or Span.* **Ca·pi·tal Federal** \ˌkäp-ə-ˌtäl-ˌfā-də-ˈräl\. The city of Buenos Aires, ✱ of Argentina, not included in province of Buenos Aires. See table at ARGENTINA.

2 Former seat of national government, SE Brazil; 451 sq. m.; coextensive with city of Rio de Janeiro.

3 Large area on plateau of SE Goiás state, cen. Brazil; 2245 sq. m.; site of Brasília, capital (since Apr. 21, 1960) of Brazil.

4 Area containing Kinshasa, ✱ of Zaire. See table at ZAIRE 1.

5 Area containing the capital of Mexico, Mexico City. See table at MEXICO.

6 Capital area, Paraguay. See table at PARAGUAY.

7 Capital area, N Venezuela. See table at VENEZUELA.

Federal Republic of Cameroon. See CAMEROON.

Federal Republic of Germany. See GERMANY, WEST.

Fed·er·als·burg \ˈfed-(ə-)rəlz-ˌbərg\. Town, Caroline and Dorchester cos., E Maryland, 25 m. NNW of Salisbury; pop. (1970c) 1917.

Federated Ma·lay States \-mə-ˈlā-, -ˈmā-(ˌ)lā-\. Former federation of the states of Pahang, Perak, Selangor, and Negri Sembilan at S extremity of Malay Penin.; ✱ Kuala Lumpur. Entered treaties providing for their protection by British government (Perak 1874, the other states later); federated 1895; occupied by Japanese 1941–45; joined Federation of Malaya 1948, Malaysia 1963. See MALAYA, FEDERATION OF and MALAYSIA.

Federated Shan States. See SHAN STATE.

Federation of Malaya. See MALAYA, FEDERATION OF.

Federation of Malaysia. See MALAYSIA.

Federative Republic of Brazil. See BRAZIL.

Fe·djadj, Chott al– \ˌshät-al-ˈfej-ˌaj\. Marshy saline lake, S cen. Tunisia, N Africa; an E extension of Chott Djerid; ab. 60 m. long.

Fe·fan \ˈfā-ˌfän\. Island in E part of Truk (*q.v.*); highest point 1026 ft.

Fehértemplom. See BELA CRKVA.

Feh·marn \ˈfā-ˌmärn\. Island, Schleswig-Holstein, West Germany; in W Baltic Sea, on NW side of entrance to Bay of Mecklenburg; 71 sq. m.; pop. (1967e) 13,268.

Fehr·bel·lin \ˌfe(ə)r-bə-ˈlēn\. Town, Potsdam dist., East Germany, NW of West Berlin; scene June 18, 1675 of victory of Elector Frederick William of Brandenburg over the Swedes under Karl Gustav Wrangel.

Feil·ding \ˈfēld-iŋ\. Borough, SW North I., New Zealand, 85 m. NNE of Wellington; pop. (1968e) 9360.

Fei·ra de San·ta·na \ˌfā-ər-ə-də-sa(ⁿ)n-ˈtan-ə\ *or formerly* **Feira.** City, Bahia state, E Brazil, 60 m. NNW of Salvador; munic. pop (1968e) 136,000.

Fe·jér \ˈfā-ˌye(ə)r\. County of W cen. Hungary. See table at HUNGARY.

Fe·la·nitx \ˌfā-lə-ˈnēch\ *or* **Fe·la·ni·che** \ˌfā-lə-ˈnē-chə\ *or anc.* **Ca·na·ti** \kə-ˈnā-ˌtī\. Commune, Baleares prov., Spain, SE Majorca I., 27 m. ESE of Palma; pop. (1970p) 12,946; pottery industry dates from 3d cent. B.C.

Feld·berg \ˈfelt-ˌbe(ə)rg\. Highest peak in Black Forest, Baden-Württemberg, West Germany, SE of Freiburg; 4905 ft.

Feld·kirch \ˈfelt-ˌki(ə)rk\ *or anc.* **Clu·nia** \ˈklü-nē-ə\. City, Vorarlberg, W Austria, on Liechtenstein frontier on Ill river 20 m. SSW of Bregenz; pop. (1961c) 17,343; castle; railroad junction, on the route over the Arlberg Pass to the E.

Félegyháza. See KISKUNFÉLEGYHÁZA.

Felicitas Julia. See LISBON 6.

Fe·li·pe Ca·rri·llo Puer·to \fā-ˈlē-pē-kə-ˌrē-(y)ō-ˈpwert-ō\ *or formerly* **San·ta Cruz de Bra·vo** \ˌsant-ə-ˌcrüs-də-ˈbräv-ō\. Town, E cen. Quintana Roo Territory, Yucatán penin., Mexico; munic. pop. (1970p) 33,704.

Fe·lix·stowe \ˈfē-lik-ˌstō\. Urban district, East Suffolk, E England; pop. (1971p) 18,888; seaside resort.

Fell·bach \ˈfel-ˌbäk\. City, Baden-Württemberg, West Germany, E of Stuttgart; pop. (1969e) 29,376.

Fel·le·tin \fel-ˈtaⁿ\. Commune, S Creuse dept., cen. France, S of Aubusson (*q.v.*); pop. (1962c) 3118; celebrated for manufacture of tapestries.

Fellin. See VILJANDI.

Fel·ling \ˈfel-iŋ\. Urban district, Durham, N England, 4 m. S of Newcastle upon Tyne; pop. (1971p) 38,595.

Felsina. See BOLOGNA 2.

Fel·sted *or* **Fel·stead** \'fel-sted\. Village, Essex, SE England, in Saffron Walden municipal borough; pop. (1961c) 2089; school, founded 1564 as grammar school, became popular with Puritans 17th cent. and a notable public school late 19th cent.

Fel·tre \'fel-(,)trā\ *or anc.* **Fel·tria** \-trē-ə\. Commune, Belluno prov., Veneto, NE Italy, 17 m. SW of Belluno; pop. (1968e) 22,671; cathedral; trades in silk, wine, oil; besieged by Austrians 1917–18.

Fe·mund *or* **Fæ·mund** \'fā-,mu̇n\. Lake, Hedmark co., E Norway, 85 m. SE of Trondheim; 78 sq. m.

Fen \'fen, 'fən\ *or* **Fen Ho** \'fen-'hō, 'fən-\. River, cen. Shansi prov., NE China; ab. 300 m. long; an E tributary of the Yellow river, flows SSE.

Fen Country. See FENS, THE.

Feng–ch'eng \'fəŋ-'chəŋ\ *or Jap.* **Feng·hwang·cheng** \'fəŋ-'hwäŋ-'chəŋ\. Town, S Liaoning prov., NE China; former treaty port; Japanese army base in Russo-Japanese War 1904–05.

Feng–chieh *or* **Feng·kieh** \,fəŋ-je-'ä\ *or formerly* **Kwei·chow** \'gwā-'jō\. City, E Szechwan, S cen. China, on N bank of Yangtze river at head of Yangtze Gorges (*q.v.*), 120 m. WNW of I-ch'ang; has long been of great strategic importance.

Feng–hua *or* **Feng·hua** \'fəŋ-'(h)wä\. Town, NE Chekiang prov., E China, ab. 10 m. SSW of Ningpo; birthplace of Generalissimo Chiang Kai-shek.

Fengkieh. See FENG-CHIEH.

Feng–t'ai \'fəŋ-'tī\. Railroad junction town, NE China, part of Peking municipality.

Feng·tien \'fəŋ-tē-'en\. **1** Province of China. See LIAONING.

2 City, China. See MUKDEN.

3 Former province (1932–45), S Manchukuo; 29,263 sq. m.; ✱ Mukden.

Feng–tu \'fəŋ-'dü\. City, SE Szechwan prov., S cen. China, on N bank of the Yangtze 85 m. ENE of Chungking; nearby (Pingtu-shan) is sacred pilgrimage center of Taoists.

Fen Ho. See FEN.

Fe·ni Islands \,fā-nē-\. Group of small islands, Bismarck Archipelago, W Pacific Ocean, ab. 40 m. off SE coast of New Ireland; administratively part of Papua New Guinea.

Fen·ni·more \'fen-ə-,mō(ə)r, -,mȯ(ə)r\. City, Grant co., SW corner of Wisconsin, 20 m. NNW of Platteville; pop. (1970c) 1861.

Fen·no·scan·dia *or* **Fen·no–Scan·dia** \,fen-ō-'skan-dē-ə\. The part of N Europe consisting of Finland, Sweden, Norway, and Denmark—specifically used in geology.

Fens, The \-'fenz\ *also* **Fen Country** \'fen-\. Low-lying districts in E England, esp. in Lincolnshire near shores of the Wash; max. length ab. 73 m.; once marshland but long since drained and cultivated.

Fen·ton \'fent-^{ə}n\. **1** Village, Genesee co., SE cen. Michigan, 15 m. S of Flint; pop. (1970c) 8284; plastics; summer resort.

2 District, England. See POTTERIES, THE.

Fen·tress \'fen-trəs\. County in Tennessee. See table at TENNESSEE.

Fen–yang \'fən-'yäŋ\. City, cen. Shansi prov., NE China, 60 m. SW of T'ai-yüan.

Fe·o·do·si·ya \,fē-ə-'dō-s(h)ē-ə\ *or Ital.* **Kaf·fa** \'käf-ə\ *or Tatar* **Ke·fe** \ke-'fā\ *or anc.* **The·o·do·sia** \,thē-ə-'dō-sh(e-)-ə\. Seaport town, SE Crimean Oblast, Ukrainian S.S.R., U.S.S.R., 55 m. WSW of Kerch; pop. (1969e) 64,000; fine harbor, rail connections with Kerch and Dzhankoi; exports grain; important esp. for its oyster fishing and preparation of caviar; health resort. Site of Greek colony founded by Milesians by 6th cent. B.C.; formed part of kingdom of Cimmerian Bosporus (*q.v.*); as Kaffa was a flourishing Genoese trading colony 13th cent.; captured by Turks 1475 and ceded to Russians 1774; bombarded by Turks Oct. 1914; held by Germans 1942–Apr. 1944.

Fer, Cape \-'fe(ə)r\ *or Fr.* **Cap de Fer** \kap-də-fer\. Cape on NE coast of Algeria, N Africa, 35 m. NW of Annaba.

Fer·dows \'fer-,dau̇s\ *or* **Fir·daus** \'fir-\ *or formerly* **Tun** \'tün\. Town, in Khorāsān prov., NE cen. Iran; pop. (1966c) 10,813.

Fère, La. See LA FÈRE.

Fère–en–Tar·de·nois \'fe(ə)r-ä^{n}-,tärd-^{ə}n-'wä\. Town, Aisne dept., N France; pop. (1962c) 2123; type station for Tardenoisian culture; nearby, at village of **Se·ringes–et–Nesles** \sə-ra^{n}zh-ā-nel\, just to the E, is the Oise-Aisne American Military Cemetery, second largest American cemetery in Europe; scene of several battles in World War I in 1914 and 1918 (July 21 taken by Allies).

Fe·ren·ti·no \,fer-ən-'tē-(,)nō\ *or anc.* **Fer·en·ti·num** \-'tī-nəm\. Commune, Frosinone prov., Latium, cen. Italy, 6 m. NW of Frosinone; pop. (1968e) 15,933; cathedral; ancient city walls; mineral baths.

Fer·ga·na *or* **Fer·gha·na** \fər-'gän-ə\. **1** Region, W cen. Asia, W of the Tien Shan; overrun by Arabs 719; conquered by Genghis Khan and Tamerlane and ruled in 15th cent. by descendants of Tamerlane; in 1513 conquered by the Uzbegs and became part of Kokand; taken by Russians 1875–76 and made a division of Russian Turkistan; under Soviet government divided bet. Uzbek S.S.R. and Kirgiz S.S.R., U.S.S.R.

2 *or formerly* **Sko·be·lev** \'skȯ-bə-,lef\. City, ✱ of Fergana Oblast, E Uzbek S.S.R., U.S.S.R., in fertile valley of region of the Alai Mts. 40 m. E of Kokand; pop. (1970p) 111,000; light industries; deposits of ferganite (a uranium mineral) in vicinity; founded 1876; built by Russians 10 m. SE of old town of Margelan and earlier known as **New Mar·ge·lan** \-,mär-gə-'län\.

Fergana Oblast \-'ȯ-bləst, -,blast\ *also* **Ferghana Oblast.** Subdivision of the Uzbek S.S.R., U.S.S.R.; 2741 sq. m.; pop. (1970p) 1,330,000; ✱ Fergana; cotton, fruit; sericulture; livestock; oil fields.

Fer·gus \'fər-gəs\. **1** County in Montana. See table at MONTANA.

2 Town, Wellington co., SE Ontario, Canada, 13 m. NW of Guelph; pop. (1971p) 5415; diversified farming.

Fergus Falls. City, ⊗ of Otter Tail co., W cen. Minnesota, 50 m. SE of Moorhead; pop. (1970c) 12,443; farm machinery; summer resort; hydroelectric power plant; Fergus Falls State Junior Coll. (1960).

Fer·gu·son \'fər-gə-sən\. City, St. Louis co., E Missouri, 10 m. NNW of St. Louis; pop. (1970c) 28,759.

Fer·gus·son \'fər-gə-sən\ *or* **Ka·lu·wa·wa** \,käl-ə-'wä-wə\. One of the D'Entrecasteaux Is., in W Pacific Ocean, 4 m. E of Goodenough I.; ab. 38 m. long and 16 m. wide; 518 sq. m.; pop. (1969e) 12,179; sugarcane; several good harbors; fumarole activity 1957.

Fer·i·ana \,fer-ē-'an-ə\. Town, W Tunisia, SSW of Kasserine Pass; pop. (1966c) 6700; taken by Germans Feb. 1943.

Fer·man·agh \fər-'man-ə\. County, SW Northern Ireland; 715 sq. m.; pop. (1971p) 49,902; ⊗ Enniskillen; chief river the Erne; agriculture, livestock grazing.

Fer·mo \'fe(ə)r-(,)mō\ *or anc.* **Fir·mum Pi·ce·num** \'fər-məm-pī-'sē-nəm\. Commune, Ascoli Piceno prov., Marches, cen. Italy, near Adriatic Sea 23 m. NNE of Ascoli Piceno; pop. (1968e) 33,713; cathedral and 14th cent. archiepiscopal palace; trades in grain, wool. Founded by Sabines before foundation of Rome; part of papal domain 1538–1860.

Fer·moy \fər-'mȯi\. Urban district, NE co. Cork, SW Eire, on Blackwater river; pop. (1971p) 3228; agricultural trading center; sport fishing.

Fer·nan·di·na \,fer-nən-'dē-nə, ,fər-\. **1** An early name of CUBA.

ə abut; ^{ə} kitten, Fr. table; ər further; a back; ā bake; ä cot, cart; á Fr. bac; au̇ out; ch chin; e less; ē easy; g gift
i trip; ī life; j joke; k̲ Ger. ich, Buch; ^{n} Fr. vin; ŋ sing; ō flow; ȯ flaw; œ Fr. bœuf; œ̄ Fr. feu; ȯi coin; th thin
t̲h̲ this; ü loot; u̇ foot; ue Ger. füllen; ue̅ Fr. rue; y yet; ^{y} Fr. digne \dēn^{y}\, nuit \nwyē\; yü few; yu̇ furious; zh vision

2 *also* **Nar·bor·ough Island** \ˌnär-b(ə-)rə-\. One of the Galápagos Is. (*q.v.*).

Fernandina Beach \ˌfər-nən-ˌdē-nə-\. City, ⊗ of Nassau co., NE corner of Florida, on Atlantic Ocean 25 m. NE of Jacksonville; pop. (1970c) 6955; shrimp packing.

Fer·nan·do de No·ro·nha \fər-ˈnan-(ˌ)dō-də-nə-ˈrōn-yə\. Brazilian island in Atlantic Ocean ab. 250 m NE of Cape São Roque; 10 sq. m.; pop. (1970p) 1239; constitutes a territory; formerly used as a penal colony; discovered c. 1501.

Fernando Póo *or* **Fernando Po** \fər-ˌnan-(ˌ)dō-ˈpō\. Island in Bight of Biafra, W Africa, ab. 60 m. SW of Douala, Cameroon; 779 sq. m.; pop. (1960c) 61,197; together with island of Annobón constitutes a province of Equatorial Guinea (*q.v.*); chief town Santa Isabel (✱ of Equatorial Guinea); exports cocoa, coffee, copra.

Fer·não Ve·lo·so Bay \fər-ˌnaůⁿ-və-ˈlō-(ˌ)zü-\. Inlet of Mozambique Channel on NE coast of Mozambique, SE Africa, S of Cape Loguno.

Fern·dale \ˈfərn-ˌdāl\. 1 Residential city, Oakland co., SE Michigan, 9 m. N of Detroit; pop. (1970c) 30,850; castings, forgings.

2 Residential borough, Cambria co., SW cen. Pennsylvania, 3 m. S of Johnstown; pop. (1970c) 2482.

Fer·ney \fer-ˈnā\ *or in full* **Ferney–Vol·taire** \-vōl-ˈta(ə)r, -väl-, -vȯl-, -ˈte(ə)r\. Town, Ain dept., E France, on shore of Lake of Geneva ab. 4 m. from Geneva; pop. (1964e) 2415; château; grew up around the colony of watchmakers established by Voltaire, who lived here 1758–78.

Fer·nie \ˈfər-nē\. City, SE British Columbia, Canada, E of Kootenay river, on W slope of Rocky Mts.; pop. (1971p) 4170; coal mines; sawmills, machine shops.

Ferns \ˈfərnz\. Village, co. Wexford, E Eire, ab. 8 m. N of Enniscorthy; once capital of kingdom of Leinster; cathedral.

Fe·rolle, Point \-fə-ˈrōl\. Cape, NW Newfoundland, Canada, on SE of entrance to Strait of Belle Isle.

Ferozepore. See FIROZPUR.

Fe·roze·shah *or also* **Fi·roz·shah** \fə-ˈrōz-(ˌ)shä\. Village, Punjab state, N India, 13 m. E of Firozpur; scene of battle of First Sikh War, a victory (but with heavy losses) of British under Sir Hugh Gough over Sikhs Dec. 21–22, 1845.

Fer·ra·ra \fə-ˈrär-ə\. 1 Province of Emilia-Romagna, N Italy. See table at ITALY.

2 *or anc.* **Fo·rum Ali·e·ni** \ˈfōr-əm-ˌal-ē-ˈē-ˌnī\. Commune, its ✱, near the Po 57 m. SW of Venice; pop. (1968e) 156,-644; chemicals, plastics, methane, sugar; seven-mile city wall; cathedral; castle; fortified citadel; art gallery, univ. (1391, suppressed 1394, reestablished 1402); birthplace of Savonarola.

History: Bestowed by pope upon margrave of Tuscany ab. end of 10th cent. A.D.; in 1240 came to be ruled by d'Este family; seat of Council of Ferrara (1438) which removed to Florence; raised to a duchy 15th cent., became seat of brilliant Renaissance court; brought under direct rule of papacy 1598; ceded to French 1797; restored to pope 1815; joined kingdom of Sardinia (see SAVOY) 1859; scene of severe fighting Apr. 1945, taken by Allies Apr. 23.

Fer·ri·day \ˈfer-ə-ˌdā\. Town, Concordia parish, E cen. Louisiana, 10 m. NW of Natchez, Miss.; pop. (1970c) 5239; timber, corn.

Ferro. See HIERRO.

Ferrol, El. See EL FERROL DE CAUDILLO.

Fer·ry \ˈfer-ē\. County in Washington. See table at WASHINGTON.

Fer·ry·land \ˈfer-ē-ˌland\. Town, SE Newfoundland, Canada, on Atlantic Ocean 38 m. S of St. John's; pop. (1966c) 723; harbor; site of colony established 1621–29 by Sir George Calvert, Lord Baltimore.

Ferryville. See MENZEL BOURGUIBA.

Ferté–Bernard, La. See LA FERTÉ-BERNARD.

Ferté–Milon, La. See LA FERTÉ-MILON.

Fertile Crescent. A semicircle of fertile land, stretching from SE coast of the Mediterranean around Syrian Desert N of Arabian Penin. to Persian Gulf; term sometimes expanded to include Nile valley; scene of struggles and migrations of some of the earliest known peoples (Sumerians, Assyrians, Semitic tribes)—a term used by some historians of the prehistory of SW Asia.

Fertő tó. See NEUSIEDLER, LAKE.

Fès \ˈfes\ *or* **Fez** \ˈfez\ *or Arab.* **Fas** \ˈfas\. Commercial city, N cen. Morocco, ab. 150 m. NE of Casablanca; pop. (1970e) 290,000; leather and metal goods; one of the sacred cities of Islam, founded 790; many mosques, incl. Qarawiyin (founded c. 850); for many years a traditional capital of Morocco.

Fes·sen·den \ˈfes-ən-dən\. City, ⊗ of Wells co., cen. North Dakota; pop. (1970c) 815; wheat.

Festiniog. See FFESTINIOG.

Fes·tu·bert \ˌfes-tə-ˈbe(ə)r\. Village, Pas-de-Calais dept., N France, near Béthune; pop. (1962c) 409; destroyed during World War I, in battles 1914, 1915, 1918.

Fes·tus \ˈfes-təs\. Commercial and residential city, Jefferson co., E Missouri, on Mississippi river 29 m. S of St. Louis; pop. (1970c) 7530; footwear; flour.

Fe·teşti \fə-ˈtesht\. Town, Ialomiţa co., SE Romania; pop. (1970e) 23,475.

Fet·lar \ˈfet-ˌlär\. One of Shetland Is., NE of Scotland.

Fetzara. See FEZZARA.

Fez. See FÈS.

Fezara. See FEZZARA.

Fé·zen·sac \ˌfā-ˌzäⁿ-ˈsak\. See ARMAGNAC.

Fez·zan \fe-ˈzan\ *or anc.* **Pha·za·nia** \fə-ˈzā-nē-ə\. Region of desert and oases in SW Libya, N Africa; area ab. 212,807 sq. m.; pop. (1964c) 78,326; date palms; under Turkish control from 16th cent. to 1912; made part of Tripoli by Italians 1912; invaded by Free French forces Mar. 1942; province of Libya 1949–63.

Fez·za·ra *or* **Fe·za·ra** \fə-ˈzär-ə\ *or* **Fet·za·ra** \fət-\. Lake, Algeria, N Africa, SW of Annaba; ab. 30 m. long.

Ffes·tin·i·og *or* **Fes·tin·i·og** \fes-ˈtin-ē-ˌäg\. Urban district, Merionethshire, W Wales; pop. (1971p) 5751; slate quarries.

Fia·na·ran·tsoa \ˌfē-ə-ˌnär-ən-ˈtsō-ə\. Commune, SE Malagasy Republic; pop. (1968e) 45,790; in rich agricultural region.

Fich·tel·berg \ˈfik-təl-ˌbe(ə)rg\. Mountain, Erzgebirge, East Germany; 3982 ft.; highest peak in East Germany.

Fich·tel·ge·bir·ge \ˈfik-tᵊl-gə-ˌbir-gə\ *or Czech* **Smr·či·ny** \ˈsmər-chə-nē\. Mountain range in NE Bavaria, West Germany; highest peak Schneeberg 3453 ft.

Ficks·burg \ˈfiks-ˌbərg\. Town, E Orange Free State, E cen. Rep. of South Africa, on Caledon river 105 m. ENE of Bloemfontein; pop. (1967e) 10,300; center of wheat region.

Fi·den·za \fi-ˈden-zə, -ˈden(t)-sə\ *or before 1927* **Bor·go San Don·ni·no** \ˈbȯ(ə)r-(ˌ)gō-ˌsän-də-ˈnē-(ˌ)nō\; *anc.* **Fi·den·tia** \fī-ˈden-ch(ē-)ə, fə-\ *or later* **Fi·den·ti·o·la** \-ˌden-chē-ˈō-lə\. Commune, Parma prov., Emilia-Romagna, N Italy, 14 m. WNW of Parma; pop. (1968e) 23,517; site of victory of Metellus Pius over Carbo 82 B.C.; St. Domninus said to have been beheaded here 304 A.D.—whence its former name; part of duchy of Parma 1545–1859.

Fiel·dale \ˈfēl-ˌdāl\. Town, Henry co., S Virginia, ab. 4 m. W of Martinsville; pop. (1970c) 1337.

Fi·er \fē-ˈe(ə)r\. 1 Province of SW Albania. See table at ALBANIA.

2 Town, its ✱; pop. (1967e) 19,681.

Fier \ˈfye(ə)r\. River, Haute-Savoie dept., E France; 41 m. long; flows W through Annecy to the Rhone; connected with Lake Annecy by Thiou canal which runs through Annecy; noted for scenery of its gorges.

Fie·scher Glacier \ˈfēsh-ər-\. Glacier, S cen. Switzerland, S side of Bernese Alps; 10 m. long.

Fie·so·le \fē-ˈā-zə-lā\ *or anc.* **Fae·su·lae** \ˈfē-zyů-(ˌ)lē\. Commune, Firenze prov., Tuscany, cen. Italy, 4 m. NE of Florence; pop. (1968e) 13,401; health resort; Romanesque cathedral (1028); episcopal palace; ruins of Etruscan city walls, Roman baths and theater; home of Fra Angelico. Ancient Etruscan town; withstood siege by Byzantine general, Belisarius, in 6th cent. A.D.; eclipsed by rise of Florence (*q.v.*), which overcame it in 11th cent.

Fife \'fīf\ *or* **Fife·shire** \-ˌshi(ə)r, -shər\. County, E Scotland, bet. firths of Tay and Forth; 505 sq. m.; pop. (1971p) 326,989; ⊗ Cupar; rivers Eden and Leven; oats, barley, turnips, wheat, sugar beets; livestock; quarrying (limestone), coal mining, linen manufacture; fisheries, engineering works; shipbuilding; coal; chief towns incl. Kirkcaldy, Dunfermline, Cowdenbeath, St. Andrews.

Fife Ness \-'nes\. Headland on E coast of Fife co., E Scotland.

Figig. See FIGUIG.

Fi·gli·ne Val·dar·no \fil-ˌyē-nə-väl-'där-nō\. Commune, Firenze prov., Tuscany, cen. Italy, on Arno river 17 m. SE of Florence; pop. (1968e) 12,868.

Fi·gue·ras \fi-'ger-əs\. City, Gerona prov., NE Spain, in E Pyrenees Mts. 24 m. N of Gerona; pop. (1970p) 22,087; iron goods; citadel built by Ferdinand VI; occupied by French 1794, 1808, 1811, 1823.

Fi·guig *also* **Fi·gig** \fi-'gig\. Commune, SE Morocco; pop. (1960c) 13,241.

Fi·ji \'fē-(ˌ)jē\ *also* **Fiji Islands.** Independent state, consisting of an island group in the SW Pacific Ocean, E of the New Hebrides and SW of Samoa, bet. 16° and 19°20′S lat. and 178°W and 177°E long.; includes Rotuma (*q.v.*); 6938 sq. m.; pop. (1970e) 524,457; ✱ Suva (on Viti Levu I.); crossed by 180th meridian but lies W of date line; group contains over 800 islands and islets, of which ab. 100 are inhabited; chief islands Viti Levu, Vanua Levu, Taveuni, Kandavu, Koro, Ngau, and Ovalau; important groups Lau Group (including Lakemba Is.), Yasawa Is. Volcanic in origin, with fertile soil; highest point Mt. Tomaniivi, on Viti Levu, 4341 ft.; chief products for export sugar, copra, and fruit; chief occupations fishing and agriculture; tourism.

History: Discovered by Tasman 1643; visited by Capt. Cook 1774; used by escaped convicts from Australia as early as 1804; surveyed by Commander Charles Wilkes of U.S. 1840; offered to Great Britain 1858 by native ruler who was pressed by dispute with U.S.; annexed by Great Britain 1874; achieved independence 1970.

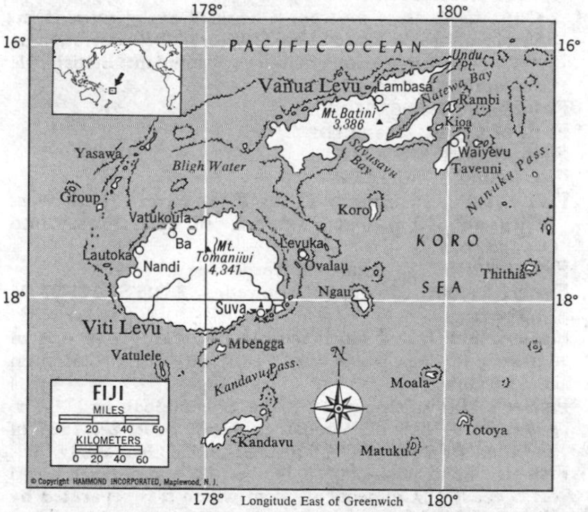

Filch·ner, Cape \-'filk-nər\. Point on coast of Antarctica extending into Indian Ocean at 91°53′E long. and ab. 66°27′S lat.; forms dividing point bet. Queen Mary Coast and Wilhelm II Coast.

Filchner Ice Shelf. Large area of shelf ice at head of Weddell Sea, Antarctica, at W end of Coats Land, ab. 79°S, 40°W; discovered 1912.

Filipinas, Islas *or* **Filipinas, Republica de.** See PHILIPPINES.

Fílippoi. See PHILIPPI.

Filitrá. See PHILIATRA.

Fill·more \'fil-mō(ə)r, -mȯ(ə)r\. **1** Name of counties in two states of the U.S. See tables at MINNESOTA and NEBRASKA.
2 City, Ventura co., SW California, 43 m. WNW of Los Angeles; pop. (1970c) 6285; fruit; oil wells.
3 City, ⊗ of Millard co., W Utah, 20 m. NW of Richfield; pop. (1970c) 1411; capital of Utah territorial government 1851–56.

Fi·lot·tra·no \ˌfē-lət-'trä-nō\. Commune, Ancona prov., Marches, cen. Italy, 16 m. SSW of Ancona; pop. (1968e) 8488.

Fi·mi \'fē-mē\ *or* **Fi·ni** \'fē-nē\ *or* **Mfi·ni** \em-'fē-nē\. River, W Zaire, cen. Africa; the section of Lukenie river bet. Lake Leopold II outlet and Kasai river.

Fi·na·le Emi·lia \fi-'näl-ē-ə-'mēl-yə\. Commune, Modena prov., Emilia-Romagna, N Italy, on Panaro river 22 m. NE of Modena; pop. (1968e) 15,165; manufactures silk.

Finale Li·gu·re \-li-'gu̇r-ē\. Commune, Savona prov., Liguria, NW Italy, on Ligurian Sea 11 m. SW of Savona; pop. (1968e) 13,785; fish processing; health resort.

Fin·cas·tle \'fin-(ˌ)kas-əl\. Town, ⊗ of Botetourt co., W cen. Virginia; pop. (1970c) 397.

Find·horn \'find-ˌhȯ(ə)rn\. River, NE Scotland; 62 m. long; flows NE in Nairn and W Moray cos. to empty into Moray Firth.

Find·lay \'fin-(d)lē\. City, ⊗ of Hancock co., NW Ohio, 40 m. S of Toledo; pop. (1970c) 35,800; in heart of petroleum and gas producing region of state; manufactures petroleum, foundry, and clay products, tires and machinery; Findlay Coll. (1882); incorporated 1890.

Fin·gal \ˌfiŋ-gəl\. Town and municipality, NE Tasmania, Australia, 50 m. ESE of Launceston; munic. pop. (1970e) 3580.

Fingal's Cave. See STAFFA.

Fin·ger Lakes \ˌfiŋ-gər-\. Group of long narrow lakes in W New York, including notably lakes Seneca, Cayuga, Keuka, Canandaigua, Owasco, and Skaneateles (*qq.v.*).

Fin·go·land \'fiŋ-gō-ˌland\. A district of Transkei (*q.v.*), Cape Province, Rep. of South Africa, E of Great Kei river.

Fini. See FIMI.

Fi·niels, Pic de \ˌpēk-də-fē-'nyels\. Mountain in Lozère dept., S France; 5585 ft.; highest peak in Lozère range of the Cévennes Mts.

Fin·is·tère \ˌfin-ə-'ste(ə)r\. Department of France. See table at FRANCE.

Fin·is·terre, Cape \-ˌfin-ə-'ste(ə)r\ *or anc.* **Ne·ri·um Pro·mon·to·ri·um** \'nir-ē-əm-ˌpräm-ən-'tōr-ē-əm, -'tȯr-\. Point on coast of La Coruña prov., NW Spain, 9°16′W.

Finisterre Range. Mountain range, E New Guinea I., Papua New Guinea, bet. coast and Markham valley, extending NW from W part of Huon Penin. to near Madang; scene of fighting Jan.–Feb. 1944.

Finke \'fiŋk\. River, Australia; ab. 400 m. long; flows SE in S Northern Territory and N South Australia; in some seasons joins Alberga river to flow into Lake Eyre.

Fin·land \'fin-lənd\; *Finnish* **Suo·mi** \'swȯ-mē\ *or* **Suo·men Ta·sa·val·ta** \'swȯ-mən-'tas-ə-ˌval-tə\. Republic, N Europe, bounded on the N by Norway, on the E by U.S.S.R., on the S by the Gulf of Finland, and on the W by the Gulf of Bothnia and Sweden; 130,128 sq. m. (land area 117,944 sq. m.); pop. (1970p) 4,596,958; ✱ Helsinki.

Physical features: Land of few hills or mountains (highest peak Haltiatunturi 4343 ft., in NW on Norwegian border) but of many lakes (nearly 1/10 of total area) and streams (esp. Oulu and Kemi in the N). Chief lakes Oulujärvi, Saimaa, Näsijärvi, Keitele, Pielinen (all in S or cen. part), and Inari (in the N). Has long coastline with several excellent ports; chief islands the Ahvenanmaa group (formerly Swedish), and Kimito, Vallgrund, and Karlö, in Gulf of Bothnia. *Chief products:* Timber, oats, barley, potatoes, rye; copper, iron ore; fishing, livestock raising; manufacturing: lumber, textiles, chemicals; food processing, shipbuilding. *Chief cities:* Helsinki, Tampere, Turku, Lahti, Espoo, Oulu. Divided into the following 12 provinces (for pronunciation of their names, see their individual entries):

NAME	AREA (sq. m.)	POP. (1970p)	CAPITAL
Ahvenanmaa	581	20,494	Maarianhamina
Häme	7,499	637,194	Hämeenlinna
Keski-Suomi	7,080	238,111	Jyväskylä
Kuopio	7,727	255,138	Kuopio
Kymi	4,960	344,456	Kouvola
Lappi	38,326	195,965	Rovaniemi
Mikkeli	8,363	220,444	Mikkeli
Oulu	23,583	399,970	Oulu
Pohjois-Karjala	8,278	182,287	Joensuu
Turku ja Pori	8,886	675,204	Turku
Uusimaa	4,000	1,011,134	Helsinki
Vaasa	10,845	416,561	Vaasa

History: Region settled by Finnish people by the beginning of the 8th century A.D.; conquered and converted by Swedes in 12th cent.; E part (see KARELIAN AUTONOMOUS SOVIET SOCIALIST REPUBLIC) ceded to Russia 1721; ceded to Russia by Sweden which had been defeated in War of Third Coalition 1809; organized as autonomous grand duchy in personal union with tsar; 1899–1917 suffered from policy of Russification which took away constitution and other rights; proclaimed independence 1917; after civil war in which Germans helped drive out Russian forces 1918–19, ended war with U.S.S.R. 1920; awarded Åland Is. 1922 after dispute with Sweden; forced to cede Karelian Isthmus and other border districts to U.S.S.R. as result of defeat in war 1939–40; joined Germany against U.S.S.R. June 1941; regained lost territory temporarily 1941–44 but again forced to yield to U.S.S.R. the same territory, with slight changes (retention of Hangö by Finland in exchange for Porkkala Penin. near Helsinki and loss of Pechenga territory); Porkkala Penin. returned to Finland 1955; member of UN and Nordic Council 1955; associate member of the European Free Trade Association 1961.

Finland, Gulf of. Arm of Baltic Sea, S of Finland and N of Estonian S.S.R., U.S.S.R.; 260 m. long, from 45 to 85 m. wide; chief islands Hogland, Lavansaari, and Kotlin; chief cities on it Helsinki and Kotka (Finland), Vyborg, Leningrad, Narva, and Tallinn (U.S.S.R.).

Fin·lay \ˈfin-lē\. River, N British Columbia, Canada; 250 m. long; from N cen. British Columbia flows S and E to unite with Parsnip river at 56°N and form Peace river; regarded as ultimate headstream of Mackenzie river.

Fin·ley \ˈfin-lē\. City, ⊗ of Steele co., E North Dakota; pop. (1970c) 809.

Finmarken. See FINNMARK.

Finn \ˈfin\. **1** River, co. Donegal, N Eire; 25 m. long; flows E out of **Lough Finn** across co. Donegal to unite with Mourne river on Northern Ireland border and form Foyle river.

2 River, N Ireland; flows from SE co. Fermanagh, Northern Ireland, into cos. Monaghan and Cavan in Eire and into Upper Lough Erne, Northern Ireland.

Fin·ney \ˈfin-ē\. County in Kansas. See table at KANSAS.

Finn·mark \ˈfin-ˌmärk\ *also* **Fin·mark·en** \-ˌmärk-ən\. County of N Norway. See table at NORWAY.

Finsch·ha·fen \ˈfinch-ˌhäf-ən\. Settlement on SE coast of New Guinea I., Papua New Guinea, at extremity of Huon Penin. 65 m. ENE of Lae; early headquarters of German trading company; occupied by Japanese Mar. 8, 1942; retaken by Australians Oct. 2, 1943.

Fin·ster·aar·horn \ˌfin(t)-stə-ˈrär-ˌhȯ(ə)rn\. Peak, S Switzerland; 14,019 ft.; highest of the Bernese Alps.

Fin·ster·wal·de \ˌfin(t)-stər-ˈväl-də\. Manufacturing city, Cottbus dist., East Germany, 61 m. SSE of Berlin; pop. (1970e) 22,782; textiles, machinery, furniture; 16th cent. Gothic church; founded 13th cent.; to Bohemia 1373, Electorate of Saxony 1635, Prussia 1815; taken by U.S.S.R. May 1945.

Fiord·land National Park \fē-ˈȯ(ə)rd-ˌland-, ˈfyȯ(ə)rd-\ *or* **Sounds National Park** \ˈsau̇n(d)z-\. National park, SW corner of South I., New Zealand; 4725 sq. m.; extends 200 m. along the coast, here indented with many sounds that resemble Norwegian fjords.

Fio·ren·zuo·la d'Ar·da \ˌfyo-rənt-ˈswō-lə-ˈdär-də\. Commune, Piacenza prov., Emilia-Romagna, N Italy, 13 m. SE of Piacenza; pop. (1968e) 13,881.

Firat. See EUPHRATES.

Fir·crest \ˈfər-ˌkrest\. Town, Pierce co., W cen. Washington, just W of Tacoma; pop. (1970c) 5651.

Firdaus. See FERDOWS.

Fire·baugh \ˈfī(ə)r-ˌbȯ\. City, Fresno co., S cen. California, 35 m. WNW of Fresno; pop. (1970c) 2517; diversified agriculture.

Fire Island \fī(ə)r-\ *or* **Fire Island Beach.** Long narrow sandy spit of land off S cen. Long I., New York, bet. Great South Bay and Atlantic Ocean; ab. 30 m. long, 1/4 to 1/2 m. wide; lighthouse and signal station for reporting transatlantic liners approaching New York; summer resort.

Fi·ren·ze \fē-ˈrent-sā\. **1** Province of Tuscany, Italy. See table at ITALY.

2 Commune, its ✱. See FLORENCE 9.

Fi·ren·zuo·la \ˌfir-ənt-ˈswō-lə\. Commune, Firenze prov., Tuscany, cen. Italy, on N slope of Apennines 24 m. NNE of Florence; pop. (1968e) 6372; summer resort.

Fir·mi·ny \ˌfi(ə)r-mə-ˈnē\. Commune, Loire dept., SE cen. France, 6 m. WSW of St-Étienne; pop. (1968c) 24,924; coal; manufactures railroad supplies.

Firmum Picenum. See FERMO.

Fi·roz·a·bad \fə-ˈrōz-ə-ˌbäd\. **1** One of the earlier cities on site of modern Delhi (*q.v.*), India; founded 1354 by Firuz Shah III, king of Delhi; abandoned after Tamerlane's invasion 1398–99.

2 Town, W Uttar Pradesh, N India, on railroad N of Yamuna river 22 m. E of Agra; pop. (1961c) 98,000.

Fi·roz·pur \fə-ˈrōz-(ˌ)pu̇(ə)r\ *also* **Fe·roze·pore** \-(ˌ)pō(ə)r, -(ˌ)pȯ(ə)r\. **1** District, Punjab, N India; 3888 sq. m.; pop. (1961c) 1,619,116; ✱ Firozpur.

2 City, its ✱, ab. 4 m. from S bank of Sutlej river 45 m. SSE of Lahore, Pakistan; pop. (1961c) 47,060; cotton market; two colleges; site of a military cantonment; British rule first established here 1835.

Firozshah. See FEROZESHAH.

Firth of Clyde. See CLYDE 5.

Firth of Forth. See FORTH.

Fiscamnum. See FÉCAMP.

Fish \ˈfish\ *or formerly* **Great Fish.** River, South-West Africa; ab. 300 m. long; rises in S cen. part, flows S into Orange river.

Fish·er \ˈfish-ər\. County in Texas. See table at TEXAS.

Fisher, Mount. Mountain, Antarctica, 85°06′S, 171°03′W; 13,386 ft.

Fish·er·mans Island \ˌfish-ər-mənz-\. Island at N side of entrance to Chesapeake Bay, S extremity of Northampton co., Virginia.

Fish·er's Hill \ˌfish-ərz-\. Village, Shenandoah co., N Virginia, 8 m. NNE of Woodstock; scene Sept. 22, 1864 of Sheridan's defeat of Confederates under Gen. Early.

Fish·ers Island \ˌfish-ərz-\. Island off NE end of Long I. and off S coast of Connecticut, from which it is separated by **Fishers Island Sound;** ab. 8 m. long, ab. 1 m. wide; a part of New York state; resort.

Fisher Strait. Channel bet. S Southampton I. and Coats I. in E Keewatin dist., Northwest Territories, Canada; ab. 50 m. wide.

Fish·guard and Good·wick \ˈfish-ˌgärd . . . ˈgu̇d-(ˌ)wik\. Urban district and commercial seaport, Pembrokeshire, SW

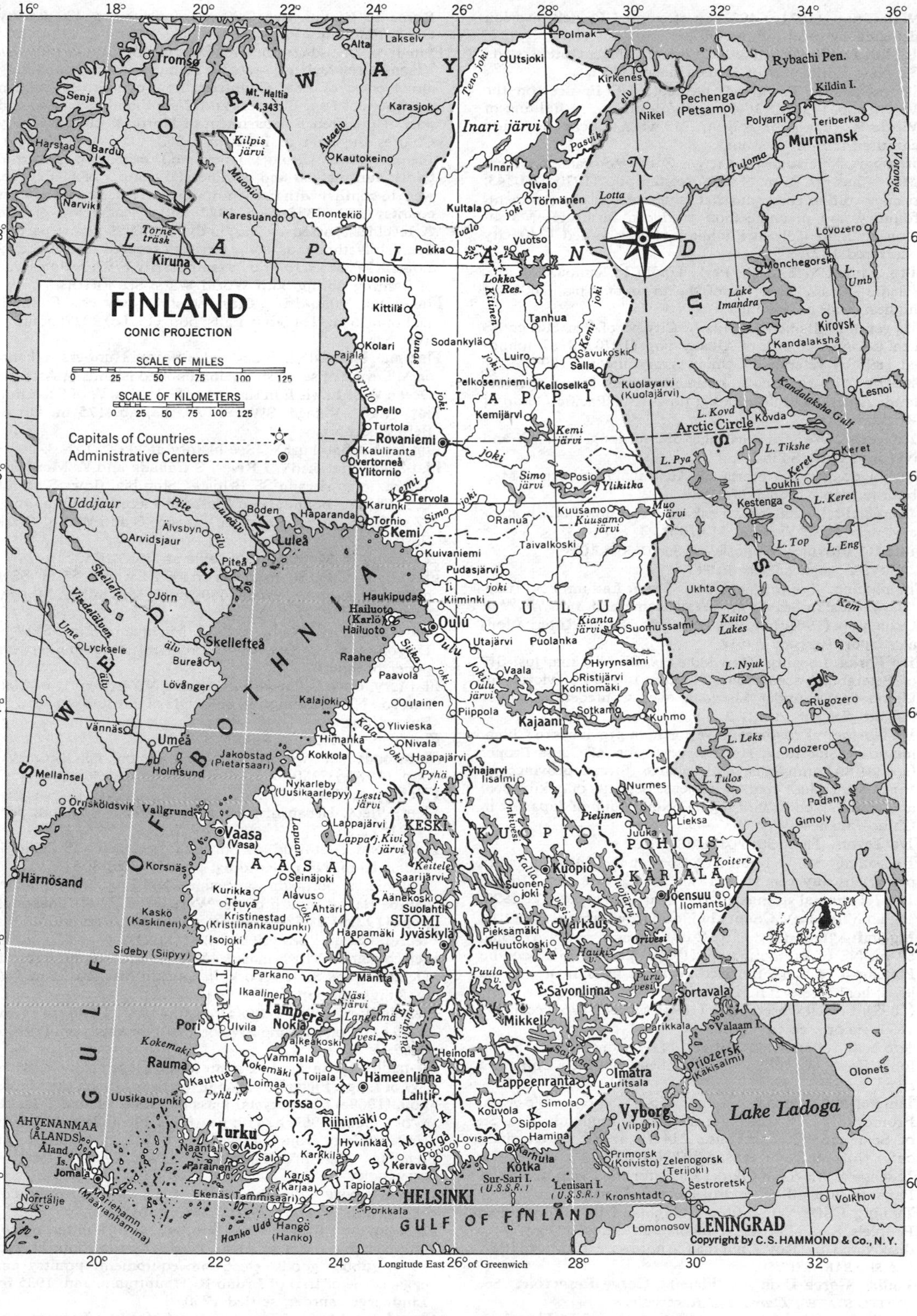

FINLAND
CONIC PROJECTION
SCALE OF MILES
0 25 50 75 100 125
SCALE OF KILOMETERS
0 25 50 75 100 125
Capitals of Countries
Administrative Centers
16° 18° 20° 22° 24° 26° 28° 30° 32° 34° 36°
68° 66° 64° 62° 60°
20° 22° 24° 26° 28° 30° 32°
Longitude East 26° of Greenwich
N O R W A Y
L A P P L A N D
U. S. S. R.
S W E D E N
G U L F O F B O T H N I A
G U L F
GULF OF FINLAND
L A P P I
O U L U
K U O P I O
POHJOIS-KARJALA
V A A S A
KESKI-SUOMI
T U R K U J A P O R I
H Ä M E
U U S I M A A
M I K K E L I
K Y M I
Alta
Lakselv
Polmak
Tromsø
Senja
Harstad
Bardu
Narvik
Mt. Haltia 4,343'
Kilpis järvi
Karasjok
Kautokeino
Utsjoki
Teno joki
Altaelv
Inari järvi
Kirkenes
Pechenga (Petsamo)
Nikel
Rybachi Pen.
Kildin I.
Polyarni
Teriberka
Murmansk
Tuloma
Voronya
Pasvik elv
Inari
Ivalo
Törmänen
Lotta
Kultala
Ivalo joki
Enontekiö
Karesuando
Muonio
Torne-träsk
Kiruna
Pokka
Vuotso
Lokka Res.
Kitinen
Muonio
Kittilä
Tanhua
Kemi joki
Lovozero
Monchegorsk
L. Umb
Lake Imandra
Kirovsk
Kandalaksha
Kandalaksha Gulf
Lesnoi
Kolari
Ounas
Sodankylä
Savukoski
Luiro
Salla
Pajala
Tornio
Pelkosenniemi
Kelloselkä
Kuolayarvi (Kuolajärvi)
Kemijärvi
Kemi järvi
L. Kovd
Kovda
Arctic Circle
Pello
Turtola
Rovaniemi
Kauliranta
Overtorneå
Ylitornio
joki
L. Pya
L. Tikshe
Keret
Simo järvi
Posio
Ylikitka
Keret
Loukhi
Uddjaur
Pite
Luleälv
Boden
Haparanda
Kemi
Tervola
Karunki
Tornio
Kemi
Simo joki
Ranua
Kuusamo
Kuusamo järvi
Muo järvi
Kestenga
L. Keret
Älvsbyn
Arvidsjaur
Luleå
Piteå
Kuivaniemi
Taivalkoski
L. Top
L. Eng
Skellefte
Vindelälven
Jörn
Pudasjärvi
Ii
Haukipudas
Kiiminki
Ii joki
Hailuoto (Karlö)
Hailuoto
Oulu
Ukhta
Kem
Kuito Lakes
Ume
Lycksele
älv
Skellefteå
Bureå
Raahe
Siikajoki
Oulu joki
Utajärvi
Puolanka
Kianta järvi
Suomussalmi
Hyrynsalmi
L. Nyuk
Lövånger
Paavola
Vaala
Oulu järvi
Ristijärvi
Kontiomäki
Kalajoki
Oulainen
Piippola
Kajaani
Sotkamo
Kuhmo
Rugozero
Vännäs
Umeå
Himanka
Kala joki
Ylivieska
Nivala
L. Leks
Ondozero
Jakobstad (Pietarsaari)
Kokkola
Haapajärvi
Holmsund
Mellansel
Nykarleby (Uusikaarlepyy)
Pyhä j.
Pyhajarvi
Iisalmi
Nurmes
L. Tulos
Örnsköldsvik
Vallgrund
Lesti järvi
Onkivesi
Pielinen
Lieksa
Padany
Gimoly
Vaasa (Vasa)
Lapuan
Lappajärvi
Lappaj.
Kivij. järvi
Juuka
Korsnäs
Härnösand
Seinäjoki
Keitele
Saarijärvi
Kuopio
Kalla
Koitere
Kurikka
Teuva
Alavus
Ähtäri
Äänekoski
Suolahti
Suonen joki
Joensuu
Ilomantsi
Kaskö (Kaskinen)
Kristinestad (Kristiinankaupunki)
Isojoki
Haapamäki
Jyväskylä
Pieksamäki
Varkaus
Orivesi
Sideby (Siipyy)
Huutokoski
Hauki v.
Parkano
Mänttä
Puula v.
Puru vesi
Sortavala
Ikaalinen
Näsi järvi
Längelmä
Tampere
Nokia
Savonlinna
Pori
Ulvila
vesi
Valkeakoski
Päijänne
Mikkeli
Parikkala
Valaam I.
Kokemäki
Vammala
Heinola
Saimaa
Rauma
Kokemäki
Toijala
Hämeenlinna
Imatra
Priozersk (Käkisalmi)
Olonets
Kauttua
Loimaa
Lahti
Lappeenranta
Lauritsala
Pyhä j.
Forssa
Simola
Uusikaupunki
Riihimäki
Kouvola
Sippola
Vyborg (Viipuri)
Lake Ladoga
AHVENANMAA (ÅLANDS)
Åland Is.
Turku (Åbo)
Naantali
Hyvinkää
Hamina
Salo
Karkkila
Borgå (Porvoo)
Lovisa
Karhula
Kotka
Primorsk (Koivisto)
Zelenogorsk (Terijoki)
Jomala
Parainen
Karis (Karjaa)
Kerava
Tapiola
Sur-Sari I. (U.S.S.R.)
Lenisari I. (U.S.S.R.)
Kronshtadt
Sestroretsk
Volkhov
Norrtälje
Mariehamn (Maarianhamina)
Ekenäs (Tammisaari)
HELSINKI
Porkkala
Hanko Udd
Hangö (Hanko)
Lomonosov
LENINGRAD
Copyright by C.S. HAMMOND & Co., N.Y.

Wales; pop. (1971p) 4933; an attempted French invasion defeated by local militia 1797.

Fish·kill Landing \'fish-ˌkil-\. Former village, Dutchess co., SE New York; part of Beacon since 1913.

Fismes \'fēm\. Town, Marne dept., NE France, on the Vesle; pop. (1962c) 3645; nearly destroyed in fighting of World War I, esp. on Aug. 4, 1918 when Americans finally captured it from Germans.

Fitch·burg \'fich-ˌbərg\. City, a ⊗ of Worcester co., cen. Massachusetts, 22 m. N of Worcester; pop. (1970c) 43,343; transportation and industrial center; electrical equipment, foundry and machine-shop products, furniture; Massachusetts State Coll. at Fitchburg (1894); settled 1740; city chartered 1872.

Fi·to, Mount \-'fē-(ˌ)tō\. Peak, Upolu I., Samoa, SW cen. Pacific Ocean, 9 m. SE of the town of Apia; 3608 ft.; highest peak on Upolu I.

Fitz·ger·ald \fits-'jer-əld, 'fits-ˌ\. City, ⊗ of Ben Hill co., S cen. Georgia, 50 m. E of Albany; pop. (1970c) 8187; founded 1895 by veterans of Union Army, incorp. 1896.

Fitz·roy \'fits-ˌrȯi, fits-'\. 1 Perennial river, E cen. Queensland, Australia; 180 m. long; flows E to Pacific Ocean at Rockhampton.

2 River, N Western Australia; 350 m. long; flows W and NW into King Sound.

3 Municipality, S Victoria, SE Australia, N suburb of Melbourne; pop. (1966c) 27,219.

4 *or* **Chal·tel** \chäl-'tel\. Peak on Argentina-Chile boundary, near Lake Viedma; 11,070 ft.

Fiume. 1 Province, Yugoslavia. See CARNARO.

2 City, Yugoslavia. See RIJEKA.

Fiu·mi·ci·no \ˌfyü-mə-'chē(ˌ)nō\. Town, Latium, cen. Italy, on Tyrrhenian Sea 15 m. SW of Rome and 3 m. WNW of Ostia; pop. (1961c) 11,300; Leonardo da Vinci International Airport (opened 1961).

Five Forks. Locality, Dinwiddie co., SE Virginia, just SW of Petersburg; scene Mar. 31–Apr. 1, 1865 of victory of Union forces under Sheridan over Confederates under Pickett. See DINWIDDIE 2.

Five Northern Provinces. Five northern provinces of China, including Shantung, Hopeh, and Shansi of China Proper (see CHINA) and Cahar and Suiyuan (former provinces of Inner Mongolia); contain immense deposits of coking coal and iron ore; control of region primary aim of Japanese in Chino-Japanese War 1937–45.

Five Towns, The. See POTTERIES, THE.

Fi·viz·za·no \ˌfi-vēd-'zän-ō\. Commune, Massa-Carrara prov., Tuscany, cen. Italy, 15 m. N of Carrara; pop. (1968e) 11,976; mineral springs; marble quarries; earthquake 1920.

Flag·ler \'flag-lər\. County in Florida. See table at FLORIDA.

Flag·staff \'flag-ˌstaf\. City, ⊗ of Coconino co., N Arizona, 63 m. NE of Prescott; pop. (1970c) 26,117; in Coconino Plateau S of San Francisco Peaks at 6907 ft. above sea level; health resort; lumber mills; Northern Arizona Univ. (1899), Lowell Observatory (1894); settled 1876, became ⊗ 1891, incorp. as city 1928.

Flam·beau \'flam-(ˌ)bō\. River, N Wisconsin; ab. 150 m. long; flows out of Lac du Flambeau SW into Chippewa river.

Flam·bor·ough Head \ˌflam-ˌbər-ə-, -ˌbə-rə-, -b(ə-)rə-\. Promontory on E coast of Yorkshire, N England, 18 m. SE of Scarborough; lighthouse, 214 ft. above water; chalk cliffs with many caverns; 54°07'N, 0°05'W.

Fla·men·co \flə-'məŋ-(ˌ)kō\. Small fortified island, Bay of Panama, just off SE end of Panama Canal.

Flam·ing Cliffs \ˌflā-miŋ-\. A highland in S Mongolian People's Republic, where fossils and dinosaur eggs were discovered by Roy Chapman Andrews expedition 1925. See SHABARAKH USU.

Flaming Gorge Dam *and* **Flaming Gorge Reservoir.** See UNITED STATES, *Dams and Reservoirs.*

Fla·min·i·an Way \flə-ˌmin-ē-ən-\ *or Lat.* **Via Fla·min·ia** \ˌvī-ə-flə-'min-ē-ə\. Ancient road, Italy; ran due N from Rome to Rimini, over 200 m.; constructed 220 B.C. by Gaius Flaminius.

Flan·ders \'flan-dərz\ *or Fr.* **Flan·dre** \flän͏dr͏ə\ *or Flemish* **Vlaan·de·ren** \'vlän-də-rə(n)\. Medieval county extending along coast of Low Countries; now constitutes Belgian provinces of East Flanders and West Flanders (*qq.v.*) and part of the French department of Nord; ✱ Lille; given by Charles the Bald to Baldwin I 862 A.D.; by 14th cent. Flemish towns (Brugge, Ieper, etc.), becoming industrial (cloth and metals) and commercial centers of N Europe, were in conflict with French-dominated rulers; rose against counts 1302, 1337, and 1382 under leadership of van Arteveldes; passed to Burgundy by marriage; as part of Spanish Netherlands, some territory secured for France by Louis XIV; ceded to France temporarily 1797; region scene of fighting during both World Wars. See ARTOIS.

Flan·dreau \'flan-drü\. City, ⊗ of Moody co., E South Dakota, 35 m. N of Sioux Falls; pop. (1970c) 2027; poultry, livestock.

Flan·nan Islands \ˌflan-ən-\ *also* **Seven Hunt·ers** \-'hənt-ərz\. Group of seven small uninhabited islands in Atlantic Ocean W of Lewis I. in the Outer Hebrides, W of Scotland.

Flat \'flat\. Village, SW cen. Alaska, ab. 175 m. NE of Bethel; airport.

Flat·bush \'flat-ˌbu̇sh\. See history at BROOKLYN 3.

Flat·head \'flat-ˌhed\. 1 River, S Canada and W Montana; 245 m. long; rises in SE British Columbia, flows S across U.S.-Canada boundary to **Flathead Lake** (ab. 30 m. long, 12 to 14 m. wide; 197 sq. m.), thence S and W into Clark Fork.

2 County in Montana. See table at MONTANA.

Flat River. City, St. Francois co., E Missouri, 55 m. SSW of St. Louis; pop. (1970c) 4550; grain; lead mines; Mineral Area Coll. (1922).

Flat Rock. City, Wayne co., SE Michigan, 22 m. SSW of Detroit; pop. (1970c) 5643; oil refinery; automobile parts, paper products.

Flat·tery, Cape \-'flat-ə-rē\. Cape on NW extremity of Clallam co., NW Washington, on S side of entrance to Juan de Fuca Strait.

Flat Top. See OTTER, PEAKS OF.

Flat·woods \'flat-wu̇dz\. City, Greenup co., NE Kentucky; pop. (1970c) 7380.

Flèche, La. See LA FLÈCHE.

Fleet \'flēt\. Urban district, Hampshire, S England; pop. (1971p) 21,362.

Fleet·wood \'flēt-ˌwu̇d\. 1 Borough, Berks co., SE Pennsylvania, 10 m. NE of Reading; pop. (1970c) 3064.

2 Municipal borough, Lancashire, NW England, on Morecambe Bay at mouth of the Wyre 20 m. N of Blackpool; pop. (1971p) 28,584; trading port; seaside resort.

Flegrei, Campi. See PHLEGRAEAN FIELDS.

Fleisch·manns \'flīsh-mənz\. Village and summer resort, Delaware co., S New York, in Catskill Mts. ab. 32 m. NW of Kingston; pop. (1970c) 434.

Flek·ke·fjord \'flek-ə-ˌfyō(ə)r, -ˌfyȯ(ə)r\. Town in Vest-Agder co., on extreme SW coast of Norway; pop. (1970p) 8659.

Flé·malle \flā-'mäl\. Two communes, Liège prov., Belgium, SW of Liège: **Flémalle–Grande** \-'grän(n)d\, on the Meuse, pop. (1969e) 6254; crystal-glass factories; **Flémalle–Haute** \-'ōt\, pop. (1969e) 8410; nearby is Flémalle fort, one of circle of forts around Liège.

Flem·ing \'flem-iŋ\. County in Kentucky. See table at KENTUCKY.

Flem·ings·burg \'flem-iŋz-ˌbərg\. City, ⊗ of Fleming co., NE Kentucky; pop. (1970c) 2483; tobacco.

Flem·ing·ton \'flem-iŋ-tən\. Borough, ⊗ of Hunterdon co., NW cen. New Jersey, 21 m. N of Trenton; pop. (1970c) 3917; rubber goods, electronic equipment; poultry and eggs; scene of trial of Bruno R. Hauptmann Jan. 1935 for Lindbergh murder; settled 1750.

Flens·burg \'flenz-ˌbərg, 'flen(t)s-ˌbu̇(ə)rk\. Seaport and manufacturing city, Schleswig-Holstein, West Germany, at head of a 30-mile-long inlet (**Flens·burg·er För·de** \-ˌbər-gər-ˌfərd-ə, -ˌbu̇r-\) of Baltic Sea near Danish border 20 m. N of Schleswig; pop. (1969e) 95,488; shipbuilding; iron foundries, rolling mills, woodworking plants; rum production; 13th cent. late-Gothic church, 12th cent. Romanesque church. Founded c. 1200; became city 1284; conquered by Imperial forces 1627 and by Swedish forces 1643; by plebiscite Mar. 1920 voted to remain in Germany; in World War II a naval base, frequently bombed.

Flers \ˈfle(ə)r\. Industrial commune, Orne dept., NW France, 38 m. NW of Alençon; pop. (1968c) 17,683; textiles.

Fletsch·horn \ˈflech-ˌhȯ(ə)rn\ *or* **Ross·bo·den·horn** \ˈrȯs-ˌbōd-ᵊn-ˌhȯ(ə)rn\. Peak in Pennine Alps, S Switzerland, S of Simplon Pass; 13,107 ft.

Fleu·rus \flər-ˈ(y)üs\. Commune, Hainaut prov., SW Belgium; pop. (1969e) 8550; scene of battle June 26, 1794 in which French under Marshal Jourdan defeated Austrians under Prince of Saxe-Coburg.

Fleu·ry \flər-ˈē\ *or in full* **Fleury–de·vant–Dou·au·mont** \-də-ˌvänⁿ-dwō-ˈmōⁿ\. Commune, Meuse dept., NE France; 2 m. NE of Verdun; one of defenses of Verdun in World War I; severe fighting 1916.

Flevo Lacus. See ZUIDER ZEE.

Flin·ders \ˈflin-dərz\. 1 Largest island of the Furneaux Group off NE Tasmania, Australia; 769 sq. m.; 20 m. wide by 40 m. long; place where aboriginal Tasmanians were forced to take refuge 1831.

2 River, N Queensland, Australia; 520 m. long; flows NW to Gulf of Carpentaria.

Flinders Reefs. Group of reefs outside Great Barrier Reef, Queensland, Australia, 17°37′S.

Flin Flon \ˈflin-ˌflän\. Mining town, on Manitoba-Saskatchewan border, Canada, ab. 148 m. NE of Prince Albert; pop. (1971p) 9307; zinc refining; copper and zinc deposits.

Flinsch Peak \ˈflinch-\. Mountain on Continental Divide in Glacier National Park, NW Montana; 9225 ft.

Flint \ˈflint\. 1 River, W Georgia; 265 m. long; formed by junction of Mud and Camp creeks in Fayette co., flows into Lake Seminole.

2 River, SE Michigan; flows NW to unite with Shiawassee river to form Saginaw river.

3 City, ⊗ of Genesee co., SE cen. Michigan, 58 m. NNW of Detroit; pop. (1970c) 193,317; manufactures automobiles, airplane engines, paints and varnishes, automobile accessories; Flint Community Junior Coll. (1923); settled 1819, chartered as city 1855; automobile industry first established 1904.

4 Small British island at S end of Line Is. in cen. Pacific Ocean S of Hawaii, ab. 450 m. NNW of Tahiti; large coconut plantation.

5 County of Wales. See FLINTSHIRE.

6 Municipal borough and seaport, Flintshire, NE Wales; pop. (1971p) 14,660; coal and lead deposits; manufactures rayon; received first charter 1284; scene of Richard II's submission to Bolingbroke 1399.

Flint·shire \ˈflint-ˌshi(ə)r, -shər\ *or* **Flint.** County, NE Wales; 256 sq. m.; pop. (1971p) 175,396; ⊗ Mold; rivers Dee, Clwyd; wheat, oats; livestock raising, dairying; coal; aircraft, iron and steel, chemicals; chief towns incl. Rhyl, Flint; contains several prehistoric sites.

Flod·den \ˈfläd-ᵊn\. Hill in N Northumberland, N England, 12 m. E of Kelso near Scottish border; site of battle (also known as **Flodden Field**) Sept. 9, 1513 in which English under Earl of Surrey defeated with great slaughter Scots under James IV, who was killed.

Flo·ra \ˈflōr-ə, ˈflȯr-\. City, Clay co., SE cen. Illinois, 33 m. NE of Mt. Vernon; pop. (1970c) 5283; manufactures shoes, furniture; dairy products; soybeans.

Flor·ala \flə-ˈral-ə\. City, Covington co., S Alabama, on Florida border; pop. (1970c) 2701; sawmills.

Flo·ral Park \ˈflōr-əl-, ˈflȯr-\. Residential village, Nassau co., SE New York, on Long I. 15 m. E of New York City; pop. (1970c) 18,422; flower culture.

Flor·ence \ˈflȯr-ən(t)s, ˈflär-\. 1 Name of counties in two states of the U.S. See tables at SOUTH CAROLINA and WISCONSIN.

2 Industrial city, ⊗ of Lauderdale co., NW corner of Alabama, on Tennessee river by Wilson Dam; pop. (1970c) 34,031; manufactures textiles, fertilizer; food-packing plants, lumber mills; Florence State Coll. (1830); founded 1818, incorp. 1826, chartered as city 1889.

3 Town, ⊗ of Pinal co., S Arizona, on Gila river 50 m. SE of Phoenix; pop. (1970c) 2173; copper mines; founded 1866.

4 City, Fremont co., S cen. Colorado, on Arkansas river 35 m. SSW of Colorado Springs; pop. (1970c) 2846; in oil producing region; founded as coal-mining center 1860, incorp. as city 1887.

5 City, Boone co., N Kentucky, SW of Cincinnati, Ohio; pop. (1970c) 11,661.

6 Manufacturing village, Burlington co., S cen. New Jersey, on Delaware river 7 m. SSW of Trenton; pop. (with Roebling, 1970c) 7551.

7 Manufacturing city, ⊗ of Florence co., E South Carolina, 40 m. ENE of Sumter; pop. (1970c) 25,977; transportation and trade center; dairy products, fertilizer; in Civil War shipping center and point of embarkation for troops, hospital town, and prison.

8 Town, ⊗ of Florence co., NE Wisconsin; pop. (1970c) 1262.

9 *or Ital.* **Fi·ren·ze** \fē-ˈrent-sā\ *or anc.* **Flo·ren·tia** \flə-ˈren-ch(ē-)ə\. Commune, ✱ of Firenze prov. and of Tuscany, cen. Italy, at head of navigation on Arno river at foot of Apennines, 146 m. NNW of Rome; pop. (1968e) 457,659; ornamental glass and pottery, furniture, precision instruments; tourism; archiepiscopal see; univ. (1321); seat of Accademia della Crusca; contains ab. 40 museums. Notable structures include 13th cent. Duomo or Cathedral of Santa Maria del Fiore, churches of Santa Croce (13th cent.), Santa Maria Novella (13th cent.), the 14th cent. Ponte Vecchio, the Campanile, the Bargello or Palazza del Podestà (national museum), the Strozzi palace, the Pitti palace, the Loggia dei Lanzi, the Uffizi gallery, the Laurentian library, the Medici-Riccardi palace, the Accademia delle Belle Arti, the Magliabechiana library, and the Palazzo Vecchio.

History: Founded at foot of hill on top of which stood Etruscan town of Faesulae (see FIESOLE); in Roman times located on Cassian Way; escaped capture by Goths 5th cent. A.D.; in medieval margraviate of Tuscany (*q.v.*); by end of 12th cent. a flourishing trade and industrial center; came to be governed chiefly by members of wealthy guilds; torn by bitter civil strife which reflected Guelph-Ghibelline struggle in Italy; republic gradually secured control of extensive surrounding territory, including Pistoia 1331, Arezzo 1337, Volterra, Pisa 1406, and Leghorn; after 1434 ruled by the Medici (Cosimo 1434–64, Lorenzo the Magnificent 1469–92), members of powerful banking family, who fostered development of Italian Renaissance in which Florence was a leader; republic under Savonarola 1494–98; final expulsion of Medici occurred 1527 but they were restored as dukes of Florence 1531 and as grand dukes of Tuscany 1569; probably greatest cultural and artistic center of W Europe (14th–16th cents.); its language diffused throughout Italy, subsequently becoming standard language of the country; capital of Italy 1865–70. In World War II abandoned July 29, 1944 by Germans, who destroyed all but one of the Arno bridges; entered by

British Aug. 4–10, 1944; suffered severe flood damage 1966.

Florence Lake *and* **Florence Lake Dam.** See SAN JOAQUIN 1.

Flo·ren·cia \flə-'ren(t)-sē-ə\. Town, ✱ of Caquetá intendancy, S Colombia, 120 m. ENE of Pasto; munic. pop. (1968e) 36,798.

Flo·ren·cio Va·re·la \flə-'ren(t)-sē-ˌō-və-'rel-ə\. Town, Buenos Aires prov., E Argentina, ab. 15 m. SE of Buenos Aires; pop. (1960c) 41,707.

Florentia. See FLORENCE 9.

Flo·res \'flōr-əs, 'flȯr-\. 1 Island, NW Azores (*q.v.*), in district of Horta; 58 sq. m.; pop. (1960c) 6556; discovered by Portuguese 1452.

2 Municipality, Pernambuco state, E Brazil, on a tributary of the São Francisco 200 m. W of Recife; pop. (1968e) 19,569.

3 Town, ✱ of Petén dept., N Guatemala, on an island in a lake; munic. pop. (1964p) 3690; produces chicle and timber; stronghold of Itza Indians who preserved it from Spaniards until 1697.

4 Island of the Lesser Sunda Is., Indonesia; ab. 224 m. long; 37 m. wide near W end; 6622 sq. m.; pop. (1961c) 803,000; largest island in the chain extending from Java to Timor, lies E of Sumbawa and bet. Flores Sea and Savu Sea; chief towns Ende and Ruteng. Volcanic in origin; several isolated peaks above 5000 ft., highest 7872 ft. in W cen. part; coastline has few inlets; no large rivers; exports chiefly copra, grows maize and rice. In early times subject to the princes of Celebes; came partly under Dutch influence c. 1667, although the E end, around Larantuka, was claimed and held by Portugal until 1851; entire island came under Dutch control 1907; under Japanese control 1942–45; to Indonesia 1949.

5 Department of SW Uruguay. See table at URUGUAY.

Flores, Laguna de. See PETÉN ITZA.

Flores, Las. See LAS FLORES.

Flores Sea. Body of water bet. E end of Java Sea and W end of Banda Sea, bet. S Celebes and Lesser Sunda Is. in Indonesia; ab. 150 m. wide; in SW merges with Bali Sea.

Flo·res·ville \'flōr-əs-ˌvil, ˌflȯr-\. City, ⊗ of Wilson co., S cen. Texas, 30 m. SSE of San Antonio; pop. (1970c) 3707.

Flor·ham Park \ˌflor-əm-, ˌflär-\. Borough, Morris co., N New Jersey, 4 m. E of Morristown; pop. (1970c) 8094.

Flo·ri·a·na \ˌflōr-ē-'än-ə, ˌflȯr-, -'an-ə\. Suburb of Valletta, on island of Malta.

Flo·ri·a·nó·po·lis \ˌflōr-ē-ə-'näp-ə-ləs, ˌflȯr-\ *or formerly* **Des·têr·ro** \dēsh-'ter-ü\. City, ✱ of Santa Catarina state, S Brazil, on Santa Catarina I.; munic. pop. (1970p) 143,101; univ. 1955; excellent harbor; considerable coastwise trade.

Flor·i·da \'flȯr-əd-ə, 'flär-, 'flōr-\. 1 Southeast state of U.S.A., bounded on N by Alabama and Georgia, on E by Atlantic Ocean, on S by Straits of Florida and the Gulf of Mexico, on W by Gulf of Mexico and Alabama; 22d state in area, 58,560 sq. m. (land area 54,136 sq. m.); 9th state in population, (1970c) 6,789,443; ✱ Tallahassee; 27th state admitted to Union (1845).

Nicknames: Sunshine State; Peninsular State. *State flower:* Orange blossom. *Motto:* In God We Trust. *Rivers:* St. Johns, rising in E cen. part and flowing N into Atlantic Ocean; Caloosahatchee, outlet of Lake Okeechobee in the S flowing W; Indian River (actually a tidal inlet) in the E extending 165 m. along the coast; Kissimmee, chief headstream of the lake of same name; Withlacoochee, in the W; Suwannee and Apalachicola in the N, and the boundary rivers Perdido in the NW and St. Marys in the NE. *Highest point:* 345 ft., located in Walton co. *Chief products:* Citrus fruits, dairy products; phosphates, clays; manufacturing; chemicals, electrical machinery, paper products; tourism. *Chief cities:* Jacksonville, Miami, Tampa, St. Petersburg, Fort Lauderdale. See *Table of States* at UNITED STATES. Divided into the following 67 counties (for pronunciation of their names see their individual entries):

NAME	LOCATION	AREA[1] (sq. m.)	POP. (1970c)	CO. SEAT
Alachua	N penin.	916	104,764	Gainesville
Baker	NE	585	9,242	Macclenny
Bay	NW coast	747	75,283	Panama City
Bradford	NE	294	14,625	Starke
Brevard[2]	cen. E coast	1,011	230,006	Titusville
Broward[3]	SE coast	1,219	620,100	Fort Lauderdale
Calhoun[4]	NW	561	7,624	Blountstown
Charlotte	SW coast	703	27,559	Punta Gorda
Citrus	W penin. coast	560	19,196	Inverness
Clay	NE	593	32,059	Green Cove Springs
Collier[3]	SW coast	2,006	38,040	East Naples
Columbia	N	784	25,250	Lake City
Dade[3,5]	SE corner; coastal	2,042	1,267,792	Miami
De Soto	SW cen. penin.	648	13,060	Arcadia
Dixie	NW penin. coast	692	5,480	Cross City
Duval	NE coast	766	528,865	Jacksonville
Escambia	NW corner; coastal	665	205,334	Pensacola
Flagler	NE coast	487	4,454	Bunnell
Franklin[6]	NW coast	536	7,065	Apalachicola
Gadsden[6]	N	512	39,184	Quincy
Gilchrist	NW penin.	346	3,551	Trenton
Glades	S cen. penin.	753	3,669	Moore Haven
Gulf[4]	NW coast	565	10,096	Wewahitchka
Hamilton	N	514	7,787	Jasper
Hardee	cen. penin.	629	14,889	Wauchula
Hendry	S	1,187	11,859	La Belle
Hernando	W penin. coast	484	17,004	Brooksville
Highlands	cen. penin.	1,043	29,507	Sebring
Hillsborough	cen. W penin. coast	1,038	490,265	Tampa
Holmes	NW	482	10,720	Bonifay
Indian River[2]	cen. E coast	507	35,992	Vero Beach
Jackson[4]	NW	935	34,434	Marianna
Jefferson	N coast	605	8,778	Monticello
Lafayette	NW penin.	549	2,892	Mayo
Lake	cen. penin.	961	69,305	Tavares
Lee	SW coast	785	105,216	Fort Myers
Leon	N	670	103,047	Tallahassee
Levy	NW penin. coast	1,183	12,756	Bronson
Liberty[6]	NW	839	3,379	Bristol
Madison	N	703	13,481	Madison
Manatee	cen. W penin. coast	739	97,115	Bradenton
Marion	N cen. penin.	1,599	69,030	Ocala
Martin	SE coast	556	28,035	Stuart
Monroe[3,5]	SW corner; coastal	1,034	52,586	Key West
Nassau[7]	NE corner; coastal	650	20,626	Fernandina Beach
Okaloosa	NW coast	944	88,187	Crestview
Okeechobee	SE cen. penin.	777	11,233	Okeechobee
Orange	cen. penin.	910	344,311	Orlando
Osceola	cen. penin.	1,310	25,267	Kissimmee
Palm Beach[3]	SE coast	1,978	348,753	West Palm Beach
Pasco	cen. W penin. coast	742	75,955	Dade City
Pinellas	cen. W penin. coast	265	522,329	Clearwater
Polk	cen. penin.	1,861	227,697	Bartow
Putnam	NE penin.	779	36,424	Palatka
Saint Johns	NE coast	605	30,727	St. Augustine
Saint Lucie[2]	cen. E coast	584	50,836	Fort Pierce
Santa Rosa	NW coast	1,032	37,741	Milton
Sarasota	cen. W penin. coast	587	120,413	Sarasota
Seminole	cen. penin.	305	83,692	Sanford
Sumter	cen. penin.	555	14,839	Bushnell
Suwannee	N	686	15,559	Live Oak
Taylor	N coast	1,051	13,641	Perry
Union	NE	241	8,112	Lake Butler
Volusia	E coast	1,062	169,487	De Land
Wakulla	NW coast	601	6,308	Crawfordville
Walton	NW coast	1,053	16,087	De Funiak Springs
Washington	NW	585	11,453	Chipley

[1]Area = land area.
[2]Indian River (inlet) along full extent of shoreline.
[3]These counties include Everglades region.
[4]On E bounded by Apalachicola river, former boundary of old colonies of East and West Florida.
[5]Includes part of Florida Keys (island chain).
[6]On W bounded by Apalachicola river.
[7]Includes Amelia I., S end of Sea Is. chain.

History: Spanish Florida, which included SE part of present U.S., discovered by Ponce de León 1513; St. Augustine (*q.v.*) settled 1565; ceded to England 1763; divided into two provinces (known as the **Flor·i·das** \-ə-dəz\), East and West Florida; retroceded to Spain

1783; West Florida claimed by U.S. as part of Louisiana Purchase 1803 and occupied 1813; border crossed by Jackson in raid on Seminoles 1818; purchase for $5,000,000 by U.S. completed in Adams-Onís Treaty 1819; organized as territory 1822; admitted to Union as state Mar. 3, 1845; passed ordinance of secession Jan. 10, 1861; annulled ordinance of secession Oct. 28, 1865 and abolished slavery; readmitted to Union 1868; adopted present constitution 1885.

2 Village, Monroe co., NE Missouri, on Salt River 28 m. SW of Hannibal; birthplace of Mark Twain.

Flo·ri·da \flə-'rēd-ə\. 1 Municipality, Camagüey prov., Cuba, 23 m. NW of Camagüey; pop. (1967e) 73,640.

2 Department of S cen. Uruguay. See table at URUGUAY.

3 Town, ✱ of Florida dept., S cen. Uruguay, 60 m. N of Montevideo; pop. (1963c) 20,923; grain-trading center.

Flor·i·da, Cape \-'flȯr-əd-ə, -'flär-, -'flōr-\. Point, SE end of Key Biscayne, Biscayne Bay, off SE coast of Florida; lighthouse.

Florida, Straits of *also* **Florida Strait.** Channel bet. Florida Keys (S end of Florida) and N coast of Cuba; ab. 90 m. wide; connects Atlantic Ocean and Gulf of Mexico.

Florida Bay. Body of water bet. S tip of Florida mainland and Florida Keys.

Flo·ri·da·blan·ca \flə-ˌrēd-ə-'bläŋ-kə\. Municipality, W Pampanga prov., Luzon, Phil.; pop. (1969e) 38,800.

Florida City. City, Dade co., SE Florida, 25 m. SSW of Miami; pop. (1970c) 5133.

Florida Island \ˌflȯr-əd-ə-, ˌflär-; flə-ˌrēd-ə-\ *or* **N'Ge·la Island** \en-'gā-lə-, eŋ-\. Island in SE Solomon Is. in SW Pacific Ocean, N of cen. Guadalcanal and W of Malaita I.; 22 m. long and ab. 6 m. wide; part of British Solomon Islands protectorate; off its W shore is Olevuga I. and close to its S shore are the three islands of Tulagi (*q.v.*), Gavutu, and Tanambogo; off SE coast stretching across to Guadalcanal are shoals and reefs, interrupted in center by Sealark Channel. Occupied by Japanese May 4, 1942, taken by Americans Aug. 7 (see also SAVO).

Florida Keys. A chain of islands extending in a curve to the SW off S tip of Florida, on N side of Straits of Florida; partly in Dade co. but chiefly in Monroe co., Florida; more important islands Key Largo, Upper Matecumbe Key, Lower Matecumbe Key, Long Key, Vaca Key, Big Pine Key, Sugarloaf Key, and Key West at SW extremity of the group; devastated by hurricane 1935; traversed by Overseas Highway, completed 1938, which crosses Card Sound from the mainland to Key Largo and extends to Key West over many miles of causeways and bridges. See KEY WEST.

Florida Strait. See FLORIDA, STRAITS OF.

Flo·ri·dia \flə-'rēd-ē-ə\. Commune, Siracusa prov., SE Sicily, Italy, 8 m. W by N of Syracuse; pop. (1968e) 16,717.

Flo·ri·na \'flȯr-ə-nə\. 1 Department of Macedonia, Greece. See table at GREECE.

2 *also* **Fló·ri·na** *or* **Phló·ri·na** \'flȯr-ə-nə\ *or Serb.* **Le·rin** \lə-'rēn\. City, its ✱, near Yugoslav border; pop. (1971p) 11,180; seized by Germans Apr. 1941.

Flor·is·sant \'flōr-ə-sənt, 'flȯr-\. City, St. Louis co., E Missouri, NW of St. Louis; pop. (1970c) 65,908.

Florissant Fossil Beds National Monument. See UNITED STATES, *National Monuments.*

Floss·moor \'fläs-(ˌ)mu̇(ə)r, 'flȯs-\. Village, Cook co., NE Illinois, 23 m. S of Chicago; pop. (1970c) 7846.

Flow·er Hill \ˌflau̇(-ə)r-\. Village, Nassau co., SE New York; pop. (1970c) 4236.

Flowery Kingdom. See CHINA.

Floyd \'flȯid\. 1 River, NW Iowa; ab. 80 m. long; rises in O'Brien co., flows SW into Missouri river at Sioux City.

2 Name of counties in six states of the U.S. See tables at GEORGIA, INDIANA, IOWA, KENTUCKY, TEXAS, VIRGINIA.

3 Town, ⊗ of Floyd co., SW Virginia; pop. (1970c) 474.

Floyd·a·da \flȯi-'dā-də\. Town, ⊗ of Floyd co., NW Texas, 28 m. SE of Plainview; pop. (1970c) 4109; cotton, wheat; livestock.

Fluchthorn. See SILVRETTA.

Flume Mountain \'flüm-\. Peak in Franconia Mts., Grafton co., New Hampshire, E of Franconia Notch; 4327 ft.; on W side is the **Flume,** a canyon, 12 ft. wide at narrowest point, ab. 70 ft. deep.

Flu·men·do·sa \ˌflü-mən-'dō-sə\. River, SE Sardinia, Italy; 79 m. long; flows into Tyrrhenian Sea.

Flu·mi·ni Man·nu \ˌflü-mə-nē-'män-(ˌ)ü\. River, S Sardinia, Italy; ab. 50 m. long; enters Gulf of Cagliari at Cagliari.

Flush·ing \'fləsh-iŋ\. 1 Village, Genesee co., SE cen. Michigan, 10 m. WNW of Flint; pop. (1970c) 7190; dies; dairy products.

2 Former village, Queens co., SE New York, on Long I.; since 1898 part of borough of Queens, New York City; mostly residential; one of oldest nursery centers in U.S.; seat of Queens Coll. (1937), York Coll. (1967); N.Y. World's Fair of 1939–40 held in **Flushing Meadow,** now site of **Flushing Meadow Park;** temporary headquarters of United Nations (1946–49). See also QUEENS 2.

3 Commune and seaport, Netherlands. See VLISSINGEN.

Flushing Bay. Inlet of East river, N shore of Long I., New York.

Flu·van·na \flü-'van-ə\. County in Virginia. See table at VIRGINIA.

Fly \'flī\. River, Papua New Guinea, SE New Guinea I.; ab. 650 m. long; one of the largest rivers in New Guinea, navigable for more than 500 m.; flows S and SE into Gulf of Papua in wide estuary; part of its middle course forms boundary with Irian Barat, Indonesia.

Foa \'fō-ə\. Island in Haapai group, Tonga, SW cen. Pacific Ocean.

Foard \'fō(ə)rd, 'fȯ(ə)rd\. County in Texas. See table at TEXAS.

Fo·ça *or* **Fo·cha** \fō-'chä\. Two seaports on Gulf of İzmir, İzmir prov., W Turkey, Asia: (1) **Ye·ni·fo·ça**\ye-'nē-fō-'chä\ (New Foça), founded 1421 by Genoese. (2) **Foça** *formerly* **Es·ki Foça** \es-'kē-\ (Old Foça) *or anc.* **Pho·caea** \fō-'sē-ə\, ab. 5 m. S of Yenifoça; most northerly of the 12 Ionian Cities on W coast of Asia Minor; a flourishing maritime state c. 800–600 B.C.; established Massilia colony (Marseilles) 600 B.C.; conquered by Persians 540 B.C.

Foc·şa·ni \fȯk-'shän(-ē)\. City, ⊗ of Vrancea co., E cen. Romania; pop. (1970e) 39,629; scene of battles: (1) Aug. 1, 1789 in which a combined Austrian-Russian army defeated the Turks; (2) Jan. 8, 1917 when it was taken by Austrian and German forces; truce signed here Dec. 6, 1917.

Fog·gia \'fō-jə\. 1 Province of Apulia, SE Italy. See table at ITALY.

2 Commune, its ✱, 162 m. ESE of Rome; pop. (1968e) 138,253; cellulose; wool market; in region producing olives, grapes, tobacco, wheat; center of great Apulian plain or "tavoliere"; ruins of castle of Frederick II who held parliament here 1240; extensive airfields, captured by British Army Sept. 27, 1943.

Fo·go \'fō (ˌ)gü\. One of Cape Verde Is., in S part of group; ab. 190 sq. m.; pop. (1960c) 25,457; contains volcano 9281 ft., highest point in islands; eruption 1847.

Fogo \'fō-(ˌ)gō\. Seaport town, E Newfoundland, Canada, on N shore of **Fogo Island,** E of entrance to Notre Dame Bay; pop. (1971p) 1155.

Föhr \'fər\. Island off W coast of Schleswig-Holstein, West Germany, one of North Frisian Is.; 32 sq. m.; pop. (1966e) 8400; chief town Wyk.

Foix \'fwä\. Commune, ✱ of Ariège dept., S France, at foot of the Pyrenees 47 m. S of Toulouse; pop. (1968c) 9331; textiles.

FLORIDA
MILES
0 25 50 75
KILOMETERS
0 25 50 75
State Capital
County Seats
Counties indicated by numbers:
1 ESCAMBIA
2 GADSDEN
3 GILCHRIST
4 HILLSBOROUGH
5 JEFFERSON
6 PINELLAS
7 SEMINOLE
8 SUMTER
GEORGIA
ALA.
ATLANTIC OCEAN
GULF OF MEXICO
Straits of Florida
FLORIDA KEYS
Tallahassee
Jacksonville
Jacksonville Beach
St. Augustine
Gainesville
Ocala
Daytona Beach
Orlando
Lakeland
Tampa
St. Petersburg
Clearwater
Sarasota
Ft. Myers
Ft. Pierce
W. Palm Beach
Ft. Lauderdale
Hollywood
Miami
Miami Beach
Hialeah
Coral Gables
Key West
Okefenokee Swamp
L. Okeechobee
Big Cypress Swamp
EVERGLADES NATIONAL PARK
Florida Bay
Dry Tortugas
Marquesas Keys
WESTERN PART OF FLORIDA
Same scale as main map
GULF OF MEXICO
Pensacola
Panama City
84°
82°
80°
30°
28°
26°
Longitude West of Greenwich
© Copyright HAMMOND INCORPORATED, Maplewood, N. J.

Foix, Countship of. Historical region of S cen. France; bordered anciently on N and E by Languedoc, SE by Roussillon, S by the Pyrenees, W by Gascony; capitals Foix and Pamiers; watered by Ariège river; made countship 1012; joined to French crown at ascension of Henry IV to throne of France.

Fol·croft \'fäl-ˌkrȯft\. Borough, Delaware co., SE Pennsylvania, 7 m. WSW of Philadelphia; pop. (1970c) 9610.

Fo·ley \'fō-lē\. 1 Town, Baldwin co., SW Alabama, 30 m. SE of Mobile; pop. (1970c) 3368; potatoes; fertilizer factory.

2 Village, ⊗ of Benton co., cen. Minnesota, 15 m. ENE of St. Cloud; pop. (1970c) 1271.

Fo·li·gno \fə-'lēn-(ˌ)yō\ *or anc.* **Ful·gin·i·um** \ˌfu̇l-'jin-ē-əm, ˌfəl-\. Manufacturing commune, Perugia prov., Umbria, cen. Italy, 18 m. SE of Perugia; pop. (1968e) 50,237; paper, sugar; cathedral; two Renaissance palaces. Founded 8th cent.; devastated by Perugians 1281; ruled by the Guelph Trinci family 1305–1439; part of Papal States 1439–1860, of Italy from 1860.

Folke·stone \'fōk-stən\. Municipal borough, Kent, SE England, on Strait of Dover 6 m. WSW of Dover; pop. (1971p) 43,760; seaport, summer resort; fisheries; dates back to Roman and Saxon times.

Folk·ston \'fōk-stən\. City, ⊗ of Charlton co., SE Georgia; pop. (1970c) 2112; cotton, corn.

Fol·lans·bee \'fäl-ənz-bē\. City, Brooke co., N West Virginia, on Ohio river 19 m. N of Wheeling; pop. (1970c) 3883; steel products; oil wells.

Fol·som \'fōl-səm\. 1 City, Sacramento co., California, NE of Sacramento; pop. (1970c) 5810; livestock; state penitentiary.

2 Village, Union co., NE New Mexico, E of Raton; pop. (1970c) 75; nearby in 1925 were found artifacts, esp. chipped stone projectile points (*Folsom points*), considered as representative of culture of a Stone Age people supposed to have lived in North America at end of last glacial period (late Pleistocene).

Fom·bo·ni \fȯm-'bō-nē\. See MOHÉLI.

Fo·men·to \fō-'ment-(ˌ)ō\. Town and municipality, Las Villas prov., W cen. Cuba; munic. pop. (1967e) 40,050.

Fon·da \'fänd-ə\. Manufacturing village, ⊗ of Montgomery co., E New York, on Mohawk river 12 m. W of Amsterdam; pop. (1970c) 1120; settled by Dutch c. 1775; burned by Loyalist troops 1780; became ⊗ 1836.

Fond du Lac \'fän-dᵊl-ˌak, 'fän-jə-ˌlak\. 1 County in E Wisconsin. See table at WISCONSIN.

2 Manufacturing city and resort, its ⊗, at S end of Lake Winnebago; pop. (1970c) 35,515; machine tools, paper boxes, outboard motors; settled 1836.

3 River, N Saskatchewan, Canada; ab. 100 m. long; flows W to Lake Athabaska.

Fon·di \'fōn-dē, 'fän-\ *or anc.* **Fun·di** \'fən-ˌdī\. Commune, Latina prov., Latium, cen. Italy, 29 m. E by S of Latina; pop. (1968e) 24,417; on ancient Appian Way; ruins of castle of Colonna family; Gothic cathedral.

Fon·douk al–Aou·a·reb \'fän-ˌdu̇k-ˌal-ə-'wär-əb, 'fün-\. Town, N cen. Tunisia, 20 m. SW of Kairouan; near mountain pass whose capture by Allies Apr. 12, 1943 resulted in capture of Kairouan.

Fon·sa·gra·da \ˌfän-sə-'grä-t͟hə\. Commune, Lugo prov., NW Spain, 27 m. ENE of Lugo; pop. (1960c) 12,423.

Fon·se·ca, Gulf of \-fän-'sā-kə\ *or* **Fonseca Bay.** Large inlet of Pacific Ocean with El Salvador on N, Honduras on E, and Nicaragua on S.

Fon·taine \fōⁿ-'ten\. Commune, Isère dept., France; pop. (1968c) 22,326.

Fon·taine·bleau \'fänt-ᵊn-ˌblō\. Commune, Seine-et-Marne dept., N France, near left bank of the Seine 35 m. SSE of Paris; pop. (1968c) 18,094; in forest of Fontainebleau; barracks, military college, communal college, school of designing and engineering; famous for its château (SE of town), former residence of French kings, now summer residence of presidents of France; place where revocation of Edict of Nantes was signed 1685 and where Pius VII was held prisoner by Napoleon 1812–14.

Fon·tana \fän-'tan-ə\. City, San Bernardino co., S California, W of San Bernardino; pop. (1970c) 20,673; electronic equipment, steel, apparel; citrus fruit.

Fontana Dam. See table at TENNESSEE VALLEY AUTHORITY.

Fontanet. See FONTENOY 2.

Fontarabia. See FUENTERRABIA.

Font–de–Gaume. See EYZIES, LES.

Fon·te·nay–aux–Roses \fōⁿ(n)t-ˌnā-ō-'rōz\. Commune, Hauts-de-Seine dept., N France; suburb of Paris; pop. (1968c) 23,355.

Fontenay–le–Comte \-lə-kōⁿt\. Town, SE Vendée dept., W France, 25 m. NE of La Rochelle; pop. (1968c) 12,199; dates from time of the Gauls; belonged to English 1360–72; scene of much fighting during 16th cent. and in 1793; capital of department of Vendée 1790–1806.

Fontenay–sous–Bois \-sü-'bwä\. Commune, Val-de-Marne dept., N France, SE suburb of Paris; pop. (1968c) 38,962.

Fon·te·noy \fōⁿ(n)t-'nwä\. 1 Commune, Hainaut prov., SW Belgium, 5 m. ESE of Tournai; pop. (1969e) 655; scene of battle May 11, 1745 in which Marshal Saxe with help of Irish Brigade defeated a combined force of British, Hanoverians, Austrians, and Dutch under duke of Cumberland.

2 *or formerly* **Fon·ta·net** \ˌfōⁿ-tə-'nā\. Town, Yonne dept., NE cen. France, S of Sens; pop. (1962c) 455; scene of defeat of Emperor Lothair by his brothers Charles the Bald and Louis the German 841.

Fon·te·vrault–l'Ab·baye \ˌfōⁿ(n)-təv-'rō-la-'bā\. Town, Maine-et-Loire dept., W France, ESE of Saumur; pop. (1962c) 2157; abbey, founded 1099, where early Plantagenet kings were buried, since 1804 a prison.

Font·hill \'fänt-ˌhil\. Village, Welland co., SE Ontario, Canada, 12 m. W of Niagara Falls; pop. (1968e) 2937; truck farming; gravel pits.

Foo·chow *or* **Fu·chau** \'fü-'jō, -'chau̇\ *or formerly* **Min·how** \'min-'hō\. Seaport, ✱ of Fukien prov., SE China, on Min river 34 m. from its mouth, ab. halfway bet. Hong Kong (455 m. by sea) and Shanghai; pop. (1970e) 900,000; chief part is walled city ab. 2 m. from N bank of river; former foreign settlement at **Nan–t'ai** \'nän-'tī\ on S bank opposite. For years famous as chief port for export of black tea (*bohea*); has developed several industries but trade now chiefly local or coastal. In the city and on nearby hills are beautiful examples of Chinese architecture—pagodas, temples, monasteries. First appeared in Chinese history during T'ang dynasty; one of the first five treaty ports opened to trade by Treaty of Nanking 1842; in World War II captured and recaptured several times 1944–45 by Japanese and Chinese.

Foots·cray \'fu̇ts-ˌkrā\. Municipality, S Victoria, SE Australia, W suburb of Melbourne; pop. (1966c) 58,823; bluestone quarries; dry docks.

For·a·ker, Mount \-'fȯr-i-kər, -'fär-\. Mountain in Alaska Range in Mount McKinley National Park, S cen. Alaska, SW of Mt. McKinley; 17,400 ft.

For·bach \fȯr-'bäk, 'fō(ə)r-ˌbäk\. Commune, Moselle dept., NE France, 32 m. E of Metz; pop. (1968c) 23,120; paper; coal mines; scene of battle Aug. 6, 1870 in which General Frossard was defeated by the Prussians.

Forbes \'fōrbz\. Town, E cen. New South Wales, SE Australia, 185 m. WNW of Sydney; pop. (1966c) 7369; flour mills, sawmills, breweries.

Forbes, Mount. Peak in Banff National Park, SW Alberta, Canada; 11,852 ft.

Forbidden City. 1 City, Tibet, China. See LHASA.

2 The walled enclosure, Peking, China (ab. 1/3 of a sq. m.), containing the Imperial Palace, with its pleasure grounds, reception halls, pavilions, and offices of state—so called because it was formerly closed to the public.

For·ca·dos \fȯr-'säd-əs\. 1 The main navigable channel of Niger river, S Nigeria.

2 Town, Mid-Western State, Nigeria, on coast 160 m. SE of Lagos; main port of entry at mouth of Niger river.

Forch·heim \'fōrk-ˌhīm, 'fōrk̲-\. City, Bavaria, West Germany, 20 m. N of Nürnberg; pop. (1969e) 21,500; machine shops, textiles; 14th cent. bishop's palace and remains of 16th–17th cent. fortifications; first mentioned 805; to Bavaria 1802.

Ford \'fō(ə)rd, 'fȯ(ə)rd\. Name of counties in two states of the U.S. See tables at ILLINOIS and KANSAS.

Ford City. Borough, Armstrong co., W Pennsylvania, on Allegheny river 34 m. NE of Pittsburgh; pop. (1970c) 4749; manufactures plate glass.

Ford·ham \'fōrd-əm, 'fȯrd-\. Former village now included in Bronx borough, New York City; Fordham Univ. (1841).

Ford Island. Island in Pearl Harbor, S Oahu, Hawaiian Is., N Pacific Ocean; naval station.

Ford·lan·dia \ˌfōrd-'lan-dē-ə, ˌfȯrd-\. Town, now abandoned, Pará state, NE Brazil, on right bank of Tapajós river ab. 110 m. S of Santarém; formerly one of the Ford rubber plantations.

Ford Ranges *or formerly* **Ed·sel Ford Ranges** \ˌed-səl-\. Mountain groups and ranges, NW Marie Byrd Land, Antarctica; extend S from shelf ice at long. 140° to 145°W and lat. 76° to 78°S; highest peak ab. 14,000 ft.

For·dyce \'fōr-ˌdīs, 'fȯr-\. City, ⊗ of Dallas co., S cen. Arkansas, 30 m. NE of Camden; pop. (1970c) 4837; lumber; fruit; livestock.

Fo·rel, Mount \-fə-'rel\. Mountain, E Greenland, near coast N of Angmagssalik; 11,024 ft.

Fore·land, North \-'fō(ə)r-lənd, -'fȯ(ə)r-\ *and* **South Foreland.** Two headlands in Kent, SE England: North Foreland, 2½ m. SE of Margate, has one lighthouse; South Foreland, 3 m. NE of Dover, has two lighthouses.

Foreland Sound. See PRINCE CHARLES FORELAND.

Fore River \'fō(ə)r-, 'fȯ(ə)r-\ *or in full* **Wey·mouth Fore River** \'wā-məth-\. Inlet of Boston Bay on coast of Norfolk co., E Massachusetts; large Fore River shipyards on it at Quincy.

For·est \'fȯr-əst, 'fär-\. 1 Name of counties in two states of the U.S. See tables at PENNSYLVANIA and WISCONSIN.

2 City, ⊗ of Scott co., cen. Mississippi, 41 m. E of Jackson; pop. (1970c) 4085; timber.

3 Town, Lambton co., SE Ontario, Canada, 23 m. ENE of Sarnia, near S end of Lake Huron; pop. (1971p) 2351.

Fo·rest \fȯ-'re\. Commune, Belgium. See VORST.

For·est Acres \'fȯr-əst-, 'fär-\. Town, Richland co., W cen. South Carolina, 6 m. W of Columbia; pop. (1970c) 6808.

Forest Can·tons, The Four \-'kant-ᵊnz, -'kan-ˌtänz\ *or Ger.* **Die Vier Wald·stät·ter** \dē-'fi(ə)r-'vält-ˌs(h)tet-ər\. Uri, Schwyz, Unterwalden, and Lucerne cantons, Switzerland, surrounding Lake of Lucerne (Lake of the Four Forest Cantons); Uri, Schwyz and Unterwalden, first to unite against Hapsburgs 1291, were nucleus of Swiss confederation. See SWITZERLAND.

Forest City. 1 City, ⊗ of Winnebago co., N Iowa, 25 m. WNW of Mason City; pop. (1970c) 3841; Waldorf Coll. (1903).

2 Town, Rutherford co., SW North Carolina, 20 m. W of Shelby; pop. (1970c) 7179; textiles, lumber, bricks.

3 Borough, Susquehanna co., NE Pennsylvania, 20 m. NNE of Scranton; pop. (1970c) 2322; textiles; fruit farms.

Forest Grove. City, Washington co., NW Oregon, 22 m. W of Portland; pop. (1970c) 8275; sawmills; Pacific Univ. (1849).

Forest Heights. Town, Prince Georges co., S cen. Maryland, 5 m. SSE of Washington, D.C.; pop. (1970c) 3600.

Forest Hill. 1 Village, Tarrant co., Texas, 6 m. SE of Fort Worth; pop. (1970c) 8236.

2 Village, York co., SE Ontario, Canada, in Greater Toronto area; pop. (1966c) 23,135.

Forest Hills. 1 Residential community in Queens borough, New York City, on Long I.; scene of national lawn tennis (grass-court) tournaments.

2 Borough, Allegheny co., SW Pennsylvania, 8 m. E of Pittsburgh; pop. (1970c) 9561.

Forest Lake. Village, Washington co., E Minnesota, 25 m. N of St. Paul; pop. (1970c) 3207; aluminum utensils and fixtures; truck farming; resort.

Forest Park. 1 Town, Clayton co., NW cen. Georgia, SSE suburb of Atlanta; pop. (1970c) 19,994; sheet metal works; potatoes.

2 Residential village, Cook co., NE Illinois, W suburb of Chicago; pop. (1970c) 15,472.

3 Residential suburb, Hamilton co., SW Ohio, 12 m. N of Cincinnati; pop. (1970c) 15,139.

For·est·ville \'fȯr-əst-ˌvil, 'fär-\. Subdivision of town of Bristol, Connecticut. See BRISTOL 2.

Fo·rez \fə-'rez\. Ancient region, cen. France, a plain bet. the upper Loire and the Allier, W of Lyons; bordered on W by **Forez Mountains;** medieval countship dependent on Burgundy; united with France 1531.

For·far \'fȯr-fər\. 1 *or* **For·far·shire** \-ˌshi(ə)r, -shər\. County of Scotland. See ANGUS.

2 Burgh, ⊗ of Angus co., E Scotland; pop. (1971p) 10,500; jute, linen goods; site of castle, scene of several Scottish parliaments (11th–14th cents.).

Fork·ed Deer \ˌfȯr-kəd-'di(ə)r\. River, W Tennessee; ab. 15 m. long; formed by confluence of long north and south forks in S Dyer co.; flows W into Mississippi river. See OBION 1.

For·lì \fȯr-'lē\. 1 Province of Emilia-Romagna, N Italy. See table at ITALY.

2 *or anc.* **Fo·rum Liv·ii** \ˌfōr-əm-'liv-ē-ˌī, ˌfȯr-\. Commune, its ✻, 168 m. SE of Milan; pop. (1968e) 103,156; household appliances, furniture; episcopal see; old citadel; 14th cent. Palazzo Communale; allied with Ravenna 12th cent.; taken by Martin IV 1282; became part of Papal States 1504; to Italy 1861.

For·man \'fōr-mən, 'fȯr-\. City, ⊗ of Sargent co., SE North Dakota; pop. (1970c) 596; grain farms.

Form·by \'fȯrm-bē\. Urban district, Lancashire, NW England, on Irish Sea 10 m. N of Liverpool; pop. (1971p) 23,501.

For·men·te·ra \ˌfȯr-mən-'ter-ə\ *or anc.* **Oph·i·u·sa** \ˌäf-ē-'(y)ü-sə, ˌōf-\. Fourth largest island of the Balearic group, Baleares prov., Spain, in W Mediterranean Sea S of Ibiza I. and 82 m. SW of Majorca; 40 sq. m.; pop. (1970p) 2965; fisheries, salt making. See BALEARIC ISLANDS.

For·men·tor, Cape \-ˌfȯr-mən-'tȯ(ə)r\. Cape on N extremity of island of Majorca, W Mediterranean Sea.

For·mia \'fȯr-mē-ə\ *or formerly* **Mo·la di Ga·e·ta** \'mō-lə-di-gä-'et-ə, ˌmō-, -'āt-ə\ *or anc.* **For·mi·ae** \'fȯr-mē-ˌē\. Commune, Latina prov., Latium, cen. Italy, on Gulf of Gaeta 41 m. ESE of Latina; pop. (1968e) 23,348; summer resort; active seaport. Ancient town of the Volsci; on Appian Way; received limited citizenship rights from Rome 322 B.C. and full rights 188 B.C.; site of a summer villa of Cicero, who was murdered nearby (see ASTURA); in World War II taken by Americans May 18, 1944.

For·mi·ga \fȯr-'mē-gə, fůr-\. City, Minas Gerais state, E Brazil, 100 m. WSW of Belo Horizonte; munic. pop. (1968e) 46,140.

For·mi·gi·ne \fȯr-'mē-ji-nə\. Commune, Modena prov., Emilia-Romagna, N Italy, 7 m. SW of Modena; pop. (1968e) 15,259.

For·mi·gny \ˌfȯr-mē-'nyē\. Village, Calvados dept., NW France, ab. 27 m. WNW of Caen; pop. (1962c) 324; scene of battle Apr. 15, 1450 in which French defeated English in next-to-last battle of Hundred Years' War (see CASTILLON).

For·mo·sa \fȯr-'mō-sə\. 1 Province of N Argentina. See table at ARGENTINA.

2 Town, its ✱, on a tributary of the Paraguay river; pop. (1960c) 36,499.

Formosa. See TAIWAN.

Formosa Bay \fȯr-'mō-sə-, fər-, -zə-\. Inlet of Indian Ocean on SE coast of Kenya, E Africa; receives Tana river.

Formosa Strait *or* **Tai·wan Strait** \tī-'wän-\. Channel bet. Fukien prov., SE China, and Taiwan; connects East China Sea with South China Sea; ab. 115 m. wide.

For·mo·so, Cape \-fȯr-'mō-(,)sō, -fər-, -(,)zō\. Cape on coast of Nigeria, W Africa, near Nun mouth of Niger river.

For·res \'fȯr-əs, 'fär-, -əz\. Burgh, Moray co., NE Scotland, 11 m. SW of Elgin; pop. (1971p) 4710; site of castle at which Macbeth is said to have killed Duncan; nearby is the heath where, in the Shakespeare play, Macbeth met the three witches.

For·rest \'fȯr-əst, 'fär-\. County in Mississippi. See table at MISSISSIPPI.

Forrest City. Commercial city, ⊗ of St. Francis co., E Arkansas; pop. (1970c) 12,521; timber, corn, sweet potatoes; cotton gins.

Forst \'fō(ə)rst\ *or in full* **Forst in der Lau·sitz** \-in-der-'laù-zəts\. Industrial city, Cottbus dist., East Germany, on Neisse river 14 m. E of Cottbus; pop. (1970e) 29,284; important textile center; foundry.

For·syth \'fō(ə)r-,sīth, fō(ə)r-'sīth\. 1 Name of counties in two states of the U.S. See tables at GEORGIA and NORTH CAROLINA.

2 City, ⊗ of Monroe co., cen. Georgia, 22 m. NW of Macon; pop. (1970c) 3736; cotton gins, lumber mills; Tift Coll. (1847).

3 City, ⊗ of Taney co., S Missouri; pop. (1970c) 803; diversified agriculture.

4 City, ⊗ of Rosebud co., SE Montana; pop. (1970c) 1873; livestock.

Fort Al·ba·ny \-'ȯl-bə-nē\. Trading post, Cochrane dist., E Ontario, Canada, on James Bay at mouth of Albany river; established ab. 1670 by Hudson's Bay Company.

Fort Aleksandrovsk. See FORT SHEVCHENKO.

For·ta·le·za \fȯrt-ᵊl-'ā-zə\ *also* **Ce·a·rá** \,sā-ə-'rä\. City and port, ✱ of Ceará state, NE Brazil, ab. 270 m. NW of Natal; munic. pop. (1970p) 842,231; port works at Point Mucuripe 5 m. E; exports sugar, coffee, cotton, hides; univ. (1954); founded early in 17th cent.; made capital 1810.

Fort Am·herst National Historic Park \-'am-(,)ərst-\. See CANADA, *National Historic Parks.*

Fort An·cient \-'ān-shənt, -chənt\. Prehistoric Indian fortification, Warren co., SW Ohio; overlooks Little Miami river; earth wall over 3½ m. long, 6–10 ft. high, encloses ab. 100 acres in two divisions, the Old Fort and the New Fort.

Fort Anne National Park \-'an-\. See CANADA, *National Historic Parks.*

Fort–Ar·cham·bault \fȯr-'är-shəm-,bō\. Town on Chari river, S Chad, 300 m. SE of Fort-Lamy; pop. (1968e) 36,-749; cotton.

Fort At·kin·son \-'at-kən-sən\. City, Jefferson co., SE Wisconsin; pop. (1970c) 9164; farm and dairy equipment; truck farms.

Fort Bat·tle·ford National Historic Park \-'bat-ᵊl-fō(ə)rd-, -fȯ(ə)rd-\. See CANADA, *National Historic Parks.*

Fort Beau·fort \-'bō-fərt\. Town, SE Cape Province, S Rep. of South Africa, 105 m. NE of Port Elizabeth; pop. (1967e) 9900.

Fort Beau·sé·jour National Historic Park \-,bō-,sā-'zhü(ə)r-\. See CANADA, *National Historic Parks.*

Fort Bel·voir \-'bel-,vȯr\ *or formerly* **Fort Hum·phreys** \-'həm-frēz\. Military post, SE Fairfax co., NE Virginia, on the Potomac; Engineer School.

Fort Bend \-'bend\. County in Texas. See table at TEXAS.

Fort Ben·ja·min Har·ri·son \-,ben-jə-mən-'har-ə-sən\. Military post, Indianapolis, Marion co., cen. Indiana; 2030 acres; estab. 1903.

Fort Ben·ning \-'ben-iŋ\. Military post, Muscogee co., W Georgia, 8 m. S of Columbus; 97,000 acres; largest infantry post in the U.S.; established during World War I, infantry school from 1919.

Fort Ben·ton \-'bent-ᵊn\. City, ⊗ of Chouteau co., N cen. Montana, on Missouri river; pop. (1970c) 1863; in early days head of navigation at low water.

Fort Bliss \-'blis\. Military post, El Paso, El Paso co., W Texas; 50 sq. m.; cavalry and antiaircraft artillery; air corps.

Fort Bragg \-'brag\. 1 City, Mendocino co., W California, on Pacific coast 96 m. S of Eureka; pop. (1970c) 4455; redwood lumber; founded 1850; army post founded 1857.

2 Military reservation, Cumberland co., S cen. North Carolina, ab. 10 m. NW of Fayetteville; estab. 1918; field artillery training center; includes Pope Field, U.S. Air Force base; site of battle of Monroes Crossroads 1865.

Fort Branch \-'branch\. Town, Gibson co., SW Indiana, 18 m. N of Evansville; pop. (1970c) 2535.

Fort Bridg·er \-'brij-ər\. Village, Uinta co., SW Wyoming; nearby is the site of trading post built 1843 by James Bridger, an important station on Oregon Trail and a U.S. Army post 1858–90, site now a state park.

Fort Brown \-'braùn\. Military reservation, Cameron co., Texas, just E of Brownsville; 288 acres; fort established 1846; military post 1865–1944.

Fort Car·il·lon \-'kar-ə-,län\. See TICONDEROGA.

Fort Car·o·line National Memorial \-'kar-ə-,līn-, -lən-\. Fortified settlement, NE Florida, on S side of mouth of St. Johns river, established by French Huguenots 1564, destroyed the next year by the Spanish under Menéndez de Avilés; memorial authorized 1950.

Fort Cham·bly National Historic Park \-'sham-blē-, -shä^{n}-'blē-\. See CANADA, *National Historic Parks.*

Fort Christiansborg. See ACCRA.

Fort Chris·ti·na \-kris-'tē-nə\. Swedish settlement on site of Wilmington, Delaware; established by Peter Minuit 1638. See WILMINGTON 1.

Fort Clay·ton \-klāt-ᵊn\. Army reservation on E shore of Miraflores Lake, Canal Zone, ab. 5 m. from Pacific terminus of Panama Canal.

Fort Col·lins \-'käl-ənz\. Residential and industrial city, ⊗ of Larimer co., N Colorado, 40 m. NNE of Boulder; pop. (1970c) 43,337; canned goods, sugar, plastics; timber; dairy farming; Colorado State Univ. (1870); founded 1864, incorp. 1879.

Fort Con·ger \-käŋ-gər\. Arctic post on Hall Basin, Grant Land, Ellesmere I., N Canada, ab. 81°45′N; station used by A.W. Greely 1881–84; a monthly average (Feb.) of 40° below zero has been recorded. See VERKHOYANSK and OIMYAKON.

Fort Crève·cœur \-'krēv-'kü(ə)r\. 1 See ILLINOIS 3.

2 Seaport, Ghana. See ACCRA.

Fort–Dau·phin \-'dō-fən\. Town and seaport, SE Malagasy Republic; pop. (1960e) 12,000; timber; founded by French 1766.

Fort Da·vis \-'dā-vəs\. Village, ⊗ of Jeff Davis co., W Texas.

Fort Dearborn. See CHICAGO.

Fort de Char·tres \-də-'shärt-ərz\. Old fort, SW Illinois, near Kaskaskia, on the Mississippi; founded 1720; in state park.

Fort–de–France \,fȯr-də-'frä^{n}s\. City, ✱ of the French overseas department of Martinique, West Indies, on large **Fort–de–France Bay** on SW coast of island; pop. (1967e) 99,051; partially destroyed by earthquake 1839 and by fire 1890.

Fort de Kock. See BUKITTINGGI.

Fort De·pos·it \-di-ˈpäz-ət\. Town, Lowndes co., S cen. Alabama, 30 m. SW of Montgomery; pop. (1970c) 1438; established as military post c. 1813.

Fort Des Moines. See DES MOINES 3.

Fort Dev·ens \-ˈdev-ənz\. Military post, Ayer, Middlesex co., Massachusetts; WAC training center in World War II; headquarters, 13th U.S. Army Corps.

Fort Dix \-ˈdiks\. Military reservation in Burlington and Ocean cos., S cen. New Jersey, ab. 10 m. NNE of Mount Holly, near Wrightstown; 13½ sq. m.

Fort Dodge \-ˈdäj\. City, ⊗ of Webster co., N cen. Iowa, 68 m. NW of Des Moines; pop. (1970c) 31,263; chemicals, farm equipment; meat packing; Iowa Central Community Coll. (1921); near gypsum deposits from which the Cardiff giant was carved (see CARDIFF 1).

Fort Don·el·son National Military Park \-ˈdän-əl-sən-\. See UNITED STATES, *National Historical Parks.*

Fort Drum \-ˈdrəm\. See CORREGIDOR.

Fort Duf·fer·in \-ˈdəf-(ə-)rən\. See MANDALAY.

Fort Du·quesne \-dü-ˈkān\. French fort on site of modern Pittsburgh, Pennsylvania; captured by British 1758 and renamed Fort Pitt.

Fort Eben Emael \-ˌā-bən-ˈā-ˌmäl\. Fort, N of Liège, Belgium, on Albert Canal; captured by Germans May 11, 1940.

Fort Ed·ward \-ˈed-wərd\. Village, Washington co., E New York, on Hudson river 38 m. N of Troy; pop. (1970c) 3733; on site of colonial Fort Edward; pulp and paper mills.

Fort Erie \-ˈi(ə)r-ē\. Town, Welland co., SE Ontario, Canada, on Lake Erie as it empties into Niagara river; pop. (1971p) 23,099; connected with Buffalo, N.Y., by International Bridge (railroad), by Peace Bridge (dedicated 1927), and by ferries; manufactures aircraft, auto accessories, paint; gold refining. Formed 1932 by amalgamation of Bridgeburg town and Fort Erie village; on site of old Fort Erie, which was captured by American forces July 13, 1813, besieged by British Aug. 7 to 14, and destroyed by American troops Nov. 1814.

For·tes·cue \ˈfȯrt-ə-ˌskyü\. River, W Western Australia; 340 m. long; in flood seasons flows NW to Indian Ocean near Dampier Archipelago.

Fort Es·te·ros \-e-ˈster-əs\. Former Bolivian post in the Chaco, on Pilcomayo river; now in Paraguay.

Fort Ethan Al·len \-ˌē-thə-ˈnal-ən\. See ESSEX JUNCTION.

Fort Fair·field \-ˈfa(ə)r-ˌfēld, -ˈfe(ə)r-\. Town and village, Aroostook co., N Maine, on Aroostook river 10 m. NE of Presque Isle; pop. (1970c) 4859; port of entry.

Fort Fish·er \-ˈfish-ər\. Fort, S New Hanover co., SE North Carolina, near Cape Fear; designed to protect port of Wilmington; captured by Union forces Jan. 15, 1865.

Fort Fran·ces \-ˈfran(t)-səs, -səz\. Town, ⊗ of Rainy River dist., SW Ontario, Canada, on Rainy river across from International Falls, Minnesota; pop. (1971p) 9698; lumber and paper mills, large power plant.

Fort Fran·cis E. War·ren \-ˌfran(t)-səs-ˌē-ˈwȯr-ən, -ˈwär-\. Military post, Laramie co., SE Wyoming, adjoining Cheyenne; maneuver reservation; intercontinental ballistic missile support base; U.S. Air Force base (U.S. Air Force Technical School); estab. ab. 1867.

Fort Frank \-ˈfraŋk\. See CORREGIDOR.

Fort Fred·er·i·ca National Monument \-fred-(ə-)ˈrē-kə-\. See UNITED STATES, *National Monuments.*

Fort Fron·te·nac \-ˈfränt-ᵊn-ˌak, -ˈfrənt-\. French fort on site of modern Kingston (*q.v.*), Ontario, Canada; captured by British 1758.

Fort Gaines \-ˈgānz\. City, ⊗ of Clay co., SW Georgia; pop. (1970c) 1255; cotton, lumber.

Fort Gar·ry \-ˈga(ə)r-ē, -ˈge(ə)r-ē\. Fort and post of Hudson's Bay Company in Canada, established 1821 at junction of Assiniboine and Red rivers; now Winnipeg (*q.v.*).

Fort George \-ˈjȯ(ə)rj\. River, cen. and W Quebec, Canada; 480 m. long; flows W into lower James Bay.

Fort George G. Meade \-ˌjȯ(ə)rj-jē-ˈmēd\. Military reservation, NW Anne Arundel co., Maryland; 7500 acres; estab. 1917; during World War II site of a WAC training school.

Fort Good Hope *or* **Good Hope.** Trading station on lower Mackenzie river, NW Mackenzie dist., Northwest Territories, Canada, ab. 130 m. NW of Norman Wells; pop. (1966c) 335.

Forth \ˈfō(ə)rth, ˈfȯ(ə)rth\. River, S cen. Scotland; 116 m. long; rises on NE slope of Ben Lomond, flows E into **Firth of Forth** *or anc.* **Bo·do·tria** \bə-ˈdō-trē-ə\, an estuary extending inland from North Sea 48 m. and varying in width from 1½ to 17½ m. The Firth is spanned by a cantilever bridge 5330 ft. long from Dalmeny (on S side ab. 9 m. W of Edinburgh) to Queensferry.

Fort Hall \-ˈhȯl\. **1** Former fort at a junction point on the Oregon Trail, on Snake river N of Pocatello, SE Idaho; original fort built 1834. Present village of Fort Hall nearby (to E) is seat of Fort Hall Indian Reservation agency. **2** Town and post, S cen. Kenya, E Africa, on Tana river 56 m. NE of Nairobi; pop. (1962c) 5389; alt. 4410 ft.

Fort Hen·ry \-ˈhen-rē\. Locality, Stewart co., NW Tennessee, on Tennessee river S of Fort Donelson National Military Park; site of Fort Henry, captured by Grant Feb. 6, 1862.

Fort Hertz. See PUTAO.

Fort Hughes \-ˈhyüz\. See CORREGIDOR.

Fort Humphreys. See FORT BELVOIR.

For·tín Bo·que·rón \fȯr-ˌtēn-ˌbō-kə-ˈrän\. Fort in S Boquerón dept., W Paraguay, in the Chaco Boreal.

Fort Jameson. See CHIPATA.

Fort Jef·fer·son National Monument \-ˈjef-ər-sən-\. See UNITED STATES, *National Monuments.*

Fort Johnston. See MANGOCHE.

Fort Kent \-ˈkent\. Town, Aroostook co., N Maine, on St. John river across from New Brunswick, Canada; pop. (1970c) 4575; port of entry.

Fort Knox \-ˈnäks\. Military reservation, N Hardin co., N cen. Kentucky; 33,000 acres; established 1917 as training camp, permanent military post since 1932; cavalry; Godman Air Force Base; location since 1936 of U.S. Gold Bullion Depository.

Fort–La·my \ˌfȯr-lə-ˈmē\. Town, ✱ of Chad, N cen. Africa, on Chari river in SW part of republic; pop. (1968c) 135,502; livestock market; handicraft industries; coll. of veterinary science (1962).

Fort Lang·ley National Historic Park \-ˈlaŋ-lē-\. See CANADA, *National Historic Parks.*

Fort Lau·der·dale \-ˈlȯd-ər-ˌdāl\. City, ⊗ of Broward co., SE Florida, on Atlantic Ocean 25 m. N of Miami; pop. (1970c) 139,590; Fort Lauderdale Univ. (1940), Broward Junior Coll. (1960); yachting and fishing resort; deepwater harbor of Port Everglades is just S; established as a military post 1838.

Fort Leav·en·worth \-ˈlev-ən-ˌwərth\. Military reservation, Leavenworth co., E Kansas, adjoining Leavenworth; 8000 acres; one of oldest military posts W of the Mississippi, estab. 1827; federal penitentiary; Command and General Staff School.

Fort Le·Boeuf \-lə-ˈbəf\. Fort erected by the French 1753 on site of Waterford, Pennsylvania, just S of Erie; visited 1753 by Washington with message from Gov. Dinwiddie of Virginia.

Fort Lee \-ˈlē\. Borough, Bergen co., NE corner of New Jersey, on Hudson river 10 m. NNE of Jersey City; pop. (1970c) 30,631; motion picture film processing; site of fort built, with Fort Washington, to defend West Point in Revolutionary War, and abandoned after fall of Fort Washington 1776; one of the cradles of motion picture industry; George Washington Bridge (completed 1931).

Fort Len·nox National Historic Park \-ˈlen-əks-\. See CANADA, *National Historic Parks.*

Fort Lew·is \-ˈlü-əs\. Military post, Pierce co., W cen. Washington, SW of Tacoma; 62,000 acres; established 1917.

Fort Li·ard \-ˈlē-ˌärd\ *or* **Liard.** Trading post, SW Mackenzie dist., Northwest Territories, Canada, on the Liard river ab. 130 m. SSW of Fort Simpson; pop. (1966c) 177.

Fort Lou·doun Dam \-ˈlau̇d-ᵊn-\. See table at TENNESSEE VALLEY AUTHORITY.

Fort Lup·ton \-ˈləp-tən\. Town, Weld co., N Colorado, on South Platte river 25 m. N of Denver; pop. (1970c) 2489; sugar beets.

Fort Mc·Clel·lan \-mə-ˈklel-ən\. Military reservation, Calhoun co., NE Alabama; 20,000 acres; infantry; National Guard.

Fort Mc·Hen·ry National Monument \-mək-ˈhen-rē-, -mə-ˈken-\. See UNITED STATES, *National Monuments.*

Fort Mac·leod \-mə-ˈklau̇d\ *also* **Macleod.** Town, Alberta, Canada, on Oldman river 28 m. W of Lethbridge; pop. (1971p) 2725; wheat; livestock.

Fort Mc·Mur·ray \-mək-ˈmər-ē\. Town, NE Alberta, W Canada, on Athabaska river; pop. (1971p) 6749.

Fort Mc·Pher·son \-mək-ˈfər-sən\ *or* **McPherson.** Trading station, NW Mackenzie dist., Northwest Territories, Canada, on Peel river S of Aklavik; pop. (1966c) 654.

Fort Mad·i·son \-ˈmad-ə-sən\. City, a ⊗ of Lee co., SE corner of Iowa, on the Mississippi; pop. (1970c) 13,996; truck trailers, cement, paper products.

Fort Malden. See AMHERSTBURG.

Fort Mal·den National Historical Park \-ˈmȯl-dən-\. See CANADA, *National Historic Parks.*

Fort Mar·i·on National Monument \-ˈmer-ē-ən-, -ˈmar-\. See SAINT AUGUSTINE.

Fort Ma·tan·zas National Monument \-mə-ˈtan-zəs-\. See UNITED STATES, *National Monuments.*

Fort Max·im Gor·ki \-ˌmak-səm-ˈgȯr-kē\. Former defense fort of Sevastopol, Crimean Oblast, Ukrainian S.S.R., U.S.S.R.; after fierce fighting taken by Germans June 17, 1942.

Fort Meade \-ˈmed\. City, Polk co., cen. Florida penin., 25 m. S of Lakeland; pop. (1970c) 4374; site of military post during Seminole War.

Fort Meigs \-ˈmegz\. Former fort at rapids in Maumee river, NW Ohio; besieged unsuccessfully May 1–9, 1813 by force of British and Indians.

Fort Mill \-ˈmil\. Town, York co., N South Carolina, 7 m. NNE of Rock Hill; pop. (1970c) 4503; textile mills; corn, wheat.

Fort Mills \-ˈmilz\. Former fort on Corregidor I. at entrance to Manila Bay, Phil.

Fort Mims \-ˈmimz\. Temporary stockade erected near junction of Alabama and Tombigbee rivers, Alabama; scene of a massacre of settlers by Creek Indians under their chief, William Weatherford, Aug. 30, 1813.

Fort Mitch·ell \-ˈmich-əl\. City, Kenton co., N Kentucky, 3 m. S of Cincinnati, Ohio; pop. (1970c) 6982.

Fort Mon·mouth \-ˈmän-məth\. Military post, E Monmouth co., E cen. New Jersey, SE of Red Bank; Signal School.

Fort Mon·roe \-mən-ˈrō\ *or* **Fortress Monroe.** Military post and post office, Hampton, SE Virginia, at Old Point Comfort at entrance to Hampton Roads; before 1946 site of coast artillery school; Jefferson Davis held prisoner here 1865–67 after Civil War.

Fort Mor·gan \-ˈmȯr-gən\. City, ⊗ of Morgan co., NE Colorado, on South Platte river 70 m. ENE of Denver; pop. (1970c) 7594; auto accessories; refines beet sugar; creamery.

Fort Moul·trie \-ˈmül-trē, -ˈmōl-\. Fort in Charleston harbor, SE South Carolina, on N side of entrance, on Sullivans I.; evacuated by Union garrison Dec. 26, 1860 to strengthen Fort Sumter; seized by state authorities Dec. 27, 1860.

Fort My·er \-ˈmī(-ə)r\. U.S. military reservation, N Virginia, 6 m. N of Alexandria.

Fort My·ers \-ˈmī(-ə)rz\. City, ⊗ of Lee co., SW Florida, on estuary of Caloosahatchee river just S of Charlotte Harbor; pop. (1970c) 27,351; electronic equipment, lumber, cigars; ships fruit and vegetables; Edison Junior Coll. (1962); fort established 1850 and used as a Union base in Civil War.

Fort Nas·sau \-ˈnas-ˌȯ\. 1 Fort built 1623 by the Dutch on left bank of Delaware river opp. site of Philadelphia, Pa.; used as trading post; abandoned 1651.

2 Fort built 1614 by the Dutch on Hudson river just S of present city of Albany, N.Y.; destroyed 1617 by flood; replaced by Fort Orange 1624 (see ALBANY 7).

Fort–National. See L'ARBAA NAÏT IRATHEN.

Fort Ne·ces·si·ty \-ni-ˈses-ə-tē\. Small fortification erected 1754 by English colonial expeditionary force under Major George Washington in Great Meadows (*q.v.*); attacked by French and Indians, forced to surrender July 3, 1754; site has been set aside as **Fort Necessity Battlefield Site:** see UNITED STATES, *National Historical Parks.*

Fort Nel·son \-ˈnel-sən\. 1 River, N British Columbia, Canada; 260 m. long; has several headstreams rising on E slopes of Rocky Mts. in N British Columbia; flows NW into Liard river.

2 Station, NE British Columbia, Canada, 225 m. N of Dawson Creek on Fort Nelson river, 58°49′N, 122°39′W; pop. (1966c) 954; formerly a Hudson's Bay Company post, now an important station on Alaska Highway; gas fields.

Fort Ni·ag·a·ra \-nī-ˈag-(ə-)rə\. Fort at mouth of Niagara river, New York; successively French, British, and American; again captured by British 1813 and returned to United States 1815.

Fort Nor·man \-ˈnȯr-mən\ *or* **Norman.** Trading station on right bank of Mackenzie river, W Mackenzie dist., Northwest Territories, Canada, at mouth of Great Bear river SE of Norman Wells; pop. (1966c) 216.

Fort Ogle·thorpe \-ˈōg-əl-ˌthȯrp\. Town, Catoosa and Walker cos., NW Georgia, 20 m. NW of Dalton; pop. (1970c) 3869.

Fort Olimpo. See FUERTE OLIMPO.

Fort Or·ange \-ˈȯr-inj, -ˈär-, -ənj\. Former Dutch fort on site of modern Albany, N.Y. (*q.v.*).

Fort Pat·rick Hen·ry Dam \-ˌpat-rik-ˈhen-rē-\. See table at TENNESSEE VALLEY AUTHORITY.

Fort Payne \-ˈpān\. City, ⊗ of De Kalb co., NE Alabama, 35 m. NE of Gadsden; pop. (1970c) 8435; brick, lumber; cotton; poultry.

Fort Pick·ens \-ˈpik-ənz\. Fort on Santa Rosa I. at entrance to Pensacola harbor, Florida; held by Union troops during Civil War (1861–65).

Fort Pierce \-ˈpi(ə)rs\. City, ⊗ of St. Lucie co., E Florida, on Indian River (lagoon) 30 m. NE of Lake Okeechobee; pop. (1970c) 29,721; fertilizer, lumber; fruit canning; Indian River Junior Coll. (1960); fort built originally 1838 as a defense against Indians; amphibious training base in World War II.

Fort Pierre \-ˈpi(ə)r\. City, ⊗ of Stanley co., cen. South Dakota; pop. (1970c) 1449; settled 1817 (see SOUTH DAKOTA).

Fort Pil·low \-ˈpil-ō\. Fort on Mississippi river 40 m. N of Memphis, Tennessee; scene of Union defeat Apr. 12, 1864.

Fort Pitt \-ˈpit\. Name given Fort Duquesne after capture by British 1758. See PITTSBURGH.

Fort Plain \-ˈplān\. Village, Montgomery co., E New York, on Mohawk river 23 m. W of Amsterdam; pop. (1970c) 2809; settled by German Palatines 1722; textiles; site of Fort Plain (1776) nearby.

Fort Pont·char·train du Dé·troit \-ˌpän-chər-ˌtrān-dü-dē-ˈtrȯit\. See DETROIT 2.

Fort Por·tal \-ˈpōrt-ᵊl, -ˈpȯrt-\. Town, Uganda, E Africa, 160 m. W of Entebbe; pop. (1969c) 8300.

Fort Presque Isle \-pre-ˈskī(ə)l, -ˈskē(ə)l\. French fort on site of Erie, Pennsylvania; built 1753, burned by Indians 1763.

Fort Prince of Wales National Historic Park \-ˌprins-əv-ˈwālz-\. See CANADA, *National Historic Parks.*

Fort Prov·i·dence \-ˈpräv-əd-ən(t)s\ *or* **Providence.** Trading post, S Mackenzie dist., Northwest Territories, Canada, on Mackenzie river at its outlet from Great Slave Lake; pop. (1966c) 378.

Fort Pu·las·ki National Monument \-pə-ˈlas-kē-, -pyü-\. See UNITED STATES, *National Monuments.*

Fort Ran·dolph \-ˈran-ˌdälf\. U.S. fort at Caribbean terminus of Panama Canal, Canal Zone, on E side of entrance to Limon Bay.

Fort Re·cov·ery \-ri-ˈkəv-(ə-)rē\. Village, Mercer co., W Ohio, 41 m. SW of Lima; pop. (1970c) 1348; on site of Gen. Arthur St. Clair's defeat by Indians 1791 and of Gen. Anthony Wayne's "recovery" of the area 1793.

Fort Res·o·lu·tion \-rez-ə-ˈlü-shən\ *or* **Resolution.** Trading post, S Mackenzie dist., Northwest Territories, Canada, at mouth of Slave river on S shore of Great Slave Lake; formerly a fort of Hudson's Bay Company.

Fortress Monroe. See FORT MONROE.

Fort·ress Mountain \ˈfȯr-trəs-\. Peak, cen. Park co., NW Wyoming; 12,073 ft.

Fortress of Lou·is·bourg National Historic Park \-ˈlü-əs-ˌbərg-\. See CANADA, *National Historic Parks.*

Fort Ri·ley \-ˈrī-lē\. Military reservation, Riley and Geary cos., E Kansas; 24,000 acres; Cavalry School, organized 1891.

Fort Rodd Hill National Historic Park \-ˈräd-\. See CANADA, *National Historic Parks.*

Fort Rosebery. See MANSA.

Fort Saint Da·vid \-sānt-ˈdā-vəd, -sənt-\. Ruins of British fort on Coromandel Coast, Tamil Nadu, SE India, just N of town of Cuddalore; at first a small fort (Tegnapatam) built by a Hindu merchant; 1677 became possession of Marathas, who sold it to the English 1690; 1746 became British headquarters for southern India; Clive appointed its governor 1756; captured by French 1758, 1782; finally passed to British 1785.

Fort Sainte Anne \-sānt-ˈan, -sənt-\. Fort on Isle La Motte, Lake Champlain, NW Vermont; built by French; first settlement in Vermont (only temporary).

Fort Saint Fré·dér·ic \-sānt-ˈfrəd-(ə)rik, -sənt-\. See CROWN POINT 2.

Fort Saint George. See MADRAS.

Fort Saint John \-sānt-ˈjän, -sənt-\. Town, NE British Columbia, Canada, ab. 40 m. NW of Dawson Creek on Peace river; pop. (1971p) 8243; oil wells.

Fort San Lo·ren·zo \-ˌsan-lə-ˈrenz-ō\. United States fort at mouth of Chagres river, Canal Zone, W of Limon Bay.

Fort Sas·katch·e·wan \-sə-ˈskach-ə-wən, -sa-, -ˌwän\. Town, Alberta, Canada, 18 m. NE of Edmonton; pop. (1971p) 5743; glass; nickel refining; agriculture.

Fort Schuy·ler \-ˈskī-lər\. 1 Military post at Throgs Neck, New York; one of N defenses of New York harbor; estab. 1856.

2 Fort, Rome, New York. See FORT STANWIX.

Fort Scott \-ˈskät\. Industrial city, ⊗ of Bourbon co., SE Kansas, 85 m. S of Kansas City; pop. (1970c) 8967; coal mines, stone quarries; Fort Scott Community Junior Coll. (1919).

Fort Sher·i·dan \-ˈsher-əd-ᵊn\. Village in Lake co., Illinois, on Lake Michigan 27 m. N of Chicago; U.S. military post; in World War II WAC (Women's Army Corps) Training School.

Fort Sher·man \-ˈshər-mən\. U.S. fort at Caribbean terminus of Panama Canal, Canal Zone, on W side of entrance to Limon Bay.

Fort Shev·chen·ko \-shif-ˈcheŋk-ə\ *or formerly* **Fort Aleksan·drovsk** \-ˌal-ek-ˈsan-ˌdrəvsk\. Soviet military station, Guryev Oblast, SW Kazakh S.S.R., U.S.S.R., at tip of Mangyshlak Penin. on NE shore of Caspian Sea; pop. (1963e) 22,400.

Fort Sill \-ˈsil\. Military post and reservation, Comanche co., SW Oklahoma, ab. 5 m. N of Lawton; estab. 1869; field artillery school; scene of surrender of the Comanches and Kiowa Indians c. 1875.

Fort Simp·son \-ˈsim(p)-sən\ *or* **Simpson.** Trading post, SW Mackenzie dist., Northwest Territories, Canada, on Mackenzie river where it is joined by the Liard.

Fort Smith \-ˈsmith\. 1 City, a ⊗ of Sebastian co., W Arkansas, at confluence of Arkansas and Poteau rivers on Oklahoma border; pop. (1970c) 62,802; auto bodies, sheet metal, optical equipment, refrigerators, glass; Westark Junior Coll. (1928); U.S. Army post 1817–71; incorp. as city 1851.

2 Town, S Mackenzie dist., Northwest Territories, Canada, on Slave river at Alberta boundary; pop. (1971p) 2372; former headquarters of Northwest Territories.

Fort Snel·ling \-ˈsnel-iŋ\. Military post in Minnesota, bet. Minnesota and Mississippi rivers S of Minneapolis; site acquired by Zebulon Pike 1805; fort, called Fort St. Anthony until 1825, built by Josiah Snelling 1820.

Fort Stan·wix \-ˈstan-wiks\. Fort on site of Rome, New York, built 1756, rebuilt 1758, by Gen. John Stanwix; called **Fort Schuy·ler** \-ˈskī-lər\ from 1776; treaty with Iroquois Indians signed here 1784.

Fort Stock·ton \-ˈstäk-tən\. City, ⊗ of Pecos co., W Texas, 73 m. SSW of Odessa; pop. (1970c) 8283; gas refining; oil wells.

Fort Sum·ner \-ˈsəm-nər\. Village, ⊗ of De Baca co., E cen. New Mexico, 58 m. W of Clovis; pop. (1970c) 1615; livestock; grave of Billy the Kid nearby.

Fort Sum·ter \-ˈsəm(p)-tər\. Fort on S side of entrance to Charleston harbor, South Carolina; object of Confederate attack Apr. 12–13, 1861 which began the Civil War; **Fort Sumter National Monument** established 1948: see UNITED STATES, *National Monuments.*

Fort Thom·as \-ˈtäm-əs\. Residential city, Campbell co., N Kentucky, 5 m. SE of Covington; pop. (1970c) 16,338.

Fort Ticonderoga. See TICONDEROGA.

For·tu·na \fȯr-ˌt(y)ü-nə-, fər-\. City, Humboldt co., NW California, 14 m. S of Eureka; pop. (1970c) 4203; lumber mills; sheep and cattle ranching; dairy farming.

Fortuna Bay. Bay S of W end of St. Thomas I., U.S. Virgin Is., West Indies.

For·tu·nate Islands \ˌfȯrch-(ə-)nət-\ *or anc.* **For·tu·na·tae In·su·lae** \ˌfȯr-chə-ˌnāt-ē-ˈin(t)-sə-ˌlē\. In early times a name applied to Canary Is.

For·tune \ˈfȯr-chən\. Seaport, S Newfoundland, Canada, on S shore at mouth of Fortune Bay; pop. (1971p) 2138.

Fortune Bay. Inlet of Atlantic Ocean in S Newfoundland, Canada; ab. 80 m. long; extensive fishing grounds; scene 1878 of conflict bet. Newfoundland and Gloucester fishermen.

Fortune Island. See LONG CAY.

Fort Un·ion \-ˈyü-nyən\. Trading post, NE Montana on Missouri river near mouth of the Yellowstone; built 1828 by Kenneth McKenzie of the American Fur Company and orig. called Fort Floyd; dismantled 1868.

Fort Union National Monument. Ruined fort, S Mora co., NE New Mexico, N of Watrous; established 1851, became one of most important military posts in SW United States; a Confederate objective (not reached) in Civil War; evacuated 1891. See table at UNITED STATES, *National Monuments.*

Fort Valley. City, ⊗ of Peach co., cen. Georgia; pop. (1970c) 9251; chemicals, truck bodies; corn, peaches; Fort Valley State Coll. (1895).

Fort Van·cou·ver \-van-ˈkü-vər\. Western terminal of Oregon Trail, now the city of Vancouver, Washington, on Columbia river.

Fort Victoria. See VICTORIA 16.

Fort Wads·worth \-ˈwädz-ˌwərth\. Military post on Staten I. at entrance to New York Bay; estab. 1827.

Fort Wag·ner \-ˈwag-nər\. Fort on Morris I. in Charleston harbor, South Carolina; attacked by Union forces July 11 and 18, 1863; captured Sept. 7, 1863.

Fort Wal·ton Beach \-ˌwȯlt-ᵊn-\. City, Okaloosa co., NW Florida, E of Pensacola; pop. (1970c) 19,994.

Fort Wash·ing·ton \-ˈwȯsh-iŋ-tən, -ˈwäsh-\. Military post during American Revolution, on upper Manhattan I., New York, on Hudson; captured by British Nov. 16, 1776.

Fort Wayne \-ˈwān\. City, ⊗ of Allen co., NE Indiana, 105 m. NE of Indianapolis; pop. (1970c) 178,021; railroad center; manufactures electrical equipment, car wheels, motor trucks, tires, gasoline pumps, cranes and dredges; Concordia Senior Coll. (1839), Indiana Inst. of Technology (1930), Saint Francis Coll. (1890). Site originally occupied by Miami Indians and visited by La Salle 1670; French fur-trading post 1680; French fort built 1686, seized by British 1760, and lost to Indians under Pontiac; new fort built 1794 by Gen. Anthony Wayne, abandoned 1819; city chartered 1840.

Fort Wel·ling·ton \-ˈwel-iŋ-tən\. Town, NE Guyana, 51 m. by rail SE of Georgetown.

Fort Wellington National Historic Park. See CANADA, *National Historic Parks.*

Fort Wil·liam \-ˈwil-yəm\. 1 City, Ontario, Canada. See THUNDER BAY 5.

2 Burgh, Inverness co., NW Scotland, on Loch Linnhe; pop. (1971p) 4195; tourist center.

Fort Wood \-ˈwu̇d\. The Statue of Liberty National Monument on Liberty I., New York harbor, New York.

Fort Worth \-ˈwərth\. City, ⊗ of Tarrant co., N Texas, on Trinity river ab. 33 m. W of Dallas; pop. (1970c) 393,476; commercial and transportation center of stock-raising, agricultural, and oil-producing region; manufactures chemicals, flour, feed, oil-field equipment, metal products, aircraft, clothing; meat packing; Carswell Air Force Base; Texas Christian Univ. (1873), Texas Wesleyan Coll. (1890), Fort Worth Christian Coll. (1956), Tarrant County Junior Coll. (1965); Noble planetarium; settled around military post founded 1849.

Fort Wright–Look·out Heights \-ˈrīt-ˌlu̇k-au̇t-ˈ\. City, Kenton co., N Kentucky; pop. (1970c) 4819.

Fort Yates \-ˈyāts\. City, Sioux co., extreme S North Dakota, on Missouri river 50 m. S of Bismarck; pop. (1970c) 1153; Indian Agency headquarters for North and South Dakota.

For·ty Fort \ˈfȯrt-ē-\. Residential borough, Luzerne co., E Pennsylvania, 3 m. N of Wilkes-Barre; pop. (1970c) 6114. See WYOMING VALLEY.

Fort Yu·kon \-ˈyü-ˌkän\. Village and old trading station, E Alaska, at junction of Porcupine river with the Yukon.

Fort Zea·lan·dia \-zi-ˈlan-dē-ə\. Fort built by the Dutch near T'ai-nan on SW coast of Taiwan; besieged and captured by Koxinga 1662.

Forum Alieni. See FERRARA 2.

Forum Julii. 1 Commune, SE France. See FRÉJUS.

2 Former duchy, NE Italy. See FRIULI.

Forum Livii. See FORLÌ 2.

Fo–shan \ˈfō-ˈshän\ *or* **Nam·hoi** \ˈnäm-ˈhȯi\ *or* **Fat·shan** \ˈfät-ˈshän\. Commercial and industrial city, cen. Kwangtung prov., SE China, ab. 12 m. above Canton in Hsi delta; pop. (1958e) 120,000.

Fossa Claudia. See CHIOGGIA.

Fos·sa·no \fə-ˈsän-(ˌ)ō\. Commune, Cuneo prov., Piedmont, NW Italy, 13 m. NE of Cuneo; pop. (1968e) 21,465; episcopal see; mineral baths.

Fosse Way *or* **Foss Way** \ˈfäs-\. Ancient Roman road in Britain; extended from Lincoln in E cen. part to Exeter in SW, passing through Leicester and Bath and intersecting Watling Street in S cen. Britain.

Fos·sil \ˈfäs-əl\. Town, ⊗ of Wheeler co., N cen. Oregon, ab. 17 m. S of Condon; pop. (1970c) 511.

Fossil Mountain. Peak in Teton Range, W Teton co., NW Wyoming; 10,912 ft.

Fos·som·bro·ne \ˌfōs-ōm-ˈbrō-nā\. Commune, Pesaro e Urbino prov., Marches, cen. Italy, near Metauro river 18 m. SSE of Pesaro; pop. (1968e) 10,154; episcopal see.

Foss Way. See FOSSE WAY.

Fos·ter \ˈfȯs-tər, ˈfäs-\. 1 County in North Dakota. See table at NORTH DAKOTA.

2 Town, Providence co., N Rhode Island; pop. (1970c) 2626.

Foster Village. Town, Honolulu co., Hawaii; pop. (1970c) 3755.

Fos·to·ria \fō-ˈstōr-ē-ə, -ˈstȯr-\. Manufacturing city, Hancock, Seneca, and Wood cos., NW Ohio, 15 m. NE of Findlay; pop. (1970c) 16,307; iron castings; flour; stockyards, stone quarries; Fostoria glass first made here 1887 (company moved soon after its founding to Moundsville, West Virginia).

Foth·er·in·ghay \ˈfat͟h-ə-riŋ-ˌgā\. Village, Northamptonshire, England; castle where Mary, Queen of Scots was imprisoned Sept. 1586 to her execution Feb. 8, 1587.

Fou·gères \fü-ˈzhe(ə)r\. Manufacturing city, Ille-et-Vilaine dept., NW France, 29 m. NE of Rennes; pop. (1968c) 26,-045; granite quarries; one of chief centers of the Chouans during the Revolution.

Fou·ge·rolles \ˌfüzh-(ə-)ˈrȯl\. Town, Haute-Saône dept., E France, SW of Remiremont; pop. (1962c) 4234; manufactures kirsch.

Fou–hsin *or* **Fu·sin** \ˈfü-ˈshin\. City, Liaoning prov., NE China, WNW of Mukden.

Fou·la \ˈfü-lə\. One of Shetland Is., NE of N Scotland; pop. (1961c) 149; Old Norse language survived here until the early 19th cent.

Foul Bay \ˈfau̇(ə)l-\. Inlet of Red Sea on E coast of Egypt, at Tropic of Cancer.

Fou–ling *or* **Fow·ling** \ˈfō-ˈliŋ\. Town, SE Szechwan, S cen. China, on S bank of Yangtze, ab. 50 m. E of Chungking.

Foul·ness Point \ˌfau̇l-ˌnes-\. Cape on **Foulness Island,** Essex, SE coast of England, N of entrance to the Thames estuary; island has atomic weapons research station.

Foul·wind, Cape \-ˈfau̇(ə)l-ˌwind\. Cape on NW coast of South I., New Zealand, forming S side of Karamea Bight.

Foun·tain \ˈfau̇nt-ᵊn\. 1 County in Indiana. See table at INDIANA.

2 Town, El Paso co., E cen. Colorado, 11 m. SSE of Colorado Springs; pop. (1970c) 3515; stock raising.

Fountain City. Town, Wayne co., E Indiana, 9 m. N of Richmond; pop. (1970c) 2643.

Fountain Hill. Borough, Lehigh co., E Pennsylvania, on Lehigh river 4 m. E of Allentown; pop. (1970c) 5384.

Fountain Inn. Town, Greenville and Laurens cos., NW South Carolina, 16 m. SE of Greenville; pop. (1970c) 3391; agriculture; cotton mills.

Fountain Valley. City, Orange co., SW California, 28 m. SE of Los Angeles; pop. (1970c) 31,886.

Four Corners. Locality in SW United States, the point of intersection of 37°N with 109°W, the only place in U.S. where boundaries of four states—Colorado, New Mexico, Arizona, and Utah—come together.

Four Forest Cantons, Lake of the. See LUCERNE, LAKE OF.

Four Forest Cantons, The. Cantons, Switzerland. See FOREST CANTONS, THE FOUR.

Four Lakes. Chain of four connected lakes in Dane co., S Wisconsin, named Mendota (or Fourth Lake), Monona (or Third Lake), Waubesa (or Second Lake), and Kegonsa (or First Lake).

Four League Bay \-ˈlēg-\. Inlet of Gulf of Mexico on W coast of Terrebonne parish, SE Louisiana.

Four·mies \fu̇(ə)r-ˈmē\. Commune, Nord dept., N France, SE of Lille; pop. (1968c) 15,117; manufacturing of glass, textiles, shoes.

Four Mountains, Islands of the. See ISLANDS OF THE FOUR MOUNTAINS.

Foúrnoi. See PHOURNOI.

Four Peaks. Mountain, E Maricopa co., S cen. Arizona; 7645 ft.

Fou·ta Djal·lon *also* **Fu·ta Jal·lon** \ˌfüt-ə-jə-ˈlōn\. Mountainous district, W Guinea, W Africa; highest point 4970 ft.; ab. 30,000 sq. m.; source of many streams, esp. the Niger and Senegal; inhabitants chiefly Fulahs; chief towns Labé and Timbo.

Foux, Cap à. See CHEVAL BLANC, POINTE DU.

Fo·veaux Strait \ˌfō-(ˌ)vō-, fə-ˌvō-\. Channel bet. South I. and Stewart I., New Zealand; 18 to 20 m. wide.

Fowl·er \ˈfaủl-ər\. 1 Town, Fresno co., S cen. California, 10 m. SE of Fresno; pop. (1970c) 2239; fruit packing.
2 Town, ⊗ of Benton co., W Indiana, 25 m. NW of Lafayette; pop. (1970c) 2643.

Fowliang. See CHING-TE-CHEN.

Fowling. See FOU-LING.

Fox \ˈfäks\. 1 River, SE Wisconsin and NE Illinois; ab. 220 m. long; flows S to the Illinois river at Ottawa in La Salle co., N Illinois.
2 River, SE cen. Wisconsin; 175 m. long; rises in N Columbia co., flows SW to a point ab. 1½ m. from Wisconsin river with which it is connected by canal (see PORTAGE 5), then N and NE into Lake Winnebago and out of N end of lake into Green Bay at city of Green Bay.

Fox Basin. See FOXE BASIN.

Fox·boro \ˈfäks-ˌbər-ə, -ˌbə-rə\. Town, Norfolk co., E Massachusetts, 11 m. W of Brockton; pop. (1970c) 14,218; manufactures time recording and controlling devices.

Fox Channel. See FOXE BASIN.

Fox Chapel. Borough, Allegheny co., SW Pennsylvania, 9 m. NE of Pittsburgh; pop. (1970c) 5310.

Foxe Basin \ˈfäks-\ *or formerly* **Fox Basin.** Large body of water bet. Melville Penin. and W Baffin I., E Franklin dist., Northwest Territories, Canada; connects with N end of Hudson Bay by **Foxe Channel** (*formerly* **Fox Channel;** ab. 110 m. wide), bet. Southampton I. and **Foxe Peninsula** (*formerly* **Fox Peninsula**), SW part of Baffin I.

Fox Islands. 1 Island group off SW tip of Alaska Penin., E Aleutian Is.; includes Unimak, Akutan, Unalaska, and Umnak Is.: chief settlements Unalaska and Dutch Harbor (*q.v.*).
2 Two islands, **North Fox Island** and **South Fox Island,** in N Lake Michigan, forming part of Leelanau co., NW Michigan.

Fox Lake. Village, Lake co., NE Illinois, 16 m. W of Waukegan; pop. (1970c) 4511; beverages, cement blocks, plastics; diversified agriculture.

Fox Peninsula. See FOXE BASIN.

Fox Point. Village, Milwaukee co., Wisconsin, on Lake Michigan, 10 m. N of Milwaukee; pop. (1970c) 7939.

Foyle \ˈfȯi(ə)l\. River, N Ireland; 16 m. long; formed by confluence of Finn and Mourne rivers on border bet. Eire and Northern Ireland; flows N past Londonderry and expands into the estuary **Lough Foyle** \ˈläk-, ˈläḵ-\, 18 m. long, on boundary bet. co. Derry, Northern Ireland, and co. Donegal, Eire.

Foynes \ˈfȯinz\. Village, NW coast of co. Limerick, SW Eire, on S shore of Shannon estuary 22 m. W of Limerick; pop. (1961c) 360; former airfield, now largely superseded for transatlantic flights by Shannon airfield at Rineanna.

Frack·ville \ˈfrak-ˌvil\. Borough, Schuylkill co., E cen. Pennsylvania, 7 m. N of Pottsville; pop. (1970c) 5445.

Fra·go·so Cay \frə-ˌgō-sə-ˈkē, -zə-, -ˈkā\. Island off NE coast of Las Villas prov., W cen. Cuba.

Fraile, El. See EL FRAILE.

Frakes, Mount \-ˈfrāks\. Mountain, Antarctica, 76°48′S, 117°42′W; 12,064 ft.

Fra·me·ries \fram-ˈrē\. Commune, Hainaut prov., SW Belgium, ab. 5 m. SSW of Mons; pop. (1969e) 11,452.

Fra·ming·ham \ˈfrā-miŋ-ˌham\. Manufacturing town, Middlesex co., NE Massachusetts, 18 m. WSW of Boston; pop. (1970c) 64,048; chemicals, automobiles, footwear; poultry farms; Massachusetts State Coll. at Framingham (1839), Cushing General Hospital.

Fran·ca \ˈfraŋ-kə\. City, NE São Paulo state, SE Brazil, on railroad 160 m. N of Campinas; munic. pop. (1968e) 67,284.

Fran·ca·vil·la Fon·ta·na \ˌfraŋ-kə-ˈvil-ə-fən-ˈtän-ə, ˌfräŋ-kə-ˈvēl-\. Commune, Brindisi prov., Apulia, SE Italy, 20 m. WSW of Brindisi; pop. (1968e) 31,241; cathedral; imperial palace.

France \ˈfran(t)s\ *or officially* **Ré·pu·blique fran·çaise** \rā-pü-blēk-fräⁿ-sāz\; *Ital.* **Fran·cia** \ˈfrän-ˌchä\ *or Span.* **Francia** \ˈfrän-(ˌ)thyä, -(ˌ)syä\; *earlier* **Gaul** \ˈgȯl\ *or Fr.* **Gaule** \ˈgōl\ *or Lat.* **Gal·lia** \ˈgal-ē-ə\. Republic of W Europe, bounded on N by English Channel, on NE by Belgium and Luxembourg, on E by West Germany, Switzerland, and Italy, on S by the Mediterranean Sea, Spain, and Andorra, and on W by Bay of Biscay; principality of Monaco forms an enclave on Mediterranean coast; 210,038 sq. m.; pop. (1971e) 51,027,000, (1968c) 49,778,540; ✱ Paris. *Chief mountains:* Alps (*q.v.*) on SE (Italian border), Pyrenees on S (Spanish border), Jura Mts. on E (Swiss border), Vosges in NE, Massif Central and Auvergne Mts. in SE cen. part; highest point Mont Blanc 15,781 ft., in the Alps. *Chief rivers:* Seine, with its tributaries the Yonne, Marne, and Oise, flowing into English Channel; Loire, Garonne, and Adour, flowing into Bay of Biscay; Rhone, with its chief tributary the Saône, flowing S into Mediterranean Sea. *Islands:* Île d'Ouessant (Ushant) off tip of Brittany; Belle-Île, Noirmoutier, Yeu, Ré, and Oléron in Bay of Biscay; Hyères Is. in Mediterranean Sea. *Chief products:* Wheat, barley, potatoes, wine; livestock; bauxite, coal, iron ore, oil, natural gas; manufacturing: iron and steel, chemicals, textiles, transportation equipment; engineering and metallurgical industries; food processing, power production; tourism. *Chief cities:* Paris, Marseilles, Lyons, Toulouse, Nice, Bordeaux, Nantes, Strasbourg, Saint-Étienne, Lille. Divided into the following 95 departments (for pronunciation of their names, see their individual entries):

NAME	AREA (sq. m.)	POP. (1968c)	CAPITAL
Ain	2,222	339,262	Bourg
Aisne	2,849	526,346	Laon
Allier	2,829	386,533	Moulins
Alpes-de-Haute Provence	2,681	104,813	Digne
Alpes-Maritimes	1,658	722,070	Nice
Ardèche	2,132	256,927	Privas
Ardennes	2,014	309,380	Mézières
Ariège	1,888	138,478	Foix
Aube	2,317	270,325	Troyes
Aude	2,406	278,323	Carcassonne
Aveyron	3,372	281,568	Rodez
Bas-Rhin	1,848	827,367	Strasbourg
Belfort, Territoire de	235	118,450	Belfort
Bouches-du-Rhône	1,974	1,470,271	Marseilles
Calvados	2,137	519,695	Caen
Cantal	2,217	169,330	Aurillac
Charente	2,298	331,016	Angoulême
Charente-Maritime	2,644	483,622	La Rochelle
Cher	2,791	304,601	Bourges
Corrèze	2,263	237,858	Tulle
Corse	3,352	269,831	Ajaccio
Côte-d'Or	3,384	421,192	Dijon
Côtes-du-Nord	2,655	506,102	Saint-Brieuc
Creuse	2,146	156,876	Guéret
Deux-Sèvres	2,318	326,462	Niort
Dordogne	3,546	374,073	Périgueux
Doubs	2,019	426,363	Besançon
Drôme	2,519	342,891	Valence
Essonne	699	674,157	Évry
Eure	2,318	383,385	Évreux
Eure-et-Loir	2,269	302,207	Chartres
Finistère	2,620	768,929	Quimper
Gard	2,258	478,544	Nîmes
Gers	2,415	181,577	Auch
Gironde	3,861	1,009,390	Bordeaux
Haute-Garonne	2,433	690,712	Toulouse
Haute-Loire	1,917	208,337	Le Puy
Haute-Marne	2,400	214,336	Chaumont
Hautes-Alpes	2,131	91,790	Gap
Haute-Saône	2,063	214,176	Vesoul
Haute-Savoie	1,696	378,550	Annecy
Hautes-Pyrénées	1,740	225,730	Tarbes

NAME	AREA (sq. m.)	POP. (1968c)	CAPITAL
Haute-Vienne	2,128	341,589	Limoges
Haut-Rhin	1,360	585,018	Colmar
Hauts-de-Seine	63	1,461,619	Nanterre
Hérault	2,360	591,397	Montpellier
Ille-et-Vilaine	2,609	652,722	Rennes
Indre	2,617	247,178	Chateâuroux
Indre-et-Loire	2,364	437,870	Tours
Isère	2,886	768,450	Grenoble
Jura	1,934	233,547	Lons-le-Saunier
Landes	3,566	277,381	Mont-de-Marsan
Loire	1,843	722,383	Saint-Étienne
Loire-Atlantique	2,661	861,452	Nantes
Loiret	2,603	430,629	Orléans
Loir-et-Cher	2,438	267,896	Blois
Lot	2,019	151,198	Cahors
Lot-et-Garonne	2,069	290,592	Agen
Lozère	1,995	77,258	Mende
Maine-et-Loire	2,753	584,709	Angers
Manche	2,296	451,939	Saint-Lô
Marne	3,152	485,388	Châlons-sur-Marne
Mayenne	1,997	252,762	Laval
Meurthe-et-Moselle	2,021	705,413	Nancy
Meuse	2,402	209,513	Bar-le-Duc
Morbihan	2,611	540,474	Vannes
Moselle	2,399	971,314	Metz
Nièvre	2,640	247,702	Nevers
Nord	2,216	2,417,899	Lille
Oise	2,261	540,988	Beauvais
Orne	2,355	288,524	Alençon
Paris, Ville-de-	41	2,590,771	Paris
Pas-de-Calais	2,563	1,397,159	Arras
Puy-de-Dôme	3,071	547,743	Clermont-Ferrand
Pyrénées-Atlantiques	2,946	508,734	Pau
Pyrénées-Orientales	1,578	281,976	Perpignan
Rhône	1,241	1,325,611	Lyons
Saône-et-Loire	3,307	550,362	Mâcon
Sarthe	2,397	461,839	Le Mans
Savoie	2,330	288,921	Chambéry
Seine-et-Marne	2,284	604,340	Melun
Seine-Maritime	2,415	1,113,977	Rouen
Seine-St-Denis	91	1,251,792	Bobigny
Somme	2,384	512,113	Amiens
Tarn	2,221	332,011	Albi
Tarn-et-Garonne	1,435	183,572	Montauban
Val-de-Marne	94	1,121,340	Créteil
Val-d'Oise	482	693,269	Pontoise
Var	2,316	555,926	Draguignan
Vaucluse	1,377	353,966	Avignon
Vendée	2,594	421,250	La Roche-sur-Yon
Vienne	2,697	340,256	Poitiers
Vosges	2,267	388,201	Épinal
Yonne	2,867	283,376	Auxerre
Yvelines	877	853,386	Versailles

French overseas departments include: French Guiana, Guadeloupe, Martinique, and Réunion (*qq.v.*).

History: S part (Gallia Narbonensis) Roman province from 121 B.C.; N and cen. part conquered by Julius Caesar 58–51 B.C. See GAUL 2. Almost all came under kingdom established 481 A.D. by Salian Franks under Clovis (Merovingians); as Frankish empire under Charlemagne (768–814) included much of Saxon lands to E, but after his death new conquests given up by Partition of Verdun 843. During medieval feudal period, in which central authority was merely nominal, divided into domains (Normandy, Aquitaine, Burgundy, Flanders, etc.); after Norman Conquest of England 1066 duchy of Normandy in personal union with England; later also lost (to English Angevin kings, 1154–1399) Maine, Brittany, and most of Aquitaine; in course of Hundred Years' War (1337–1453) regained all of these lands except Calais (regained 1558); at end of Thirty Years' War (Treaty of Westphalia 1648) territory did not include Netherlands and Franche-Comté (both Spanish), Lorraine or Savoy; power decreased by Treaty of Paris ending Seven Years' War 1763. Royal government overthrown by French Revolution 1789, country becoming in turn a republic (First Republic 1792–99), the Consulate (1799–1804), an empire (First Empire 1804–15); during period of Napoleonic Wars (1796–1815), acquired by conquest most of W and cen. Europe, but lost all after final defeat of Napoleon at Waterloo 1815. Again became monarchy under Bourbons, but monarchy overthrown by revolution of 1848 and succeeded in turn by Second Republic (1848–52), Second Empire (1852–70), and Third Republic, established 1870, a result of French defeat in Franco-Prussian War (1870–71); N part of country ravaged by fighting in World War I (1914–18). In World War II conquered and controlled 1940–44 by Germans who divided it into "occupied" (N and W) and "unoccupied" (S) zones, the latter nominally under a French government with capital at Vichy, repudiated by the Fighting French (called Free French prior to July 14, 1942) under Charles de Gaulle, head of the French National Committee, which actively continued resistance to Axis forces and assumed authority over liberated French territories; country invaded by Allies (in Normandy June 6, 1944, on Mediterranean coast Aug. 15, 1944) and completely liberated by Sept. 1944; under provisional government until establishment of Fourth Republic 1945; member of UN 1945, NATO 1949, EEC 1958; intervened militarily in Egypt (Suez Crisis) 1956; Fifth Republic established under the constitution of Oct. 4, 1958 (see FRENCH COMMUNITY); relinquished control over Algeria 1962 following nationalist rebellion against French rule 1954–61; withdrew from integrated NATO command system 1966; resignation of President Charles de Gaulle April 1969, following defeat of referendum on constitutional reforms.

Fran·cés, Cape \-frän-ˈses\. Cape on SW coast of Pinar del Río prov., W Cuba, S of Cortés Bay.

Francés, Point. Cape on SW coast of Isle of Pines, Caribbean Sea; encloses Siguanea Bay.

Francés Vie·jo, Cape \-frän-ˌses-vē-ˈe-(ˌ)hō\. Cape, N coast of Hispaniola I., in Dominican Republic.

France·ville \fräⁿs-ˈvēl, ˈfran(t)s-ˌvil\. Town, SE Gabon, on a tributary of the Ogooué river.

Franche–Com·té \ˌfräⁿsh-kōⁿ-ˈtā\. Historical region of E cen. France; bounded anciently on N by Lorraine, E by Swiss Confederation, W by duchy of Burgundy and S by Savoy; ✱ Besançon; included in original kingdom of Burgundy founded 5th cent. A.D.; later became county of Burgundy as distinct from duchy of Burgundy; part of kingdom of Arles; belonged to Holy Roman Empire from 12th cent.; brought under control of duchy of Burgundy by Philip the Bold 1384; passed to Spanish Hapsburgs by marriage; occupied 1667 and 1674 by Louis XIV of France to whom Spain finally ceded it 1678; a province of France until the Revolution.

Franchise. See ARRAS.

Fran·cia \ˈfran-chē-ə\. 1 The kingdom of the Franks (Austrasia, Neustria, and Aquitaine), from c. 481 to 768.

2 Duchy of N cen. France, c. 1000; chief towns Paris, Orléans, and Tours.

Francia. See FRANCE.

Franciade. See SAINT-DENIS 1.

Fran·cis, Cape \-ˈfran(t)-səs\ *also* **Cape Saint Francis.** Cape, SE Newfoundland, Canada, E of entrance to Conception Bay N of St. John's.

Fran·cis·co I. Ma·de·ro \fran-ˌsis-kō-ē-mə-ˈder-ō\. Municipality, Coahuila state, Mexico, 24 m. NE of Torreón; pop. (1970p) 38,920; cattle raising, viniculture.

Francisco Mo·ra·zán \fran-ˌsis-kō-ˌmōr-ə-ˈzän, -ˌmȯr-\ *or formerly* **Te·gu·ci·gal·pa** \tə-ˌgü-sə-ˈgal-pə\. Department of S cen. Honduras. See table at HONDURAS.

Fran·cis·town \ˈfran(t)-sə-ˌstau̇n\. Chief town of N Botswana, S Africa, near Rhodesia border; pop. (1969e) 11,000.

Fran·co·fon·te \ˌfraŋ-kə-ˈfänt-ē\. Commune, Siracusa prov., Sicily, Italy, 21 m. WNW of Syracuse; pop. (1968e) 15,920.

Fran·co·nia \fraŋ-ˈkō-nē-ə, -nyə\. 1 Resort village, Grafton co., W New Hampshire, in Franconia Mts. ab. 5 m. S of Littleton; pop. (1970c) 655; Franconia Coll. (1962).

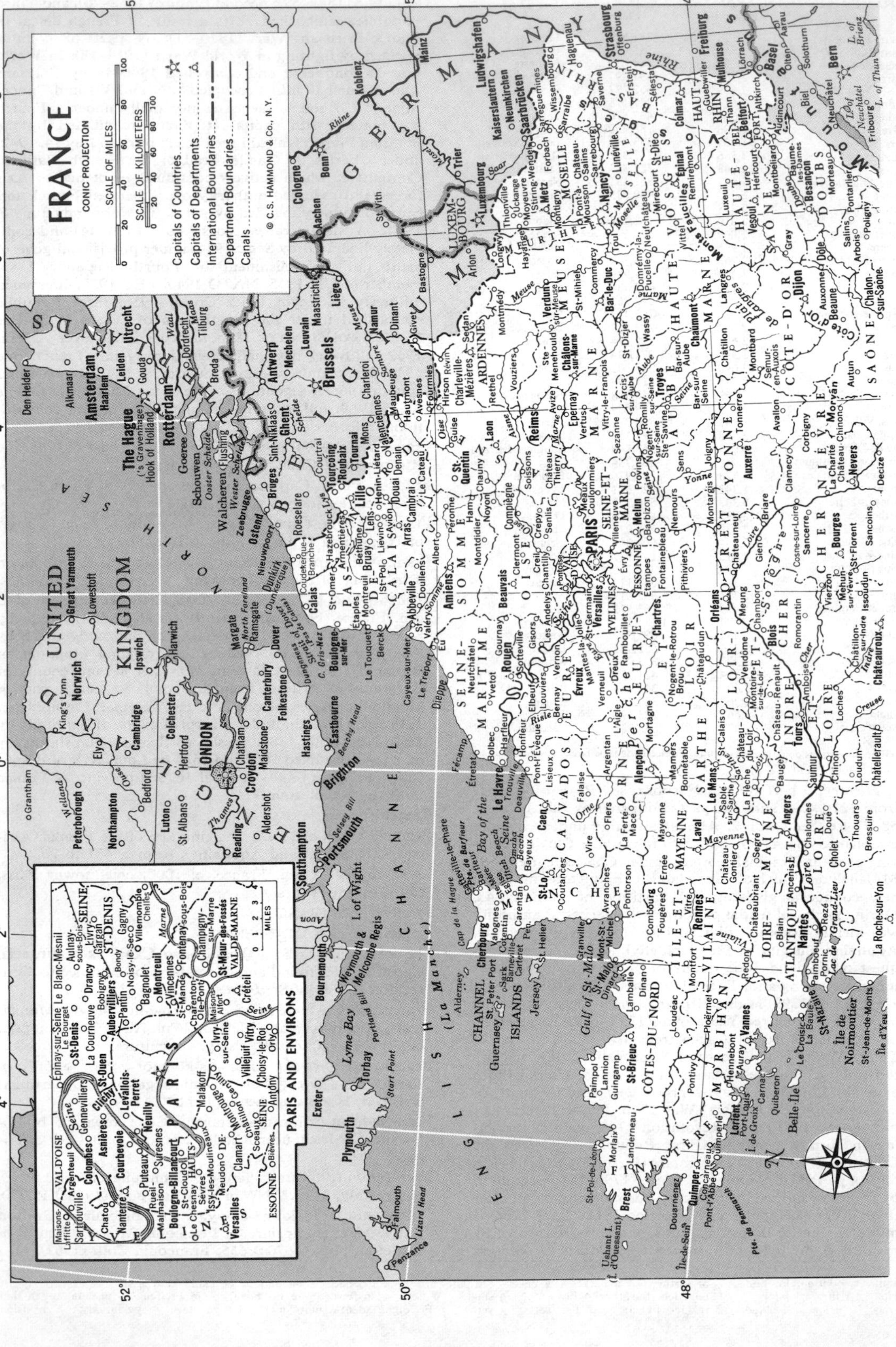
FRANCE
CONIC PROJECTION
SCALE OF MILES
0 20 40 60 80 100
SCALE OF KILOMETERS
0 20 40 60 80 100
Capitals of Countries
Capitals of Departments
International Boundaries
Department Boundaries
Canals
© C.S. HAMMOND & Co., N.Y.
PARIS AND ENVIRONS
MILES
0 1 2 3
Maisons-Laffitte
Sartrouville
Argenteuil
Chatou
Colombes
Gennevilliers
Asnières
Nanterre
Courbevoie
Puteaux
Rueil-Malmaison
Suresnes
Boulogne-Billancourt
St-Cloud
Le Chesnay
Versailles
Sèvres
Issy-les-Moulineaux
Meudon
Clamart
Châtillon
Sceaux
Bièvres
ESSONNE
Antony
Montrouge
Malakoff
Villejuif
Vitry
Choisy-le-Roi
Orly
Ivry-sur-Seine
Créteil
Maisons-Alfort
Charenton-le-Pont
Vincennes
St-Mandé
Fontenay-sous-Bois
Champigny-sur-Marne
St-Maur-des-Fossés
VAL-DE-MARNE
Montreuil
Bagnolet
Pantin
Noisy-le-Sec
Bondy
Villemomble
Chelles
Gagny
Livry-Gargan
Aulnay-sous-Bois
Le Blanc-Mesnil
Le Bourget
Drancy
Bobigny
Aubervilliers
La Courneuve
St-Denis
ST-DENIS
Épinay-sur-Seine
St-Ouen
Clichy
Levallois-Perret
Neuilly
PARIS
VAL-D'OISE
HAUTS-DE-SEINE
YVELINES
SEINE
Marne
UNITED KINGDOM
NORTH SEA
NETHERLANDS
BELGIUM
LUXEMBOURG
GERMANY
ENGLISH CHANNEL (La Manche)
CHANNEL ISLANDS
Bay of the Seine
Gulf of St-Malo
Strait of Dover
London
Amsterdam
The Hague ('s Gravenhage)
Rotterdam
Brussels
Antwerp
Ghent
Bruges
Ostend
Liège
Namur
Luxembourg
Cologne
Bonn
Koblenz
Aachen
Trier
Saarbrücken
Kaiserslautern
Ludwigshafen
Mainz
Strasbourg
Freiburg
Basel
Bern
Mulhouse
Colmar
Belfort
Besançon
Dijon
Nancy
Metz
Reims
Laon
Amiens
Lille
Calais
Dunkirk (Dunkerque)
Boulogne-sur-Mer
Abbeville
Arras
Rouen
Le Havre
Dieppe
Caen
Cherbourg
St-Lô
Rennes
St-Malo
Brest
Quimper
Lorient
Vannes
St-Brieuc
Nantes
St-Nazaire
Angers
Le Mans
Laval
Alençon
Chartres
Orléans
Tours
Blois
Bourges
Nevers
Auxerre
Troyes
Chaumont
Bar-le-Duc
Épinal
Vesoul
Châlons-sur-Marne
Beauvais
Évreux
Melun
Versailles
Châteauroux
La Roche-sur-Yon
Plymouth
Portsmouth
Southampton
Brighton
Dover
Canterbury
Norwich
Ipswich
Cambridge
Colchester
NORD
PAS-DE-CALAIS
SOMME
AISNE
OISE
ARDENNES
MARNE
MEUSE
MOSELLE
MEURTHE-ET-MOSELLE
BAS-RHIN
HAUT-RHIN
VOSGES
HAUTE-MARNE
HAUTE-SAÔNE
DOUBS
CÔTE-D'OR
SAÔNE-ET-LOIRE
AUBE
YONNE
NIÈVRE
CHER
LOIRET
LOIR-ET-CHER
EURE-ET-LOIR
SEINE-ET-MARNE
ESSONNE
YVELINES
EURE
SEINE-MARITIME
CALVADOS
MANCHE
ORNE
SARTHE
MAYENNE
ILLE-ET-VILAINE
CÔTES-DU-NORD
FINISTÈRE
MORBIHAN
LOIRE-ATLANTIQUE
MAINE-ET-LOIRE
INDRE-ET-LOIRE
INDRE
Rhine
Seine
Loire
Marne
Meuse
Moselle
Oise
Somme
Aisne
Yonne
Cher
Indre
Vienne
Sarthe
Mayenne
Orne
Vilaine
Thames
Ushant I. (Î. d'Ouessant)
Belle Île
Île de Noirmoutier
Île d'Yeu
Jersey
Guernsey
Alderney
Sark
I. of Wight
Monts Faucilles
Plateau de Langres
Morvan
Côte d'Or
L. of Neuchâtel
L. of Thun
L. of Brienz
2° 0° 2° 4° 6° 8°
48° 50° 52°

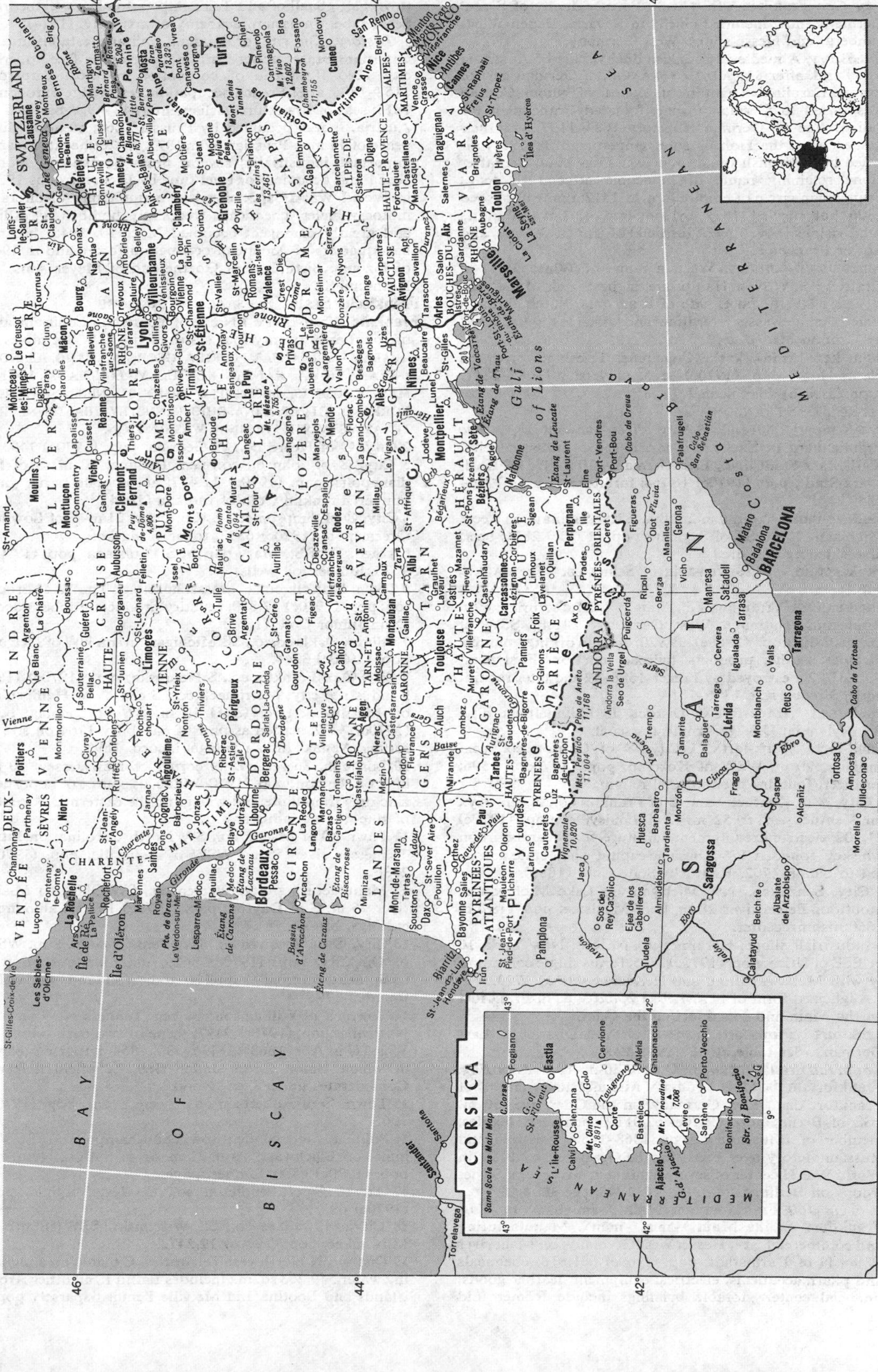
BAY OF BISCAY
MEDITERRANEAN SEA
Gulf of Lions
SWITZERLAND
SPAIN
ANDORRA
MONACO
CORSICA
Same Scale as Main Map
BARCELONA
Marseille
Lyon
Bordeaux
Toulouse
Turin
Geneva
Longitude West of Greenwich
Longitude East of Greenwich

2 *or Ger.* **Fran·ken** \ˈfräŋ-kən\. Former duchy of S cen. Germany, now included chiefly in Bavaria, Baden-Württemberg, and Hesse states, West Germany.

History: A medieval Frankish duchy, part of Austrasia (*q.v.*) and, after 843 A.D. (see FRANCE), of German part of former Carolingian empire; its dukes, of whom Conrad was raised to German throne, founded Franconian (or Salian) line of German emperors 1024–1137 and their descendants, the Hohenstaufen emperors 1138–1254; divided into Rhenish (west) and East Franconia, the latter alone retaining name of Franconia after 12th cent.; Franconian circle of empire formed 1512; name abolished 1806 but revived 1837 by kingdom of Bavaria in its subdivisions (government districts) of Upper, Middle, and Lower Franconia.

Franconia Mountains. Western range of White Mts., in Grafton co., W New Hampshire; highest peak Mount Lafayette 5249 ft., on E side of **Franconia Notch** through which Pemigewasset river flows and which is flanked on W by Cannon Mt. (*q.v.*).

Fra·ne·ker \ˈfrän-ə-kər\. Commune, Friesland prov., N Netherlands; pop. (1970e) 9575; university (1585–1811) suppressed by Napoleon I.

Franken. See FRANCONIA 2.

Fran·ken·berg \ˈfraŋ-kən-ˌbərg, ˈfräŋ-kən-ˌbu̇(ə)rg\ *also* **Frankenberg in Sach·sen** \-in-ˈzäk-sən\. Industrial city, Karl-Marx-Stadt dist., East Germany, 10 m. NE of Karl-Marx-Stadt; pop. (1970e) 16,764; furniture; church 1286–1359.

Frank·en·muth \ˈfraŋ-kən-ˌmüth\. City, Saginaw co., cen. Michigan, 15 m. SE of Saginaw; pop. (1970c) 2834; beer; diversified agriculture.

Frankenstein *or* **Frankenstein in Schlesien.** See ZABKOWICE.

Fran·ken·thal \ˈfraŋ-kən-ˌtäl, ˈfräŋ-\. Manufacturing city, Rhineland-Palatinate, West Germany, 28 m. SSW of Darmstadt; pop. (1969e) 39,920; metalworking; pumps, turbines, leather products; railroad junction. First mentioned 772; destroyed by French 1688–89 and later rebuilt; under French rule 1796–1814.

Frank·ford \ˈfraŋk-fərd\. District, E Philadelphia city, Pennsylvania; U.S. government arsenal.

Frank·fort \ˈfraŋk-fərt\. 1 City, ⊗ of Clinton co., cen. Indiana, 20 m. WSW of Kokomo; pop. (1970c) 14,596; fertilizer, foundry products; oil refining.

2 City, ✱ of Kentucky and ⊗ of Franklin co., N cen. Ky., on Kentucky river 52 m. E of Louisville; pop. (1970c) 21,902; electronic equipment, furniture, footwear, bourbon whiskey; founded 1786; became capital when state admitted to Union 1792. Kentucky State Coll. (1886).

3 City, Benzie co., NW Michigan, on Lake Michigan at mouth of Betsie river 28 m. N of Manistee; pop. (1970c) 1660; fishing center.

4 Industrial village, Herkimer co., NE cen. New York, 10 m. ESE of Utica; pop. (1970c) 3305; forms single community with Mohawk, Ilion, and Herkimer; settled 1723.

5 Anglicized form of FRANKFURT 2 *and* 3 as in **Frankfort on the Main** and **Frankfort on the Oder.**

Frank·furt \ˈfraŋk-fərt, ˈfräŋk-ˌfu̇(ə)rt\. 1 District of East Germany. See table at GERMANY, EAST.

2 *or in full* **Frankfurt an der Oder** \-ˌän-də-ˈrōd-ər\ *or Eng.* **Frankfort on the Oder** \-ˈōd-ər\. Manufacturing city, ✱ of Frankfurt dist., East Germany, on the Oder river 50 m. ESE of Berlin; pop. (1970e) 62,011; machinery, textiles; member of Hanseatic League 1368–1450; Austrian and Russian victory over Frederick the Great nearby 1759; in World War II center of severe fighting in advance of Soviet troops on Berlin, taken Apr. 24, 1945. See SŁUBICE.

3 *or in full* **Frankfurt am Main** \-äm-ˈmīn\ *or Eng.* **Frank·fort on the Main** \-ˈmīn, -ˈmān\. Manufacturing and commercial city, Hesse, West Germany, on Main river 17 m. N of Darmstadt; pop. (1969e) 661,816; chemicals and pharmaceuticals, electrical equipment, leather goods; financial center; notable buildings include Römer (old town hall), Saalhof and Taxis imperial palaces, cathedral, Senckenberg museum, academy of art; univ. (1914).

History: On site of Roman military establishment; important center under Carolingian empire; free imperial city 1245 ff.; scene of coronation of most emperors 1152–1806; after French occupation, restored to autonomy 1815; seat of Frankfurt Parliament 1848–49; a partisan of Austria, it was occupied by Prussia 1866; scene of final peace of Franco-Prussian War 1871. In 20th cent. became important industrially; several times bombed in World War I and occupied for brief time by French troops 1920; in World War II specialized in manufacture of aircraft, motor vehicles, chemicals; frequently bombed by Allies and greatly damaged; occupied Mar. 30, 1945, became headquarters of American occupation forces and in 1948 of Bizonia. Birthplace of Goethe and of Meyer Amschel Rothschild.

Fränkische Saale. See SAALE, FRÄNKISCHE.

Frank·lin \ˈfraŋ-klən\. 1 Name of a parish in Louisiana and of counties in twenty-four states of the U.S. See tables at ALABAMA, ARKANSAS, FLORIDA, GEORGIA, IDAHO, ILLINOIS, INDIANA, IOWA, KANSAS, KENTUCKY, LOUISIANA, MAINE, MASSACHUSETTS, MISSISSIPPI, MISSOURI, NEBRASKA, NEW YORK, NORTH CAROLINA, OHIO, PENNSYLVANIA, TENNESSEE, TEXAS, VERMONT, VIRGINIA, WASHINGTON.

2 City, ⊗ of Heard co., W Georgia; pop. (1970c) 749.

3 City, ⊗ of Johnson co., cen. Indiana, 20 m. S of Indianapolis; pop. (1970c) 11,477; automobile parts, glue, lumber; Franklin Coll. of Indiana (1834).

4 City, ⊗ of Simpson co., S Kentucky, 21 m. S of Bowling Green; pop. (1970c) 6553; tobacco market.

5 Town, ⊗ of St. Mary parish, S Louisiana; pop. (1970c) 9325; lumber; oil wells.

6 Town, Norfolk co., E Massachusetts, 19 m. W of Brockton; pop. (1970c) 17,830; foundry products, rubber goods; Dean Junior Coll. (1865).

7 Village, Oakland co., SE Michigan, 20 m. NW of Detroit; pop. (1970c) 3344.

8 City, ⊗ of Franklin co., S Nebraska; pop. (1970c) 1193.

9 Industrial city, Merrimack co., S cen. New Hampshire, on Merrimack river (*q.v.*) 10 m. SW of Laconia; pop. (1970c) 7292; settled as part of Salisbury 1764 on site of former Abnaki Indian village; incorp. 1895.

10 Borough, Sussex co., N corner of New Jersey, 10 m. ENE of Newton; pop. (1970c) 4236; as source of important zinc ores franklinite and willemite, the eastern U.S. center of zinc-mining industry.

11 Town, ⊗ of Macon co., SW North Carolina, on Little Tennessee river 55 m. WSW of Asheville; pop. (1970c) 2336.

12 Manufacturing city, Warren co., SW Ohio, on Miami river 15 m. S of Dayton; pop. (1970c) 10,075; aluminum castings, brass.

13 City, ⊗ of Venango co., NW Pennsylvania, 8 m. WSW of Oil City; pop. (1970c) 8629; manufactures oil well equipment, railroad supplies, tools; oil and gas wells; founded 1795.

14 Town, ⊗ of Williamson co., cen. Tennessee, 19 m. S of Nashville; pop. (1970c) 9497; scene of two battles in Civil War: (1) in Apr. 1863; (2) Nov. 30, 1864, important battle in which Union forces under Gen. Schofield defeated Confederates under Gen. Hood.

15 Town, ⊗ of Robertson co., E cen. Texas; pop. (1970c) 1063.

16 Politically independent town, Southampton co., SE Virginia, on Blackwater river 21 m. W of Suffolk; 4 sq. m.; pop. (1970c) 6880; lumber, paper.

17 Town, ⊗ of Pendleton co., E West Virginia; pop. (1970c) 695.

18 City, Milwaukee co., SE Wisconsin, SSW suburb of Milwaukee; pop. (1970c) 12,247.

19 District, N Northwest Territories, Canada; area including water 549,253 sq. m.; includes Baffin I., all other Arctic islands and Boothia and Melville Penins.; sparsely popu-

lated; administered from Ottawa. Formed 1895, boundaries defined 1918.

Franklin, Mount. 1 Peak of White Mts., in S Coos co., N New Hampshire, SSW of Mt. Washington; 5004 ft.

2 Peak, New South Wales, Australia, 24 m. SW of Canberra; 5392 ft.

Franklin, State of. A temporary state organized 1784 in W lands of North Carolina (now part of E Tennessee) which it had ceded to the United States (act of cession repealed 1785); first legislative sessions at Jonesboro; capital established at Greenville 1785; last legislative session 1787; ceased to exist Feb. 1788.

Franklin Bay. Inlet of Amundsen Gulf, coast of Northwest Territories, Canada.

Franklin D. Roo·se·velt Lake \-ˌrō-zə-ˌvelt-, -vəlt- *also* -ˌrü-\ *also infrequently* **Grand Cou·lee Reservoir** \-ˈkü-lē-\. Lake, N cen. Washington; formed in Columbia river by Grand Coulee Dam, N end near Canada border; 151 m. long; named Apr. 18, 1945.

Franklin Falls Dam. Dam across Pemigewasset river near Franklin, S cen. New Hampshire; height 146 ft.; completed 1943; impounds water for flood control.

Franklin Lake. Dry salt lake in S Elko co., NE Nevada.

Franklin Lakes. Borough, Bergen co., NE New Jersey, 5 m. NW of Paterson; pop. (1970c) 7550.

Franklin Mountains. Range, in W cen. Mackenzie dist., Northwest Territories, Canada, W of Great Bear Lake; highest peak Mt. Clark 4798 ft.

Franklin Park. 1 Village, Cook co., NE Illinois, suburb of Chicago; pop. (1970c) 20,497.

2 Borough, Allegheny co., SW Pennsylvania, 12 m. NW of Pittsburgh; pop. (1970c) 5310.

Franklin Square. Urban community, Nassau co., New York, in SE Long I. W of Hempstead; pop. (1970c) 32,156.

Franklin Strait. Channel bet. SE Prince of Wales I. and Boothia Penin., S Franklin dist., Northwest Territories, Canada.

Frank·lin·ton \ˈfraŋ-klən-tən\. 1 Town, ⊗ of Washington parish, E Louisiana, N of New Orleans; pop. (1970c) 3562; timber.

2 City, Ohio. See COLUMBUS 11.

Franklin Tunnel. Railroad tunnel ab. 30 m. E of San Francisco, California; 5600 ft. long.

Frank·lin·ville \ˈfraŋ-klən-ˌvil\. Village, Cattaraugus co., SW New York, 16 m. N of Olean; pop. (1970c) 1948.

Franks Peak \ˈfraŋ(k)s-\. Highest peak in the Absaroka Range, at S end in S Park co., NW Wyoming; 13,140 ft.

Fran·tiš·ko·vy Láz·ně \ˌfrän-tish-ˌkȯ-vē-ˈläz-nē-ˌä\ *or Ger.* **Fran·zens·bad** \ˈfrän(t)-sənz-ˌbät, -sən(t)s-\. Village, Czech S.R., W Czechoslovakia, ab. 24 m. WSW of Karlovy Vary; mineral baths and springs.

Franz Jo·sef Fjord \ˌfran(t)s-ˌjō-zəf- *also* -səf-; ˌfrän(t)s-ˌyō-zəf-\ *also* **Kej·ser Franz Jo·sephs Fjord** \ˌkī-sər-ˌfrän(t)s-ˈyō-sefs-ˌfyȯr\. Inlet of Greenland Sea, NE coast of Greenland, ab. 73°15′N; 125 m. long.

Franz Josef Land *or Russ.* **Zem·lya Fran·tsa Io·si·fa** \ˌzem-lē-ˈä-ˌfrän(t)-sə-ˈyȯ-sə-fə\ *also* **Fridt·jof Nan·sen Land** \ˌfrit-ˌyȯf-ˈnan(t)-sən-\. Archipelago in Arctic Ocean, part of Arkhangelsk Oblast, Russian S.F.S.R., U.S.S.R.; 80° to 82°N, 43° to 65°E, N of Novaya Zemlya; ab. 8000 sq. m.; consists of ab. 187 islands, largest: Aleksandra Land, George Land, Wilczek Land, and Graham Bell I.; most northerly land of E hemisphere; covered with ice. Discovered 1873 by Austrian expedition of Payer and Weyprecht; visited by several explorers since 1881, esp. by F. G. Jackson and Fridtjof Nansen 1896, Walter Wellman 1898, and the duke of the Abruzzi 1899; after Revolution 1917 explored by Russians, who claimed and renamed it 1928; has world's most northern meteorological station (estab. 1929 by U.S.S.R.). See ARCTIC, THE.

Franz Josef–Spitze. See GERLACHOVKA.

Fra·sca·ti \fra-ˈskät-ē, frä-\. Commune, Roma prov., Latium, cen. Italy, on NW side of Alban Hills 11 m. SE of Rome; pop. (1968e) 18,023; cathedral; summer resort; ancient Roman ruins, including villa of Cicero; near ruins of ancient Tusculum.

Fra·ser \ˈfrā-zer, -zhər\. 1 Town, Grand co., N Colorado, NNW of Berthoud Pass; pop. (1970c) 221; alt. 8568 ft.; often called "the Nation's icebox."

2 City, Macomb co., SE Michigan, NE suburb of Detroit; pop. (1970c) 11,868.

3 River, S cen. British Columbia, Canada; 850 m. long; drainage area ab. 84,100 sq. m.; rises in Rocky Mts. near Yellowhead Pass, flows NW bet. Rocky and Cariboo ranges, then in sharp turn S around N of Cariboo Mts. nearly to U.S. border and finally W, breaking through Coast Mts. in long canyon, to empty into Strait of Georgia just S of Vancouver; navigable for ab. 90 m.; chief tributaries the Nechako, Chilcotin, Thompson, Blackwater, and Lillooet. Discovered by Alexander Mackenzie 1793, explored by Simon Fraser 1808.

Fra·ser·burgh \ˈfrā-zər-ˌbər-ə, -zhər-, -ˌbə-rə, -b(ə-)rə\. Seaport burgh, Aberdeen co., NE Scotland, near Kinnairds Head on NE coast 57°40′N, 2°W; pop. (1971p) 10,605; herring fisheries.

Fraser Island *or* **Great Sandy Island.** Island off SE coast of Queensland, Australia; 70 m. long; 66 sq. m.

Frat·ta·mag·gio·re \ˌfrät-ə-mə-ˈjōr-ē, -ˈjȯr-\. Commune, Napoli prov., Campania, S Italy, 7 m. N by E of Naples; pop. (1968e) 34,844; resort.

Frauenburg. See FROMBORK.

Frau·en·feld \ˈfrau̇(-ə)n-ˌfelt\. Commune, ✱ of Thurgau canton, NE Switzerland, 21 m. NE of Zurich; pop. (1970c) 17,576; textiles; publishing; old castle; armory; became city in middle of 13th cent.

Fray Ben·tos \frī-ˈbent-əs\. Town and river port, ✱ of Río Negro dept., W Uruguay, on E bank of Uruguay river ab. 175 m. NW of Montevideo; pop. (1963c) 20,755; meatpacking; Uruguay's first industrialized meat-packing plant estab. here 1861.

Fray·ser's Farm \ˌfrā-zərz-, -zhərz-\ *or* **Glen·dale** \ˈglen-ˌdāl\. Battlefield near Richmond, Virginia, where Longstreet and A. P. Hill lost 3000 men in an encounter with Union forces June 30, 1862.

Fre·chen \ˈfrek-ən\. Town, North Rhine-Westphalia, West Germany, SW suburb of Cologne; pop. (1969e) 30,604; artificial fibers; coal mining.

Fred·er·i·cia \ˌfred-ə-ˈrish-ē-ə\. Seaport, Vejle co., SE Jutland Penin., Denmark; pop. (1970e) 43,513; textiles, chemicals; oil refinery; scene of battle July 6, 1849 in which Danes defeated Prussians.

Fred·er·ick \ˈfred-(ə-)rik\. 1 Name of counties in two states of the U.S. See tables at MARYLAND and VIRGINIA.

2 City, ⊗ of Frederick co., N Maryland, 24 m. SE of Hagerstown; pop. (1970c) 23,641; in agricultural region; canneries; residence of Francis Scott Key and Barbara Fritchie; Hood Coll. (1893), Frederick Community Coll. (1957). See MONOCACY 2.

3 City, ⊗ of Tillman co., SW Oklahoma, 25 m. SE of Altus; pop. (1970c) 6132; cotton.

Frederick Henry. See DOLAK ISLAND.

Fred·er·icks·burg \ˈfred-(ə-)riks-ˌbərg\. 1 Town, ⊗ of Gillespie co., cen. Texas; pop. (1970c) 5326; granite, limestone.

2 Industrial city, NE Virginia, in Spotsylvania co. but politically independent, on Rappahannock river 41 m. SW of Alexandria; 6 sq. m.; pop. (1970c) 14,450; settled 1671; incorp. as city 1879; scene of battle Dec. 11–15, 1862, when Union army under Burnside was defeated by Confederates under Robert E. Lee. Mary Washington College (1908; women) of the Univ. of Virginia.

Fredericksburg and Spot·syl·va·nia County Battlefields Memorial National Military Park \-ˌspät-səl-ˈvān-yə-, -ˈvān-ē-ə-\. See UNITED STATES, *National Historical Parks.*

Fred·er·ick·town \ˈfred-(ə-)rik-ˌtau̇n\. City, ⊗ of Madison co., SE Missouri, 45 m. WNW of Cape Girardeau; pop. (1970c) 3799; lead deposits nearby.

Frederick Wil·liam IV Falls \ˌfred-rik-ˌwil-yəm-thə-ˈfō(ə)rth-, -ˈfȯ(ə)rth-\. Falls on Courantyne river, on boundary bet. Guyana and Surinam.

Fred·er·ic·ton \ˈfred-(ə-)rik-tən\. City, ✱ of New Brunswick and ⊗ of York co., New Brunswick, Canada, in SW part of province at head of navigation of St. John river 55 m. NNW of St. John; pop. (1971p) 23,612; trades extensively in lumber; footwear; railroad center; Univ. of New Brunswick (1859). Laid out as provincial capital 1785 across river from village of **Sainte Anne's Point** \sānt-ˈanz-, sent-\, which was settled by French 1740, earliest settlement in region, and received many Acadian refugees.

Frederik Hendrik. See DOLAK ISLAND.

Fred·er·iks·berg \ˈfred-(ə-)riks-ˌbərg\. Commune, Sjælland I., Denmark; 3 sq. m.; pop. (1971c) 101,970; a suburb of Copenhagen; Royal Copenhagen Porcelain factory; founded 1651.

Fre·de·riks·borg \ˈfred-(ə-)riks-ˌbȯrg\. County of Denmark. See table at DENMARK.

Fre·de·riks·håb \ˈfred-(ə-)riks-ˌhȯp\. Settlement on S coast of Greenland, NNW of Ivigtut; pop. (1968e) 2436.

Fre·de·riks·havn \ˌfred-(ə-)riks-ˈhau̇n\. Seaport, Nordjylland co., NE Jutland Penin., Denmark, on the Kattegat 37 m. NE of Ålborg; pop. (1970e) 32,826; exports meat and fish.

Frederiksnagar. See SERAMPORE.

Fred·er·ik·sted \ˈfred-(ə-)rik-ˌsted\. City on W coast of St. Croix I., Virgin Islands of the United States, West Indies; pop. (1970p) 1548.

Fre·do·nia \fri-ˈdō-nē-ə, -nyə\. 1 City, ⊗ of Wilson co., SE Kansas, N of Independence; pop. (1970c) 3080; oil, gas. 2 Village, Chautauqua co., SW corner of New York, near Lake Erie 23 m. N of Jamestown; pop. (1970c) 10,326; manufactures grape juice, wine, shovels, coal-handling machinery; State Univ. of New York at Fredonia (1866).

Fredrikshald. See HALDEN.

Fredrikshamn. See HAMINA.

Fred·rik·stad \ˈfred-rik-ˌstäd\. Seaport, Østfold co., SE Norway, on E shore of Oslo Fjord at mouth of Glåma river; pop. (1970e) 29,912; shipping point for lumber, chemicals, granite, feldspar.

Free·born \ˈfrē-ˌbȯ(ə)rn\. County in Minnesota. See table at MINNESOTA.

Free·burg \ˈfrē-ˌbərg\. Village, St. Clair co., SW Illinois, 18 m. SE of East St. Louis; pop. (1970c) 2495.

Free City of Danzig. See history at GDAŃSK 2.

Free·dom \ˈfrēd-əm\. Borough, Beaver co., W Pennsylvania, on Ohio river 21 m. NW of Pittsburgh; pop. (1970c) 2643; Community Coll. of Beaver County (1966); founded 1832.

Free·hold \ˈfrē-ˌhōld\. Industrial borough, ⊗ of Monmouth co., E cen. New Jersey, 18 m. S of Perth Amboy; pop. (1970c) 10,545; first white settlement 1650; settled by Scots 1715, called Monmouth Court House, later (1795) Monmouth, changed to Freehold 1801; incorp. 1869. See MONMOUTH COURT HOUSE.

Free·land \ˈfrē-lənd\. Borough, Luzerne co., E Pennsylvania, S of Wilkes-Barre; pop. (1970c) 4784; coal.

Freels, Cape \-ˈfrē(ə)lz\. Cape on E coast of Newfoundland, Canada, marking NW point of Bonavista Bay, 49°15′N.

Freels Peak. Mountain, E El Dorado co., E California; 10,880 ft.

Free·man Lake \ˌfrē-mən-\. Lake, NW cen. Indiana, formed in Tippecanoe river by Oakdale Dam (completed 1935). See SHAFER LAKE.

Free·man's Farm \ˌfrē-mənz-\. Locality, near Bemis Heights on W bank of Hudson river bet. villages of Saratoga and Stillwater, Saratoga co., New York; center of fighting in two battles of Saratoga (*q.v.*) 1777.

Free·port \ˈfrē-ˌpō(ə)rt, -ˌpȯ(ə)rt\. 1 City, ⊗ of Stephenson co., N Illinois, 28 m. W of Rockford; pop. (1970c) 27,736; farm machinery, plastics, cosmetics; foundries; settled 1835, chartered 1855; scene of Lincoln-Douglas debate (1858) in which Douglas expounded his "Freeport Doctrine" that local legislation could be effective against slavery despite the Supreme Court's Dred Scott decision.
2 Town, Cumberland co., SW Maine, 16 m. NNE of Portland; pop. (1970c) 4781; incorporated 1789; final papers for separation of Maine from Massachusetts signed here 1820, establishing Maine as an independent state.
3 Residential village, Nassau co., SE New York, on S shore of Long I. 25 m. ESE of New York; pop. (1970c) 40,374; fisheries, esp. oysters.
4 Borough, Armstrong co., W Pennsylvania, on Allegheny river 24 m. NE of Pittsburgh; pop. (1970c) 2375; coal.
5 City and port of entry, Brazoria co., SE Texas, at mouth of Brazos river on Gulf of Mexico 40 m. WSW of Galveston; pop. (1970c) 11,997; mines, processes, and ships sulfur; Brazosport Junior Coll. (1968); Dow Chemical Company plant, built 1940, for extracting magnesium from seawater.
6 Town on SW coast of Grand Bahama I., Bahama Is.; pop. (1970c) 25,859; tourism.

Freer \ˈfri(ə)r\. City, Duval co., S Texas, 60 m. ENE of Laredo; pop. (1970c) 2804; oil wells.

Free·stone \ˈfrē-ˌstōn\. County in Texas. See table at TEXAS.

Free Territory of Trieste. See TRIESTE 3.

Free·town \ˈfrē-ˌtau̇n\. 1 Town, Bristol co., SE Massachusetts, 10 m. N of New Bedford; pop. (1970c) 4270.
2 Seaport town, ✱ of Sierra Leone, W Africa, on N shore of Sierra Leone Penin.; pop. (1970e) 178,600; best harbor in W Africa, at mouth of Sierra Leone river; cathedral (1852), univ. (1967); founded 1787 chiefly by freed or rescued Negro slaves who were granted land by a native chieftain.

Fre·gel·lae \fri-ˈjel-ē\. Ancient Volscian town, Latium, Italy; a few ruins near modern Ceprano; near the Liris (*mod.* Liri); Latin colony established 328 B.C.; revolted against Rome 125 B.C.; destroyed, but existed as a village under the empire.

Fre·ge·nal de la Sie·rra \ˌfrā-hə-ˈnäl-ˌdel-ə-sē-ˈer-ə\. Commune, Badajoz prov., SW Spain, 47 m. SSE of Badajoz; pop. (1970p) 7706.

Fré·hel, Cape \-frā-ˈ(h)el\. Cape on coast of Côtes-du-Nord dept., NW France, 15 m. W by N of Saint-Malo.

Frei·berg \ˈfrī-bərg, -berk\. Manufacturing and mining city, Karl-Marx-Stadt dist., East Germany, 21 m. SW of Dresden near W bank of Mulde river; pop. (1970e) 50,272; precision instruments, leather, porcelain, textiles; lead and zinc mines; mining academy (founded 1765, univ. status 1905); 13th cent. relic called the Golden Portal; 15th cent. Gothic cathedral. Founded 12th cent. as silver-mining camp; scene of victory of Prussians over Austrians and Saxons 1762.

Frei·burg \ˈfrī-ˌbu̇(ə)rg, -ˌbərg, -ˌbu̇(ə)rk\. 1 Canton and commune, Switzerland. See FRIBOURG.
2 *also* **Freiburg im Breis·gau** \-im-ˈbrīs-ˌgau̇\. Manufacturing city, Baden-Württemberg, West Germany, at W foot of Black Forest 80 m. SW of Stuttgart; pop. (1969e) 163,509; chemicals, electronic equipment, optical instruments; textiles; Gothic cathedral, univ. (1457), ducal palace. Founded 1120; Austrian 1368–1806; scene of close battle Aug. 3 and 5, 1644 in which French under Enghien and Turenne were defeated by Bavarians under General Mercy.

Frei·en·wal·de \ˌfrī-ən-ˈväl-də\ *also* **Bad Freienwalde** \ˈbät-\ *or* **Freienwalde an der Oder** \-ˌän-də-ˈrōd-ər\. City, Frankfurt dist., East Germany, near Oder river 33 m. NE of Berlin; pop. (1967e) 11,900; health resort; warm mineral springs.

Frei·sing \ˈfrī-ziŋ\. City, Bavaria, West Germany, 20 m. NNE of Munich; pop. (1969e) 29,788; 12th cent. cathedral; manufactures agricultural machines, pottery, glass. Founded by Romans; episcopal see 724–1803.

Frei·tal \ˈfrī-ˌtäl\. Industrial city, Dresden dist., East Germany, 6 m. SW of Dresden; pop. (1970e) 42,159; manufactures steel, leather, and glass goods; coal mining; founded 1921.

Fré·jus \frā-ˈzhüs\ *or anc.* **Fo·rum Ju·lii** \ˌfōr-əm-ˈjü-lē-ˌī, ˌfȯr-\. Commune, Var dept., SE France; pop. (1968c) 23,629; Roman remains; cathedral; founded by Julius Caesar.

Fréjus, Pointe de \ˌpwa^{n}t-də-\. Mountain mass at SW end of Graian Alps bet. France and Italy; crossed by **Col de Fréjus** \ˌkȯl-də-, ˌkəl-\, pass ab. 16 m. SW of Mont Cenis Pass, pierced by Mont Cenis Tunnel (see ALPS).

Fre·man·tle \frē-ˈmant-^{ə}l\. City, SW Western Australia, on Indian Ocean at mouth of Swan river, part of the Perth met. area; pop. (1966c) 25,284; founded 1829; seaport for Perth; exports chiefly wool, wheat; suburbs are **East Fremantle** and **North Fremantle.**

Fre·mont \ˈfrē-ˌmänt\. 1 Name of counties in four states of the U.S. See tables at COLORADO, IDAHO, IOWA, WYOMING.
2 City, Alameda co., W California, SSE of Oakland; pop. (1970c) 100,869; automobiles, switch gears; brewing; ships fruit and vegetables; Holy Family Junior Coll. (1952), Ohlone Coll. (1966).
3 City, Newaygo co., W Michigan, 22 m. NE of Muskegon; pop. (1970c) 3465; fruit, poultry.
4 City, ⊗ of Dodge co., E Nebraska, on Platte river 33 m. WNW of Omaha; pop. (1970c) 22,962; cement, foundry products; flour mills, canneries; Midland Lutheran Coll. (1887).
5 Manufacturing city, ⊗ of Sandusky co., N Ohio, 21 m. WSW of Sandusky; pop. (1970c) 18,490; sugar beet and cannery center; on site of Fort Stevenson (built 1812), scene of Maj. Croghan's defeat of English and Indians 1813.

Fremont Peak. 1 Mountain peak, N Arizona. See SAN FRANCISCO PEAKS.
2 Mountain in Wind River Range, W cen. Wyoming; 13,730 ft.

French \ˈfrench\. River, SE Ontario, Canada, bet. Sudbury and Parry Sound dists.; 60 m. long; outlet of Lake Nipissing to Georgian Bay.

French Antilles. See FRENCH WEST INDIES.

French Broad \-ˈbrȯd\. River, E United States; 210 m. long; formed by junction of N and W forks in Transylvania co., SW North Carolina, flows NW through Great Smoky Mts. across Tennessee border, turns W to unite with Holston river near Knoxville and form Tennessee river; near this junction is Douglas Dam, one of dams of Tennessee Valley Authority (*q.v.*).

French·burg \ˈfrench-ˌbərg\. City, ⊗ of Menifee co., E Kentucky; pop. (1970c) 467.

French Community *or Fr.* **Com·mu·nau·té fran·çaise** \kȯ-mūē-nō-tā-frä^{n}-sez, -sāz\. The federation comprising metropolitan France, its overseas departments and territories, and those of its former African territories (Central African Republic, Chad, Congo, Gabon, Malagasy Republic, and Senegal) which, on becoming republics, chose to maintain their ties with France; formed under the Constitution of the Fifth Republic promulgated Oct. 5, 1958, and superseding the French Union.

French Congo. See FRENCH EQUATORIAL AFRICA.

French Creek. River, New York and Pennsylvania; ab. 140 m. long; flows from SW New York SW and SE into Allegheny river at Franklin, cen. Venango co., NW Pennsylvania.

French Equatorial Africa *or Fr.* **Afrique Equa·to·ri·ale fran·çaise** \á-frēk-ā-kwä-tȯr-yäl-frä^{n}-sez, -sāz\; *occas. shortened to* **Equatorial Africa** *or earlier* **French Congo.** Former federation of French possessions, W cen. Africa, consisting of Chad, Gabon, Middle Congo (now Congo), and Ubangi-Shari (now Central African Republic); 969,112 sq. m.; ✱ Brazzaville.

History: Coast discovered by Portuguese 1470; Lake Chad explored by English 1823; not settled by Europeans until French settled on Gabon river 1841 and founded Libreville 1849; after settlement of Brazzaville 1880 French penetrations inland extended to Ubangi region and finally to Lake Chad 1897; borders of French possessions determined by series of agreements with Powers from 1885; three colonies, Gabon, Middle Congo, and Ubangi-Shari-Chad, designated 1910 divisions of the region whose name was changed from French Congo (Chad made a separate colony 1920); ab. 100,000 sq. m. which were ceded to Germany in return for her agreement on Morocco (Agadir crisis) 1911 were recovered 1919; declared its independence of Vichy government 1940; Brazzaville became center of operations of Free French in Africa; by the new French constitution of Oct. 1946 status of the colonies changed to that of overseas territories of France; territories became autonomous republics within French Community 1958, and achieved total independence 1960.

French Frig·ate Shoal \-ˈfrig-ət-\. Group of islets, Hawaiian Is., 100 m. W of Necker I., lat. 23°45′N, long. 166°10′W.

French Gui·a·na \-gē-ˈan-ə, -ˈän-ə, -gī-ˈan-ə\ *or Fr.* **Guy·ane fran·çaise** \gwē-yán-frä^{n}-sez, -sāz\. French overseas department on NE coast of South America, having Surinam on the W and Brazil on E and S; 34,749 sq. m.; pop. (1970e) 51,000; ✱ Cayenne; divided into two *arrondissements,* the coastal region (**Cay·enne** \kī-ˈen, kā-\, 19,112 sq. m.) and the hinterland (**Ini·ni** \ē-ni-ˈnē\, 15,637 sq. m.); chief mountains the Tumuc-Humac Mts. on the S border separating it from Brazil; Inini hinterland largely plateau. Chief rivers the Maroni, forming boundary with Surinam on W, the Oyapock, forming boundary with Brazil on E, and the Mana and Sinnamary rivers. *Chief exports:* Timber, shrimp, rum; other products rice, corn, bananas.

History: First French settlement at Cayenne 1604; neglected until 18th cent. when French made unsuccessful attempts to settle; occupied by British 1809 but restored to France after 1817; early development hindered because of presence of penal colony; boundary with Brazil settled by arbitration 1900; reconstituted as overseas department of France 1946; penal colonies closed 1947.

French Guinea. See GUINEA 2.

French India *or officially* **Éta·blisse·ments fran·çais dans l'Inde** \ā-táb-lē-ˈsmä^{n}-frä^{n}-se-dä^{n}-la^{n}d, -sā-\. Five settlements in India that formerly constituted a territory of France: Chandernagor, Pondicherry (Pondichéry), Karikal, Yanam, on E coast, Mahé on W coast; 197 sq. m.; ✱ Pondicherry.

History: French stations in India founded by French East India Co. (chartered 1664); under leadership of Dupleix and La Bourdonnais, Deccan and Carnatic (*qq.v.*) came to be controlled by France 1751 until Clive's victory at Plassey 1757 gave British ascendancy in India (see INDIA 1); Pondicherry and other ports captured and restored several times, until by treaties of 1814 and 1815 French possessions in India were returned and (1816 and 1817) permanently established; restored to India 1949–54.

French Indochina. See INDOCHINA 2.

French Lick \ˈfrench-ˈlik\. Resort town, Orange co., S Indiana, SSW of Bedford; pop. (1970c) 2059; sulfur springs.

French·man Bay \ˌfrench-mən-\. Inlet of Atlantic Ocean on SE coast of Maine, E of Mt. Desert I.

French Morocco. See MOROCCO 1.

French Pol·y·ne·sia \-ˌpäl-ə-ˈnē-zhə, -shə\ *or Fr.* **Po·ly·né·sie fran·çaise** \pəl-ə-nā-zē-frä^{n}-sez, -sāz\; *formerly* **French Oce·an·ia** \-ˌō-shē-an-ē-ə, -ā-nē-ə\ *or Fr.* **Éta·blisse·ments (fran·çais) de l'Océ·a·nie** \ˌā-ˌtáb-lē-smä^{n}-(frä^{n}-se)-də-lō-sā-ə-nē\. French overseas territory in South Pacific Ocean, comprising Marquesas, Society, Gambier, and Tubuai Is. and Tuamotu Archipelago; 1261 sq. m.; pop. (1971e) 114,000; ✱ Papeete on Tahiti, Society Is.; covers wide area,

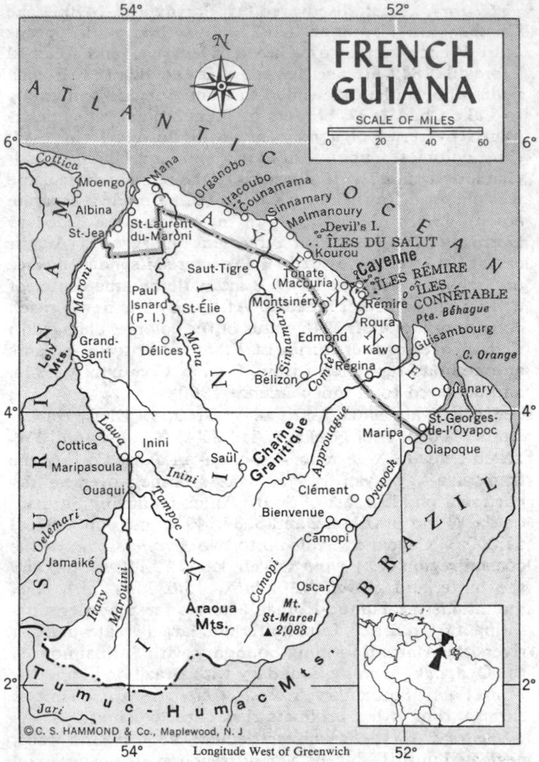

approx. from 7°S to 29°S and 132°W to 156°W; exports include phosphates, copra, vanilla.

History: Tahiti explored by Louis de Bougainville 1766 and Marquesas visited by French missionaries in late 18th cent.; Oceania visited by Dumont d'Urville 1837–40; annexation of Marquesas and protection of Society group accomplished by French in 1842 and remainder taken over by close of 19th cent.; placed under single administration 1903; administration reorganized 1946; French nuclear tests conducted in region 1966 and 1968.

French River. See FRENCH.

French Shore. Neutralized territory on W and N coasts of Newfoundland, Canada, from Cape Ray in SW to Cape St. John (50°N); established 1713 when Newfoundland was ceded to Great Britain with certain rights granted to French fishermen, esp. that of drying fish on land; above limits defined 1783; source of much friction 19th cent. bet. England and France and of trouble with American fishermen (settled by convention 1909).

French Somaliland. See AFARS AND ISSAS.

French Southern and Antarctic Territories *or Fr.* **Terres Au·strales et Ant·arc·tiques fran·çaises** \ter-ō-strȧl-zā-ȧnt-ärk-tēk-fräⁿ-sez, -sāz\. French overseas territory, consisting of Adélie Coast and the following S Indian Ocean islands: Amsterdam I., Crozet Is., Kerguelen Is., and St. Paul I. (*qq.v*); established 1955.

French Sudan. See MALI.

French Territory of the Afars and the Issas. See AFARS AND ISSAS.

French Togo. See TOGO 1.

French Union *or Fr.* **Union fran·çaise** \yü-nyōⁿ-fräⁿ-sez, -sāz\. The French federation formed by the Constitution of the Fourth Republic of Sept. 29, 1946 (confirmed by referendum of Oct. 13, 1946), comprising France with its overseas departments and territories and the associated states; superseded 1958 by the French Community (*q.v.*).

French·ville \ˈfrench-ˌvil\. Town, Aroostook co., N Maine, on St. John river E of Fort Kent; pop. (1970c) 1375.

French West Africa *or Fr.* **Afrique Oc·ci·den·tale fran·çaise** \ȧ-frēk-ōk-si-däⁿ-tȧl-fräⁿ-sez, -sāz\. Former federation of French dependencies, W Africa, consisting of what are now the independent republics of Dahomey, Guinea, Ivory Coast, Mali, Mauritania, Niger, and Senegal; 1,739,034 sq. m.; ✱ Dakar; established 1895, reorganized 1904 and 1946; federation abolished Jan. 21, 1959.

French West Indies; *also* **French An·til·les** \-an-ˈtil-ēz\ *or Fr.* **An·tilles fran·çaises** \äⁿ-tēl-fräⁿ-sez, -sāz\. Islands of the Lesser Antilles, West Indies; pop. (1961c) 575,285; comprise Martinique and Guadeloupe (formerly French colonies, since 1946 overseas departments) and the five dependencies of Guadeloupe: Désirade, Les Saintes, Marie Galante, Saint Barthélemy, and part of Saint Martin.

Fresh·wa·ter \ˈfresh-ˌwȯt-ər, -ˌwät-\. Village, W Isle of Wight, England; resort; site of Farringford estate, Lord Tennyson's home from 1853.

Fresnes \ˈfren\. Commune, Val-de-Marne dept., N France; pop. (1968c) 26,847.

Fres·ni·llo \frez-ˈnē-(ˌ)(y)ō\ *or in full* **Fresnillo de Gon·zá·lez Eche·ve·rría** \-ˌdā-gən-ˌzäl-əz-ˌech-ə-və-ˈrē-ə\. Municipality, Zacatecas state, cen. Mexico; pop. (1970p) 101,316; school of mines (1853); near silver mines; founded 1554.

Fres·no \ˈfrez-(ˌ)nō\. **1** County in S cen. California. See table at CALIFORNIA.

2 City, its ⊗, 155 m. SE of San Francisco, in San Joaquin valley; pop. (1970c) 165,972; marketing and shipping center; livestock feed; fruit packing (esp. raisins); Fresno City Coll. (1910), Fresno State Coll. (1911), Pacific Coll. (1944); founded 1872, made ⊗ 1874, incorp. as city 1885.

Fresno Dam. Dam across Milk river, N Montana; height 111 ft.; completed 1939; impounds water for irrigation.

Fretum Gaditanum. See GIBRALTAR, STRAIT OF.

Fretum Gallicum. See DOVER, STRAIT OF.

Frey·ci·net Peninsula \ˌfrās-ᵊn-ˌā-\. Peninsula on E coast of Tasmania, Australia, 42°13′S; ab. 20 m. long.

Fria, Cape \-ˈfrē-ə\. Cape extending into Atlantic Ocean on NW coast of South-West Africa, S of Angola boundary.

Fri·ant Dam \ˌfrī-ənt-\. See SAN JOAQUIN 1.

Friaul. See FRIULI.

Fri·bourg \frē-ˈbu̇(ə)r\ *or Ger.* **Frei·burg** \ˈfrī-ˌbu̇(ə)rg, -ˌbərg, -ˌbu̇(ə)rk\. **1** Swiss canton; 645 sq. m.; pop. (1970c) 180,309; ✱ Fribourg; dairy products; tourism. In ancient times inhabited by the Helvetii; conquered by Franks in 6th cent.; to Holy Roman Empire 1032; remained Catholic during Reformation; under French rule 1798–1814.

2 Commune, its ✱, on peninsula in Saane river 17 m. SW of Bern; pop. (1970c) 39,659; food processing, metalworking; chemicals; 13th cent. cathedral, univ. (1889); founded as military post 1157; became member of Swiss confederation 1481.

Fri·court \frē-ˈku̇(ə)r\. Village, Somme dept., N France, near Albert; destroyed in World War I.

Fri·day Harbor \ˌfrī-dē-\. Town and resort, ⊗ of San Juan co., NW Washington; pop. (1970c) 803.

Frid·ley \ˈfrid-lē\. City, Anoka co., E Minnesota, SE of Anoka; pop. (1970c) 29,233.

Fridt·jof Nan·sen, Mount \-ˌfrit-yȯf-ˈnan-sən\. Mountain, Antarctica, 85°21′S, 167°33′W; 13,087 ft.

Fridtjof Nansen Land. See FRANZ JOSEF LAND.

Fried·berg \ˈfrēd-ˌbərg, ˈfrēt-berk\. City, Hesse, West Germany, near Usa river 15 m. N of Frankfurt am Main; pop. (1968e) 17,522; sugar; apparel.

Friedek–Mistek. See FRÝDEK-MÍSTEK.

Friedland. See PRAVDINSK.

Fried·ling·en \ˈfrēt-liŋ-ən\. Battlefield in SW corner of Baden, West Germany, on the Rhine N of Basel and SE of Mulhouse; scene of victory of duc de Villars over Louis William of Baden 1702 (War of Spanish Succession).

Frie·drichs·ha·fen \ˌfrē-driks-ˈhäf-ən\ *or before 1811* **Buchhorn** \ˈbük-ˌhȯ(ə)rn\. City, SE Baden-Württemberg, West Germany, on Lake Constance 14 m. E of Konstanz; pop. (1969e) 41,853; precision instruments; tourism; important harbor; passed to Bavaria 1802, to Württemberg 1810.

Chief center of manufacture of Zeppelins during and for some years after World War I.

Frie·drichs·ruh \ˌfrē-driks-ˈrü\. Village, Schleswig-Holstein, West Germany, 15 m. SE of Hamburg; home of Bismarck on his retirement 1890.

Friedrichstadt. See YAUNYELGAVA.

Frie·drichs·thal \ˈfrē-driks-ˌtäl\. Mining and manufacturing town, Saarland, West Germany, ab. 8 m. N of Saarbrücken; pop. (1967e) 14,400; coal mining.

Friedrich–Wilhelmshafen. See MADANG 2.

Friendly Islands. See TONGA.

Friend·ship \ˈfren(d)-ship\. Village, ⊗ of Adams co., cen. Wisconsin; pop. (1970c) 641.

Friends·wood \ˈfren(d)z-ˌwu̇d\. City, Galveston co., SE Texas, 20 m. SE of Houston; pop. (1970c) 5675.

Fries \ˈfrēz\. Town, Grayson co., SW Virginia, 26 m. SSW of Pulaski; pop. (1970c) 885.

Friesche Eilanden. See FRISIAN ISLANDS.

Fries·land \ˈfrēz-lənd, ˈfrēs-, -ˌland\ *also* **Vries·land** \ˈvrēz-, ˈvrēs-\. Province, N Netherlands; 1464 sq. m.; pop. (1970e) 521,751; ✱ Leeuwarden; dairy farming, livestock raising.

Frim·ley and Cam·ber·ley \ˈfrim-lē . . . ˈkam-bər-lē\. Urban district, Surrey, S England, N of Aldershot; pop. (1971p) 44,784; nearby is Bisley (*q.v.*), well-known rifle range.

Frin·ton and Wal·ton \ˈfrint-ᵊn . . . ˈwȯlt-ən\. Urban district, Essex, SE England; pop. (1971p) 12,431; seaside resort.

Frio \ˈfrē-(ˌ)ō\. **1** River, Live Oak co., S Texas; 220 m. long; flows into Nueces river.

2 County in Texas. See table at TEXAS.

Frio, Cape. Cape extending into Atlantic Ocean from coast of Rio de Janeiro state, SE Brazil.

Fri·o·na \frē-ˈō-nə\. City, Parmer co., NW Texas, 65 m. SW of Amarillo; pop. (1970c) 3111; cattle and grain shipping; diversified agriculture.

Frische Nehrung *or* **Frisches Haff.** See VISLINSKI ZALIV.

Fri·sia \ˈfrizh-(ē-)ə, ˈfrē-zh(ē-)ə\. Country along SE coast of North Sea at time of Frankish empire; corresponded approximately to modern Netherlands.

Fri·sian Islands \ˈfrizh-ən-, ˈfrē-zhən-\ *or Du.* **Frie·sche Ei·lan·den** \ˌfrē-sə-ˈī-ˌlän-dən\. Chain of islands in North Sea, bet. 3 and 20 m. from European mainland, including: (1) **North Frisian Islands** off NW coast of Schleswig-Holstein, West Germany, and the SW coast of Denmark; chief islands (German) Sylt, Föhr, Nordstrand, Pellworm, and Amrum; (Danish) Rømø, Fanø, and Mandø. (2) **East Frisian Islands** off Lower Saxony state, West Germany; chief islands Borkum, Juist, Norderney, Langeoog, Spiekeroog, and Wangerooge. (3) **West Frisian Islands** off Wadden Zee and N Netherlands coast; chief islands Texel, Vlieland, Terschelling, Ameland, and Schiermonnikoog. Helgoland (*q.v.*) belongs to German group of North Frisian Is.

Fris·sell, Mount \-frə-ˈzel\. Mountain, Litchfield co., NW Connecticut; 2380 ft.; highest point in the state.

Fritz·lar \ˈfrits-(ˌ)lär\. Town, N Hesse, West Germany, on the Eder; pop. (1967e) 8900; church of St. Peter and monastery, both founded 723 by Boniface.

Fri·u·li \ˈfrē-ə-ˌlē, frē-ˈü-lē\ *or Ger.* **Fri·aul** \frē-ˈau̇(ə)l\ *or anc.* **Fo·rum Ju·lii** \ˌfōr-əm-ˈjü-lē-ˌī, ˌfȯr-\. Former duchy in NE Italy; became Lombard duchy 6th cent.; made Charlemagne's Friulian March; at close of 11th cent., part of patriarchate of Aquileia (*q.v.*); W part occupied by Venice in 15th cent.; E part (under Gorizia) acquired 1500 by Austria who received rest 1797; in Napoleon's Illyrian Provinces (*q.v.*); Venetian part returned to Italy during unification and rest after World War I; now part of Friuli-Venezia Giulia.

Friuli–Ve·ne·zia Giu·lia \-və-ˌnet-sē-ə-ˈjül-yə\. Autonomous region, NE Italy; 3028 sq. m.; pop. (1968e) 1,225,894; ✱ Trieste; dairy products, textiles, ceramics; shipyards; was granted limited autonomy 1963. See VENEZIA GIULIA.

Fro·bish·er Bay \ˌfrō-bi-shər-\. Inlet extending NW in SE Baffin I., E Franklin dist., Northwest Territories, N Canada, S of Hall Penin.; first entered by Martin Frobisher 1576; airfield at its head.

From·bork \ˈfrȯm-ˌbȯrk\ *or Ger.* **Frau·en·burg** \ˈfrau̇-ən-ˌbu(ə)rg, -ˌbərg, -ˌbu̇(ə)rk\. Town, Olsztyn prov., N Poland, on the Vislinski Zaliv, ab. 40 m. E of Gdańsk; pop. (1966e) 1454; cathedral (1329–88); monument to Copernicus who was canon of cathedral; formerly in East Prussia.

Frome \ˈfrüm\. **1** River, Herefordshire, W England; 20 m. long; flows into the Lugg.

2 Urban district, Somersetshire, SW England, on the **Frome River** (tributary of the Avon) 20 m. SSE of Bristol; pop. (1971p) 13,384; wool, paper, art metalwork; first mentioned A.D. 689.

Frome, Lake \-frōm\. Shallow lake, E South Australia, E of Lake Torrens; ab. 60 m. long.

Fron·te·nac \ˈfränt-ə-ˌnak\. **1** City, Crawford co., SE Kansas, 4 m. N of Pittsburg; pop. (1970c) 2223.

2 City, St. Louis co., E Missouri, 9 m. W of St. Louis; pop. (1970c) 3920.

3 County, Ontario, Canada. See table at ONTARIO.

4 County, Quebec, Canada. See table at QUEBEC.

Frontenac, Lac. See ONTARIO, LAKE.

Fron·te·ra \ˌfrən-ˈter-ə, frän-\ *or formerly* **Ál·va·ro Obre·gón** \ˈäl-və-(ˌ)rō-ˌō-bri-ˈgōn\. Town, Tabasco state, SE Mexico, on Grijalva river near its mouth; pop. (1960c) 8375.

Fron·tier \frən-ˈti(ə)r\. County in Nebraska. See table at NEBRASKA.

Fron·ti·gnan \ˌfrōⁿ-tē-ˈnyäⁿ\. Commune, Hérault dept., S France, on a narrow lagoon just E of Étang de Thau; pop. (1968c) 11,141; manufactures muscatel.

Front Range \ˈfrənt-\. A range of Rocky Mts. in N cen. Colorado; highest peak Grays Peak 14,270 ft.

Front Royal \-ˈrȯi(-ə)l\. Town, ⊗ of Warren co., N Virginia, 20 m. S of Winchester; pop. (1970c) 8211; scene of capture of Union troops by Confederates 1862.

Fröschwiller. See WÖRTH.

Fro·si·no·ne \ˌfrō-zə-ˈnō-nē\. **1** Province of Latium, cen. Italy. See table at ITALY.

2 *or anc.* **Fru·si·no** \ˈfrüz-ᵊn-ˌō, ˈfrüs-\. Commune, its ✱, 48 m. ESE of Rome; pop. (1968e) 37,024; wine; remains of ancient Volscian town.

Frost·burg \ˈfrȯst-ˌbərg\. City, Allegany co., NW Maryland, 9 m. W of Cumberland; pop. (1970c) 7327; aluminum, chemicals; dairy and truck farms; Frostburg State Coll. (1898).

Frost·proof \ˈfrȯst-ˌprüf\. City, Polk co., cen. Florida penin., 35 m. SE of Lakeland; pop. (1970c) 2814; citrus fruit.

Fro·ward, Cape \-ˈfrō-(w)ərd\. South tip of Brunswick Penin., Chile, on N side of Strait of Magellan; most S point of mainland of South America, 53°54′S, 71°18′W.

Frøya \ˈfrȯi-ə\. Island in Norwegian Sea off W coast of Norway, W of Trondheim Fjord and N of Hitra I.

Frun·ze \ˈfrün-zə\ *or formerly* **Pish·pek** \pish-ˈpek\. City, ✱ of Kirgiz S.S.R., U.S.S.R., on Chu river on Kazakh border 125 m. WSW of Alma-Ata; pop. (1970p) 431,000; agricultural machinery; leather, textiles; meat packing; univ. (1951); birthplace of Gen. Mikhail V. Frunze, for whom it was renamed; taken by Russians 1862.

Frusino. See FROSINONE 2.

Frý·dek–Mís·tek \ˈfrē-(ˌ)dek-ˈmis-(ˌ)tek\ *or Ger.* **Frie·dek–Mis·tek** \ˈfrē-(ˌ)dek-ˈmis-(ˌ)tek\. Town, Czech S.R., cen. Czechoslovakia, just S of Ostrava; pop. (1968e) 35,800; textiles, timber.

Frye·burg \ˈfrī-ˌbərg\. Town, Oxford co., W Maine, on New Hampshire border 38 m. W of Lewiston; pop. (1970c) 2208; Fryeburg Academy (1791).

Fu·cec·chio \fü-ˈchek-ē-ˌō\. Commune, Firenze prov., Tuscany, cen. Italy, on Arno river 23 m. W by S of Florence; pop. (1968e) 17,930; textiles.

Fuchau. See FOOCHOW.

Fu–ch'un \ˈfü-ˈchùn\ *or* **Tsien Tang** \chē-ˈen-ˈtäŋ\. Navigable river, Chekiang prov., E China; ab. 140 m. long; flows NE into Hangchow Bay; remarkable for its tidal bore.

Fu·ci·no \ˈfü-chi-ˌnō\ *or anc.* **Fu·ci·nus** \ˈfyüs-ᵊn-əs\ *or mod.* **Ce·la·no** \chā-ˈlän-ō\. Former lake in Aquila prov., cen. Italy; 60 sq. m.; drained 1854–75, providing 42,000 acres for cultivation (vineyards).

Fue·go \f(y)ù-ˈā-(ˌ)gō\. Volcano, Guatemala, SW of Guatemala city; 12,346 ft.; eruption 1880.

Fuen·te de Can·tos \ˈfwān-tə-də-ˈkän-tōs\. Commune, Badajoz prov., SW Spain, 53 m. SE of Badajoz; pop. (1970p) 5967.

Fuente Obe·ju·na *or formerly* **Fuen·te·o·ve·ju·na** \ˈfwān-tə-ˌō-bə-ˈhü-nə, -ō-və-\. City, Córdoba prov., S Spain, 46 m. NW of Córdoba; pop. (1970p) 9247; coal, lead, and mica mines; formerly seat of Knights of Calatrava.

Fuen·te·rra·bía \ˌfwān-tə-ˈräb-yə, -ˈräv-\ *or Eng.* **Fon·ta·ra·bia** \ˌfòn-tə-ˈrā-bē-ə\. Town, Guipúzcoa prov., N Spain, at mouth of Bidassoa just N of Irún; pop. (1960c) 858; medieval town with interesting ruins; often a scene of conflict 12th to 19th cents.

Fuer·te, Rio del \ˈrē-ō-ˌdel-fü-ˈert-ē\. River, SW Chihuahua and N Sinaloa states, Mexico; ab. 180 m. long; flows into Gulf of California.

Fuerte Olim·po \ˌfwər-tē-ō-ˈlim-pō\ *or Eng.* **Fort Olimpo.** Town, ✱ of Olimpo dept., N Paraguay, on Paraguay river; pop. (1970e) 4940.

Fuer·te·ven·tu·ra \fü-ˌert-ē-ven-ˈtùr-ə\. One of the Canary Islands (*q.v.*), Las Palmas prov., Spain, 75 m. ENE of Grand Canary I.; 668 sq. m.; pop. (1970p) 18,192; extinct volcanoes.

Fu·ga \ˈfü-gə\. Island in Babuyan group, N of Luzon, Phil.; 36 sq. m.; good anchorage.

Fuhkien. See FUKIEN.

Fu–hsing–chen \ˈfü-ˈshin-ˈchən\ *or formerly* **Sze·mao** \ˈsə-ˈmaù\. Town, S cen. Yunnan prov., S China, on Mekong river; former treaty port.

Fu·jai·rah \fə-ˈjīr-ə\. 1 Emirate. See UNITED ARAB EMIRATES.

2 Coastal town, its ✱; pop. (1968c) 761.

Fu·ji \ˈf(y)ü-(ˌ)jē\. 1 *or* **Fu·ji·ya·ma** \ˌf(y)ü-jē-ˈ(y)äm-ə\ *or more correctly* **Fu·ji–no–Ya·ma** \-(ˌ)nō-\ *or* **Fu·ji·san** \ˌf(y)ü-(ˌ)jē-ˈsän\. Sacred mountain in S cen. Honshū, Japan, ab. 70 m. WSW of Tokyo; 12,388 ft.; an isolated peak, highest in Japan; almost a perfect cone; its crater has diameter of nearly 2000 ft.; a quiescent volcano, last eruption 1707.

2 City, Shizuoka prefecture, Honshū, Japan; pop. (1970c) 180,639.

Fu·ji·eda \ˌfü-jē-ˈā-də\. City, Shizuoka prefecture, Honshū, Japan, 12 m. SW of Shizuoka; pop. (1970c) 78,750.

Fu·ji·no·me·ya \ˌfü-jē-nō-ˈmā-yə\. City, Shizuoka prefecture, Honshū, Japan, 22 m. NE of Shizuoka; pop. (1970c) 88,880.

Fu·ji·sa·wa \ˌfü-jē-ˈsä-wə\. City, Kanagawa prefecture, Honshū, Japan; pop. (1970c) 228,978; iron goods.

Fukae. See FUKUE.

Fu·ka·ya \fü-ˈkä-yə\. City, Saitama prefecture, Honshū, Japan, 46 m. NW of Tokyo; pop. (1970c) 60,609.

Fu·kien *also* **Fuh·kien** \ˈfü-ˈkyen, -kē-ˈen. Maritime province, SE China, bounded on N by Chekiang prov., on E and SE by East China Sea and Formosa Strait, on SW by Kwangtung, and on W by Kiangsi; 47,529 sq. m.; pop. (1968e) 17,000,000; ✱ Foochow; chief river the Min flowing SE to East China Sea near Foochow; subtropical climate; important agriculturally, tea and rice the chief crops; extensive forests from which in earlier times camphor was an important product; coal, iron ore, gold, graphite; chief cities Foochow, Amoy, Ch'üan-chou, Chang-chou, Nan-p'ing. In early times home of barbaric tribes; part of Southern Sung empire in 5th cent. A.D. and under Liang dynasty in 6th cent.; according to Marco Polo, under Kublai Khan (13th cent.) it had an immense trade through the port of Zayton.

Fu·ku·chi·ya·ma \fù-ˌkü-chē-ˈyä-mə\. City, Kyōto prefecture, Honshū, Japan, 35 m. NW of Kyōto; pop. (1970c) 57,174.

Fu·kue \ˈfü-kü-ā\ *or* **Fu·kae** \ˈfü-ˌkī\. 1 Largest island of Gotō Archipelago, off W coast of Kyūshū, Japan; 1342 sq. m.

2 Town, on E coast of Fukue I.; pop. (1970c) 33,442; largest town of Gotō Archipelago.

Fu·kui \fü-ˈkü-ē, ˈfü-ˌ\. 1 Prefecture, Honshū, Japan; 1617 sq. m.; pop. (1970c) 744,230; ✱ Fukui; textiles.

2 City, its ✱, near the coast ab. 70 m. NNW of Nagoya; pop. (1970c) 200,509; in feudal period seat of a daimyo; after restoration became large industrial center, producing textiles, esp. habutai (a thin, soft, Japanese silk), and paper; univ. (1949); destroyed by earthquake June 28, 1948, since rebuilt.

Fu·ku·o·ka \ˌfü-kə-ˈwō-kə\. 1 Prefecture, N Kyūshū, Japan; pop. (1970c) 4,027,416; ✱ Fukuoka; coal, chemicals.

2 Seaport city, its ✱, on Hakata Bay; pop. (1970c) 853,270; manufactures iron and steel, electrical equipment; fishing, shipbuilding; Kyūshū Univ. (1910). In ancient times one of the three trade ports of Japan; at time (1274–81) of attempted invasions of Kublai Khan, the scene of much fighting; heavily bombed 1945.

Fu·ku·shi·ma \ˌfü-kə-ˈshē-mə\. 1 Prefecture, N cen. Honshū, Japan; 5321 sq. m.; pop. (1970c) 1,946,077; ✱ Fukushima; mountainous region; rice, tobacco; fishing.

2 City, its ✱, pop. (1970c) 227,451; railroad junction; trade center (agricultural products, silk and silk goods). In feudal times the castle town of a daimyo.

Fu·ku·ya·ma \ˌfü-kə-ˈyäm-ə\. 1 City, Hiroshima prefecture, SW Honshū, Japan, on Inland Sea 33 m. W of Okayama; pop. (1970c) 255,086.

2 Town, Hokkaidō, Japan. See MATSUMAE.

Fu·lah Empire \ˈfü-lə-, ˈfùl-\. See SOKOTO.

Ful·da \ˈfùl-də\. 1 River, West Germany; 135 m. long; flows N from E Hesse state to unite with Werra river at Münden and form the Weser river.

2 Manufacturing city, E Hesse, West Germany, on Fulda river 54 m. NE of Frankfurt am Main; pop. (1969e) 44,365; textiles, candles, ball bearings, tires, agricultural machinery; cathedral (a smaller-scale replica of St. Peter's in Rome); abbey (founded 8th cent.; in 10th cent. abbot became primate of Germany); formerly seat of university (1734–1803); passed to Prussia 1866; in World War II taken by American army Apr. 4, 1945.

Fulginium. See FOLIGNO.

Ful·ler·ton \ˈfùl-ərt-ᵊn\. 1 City, Orange co., SW California, 17 m. NE of Long Beach; pop. (1970c) 85,987; transportation equipment, aircraft parts, paper products; oil wells; Fullerton Junior Coll. (1913), California State Coll. at Fullerton (1957).

2 City, ⊗ of Nance co., E cen. Nebraska; pop. (1970c) 1444.

Ful·ton \ˈfùlt-ᵊn\. 1 Name of counties in eight states of the U.S. See tables at ARKANSAS, GEORGIA, ILLINOIS, INDIANA, KENTUCKY, NEW YORK, OHIO, PENNSYLVANIA.

2 City, Whiteside co., NW Illinois, on Mississippi river 35 m. N of Rock Island; pop. (1970c) 3630; dairy products, lumber.

3 City, Fulton co., SW corner of Kentucky, on Tennessee border 23 m. SW of Mayfield; pop. (1970c) 3250.

4 Town, ⊗ of Itawamba co., NE Mississippi; pop. (1970c) 2899; Itawamba Junior Coll. (1948).

5 City, ⊗ of Callaway co., cen. Missouri, 25 m. NNE of Jefferson City; pop. (1970c) 12,248; wheat, oats; mineral

springs; Westminster Coll. (1851), William Woods Coll. (1890).

6 Manufacturing city, Oswego co., cen. New York, 24 m. NNW of Syracuse; pop. (1970c) 14,003; paper products; poultry and fruit farms.

Fulton Chain Lakes. Chain of small lakes in NE cen. New York, chiefly in Herkimer co.

Ful·ton·dale \ˈfu̇lt-ᵊn-ˌdāl\. City, Jefferson co., cen. Alabama, 5 m. N of Birmingham; pop. (1970c) 5163.

Ful·wood \ˈfu̇l-wu̇d\. Urban district, Lancashire, NW England, NE suburb of Preston; pop. (1971p) 21,741.

Fu·na·bashi \ˌfü-nə-ˈbäsh-ē\. City, Chiba prefecture, Honshū, Japan; pop. (1970c) 325,426; suburb of Tokyo; fish market.

Fu·na·fu·ti \ˌf(y)ü-nə-ˈf(y)üt-ē\. Atoll, cen. Ellice Is., W Pacific Ocean, 8°31′S lat. and 179°13′E long.; 30 islets; lagoon area 84 sq. m., land area 17 sq. m.; contains chief village and government headquarters of the group. Occupied by U.S. Marines Apr. 23, 1943 and converted into a U.S. base.

Fun·chal \fün-ˈshäl, fən-\. 1 District of Portugal. See table at PORTUGAL.

2 Seaport commune, its ✱, at head of large bay on SE coast of Madeira I.; munic. pop. (1970p) 105,791; winter resort; cathedral (1485–1514); tomb of Zarco, discoverer of island.

Fun·dão \fü(ⁿ)-ˈdau̇(ⁿ)\. Commune, Castelo Branco dist., E cen. Portugal, 24 m. N of Castelo Branco; pop. (1970p) 5081; scene of insurrection 1903.

Fundi. See FONDI.

Fun·dy, Bay of \-ˈfən-dē\. Inlet of Atlantic Ocean in SE Canada, extending bet. S New Brunswick and Nova Scotia; 94 m. long, 32 m. wide at its mouth; at upper end branches into Chignecto Bay and Minas Basin; remarkable for swift tidal currents; tides reaching 70 ft. recorded at head of bay; St. John (New Brunswick) on it.

Fundy National Park. See CANADA, *National Parks.*

Fünen. See FYN.

Fünfkirchen. See PÉCS.

Fung, Al–. See AL-FUNG.

Fu Niu Shan \ˌfü-ˌnyü-ˈshän\. Mountain range in E cen. China, chiefly in N Honan prov., an E extension of Ch'in Ling Shan; includes peaks ab. 9000 ft. high.

Funza. See BOGOTÁ 1.

Fu·quay–Va·ri·na \ˈf(y)ü-(ˌ)kwā-və-ˈrī-nə\. Town, Wake co., E cen. North Carolina, 18 m. SW of Raleigh; pop. (1970c) 3576; baby clothing; agriculture.

Füred. See BALATONFÜRED.

Fur·ka Pass \ˌfu̇(ə)r-kə-\. Mountain pass bet. Uri and Valais cantons, S cen. Switzerland; 7994 ft.

Fur·nas \ˈfərn-əs\. County in Nebraska. See table at NEBRASKA.

Fur·neaux Islands \ˈfər-(ˌ)nō-\. Island group off NE Tasmania, Australia, at E end of Bass Strait; separated from Tasmania by Banks Strait; ab. 900 sq. m.; pop. (1969e) 1240; largest Flinders I. and Cape Barren I. Discovered 1773 by Capt. T. Furneaux in command of the *Adventure,* one of Capt. Cook's ships.

Furnes \ˈfu̇(ə)rn\ *or Flem.* **Veur·ne** \ˈvər-nə\. Commune, West Flanders prov., NW Belgium; pop. (1969e) 7516; Belgian headquarters in World War I, 6 m. behind the Yser front.

Fur·ness \ˈfər-nəs\. District, NW Lancashire, NW England, N of Morecambe Bay; S portion a peninsula with Barrow-in-Furness the chief town, N portion in Lake District; iron ore in SW; famous abbey, founded 1127 by a Benedictine order which joined Cistercian order 1148, became largest Cistercian abbey in England.

Fur Seal Islands. See PRIBILOF ISLANDS.

Fürst·en·feld·bruck \ˌf(y)u̇r-stən-ˈfelt-ˌbru̇k\. City, Bavaria, West Germany, 15 m. W of Munich; pop. (1969e) 22,045; clothing; 15th and 17th cent. churches.

Fürstentum Liechtenstein. See LIECHTENSTEIN.

Für·sten·wal·de \ˌf(y)u̇r-stən-ˈväl-də\. Industrial city, Frankfurt dist., East Germany, on Spree river 24 m. ESE of East Berlin; pop. (1970e) 30,830; metalworking. Received municipal privileges 1285; episcopal see 1385–1571; bombed during World War II.

Fürth \ˈfu̇(ə)rt, ˈfi(ə)rt\. Manufacturing city, Bavaria, West Germany, at confluence of Regnitz and Pegnitz rivers 5 m. NW of Nürnberg; pop. (1969e) 94,252; electronic equipment, toys; city hall (1840–50); in World War II had airplane factories; bombed by Allies 1944–45.

Fu·ry and Hec·la Strait \ˌfyu̇(ə)r-ē . . . ˌhek-lə-\. Passage from Gulf of Boothia to Foxe Basin, bet. Melville Penin. and NW Baffin I., Canada; ab. 100 m. long.

Fusan. See PUSAN.

Fu·sa·ro \fü-ˈsär-(ˌ)ō, -ˈzär-\ *or anc.* **Pa·lus Ach·e·ru·sia** \ˌpā-lə-ˌsak-ə-ˈrü-zh(ē-)ə\. Small lake, Campania, Italy, on peninsula bet. Gulf of Gaeta and Bay of Pozzuoli; oyster cultivation, hydrobiological station.

Fushih. See YEN-AN.

Fu·shi·mi \ˈfü-shə-(ˌ)mē\. Suburb of Kyōto, Kyōto prefecture, Honshū, Japan; historically important as residence (1594–98) of the shogun Toyotomi Hideyoshi.

Fu–shun \ˈfü-ˈshu̇n\. City, Liaoning prov., NE China, 30 m. E of Mukden; pop. (1970e) 1,700,000; on rich bituminous coalfield. Mines known to Chinese since 13th cent. A.D.; modern development begun by Russians 1902.

Fusin. See FOU-HSIN.

Füs·sen \ˈf(y)üs-ᵊn\. Commune, SW Bavaria, West Germany, near Tirol border; pop. (1968e) 10,778; castle; treaty signed Apr. 22, 1745 bet. Elector Maximilian III Joseph of Bavaria and Maria Theresa.

Fustāt, Al–. City, Egypt. See CAIRO 2.

Futa Jallon. See FOUTA DJALLON.

Futa Pass. See table at APENNINES.

Fu·tu·na Islands \fə-ˈtü-nə-\ *or* **Hoorn Islands** \ˈhō(ə)rn-, ˈhȯ(ə)rn-\. Island group in SW Pacific Ocean, NE of Fiji; 35 sq. m.; pop. (1965e) 2945; a part of Wallis and Futuna Islands group, a French overseas territory; before 1958 a dependency of the French overseas territory of New Caledonia; comprises **Futuna** (8 m. by 5 m.) and Alofi (6 m. by 3 m.) islands; annexed by France 1887.

Fu–yü \ˈfü-ˈyü\ *or* **Pe·tu·na** \pi-ˈt(y)ü-nə\. Town, Kirin prov., NE China, 100 m. SW of Harbin.

Fyn \ˈfin\ *or Ger.* **Fü·nen** \ˈf(y)ü-nən\. One of the islands of Denmark, bet. Sjælland on E and lower Jutland Penin. on W; with small adjacent islands constitutes a county (area 1346 sq. m.; pop. [1971c] 433,765); wheat, dairy products.

Fyne, Loch \läk-ˈfin, läk̲-\. Inlet of Firth of Clyde, W Scotland, in Argyll co.; 40½ m. long; herrings.

Fyzabad. 1 Town, Afghanistan. See FAIZĀBĀD 1.

2 City, India. See FAIZĀBĀD 2.

G

Gab·a·rus Bay \ˌgab-ə-ˌrüs-\. Inlet of Atlantic Ocean, E coast of Cape Breton I., Nova Scotia, Canada, SW of Louisburg.

Gabelhorn. See OBER-GABELHORN.

Gabe Rock \ˈgāb-\. Height, SW Banner co., W Nebraska; 5006 ft.

Gaberones. See GABORONE.

Ga·bès \ˈgäb-əs, -ˌes\ *also* **Qa·bes** \ˈkäb-ˌes\ *or anc.* **Tac·a·pe** \ˈtak-ə-ˌpē\. Seaport town and oasis, SE Tunisia, on the **Gulf of Gabès** (*or anc.* **Syr·tis Mi·nor** \ˌsərt-ə-ˈsmī-nər\); pop. (1966c) 32,300; export trade in dates, skins, wool; peaches; fishing.

Ga·bii \ˈgā-bē-ˌī\. Ancient city, Latium, Italy, 12 m. E of Rome, on shore of a lake which has dried up; well-known baths; temple of Juno; medieval fortress.

Ga·ble, Great \-ˈgā-bəl\. Mountain, W Cumberland, NW England, in the Lake District; 2949 ft.

Gable Mountain. Peak in Glacier National Park, NW Montana; 9200 ft.

Gablonz. See JABLONEC NAD NISOU.

Ga·bon \ga-ˈbōⁿ\ *or* **Ga·bun** \gə-ˈbün\ *or Eng.* **Ga·boon** \gə-ˈbün\. 1 *or officially* **Gabon Republic** *or Fr.* **Ré·pu·blique Ga·bo·naise** \rā-pə-blēk-gab-ə-nez, -nāz\. Republic, W equatorial Africa, bounded on NW by Equatorial Guinea, on N by Cameroon, on E and S by Congo, and on W by the Atlantic Ocean; 102,317 sq. m.; pop. (1970e) 500,000; ✻ Libreville. *Physical features:* Narrow coastal plain; hilly in S and on N border; highest point Mt. Iboundji 5167 ft. in N. Chief river the Ogooué, whose basin covers most of the republic. *Chief products:* Cocoa, coffee, cassava, palm oil; manganese, iron ore, uranium, oil. *Chief towns:* Libreville, Port-Gentil.

History: First part of French Equatorial Africa to be settled by the French (1841); Libreville founded 1849; became a colony 1903 and part of French Equatorial Africa 1910; changed to a territory 1946; became a republic within the French Community 1958; achieved independence 1960; government overthrown by army, restored with aid of French troops 1964; adopted new constitution 1966; initiated major economic development program 1971.

2 Estuary, Gabon Republic; 7 m. wide, extending ab. 40 m. inland; Libreville is at its mouth; discovered by Portuguese at end of 15th cent.

Ga·bo·ro·ne \ˌgäb-ə-ˈrō-nē\ *or formerly* **Ga·be·ro·nes** \ˌgäb-ə-ˈrō-nəs\. Town, ✻ of Botswana, S Africa; pop. (1971e) 14,467.

Ga·bro·vo \ˈgäb-rə-ˌvō\. 1 Province of cen. Bulgaria. See table at BULGARIA.

2 Town, its ✻, on upper Yantra river; pop. (1968e) 67,887; textiles, leather goods; first Bulgarian national school opened here 1835.

Gabun. See GABON.

Ga·dag \ˈgəd-əg\. Town, Mysore, SW India, 310 m. SE of Bombay; pop. (1961c) 76,600; important rail junction; old Hindu temples with noteworthy carving, especially the Temple of Trimbakeshwar and a temple to Vishnu.

Ga·dà·mes \gə-ˈdam-əs, -ˈdäm-\ *or* **Ghu·dā·mis** \gə-ˈdäm-əs\ *also* **Rha·da·mes** \rə-ˈdam-əs\. Oasis and town, NW Libya, on Libya-Algeria boundary.

Gad·a·ra \ˈgad-ə-rə\. Greek town of the Decapolis (*q.v.*), NE Palestine, ab. 6 m. SE of Sea of Galilee; gave its name to the Gadarenes (*Mark* v. 1; *Luke* viii. 26).

Gades, Gadier, Gadir, Gadire. See CÁDIZ 2.

Gaditan Strait. See GIBRALTAR, STRAIT OF.

Gaditanum, Fretum. See GIBRALTAR, STRAIT OF.

Gads·den \ˈgadz-dən\. 1 County in Florida. See table at FLORIDA.

2 Industrial city, ⊗ of Etowah co., NE Alabama, on Coosa river 60 m. ENE of Birmingham; pop. (1970c) 53,928; steel, textiles, automobile tires; in area rich in manganese, iron ore, coal, limestone, bauxite, sandstone, timber; settled 1840.

Gadsden Purchase. A tract of land, now in New Mexico and Arizona; 29,640 sq. m.; purchased 1853 by U.S. from Mexico for $10,000,000 after negotiations conducted by James Gadsden, U.S. minister to Mexico.

Gads·hill \ˈgadz-ˌhil\. Low hill in Kent, SE England, 3 m. WNW of Rochester; home of Charles Dickens.

Ga·e·ta \gä-ˈāt-ə\ *or anc.* **Ca·ie·ta** \kā-ˈ(y)ēt-ə, kī-ˈēt-\. Fortified seaport, Latina prov., Latium, cen. Italy, on Gulf of Gaeta 41 m. ESE of Littoria; pop. (1968e) 22,799; fisheries; ancient ruins, including a Roman theater, a Roman amphitheater, and a campanile. Center of commercial prosperity after dissolution of Roman and Eastern empires; withstood numerous invasions, esp. by Lombards and Saracens; fell to Norman Sicily 1134; papal refuge 1848–50 from Roman revolutions; last stronghold of Neapolitan Bourbons in Italy; fell to General Cialdini after long siege 1861.

Gaeta, Gulf of. Inlet of Tyrrhenian Sea on W coast of Italy, N of Bay of Naples and E of Ponza Is.; its coast occupied by Allies May 1944.

Gae·tu·lia \ji-ˈt(y)ü-lē-ə\. Ancient district, N Africa, N part of Libya and of Sahara region; inhabited by nomad tribes which belonged to Numidian Berber race.

Gaff·ney \ˈgaf-nē\. City, ⊗ of Cherokee co., N South Carolina, 19 m. ENE of Spartanburg; pop. (1970c) 13,253; textile mills; limestone; diversified farming; Limestone Coll. (1845).

Gäfle. See GÄVLE.

Gäfleborg. See GÄVLEBORG.

Gaf·sa \ˈgaf-sə\ *or anc.* **Cap·sa** \ˈkap-sə\. Town and oasis, W cen. Tunisia, ab. 115 m. W of Sfax; pop. (1966c) 32,408; olives, dates; thermal springs; prehistoric discoveries nearby have given name (*Capsian*) to a Paleolithic culture of N Africa and S Europe regarded as contemporaneous with the Aurignacian. In World War II scene of some of first fighting by American troops in African campaign; taken by Germans last week of Feb. 1943 (see AL-QASRAYN), retaken by Americans Mar. 17, 1943.

Ga·ga·rin \gə-'gär-ən\ *or formerly* **Gzhatsk** \gə-'zhatsk\. Town, NE Smolensk Oblast, Russian S.F.S.R., U.S.S.R., 90 m. W of Moscow, on main Moscow-Smolensk highway and railroad; in World War II held a few months of 1941–42 by the Germans.

Gage \'gāj\. County in Nebraska. See table at NEBRASKA.

Gage·town \'gāj-ˌtau̇n\. Town (unincorporated), ⊗ of Queens co., S New Brunswick, Canada, on St. John river 36 m. N of St. John; pop. (1966c) 618.

Ga·gnon \gä-'nyō^{n}\. Town, Saguenay co., SE Quebec, Canada; pop. (1971p) 3773.

Ga·gny \gä-'nyē\. Commune, Seine-St-Denis dept., N France, 6 m. ENE of Paris; pop. (1968c) 35,780.

Ga·han·na \gə-'han-ə\. Village, Franklin co., cen. Ohio, 5 m. NE of Columbus; pop. (1970c) 12,400; diversified agriculture.

Gaidaro. See ANGATHONÍSI.

Gail \'gāl\. Town, ⊗ of Borden co., NW Texas; pop. (1970c) 178.

Gail·lac \ga-'yák\ *or* **Gaillac–sur–Tarn** \-s(y)ür-'tärn\. Manufacturing commune, Tarn dept., S France, on Tarn river ab. 12 m. W of Albi; pop. (1968c) 10,315; Benedictine abbey founded 960; noted for sparkling white wine.

Gail·lard Cut \gil-ˌyärd-, ˌgāl-ˌ(y)ärd-\ *or formerly* **Cu·le·bra Cut** \k(y)ü-ˌlā-brə-, -ˌleb-rə-\. Southeast section of Panama Canal, Canal Zone, ab. 8 m. through Culebra Mt., from Gamboa to locks at Pedro Miguel; 45 ft. deep, width at bottom 300 ft.; name changed by Pres. Wilson in honor of David Du Bose Gaillard (d. 1913) who had charge of excavation of this most difficult part in construction of the canal.

Gain·er Memorial Dam \'gān-ər-\ *or formerly* **Scit·u·ate Dam** \'sich-ə-ˌwāt-\. Dam across Pawtuxet river, N cen. Rhode Island; height 180 ft.; completed 1928; impounds water, **Scituate Reservoir,** for water supply of Providence.

Gaines \'gānz\. County in Texas. See table at TEXAS.

Gaines·boro \'gānz-ˌbər-ə, -ˌbə-rə\. Town, ⊗ of Jackson co., N Tennessee; pop. (1970c) 1101; oil wells.

Gaines' Mill \'gānz-\. Battlefield just ENE of Richmond, Virginia; scene June 27, 1862 of defeat of Union forces under General Fitz-John Porter by Lee's Confederates; sometimes known as Cold Harbor (*q.v.*).

Gaines·ville \'gānz-ˌvil, -vəl\. **1** City, ⊗ of Alachua co., N Florida penin., 65 m. SW of Jacksonville; pop. (1970c) 64,510; electronic equipment; meat-packing; sawmills, naval stores; Univ. of Florida (1853), Santa Fe Junior Coll. (1965).

2 City, ⊗ of Hall co., N Georgia, 35 m. NW of Athens; pop. (1970c) 15,459; textile mills; Brenau Coll. (1878), Gainesville Junior Coll. (1965); incorp. 1821.

3 City, ⊗ of Ozark co., S Missouri; pop. (1970c) 627.

4 City, ⊗ of Cooke co., N Texas, 30 m. W of Sherman; pop. (1970c) 13,830; food processing, oil refining; settled c. 1851 on route of the 1849 gold seekers; chartered as city 1879.

5 Village, Prince William co., NE Virginia; battle Aug. 28, 1862, a part of second battle of Bull Run.

Gains·bor·ough \'gānz-ˌbər-ə, -ˌbə-rə, -b(ə-)rə\. Urban district, Parts of Lindsey, Lincolnshire, E England, on the Trent 30 m. SW of Hull; pop. (1971p) 17,420; the St. Ogg's of George Eliot's *Mill on the Floss;* Sweyn Forkbeard landed here 1013 with his Danish marauders.

Gaïon. See PAXOS.

Gaird·ner, Lake \-'ga(ə)rd-nər, -'ge(ə)rd-\. Lake, S South Australia, N of Eyre Penin.; ab. 90 m. long; 1840 sq. m.

Gair Loch \'ga(ə)r-läk, 'ge(ə)r-, läk-\. Inlet of Atlantic Ocean in Ross and Cromarty co., NW coast of Scotland; the village of **Gair·loch** is at its head.

Gai·thers·burg \'gā-thərz-ˌbərg\. Town, Montgomery co., W Maryland, 20 m. NW of Washington; pop. (1970c) 8344; precision equipment.

Gajac. See VILLENEUVE-SUR-LOT.

Ga·la \'gäl-ə\ *or* **Gala Water.** River, SE Scotland; 21 m. long; rises in Moorfoot Hills, S of Edinburgh; flows SSW into the Tweed 2½ m. W of Melrose.

Ga·la·na \gə-'län-ə\. River, E Africa; 340 m. long; rises in S Kenya, flows SE across S Kenya into Indian Ocean S of Formosa Bay.

Ga·lá·pa·gos Islands \gə-ˌläp-ə-gəs-, -ˌlap-\ *or* **Co·lón Archipelago** \kə-ˌlōn-\ *or Span.* **Ar·chi·pié·la·go de Colón** \ˌär-chi-'pyel-ə-(ˌ)gō-ˌdā-\ *also* **Tor·toise Islands** \ˌtȯrt-əs-\. Island group constituting a territory of Ecuador, in Pacific Ocean on the equator ab. 600 m. W of mainland; 3075 sq. m.; pop. (1970e) 3600; ✱ San Cristóbal; coffee, lemons; fishing; comprises many small islands and ab. 15 large ones; interesting specimens of wildlife peculiar to the islands, on which exploration without official permission is prohibited; noted esp. for species of giant tortoise (*Span.* galápago), now almost extinct, which includes perhaps the largest living form now known, found on Isabel (Albemarle) I. Discovered 1535 by Spanish; taken possession of by Ecuador 1832; measures for protection of wildlife passed by Ecuador government 1935 and 1959; during World War II one of islands, Seymour, site of air base established by U.S. forces Dec. 1941, evacuated July 1946; biological research center opened 1964.

Gal·a·shiels \ˌgal-ə-'shēlz\. Burgh, Selkirk co., SE Scotland; pop. (1971p) 12,605; manufactures tweeds.

Gal·a·ta \'gal-ə-tə, ˌgäl-ə-'tä\. Seaport suburb, chief business section of İstanbul, Turkey, on the Golden Horn S of Pera; in 1265 assigned by Michael Palaeologus to Genoese merchants; fortified by them but taken over by the Turks 1453.

Ga·la·ți \gə-'läts(-ē)\ *or formerly* **Ga·latz** \'gäl-ˌäts\. **1** County of E Romania. See table at ROMANIA.

2 City, its ⊗, on lower Danube ab. 115 m. NE of Bucharest; pop. (1970e) 179,189; port, exporting esp. timber and grain; shipyards, iron and steel plant; chemicals, textiles; technical inst. (1948); seat of European Danube Commission 1856–1945.

Ga·la·tia \gə-'lā-sh(ē-)ə\. Ancient country of cen. Asia Minor, originally including parts of Phrygia and Cappadocia; settled by Gauls in 3d cent. B.C.; expanded by them until checked by Attalus I of Pergamum c. 230 B.C.; became dependent upon Romans in 2d cent. B.C. and Roman province 25 B.C.; visited by St. Paul (*Epistle to the Galatians*). See ANKARA.

Ga·la·ti·na \ˌgal-ə-'tē-nə\. Commune, Lecce prov., Apulia, SE Italy, 10 m. S of Lecce; pop. (1968e) 26,550.

Ga·la·to·ne \ˌgäl-ə-'tō-nē\. Commune, Lecce prov., Apulia, SE Italy, 13 m. SSW of Lecce; pop. (1968e) 15,048; cathedral.

Galatz. See GALAȚI.

Gala Water. See GALA.

Ga·lax \'gā-(ˌ)laks\. City, SW Virginia, in Carroll and Grayson cos. but politically independent; 3 sq. m.; pop. (1970c) 6278; furniture, flour.

Gald·hø·pig·gen \'gäl-ˌhə(r)-ˌpig-ən\. Peak in the Jotunheimen, S cen. Norway, S of Glittertind; 8100 ft.

Ga·le·a·na \ˌgäl-ē-'än-ə\. Municipality, Nuevo León state, Mexico, 70 m. S of Monterrey; pop. (1970p) 39,143; lumber; corn, wheat, fruit.

Ga·le·ka·land \gə-'lā-kə-ˌland\. A district of Transkei (*q.v.*), Rep. of South Africa, along the coast bet. Great Kei and Umtata rivers, inhabited by the Galeka.

Ga·le·na \gə-'lē-nə\. **1** City, ⊗ of Jo Daviess co., NW corner of Illinois, on Galena river; pop. (1970c) 3930; in zinc and lead mines region; marble and granite works; home of Ulysses S. Grant.

2 City, Cherokee co., SE corner of Kansas, 22 m. S of Pittsburg; pop. (1970c) 3712; lead and zinc deposits; smelters.

3 City, ⊗ of Stone co., SW Missouri; pop. (1970c) 391.

Galena Park. City, Harris co., SE Texas; pop. (1970c) 10,479.

Ga·len·stock \'gäl-ən-ˌshtȯk, 'gal-ən-ˌstäk\. Peak in Valais and Uri cantons, S cen. Switzerland; 11,755 ft.

Ga·le·ra Point \gə-ˌlir-ə-\. Cape at NE tip of island of Trinidad.

Ga·le·ras \gə-'ler-əs\ *or* **Pas·to** \'päs-(ˌ)tō\. Volcano at S end of Cordillera Occidental in SW Colombia, near Ecuador border; 13,996 ft.

Gales·burg \'gā(ə)lz-ˌbərg\. Industrial city, ⊗ of Knox co., W Illinois, 45 m. WNW of Peoria; pop. (1970c) 36,290; auto parts, refrigerators, air conditioners, paint; Knox Coll. (1837), Carl Sandburg Coll. (1967); settled 1836 by pioneers from Whitesboro, N.Y.; incorporated as city 1857.

Gales Ferry \ˌgā(ə)lz-\. Subdivision of town of Connecticut. See LEDYARD.

Ga·li·cia \gə-'lish-(ē-)ə\. 1 *or Pol.* **Ha·licz** \'häl-ich\ *or Russ.* **Ga·lich** \'gäl-(y)ich\ *or* **Ga·li·tsi·ya** \gə-'lēt-sē-(y)ə\. Former Austrian crownland in E cen. Europe; 30,645 sq. m.; included N slopes of Carpathian Mts. and the valleys of upper Vistula and of upper Dniester, Bug, and Seret rivers.

History: From 6th cent. A.D., inhabited by Slavs; medieval principalities of Halicz and Lodomeria emerged about 12th cent. and were united in 13th cent.; E part, once attached to principality of Kiev, separated from Russian territory by Mongol invasion; ultimately became part of Poland 1386; in partitions of Poland 1772 and 1795, annexed to Austria; Western Galicia included in grand duchy of Warsaw 1809; scene of rising after which Kraków (*q.v.*) returned to Austria (1846); in World War I scene of fighting bet. Russians and Austrians and Germans; ceded by Austria 1919; after the war Poland conquered E part which had joined Ukraine, and in 1923, was confirmed in her possession of it; became Polish departments of Kraków, Lwów, Stanisławów, and Ternopol (*qq.v.*); divided bet. Germany and U.S.S.R. 1939 until outbreak of German war against U.S.S.R. 1941 (World War II); E half returned to U.S.S.R. and made part of Ukrainian S.S.R. after World War II, W half to Poland.

2 *or anc.* **Gal·lae·cia** \gə-'lē-sh(ē-)ə\. Region and ancient kingdom, NW Spain, bounded N and W by Atlantic Ocean, S by Portugal, SE by León, NE by Asturias; comprises modern provinces of La Coruña, Lugo, Orense, Pontevedra; deeply indented coastline with good harbors; mountainous; chief river the Miño; lead, tin, iron pyrites, and copper mines. Independent kingdom under the Suevi 411–585; overthrown first by Visigoths, later by Moors; became part of kingdom of Asturias and later of León and Castile.

Ga·li·či·ca National Park \ˌgäl-ə-'chēt-sə-\. National park, Yugoslavia; 93 sq. m.; high-altitude forests; established 1958.

Gal·i·lee \'gal-ə-ˌlē, ˌgal-ə-'\. Hilly region, coextensive with N part of modern Israel, bounded on E by Jordan river and Sea of Galilee, and extending S to Plain of Esdraelon; in early times corresponded to land of tribe of Naphtali; in 1st cent. B.C. a Roman province, divided into Upper Galilee and Lower Galilee, and forming a tetrarchy under rule of Herod family; chief scene of Christ's ministry. Ancient capital Sepphoris, Roman capital Tiberias, other important town Nazareth.

Galilee, Sea of; *usual name in Gospels for mod.* **Bahr Ta·ba·ri·ya** \ˌba(ə)r-ˌtäb-ə-'rē-(y)ə\; *in Bible also called* **Sea of Chin·ne·reth** \-'kin-ə-ˌreth\ [*Deut.* iii. 17], **Lake of Gen·nes·a·ret** \-gə-'nes-ə-ˌret, -rət\ [*Luke* v. 1], *or* **Sea of Ti·be·ri·as** \-tī-'bir-ē-əs\ [*John* vi. 1]. Freshwater lake, N Israel; 13 m. long, 7½ m. wide; 696 ft. below sea level; derives ab. 75 percent of its inflow from the Jordan river; economically significant (irrigation, fishing); rich in biblical associations; numerous archaeological sites in region.

Ga·li·na Point \gə-ˌlē-nə-\. Cape on NE coast of island of Jamaica, West Indies.

Gal·ion \'gal-yən\. Manufacturing city, Crawford co., N cen. Ohio, 15 m. W of Mansfield; pop. (1970c) 13,123; steel abrasives, telephone equipment; settled 1831.

Galitsiya. See GALICIA 1.

Gal·la·bat \'gal-ə-ˌbat\. Town, S Kassala prov., E Sudan, on Ethiopian border NW of Lake Tana.

Gallaecia. See GALICIA 2.

Gal·la·ra·te \ˌgal-ə-'rät-ē\. Industrial commune, Varese prov., Lombardy, N Italy, 10 m. S of Varese; pop. (1968e) 41,208; produces cotton cloth.

Gal·la·tin \'gal-ət-ᵊn\. 1 River, Wyoming and S Montana; 125 m. long; rises in NW corner of Wyoming, flows N into Montana to unite with Jefferson and Madison rivers and form the Missouri river; has formed a deep narrow canyon ab. 70 m. long, at entrance to which is a small village **Gallatin Gateway,** cen. Gallatin co., the canyon being one of the entrances to Yellowstone National Park.

2 Name of counties in three states of the U.S. See tables at ILLINOIS, KENTUCKY, MONTANA.

3 City, ⊗ of Daviess co., NW Missouri, 25 m. WNW of Chillicothe; pop. (1970c) 1883; diversified farming.

4 City, ⊗ of Sumner co., N Tennessee, 26 m. NE of Nashville; pop. (1970c) 13,271; burley tobacco market.

Gallatin Peak *or* **Gallatin Mountain.** Peak, S cen. Gallatin co., S Montana; 11,015 ft.

Gallatin Range. Mountains, Gallatin and Park cos., S Montana and NW Wyoming, bet. the Gallatin and Yellowstone rivers; highest point Electric Peak 11,155 ft., in NW corner of Yellowstone National Park.

Galle \'gäl, 'gal\ *or formerly* **Point de Galle** \ˌpȯint-də-\. Town, Ceylon, on Indian Ocean ab. 55 m. SSE of Colombo; pop. (1968e) 73,000; fortified seaport on rocky promontory. Occupied by Portuguese 1597; taken 1643 by Dutch, who erected fort; many curious old Buddhist monasteries.

Ga·lle·gos \gä-'yā-gəs, gī-'ā-\. 1 River, S Argentina; 180 m. long; flows E across S Santa Cruz prov. into **Gallegos Bay** opp. Falkland Is.

2 *or* **Río Gallegos** \ˌrē-ō-\ *also* **Puer·to Gallegos** \ˌpwer-tō-\. River port, ✱ of Santa Cruz prov., S Argentina, near mouth of Gallegos river; pop. (1960c) 14,439.

Gal·ley·head \'gal-ē-ˌhed\. Cape on SW coast of Ireland, E of Cape Clear; lighthouse.

Gal·lia \'gal-ē-ə\. County in Ohio. See table at OHIO.

Gallia, Gallia Cisalpina, Gallia Cispanada, etc. See GAUL.

Gal·lia·te \gäl-'yä-tā\. Commune, Novara prov., Piedmont, NW Italy, 5 m. NE of Novara; pop. (1968e) 13,305.

Gallim. See BEIT JALA.

Ga·lli·nas, Point \-gə-'yē-nəs\. Northernmost point of South America, La Guajira Penin., N Colombia; 12°25′N.

Gal·lip·o·li \gə-'lip-ə-lē\. 1 Fortified seaport and manufacturing commune, Lecce prov., Apulia, SE Italy, on E shore of Gulf of Taranto 21 m. SSW of Lecce; pop. (1968e) 17,739.

2 Seaport, Turkey. See GELİBOLU.

Gallipoli Peninsula *or Turk.* **Ge·li·bo·lu Ya·rı·ma·da·sı** \ˌgel-ə-bə-'lü-ˌyär-ə-ˌmäd-ə-'sē\. Narrow tongue of land extending SW from S coast of Turkey, Europe, bet. the Dardanelles on the SE and Saros Gulf and Aegean Sea on the NW and W; 63 m. long. Scene of battles 1915–16 in Allied campaign in World War I, in conjunction with naval bombardment of Dardanelles forts; troops, mainly Anzacs, landed Apr. 25, 1915; severe fighting at Kirte, Sari Bair, Suvla Bay (now called Anafarta Bay), etc.; unsuccessful issue led to withdrawal (last troops left Jan. 8, 1916).

Gal·li·po·lis \ˌgal-ə-pə-'lēs\. Industrial city, ⊗ of Gallia co., S Ohio, on Ohio river 30 m. NE of Ironton; pop. (1970c) 7490; settled by French colonists 1790.

Gal·li·tzin \gə-'lit-sən\. Borough, Cambria co., SW cen. Pennsylvania, 10 m. W of Altoona; pop. (1970c) 2496; railroad tunnel at crest of Alleghenies above Altoona.

Gäl·li·va·re *also* **Gel·li·vare** \'yel-ə-ˌvär-ə\. Rural commune, Norrbotten co., N Sweden, in the Arctic Circle; pop. (1970e) 25,633; hydroelectric power plant; iron mines.

Gal·lo, Cape \-'gäl-(ˌ)ō\. 1 *or Gk.* **Akrí·tas** \ə-'krēt-əs\. Cape on SW coast of Peloponnesus, S Greece, on W side of Gulf of Messenia.

2 Point on NW coast of Sicily, Italy, NW of Palermo.

Gal·lon Head \ˌgal-ən-\. Cape on W coast of island of Lewis with Harris, in the Outer Hebrides, off NW coast of Scotland.

Gal·loo Island \ˌgal-(ˌ)ü-\. Island in NE Lake Ontario, off W cen. coast of Jefferson co., N New York.

Gal·lo·way \'gal-ə-ˌwā\. District in SW Scotland, comprising Wigtown and Kirkcudbright cos.

Galloway, Mull of \ˌməl-\. Cape on SW extremity of Scotland, projecting into Irish Sea W of entrance to Luce Bay; lighthouse.

Gal·lup \'gal-əp\. Town, ⊗ of McKinley co., NW New Mexico, bet. Southern Navajo and Zuñi Indian Reservations; pop. (1970c) 13,779; railroad division point; coal mines; wool combing and packing, sheep and cattle raising; incorp. 1891, made ⊗ 1901.

Gal·lups Islands \ˌgal-əps-\. One of the smaller and outer islands in Boston Harbor, Massachusetts.

Galoenggoeng. See GALUNGGUNG.

Ga·lo·fa·lo \gə-'lō-fə-ˌlō\ *or anc.* **Cha·ryb·dis** \kə-'rib-dəs\. Famous whirlpool near Cape Faro, Sicily, Italy.

Gal Oya National Park \gä-'lō-yə-\. National park, Ceylon; 98 sq. m.; habitat of wide variety of wildlife, incl. bear, elephant, leopard; established 1954.

Galt \'gȯlt\. 1 City, Sacramento co., N cen. California, 22 m. SSW of Sacramento; pop. (1970c) 3200; winery, seed mill; diversified agriculture.

2 City, Waterloo co., SE Ontario, Canada, on Grand river 11 m. SE of Kitchener; pop. (1971p) 38,134; mining equipment, plastics, textiles; foundries; in rich farming area; varied manufactures. Founded as **Shade's Mills** \'shādz-ˌmilz\ 1816; many early settlers were Scottish; renamed 1827 after John Galt, Scottish novelist.

Gal·ty Mountains *or* **Gal·tee Mountains** \'gȯl-tē-\. Range, extending E to W in cos. Tipperary and Limerick, Eire; ab. 15 m. long; highest peak **Gal·ty·more** \ˌgȯl-tē-'mō(ə)r, -'mȯ(ə)r\, 3018 ft., in SW co. Tipperary.

Ga·lung·gung *or Du.* **Ga·loeng·goeng** \gä-'lu̇ŋ-ˌgu̇ŋ\. Volcanic peak, W Java, Indonesia, ab. 10 m. E of Garut; 7113 ft.; destructive eruption 1822.

Gal·va \'gal-və\. City, Henry co., NW Illinois, 35 m. SE of Rock Island; pop. (1970c) 3061.

Gal·ves·ton \'gal-və-stən\. 1 County in SE Texas. See table at TEXAS.

2 City and port of entry, its ⊗, on E end of **Galveston Island** (30 m. long) at S side of entrance to **Galveston Bay** (inlet of Gulf of Mexico) 48 m. SSE of Houston; pop. (1970c) 61,809; connected with mainland by causeway and bridge; extensive port facilities, exports esp. cotton, sulfur, oil, grain; manufactures wire and nails, petrochemicals, food products, cement, clothing; fisheries; Galveston Community Coll. (1967).

History: Used as rendezvous by Jean Laffite 1817–21; made naval base during Texas revolt against Mexico 1835; temporary capital of the republic before and after battle of San Jacinto 1836; incorporated as city 1839; scene of Civil War battle 1863; suffered from severe hurricanes and floods (esp. 1900); first city to adopt (1901) commission plan of municipal government, later called Galveston plan.

Gal·way \'gȯl-ˌwā\. 1 County, Connacht prov., W Eire; 2293 sq. m.; pop. (1971p) 148,220; ⊗ Galway; mountainous; chief river the Shannon; agriculture, fishing, quarrying (marble), manufacturing linen and woolen goods.

2 Municipal borough and seaport, its ⊗, at head of **Galway Bay** (extends inland ab. 20 m. on border bet. cos. Galway and Clare); pop. (1971p) 26,896; black marble quarrying, distilling, iron founding, fishing. Ruins of a 13th cent. Franciscan friary; seat of University College (1845).

Ga·ma·gō·ri \ˌgäm-ə-'gȯr-ē, gə-'mäg-ə-rē\. City, Aichi prefecture, Honshū, Japan, 32 m. SE of Nagoya; pop. (1970c) 82,868.

Gam·be·la *or* **Gam·bei·la** \gam-'bā-lə\. Town, Ilubabor prov., W Ethiopia; pop. (1970e) 2043.

Gam·bell \'gam-bəl\. City on coast at NW point of St. Lawrence I. in Bering Sea, Alaska; pop. (1970c) 372.

Gam·bia \'gam-bē-ə\. 1 *or in full* **Republic of the Gambia.** Republic, W Africa; 4003 sq. m.; pop. (1971e) 374,770; ✻ Bathurst; consists of a strip of land extending ab. 6 m. on both sides of the Gambia river and ab. 200 m. inland from river mouth; constitutes an enclave in Senegal. *Chief products:* Peanuts, palm kernels, hides, fish. *Chief towns:* Bathurst, Georgetown.

History: River mouth discovered by Portuguese in 1455 and river ascended by agent of English trading company 1618–19; Fort James, built on small island ab. 20 m. from mouth of Gambia, established 1664, captured by French 1779; British claims to region recognized by Treaty of Versailles 1783; Gambia settlement placed under government of Sierra Leone 1807–43; became a British colony 1843; reverted to former status under Sierra Leone 1866; again made a separate colony 1888; boundaries settled 1889; territory upstream made a British protectorate 1894; achieved independence 1965; became a republic 1970.

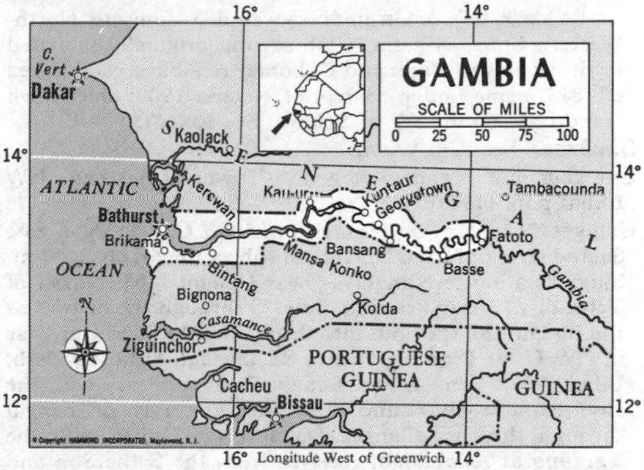

2 River, W Africa; ab. 700 m. long; rises in Fouta Djallon, Guinea; flows NW through Senegal and W into Atlantic Ocean at Bathurst; lower 200 m., which are navigable at all seasons, are in Republic of the Gambia.

Gam·bier \'gam-ˌbi(ə)r\. Village, Knox co., cen. Ohio, ab. 5 m. E of Mount Vernon; pop. (1970c) 1571; Kenyon Coll. (1824).

Gambier Islands. Island group, French Polynesia, S Pacific Ocean, SE of Tuamotu Archipelago; lat. 23°09′S and long. 134°58′W; 12 sq. m.; chief island Mangareva; nearly enclosed by barrier reef 40 m. in circumference; generally considered a part of the Tuamotu Archipelago.

Gam·boa \gam-'bō-ə\. Town on Panama Canal at SE corner of Gatun Lake, Canal Zone; pop. (1970p) 2137; channel (8 m.) of canal in arm of Gatun Lake W of Gamboa known as **Gamboa Reach.**

Ga·me·lei·ra, Cape *or* **Cape Ga·me·llei·ra** \-ˌgam-ə-'le(ə)r-ə\. Cape extending into Atlantic Ocean on NE coast of Rio Grande do Norte state, NE Brazil.

Gam·ka \'gam-kə\. River, Great Karroo region of Cape Province, Rep. of South Africa; 160 m. long; unites with the Olifants river to form the Gourits.

Ga·mō·da, Cape \-gə-'mōd-ə\. Cape on E coast of Shikoku, Japan, projecting into Kii Channel.

Gam·toos \gam-'tüs\. River in S Cape Province, Rep. of South Africa; including Groot river, its main headstream, ab. 300 m. long; flows SE to Indian Ocean.

Ga·mu \gä-ˈmü\. Municipality, W cen. Isabela prov., Luzon, Phil., 7 m. S of Ilagan; pop. (1969e) 25,700.

Gana. See GHANA.

Ganale Dorya. See GENALE.

Gan·a·noq·ue \ˌgan-ə-ˈnäk-wē\. Town, Leeds co., SE Ontario, Canada, on St. Lawrence river 20 m. E of Kingston; pop. (1971p) 5072; adjacent to the Thousand Is.

Gand. See GENT.

Gan·dak \ˈgən-(ˌ)dək\. River, Nepal and N India; 475 m. long; formed by union of several streams in cen. Nepal W of Katmandu, flows SW and SE through NW Bihar, India, to the Ganges opp. Patna.

Gan·der \ˈgan-dər\. River, E Newfoundland, Canada; 102 m. long; rises in S cen. section of the island, flows NE into **Gander Bay,** inlet of Atlantic Ocean W of Cape Freels; flows through **Gander Lake** on N shore of which at town of Gander (pop. [1971p] 7720), 215 m. NW of St. John's, is air base, take-off point for transatlantic flights.

Gan·dha·ra \gən-ˈdär-ə\. Region, NW Pakistan and part of E Afghanistan — loosely so called from ab. 6th cent. B.C. to 5th cent. A.D.; name preserved in modern *Kandahār.*

Gan·dia \gän-ˈdē-ə\. Seaport commune, Valencia prov., E Spain, on Mediterranean 38 m. SSE of Valencia; pop. (1970p) 36,342; manufactures silk, velvet, leather.

Gandja. See KIROVABAD.

Gan·do \ˈgän-dō\ *or* **Gwan·du** \ˈgwän-dü\. Emirate, North-Western State, Nigeria; 6208 sq. m.; originally included territory now in Niger and Dahomey republics; established c. 1819, came under control of Nigeria 1903; chief town Gando ab. 60 m. SW of Sokoto. See SOKOTO.

Gandzha. See KIROVABAD.

Gan·ga·na·gar \ˈgəŋ-gə-ˌnəg-ər\. Town, Rajasthan, NW India; pop. (1961c) 63,854.

Gan·ges \ˈgan-ˌjēz\ *or Sanskrit and Hind.* **Gan·ga** \ˈgəŋ-gə\. Sacred river of N and NE Indian subcontinent; ab. 1557 m. long; rises in the Himalayas near Gangotri, NE border of Tehri dist., Uttar Pradesh; flows S through the district as the Bhagirathi, then out into the plain of India at Hardwar in NW Uttar Pradesh, thence SE through Uttar Pradesh, Bihar, West Bengal, and Bangla Desh to merge with the Brahmaputra river and flow into the Bay of Bengal through the vast Ganges Delta (*q.v.*). Unites with the Yamuna at Allahabad; receives from the S the Son and from the N the tributaries Somati, Ghaghara, and Gandak; in upper course is source of extensive irrigation canals. On its banks are the sacred cities of Allahabad and Varanasi.

Ganges Delta *or* **Ganges–Brah·ma·pu·tra Delta** \-ˌbräm-ə-ˈp(y)ü-trə-\. Region in Bangla Desh and West Bengal, India; ab. 220 m. wide along Bay of Bengal; covered by the streams forming the mouths of the Ganges and Brahmaputra rivers. On entering Bangla Desh the Brahmaputra is joined by the Tista from the NW and from there to Rajbari is known as the Jamuna. The main streams, Ganges and Jamuna, united at Rajbari form the **Pad·ma** \ˈpəd-mə\, which below Dacca is joined by the Meghna; from this point to the Bay of Bengal the E mouth of the delta is known as the Meghna; the W outlet of the Meghna, W of Dakhin Shahbazpur I., is the **Te·tu·lia** \ti-ˈtül-yə\. Above Rajbari the **Mad·hu·ma·ti** \ˌməd-ə-ˈmət-ē\ leaves the Ganges entering the Bay of Bengal at the **Ba·les·war** \bə-ˈles-wər\ mouth. The stream farthest W is the Hooghly which leaves the Ganges near Murshidabad, passing Calcutta (90 m. from the sea) and entering the Bay of Bengal by the largest mouth of the delta; its upper course above Santipur is an old channel of the Ganges, generally known as the **Bha·gi·ra·thi** \bä-ˈgir-ət-ē\. Many smaller streams of the delta bet. the Tetulia and Hooghly mouths form a swamp region (ab. 6526 sq. m.) known as the **Sun·dar·bans** \ˈsu̇n-dər-ˌbənz\ *also* **Sun·der·bunds** \-ˌbən(d)z\.

Gan·gi \ˈgän-jē\ *or anc.* **En·gy·um** \ˈen-jē-əm\. Commune, Palermo prov., NW cen. Sicily, Italy, 52 m. ESE of Palermo; pop. (1968e) 10,496; castle.

Gan·go·tri \ˈgəŋ-gə-ˌtrē\. Mountain temple, NW Uttar Pradesh, N India, near source of Bhagirathi river; elev. 10,319 ft.

Gangra. See ÇANKIRI 2.

Gan·gri \ˈgäŋ-(ˌ)grē, ˈgəŋ-\. Mountain in the Himalayas, Bhutan; 24,742 ft.

Gang·tok \ˈgəŋ-ˌtäk\. Town, ✱ of Sikkim, NE Indian subcontinent; 28 m. NE of Darjeeling; pop. (1968e) 9000.

Gan·nett Peak \ˌgan-ət-\. Mountain, Fremont co., cen. Wyoming, in Wind River Range; 13,785 ft.; highest point in the state.

Gann·val·ley \ˈgan-ˈval-ē\. Village, ⊗ of Buffalo co., S cen. South Dakota; pop. (1970c) 78.

Ga·nong·ga \gə-ˈnäŋ-gə\. Small island of the New Georgia Is., cen. Solomon Is., W Pacific Ocean; S of Vella Lavella I.

Gan·sho·ren \ˈgäns-ˌhȯr-ən\. Commune, suburb of Brussels, Brabant prov., Belgium; pop. (1969e) 20,497.

Gap \ˈgäp\ *or anc.* **Va·pin·cum** \və-ˈpiŋ-kəm\. Commune, ✱ of Hautes-Alpes dept., SE France, 96 m. NNE of Marseilles; pop. (1968c) 23,994; episcopal see; manufactures gloves, textiles.

Ga·pan \gə-ˈpän\. Municipality, S Nueva Ecija prov., Luzon, Phil., S of Cabanatuan; pop. (1969e) 44,200.

Ga·ra Gor·fu \ˌgär-ə-gȯr-ˈfü\. Peak, cen. Ethiopia, N of Addis Ababa; 11,482 ft.

Ga·ra·ka·yo \ˌgär-ə-ˈkī-(ˌ)ō\. Island, S Palau Is., SW Pacific Ocean, near Peleliu, 1 m. in diameter; occupied by U.S. forces Oct. 9, 1944.

Garam. See HRON.

Garam Bi, Cape. See O-LUAN, CAPE.

Ga·ra·nhuns \ˌgar-ə-ˈnyü(^{n})s\. City, Pernambuco state, E Brazil, 120 m. SW of Recife; munic. pop. (1968e) 69,093.

Gar·a·pan \ˌgar-ə-ˈpan\. Town on W coast of Saipan, Mariana Is., W Pacific Ocean; administrative center of the Marianas under Japanese mandate. Captured by American forces July 1944.

Garbieh. See GHARBĪYA.

Garb·sen \ˈgärb-sən\. Municipality, Lower Saxony, West Germany, 8 m. W of Hannover; pop. (1969e) 26,576; formed 1967.

Garches \ˈgärsh\. Commune, Hauts-de-Seine dept., N France, ab. 8 m. W of Paris; pop. (1968c) 14,213; Lafayette Escadrille monument in memory of American aviators killed in World War I.

Gar·cía Caves \gär-ˌsē-ə-\. Large natural caves, Nuevo León state, NE Mexico, near Monterrey; stalactites and an underground lake.

Gard \ˈgär\. Department of S France. See table at FRANCE.

Gar·da, Lake \-ˈgärd-ə\ *or anc.* **La·cus Be·na·cus** \ˌlā-kəs-bə-ˈnā-kəs\. Lake in E Lombardy, N Italy, its E shore on Veneto boundary; 32 m. long and 2 to 11 m. wide; 143 sq. m.; drains S through Mincio river into the Po.

Gardaia. See GHARDAÏA.

Gar·den \ˈgard-^{ə}n\. County in Nebraska. See table at NEBRASKA.

Gar·de·na \gär-ˈdē-nə\. City, Los Angeles co., SW California, S suburb of Los Angeles; pop. (1970c) 41,021.

Gardena, Val di \ˌväl-dē-gär-ˈden-ə, -ˈdā-nə\ *or Ger.* **Gröd·ner·tal** \ˈgrəd-nər-ˌtäl\. Valley, Trentino-Alto Adige, NE Italy; 18 m. long.

Garden City. 1 Town, Chatham co., SE Georgia, 2 m. N of Savannah; pop. (1970c) 5790.

2 City, ⊗ of Finney co., W Kansas, on Arkansas river; pop. (1970c) 14,790; Garden City Community Coll. (1919).

3 City, Wayne co., SE Michigan, 15 m. W of Detroit; pop. (1970c) 41,864.

4 Residential village, Nassau co., SE New York, on Long I. 18 m. E of New York; pop. (1970c) 25,373; Protestant Episcopal Cathedral of the Incarnation; Adelphi Univ. (founded 1896 in Brooklyn), Nassau Community Coll. (1960); Roosevelt Field, airport from which Charles A. Lindbergh took off in 1927; printing and publishing center.

5 Village, ⊗ of Glasscock co., W Texas; pop. (1970c) 286.

Gar·den·dale \'gärd-ᵊn-ˌdāl\. City, Jefferson co., cen. Alabama, 10 m. N of Birmingham; pop. (1970c) 6537.

Garden Grove. City, Orange co., SW California, S of Anaheim; pop. (1970c) 120,967; citrus fruit, beans.

Garden Island. Island in N Lake Michigan N of Beaver I.; part of Charlevoix co., NW Michigan.

Garden of the Gods. A region near Colorado Springs, Colorado; ab. 500 acres; noted for numerous rock formations of red and white sandstone.

Garden Reach \-'rēch\. SW suburb of Calcutta, West Bengal, NE India, on E bank of Hooghly river; pop. (1961c) 130,800.

Garden Wall. Mountain in Glacier National Park, NW Montana; 8600 ft.; a narrow ridge with glaciers on either side.

Gar·dez\gär-'dez, gər-, -'dāz\. Town, ✱ of Paktīā prov., E Afghanistan; pop. (1969e) 39,142; elev. 7500 ft.; lumbering.

Gardinas. See GRODNO.

Gar·di·ner \'gärd-nər, -ᵊn-ər\. 1 City, Kennebec co., SW Maine, on Kennebec river 8 m. S of Augusta; pop. (1970c) 6685; shoe factories, paper mills, woodworking shops.

2 Town, S Park co., S Montana; N entrance to Yellowstone National Park; alt. 5287 ft.; nearby are **Gardiner River** and **Gardiner Canyon.**

Gar·di·ners Bay \ˌgärd-nərz-, -ᵊn-ərz-\. Inlet of Long Island Sound on E end of Long I., New York.

Gardiners Island. Island in Gardiners Bay, E Long I., New York, W of Montauk Point; settled 1639; made part of Long I. and of East Hampton township 1683; reputed burial place of pirate loot by Captain Kidd.

Gard·ner \'gärd-nər\. 1 City, Worcester co., cen. Massachusetts, 9 m. W of Fitchburg; pop. (1970c) 19,748; manufactures chairs, upholstered furniture; Mount Wachusett Community Coll. (1963).

2 One of the Phoenix Is. (*q.v.*), cen. Pacific Ocean, 4°40′S lat. and 174°32′W long.; ab. 2 m. long; large coconut plantations.

Gardner, Mount. Mountain, Antarctica, 78°23′S, 86°02′W; 15,375 ft.

Gardner Canal *or* **Gardner Channel.** Inlet of Pacific Ocean, W British Columbia, Canada, joining Douglas Channel at its mouth; ab. 80 m. long.

Gardner Lake. Lake in W cen. New London co., SE Connecticut.

Gardner Pinnacles. Group of islets, Hawaiian Is., in cen. Pacific Ocean 25°N, 167°55′W; consists of lava rock columns 170 ft. high; in Hawaiian Is. Bird Reservation.

Gare Loch \'ga(ə)r-'läk, 'ge(ə)r-, -'läk\. Branch of the Firth of Clyde, SW Scotland; 7 m. long.

Garenne–Colombes, La. See LA GARENNE-COLOMBES.

Gar·field \'gär-ˌfēld\. 1 Name of counties in six states of the U.S. See tables at COLORADO, MONTANA, NEBRASKA, OKLAHOMA, UTAH, WASHINGTON.

2 Industrial city, Bergen co., NE corner of New Jersey, on Passaic river 5 m. SE of Paterson; pop. (1970c) 30,797; printing machinery, clothing, paper products, rubber goods.

Garfield, Mount. 1 Peak, San Juan co., SW Colorado; 13,072 ft.

2 Peak, Franconia Mts., N cen. New Hampshire, in N Grafton co.; 4488 ft.

Garfield Heights. City, Cuyahoga co., N Ohio, 6 m. SSE of Cleveland; pop. (1970c) 41,417; manufactures iron, steel, abrasives; oil refineries.

Garfield Mountain. 1 Peak, Chaffee and Pitkin cos., W cen. Colorado; 13,800 ft.

2 Peak in Bitterroot Range on Idaho-Montana state boundary; 10,961 ft.

Gar·forth \'gär-ˌfō(ə)rth, -ˌfȯ(ə)rth\. Urban district, West Riding, Yorkshire, N England; pop. (1971p) 25,296.

Gar·ga·no, Mount \-gär-'gän-(ˌ)ō\ *or anc.* **Gar·ga·nus Mons** \gär-ˌgā-nə-'smänz\. Promontory extending into Adriatic Sea from E coast of Foggia prov., Apulia, SE Italy; ab. 30 m. long; highest point 3465 ft.; easternmost point is **Te·sta del Gargano** \'tes-tə-ˌdel-\.

Garges–lès–Go·nesse \ˌgärzh-le-gō-'nes\. Commune, Val-d'Oise dept., N France; pop. (1968c) 27,312.

Garh·wal *also* **Gurh·wal** \gər-'wäl\. District, N Uttar Pradesh, N India; 2106 sq. m.; pop. (1961c) 482,327; ✱ Pauri; includes some of the highest peaks of the Himalayas: Kamet, Trisul, Badrinath, and Nanda Devi.

Gar·i·bal·di Park \ˌgar-ə-'bȯl-dē-\. Canadian provincial park in SW British Columbia, N of Vancouver; 966 sq. m.; peaks, glaciers, snowfields.

Ga·ri·glia·no \ˌgär-əl-'yän-(ˌ)ō\. River, SE Latium, cen. Italy; ab. 100 m. long; flows SE, then SW on Campania border to Gulf of Gaeta; its main headstream the Liri; in World War II formed German defense line 1943–44; crossed by Allies May 1944 after long and severe fighting.

Ga·rin \'gär-ən\. Town, Buenos Aires prov., E Argentina, ab. 25 m. NW of Buenos Aires; pop. (1960c) 6341.

Gar·land \'gär-lənd\. 1 County in Arkansas. See table at ARKANSAS.

2 City, Dallas co., NE Texas, 14 m. NE of Dallas; pop. (1970c) 81,437; oil-field equipment, steel fabricators, electronic equipment, dairy products.

Gar·misch–Par·ten·kir·chen \ˌgär-mish-ˌpärt-ᵊn-'ki(ə)r-kən, -'pärt-ᵊn-ˌ\. Commune, Bavaria, West Germany, in foothills of Bavarian Alps near Oberammergau; pop. (1969e) 27,367; noted as resort and center for winter sports; scene of winter Olympics Feb. 7–16, 1936. In World War II supposed to be a last retreat for Nazi leaders; taken by Allies Apr. 30, 1945.

Garmo Peak. See COMMUNISM PEAK.

Gar·ner \'gär-nər\. 1 Town, ⊗ of Hancock co., N Iowa, 21 m. W of Mason City; pop. (1970c) 2257; in farming and dairying region.

2 Town, Wake co., E cen. North Carolina, 5 m. SSE of Raleigh; pop. (1970c) 4923.

Gar·nett \'gär-nət\. City, ⊗ of Anderson co., E Kansas, 42 m. NW of Fort Scott; pop. (1970c) 3169; flour mills, oil wells.

Garoet. See GARUT.

Ga·ro Hills \ˌgär-ō-\. Hilly region, Meghalaya, NE India, in bend of Brahmaputra; highest point ab. 5000 ft.

Ga·ronne \gə-'rän, -'rōn\ *or anc.* **Ga·rum·na** \gə-'rəm-nə\. River, SW France; 357 m. long; rises on slopes of the Pyrenees, in Spain; flows NW past Toulouse and Bordeaux to unite with Dordogne river 13 m. N of Bordeaux and form Gironde estuary.

Garonne, Haute– \'ōt-\. Department of S France. See *Haute-Garonne* in table at FRANCE.

Ga·roua *or* **Ga·rua** \gə-'rü-ə\. Commercial town, N Cameroon, on the Benue at head of navigation in the summertime; pop. (1970e) 28,000; belonged to Germany 1894–1915; besieged and captured by British and French 1915.

Gar·rard \'gar-əd\. County in Kentucky. See table at KENTUCKY.

Gar·rett \'gar-ət\. 1 County in Maryland. See table at MARYLAND.

2 City, De Kalb co., NE Indiana, 20 m. N of Fort Wayne; pop. (1970c) 4715; electric motors.

Gar·ri·son \'gar-ə-sən\. City, McLean co., W cen. North Dakota, 40 m. S of Minot; pop. (1970c) 1614; lignite mines.

Garrison Dam. Dam in Missouri river near Riverdale, North Dakota; earth embankment over 2 m. long, 210 ft. high; for flood control, irrigation, power; completed 1956; forms **Garrison Reservoir** (ab. 200 m. long).

Gar·ron Point \ˌgar-ən-\. Headland in co. Antrim, NE Northern Ireland, on the Irish Sea.

Gar·ry, Lake \-ˈgar-ē\. Lake, NW Keewatin dist., Northwest Territories, Canada; 980 sq. m.; traversed by Black river.

Gar·stedt \ˈgär-(ˌ)s(h)tet\. City, Schleswig-Holstein, West Germany, 9 m. N of Hamburg; pop. (1969e) 20,682; shoes, textiles, paper.

Gartok. See KA-ERH.

Garua. See GAROUA.

Garumna. See GARONNE.

Ga·rut *or Du.* **Ga·roet** \ˈgä-(ˌ)rüt\. Town, West Java prov., Indonesia, ab. 32 m. SE of Bandung; pop. (1961c) 76,244; on plateau (alt. 2300 ft.) surrounded by mountains; resort.

Garvelloch Isles. See ISLES OF THE SEA.

Gar·vin \ˈgär-vən\. County in Oklahoma. See table at OKLAHOMA.

Gar·wood \ˈgär-ˌwu̇d\. Manufacturing borough, Union co., NE New Jersey, 6 m. W of Elizabeth; pop. (1970c) 5260.

Gary \ˈgar-ē, ˈger-\. Industrial city, Lake co., NW corner of Indiana, on Lake Michigan; pop. (1970c) 175,415; important steel-producing center; scene of origin and development of the platoon school (*Gary plan*); site purchased and laid out by U.S. Steel Corp. 1905 (see also FAIRFIELD 2); incorporated 1906.

Gar·za \ˈgär-zə\. County in Texas. See table at TEXAS.

Garza Dam *or* **Lake Dal·las Dam** \-ˈdal-əs-, -is-\. Dam across Elm Fork of Trinity river, Denton co., N Texas; height 80 ft.; completed 1927; impounds water, **Lake Dallas,** for water supply of Dallas.

Garza Gar·cía \ˌgär-zə-gär-ˈsē-ə, ˌgär-sə-\. City, Nuevo León state, Mexico, 8 m. SW of Monterrey; munic. pop. (1970p) 46,346; oranges.

Ga·san \gä-ˈsän\. Municipality, SW coast of Marinduque I., Phil., 11 m. S of Boac; pop. (1969e) 19,900; an old town.

Gas City \ˈgas-\. Industrial city, Grant co., N cen. Indiana, 5 m. SSE of Marion; pop. (1970c) 5742; manufactures glass.

Gascogne. See GASCONY.

Gascogne, Golfe de. See BISCAY, BAY OF.

Gas·con·ade \ˌgas-kə-ˈnād\. 1 River, S cen. Missouri; ab. 265 m. long; rises in Ozark Plateau, flows N into Missouri river in N Gasconade co.

2 County in Missouri. See table at MISSOURI.

Gas·co·ny \ˈgas-kə-nē\ *or Fr.* **Gas·cogne** \gȧ-skȯnʸ\ *or Lat.* **Vas·co·nia** \vas-ˈkō-nē-ə, -nyə\. Historical region of SW France; bounded anciently on N by Guienne, E by Languedoc, SE by Countship of Foix, S by Béarn and Pyrenees, W by Atlantic Ocean; ✱ Auch. Part of Roman Aquitania Tertia; settled in 6th cent. A.D. by Basques from S of Pyrenees; conquered by Franks who erected duchy of Gascony; became attached to Aquitaine (*q.v.*) in 11th cent., and was long a stronghold of English allegiance on Continent; up to 1789, formed with Guienne (*q.v.*), part of French *gouvernement* of Guienne and Gascony.

Gascony, Gulf of. See BISCAY, BAY OF.

Gas·coyne \ˈgas-ˌkȯin\. River, W Western Australia; 475 m. long; upper course in desert, flows W to Geographe Channel; nearly dry except in flood time.

Gash. See MAREB.

Ga·sher·brum \ˈgəsh-ər-ˌbrüm, -ˌbru̇m\ *also* **Gu·shar·brum** \ˈgu̇sh-\. Peak in the Himalayas, Jammu and Kashmir, in region controlled by Pakistan, just SE of Mt. Godwin Austen; 26,470 ft.; first scaled 1958.

Gashiun Nor. See KA-SHUN-NO-ERH.

Gas·ma·ta \gaz-ˈmät-ə\. Coastal town and government station, S New Britain I., Bismarck Archipelago, ab. 200 m. SW of Rabaul; Japanese base in World War II; often bombed by Allies 1943–44.

Gas·pa·ril·la Island \ˌgas-pə-ˌril-ə-\. Island in Gulf of Mexico, at N of entrance to Charlotte Harbor, off W coast of Charlotte co., SW Florida.

Gaspar Strait. See KELASA STRAIT.

Gas·pé \ga-ˈspā\. Town, Gaspé-Est co., SE Quebec, Canada, on Gaspé Peninsula, 115 m. NE of Dalhousie, N.B.; pop. (1971p) 16,842.

Gaspé, Cape. East tip of Gaspé Penin., at NE of entrance to Gaspé Bay, SE Quebec, Canada.

Gaspé Bay. Inlet of Gulf of St. Lawrence at E end of Gaspé Penin., SE Quebec, Canada; ab. 18 m. long.

Gaspé–Est \-ˈest\ *or* **East Gaspé.** County, Quebec, Canada. See table at QUEBEC.

Gaspé–Ouest \-ˈwest\ *or* **West Gaspé.** County, Quebec, Canada. See table at QUEBEC.

Gaspé Park. Canadian provincial park, West Gaspé co., N cen. Gaspé Penin., SE Quebec; 514 sq. m.; Mt. Jacques Cartier, fishing lakes and streams.

Gaspé Peninsula. Peninsula in SE Quebec, Canada, N of New Brunswick and Chaleur Bay and S of mouth of St. Lawrence river; ab. 11,390 sq. m., 170 m. long; comprises Gaspé-Est, Gaspé-Ouest, Bonaventure, Matane, and Matapédia cos.; a tableland (highest peak 4159 ft.), thickly forested with many lakes and rivers; excellent hunting and fishing; famous for its scenery.

Ga·stein \gä-ˈstīn\ *also* **Bad·ga·stein** \ˌbät-\. Village, Salzburg, Austria, 47 m. S of Salzburg in N foothills of Hohe Tauern on the Gasteiner Ache; pop. (1961c) 5742; health resort. By Convention of Gastein Aug. 14, 1865, differences over Schleswig-Holstein bet. Prussia and Austria temporarily adjusted.

Ga·stein·er Ache \gä-ˌstī-nər-ˈäk-ə, -ˈä-k̲ə\. Stream, Salzburg, Austria; ab. 25 m. long; flows N from Hohe Tauern to Salzach river through beautiful valley (alt. 3000–3500 ft.) noted for its mineral springs; contains two notable waterfalls: **Upper Ga·stein** \-gä-ˈstīn\ 207 ft. and **Lower Gastein** 279 ft.

Gas·ti·neau Channel \ˌgas-tə-ˌnō-\. Short channel, SE Alaska, bet. mainland and Douglas I. Both Juneau and Douglas are situated on it.

Gas·ton \ˈgast-ᵊn\. County in North Carolina. See table at NORTH CAROLINA.

Gas·to·nia \ga-ˈstō-nē-ə, -nyə\. Industrial city, ⊗ of Gaston co., SW North Carolina, 20 m. W of Charlotte; pop. (1970c) 47,142; chemicals, plastics; bottling works, foundries; Gaston Coll. (1963).

Gat *or* **Ghāt** \ˈgät\. Town and oasis, SW Libya, near Algerian border.

Ga·ta, Cape \-ˈgät-ə\. 1 Southern point of Cyprus, tip of peninsula W of Akrotiri Bay.

2 *or Span.* **Ca·bo de Gata** \ˌkäb-ō-dā-\. Cape on SE coast of Spain, forming E side of Gulf of Almería; naval engagement 1643 bet. French and Spanish.

Gata, Sierra de. See SIERRA DE GATA.

Gat·chi·na \ˈgach-ə-nə\; *formerly* **Kras·no·gvar·deisk** \ˌkräs-nəg-vər-ˈdāsk\ *also (1923–29)* **Trot·sko·ye** \ˈträt-skə-yə, ˈtrȯt-\. Town, Leningrad Oblast, Russian S.F.S.R., U.S.S.R., 25 m. SSW of Leningrad; pop. (1969e) 57,000; originally a Swedish estate; has castle and palace (now a museum), former summer residence of tsars. A military base during Revolution 1917–19; held by Germans in World War II.

Gate City \ˈgāt-\. Town, ⊗ of Scott co., SW Virginia, 24 m. W of Bristol; pop. (1970c) 1914; coal mines; timber.

Gates \ˈgāts\. County in North Carolina. See table at NORTH CAROLINA.

Gates·head \ˈgāts-ˌhed\. County borough, Durham, N England, on the Tyne opp. Newcastle; pop. (1971p) 94,457; shipbuilding yards, locomotive works, glass and chemical manufactures; coal mines; technical college.

Gates·ville \ˈgāts-ˌvil, -vəl\. 1 Town, ⊗ of Gates co., NE North Carolina; pop. (1970c) 338.

2 City, ⊗ of Coryell co., cen. Texas, 35 m. W of Waco; pop. (1970c) 4683; cotton-processing and feed plants.

Gath \ˈgath\. City of ancient Philistia, Palestine, ab. 12 m. E of Ashdod; one of five Philistine city-kingdoms; residence of Goliath and the Anakim.

Ga·ti·co \gə-'tē-kō\. Port, Antofagasta prov., N Chile; formerly belonged to Bolivia and was its only seaport; damaged by earthquake and tidal wave 1877; ceded to Chile 1883; exports copper.

Gat·i·neau \ˌgat-ᵊn-'ō\. 1 River, SW Quebec, Canada; 240 m. long; rises in chain of lakes S of the height of land, flows S through Lake Baskatong into the Ottawa river at Hull opp. Ottawa; source of waterpower.
2 County in Quebec, Canada. See table at QUEBEC.
3 Town, Hull co., SW Quebec, Canada, just NE of Hull near mouth of Gatineau river; pop. (1966c) 17,727; cement, chemicals.

Ga·too·ma \gə-'tü-mə\. Town, NE Rhodesia, 85 m. SW of Salisbury; met. area pop. (1970e) 23,000; center of richest gold-mining region of Rhodesia.

Gat·ta·ran \ˌgät-ə-'rän\. Municipality, W cen. Cagayan prov., Luzon, Phil., on Cagayan river 20 m. S of Aparri; pop. (1969e) 28,200.

Ga·tu·kai \ˌgat-ə-'kī\. Small island of the New Georgia Is., cen. Solomon Is., W Pacific Ocean, off SE coast of Vangunu I.

Ga·tun *or Span.* **Ga·tún** \gə-'tün\. Town, Cristobal dist., Canal Zone, 7 m. S of Colón; nearby are the **Gatun Locks** and **Gatun Dam** (across Chagres river; completed 1913; maximum height 115 ft.; length of crest 8324 ft.), the latter forming **Gatun Lake** (area 166 sq. m.).

Ga·tun·ci·llo \gä-ˌtün-'sē-(ˌ)(y)ō\. River in Panama E of the Panama Canal; flows S into the Canal Zone, joins Chagres river near Madden Dam.

Gaua. Island, New Hebrides. See SANTA MARÍA 5.

Gaud–i–Zirreh. See GAWD-I-ZIRREH.

Gau·ga·me·la \ˌgȯ-gə-'mē-lə\. Ancient village in Assyria, ab. 18 m. NE of Nineveh and ab. 32 m. W of Arbela (see ERBIL); scene of battle 331 B.C. in which Alexander the Great defeated Persians under Darius, erroneously called the battle of Arbela.

Gau·ha·ti \gaů-'hät-ē\. Town, NW Assam, NE India, on Brahmaputra river 335 m. NE of Calcutta; pop. (1970e) 223,741; commercial center; univ. (1948); nearby temple of Kamakhya and the island of Umananda in the Brahmaputra are places of Hindu pilgrimage. Ceded to British 1826; British seat of administration for Assam 1826–74.

Gau·ja *or Russ.* **Gau·ya** \'gaů-yä\ *or Ger.* **Aa** \'ä\. River, Latvian S.S.R., U.S.S.R.; 260 m. long; rises SE of Cēsin, flows in wide bend to Gulf of Riga NE of Riga; longest river in Latvian S.S.R.

Gaul \'gȯl\ *or Fr.* **Gaule** \gōl\ *or Lat.* **Gal·lia** \'gal-ē-ə\. Ancient country of Europe, commonly the part S and W of the Rhine, W of Alps, and N of Pyrenees, inhabited from ab. 600 B.C. by Celtic race (Lat. *Galli*); in earliest times also N Italy.

Early divisions: 1 **Cis·al·pine Gaul** \sis-ˌal-ˌpīn-\; *Lat.* **Gallia Cis·al·pi·na** \-ˌsis-ˌal-'pī-nə\ *also* **Gallia Ci·te·ri·or** \-sə-'tir-ē-ər, -sī-\. N Italy in valley of Po N of Apennines; settled by Celts c. 4th–3d cents. B.C.; conquered by Rome c. 222 B.C.; made Roman province c. 42 B.C., its SE boundary being the Rubicon (*q.v.*). Divided c. 1st cent. B.C. into: (a) **Cis·pa·dane Gaul** \ˌsis-pə-ˌdān-, sis-'pā-ˌdān-\ *or Lat.* **Gallia Cis·pa·da·na** \-ˌsis-pə-'dā-nə\. Region S of lower Po, ab. coextensive with modern Emilia-Romagna autonomous region. (b) **Trans·pa·dane Gaul** \ˌtran(t)s-pə-ˌdān-, tran(t)s-'pā-ˌdān-\ *or Lat.* **Gallia Trans·pa·da·na** \ˌtran(t)s-pə-'dā-nə\. Region N of upper Po, ab. coextensive with modern W Lombardy and N Piedmont. See CISALPINE REPUBLIC, CISPADANE REPUBLIC, TRANSPADANE REPUBLIC.
2 **Trans·al·pine Gaul** \tran(t)s-ˌal-ˌpīn-, tranz-\; *Lat.* **Gallia Trans·al·pi·na** \-ˌtran(t)s-ˌal-'pī-nə, -ˌtranz-\ *also* **Gallia Ul·te·ri·or** \-ˌəl-'tir-ē-ər\ *or later* **Gallia Cel·ti·ca** \-'sel-ti-kə, -'kel-\; *also known as* **Gallia Proper** *or Fr.* **Gaule.** Practically all of region of modern France including Gallia Narbonensis. Conquered by Julius Caesar 58–51 B.C.; divided into three parts according to native peoples inhabiting the regions—Aquitania (in SW), Gallia (W and center), Belgica (NE)—which under Augustus and Tiberius were regrouped into 5 administrative areas: Narbonensis, Aquitania, Lugdunensis, Belgica, and Rhine Military Frontier dist. (Germania Inferior and Germania Superior).
3 **Gallia Nar·bo·nen·sis** \-ˌnär-bə-'nen-səs\ *or* **Narbonensis.** SE part of Gallia Proper, formed as Roman province c. 121 B.C., with chief settlement at Narbo Martius (see NARBONNE); later named **Pro·vin·cia Ro·ma·na** \prə-ˌvin-sh(ē-)ə-rō-'män-ə\, which became Provence (*q.v.*).

Gau·la·ni·tis \ˌgȯl-ə-'nīt-əs\. District of Decapolis, NE ancient Palestine, along E shore of Sea of Galilee.

Gaule. See GAUL.

Gau·ley \'gȯ-lē\. River, cen. West Virginia; 104 m. long; rises in Pocahontas co., flows W and S, joins New river in N Fayette co. to form Kanawha river.

Gaulus. See GOZO.

Gaur \'gaů(ə)r\ *or* **Lakh·nau·ti** \lək-'naůt-ē\. Ancient city, former ✱ (c. 1200–1340, 1455–1563) of Bengal, in West Bengal, NE India, 8 m. S of English Bazar and ab. 163 m. N of Calcutta. As Muslim seat of government, famed for its size and splendor. Now has ruins of mosques, citadel, towers, etc.

Gau·ri San·kar *or* **Gau·ri·san·kar** \ˌgaů(ə)r-ē-'səŋ-kər\. Peak in the Himalayas, on the Nepal-China border; ab. 35 m. W of Mount Everest; 23,440 ft.

Gauss·berg \'gaůs-ˌbərg\ *or* **Mount Gauss** \-'gaůs\. Extinct volcano on Wilhelm II coast, Antarctica, 66°48′S, 89°12′E; 1120 ft.; discovered Feb. 1902 by expedition under Dr. Erich von Drygalski and named for its ship, the *Gauss.*

Gau·sta \'gaů-stə\. Peak, Telemark co., S Norway; 6178 ft.

Gauya. See GAUJA.

Ga·var·nie \ˌgav-ər-'nē\. Village, Hautes-Pyrénées dept., SW France, near the Spanish border at head of the Gave de Pau whose valley here forms the **Cirque de Gavarnie** \ˌsirk-də-\, most famous of the characteristic cirques of the Pyrenees, a vast amphitheater 2 m. wide with steep wall, in places reaching 5600 ft., over which the *gave* (mountain torrent) comes in a spectacular waterfall 1384 ft. high.

Ga·vā·ter Bay \gə-ˌvät-ər-\ *also* **Gwā·tar Bay** \ˌgwät-ər-\. Inlet of Arabian Sea on Iran-Pakistan border; ab. 20 m. long.

Gav·dos \'gäv-dəs\ *or* **Gāv·dhos** \-(ˌ)dȯs\; *anc.* **Cau·da** \'kȯd-ə\ *or* **Clau·da** \'klȯd-ə\. Small island, E Mediterranean Sea, 22 m. S of W end of Crete, Greece; belongs to Greece; refuge of St. Paul's ship during tempest (*Acts* xxvii. 16).

Gave de Pau. See PAU, GAVE DE.

Gäv·le *also* **Gäf·le** *or* **Gef·le** \'yev-lə\. Seaport city, ⊗ of Gävleborg co., E Sweden, NNW of Stockholm; pop. (1970e) 72,987; exports iron ore and wood pulp; textile mills, chemical factories; received city charter 1446.

Gäv·le·borg *also* **Gäf·le·borg** *or* **Gef·le·borg** \'yev-lə-ˌbȯr\. County of E Sweden. See table at SWEDEN.

Ga·vor·ra·no \ˌgäv-ə-'rän-ō\. Commune, Grosseto prov., Tuscany, cen. Italy, 16 m. NW of Grosseto; pop. (1968e) 9437.

Ga·vrelle \gə-'vrel\. Village, Pas-de-Calais dept., NE France, E of Arras; pop. (1962c) 385; taken by British naval division Apr. 1917 in battle of Arras.

Ga·vu·tu \gə-'vüt-(ˌ)ü\. Small island in SE Solomon Is., in W Pacific Ocean, off S coast of Florida I. just E of Tulagi I. Key point (principal seaplane base) in Japanese defense of S Solomon Is.; seized by U.S. Marines Aug. 7–8, 1942. See TANAMBOGO.

Gawd–i–Zir·reh *or* **Gaud–i–Zirreh** \ˌgȯd-ē-'zir-ə\. Lake and swamp, SW Afghanistan, near Pakistan and Iran borders; in wet season connected with Lake Helmand to NW.

Gaw·ler \'gȯl-ər\. Town, SE South Australia, 20 m. NNE of Adelaide; pop. (1966c) 5700; wheat; gold, silver, copper, and lead mines.

Ga·ya \gə-'yä\. City, cen. Bihar, NE India, 57 m. S of Patna; pop. (1970e) 169,464; large trade with Calcutta; numerous Hindu temples; ab. 7 m. S is Buddh Gaya (*q.v.*), one of the holiest sites of Buddhism.

Gay Head \'gā-\. Promontory, W end of Martha's Vineyard, Massachusetts.

Gay·lord \'gāl-ərd, 'gā-ˌlȯ(ə)rd\. 1 City, ⊗ of Otsego co., N Michigan, 43 m. S of Cheboygan; pop. (1970c) 3012; in potato-growing section.

2 City, ⊗ of Sibley co., S cen. Minnesota, 30 m. NNW of Mankato; pop. (1970c) 1720; grain farms.

Ga·za \'gäz-ə, 'gaz-, 'gāz-\; *Arab.* **Ghaz·ze** \'gäz-ē, 'gəz-\ *or* **Ghaz·zah** \'gäz-ə, 'gəz-\. 1 Strip of land on SE Mediterranean Sea; ab. 26 m. long, 4 to 5 m. wide. For history, see 2 below.

2 Seaport, its commercial and administrative center, near coast, with small harbor 3 m. distant; pop. (1968e) 118,300.

History: Most southerly of the five city-kingdoms of the Philistines, in early times a junction point of trade routes; a base for campaign of Egyptian king, Thutmose III, against Syria c. 1480 B.C.; seat of Philistine worship of Dagon, whose temple Samson overthrew (*Judges* xvi. 23–31); taken by Sargon 720 B.C. and by Alexander the Great 332 B.C. after five months' siege; prominent in Wars of the Maccabees and several times captured or devastated by Syrians, Romans, Jews, and Arabs (634 A.D.); taken by Napoleon 1799. In World War I scene of three battles: Mar. 26–27, 1917, Apr. 19, 1917 (both British defeats), and Nov. 7, 1917 when Gen. Allenby forced evacuation of Turks; part of British mandate 1917–48; under Egyptian control 1948–67 (except for a period of Israeli occupation, Nov. 1956–Mar. 1957); occupied by Israel 1967.

Gaz·a·ca \'gaz-ə-kə\. Ancient city of Media, ✻ of Media Atropatene, in mountains SE of Lake Matianus (*mod.* Urmia) and W of Zanjān—exact location not known.

Gazala, Al–. See AL-GAZALA.

Ga·zelle Peninsula \gə-'zel-\. Peninsula at NE end of New Britain I., Bismarck Archipelago, W Pacific Ocean; site of Rabaul.

Ga·zi·an·tep *or* **Gazi Antep** \ˌgäz-ē-än-'tep\. 1 Province of S Turkey, Asia. See table at TURKEY.

2 *or formerly* **Ain·tab** \in-'tab\. Town, its ✻, ab. 60 m. N of Aleppo, Syria; pop. (1965c) 160,152; strong castle in time of Crusades; base for successful campaign of Ibrahim Pasha against Turks 1839; center of Turkish resistance against French 1920–21.

Gdańsk \gə-'dän(t)sk, -'dan(t)sk\ *or Ger.* **Dan·zig** \'dan(t)-sig, 'dän(t)-\ *or Fr.* **Dant·zig** \däⁿt-sēk\. 1 Province of N Poland. See table at POLAND.

2 City and commercial seaport, its ✻, on Gulf of Danzig just W of mouth of the Vistula, situated on delta arm of the Vistula; pop. (1970p) 364,300; shipyards; chemicals, lumber; food processing, metalworking.

History: Mentioned in 10th cent. A.D. as Polish town of Gdańsk; capital of dukes of Pomerania 13th cent.; ruled by Teutonic Order 1309–1454; joined Hanseatic League and became one of leading centers for Hanseatic trade and monopolized Polish foreign trade; in 1466, after revolt of part of W Prussia, became free city under Polish protection; captured by Russia 1734; ceded to Prussia in 3d partition of Poland 1793; by Article 102 of Treaty of Versailles (1919), the city, with adjoining territory (731 sq. m.), established as free state (**Free City of Danzig**) under League of Nations; within Polish customs union, it served as Polish outlet to sea; in continuous postwar friction with Poland; after 1933, threatened by competition of Gdynia (*q.v.*) and by rise of Nazis in Germany; cession of city to Germany the immediate issue of conflict bet. Poland and Germany which precipitated World War II; incorporated in Germany 1939; named **Hanseatic City of Danzig** 1940; recovered 1945 by Allies, and made part of Poland.

Gdy·nia \gə-'din-ē-ə\ *or Ger.* **Gding·en** \gə-'diŋ-ən\. Seaport city, N Gdańsk prov., Poland, on Gulf of Danzig 10 m. NNW of Gdańsk; pop. (1970p) 190,100; one of Poland's chief ports; naval base; until 1920 an insignificant fishing village (pop. ab. 300); made city 1926; occupied by Germany Sept. 1939; restored to Poland 1945.

Gé·ant, Ai·guille du \ā-'gwēd-ə-zhā-'äⁿ\. Peak in the Savoy Alps, Haute-Savoie dept., E France, NE of Mont Blanc; 13,166 ft.; nearby is the **Col du Géant** \ˌkȯl-də-, ˌkəl-\, mountain pass, alt. 11,145 ft., through the Alps from Chamonix-Mont-Blanc SE to Italy.

Gea·ry \'gi(ə)r-ē\. 1 County in Kansas. See table at KANSAS.
2 City, Blaine and Canadian cos., W cen. Oklahoma, 49 m. W of Oklahoma City; pop. (1970c) 1380; cotton gins.

Ge·au·ga \jē-'ȯg-ə\. County in Ohio. See table at OHIO.

Gê·ba \'gā-bə\. River, W Africa; ab. 190 m. long; rises in Guinea; flows into Atlantic Ocean in Portuguese Guinea.

Gebal. See JUBAYL.

Gebala. See YEBALA.

Gebel. See JEBEL.

Gebweiler. See GUEBWILLER.

Geb·ze \geb-'zä\. Town, Kocaeli prov., NW Turkey in Asia, on NE coast of Sea of Marmara ab. 30 m. SE of İstanbul.

Ge·da·ref \gə-'där-əf\ *or* **Al–Qa·ḍā·rif** \ˌal-kə-'där-if\. Town, S Kassala prov., E Sudan; on Port Sudan-Sennar railroad; pop. (1969e) 55,430.

Gedda. See JIDDA.

Ged·ding·ton \'ged-iŋ-tən\. Village, N Northamptonshire, cen. England; Eleanor Cross marking a stage of the funeral procession of Eleanor, queen of Edward I.

Ge·de *or* **Ge·deh** \'gād-ə\. Volcano, W Java, Indonesia, 45 m. SE of Djakarta; 9705 ft.; many eruptions since 1832, the most severe in 1840; twin peak of Mt. Pangrango (*q.v.*).

Gedi. See MALINDI.

Ge·diz \gə-'dēz\ *or* **Sa·ra·bat** \ˌsär-ə-'bät\ *or anc.* **Her·mus** \'hər-məs\. River, W Turkey in Asia; 217 m. long; rises in mountains S of Kütahya, flows W into Gulf of İzmir.

Ge·dro·sia \jə-'drō-zh(ē-)ə\. Ancient country of SW Asia, a subdivision of Ariana and a province of the Persian and Alexandrian empires, bounded on N by Drangiana and Arachosia, on E by India, on S by Arabian Sea, and on W by Carmania; largely desert; known in history chiefly for the hardships experienced by Alexander's army crossing it on his return from India 325–324 B.C.; region now in SE Iran and Pakistan.

Geel *or* **Gheel** \'gā(ə)l\. Commune, Antwerp prov., N Belgium; pop. (1969e) 29,117; noted for its system of care of mentally retarded persons; Central Nuclear Measurements Bureau; scene 7th cent. of murder of the Irish princess Saint Dympna.

Gee·long \jə-'lȯŋ\. Seaport, S Victoria, SE Australia, at W end of Port Phillip Bay 50 m. SW of Melbourne; pop. (1968e) 18,190, statistical dist. 115,500; auto castings, safety glass, fertilizers; ships esp. wool; tourism.

Geelvink Bay. See SARERA BAY.

Geel·vink Channel \ˈgā(ə)l-ˌviŋk-\. Channel bet. W Western Australia and Houtman Rocks.

Gee·raards·ber·gen \'gā(ə)r-ərtz-ˌber-gə(n)\ *or* **Gram·mont** \grä-'mōⁿ\. Commune, East Flanders prov., NW cen. Belgium, 22 m. W of Brussels; pop. (1969e) 8878.

Gefle. See GÄVLE.

Gefleborg. See GÄVLEBORG.

Gehenna. See HINNOM.

Geis·ling·en an der Stei·ge \'gī-sliŋ-ən-ˌän-dər-'s(h)tī-gə\. Manufacturing city, Baden-Württemberg, West Germany, 34 m. ESE of Stuttgart; pop. (1969e) 26,969; metal goods, machinery, cotton goods; 15th cent. church; to Württemberg 1810.

Geis·town \'gīs-ˌtau̇n\. Borough, Cambria co., SW cen. Pennsylvania, 4 m. SE of Johnstown; pop. (1970c) 3633.

Ge·la \'jā-lə\ *or formerly* **Ter·ra·no·va di Si·ci·lia** \ˌter-ə-'nō-və-ˌdē-sə-'chēl-(ˌ)yä\ *or anc.* **Gela** \'jē-lə\. Commune,

Caltanissetta prov., Sicily, Italy, on S coast 30 m. SSE of Caltanissetta; pop. (1968c) 65,289; petrochemicals; fisheries; remains of ancient city nearby. Founded 689 B.C. by Greek colonists from Rhodes and Crete; flourished under the tyrant Hippocrates; home of the poet Aeschylus; destroyed by Carthaginians; rebuilt by Timoleon 340 B.C. and again destroyed 282 B.C. In World War II scene of American landings July 11, 1943.

Gel·der·land *also* **Guel·der·land** \ˈgel-dər-ˌland\. Province, E Netherlands; 1981 sq. m.; pop. (1970e) 1,505,760; ✱ Arnhem; livestock raising; bricks, cellulose, electrical equipment, textiles.

History: The larger part of the county including Zutphen, Nijmegen, Arnhem (3 divisions known as Lower Gelderland), and Roermond (Upper Gelderland) which had grown up around the county of Gelder (or Gelre) of the Holy Roman Empire and which became duchy 1339, united with Jülich 1377, was held by Charles the Bold of Burgundy 1473–77, and inherited by Charles V of Spain; province originated when Lower Gelderland joined revolt of Netherlands (*q.v.*) 1579, while Upper Gelderland remained Spanish; Upper Gelderland claimed by Frederick of Prussia, awarded to Prussia 1713, and divided between kingdom of Netherlands and Prussia 1815.

Gel·dern \ˈgel-dərn\. Town, North Rhine-Westphalia, West Germany, 28 m. NW of Düsseldorf; pop. (1968e) 22,346; manufactures metalware, shoes, furniture, textiles; received municipal charter c. 1229; seat of counts and dukes of Gelder (see GELDERLAND) to 1371; to Prussia 1713.

Gel·drop \ˈgel-ˌdräp\. Commune, North Brabant prov., SE Netherlands, 4 m. SE of Eindhoven; pop. (1970e) 26,909; woolen manufacturing.

Ge·leen \gə-ˈlān\. Commune, Limburg prov., SE Netherlands, NE of Maastricht; pop. (1970e) 36,121; coal mining; textiles.

Ge·li·bo·lu \ˌgel-ə-bə-ˈlü\ *or angl.* **Gal·lip·o·li** \gə-ˈlip-ə-lē\ *or anc.* **Cal·lip·o·lis** \kə-ˈlip-ə-ləs\. Seaport and manufacturing town, Çanakkale prov., Turkey, Europe, at entrance to Sea of Marmara on narrow neck of Gallipoli Penin.; pop. (1965c) 12,945. Ancient Callipolis colonized by Greeks; medieval trading center; first European conquest of Turks 1354.

Gelibolu Yarımadası. See GALLIPOLI PENINSULA.

Gel·i·do·nya, Cape \-ˌgel-ə-ˈdō-nyə, -də-ˈnyä\ *or Turk.* **Ge·li·do·nya Bu·run** \-bə-ˈrün\. Cape on S coast of Turkey, Asia, on W side of entrance to Gulf of Antalya.

Gel·li·gaer \ˌgel-ə-ˈgī(ə)r\. Urban district, Glamorganshire, SE Wales; pop. (1971p) 33,670; manufacturing and coal mining center; rubber works.

Gellivare. See GÄLLIVARE.

Gel·sen·kir·chen \ˌgel-zən-ˈki(ə)r-kən\. Industrial city, North Rhine-Westphalia, West Germany, 15 m. W of Dortmund; pop. (1969e) 360,981; in Ruhr coal-mining region; chemicals, glass, soap, flour; steel works, foundries; includes since 1928 the city of Buer and the commune of Horst an der Emscher; Buer town hall, 16th cent. Horst castle; incorporated as city in Arnsberg govt. dist. 1875; often bombed 1943–45.

Geluveld. See GHELUVELT.

Gem \ˈjem\. County in Idaho. See table at IDAHO.

Ge·mas \je-ˈmäs\. Town, SE Negri Sembilan state, Malaysia, near border of Johore 35 m. NE of Malacca; railroad junction. Severe fighting bet. Japanese and British Jan. 1942.

Gem·bloux \zhäⁿ-ˈblü\. Commune, Namur prov., S Belgium, 10 m. NW of Namur; pop. (1969e) 11,384; manufactures cutlery; state institute of agriculture; scene Jan. 31, 1578 of defeat of Dutch by Don John of Austria.

Gem·i·ni Peaks \ˌjem-ə-ˌnī-\. Mountain, Lake and Park cos., cen Colorado; 13,900 ft.

Gem·lik Gulf \gem-ˌlēk-\. Inlet of SE Sea of Marmara, Turkey, Europe; Mudanya is on it.

Gem·mi Pass \ˌgem-ē-\. Mountain pass in the Bernese Alps, SW cen. Switzerland, 25 m. S of Thun; 7598 ft.

Ge·mu Ge·fa \ˌgā-mü-ˈgā-fə\ *also* **Gemu Gof·fa** \-ˈgäf-ə\. Province of NE Ethiopia. See table at ETHIOPIA.

Ge·na·den·dal \gə-ˈnäd-ᵊn-ˌdäl\. Town, SW Cape Province, Rep. of South Africa, 68 m. E of Capetown; Moravian mission station founded 1737, oldest mission station in republic.

Ge·na·le \gə-ˈnä-lē\ *also* **Ga·na·le Dor·ya** \-ˈdȯr-yə\. River, S Ethiopia, ab. 225 m. long; flows SE, then S to join the Weyib and Dawa and form the Juba.

Ge·nappe \zhə-ˈnap, jə-\ *or* **Ge·ne·pi·ën** \ˈgə-ˈnā-pē-ən\. Town, Brabant prov., Belgium, SSE of Brussels; pop. (1969e) 1716; ab. 2½ m. S is Quatre Bras (*q.v.*).

Genck. See GENK.

Gen·dring·en \ˈgen-driŋ-ən\. Commune, Gelderland prov., E Netherlands, 20 m. ESE of Arnhem on West German border; pop. (1970e) 18,028.

Geneina, Al–. See AL-GENEINA.

Genepiën. See GENAPPE.

Ge·ne·ral Al·va·ra·do \ˌjen-(ə-)rəl-ˌal-və-ˈräd-(ˌ)ō, ˌhen-ə-ˈral-\ *or* **Mi·ra·mar** \ˌmir-ə-ˈmär\. Seaside resort, E Buenos Aires prov., E Argentina, S of Mar del Plata; pop. (1960c) 7782.

Gen·er·al Grant National Park \ˌjen-(ə-)rəl-ˈgrant-\. Former national park, SE cen. California; 4 sq. m.; included two groves of giant sequoias; estab. 1890; since 1940 known as **General Grant Grove Section** of Kings Canyon National Park (see UNITED STATES, *National Parks*).

General J. F. Uriburu. See ZÁRATE.

General Manuel Belgrano. See SIERRA DE FAMATINA.

Ge·ne·ral Pi·co \ˌjen-(ə-)rəl-ˈpē-kō, ˌhen-ə-ˈral-\. Town, La Pampa prov., S cen. Argentina, 290 m. WSW of Buenos Aires; pop. (1960c) 18,133.

General Ro·ca \-ˈrō-kə\. Town, Río Negro prov., Argentina; pop. (1960c) 21,960.

General San Mar·tín \-ˌsan-mär-ˈtēn\ *also* **San Martín.** City, Buenos Aires prov., E Argentina, a suburb of Buenos Aires; pop. (1960c) 278,751.

Ge·ne·ral San·tos \-ˈsan-təs, -ˈsän-\. Chartered city, Cotabato del Sur prov., Mindanao, Phil.; pop. (1970e) 121,200.

General Sar·mien·to \-ˌsär-mē-ˈen-(ˌ)tō\ *also* **Sarmiento.** Town, Buenos Aires prov., E Argentina, a W suburb of Buenos Aires; pop. (1960c) 167,160.

General Tri·as \-ˈtrē-əs\. Municipality, Cavite prov., Luzon, Phil., 7 m. S of Cavite; pop. (1969e) 29,600.

Gen·e·see \ˌjen-ə-ˈsē, ˈjen-ə-ˌ\. **1** River, Pennsylvania and New York; 144 m. long; rises in Potter co., N Pennsylvania, flows N into Lake Ontario near Rochester, W New York.

2 Name of counties in two states of the U.S. See tables at MICHIGAN and NEW YORK.

Gen·e·seo \ˌjen-ə-ˈsē-(ˌ)ō\. **1** City, Henry co., NW Illinois, 24 m. E of Rock Island; pop. (1970c) 5840.

2 Village, ⊗ of Livingston co., W New York, on Genesee river 26 m. SSW of Rochester; pop. (1970c) 5714; fruit and vegetable raising; State Univ. of New York Coll. (1867).

Ge·ne·va \jə-ˈnē-və\. **1** County in Alabama. See table at ALABAMA.

2 City, ⊗ of Geneva co., SE Alabama, 2 m. N of Florida border; pop. (1970c) 4398.

3 City, ⊗ of Kane co., NE Illinois, 36 m. W of Chicago; pop. (1970c) 9115; farm machinery, foundry products; founded ab. 1835, incorp. as city 1887.

4 City, ⊗ of Fillmore co., SE Nebraska, 44 m. E of Hastings; pop. (1970c) 2275; grain farms.

5 City, Ontario co., W New York, at N end of Seneca Lake; pop. (1970c) 16,793; vegetable and fruit canning; furnaces, radiators, enamelware, optical goods; Hobart and William

Smith Colleges (1822); settled c. 1785 on site of Indian village.
6 City, Ashtabula co., NE corner of Ohio, 8 m. WSW of Ashtabula; pop. (1970c) 6449; manufactures farm implements, builders' hardware; greenhouses, apiaries.

Geneva *or Fr.* **Ge·nève** \zhə-nev, -nāv\ *or Ger.* **Genf** \'genf\ *or Ital.* **Gi·ne·vra** \ji-'nev-rə\. 1 Swiss canton. See table at SWITZERLAND.
2 City, ✱ of Geneva canton, SW Switzerland, at S tip of Lake of Geneva on Rhone river; pop. (1970c) 173,618; manufactures clocks, watches, jewelry, precision instruments, iron goods, chemicals, scientific and surgical appliances; banking; tourism; cultural center; buildings include the Palais des Nations (originally headquarters of the League of Nations, now offices of the United Nations), 10th–12th cent. Gothic cathedral, university (see below).
History: A center of Allobroges, a Celtic-speaking people conquered by Romans; seat of Burgundian kingdom until latter conquered by Franks c. 534 A.D.; obtained privileges as result of struggle bet. bishop and Savoyards who constantly threatened the city's independence; in 16th cent., alliance with Bern and Fribourg protected it from Savoy; home of John Calvin, who established a theocratic state (1541) and made 16th cent. Geneva the intellectual center of Protestant Europe; Calvin's Academy, founded 1559, became university 1873; united with France 1798; in 1815, with expanded territory, joined Swiss Confederation as canton of Geneva; scene of conference which drew up Geneva (Red Cross) Convention 1864; from 1920 to Apr. 18, 1946 seat of League of Nations, its buildings later taken over by UN; site of many international conferences incl. those dealing with political developments in Vietnam (1954) and Laos (1962).

Geneva, Lake of *or* **Lake Le·man** \-'lē-mən, -'lem-ən, -lə-'man\; *anc.* **Le·man·nus** \li-'man-əs\ *or* **Le·ma·nus** \li-'mān-əs\. Lake in SW Switzerland and E France, extending in an arc along the boundary, only its S shore in France; 45 m. long, 1½ to 9 m. wide; 224 sq. m.; traversed E to W by Rhone river.

Ge·nè·vre, Col de \ˌkȯl-də-zhə-'nevrᵊ\. Mountain pass, N part of Cottian Alps, bet. France and Italy, E of Briançon; 6102 ft.

Genf. German form of Geneva, Switzerland. See GENEVA.

Ge·nil *or* **Je·nil** \hā-'nē(ə)l\. River, S Spain; flows into Guadalquivir river 33 m. SW of Córdoba; 209 m. long.

Ge·ni·tsa \ˌyen-it-'sä\ *or* **Gia·ni·tsà** \ˌyän-\ *or Gk.* **Yan·ni·tsà** \ˌyän-\ *or Serb.* **Ja·ni·ca** \'yän-it-ˌsä\. City, Pella dept., W Macedonia, N Greece, ab. 20 m. E of Edessa.

Genk *or* **Genck** \'geŋk\. Commune, Limburg prov., NE Belgium, 11 m. N of Liège; pop. (1969e) 57,375; automobiles; in coal-mining region.

Gen·nar·gen·tu \ˌjen-är-'jen-(ˌ)tü\. Mountain group, E cen. Sardinia, Italy; highest point 6017 ft.

Gennesaret, Lake of. See GALILEE, SEA OF.

Gen·ne·vil·liers \ˌzhen-vēl-'yā\. Commune, Hauts-de-Seine dept., N France, NNW suburb of Paris; pop. (1968c) 46,074; site of large U.S. camp in World War II.

Ge·noa \jə-'nō-ə\. 1 City, De Kalb co., N Illinois, 22 m. SE of Rockford; pop. (1970c) 3003; power mowers, hand tools, cabinets; diversified agriculture.
2 Town, Douglas co., W Nevada, 12 m. SSW of Carson City; oldest permanent settlement in Nevada.

Ge·noa \'jen-ə-wə\ *or Ital.* **Ge·no·va** \'jen-ə-və\ *or anc.* **Gen·ua** \'jen-yə-wə\. Seaport, ✱ of Genova prov. and ✱ of Liguria, NW Italy, at head of Gulf of Genoa at foot of Apennines 71 m. SSW of Milan; pop. (1968e) 842,764; archiepiscopal see; one of most important Italian seaports; exports chiefly rice, wine, olive oil, silk goods, coral, paper, macaroni, marble; manufactures include iron and steel, textiles, fertilizers, soap; oil refining, shipbuilding; cathedral of San Lorenzo, 16th cent. church of Sant'Ambrogio, 16th cent. Palazzo Doria, the Doges' palace, univ. (1471), Academy of Fine Arts (1751), Verdi Institute of Music; birthplace of Christopher Columbus.
History: Ancient settlement on Ligurian coast, first mentioned by Romans 218 B.C.; trading center of Liguria even in Roman times; captured by Burgundians 539 A.D. and by Lombards 670; as independent city, soon became chief commercial city of Mediterranean and Levant, defeating its rival, Pisa, 1284; early European banking center (Bank of St. George); in return for its assistance against Venice 1261, rewarded by Palaeologi (see BYZANTINE EMPIRE) with special privileges at Constantinople and colonies at Chios, Lesbos, Samos, Kaffa (see FEODOSIYA), and Azov; in War of Chioggia 1378–81, lost century-long struggle with Venice for control of Levant; declined commercially, but became object of French rivalry with Milan (*q.v.*); under Andrea Doria threw off French rule 1528; lost Chios 1566 and sold Corsica (*q.v.*) 1768; with surrounding coastal strip set up as Ligurian Republic by Napoleon 1797 and incorporated with France 1805; given to kingdom of Sardinia 1815; scene of international conference which failed to settle Russian debt question 1922; in World War II badly damaged by Allied bombings 1942–44; entered by Allies Apr. 25, 1945.

Genoa, Gulf of. Inlet on Ligurian coast, NW Italy; N part of Ligurian Sea.

Ge·no·va \'jen-ə-və\. 1 Province of Liguria, Italy. See table at ITALY.
2 Seaport, Italy. See GENOA.

Ge·no·ve·sa \ˌhā-nə-'vā-sə\ *also* **Tow·er Island** \'taů(-ə)r-\. One of the Galápagos Is. (*q.v.*).

Gent \'gent\ *or Eng.* **Ghent** \'gent\ *or Fr.* **Gand** \gäⁿ\. Commercial and manufacturing fortified city, ✱ of East Flanders prov., NW cen. Belgium, at confluence of Schelde and Lys rivers and at junction of several canals; pop. (1970e) 149,265; metallurgical industries; occupies a number of islands connected by bridges; important port; a center of flower-seed and bulb market; univ. (1817). Scene of signing of Pacification of Gent Nov. 8, 1576, which united the provinces against Spain, and of a treaty Dec. 24, 1814 marking end of War of 1812 bet. Great Britain and United States; occupied by Germans in both World Wars.

Gent·brug·ge \'gent-ˌbrəg-ə, -ˌbrůg-\. Commune, East Flanders prov., NW cen. Belgium; pop. (1969e) 22,467.

Gente Hermosa. See SWAINS.

Gen·til·ly \ˌzhäⁿ-tē-'yē\. Commune, Val-de-Marne dept., N France, S suburb of Paris; pop. (1968c) 18,812.

Gen·tof·te \'gen-ˌtəf-tə\. City, Copenhagen co., island of Sjælland, Denmark; pop. (1970e) 77,970; part of Greater Copenhagen.

Gen·try \'jen-trē\. County in Missouri. See table at MISSOURI.

Genua. See GENOA.

Genzan. See WŎNSAN.

Ge·og·ra·phe Bay \jē-ˌäg-rə-fē-\. Inlet of Indian Ocean, SW Western Australia, just E of Cape Naturaliste.

Geographe Channel. Passage bet. Bernier I. and mainland, W Western Australia; connects with Shark Bay on S.

Geok–Te·pe *or* **Gök–Té·pé** \ˌgək-tə-'pā\. Town, S Turkmen S.S.R., U.S.S.R., ab. 40 m. NW of Ashkhabad; scene of victory of Russians over Tekke tribe of Turkmen 1881.

George \'jȯ(ə)rj\. 1 County in Mississippi. See table at MISSISSIPPI.
2 River, NE Quebec, Canada; 365 m. long; flows N to Ungava Bay.
3 Town, S Cape Province, Rep. of South Africa, 235 m. E of Cape Town; pop. (1967e) 19,600; founded 1811; residential.

George, Cape. Cape on N Nova Scotia, Canada, at W entrance to George Bay.

George, Lake. 1 Lake in SE Putnam co., NE Florida penin.; an expansion of St. Johns river.
2 Lake bet. Warren and Washington cos., E New York; ab. 33 m. long, ¾ to 3 m. wide; outlet to N into Lake Champlain; scene of a number of engagements in French and Indian War 1754–63. Called **Lake Hor·i·con** \-'hȯr-i-kən, -'här-\ by James Fenimore Cooper.

3 Small lake, SW Uganda, SE cen. Africa, NE of Lake Edward.

George Bay. Inlet of Gulf of St. Lawrence, NE Antigonish co., N Nova Scotia, Canada, bet. Nova Scotia and SW Cape Breton I.

George V Coast \-thə-'fif(t)th-\ *also* **King George V Land.** Section of coast of Antarctica E of Wilkes Land; 142° to 153°E and bet. 67° and 71°S; part of Australian Antarctic claim.

George Hill. Elevation in Garrett co., NW corner of Maryland; 3004 ft.

George Land. See FRANZ JOSEF LAND.

George Rog·ers Clark National Historical Park \-ˌräj-ərz-'klärk-\. See UNITED STATES, *National Historical Parks.*

Georg·es \'jȯr-jəz\. River, SE New South Wales, SE Australia; flows into Botany Bay S of Sydney.

Georges Island. Island in outer Boston Harbor, Massachusetts, NNW of Hull; Fort Warren on it.

Georges Islands. Group of small islands, in Knox co., S Maine, at mouth of Muscongus Bay.

George·town \'jȯ(ə)rj-ˌtau̇n\. **1** County in South Carolina. See table at SOUTH CAROLINA.

2 Town, ⊗ of Clear Creek co., N cen. Colorado; pop. (1970c) 542.

3 Town, ⊗ of Sussex co., S Delaware, 33 m. S of Dover; pop. (1970c) 1844; bricks; sawmill.

4 Former town in District of Columbia (*q.v.*), now part of city of Washington. Settled as early as 1665; town laid out 1751, incorp. 1789; lost charter 1871, annexed to Washington 1878. Georgetown Univ. (1789).

5 Town, ⊗ of Quitman co., SW Georgia; pop. (1970c) 578.

6 City, Vermilion co., E Illinois, 10 m. S of Danville; pop. (1970c) 3984; truck farms; coal mining.

7 City, ⊗ of Scott co., N cen. Kentucky, 12 m. N of Lexington; pop. (1970c) 8269; horse breeding; Georgetown Coll. (1787).

8 Town, Essex co., NE Massachusetts, NE of Lowell; pop. (1970c) 5290.

9 Village, ⊗ of Brown co., SW Ohio, 35 m. ESE of Cincinnati; pop. (1970c) 2949; manufactures shoes; boyhood home of Ulysses S. Grant.

10 City and port of entry, ⊗ of Georgetown co., E South Carolina, at head of Winyah Bay 57 m. NE of Charleston; pop. (1970c) 10,449; ships esp. fish, lumber, cotton; settled 1735.

11 City, ⊗ of Williamson co., cen. Texas, 27 m. N of Austin; pop. (1970c) 6395; cotton; mineral springs, limestone quarries; Southwestern Univ. (1840).

12 Settlement on W coast of Ascension I.

13 Town, Halton co., SE Ontario, Canada, 28 m. W of Toronto; pop. (1971p) 15,793; electronic instruments, dairy products; founded 1837.

14 Coast town, ⊗ of Kings co., E Prince Edward I., Canada; pop. (1966c) 828.

15 Town, ✱ of Cayman Is., on Grand Cayman I., West Indies; pop. (1970c) 3975.

16 Town, Gambia, W Africa, near mouth of the Gambia river; pop. (1970e) 1958.

17 City, ✱ of Guyana, at mouth of Demerara river; pop. (1970p) 66,070; chief port of Guyana; exports include sugar, bauxite, rice, diamonds; cathedral, univ. (1963), botanical gardens. Founded by English 1781; called **Sta·broek** \'stä-ˌbru̇k\ during Dutch occupation when it was made seat of government of combined colonies of Essequibo and Demerara 1784; renamed Georgetown 1812.

18 Town on island of St. Vincent, Windward Is., West Indies.

George Town \'jȯ(ə)rj-ˌtau̇n\. **1** Municipality, N Tasmania, Australia, near mouth of Tamar river 35 m. NNW of Launceston; pop. (1970e) 5690; resort; harbor.

2 Town on Exuma I., Bahama Is., West Indies; good harbor.

3 City, Malaysia. See PENANG 3.

George Wash·ing·ton Birthplace National Monument \-'wȯsh-iŋ-tən-\. See UNITED STATES, *National Monuments;* WAKEFIELD 4.

George Washington Car·ver National Monument \-kär-vər-\. See UNITED STATES, *National Monuments.*

George West \jȯ(ə)rj-'west\. City, ⊗ of Live Oak co., S Texas; pop. (1970c) 2022; diversified farming.

Geor·gia \'jȯr-jə\. A southern state of U.S.A., bounded on N by Tennessee and North Carolina, on E by South Carolina and the Atlantic Ocean, on S by Florida, and on W by Alabama; 21st state in area, 58,876 sq. m. (land area 58,197 sq. m.); 15th state in population, (1970c) 4,589,575; ✱ Atlanta; an original state of the Union, the 4th to ratify the Federal Constitution, Jan. 2, 1788.

Nicknames: Empire State of the South; Peach State. *State flower:* Cherokee rose. *Motto:* Wisdom, Justice, Moderation. *Rivers:* Chattahoochee and Flint, uniting in SW to form the Apalachicola; Ocmulgee and Oconee, uniting in SE to form the Altamaha; Savannah, forming E boundary bet. Georgia and South Carolina. *Highest point:* Brasstown Bald 4784 ft. on boundary of Towns and Union cos. *Other important natural feature:* Okefenokee Swamp 660 sq. m. in SE. *Chief products:* Corn, peanuts, pecans, peaches, tobacco; poultry, livestock; clays, limestone, barite; manufacturing: textiles, pulp and paper products, chemicals. *Chief cities:* Atlanta, Columbus, Macon, Savannah, Albany, Augusta. See *Table of States* at UNITED STATES. Divided into the following 159 counties (for pronunciation of their names, see their individual entries):

NAME	LOCATION	AREA[1] (sq. m.)	POP. (1970c)	CO. SEAT
Appling	SE	513	12,726	Baxley
Atkinson	S	318	5,879	Pearson
Bacon	SE	293	8,233	Alma
Baker	SW	355	3,875	Newton
Baldwin	cen.	255	34,240	Milledgeville
Banks	NE	231	6,833	Homer
Barrow	N	171	16,859	Winder
Bartow	NW	461	32,663	Cartersville
Ben Hill	S cen.	255	13,171	Fitzgerald
Berrien	S	468	11,556	Nashville
Bibb	cen.	254	143,418	Macon
Bleckley	cen.	219	10,291	Cochran
Brantley	SE	447	5,940	Nahunta
Brooks	S	490	13,743	Quitman
Bryan	SE; coastal	443	6,539	Pembroke
Bulloch	E	685	31,585	Statesboro
Burke	E	831	18,255	Waynesboro
Butts	cen.	185	10,560	Jackson
Calhoun	SW	289	6,606	Morgan
Camden[2]	SE corner; coastal	653	11,334	Woodbine
Candler	E cen.	250	6,412	Metter
Carroll	W	495	45,404	Carrollton
Catoosa	NW	167	28,271	Ringgold
Charlton	SE	796	5,680	Folkston
Chatham[2]	SE; coastal	445	187,816	Savannah
Chattahoochee	W	253	25,813	Cusseta
Chattooga	NW	317	20,541	Summerville
Cherokee	NW	415	31,059	Canton
Clarke	NE	125	65,177	Athens
Clay	SW	224	3,636	Fort Gaines
Clayton	NW cen.	149	98,043	Jonesboro
Clinch	S	797	6,405	Homerville
Cobb	NW	343	196,793	Marietta
Coffee	S	612	22,828	Douglas
Colquitt	S	563	32,298	Moultrie
Columbia	E	290	22,327	Appling
Cook	S	233	12,129	Adel
Coweta	W	442	32,310	Newnan
Crawford	cen.	315	5,748	Knoxville
Crisp	SW cen.	292	18,087	Cordele
Dade	NW corner	168	9,910	Trenton
Dawson	N	211	3,639	Dawsonville
Decatur	SW	575	22,310	Bainbridge
De Kalb	NW cen.	269	415,387	Decatur
Dodge	S cen.	498	15,658	Eastman
Dooly	SW cen.	394	10,404	Vienna

NAME	LOCATION	AREA[1] (sq. m.)	POP. (1970c)	CO. SEAT
Dougherty	SW	324	89,639	Albany
Douglas	W	202	28,659	Douglasville
Early	SW	525	12,682	Blakely
Echols	S	425	1,924	Statenville
Effingham	E	480	13,632	Springfield
Elbert	NE	358	17,262	Elberton
Emanuel	E cen.	686	18,357	Swainsboro
Evans	SE cen.	186	7,290	Claxton
Fannin	N	394	13,357	Blue Ridge
Fayette	W	199	11,364	Fayetteville
Floyd	NW	514	73,742	Rome
Forsyth	N	218	16,928	Cumming
Franklin	NE	269	12,784	Carnesville
Fulton	NW cen.	530	607,592	Atlanta
Gilmer	N	439	8,956	Ellijay
Glascock	E cen.	143	2,280	Gibson
Glynn[2]	SE; coastal	412	50,528	Brunswick
Gordon	NW	358	23,570	Calhoun
Grady	SW	466	17,826	Cairo
Greene	NE cen.	403	10,212	Greensboro
Gwinnett	N	437	72,349	Lawrenceville
Habersham	NE	282	20,691	Clarkesville
Hall	N	378	59,405	Gainesville
Hancock	cen.	478	9,019	Sparta
Haralson	W	285	15,927	Buchanan
Harris	W	465	11,520	Hamilton
Hart	NE	256	15,814	Hartwell
Heard	W	302	5,354	Franklin
Henry	NW cen.	331	23,724	McDonough
Houston	cen.	380	62,924	Perry
Irwin	S	372	8,036	Ocilla
Jackson	NE	337	21,093	Jefferson
Jasper	cen.	373	5,760	Monticello
Jeff Davis	SE cen.	331	9,425	Hazlehurst
Jefferson	E cen.	530	17,174	Louisville
Jenkins	E	351	8,332	Millen
Johnson	cen.	313	7,727	Wrightsville
Jones	cen.	402	12,218	Gray
Lamar	W cen.	181	10,688	Barnesville
Lanier	S	177	5,031	Lakeland
Laurens	cen.	810	32,738	Dublin
Lee	SW	355	7,044	Leesburg
Liberty[2]	SE; coastal	514	17,569	Hinesville
Lincoln	E	193	5,895	Lincolnton
Long	SE	402	3,746	Ludowici
Lowndes	S	507	55,112	Valdosta
Lumpkin	N	292	8,728	Dahlonega
McDuffie	E	253	15,276	Thomson
McIntosh[2]	SE; coastal	426	7,371	Darien
Macon	SW cen.	403	12,933	Oglethorpe
Madison	NE	281	13,517	Danielsville
Marion	W	365	5,099	Buena Vista
Meriwether	W	499	19,461	Greenville
Miller	SW	287	6,424	Colquitt
Mitchell	SW	509	18,956	Camilla
Monroe	cen.	398	10,991	Forsyth
Montgomery	SE cen.	237	6,099	Mount Vernon
Morgan	N cen.	356	9,904	Madison
Murray	N	342	12,986	Chatsworth
Muscogee	W	220	167,377	Columbus
Newton	N cen.	271	26,282	Covington
Oconee	NE cen.	186	7,915	Watkinsville
Oglethorpe	NE	435	7,598	Lexington
Paulding	NW	318	17,520	Dallas
Peach	cen.	151	15,990	Fort Valley
Pickens	N	225	9,620	Jasper
Pierce	SE	342	9,281	Blackshear
Pike	W	230	7,316	Zebulon
Polk	NW	312	29,656	Cedartown
Pulaski	S cen.	253	8,066	Hawkinsville
Putnam	cen.	340	8,394	Eatonton
Quitman	SW	171	2,180	Georgetown
Rabun	NE corner	368	8,327	Clayton
Randolph	SW	436	8,734	Cuthbert
Richmond	E	323	162,437	Augusta
Rockdale	N cen.	128	18,152	Conyers
Schley	SW cen.	162	3,097	Ellaville
Screven	E	651	12,591	Sylvania
Seminole	SW corner	246	7,059	Donalsonville
Spalding	W cen.	201	39,514	Griffin
Stephens	NE	180	20,331	Toccoa
Stewart	W	463	6,511	Lumpkin
Sumter	SW cen.	489	26,931	Americus
Talbot	W	390	6,625	Talbotton
Taliaferro	NE cen.	195	2,423	Crawfordville
Tattnall	SE cen.	490	16,557	Reidsville
Taylor	W cen.	403	7,865	Butler
Telfair	S cen.	440	11,394	McRae
Terrell	SW	329	11,416	Dawson
Thomas	S	541	34,562	Thomasville
Tift	S	266	27,288	Tifton
Toombs	SE cen.	368	19,151	Lyons
Towns	N	166	4,565	Hiawassee
Treutlen	E cen.	194	5,647	Soperton
Troup	W	446	44,466	La Grange
Turner	S	293	8,790	Ashburn
Twiggs	cen.	364	8,222	Jeffersonville
Union	N	309	6,811	Blairsville
Upson	W cen.	334	23,505	Thomaston
Walker	NW	445	50,691	La Fayette
Walton	N cen.	330	23,404	Monroe
Ware	SE	912	33,525	Waycross
Warren	E cen.	284	6,669	Warrenton
Washington	cen.	674	17,480	Sandersville
Wayne	SE	645	17,858	Jesup
Webster	W	195	2,362	Preston
Wheeler	SE cen.	306	4,596	Alamo
White	NE	243	7,742	Cleveland
Whitfield	NW	281	55,108	Dalton
Wilcox	S cen.	383	6,998	Abbeville
Wilkes	NE	468	10,184	Washington
Wilkinson	cen.	458	9,393	Irwinton
Worth	S	579	14,770	Sylvester

[1] Area = land area.
[2] Includes islands of Sea Islands chain.

History: Discovered by Spanish and penetrated by Spanish missions; English colony, last of original 13 colonies to be founded, chartered 1732 and settled 1733 at Savannah by Oglethorpe as refuge for debtors and buffer state bet. Spanish Florida and the Carolinas; surrendered charter to crown 1754; Savannah held by British 1778–82; chartered University of Georgia 1785, the oldest state university; first southern state to ratify federal constitution Jan. 2, 1788; ceded claims to western lands (now Alabama and Mississippi) 1802; in dispute over southern boundary from colonial days until 1866 when it accepted line based upon Joseph Ellicott's points; seceded from Union Jan. 19, 1861; scene of battle of Chickamauga 1863, campaign bet. Chattanooga and Atlanta, and Sherman's "March to the Sea" 1864; ordinance of secession repealed Oct. 30, 1865 and slavery abolished; last state to be readmitted to Union July 15, 1870; adopted present constitution 1945.

Georgia. See GEORGIAN SOVIET SOCIALIST REPUBLIC.

Georgia, Strait of. Channel in SW Canada and NW U.S.; has Vancouver I. on the W and mainland of SW British Columbia and Whatcom co., Washington on the E; 150 m. long, 30 m. wide at its widest part; connects by Johnstone Strait with Queen Charlotte Strait and extends S to Haro Strait (*q.v.*); forms part of inland steamship passage from U.S. to Alaska.

Geor·gi·ana \ˌjȯr-jē-ˈan-ə\. Town, Butler co., S Alabama, 60 m. SW of Montgomery; pop. (1970c) 2148.

Geor·gi·an Bay \ˌjȯr-jən-\. Inlet of Lake Huron, SE Ontario, Canada; ab. 125 m. long, 50 m. wide; 860 sq. m.; has entrance ab. 20 m. wide bet. E Manitoulin I. and Cape Hurd. Thirty islands in SE included in **Georgian Bay Islands National Park** (see CANADA, *National Parks*).

Georgian Soviet Socialist Republic \ˈjȯr-jən-\ *also* **Geor·gia** \ˈjȯr-jə\ *or Georgian* **Sa·kart·ve·lo** \sä-ˈkärt-və-ˌlō\ *or Russ.* **Gru·zi·ya** \ˈgrü-zē-(y)ə\ *or anc.* **Ibe·ria** \ī-ˈbir-ē-ə\. A constituent republic of the U.S.S.R., bounded on SE by Azerbaijan S.S.R., on S by Armenian S.S.R. and Turkey, and on W by the Black Sea; 26,911 sq. m.; pop. (1970p) 4,688,000; ❋ Tbilisi; includes Abkhazian and Adzhar Autonomous Republics and South Ossetian Autonomous Oblast. Separated from Russian S.F.S.R. on N and NE by main range of Caucasus Mts.; comprises mainly the S slopes of W and cen. Caucasus, and valleys of the Rioni and upper Kura rivers. *Chief products:* Wheat, sugar beets, barley, tea, citrus fruit; livestock; manufacturing: textiles, chemicals, steel products; hydroelectric power plants. *Chief towns:* Tbilisi Kutaisi, Batumi.

History: Region contained ancient kingdoms of Colchis and Iberia; dependent upon Rome after 1st cent. B.C. but retained autonomy; Christianized in 4th cent. A.D.; E part, esp. under Sassanidae, became Persian, and, in 8th cent., was conquered by Arabs; reunited with W part 11th cent.; expanded to include region from Black Sea to Caspian and parts of Armenia and Persia before its disintegration under impact of Mongol and Turkish invasions; under Armenian, Turkish, and Persian control until it sought Russian protection in 18th cent.; annexation to Russia 1801 caused

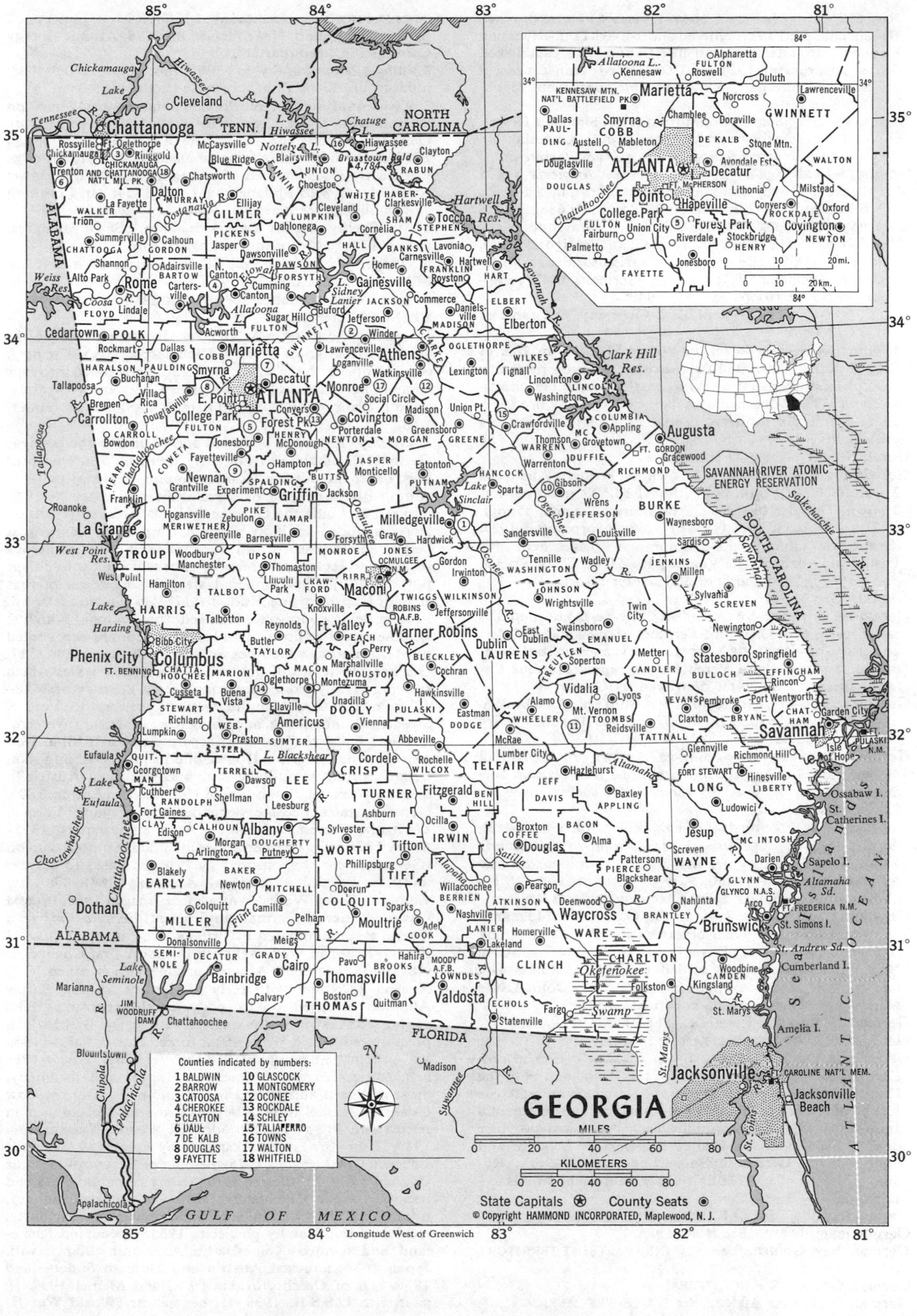
GEORGIA
Counties indicated by numbers:
1 BALDWIN
2 BARROW
3 CATOOSA
4 CHEROKEE
5 CLAYTON
6 DADE
7 DE KALB
8 DOUGLAS
9 FAYETTE
10 GLASCOCK
11 MONTGOMERY
12 OCONEE
13 ROCKDALE
14 SCHLEY
15 TALIAFERRO
16 TOWNS
17 WALTON
18 WHITFIELD
MILES
0 20 40 60 80
KILOMETERS
0 20 40 60 80
State Capitals
County Seats
© Copyright HAMMOND INCORPORATED, Maplewood, N. J.
Longitude West of Greenwich
85° 84° 83° 82° 81°
35° 34° 33° 32° 31° 30°
ATLANTA
Augusta
Macon
Columbus
Savannah
Albany
Athens
Chattanooga
Jacksonville
Valdosta
Brunswick
Waycross
Rome
Marietta
Decatur
Gainesville
Milledgeville
Thomasville
Warner Robins
Dalton
Griffin
La Grange
Phenix City
Dothan
NORTH CAROLINA
SOUTH CAROLINA
ALABAMA
FLORIDA
TENN.
GULF OF MEXICO
ATLANTIC OCEAN
Sea Islands
Okefenokee Swamp
SAVANNAH RIVER ATOMIC ENERGY RESERVATION
Clark Hill Res.
Hartwell Res.
Lake Sinclair
L. Sidney Lanier
Allatoona L.
L. Blackshear
Lake Seminole
Savannah R.
Altamaha R.
Chattahoochee R.
Flint R.
Ocmulgee R.
Oconee R.
Ogeechee R.
Satilla R.
Suwannee R.

Russian war with Persia 1804–13 (see GULISTAN); when Russia collapsed 1917, entered short-lived Transcaucasian Republic; declared independent republic 1918; established Soviet government 1921; in 1922 joined Transcaucasian S.F.S.R. and entered U.S.S.R.; became constituent republic 1936.

Geor·gi·na \jȯr-ˈjē-nə\. Intermittent river, Simpson Desert, E Northern Territory and W Queensland, Australia; ab. 700 m. long; in some seasons flows to the Warburton.

Ge·or·giu–Dezh \gē-ˌȯr-gyü-ˈd(y)ezh\ *or formerly* **Lis·ki** \ˈl(y)ē-skē\. Town, Voronezh Oblast, Russian S.F.S.R., U.S.S.R., ab. 50 m. SSE of Voronezh; pop. (1968e) 55,000.

Ge·or·giy·evsk \gē-ˌȯr-gē-ˈefsk\. Town, S Stavropol Krai, Russian S.F.S.R., U.S.S.R., 18 m. E of Pyatigorsk; pop. (1967e) 41,000; trade center for agricultural and cattle products. Founded 1777; taken by Germans 1942, recaptured by Soviet troops Jan. 10, 1943.

Ge·ra \ˈger-ə\. 1 District of East Germany. See table at GERMANY, EAST.

2 Industrial city, its ✱, on the Weisse Elster 47 m. ESE of Erfurt; pop. (1970e) 111,099; textiles, tobacco products; food processing, metal-working; castle, church (Trinitatiskirche, 1611), 16th cent. town hall; destroyed by fire 1639, 1686, and 1780; formerly capital of Reuss-Schleiz-Gera principality.

Geral, Serra. See SERRA GERAL.

Ger·ald·ton \ˈjer-əl(d)-tən\. 1 Town, W Western Australia, 210 m. NNW of Perth; pop. (1968e) 13,500; good harbor.

2 Town, Thunder Bay dist., SW Ontario, Canada, 55 m. E of Lake Nipigon; pop. (1971p) 3145; incorporated 1937.

Gé·rard·mer \ˌzhā-ˌrär-ˈmā\. Commune, Vosges dept., NE France, on a lake in the Vosges Mts. 20 m. SE of Épinal; pop. (1962c) 9626; summer and winter resort.

Gerasa. See JERASH.

Ger·go·vie \ˌzher-gə-ˈvē\. Plateau, Puy-de-Dôme dept., S cen. France, S of Clermont-Ferrand; above village of Gergovie; site of **Ger·go·via** \ jər-ˈgō-vē-ə\, ancient settlement of the Arverni where Vercingetorix repulsed Julius Caesar's forces 52 B.C., later destroyed by Caesar.

Ge·ring \ˈgi(ə)r-iŋ\. City, ⊗ of Scotts Bluff co., W Nebraska, on N Platte river opp. Scottsbluff; pop. (1970c) 5639; dairy farms; beet sugar.

Ger·i·zim, Mount \-ˈger-ə-ˌzim, -gə-ˈrī-zəm\ *or Arab.* **Je·bel at Tur** \ˌjeb-əl-at-ˈü(ə)r\. Mountain just S of Nablus, Jordan, in region occupied by Israel 1967; sacred place for Samaritans.

Ger·la·chov·ka \ˈge(ə)r-lə-ˌkȯf-kə, -ˌkȯv-\ *or Ger.* **Gerls·dor·fer Spit·ze** \ˌge(ə)rls-ˌdȯr-fər-ˈs(h)pit-sə\; *formerly* **Franz Jo·sef–Spitze** \ˌfrän(t)s-ˌyō-zəf-ˈs(h)pit-sə\ *or* **Sta·lin Peak** \ˌstäl-ən-, ˌstal-, -ˌēn-\. Peak in Tatra Mts., Carpathians, N Slovak S.R., Czechoslovakia; 8711 ft.

Ger·man Coast \ˌjər-mən-\ *or Fr.* **Côte des Al·le·mands** \kōt-dāz-al-ə-mäⁿ\. District extending ab. 40 m. along right bank of Mississippi river from a point ab. 30 m. above New Orleans, Louisiana; settled 1721 by Alsatians who had come to America under inducements of John Law's Mississippi Scheme, which collapsed 1720.

German Democratic Republic. See GERMANY, EAST.

German East Africa. See TANZANIA.

Ger·ma·nia \(ˌ)jər-ˈmā-nē-ə, -nyə\. Ancient region of cen. Europe, comprising territory E of the Rhine and N of the Danube which never became part of Roman Empire. Areas just W of Rhine conquered by Romans became: **Germania In·fe·ri·or** \(ˌ)jər-ˌmān-yə-in-ˈfir-ē-ər\, a Roman province of E Gallia (mod. NE France and part of Belgium and Netherlands); **Germania Su·pe·ri·or** \-sü-ˈpir-ē-ər\, Roman province of NE Gallia (nearly equivalent to Alsace-Lorraine).

Germanicopolis. See ÇANKIRI 2.

Germanicum, Mare. See NORTH SEA.

German New Guinea. See NEW GUINEA, TRUST TERRITORY OF.

German Ocean. See NORTH SEA.

German Southwest Africa. See SOUTH-WEST AFRICA.

Ger·man·town \ˈjər-mən-ˌtau̇n\. 1 Village, Montgomery co., SW cen. Maryland, NW of Rockville; U.S. Atomic Energy Commission headquarters.

2 Village, Montgomery co., SW Ohio; pop. (1970c) 4088; tobacco products, flour, concrete products.

3 Residential section of Philadelphia, Pennsylvania, on Wissahickon Creek; originally settled as township by German colonists 1683–84; battle of Germantown Oct. 4, 1777 in which Washington tried unsuccessfully to dislodge British troops stationed there under Sir Wm. Howe; consolidated with Philadelphia (*q.v.*) 1854; early printing and publishing center.

4 City, Shelby co., SW Tennessee, 14 m. ESE of Memphis; pop. (1970c) 3474; draperies; agriculture.

5 Village, Washington co., SE Wisconsin, 17 m. NW of Milwaukee; pop. (1970c) 6974.

German Volga Republic. See VOLGA GERMAN AUTONOMOUS SOCIALIST REPUBLIC.

Ger·ma·ny \ˈjərm-(ə-)nē\; *or Ger.* **Deutsch·land** \ˈdȯich-ˌlänt\ *or* **Deut·sches Reich** \ˌdȯich-əs-ˈrīk, -ˈrīk̲\. Country, cen. Europe; 182,426 sq. m.; ✱ Berlin; partitioned into four zones of occupation (1945) which in 1949 were reconstituted into two republics. See GERMANY, EAST and GERMANY, WEST.

History: Region E of Rhine and N of Danube (ancient Germania), inhabited from early times by Teutonic peoples, never included in Roman Empire; began as political entity with the division of Carolingian empire (see FRANCE) allotted to Louis the German 843 A.D.; Germany, with N Italy, included in Holy Roman Empire (*q.v.*); even at height of Emperor's influence divided into numerous secular and ecclesiastical feudal units which increased their power during papal-imperial struggle; accession of first ruler of Hapsburg line, Rudolf I, 1273; expanded eastward, Prussia being conquered 13th cent. by Teutonic Knights; weakness and political dissolution of Empire accelerated by Reformation which began with Lutheran revolt 1517; Germany split into Catholic and Protestant states which suffered greatly from disastrous Thirty Years' War 1618–48 (see BOHEMIA); Empire yielded territory to France, Sweden, Brandenburg, and recognized practical sovereignty (Ger. *Landeshoheit*) of its separate states 1648; in 18th cent. Prussia under the Hohenzollerns prospered and soon became strongest military state and weakened Austria in Silesian Wars; on dissolution of Holy Roman Empire 1806, German states became dependents of France. Formed *Germanic Confederation* under Austrian hegemony 1815–66; by 1866 most German states included in customs union (Ger. *Zollverein*) sponsored by Prussia; failed to achieve unity in Frankfurt National Assembly 1848–49; after victory in Seven Weeks' War against Austria 1866, Prussia became leader of German unification; *German Empire*, a federal state dominated by Prussia, proclaimed at close of Franco-Prussian War 1871 with Bismarck first Chancellor (1871–90); acquired Alsace-Lorraine (*q.v.*); allied with Austria 1879 and with Italy 1882, thus forming Triple Alliance; adopted policy of colonial expansion 1884; supported Austria in the quarrel with Serbia (*q.v.*) which precipitated World War I 1914; forced Kaiser's abdication and proclaimed republic 1918; by Versailles Treaty 1919 lost Alsace-Lorraine, Moresnet, Eupen, and Malmédy, most of Posen and West Prussia (including Danzig, now Gdańsk), Memel (now Klaipėda), and all her colonies in Africa and in the Pacific; adopted Weimar Constitution 1919; Ruhr (*q.v.*) region occupied by French 1923; signed Locarno (*q.v.*) treaties 1925; member of League of Nations Council 1926–33. Ceased to be federal republic 1933 and became, under Chancellor Hitler, centralized, unitary, totalitarian state dominated by National Socialist party; recovered the Saar by plebiscite 1935; reoccupied Rhineland and formed Rome-Berlin Axis and alliance with Japan 1936; annexed Austria and German Sudetenland 1938, rest of Czechoslovakia (*q.v.*) and Memel 1939. In pact with U.S.S.R. 1939–41, began war (World War II) with Poland and with Great Britain and France Sept. 1939; conquered Norway Apr. 1940; overran Netherlands and Belgium May–June 1940; forced surrender of France June 1940; attacked U.S.S.R. June 22, 1941, defeated at Stalingrad (now Volgograd) Jan. 1943, gradually forced out of U.S.S.R. 1943–44; driven out of North Africa May 1943; driven out of France and finally forced to surrender to Allies May 8, 1945; by Potsdam Conference July 17–Aug. 2, 1945, lost territory in E to Poland and the U.S.S.R. (see EAST PRUSSIA); divided 1945 into four zones of occupation: American, British, French, and Russian; in 1949 American, British, and French zones were reconstituted forming West Germany, Russian zone forming East Germany.

Germany, East; *officially* **German Democratic Republic** *or Ger.* **Deutsche De·mo·krat·ische Re·pu·blik** \ˌdȯi-chə-ˌdā-mō-ˈkrät-ish-ə-ˌrā-pü-ˈblēk\. Republic, N cen. Europe, bounded on N by the Baltic Sea, on E by Poland, on S by Czechoslovakia and West Germany, and on W by West Germany; 41,766 sq. m.; pop. (1970e) 17,056,983; ✱ East Berlin. *Physical features:* N part characterized by morainic hills (parallel to Baltic coast) and numerous lakes; cen. and S regions progressively more mountainous, with greatest elevations reached in the Erzgebirge along border with Czechoslovakia, and in the Thuringian Forest in SW part; highest peak Fichtelberg 3982 ft. *Chief rivers:* Elbe, Oder (forms section of boundary with Poland), Saale, Havel, Spree. *Chief products:* Wheat, barley, rye, potatoes, sugar beets; lignite, potash, rock salt, copper, and iron ore; manufacturing: chemicals, textiles, building materials, motor vehicles, textile machinery, optical instruments, electrical apparatus. *Chief cities:* East Berlin, Leipzig, Dresden, Karl-Marx-Stadt, Magdeburg, Halle, Erfurt, Rostock. Divided into the following 15 districts (*Bezirke*) —for pronunciation of their names, see their individual entries:

NAME	AREA (sq. m.)	POP. (1970e)	CAPITAL
Cottbus	3,190	861,061	Cottbus
Dresden	2,602	1,837,069	Dresden
East Berlin	156	1,085,441	East Berlin
Erfurt	2,837	1,255,536	Erfurt
Frankfurt	2,774	680,576	Frankfurt
Gera	1,546	738,451	Gera
Halle	3,386	1,925,988	Halle
Karl-Marx-Stadt	2,320	2,047,854	Karl-Marx-Stadt
Leipzig	1,917	1,490,611	Leipzig
Magdeburg	4,450	1,317,511	Magdeburg
Neubrandenburg	4,167	638,842	Neubrandenburg
Potsdam	4,853	1,132,799	Potsdam
Rostock	2,731	858,846	Rostock
Schwerin	3,348	597,378	Schwerin
Suhl	1,489	553,020	Suhl

History: For history prior to 1945, see GERMANY. Following the partition of Germany (1945), region administered as occupation zone by U.S.S.R.; initial postwar period marked by the establishment of Soviet-type institutions and the confiscation of private property. Republic established as Communist state 1949; recognized frontier (Oder-Neisse line) with Poland as final German boundary in cen. Europe 1950; initiated collectivization of agriculture 1952; anti-Communist demonstrations suppressed with aid of Soviet forces 1953; was declared a sovereign state in treaty with U.S.S.R. 1955, becoming a member of the Warsaw Pact in same year; constructed wall along East Berlin-West Berlin border in order to stem flight of its citizens to West; signed 20-year friendship treaty with U.S.S.R. 1964; participated with other Warsaw Pact members in invasion of Czechoslovakia 1968; its repeated demands for diplomatic recognition not acceded to by most non-Communist governments.

Germany, West; *officially* **Federal Republic of Germany** *or Ger.* **Bun·des·re·pu·blik Deutsch·land** \ˌbu̇n-dəs-ˌrā-pü-ˈblēk-ˈdȯich-ˌlänt\. Republic, W cen. Europe, bounded on N by North Sea and Denmark, on E by East Germany and Czechoslovakia, on SE by Austria, on S by Austria and Switzerland, on SW by France, and on W by Luxembourg, Belgium, and the Netherlands; 95,781 sq. m., pop. (1970e) 59,214,400 (area and pop. figures exclusive of West Berlin); ✱ Bonn. *Physical features:* Generally flat in N, hilly in cen. region and mountainous in S (highest peak Zugspitze 9720 ft., in Bavarian Alps). *Chief rivers:* Rhine, Danube, Ems, Weser, and Elbe. *Chief products:* Wheat, rye, barley, potatoes; coal, iron ore, lead, potash; manufacturing: iron and steel, heavy machinery, motor vehicles, precision tools, optical instruments, electronic equipment, chemicals, textiles. *Chief cities:* Hamburg, Munich, Cologne, Essen, Düsseldorf, Frankfurt, Dortmund, Stuttgart, Bremen. Divided into the following ten states (*Länder*)—for pronunciation of their names, see their individual entries:

NAME	AREA (sq. m.)	POP. (1970e)	CAPITAL
Baden-Württemberg	13,803	8,959,700	Stuttgart
Bavaria	27,239	10,603,200	Munich
Bremen	156	754,400	Bremen
Hamburg	289	1,814,100	Hamburg
Hesse	8,151	5,441,300	Wiesbaden
Lower Saxony	18,305	7,109,000	Hannover
North Rhine-Westphalia	13,142	17,167,500	Düsseldorf
Rhineland-Palatinate	7,659	3,677,000	Mainz
Saarland	991	1,127,000	Saarbrücken
Schleswig-Holstein	6,046	2,561,200	Kiel
Berlin, West*	185	2,130,900	

*Not a constitutional part of West Germany.

History: For history prior to 1945, see GERMANY. Establishment of federal republic 1949; gained sovereignty and became member of NATO 1955; Saarland united with West Germany as 10th state 1957; member of the European Economic Community and of the European Atomic Energy Community 1958; cultural, military, and political relations with France codified in treaty 1963; in nonaggression treaty with U.S.S.R. (1970) recognized inviolability of existing European frontiers.

Ger·mers·heim \ˈger-mərs-ˌhīm\ *or anc.* **Vi·cus Ju·lii** \ˌvī-kəs-ˈjü-lē-ˌī\. Commune, SE Rhineland-Palatinate, West Germany, on the Rhine 8 m. SSW of Speyer; pop. (1967e) 8500; bet. 1644 and 1815 belonged alternately to France and the Palatinate.

Ger·mis·ton \ˈjər-mə-stən\. City, S Transvaal, NE Rep. of South Africa, 9 m. E of Johannesburg; pop. (1968e) 197,-020; goldfields; world's largest gold refinery; engineering industries.

Ge·rol·stein \ˈger-əl-s(h)tīn\. Village, Rhineland-Palatinate, West Germany, 28 m. N of Trier; pop. (1967e) 4600; health resort.

Ge·ro·na \jə-ˈrō-nə\. 1 Municipality, NE cen. Tarlac prov., Luzon, Phil., 10 m. N of Tarlac; pop. (1969e) 44,500.
2 Province of NE Spain. See table at SPAIN.
3 *or anc.* **Ge·run·da** \jə-ˈrən-də\. Fortified commune, ✱ of Gerona prov., NE Spain, 52 m. NE of Barcelona; pop. (1970p) 50,338; textiles, chemicals, electronic equipment, soap; 14th cent. Gothic cathedral, 13th cent. collegiate church; under Moorish rule c. 713–785 and 795–1015; became principality under kingdom of Aragon; often besieged, esp. by French 1809.

Ger·ra *or* **Ger·rha** \ˈjer-ə\. Ancient port on SW coast of Sinus Persicus (Persian Gulf); mentioned by Strabo and Pliny; site probably at modern Oqair, Saudi Arabia.

Gers \ˈzhe(ə)r\. 1 River, SW France; 111 m. long; flows N into Garonne river near Agen.
2 Department of SW France. See table at FRANCE.

Ger·sau \ˈge(ə)r-ˌzau̇\. Village, Schwyz canton, E cen. Switzerland, on Lake of Lucerne; pop. (1970c) 1753; resort; independent state 1390–1817.

Ger·sop·pa, Falls of \-jər-ˈsäp-ə\ *also* **Jog Falls** \ˈjōg-\. Cataract in small stream (Sharavati) ab. 18 m. from its mouth, on border of NW Mysore, India; 830 ft. high.

Gerunda. See GERONA 3.

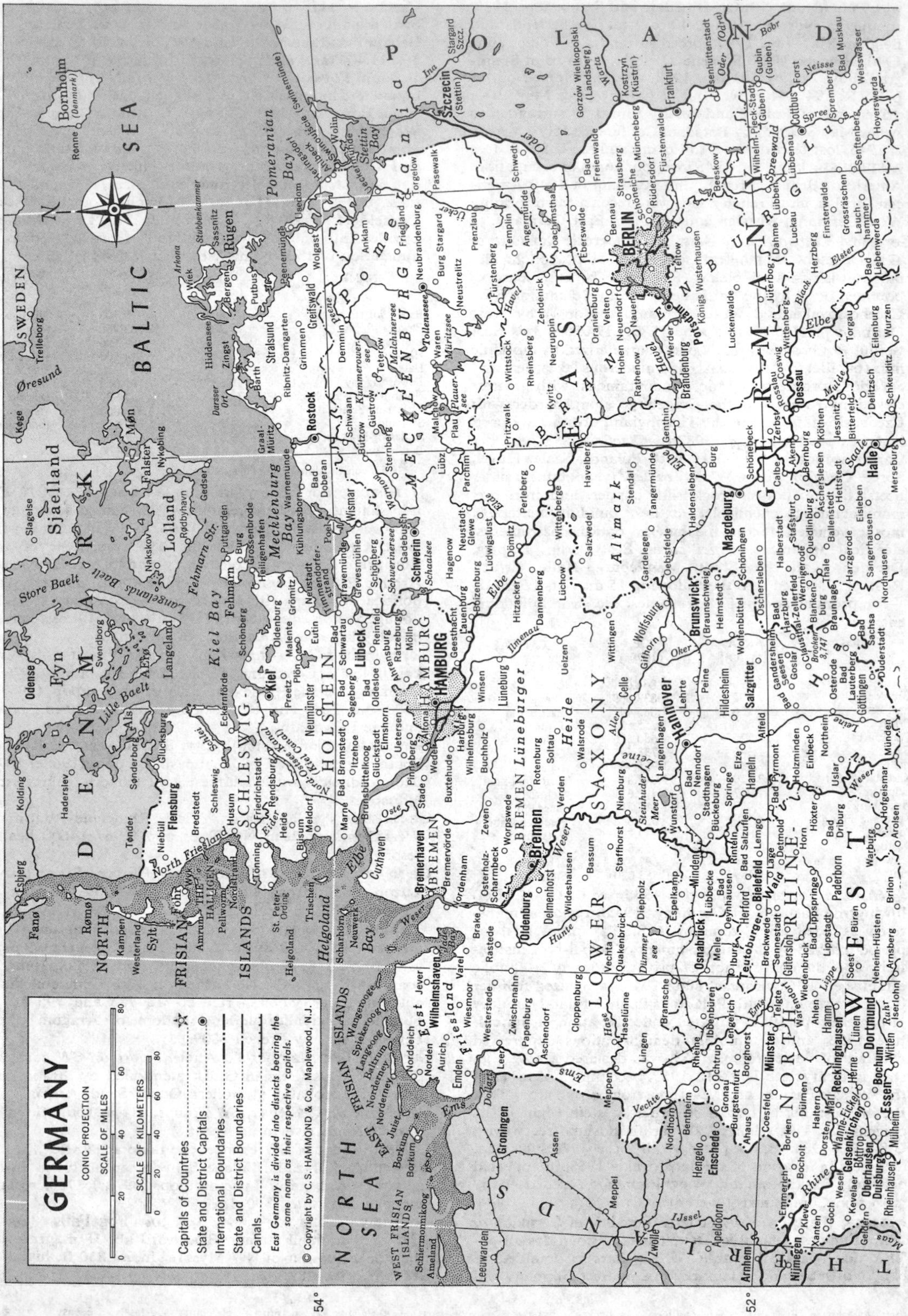
GERMANY
CONIC PROJECTION
SCALE OF MILES
0 20 40 60 80
SCALE OF KILOMETERS
0 20 40 60 80
Capitals of Countries
State and District Capitals
International Boundaries
State and District Boundaries
Canals
East Germany is divided into districts bearing the same name as their respective capitals.
© Copyright by C.S. HAMMOND & Co., Maplewood, N.J.
NORTH SEA
BALTIC SEA
DENMARK
SWEDEN
POLAND
NETHERLANDS
WEST GERMANY
EAST GERMANY
SCHLESWIG-HOLSTEIN
HAMBURG
BREMEN
LOWER SAXONY
NORTH RHINE-WESTPHALIA
MECKLENBURG
BRANDENBURG
Pomerania
Altmark
Lüneburger Heide
Harz
Teutoburger Wald
East Friesland
NORTH FRISIAN ISLANDS
EAST FRISIAN ISLANDS
WEST FRISIAN ISLANDS
Helgoland Bay
Kiel Bay
Mecklenburg Bay
Pomeranian Bay
Stettin Bay
Fehmarn Str.
Store Baelt
Lille Baelt
Langelands Baelt
Øresund
Sjaelland
Lolland
Falster
Fyn
Langeland
Bornholm (Denmark)
Rügen
Fehmarn
Sylt
Berlin
Hamburg
Bremen
Hannover
Kiel
Schwerin
Rostock
Magdeburg
Potsdam
Frankfurt
Cottbus
Halle
Dessau
Lübeck
Brunswick
Szczecin (Stettin)
Elbe
Weser
Ems
Oder
Havel
Spree
Rhine
Aller
Leine
Saale
Mulde
Neisse
Nord-Ostsee-Kanal (Kiel Canal)
54°
52°
6°
8°
10°
12°
14°

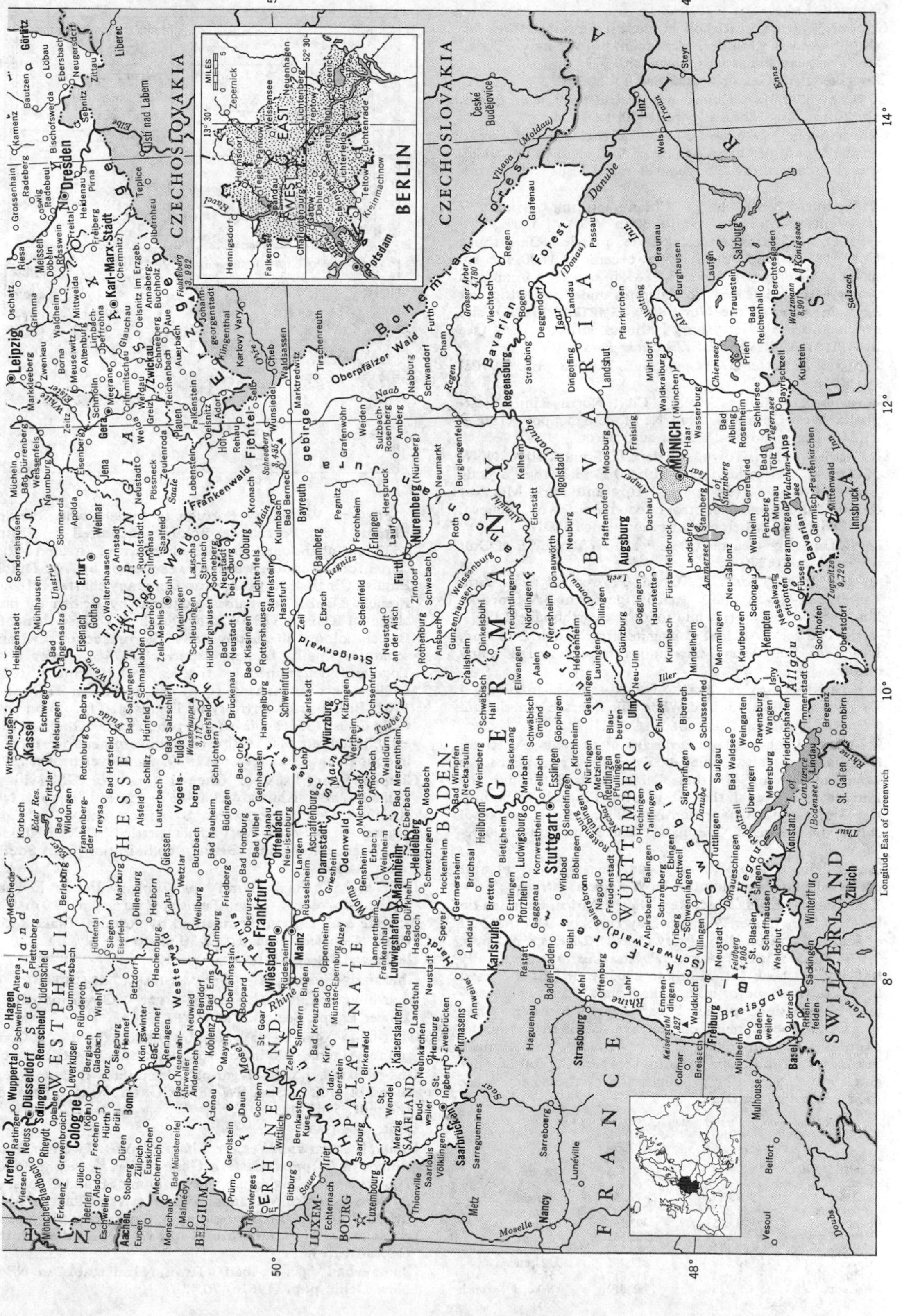

GERMANY
BAVARIA
WESTPHALIA
HESSE
THURINGIA
SAXONY
RHINELAND
PALATINATE
SAARLAND
BADEN-WÜRTTEMBERG
CZECHOSLOVAKIA
AUSTRIA
SWITZERLAND
FRANCE
BELGIUM
LUXEMBOURG
BERLIN
WEST
EAST
Potsdam
MILES
Bohemian Forest
Bavarian Forest
Oberpfälzer Wald
Fichtelgebirge
Frankenwald
Thüringer Wald
Erzgebirge
Westerwald
Schwarzwald
Bavarian Alps
Allgäu
Steigerwald
Odenwald
Rhine
Main
Danube
Elbe
Moselle
Saar
Isar
Inn
Munich
Nuremberg
Stuttgart
Frankfurt
Cologne
Düsseldorf
Leipzig
Dresden
Karl-Marx-Stadt
Erfurt
Kassel
Würzburg
Regensburg
Augsburg
Mannheim
Karlsruhe
Wiesbaden
Mainz
Bonn
Koblenz
Strasbourg
Zürich
Linz
Salzburg
Innsbruck
Longitude East of Greenwich
50°
48°
8°
10°
12°
14°

Geserich, Lake. See JEZIORAK.

Ge·shur \'gē-shər\. Region in ancient Palestine from NE shore of Sea of Galilee E to Bashan; in the time of David an Aramaean kingdom (*2 Sam.* xiii. 37).

Gesoriacum *or* **Gessoriacum.** See BOULOGNE.

Ge·ta·fe \hā-'tä-fā\. Commune, Madrid prov., cen. Spain, ab. 20 m. S of Madrid; pop. (1970p) 69,424.

Geth·sem·a·ne \geth-'sem-ə-nē\. The enclosure or garden on the Mount of Olives outside of Jerusalem (*q.v.*) which was the scene of the agony and arrest of Jesus (*Matt.* xxvi. 36–47).

Get·tys·burg \'get-ēz-ˌbərg\. **1** Manufacturing borough, ⊗ of Adams co., S Pennsylvania, 30 m. WSW of York; pop. (1970c) 7275; iron mines, granite quarries; Gettysburg Coll. (1832). Laid out in 1780's, became ⊗ 1800, incorp. 1806; scene of battle July 1–3, 1863, in which Union forces under Meade defeated Confederates under Lee, stopping Lee's invasion of the North (see CEMETERY RIDGE), site now comprising **Gettysburg National Military Park** (see UNITED STATES, *National Historical Parks*).
2 City, ⊗ of Potter co., N cen. South Dakota; pop. (1970c) 1915.

Ge·vels·berg \'gā-fəls-ˌbe(ə)rg\. City, North Rhine-Westphalia, West Germany, 32 m. NE of Cologne; pop. (1969e) 31,419; iron products, stoves, auto parts.

Gex \'zheks, 'zhā\. Town, Ain dept., E France, 10 m. NNW of Geneva, Switzerland; pop. (1966e) 2766; in the **Pa·ys de Gex** \pā-ˌēd-ə-\, region bet. Alps and Jura Mts., at different times under control of counts of Savoy, Geneva, and Switzerland, belongs to France since 1601.

Ge·yik Da·ğı \ge-ˌyēk-dä-'(g)ē\. Peak, SW Turkey, E of Gulf of Antalya; 10,270 ft.

Gey·sir \'gī-zər\ *or Eng.* **Great Gey·ser** \-'gī-zər, *Brit. sometimes* -'gā- *or* -'gē-\. Inactive geyser in SW cen. Iceland; active for short while following earthquake 1896.

Ge·zer \'gē-zər\. Ancient Canaanite city; ab. 6 m. S of Lod, Israel, at Tell Jezar; excavations have revealed many cultures.

Ge·zi·ra \jə-'zir-ə\ *or Arab.* **Al–Ja·zi·rah** \ˌal-jə-'zir-ə\. **1** District bet. Blue Nile and White Nile rivers, E cen. Sudan. **2** Province, Sudan. See BLUE NILE 2.

Ghā·gha·ra \'gäg-ə-rə\ *or formerly* **Gog·ra** \gäg-rə\. River, N India, Nepal, and China; ab. 570 m. long; rises near Lake Manasarowar in SW Tibet, China, flows S through the Himalayas in Nepal, then SE in Uttar Pradesh, India into the Ganges near Chapra on NW Bihar border. In Nepal called the **Kar·na·li** \kär-'näl-ē\ *also* **Kau·ri·ala** \ˌkau̇-rē-'äl-ə\.

Gha·na \'gän-ə, 'gan-ə\. **1** *or* **Ga·na** \'gän-ə\. Ancient and medieval Sudanese kingdom in W Sahara, Africa.
2 *or formerly* **Gold Coast.** Republic, W Africa, bounded on NW and N by Upper Volta, on E by Togo, on S by the Gulf of Guinea, and on W by Ivory Coast; 92,100 sq. m.; pop. (1970p) 8,545,561; ✱ Accra. *Physical features:* Generally flat; highest peak Mt. Afadjato 2905 ft., in SE; traversed by Volta river; major lake: Lake Volta; N area characterized by grassland plains, S part heavily forested. *Chief products:* Cocoa, palm oil, cassava, corn; fish; bauxite, diamonds, gold, manganese. *Chief towns:* Accra, Kumasi, Sekondi-Takoradi. Divided into the Accra Capital District and eight regions (for pronunciation of their names, see their individual entries):

NAME	AREA (sq. m.)	POP. (1970p)	CAPITAL
Capital District	995	848,825	Accra
Regions			
Ashanti	9,417	1,477,397	Kumasi
Brong-Ahafo	15,273	762,673	Sunyani
Central	3,815	892,593	Cape Coast
Eastern	7,698	1,262,882	Koforidua
Northern	27,175	728,572	Tamale
Upper	10,548	857,295	Bolgatanga
Volta	7,943	947,012	Ho
Western	9,236	768,312	Sekondi-Takoradi

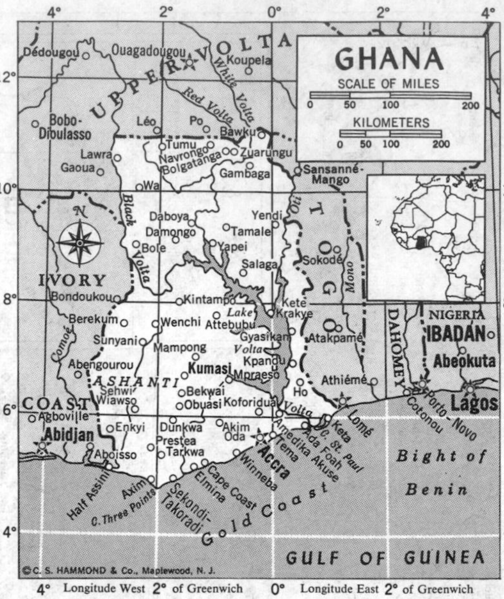

History: Visited by Portuguese traders who founded Elmina 1482; Portuguese holdings captured by Dutch 1637 and abandoned as price of return of Brazil 1642; a center for slave trade which was carried on by rival Dutch, English (English Royal African Company chartered 1672), French, Danish companies; acquired by British by purchase of Danish (1850) and Dutch (1871) settlements; British colony, alternately under Sierra Leone (*q.v.*) and separate, finally became separate 1874; frontier with Togoland determined by treaties with Germany 1886, 1899; took over Ashanti (*q.v.*) and Northern Territories 1901; British trust territory of Togo voted for union with Gold Coast 1956; achieved independence (as Ghana) 1957; established republic 1960; civilian government overthrown in coup d'état 1966, restored 1969, again overthrown 1972.

Ghan·si \'gän(t)-sē\ *or* **Ghan·zi** \-zē\ *or* **Ghan·si·land** \-ˌland\ *also* **Khan·zi** \'kän-zē\. Plateau region, NW Kalahari Desert, Botswana, S Africa; on NE is Lake Ngami, on W South-West Africa; settled by Cecil Rhodes as buffer state against German colonization from South-West Africa.

Ghār al–Milḥ \ˌgär-al-'mil\ *or formerly* **Por·to Fa·ri·na** \ˌpȯrt-ə-fə-'rē-nə\. Town, Tunisia, N Africa, ab. 20 m. E of Bizerte on a lagoon; bombarded by Admiral Blake 1655; ruins of ancient Utica (*q.v.*) 10 m. to the SE.

Gharapuri. See ELEPHANTA.

Gharaq as–Sultani, Al–. See AL-GHARAQ AS-SULTANI.

Ghar·bī·ya *or* **Gar·bi·eh** \gär-'bē-ə, gər-\. Governorate of N Lower Egypt. See table at EGYPT.

Ghar·da·ïa \gär-'dä-yə\ *also* **Gar·daia** \gär-'dī-ə\. Commune, Algeria, 300 m. S of Algiers; pop. (1966c) 30,167.

Ghā·rib, Ge·bel \ˌjeb-əl-'gar-əb\. Mountain, E Egypt, near S end of Gulf of Suez SW of **Ras Ghārib** \räs-\, point on the gulf; 5745 ft.

Ghāt. See GAT.

Ghats, Eastern *and* **Western Ghats** \-'gȯts\. Two mountain ranges in S India: **Eastern Ghats** (average height 1500–2000 ft.) extending for ab. 500 m. along SE and E coast as far N as mouth of Mahanadi river; **Western Ghats** (average height 3000–5000 ft.) extending 800 m. along SW and W coast as far N as mouth of Tapti river; bet. them is the Deccan (*q.v.*).

Gha·zi·a·bad \'gäz-ē-ə-ˌbäd\. Town, N India, ab. 7 m. NE of New Delhi; pop. (1961c) 70,438.

Gha·zi·pur \'gäz-i-ˌpu̇(ə)r\. Town, SE Uttar Pradesh, N India, on Ganges river 40 m. ENE of Varanasi; pop. (1961c) 37,100; former licensed center for collecting and processing opium; has scent distilleries; founded 1330.

Ghaz·ni \'gäz-nē\. 1 Province of E Afghanistan. See table at AFGHANISTAN.

2 City, its ✻, 92 m. SW of Kabul; pop. (1969e) 43,423; trades in corn, fruit, and wool.

History: Became Muslim in 9th cent.; made capital of Ghaznevid dynasty by Subuktigin 977; its most famous ruler was Mahmud of Ghazni (998–1030) who conquered neighboring regions and made the city capital of a kingdom extending from the Tigris to the Ganges which endured until 1173 when it was finally overcome by Mohammed of Ghor; taken by Ogadai, son of Genghis Khan, c. 1238. Declined politically under the Moguls of India until 1738 when it became part of new Afghan kingdom; in Afghan Wars of 19th cent. captured by British July 23, 1839; later besieged for four months by Afghans and surrendered Mar. 6, 1842; retaken and partly destroyed by British Sept. 1842.

Ghazzah *or* **Ghazze.** See GAZA.

Gheel. See GEEL.

Ghe·lu·velt \'gā-lə-ˌvelt\ *or Flem.* **Ge·lu·veld** \'gā-\. Small commune, West Flanders prov., NW Belgium, 5 m. E of Ieper (Ypres); pop. (1969e) 1520; battlefield 1914, 1917.

Ghent. See GENT.

Gheor·ghe Gheor·ghiu–Dej \ˌgyȯr-gyə-'gyȯr-gyü-'dezh\. Town, Bacău co., E cen. Romania, ab. 25 m. SSW of Bacău; pop. (1970e) 40,563.

Ghe·ri·ah \'gar-ē-ə\. Locality, Maharashtra state, India, S of Bombay; site of pirate stronghold reduced by Clive 1756.

Ghilan. See GĪLĀN.

Ghor \'gȯ(ə)r\ *or* **Ghur** \'gu̇(ə)r\. 1 Ancient kingdom, SW Asia, in what is now NW Afghanistan; its princes, first mentioned in 11th cent. A.D., closely connected with Ghaznevid dynasty; their greatest ruler Mohammed of Ghor, who captured Ghazni 1173 and conquered all northern India (1186–1206).

2 Province of NW cen. Afghanistan. See table at AFGHANISTAN.

Ghor, The \-'gȯ(ə)r\. The valley of the Dead Sea and lower Jordan, Israel and Jordan; 4 to 12 m. wide, ab. 65 m. long.

Ghudāmis. See GADÀMES.

Ghur·da·qah \gər-'däk-ə\. Town, ✻ of Red Sea governorate, Egypt; pop. (1970e) 4400.

Gia Dinh \'zhä-'din\. Town, South Vietnam, just N of Saigon; pop. (1968e) 51,113.

Gianitsà. See GENITSA.

Gian·nu·tri \jä-'nü-trē\. Small island in Tyrrhenian Sea off SW coast of Tuscany, cen. Italy.

Gi·ant Mountain \ˌjī-ənt-\. Peak in the Adirondack Mts., Essex co., NE New York; 4622 ft.

Giant Mountains. See RIESENGEBIRGE.

Gi·ant's Castle \ˌjī-ənts-\. Peak in Drakensberg Mts., E Rep. of South Africa, on border bet. Lesotho and Natal; 10,902 ft.

Giant's Causeway. Formation of prismatic basaltic columns on N coast of co. Antrim, Northern Ireland, making a rough platform extending for 300 yards along coast and at one point ab. 500 ft. into the sea.

Giar·re \'jär-ē\. Commune, Catania prov., E Sicily, Italy, at E foot of Mt. Etna; pop. (1968e) 22,563.

Gia·ve·no \jä-'vē-nō\. Commune, Torino prov., Piedmont, NW Italy, 17 m. SW of Turin; pop. (1968e) 9794.

Gi·ba·ra \hē-'vär-ə\. Town and municipality, N coast of Oriente prov., E Cuba; munic. pop. (1967e) 44,890; exports esp. bananas; port opened to commerce 1827. See HOLGUÍN.

Gib·bon Falls \ˌgib-ən-\. Waterfall on **Gibbon River,** Yellowstone National Park, NW Wyoming; 84 ft. high.

Gibbs·boro \'gibz-ˌbər-ə, -ˌbə-rə\. Borough, Camden co., SW New Jersey, 8 m. SE of Camden; pop. (1970c) 2634.

Gib·e·ah \'gib-ē-ə\. Town, S ancient Palestine, site now in Israeli-occupied Jordan; political capital of Saul, first king of Israel (*1 Sam.* xxii. 6).

Gib·e·on \'gib-ē-ən\. 1 City of Canaan, 6 m. NW of Jerusalem; the modern village of Al-Jib in Israeli-occupied Jordan; its inhabitants (Gibeonites) made an alliance with Joshua but were made slaves (*Josh.* ix. 3–27).

2 Town, S cen. South-West Africa, on Fish river 180 m. SSE of Windhoek; scene of fighting bet. German and South African forces during World War I.

Gi·bral·tar \jə-'brȯl-tər\. 1 City, Wayne co., SE Michigan, 20 m. S of Detroit; pop. (1970c) 3842.

2 British colony, a peninsula in S part of Spain; 2½ m. long, 2¼ sq. m.; pop. (1970c) 26,833; administrative center Gibraltar (town); British naval and air base.

History: Captured 711 A.D. and fortified by Tariq, Moorish invader of Spain; finally taken by Spanish 1462; captured by British 1704 during War of Spanish Succession and retained by treaty 1713; unsuccessfully besieged by French and Spanish 1779–83; made a British colony 1830; adopted new constitution 1964; Spanish claims to colony rejected by Great Britain.

Gibraltar, Bay of *also* **Bay of Al·ge·ci·ras** \-ˌal-jə-'sir-əs\. Bay in S extremity of Spain, bet. Algeciras and Gibraltar.

Gibraltar, Rock of *or anc.* **Cal·pe** \'kal-pē\. Mountain on E end of Strait of Gibraltar, constituting with S part of isthmus linking it with Spain the British colony of Gibraltar; highest point 1398 ft.

Gibraltar, Strait of *also* **Straits of Gibraltar;** *Lat.* **Fre·tum Gad·i·ta·num** \'frēt-əm-ˌgad-ə-'tā-nəm\ *or angl.* **Gad·i·tan Strait** \ˌgad-ə-tən-, -ˌtan-\; *Arab.* **Bab al–Za·kak** \ˌbab-ˌaz-ə-'käk, ˌbab-ˌal-zə-\. Passage connecting Mediterranean Sea and Atlantic Ocean, bet. Spain and Africa, with Gibralter and Ceuta on either side at E end, capes Trafalgar and Spartel at W end; 36 m. long; ab. 8 m. wide in narrowest part, ab. 23 m. in widest. See PILLARS OF HERCULES.

Gibraltar Point. Cape on N side of entrance to the Wash, E cen. England, S of Skegness.

Gib·son \'gib-sən\. 1 Name of counties in two states of the U.S. See tables at INDIANA and TENNESSEE.

2 *or* **Gibson City.** City, ⊗ of Glascock co., E cen. Georgia; pop. (1970c) 701; lumber.

3 Residential city, Ford co., NE cen. Illinois, 32 m. E of Bloomington; pop. (1970c) 3454.

Gib·son·burg \'gib-sən-ˌbərg\. Village, Sandusky co., N Ohio, 20 m. SSE of Toledo; pop. (1970c) 2585; flour mills; oil and gas wells.

Gibson Desert. Desert, cen. and E Western Australia, S of Great Sandy Desert; N–S extent ab. 250 m., E–W extent ab. 520 m.; salt lakes.

Gibson Peak. Mountain in Custer and Saguache cos., S cen. Colorado; 13,729 ft.

Gib·son·ville \'gib-sən-ˌvil\. Town, Alamance and Guilford cos., N cen. North Carolina; pop. (1970c) 2019; food processing plants, cottonseed oil and feed mills.

Gid·dings \'gid-iŋz\. City, ⊗ of Lee co., cen. Texas, 30 m. W of Brenham; pop. (1970c) 2783; cotton.

Gid·e·on \'gid-ē-ən\. City, New Madrid co., SE Missouri, 24 m. NNW of Caruthersville; pop. (1970c) 1112; soybeans, corn.

Gien \zhē-'aⁿ\. Commune, Loiret dept., N cen. France, on the Loire 38 m. ESE of Orléans; pop. (1962c) 10,254; castle, rebuilt 1494 by Anne of Beaujeu; manufactures faience.

Giens \zhē-'aⁿ\. Peninsula on SE coast of Var dept., S France, S of Hyères; forms E side of the **Gulf of Giens.**

Giess·bach \'gēs-ˌbäk\. Waterfall, SE Bern canton, Switzerland, E of Lake of Brienz; total drop 1312 ft.

Gies·sen \'gēs-ᵊn\. City, cen. Hesse, West Germany, on Lahn river 35 m. N of Frankfurt am Main; pop. (1969e) 74,380; rubber goods, tobacco; brewing; castle ruins (14th cent.), univ. (1607). Chartered as city 1248; passed to Hesse 1265; in World War II entered by American troops Mar. 28, 1945.

Gif·fard \'zhē-ˌfär, zhē-'\. Village, Quebec co., S Quebec, Canada, on St. Lawrence river 2 m. N of Quebec; pop. (1971p) 13,087.

Gif·horn \'gif-ˌhȯ(ə)rn\. City, Lower Saxony, West Germany, 16 m. N of Brunswick; pop. (1969e) 22,415; residential; 14th–16th cent. castle; founded 1265.

Gi·fu \'gē-(ˌ)fü\. **1** Prefecture, cen. Honshū, Japan; 4092 sq. m.; pop. (1970c) 1,758,954; ✱ Gifu; automobiles, chemicals, machinery, textiles.

2 City, its ✱, 20 m. NNW of Nagoya on Nagara river; pop. (1970c) 385,727; manufactures paper wares (umbrellas, lanterns, fans, napkins, crape, etc.). A castle town in medieval Japan; captured 1564 by Oda Nobunaga; a center of civil conflict until about 1600; famous as scene of cormorant fishing on the Nagara.

Gi·gan·te \hē-'hän-(ˌ)tā\. Mountain, Guanajuato state, cen. Mexico; 10,653 ft.

Gi·gha \'gē-ə\. Small island of the Inner Hebrides, SW Scotland, ab. 3½ m. W of Kintyre Penin.

Gi·glio \'jēl-(ˌ)yō\ *or anc.* **Igil·i·um** \ī-'jil-ē-əm\. Italian island in Mediterranean Sea off SW coast of Tuscany, cen. Italy; ab. 15 sq. m., highest point 1634 ft.; has two towns: **Giglio Ca·stel·lo** \-kä-'stel-(ˌ)ō\, on the height, and the port of **Giglio Por·to** \-'pōrt-(ˌ)ō, -'pȯrt-\; granite quarries since Roman times.

Gi·hei·na \jē-'hā-nə\ *or* **Ju·hay·nah** \jə-\. Town, Sawhaj gov., Upper Egypt, near Nile; pop. (1966c) 24,200.

Gi·hulng·an \hē-'hu̇lŋ-ˌän\. See GUIHULNGAN 2.

Gi·jón \hē-'hōn\. Seaport, Oviedo prov., NW Spain, on Bay of Biscay 16 m. NE of Oviedo; pop. (1970p) 187,612; good harbor (founded 1552 by Charles V); commercial fishing; manufactures glass, pottery, soap, chocolates, tobacco; exports incl. iron ore and coal. Founded before Roman times; captured by Moors, 8th cent.; port of refuge of Spanish Armada after its defeat by British 1588.

Gi·la \'hē-lə\. **1** River, New Mexico and Arizona; 500 m. long; flows from SW New Mexico W across S Arizona to Colorado river near Yuma, SW corner of Arizona; its valley is chief habitat of the Gila monster, a large poisonous lizard.

2 County in Arizona. See table at ARIZONA.

Gila Cliff Dwellings National Monument. See UNITED STATES, *National Monuments.*

Gī·lān *or* **Ghi·lan** *also* **Gui·lan** \gē-'län\. Province of NW Iran, SW of Caspian Sea. See table at IRAN.

Gil·bert \'gil-bərt\. **1** City, St. Louis co., NE Minnesota, 3 m. ESE of Virginia; pop. (1970c) 2287; former iron-mining center.

2 River, N Queensland, Australia; 320 m. long; flows NW into Gulf of Carpentaria; seasonal.

Gilbert and El·lice Islands Colony \-'el-əs-\. British colony in W Pacific Ocean, consisting of the Gilbert Is., Ellice Is., Ocean I., three islands (Fanning, Washington, and Christmas) of the Line Is., and the Phoenix Is.; 283 sq. m.; pop. (1970e) 56,400; ✱ Tarawa. The two main groups proclaimed a British protectorate 1892 and made a colony 1915; Fanning I., Washington I., and Ocean I. added 1916, Christmas I. in 1919, and the Phoenix group 1937; inaugurated new constitution 1971.

Gilbert Grosvenor Range. See GROSVENOR MOUNTAINS.

Gilbert Islands. Island group containing 16 atolls in the W Pacific Ocean on the equator, SSE of Marshall Is. and NE of Solomon Is.; 102 sq. m.; pop. (1968p) 44,206; forms main part of British Gilbert and Ellice Islands Colony; most important islands Tarawa (largest), Makin, Abaiang, Abemama, Tabiteuea, Nonouti, and Beru. Islands have long been densely populated.

History: Probably first sighted by Mendaña in 1567; various islands visited by British navigators bet. 1767 and 1824; visited by Commander Wilkes 1846; scene of missionary labors of Hiram Bingham 1857–64, 1873–75. Proclaimed a British protectorate 1892, made part of Gilbert and Ellice Islands Colony 1915; occupied by Japanese Dec. 1941–Nov. 1943 (see TARAWA).

Gil·ber·ton \'gil-bərt-ᵊn\. Borough, Schuylkill co., E cen. Pennsylvania, 8 m. N of Pottsville; pop. (1970c) 1923; coal mining.

Gilbert Peak. Mountain, NE Utah, bet. Summit and Duchesne cos.; in Unita Mts.; 13,422 ft.

Gil·boa, Mount \-gil-'bō-ə\. Mountain, Israel, W of the Jordan and S of the Plain of Esdraelon near source of the Qishon; 1631 ft.; place where Saul was defeated by the Philistines and slew himself (*1 Sam.* xxxi. 1, 4).

Gil·christ \'gil-krəst\. County in Florida. See table at FLORIDA.

Gil·e·ad \'gil-ē-əd\. **1** Mountainous region E of Jordan river in ancient Palestine, extending approximately from the Yarmuk to the Wadi al-Mawjib; now in NW Jordan.

2 Ancient city of the Gilead, S of the Zarqa.

Gilead, Mount. Peak, NNE of the Dead Sea, Jordan; 3597 ft.; in ancient Palestine in cen. Gilead.

Giles \'jīlz\. Name of counties in two states of the U.S. See tables at TENNESSEE and VIRGINIA.

Gil·gal \'gil-ˌgal\. Name of several places in ancient Palestine, some yet unidentified; esp. village near Jericho, the first encampment of the Israelites W of Jordan (*Josh.* iv. 19–24).

Gil·git \'gil-gət\. **1** Region in NW Himalayas, under Pakistani control; 3118 sq. m.; prior to the partition of India was a district.

2 Town in the region, on **Gilgit River** (tributary of the Indus, ab. 150 m. long) at elevation of 4890 ft.; once a Buddhist center, now an important strategic station on the highway to Chitral on W and to Hunza and Hindu Kush passes on N.

Gil·les·pie \gi-'les-pē\. **1** County in Texas. See table at TEXAS.

2 City, Macoupin co., SW cen. Illinois, 27 m. NE of Alton; pop. (1970c) 3457; grain farms; coal mining.

Gil·lette \jə-'let\. Town, ⊗ of Campbell co., NE Wyoming, 80 m. ESE of Sheridan; pop. (1970c) 7194; grain, livestock; oil wells.

Gil·li·am \'gil-yəm\. County in Oregon. See table at OREGON.

Gil·ling·ham \'jil-iŋ-əm\. Municipal borough, Kent, SE England, on the Medway 30 m. ESE of London; pop. (1971p) 86,714; dockyard; light industries.

Gillis Island. See KVITØYA.

Gil·ly \zhē-'yē\. Commune, Hainaut prov., SW Belgium, on the Sambre just E of Charleroi; pop. (1969e) 23,861; glass, textiles.

Gil·man \'gil-mən\. City, Iroquois co., E Illinois, 27 m. S of Kankakee; pop. (1970c) 1786; dairy farms.

Gil·mer \'gil-mər\. **1** Name of counties in two states of the U.S. See tables at GEORGIA and WEST VIRGINIA.

2 City, ⊗ of Upshur co., NE Texas, 34 m. NE of Tyler; pop. (1970c) 4196; timber; oil wells.

Gi·lo \'jē-(ˌ)lō\. River, SW Ethiopia; flows NW into the Pibor river on Sudan border.

Gilolo. See HALMAHERA.

Gil·pin \'gil-pən\. County in Colorado. See table at COLORADO.

Gilpin Peak. Mountain, Ouray and San Miguel cos., SW Colorado; 13,682 ft.

Gil·roy \'gil-ˌrȯi\. City, Santa Clara co., W California, 30 m. SE of San Jose; pop. (1970c) 12,665; fruits, vegetables, livestock, poultry; Gavilan Coll. (1919).

Gimma. See JIMA.

Gin·chy \zha^n-'shē\. Village, Somme dept., N France, 25 m. NE of Amiens; pop. (1962c) 89; captured by British in battle of the Somme Sept. 9, 1916.

Ginevra. Italian form of Geneva, Switzerland. See GENEVA.

Gin·go·og \hēŋ-'gō-ˌäg\. Chartered city, E Misamis Oriental prov., N Mindanao, Phil; pop. (1970e) 74,700; on S shore of **Gingoog Bay,** inlet of Mindanoa Sea ab. 22 m. wide at mouth.

Gi·no·sa \jə-'nō-sə\. Commune, Taranto prov., Apulia, SE Italy, 26 m. WNW of Taranto; pop. (1968e) 18,100.

Gin·seng Mountain \ˌjin-ˌseŋ-\. Peak in the Catskill Mts., SE New York; 3790 ft.

Gio·fra \'jō-frə, jē-'ō-\. Oasis, NW cen. Libya.

Gio·ia del Col·le \ˌjȯ-yə-del-'kȯ-(ˌ)lā\. Commune, Bari prov., Apulia, SE Italy, 20 m. SE of Bari; pop. (1968e) 27,324; Norman castle.

Gio·io·sa Io·ni·ca \jə-ˌyō-sə-'yȯ-ni-kə\. Commune, Reggio di Calabria prov., S Calabria, S Italy, on Ionian Sea; pop. (1968e) 7629; sea bathing.

Gior·ni·co \'jȯr-ni-ˌkō\. Village, Ticino canton, SE Switzerland, on Ticino river; pop. (1970c) 1389; scene of victory of greatly outnumbered Swiss forces over the Milanese Dec. 28, 1478.

Gio·vi·naz·zo \ˌjō-vi-'nät-(ˌ)sō\. Seaport, Bari prov., Apulia, SE Italy, on Adriatic 10 m. WNW of Bari; pop. (1968e) 16,165; episcopal see (from 951).

Gio·vi·net·to, Mount \-ˌjō-və-'net-ˌō\. Mountain, Antarctica, 78°16′S, 86°10′W; 13,412 ft.

Giovi Pass. See table at APENNINES.

Gipps·land \'gip-ˌsland\. Region, SE coast of Victoria, SE Australia; ab. 14,000 sq. m.; chief town Sale; fertile, rich in minerals; includes **Gippsland Lakes.**

Gi–ran. See I-LAN 2.

Gi·rard \jə-'rärd\. 1 City, Macoupin co., SW cen. Illinois, 22 m. SSW of Springfield; pop. (1970c) 1881.

2 City, ⊗ of Crawford co., SE Kansas, 10 m. NW of Pittsburg; pop. (1970c) 2591; grain farms.

3 City, Trumbull co., NE Ohio, NW of Youngstown; pop. (1970c) 14,119; manufactures steel, iron, leather.

4 Borough, Erie co., NW corner of Pennsylvania, on Lake Erie 16 m. WSW of Erie; pop. (1970c) 2613; iron castings; truck farms.

Gi·rar·dot \ˌhē-ˌrär-'dȯt\. City, Cundinamarca dept., cen. Colombia, ab. 50 m. SE of Bogotá; pop. (1968e) 82,310; synthetic fiber; cattle market.

Gi·rard·ville \jə-'rärd-ˌvil\. Borough, Schuylkill co., E cen. Pennsylvania, 9 m. NNW of Pottsville; pop. (1970c) 2450; coal mining.

Gir·dle Ness \ˌgərd-ᵊl-'nes\. Headland on E cen. coast of Scotland, 2 m. S of Aberdeen; lighthouse.

Gi·re·sun \ˌgir-ə-'sün\ *or* **Ke·ra·sun** \ˌker-ə-\. 1 Province of NE Turkey, Asia. See table at TURKEY.

2 *or anc.* **Cer·a·sus** \'ser-ə-səs\ *or later* **Phar·na·cia** \fär-'nā-sh(ē-)ə\. Seaport, its ✱, on the Black Sea 70 m. W of Trabzon; pop. (1965c) 25,331; exports hides, nuts, timber; site of Byzantine fortress.

Gir·ga *or* **Gir·geh** \'gi(ə)r-gə\. City, Egypt, on the Nile SE of Sawhaj; pop. (1966c) 44,300; noted for pottery; ancient Roman Catholic monastery.

Girgenti. See AGRIGENTO.

Gi·ri·dih \'gir-əd-ē\. Town, E Bihar, NE India, 170 m. NW of Calcutta; pop. (1961c) 36,881.

Girin. See KIRIN.

Gi·rishk \gə-'rishk\. Town, S cen. Afghanistan, on Helmand river 75 m. WNW of Kandahār; center of rich agricultural district.

Gir·nar Hills \gi(ə)r-'när-\. Mountains, India. See JUNAGADH.

Gi·rón \hē-'rōn\. Town, Azuay prov., S Ecuador; met. area pop. (1962c) 10,020.

Gi·ronde \jə-'ränd, zhē-'rō^{n}d\. 1 Estuary on W coast of France, formed by confluence of Garonne and Dordogne rivers near Bordeaux; extends 45 m. inland.

2 Department of SW France. See table at FRANCE.

Gir·van \'gər-vən\. Seaport burgh, Ayr co., SW Scotland, 17 m. SSW of Ayr at mouth of Firth of Clyde; pop. (1971p) 7405; tourism; fishing port.

Gis·borne \'giz-bərn\. Seaport city, E North I., New Zealand, on Poverty Bay; pop. (1970e) 26,500; nearby is place where Capt. Cook landed 1769.

Gi·sors \zhē-'zȯ(ə)r\. Commune, Eure dept., N France, 20 m. NW of Paris; pop. (1962c) 6734; as medieval capital of the Vexin dist. on frontier of Normandy was subject of many disputes bet. English and French; ruins of castle begun 1097 by William Rufus.

Gitschin. See JIČÍN.

Giuba. See JUBA.

Giu·dec·ca \jü-'dek-ə\ *or* **La Giudecca** \lä-\. Long, narrow island, forming S part of city of Venice, Italy; separated from main island by channel, **Ca·na·le del·la Giudecca** \kə-'näl-ē-ˌdel-ə-\; in early times inhabited by Jews (hence its name); later made a pleasure resort, now suburb for workers.

Giu·lia·no in Cam·pa·nia \jül-'yän-ō-in-käm-'pän-yə\. Commune, Napoli prov., Campania, S Italy, 6 m. NNW of Naples; pop. (1968e) 34,952.

Giu·lia·no·va \ˌjül-yə-'nȯ-və\. Commune, Teramo prov., Abruzzi, cen. Italy, on Adriatic Sea 16 m. ENE of Teramo; pop. (1968e) 18,264.

Giur·giu \'jü(ə)r-(ˌ)jü\ *or Bulg.* **Giur·ge·vo** \'zhu̇r-zhə-ˌvō\. City, S Romania, on the Danube; munic. pop. (1970e) 43,701; shipyards; food processing; ruins of 14th cent. fort.

Gi·ven·chy–en–Go·helle \ˌzhē-vä^n-'shē-ä^n-gō-'el\. Commune, Pas-de-Calais dept., N France, 7 m. NNW of Arras; pop. (1962c) 1508; fighting Sept.–Nov. 1915, taken by Canadians Apr. 12, 1917.

Gi·vet \zhē-'vā\. Commune, Ardennes dept., NE France, near Belgian frontier; pop. (1962c) 7925; divided by the Meuse into **Grand–Givet** \'grä^n- \, with church built 1682 by Vauban, and **Pe·tit–Givet** \pə-'tē-\; formerly an important fortress; occupied by Germans Aug. 1914–Nov. 1918.

Gi·vors \zhē-'vȯ(ə)r\. Commune, Rhône dept., E cen. France, on Rhone river 13 m. S of Lyons; pop. (1968c) 19,048; metal and glassworks.

Gi·za *or* **Al–Gi·zeh** \al-'gē-zə\ *or* **Al–Jī·zah** \-'jē-zə\. 1 Governorate of Upper Egypt. See table at EGYPT.

2 City, its ✱, on W bank of the Nile near Cairo; pop. (1966c) 345,261; cotton textiles, footwear; brewing; motion-picture industry; 5 m. W lie the great pyramids and famous Sphinx. See PYRAMIDS.

Gi·zo \'gē-(ˌ)zō\. Small island of the New Georgia Is., cen. Solomon Is., W Pacific Ocean, bet. Ganongga I. and Kolombangara I.; government station for the New Georgia Is.

Gi·życ·ko \gə-'zhit-(ˌ)skō\ *or Ger.* **Löt·zen** \'lə(r)t-sən\. City, E Olsztyn prov., N Poland, at S end of Lake Mamry; pop. (1968e) 17,700.

Gjels·vik Peak \ˌgēls-vik-\. Peak, Antarctica, 85°19′S, 167°54′W; 12,008 ft.

Gji·ro·kas·tër \ˌgir-ə-'käs-tər\ *or* **Gji·no·kas·tër** \ˌgē-nə-\ *or Gk.* **Ar·gy·ro·ka·stron** \ˌär-yi-'rō-kə-ˌstrōn\ *or Ital.* **Ar·gi·ro·ca·stro** \ˌär-ji-'rō-kə-ˌstrō\. 1 Province of S Albania. See table at ALBANIA.

2 Town, its ✱; pop. (1967e) 15,590; under Turkish rule 1420–1913; held by Greeks Dec. 1940–Apr. 1941 in war with Italy.

Gjø·vik \'yər-vik\. Town, Oppland co., S cen. Norway, on Lake Mjøsa; pop. (1970e) 25,164; dairy farming.

Gju·hë·zës, Cape \-ˌjü-'hə-ˌzəs\; *formerly* **Cape Lin·guet·ta** \-liŋ-'gwet-ə\ *or* **Cape Glos·sa** \-'gläs-ə\. Cape and promontory, SW Albania, 40°25′N, 19°18′E.

Glace Bay \'glās-\. Town, Cape Breton co., E Nova Scotia, Canada, on Atlantic Ocean 12 m. E of Sydney; pop. (1971p) 22,276; fishing; produces coal.

Gla·cier \'glā-shər\. County in Montana. See table at MONTANA.

Glacier Bay. Narrow inlet of Pacific Ocean in N part of SE Alaska, NE extension of Cross Sound; ab. 60 m. long; in center of **Glacier Bay National Monument** (see UNITED STATES, *National Monuments*).

Glacier National Park. 1 See UNITED STATES, *National Parks.*

2 See CANADA, *National Parks.*

Glacier Peak. Mountain, E Snohomish co., NW cen. Washington; 10,436 ft.

Gla·ciers, Ai·guille des \ā-'gwē-ˌdā-glas-'yā\. Mountain in the French Alps, just SW of Mont Blanc; 12,517 ft.

Glad·beck \'glät-ˌbek, 'glad-\. City, North Rhine-Westphalia, West Germany, 22 m. WNW of Dortmund; pop. (1969e) 82,810; metalworking, electrical machinery, apparel; coal mining; became city 1919.

Glades \'glādz\. County in Florida. See table at FLORIDA.

Glade·wa·ter \'glād-ˌwȯt-ər, -ˌwät-\. City, Gregg and Upshur cos., NE Texas, 25 m. ENE of Tyler; pop. (1970c) 5574; oil refining; timber.

Glad·stone \'glad-ˌstōn\. **1** City, Delta co., S Michigan penin., on W side of Little Bay de Noc 8 m. N of Escanaba; pop. (1970c) 5237; sporting goods.

2 City, Clay co., NW Missouri, N of Kansas City; pop. (1970c) 23,422.

3 City, Clackamas co., NW Oregon, on Clackamas river 9 m. S of Portland; pop. (1970c) 6237; fruit farms.

Gladstone \'glad-ˌstōn, -stən\. Town, E Queensland, Australia, on Pacific Ocean 270 m. NNW of Brisbane; pop. (1968e) 12,400; founded on site of unsuccessful colony sponsored by Gladstone.

Gladstone Peak \ˌglad-ˌstōn-\. Mountain, Dolores and San Miguel cos., SW Colorado; 13,900 ft.

Glad·win \'glad-win\. **1** County in cen. Michigan. See table at MICHIGAN.

2 City, its ⊗, 30 m. NNE of Mt. Pleasant; pop. (1970c) 2071; lake resort.

Glå·ma \'glȯ-mə\. River, E Norway; 380 m. long; rises in Dovrefjell plateau; flows S into Skagerrak at Fredrikstad; longest river in Norway.

Gla·mis \'glām-əs, 'glam-; 'glämz\. Village, S Angus co., E Scotland, N of Dundee; 17th cent. castle on site of an 11th cent. structure.

Gla·mor·gan·shire \glə-'mȯr-gən-ˌshi(ə)r, -shər\ *or* **Gla·mor·gan.** County, S Wales; 818 sq. m.; pop. (1971p) 1,202,591; ⊗ Cardiff; rivers Taff, Neath, Tawe; coal mining, iron and steel manufacture; aluminum, paint, paper; oil refining; livestock.

Gla·mu·jö·kull \'glaù-mə-ˌyər-ˌkət-ᵊl\. Glacier in NW Iceland.

Gla·rus \'glär-əs\. **1** Swiss canton. See table at SWITZERLAND.

2 Commune, its ✱, E cen. Switzerland, 36 m. E of Lucerne; pop. (1970c) 6189; furniture; destroyed by fire May 1861; Zwingli parish priest here 1506–16.

Glas·cock \'glas-ˌkäk\. County in Georgia. See table at GEORGIA.

Glas·gow \'glas-(ˌ)kō, -(ˌ)gō\. **1** City, ⊗ of Barren co., S Kentucky, 30 m. E of Bowling Green; pop. (1970c) 11,301; dairy products, tobacco, timber.

2 City, ⊗ of Valley co., NE Montana, 15 m. NNW of Fort Peck Dam on Missouri river; pop. (1970c) 4700; flour mills, truck farms; gas wells.

Glasgow \'glas-(ˌ)kō, 'glas-(ˌ)gō, 'glaz-(ˌ)gō\. City, geographically in Lanark co., W cen. Scotland, on both banks of the Clyde; pop. (1971p) 896,958; the largest city in Scotland; seaport, extensive docks; manufactures heavy iron and steel products, textiles, chemicals; shipbuilding; ships coal; 13th cent. cathedral, Univ. of Glasgow (1451), Univ. of Strathclyde (1964), museums, libraries, art galleries, botanical gardens.

History: Although date of origin uncertain, probably had been settled for some centuries when its bishop received rights of royal burgh 1175–78; as prominent Scottish ecclesiastical center, declined for a time after the Reformation; became free royal burgh 1636; prosperous commercial center from 18th cent., developed shipbuilding and iron industries 19th cent.

Glass·boro \'glas-ˌbər-ə, -ˌbə-rə\. Borough, Gloucester co., SW New Jersey, 17 m. S of Camden; pop. (1970c) 12,938; settled by German glassmakers 1775; Glassboro State Coll. (1923); scene of meeting between U.S. President Johnson and Soviet Premier Kosygin 1967.

Glass·cock \'glas-ˌkäk\. County in Texas. See table at TEXAS.

Glass Mountains \ˌglas-\. Range, N Brewster co., W Texas; highest peak 6487 ft.

Glass·port \'glas-ˌpō(ə)rt, -ˌpȯ(ə)rt\. Borough, Allegheny co., SW Pennsylvania, on Monongahela river 10 m. SSE of Pittsburgh; pop. (1970c) 7450; glass, steel hoops, tools.

Glas·ten·bury Mountain \'glas-tən-ˌber-ē-\. Mountain, Bennington co., SW Vermont; 3764 ft.

Glas·ton·bury. 1 \'glas-(t)ən-ˌber-ē\. Town, SE Hartford co., N Connecticut, 5 ½ m. SE of Hartford; pop. (1970c) 20,651; aluminum wire, fire extinguishers; fruit farms; settled 1650, incorp. 1690.

2 \'glas-(t)ən-ˌber-ē, -b(ə-)rē\. Municipal borough, Somersetshire, SW England; pop. (1971p) 6571; ancient abbey, ancient Celtic settlement, extensive finds of pre-Roman metal objects.

Glatz. See KŁODZKO.

Glatzer Neisse. See NYSA 1.

Glau·chau \'glaù-ˌkaù\. Manufacturing city, Karl-Marx-Stadt dist., East Germany, on Mulde river 16 m. W of Karl-Marx-Stadt; pop. (1970e) 32,127; metalworking; two 16th cent. castles.

Gla·zov \'glaz-əf\. Town, N Udmurt A.S.S.R., Russian S.F.S.R., U.S.S.R., ab. 120 m. E of Kirov; pop. (1969e) 67,000.

Gleiwitz. See GLIWICE.

Glen·ar·den \glen-'ärd-ən\. Town, Prince Georges co., S cen. Maryland; pop. (1970c) 4502.

Glen·brook \'glen-ˌbrùk\. Subdivision of town of Stamford, Connecticut; residential. See STAMFORD 1.

Glen Canyon \ˌglen-\. Gorge along the Colorado river, S Utah and N Arizona, above Marble Canyon; site of **Glen Canyon Dam** in Colorado river (see UNITED STATES, *Dams and Reservoirs*).

Glen·coe \'glen-ˌkō\. **1** Town, Etowah co., NE Alabama, 6 m. E of Gadsden; pop. (1970c) 2901.

2 Residential village, Cook co., NE Illinois, 22 m. N of Chicago; pop. (1970c) 10,675.

3 City, ⊗ of McLeod co., S cen. Minnesota, 45 m. WSW of Minneapolis; pop. (1970c) 4217; dairying; ships cattle.

4 Town, Natal, Rep. of South Africa, NW of Durban; pop. (1967e) 10,000.

Glencoe \glen-'kō\ *or* **Glen Coe.** Glen in N Argyll co., W Scotland; site of notorious massacre of Macdonalds of Glencoe by soldiers of Campbell of Glenlyon 1692.

Glen Cove \'glen-'kōv\. Residential city, Nassau co., SE New York, on N shore of Long I. 22 m. ENE of New York; pop. (1970c) 25,770.

Glen·dale \'glen-ˌdāl\. **1** City, Maricopa co., SW cen. Arizona, 8 m. NW of Phoenix; pop. (1970c) 36,228; cotton ginning; cottonseed oil, flour, feed; Glendale Community Coll. (1965).

2 City, Los Angeles co., SW California, 6 m. N of Los Angeles; pop. (1970c) 132,752; occupies part of first Spanish land grant in California (Rancho San Rafael 1784); manufactures airplanes, airplane engines, tools and dies, furniture, pottery and tile, and medical supplies; Glendale Coll. (1927); founded 1886.

3 City, St. Louis co., E Missouri, 11 m. SW of St. Louis; pop. (1970c) 6891.

4 Village, Hamilton co., SW corner of Ohio, 12 m. N of Cincinnati; pop. (1970c) 2690.

5 Battlefield, Virginia. See FRAYSER'S FARM.

6 City, Milwaukee co., SE Wisconsin; pop. (1970c) 13,426.

Glendale Heights. Village, Du Page co., NE Illinois, 22 m. W of Chicago; pop. (1970c) 11,406.

Glen·da·lough, Vale of \-'glen-də-ˌläk, -ˌläk\. Valley in co. Wicklow, E Eire, containing two small lakes; ruins of several ecclesiastical structures, esp. the monastery founded by St. Kevin 6th cent.

Glen·dive \'glen-ˌdīv\. City, ⊗ of Dawson co., E Montana, on Yellowstone river 72 m. NE of Miles City; pop. (1970c) 6305; grain, forage; lignite, oil and gas wells; Dawson Coll. (1940).

Glen·do·ra \glen-'dōr-ə, -'dȯr-\. City, Los Angeles co., SW California, 22 m. ENE of Los Angeles; pop. (1970c) 31,349; ships fruit.

Glen·elg \gle-'nelg\. 1 River, W Victoria, SE Australia; 290 m. long; flows into Discovery Bay just over the border in South Australia.

2 Suburb of Adelaide, SE South Australia, on Gulf of St. Vincent; pop. (1966c) 14,800; irrigation equipment; fruit packing. South Australia first declared a British colony here 1836.

3 Town, Inverness co., NW Scotland, on Sound of Sleat.

Glen El·lyn \gle-'nel-ən\. Village, Du Page co., NE Illinois, 23 m. W of Chicago; pop. (1970c) 21,909; Maryknoll Coll. (1949).

Glen·gar·riff \glen-'gar-əf\. Town, SW co. Cork, SW Eire, on N inlet of Bantry Bay; resort.

Glen·gar·ry \glen-'gar-ē\. County, Ontario, Canada. See table at ONTARIO.

Glen In·nes \-'in-əs\. Town, NE New South Wales, SE Australia, in New England Range; munic. pop. (1966c) 5737.

Glen·ly·on \glen-'lī-ən\. Narrow valley, Perth co., cen. Scotland, N of Loch Tay; ab. 30 m. long; near E end is Glenlyon House, ancient seat of the Campbells of Glenlyon.

Glenn \'glen\. County in California. See table at CALIFORNIA.

Glenn Highway. Highway, S Alaska; running ENE from Anchorage to Copper Center on Richardson Highway; ab. 170 m. long.

Glenn·ville \'glen-ˌvil\. City, Tattnall co., SE cen. Georgia, 50 m. W of Savannah; pop. (1970c) 2965; cotton gins; potatoes.

Glen·ol·den \gle-'nōl-dən\. Borough, Delaware co., SE Pennsylvania, 8 m. WSW of Philadelphia; pop. (1970c) 8697.

Glen·or·chy \gle-'nȯr-kē\. City, SE Tasmania, Australia, N suburb of Hobart; pop. (1970e) 42,740.

Glen Ridge \'glen-'rij\. Residential borough, Essex co., NE New Jersey, 5 m. NNW of Newark; pop. (1970c) 8518.

Glen·rock \'glen-ˌräk\. Town, Converse co., E Wyoming, on North Platte river; pop. (1970c) 1515.

Glen Rock. Borough, Bergen co., NE corner of New Jersey, 4 m. NNE of Paterson; pop. (1970c) 13,011.

Glen Rose \'glen-ˌrōz\. City, ⊗ of Somervell co., N cen. Texas, 40 m. SSW of Fort Worth; pop. (1970c) 1554; cotton, peanuts.

Glen Roy \glen-'rȯi\. Narrow valley in Inverness co., NW Scotland, NE of Fort William; noted for its *parallel roads,* a geological formation.

Glens Falls \'glenz-\. City, Warren co., E New York, at falls (60 ft.) in Hudson river 38 m. NE of Amsterdam; pop. (1970c) 17,222; paper and pulp, clothing, cement and brick, chemicals; limestone and black marble quarries; Adirondack Community Coll. (1961); settled c. 1763; destroyed by British 1780. Cooper's Cave (at foot of falls), named for James Fenimore Cooper, setting for an episode of his *Last of the Mohicans.*

Glen·side \'glen-ˌsīd\. Locality, Montgomery co., SE Pennsylvania, ab. 10 m. N of Philadelphia; pop. (1970c) 17,353; paints, toys, rubber and wood products; stone quarries; Beaver Coll. (1853).

Glens of An·trim \ˌglenz . . . 'an-trəm\ *also* **Glynns of Antrim** \ˌglinz-\. Series of valleys on NE coast of co. Antrim, Northern Ireland.

Glen·view \'glen-ˌvyü\. Village, Cook co., NE Illinois, 18 m. NNW of Chicago; pop. (1970c) 24,880; U.S. Naval Air Station.

Glen·ville \'glen-ˌvil\. 1 Subdivision of town of Greenwich, Connecticut. See GREENWICH.

2 Town, ⊗ of Gilmer co., cen. West Virginia; pop. (1970c) 2183; Glenville State Coll. (1872).

Glen·wood \'glen-ˌwu̇d\. 1 Village, Cook co., NE Illinois, 21 m. S of Chicago; pop. (1970c) 7416.

2 City, ⊗ of Mills co., SW Iowa, 18 m. SSE of Council Bluffs; pop. (1970c) 4421; grain farms.

3 City, ⊗ of Pope co., W cen. Minnesota, at N end of Lake Minnewaska; pop. (1970c) 2584; summer resort.

Glenwood Springs. City, ⊗ of Garfield co., W Colorado, on Colorado river; pop. (1970c) 4106; Colorado Mountain Coll. (1967); thermal mineral springs.

Glevum. See GLOUCESTER 6.

Glit·ter·tind \'glit-ər-ˌtin\. Peak in the Jotunheimen, S cen. Norway; 8110 ft.; highest peak in Norway.

Gli·wi·ce \gli-'vēt-sə\ *or Ger.* **Glei·witz** \'glī-(ˌ)vits\. Manufacturing city, Katowice prov., SW Poland, 14 m. W of Katowice; pop. (1970p) 170,900; blast furnaces, coal mines; chemicals; technical univ. (1945); chartered as city 1276; passed to Prussia 1742; in World War II taken by U.S.S.R. Jan. 25, 1945; assigned to Poland by Potsdam Conference 1945.

Globe \'glōb\. City, ⊗ of Gila co., E cen. Arizona, 70 m. E of Phoenix; pop. (1970c) 7333; important copper mines; also silver, gold, asbestos, manganese, vanadium, and tungsten in vicinity; incorporated 1907.

Gloces·ter \'gläs-tər, 'glȯs-\. Town, Providence co., N Rhode Island, near Connecticut border; pop. (1970c) 5160; governmental center Chepachet.

Gło·gów \'glȯ-ˌgüf\ *or Ger.* **Glo·gau** \'glō-ˌgau̇\. Manufacturing city, Zielona Góra prov., SW Poland, on Odra (Oder) river; pop. (1970p) 20,200; copper refining; founded c. 1010; to Prussia 1742; in World War II taken by U.S.S.R. Feb. 1945; assigned to Poland by Potsdam Conference 1945.

Glo·mach, Falls of \-'gläm-ək\. Waterfall in headstream of the Elchaig, Ross and Cromarty co., Scotland; 370 ft. high.

Glo·rieuses, Îles \'ē(ə)l-ˌglōr-ē-'əz, -ˌglȯr-\ *or Eng.* **Glo·ri·o·so Islands** \ˌglōr-ē-ˌō-sō-, -zō-\. Group of small French islands in Indian Ocean, WNW of N Malagasy Republic.

Glossa, Cape. See GJUHËZËS, CAPE.

Glos·sop \'gläs-əp\. Municipal borough, Derbyshire, N cen. England, 16 m. ESE of Manchester; pop. (1971p) 24,147; cotton mills, paper mills.

Glouces·ter \'gläs-tər, 'glȯs-\. 1 Counties in two states of the U.S. See tables at NEW JERSEY and VIRGINIA.

2 City, Essex co., NE Massachusetts, on coast of Cape Ann 27 m. NE of Boston; pop. (1970c) 27,941; port of entry; summer resort; important fishing port; granite quarries. Visited by Champlain 1605, settled 1623, chartered as city 1874; has bronze statue, "Fisherman at the Wheel," by Leonard Craske.

3 Village, ⊗ of Gloucester co., E Virginia; pop. (1971e) 500.

4 County, New Brunswick, Canada. See table at NEW BRUNSWICK.

5 County in England. See GLOUCESTERSHIRE.

6 *or anc.* **Gle·vum** \'glē-vəm\. County borough, ⊗ of Gloucestershire, SW cen. England, on the Severn 94 m. WNW of London; pop. (1971p) 90,134; aircraft parts, insulating material; fishing; has cathedral, on site of an abbey founded 681. Founded by Nerva (emperor 96–98 A.D.); began early to trade in iron and cloth; scene of first Sunday School, founded by Robert Raikes 1780.

Gloucester, Cape. Cape at NW corner of New Britain I., Bismarck Archipelago, on Dampier Strait; landing place of U.S. Marines Dec. 26, 1943.

Gloucester City. Manufacturing city, Camden co., SW New Jersey, on Delaware river 3 m. S of Camden; pop. (1970c) 14,707; settled by Irish Quakers 1682; scene of skirmishes during Revolution; incorporated 1868.

Glouces·ter·shire \'gläs-tər-ˌshi(ə)r, 'glȯs-, -shər\ *or* **Gloucester.** County, SW cen. England; 1259 sq. m.; pop. (1971p) 1,069,454; ⊗ Gloucester; rivers Severn, Avon, Wye; barley, winter wheat; sheep grazing; manufacturing (aircraft, paper, woolen goods, tobacco, chemicals); other towns Bristol, Tewkesbury, Cheltenham, Stroud.

Glous·ter \'gläs-tər, 'glȯs-\. Village, Athens co., SE Ohio, 30 m. S of Zanesville; pop. (1970c) 2121; brickmaking.

Glov·ers·ville \'gləv-ərz-ˌvil\. City, Fulton co., E New York, 12 m. NW of Amsterdam; pop. (1970c) 19,677; glovemaking center of U.S.; leather, silks, knit goods, wood products; settled c. 1760 by Scots.

Głub·czy·ce \glüp-'chit-sə\ *or Ger.* **Le·ob·schütz** \'lā-əp-ˌshüts\. City, Opole prov., SW Poland; pop. (1968e) 10,300; formerly in Germany.

Glück·stadt \'glük-ˌs(h)tät\. Town, Schleswig-Holstein, West Germany, on the Elbe river 28 m. NW of Hamburg; pop. (1968e) 16,093; fishing; founded 1616 and fortified by Christian IV of Denmark; fortifications destroyed 1814.

Glu·gor \glü-'gȯr\. Town, Penang state, Malaysia; pop. (1970c) 9190; univ. (1969).

Glu·khov \'glü-kəf\. Town, NE Ukrainian S.S.R., U.S.S.R., ab. 65 m. NW of Sumy; pop. (1967e) 28,000.

Gly·der Fach \'glid-ər-ˌväk\ *or* **Gly·der–fach.** Mountain, Caernarvonshire, NW Wales; 3262 ft.

Glyder Fawr \'glid-ər-ˌvaù(ə)r\ *or* **Glyder–fawr.** Mountain, Caernarvonshire, NW Wales; 3279 ft.

Glynn \'glin\. County in Georgia. See table at GEORGIA.

Glynns of Antrim. See GLENS OF ANTRIM.

Gmünd. See SCHWÄBISH-GMÜND.

Gmun·den \gə-'mün-dən\. Commune, Upper Austria, on Lake Traun at outlet into Traun river; pop. (1961c) 12,518; cement, textiles; summer resort.

Gmundner See. See TRAUN, LAKE.

Gna·den·hut·ten \jə-'näd-ən-ˌhət-ən\. Village, Tuscarawas co., E Ohio, on Tuscarawas river; pop. (1970c) 1466; founded 1772 under leadership of Moravians by Christian Indians who had to move to Sandusky 1781; scene Mar. 7, 1782 of massacre by white men of a group of the Indians who had returned.

Gniez·no \gə-'nyez-(ˌ)nō\ *or Ger.* **Gne·sen** \gə-'nāz-ᵊn\. Commune, Poznań prov., Poland, 28 m. ENE of Poznań; pop. (1970p) 50,600; manufactures cloth, iron goods, sugar, leather, beer, oil; ancient cathedral containing relics of St. Adalbert (*Pol.* Wojciech), patron saint of Poland. First king of Poland (Boleslav the Mighty) crowned here 1025 for second time; coronation place of kings of Poland to 1320; to Prussia 1793, to Poland 1919.

Gnossus. See KNOSSOS.

Goa *or Port.* **Gôa** \'gō-ə\. **1** A constituent part of the centrally administered territory of Goa, Daman, and Diu, on W coast of India, ab. 250 m. S of Bombay; 1404 sq. m.; pop. (1960c) 626,978; 62 miles of coastline; traversed by a spur of the Western Ghats ab. 4000 ft. high, from which several short but navigable streams flow to the marshy coast, the two largest the Mandavi and the Juari; rice, fruit, iron ore, manganese. Former Portuguese possession; annexed by India 1962.

2 *or* **Old Goa.** Seaport, its former ✱; founded 1440; at first under Bahmani dynasty (see DECCAN); under king of Bijapur 1482–1510; taken by Portuguese under Albuquerque 1510 and made capital of Portuguese India; scene of beginning of St. Francis Xavier's missionary labors 1542; besieged by ruler of Bijapur 1570; a city of 200,000 at height of its prosperity (1575–1625); blockaded by Dutch fleets 1603, 1639; site abandoned for New Goa (see PANAJI) by most Portuguese inhabitants early 18th cent. as result of cholera epidemics; now mostly in ruins but has cathedral (founded 1511) and several churches and convents still standing.

3 Municipality, E Camarines Sur prov., Luzon, Phil., near head of Lagonoy Gulf; pop. (1969e) 34,300; at foot of Mt. Isarog.

Goa, Da·man, and Diu \-də-'man . . . 'dē-(ˌ)ü\. A centrally administered territory of India, consisting of the former Portuguese possessions of Goa, Daman, and Diu; 1441 sq. m.; pop. (1971p) 857,180; ✱ Panaji; formally annexed by India 1962. See GOA 1, DAMAN 1, DIU.

Goalanda. See RAJBARI.

Go·al·pa·ra \ˌgō-əl-'pär-ə\. Town, NW Assam, NE India, on S bank of Brahmaputra; pop. (1961c) 13,700; a district capital before 1879.

Goat Haunt Mountain \ˌgōt-ˌhȯnt-, -ˌhänt-\. Peak in Glacier National Park, NW Montana; 8613 ft.

Goat Island. **1** Island in Niagara river, W New York, just above Niagara Falls; 3/4 m. long; divides Niagara Falls (*q.v.*) into American Fall and Horseshoe Fall.

2 Island, California. See YERBA BUENA ISLAND.

3 Island, Chile. See JUAN FERNÁNDEZ.

Goat Mountain. **1** Peak in Glacier National Park, NW Montana; 8790 ft.

2 Peak, Culberson co., W Texas; 8600 ft.

Go·ba \'gō-bə\. Town, ✱ of Bale prov., Ethiopia; pop. (1970e) 11,777.

Go·ba·bis \gō-'bäb-əs\. Town, E South-West Africa, 130 m. E of Windhoek; pop. (1960c) 4316; alt. 4740 ft.; in pastoral region.

Gobannium. See ABERGAVENNY.

Gö·bels·berg \'gər-bəlz-ˌbe(ə)rg\. Highest peak in the Hausruck Mts., Upper Austria; 2625 ft.

Go·bi \'gō-(ˌ)bē\ *or Chin.* **Sha·mo** \'shäm-'ō\. Desert, mostly in the Mongolian People's Republic and Inner Mongolia, China, cen. Asia; ab. 500,000 sq. m.; a broad depression (average alt. 3000 to 5000 ft.) in plateau region, bounded on S by ranges of N Tibetan plateau (Nan Shan in Tsinghai and A-la Shan in Ningsia Hui), on W and NW by Altai Mts., on E by mountains of Inner Mongolia and the Mongolian People's Republic; SW part entirely sand but on other borders is steppe land; by some, taken to include Tarim basin also. See HAN-HAI.

Goch \'gȯk\. City, NW North Rhine-Westphalia, West Germany, on Dutch border 66 m. WSW of Münster; pop. (1968e) 27,408; manufactures shoes, leather, brushes; chartered 1250; belonged to dukes of Gelder (see GELDERLAND); in World War II scene of severe fighting Feb. 18–21, 1945.

God·al·ming \'gäd-ᵊl-miŋ\. Municipal borough, Surrey, S England, on the Wey 30 m. SW of London; pop. (1971p) 18,634; light engineering; became borough 1574; since 1872 seat of Charterhouse School, founded in London in 17th cent.

Go·da·va·ri \gə-'däv-ə-rē\. River, cen. India; ab. 900 m. long; rises in NW Maharashtra state, flows SE across the Deccan, crossing N Andhra Pradesh, and thence SE into Bay of Bengal through several mouths; its chief tributaries Dudna, Pranhita, Indravati, and Sabari on the N and Manjra on the S; navigable in lower course; source of reservoirs, canals, and irrigation systems; a sacred river of the Hindus.

God·dard, Mount \-'gäd-ərd\. Peak in Sierra Nevada, in E Fresno co., S cen. California; 13,555 ft.

Gode·rich \'gäd-(ˌ)rich\. Resort town, ⊗ of Huron co., SE Ontario, Canada, on SE shore of Lake Huron 65 m. NNE of Sarnia; pop. (1971p) 6804; harbor; lumbering; makes salt, road machinery; grain elevator; founded 1828.

Godesberg. See BAD GODESBERG.

God·havn \'gäd-ˌhaůn\. Town, W Greenland, on Davis Strait on S coast of Disko I., 69°15'N, 53°33'W; pop. (1968e) 971; an administrative center; formerly important in whaling industry; has radio and other scientific stations.

Godh·ra \'gäd-rə\. Town, Gujarat, W India, 68 m. ESE of Ahmadabad; pop. (1961c) 52,167; tanneries; trades in timber.

Göding. See HODONÍN.

Gö·döl·lö \'gərd-ᵊl-ˌər\. Commune, 12 m. NE of Budapest, cen. Hungary; pop. (1970p) 20,953; former royal palace (now part of university).

Go·doy Cruz \gə-'dȯi-'krüz\. Town, Mendoza prov., W Argentina; S suburb of Mendoza; pop. (1960c) 80,024; wine making.

Gods Lake \'gädz-\. Lake, E Manitoba, Canada; 319 sq. m.; its outlet is **Gods River,** a tributary of Hayes river.

Godt·håb *or* **Godt·haab** \'gȯt-ˌhȯb, 'gät-\. Town, ✱ of Greenland, on SW coast, 64°11'N, 51°44'W; pop. (1968e) 6104; fish processing; oil and liquid gas bunker station; scientific stations; oldest Danish settlement in Greenland, founded 1721.

God·win Aus·ten \ˌgäd-wə-'nȯ-stən, -'näs-tən\ *or* **Dap·sang** \'dap-ˌsaŋ, 'dəp-ˌsəŋ\ *or* **K2** \'kā-'tü\. Highest peak in Karakoram Range, N Jammu and Kashmir, in region controlled by Pakistan; 28,250 ft.; 2d highest mountain in the world; first scaled 1954.

Godwin Island \'gäd-win-\. Island in Atlantic Ocean, SE coast of Northampton co., Virginia.

Goenoeng Agoeng. See AGUNG, GUNUNG.

Goenoeng Api. See GUNUNG API.

Goenoeng Awoe. See AWU, GUNUNG.

Goenoengsitoli. See GUNUNGSITOLI.

Goentoer. See GUNTUR 2.

Goe·ree \gü-'rā\. Island, South Holland prov., Netherlands, in estuary of the Maas (Meuse) river; 83 sq. m.; pop. (1964e) 34,000; W section is called Goeree and E section **Over·flak·kee** \ˌō-vər-flä-'kā\; wheat, sugar beets.

Goes \'güs\. Commune, Zeeland prov., SW Netherlands, on South Beveland I.; pop. (1970e) 25,822.

Goffs·town \'gäf-ˌstaůn\. Town, Hillsborough co., S New Hampshire, 5 m. WNW of Manchester; pop. (1970c) 9284.

Go·ge·bic \gō-'gē-bik\. County in Michigan. See table at MICHIGAN.

Gogebic Lake. Lake, Ontonagon and Gogebic cos., NW Michigan penin.; ab. 12 m. long.

Gogebic Range. Iron range, N Wisconsin and W Upper Peninsula of Michigan, extending E-W in Gogebic co., Michigan, and Bayfield, Ashland, and Iron cos., Wisconsin; highest point 1823 ft., in Gogebic co.

Gogra. See GHĀGHARA.

Goi·â·nia *or formerly* **Goy·a·nia** \gȯi-'an-ē-ə\. City, ✱ of Goiás state, SE cen. Brazil; munic. pop. (1970p) 388,926; in livestock-raising region; Catholic univ. (1959), federal univ. (1964); inaugurated as capital 1942.

Goi·ás *formerly* **Goi·az** *or* **Goy·az** \gȯi-'äs\. **1** State, cen. Brazil; 247,912 sq. m.; pop. (1970p) 2,989,414; ✱ Goiânia; produces diamonds, chromium, nickel, titanium; first explored by Portuguese in 17th cent.

2 Town, Goiás state, cen. Brazil, 75 m. NW of Goiânia; munic. pop. (1968e) 37,885; formerly ✱ of Goiás state.

Goil, Loch \läk-'gȯi(ə)l, läk̲-\. Inlet of Firth of Clyde in Argyll co., W cen. coast of Scotland, an arm of Loch Long.

Go·ing–to–the–Sun Mountain \ˌgō-iŋ-\. Peak in Glacier National Park, NW Montana, N of **Going–to–the–Sun Highway** which crosses the park; 9615 ft.

Go·jam *also* **Goj·jam** \'gō-ˌjam\. Province of W Ethiopia. See table at ETHIOPIA.

Gök \'gərk\. River in N Turkey in Asia; flows E into Kızıl Irmak.

Gökcha. See SEVAN.

Gök·su \ˌgərk-'sü\. **1** *or anc.* **Cal·y·cad·nus** \ˌkal-ə-'kad-nəs\. River, S Turkey in Asia (Cilicia); flows into Mediterranean at ruins of ancient Seleucia (Tracheotis) SW of İçel; 155 m. long; the river in which Frederick Barbarossa drowned 1190.

2 River, E cen. Turkey in Asia; rises in Anti-Taurus Mts.; flows SW into Seyhan river; 125 m. long; by some considered the main stream of the Seyhan.

Gök–Tépé. See GEOK-TEPE.

Go·lan Heights \ˌgō-ˌlän-, -lən-\ *or Arabic* **Jaw·lan** \'jä-lən\. Hilly region, SW Syria; highest point 7297 ft.; since 1967 under Israeli control.

Go·la·sec·ca \ˌgō-lə-'sek-ə\. Village, W Lombardy, N Italy, near S end of Lake Maggiore; pop. (1968e) 2327; nearby lived a prehistoric group of Iron Age people.

Gol·borne \'gōl-bərn\. Urban district, Lancashire, NW England, 15 m. W of Manchester; pop. (1971p) 28,178.

Gol·con·da \gäl-'kän-də\. **1** City, ⊗ of Pope co., SE corner of Illinois; pop. (1970c) 922; fluorite deposits.

2 Ruined town and fortress, W Andhra Pradesh, S cen. India, 5 m. W of Hyderabad city. Capital 1512–1687 of ancient kingdom ruled by Kutb Shahi dynasty, one of the five Muslim kingdoms of the Deccan (*q.v.*) conquered by Aurangzeb 1687–88 and annexed to Delhi empire; famous for its diamonds.

Gold Beach \'gōld-\. City, ⊗ of Curry co., SW corner of Oregon, on Pacific Ocean; pop. (1970c) 1554.

Gold Coast \-ˌkōst\. **1** Republic, W Africa. See GHANA.

2 Coastal city, Queensland, Australia; pop. (1968e) 56,500; tourism.

3 Coast of the Gulf of Guinea, along shore of Ghana, W of the Slave Coast— so called from large quantities of gold formerly taken from sands and mines along the coast.

Gold Coast Colony. Former British colony on the Gold Coast; now part of Ghana; area now divided into two administrative units, the Western Region and the Eastern Region; ✱ Accra; on N bordered on Ashanti and on W on Ivory Coast.

Gold Dust Peak \-ˌdəst-\. Mountain, Eagle co., NW cen. Colorado; 13,500 ft.

Gold·en \'gōl-dən\. **1** City, ⊗ of Jefferson co., cen. Colorado, 10 m. W of Denver; pop. (1970c) 9817; summer resort; in region producing coal, gold, clay, wheat, sugar beets; Colorado School of Mines (1874); founded 1859 as mining camp; capital of Colorado Territory 1862–67.

2 Town, SE British Columbia, Canada, on Canadian Pacific R.R. and on Columbia river; pop. (1971p) 2929; alt. 2585 ft.

Golden Bay. West arm of upper Tasman Bay on N coast of South I., New Zealand.

Golden Chersonese. See MALAY PENINSULA.

Gold·en·dale \'gōl-dən-ˌdāl\. City, ⊗ of Klickitat co., S Washington, 57 m. SSW of Yakima; pop. (1970c) 2484; lumber; diversified farming.

Golden Fall. See GULLFOSS.

Golden Gate. Strait leading from Pacific Ocean into San Francisco Bay; San Francisco on its S shore; ab. 2 m. wide; named 1849 during the gold rush; crossed by bridge, central span 4200 ft. (second longest in world), built 1933–37.

Golden Gate Highlands National Park. National park, Orange Free State, Rep. of South Africa; ab. 17 sq. m.; wildlife reserve; established 1963.

Golden Hinde \-'hīnd\. Mountain, cen. Vancouver I., British Columbia, Canada; 7219 ft.; highest mountain on Vancouver I.

Golden Horn. **1** Peak, San Juan and San Miguel cos., SW Colorado; 13,600 ft.

2 *or Turk.* **Ha·liç** \hä-ˈlēch\. Inlet of the Bosporus, Turkey in Europe, forming harbor of İstanbul; ab. 5 m. long; separates Pera and Galata from older part of city.
3 *or Russ.* **Zo·lo·toi Rog** \ˌzȯ-lə-ˌtȯi-ˈrȯk\. Harbor of Vladivostok, Primorski Krai, Russian S.F.S.R., U.S.S.R.; an inlet of Amur Bay.

Golden Meadow. Town, Lafourche parish, SE Louisiana, on Bayou Lafourche 35 m. S of New Orleans; pop. (1970c) 2681; boatbuilding.

Golden Throne \-ˈthrōn\. Peak in Karakoram Range of the Himalayas, N Jammu and Kashmir, in region controlled by Pakistan, SE of Godwin Austen; 23,600 ft.

Golden Valley. 1 Name of counties in two states of the U.S. See tables at MONTANA and NORTH DAKOTA.
2 Village, Hennepin co., SE cen. Minnesota, 5 m. W of Minneapolis; pop. (1970c) 24,246.

Gold·field \ˈgōl(d)-ˌfēld\. Village, ⊗ of Esmeralda co., SW Nevada, 26 m. S of Tonopah; formerly active (esp. 1910–11) gold-mining center.

Golds·boro \ˈgōl(d)z-ˌbər-ə, -ˌbə-rə\. City, ⊗ of Wayne co., E North Carolina, on Neuse river 46 m. SE of Raleigh; pop. (1970c) 26,810; processes tobacco, manufactures textiles, furniture, brick; Wayne Community Coll. (1957), William Carter Coll. (1963).

Gold·stone Mountain \ˌgōl(d)-ˌstōn-\. Peak on NE boundary of Lemhi co., E cen. Idaho; 9892 ft.

Gold·thwait, Mount \-ˈgōl(d)-(ˌ)thwāt\. Mountain, Antarctica, 77°59′S, 86°03′W; 12,510 ft.

Gold·thwaite \ˈgōl(d)-ˌthwāt\. City, ⊗ of Mills co., cen. Texas; pop. (1970c) 1693; ships wool.

Go·le·niów \gə-ˈlen-ˌyüf\ *or Ger.* **Goll·now** \ˈgȯl-(ˌ)nō\. Manufacturing city, W Szczecin prov., NW Poland, 16 m. NE of Szczecin; pop. (1968e) 13,400; cement; founded 1268; to Sweden 1648, to Prussia 1720; in World War II taken by Soviet troops Mar. 8, 1945; assigned to Poland by Potsdam Conference 1945.

Goletta. See HALQ AL-WADI.

Golf Manor \ˌgälf-, ˌgȯlf-, ˌgäf-, ˈgȯf-\. Village, Hamilton co., SW Ohio, 7 m. NE of Cincinnati; pop. (1970c) 5170.

Golgotha. See CALVARY.

Go·li·ad \ˈgō-lē-ˌad\. 1 County in S Texas. See table at TEXAS.
2 City, its ⊗, 22 m. W of Victoria; pop. (1970c) 1709; historic resort, built up around mission and presidio estab. by Spaniards in 1749; figured in the Mexican revolt against Spain 1812–13, and in the revolt of Texas 1835 ff.

Gol·ling·er \ˈgȯl-iŋ-ər\. Waterfall in Salzach river, Salzburg, Austria, ab. 10 m. S of Salzburg near village of **Gol·ling** \-iŋ\; 200 ft. high.

Gollnow. See GOLENIÓW.

Golodnaya Step. See BETPAK-DALA.

Gol·pāy·e·gān \ˌgōl-pī-(ə-)ˈgän\ *or* **Gul·pai·gan** \ˌgu̇l-pī-ˈgän\. Town, W cen. Iran, 90 m. NW of Eşfahān; pop. (1966c) 20,515; wood carving; many orchards in surrounding area.

Gomal. See GUMAL.

Gomal Pass. See GUMAL PASS.

Go·ma·ti \ˈgäm-ə-tē\ *or formerly* **Gum·ti** \ˈgüm-tē\. River, N India; ab. 500 m. long; rises in NE Uttar Pradesh, flows SE past Lucknow to the Ganges below Varanasi; navigable for small vessels.

Gombroon. See BANDAR ʻABBĀS.

Go·mel \ˈgō-məl, ˈgȯ-\ *also* **Ho·mel** \ˈhō-məl, ˈhȯ-\. City, ✱ of Gomel Oblast, Belorussian S.S.R., U.S.S.R., on the Sozh 140 m. N of Kiev; pop. (1970p) 272,000; railroad junction; trades in wool, flax, lumber; agricultural machinery; ship repair; has steamer traffic connections with towns on the Dnieper. A historical and cultural center, first mentioned 1142; alternately a possession of Poland and Russia, finally becoming Russian 1772; held by Germans Aug. 21, 1941 to Nov. 25, 1943.

Gomel Oblast \-ˈȯ-bləst, -ˌblast\. Subdivision of the Belorussian S.S.R., U.S.S.R.; 15,598 sq. m.; pop. (1970p) 1,534,000; ✱ Gomel; parts of W section swampy; potatoes, flax, timber.

Go·me·ra \gō-ˈmer-ə\. One of Canary Is. (*q.v.*), in Santa Cruz de Tenerife prov., Spain; 22 m. W of Tenerife I.; 146 sq. m.; pop. (1970p) 19,389; chief town and port San Sebastián.

Gó·mez Pa·la·cio \ˈgō-ˌmez-pə-ˈläs-ē-ˌō\. Municipality, Durango state, NW cen. Mexico, 195 m. W of Monterrey; pop. (1970p) 139,743.

Gom·me·court \gȯm-ˈku̇(ə)r, gəm-\. Village, Pas-de-Calais dept., N France, 9 m. N of Albert; pop. (1962c) 150; scene of much fighting 1916–18.

Go·mor·rah \gə-ˈmȯr-ə, -ˈmär-\. See SODOM.

Go·na \ˈgō-nə\. Settlement and mission station on SE coast of New Guinea I., Papua New Guinea, on Holnicote Bay just NNW of Buna; scene of much fighting 1942–43; see BUNA.

Go·na·ïves \ˌgō-nə-ˈēv\ *or* **Les Gonaïves** \lā-\. Commercial town, W Haiti, on **Gulf of Go·nave** \-gə-ˈnav\ 68 m. NNW of Port-au-Prince; pop. (1971e) 25,925; harbor; exports cotton, coffee, cabinet woods. Independence of Haiti proclaimed here Jan. 1, 1804.

Go·nave Island \gə-ˌnav-\ *also* **Go·na·ïve Island** \ˌgän-ə-ˌēv-\. Island of the West Indies, in Gulf of Gonave, Haiti; 287 sq. m.; highest point 984 ft.

Gon·bad–e Kā·vūs \gōn-ˌbäd-ə-kä-ˈvüs\. Town, Māzandarān prov., N Iran; pop. (1971e) 44,000.

Gon·da \ˈgōn-də\. Town, E Uttar Pradesh, N India, 65 m. ENE of Lucknow; pop. (1961c) 43,496.

Gon·dal \ˈgōn-dᵊl\. 1 Former Indian state, cen. Kathiawar, now part of Gujarat, W India; 1024 sq. m.
2 Town, its ✱, Gujarat state, on tributary of the Bhadar ab. 250 m. NNW of Bombay; pop. (1961c) 45,069.

Gon·der \ˈgän-dər\ *or* **Gon·dar** \-dər, -ˌdär\. City, ✱ of Begemdir and Simen prov., NW Ethiopia, 21 m. N of Lake Tana; pop. (1970e) 35,331; alt. 7500 ft.; leather goods; cotton, copperware; made Abyssinian capital early 16th cent., reached height of power middle 18th cent., afterward sacked several times; has castles and other royal buildings which through Portuguese influence resemble European medieval fortresses.

Gon·dia \ˈgän-dē-ə, ˈgän-dyə\. Town, Maharashtra, cen. India; pop. (1961c) 56,320.

Gon·do·ko·ro \gən-ˈdȯ-kə-ˌrō\. Town, Equatoria prov., S Sudan; on right bank of Nile (White Nile) just S of Mongalla; became ivory and slave-trading center after first visit by Europeans 1841; occupied by British after 1898, made part of Uganda protectorate; made part of Sudan 1914.

Gond·wa·na \gän-ˈdwän-ə\. Region of India, now divided between Andhra Pradesh, Madhya Pradesh, and Maharashtra; inhabited chiefly by the Gonds, a Dravidian (or pre-Dravidian) people, formerly noted for the practice of human sacrifices, who formed several kingdoms 12th–18th cents.; in geology has given its name to the hypothetical land area, **Gondwana Land** *or* **Gond·wa·na·land** \-ˌland\, believed to have connected South Africa and India at one time.

Go·nesse \gȯ-ˈnes\. Commune, Val-d'Oise dept., N France; pop. (1968c) 21,187.

Gon·za·ga \gən-ˈzäg-ə\. Commune, Mantova prov., Lombardy, N Italy, 14 m. S of Mantua; pop. (1968e) 7256.

Gon·zal·es \gən-ˈzal-əs, -ˈzäl-\. 1 County in Texas. See table at TEXAS.
2 Town, Ascension parish, SE Louisiana, 22 m. SE of Baton Rouge; pop. (1970c) 4512; truck farming; oil wells.
3 City, ⊗ of Gonzales co., S cen. Texas, 60 m. E of San Antonio; pop. (1970c) 5854; clay pits; cotton; scene of first battle in Texas Revolution 1835.

Gooch·land \ˈgüch-lənd\. 1 County in E cen. Virginia. See table at VIRGINIA.
2 Village, its ⊗.

Good·e·nough \ˈgu̇d-ᵊn-ˌəf\ *or* **Mo·ra·ta** \mə-ˈrät-ə\. Island, W D'Entrecasteaux Is., in W Pacific Ocean off E extremity of New Guinea I., ab. 20 m. long and 10 to 12 m. wide;

pop. (1969e) 10,375; administratively part of Papua New Guinea; has central peak, **Mount Goodenough,** 8419 ft.

Goodenough Bay. Inlet at NW end of Ward Hunt Strait (Solomon Sea), on N coast of E extremity of New Guinea I.

Good Harbor Bay. Inlet of Lake Michigan on N shore of Leelanau co., NW Michigan.

Good Hope. See FORT GOOD HOPE.

Good Hope, Cape of. 1 Cape, Indonesia. See JAMURSBA, CAPE.

2 *or Port.* **Ca·bo da Boa Es·pe·ran·ça** \ˈkab-(ˌ)ü-də-ˌbō-ə-ˌēsh-pə-ˈran(t)-sə\. Cape on SW coast of Cape Province, S Rep. of South Africa, W of False Bay and 30 m. S of Cape Town; alt. 840 ft. First rounded 1488 by Bartholomeu Dias who named it **Cabo Tor·men·to·so** \-ˌtu̇r-mən-ˈtō-(ˌ)zü\ ("Cape of Storms"); passed by Vasco da Gama 1497 on voyage to India; first Dutch settlement at Table Bay nearby 1652.

3 Province, Rep. of South Africa. See CAPE PROVINCE.

Good·hue \ˈgu̇d-(ˌ)hyü\. County in Minnesota. See table at MINNESOTA.

Good·ing \ˈgu̇d-iŋ\. 1 County, S Idaho. See table at IDAHO.

2 City, its ⊗, ab. 12 m. E of junction of Big Wood river with the Snake; pop. (1970c) 2599; creamery; fruit farms; founded 1883 as Toponis, name changed to Gooding 1896.

Good·land \ˈgu̇d-lənd\. City, ⊗ of Sherman co., NW Kansas, 20 m. E of Colorado border; pop. (1970c) 5510; wheat growing, livestock raising.

Good·news Bay \ˈgu̇d-ˌn(y)üz-\. Village, SW Alaska, on inlet of Bering Sea just S of Kuskokwim Bay.

Good·well \ˈgu̇d-ˌwel\. Town, Texas co., NW Oklahoma, in panhandle ab. 12 m. SW of Guymon; pop. (1970c) 1467; Oklahoma Panhandle State Coll. (1909).

Good·win Sands \ˌgu̇d-wən-\. Dangerous shoals in N Strait of Dover, ab. 7 m. E of Deal, England; 10 m. long; encloses the Downs, famous roadstead where Dutch fleet under van Tromp was defeated by English 1652.

Goole \ˈgül\. Municipal borough, West Riding, Yorkshire, N England, at confluence of Ouse and Don rivers 25 m. W of Hull; pop. (1971p) 18,066; shipbuilding and shipping center; exports coal.

Goose \ˈgüs\. River, E North Dakota; ab. 85 m. long; formed by confluence of forks in Steele co., flows E into Red river in E Traill co.

Goose Creek. Town, Berkeley co., SE South Carolina, 15 m. NNW of Charleston; pop. (1970c) 2657.

Goose Creek Dam *and* **Goose Creek Reservoir.** See OAKLEY DAM.

Goose Island. Island in Long Island Sound off SE coast of New Haven co., Connecticut.

Goose Lake. Dry lake on Oregon-California boundary; once ab. 30 m. long by 10 m. wide.

Goo·ty *also* **Gu·ti** \ˈgüt-ē\. Town, SW cen. Andhra Pradesh, S India, 48 m. E of Bellary; pop. (1961c) 19,100; has citadel, a Maratha stronghold in 18th cent.

Göp·ping·en \ˈgə(r)p-iŋ-ən\. City, Baden-Württemberg, West Germany, 24 m. ESE of Stuttgart; pop. (1969e) 47,119; pharmaceuticals, toys, leather goods; 15th cent. church, 16th cent. castle; burned 1782 and later rebuilt.

Go·rakh·pur \ˈgōr-ək-ˌpu̇(ə)r, ˈgȯr-\. 1 District, NE Uttar Pradesh, N India; 2439 sq. m.; pop. (1961c) 2,565,182; rice, barley, sugarcane.

2 City, SE Uttar Pradesh, N India, on Rapti river 100 m. N of Varanasi; pop. (1970e) 241,001; textiles, dyes; railroad divisional point, railroad workshops; univ. (1956); founded c. 1400.

Gora Zaozernaya. See CHANG-KU FENG.

Gor·da, Pun·ta \ˌpün-tə-ˈgȯrd-ə\. Cape on W tip of Zapata Penin., SW Matanzas prov., W cen. Cuba, at S of entrance to Broa Bay.

Gor·di·um \ˈgȯrd-ē-əm\. Ancient city, ✻ of Phrygia; according to tradition founded by Gordius, mythical king of Phrygia; scene of episode of the cutting of the Gordian knot by Alexander; now ruins on right bank of the Sakarya 50 m. WSW of Ankara, Turkey in Asia.

Gor·don \ˈgȯrd-ᵊn\. 1 County in Georgia. See table at GEORGIA.

2 Town, Wilkinson co., cen. Georgia, 20 m. E of Macon; pop. (1970c) 2553.

3 City, Sheridan co., NW Nebraska; pop. (1970c) 2106.

4 River, SW Tasmania, Australia; ab. 85 m. long; rises in central highlands, flows S, then W, to Macquarie Harbour.

Gor·dons Bay \ˌgȯrd-ᵊnz-\. Inlet of South Pacific Ocean, New South Wales, SE Australia, on SE edge of Sydney.

Gor·dy·e·ne \ˌgȯrd-ē-ˈē-nē\ *also* **Cor·du·e·ne** \ˌkȯr-jə-ˈwē-nē\. Mountainous region of ancient Armenia, in S part S of Lake Thospitis (Van); its inhabitants were the Gordyaeans, probably ancestors of the modern Kurds.

Gore \ˈgō(ə)r, ˈgȯ(ə)r\. 1 Town, ✻ of Ilubabor prov., SW Ethiopia; pop. (1970e) 8381.

2 Borough, S South I., New Zealand, 30 m. NE of Invercargill; pop. (1968e) 8380.

Gore, The. NE tip of Vermont, E of Halls stream; 1 sq. m.; projects E into New Hampshire ab. 2 m.

Gore Bay. Town, ⊗ of Manitoulin dist., S Ontario, Canada, on N shore of Manitoulin I.; pop. (1971p) 770.

Go·rée \gȯ-ˈrā\. Island and town, Senegal, W Africa, formerly in the circumscription of Dakar and Dependencies, which was united with Senegal 1946; in the harbor formed by peninsula of Cape Vert; first capital of French West Africa; first occupied by Dutch; captured by French in behalf of Senegal Company 1677; slave-trading center; held by British during Napoleonic Wars but restored to France 1817; lost importance with foundation of Dakar (*q.v.*).

Gore Mountain. Peak in the Adirondack Mts., Warren co., E New York; 3595 ft.

Gor·gān \gȯr-ˈgän\ *also* **Gur·gan** \gu̇r-\. River, N Iran; 150 m. long; flows W into SE Caspian Sea N of Bander-e Shāh.

Gorgān *also* **Gurgan** *or formerly* **As·ter·a·bad** *or* **As·tar·a·bad** \ˌäs-t(ə)rə-ˈbäd, ˈas-t(ə-)rə-ˌbad\ *or* **As·tra·bad** \ˌäs-trə-ˈbäd, ˈas-trə-ˌbad\. 1 Former province of Iran, now part of Māzandarān prov., N Iran; its anc. name **Hyr·ca·nia** \hər-ˈkā-nē-ə\.

2 City, Māzandarān prov., N Iran, ab. 23 m. inland from Caspian Sea; pop. (1971e) 55,000; trades in cotton, wheat, salt.

Gor·go·na \gȯr-ˈgō-nə\. Italian island in Ligurian Sea bet. Leghorn and N tip of Corsica; ab. 2 sq. m.

Gor·gon·zo·la \ˌgȯr-gən-ˈzō-lə\. Town, Milano prov., SW cen. Lombardy, N Italy, 12 m. ENE of Milan; pop. (1968e) 11,077; produces Gorgonzola cheese.

Gor·ham \ˈgȯr-əm\. 1 Town, Cumberland co., SW Maine, 10 m. W of Portland; pop. (1970c) 7839; Univ. of Maine Gorham State Coll. (1878).

2 Town, Coos co., N New Hampshire, at confluence of Androscoggin and Peabody rivers 5 m. S of Berlin; pop. (1970c) 2998; tourist center; lumbering.

Gori \ˈgȯ(ə)r-ē\. Town, E cen. Georgian S.S.R., U.S.S.R., on Kura river ab. 40 m. NW of Tbilisi; pop. (1967e) 43,000; altitude 2010 ft.; center of a district producing corn, wine, and lumber; summer resort; birthplace of Josef Stalin. Founded in 12th cent. as a fortress for Armenian refugees; destroyed by Nadir Shah in 18th cent.; in recent years has suffered from earthquakes.

Go·rin·chem \ˈgōr-iŋ-kəm, ˈgȯr-\ *or* **Gor·kum** \ˈgȯr-kəm\. Commune, South Holland prov., SW Netherlands, at confluence of the Waal and Maas (Meuse) rivers; pop. (1970e) 26,380; metalworking; nearby is castle where Hugo Grotius was imprisoned 1619–21.

Go·ri·zia \gə-ˈrēt-sē-ə\. 1 Province of NW Friuli-Venezia Giulia, NE Italy. See table at ITALY.
2 *or Ger.* **Görz** \ˈgərts\. Commune, its ✱, on Isonzo river on new Yugoslav border, 74 m. ENE of Venice; pop. (1968e) 43,663; bricks, machinery, textiles; 14th cent. Gothic cathedral; tourist resort; capital of former Austrian crownland of Görz and Gradisca; strategic point in Isonzo campaign in World War I; captured by Italians 1916; recaptured by German-Austrian offensive 1917; ceded to Italy by Treaty of St-Germain 1919.

Gorj \ˈgȯrzh\. County of SW Romania. See table at ROMANIA.

Gor·ki \ˈgȯr-kē\ *or before 1932* **Nizh·ni Nov·go·rod** \ˌnizh-nē-ˈnäv-gə-ˌräd\. City, ✱ of Gorki Oblast, Russian S.F.S.R., U.S.S.R., on S bank of Volga at its confluence with the Oka 250 m. E of Moscow; pop. (1970p) 1,170,000; 7th city in size in U.S.S.R.; one of the major industrial cities of the U.S.S.R.; aircraft, automobiles, electrical equipment, agricultural machinery, plastics, textiles, leather products; oil refining; univ. (1918).

History: First established as a fort 1221 by Prince Yuri Vsevolodovich; as Nizhni Novgorod famous for centuries for its fair, held (Aug. and Sept.) at irregular intervals from 1817 to 1914, which was market for barter trade with the Orient through Siberia and Turkistan; contains memorials of early Russia from 13th and 14th cents.: the ancient citadel (kremlin), cathedrals, convents, and palace of ruling family. Plundered by Tatars 1377–78; annexed to Moscow 1417; in 17th cent. a center of political and religious disturbance; in 18th and 19th cents. became a cultural center.

Gorki Oblast \-ˈō-bləst, -ˌblast\. Subdivision of the Russian S.F.S.R., U.S.S.R.; 28,880 sq. m.; pop. (1970p) 3,683,000; ✱ Gorki; crossed by the Volga; N part along the Vetluga covered with pine forests; S part fertile black-earth area; wheat, rye, oats; iron ore.

Gorkum. See GORINCHEM.

Gor·li·ce \gȯr-ˈlēt-sə\. Commune, SW Rzeszów prov., SE Poland, 58 m. ESE of Kraków; pop. (1968e) 14,400; center of petroleum industry. Battle May 1915 of the Dunajec campaign in which Russians were driven back by Austro-German armies.

Gör·litz \ˈgər-ˌlits, -ləts\. City, Dresden dist., East Germany, 54 m. E of Dresden chiefly on W bank of the Neisse river; pop. (1970e) 87,308; furniture, railway cars, electronic equipment; lignite mined nearby; since 1945 the small part (pop. [1970p] 28,400) on E bank of the river belongs to Poland (Wrocław prov.) and is called **Zgor·ze·lec** \zə-gȯr-ˈzel-əts\; first mentioned 11th cent.

Gor·lov·ka \gȯr-ˈlȯf-kə, -ˈlȯv-\. City, E Donetsk Oblast, E Ukrainian S.S.R., U.S.S.R., just N of Donetsk; pop. (1970p) 335,000; chemicals; coal mining center.

Gor·na–Or·ya·kho·vit·sa \ˌgȯr-nə-ȯr-ˈyäk-ə-ˌvet-sə\. Town, Veliko Tŭrnovo prov., N Bulgaria; pop. (1968e) 27,941; sugar refining.

Gor·ner Grat \ˈgȯr-nər-ˌgrät\. Ridge, Valais canton, SW cen. Switzerland, 3 m. SE of Zermatt; 10,289 ft.; affords one of the finest views in the Alps.

Gor·no–Al·tai Autonomous Oblast \ˌgȯr-(ˌ)nō-ˈal-ˈtī . . . ˈō-bləst, -ˌblast\ *or formerly* **Oi·rot Autonomous Oblast** \ˈȯi-rət-\. Autonomous subdivision of the Russian S.F.S.R., U.S.S.R., bordering on the Mongolian People's Republic; 35,753 sq. m.; pop. (1970p) 168,000; ✱ Gorno-Altaisk; a mountainous region, comprising the ranges of the NW Altai Mts.; on the S on Kazakh border is Mt. Belukha, 15,157 ft., highest of the Altais; its two main streams are the Katun and Biya which join to form the Ob in SE Altai Krai; livestock raising; oats, barley, wheat, potatoes; gold, mercury; first colonized in 18th cent.; created an autonomous oblast 1922.

Gorno–Al·taisk \-al-ˈtīsk\; *formerly* **Oi·rot Tu·ra** \ˌȯi-rət-tü-ˈrä\ *or* **Ula·la** \ü-ˈlä-lə\. Town, ✱ of Gorno-Altai Autonomous Oblast, Russian S.F.S.R., U.S.S.R., on Katun river; pop. (1970p) 34,000; bricks, footwear, furniture, meat processing.

Gorno–Ba·dakh·shan Autonomous Oblast \-ˌbäd-ək-ˈshän . . . ˈō-bləst, -ˌblast\. Autonomous subdivision of the Tadzhik S.S.R., U.S.S.R., bordering on Afghanistan and Sinkiang Uighur, China; 24,595 sq. m.; pop. (1970p) 98,000; ✱ Khorog; wheat, fruit; livestock raising; Pamir Biological Research station.

Go·ro·dok \ˌgȯr-ə-ˈdäk\ *or* **Gorodok Ya·gel·lon·ski** \-ye-ˈgel-ən-skē\ *or Pol.* **Gró·dek Ja·giel·loń·ski** \ˈgrü-ˌdek-ˌyäg-ə-ˈlȯn(t)-skē\. Town, Lvov Oblast, W Ukrainian S.S.R., U.S.S.R., 16 m. WSW of Lvov (formerly in Poland); trades in flax, grain. Important Russian fortification in World War I; battle June 12, 1915 in which Russians were defeated.

Go·rong Islands \ˌgō-ˌrȯŋ-\. See CERAM.

Go·ron·go·sa National Park \ˌgōr-ən-ˈgō-sə-\. National park, Mozambique; 2135 sq. m.; abundant wildlife (including buffalo, eland, elephant, hippopotamus, kudu, zebra).

Go·ron·ta·lo \ˌgōr-ən-ˈtäl-(ˌ)ō, ˌgȯr-\. Town on S coast of N peninsula of Celebes I., Indonesia; pop. (1961c) 71,378; harbor; important trade center.

Gorontalo, Gulf of. See TOMINI, GULF OF.

Gor·ty·na \gȯr-ˈtī-nə\. Ruins of ancient town, S cen. Crete, Greece, SW of Candia and ancient Knossos near S coast; many temples; long a rival of Knossos; its legal code, longest existing Greek inscription, found here 1884.

Go·ryn \ˈgȯr-ən\ *or Pol.* **Ho·ryń** \ˈhȯr-ən(-yə)\. River, W Ukrainian S.S.R. and Belorussian S.S.R., U.S.S.R.; 404 m. long; flows N into Pripyat river in the Polesye.

Góry Tarnowskie. See TARNOWSKIE GÓRY.

Görz. See GORIZIA 2.

Gor·zów Wiel·ko·pol·ski \ˌgȯr-züf-ˌvyel-kə-ˈpȯl-skē\; *Ger.* **Lands·berg** \ˈlän(t)s-ˌbe(ə)rg\ *also* **Landsberg an der Warthe** \-ˌän-dər-ˈvärt-ə\. Industrial city, Zielona Góra prov., W Poland, on Warta river; pop. (1970p) 74,300; chemical and timber industries; 13th cent. church; 18th cent. church; founded as German city 1257; battle Feb. 1813 in which French and Poles were defeated by Russians; assigned to Poland by Potsdam Conference 1945.

Go·sain·than \ˌgō-ˌsīn-ˈtän\. Peak in the Himalayas, in S Tibet, China, near border of Nepal, ab. 55 m. NE of Katmandu; 26,291 ft.; first scaled 1964.

Gösch·e·nen \ˈgə(r)sh-ən-ən\. Village, Uri canton, cen. Switzerland, at N entrance to St. Gotthard Tunnel; pop. (1970c) 888.

Go·schen Strait \ˌgō-shən-\. Channel bet. East Cape, SE New Guinea I. and Normanby I. of the D'Entrecasteaux Is., Papua New Guinea; ab. 10 m. wide.

Gos·ford \ˈgäs-fərd\. Town, New South Wales, Australia, 35 m. N of Sydney; pop. (1966c) 11,310; food processing; building materials.

Gos·forth \ˈgäz-ˌfō(ə)rth, -fərth\. Urban district, Northumberland, N England, N suburb of Newcastle upon Tyne; pop. (1971p) 26,826; residential.

Go·shen \ˈgō-shən\. 1 County in Wyoming. See table at WYOMING.
2 City, ⊗ of Elkhart co., N Indiana, 22 m. ESE of South Bend; pop. (1970c) 18,004; timber, rubber products, hydraulic presses; Goshen Coll. (1894).
3 Village, ⊗ of Orange co., SE New York, 18 m. WSW of Newburgh; pop. (1970c) 4342; racing center for harness horses. While teaching school here 1782 Noah Webster worked on his "blue-backed" spelling book (pub. 1783).
4 District of ancient Egypt E of the Nile delta; granted to Jacob and his family by the king of Egypt; place where Jacob's descendents lived until the Exodus (*Gen.* xlvi–xlvii).
5 Boer republic, S Africa, now part of Rep. of South Africa; established in W Transvaal 1882 as part of westward expansion of Boers; became part of British Bechuanaland 1885. See STELLALAND.

Goshen Point. Point, New London co., SE Connecticut, W of mouth of Thames river.

Gos·lar \'gȯs-ˌlär\. Manufacturing city, SE Lower Saxony, West Germany, 23 m. S of Brunswick in N Harz Mts.; pop. (1969e) 41,101; chemicals, optical instruments. Founded 922; joined Hanseatic League c. 1350; promulgated *Goslar statutes*, a famous code of laws, in middle of 14th cent.; passed to Prussia 1802, to Westphalia 1807; again became part of Prussia 1866.

Gos·per \'gäs-pər\. County in Nebraska. See table at NEBRASKA.

Gos·port \'gäs-ˌpō(ə)rt, -ˌpȯ(ə)rt\. Municipal borough, Hampshire, S England, on Portsmouth harbor opp. Portsmouth; pop. (1971p) 75,947; naval establishments; shipbuilding; radar.

Gos·sau \'gȯs-au̇\. Commune, St. Gallen canton, Switzerland, 6 m. W of St. Gallen; pop. (1970c) 12,793; rubber goods.

Gos·se·lies \gȯs-'lē\. Commune, Hainaut prov., SW Belgium, 4 m. N of Charleroi; pop. (1969e) 10,754; enamelware; coal mining, brewing; foundries.

Gö·ta \'yə(r)t-ə, 'yāt-\. Navigable river, S Sweden; 58 m. long; drains Lake Vänern and flows SSW into the Kattegat; locks at the falls of Trollhättan (*q.v.*); part of **Göta Canal** connecting Göteborg on the W with Stockholm on the E; 58 locks, highest point 300 ft., uses many lakes (total distance ab. 360 m., constructed part ab. 54 m.).

Gö·ta·land \'yə(r)t-ə-ˌland, 'yāt-\ *or* **Gö·ta·ri·ke** \-ˌrē-kə\. The southern division of Sweden; 35,762 sq. m.; pop. (1970e) 3,819,757; comprises the 12 counties of Älvsborg, Blekinge, Göteborg and Bohus, Gotland, Halland, Jönköping, Kalmar, Kristianstad, Kronoberg, Malmöhus, Östergötland, and Skaraborg.

Gö·te·borg \ˌyə(r)t-ə-'bȯ(ə)r(-yə), ˌyāt-\ *or* **Goth·en·burg** \'gäth-ən-ˌbərg, 'gät-ᵊn-\. Seaport, ⊗ of Göteborg and Bohus co., SW Sweden, at mouth of Göta river on the Kattegat; pop. (1970e) 446,875; 2d largest city in Sweden; Sweden's chief seaport; shipbuilding, fishing; manufactures textiles, matches, porcelain, timber and wood products, iron and steel products; cathedral (1633, restored 1956–57), univ. (1891), technical univ. (1829); founded 1619 by Gustavus Adolphus; originated 1865 what is known as the Gothenburg system for the regulation of the sale of intoxicating liquors; became a free port 1921.

Göteborg and Bo·hus \-'bü-hüs\. County of SW Sweden. See table at SWEDEN.

Go·tem·ba \gō-'tām-bə\. City, Shizuoka prefecture, Honshū, Japan, 40 m. NE of Shizuoka; pop. (1970c) 55,-997.

Go·tha \'gōt(h)-ə\. City, Erfurt dist., East Germany, 15 m. W of Erfurt; pop. (1970e) 57,328; chemicals, precision instruments, textiles; 11th cent. town hall, 12th cent. church, 17th cent. castle; publishing (incl. the geographical house of Hermann Haack [formerly Justus Perthes]); first mentioned 10th cent.; received charter 1189; residence of dukes of Saxony-Gotha 1640–1825, and of dukes of Saxe-Coburg-Gotha 1826–1918.

Go·tham \'gäth-əm, 'gō-thəm; *Brit.* 'gōt-əm *also* 'gät-əm\. 1 Village, Nottinghamshire, England, 7 m. SW of Nottingham; inhabitants obtained the name "the wise men of Gotham" for their reputed simplicity, since according to tradition when King John visited the village to select a site for a palace, the people not wishing to support such a royal residence, feigned stupidity.

2 The city of New York— first popularly so called in *Salmagundi* (1807–08), a humorous work by Washington Irving, William Irving, and James Kirke Paulding, because the inhabitants were such wiseacres.

Goth·en·burg \'gäth-ən-ˌbərg\. 1 City, Dawson co., S cen. Nebraska, on Platte river 36 m. ESE of North Platte; pop. (1970c) 3154; grain farms.

2 Seaport, Sweden. See GÖTEBORG.

Goth·ic Line \ˌgäth-ik-\. German defense line in World War II, in N cen. Italy, extending from Pisa to Rimini along heights above the Arno, 150 m. N of Rome; attacked by Allies Sept. 1944; penetrated after severe fighting by Dec. 1944.

Gothland. See GOTLAND.

Got·land *or* **Gott·land** \'gät-ˌland, -lənd\ *or* **Goth·land** \'gäth-\. Island in Baltic Sea off SE coast of Sweden; with several islands (incl. Farön and Karlsö), constitutes a county of Sweden, 1225 sq. m.; pop. (1970e) 54,093, ⊗ Visby; barley, rye; sugar beet processing; sheep raising; fisheries, cement works.

History: Center of trade since early times as evidenced by large number of Roman, Byzantine, and Arabic coins found; belonged to Sweden in 13th cent., at height of importance 14th cent. when Visby (*q.v.*) belonged to Hanseatic League; attacked by Danish 1361; became abode of pirates; to Denmark by Peace of Stettin 1570; to Sweden by Treaty of Brömsebro 1645; occupied temporarily by Danes 1676–79, 1808.

Go·tō Archipelago \ˌgōt-(ˌ)ō-\ *or Jap.* **Go·tō–ret·tō** \ˌgōt-ō-'ret-(ˌ)ō\. Chain of islands extending for ab. 100 m. SW from NW Kyūshū, Japan; five main islands Fukue, Uku, Nakadōri, Naru, Hisaka; part of Nagasaki prefecture; ✱ Fukue; fishing.

Gottesberg. See BOGUSZÓW.

Göt·ting·en \'gə(r)t-iŋ-ən, 'get-\. Manufacturing city, S Lower Saxony, West Germany, on the Leine river 55 m. SSW of Brunswick; pop. (1969e) 113,963; optical and scientific instruments; univ. (1737); headquarters of Max Planck Society; first mentioned 953.

Gottland. See GOTLAND.

Got·torp \'gät-ˌȯ(ə)rp\ *also* **Got·torf** \'gȯt-ˌȯrf\. Castle, Schleswig-Holstein, West Germany, just NW of the city of Schleswig; gave its name to Gottorp or Holstein-Gottorp line of Oldenburg family, founded 1586 by Duke Adolf, a younger son of King Frederick I of Denmark; residence of dukes of Schleswig 1268; became a museum 1948.

Gottschee. See KOČEVJE.

Gott·wald·ov \'gät-vəl-ˌdȯf, -ˌdȯv\; *formerly* **Zlín** *or Ger.* **Zlin** \zə-'lēn\. Town, Czech S.R., Czechoslovakia; pop. (1968e) 64,499; footwear.

Gou·da \'gau̇d-ə, 'güd-, 'hau̇d-\. Commune, South Holland prov., SW Netherlands, NE of Rotterdam; pop. (1970e) 45,990; manufactures pottery; cheese market (Gouda cheese); Groote Kerk, known esp. for its 40 stained glass windows, mostly made by Dirck Crabeth; received charter 1272.

Gough Island \'gäf-\ *or* **Gough's Island** \'gäfs-\. Small island in South Atlantic Ocean, one of the Tristan da Cunha group, 40°20′S, 10°W; a British claim, attached Jan. 12, 1938 to St. Helena I.

Gou·in Reservoir \'gwaⁿ-\. Lake in SW Quebec, Canada, NW of city of Quebec; its outlet Saint-Maurice river.

Goul·burn \'gōl-bərn\. 1 River, E cen. Victoria, SE Australia; 280 m. long; flows NW to Murray river.

2 City, SE New South Wales, SE Australia, 50 m. NE of Canberra; pop. (1968e) 21,090; made a city 1864.

Gould, Mount \-'güld\. Peak in Glacier National Park, NW Montana; 9551 ft.

Goulette, La. See HALQ AL-WADI.

Gou·li·mime \ˌgü-lə-'mēm\. Town, SW Morocco; pop. (1960c) 10,317.

Goumenitsa. See HEGOUMENITSA.

Goun·dam \gün-'dam\. Town, Mali, W Africa, near Lake Faguibine SW of Tombouctou.

Gou·rin \gü-'raⁿ\. Commune, Morbihan dept., NW France, 25 m. NE of Quimper; pop. (1962c) 5662; 16th cent. Gothic church and chapel.

Gou·rits \ˈgaů-rəts\. River, Cape Province, Rep. of South Africa; 80 m. long; formed by confluence of Groot and Olifants rivers, flows S into Indian Ocean near Mossel Bay.

Gour·nia \ˈgůr-nē-ə\. Ancient town, NE Crete, Greece, at head of Mirabella Bay; on a low hill, streets 5 ft. wide, some with steps; ruins of palace and shrine.

Gour·ock \ˈgůr-ək\. Burgh, Renfrew co., SW Scotland, on S shore of Firth of Clyde; pop. (1971p) 10,922; seaport; summer resort, yachting center. During World War II debarkation point for U.S. forces (in 2½ years after May 1942, ab. 1,317,000 Americans landed here).

Gouv·er·neur \ˌgəv-ə(r)-ˈnůr, ˌgův-, -ˈnər\. Village, St. Lawrence co., N New York, 24 m. S of Ogdensburg; pop. (1970c) 4574; talc, lead, and zinc mines; marble works.

Gou·yave \gü-ˈyäv\ *or* **Char·lotte Town** \ˈshär-lət-\. Town, W coast of Grenada I., Windward Is., West Indies; pop. (1960c) 2356.

Gove \ˈgōv\. 1 County in W Kansas. See table at KANSAS.
2 *or* **Gove City.** City, its ⊗; pop. (1970c) 379.

Gove Peninsula. Peninsula, Arnhem Land, Northern Territory, Australia; bauxite deposits.

Go·ver·na·dor Island \ˌgəv-ər-nə-ˌdȯ(ə)r-, ˌgō-vər-\. Island in Guanabara Bay, N of Rio de Janeiro, Brazil; 12 sq. m.; airport.

Governador Va·la·dar·es \-ˌval-ə-ˈdär-əs\. Municipality, Minas Gerais state, E Brazil, 150 m. NE of Belo Horizonte; pop. (1968e) 124,606.

Gov·ern·ment Mountain \ˌgəv-ər(n)-mənt-\. Peak, cen. Coconino co., N cen. Arizona; 8347 ft.

Gov·er·nor's Harbour \ˈgəv-(ə-)nərz-, ˈgəv-ər-nərz-\. Town on Eleuthera I. in Bahama Is.

Governors Island. 1 Island in inner part of Boston Harbor, Massachusetts; site of Fort Winthrop.
2 Fortified island in New York Bay, off end of East river; 173 acres; old fort, Castle William, built 1807–11.

Go·wan·da \gə-ˈwän-də\. Village, Cattaraugus and Erie cos., SW New York, 28 m. S of Buffalo; pop. (1970c) 3110; machine tools, leather, glue. Settled 1810, called Lodi until 1848; State Homeopathic Hospital in nearby **Hel·muth** \ˈhel-məth\ in Erie co.

Go·wa·nus Bay \gə-ˌwän-əs-\. Inlet of Upper New York Bay extending into S Brooklyn, W Long I., New York.

Gow·er \ˈgaů(-ə)r\. Peninsula extending S into Bristol Channel from S cen. coast of Wales.

Go·ya \ˈgō-yə, ˈgȯi-ə\. Town, Corrientes prov., NE Argentina, on E bank of Paraná river 112 m. S of Corrientes; pop. (1960c) 30,011.

Goyania. See GOIÂNIA.

Goyaz. See GOIÁS.

Go·zo \ˈgȯt-(ˌ)sō\ *or anc.* **Gau·lus** \ˈgȯ-ləs\. Island of Malta group in Mediterranean Sea 58 m. S of Sicily; 26 sq. m.; pop. (1961e) 27,506; chief town Victoria. See MALTA.

Graaff Rei·net \ˈgräf-ˈrī-nət\. Town, S Cape Province, S Rep. of South Africa, on Sunday river 135 m. NNW of Port Elizabeth, in center of the Great Karroo; pop. (1967e) 17,700; produces fine quality wood and angora hair; founded by the Dutch in 1786.

Grace·ville \ˈgräs-ˌvil\. City, Jackson co., NW Florida, 16 m. NW of Marianna; pop. (1970c) 2560; lumbering; agriculture.

Gra·cias \ˈgräs-ē-əs\. 1 See LEMPIRA.
2 Town, ✱ of Lempira dept., W Honduras, 100 m. WNW of Tegucigalpa; pop. (1961c) 1854.

Gracias a Dios \-ˌäd-ē-ˈōs\. Department of E Honduras. See table at HONDURAS.

Gracias a Dios, Cape. Northeast extremity of Nicaragua, extending into Caribbean Sea near Honduras border.

Gra·cio·sa \ˌgräs-ē-ˈō-zə\. Island in cen. Azores, NW of Terceira; 24 sq. m.; pop. (1960c) 8700; in Angra do Heroísmo dist.; chief town Santa Cruz da Graciosa.

Graciosa Bay \ˌgräs-ē-ˌō-sə-\. Inlet on NW coast of Ndeni I., Santa Cruz Is., SW Pacific Ocean; good harbor; Mendaña died here 1595.

Gra·di·sca d'Ison·zo \grä-ˌdēs-kə-dē-ˈzōn(t)-ˌsō\. Commune, Gorizia prov., Friuli-Venezia Giulia, NE Italy, SW of Gorizia on opp. side of the Isonzo; pop. (1968e) 5820; Venetian fortress ceded to Austria 1511 and became part of Austrian crownland of Görz and Gradisca (see GORIZIA); taken by Italians June 1915 and made part of Italy 1918.

Gra·do \ˈgräd-(ˌ)ō\. Commune, Friuli-Venezia Giulia, NE Italy, on a small island in NW part of Gulf of Trieste, N Adriatic Sea; pop. (1968e) 10,065; resort; founded by refugees from Aquileia in time of Attila; has fine cathedral, rebuilt 571–586 with a mosaic pavement.

Grado \ˈgräd-(ˌ)ō, ˈgrä-t͟hō\. Commune, Oviedo prov., NW Spain, 12 m. WNW of Oviedo; pop. (1970p) 13,990; iron founding; ordnance works.

Gra·dy \ˈgrād-ē\. Name of counties in two states of the U.S. See tables at GEORGIA and OKLAHOMA.

Graecia Magna. See MAGNA GRAECIA.

Gra·fen·wöhr \ˈgräf-ən-ˌvər\. Village, Bavaria, West Germany, ab. 21 m. SE of Bayreuth; pop. (1968e) 5800; formerly site of Nazi concentration camp.

Graf·ton \ˈgraf-tən\. 1 County in New Hampshire. See table at NEW HAMPSHIRE.
2 Town, Worcester co., cen. Massachusetts, 6 m. ESE of Worcester; pop. (1970c) 11,659; residential. Site of an Indian village established by John Eliot 1654.
3 City, ⊗ of Walsh co., NE North Dakota, 38 m. NNW of Grand Forks; pop. (1970c) 5946; livestock; grain farms; settled 1877.
4 City, ⊗ of Taylor co., N West Virginia, on Tygart river 12 m. SSE of Fairmont; pop. (1970c) 6433; foundry, granite works.
5 Village, Ozaukee co., E Wisconsin, 22 m. E of Milwaukee; pop. (1970c) 5998.
6 Town, NE New South Wales, SE Australia, on Clarence river 45 m. from its mouth and 150 m. S of Brisbane; pop. (1968e) 16,150; port.

Gra·gna·no \grä-ˈnyän-(ˌ)ō\. Commune, Napoli prov., Campania, S Italy, 18 m. SE of Naples; pop. (1968e) 22,961; macaroni factories.

Gra·ham \ˈgrā-əm, ˈgra(-ə)m\. 1 Name of counties in three states of the U.S. See tables at ARIZONA, KANSAS, NORTH CAROLINA.
2 Town, ⊗ of Alamance co., N cen. North Carolina, 21 m. E of Greensboro; pop. (1970c) 8172; textile center; furniture.
3 City, ⊗ of Young co., N Texas, 57 m. S of Wichita Falls; pop. (1970c) 7477; oil refineries, flour and feed mills; wheat, cotton.

Graham, Mount. 1 Peak, Arizona. See GRAHAM PEAK.
2 Peak in Catskill Mts., Ulster co., SE New York; 3868 ft.

Graham Bell Island \ˌgrā-əm-ˌbel-, ˌgra(-ə)m-\. See FRANZ JOSEF LAND.

Graham Coast. See GRAHAM LAND.

Graham Island. Northernmost and largest of the Queen Charlotte Is., off W British Columbia, Canada; 2491 sq. m.

Graham Land *or formerly* **Graham Coast.** Part of the Antarctic Peninsula, British Antarctic Territory, extending from ab. 65°S to 66°15′S; once known as **North Graham Island** and **South Graham Island** but on later exploration found to be part of the mainland; annexed to Great Britain by John Biscoe 1831–32; claimed by Argentina and Chile.

Graham Peak *or* **Mount Graham.** Peak in Pinaleno Mts., Graham co., SE Arizona; 10,713 ft.

Gra·hams·town \ˈgrā-əmz-ˌtaůn, ˈgra(-ə)mz-\ *or Afrikaans* **Gra·hams·tad** \-ˌstät\. Residential town, SE Cape Province, S Rep. of South Africa, 75 m. ENE of Port Elizabeth; pop. (1967e) 37,600; summer resort; important legal and educational center; cathedral, Rhodes Univ. (1904, before 1951 part of Univ. of South Africa). Founded 1812 as a British military outpost in a region which for many years was scene of almost constant struggle bet. whites and natives; besieged by Kafirs in 1819; chief town of British settlers of 1820.

Graian Alps. See table at ALPS.

Grain Coast \'grān-\. Section of coast of Upper Guinea, W Africa, now Liberia, from Cape Palmas to Sierra Leone border— so called from the old trade in grains of paradise (*Amomum melegueta*), a kind of pepper (melegueta pepper).

Grain·ger \'grān-jər\. County in Tennessee. See table at TENNESSEE.

Gra·jaú \'grazh-ə-'ü\. River, Maranhão state, NE Brazil; ab. 300 m. long; flows NNE to Mearim river.

Grajaú, Lake. Lake in N cen. Maranhão state, NE Brazil, bet. the Pindaré and Grajaú rivers.

Gram·bling \'gram-bliŋ\. Village, Lincoln parish, N Louisiana, 34 m. W of Monroe; pop. (1970c) 4407.

Gra·mer·cy \grə-'mər-sē\. Town, St. James parish, SE Louisiana, 39 m. SE of Baton Rouge; pop. (1970c) 2567.

Gram·mi·che·le \ˌgräm-(m)i-'kā-lē, -'kel-ē\. Commune, Catania prov., E Sicily, Italy, 32 m. SW of Catania; pop. (1968e) 13,681; stone quarries; on site of Occhialà, which was destroyed 1693 by earthquake.

Grammont. See GEERAARDSBERGEN.

Gram·pi·ans, The \-'gram-pē-ənz\. 1 Mountain range, W Victoria, SE Australia; highest Mt. William 3829 ft.

2 *or* **Gram·pi·an Hills** \-ən-\. Mountain system of Scotland, extending NE to SW across cen. Scotland, forming a natural boundary bet. the Scottish Highlands and the Scottish Lowlands; highest peak Ben Nevis 4406 ft., highest mountain in Great Britian. See GRAUPIUS, MOUNT.

Gramsh \'grämsh\. 1 Province of cen. Albania. See table at ALBANIA.

2 Town, its ❋; pop. (1967e) 1945.

Gran. 1 River, Czechoslovakia. See HRON.

2 City, Hungary. See ESZTERGOM.

Gra·na·da \grə-'näd-ə\. 1 Department of SW Nicaragua. See table at NICARAGUA.

2 City, ❋ of Granada dept., SW Nicaragua, on NW shore of Lake Nicaragua; pop. (1970e) 51,363; hides, coffee, sugar; oldest city in Nicaragua, founded by Córdoba 1523.

3 Ancient kingdom, Upper Andalusia, S Spain; 11,100 sq. m.; divided 1833 into modern provinces of Granada, Almería, and Málaga. For its history, see GRANADA 5 and ANDALUSIA 2.

4 Province of S Spain. See table at SPAIN.

5 City, ❋ of Granada prov., S Spain, in Sierra Nevada Mts. 80 m. SE of Córdoba; pop. (1970p) 190,429; divided into three sections: Antequeruela (founded 1410), Albaicín, and Granada; manufactures textiles, paper, soap, woolens, liqueurs; archiepiscopal see (from 1493); univ. (1531); the Alhambra (built 1248–1354), one of finest examples of Moorish architecture in Spain; Renaissance cathedral (begun 1529), containing tombs of Ferdinand and Isabella of Castile; the Cartuja, a Carthusian monastery; Moorish remains, among them the Alcazaba (citadel).

History: Founded by Moors in 8th cent.; part of Caliphate of Córdoba 1031–1229; became capital 1238 of independent Moorish kingdom of Granada founded by Nasrid dynasty; attained greatest prosperity in 13th cent.; after Spanish reconquest, remained for 250 years the last Moorish stronghold in Spain; captured 1492 by Ferdinand and Isabella of Castile, completely destroying Moorish power in Spain.

Gran·bury \'grän-ˌber-ē\. City, ⊗ of Hood co., N cen. Texas; pop. (1970c) 2473; cotton.

Gran·by \'gran-bē, 'gram-bē\. 1 Town, NW Hartford co., N Connecticut; pop. (1970c) 6150; settled 1664, incorp. 1786.

2 Town, Hampshire co., W Massachusetts, 20 m. NNE of Springfield; pop. (1970c) 5473.

3 Industrial city, Shefford co., S Quebec, Canada, 45 m. E of Montreal; pop. (1971p) 33,958; lumber, rubber goods; dairy products.

Gran Canaria. See GRAND CANARY.

Gran Chaco. See CHACO.

Gran Colombia. See GREAT COLOMBIA.

Grand \'grand\. 1 Former name of Colorado river from its source to its junction with Green river in SE Utah.

2 River in Iberville parish, S Louisiana; empties into Atchafalaya river.

3 River, SW Michigan; 260 m. long; flows from Jackson co. N and W into Lake Michigan at Grand Haven; furnishes waterpower; navigable 40 m. from mouth.

4 River, NW Missouri; 300 m. long; rises in Adair co., SW cen. Iowa, flows SE across NW Missouri into Missouri river.

5 River, N South Dakota; ab. 200 m. long; formed by confluence of North and South Forks in N Perkins co., flows E into Missouri river.

6 The lower course of the Neosho river (*q.v.*) in Oklahoma. See PENSACOLA DAM.

7 Name of counties in two states of the U.S. See tables at COLORADO and UTAH.

8 River, SE Ontario, Canada; 140 m. long; rises in Grey co. and flows S and SE to Lake Erie.

Grand Andely, Le. See LES ANDELYS.

Grand Atlas. See ATLAS MOUNTAINS.

Grand Ba·ha·ma \ˌgran(d)-bə-'häm-ə, *by outsiders also* -'hā-mə\. One of the Bahama Is.; 530 sq. m.; pop. (1963c) 8230.

Grand Bank. Seaport, S Newfoundland, Canada, on S shore and near mouth of Fortune Bay; pop. (1971p) 3465; is a supply depot for fishing fleets.

Grand Banks. Shoal or banks in Atlantic Ocean E and S of Newfoundland, Canada; extends ab. 350 m. from W to E, ab. 200 m. wide; average depth 50 fathoms; crossed by the Labrador Current from the N mingling with the Gulf Stream along its E edge; greatest cod-fishing region in the world, for centuries has been frequented by fishing fleets of Canada, Great Britain, France, and U.S.; made dangerous by fog, icebergs, and the fact that it is in the path of the transatlantic liners.

Grand Bassa. See BUCHANAN 5.

Grand Bas·sam \-bə-'sam\ *or* **Bassam.** Seaport, Ivory Coast, W Africa, adjoining Bingerville and just E of Abidjan; pop. (1963e) 22,994; customs station.

Grand Blanc \ˌgran(d)-'blaŋk\. City, Genessee co., SE cen. Michigan, 7 m. SSE of Flint; pop. (1970c) 5132.

Grand Bourg *or* **Grand–Bourg** \grän-'bü(ə)r\. Commune, ❋ of Marie Galante I., Guadeloupe dept., West Indies; on SW coast of the island.

Grand Caicos. See TURKS AND CAICOS ISLANDS.

Grand Caillou Bayou. See CAILLOU LAKE.

Grand Canal. 1 *or* **Yün Ho** \'yün-'hō\. Inland waterway, NE China; ab. 1000 m. long, from Tientsin, Hopeh prov., to Hangchow, Chekiang prov. (airline distance ab. 650 m.). Central part from the Yangtze (at Chen-chiang) to Yellow river finished 486 B.C.; extended S to Hangchow 605–618 A.D.; N section finished by Kublai Khan 1282–92; later extended to T'ung-hsien and Peking. Called by the Chinese "Imperial river" (*Yu-ho*) or "Transport river" (*Yün Ho*). Now silted up in part and superseded somewhat by coast transport and the Tientsin-P'u-k'ou railroad.

2 *or Ital.* **Il Ca·na·le Gran·de** \ˌēl-kə-ˌnäl-ā-'grän-dā\. Main water thoroughfare of Venice, in winding course, 80 to 175 ft. wide; crossed by Rialto and other bridges; lined with palaces and fine buildings.

Grand Ca·nary \-kə-'ne(ə)r-ē\ *or Span.* **Gran Ca·na·ria** \ˌgräŋ-kä-'när-yä\. One of the Canary Is. (*q.v.*), Las Palmas prov., Spain, 40 m. ESE of Tenerife I.; 592 sq. m.; pop. (1970p) 519,606; chief city Las Palmas; bananas, tomatoes, tobacco.

Grand Canyon. 1 Gorge in the Colorado river where it flows across NW corner of Arizona; usually taken as extending from mouth of Little Colorado river to Grand Wash Cliffs near Arizona-Nevada boundary but sometimes taken as also including Marble Canyon, above, and when measured thus, ab. 280 m. long; 4–18 m. wide, in places more than a mile deep; many peaks and smaller canyons within the main canyon; surrounding plateau 5000 to 9000 ft. above sea level; an area mostly N of the canyon in NE Mohave co. set aside 1932 as **Grand Canyon National Monument** (see UNITED STATES, *National Monuments*); E of the National Monument in Coconino co. is **Grand Canyon National Park** (see UNITED STATES, *National Parks*).

2 Village (unincorp.), Coconino co., N Arizona, in Grand Canyon National Park; pop. (1970c) 1011; park administration building.

Grand Canyon of the Snake. See HELLS CANYON.

Grand Canyon of the Tuolumne. See TUOLUMNE 1.

Grand Canyon of the Yellowstone. See YELLOWSTONE 1.

Grand Cayman \-'kā-ˌman, -mən\. See CAYMAN ISLANDS.

Grand Cess \-'ses\. Coastal town, SE Liberia, W Africa, 40 m. WNW of Cape Palmas.

Grand'Combe, La. See LA GRAND'COMBE.

Grand Com·bin \ˌgräⁿ-kōⁿ-'baⁿ\. Peak in Pennine Alps, S Switzerland; 14,154 ft.

Grand Cor·nier \ˌgräⁿ-kȯr-'nyā\. Peak in Pennine Alps, S Switzerland; 13,008 ft.

Grand Cou·lee \-'kü-lē\. 1 Valley bet. ranges of cliffs in cen. Washington, extending N to S in Douglas co.

2 City, Grant co., cen. Washington, at site of Grand Coulee Dam on Columbia river 78 m. WNW of Spokane; pop. (1970c) 1302; comprised of former towns of Coulee Heights, Coulee Center, and Grand Coulee.

Grand Coulee Dam. See UNITED STATES, *Dams and Reservoirs.*

Grand Coulee Reservoir. See FRANKLIN D. ROOSEVELT LAKE.

Grand Cou·ron·né \ˌgräⁿ-ˌku̇r-ə-'nā\. Wooded heights E and NE of Nancy, France; battle Sept. 5–12, 1914 in which Germans attempted to capture Nancy but were driven back by Castelnau.

Grand·court \gräⁿ-'kü(ə)r\. Village, Somme dept., N France, N of Albert; severe fighting during battle of the Somme 1916; taken by British Feb. 7, 1917.

Grand–Duché de Luxembourg *or* **Grand Duchy of Luxembourg.** See LUXEMBOURG 2.

Gran·de, Ilha \ˌēl-yə-'gran-də\. Island in Atlantic Ocean off S coast of Rio de Janeiro state, SE Brazil; 15 m. long, 8 m. wide.

Grande, Rio \ˌrē-ō-'grand(-ē), ˌrē-ə-; *also* ˌrī-ō-'grand\. River in S United States. See RIO GRANDE.

Gran·de, Rio \ˌrē-ō-'gran-də, ˌrē-ə-, -dē\. 1 River, W Africa; ab. 250 m. long; rises in Fouta Djallon, W Guinea, flows by winding course W into Gêba estuary, Portuguese Guinea; lower course sometimes called **Co·ru·bal** \ˌkȯr-ə-'bäl\, upper course in French Guinea, the **Kom·ba** \'käm-bə\.

2 River, W Bahia state, E Brazil; ab. 300 m. long; flows NE into São Francisco river.

3 River, SW Minas Gerais state, E Brazil; ab. 680 m. long; flows W to unite with Paranaíba river and form Paraná river; forms section of boundary bet. Minas Gerais and São Paulo states.

Gran·de, Río \ˌrē-ō-'grän-(ˌ)dā\. 1 River, Mendoza prov., W cen. Argentina; ab. 80 m. long; rises near Chilean border, flows SE to unite with Barrancas river and form Colorado river.

2 A name of the Mamoré (*q.v.*) in its upper course, Bolivia.

3 *or* **Río Grande de Santiago.** River, Mexico. See SANTIAGO 10.

4 River, Nicaragua; ab. 200 m. long; flows E to Caribbean Sea.

Gran·de Añas·co \ˌgrän-dā-än-'yäs-(ˌ)kō\. River in W Puerto Rico; flows W into Añasco Bay.

Grande Casse, Pointe de la \ˌpwaⁿt-də-lä-'gräⁿd-'käs\. Peak, W Graian Alps, Savoie dept., E France; 12,638 ft.

Grande Chartreuse, La. See CHARTREUSE, LA GRANDE.

Grande–Comore. See GREAT COMORO.

Gran·de de Are·ci·bo \'grän-dā-dā-ˌär-ə-'sē-(ˌ)bō\. River in N Puerto Rico; 40 m. long; flows N through Arecibo municipality into Atlantic Ocean.

Gran·de de Lo·í·za \-dā-lō-'ē-zə\. River in NE Puerto Rico; flows N and NE into Atlantic Ocean.

Gran·de Island \ˌgrän-dā-\. Island, S Zambales prov., Luzon, Phil., in center of entrance to Subic Bay (*q.v.*); ½ sq. m.; strongly fortified; retaken from Japanese Feb. 1, 1945.

Grande Prai·rie \'gran(d)-'pre(ə)r-ē\. City, W Alberta, Canada, 235 m. WNW of Edmonton; pop. (1971p) 12,797; timber; livestock.

Grand Erg Occidental *and* **Grand Erg Oriental.** See ERG, AL-.

Grande Ronde \'gran-'dränd\. River, NE Oregon; 175 m. long; rises in SW Union co., flows NE across Washington border and into Snake river.

Grandes Jo·rasses \ˌgräⁿ-jə-'ras\. Mountain having two peaks (higher one 13,799 ft.) in Pennine Alps, on France-Italy boundary, NE of Mont Blanc.

Grande Soufrière. See SOUFRIERE 1.

Grande Terre \gran-'te(ə)r\. Island forming E part of Guadeloupe, West Indies.

Grand Falls. 1 Waterfall, Canada. See CHURCHILL FALLS.

2 Town, Victoria co., W New Brunswick, Canada, on St. John river 35 m. SE of Edmundston; pop. (1971p) 4364; soap, lumber; dairying.

3 Town, cen. Newfoundland, Canada, on N bank of Exploits river; pop. (1971p) 7659; pulp and paper mills.

Grand Forks. 1 County in E North Dakota. See table at NORTH DAKOTA.

2 City, its ⊗, on Red river 73 m. N of Fargo; pop. (1970c) 39,008; industrial center in hard wheat belt; manufactures flour, feed, beet sugar; meat-packing; livestock raising; Univ. of North Dakota (1883). Established as fur-trading post 1801, settled 1871, incorporated as city 1881, established council-manager form of government 1947.

3 City, British Columbia, Canada, 60 m. SW of Nelson; pop. (1971p) 3169; diversified agriculture; gold and copper mines; sawmill.

Grand–Fort–Phi·lippe \ˌgräⁿ-fȯr-fi-'lēp\. Coastal commune, Nord dept., N France, ab. 11 m. ENE of Calais; pop. (1962c) 4707.

Grand Haven. City, ⊗ of Ottawa co., W Michigan, on Lake Michigan at mouth of Grand river 12 m. S of Muskegon; pop. (1970c) 11,844; summer resort; port of entry; pneumatic tools, auto parts.

Grand Island. 1 Island in upper Niagara river; part of Erie co., W New York; 8 m. long.

2 City, ⊗ of Hall co., SE cen. Nebraska, on Platte river 90 m. W of Lincoln; pop. (1970c) 31,269; farm implements; flour mills, packinghouses, dairies.

Grand Isle \'gran-'dī(ə)l\. 1 Island in Jefferson parish, off coast of SE Louisiana, at SW entrance to Barataria Bay.

2 Island in Lake Champlain, Grand Isle co., NW corner of Vermont; ab. 10 m. long.

3 County in Vermont. See table at VERMONT.

4 Town, Aroostook co., N Maine, on St. John river 22 m. E of Fort Kent; pop. (1970c) 797.

Grand Junction. City, ⊗ of Mesa co., W Colorado, at junction of Gunnison and Colorado rivers; pop. (1970c) 20,170; trade center and distributing point for irrigated valley; peach orchards; Mesa Coll. (1925); incorporated 1881.

Grand Lac. See TONLE SAP.

Grand La·hou \ˌgräⁿ-lä-'(h)ü\ *also* **Grand La·hu** \-lä-'hü\. Seaport, Ivory Coast, W Africa, 70 m. W of Abidjan; pop. (1963e) 2900.

Grand Lake. 1 Lake, NE Grand co., N Colorado, on SW border of Rocky Mountain National Park; the town of Grand Lake (pop. [1970c] 189) is on it.

2 Lake in NE Cameron parish, SW Louisiana; outlet SW into Gulf of Mexico.

3 Lake, chiefly in Iberia and St. Mary parishes, S Louisiana; ab. 30 m. long, 9 m. wide; drains through Atchafalaya river into Atchafalaya Bay.

4 Lake, Maine. See WEST GRAND LAKE.

5 *or* **Grand Reservoir.** Lake, Ohio. See ST. MARYS, LAKE.

6 Dam, Oklahoma. See PENSACOLA DAM.

7 Lake, Queens co., S New Brunswick, Canada; 65 sq. m.; outlet St. John river.

8 *or formerly* **East Grand Lake.** Largest of the Chiputneticook Lakes, on SW border of York co., SW New Brunswick, Canada; borders on Maine.

9 Lake, W Newfoundland, Canada; ab. 56 m. long; 205 sq. m.; outlet through Humber river.

Grand Lake Métascouac. See MÉTASCOUAC.

Grand Ledge \-'lej\. Industrial city, Eaton co., S Michigan, W of Lansing; pop. (1970c) 6032; chemicals, clay products; livestock.

Grand Liban. See LEBANON 1.

Grand Ma·nan Island \-mə-'nan-\. Island at entrance to Bay of Fundy and S of Passamaquoddy Bay, off SW coast of New Brunswick, SE Canada; ab. 20 m. long; separated from coast of Maine by **Grand Manan Channel** (ab. 8 m. wide), which has strong currents; fine cliff scenery; summer resort; chief village North Head; fishing.

Grand Manitoulin. See MANITOULIN ISLAND.

Grand Ma·rais \-mə-'rā\. Village, ⊗ of Cook co., NE corner of Minnesota, on Lake Superior 23 m. S of Canadian border; pop. (1970c) 1301; timber.

Grand'Mère \grä^{n}-'me(ə)r\. City, Champlain co., S Quebec, Canada, on Saint-Maurice river 20 m. NNW of Three Rivers; pop. (1971p) 17,144; paper and pulp mills; manufactures shirts, shoes, textiles.

Grand Monadnock. See MONADNOCK, MOUNT.

Grand–Montrouge, Le. See MONTROUGE.

Grand Paradis. See GRAN PARADISO.

Grand Pass. See BARATARIA PASS.

Grand Po·po \gran(d)-'pō-(,)pō\. Seaport, SW Dahomey, W Africa, at mouth of the Mono river; on coastal railroad bet. Porto-Novo and Lomé.

Grand Port·age National Monument \-'pōrt-ij-, -'pȯrt-\. See UNITED STATES, *National Monuments.*

Grand Prairie. City, Dallas and Tarrant cos., NE Texas, 13 m. W of Dallas; pop. (1970c) 50,904; aircraft, rubber goods; incorp. 1909.

Grand·pré \grä^{n}-'prā\. Village, Ardennes dept., NE France, on Aire river 10 m. SE of Vouziers; pop. (1962c) 616; center of fighting Oct. 1918 in the Meuse-Argonne offensive (see ARGONNE).

Grand Pré \'gran-'prā\. Village, Kings co., W Nova Scotia, Canada, on S shore of Minas Basin near Wolfville; founded c. 1675; early home of the Acadians; scene of Longfellow's *Evangeline.* See ACADIA 2.

Grand Pré National Historic Park. See CANADA, *National Historic Parks.*

Grand Rapids. 1 City, ⊗ of Kent co., W Michigan, on Grand river 61 m. WNW of Lansing; pop. (1970c) 197,649; manufactures esp. furniture, business machinery, auto parts, chemicals, paper products; petroleum refineries; Calvin College (1876), Aquinas Coll. (1886), Grand Rapids Junior Coll. (1914), Reformed Bible Inst. (1940), Grace Bible Inst. (1946). Originally site of an Ottawa Indian village; trading post 1826; became lumbering center; chartered as city 1850.

2 Village, ⊗ of Itasca co., N Minnesota, 32 m. WSW of Hibbing; pop. (1970c) 7247; paper mills; Itasca State Junior Coll. (1922).

Grand Reservoir. See SAINT MARYS, LAKE.

Grand River. See GRAND.

Grand River Dam. See PENSACOLA DAM.

Grand–Saint–Ber·nard \,grä^{n}-,sa^{n}-bər-'när\. Alpine pass. See ALPS.

Grand Sa·line \-sə-'lēn\. City, Van Zandt co., NE Texas, 30 m. NW of Tyler; pop. (1970c) 2257; salt mining and processing.

Grand Sen·ti·nel \-'sent-nəl, -ᵊn-əl\. Peak in Sierra Nevada, E Fresno co., S cen. California; 8514 ft.

Grand·son *or* **Gran·son** \grä^{n}-'sō^{n}\. Commune, Vaud canton, W Switzerland, SW of Neuchâtel; pop. (1970c) 2135; castle, 12th cent. church; garrison surrendered and put to death Feb. 1476 by Charles the Bold who with heavy loss was defeated in battle Mar. 2 by Swiss Confederates.

Grand Terre Island \,gran-,te(ə)r-\. Island in Jefferson parish at entrance to Barataria Bay off coast of SE Louisiana; Barataria lighthouse.

Grand Te·ton \-'tē-,tän\. Peak in cen. Grand Teton National Park, Teton co., NW Wyoming; 13,766 ft.; highest point in Teton Range.

Grand Teton National Park. See UNITED STATES, *National Parks.*

Grand Trav·erse \-'trav-ərs\. County in Michigan. See table at MICHIGAN.

Grand Traverse Bay. Inlet of Lake Michigan, bet. Leelanau and Antrim cos., NW Michigan.

Grand Trianon. See VERSAILLES.

Grand Turk \-'tərk\. Island and town (pop. [1970c] 2330), ✱ of Turks and Caicos Is., West Indies; 7 m. long.

Grand·view \'gran(d)-,vyü\. City, Jackson co., W Missouri, 5 m. S of Kansas City; pop. (1970c) 17,456; diversified farming.

Grand View. City, Yakima co., S Washington, 39 m. SE of Yakima; pop. (1970c) 3605; cement products; diversified agriculture.

Grandview Heights. City, Franklin co., cen. Ohio, 6 m. NNW of Columbus; pop. (1970c) 8460.

Grand·ville \'gran(d)-,vil\. City, Kent co., W Michigan, 5 m. SW of Grand Rapids; pop. (1970c) 10,764.

Grand Wash Cliffs. Chain of cliffs in NW Mohave co., NW Arizona, near Lake Mead.

Grange·mouth \'grānj-məth, -,mau̇th\. Seaport burgh, Stirling co., cen. Scotland, on Forth estuary at terminus of the Forth and Clyde Canal 3 m. NE of Falkirk; pop. (1971p) 24,572; shipbuilding yards, oil refinery.

Gran·ger \'grān-jər\. City, Williamson co., cen. Texas, 26 m. S of Temple; pop. (1970c) 1256.

Granges. See GRENCHEN.

Grange·ville \'grānj-,vil\. City, ⊗ of Idaho co., N cen. Idaho; pop. (1970c) 3636; wheat, livestock; timber; gold mines.

Gra·ni·cus \grə-'nī-kəs\ *or mod.* **Ko·ca·baş** \'käj-ə-,bäsh\. River in Turkey; 56 m. long; flowing N into the Propontis (Sea of Marmara); near its mouth Alexander defeated the Persians 334 B.C.

Gran·ite \'gran-ət\. County in Montana. See table at MONTANA.

Granite City. Industrial city, Madison co., SW Illinois, 7 m. N of East St. Louis; pop. (1970c) 40,440; sheet steel, tin plate, auto frames, lubricants.

Granite Dome. Peak in Sierra Nevada, in NE Tuolumne co., cen. California; 10,321 ft.

Granite Falls. 1 Waterfall in Mount Rainier National Park, W cen. Washington; 350 ft. high.

2 City, ⊗ of Yellow Medicine co., Chippewa and Yellow Medicine cos., SW Minnesota, on Minnesota river 13 m. SE of Montevideo; pop. (1970c) 3225; hydroelectric power plant.

3 Town, Caldwell co., W North Carolina, 10 m. SSE of Lenoir; pop. (1970c) 2388; textiles, hosiery, lumber.

Granite Peak. 1 Mountain, SE Park co., S Montana; 12,799 ft.; highest point in state.

2 Mountain, cen. Washoe co., NW Nevada; 8990 ft.

ə abut; ᵊ kitten, Fr. table; ər further; a back; ā bake; ä cot, cart; ȧ Fr. bac; au̇ out; ch chin; e less; ē easy; g gift
i trip; ī life; j joke; k̲ Ger. ich, Buch; ^{n} Fr. vin; ŋ sing; ō flow; ȯ flaw; œ Fr. bœuf; œ̄ Fr. feu; ȯi coin; th thin
th̲ this; ü loot; u̇ foot; ue Ger. füllen; ue̅ Fr. rue; y yet; ^{y} Fr. digne \dēn^{y}\, nuit \nw^{y}ē\; yü few; yu̇ furious; zh vision

Gran·ite·ville \'gran-ət-ˌvil\. Village (unincorp.), Aiken co., W South Carolina, ab. 5 m. NW of Aiken; pop. (1970c) 1127; textiles.

Granja, La. See SAN ILDEFONSO 2.

Gran Malindang. See MALINDANG, MOUNT.

Gra·nol·lérs \ˌgrän-ō(l)-'ye(ə)rs\. Commune, Barcelona prov., NE Spain, 16 m. NNE of Barcelona; pop. (1960c) 20,194.

Gran Pa·ra·di·so \ˌgrän-ˌpär-ə-'dē-(ˌ)zō\ *or Fr.* **Grand Pa·ra·dis** \grän-pär-ə-dē\. Peak, highest of the Graian Alps, in Gran Paradiso National Park, NW Piedmont, NW Italy; 13,323 ft.

Gran Paradiso National Park. National park, Piedmont, NW Italy; 240 sq. m.; alpine vegetation, glaciers; established 1922.

Gran Piedra, La. See LA GRAN PIEDRA.

Gran Qui·vi·ra National Monument \ˌgran-kə-'vir-ə-\. See QUIVIRA; UNITED STATES, *National Monuments.*

Gran Salar de Uyuni. See SALAR DE UYUNI.

Gran Sas·so d'Ita·lia \grän-ˌsäs-ō-dē-'täl-yə\. Mountain group, N Abruzzi, cen. Italy; includes Monte Corno 9560 ft., highest peak in the Apennines.

Granson. See GRANDSON.

Grant \'grant\. 1 Name of a parish in Louisiana and of counties in fourteen states of the U.S. See tables at ARKANSAS, INDIANA, KANSAS, KENTUCKY, LOUISIANA, MINNESOTA, NEBRASKA, NEW MEXICO, NORTH DAKOTA, OKLAHOMA, OREGON, SOUTH DAKOTA, WASHINGTON, WEST VIRGINIA, WISCONSIN.

2 City, ⊗ of Perkins co., SW Nebraska; pop. (1970c) 1099; wheat; livestock.

Grant, Mount. 1 Peak, Flathead co., NW Montana; 8620 ft.

2 Peak, E Churchill co., W Nevada; 8854 ft.

3 Peak, W Mineral co., SW Nevada; 11,245 ft.; highest in Wassuk Range.

Grant City. City, ⊗ of Worth co., NW Missouri; pop. (1970c) 1095; diversified farming.

Gran·tham \'gran-thəm\. Municipal borough, Parts of Kesteven, Lincolnshire, E England, on the Witham 23 m. E of Nottingham; pop. (1971p) 27,913; agricultural implements; battlefield where Oliver Cromwell won his first victory (Mar. 1643) over Royalists.

Grant Land. North section of Ellesmere I., N Franklin dist., Northwest Territories, Canada—a former designation.

Grant Peak. Mountain, E Yellowstone National Park, NW Wyoming; 11,015 ft.

Grants \'gran(t)s\. Town, Valencia co., W New Mexico, ab. 70 m. NW of Belen; pop. (1970c) 8768; sawmills; truck farming.

Grants·burg \'gran(t)s-ˌbərg\. Village, ⊗ of Burnett co., NW Wisconsin; pop. (1970c) 930.

Grants Pass. City, ⊗ of Josephine co., SW Oregon, on Rogue river 25 m. WNW of Medford; pop. (1970c) 12,455; fruit growing, dairying, lumbering, mining (gold, silver, copper), salmon fishing and canning.

Grants·ville \'gran(t)s-ˌvil\. 1 City, Tooele co., NW Utah, 45 m. SW of Salt Lake City; pop. (1970c) 2931.

2 Town, ⊗ of Calhoun co., cen. West Virginia; pop. (1970c) 795.

Gran Valira. See VALIRA.

Gran·ville \'gran-(ˌ)vil, -vəl\. 1 County in North Carolina. See table at NORTH CAROLINA.

2 Village, Washington co., E New York, on Vermont border 50 m. NNE of Troy; pop. (1970c) 2748; slate quarries; potatoes.

3 Village, Licking co., cen. Ohio, 6 m. W of Newark; pop. (1970c) 3963; Denison Univ. (1831).

Granville \grän-'vēl\. Fortified seaport and manufacturing commune, Manche dept., NW France, on Gulf of Saint-Malo 30 m. SW of Saint-Lô; pop. (1968c) 12,715; 12th cent. church. Besieged by Vendeans 1793 and by English 1808; in World War II taken by Americans July 30, 1944.

Granville Lake \ˌgran-vil-\. Lake, NW Manitoba, Canada; 392 sq. m.; an expansion of Churchill river.

Grape·vine \'grāp-ˌvīn\. City, Tarrant co., N Texas, 20 m. NE of Fort Worth; pop. (1970c) 7023; oil refining; trailers, cottonseed oil; diversified agriculture.

Grap·pa, Mount \-'gräp-ə\ *or Ital.* **Mon·te Grappa** \ˌmōn-tē-\. Peak, Veneto, NE Italy, 10 m. N of Bassano; 5823 ft.; severe fighting Oct. 24–30, 1918.

Gras, Lac de \ˌlak-də-'grä\. Lake, cen. Mackenzie dist., Northwest Territories, Canada; 345 sq. m.; a source of the Coppermine river.

Graslitz. See KRASLICE.

Gras·mere \'gras-ˌmi(ə)r\. 1 Lake in the Lake District, Westmorland, NW England; 1 m. long.

2 Former urban district on the lake, now in Lakes urban district; Wordsworth's home for many years.

Gras·moor \'gras-ˌmu̇(ə)r\ *or* **Grass·moor** *also* **Grasmoor Hill.** Mountain, Cumberland, NW England, in Lake District; 2791 ft.

Gräsö \'gres-ˌər, 'grās-\. Island off SE coast of Sweden, in Gulf of Bothnia N of Väddö I.; 34 sq. m.

Grasse \'gras, 'gräs\. Manufacturing commune, Alpes-Maritimes dept., SE France, 17 m. W of Nice; pop. (1968c) 30,907; winter resort; manufactures perfumes and essences. Independent republic in 12th cent.; became part of countship of Provence 1227.

Grassmoor. See GRASMOOR.

Grass Valley \ˌgras-\. City, Nevada co., E California, 45 m. W of Lake Tahoe; pop. (1970c) 5149; sheet metal; sawmills; ships fruit.

Grassy Bay \ˌgras-ē-\. Bay off NW coast of Bermuda I.

Grassy Knob. Peak, Union co., N Georgia; 4768 ft.

Grå·sten \'grō-stən\ *or Ger.* **Grav·en·stein** \'grav-ən-ˌstīn, 'gräv-ən-ˌs(h)tīn\. Village, Sønderjylland co., SE Jutland, Denmark, SSE of Åbenrå; pop. (1970e) 6332; summer residence of Danish monarch; formerly in Germany.

Gratianopolis. See GRENOBLE.

Gra·tiot \'grash-ət\. County in Michigan. See table at MICHIGAN.

Gratz. See GRAZ.

Grau·bün·den \grau̇-'bin-dən, -'bu̇n-\ *or Fr.* **Gri·sons** \grē-'zōn\. Canton, E Switzerland; 2745 sq. m.; pop. (1970c) 162,086; ✱ Chur; in Alps (Rhaetian Alps in E); includes Engadine valley and sources of Rhine and Inn rivers; numerous mountain passes (Bernina, Oberalp, etc.); corn, wine; tourism. Formed largest part of ancient Roman province of Raetia (*q.v.*); conquered by Franks 6th cent.; became part of Germany early 10th cent.; accepted Reformation 1526; joined Swiss Confederation 1803.

Graudenz. See GRUDZIĄDZ.

Grau·pi·us, Mount \-'grō-pē-əs\ *or Lat.* **Mons Graupius** \mänz-\. Mountain in ancient Caledonia, of uncertain location; scene of battle in which Galgacus was defeated 84 A.D. by Romans under Agricola, mentioned by Tacitus in his *Agricola;* has also been called, erroneously, Mount Grampius, the name which became applied to the Grampians of Scotland.

Grave Creek Mound. See MOUNDSVILLE.

Gra·ve·lines \ˌgrav-(ə-)'lēn\. Seaport commune, Nord dept., N France, 15 m. SW of Dunkerque; pop. (1962c) 7731; produces paper, sugar, salt; cans vegetables, cures fish.

Grav·el Mountain \ˌgrav-əl-\. Peak, Hinsdale co., SW Colorado; 13,600 ft.

Gra·ve·lotte \ˌgrav-(ə-)'lät\. Village, Moselle dept., NE France, near Metz; pop. (1962c) 375; scene of one of most important battles of Franco-Prussian War 1870 in which the French under Marshal Bazaine were forced to retreat into Metz by the Germans under King William.

Gravenhage, 's. See HAGUE, THE.

Gra·ven·hurst \'grāv-ən-ˌhərst\. Town, Muskoka dist., SE Ontario, Canada, at foot of Lake Muskoka 10 m. SSW of Bracebridge; pop. (1971p) 7101; center for campers and sportsmen.

Gravenstein. See GRÅSTEN.

Graves \'grāvz\. County in Kentucky. See table at KENTUCKY.

Graves \'gräv\. District, Gironde dept., SW France; extends ab. 25 m. along the Garonne W and S of Bordeaux; gravelly soil, hence the name; famous red and white wines; adjoining on the SE is Sauternes (*q.v.*).

Graves·end \'grāv-'zend\. Municipal borough, Kent, SE England, on Thames estuary 22 m. E of London; pop. (1971p) 54,044; shipbulding yards; paper mills, fisheries, iron foundries, engineering works; here (1617) Pocahontas died and was buried.

Gravesend Bay. Inlet of Lower New York Bay, SW Long I.

Gra·vi·na in Pu·glia \grä-ˌvē-nə-in-'pül-yə\. Commune, Bari prov., Apulia, SE Italy, 30 m. SW of Bari; pop. (1968e) 33,152; cathedral; catacombs; castle built by Frederick II; limestone quarries.

Gray \'grā\. **1** Name of counties in two states of the U.S. See tables at KANSAS and TEXAS.

2 Town, ⊗ of Jones co., cen. Georgia; pop. (1970c) 2014; cotton, peaches.

3 Town, Cumberland co., SW Maine, 11 m. N of Portland; pop. (1970c) 2939.

4 Commune, Haute-Saône dept., E France, river port on Saône 30 m. SW of Vesoul; pop. (1962c) 8150; founded in 7th cent.; gave its name to distinguished English family of Grey, or de Grey; church of 13th–15th cents., 17th cent. château.

Gray Kaweah. See KAWEAH PEAKS.

Gray·ling \'grā-liŋ\. City, ⊗ of Crawford co., N Michigan, 45 m. E of Traverse City; pop. (1970c) 2143; timber; resort.

Gray Peak. **1** Mountain in Adirondack Mts., Essex co., NE New York; 4840 ft.

2 Mountain in Yellowstone National Park, NW Wyoming; 10,300 ft.

Grays Harbor \'grāz-\. **1** Inlet of Pacific Ocean on SW coast of Grays Harbor co., W Washington.

2 County in Washington. See table at WASHINGTON.

Grays·lake \'grāz-'lāk\. Village, Lake co., NE Illinois, 11 m. W of Waukegan; pop. (1970c) 4907.

Grays Lake. Lake bet. Bonneville and Caribou cos., SE Idaho.

Grays Landing. Locality, Fayette co., SW Pennsylvania, on Monongahela river ab. 12 m. SW of Uniontown.

Gray·son \'grā-sən\. **1** Name of counties in three states of the U.S. See tables at KENTUCKY, TEXAS, VIRGINIA.

2 City, ⊗ of Carter co., NE Kentucky; pop. (1970c) 2184; sawmill; wheat, tobacco; Kentucky Christian Coll. (1919).

Grays Peak. Mountain, Clear Creek co., cen. Colorado; 14,270 ft.; highest peak in Front Range.

Grays·ville \'grāz-ˌvil\. City, Jefferson co., cen. Alabama; pop. (1970c) 3182.

Gray·ville \'grā-ˌvil\. City, Edwards and White cos., SE Illinois, on Wabash river; pop. (1970c) 2035.

Graz *or earlier* **Gratz** \'gräts\. City, ✱ of Styria, Austria, on left bank of Mur river 87 m. SSW of Vienna, in Styrian Alps; pop. (1971p) 249,200; railroad shops; steel, machinery, paper, glass, leather, textiles; medieval fortifications converted into promenades; 11th cent. castle, 15th cent. Gothic cathedral, univ. (1585), 17th cent. arsenal, technical univ. (1811); residence of early rulers of Styria; home of the astronomer Johannes Kepler 1594–1600.

Great Abaco. See ABACO.

Great Admiralty Island. See MANUS 2.

Great American Desert. Originally, a vaguely defined region, W United States, W of the Missouri river and sometimes including region W of the Rocky Mts.— so named from reports of early explorers to whom the territory appeared uninhabitable; later, the semiarid region bet. the Sierra Nevada and the Rockies, including the Great Basin; now, the region of deserts in SW Arizona and SE California.

Great Australian Bight. Bay on S coast of Australia; part of Indian Ocean; ab. 600 m. wide.

Great Bahama Bank. See BAHAMA BANKS.

Great Ban·da \-'bän-də, -'ban-\ *or* **Lon·tor** \'lȯn-ˌtȯ(ə)r\ *or* **Ban·dar Be·sar** \bän-'där-bə-'sär\. Largest of the Banda Is., Indonesia; 7½ m. long; volcanic in origin; with Bandanaira and Gunung Api encloses a small inland sea that forms the harbor of Bandanaira, one of best in the Malay Archipelago.

Great Banjak. See BANJAK ISLANDS.

Great Barrier Island *or* **Otea** \ō-'tā-ə\. Island off E coast of N extension of North I., New Zealand, at E entrance to Hauraki Gulf.

Great Barrier Reef also **Barrier Reef.** Coral reef, the largest deposit of coral in the world, off NE coast of Queensland, Australia; ab. 1250 m. long; N end close to coast, S end ab. 150 m. out to sea; shallow waters inside reef strewn with coral islets or atolls, outside in Coral Sea waters of great depth; high tides and tremendous surf on outer edge.

Great Bar·ring·ton \-'bar-iŋ-tən\. Town, Berkshire co., W Massachusetts, on Housatonic river 18 m. S of Pittsfield; pop. (1970c) 7537; summer resort; William Cullen Bryant town clerk here 1815–25.

Great Basin. Elevated region bet. the Wasatch and Sierra Nevada Mts., including most of Nevada and parts of Utah, California, Idaho, Wyoming, and Oregon; 189,000 sq. m.; chief rivers the Humboldt, N Nevada, and the Sevier, SW cen. Utah; has no drainage to the ocean, chief drainage center Great Salt Lake; includes Great Salt Lake Desert, Carson Sink, Mojave Desert (*qq.v.*) and Death Valley (see UNITED STATES, *National Monuments*).

Great Bay. Inlet at extreme S tip of Ocean co., New Jersey; connecting with Atlantic Ocean through Little Egg Inlet.

Great Bear Lake \-'ba(ə)r-, -'be(ə)r-\. Lake, NW cen. Mackenzie dist., Northwest Territories, Canada; 12,275 sq. m.; of very irregular shape, with several long arms, its greatest length 192 m.; max. depth 1356 ft.; its outlet is **Great Bear River** (70 m. long), flowing W to the Mackenzie; frozen ab. 8 months in the year; abounds in fish. Discovered ab. 1800 and explored by Sir John Franklin 1825; radium ores discovered on its E shore 1929.

Great Belt \-'belt\. Strait bet. Sjælland and Fyn Is., Denmark, connecting the Kattegat with the Baltic Sea; 40 m. long, averages 10 m. wide. See LITTLE BELT.

Great Bend. City, ⊗ of Barton co., cen. Kansas, on Arkansas river 53 m. WNW of Hutchinson; pop. (1970c) 16,133; Barton County Community Coll. (1965); on old Santa Fe trail; Coronado's Quivira (*q.v.*) generally located nearby.

Great Benin. See BENIN 3.

Great Berg \-'bərg\. River, SW Cape Province, S Rep. of South Africa; 140 m. long; rises E of Cape Town, flows N and W into St. Helena Bay.

Great Berkhampstead. See BERKHAMPSTEAD.

Great Bermuda. See BERMUDA.

Great Bitter Lake. See BITTER LAKES.

Great Black. See BIG BLACK 1.

Great Blasket. See BLASKET ISLANDS.

Great Brit·ain \-'brit-ᵊn\. Kingdom, W Europe, comprising England, Scotland, and Wales; together with Northern Ireland constitutes the **United Kingdom of Great Britain and Northern Ireland** (93,598 sq. m.; pop. [1971p] 55,346,-551; ✱ London); largest island in Europe. For natural features, chief cities, and other data, see ENGLAND; IRELAND, NORTHERN; SCOTLAND; WALES.

History: (1) *Britain:* Inhabited in pre-Roman times by Celtic-speaking peoples whose early religion was druidism, its chief tribe in the S being the Britons (*Lat.* Brittones); invaded by Julius Caesar 55 and 54 B.C. but not subjugated until Roman conquest in 1st cent. A.D. (first attack by Claudius 43 A.D., last serious opposition the revolt of 60 A.D. under Boadicea, Queen of the Iceni). In Roman times divided into southern Britain (corresponding to modern England and Wales), part of Roman Empire as province of Britannia, and northern Britain by Hadrian's Wall, constructed 120–123 A.D., extending from Solway Firth to mouth of the Tyne; southern Britain saw building of roads (see FOSSE WAY; WATLING STREET), establishment of cities, and introduction of Christianity; attacked by various barbarian tribes; gradually abandoned by Romans during first half of 5th cent., garrisons being withdrawn 410; invaded by Nordic tribes, the Angles, Saxons, and Jutes, who drove Celtic inhabitants into SW and W parts (Cornwall and Wales) and into Armorica (*q.v.*) on the Continent.

(2) *England:* After Anglo-Saxon invasions of 5th cent., southern Britain (except Wales in W and Strathclyde in NW) became divided into seven petty kingdoms, the Heptarchy (*q.v.*), which, beginning with Kent in 6th cent., were converted to Christianity; by end of 8th cent. dominated by Wessex, whose king Egbert (775?–839) was first to bring all English peoples under one overlord and whose king Alfred the Great (849–899) defeated the Danes under Guthrum. By Peace of Wedmore 878 Danes left only in NE part of England N of Watling Street (the Danelaw, reconquered by c. 954); English kingdom part of empire of Canute of Denmark 1017–35. Conquered 1066 by William of Normandy, who introduced centralized government; began conquest of Ireland under Henry II; by inheritance of its Norman rulers and by marriage 1152 of Henry II with Eleanor of Aquitaine acquired holdings in France, which, beginning with John's forfeiture of Normandy 1204 and ending with fall of Calais 1558, were gradually lost during a period of many conflicts with the French including the Hundred Years' War 1337–1453 (see CRÉCY, POITOU, AGINCOURT, ORLÉANS); medieval England saw foundation of political and personal liberty in Magna Carta, signed June 15, 1215 by King John, and establishment of parliamentary system by Edward I, who summoned first parliament Nov. 27, 1295; subdued Wales 1284; torn by Wars of the Roses 1455–85 bet. houses of Lancaster and York, terminated with accession of Henry VII, first of the Tudor sovereigns. Broke with Rome under Henry VIII and established Church of England as state church; entered period of maritime and colonial expansion accelerated by defeat of Spanish Armada 1588; with exception of years as a Commonwealth (1649–60) ruled 1603–1714 by the Stuarts, who were rulers also of Scotland; effected formal union with Scotland 1707, *Great Britain* being adopted as official name of both island and kingdom.

(3) *Great Britain:* In 18th cent. completed evolution of modern party system and cabinet government, engaged in series of wars with Spain and France which resulted in imperial gains (esp. Canada and India), led in developments of Industrial Revolution, and lost American colonies. In 19th cent. enacted legislative union with Ireland 1801, thus forming the **United Kingdom of Great Britain and Ireland;** participated in wars to liberate Continent from French control 1793–1815 (see PENINSULA, THE 2; WATERLOO 4); passed 1832 first of series of Reform Bills (others 1867, 1884–85, 1918) leading to universal suffrage; repealed Corn Laws 1846, removing last barrier to free trade; as an ally of Turkey fought in Crimean War 1854–56; put down Sepoy Mutiny 1857–58 in India; fought Boer War 1899–1902 with the Transvaal and Orange Free State. Participated as one of the Allies in World War I Aug. 4, 1914–Nov. 11, 1918. Granted dominion status to Ireland 1922, establishing Irish Free State, and forming with Northern Ireland the **United Kingdom of Great Britain and Northern Ireland** (new name officially adopted 1927); as result of Imperial Conferences, esp. of 1918, 1926, and 1930, agreed 1931 to the Statute of Westminster granting to the self-governing dominions equality of status within the British Commonwealth of Nations (now Commonwealth of Nations [*q.v.*]); abandoned policy of free trade 1932. Participated as one of the Allies in World War II Sept. 3, 1939–Aug. 14, 1945; after the fall of France 1940, threatened with invasion by the Germans until German defeat in air war ("Battle of Britain") Aug. 8–Oct. 31, 1940; base for the Allied invasion of Normandy, NW France, June 1944; member of UN 1945; gave up rule over India 1947; joined NATO 1949; participated with other UN forces in Korean War 1950–53; coronation of Queen Elizabeth II 1953; intervened militarily in Egypt (Suez Crisis) 1956; during period 1957–70 relinquished control over most of its colonies and other overseas dependencies; signed treaty of accession to European Economic Community 1972.

Great Central Plain. A region in the interior of the United States including a large portion of the upper Mississippi drainage basin; bounded on E by the Appalachian Plateau, on S by Gulf Plain and the Interior Highlands, on W by the Great Plains, and on N by Laurentian Highlands.

Great Cha·zy \-shā-ˈzē\. River, Clinton co., NE corner of New York; flows out of Chazy Lake NE into Lake Champlain.

Great Co·co \-ˈkō-(ˌ)kō\. Small island of the Andaman Is., separated from North Andaman I. by Coco Channel.

Great Co·lom·bia \-kə-ˈləm-bē-ə, -ˈlōm-\ *or Span.* **Gran Colombia** \ˌgrän-\. Country of NW South America, 1819–30; formed as result of wars of Latin American states against Spain for independence, chiefly by activities of Gen. Simón Bolívar. Created by proclamation of Congress of Angostura Aug. 17, 1819; comprised what is now Colombia, Panama, Venezuela, and Ecuador (not completely independent of Spain until May 1822); at first known as Republic of Colombia but soon after as Great Colombia; ✱ Bogotá; terminated by secession of Venezuela 1829 and by establishment of Ecuador as independent state 1830. See COLOMBIA.

Great Com·o·ro \-ˈkäm-ə-ˌrō\ *or Fr.* **Grande–Co·more** \gräⁿ(n)d-kə-mȯ(ə)r\. Largest of the Comoro Is., N Mozambique Channel; 443 sq. m.; pop. (1970e) 132,000; N part a plateau, alt. ab. 2000 ft.; in S is Karthala volcano; chief town Moroni.

Great Corn Island. See CORN ISLANDS.

Great Crag·gy Mountains \-ˈkrag-ē-\. Range, W North Carolina; includes **Craggy Dome** 6105 ft., Buncombe co., and nearby **Craggy Pinnacle** 5944 ft. Extending 10 m. along crest of the range are the **Craggy Gardens,** a dense stand of purple rhododendron.

Great Crosby. See CROSBY 4.

Great Cumbrae Island. See CUMBRAES, THE.

Great Dayak. See KAHAJAN.

Great Divide. 1 Mountain range, North America. See CONTINENTAL DIVIDE.

2 Mountain range, Australia. See GREAT DIVIDING RANGE.

Great Dividing Range *or* **Great Divide** *or* **Eastern Highlands.** Entire extent of mountain ranges in Queensland, New South Wales, and Victoria, along E border of Australia; from 100 to 200 m. wide; includes Australian Alps (*q.v.*) in SE part, with highest summit in Australia (Mt. Kosciusko 7316 ft.); at N end is Atherton Plateau (*q.v.*).

Great Driffield. See DRIFFIELD.

Great Egg Harbor Inlet \-ˌeg-, -ˌäg-\. Narrow strait bet. Cape May and Atlantic cos., S New Jersey, leading from

UNITED KINGDOM
BONNE PROJECTION
Copyright by C. S. HAMMOND & Co., N.Y.
SCALE OF MILES
0 10 20 40 60 80
KILOMETERS
0 10 20 40 60 80
Capitals of Countries
Canals
Loch Lomond
Loch Long
R. Forth
Alloa
Kirkcaldy
Stirling
Dunfermline
Dumbarton
Falkirk
Firth of Forth
Clydebank
Forth & Clyde Canal
Bo'ness
Greenock
Port Glasgow
Glasgow
Edinburgh
Musselburgh
Paisley
R. Clyde
Airdrie
Coatbridge
Largs
Rutherglen
Motherwell
Hamilton
MILES
0 4 8 12 16
SHETLAND ISLANDS
Lerwick
Fair I.
SHETLAND ISLANDS
Same scale as main map
Yell
Unst
Fetlar
Papa Stour
Whalsay
Foula
Lerwick
Westray
Sanday
ORKNEY ISLANDS
Stronsay
Kirkwall
Hoy
Scapa Flow
Pentland Firth
C. Wrath
Strathy Pt.
Thurso
Wick
Lewis
Stornoway
HEBRIDES
North Minch
Loch Shin
Harris
Little Minch
Dornoch
Tain
Moray Firth
Invergordon
Fraserburgh
North Uist
Dingwall
Elgin
Buckie
Nairn
Peterhead
Skye
Inverness
R. Spey
South Uist
Loch Ness
Inverurie
Loch Arkaig
Caledonian Canal
Ballater
R. Dee
Aberdeen
Barra Isles
Rum I.
L. Shiel
Stonehaven
Sea of the Hebrides
Fort William
Ben Nevis 4,406
Brechin
Montrose
Coll
L. Linnhe
Forfar
Tiree
Dundee
Arbroath
Tobermory
Loch Tay
Perth
Mull
Oban
Firth of Tay
Kirkcaldy
St. Andrews
Inveraray
ATLANTIC
Firth of Lorne
Lochgilphead
Dunfermline
Firth of Forth
Falkirk
Greenock
Jura
Dunoon
Glasgow
Edinburgh
Berwick-upon-Tweed
Islay
Paisley
R. Clyde
OCEAN
Kilmarnock
Galashiels
Arran
Prestwick
Hawick
Alnwick
Malin Head
Campbeltown
L. Swilly
Ayr
R. Nith
Tory I.
Buncrana
Lough Foyle
Firth of Clyde
Maybole
Lockerbie
Blyth
Coleraine
North Channel
Girvan
Dumfries
Annan
Newcastle upon Tyne
South Shields
Aran I.
Londonderry
Limavady
Stranraer
Castle Douglas
Gateshead
Sunderland
Letterkenny
Ballymena
Carlisle
Bishop Auckland
Hartlepool
Ballyshannon
Strabane
NORTHERN
Larne
Luce Bay
Solway Firth
Workington
Rossan Pt.
Omagh
Lough Neagh
Belfast
Teesside
Donegal Bay
L. Erne
IRELAND
Lisburn
Whitehaven
Darlington
Whitby
Scarborough
Erris Head
Sligo Bay
Sligo
Enniskillen
Monaghan
Craigavon
Isle of Man
Northallerton
Malton
Flamborough Hd.
Ballina
Newry
Barrow-in-Furness
Kendal
Lancaster
Bridlington
Lough Conn
Lough Allen
Clones
Douglas
Morecambe Bay
Harrogate
York
Achill I.
Castlebar
Boyle
Cavan
Dundalk
Dundalk Bay
Bradford
Leeds
Beverley
Hull
NORTH
Clare I.
Westport
Longford
IRISH SEA
Blackpool
Preston
Wakefield
R. Aire
Grimsby
Lough Mask
Roscommon
Kells
An Uaimh
Drogheda
Blackburn
Manchester
Scunthorpe
SEA
Tuam
Lough Ree
Balbriggan
Doncaster
Slyne Head
Lough Corrib
IRELAND
Trim
Dublin
Anglesey
Liverpool
Sheffield
Rotherham
Ballinasloe
Athlone
Edenderry
Birkenhead
Worksop
Lincoln
Galway
Holyhead
Bangor
Colwyn Bay
Chesterfield
Galway Bay
Tullamore
Naas
Kingstown
Caernarvon
Chester
Crewe
Mansfield
Nottingham
Boston
The Wash
Loughrea
Bray
Snowdon 3,560
Hunstanton
Aran Is.
Lough Derg
Birr
Athy
Wicklow
Caernarvon Bay
Wrexham
Stoke-on-Trent
Derby
Grantham
King's Lynn
Great Yarmouth
Ennis
Nenagh
R. Barrow
Carlow
Wicklow Head
Ffestiniog
Stafford
R. Trent
Loughborough
Kilrush
Thurles
Kilkenny
Arklow
Wolverhampton
Leicester
Peterborough
Norwich
Limerick
Gorey
Barmouth
Shrewsbury
Walsall
Lowestoft
R. Shannon
Foynes
Enniscorthy
Tywyn
Dudley
Nuneaton
Kettering
Newmarket
Tipperary
Clonmel
New Ross
Cardigan Bay
Newtown
Birmingham
Coventry
R. Ouse
Bury St. Edmunds
Listowel
R. Suir
Wexford
Wexford Har.
Aberystwyth
Cambridge
Ipswich
Mallow
Waterford
Llandrindod Wells
Worcester
Northampton
Bedford
Colchester
Tralee
Blackwater
Dungarvan
Fishguard
Cardigan
WALES
Hereford
Luton
Dingle Bay
Killarney
Youghal
St. George's Channel
Cheltenham
Oxford
Hertford
Bandon
Cork
Cobh
Youghal Bay
Carmarthen
Brecknock
Ross-on-Wye
Gloucester
St. Albans
Romford
Southend-on-Sea
Cork Harbor
Milford Haven
Llanelli
Merthyr Tydfil
R. Severn
Stroud
Swindon
LONDON
Margate
Bantry Bay
Rosscarbery Bay
Pembroke
Swansea
Rhondda
Bristol
Newbury
R. Thames
Chatham
Canterbury
Cape Clear
Cardiff
Newport
Chippenham
Reading
Croydon
Dover
Bristol Channel
Bath
Aldershot
Reigate
Maidstone
Lundy I.
Salisbury
Winchester
Folkestone
Ilfracombe
Bridgwater
Southampton
Hastings
Strait of Dover
Calais
Barnstaple
Taunton
Yeovil
Gosport
Hove
Tiverton
Lymington
Portsmouth
Brighton
Eastbourne
Boulogne-sur-Mer
R. Exe
Bridport
Poole
Worthing
Okehampton
Exeter
Bournemouth
Isle of Wight
Tavistock
Torbay
Lyme Bay
Portland Bill
ENGLAND
Bodmin
St. Austell with Fowey
Camborne-Redruth
Devonport
Plymouth
Prawle Pt.
Land's End
Falmouth
Eddystone Rocks
Dieppe
Lizard Head
Scilly Is.
ENGLISH CHANNEL
Alderney
CHANNEL ISLANDS
Guernsey
Jersey
Baie de la Seine
Cherbourg
Le Havre
Rouen
FRANCE
Blackpool
Preston
Keighley
Bradford
Burnley
IRISH SEA
Blackburn
Halifax
Huddersfield
Southport
Bolton
Dewsbury
Manchester
Rochdale
Wigan
St. Helens
Oldham
Bootle
Salford
Hyde
Wallasey
Liverpool
Warrington
Stockport
R. Mersey
R. Dee
Ellesmere Port
Macclesfield
Chester
Crewe
MILES
0 4 8 12 16 20
Watford
Enfield
Cheshunt
Barnet
Brentwood
Haringey
Redbridge
R. Colne
Harrow
Havering
GREATER
Westminster
Newham
Barking
Ealing
R. Thames
Thurrock
Greenwich
Hounslow
LONDON
Bexley
Egham
Kingston upon T.
Bromley
Gravesend
Croydon
Esher
Woking
Epsom & Ewell
MILES
0 5 10
12°
10°
8°
6°
4°
2°
0°
2°
60°
58°
56°
54°
52°
50°
6° Longitude West of Greenwich 4°

Atlantic Ocean into **Great Egg Harbor;** receives the **Great Egg River** *or* **Great Egg Harbor River** (ab. 40 m. long, flows SE, lower part in Atlantic co.).

Great Elobey. See ELOBEY, GREAT.

Great End. Mountain, Cumberland, NW England, in Lake District; 2984 ft.

Greater An·chor·age Area \-'aŋ-k(ə-)rij-\. Borough in Alaska. See table at ALASKA.

Greater Antilles. See WEST INDIES.

Greater Armenia. See ARMENIA, GREATER.

Greater Athens. See ATHENS 10.

Greater Bombay. See BOMBAY 2.

Greater Copenhagen. See COPENHAGEN 2.

Greater Khingan Range. See KHINGAN 2.

Greater London. See LONDON 4.

Greater Montreal. See MONTREAL 2.

Greater New York. See NEW YORK 3.

Greater Phrygia. See PHRYGIA.

Greater Sit·ka \-'sit-kə\. Borough in Alaska. See table at ALASKA.

Greater Sunda Islands. See SUNDA ISLES.

Greater Tunb. See TUNB.

Greater Walachia. See MUNTENIA.

Greater Wollongong. See WOLLONGONG.

Great Exuma. See EXUMA.

Great Falls. 1 Falls, Kentucky. See CUMBERLAND 1.

2 Cataract in the Potomac river on boundary bet. Maryland and Virginia; in a series of rapids ab. 15 m. above Washington, D.C. where the river descends ab. 90 ft.; 35 ft. high.

3 Dam in Caney Fork river, forming **Great Falls Lake** bet. White and Warren cos., cen. Tennessee. See table at TENNESSEE VALLEY AUTHORITY.

4 City, ⊗ of Cascade co., cen. Montana, on Missouri river 12 m. N of the **Great Falls of the Missouri** (92 ft.); pop. (1970c) 60,091; copper refining and smelting; coal, natural gas, silver, and lead deposits; aluminum rolling mills; College of Great Falls (1932).

5 Town, Chester co., N South Carolina, ab. 22 m. SE of Chester; pop. (1970c) 2727; textile manufacturers.

Great Fish \-'fish\. 1 River in Canada. See BACK RIVER.

2 River, SE Cape Province, Rep. of South Africa; 400 m. long; flows SSE into Indian Ocean NE of Port Alfred.

3 River in South-West Africa. See FISH.

Great Gable. See GABLE, GREAT.

Great Geyser. See GEYSIR.

Great Grimsby. See GRIMSBY 2.

Great Gua·na Cay \-ˌgwän-ə-'kē, -'kā\. One of the Bahama Is., in Atlantic Ocean bet. SE Andros I. and Cat I.

Great Gull Island \-'gəl-\. Island at E end of Long Island Sound, New York, just NE of Plum I.

Great Har·wood \-'här-wu̇d\. Urban district, Lancashire, NW England, 22 m. N of Manchester; pop. (1971p) 11,000.

Great Inagua. See INAGUA.

Great Indian Desert. See THAR DESERT.

Great Isaacs \-'ī-ziks, -zəks\. Lighthouse (estab. 1859) on small cay in NW Bahama Is., NE of the Bimini.

Great Island. Island in Cork Harbour, S coast of Ireland; site of city of Cobh (Queenstown), Eire.

Great Kai Island. See KAI ISLANDS.

Great Kanawha. See KANAWHA.

Great Kapela. See KAPELA, GREAT.

Great Karimata. See KARIMATA ISLANDS.

Great Karroo. See KARROO.

Great Kei \-'kā, -'kī\. River, Cape Province, S Rep. of South Africa; ab. 150 m. long; flows SE to Indian Ocean.

Great Lake. Largest lake in Tasmania, Australia, in cen. part S of the Great Western Tiers; 44 sq. m.; ab. 15 m. long; 2880 ft. above sea level; largest natural freshwater lake in Australia; drained by Ouse river, a tributary of the Derwent; dam and hydroelectric plant; discovered 1815.

Great Lakes. 1 Chain of five lakes, Superior, Michigan, Huron, Erie, and Ontario (*qq.v.*), cen. North America; through the chain (except for Lake Michigan, which is wholly within the U.S.) runs the U.S.-Canada boundary; drained by St. Lawrence river. Discovered and explored in 17th cent. by French, Champlain probably being first to reach upper lakes 1615; Lake Michigan explored by Nicolet 1634; founding of Detroit (*q.v.*) 1701 assured French control of region until Canada was ceded to British 1763; lakes Ontario and Erie scenes of naval warfare bet. U.S. and British during War of 1812; disarmament effected under terms of Rush-Bagot Agreement 1817; came to be of great importance as commercial link bet. eastern and northwestern U.S., especially after building of steamships and of Erie Canal 1825.

2 Group of large lakes chiefly in Great Rift Valley, E cen. Africa, including esp. Lakes Rudolf, Albert, Victoria, Tanganyika, and Nyasa.

Great Lakes Naval Training Center. See WAUKEGAN.

Great Lyakhov. See LYAKHOV ISLANDS.

Great Mar·low \-'mär-(ˌ)lō\. Parish, part of Marlow urban dist., Buckinghamshire, S cen. England, near Windsor; residence of Shelley and Peacock.

Great Meadows. Level area on the Youghiogheny river, SW Pennsylvania, ab. 10 m. E of present Uniontown; site of Fort Necessity, built 1754 under Washington's supervision in campaign against French at Fort Duquesne.

Great Miami. See MIAMI 1.

Great Miquelon. See MIQUELON ISLAND.

Great Namaqualand. See NAMAQUALAND.

Great Natoena. See NATUNA ISLANDS.

Great Neck \'grāt-ˌnek\. Residential village, Nassau co., SE New York, on N shore of Long I.; pop. (1970c) 10,724.

Great Neck Estates. Residential village, Nassau co., SE New York, on N shore of Long I.; pop. (1970c) 3131.

Great Neck Plaza. Residential village, Nassau co., SE New York, on N shore of Long I., near Great Neck; pop. (1970c) 5921.

Great Nemaha. See NEMAHA.

Great Nethe. See NETHE.

Great Nic·o·bar \-'nik-ə-ˌbär\. One of the Nicobar Is. (*q.v.*).

Great Novgorod. See NOVGOROD 2.

Great Ormes Head \-'ó(ə)rmz-\. Cape extending into Irish Sea on N coast of Wales, E of Anglesey I.; lighthouse.

Great Ouse. See OUSE 1.

Great Pat·er·nos·ter Point \-ˌpat-ər-ˌnäs-tər-, -ˌpät-\. Cape on W coast of Cape Province, Rep. of South Africa, S of Saint Helena Bay.

Great Peconic Bay. See PECONIC BAY.

Great Plains. The continental slope of cen. North America (United States and Canada) extending E from the Rocky Mts. to the margin of the Central Plains in the U.S. and to the margin of the Laurentian Highlands in Canada; N to S extent is from delta of Mackenzie river to S Texas; characterized by smooth, treeless plains traversed by broad, shallow valleys of rivers rising in Rocky Mts., but in some sections with sand hills (esp. in NW Nebraska), buttes, and badlands.

Great Point. Northeastern point of Nantucket I., Massachusetts.

Great Rann of Kutch. See KUTCH, RANN OF.

Great Re·dang \-'rā-ˌdäŋ\ *or* **Redang.** Island off E coast of Malay Penin. in South China Sea.

Great Rift Valley \-'rift-\. A great depression extending from valley of the Jordan in SW Asia S to Mozambique, SE Africa— a geological rather than a geographical term; marks a series of geological faults which are the result of great volcanic action; includes Dead Sea, Gulf of 'Aqaba, Red Sea, the chain of lakes in S Ethiopia, Lake Rudolf and the chain of small lakes S of it in Kenya and Tanzania which are in eastern rift valley, and Lakes Albert, Edward, Kivu, Tanganyika, and Nyasa in western rift valley. Below sea level at Dead Sea but in Africa in some places at over 6000 ft. (as at Lake Naivasha in the eastern rift which has elevation of 6135 ft.); esp. marked in cen. Kenya in the eastern rift valley bet. 1°N and 1°S where it has perpendicular cliffs several thousand feet high.

Great Ru·a·ha \-rü-ˈä-(ˌ)hä\. River in cen. Tanzania, E Africa; ab. 300 m. long; flows E into Rufiji river.

Great Sac·an·da·ga Reservoir \-ˌsak-ən-ˈdȯ-gə-\. Reservoir in Sacandaga river, E Fulton and W Saratoga cos., E New York; 42 sq. m. and 27 m. long; formed by Conklingville Dam; completed 1930; regulates flow of upper Hudson. Now a summer resort.

Great Saint Ber·nard \-ˌsānt-bər-ˈnärd\. Alpine pass. See ALPS.

Great Salt Desert \-ˌsȯlt-\. See DASHT-E-KAVĪR.

Great Salt Lake. Lake in Great Basin of United States, in Box Elder, Tooele, Salt Lake, Davis, and Weber cos., N Utah; ab. 83 m. long, 51 m. wide; ab. 2000 sq. m.; max. depth ab. 35 ft.; waters strongly saline; mean elevation, 4200 ft.; receives Bear, Jordan, and Weber rivers from E; no outlet; has a number of islands, including Antelope Island (36 sq. m.). Discovered by James Bridger 1824.

Great Salt Lake Desert. Broad, flat, low area SW of Great Salt Lake, N Utah; ab. 110 m. long; barren and uncultivated.

Great Salt Plains Dam. Dam across Salt Fork of Arkansas river in Grant co., N Oklahoma, forming reservoir 10 m. long for flood control and conservation.

Great Sand Dunes National Monument. See UNITED STATES, *National Monuments.*

Great Sandy Desert \-ˌsan-dē-\. 1 Desert, Arabian Penin. See RUBʻ AL-KHALI.
2 Tract of arid country, N cen. Western Australia. See CANNING BASIN.

Great Sandy Island. See FRASER ISLAND.

Great Sangir. See SANGIHE ISLANDS.

Great Sark. See SARK 1.

Great Scheidegg. See SCHEIDEGG.

Great Schütt \-ˈshüt\ *or Slovak* **Os·trov** \ˈȯs-(ˌ)trȯf\ *or formerly* **Vel'·ký Žit·ný** \ˌvel-kē-ˈzhit-nē\ *or Hung.* **Csal·ló·köz**\ˈchȯ-lō-ˌkərz\. Island, Slovak S.R., Czechoslovakia; 728 sq. m.; formed by arms of Danube river to the N of the main stream extending from Bratislava to Komárom; 53 m. long, bet. 9 and 18 m. wide.

Great Sea, The. The Mediterranean— esp. in Biblical usage (as in *Num.* xxxiv. 6).

Great Ser·pent Mound \-ˈsər-pənt-\. Prehistoric earthwork, Adams co., S Ohio; ab. 1330 ft. long; 20 ft. wide at base, averages ab. 3 ft. high; walls indicate possibility it was used for defense; probably mostly used in religious worship; in Serpent Mound State Park.

Great Sit·kin \-ˈsit-kən\. Small island NE of Adak I. in Andreanof Is., Aleutian Is.

Great Skellig. See SKELLIGS.

Great Slave Lake \-ˈslāv-\. Lake in S Mackenzie dist., Northwest Territories, Canada; 10,980 sq. m.; 298 m. long; max. depth 2015 ft.; of irregular shape, with several long arms; outlet the Mackenzie, flowing from its W end; on S receives Slave river, the outlet of Lake Athabaska, and on SW the Hay river. Discovered 1771.

Great Slave River. See SLAVE.

Great Smoky Mountains \-ˈsmō-kē-\ *or* **Great Smok·ies** \-kēz\. Range of the Appalachian Mts. extending along North Carolina-Tennessee boundary; highest peak Clingmans Dome 6643 ft.; remarkable for its flora, includes largest tract of hardwood in America and largest virgin forest of red spruce. Has been set aside as **Great Smoky Mountains National Park:** see UNITED STATES, *National Parks.*

Great Sound. Body of water enclosed by curve at W end of Bermuda I.

Great South Bay. Long narrow inlet of Atlantic Ocean bet. Fire I. and S shore of Long I., New York.

Great Trail. Indian trail from Fort Pitt at junction of Allegheny and Monongahela rivers to present site of Detroit; used by white men until Cumberland Road opened.

Great Tupper Lake. See TUPPER LAKES.

Great Vic·to·ria Desert \-vik-ˌtōr-ē-ə-, -ˌtȯr-\. Desert region in SE Western Australia and W South Australia; ab. 450 m. E to W; average height 500 to 1000 ft., sloping to Nullarbor Plain on S.

Great Wall *or* **Chinese Wall** *or Chin.* **Chang–chêng** \ˈjäŋ-ˈchəŋ\. Defensive wall with towers at intervals, N China, extending for ab. 1500 m. from Kansu prov. to the Gulf of Chihli (Po Hai); 20 to 50 ft. high, 15 to 25 ft. thick; built in the 3d cent. B.C. (completed 204 B.C.) by the emperor Shih Huang Ti; actual length, including branches and windings, more than 2000 m.; built by 300,000 men, mostly criminals; had four important gates: Shan-hai-kuan (at E end), Nankow (leading to Kalgan), Yen-man (N Shansi), and Chia-yü-kuan (Kiayukwan at extreme W in Kansu).

Great Wass \-ˈwäs\. Island in Atlantic Ocean off coast of Washington co., SE Maine.

Great Western Tiers \-ˈti(ə)rz\. Mountain range in N cen. Tasmania, Australia, extending NW and SE along N border of the lake region; highest peak ab. 4200 ft.

Great Whale \-ˈhwā(ə)l, -ˈwā(ə)l\. River, cen. and W Quebec, Canada; 230 m. long; flows W into SE Hudson Bay; outlet of Bienville Lake.

Great Yarmouth. See YARMOUTH 5.

Great Zab. See ZAB, GREAT.

Great Zimbabwe. See ZIMBABWE.

Gre·co, Cape \-ˈgrek-(ˌ)ō, -ˈgrāk-, -ˈgrēk-\. Southeastern point of Cyprus, at S end of Famagusta Bay.

Gredos, Sierra de. See SIERRA DE GREDOS.

Greece \ˈgrēs\ *or Gk.* **El·lás** \e-ˈläs\ *or anc.* **Hel·las** \ˈhel-əs\. Kingdom, S Europe, SW part of Balkan Penin., bounded on N by Albania, Yugoslavia, and Bulgaria, on NE by Turkey, on E by Aegean Sea, on S by Mediterranean, and on W by Ionian Sea; 50,944 sq. m.; pop. (1971p) 8,745,084; ✱ Athens; incl. Aegean Is., Ionian Is., and Crete. *Physical features:* Forms a peninsula of irregular shape, with many deep indentations in coastline and two large peninsulas projecting from it: in NE Chalcidice with its three long projections, in S the Peloponnesus (in medieval times Morea), joined to N part by Isthmus of Corinth and ending in three long peninsulas, the cen. one ending in Cape Taínaron, the southernmost point of the mainland. *Islands:* Near coast the Ionian Is. on W and S and Euboea on E; in Aegean Sea the large groups of Cyclades, North and South Sporades, and Dodecanese (*q.v.*); Thasos, Samothrace, and Lemnos in N Aegean; Lesbos, Chios, and Samos in E Aegean off W coast of Turkey in Asia; Crete to the SE in the Mediterranean. *Mountains:* Pindus Mts. in Epirus; peaks of Olympus and Ossa on E coast; Othrys range, Oeta and Parnassus in cen. part; and Cyllene and Erymanthus, with many ranges, in the Peloponnesus. *Chief rivers:* Peneus, Achelous, Arakhthos, Cephisus, and Alpheus; most rivers short. *Chief products:* Wheat, tobacco, olives, corn; viticulture; ab. 25 percent of total land area is cultivable; fishing; iron ore, bauxite, magnesite, zinc; manufacturing: textiles, cement, chemicals; tourism. *Chief cities:* Athens, Salonika, Piraeus, Patras, Nikhía, Peristéri, Candia.

In ancient times divided into regions which were at times independent kingdoms: Thrace, Macedonia, Epirus, Thessaly, Peloponnesus, and which were, esp. in S Greece, made up of many subdivisions (provinces or states), some of great historical importance in the classic period, as, Attica, Boeotia, Phocis, Aetolia, Achaea, Corinth, Elis, Arcadia, Laconia, and Messenia.

[In modern Greece many names are somewhat changed in form because of difference in transliteration systems of ancient and modern Greek. In this book the form preferred for the more important ancient names is generally the common, well-known spelling.] Divided into the following ten regions (*dhiamérismata*) which in turn are subdivided into a number of departments (*nomói*)— for pronunciation of their names, see their individual entries:

NAME	AREA (sq. m.)	POP. (1971p)	CAPITAL
Aegean Islands			
Chios	349	53,942	Chios
Cyclades	993	86,084	Hermoupolis
Dodecanese	1,028	120,258	Rhodes
Lesbos	832	114,504	Mytilene
Samos	300	41,687	Vathy
Central Greece and Euboea			
Aetolia and Acarnania	2,103	228,719	Mesolóngion
Attica	964	201,460*	Athens
Boeotia	1,240	114,288	Lebadea
Euboea	1,509	165,822	Chalcis
Eurytania	790	29,476	Karpenision
Phocis	819	41,530	Amphissa
Phthiotis	1,686	154,720	Lamia
Piraeus	339	55,672	Piraeus
Crete			
Canea	917	119,595	Canea
Hērákleion	1,020	209,652	Candia
Lasithion	702	66,105	Hagios Nikólaos
Rethýmnē	578	60,856	Rethymnon
Epirus			
Arta	622	78,039	Arta
Ioannina	1,927	139,356	Ioannina
Preveza	419	56,616	Preveza
Thesprotia	585	40,547	Egoumenitsa
Greater Athens	167	2,530,207	Athens
Ionian Islands			
Cephalonia	339	36,657	Argostolion
Corfu	247	92,261	Corfu
Leukas	125	24,559	Leukas
Zante	157	30,156	Zante
Macedonia			
Chalcidice	1,267	75,564	Polygyros
Drama	1,339	91,015	Drama
Florina	719	52,213	Florina
Grevená	903	35,385	Grevená
Hematheia	656	118,000	Veroia
Kastoria	651	45,628	Kastoria
Kavalla	814	121,491	Kavalla
Kilkís	1,003	84,539	Kilkís
Kozánē	1,375	135,619	Kozánē
Pella	968	126,201	Edessa
Pieria	598	91,380	Katerínē
Serrai	1,539	202,771	Serrai
Thessalonike	1,375	703,350	Salonika
Peloponnese			
Achaea	1,239	238,594	Patras
Arcadia	1,706	122,068	Tripolis
Argolis	855	89,044	Nauplia
Corinth	884	112,404	Corinth
Elis	1,035	164,860	Pyrgos
Laconia	1,404	95,800	Sparta
Messenia	1,155	172,850	Kalamata
Thessaly			
Karditsa	995	133,756	Karditsa
Larissa	2,067	232,157	Larissa
Magnesia	1,018	161,510	Volos
Trikkala	1,289	131,820	Trikkala
Thrace			
Evros	1,638	141,002	Alexandroúpolis
Rhodope	982	107,618	Komotinē
Xanthe	692	80,677	Xanthe

*Does not incl. pop. of Greater Athens.

History: Mainland site of early civilizations of Aegean origin (see MYCENAE, TIRYNS); c. 1500–1000 B.C. invaded by Greeks, a people from NW of Balkan Mts., who soon formed many small independent city-kingdoms; in age of commercial and industrial advance c. 750–550 B.C., Greek city-states founded colonies in N Aegean, on shores of Black Sea, in S Asia Minor and Cyprus, in Nile delta and near Cyrene, in N shores of W Mediterranean, and, most important, in S Italy (see MAGNA GRAECIA) and Sicily; ancient Greece never achieved political unity, but Sparta in Peloponnesus and Athens in Attica became predominant states while all states participated in shifting and loosely organized leagues; finally repulsed Persian invasions at Plataea in 479 B.C.; Athenian empire developed in 5th cent. B.C. and was broken by Peloponnesian Wars 460–404 B.C.; in 4th cent. B.C., Greek states became dependent upon Macedon until liberated by Rome at Cynoscephalae 197 B.C.; gradually conquered by Rome which set up provinces of Epirus, Achaea, and Macedonia; part of Byzantine Empire until 1204 when Constantinople was captured at end of Fourth Crusade and Baldwin I became first of the Latin emperors; again part of Byzantine Empire (*q.v.*) 1261 until its fall 1453; became part of Ottoman Empire when conquered by Turks 1456; modern Greek kingdom won independence from Turkey in war 1821–29; received Ionian Is. 1864, Thessaly and part of Epirus 1881; defeated by Turkey in brief war over Crete (*q.v.*) which Greece finally annexed 1913; as result of Balkan Wars 1912–13, gained several islands in Aegean and territory in Macedonia; declared war on Germany 1916; at close of war with Turkey 1920–22, gave back E Thrace, İmroz, and Bozcaada and claim to Dodecanese (former gains by Treaty of Sèvres 1920); exchanged population with Turkey 1923–30; republic 1924–35; joined Balkan Pact 1934; restored monarchy 1935; invaded by Italy 1940 and conquered by Germany 1941; liberated by Greek and British troops Sept. 24–Oct. 30, 1944; recalled King George to throne by plebiscite 1946; fought civil war 1946–49; received Dodecanese 1947; became a member of NATO 1951, and an associate member of the European Economic Community 1962; civilian government overthrown in *coup d'état* 1967.

Gree·ley \'grē-lē\. 1 Name of counties in two states of the U.S. See tables at KANSAS and NEBRASKA.

2 City, ⊗ of Weld co., N Colorado; pop. (1970c) 38,902; food processing; Colorado State Coll. (1889), Aims Coll. (1967); incorporated as a city 1885.

3 *or* **Greeley Center.** Village, ⊗ of Greeley co., E cen. Nebraska; pop. (1970c) 580.

Green \'grēn\. 1 River, N Illinois; 120 m. long; flows SW out of Lee co. to Rock river.

2 Navigable river, E cen. Kentucky; 360 m. long; flows from cen. Lincoln co., W and NW into Ohio river.

3 River, W cen. Washington; flows W through S King co. to unite with White river and form Duwamish river.

4 River, W United States; 730 m. long; flows from Wind River Range, NE Sublette co., W Wyoming, S into Utah where it turns E, makes a loop in NW corner of Colorado, then turns SW and S in Utah to enter Colorado river on boundary bet. Wayne and San Juan cos., SE Utah.

5 Name of counties in two states of the U.S. See tables at KENTUCKY and WISCONSIN.

Green Bank. Locality, Pocahontas co., E West Virginia, ab. 20 m. NE of Marlinton; site of National Radio Astronomy Observatory.

Green Bay. 1 Inlet of NW Lake Michigan, on shore of S Michigan penin. and NE Wisconsin; ab. 120 m. long; 10 to 20 m. wide; average depth ab. 100 ft.; from early visits by French explorers (see WISCONSIN) was head of important portage route bet. Great Lakes and Mississippi river by way of Fox and Wisconsin rivers (*qq.v.*).

2 City, ⊗ of Brown co., E Wisconsin, on S end of Green Bay at mouth of Fox river; pop. (1970c) 87,809; port for river and lake steamers; meat-packing plants, fisheries, shipyard, limestone quarries; manufactures paper, iron and steel, auto parts; dairy products. Visited by Jean Nicolet 1634; settled by Langlade 1745, oldest settlement in Wisconsin; in region controlled by British 1763; ceded to U.S. 1783; fur-trading center; occupied by British in War of 1812; Fort Howard, U.S. military post, built 1816; incorp. as city 1854.

Green·belt \'grēn-ˌbelt\. City, Prince Georges co., S cen. Maryland; pop. (1970c) 18,199; built 1935–38 by U.S. government to provide low-priced housing for families of moderate income.

Green·bri·er \'grēn-ˌbrī(-ə)r\. 1 River, SE West Virginia; ab. 175 m. long; rises in N Pocahontas co., flows SW into New river near Hinton.

2 County in West Virginia. See table at WEST VIRGINIA.

Green·cas·tle \'grēn-ˌkas-əl\. 1 City, ⊗ of Putnam co., W cen. Indiana, 32 m. ENE of Terre Haute; pop. (1970c) 8852;

GREECE
CONIC PROJECTION
SCALE OF MILES
0 25 50 75 100 125 150
SCALE OF KILOMETERS
0 25 50 75 100 125 150
Capitals of Countries
Administrative Centers
© Copyright HAMMOND INCORPORATED, Maplewood, N. J.
Longitude East of Greenwich
20° 22° 24° 26° 28°
42° 40° 38° 36° 34°
YUGOSLAVIA
ALBANIA
BULGARIA
TURKEY
MACEDONIA
THRACE
EPIRUS
THESSALÍA
CENTRAL GREECE AND EUBOEA
PELOPONNISOS
IONIAN SEA
IONIAN IS.
AEGEAN SEA
SEA OF MARMARA
BLACK SEA
SEA OF CRETE
MIRTÓÖN SEA
CYCLADES ISLANDS
NORTHERN SPORADES
DODECANESE IS.
Balkan Mts.
Rhodope Mts.
Pindus Mts.
Athens
Thessaloníki
(Salonika)
Pátrai
(Patras)
Piraiévs
Iráklion
(Candia)
Khaniá
(Canea)
Crete
Rhodes
Sofia
Tiranë (Tirana)
Skopje
Edirne
Izmir
(Smyrna)
Kérkira
(Corfu)
Lárisa
Vólos
Kaválla
Xánthi
Komotiní
Alexandroúpolis
Kalámai
Trípolis
Kórinth
Lamía
Khíos
Mitilíni
Lésvos
Límnos
Sámos
Náxos
Kos
Kárpathos
Ródhos
(Rhodes)
Olympus 9,570
Athos 6,667
Musalá 9,596
Smólikas 8,352
Taíyetos 7,897
Ídhi 8,058
A
GREATER ATHENS
Athens
(Athínai)
Lycabettus 909
Acropolis
Piraiévs
Níkaia
Áyios Yeóryios
Salamis
Bay of Elevsís
Bay of Salamis
Bay of Fáliron
Kifisiá
Amaroúsion
Néa Ionía
Khalándri
Peristéri
Kallithéa
Moskháton
Néa Smírni
Áyios Dhimítrios
Víron
Kaisarianí
Imittós
MILES
0 1 2 3 4 5

dairy farming, lumbering; limestone quarries; DePauw Univ. (1837).

2 Borough, Franklin co., S Pennsylvania, 12 m. S of Chambersburg; pop. (1970c) 3293; canned goods.

Green Cove Springs \ˈgrēn-ˌkōv-\. City, ⊗ of Clay co., NE Florida, on St. Johns river 25 m. S of Jacksonville; pop. (1970c) 3857; health resort; sport fishing.

Green·dale \ˈgrēn-ˌdāl\. 1 Town, Dearborn co., SE Indiana, suburb of Lawrenceburg on Ohio river; pop. (1970c) 3783; distilleries.

2 Residential village, Milwaukee co., SE Wisconsin; pop. (1970c) 15,809; built by U.S. government as experiment in city planning and low-cost housing; incorp. 1938.

Greene \ˈgrēn\. Name of counties in fourteen states of the U.S. See tables at ALABAMA, ARKANSAS, GEORGIA, ILLINOIS, INDIANA, IOWA, MISSISSIPPI, MISSOURI, NEW YORK, NORTH CAROLINA, OHIO, PENNSYLVANIA, TENNESSEE, VIRGINIA.

Greene·ville \ˈgrēn-ˌvil, -vəl\. Town, ⊗ of Greene co., NE Tennessee, 30 m. WSW of Johnson City; pop. (1970c) 13,722; burley tobacco market; electronic equipment, fertilizer; Tusculum Coll. (1794). Capital of State of Franklin 1785–87; home of Andrew Johnson, his homestead, tailor shop, and burial place set aside as a national historic site.

Green·field \ˈgrēn-ˌfēld\. 1 City, Monterey co., W California, 32 m. SE of Salinas; pop. (1970c) 2608; diversified agriculture.

2 City, ⊗ of Hancock co., cen. Indiana, 20 m. E of Indianapolis; pop. (1970c) 9986; cans tomatoes; birthplace of James Whitcomb Riley.

3 City, ⊗ of Adair co., SW cen. Iowa, 50 m. WSW of Des Moines; pop. (1970c) 2212; livestock.

4 Town, ⊗ of Franklin co., NW Massachusetts, on Connecticut river 34 m. N of Springfield; pop. (1970c) 18,116; manufactures taps and dies and other hardware, silverware; Greenfield Community Coll. (1962); founded 1686, originally part of Deerfield.

5 City, ⊗ of Dade co., SW Missouri; pop. (1970c) 1172; fruit; livestock.

6 Industrial village, Highland co., S Ohio, 21 m. W of Chillicothe; pop. (1970c) 4780; stone quarries.

7 Town, Weakley co., NW Tennessee, 30 m. WSW of Paris; pop. (1970c) 2050; cotton; dairying.

8 City, Milwaukee co., W Wisconsin, SE of Winona, Minnesota; pop. (1970c) 24,424; residential.

Greenfield Park. Town, Chambly co., S Quebec, Canada, 4 m. E of Montreal on opp. side of St. Lawrence; pop. (1971p) 15,277.

Green·hills \ˈgrēn-ˌhilz\. Village, Hamilton co., SW corner of Ohio, near Cincinnati; pop. (1970c) 6092; completed 1937 as a federal government project in low-cost housing.

Green Island. Industrial village, Albany co., E New York, on an island in Hudson river 8 m. N of Albany; pop. (1970c) 3297; automobile assembly plant.

Green Islands. Group of small islands in extreme N Solomon Is., W Pacific Ocean, 45 m. NNW of Buka I.; largest Nissan I., ab. 30 sq. m.; administratively part of Papua New Guinea.

Green Lake. 1 Lake, Green Lake co., cen. Wisconsin, 25 m. W of Fond du Lac; ab. 7 m. long.

2 County in Wisconsin. See table at WISCONSIN.

3 Village, ⊗ of Green Lake co., cen. Wisconsin, at NE end of Green Lake; pop. (1970c) 1109; resort.

Green·land \ˈgrēn-lənd, -ˌland\ or *Dan.* **Grøn·land** \ˈgrœn-ˌlän\. Island, NE North America; 839,999 sq. m. (of which ab. 135,000 sq. m. are ice-free); pop. (1970e) 46,331; ❋ Godthåb; an integral part of the Danish realm. *Physical features:* Largest island in the world (exclusive of Australia); greater part lies within Arctic Circle; max. length ab. 1650 m., max. breadth ab. 800 m.; max. ice thickness ab. 11,000 ft.; numerous islands (largest is Disko) along coastline, which is deeply indented with fjords; highest peak is Mt. Gunnbjørn 12,139 ft. *Chief products:* Cryolite (largest deposits in the world), coal, lead, zinc; fishing, hunting. *Chief communities:* Godthåb, Holsteinsborg, Sukkertoppen, Egedesminde, Julianehåb.

History: Discovered and colonized in 10th cent. A.D. by Eric the Red, Norse leader, whose son, Leif Ericson, was traditional discoverer of North America; visited by Davis, Hudson, Baffin ab. end of 16th cent.; from 19th cent., explored by Kane, Hall, Nordenskjøld, by Nansen who made first crossing of Greenland 1888, Peary, and other expeditions of Danish, American, Norwegian, German, and British nationality; visited by Danish expedition of Mylius-Erichsen 1902–07; Danish East Greenland Company, founded 1919, established posts; made crown colony 1924 by Denmark which claimed full sovereignty 1921; eastern Greenland, annexed by Norway 1931, awarded to Denmark by decision of World Court 1933; after occupation of Denmark by Germans in 1940, subject of an agreement Apr. 9, 1941 (ratified by Danish Rigsdag May 1945) by which U.S. was permitted to establish air bases, weather stations, etc., necessary for protection of the island and preservation of Danish sovereignty there during World War II; conclusion of U.S.-Danish treaty (1951) providing for joint defense of Greenland; status changed from colony to (Danish) province 1953; initiation of major development program (financed by Denmark) 1966.

Greenland Sea. Section of Arctic Ocean off NE coast of Greenland; now generally considered as part of Norwegian Sea.

Green·lawn \ˈgrēn-ˌlȯn, -ˌlän\. Urban community (unincorporated), Suffolk co., New York, on Long I. E of Huntington; pop. (1970c) 8178.

Green·lee \ˈgrēn-(ˌ)lē\. County in Arizona. See table at ARIZONA.

Green Lowther. See LOWTHERS, THE.

Green·ly \ˈgrēn-lē\. Small island in Quebec, Canada, at W end of Strait of Belle Isle opp. the Labrador line.

Green Mountain. 1 Peak, Lawrence co., W South Dakota; 5101 ft.

2 Crater, Ascension. See ASCENSION 2.

Green Mountains. A range of the Appalachian system, extending from Canada through Vermont into W Massachusetts; highest peak Mount Mansfield 4393 ft.

Green·ock \ˈgrēn-ək, ˈgrin-, ˈgren-\. Seaport and manufacturing burgh, Renfrew co., SW Scotland, on S shore of the Firth of Clyde; pop. (1970e) 69,004; shipbuilding; iron foundries, distilleries, sugar refineries, textile and paper mills; birthplace of James Watt.

Green Pe·ter Dam *and* **Green Peter Reservoir** \-ˌpēt-ər-\. See UNITED STATES, *Dams and Reservoirs.*

Green·point \ˈgrēn-ˌpȯint\. District, N Brooklyn borough, New York City, bounded on W by the East river; formerly a shipbuilding center, place where *Monitor* was built (launched Jan. 30, 1862).

Green Point. Town, W suburb of Cape Town, Cape Province, Rep. of South Africa. See SEA POINT.

Green·port \ˈgrēn-ˌpō(ə)rt, -ˌpȯ(ə)rt\. Village, Suffolk co., SE New York, on N extension of Long I. bet. Long Island Sound and Gardiners Bay; pop. (1970c) 2481; summer resort; oyster and fishing industries; shipbuilding.

Green River. 1 For rivers. See GREEN.

2 Town, ⊗ of Sweetwater co., SW Wyoming, on Green river 15 m. W of Rock Springs; pop. (1970c) 4196; lumbering, coal mining; livestock.

Green River Mountain. Peak, N Sublette co., W Wyoming; 10,175 ft.

Green Rock. City, Henry co., NW Illinois; pop. (1970c) 2744.

Greens·boro \ˈgrēnz-ˌbər-ə, -ˌbə-rə\. 1 Town, ⊗ of Hale co., W Alabama, 35 m. S of Tuscaloosa; pop. (1970c) 3371; lumber mills; settled 1816, incorp. 1823; former site (1856–1918) of Southern Univ. (now Birmingham-Southern Coll. at Birmingham); antebellum mansions.

2 City, ⊗ of Greene co., NE cen. Georgia, 29 m. SSE of Athens; pop. (1970c) 2583; cotton mills.

3 City, ⊗ of Guilford co., N cen. North Carolina, 26 m. E of Winston-Salem; pop. (1970c) 144,076; cellophane products, chemicals; textile mills, terra-cotta works, foundries, machine shops; Guilford Coll. (1834), Greensboro Coll. (1838), Bennett Coll. (1873), Univ. of North Carolina at Greensboro (1891), North Carolina Agricultural and Technical State Univ. (1891); made ⊗ 1808; Guilford Courthouse National Military Park (see UNITED STATES, *National Historical Parks*) nearby.

Greens·burg \'grēnz-ˌbərg\. 1 City, ⊗ of Decatur co., SE cen. Indiana, 18 m. SE of Shelbyville; pop. (1970c) 8620; auto accessories, cement blocks.

2 City, ⊗ of Kiowa co., S Kansas; pop. (1970c) 1907; wheat; livestock.

3 City, ⊗ of Green co., cen. Kentucky; pop. (1970c) 1990; timber, tobacco.

4 Town, ⊗ of Saint Helena parish, E Louisiana; pop. (1970c) 652.

5 City, ⊗ of Westmoreland co., SW Pennsylvania, 27 m. ESE of Pittsburgh; pop. (1970c) 15,870; glass, metal products; oil refining; coal mines; Seton Hill Coll. (1883); founded 1785.

Greens Peak \'grēnz-\. Mountain, S Apache co., E Arizona; 10,115 ft.

Greens·ville \'grēnz-ˌvil, -vəl\. County in Virginia. See table at VIRGINIA.

Green·tree \'grēn-ˌtrē\. Borough, Allegheny co., SW Pennsylvania, 4 m. W of Pittsburgh; pop. (1970c) 6441.

Green·up \'grēn-əp\. 1 County in NE Kentucky. See table at KENTUCKY.

2 City, its ⊗; pop. (1970c) 1284; sawmills; truck farming.

Green·ville \'grēn-ˌvil, -vəl\. 1 County in South Carolina. See table at SOUTH CAROLINA.

2 Commercial city, ⊗ of Butler co., S Alabama, 42 m. SW of Montgomery; pop. (1970c) 8033; fertilizer; lumber; feed mills; settled 1819, incorp. 1889.

3 City, ⊗ of Meriwether co., W Georgia; pop. (1970c) 1085.

4 City, ⊗ of Bond co., SW cen. Illinois, 47 m. ENE of East St. Louis; pop. (1970c) 4631; alfalfa; Greenville Coll. (1855).

5 City, ⊗ of Muhlenberg co., W Kentucky, 30 m. NNE of Hopkinsville; pop. (1970c) 3875; tobacco; coal mining.

6 Town, Piscataquis co., N cen. Maine, on Moosehead Lake 60 m. NW of Bangor; pop. (1970c) 1894.

7 City, Montcalm co., cen. Michigan, 25 m. ENE of Grand Rapids; pop. (1970c) 7493; auto bearings, farm implements.

8 City, ⊗ of Washington co., W Mississippi, on Mississippi river; pop. (1970c) 39,648; auto parts, concrete products, lumber; fisheries.

9 City, ⊗ of Wayne co., SE Missouri; pop. (1970c) 328.

10 City, ⊗ of Pitt co., E North Carolina, 33 m. SE of Rocky Mount; pop. (1970c) 29,063; market for tobacco, cotton, corn; East Carolina Univ. (1907).

11 City, ⊗ of Darke co., W Ohio, 32 m. NW of Dayton; pop. (1970c) 12,380; manufactures stoves, concrete, medicines; gravel pits. On site of Fort Greenville (built 1793) where Anthony Wayne's treaty with Indians was signed 1795, and of Shawnee Indian village, home of Tecumseh; became county seat 1809.

12 Borough, Mercer co., W Pennsylvania, 27 m. N of New Castle; pop. (1970c) 8704; railroad cars, aluminum products; truck farms; Thiel Coll. (1866); settled 1796.

13 City, ⊗ of Greenville co., NW South Carolina, 100 m. NW of Charleston; pop. (1970c) 61,438; textile center; manufactures cotton, rayon, and worsted goods, textile machinery, clothing, cottonseed oil, peanut products; chemicals and patent medicines; tourist resort in piedmont region of Blue Ridge; Furman Univ. (1825), Bob Jones Univ. (1927).

14 City, ⊗ of Hunt co., NE Texas, 43 m. NE of Dallas; pop. (1970c) 22,043; manufactures cottonseed oil, flour, foundry products; oil refinery, cotton compress.

Greenville \'grēn-ˌvil\ *also* **Si·no** \'sē-ˌnō\. Coastal town, SE Liberia, W Africa, 105 m. NW of Cape Palmas; pop. (1962c) 3962.

Green·wa·ter Lake Park \'grēn-ˌwȯt-ər-, -ˌwät-\. Canadian provincial park, E cen. Saskatchewan, SE of Prince Albert; 35 sq. m.; virgin forests, many lakes.

Green·wich. 1 \'gren-ich, 'grēn-ˌwich, 'grin-ˌwich\. Residential town, SW Fairfield co., SW Connecticut, on Long Island Sound on New York border; pop. (1970c) 59,775; settled 1640; annexed to Connecticut 1656.

2 \'grēn-ˌwich\. Village, Washington co., E New York, 27 m. NNE of Troy; pop. (1970c) 2092; manufactures paper, thread.

3 \'grin-ij, 'gren-, -ich\. A borough of Greater London, SE England. See table at LONDON 4. Site of Royal Greenwich Observatory 1675–1958; the Greenwich meridian serves as the basis for standard time throughout the world and for reckonings of longitude.

4 \'gren-ich, 'grin-, -ij\. Island in South Shetland Is. (*q.v.*).

Greenwich Village \ˌgren-ich-, ˌgrin-, -ij-\. Formerly a village on Manhattan I., now a part of Manhattan borough, New York City, bounded approximately by W 14th St., Spring St., Broadway, and the Hudson river; long frequented by authors, artists, and students.

Green·wood \'grēn-ˌwu̇d\. 1 Name of counties in two states of the U.S. See tables at KANSAS and SOUTH CAROLINA.

2 Town, a ⊗ of Sebastian co., W Arkansas; pop. (1970c) 2156; coal mines.

3 City, Johnson co., cen. Indiana, 10 m. S of Indianapolis; pop. (1970c) 11,408; auto accessories; grain farms; livestock.

4 City, ⊗ of Leflore co., W Mississippi, 50 m. E of Greenville; pop. (1970c) 22,400; long-staple cotton.

5 City, ⊗ of Greenwood co., W South Carolina, 36 m. SE of Anderson; pop. (1970c) 21,069; manufactures cottons, cheese, clothing, lumber, foundry and machine-shop products; Lander Coll. (1872).

Greenwood Lake. Lake in N Passaic co., N New Jersey, and Orange co., SE New York; ab. 9 m. long; summer resort.

Greenwood Village. Town, Arapahoe co., NE cen. Colorado, 5 m. S of Denver; pop. (1970c) 2578.

Greer \'gri(ə)r\. 1 Former county, Oklahoma, coextensive with present Beckham (S part), Greer, Harmon, and Jackson cos.; subject of long dispute between Texas and U.S., which was settled by the Supreme Court 1896.

2 County in Oklahoma. See table at OKLAHOMA.

3 Town, Greenville and Spartanburg cos., NW South Carolina, 12 m. ENE of Greenville; pop. (1970c) 10,642; textile mills.

Gregg \'greg\. County in Texas. See table at TEXAS.

Greg·o·ry \'greg-(ə-)rē\. 1 County in South Dakota. See table at SOUTH DAKOTA.

2 City, Gregory co., S South Dakota; pop. (1970c) 1756; livestock.

Gregory, Lake. Shallow salt lake, NE South Australia, ESE of Lake Eyre.

Greifenberg. See GRYFICE.

Greifs·wald \'grīfs-ˌvält\. City, Rostock dist., East Germany, 19 m. SE of Stralsund; pop. (1970e) 47,083; trades in coal and lumber; city hall (1350), univ. (1456), observatory (1946); incorporated as city 1250; to Sweden 1648, to Prussia 1815.

Greiz \'grīts\. City, Gera dist., East Germany, 14 m. WSW of Zwickau; pop. (1970e) 39,058; textiles, paper; metalworking; old castle, residence of former prince of Reuss; until 1918 capital of principality of Reuss-Greiz.

Gre·na·da \grə-'nād-ə\. 1 County in N cen. Mississippi. See table at MISSISSIPPI.

2 City, its ⊗, 28 m. NE of Greenwood; pop. (1970c) 9944; cotton growing.
3 Island, southernmost of the Windward Is., West Indies, 90 m. N of Trinidad; 120 sq. m.; pop. (1970e) 87,300; ✱ St. George's on SW coast; of volcanic origin; has many short streams; mountainous, highest point Mt. St. Catherine 2757 ft.; chief exports cocoa, nutmegs, lime oil, bananas.

History: Discovered 1498 by Columbus, who named it **Con·cep·ci·ón** \kən-ˌsep-sē-ˈōn, -ˈsep-shən\; colonized by French governor of Martinique 1650; finally passed to French crown 1674; captured by British 1762 and ceded to them 1763; held by French 1779–83; scene of native rising suppressed by British 1795; member of West Indies Federation 1958–62; became (with dependent islands) an associate state of Great Britain 1967.
4 Self-governing state in Windward Is., West Indies; comprises Grenada I. (see 3, above) and the southern Grenadines (including Carriacou); 133 sq. m.; pop. (1970e) 94,500; ✱ St. George's on Grenada I.

Gren·a·dier Island \ˌgren-ə-ˌdi(ə)r-\. Island in NE Lake Ontario, Jefferson co., N New York, NW of Sackets Harbor.

Gren·a·dines \ˌgren-ə-ˈdēnz\. Group of 600 small islands, Windward Is., at E end of Caribbean Sea, bet. Grenada and St. Vincent; 30 sq. m.; largest Carriacou; S part (13 sq. m.; pop. [1968e] 8179) to Grenada, N part (17 sq. m.; pop. [1960c] 5068, including Bequia and Union Is.) to St. Vincent.

Gren·chen \ˈgren-kən\ *or Fr.* **Granges** \gräⁿzh\. Commune, Solothurn canton, NW Switzerland, 7 m. W of Solothurn; pop. (1970c) 17,708; manufactures clocks.

Gre·no·ble \grə-ˈnō-bəl, -ˈnȯblᵊ\; *anc.* **Cu·la·ro** \ˌc(y)ü-lə-ˌrō\ *or later* **Gra·ti·an·op·o·lis** \ˌgrā-sh(ē-)ə-ˈnäp-ə-ləs\. Commercial and manufacturing city, ✱ of Isère dept., SE France, on Isère river 133 m. NNE of Marseilles; pop. (1968c) 161,616; electrical machinery, gloves, cement; tourism; 10th cent. cathedral; Renaissance law court; univ. (1339); nuclear research center (1959); site of Winter Olympic Games 1968. La Grande Chartreuse ab. 12½ m. N of here; capital of the Dauphiné until 1450.

Gren·ville \ˈgren-ˌvil, -vəl\. 1 County, Ontario, Canada. See table at ONTARIO.
2 Town, E coast of Grenada I., West Indies; pop. (1960c) 1747.

Grenz·mark Po·sen–West·preus·sen \ˈgren(t)s-ˌmärk-ˈpōz-ᵊn-vest-ˈprȯis-ᵊn\. Former Prussian province, E Germany, on border of Poland; formed 1919 out of parts of former Posen and West Prussia provs.; since 1945 divided among several provinces of W Poland.

Gresh·am \ˈgresh-əm\. City, Multnomah co., NW Oregon, 14 m. E of Portland; pop. (1970c) 10,030; Mount Hood Community Coll. (1965).

Gre·sik \gre-ˈsēk\; *formerly* **Gris·see** *or* **Gri·see** \gri-ˈsē\. Seaport, East Java prov., Indonesia, ab. 8 m. NW of Surabaja, on Surabaja Strait opp. Madura I.; pop. (1961c) 38,998.

Gret·na \ˈgret-nə\. 1 Industrial city, ⊗ of Jefferson parish, SE Louisiana, on Mississippi river opp. New Orleans; pop. (1970c) 24,875; molasses, industrial alcohol, cottonseed oil, petroleum products.
2 District, Dumfries co., S Scotland, on English border; pop. (1970e) 5254; 1 m. SE of **Gretna Green,** village on the Sark, long famous as marrying place of runaway couples from England.

Gre·ve \ˈgrev-(ˌ)ā, ˈgrāv-\. Commune, Firenze prov., Tuscany, cen. Italy, 15 m. SE of Florence; pop. (1968e) 10,296.

Gre·ve·ling·en \ˈgrā-və-ˌliŋ-ən\. Inlet on SW coast of the Netherlands bet. Schouwen and Goeree Is.

Gre·ven \ˈgrā-vən\. City, North Rhine-Westphalia, West Germany, 10 m. N of Munster; pop. (1969e) 26,293; center of textile industry; shoes, furniture.

Gre·ve·ná \ˌgrev-ə-ˈnä\. 1 Department of Macedonia, Greece. See table at GREECE.
2 Town, its ✱; pop. (1971p) 8387.

Gre·ven·broich \ˌgrā-vən-ˈbrōk\. Town, North Rhine-Westphalia, West Germany; pop. (1969e) 27,996; railroad junction; aluminum products, textiles; taken by Allies Mar. 1945.

Grey \ˈgrā\. 1 County, Ontario, Canada. See table at ONTARIO.
2 River, NW South I., New Zealand; 75 m. long; flows SW into Tasman Sea at Greymouth.

Grey·beard \ˈgrā-ˌbi(ə)rd\. Mountain, Buncombe co., W North Carolina; 5448 ft.

Grey·bull \ˈgrā-ˌbu̇l\. 1 River, NW Wyoming; ab. 100 m. long; rises in S Park co., flows NE into Bighorn river.
2 Town, Big Horn co., N Wyoming, on Bighorn river 33 m. N of Worland; pop. (1970c) 1953; oil refineries.

Greyerz. See GRUYÈRES.

Grey·lock, Mount \-ˈgrā-ˌläk\. Peak in Berkshire Hills, Berkshire co., NW Massachusetts; 3491 ft.; highest point in state; memorial tower 105 ft. high on summit dedicated to soldiers and sailors of Massachusetts.

Greylock Mountain. 1 Peak, La Plata co., SW Colorado; 13,578 ft.
2 Peak, N Elmore co., SW cen. Idaho; 9317 ft.
3 Peak, SW Klamath co., S Oregon; 7850 ft.

Grey·mouth \ˈgrā-ˌmau̇th, -məth\. Seaport borough, W South I., New Zealand, at mouth of Grey river 138 m. SW of Nelson; pop. (1968e) 8590; exports coal and timber.

Greys \ˈgrāz\. River, W Wyoming; ab. 65 m. long; flows N in N Lincoln co. into Snake river.

Grey·town \ˈgrā-ˌtau̇n\. 1 Seaport, Nicaragua. See SAN JUAN DEL NORTE.
2 Town, cen. Natal, E Rep. of South Africa, 58 m. NNW of Durban; pop. (1967e) 9800; sheep and cattle; wattle.

Grid·ley \ˈgrid-lē\. City, Butte co., N California, 55 m. N of Sacramento; pop. (1970c) 3534; diversified farming.

Gridley Mountain. Mountain in Salisbury, extreme NW Connecticut; 2200 ft.

Gries Pass \ˈgrēs-\. Mountain pass in Alps bet. Piedmont, NW Italy, and Valais canton, Switzerland; 8089 ft.

Grif·fin \ˈgrif-ən\. City, ⊗ of Spalding co., W cen. Georgia, 42 m. SSE of Atlanta; pop. (1970c) 22,734; textile mills, fruit and dairy farms.

Grif·fith \ˈgrif-əth\. Town, Lake co., NW corner of Indiana, 8 m. S of Gary; pop. (1970c) 18,168; metal products.

Griggs \ˈgrigz\. County in North Dakota. See table at NORTH DAKOTA.

Gri·jal·va \grē-ˈhäl-və\ *also* **Ta·bas·co** \tə-ˈbas-(ˌ)kō\. River, Chiapas and Tabasco states, SE Mexico; ab. 300 m. long; flows N into Bay of Campeche.

Grim, Cape \-ˈgrim\. Northwest point of Tasmania, Australia.

Gri·mal·di \grə-ˈmäl-dē\. Caves in commune of Ventimiglia, Imperia prov., W Liguria, NW Italy, just across the border from Menton, France; remains of a prehistoric race of men (Grimaldi race, a Negroid type, late Paleolithic) have been discovered here.

Grimes \ˈgrīmz\. County in Texas. See table at TEXAS.

Grim·ma \ˈgrim-ə\. Manufacturing city, Leipzig dist., East Germany, on left bank of the Mulde river 16 m. SE of Leipzig; pop. (1970e) 16,763; machinery; 13th cent. castle, 15th cent. town hall; founded c. 1170.

Grims·by \ˈgrimz-bē\. 1 Town, Lincoln co., SE Ontario, Canada, on SW shore of Lake Ontario 18 m. E of Hamilton; pop. (1971p) 15,742; electric appliances, printing materials; cans fruit.
2 *or formerly* **Great Grimsby.** County borough, Parts of Lindsey, Lincolnshire, E England, near mouth of the Humber 18 m. SSE of Hull; pop. (1971p) 95,685; has harbor; fisheries, shipbuilding yards; produces titanium oxide; breweries.

Grim·sel Pass \ˌgrim-zəl-\. Mountain pass in Bernese Alps, SW cen. Switzerland; 7159 ft.

Gríms·ey \ˈgrēm(p)s-ˌā\. Island NE of Eyja Fjord, N Iceland, in Arctic Ocean.

Grin·del·wald \'grin-dᵊl-ˌwȯld, -ˌvält\. Valley and town (pop. [1970c] 3511), in Bernese Alps, cen. Switzerland, N of the Wetterhorn and E of Interlaken; cattle raising; tourist resort; elevation of valley 3400–3500 ft., town at 3412 ft.

Grin·nell \grə-'nel\. City, Poweshiek co., SE cen. Iowa, 23 m. SSE of Marshalltown; pop. (1970c) 8402; gloves, farm implements; livestock; Grinnell Coll. (1846); settled 1854, incorp. as town 1865, as city 1882.

Grinnell, Mount. Peak in Glacier National Park, NW Montana; 8848 ft.

Grinnell Land. Central section of Ellesmere I., N Franklin dist., Northwest Territories, Canada.

Grinnell Peninsula. Northwest portion of Devon I., Franklin dist., Northwest Territories, Canada, SW of Ellesmere I.

Gri·qua·land East \'grē-kwə-ˌland-, 'grik-wə-\. Historical division, E Cape Province, S Rep. of South Africa; 7722 sq. m.; chief town Kokstad; agricultural and sheep-raising country; settled 1862 by Griquas, a people of Bushman and Hottentot descent, under their leader, Adam Kok; annexed to Cape Colony 1879.

Griqualand West. Historical division, N Cape Province, S Rep. of South Africa, N of Orange river and W of Orange Free State; 15,444 sq. m.; chief town Kimberley; dry, desert country, noted for its diamond fields. Following the discovery of diamonds (1867), region, settled earlier by Griquas, became subject of dispute bet. Orange Free State and British, who annexed it 1871; joined to Cape Colony 1880.

Gri·qua·town \'grē-kwə-ˌtau̇n, 'grik-wə-\. Town, N cen. Cape Province, Rep. of South Africa, 90 m. W of Kimberley; in district yielding diamonds, asbestos, galena, crocidolite, wool, mohair, and cereals; occupied several times by Boers during Boer War; remains of old fort.

Grisee. See GRESIK.

Gris–Nez, Cape \-grē-'nā\. Headland, Pas-de-Calais dept., N France, extending into Strait of Dover 15 m. SW of Calais; point nearest to Great Britain; lighthouse. See BLANC-NEZ.

Grisons. See GRAUBÜNDEN.

Grissee. See GRESIK.

Gris·wold \'griz-wəld, -ˌwȯld\. Town, NE New London co., SE corner of Connecticut, on E bank of Quinebaug river; pop. (1970c) 7763; agriculture, dairying; includes borough of Jewett City (*q.v.*); incorporated 1815.

Gri·ve·gnée \ˌgrēv-(ə-)'nyā\. Manufacturing commune, Liège prov., E Belgium, a suburb of Liège; pop. (1969e) 23,232; coal mines; metallurgical works.

Griz·zly Mountain \ˌgriz-lē-\. 1 Peak, Chaffee co., cen. Colorado; 13,800 ft.

2 Peak, Pitkin and Chaffee cos., W cen. Colorado; 13,988 ft.

3 Peak in Glacier National Park, NW Montana; 9070 ft.

Grizzly Peak. 1 Mountain in Sierra Nevada, on boundary bet. Tuolumne and Mono cos., E cen. California; 10,369 ft.

2 Peak, Dolores and San Juan cos., SW Colorado; 13,738 ft.

3 Peak, La Plata co., SW Colorado; 13,695 ft.

Gro·chów \'grȯ-ˌküf\. Village, an E suburb of Warsaw, Poland, on right bank of the Vistula; scene of battle Feb. 25, 1831 bet. Poles and Russians under Diebitsch, in Polish Revolution.

Gródek Jagielloński. See GORODOK.

Grödnertal. See GARDENA, VAL DI.

Grod·no \'gräd-(ˌ)nō, 'grȯd-\ *or Lithuanian* **Gar·di·nas** \gär-'din-əs\. City, ✻ of Grodno Oblast, Belorussian S.S.R., U.S.S.R., on Neman river; pop. (1970p) 132,000; electrical equipment, textiles, tobacco, leather; trades in lumber, agricultural products.

History: First mentioned 1126; at various times in its history under Lithuanian, Russian, and Polish rule; sacked by Tatars 1241, by Teutonic Knights 1284 and 1391; capital of Lithuania in 14th cent.; seat of Polish Sejm 1795 which ratified third Partition of Poland; captured by Germans Sept. 1915, and again, in World War II, in June 1941; retaken by Soviet troops July 16, 1944.

Grodno Oblast \-'ȯ-bləst, -ˌblast\. Subdivision of the Belorussian S.S.R., U.S.S.R., bounded on N by Lithuanian S.S.R. and on W by Poland; 9652 sq. m.; pop. (1970p) 1,121,000; ✻ Grodno; sugar beet, tobacco, rye; livestock.

Gro·dzisk Ma·zo·wiec·ki \'grȯ-(ˌ)jisk-ˌmäz-əv-'yet-skē\. Commune, Warszawa prov., NE cen. Poland, 12 m. SW of Warsaw; pop. (1970e) 20,400.

Groes·beck \'grōs-(ˌ)bek\. City, ⊗ of Limestone co., E cen. Texas, 33 m. E of Waco; pop. (1970c) 2396; bricks; livestock raising.

Groes·beek \'grüs-bāk\. Commune, Gelderland prov., E Netherlands, near West German border; pop. (1970e) 17,308; frontier and customs station.

Groix, Île de \ˌēl-də-grə-'wä, -'grwä\. Island in Bay of Biscay off Morbihan dept., NW France, 9 m. S of Lorient; 6 sq. m.; sea caves, dolmens; fishing.

Grom·bal·ia \gräm-'bal-yə\. Town, NE Tunisia, at base of Cape Bon Penin. ab 25 m. SE of Tunis; pop. (1966c) 7300.

Gro·nau \'grō-ˌnau̇\ *also* **Gronau in West·fa·len** \-in-vest-'fäl-ən\. City, North Rhine-Westphalia, West Germany, near Dutch border 32 m. NW of Münster; pop. (1969e) 26,626; textiles.

Gron·gar Hill \ˌgräŋ-gər-\. Hill, Carmarthenshire, S Wales; celebrated by John Dyer, English poet.

Gro·ning·en \'grō-niŋ-ən\. 1 Province, NE Netherlands; 934 sq. m.; pop. (1970e) 517,305; ✻ Groningen; wheat, oats, barley, potatoes, sugar beet; horse breeding, dairy farming.

2 City, ✻ of Groningen prov., NE Netherlands; pop. (1970e) 168,843; sugar refining, book printing; commercial center; univ. (1614), Church of St. Martin, dating in part from 13th cent., Museum van Oudheden. First mentioned 1006; place of internment of British Royal Naval Brigade after fall of Antwerp Oct. 1914; in World War II taken by Allies Apr. 1945.

3 Town, N Surinam, on Saramacca river ab. 22 m. W of Paramaribo; pop. (1960e) 600.

Grønland. See GREENLAND.

Grøn·sund \'grə(r)n-ˌsu̇n\. Channel bet. Falster and Møn Is., SE Denmark.

Groot \'grüt\. 1 River, Cape Province, Rep. of South Africa; joins Gourits river.

2 River, Cape Province, Rep. of South Africa, main headstream of the Gamtoos (*q.v.*).

Groo·te Ey·landt \grüt-'ī-lənd\. Island, W Gulf of Carpentaria, Northern Territory, Australia; 950 sq. m.; tropical fruit, manganese.

Groot·fon·tein \'grüt-ˌfän-ˌtān\. Town, N South-West Africa, 220 m. NNE of Windhoek; pop. (1960c) 3725; copper and lead mining center; large meteorite is on nearby farm.

Gros Is·let Bay \ˌgrō-ˌsī-lət-\. Inlet of Caribbean Sea, NW coast of Saint Lucia I., West Indies, ab. 5 m. N of Castries; 120 acres; seaplane base leased for 99 years to U.S. by Great Britain Sept. 3, 1940.

Gros Morne \grō-'mȯ(ə)rn\. Peak, W Newfoundland I., Canada; 2644 ft.

Gross·bee·ren \grōs-'bā-rən, -'ber-ən\. Village, Potsdam dist., East Germany; pop. (1965e) 2800; scene of battle Aug. 23, 1813 in which French were defeated by Prussians under von Bülow and Berlin was thereby saved.

Grosse Mythe. See MYTHEN.

Gros·sen·hain \'grōs-ᵊn-ˌhīn\. City, Dresden dist., East Germany, 19 m. WNW of Dresden; pop. (1970e) 19,339; manufactures machinery, tinware, paper, cloth.

Grosse Pointe \ˈgrō-ˈspȯint\. Residential city, Wayne co., SE Michigan, on Lake St. Clair 9 m. E of Detroit; pop. (1970c) 6637.

Grosse Pointe Farms. Residential city, Wayne co., SE Michigan, on Lake St. Clair 10 m. E of Detroit; pop. (1970c) 11,701.

Grosse Pointe Park. Residential city, Wayne co., SE Michigan, on Lake St. Clair; pop. (1970c) 15,585.

Grosse Pointe Shores. Village, Macomb and Wayne cos., SE Michigan, 12 m. ENE of Detroit; pop. (1970c) 3042.

Grosse Pointe Woods. Village, Wayne co., SE Michigan; pop. (1970c) 21,878; residential suburb of Detroit.

Gros·ser Aletsch \ˈgrōs-ər-ˈä-lech\. Glacier in the Bernese Alps, Switzerland; ab. 14 m. long, ab. 1 m. wide near its terminus.

Grosser Belchen. See GUEBWILLER, BALLON DE.

Gros·ser Feld·berg \ˌgrō-sər-ˈfelt-ˌbe(ə)rg\. Highest peak in Taunus range, West Germany; 2886 ft.

Grosser Plöner See. See PLÖN.

Grosse Scheidegg. See SCHEIDEGG.

Gros·se·to \grō-ˈsāt-(ˌ)ō\. 1 Province of Tuscany, cen. Italy. See table at ITALY.

2 Commune, its ✻, 94 m. NW of Rome; pop. (1968e) 60,116; 13th cent. Gothic cathedral; fortified citadel; museum of Etruscan antiquities; ruins of **Ru·sel·lae** \rü-ˈsel-ē\, an ancient Etruscan city deserted in 12th cent.; sulfur baths.

Gross·glock·ner \ˈgrōs-ˈgläk-nər\. Peak in the Hohe Tauern range in the Tirol Alps, S Austria, bet. E Tirol and Carinthia; 12,470 ft.; highest point in Austria.

Gross·gör·schen \grōs-ˈgər-shən\. Village, Halle dist., East Germany; pop. (1965e) 1300; formerly in Saxony prov., Prussia, near Lützen; battle, often called battle of Lützen (*q.v.*), May 2, 1813.

Grossherzogtum Luxemburg. See LUXEMBOURG.

Gross–Jä·gers·dorf \ˈgrōs-ˈyā-garz-ˌdȯrf, -ˌdȯrf\ *or* **Gross–Jä·gern·dorf** \-gərn-\. Village, formerly in Prussia, Germany, now in U.S.S.R., W of Chernyakhovsk; scene of battle July 30, 1757 in which Russians under Apraksin defeated Prussians under Lehwald; assigned to U.S.S.R. by Potsdam Conference 1945.

Gross Schreckhorn. See SCHRECKHORN, GROSS.

Gross Strehlitz. See STRZELCE OPOLSKIE.

Gross·ve·ne·di·ger \ˌgrōs-və-ˈnā-di-gər\. Peak in Hohe Tauern range in the Tirol Alps, bet. E Tirol and Carinthia, Austria, and near Italian border; 12,054 ft.

Grosswardein. See ORADEA.

Gros·ve·nor Dale \ˌgrōv-(ə-)nər-\. Subdivision of town in Connecticut. See THOMPSON 1.

Grosvenor Mountains *also* **Grosvenor Range** *or formerly* **Gil·bert Grosvenor Range** \ˌgil-bərt-\. Mountain range, Antarctica, S of Ross Ice Shelf, bet. it and the South Pole; 86°S lat., crossed by 178th meridian; on the W touches Queen Alexandra Range and on E the Queen Maud Mountains.

Gros Ventre \ˈgrō-ˌvänt\. River, W Wyoming; ab. 100 m. long; rises in Wind River Range, N Sublette co., flows W into Snake river in cen. Teton co.

Grot·on \ˈgrät-ᵊn\. 1 Town, S New London co., SE corner of Connecticut, on Long Island Sound at mouth of Thames river opp. New London; pop. (1970c) 38,244; settled 1649, incorp. 1704; agriculture, commercial fishing; shipbuilding; U.S. submarine base; site of Fort Griswold which was attacked and taken by British under Benedict Arnold 1781. Includes borough of Groton (pop. [1970c] 8933).

2 Town, Middlesex co., NE Massachusetts, 11 m. E of Fitchburg; pop. (1970c) 5109; Groton School (boys preparatory school; 1884).

3 Industrial village, Tompkins co., S cen. New York, 26 m. SSE of Auburn; pop. (1970c) 2112.

Grot·ta·glie \grō-ˈtäl-(ˌ)yā\. Commune, Taranto prov., Apulia, SE Italy, 11 m. ENE of Taranto; pop. (1968e) 24,775; pottery.

Grouse Hill \ˈgrau̇s-\. Peak, W Klamath co., S Oregon, N of Crater Lake; 7401 ft.

Grouse Mountain. Peak, SW Catron co., W New Mexico; 10,132 ft.

Grove City \ˈgrōv-\. 1 Village, Franklin co., cen. Ohio, 8 m. SSW of Columbus; pop. (1970c) 13,911; diversified agriculture.

2 Borough, Mercer co., W Pennsylvania, 18 m. ENE of New Castle; pop. (1970c) 8312; gas and diesel engines, iron castings; Grove City Coll. (1876); settled 1798.

Grove Hill. Town, ⊗ of Clarke co., SW Alabama; pop. (1970c) 1825; timber.

Grove·land \ˈgrōv-lənd\. Town, Essex co., NE corner of Massachusetts, 16 m. ENE of Lowell; pop. (1970c) 5382.

Grove·port \ˈgrōv-ˌpō(ə)rt, -ˌpȯ(ə)rt\. Village, Franklin co., cen. Ohio, 10 m. SE of Columbus; pop. (1970c) 2490.

Gro·ver \ˈgrō-vər\. City, San Luis Obispo co., SW California, S of San Luis Obispo; pop. (1970c) 5939.

Groves \ˈgrōvz\. City, Jefferson co., SE coastal Texas, E of Port Arthur; pop. (1970c) 18,067.

Grove·ton \ˈgrōv-tən\. 1 Town in Northumberland township, Coos co., N New Hampshire, ab. 19 m. NW of Berlin; pop. (1970c) 1597; paper and pulpwood mills.

2 City, ⊗ of Trinity co., E Texas; pop. (1970c) 1219; timber.

3 Stream, Virginia. See BULL RUN.

Grove·town \ˈgrōv-ˌtau̇n\. City, Columbia co., E Georgia, 20 m. W of Augusta; pop. (1970c) 3169.

Groz·ny \ˈgrȯz-nē, ˈgräz-\. City, ✻ of Checheno-Ingush A.S.S.R., Russian S.F.S.R., U.S.S.R., on a tributary of the Terek river 50 m. ENE of Ordzhonikidze; pop. (1970p) 341,000; a major oil center, connected by pipelines with Makhachkala on the Caspian Sea and with Tuapse and Rostov-na-Donu to the NW; petrochemicals; food processing. Originally a Russian frontier fortress, established 1818; oil discovered 1893; goal, but never reached, of German drive in Caucasus 1942.

Grubeshov. See HRUBIESZÓW.

Gru·dziądz \ˈgrü-ˌjōⁿts, -ˌjȯn(t)s\ *or Ger.* **Grau·denz** \ˈgrau̇-den(t)s\. City, Bydgoszcz prov., N cen. Poland, on Vistula river 30 m. N of Toruń; pop. (1970p) 75,500; important agricultural center; manufactures iron goods, machinery, tile, shoes. Founded by Teutonic Knights 1291; to Poland 1466; seized by Prussia 1772, and in 1920 again assigned to Poland; held by Germany in World War II.

Gru·gli·ano \grül-ˈyän-(ˌ)ō\. Commune, Torino prov., Piedmont, NW Italy, 5 m. W of Turin; pop. (1968e) 30,118.

Gruin·ard Bay \ˌgrin-yərd-\. Bay on NW coast of Ross and Cromarty co., N Scotland.

Grullo, El. See EL GRULLO.

Gru·mo Ap·pu·la \ˌgrü-mō-ˈäp-ə-lə\. Commune, Bari prov., Apulia, SE Italy, SW of Bari; pop. (1968e) 11,358.

Grünberg *or* **Grünberg in Schlesien.** See ZIELONA GÓRA 2.

Grun·dy \ˈgrən-dē\. 1 Counties in four states of the U.S. See tables at ILLINOIS, IOWA, MISSOURI, TENNESSEE.

2 Town, ⊗ of Buchanan co., SW Virginia; pop. (1970c) 2054.

Grundy Center. City, ⊗ of Grundy co., NE cen. Iowa, 25 m. WSW of Waterloo; pop. (1970c) 2712.

Grütli. See RÜTLI.

Gru·yère \grü-ˈye(ə)r, grē-ˈ(y)e(ə)r\. District, SE Fribourg canton, W cen. Switzerland; 192 sq. m.; noted esp. for its cheese (Gruyère cheese) originally made here.

Gru·yères \grü-ˈye(ə)r, grē-ˈ(y)e(ə)r\ *or Ger.* **Grey·erz** \ˈgrī-ərts\. Commune, Fribourg canton, Switzerland, 16 m. SW of Fribourg; pop. (1970c) 1234; old castle, seat of counts of Gruyère.

Gruziya. See GEORGIAN SOVIET SOCIALIST REPUBLIC.

Gry·fi·ce \gri-ˈfēt-sə\; *Ger.* **Grei·fen·berg** \ˈgrī-fən-ˌbərg, ˌbe(ə)rg\ *or* **Greifenberg in Pom·mern** \-in-ˈpȯm-ərn\. Town, NW Szczecin prov., NW Poland, NE of Szczecin; pop. (1968e) 12,700; founded 1262.

Gry·nei·on \grin-ˈī-än\. Ancient Aeolian town, on NW coast of Asia Minor, near Cyme; a religious center, noted for its worship of Apollo.

Gryt·vi·ken Harbour \ˌgrit-ˌvē-kən-, ˌgrüt-\. See SOUTH GEORGIA.

Gua·ca·na·ya·bo Bay \ˌgwäk-ə-nə-ˌyäb-ō-\. Bay in W coast of Oriente prov. and S coast of Camagüey prov., E Cuba.

Gua·chi·ría \ˌgwäch-ə-'rē-ə\. River, NE cen. Colombia; ab. 110 m. long; flows E into Meta river.

Gua·da·la·ja·ra \ˌgwäd-ə-lə-'här-ə, ˌgwäth-\. 1 Province of cen. Spain. See table at SPAIN.

2 *or anc.* **Ar·ri·a·ca** \ˌar-ē-'ā-kə\. Commune, ✻ of Guadalajara prov., cen. Spain, 34 m. NE of Madrid; pop. (1970p) 31,917; manufactures woolens, leather, soap; palace of Mendoza family; Roman bridge and aqueduct; held by Moors 714–1081.

3 City, ✻ of Jalisco state, W cen. Mexico, 280 m. WNW of Mexico City; munic. pop. (1970p) 1,196,218; altitude 5141 ft.; center of rich agricultural and industrial area; important mining center; produces chemicals, footwear, textiles; noted for its pottery, clay figures, and drawn work; cathedral (built 1561–1618), Univ. of Guadalajara (1792), Autonomous Univ. of Guadalajara (1935).

Gua·da·la·viar \ˌgwäd-ᵊl-ə-'vyär\ *also* **Tu·ria** \'tu̇r-ē-ə\. River, E Spain; 174 m. long; flows S and SE into Mediterranean Sea 3 m. E of Valencia.

Gua·dal·ca·nal \ˌgwäd-ᵊl-kə-'nal, ˌgwäd-ə-kə-\. Island, British Solomon Is., W Pacific Ocean, ab. 300 m. SE of Bougainville, 100 m. SE of New Georgia, and 35 m. SW of Malaita; 2180 sq. m.; 92 m. long and 33 m. wide at its widest part; pop. (1970p) 23,922; has no good harbors and only a few at all usable; traversed lengthwise by Kavo Mts.; highest peak Popomanasiu 7648 ft.; many short streams are along coast, the best known the Mataniko, Lunga, and Tenaru rivers in N. Has many coconut plantations; in some of the low coast regions mangrove swamps.

History: First visited by English navigator 1788; gradually settled by white traders after 1860; taken as part of protectorate by British 1893. In World War II occupied 1942 by Japanese who built airfield on N coast which was seized by U.S. Marines Aug. 7, 1942, the first episode in the "Battle of Guadalcanal" (Aug. 7–Nov. 13, 1942) which included several naval battles (see SAVO) and several bitterly contested land battles (see MATANIKO, TENARU, LUNGA); evacuated by Japanese Feb. 1943.

Gua·da·le·te \ˌgwäd-ᵊl-'at-e\. River, SW Spain; 86 m. long; flows SW into Gulf of Cádiz through 2 mouths.

Gua·da·li·mar \ˌgwäd-ᵊl-i-'mär\. River, S Spain; 104 m. long; flows into the Guadalquivir, 14 m. N of Jaén.

Gua·dal·quiv·ir \ˌgwäd-ᵊl-'kwiv-ər, -ki-'vi(ə)r\ *or Arab.* **Wa·di al–Ke·bir** \ˌwäd-ē-ˌal-kə-'bi(ə)r\ *or anc.* **Bae·tis** \'bēt-əs\. River in S Spain; 408 m. long; flows W and SW into Gulf of Cádiz at Sanlúcar de Barrameda.

Gua·da·lu·pe \'gwäd-ᵊl-ˌüp, ˌgwäd-ᵊl-'üp-ē\. 1 River, SE Texas; ab. 250 m. long; rises in Kerr co., flows SE into San Antonio river ab. 9 m. from its mouth.

2 Name of counties in two states of the U.S. See tables at NEW MEXICO and TEXAS.

3 City, Santa Barbara co., SW California, 50 m. NW of Santa Barbara; pop. (1970c) 3145.

4 City, Costa Rica, suburb of San José; pop. (1968e) 26,750.

5 Island in Pacific Ocean 180 m. off coast of W cen. Baja California, Mexico; 80 sq. m.; an extinct volcano, height ab. 4500 ft.; set aside ab. 1923 by Mexican government as a game reservation, esp. for protection of elephant seals.

6 City, Nuevo León state, Mexico, 10 m. E of Monterrey; munic. pop. (1970p) 153,454; livestock raising; wheat; 18th cent. basilica.

7 Municipality, Zacatecas state, Mexico, 4 m. SE of Zacatecas; pop. (1970p) 31,976; commercial center; brickworks, handicrafts; livestock farming; diversified agriculture.

8 Town, Uruguay. See CANELONES 2.

Guadalupe Hi·dal·go \-hi-'dal-(ˌ)gō, -ē-'thäl-\ *or officially* **Gus·ta·vo A. Ma·de·ro** \gu̇-ˌstäv-ō-ˌäm-ə-'de(ə)r-(ˌ)ō\. City, Federal District, cen. Mexico; munic. pop. (1970p) 1,182,895; printing, metalworking; textiles, chemicals; large church containing a portrait of the Virgin Mary, object of pilgrimage for many Indians in Mexico. Treaty signed here Feb. 2, 1848 terminating Mexican War.

Guadalupe Mountains. 1 Mountain range, S New Mexico and SW Texas; highest Guadalupe Peak 8751 ft.; contains **Guadalupe Mountains National Park.** See UNITED STATES, *National Parks.*

2 *or* **Sie·rra de Guadalupe** \sē-ˌer-əd-ə-\. Range, mostly in S Cáceres prov., SW cen. Spain; highest peak Cabeza del Moro 5695 ft.

Guadalupe Peak. Mountain, Culberson co., W Texas, in Guadalupe Mts.; 8751 ft.; highest point in Texas.

Guadalupe y Cal·vo \-ē-'käl-vō\. Municipality, Chihuahua state, Mexico, 40 m. SE of Ciudad Juárez; pop. (1970p) 31,131; cattle raising, lumbering; diversified agriculture.

Guadarrama, Sierra de. See SIERRA DE GUADARRAMA.

Gua·da·rra·ma Pass \ˌgwäd-ə-ˌräm-ə-\. Mountain pass in the Sierra de Guadarrama, cen. Spain, S of Segovia; elev. ab. 4151 ft.

Gua·de·loupe \'gwäd-ᵊl-ˌüp, ˌgwäd-ᵊl-'\. Name applied to 2 islands, Basse-Terre (or Guadeloupe proper) and Grande Terre, E West Indies, separated by narrow channel; 583 sq. m.; with dependencies Marie Galante, Désirade, Les Saintes, St. Barthélemy, and part of St. Martin, constitutes **Guadeloupe** department of France, 683 sq. m., pop. (1970e) 327,000; ✻ Basse-Terre; highest peak Soufrière 4813 ft.; exports sugar, rum, bananas, coffee.

History: Discovered by Columbus 1493; occupied by French 1635; held by British 1759–63, 1794, 1810–13; transferred to Sweden 1813 and restored to France 1816; in World War II held under Vichy control until July 1943; status changed from colony to overseas department 1946.

Gua·di·a·na \ˌgwäd-ē-'än-ə, -'an-\ *or anc.* **Anas** \'ā-nəs\. River, Spain and Portugal; 515 m. long; rises in S cen. Spain; flows W to Portuguese border; turns S, forming 2 sections of the boundary bet. Spain and Portugal, and empties into Gulf of Cádiz.

Guadiana Bay. Bay in N coast of W tip of Pinar de Río prov., W Cuba, E of Cape San Antonio.

Guadiana Me·nor \-mā-'nȯ(ə)r\. River, S Spain; 58 m. long; unites with the Guadalquivir 4 m. ESE of Úbeda.

Gua·di·a·ro \ˌgwäd-ē-'är-(ˌ)ō\. River, S Spain; 49 m. long; flows S into Mediterranean Sea 11 m. NE of Gibraltar.

Gua·di·a·to \ˌgwäd-ē-'ät-(ˌ)ō\. River, S Spain; ab. 70 m. long; flows into the Guadalquivir 17 m. WSW of Córdoba.

Gua·dix \gwä-'dēsh\. City, Granada prov., S Spain, 26 m. ENE of Granada; pop. (1970p) 19,840; in wheat and olive producing region; Roman remains, Moorish castle, 18th cent. cathedral; one of oldest episcopal sees in Spain.

Gua·fo \'gwäf-(ˌ)ō\. Island off SW coast of Chile, SW of Chiloé I. and W of **Gulf of Guafo.**

Gua·gua \'gwäg-(ˌ)wä\. Municipality, S cen. Pampanga prov., Luzon, Phil., on N edge of Pampanga delta 7 m. SW of San Fernando; pop. (1969e) 55,200.

Guahan. See GUAM.

Guái·ma·ro \'gwī-mə-ˌrō\. Municipality, E Camagüey prov., E cen. Cuba, 44 m. SE of Camagüey near border of Oriente prov.; pop. (1967e) 70,520.

Guai·nía \gwī-'nē-ə\. 1 River, South America. See NEGRO, RIO 3.

2 Commissary of E Colombia. See table at COLOMBIA.

Guai·rá \gwī-'rä\. Department of S cen. Paraguay. See table at PARAGUAY.

Guaíra. See SETE QUEDAS.

Guaira, La. See LA GUAIRA.

Guai·te·cas Islands *or* **Guay·te·cas Islands** \gwī-ˌtek-əs-\. Group of islands in Pacific Ocean off SW coast of Chile, comprising N part of Chonos Archipelago.

Gua·ja·ba Cay \gwä-ˌhäb-ə-ˈkē, -ˈkā\. Island, Camagüey Archipelago, off N coast of Camagüey prov., E cen. Cuba.

Guajira, La. See LA GUAJIRA.

Gua·la·ceo \ˌgwä-lə-ˈsā-(ˌ)ō\. Town, Azuay prov., S Ecuador, 15 m. E of Cuenca; pop. (1962c) 3065; manufactures straw hats.

Gua·lán \gwä-ˈlän\. Town, Zacapa dept., E Guatemala, on the Montagua ab. 15 m. NE of Zacapa; munic. pop. (1964p) 22,914.

Gual·do Ta·di·no \ˌgwäl-dō-tä-ˈdē-(ˌ)nō\. Commune, Perugia prov., Umbria, cen. Italy, 20 m. ENE of Perugia; pop. (1968e) 13,294; cathedral; pottery.

Gua·le·guay \ˌgwäl-ə-ˈgwī\. 1 River, Entre Ríos prov., E Argentina, ab. 220 m. long; flows S into the Paraná.
2 Town, Entre Ríos prov., E Argentina, 80 m. ESE of Rosario; pop. (1960c) 16,542.

Gua·le·guay·chú \ˌgwäl-ə-gwī-ˈchü\. Town, Entre Ríos prov., E Argentina, near Uruguay river 125 m. E of Rosario; pop. (1960c) 29,863.

Gua·lla·ti·ri \ˌgwä-yə-ˈtir-e, ˌgwī-ə-\. Volcano, N Chile; 19,882 ft.; erupted 1959.

Guam \ˈgwäm\ *or* **Gua·han** \gwä-ˈhän\. Unincorporated U.S. territory, largest and southernmost of Mariana Is., W Pacific Ocean; 32 m. long, bet. 4 and 10 m. wide; 209 sq. m.; pop. (1970p) 86,926; ✻ Agana; in S half are hills (highest 1329 ft.) with several streams and fertile areas, N half mainly plateau ab. 500 ft.; has reef along much of the coast; on W coast is best anchorage, Apra Harbor, bet. Orote Penin. and Cabras I.; visited occasionally by earthquakes and typhoons; extensive naval facilities; chief crops bananas, beans, melons, papayas.
History: Discovered by Magellan 1521; occupied by Spain 1565 but not completely subjected until 130 years later; ceded to U.S. by Spain Dec. 1898 and occupied 1899; developed by U.S. as naval station and in 1936 as civil aviation stop; seized by Japanese Dec. 11, 1941; retaken by American forces July 20–Aug. 10, 1944; made headquarters of U.S. Navy in the Pacific Jan. 28, 1945; administration transferred to U.S. Department of the Interior 1950.

Gua·ma·ca·ro \ˌgwäm-ə-ˈkär-(ˌ)ō\. Municipality, Matanzas prov., W cen. Cuba, SW of Cárdenas; pop. (1967e) 18,180.

Guam·blin \ˈgwäm-ˌblēn\ *or* **So·cor·ro** \sə-ˈkȯr-ō\. Island off SW coast of Chile, NW of Chonos Archipelago.

Gua·na·ba·coa \ˌgwän-ə-bə-ˈkō-ə\. Town and municipality, La Habana prov., W Cuba, just E of Havana; munic. pop. (1967e) 203,010.

Gua·na·ba·ra \ˌgwän-ə-ˈbar-ə\. State, SE Brazil; 524 sq. m.; pop. (1970p) 4,296,782; ✻ Rio de Janeiro; created from former federal district 1960.

Guanabara Bay *also* **Rio de Ja·nei·ro Bay** \ˈrē-(ˌ)ō-ˌdā-zhəˌne(ə)r-(ˌ)ō-, -ˌdē-, -də-, -jə-, -ˈni(ə)r-\. Inlet of Atlantic Ocean in SE Brazil; the city of Rio de Janeiro is on its SW shore; 16½ m. long, 11 m. wide, entrance ab. 1 m. wide.

Gua·na·cas·te \ˌgwän-ə-ˈkäs-(ˌ)tā\. Province of NW Costa Rica. See table at COSTA RICA.

Guanacaste, Cor·dil·le·ra \ˌkȯrd-ᵊl-ˈ(y)er-ə-, ˈkȯrd-ē-ˈer-ə-\. Range, NW Costa Rica; highest peak 6627 ft.

Guanahani. See SAN SALVADOR 1.

Gua·na·ja \gwä-ˈnä-(ˌ)hä\ *or* **Bo·nac·ca** \bō-ˈnäk-ə\. One of the Islas de la Bahía, N of N cen. Honduras in the Caribbean Sea.

Gua·na·jay \ˌgwän-ə-ˈhī\. Town and municipality, Pinar del Río prov., W Cuba, 25 m. SW of Havana; munic. pop. (1967e) 22,920.

Gua·na·jua·to \ˌgwän-ə-ˈ(h)wät-(ˌ)ō\. 1 State of cen. Mexico. See table at MEXICO.
2 City, its ✻, 170 m. NW of Mexico City; munic. pop. (1970p) 65,258; altitude 6726 ft.; in mountainous region noted for centuries for its gold and silver mines, still being worked; univ. (1732, univ. status 1945); famous for its catacombs.

Gua·nal, Point \-gwä-ˈnäl\. Cape on S coast of Isle of Pines, West Indies.

Gua·na·re \gwä-ˈnär-ē\. 1 River, W Venezuela; flows ESE to join the Portuguesa river.
2 Town, ✻ of Portuguesa state, W cen. Venezuela, ab. 75 m. SSW of Barquisimeto; pop. (1970e) 33,379; in coffee-producing region.

Gua·ne \ˈgwän-(ˌ)ā\. Municipality, Pinar del Río prov., W Cuba, 28 m. SW of Pinar del Río; pop. (1967e) 49,680.

Guá·ni·ca \ˈgwän-i-kə\. Town and municipality, SW Puerto Rico; pop. (1970p) 8538 (town), 14,884 (munic.); town is on Guánica Harbor 25 m. W of Ponce.

Guánica Harbor. Bay on S coast of Mayagüez municipality, W Puerto Rico; landing place of American troops in Spanish-American War 1898.

Gua·ni·qui·lla Point \ˌgwän-ə-ˈkē-(y)ə-\. Cape on SW coast of Puerto Rico, N of Boquerón Bay.

Gua·no \ˈgwän-(ˌ)ō\. Town, Chimborazo prov., cen. Ecuador, just N of Riobamba; pop. (1962c) 4455.

Guan·tá·na·mo \gwän-ˈtän-ə-ˌmō\. Town and municipality, SE Oriente prov., E Cuba; munic. pop. (1967e) 238,700; sugar center; town, ab. 10 m. N of Guantánamo Bay; municipality includes seaport barrio Caimanera on W side of Guantánamo Bay.

Guantánamo Bay. Bay on SE coast of Oriente prov., E Cuba; 30 sq. m.; site of U.S. naval station (leased 1903); in Spanish-American War its shores landing place of U.S. naval units June 1898.

Guapay. See MAMORÉ.

Gua·po·ré \ˌgwäp-ə-ˈrā\. 1 *or* **Ité·nez** \ē-ˈtā-nəs\. River, W cen. South America; 1087 m. long; rises in W Mato Grosso state, SW Brazil, flows NW, forming section of Brazil-Bolivia boundary, to join the Mamoré river.
2 Territory, Brazil. See RONDÔNIA.

Gua·qui \ˈgwäk-ē\. Lake port, La Paz dept., W Bolivia, at S end of Lake Titicaca near mouth of Desaguadero river; railroad terminus 61 m. from La Paz.

Gua·ram·ba·ré \gwä-ˌräm-bə-ˈrā\. Town, Central dept., SW cen. Paraguay; pop. (1970e) 7251.

Gua·ran·da \gwä-ˈrän-də\. City, ✻ of Bolívar prov., W Ecuador, 72 m. NE of Guayaquil; pop. (1970e) 11,900.

Gua·ra·pua·va \ˌgwar-ə-ˈpwäv-ə\. Town, S cen. Paraná state, S Brazil, 140 m. W of Curitiba; munic. pop. (1968e) 126,080.

Gua·ra·tin·gue·tá \ˌgwar-ə-ˌtēŋ-gə-ˈtä\. City, São Paulo state, SE Brazil, 125 m. W of Rio de Janeiro; munic. pop. (1968e) 62,077; commercial center of agricultural district producing esp. coffee.

Guar·da \ˈgwärd-ə\. 1 District of NE Portugal. See table at PORTUGAL.
2 Commune, its ✻, 65 m. ENE of Coimbra; munic. pop. (1970p) 40,529; cathedral.

Guardafui, Cape. See ASIR, RAS.

Guard·house, The \-ˈgärd-ˌhau̇s\. Mountain in Glacier National Park, NW Montana; 9300 ft.

Guar·dia·gre·le \ˌgwärd-ē-ə-ˈgrel-ē, -ˈgrā-lē\. Commune, Chieti prov., Abruzzi, cen. Italy, 12 m. S of Chieti; pop. (1968e) 9977; summer resort.

Guard·i·an, The \-ˈgärd-ē-ən\. Peak, San Juan co., SW Colorado; 13,624 ft.

Guá·ri·co \ˈgwär-i-ˌkō\. 1 River, W Venezuela; ab. 300 m. long; flows SW and S into Apure river.
2 State of N cen. Venezuela. See table at VENEZUELA.

Gua·ri·ti·co \ˌgwär-ə-ˈtē-(ˌ)kō\. River, W Venezuela; ab. 160 m. long; flows ENE into Apure river.

Gua·ru·já \ˌgwar-ə-ˈzhä\. See SANTOS.

Gua·ru·lhos \gwə-ˈrül-yu̇s\. Municipality, São Paulo state, SE Brazil, 9 m. NE of São Paulo; pop. (1968e) 119,572.

Gua·sa·ve \gwä-ˈsä-vā\. Municipality, Sinaloa state, Mexico, 95 m. NE of Culiacán; pop. (1970p) 148,475; fishing, livestock raising; wheat, cotton.

Guásimas, Las. See LAS GUÁSIMAS.

Guaso Nyiro. See EWASO NG'IRO.

Gua·stal·la \gwä-ˈstäl-ə\ *or anc.* **War·da·stal·la** \ˌwȯrd-ə-ˈstal-ə\. Commune, Reggio nell'Emilia prov., Emilia-Romagna, N Italy, on Po river 14 m. NE of Reggio; pop. (1968e) 14,267; cathedral; palace of Gonzaga family; produces spun silk, leather, cheese.

History: Founded by Lombards in 7th cent.; belonged successively to Reggio, Cremona, and Milan; became center of countship of same name 1406; to Gonzaga family 1538; made center of duchy 1621; to Spanish duke of Parma 1748; ruled by members of Napoleonic family 1805–47, by duke of Modena 1847–60; became part of kingdom of Italy 1860.

Gua·ta·vi·ta \ˌgwät-ə-ˈvēt-ə\. Town, Cundinamarca dept., cen. Colombia, near Bogotá; munic. pop. (1968e) 5537; ancient city of the Chibchas.

Gua·te·ma·la \ˌgwät-ə-ˈmäl-ə\. **1** Republic, Central America, bounded on W and N by Mexico, on E by British Honduras and the Gulf of Honduras, on SE by Honduras and El Salvador, and on S by the Pacific Ocean; 42,042 sq. m.; pop. (1970e) 5,110,000, (1968e) 4,738,956; ✱ Guatemala. *Physical features:* Mountainous; main range the SE extension of the Sierra Madre of Mexico, roughly parallel with Pacific coast ab. 40 m. distant; highest peaks incl. Tajumulco 13,845 ft., Tacaná 13,428 ft., Acatenango 13,044 ft., Santa María 12,375 ft., Atitlán 11,604 ft.; interior is extensive tableland 2000 to 5000 ft.; regions on both Pacific and Atlantic coasts are hot lowlands. Chief rivers the Usumacinta in NW on Mexican border, the Sarstoon flowing E into Amatique Bay, the Polochic (through Lake Izabal) and Motagua flowing to Gulf of Honduras. Chief lakes Lake Izabal in E, Petén Itza in N, and Atitlán in SW cen. part. *Chief products:* Coffee, cotton, bananas, corn, rice, timber; lead, zinc. *Chief towns:* Guatemala, Tiquisate, San Pedro Carchá, Quezaltenango, Escuintla, Jutiapa, Totonicapán. Divided into the following 22 departments (for pronunciation of their names, see their individual entries):

NAME	AREA (sq. m.)	POP. (1968e)	CAPITAL
Alta Verapaz	3,354	280,367	Cobán
Baja Verapaz	1,206	105,653	Salamá
Chimaltenango	764	185,281	Chimaltenango
Chiquimula	917	166,072	Chiquimula
El Progreso	742	74,386	El Progreso
Escuintla	1,693	300,103	Escuintla
Guatemala	821	914,780	Guatemala
Huehuetenango	2,857	318,426	Huehuetenango
Izabal	3,490	129,412	Puerto Barrios
Jalapa	797	110,147	Jalapa
Jutiapa	1,243	217,233	Jutiapa
Petén	13,843	29,679	Flores
Quezaltenango	753	295,874	Quezaltenango
Quiché	3,235	271,811	Santa Cruz del Quiché
Retalhuleu	717	127,458	Retalhuleu
Sacatepéquez	180	90,828	Antigua
San Marcos	1,464	336,339	San Marcos
Santa Rosa	1,141	174,763	Cuilapa
Sololá	410	117,398	Sololá
Suchitepéquez	969	200,646	Mazatenango
Totonicapán	410	155,363	Totonicapán
Zacapa	1,039	106,937	Zacapa

History: Conquered by Alvarado 1524; Guatemala City founded and captaincy general of Guatemala established (included present Guatemala, El Salvador, Honduras, Nicaragua, Costa Rica) 1527; revolted against Spain 1821 and joined Iturbide's Mexican empire 1822–23; withdrew from United Provinces (see CENTRAL AMERICA) and became independent republic 1839; dominated by Carrera 1840–65; under President Barrios 1873–85, tried by force to form a union of Central American states; ruled by Estrada Cabrera 1898–1920; declared war on Germany 1918; in 1933 settled century-old boundary dispute with Honduras; in World War II declared war on Axis powers 1941; promulgated new constitution 1965.

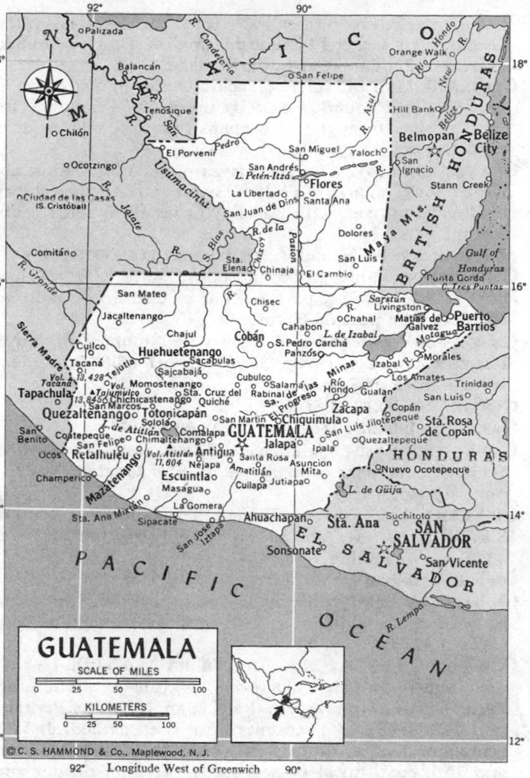

2 Department of S cen. Guatemala. See table at GUATEMALA 1.

3 *or* **Guatemala City.** City, ✱ of Guatemala and of Guatemala dept.; met. area pop. (1971e) 730,991; altitude ab. 5000 ft.; largest city in Central America; in volcanic area; center of fertile agricultural region; several colleges incl. San Carlos Univ. of Guatemala (1676). Founded by Alvarado 1527 as Santiago de los Cabelleros, destroyed 1541 by floods; capital moved to Antigua, which was destroyed by earthquake 1773; rebuilt on present site 1776, became capital 1779; severely damaged 1917–18 by earthquakes.

Guatemala Antigua. City, Guatemala. See ANTIGUA.

Guaura. See HUAURA.

Gua·via·re \gwäv-ˈyär-ē, ˌgwäv-ē-ˈär-\. River, Colombia; ab. 650 m. long; flows E from its source in Andes Mts. in SW cen. Colombia; empties into Orinoco river on Colombia-Venezuela boundary.

Gua·ya·ma \gwə-ˈyäm-ə\. Town and municipality, SE Puerto Rico, near coast 32 m. E of Ponce; pop. (1970p) 20,227 (town), 36,159 (munic.); its port is Arroyo.

Guayana. See GUIANA.

Gua·ya·ne·co Islands \ˌgwī-ə-ˌnek-ō-\. Group of small islands in Pacific Ocean off SW coast of Chile, S of Gulf of Penas.

Gua·ya·ni·lla \ˌgwī-ə-ˈnē-(y)ə\. Town and municipality, SW Puerto Rico; pop. (1970p) 5156 (town), 18,054 (munic.); town on coast 12 m. W of Ponce on **Guayanilla Harbor.**

Gua·ya·quil \ˌgwī-ə-ˈkē(ə)l, -ˈkil\ *or officially* **San·tia·go de Guayaquil** \ˌsant-ē-ˈäg-ō-də-, ˌsänt-\. Seaport, ✱ of Guayas prov., SW Ecuador, its old part on Guayas river ab. 40 m. from the coast; munic. pop. (1970e) 794,300; chief port of Ecuador; sugar refineries, iron foundries, tanneries; Univ. of Guayaquil (1867), technical coll. (1958); cathedral. Founded July 25, 1535, St. James's day, hence its official name; attacked by pirates 1624, 1683, and 1709; has often been burned; scene of historic meeting bet. Bolívar and San Martín 1822; damaged by earthquake 1942.

Guayaquil, Gulf of. Inlet of Pacific Ocean in SW coast of Ecuador, and bounded on S by tip of NW Peru; receives Guayas river from the N; contains many islands in inner part, the largest Puná I.

Gua·yas \ˈgwī-əs\. 1 River, Guayas prov., W Ecuador; ab. 180 m. long; an arm of Gulf of Guayaquil and the estuary of Babahoyo river; with Babahoyo river navigable for ab. 200 m.

2 Province of W Ecuador. See table at ECUADOR.

Guay·mas \ˈgwī-məs\. Town, Sonora state, NW Mexico; pop. (1969e) 60,981; port on Gulf of California; railroad terminus; the port of Hermosillo.

Guay·na·bo \gwī-ˈnäb-(ˌ)ō\. Town and municipality, NE Puerto Rico; pop. (1970p) 53,785 (town), 65,557 (munic.); town 8 m. S of San Juan.

Guayra. See SETE QUEDAS.

Guaytecas Islands. See GUAITECAS ISLANDS.

Gua·za·ca·pán \ˌgwäz-ə-kə-ˈpän\. Town, Santa Rosa dept., S Guatemala, near coast ab. 40 m. S of Guatemala City; pop. (1964p) 7657.

Gu·ba·kha \gü-ˈbäk-ə\. Town, Perm Oblast, Russian S.F.S.R., U.S.S.R., ab. 35 m. NE of Perm; pop. (1967e) 43,000; coal mining.

Gu·ban \ˈgü-ˌbän\. Plateau region, NW Somalia.

Gu·bat \ˈgü-ˌbät\. Municipality and port, NE Sorsogon prov., Luzon, Phil., ab. 10 m. ESE of Sorsogon; pop. (1969e) 42,500.

Gub·bio \ˈgü-bē-ˌō\; *anc.* **Eu·gu·bi·um** \yü-ˈg(y)ü-bē-əm\ *also* **Igu·vi·um** \ig-ˈ(y)ü-vē-əm, ī-ˈg(y)ü-\. Commune, Perugia prov., Umbria, cen. Italy, 23 m. N by E of Perugia; pop. (1968e) 31,085; ceramics; 13th cent. cathedral, 13th cent. church of St. Francis, 14th cent. Palazzo dei Consoli, and 15th cent. ducal palace; ancient Roman theater and mausoleum. See UMBRIA.

Gu·bin \ˈgü-ˌbēn\ *or Ger.* **Gu·ben** \ˈgü-bən\. Manufacturing city, Zielona Góra prov., W Poland, on Nysa river.

History: In origin a Wendish town; successively a possession of Brandenburg 1311, Bohemia 1367, Saxony 1635, and Prussia 1815; in World War II in area of considerable fighting Feb.–Apr. 1945; following Potsdam Conference (1945) city became part of Poland, its W section being assigned to East Germany. See WILHELM-PIECK-STADT GUBEN.

Gub·kin \ˈgüp-kin\. Town, Belgorod Oblast, Russian S.F.S.R., U.S.S.R., ab. 65 m. NE of Belgorod; pop. (1967e) 42,000; iron ore deposits nearby.

Gud·brands·dal \ˈgu̇b-ˌrän(t)s-ˌdäl\. Valley in Oppland co., S cen. Norway; ab. 140 m. long; extends NW and SE above Lake Mjøsa and Lillehammer, N part bet. the Jotunheimen and Dovrefjell; scene of severe fighting Apr. 1940 when British were driven N by Germans.

Gu·de·nå \ˈgü-t͟hən-(ˌ)ȯ\. Longest river in Denmark; 98 m. long; rises in N cen. Jutland, empties into Randers Fjord, an inlet of the Kattegat on E coast.

Gu·di·ya·ttam \ˌgu̇d-ē-ˈ(y)ät-əm\. Town, N Tamil Nadu, S India, near Palar river 100 m. W of Madras; pop. (1961c) 50,384.

Gueb·wil·ler \ˌgeb-vē-ˈle(ə)r\ *or Ger.* **Geb·wei·ler** \ˈgāp-ˌvī-lər\. Commune, Haut-Rhin dept., NE France, 15 m. SSW of Colmar; pop. (1968c) 10,840.

Guebwiller, Bal·lon de \ba-ˌlōⁿ-də-\ *or Ger.* **Gros·ser Bel·chen** \ˌgrō-sər-ˈbel-kən\ *or* **Sul·zer Belchen** \ˌzu̇lt-sər-\. Mountain in Haut-Rhin dept., NE France, W of Guebwiller; highest in Vosges Mts.; 4672 ft.

Gue·cho \ˈgwā-(ˌ)chō\. Commune, Vizcaya prov., N Spain, on Bay of Biscay 8 m. NW of Bilbao; pop. (1970p) 39,153.

Guelderland. See GELDERLAND.

Guel·ma \gel-ˈmä\. Commune, Annaba dept., NE Algeria, ab. 40 m. E of Constantine; pop. (1966c) 36,113.

Guelph \ˈgwelf\. Manufacturing city, ⊗ of Wellington co., SE Ontario, Canada, 15 m. ENE of Kitchener; pop. (1971p) 58,364; rubber goods, electrical apparatus, paint, manufactures iron and steel products, woolen goods, carpets, cotton and linen goods; foundries, tobacco warehouses; Univ. of Guelph (1964); Ontario Reformatory; founded 1827.

Gué·mappe \gā-ˈmap\. Village, Pas-de-Calais dept., N France, 7 m. ESE of Arras; pop. (1962c) 649; battles in region Apr.–May 1917 and Mar. 1918.

Gué·rande \gā-ˈräⁿ(n)d\. Commune, Loire-Atlantique dept., NW France, ab. 10 m. W of St-Nazaire; pop. (1962c) 6688; greater part of stone walls built by John V of Brittany 1431 still preserved; 12th–16th cent. church.

Gué·ret \gā-ˈrā\. Commune, ✱ of Creuse dept., cen. France, 124 m. S of Orléans; pop. (1968c) 12,849.

Guer·ni·ca \ger-ˈnē-kə\ *or* **Guernica y Lu·no** \-ē-ˈlü-nō\. Town, E Vizcaya prov., N Spain, ENE of Bilbao; pop. (1970p) 14,678; once seat of a Basque parliament; bombed 1937 by German planes in Spanish civil war; its destruction the subject of a noted painting by Pablo Picasso.

Guern·sey \ˈgərn-zē\. 1 County in Ohio. See table at OHIO.

2 One of the Channel Is., in the English Channel; 24 sq. m.; pop. (1968e) 46,182; constitutes, with Alderney, Sark, and adjacent islands, a bailiwick with area 30 sq. m., pop. (1971p) 53,734, and ✱ St. Peter Port; market gardening, cattle breeding (the *Guernsey* breed of cattle originating here).

Guernsey Dam. Dam across North Platte river, NE Platte co., SE Wyoming; height 135 ft.; forms **Guernsey Reservoir** or **Guernsey Lake;** completed 1927.

Guer·re·ro \gə-ˈre(ə)r-(ˌ)ō\. 1 State of S Mexico. See table at MEXICO.

2 Municipality, Chihuahua state, Mexico, 95 m. W of Chihuahua; pop. (1970p) 35,631; horses; wheat, barley, fruit.

Guettar, Al–. See AL-GUETTAR.

Gueu·de·court \ˌgərd-(ə-)ˈku̇(ə)r\. Village, Somme dept., N France, 3 m. SSW of Bapaume; pop. (1962c) 137; taken by British Sept. 1916.

Gü·fer·horn \ˈg(y)ü-fər-ˌhȯ(ə)rn\. Peak in the Adula group, on Swiss-Italian border; 11,103 ft.

Gu·gu \ˈgü-(ˌ)gü\. Mountain range, cen. Ethiopia, E of Addis Ababa; highest peak Gugu 11,886 ft.

Gu·guan \gü-ˈgwän\. Island, cen. Mariana Is., W Pacific Ocean; ab. 2½ m. by 1 m.

Guía \ˈgē-ə\. Commune, N coast of Grand Canary I., Canary Is.; pop. (1960c) 11,963.

Gui·a·na \gē-ˈan-ə, -ˈän-ə, gī-ˈan-ə\ *also* **Gua·ya·na** \gwə-ˈyän-ə\. 1 Region bet. the Orinoco, Negro, and Amazon rivers and the Atlantic Ocean, N South America, including Surinam, Guyana, French Guiana, S and E Venezuela, and N Brazil; ab. 690,000 sq. m. Coast discovered by Spanish explorers 1499–1500; originally name Guiana referred to region extending farther west than present boundaries and was thought to include El Dorado; see FRENCH GUIANA, GUYANA, and SURINAM.

2 Coastal strip of French Guiana. See FRENCH GUIANA.

Guiana Massif *or* **Guiana Highlands.** Highland area in N South America, extending from E Venezuela E across N Brazil, Guyana, Surinam, and French Guiana.

Gui·do·nia Mon·te·ce·lio \gwē-ˈdȯn-yə-ˌmȯn-tə-ˈchāl-(ˌ)yō\. Commune, Roma prov., Latium, W cen. Italy; pop. (1968e) 26,570.

Gui·enne *or* **Guy·enne** \gē-ˈen\ *or Lat.* **Aq·ui·ta·nia** \ˌak-wə-ˈtā-nē-ə, -nyə\. Historical region of SW France; bounded anciently on N by Limousin, NE by Auvergne, E and SE by Languedoc, S by Gascony, W by Atlantic Ocean, NW by Angoumois; ✱ Bordeaux; old duchy near Garonne and Dordogne rivers, part of Aquitaine (*q.v.*); name, Guienne, often used interchangeably with Aquitaine; after French crown recovered it from English at close of Hundred Years' War, reestablished as duchy separate from Gascony, etc.; from 17th cent. to 1789, part of French *gouvernement* of Guienne and Gascony. See AQUITANIA.

Gui·hulng·an \gē-ˈhu̇lŋ-ˌän\. 1 Municipality, Negros Oriental prov., Negros, Phil., on coast, ab. 45 m. SE of Bacolod; pop. (1969e) 126,200.

2 *also* **Gi·hulng·an** \hē-\. Municipality, NE Negros Oriental, Negros, Phil., on Tanon Strait; pop. (1969e) 126,200; largest town in province; founded 1800.

Gui·ja \ˈgē-(ˌ)hä\. Lake on border bet. El Salvador and Guatemala; 20 m. long; traversed by Lempa river.

Guilan. See GILAN.

Guild·ford \ˈgil-fərd\. Municipal borough, Surrey, S England, on the Wey 28 m. SW of London; pop. (1971p) 56,887; light engineering; ruins of Norman castle; grammar school founded 1509; Anglican cathedral (begun 1936, consecrated 1961), Univ. of Surrey (1966).

Guild·hall \ˈgild-ˌhȯl\. Town, ⊗ of Essex co., NE corner of Vermont; pop. (1970c) 169.

Guil·ford \ˈgil-fərd\. 1 County in North Carolina. See table at NORTH CAROLINA.

2 Town, SE New Haven co., S Connecticut; on Long Island Sound E of New Haven; pop. (1970c) 12,033; settled 1639.

3 Town, Piscataquis co., N cen. Maine; pop. (1970c) 1694.

Guilford College. Town, Guilford co., N cen. North Carolina, ab. 6 m. NW of Greensboro; pop. (1970c) 61; Guilford Coll. (1834); settled by Quakers 1750.

Guilford Courthouse. Locality, Guilford co., N cen. North Carolina, near Greensboro; scene of battle Mar. 15, 1781 in which Americans under Greene defeated British troops under Cornwallis, ending British control of the Carolinas; area now set aside as **Guilford Courthouse National Military Park** (see UNITED STATES, *National Historical Parks*).

Guil·le·mont \ˌge-yə-ˈmōⁿ\. Village, Somme dept., N France; pop. (1962c) 198; captured by Germans 1914, became center of German resistance; taken by British Sept. 3, 1916.

Güí·mar \ˈgwē-ˌmär\. Village, E coast of Tenerife, Canary Is.; pop. (1970p) 12,131; resort.

Gui·ma·rães \ˌgē-mə-ˈrāⁿsh\. Commune, Braga dist., NW Portugal, 12 m. SE of Braga; pop. (1960c) 23,598; birthplace of Alfonso, first king of Portugal; besieged and taken 1127 by Alfonso VII of León.

Gui·ma·ras \ˌgē-mə-ˈräs\. Island off S coast of Panay I., cen. Phil., separated from it by narrow Iloilo Strait; 223 sq. m.; chief town Jordan; part of Iloilo prov.

Guimaras Strait. Channel, extending NE and SW bet. SE Panay I. and NW Negros I., cen. Phil.; connects Visayan Sea with Sulu Sea; width varies from 7 m. to 20 m.

Guim·ba \gēm-ˈba\. Municipality, W Nueva Ecija prov., Luzon, Phil., 17 m. NW of Cabanatuan; pop. (1969e) 52,000; on main highway bet. Pangasinan and Nueva Ecija provs.

Gui·na·yang·an \ˌgē-nə-ˈyäŋ-ən\. Municipality, SE Quezon prov., SE Luzon, Phil., on coast at head of Ragay Gulf; pop. (1969e) 22,500.

Guin·ea \ˈgin-ē\ *or Fr.* **Gui·née** \gē-nā\ *or Span.* **Gui·nea** \gē-ˈnā-ə\ *or Port.* **Gui·né** \gē-ˈnā\. 1 Term applied to coastal region of W Africa bet. lat. 15°N and lat. 15°S; bet. Gambia and Cameroon (**Upper Guinea**) and bet. Cameroon and S Angola (**Lower Guinea**), name, from an ancient kingdom, not in general European use until after 1500. See EQUATORIAL GUINEA, PORTUGUESE GUINEA. Various sections of coast of Upper Guinea given different names by early traders: Slave Coast, Gold Coast, Ivory Coast, Grain Coast (*qq.v.*).

2 *or formerly* **French Guinea** *or Fr.* **Guinée fran·çaise** \-fräⁿ-sāz, -sez\. Republic, W Africa, bounded on N by Senegal and Mali, on E by Mali and Ivory Coast, on S by Liberia and Sierra Leone, on W by the Atlantic Ocean, and on NW by Portuguese Guinea; 94,925 sq. m.; pop. (1970e) 3,920,000; ✱ Conakry, on Tombo I. *Physical features:* Includes Los Is. group opp. Conakry. Has marshy seacoast, ab. 170 m. long, the coastal plain rising to hilly and plateau regions in the interior which form a tableland that is source of upper tributaries of Niger and Senegal rivers, also of many streams flowing SW to Atlantic. In N is Fouta Djallon tableland and on S borders are ranges that reach 3500 ft. near coast and 6000 ft. on Liberia border. *Chief products:* Rice, sorghum, bananas, coffee, pineapples, peanuts; bauxite, iron ore, diamonds. *Chief towns:* Conakry, Boké, Labé, Kankan, Dubréka.

History: Coastal region proclaimed French protectorate 1849; boundary agreements with Great Britain 1882 and Portugal 1886; administered with Senegal under name of **Ri·vières du Sud** \ˌrē-vē-ˌe(ə)r-dəs-ˈ(y)üd\ until its establishment as a separate colony 1893; became part of French West Africa 1895; status changed to that of overseas territory of France 1946; achieved independence 1958; charged Portugal with responsibility for attempted overthrow of government 1970.

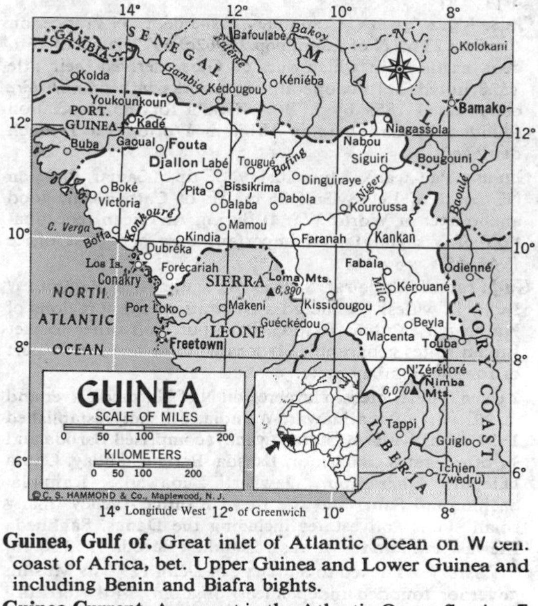

Guinea, Gulf of. Great inlet of Atlantic Ocean on W cen. coast of Africa, bet. Upper Guinea and Lower Guinea and including Benin and Biafra bights.

Guinea Current. A current in the Atlantic Ocean flowing E along the Guinea coast, W Africa.

Guinée. See GUINEA 1.

Guinée française. See GUINEA 2.

Guinegaste *or* **Guinegate.** See ENGUINEGATTE.

Güi·nes \ˈgwē-(ˌ)nās\. Town and municipality, La Habana prov., W Cuba; munic. pop. (1967e) 56,040; in tobacco-producing region; railroad junction 30 m. SE of Havana; terminus of first railroad built in Cuba (1835–38).

Guînes \ˈgēn\. Commune, Pas-de-Calais dept., N France, 7 m. SE of Calais; pop. (1962c) 4749; held by English 1352–1558; residence of Henry VIII in 1520 during meeting of "Field of the Cloth of Gold" bet. him and Francis I. See ARDRES.

Guin·gamp \gaⁿ-ˈgäⁿ\. Commune, Côtes-du-Nord dept., NW France, 17 m. WNW of St-Brieuc; pop. (1962c) 10,571; tourist center; former capital of county, later the duchy, of Penthièvre; ruins of 15th cent. castle and of town walls; noted for church (14th–16th cents.) where annual pardons are granted to pilgrims.

Gui·no·ba·tan \ˌge-nə-ˈbä-ˌtän\. Municipality, E cen. Albay prov., Luzon, Phil., ab. 9 m. WNW of Legaspi; pop. (1969e) 66,300; in region producing hemp (abacá).

Gui·o·nes, Point \-gē-'ō-nəs\. Cape on W coast of Nicoya Penin., W Costa Rica.

Gui·púz·coa \gē-'püth-kə-wə, -'püs-\. Province of N Spain. See table at SPAIN.

Guir, Cape. See RHIR, CAPE.

Güi·ra de Me·le·na \ˌgwir-ə-də-mə-'lā-nə\. Town and municipality, La Habana prov., W Cuba, 25 m. SSW of Havana; munic. pop. (1967e) 28,600.

Güi·ria \'gwir-ē-ə\. Town, Sucre state, N Venezuela, on Gulf of Paria on S coast of Paria Penin.; pop. (1961c) 11,061.

Guis·bor·ough \'giz-b(ə-)rə\. Urban district, North Riding, Yorkshire, N England, 10 m. ESE of Middlesbrough; pop. (1971p) 13,852; remains of a priory founded by Robert de Bruce (an ancestor of Robert the Bruce) 1119.

Guis·card \gē-'skär\. Commune, Oise dept., N France, 19 m. NNE of Compiègne; pop. (1962c) 1135; held by Germans Aug. 1914–Mar. 1917; again lost, but finally freed Sept. 1918.

Guise \'gēz, 'gwēz\. Commune, Aisne dept., N France, on the Oise 23 m. N of Laon; pop. (1962c) 6972; ruins of 16th cent. castle from which ducs de Guise derived their title 1528; noted for its cooperative ironworks with a *familistère* constructed 1859 by J. B. A. Godin for the association founded by him here in 1846; in World War I much damaged.

Gui·uan \'gē-ˌwän\. Municipality, SE tip of Samar, Phil., on NE coast of Leyte Gulf 76 m. SE of Catbalogan; good anchorage; in World War II during American reoccupation of Visayan Is. an important base and post office 1944–45.

Gu·ja·rat *or* **Gu·je·rat** \ˌgü-je-'rät, ˌgu̇j-ə-\. 1 Region, W India, in widest use includes Gujarati-speaking regions of Kathiawar, Kutch, Baroda, Palanpur, and other former Indian states geographically located in or near the N part of former Bombay state.

2 Usually restricted to level region N of Narmada river and in NE part of Kathiawar, W India; officially established 1937–39 as **Gujarat States Agency;** comprised Baroda and 11 other states (Balasinor, Bansda, Baria, Cambay, Chota Udepur, Dharampur, Jawhar, Lunawada, Rajpipla, Sachin, and Sant) and the Rewa Kantha Agency (many small states and estates including the Dangs, Sankheda Mewas, and Pandu Mewas); excluding Baroda 7352 sq. m.

History: Annexed to Sultanate of Delhi 1297; its Muslim governor founded independent kingdom, 1401; territory extended by Ahmad I (1411–41) who built Ahmadabad; annexed 1572–73 by Mogul Emperor Akbar; in 18th cent., overrun by Marathas who later ceded to British much of old kingdom of Gujarat. Formerly these states were grouped in the Rewa Kantha Agency, Kaira Agency, Surat Agency, Nasik Agency, and Thana Agency; became part of Republic of India 1947.

3 State, W India; 72,236 sq. m.; pop. (1971p) 26,660,929; ✱ Ahmadabad; comprises the Gujarati-speaking NW portion of the former Bombay state (*q.v.*); rice, cotton, wheat, salt, manganese. *Largest towns:* Ahmadabad, Baroda, Rajkot. Formed 1960. See MAHARASHTRA 2.

Guj·ran·wa·la \ˌgu̇j-rən-'wäl-ə, ˌgu̇j-\. 1 District, Lahore division, Punjab, Pakistan; 2312 sq. m.; pop. (1961c) 1,291,886; ✱ Gujranwala; cotton, wheat.

2 Town, its ✱, 42 m. N of Lahore; pop. (1969e) 289,300; grain trade; brass and copper utensils; tanneries. Birthplace of Ranjit Singh; capital of Sikh power in its early period; included in territory annexed by British after Second Sikh War (1848–49).

Guj·rat \'gu̇j-ˌrät\. Town, Punjab, Pakistan, near Chenab river 68 m. N of Lahore; pop. (1969e) 73,000; known for work in gold and silver inlay; ceramics, electric fans. Present town founded c. 1500, traditionally the third in a series on this site; scene of battle 1849 in which Sikh power was broken.

Gu·ko·vo \'gü-kə-və\. Town, Rostov Oblast, Russian S.F.S.R., U.S.S.R., ab. 60 m. NNE of Rostov-na-Donu; pop. (1969e) 70,000; coal mining.

Gul·bar·ga \'gu̇l-bər-ˌgä\. Town, N cen. Mysore, S cen. India, 120 m. W of Hyderabad; pop. (1961c) 97,069; manufactures cotton, flour, paint, and oil. Seat of Bahmani kings of the Deccan 1347–1422; many interesting remains of this era, notably a mosque patterned after that of Córdoba in Spain.

Gülek Bogaz. See CILICIAN GATES.

Gulf \'gəlf\. County in Florida. See table at FLORIDA.

Gulf Breeze \-ˌbrēz\. City, Santa Rosa co., NW Florida, 5 m. SE of Pensacola; pop. (1970c) 4190; residential suburb of Pensacola.

Gulf Intracoastal Waterway. System of inland waterways including rivers, bays and canals from Apalachee Bay, Florida, to Brownsville, Texas; ab. 1100 m. long; includes Mobile Bay and Mississippi Sound, goes through New Orleans, takes in the Sabine-Neches Waterway (*q.v.*) and the ship canal at Houston, Texas.

Gulf Plain. Lowland bordering the Gulf of Mexico, S United States.

Gulf·port \'gəlf-ˌpō(ə)rt, -ˌpȯ(ə)rt\. 1 City, Pinellas co., W Florida penin.; suburb of St. Petersburg; pop. (1970c) 9730.

2 City, ⊗ of Harrison co., SE Mississippi, on Gulf of Mexico; pop. (1970c) 40,791; resort; ships cotton, lumber; seafood canneries.

Gulf States. The states of the United States bordering on the Gulf of Mexico: Florida, Alabama, Mississippi, Louisiana, and Texas.

Gulf Stream. Warm ocean current in North Atlantic Ocean; flows out of Gulf of Mexico through Straits of Florida, where it is a current 50 m. wide and more than 2000 ft. deep, continues NE along coast of United States to Nantucket I. and thence eastward; in N mid-Atlantic (40°N, 45°W) merges with North Atlantic Drift Current, a warm current flowing NE to the Barents Sea and influencing climate of W Europe as far as Norway; at ab. 30°W sends off Southeast Drift Current touching coasts of Iberian Penin. and NW Africa; rate of flow, more than 4 m. an hour in the S and between 10 and 15 m. a day farther N. Strictly, the term *Gulf Stream* does not apply beyond 60°W.

Gu·lis·tan \ˌgü-lə-'stan, -'stän\. 1 Village, Baluchistan, Pakistan, 40 m. NW of Quetta; pop. (1961c) 128.

2 Village, cen. Azerbaijan S.S.R., U.S.S.R.; treaty bet. Russia and Persia signed here Oct. 12, 1813 by which Persia gave up Georgia and neighboring districts.

Gul·kana \gəl-'kan-ə\. Village on Copper river, SE Alaska, on Richardson and Glenn Highways; pop. (1970c) 53; junction for cutoff to Tanacross on Alaska Highway.

Gull·foss \'g(y)üt-ᵊl-ˌfȯs\ *or Eng.* **Golden Fall.** Waterfall in Hvítá river, SW Iceland, near Geysir; 101 ft. high.

Gull Lake \'gəl-\. Lake, Cass and Crow Wing cos., N cen. Minnesota; resort.

Gul·marg \'gəl-ˌmärg\. Village, Jammu and Kashmir, N India, 30 m. W of Srinagar; pop. (1961c) 200.

Gulpaigan. See GOLPĀYEGĀN.

Gu·mal \gə-'məl\ *or* **Go·mal** \gō-\. River, S North-West Frontier Province, Pakistan; provides water for irrigation; flows from E Afghanistan E and SE to the Indus near Dera Ismail Khan; chief tributary the Zhob.

Gumal Pass *or* **Gomal Pass.** Mountain pass at N end of Sulaiman Range, in S North-West Frontier Province, Pakistan, WNW of Dera Ismail Khan; elev. 7500 ft.

Gumbinnen. See GUSEV.

Gum·ma \'gu̇m-(ˌ)ä\. Prefecture, Honshū, Japan; 2452 sq. m.; pop. (1970c) 1,658,909; ✱ Maebashi; mountainous region; sericulture; sulfur, manganese.

Gum·mers·bach \'gu̇m-ərz-ˌbäk\. City, North Rhine-Westphalia, West Germany, 28 m. E of Cologne; pop. (1969e) 32,957; manufactures textiles, leather, lumber.

Gumry. See LENINAKAN.

Gumti. See GOMATI.

Gümüljina. See KOMOTINÉ.

Gü·müşh·a·ne *or* **Gü·müş·a·ne** \ˌg(y)ü-mə-shə-ˈnā\ *or* **Gü·müsh Kha·neh** \ˌgü-mu̇sh-kä-ˈnā\. 1 Province of NE Turkey, Asia. See table at TURKEY.

2 Town, its ✻, 40 m. SSW of Trabzon; pop. (1965c) 8092; noted for its silver mines.

Gu·na \ˈgü-nə\. Peak, N cen. Ethiopia, E of Lake Tana; 13,878 ft.

Gun Cay \ˈgən-ˈkē, -ˈkā\. Island in the Bahama Is., S of the Biminis; lighthouse on S end (estab. 1836).

Gun·flint \ˈgən-ˌflint\. Village, Cook co., NE Minnesota, at W end of **Gunflint Lake** on the U.S.-Canada boundary; iron ore in the region to the S, first to be discovered in the state but never mined because of its high titanium content.

Gu·nib \gü-ˈnib\. Village, W Dagestan A.S.S.R., Russian S.F.S.R., U.S.S.R., in E Caucasus Mts.; scene of capture 1859 of the Caucasian leader, Shamyl, which ended resistance of mountain tribes to Russian domination.

Gunn·bjørn, Mount \-ˈgu̇n-ˌbyȯrn\. Mountain, near coast of E cen. Greenland; 12,139 ft.; highest peak in Greenland.

Gun·ni·son \ˈgən-ə-sən\. 1 River, W cen. Colorado; 150 m. long; rises in SE Gunnison co., flows W and NW into Colorado river in cen. Mesa co. Black Canyon of the Gunnison is a national monument (see UNITED STATES, *National Monuments*). See also BLACK CANYON 2.

2 Island in NW Great Salt Lake, Utah; bird rookery.

3 County in Colorado. See table at COLORADO.

4 Town, ⊗ of Gunnison co., W cen. Colorado, on Gunnison river 50 m. W of Salida; pop. (1970c) 4613; founded 1879 as mining center; resort; Western State Coll. of Colorado (1911).

Gunong. See GUNUNG.

Gun·pow·der \ˈgən-ˌpau̇d-ər\. River, N Maryland; rises in NE Carroll co., flows SE into upper Chesapeake Bay; ab. 60 m. long.

Gunsan. See KUNSAN.

Gun·sight, Mount \-ˈgən-ˌsīt\. Peak in Glacier National Park, NW Montana; 9250 ft.

Gun·ters·ville \ˈgənt-ərz-ˌvil\. Industrial town, ⊗ of Marshall co., NE Alabama, on Tennessee river, 30 m. NW of Gadsden; pop. (1970c) 6491; river port.

Guntersville Dam. See table at TENNESSEE VALLEY AUTHORITY.

Gun·tur \gu̇n-ˈtu̇(ə)r\. 1 City, cen. Andhra Pradesh, E India, NW of mouths of Krishna river, 220 m. N of Madras; pop. (1970e) 273,385; important cotton and tobacco trade. Apparently founded in 18th cent. by French; ceded to British 1788, cession confirmed 1823.

2 *or Du.* **Goen·toer** \gu̇n-ˈtu̇(ə)r\. Volcano, W cen. Java, Indonesia; 7377 ft.

Günük. See XANTHUS 2.

Gu·nung \ˈgü-ˌnu̇ŋ\ *or* **Gu·nong** \-ˌnȯŋ\. Malay term meaning "mountain," *Dutch* **Goe·noeng** \-ˌnu̇ŋ\; as in **Gunong Ta·han** \-tə-ˈhän\, **Gunong Ker·bau** \-kər-ˈbau̇\, **Gunung Awu** \-ˈä-(ˌ)wü\. See second element of the name.

Gunung Api *or Du.* **Goe·noeng Api** \-ˈä-pē\. Volcanic island, one of the Banda Is., Malay Archipelago, Indonesia; with Great Banda (*q.v.*) and Bandanaira I. forms harbor of Bandanaira; an active volcano, 1858 ft. high; eruptions 1820, 1852.

Gunung Awu. See AWU, GUNUNG.

Gu·nung·si·to·li *or Du.* **Goe·noeng·si·to·li** \ˌgü-ˌnu̇ŋ-sə-ˈtȯl-ə\. Chief village of Nias I. off W coast of Sumatra, Indonesia.

Gunzan. See KUNSAN.

Gur, Lough \läk-ˈgu̇(ə)r\. Small lake, co. Limerick, S Eire, S of Limerick; prehistoric stone monuments; castle ruins.

Gu·ra·bo \gu̇-ˈräb-(ˌ)ō\. Town and municipality, E Puerto Rico; pop. (1970p) 6255 (town), 18,219 (munic.); town 17 m. SE of San Juan.

Gur·das·pur \gu̇r-ˈdäs-ˌpu̇(ə)r\. 1 District, formerly entirely in Lahore division, N Punjab, NW India; 1889 sq. m.; divided 1947 with 1360 sq. m. in Punjab state, India (see 2 below), and 529 sq. m. in Punjab, Pakistan.

2 District, Punjab, N India; 1360 sq. m.; pop. (1961c) 987,994.

3 Town, Punjab, N India, bet. Beas and Ravi rivers; pop. (1961c) 27,665.

Gur·don \ˈgər-dən\. City, Clark co., SW Arkansas, 15 m. SSW of Arkadelphia; pop. (1970c) 2075; cotton, lumber.

Gurev. See GURYEV.

Gurev Oblast. See GURYEV OBLAST.

Gurgan. See GORGĀN.

Gurhwal. See GARHWAL.

Gurk \ˈgu̇(ə)rk\. River, Carinthia, S Austria; 99 m. long; flows E and S into Drau (Drava) river 10 m. E of Klagenfurt.

Gur·kha \ˈgu̇(ə)r-kə\. Village, E cen. Nepal, 50 m. WNW of Katmandu; ancestral home of Nepal's ruling house.

Gurla Mandhata. See KUA-LA-MAN-TA-T'A.

Gur·nards Head \ˌgər-nərdz-\. Promontory on SE coast of Cornwall, SW England, N of Lands End.

Gur·net Point \ˌgər-nət-\. Cape on N side of Plymouth Bay, Massachusetts; 2 fixed lights.

Gu·ru·pi \ˌgu̇r-ə-ˈpē\. River, NE Brazil; ab. 300 m. long; flows N from W Maranhão state, forming boundary bet. Pará and Maranhão; empties into Atlantic Ocean.

Gu·ryev *or* **Gu·rev** \ˈgu̇r-yəf\. Seaport town, ✻ of Guryev Oblast, SW Kazakh S.S.R., U.S.S.R., at N end of Caspian Sea at mouth of Ural river; pop. (1970p) 113,000; terminus of oil pipeline NE to Aktyubinsk and Orsk.

Guryev Oblast *or* **Gurev Oblast** \-ˈo-bləst, -ˌblast\. Subdivision of Kazakh S.S.R., U.S.S.R., bounded on S by Turkmen S.S.R. and on W by Caspian Sea and Astrakhan Oblast of the Russian S.F.S.R.; 107,567 sq. m.; pop. (1970p) 499,000; ✻ Guryev; largely marsh and desert; has long coastline on the Caspian, including Buzachi Penin. and Mangyshlak Penin. crossed by lower courses of Ural and Emba rivers; oil; livestock raising, fishing.

Gu·sau \gü-ˈzau̇\. Town, North-Western State, NW Nigeria, 130 m. W of Kano; pop. (1969e) 80,286.

Gu·sev \ˈgü-səf\ *or Ger.* **Gum·bin·nen** \gu̇m-ˈbin-ən\. Manufacturing city, Kaliningrad Oblast, Russian S.F.S.R., U.S.S.R., 68 m. E of Kaliningrad; pop. (1967e) 20,000; agricultural machinery, steam and water mills, electrical goods. Scene of Russian victory over Germans Aug. 19–20, 1914; assigned to U.S.S.R. by Potsdam Conference 1945.

Gusharbrum. See GASHERBRUM.

Gus–Khru·stal·ny \ˌgu̇s-kru̇-ˈstäl-nē\. Town, Vladimir Oblast, Russian S.F.S.R., U.S.S.R., ab. 40 m. SSE of Vladimir; pop. (1969e) 65,000.

Gus·tav Line \ˌgu̇s-täf-\. In World War II the main German defense line across Italy S of Rome; its key position Cassino with the Liri valley behind it; reached by Allies Feb. 1944, not taken until May 1944.

Gustavo A. Madero. See GUADALUPE HIDALGO.

Gus·ta·vus \gəs-ˈtā-vəs\. Village, SE Alaska, on Cross Sound N of Chichagof I. and W of Juneau; pop. (1970c) 64; entrance to Glacier Bay National Monument; airport.

Gus·tine \gəs-ˈtēn\. City, Merced co., cen. California, 27 m. W of Merced; pop. (1970c) 2793; butter, feed; diversified agriculture.

Gü·strow \ˈg(y)ü-(ˌ)strō\. Manufacturing city, Schwerin dist., East Germany, 50 m. SW of Stralsund; pop. (1970e) 37,213; machinery, food processing; 13th cent. cathedral; 16th cent. ducal castle; received city rights 1228.

Gü·ters·loh \ˈg(y)üt-ərz-ˌlō\. City, NE North Rhine-Westphalia, West Germany, 31 m. E of Münster; pop. (1969e) 56,000; manufactures foodstuffs, textiles, iron goods; botanical gardens; made city 1825.

Guth·rie \'gəth-rē\. 1 County in Iowa. See table at IOWA.
2 City, ⊗ of Logan co., cen. Oklahoma, 28 m. N of Oklahoma City; pop. (1970c) 9575; manufactures steel, concrete, wooden products; oil wells; founded 1889; capital of Oklahoma territory and state 1890–1910.
3 Village, ⊗ of King co., NW Texas.

Guthrie Center. City, ⊗ of Guthrie co., SW cen. Iowa, 50 m. W of Des Moines; pop. (1970c) 1834.

Guti. See GOOTY.

Gut·ten·berg \'gət-ᵊn-ˌbərg\. 1 City, Clayton co., NE Iowa, on Mississippi river 30 m. NW of Dubuque; pop. (1970c) 2177; settled 1834, colonized by German immigrants 1845.
2 Town, Hudson co., NE New Jersey, on Hudson river 5 m. N of Jersey City; pop. (1970c) 5754.

Guy·ana \gī-'an-ə\ *or formerly* **British Gui·a·na** \-gē-'an-ə, -'än-ə; -gī-'an-ə\. Republic, N South America, bounded on N and NE by the Atlantic Ocean, on E and SE by Surinam, on S and SW by Brazil, and on W by Brazil and Venezuela; 83,000 sq. m.; pop. (1970p) 714,233; ✱ Georgetown. *Physical features:* Has low-lying, marshy coastal region (coastline ab. 270 m.) with inland plains sloping up to mountain ranges on W and S; highest range Pacaraima Mts., the NE extension of the Serra Pacaraima along the Venezuela-Brazil boundary, culminating in Roraima 9219 ft. near the junction of the Venezuela-Brazil-Guyana boundaries; in S is Serra Acaraí, highest peak ab. 2000 ft., densely wooded, and the W extension of the Tumuc-Humac Mountains along the Brazilian border. Has many rivers, all flowing to the Atlantic; among them the Essequibo, in cen. part with main tributaries: Cuyuni, Mazaruni, and Potaro (containing the Kaieteur Falls); the Courantyne on Surinam boundary in E; and the commercially important, but shorter streams, Demerara and Berbice, in the NE . *Chief products:* Bauxite, gold, sugar, rice, coffee. *Chief towns:* Georgetown, New Amsterdam, Mackenzie.
History: For history of region, see GUIANA; colony of Essequibo founded by Dutch probably c. 1620; Berbice founded 1624 under auspices of Dutch West India Company and Demerara 1645, an offshoot of Berbice; in 18th cent., settled by non-Dutch, including many English; first captured by British and Georgetown (see GEORGETOWN 17) founded 1781; after final recapture from Dutch 1803, ceded to British 1814; Essequibo, Berbice, and Demerara united as crown colony of British Guiana 1831; its boundary with Venezuela, long subject of controversy, became serious issue, involving U.S. (Olney Doctrine) in 1895; in arbitration award 1899, most of British claims upheld; boundary with Brazil arbitrated 1904; sites (on Demerara river and near Suddie) for military and naval bases leased to U.S. 1940; achieved independence 1966; became republic 1970.

Guy·an·dotte \'gī-ən-ˌdät\. River, SW West Virginia; ab. 150 m. long; rises in Wyoming co., flows NW into Ohio river near Huntington.

Guyane française. See FRENCH GUIANA.

Guyenne. See GUIENNE.

Guy·mon \'gī-mən\. City, ⊗ of Texas co., NW Oklahoma; pop. (1970c) 7674; oil and gas wells; livestock.

Guy·ot, Mount \-'gē-(ˌ)ō\. 1 Mountain on E boundary of Tulare co., California, SW of Mt. Whitney; 12,300 ft.
2 Peak, Grafton co., N cen. New Hampshire; 4589 ft.
3 Peak in Great Smoky Mts., on boundary bet. Tennessee and North Carolina; 6621 ft.

Guys·bor·ough \'gīz-ˌbər-ə, -ˌbə-rə\. 1 County, E Nova Scotia, Canada. See table at NOVA SCOTIA.
2 Town (unincorporated), its ⊗, at head of Chedabucto Bay; pop. (1966c) 502.

Gwa·dar *or* **Gwa·dur** \'gwäd-ər\. Port on Makran coast, SW Baluchistan, Pakistan; pop. (1961c) 8146; with ab. 300 sq. m. of adjoining territory belonged to Oman from beginning of 19th cent. until ceded to Pakistan 1958.

Gwa·li·or \'gwäl-ē-ˌȯ(ə)r\. 1 Former state, India, now part of Madhya Pradesh state; 26,367 sq. m.; ✱ Lashkar; one

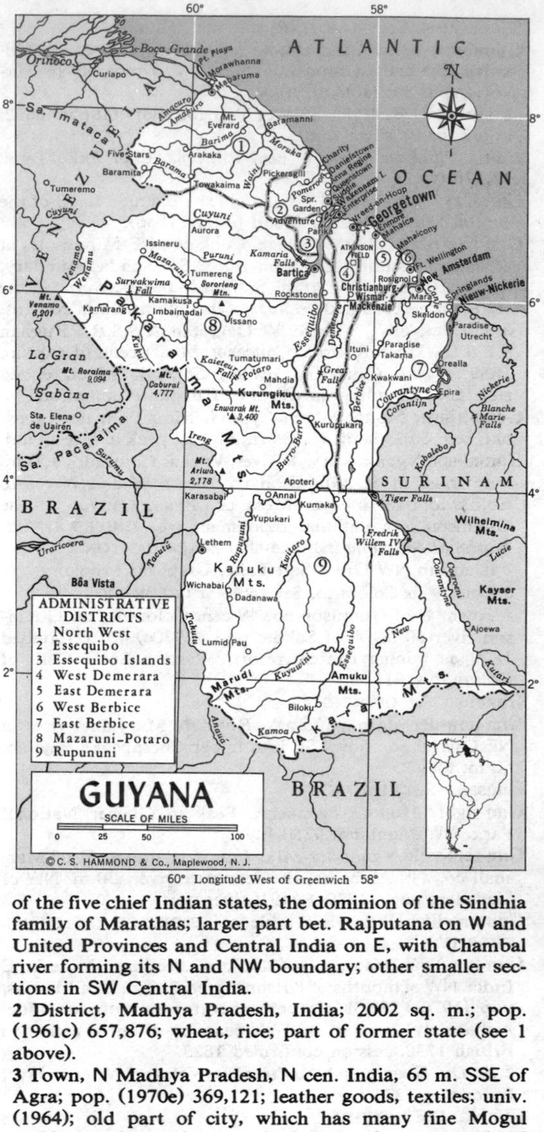

of the five chief Indian states, the dominion of the Sindhia family of Marathas; larger part bet. Rajputana on W and United Provinces and Central India on E, with Chambal river forming its N and NW boundary; other smaller sections in SW Central India.
2 District, Madhya Pradesh, India; 2002 sq. m.; pop. (1961c) 657,876; wheat, rice; part of former state (see 1 above).
3 Town, N Madhya Pradesh, N cen. India, 65 m. SSE of Agra; pop. (1970e) 369,121; leather goods, textiles; univ. (1964); old part of city, which has many fine Mogul architectural remains, overlooked by famous medieval Hindu fort of Gwalior, on a sandstone cliff 300 ft. high and including within its walls the palace of Man Singh, the citadel, temples, and reservoirs. Fort annexed by Mahadaji Sindhia, Maratha leader of 18th cent. who expanded his territory from vicinity of Ujjain to include large part of cen. India; fort lost to English as result of Maratha Wars, the Maratha kingdom, reduced in territory, being allowed to stand; fort restored to ruler by Lord Dufferin 1886. To the S is the new city, **Lash·kar** \'ləsh-kər\, founded c. 1800.

Gwandu. See GANDO.

Gwātar Bay. See GAVĀTER BAY.

Gwee·bar·ra Bay \gwē-'bar-ə-\. Inlet of Atlantic Ocean in W co. Donegal, N Eire, N of Donegal Bay.

Gwee·dore \gwē-'dō(ə)r, -'dȯ(ə)r\. Village, co. Donegal, N Eire, 20 m. NW of Letterkenny; tourist resort; fishing.

Gwe·lo \'gwā-(ˌ)lō\. Town, SW Rhodesia, S Africa, 90 m. ENE of Bulawayo; pop. (1970e) 19,000; center in district producing gold, chrome ore, asbestos fiber.

Gwin·nett \gwin-'et\. County in Georgia. See table at GEORGIA.

Gwy·dir \'gwīd-ər\. River, NE New South Wales, SE Australia; 415 m. long; flows W into Barwon river.

Gwyn·edd *or* **Gwyn·eth** \'gwin-ˌeth\. Ancient region in NW Wales, now included in Caernarvonshire, Denbighshire, and Merionethshire.

Gya·la Pe·ri \ˌgyäl-ə-pə-'rē\. Mountain in the Himalayas, Tibet, China; 24,443 ft.

Gy·a·ros \'yē-ə-ˌrȯs\ *or Gk.* **Yi·oú·ra** \yē-'u̇r-ə\. Mountainous island, NW Cyclades, S Aegean Sea, NW of Syros; 7 sq. m.; in Cyclades dept., Greece.

Gym·pie \'gim-pē\. Town, E Queensland, Australia, 90 m. N of Brisbane; pop. (1968e) 11,350; in region producing gold, silver, coal, antimony, and copper.

Gyō·da \gē-'ōd-ə\. City, Saitama prefecture, Honshū, Japan, 35 m. NW of Tokyo; pop. (1970c) 60,135.

Gyo·ma \'jō-(ˌ)mȯ\. Commune, SE Hungary, 55 m. SW of Debrecen; pop. (1970p) 10,650.

Gyön·gyös \'jərn-ˌjərsh\. City, N cen. Hungary, 45 m. NE of Budapest; pop. (1970p) 33,149; trade center in area producing wool and wines.

Győr \'jər\ *or Ger.* **Raab** \'räp\. City, ⊗ of Győr-Sopron co., NW Hungary, 67 m. WNW of Budapest; pop. (1970p) 100,065; textiles; flour milling, distilling; 12th cent. cathedral, 15th cent. episcopal palace.

Győr–So·pron \-'shō-ˌprōn\. County of NW Hungary. See table at HUNGARY.

Gy–Paraná. See JIPARANÁ.

Gyth·i·um \jith-ē-əm\ *or Gk.* **Yí·thi·on** \'yē-thē-ˌȯn\. Seaport town, S Laconia dept., SE Peloponnesus, Greece, near head of Gulf of Laconia; pop. (1961c) 4922; important Spartan base in Greek wars.

Gyu·la \'jül-ˌȯ\. City, SE Hungary, NE of Szeged near Romanian border; pop. (1970p) 26,266; under Turkish rule 1566–1694.

Gyulafehérvár. See ALBA IULIA.

Gzhatsk. See GAGARIN.

Gzi·ra \gə-'zi(ə)r-ə\. Town, E Malta, across bay NW of Valletta; pop. (1968e) 9744.

H

Haabai. See HAAPAI.

Haa·kon \'hak-ən\. County in South Dakota. See table at SOUTH DAKOTA.

Haan \'hän\. City, North Rhine-Westphalia, West Germany, NW suburb of Solingen; pop. (1969e) 20,739; manufactures steel, tools, chemicals.

Ha·a·no \'hän-(,)ō\. Island in NE Haapai group, Tonga, SW cen. Pacific Ocean.

Ha·a·pai \hä-'pī\ *or* **Ha·a·bai** \-'bī\. Island group in cen. Tonga (*q.v.*), SW cen. Pacific Ocean, ab. 60 m. S of Vavau group; pop. (1966c) 13,533; ab. 50 islands, including Haano, Foa, Lifuka, Uiha, and Tofua; chief village Pangai on Lifuka I.

Haar·lem *or formerly* **Har·lem** \'här-ləm\. City, ✱ of North Holland prov., W Netherlands, 12 m. W of Amsterdam; pop. (1970e) 172,235; electronic equipment, machinery; center of tulip-growing and exporting region; 15th cent. Groote Kerk of St. Bavo; Frans Hals Museum; Teyler Museum (science). Forced to yield to Spaniards after siege of 7 months 1572–73; recaptured 1577 by William of Orange.

Haar·lem·mer·meer \'här-lə-mər-,me(ə)r\. Commune, North Holland prov., W Netherlands; pop. (1970e) 58,966; built on land reclaimed from the former **Haarlem Lake,** a branch of Zuider Zee; in agricultural region.

Hab \'həb\. River, Pakistan; ab. 250 m. long; flows S into Arabian Sea, in its lower course forming boundary bet. Baluchistan and Sind.

Habana, La. See LA HABANA and HAVANA 2.

Habarovsk. See KHABAROVSK.

Hab·ba·ni·ya, Lake \-hə-'ban-ē-(y)ə\ *or Arab.* **Hawr al–Hab·bā·ni·yah** \'här-al-\. Lake along S bank of the Euphrates, cen. Iraq, 50 m. W of Baghdad; 54 sq. m.; scene of brief fighting Apr.–May 1941 for control of large British airfield established near its N shore during World War II.

Hab·er·sham \'hab-ər-,sham, -shəm\. County in Georgia. See table at GEORGIA.

Habesha, Al-. See ETHIOPIA.

Ha·bi·ki·no \,häb-i-'kē-nō\. City, Ōsaka prefecture, Honshū, Japan, 11 m. SSE of Ōsaka; pop. (1970c) 77,134.

Ha·bor \'hā-,bȯ(ə)r\. Biblical name (*2 Kings* xvii. 6) for the Khabur river.

Habs·burg \'haps-,bərg, 'häps-,bu̇(ə)rg\. Hamlet in Aargau canton, N cen. Switzerland, NE of Aarau; pop. (1970c) 150; original seat of the Hapsburgs (*Ger.* Habsburg).

Ha·chi·jō \'häch-ē-,jō\. 1 Group of islands off SE Honshū, Japan, ab. 180 m. S of Tokyo; ab. 32 sq. m.; pop. (1970c) 10,550; forms an administrative unit of Tokyo prefecture; consists of Hachijō I. and three islets.

2 Chief island of the group; 27 sq. m.; pop. (1970c) 10,316; sericulture, stock raising.

Ha·chi·no·he \,häch-i-'nō-(,)hā\. Coastal town, Aomori prefecture, N Honshū, Japan; pop. (1970c) 208,801; chemicals; fisheries.

Ha·chi·ō·ji \,häch-ē-'ō-jē\. City, Tokyo prefecture, SE cen. Honshū, Japan, 27 m. W of Tokyo; pop. (1970c) 253,527; since early 18th cent. noted for its weaving industry, esp. of silk fabrics for Japanese wear; produces habutai, pongee, and silk-cotton mixtures.

Hack·en·sack \'hak-ən-,sak\. 1 River, New York and New Jersey; ab. 40 m. long; flows from Rockland co., SE New York, S across New Jersey border and into Newark Bay.
2 City, ⊗ of Bergen co., NE corner of New Jersey, on Hackensack river 7 m. ESE of Paterson; pop. (1970c) 36,008; foundry products, furniture, chemicals. Settled by Dutch 1647, by English 1668; served as Revolutionary camping ground in turn for Americans and British; incorp. 1868, chartered as city 1921.

Hack·etts·town \'hak-ət-,stau̇n\. Town, Warren co., NW New Jersey, 19 m. W of Morristown; pop. (1970c) 9472; manufactures silk goods, leather; lake resort; Centenary Coll. for Women (1867).

Hack·ney \'hak-nē\. A borough of Greater London, SE England. See table at LONDON 4.

Ha·da·mar \'häd-ə-,mär\. Town, Hesse, West Germany, 27 m. N of Wiesbaden; pop. (1968e) 6300; textiles; first mentioned 832; site of concentration camp during World War II.

Ha·da·no \hä-'dä-nō\. City, Kanagawa prefecture, Honshū, Japan, 37 m. SW of Tokyo; pop. (1970c) 75,226.

Ha·dar·ba, Ras \,räs-hə-'där-bə\ *or formerly* **Cape El·ba** \-'el-bə\. Cape extending into Red Sea, NE Sudan.

Hadd, Cape \-'had\ *or Arab.* **Ras al–Hadd** \,räs-,al-\. East extremity of Oman, SE Arabian Penin., projecting into the Arabian Sea.

Had·dam \'had-əm\. Agricultural town, cen. Middlesex co., S Connecticut, on Connecticut river; pop. (1970c) 4934; incorporated 1668.

Had·ding·ton \'had-iŋ-tən\ *or* **Had·ding·ton·shire** \-,shi(ə)r, -shər\. 1 County, SE Scotland. See EAST LOTHIAN.

2 Burgh, ⊗ of East Lothian co., SE Scotland; pop. (1971p) 6505; includes Giffordgate, birthplace of John Knox.

Had·don \'had-ᵊn\. Urban township, Camden co., SW New Jersey, SSE of Camden; pop. (1970c) 18,192.

Had·don·field \'had-ᵊn-,fēld\. Residential borough, Camden co., SW New Jersey, 6 m. SE of Camden; pop. (1970c) 13,118; founded c. 1710 by Elizabeth Haddon, an English Quaker; scene of Revolutionary skirmishes; meeting place of New Jersey's first legislature 1777.

Haddon Heights. Borough, Camden co., SW New Jersey, 5 m. SSE of Camden; pop. (1970c) 9365.

Ha·de·jia \hə-'dā-jē-ə\. 1 River, N Nigeria; 375 m. long; rises W of Kano and flows ENE to the Yobe on Nigerian border.

2 Town, Kano State, NE Nigeria, on Hadejia river 110 m. E of Kano; chief town of former emirate of Katagum.

Ha·de·ra \hə-'dār-ə\. Town, W Israel, near coast 26 m. S of Haifa; pop. (1970e) 30,700; paper.

Ha·ders·lev \'hath-ərz-,lev\ *or Ger.* **Ha·ders·le·ben** \'häd-ərz-,lā-bən\. Seaport, Sønderjylland co., Denmark, SE Jutland; pop. (1970e) 29,647; railroad center; iron foundries, breweries, tanneries, fisheries; 13th cent. cathedral; first mentioned 1228; under German rule 1864–1920.

Hadhr, Al–. See AL-HADHR.

Ha·dhra·maut *or* **Ha·dra·maut** *or* **Ha·dra·mawt** \,häd-rə-'mu̇t, -'mau̇t\. Coastal region, E Yemen (✱ Aden), S Arabian Penin.; ab. 58,000 sq. m.; pop. (1961e) 240,000; parallel to coast is mountain range with av. alt. of 3500 ft. (highest peak ab. 8000 ft.); central part contains fertile valley along **Wa·di Hadhramaut** \,wäd-ē-\ (ab. 400 m. long); produces dates, honey, tobacco; chief town port of Mukalla.

History: In ancient times had advanced civilization as indicated by extensive ruins; little known before end of 19th cent. as the inhabitants (Hadhramautians or Hadhrumi) have resisted entry by foreigners; formerly divided into several sultanates and sheikhdoms in the more important of which the British had resident advisers (since 1882, by treaty); Arab rulers overthrown and region made part of Yemen 1967.

Hadibu. See TAMRIDAH.

Ha·di·tha \hə-'dē-thə\ *or* **Al–Ha·di·thah** \al-\. Town, W cen. Iraq, on W bank of the Euphrates above Hit.

Had·ley \'had-lē\. Town, Hampshire co., W Massachusetts, on Connecticut river 16 m. N of Springfield; pop. (1970c) 3750; birthplace of Gen. Joseph Hooker; settled 1659, incorporated 1661.

Hadley Falls Dam. See HOLYOKE DAM.

Hadramaut *or* **Hadramawt.** See HADHRAMAUT.

Hadranum. See ADRANO.

Hadria. See ADRIA.

Hadrianopolis. See EDİRNE.

Hadria Picena. See ATRI.
Hadrumetum. See SOUSSE.
Hae·ju \'hī-(,)jü\ *or Jap.* **Kai·shu** \'kī-(,)shü\. Town, ✱ of South Hwanghae prov., North Korea; pop. (1960e) 70,000.
Haelen. See HALEN.
Haemus. See BALKAN MOUNTAINS.
Ha–erh–pin. See HARBIN.
Haf·fe \'haf-ə\ *or* **Al–Haf·fah** \al-\. Town, N Latakia, Syria, ab. 15 m. NE of Latakia.
Haf·nar·fjör·dhur \'häp-när-,fyər-thu̇r\. Town, SW Iceland, ab. 10 m. S of Reykjavík; pop. (1970c) 9696; fishing port.
Ha·fun, Cape \-ha-'fün\ *or Arab.* **Ras Hafun** \,räs-\. Cape on coast of NE Somalia; the E extremity of Africa, 10°27′N and 51°26′E.
Hafun Bay North. Inlet of Indian Ocean on NE coast of Somalia, N of Cape Hafun; S of cape is **Hafun Bay South.**
Ha·gen \'häg-ən\. Industrial city, North Rhine-Westphalia, West Germany, 30 m. ENE of Düsseldorf; pop. (1969e) 201,512; iron and steel, machinery, chemicals, paper; received municipal rights 1746.
Ha·gers·town \'hā-gərz-,tau̇n\. City, ⊗ of Washington co., N Maryland, 68 m. WNW of Baltimore; pop. (1970c) 35,862; manufactures organs, furniture, flour, cement, aircraft.
Ha·gi \'häg-ē\. Coastal town, Yamaguchi prefecture, SW Honshū, Japan, in N part on Sea of Japan; pop. (1970c) 52,541; former ✱ of Yamaguchi prefecture.
Ha·gia Tri·a·da \ä-,yē-ə-trē-'äth-ə\. Ruins of ancient town, near Tympákion and shore of Bay of Messara, S Crete, Greece; important archaeological site.
Hagion *or* **Hagios.** See SAINT.
Hagion Oros. Department, Greece. See MOUNT ATHOS.
Ha·gi·os Eli·as, Mount \-ä-yȯs-ē-'l(y)ē-əs\ *or* **Mount Ayi·os·ilí·as** \-ä-yȯ-si-'lē-əs\ *also* **Mount Saint Elias** \-,sānt-\. Name of several mountains in Greece; including: (1) a peak 7904 ft. in the Taygetus Mts., W Laconia, S Peloponnesus; (2) *or* **Ókhi·ó·ros** \ȯk-ē-'ȯr-ȯs\ *or anc.* **Ocha** \'ō-kə\, a peak 4839 ft. in S Euboea I.; (3) a peak 5663 ft. in Othrys Mts., S Thessaly.
Hagios Ev·strá·ti·os *also* **Áyi·os Ev·strá·ti·os** \'ä-yȯ-sef-'strät-ē-əs\. Island in N cen. Aegean Sea, ab. 25 m. S of Lemnos; chief town Hagios Evstrátios, near NW tip of island; part of Lesbos dept., Greece.
Hagios Ni·kó·la·os \'ä-yȯ-sni-'kȯ-lə-,ȯs\. Seaport town, ✱ of Lasithion dept., E Crete, Greece; on W shore of Mirabella Bay; pop. (1971p) 5170.
Ha·go·noy \,hä-gə-'nȯi\. Municipality, SW Bulacan prov., Luzon, Phil., in Pampanga delta 7 m. W of Malolos; pop. (1969e) 64,300.
Hague, Cape La. See LA HAGUE, CAPE.
Hague, The \thə-'hāg\ *or Du.* **'s Gra·ven·ha·ge** \,s(k)räv-ən-'häg-ə\. City, de facto seat of the Dutch government and ✱ of South Holland prov., SW Netherlands, 33 m. SW of Amsterdam and 4 m. inland from North Sea; pop. (1970e) 550,613; metallurgical industries; chemicals, glass; food processing, printing; site of headquarters of many international companies; meeting place of the International Peace Conference 1899 and the Second International Peace Conference 1907; site of the international courts of arbitration and justice, housed in the Peace Palace (gift of Andrew Carnegie); Royal Palace, Groote Kerk, Municipal Museum, Mauritshuis. Originally a hunting seat of the counts of Holland, since 1250 the royal residence; in World War II occupied by Germans May 16, 1940.
Ha·gue·nau \ag-(ə-)'nō\. Commune, Bas-Rhin dept., NE France, 11 m. N of Strasbourg; pop. (1968c) 22,944; textiles, glass; breweries; 13th cent. church; 15th cent. chancellery (now a municipal library); built around hunting lodge of duke of Swabia 11th cent.; site of Hohenstaufen imperial tribunal (before which Richard the Lion-Hearted appeared); became free city 1255, French 1634; fortresses razed by Louis XIV; in World War II taken by Americans Mar. 1945.
Ha·ha·ji·ma \,hä-hä-'jē-mə\ *also* **Mother Island.** Island group of the Bonin Is., Japan.
Ha–ha–Ji·ma. Largest island of the Hahajima island group, Japan.
Hahn·ville \'hän-,vil\. Village, ⊗ of Saint Charles parish, SE Louisiana; pop. (1970c) 2483.
Hai \'hī\ *or* **Hai Ho** \'hī-'hə\. The lower course of the Pai river, China, from its junction at Tientsin with the Grand Canal to its mouth on Gulf of Chihli.
Hai·bak \'hī-(,)bək\. Town, ✱ of Samāngan prov., N Afghanistan; pop. (1969e) 38,350.
Haidarabad. See HYDERABAD.
Hai·ding·er \'hīd-iŋ-ər\. Mountain, Southern Alps, South I., New Zealand; N of Mt. Cook; 10,059 ft.
Haï·dra \'hī-drə\ *or anc.* **Am·moe·da·ra** \a-'mēd-ə-rə\. Town, W Tunisia, on boundary of Algeria; phosphates; ruins of ancient town include two arches and a mausoleum.
Hai·fa \'hī-fə\ *also* **Kaif·fa** *or* **Khai·fa** \'kī-fə\. **1** District of NW Israel. See table at ISRAEL.
2 *or anc.* **Syc·a·mi·num** \,sik-ə-'mī-nəm\. Seaport, its ✱, at S end of Bay of Haifa at foot of Mt. Carmel; pop. (1970e) 217,100, met. area pop. 463,500; Israel's chief port; steel mill, chemical plants, oil refinery; textiles, glass, cement; naval base; technical inst. (1924), univ. (1963).
Haifong. See HAIPHONG.
Hai–k'ou \'hī-'kau̇, -'kō\ *or* **Hoi·how** \'hȯi-'hau̇, 'hī-'kō\ *or Fr.* **Hoï–Hao** \ō-ē-au̇\. Port, NE coast of Hainan I., Kwangtung prov., SE China; pop. (1970e) 500,000; made an open port 1876.
Hail \'hīl\ *or* **Hā'il** \'hī(ə)l\. Town and oasis, N Nejd, Saudi Arabia, 250 m. NE of Medina.
Hai·lar \'hī-'lär\ *or* **Hai–la–erh** \-'lä-'e(ə)r\. **1** River, Inner Mongolia, China; ab. 240 m. long; upper course of the Argun (*q.v.*).
2 *or formerly* **Hu·lun** \'hü-'lün\. Town, Inner Mongolia, China, on Hailar river; ✱ of former North Hsingan prov., Manchukuo.
Hai·ley \'hā-lē\. City, ⊗ of Blaine co., S cen. Idaho; pop. (1970c) 1425; timber.
Hai·ley·bury \'hā-lē-,ber-ē\. Residential town, ⊗ of Timiskaming dist., SE Ontario, Canada, on W shore of Lake Timiskaming 80 m. N of North Bay; pop. (1971p) 5257; founded c. 1873.
Hai–lun \'hī-'lün\. Town, SE cen. Heilungkiang prov., NE China, ab. 110 m. N of Harbin.
Hai·nan \'hī-'nän\ *or* **Hai–nan Tao** \-'tau̇\. Island in South China Sea off S coast of Kwangtung prov., SE China, and E of Gulf of Tonkin; a part of Kwangtung prov.; 13,124 sq. m.; pop. (1953c) 2,800,000 (ab. 2/3 Chinese); its administrative center is Hai-k'ou; separated from Luichow Penin. by **Hainan Strait** (15 m. wide). Mountainous (central range, 2500 to 5100 ft.), much of area thickly forested; products incl. bananas, coffee, pepper; chief towns Ch'iung-shan and its port Hai-k'ou. Chinese since 2d cent. B.C.; not closely controlled until Yüan dynasty (1280–1368); Ch'iung-shan (*q.v.*) opened to foreign trade 1858; occupied by Japanese 1939–45; came under Chinese Communist control April 1950.
Hainau. See CHOJNÓW.
Hai·naut \(h)ā-'nō\ *or Flem.* **He·ne·gou·wen** \'hā-nə-,gau̇-ən\. **1** Medieval county in the Low Countries, now included in Belgium (Hainaut prov.) and N France (Nord dept.); erected in 9th cent. A.D.; united by marriage with county of Flanders and later with Holland; in 14th cent. came to be held by Wittelsbach house of Bavaria; taken by Philip of Burgundy 1433; became in turn part of Spanish and Austrian Netherlands and a province of kingdom of Belgium.

2 Province, SW Belgium; 1463 sq. m.; pop. (1970e) 1,330,-789; ✱ Mons; wheat, sugar beet; livestock raising, coal mining; steel, textiles, chemicals, glass, wire, machine tools.

Hain·burg \'hīn-ˌbu̇(ə)rg\ *or in full* **Hainburg an der Do·nau** \-än-dər-'dō-nau̇\. Town, Lower Austria, on the Danube near its confluence with the Morava W of Bratislava; pop. (1967e) 6400; manufactures tobacco. A very old town, has many Roman remains including an aqueduct still in use; captured by Turks 1529, 1683.

Haine \'an, 'en\. River, S Hainaut prov., Belgium; 40 m. long; flows W into Schelde river in France.

Haines \'hānz\. 1 Borough in Alaska. See table at ALASKA.
2 City, its ⊗, on W side of Lynn Canal ab. 20 m. S of Skagway; pop. (1970c) 463; former U.S. Army base.

Haines City. City, Polk co., cen. Florida penin., 20 m. E of Lakeland; pop. (1970c) 8956; citrus center; incorporated 1920.

Hai·phong *or* **Hai Phong** *also* **Hai·fong** \'hī-'fŏŋ\. Seaport, North Vietnam, in the delta of the Red river ab. 20 m. from the Gulf of Tonkin and ab. 60 m. E of Hanoi; pop. (1960c) 182,496; harbor suffers from silting in its channels but has sizable export trade; manufactures cement, glass, chemicals, and cotton; fish processing; naval station; connected by railway with K'un-ming in Yunnan, China. Established 1874; occupied by Japanese Sept. 26, 1940–Aug. 1945; port facilities heavily damaged by U.S. bombing 1965–68.

Hai·ti \'hāt-ē\ 1 *or Fr.* **Ha·ï·ti** \á-ē-tē\. Republic occupying W third of Hispaniola I., West Indies; 10,714 sq. m.; pop. (1971e) 4,969,113; ✱ Port-au-Prince. *Physical features:* NW separated from E tip of Cuba by Windward Passage; coastline irregular with large indentation (Gulf of Gonave) on W coast enclosed by two peninsulas (the one on the S being the long, mountainous Tiburon Penin.) and containing Gonave I.; off N coast is Tortuga I. Highest point in SE, in La Selle Mts., 8793 ft.; only large river the Artibonite. *Chief exports:* Coffee, cotton, sugar, bananas, sisal; bauxite, copper. *Chief towns:* Port-au-Prince, Cap Haitien, Cayes, Gonaïves. Population chiefly Negroes; official language French.

History: West part of island of Hispaniola belonged to French from Treaty of Ryswick 1697; French rule not challenged until slave insurrection 1791 which was succeeded by stormy period under native rulers who at times dominated entire island, as did Toussaint L'Ouverture 1801–02, Dessalines 1804–06, and Boyer 1822–43; republic since 1820; because of financial and civil disorder, subject to occupation by American marines and a virtual protectorate of U.S. 1915–34; adopted present constitution 1964, amended it 1971.
2 Original name for Hispaniola island. See HISPANIOLA.

Hai–yang \'hī-'yäŋ\. Island in Korea Bay, China, SE of Liaotung Penin. and 90 m. ENE of Dairen; naval battle Sept. 17, 1894 in which Japanese decisively defeated the Chinese.

Ha·ja·ra, Al– \al-'haj-ə-rə\ *or* **Al–Hi·jā·rah** \al-hi-'jär-ə\. Extensive desert region, S Iraq, bet. the Euphrates and border of Saudi Arabia.

Haj·dú–Bi·har \'hȯi-dü-ˌbē-(ˌ)hȯ(ə)r\. County of E Hungary. See table at HUNGARY.

Haj·dú·bö·ször·mény \'hȯi-dü-ˌbər-sər-ˌmān(-yə)\. City, E Hungary, 10 m. NW of Debrecen; pop. (1970p) 30,448; 16th cent. church.

Haj·du·do·rog \'hȯi-dü-ˌdō-ˌrōg\. Commune, E Hungary, ab. 20 m. N of Debrecen; pop. (1970p) 10,224; in agricultural region.

Haj·du·had·ház \'hȯi-dü-ˌhäd-(ˌ)häz\. City, E Hungary, 11 m. N of Debrecen; pop. (1970p) 13,610; in agricultural region.

Haj·du·ná·nás \'hȯid-ə-ˌnän-əsh\. City, E Hungary, 25 m. NNW of Debrecen; pop. (1970p) 17,824.

Haj·du·szo·bosz·ló \'hȯi-dü-ˌsō-bə-ˌslō\. City, E Hungary, 13 m. SW of Debrecen; pop. (1970p) 21,793; health resort.

Ha·ka·lau \ˌhä-kä-'lä-ü\. Village, South Hilo div., Hawaii co., Hawaii, on E coast of Hawaii I. N of Hilo; pop. (1970c) 742.

Ha·ka·pe·hi \ˌhäk-ə-'pā-(ˌ)hē\ *or* **Ta·i·o·hae** *or* **Tai–o–hae** \ˌtī-ō-'hī\. Town, ✱ of the Marquesas Is., on S shore of Nuku Hiva I., French Polynesia; pop. (1967e) 687; huge prehistoric stone platforms of unknown origin nearby.

Ha·ka·ta Bay \'hä-ˌkät-ə-\. Inlet of Sea of Japan, NW coast of Kyūshū, Japan; forms outer harbor of Fukuoka.

Hak·kâ·rı *or formerly* **Ha·kâ·ri** \ˌhäk-(y)ä-'rē\. 1 Province of SE Turkey, Asia. See table at TURKEY.
2 Town, SE Turkey. See CÖLEMERIK.

Ha·ko·da·te \ˌhäk-ə-'dät-ē\. Seaport city, SW Hokkaidō, Japan, on Tsugaru Strait; pop. (1970e) 241,663; for many years chief city of the island and capital of Hokkaidō prefecture, now replaced by Sapporo; built on rocky peninsula; excellent harbor; first opened to foreign trade 1854.

Ha·ko·ne \hä-'kō-nē\. Village and mountain resort in SE Honshū, Japan, in Kanagawa prefecture 23 m. ESE of Fuji and ab. 35 m. SW of Yokohama; on **Lake Hakone**; numerous hot springs; good views of Fuji.

Ha·ku·san \ˌhäk-ə-'sän\. Mountain, Ishikawa prefecture, W Honshū, Japan, on Gifu border; 8862 ft.; an extinct volcano, last eruption recorded 1554; comprises 5 peaks.

Hakusan National Park. National park, Honshū, Japan; 183 sq. m.; contains Hakusan Mt.; established 1962.

Hal. See HALLE 1.

Ha·la \'həl-ə\. Town, Sind prov., Pakistan, 30 m. N of Hyderabad; pop. (1961c) 11,956; noted for its glazed pottery.

Halab. See ALEPPO.

Hala Mountains. See KIRTHAR RANGE.

Halas. See KISKUNHALAS.

Ha·la·wa Bay \hə-'lä-və-, -wə-\. Bay on NE coast of Molokai I., Hawaii, W of Halawa Point.

Halawa Heights. Town, Honolulu co., Hawaii, 6 m. NW of Honolulu; pop. (1970c) 5809.

Halawa Point. Cape at NE end of Molokai I., Hawaii.

Hal·ba \'hal-bə\. Town, N Lebanon, 15 m. NE of Tripoli.

Hal·ber·stadt \'häl-bər-ˌs(h)tät\. City, Magdeburg dist., East Germany, 33 m. SE of Brunswick; pop. (1970e) 46,-774; agricultural machinery, asbestos; metalworking, food processing; founded in 12th cent.; in World War II center for manufacture of bombers.

Hal·con, Mount \-häl-'kȯn\. Highest peak in Mindoro I., Phil., in N part ab. 15 m. SW of Calapan; 8469 ft.

Hal·cott, Mount \-'hȯl-kət\. Peak in Catskill Mts., Greene co., SE New York; 3537 ft.

Hal·den \'häl-dən\ *or formerly* **Fred·riks·hald** \'fred-riks-ˌhäl\. Seaport, Østfold co., SE Norway, on the Skagerrak near Swedish border; pop. (1970e) 26,721; lumber-manufacturing center; quarrying; textile mills.

Hal·di·mand \'hȯl-də-mənd\. County, Ontario, Canada. See table at ONTARIO.

Halditjokko. See HALTIATUNTURI.

Hale \'hāl\. 1 Name of counties in two states of the U.S. See tables at ALABAMA and TEXAS.

2 Urban district, Cheshire, NW England, 10 m. S of Manchester; pop. (1971p) 17,030.

Ha·le·a·ka·la Crater \ˌhäl-ē-ˌäk-ə-'lä-\. Crater in E Maui I., Hawaii; present crater (area 19 sq. m., depth 2720 ft.) chiefly a result of stream erosion. Area, formerly part of Hawaii National Park, was in 1961 made a separate park, **Haleakala Volcanoes National Park.** See UNITED STATES, *National Parks.*

Haleb. See ALEPPO.

Hale·don \'hā(ə)l-dən\. Borough, Passaic co., N New Jersey, 2 m. N of Paterson; pop. (1970c) 6767.

Ha·le·i·wa \ˌhä-lā-'ē-və\. City, Honolulu co., Hawaii, on Waialua Bay on N coast of Oahu; pop. (1970c) 2626.

Ha·le·mau·mau \ˌhäl-ə-'mau̇-ˌmau̇\. The fire pit of Kilauea crater on the slope of Mauna Loa volcano, Hawaii I., Hawaii; ab. 470 ft. deep; when active, contains from 48 to 190 acres of red-hot lava.

Ha·len *also* **Hae·len** \'häl-ən\. Commune, Limburg prov., NE Belgium; pop. (1969e) 5341; scene of Belgian victory over Germans Aug. 12, 1914.

Ha·le·pa \hä-'lep-ə\ *or Gk.* **Kha·lé·pa** \ˌkä-\. Eastern suburb of Canea, on island of Crete, Greece; Pact of Halepa signed here Oct. 1878.

Hales Corners \'hālz-\. Village, Milwaukee co., SE Wisconsin, SW of Milwaukee; pop. (1970c) 7771.

Hales·ow·en \'hā-(ə)l-ˌzō-ən\. Municipal borough, Worcestershire, W cen. England, on the Stour 8 m. SW of Birmingham; pop. (1970e) 53,933; manufactures iron and steel, electronic equipment, brick.

Ha·ley·ville \'hā-lē-ˌvil\. City, Winston co., NW Alabama, 46 m. SW of Decatur; pop. (1970c) 4190; lumber; coal mines.

Halfa. See WADI HALFA.

Hal·fa·ya Pass \hal-ˌfī-ə-\ *or Arab.* **Nagb al–Halfayah** \ˌnäk-əb-al-\. Pass through the coast range of hills just S of Salūm, extreme NW Egypt; battles Jan. and Nov. 1942; called "Hellfire Pass" by British soldiers.

Half Dome. Peak in Sierra Nevada, in E Mariposa co., cen. California; 8842 ft.

Half Moon Bay. City, San Mateo co., W California, on Half Moon Bay (inlet); pop. (1970c) 4023; packs fruit and vegetables.

Haliacmon. See VISTRITSA.

Hal·i·ar·tus \ˌhal-ē-'ärt-əs\. Ancient town, Boeotia, Greece, 15 m. NW of Thebes; place where Spartan commander Lysander was killed 395 B.C.

Hal·i·bur·ton \'hal-ə-ˌbərt-ᵊn\. County, Ontario, Canada. See table at ONTARIO.

Haliç. See GOLDEN HORN 2.

Hal·i·car·nas·sus \ˌhal-ə-(ˌ)kär-'nas-əs\ *or mod.* **Bo·drum** \bō-'drüm\. Ancient city in SW Caria, Asia Minor (now in Turkey), on S coast of a peninsula; site of tomb of Mausolus (Mausoleum of Halicarnassus), erected c. 350 B.C. by Queen Artemisia, which ranked among Seven Wonders of the World in ancient times (its remains in the British Museum); birthplace of Herodotus.

Ha·licz \'häl-ich\. 1 Polish name of GALICIA.

2 Medieval principality, E Galicia, 12th and 13th cents.; then part of Russia, comprising lands about the upper courses of Dniester and Prut rivers; chief town Halicz. United with Lodomeria in 13th cent., later belonged for varying periods to Poland, Austria, Russia, and Germany; now in SW Ukrainian S.S.R., U.S.S.R.

Hal·i·don Hill \ˌhal-əd-ᵊn-\. Hill near Berwick-upon-Tweed, N England; battle July 19, 1333 in which Edward III, assisting Edward de Baliol, claimant to the throne of David Bruce, defeated the Scots.

Hal·i·fax \'hal-ə-ˌfaks\. 1 Counties in two states of the U.S. See tables at NORTH CAROLINA and VIRGINIA.

2 Town, Plymouth co., Massachusetts, 10 m. WNW of Plymouth; pop. (1970c) 3537.

3 Town, ⊗ of Halifax co., NE North Carolina, 29 m. NNE of Rocky Mount; pop. (1970c) 335; settled c. 1723; scene of North Carolina's first constitutional convention.

4 Town, ⊗ of Halifax co., S Virginia; pop. (1970c) 899.

5 County, Nova Scotia, Canada. See table at NOVA SCOTIA.

6 Commercial city, ✻ of Nova Scotia, Canada, and ⊗ of Halifax co., on Atlantic Ocean in cen. part of S coast of province; pop. (1971p) 121,086, met. area pop. 220,350; natural harbor; dry docks, dockyards; in winter Canada's most active port; used by fishing fleets; iron foundries, soap, boot and shoe factories, machine shops, breweries; oil refining; railroad terminus; old fortress; Dalhousie Univ. (1818), Saint Mary's Univ. (1841), Nova Scotia Technical Coll. (1907), Mount Saint Vincent Univ. (1873).

History: Founded 1749 as British stronghold to rival French Louisburg; made capital of Nova Scotia in place of Annapolis Royal 1750; incorporated as city 1842; garrisoned by British troops until its defense was taken over by dominion forces 1906; Canadian naval base since 1910; greatly damaged by an explosion caused by a harbor collision 1917; in World War II an important embarkation port.

7 County borough, West Riding, Yorkshire, N England, on the Hebble 22 m. NE of Manchester; pop. (1971p) 91,171; has manufactures of cotton, wool, and worsted goods, iron and steel. Defoe is reputed to have written part of *Robinson Crusoe* at an inn here.

Halifax Bay. Inlet of Pacific Ocean on E coast of Queensland, Australia, 18°50′S, 146°30′E; Townsville on it.

Halifax Citadel National Historic Park. See CANADA, *National Historic Parks.*

Ha·li·sa·har \'häl-ə-sə-ˌhər\. Town, West Bengal, NE India; pop. (1961c) 51,423.

Hall \'hȯl\. Name of counties in three states of the U.S. See tables at GEORGIA, NEBRASKA, TEXAS.

Hall. See SCHWÄBISCH-HALL.

Hal·la \'hä-'lä\ *or Jap.* **Kan·ra** \'kän-ˌrä\. Extinct volcano on Cheju I., in East China Sea off S coast of South Korea; 6398 ft.

Hal·land \'häl-ənd\. County of SW Sweden. See table at SWEDEN.

Hal·lan·dale \'hal-ən-ˌdāl\. City, Broward co., SE Florida, on Atlantic Ocean 15 m. N of Miami; pop. (1970c) 23,849; chemicals, canned goods, furniture; citrus fruit, vegetables.

Hal·la·ni·ya \ˌhal-ə-'nē-(y)ə\. Largest of the Kuria Muria Is. (*q.v.*); pop. (1967e) 85.

Hall Basin. Expansion of passage bet. Ellesmere I. and NW Greenland; connects Kennedy Channel with Robeson Channel.

Hal·le \'häl-ə\. 1 *or Fr.* **Hal** \ål\. Commune, Brabant prov., Belgium; pop. (1969e) 20,183; paper.

2 District of East Germany. See table at GERMANY, EAST.

3 Commercial and industrial city, ✻ of Halle dist., East Germany, on the Saale 31 m. WNW of Leipzig; pop. (1970e) 257,300; machinery, electronic equipment; coal mining, food processing; important railroad junction; medieval town hall; 15th cent. tower; former archiepiscopal residence; univ. (formed 1817 through merger of two older universities). Existed in 9th cent.; member of Hanseatic League in 13th and 14th cents.; captured by French

1806; to Prussia 1813; in World War II frequently bombed 1944–45; taken by Allies Apr. 17–19, 1945.

Hal·letts·ville \'hal-əts-ˌvil\. City, ⊗ of Lavaca co., SE cen. Texas, 45 m. N of Victoria; pop. (1970c) 2712; ships livestock, cotton, cottonseed oil.

Hal·li·gen \'häl-i-gən\. Island group off W coast of Schleswig-Holstein, West Germany; pop. (1966e) 374; consists of the southern islands of the North Frisian group; largest islands Nordstrand and Pellworm.

Hal·lock \'hal-ək\. Village, ⊗ of Kittson co., NW corner of Minnesota, 55 m. NW of Thief River Falls; pop. (1970c) 1477.

Hal·lo·well \'häl-ə-ˌwel, -wəl\. City, Kennebec co., SW Maine, on Kennebec river 3 m. S of Augusta; pop. (1970c) 2814; potatoes, beans.

Hall Peninsula. Peninsula, N of Frobisher Bay, SE Baffin I., E Franklin dist., Northwest Territories, Canada.

Halls \'hölz\. Town, Lauderdale co., W Tennessee, 11 m. S of Dyersburg; pop. (1970c) 2323; cotton, lumber.

Halls Stream. Tributary of the Connecticut river; running bet. province of Quebec, Canada, and state of New Hampshire, U.S.; 20 m. long.

Hall·statt \'höl-ˌstat, 'häl-ˌs(h)tät\. Village, Austria, on shore of **Hall·stät·ter Lake** \ˌhöl-ˌstet-ər-, ˌhäl-ˌs(h)tet-\ (ab. 3 sq. m., max. depth 410 ft.); pop. (1964e) 1340; site of an early Iron-Age culture, known from discovery 1846–99 of more than 2000 graves from which many cultural and art objects were taken dating back to as early as 900 B.C.

Hal·luin \al-'waⁿ\. Commune, Nord dept., N France, on Belgian border 13 m. N of Lille; pop. (1968c) 14,829.

Hall·wil, Lake \-'häl-ˌvil, -vəl\ *or Ger.* **Hall·wi·ler See** \ˌhäl-ˌvil-ər-'zā\. Lake, Aargau canton, N cen. Switzerland; ab. 4 sq. m., max. depth 154 ft.; formed by expansion of the Aa river.

Hal·ma·he·ra \ˌhal-mə-'hər-ə, ˌhäl-\; *Du.* **Djai·lo·lo** \jī-'lō-(ˌ)lō\ *also* **Gi·lo·lo** \ji-'lō-(ˌ)lō\. Largest island of the Moluccas, in Indonesia, lying on the equator; 6928 sq. m.; pop. (1954e) 54,000; no towns of importance; in NE is a steamer port Galela. On E has four peninsulas enclosing three large bays; on W coast are the small islands of Ternate and Tidore (*qq.v.*); all peninsulas have mountains, 3000 to 5000 ft., those in W being volcanic; some trade in coconuts, dammar, spices. Known early to Spanish and Portuguese; under Sultan of Ternate who yielded it to Dutch 1683; in latter part of 19th cent. scene of insurrections and piracy; taken 1942 by Japanese whose bases were frequently bombed by Allies 1944.

Halm·stad \'hälm-ˌstä(d)\. Seaport, ⊗ of Halland co., SW Sweden, on the Kattegat; pop. (1970e) 46,723; steel plant, paper mills, shipbuilding yards, fisheries, breweries; 14th cent. church.

Ha–lo–hsin \'hä-'lō-'shin\ *or formerly* **Khal·ka** \'käl-kə\. River, NE China; ab. 240 m. long; its banks scene of fighting 1939.

Halq al–Wa·di \'halk-al-'wäd-ē\; *formerly* **La Gou·lette** \ˌlä-gü-'let\ *or* **Go·let·ta** \gō-'let-ə\. Seaport town, NE Tunisia; pop. (1966c) 31,830; the port of Tunis.

Häl·sing·borg *or* **Hel·sing·borg** \'hel-siŋ-ˌbȯ(ə)r\. Seaport, Malmöhus co., SW Sweden, on Øresund opp. Helsingør, Denmark; pop. (1970e) 82,137; ships grain; sugar refineries, copper smelters, rubber factories, breweries, potteries; coal and clay deposits; first mentioned 1085; belonged to Denmark before 1658.

Hal·stead \'höl-(ˌ)sted\. Urban district, Essex, SE England, on the Colne 46 m. NE of London; pop. (1971p) 7621; 16th cent. grammar school.

Hal·tem·price \'höl-təm-ˌprīs\. Urban district, East Riding, Yorkshire, NE England; pop. (1971p) 52,239; horticulture, precision engineering.

Hal·tia·tun·tu·ri \ˌhäl-tē-ə-'tün-tə-rē\ *or* **Hal·tia** \'häl-tē-ə\ *also* **Hal·dit·jok·ko** \'häl-dət-ˌyō-(ˌ)kō\. Peak, NW Finland, on Norwegian border; 4343 ft.; highest point in Finland.

Hal·tom City \ˌhöl-təm-\. Village, Tarrant co., N Texas, NE of Fort Worth; pop. (1970c) 28,127.

Hal·ton \'hölt-ᵊn\. County, Ontario, Canada. See table at ONTARIO.

Halys. See KIZIL IRMAK.

Ham \'(h)am, '(h)äm\. Village, Somme dept., N France, on the Somme 35 m. SE of Amiens; pop. (1962c) 4193; ruins of medieval castle which frequently served as state prison for political offenders, including Joan of Arc and esp. Louis Napoleon (imprisoned 1840–46); 12th–13th cent. church with ancient crypt; suffered greatly during World War I, esp. during German retreat Mar. 1917.

Ha·ma *or* **Ha·māh** \'ham-ə\ *or Bib.* **Ha·math** \'hā-ˌmath\ *or classical* **Ep·i·pha·nia** \ˌep-ə-fə-'nī-ə\. Commercial city, W Syria, 75 m. SSW of Aleppo; pop. (1970e) 137,000; on railroad; in rich agricultural region; noted for its picturesque huge waterwheels used in Middle Ages for irrigation. An old city of Hittite origin and frequently mentioned in the Bible as on the N boundary of Israel; several times captured by Assyrian kings (*2 Kings* xviii. 34; *Isaiah* xi. 11); also figured in Muslim conquest and wars of the Crusades; home of famous Arab historian Abulfeda, who was its prince 1310–31.

Hama. See TIHAMA.

Hamad, Al–. See SYRIAN DESERT.

Ha·ma·dān \ˌham-ə-'dan, -'dän\. **1** Governorship of W Iran. See table at IRAN.

2 *or anc.* **Ec·bat·a·na** \ek-'bat-ᵊn-ə\. City, its ✱, in plain at foot of Mt. Alwand ab. 180 m. WSW of Tehran; pop. (1971e) 130,000; important commercial city noted esp. for its leather goods and rugs; residence and burial place of Arab philosopher Avicenna.

History: Ancient Ecbatana capital of Media Magna and summer residence of Persian and Parthian kings; taken by Cyrus from Astyages 550 B.C.; captured by Alexander 330 B.C., by Arabs 645 A.D. The **Ach·me·tha** \ak-'mē-thə\ of the Bible (*Ezra* vi. 2), in the palace of which the decree of Cyrus was found; site of the traditional tomb of Mordecai and Esther.

Hamāh. City, Syria. See HAMA.

Ha·ma·ki·ta \ˌhäm-ə-'kē-tə\. City, Shizuoka prefecture, Honshū, Japan, 12 m. NE of Hamamatsu; pop. (1970c) 59,592.

Ha·ma·ma·tsu \ˌhäm-ə-'mät-(ˌ)sü\. Industrial city, Shizuoka prefecture, S Honshū, Japan, near coast 56 m. SE of Nagoya; pop. (1970c) 432,221; chief products tea, musical instruments; an old daimio castle town; bombed by Allies May–June 1945.

Ha·mar \'häm-ˌär\. City, ⊗ of Hedmark co., E Norway, on W shore of Lake Mjøsa N of Oslo; pop. (1970e) 15,189; foundry, dairies; seat of bishopric. Original town, destroyed by the Swedes 1567, founded 1152 by the English pope, Adrian IV; scene of fighting Apr. 1940.

Hamath. City, Syria. See HAMA.

Ham·bach \'häm-ˌbäk\. Commune, Rhineland-Palatinate, West Germany, 15 m. W of Speyer; pop. (1967e) 4400; produces wine; to SW lie ruins of Hambach Castle, scene of the Hambacher Fest May 1832, a gathering of ab. 25,000 persons demanding a republic and national unity of Germany.

Ham·ber Park \ˌham-bər-\. Canadian provincial park, SE British Columbia, on W slope of Rocky Mts. NW of Golden; 3800 sq. m.

Ham·blen \'ham-blən\. County in Tennessee. See table at TENNESSEE.

Ham·born \häm-'bȯ(ə)rn\. Former city, Prussia, Germany; became part of Duisburg-Hamborn 1929. See DUISBURG.

Ham·burg \'ham-ˌbərg\. **1** City, ⊗ of Ashley co., SE Arkansas; pop. (1970c) 3102; sawmills.

2 Village, Erie co., W New York, 10 m. S of Buffalo; pop. (1970c) 10,215; truck farming; manufactures optical goods; Immaculata Coll. (1928).

3 Borough, Berks co., SE Pennsylvania, on Schuylkill river 15 m. N of Reading; pop. (1970c) 3909; aluminum and steel castings, motor trucks; dairy products; founded 1779.
4 \ *also* ˈhäm-ˌbu̇(ə)rg, -ˌbu̇(ə)rk\. Maritime commercial city, constituting a state of West Germany, on Elbe river ab. 68 m. from its mouth at Cuxhaven; 289 sq. m.; pop. (1970e) 1,814,100; one of Europe's major ports; shipbuilding, oil refining, chemicals, heavy machinery, electronic equipment; exports incl. industrial equipment, metal goods, glass, chemicals, vehicles; has extensive harbor and dock installations and outport at Cuxhaven; noteworthy buildings include the Exchange, commercial library, modern Rathaus in Renaissance style, theater, 19th cent. Gothic-style church, and an 18th cent. Renaissance-style church; univ. (1919); hydrographic institute; birthplace of Brahms and Mendelssohn.
History: Founded by Charlemagne who built citadel here against Slavs bet. 808 and 811; made episcopal see 831, archiepiscopal see 834; served as missionary center for northern Europe; alliance with Lübeck 1241 and 1249 led to formation of Hanseatic League; became independent 1292; made imperial city 1510; accepted Reformation 1521–29; joined Schmalkaldic League 1536; under French rule 1806–15; became member of German Federation as free city 1815; devastated by fire 1842; received new constitution 1861 and 1921; scene of Communist rioting 1923; lost special privileges as free state 1933; by decree of Jan. 26, 1937 reorganized along lines making it a geographical unit, including a strip of land on the left (south) bank of the Elbe river and incorporating the cities of Altona, Harburg-Wilhelmsburg, and Wandsbek; laid waste by numerous bombing attacks by Allies in World War II; taken by British forces on May 3, 1945.

Ham·den \ˈham-dən\. Suburban residential town, cen. New Haven co., S Connecticut; pop. (1970c) 49,357; Quinnipiac Coll. (1929), Mount Sacred Heart Coll. (1954), South Central Community Coll. (1967).

Hä·me \ˈham-ə\ *or Swed.* **Ta·vas·te·hus** \tə-ˈvas-tə-ˌhüs, -ˈväs-\. Province of S Finland. See table at FINLAND.

Hä·meen·lin·na \ˈham-ˌān-ˌlin-ə\ *or Swed.* **Tavastehus.** City, Häme prov., SW Finland; pop. (1970p) 38,100; textiles; developed around a castle built 1249 by Birger of Bjälbo; incorporated 1638; fortress held by Russians 1918 until recovered by Finnish troops with German aid.

Ha·meln *or formerly* **Ham·e·lin** \ˈham-(ə-)lən\. Manufacturing city, Lower Saxony, West Germany, on Weser river 25 m. SW of Hannover; pop. (1969e) 46,986; metalworking; carpets; famous as scene of legend of *Pied Piper of Hamelin.*

Ham·ers·ley Range \ˌham-ərz-lē-\. Mountain range, NW Western Australia; its highest peak (also highest peak in the state) is Mt. Bruce (*q.v.*).

Ham·hŭng \ˈhäm-ˌhu̇ŋ\ *or Jap.* **Kan·ko** \ˈkän-ˌkō\. City, ❋ of South Hamgyŏng prov., North Korea; pop. (1962e) 125,000; fertilizers.

Ha–mi \ˈhä-ˈmē\ *or formerly* **Qo·mul** \kō-ˈmül\. Town and oasis, E Sinkiang Uighur, W China; ancient frontier trading center.

Ha·mid \ˈhä-ˈmēt\. District of the Ottoman Empire, S Asia Minor, W of Karaman; roughly equivalent to modern İsparta province and W Konya.

Ham·il·ton \ˈham-əl-tən, -əlt-ᵊn\. 1 Counties in ten states of the U.S. See tables at FLORIDA, ILLINOIS, INDIANA, IOWA, KANSAS, NEBRASKA, NEW YORK, OHIO, TENNESSEE, TEXAS.
2 Town, ⊗ of Marion co., NW Alabama; pop. (1970c) 3088.
3 City, ⊗ of Harris co., W Georgia; pop. (1970c) 357.
4 City, Hancock co., W Illinois, on Mississippi river 33 m. N of Quincy; pop. (1970c) 2764; stock farms.
5 Town, Essex co., NE corner of Massachusetts, 21 m. NE of Boston; pop. (1970c) 6373.
6 City, ⊗ of Ravalli co., W Montana, 45 m. S of Missoula; pop. (1970c) 2499; lumber mills, creamery, cannery.
7 *or* **Hamilton Square.** Urban township, Mercer co., W cen. New Jersey, E of Trenton; pop. (1970c) 79,609.
8 Village, Madison co., cen. New York, 26 m. SW of Utica; pop. (1970c) 3636; settled 1792; canning and quarrying industries; Colgate Univ. (chartered 1819).
9 Industrial city, ⊗ of Butler co., SW Ohio, 20 m. N of Cincinnati; pop. (1970c) 67,865; automobile parts, chemicals, paper-mill machinery, paper products; on site of Fort Hamilton, built by St. Clair 1791, used as garrison post in Wayne's campaign of 1793–94; settled c. 1803, and became ⊗; incorporated 1810.
10 City, ⊗ of Hamilton co., cen. Texas, 47 m. E of Brownwood; pop. (1970c) 2760; cotton gins, flour and cottonseed-oil mills; clay and limestone deposits.
11 Town, SW Victoria, SE Australia, 160 m. W of Melbourne; pop. (1968e) 10,160; freezes and exports mutton.
12 Seaport town, ❋ of Bermuda, on Bermuda I.; pop. (1970e) 2127; tourism; founded 1790, made capital 1815; made free port 1956.
13 River, Canada. See CHURCHILL 4.
14 City, ⊗ of Wentworth co., SE Ontario, Canada, at W end of Lake Ontario ab. 40 m. SW of Toronto; pop. (1971p) 307,473, met. area pop. 495,864; important transportation center: harbor, railroad terminus, airport; manufactures steel, iron, electrical equipment, textiles. McMaster Univ. (1887) in nearby Westdale; Royal Botanical Gardens (established 1941). Visited by La Salle 1669; first settled 1813.
15 City, cen. North I., New Zealand; on Waikato river 70 m. SSE of Auckland; pop. (1970e) 71,600; center of farming, cattle, and sheep district; Univ. of Waikato (1964).
16 Burgh, ⊗ of Lanark co., S cen. Scotland; pop. (1971p) 46,347; coal and iron mines, quarries, iron foundries.

Hamilton, Lake. 1 Lake in S Garland and NW Hot Spring cos., SW cen. Arkansas, formed by **Car·pen·ter Dam** \ˌkär-pən-tər-\across Ouachita river.
2 Lake in cen. Texas. See BUCHANAN DAM.

Hamilton, Mount. 1 Peak, Santa Clara co., W California, 13 m. E of San Jose; 4261 ft.; site of Lick Observatory.
2 Peak, White Pine co., E Nevada; 10,741 ft.

Hamilton Dam. See BUCHANAN DAM.

Hamilton Inlet. Inlet of Atlantic Ocean, SE Labrador, Newfoundland, Canada, estuary of Churchill river; with Lake Melville ab. 150 m. long; one of the largest fjords on the Labrador coast, 14 to 25 m. wide. Visited by early explorers (John Davis, 1586); site of French and English trading posts in 18th cent.; at its head Rigolet was established 1837 by Hudson's Bay Company.

Hamilton Square. Township, New Jersey. See HAMILTON 7.

Ha·mi·na \ˈham-ə-nə\ *or Swed.* **Fre·driks·hamn** \ˈfrā-driks-ˌham-ən\. Town, Kymi prov., SE Finland, on Gulf of Finland; pop. (1967e) 10,770; scene of signing of treaty of peace 1809 by which Sweden ceded Finland to Russia.

Ha·mir·pur \hə-ˈmi(ə)r-ˌpu̇(ə)r\. Town, SW Uttar Pradesh, N India, on the Yamuna 38 m. SSW of Kanpur; pop. (1961c) 10,921; traditionally founded by a Rajput chieftain in 11th cent.

Ham·let \ˈham-lət\. Town, Richmond co., S North Carolina, 48 m. WSW of Fayetteville; pop. (1970c) 4627; peaches; timber.

Ham·lin \ˈhəm-lən\. 1 County in South Dakota. See table at SOUTH DAKOTA.
2 City, Fisher and Jones cos., NW cen. Texas, 40 m. NNW of Abilene; pop. (1970c) 3325; gypsum, sand, gravel deposits.
3 Town, ⊗ of Lincoln co., W West Virginia; pop. (1970c) 1024.

Hamm \ˈhäm, ˈham\ *also* **Hamm in West·fa·len** \-in-vest-ˈfäl-ən\. Commercial and manufacturing city, North

Rhine-Westphalia, West Germany, on Lippe river 21 m. SSE of Münster; pop. (1969e) 84,266; iron and wire mills; textiles, office equipment; 15th cent. town hall; in World War II a traffic, power, and supply center. Founded 1227; one of Hanse Towns 1417 ff.; passed to Brandenburg 1666; frequently bombed by Allies 1944–45, taken Apr. 3–4, 1945.

Hamma, Al–. See AL-HAMMA.

Ham·ma·da al–Ham·ra \ha-ˌmad-ə-al-ˈham-rə\. Plateau and desert region, NW Libya, on border of Algeria; ab. 40,000 sq. m.; explored by J. Richardson and H. Barth 1850–55.

Hammām, Al–. See AL-HAMMĀM.

Ham·mam–bou–Ha·djar \hə-ˌmam-bü-ˈhaj-ˌär\. Commune, Oran dept., NW Algeria, SW of Oran; pop. (1966c) 11,219.

Ham·ma·met \ˌham-ə-ˈmet\. Coastal town, NE Tunisia, on the **Gulf of Hammamet,** an inlet of the Mediterranean, at S base of peninsula ending in Cape Bon; pop. (1966c) 12,500; seized May 10, 1943 by British in pursuit of German forces retreating into the peninsula.

Hammam Lif \hə-ˈmäm-ˈlēf\. Town, Tunisia, on Gulf of Tunis; pop. (1966c) 25,091.

Ham·mar, Hor al– \ˌhȯr-ˌal-ˈham-ər\. Lake or marshland region, SE Iraq, S of the Euphrates before it joins the Tigris at Al-Qurna; ab. 70 m. long; has connection with the Euphrates and with the Shatt-al-Arab above Basra.

Ham·me \ˈhäm-ə\. Commune, East Flanders prov., NW cen. Belgium, 14 m. SW of Antwerp; pop. (1969e) 17,493; brewing; carpets.

Ham·me·ren, Cape \-ˈham-ə-rən, -ˈhäm-\. Cape on N tip of Bornholm I., Denmark; lighthouse.

Ham·mer·fest \ˈham-ər-ˌfest, ˈhäm-\. Northernmost city in Europe, Finnmark co., N Norway; located on Kvaløy I., 70°40′N, 23°42′E; pop. (1970e) 7062; manufactures cod-liver oil; exports furs, smoked and salted fish; has uninterrupted daylight May 17 to July 29; sun not visible Nov. 21 to Jan 21; received charter 1789.

Ham·mer·smith \ˈham-ər-ˌsmith\. A borough of Greater London. See table at LONDON 4.

Hamm in Westfalen. See HAMM.

Ham·mo·nas·set \ˌham-ə-ˈnas-ət\. River, S Connecticut; ab. 18 m. long; forms S part of boundary bet. New Haven and Middlesex cos. and empties into Long Island Sound just E of **Hammonasset Point.**

Ham·mond \ˈham-ənd\. 1 Industrial city, Lake co., NW corner of Indiana, on Illinois border adjacent to Calumet City; pop. (1970c) 107,790; railroad equipment and supplies, steel, hospital supplies; oil refineries, packing plants; printing industry; incorporated as city 1884.

2 City, Tangipahoa parish, SE Louisiana, 45 m. E of Baton Rouge; pop. (1970c) 12,847; steel mill, truck farms; Southeastern Louisiana Coll. (1925).

Ham·monds·port \ˈham-ən(d)z-ˌpō(ə)rt, -ˌpȯ(ə)rt\. Village, Steuben co., S New York, at S end of Keuka Lake 25 m. E of Hornell; pop. (1970c) 1066; vineyards; wine and champagne making center; birthplace of Glenn H. Curtiss.

Ham·mon·ton \ˈham-ən-tən\. Town, Atlantic co., SE New Jersey, 27 m. SE of Camden; pop. (1970c) 11,464; furniture; ships fruit.

Hamp·den \ˈham-dən\. 1 County in Massachusetts. See table at MASSACHUSETTS.

2 Town, Penobscot co., E cen. Maine, on Penobscot river 7 m. S of Bangor; pop. (1970c) 4693; footwear; potatoes.

Hampden–Syd·ney \-ˈsid-nē\. Town, Prince Edward co., S cen. Virginia, ab. 5 m. SW of Farmville; Hampden-Sydney Coll. (1776).

Ham·pi \ˈhəm-pē\. See VIJAYANAGAR 2.

Ham·pole \ˈham-ˌpōl\. Village, West Riding, Yorkshire, N England, 6 m. NW of Doncaster; home of Richard Rolle de Hampole, the hermit (d. 1349).

Hamp·shire \ˈham(p)-ˌshi(ə)r, -shər\. Counties in two states of the U.S. See tables at MASSACHUSETTS and WEST VIRGINIA.

Hampshire; *abbr.* **Hants** \ˈhan(t)s\. 1 Formerly a county in S England, comprising the modern administrative counties of Hampshire (see 2, below) and the Isle of Wight (*q.v.*); 1650 sq. m.

2 Administrative county, S England, mainland part of former county of Hampshire (see 1, above); 1503 sq. m.; pop. (1971p) 1,561,605; ⊗ Winchester; naval establishments; oil refining, aircraft engineering; major towns incl. Portsmouth, Southampton, Bournemouth, Gosport, Aldershot, Eastleigh.

Hamp·stead \ˈham(p)-stəd, -ˌsted\. 1 Residential town, Montreal I., S Quebec, Canada, W of Montreal city; pop. (1971p) 7035.

2 Former metropolitan borough of London, SE England, now part of the borough of Camden; includes **Hampstead Heath.**

Hamp·ton \ˈham(p)-tən\. 1 County in South Carolina. See table at SOUTH CAROLINA.

2 City, ⊗ of Calhoun co., S Arkansas; pop. (1970c) 1252; sawmills.

3 City, ⊗ of Franklin co., N cen. Iowa, 27 m. S of Mason City; pop. (1970c) 4376; corn canneries.

4 Town, Rockingham co., SE New Hampshire, on Atlantic Ocean 10 m. S of Portsmouth; pop. (1970c) 8011; shoe manufacturing. Incorporated 1639; outpost of Massachusetts Bay Colony. **Hampton Beach** (resort on Atlantic) nearby.

5 Town, ⊗ of Hampton co., SW South Carolina; pop. (1970c) 2845; cotton gins.

6 Independent city, SE Virginia, on Hampton Roads 7 m. NE of Newport News; 57 sq. m.; pop. (1970c) 120,779; fisheries, packing plants (oysters, crabs). Hampton Institute (1868), Langley Field (*q.v.*), Old Point Comfort, and Fort Monroe in environs. Settled by colonists from Jamestown 1610 (oldest continuous English community in America); burned by British in War of 1812 and by its own inhabitants to prevent occupation by Union troops 1861; incorp. as city 1908; consolidated with Elizabeth City co. 1952.

7 Town (unincorp.), ⊗ of Kings co., S New Brunswick, Canada, 22 m. NNE of St. John; pop. (1966c) 829.

8 Former urban district, SE England, SW of London on the Thames, now part of the Greater London borough of Richmond upon Thames; nearby is Hampton Court Palace, one of largest of the royal residences, built by Cardinal Wolsey 1515, and given to Henry VIII 1526.

Hampton Bay. Inlet of Atlantic Ocean on S side of E Long I., New York.

Hampton Roads. Channel through which the James, Elizabeth, and Nansemond rivers flow into Chesapeake Bay; 40 ft. deep, 4 m. wide; naval battle bet. *Merrimac* and *Monitor* Mar. 9, 1862. The **Port of Hampton Roads,** comprising harbors of Newport News, Norfolk, and Portsmouth, is under local jurisdiction of State Port Authority of Virginia, created 1926.

Ham·run \ham-ˈrün\. Town, E cen. Malta I., just W of Valletta; pop. (1968e) 14,980.

Ham–Sud \am-ˈsüd\. Village (unincorporated), ⊗ of Wolfe co., S Quebec, Canada, 28 m. NE of Sherbrooke; pop. (1966c) 58.

Ham·tramck \ham-ˈtram-ik\. City, Wayne co., SE Michigan, entirely within city of Detroit; pop. (1970c) 27,245; automobile manufacturing.

Ha·mun–i–Lo·ra \hä-ˌmün-ē-lō-ˈrä\. Large lake (***hamun***) with no outlet, Chagai, NW Baluchistan, Pakistan; receives the Pishin Lora.

Hamun–i–Mash·kel \-mash-ˈkel\ *or anc.* **Ar·ia Pa·lus** \ˌar-ē-ə-ˈpā-ləs, ˌer-\. Lake (*hamun*), morass, and desert region, Chagai, NW Baluchistan, Pakistan, on Iranian border; receives Mashkel river from the SE.

Han \ˈhän\ *or Chin.* **Han Kiang** \-jē-ˈäŋ\. 1 River, Shensi and Hupeh provs., E cen. China, flowing SE into Yangtze river at Hankow; ab. 750 m. long; navigable for large vessels for ab. 370 m.

2 Lower course of river system, E Kwangtung prov., SE China; ab. 100 m. long; flows S past Ch'ao-an to South China Sea at Swatow.

3 *or formerly* **Kan** \ˈkän\. River, South Korea, flowing WNW into Yellow Sea N of Inch'ŏn; 292 m. long.

Ha·na·lei Bay \ˌhän-ə-ˌlā-ē-\. Bay on N coast of Kauai I., Hawaii.

Ha·na·ma·ki \ˌhä-nə-ˈmäk-ē\. City, Iwate prefecture, Honshū, Japan, 23 m. S of Morioka; pop. (1970c) 63,753.

Ha·na·ma·ni·oa, Cape \-ˌhän-ə-ˌmän-ē-ˈō-ə\. Cape on S coast of Maui I., Hawaii, on Alalakeiki Channel opp. Kahoolawe I.

Ha·na·ma·u·lu \ˌhä-nə-ˈmä-ü-ˌlü\. Village, Lihue div., E coast of Kauai I., Hawaii, N of Nawiliwili Bay; pop. (1970c) 2461.

Ha·na·pe·pe \ˌhä-nə-ˈpā-pā\. Town, Waimea div., S coast of Kauai I., Hawaii; pop. (1970c) 1388; on **Hanapepe Bay** (W of Wahiawa Bay) adjoining Port Allen.

Ha·nau \ˈhän-ˌau̇\. City, Hesse, West Germany, on Main river 11 m. E of Frankfurt am Main; pop. (1969e) 54,868; diamond polishing; manufactures jewelry, rubber goods, chemicals; St. Mary's church (14th. cent.), Dutch-Walloon church (1600–08), castle (1701–12). Became city 1303; Napoleonic victory over Bavarians and Prussians under Wrede nearby 1813.

Han–chung \ˈhän-ˈju̇ŋ\ *or formerly* **Nan·cheng** \ˈnän-ˈjəŋ\. City, S Shensi prov., NE cen. China, on N bank of the Han 135 m. SW of Sian; pop. (1970e) 120,000; important commercial center.

Han·cock \ˈhan-ˌkäk\. 1 Counties in ten states of the U.S. See tables at GEORGIA, ILLINOIS, INDIANA, IOWA, KENTUCKY, MAINE, MISSISSIPPI, OHIO, TENNESSEE, WEST VIRGINIA.

2 Town, Berkshire co., W Massachusetts, 7 m. NW of Pittsfield; pop. (1970c) 4572.

3 City, Houghton co., NW Michigan penin., 70 m. NW of Marquette; pop. (1970c) 4820; copper mines; manufactures mining machinery; iron and brass products; Suomi Coll. (1896).

Hancock, Mount. Peak, near S boundary of Yellowstone National Park, NW Wyoming; 10,100 ft.

Hand \ˈhand\. County in South Dakota. See table at SOUTH DAKOTA.

Han·da \ˈhän-də\. City, Aichi prefecture, Honshū, Japan, 20 m. S of Nagoya; pop. (1970c) 80,663.

Han·dies Peak \ˌhan-dēz-\. Peak, Hinsdale co., SW Colorado; 14,048 ft.

Han·dlo·vá \ˈhän-dlə-ˌvä\ *or Hung.* **Nyi·tra·bán·ya** \ˈnyi-trə-ˌbän-ˌyò\. Town, Slovak S.R., E cen. Czechoslovakia, in mountains 90 m. NE of Bratislava; pop. (1968e) 16,324.

Hand·öl \ˈhan-ˌdər(-ə)l, ˈhän-\. Waterfall on **Handöl Creek,** W Jämtland, W Sweden; total drop 345 ft.; highest waterfall in Sweden.

Han·ford \ˈhan-fərd\. 1 City, ⊗ of Kings co., SW cen. California, 30 m. S of Fresno; pop. (1970c) 15,179; fruit canneries; oil refineries; settled 1871.

2 Village, part of Richland town, Benton co., S Washington, on Columbia river ab. 20 m. N of Richland center; made site 1943 of industrial plant (Hanford Engineer Works) of the Manhattan District. See RICHLAND 3.

Hang·chow *or* **Hang–chou** \ˈhaŋ-ˈchau̇, ˈhäŋ-ˈjō\. City, ✱ of Chekiang prov., E China, at mouth of Fu-ch'un river at head of Hangchow Bay ab. 110 m. SW of Shanghai; pop. (1970e) 1,100,000; iron and steel, machinery; important coastal trade; center of rice culture and silk manufacture; S terminus of Grand Canal; technical univ. (1927), univ. (1959); for centuries considered one of finest cities of China. Founded 606 A.D.; capital of China during later Sung dynasty (12th cent.). Known to Marco Polo as **Kin·sai** \ˈkin-ˈsā\. Devastated in Taiping Rebellion 1861; opened to foreign trade 1896; under Japanese control 1937–45; fell to Chinese Communist forces 1949.

Hangchow Bay. Funnel-shaped bay at mouth of the Fu-ch'un river, Chekiang prov., E China; 60 m. wide at entrance, extends inland 70 m.; famous for its bore. Chou-shan archipelago lies across S entrance.

Hang·klip, Cape \-ˈhaŋ-ˌklip\. Cape on SW coast of Cape Province, Rep. of South Africa, on SE side of entrance to False Bay.

Hangö \ˈhäŋ-ˌər\ *or Finnish* **Han·ko** \-kò\. Seaport and peninsula, Uusimaa prov., S Finland, on Baltic Sea; pop. (1966e) 9418; resort; exports lumber, fish, dairy products; founded 1874; ceded to U.S.S.R. as a military base Mar. 12, 1940; regained by Finns and Germans 1941; after World War II relinquished by U.S.S.R. in exchange for Porkkala Penin.

Han–hai \ˈhän-ˈhī\. Chinese name for the vast Gobi and Sinkiang Uighur desert area in cen. Asia.

Hanka. See KHANKA.

Han Kiang. See HAN.

Hanko. See HANGÖ.

Han·kow \ˈhaŋ-ˈkau̇, -ˈkō, ˈhän-ˈkō\. Port of the tri-city conurbation of Wuhan, SE Hupeh prov., E cen. China, on N bank of the Yangtze E of the Han and opp. Wu-ch'ang, 585 m. by river from Shanghai; iron and steel works, textile manufactures, rice and flour mills; extensive river trade. For centuries during prominence of Wu-ch'ang a neglected fishing village; opened to trade 1861; grew rapidly after 1900; in Revolution 1911 burned by Imperial troops; captured by Nationalists Dec. 1926, by Japanese Oct. 1938.

Han·ley \ˈhan-lē\. Former county borough, Staffordshire, W cen. England, since 1910 part of Stoke-on-Trent; manufactures earthenware and porcelain; birthplace of Arnold Bennett. See POTTERIES, THE.

Hanley Hills. Village, St. Louis co., E Missouri; pop. (1970c) 2726.

Hann, Mount \-ˈhan\. Mountain in Kimberleys, NE Western Australia; 2800 ft.

Han·na \ˈhan-ə\. Town, SE Alberta, Canada, 100 m. ENE of Calgary; pop. (1971p) 2561; coal mines, dairy farms.

Han·nas·town \ˈhan-əz-ˌtau̇n\. Locality, Westmoreland co., SW Pennsylvania, ab. 5 m. NNE of Greensburg; coal mining; pre-Revolutionary capital of W Pennsylvania.

Han·ni·bal \ˈhan-ə-bəl\. City, Marion and Ralls cos., NE Missouri, on Mississippi river; pop. (1970c) 18,698; river port; manufactures shoes, stoves, railroad-car wheels; boyhood home of Mark Twain.

Han·no·ver \ˈhan-ˌō-vər, ˈhan-ə-vər, *Ger.* hä-ˈnō-vər, -ˈnō-fər\ *or Eng.* **Han·o·ver** \ˈhan-ˌō-vər, ˈhan-ə-vər\. 1 Former state of NW Germany; an electorate of the Holy Roman Empire 1692–1806; kingdom 1814–66; province of Prussia 1866–1945; state of West Germany 1946, in same year made part of Lower Saxony state.

2 Commercial and industrial city, ✱ of Lower Saxony and of the former state, West Germany, on the Leine river 35 m. WNW of Brunswick; pop. (1970c) 523,941; machinery, transportation equipment, steel and rubber works; electronic apparatus, textiles, chemicals; railway junction; zoological gardens, palace (1829), technical univ. (1831, univ. status 1880), medical school 1963.

History: First mentioned 1100; chartered 1241; became residence 1636 of dukes of Brunswick-Lüneburg, the duke being raised to rank of elector of Hannover 1692, the elector succeeding to English throne as George I 1714 (first of House of Hanover); acquired Bremen and Verden from Sweden 1719; in Seven Years' War supported by England as ally of Prussia; occupied by French 1803 and made part of Napoleon's kingdom of Westphalia 1807–13; with accession of Victoria to English throne 1837, became separate from England with which it had had a personal union since 1714; received 1833 constitution which was suspended by King Ernest Augustus (1837–51); kingdom extinguished and incorporated with Prussia as result of Austro-Prussian War 1866; frequently bombed in World War II; became ✻ of Lower Saxony 1946.

Hannoversch–Münden. See MÜNDEN.

Hanö Bay \ˌhän-ˌə-\. Inlet of Baltic Sea on SE coast of Sweden.

Ha·noi \ha-ˈnȯi, hə-\ *or Fr.* **Ha·noï** \á-nȯ-ē\. City, ✻ of North Vietnam, on Red river ab. 75 m. from the sea; its port is Haiphong; met. area pop. (1965e) 850,000; metal-working; textiles, rubber goods, enamelware; univ. (1956). Dates back to era before Chinese invasions; occupied by French 1883 and made capital of Tonkin; capital of French Indochina 1887–1946; after occupation by Japanese frequently bombed by Allies 1943–45; became ✻ of North Vietnam 1954.

Han·o·ver \ˈhan-ˌō-vər\. **1** County in Virginia. See table at VIRGINIA.

2 Town, Jefferson co., SE Indiana, on Ohio river; pop. (1970c) 3018; Hanover Coll. (1827).

3 Town, Plymouth co., SE Massachusetts, 10 m. E of Brockton; pop. (1970c) 10,107.

4 Town, Grafton co., W New Hampshire, on Connecticut river 5 m. NNW of Lebanon; pop. (1970c) 8494; chartered 1761; settled 1765; Dartmouth Coll. (chartered 1769, opened 1770).

5 Borough, York co., S Pennsylvania, 18 m. SW of York; pop. (1970c) 15,623; manufactures shoes, wire cloth, jute products; settled 1733; battle bet. Union and Confederate cavalry 1863.

6 Village, ⊗ of Hanover co., E cen. Virginia; home of Patrick Henry, Henry Clay, Thomas Nelson Page.

7 Town, Grey co., SE Ontario, Canada, 30 m. S of Owen Sound; pop. (1966c) 4665; timber.

8 English form of Hannover. See HANNOVER.

Hanover Island. Island off SW coast of Chile, S of Concepción Strait.

Hanover Park. Village, Cook and Du Page cos., NE Illinois, 27 m. WNW of Chicago; pop. (1970c) 11,916.

Han·pan, Cape \-ˈhan-(ˌ)pan\. Northernmost point of Buka I., NW Solomon Is., W Pacific Ocean; 5°01′S, 154°37′E.

Han·sa Bay \ˌhan(t)-sə-\. Inlet on NE coast of New Guinea I., Papua New Guinea, halfway bet. Madang and Wewak; occupied by Australian forces June 15, 1944.

Han·ság \ˈhȯn-ˌshäg\. Marshy region, E Austria and W Hungary, SE of Neusiedler Lake; 147 sq. m.

Hanseatic City of Danzig. See GDAŃSK 2.

Hanse Towns \ˈhan(t)s-\ *or* **Han·se·at·ic League** \ˌhan(t)-sē-ˌat-ik-\. A defensive commercial confederacy in the Middle Ages, originating in a league of merchants of various free Germanic cities trading abroad; earliest date of any union 1241 when Lübeck and Hamburg made agreements for mutual defense in trading; at first meeting 1256 included Lübeck, Hamburg, Lüneburg, Wismar, Rostock, and Stralsund; joined later by other towns, the league reached height of its power 14th and 15th cents. when it contributed to defeat of Waldemar IV of Denmark 1367–68 and secured control of Baltic trade by Peace of Stralsund 1370; included such widely separated places as Novgorod, Reval, Riga, Danzig (Gdańsk), Magdeburg, Cologne, Bruges, and London; gave trading privileges to merchants of many other towns; held last general assembly 1669; name of Hanseatic towns retained by Lübeck, Hamburg, and Bremen as long as they were free cities.

Hans·ford \ˈhan(t)s-fərd, ˈhanz-\. County in Texas. See table at TEXAS.

Hans Lol·lik Island \ˌhanz-ˌläl-ik-\. One of the Virgin Islands of the United States, West Indies, N of St. Thomas and separated from it by Leeward Passage.

Han·son \ˈhan(t)-sən\. **1** County in South Dakota. See table at SOUTH DAKOTA.

2 Town, Plymouth co., SE Massachusetts, 8 m. ESE of Brockton; pop. (1970c) 7145.

Han–tan \ˈhän-ˈtän\. Town, Hopeh prov., NE China, ab. 100 m. S of Shin-chia-chuang; pop. (1970e) 500,000.

Han·tha·wad·dy \ˌhan(t)-thə-ˈwäd-ē\. District, Pegu division, Lower Burma; 1927 sq. m.; pop. (1962e) 587,362; marshland; produces rice.

Hants \ˈhan(t)s\. **1** County, Nova Scotia, Canada. See table at NOVA SCOTIA.

2 County, England. See HAMPSHIRE.

Han–yang \ˈhän-ˈyäŋ\. Part of the tri-city conurbation of Wuhan, SE Hupeh prov., E cen. China, on N bank of the Yangtze W of Han river mouth and opp. Hankow and Wu-ch'ang; has grown rapidly since 1900 as part of industrial development of Hankow; iron and steel works.

Hao \ˈhau̇\ *also* **Bow Island** \ˈbō-\. Atoll in cen. Tuamotu Archipelago, French Polynesia, S Pacific Ocean, 18°15′S, 140°54′W; 30 m. long, 5 to 9 m. wide; called Bow Island by Captain Cook 1769.

Hao–kang \ˈhau̇-ˈkäŋ\. Town, Heilungkiang prov., NE China, ab. 40 m. N of Chia-mu-ssu; pop. (1970e) 350,000.

Hapar. See HAPUR.

Ha·pa·ran·da \ˌhäp-ə-ˈrän-də\. Seaport, Norrbotten co., NE Sweden, at mouth of Torne river on Gulf of Bothnia opp. Finnish town of Tornio; pop. (1970e) 8963; exports lumber products, tar, and articles made by the Lapps; founded 1812.

Hape·ville \ˈhāp-ˌvil, -vəl\. Residential city, Fulton co., NW cen. Georgia, 8 m. S of Atlanta; pop. (1970c) 9567.

Hap·py Valley \ˌhap-ē-\. Town, Newfoundland, E Canada; pop. (1966c) 4215.

Ha·pur \ˈhäp-ər, -ˌu̇(ə)r\ *or formerly* **Ha·par** \ˈhäp-ər\. Town, W Uttar Pradesh, N India, 35 m. E of Delhi; pop. (1961c) 55,248; trades in sugar, grain, brassware, timber, cotton; supposedly founded in 10th cent.

Har·a·han \ˈhar-ə-ˌhan\. City, Jefferson parish, SE Louisiana, W of New Orleans; pop. (1970c) 13,037.

Har·al·son \ˈhar-əl-sən\. County in Georgia. See table at GEORGIA.

Ha·ra·mosh \ˌhär-ə-ˈmōsh\. Mountain in the Karakoram Range, in Pakistani controlled sector of Jammu and Kashmir; 24,270 ft.

Ha·ra·muk \ˈhär-ə-ˌmu̇k\. Peak in the Himalayas, N India, 25 m. N of Srinagar; 16,015 ft.

Ha·ran *or* **Har·ran** \hə-ˈrän\; *anc.* **Car·rhae** *also* **Car·rae** \ˈkar-(ˌ)ē\. Town, Urfa prov., SE Turkey, ab. 22 m. SSE of Urfa. In ancient times an important city (**Char·ran** \ˈkar-ˌan\ in *Acts* vii. 2) of N Mesopotamia, on the main trade routes from Babylonia to the Mediterranean; residence of Terah and Abraham (*Gen.* xi. 31, 32). Scene of two Roman defeats: (1) 53 B.C., Crassus defeated and killed by Parthians; (2) 296 A.D., Galerius defeated by the Persians.

Ha·rap·pa \hə-ˈrap-ə\. Locality, Punjab, Pakistan, in the Indus valley; site of an early (Chalcolithic) culture, perhaps dating back to 3300 B.C., and indicating in its archaeological remains an early connection bet. Indian and Sumerian cultures. See MOHENJO-DARO.

Harar. See HARER.

Har·bin \ˈhär-bən, här-ˈbin\ *or* **Ha–erh–pin** \ˈhä-ˈer-ˈbin\ *also* **Khar·bin** \här-ˈbin, kär-\; *formerly* **Pin·kiang** \ˈbin-jē-ˈäŋ\ *or* **Ping·kiang** \ˈbiŋ-\. City, ✻ of Heilungkiang prov., NE China, on Sungari river 145 m. NNE of Ch'ang-ch'un; pop. (1970e) 2,750,000; ball bearings, wire and cable, tractors; food processing; almost in exact center of Manchuria. Only a village in 1896, began to grow rapidly with completion 1898 of railroad to Port Arthur. Russian administrative headquarters 1898–1905; Chinese 1905–32, part of the time under warlords; seized by Japanese 1932; taken by U.S.S.R. Aug. 1945.

Har·bor Beach \ˌhär-bər-\. City, Huron co., E Michigan, on Lake Huron 20 m. S of mouth of Saginaw Bay; pop. (1970c) 2134; fishing; summer resort.

Har·bour Grace \ˌhär-bər-ˈgrās\. Seaport, SE Newfoundland, Canada, on W shore of Conception Bay 27 m. W of

St. John's; pop. (1971p) 2726; has been the take-off point for several important transatlantic airplane flights.

Harbour Island. One of the Bahama Is., just off N Eleuthera I.; 2 sq. m.; pop. (1963e) 997.

Har·burg–Wil·helms·burg \ˈhär-ˌbu̇(ə)rg-ˈvil-əmz-ˌbu̇(ə)rg, -ˈvil-ˌhelmz-\. Former city, Prussia, Germany; since 1937 part of Hamburg. See HAMBURG 4.

Har·dang·er Fjord \här-ˌdäŋ-ər-\. Inlet of North Sea, Hordaland co., on SW coast of Norway; extends inland NE and E 114 m.

Har·dang·er·vid·da \här-ˈdäŋ-ər-ˌvid-ə\. Large plateau in S Norway, E of Hardanger Fjord.

Har·dee \ˈhärd-ē\. County in Florida. See table at FLORIDA.

Har·de·man \ˈhärd-ə-mən\. Name of counties in two states of the U.S. See tables at TENNESSEE and TEXAS.

Har·den·berg \ˈhärd-en-ˌbe(ə)rg\. Commune, Overijssel prov., E Netherlands; pop. (1970e) 26,011.

Har·der·wijk \ˈhärd-ər-ˌvīk\. Commune and seaport, Gelderland prov., E Netherlands, on the IJsselmeer (*q.v.*); pop. (1970e) 24,895; metalworking; rubber goods; formerly one of Hanse Towns; has declined in importance since start of planning for reclamation of the Zuider Zee.

Har·din \ˈhärd-ᵊn\. **1** Name of counties in six states of the U.S. See tables at ILLINOIS, IOWA, KENTUCKY, OHIO, TENNESSEE, TEXAS.

2 Village, ⊗ of Calhoun co., W Illinois; pop. (1970c) 1035; wheat.

3 City, ⊗ of Big Horn co., S Montana, 45 m. E of Billings; pop. (1970c) 2733; gas wells.

Har·ding \ˈhärd-iŋ\. Counties in two states of the U.S. See tables at NEW MEXICO and SOUTH DAKOTA.

Har·dins·burg \ˈhärd-ᵊnz-ˌbərg\. City, ⊗ of Breckenridge co., NW cen. Kentucky; pop. (1970c) 1547; timber, tobacco, corn.

Har·doi \ˈhär-ˌdȯi\. Town, cen. Uttar Pradesh, N India, 60 m. NW of Lucknow; pop. (1961c) 36,725.

Har·dwar \ˈhär-ˌdwär, ˈhər-\. Town, NW Uttar Pradesh, N India, on the Ganges 110 m. NNE of Delhi; pop. (1961c) 58,500; railroad center; place where the main Ganges canal begins; the temple of Gangadwara and the bathing ghat with its footprint of Vishnu, visited annually by over 2 million pilgrims; every twelve years scene of an especially large bathing festival, the Kumbh-Mela, attracting more than 500,000 pilgrims; very old, has had many names.

Hard·wick \ˈhärd-(ˌ)wik\. **1** Town, Worcester co., cen. Massachusetts, 21 m. WNW of Worcester; pop. (1970c) 2379; in agricultural and livestock-raising region.

2 Village in Hardwick town, Caledonia co., NE Vermont, 20 m. NNE of Montpelier; pop. (1970c) 1503 (village), 2466 (town); settled 1797; granite, lumber; manufactures furnaces.

Hard·wicke Bay \ˌhärd-(ˌ)wik-\. Inlet in Yorke Penin., SE Spencer Gulf, South Australia.

Har·dy \ˈhärd-ē\. **1** County in West Virginia. See table at WEST VIRGINIA.

2 Town, a ⊗ of Sharp co., N Arkansas, on Spring river; pop. (1970c) 692; resort.

Hardy Dam. Dam across Muskegon river, W Michigan; height 130 ft.; completed 1931; impounds water for water-power, forming **Hardy Dam Pond** in Newaygo and Mecosta cos.

Hare Bay \ˈha(ə)r-, ˈhe(ə)r-\. Inlet of Atlantic Ocean near N tip of Newfoundland, Canada.

Hare Island. Island in St. Lawrence river opp. Rivière du Loup, S Quebec, Canada.

Ha·rel·be·ke \ˈhar-əl-ˌbā-kə\ *or* **Har·le·beke** \ärl-ˈbek, -ˈbāk\. Commune, West Flanders prov., NW Belgium, on Lys river 22 m. SW of Gent; pop. (1968e) 18,410; in tobacco-growing area.

Ha·rer *or* **Ha·rar** *also* **Har·rar** \ˈhär-ər\. **1** Province of E Ethiopia. See table at ETHIOPIA.

2 City, its ✱; pop. (1970e) 45,033; trades in coffee; agricultural coll. (1956).

Har·fleur \(h)är-ˈflər\. Seaport, Seine-Maritime dept., N France, 4 m. E of Le Havre; pop. (1968c) 15,598; before rise of Le Havre, a chief port of France; captured by Henry V 1415, retaken by French 1435, again held by English 1445–49 but recovered by Dunois; pillaged by Huguenots 1562; has late 15th cent. church.

Har·ford \ˈhär-fərd\. County in Maryland. See table at MARYLAND.

Har·gey·sa *or* **Har·gei·sa** \här-ˈgā-sə\. Town, N Somalia, 50 m. SW of Berbera; pop. (1963e) 40,255; ✱ of former British Somaliland.

Har·ghi·ta \ˌhər-ˈgē-tə\. County of N cen. Romania. See table at ROMANIA.

Har·gi·court \ˌär-zhē-ˈku̇(ə)r\. Village, Aisne dept., N France, 9 m. NW of St-Quentin; pop. (1962c) 618; fighting in 1917, destroyed by Germans Mar. 21, 1918.

Har HaZofim. See SCOPUS, MOUNT.

Har Horih. See KARAKORUM.

Ha·ri \ˈhär-ē\ *or formerly* **Djam·bi** \ˈjäm-bē\. River, S cen. Sumatra, Indonesia; ab. 450 m. long; rises in Barisan Mts., flows E to Berhala Strait.

Hariana. See HARYANA.

Ha·ri·ma Sea \ˌhär-i-mə-\. Body of water at E end of Inland Sea bet. S Honshū and N Shikoku, Japan; bounded on E by Awaji I. and on W by Shōdo I.

Harimukotan. See KHARIMKOTAN.

Har·in·gey \ˈhar-iŋ-(ˌ)gā\. A borough of Greater London, SE England. See table at LONDON 4.

Har·ing·vliet \ˈhar-iŋ-və-ˌlēt, -ˌvlēt\. Inlet of North Sea on SW coast of Netherlands; ab. 2½ m. wide; the W extension of Hollandsch Diep to the sea.

Ha·ri Rud \ˌhar-ē-ˈrüd\ *also* **He·ri Rud** \ˌher-\ *or anc.* **Ar·i·us** \ˈar-ē-əs, ˈer-, ə-ˈrī-əs\. River, NW Afghanistan and S Turkmen S.S.R., U.S.S.R.; 700 m. long; rises in mountains (Koh-i-Baba) W of Kabul, flows W through fertile valley at Herāt, turns N forming part of boundary bet. Afghanistan and Turkmen S.S.R. on E and Iran on W, and then is lost in sands of Kara Kum desert of S Turkmen S.S.R. Its lower course called by the Turkmenian name, Tedzhen (*q.v.*), by Russians.

Har·kány \ˈhär-kän-yə\. Town, S Hungary, S of Pécs and SW of Mohács; pop. (1960c) 1600; mineral springs; scene of battle (often called "Second battle of Mohács") Aug. 12, 1687 in which Charles of Lorraine defeated the Turks.

Har·ker Heights \ˌhär-kər-\. Town, Bell co., cen. Texas, 20 m. W of Temple; pop. (1970c) 4216.

Har·lan \ˈhär-lən\. **1** Name of counties in two states of the U.S. See tables at KENTUCKY and NEBRASKA.

2 City, ⊗ of Shelby co., W Iowa, 40 m. NE of Council Bluffs; pop. (1970c) 5049; farm implements, cement; livestock raising.

3 City, ⊗ of Harlan co., SE Kentucky, 28 m. NE of Middlesborough; pop. (1970c) 3318; coal mining.

Harlebeke. See HARELBEKE.

Har·lech \ˈhär-lek\. Village, W Wales, on coast 8 m. N of Barmouth; ancient capital of Merionethshire. Harlech Castle an excellent example of Edwardian concentric fortification, founded by Edward I 1285, captured by Glendower 1404; last Welsh fortress to be held for King Charles until its fall 1647.

Har·lem \ˈhär-ləm\. **1** River channel, NE of Manhattan I., New York; with Spuyten Duyvil creek connects the Hudson and East rivers.

2 District of Manhattan borough, New York City, N of Central Park bet. Eighth Ave. and the East and Harlem rivers; a former village created 1658 and named New Haarlem; annexed to New York City 1731; small group of Negroes settled here 1900; now the chief Negro quarter of

New York; includes also Italian and Spanish (Latin American) sections.

3 City, Netherlands. See HAARLEM.

Har·lin·gen \'här-lən-jən\. City, Cameron co., S Texas, 21 m. NNW of Brownsville; pop. (1970c) 33,503; ships fruits (esp. citrus fruit), vegetables; cotton processing.

Har·ling·en \'här-liŋ-ən\. Commune and seaport, Friesland prov., N Netherlands, on Wadden Zee 16 m. W of Leeuwarden; pop. (1970e) 12,552; leather goods; ships dairy products.

Har·low \'här-(,)lō\. Urban district, Essex, S England; pop. (1971p) 77,666; scientific apparatus, glass; printing; founded 1947.

Har·low·ton \'här-lō-,taun, -tən\. City, ⊗ of Wheatland co., cen. Montana, 48 m. SSW of Lewistown; pop. (1970c) 1375.

Har·mon \'här-mən\. County in Oklahoma. See table at OKLAHOMA.

Har·mo·ny \'här-mə-nē\. Borough, Butler co., W Pennsylvania, NW of Pittsburgh; pop. (1970c) 1207.

Harmozia. See HORMUZ 2.

Harnes \'(h)ärn\. Commune, Pas-de-Calais dept., N France, 11 m. NNE of Arras; pop. (1968c) 14,622; coal mines.

Har·nett \'här-nət\. County in North Carolina. See table at NORTH CAROLINA.

Har·ney \'här-nē\. County in Oregon. See table at OREGON.

Harney Basin. Former lake bottom, Harney co., SE Oregon; 2500 sq. m.

Harney Lake. Lake, Harney Basin, cen. Harney co., SE Oregon; ab. 10 m. long; connected with Malheur Lake.

Harney Peak. Mountain in Black Hills, Pennington co., SW South Dakota; 7242 ft.; highest point in state and highest point in United States E of Rocky Mts., although by some the Black Hills are considered a part of the Rocky Mountain system.

Härn·ö·sand *or* **Hern·ö·sand** \,här-nə-'sand\. Seaport, ⊗ of Västernorrland co., E Sweden, at mouth of Ångerman river; pop. (1970e) 27,032; ships forest products, as tar, timber, cellulose, wood pulp; plundered and burned by Russians 1721.

Har Nuur \'här-'nu̇(ə)r\ *or* **Kha·ra Nur** \'kär-ə-\. Salt lake (*nuur, nur*), W Mongolian People's Republic, just E of the larger lake Har Us Nuur.

Haro Strait \,har-ō-, ,her-\. Strait SE of Vancouver I., in W part of Washington Sound, connecting Juan de Fuca Strait with Strait of Georgia, the three straits being traversed by the United States-Canadian boundary.

Har·pen·den \'här-pən-dən\. Urban district, Hertfordshire, SE England, 25 m. NNW of London; pop. (1971p) 24,161; site of the Rothamsted Experimental Station (founded 1843), noted for biological and agricultural research.

Har·per \'här-pər\. 1 Name of counties in two states of the U.S. See tables at KANSAS and OKLAHOMA.

2 Commercial seaport, extreme SE Liberia, W Africa, at Cape Palmas; pop. (1962c) 6095.

Har·pers Ferry \,här-pərz-\. Residential town and tourist resort, Jefferson co., NE West Virginia, in Blue Ridge Mts. at confluence of Potomac and Shenandoah rivers ab. 55 m. NW of Washington, D.C.; pop. (1970c) 423; settled c. 1747; site of U.S. arsenal estab. 1796 and seized in John Brown's raid 1859; strategic base in Civil War. See *Harpers Ferry National Historical Park* at UNITED STATES, *National Historical Parks.*

Harper Woods. City, Wayne co., SE Michigan, NE of Detroit; pop. (1970c) 20,186.

Har·peth \'här-pəth\. River, W cen. Tennessee; ab. 90 m. long; rises in SW Rutherford co., flows NW into Cumberland river.

Harps·well \'härp-,swel, 'härps-wəl\. Town, Cumberland co., SW Maine, 22 m. NE of Portland; pop. (1970c) 2552; seaside resort.

Har·put \här-'püt\ *or formerly* **Khar·put** \kär-\. Town, Elâzığ prov., E cen. Turkey, near banks of upper Euphrates; trades in cotton, oil, wine; bazaars, Jacobite convent, ancient church; scene of Armenian massacre 1895.

Harran. See HARAN.

Harrar. See HARER.

Harrat ar Raha *or* **Harrat ar–Rahā.** See RAHA, HARRAT AR.

Har·ri·can·aw \,har-i-'kan-(,)ȯ\. River, SW Quebec, Canada; ab. 250 m. long; flows NNW to S end of James Bay in Ontario.

Har·ri·man \'har-ə-mən\. City, Roane co., E Tennessee, 38 m. W of Knoxville; pop. (1970c) 8734; hosiery, woolens, farm implements; coal and iron ore deposits; dairying; tobacco.

Harriman, Mount. Peak, SW Klamath co., S Oregon; 7950 ft.

Harriman Dam *also* **Davis Bridge Dam** \'dā-vəs-\. Dam across Deerfield river in S Vermont; height 220 ft.; completed 1924; impounds water for power.

Har·ring·ton \'har-iŋ-tən\. City, Kent co., cen. Delaware, 17 m. S of Dover; pop. (1970c) 2407; canneries; dairying; wheat.

Harrington Park. Borough, Bergen co., NE New Jersey, 12 m. NE of Paterson; pop. (1970c) 4841.

Harrington Sound. Body of water in NE cen. Bermuda I.

Har·ris \'har-əs\. 1 Name of counties in two states of the U.S. See tables at GEORGIA and TEXAS.

2 Southern section of island of Lewis with Harris, a part of Inverness co., in Outer Hebrides, off NW coast of Scotland; 195 sq. m.; pop. (1961c) 5276; place where Harris tweed was originally made.

Harris, Sound of. Channel bet. Lewis with Harris I. and North Uist I. in the Outer Hebrides, NW Scotland.

Har·ris·burg \'har-əs-,bərg\. 1 City, ⊗ of Poinsett co., NE Arkansas; pop. (1970c) 1931; rice mills.

2 City, ⊗ of Saline co., SE Illinois, 22 m. E of Marion; pop. (1970c) 9535; coal mining; flour and lumber mills; Southeastern Illinois Coll. (1961).

3 Village, ⊗ of Banner co., W Nebraska; pop. (1972e) 85.

4 City, ✻ of Pennsylvania and ⊗ of Dauphin co., SE cen. Pennsylvania, on Susquehanna river 98 m. WNW of Philadelphia; pop. (1970c) 68,061; manufactures steel and iron products, machinery, meat and lumber products, building materials, airplane parts; Harrisburg Area Community Coll. (1964). Settled c. 1718; known as Harris' Ferry until 1785 when it became ⊗ ; scene of noted conventions, esp. Harrisburg Convention of 1788; became borough 1791, state capital 1812, city 1860; site of Camp Curtin, first camp for Union forces during Civil War.

Har·ri·smith \'har-ə-,smith\. Town, NE Orange Free State, E cen. Rep. of South Africa, 153 m. NW of Durban; pop. (1967e) 16,200; important trade center; health resort; Bushman paintings in nearby caves.

Har·ri·son \'har-ə-sən\. 1 Name of counties in eight states of the U.S. See tables at INDIANA, IOWA, KENTUCKY, MISSISSIPPI, MISSOURI, OHIO, TEXAS, WEST VIRGINIA.

2 City, ⊗ of Boone co., N Arkansas, ab. 64 m. ENE of Fayetteville; pop. (1970c) 7239; ships lumber; deposits of lead, zinc, marble, silicon. Diamond Cave (stalactite and stalagmite cavern) in vicinity.

3 City, ⊗ of Clare co., cen. Michigan; pop. (1970c) 1460; poultry; summer resort; Mid Michigan Community Coll. (1965).

4 Village, ⊗ of Sioux co., NW Nebraska; pop. (1970c) 377.

5 Industrial town, Hudson co., NE New Jersey, on Passaic river opp. Newark; pop. (1970c) 11,811; steelworks, foundries; manufactures pumps, elevators, electron tubes.

6 Village, Hamilton co., SW corner of Ohio, on Indiana border 18 m. WNW of Cincinnati; pop. (1970c) 4408; iron castings, shoes, pottery.

7 Urban township, Allegheny co., SW Pennsylvania, NE suburb of Pittsburgh; pop. (1970c) 14,448.

Harrison Bay. Inlet of Arctic Ocean N coast of Alaska, E of Point Barrow, 70°30′N, 151°30′W.

Har·ri·son·burg \ˈhar-ə-sən-ˌbərg\. 1 Village, ⊗ of Catahoula parish, cen. Louisiana; pop. (1970c) 626; cotton, timber; poultry.

2 Industrial city, ⊗ of Rockingham co. but politically independent, N Virginia, 23 m. NNE of Staunton; 3 sq. m.; pop. (1970c) 14,605; manufactures shoes, rayon, automobile parts; Madison Coll. (1908), Eastern Mennonite Coll. (1917); estab. 1780.

Harrison Lake. See LILLOOET.

Harrison's Landing. See BERKELEY 5.

Harrison Stickle. See LANGDALE PIKES.

Har·ri·son·ville \ˈhar-ə-sən-ˌvil\. City, ⊗ of Cass co., W Missouri, 30 m. S of Independence; pop. (1970c) 4928; livestock.

Har·ris·ville \ˈhar-əs-ˌvil\. 1 City, ⊗ of Alcona co., NE Michigan; pop. (1970c) 541.

2 Village (unincorp.), Providence co., N Rhode Island, ab. 17 m. NW of Providence; pop. (1970c) 1053; administrative center of Burrillville town.

3 Town, ⊗ of Ritchie co., NW West Virginia; pop. (1970c) 1464.

Har·rods·burg \ˈhar-ədz-ˌbərg\. City, ⊗ of Mercer co., cen. Kentucky, 9 m. NNW of Danville; pop. (1970c) 6741; optical glass; dairying; wheat; founded 1774, settled 1775, oldest city in the state; site of cabin in which Nancy Hanks and Thomas Lincoln were married. See SPRINGFIELD 5.

Har·ro·gate \ˈhar-ə-ˌgāt\. Village, Claiborne co., NE Tennessee, on Kentucky border ab. 48 m. NE of Knoxville; formerly a summer resort; Lincoln Memorial Univ. (1897).

Harrogate \ˈhar-ə-gət, -ˌgāt\. Municipal borough, West Riding, Yorkshire, N England, 13 m. N of Leeds; pop. (1971p) 62,290; fashionable resort; many mineral springs.

Har·row \ˈhar-(ˌ)ō\. A borough of Greater London, SE England. See table at LONDON 4.

Har·språng·et \ˈhär-ˌsprȯŋ-ət\ *or Lapp* **Njom·mel·sas·ka** \ˈnyȯm-əl-ˌsäs-kə\. Waterfall in Luleälv river, Norrbotten co., N Sweden; 110 ft. high.

Hart \ˈhärt\. 1 Name of counties in two states of the U.S. See tables at GEORGIA and KENTUCKY.

2 City, ⊗ of Oceana co., W Michigan, 18 m. S of Ludington; pop. (1970c) 2139; fruit growing; canneries.

Hart·ford \ˈhärt-fərd\. 1 County in Connecticut. See table at CONNECTICUT.

2 Town, Geneva co., SE Alabama, 20 m. SW of Dothan; pop. (1970c) 2648; wood products; peanuts, cotton.

3 Industrial and commercial city, ✱ of Connecticut, at head of navigation on Connecticut river 36 m. NNE of New Haven; pop. (1970c) 158,017; largest city in the state; port of entry; a major insurance center; automobile parts, electrical equipment, precision instruments, typewriters; numerous parks with excellent recreational facilities; State Capitol, Old State House, State Arsenal and Armory, Atheneum, Colt and Morgan memorials; Trinity Coll. (1823), Morse Coll. (1860), Hartford Coll. for Women (1933), Hartford State Technical Coll. (1946), Greater Hartford Community Coll. (1967).

History: Established as trading post and fort by Dutch 1633; settled by band of colonists from Massachusetts Bay 1635–36; given present name 1637; first constitution of Connecticut Colony drawn up 1639; according to tradition royal charter protected from Governor Andros in famous Charter Oak incident 1687; capital of Connecticut (*q.v.*) although shared honor with New Haven 1701–1875; during Revolution important and rich military supply depot; incorporated as city 1784; home of the "Hartford wits" in 18th cent.; site of Hartford Convention 1814. The town (incorporated 1784) and the city were made coextensive 1881 and consolidated 1896.

4 Village, Madison co., SW Illinois, on Mississippi river 15 m. N of East St. Louis; pop. (1970c) 2243.

5 City, ⊗ of Ohio co., W cen. Kentucky; pop. (1970c) 1868; tobacco.

6 Village, Van Buren co., SW Michigan, 32 m. W of Kalamazoo; pop. (1970c) 2508; fruit growing.

7 Town, Windsor co., E Vermont; pop. (1970c) 6477.

8 City, Washington co., SE Wisconsin, 30 m. NW of Milwaukee; pop. (1970c) 6499; automobile parts.

Hartford City. City, ⊗ of Blackford co., E Indiana, 17 m. ESE of Marion; pop. (1970c) 8027; natural gas and oil fields.

Har·ting·ton \ˈhärt-iŋ-tən\. City, ⊗ of Cedar co., NE Nebraska, 42 m. N of Norfolk; pop. (1970c) 1581; corn; hogs.

Hart Island \ˌhärt-\ *or* **Hart's Island** \ˈhärts-\. Island in Long Island Sound off E coast of the Bronx, New York City; attached to Bronx borough; New York City's potter's field; United States naval prison.

Hart·land \ˈhärt-lənd\. Village, Waukesha co., SE Wisconsin; pop. (1970c) 2763.

Hartland Point. Cape on W coast of Devonshire, SW England, on S side of entrance to Bristol Channel; lighthouse.

Har·tle·pool \ˈhärt-lē-ˌpül, ˈhärt-ᵊl-\. Municipal borough, Durham, N England, on North Sea 26 m. SSE of Newcastle upon Tyne; pop. (1971p) 96,898; extensive docks; manufactures iron, steel, and cement; received charter 1201.

Hart·ley \ˈhärt-lē\. 1 County in Texas. See table at TEXAS.

2 Town, NE Rhodesia, 70 m. WSW of Salisbury; pop. (1969p) 8640; center of agricultural and gold mining region.

Hart·manns·wei·ler·kopf \ˌärt-mänz-ˌvāl-ər-ˈkȯf, ˈhärt-mäns-ˌvī-lər-ˌkȯpf\. Commanding height in the Vosges Mts., Haut-Rhin dept., NE France, 8 m. NW of Mulhouse; 3700 ft.; severe fighting for its control 1915.

Hart·selle \ˈhärt-səl\. City, Morgan co., N Alabama, 11 m. S of Decatur; pop. (1970c) 7355; cotton ginning; founded 1870.

Harts·horne \ˈhärts-ˌhȯ(ə)rn\. City, Pittsburg co., SE Oklahoma, 15 m. ESE of McAlester; pop. (1970c) 2121; coal mining, lumbering.

Hart's Island. See HART ISLAND.

Harts·ville \ˈhärts-ˌvil, -vəl\. 1 Town, Darlington co., NE South Carolina, 21 m. NW of Florence; pop. (1970c) 8017; manufactures cotton, rayon, and silk textiles; Coker Coll. (1894).

2 City, ⊗ of Trousdale co., N Tennessee; pop. (1970c) 2243; tobacco.

Hart·ville \ˈhärt-ˌvil\. City, ⊗ of Wright co., S Missouri; pop. (1970c) 524.

Hart·well \ˈhärt-(ˌ)wel, -wəl\. City, ⊗ of Hart co., NE Georgia, 37 m. NE of Athens; pop. (1970c) 4865; textile mills; incorporated 1856.

Haru. See MOEN.

Hārūn, Jabal. See HOR, MOUNT.

Har Us Nuur \ˈhär-üs-ˈnu̇(ə)r\ *or* **Kha·ra Usu Nur** *also* **Ka·ra Usu Nur** \ˌkär-ə-ˌüs-ü-ˈnu̇(ə)r\. Salt lake (*nuur, nur*), W Mongolian People's Republic, E of Hovd; 40 m. long.

Har·vard \ˈhär-vərd\. 1 City, McHenry co., N Illinois, 28 m. ENE of Rockford; pop. (1970c) 5177; in lake region.

2 Town, Worcester co., cen. Massachusetts, 11 m. ESE of Fitchburg; pop. (1970c) 12,536; Harvard Astronomical Observatory; in vicinity are remains of New Eden, the Utopian community established 1844 by Bronson Alcott.

Harvard, Mount. Peak in Sawatch Range, in Chaffee co., cen. Colorado; 14,420 ft.

Har·vey \ˈhär-vē\. 1 County in Kansas. See table at KANSAS.

2 Industrial city, Cook co., NE Illinois, 18 m. S of Chicago; pop. (1970c) 34,636; diesel engines, railroad equipment, steel castings, gears.

3 City, Wells co., cen. North Dakota, 58 m. WSW of Devils Lake (city); pop. (1970c) 2361; dairying.

Har·well \'här-ˌwel, -wəl\. Village, Berkshire, S England, ab. 12 m. S of Oxford; pop. (1961c) 669; airfield in World War II; site of first chain-reacting pile established in England.

Har·wich \'här-(ˌ)wich\. Town, Barnstable co., SE Massachusetts, 12 m. E of Barnstable; pop. (1970c) 5892; summer resort.

Harwich \'har-ij, -ich, *U.S. also* 'här-(ˌ)wich\. Municipal borough, Essex, SE England, on North Sea 68 m. ENE of London; pop. (1971p) 14,892; light engineering, fishing.

Harwich Port \'här-wich-ˌpō(ə)rt, -pȯ(ə)rt\. Village, Barnstable co., SE Massachusetts, on Atlantic Ocean; summer resort.

Har·win·ton \'här-wən-tən\. Town, Litchfield co., NW Connecticut, 15 m. W of Hartford; pop. (1970c) 4318.

Har·wood Heights \ˌhär-ˌwu̇d-\. Village, Cook co., NE Illinois, NW suburb of Chicago; pop. (1970c) 9060.

Ha·ry·a·na *or* **Ha·ri·a·na** \ˌhär-ē-'än-ə\. State, N India; 17,010 sq. m.; pop. (1971p) 9,971,165; provisional ✱ Chandigarh; largely part of Indo-Gangetic plain; corn, rice, millet; cattle; sugar refining; formed 1966.

Harz \'härts\. Mountain group crossing border bet. West Germany and East Germany, bet. Elbe and Weser rivers S of Brunswick; highest peak Brocken 3747 ft.; has many summer resorts; well forested; profitable mines of varied kinds; region, long a stronghold of paganism, has been source of many legends.

Harzburg. See BAD HARZBURG.

Hasa, Al– *or* **Hasa, El.** See AL-HASA.

Ha·san Dağ \ˌhäs-än-'dä(g)\. Peak, cen. Turkey, Asia, SE of Tuz Lake; 10,670 ft.

Has·be·ya \'haz-bē-ə, -bā-\ *or* **Haş·bay·yā** \-'bā-\. Town, Lebanon, just W of Mt. Hermon; castle held for a time by the Crusaders.

Has·brouck Heights \ˌhaz-bru̇k-\. Residential borough, Bergen co., NE corner of New Jersey, 7 m. SE of Paterson; pop. (1970c) 13,651; founded 1685.

Hashemite Kingdom of Jordan. See JORDAN 1.

Has·kell \'has-kəl\. 1 Name of counties in three states of the U.S. See tables at KANSAS, OKLAHOMA, TEXAS.

2 Town, Muskogee co., E Oklahoma on Arkansas river 19 m. W of Muskogee; pop. (1970c) 2063; cotton gins, oil wells.

3 City, ⊗ of Haskell co., N Texas, 50 m. N of Abilene; pop. (1970c) 3655; ships cotton and livestock.

Haskovo. See KHASKOVO.

Ha·sle·mere \'hā-zəl-ˌmi(ə)r\. Urban district, Surrey, S England, 11 m. S of Aldershot; pop. (1971p) 13,252; in high valley bet. two ridges: Hindhead, on N side of which is "Devil's Punch Bowl," a curious depression, and Blackdown, on E slope of which is Aldworth, a house built by Tennyson 1868–69 and in which he died 1892.

Has·li \'häs-lē\. Valley, SE Bern canton, W cen. Switzerland, E of the Grindelwald, through which passes upper course of the Aare (*q.v.*).

Has·ling·den \'haz-liŋ-dən\. Municipal borough, Lancashire, NW England, 17 m. N of Manchester; pop. (1971p) 14,953; bricks, cotton textiles.

Has·san \'həs-ᵊn\. Town, S Mysore, S India, 63 m. NW of Mysore; pop. (1961c) 32,200.

Has·selt \'häs-əlt\. Commune, ✱ of Limburg prov., NE Belgium, 42 m. E of Brussels; pop. (1970e) 39,673; agricultural machinery; distilleries; received charter 1232; scene of septennial fete on Assumption Day, Aug. 15, when it is visited by throngs of pilgrims; battle Aug. 6, 1831 in which Dutch defeated Belgian nationalists.

Has·su·na \ha-'sü-nə\. Archaeological site, N Iraq, on W bank of Tigris 25 m. S of Mosul; village uncovered (1945) is one of oldest in the world, dating back probably to bet. 6000 and 5000 B.C.

Hasta Colonia. See ASTI 2.

Hasta Pompeia. See ASTI 2.

Ha·sten·beck \'häs-tən-ˌbek\. Village, Lower Saxony, West Germany, 3 m. SE of Hameln; pop. (1968e) 950; scene of French victory over the English July 26, 1757 which led to convention of Kloster-Zeven (see ZEVEN).

Has·tings \'hā-stiŋz\. 1 City, ⊗ of Barry co., SW Michigan, 29 m. NE of Kalamazoo; pop. (1970c) 6501; sprinkler equipment, aluminum die castings.

2 City, ⊗ of Dakota co., SE Minnesota, on Mississippi river 20 m. SE of St. Paul; pop. (1970c) 12,195; manufactures flour-milling accessories, paper, clay products; dairy products.

3 City, ⊗ of Adams co., S Nebraska, 23 m. S of Grand Island; pop. (1970c) 23,580; manufactures building materials, farm implements; flour and feed mills, creameries; Hastings Coll. (1882).

4 River, New South Wales, Australia; 108 m. long.

5 County, Ontario, Canada. See table at ONTARIO.

6 County borough, East Sussex, S England, on English Channel at entrance to Strait of Dover; pop. (1971p) 72,169; one of the Cinque Ports; scene of the battle of Hastings Oct. 14, 1066 in which William the Conqueror defeated Saxons under King Harold.

7 City, E North I., New Zealand, near Napier 160 m. NE of Wellington; pop. (1970e) 29,100.

Hastings–on–Hud·son \-'həd-sən\. Residential village, Westchester co., SE New York, on Hudson river 18 m. N of New York, opp. the Palisades; pop. (1970c) 9479; manufactures copper wire, chemicals; produced mustard gas for American troops in World War I.

Ha·tay \hä-'tī\. Province of S Turkey, Asia, on Mediterranean coast; 2086 sq. m.; pop. (1969e) 560,100; ✱ Antakya; coextensive with former Sanjak of Alexandretta (*q.v.*); created 1938 as a republic, an autonomous unit among the Levant States, with Turkish majority in its assembly; became an integral part of Turkey June 23, 1939 by agreement bet. France and Turkey.

Hat·boro \'hat-ˌbər-ə, -ˌbə-rə\. Borough, Montgomery co., SE Pennsylvania, 15 m. NNE of Philadelphia; pop. (1970c) 8880; radio tubes, ball bearings, machine tools.

Hatch·ie \'hach-ē\. River, flowing from N Mississippi NW into Mississippi river on NW boundary of Tipton co., Tennessee; ab. 180 m. long.

Hat·field \'hat-ˌfēld\. Town, Hampshire co., W Massachusetts, on Connecticut river 18 m. N of Springfield; pop. (1970c) 2825; attacked by Indians 1675 and 1677; home of: Sophia Smith, founder of Smith College; Col. Ephraim Williams, founder of Williams College; Rev. Jonathan Dickinson, first president of the College of New Jersey (Princeton); and Elisha Williams, president of Yale 1726–39.

Ha·thras \'hät-rəs\. Town, W Uttar Pradesh, N India, 85 m. SSE of Delhi; pop. (1961c) 64,045; railroad center; has ruined Jat fort.

Ha·tia *or* **Ha·tya** \'hät-ē-ə\. Island group, formerly one island, Bangla Desh, in main E mouth of the Ganges; 171 sq. m.; suffered severe cyclone damage 1970.

Ha·ti·llo \ä-'tē-(ˌ)(y)ō\. Town and municipality, NW Puerto Rico; town near coast just W of Arecibo; pop. (1970p) 2791 (town), 21,549 (munic.).

Hatra. See AL-HADHR.

Hatria. See ADRIA.

Hatria Picena. See ATRI.

Hat·ten·heim \'hät-ᵊn-ˌhīm\. Village, W Hesse, West Germany, in the Rheingau; pop. (1968e) 1800; noted wine-producing region; Steinberger white wine made nearby.

Hat·ter·as, Cape \-'hat-ə-rəs, -'ha-trəs\. Cape, SE **Hatteras Island,** Dare co., North Carolina; a long, narrow sand bar, one of the chain of islands off E coast of North Carolina; extends into Atlantic Ocean at a dangerous navigation point; lighthouse, 193 ft. high, abandoned 1936 because the sea had come too close, replaced by new light on a tower farther inland; much of area included in **Cape Hatteras National Seashore** (authorized 1937); to the SW, near S tip of the island, is village of **Hatteras.**

Hatteras Inlet. Narrow strait leading from Atlantic Ocean into Pamlico Sound bet. S tip of Hatteras I. and Ocracoke

I.; during Civil War guarded by two forts built by Confederates but captured by Union forces Aug. 28–29, 1861.

Hat·ties·burg \'hat-ēz-ˌbərg\. Industrial city, ⊗ of Forrest co., SE Mississippi, 28 m. SSW of Laurel; pop. (1970c) 38,272; chemicals, concrete; oil refinery, railroad shops; Mississippi Southern Coll. (1910).

Hat·ting·en \'hät-iŋ-ən\ *also* **Hattingen an der Ruhr** \-ˌän-də(r)-'rü(ə)r\. Industrial city, cen. North Rhine-Westphalia, West Germany, SE suburb of Essen on Ruhr river; pop. (1969e) 32,876; machinery, flanges, rivets, screws, locomotives; ruins of 13th cent. castle (Isenburg); first mentioned 1019.

Hattushash. See BOGAZKÖY.

Ha·tu·tu \hä-'tüt-(ˌ)ü\. Island, Marquesas Is., French Polynesia, S Pacific Ocean, 10 m. NE of Eïao I.; 4 sq. m.

Hat·van \'hȯt-ˌvȯn\. Commune, cen. Hungary, 30 m. E of Budapest; pop. (1970p) 21,958; railroad center.

Hatya. See HATIA.

Hatzfeld. See JIMBOLIA.

Hau·bour·din \ˌō-ˌbu̇r-'daⁿ\. Commune, Nord dept., N France, 6 m. SW of Lille; pop. (1968c) 12,106; textiles.

Haud \'hau̇d\. Region, SE Ethiopia and SW Somalia; semidesert, also has grassy plains.

Hau·dio·mont \ˌōd-ē-ə-'mōⁿ\. Commune, Meuse dept., NE France, 8 m. SE of Verdun; pop. (1962c) 273; held by Germans Feb. 1916–Sept. 1918.

Hau·ge·sund \'hau̇-gə-ˌsu̇n\. Seaport, Rogaland co., SW Norway, on a fjord opp. Stavanger; pop. (1970e) 27,603; exports fish; shipbuilding yards, woolen mills, aluminum plant; place where American ship *City of Flint* under a German crew anchored Oct. 20, 1939 when it was returned to Americans by the Norwegians.

Hau·ki·ve·si, Lake \-'hau̇-kə-ˌves-ə\. Lake, SE Finland. See LINNANSAARI NATIONAL PARK.

Haul·bow·line \hȯl-'bō-lən\. Small island, Cork Harbour, SE co. Cork, SW Eire; pop. (1961c) 431; formerly an important British naval base.

Haun·stet·ten \'hau̇n-ˌs(h)tet-ən\. City, Bavaria, West Germany, 5 m. S of Augsburg; pop. (1969e) 21,958; residential; textiles, woodworking; became city 1952.

Hau·raki Gulf \hau̇-ˌrak-ē-, -ˌräk-\. Large bay, inlet of Pacific Ocean, on N coast of North I., New Zealand; in SW has inlet, Waitemata Harbor, on which Auckland is situated.

Hau·ran *or* **Haw·rān** \hau̇-'rän\. Plateau region in S Syria, S of Damascus and E of Jordan river; fertile, produces much grain. In Greco-Roman period a part of it known as Auranitis (*q.v.*).

Hauran, Wa·di *or* **Wā·di Hawrān** \ˌwäd-ē-\. River (*wadi*) in Syrian Desert, W Iraq; ab. 240 m. long; flows ENE to the Euphrates near Khan Baghdadi.

Hau·sa·land *or* **Hausa Land** \'hau̇-sə-ˌland, -zə-\. Strictly, an ethnological term; the region in Africa N of the Niger and Benue rivers, now corresponding to N Nigeria; chief town Kano; inhabited by the Hausa, a Negroid people of the Sudan. Early kingdom conquered 1801 by Muslim Fulah Empire (see SOKOTO 1); incorporated in Nigeria 1900.

Haus·ruck Mountains \ˌhau̇s-ˌru̇k-\. Range, Austria, S of the Danube and SE of the Inn; highest peak Göbelsberg 2625 ft.

Hau·ta \'hau̇t-ə, 'hau̇-ˌtä\ *or* **Al–Haw·tah** \al-'hȯ-\. Town, cen. Nejd, Saudi Arabia, 80 m. S of Riyadh.

Haute–Ga·ronne \ˌōt-gə-'rän, -'rōn\. Department of S France. See table at FRANCE.

Haute–Loire \ōt-lə-'wär\. Department of S cen. France. See table at FRANCE.

Haute–Marne \ōt-'märn\. Department of NE France. See table at FRANCE.

Haute·rive \ō-'trēv\. Town, Saguenay co., SE Quebec, Canada, 57 m. NE of Chicoutimi; pop. (1966c) 11,366.

Hautes–Alpes \ōt-'zalp\. Department of SE France. See table at FRANCE.

Haute–Saône \ōt-'sōn\. Department of E France. See table at FRANCE.

Haute–Sa·voie \ˌōt-sə-'vȯi, -sȧ-'vwȧ\. Department of E France. See table at FRANCE.

Hautes Fagnes. See HOHE VENN MOUNTAINS.

Hautes–Py·ré·nées \ōt-ˌpir-ə-'nā\. Department of SW France. See table at FRANCE.

Haute–Vienne \ˌōt-vē-'en\. Department of W cen. France. See table at FRANCE.

Haute–Volta. See UPPER VOLTA.

Haut·mont \ō-'mōⁿ\. Commune, Nord dept., N France, 46 m. SE of Lille; pop. (1968c) 17,870; produces iron, steel, chemicals.

Haut–Rhin \ō-'raⁿ\. Department of NE France. See table at FRANCE.

Hauts–de–Seine \ˌō-də-'sān, -'sen\. Department of N France. See table at FRANCE.

Haut–Za·ïre \'ō-zä-'i(ə)r\ *or formerly* **Ori·en·tale** \ˌȯr-ē-äⁿ-'täl\. Province of NE Zaire. See table at ZAIRE.

Ha·vana \hə-'van-ə\. 1 City, ⊗ of Mason co., cen. Illinois, on Illinois river 38 m. SW of Peoria; pop. (1970c) 4376; flour, farm implements, gasoline engines.

2 *or Span.* **La Ha·ba·na** \ˌlä-(ä-)'vän-ə\. Seaport, ✱ of Cuba and ✱ of La Habana prov., on NW coast of Cuba, 90 m. SSW of Key West, Florida; pop. (1967e) 1,008,500, met. area pop. 1,700,300; met. area 1,700,300; largest city of the West Indies; harbor (ab. 3 m. by 1½ m.), one of best in W hemisphere, its entrance through narrow channel having El Morro castle (erected 1589–97) and lighthouse on E and La Punta Fort (or castle) in old city on W; old city or commercial section on peninsula bet. harbor and ocean, new city, largely residential, on hills to W and S; railroad center; exports sugar, tobacco, cigars, cigarettes, coffee; textile mills, packing plants; prior to 1961 tourism a major source of revenue; cathedral (1704), palace of old captains general, Univ. of Havana (1728); fine squares and drives, esp. the Prado boulevard and the Malecón along N shore.

History: Founded by Diego Velásquez 1519 (removed from another site of 1515); burned 1528 but soon rebuilt; chief naval station of Spain in New World and suffered esp. in 16th cent. in wars bet. Spain and England; captured by English 1762, restored 1763; since 1700 its history the same generally as that of Cuba (*q.v.*); its outer harbor scene of blowing up of U.S. battleship *Maine* Feb. 15, 1898, immediate cause of Spanish-American War; since 1898 capital of independent Cuba.

Ha·van·nah \hə-'van-ə\. Village on N coast of Efate I., New Hebrides, SW Pacific Ocean; good harbor.

Hav·ant and Wa·ter·loo \'hav-ənt . . . ˌwȯt-ər-'lü, -ˌwät-\. Urban district, Hampshire, S England; pop. (1971p) 108,-999; electronic equipment, gloves.

Ha·vel \'häf-əl\. River, East Germany; 212 m. long; flows S out of Mecklenburg to Spandau, where it is joined by the Spree, and on into Elbe river.

Have·lock \'hav-ˌläk, -lək\. 1 Former city, Lancaster co., SE Nebraska, now part of Lincoln; railroad repair shops. 2 Town, Craven co., SE North Carolina, 16 m. SSE of New Bern; pop. (1970c) 5283; cotton, tobacco.

Havelock Island. See RITCHIE'S ARCHIPELAGO.

Hav·er·ford \'hav-ə(r)-fərd\. 1 Urban township, Delaware co., SE Pennsylvania; pop. (1970c) 55,132; residential. 2 Residential community in Lower Merion township (pop. [1970c] 63,392), Montgomery co., SE Pennsylvania, NW of Philadelphia; settled by Welshmen in 1680's; Haverford Coll. (1833).

Hav·er·ford·west \ˌhav-ər-fərd-ˈwest\. Municipal borough and seaport, Pembrokeshire, SW Wales; pop. (1971p) 9101; ruins of 12th cent. castle and of 12th cent. Augustinian priory.

Hav·er·hill \ˈhāv-(ə-)rəl\. 1 Industrial city, Essex co., NE corner of Massachusetts, on Merrimack river 15 m. NE of Lowell; pop. (1970c) 46,120; shoes, electric coils; Northern Essex Community Coll. (1961); birthplace of John Greenleaf Whittier.

2 Town, Grafton co., W New Hampshire, on Connecticut river 22 m. SSW of Littleton; pop. (1970c) 3090; dairying, farming, granite quarrying; chartered 1763.

3 Urban district, West Suffolk, E England; pop. (1971p) 12,430.

Hav·er·ing \ˈhāv-(ə-)riŋ\. A borough of Greater London, SE England. See table at LONDON 4.

Hav·er·straw \ˈhav-ər-ˌstrȯ\. Village, Rockland co., SE New York, on W shore of Hudson river 32 m. N of New York; pop. (1970c) 8198; traprock quarries, brickyards, cement works; hardware, leather; artist's colony.

Ha·ví·řov \ˈhäv-ə-ˌrȯf\. Town, Czech S.R., Czechoslovakia, E of Ostrava; pop. (1968e) 80,855.

Hav·líč·kův Brod \ˌhäv-lēch-ˌküf-ˈbrȯt\; *formerly* **Ně·mec·ký Brod** \ˌnyem-ət-skē-\ *or Ger.* **Deutsch–Brod** \ˈdȯich-ˈbrōt\. City, Czech S.R., W Czechoslovakia, 60 m. SE of Prague; pop. (1968e) 17,543.

Hav·re \ˈhav-ər\. City, ⊗ of Hill co., N Montana, 108 m. NE of Great Falls; pop. (1970c) 10,558; ships livestock, wheat, potatoes; gas wells; Northern Montana Coll. (1913).

Havre, Le. See LE HAVRE.

Ha·vre–Au·bert \ˌav-rō-ˈbe(ə)r\. Chief village of Magdalen Is., Quebec, Canada, on Amherst I.; pop. (1966c) 459.

Hav·re de Grace \ˌhav-ər-də-ˈgras, -ˈgrās\. City, Harford co., NE Maryland, at mouth of Susquehanna river; pop. (1970c) 9791; aircraft parts, chemicals; resort; duck hunting.

Ha·vrin·court \ˌav-ˌraⁿ-ˈku̇(ə)r\. Village, Pas-de-Calais dept., N France, 19 m. SE of Arras; pop. (1962c) 422; severe fighting Apr., May, and Sept. 1918.

Haw \ˈhȯ\. River, N cen. North Carolina; ab. 130 m. long; formed by forks uniting in Alamance co., flows SE and unites with Deep river to form Cape Fear river.

Ha·waii \hə-ˈwä-(ˌ)(y)ē, -ˈwī-(ˌ)(y)ē, -ˈwȯ-(ˌ)(y)ē, -ˈwä-yə, -wȯ-yə, -ˈwī-(y)ə\. 1 Largest of the Hawaiian Is. (see 2, below), southernmost large island of the group, constituting a county of the state of Hawaii; 4021 sq. m.; pop. (1970c) 63,468; ⊗ Hilo; top of a gigantic submarine mountain; contains four volcanic mountains: Mauna Kea, Hualalai, Mauna Loa, and Kilauea (the last two in Hawaii Volcanoes National Park). Chief towns Keaau, Pahala, Papaikou, and Honokaa.

2 *also* **Ha·wai·ian Islands** \hə-ˌwä-yən-, -ˌwī-(y)ən-, -ˌwȯ-yən-\ *or formerly* **Sand·wich Islands** \ˈsan-(ˌ)(d)wich-\. A state of U.S.A.; chain of volcanic and coral islands in N cen. Pacific Ocean, comprising eight major and 114 minor islands; 2090 m. WSW of San Francisco; 47th state in area, 6450 sq. m. (land area 6415 sq. m.); 40th state in population, (1970c) 769,913; ✱ Honolulu (on Oahu I.); admitted to Union 1959 as 50th state, including entire chain except Midway Is.

Nicknames: Aloha State; Paradise of the Pacific. *State flower:* Red hibiscus. *Motto:* Ua Mau Ke Ea O Ka Aina I Ka Pono (The Life of the Land is Perpetuated in Righteousness). *Highest point:* Mauna Kea 13,796 ft. on Hawaii I. *Chief products:* Sugarcane, pineapples, coffee; livestock; manufacturing: food processing; apparel; chemicals; tourism. *Chief cities:* Honolulu, Kailua, Kaneohe, Hilo. See *Hawaiian Islands Bird Reservation* at LEEWARD ISLANDS 2 and *Hawaii Volcanoes National Park* and *Haleaka National Park* at UNITED STATES, *National Parks.* See *Table of States* at UNITED STATES. Divided into the following 4 counties (for pronunciation of their names, see their individual entries):

COUNTY	ISLAND	AREA[1] (sq. m.)	POP. (1970c)	CO. SEAT
Hawaii	Hawaii	4,021	63,468	Hilo
Honolulu[2]	Oahu	598[2]	630,528	Honolulu
Kauai	Kauai Niihau	623	29,761	Lihue
Maui	Kahoolawe Lanai Maui Molokai[3]	1,173	46,156	Wailuku

[1]Area = land area.
[2]Includes the uninhabited islands of the archipelago (Kaula, Kure, Necker, French Frigate Shoal, Gardner Pinnacles, etc.).
[3]Includes Kalawao district which, although officially designated as a county, consists only of Kalaupapa leper settlement and has no local government.

History: By tradition first reached by Polynesians when small group arrived from S ab. 500 A.D.; received other immigrants in 12th and 13th cents.; discovered and named Sandwich Is. 1778 by Capt. Cook who was killed here 1779; islands united under rule (1795–1819) of King Kamehameha I; frequented by American whalers from early 19th cent.; first visited by Christian missionaries (Americans) 1820; by 1844 recognized as independent by U.S., Great Britain, and France; when dynasty founded by Kamehameha I terminated 1872 had made much progress; secured reciprocity treaty with U.S. 1876; under last two native rulers 1874–1893 subjected to misrule which led to deposition of Queen Liliuokalani and request for annexation to U.S. 1893 (annexation treaty withdrawn from U.S. Senate by President Cleveland); set up provisional government 1893, republic 1894; annexed to U.S. by joint resolution 1898; established as U.S. territory Apr. 30, 1900; began to use Pearl Harbor (*q.v.*) as coaling and repair station 1908; received jurisdiction over Midway Is. 1909; after 1920 extensively developed as U.S. Pacific naval and military base; scene of Japanese attack on Pearl Harbor Dec. 7, 1941; admitted as a state Aug. 21, 1959.

3 County in Hawaii. See 1 above and table at HAWAII.

Ha·wai·ian Gardens \hə-ˌwä-yən-, -ˌwī-(y)ən-, -ˌwȯ-yən-\. City, Los Angeles co., SW California, 19 m. SE of Los Angeles; pop. (1970c) 9019.

Hawaiian Islands Bird Reservation. See LEEWARD ISLANDS 1.

Hawaii Volcanoes National Park. See UNITED STATES, *National Parks.*

Ha·wal·li \hə-ˈwäl-ē\. Town, Kuwait, ab. 5 m. SE of Al-Kuwait; pop. (1970c) 106,507.

Ha·wa·ra \hə-ˈwär-ə\. Site of a pyramid, SE of Birket Qārūn, Lower Egypt, probably built by Amenemhet III of XIIth dynasty, also site of remains of the Labyrinth, which was a huge funerary temple.

Ha·war·den \ˈhā-ˌwȯrd-ᵊn\. City, Sioux co., NW Iowa, on Big Sioux river 35 m. N of Sioux City; pop. (1970c) 2789; livestock shipping; Sioux Empire Coll. (1967).

Haw·ar·den \ˈhärd-ᵊn, ˈhȯ-ər-dən\. Parish, Flintshire, N Wales, near Chester, England; site of the Hawarden Castle, built 1752 near ruins of medieval castle, long residence of Gladstone; St. Deniol's Library, founded by Gladstone 1895, in building erected 1902.

Hawash. See AWASH.

Ha·wea, Lake \-ˈhä-wē-ə\. Lake, S cen. South I., New Zealand; 46 sq. m.; 19 m. long; max. depth 1285 ft.

Ha·we·ra \ˈhä-wə-rə\. Seaport, W North I., New Zealand, on South Taranaki Bight 120 m. N of Wellington; pop. (1970e) 8320.

Hawes·ville \ˈhȯz-ˌvil\. City, ⊗ of Hancock co., NW cen. Kentucky; pop. (1970c) 1262; tobacco; coal mining; oil wells.

Hawes Water \ˈhȯz-\. Lake in Lake District, NW England, in Westmorland 5 m. N of Kendal; 2½ m. long; maximum depth 103 ft.; provides part of Manchester water supply.

Ha·wi \ˈhä-wē\. Village, Hawaii co., Hawaii, near Upolu Point on N coast of Hawaii I.; pop. (1970c) 797.

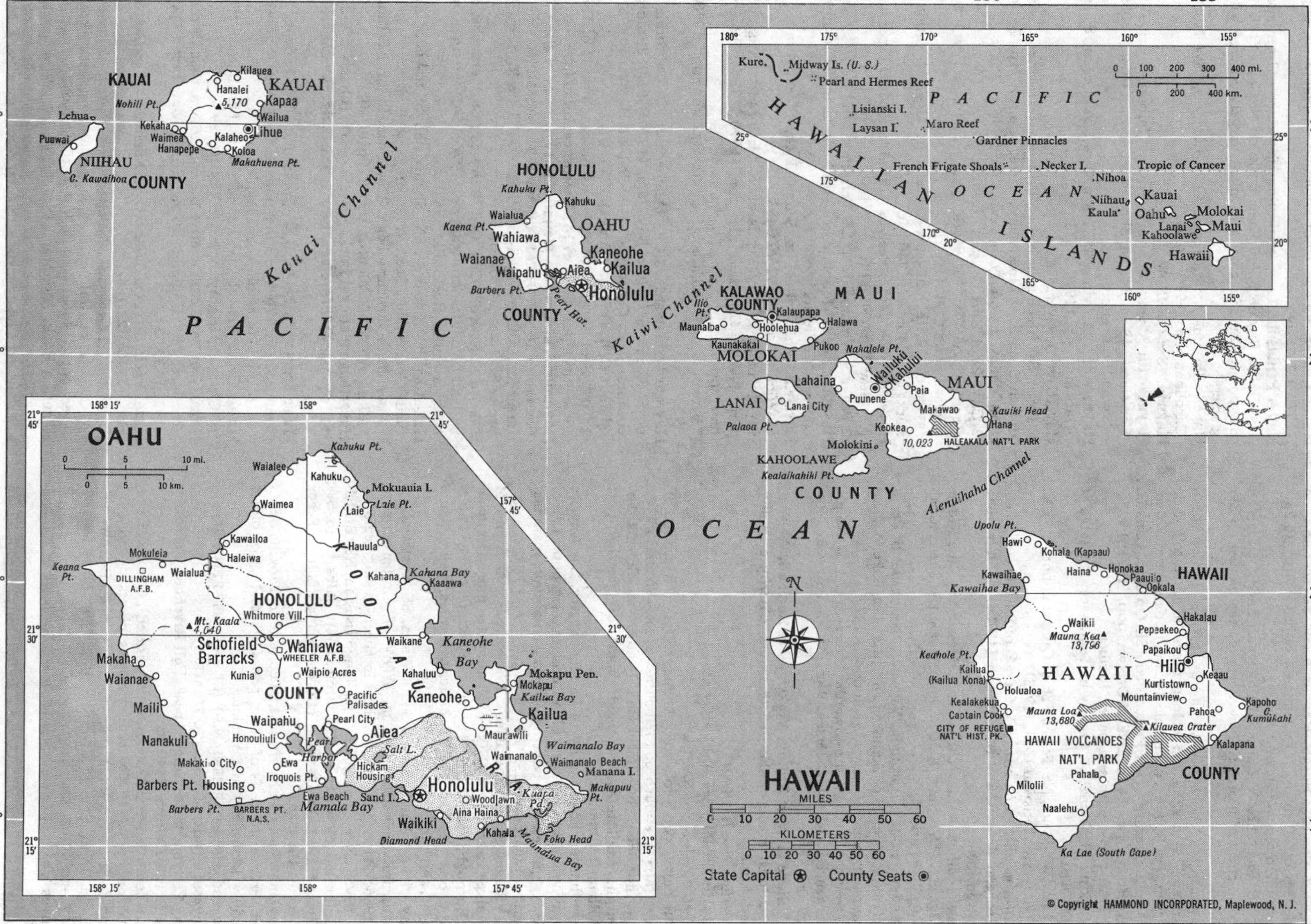
HAWAII
KAUAI
NIIHAU
COUNTY
HONOLULU
COUNTY
KALAWAO COUNTY
MAUI
COUNTY
HAWAII
COUNTY
PACIFIC
OCEAN
Kauai Channel
Kaiwi Channel
Alenuihaha Channel
OAHU
MOLOKAI
LANAI
KAHOOLAWE
Lihue
Honolulu
Wailuku
Hilo
Mauna Kea 13,796
Mauna Loa 13,680
HAWAII VOLCANOES NAT'L PARK
HALEAKALA NAT'L PARK
CITY OF REFUGE NAT'L HIST. PK.
HAWAIIAN ISLANDS
Tropic of Cancer
Midway Is. (U. S.)
MILES
KILOMETERS
State Capital
County Seats
Longitude West of Greenwich
© Copyright HAMMOND INCORPORATED, Maplewood, N. J.

Ha·wick \'hȯ-ik\. Burgh, Roxburgh co., SE Scotland, on the Teviot 40 m. NE of Dumfries; pop. (1971p) 16,286; manufactures tweeds and hosiery.

Hawke Bay \'hȯk-\. Large inlet of South Pacific Ocean on E cen. coast of North I., New Zealand; has Napier on SW shore.

Hawkes·bury \'hȯks-ˌber-ē, -b(ə-)rē\. 1 River, E New South Wales, SE Australia; 293 m. long; flows NE and E to Pacific Ocean N of Sydney; navigable for small boats for ab. 70 m.
2 Manufacturing town, Prescott co., SE Ontario, Canada, on Ottawa river 54 m. ENE of Ottawa; pop. (1971p) 9256; aircraft parts, pulp and paper, lumber.

Haw·kins \'hȯk-ənz\. 1 County in Tennessee. See table at TENNESSEE.
2 City, Wood co., NE Texas, ESE of Quitman; pop. (1970c) 977; Jarvis Christian Coll. (1912).

Haw·kins·ville \'hȯk-ənz-ˌvil\. City, ⊗ of Pulaski co., S cen. Georgia, 38 m. SSE of Macon; pop. (1970c) 4077; lumber; cotton, peanuts.

Hawks·bill Mountain \ˌhȯks-ˌbil-\. Peak in the Blue Ridge, Page co., N Virginia; 4050 ft.; highest point in Shenandoah National Park.

Haw·ley \'hȯ-lē\. Borough, Wayne co., NE corner of Pennsylvania, 27 m. E of Scranton and just N of Lake Wallenpaupack; pop. (1970c) 1331; founded 1827.

Ha·worth \'hȯ-ərth, 'hȯ-(ˌ)wərth, 'hau̇-ərth\. 1 Borough, Bergen co., NE New Jersey, 9 m. NE of Paterson; pop. (1970c) 3760.
2 Village in West Riding, Yorkshire, N England, WNW of Bradford; home of the Brontë sisters, Charlotte, Emily, and Anne.

Hawrān. See HAURAN.

Hawrān, Wādi. See HAURAN, WADI.

Hawtah, Al–. See HAUTA.

Haw·thorn \'hȯ-ˌthȯ(ə)rn\. Municipality, S Victoria, SE Australia, E suburb of Melbourne; pop. (1966c) 36,728.

Haw·thorn·den \'hȯ-ˌthȯrn-dən\. Estate, 8 m. SE of Edinburgh, Midlothian, Scotland; home of Scottish poet William Drummond.

Haw·thorne \'hȯ-ˌthȯ(ə)rn\. 1 Residential city, Los Angeles co., SW California, 12 m. SW of Los Angeles; pop. (1970c) 53,304; in region producing oil and gas; aircraft manufacturing; incorporated 1922.
2 Village, ⊗ of Mineral co., SW Nevada, on S end of Walker Lake; pop. (1970c) 3539; tungsten mines; tourism.
3 Borough, Passaic co., N New Jersey, 2 m. NNE of Paterson; pop. (1970c) 19,173; hosiery, textiles, paint, glass, television tubes; dye works.

Hay \'hā\. 1 Town, S New South Wales, SE Australia, on Murrumbidgee river 230 m. WNW of Canberra; pop. (1966c) 4180; railroad terminus in sheep-raising region.
2 River, NW Canada; 530 m. long; rises in NE British Columbia, flows E and N through NW Alberta to SW Great Slave Lake; its valley affords highway N from Peace river to the lake.

Hay·ange \ā-'(y)äⁿzh\. Industrial commune, Moselle dept., NE France, 16 m. N of Metz; pop. (1968e) 10,305; oldest iron-working city in Lorraine.

Hayasdan. See ARMENIAN SOVIET SOCIALIST REPUBLIC.

Hayasui Strait. See BUNGO STRAIT.

Hay Canyon Butte. Isolated peak, Fall River co., SW corner of South Dakota; 3440 ft.

Hay·den \'hād-ᵊn\. Town (unincorporated), Gila co., E cen. Arizona; pop. (1970c) 1283; smelting plants.

Hay·dock \'hā-ˌdäk\. Urban district, Lancashire, NW England, 15 m. ENE of Liverpool; pop. (1971p) 14,180.

Haye–du–Puits, La. See LA HAYE-DU-PUITS.

Hayes \'hāz\. 1 County in Nebraska. See table at NEBRASKA.
2 River, E Manitoba, Canada; 300 m. long; rises in chain of lakes and flows NE to Hudson Bay at York Factory.

Hayes, Mount. Mountain, E Alaska, at E end of Alaska Range, 63°37′N, 146°43′W; 13,700 ft.

Hayes Center. Village, ⊗ of Hayes co., S Nebraska; pop. (1970c) 237; livestock.

Hayes Peninsula. Large projection of land, NW Greenland, bet. Baffin Bay on S and Kane Basin on N; Cape York its SW point, Thule its chief settlement; largely covered with glaciers.

Hayes·ville \'hāz-ˌvil\. Town, ⊗ of Clay co., SW North Carolina; pop. (1970c) 428.

Haynau. See CHOJNÓW.

Haynes·ville \'hānz-ˌvil, -vəl\. Town, Claiborne parish, N Louisiana, 48 m. NE of Shreveport; pop. (1970c) 3055; plywood; oil refining.

Hayne·ville \'hān-vil, -vəl\. Town, ⊗ of Lowndes co., S cen. Alabama; pop. (1970c) 473.

Hay River. 1 River, Canada. See HAY 2.
2 Town, SW Mackenzie dist., Northwest Territories, Canada, on S shore of Great Slave Lake; pop. (1971p) 2420.

Hays \'hāz\. 1 County in Texas. See table at TEXAS.
2 City, ⊗ of Ellis co., cen. Kansas, 48 m. NW of Great Bend; pop. (1970c) 15,396; flour mills, oil fields; Fort Hays Kansas State Coll. (1902).

Hay·stack Butte \ˌhā-ˌstak-\. Peak in Glacier National Park, NW Montana; 7405 ft.

Haystack Mountain. 1 Peak in Adirondack Mts., Essex co., NE New York; 4960 ft.
2 Peak, S Windham co., SE Vermont; 3462 ft.

Haystack Peak. Mountain in Sierra Nevada, in E Tuolumne co., cen. California; 9966 ft.

Hays·ville \'hāz-ˌvil\. City, Sedgwick co., S cen. Kansas, S of Wichita; pop. (1970c) 6483.

Hay·ti \'hā-ˌtī\. 1 City, Pemiscot co., SE corner of Missouri, 5 m. NW of Caruthersville; pop. (1970c) 3841; lumber, dairy products.
2 Town, ⊗ of Hamlin co., E South Dakota; pop. (1970c) 393.

Hay·ward \'hā-wərd\. 1 City, Alameda co., W California, 5 m. E of San Francisco Bay; pop. (1970c) 93,058; motor coaches, steel; California State Coll. at Hayward (1957), Chabot Coll. (1961); founded 1854.
2 City, ⊗ of Sawyer co., NW Wisconsin, 38 m. N of Rice Lake (city); pop. (1970c) 1427; resort center in lake region.

Hay·wood \'hā-(ˌ)wu̇d\. Counties in two states of the U.S. See tables at NORTH CAROLINA and TENNESSEE.

Hā·zār·ān, Kuh–e– \ˌkü-(h)ē-hə-'zär-ən\. Peak, Kermān prov., SE Iran; 14,500 ft.

Haz·ard \'haz-ərd\. City, ⊗ of Perry co., SE Kentucky, 53 m. NE of Middlesborough; pop. (1970c) 5459; natural gas, coal; sawmills, steel mill.

Haz·ard·ville \'haz-ərd-ˌvil\. Subdivision of town of Enfield, Connecticut. See ENFIELD 1.

Ha·za·ri·bagh \hə-'zär-i-ˌbäg\. Town, cen. Bihar, NE India, 210 m. WNW of Calcutta; pop. (1961c) 40,958.

Hazaribagh National Park. National park, Bihar, NE India; 150 sq. m.; wildlife refuge (bear, leopard, tiger); established 1955.

Ha·ze·brouck \ˌaz-ə-'brük\. Commune, Nord dept., N France, 24 m. WNW of Lille; pop. (1968c) 19,037; breweries; manufactures oil, soap, textiles.

Ha·zel Crest \'hā-zəl-\. Village, Cook co., NE Illinois, NNW of Chicago Heights; pop. (1970c) 10,329.

Hazel Grove and Bram·hall \-'bram-(ˌ)hȯl\. Urban district, Cheshire, NW England, 10 m. SE of Manchester; pop. (1971p) 39,534.

Hazel Park. City, Oakland co., SE Michigan, N of Detroit; pop. (1970c) 23,784.

Ha·zel·ton \'hā-zəl-tən\. Village, N cen. British Columbia, W Canada, on Bulkley river at its junction with Skeena river; pop. (1966c) 403; end of Cariboo Road.

Hazelton Peak. Mountain, W Johnson co., N Wyoming; 10,552 ft.

Ha·zel·wood \'hā-zəl-ˌwu̇d\. 1 Village, St. Louis co., E Missouri, NW of St. Louis; pop. (1970c) 14,082.
2 Town, Haywood co., W North Carolina, 28 m. WSW of Asheville; pop. (1970c) 2057.

Ha·zle·hurst \ˈhā-zəl-ˌhərst\. 1 City, ⊗ of Jeff Davis co., SE cen. Georgia, 48 m. NNW of Waycross; pop. (1970c) 4065; cotton, tobacco.

2 City, ⊗ of Copiah co., SW Mississippi, 32 m. SSW of Jackson; pop. (1970c) 4577; lumber; diversified farming.

Ha·zle·ton \ˈhā-zəl-tən\. City, Luzerne co., E Pennsylvania, 20 m. S of Wilkes-Barre; pop. (1970c) 30,429; coal; knit goods, clothing, iron and steel products.

Head·land \ˈhed-lənd\. City, Henry co., SE Alabama, 10 m. N of Dothan; pop. (1970c) 2545; fertilizer, lumber; founded 1817.

Healds·burg \ˈhēl(d)z-ˌbərg\. City, Sonoma co., W California, 14 m. NNW of Santa Rosa; pop. (1970c) 5438; fruit growing; founded 1852.

Heald·ton \ˈhēl(d)-tən\. Town, Carter co., S Oklahoma, 22 m. W of Ardmore; pop. (1970c) 2324; asphalt deposits; oil wells.

Hea·nor \ˈhē-nər, ˈhā-\. Urban district, Derbyshire, N cen. England, 10 m. WNW of Nottingham; pop. (1971p) 24,352.

Heard \ˈhərd\. County in Georgia. See table at GEORGIA.

Heard Island. Island in S Indian Ocean, ab. 310 m. SE of Kerguelen I., 53°10′S, 74°35′E; highest point ab. 6000 ft.; discovered by American navigator 1853; claimed by Australia 1947; together with the McDonald Is. (53°02′S, 72°36′E) constitutes the Australian external territory **Heard and McDonald Is.** \-mək-ˈdän-ᵊld-\ (total area 113 sq. m.).

Hearne \ˈhərn\. City, Robertson co., E cen. Texas, 18 m. NNW of Bryan; pop. (1970c) 4982; cotton.

Hearst \ˈhərst\. Town, Cochrane district, SE Ontario, Canada, 130 m. NW of Cochrane; pop. (1971p) 3484.

Hearst Island. Island in Weddell Sea, Antarctica, off E coast of Antarctic Penin.; centers ab. 69°25′S, 62°10′W; ab. 42 m. long, ab. 12 m. wide; highest point 1200 ft.; first sighted and named Hearst Land by Sir Hubert Wilkins Dec. 20, 1928.

Heart \ˈhärt\. River, SW North Dakota; ab. 200 m. long; rises in S Billings co., flows E into Missouri river opp. Bismarck.

Heart Lake. Lake in Yellowstone National Park, NW Wyoming; S of Yellowstone Lake.

Heart's Con·tent \ˈhärts-kən-ˈtent\. Town, SE Newfoundland, Canada, on E shore of Trinity Bay 35 m. WNW of St. John's; pop. (1966c) 592; terminus of several transatlantic cables.

Heath \ˈhēth\. 1 City, Licking co., cen. Ohio, 30 m. E of Columbus; pop. (1970c) 6768.

2 River forming part of boundary bet. Peru and Bolivia; flows N to the Madre de Dios.

Heath Point. Eastern tip of Anticosti I., at mouth of St. Lawrence river, E Canada.

Heaths·ville \ˈhēths-ˌvil\. Village, ⊗ of Northumberland co., E Virginia.

Heave·ner \ˈhēv-(ə-)nər\. City, Le Flore co., E Oklahoma, 13 m. S of Poteau; pop. (1970c) 2566; coal mines; timber; livestock.

Heav·ens Peak \ˌhev-ənz-\. Mountain in Glacier National Park, NW Montana; 9008 ft.

Heb·bron·ville \ˈheb-rən-ˌvil\. Town, ⊗ of Jim Hogg co., S Texas, 50 m. ESE of Laredo; pop. (1970c) 4079; oil wells; cattle ranches.

Heb·burn \ˈheb-ərn\. Urban district, Durham, N England, on the Tyne 7 m. E of Newcastle upon Tyne; pop. (1971p) 23,597; chemicals; shipbuilding; engineering works.

He·ber \ˈhē-bər\. City, ⊗ of Wasatch co., N cen. Utah, 30 m. SE of Salt Lake City; pop. (1970c) 3245; lead and zinc mines.

Heber Springs. City, ⊗ of Cleburne co., N cen. Arkansas, 50 m. NNE of Little Rock; pop. (1970c) 2497; numerous mineral springs of curative value.

Heb·gen Dam \ˌheb-gən-\. Dam across Madison river, S Gallatin co., S Montana; forming **Hebgen Lake** 21 m. long.

Heb·ri·des \ˈheb-rə-ˌdēz\ *or* **Western Islands;** *anc.* **Ebu·dae** \i-ˈbyüd-ē\ *or* **He·bu·dae** \hi-\. Islands in the Atlantic Ocean W of Scotland; 2900 sq. m.; pop. (1961e) 60,000; divided by the Little Minch into two groups: **Outer Hebrides** *or* **Long Island,** principal islands Lewis with Harris, North Uist, South Uist, and Barra; **Inner Hebrides,** principal islands Skye, Mull, and Islay. Scene of frequent incursions of Scandinavian settlers from 6th cent. A.D.; ceded by Norway to Scotland in 13th cent.

Hebrides, Sea of the *also* **Gulf of the Hebrides.** Body of water off NW coast of Scotland, bet. S part of Outer Hebrides and the N part of Inner Hebrides.

He·bron \ˈhē-brən\. 1 Town, Tolland co., N Connecticut, 17 m. SE of Hartford; pop. (1970c) 3815.

2 City, ⊗ of Thayer co., S Nebraska, 47 m. W of Beatrice; pop. (1970c) 1667.

3 City, Morton co., SW cen. North Dakota, 37 m. E of Dickinson; pop. (1970c) 1103; clay deposits, brick plant.

4 *or Arab.* **Al–Kha·līl** \ˌal-kä-ˈlē(ə)l\ *or anc.* **Kir·jath–Ar·ba** \ˌkər-jath-ˈär-bə, ˌkir-\. Town, Jordan, in region occupied by Israel 1967; 20 m. SSW of Jerusalem; pop. (1968e) 38,300; tanning.

History: One of the four holy cities of the Talmud; believed to be one of the oldest cities in the world; home of Abraham; contains the structure, the Haram, enclosing the mosque built over the **Cave of Mach·pe·lah** \-mak-ˈpē-lə\ (*Gen.* xxv. 9–10) where, according to tradition, Abraham and Sarah were buried. Taken by Joshua; for a time the home of David; captured by Judas Maccabaeus; figured in wars of the Romans, Muslims, and Crusaders.

Heb·ros \ˈev-ˌrȯs\. Modern Greek form of *Evros* department of Thrace, Greece: see table at GREECE.

Hebrus. See MARITSA.

Hebudae. See HEBRIDES.

Hec·ate Strait \ˌhek-ət-\. Channel bet. mainland of W British Columbia, Canada, and the Queen Charlotte Is., connecting Dixon Entrance with Queen Charlotte Sound; 35 to 80 m. wide.

Hec·a·tom·py·los \ˌhek-ə-ˈtäm-pə-ˌläs\. Ancient city, for a time ✱ of kingdom of Parthia, at foot of S slope of E Elburz Mts.; center of ancient highways, hence, its name (literally, Greek, "hundred-gated"); ruins near modern Dāmghān, NW Khorāsān prov., NE Iran.

Hech·ing·en \ˈhek-iŋ-ən\. Commune, cen. Baden-Württemberg, West Germany, 25 m. SSW of Stuttgart; pop. (1968e) 10,000; textiles, wood products; church (1779–83).

Heck·mond·wike \ˈheck-mən-ˌdwīk\. Urban district, West Riding, Yorkshire, N England, SW of Leeds; pop. (1971p) 9361; blankets, carpets; dyeworks, iron foundries.

Hecla. See HEKLA.

Hec·la and Gri·per Bay \ˌhek-lə . . . ˌgrī-pər-\. Bay, Melville I., W Franklin dist., Northwest Territories, Canada; 75°40′N, 111°W.

Hecla Island. Island in S Lake Winnipeg, SE Manitoba, S Canada.

Hedemarken. See HEDMARK.

Hedge·hope Hill \ˌhej-əp-\. Peak in Cheviot Hills along border bet. England and Scotland; 2348 ft.

Hedjaz. See HEJAZ.

Hed·mark \ˈhed-ˌmärk, ˈhād-\ *or formerly* **He·de·mar·ken** \ˈhād-ə-ˌmär-kən\. County of SE Norway. See table at NORWAY.

Hed·on \ˈhed-ᵊn\. Municipal borough, East Riding, Yorkshire, N England, ab. 5 m. E of Hull; pop. (1971p) 2600; in 13th cent. an important port; notable church of St. Augustine.

Hed·wig Village \ˌhed-wig-\. City, Harris co., SE Texas, 10 m. W of Houston; pop. (1970c) 3255.

Heems·kerk \'hāms-(,)kerk\. Commune, North Holland prov., Netherlands; pop. (1970e) 28,152.

Heem·ste·de \'hām-,stād-ə\. Commune, North Holland prov., W Netherlands, S suburb of Haarlem; pop. (1970e) 26,507.

Hee·ren·veen \'her-ən-,vān\. Commune, Friesland prov., N Netherlands, 17 m. SSE of Leeuwarden; pop. (1970e) 31,-434; apparel.

Heer·len \'he(ə)r-lə(n)\. Commune, Limburg prov., SE Netherlands, just NE of Maastricht 5 m. from West German border; pop. (1970e) 75,147; steel, electronic equipment, coal mining.

Hef·lin \'hef-lən\. Town, ⊗ of Cleburne co., NE Alabama; pop. (1970c) 2872; lumber; settled 1883.

He·gou·me·ni·tsa \,ē-gů-mə-'nēt-sə, -'nit-\ *or* **Gou·me·ni·tsa** \,gü-mə-\ *or Gk.* **Igou·me·ní·tsa** \,ē-gů-mə-\. Commune, Ioannina dept., N Epirus, Greece; on coast opp. S Corfu I.

Heian–kyo. See KYŌTO.

Hei·de \'hīd-ə\ *also* **Heide in Hol·stein** \-in-'hōl-,stīn, -,stēn\. City, Schleswig-Holstein, West Germany, 28 m. SW of Schleswig; pop. (1969e) 23,352; important cattle market; produces furniture.

Hei·del·berg \'hīd-ᵊl-,bərg, -,be(ə)rg\. **1** Borough, Allegheny co., SW Pennsylvania, 6 m. WSW of Pittsburgh; pop. (1970c) 2034.

2 Town, S Transvaal, NE Rep. of South Africa, 30 m. ESE of Johannesburg; pop. (1967e) 12,200; peace treaty at close of Boer war of 1880 signed here.

3 City, Baden-Württemberg, West Germany, on Neckar river 11 m. ESE of Mannheim; pop. (1969e) 122,004; electrical appliances, suitcases, metalware; tourism; univ. (1386); ruins of 13th cent. castle; first mentioned 1196; capital of the Palatinate until 1719; center of German Calvinism in 16th cent. (*Heidelberg Catechism* 1563); passed to Baden 1803; in 1947 became site of U.S. military headquarters in Europe.

Hei·de·nau \'hīd-ᵊn-,au̇\. Industrial city, Dresden dist., East Germany, SE suburb of Dresden on Elbe river; pop. (1970e) 19,840; printing equipment, cellulose; founded 1920.

Hei·den·heim \'hīd-ᵊn-,hīm\. City, Baden-Württemberg, West Germany, 41 m. NW of Augsburg; pop. (1969e) 50,-007; partly ruined 11th cent. castle (Hellenstein); manufactures machinery, textiles; place where Saint Walburga died 777.

Hei·ho \'hā-'hə\. **1** Former province (1932–45), N Manchukuo; 42,388 sq. m.

2 Town, N Manchuria. See AI-HUI.

Heijo. See P'YŎNGYANG.

Heil·bron \'hī(ə)l-,brän\. Town, N Orange Free State, E cen. Rep. of South Africa, 73 m. S of Johannesburg; pop. (1967e) 7900; center of republic's main corn district; capital of Orange Free State May 13–20, 1900.

Heil·bronn \'hī(ə)l-,brän, hīl-'brȯn\. Industrial city, Baden-Württemberg, West Germany, on Neckar river 27 m. N of Stuttgart; pop. (1969e) 98,481; chemicals, leather, ironware, paper; railroad junction; old fortifications converted into promenades; belonged to Frankish crownlands 8th cent.; first charter 1281; passed to Württemberg 1802; severely damaged during World War II.

Hei·lig·en·haus \'hī-li-gən-,hau̇s\. City, North Rhine-Westphalia, West Germany, 9 m. NE of Düsseldorf; pop. (1969e) 28,196; electronic equipment; foundries.

Heilsberg. See LIDZBARK WARMIŃSKI.

Hei–lung chiang. See AMUR.

Hei·lung·kiang \'hā-'lu̇ŋ-jē-'äŋ\. Province, NE China, in N part bordering on Amur river; 178,996 sq. m.; pop. (1967e) 21,000,000; ✱ Harbin; wheat, sugar beets, flax, timber; coal, gold; under Japanese control 1932–45.

He·jaz *also* **He·djaz** \he-'jaz, hij-'az\ *or Arab.* **Al–Hi·jaz** \,al-hij-'az\. W province of Saudi Arabia, extending along Red Sea coast, bounded on the N by Jordan, on E by Nejd, on S by Asir, and on W by Red Sea; 134,600 sq. m.; pop. (1963e) 2,000,000; NW coast extends along Gulf of 'Aqaba. Its coastal plain generally desolate; on its E edge is mountain range (highest point Harrat ar Raha in N 7000 ft.) with inland basins that have little drainage. Chief products dates, millet, wheat. Most fertile part in S around Mecca and Medina, its chief towns; other towns Taif and the ports of Jidda, Yenbo', and Wejh.

History: Seat of Mecca and Medina (*qq.v.*), original centers of Islam; as province of Arabia, fell under Egyptian domination after end of Abbasside caliphate 1258; became Ottoman dependency after conquest of Egypt 1517; restored to order 1811–20 by Mehemet Ali, viceroy of Egypt, after Wahabi revolt; resisted building of railroad by Turks before World War I; revolted and proclaimed independence under Husein ibn-Ali 1916; its independence guaranteed by Great Britain in contradiction to latter's promises to ibn-Saud; defeat of Husein by ibn-Saud 1919; independence guaranteed by Treaty of Sèvres 1920; consolidated as dual kingdom with Nejd 1926 after Husein driven out 1924; from 1932 part of single kingdom of Saudi Arabia (*q.v.*).

He·ki·nan \,hā-ki-'nän\. City, Aichi prefecture, Honshū, Japan, 23 m. S of Nagoya; pop. (1970c) 56,933.

Hek·la *or* **Hec·la** \'hek-lə\. Volcano in SW Iceland; 4747 ft.; largest crater ab. 1¼ m. in circumference and 200 to 300 ft. deep; 21 eruptions recorded since 12th cent.

Helder, Den. See DEN HELDER.

Hel·der·berg Mountains \,hel-dər-,bərg-\. Range of hills in Albany and Schoharie cos., E New York; ab. 1000 ft. high.

Hel·en, Mount \-'hel-ən\. Peak, Flathead and Glacier cos., NW Montana; 8540 ft.

Hel·e·na \'hel-ə-nə\. **1** City, ⊗ of Phillips co., E Arkansas, on Mississippi river 88 m. ENE of Pine Bluff; pop. (1970c) 10,415; lumber, fertilizer; river port and railroad terminus; Phillips County Community Coll. (1965); settled 1820; scene of battle July 4, 1863 won by Union forces under General B.M. Prentiss.

2 City, ✱ of Montana and ⊗ of Lewis and Clark co., W cen. Montana, 48 m. NNE of Butte; pop. (1970c) 22,730; alt. 4155 ft.; machine parts, ceramics, paints; Carroll Coll. (1910); founded 1864 on a site where gold had been discovered; incorporated as town 1870, as city 1881; capital of Montana Territory 1875, and of the state 1889.

Hel·ens·burgh \'hel-ənz-,bər-ə, -,bə-rə, -b(ə-)rə\. Coastal burgh, Dunbarton co., W cen. Scotland, on N shore of Firth of Clyde; pop. (1971p) 12,874; resort.

Hel·ford \'hel-fərd\. Stream in S Cornwall, England; 10 m. long; flows S and E to English Channel; marks N limit of the Lizard.

Hel·go·land \'hel-gō-,land\ *or Eng.* **Hel·i·go·land** \'hel-ə-gō-\. Island in North Sea off W coast of Schleswig-Holstein, West Germany, 28 m. from nearest mainland; ¼ sq. m.; pop. (1967e) 3200; attached to North Frisian Is. and a part of Schleswig-Holstein state. Danish to 1807 when it was seized by British (formal cession 1814); ceded to Germany 1890; fortifications dismantled after World War I but rebuilt by Hitler; in World War II surrendered to Allies May 5, 1945; under British control 1945–52.

Helgoländer Bucht. See HELIGOLAND BIGHT.

Hel·i·ce \'hel-ə-(,)sē\. Ancient city, one of chief cities of Achaea, N Peloponnesus, S Greece, in N part on shore of Gulf of Corinth; noted for its temple and worship of Poseidon; destroyed 373 B.C. by earthquake and tidal wave.

Hel·i·con \'hel-ə-,kän, -i-kən\ *or Gk.* **Eli·kón** \,el-ə-'kȯn\. Mountain, E cen. Greece, near Gulf of Corinth; 5738 ft.; was in SW part of ancient Boeotia on border of Phocis; supposed by ancient Greeks to be the abode of Apollo and the Muses; on it were the fountains of Aganippe and Hippocrene.

Hel·i·go·land Bight \,hel-ə-gō-,land-\ *or Ger.* **Hel·go·län·der Bucht** \,hel-gə-,len-dər-'bu̇kt\. Arm of the North Sea extending S and E of the island of Helgoland; scene of naval battle Aug. 28, 1914 bet. British and German lighter craft, resulting in definite advantage to British.

He·li·op·o·lis \ˌhē-lē-ˈäp-ə-ləs\. **1** *or Bib.* **On** \ˈän\. Ancient holy city in Lower Egypt; its ruins lie 6 m. NE of Cairo; dedicated to worship of the sun god, Ra, who was supposed to be incarnate in the Mnevis, a black bull, its temple becoming depository for historical records; its obelisks later taken by Romans to decorate Rome and other cities in Egypt; two of these obelisks, Cleopatra's Needles, being removed (1)1878 to the Thames Embankment, London, (2) 1880 to Central Park, New York City.

2 Ancient city of Egypt, its site recently discovered at the necropolis of Hilwān, on right bank of the Nile 15 m. S of Cairo; said to be of the late Stone Age and destroyed ab. 5000 B.C.; not the On of the Bible (see sense 1, above).

3 Village, Lebanon. See BAALBEK.

Hellas. See GREECE.

Hel·lemmes–Lille \e-lem-ˈlē(ə)l\. Commune, Nord dept., N France, E suburb of Lille; pop. (1968c) 18,670; 17th cent. pilgrimage church.

Hel·len·doorn \ˈhel-ən-ˌdō(ə)rn, -ˌdȯ(ə)rn\. Commune, Overijssel prov., E Netherlands, 17 m. SE of Zwolle; pop. (1970e) 29,410; textile manufactures.

Hel·ler·town \ˈhel-ər-ˌtaůn\. Borough, Northampton co., E Pennsylvania, 8 m. ESE of Allentown; pop. (1970c) 6613.

Hellespont *or* **Hellespontus.** See DARDANELLES.

Hell·fire Pass \ˌhel-ˌfī(ə)r-\. See HALFAYA PASS.

Hell Gate \ˈhel-\. A narrow part of the East River, New York City, bet. Long I. and Manhattan I., and also bet. Ward's I. and Long I. and bet. Ward's I. and Manhattan I.; made safe for navigation by removal, begun 1851, of rock reefs and by dredging; channel 200 ft. wide at narrowest part, 26 ft. deep; spanned by the Hell Gate Bridge (railroad, completed 1917) and the Triborough Bridge (highway, completed 1936).

Hel·lín \ā-ˈyēn\. Manufacturing commune, Albacete prov., SE Spain, 35 m. SSE of Albacete; pop. (1970p) 22,152; sulfur mining and refining.

Hells Canyon \ˈhelz-\ *or* **Grand Canyon of the Snake** \-ˈsnāk\. Canyon of the Snake river on Idaho-Oregon border; 40 m. long; max. height 8032 ft.

Hel·mand *or* **Hel·mund** \ˈhel-mənd\. **1** *or anc.* **Et·y·man·der** \ˌet-ə-ˈman-dər\. River, SW Afghanistan; 870 m. long; flows SW and W into **Lake Helmand** (*Pers.* **Dar·yā·cheh–ye Sī·stān** \ˌdär-yə-ˈchā-(y)ə-si-ˈstän\), swampy region on border bet. Iran and Afghanistan. See GAWD-I-ZIRREH.

2 Province of S Afghanistan. See table at AFGHANISTAN.

Helmantica. See SALAMANCA.

Hel·mond \ˈhel-ˌmȯnt\. Manufacturing commune, North Brabant prov., S Netherlands, 9 m. ENE of Eindhoven; pop. (1970e) 57,889; furniture; metalworking, food processing; castle, built 1402.

Helm·stedt \ˈhelm-ˌs(h)tet\. City, Lower Saxony, West Germany, 21 m. E of Brunswick; pop. (1969e) 27,267; foundries, brick works; precision instruments; city rights confirmed 1228; 11th cent. church; seat of university 1576–1810.

Helmund. See HELMAND.

Helmuth. See GOWANDA.

Hel Peninsula \ˈhel-\. Spit of land, Gdańsk prov., N Poland, on W side of Gulf of Danzig; ab. 22 m. long.

Hel·per \ˈhel-pər\. City, Carbon co., E cen. Utah, on Price river 7 m. N of Price; pop. (1970c) 1964; coal mining.

Helsingborg. See HÄLSINGBORG.

Hel·sing·ør \ˌhel-siŋ-ˈər\ *or Eng.* **El·si·nore** \ˈel-sə-ˌnō(ə)r, -ˌnȯ(ə)r\. Seaport, Frederiksborg co., N Sjælland I., Denmark; pop. (1970e) 30,211; shipbuilding; textile manufacturing, brewing; site of Kronborg Castle, dating from 16th cent. and famous as scene of Shakespeare's *Hamlet.*

Hel·sin·ki \ˈhel-ˌsiŋ-kē, hel-ˈ\ *or Swed.* **Hel·sing·fors** \ˈhel-siŋ-ˌfȯ(ə)rz\. Seaport, ❋ of Finland and ❋ of Uusimaa prov., S Finland, on Gulf of Finland on a peninsula surrounded by islands and protected by fortifications at Suomenlinna; pop. (1970p) 517,000; chemicals, clothing, metal goods, foodstuffs; Univ. of Helsinki (transferred from Turku 1828), Technical Univ. (1849, univ. status 1908), cathedral (completed 1852).

History: Founded N of present site by Gustavus I of Sweden 1550; removed to present site 1640; fortified 1748; with Finland (*q.v.*) became Russian 1809; made Finnish capital instead of Turku (see ÅBO) 1812; damaged in bombings by U.S.S.R. 1939–40; site of Olympic Games 1952; scene of U.S.-Soviet Strategic Arms Limitation Talks (initiated 1969).

Hel·ston \ˈhel-stən\. Municipal borough, Cornwall, SW England, 11 m. WSW of Falmouth; pop. (1971p) 9827; formerly a tin-mining center; tourist resort for visitors to the Lizard S of it; noted for annual holiday, May 8, when dancers perform in the streets and gardens.

Hel·vel·lyn \hel-ˈvel-ən\. Mountain in SE Cumberland, NW England, in Lake District 9 m. SE of Keswick; 3118 ft.

Helvetia. See SWITZERLAND.

Hel·vick Head \ˌhel-vik-\. Cape on S coast of Eire, S of entrance to Dungarvan Harbour.

Hel·ville \el-ˈvēl\. Town on island of Nossi-Bé, NW Malagasy Republic.

He·ma·theia \ˌē-mə-ˈthē-ə\. Department of Macedonia, Greece. See table at GREECE.

Hem·el Hemp·stead \ˌhem-əl-ˈhem(p)-stəd\. Municipal borough, Hertfordshire, SE England, near the Gade 23 m. NW of London; pop. (1971p) 69,371; light engineering; paper mills.

He·mer \ˈhā-mər\. City, North Rhine-Westphalia, West Germany, 35 m. E of Essen; pop. (1969e) 25,018; iron foundries, wire, brass. First mentioned 1072; became city 1647.

Hem·et \ˈhem-ət\. City, Riverside co., SE California, 31 m. SE of San Bernardino; pop. (1970c) 12,252; aluminum castings; ancient rock paintings and carvings.

Hem·lock Lake \ˌhem-ˌläk-\. Lake, W New York, bet. Ontario and Livingston cos.; ab. 7 m. long, 1 m. wide; outlet from N end joins outlet from Honeoye Lake and flows into Genesee river.

Hemp·field \ˈhem(p)-ˌfēld\. Urban township, Westmoreland co., SW Pennsylvania, SE of Pittsburgh; pop. (1970c) 39,196.

Hemp·hill \ˈhemp-ˌhil\. **1** County in Texas. See table at TEXAS.

2 City, ⊗ of Sabine co., E Texas; pop. (1970c) 1005.

Hemp·stead \ˈhem(p)-ˌsted, -stəd\. **1** County in Arkansas. See table at ARKANSAS.

2 Residential village, Nassau co., SE New York, on Long I. 20 m. E of New York; pop. (1970c) 39,411; precision tools, drugs; Hofstra Univ. (1935; before 1940 an affiliate of N.Y. Univ.); settled c. 1643.

3 Town, ⊗ of Waller co., SE Texas, 20 m. E of Brenham; pop. (1970c) 1891; nearby is Prairie View Agricultural and Mechanical Coll. (1876).

Hems·worth \ˈhemz-(ˌ)wərth\. Urban district, West Riding, Yorkshire, N England, SE of Wakefield; pop. (1971p) 14,856.

He·na·res \(h)ā-ˈnär-əs\. River, cen. Spain; ab. 75 m. long; flows SW into Jarama river 10 m. ESE of Madrid.

Hen·daye \äⁿ-ˈdī\. Commune, Pyrénées-Atlantiques dept., SW France; on the Bidassoa 13 m. SW of Biarritz; pop. (1962c) 7936; frontier town, resort.

Hen·der·son \ˈhen-dər-sən\. **1** Name of counties in five states of the U.S. See tables at ILLINOIS, KENTUCKY, NORTH CAROLINA, TENNESSEE, TEXAS.

2 Commercial city, ⊗ of Henderson co., NW Kentucky, on Ohio river 10 m. S of Evansville, Indiana; pop. (1970c)

22,976; manufactures furniture, clothing, and hardware; settled 1784, became a city 1854.
3 City, Clark co., SE corner of Nevada, S of Las Vegas; pop. (1970c) 16,395; titanium plant.
4 Industrial city, ⊗ of Vance co., N North Carolina, 40 m. NNE of Raleigh; pop. (1970c) 13,896; cotton and tobacco market; manufactures cotton and tobacco products.
5 City, ⊗ of Chester co., W Tennessee, 17 m. SW of Jackson; pop. (1970c) 3581; cotton gin; Freed-Hardeman Coll. (1908).
6 City, ⊗ of Rusk co., E Texas, 31 m. ESE of Tyler; pop. (1970c) 10,187; oil wells and industries; manufactures cottonseed oil, foundry and lumber products.

Henderson Island *or* **Eliz·a·beth Island** \i-ˌliz-ə-bəth-\. Uninhabited British coral island in S Pacific Ocean, SE of Tuamotu Archipelago, 24°22′S, 128°16′W; ab. 120 m. NE of Pitcairn I.; 12 sq. m.; attached to Pitcairn I. colony.

Henderson Lake. Lake, W Essex co., NE New York; ab. 2½ m. long; a source of Hudson river.

Hen·der·son·ville \ˈhen-dər-sən-ˌvil\. City, ⊗ of Henderson co., SW North Carolina, in Blue Ridge Mts. 21 m. SSE of Asheville; pop. (1970c) 6443; summer and health resort; textile mills.

Hen·dricks \ˈhen-driks\. County in Indiana. See table at INDIANA.

Hen·dry \ˈhen-drē\. County in Florida. See table at FLORIDA.

Hen Egg Mountain \ˌhen-ˌeg-, -ˌāg-\. Peak, W Brewster co., W Texas; 5002 ft.

Henegouwen. See HAINAUT.

Heng \ˈhəŋ\ *or* **Heng Shan** \-ˈshän\. Mountain, E cen. Hunan prov., China, N of Heng-yang; 2953 ft.; has many Buddhist temples on its summit.

Heng·e·lo \ˈheŋ-ə-ˌlō\. Commune, Overijssel prov., E Netherlands, near German border; pop. (1970e) 69,618; chemicals, textiles, electronic apparatus; brewing.

Heng–feng \ˈhəŋ-ˈfəŋ\. Town, NE Kiangsi prov., SE China, on railroad E of Nan-ch'ang.

Heng–yang \ˈhəŋ-ˈyäŋ\ *or formerly* **Heng·chow** \-ˈjō\. Town, S cen. Hunan prov., SE cen. China, ab. 150 m. S of Ch'ang-sha; pop. (1970e) 240,000; important rail and river junction point; American air base, scene of severe fighting 1944, taken by Japanese Aug. 8 but recovered.

Hé·nin–Lié·tard \ā-ˈnaⁿ-ˌlē-ā-ˈtär\. Commune, Pas-de-Calais dept., N France, 4 m. N of Arras; pop. (1968c) 25,067; coal mines; metal works; ancient capital of a principality estab. 1579 by Charles of Alsace; damaged in World War I.

Hénin–sur–Co·jeul \-ˌsu̇(ə)r-kō-ˈzhər(-ə)l\. Village, Pas-de-Calais dept., N France, SE of Arras; pop. (1962c) 310; battles Apr. 1917 and Aug. 1918.

Hen·kel Mountain \ˌheŋ-kəl-\. Peak in Glacier National Park, NW Montana; 8700 ft.

Hen·ley \ˈhen-lē\ *or* **Henley–on–Thames** \-ˈtemz, -ˈthāmz, -ˈtāmz\. Municipal borough, Oxfordshire, cen. England, 35 m. W of London; pop. (1971p) 31,744; known esp. as scene of annual Henley rowing regatta, estab. 1839.

Hen·lo·pen, Cape \-hen-ˈlō-pən\. Cape on E coast of Sussex co., Delaware, at S of entrance to Delaware Bay.

Henna. See ENNA 2.

Hen·ne·bont \ˌen-(ə-)ˈbōⁿ\. Commune, Morbihan dept., NW France, on the Blavet 6 m. NE of Lorient; pop. (1968c) 11,799; famous for its defense by Jeanne de Montfort when besieged by Charles de Blois 1342; Gothic church built 1513–30; nearby is Cistercian abbey founded 1270.

Hen·ne·pin \ˈhen-ə-pən\. 1 County in Minnesota. See table at MINNESOTA.
2 Village, ⊗ of Putnam co., N cen. Illinois; pop. (1970c) 535.

Hen·ri·co \hen-ˈrī-kō\. County in Virginia. See table at VIRGINIA.

Hen·ri·et·ta \ˌhen-rē-ˈet-ə\. Town, ⊗ of Clay co., N Texas, 19 m. ESE of Wichita Falls; pop. (1970c) 2897; manufactures flour, lumber; oil and gas wells.

Henrietta Ma·ria, Cape \-mə-ˈrē-ə\. Cape, N coast of Ontario, Canada, at W of entrance to James Bay.

Hen·ry \ˈhen-rē\. 1 Name of counties in ten states of the U.S. See tables at ALABAMA, GEORGIA, ILLINOIS, INDIANA, IOWA, KENTUCKY, MISSOURI, OHIO, TENNESSEE, VIRGINIA.
2 City, Marshall co., N cen. Illinois, on Illinois river 30 m. N of Peoria; pop. (1970c) 2610.

Henry, Cape. Cape on E coast of Virginia, S of entrance to Chesapeake Bay, opp. Cape Charles.

Henry, Mount. 1 Peak in Sierra Nevada, E Fresno co., S cen. California; 12,196 ft.
2 Peak in Glacier National Park, NW Montana; 7247 ft.

Hen·ry·et·ta \ˌhen-rē-ˈet-ə\. City, Okmulgee co., E cen. Oklahoma, 13 m. S of Okmulgee; pop. (1970c) 6430; foundry products; zinc smelters, coal mines, gas and oil wells.

Hens·low, Cape \-ˈhenz-(ˌ)lō\. Cape, SE extremity of Guadalcanal, Solomon Is., W Pacific Ocean.

Hen·tiyn Nu·ruu \hen-ˈtēn-ˈnu̇(ə)r-ü\ *or* **Ken·tei Shan** \ˈ-gen-ˈtā-ˈshän\. Mountain range, N Mongolian People's Republic, NE of Ulan Bator, in part parallel with U.S.S.R. border; highest peak 8494 ft.

Hen·za·da \ˌhen-zə-ˈdä\. 1 District, Irrawaddy division, Lower Burma; 2807 sq. m.; pop. (1962e) 896,836; ✱ Henzada.
2 Town, its ✱, on the Irrawaddy 75 m. NNW of Rangoon; pop. (1953c) 61,972; at head of Irrawaddy delta; connected by rail with Bassein; center of rice and tobacco cultivation.

Hep·pen·heim \ˈhep-ən-ˌhīm\. Commune, SE Hesse, West Germany, 18 m. S of Darmstadt; pop. (1969e) 16,249; textiles, precision tools; first mentioned 755; nearby are ruins of Starkenburg castle built 1066 by the abbot Ulrich von Lorsch.

Hepp·ner \ˈhep-nər\. City, ⊗ of Morrow co., N Oregon, 45 m. WSW of Pendleton; pop. (1970c) 1429; timber; livestock.

Heptanesus. See IONIAN ISLANDS.

Hep·tarchy, The \ˈhep-ˌtär-kē\. The seven Anglo-Saxon kingdoms of Britain: Kent, Sussex, Wessex, Essex, Northumbria, East Anglia, Mercia. See these names.

Her·a·clea \ˌher-ə-ˈklē-ə\. 1 Ancient city, Lucania, Italy, near Gulf of Taranto; founded by Greeks from Tarentum (*mod.* Taranto); battle 280 B.C. in which Pyrrhus, King of Epirus, defeated the Romans but with heavy losses, hence, a "Pyrrhic victory."
2 Town, Turkey. See AYVALIK.

Heraclea Lyncestis. See BITOLA.

Heraclea Pontica. See EREĞLİ 2.

Her·a·cle·op·o·lis \ˌher-ə-klē-ˈäp-ə-ləs\. Ancient city in Egypt; site in Faiyūm gov. near the Nile; capital for one period of the Middle Kingdom in Egypt, IXth and Xth Dynasties ruling at this time (c. 2445–2160 B.C.) being called the Heracleopolitan Dynasties.

Heracleum. See CANDIA 2.

He·radhs·vötn \ˈher-əths-ˌvə(r)-tən\. River, N Iceland, flowing N into Skaga Fjord.

Hē·rá·klei·on \hi-ˈrak-lē-ən\. Department of Greece. See table at GREECE.

Heraklion. See CANDIA 2.

Her·ald Island \ˌher-əld-\. Small island in Chukchi Sea, Arctic Ocean, 40 m. E of Wrangel I.

He·rāt \he-ˈrät, hə-\. 1 A province of NW Afghanistan. See table at AFGHANISTAN.
2 *or anc.* **Ar·ia** \ˈar-ē-ə, ˈer-, ə-ˈrī-ə\. City, its ✱, on the Hari Rud; pop. (1970e) 101,579; carpets; commercial center; remarkable for its huge earthworks and defense walls and for its palaces, mosques, and tombs, some partly in ruins.
History: An old city, for centuries on trade route from India to Persia, Mesopotamia, and Europe; subject at different times to Khurasan, Seistan, Bukhara, and to Turkmen; obscured by Ghazni during Middle Ages and although recovered under rulers of Ghor practically destroyed twice by the Mongols, 1221 and 1383; rebuilt, prospered as independent Afghan kingdom; in modern

times has undergone many revolutions; attacked by Persia 1856; taken by Dost Mohammed Khan 1863.

Hé·rault \ā-'rō\. 1 River, S France; 100 m. long; rises in Cévennes Mts., flows SSW into Gulf of Lions near Agde.
2 Department of S France. See table at FRANCE.

Her·bert Hoo·ver Lake \ˌhər-bərt-'hü-vər-\. Small lake, New Guinea I., on border bet. Papua New Guinea and Irian Barat, W of Fly river.

Herbertshöhe. See KOKOPO.

Her·ceg·no·vi \ˌhert-sek-'nȯ-vē, ˌk̲ert-\ *or Ital.* **Ca·stel·nuo·vo** \käs-ˌtel-nü-'ō-vō\. Seaport, Montenegro, S Yugoslavia, on N shore of Gulf of Kotor.

Hercegovina. See HERZEGOVINA.

Her·cu·la·ne·um \ˌhər-kyə-'lā-nē-əm\. Ancient city, Campania, Italy, on coast SE of Neapolis, at NW foot of Mt. Vesuvius; with Pompeii, just S of the mountain, destroyed by eruption of 79 A.D. See RESINA.

Hercules, Pillars of. See PILLARS OF HERCULES.

He·re·dia \ā-'rād-ē-ə\. 1 Province of cen. Costa Rica. See table at COSTA RICA.
2 Town, its ✱, just NW of San José; pop. (1970p) 24,021; center of coffee industry.

Her·e·ford \'hər-fərd\. City, ⊗ of Deaf Smith co., NW Texas, 40 m. SW of Amarillo; pop. (1970c) 13,414; fertilizer; sugar beet processing; cattle.

Hereford \'her-ə-fərd, *US also* 'hər-fərd\. 1 County, W England. See HEREFORDSHIRE.
2 Municipal borough, ⊗ of Herefordshire, W England, on the Wye 47 m. SW of Birmingham; pop. (1971p) 46,503; glass, furniture, nickel alloys; founded by West Saxons in 7th cent. as an outpost near Welsh marches; incorporated 1186; trade center of agricultural and livestock-raising section; 11th cent. cathedral.

Hereford Inlet. Narrow strait leading from Atlantic Ocean through barrier reefs in SE Cape May co., S New Jersey.

Her·e·ford·shire \'her-ə-fərd-ˌshi(ə)r, -shər\ *or* **Hereford.** County, W England, on border of Wales; 842 sq. m.; pop. (1971p) 138,425; ⊗ Hereford; rivers Wye, Teme, Frome; fruit, hops; livestock raising (Hereford cattle), quarrying; chief towns Hereford, Leominster.

Hé·rens, Dent d' \'däⁿ-dā-'räⁿ\. Peak in Pennine Alps, on Swiss-Italian boundary; 13,715 ft.

He·rent·hals *or* **He·rent·als** \'her-ənt-ˌhäls\. Manufacturing commune, Antwerp prov., N Belgium, 18 m. E of Antwerp; pop. (1969e) 18,684; furniture, cement.

Her·ford \'he(ə)r-ˌfȯ(ə)rt\. Manufacturing city, North Rhine-Westphalia, West Germany, 43 m. ENE of Münster; pop. (1969e) 67,377; carpets, furniture; food processing; church (14th cent.).

Hé·ri·court \ˌer-i-'kü(ə)r\. Commune, Haute-Saône dept., E France, near Belfort; pop. (1962c) 7175; battles: (1) 1474 in which the Swiss were victorious over Charles the Bold; (2) Jan. 1871, in Franco-Prussian War, in which Bourbaki tried unsuccessfully to raise the siege of Belfort.

Her·ing·ton \'her-iŋ-tən\. City, Dickinson co., E cen. Kansas, 40 m. ESE of Salina; pop. (1970c) 3165; corn; oil wells.

Heri Rud. See HARI RUD.

He·ri·sau \'her-ə-ˌzau̇\ *or Fr.* **Hé·ri·sau** \ā-rē-zō\. Commune, ✱ of Appenzell Outer Rhodes demicanton, NE Switzerland, 5 m. SW of St. Gallen; pop. (1970c) 14,597; railroad junction; textiles (esp. cotton goods), embroidery.

Héristal. See HERSTAL.

Her·it·age Range \ˌher-ət ij \. Mountain range, Antarctica. See ELLSWORTH MOUNTAINS.

Her·je·da·len \'her-yə-ˌdäl-ən\. Former district, cen. Sweden; belonged to Norway before 1645 when it was ceded to Sweden as result of the war 1643–45.

Her·ki·mer \'hər-kə-mər\. 1 County in NE cen. New York. See table at NEW YORK.
2 Industrial village, its ⊗, on Mohawk river 14 m. ESE of Utica; pop. (1970c) 8960; forms single community with Mohawk, Ilion, and Frankfort across river; manufactures office furniture, metal specialties, knit goods. Settled by Palatines c. 1725; raided in French and Indian War; site of Fort Dayton (1776), from which Gen. Herkimer marched to battle of Oriskany; attacked by Indians under Brant 1778.

Herlen Go. See KERULEN.

Herm \'hərm\. One of the Channel Is., 3 m. E of Guernsey; in Guernsey bailiwick; ½ sq. m.

Her·mann \'hər-mən\. City, ⊗ of Gasconade co., E cen. Missouri, on Missouri river 44 m. E of Jefferson City; pop. (1970c) 2658; settled 1837 by colonists sent out by German Settlement Society of Philadelphia, Pa.

Hermanos, Los. See LOS HERMANOS.

Her·mans·verk \'hər-məns-ˌverk\. Commune, ⊗ of Sogn og Fjordane co., Norway.

Her·man·us \hər-'man-əs\. Town, SW Cape Province, S Rep. of South Africa, 60 m. ESE of Cape Town; pop. (1967e) 5200; seaside resort, one of world's finest angling centers.

Her·mit·age \'hər-mət-ij\. City, ⊗ of Hickory co., SW cen. Missouri; pop. (1970c) 284.

Hermitage Bay. Inlet of Atlantic Ocean, S coast of Newfoundland, Canada; ab. 25 m. long; has several long arms.

Her·mit Islands \ˌhər-mət-\. See NORTHWESTERN ISLANDS.

Her·mon, Mount \-'hər-mən\ *or Arab.* **Ja·bal ash–Shaykh** \ˌjab-əl-ash-'shīk, -'shāk\. Mountain, on boundary bet. Lebanon and SW Syria 28 m. WSW of Damascus, Syria; 9232 ft.; highest point in Anti-Lebanon Range; has snow-covered crest; the N limit of Israelite conquests; figures in Hebrew poetry (*Ps.* lxxxix. 12; cxxxiii. 3).

Her·mon·this \(ˌ)hər-'män(t)-thəs\. Ancient city in Upper Egypt, on W bank of Nile near Thebes.

Hermopolis. See HERMOUPOLIS.

Hermopolis Magna. See AL-ASHMŪNEIN.

Hermopolis Parva. See DAMANHŪR.

Her·mo·sa \er-'mō-sə, hər-\. Municipality, NE Bataan prov., Luzon, Phil., ab. 2 m. from NW coast of Manila Bay; pop. (1969e) 17,200; severe fighting early in Bataan campaign Jan. 1942.

Hermosa Beach \hər-ˌmō-sə-\. Resort city, Los Angeles co., SW California, on Pacific Ocean 15 m. SSW of Los Angeles; pop. (1970c) 17,412; oil wells.

Her·mo·si·llo \ˌer-mə-'sē-(ˌ)(y)ō\. Town, ✱ of Sonora state, NW Mexico, on Sonora river ab. 65 m. from Gulf of California; munic. pop. (1970p) 206,663; gold, copper, and silver mines; univ. (1938).

Her·mou·po·lis \hər-'mü-pə-ləs\ *also* **Her·mop·o·lis** \-'mäp-ə-ləs\ *or* **Sy·ros** \'sī-ˌräs, 'sē-ˌrȯs\. Commercial seaport city, ✱ of Cyclades dept., Cyclades Is., Greece, on E coast of Syros I.; pop. (1971p) 13,460.

Hermus. See GEDİZ.

Her·nád \'he(ə)r-ˌnäd\ *or* **Hor·nad** \'hȯr-\. River in Czechoslovakia and Hungary; 165 m. long; rises in Slovak S.R., Czechoslovakia, flows E and S into the Sajó (tributary of the Tisza).

Her·nan·da·rias \ˌer-nän-'där-yəs\ *or formerly* **Ta·cu·ru·pu·cú** \ˌtäk-ə-ˌrü-pə-'kü\. Town, ✱ of Alto Paraná dept., E Paraguay, on the Paraná river; pop. (1970e) 2100.

Her·nan·do \hər-'nan-dō\. 1 County in Florida. See table at FLORIDA.
2 Town, ⊗ of De Soto co., NW corner of Mississippi; pop. (1970c) 2499.

Hern·don \'hərn-dən\. Town, Fairfax co., NE Virginia, 20 m. NW of Washington, D.C.; pop. (1970c) 4301.

Her·ne \'he(ə)r-nə\. Industrial city, North Rhine-Westphalia, West Germany, in the Ruhr 33 m. SSW of Münster; pop. (1969e) 101,514; coal mines; chemicals, machinery, cable, hardware; became city 1897.

Herne Bay \ˈhərn-\. Urban district, Kent, SE England, on North Sea 53 m. E of London; pop. (1971p) 25,117; seaside resort.

Her·ning \ˈhe(ə)r-niŋ, ˈha(ə)r-\. Commercial city, Ringkøbing co., W cen. Jutland, Denmark, E of Ringkøbing; pop. (1970e) 32,512; machinery, textiles.

Hernösand. See HÄRNÖSAND.

He·ro·op·o·lis \ˌhē-rō-ˈäp-ə-ləs, ˌhir-ō-\. Ancient town on E edge of Nile delta, N Egypt; terminus of canal from Bubastis on the Nile and port at head of **Gulf of Heroopolis** (now Bitter Lakes and Gulf of Suez).

He·rre·ra \e-ˈrer-ə\. Province on the Azuero Penin., S Panama. See table at PANAMA.

He·rre·ro \e-ˈre(ə)r-(ˌ)ō\. Cape on E cen. coast of Yucatán penin., SE Mexico, at S of entrance to Espíritu Santo Bay.

Herreroland. See DAMARALAND.

Her·rin \ˈher-ən\. City, Williamson co., S Illinois, 5 m. NE of Marion; pop. (1970c) 9623; trading center in coal-mining section; scene of so-called Herrin Massacre during a miners' strike 1922.

Herrn·hut \ˈhe(ə)rn-ˈhüt\. Town, Dresden dist., East Germany, 18 m. SE of Bautzen; pop. (1965e) 1800; seat of a persecuted colony of Moravians, hence called Herrnhuters, who settled here 1722 on estate of Count von Zinzendorf.

Her·schel \ˈhər-shəl\. Small island in NW Mackenzie Bay, off coast of N Yukon Territory, Canada.

Hersfeld. See BAD HERSFELD.

Her·shey \ˈhər-shē\. Unincorporated community, Dauphin co., SE cen. Pennsylvania, ab. 13 m. E of Harrisburg; pop. (1970c) 7407; privately developed as workers' community by Hershey Chocolate Corporation 1903.

Her·stal \ˈhe(ə)r-ˌstäl, -ˌstȯl\ *or Fr.* **Hé·ris·tal** \(h)er-ə-stál\. Commune, Liège prov., E Belgium; pop. (1969e) 29,711; manufactures iron and steel; birthplace of Pepin II (Pepin of Herstal) and often the residence of Charlemagne.

Herstmonceux. See HURSTMONCEUX.

Her·ten \ˈhe(ə)rt-ᵊn\ *also* **Herten in West·fa·len** \-ˌin-vest-ˈfäl-ən\. Commune, North Rhine-Westphalia, West Germany, 10 m. N of Essen; pop. (1969e) 52,258; coal mining; manufactures machinery.

Hert·ford \ˈhərt-fərd\. 1 County in North Carolina. See table at NORTH CAROLINA.

2 Town, and port of entry, ⊗ of Perquimans co., NE North Carolina, on arm of Albemarle Sound 17 m. WSW of Elizabeth City; pop. (1970c) 2023; manufactures lumber, cotton products; fisheries.

Hertford \ˈhär-fərd *also* ˈhärt-\. 1 County, SE England. See HERTFORDSHIRE.

2 Municipal borough, ⊗ of Hertfordshire, SE England, on the Lea 22 m. N of London; pop. (1971p) 20,379; site of synod held 673 by Theodore of Tarsus.

Hert·ford·shire \ˈhär-fərd-ˌshi(ə)r, ˈhärt-, -shər\ *or* **Hertford** *or* **Herts** \ˈhärts, ˈhərts\. County, SE England; 631 sq. m.; pop. (1971p) 922,188; ⊗ Hertford; rivers Lea, Colne; wheat; dairying; paper, electrical equipment; towns incl. Hertford, Watford, St. Albans, Hemel Hempstead, Hitchin.

Hertogenbosch, 's. See 'S HERTOGENBOSCH.

Hertseliya. See HERZLIYYA.

Her·vey Bay \ˌhər-vē-\. Inlet of Pacific Ocean in SE Queensland, Australia, N of Brisbane, bet. Fraser I. and mainland.

Her·ze·go·vi·na \ˌhert-sə-gō-ˈvē-nə, ˌhərt-\ *or Serb.* **Her·ce·go·vi·na** \ˈkert-sə-gō-ˌvē-nə, ˈhert-\. Region, part of the constituent republic of Bosnia and Herzegovina, Yugoslavia. See BOSNIA.

History: As principality of the Huns, independent, except for brief intervals, from 10th–14th cents.; conquered by Bosnia 14th cent.; became independent duchy (origin of name Herzegovina), early 15th cent.; overcome by Turks 1482; by Treaty of Berlin 1878, placed under control of Austria-Hungary which made it part of new province of Bosnia and Herzegovina; became part of Serb-Croat-Slovene State 1918 and part of Zetska co., Yugoslavia, 1929; made part of Bosnia and Herzegovina federated republic 1946.

Her·zliy·ya *also* **Her·tsel·i·ya** \ˌhert-sə-ˈlē-(y)ə\. Town, W Israel, on Mediterranean Sea, 35 m. NW of Jerusalem; pop. (1970e) 38,500; residential; named after Theodor Herzl.

Hes·din \ā-ˈdaⁿ\. Town, Pas-de-Calais dept., N France, NE of Abbeville; pop. (1962c) 3598; founded by Charles V; birthplace of Abbé Prévost.

Heshbon. See ḤISBĀN.

Hes·pe·ler \ˈhes-pə-lər\. Town, Waterloo co., SE Ontario, Canada, 10 m. E of Kitchener; pop. (1971p) 6252; electric washers, tools; livestock.

Hes·pe·rus Peak \ˌhes-p(ə-)rəs-\. Mountain, NE Montezuma co., SW Colorado; 13,225 ft.; highest in La Plata Mts.

Hesse \ˈhes, ˈhes-ē\ *or Ger.* **Hes·sen** \ˈhes-ᵊn\. 1 Region in SW Germany, comprising the state of Hesse and the former Prussian province of Hesse-Nassau.

2 Former state of Germany; 2969 sq. m.; ✱ Darmstadt; now part of West German states of Hesse and Rhineland-Palatinate.

3 A state of West Germany; 8151 sq. m.; pop. (1970e) 5,441,300; ✱ Wiesbaden; electrical equipment, motor vehicles, chemicals, textiles; iron ore, natural gas.

History: (1) Medieval landgraviate expanded from original holdings W to the Rhine and S to the Main; 1567, according to will of Landgrave Philip I, divided bet. four sons, two of whom founded houses of **Hesse–Darm·stadt** \-ˈdärm-ˌstat\ and **Hesse–Cas·sel** \-ˈkas-əl, -ˈkäs-\; (2) Hesse-Darmstadt (*Ger.* **Hessen–Darmstadt** \-ˈdärm-ˌs(h)tät\) inherited by George I in 1567, extended its territory and became grand duchy of Hesse in Napoleon's Confederation of the Rhine 1806; joined Prussian customs union 1828; in 1866, after supporting Austria in Seven Weeks' War forced to cede to Prussia **Hesse–Hom·burg** \-ˈhäm-ˌbərg\ and part of Upper Hesse; joined North German Confederation 1867; republic 1918; came under (Ger.) *Statthalter* appointed by Hitler 1935; following World War II partitioned between newly formed states of Hesse and Rhineland-Palatinate. (3) Hesse-Cassel (*Ger.* **Hessen–Kas·sel** \-ˈkäs-əl\), or electoral Hesse, came from line of William IV, eldest son of Landgrave Philip I; its ruler, as Frederick I King of Sweden 1720–51; part of kingdom of Westphalia 1807–13; restored as independent state 1815; joined Prussian customs union 1831; its liberal reforms of 1848 overthrown with aid of intervention 1850; occupied by and united with Prussia in 1866 as result of siding with Austria; (4) **Hesse–Nas·sau** \-ˈnas-ˌȯ\ (*Ger.* **Hessen–Nassau** \-ˈnäs-ˌau̇\) formerly a Prussian province formed from territories annexed in 1866: electoral Hesse, duchy of Nassau, part of landgraviate of Hesse-Homburg, free city of Frankfurt am Main, etc., and after 1929, former republic of Waldeck; lost sovereignty at accession of National Socialists 1934; reconstituted 1945, with most of area becoming part of new state (*Land*).

Hest·mona \ˈhest-ˌmän-ə\. Small island in Norwegian Sea, off W coast of Norway.

Hetch Hetchy Dam *and* **Hetch Hetchy Reservoir** \ˈhech-ˌhech-ē\. See *O'Shaughnessy Dam* at UNITED STATES, *Dams and Reservoirs;* TUOLUMNE 1.

Het·ting·er \ˈhet-ən-jər\. 1 County in North Dakota. See table at NORTH DAKOTA.

2 City, ⊗ of Adams co., SW North Dakota; pop. (1970c) 1655.

Het·ton \ˈhet-ᵊn\. Urban district, Durham, N England, 13 m. SSE of Newcastle upon Tyne; pop. (1971p) 16,871.

Hett·stedt \ˈhet-ˌs(h)tet\. City, Halle dist., East Germany, 23 m. NW of Halle; pop. (1970e) 20,160; a major center of the East German copper industry; founded 1394; to Prussia 1815.

Heumar. See PORZ AM RHEIN.

Heuvelton. See OGDENSBURG.

Hé·ver·lé \ˌā-ver-ˈlā\. Commune, Brabant prov., cen. Belgium, S of Louvain; pop. (1969e) 18,489; market gardens.

He·ves \'hev-esh\. County of N Hungary. See table at HUNGARY.

Hev·ros \'ev-ˌrȯs\. Modern Greek form of *Evros* department of Thrace, Greece: see table at GREECE.

Hex·ham \'hek-səm\. Urban district, Northumberland, N England, on the Tyne 20 m. W of Newcastle upon Tyne; pop. (1971p) 9799; present abbey church of St. Andrew dates from 12th cent.

Hex·ham·shire \-ˌshi(ə)r, -shər\. District around Hexham, S Northumberland, N England, one of original counties palatine until close of 16th cent.

Hey·wood \'hā-(ˌ)wu̇d\. Municipal borough, Lancashire, NW England, 9 m. NNW of Manchester; pop. (1969e) 30,360; cotton mills; engineering.

Hi·a·le·ah \ˌhī-ə-'lē-ə\. City, Dade co., SE Florida, 5 m. NW of Miami; pop. (1970c) 102,452; aluminum, chemicals, electronic products; incorporated 1925; Hialeah Park race track.

Hi·a·was·see \ˌhī-ə-'wäs-ē\. 1 River, United States. See HIWASSEE.

2 Town, ⊗ of Towns co., N Georgia; pop. (1970c) 415.

Hi·a·wa·tha \ˌhī-ə-'wȯ-thə, -wä-\. City, ⊗ of Brown co., NE Kansas, 28 m. NW of Atchison; pop. (1970c) 3365; corn, wheat, apples.

Hib·bing \'hib-iŋ\. Village, St. Louis co., NE Minnesota, 58 m. NW of Duluth, in the Mesabi Range; pop. (1970c) 16,104; foundry; iron ore deposits.

Hibernia. See IRELAND.

Hibernicus, Oceanus. See IRISH SEA.

Hick·man \'hik-mən\. 1 Name of counties in two states of the U.S. See tables at KENTUCKY and TENNESSEE.

2 City, ⊗ of Fulton co., SW corner of Kentucky, on Mississippi river; pop. (1970c) 3048.

Hick·o·ry \'hik-(ə-)rē\. 1 County in Missouri. See table at MISSOURI.

2 City, Catawba co., W cen. North Carolina, 25 m. W of Statesville; pop. (1970c) 20,569; manufactures wagons, cordage, cotton and knit goods, furniture; Lenoir-Rhyne Coll. (1891); annexed West Hickory 1931.

Hickory Hills. Village, Cook co., NE Illinois, 15 m. SW of Chicago; pop. (1970c) 13,176.

Hicks·ville \'hiks-ˌvil\. 1 Village, Nassau co., SE New York, on Long I. NE of Mineola; pop. (1970c) 48,075.

2 Village, Defiance co., NW Ohio, 50 m. NW of Lima; pop. (1970c) 3461.

Hi·da·ka Mountains \hi-ˌdäk-ə-\. Range in S Hokkaidō, Japan; highest peak Horoshiri 6730 ft.

Hi·dal·go \hid-'al-(ˌ)gō\. 1 Counties in two states of the U.S. See tables at NEW MEXICO and TEXAS.

2 \or *Span.* ē-'thäl-gō\. State of cen. Mexico. See table at MEXICO.

Hidalgo del Parral. See PARRAL 2.

Hiddekel. See TIGRIS.

Hi·ei–zan \hē-'ā-ˌzän\. Mountain, Kyōto prefecture, W cen. Honshū, Japan, just N of Kyōto and near SW shore of Lake Biwa; 2800 ft.; place of pilgrimage; monastery built by Saicho.

Hien·ghene \yen-'gen\. Town on E coast of New Caledonia I., SW Pacific Ocean, near N end; pop. (1969c) 1846.

Hiera. See VULCANO.

Hi·e·ra·kon·po·lis \ˌhī-(ə-)rə-'kän-pə-ləs\. Ancient city of Upper Egypt, on left bank of Nile, S of Thebes; important tombs and relics found in its ruins.

Hie·rá·pe·tra *or Gk.* **Ie·rá·pet·ra** \ye-'räp-ə-trə\. Seaport town, Lasithion dept., E Crete, Greece.

Hi·er·ap·o·lis \ˌhī-(ə-)'rap-ə-ləs\. Ancient city of Phrygia, Asia Minor, near Maeander river just N of Laodicea; an early seat of Christianity.

Hierosolyma. See JERUSALEM 2.

Hie·rro \'ye(ə)r-(ˌ)ō\ *or formerly* **Fer·ro** \'fe(ə)r-(ˌ)ō\. Westernmost of the Canary Is. (*q.v.*), 78 m. WSW of Tenerife I., in Santa Cruz de Tenerife prov., Spain; 107 sq. m.; pop. (1970p) 5503; chief town Valverde; volcanic in origin; rocky, unfertile soil; warm springs; produces figs, wines, and brandies. Thought by ancient geographers to mark W limit of world and hence they reckoned longitude from it.

Hi·ga·shi·mu·ra·ya·ma \hē-'gä-shē-ˌmu̇r-ə-'yäm-ə\. City, Tokyo prefecture, Honshū, Japan, 18 m. NW of Tokyo; pop. (1970c) 96,545.

Hi·ga·shi·ōsa·ka \hē-ˌgä-shē-ō-'säk-ə\. City, Ōsaka prefecture, Honshū, Japan, suburb of Ōsaka; pop. (1970c) 500,173.

Hig·ga·num \'hig-ə-nəm\. Subdivision of town of Haddam, Connecticut. See HADDAM.

Hig·gins Lake \ˌhig-ənz-\. Lake, N Roscommon co., N cen. Michigan; ab. 7 m. long; has outlet into Houghton Lake to the S.

Hig·gins·ville \'hig-ənz-ˌvil\. City, Lafayette co., W Missouri, 39 m. NW of Sedalia; pop. (1970c) 4318; coal; manufactures incubators, brick and tile.

High Atlas. See ATLAS MOUNTAINS.

High Bridge. Borough, Hunterdon co., NW cen. New Jersey, 15 m. E of Phillipsburg; pop. (1970c) 2606; iron and steel.

High·gate \'hī-ˌgāt\. Town, Franklin co., NW Vermont, near Canadian boundary; pop. (1970c) 1936; settled 1787; customs station.

Highgate \'hī-gət\. Part of Heringey, London, England, NE of Hampstead Heath in Hornsey; residence of Coleridge and Andrew Marvell; place where, the legend has it, Dick Whittington heard Bow bells and decided to go on to London.

High Island. Island in N Lake Michigan, NW of Beaver I., part of Charlevoix co., NW Michigan.

High Knob. Peak, Wise co., SW Virginia; 4162 ft.

High·land \'hī-lənd\. 1 Counties in two states of the U.S. See tables at OHIO and VIRGINIA.

2 City, Madison co., SW Illinois, 27 m. ESE of East St. Louis; pop. (1970c) 5981; electronic equipment, transformers.

3 Town, Lake co., NW corner of Indiana, 7 m. S of Lake Michigan; pop. (1970c) 24,947; concrete blocks, metal goods; truck farms.

Highland Falls. Village, Orange co., SE New York, on Hudson river 5 m. SSW of Newburgh; pop. (1970c) 4638; adjoins West Point; Ladycliff Coll. (1933).

Highland Heights. 1 City, Campbell co., N Kentucky; pop. (1970c) 4400.

2 City, Cuyahoga co., N Ohio, 14 m. NE of Cleveland; pop. (1970c) 5926.

Highland Lake. Lake in NE Litchfield co., NW Connecticut, W of Winsted.

Highland Park. 1 Residential city, Lake co., NE corner of Illinois, on Lake Michigan 25 m. N of Chicago; pop. (1970c) 32,263.

2 City, Wayne co., SE Michigan, entirely within city of Detroit; pop. (1970c) 35,444; tractors, automobiles.

3 Borough, Middlesex co., cen. New Jersey, on Raritan river 2 m. E of New Brunswick; pop. (1970c) 14,385; nonmetallic station of U.S. Bureau of Mines.

4 Town, Dallas co., NE Texas, entirely within the city of Dallas; pop. (1970c) 10,133.

Highland Peak. Mountain, N cen. Lincoln co., E Nevada; 9395 ft.

High·lands \'hī-lən(d)z\. 1 County in Florida. See table at FLORIDA.

2 Borough, Monmouth co., E cen. New Jersey, on Sandy Hook Bay 17 m. ESE of Perth Amboy; pop. (1970c) 3916; fishing village, summer resort; first U.S. Navy wireless station erected on nearby Monmouth Hills 1903; place where Henry Hudson first landed 1609.

Highlands, The. That portion of Scotland lying NW of a line drawn from Dumbarton to Stonehaven; term sometimes includes the county of Bute and the Hebrides, but excludes the Orkney Is., Shetland Is., Caithness, the flat coastal regions of Nairn, Elgin, Banff, and E Aberdeenshire. The area below the Dumbarton-Stonehaven line is known as **The Low·lands** \-ˈlō-lan(d)z\.

Highlands of Nav·e·sink \-ˈnav-ə-ˌsiŋk, -ˈnāv-, -ˈnev-\ *also* **Navesink Highlands** *or* **Navesink Hills.** Range of hills in NE New Jersey, extending from near Sandy Hook to Raritan Bay.

Highlands of the Hud·son \-ˈhəd-sən\. Hilly region on both sides of Hudson river in Rockland, Orange, Putnam, and Dutchess cos., SE New York.

High·more \ˈhī-ˌmō(ə)r, -ˌmȯ(ə)r\. City, ⊗ of Hyde co., cen. South Dakota; pop. (1970c) 1173; livestock.

High Peak. 1 Mountain in the Catskill Mts., Greene co., SE New York; 3654 ft.

2 Highest peak of Zambales Mts., in N cen. Zambales prov., Luzon, Phil., ab. 17 m. NE of Iba; 6683 ft.

High Plains. The Great Plains esp. from Nebraska southward.

High Point. 1 Elevation in N Sussex co., N New Jersey; 1803 ft.; highest point in New Jersey, in High Point (State) Park; New Jersey War Memorial, stone tower 225 ft. high.

2 Industrial city, Guilford co., N cen. North Carolina, 14 m. WSW of Greensboro; pop. (1970c) 63,259; in Piedmont Region; furniture-manufacturing center; hosiery; High Point Coll. (1924); incorporated 1859.

High Rock Lake. Reservoir for water power in Yadkin river (*q.v.*) bet. Rowan and Davidson cos., cen. North Carolina; formed by **High Rock Dam.**

High Sierra. The Sierra Nevada in California. See SIERRA NEVADA.

High·spire \ˈhī-ˌspī(ə)r\. Borough, Dauphin co., SE cen. Pennsylvania, on Susquehanna river 7 m. SE of Harrisburg; pop. (1970c) 2947.

High Springs. City, Alachua co., N Florida penin., 22 m. NW of Gainesville; pop. (1970c) 2787; phosphate mine; tobacco; founded 1885.

High Tatra Mountains. See TATRA MOUNTAINS.

High·tow·er Bald \ˌhī-ˌtau̇(-ə)r-ˈbȯld\. Peak, Towns co., N Georgia; 4517 ft.

Hights·town \ˈhīts-ˌtau̇n\. Borough, Mercer co., W cen. New Jersey, 13 m. ENE of Trenton; pop. (1970c) 5431; truck farms; Peddie School (1864); founded 1721.

High Will·hays \-ˈwil-ēz\. Highest point in Dartmoor, Devonshire, SW England; 2039 ft.

High·wood \ˈhī-(ˌ)wu̇d\. City, Lake co., NE corner of Illinois, on Lake Michigan 12 m. S of Waukegan; pop. (1970c) 4973.

High Wyc·ombe \hī-ˈwik-əm\; *formerly* **Chep·ping Wyc·ombe** *or* **Chip·ping Wycombe** \ˈchip-iŋ-\. Municipal borough, Buckinghamshire, SE cen. England, on the Wye 29 m. WNW of London; pop. (1971p) 59,298; paper mills, printing works.

Higuera, La. Commune, cen. Chile. See CRUZ GRANDE.

Hi·güe·ro, Point \-ē-ˈgwer-ō\ *also* **Point Ji·güe·ro** \-hē-\. Cape at NW end of Puerto Rico, SW of Point Borinquén and on E side of Mona Passage.

Hi·güey \ē-ˈgwā\. Town, ✻ of La Altagracia prov., E Dominican Republic; pop. (1970p) 13,031.

Hii·u·maa \ˈhē-ə-(ˌ)mä\ *or Russ.* **Khi·u·ma** \ˈkē-ə-mə\ *or Swed.* **Dagö** \ˈdäg-ə\. Island in Baltic Sea off W coast of Estonian S.S.R., U.S.S.R.; 373 sq. m.

Hijārah, Al–. See HAJARA, AL-.

Hijaz, Al–. See HEJAZ.

Hi·ko·ne \hi-ˈkō-nē\. Town on E shore of Lake Biwa, W cen. Honshū, Japan, in Shiga prefecture; pop. (1970c) 78,753; noted for its scenery. Castle town of a daimio 1623–1868, one of strongest supporters of the Tokugawas; residence in 19th cent. of Baron Ii Naosuke who signed Japan's first treaties with U.S., England, and Russia.

Hi·ko Range *or* **Hy·ko Range** \ˌhī-kō-\. Small range in cen. Lincoln co., E Nevada.

Hi·kue·ru \hi-ˈkwe(ə)r-(ˌ)ü\. Island, cen. Tuamotu Archipelago, French Polynesia, S Pacific Ocean, 17°36′S, 142°37′W.

Hild·burg·hau·sen \ˈhilt-ˌbu̇(ə)rg-ˌhau̇z-ᵊn\. Town, Suhl dist., East Germany, on the Werra SE of Meiningen; pop. (1970e) 10,882; capital of a principality 1683 which was united to Saxe-Meiningen 1826; late 17th cent. ducal palace.

Hil·den \ˈhil-dən\. Manufacturing city, North Rhine-Westphalia, West Germany, near Rhine river 7 m. SE of Düsseldorf; pop. (1969e) 49,168; textiles, pipes, varnish.

Hil·des·heim \ˈhil-dəs-ˌhīm\. Manufacturing city, Lower Saxony, West Germany, 18 m. SSE of Hannover; pop. (1969e) 96,018; rubber goods, dairy and agricultural machinery; iron founding; received charter 1300.

Hill \ˈhil\. Name of counties in two states of the U.S. See tables at MONTANA and TEXAS.

Hill 60. Height, West Flanders prov., NW Belgium, ab. 3 m. SE of Ieper (Ypres); scene of bitter fighting Apr. 17–May 5, 1915.

Hill 70. Hill, ab. 3 m. N of Lens, France; fighting Sept. 1915; captured by Canadians Aug. 15, 1917.

Hill 102 *or* **Ma·mai Kur·gan** \mə-mī-ˈku̇(ə)r-gən\. Height in city of Volgograd (formerly Stalingrad), Russian S.F.S.R., U.S.S.R.; severe fighting Sept. 14, 1942 in which U.S.S.R. was unable to retake it from Germany.

Hill 192. Height in Normandy, NW France, N of Carentan, commanding road from St-Lô to Bayeux; taken by Americans July 11, 1944.

Hill 193. See CASTLE HILL.

Hill 295. See LE MORT HOMME.

Hill 304. Height, NE France, 10 m. NW of Verdun and near Le Mort Homme; fighting May 1916 and Aug. 1917.

Hill 516. Height, Cassino, Italy; site of Monte Cassino (*q.v.*), Benedictine monastery.

Hill 609 *or* **Djeb·el Ta·hent** \ˌjeb-əl-ta-ˈhent\. Height commanding Mateur, N Tunisia; severe fighting Apr. 28–29, 1943; captured by Americans May 1, 1943.

Hill 660. See BORGEN BAY.

Hil·la \ˈhil-ə\. Town, cen. Iraq, near the Euphrates 58 m. S of Baghdad; pop. (1965c) 84,717; near site of ancient Babylon.

Hil·la·by, Mount \-ˈhil-ə-bē\. Peak, Barbados; 1104 ft.; highest peak in Barbados.

Hill City. City, ⊗ of Graham co., NW cen. Kansas; pop. (1970c) 2071.

Hil·le·gom \ˈhil-ə-ˌkȯm\. Commune, South Holland prov., SW Netherlands, 8 m. S of Haarlem; pop. (1970e) 16,963.

Hil·le·rød \ˈhil-ə-ˌrə(r)th\. Town, ⊗ of Frederiksborg co., N Sjælland, Denmark, 19 m. NW of Copenhagen; pop. (1970e) 23,500; museum; tourism.

Hil·lers, Mount \-ˈhil-ərz\. Peak, E Garfield co., S Utah; 10,650 ft.

Hill·gard, Mount \-ˈhil-ˌgärd\. Peak, Sevier co., cen. Utah; 11,527 ft.

Hil·liard \ˈhil-yərd\. Village, Franklin co., cen. Ohio, NW of Columbus; pop. (1970c) 8369.

Hil·ling·don \ˈhil-iŋ-dən\. A borough of Greater London, SE England. See table at LONDON 4.

Hill·man Peak \ˌhil-mən-\. Mountain, W Klamath co., S Oregon; 8156 ft.; highest point on rim of Crater Lake.

Hills·boro \ˈhilz-ˌbər-ə, -ˌbə-rə\. 1 City, ⊗ of Montgomery co., S cen. Illinois, 48 m. SSE of Springfield; pop. (1970c) 4267; coal mining, zinc smelting.

2 City, Marion co., E cen. Kansas; pop. (1970c) 2730; Tabor Coll. (1908).

3 Town, ⊗ of Jefferson co., E Missouri; pop. (1970c) 2599; diversified farming.

4 Industrial town, ⊗ of Orange co., N North Carolina, 13 m. WNW of Durham; pop. (1970c) 1444; summer capital of the state in second half of 18th cent.; meeting place of Provincial Congress 1775 and of general assemblies 1778,

1780, 1783, 1784; center of Regulator disturbances 1768–71; occupied by Cornwallis 1781; raided by Tories 1781.

5 City, ⊗ of Traill co., E North Dakota; pop. (1970c) 1309; wheat; poultry.

6 City, ⊗ of Highland co., S Ohio, 32 m. WSW of Chillicothe; pop. (1970c) 5584; foundry products.

7 City, ⊗ of Washington co., NW Oregon, 15 m. W of Portland; pop. (1970c) 14,675; lumber; diversified farming; settled 1841.

8 City, ⊗ of Hill co., NE cen. Texas, 33 m. N of Waco; pop. (1970c) 7224; stock raising; cotton.

Hillsboro Bay. Inlet of Northumberland Strait, in S Prince Edward I., SE Canada.

Hills·bor·ough \ˈhilz-ˌbər-ə, -ˌbə-rə\. 1 River, W Florida; flows SW into Tampa Bay.

2 County in Florida. See table at FLORIDA.

3 County in New Hampshire. See table at NEW HAMPSHIRE.

4 Residential town, San Mateo co., W California, 10 m. S of San Francisco; pop. (1970c) 8753.

5 Town, Hillsborough co., S New Hampshire, 18 m. WSW of Concord; pop. (1970c) 2775; birthplace of Franklin Pierce, 14th president of U.S.

Hills·dale \ˈhilz-ˌdāl\. 1 County in Michigan. See table at MICHIGAN.

2 City, ⊗ of Hillsdale co., S Michigan, 25 m. SSW of Jackson; pop. (1970c) 7728; auto parts, dies; lake resort; Hillsdale Coll. (1844).

3 Village, St. Louis co., E Missouri; pop. (1970c) 2599.

4 Borough, Bergen co., NE corner of New Jersey, 9 m. ENE of Paterson; pop. (1970c) 11,768; corn, apples.

Hill·side \ˈhil-ˌsīd\. 1 Village, Cook co., NE Illinois, WSW of Oak Park; pop. (1970c) 8888.

2 Township, Union co., NE New Jersey, 2 m. N of Elizabeth; pop. (1970c) 21,636; aluminum castings, cork, insulated wire.

Hills·ville \ˈhilz-ˌvil\. Town, ⊗ of Carroll co., S Virginia; pop. (1970c) 1149.

Hill Tippera. See TRIPURA.

Hill X \-ˈeks\. Height on Attu I., Aleutian Is.; held by Japanese and captured by Americans after sharp fighting in May 1943.

Hi·lo \ˈhē-(ˌ)lō\. 1 Division, Hawaii co., Hawaii. See NORTH HILO.

2 City, ⊗ of Hawaii co., Hawaii, on **Hilo Bay** on E coast of Hawaii I.; pop. (1970c) 26,353; excellent harbor; exports sugar, coffee, fruits, orchids; tourist center for volcanoes Mauna Kea and Mauna Loa and Kilauea in Hawaii Volcanoes National Park. Important in early wars of the kingdom; nearby in 1796 Kamehameha I crushed the last serious revolt on Hawaii I.; American mission established ab. 1820.

Hi·long·hi·long, Mount \-ˈhē-ˌlȯŋ-ˈhē-ˈlȯŋ\. Mountain, NE Agusan del Norte prov., Mindanao, Phil.; 6599 ft.; highest point of Diuata Mts.

Hi·long·os \hē-ˈlȯŋ-əs\. Municipality on SW coast of Leyte I., Phil., 62 m. SSW of Tacloban; pop. (1969e) 37,100.

Hil·ton Head Island \ˌhilt-ᵊn-ˌhed-\. Island, Atlantic Ocean off South Carolina coast S of mouth of Broad river; 42 sq. m.

Hil·ver·sum \ˈhil-vər-səm\. Commune, North Holland prov., W Netherlands; pop. (1970e) 99,792; radio stations; electrical machinery, pharmaceutical products.

Hil·wān \hil-ˈwän, -ˈwan\ *or* **Hul·wān** \hul-ˈwän\. Town and baths on Nile river S of Cairo, Lower Egypt, opp. ruins of Memphis; pop. (1966c) 203,500; iron and steel plant; cement. See HELIOPOLIS 2.

Hi·ma·chal Pra·desh \hə-ˌmäch-əl-prə-ˈdesh\. State, N India, in the Himalayas NW of Uttar Pradesh, bordering on Tibet, China; 21,490 sq. m.; pop. (1971p) 3,424,332; ✱ Simla; mountainous region, with highest peak ab. 22,000 ft.; wheat, corn, rice, tea; established as a union territory 1948, reconstituted 1966, made a state 1970.

Hi·ma·la·yas, The \ˌhim-ə-ˈlā-əz, -ˈmäl-(ə-)yəz\ *or more correctly* **The Hi·ma·la·ya** \-(y)ə\. Mountain system, S Asia, bordering the Indian subcontinent on the N in a 1500-mile long arc extending from Jammu and Kashmir in the W to Assam in the E and covering most of Nepal, Sikkim, Bhutan, and the S edge of Tibet; separated from the Karakoram Range in the NW by the Indus river and bounded on the N and E by the Brahmaputra river; divided into three main ranges, the Greater Himalayas in the N, having an average elevation of 20,000 ft. and including Everest, 29,028 ft., the Lesser Himalayas in the center, and the Outer Himalayas in the S, including Siwalik Range. Besides Everest includes numerous other high peaks including Kanchenjunga, Dhaulagiri, Nanga Parbat, Nanda Devi; crossed in E from Kalimpong to Chiang-tzu by pass through Ch'u-mu-pi valley and in W from Srinagar to Gilgit by Burzil Pass.

Hi·mal·chu·li \ˌhē-mäl-ˈchü-lē\. Peak in the Himalayas, Nepal, 28°25′N, 84°39′E; 25,801 ft.

Hi·ma·may·lan \ˌhē-mə-ˈmī-ˌlän\. Municipality, W Negros Occidental, Negros, Phil., at S end of Guimaras Strait 40 m. S of City of Bacolod; pop. (1969e) 57,100.

Hi·me·ji \hi-ˈmej-ē\. Industrial city, Hyōgo prefecture, W Honshū, Japan, 34 m. WNW of Kōbe near N shore of Inland Sea; pop. (1970c) 408,353; textiles; castle (1346, reconstructed 1601 and 1956), large Buddhist shrine.

Him·era \ˈhim-ə-rə\. Ancient Greek city on N coast of Sicily; home of Greek lyric poet Stesichorus; scene of battle in which Gelon of Syracuse defeated the Carthaginians 480 B.C.; destroyed by Hannibal 409 B.C. and a new city founded at Termini Imerese.

Hi·mi \ˈhē-mē\. City, Toyama prefecture, Honshū, Japan, 18 m. NW of Toyama; pop. (1970c) 60,883.

Ḥimṣ. City, Syria. See HOMS.

Hi·na·tuan \hi-ˈnä-ˌtwän\. Municipality, SE Surigao del Sur prov., Mindanao, Phil., on coast 115 m. SE of Surigao; pop. (1969e) 29,900.

Hinatuan Passage. Channel bet. Bucas Grande I. and mainland of NE Mindanao, Phil.; ab. 8 m. wide; by some extended to include the channel bet. NE Mindanao and S Dinagat I.

Hin·chin·brook \ˈhin-chən-ˌbru̇k\. 1 Island on E side of entrance to Prince William Sound, S Alaska; on its W side is Nuchek village.

2 Island on NE coast of Queensland, Australia, bet. Townsville and Cairns.

Hinck·ley \ˈhiŋ-klē\. Urban district, Leicestershire, cen. England, 23 m. ENE of Birmingham; pop. (1970e) 47,982; hosiery; engineering works.

Hindenburg *or* **Hindenburg in Oberschlesien.** See ZABRZE.

Hin·den·burg Line \ˈhin-dən-ˌbərg-\. A line of defensive fortifications established 1916 by Germans across NE France, extending S from near Lille, past Cambrai and Saint-Quentin, turning E near Laon and reaching nearly to Metz; had many branch lines; scene of severe fighting in World War I, esp. 1917.

Hin·di·ya \hin-ˈdē-(y)ə\. 1 River in S cen. Iraq; leaves the Euphrates river at **Hindiya Barrage** (dam in the Euphrates ab. 45 m. S of Baghdad) and after flowing SE past Babylon and Hilla returns to it lower in its course; flows through Shinafiya marsh region; important in ancient irrigation system.

2 *or* **Al–Hin·di·yah** \al-\. Town, Iraq, on E bank of main stream of Euphrates ab. 10 m. S of Hindiya Barrage.

Hind·ley \ˈhin-dlē\. Urban district, Lancashire, NW England, 14 m. WNW of Manchester; pop. (1971p) 24,307; cotton mills; coal mines.

Hind·man \ˈhīn(d)-mən\. City, ⊗ of Knott co., SE Kentucky; pop. (1970c) 808.

Hind·marsh, Lake \-'hin(d)-ˌmärsh\. Lake, W Victoria, SE Australia; 47 sq. m.; receives the Wimmera river.

Hin·dol \hin-'dōl\. Former Indian state, now part of Orissa state, NE India.

Hindostan. See HINDUSTAN.

Hinds \'hīn(d)z\. County in Mississippi. See table at MISSISSIPPI.

Hin·du Kush \ˌhin-dü-'ku̇sh, -'kəsh\ *known to historians of Alexander's time as* **Par·o·pa·mi·sus** \ˌpar-ə-pə-'mī-səs\ *or* **Cau·ca·sus In·di·cus** \ˌkȯ-kə-sə-'sin-di-kəs\. Mountain range, cen. Asia, extending ab. 600 m. along N Jammu and Kashmir border and W and SW into Afghanistan to the Koh-i-Baba range W of Kabul; on E extends to the Pamirs and the Karakoram Range; watershed bet. Kabul river on S and tributaries of the Amu Darya on N. In cen. part peaks above 20,000 ft., highest point Tirich Mir 25,260 ft.; crossed by passes (up to 17,500 ft.) from Chitral to Turkistan, one of most important being Baroghil Pass at 12,457 ft.

Hindur. See NALAGARH.

Hin·du·stan *or* **Hin·do·stan** \ˌhin-(ˌ)dü-'stan, -də-, -'stän\. The Persian name of India, variously applied to: (1) The whole Indian peninsula N of the Deccan (*q.v.*); *i.e.* the region bounded on N by the Himalayas and on S by the Vindhya Mts. and Narmada river, comprising Ganges valley from the Punjab to Assam; chief languages Hindi and Urdu, and the dialect Hindustani. (2) A smaller area comprising the upper basin of the Ganges. (3) An occasional name for the Republic of India.

Hines·ville \'hīnz-ˌvil, -vəl\. Town, ⊗ of Liberty co., SE Georgia; pop. (1970c) 4115; timber; tobacco.

Hin·gan·ghat \'hiŋ-gən-ˌgät\. Town, NE Maharashtra state, cen. India, on tributary of Wardha river 50 m. S of Nagpur; pop. (1961c) 36,890; cotton mills, presses, and ginning factories; has given its name to one of the best indigenous cotton staples of India.

Hing·ham \'hiŋ-əm\. Town, Plymouth co., SE Massachusetts, on Massachusetts Bay 11 m. SE of Boston; pop. (1970c) 18,845; summer resort.

Hin·gol \'hiŋ-ˌgōl\. River, Pakistan; ab. 350 m. long; flows S into Arabian Sea; its upper course also known as the **Nal** \'nəl\.

Hi·ni·ga·ran \ˌhē-ni-'gär-ən\. Municipality, W Negros Occidental, Negros, Phil., at S end of Guimaras Strait; pop. (1969e) 49,300.

Hink·ley Reservoir \'hiŋ-klē-\. Reservoir in W Herkimer co., NE cen. New York.

Hin·lo·pen Strait \ˌhin-ˌlō-pən-\. Channel bet. Spitsbergen I. and Northeast Land, Svalbard.

Hin·nom \'hin-əm\. A valley near ancient Jerusalem; its identification uncertain, but believed to be the shallow wadi S of the city. In Old Testament times place where the refuse of the city was deposited and perpetual fires kept burning to Moloch; hence, later, its Greek form **Ge·hen·na** \gi-'hen-ə\ became the New Testament word for "hell."

Hinn·øy \'hin-ˌȯi\. Largest island of the Verterålen, in Norwegian Sea off NW coast of Norway; 848 sq. m.

Hi·no \'hē-(ˌ)nō\. City, Tokyo prefecture, Honshū, Japan, 21 m. W of Tokyo; pop. (1970c) 98,557.

Hi·no·jo·sa del Du·que \ˌē-nə-'hō-sə-del-'dü-(ˌ)kā\. Commune, Córdoba prov., S Spain, 48 m. NNW of Córdoba; pop. (1970p) 10,190; agricultural products; copper mines; manufactures textiles, metal products.

Hins·dale \'hinz-ˌdāl\. 1 County in Colorado. See table at COLORADO.

2 Village, Cook and Du Page cos., NE Illinois, 17 m. W of Chicago; pop. (1970c) 15,918.

3 Manufacturing town, Cheshire co., SW corner of New Hampshire, on Ashuelot river near its junction with the Connecticut 14 m. SSW of Keene; pop. (1970c) 3276; scene of Indian attack 1748.

Hinterpommern. See POMERANIA 1.

Hin·ter·rhein \ˌhin-tə(r)-'rīn\. River in SE Switzerland; rises in glaciers on the Rheinwaldhorn and flows NE to join the Vorderrhein and form the Rhine river.

Hin·ton \'hint-^{ə}n\. 1 City, ⊗ of Summers co., S West Virginia, on New river 20 m. ESE of Beckley; pop. (1970c) 4503; mineral springs.

2 Town, Alberta, Canada, 165 m. E of Edmonton; pop. (1971p) 4916; pulp mills.

Hiogo. See HYŌGO.

Hippo *or* **Hippo Regius.** See ANNABA 2.

Hipponiates, Gulf of. See SANT'EUFEMIA, GULF OF.

Hipponium. See VIBO VALENTIA.

Hippo Zarytus. See BIZERTE.

Hips·well \'hips-ˌwel, -wəl\. Village, North Riding, Yorkshire, England, near Richmond; generally considered to be birthplace of John Wycliffe.

Hi·ra \'hi(ə)r-ə\ *or Arab.* **Al–Hī·rah** \al-\. 1 Ancient kingdom of the Lakhmid dynasty (3d cent. A.D. to 602) comprising lower Euphrates valley and upper part of Persian Gulf, subordinate to the Sassanidae of Persia.

2 Its chief town, 4 m. SE of modern An Najaf, Iraq, captured by Arabs under Khalid ab. 633 and declined rapidly after founding of Al-Kufa 638.

Hi·ra·do \hi-'räd-(ˌ)ō\. Island off NW coast of Kyūshū, Japan; ab. 66 sq. m., 19½ m. long and 6 m. wide; pop. (1960c) 40,879; chief town and harbor Hirado. Important in feudal period; first trading port opened to foreign vessels: to Portuguese c. 1550–1639 when they were driven out by Iyemitsu; to Dutch 1610–41 when they were transferred to Deshima; to English, who had a factory 1613–24.

Hi·ra·ka·ta \ˌhir-ə-'kät-ə\. City, Ōsaka prefecture, Honshū, Japan; pop. (1969e) 172,000.

Hi·ram \'hī-rəm\. Village in Hiram township, Portage co., NE Ohio, ab. 30 m. SE of Cleveland; pop. (1970c) 1484; Hiram Coll. (1849).

Hirata Gunto. See PARACEL ISLANDS.

Hi·ra·tsu·ka \hi-'räts-(ə-)ˌkä\. City, Kanagawa prefecture, SE Honshū, Japan; on N shore of Sagami Sea 18 m. SW of Yokohama; pop. (1970c) 163,671; textiles.

Hi·ro·sa·ki \hi-'rȯ-sə-kē, ˌhir-ə-'säk-ē\. City, Aomori prefecture, N Honshū, Japan; in plain of the Iwaki river 23 m. SW of Aomori and near Mt. Iwaki; pop. (1970c) 157,603; center for silk culture, fruit growing, and manufacture of a special kind of lacquer; univ. (1949).

Hi·ro·shi·ma \ˌhir-ə-'shē-mə, hə-'rō-shə-mə\. 1 Prefecture of Honshū, Japan; 3258 sq. m.; pop. (1970c) 2,436,135; ✱ Hiroshima; rice, oranges, textiles; shipyards.

2 City, its ✱, at W end of Inland Sea; pop. (1970c) 541,998; has rail, river, and canal connections; manufactures trucks; shipbuilding, brewing; Hiroshima Univ. (1949). Founded at end of 16th cent.; a military headquarters in wars of 1894–95, 1900, and 1904–05; about 60 percent destroyed Aug. 6, 1945 by explosion of first atomic bomb used in warfare (dropped by U.S. plane) which caused an estimated loss of 80,000 lives, this event being one of immediate causes of surrender of Japan Aug. 14, 1945; largely rebuilt since 1950. See also ITSUKU-SHIMA.

Hirschberg *or* **Hirschberg in Schlesien** *or* **Hirschberg im Riesengebirge.** See JELENIA GÓRA.

Hir·son \ir-'sō^{n}\. Manufacturing commune, Aisne dept., N France, on Oise river 34 m. NE of Laon; pop. (1968c) 11,858; foundries.

Hi·sa·ka \'hē-sä-kə, hi-'säk-ə\. Island in Gotō Archipelago (*q.v.*), Japan.

Ḥis·bān \'his-bən, -ˌban\ *or anc.* **Hesh·bon** \'hesh-bən\. Town, Jordan, 13 m. SW of Amman; a Moabite town; in Old Testament times in ancient Palestine.

Hispalis. See SEVILLE.

Hispania. See SPAIN.

Hispania Tarraconensis. See TARRACONENSIS.

His·pan·io·la \ˌhis-pən-'yō-lə\ *or orig. Span.* **Es·pa·ño·la** \ˌes-ˌpän-'yō-lə\ *or formerly* **Hai·ti** \'hāt-ē\. Island of the cen. West Indies, in N cen. Caribbean Sea E of Cuba and

W of Puerto Rico; 29,371 sq. m.; pop. (1969e) 8,600,000; divided bet. republic of Haiti on W and Dominican Republic on E.

History: Visited by Columbus 1492 and settled 1493; became center of Spanish rule in West Indies (see also history at WEST INDIES); natives soon exterminated by the Spanish and replaced by Negro slaves; W part of island, occupied in 17th cent. by buccaneers and ceded to France by Spain 1697, came to be known as colony of (Fr.) Saint Domingue, while E part (Santo Domingo) remained under the Spanish; island thus divided until latter part of 18th cent. when slave insurrection (1791) introduced period of conflict; occupied 1793–98 by British who were driven out by Toussaint L'Ouverture; entire island under Toussaint 1801–02; scene of struggle against domination of French 1802–04 when independence declared under Dessalines and the island became republic of Haiti; divided again 1807–21 with Spanish ruling E part; entire island ruled by Boyer from 1822 until E part revolted 1843 and formed the Dominican Republic 1844. See DOMINICAN REPUBLIC and HAITI.

His·par Glacier \his-'pär-\. Glacier in Karakoram Range, in area controlled by Pakistan; 38 m. long, 2 m. wide near its terminus.

His·sar \his-'är\. Town, Haryana, N India, 100 m. WNW of Delhi; pop. (1961c) 60,222; founded 1356 by Firuz Shah III of Delhi; almost depopulated by famine 1783, but fort constructed shortly thereafter by Irish adventurer George Thomas and population restored.

His·sar·lik \ˌhis-ər-'lik\. Site of ancient Troy (*q.v.*), Çanakkale prov., NW Turkey, Asia, 4 m. SE of mouth of the Dardanelles.

Hissar Mountains \his-'är-\. Mountain range in NW Tadzhik S.S.R., U.S.S.R., a branch of the Alai Mts.

Histonium. See VASTO.

Hit \'hit\ *or anc.* **Is** \'is\. Town, W cen. Iraq, on W bank of the Euphrates river at head of navigation ab. 90 m. W of Baghdad; in oil-producing region; in ancient times source of bitumen used in construction of walls and buildings of Babylon.

Hi·ta \'hē-tə\. City, Ōita prefecture, Kyūshū, Japan, 40 m. W of Ōita; pop. (1970c) 64,866.

Hi·ta·chi \hi-'täch-ē\. Coastal city, NE Ibaraki prefecture, Honshū, Japan, 83 m. NE of Tokyo; pop. (1970c) 193,210; center of important industrial area; bombarded by American fleet July 17–18, 1945.

Hitch·cock \'hich-ˌkäk\. **1** County in Nebraska. See table at NEBRASKA.

2 City, Galveston co., SE Texas, NW of Galveston; pop. (1970c) 5565; oil.

Hitch·in \'hich-ən\. Urban district, Hertfordshire, SE England, on the Hiz 32 m. N of London; pop. (1971p) 28,680; engineering.

Hither Pomerania. See POMERANIA 1.

Hit·ler Line \ˌhit-lər-\. In World War II a German defense line, W Italy, from Terracina on W coast to Aquino in mountains W of Cassino; a support for the Gustav Line; taken by Allies May 1944.

Hit·ra \'hi-(ˌ)trä\ *or formerly* **Hit·te·ren** \'hit-ə-rən\. Island in Norwegian Sea off W coast of Norway, WSW of entrance to Trondheim Fjord; 218 sq. m.

Hiu \'hē-(ˌ)ü\. Largest of the Torres Is. (*q.v.*).

Hi·va Oa *or* **Hi·va·oa** \ˌhē-və-'ō-ə\. One of the Marquesas Is., French Polynesia, S Pacific Ocean; 23 m. long, 77 sq. m.; pop. (1967e) 1027; chief village Atuona, administrative center of the group. Of volcanic origin; has high central ridge, highest point Mt. Temetiu 4134 ft.; produces esp. copra, grows some cotton and sugar; place where Gauguin is buried.

Hi·was·see \hī-'wäs-ē\ *or* **Hi·a·was·see** \ˌhī-ə-'wäs-ē\. River, SE United States; ab. 150 m. long; rises in NE Georgia, flows across W extremity of North Carolina and into SE Tennessee to empty into Tennessee river ab. 10 m. SW of Decatur; in its course are three great dams, Apalachia, Hiwassee, and Chatuge, of the Tennessee Valley Authority (*q.v.*).

Hiwassee Dam. See table at TENNESSEE VALLEY AUTHORITY.

Hjäl·ma·ren \'yel-mə-rən\. Lake in Örebro and Södermanland cos., S cen. Sweden, E of N Lake Vänern and N of Lake Vättern; 187 sq. m.

Hjør·ring \'yər-iŋ\. City, Nordjylland co., NE Jutland, Denmark; pop. (1970e) 15,699; textiles; food processing.

Hkamti Long. See MYITKYINA.

Hlu·čín \hə-'lüch-ˌēn, 'hlüch-\ *or Ger.* **Hul·tschin** \'hül-ˌchēn\. **1** District, Czech S.R., Czechoslovakia, just NW of Ostrava; 127 sq. m.; obtained by Czechoslovakia from Germany by Treaty of Versailles 1919—the only part of the Sudeten area (Sudetenland) originally German; population was 82 percent Czechoslovak.

2 Town, its chief urban center, ab. 6 m. NW of Ostrava; pop. (1968e) 12,229.

Ho \'hō\. Town, ✱ of Volta Region, SE Ghana; pop. (1970p) 22,446.

Ho·back Peak \ˌhō-bak-\. Mountain, NW Sublette co., W Wyoming; 10,864 ft.

Ho·bart \'hō-bərt\. **1** City, Lake co., NW corner of Indiana, 8 m. S of Lake Michigan; pop. (1970c) 21,485; residential; settled 1849; incorp. 1921.

2 City, ⊗ of Kiowa co., SW Oklahoma, 31 m. NNE of Altus; pop. (1970c) 4638; cotton; dairying, poultry and stock raising.

Hobart \'hō-ˌbärt\. City, ✱ of Tasmania, Australia, in SE part on Derwent river 12 m. from the sea, at base of Mt. Wellington; pop. (1970e) 52,900; met. area pop. 150,000; deep sheltered harbor; exports fruit, grain, wool, timber, and minerals; electrolytic zinc, sulfuric acid; has iron foundries, sawmills, flour mills; University of Tasmania (1890). See RISDON. Founded in 1804 as a penal colony; made the capital of Tasmania 1812; called **Hobart Town** up to 1881, also, for a time, **Ho·bar·ton** \'hō-ˌbärt-ᵊn, -bərt-\; became a city 1842.

Hobbs \'häbz\. City, Lea co., SE corner of New Mexico, near Texas border ab. 18 m. N of Eunice; pop. (1970c) 26,025; expanded following discovery of oil in 1927; headquarters for oil-well supplies; New Mexico Junior Coll. (1965); founded 1907.

Hobbs Coast. Section of coast of West Antarctica, lying along N Marie Byrd Land, from 131° to 140°30′W.

Hob·do Gol \ˌhäb-dō-'gäl\ *or* **Kob·do** \'käb-\. River in extreme W Mongolian People's Republic; rises on N slope of Altai Mts., flows NE and SE to salt lakes Har Us Nuur and Har Nuur.

Hobe Sound \'hōb-\. Town, Martin co., E Florida, 12 m. SE of Stuart; pop. (1970c) 2029; resort.

Hob·kirk's Hill \ˌhäb-kərks-\. Locality, South Carolina, 2 m. N of Camden; battle Apr. 25, 1781 in which Continentals, during their strategic retreat under Nathanael Greene, were defeated by British under Francis Rawdon-Hastings who was in command of British post at Camden.

Ho·bo·ken \'hō-ˌbō-kən\. **1** City, Hudson co., NE New Jersey, on Hudson river 2 m. N of and adjoining Jersey City and opp. New York City (with which it is connected by ferries and tunnels); pop. (1970c) 45,380; railroad center, with long waterfront; port of entry and departure for steamship lines; electronic equipment, precision instruments, chemicals; shipbuilding. Stevens Institute of Technology (1867). Land purchased from Indians by Dutch 1630 and named New Amsterdam; bought by Peter Stuyvesant 1658; sold to Samuel Bayard 1711; purchased 1784 by John Stevens, who laid out town 1804; became pleasure resort, esp. for New Yorkers; incorporated as town 1849, as city 1855.

2 Commune, Antwerp prov., N Belgium, a suburb of Antwerp; pop. (1969e) 33,278; shipbuilding yards; first mentioned 1135.

Hoch·e·laga \ˌhäsh-ə-'lag-ə\. 1 Early name, given by Cartier 1535 on maps of the St. Lawrence river and of the region above the village (see 2, below).

2 Indian (Huron) village, E end of island (now Montreal I.) in St. Lawrence river, Canada, found by Cartier 1535; it had disappeared, probably destroyed by hostile tribes, when place was visited by Champlain 1603.

Hoch·fei·ler \'hōk-ˌfī-lər\. Peak, highest point of the Zillertaler Alps, S Tirol, on Austria-Italy boundary; 11,513 ft.

Hoch·heim \'häk-ˌhīm, 'hōk-, 'hȯk-\. Commune, Hesse, West Germany, on the Main near its confluence with the Rhine; pop. (1968e) 9700; noted for its production of a white wine, called *Hochheimer,* or *hock.*

Ho–ch'ih \'hə-'chir\. Town, NW Kwangsi Chuang, SE China 95 m. W of Liu-chou; held by Japanese through latter part of World War II; taken by Chinese May 21, 1945.

Hoch·kirch \'hōk-ˌki(ə)rk\. Village, Dresden dist., East Germany, NW of Löbau; pop. (1965e) 900; in Seven Years' War scene of victory Oct. 14, 1758 of Austrians over Prussians under Frederick the Great.

Höch·städt \'hə(r)k-ˌs(h)tet\ *also* **Höchstädt an der Do·nau** \-än-dər-'dō-ˌnaü\. Town, Bavaria, West Germany, on Danube NE of Ulm; pop. (1968e) 3600; scene of battles in War of the Spanish Succession in which the Imperialists were routed by the French and Bavarians Sept. 30, 1703 and in which the French and Bavarians were overwhelmed by Marlborough and Prince Eugene Aug. 13, 1704 (often called the battle of Blenheim, *q.v.*); in Napoleonic Wars scene of victory of Moreau's army of the Rhine over the Austrians under Kray von Krajowa June 19, 1800.

Hoch·stuhl \'hōk-ˌs(h)tül\. Mountain on border bet. S Austria and NW Yugoslavia; 7341 ft.; highest point in the Karawanken Alps.

Hoch·vo·gel \'hōk-ˌfō-gel\. Peak in the Algäu Alps, on the border bet. West Germany and Austria E of Lake Constance; 8505 ft.

Hock·ing \'häk-iŋ\. 1 River, Ohio and West Virginia, ab. 80 m. long; rises in Fairfield co., S cen. Ohio, and flows SE into Ohio river below Parkersburg, West Virginia.

2 County in Ohio. See table at OHIO.

Hock·ley \'häk-lē\. County in Texas. See table at TEXAS.

Hoddes·don \'hädz-dən\. Urban district, Hertfordshire, SE England, at confluence of Lea and Stort rivers 19 m. N of London; pop. (1971p) 26,071; a favorite angling place of Izaak Walton.

Ho·dei·da \hō-'dād-ə\ *also* **Al–Hu·day·dah** \ˌal-hü-'dā-də\. Industrial and commercial seaport, W Yemen (✱ San'a), on the Red Sea; pop. (1960e) 40,000; the port of San'a; chief exports coffee and dates.

Hodge·man \'häj-mən\. County in Kansas. See table at KANSAS.

Hodg·en·ville \'häj-ən-ˌvil\. City, ⊗ of Larue co., cen. Kentucky, 47 m. S of Louisville; pop. (1970c) 2562; sawmills, gas wells.

Hód·me·ző·vá·sár·hely \'hōd-mə-ˌzə(r)-'väsh-ər-ˌhā\. City, Csongrád co., SE Hungary; pop. (1970p) 52,797; textiles.

Hod·na, Chott el \ˌshät-el-'häd-nə\ *or Arab.* **Shatt al–Hodna** \ˌshät-al-\. Marshy saline lake in NE Algeria.

Hodna Mountains. Range of the Little Atlas Mts. in NE Algeria.

Ho·do·nín \'hȯd-ᵊn-ˌyēn\ *or Ger.* **Gö·ding** \'gə(r)-diŋ\. Town, Czech S.R., cen. Czechoslovakia, on the Morava river 50 m. N of Bratislava; pop. (1968e) 20,777.

Hoei. See HUY.

Hoeksche Waard. See BEIJERLAND.

Hoek van Holland. See HOOK OF HOLLAND.

Hoek van Mandar. See MANDAR, GULF OF.

Hoens·broek \'hünz-ˌbrük\. Commune, Limburg prov., SE Netherlands, NE of Maastricht; pop. (1970e) 22,703.

Hoet·jes Bay \ˌhüt-yəs-\. Village on N shore of Saldanha Bay, Cape Province, S Rep. of South Africa, 70 m. NNW of Cape Town; harbor.

Hof \'hōf, 'hȯf\. City, NE Bavaria, West Germany, on Saale river 31 m. NNE of Bayreuth; pop. (1969e) 54,964; railroad junction; manufactures woolens, carpets, iron goods, machinery, porcelain; brewing; first mentioned 1214; to Prussia 1792, to Bavaria 1810.

Ho–fei \'hə-'fā\ *or formerly* **Lu·chow** \'lü-'jō\. City, ✱ of Anhwei prov., E China; pop. (1970e) 400,000; food processing.

Hoff·man Estates \ˌhäf-mən-, ˌhȯf-\. Village, Cook co., NE Illinois, 25 m. NW of Chicago; pop. (1970c) 22,238.

Hoffman Island. Island off E coast of Staten I., New York, in Lower New York Bay; part of Richmond borough.

Hoff·mann, Mount \-'häf-mən, -'hȯf-\. Peak in Sierra Nevada, in E Tuolumne co., cen. California; 10,836 ft.

Hoffmann Mountain. Peak in Adirondack Mts., Essex co., NE New York; 3715 ft.

Hō·fu \'hō-ˌfü\ *also* **Bō·fu** \'bō-\. City, Yamaguchi prefecture, Honshū, Japan, 56 m. SW of Hiroshima; pop. (1970c) 97,009.

Ho·fuf \hü-'füf\ *or* **Al–Hu·fuf** \al-\. Oasis, Nejd, Saudi Arabia, in S part on caravan route from Riyadh to the United Arab Emirates; pop. (1960e) 100,000; great mosque (19th cent.); active market.

Ho·gans·ville \'hō-gənz-ˌvil\. City, Troup co., W Georgia, 10 m. NE of La Grange; pop. (1970c) 3075; cotton mills; incorporated 1870.

Hog·back Mountain \ˌhȯg-bak-, ˌhäg-\. Peak in Banner co., W Nebraska; 5084 ft.

Hogback Peak. Mountain in Sierra Nevada, in E Fresno co., S cen. California; 10,500 ft.

Hoggar Mountains. See AHAGGAR MOUNTAINS.

Hog Island \ˌhȯg-, ˌhäg-\. 1 Island in N Lake Michigan, part of Charlevoix co., NW Michigan, NE of Beaver I.

2 Island in Delaware river below Philadelphia, Pennsylvania; great shipyards.

3 Island in Atlantic Ocean, N Northampton co., Virginia.

Hog·land \'hȯg-ˌland\ *or* **Suur·saa·ri** \'sü(ə)r-sə-rē\. Island in Gulf of Finland, S of seaport of Kotka and ab. 110 m. W of Leningrad, U.S.S.R.

Hogoleu Islands. See TRUK ISLANDS.

Hogue, La. See LA HOGUE.

Hohenfriedeberg. See DĄBROMIERZ.

Ho·hen·lim·burg \ˌhō-ən-'lim-ˌbərg, -ˌbü(ə)rg\. City, North Rhine-Westphalia, West Germany, 40 m. NE of Cologne; pop. (1969e) 26,176; rolling mills; first mentioned 1243.

Ho·hen·lin·den \'hō-ən-ˌlin-dən, ˌhō-ən-'\. Village, Bavaria, West Germany, 20 m. E of Munich; pop. (1968e) 1800; scene of battle Dec. 3, 1800 in which French under Moreau defeated Austrians under Archduke John, a victory which together with that of Napoleon at Marengo led to Peace of Lunéville 1801.

Hohenmauth. See VYSOKÉ MÝTO.

Hohensalza. See INOWROCŁAW.

Ho·hen·stau·fen \'hō-ən-ˌs(h)taü-fən\. Mountain near Göppingen, cen. Baden-Württemberg, West Germany; 2240 ft.; contains ruins of ancestral castle of Hohenstaufen family.

Ho·hen·stein–Ernst·thal \'hō-ən-ˌs(h)tīn-'e(ə)rnst-ˌtäl\. Industrial city, Karl-Marx-Stadt dist., East Germany, on N edge of Erzgebirge 9 m. W of Karl-Marx-Stadt; pop. (1970e) 16,800; textiles, metal goods; received city rights 1521.

Ho·hen·twiel \'hō-ən-ˌtfēl\. Conical mountain in S Baden-Württemberg, West Germany, near Singen; 2260 ft.; contains ruins of a fortress.

Ho·hen·wald \'hō-ən-ˌwȯld\. Town, ⊗ of Lewis co., SW cen. Tennessee; pop. (1970c) 3385.

Ho·hen·zol·lern \'hō-ən-ˌzäl-ərn, ˌhō-ən-'\. 1 Historical region and province of Prussia, Germany, now part of Baden-Württemberg, West Germany.

History: Formed in 1849 from territories of Hohenzollern-Hechingen and Hohenzollern-Sigmaringen; derived from ancient family seat of Hohenzollerns of whom the Franconian branch were rulers of Prussia and emperors of Germany 1871–1918; ceded to Prussian king by their rulers, members of (Swabian) line of Hohenzollerns; since 1952 part of Baden-Württemberg.

2 Castle in this region of Hohenzollern; on Mount Zollern, near Hechingen.

Ho·hes Licht \ˈhō-ə-ˌslikt\. Peak in the Algäu Alps (*q.v.*), on border bet. Bavaria and Tirol, N of Lech valley; 8706 ft.

Hohe Tauern. See table at ALPS.

Ho·he Venn Mountains \ˌhō-ə-ˈfen-\ *or Fr.* **Hautes Fagnes** \ōt-fänʸ\. Range in Liège prov., E Belgium; highest peak Botrange 2277 ft.

Ho·ho·kus \hō-ˈhōk-əs\. Borough, Bergen co., NE corner of New Jersey, on Hohokus river 7 m. NNE of Paterson; pop. (1970c) 4348.

Ho Hu \ˈhō-ˈhü\ *also* **Ko Hu** \ˈkō-\. Lake, S Kiangsu prov., E China.

Hoi An \ˈhȯi-ˈän\ *or formerly* **Fai·fo** \ˈfī-ˈfō\. Coastal town, 14 m. S of Danang, South Vietnam; pop. (1968e) 36,663.

Hoihow *or* **Hoï–Hao.** See HAI-K'OU.

Hoi·sing·ton \ˈhȯi-ziŋ-tən\. City, Barton co., cen. Kansas, 10 m. N of Great Bend; pop. (1970c) 3710; wheat growing, livestock raising.

Hoke \ˈhōk\. County in North Carolina. See table at NORTH CAROLINA.

Ho·kiang \ˈhə-jē-ˈäŋ\. Former province, E Manchuria, NE China, on the lower Sungari river; 50,816 sq. m.; now part of Heilungkiang prov.

Ho·ki·anga Harbor *or* **Hokianga River** \ˌhō-kē-ˌäŋ-ə-\. Broad inlet or harbor on W coast of N peninsula of North I., New Zealand, 125 m. NW of Auckland.

Ho·ki·ti·ka \ˌhō-ki-ˈtē-kə, ˌhäk-i-ˈtik-ə\. Borough, W South I., New Zealand, 160 m. SW of Nelson; pop. (1968e) 3310; seaport; gold and coal in vicinity.

Hok·kai·dō \hä-ˈkīd-(ˌ)ō\; *formerly* **Ye·zo** *also* **Ye·so** \ˈyez-(ˌ)ō\ *or* **Ezo** \ˈez-(ˌ)ō\. 1 Northernmost of the four main islands of Japan, in Pacific Ocean off E coast of Asia, N of island of Honshū; separated from S Sakhalin on N by Sōya Strait, from Honshū on S by Tsugaru Strait, and from the Kuril Is. on NE by Nemuro Strait. Has several high peaks, esp. Asahi (formerly Ishikari Dake) 7513 ft., Horoshiri 6732 ft., and Tokachi 6814 ft.; rivers include Ishikari, longest in Japan, and the Tokachi; fishing; produces rice, barley, corn, potatoes; has substantial resources in timber and coal. Chief cities Sapporo (capital of Hokkaidō prefecture), Utashinai, Asahikawa, Hakodate.

History: In early times inhabited by Ainus; not made part of Japan until medieval period (ab. 1604); scene of conflicts bet. Shogun's representatives and Russian adventurers; its modern development begun 1871–81 when government was assisted by American engineers and agriculturists; after 1881 given over to private interests.

2 Prefecture, N Japan, including Hokkaidō (see 1, above), adjacent small islands and (formerly) the Kuril Is. (Chishima Retto); 30,313 sq. m.; pop. (1970c) 5,184,287; ❋ Sapporo. Since 1945 does not include Kuril Is., which were transferred to U.S.S.R.

Hoko Shoto *or* **Hoko Gunto.** See PESCADORES.

Hokou. Town, Kiangsi prov., China. See HU-K'OU.

Ho–k'ou *or* **Ho·kow** \ˈhō-ˈkau̇, ˈhə-ˈkō\. Frontier town, SE Yunnan prov., S China, on Yüan river opp. Lao Cai in North Vietnam; connected by rail with Hanoi.

Ho–lan Shan. See A-LA SHAN.

Hol·bæk \ˈhəl-ˌbek\. Town, Vestsjælland co., NW Sjælland, Denmark, 33 m. W of Copenhagen; pop. (1970e) 17,892; iron foundries; shipbuilding.

Hol·beach \ˈhōl-ˌbēch\. Market town, Parts of Holland, Lincolnshire, E England, 51 m. ESE of Nottingham.

Hol·born Head *or* **Hol·burn Head** \ˌhäl-bərn-, ˌhōl-\. Cape on NE coast of Scotland; lighthouse.

Hol·brook \ˈhōl-ˌbru̇k\. 1 Town, ⊗ of Navajo co., NE Arizona; pop. (1970c) 4759; tourism.

2 Town, Norfolk co., E Massachusetts, 5 m. N of Brockton; pop. (1970c) 11,755.

Hol·den \ˈhōl-dən\. Town, Worcester co., cen. Massachusetts, 8 m. NNW of Worcester; pop. (1970c) 12,564.

Hol·den·ville \ˈhōl-dən-ˌvil\. City, ⊗ of Hughes co., E cen. Oklahoma, 28 m. NE of Ada; pop. (1970c) 5181; oil and gas wells; coal deposits.

Hol·der·ness. 1 \ˈhōl-dər-nəs\. Town, Grafton co., W New Hampshire, on Squam Lake; pop. (1970c) 1048; summer resort.

2 \ˌhōl-dər-ˈnes\. Peninsula in SE East Riding, Yorkshire, N England, bet. Humber river and the North Sea; 309 sq. m.

Hol·drege \ˈhōl-drij\. City, ⊗ of Phelps co., S Nebraska, 24 m. SW of Kearney; pop. (1970c) 5635; flour mills; dairying.

Hol·guín \(h)ȯl-ˈgēn\. Town and municipality, N cen. Oriente prov., E Cuba, in plateau region 65 m. NW of Santiago de Cuba; munic. pop. (1967e) 350,250; through its port, Gibara, exports tobacco and cattle products; settled c. 1720; insurgent center 1868–78 and 1895–98.

Hol·la \ˈhäl-ə\. Peak, Kefa prov., SW Ethiopia, NW of Lake Abaya; 12,093 ft.

Hol·la·brunn \ˌhȯl-ə-ˈbrün\ *also* **Ober·hol·la·brunn** \ˈō-bər-\. Town, Lower Austria, N of Vienna; pop. (1961c) 6773; scene of battle Nov. 16, 1805 in which Prince Bagration successfully resisted greatly superior French force.

Hol·land \ˈhäl-ənd\. 1 Kingdom. See NETHERLANDS.

2 City, Allegan and Ottawa cos., W Michigan, on Lake Michigan 25 m. WSW of Grand Rapids; pop. (1970c) 26,337; summer resort; manufactures furnaces and furnace equipment, chemicals, glass; ships poultry; Hope Coll. (1851); settled 1847.

3 Medieval county of Holy Roman Empire on North Sea coast, now in North and South Holland provs., Netherlands; established 1018 when it became independent of Lorraine; in 1247 its Count William II elected emperor during struggle against Frederick II; united with Zeeland and Hainaut in 14th cent.; ceded to Burgundy (*q.v.*) by Countess Jacqueline 1433; see NETHERLANDS.

Holland, The Parts of. See LINCOLNSHIRE.

Hol·lan·dale \ˈhäl-ən-ˌdāl\. City, Washington co., W Mississippi, 21 m. SE of Greenville; pop. (1970c) 3260.

Hollandia. See DJAJAPURA.

Hol·landsch Diep \ˌhäl-ən(t)s-ˈdēp\. Estuary of the Maas (Meuse) river in SW Netherlands, on border bet. South Holland and North Brabant provs.

Holland Tunnel \ˌhäl-ən(d)-\. Vehicular tunnel under Hudson river from Manhattan I., New York, to Jersey City, New Jersey; 9250 ft. long.

Hol·le·be·ke \ˈhäl-ə-ˌbā-kə\. Commune, West Flanders prov., Belgium, near Ieper (Ypres); pop. (1969e) 723; fiercely contested bet. British and Germans 1914–18, almost wholly destroyed.

Hol·li·days·burg \ˈhäl-ə-ˌdāz-ˌbərg, -dēz-\. Borough, ⊗ of Blair co., S cen. Pennsylvania, 6 m. S of Altoona; pop. (1970c) 6262; explosives, boilers; became railroad and canal terminus in 1830's; founded 1768.

Hol·li·days Cove \ˌhäl-ə-dāz-\. A former city in Brooke and Hancock cos., N West Virginia, 25 m. NNE of Wheeling; since 1947 part of Weirton.

Hol·lins College \ˈhäl-ənz-\. Town (unincorp.), Roanoke co., W cen. Virginia, ab. 7 m. N of Roanoke; Hollins Coll. (1842).

Hol·lis \'häl-əs\. 1 Town, Hillsborough co., S New Hampshire, 16 m. SSW of Manchester; pop. (1970c) 2616.
2 Residential community in Queens borough of New York City, Queens co., SE New York, on Long I.
3 City, ⊗ of Harmon co., SW Oklahoma, 35 m. W of Altus; pop. (1970c) 3150; flour mills.

Hol·lis·ter \'häl-ə-stər\. City, ⊗ of San Benito co., W California, 20 m. E of Monterey Bay; pop. (1970c) 7663; fruit and vegetable canning; settled 1868.

Hol·lis·ton \'häl-ə-stən\. Town, Middlesex co., NE Massachusetts, 18 m. ESE of Worcester; pop. (1970c) 12,069.

Holl·man, Cape \-'hōl-mən\. Cape at N end of Willaumez Penin., N New Britain, Bismarck Archipelago.

Holloman Air Force Base. See ALAMOGORDO.

Hol·ly \'häl-ē\. Village, Oakland co., SE Michigan, 16 m. S of Flint; pop. (1970c) 4355; tools and dies.

Holly Hill. City, Volusia co., E Florida, on Atlantic Ocean 5 m. N of Daytona Beach; pop. (1970c) 8191.

Holly Springs. City, ⊗ of Marshall co., N Mississippi, 54 m. NW of Tupelo; pop. (1970c) 5728; ships cotton and dairy products; Rust Coll. (1866), Mississippi Industrial Coll. (1905).

Hol·ly·wood \'häl-ē-ˌwu̇d\. 1 District in city of Los Angeles, California, E of Beverly Hills; major center of U.S. motion-picture and television industries; became a district of Los Angeles 1910.
2 City, Broward co., SE Florida, on Atlantic Ocean 18 m. N of Miami; pop. (1970c) 106,873; electronic equipment, cement; tourism; incorporated 1926.

Holmes \'hōmz\. Counties in three states of the U.S. See tables at FLORIDA, MISSISSIPPI, OHIO.

Holmes, Mount. Peak in Yellowstone National Park, NW Wyoming; 10,336 ft.

Holmes Beach. City, Manatee co., W cen. Florida, 17 m. NW of Sarasota; pop. (1970c) 2699.

Holmes·burg \'hōmz-ˌbərg\. Suburban district, NE Philadelphia, Pennsylvania, near Delaware river.

Holmes Reefs. Group of coral islets in W Coral Sea outside Great Barrier Reef, 16°27′S, 148°E.

Holm·firth \'hōm-ˌfərth\. Urban district, West Riding, Yorkshire, N England, 6 m. S of Huddersfield; pop. (1970e) 19,319; woolens, stone quarries.

Holm·ön \'hȯl-ˌmərn\. Swedish island in Gulf of Bothnia off coast of Västerbotten co., N Sweden.

Holm·sjön \'hȯlm-ˌshərn\. Lake, Västernorrland co., E Sweden; drained by Ljungan river.

Hol·ni·cote Bay \ˌhäl-ni-kōt-\. Inlet of Solomon Sea, on coast of New Guinea I., Papua New Guinea.

Ho·lon \hō-'lōn\. Town, cen. Israel, a part of the Tel Aviv-Jaffa metropolitan area; pop. (1970e) 88,500; textiles, silverware; became a city 1941.

Hol·ste·bro \ˌhəl-stə-'brō\. Town, Ringkøbing co., W Jutland, Denmark, 24 m. NE of Ringkøbing; pop. (1970e) 24,009; textiles; tobacco processing.

Hol·stein \'hōl-ˌstīn, -ˌstēn\. The S part of the West German state of Schleswig-Holstein (*q.v.*).
History: From ab. 800 A.D., part of German duchy of Saxony in Carolingian empire; German duke of Holstein came to rule Schleswig (*q.v.*), a fief of Denmark; in 1460, in dynastic union with Schleswig under Oldenburg kings of Denmark; raised to a duchy 1474; thoroughly Germanized, but a Danish holding; duke of Holstein (king of Denmark) became member of German Confederation 1815; its status, as part of Schleswig-Holstein, caused friction bet. Germanic Confederation and Denmark; by agreement bet. Austria and Prussia, after war with Denmark 1864, Holstein administered by Austria; incorporated by Prussia as part of Schleswig-Holstein (1866), which in 1946 was made a state of West Germany.

Hol·steins·borg \'həl-ˌstīnz-ˌbȯ(ə)rg\. Settlement on W coast of Greenland, just N of Arctic Circle; pop. (1968e) 4043; fishing.

Hol·ston \'hōl-stən\. River, E Tennessee; 140 m. long; formed by junction of north and south forks in Sullivan co., flows SW to unite with French Broad river near Knoxville and form the Tennessee river; in its course are two great dams, Cherokee and South Holston, of the Tennessee Valley Authority (*q.v.*). See WATAUGA.

Holston High Knob *or* **Holston Mountain.** Peak, Carter and Sullivan cos., NE Tennessee; 4350 ft.

Holt \'hōlt\. Name of counties in two states of the U.S. See tables at MISSOURI and NEBRASKA.

Hol·ton \'hōlt-ᵊn\. City, ⊗ of Jackson co., NE Kansas, 28 m. N of Topeka; pop. (1970c) 3063; corn, fruit.

Holt·ville \'hōlt-ˌvil\. City, Imperial co., SE corner of California, 10 m. E of El Centro; ab. 10 ft. below sea level; pop. (1970c) 3496; ships dairy products, fruits, and vegetables.

Holtz Bay \'hōlts-\. Inlet, NE Attu I., Aleutian Is.; one of landing places of American forces May 11, 1943 (see also MASSACRE BAY).

Ho·ly Cross \ˌhō-lē-'krȯs\. City, W Alaska, on lower Yukon 115 m. NNE of Bethel; pop. (1970c) 199.

Holy Cross, Mount of the. Peak in Sawatch Range, Eagle co., NW cen. Colorado; 14,005 ft.

Hol·y·head \'häl-ē-ˌhed\. 1 Island in NE St. George's Channel, in Anglesey co., NW Wales, off W coast of island of Anglesey; 8 m. long, 3½ m. wide; connected with Anglesey I. by a long causeway; mostly barren rock.
2 *or Welsh* **Caer Gy·bi** \'kī(ə)r-'gəb-ē\. Urban district and seaport on N coast of Holyhead I.; pop. (1971p) 10,608; seaside resort; harbor protected by breakwater more than a mile long; nearest British port to Dublin (61 m.); church, reputedly founded 7th cent. by one St. Gybi.

Holy Island *or* **Lin·dis·farne** \'lin-dəs-ˌfärn\. Peninsula, which becomes an island at high water, off NE coast of Northumberland, N England; 3 m. long by 1¾ m. wide; site of monastery founded 635 by St. Aidan and destroyed by Danes 793; ruins of late 11th cent. priory; 16th cent. castle.

Holy Land. Palestine—so-called first in *Zech.* ii. 12.

Holy Loch \-'läk, -läk\. Small inlet on W shore of Firth of Clyde, W Scotland, opp. mouth of Clyde river; U.S. submarine base.

Hol·yoke \'hōl-ˌyōk\. 1 Town, ⊗ of Phillips co., NE Colorado, 48 m. E of Sterling; pop. (1970c) 1640.
2 Industrial city, Hampden co., SW Massachusetts, on Connecticut river 8 m. N of Springfield; pop. (1970c) 50,112; leading manufacturing city in the U.S. in fine writing and envelope papers; electronic equipment, fabricated steel; brewing. Originally part of Springfield and of West Springfield after 1774; incorporated as town 1850, as city 1873; large power dam (see HOLYOKE DAM).

Holyoke, Mount. Peak, Hampshire co., near Holyoke, W Massachusetts; 878 ft.

Holyoke Dam *or* **Had·ley Falls Dam** \'had-lē-\. Dam at Hadley Falls across Connecticut river above Holyoke, SW Massachusetts; completed 1900; impounds water for water-power.

Holy Roman Empire. A realm of cen. Europe in medieval and modern periods, originating 800 A.D. when Charlemagne was crowned Emperor of the West (sometimes called the First Reich); revived as Roman Empire of the German Nation with coronation 962 of Otto the Great as emperor of an area including Germany and N Italy; at its height in mid-11th cent. before emperors began great struggle with papacy for dominance; under Hohenstaufens 1138–1254, imperial power absorbed by renewed struggle with popes over control of Italy; had no emperor 1250–73 (Great Interregnum) when German unity collapsed and seeds of later particularism of princes were planted; under Rudolf of Hapsburg 1273–91 who consolidated dynastic monarchy (see AUSTRIA) at expense of imperial strength; seven imperial electors set up by Golden Bull 1356: archbishops of Mainz, Trier, Cologne, king of Bohemia, count Palatine of Rhine, duke of Saxony, and margrave of Brandenburg; lost most Italian holdings by 16th cent. (see ITALY); from 15th cent. to 1806, emperor's crown almost hereditary in Hapsburg family; formally dissolved during Napoleonic Wars 1806 (see GERMANY).

Hol·y·rood \'häl-ē-,rüd\. Royal palace, E Edinburgh city, Scotland; residence of Mary, Queen of Scots, 1561–67; not much used by royalty since ascension of James VI to throne of England 1603; adjoining the palace is abbey which was scene of coronations of James II of Scotland and Charles I of England, and of Mary's marriage to Darnley 1565 and which contains burial vault of Scottish kings and burial places of Darnley and Rizzio.

Holy See. See VATICAN CITY.

Hol·y·well \'häl-ē-,wel, -wəl\. Manufacturing urban district, Flintshire, NE Wales; pop. (1971p) 8536; site of St. Winifred's Well, reputed to have burst forth on spot where her head fell when St. Winifred was beheaded by the pagan prince Caradoc (c. 634), now a place of pilgrimage for Roman Catholics and sometimes called "the Lourdes of Wales."

Hol·y·wood \'häl-ē-,wu̇d\. Urban district, co. Down, SE Northern Ireland; on Belfast Lough 6 m. NE of Belfast; pop. (1971p) 7715.

Holz·min·den \'hȯlts-,min-dən\. City, Lower Saxony, West Germany, on Weser river 55 m. SW of Brunswick; pop. (1969e) 22,248; electronic equipment, glass; tourism; founded c. 1197.

Homalig. See JOMALIG.

Ho·ma·lin \'hō-mə-,lin\. Town, W Upper Burma, on Chindwin river near Manipur border.

Ho·māy·un·shahr \hō-,mī-(y)ün-'shär\. Town, Eşfahān prov., W cen. Iran, ab. 6 m. NW of Eşfahān; pop. (1971e) 48,000.

Hom·berg \'häm-,bərg, -,be(ə)rg\ *also* **Homberg am Nie·der·rhein** \-äm-,nē-də(r)-'rīn\. Manufacturing town, North Rhine-Westphalia, West Germany, on Rhine river opp. Duisburg; pop. (1969e) 35,063; coal mining; refractory goods, machinery; iron founding.

Homburg. See BAD HOMBURG.

Homel. See GOMEL.

Ho·mer \'hō-mər\. **1** City, S Alaska, on Cook Inlet SW of Seward; pop. (1970c) 1083; seaport.

2 Town, ⊗ of Banks co., NE Georgia; pop. (1970c) 365.

3 Town, ⊗ of Claiborne parish, N Louisiana, 47 m. ENE of Shreveport; pop. (1970c) 4483; trading center of timber section; petroleum deposits.

4 Village, Cortland co., cen. New York, 28 m. S of Syracuse; pop. (1970c) 4143; in dairying region; bean canneries; settled 1791.

Homer City. Borough, Indiana co., W cen. Pennsylvania, 20 m. NW of Johnstown; pop. (1970c) 2465.

Ho·mer·ville \'hō-mər-,vil\. City, ⊗ of Clinch co., S Georgia; pop. (1970c) 3025; timber.

Home·stead \'hōm-,sted\. **1** City, Dade co., SE Florida, 28 m. SW of Miami; pop. (1970c) 13,674; trade center for region producing citrus fruits, vegetables; incorp. 1923.

2 Industrial borough, Allegheny co., SW Pennsylvania, on Monongahela river 6 m. ESE of Pittsburgh; pop. (1970c) 6309; steel, iron products, glass, machinery; settled 1871, incorp. 1880; scene of serious strike 1892.

Homestead National Monument. See UNITED STATES, *National Monuments.*

Home·town \'hōm-,tau̇n\. City, Cook co., NE Illinois, SW suburb of Chicago; pop. (1970c) 6729.

Home·wood \'hōm-,wu̇d\. **1** City, Jefferson co., cen. Alabama, 2 m. SE of Birmingham; pop. (1970c) 21,223.

2 Village, Cook co., NE Illinois, 22 m. S of Chicago; pop. (1970c) 18,871.

Hom·il·don Hill \,häm-əl-dən-\ *or* **Hum·ble·don Hill** \,həm-bəl-dən-\ *or* **Hum·ble·ton Hill** \-tən-\. Small hill, N Northumberland, N England, SE of Flodden; scene of victory of Sir Henry Percy (Hotspur) and George Dunbar, Earl of March, over the Scots 1402.

Hom·i·ny \'häm-ə-nē\. City, Osage co., N Oklahoma, 30 m. NW of Tulsa; pop. (1970c) 2274; cotton, livestock, poultry; oil and gas wells.

Ho·mon·hon \,hō-mən-'hȯn\ *or* **Jo·mon·jol** \,hō-mən-'hȯl\ *or* **Mal·hon** \mäl-'hȯn\. Island, S of Samar, Phil., in entrance to Leyte Gulf; 40 sq. m.; belongs to Guiuan municipality of Samar Oriental prov.; place of first landing of Magellan on Philippine Is. Mar. 17, 1521; also, with Suluan (*q.v.*), first landing of MacArthur and Americans on invasion of Philippines Oct. 19, 1944.

Homs \'hȯmz, 'hȯm(p)s\ *or* **Ḥimş** \'him(p)sh\ *or anc.* **Em·e·sa** \'em-ə-sə\. City, W Syria, on the Orontes 85 m. N of Damascus; pop. (1970e) 216,000; oil and sugar refineries; in fertile area with gardens and orchards; manufactures silk goods; on ancient highway N from Egypt; nearby is battleground of Kadesh (*q.v.*).

History: As Emesa devoted to worship of Sun god (Elagabal) and birthplace of Heliogabalus, one of its priests who became Roman emperor 218 A.D.; scene of defeat of Zenobia 272 by Emperor Aurelian; seized by Arabs 636; its walls destroyed 745 in revolt against the Ommiad caliph Marwan II; held by Egyptians under Ibrahim Pasha 1831–40 and scene of a revolt 1832; taken by British and Arabs Oct. 15, 1918.

Homs \'hȯmz, 'hȯm(p)s\ *or* **Khoms** \'kȯm(p)s\ *or* **Al-Khums** \al-'ku̇ms\. Seaport, Libya, 65 m. ESE of Tripoli; pop. (1964c) 13,900; cement; ruins of ancient Leptis Magna, an important Roman walled city, ab. 2 m. to the E.

Hon \'hən\. Town, N cen. Libya, in oasis ab. 220 m. S of Misurata.

Ho·nan \'hō-'nan\. **1** Province, E cen. China, bounded on N by Shansi, Hopeh, and Shantung provs., on E by Kiangsu and Anhwei, on S by Hupeh, and on W by Shensi; 64,479 sq. m.; pop. (1968e) 50,000,000; ✱ Cheng-Chou; one of China's most densely populated provinces. Rivers include the Yellow, forming NW boundary and flowing SE, the Lo in NW, and the upper course of the Huai. In the SW are the most easterly spurs of the Kunlun Mts. with highest point at 7800 ft. Has rich agricultural regions; wheat, cotton, tobacco, peanuts. Chief cities Cheng-chou, Lo-yang, K'ai-feng. Region of earliest settlements in China from which its culture spread; its geographical location controlled movements of early tribes; Lo-yang (or Honan) capital of China in the Eastern Han, Chin, and T'ang dynasties and K'ai-feng of the Sung dynasty (10th cent. A.D.).

2 City, China. See LO-YANG.

Hon·da \'hän-də\. Town, Tolima dept., W cen. Colombia, ab. 50 m. NW of Bogotá; pop. (1968e) 22,315.

Honda Rapids. Rapids in Magdalena river in NW cen. Colombia, stopping navigation at that point.

Hon·do \'hän-(,)dō\. **1** City, ⊗ of Medina co., S cen. Texas, 37 m. W of San Antonio; pop. (1970c) 5487; corn, livestock.

2 Island of Japan. See HONSHŪ.

3 River, rising in N Guatemala and flowing NE into Chetumal Bay; ab. 150 m. long; forms boundary bet. British Honduras and Mexico (Quintana Roo territory).

Hon·du·ras \hän-'d(y)u̇r-əs\. Republic, Central America, bounded on N by the Gulf of Honduras and the Caribbean Sea, on E by the Caribbean Sea, on S by Nicaragua and the Gulf of Fonseca, on SW by El Salvador, and on W by Guatemala; 43,277 sq. m.; pop. (1970e) 2,582,000; ✱ Tegucigalpa. *Physical features:* Coastline ab. 400 m. on the Caribbean and ab. 40 m. on the Pacific (Gulf of Fonseca) bet. El Salvador and Nicaragua; most easterly point Cape Gracias a Dios; off N coast are Islas de la Bahía. Generally mountainous with many ranges much varied in extent and direction; highest in S above 10,000 ft. Chief rivers Chamelecón and Ulúa in W, Aguán in N, Patuca in E,

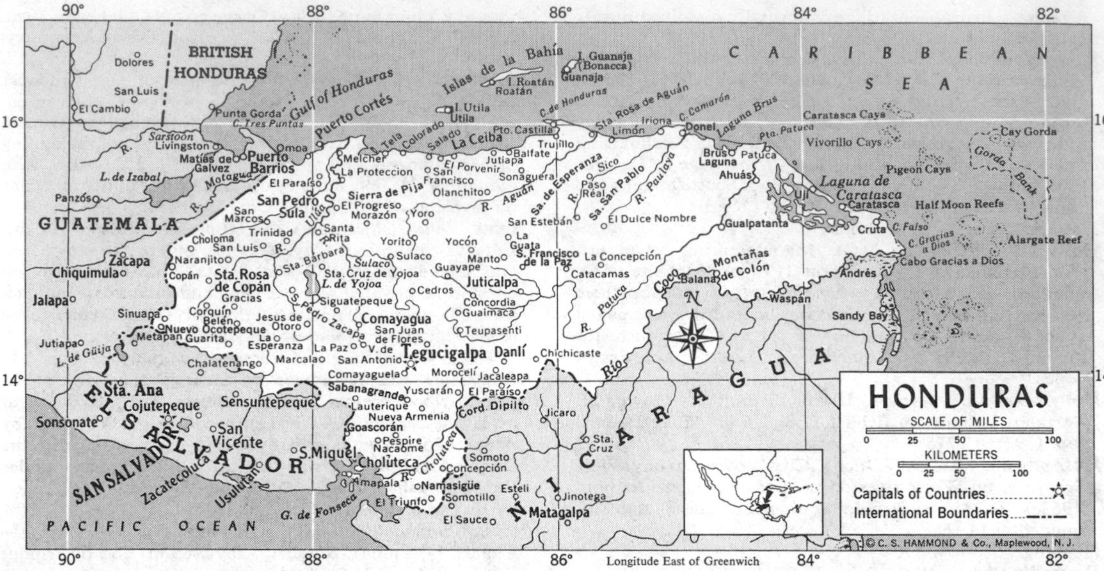

Choluteca in S; the Coco (*q.v.*) claimed as the border with Nicaragua; only large inland lake Yojoa in W with outlet to Ulúa river. *Chief products:* Coffee, bananas, tobacco, corn; livestock; silver, gold, lead; ab. 65 percent of labor force is engaged in agriculture. *Chief cities:* Tegucigalpa, San Pedro Sula, La Ceiba, Choluteca, Comayagua. Divided into the following 18 departments (for pronunciation of their names, see their individual entries):

NAME	AREA (sq. m.)	POP. (1970e)	CAPITAL
Atlántida	1,641	132,600	La Ceiba
Choluteca	1,625	207,700	Choluteca
Colón	3,426	60,500	Trujillo
Comayagua	2,006	134,800	Comayagua
Copán	1,236	166,700	Santa Rosa
Cortés	1,526	293,800	San Pedro Sula
El Paraíso	2,786	138,600	Yuscarán
Francisco Morazán	3,068	425,500	Tegucigalpa
Gracias a Dios	6,420	15,800	Puerto Lempira
Intibucá	1,186	91,400	La Esperanza
Islas de la Bahía	100	9,900	Roatán
La Paz	899	72,500	La Paz
Lempira	1,656	138,500	Gracias
Ocotepeque	648	61,400	Nueva Ocotepeque
Olancho	9,401	142,200	Juticalpa
Santa Bárbara	1,975	216,300	Santa Bárbara
Valle	604	101,400	Nacaome
Yoro	3,065	172,400	Yoro

History: Coast discovered by Columbus 1502; Trujillo and Puerto Cortés founded c. 1525; included in captaincy general of Guatemala 1539; proclaimed independence 1821; part of United Provinces of Central America 1823–38; from 1842, participant in several unsuccessful efforts to federate Honduras, Nicaragua, and El Salvador; 1859 received Bay Is. (Islas de la Bahía), former subject of dispute with Great Britain; scene of incessant civil war and of intervention of U.S. on several occasions; in World War I declared war on Germany July 19, 1918 and in World War II on Axis powers Dec. 1941. Coco (Segovia) river confirmed as SE boundary by International Court of Justice 1961 in settlement of dispute with Nicaragua; adopted new constitution 1965; fought brief border war with El Salvador 1969.

Honduras, British. See BRITISH HONDURAS.

Honduras, Cape *or Span.* **Ca·bo de Honduras** \ˈkäb-ō-ˌdā-ȯn-ˈdu̇r-əs\. Cape, N coast of Honduras, extending into Caribbean Sea.

Honduras, Gulf of. Inlet of Caribbean Sea, bet. S British Honduras, E Guatemala, and N Honduras.

Hon·ea Path \ˈhən-ē-ˌpath\. Town, Abbeville and Anderson cos., W South Carolina; pop. (1970c) 3707; textiles; corn.

Hon·e·oye Lake \ˌhən-ē-ˌȯi-\. Lake, W Ontario co., W New York; outlet from N end flows into Genesee river; ab. 5 m. long.

Hones·dale \ˈhōnz-ˌdāl\. Borough, ⊗ of Wayne co., NE corner of Pennsylvania, 25 m. ENE of Scranton; pop. (1970c) 5224; coal mining and shipping; manufactures silk and woolen goods, shoes; starting point of trial run of first locomotive in U.S. Aug. 9, 1829.

Hon·ey Island *or* **Honey Island Swamp** \ˌhən-ē-\. Swamp, SE Louisiana and SW Mississippi, in delta of Pearl river; in 19th cent. a hideout for pirates and during Civil War for deserters from Confederate Army.

Honey Lake. Lake, SE Lassen co., NE California; ab. 20 m. long; altitude 3949 ft.; no outlet.

Hon·fleur \ōⁿ-ˈflər\. Seaport, Calvados dept., NW France, on Seine estuary opp. Le Havre; pop. (1962c) 9132; chemicals; tourism; founded in 11th cent.; frequently taken and retaken in wars bet. France and England and not finally acquired by France until 1450; center for exploration in 16th and 17th cents.; in 18th cent. supplanted by Le Havre in commercial importance.

Hong. See RED 4.

Hon·ga River \ˌhäŋ-gə-\. Inlet of Chesapeake Bay on SW shore of Dorchester co., SE Maryland.

Hong Kong \ˈhäŋ-ˌkäŋ, -ˈkäŋ; ˈhȯŋ-ˌkȯŋ, -ˈkȯŋ\ *also* **Hongkong.** British crown colony, SE China, E of mouth of the Pearl river ab. 90 m. S of Canton; 398 sq. m.; pop. (1971p) 3,950,000; ✱ Victoria. Comprises (1) *British owned:* (a) **Hong Kong Island;** 29 sq. m.; pop. (1971p) 997,555; irregular with broken ridge; highest point Victoria Peak 1805 ft. in NW; coast much indented; separated (1 m. across) from British Kowloon by spacious Hong Kong harbor and from mainland farther E by Lei U Mun Pass; on NW shore is Victoria (see VICTORIA 13) city. (b) **Kowloon Peninsula** \ˌkau̇-ˌlün-\, part of mainland opp. Hong Kong I.; 3 sq. m.; chief town Kowloon (*q.v.*). (2) *Leased:* **New Territories,** enclave of Kwangtung prov. comprising area N of Kowloon Penin. from Mirs Bay on E to Deep Bay, inlet of Pearl river, on W; 366 sq. m.; includes also Lan Tao and other islands. Colony an important center of world commerce in the Far East; has steamship connections with all principal ports of the world; electronic equipment, textiles, ceramics, plastic; food processing, shipbuilding; tourism; two universities.

History: Island occupied by British 1839, ceded to them by Chinese in 1841, cession confirmed by Treaty of Nanking 1842; Kowloon Penin. ceded by China to British 1860; New Territories leased to Great Britain for 99 years 1898; bombed by Japanese, December 18–24, 1941 and surrendered Dec. 25. Reoccupied by British forces Sept. 1945; scene of Communist-organized rioting 1967.

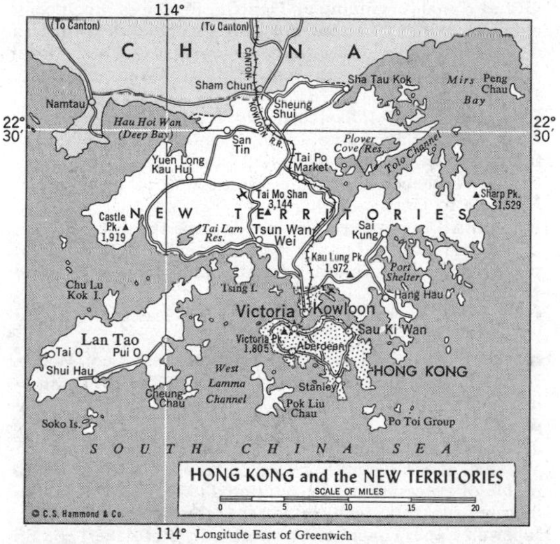

Ho·ni·a·ra \ˌhō-nē-ˈär-ə\. Town, ✱ of British Solomon Is., on NW Guadalcanal I.; pop. (1971e) 13,350.

Hon·is·ter Hause \ˌhän-ə-stər-ˈhȯs\ *or* **Honister Pass.** Mountain pass near Keswick, Cumberland, NW England; 1190 ft.

Hon·i·ton \ˈhän-ə-tən, ˈhən-\. Municipal borough, Devonshire, SW England, 16 m. NE of Exeter; pop. (1971p) 5058; famous for its manufacture of Honiton lace, introduced by refugees from Flanders 16th cent.

Ho·no·kaa \ˌhō-nə-ˈkä-ə\. Town, Hawaii co., Hawaii, on NE coast of Hawaii I.; N of Mauna Kea; pop. (1970c) 1555.

Ho·no·ka·la Point \ˌhō-nə-ˌkäl-ə-\. Point on NE coast of Maui I., Hawaii.

Ho·no·ka·o·pe Bay \ˌhō-nə-kə-ˌō-pē-\. Bay on NW coast of Hawaii I., bet. Keawaiki Bay and Kawaihae Bay.

Hon·o·lu·lu \ˌhän-ᵊl-ˈü-(ˌ)lü, ˌhōn-ᵊl-\. **1** County, Hawaii. See table at HAWAII. Its legal designation established by Municipal Act of 1907, is **City and County of Honolulu;** comprises Oahu I. and the small uninhabited islands of the Hawaiian group.

2 Seaport city, ✱ of the state of Hawaii and ⊗ of Honolulu co.; forms a division of City and County of Honolulu; SE Oahu I., Hawaii; pop. (1970c) 324,871; has protected harbor; tourism; sugar processing, pineapple canning; its position in center of North Pacific Ocean (2090 naut. m. from San Francisco, 4711 m. from Panama, 4483 m. via Suva from Sydney, 4767 m. from Manila, 3380 from Yokohama, and 1304 statute m. by air from Midway) makes it a port of exceptional importance; at mouth of Nuuanu valley with mountains immediately behind it (Punchbowl 500 ft. and Mt. Tantalus 2013 ft.) and farther to NE the Koolau Range with peaks above 3000 ft. (see NUUANU PALI); to SE is suburb of Waikiki with excellent beach; government executive building, former royal palace, completed 1882; Univ. of Hawaii (1907), Jackson Coll. (1949), Chaminade Coll. of Honolulu (1955), Hawaii Loa Coll. (1963), Bishop Museum, state capitol (dedicated 1969). Harbor first discovered 1794 by Capt. William Brown; city began 1816; became capital 1820.

Ho·no·pu Point \hə-ˌnō-pü-\. Cape on NW coast of Lanai I., Hawaii.

Hon·shū \ˈhän-(ˌ)shü\ *or* **Hon·do** \-(ˌ)dō\. Largest of the four chief islands of Japan; area with adjacent small islands 86,246 sq. m.; pop. (1970c) 82,569,581; considered as the mainland of Japan. For administrative divisions, history, physical features, etc., see JAPAN.

Honte. See WEST SCHELDE ESTUARY.

Honto. See NEVELSK.

Hood \ˈhu̇d\. County in Texas. See table at TEXAS.

Hood, Mount. Peak in Cascade Range, in Clackamas and Hood River cos., NW Oregon; 11,235 ft.; highest mountain in Oregon.

Hood Canal. Navigable inlet of Puget Sound, W Washington; extends SW of Admiralty Inlet; ab. 80 m. long, bet. 2 and 3 m. wide.

Hood Island. See ESPAÑOLA 1.

Hoo·doo Peak \ˌhüd-(ˌ)ü-\. Mountain, W Park co., NW Wyoming; 10,522 ft.

Hood River. 1 County in N Oregon. See table at OREGON.

2 City, its ⊗, on Columbia river ab. 17 m. NW of the Dalles; pop. (1970c) 3991; ships fruits (esp. apples, pears, cherries) and berries; fruit-packing plants and canneries; settled 1854.

Hoo·ge \ˈhō-gə\. Former château E of Ieper (Ypres), West Flanders prov., NW Belgium; scene of several battles in World War I; liquid fire first used here in the German attack of July 30, 1915.

Hoo·ge·veen \ˌhō-gə-ˈvān\. Commune, Drenthe prov., NE Netherlands, 23 m. NE of Zwolle; pop. (1970e) 37,485; market for agricultural products; founded in 17th cent.

Hoo·ge·zand–Sap·pe·meer \ˌhō-gə-ˈzänt-ˈsäp-ə-ˌmā(ə)r\. Commune, Groningen prov., NE Netherlands, on canal 9 m. ESE of Groningen; pop. (1970e) 30,189.

Hoogh·ly *or* **Hug·li** \ˈhü-glē\. Most westerly and commercially the most important channel of Ganges river in Ganges Delta (*q.v.*), West Bengal, NE India; ab. 120 m. long from Santipur to Bay of Bengal; nearly 10 m. wide at mouth; navigable to Calcutta; formed by confluence at Nabadwip and Santipur of its headwaters, several distributaries of the Ganges, the most important being the Bhagirathi, an old channel of the Ganges.

Hooghly–Chin·su·ra \-ˈchin(t)-sə-rə\. Town, West Bengal, NE India, on Hooghly river 22 m. N of Calcutta; pop. (1961c) 83,104; joint municipality; trading post established by Portuguese 1537, by the English at Hooghly 1651, and by the Dutch at Chinsura 1656; British forced out temporarily 1685 by Nawab of Bengal; sacked by Marathas 1742.

Hook·er \ˈhu̇k-ər\. County in Nebraska. See table at NEBRASKA.

Hooker Island. Island in Arctic Ocean, S cen. Franz Josef Land, U.S.S.R.; discovered 1896.

Hook Head \ˈhu̇k-\. Cape on SE coast of Ireland, at E of entrance to Waterford Harbour.

Hook of Hol·land \-ˈhäl-ənd\ *or Du.* **Hoek van Holland** \ˌhük-vän-ˈhȯl-(ˌ)änt\. **1** Cape on SW coast of South Holland prov., SW Netherlands, N of mouth of Nieuwe Maas river; scene of naval battle 1914.

2 Seaport on the cape ab. 6 m. NW of Rotterdam; pop. (1966e) 5200; belongs to Rotterdam.

Hooks \ˈhu̇ks\. Town, Bowie co., NE Texas, 16 m. WNW of Texarkana; pop. (1970c) 2545.

Hook·sett \ˈhu̇k-sət\. Town, Merrimack co., S cen. New Hampshire, on Merrimack river 7 m. S of Concord; pop. (1970c) 5564; manufactures furniture. Mount St. Mary Coll. (1934).

Hoo·nah \ˈhü-nə\. City on NE coast of Chichagof I., SE Alaska, 20 m. WSW of Juneau; pop. (1970c) 748.

Hoo·per Islands \ˌhü-pər-, ˌhu̇p-ər-\. Island group, SW Dorchester co., Maryland, on E side of lower Chesapeake Bay.

Hooper Strait. Strait bet. Bloodsworth I. and mainland of Dorchester co., SE Maryland.

Hoopes·ton \ˈhüp-stən, ˈhu̇p-\. City, Vermilion co., E Illinois, 25 m. N of Danville; pop. (1970c) 6461; cable and wire; in agricultural region.

Hoorn \ˈhō(ə)rn, ˈhȯ(ə)rn\. Commune, North Holland prov., W Netherlands, on an inlet of IJsselmeer; pop. (1970e) 18,574; important agricultural market; has two medieval gates; scene of Dutch naval victory over Spanish 1573. Birthplace of Willem C. Schouten, mariner, first to double Cape Horn (named after this town), and of Abel J. Tasman, explorer and discoverer of Tasmania.

Hoorn Islands. See FUTUNA ISLANDS.

Hoo·sac Mountains \ˌhü-sək-, -sik-\. A range of the Green Mts. in Berkshire co., W Massachusetts; highest peak Spruce Hill 1974 ft.

Hoosac Tunnel. Railroad tunnel, Berkshire co., W Massachusetts, in Hoosac Mts.; 4¾ m. long; completed 1875 after 24 years of work.

Hoo·sic \ˈhü-sik\. River, E United States; ab. 70 m. long; rises in N cen. Berkshire co., Massachusetts, flows N and NW across SW extremity of Vermont into New York, and empties into Hudson river 14 m. N of Troy, Rensselaer co., E New York.

Hoo·sick Falls \ˌhü-sik-\. Village, Rensselaer co., E New York, on Hoosic river near Vermont border 21 m. ENE of Troy; pop. (1970c) 3897; manufactures paper and papermaking machinery, electrical appliances, agricultural implements; Bennington Battlefield (state park), site of British entrenchments at battle of Bennington 1777 nearby.

Hoo·sier Pass \ˌhü-zhər-\. Mountain pass, Park and Summit cos., cen. Colorado, in Park Range of the Rocky Mts.; 11,541 ft.; highway.

Hoo·ver Dam \ˌhü-vər-\. See UNITED STATES, *Dams and Reservoirs.*

Hop \ˈhäp\. River, E cen. Connecticut; rises in W Tolland co., flows SE into the Willimantic river near Willimantic.

Ho Pa Shan \ˌhō-ˌbä-ˈshän\. Mountain range on border bet. S Shensi and NE Szechwan provs., cen. China.

Ho·pat·cong \hə-ˈpat-ˌkän, -ˌkäŋ\. Borough, Sussex co., N New Jersey, 14 m. NW of Morristown; pop. (1970c) 9052.

Hopatcong, Lake. Lake on boundary bet. Morris and Sussex cos., N New Jersey; ab. 8 m. long; summer resort.

Hope \ˈhōp\. **1** Commercial city, ⊗ of Hempstead co., SW Arkansas, 32 m. NE of Texarkana; pop. (1970c) 8810; distributing point for truck-gardening, fruit-growing, and cotton region; county seat moved here from Washington 1939.

2 Town, British Columbia, Canada, 75 m. E of Vancouver; pop. (1966c) 2948; lumber, bricks, tiles; agriculture.

Hope, Mount. Peak, Chaffee co., cen. Colorado; 13,943 ft.

Hope, Point *or* **Tig·a·ra** \ˈtig-ə-rə\. Cape and village, NW Alaska, on Arctic Ocean N of Bering Strait, 68°21′N, 166°50′W; Eskimo center for whale catching. Nearby is Ipiutak, site of ancient city that flourished probably 2000 years ago, discovered 1939–40 by Department of Anthropology of Univ. of Alaska; tombs yielded skeletons buried with beautiful ivory carvings and many engraved implements of a culture definitely not Eskimo or Indian.

Hope·dale \ˈhōp-ˌdāl\. **1** Town, Worcester co., cen. Massachusetts, 16 m. ESE of Worcester; pop. (1970c) 4292; location of a Utopian religious community established 1841 by a joint-stock company under leadership of Adin Ballou, Universalist minister; experiment ended by Ballou's successor E. D. Draper, who bought 75 percent of the stock, dissolved the company 1856, and founded the Draper Corp., manufacturers of textile machinery and textiles.

2 Village and harbor, E coast of Labrador, Newfoundland, Canada.

Ho·peh *also* **Ho·pei** \ˈhō-ˈpā, ˈhə-ˈbā\ *or formerly* **Chih·li** \ˈchē-ˈlē\. Province, NE China, bounded on NE by Liaoning, on E by the Gulf of Chihli and Shantung, on S by Honan, on W by Shansi, and on NW by Inner Mongolia; 81,479 sq. m.; pop. (1968e) 47,000,000; ✱ Shih-chia-chuang; mostly a level plain; N and NW boundary closely coincides with E part of Great Wall; E part crossed by the Grand Canal, beginning at Tientsin. Produces much coal, also iron ore and cotton. For centuries chief defense area against Mongols and Manchus to the N. Chief cities: Shih-chia-chuang, T'ang-shan, Kalgan, Ch'in-huang-tao, Pao-ting.

Hope Island. Island, Svalbard, Norway, in Barents Sea ab. 60 m. SE of Edge I.; ab. 20 m. long.

Hopes Ad·vance, Cape \-ˌhōp-səd-ˈvans\. Cape, N Ungava Penin., N Quebec, Canada, on Hudson Strait at W side of entrance to Ungava Bay.

Hope·town \ˈhōp-ˌtau̇n\. Town, NE Cape Province, S Rep. of South Africa, on Orange river 70 m. SSW of Kimberley; place where first South African diamonds were found 1867.

Hope Town. Town on small island off E coast of Great Abaco I., Bahama Is.

Hope·well \ˈhōp-ˌwel, -wəl\. **1** Borough, Mercer co., W cen. New Jersey, 13 m. N of Trenton; pop. (1970c) 2271; camping ground of Washington's army before battle of Monmouth.

2 City in Prince George co. but politically independent, SE Virginia, at confluence of James and Appomattox rivers 10 m. NE of Petersburg; 7 sq. m.; pop. (1970c) 23,471; manufactures synthetic textiles, pottery, chemicals.

Hopewell Cape. Town (unincorporated), ⊗ of Albert co., SE New Brunswick, Canada, at mouth of Petitcodiac estuary; pop. (1966c) 171.

Hop·kins \ˈhäp-kənz\. **1** Counties in two states of the U.S. See tables at KENTUCKY and TEXAS.

2 City, Hennepin co., SE cen. Minnesota, 8 m. WSW of Minneapolis; pop. (1970c) 13,428; truck gardening; manufactures farm machinery.

Hop·kins·ville \ˈhäp-kənz-ˌvil\. City, ⊗ of Christian co., SW Kentucky, 68 m. S of Henderson; pop. (1970c) 21,250; tobacco and livestock market.

Hop·kin·ton \ˈhäp-kən-tən\. **1** Town, Middlesex co., NE Massachusetts, 13 m. ESE of Worcester; pop. (1970c) 5981.

2 Agricultural town, Merrimack co., S cen. New Hampshire, 7 m. W of Concord; pop. (1970c) 3007; chartered and settled 1735.

3 Town, Washington co., S Rhode Island, 23 m. W of Newport; pop. (1970c) 5392; taken from Westerly and incorporated 1757.

Ho·qui·am \ˈhō-kwē-əm\. Seaport city, Grays Harbor co., W Washington, on Grays Harbor adjacent to Aberdeen ab. 50 m. W of Olympia; pop. (1970c) 10,466; lumber center, manufactures lumber products; salmon and tuna fisheries, fish and oyster canneries.

Hor, Mount \-ˈhȯ(ə)r\ *or Arab.* **Ja·bal Hā·rūn** \ˌjab-əl-hä-ˈrün\. Mountain, E of Wadi al-'Araba, Jordan, highest of the Seir Mts. of ancient Edom; ruined city of Petra (*q.v.*) is on its NE slope; by tradition the mountain on which Aaron died and was buried (*Num.* xx. 22–29).

Hor·bury \ˈhȯr-b(ə-)rē\. Urban district, West Riding, Yorkshire, N England, just SW of Wakefield; pop. (1971p) 8914.

Hor·da·land \ˈhȯrd-ə-ˌlän\. County of SW Norway. See table at NORWAY.

Ho·reb \ˈhōr-ˌeb, ˈhȯr-\. Mountain, identity unknown, perhaps in Sinai Penin. See SINAI, MOUNT.

Hor·gen \ˈhȯr-gən\. Commune, Zurich canton, NE cen. Switzerland, on Lake of Zurich 9 m. SSE of Zurich; pop. (1970c) 15,691; electronic equipment; church (1780).

Hor·i·con \ˈhȯr-ə-ˌkän\. City, Dodge co., SE cen. Wisconsin, 25 m. S of Fond du Lac; pop. (1970c) 3356; manufactures farm equipment, furniture.

Horicon, Lake. See GEORGE, LAKE 2.

Hor·mi·gue·ros \ˌōr-mi-ˈger-əs\. Town and municipality, W Puerto Rico; town on railroad 4 m. S of Mayagüez; pop. (1970p) 6428 (town), 10,803 (munic.).

Hor·muz \ˈhȯr-ˌməz, hȯr-ˈmüz\ *also* **Or·muz** \ˈȯr-ˌməz, ȯr-ˈmüz\. 1 Island in Strait of Hormuz; belongs to Iran; under Portuguese control 1514–1622.

2 *or anc.* **Har·mo·zia** \här-ˈmō-zh(ē-)ə\. Ancient Persian town, near modern Bandar ʻAbbās on Strait of Hormuz, S Iran.

History: Scene of battle in which Parthian Empire was overthrown by Ardashir I (see IRAN) 226 A.D.; conquered by Arabs and later the seat of small Arabian kingdom; trade center for overland route to India; removed to island (11 m. SE of Bandar ʻAbbās), probably in 14th cent.; 14th–16th cents. the leading mart in Persian Gulf; held by Portuguese 1514–1622; captured by Persian ruler aided by forces of English East India Co. 1622; declined after removal of its trade to Bandar ʻAbbās on mainland.

Hormuz, Strait of *also* **Strait of Ormuz.** Strait bet. the N tip of Oman, SE Arabian Penin., and the S coast of Iran; connects the Persian Gulf with the Gulf of Oman.

Horn \ˈhȯ(ə)rn\ *or* **North Cape.** Cape, NW Iceland, W of Húna Bay.

Horn, Cape *or Span.* **Ca·bo de Hor·nos** \ˈkäb-ō-dā-ˈȯr-nəs\. Cape, at S extremity of South America, 56°S, 67°16′W, on **Horn Island** of Wollaston group, S Tierra del Fuego Archipelago (*q.v.*), projecting S into Drake Passage; first sighted by Sir Francis Drake 1578; named 1616 by Dutch navigators, J. Le Maire and W. C. Schouten, after Hoorn in Holland; further explored by Nodal brothers 1619.

Hornad. See HERNÁD.

Hor·na Fjord \ˈhär-nə-\. Inlet of Atlantic Ocean on SE coast of Iceland; good harbor.

Horn·a·van \ˈhu̇(ə)r-ˌnäv-ən\. Lake, Västerbotten co., N Sweden; 89 sq. m.; drained by Skellefte river.

Horn·cas·tle \ˈhȯ(ə)rn-ˌkas-əl\. Urban district, the Parts of Lindsey, Lincolnshire, E England; pop. (1971p) 4096; malting, tanning.

Hor·ne·len \hȯr-ˈnā-lən\. Island off SW coast of Norway, near entrance to Nord Fjord; shores rise abruptly to a height of ab. 3000 ft.

Hor·nell \hȯr-ˈnel\. City, Steuben co., S New York, 56 m. S of Rochester; pop. (1970c) 12,144; railroad center; manufactures textiles, hosiery, brick and tile, leather, wagons, farm tools, electrical machinery; settled 1790.

Horn Island. 1 Island, off SE Mississippi coast, bet. Mississippi Sound and Gulf of Mexico.

2 Small island off Cape York, N Queensland, Australia, E of Thursday I.

3 Island, South America. See HORN, CAPE.

Hornos, Cabo de. See HORN, CAPE.

Horn Peak. 1 Mountain, Custer and Saguache cos., S cen. Colorado; 13,400 ft.

2 Mountain in Blue Mts., NE Oregon; 8922 ft.

Horn·sund·tind \ˈhȯ(ə)rn-sən-ˌtin\. Mountain, at S end of Spitsbergen I., near **Horn Sound** (*Norw.* **Horn·sund** \ˈhȯ(ə)rn-ˌsün\), inlet on SW coast.

Hor·nu \(h)ȯr-ˈn(y)ü\. Commune, Hainaut prov., SW Belgium, just W of Mons; pop. (1969e) 10,920.

Hör·num \ˈhər-nəm\. Southern part of island of Sylt, West Germany, off W coast of Schleswig-Holstein; sandy region; incl. village of Hörnum, pop. (1968e) 1400.

Ho·ro·shi·ri \hə-ˈrō-shə-rē\. Mountain peak, Hidaka Mts., S Hokkaidō I., Japan; 6732 ft.

Hor·que·ta \ȯr-ˈkāt-ə\. Town, SE Concepción dept., Paraguay, E of Concepción; munic. pop. (1970e) 29,090.

Hor·ry \ˈhȯ(ə)r-ē\. County in South Carolina. See table at SOUTH CAROLINA.

Horse·head Lake \ˌhȯrs-ˌhed-\. Lake in cen. Kidder co., S cen. North Dakota.

Horse·heads \ˈhȯrs-ˌhedz\. Village, Chemung co., S New York, 5 m. N of Elmira; pop. (1970c) 7989; manufactures bricks, optical goods.

Hör·sel·ber·ge \ˈhər-zəl-ˌbe(ə)r-gə\ *or* **Ve·nus·berg** \ˈvē-nəs-ˌbərg\. Mountains, Erfurt dist., East Germany, bet. Gotha and Eisenach; contains the cave in which, according to medieval legend, Venus held her court.

Hor·sens \ˈhȯr-sənz, -sən(t)s\. Seaport, Vejle co., E Jutland, Denmark, at head of **Horsens Fjord;** pop. (1970e) 35,621; ships dairy products; manufactures textiles, electrical equipment, tobacco products.

Horse·shoe Bend National Military Park \ˌhȯrs(h)-ˌshü-\. See UNITED STATES, *National Historical Parks.*

Horseshoe Curve. Construction and scenic feature of Pennsylvania Railroad, Pennsylvania, just W of Altoona; 2375 ft. long, and graded 91 ft. to the mile; of exceptional engineering interest; completed 1852.

Horseshoe Fall. See NIAGARA FALLS.

Horseshoe Mountain. Peak, Park and Lake cos., cen. Colorado; 13,902 ft.

Horse Trough \-ˌtrȯf\. Peak, Union co., N Georgia; 4052 ft.

Hors·forth \ˈhȯrs-fərth\. Urban district, West Riding, Yorkshire, N England, 5 m. NW of Leeds; pop. (1971p) 19,366.

Hor·sham \ˈhȯr-shəm\. 1 Town, W Victoria, SE Australia, 115 m. W of Bendigo; pop. (1968e) 10,900.

2 Urban district, West Sussex, S England; pop. (1971p) 26,378; to NW is Field Place, birthplace of Percy Bysshe Shelley; Christ's Hospital (transferred from London 1902).

Hor·ta \ˈ(h)ȯrt-ə\. 1 District of Portugal in the Azores. See table at PORTUGAL.

2 Seaport commune, its ✱, in Azores, on SE coast of Faial I.; pop. (1970p) 17,474; radio station; telegraph center; exports wine, oranges, grain; air base.

Hor·ten \ˈhȯrt-ᵊn\. Seaport, Vestfold co., SE Norway, on W side of Oslo Fjord; pop. (1970e) 14,050; shipbuilding yards, arsenal; naval museum. In World War II naval battle Apr. 9, 1940 occurred nearby in which the Norwegians sank some German transports and damaged the cruiser *Emden.*

Hor·ton \ˈhȯrt-ᵊn\. 1 River, NW Mackenzie dist., Northwest Territories, Canada, E of Anderson river; 275 m. long; flows NW into W side of Franklin Bay.

2 Parish, Buckinghamshire, SE England, 3 m. ESE of Windsor; pop (1961c) 1504; residence 1632–38 of John Milton.

Hor·wich \ˈhär-ich, -ij\. Urban district, Lancashire, NW England, 15 m. NW of Manchester; pop. (1971p) 16,433; locomotives, cotton textiles.

Horyń. See GORYN.

Ho·ryu·ji \ˈhȯr-yə-(ˌ)jē\. Town, Nara prefecture, W cen. Honshū, Japan, ab. 7 m. SW of Nara; site of oldest existing Buddhist shrine in Japan, built ab. 607 A.D.

Ho·shang·a·bad \hō-ˈshəŋ-ə-ˌbäd\. Town, cen. Madhya Pradesh, India, on Narmada river; pop. (1961c) 19,300; founded 15th cent.; bet. 1720 and 1818 scene of conflicts bet. Marathas and Bhopal rulers.

Ho·shi·ar·pur \ˌhō-shē-ˈär-(ˌ)pu̇(ə)r\. Town, cen. Punjab, NW India; pop. (1961c) 50,739; produces inlaid ivory, metal, and inlaid woodwork, furniture. Founded early 14th cent.; occupied 1809 by Ranjit Singh; annexed by British 1849.

Hos·pet \ˈhōsh-ˌpet\. Town, Mysore, India, on Tungabhadra river 37 m. W of Bellary; pop. (1961c) 53,242.

Hos·pi·ta·let \ˌ(h)äs-ˌpit-ᵊl-ˈet\. City, Barcelona prov., NE Spain, SW suburb of Barcelona; pop. (1970p) 241,978; steel, textiles; agricultural institute.

Hos·te \ˈ(h)ō-(ˌ)stā\. Chilean island in Tierra del Fuego Archipelago (*q.v.*), S of W Tierra del Fuego I.; 90 m. long, 50 m. wide.

Hoth·am, Mount \-'häth-əm\. Mountain in the Darg Plateau, E Victoria, SE Australia, SW of Mt. Kosciusko; 6108 ft.

Ho–t'ien \'hō-'tyen\ *also* **Kho·tan** \'kō-'tän\. 1 River, W Sinkiang Uighur, W China; joins the Yarkand to form Tarim river, but dry much of the year.
2 Town, China. See KHOTAN 2.

Hotin. See KHOTIN.

Hot Spring. County in Arkansas. See table at ARKANSAS.

Hot Springs. 1 County in Wyoming. See table at WYOMING.
2 City, ⊗ of Garland co., W cen. Arkansas, in Ouachita Mts. 47 m. WSW of Little Rock; pop. (1970c) 35,631; health and tourist resort noted for its 47 thermal springs. Settled 1807; made, with surrounding area, a U.S. Government reservation 1832, **Hot Springs National Park** 1921 (see UNITED STATES, *National Parks*).
3 City, New Mexico. See TRUTH OR CONSEQUENCES.
4 City, ⊗ of Fall River co., SW corner of South Dakota, in foothills of Black Hills 48 m. S of Rapid City; pop. (1970c) 4434; health resort; thermal and mineral springs; sandstone quarries; mica, feldspar, gold, silver mines.
5 Village, Bath co., W Virginia, 5 m. SW of Warm Springs; mineral springs; Japanese diplomats interned here 1942 at beginning of war with Japan; scene of United Nations Conference on Food and Agriculture 1943.

Hot Springs Peak. Mountain, Humboldt co., NW Nevada; 6450 ft.

Hot Sul·phur Springs \-'səl-fər-\. Town, ⊗ of Grand co., N Colorado; pop. (1970c) 220; hot sulfur springs.

Hotte, Massif de la. See SUD, MASSIF DU.

Hot·ten·tot Point \ˌhät-^{ə}n-ˌtät-\. Cape on SW coast of South-West Africa, N of Lüderitz.

Hou·dain \ü-'da^{n}\. Commune, Pas-de-Calais dept., N France, near Béthune; pop. (1962c) 8869; coal; has church (12th and 16th cents.); destroyed in World War I and rebuilt.

Hou·dan \ü-'dä^{n}\. Village, Yvelines dept., N France; pop. (1962c) 2358; has 15th–16th cent. church and keep of an early 12th cent. castle; noted for its poultry market, the Houdan breed of domestic fowl originating here.

Hou·deng–Goe·gnies \ü-ˌdä^{n}-gər-'nyē\. Commune, Hainaut prov., SW Belgium, on a tributary of the Haine, E of Mons; pop. (1969e) 8947; coal mines, smelting, woodworking, rope making, glassworks.

Houf·fa·lize \ü-fə-'lēz\. Village, Luxembourg prov., SE Belgium, 10 m. N of Bastogne; pop. (1969e) 1346; taken by Germans in early phase of Battle of the Bulge Dec. 1944; retaken by Allies Jan. 16, 1945.

Hough·ton \'hō-tən\. 1 County in Michigan. See table at MICHIGAN.
2 Village, ⊗ of Houghton co., NW Michigan penin., 70 m. NW of Marquette; pop. (1970c) 6067; in copper-mining region; distribution center for Keweenaw Penin.; Michigan Technological Univ. (1885).
3 Village, Allegany co., SW New York, 65 m. SE of Buffalo; pop. (1970c) 1620; Houghton Coll. (1883).

Houghton Lake. Lake in cen. Roscommon co., N cen. Michigan; 31 sq. m.; 16 m. long; largest inland lake in the state; source of Muskegon river.

Houghton–le–Spring \ˌhōt-^{ə}n-lə-'spriŋ\. Urban district, Durham, N England, 11 m. SSE of Newcastle upon Tyne; pop. (1971p) 32,666; limestone quarrying, coal mining.

Hou·gou·mont \ˌü-gə-'mō^{n}\. Château on the battlefield of Waterloo, Belgium; held by British throughout the battle, June 18, 1815, against repeated attacks.

Hougue, La. See LA HOGUE.

Hou·illes \'ü-yə\. Commune, Yvelines dept., N France, NW of Paris on Seine river; pop. (1968c) 29,338; metalworking.

Houl·ton \'hōlt-^{ə}n\. Town, ⊗ of Aroostook co., N Maine, on Canadian border 22 m. N of Grand Lake; pop. (1970c) 8111; ships potatoes, lumber; wood products.

Hou·ma \'hō-mə, 'hü-\. City, ⊗ of Terrebonne parish, SE Louisiana, 49 m. WSW of New Orleans on the Intracoastal Waterway; pop. (1970c) 30,922; packinghouses for shrimp, oysters, crabs; fisheries; sugar and molasses; founded 1810, incorp. as city 1898.

Houns·low \'hau̇nz-(ˌ)lō\. A borough of Greater London, SE England. See table at LONDON 4; incl. **Hounslow Heath,** site of a Roman camp, once a resort of highwaymen.

Hou·plines \ü-'plēn\. Commune, Nord dept., N France, on Belgian frontier just E of Armentières; pop. (1962c) 5934; battle Apr. 9, 1918 when it was taken by British.

Hourn, Loch \läk-'hu̇(ə)rn, läk-\. Inlet of Sound of Sleat, Inverness co., on NW coast of Scotland; extends inland ab. 13 m.

Hou·sa·ton·ic \ˌhü-sə-'tän-ik, ˌhü-zə-\. River, Berkshire co., W Massachusetts; 148 m. long; formed by junction of E and W branches S of Pittsfield, and flowing S, across W Connecticut, into Long Island Sound at Stratford.

Hous·ton \'(h)yü-stən, *in Georgia* 'hau̇s-tən\. 1 Name of counties in five states of the U.S. See tables at ALABAMA, GEORGIA, MINNESOTA, TENNESSEE, TEXAS.
2 Town, a ⊗ of Chickasaw co., NE Mississippi, 30 m. SW of Tupelo; pop. (1970c) 2720; dairying.
3 City, ⊗ of Texas co., S Missouri, 42 m. N of West Plains; pop. (1970c) 2178; lumber.
4 City and port of entry, ⊗ of Harris co., SE Texas, ab. 25 m. NW of Galveston Bay; pop. (1970c) 1,232,802; connected with Gulf of Mexico by **Houston Ship Canal** *or* **Houston Ship Channel** (through former Buffalo Bayou and Galveston Bay, 57.3 m. long, 200 ft. wide, 34 ft. deep); largest city in the state and its leading industrial center; ships esp. petroleum products, cotton, sulfur, lumber, rice; petroleum refining, meat-packing, printing and publishing; sugar and rice mills; manufactures chemicals, steel, electronic and geophysical equipment, cotton and cottonseed oil products, oil-well machinery; sulfur, salt, limestone deposits; Ellington Air Force Base, Manned Spacecraft Center (established 1961); Astrodome (1965); William Marsh Rice University (1891), Texas Southern Univ. (1927), Univ. of Houston (1934), Univ. of St. Thomas (1947), South Texas Junior Coll. (1948), Gulf-Coast Bible Coll. (1953), Houston Baptist Coll. (1960); founded 1836; incorporated and became ⊗ 1837; capital of Republic of Texas 1837–39, 1842–45; developed rapidly since completion of ship canal 1914.

Hout·man Rocks \ˌhau̇t-mən-\ *or* **Houtman Abro·lhos** \-ə-'brōl-ˌyüsh\. Rocky islets, in Indian Ocean ab. 80 m. W of Geraldton, W Western Australia.

Hovd \'hȯv-də\ *or* **Kob·do** *or* **Khob·do** \'kȯb-dō\ *or* *formerly* **Dzhir·ga·lan·tu** \ˌjir-gə-län-'tü\. Town, chief trading center of W Mongolian People's Republic, SW of the Hobdo Gol at foot of Altai Mts., ab. 260 m. W of Uliastay; market for cattle, sheep, skins, and wool.

Hove \'hōv\. Municipal borough, East Sussex, S England, W suburb of Brighton on English Channel; pop. (1971p) 72,659.

Ho·ven·weep National Monument \'hō-vən-ˌwēp-\. See UNITED STATES, *National Monuments.*

Hövs·göl \'həfs-'gəl, 'kəfs-\ *also* **Ko·so Gol** *or* **Kos·so–gol** \'kȯs-ō-'gəl\. Lake, N Mongolian People's Republic, near U.S.S.R. border E of Tuva A.S.S.R.; elevation 5620 ft.

How·ard \'hau̇-ərd\. 1 Name of counties in seven states of the U.S. See tables at ARKANSAS, INDIANA, IOWA, MARYLAND, MISSOURI, NEBRASKA, TEXAS.
2 City, ⊗ of Elk co., SE Kansas; pop. (1970c) 918.
3 City, ⊗ of Miner co., E South Dakota; pop. (1970c) 1175.
4 Village, Brown co., E Wisconsin, 5 m. NW of Green Bay; pop. (1970c) 4911.

Howe, Cape \-'hau̇\. Extreme SE point of Australia, on border of New South Wales and Victoria.

How·ell \'hau̇(-ə)l\. 1 County in Missouri. See table at MISSOURI.
2 City, ⊗ of Livingston co., SE Michigan, 25 m. NNW of Ann Arbor; pop. (1970c) 5224; metal castings; cattle; dairy products.

Howe Sound. Inlet of Strait of Georgia, Canada, extending N into British Columbia, N of Vancouver.

How·ick \'hau̇-ik\. 1 Borough, North I., New Zealand; pop. (1970e) 10,850.
2 Resort, Natal, E Rep. of South Africa, NW of Pietermaritzburg; at the falls (364 ft. high) in the Mgeni river.

How·land Island \ˌhau̇-lənd-\. Small island in cen. Pacific Ocean, near the equator NW of Phoenix Is.; 1 sq. m.; belongs to the United States; has airport, constructed 1937. Visited for guano bet. 1856 and 1890.

How·rah \'hau̇-rə\. City, West Bengal state, NE India, on Hooghly river opp. Calcutta; pop. (1970e) 599,740; important industrial community; iron and steel rolling mills; jute and cotton mills, railroad workshops, paper factories; Bengal engineering school; botanical gardens (established 1787).

Hox·ie \'häk-sē\. City, ⊗ of Sheridan co., NW Kansas; pop. (1970c) 1419.

Hox·ne \'häk-sən—*sic*\. Village, N Suffolk, England; Stone Age deposits; scene of defeat of St. Edmund by the Danes in 870.

Hoy \'hȯi\. One of the Orkney Is., off N coast of Scotland; 13 m. long; its highest point (1564 ft.) is highest in the Orkneys.

Hoy·ers·wer·da \ˌhȯi-ərz-'ver-də\. City, Cottbus dist., East Germany; pop. (1970e) 58,663; glass; received municipal rights 1371.

Hoy·lake \'hȯi-ˌlāk\. Urban district, Cheshire, NW England, on Irish Sea 9 m. W of Liverpool; pop. (1971p) 32,196; yachting; famous golf links, scene of many championship matches.

Hoy·land Neth·er \ˌhȯi-lən(d)-'neth-ər\. Urban district, West Riding, Yorkshire, N England, near Barnsley; pop. (1971p) 15,812; brickworks, coal mines.

Hoy·ran, Lake \-hȯi-'rän\ *or Turk.* **Hoyran Gö·lü** \-gəl-'(y)ü\. Lake (*gölü*) in W Turkey, Asia, S of Afyonkarahisar; forms the N part of Eğridir Lake.

Hoy Sound \ˌhȯi-\. Body of water bet. islands of Pomona (Mainland) on N and Hoy on S in the Orkney Is., off N coast of Scotland.

Hoyt Lakes \ˌhȯit-\. Village, St. Louis co., NE Minnesota, 50 m. N of Duluth; pop. (1970c) 3634.

Hoyt Peak. Mountain, S Summit co., NE Utah; 10,248 ft.

Ho·zu \'hō-(ˌ)zü\. River, Honshū, Japan; joins Uji river to form the Yodo river.

Hra·dec Kra·lo·vé \ˌ(h)räd-ets-'kräl-ə-və\ *or Ger.* **Kö·nig·grätz** \'kā-nig-ˌgrāts, 'kə(r)n-ig-\. Town, Czech S.R., Czechoslovakia, on Labe (Elbe) river, 60 m. E of Prague; pop. (1968e) 66,744; battle July 3, 1866 in which Prussians under Count von Moltke decisively defeated the Austrians under Gen. Benedek in Austro-Prussian War.

Hra·ni·ce \'hrän-yət-(ˌ)sä\ *or Ger.* **Mäh·risch–Weiss·kir·chen** \ˌmā-rish-'vīs-ˌki(ə)r-kən, ˌme(ə)r-ish-\. Town, Czech S.R., cen. Czechoslovakia, 24 m. E of Olomouc; pop. (1968e) 12,262.

Hron \'hrȯn\ *or Hung.* **Ga·ram** \'gȯr-ˌȯm\ *or Ger.* **Gran** \'grän\. River, Czechoslovakia; ab. 170 m. long; flows W, then S into Danube river opp. Esztergom, Hungary.

Hru·bie·szów \hrü-'byesh-əf\ *or Russ.* **Gru·be·shov** \ˌgrüb-yə-'shȯf\. Commune, Lublin prov., Poland; 64 m. ESE of Lublin just W of the Bug; pop. (1968e) 13,900; agriculture; scene of battle July 1915 bet. Germans and Russians.

Hrvatska. See CROATIA.

Hsen·wi \'sen-'wē\. Town, ✱ of former North Hsenwi state, Burma, 25 m. NNE of Lashio.

Hsi *or* **Si** \'shē\ *also* **Hsi Chiang** \-chē-'äŋ\ *or Eng.* **West River.** River, SE China; 1200 m. long; commercial waterway; known in its upper course as the Hung-shui (*q.v.*); the Hsi proper begins in E Kwangsi Chuang where the Hung-shui unites with the Hsiang, then flows W ab. 300 m. through Kwangtung prov. into China Sea near Macao and W of the island of Hong Kong; the city of Canton is in its delta (see PEARL 2). Navigable for large vessels to Wu-chou and for smaller vessels beyond; receives the tributaries Kuei and Pei from the N.

Hsia–men. See AMOY.

Hsiang *or* **Siang** \shē-'äŋ\. Navigable river, cen. Hunan prov., SE cen. China; rises in NE Kwangsi Chuang and flows N into Tung-t'ing Hu (lake); its valley highly developed agriculturally and for centuries has been a north-south trade route; also has important mineral resources in coal, antimony, and lead.

Hsiang–shan *or* **Siang·shan** \shē-'äŋ-'shän\. Town, Chekiang prov., E China, 120 m. S of Shanghai on S shore of **Hsiang–shan Bay,** long narrow inlet of East China Sea S of Ning-po; Japanese naval supply base in latter part of Chino-Japanese War 1943–45.

Hsiang–t'an *or* **Siang·tan** \shē-'äŋ-'tän\. Town, Hunan prov., SE China, on Siang river ab. 20 m. SSW of Ch'ang-sha; pop. (1970e) 300,000.

Hsiang–yang *or* **Siang·yang** \shē-'äŋ-'yäŋ\. Town, N Hupeh prov., E cen. China, on right bank of the Han 170 m. NW of Hankow.

Hsiang–yün *or* **Siang·yun** \shē-'äŋ-'yün\. Town, cen. Yunnan prov., S China, 30 m. SE of Ta-li; junction point.

Hsiao–hsing–an–ling Shan–mo. See KHINGAN 2.

Hsi–ch'ang *also* **Si·chang** \'shē-'chäŋ\. Town, S China, on a tributary of the Yangtze, ab. 285 m. SW of Chungkiang.

Hsi Chiang. See HSI.

Hsien–yang *or* **Sien·yang** \shē-'en-'yäŋ\. 1 City, NE cen. China. See SIAN.
2 Town, Shensi prov., NE cen. China, ab. 15 m. NW of Sian; pop. (1970e) 120,000.

Hsikang. See SIKANG.

Hsin–feng *or* **Sin·feng** \'shin-'fəŋ\. Town, S Kiangsi prov., SE China, ab. 33 m. S of Kan-chou; an American airfield in World War II, taken by the Japanese but recovered July 1945.

Hsing·an \'shiŋ-'än\. One of nine former provinces of Manchuria, in NW part; 103,918 sq. m.; created Sept. 1945; now part of Inner Mongolia.

Hsiang–K'ai Hu. See KHANKA.

Hsin–hsiang *or* **Sin·siang** \ˌshin-shē-'äŋ\. Town, Honan prov., E cen. China, ab. 35 m. N of Cheng-chou; pop. (1970e) 300,000.

Hsi–ning *or* **Hsi·ning** *or* **Si·ning** \'shē-'niŋ\. City, ✱ of Tsinghai prov., W cen. China, on Hsi-ning river; pop. (1970e) 250,000.

Hsin–kao \'shin-'gau̇\ *or Jap.* **Ni·i·ta·ka·ya·ma** \ˌnē-ə-ˌtäk-ə-'yäm-ə\ *also* **Mount Mor·ri·son** \-'mȯr-ə-sən, -'mär-\. Peak, S cen. Taiwan; 13,113 ft.; highest peak in Taiwan.

Hsinking. See CH'ANG-CH'UN.

Hsin·king Special Municipality \'shin-'kiŋ-\. Former province (1932–45), S cen. Manchukuo, comprising the capital city Hsinking (Ch'ang-ch'un); 169 sq. m.

Hsin–min *or* **Sin·min** \'shin-'min\. Town, SW Liaoning prov., NE China, 35 m. W of Mukden; former treaty port W of the Liao on the Mukden-Tientsin railroad.

Hsin–yang *or* **Sin·yang** \'shin-'yäŋ\. Town, Honan prov., E cen. China, ab. 180 m. SSE of Cheng-chou; pop. (1970e) 125,000; center of fighting in Chino-Japanese War, esp. in Jan. 1943.

Hsi·paw \'sē-'pȯ\. 1 One of the former Shan States, NE of Mandalay, E cen. Burma; 4591 sq. m.
2 Town, its ✱, on railroad ab. 90 m. NE of Mandalay.

Hsü–ch'ang \'sü-'chäŋ\ *or formerly* **Hsu·chow** \'sü-'jō\. Town, N Honan prov., E cen. China, S of Cheng-chou; scene of hard battle May 1938 after which Japanese gained control of Lunghai railroad.

Hsü–chou. See SÜCHOW.

Hua·cas Point \ˌwäk-əs-\. Cape on W cen. coast of Peru, S of Callao.

Hua·cho \'wäch-(,)ō\. Seaport, Lima dept., cen. Peru, 70 m. N of Callao; pop. (1969e) 28,700; shipping point for cotton and sugar district.

Hua·chu·ca \wə-'chü-kə\. Town, Cochise co., SE Arizona; pop. (1970c) 1241.

Huachuca Peak. Mountain, SW Cochise co., SE Arizona; 8406 ft.

Hua·hi·né \wä-'hē-nē\. One of the Leeward Is. group of Society Is., French Polynesia, S Pacific Ocean, ab. 80 m. WNW of Tahiti; 7 m. N to S by 4 m. wide; pop. (1962) 3214; produces copra, tropical fruits, and vegetables; highest point 2331 ft.

Huai *or* **Hwai** \'(h)wī\. River, S Honan and NW Anhwei provs., E China; ab. 350 m. long; flows into the Yellow river above Hungtse Hu (lake); has many tributaries watering a rich agricultural region. See YELLOW 4.

Huai·llas \'wī-yäs\. Peak, W Bolivia, N of Lake Poopó; 18,045 ft.

Huai–nan *or* **Hwai·nan** \'(h)wī-'nän\. Town, Anhwei prov., E China, ab. 50 m. NNW of Ho-fei; pop. (1970e) 350,000.

Huai·na Po·to·sí \'wī-nə-,pōt-ə-'sē\. Andean mountain peak in Bolivia, 20 m. N of La Paz; 20,340 ft.

Huaina–Putina. See OMATE.

Hua·jua·pan de Le·ón \wä-,hwä-pän-,dā-lā-'ōn\. Municipality, Oaxaca state, Mexico, 90 m. NW of Oaxaca; pop. (1970p) 83,939; commercial center; ceramics, palm products; lumber; diversified agriculture.

Hua–jung *or* **Hwa·jung** \'(h)wä-'ru̇ŋ\. City, N Hunan, SE cen. China; scene of fighting bet. Japanese and Chinese Mar. 1943.

Hu·a·la·lai \,hü-ə-lə-'lī\. Volcano, W Hawaii I.; 8276 ft.; dormant since 1801.

Hual·cán \wäl-'kän\. Peak in Cordillera Occidental, Peru; 21,000 ft.

Hua·lla·ga \wä-'yäg-ə\. River, W and N Peru; ab. 700 m. long; rises in Andes Mts., flows N into Marañón river in N Peru.

Hual·pai Peak \,wäl-,pī-\. Mountain in **Hualpai Mountains,** S cen. Mohave co., W Arizona; 8266 ft.

Hua·man·tla \wä-'män-tlä\. Municipality, Tlaxcala state, 80 m. E of Mexico City; pop. (1970p) 26,191; grain, fruit.

Huambo. See NOVA LISBOA.

Hua·mi·na \wä-'mē-nə\. Peak, Apurímac dept., S Peru; 14,-435 ft.

Huan·ca·ve·li·ca \,wäŋ-kə-və-'lē-kə\. **1** Department of S cen. Peru. See table at PERU.

2 Town, its ✻, 140 m. SE of Lima; pop. (1961c) 11,039; altitude ab. 12,500 ft.; mining; founded by Francisco de Toledo 1572.

Huan·ca·yo \wäŋ-'kī-(,)ō\. City, ✻ of Junín dept., cen. Peru, on Mantaro river ab. 122 m. E of Lima; met. area pop. (1969e) 91,200; altitude 10,958 ft.; univ. (1962); noted for its marketplace to which Indians come from surrounding districts.

Huan·cha·ca \wän-'chäk-ə\. Town, Potosí dept., SW Bolivia, ab. 20 m. NE of Uyuni; silver mining.

Huan·doy \wän-'dȯi\. Peak, Ancash dept., W Peru; 20,852 ft.

Huang–pu \'(h)wäŋ-'pü\ *or* **Wham·poa** \'(h)wäm-'pō-'ä\. Seaport town, Kwangtung, SE China, on island on S side of upper Pearl river in Hsi delta, 12 m. below Canton; outport of Canton where in early trade British and American clippers anchored.

Huang–p'u *or* **Hwang Pu** *or formerly* **Whang·poo** \'(h)wäŋ-'pü\. River, S Kiangsu prov., E China; flows NE past Shanghai to enter mouth of the Yangtze at Wu-sung.

Huang–shih *or* **Hwang·shih** \'hwäŋ-'shē\. Town, Hupeh prov., E cen. China, ab. 50 m. ESE of Hankow; pop. (1970e) 200,000.

Huá·nu·co \'wän-ü-,kō\. **1** Department of cen. Peru. See table at PERU.

2 Town, its ✻, near Huallaga river ab. 170 m. NE of Lima; pop. (1969e) 33,300; altitude 6273 ft.; univ. (1964); founded by Gómez Alvarado 1539; former capital of Junín dept. (until 1855); nearly destroyed by Chilean riots and massacres 1881, 1883; 35 m. to the W is Inca town **Huánuco Vie·jo** \-vē-'e-(,)hō\, settled by Spanish 1535, now almost abandoned.

Hua·ra \'wär-ə\. Commune, Tarapacá prov., N Chile, ab. 25 m. N of Iquique; pop. (1960c) 885.

Hua·rás *or formerly* **Hua·raz** \wä-'räs\. Town, ✻ of Ancash dept., W Peru, on Santa river 190 m. N of Lima; pop. (1961c) 20,345; altitude 9932 ft.; silver, copper, gold, coal; severe earthquake damage 1970.

Huas·ca·rán \,wäs-kə-'rän\ *or* **Huas·cán** \wä-'skän\. Peak, Ancash dept., W Peru; 22,205 ft.; highest mountain in Peru.

Huas·co \'wäs-(,)kō\. Port, Atacama prov., N cen. Chile, midway bet. Coquimbo and Caldera; pop. (1960c) 1902; exports copper, silver, cattle.

Hua Shan *or* **Hwa Shan** \'(h)wä-'shän\. Mountain in S cen. Shensi prov., NE China; ab. 3000 ft.; traditionally one of the five sacred mountains of China.

Hua·ta·bam·po \,wät-ə-'bäm-(,)pō\. Town, S Sonora state, NW Mexico, near coast; munic. pop. (1970p) 43,963.

Hua·tus·co \wä-'tüs-(,)kō\. Town, Veracruz state, E Mexico, ab. 50 m. W of Veracruz; munic. pop. (1970p) 20,621.

Huau·chi·nan·go \,wau̇-chi-'näŋ-(,)gō\. Town, Puebla state, SE cen. Mexico, 45 m. E of Pachuca; munic. pop. (1970p) 37,211.

Huau·ra \'wau̇-rə\ *or* **Guau·ra** \'gwau̇-\. River, cen. Peru; ab. 85 m. long; flows W into Pacific Ocean N of Lima.

Huayhuash, Cordillera. See ANDES.

Hub·bard \'həb-ərd\. **1** County in Minnesota. See table at MINNESOTA.

2 Village, Trumbull co., NE Ohio, 6 m. NE of Youngstown; pop. (1970c) 8583; manufactures steel, slag products.

3 City and health resort, Hill co., NE cen. Texas, 28 m. NNE of Waco; pop. (1970c) 1572; mineral springs.

Hubbard, Mount. Peak in Coast Mountains on Alaska-Yukon boundary, SE of Mt. Logan; 15,013 ft.

Hubbard Glacier. Glacier in the St. Elias Mountains, on Alaska-Yukon border; 71 m. long, ab. 6 m. wide near its terminus.

Hubbard Lake. Lake, N Alcona co., NE Michigan; ab. 10½ sq. m.; outlet N into Thunder Bay.

Hub·bard·ton \'həb-ər(d)-tən\. Town, Rutland co., Vermont; pop. (1970c) 228; scene of battle July 7, 1777 in which British under Gen. Fraser defeated Americans under Seth Warner.

Hu·ber·tus·burg \hyü-'bərt-əs-,bərg, hü-'bert-əs-,bu̇(ə)rg\ *or* **Hu·berts·burg** \'hyü-bərts-,bərg, 'hü-bərts-,bu̇(ə)rg\. Castle near Oschatz, Leipzig dist., East Germany; here on Feb. 15, 1763 treaty was signed ending the Seven Years' War.

Hub·li–Dhar·war \,hu̇b-lē-där-'wär\. Municipality, NW Mysore, India, 290 m. SSE of Bombay; pop. (1970e) 222,-775; joint municipality formed 1961.

Huchow. See WU-HSING.

Hück·el·ho·ven–Rat·heim \'h(y)ü-kəl-,hō-vən-'rät-,hīm\. City, North Rhine-Westphalia, West Germany, 22 m. NNE of Aachen; pop. (1969e) 24,857; coal mines; shoes, cushions.

Huck·nall \'hək-nᵊl\. Urban district, Nottinghamshire, N cen. England, 5 m. NNW of Nottingham; pop. (1971p) 26,349; manufactures hosiery; coal mines; burial place of Lord Byron.

Hudaydah, Al–. See HODEIDA.

Hud·ders·field \'həd-ərz-,fēld\. County borough, West Riding, Yorkshire, N England, 24 m. NE of Manchester; pop. (1971p) 130,964; has woolen mills, engineering plants, ironworks.

Hud·son \'həd-sən\. **1** River, New York; 306 m. long; rises in Essex co., in Adirondack Mts., E New York; flows S into Upper New York Bay, at its S end forming boundary bet. New York and New Jersey; has New York City at its mouth; navigable to Troy. Explored 1609 by Henry Hudson.

2 County in New Jersey. See table at NEW JERSEY.

3 Industrial town, Middlesex co., NE Massachusetts, 15 m. NE of Worcester; pop. (1970c) 16,084; electronic equipment, aircraft parts, machine parts.

4 City, Lenawee co., S Michigan, 27 m. S of Jackson; pop. (1970c) 2618; flour mills.

5 Residential town, Hillsborough co., S New Hampshire, on Merrimack river opp. Nashua; pop. (1970c) 10,638; Saint Anthony Seminary (1956).

6 Industrial city, ⊗ of Columbia co., SE New York, on E bank of Hudson river 28 m. S of Albany; pop. (1970c) 8940· cement, machinery, woolen goods; canned vegetables. First permanently settled 1783; home port of schooners in whaling, seal, and West Indies ocean trade c. 1790.

7 Town, Caldwell co., W North Carolina, SE of Lenoir; pop. (1970c) 2820.

8 Village, Summit co., NE Ohio, 12 m. NNE of Akron; pop. (1970c) 3933; earth-moving vehicles; agriculture.

9 City, ⊗ of St. Croix co., W Wisconsin, on St. Croix river 15 m. N of its confluence with Mississippi river; pop. (1970c) 5049; creameries.

Hudson Bay. Inland sea in Keewatin dist., E Northwest Territories, Canada, bounded on SW by Manitoba, on S by Ontario, and on E by Quebec; 480,000 sq. m. (incl. James Bay, Hudson Strait, Ungava Bay); max. depth 2846 ft.; connected with Atlantic Ocean by Hudson Strait and with Foxe Basin to N by Foxe Channel; on S has large shallow extension, James Bay; contains islands, largest Southampton I. in N, all of which are administratively a part of Keewatin dist.; on its NW shore are two large inlets Wager Bay and Chesterfield Inlet. East coast navigated by Hudson 1610; explored bet. 1612 and 1632 by Button, Fox, and James; surrounding land, known as Prince Rupert's Land (*q.v.*), controlled by Hudson's Bay Company 1670–1869; definitely declared as within Keewatin by Order in Council 1918.

Hudson Falls. Village, ⊗ of Washington co., E New York, on Hudson river 40 m. N of Troy; pop. (1970c) 7917; paper; settled in 1760's; in line of Burgoyne's march 1777; burned by Sir Guy Carleton 1780.

Hudson Strait. Strait bet. S Baffin I. and N Quebec, NE Canada, connecting Atlantic Ocean with Hudson Bay; 50 to 100 m. wide, 450 m. long; max. depth 2886 ft. Entered by Frobisher 1576–78; navigated by Hudson 1607–11.

Hud·son·ville \'həd-sən-ˌvil\. City, Ottawa co., W Michigan, 15 m. SW of Grand Rapids; pop. (1970c) 3523; condensed milk.

Hud·speth \'həd-spəth\. County in Texas. See table at TEXAS.

Hue *or* **Hué** \h(y)ü-'ā, 'wā\. City, South Vietnam; pop. (1968e) 156,537; in flat alluvial region surrounded by hills; a native market town, trades esp. in rice; univ. (1957); former ✱ of Annam; captured by French 1883; palace and tombs of Annamese rulers destroyed 1968 during fighting in Vietnam War.

Hue·chu·cui·cui, Point \-ˌwā-chə-'kwē-kwē\. Cape on NW tip of Chiloé I. off SW coast of Chile.

Hue·co Mountains \ˌwā-(ˌ)kō-\. Range in S New Mexico and W Texas; highest point 6717 ft.

Hue·hue·te·nan·go \ˌwā-ˌwā-tə-'näŋ-(ˌ)gō\. 1 Department of W Guatemala. See table at GUATEMALA.

2 Town, its ✱; pop. (1964p) 25,279; mining center (lead, silver, copper).

Hue·ju·tla de Cres·po \wā-ˌhü-tlə-dā-'kres-(ˌ)pō\. City, Hidalgo state, Mexico, 85 m. NNE of Pachuca; munic. pop. (1970p) 45,771; livestock raising; wheat, coffee; founded by Augustinians c. 1544.

Huel·va \'wel-və\. 1 Province of SW Spain. See table at SPAIN.

2 Commune, its ✱, on Odiel river 10 m. from the Atlantic Ocean and 53 m. WSW of Seville; pop. (1970p) 96,689; fisheries, machine shops, shipyards; copper, manganese, and iron mining. Founded by Carthaginians; colonized by Romans; Roman aqueduct; monastery in which Columbus resided for a time; large statue of Columbus.

Hueneme. See PORT HUENEME.

Huér·cal–Ove·ra \'wer-käl-ō-'vär-ə\. Commune, Almería prov., SE Spain, 45 m. NE of Almería; pop. (1970p) 11,607; agriculture; lead, copper, silver mines.

Huer·fa·no \'ór-fə-ˌnō, 'wər-, 'wer-\. 1 River, S Colorado; ab. 90 m. long; flows E and NE from Sangre de Cristo Range into Arkansas river.

2 County in Colorado. See table at COLORADO.

Hues·ca \'wes-kə\. 1 Province of NE Spain. See table at SPAIN.

2 *or anc.* **Os·ca** \'äs-kə\. Commune, its ✱, 208 m. NE of Madrid; pop. (1970p) 33,185; episcopal see; manufactures agricultural machinery, cloth, pottery, bricks, leather; 15th cent. Gothic cathedral; 12th cent. Romanesque church; episcopal palace and old palace of kings of Aragon; formerly site of university of Saragossa. Important Roman town; site of school for native chiefs founded by Quintus Sertorius c. 76 B.C.; taken and fortified by Moors 8th cent.; recaptured 1096 by Pedro I of Aragon; made capital of kingdom of Aragon 1096–1118.

Hue·ta·mo \wā-'täm-(ˌ)ō\. Municipality, Michoacan state, Mexico, 70 m. S of Morelia; pop. (1970p) 35,414; corn, tropical fruits.

Hu·ey·town \'hyü-ē-ˌtau̇n\. City, Jefferson co., cen. Alabama, NW of Bessemer; pop. (1970c) 8673.

Hufaf, Al–. See HOFUF.

Hug·gins, Mount \-'həg-ənz\. Peak, Antarctica, 78°17'S, 162°28'E; 12,247 ft.

Hughes \'hyüz\. 1 River, W West Virginia; ab. 15 m. long; formed by confluence of forks on W boundary of Ritchie co., flows W into Little Kanawha river.

2 Name of counties in two states of the U.S. See tables at OKLAHOMA and SOUTH DAKOTA.

Hughesovka. See DONETSK.

Hugh Town \'hyü-\. See SCILLY ISLES 1.

Hugli. See HOOGHLY.

Hu·go \'hyü-(ˌ)gō\. 1 Town, ⊗ of Lincoln co., E Colorado; pop. (1970c) 759; stock and dairy farms.

2 City, ⊗ of Choctaw co., SE Oklahoma, 54 m. E of Durant; pop. (1970c) 6585; creosoting plant, lumber mills.

Hu·go·ton \'hyü-gō-tən\. City, ⊗ of Stevens co., SW Kansas; pop. (1970c) 2739; gas wells.

Hu·he·hot \'hü-hā-'hōt\ *also* **Hu·ho·hao·t'e** \'hü-hō-'hau̇-(ˌ)tā\ *or Mongol.* **Ku·ku·kho·to** \ˌkü-(ˌ)kü-'kōt-(ˌ)ō, -'hōt-\ *or formerly* **Kwei·sui** \'gwā-'swā\. Town, ✱ of Inner Mongolia, China; pop. (1970e) 700,000; cotton; sugar refineries; univ. (1957).

Hui–chou \'(h)wā-'jō, -'chau̇\ *or formerly* **Wai·yeung** \'wī-'yəŋ\. City, Kwangtung prov., SE China, on Tung river 70 m. E of Canton; pop. (1958c) 73,000.

Hui·la \'wē-(ˌ)lä\. 1 Volcano, W cen. Colombia, ab. 60 m. NE of Popayán; 18,865 ft.

2 Department of S cen. Colombia. See table at COLOMBIA.

Hui–li *or* **Hwei·li** \'(h)wā-'lē\. Town, Szechwan, S China.

Hui·man·gui·llo \ˌwē-mäŋ-'gē-(ˌ)yō\. Municipality, Tabasco state, Mexico, 35 m. SW of Villahermosa; pop. (1970p) 70,525; fishing; diversified agriculture.

Hui–tse *or* **Hwei·tseh** \'(h)wā-'dzə\ *or formerly* **Tung-chwan** \'du̇ŋ-chə-'wän\. City, NE Yunnan, S China, near the Yangtze.

Hui·tzu·co \wēt-'sü-(ˌ)kō\. Municipality, Guerrero state, Mexico, 20 m. SE of Iguala; pop. (1970p) 28,159; mercury, lead, silver; diversified agriculture.

Huix·qui·lu·can \ˌwēs-ki-'lü-(ˌ)kän\. Municipality, México state, Mexico, 14 m. W of Mexico City; pop. (1970p) 34,-933.

Huix·tla \'wēs-tlä\. Town, S Chiapas state, SE Mexico, near Guatemala border; munic. pop. (1970p) 25,884.

Hui·zen \'hȯiz-ᵊn, 'hīz-\. Commune, North Holland prov., W Netherlands, on the IJsselmeer ESE of Amsterdam; pop. (1970e) 20,554; fishing; radio station.

Hu·kawng *or* **Hu·kong** \'hü-'kȯŋ\. Valley, N Burma; lies in course of upper Chindwin river bet. Kumon Range and foothills of Patkai Range; 5586 sq. m.; amber mines. Scene of fierce fighting 1943–44 in World War II.

Hu–k'ou *or* **Hu·kow** \'hü-'kau̇, -'kō\ *or* **Ho·kou** \'hō-'kau̇\. Town, N Kiangsi prov., SE China, on the Yangtze ab. 140 m. SSE of Hankow.

Hu·kwang \'hü-'gwäŋ\. Former political division of SE China set up under Yüan dynasty (1260–1368) and comprising territory of three modern provinces of Hupeh, Hunan, and Kwangtung and Kwangsi Chuang Autonomous Region; ✻ Wu-ch'ang; first reduced under the Mings (1368–1644). See HUPEH.

Hu–lan \'hü-'län\. Town, S Heilungkiang prov., NE China, on a tributary of the Sungari ab. 20 m. N of Harbin.

Hull \'həl\. **1** Town, Plymouth co., SE Massachusetts, on point of peninsula in Massachusetts Bay 9 m. ESE of Boston; pop. (1970c) 9961; summer resort.

2 County, SW Quebec, Canada. See table at QUEBEC.

3 City, ⊗ of Hull co., Quebec, on Ottawa river opp. Ottawa, Ontario, Canada, and at mouth of Gatineau river; pop. (1966c) 60,176; produces lumber, pulp, paper, and cement; mica, feldspar, and iron mines in vicinity; Coll. Marguerite d'Youville (1945); founded 1800, incorporated 1875.

4 *or* **Kings·ton upon Hull** \'kiŋ(k)-stən-\. County borough, East Riding, Yorkshire, N England, on the Humber where it is joined by the Hull river 157 m. N of London; pop. (1971p) 285,472; is an important seaport, forming outlet for products of Yorkshire and Lancashire; manufactures chemicals, flour, engineering equipment, pharmaceutical products, paper, iron and steel; shipbuilding; fisheries; Univ. of Hull (1954). Known in 12th cent., received charter 1299; its grammar school founded 1486; repeatedly bombed by Germans in spring of 1941.

Hull Island. **1** One of the smaller islands of the Phoenix Is. (*q.v.*), in S part, cen. Pacific Ocean, 4°29'S and 172°10'W, SSW of Canton I.

2 Island, Tubuai Is., French Polynesia. See MARIA ISLAND 3.

Hultschin. See HLUČÍN.

Hulun. See HAILAR 2.

Hu–lun \hü-'lün\ *or formerly* **Da·lai** \'dä-ˌlī\. Lake, Inner Mongolia, China; 425 sq. m.; receives Kerulen river; source of Argun river, a headstream of the Amur; ab. 40 m. in circumference, alt. 4200 ft.

Hu–lun–pei–erh \'hü-'lün-'pā-'e(ə)r\ *or formerly* **Bar·ga** \'bär-gə\. Region, NE China, W of the Greater Khingan Range; traditionally inhabited by Mongols.

Hu–lu–tao \'hü-'lü-'dau̇\. Town and seaport on Gulf of Liaotung, Liaoning prov., NE China.

Hulwān. See HILWAN.

Hu·ma·cao \ˌüm-ə-'kau̇\. Town and municipality, E Puerto Rico; town near coast 28 m. SE of San Juan; pop. (1970p) 12,332 (town), 35,655 (munic.); in region producing sugar, coconuts, fruit, and tobacco.

Hu–ma–erh Ho \'hü-'mä-'e(ə)r-'hō\ *also* **Ku·ma·ra** \kü-'mär-ə\. River, N China; 230 m. long; flows E into Amur river N of the I-lo-hu-li Range.

Hu·mans·dorp \'hü-məns-ˌdȯ(ə)rp\. Town, near S coast of Cape Province, S Rep. of South Africa, W of Port Elizabeth.

Hum·ber \'həm-bər\. **1** River, W Newfoundland, Canada; 75 m. long; flows SW to the Bay of Islands at Corner Brook; one branch flows from Grand Lake.

2 *or anc.* **Abus** \'ā-bəs\. Estuary on E coast of England, formed by confluence of Ouse and Trent rivers 8 m. E of Goole; flows E and SE into North Sea; navigable for large vessels as far as Hull.

Hum·ble \'həm-bəl\. City, Harris co., SE Texas, 20 m. NNE of Houston; pop. (1970c) 3278; oil and gas wells.

Humbledon Hill *or* **Humbleton Hill.** See HOMILDON HILL.

Hum·boldt \'həm-ˌbōlt\. **1** River, N Nevada; 290 m. long; rises in Elko co., flows W, NW and SW into Humboldt Lake.

2 Counties in three states of the U.S. See tables at CALIFORNIA, IOWA, NEVADA.

3 City, Humboldt co., NW cen. Iowa, 16 m. N of Fort Dodge; pop. (1970c) 4665; concrete products, sporting goods.

4 City, Gibson co., NW Tennessee, 15 m. NNW of Jackson; pop. (1970c) 10,066; diversified farming; granite works.

5 Town, S cen. Saskatchewan, Canada, 68 m. E of Saskatoon; pop. (1971p) 3889; flour mill.

Humboldt, Mount. Peak on island of New Caledonia, SW Pacific Ocean, near SE coast; 5308 ft.

Humboldt Bay. **1** Inlet of Pacific Ocean on W cen. coast of Humboldt co., NW California.

2 Bay, Indonesia. See KAYO BAY.

Humboldt Current. See PERUVIAN CURRENT.

Humboldt Glacier. Glacier, NW Greenland; 71 m. long, 59 m. wide near its terminus.

Humboldt Lake *or* **Humboldt Sink.** Lake in S Pershing and N Churchill cos., W Nevada; ab. 20 m. long, from 8 to 10 m. wide at greatest extent; receives Humboldt river from the N; no outlet.

Humboldt Peak. Mountain, Custer co., S cen. Colorado; 14,064 ft.

Humboldt Range. Range in cen. Pershing co., NW Nevada; in Great Basin.

Humboldt Salt Marsh. Marsh in NE Churchill co., W Nevada.

Humboldt Sink. See HUMBOLDT LAKE.

Hum·mels·town \'həm-əlz-ˌtau̇n\. Borough, Dauphin co., SE cen. Pennsylvania, 9 m. E of Harrisburg; pop. (1970c) 4723.

Humphrey. See MANAHIKI.

Hum·phreys \'həm(p)-frēz\. Counties in two states of the U.S. See tables at MISSISSIPPI and TENNESSEE.

Humphreys, Mount. **1** Peak in Sierra Nevada, on boundary bet. Fresno and Inyo cos., SE cen. California; 13,986 ft.

2 Peak in Yellowstone National Park, NW Wyoming; 11,-050 ft.

Humphreys Peak. Highest point in Arizona, Coconino co.; 12,633 ft. See SAN FRANCISCO PEAKS.

Hu·mu·ya \ü-'mü-yə\. River of W Honduras; an important tributary of the Ulúa river.

Hun \'hu̇n\. **1** River, NE China, mostly in Liaoning prov.; ab. 240 m. long; flows SW to the Liao near its mouth.

2 River, N Shansi prov., NE China. See YUNG-TING.

Hú·na Bay \ˌhü-nə-\ *or Icel.* **Hú·na·flói** \'hü-nə-ˌflȯi\. Inlet of Arctic Ocean on NW cen. coast of Iceland.

Hu·nan \'hü-'nän\. Province, SE cen. China, bounded on N by Hupeh prov., on E by Kiangsi, on S by Kwangtung and Kwangsi Chuang, and on W by Kweichow and Szechwan; 81,274 sq. m.; pop. (1968e) 38,000,000; ✻ Ch'ang-sha; lies S of the Yangtze which forms part of its boundary on NE; in NE is Tung-t'ing Lake into which flow Yüan, Hsiang, and Tzu rivers; along its W and SW borders is the Nan Ling mountain range (highest ab. 5000 ft.); in E cen. part is Heng, one of the traditionally sacred mountains of China (2953 ft.). Products incl. rice, beans, wheat, cotton, tea, tobacco; important mineral reserves (coal, antimony, tungsten, manganese). Chief cities Ch'ang-sha, Chu-chou, Hsiang-t'an, Ch'ang-te. Western mountainous part still inhabited by members of non-Chinese aboriginal tribes; central region of early kingdoms of S China, but has taken only small part in its history; invaded 1852 by Taiping rebels who failed to take Ch'ang-sha; scene of much fighting 1944–45 in World War II. See HUPEH.

Hun–ch'un \'hu̇n-'chu̇n\. Town, Kirin prov., NE China, near Tumen river not far from its mouth and 40 m. E of Yen-chi; near point where Russian, North Korean, and Chinese boundaries meet, NW of Chang-ku Feng.

Hu·ne·doa·ra \ˌhü-nə-ˈdwär-ə\. **1** County of W Romania. See table at ROMANIA.

2 Town, Hunedoara co., Romania, ab. 10 m. S of Deva; pop. (1970e) 77,292; iron and steel.

Hun·ga·ry \ˈhəŋ-g(ə-)rē\ *or officially* **Hun·gar·i·an People's Republic** \həŋ-ˈger-ē-ən-\; *Hung.* **Ma·gyar Nép·köz·tár·sa·ság** \ˈmäj-ˌär-ˌnāp-kerz-ˌtär-sə-ˈsäj\ *or* **Ma·gyar·or·szág** \ˈmäj-ˌär-ˌór-ˌsäg\ *or Ger.* **Un·garn** \ˈůŋ-ˌgärn\. Republic, cen. Europe, bounded on N by Czechoslovakia, on NE by the U.S.S.R., on E and SE by Romania, on S and SW by Yugoslavia, and on W by Austria; 35,919 sq. m.; pop. (1970p) 10,315,597; ✱ Budapest. *Physical features:* Consists mainly of a plain, the Great Alföld, with fertile agricultural land; in N are S spurs of Carpathian Mts., highest point ab. 3300 ft.; bisected by the Danube flowing N to S; in W is Lake Balaton, largest lake in cen. Europe; in E is the Tisza, large tributary of the Danube, flowing across the Great Alföld N to S. *Chief products:* Wheat, corn, barley, sugar beets; livestock; viticulture; bauxite, coal, manganese, oil, natural gas; manufacturing: chemicals, textiles, electronic instruments, motor vehicles, diesel engines. *Chief cities:* Budapest, Miskolc, Debrecen, Pécs, Szeged, Győr, Kecskemét, Székesfehérvár. Divided into the following 19 counties and 5 cities (having county rank)—for pronunciation of their names, see their individual entries:

NAME	AREA (sq. m.)	POP. (1970p)	CAPITAL
Cities with county rank*			
Budapest	203	1,940,212	
Debrecen	172	155,122	
Miskolc	86	172,952	
Pécs	56	145,307	
Szeged	43	118,490	
Counties			
Bács-Kiskun	3,229	572,988	Kecskemét
Baranya	1,694	279,715	Pécs
Békés	2,189	447,196	Békéscsaba
Borsod-Abaúj-Zemplén	2,712	608,368	Miskolc
Csongrád	1,602	323,229	Szeged
Fejér	1,689	388,910	Székesfehérvár
Győr-Sopron	1,549	404,698	Győr
Hajdú-Bihar	2,226	375,371	Debrecen
Heves	1,405	348,395	Eger
Komárom	869	301,853	Tatabánya
Nógrád	982	241,122	Salgótarján
Pest	2,468	869,864	Budapest
Somogy	2,349	363,510	Kaposvár
Szabolcs-Szatmár	2,292	592,186	Nyíregyháza
Szolnok	2,151	449,827	Szolnok
Tolna	1,393	259,267	Szekszárd
Vas	1,290	280,842	Szombathely
Veszprém	2,003	408,989	Veszprém
Zala	1,268	267,184	Zalaegerszeg

*Area and population of these cities not included in county list.

History: Valleys of mid-Danube and of Tisza, formerly Slavic, occupied by Magyars c. 893–901 A.D.; Magyar westward advance defeated by German Emperor Otto I 955; c. 1000 became independent kingdom and completed conversion to Latin Christianity; acquired Dalmatia, Slavonia, and Croatia in 11th cent.; received grant of Golden Bull, comparable to Magna Carta, 1222; invaded by Mongols 1241; after Árpád dynasty (997–1301) died out, crown became elective; ruled by house of Anjou 1308–82 and by Sigismund (Emperor of Germany) 1387–1437; under Hunyadi (d. 1456) resisted first wave of Turkish invasion; in reign of Matthias Corvinus (1458–90), who conquered Silesia, Moravia, and lower Austria (including Vienna), Hungary leading power of cen. Europe; broken by Turks at battle of Mohács 1526; in 16th cent., Transylvania (*q.v.*) became independent, and most of Hungary was divided bet. Turks (see OTTOMAN EMPIRE) and Austria (*q.v.*); recaptured Buda from Turks 1686; came under Hapsburgs 1687; with Slavonia and Transylvania, all Hungary except Banat ceded to Austrian crown 1699; scene of revolt under Lajos Kossuth 1848, revolt suppressed 1849; part of "dual monarchy" of Austria-Hungary (*q.v.*) 1867–1918; proclaimed independent republic 1918, soviet government under Béla Kun 1919, and monarchy with vacant throne under Regent Horthy 1920; lost about two thirds of territory by Treaty of Trianon 1920, including Slovakia, Western Hungary, Fiume, Croatia, Slavonia, Banat, Transylvania; received Sopron (*q.v.*) by plebiscite 1921; as sympathetic partner of the Axis, acquired territory in S Slovakia and Ruthenia 1938, Carpatho-Ukraine 1939, and N half of Transylvania (see ROMANIA) 1940, but lost these regions when Axis powers were defeated 1945; established republic 1946; proclaimed itself a people's republic 1949; joined Warsaw Pact 1955; popular anti-Communist uprising suppressed by U.S.S.R. 1956; participated with other Warsaw Pact forces in invasion of Czechoslovakia 1968.

Hungersteppe. See BETPAK-DALA.

Hun·gry Horse Dam *and* **Hungry Horse Reservoir** \ˌhəŋ-grē-ˌhórs-\. See UNITED STATES, *Dams and Reservoirs.*

Hung–shui \ˈhůŋ-ˈshwā\. River, S China; ab. 700 m. long; rises in E Yunnan, flows S and E forming part of boundary bet. Kweichow and Kwangsi Chuang, then in E Kwangsi Chuang unites with Hsiang river at Kuei-p'ing to form Hsi river; navigable for small vessels only.

Hung–t'ou \ˈhůŋ-ˈtō\; *formerly* **Ko·to·sho** *or* **Ko·to Sho** \ˌkō-tō-ˈshō\. Island in Pacific Ocean, ab. 40 m. E of the S tip of Taiwan.

Hung–tse Hu \ˈhůŋ-ˈtsē-ˈhü, -ˈtsə-\. Lake in Anhwei and Kiangsu provs., E China; 502 sq. m.; traversed by the Yellow river.

Huns·rück \ˈhůn(t)s-ˌrůk\. Mountainous region, North Rhine-Westphalia, West Germany, bet. Moselle and Nahe rivers, extending SW from the Rhine to French border; highest peak 2677 ft. Occupied by Allies Mar. 1945.

Hunt \ˈhənt\. County in Texas. See table at TEXAS.

Hunt, Mount. Peak in S Grand Teton National Park, NW Wyoming; 10,775 ft.

Hun·te \ˈhůn-tə\. River, Lower Saxony, West Germany; 117 m. long; rises in hills E of Osnabrück and flows into Weser river near Bremen.

Hun·ter \ˈhənt-ər\. Navigable river, E New South Wales, SE Australia; 287 m. long; flows E to South Pacific Ocean at Newcastle.

Hunter, Cape. Cape on SW coast of Guadalcanal I., SE Solomon Is., W Pacific Ocean.

Hun·ter·don \ˈhənt-ər-dən\. County in New Jersey. See table at NEW JERSEY.

Hunter Island. 1 Island off NW Tasmania, Australia. See HUNTERS ISLANDS.

2 Island off W coast of British Columbia, Canada, opp. mouth of Dean Channel; 137 sq. m.

3 Tract of land surrounded by rivers in W Ontario, Canada, on Minnesota border E of Rainy Lake, in Quetico Provincial Park.

Hunter Mountain. Peak in Catskill Mts., Greene co., SE New York; 4040 ft.

Hunter Peak. Mountain, E boundary of Idaho co., N cen. Idaho; 8442 ft.

Hunt·er's Bay \ˌhənt-ərz-\. Inlet of Bay of Bengal on W coast of Burma, SE of Sittwe and E of Boronga Is.

Hunt·ers Creek Village \ˈhənt-ərz-\. City, Harris co., SE Texas, 9 m. W of Houston; pop. (1970c) 3959.

Hunter's Hill. Municipality, E New South Wales, SE Australia, NW suburb of Sydney, N of Parramatta river; pop. (1966c) 14,233.

Hunter's Island. Former island in Long Island Sound off E coast of the Bronx, New York City; attached to Bronx borough, made part of mainland by filled-in area.

Hunters Islands. Group of islands off Cape Grim, the NW point of Tasmania, Australia; comprises Hunter, Three Hummock, and Robbins Is. and many islets.

Hun·ting·burg \'hənt-iŋ-ˌbərg\. Industrial city, Dubois co., SW Indiana, 38 m. ENE of Evansville; pop. (1970c) 4794; clay deposits; pottery, wagons.

Hun·ting·don \'hənt-iŋ-dən\. 1 County in Pennsylvania. See table at PENNSYLVANIA.

2 Industrial borough, ⊗ of Huntingdon co., S cen. Pennsylvania, 22 m. E of Altoona; pop. (1970c) 6987; machines, boilers, sewer pipe, radiators, stationery; Juniata Coll. (1876); platted 1767.

3 Town, ⊗ of Carroll co., W Tennessee; pop. (1970c) 3661.

4 County, Quebec, Canada. See table at QUEBEC.

5 Town, ⊗ of Huntingdon co., S Quebec, Canada, 40 m. SW of Montreal; pop. (1971p) 3069.

Huntingdon and God·man·ches·ter \-'gäd-mən-ˌches-tər\. Municipal borough, ⊗ of Huntingdon and Peterborough co., E cen. England, on the Great Ouse 58 m. N of London; pop. (1971p) 16,540; breweries, engineering works, market gardens; birthplace of Oliver Cromwell.

Huntingdon and Pe·ter·bor·ough \-'pēt-ər-bər-ə, -bə-rə, -b(ə-)rə\. County, E cen. England; 486 sq. m.; pop. (1971p) 202,337; ⊗ Huntingdon and Godmanchester; rivers Nene and Ouse; wheat, barley, potatoes, fruit; towns incl. Huntingdon and Godmanchester, St. Ives, Ramsey, Old Fletton; formed 1965 by amalgamation of former counties of **Hunt·ing·don·shire** \-ˌshi(ə)r, -shər\ and the Soke of Peterborough.

Hun·ting·ton \'hənt-iŋ-tən\. 1 County in Indiana. See table at INDIANA.

2 City, ⊗ of Huntington co., NE Indiana, 22 m. SW of Fort Wayne; pop. (1970c) 16,217; grain elevators, limestone quarries; Huntington Coll. (1897).

3 Residential village (pop. [1970c] 12,130), with **Huntington Station** (pop. 28,817) included in **Huntington** town (pop. 200,172; settled 1653), Suffolk co., SE New York, on N shore of Long I.; Nathan Hale captured near here by British 1776.

4 City, Cabell and Wayne cos., ⊗ of Cabell co., W West Virginia, on Ohio river ab. 50 m. W of Charleston; pop. (1970c) 74,315; tobacco and agricultural (esp. apples) market; railroad terminus; coal mines, gas wells; manufactures airplane parts, chemicals, insulators, nickel and nickel alloys; Marshall Univ. (1837); founded 1871.

Huntington Bay. Village, Suffolk co., SE New York; pop. (1970c) 3258.

Huntington Beach. City, Orange co., SW California, on Pacific Ocean 14 m. SE of Long Beach; pop. (1970c) 115,960; oil-well equipment; oil wells and refineries; truck farming; Golden West Coll. (1966).

Huntington Lake. See SAN JOAQUIN 1.

Huntington Park. Industrial city, Los Angeles co., SW California, 4 m. S of Los Angeles; pop. (1970c) 33,744; chemicals, steel castings, truck bodies; incorporated as city 1906.

Huntington Station. See HUNTINGTON 3.

Huntington Woods. Residential city, Oakland co., SE Michigan, 11 m. from Detroit; pop. (1970c) 8536.

Hunt Mountain. 1 Peak in Blue Mts., Baker co., E Oregon; 8232 ft.

2 Peak, E Big Horn co., N Wyoming; 10,162 ft.

Hunts Peak \'hənts-\. 1 Mountain, Sangre de Cristo Mts., S Colorado, on boundary bet. Fremont and Saguache cos. S of Salida; 12,466 ft.

2 Mountain, Colorado. See OURAY PEAK.

Hunts·ville \'hən(t)s-ˌvil, -vəl\. 1 City, ⊗ of Madison co., N Alabama, 23 m. NE of Decatur; pop. (1970c) 137,802; sheet-metal goods, farm implements; natural-gas wells; Marshall Space Flight Center nearby (to SW). Oakwood Coll. (1896). Settled 1805 around Big Spring (now in center of city); chartered as town 1811, first settlement in Alabama to receive charter, and as city 1844; site of Alabama constitutional convention and temporary ❋ 1819; burned by Union troops 1862.

2 City, ⊗ of Madison co., NW Arkansas; pop. (1970c) 1287.

3 City, ⊗ of Randolph co., N cen. Missouri, 7 m. W of Moberly; pop. (1970c) 1442.

4 Town, ⊗ of Scott co., N Tennessee; pop. (1970c) 337.

5 City, ⊗ of Walker co., E Texas, 47 m. E of Bryan; pop. (1970c) 17,610; manufactures cottonseed oil, lumber, furniture; Sam Houston State Coll. (1879); home and grave of Gen. Sam Houston.

6 Town, Muskoka dist., SE Ontario, Canada, 20 m. N of Bracebridge; pop. (1971p) 9577; fishing and summer resort.

Hun·za \'hu̇n-zə\. 1 River, Jammu and Kashmir, in region controlled by Pakistan; ab. 120 m. long; flows W from E Karakoram Range, then S to join the Gilgit at Gilgit.

2 District, N Jammu and Kashmir, in region controlled by Pakistan; 8000 sq. m.; with Nagar constituted two small states that in frontier troubles with Russia (end of 19th cent.) were occupied by British (Hunza-Nagar expedition of 1891); inhabited by a Dard race.

Hunza Kun·ji \-'ku̇n-jē\. Mountain in the Karakoram Range, in region of Jammu and Kashmir under Pakistani control; 25,543 ft.

Hu·on \'hyü-ən\. 1 River, S Tasmania, Australia; 100 m. long; flows E and S through wide estuary to D'Entrecasteaux Channel; navigable to Huonville; its banks the home of the Huon pine (*Dacrydium franklinii*).

2 Municipality, SE Tasmania. See HUONVILLE.

Huon Gulf. Large inlet of Solomon Sea on E coast of New Guinea I., Papua New Guinea, S of Huon Penin.; site of Lae, Salamaua, and Morobe.

Huon Islands. Small group of barren islands in E Coral Sea, 170 m. NNW of New Caledonia; dependency of New Caledonia; guano deposits.

Huon Peninsula. Peninsula on E coast of New Guinea I., Papua New Guinea; bordered by Huon Gulf on S; scene of severe fighting, esp. around Finschhafen and Sattelberg, Sept.–Nov. 1943.

Hu·on·ville \'hyü-ən-ˌvil\. Town in Huon municipality, SE Tasmania, Australia, at head of navigation on Huon river 17 m. SW of Hobart; munic. pop. (1968e) 5200; fruit-growing center.

Hu·peh *or* **Hu·pei** \'hü-'pā, -'be\. Province, E cen. China, bounded on N by Honan, on E by Anhwei, on S by Kiangsi and Hunan, and on W by Szechwan and Shensi; 72,394 sq. m.; pop. (1968e) 32,000,000; ❋ Wu-ch'ang. In S crossed from W to E by the Yangtze; contains Yangtze Gorges (*q.v.*) in W; in center crossed by the Han flowing SE to the Yangtze. Hilly, with lakes and swamps in the two river valleys; bordered on N, W, and SW by mountain ranges 7000 to 10,000 ft. Products include rice, wheat, corn, tea, tobacco, coal, iron ore, gypsum. Chief cities Wu-ch'ang, Hankow, Han-yang, Huang-shih. In early times roughly coextensive with state of Chu; later formed N part of Hukwang which was divided by the Emperor K'ang-hsi (reigned 1662–1722) into the modern provinces of Hupeh and Hunan.

Hurd, Cape \-'hərd\. Cape, SE Ontario, Canada, at end of Bruce Penin., on S side of channel connecting Georgian Bay and Lake Huron.

Hur·ley \'hər-lē\. City, ⊗ of Iron co., N Wisconsin, on Michigan border 32 m. ESE of Ashland; pop. (1970c) 2418; formerly important logging town, locale for Edna Ferber's *Come and Get It;* ships iron ore.

Hur·ling·ham \'hər-liŋ-ˌham, ˌu̇r-liŋ-'än\. Town in Argentina, a suburb of Buenos Aires.

Hu·ron \'hyu̇r-ən, 'hyu̇(ə)r-ˌän\. 1 River, SE Michigan; ab. 97 m. long; flows from Oakland co. SW, then curves SE into Lake Erie at SE corner of Wayne co.

2 Name of counties in two states of the U.S. See tables at MICHIGAN and OHIO.

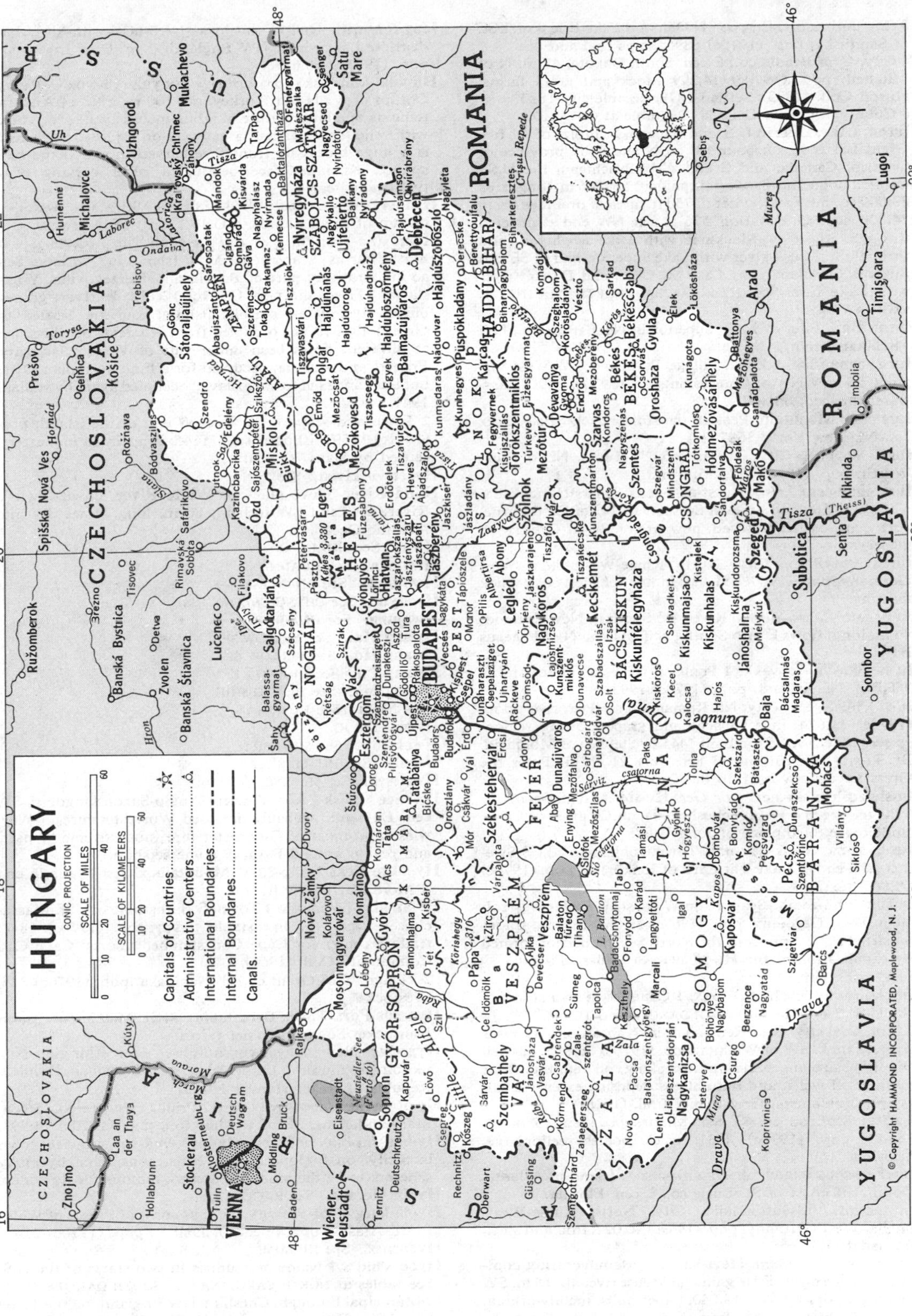
HUNGARY
CONIC PROJECTION
SCALE OF MILES
0 10 20 40 60
SCALE OF KILOMETERS
0 10 20 40 50
Capitals of Countries
Administrative Centers
International Boundaries
Internal Boundaries
Canals
CZECHOSLOVAKIA
ROMANIA
YUGOSLAVIA
AUSTRIA
U.S.S.R.
BUDAPEST
VIENNA
GYŐR-SOPRON
KOMÁROM
VESZPRÉM
FEJÉR
PEST
NÓGRÁD
HEVES
BORSOD-ABAÚJ-ZEMPLÉN
SZABOLCS-SZATMÁR
HAJDÚ-BIHAR
SZOLNOK
BÁCS-KISKUN
CSONGRÁD
BÉKÉS
TOLNA
BARANYA
SOMOGY
ZALA
VAS
Danube
Tisza
Drava
L. Balaton
Longitude East of Greenwich
© Copyright HAMMOND INCORPORATED, Maplewood, N. J.

3 City and resort, Erie co., N Ohio, on Lake Erie 8 m. ESE of Sandusky; pop. (1970c) 6896; ships coal and ore.

4 City, ⊗ of Beadle co., E cen. South Dakota, 47 m. N of Mitchell; pop. (1970c) 14,299; stock and grain farms; Huron Coll. (1883); settled 1879, became city 1883.

5 County, Ontario, Canada. See table at ONTARIO.

Huron, Lake. Lake in U.S. and Canada, 2d in size of the five Great Lakes (*q.v.*); bounded on N and E by province of Ontario, Canada, and S and W by Michigan, the U.S.-Canada boundary passing through it; ab. 206 m. long, area 23,000 sq. m.; greatest depth 750 ft.; area of drainage basin 74,800 sq. m.; elevation 576 ft.; at NW end connected through Straits of Mackinac with Lake Michigan, and through St. Marys river with Lake Superior, and at SE end through St. Clair river, Lake St. Clair, and Detroit river with Lake Erie. See GEORGIAN BAY; NORTH CHANNEL 1; SAGINAW BAY.

Huron Bay. Inlet of Lake Superior in NE Baraga co., NW Michigan Penin.

Hur·ri·cane \'hər-ə-ˌkān\. Village, Putnam co., W West Virginia, 25 m. WNW of Charleston; pop. (1970c) 3491; glassware; tobacco; oil wells.

Hurricane Mountain. Peak in the Adirondack Mts., Essex co., NE New York; 3687 ft.

Hurst \'hərst\. City, Tarrant co., N Texas, NE of Fort Worth; pop. (1970c) 27,215; fruit.

Hurst·mon·ceux *also* **Herst·mon·ceux** \ˌhərs(t)-mən-'sü\. Village, S England, in East Sussex 9 m. NE of Eastbourne; 15th cent. castle, restored, now site of Royal Greenwich Observatory.

Hürth \'h(y)ürt\. City, North Rhine-Westphalia, West Germany; pop. (1969e) 51,421; motor vehicles; coal; truck farming.

Hu·ru·nui \ˌhu̇r-ə-'nü-ē\. River, NE South I., New Zealand; 86 m. long; flows E into South Pacific Ocean N of Pegasus Bay.

Hú·sa·vík \'hü-sə-ˌvēk\. 1 Point on NE coast of Iceland.

2 Town, NE Iceland; pop. (1970c) 1993.

Hu·şi \'hüsh(-ē)\. City, NE Romania, near Prut river; pop. (1970e) 21,674; in a tobacco and grape-growing region; episcopal see; cathedral built 1441 by Stephen of Moldavia. By Treaty of Prut signed here July 21, 1711, Peter the Great gave Azov back to the Turks.

Hu·si·nec \'hüs-ə-ˌnets\ *or Ger.* **Hu·si·netz** \'hüz-ə-ˌnets\. Village, Czech S.R., Czechoslovakia, ab. 20 m. W of České Budějovice; birthplace of John Huss.

Hus·kvar·na \'hüsk-ˌvär-nə\. Town, Jönköping co., S Sweden, at S end of Lake Vättern E of Jönköping; pop. (1970e) 18,886; textiles.

Hu·sum \'hü-zəm\. Seaport on W coast of Schleswig-Holstein, West Germany; pop. (1969e) 25,069; fishing; trades in cattle; ab. 2½ m. from the North Sea, its harbor formed by canalization of the **Hu·su·mer Au** \ˌhü-zə-mə-'rau̇\.

Huszt. See KHUST.

Hutch·in·son \'həch-ə(n)-sən\. 1 Counties in two states of the U.S. See tables at SOUTH DAKOTA and TEXAS.

2 Industrial city, ⊗ of Reno co., cen. Kansas, on Arkansas river 42 m. WNW of Wichita; pop. (1970c) 36,885; oil-well supplies, airplane parts; meat-packing, oil refining, flour milling; oil wells, and natural gas deposits; extensive salt mines; Hutchinson Community Coll. (1928).

3 City, McLeod co., S cen. Minnesota, 48 m. S of St. Cloud; pop. (1970c) 8031; truck bodies, cellophane; dairying.

Hutch·in·sons Island \ˌhəch-ə(n)-sənz-\. Island in Atlantic Ocean, off coast of St. Lucie co., E cen. Florida.

Hüt·ten·tal \'h(y)üt-ən-ˌtäl\. City, North Rhine-Westphalia, West Germany; pop. (1969e) 40,027; iron and steel; formed 1966.

Huy \ü-'wē\ *or Flem.* **Hoei** \hü-'ē\. Manufacturing commune, Liège prov., E Belgium, on Meuse river ab. 15 m. SW of Liège; pop. (1969e) 13,040; paper mills; metalworking; ruins of abbey of Neufmoustier founded by Peter the Hermit.

Huy·ton–with–Ro·by \ˌhīt-ᵊn-wit͟h-'rō-bē, -with-\. Urban district, Lancashire, NW England, 7 m. E of Liverpool; pop. (1971p) 66,629.

Hü·yük \hü-'yu̇k\ *or formerly* **Eu·yuk** \ü-'yu̇k\. Ruins, Çorum prov., N cen. Turkey, ab. 100 m. ENE of Ankara; remains of a large Hittite building include walls decorated with relief carvings and a gateway on each side of which is a huge block, its front face carved in the shape of a sphinx, its inner face bearing a relief carving of a two-headed eagle.

Hva·ler \'väl-ər\ *also* **Whale Islands** \'hwā(ə)l-, 'wā(ə)l-\. Group of small islands in Oslo Fjord, SE Norway.

Hvar \(hə-)'vär, 'fär\ *or Ital.* **Le·si·na** \'lez-i-nə, 'lā-zi-\ *or anc.* **Phar·us** \'far-əs, 'fer-\. 1 Island in Adriatic Sea, administratively part of Bosnia and Herzegovina, Yugoslavia; 111 sq. m.; pop. (1961c) 12,132; ✱ Hvar; grapes, olives, figs, dates; marble; fishing; tourism. Settled by Greeks ab. 390 B.C.; occupied from 7th cent. by Slavs; has at different times been under rule of Venice, Hungary, France, and Austria; occupied for a time by Italians 1918 but later annexed to Yugoslavia; occupied again by Italians 1941.

2 Town and seaport, its ✱, at W end of the island; pop. (1961c) 1959; bishopric since 1145; Franciscan monastery; settled by Slavs 7th cent.

Hveen *or* **Hven.** See VEN.

Hvítá River \'hwē-ˌtau̇-\ *or* **White River** \'hwīt-, 'wīt-\. River, cen. and SW Iceland; 80 m. long; flows SW into Atlantic Ocean.

Hwai. See HUAI.

Hwainan. See HUAI-NAN.

Hwaining. See AN-CH'ING.

Hwaiyin. See CH'ING-CHIANG.

Hwajung. See HUA-JUNG.

Hwang Hai. See YELLOW SEA.

Hwang Ho. See YELLOW 4.

Hwang Pu. See HUANG-P'U.

Hwangshih. See HUANG-SHIH.

Hwa Shan. See HUA SHAN.

Hwei. See JO.

Hweichow. See SHE-HSIEN.

Hweili. See HUI-LI.

Hweitseh. See HUI-TSE.

Hwic·ce \'hwik-(ˌ)kā\. Ancient Anglo-Saxon kingdom, SW cen. England; probably included Worcestershire, S Warwickshire, most of Gloucestershire (not extreme W part) and region around Bath, N Somersetshire.

Hy·a·lite Peak \ˌhī-ə-ˌlīt-\. Mountain, S cen. Gallatin co., S Montana; 10,299 ft.

Hy·an·nis \hī-'an-əs\. 1 Town, S Barnstable co., SE Massachusetts; part of Barnstable town; pop. (1970c) 6847; trading center for Cape Cod summer resorts; Cape Cod Community Coll. (1961).

2 Village, ⊗ of Grant co., W Nebraska; pop. (1970c) 345; livestock.

Hyannis Port. Town, Barnstable co., SE Massachusetts, on Nantucket Sound; summer resort.

Hyar·gas Nuur \ˌhyär-gəs-'nu̇(ə)r\ *also* **Khir·gis Nur** \ˌki(ə)r-gis-'nu̇(ə)r\. Large lake, W Mongolian People's Republic, NNE of Har Us Nuur.

Hy·atts·ville \'hī-əts-ˌvil\. City, Prince Georges co., S cen. Maryland, 7 m. NE of Washington; pop. (1970c) 14,998.

Hy·bla \'hī-blə\ *or* **Hybla Ma·jor** \-'mā-jər\. Ancient town in Sicily, on S slope of Mt. Etna; considered by many scholars to be the modern Paternò; famous for its honey.

Hybla Heraea. See RAGUSA 2.

Hy·da·burg \'hīd-ə-ˌbərg\. City, W coast of Prince of Wales I., SE Alaska, opp. N end of Dall I.; pop. (1970c) 214.

Hydaspes. See JHELUM.

Hyde \'hīd\. 1 Name of counties in two states of the U.S. See tables at NORTH CAROLINA and SOUTH DAKOTA.

2 Municipal borough, Cheshire, NW England, on the Tame 9 m. ESE of Manchester; pop. (1971p) 37,075; engineering; textile mills.

Hy·den \'hīd-ᵊn\. City, ⊗ of Leslie co., SE Kentucky; pop. (1970c) 482.

Hyde Park. 1 Former town, Norfolk co., E Massachusetts; since 1912 part of Boston.
2 Residential village, Dutchess co., SE New York, on E bank of Hudson river ab. 6 m. N of Poughkeepsie; pop. (1970c) 2805; settled by Dutch 1741; Franklin D. Roosevelt Library (opened 1941); birthplace of Franklin Delano Roosevelt, 32d president of the U.S.
3 Village, ⊗ of Lamoille co., N Vermont; pop. (1970c) 418.
4 Park in W cen. London, England; area ab. 364 acres; recreation center; known esp. as place for open-air meetings.

Hy·der·a·bad *or* **Hai·dar·a·bad** \'hīd-(ə-)rə-ˌbad, -ˌbäd\. 1 *or formerly often called* **Ni·zam's Dominions** \ni-ˌzämz-, 'nī-ˌzamz-, nī-ˌzamz-\. Former Indian state, its territory now divided among the states Andhra Pradesh, Mysore, and Maharashtra, S cen. India; bounded on N and NE by Berar, on S and SE by Tamil Nadu, and on W by Maharashtra; mountainous in some parts, has many fertile plains; chief rivers Godavari, Wardha, Penganga, Krishna, and Tungabhadra.
History: In ancient kingdom of Golconda (*q.v.*); on overthrow of Golconda by Aurangzeb 1687, became part of Mogul Empire; ruled since 1713 by nizams, beginning with Asaf Jah, Mogul governor of the Deccan, who founded independent kingdom in 1724; after 1748 scene of rivalry over succession in which British and French supported different candidates; ceded to British Northern Circars 1766 and, in 1853, the "Assigned Districts" which later became Berar (*q.v.*). Refused to become part of India 1947 but yielded under threat of force 1948; reorganized and divided among Andhra Pradesh, Mysore, and Maharashtra 1956.
2 Walled city, ✱ of Andhra Pradesh, India, on Musi river 310 m. NNW of Madras; pop. (1970e), incl. cantonment, 1,316,802; pottery works, paper factories, and carpet and textile mills; sugar refining; nizam's palace, the Char Minar (or Four Minarets), and several mosques and tombs; univ. (1918); was ✱ of Hyderabad state. At adjacent Secunderabad is a large military cantonment. Founded 1589 by ruler of Golconda; suffered a disastrous flood 1908 and serious depopulating pestilences and influenza epidemics since 1911.
3 City, Sind, Pakistan, on E bank of Indus river 120 m. N of its mouths and 90 m. ENE of Karachi; pop. (1969e), with cantonment 698,100; rail center; noted for handicrafts: silk, gold, and silver embroidery, lacquer- and enamelware, and pottery; univ. (1947). In its fort are mosques, palaces, and the arsenal. Founded 1768 by Ghulam Shah Kalhora; capital of Sind till 1843 when it surrendered to the British.

Hy·dra \'hī-drə\ *or Gk.* **Idhra** \'ē-t͟hrä\ *or anc.* **Hyd·rea** \'hid-rē-ə\. 1 Greek island in S Aegean Sea 4 m. off E coast of Peloponnesus; ab. 11 m. long, area 20 sq. m.; pop. (1961c) 2766; sponge fishing; refuge in 16th and 17th cents. of persecuted peoples from the mainland, who developed shipbuilding and commerce; fleets and patriotism of Hydriotes in War of Independence (1812–29) of great value to Greek cause.
2 Its chief town, port on N coast of island; pop. (1961c) 2546.

Hydraotes. See RAVI.

Hydruntum. See OTRANTO.

Hy·ères \'ye(ə)r\. Commune, Var dept., SE France, near the Mediterranean 32 m. S of Draguignan; pop. (1968c) 34,875; winter resort; market gardens; founded 10th cent.

Hyères Islands *or Fr.* **Îles d'Hy·ères** \ēl-dye(ə)r\. French island group in the Mediterranean Sea off SE coast of France, SE of Toulon; group includes Port Cros, Île du Levant, and the fortified island of Porquerolles. Occupied by Allies Aug. 14–15, 1944.

Hye·san \(h)yā-'sän\. Town, ✱ of Yanggang prov., North Korea.

Hyko Range. See HIKO RANGE.

Hy·met·tus \hī-'met-əs\. Mountain ridge just E and SE of Athens, Greece; highest point 3366 ft.; noted for a marble used in building ancient Athens.

Hynd·man Peak \ˌhīn(d)-mən-\. Mountain, S Custer co., cen. Idaho; 12,078 ft.

Hyō·go *or* **Hio·go** \'hyō-(ˌ)gō\. 1 Prefecture, Honshū, Japan; 3221 sq. m.; pop. (1970c) 4,667,928; ✱ Kōbe; textiles; food processing, lumbering.
2 City, Japan. See KŌBE.

Hypanis. 1 River, Russian S.F.S.R., U.S.S.R. See KUBAN.
2 River, Ukrainian S.S.R., U.S.S.R. See BUG 2.

Hyphasis. See BEAS.

Hyrcania. See GORGĀN 1.

Hyrcanum Mare. See CASPIAN SEA.

Hy·rum \'hī-rəm\. City, Cache co., N Utah, 8 m. S of Logan; pop. (1970c) 2340; farming.

Hy·sham \'hī-shəm\. Town, ⊗ of Treasure co., SE cen. Montana; pop. (1970c) 373.

Hythe \hīt͟h\. Municipal borough, Kent, SE England, on Strait of Dover 10 m. WSW of Dover; pop. (1971p) 11,949; one of the Cinque Ports; market town for agricultural region; summer resort.

Hy·vin·kää \'hü-viŋ-ˌkä\ *or Swed.* **Hy·vin·ge** \'hü-viŋ-ə\. Town, Uusimaa prov., S Finland, ab. 30 m. N of Helsinki; pop. (1967e) 25,281; textiles, rubber goods.

Iadera. See ZADAR.

Ia·lo·mi·ţa *also* **Ja·lo·mi·tsa** \ˌyäl-ə-ˈmēt-sə\. 1 *or* **Ia·lo·mi·tsa** \ˌyäl-ə-ˈmēt-sə\. River, SE Romania; 200 m. long; rises in the Transylvanian Alps NW of Ploieşti and flows S and E into Danube river.
2 County of SE Romania. See table at ROMANIA.

Ialpug. See YALPUKH.

Ial·y·sus \ī-ˈal-ə-səs\. Ancient city, N Rhodes, SE Aegean Sea; ruins just SW of town of Rhodes; a city of the Pentapolis of Asia Minor.

Iao Valley \ē-ˌaů-\ *or* **Wai·lu·ku Valley** \wī-ˌlü-kü-\. Canyon on slope of Mt. Puu Kukui, W Maui I., Hawaii; ab. 5 m. long, 4000 ft. deep.

Ia·pyg·ia \ˌī-ə-ˈpij-ē-ə\. Ancient Greek name of SE Italy; the S part of the Salentina Peninsula.

Ia·şi \ˈyäsh(-ē)\ *or Ger.* **Jas·sy** *also* **Yas·sy** \ˈyäs-ē\. 1 County of NE Romania. See table at ROMANIA.
2 Commercial city, its ⊗, on a tributary of Prut river; pop. (1970e) 183,776; chemicals, pharmaceutical products, textiles, machinery, timber.
History: First mentioned 1408; capital of Romania before 1861 when government was moved to Bucharest; suffered in various wars; burned by Tatars 1513, by Turks 1538, and by Russians 1686; Treaty of Jassy ending Catherine the Great's second war with Turkey signed here Jan. 9, 1792; temporary capital of Romania in World War I; taken by U.S.S.R. Aug. 25, 1944 in World War II.

Iaxartes. See JAXARTES.

Iba \ˈē-bə\. 1 Mountain, E Zambales prov., Luzon, Phil.; 5265 ft.
2 Municipality, its ✱, on coast 85 m. NW of Manila; pop. (1969e) 19,900; good anchorage at mouth of river.

Iba·dan \ē-ˈbäd-ᵊn\. City, ✱ of Western State, Nigeria, 89 m. NNE of Lagos; pop. (1971e) 758,332; cigarettes, furniture, plastics; univ. (1948, univ. status 1962).

Iba·gué \ˌē-bə-ˈgā\. City, ✱ of Tolima dept., W cen. Colombia; pop. (1968e) 172,091; on high plain (alt. 4300 ft.); univ. (1954); founded 1550.

Iba·jay \ˌē-bə-ˈhī\. Municipality, Panay, Phil., on coast 43 m. WNW of Roxas; pop. (1969e) 34,200.

Ibañeta, Puerto. See RONCESVALLES.

Ibar \ˈē-ˌbär\. River, Serbia, cen. Yugoslavia; ab. 150 m. long; rises in North Albanian Alps in Montenegro and flows N to the Western Morava near Kraljevo.

Iba·ra·ki \ˌē-bə-ˈräk-e, i-ˈbär-ə-kē\. 1 Prefecture, Honshū, Japan; 2351 sq. m.; pop. (1970c) 2,143,551; ✱ Mito; tobacco, cereals, coal, copper.
2 Town, Ōsaka prefecture, Honshū, Japan; pop. (1970c) 163,903.

Iba·rra \i-ˈbär-ə\ *also* **San Mi·guel de Ibarra** \ˌsän-mi-ˈgel-dā-\. Town, ✱ of Imbabura prov., N Ecuador, 55 m. NNE of Quito; pop. (1970e) 37,100; alt. 7340 ft.; founded by Alvaro de Ibarra, president of Quito, 1597; has suffered from volcanic eruptions of Imbabura and from earthquakes; nearby Huayna Capac, father of Atahualpa, won two decisive victories, adding to his realm a large part of Ecuador.

Ib·ben·bür·en \ˈib-ən-ˌbyür-ən\. City, North Rhine-Westphalia, West Germany, 21 m. N of Münster; pop. (1968e) 17,500; chemicals, textiles; received charter 1721.

Ibe·ria \ī-ˈbir-ē-ə\. 1 Parish in Louisiana. See table at LOUISIANA.
2 Ancient Hispania; the Iberian Penin.
3 Ancient region S of the Caucasus Mts., approx. coextensive with modern Georgian S.S.R. (*q.v.*), U.S.S.R.; Iberians, as allies of Mithridates VI, were defeated by Pompey.

Ibe·ri·an Peninsula \ī-ˈbir-ē-ən-\. Peninsula, SW Europe, occupied by Spain and Portugal; in Roman times, Hispania; so-called from name applied by early Greeks to people dwelling by the river Iberus (*mod.* Ebro) in Spain.

Iberus. See EBRO.

Iber·ville. 1 \ˈī-bər-ˌvil\. Parish in Louisiana. See table at LOUISIANA.
2 \ˈē-bər-ˌvil\. County, Quebec, Canada. See table at QUEBEC.
3 \ˈē-bər-ˌvil\. Town, ⊗ of Iberville co., Quebec, Canada, on Richelieu river 23 m. SE of Montreal; pop. (1971p) 9300; agricultural implements, artificial silks, carriages.

Ibi·cuí *or* **Ibi·cu·hy** \ˌē-bi-ˈkwē\. 1 River, Rio Grande do Sul state, S Brazil; ab. 300 m. long; flows W to Uruguay river on Argentina boundary.
2 Town, Paraguay. See YBYCUÍ.

Ibi·za *also* **Ivi·za** \ē-ˈvē-zə\ *or anc.* **Eb·u·sus** \ˈeb-yə-səs\. 1 Third largest island of Balearic group, Baleares prov., Spain; in W Mediterranean SW of Majorca and ab. 80 m. E of coast of Spain; 209 sq. m.; pop. (1970p) 45,075; agricultural products; tourism. See BALEARIC ISLANDS.
2 Seaport, its ✱, 80 m. SW of Palma; munic. pop. (1970p) 16,943; exports figs, raisins, pine lumber, salt.

Ibo \ˈē-(ˌ)bō, -(ˌ)bü\. 1 Small Portuguese island off NE coast of Mozambique.
2 Site, on island, of former capital of Cabo Delgado dist., N Mozambique.

Iboun·dji, Mount \-ē-ˈbün-jē\. Mountain, S cen. Gabon; 5167 ft.; highest peak in Gabon.

Ib·ra \ˈib-rə\. Inland town, Oman, SE Arabian Penin., WNW of Sur.

Ibu·su·ki \i-ˈbü-sə-kē\. Town, Kagoshima prefecture, S Kyūshū I., Japan, on W side of entrance to Kagoshima Bay; pop. (1970c) 55,944.

Ibycuí. See YBYCUI.

Ica \ˈē-kə, -(ˌ)kä\. 1 River, Ica dept., SW Peru; ab. 100 m. long; flows SW into Pacific Ocean.
2 Department of SW Peru. See table at PERU.
3 City, its ✱, on Ica river, 170 m. SE of Lima; pop. (1969e) 69,400; cotton, sheep; vineyards; univ. (1961); original city founded 1563, twice destroyed by earthquakes.

Içá \ē-ˈsä\. Name of Putumayo river in Brazil.

Ica·cos Point \i-ˌkäk-əs-\. Tip of peninsula at SW corner of island of Trinidad.

Iça·na \i-ˈsan-ə\ *or in Colombia* **Isa·na** \i-ˈsän-ə\. River, Colombia and Brazil; rises in E Colombia and flows E and SE into the Rio Negro, NW Brazil, above confluence of the Uaupés with the Rio Negro.

Icar·ia \ī-ˈker-ē-ə, -ˈkar-; ik-ˈer-, -ˈar-\. 1 Island, Greece. See IKARIA.
2 Ancient town, Attica, Greece; ruins on N slope of Mt. Pendelikon.

Icar·i·an Sea \ī-ˌker-ē-ən-, -ˌkar-; ik-ˌer-, -ˌar-\ *or Lat.* **Icar·i·um Ma·re** \-ē-əm-ˈmā-(ˌ)rē, -ˈmär-(ˌ)ē\. The part of the Aegean Sea bet. the islands of Patmos and Leros and the coast of Asia Minor. According to legend Icarus fell into the sea here.

Ice Bay. See AMUNDSEN BAY.

Ice Fjord \ˈīs-\. Inlet of Arctic Ocean, W coast of Spitsbergen, Norway; ab. 70 m. long. See ADVENT BAY.

İçel \ē-ˈchel\ *also* **Ichi·li** \ˌē-chi-ˈlē\. 1 Province of S Turkey, Asia. See table at TURKEY.
2 City, Turkey. See MERSIN.

Ice·land \ˈī-slənd, ˈī-ˌsland\ *or Dan.* **Is·land** \ˈē-ˌslän\ *or Icelandic* **Ís·land** \ˈē-ˌslänt\. Island bet. North Atlantic and Arctic oceans, 155 m. SE of Greenland and 570 m. W of Norway; separated from Greenland by Denmark Strait and from Norway by Norwegian Sea; 39,702 sq. m.; pop. (1971e) 210,000; ✱ Reykjavík. *Physical features:* Roughly oval with coastline ab. 3730 m. long; max. E-W length ab. 290 m.; indented by many long fjords; Faxa Bay on W coast and Húna Bay and Breidha Fjord on either side of base of large peninsula (average alt. 2000 ft.) on NW; mostly tableland, esp. in SE where great snowfield of Vatnajökull (average elevation 2000–3000 ft.) covers 3247 sq.

m.; highest point Öraefajökull 6952 ft.; more than 100 volcanoes, which have created great lava fields, most noted Mt. Hekla 4747 ft.; 120 glaciers; lowland forms ab. ¼ of area and is only partly habitable and only ab. ⅐ of land is productive; has suffered from destructive earthquakes; many small streams, lakes, and hot springs. *Chief products:* Fishing and fish processing constitute the major industry; livestock raising; potatoes, turnips; greenhouse cultivation; manufacturing: clothing, shoes, chemicals, cement, paints. *Chief towns:* Reykjavík, Kópavogur, Akureyri, Hafnarfjördhur, Keflavík, Vestmannaeyjar.

History: Settled by Norwegians in second half of 9th cent. A.D. (date usually given as 874); founded the Althing (national assembly) 930; adopted Christianity 1000; united with Norway 1262, with Denmark 1380; by Act of Union 1918, became independent kingdom in personal union with Denmark; placed under British and American military occupation in World War II; British forces landed May 10, 1940, American marines July 7, 1941, both with permission; American North Atlantic naval base for rest of war. Proclaimed intention not to renew 1918 Act of Union with Denmark, the action being voted in plebiscite May 24, 1944; independent republic proclaimed June 17, 1944; became a member of NATO 1949; signed defense treaty with U.S. 1951; extended its fishing limits from 4 to 12 miles (1958), thereby precipitating serious dispute with Great Britain (settled 1961); joined European Free Trade Association 1970.

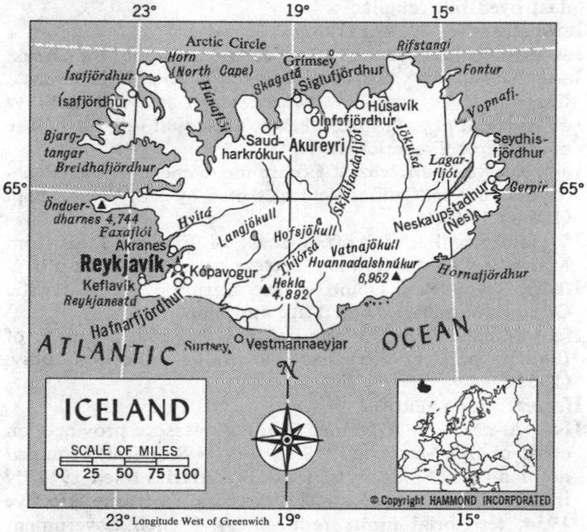

Ichal·ka·ran·ji \ˌi-chəl-ˈkər-ən-jē\. Town, Maharashtra, India; pop. (1961c) 50,978.

I–ch'ang \ˈē-ˈchäŋ\. Walled city, S Hupeh prov., E cen. China, at head of navigation of the Yangtze 1000 m. from the East China Sea and 170 m. W of Hankow (387 m. by river); pop. (1970e) 160,000; food processing; made treaty port by Chefoo Convention 1876; transshipment point for goods to and from Szechwan through Yangtze Gorges (*q.v.*).

Ichi·ha·ra \i-ˈchē-ˌhär-ə\. City, Chiba prefecture, Honshū, Japan; pop. (1970c) 156,016.

Ichi·ka·wa \i-ˈchē-ˌkä-wə\. City, Chiba prefecture, Honshū, Japan; pop. (1970c) 261,055.

Ichili. See İÇEL.

Ichi·no·mi·ya \ˌē-chi-ˈnō-mē-ˌ(y)ä\. Town, Aichi prefecture, SE Honshū, Japan, ab. 11 m. NNW of Nagoya; pop. (1970c) 219,274; textiles; 7th cent. Shinto shrine.

Ichi·no·se·ki \ˌē-chi-ˈnō-sā-kē\. City, Iwate prefecture, Honshū, Japan, 50 m. N of Sendai; pop. (1970c) 55,830.

Ichin·ska·ya Sop·ka \i-ˈchēn-skə-yə-ˈsȯp-kə, -ˈchin-\. Volcano (*sopka*) in cen. part of Central Range, Kamchatka Penin., Russian S.F.S.R., U.S.S.R.; 11,880 ft.

Ichow. See LIN-I.

I–ch'un \ˈē-ˈchu̇n\. Town, Heilungkiang prov., NE China, ab. 90 m. NW of Chia-mu-ssu; pop. (1970e) 200,000.

Ick·nield Street \ˌik-nē(ə)l(d)-\. Ancient highway of S cen. England, probably a Roman road; extended W from near Bury St. Edmunds through Wantage to Cirencester and Gloucester.

Icod de los Vi·nos \ē-ˌkōth-del-əs-ˈvē-nəs\ *or* **Icod.** Commune on NW Tenerife I., W Canary Is., in Santa Cruz de Tenerife prov., Spain, 28 m. WSW of Santa Cruz de Tenerife; pop. (1970p) 18,883; agricultural products; silk.

Iconium. 1 City, Turkey. See KONYA 2.

2 Seljuk sultanate, Asia Minor. See RUM.

Icosium. See ALGIERS 2.

Iculisma. See ANGOULÊME.

Icu·tú, Mount \-ˌē-kə-ˈtü\. Peak, cen. Venezuela; ab. 11,000 ft.

Icy Bay \ˌī-sē-\. Inlet of Gulf of Alaska, SE Alaska, W of Yakutat Bay.

Icy Cape. Cape on NW coast of Alaska, ab. 161°31′W, 70°15′N.

Icy Strait. Strait, SE Alaska; joins Chatham Strait and Glacier Bay.

Ida \ˈīd-ə\. 1 County in Iowa. See table at IOWA.

2 *or mod.* **Kaz·da·ğı** \ˌkäz-dä-ˈ(g)ē\. Famous mountain in NW Asia Minor, SE of site of ancient Troy and along N shore of Gulf of Adramyttium; actually a range (**Ida Mountains**), highest point 5797 ft.; in Homeric legend an abode of the gods.

3 *or* **Psi·lo·ri·ti** \ˌ(p)sē-lə-ˈrēt-ē\ *or Gk.* **Ídhi** \ˈē-t͟hē\. Highest mountain in Crete, Greece, in cen. part; 8058 ft.; in early times closely connected with worship of Zeus.

Ida·bel \ˈīd-ə-ˌbel\. City, ⊗ of McCurtain co., SE corner of Oklahoma; pop. (1970c) 5946; farming, lumbering.

Ida Grove \ˌīd-ə-\. City, ⊗ of Ida co., W Iowa, 28 m. S of Cherokee; pop. (1970c) 2261; corn; livestock.

Ida·ho \ˈīd-ə-ˌhō\. 1 A northwest state of U.S.A., bounded on N by British Columbia in Canada, on E by Montana and Wyoming, on S by Utah and Nevada, on W by Oregon and Washington; 13th state in area, 83,557 sq. m. (land area 82,677 sq. m.); 42d state in population, (1970c) 713,008; ✱ Boise; 43d state admitted to Union (1890).

Nicknames: Gem State; Gem of the Mountains. *State flower:* Syringa. *Motto:* Esto Perpetua (May She Endure Forever). *Rivers:* Snake, flowing from SE region W to Oregon border, then N forming boundary bet. Idaho and Oregon; Salmon, rising in cen. region, flowing N and then W across the state and emptying into the Snake. *Lakes:* Pend Oreille and Coeur d'Alene in N, American Falls Reservoir in SE. *Highest peak:* Borah Peak, 12,662 ft., in Custer co. *Chief products:* Potatoes, sugar beets, barley; livestock; silver, phosphates, lead; manufacturing: wood products, chemicals. *Chief cities:* Boise, Pocatello, Idaho Falls, Lewiston, Twin Falls, Nampa. See *Table of States* at UNITED STATES. Divided into the following 44 counties (for pronunciation of their names, see their individual entries):

NAME	LOCATION	AREA[1] (sq. m.)	POP. (1970c)	CO. SEAT
Ada	SW	1,043	112,230	Boise
Adams	W	1,371	2,877	Council
Bannock	SE	1,122	52,200	Pocatello
Bear Lake	SE corner	984	5,801	Paris
Benewah	NW	788	6,230	St. Maries
Bingham	SE	2,084	29,167	Blackfoot
Blaine	S cen.	2,648	5,749	Hailey
Boise	W cen.	1,910	1,763	Idaho City
Bonner	N	1,733	15,560	Sandpoint
Bonneville	SE	1,836	52,457	Idaho Falls
Boundary[2]	N	1,275	5,484	Bonners Ferry
Butte	SE cen.	2,239	2,925	Arco

ə abut; ᵊ kitten, Fr. table; ər further; a back; ā bake; ä cot, cart; à Fr. bac; au̇ out; ch chin; e less; ē easy; g gift
i trip; ī life; j joke; k̲ Ger. ich, Buch; ⁿ Fr. vin; ŋ sing; ō flow; ȯ flaw; œ Fr. bœuf; œ̄ Fr. feu; ȯi coin; th thin
t͟h this; ü loot; u̇ foot; ue Ger. füllen; ǖ Fr. rue; y yet; ʸ Fr. digne \dēnʸ\, nuit \nwʸē\; yü few; yu̇ furious; zh vision

NAME	LOCATION	AREA[1] (sq. m.)	POP. (1970c)	CO. SEAT
Camas	S cen.	1,054	728	Fairfield
Canyon	SW	578	61,288	Caldwell
Caribou	SE	1,746	6,534	Soda Springs
Cassia	S	2,544	17,017	Burley
Clark	E	1,751	741	Dubois
Clearwater	NE	2,521	10,871	Orofino
Custer	cen.	4,929	2,967	Challis
Elmore	SW cen.	3,048	17,479	Mountain Home
Franklin	SE	664	7,373	Preston
Fremont	E	1,864	8,710	St. Anthony
Gem	SW	555	9,387	Emmett
Gooding	S	720	8,645	Gooding
Idaho	N cen.	8,516	12,891	Grangeville
Jefferson	E	1,096	11,619	Rigby
Jerome	S	595	10,253	Jerome
Kootenai	N	1,249	35,332	Coeur d'Alene
Latah	NW	1,090	24,891	Moscow
Lemhi	E cen.	4,580	5,566	Salmon
Lewis	W	476	3,867	Nezperce
Lincoln	S	1,203	3,057	Shoshone
Madison	E	473	13,452	Rexburg
Minidoka	S	750	15,731	Rupert
Nez Perce	W	844	30,376	Lewiston
Oneida	S	1,191	2,864	Malad City
Owyhee	SW corner	7,641	6,422	Murphy
Payette	SW	402	12,401	Payette
Power	SE	1,413	4,864	American Falls
Shoshone	NE	2,609	19,718	Wallace
Teton	E	457	2,351	Driggs
Twin Falls	S	1,947	41,807	Twin Falls
Valley	W cen.	3,676	3,609	Cascade
Washington	W	1,462	7,633	Weiser
Yellowstone National Park (part)	E	58[3]		

[1]Area = land area.

[2]Northernmost county, bordering Canada (Brit. Columbia) on N, Montana on E, Washington on NW.

[3]Main part of Yellowstone National Park is within Wyoming state boundaries (2930.8 sq. m.), with adjacent strips in Montana (268.9 sq. m.) and Idaho (57.6 sq. m.). Total area with inland water 3419 sq. m.

History: First white exploration by Lewis and Clark expedition 1805; held by United States and Great Britain jointly until by treaty 1846 Great Britain gave United States sole possession S of 49th parallel; included in Oregon Territory 1848; part N of 46° included in Washington Territory 1853; gold discovered 1860; crossed by Oregon Trail; organized as separate territory 1863; admitted to Union July 3, 1890.

2 County in Idaho. See table at IDAHO.

Idaho City. Village, ⊗ of Boise co., W cen. Idaho; pop. (1970c) 164; founded 1862 during a gold rush; said to have had at one time a population of 30,000, which declined as mining claims were worked out.

Idaho Falls. City, ⊗ of Bonneville co., SE Idaho, on Snake river 50 m. NNE of Pocatello; pop. (1970c) 35,776; ships esp. potatoes, wheat, and sugar beets.

Idaho Springs. Resort city, Clear Creek co., N cen. Colorado, 30 m. W of Denver; pop. (1970c) 2003; mining center; thermal mineral springs.

Idalia. See YALIAS.

Ida·li·um \ī-ˈdā-lē-əm\ *or mod.* **Da·li** \ˈdäl-ē\. Village, E cen. Cyprus, on Yalias river; site of ancient temple, sacred to Aphrodite.

Ida Mountains. See IDA 2.

Idar \ˌē-ˌdär\. 1 Former Indian state, now part of Gujarat state, W India; 1668 sq. m.; at one time in Mahi Kantha Agency; joined Union of Rajasthan June 26, 1947.

2 Town, its ✱, 55 m. NNE of Ahmadabad; pop. (1961c) 10,800.

Idar–Ober·stein \ˈē-dər-ˈō-bər-ˌs(h)tīn\. City, Rhineland-Palatinate, West Germany, in Nahe river valley; pop. (1969e) 40,063; jewelry, leather goods, aluminum; formed 1933.

Idenburg. 1 Peaks, Indonesia. See PILIMSIT.

2 River, Indonesia. See TARITATU.

Id·fu \ˈid-(ˌ)fü\ *or* **Ed·fu** \ˈed-\. Town on Nile river, Aswān gov., Egypt; pop. (1966c) 27,300; ancient ruins; famous for its temple of Horus, almost wholly preserved, begun by Ptolemy III Euergetes 237 B.C. and not finally completed until 57 B.C.

Ídhi. See IDA 3.

Ídhra. See HYDRA.

Idjen *or* **Ijen** \ē-ˈjen\. Old crater forming a plateau with many volcanoes on E end of Java, Indonesia; highest points Raung 10,932 ft. and Merapi, an active volcano 9551 ft.

Id·lib \ˈid-ˌlib\. Commercial town, NW Syria, 35 m. SW of Aleppo; pop. (1961e) 36,361.

Idri·ja *or Ital.* **Idria** \ˈid-rē-ə, ˈē-drē-ə\. Mining commune, W Slovenia, NW Yugoslavia; pop. (1961c) 6500; formerly in Italy; 16th cent. castle; mercury mines (discovered 1490); produces cinnabar.

Id·u·maea *or* **Id·u·mea** \ˌij-ə-ˈmē-ə\. Name given by Greeks and Romans to the country of the Edomites (see EDOM) who, after being driven westward by the Nabataeans c. 300 B.C., settled in S Judaea.

Idu·ty·wa Reserve \ˌēd-ə-ˌtī-wə-\. A district of Transkei (*q.v.*), E Cape Province, S Rep. of South Africa; chief town **Idutywa.**

Ie·per \ˈyā-pər\ *or Fr.* **Ypres** \ēprᵊ\. Commune, West Flanders prov., NW Belgium; pop. (1969e) 18,696; famous as a commercial center in medieval times, esp. in the cloth-weaving industry; said to have a population of 200,000 in 13th cent., when the Cloth Hall (Les Halles) and church of St. Martin were built; a border town, subject to many sieges, and therefore gradually declined; in World War I in one of most fiercely contested areas of entire war and scene of three great battles: Oct. 19–Nov. 22, 1914, Apr. 22–May 25, 1915, and July 31–Nov. 1917; completely destroyed but rebuilt.

Ierápetra. See HIERÁPETRA.

Ier·ne \ī-ˈər-nē\. Ancient name of Ireland, from the Greek.

Ie·si \ˈyez-ē, ˈyāz-\ *also* **Je·si** \ˈyā-zē\ *or anc.* **Æsis** \ˈē-səs\. Commune, Ancona prov., Marches, cen. Italy, 16 m. WSW of Ancona; pop. (1968e) 38,346; episcopal see; birthplace of Emperor Frederick II.

Ie·so·lo \ˈyez-ə-ˌlō, ˈyāz-\. Commune, Venezia prov., Veneto, NE Italy, on Gulf of Venice 20 m. E by N of Venice; pop. (1968e) 19,987.

If \ˈēf\. Small island off S coast of France, 2 m. from Marseilles; site of famous fortress prison Château d'If.

Ifa·lik \ˈē-fə-ˌlēk\. Island of the Caroline Is., W Pacific Ocean, ab. halfway bet. Truk and Yap.

Ife \ˈē-(ˌ)fā\. Town, Western State, Nigeria, 54 m. E of Ibadan; pop. (1969e) 150,818; trades in cocoa; univ. (1961).

Iferten. See YVERDON.

If·ni \ˈif-nē, ˈēf-\. A former Spanish overseas province, on coast of SW Morocco; 579 sq. m.; ✱ Sidi Ifni; occupied nominally by Spain from 1860; boundaries fixed 1912 by treaty with France; Spanish occupation became effective 1934; territorial limits reduced by French government 1935; ceded to Morocco 1969.

Iforas, Adrar des. See ADRAR.

Ifu·gao \ˌē-fü-ˈgaů\. Province, Luzon, Phil.; 972 sq. m.; pop. (1970p) 92,896; ✱ Lagawe; W and NW mountainous; E third sloping to Magat river on SE border thinly inhabited; chief product rice; under Spaniards region known as Kiangan; part of Nueva Vizcaya prov. 1902–08; created a subprovince of Mountain Province 1908.

Igabrum. See CABRA.

Igidi, Erg. See ERG, AL-.

Igilgili. See DJIDJELLI.

Igilium. See GIGLIO.

Iglau. See JIHLAVA.

Igle·sias \i-ˈglez-ē-əs, -ˈglāz-\. Commune, Cagliari prov., S Sardinia, Italy, near W coast 32 m. WNW of Cagliari; pop. (1968e) 28,316.

Igló. See SPIŠSKÁ NOVÁ VES.

Igoumenítsa. See HEGOUMENITSA.

Igridir. See EĞRIDIR.

Igua·çu \ˌē-gwə-ˈsü\ *or Span.* **Igua·zú** \-ˈsü, -ˈzü\. River, S Brazil; 745 m. long; flows W in Paraná state and empties into the Alto Paraná on border of NE Argentina, forming small section of Argentina-Brazil boundary; ab. 16 m.

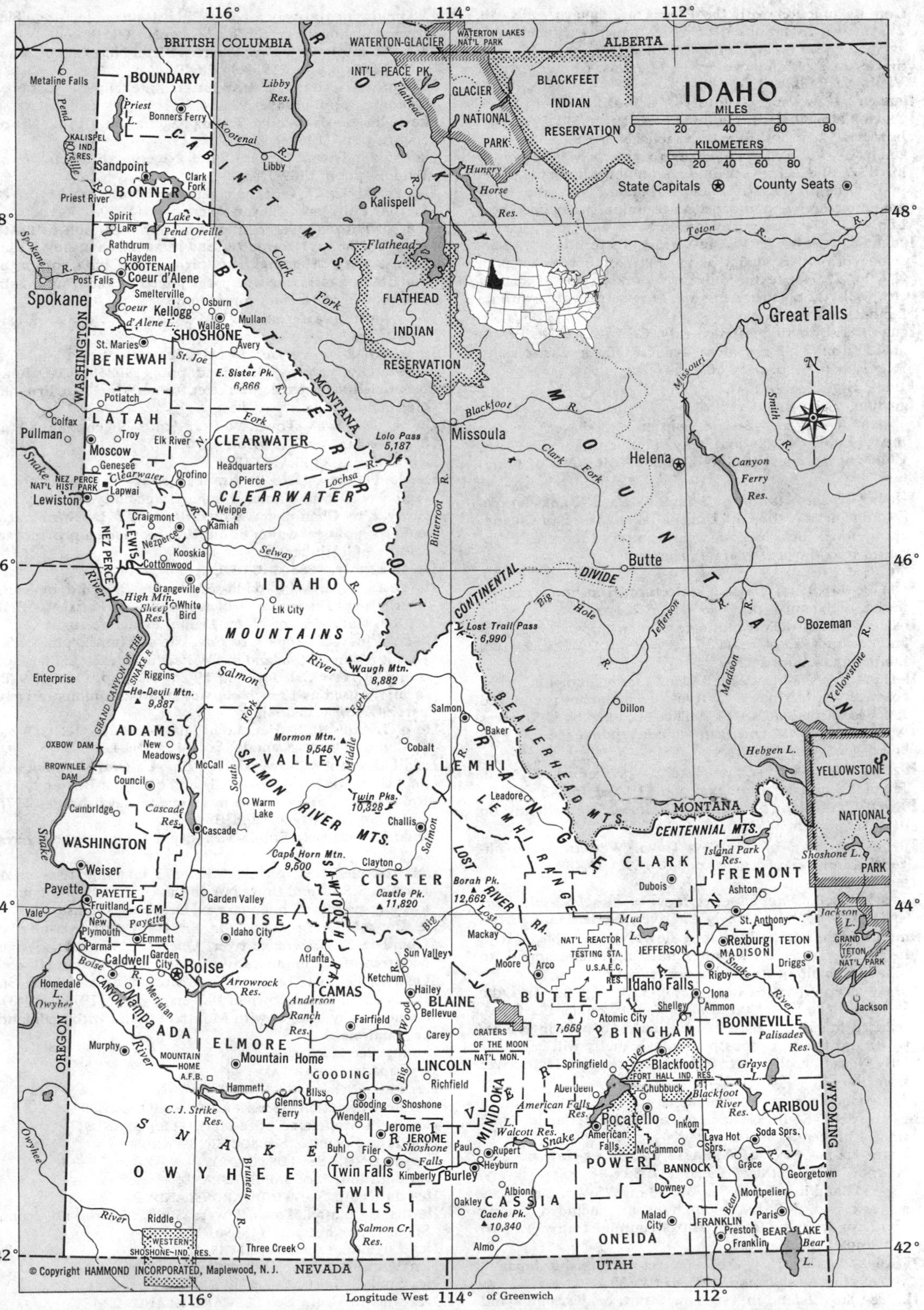
IDAHO
MILES
0 20 40 60 80
KILOMETERS
0 20 40 60 80
State Capitals
County Seats
116°
114°
112°
48°
46°
44°
42°
BRITISH COLUMBIA
ALBERTA
WATERTON-GLACIER
WATERTON LAKES NAT'L PARK
INT'L PEACE PK.
GLACIER
NATIONAL
PARK
BLACKFEET
INDIAN
RESERVATION
FLATHEAD
INDIAN
RESERVATION
ROCKY MOUNTAINS
BITTERROOT RANGE
CABINET MTS.
BEAVERHEAD MTS.
CONTINENTAL DIVIDE
MONTANA
WASHINGTON
OREGON
NEVADA
UTAH
WYOMING
YELLOWSTONE
NATIONAL
PARK
Metaline Falls
Pend Oreille
KALISPEL IND. RES.
BOUNDARY
Priest L.
Bonners Ferry
Kootenai R.
Libby Res.
Libby
Flathead
Hungry Horse Res.
Kalispell
Flathead L.
Sandpoint
Clark Fork
BONNER
Priest River
Spirit Lake
Lake Pend Oreille
Rathdrum
Hayden
KOOTENAI
Coeur d'Alene
Post Falls
Spokane R.
Spokane
Smelterville
Kellogg
Osburn
Mullan
Wallace
Coeur d'Alene L.
SHOSHONE
Avery
St. Maries
BENEWAH
St. Joe
E. Sister Pk. 6,866
Clark Fork
Potlatch
LATAH
Colfax
Pullman
Troy
Elk River
N. Fork
Moscow
CLEARWATER
Lolo Pass 5,187
Missoula
Blackfoot R.
Clark Fork
Helena
Canyon Ferry Res.
Great Falls
Missouri
Smith R.
Teton R.
Genesee
Headquarters
Pierce
Orofino
Lochsa R.
NEZ PERCE NAT'L HIST PARK
Clearwater
Lapwai
Lewiston
Snake
CLEARWATER
Weippe
Craigmont
Kamiah
Nezperce
LEWIS
Kooskia
Cottonwood
NEZ PERCE
Selway
Bitterroot R.
Butte
Grangeville
IDAHO
High Mtn. Sheep Res.
White Bird
Elk City
MOUNTAINS
Lost Trail Pass 6,990
Big Hole R.
Jefferson R.
Madison R.
Bozeman
Yellowstone R.
Enterprise
Riggins
Salmon River
Waugh Mtn. 8,882
GRAND CANYON OF THE SNAKE R.
He-Devil Mtn. 9,387
South Fork
Middle Fork
Salmon
Baker
Dillon
ADAMS
OXBOW DAM
New Meadows
Mormon Mtn. 9,545
VALLEY
Cobalt
LEMHI
BROWNLEE DAM
McCall
Council
SALMON RIVER MTS.
Twin Pks. 10,328
Leadore
LEMHI RANGE
Hebgen L.
Cambridge
Cascade Res.
Warm Lake
Challis
MONTANA
CENTENNIAL MTS.
Island Park Res.
Cascade
WASHINGTON
Cape Horn Mtn. 9,500
SAWTOOTH RA.
LOST RIVER RA.
CLARK
Shoshone L.
Weiser
Clayton
CUSTER
Borah Pk. 12,662
Dubois
FREMONT
Payette
PAYETTE
Castle Pk. 11,820
Ashton
Vale
Fruitland
GEM
Garden Valley
BOISE
Big Lost
Mud L.
St. Anthony
Jackson L.
New Plymouth
Payette
Idaho City
Mackay
NAT'L REACTOR TESTING STA. U.S.A.E.C. RES.
JEFFERSON
Rexburg
MADISON
TETON
GRAND TETON NAT'L PARK
Parma
Emmett
Caldwell
Garden City
Boise
Atlanta
Sun Valley
Ketchum
Moore
Arco
Driggs
Rigby
Homedale
Boise R.
CANYON
Arrowrock Res.
CAMAS
Hailey
BLAINE
BUTTE
Idaho Falls
Iona
Ammon
Owyhee L.
Nampa
Meridian
Anderson Ranch Res.
Bellevue
Atomic City
Shelley
Jackson
ADA
Fairfield
Wood R.
Carey
CRATERS OF THE MOON NAT'L MON.
7,659
BINGHAM
BONNEVILLE
Palisades Res.
Murphy
ELMORE
Mountain Home
Springfield
Blackfoot
MOUNTAIN HOME A.F.B.
GOODING
LINCOLN
Richfield
Grays L.
River
FORT HALL IND. RES.
Hammett
Bliss
Aberdeen
Chubbuck
Blackfoot River Res.
CARIBOU
Glenns Ferry
Gooding
Shoshone
MINIDOKA
American Falls Res.
C. J. Strike Res.
Wendell
Jerome
JEROME
Walcott Res.
Pocatello
Inkom
Soda Sprs.
SNAKE RIVER PLAIN
Owyhee
Buhl
Filer
Shoshone Falls
Paul
Rupert
Heyburn
American Falls
McCammon
Lava Hot Sprs.
OWYHEE
Twin Falls
Kimberly
Burley
POWER
BANNOCK
Grace
Georgetown
Bruneau R.
TWIN FALLS
Albion
CASSIA
Downey
Montpelier
River
Oakley
Cache Pk. 10,340
Bear R.
Paris
Riddle
Malad City
FRANKLIN
WESTERN SHOSHONE IND. RES.
Salmon Cr. Res.
Preston
BEAR LAKE
Three Creek
Almo
ONEIDA
Franklin
Bear L.
© Copyright HAMMOND INCORPORATED, Maplewood, N.J.
Longitude West 114° of Greenwich

from its junction with the Paraná are **Iguaçu Falls,** ab. $2^1/_2$ m. wide, composed of more than twenty cataracts averaging 200 ft. high and separated from each other by masses of rock and tree-covered islands; formerly called **Vic·to·ria Falls** \vik-ˌtōr-ē-ə-\.

Igua·çú \ˌē-gwə-ˈsü\. Territory of S Brazil 1943–46.

Iguaçu National Park. National park, Brazil, on Argentina border; 792 sq. m.; forests; established 1939.

Igua·la \i-ˈgwäl-ə\. Town, Guerrero state, S Mexico, ab. 50 m. SSW of Cuernavaca in silver-mining district; munic. pop. (1970p) 60,980. Plan of Iguala, with the three guarantees: religion, independence, union, proclaimed here Feb. 24, 1821 by Agustín de Iturbide.

Igua·la·da \ˌēg-wə-ˈläd-ə, ˌig-\. Manufacturing city, Barcelona prov., NE Spain, 32 m. WNW of Barcelona; pop. (1970p) 27,941; textile mills, ironworks; ruins of ancient city walls; 12 m. to the E is the Montserrat (*q.v.*) with its famous monastery.

Igua·tu \ˌē-gwə-ˈtü\. Municipality, Ceará state, NE Brazil, ab. 200 m. S of Fortaleza, on R.R. from Fortaleza to Recife; pop. (1968e) 54,661.

Iguidi, Erg. See ERG, AL-.

Iguvium. See GUBBIO.

I–hsien \ˈē-shē-ˈen, ˈyē-\ *or* **Ye·hsien** \ˈyā-shē-ˈen\ *or formerly* **Lai·chow** \ˈlī-ˈjō\. City, N Shantung prov., NE China, near S coast of Gulf of Chihli 80 m. NNW of Tsingtao.

I–hsing \ˈē-ˈshiŋ\ *or* **Ihing** \ˈē-ˈhiŋ\. Town, S Kiangsu prov., E China, near W shore of T'ai Hu (lake) 28 m. S of Ch'angchou; noted for a reddish-yellow pottery (boccaro) introduced into Europe by the Portuguese.

Ihú. See YHÚ.

Ii·da \ˈē-də\. City, Nagano prefecture, Honshū, Japan, 58 m. NE of Nagoya; pop. (1970c) 77,261.

Ii·sal·mi \ˈē-ˌsäl-mē\. Commune, Kuopio prov., S cen. Finland, on railroad 50 m. N of Kuopio; pop. (1970e) 21,164; lumbering; founded 1891.

Ii–shi·ma \ē-ˈshē-mə\. Small island (*shima*) ab. 4 m. off W coast of cen. Okinawa I., Ryukyu Is., Japan; island and Japanese airfield at **Ii** \ˈē-ə\ village occupied by U.S. forces Apr. 16–20, 1945; American war correspondent Ernie Pyle killed here Apr. 18.

Ii·zu·ka \ˈē-zu̇-kə\. City, Fukuoka prefecture, Kyūshū, Japan, 18 m. E of Fukuoka; pop. (1970c) 75,643.

IJ *or* **Y** \ˈī\. Inland arm of the IJsselmeer, Netherlands; on its S side is Amsterdam.

Ije·bu–Ode \i-ˈjā-bü-ˈō-(ˌ)dā\. Town, Western State, Nigeria, 45 m. NE of Lagos; pop. (1969e) 79,489.

Ijen. See IDJEN.

IJs·sel \ˈī-səl\; *Eng.* **Ijssel** *or* **Is·sel** *or* **Ys·sel** \ˈī-səl\; *anc.* **Sa·la** \ˈsal-ə, ˈsäl-\. Navigable river, Netherlands, the N mouth of the Rhine; 70 m. long; flows N out of Neder Rijn in E Netherlands to IJsselmeer; its ancient name applied to inhabitants along its banks, the *Salian* Franks.

IJs·sel·meer \ˈī-səl-ˌme(ə)r\; *Eng.* **Lake Ijs·sel** *or* **Lake Is·sel** *or* **Lake Ys·sel** \ˈī-səl\. The former Zuider Zee (*q.v.*), reduced in size as result of reclamation of Wieringermeer (*q.v.*) and the Noordoostpolder; eventually will comprise only N section of former Zuider Zee; receives IJssel river from the SE.

IJs·sel·mon·de *also* **Ijsselmonde** \ˌī-səl-ˈmȯn-də\. Island in Meuse delta, South Holland prov., SW Netherlands; diked since 13th cent.

Ika·ria \ˌē-kə-ˈrē-ə\ *or* **Ni·ka·ria** *also* **Ni·ca·ria** \ˌnē-\ *or* **Ka·ri·ot** \ˌkär-ē-ˈōt\; *anc.* **Icar·ia** \ī-ˈker-ē-ə, -ˈkar-; ik-ˈer-, -ˈar-\. Island in Aegean Sea, ab. 13 m. WSW of Samos; 99 sq. m.; pop. (1961c) 9600; by some included among Southern Sporades (see SPORADES); administratively a part of Samos dept., Greece.

Ike·da \i-ˈkād-ə\. City, Ōsaka prefecture, Honshū, Japan, 8 m. NNW of Ōsaka; pop. (1970c) 94,333.

Iki \ˈē-(ˌ)kē\. Island in Tsushima Strait, bet Tsushima and NW coast of Kyūshū, Japan; 53 sq. m.; pop. (1970c) 42,983; administratively a part of Nagasaki prefecture; chief town Mushozu; overrun by Mongols in 13th cent.

Iki·re \i-ˈki(ə)r-ē\. Town, Western State, Nigeria, ab. 20 m. E of Ibadan; pop. (1969e) 62,649.

Iki·run \ˌē-ki-ˈrün\. Town, Western State, Nigeria, just N of Oshogbo; pop. (1969e) 92,214.

Iko·ro·du \ˌē-kə-rə-ˈdü\. Town, Nigeria, ab. 10 m. NE of Lagos; pop. (1969e) 93,963.

Ila \ˈē-lə\. Town, Western State, Nigeria, ab. 90 m. NE of Ibadan; pop. (1969e) 133,003.

Ila·gan \i-ˈläg-ˌän\. Municipality, ✻ of Isabela prov., Luzon, Phil., on Cagayan river; pop. (1969e) 66,100.

Īlām \ē-ˈläm\. Governorship of W Iran. See table at IRAN.

I–lan \ˈē-ˈlän\. 1 *formerly* **San·hsing** *or* **San·sing** \ˈsän-ˈshiŋ\. City, Heilungkiang prov., NE China, on right bank of Sungari river where it is joined by the Mu-tan, ab. 190 m. NE of Harbin; furs, lumber.
2 *or formerly* **Gi–ran** \ˈgē-ˈrän\. Town, NE coast of Taiwan.

Iła·wa \i-ˈlä-və\ *or Ger.* **Deutsch–Ey·lau** \ˈdȯich-ˈī-(ˌ)lau̇\. Town, Olsztyn prov., N Poland; pop. (1968e) 15,200; lumber, machinery; cattle markets; formerly in East Prussia, Germany.

Ila·we \ˌē-lə-ˈwā\. Town, Western State, Nigeria, ab. 80 m. E of Ibadan; pop. (1969e) 93,741.

Ilebo. See PORT FRANCQUI.

Île–de–France *or* **Isle–de–France** \ˌēl-də-ˈfräⁿs\. Historical region of N cen. France; bounded anciently on N by Picardy, E by Champagne, S by Orléanais, W by Normandy; ✻ Paris; political center of old France; made a province in middle of 15th cent.

Île de France. See MAURITIUS.

Île de la Ci·té \ˌē(ə)l-də-lä-sē-ˈtā\. Small island in Seine river, Paris, France, on which the city of Paris was first settled; Cathedral of Notre Dame, Palais de Justice.

Île des Pins \ˌēl-dā-ˈpaⁿ\ *or Eng.* **Isle of Pines** \-ˈpīnz\ *also* **Ku·nie** \ˈkün-yā\. Island in SW Pacific Ocean, 32 m. SE of S end of New Caledonia I.; 59 sq. m.; pop. (1969c) 978; formerly used as French convict station; administratively part of New Caledonia.

Île d'Orléans. 1 District, Louisiana. See ORLEANS, ISLE OF.
2 Island, Quebec, Canada. See ORLEANS, ISLAND OF.

Île d'Oues·sant \ˌēl-dwe-ˈsäⁿ\ *or Eng.* **Ush·ant** \ˈəsh-ənt\ *or anc.* **Ux·an·tis** \ək-ˈsant-əs\. Island off tip of Brittany, NW France; 6 sq. m.; $4^1/_2$ m. long; scene of naval battles 1778 and 1794 bet. French and English.

Île du Le·vant \ˌē(ə)l-də-lə-ˈväⁿ, -d(y)ü-\. One of the Hyères Is. (*q.v.*).

Ilek \il-ˈ(y)ek\. River, U.S.S.R.; 373 m. long; rises in W Kazakh S.S.R. and flows NW to the Ural, its lower course forming part of S boundary of Orenburg Oblast.

Ile Per·rot \ˌē(ə)l-pə-ˈrō\ *or Fr.* **Île Perrot** \ēl-pe-rō\. Island in St. Lawrence river, Quebec, E Canada, SW of Montreal I.; administratively a part of Vaudreuil co., Quebec; lies bet. Lake of Two Mountains and Lake St. Louis; in SE part is town of Ile Perrot (pop. [1971p] 4043); connected by bridges with Montreal I. and with mainland at Vaudreuil.

Ilerda. See LÉRIDA 2.

Île Rouad. See ARWAD.

Île Rousse. See L'ÎLE ROUSSE.

Îles de Désolation. See KERGUELEN ISLANDS.

Îles de la Madeleine. See MAGDALEN ISLANDS.

Îles de la Société. See SOCIETY ISLANDS.

Îles de Loos. See LOS ISLANDS.

Îles du Salut. See SAFETY ISLANDS.

Îles du Vent. See WINDWARD ISLANDS 2.

Ile·sha \i-ˈlesh-ə\. Town, Kwara State, Nigeria, ab. 15 m. SE of Oshogbo; pop. (1969e) 192,302.

Îles Loyauté. See LOYALTY ISLANDS.

Îles Marquises. See MARQUESAS ISLANDS.

Îles Scilly. See SCILLY ISLES 2.

Îles sous le Vent. See LEEWARD ISLANDS 2.

Iletsk *or* **Iletskaya Zashchita.** See SOL-ILETSK.

Il·fov \ēl-ˈfȯv\. County of S Romania. See table at ROMANIA.

Il·fra·combe \ˈil-frə-ˌküm\. Urban district, Devonshire, SW England, on Bristol Channel 57 m. N of Plymouth; pop. (1971p) 9846; seaside resort.

Ilha Gran·de Bay \ˌēl-yə-ˌgran-də-\. Inlet of Atlantic Ocean on S coast of Rio de Janeiro state, SE Brazil.

Ilhas do Cabo Verde. See CAPE VERDE ISLANDS.

Ilha·vo \il-ˈyav-(ˌ)ü\. Commune, Aveiro dist., NW Portugal, on coastal lagoon 3 m. SW of Aveiro; munic. pop. (1970p) 22,771; fisheries, saltworks; glass, china.

Ilhé·us \il-ˈyā-əs\. City, SE coast of Bahia state, E Brazil, 140 m. SSW of Salvador; munic. pop. (1968e) 100,687; exports large percentage of Brazil's cacao crop.

I–li \ˈē-ˈlē\. 1 River, China and U.S.S.R.; ab. 800 m. long; from NW Sinkiang Uighur, W China, flows into SW end of Lake Balkhash, Kazakh S.S.R., U.S.S.R.; formed by K'ung-chi-ssu and T'e-k'o-ssu rivers in N ranges of the Tien Shan; in China flows through fertile valley, settled since early times; in U.S.S.R. chief town on its banks is **Ili**, above which it is navigable for ab. 280 m. in rainy season.
2 Formerly a district, its E part now in Sinkiang Uighur; contested for by Russia and China but became Chinese by treaty 1881.

Il·i·am·na \ˌil-ē-ˈam-nə\. Village at NE end of Iliamna Lake, SW Alaska; pop. (1970c) 48.

Iliamna Lake. Lake, SW Alaska, W of Cook Inlet; 1033 sq. m.

Iliamna Peak. Volcano, SW Alaska, on W side of Cook Inlet; 10,016 ft.

Ilici. See ELCHE.

Ili·gan \i-ˈlē-ˌgän\. Chartered city, * of Lanao del Norte prov., Mindanao, Phil., on SE shore of Iligan Bay; pop. (1970e) 82,900; tinplate mill; chief port on N coast; scene of uprising in Philippine Revolution 1896.

Iligan Bay. Inlet of S Mindanao Sea, N coast of Mindanao, Phil.; 25 to 40 m. wide; its SW arm is the long Panguil Bay.

Ilimsk \il-ˈ(y)ēm(p)sk, -ˈ(y)im(p)sk\. Town, cen. Irkutsk Oblast, Russian S.F.S.R., U.S.S.R., on **Ilim** \il-ˈ(y)ēm, -ˈ(y)im\ river (tributary of Angara, ab. 240 m. long).

Ilin Island \i-ˌlēn-\. Island off SW coast of Mindoro, Phil.; S of Mangarin Bay, 30 sq. m.; U.S. forces landed Dec. 15, 1944.

Ilio·dhró·mia \ˌēl-yȯ-ˈt͟hrō-mē-ə\ *or formerly* **Alón·ni·sos** \ə-ˈlōn-i-ˌsȯs\. Island of the Northern Sporades, NW Aegean Sea, part of Magnesia dept., Greece, NE of Skopelos.

Il·i·on \ˈil-ē-ən\. Village, Herkimer co., NE cen. New York, on Mohawk river 11 m. ESE of Utica; pop. (1970c) 9808; forms single community with Mohawk, Herkimer, and Frankfort; firearms and ammunition, typewriters, office equipment; Herkimer County Community Coll. (1966).

Ilion. See TROY 8.

Ilio Point \i-ˌlē-(ˌ)ō-\. Point, NW Molokai I., Hawaii, on Kaiwi Channel.

Il·i·pa \ˈil-ə-pə\. Town of ancient Baetica, S Spain, ab. 60 m. N of Hispalis (*mod.* Seville); scene 206 B.C. of victory of Scipio Africanus over the Carthaginians whose power in Spain was broken; battle famous for superb military tactics.

Ilis·sus \ī-ˈlis-əs, īl-ˈis-\ *or* **Ilis·sós** \ˌil-ə-ˈsȯs\. Short river, Attica dept., E cen. Greece, S of Athens; flows into the Cephisus.

Ilium. See TROY 8.

Il·kes·ton \ˈil-kə-stən\. Municipal borough, Derbyshire, N cen. England, 8 m. WNW of Nottingham; pop. (1971p) 34,123; hosiery, earthenware; coal mines.

Ilk·ley \ˈil-klē\. Urban district, West Riding, Yorkshire, N England; pop. (1971p) 21,828; health resort; Roman remains.

Ilkuri Shan. See I-LO-HU-LI RANGE.

Ill \ˈil\. River, Vorarlberg, SW Austria, flowing NW into Rhine NW of Feldkirch; 45 m. long.

Ill \ˈē(ə)l\. River, Haut-Rhin and Bas-Rhin depts., NE France; 129 m. long; flows into Rhine.

Illam·pu \ē-ˈ(y)äm-(ˌ)pü\. Peak, W Bolivia; 20,867 ft. See ANCOHUMA.

Illa·na Bay \i-ˌyän-ə-\. Inlet of Moro Gulf on W coast of Mindanao, Phil.; receives in SE the waters of the Rio Grande de Mindanao; ab. 45 m. wide at mouth.

Illa·pel \ˌē-yə-ˈpel\. Inland city, Coquimbo prov., cen. Chile, 100 m. N of Valparaíso; pop. (1960c) 10,395.

Il·la·war·ra \ˌil-ə-ˈwär-ə\. District, SE New South Wales, SE Australia; extends along the coast 40 m. from ab. 30 m. S of Sydney; pop. (1967e) 215,000; dairying, fishing; coal and iron; bet. its chief towns, Kiama and Wollongong, is **Illawarra Lake,** a salt lagoon 9 m. long and 3 m. wide, connected with the sea by narrow channel.

Ille \ˈē(ə)l\. River, Ille-et-Vilaine dept., NW France, flowing S to the Vilaine at Rennes.

Il·le·cil·le·waet \ˌil-ə-ˈsil-ə-wət\. 1 Glacier in Selkirk Mts. in Glacier National Park, British Columbia, Canada; its ice field drops 3600 ft. into the valley.
2 River flowing from its foot into Columbia river near Revelstoke.

Ille–et–Vi·laine \ˈē(ə)l-ā-vi-ˈlān, -ˈlen\. Department of NW France. See table at FRANCE.

Il·ler \ˈil-ər\. River, West Germany; 91 m. long; rises in Algäu Alps and flows N through Bavaria and along boundary of Baden-Württemberg into the Danube near Ulm.

Illiberis. See ELNE.

Il·li·lou·ette Falls \ˌil-i-lü-ˌet-\. Waterfall in Yosemite National Park, E cen. California; 370 ft. high.

Illi·ma·ni \ˌē-(y)ə-ˈmän-ē\. Mountain in W Bolivia, E of La Paz; its highest peak 21,201 ft.

Illi·ni·za \ˌil-ə-ˈnē-zə, ˌēl-, -sə\. Peak in Andes Mts., Ecuador; 17,394 ft.

Il·li·nois \ˌil-ə-ˈnȯi *also* -ˈnȯiz\. 1 River, Arkansas and Oklahoma; 145 m. long; rises in Benton co., Arkansas, flows W and NW, joining Arkansas river in Oklahoma.
2 Navigable river, Illinois; 273 m. long; formed by confluence of Des Plaines and Kankakee rivers in Grundy co., SW of Joliet, NE Illinois, flows diagonally SW across Illinois to empty into the Mississippi in W Illinois; upper waters (Des Plaines river) connected by ship canal with Lake Michigan (see ILLINOIS WATERWAY).
3 A north central state of U.S.A., bounded on N by Wisconsin, on E by Lake Michigan and Indiana, on SE and S by Kentucky, on SW by Missouri, and on W by Missouri and Iowa; 24th state in area, 56,400 sq. m., not including 1526 sq. m. of water of the Great Lakes (land area 55,875 sq. m.); 5th state in population, (1970c) 11,113,976; * Springfield; 21st state admitted to Union (1818).

Nicknames: Prairie State; Sucker State. *State flower:* Violet. *Motto:* State Sovereignty—National Union. *Rivers:* Mississippi, forming W boundary; Ohio, forming SE boundary; Wabash, forming lower section of E boundary; Illinois (see 2 above). *Highest point:* Charles Mound, 1235 ft., in Jo Daviess co. *Chief products:* Corn, soybeans, dairy products, livestock; oil, coal, gravel; manufacturing: iron and steel, electrical machinery, chemicals, metal products. *Chief cities:* Chicago, Rockford, Peoria, Springfield, East St. Louis. See *Table of States* at UNITED STATES. Divided into the following 102 counties (for pronunciation of their names, see their individual entries):

NAME	LOCATION	AREA' (sq. m.)	POP. (1970c)	CO. SEAT
Adams	W	862	70,861	Quincy
Alexander	SW corner	229	12,015	Cairo
Bond	SW cen.	383	14,012	Greenville
Boone	N	283	25,440	Belvidere

NAME	LOCATION	AREA[1] (sq. m.)	POP. (1970c)	CO. SEAT
Brown	W	306	5,586	Mount Sterling
Bureau	N	866	38,541	Princeton
Calhoun	W	247	5,675	Hardin
Carroll	NW	456	19,276	Mount Carroll
Cass	W cen.	371	14,219	Virginia
Champaign	E cen.	1,000	163,281	Urbana
Christian	cen.	709	35,948	Taylorville
Clark	E	505	16,216	Marshall
Clay	SE cen.	464	14,735	Louisville
Clinton	SW cen.	499	28,315	Carlyle
Coles	E cen.	506	47,815	Charleston
Cook	NE	954	5,493,529	Chicago
Crawford	E	443	19,824	Robinson
Cumberland	SE cen.	347	9,772	Toledo
De Kalb	N	636	71,654	Sycamore
De Witt	cen.	399	16,975	Clinton
Douglas	E cen.	420	18,997	Tuscola
Du Page	NE	331	492,181	Wheaton
Edgar	E	628	21,591	Paris
Edwards	SE	225	7,090	Albion
Effingham	SE cen.	481	24,608	Effingham
Fayette	S cen.	719	20,752	Vandalia
Ford	NE cen.	488	16,382	Paxton
Franklin	S	434	38,329	Benton
Fulton	W cen.	877	41,900	Lewistown
Gallatin	SE	328	7,418	Shawneetown
Greene	W	543	17,014	Carrollton
Grundy	NE	432	26,535	Morris
Hamilton	SE	435	8,665	McLeansboro
Hancock	W	797	23,664	Carthage
Hardin	SE	183	4,914	Elizabethtown
Henderson	W	376	8,451	Oquawka
Henry	NW	826	53,217	Cambridge
Iroquois	E	1,122	33,532	Watseka
Jackson	SW	605	55,008	Murphysboro
Jasper	SE cen.	495	10,741	Newton
Jefferson	S	573	31,848	Mount Vernon
Jersey	W	376	18,492	Jerseyville
Jo Daviess	NW corner	608	21,766	Galena
Johnson	S	345	7,550	Vienna
Kane	NE	520	251,005	Geneva
Kankakee	NE	678	97,250	Kankakee
Kendall	NE	320	26,374	Yorkville
Knox	W	728	60,939	Galesburg
Lake	NE corner	457	382,638	Waukegan
La Salle	N	1,150	111,409	Ottawa
Lawrence	SE	374	17,522	Lawrenceville
Lee	N	728	37,947	Dixon
Livingston	NE cen.	1,043	40,690	Pontiac
Logan	cen.	622	33,538	Lincoln
McDonough	W	582	36,653	Macomb
McHenry	N	610	111,555	Woodstock
McLean	cen.	1,173	104,389	Bloomington
Macon	cen.	578	125,010	Decatur
Macoupin	SW cen.	872	44,557	Carlinville
Madison	SW	733	250,934	Edwardsville
Marion	S cen.	579	38,986	Salem
Marshall	N cen.	391	13,302	Lacon
Mason	cen.	541	16,180	Havana
Massac	S	245	13,889	Metropolis
Menard	cen.	312	9,685	Petersburg
Mercer	NW	556	17,294	Aledo
Monroe	SW	382	18,831	Waterloo
Montgomery	S cen.	705	30,260	Hillsboro
Morgan	W cen.	561	36,174	Jacksonville
Moultrie	cen.	345	13,263	Sullivan
Ogle	N	758	42,867	Oregon
Peoria	NW cen.	623	195,318	Peoria
Perry	SW	439	19,757	Pinckneyville
Piatt	cen.	437	15,509	Monticello
Pike	W	828	19,185	Pittsfield
Pope	SE corner	381	3,857	Golconda
Pulaski	S	204	8,741	Mound City
Putnam	N cen.	160	5,007	Hennepin
Randolph	SW	594	31,379	Chester
Richland	SE	364	16,829	Olney
Rock Island	NW	424	166,734	Rock Island
Saint Clair	SW	673	285,199	Belleville
Saline	SE	383	25,721	Harrisburg
Sangamon	cen.	879	161,335	Springfield
Schuyler	W	434	8,135	Rushville
Scott	W	251	6,096	Winchester
Shelby	cen.	772	22,589	Shelbyville
Stark	NW cen.	291	7,510	Toulon
Stephenson	N	568	48,861	Freeport
Tazewell	cen.	652	118,649	Pekin
Union	SW	416	16,071	Jonesboro
Vermilion	E	899	97,047	Danville
Wabash	SE	222	12,841	Mount Carmel
Warren	W	541	21,595	Monmouth
Washington	SW	564	13,780	Nashville
Wayne	SE	715	17,004	Fairfield
White	SE	502	17,312	Carmi
Whiteside	NW	687	62,877	Morrison
Will	NE	847	247,825	Joliet
Williamson	S	429	49,021	Marion
Winnebago	N	519	246,623	Rockford
Woodford	N cen.	528	28,012	Eureka

[1] Area = land area.

History: Explored by Marquette and Jolliet 1673 and by La Salle who erected Fort Crèvecœur on Illinois river 1680; included in French Louisiana; ceded by France to England 1763 and by England to U.S. 1783; Virginia, Massachusetts, and Connecticut claims to territory given up by 1786; part of Northwest Territory 1787 and of Indiana Territory 1800; organized as separate territory which included present Wisconsin and eastern part of Minnesota 1809; admitted to Union as state Dec. 3, 1818 with capital at Kaskaskia (capital transferred to Vandalia 1820 and to Springfield 1837); adopted present constitution 1970.

Illinois Bayou. Bayou, Pope co., NW cen. Arkansas, draining SW into Arkansas river; ab. 75 m. long; has three headstreams (middle, east, and west forks).

Illinois Waterway. Combined system of rivers, canals, and state recreation areas, NE Illinois, with Chicago at N end; comprises: **Illinois and Michigan Canal** 96 m. long, from Chicago river to La Salle on Illinois river, opened 1848, discontinued 1900; South Branch of Chicago river, connected by **Chicago Drainage Canal** 28 m. long with Lockport on Des Plaines river, opened 1900, by which current was reversed and the flow of sewage directed into the Illinois river; **Sanitary and Ship Canal,** new name of improved Chicago Drainage Canal after its acquisition 1930 by the Federal government.

Illiturgis. See ANDÚJAR.

Ill·kirch–Graf·fen·sta·den \ˈil-ˌki(ə)rk-ˌgräf-ən-ˈs(h)täd-ᵊn, -ˌki(ə)rsh-\. Commune, Bas-Rhin dept., suburb of Strasbourg, NE France, on Ill river; pop. (1962c) 9607; scene of signing of capitulation of Strasbourg to Louis XIV 1681.

Íllo·ra \ˈē-yōr-ə\. Commune, Granada prov., S Spain, 15 m. WNW of Granada; pop. (1970p) 10,775; textiles, soap, liquors; Moorish castle.

Il·lyr·i·a \ə-ˈlir-ē-ə\. Ancient country comprising E Adriatic coast and its hinterland; inhabited by Illyrians, a Balkan people, loosely united, who practiced piracy on Roman shipping; after series of wars beginning with one in 229–228 B.C., finally overthrown 35–33 B.C. by Romans who established large province of Illyricum; furnished many soldiers for the Roman legions, several of whom became emperor (Claudius II, Diocletian, etc.); prefecture of Illyricum (*q.v.*) erected by Diocletian (d. 313 A.D.); region occupied by south Slavs in 6th cent. (see BALKAN STATES); practically coextensive with Illyrian Provinces (*q.v.*); kingdom of Illyria, comprising Carinthia, Carniola, and Küstenland, a division of Austria 1816–49.

Il·lyr·i·an Provinces \ə-ˈlir-ən-\. The division of the empire formed by Napoleon from the Austrian lands (beyond the Sava river) which France acquired by Treaty of Schönbrunn 1809; included Carinthia, Carniola, Gorizia, Istria, part of Croatia, Dalmatia, Ragusa (see DUBROVNIK), and the Ionian Is.; ✱ Ljubljana; although reconquered by Austria in 1813 and formally restored to her in 1815, reformed government aroused Illyrian (later Yugoslav) nationalism.

Il·lyr·i·cum \ə-ˈlir-i-kəm\. **1** Roman province with shifting boundaries, in ancient Illyria; roughly coextensive with W Yugoslavia; established 9 A.D. by Tiberius. See ILLYRIA. **2** Roman prefecture of 4th cent. A.D. including most of the Balkan Penin. (Dacia, Macedonia, Epirus, Thessaly, Achaea) and Crete.

Il·men \ˈil-mən\. Shallow lake, Novgorod Oblast, Russian S.F.S.R., U.S.S.R.; 425 to 850 sq. m.; receives Lovat and Msta rivers; outlet the Volkhov; in World War II came under control of Germans Aug. 21, 1941; recovered by U.S.S.R. Jan.–Feb. 1944.

Il·me·nau \ˈil-mə-ˌnau̇\. City, Suhl dist., East Germany, 24 m. S of Erfurt; pop. (1970e) 19,376; resort; manufactures

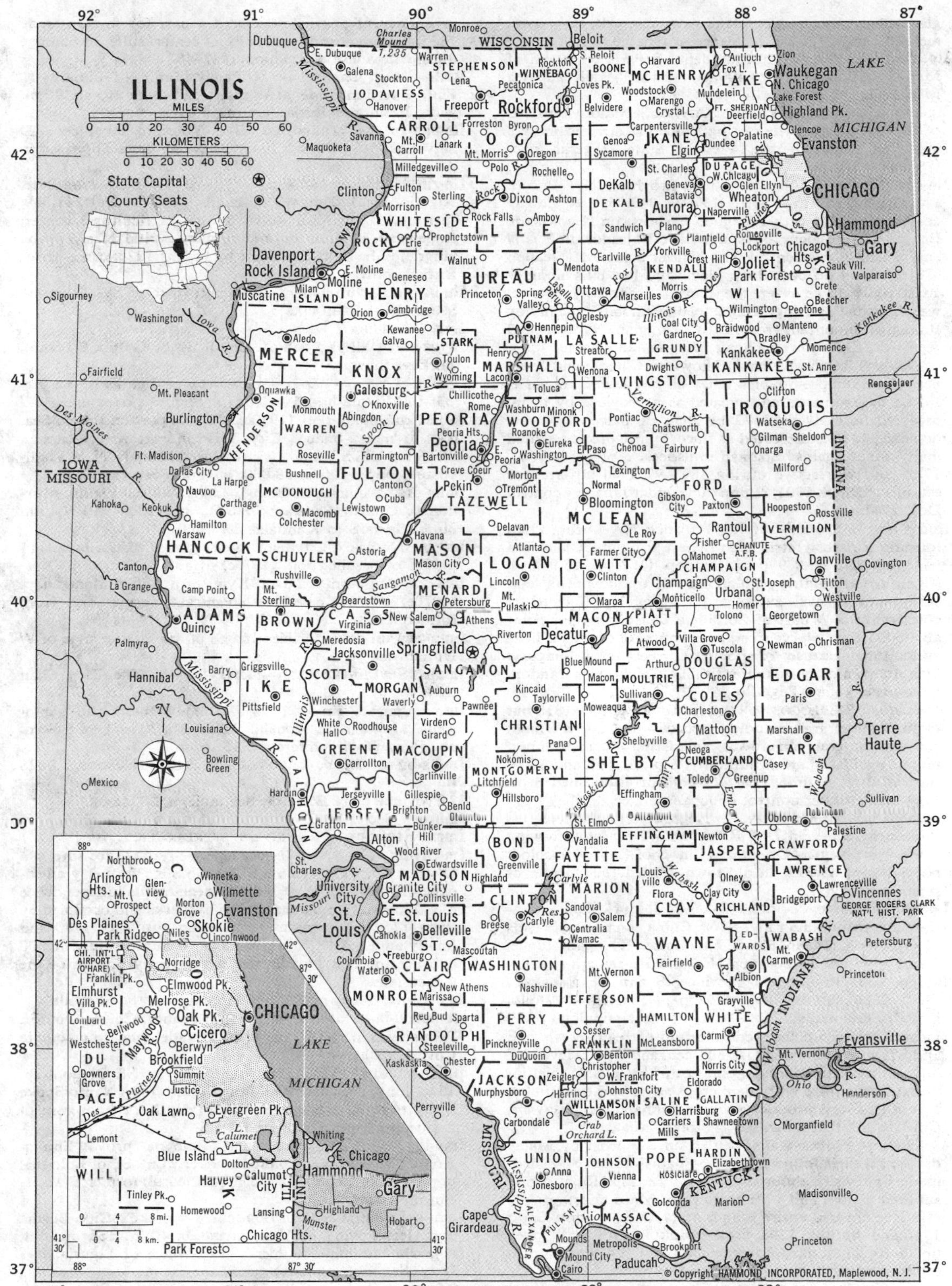
ILLINOIS
MILES
0 10 20 30 40 50 60
KILOMETERS
0 10 20 30 40 50 60
State Capital
County Seats
92° 91° 90° 89° 88° 87°
42° 41° 40° 39° 38° 37°
WISCONSIN
IOWA
MISSOURI
INDIANA
KENTUCKY
LAKE MICHIGAN
Charles Mound 1,235
JO DAVIESS
STEPHENSON
WINNEBAGO
BOONE
MC HENRY
LAKE
CARROLL
OGLE
DE KALB
KANE
DU PAGE
COOK
WHITESIDE
LEE
ROCK ISLAND
HENRY
BUREAU
LA SALLE
KENDALL
GRUNDY
WILL
KANKAKEE
MERCER
KNOX
STARK
PUTNAM
MARSHALL
LIVINGSTON
IROQUOIS
HENDERSON
WARREN
PEORIA
WOODFORD
FORD
HANCOCK
MC DONOUGH
FULTON
TAZEWELL
MC LEAN
VERMILION
SCHUYLER
MASON
LOGAN
DE WITT
CHAMPAIGN
ADAMS
BROWN
CASS
MENARD
MACON
PIATT
DOUGLAS
EDGAR
PIKE
SCOTT
MORGAN
SANGAMON
CHRISTIAN
MOULTRIE
COLES
CLARK
CALHOUN
GREENE
MACOUPIN
MONTGOMERY
SHELBY
CUMBERLAND
JERSEY
BOND
FAYETTE
EFFINGHAM
JASPER
CRAWFORD
MADISON
CLINTON
MARION
CLAY
RICHLAND
LAWRENCE
ST. CLAIR
WASHINGTON
WAYNE
EDWARDS
WABASH
MONROE
RANDOLPH
PERRY
JEFFERSON
HAMILTON
WHITE
FRANKLIN
JACKSON
WILLIAMSON
SALINE
GALLATIN
UNION
JOHNSON
POPE
HARDIN
ALEXANDER
PULASKI
MASSAC
Mississippi R.
Rock R.
Illinois R.
Fox R.
Des Plaines R.
Kankakee R.
Vermilion R.
Spoon R.
Sangamon R.
Iowa R.
Des Moines R.
Missouri R.
Kaskaskia R.
Little Wabash R.
Embarras R.
Wabash R.
Ohio R.
Carlyle Res.
Crab Orchard L.
Monroe
Beloit
S. Beloit
Dubuque
E. Dubuque
Galena
Warren
Stockton
Lena
Hanover
Freeport
Rockton
Pecatonica
Rockford
Loves Pk.
Belvidere
Harvard
Woodstock
Marengo
Crystal L.
Antioch
Fox L.
Zion
Waukegan
N. Chicago
Mundelein
Lake Forest
Highland Pk.
Deerfield
Glencoe
Evanston
Savanna
Mt. Carroll
Lanark
Forreston
Byron
Mt. Morris
Oregon
Polo
Rochelle
Carpentersville
Dundee
Elgin
Palatine
Genoa
Sycamore
DeKalb
St. Charles
Geneva
Batavia
W. Chicago
Glen Ellyn
Wheaton
Aurora
Naperville
CHICAGO
Hammond
Gary
Maquoketa
Milledgeville
Clinton
Fulton
Morrison
Sterling
Rock Falls
Dixon
Ashton
Amboy
Prophetstown
Erie
Sandwich
Plano
Yorkville
Plainfield
Romeoville
Lockport
Joliet
Crest Hill
Chicago Hts.
Sauk Vill.
Park Forest
Valparaiso
Davenport
Rock Island
E. Moline
Moline
Milan
Geneseo
Walnut
Princeton
Mendota
Earlville
Spring Valley
Ottawa
Marseilles
Morris
Crete
Beecher
Muscatine
Orion
Cambridge
Kewanee
Galva
Oglesby
Hennepin
Coal City
Gardner
Braidwood
Wilmington
Peotone
Manteno
Bradley
Kankakee
Momence
St. Anne
Sigourney
Washington
Aledo
Toulon
Henry
Wyoming
Lacon
Wenona
Streator
Dwight
Fairfield
Mt. Pleasant
Oquawka
Monmouth
Galesburg
Knoxville
Abingdon
Chillicothe
Rome
Washburn
Minonk
Toluca
Pontiac
Chatsworth
Fairbury
Watseka
Gilman
Sheldon
Onarga
Clifton
Rensselaer
Burlington
Roseville
Farmington
Peoria Hts.
Peoria
Bartonville
E. Peoria
Roanoke
Eureka
Washington
El Paso
Chenoa
Lexington
Milford
Ft. Madison
Dallas City
La Harpe
Nauvoo
Bushnell
Canton
Cuba
Creve Coeur
Pekin
Morton
Tremont
Normal
Bloomington
Gibson City
Paxton
Hoopeston
Rossville
Kahoka
Keokuk
Carthage
Hamilton
Warsaw
Macomb
Colchester
Lewistown
Havana
Delavan
Le Roy
Rantoul
Fisher
CHANUTE A.F.B.
Canton
La Grange
Camp Point
Rushville
Astoria
Mason City
Atlanta
Lincoln
Farmer City
Clinton
Mahomet
Champaign
Urbana
St. Joseph
Danville
Covington
Tilton
Westville
Mt. Sterling
Beardstown
Petersburg
Mt. Pulaski
Monticello
Homer
Tolono
Georgetown
Quincy
Virginia
New Salem
Athens
Maroa
Bement
Meredosia
Jacksonville
Springfield
Riverton
Decatur
Atwood
Villa Grove
Tuscola
Newman
Chrisman
Palmyra
Barry
Griggsville
Hannibal
Pittsfield
Winchester
Auburn
Waverly
Kincaid
Taylorville
Blue Mound
Macon
Arthur
Arcola
Sullivan
Moweaqua
Paris
Pawnee
White Hall
Roodhouse
Virden
Girard
Charleston
Mattoon
Louisiana
Shelbyville
Pana
Marshall
Terre Haute
Bowling Green
Carrollton
Carlinville
Nokomis
Litchfield
Hillsboro
Neoga
Casey
Toledo
Greenup
Mexico
Hardin
Jerseyville
Gillespie
Brighton
Benld
Staunton
Effingham
Altamont
St. Elmo
Vandalia
Oblong
Robinson
Palestine
Sullivan
Grafton
Alton
Bunker Hill
Wood River
Edwardsville
Greenville
Newton
St. Charles
University City
Granite City
Highland
Collinsville
Carlyle
Louisville
Flora
Olney
Clay City
Lawrenceville
Vincennes
GEORGE ROGERS CLARK NAT'L HIST. PARK
Bridgeport
St. Louis
E. St. Louis
Belleville
Cahokia
Breese
Sandoval
Salem
Centralia
Wamac
Petersburg
Columbia
Waterloo
Freeburg
Mascoutah
Nashville
Mt. Vernon
Fairfield
Albion
Mt. Carmel
Princeton
New Athens
Marissa
Red Bud
Sparta
Grayville
Carmi
Steeleville
Pinckneyville
Sesser
McLeansboro
Benton
Christopher
Kaskaskia
Chester
DuQuoin
Evansville
Mt. Vernon
Zeigler
W. Frankfort
Norris City
Henderson
Perryville
Murphysboro
Herrin
Johnston City
Eldorado
Marion
Harrisburg
Carriers Mills
Shawneetown
Morganfield
Carbondale
Anna
Jonesboro
Vienna
Rosiclare
Elizabethtown
Golconda
Marion
Madisonville
Cape Girardeau
Mounds
Mound City
Cairo
Metropolis
Brookport
Paducah
Princeton
88° 42° 87° 30' 41° 30'
Northbrook
Arlington Hts.
Mt. Prospect
Glenview
Winnetka
Wilmette
Morton Grove
Evanston
Des Plaines
Skokie
Park Ridge
Niles
Lincolnwood
CHI. INT'L AIRPORT (O'HARE)
Norridge
Franklin Pk.
Elmwood Pk.
Elmhurst
Villa Pk.
Melrose Pk.
Oak Pk.
Lombard
Bellwood
Maywood
Cicero
Westchester
Berwyn
Brookfield
Summit
Downers Grove
Justice
DU PAGE
COOK
Oak Lawn
Evergreen Pk.
Lemont
L. Calumet
Whiting
E. Chicago
Blue Island
Dolton
Calumet City
Harvey
Hammond
WILL
Tinley Pk.
Homewood
Lansing
Highland
Munster
Hobart
Gary
0 4 8 mi.
0 4 8 km.
Chicago Hts.
Park Forest
LAKE MICHIGAN
ILL.
IND.
Longitude West of Greenwich
© Copyright HAMMOND INCORPORATED, Maplewood, N. J.

glass, thermometers, porcelain, wooden goods, toys, dyes; technical univ. (1953); residence of Goethe.

Ilo \ˈē-(ˌ)lō\. Port, Moquegua dept., S Peru, 53 m. SE of Mollendo; pop. (1961c) 6400; connected by railroad with Moquegua, 60 m. N.

Ilo·bas·co \ˌēl-ə-ˈbäs-(ˌ)kō, ˌil-\. City, El Salvador, 40 m. NE of San Salvador; cattle raising, coffee, sugar, and indigo.

Ilo·bu \ˌē-lə-ˈbü\. Town, Western State, Nigeria; pop. (1969e) 101,152.

Ilo·cos Nor·te \i-ˌlō-kə-ˈsnȯr-ˌtā\. Province, NW Luzon, Phil.; 1312 sq. m.; pop. (1970p) 343,051; ✱ Laoag; coastline regular with few good harbors; on N coast are Bangui and Pasaleng bays and Cape Bojeador; in E is N end of Cordillera Central with highest point, Mt. Sicapoo (7716 ft.), on SE boundary; plains and low hills along W coast; only large river the Laoag; produces esp. rice; weaving, stock raising, fishing; plains inhabited mainly by Ilokanos, mountain region by Tinggian, Igorot, and Apayaos. Chief towns Laoag, Dingras, and Batac.

History: Region probably known to Chinese and Japanese traders in pre-Spanish times; all NW Luzon known as Ilocos by Spaniards and created as a province by them; explored as early as 1572 by Juan de Salcedo; N part detached 1818 and created as Ilocos Norte prov.; revolted many times against Spanish injustices, esp. 1589, 1660, 1788, and was active during 1898–99; civil government established Sept. 1901; region came under Japanese control Dec. 1941.

Ilocos Sur \i-ˌlō-kə(s)-ˈsu̇(ə)r\. Province, NW Luzon, Phil., forming a narrow strip along coast of South China Sea widening at S end; 996 sq. m.; pop. (1970p) 385,945; ✱ Vigan; coastline fairly regular, but with frequent reefs; land comparatively level, except in SE; E boundary formed by coast range, a W part of Cordillera Central; highest point ab. 3600 ft.; only large river lower course of the Abra; little agriculture because of poor soil; best crop maguey; inhabitants mostly Ilokanos; fishing. Chief towns Candon, Narvacan, Vigan, Tagudin.

History: See ILOCOS NORTE; created a province 1818 but of much larger area including parts of Abra and La Union; contains several old towns antedating Spanish times; revolts against Spanish authority, esp. in 1660 and 1763, successful for a time; civil government established Sept. 1901; came under control of Japanese Dec. 1941.

Ilog \ˈē-ˌlȯg\. Municipality, SW Negros Occidental, Negros, Phil., near coast on **Ilog River** (ab. 40 m. long, flowing NNW from Negros Oriental) 45 m. S of City of Bacolod; pop. (1969e) 33,000; an old town, settled 1584; center of sugar industry.

I–lo–hu–li Range \ˈē-ˈlō-ˈhü-ˈlē-\ *also* **Il·ku·ri Shan** \ˌil-kə-rē-ˈshän\. Mountain range in NE China connecting N ends of Greater Khingan Range and Lesser Khingan Range; forms a watershed between Nen and Hu-ma-erh rivers.

Ilo·i·lo \ˌē-lə-ˈwē-(ˌ)lō\. **1** Province, S and NE Panay I., Phil.; 2056 sq. m.; pop. (1970p) 1,168,454; ✱ Iloilo; includes Guimaras I. (*q.v.*); one of most populous provinces of the archipelago; coastline quite irregular, esp. in E and SE, with many small islands; cen. and E parts level, NE hilly, W mountainous; largest stream the Jalaud; chief industry agriculture with main crops sugar and rice; timber and other forest products; weaving; inhabitants Visayans. Chief towns Iloilo, Janiuay, Pototan, Miagao.

History: Probably first settled on SW coast by Malay datos and their followers in pre-Spanish times; Spaniards made first visits about the time of Legaspi 1565; region suffered in 16th and 17th cents. from Moro raids; original province covered entire island; parts taken to form Capiz 1716 and Antique 1798; grew rapidly in 19th cent.; given up to Revolutionary government 1898; civil government established Apr. 1901.

2 *or officially* **City of Iloilo.** Chartered city, ✱ of Iloilo prov., Phil., in SE part of Iloilo Strait; pop. (1970e) 213,000; commercial center; did not acquire a leading position until 1688; often raided by Moro pirates but because of prosperity of province declared a port for foreign trade 1855; manufacturing and cultural center; suffered damage during Japanese occupation 1942–45.

Iloilo Strait. Channel bet. S Panay I. and N Guimaras I., Phil.; 1 to 5 m. wide; at W end broadens out to ab. 25 m. wide; Iloilo and Jordan are on it.

Ilo·pan·go \ˌēl-ə-ˈpäŋ-(ˌ)gō, ˌil-\. Volcanic lake, cen. El Salvador; 5½ m. long; islands have at times appeared in it.

Ilo·rin \ˌē-lə-ˈrēn, i-ˈlȯr-ən\. Town, ✱ of Kwara State, Nigeria, ab. 170 m. NE of Lagos; pop. (1969e) 241,849; surrounded by mud walls; Yoruba agricultural center; trades esp. in palm oil and rubber; capital of a Yoruba kingdom ab. 1800; overcome by Fulahs 1825; came under British control 1900.

Ilu·ba·bor \i-ˈlüb-ə-ˌbȯr, -ˈlu̇b-\. Province of SW Ethiopia. See table at ETHIOPIA.

Ilva. See ELBA 2.

İl·yas·ba·ba \il-yäs-ˈbäb-ə\. South tip of Gallipoli Penin., Turkey, Europe.

Ima·ba·ri \ˌē-mə-ˈbär-ē, i-ˈmäb-ə-rē\ *or* **Ima·ha·ru** \ˌē-mə-ˈhär-(ˌ)ü, i-ˈmä-hə-ˌrü\. Town, Ehime prefecture, NW Shikoku, Japan; pop. (1970c) 111,125; port on Inland Sea.

Iman \i-ˈman, -ˈmän\. City, W Primorski Krai, Russian S.F.S.R., U.S.S.R., on Ussuri River 212 m. NNE of Vladivostok; pop. (1967e) 28,000; on Trans-Siberian R.R.

Iman·dra \i-ˈman-drə, -ˈmän-\. Lake, W Kola Penin., Murmansk Oblast, Russian S.F.S.R., U.S.S.R.; 340 sq. m.; outlet flows S to Kandalaksha Gulf.

Ima·ri \i-ˈmär-ē\. City, Saga prefecture, Kyūshū, Japan, 11 m. NE of Sasebo; pop. (1970c) 61,561.

Ima·tra \ˈim-ə-ˌträ\. Town, Kymi prov., SE Finland; pop. (1970e) 34,985; cellulose, chemicals; copper and iron; formed 1948.

Im·a·us \ˈim-ē-əs\. Ancient name of mountain range of W Himalayas.

Imaus Scyth·i·cus \-ˈsith-i-kəs, -ˈsi<u>th</u>-\. The Tien Shan (Mts.).

Im·ba \ˈim-bə, ˈēm-(ˌ)bä\ *or Jap.* **Im·ba·nu·ma** \im-ˈbän-ə-(ˌ)mä\. Lake in SE Honshū, Japan, ab. 30 m. E of Tokyo; ab. 44 m. in circumference; 15 sq. m.

Im·ba·bu·ra \ˌim-bə-ˈbu̇r-ə\. **1** Volcano, N Ecuador; 15,028 ft.

2 Province of N Ecuador. See table at ECUADOR.

Imbros. See İMROZ.

Imeni Svedlova Rudnik. See SVERDLOVSK 2.

Im·e·ri·tia \ˌim-ə-ˈrish-(ē-)ə\ *or* **Im·e·re·tia** \-ˈrē-sh(ē-)ə\. District of W Georgian S.S.R., U.S.S.R.; formerly an independent kingdom, ✱ Kutaisi; declared its independence c. 1424; in 18th cent. threatened by Turks and occupied by them 1750–70; came under Russian authority 1770 and finally annexed 1810. Imeritians now number ab. 500,000 and are thought to represent a very early branch of the Caucasians.

Imi \ˈē-mē\. Town, SE cen. Ethiopia, on the Shebelle.

Im·mac·u·la·ta \im-ˌak-yə-ˈlät-ə\. Locality, Chester co., SE Pennsylvania, ab. 25 m. W of Philadelphia; Immaculata Coll. (1920).

Im·na·ha \im-ˈnȯ-(ˌ)hȯ, ˈim-nə-ˌhȯ\. River, NE Oregon; ab. 75 m. long; rises in S Wallowa co., and flows N into Snake river; its gorge averages 5500 ft. in depth for 40 m., one of the deepest and narrowest in U.S.

Imo·la \ˈē-mə-ˌlä\. Commune, Bologna prov., Emilia-Romagna, N Italy, on Santerno river 21 m. SE of Bologna; pop. (1968e) 55,580; 12th cent. cathedral; former Franciscan monastery.

Imot·ski \ˈē-mət-skē\ *or* **Imo·schi** \i-ˈmȯ-skē\. City, Bosnia and Herzegovina, W Yugoslavia, ab. 40 m. ESE of Split.

Im·pe·ria \im-ˈpir-ē-ə, -ˈper-\. **1** Province of Liguria, NW Italy. See table at ITALY.

2 Seaport, its ✱, on Ligurian Sea 60 m. SW of Genoa; pop. (1968e) 39,307; formed 1923 by union of former communes Oneglia and Porto Maurizio; 18th cent. church; health resort.

Im·pe·ri·al \im-ˈpir-ē-əl\. 1 County in California. See table at CALIFORNIA.

2 City, Imperial co., SE corner of California, in Imperial Valley 5 m. N of El Centro; pop. (1970c) 3094; headquarters of Imperial Irrigation District; 67 ft. below sea level; grapefruit, cantaloupe, dates, strawberries, asparagus; founded 1902.

3 City, ⊗ of Chase co., S Nebraska; pop. (1970c) 1589.

Imperial Beach. City, San Diego co., SW California, on San Diego Bay near Mexican border; pop. (1970c) 20,244; residential.

Imperial Dam. Dam across Colorado river on S California-Arizona boundary, N of Yuma, Ariz.; height 85 ft.; completed 1938; impounds water for irrigation in **Imperial Reservoir** N of and adjoining Laguna Reservoir.

Imperial Valley. Valley in Imperial co., SE corner of California, and partly in Baja California; mostly below sea level; formerly desert, uninhabited, a part of Colorado Desert; includes Salton Sea; first irrigation project completed 1902; region now watered by the All-American Canal, 80 m. long, 200 ft. wide, which is fed by the Imperial Reservoir; market gardens; cotton and alfalfa.

Imp·hal \ˈimp-ˌhəl\. City, ✱ of Manipur state, NE India, 400 m. ENE of Calcutta; in **Imphal Plain** of cen. Manipur; pop. (1961c) 67,717; has military cantonment; object of Japanese attack and siege Mar.–June 1944; siege raised June 30.

Im·pru·ne·ta \ˌim-prü-ˈnāt-ə\. Commune, Firenze prov., Tuscany, cen. Italy, 6 m. S of Florence; pop. (1968e) 12,885.

İm·roz \im-ˈrȯz\ *or Gk.* **Im·bros** \ˈim-brəs, ˈēm-ˌvrȯs\. Turkish island in NE Aegean Sea, W of Gallipoli Penin. and NW of entrance to Dardanelles; 110 sq. m.; pop. (1965e) 1856; in ancient times a seat of worship of the Cabiri; Byzantine and Turkish island to 1912; occupied by Greece 1912–14 and then by British during Gallipoli campaign (see GALLIPOLI PENINSULA); given back to Turkey and demilitarized 1923.

Imus \ˈē-(ˌ)müs, -məs\. Municipality, Cavite prov., Luzon, Phil., 7 m. SE of Cavite; pop. (1969e) 43,400.

ʽImwas. See EMMAUS 3.

Ina \ˈē-nə\. City, Nagano prefecture, Honshū, Japan, 75 m. NE of Nagoya; pop. (1970c) 51,922.

Ina·banga \ˌē-nə-ˈbäŋ-ə\. Municipality on NW coast of Bohol I., Phil., on Bohol Strait; pop. (1969e) 38,700.

In·ac·ces·si·ble \ˌin-ik-ˈses-ə-bel, ˌin-(ˌ)ak-\. Westernmost of the Tristan de Cunha Is., S Atlantic Ocean.

In·a·chus \ˈin-ə-kəs\ *or Gk.* **Ína·khos** \ˈē-nə-ˌkȯs\. River, a headstream of the Achelous in SE Epirus, NW Greece; ab. 75 m. long.

In·a·du Knob \ˌin-ə-dü-\. Peak, Cocke co., E Tennessee; 5941 ft.

Ina·gua \in-ˈäg-wə\. Either one of two islands of the Bahama Is.: **Great Inagua** (50 m. long and 25 m. wide; lighthouse on its SW point) or **Little Inagua** (8 m. long), both in Atlantic Ocean N of W Haiti; together constitute a district, 600 sq. m., pop. (1963c) 1240.

Ina·ri \ˈē-nə-rē, -ˌnär-ē\ *or Swed.* **Ena·re** \ˈān-ə-rē, ˈā-ˌnär-ē\. Town, Lappi prov., N Finland, on SW shore of Lake Inari; pop. (1970e) 7517.

Inari, Lake *or* **Lake Ena·re** \-ˈān-ər-ē, -ˈā-ˌnär-ē\. Lake, N Finland; 535 sq. m.; receives Ivalo river from the S; outlet into Arctic Ocean.

Ina·wa·shi·ro \ˌē-nə-ˈwäsh-ə-ˌrō\. Lake, Fukushima prefecture, N cen. Honshū, Japan, SW of Mt. Bandai; 40 sq. m.; alt. 1920 ft.

Ina·za·wa \ē-ˈnäz-ə-wə\. City, Aichi prefecture, Honshū, Japan, 9 m. NW of Nagoya; pop. (1970c) 78,180.

In·ca \ˈiŋ-kə\. Commune, Baleares prov., Spain, N cen. Majorca I., 16 m. ENE of Palma; pop. (1970p) 16,930.

Inca, Pa·so del \ˈpäs-ō-de-ˈliŋ-kə\. Andean pass on border bet. La Rioja prov., NE Argentina, and S Atacama prov., N cen. Chile; alt. 15,518 ft.

In·ca·huá·si, Cerro de \ˌser-ō-dā-ˌēŋ-kə-ˈwä-sē\ *also* **Cerro de In·ca·guas·si** \-ˈgwä-\. Peak, NW Catamarca prov., NW Argentina, on border of Chile; 21,720 ft.

In·ce, Cape \-in-ˈjā\ *or Turk.* **İn·ce·bu·run** \in-ˌjā-bə-ˈrün\. Cape (*burun*) on N coast of Turkey in Asia, projecting into Black Sea W of Sinop.

Ince–in–Ma·ker·field \ˈin(t)s . . . ˈmā-kər-ˌfē(ə)ld\ *or* **Ince.** Urban district, Lancashire, NW England, 16 m. WNW of Manchester; pop. (1971p) 15,925; coal mining, textiles, ironworks.

Inch·cape Rock \ˌinch-kāp-\ *or* **Bell Rock** \ˈbel-\. Rock in North Sea, Scotland, 12 m. SE of Arbroath; covered by sea at high tide; has lighthouse built 1807–11 by Robert Stevenson, grandfather of R. L. Stevenson; subject of legends.

Inch·colm \ˈinch-kəm\. Small island in Firth of Forth, E Scotland, NW of Leith; ruins of 12th cent. abbey.

Inch·keith \ˈinch-ˌketh\. Small island, Firth of Forth, E Scotland, 4 m. N of Leith; lighthouse.

In·ch'ŏn \ˈin-ˌchän\; *formerly* **Jin·sen** \ˈjin-ˌsen\ *or* **Che·mul·po** \jə-ˈmu̇l-(ˌ)pō\. Seaport city, South Korea, 25 m. WSW of Seoul; pop. (1970e) 646,013; iron and steel plant; chemicals, lumber; opened 1883 as treaty port.

In·cu·dine, Mont l' \ˈmōⁿ-ˌlaⁿ(ŋ)-kyə-ˈdēn\. Mountain, S Corsica, ESE of Ajaccio; 7008 ft.

In·dal \ˈin-ˌdäl\ *or Swed.* **In·dals·älv** \-däl-ˌselv\. River (*älv*), N cen. Sweden; 261 m. long; flows SE into Gulf of Bothnia.

In·dang \in-ˈdäŋ\. Municipality, Cavite prov., Luzon, Phil.; road center 21 m. S of City of Cavite; pop. (1969e) 27,000.

In·daw \ˈin-(ˌ)dȯ\. Town, Sagaing division, N cen. Burma, 140 m. NW of Mandalay; taken by Allies Dec. 10, 1944.

In·daw·gyi, Lake \-ˈin-(ˌ)dȯ-ˌjē\. Lake, Kachin State, N Burma, ab. 60 m. W of Myitkyina.

Indefatigable Island. Island, Galápagos Is. See SANTA CRUZ 6.

In·de·pend·ence \ˌin-də-ˈpen-dən(t)s\. 1 County in Arkansas. See table at ARKANSAS.

2 Town, ⊗ of Inyo co., E California, 82 m. E of Fresno; lead and mercury mines.

3 City, ⊗ of Buchanan co., E Iowa, 25 m. E of Waterloo; pop. (1970c) 5910; farm elevators; dairying.

4 City, ⊗ of Montgomery co., SE Kansas, 58 m. WSW of Pittsburg; pop. (1970c) 10,347; corn, wheat; oil wells, natural-gas fields; cement; Independence Community Junior Coll. (1925).

5 City, a ⊗ of Kenton co., N Kentucky; pop. (1970c) 1784.

6 City, ⊗ of Jackson co., W Missouri, 9 m. E of Kansas City; pop. (1970c) 111,630; residential suburb of Kansas City; home of Mormon colony 1831–33; now center of Reorganized Church of Jesus Christ of Latter Day Saints; starting point of Santa Fe and Oregon Trails during Gold Rush (1849); in Civil War scene of first phase of battle of Westport Oct. 21, 1864. Home of Harry S. Truman; Harry S. Truman library (dedicated 1957).

7 City, Cuyahoga co., N Ohio, 9 m. S of Cleveland; pop. (1970c) 7034.

8 City, Polk co., NW Oregon, S of Salem; pop. (1970c) 2594.

9 Town, ⊗ of Grayson co., SW Virginia, WSW of Galax; pop. (1970c) 673.

Independence Mountains. See INDEPENDENCE RANGE.

Independence National Historical Park. See UNITED STATES, *National Historical Parks.*

Independence Pass. Mountain pass, Lake and Pitkin cos., W cen. Colorado, in Sawatch Range of the Rocky Mts.; elev. 12,095 ft.; highway, highest automobile pass in the state.

Independence Range *or* **Independence Mountains.** Range, chiefly in W Elko co., in N Nevada.

Independence Rock. Granite boulder in S Natrona co., cen. Wyoming, on N bank of Sweetwater river; 1950 ft. long, 850 ft. wide, 193 ft. high at N end; a landmark on the old Oregon Trail.

In·de·pen·den·cia \ˌin-də-pen-ˈden(t)-sē-ə\. Province, SW Dominican Republic. See table at DOMINICAN REPUBLIC.

Inderagiri. See INDRAGIRI.

In·dex Mountain \ˌin-deks-\. Mountain, King co., W Washington, in Cascade Mts. ENE of Seattle; 5978 ft.

Index Peak. 1 Mountain, Carbon co., S Montana; 11,977 ft. 2 Mountain in the Absaroka Range, NW Wyoming; 11,500 ft.

In·dia \ˈin-dē-ə\. **1** Subcontinent, S Asia; ab. 1,704,300 sq. m.; political divisions: Bangla Desh, Bhutan, the Republic of India (2 below), Nepal, Pakistan, Sikkim (*qq.v.*).

History: Invaded from Iranian plateau c. 1700–1200 B.C. by Aryans, who pushed to S and SE the earlier Dravidian and Munda inhabitants; developed important religious systems; Buddhism and Jainism, both founded in late 6th cent. B.C.; Brahmanism, with its accompanying social caste system, evolved from the Vedic religion of Aryan invaders; invaded across Indus in NW (Punjab) by Alexander the Great 327–325 B.C. Northern part consolidated (with Afghanistan) into an empire by Chandragupta, Hindu founder of Maurya dynasty (c. 322–185 B.C.), whose grandson Asoka (d. 232 B.C.) extended his empire by addition of kingdoms of Bengal and Orissa to include over two thirds of peninsula, all but extreme S part; N part again united by rulers of Gupta dynasty (320–480 A.D.); divided politically into states of varying size and power. Muslim invasions begun ab. 1000 A.D. by raid in N by the Afghan Mahmud of Ghazni; earliest Muslim kingdom, Sultanate of Delhi, including N India and part of Coromandel Coast, founded 1206 by Mohammed Tughlak but soon split up; a Muslim dynasty, the Bahmani, flourished in the Deccan from 14th cent.; for chief contemporary Hindu kingdom in S, see VIJAYANAGAR; peninsula opened by Vasco da Gama's voyage 1497–98 to direct European trade, which Portuguese monopolized in 16th cent. and for which Dutch, English, and French competed in 17th cent. Gradually conquered 1526–1707 by Mogul emperors, of whom the first was Babur and the most famous Akbar (1556–1605), until their power was challenged in late 17th cent. by the Marathas, a Hindu people whose powerful confederacy was broken by Afghans at Panipat (*q.v.*) 1761; torn by dynastic conflicts with decline of Mogul power after 1707, thus opening way for European intervention and territorial acquisition.

Period of British control: Establishment of trading posts ("factories") in 17th cent. by rival British and French East India companies (chartered 1600 and 1664, respectively) led in 18th cent. to war bet. England and France culminating in French defeat at Plassey 1757 (see CALCUTTA, DECCAN, FRENCH INDIA); ascendancy of British East India Company resulted in first extensive territorial acquisitions (Bengal and Bihar 1765, the Circars 1766) but alleged misrule by Company caused British Parliament to pass Regulating Act 1773 and Pitt's Act 1784 establishing "dual control" of Company and Crown; after wars with Mysore (*q.v.*) and Marathas, British acquired Malabar Coast 1792, Kanara 1799, Carnatic 1801, Orissa 1803, and Maratha lands (see POONA); Company's monopoly of trade abolished 1813; annexed Burma 1826–86, Sind 1843, Punjab 1849, Berar 1853, Nagpur 1854, Oudh 1856, and Baluchistan 1887 (*qq.v.*); by 1887 the parts of India not under direct British control were protected states, under native rulers, with varying degrees of dependence upon British; government modified (1861, 1909, 1919) in direction of limited self-rule. After World War I, scene of bitter struggle bet. British rulers and Indian Nationalists, under Gandhi's leadership; eventual federation of all India the goal of Act of 1935 which separated Burma and Aden from India. Areas under direct British control (i.e. **British India**) divided 1935 into eleven provinces each under a governor: Assam, Bengal, Bihar, Bombay, Central Provinces and Berar, Madras, North-West Frontier Province, Orissa, Punjab, Sind, United Provinces of Agra and Oudh and 6 provinces each under a chief commissioner responsible directly to the governor-general (Ajmer-Merwara, Andaman and Nicobar Islands, British Baluchistan, Coorg, Delhi, Panth Piploda). British rule terminated with creation of sovereign states of India (see INDIA 2) and PAKISTAN 1947.

2 *officially* **Republic of India** *also* **Indian Union** *or* **Union of India;** *Sanskrit* **Bha·rat** \ˈbər-ət, ˈbə-rət\. Republic, S Asia, bounded on N by China, Nepal, Sikkim, and Bhutan, on E by Burma, Bangla Desh, and the Bay of Bengal, on S by the Indian Ocean, and on W by the Arabian Sea and Pakistan; 1,229,424 sq. m.; pop. (1971p) 546,955,945; ✻ New Delhi. *Physical features:* May be divided into three well defined regions (a) Himalayan region in the N (b) Indo-Gangetic Plain bet. foothills of the Himalayas and the Vindhya Mts. (c) plateau region in the S and cen. part. *Chief mountains:* The Himalayas (*q.v.*) in N, containing highest peaks in the world, and in NW the borders of the Hindu Kush, Safed Koh, and Sulaiman Range, this mountain barrier bet. India and the rest of Asia being crossed by several famous passes, esp. the Khyber (*q.v.*), Bolan (5900 ft.), and Gumal (7500 ft.); passes in NW; Vindhya Mts. bet. Ganges valley and the Deccan (*q.v.*); Eastern and Western Ghats along E and W coasts; Nilgiri Hills in S. *Chief rivers:* Ganges with its chief tributary, the Yamuna, in extensive river plain of the N ; Indus system in NW with tributaries (Chenab, Jhelum, Sutlej, Beas, and Ravi); Brahmaputra in the NE flowing into the Ganges delta; Narmada and Tapti in N Deccan; Godavari and Krishna in cen. Deccan. *Chief products:* Wheat, rice, corn, cotton, tea; iron ore, coal, manganese, bauxite, mica. *Chief cities:* Bombay, Calcutta, Delhi, Madras, Ahmadabad, Hyderabad, Kanpur, Bangalore, Poona, Nagpur. Divided into the following states and territories (for pronunciation of their names and other information, see their individual entries):

NAME	AREA (sq. m.)	POP. (1971p)	CAPITAL
States			
Andhra Pradesh	106,272	43,394,951	Hyderabad
Assam[1]	69,867	14,857,314	Shillong
Bihar	67,184	56,387,296	Patna
Gujarat	72,236	26,660,929	Ahmadabad
Haryana	17,010	9,971,165	Chandigarh
Himachal Pradesh	21,490	3,424,332	Simla
Jammu and Kashmir[2]	53,665	4,615,176	Srinagar[3]
Kerala	15,007	21,280,397	Trivandrum
Madhya Pradesh	171,220	41,449,729	Bhopal
Maharashtra	118,637	50,295,081	Bombay
Manipur	8,628	1,069,555	Imphal
Meghalaya	8,665	983,336	Shillong
Mysore	74,037	29,224,046	Bangalore
Nagaland	6,366	515,561	Kohima
Orissa	60,178	21,934,827	Bhubaneswar
Punjab	19,495[4]	13,472,972	Chandigarh
Rajasthan	132,149	25,724,142	Jaipur
Tamil Nadu	50,180	41,103,125	Madras
Tripura	4,035	1,556,822	Agartala
Uttar Pradesh	113,655	88,299,453	Lucknow
West Bengal	33,852	44,440,095	Calcutta
Union Territories			
Andaman and Nicobar	3,202	115,090	Port Blair
Arunachal Pradesh[1]	. . .	. . .	Ziro
Chandigarh	. . .	256,979	Chandigarh
Dadra and Nagar Haveli	189	74,165	Silvassa
Delhi	573	4,044,338	Delhi
Goa, Daman, and Diu	1,441	857,180	Panaji
Laccadive, Minicoy, and Amindivi Is.	11	31,798	Kavaratti
Mizoram[1,5]	. . .	. . .	. . .
Pondicherry	183	471,347	Pondicherry

[1]Assam includes area and population of Arunachal Pradesh and Mizoram.
[2]Figures apply to Indian-controlled area only.
[3]Summer capital. Jammu is the winter capital.
[4]Punjab includes area of Chandigarh.
[5]Capital not official.

History: For history of region prior to 1947, see 1 above. Established Aug. 15, 1947 by Act of British Parliament; (July 18, 1947) military clash with Pakistan over possession of Jammu and Kashmir 1947–49; inaugurated republic 1950; annexed Portuguese territories of Goa, Daman, and Diu 1962; military clash with China 1959 and 1962, with Pakistan 1965 and 1971; its defeat of Pakistan (1971) decisive in establishment of Bangla Desh.

India, Bas·sas da \ˌbas-əz-də-ˈin-dē-ə\. Small islands in cen. Mozambique Channel bet. SW Malagasy Republic and SE Mozambique; belong to Malagasy Republic.

India, Farther. See INDOCHINA 1.

In·di·a·lan·tic \ˌin-dē-ə-ˈlant-ik\. City, Brevard co., E Florida, 20 m. ESE of Cocoa; pop. (1970c) 2685.

In·di·ana \ˌin-dē-ˈan-ə\. **1** A north central state of U.S.A., bounded on N by Michigan and Lake Michigan, on E by Ohio, on S by Kentucky, and on W by Illinois; 38th state in area, 36,291 sq. m., not including 228 sq. m. of water of the Great Lakes (land area 36,189 sq. m.); 11th state in population, (1970c) 5,193,669; ✱ Indianapolis; 19th state admitted to Union (1816).

Nickname: Hoosier State. *State flower:* Peony. *Motto:* The Crossroads of America. *Rivers:* Wabash, flowing from middle Ohio border W across state and then S to form lower section of boundary with Illinois; Ohio, forming SE and S boundary with Kentucky; White, with East and West Forks, flowing from central and S area SW into the Wabash. *Highest point:* Franklin township 1257 ft., in Wayne co. *Chief products:* Corn, soybeans, wheat; livestock; coal, oil, gravel; manufacturing: steel, electrical machinery, primary metal products, chemicals. *Chief cities:* Indianapolis, Fort Wayne, Gary, Evansville, South Bend, Hammond. See *Table of States* at UNITED STATES. Divided into the following 92 counties (for pronunciation of their names, see their individual entries):

NAME	LOCATION	AREA[1] (sq. m.)	POP. (1970c)	CO. SEAT
Adams	E	345	26,871	Decatur
Allen	NE	671	280,455	Fort Wayne
Bartholomew	S cen.	402	57,022	Columbus
Benton	W	409	11,262	Fowler
Blackford	E cen.	167	15,888	Hartford City
Boone	cen.	427	30,870	Lebanon
Brown	S cen.	324	9,057	Nashville
Carroll	NW cen.	374	17,734	Delphi
Cass	N cen.	415	40,456	Logansport
Clark	S	384	75,876	Jeffersonville
Clay	W	364	23,933	Brazil
Clinton	cen.	407	30,547	Frankfort
Crawford	S	312	8,033	English
Daviess	SW	430	26,602	Washington
Dearborn	SE	306	29,430	Lawrenceburg
Decatur	SE cen.	370	22,738	Greensburg
De Kalb	NE	366	30,837	Auburn
Delaware	E cen.	398	129,219	Muncie
Dubois	SW	433	30,934	Jasper
Elkhart	N	468	126,529	Goshen
Fayette	E	215	26,216	Connersville
Floyd	S	149	55,622	New Albany
Fountain	W	397	18,257	Covington
Franklin	E	394	16,943	Brookville
Fulton	N	368	16,984	Rochester
Gibson	SW	498	30,444	Princeton
Grant	N cen.	421	83,955	Marion
Greene	SW	549	26,894	Bloomfield
Hamilton	cen.	401	54,532	Noblesville
Hancock	cen.	305	35,096	Greenfield
Harrison	S	479	20,423	Corydon
Hendricks	cen.	417	53,974	Danville
Henry	E cen.	400	52,603	New Castle
Howard	N cen.	293	83,198	Kokomo
Huntington	NE	390	34,970	Huntington
Jackson	S	520	33,187	Brownstown
Jasper	NW	562	20,429	Rensselaer
Jay	E	386	23,575	Portland
Jefferson	SE	366	27,006	Madison
Jennings	SE	377	19,454	Vernon
Johnson	cen.	315	61,138	Franklin
Knox	SW	517	41,546	Vincennes
Kosciusko	N	540	48,127	Warsaw
Lagrange	N	381	20,890	Lagrange
Lake	NW corner	513	546,253	Crown Point
La Porte	N	607	105,342	La Porte
Lawrence	S	459	38,038	Bedford
Madison	cen.	453	138,451	Anderson
Marion	cen.	400	793,590	Indianapolis
Marshall	N	443	34,986	Plymouth
Martin	SW	345	10,969	Shoals
Miami	N cen.	380	39,246	Peru
Monroe	S cen.	410	84,849	Bloomington
Montgomery	W cen.	507	33,930	Crawfordsville
Morgan	cen.	406	44,176	Martinsville
Newton	NW	413	11,606	Kentland
Noble	NE	412	31,382	Albion
Ohio	SE	87	4,289	Rising Sun
Orange	S	405	16,968	Paoli
Owen	SW cen.	390	12,163	Spencer
Parke	W	451	14,600	Rockville
Perry	S	384	19,075	Cannelton
Pike	SW	335	12,281	Petersburg
Porter	NW	425	87,114	Valparaiso
Posey	SW corner	412	21,740	Mount Vernon
Pulaski	NW	433	12,534	Winamac
Putnam	W cen.	490	26,932	Greencastle
Randolph	E	457	28,915	Winchester
Ripley	SE	442	21,138	Versailles
Rush	E cen.	409	20,352	Rushville
Saint Joseph	N	466	245,045	South Bend
Scott	SE	193	17,144	Scottsburg
Shelby	cen.	409	37,797	Shelbyville
Spencer	SW	396	17,134	Rockport
Starke	NW	310	19,280	Knox
Steuben	NE corner	309	20,159	Angola
Sullivan	SW	457	19,889	Sullivan
Switzerland	SE	221	6,306	Vevay
Tippecanoe	W cen.	500	109,378	Lafayette
Tipton	cen.	261	16,650	Tipton
Union	E	168	6,582	Liberty
Vanderburgh	SW	241	168,772	Evansville
Vermillion	W	263	16,793	Newport
Vigo	W	415	114,528	Terre Haute
Wabash	N	421	35,553	Wabash
Warren	W	368	8,705	Williamsport
Warrick	SW	391	27,972	Boonville
Washington	S	516	19,278	Salem
Wayne	E	405	79,109	Richmond
Wells	NE	368	23,821	Bluffton
White	NW	497	20,995	Monticello
Whitley	NE	337	23,395	Columbia City

[1]Area = land area.

History: French settlement at Vincennes c. 1700; included in territory ceded by France to England 1763; ceded by England to United States by Treaty of Paris 1783; included in Northwest Territory 1787 and 1800 in Indiana Territory (see NORTHWEST TERRITORY); admitted to Union Dec. 11, 1816; capital removed from Corydon to Indianapolis 1825; adopted present constitution 1851.

2 County in W cen. Pennsylvania. See table at PENNSYLVANIA.

3 Borough, its ⊗, 25 m. NW of Johnstown; pop. (1970c) 16,100; leather products, tires; coal mines; Indiana Univ. of Pennsylvania (1875).

Indiana Harbor. Harbor district, East Chicago, NW Indiana, on Lake Michigan.

In·di·an·ap·o·lis \ˌin-dē-ə-ˈnap-(ə-)ləs\. City, ✱ of Indiana and ⊗ of Marion co., cen. Indiana; pop. (1970c) 745,739; largest city in the state; chemicals, electrical machinery, transportation equipment; railroad center; meat-packing houses, flour mills; War Memorial (buildings, parkways, plazas); Fort Benjamin Harrison (*q.v.*); Stout Field, with U.S. Air Force Reserve Training Center; Butler Univ. (1850), Indiana Central Coll. (1902), Marian Coll. (1937); settled 1820, made capital 1825.

In·di·an Countercurrent \ˌin-dē-ən-\. The equatorial countercurrent in the N Indian Ocean.

Indian Empire. Those parts of India formerly (until Aug. 15, 1947) under British rule or protection; consisted of British India and 562 Indian States; after April 1937 exclusive of Aden and Burma. See history at INDIA 1.

Indian Harbour. Settlement on island on N side of entrance to Hamilton Inlet, SE Labrador, Canada; one of earliest hospitals of Grenfell Mission located here 1894.

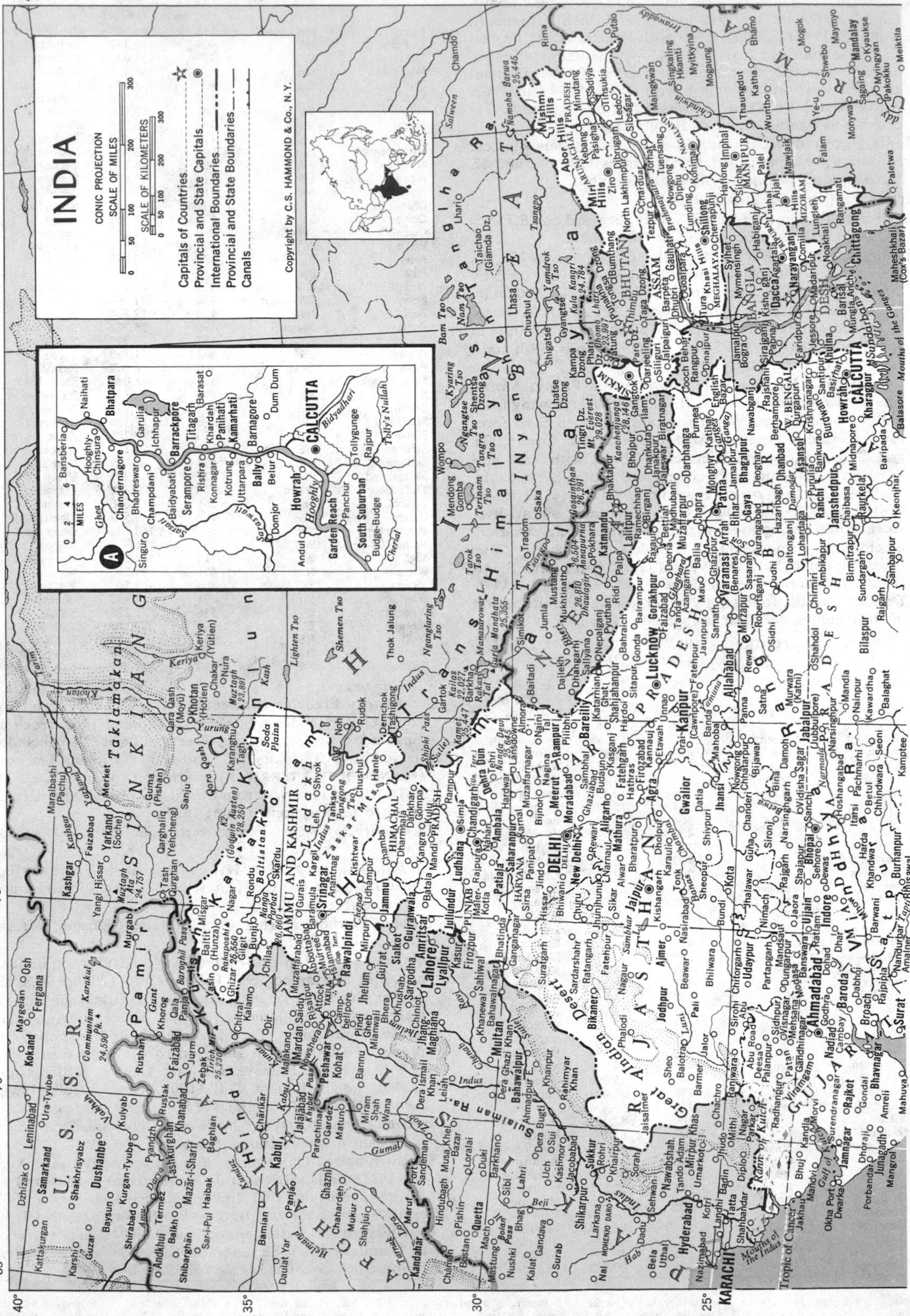
INDIA
CONIC PROJECTION
SCALE OF MILES
0 50 100 200 300
SCALE OF KILOMETERS
0 50 100 200 300
Capitals of Countries
Provincial and State Capitals
International Boundaries
Provincial and State Boundaries
Canals
Copyright by C.S. HAMMOND & Co., N.Y.
A
MILES
0 2 4 6
CALCUTTA
Howrah
Barrackpore
Serampore
Chandernagore
Bhatpara
Garden Reach
South Suburban
Dum Dum
Tollygunge

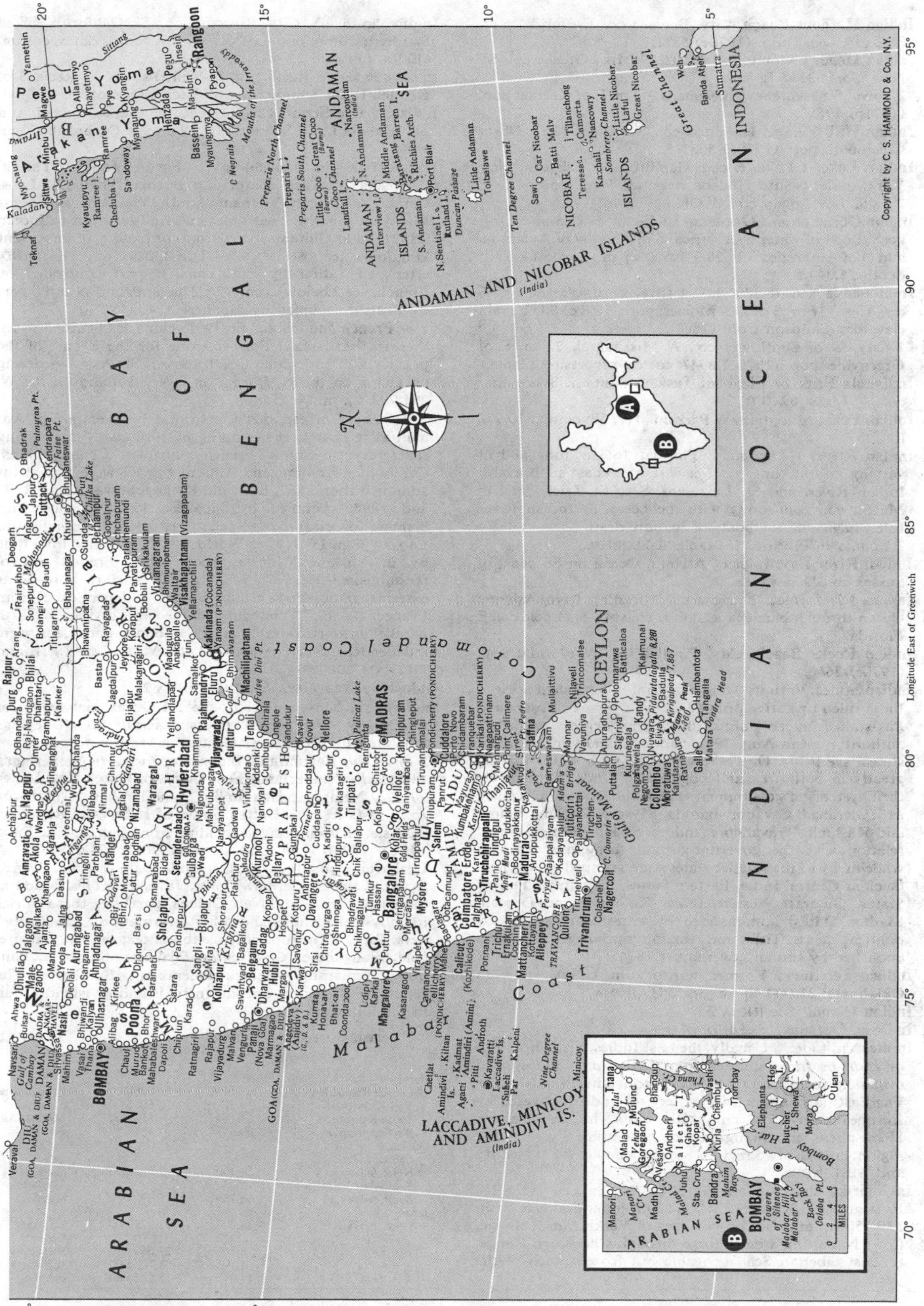

ARABIAN SEA
BAY OF BENGAL
INDIAN OCEAN
ANDAMAN SEA
ANDAMAN AND NICOBAR ISLANDS (India)
LACCADIVE, MINICOY AND AMINDIVI IS. (India)
CEYLON
INDONESIA
ANDHRA PRADESH
MADRAS
BOMBAY
Hyderabad
Bangalore
Mysore
Rangoon
Colombo
Trivandrum
Malabar Coast
Coromandel Coast
Gulf of Mannar
Palk Strait
Ten Degree Channel
Nine Degree Channel
Preparis North Channel
Preparis South Channel
Coco Channel
Duncan Passage
Sombrero Channel
Great Channel
Mouths of the Irrawaddy
Port Blair
Car Nicobar
Great Nicobar
Little Andaman
Sumatra
Jaffna
Trincomalee
Kandy
Galle
Madurai
Cochin
Calicut
Mangalore
Goa
Nagpur
Poona
Vijayawada
Visakhapatnam (Vizagapatam)
Cuttack
Pondicherry
Tiruchirapalli
Salem
Coimbatore
Kolhapur
Sholapur
Belgaum
Hubli
Kurnool
Guntur
Nellore
Vellore
Tanjore
Tuticorin
Alleppey
Quilon
Nagercoil
Sittwe
Bassein
Minicoy
Kavaratti
B
ARABIAN SEA
BOMBAY
Salsette I.
Elephanta
Thana
Bandra
Colaba Pt.
Back Bay
Malabar Hill
Towers of Silence
MILES
A
B
Longitude East of Greenwich
Copyright by C. S. HAMMOND & Co., N.Y.

Indian Harbour Beach. City, Brevard co., E Florida, 6 m. ESE of Cocoa; pop. (1970c) 5371.

Indian Head. 1 Mountain in Catskill Mts., Greene co., SE New York; 3585 ft.

2 Town, S Saskatchewan, Canada, 44 m. E of Regina; pop. (1971p) 1789.

Indian Hill. Village, Hamilton co., SW Ohio, 12 m. NE of Cincinnati; pop. (1970c) 5651.

Indian Lake. 1 Lake, E cen. Hamilton co., NE cen. New York; outlet N into Hudson river; ab. 7 m. long.

2 Lake, NW Logan co., W Ohio.

Indian Ocean *or anc.* **Oce·a·nus In·di·cus** \ō-ˌsē-ə-nə-ˈsin-di-kəs\. Body of water E of Africa, S of Asia, W of Australia, and N of Antarctica; ab. 28,350,500 sq. m.; greatest known depth 25,344 ft.

In·di·a·no·la \ˌin-dē-ə-ˈnō-lə\. 1 City, ⊗ of Warren co., S cen. Iowa, 16 m. S of Des Moines; pop. (1970c) 8852; grain elevators; Simpson Coll. (1860).

2 City, ⊗ of Sunflower co., W Mississippi, 23 m. E of Greenville; pop. (1970c) 8947; cotton-processing plants.

Indianola Peak *or* **Elephant Tusk.** Mountain, S Brewster co., W Texas; 5240 ft.

Indian Peak. Mountain, W Park co., NW Wyoming; 10,923 ft.

Indian River. 1 Lagoon, E Florida; 165 m. long and of varying width; runs parallel with the coast in Brevard, Indian River, and St. Lucie cos. S to St. Lucie Inlet in Martin co., connecting with the ocean at Indian River Inlet; navigable for boats of shallow draft.

2 County in Florida. See table at FLORIDA.

Indian River Bay. Inlet of Atlantic Ocean on SE coast of Sussex co., Delaware.

Indian River Inlet. Narrow strait leading from Atlantic Ocean through barrier reefs off E coast of St. Lucie co., E Florida.

Indian Rocks Beach. City, Pinellas co., W Florida; pop. (1970c) 2666.

Indian States. Various (formerly) semi-independent areas in India ruled by native princes; areas now part of India and Pakistan; formerly subject in varying degrees to British authority, but in Aug. 1947 made nominally independent states (see INDIA 1). There were 562 such states varying greatly in both area and population. Under British rule their systems of government varied, the larger states (such as Hyderabad, Gwalior, Baroda, Mysore, Cochin, Jammu and Kashmir, Travancore, Indore, Sikkim) were in direct relation with the governor-general through a resident, while many of the smaller states were grouped in Agencies (such as Central India, Eastern States, Rajputana, Punjab States, Gujarat, Western India, Kolhapur and Deccan, Madras States) administered by a resident assisted by political agents. Titles and remaining privileges of princes abolished by Indian government 1971.

Indian Territory. Former territory in U.S.A., now in Oklahoma; 31,000 sq. m. See OKLAHOMA.

Indian Union. See INDIA 2.

Indicus, Oceanus. See INDIAN OCEAN.

In·dies \ˈin-(ˌ)dēz\. Usually, the East Indies; the plural form of *Indie* or *Indy,* adapted from Latin *India* and applied originally to India and adjacent lands and islands in the Far East; later applied by writers to lands discovered by Europeans in 15th and 16th cents. in the Western Hemisphere, and thought to be geographically the same region; later the two regions became known as EAST INDIES and WEST INDIES.

In·di·gir·ka \ˌin-də-ˈgi(ə)r-kə\. River, NE Yakutsk A.S.S.R., Russian S.F.S.R., U.S.S.R.; 1112 m. long; drainage basin 139,150 sq. m.; rises on N slopes of Verkhoyansk Range, flows N, cutting a deep gorge through Cherskogo Range, to East Siberian Sea; navigable but frozen much of the year.

In·dio \ˈin-dē-ˌō\. City, Riverside co., SE California, SE of San Bernardino; pop. (1970c) 14,459; resort; dates, cotton, alfalfa; founded 1876.

In·dis·pen·sa·ble Reefs \ˌin-dis-ˈpen(t)-sə-bəl-\. Reefs S of Rennell I., SE Solomon Is., W Pacific Ocean; ab. 11°S lat.

Indispensable Strait. Channel bet. NE Guadalcanal I. and SW Malaita I., SE Solomon Is., W Pacific Ocean; ab. 35 m. wide.

In·do·chi·na \ˈin-(ˌ)dō-ˈchī-nə\ *or* **Farther India.** 1 The SE peninsula of Asia, comprising Burma, Thailand, Laos, Cambodia, North Vietnam, South Vietnam, and West Malaysia. Since ancient times culturally subject to Indian (Hindu) and Chinese civilization; for history of important kingdoms, see ANNAM, BURMA, CAMBODIA, and THAILAND; after penetration by Europeans, E part controlled by French (see 2 below), center by Thailand, and W and S part by British; occupied by Japanese 1940–45.

2 *or* **French Indochina;** *Fr.* **In·do·chine fran·çaise** \aⁿ-dō-shēn-fräⁿ-sez, -säz\. Former name for the E part of the peninsula of Indochina (see 1 above), SE Asia, bordering on China on the N, Burma on NW, Thailand on the W; 291,793 sq. m.; ✱ Hanoi.

History: Corresponds approximately to empire of Annam as it existed at beginning of 19th cent., then owing suzerainty to China. French-controlled Cochin China, Cambodia, Annam, and Tonkin (*qq.v.*) were united for administration 1887, Laos and Kwangchowan added 1893 and 1898; occupied by Japanese 1940; clashed with Siamese forces; forced to cede territory in Cambodia and Laos to Siam 1941; after World War II occupied for a time by British and Chinese troops until French control reestablished Mar. 4, 1946; scene of warfare 1946–54 as extreme nationalist group sought independence from France; by 1955 Vietnam had become divided at 17th parallel into two states and Cambodia and Laos were independent. See CAMBODIA; LAOS; VIETNAM, NORTH and VIETNAM, SOUTH.

Indochine française. See INDOCHINA 2.

In·do·ne·sia \ˌin-də-ˈnē-zhə, -shə\. 1 Occasional name for the Malay Archipelago; refers generally to all regions inhabited by peoples related to the Malays proper.

2 *or in full* **Republic of Indonesia;** *formerly* **Netherlands Indies** *also* **Netherlands East Indies** *or* **Dutch East Indies** *or Du.* **Ne·der·landsch–In·dië** \ˌnā-dər-ˌlän(t)s-ˈin-dē-ə\; *from 1949 to 1950* **United States of Indonesia.** Republic, SE Asia, an archipelago extending from long. 95°E to long. 141°E; 779,675 sq. m.; pop. (1970e) 121,089,000; ✱ Djakarta. Constituent parts include: Bali, Bangka, Borneo (part), Celebes, Ceram, Flores, Java, Lombok, Madura, Sumatra, Timor, and New Guinea (part) [see these entries for physical features and other information]. *Chief products:* Rice, corn, root crops, rubber, tea; oil, tin, bauxite, coal, manganese. *Chief cities:* Djakarta, Surabaja, Bandung, Semarang, Medan, Palembang, Surakarta. The republic's provinces are shown by island or island group in the following table:

NAME	AREA (sq. m.)	POP. (1970e)	CAPITAL
Borneo			
Central Kalimantan	60,445	626,000	Palangkaraja
East Kalimantan	78,231	695,000	Samarinda
South Kalimantan	13,144	1,857,000	Bandjarmasin
West Kalimantan	60,643	1,994,000	Pontianak
Celebes			
Central Sulawesi			Palu
North Sulawesi	34,200[1]	2,526,000[2]	Manado
South-East Sulawesi			Kendari
South Sulawesi	38,786[3]	6,399,000[4]	Makasar
Java			
Central Java	13,207	22,827,000	Semarang
Djakarta[5]	228		Djakarta
East Java	18,503	27,063,000	Surabaja
Jogjakarta[6]	1,193	2,779,000	Jogjakarta
West Java	17,876	25,532,000[7]	Bandung

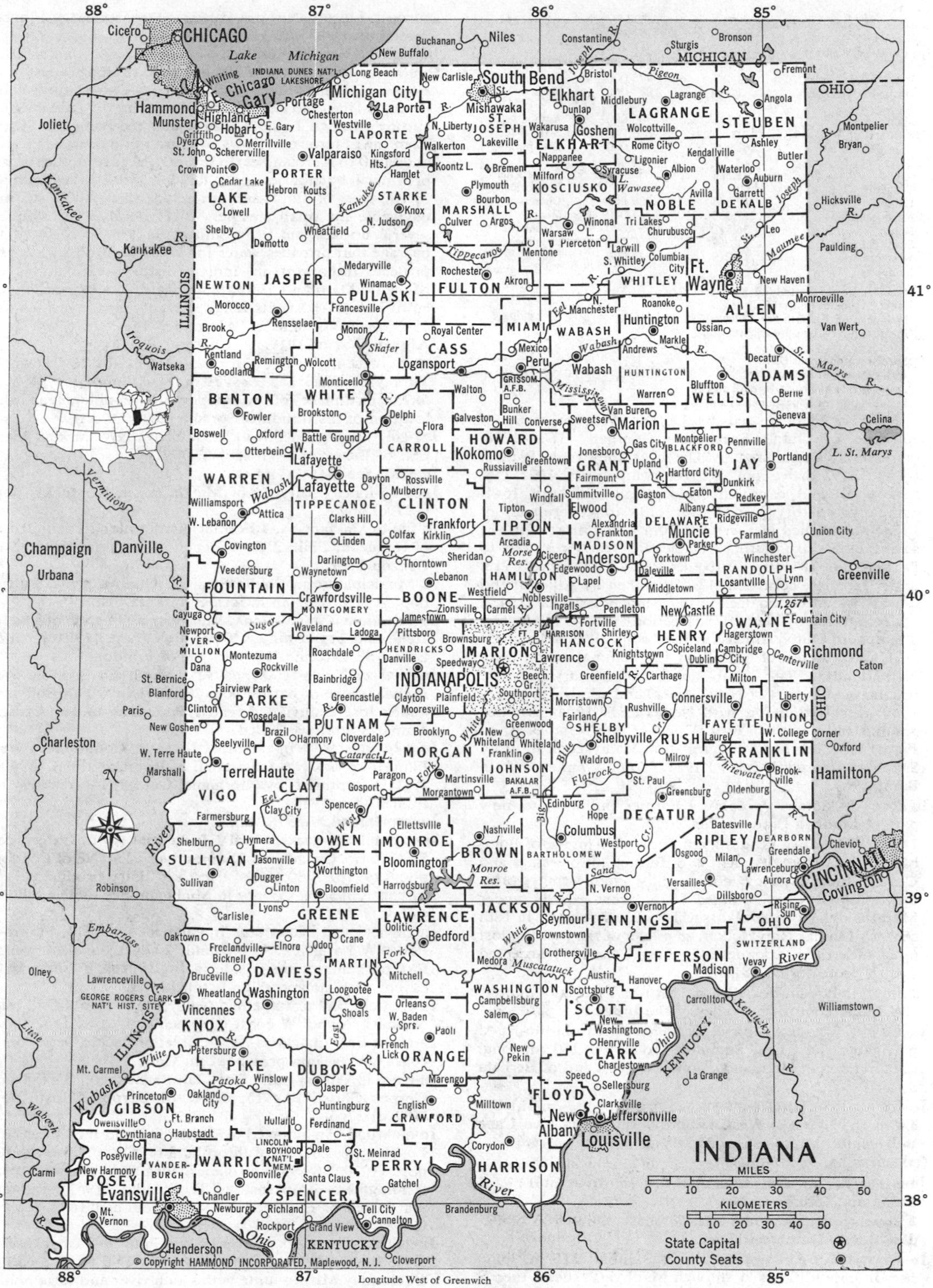
INDIANA
MILES
0 10 20 30 40 50
KILOMETERS
0 10 20 30 40 50
State Capital
County Seats
88° 87° 86° 85°
41° 40° 39° 38°
Longitude West of Greenwich
© Copyright HAMMOND INCORPORATED, Maplewood, N. J.
N
CHICAGO
Cicero
Lake Michigan
MICHIGAN
ILLINOIS
OHIO
KENTUCKY
INDIANA DUNES NAT'L LAKESHORE
LINCOLN BOYHOOD NAT'L MEM.
GEORGE ROGERS CLARK NAT'L HIST. SITE
GRISSOM A.F.B.
BAKALAR A.F.B.
INDIANAPOLIS
LAKE
PORTER
LAPORTE
ST. JOSEPH
ELKHART
LAGRANGE
STEUBEN
NOBLE
DEKALB
KOSCIUSKO
MARSHALL
STARKE
NEWTON
JASPER
PULASKI
FULTON
WHITLEY
ALLEN
HUNTINGTON
WABASH
MIAMI
CASS
WHITE
BENTON
CARROLL
HOWARD
GRANT
BLACKFORD
WELLS
ADAMS
JAY
WARREN
TIPPECANOE
CLINTON
TIPTON
MADISON
DELAWARE
RANDOLPH
FOUNTAIN
MONTGOMERY
BOONE
HAMILTON
HANCOCK
HENRY
WAYNE
VERMILLION
PARKE
HENDRICKS
MARION
SHELBY
RUSH
FAYETTE
UNION
PUTNAM
MORGAN
JOHNSON
FRANKLIN
VIGO
CLAY
OWEN
MONROE
BROWN
BARTHOLOMEW
DECATUR
RIPLEY
DEARBORN
SULLIVAN
GREENE
LAWRENCE
JACKSON
JENNINGS
OHIO
SWITZERLAND
JEFFERSON
KNOX
DAVIESS
MARTIN
WASHINGTON
SCOTT
CLARK
ORANGE
PIKE
DUBOIS
CRAWFORD
FLOYD
HARRISON
GIBSON
WARRICK
PERRY
POSEY
VANDERBURGH
SPENCER
Joliet
Hammond
Munster
Highland
Griffith
Dyer
St. John
Crown Point
Cedar Lake
Lowell
Whiting
E. Chicago
Gary
E. Gary
Hobart
Merrillville
Schererville
Portage
Chesterton
Westville
Valparaiso
Hebron
Kouts
Michigan City
La Porte
Long Beach
New Buffalo
Buchanan
Niles
New Carlisle
South Bend
Mishawaka
N. Liberty
Walkerton
Lakeville
Kingsford Hts.
Hamlet
Koontz L.
Bremen
Plymouth
Bourbon
Culver
Argos
Knox
N. Judson
Wheatfield
Demotto
Shelby
Kankakee
Constantine
Sturgis
Bronson
Fremont
Bristol
Elkhart
Middlebury
Dunlap
Wakarusa
Goshen
Nappanee
Lagrange
Wolcottville
Rome City
Kendallville
Ligonier
Albion
Angola
Ashley
Butler
Waterloo
Auburn
Garrett
Avilla
Syracuse
Milford
Wawasee
Warsaw
Winona L.
Pierceton
Mentone
Tri Lakes
Churubusco
Larwill
S. Whitley
Columbia City
Ft. Wayne
Leo
New Haven
Montpelier
Bryan
Hicksville
Paulding
Monroeville
Van Wert
Rochester
Akron
Medaryville
Winamac
Francesville
Morocco
Brook
Rensselaer
Kentland
Goodland
Remington
Watseka
Monon
L. Shafer
Royal Center
Logansport
Wolcott
Monticello
Mexico
Peru
Wabash
N. Manchester
Roanoke
Huntington
Ossian
Markle
Andrews
Decatur
Bluffton
Warren
Berne
Geneva
Celina
L. St. Marys
Fowler
Boswell
Oxford
Otterbein
Brookston
Delphi
Flora
Walton
Galveston
Bunker Hill
Converse
Sweetser
Van Buren
Marion
Battle Ground
W. Lafayette
Lafayette
Kokomo
Russiaville
Greentown
Jonesboro
Gas City
Upland
Fairmount
Hartford City
Montpelier
Pennville
Portland
Dayton
Rossville
Mulberry
Windfall
Summitville
Gaston
Eaton
Dunkirk
Redkey
Albany
Williamsport
W. Lebanon
Attica
Clarks Hill
Frankfort
Kirklin
Tipton
Elwood
Alexandria
Frankton
Muncie
Parker
Ridgeville
Farmland
Union City
Winchester
Lynn
Greenville
Champaign
Urbana
Danville
Covington
Veedersburg
Linden
Colfax
Darlington
Thorntown
Waynetown
Lebanon
Sheridan
Arcadia
Cicero
Morse Res.
Anderson
Edgewood
Lapel
Yorktown
Daleville
Middletown
Losantville
Crawfordsville
Westfield
Noblesville
Zionsville
Carmel
Ingalls
Pendleton
New Castle
Fountain City
Cayuga
Newport
Jamestown
Waveland
Ladoga
Pittsboro
Brownsburg
Fortville
Shirley
Hagerstown
Richmond
Montezuma
Rockville
Dana
Roachdale
Danville
Speedway
Lawrence
Knightstown
Spiceland
Dublin
Cambridge City
Centerville
Eaton
St. Bernice
Blanford
Fairview Park
Bainbridge
Greencastle
Clayton
Plainfield
Beech Gr.
Southport
Greenfield
Carthage
Milton
Paris
Clinton
Rosedale
Mooresville
Morristown
Rushville
Connersville
Liberty
New Goshen
Brazil
Harmony
Cloverdale
Brooklyn
New Whiteland
Whiteland
Greenwood
Franklin
Fairland
Shelbyville
Laurel
W. College Corner
Oxford
Charleston
W. Terre Haute
Seelyville
Terre Haute
Cataract L.
Martinsville
Waldron
Milroy
Brookville
Hamilton
Marshall
Paragon
Gosport
Morgantown
St. Paul
Greensburg
Oldenburg
Farmersburg
Clay City
Spencer
Edinburg
Hope
Batesville
Shelburn
Hymera
Ellettsville
Nashville
Columbus
Westport
Osgood
Milan
Greendale
Cheviot
Jasonville
Worthington
Bloomington
Monroe Res.
Lawrenceburg
Aurora
CINCINNATI
Covington
Robinson
Sullivan
Dugger
Linton
Bloomfield
Harrodsburg
N. Vernon
Versailles
Dillsboro
Rising Sun
Carlisle
Lyons
Oolitic
Bedford
Seymour
Vernon
Oaktown
Freelandville
Elnora
Odon
Crane
Brownstown
Crothersville
Vevay
Bicknell
Medora
Madison
Olney
Lawrenceville
Bruceville
Wheatland
Washington
Loogootee
Mitchell
Austin
Hanover
Carrollton
Vincennes
Shoals
Orleans
W. Baden Sprs.
French Lick
Paoli
Campbellsburg
Salem
Scottsburg
New Washington
Henryville
Williamstown
Petersburg
Mt. Carmel
New Pekin
Charlestown
Winslow
Jasper
Marengo
Speed
Sellersburg
La Grange
Princeton
Oakland City
Huntingburg
English
Milltown
Clarksville
Jeffersonville
Owensville
Ft. Branch
Haubstadt
Cynthiana
Hulland
Ferdinand
New Albany
Louisville
Poseyville
Dale
St. Meinrad
Corydon
New Harmony
Boonville
Santa Claus
Gatchel
Carmi
Chandler
Newburgh
Richland
Tell City
Cannelton
Brandenburg
Evansville
Mt. Vernon
Rockport
Grand View
Henderson
Cloverport
1,257
Kankakee R.
Iroquois R.
Vermilion
Wabash
Sugar
Eel
White
West Fork
East Fork
Embarrass
Little Wabash
Patoka
Big Blue
Flatrock
Sand
Muscatatuck
Whitewater
Pigeon
St. Joseph R.
Maumee
St. Marys R.
Tippecanoe
Mississinewa
Salamonie
Ohio River
Kentucky R.

NAME	AREA (sq. m.)	POP. (1970e)	CAPITAL
Lesser Sunda Islands			
Bali	2,147	2,247,000	Denpasar
East Nusa Tenggara	18,485	2,475,000	Kupang
West Nusa Tenggara	7,790	2,277,000	Mataram
Moluccas			
Maluku	28,766	995,000	Ambon
New Guinea			
Irian Barat	162,927	957,000	Djajapura
Sumatra			
Atjeh[6]	21,387	2,055,000	Banda Atjeh
Bengkulu			Bengkulu
Djambi	17,345	939,000	Djambi
North Sumatra	27,331	6,257,000	Medan
Riau	36,510	1,557,000	Pakanbaru
South Sumatra	61,067[8]	6,107,000[9]	Palembang
West Sumatra	19,219	2,925,000	Padang
Lampung			Tandjungkarang

[1]Includes area of Central Sulawesi.
[2]Includes pop. of Central Sulawesi.
[3]Includes area of South-East Sulawesi.
[4]Includes pop. of South-East Sulawesi.
[5]Capital Territory.
[6]Special Autonomous District.
[7]Includes pop. of Djakarta.
[8]Includes area of Bengkulu and Lampung.
[9]Includes pop. of Bengkulu and Lampung.

History: First visited by Dutch 1595–96; scene of activities of Dutch East India Company 1602–1798; increasingly dominated by Dutch as they built Batavia (*q.v.*) 1619, drove out English competitors 1623 (see AMBON 3), and captured Malacca on mainland 1641; company territory turned over 1798 to government of French-controlled Netherlands from which most of it was seized by British during Napoleonic Wars; restored to Netherlands 1816; legislative assembly established 1918; under Japanese control 1942–45; retaken by Allies at end of war 1945; declared itself an independent republic (1945), not recognized by Netherlands; period 1945–49 marked by attempts of Dutch to reassert their control; establishment of United States of Indonesia (in nominal union with Netherlands) 1949; establishment of unitary republic (exclusive of W part of New Guinea) and admission to UN 1950; dissolved union with Netherlands 1954; assumed administrative control over W part of New Guinea (Irian Barat) 1963; reached settlement with Malaysia on status of Sabah and Sarawak (*qq.v.*) 1966; formally annexed Irian Barat 1969.

In·dore \in-'dō(ə)r, -'dȯ(ə)r\. 1 Former Indian state, now part of Madhya Pradesh, cen. India.

2 City, W Madhya Pradesh, cen. India, 340 m. NE of Bombay; pop. (1970e) 494,664; ✱ of former Indore state and Central India Agency; cotton mills; engineering works; univ. (1964). City, founded 1715, grew rapidly under Maratha dynasty of Holkars which was established in 18th cent. by Malhar Rao Holkar, an officer of the peshwa; lost much of territory after defeat by Lord Lake 1804; accepted British protectorate 1818.

In·do·scyth·ia \ˌin-dō-'sith-ē-ə, -'sit͟h-\. Ancient country, NW India, comprising valley of the Indus.

In·dra·gi·ri \ˌin-drə-'gi(ə)r-ē\ *or* **In·de·ra·gi·ri** \ˌin-d(ə-)rə-\. Navigable river, cen. Sumatra, Indonesia; 250 m. long; rises in Padang Highlands, flows E into N end of Berhala Strait.

In·dra·ma·ju *or* **In·dra·ma·yu** \ˌin-drə-'mī-(ˌ)ü, -'mä-(ˌ)yü\. Town on N coast of West Java prov., Indonesia, near **Cape Indramaju;** pop. (1961c) 25,710.

Indraprastha. See DELHI 2.

In·dra·pu·ra *or Du.* **In·dra·poe·ra** \ˌin-drə-'pu̇(ə)r-ə\. 1 Mountain, Indonesia. See KERENTJI 2.

2 Town, Sumatra, Indonesia; on coast 90 m. SSE of Padang; early Dutch settlement.

In·dra·va·ti \in-'dräv-ət-ē\. River, S India; 315 m. long; rises in Orissa, flows W through Madhya Pradesh, then S to the Godavari on border of Andhra Pradesh.

In·dre \'a^{n}(n)dr^{ə}\. 1 River, cen. France; 165 m. long; flows NW in Indre and Indre-et-Loire depts. into the Loire river.

2 Department of cen. France. See table at FRANCE.

Indre–et–Loire \ˌa^{n}(n)-drā-lə-'wär\. Department of France. See table at FRANCE.

Indreville. See CHÂTEAUROUX.

In·dus \'in-dəs\. River, Asia; ab. 1800 m. long; rises on N slopes of Kailas Range, SW Tibet, China, flows NW through Tibet and Jammu and Kashmir (*q.v.*) ab. 680 m., cutting through Ladakh Range and receiving the Shyok from the E; turns and flows SW through Pakistan (Punjab and Sind) to Arabian Sea; in several places its course forms provincial boundaries; only large tributary the Panjnad (*q.v.*); area of its basin estimated at 372,000 sq. m.; navigable for small steamers to Hyderabad; crossed by several bridges and in N Sind at Sukkur (*q.v.*) by great barrage that provides water for vast irrigation and power project. Important in Indian history: excavations at Mohenjo-Daro and Harappa indicate an advanced Indus culture ab. 2500 B.C.; its valley scene of many invasions and conflicts from time of Alexander the Great to Third Afghan War of 1919.

Ine·bo·lu \ˌē-nə-bə-'lü\ *or formerly* **Ine·bo·li** \-'lē\. Town, N Turkey, on Black Sea coast 70 m. W of Sinop; pop. (1960c) 5873; birthplace of Alexander the Paphlagonian and location of his fraudulent oracle (2d cent. A.D.).

İne·göl \ˌēn-ə-'gəl\. Town, Bursa prov., NW Turkey, 25 m. ESE of Bursa; pop. (1965c) 27,777.

Inessa. See BIANCAVILLA.

Inez \'ī-(ˌ)nez\. City, ⊗ of Martin co., E Kentucky; pop. (1970c) 469.

In·fan·ta \in-'fant-ə\. 1 Former district along Pacific coast of E Luzon, Phil., a dependency of Laguna; annexed to Quezon 1902.

2 Municipality on Polillo Strait, E Quezon prov., Luzon; pop. (1969e) 29,800; in former Infanta dist.

In·gate·stone \'iŋ-gət-stən\. Village in civil parish of **Ingatestone and Fry·er·ning** \-'frī-ər-niŋ\ (pop. [1961c] 2012), Essex, SE England, 23½ m. NE of London.

In·ga·ví *or* **Yn·ga·ví** \ˌēŋ-gä-'vē\. Mountain S of La Paz, Bolivia; scene of battle Nov. 20, 1841 in which Bolivians under José Ballivián defeated Peruvians under Agustín Gamarra who was killed.

In·gel·mun·ster \'iŋ-gəl-ˌmən(t)-stər\. Commune, West Flanders prov., NW Belgium, E of Roeselare; pop. (1969e) 10,213; captured by Germans Oct. 1914, retaken by French Oct. 1918.

Ingermanland. See INGRIA.

In·ger·soll \'iŋ-gər-ˌsȯl, -səl\. Industrial town, Oxford co., SE Ontario, Canada, on Thames river 18 m. NE of London; pop. (1971p) 7780; tools; livestock; dairy products.

Ing·ham \'iŋ-əm\. County in Michigan. See table at MICHIGAN.

In·gle·bor·ough Mountain \'iŋ-gəl-ˌbər-ə-, -ˌbə-rə-, -b(ə-)rə-\. Peak, W Yorkshire, N England; 2373 ft.; ancient walled fort on summit; on S side is **Ingleborough Cave,** large cavern with stalactites and stalagmites.

In·gle·field Bay *or* **Inglefield Gulf** \ˌiŋ-gəl-ˌfē(ə)l(d)-\. Inlet of Smith Sound, W coast of Greenland.

In·gle·sa Bay \iŋ-ˌglā-sə-, -zə-\. Inlet of Pacific Ocean on W coast of Atacama prov., N cen. Chile.

In·gle·side \'iŋ-gəl-ˌsīd\. City, San Patricio co., S Texas, on Corpus Christi Bay 15 m. NE of Corpus Christi; pop. (1970c) 3763.

In·gle·wood \'iŋ-gəl-ˌwu̇d\. Residential and industrial city, Los Angeles co., SW California, 8 m. SW of Los Angeles; pop. (1970c) 89,985; airplanes, furniture, plastics; truck farming; Northrop Inst. of Technology (1942), Western State Coll. of Engineering (1946); founded 1873, incorp. (1908).

In·go·da \'iŋ-gəd-ə\. River, SW Chita Oblast, Russian S.F.S.R., U.S.S.R.; 360 m. long; flows NE from S end of Yablonovy Mts. to unite with Onon river and form Shilka river.

In·gol·stadt \'iŋ-gəl-ˌs(h)tät\. City, Bavaria, West Germany, on left bank of Danube river 43 m. N of Munich; pop. (1969e) 70,841; automobiles, machinery, textiles, electron-

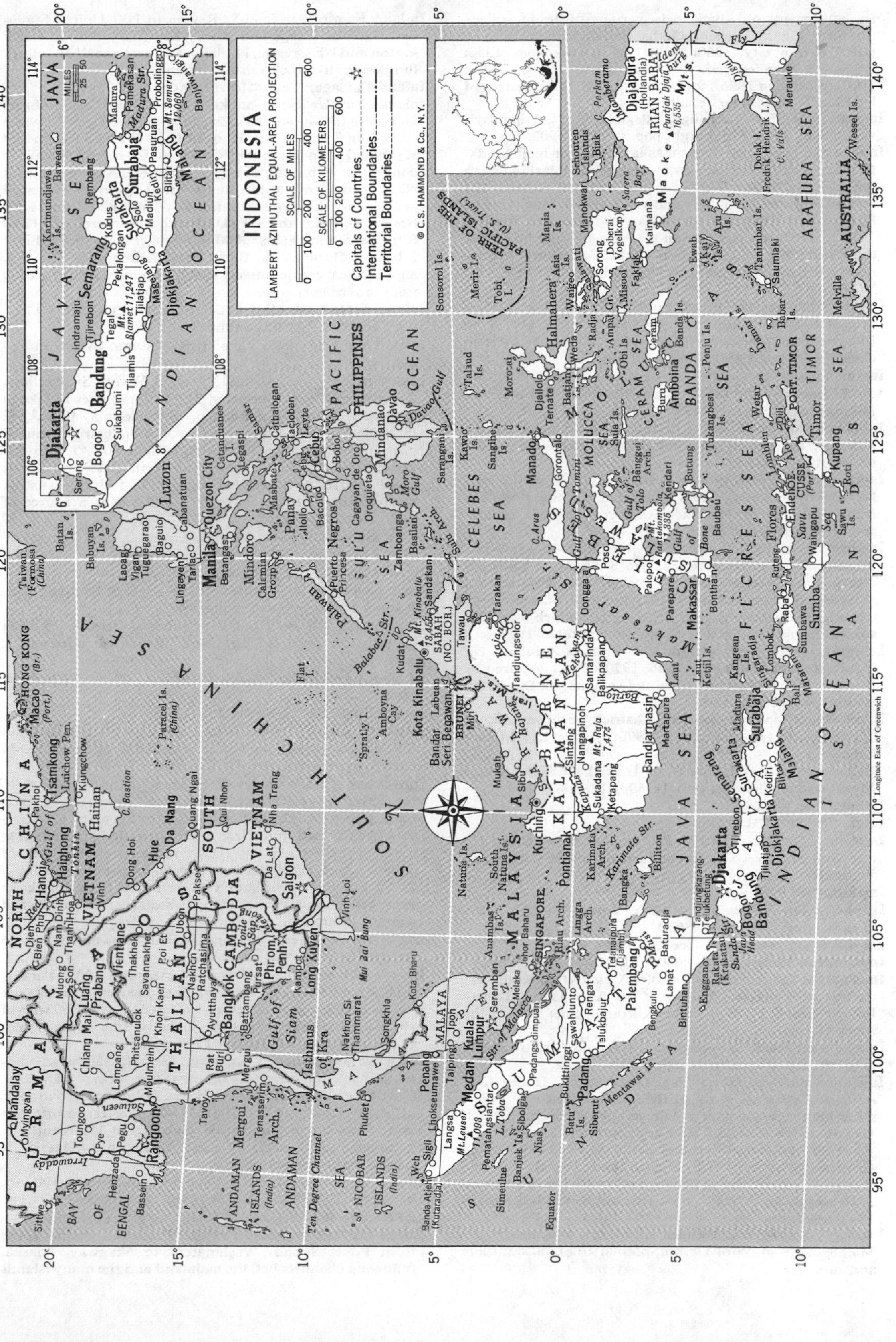
INDONESIA
LAMBERT AZIMUTHAL EQUAL-AREA PROJECTION
SCALE OF MILES
0 100 200 400 600
SCALE OF KILOMETERS
0 100 200 400 600
Capitals of Countries
International Boundaries
Territorial Boundaries
© C.S. HAMMOND & Co., N.Y.
JAVA
INDIAN OCEAN
JAVA SEA
SOUTH CHINA SEA
PACIFIC OCEAN
CELEBES SEA
SULU SEA
MOLUCCA SEA
CERAM SEA
BANDA SEA
FLORES SEA
TIMOR SEA
ARAFURA SEA
BAY OF BENGAL
ANDAMAN SEA
PHILIPPINES
MALAYSIA
KALIMANTAN
BORNEO
SUMATRA
CELEBES
IRIAN BARAT
THAILAND
CAMBODIA
BURMA
NORTH VIETNAM
SOUTH VIETNAM
AUSTRALIA
Djakarta
Longitude East of Greenwich

ics equipment; old ducal palace; ruins of Jesuit college (founded 1555); 15th cent. Gothic church. First mentioned 806; became city 1250, capital of a dukedom 1350; university founded here 1472 (transferred to Landshut 1800, to Munich 1826); fortifications built 1539, destroyed by French 1800, later rebuilt.

In·gram \ˈiŋ-grəm\. Borough, Allegheny co., SW Pennsylvania, 4 m. W of Pittsburgh; pop. (1970c) 4902.

In·gria \ˈiŋ-grē-ə\ *or* **In·ger·man·land** \ˈiŋ-gər-mən-ˌland\. District of early Russia, now in Leningrad Oblast, Russian S.F.S.R., U.S.S.R., S of E end of Gulf of Finland; for several centuries nominally under Novgorod; fought for by Sweden and Russia 14th to 17th cents.; became Swedish 1617 to 1703; its chief fort on the Neva captured by Peter the Great 1703 who there founded St. Petersburg; permanently Russian by Treaty of Nystad (see UUSIKAUPUNKI) 1721.

In·grid Chris·ten·sen Coast \ˌiŋ-grəd-ˌkris-tən-sən-\. Section of coast of Antarctica, on Indian Ocean, ab. 74° to 81°E, bet. Lars Christensen Coast and Luitpold and Astrid Coast; discovered and claimed by Norway 1935.

In·gul \in-ˈgül, iŋ-\. River, S Ukrainian S.S.R., U.S.S.R.; ab. 220 m. long; flows S into Bug river near its mouth, at Nikolayev.

In·gu·lets \ˌiŋ-gəl-ˈ(y)ets\. River, S Ukrainian S.S.R., U.S.S.R.; ab. 341 m. long; flows S into Dnieper river near its mouth.

In·gu·ri \in-ˈgu̇(ə)r-ē, iŋ-\ *or* **In·gur** \in-ˈgu̇(ə)r, iŋ-\. River, NW Georgian S.S.R., U.S.S.R.; ab. 132 m. long; flows SW from Caucasus Mts. to Black Sea; forms part of E boundary of Abkhazian A.S.S.R.

In·gush \in-ˈgüsh, iŋ-\ *or* **In·gu·she·tia** \ˌiŋ-gə-ˈshē-sh(ē-)ə\. Former autonomous area, Russian S.F.S.R., U.S.S.R., N of Caucasus Mts. and W of Chechen area; 1242 sq. m.; ✱ Ordzhonikidze; in Nov. 1920 joined with Chechen area to form Checheno-Ingush A.S.S.R. (*q.v.*) which was dissolved during World War II but reconstituted 1957.

Ing·wa·vu·ma \ˌiŋ-(g)wə-ˈvü-mə\. District, N Zululand, NE Natal, Rep. of South Africa; ab. 1950 sq. m.; acquired by Great Britain 1895; chief town Ingwavuma, on Swaziland border. See TONGALAND.

Inham·ba·ne \ˌin-yəm-ˈban-ə\. 1 District, SE Mozambique, SE Africa; 26,436 sq. m.; pop. (1970p) 745,911; ✱ Inhambane.

2 Commercial seaport, its ✱, on **Inhambane Bay,** inlet of Mozambique Channel; pop. (1960p) 22,108.

I–ning. See KULDJA.

Inini. See FRENCH GUIANA.

Iní·ri·da \i-ˈnir-əd-ə\. River, E Colombia; flows E and NE into Guaviare river near its confluence with the Orinoco on Venezuelan border.

Inisfail. See INNISFAIL 2.

Ini·sha \ə-ˈnē-shə\ *or* **Ini·sa** \-sə\. Town, Western State, Nigeria; pop. (1969e) 60,863.

Ini·sheer \ˌin-ə-ˈshi(ə)r\. See ARAN ISLANDS.

In·ish·maan \ˌin-ish-ˈman, -ˈmän\. See ARAN ISLANDS.

In·ish·more \ˌin-ish-ˈmō(ə)r, -ˈmȯ(ə)r\ *also* **Ar·an·more** \ˌar-ən-ˈmō(ə)r, -ˈmȯ(ə)r\. Largest of the Aran Is., in Galway Bay, W Eire; 9 m. long; on it is Kilronan, chief town of the Aran Is.

In·ish·ow·en Head \ˌin-i-ˌshō-ən-\. Cape on N coast of Ireland, W of entrance to Lough Foyle.

In·ish·tra·hull \ˌin-ish-trə-ˈhəl\. Island in co. Donegal, in Atlantic Ocean off N tip of Ireland; lighthouse.

In·ker·man \ˈiŋ-kər-mən\. Village, SW Crimean Oblast, Ukrainian S.S.R., U.S.S.R., near mouth of Chernaya river, just E of Sevastopol; scene of battle Nov. 5, 1854 during Crimean War in which English and French defeated Russians under General Dannenberg, with heavy losses on both sides; in World War II occupied by Germans 1942–1944.

Ink·ster \ˈiŋ(k)-stər\. Residential village, Wayne co., SE Michigan, 13 m. W of Detroit; pop. (1970c) 38,595; tools and dies.

In·land Empire \ˌin-lənd-\. Region in NW United States, bet. Cascade Range and Rocky Mts., including E Washington and NE Oregon, N Idaho, and extreme W Montana; lumbering, livestock raising, mining.

Inland Passage. See INSIDE PASSAGE.

Inland Sea; *Jap.* **Se·to–nai·kai** \ˌse-ˌtō-nī-ˈkī\ *also* **Seto no Uchi** \ˈse-(ˌ)tō-ˌnō-ə-ˈchē\. Irregular-shaped body of water extending E and W bet. Honshū I. on N and Shikoku and Kyūshū Is. on S, Japan; closed at E end by Awaji I.; connected with outer sea by 4 channels: Akashi Strait at NE, Naruto Strait at SE, Bungo Strait (formerly Hayasui) at SW, and Shimonoseki Strait at W end; noted for scenic beauty: contains ab. 300 islands and is bordered on N and S by mountain chains, 3000 to 6000 ft. high; divided into 5 basins: Harima Sea, Bingo Sea, Mishima Sea, Iyo Sea, and Suō Sea; comparatively shallow and marked by strong tidal movements.

Inland Waterway. See ATLANTIC INTRACOASTAL WATERWAY and GULF INTRACOASTAL WATERWAY.

In·le, Lake \-ˈin-(ˌ)lā\. Lake in cen. Burma, SW of Taunggyi.

Inn \ˈin\ *or anc.* **Ae·nus** \ˈē-nəs\. River, Switzerland, Austria, and West Germany; 317 m. long; rises in lake in Rhaetian Alps, Graubünden, Switzerland, flows NE through Engadine valleys into Tirol, SW Austria; thence E past Innsbruck, then NE through Bavarian Alps to Bavaria, West Germany, entering the Danube at Passau; in its lower course, boundary bet. Bavaria and Upper Austria, receives the Salzach. Extensively utilized as a source of hydroelectric power.

Inner Hebrides. See HEBRIDES.

Inner Mongolia. See MONGOLIA, INNER.

Inner Rhodes. See APPENZELL.

Inner Sound. Body of water off NW coast of Scotland, bet. Raasay I. and Scottish mainland.

In·nis·fail. 1 \ˈin-əs-ˌfāl\. Town, Alberta, Canada, 75 m. N of Calgary; pop. (1971p) 2468; diversified agriculture; creamery.

2 *also* **In·is·fail** \ˈin-ish-ˌfȯl, ˈin-əs-ˌfāl\. Ireland—poetical name.

Inniskilling. See ENNISKILLEN.

In·no·ko \ˈin-ə-ˌkō\. River, W Alaska; ab. 450 m. long; flows SW, almost parallel to Yukon river which it enters at ab. 160°W.

Inns·bruck \ˈinz-ˌbru̇k, ˈin(t)s-\. Manufacturing city, ✱ of the Tirol, W Austria, on Inn river ab. 85 m. SW of Salzburg; pop. (1969e) 112,824; tourist resort; textiles, chemicals, boats; bell founding, metalworking, bookbinding; univ. (1669); made city 1239; residence 1363–1665 of collateral line of Hapsburgs; capital of the Tirol from c. 1420; center of uprising of Tirolese peasants 1809; heavily damaged during World War II; headquarters of French zone of occupation 1945–55.

In·ny \ˈin-ē\. River, NE cen. Ireland, flowing SW from Lough Sheelin into Lough Ree.

İnö·nü \ˌin-ə-ˈn(y)ü\. Village, Bilecik prov., NW Turkey, Asia, on railroad ab. 20 m. WNW of Eskişehir; here İsmet Paşa, Turkish general, twice defeated Greeks in war of 1919–22 and took name of village as last name (İsmet İnönü, president of Turkey 1938–50).

Ino·wroc·ław \ˌē-nəv-ˈrȯt-ˌsläf\ *or Ger.* **Ho·hen·sal·za** \ˌhō-ən-ˈzält-sə\; *before 1905* **Ino·wraz·law** \ˌē-nəv-ˈrät-ˌsläf\. Commune, Bydgoszcz prov., N cen. Poland, ab. 25 m. SSE of Bydgoszcz; pop. (1970p) 54,800; health resort; salt mining; machinery; industrial center from 15th cent.

In Sa·lah \ˌin(t)-sə-ˈlä\. Oasis, Oasis dept., Algeria, N Africa; pop. (1966c) 6331.

In·sein \ˈin-ˌsān\. 1 District, Pegu division, Burma; 1903 sq. m.; pop. (1962e) 537,291; ✱ Insein.

2 Town, its ✱, 10 m. NW of Rangoon; pop. (1953c) 27,030.

Inside Passage *or* **Inland Passage.** Protected steamer route from Puget Sound, Washington, to Skagway, Alaska, following channels bet. the mainland and the many islands along the coast in this region; chief ports Ketchikan, Wrangell, Juneau.

Insterburg. See CHERNYAKHOVSK.

In·sti·tute \ˈin(t)-stə-ˌt(y)üt\. Village, Kanawha co., West Virginia, W of Charleston; West Virginia State Coll. (1891).

Insula. See LILLE.

In·ta \ˈēn-tə\. Town, Komi A.S.S.R., Russian S.F.S.R., U.S.S.R., ab. 150 m. SW of Vorkuta; pop. (1969e) 51,000; coal mining; formed 1940.

Inter–American Highway. See PAN-AMERICAN HIGHWAY.

Interamna. See TERAMO 2.

Interamna Nahars. See TERNI 2.

In·ter·la·ken \ˌint-ər-ˈläk-ən\. Commune, Bern canton, Switzerland, on Aare river bet. Lake of Thun and Lake of Brienz 26 m. SE of Bern; pop. (1970c) 4735; health resort; textiles, shirts, clocks and watches; founded c. 1128; valley region famous for view of the Jungfrau.

In·ter·loch·en \ˈint-ər-ˌläk-ən\. Village, Grand Traverse co., Michigan, on Green Lake in NW southern penin.; National Music camp.

International Date Line. See DATE LINE.

In·ter·na·tion·al Falls \ˌint-ər-ˌnash-nəl-, -ən-ᵊl-\. City, ⊗ of Koochiching co., N Minnesota, on Rainy river near Rainy Lake; pop. (1970c) 6439; railroad center, summer resort; paper mills, truck and dairy farms; lumbering.

International Peace Garden. International park area, N North Dakota and SW Manitoba, Canada, near Whitewater Lake (Canada); 888 acres in U.S.

International Zone. See TANGIER.

Internum, Mare. See MEDITERRANEAN SEA.

In·ti·bu·cá \ˌint-i-bu̇-ˈkä\. Department of W cen. Honduras. See table at HONDURAS.

In·tra \ˈēn-trə\. Former commune, now a subdivision of the commune of Verbania, Italy. See VERBANIA.

Intracoastal Waterway. See ATLANTIC INTRACOASTAL WATERWAY and GULF INTRACOASTAL WATERWAY.

Inu·bo, Cape \-ˈē-nu̇-ˌbō\ *or Jap.* **Inu·bō–sa·ki** \-ˈsäk-ē\. Cape on SE coast of Honshū, Japan, in Chiba prefecture, E of Tokyo; lighthouse, 35°42′N, 140°53′E.

In·ú·til Bay \i-ˈnü-tēl-, in-ˈüt-ᵊl-\ *or Eng.* **Use·less Bay** \ˌyüs-ləs-\. Large inlet on NW coast of Tierra del Fuego I., Chile; opens into Strait of Magellan.

In·ver·ar·ay \ˌin-və-ˈra(ə)r-ē, -ˈre(ə)r-\. Burgh, Argyll co., W Scotland; pop. (1971p) 438; herring fishing; castle.

In·ver·car·gill \ˌin-vər-ˈkär-gəl\. City, S South I., New Zealand, on estuary of Foveaux Strait 110 m. WSW of Dunedin; pop. (1970e) 46,700; Bluff, its port; wheat, oats, wool, meat, dairy products; woolen and lumber mills, foundries, breweries; founded 1856.

In·ver·ell \ˌin-və-ˈrel\. Town, NE New South Wales, SE Australia, 280 m. N of Sydney; pop. (1966c) 8413; wheat, grapes, corn; silver, tin, diamond mines; cattle and sheep raising.

In·ver Grove Heights \ˌin-vər-ˌgrōv-\. Village, Dakota co., SE Minnesota, 3 m. SE of St. Paul; pop. (1970c) 12,148; residential suburb of St. Paul.

In·ver·ness \ˈin-vər-ˌnes\. Town, ⊗ of Citrus co., W Florida penin.; pop. (1970c) 2299; timber, citrus fruits.

Inverness \ˌin-vər-ˈnes\. **1** County, Nova Scotia, Canada. See table at NOVA SCOTIA.

2 Coastal town, Inverness co., NE Nova Scotia, Canada, on W coast of Cape Breton I. on Gulf of St. Lawrence; pop. (1966c) 2022; copper, gypsum, and clay deposits.

3 *or* **Inverness–shire** \-ˌshi(ə)r, -shər\. County, NW Scotland; 4211 sq. m.; pop. (1971p) 89,545; ⊗ Inverness; includes several of Inner and Outer Hebrides, as Harris, North Uist, South Uist, Skye, and Eigg; mountainous region, including Ben Nevis 4406 ft., highest peak in British Isles; livestock raising, fishing, lumbering; hydroelectric power production.

4 Burgh, ⊗ of Inverness co., NW Scotland, on the Ness at NE terminus of Caledonian Canal; pop. (1971p) 34,870; metalworking; fishing; machine tools; chartered c. 1200.

In·ves·ti·ga·tor Strait \in-ˈves-tə-ˌgāt-ər-\. Channel bet. N Kangaroo I. and mainland, South Australia; forms SW entrance to Gulf of St. Vincent.

In·wood \ˈin-wu̇d\. Village, Nassau co., SE New York, on Long I. on shore of Jamaica Bay, ab. 12 m. E of Brooklyn; pop. (1970c) 5878.

In·yo \ˈin-(ˌ)yō\. County in California. See table at CALIFORNIA.

In·yo·kern \ˌin-yō-ˈkərn\. Town, Kern co., E California, 30 m. W of Death Valley and NE of Bakersfield; naval ordnance research station.

Inyo Mountains. Range in W cen. Inyo co., E California.

Io·an·ni·na *or* **Io·án·ni·na** \yō-ˈän-ē-(ˌ)nä\. **1** Department of Greece. See table at GREECE.

2 *also* **Yan·ni·na** *or Serb.* **Ja·ni·na** \ˈyän-ē-(ˌ)nä\. City, its ✱, N Epirus, NW Greece, near Albanian frontier on **Lake Ioannina;** pop. (1971p) 39,814; univ. (1966); 11th cent. Byzantine city; captured by Turks 1430; famous in late 18th cent. as seat of Ali Pasha, the Lion of Janina; taken by Greeks 1913; during World War II occupied by Germans, Apr. 1941–Aug. 1944.

Io·la \ī-ˈō-lə\. City, ⊗ of Allen co., SE Kansas, 15 m. N of Chanute; pop. (1970c) 6493; cement works; Allen County Community Junior Coll. (1923).

Iol·cus \ī-ˈäl-kəs\. Ruined city, SE Thessaly, NE Greece, near modern Volos; legendary home of Jason and port from which Argonauts set out.

Io·na \ī-ˈō-nə\. Island of the Inner Hebrides, Scotland, off SW tip of Mull I.; 6 sq. m.; early center of the Celtic church; St. Columba and his disciples landed here from Ireland c. 563.

Iô·na National Park \ē-ˈōn-ə-\. National park, Angola; 6148 sq. m.; abundant wildlife; established 1937.

Io·nia \ī-ˈō-nē-ə\. **1** County in S cen. Michigan. See table at MICHIGAN.

2 City, its ⊗, 32 m. E of Grand Rapids; pop. (1970c) 6361; auto body parts, flour.

3 Ancient district on W coast of Asia Minor bordering on Aegean Sea and extending from a point near mouth of Hermus river S to the Halicarnassus Penin.; mountainous country 90 m. long and 20 to 30 m. wide; included some of islands of E Aegean Sea (Chios, Samos, etc.); its hinterland was Lydia and Caria; received name from Ionians, a branch of ancient Greeks, who probably migrated from Greek mainland to Asia Minor c. 1000 B.C.; never a political unit, had religious league of **12 Ionian Cities** (N to S): Phocaea, Clazomenae, Erythrae, Teos, Lebedos, Colophon, Ephesus, Priene, Myus, Miletus, and the two island cities of Chios and Samos; became subject to Lydia (*q.v.*) and later, to Persia c. 547 B.C.; produced Ionic school of philosophy and architectural advances (Ionic order); revolt of Miletus (*q.v.*) brought on Greek wars with Persia; freed from Persia by Alexander of Macedon 334 B.C.; became part of the Roman province of Asia; ruined during the Turkish conquest of Asia Minor.

Io·ni·an Islands \ī-ˈō-nē-ən-\ *or anc.* **Hep·ta·ne·sus** \ˌhep-tə-ˈnē-səs\. Group of seven Greek islands in Ionian Sea: Corfu, Paxos, Leukas, Ithaca, Cephalonia, and Zante off W coast of Greece, and Cerigo off S coast of Peloponnesus; 868 sq. m.; pop. (1971p) 183,633; islands constitute an administrative region of Greece consisting of departments of Cephalonia, Corfu, Leukas, and Zante (see table at GREECE); generally mountainous; fruits (esp. currants), olive oil, grain, wine. Colonized by ancient Greeks; part of Roman and Byzantine Empires; Corfu occupied by Venetians 1386–1797; taken by French 1797 but surrendered to Russians 1799; organized as Septinsular Republic under

Russian protection 1800–07; British protectorate 1815–64; annexed to Greece 1864.

Ionian Sea *or Lat.* **Ma·re Io·ni·um** \ˌmā-(ˌ)rē-ī-ˈō-nē-əm, ˌmär-(ˌ)ā-\. Part of Mediterranean Sea bet. SE coast of Italy and W Greece, connected with Adriatic Sea by Strait of Otranto; along its E shore are the Ionian Is. and on NW is the Gulf of Taranto.

Io·ri·bai·wa \ˌyȯr-ə-ˈbī-wə\. Village, Papua New Guinea, SE New Guinea I., in mountains 30 m. E of Port Moresby; Japanese advance from Buna and Gona stopped here by Australians Sept. 1942.

Ios \ˈī-ˌäs, ˈē-ˌȯs\. 1 *or* **Nio** \ˈnē-(ˌ)ō\. Island in Aegean Sea, in S cen. Cyclades; 46 sq. m.; belongs to Cyclades dept., Greece.

2 Town on W coast of island.

Ios·co \ī-ˈäs-(ˌ)kō\. County in Michigan. See table at MICHIGAN.

Ioshkar Ola. See YOSHKAR-OLA.

Io·wa \ˈī-ə-wə\. 1 River, Iowa; 291 m. long; formed by confluence of branches in N cen. Iowa and flowing SE into the Mississippi in SE Iowa.

2 A north central state of U.S.A., bounded on N by Minnesota, on E by Wisconsin and Illinois, on S by Missouri, and on W by Nebraska and South Dakota; 25th state in area, 56,290 sq. m. (land area 56,044 sq. m.); 25th state in population, (1970c) 2,825,041; ✱ Des Moines; 29th state admitted to Union (1846).

Nickname: Hawkeye State. *State flower:* Wild rose. *Motto:* Our Liberties We Prize, and Our Rights We Will Maintain. *Rivers:* Des Moines, flowing diagonally across state NW to SE, forming in its lower course the boundary with Missouri, and emptying into the Mississippi; Mississippi, forming E boundary; Missouri, forming W boundary bet. Iowa and Nebraska; Big Sioux, forming W boundary bet. Iowa and South Dakota. *Highest point:* Ocheyedan Mound 1675 ft., in Osceola co. *Chief products:* Corn, soybeans, oats; cattle, hogs; cement, limestone; manufacturing: electronic equipment, farm machinery, chemicals. *Chief cities:* Des Moines, Cedar Rapids, Davenport, Sioux City, Waterloo, Dubuque. See *Table of States* at UNITED STATES. Divided into the following 99 counties (for pronunciation of their names, see their individual entries):

NAME	LOCATION	AREA[1] (sq. m.)	POP. (1970c)	CO. SEAT
Adair	SW cen.	569	9,487	Greenfield
Adams	SW	426	6,322	Corning
Allamakee	NE corner	636	14,968	Waukon
Appanoose	S	523	15,007	Centerville
Audubon	W	448	9,595	Audubon
Benton	E cen.	718	22,885	Vinton
Black Hawk	NE cen.	568	132,916	Waterloo
Boone	cen.	573	26,470	Boone
Bremer	NE	439	22,737	Waverly
Buchanan	E	568	21,762	Independence
Buena Vista	NW	572	20,693	Storm Lake
Butler	NE cen.	582	16,953	Allison
Calhoun	NW cen.	571	14,287	Rockwell City
Carroll	W cen.	574	22,912	Carroll
Cass	SW	559	17,007	Atlantic
Cedar	E	585	17,655	Tipton
Cerro Gordo	N	575	49,223	Mason City
Cherokee	NW	573	17,269	Cherokee
Chickasaw	NE	505	14,969	New Hampton
Clarke	S	429	7,581	Osceola
Clay	NW	570	18,464	Spencer
Clayton	NE	779	20,606	Elkader
Clinton	E	693	56,749	Clinton
Crawford	W	716	19,198	Denison
Dallas	S cen.	597	26,085	Adel
Davis	SE	509	8,207	Bloomfield
Decatur	S	530	9,737	Leon
Delaware	E	572	18,770	Manchester
Des Moines	SE	408	46,982	Burlington
Dickinson	NW	380	12,565	Spirit Lake
Dubuque	E	612	90,609	Dubuque
Emmet	N	394	14,009	Estherville
Fayette	NE	728	26,898	West Union
Floyd	N	503	19,860	Charles City
Franklin	N cen.	586	13,255	Hampton
Fremont	SW corner	524	9,282	Sidney
Greene	W cen.	569	12,716	Jefferson
Grundy	NE cen.	501	14,119	Grundy Center
Guthrie	SW cen.	596	12,243	Guthrie Center
Hamilton	N cen.	577	18,383	Webster City
Hancock	N	570	13,492	Garner
Hardin	N cen.	574	22,248	Eldora
Harrison	W	696	16,240	Logan
Henry	SE	440	18,114	Mount Pleasant
Howard	N	471	11,442	Cresco
Humboldt	NW cen.	435	12,519	Dakota City
Ida	W	431	9,283	Ida Grove
Iowa	E cen.	584	15,419	Marengo
Jackson	E	644	20,839	Maquoketa
Jasper	S cen.	734	35,425	Newton
Jefferson	SE	436	15,774	Fairfield
Johnson	E	619	72,127	Iowa City
Jones	E	585	19,868	Anamosa
Keokuk	SE cen.	579	13,943	Sigourney
Kossuth	N	979	22,937	Algona
Lee	SE corner	528	42,996	Keokuk & Fort Madison
Linn	E	717	163,213	Cedar Rapids
Louisa	SE	403	10,682	Wapello
Lucas	S	434	10,163	Chariton
Lyon	NW corner	588	13,340	Rock Rapids
Madison	S cen.	564	11,558	Winterset
Mahaska	SE cen.	572	22,177	Oskaloosa
Marion	S cen.	567	26,352	Knoxville
Marshall	cen.	574	41,076	Marshalltown
Mills	SW	447	11,832	Glenwood
Mitchell	N	467	13,108	Osage
Monona	W	699	12,069	Onawa
Monroe	S	435	9,357	Albia
Montgomery	SW	422	12,781	Red Oak
Muscatine	E	443	37,181	Muscatine
O'Brien	NW	575	17,522	Primghar
Osceola	NW	398	8,555	Sibley
Page	SW	535	18,537	Clarinda
Palo Alto	N	561	13,289	Emmetsburg
Plymouth	NW	863	24,322	Le Mars
Pocahontas	NW cen.	581	12,757	Pocahontas
Polk	S cen.	594	286,101	Des Moines
Pottawattamie	SW	963	86,991	Council Bluffs
Poweshiek	SE cen.	589	18,803	Montezuma
Ringgold	S	538	6,373	Mount Ayr
Sac	W	578	15,573	Sac City
Scott	E	454	142,687	Davenport
Shelby	W	587	15,528	Harlan
Sioux	NW	766	27,996	Orange City
Story	cen.	568	62,783	Nevada
Tama	E cen.	720	20,147	Toledo
Taylor	SW	528	8,790	Bedford
Union	S	425	13,557	Creston
Van Buren	SE	487	8,643	Keosauqua
Wapello	SE	437	42,149	Ottumwa
Warren	S cen.	572	27,432	Indianola
Washington	SE	568	18,967	Washington
Wayne	S	532	8,405	Corydon
Webster	NW cen.	718	48,391	Fort Dodge
Winnebago	N	401	12,990	Forest City
Winneshiek	NE	688	21,758	Decorah
Woodbury	W	871	103,052	Sioux City
Worth	N	400	8,968	Northwood
Wright	N cen.	577	17,294	Clarion

[1]Area = land area.

History: Became part of U.S. by Louisiana Purchase 1803; part of Missouri Territory 1812–21, unorganized 1821–34, part of territories of Michigan 1834–36 and of Wisconsin 1836–38; first permanent settlement made 1833 at Dubuque; organized in 1838 as Iowa Territory which included parts of Minnesota, North Dakota, and South Dakota; held first constitutional convention 1844; present constitution dates from 1851. Admitted to Union Dec. 28, 1846; capital removed from Iowa City to Des Moines 1857.

3 Name of counties in two states of the U.S. See tables at IOWA and WISCONSIN.

Iowa City. City, ⊗ of Johnson co., E Iowa, 25 m. S of Cedar Rapids; pop. (1970c) 46,850; sheet metal goods, drugs; creameries, hatcheries; Univ. of Iowa (1847); settled 1838; capital of Iowa Territory 1839–57.

Iowa Falls. City, Hardin co., N cen. Iowa, 37 m. NW of Marshalltown; pop. (1970c) 6454; Ellsworth Junior Coll. (1890).

Iowa Park. Town, Wichita co., N Texas, 10 m. W of Wichita Falls; pop. (1970c) 5796.

Ipa·me·ri \ˌēp-ə-mə-ˈrē\. Municipality, Goiás state, cen. Brazil, 100 m. SE of Goiânia; pop. (1968e) 24,615.

Ipek. See PEĆ.

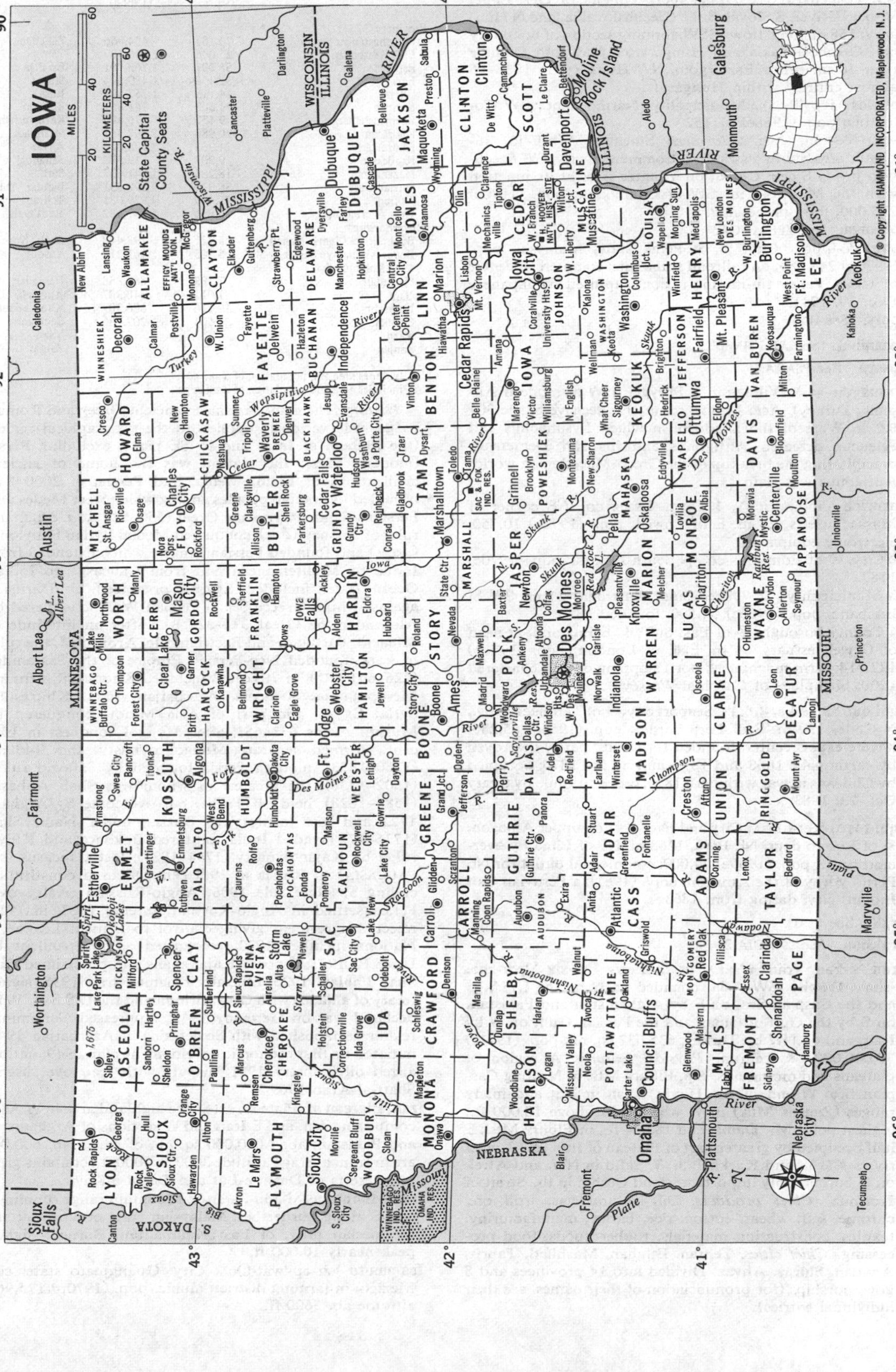
IOWA
MILES
0 20 40 60
KILOMETERS
0 20 40 60
State Capital
County Seats
MINNESOTA
WISCONSIN
ILLINOIS
MISSOURI
NEBRASKA
S. DAKOTA
MISSISSIPPI RIVER
Missouri River
Des Moines
Cedar Rapids
Davenport
Dubuque
Sioux City
Council Bluffs
Omaha
Waterloo
Iowa City
Ames
Burlington
Ottumwa
Mason City
Clinton
Ft. Dodge
Keokuk
Moline
Rock Island
Galesburg
LYON
OSCEOLA
DICKINSON
EMMET
KOSSUTH
WINNEBAGO
WORTH
MITCHELL
HOWARD
WINNESHIEK
ALLAMAKEE
SIOUX
O'BRIEN
CLAY
PALO ALTO
HANCOCK
CERRO GORDO
FLOYD
CHICKASAW
FAYETTE
CLAYTON
PLYMOUTH
CHEROKEE
BUENA VISTA
POCAHONTAS
HUMBOLDT
WRIGHT
FRANKLIN
BUTLER
BREMER
BLACK HAWK
BUCHANAN
DELAWARE
DUBUQUE
WOODBURY
IDA
SAC
CALHOUN
WEBSTER
HAMILTON
HARDIN
GRUNDY
TAMA
BENTON
LINN
JONES
JACKSON
MONONA
CRAWFORD
CARROLL
GREENE
BOONE
STORY
MARSHALL
IOWA
JOHNSON
CEDAR
CLINTON
SCOTT
HARRISON
SHELBY
AUDUBON
GUTHRIE
DALLAS
POLK
JASPER
POWESHIEK
MUSCATINE
POTTAWATTAMIE
CASS
ADAIR
MADISON
WARREN
MARION
MAHASKA
KEOKUK
WASHINGTON
LOUISA
MILLS
MONTGOMERY
ADAMS
UNION
CLARKE
LUCAS
MONROE
WAPELLO
JEFFERSON
HENRY
DES MOINES
FREMONT
PAGE
TAYLOR
RINGGOLD
DECATUR
WAYNE
APPANOOSE
DAVIS
VAN BUREN
LEE
43°
42°
41°
90°
91°
92°
93°
94°
95°
96°
Longitude West of Greenwich
© Copyright HAMMOND INCORPORATED, Maplewood, N.J.

Ipel' \'ē-ˌpel(-yə)\ *or Hung.* **Ipoly** \'ip-ˌȯi\ *or Ger.* **Ei·pel** \'ī-pəl\. River, S Slovak S.R., Czechoslovakia, and N Hungary; 158 m. long; flows SSW, forming section of boundary bet. Czechoslovakia and Hungary, empties into Danube river 10 m. below Esztergom, NW Hungary; in 1938–45 almost entirely within Hungary.

Ipia·les \i-'pyäl-əs\. Municipality, Nariño dept., SW Colombia; pop. (1968e) 42,152.

I-pin \'ē-'pin, -'pēn\; *formerly* **Su·chow** \'s(h)ü-'jō, 'sü-'chau̇\ *also* **Sui·fu** \'swā-'fü\. Commercial city, SW Szechwan prov., S cen. China, on Yangtze river at its junction with the Min, 140 m. SW of Chungking; pop. (1970e) 275,000; food processing.

Ipiranga. See YPIRANGA.

Ipoh \'ē-(ˌ)pō\. City, ✱ of Perak state, Malaysia; pop. (1970p) 247,689; on railroad trunk line; commercial center of Kinta Valley tin-mining region; captured by Japanese Dec. 29, 1941.

Ipoly. See IPEL'.

Ipsambul. See ABU SIMBEL.

Ipsara. See PSARA.

Ip·sus \'ip-səs\. Village in S Phrygia (NW of modern Akşehir, Turkey), Asia Minor; scene of a decisive battle 301 B.C. in Wars of the Diadochi in which Lysimachus and Seleucus defeated Antigonus and his son Demetrius, precipitating the breakup of the Greco-Macedonian world; Antigonus was slain.

Ips·wich \'ip-(ˌ)swich\. **1** Town, Essex co., NE corner of Massachusetts, 23 m. E of Lowell; pop. (1970c) 10,750; electronic equipment.
2 City, ⊗ of Edmunds co., N South Dakota; pop. (1970c) 1187.
3 Municipality, SE Queensland, Australia, 25 m. SW of Brisbane; pop. (1966c) 54,500; founded 1829.
4 County borough, ⊗ of East Suffolk, E England, at head of Orwell estuary 64 m. ENE of London; pop. (1971p) 122,814; farm machinery; port, shipping center; chartered 1200; birthplace of Cardinal Wolsey.

Iqui·que \i-'kē-kē, -(ˌ)kā\. Seaport city, ✱ of Tarapacá prov., N Chile, 130 m. S of Peru border; pop. (1966e) 65,288; nitrate export center; founded 16th cent.; partly destroyed by earthquake 1868 and 1877, and by fire 1875; occupied by Chileans in war with Peru 1879; ceded to Chile by treaty Oct. 23, 1883.

Iqui·tos \i-'kēt-(ˌ)ōs\. City and river port on upper Amazon, ✱ of Loreto dept, NE Peru, 1268 m. NE of Lima by overland route; pop. (1969e) 74,000; commercial outlet for NE Peru by way of the Amazon; univ. (1961); a Peruvian (not Indian) city, dating from 1863.

Irak. See IRAQ.

Iráklion. See CANDIA 2.

Iran \i-'ran, -'rän; ī-'ran\ *or formerly* **Per·sia** \'pər-zhə, -shə\. Empire, SW Asia, bounded on N by the U.S.S.R. and the Caspian Sea, on E by Afghanistan and Pakistan, on S by the Gulf of Oman and the Persian Gulf, on W by Iraq, and on NW by Turkey; 635,932 sq. m.; pop. (1971e) 30,000,000, ✱ Tehran. *Physical features:* A region of plateaus and mountains, esp. Elburz Mts. in N along Caspian Sea; W end of the Hindu Kush in NE; and many ranges (Zagros Mts.) in W with peaks above 10,000 ft.; highest point Mt. Damāvand 18,934 ft., in Elburz Mts.; E half occupied by greater part of Plateau of Iran (*q.v.*); chief rivers Kārūn and Karkheh in W, Safīd in NW, and Atrek on N border; only important island Qeshm in the Strait of Hormuz. *Chief products:* Oil, natural gas, iron ore, chrome, salt; wheat, cotton, rice, barley; manufacturing: textiles, construction materials, rubber goods; food processing. *Chief cities:* Tehran, Eşfahān, Mashhad, Tabrīz, Ābādān, Shīrāz, Ahvāz. Divided into 14 provinces and 8 governorships (for pronunciation of their names, see their individual entries):

NAME	AREA (sq. m.)	POP. (1966c)	CAPITAL
Provinces			
Balūchestān va Sīstān	70,107	454,966	Zāhedān
East Azerbaijan	25,096	2,596,439	Tabrīz
Eşfahān[1]	58,609	1,703,701	Eşfahān
Fārs	51,465	1,439,804	Shīrāz
Gīlān[2]	14,115	1,752,504	Rasht
Kermān	74,508	761,851	Kermān
Kermānshāhan	9,477	776,409	Kermānshāh
Khorāsān	120,980	2,497,381	Mashhad
Khūzestān	24,962	1,578,079	Ahvāz
Kordestān	9,307	619,573	Sanandaj
Māzandarān	18,286	1,841,637	Sārī
Persian Gulf	36,374	598,331	Bandar 'Abbās
Tehran	35,335	4,979,081	Tehran
West Azerbaijan	16,856	1,087,182	Reza'īyeh
Governorships			
Bakhtīarī va Chahār Mahāll	5,721	298,448	Shahr Kord
Boyer Ahmadī-ye Sardīr va Kohkīlūyeh	5,505	161,219	Yasoof
Hamadān	7,788	889,888	Hamadān
Īlām	7,011	148,307	Ābdānān
Lorestān	12,116	686,307	Khorramābād
Semnān	31,504	207,786	Semnān
Yazd			Yazd
Zanjān			Zanjān

[1]Includes area and population of Yazd gov.
[2]Includes area and population of Zanjān gov.

History: The name *Ariana,* in ancient Greek and Roman usage, was variously applied to the geographical region (the Plateau of Iran) and to SE parts, excluding Persis (modern Fārs); the plateau was the home of ancient civilizations of Elam, Media, and Persia; c. 2000 B.C., occupied by Iranian peoples among which were Medes and Persians. Under Cyrus the Great (550–529 B.C.), originally ruler of Anshan (*q.v.*), conquered Media, Lydia, Babylonia (*qq.v.*) and founded Persian Empire which extended from Indus to Mediterranean and from Caucasus to Indian Ocean (later included Egypt); organized by Darius I against whom Greece began Persian Wars; conquered by Alexander the Great 331–327 B.C.; after an interlude of Seleucid, Parthian, and Bactrian rule, Ardashir I, the ruler of Fārs, founded Neo-Persian Empire of the Sassanidae (226–641 A.D.); in 7th cent., included Khorāsān, Kermān, Mesopotamia, Armenia, Azerbaijan, Fārs, Khūzestān, Syria, Egypt, and part of Asia Minor; conquered by Muslim Arabs 633–651; after Mongol conquest in 13th cent., formed separate Mongol dynasty, the Il-khans (1260–1353); modern Persia founded by Safawid rulers (1502–1736), the greatest of whom was Shah Abbas I (1586–1628); held off Turks, but overcome by Afghans 1722 and lost territory to Russia; under Nadir Shah (1736–47) invaded India, captured Bukhara and Khiva; ruled by Kajar dynasty (1794–1925); lost Caucasus (see CAUCASIA) to Russia in 19th cent.; secured constitution ending absolute rule 1906; Anglo-Russian rivalry over Persia settled in Anglo-Russian Entente 1907; in 1919, rejected agreement giving control to British; League of Nations member 1920; recognized as independent by U.S.S.R. 1921; deposed Kajar shahs and proclaimed Riza Shah Pahlavi 1925; officially renamed Iran 1935; signed treaty of alliance with Great Britain and the U.S.S.R. 1942; declared war on Germany 1943; suppressed Communist regime (established with Soviet aid) in Azerbaijan 1946; initiated its first economic development plan 1949; nationalized oil industry 1951; dispute with Iraq over use of Shatt-al-Arab 1969.

Iran, Plateau of. Plateau, extensive highland area in W Asia, comprising cen. and E Iran and W sections of Afghanistan and Pakistan; ab. 1,000,000 sq. m., of which ab. 600,000 are in Iran; average altitude 3000 to 5000 ft.; contains great salt deserts of Dasht-e-Lūt and Dasht-e-Kavīr.

Iran Mountains \i-ˌran-, -ˌrän-\. Mountain range running N and S along border bet. Malaysian state of Sarawak and Indonesian prov. of East Kalimantan, Borneo; highest peak nearly 10,000 ft.

Ira·pua·to \ˌir-əp-'wät-(ˌ)ō\. City, Guanajuato state, cen. Mexico, in farming district; munic. pop. (1970p) 175,966; altitude ab. 5600 ft.

Iraq \i-ˈräk, -ˈrak\ *also* **Irak** *or Arab.* **ʻIraq.** Republic, SW Asia, bounded on N by Turkey, on E by Iran, on SE by Kuwait and Persian Gulf, on S by Saudi Arabia, and on W by Jordan and Syria; 168,927 sq. m.; pop. (1970e) 9,440,098; ✻ Baghdad. *Physical features:* Comprises for most part level country drained by Euphrates and Tigris rivers which unite ab. 120 m. from Persian Gulf NNW of Basra to form the Shatt-al-Arab, and by tributaries of the Tigris from the E; includes most of Mesopotamia (*q.v.*); river region fertile with many lakes; wide desert region in W (part of Syrian Desert) and SW; mountainous in Kurdistan region of NE. *Chief products:* Wheat, barley, hides, dates, cotton; oil, sulfur; manufacturing: textiles, construction materials, cigarettes; food processing. *Chief cities:* Baghdad, Basra, Mosul, Kirkuk, An Najaf, Erbil.

History: Kingdom established 1921 after World War I out of former Turkish territory; under British mandate 1920 until Oct. 1932 when it became independent under King Faisal I; semi-independent state in alliance with Great Britain 1922; a limited monarchy according to organic law 1924; awarded Mosul (*q.v.*) by League of Nations 1925; independence and sovereignty recognized in treaties with Great Britain 1927 and 1930, the full result of which was admission to League 1932; in treaty with Saudi Arabia (*q.v.*) 1936; occupied by British Apr.–June 1941 to prevent Nazi control; joined United Nations 1945; republic established following army coup July 1958 during which King Faisal II and Crown Prince Abdul Illah were assassinated; advanced claims to Kuwait (rejected by Great Britain) 1961; participated in Arab-Israeli War 1967; announced termination of (sporadic) hostilities between central government and autonomy-seeking Kurds 1970. See MESOPOTAMIA, and for ancient history BABYLONIA and ASSYRIA.

ʻIraq ʻAra·bi \i-ˈräk-ˈär-ə-bē\. The region of lower Mesopotamia; the Tigris-Euphrates valley S of Baghdad, comprising Basra, Baghdad, and adjoining provinces in Iraq; nearly coextensive with ancient Babylonia.

ʻIraq–i–ʻAjam \i-ˈräk-ē-ˈaj-ˌam\ *or* **Iraq Aje·mi** \-ˌaj-ə-ˈmē\. Region and former province in W cen. Iran; as province, capital was Sultanabad (Arāk).

Irawadi. See IRRAWADDY.

Ira·zú \ˌir-ə-ˈzü, -ˈsü\. Volcano, cen. Costa Rica, near city of Cartago; 11,200 ft.; active 1841, 1910, and 1963; only place on North American continent where on a clear day both the Atlantic and Pacific oceans can be seen.

Ir·bid \ˈi(ə)r-bəd\. Town, N Jordan, 42 m. N of Amman; pop. (1970e) 120,000.

Irbīl. See ERBIL.

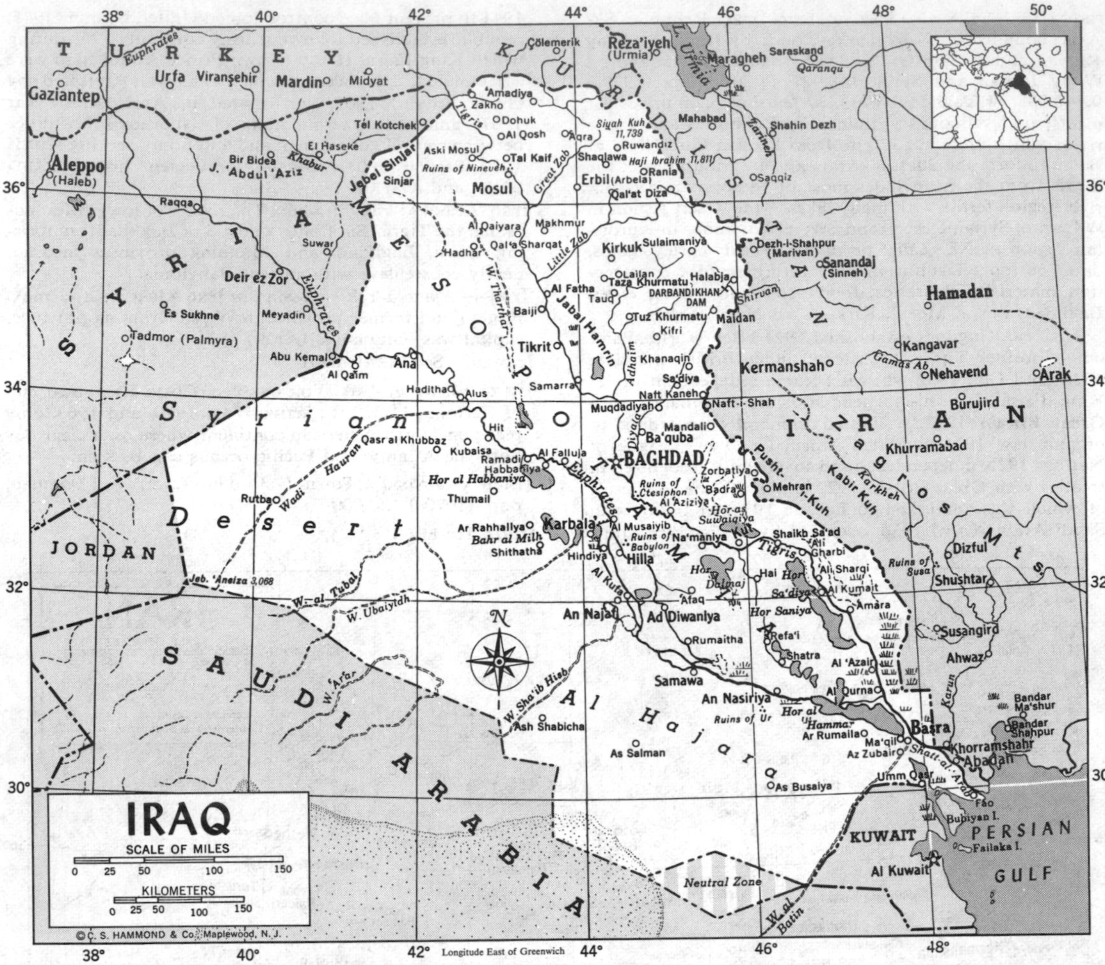

Ir·bit \i(ə)r-ˈb(y)ēt\. Commercial town, Sverdlovsk Oblast, Russian S.F.S.R., U.S.S.R., 110 m.NE of Sverdlovsk; pop. (1967e) 49,000.

Ire·dell \ˈī(ə)r-ˌdel\. County in North Carolina. See table at NORTH CAROLINA.

Ire·land \ˈī(ə)r-lənd\ *or Lat.* **Hi·ber·nia** \hī-ˈbər-nē-ə\ *also known as the* **Em·er·ald Isle** \ˌem-(ə-)rəld-\ *and* (*in poetry*) **Er·in** \ˈer-ən\. 1 The Republic of Ireland. See EIRE.

2 Island, W of England and separated from it by St. George's Channel and the Irish Sea; divided bet. the independent Republic of Ireland (Eire), which occupies the 26 counties in the S, cen., and NW part, and Northern Ireland (forming part of the United Kingdom), which occupies the six counties in the NE part; area (Eire 26,600 sq. m.; Northern Ireland 5452 sq. m.); pop. (Eire [1971p] 2,971,230; Northern Ireland [1971p] 1,525,187). Consists of central plain with lakes (*loughs*) in N, cen., and W parts, esp. Erne, Neagh, Mask, Corrib, Conn, Ree, Derg, and the small and beautiful Lakes of Killarney in SW, and with groups of hills averaging 2000 to 3000 ft. on N, W, and S; highest point Carrantuohill 3414 ft. in SW. *Rivers:* Shannon in cen. part, Bann in N, Lagan in NE, Boyne and Liffey in E, Barrow, Nore, and Suir in SE, Blackwater and Lee in S. Coastline irregular; harbors include Lough Foyle, Belfast Lough, Donegal Bay, Sligo Bay, Galway Bay, Dingle Bay, Bantry Bay, Dundalk Bay, and estuaries of the Shannon and Lee (Cork Harbour); numerous small islands, esp. Rathlin, Achill, Aran Is., Valencia, and Fastnet. For further information, see EIRE and IRELAND, NORTHERN.

History: Invaded by Celts c. 500 B.C.; according to tradition, governed as kingdoms of Ulster, Leinster, Connaught, Munster, and Meath, under which were numerous warring tribal kings; in 5th cent. A.D., converted to Christianity by St. Patrick; Irish monasticism produced outstanding scholars and missionaries, 6th–9th cents.; raided by Vikings (see CLONTARF) who founded Dublin, Waterford, and Limerick as trading stations; conquered 1169–71 by Norman lords and Henry II who established English rule over strip of coast around Dublin (later known as the Pale); Irish Parliament restricted by Poynings' Law 1494; extent of Pale varied until Cromwell, after rebellion of 1641–42, subdued all of Ireland; colonized, especially in N, by Scots, Welsh, and English; supported James II at battle of the Boyne (*q.v.*) 1690; united legislatively with Great Britain, forming United Kingdom of Great Britain and Ireland (see GREAT BRITAIN) 1801; in 19th cent., "Irish Question" (including problems of status of Catholics, land, self-government—Home Rule after 1886) became a key issue of British politics; unsuccessfully attempted to throw off British rule by Easter Rebellion (Easter Monday, Apr. 24, 1916); S Ireland refused Home Rule as provided by Act of 1920, and, after civil war 1919–21, was granted dominion status as Irish Free State 1921 (established 1922); 6 counties of Ulster formed Northern Ireland 1920.

Ireland, Northern. Division of the United Kingdom of Great Britain and Northern Ireland, occupying NE section of the island of Ireland; 5452 sq. m.; pop. (1971p) 1,525,187; ✱ Belfast. *Physical features:* Highland areas are in cos. Londonderry (Sperrin Mts.) and Tyrone; chief rivers Foyle on W boundary and the Upper Bann flowing into Lough Neagh and the Lower Bann, outlet of Lough Neagh (in E cen. part, largest lake in British Isles); other loughs are Foyle (on NW coast), Belfast (including harbor of Belfast) in E, Lough Strangford in E, and Lower and Upper Loughs Erne in SW. Coast borders on North Channel and Irish Sea. *Chief products:* Barley, oats, potatoes; livestock; manufacturing: textiles, aircraft, textile machinery, data-processing equipment; shipbuilding. *Chief cities:* Belfast, Newtownabbey, Londonderry, Newry, Armagh. Divided into the following six counties (for pronunciation of their names, see their individual entries):

NAME*	AREA (sq. m.)	POP. (1969e)	CO. SEAT
Antrim	1,200	719,700	Belfast
Armagh	512	128,200	Armagh
Down	952	300,800	Downpatrick
Fermanagh	715	49,900	Enniskillen
Londonderry	814	177,300	Londonderry
Tyrone	1,260	136,600	Omagh

*In Irish idiom, *county* precedes the name, as in *county Antrim*.

History: See ULSTER 2; accepted provisions of Government of Ireland Act 1920 which offered Home Rule to both northern and southern Ireland (see IRELAND 2); after long dispute, existing boundary with Irish Free State accepted 1925; scene of civil strife 1968 ff.; has consistently opposed union with rest of Ireland and remains part of United Kingdom (see GREAT BRITAIN).

Ireland Island. One of the Bermuda Is., W of Grassy Bay and N of Great Sound.

Ireng \ī-'reŋ\. River, Guyana; 175 m. long; tributary of the Tacutú; flows S and forms section of boundary bet. W cen. Guyana and Brazil.

Ir·giz \i(ə)r-'gēz, -'gēs\. River, W cen. Kazakh S.S.R., U.S.S.R.; ab. 270 m. long; flowing SE into Chelkar-Tengiz (lake), NE of Aral Sea.

Iri. 1 River, Greece. See EUROTAS.
2 \'ē-'rē\. Town, North Chŏlla prov., South Korea, 14 m. NW of Chŏnju; pop. (1970e) 86,770.

Irian. See NEW GUINEA.

Iri·an Ba·rat \ˌir-ē-ˈän-ˈbär-ˌät\ *or* **West Irian** *or* **West New Guinea** \-'gin-ē\; *formerly* **Dutch New Guinea** *or* **Neth·er·lands New Guinea** \'neth-ər-lən(d)z-\. A province of Indonesia, consisting of the W half of the island of New Guinea and adjacent islands off N and NW coasts, esp. Schouten Is., Japen, Numfoor, Salawati, and Waigeo and Dolak I. in the S; 162,927 sq. m.; pop. (1970e) 957,000; ✱ Djajapura. Traversed by Maoke Mts., highest peak Mt. Djaja 16,535 ft. Coastline irregular, esp. in NW where indentations of Sarera Bay and Berau Bay almost cut off large peninsula of Doberai. Has many rivers, Mamberamo largest in the N and Digul in the S, also large areas of swampland, esp. in the S. Many regions only partially explored; chief settlements on N and NW coasts: Djajapura, Manokwari, Sorong, Fakfak.

History: Islands off NW first visited by Dutch in 17th cent.; coastal regions saw gradual extension of Dutch sovereignty in 18th cent.; NW New Guinea declared a dependency of Tidore 1828; in 1884 the meridian of 141°E agreed upon with British as frontier boundary and in 1885 defined as also the frontier of German New Guinea; this line slightly altered along course of Fly river by convention with Great Britain in 1895. In World War II the N coastal areas occupied by Japanese 1942 but retaken by Allies by seizure esp. of Hollandia (now Djajapura), Wakde Is., Biak, and Numfoor 1944; remained under Dutch control when rest of the Neth. Indies became independent 1949; relinquished to United Nations administration 1962 by the Dutch and transferred to Indonesia 1963.

Iri·ga \i-'rē-gə\. 1 Extinct volcano, S Camarines Sur prov., Luzon, Phil.; 4023 ft.
2 Chartered city, S Camarines Sur prov., SW of Mt. Iriga and on railroad 22 m. SE of Naga; pop. (1970e) 107,300; largest town in province; in rich agricultural region.

Irin·ga \i-'riŋ-gə\. 1 Administrative region of S cen. Tanzania. See table at TANZANIA.
2 Town, its ✱, 255 m. SW of Dar es Salaam; pop. (1967c) 21,746.

Iri·o·mo·te \ˌir-ē-ə-'mō-(ˌ)tā\. Island in Sakishima group, SW end of Ryukyu Is., Japan; 57 m. in circumference.

Ir·i·on \'ir-ē-ən\. County in Texas. See table at TEXAS.

Iri·ri \ˌir-ə-'rē\. River, cen. Pará state, N Brazil; ab. 570 m. long; rises in N Mato Grosso and flows N into Xingu river.

Iris. See YEŞIL IRMAK.

Irish Free State. See EIRE.

Irish Sea \ˌī(ə)r-ish-\ *or anc.* **Oce·a·nus Hi·ber·ni·cus** \ō-ˌsē-ə-nəs-hī-'bər-ni-kəs\. Body of water bet. England on E and Ireland on W, connected with Atlantic Ocean on N through North Channel and on S through St. George's Channel; including St. George's Channel, extends 100 m. N-S and 125 m. E-W.

Ir·kutsk \i(ə)r-'kütsk, ər-\. City, ✱ of Irkutsk Oblast, Russian S.F.S.R., U.S.S.R., on Angara river 45 m. from SW shore of Lake Baikal; pop. (1970p) 451,000; one of chief cities on Trans-Siberian R.R.; cultural center; market for furs and skins; mica processing, timber working; machine tools, electrical equipment; hydroelectric plant; established 1652 as government station; grew because of trade with China and Amur valley and connection with Lena goldfields and with fur trade; much damaged during Russian Civil War 1918–21.

Irkutsk Oblast \-'ō-bləst, -ˌblast\. Subdivision of the Russian S.F.S.R., U.S.S.R.; 296,486 sq. m.; pop. (1970p) 2,314,000; ✱ Irkutsk; Lake Baikal forms a large part of its E border; principal streams the Angara, the upper headstreams of the Lena, the Lower Tunguska, and the Chuna, and the lower course of the Vitim; chiefly a mountain and plateau region with highest peaks in Sayan Mts. on SW boundary; most important resources mineral, esp. gold, coal, salt, iron ore, mica, but timber, fishing, and furbearing animals also valuable; large hydroelectric power plants; industrial centers Irkutsk and Cheremkhovo, both near or on the navigable Angara and the Trans-Siberian R.R., which traverses region from NW to SE; chief cities Irkutsk, Angarsk, Cheremkhovo, Bratsk. Region began to be settled in latter half of 17th cent.; long used as place of banishment for political and other exiles; in 19th cent. received many voluntary settlers; became part of East Siberia region; scene of extensive fighting during Civil War 1918–21; reorganized as subdivision of U.S.S.R. in Asia 1937; rapid industrial development since 1960.

Ir·lam \'ər-ləm\. Urban district, Lancashire, NW England, at confluence of Mersey and Irwell rivers 7½ m. W of Manchester; pop. (1971p) 20,571.

Iro, Cape \-'ē-(ˌ)rō\ *or Jap.* **Irō–Za·ki** \-'zäk-ē\. Cape on SE coast of Honshū, Japan, bet. Suruga Bay and Sagami Sea.

Iron \'ī(-ə)rn\. Name of counties in four states of the U.S. See tables at MICHIGAN, MISSOURI, UTAH, WISCONSIN.

Iron·dale \'ī(-ə)rn-ˌdāl\. City, Jefferson co., cen. Alabama, 3 m. E of Birmingham; pop. (1970c) 3166.

Iron·de·quoit Bay \ir-'än-də-ˌkwoit-, -kwät-\. Inlet of Lake Ontario, E of Rochester, W New York; rendezvous 1687 of Marquis de Denonville in his sally against the Iroquois; French post 1710.

Iron Gate *or* **Iron Gates** \ˌī(-ə)rn-\ *or Rom.* **Por·ţi·le de Fier** \pôrt-ˌsē-lə-də-'fye(ə)r\ *or Ger.* **Ei·ser·nes Tor** \ˌī-zər-nə-

ˈstō(ə)r, -ˈstȯ(ə)r\. Gorge, with rapids, in Danube river bet. Orşova and Turnu-Severin, Romania, on Yugoslav boundary; 2 m. long.

Iron Mountain. 1 Elevation, Polk co., cen. Florida penin.; 325 ft.

2 Mountain, St. Francois co., E Missouri, ab. 12 m. NE of Taum Sauk; 1077 ft.

3 Peak, Custer and Pennington cos., SW South Dakota; 5500 ft.

4 City, ⊗ of Dickinson co., S Michigan penin., 48 m. W of Escanaba; pop. (1970c) 8702; chemicals; mining machinery; dairy and fruit farming; summer resort.

Iron Mountains. Ridge, part of Unaka Mountains, extending along boundary bet. Smyth and Grayson cos. and bet. Grayson and Wythe cos., in Virginia, and SW into Tennessee; ab. 80 m. long; highest peak ab. 4200 ft.

Iron River. City, Iron co., SW Michigan penin., 34 m. WNW of Iron Mountain; pop. (1970c) 2684; lake resort; iron mining, dairy, poultry, and truck farming.

Iron·ton \ˈī(-ə)rn-tən\. 1 City, ⊗ of Iron co., SE Missouri; pop. (1970c) 1452; lead mines; diversified agriculture.

2 City, ⊗ of Lawrence co., S Ohio, on Ohio river opp. Russell, Kentucky, 21 m. SE of Portsmouth; pop. (1970c) 15,030; coke, flour, cement, clay products, steel castings; limestone quarries; founded 1848.

Iron·wood \ˈī(-ə)rn-ˌwu̇d\. City, Gogebic co., NW Michigan penin., on Wisconsin border 15 m. SE of Lake Superior; pop. (1970c) 8711; summer resort; iron mines; concrete blocks, flooring, lumber; Gogebic Community Coll. (1932).

Ir·o·quois \ˈir-ə-ˌkwȯi\. 1 River, Indiana and Illinois; ab. 120 m. long; rises in NW Indiana, and flows W across Illinois border, then N into Kankakee river in NE Illinois.

2 County in Illinois. See table at ILLINOIS.

Iroquois Falls. Town, Cochrane dist., E Ontario, Canada, 45 m. NE of Timmins; on railroad W of Lake Abitibi; pop. (1971p) 7248; pulp and paper mills.

Iroquois Point. City, Honolulu co., Hawaii; pop. (1970c) 4572.

Irō–Zaki. See IRO, CAPE.

Ir·ra·wad·dy *also* **Ira·wa·di** \ˌir-ə-ˈwäd-ē\. 1 River, cen. Burma; ab. 1300 m. long; formed by confluence of Mali and Nmai rivers just N of Myitkyina in Upper Burma, flows S through cen. Burma into Bay of Bengal through several mouths, near Rangoon; has extensive delta; navigable to Bhamo; main tributary the Chindwin which joins it 60 m. WSW of Mandalay; other branches the Shweli, Mu, and Myitnge; passes through three defiles where course is narrow and rapid; important towns on its banks Myitkina, Bhamo, Mandalay, Myingyan, Pyè, and Henzada.

2 Division of Lower Burma. See table at BURMA.

Ir·tysh *or* **Ir·tish** \i(ə)r-ˈtish, ər-\. River, NE Kazakh S.S.R., U.S.S.R., and W part of Russian S.F.S.R. (Omsk Oblast); ab. 2760 m. long; rises on W slopes of Altai Mts. in N Sinkiang Uighur, flows W across Chinese border through Zaisan Lake and then NW to join Ob river; largest tributary of the Ob and navigable for most of its course; Semipalatinsk, Pavlodar, Omsk, and Tobolsk are on its banks.

Iru·ma \i-ˈrü-mə\. City, Saitama prefecture, Honshū, Japan, 25 m. NW of Tokyo; pop. (1970c) 65,369.

Irún \ē-ˈrün\. Commune, Guipúzcoa prov., N Spain, on Bidassoa river 9 m. E of San Sebastián near French border; pop. (1970p) 45,060; port of entry; iron foundries, tanneries, paper mills, medicinal springs.

Ir·vine \ˈər-vən\. 1 City, ⊗ of Estill co., E Kentucky, 23 m. SSE of Winchester; pop. (1970c) 2918; sawmills.

2 Burgh, Ayr co., SW Scotland, on Irvine estuary 11 m. N of Ayr; pop. (1971p) 23,011; ships building materials; shipyards, brass foundries; chemicals, glass products.

Ir·ving \ˈər-viŋ\. City, Dallas co., NE Texas, NW of Dallas; pop. (1970c) 97,260; aluminum, gypsum, airplane parts; diversified farming.

Ir·ving·ton \ˈər-viŋ-tən\. 1 Town, Essex co., NE New Jersey, 3 m. WSW of and adjoining Newark; pop. (1970c) 59,743; foundries, tanneries; toys, insulators, dies, tools.

2 Residential and industrial village, Westchester co., SE New York, on Hudson river 22 m. N of New York and 3 m. S of Tarrytown; pop. (1970c) 5878; forms one community with North Tarrytown, Elmsford, and Tarrytown; manufactures greenhouses, electronic components; home of Washington Irving (Wolfert's Roost, renamed Sunnyside).

Ir·well \ˈər-ˌwel, -wəl\. River, W England; ab. 30 m. long; flows in winding course S past Rochdale, Bury, and Manchester into the Mersey at Irlam.

Ir·win \ˈər-win\. 1 County in Georgia. See table at GEORGIA.

2 Borough, Westmoreland co., SW Pennsylvania, 18 m. ESE of Pittsburgh; pop. (1970c) 4059; machine tools; diversified agriculture.

Ir·win·ton \ˈər-win-tən\. Town, ⊗ of Wilkinson co., cen. Georgia; pop. (1970c) 757; corn, peanuts.

Is. See HIT.

Isa \ˈē-sə\. Town, North-Western State, N Nigeria; 160 m. WNW of Kano.

Isabel. See SANTA ISABEL 4.

Is·a·bel, Mount \-ˈiz-ə-ˌbel\. Peak, N cen. Lincoln co., W Wyoming; 10,154 ft.

Isa·be·la \ˌiz-ə-ˈbel-ə, -ˈbāl-\. 1 Cape and port, N Dominican Republic, Hispaniola I.; Columbus's first settlement 1493.

2 Province, NE Luzon, Phil., in upper valley of Cagayan river; 4118 sq. m.; pop. (1970e) 662,891; ✱ Ilagan; on E along Pacific coast is part of Sierra Madre range; a major tobacco-producing province of the Philippines; other products corn, rice, sugar, and coffee.

History: Province created 1856 out of lands belonging to Cagayan and Nueva Vizcaya; old towns centers of missionary activities in 17th cent.; suffered from revolts 1763, 1785; civil government established Aug. 1901.

3 *or* **Isabela de Basilan.** City, Phil. See BASILAN 3.

4 Municipality, cen. Negros Occidental, Negros, Phil., 37 m. S of City of Bacolod; pop. (1969e) 40,700; important communications center and sugar town.

5 Town and municipality, NW Puerto Rico; town on coast 10 m. NE of Aguadilla; pop. (1970p) 9884 (town), 30,201 (munic.).

Isabela Island *or* **Al·be·marle Island** \ˈal-bə-ˌmärl-\. Island, largest of Galápagos Is.; in W part of the group, 0°30′S, 91°06′W, its N end crossed by equator; 1650 sq. m. See GALÁPAGOS ISLANDS.

Is·a·bel·la \ˌiz-ə-ˈbel-ə\. County in Michigan. See table at MICHIGAN.

Isach·sen Peninsula \ˈī-zik-sən-, -zək-\. Peninsula in NW Ellef Ringnes I., N Franklin dist., Northwest Territories, Canada; formerly thought to be an island.

Ísa·fjör·dhur \ˈē-sə-ˌfyər-t͟hər\. Town at tip of peninsula of NW Iceland; pop. (1970c) 2680.

Isa·ha·ya \i-ˈsä-hä-yə\. City, Nagasaki prefecture, Kyūshū, Japan, 15 m. NW of Nagasaki; pop. (1970c) 65,261.

Isana. See IÇANA.

Isan·ti \i-ˈsant-ē\. County in Minnesota. See table at MINNESOTA.

Isar \ˈē-ˌzär\. River, Bavaria, West Germany; 163 m. long; rises in Tirol and flows through Munich and past Landshut NW into the Danube; not navigable.

Isar·co \i-ˈzär-(ˌ)kō\. River, Trentino-Alto Adige, N Italy; ab. 70 m. long; flows into the Adige at Bolzano.

Isa·rog \ˌē-sə-ˈrȯg\. Volcanic mountain, E cen. Camarines Sur prov., Luzon, Phil., on isthmus bet. Lagonoy Gulf and San Miguel Bay; 6448 ft; base ab. 36 m. in circumference; source of many streams.

Isau·ria \ī-ˈsȯr-ē-ə\. Ancient district in E Pisidia, Asia Minor (Turkey), on N slope of W Taurus Mts.; in 1st cent. B.C. boundaries were changed so that it included a part of W Cilicia; furnished several rulers of Byzantine Empire.

Isca Damnoniorum. See EXETER 6.

Isca Silurum. See CAERLEON.

Is·chia \'is-kē-ə\ *or* **Iso·la D'Ischia** \ˌē-zə-lə-'dis-\ *or anc.* **Ae·nar·ia** \i-'nar-ē-ə, -'ner-\. Island in Tyrrhenian Sea bet. Gulf of Gaeta and Bay of Naples; 18 sq. m.; administratively a part of Napoli prov., Campania, S Italy; highest point the volcanic Monte Epomeo 2585 ft.; summer resort, mineral springs; suffered greatly from volcanic eruptions and earthquakes, esp. the earthquake of 1883; chief town Ischia, commune pop. (1968e) 14,139.

Ischl \'ish-əl\ *or* **Bad Ischl** \(ˈ)bät-\. Commune, Upper Austria, on Traun river S of Lake Traun 51 m. SW of Linz; pop. (1961c) 12,703; trade center; tourist and health resort; mineral springs, salt mine; metalworking.

Ise \'ē-(ˌ)sā\. 1 Old province, S coast of Honshū, Japan, now part of Mie prefecture. Name also applied to the sacred Shinto shrine to the Sun Goddess, located at Ise, in Mie prefecture; for centuries the mecca of pilgrims and of the emperor and high officials.

2 *or formerly* **Uji–ya·ma·da** \ˌü-jē-yä-'mäd-ə\. Town, Mie prefecture, Honshū, Japan; pop. (1970c) 103,576; several Shinto shrines.

Ise Bay *or* **Atsu·ta Bay** \ˌät-sü-ˌtä-\ *or formerly* **Owa·ri Bay** \ō-'wär-ē-\. Inlet of Pacific Ocean on S coast of Honshū, Japan, bet. Mie and Aichi prefectures.

Ise Fjord \ˌē-sə-\. Inlet of the Kattegat on N coast of Sjælland I., Denmark; extends S inland 20 m.; its E extension is Roskilde Fjord.

Iseghem. See IZEGEM.

Isel·le \ē-'zel-ā\. Town, NE Piedmont, NW Italy, just NW of Domodossola; S terminal of Simplon Pass and Tunnel.

Iseo, Lake \-ē-'zā-(ˌ)ō\ *or* **La·go d'Iseo** \ˌlä-gō-dē-'zā-(ˌ)ō\. Lake in Lombardy, N Italy, on border bet. Brescia and Bergamo provs.; 24 sq. m.

Iser \'ē-zər\ *or Czech* **Ji·se·ra** \'yi-sə-ˌrä\. River, Czechoslovakia; 94 m. long; flows S into Labe (Elbe) river.

Ise·ran, Col de l' \ˌkȯl-də-ˌlēz-(ə-)'räⁿ, ˌkəl-\. Mountain pass, Graian Alps, E Savoie dept., E France; 9084 ft. high; highway, completed 1937.

Isère \ē-'ze(ə)r\. 1 River, SE France; 180 m. long; rises on slopes of Graian Alps near border of Italy, flows W and SW into Rhone river 4 m. NNW of Valence.

2 Department of France. See table at FRANCE.

Iser·lohn \ˌē-zər-'lōn, 'ē-zər-ˌ\. City, North Rhine-Westphalia, West Germany, 15 m. W of Arnsberg; pop. (1969e) 57,615; heavy machinery, electrical equipment, textiles; became city mid 13th cent.

Isér·nia \i-'zer-nē-ə\ *or anc.* **Æ·ser·nia** \ē-'zər-\. 1 Province Molise, cen. Italy. See table at ITALY.

2 Commune, its ✽, 22 m. WNW of Campobasso; pop. (1968e) 14,241; cathedral; manufactures lace; has ancient remains. Came under Romans 295 B.C.; became Roman colony 263 B.C.; took part in Social War 90 B.C.

Ise·sa·ki \ˌē-sā-ˌsäk-ē\. City, Gumma prefecture, Honshū, Japan, 55 m. NW of Tokyo; pop. (1970c) 91,277.

Ise·yin \ˌē-sə-'yēn\. City, Western State, Nigeria, NNW of Ibadan; pop. (1969e) 110,426.

Isfahan. See EṢFAHĀN 2.

Ish·a·wooa Cone \ˌish-ə-wä-\. Mountain in Absaroka Range, SW Park co., NW Wyoming; 11,840 ft.

Ishi·ga·ki \ˌish-i-'gäk-ē\. Island in cen. part of Sakishima group, S Ryukyu Is., Japan.

Ishi·ka·ri \ˌish-i-'kär-ē\ *or Jap.* **Ishikari–ga·wa** \-'gä-wə\. River, W Hokkaidō I., Japan; 275 m. long; 2d longest river in Japan; flows W into **Ishikari Bay.**

Ishikari Dake. See ASAHI DAKE.

Ishi·ka·wa \ˌish-i-'kä-wə\. Prefecture, Honshū, Japan; 1620 sq. m.; pop. (1970c) 1,002,420; ✽ Kanazawa.

Ishim \i-'shim\. 1 River, N cen. Kazakh S.S.R., U.S.S.R., and W part of Russian S.F.S.R. (Omsk Oblast); ab. 1330 m. long; rises in cen. steppe region of Kazakh S.S.R. and flows N past Petropavlovsk to join the Irtysh at Ust-Ishim.

2 Town on lower Ishim river, Tyumen Oblast, on railroad 85 m. N of Petropavlovsk; pop. (1967e) 48,000.

Ishim·bay \ˌē-shim-'bī\. Town, Bashkir A.S.S.R., Russian S.F.S.R., U.S.S.R., ab. 90 m. S of Ufa; pop. (1969e) 55,000.

Ishi·no·ma·ki \ˌish-i-nō-'mäk-ē\. Town, Miyagi prefecture, N Honshū on E coast, Japan; pop. (1970c) 106,681; fair harbor; important port of call for small coastal steamers.

Ishinomaki Bay. Inlet of Pacific Ocean, Miyagi prefecture, NE coast of Honshū, Japan.

Ishi·zu·chi·no \ˌē-shi-'zü-chi-ˌnō\ *or Jap.* **Ishizuchino–mo·ri** \-'mōr-ē\. Peak, W Shikoku I., Japan; 6500 ft.; highest peak on Shikoku.

Ish·pe·ming \'ish-pə-miŋ\. City, Marquette co., N Michigan penin., 15 m. W of Marquette; pop. (1970c) 8245; iron mining.

Ishtib. See ŠTIP.

Isi·bo·ro–Se·cu·re National Park \ˌē-sə-ˌbōr-ə-sə-'kür-ə-\. National park, Bolivia; 4600 sq. m.; tropical forest; established 1965.

Isi·gny \ˌē-zi-'nyē\ *or in full* **Isigny–sur–Mer** \-sü(ə)r-'me(ə)r\. Village, NW Calvados dept., NW France, W of Bayeux and near Carentan; pop. (1962c) 2641; watering place; captured by U.S. forces June 6–10, 1944 in Normandy invasion of World War II.

Isin. See ISSIN.

Isio·lo \ˌē-zē-'ō-(ˌ)lō, -'ō-(ˌ)lō\. Town, NE Kenya, E Africa, N of Mt. Kenya; pop. (1962c) 5445.

Isis \'ī-səs\. Local name for upper course of the Thames river, in England.

Iskandarīyah, Al–. Governorate and seaport, Egypt. See ALEXANDRIA.

Iskâr. See ISKŬR.

Iskelib. See İSKİLİP.

İs·ken·de·run *or* **Is·ken·de·ron** \(ˌ)is-ˌken-də-'rün\; *formerly* **Al·ex·an·dret·ta** \ˌal-ig-zan-'dret-ə, ˌel-\ *or Fr.* **Alex·an·drette** \á-lek-säⁿ-dret\. Seaport city on SE shore of Gulf of İskenderun (Alexandretta), Hatay, S Turkey, ab. 60 m. SE of Adana; pop. (1965c) 69,382; steel plant; chief town of former sanjak of Alexandretta and of republic of Hatay; on branch railroad and on coastal highway S of site of Issus (battle 333 B.C.); founded by Alexander and named by him ("Little Alexandria") to commemorate the battle; has good harbor; chief port of Aleppo and formerly outlet for overland trade from Persia and India until opening of Suez Canal.

İskenderun, Gulf of *or Turk.* **İskenderun Kör·fe·zi** \-ˌkər-fə-'zē\ *or formerly* **Gulf of Alexandretta.** Inlet of E Mediterranean Sea on S coast of Turkey near Syrian boundary; its E coast is province (former republic) of Hatay.

Is·ker \'is-kər\. 1 River, Bulgaria. See ISKŬR.

2 *or Cossack name* **Si·bir** \sə-'bi(ə)r\. Ancient town, ✽ of a Tatar khanate in W Siberia in 16th cent., near site of city of Tobolsk, Russian S.F.S.R., U.S.S.R.; captured 1581 by Ermak Timofeev (or Yermak), a hetman of the Don Cossacks, an event which marked beginning of Russian conquest of N Asia; town gave its name to the region, Siberia.

İs·ki·lip *or* **Is·ke·lib** \ˌis-kə-'lēp, -'lip\. Town near left bank of the Kızıl, Çorum prov., N cen. Turkey, 103 m. NE of Ankara; pop. (1965c) 12,400.

Is·ki·tim \ēs-kə-'t(y)ēm\. Town, Novosibirsk Oblast, Russian S.F.S.R., U.S.S.R., ab. 30 m. SSE of Novosibirsk; pop. (1967e) 43,000.

Is·kŭr *or* **Is·kâr** *also* **Is·ker** *or* **Iskr** \'is-kər\. River, NW cen. Bulgaria; 228 m. long; rises in Rhodope Mts., flows N through Balkan Mts., into Danube river 22 m. W of Nikopol.

Is·la \'ī-lə\. River, chiefly in Angus co., E Scotland; 46 m. long; flows S and SW to the Tay in Perth co.

Isla Cris·ti·na \ˌēz-lə-kri-ˈstē-nə\. Seaport, Huelva prov., SW Spain, on the Mediterranean Sea 21 m. W of Huelva; pop. (1960c) 12,330; fisheries, esp. for tuna, sardines.

Isla de León. See LEÓN, ISLA DE.

Isla de los Estados. See ESTADOS, ISLA DE LOS.

Isla de Pinos. See ISLE OF PINES 1.

Isla Grande de Tierra del Fuego. See TIERRA DEL FUEGO 2.

Is·lam·a·bad \is-ˈläm-ə-ˌbäd, iz-ˈlam-ə-ˌbad\. City, ✱ of Pakistan, NE of Rawalpindi; pop. (1965e) 50,000; univ. (1965), mosque.

Islamic Republic of Mauritania. See MAURITANIA.

Islamic Republic of Pakistan. See PAKISTAN.

Is·land \ˈī-lənd\. County in Washington. See table at WASHINGTON.

Island *or* **Ísland.** See ICELAND.

Island Beach. Narrow sand spit off E coast of Ocean co., E New Jersey, enclosing Barnegat Bay.

Island Lake. Lake, E Manitoba, Canada; 550 sq. m.; outlet through Gods Lake and Hayes river to Hudson Bay.

Island No. 10. Former island in Mississippi river, in New Madrid co., SE corner of Missouri; scene of Civil War engagements Apr. 1862.

Island Park. Village on Long I., Nassau co., SE New York, on Atlantic Ocean 20 m. ESE of New York; pop. (1970c) 5396.

Islands, Bay of. 1 Inlet of Gulf of St. Lawrence, W Newfoundland, Canada; estuary of Humber river.

2 Inlet of Pacific Ocean on NE coast of N extension of North I., New Zealand, W of Cape Brett.

Islands of the Four Mountains. Island group in E cen. Aleutian Is., Alaska, W of Umnak; chief islands Chuginadak, Kagamil, Carlisle, and Herbert.

Islas de la Bahía. See BAHÍA, ISLAS DE LA.

Islas de Ori·en·te \ˈēz-ləs-dē-ˌōr-ē-ˈent-ə, -ˌȯr-\. Early Portuguese name of the Philippines—literally "Eastern Islands," because lying to the E within the new lands assigned to Portugal by Treaty of Tordesillas (*q.v.*) 1494.

Islas de Po·nien·te \ˈēz-ˌläs-dā-ˌpō-nē-ˈent-ē\. Early Spanish name of the Phillipines—literally "Western Islands," because lying to the W (beyond Mexico) within the lands of the Far East claimed by Spain because of Magellan's discovery.

Islas Filipinas. See PHILIPPINES.

Is·lay \ˈī-(ˌ)lā, -lə\. Most southerly island of the Inner Hebrides, off W coast of Scotland, in Argyll co.; 234 sq. m.; pop. (1961c) 5743; farming, fishing, whiskey distilling.

Isle \ˈē(ə)l\. River, SW cen. France; 145 m. long; rises in Haute-Vienne dept., flows SW into Dordogne river.

Isle au Haut \ˌī-lə-ˈhō, ē-\. Island at entrance to Penobscot Bay off S cen. Maine coast; included in Knox co.; half of it in Acadia National Park.

Isle–de–France. See ÎLE-DE-FRANCE.

Isle La Motte \ˌīl-lə-ˈmät\. Island in Lake Champlain, Grand Isle co., NW Vermont; ab. 6 m. long; settled by French (Fort Sainte Anne) 1666; black-marble quarry.

Isle of Ely. See CAMBRIDGESHIRE AND ISLE OF ELY.

Isle of Man. See MAN, ISLE OF.

Isle of Palms \-ˈpämz, -ˈpälmz\. City, Charleston co., South Carolina, 7 m. E of Charleston; pop. (1970c) 2569.

Isle of Pines \-ˈpīnz\. 1 *or Span.* **Is·la de Pi·nos** \ˌēz-lä-t͟hā-ˈpē-nōs\. Island in NW Caribbean Sea, S of W Cuba; 1182 sq. m.; pop. (1967e) 20,630; administratively, a municipality of La Habana prov.; chief town Nueva Gerona.

2 French island in Pacific Ocean. See ÎLE DES PINS.

Isle of Wight \-ˈwīt\. 1 County in SE Virginia. See table at VIRGINIA.

2 Village, its ⊗, 17 m. W of Newport News.

3 Island in English Channel. See WIGHT, ISLE OF.

Isle Roy·ale \ī(ə)l-ˈrȯi(-ə)l\. Island in NW Lake Superior, N of, and a part of, Keweenaw co., N tip of upper Michigan penin.; ab. 44 m. long by 8 m. wide; copper deposits were mined by Indians, their pits still in evidence; with surrounding islands now constitutes **Isle Royale National Park:** see UNITED STATES, *National Parks*.

Isles Der·nieres \ˌē(ə)l-der-ˈnye(ə)r\. Small group of islands in Gulf of Mexico, in Terrebonne parish, SE Louisiana.

Isles of Scilly. See SCILLY ISLES.

Isles of Shoals \-ˈshōls\. Group of nine rocky islands 10 m. SE of Portsmouth, New Hampshire; ab. 1 sq. m.; most important Star and Appledore; resort; Maine-New Hampshire boundary passes through the group.

Isles of the Sea *or* **Gar·vel·loch Isles** \gär-ˌvel-ək-\. Island group Firth of Lorn, W Scotland.

Is·le·ta \i-ˈzlāt-ə\. Indian village and pueblo, Bernalillo co., cen. New Mexico, on the Rio Grande in Isleta Pueblo Indian Reservation, S of Albuquerque; pop. (1970c) 1080; inhabited by Indians chiefly of Tanoan stock.

Is·ling·ton \ˈiz-liŋ-tən\. A borough of Greater London, SE England. See table at LONDON 4.

Islip \ˈī-sləp\. 1 Town, Suffolk co., SE New York, on Long I. on Great South Bay, ab. 10 m. W of Patchogue; pop. (1970c) 7692; resort.

2 Parish and village, Oxfordshire, cen. England, ab. 6 m. N of Oxford; parish pop. (1961c) 522; birthplace of Edward the Confessor.

Is·ly \ē-slē\. Short river, NE Morocco, N Africa.

Is·ma·il \ˈiz-mē-əl, ˌē-smä-ˈē(ə)l\. 1 *or Russ.* **Iz·ma·il** \ˈiz-mē-əl, is-mə-ˈē(ə)l\. Former department, S Bessarabia, Romania, N of Danube delta; 1626 sq. m.; now in Odessa Oblast, Ukrainian S.S.R., U.S.S.R.

2 City, its ✱. See IZMAIL 2.

Is·ma·i·lia \ˌiz-mā-ə-ˈlē-ə\ *or Arab.* **Al–Ismā·ʽīlī·yah** \ˌal-ˌis-mə-i-ˈlē-ə\. 1 Governorate of NE Egypt. See table at EGYPT.

2 Town, its ✱, on Lake Timsah; pop. (1970e) 167,500; halfway station on Suez Canal; founded 1863.

Ismailia Canal *or Arab.* **Tur·ʽat al–Ismā·ʽīlī·yah** \tu̇-ˈrät-ˌal-ˌis-mə-i-ˈlē-ə\. Canal extending from Nile river near Cairo, Egypt to Suez Canal at Ismailia on Lake Timsah.

Ismid. See İZMİT.

Ismid, Gulf of. See İZMİT, GULF OF.

Is·na \ˈis-nə\ *or* **Es·na** \ˈes-\. Commercial town on Nile river, Upper Egypt, S of the ruins of Thebes; pop. (1966c) 27,400; pottery; Ptolemaic and Coptic ruins.

Isola D'Ischia. See ISCHIA.

Isola Lunga. See DUGI OTOK.

Isole Egadi. See EGADI ISLANDS.

Isole Eolie. See LIPARI ISLANDS.

Isole Italiane dell'Egeo. See AEGEAN ISLANDS 3.

Ison·zo \ē-ˈzȯn(t)-(ˌ)sō\ *or Serbo-Croat.* **So·ča** \ˈsō-chə\ *or anc.* **Son·ti·us** \ˈsänt-ē-əs, ˈsän-sh(ē-)əs\. River, Yugoslavia and Italy; 84 m. long; rises in NW Yugoslavia, flows S into Gulf of Trieste near Monfalcone, NE Italy. Area of severe fighting in Word War I, esp. at Gorizia and Caporetto (Kobarid).

Iso·to·ro Nāl \ˌē-sə-ˌtȯr-ə-ˈnəl\. Mountain in the Hindu Kush, on Afghanistan-Pakistan boundary; 24,273 ft.

Ispahan. See EŞFAHAN.

İs·par·ta \ˌis-pär-ˈtä\ *also* **Is·bar·ta** \ˌēs-bär-ˈtä\. 1 Province of SW Turkey, Asia. See table at TURKEY.

2 Town, its ✱, 110 m. W of Konya; pop. (1965c) 42,901.

Is·ra·el \ˈiz-rē-əl\. 1 Ancient kingdom in Palestine; as first formed under Saul c. 1025 B.C. comprised the lands in Canaan (*q.v.*) which in 12th cent. B.C. were occupied by Hebrew tribes descended from the sons of Jacob (Israel) who had been led out of Egypt by Moses; consolidated by David who began to rule c. 1013 B.C. and made Jerusalem his capital and under whom it included also Galilee and land E of the Jordan; became prosperous trading nation under Solomon who erected temple at Jerusalem; after death of Solomon kingdom divided, the ten northern tribes seceding and forming c. 933 B.C. under Jeroboam the kingdom of Israel (*or* **Northern Kingdom**), while the two tribes in the S under Solomon's son Rehoboam formed kingdom of Judah (*q.v.*); Northern Kingdom (capital first at Shechem, then Tirzah, finally at Samaria which was built by Omri c. 887 B.C.) weakened by rivalry with Judah and Damascus, finally overthrown by Assyrians, who under Sargon II captured Samaria 721 B.C.

2 *or officially* **State of Israel.** Republic, SW Asia, bounded on N by Lebanon, on E by Syria and Jordan, on SW by Egypt (Sinai Penin.), and on W by the Mediterranean Sea; 7992 sq. m.; pop. (1970e) 3,000,400; ✱ Jerusalem; in extreme S has port on Gulf of ʻAqaba; hilly in N (highest peak Mt. Meron 3692 ft.); coastal plain (max. width ab. 20 m.), and Plain of Esdraelon, both below 300 ft.; in S is Negev (*q.v.*). *Chief products:* Citrus fruit, potash, magnesium, copper, bromine; manufacturing: textiles, chemicals, electrical goods; food processing, diamond-cutting; tourism. *Chief towns:* Tel Aviv-Jaffa, Jerusalem, Haifa, Ramat Gan, Bat Yam, Holon. For administrative purposes divided into the following six districts:

NAME	AREA (sq. m.)	POP. (1970e)	CAPITAL
Central	480	537,500	Ramla
Haifa	330	463,500	Haifa
Jerusalem*	215	323,700	Jerusalem
Northern	1,347	459,900	Nazareth
Southern	5,555	333,200	Beersheba
Tel Aviv	66	882,600	Tel Aviv-Jaffa

*Includes Jordanian sector of Jerusalem occupied by Israel 1967.

History: Established by decree of May 15, 1948, in the partition of Palestine between Jews and Arabs as recommended (1947) by a special committee of the United Nations. Its establishment intensified the state of civil war in Palestine (*q.v.*) bet. Arabs and Jews; invaded by Arab forces of neighboring countries; in offensive actions Oct. and Dec. 1948 regained positions in the S (the Negev) which had been lost to Egyptian forces in July; occupied new city of Jerusalem early in 1948 and on Feb. 1, 1949 declared it to be a part of the state of Israel; signed armistice agreement with Arab states retaining new city of Jerusalem but yielding to Egypt the coastal region around Gaza (*q.v.*); engaged in war with Arab countries 1956–57 (Sinai campaign); in the face of renewed Arab threats in 1967 occupied the immediately adjoining parts of Syria, the parts of Jordan W of the Jordan river, and the whole of the Sinai Peninsula in a lightning campaign June 5–10 ("the 6-day war") ending in a cease-fire but without withdrawal from occupied territories.

Issa. See VIS.

Is·sa·quah \ˈis-ə-ˌkwȯ\. City, King co., W cen. Washington, 15 m. SE of Seattle; pop. (1970c) 4313; lumbering; diversified agriculture; coal mines; resort.

Is·sa·que·na \ˌis-ə-ˈkwē-nə\. County in Mississippi. See table at MISSISSIPPI.

Issel. See IJSSEL.

Issel, Lake. See IJSSELMEER.

Is·ser \ˈis-ər, ˈē-sər\. Commune, Tizi-Ouzou dept., N Algeria, near Tizi-Ouzou; pop. (1966c) 5508.

Is·sin *or* **Is·in** \ˈis-ᵊn\. Archaeological site, a low mound with a large building on it, S Iraq, bet. the Euphrates and the Tigris 60 m. SE of Hilla; ancient city of Babylonia, of Semitic origin; conquered by Elamites 2126 B.C.; part of Babylonian empire of Hammurabi.

Issiq Köl. See ISSYK-KUL.

Is·soire \ē-ˈswär\. Commune, Puy-de-Dôme dept., S cen. France, 18 m. SSE of Clermont-Ferrand; pop. (1968c) 11,-886; 12th cent. Romanesque church.

Is·sou·dun \ˌē-sü-ˈdəⁿ\ *or anc.* **Ux·el·lo·du·num** \ək-ˌsel-ə-ˈd(y)ü-nəm\. City, Indre dept., cen. France, 19 m. NE of Châteauroux; pop. (1968c) 15,108.

Is·sus \ˈis-əs\. Ancient town, S Asia Minor, ab. 20 m. N of modern İskenderun (Turkey), in a narrow coastal plain S of passes through Taurus Mts.; scene of two battles: (1) 333 B.C., Alexander won victory over Darius and the Persians; (2) 194 A.D., Roman emperor L. Septimius Severus defeated his rival Pescennius Niger.

Is·syk–Kul \ˌis-ik-ˈkəl\ *also* **Is·siq Köl** \ˌis-ik-ˈkə(r)l\. Lake (*kul*), NE Kirgiz S.S.R., U.S.S.R.; a brackish lake lying in a basin at alt. 5279 ft. bet. W spurs of the Tien Shan; 115 m. long by 38 m. wide; 2355 sq. m.; max. depth 2303 ft.; mountain ranges to S and N have peaks 13,000 to 18,000 ft. high; sometimes receives waters from the Chu river at W end; in early times shores inhabited by Usuns and Yue-chi, later by Kara Kirghiz tribes.

Is·sy–les–Mou·li·neaux \ē-ˌsē-lā-ˌmü-lə-ˈnō\ *or* **Issy.** Commune, Hauts-de-Seine dept., N France, SW suburb of Paris on Seine river; pop. (1968c) 50,442; aircraft, electronic equipment.

İs·tan·bul \ˌis-təm-ˈbül, -täm-, -tam-, -tän-\ *or formerly* **Con·stan·ti·no·ple** \ˌkän-ˌstant-ᵊn-ˈō-pəl\. 1 Province of NW Turkey, on both sides of Bosporus. See table at TURKEY.

2 *or Bulg.* **Tsa·ri·grad** \ˈtsär-ə-ˌgrät\ *or Russ.* **Tsar·grad** \ˈtsär-ˌgrät\ *or anc.* **By·zan·ti·um** \bə-ˈzan-sh(ē-)əm, -ˈzant-ē-əm\. City, its ✱, on both sides of the Bosporus; old part of city on W side of the Bosporus; chief city and former ✱ of Turkey; pop. (1970p) 2,312,751; shipbuilding yards; textiles, leather goods, cement, pottery; tourism; contains church of Saint Sophia, erected 532–562 in time of Justinian; univ. (1453), technical univ. (1944).

History: As ancient Byzantium founded c. 660 B.C. by Greeks from Megara and Argos under Byzas; destroyed in reign (521–486) of Darius Hystaspis but recolonized by Greeks from Sparta after 478 B.C.; rose to great importance as trading port; often contended for by various states (Sparta, Macedonia, Rhodes, Rome) in 750 years bet. Peloponnesian War and time of Constantine; captured by Emperor Septimius Severus 196 A.D. Name changed 330 A.D. to Constantinople (*Lat. Constantinopolis,* from *Gk. Konstantinou polis* Constantine's city) by Constantine the Great, who chose its site for his new capital of Eastern Roman, or Byzantine, Empire (see BYZANTINE EMPIRE); official capital 395–1453; old city on Golden Horn, an arm of Bosporus, was greatly enlarged by Byzantine emperors and protected by walls; attacked many times; captured and sacked by Crusaders 1204; retaken by Byzantines 1261; captured 1453 by Turks under Mohammed II; Muslim capital 1453–1922, and seat of government (Sublime Porte) of Ottoman sultans 1453–1922, when, after its occupation by Allies 1918–23 and deposition of sultan 1922, Ankara became 1923 capital of new Turkish Republic. Following a decree of the Grand National Assembly Nov. 1928, the use of the Latin alphabet became general and the name İstanbul was officially adopted 1930. For sections or suburbs of the city, see BEYOĞLU, GALATA, ÜSKÜDAR, YESILKÖY.

Ister. See DANUBE.

Istib *or* **Istip.** See ŠTIP.

Is·tok·po·ga, Lake \-ˌis-täk-ˈpō-gə\. Lake in cen. Highlands co., cen. Florida penin.

Is·tran·ca Mountains \is-ˌträn-jə-\ *or Turk.* **Istranca Da·ğla·ri** \-ˌdä(g)-lə-ˈrē\. Mountain range along Black Sea coast, Kirklareli and İstanbul provs., Turkey, Europe; highest point 3378 ft.

Is·tria \ˈis-trē-ə\ *or* **Is·tri·an Peninsula** \-ən-\. Peninsula, NE coast of Adriatic Sea, ab. 60 m. long from Trieste at its base to its S point; 1545 sq. m.; Pula, its chief town, is near S end; Rijeka is just E of its E border; on SE is gulf of Kvarner.

History: Inhabited by Istrians who were overthrown by Romans in 177 B.C.; Carolingian march of Istria, erected c. 788 A.D., was united with duchy of Bavaria in 10th cent.; came to patriarchs of Aquileia and, in 13th cent., to Venice; N part was an Austrian crownland under the Hapsburgs, but S part was Venetian until 1797; part of Illyrian Provinces 1809–13; ceded by Austria 1919 and awarded to Italy, except for Fiume, 1920; after World War II E part claimed by Yugoslavia and all except region

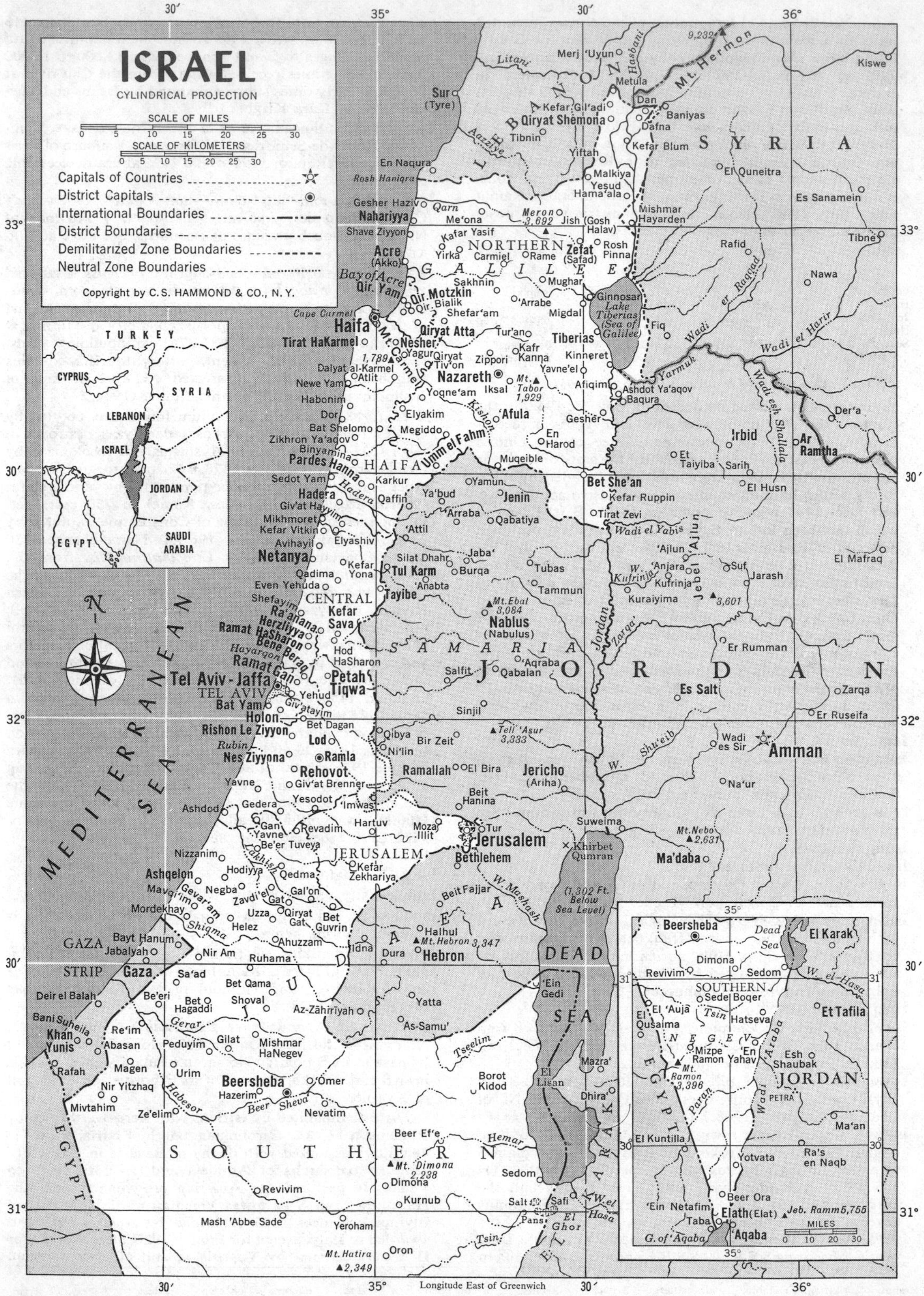
ISRAEL
CYLINDRICAL PROJECTION
SCALE OF MILES
0 5 10 15 20 25 30
SCALE OF KILOMETERS
0 5 10 15 20 25 30
Capitals of Countries
District Capitals
International Boundaries
District Boundaries
Demilitarized Zone Boundaries
Neutral Zone Boundaries
Copyright by C.S. HAMMOND & CO., N.Y.
TURKEY
CYPRUS
SYRIA
LEBANON
ISRAEL
JORDAN
EGYPT
SAUDI ARABIA
MEDITERRANEAN SEA
LEBANON
SYRIA
JORDAN
EGYPT
NORTHERN
GALILEE
HAIFA
CENTRAL
SAMARIA
TEL AVIV
JERUSALEM
JUDAEA
SOUTHERN
GAZA STRIP
DEAD SEA
(1,302 Ft. Below Sea Level)
Lake Tiberias (Sea of Galilee)
Mt. Hermon
9,232
Merj 'Uyun
Litani
Hasbani
Metula
Dan
Baniyas
Dafna
Kefar Gil'adi
Qiryat Shemona
Sur (Tyre)
Tibnin
Kefar Blum
Yiftah
Aazziye
En Naqura
Rosh Haniqra
Malkiya
Yesud Hama'ala
El Quneitra
Es Sanamein
Kiswe
Gesher Haziv
Qarn
Nahariyya
Me'ona
Meron 3,692
Jish (Gosh Halav)
Mishmar Hayarden
Shave Ziyyon
Kafar Yasif
Yirka
Carmiel
Rame
Zefat (Safad)
Rosh Pinna
Rafid
Tibne
Acre (Akko)
Bay of Acre
Qir. Yam
Sakhnin
Mughar
Nawa
Qir. Motzkin
Qir. Bialik
Shefar'am
'Arrabe
Ginnosar
Migdal
er Raqqad
Cape Carmel
Haifa
Qiryat Atta
Tur'an
Tiberias
Fiq
Wadi el Harir
Tirat HaKarmel
Nesher
Kafr Kanna
Kinneret
Mt. Carmel
1,789
Yagur
Qiryat Tiv'on
Zippori
Yavne'el
Yarmuk
Dalyat al-Karmel
Atlit
Nazareth
Mt. Tabor 1,929
Afiqim
Ashdot Ya'aqov
Baqura
Newe Yam
Iksal
Habonim
Yoqne'am
Kishon
Wadi esh Shallala
Dor
Elyakim
'Afula
Gesher
Der'a
Bat Shelomo
Megiddo
En Harod
Irbid
Ar Ramtha
Zikhron Ya'aqov
Umm el Fahm
Binyamina
Pardes Hanna
Muqeible
Et Taiyiba
Sarih
Sedot Yam
Karkur
Yamun
Bet She'an
El Husn
Hadera
Qaffin
Ya'bud
Jenin
Kefar Ruppin
Giv'at Hayyim
Tirat Zevi
Mikhmoret
Kefar Vitkin
'Arraba
Qabatiya
Wadi el Yabis
Jebel 'Ajlun
'Attil
Elyashiv
Avihayil
'Ajlun
El Mafraq
Netanya
Kefar Yona
Silat Dhahr
Jaba'
W. Kufrinja
'Anjara
Suf
Qadima
Tul Karm
Burqa
Tubas
Kufrinja
Jarash
Even Yehuda
'Anabta
Tammun
Kuraiyima
Shefayim
Tayibe
Mt. Ebal 3,084
3,601
Ra'anana
Kefar Sava
Nablus (Nabulus)
Zarqa'
Jordan
Herzliyya
Ramat HaSharon
Bene Beraq
Hod HaSharon
Er Rumman
Hayarqon
Ramat Gan
Petah Tiqwa
Aqraba
Qabalan
Salfit
Es Salt
Zarqa
Tel Aviv-Jaffa
Yehud
Bat Yam
Giv'atayim
Sinjil
Er Ruseifa
Holon
Bet Dagan
Rishon Le Ziyyon
Qibya
Tell 'Asur 3,333
Shu'eib
Wadi es Sir
Amman
Rubin
Lod
Bir Zeit
Nes Ziyyona
Ramla
Ni'lin
Rehovot
Ramallah
El Bira
Jericho (Ariha)
Na'ur
Yavne
Giv'at Brenner
Yesodot
Beit Hanina
Ashdod
Gedera
'Imwas
Suweima
Gan Yavne
Revadim
Hartuv
Moza Illit
Tur
Mt. Nebo 2,631
Be'er Tuveya
Jerusalem
Khirbet Qumran
Nizzanim
Bethlehem
Ma'daba
Lakhish
Ashqelon
Hodiyya
Qedma
Kefar Zekhariya
Mavqi'im
Gevar'am
Negba
Zavdi'el
Gal'on
Beit Fajjar
W. Mashash
Mordekhay
Gat
Uzza
Qiryat Gat
Bet Guvrin
Halhul
Shiqma
Helez
Mt. Hebron 3,347
GAZA
Bayt Hanum
Ahuzzam
Jabalyah
Nir Am
Ruhama
'Idna
Dura
Hebron
STRIP
Gaza
Sa'ad
Bet Qama
Deir el Balah
Be'eri
Bet Hagaddi
Shoval
Az-Zahiriyah
Yatta
'Ein Gedi
Bani Suheila
Khan Yunis
Re'im
'Abasan
Gerar
Peduyim
Gilat
Mishmar HaNegev
As-Samu'
Tseelim
Rafah
Magen
Urim
Borot Kidod
Mazra'
El Lisan
Nir Yitzhaq
Habesor
Beersheba
Hazerim
'Omer
Mivtahim
Ze'elim
Beer Sheva
Nevatim
Dhira'
Beer Ef'e
Hemar
Mt. Dimona 2,238
Dimona
Sedom
Revivim
Kurnub
Salt
Safi
W. el Hasa
El Ghor
Pans
Mash 'Abbe Sade
Yeroham
Tsin
Mt. Hatira 2,349
Oron
Longitude East of Greenwich
Dead Sea
El Karak
Dimona
Revivim
Sedom
W. el-Hasa
SOUTHERN
Sede Boqer
El 'Auja
El Qusaima
Tsin
Hatseva
Et Tafila
NEGEV
Mizpe Ramon
'En Yahav
Araba
Mt. Ramon 3,396
Esh Shaubak
Paran
Wadi
PETRA
Ma'an
El Kuntilla
Yotvata
Ras en Naqb
Beer Ora
'Ein Netafim
Taba
Elath (Elat)
Jeb. Ramm 5,755
G. of 'Aqaba
'Aqaba
MILES
0 10 20 30
35°
36°
30'
33°
32°
31°

around Trieste (Free City of Trieste) assigned to it by treaty of 1946.

Itá \i-'tä\. City, Central dept., S Paraguay, just SE of Asunción; pop. (1970e) 26,913.

Ita·ba·ia·na \ēt-ə-bə-'yan-ə\. Town, Paraíba state, E Brazil, on railroad WSW of João Pessoa; munic. pop. (1968e) 22,-284.

Ita·bi·ra \ēt-ə-'bir-ə\ *or formerly* **Pre·si·den·te Var·gas** \ˌprā-zi-ˌdent-ə-'vär-gəs\. Town, Minas Gerais state, SE Brazil; munic. pop. (1968e) 42,836.

Ita·bu·na \ēt-ə-'bü-nə\. City, SE Bahia state, E Brazil, W of Ilhéus; munic. pop. (1968e) 87,561.

Ita·cu·ru·bí de la Cor·di·lle·ra \ˌēt-ə-ˌkůr-ə-'bē-del-ə-ˌkȯr-di-'yer-ə\. Town, S Cordillera dept., cen. Paraguay; pop. (1962c) 2137.

Itacurubí del Ro·sa·rio \-ˌdel-rō-'zär-ē-ˌō, -'sär-\. Town, San Pedro dept., cen. Paraguay; pop. (1970e) 11,149.

Ita·jaí \ˌēt-ə-zhə-'ē\. 1 River, Santa Catarina state, S Brazil; 125 m. long; flows E into Atlantic Ocean.

2 Port at mouth of river; munic. pop. (1968e) 59,423.

Ita·ju·bá \ˌēt-ə-zhů-'bä\. City, S Minas Gerais state, E Brazil, 110 m. NE of São Paulo; munic. pop. (1968e) 50,669.

Italia. See ITALY.

Ita·lia ir·re·den·ta \ē-'täl-yə-ˌir-ə-'dent-ə\. Name given by Italians to lands near Italy (as Trentino, Trieste, Istria, Fiume, Dalmatia) once belonging to Italy and having a large Italian population, sought by Irredentists for reincorporation in Italy. Movement began c. 1878 and was especially strong in 1887 and 1910.

Italian East Africa *or Ital.* **Afri·ca Ori·en·ta·le Ita·li·a·na** \'äf-ri-kə-ˌōr-ē-en-'täl-ē-ē-ˌtäl-ē-'än-ə\. Former Italian possessions in East Africa, including Eritrea (now part of Ethiopia), Ethiopia, and Italian Somaliland (now part of Somalia).

Italian So·ma·li·land \-sō-'mäl-ē-ˌland\ *or Ital.* **So·ma·lia Ita·li·a·na** \sō-'mäl-yə-ē-ˌtäl-ē-'än-ə\. Former Italian colony, E Africa, extending S from Ras (Cape) Asir to boundary of Kenya; 178,218 sq. m.; ✻ Mogadisho.

History: Benadir coast granted to Italy by sultan of Zanzibar 1889; colony leased to a private company 1893–1905; incorporated as state in Italian East Africa 1936; invaded by British troops 1941; governed by the British after the war until in 1950 it became a UN trust territory (Trust Territory of Somalia) administered by Italy; united with former British Somaliland, it became (as Somalia) an independent republic 1960. See SOMALIA.

It·aly \'it-ᵊl-ē\ *or Ital.* **Ita·lia** \ē-'täl-yə\ *or Lat.* **Ital·ia** \ə-'tal-yə, i-\. Republic in S Europe, comprising the boot-shaped peninsula (ab. 760 m. long and from 100 to 150 m. wide) which extends S into the Mediterranean Sea, and the islands of Sicily and Sardinia (*qq.v.*), and a number of small islands, esp. Elba, Capri, Ischia, Capraia, and Lipari Is.; bounded on N by Switzerland, on NE by Yugoslavia, on E by the Adriatic and Ionian Seas, on S and SW by the Tyrrhenian Sea (Mediterranean Sea), on W by the Ligurian Sea and on NW by France; 116,313 sq. m.; pop. (1970e) 54,683,136, (1968e) 53,939,940; ✻ Rome. *Physical features:* Peninsula traversed entire length by the Apennines (*q.v.*) and bordered on NW, N, and NE by various ranges of the Alps (*q.v.*); highest points on N border Mont Blanc 15,787 ft. and Monte Rosa 15,203 ft., in the Apennines Monte Corno 9560 ft., and in Sicily Mt. Etna 10,902 ft. *Rivers:* Largest the Po, with its many tributaries forming a valley which constitutes the great plain of the N; other important streams the Tiber (Tevere) in cen. part, Arno, Volturno, and Liri in W, Adige in N, Piave and Tagliamento in NE, and Isonzo on NE border, and many shorter rivers on E side flowing to the Adriatic. *Lakes:* Large lakes in N noted for their beauty: Maggiore, Como, Garda; Trasimeno in N cen. part, Bolsena and Bracciano in W cen. part; many lagoons at N end of the Adriatic near mouths of the Po. *Coastal features:* E coastline fairly regular except for headland of Gargano near the S; separated from Albania by Strait of Otranto; in SE large Gulf of Taranto forms the "heel" (Apulia) and the "toe" (Calabria) of Italy; S tip separated from Sicily by Strait of Messina; W coast indented by gulfs of Sant' Eufemia, Salerno, and Gaeta, and Bay of Naples. *Chief products:* Wheat, rice, olives, grapes, citrus fruit; mercury, iron ore, sulfur; manufacturing: chemicals, textiles, industrial machinery, automobiles; food processing, oil refining; tourism. *Chief cities:* Rome, Milan, Naples, Turin, Genoa, Palermo, Bologna, Florence, Catania, Venice, Bari. Within its borders are two small sovereign states, San Marino and Vatican City (*qq.v.*). Divided into 20 autonomous regions, which in turn are subdivided into a number of provinces (see table below; for pronunciation of their names, see their individual entries):

NAME	AREA (sq. m.)	POP. (1968e)	CAPITAL
Abruzzi	4,168	1,205,142	Aquila
Aquila	1,944	309,181	Aquila
Chieti	999	369,883	Chieti
Pescara	473	262,785	Pescara
Teramo	752	263,293	Teramo
Apulia	7,469	3,616,086	Bari
Bari	1,980	1,343,428	Bari
Brindisi	709	370,695	Brindisi
Foggia	2,774	676,604	Foggia
Lecce	1,065	721,948	Lecce
Taranto	941	503,411	Taranto
Basilicata	3,857	633,538	Potenza
Matera	1,330	204,118	Matera
Potenza	2,527	429,420	Potenza
Calabria	5,822	2,067,154	Catanzaro
Catanzaro	2,026	743,541	Catanzaro
Cosenza	2,567	718,794	Cosenza
Reggio di Calabria	1,229	604,819	Reggio di Calabria
Campania	5,250	5,132,860	Naples
Avellino	1,082	453,897	Avellino
Benevento	796	307,701	Benevento
Caserta	1,019	699,256	Caserta
Napoli	452	2,698,665	Naples
Salerno	1,901	973,341	Salerno
Emilia-Romagna	8,543	3,815,254	Bologna
Bologna	1,429	901,652	Bologna
Ferrara	1,016	391,516	Ferrara
Forlì	1,124	558,451	Forlì
Modena	1,039	540,550	Modena
Parma	1,332	396,235	Parma
Piacenza	1,000	288,938	Piacenza
Ravenna	718	350,323	Ravenna
Reggio nell'Emilia	885	387,589	Reggio nell'Emilia
Friuli-Venezia Giulia	3,028	1,225,894	Trieste
Gorizia	180	141,195	Gorizia
Pordenone	889	254,119	Pordenone
Trieste	81	307,028	Trieste
Udine	1,878	523,552	Udine
Latium	6,642	4,565,448	Rome
Frosinone	1,251	437,905	Frosinone
Latina	869	365,039	Latina
Rieti	1,061	150,369	Rieti
Roma	2,066	3,351,816	Rome
Viterbo	1,395	260,319	Viterbo
Liguria	2,089	1,866,186	Genoa
Genova	707	1,106,855	Genoa
Imperia	446	225,884	Imperia
La Spezia	340	247,334	La Spezia
Savona	596	286,113	Savona
Lombardy	9,202	8,231,667	Milan
Bergamo	1,065	809,811	Bergamo
Brescia	1,837	941,916	Brescia
Como	798	691,079	Como
Cremona	684	338,384	Cremona
Mantova	903	379,257	Mantova
Milano	1,067	3,684,127	Milan
Pavia	1,145	529,753	Pavia
Sondrio	1,240	170,008	Sondrio
Varese	463	687,332	Varese
Marches	3,742	1,358,089	Ancona
Ancona	748	412,588	Ancona
Ascoli Piceno	806	341,361	Ascoli Piceno
Macerata	1,071	288,535	Macerata
Pesaro e Urbino	1,117	315,605	Pesaro
Molise	1,713	336,053	Campobasso
Campobasso*	1,713	336,053	Campobasso
Isérnia			Isérnia
Piedmont	9,807	4,316,466	Turin
Alessandria	1,375	485,573	Alessandria
Asti	583	218,006	Asti
Cuneo	2,665	540,443	Cuneo

NAME	AREA (sq.m.)	POP. (1968e)	CAPITAL
Novara	1,388	489,760	Novara
Torino	2,637	2,175,084	Turin
Vercelli	1,159	407,600	Vercelli
Sardinia	9,301	1,488,008	Cagliari
Cagliari	3,590	804,715	Cagliari
Nuoro	2,808	284,540	Nuoro
Sassari	2,903	398,753	Sassari
Sicily	9,925	4,867,650	Palermo
Agrigento	1,174	483,954	Agrigento
Caltanissetta	813	301,725	Caltanissetta
Catania	1,372	958,015	Catania
Enna	989	214,191	Enna
Messina	1,253	687,357	Messina
Palermo	1,937	1,172,851	Palermo
Ragusa	623	258,506	Ragusa
Siracusa	814	362,405	Syracuse
Trapani	950	428,646	Trapani
Trentino-Alto Adige	5,256	834,675	Trent
Bolzano	2,857	408,412	Bolzano
Trento	2,399	426,263	Trent
Tuscany	8,876	3,434,618	Florence
Arezzo	1,248	306,802	Arezzo
Firenze	1,498	1,112,490	Florence
Grosseto	1,736	217,332	Grosseto
Livorno	471	332,109	Leghorn
Lucca	684	378,817	Lucca
Massa-Carrara	446	204,001	Massa
Pisa	945	372,119	Pisa
Pistoia	373	249,171	Pistoia
Siena	1,475	261,777	Siena
Umbria	3,265	783,274	Perugia
Perugia	2,446	558,340	Perugia
Terni	819	224,934	Terni
Valle d'Aosta	1,260	107,861	Aosta
Aosta	1,260	107,861	Aosta
Veneto	7,096	4,054,017	Venice
Belluno	1,420	229,362	Belluno
Padova	827	744,635	Padua
Rovigo	696	256,648	Rovigo
Treviso	956	651,324	Treviso
Venezia	950	796,372	Venice
Verona	1,196	715,323	Verona
Vicenza	1,051	660,353	Vicenza

*Includes area and population data for Isérnia.

History: For earlier history, see ETRURIA, ROME, and ROMAN EMPIRE; after barbarian invasions of 4th and 5th cents. A.D., Germanic kingdoms established by Ostrogoths and by Lombards; S part remained longest under nominal Byzantine rule; in midst of disorder, Papacy at Rome founded its position as political arbiter of medieval Italy; part of Carolingian empire 774 and of Holy Roman Empire (*q.v.*) from 962; in course of struggle bet. papal and imperial authority (Guelph versus Ghibelline), the Italian communes (see MILAN, FLORENCE, etc.) obtained independence, built up petty states, and became commercial and political rivals; S Italy (see NAPLES and SICILY) ruled by foreign dynasties; c. 1000, Venice (*q.v.*) began her rise to career of territorial expansion; during period of marked political disunity, Italy produced cultural movements known as the Risorgimento (conventionally dated c. 1300–1500) and the Cinquecento (16th cent.); scene of Italian Wars 1494–1559, a struggle for power bet. Hapsburg (imperial and Spanish) and Valois (French) forces; Hapsburg predominance temporarily broken and territorial consolidation effected by Napoleon who erected kingdom of Italy (included Venice and Milan) 1805 and finally incorporated in France Piedmont, Genoa, Parma, Lucca, Tuscany, and States of the Church; from 1815–70, Lombardy and Venetia threw off Austrian rule, and with Modena, Parma, Lucca, kingdom of Naples, and States of the Church, were annexed to kingdom of Sardinia to form kingdom of Italy; member of Triple Alliance 1882–1915; undertook colonial expansion (see ERITREA, ETHIOPIA, ADWA, ITALIAN SOMALILAND, LIBYA, TRIPOLI); at war with Turkey 1911–12; entered World War I on side of Allies 1915; government seized by Fascists under Mussolini in "March on Rome" 1922; annexed Fiume (see RIJEKA) 1924; abolished parliamentary institutions for rule by Fascist Grand Council 1928; made peace with Papacy (see VATICAN CITY) 1929; at war with Ethiopia 1935–36; occupied Albania (*q.v.*) 1939; became military and political ally of Germany 1939; entered World War II 1940; invaded by Allies 1943 and its Fascist government overthrown; German resistance strong in cen. part 1943–45 (battles of Salerno, Cassino, Anzio; Rome taken June 4, 1944); became republic June 10, 1946; lost Dodecanese to Greece 1945 and territory on borders to France and Yugoslavia by treaty of Feb. 10, 1947; member of NATO 1949, UN 1955, and EEC 1958; completed process of setting up regional legislatures with limited autonomy 1970.

Ita·ny \ˌēt-ə-ˈnē\. Upper tributary of Moroni river, N South America, forming section of boundary bet. French Guiana and Surinam.

Ita·pa·ri·ca \ˌēt-ə-pə-ˈrē-kə\. Island in Atlantic Ocean, off Bahia state, Brazil, at entrance to All Saints Bay.

Ita·pe·cu·ru \ˌēt-ə-ˌpā-kə-ˈrü\. River, Maranhão state, NE Brazil; ab. 450 m. long; flows N into São José Bay.

Ita·pe·ru·na \ˌēt-ə-pə-ˈrü-nə\. City, Rio de Janeiro state, SE Brazil, 150 m. NE of Rio de Janeiro; munic. pop. (1968e) 85,874.

Ita·pe·ti·nin·ga \ˌēt-ə-ˌpāt-ə-ˈniŋ-gə\. City, São Paulo state, SE Brazil, 85 m. W of São Paulo; munic. pop. (1968e) 56,437.

Ita·pi·cu·ru \ˌēt-ə-ˌpē-kə-ˈrü\. River, Bahia state, E Brazil; ab. 250 m. long; flows SE to Atlantic Ocean.

Ita·pi·po·ca \ˌēt-ə-pi-ˈpō-kə\. Municipality, Ceará state, NE Brazil; pop. (1968e) 84,439.

Ita·pi·ra \ˌē-tə-ˈpir-ə\. City, São Paulo state, SE Brazil, ab. 40 m. NE of Campinas; munic. pop. (1968e) 42,926.

Ita·púa \ˌēt-ə-ˈpü-ə\. Department of SE Paraguay. See table at PARAGUAY.

Itas·ca \ī-ˈtas-kə\. 1 County in Minnesota. See table at MINNESOTA.

2 Village, Du Page co., NE Illinois, 20 m. WNW of Chicago; pop. (1970c) 4638.

Itasca, Lake. Lake in SE Clearwater co., N Minnesota; 2 sq. m.; elevation 1475 ft.; discovered 1832 and established as source of Mississippi river; in **Itasca State Park** (35 sq. m.).

Ita·ta \i-ˈtät-ə\. River, S cen. Chile, N of Concepción, flowing into Pacific Ocean; 110 m. long.

Ita·ti·a·ia National Park \ˌēt-ə-ˈtyī-ə-\. National Park, Brazil, on Serra da Mantiqueira, on border of Minas Gerais and Rio de Janeiro states; 46 sq. m.; mountain range, lakes; established 1937.

Itau·guá \ˌē-taù-ˈgwä\. Town, Central dept., SW Paraguay, ab. 17 m. SE of Asunción; munic. pop. (1970e) 20,289; lace making.

It·a·wam·ba \ˌit-ə-ˈwäm-bə\. County in Mississippi. See table at MISSISSIPPI.

It·ba·yat \it-ˈbī-ˌät\. Island, largest of Batan Is., N Phil.; 33 sq. m.

Iténez. See GUAPORÉ.

Ith·a·ca \ˈith-i-kə\. 1 City, ⊗ of Gratiot co., cen. Michigan, 24 m. S of Mt. Pleasant; pop. (1970c) 2749.

2 City, ⊗ of Tompkins co., S cen. New York, on S end of Cayuga Lake 29 m. NE of Elmira; pop. (1970c) 26,226; firearms, adding machines; Cornell Univ. (1865), Ithaca Coll. (1892); settled 1789; became city 1888.

3 *or Gk.* **Ithá·kí** \i-ˈthäk-ē\. One of the Ionian Is., in the Ionian Sea off W coast of Greece and just NE of Cephalonia; 37 sq. m.; with Cephalonia I. forms Cephalonia dept., Greece: see table at GREECE. Consists of two mountain groups (highest point 2650 ft.) with narrow isthmus between; chief products olive oil, currants, and wine; generally identified in Greek mythology as home of Homer's Odysseus; occupied by Germans 1941.

4 Chief town of Ithaca I., Greece; on E coast.

Ithome. See MESSENE 1.

Itō \ˈē-tō\. City, Shizuoka prefecture, Honshū, Japan, 40 m. E of Shizuoka; pop. (1970c) 63,003.

Ito·gon \i-ˈtō-ˌgän\. Municipality, Mountain prov., Luzon, Phil.; pop. (1969e) 45,200.

Itonamas. See SAN MIGUEL 1.

Itsu·ku-shi·ma \ˌit-sù-ˈkù-shi-mə\ *or* **Mi·ya·ji·ma** \ˌmē-yə-ˈjē-mə\. 1 Island in N inlet of the Inland Sea, Hiroshima

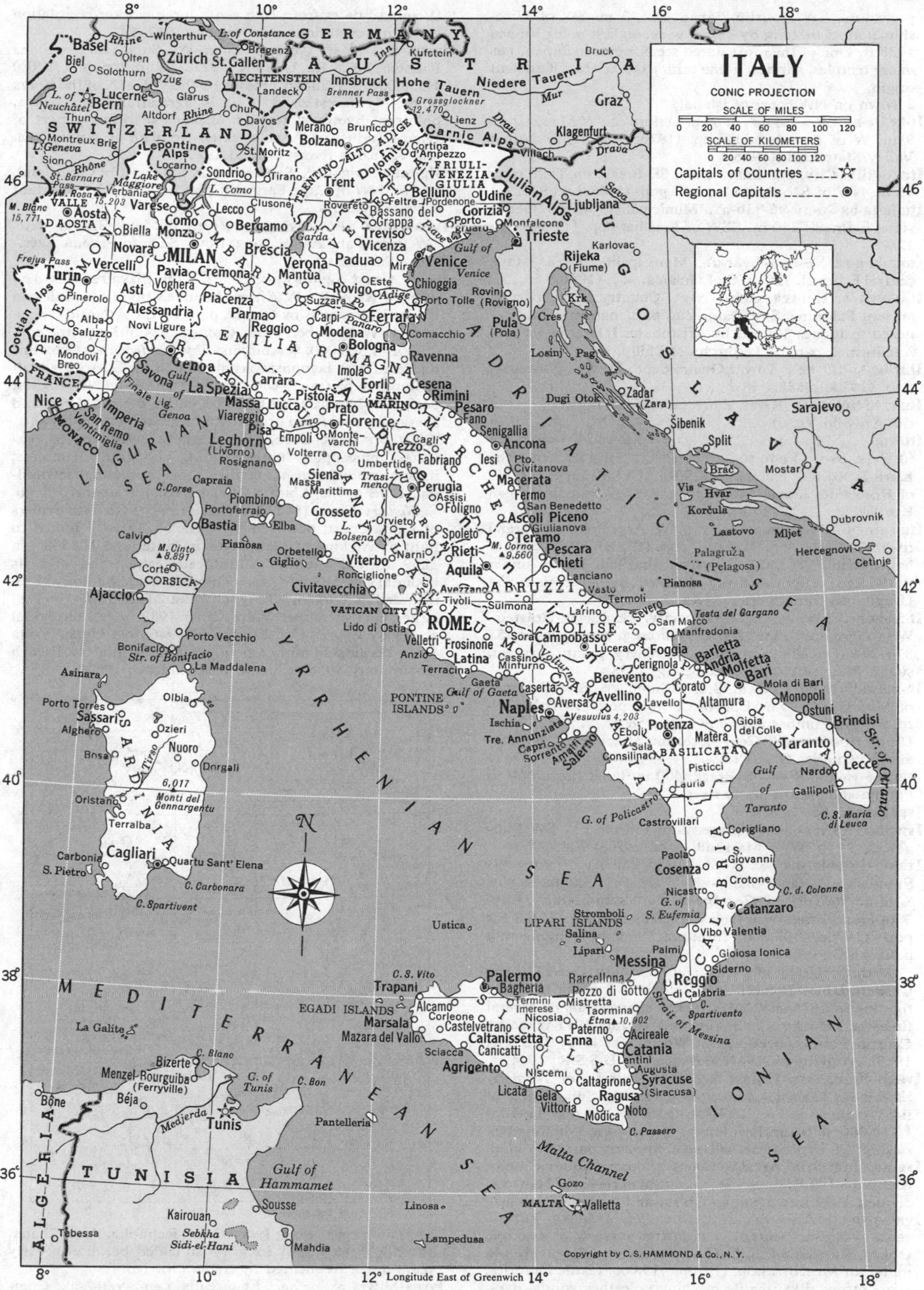
ITALY
CONIC PROJECTION
SCALE OF MILES
0 20 40 60 80 100 120
SCALE OF KILOMETERS
0 20 40 60 80 100 120
Capitals of Countries
Regional Capitals
GERMANY
AUSTRIA
SWITZERLAND
LIECHTENSTEIN
YUGOSLAVIA
FRANCE
MONACO
SAN MARINO
VATICAN CITY
CORSICA
SARDINIA
SICILY
TUNISIA
ALGERIA
MALTA
PIEDMONT
LOMBARDY
VENETIA
TRENTINO-ALTO ADIGE
FRIULI-VENEZIA GIULIA
VALLE D'AOSTA
LIGURIA
EMILIA
ROMAGNA
TUSCANY
UMBRIA
MARCHES
LATIUM
ABRUZZI
MOLISE
CAMPANIA
APULIA
BASILICATA
CALABRIA
LIGURIAN SEA
TYRRHENIAN SEA
ADRIATIC SEA
IONIAN SEA
MEDITERRANEAN SEA
Gulf of Venice
Gulf of Genoa
Gulf of Taranto
Gulf of Gaeta
G. of Policastro
G. of S. Eufemia
Gulf of Hammamet
G. of Tunis
Malta Channel
Strait of Messina
Str. of Otranto
Str. of Bonifacio
L. of Constance
L. of Neuchâtel
L. Geneva
Lake Maggiore
L. Como
Garda
L. Trasimeno
L. Bolsena
Rhine
Rhône
Inn
Drau
Drava
Mur
Sava
Po
Adige
Piave
Panaro
Arno
Tiber
Volturno
Tirso
Medjerda
Lepontine Alps
Dolomite Alps
Carnic Alps
Julian Alps
Cottian Alps
Hohe Tauern
Niedere Tauern
Brenner Pass
St. Bernard Pass
Frejus Pass
M. Blanc 15,771
M. Rosa 15,203
Grossglockner 12,470
M. Cinto 8,891
M. Corno 9,560
Vesuvius 4,203
Etna 10,902
Monti del Gennargentu 6,017
ROME
MILAN
Turin
Genoa
Venice
Florence
Naples
Bari
Palermo
Messina
Catania
Trieste
Bologna
Cagliari
Basel
Zürich
Bern
Lucerne
Innsbruck
Graz
Klagenfurt
Ljubljana
Rijeka (Fiume)
Pula (Pola)
Zadar (Zara)
Split
Šibenik
Sarajevo
Mostar
Dubrovnik
Cetinje
Nice
Ajaccio
Bastia
Tunis
Bizerte
Sousse
Kairouan
Trapani
Marsala
Agrigento
Syracuse (Siracusa)
Ragusa
Reggio di Calabria
Catanzaro
Cosenza
Taranto
Brindisi
Lecce
Foggia
Potenza
Salerno
Campobasso
Pescara
Aquila
Ancona
Perugia
Leghorn (Livorno)
Pisa
La Spezia
Parma
Verona
Padua
Trent
Bolzano
Udine
Aosta
Copyright by C. S. HAMMOND & Co., N. Y.
Longitude East of Greenwich

prefecture, SW Honshū, Japan, ab. 12 m. SW of Hiroshima; ab. 5 m. long by 2½ m. wide; highest point Mi-sen 1738 ft. One of the most noted scenic spots in Japan, has many temples, shrines, a fine torii, pagoda, etc. Of ancient origin.

2 Town on NW coast of island.

It·ta Be·na \ˌit-ə-ˈbē-nə\. Town, Leflore co., W Mississippi, 9 m. W of Greenwood; pop. (1970c) 2489; Mississippi Valley State Coll. (1946).

Itu \i-ˈtü\. City, São Paulo state, SE Brazil, on Tietê river 45 m. NW of São Paulo; munic. pop. (1968e) 43,971.

Itu·iu·ta·ba \i-ˌtü-yü-ˈtäb-ə\. Municipality, Minas Gerais state, E Brazil, 240 m. SSW of Brasília; pop. (1968e) 57,128.

Itum·bi·a·ra \ˌē-tüm-ˈbyär-ə\. Municipality, Goiás state, central E Brazil, 120 m. S of Goiânia; pop. (1968e) 65,157.

It·u·raea *or* **It·u·rea** \ˌich-ə-ˈrē-ə\. Country in NE part of ancient Palestine, S of Damascus; part conquered and annexed to Judaea 106 B.C. by Aristobulus I; later in 1st cen. A.D. formed part of Tetrarchy of Philip.

Itur·be \i-ˈtu̇r-bē\. Town, Guairá dept., SE cen. Paraguay; pop. (1970e) 9688.

Itu·ri \i-ˈtu̇(ə)r-ē\. River, Zaire, cen. Africa; upper course of the Aruwimi (*q.v.*).

Itu·rup \ˈēt-ə-ˌrəp\ *or Jap.* **Eto·ro·fu** \ˌet-ə-ˈrō-(ˌ)fü\ *also* **Ye·to·ro·fu** \ˌyet-\. Largest of the Kuril Is. (*q.v.*), Russian S.F.S.R., U.S.S.R., at S end NE of Hokkaidō, Japan; 140 m. long; 2587 sq. m.; chief town Kurilsk.

Itu·zain·gó \ˌēt-ə-sīŋ-ˈgō\. Town, NE Argentina, on Paraná river ab. 50 m. W of Posadas; pop. (1960c) 2459; scene of battle Feb. 20, 1827 in which Brazilian forces under Barbacena were decisively defeated by Argentine and Uruguayan forces under Alvear.

It·ze·hoe \ˈit-sə-ˌhō\. Seaport city, Schleswig-Holstein, West Germany, 33 m. NW of Hamburg; pop. (1969e) 35,874; commercial center; nets, machinery, pumps, cement, sugar; founded c. 810; became city 1238.

Iu·ka \ī-ˈ(y)ü-kə\. Town, ⊗ of Tishomingo co., NE corner of Mississippi, 20 m. ESE of Corinth; pop. (1970c) 2389; resort; pine timber; scene of battle Sept. 19, 1862, when Union troops under Gen. Rosecrans attacked a Confederate force under Gen. Price.

Ivaí \ˌē-və-ˈē\. River, S Brazil; 400 m. long; flows NW in Paraná state into Paraná river.

Ivangorod. See DĘBLIN.

Ivan·hoe \ˈī-vən-ˌhō\. Village, ⊗ of Lincoln co., SW Minnesota, 22 m. W of Marshall; pop. (1970c) 738.

Iva·no–Fran·kovsk \i-ˌvä-nō-fräŋ-ˈkȯfsk\; *formerly* **Sta·nis·lav** \ˌstan-ə-ˈsläf, -ˈsläv\ *or Pol.* **Sta·nis·ła·wów** \ˌstä-nə-ˈslä-vu̇f\ *or Ger.* **Sta·nis·lau** \ˈstän-əs-ˌlau̇\. City, ✱ of Ivano-Frankovsk Oblast, Ukrainian S.S.R., U.S.S.R.; pop. (1970p) 105,000; furniture, ceramics; engineering industries.

History: Capital of a Russian principality seized 1340 by Casimir III of Poland; in World War I scene of much fighting in 1915 and 1916 when it changed hands several times bet. Russians and Austrians; in July 1917 taken by Central Powers; occupied in World War II by U.S.S.R. 1939, by Germany 1941, and again by U.S.S.R. 1944.

Ivano–Frankovsk Oblast \-ˈō-bləst, -ˌblast\ *or formerly* **Sta·nis·lav Oblast** \ˌstan-ə-ˈsläf-, -ˈsläv-\. Subdivision of the Ukrainian S.S.R., U.S.S.R.; 5367 sq. m.; pop. (1970p) 1,250,000; ✱ Ivano-Frankovsk; wheat, corn, rye; livestock raising; oil, natural gas, salt, coal; formerly part of Poland.

Iva·nov Industrial Area \i-ˈvän-əf-\. Former subdivision of Russian S.F.S.R., U.S.S.R., in central part NE of Moscow; divided 1929 into Ivanovo Oblast and Yaroslavl Oblast.

Iva·no·vo \i-ˈvän-ə-və\ *or before 1932* **Ivanovo Voz·ne·sensk** \-ˌvəz-nə-ˈsen(t)sk\. Industrial city, ✱ of Ivanovo Oblast, Russian S.F.S.R., U.S.S.R., S of the Volga, ab. 145 m. NE of Moscow; pop. (1970p) 419,000; textile factories, esp. cotton; silks, textile machinery, leather goods, dyes; formed 1871 by incorporating two villages, one of which (Ivanovo) dates from 16th cent.; large worker population active in revolutionary movement 1917–18.

Ivanovo Oblast \-ˈō-bləst, -ˌblast\. Subdivision of the Russian S.F.S.R., U.S.S.R.; 9228 sq. m.; pop. (1970p) 1,338,000; ✱ Ivanovo; crossed by the Volga; N of the Volga is heavily forested, S of it is agricultural land; oats, potatoes; livestock; textiles, chemicals; formerly part of Ivanov Industrial Area, in extensive plain of Volga, Oka, and Klyazma rivers; created 1929.

Ivig·tut \ˈē-vig-ˌtüt\. Settlement on SW coast of Greenland, 175 m. NW of Cape Farewell; pop. (1968e) 73; important cryolite quarries.

Ivi·nhei·ma \ˌē-və-ˈnyā-mə\. River, S Mato Grosso state, SW Brazil; ab. 200 m. long; flows SE into Paraná river.

Iviza. See IBIZA.

Ivo·ry Coast \ˈīv-(ə-)rē-\ *or Fr.* **Côte d'Ivoire** \ˌkōt-dēv-wär\. 1 Republic, W Africa, bounded on N by Mali and Upper Volta, on E by Ghana, on S by the Atlantic Ocean, and on W by Liberia and Guinea; 124,503 sq. m.; pop. (1970e) 4,310,000; ✱ Abidjan. *Physical features:* Coastline bordered with lagoons; coastal plain in the S part gradually slopes to plateau in cen. part; hilly in W and NW; highest peak Mt. Nimba 6069 ft.; watered by the Bandama and Sassandra rivers and upper tributaries of Volta and Niger. *Chief products:* Corn, palm kernels, coffee, cocoa, bananas, pineapples, timber; gold, industrial diamonds; fishing; manufacturing: textiles; food processing; sawmilling. *Chief towns:* Abidjan, Bouaké, Man, Daloa, Korhogo.

History: From 1842 French had treaty with native rulers of Ivory Coast; occupied by French who were forced to fight native king of Mandingos in hinterland 1885–86; in 1889 formal French protectorate established and its boundary with Gold Coast delimited; made a colony 1893; included in reorganized French West Africa 1895; received larger part of Upper Volta (*q.v.*) 1933; given territorial status by French Constitution of 1946; lost Upper Volta 1947; became an autonomous republic within the French Community 1958; achieved independence 1960.

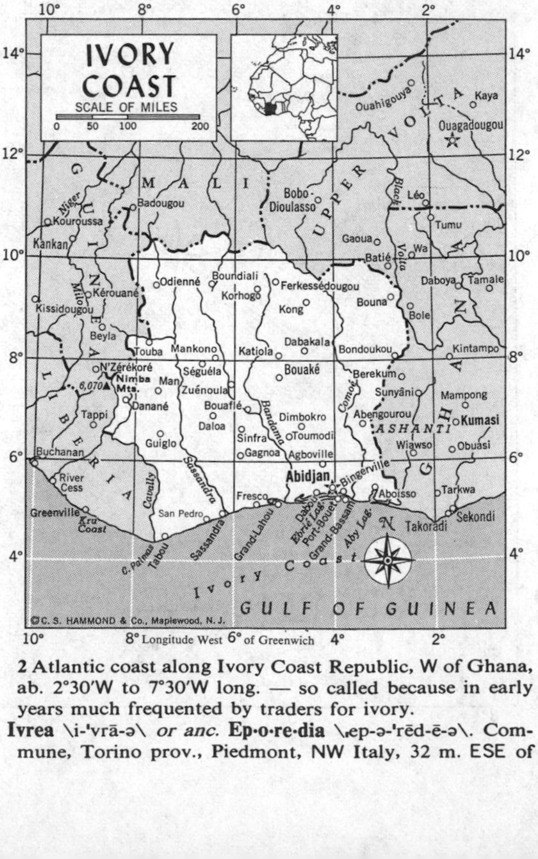

2 Atlantic coast along Ivory Coast Republic, W of Ghana, ab. 2°30′W to 7°30′W long. — so called because in early years much frequented by traders for ivory.

Ivrea \i-ˈvrā-ə\ *or anc.* **Ep·o·re·dia** \ˌep-ə-ˈrēd-ē-ə\. Commune, Torino prov., Piedmont, NW Italy, 32 m. ESE of

Aosta; pop. (1968e) 28,607; textiles, typewriters; 11th cent. cathedral; 14th cent. castle; scene of action in Napoleon's Italian campaign 1800.

Ivry–la–Ba·taille \ēv-ˌrē-ˌläb-ə-ˈtī\. Commune, Eure dept., N France, on Eure river 40 m. W of Paris; pop. (1966e) 2006; scene of decisive victory of Huguenots under Henry IV over Catholics under duke of Mayenne Mar. 14, 1590.

Ivry–sur–Seine \-ˌsü(ə)r-ˈsän, -ˈsen\. Commune and river port, Val-de-Marne dept., N France, SE suburb of Paris on Seine river; pop. (1968c) 60,455; chemicals, tiles, electrical equipment, paint, rubber, chocolate.

Ivy Lea. See THOUSAND ISLANDS 1.

Iwa·ki \i-ˈwäk-ē\. 1 River, Aomori prefecture, N Honshū, Japan; flows N to Sea of Japan; ab. 50 m. long.

2 *or formerly* **Tai·ra** \ˈtī-rä\. City, Fukushima prefecture, Honshū, Japan; pop. (1970c) 327,164.

Iwaki, Mount *or Jap.* **Iwaki–yama** \-ˈyäm-ə\. Peak, Aomori prefecture, N Honshū, Japan, NW of Hirosaki; 5330 ft.

Iwa·ku·ni \ˌē-wä-ˈkü-nē\. City, Yamaguchi prefecture, Honshū, Japan; pop. (1970c) 106,116; paper; oil refining.

Iwa·mi·za·wa \i-ˌwäm-ē-ˈzä-wə\. Town, W Hokkaidō, Japan, 25 m. ENE of Sapporo; pop. (1970c) 68,712; railroad junction and center of coalfields.

Iwa·ta \ē-ˈwät-ə\. City, Shizuoka prefecture, Honshū, Japan, 8 m. E of Hamamatsu; pop. (1970c) 63,002.

Iwa·te \i-ˈwä-(ˌ)tā\. 1 *or Jap.* **Iwa·te–ya·ma** \-ˈyäm-ə\. Mountain, Iwate prefecture, N Honshū, Japan, just N of Morioka; 6694 ft.; a dormant volcano with ancient crater in which are shrines often visited by pilgrims.

2 Prefecture, Honshū, Japan; 5898 sq. m.; pop. (1970c) 1,371,383; ✱ Morioka; rice; fishing.

Iwo \ˈē-(ˌ)wō\. City, Western State, Nigeria, on railroad just NE of Ibadan; pop. (1969e) 183,907; a Yoruba city.

Iwo Islands. See VOLCANO ISLANDS.

Iwo Ji·ma \ˌē-(ˌ)wō-ˈjē-mə\ *or* **Na·ka Iwo** \ˌnä-kə-ˈē-(ˌ)wō\ *or commonly shortened to* **Iwo** \ˌē-(ˌ)wō\. Center island of the three in the Volcano Is., 660 nautical m. S of Tokyo, Japan; small volcanic island 5½ m. long, max. width 2½ m., 8 sq. m. Scene of one of severest campaigns in U.S. history; bombed by U.S. planes Dec. 1944, Jan. and Feb. 1945; invaded by U.S. marines Feb. 19; Mt. Suribachi at S end seized Feb. 23; Motoyama airfields taken Feb. 23–26, and island finally completely taken by Mar. 15; returned to Japan 1968.

Iwo Retto. See VOLCANO ISLANDS.

Ix·elles \ēk-ˈsel\. Commune, Brabant prov., cen. Belgium, a suburb of Brussels; pop. (1969e) 88,970.

Ix·hua·tlán de Ma·de·ro \ˌēs-wä-ˌtlän-də-mə-ˈder-(ˌ)ō\. Municipality, Veracruz state, Mexico, 55 m. W of Veracruz; pop. (1970p) 40,470; wheat, sugarcane.

Ix·mi·quil·pan \ˌēs-mi-ˈkēl-ˌpän\. Municipality, Hidalgo state, Mexico, 44 m. NW of Pachuca; pop. (1970p) 35,851; agriculture; area first entered by Spanish 1530.

Ix·ta·cal·co \ˌē-stə-ˈkäl-(ˌ)kō\. Municipality, Federal District, Mexico, just S of Mexico City; pop. (1970p) 474,700; site of "Floating Gardens."

Ixtacihuatl. See IZTACCÍHUATL.

Ix·ta·pa·la·pa \ˌē-stə-pə-ˈläp-ə\. Municipality, Federal District, Mexico, 5 m. SE of Mexico City; pop. (1970p) 533,569.

Ix·tlán de Juá·rez \es-ˌtlän-də-ˈwär-əs\. Municipality, Oaxaca state, Mexico, 25 m. NE of Oaxaca; pop. (1970p) 38,776; livestock raising; beans, potatoes, fruit.

Iyo Sea \ˌē-yō-\. Open body of water forming SW part of Inland Sea, Japan, bet. Shikoku and Kyūshū, Japan; connected with Pacific Ocean by Bungo Strait.

Iza·bal \ˌē-zə-ˈbal, -sə-ˈbäl\. Department of E Guatemala. See table at GUATEMALA.

Izabal, Lake *also* **Lake Yza·bal** \-ˌē-sə-ˈbäl\ *or formerly* **Dul·ce Gulf** \ˌdül-sē-\. Lake, E Guatemala; drains through Dulce river (*q.v.*).

Izal·co \i-ˈzal-(ˌ)kō, ē-ˈsäl-\. 1 Volcano, Sonsonate dept., El Salvador, ab. 10 m. N of Sonsonate; 7828 ft.; created 1770 by eruption from side of Santa Ana; continually active.

2 Town at foot of the volcano; pop. (1961c) 7201.

Iza·mal \ˌē-zə-ˈmal, ˌē-sə-ˈmäl\. Town, Yucatán state, on Yucatán penin., SE Mexico, 38 m. E of Mérida; munic. pop. (1970p) 16,188.

Iz·ard \ˈiz-ərd\. County in Arkansas. See table at ARKANSAS.

Ize·gem \ˈē-zə-gəm\ *or formerly* **Ise·ghem** \ˈē-sə-gəm\. Commune, West Flanders prov., NW Belgium, 25 m. SW of Gent; pop. (1969e) 22,850; linens, tobacco.

Izhevsk \ˈē-ˌzhefsk\. Town, ✱ of Udmurt A.S.S.R., Russian S.F.S.R., U.S.S.R., 175 m. ENE of Kazan; pop. (1970p) 422,000; on tributary of Kama river and on branch of Kazan-Sverdlovsk R.R.; sawmills, breweries; steel, armaments, motor vehicles, machine tools, furniture; founded 1760.

Izh·ma \ˈēzh-mə, ˈizh-\. Navigable river, U.S.S.R.; ab. 180 m. long; flows N in cen. Komi A.S.S.R.; a W tributary of the Pechora.

Iz·ma·il \ˈiz-mē-əl, ˌis-mə-ˈē(ə)l\ *or Rom.* **Is·ma·il** \ˈiz-mē-əl, ˌē-smä-ˈē(ə)l\. 1 Former department, U.S.S.R. See ISMAIL 1.

2 City, Odessa Oblast, Ukrainian S.S.R., U.S.S.R., on N side of Danube delta ab. 45 m. from Black Sea; pop. (1967e) 63,000; formerly a Turkish fort; occupied by Russia 1770, 1790, and 1812; since 1812 transferred several times: Romanian 1856–78 and 1918–40; Russian 1878–1918 and since 1940 although from 1941 to 1944 held by Axis forces.

Izmail Oblast \-ˈó-bləst, ˌblast\. Former administrative subdivision, Ukrainian S.S.R., U.S.S.R., S part of former Bessarabia bordering on Black Sea SW of Odessa and on Danube delta; chief towns Izmail, its capital, and Belgorod-Dnestrovski; organized 1945, incorporated into Odessa Oblast (*q.v.*) 1954.

İz·mir \iz-ˈmi(ə)r\ *or formerly* **Smyr·na** \ˈsmər-nə\. 1 Province of W Turkey, Asia. See table at TURKEY.

2 Seaport city, its ✱, at head of Gulf of İzmir; pop. (1970p) 753,443; Turkey's 3d largest city and its most important port in Asia; large harbor; exports figs, tobacco, raisins, carpets, silk, cotton; univ (1955); connected by rail with Bandırma, İstanbul, Aydın, and through Konya with E Turkey.

History: Ancient Smyrna an Aeolian and later Ionian town; destroyed 6th cent. B.C. by Alyattes, King of Lydia; new city built by Antigonus and improved by Lysimachus 3d cent. B.C.; taken by Romans, it belonged mostly to Byzantine Empire; held for a time by Knights of St. John prior to Turkish conquest in 15th cent.; occupied by Greeks 1919 and temporarily ceded to them 1920; recaptured by Turkish Nationalists 1922; nearly destroyed by fire Sept. 14–15, 1922 and badly damaged by earthquakes 1928.

İzmir, Gulf of *or formerly* **Gulf of Smyr·na** \-ˈsmər-nə\ *or anc.* **Si·nus Smyr·nae·us** \ˌsī-nə(s)-(ˌ)smər-ˈnē-əs\. Large irregular inlet of Aegean Sea, W Turkey, N of the peninsula opp. Chios I.; extends inland ab. 40 m.; breadth at entrance 13 m.; city of İzmir is at its head.

İz·mit *or* **Is·mid** \iz-ˈmit\ *or* **Ko·ca·e·li** \kə̇-ˈjī-lē\; *anc.* **As·ta·cus** \ˈas-tə-kəs\ *or later* **Nic·o·me·dia** \ˌnik-ə-ˈmēd-ē-ə\. Town on Gulf of İzmit, ✱ of Kocaeli prov., NW Turkey, on railroad 51 m. ESE of İstanbul; pop. (1965c) 89,547; paper mills; chemicals; oil refining; 16th cent. mosque; seat of a Greek metropolitan and an Armenian archbishop; as Astacus, a celebrated city of Bithynia, destroyed by Lysimachus; on neighboring site Nicomedia built 264 B.C. by Nicomedes I as his new capital.

İzmit, Gulf of *or* **Gulf of Ismid.** Inlet of E Sea of Marmara on NW coast of Turkey in Asia.

Iz·ná·jar \ēs-'nä-här\. Commune, Córdoba prov., S Spain, 51 m. SE by S of Córdoba; pop. (1970p) 8329.

İz·nik \iz-'nik\; *anc.* **Ni·caea** \nī-'sē-ə\ *or angl.* **Nice** \'nīs\. Village, Bursa province, NW Turkey, Asia, at E end of İznik Lake, 39 m. ENE of Bursa; of slight importance but located on site of Nicaea, a great city of the Byzantine Empire; founded by Antigonus c. 316 B.C.; rival of Nicomedia as chief city of Bithynia; grew in importance after Constantinople became capital of Eastern Roman Empire; seat of first Nicene Council 325 A.D. which condemned the Arian heresy and promulgated the Nicene Creed, and of the second (seventh Ecumenical) Council 787 that defined veneration due to images; made temporary capital by the Crusaders whose Nicaean emperors of the Lascaris family ruled 1206 to 1261; remained an important city during first years of Ottoman rule.

İznik Lake *or Turk.* **İznik Gö·lü** \-gəl-'(y)ü\ *or anc.* **As·ca·nia** \as-'kā-nē-ə\. Lake (*gölü*), NW Turkey, Asia, E of Sea of Marmara; 14 m. long; outlet through a small stream into Sea of Marmara.

Iz·tac·cí·huatl \ˌēs-täk-'sē-ˌwät-ᵊl\ *or* **Ix·ta·ci·huatl** \ˌēs-tä-'sē-\. Mountain, SE of Mexico City, Mexico, N of Popocatepétl; 17,343 ft.; extinct volcano, has three summits, no crater.

Izu \'ē-(ˌ)zü\. Peninsula, S cen. Honshū, Japan, extending into Pacific Ocean bet. Suruga Bay and Sagami Sea.

Izúcar de Matamoros. See MATAMOROS 2.

Izu·mi \i-'zü-mē\. City, Ōsaka prefecture, Honshū, Japan, 15 m. SSW of Ōsaka; pop. (1970c) 95,987.

Izumi–ōt·su \-'ōt-(ˌ)sü\. City, Ōsaka prefecture, Honshū, Japan, 14 m. SW of Ōsaka; pop. (1970c) 59,437.

Izumi–sa·no \-'sän-(ˌ)ō\. City, Ōsaka prefecture, Honshū, Japan, 22 m. SW of Ōsaka; pop. (1970c) 77,000.

Izu·mo \i-'zü-(ˌ)mō\. City, Shimane prefecture, Honshū, Japan, 75 m. N of Hiroshima; pop. (1970c) 69,078.

Izu–shi·chi·tō \ˌē-(ˌ)zü-'shē-chə-ˌtō\. A group of volcanic islands, seven main ones, in Pacific Ocean off Izu Penin. on SE coast of Honshū, Japan, S of Yokohama.

Izyum \i-'zyüm\. Town, Kharkov Oblast, Ukrainian S.S.R., U.S.S.R., on the Donets 75 m. SE of Kharkov; pop. (1967e) 43,000; held by Germans May 1942–43.

Jabal. See JEBEL.
Jabal ad Durūz. See DRUZE, JEBEL.
Jabal at Tīh. See AL-TIH.
Jabal Mūsā. See SINAI, MOUNT.
Ja·bal·pur \'jəb-əl-ˌpu̇(ə)r\ *or formerly* **Jub·bul·pore** \'jəb-əl-ˌpō(ə)r, -ˌpȯ(ə)r\. 1 District, Madhya Pradesh, cen. India; 3918 sq. m.; pop. (1961c) 1,273,825; ✱ Jabalpur; rice, wheat.
2 City, its ✱, near Narmada river 150 m. NNE of Nagpur; pop. (1970e) 419,462; cement, pottery, brassware, cloth; univ. (1957); in region surrounded by rocky gorges and lakes; a trade and distribution point and rail junction; maintains large civil and military cantonment with government ordnance plants.
Jabbok. See ZARQA 1.
Ja·besh–gil·e·ad \ˌjā-besh-'gil-ē-əd\. Town of Gilead, ancient Palestine, in valley of the Jordan E of the river ab. 20 m. S of the Sea of Galilee; in days of the Judges destroyed by tribe of Benjamin (*Judges* xxi. 8–15); besieged by Ammonites and siege relieved by Saul (*1 Sam.* xi. 1–11).
Ja·blon·ec nad Ni·sou \'yäb-lə-ˌnets-näd-'nē-sü\ *or Ger.* **Ga·blonz** \'gäb-ˌlōn(t)s\. City, Czech S.R., NW Czechoslovakia, 55 m. NE of Prague; pop. (1968e) 33,722; glassware, jewelry.
Ja·blo·ni·ca Pass \ˌyäb-lə-ˌnit-sə-\ *also* **De·la·tyn Pass** \də-ˌlät-ᵊn-\ *or* **Ta·tar Pass** \ˌtät-ər-\ *or Russ.* **Pe·re·val Ya·blo·nit·ski** \ˌper-ə-'väl-'yäb-lə-ˌnēt-skē\. Pass through E Carpathian Mts., Ukrainian S.S.R., U.S.S.R., ab. 30 m. SW of Kolomyya; through it passes railroad from U.S.S.R. to upper valley of the Tisza; used by Mongols (Tatars) in their invasion and conquest of Hungary 1241; scene of heavy fighting bet. Austrians and Russians Oct. 1914 to Feb. 1917; used by U.S.S.R. 1944 in its attack on Hungary.
Ja·boa·tão \ˌzhab-wə-'tau̇\. City, Pernambuco state, E Brazil, a W suburb of Recife; munic. pop. (1968e) 114,360.
Ja·bor \'jäb-ˌȯ(ə)r\. Port and chief village on Jaluit I., Marshall Is., part of Trust Terr. of the Pacific Islands, W Pacific Ocean, at SE pass into the lagoon.
Ja·ca \'häk-ə\. Town, Huesca prov., N Spain, in S Pyrenees; pop. (1970p) 11,134; 11th cent. cathedral.
Ja·ca·reí \ˌzhak-ə-rē-'ē\. Municipality, São Paulo state, SE Brazil, 50 m. ENE of São Paulo; pop. (1968e) 41,784.
Ja·ca·ré·pa·guá \ˌzhak-ə-ˌrā-pə-'gwä\. Town, Guanabara state, Brazil, suburb of Rio de Janeiro.
Ja·ca·rè·zi·nho \ˌzhak-ə-re-'zēn-(ˌ)yü\. Municipality, Paraná state, Brazil, 210 m. WNW of São Paulo; pop. (1968e) 66,789.
Ja·ca·tra \ˌjäk-ə-'trä\. 1 Former town, Indonesia. See history at DJAKARTA.
2 Japanese name for Batavia (now Djakarta) 1942–45.
Já·chy·mov \'yäk-ə-ˌmȯf\ *or Ger.* **Sankt Jo·a·chims·thal** \zäŋ(k)t-'yō-ə-kəmz-ˌtäl, ˌzäŋ(k)t-yō-'äk-əmz-\. Commune, Czech S.R., NW Czechoslovakia, in Erzgebirge 12 m. N of Karlovy Vary; tin and tungsten mines; famous 16th cent. silver-mining center; largely destroyed in Thirty Years' War.
Ja·cin·to City \jə-ˌsint-ə-\. City, Harris co., SE Texas, on Galveston Bay, E suburb of Houston; pop. (1970c) 9563.
Jack \'jak\. County in Texas. See table at TEXAS.
Jack·field \'jak-ˌfēld\. Village, Shropshire, W England, E of Wenlock; pop. (1961c) 879; pottery, esp. Jackfield ware, made in 18th cent., distinguished by its thick, brilliant black glaze applied over a common red clay.
Jacks·boro \'jaks-ˌbər-ə, -ˌbə-rə\. 1 Village, ⊗ of Campbell co., N Tennessee; pop. (1970c) 689.
2 City, ⊗ of Jack co., N Texas, 55 m. NW of Fort Worth; pop. (1970c) 3554; oil and gas wells; oil refinery, grist mills.

Jack·son \'jak-sən\. 1 River, W Virginia; rises in Highland co., flows SW and then SE to unite with Cowpasture river in N Botetourt co. and form James river.
2 Name of a parish in Louisiana and of counties in twenty-three states of the U.S. See tables at ALABAMA, ARKANSAS, COLORADO, FLORIDA, GEORGIA, ILLINOIS, INDIANA, IOWA, KANSAS, KENTUCKY, LOUISIANA, MICHIGAN, MINNESOTA, MISSISSIPPI, MISSOURI, NORTH CAROLINA, OHIO, OKLAHOMA, OREGON, SOUTH DAKOTA, TENNESSEE, TEXAS, WEST VIRGINIA, WISCONSIN.
3 City, Clarke co., SW Alabama, on Tombigbee river 50 m. N of Mobile Bay; pop. (1970c) 5957; pulpwood mills.
4 Mining city, ⊗ of Amador co., cen. California, 40 m. ESE of Sacramento; pop. (1970c) 1924; sawmills, gold mines, claypits; truck and dairy farming.
5 City, ⊗ of Butts co., cen. Georgia, 35 m. NW of Macon; pop. (1970c) 3378; textiles.
6 City, ⊗ of Breathitt co., E Kentucky, 24 m. NNW of Hazard; pop. (1970c) 1887; diversified agriculture; Lees Junior Coll. (1883).
7 Town, East Feliciana parish, E Louisiana, 27 m. N of Baton Rouge; pop. (1970c) 4697.
8 Industrial city, ⊗ of Jackson co., S Michigan, 34 m. S of Lansing; pop. (1970c) 45,484; automobile accessories, machinery, radios, electrical equipment, aircraft parts, toys; Jackson Community Coll. (1928); settled 1829; scene of founding of the Republican party in a convention July 6, 1854.
9 City, ⊗ of Jackson co., S Minnesota, 25 m. W of Fairmont; pop. (1970c) 3550; dairy products; poultry farming.
10 City, ✱ of Mississippi and a ⊗ of Hinds co., SW cen. Mississippi, on Pearl river; pop. (1970c) 153,968; largest city in the state; railroad and cotton-shipping center; textiles, glass, electronic equipment, tile, meat products. Jackson State Coll. (1877), Millsaps Coll. (1890), Belhaven Coll. (1894), Jackson School of Law (1930). Originally a trading station known as Le Fleur's Bluff; selected as capital 1821; first session of legislature 1822; name changed to Jackson in honor of Andrew Jackson; scene of secession convention Jan. 1861; captured by Union army under Gen. Grant May 14, 1863.
11 City, ⊗ of Cape Girardeau co., SE Missouri, 10 m. NW of Cape Girardeau; pop. (1970c) 5896; hardwood timber; diversified agriculture.
12 Town, ⊗ of Northampton co., NE North Carolina; pop. (1970c) 762.
13 City, ⊗ of Jackson co., S Ohio, 25 m. SE of Chillicothe; pop. (1970c) 6843; iron pipe, bricks, pig iron; coal mines, gas wells; apple growing.
14 City, ⊗ of Madison co., W Tennessee, on south fork of Forked Deer river 80 m. ENE of Memphis; pop. (1970c) 39,996; textiles, furniture, hardwood lumber, batteries. Union Univ. (1834), Lane College (1882), Lambuth Coll. (1924), Jackson State Community Coll. (1965); settled 1819; incorp. as town 1823, as city 1845.
15 Town, ⊗ of Teton co., NW Wyoming; pop. (1970c) 2101; livestock.
Jackson, Mount. 1 Peak in Eagle co., NW cen. Colorado; 13,687 ft.
2 Peak on Continental Divide in Glacier National Park, NW Montana; 10,033 ft.
3 Peak on NE border of Grafton co., E of Crawford Notch, N cen. New Hampshire, in the Presidential Range of the White Mts.; 4052 ft.
4 *or formerly* **Mount Andrew Jackson.** Mountain at S end of Antarctic Penin., Antarctica, 71°23′S, 63°22′W; 13,745 ft.

Jackson Heights. Residential section of Queens borough, New York City. See QUEENS 2.

Jackson Hole. Valley, NW Wyoming, E of Teton Range, in Grand Teton National Park; formerly an important hunting and trapping ground.

Jackson Lake Dam. Dam across south fork of Snake river, Teton co., NW Wyoming; height 78 ft.; completed 1911; forms **Jackson Lake Reservoir.**

Jackson Peak. Mountain, S Teton co., NW Wyoming; 10,-707 ft.

Jack·son·ville \'jak-sən-ˌvil\. 1 City, Calhoun co., NE Alabama, 18 m. SE of Gadsden; pop. (1970c) 7715; sawmills; diversified agriculture; Jacksonville State Univ. (1883).
2 City, Pulaski co., cen. Arkansas, 13 m. NE of Little Rock; pop. (1970c) 19,832; nightwear; cotton, rice.
3 Seaport city, ⊗ of Duval co., NE Florida, near mouth of St. Johns river; pop. (1970c) 528,865; cigars, fertilizer, concrete products, glass, canned fruit; Edward Waters Coll. (1866), Jones Coll. (1918), Jacksonville Univ. (1934), Florida Junior Coll. at Jacksonville (1963). Settled 1816; laid out and renamed 1822; incorporated 1832; charter repealed 1840 and replaced by new charter 1851; base for Confederate blockade runners during the Civil War; severely damaged by fire 1901.
4 City, ⊗ of Morgan co., W cen. Illinois, 30 m. W of Springfield; pop. (1970c) 20,553; men's clothing, vegetable oils, plastics; Illinois Coll. (1829), MacMurray Coll. (1846). Platted 1825; incorp. 1830.
5 City, ⊗ of Onslow co., SE North Carolina; pop. (1970c) 16,289; summer resort; tobacco, potatoes.
6 City, Cherokee co., E Texas, 24 m. ENE of Palestine; pop. (1970c) 9734; bottling plant; dresses, furniture; sawmills.

Jac·mel *also* **Jaque·mel** \zhak-'mel\. Seaport, S Haiti, on coast ab. 25 m. SSW of Port-au-Prince; pop. (1961e) 10,-879.

Ja·cob \'jā-kəb\. Town, Congo; pop. (1970p) 23,600.

Ja·cob·a·bad \'jā-kəb-ə-ˌbäd\. 1 *or formerly* **Upper Sind Frontier** \-'sind-\. District, N Sind, Pakistan; 2982 sq. m.; pop. (1961c) 528,309; ✻ Jacobabad.
2 Municipality, its ✻; pop. (1961c) 35,278.

Ja·co·na \hä-'kō-nə\. Municipality, Michoacán state, Mexico, 75 m. WNW of Morelia; pop. (1970p) 26,138.

Jacques Car·tier \ˌzhak-kär-'tyā\. River, S Quebec, Canada; ab. 70 m. long; flows S into St. Lawrence river 22 m. WSW of city of Quebec.

Jacques–Cartier. City, Chambly co., S Quebec, Canada, 12 m. SW of Montreal; pop. (1966c) 52,527; truck bodies, aircraft engines, tools; sheet metal works.

Jacques Cartier, Mount. Mountain in Gaspé Park, N Gaspé Penin., Quebec, Canada; 4160 ft.; highest point in Quebec.

Jac·qui·not Bay \ˌzhak-ə-ˌnō-\. Large inlet of the Solomon Sea on S coast of New Britain I., Bismarck Archipelago, W Pacific Ocean, near E end of the island.

Ja·cuí \zhə-'kwē\. River, Rio Grande do Sul state, S Brazil; 280 m. long; flows S and E to Lagoa dos Patos.

Ja·dar \'yäd-ˌär\. Small river in NW Serbia, Yugoslavia, a tributary of Drina river; battle Aug. 1914 in which the Serbs defeated the Austrians.

Ja·de Bay \ˌyäd-ə-\ *or* **Ja·de·bu·sen** \-'bü-zən\. Inlet of North Sea on N coast of Oldenburg region of Lower Saxony, West Germany; on its W coast is Wilhelmshaven.

Jadida, Al–. See AL-JADIDA.

Jadotville. See LIKASI.

Ja·én \hä-'ān\. 1 Province of S Spain. See table at SPAIN.
2 Commune, its ✻, 178 m. S of Madrid; pop. (1970p) 78,156; leather, olive oil, alcohol, linen; 16th cent. cathedral; Moorish citadel.

Jaf·fa \'jaf-ə, 'yaf-ə\ *or Arab.* **Ya·fa** \'yaf-ə\ *or Heb.* **Ya·fo** \'yä-(ˌ)fō\; *anc.* **Jop·pa** \'jäp-ə\. Commercial seaport, part of Tel Aviv-Jaffa (*q.v.*), Israel, 35 m. NW of Jerusalem.
History: Ancient town, mentioned in Biblical history (*2 Chron.* ii. 16); destroyed by Vespasian 68 A.D.; seat of early Christian bishopric; twice captured by Crusaders, but lost to Muslims 1196; destroyed 1345 by Egyptian sultan; captured by Napoleon 1799; occupied by British 1917; center of postwar disturbance 1945–47; incorporated with Tel Aviv 1950.

Jaff·na \'jäf-nə\. 1 Peninsula, N extremity of Ceylon; ab. 50 m. long.
2 Town on penin.; pop. (1968e) 101,000; good harbor and active trade; exports cotton, tobacco, timber, and fruits; includes old Dutch fort and Hindu shrines. Taken by Tamils 204 B.C. whose rajas ruled till ousted by Portuguese 1617, who in turn were succeeded by Dutch 1658; became British 1795; was last Portuguese possession in Ceylon.

Jaf·frey \'jaf-rē\. Town in Cheshire co., SW New Hampshire, 13 m. ESE of Keene; pop. (1970c) 3353; summer resort on S shoulder of Grand Monadnock; business center is **East Jaffrey;** Queen of Peace Mission Seminary (1954) in Jaffrey Center.

Jagannath. See PURI.

Jag·dal·pur \'jəg-d^{ə}l-ˌpu̇(ə)r\. Town in SE Madhya Pradesh, E India, 125 m. NW of Vishakhapatnam; pop. (1961c) 20,412.

Jägerndorf. See KRNOV.

Ja·gers·fon·tein \'yä-(g)ərs-ˌfän-ˌtān\. Town, SW Orange Free State, E cen. Rep. of South Africa, 60 m. SW of Bloemfontein; has most important diamond mine in state.

Jag·ged Mountain \ˌjag-əd-\. Peak in San Juan co., SW Colorado; 13,829 ft.

Jag·raon \'jəg-rau̇n\. Town, Punjab, NW India; pop. (1961c) 29,617.

Jagst·hau·sen \'yäkst-ˌhau̇z-^{ə}n\. Village, N Baden-Württemberg, West Germany, NE of Heilbronn; pop. (1968e) 1200; birthplace of Götz von Berlichingen.

Ja·gua·rão \ˌzhag-wə-'rau̇^{n}\. 1 *or Span.* **Ya·gua·rón** \ˌyäg-wə-'rōn\. River, forming E section of boundary bet. Uruguay and S Brazil; ab. 135 m. long; empties into Lake Mirim.
2 City, S Rio Grande do Sul state, S Brazil, near mouth of river; munic. pop. (1968e) 21,510.

Ja·gua·ri·be \ˌzhag-wə-'rē-bə\. River, E Ceará state, NE Brazil; ab. 350 m. long; flows into Atlantic Ocean at Aracati.

Ja·güey Gran·de \ˌhäg-(ˌ)wā-'grän-dē\. Municipality, Matanzas prov., W cen. Cuba, 45 m. SE of Matanzas; pop. (1967e) 17,030.

Ja·gun·gul, Mount \-jə-'gəŋ-gəl\. Peak in Australian Alps, SE Australia; 6754 ft.

Jah·rom \yä-'(h)rōm\. City, Fārs prov., SW Iran, ab. 90 m. SE of Shīrāz; pop. (1971e) 40,000; produces dates.

Jainat. See CHAINAT.

Jaintia Hills. See UNITED KHASI AND JAINTIA HILLS.

Jai·pur \'jī-ˌpu̇(ə)r\ *also* **Jey·pore** \'jā-ˌpō(ə)r, -ˌpȯ(ə)r\. 1 Former Indian state, E Rajputana, NW India, now in Rajasthan state; 15,610 sq. m.; ✻ Jaipur; hills and desert in N and W, fertile in E and S; founded in 12th cent. (probably 1128) by Rajput chief from Gwalior; furnished famous generals to Mogul emperors; came under British protection 1818; was ruled by a maharaja.
2 City, ✻ of Rajasthan and ✻ of former Jaipur state, ab. 140 m. W of Agra; pop. (1970e) 548,684; commercial center; textiles, glass, enamel and metalwork, jewelry, ivory, marble carvings; noted for walls and fortifications; city laid out in rectangular pattern with wide streets; has maharajah's palace with open-air observatories; founded 1727 by Maharajah Jai Singh II.

Jaipur Residency. Former division of Rajputana Agency, NW India, including Indian states of Alwar, Jaipur, Kishangarh, Shahpura, and Tonk. Since 1947 these states have either joined other groups or have been assimilated with administrative units of India.

Jai·sal·mer \'jī-səl-ˌme(ə)r\. 1 Former Indian state, now a district of Rajasthan state, NW India; 14,847 sq. m.; pop. (1961c) 140,338; almost entirely a sandy waste, forming part of Thar, or Indian, Desert; has practically no crops, but some grazing; founded 1156 by a Rajput chief; entered into political relations with British 1818.

2 Town, its ✱, in desert 140 m. WNW of Jodhpur; pop. (1961c) 8362.

Jaj·ce \ˈyīt-sə\. Town, N cen. Bosnia and Herzegovina, Yugoslavia, on Vrbas river; manufactures chemicals. Held by Hungarians against Turks 1463–1526; finally surrendered to Turks 1528 and held by them until 1908 when Bosnia and Herzegovina was annexed by Austria.

Jakarta. See DJAKARTA.

Jakko, Mount. See SIMLA.

Ja·kobs·havn \ˌyäk-əps-ˈhau̇n\. Settlement on Disko Bay, W coast of Greenland; pop. (1968e) 2872.

Jakobstad. See PIETARSAARI.

Jal \ˈjal\. City, Lea co., SE New Mexico, 37 m. S of Hobbs; pop. (1970c) 2602; oil wells; livestock raising.

Ja·lāl·ā·bād *or* **Je·lal·a·bad** \jə-ˈläl-ə-ˌbäd\. Town, ✱ of Nangarhār prov., E Afghanistan, W of Khyber Pass and on Kabul river near its junction with the Kunar; pop. (1969e) 48,919; trade center; sugar processing; univ. (1963); in strategic location in river plain 70 m. E of Kabul and 80 m. W of Peshawar, Pakistan; also commands Kunar valley N to Chitral, Pakistan; site chosen by Mogul emperor Babur and town built by Akbar 1560. Defended in First Afghan War by British under Sir Robert Sale Nov. 1841–Apr. 1842.

Jalandhar. See JULLUNDUR.

Ja·la·pa \hə-ˈläp-ə\. 1 Department of SE Guatemala. See table at GUATEMALA.

2 Town, its ✱; munic. pop. (1964p) 36,157; altitude 4526 ft.; corn, tobacco, livestock.

3 *or formerly* **Xa·la·pa** \hə-\ *or in full* **Jalapa En·rí·quez** \-en-ˈrē-kəs\. City, ✱ of Veracruz state, Mexico; pop. (1969e) 84,484; altitude 4500 ft.; mountain resort; coffee, tobacco; univ. (1944).

Ja·la·pa·har \ˌjəl-ə-pə-ˈhär\. See DARJEELING.

Ja·laud \hä-ˈlau̇d\. River, NW and cen. Iloilo prov., Panay, Phil.; ab. 60 m. long; rises in mountains near Antique border, flows W and S to Iloilo Strait.

Jal·gaon \ˈjäl-ˌgau̇n\. Town, N Maharashtra state, W India, 235 m. NE of Bombay; pop. (1961c) 80,351.

Ja·lis·co \hə-ˈlis-(ˌ)kō\. State of W cen. Mexico. See table at MEXICO.

Jal·na \ˈjäl-nə\. Town, N cen. Maharashtra state, S cen. India, ab. 35 m. E of Aurangabad; pop. (1961c) 67,518.

Jalomitsa. See IALOMIŢA.

Ja·lón \hä-ˈlōn\. River, NE cen. Spain; ab. 120 m. long; flows NE into Ebro river 13 m. above Saragossa.

Ja·lo·sto·ti·tlán \hə-ˌlō-stə-ti-ˈtlän\. Municipality, Jalisco state, Mexico, 68 m. NE of Guadalajara; pop. (1970p) 19,191.

Jal·pa \ˈhäl-pə\. Municipality, Tabasco state, Mexico, 15 m. NW of Villahermosa; pop. (1970p) 29,904; lumber; coffee, cacao, sugarcane, tropical fruits.

Jal·pai·gu·ri \ˌjəl-pī-ˈgu̇(ə)r-ē\. 1 District, formerly entirely in Rajshahi division, N Bengal, NE Brit. India, on Bhutan frontier; 3050 sq. m.; divided 1947 with ab. ⅓ of area and ¼ of population assigned to East Pakistan (now Bangla Desh), the remainder to West Bengal, India.

2 District, West Bengal, NE India; 2407 sq. m.; pop. (1961c) 1,359,292; ✱ Jalpaiguri; part of earlier district (see 1, above).

3 Town, ✱ of Jalpaiguri dist., West Bengal, India; on Tista river; pop. (1961c) 48,738.

Jal·te·pec \ˌhäl-tə-ˈpek\. River on Isthmus of Tehuantepec, Mexico; 160 m. long; rises in E Oaxaca state, flows NE into Bay of Campeche.

Jal·u·it \ˈjal-(y)ə-wət\. One of the Marshall Is., in Ralik Chain, in W Pacific Ocean; atoll 38 m. long by 21 m. wide; has ab. 50 islets; harbor at Jabor, on SE side; in World War II strongly garrisoned by Japanese; bypassed by American forces in attack on Kwajalein.

Ja·mai·ca \jə-ˈmā-kə\. 1 Independent state, an island in the West Indies, 95 m. S of Cuba; ab. 145 m. long; 4471 sq. m.; pop. (1970e) 1,972,130; ✱ Kingston; includes Morant Cays and Pedro Cays; mountainous with main ridge running E and W; highest point Blue Mt. Peak 7388 ft. in Blue Mts. at E end; has many short streams; on coast are several bays with good anchorage, esp. Kingston harbor, Portland Bight, Montego Bay, Port Antonio. *Chief products:* Sugar, bananas, coffee, cocoa, bauxite; tourism. *Chief towns:* Kingston, Montego Bay, Spanish Town, May Pen, Port Antonio.

History: Discovered by Columbus 1494; a Spanish colony 1509–1655; St. Iago de la Vega founded bet. 1520–26 (see SPANISH TOWN); captured by English under Penn and Venables 1655; governed by representative council 1661–1866 when Legislative Council was substituted; Port Royal, center of its flourishing slave trade, destroyed by earthquake, and Kingston built 1692; until 19th cent., when slavery was abolished, prospered as a producer of sugar; put down several Negro insurrections, notably in 1865; Kingston severely damaged by earthquake 1907; in World War II a fleet anchorage in Old Harbour Bay, several land areas on its shores, and use of Port Royal dockyard leased to United States. A British colony 1655–1958; a territory of West Indies Federation 1958–62; achieved full independence 1962; joined Caribbean Free Trade Association 1968.

2 Former town, since 1898 part of borough of Queens in New York City, ⊗ of Queens co., SE New York, on Long I.; manufacturing and commercial center; St. John's Univ. (1870); settled by English 1655; became ⊗ 1683.

Jamaica Bay. Inlet of Atlantic Ocean at W end of Long I., New York; ab. 20 sq. m.; protected by the narrow peninsula on which Rockaway Beach is located.

Jamaica Plain. Former village in Suffolk co., Massachusetts, now a part of Boston; location of Arnold Arboretum.

Ja·mal·pur \jə-ˈmäl-ˌpu̇(ə)r\. 1 Town, N Bangla Desh, near Jamuna river ab. 83 m. NNW of Dacca; munic. pop. (1961c) 37,988.

2 Town, NE Bihar, NE India, near Ganges river 80 m. E of Patna; pop. (1961c) 57,000.

Ja·may \hä-ˈmī\. Municipality, Jalisco state, Mexico, on NE shore of Lake Chapala; pop. (1970p) 12,675.

Jambes \ˈzhäⁿ(m)b\. Commune, Namur prov., S Belgium, suburb of Namur; pop. (1969e) 16,078; glassworks.

Jambi. See DJAMBI.

Jambol. See YAMBOL.

Jam·de·na *or* **Yam·de·na** \yäm-ˈdā-nə\. Largest of the Tanimbar group of islands in S Moluccas, E Malay Archipelago, Indonesia; 70 m. long by 28 m. wide; ab. 1100 sq. m.

James \ˈjāmz\. 1 River, North Dakota and South Dakota. See DAKOTA 1.

2 River, formed by confluence of Jackson and Cowpasture rivers in N Botetourt co., cen. Virginia; 340 m. long; flows E into Chesapeake Bay through broad estuary at Hampton Roads; navigable to Richmond.

James Bay. Southern extension of Hudson Bay, Canada, bet. NE Ontario and W Quebec; ab. 280 m. long and 150 m. wide; contains Akimiski I. and several small islands; receives several large rivers, esp. the Fort George, Eastmain, Nottaway, and Harricanaw in Quebec, and the Moose, Albany, and Attawapiskat in Ontario.

James·burg \ˈjāmz-ˌbərg\. Borough, Middlesex co., cen. New Jersey, 10 m. S of New Brunswick; pop. (1970c) 4584; dresses, concrete block; diversified agriculture.

James City. County in Virginia. See table at VIRGINIA.

James Island. See SAN SALVADOR 6.

Jame·son Bay \ˌjām(p)-sən-\. See JAN MAYEN ISLAND.

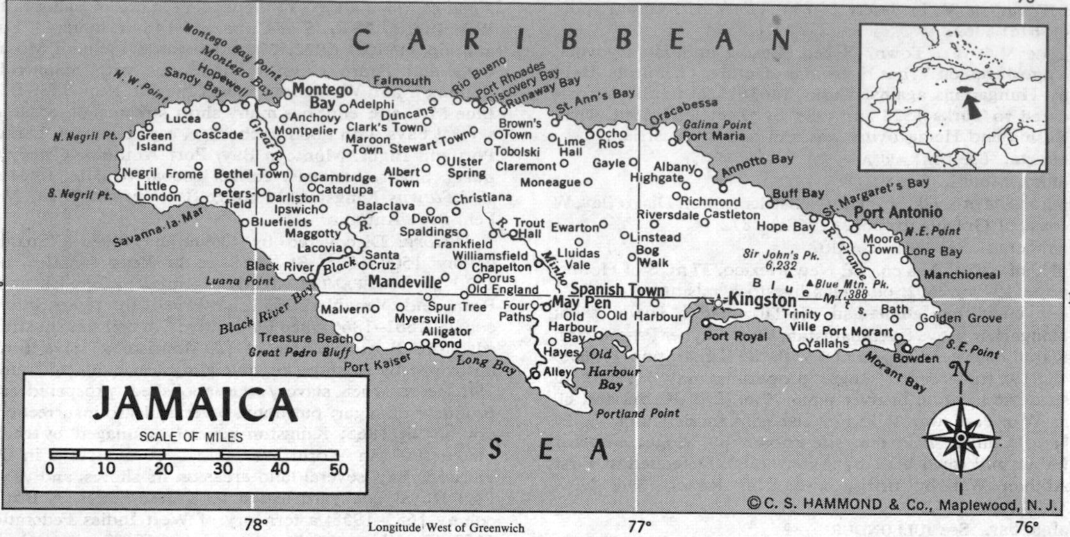

James Peak. Mountain, Clear Creek, Grand, and Gilpin cos., N cen. Colorado; 13,260 ft.; Moffat Tunnel goes through it.

James Ross Island \ˈjāmz-ˈrȯs-\ *or formerly* **Ross Island.** Island in Weddell Sea, Antarctica, British Antarctic Territory, Antarctic Penin., 64°15′S, 57°45′W.

James·town \ˈjām-ˌstau̇n\. **1** City, ⊗ of Russell co., S Kentucky; pop. (1970c) 1027; flour mills; corn, tobacco.

2 Manufacturing city, Chautauqua co., SW corner of New York, at S end of Chautauqua Lake 57 m. SSW of Buffalo; pop. (1970c) 39,975; tools, airplane and automobile parts, furniture, household appliances, textiles; truck and dairy farming; Jamestown Community Coll. (1934); settled 1810, chartered as city 1886.

3 City, ⊗ of Stutsman co., SE cen. North Dakota, 95 m. W of Fargo; pop. (1970c) 15,385; grain, dairy, poultry, and livestock farming.

4 Residential town and summer resort, Newport co., SE Rhode Island, coextensive with Conanicut I., 3 m. W of Newport; pop. (1970c) 2911.

5 City, ⊗ of Fentress co., N Tennessee; pop. (1970c) 1899; fertilizer, farm machinery; diversified agriculture.

6 Ruined village, James City co., E Virginia, on peninsula (now **Jamestown I.**) of James river almost opp. Williamsburg; in Colonial National Historical Park; first permanent English settlement in America, founded May 13, 1607; capital of Virginia 1607–98; suffered famine ("Starving Time" 1609–10) and Indian attacks; meeting place of first legislative assembly in America 1619; almost entirely destroyed by Nathaniel Bacon 1676, rebuilt, but again declined following removal of capital to Williamsburg; site of Jamestown Exposition (1907) and of Jamestown Festival Park (1957).

7 Seaport town, ✻ of British island of St. Helena, S Atlantic Ocean; pop. (1969e) 1600.

James W. Ellsworth Land. See ELLSWORTH LAND.

Ja·mil·te·pec \hä-ˈmēl-tə-ˌpek, -ˌmēl-tā-ˈpek\. Municipality, Oaxaca state, Mexico, 95 m. SW of Oaxaca; pop. (1970p) 104,275.

Jam·khan·di \jəm-ˈkən-dē\. **1** Former Indian state in Deccan and Kolhapur States, W India, now part of Maharashtra state; 522 sq. m.; formerly in Southern Maratha States.

2 Town, its ✻, 68 m. E of Kolhapur; pop. (1961c) 24,017.

Jam·mu *also* **Jum·moo** \ˈjəm-(ˌ)ü\. **1** District, Jammu and Kashmir state, N India (*q.v.*); formerly a province, occupying upper valley of Chenab river.

2 Town, Jammu and Kashmir state, N India, on Tawi river (tributary of the Chenab) 95 m. S of Srinagar; pop. (1970e) 135,522; univ. (1948); winter capital of state; has fort and a large palace of the (former) rajas; was seat of a Rajput dynasty, later acquired by the Sikhs.

Jammu and Kash·mir \-ˈkash-ˌmi(ə)r, -ˈkazh-, -kash-ˈ\ *or frequently* **Kashmir.** Former princely state, now divided into two parts: (1) Indian state of Jammu and Kashmir; 53,665 sq. m.; pop. (1971p) 4,615,176; ✻ Srinagar; (2) area under Pakistani control; 32,358 sq. m.; ✻ Muzaffarabad. Bounded on N by Afghanistan and China; mountainous, with several peaks over 20,000 ft.; major ranges: Karakoram, Ladakh, Pir Panjal; rice, corn, fruit, wool, wood carvings.

History: Became part of Mogul Empire (see INDIA) under Akbar 1587; in second half of 18th cent. included in Ahmad Shah's Afghan empire; annexed to Sikh kingdom by Ranjit Singh 1819; after Sikh wars, held by Raja of Jammu as part of British India 1846; scene of fighting between Indian and Pakistani forces 1947–49; princely state partitioned (1949) into two parts: NW area controlled by Pakistan, the remainder constituting a state of India; jurisdiction over whole territory claimed by both India and Pakistan since 1947; NE border areas in Indian territory occupied by China 1959; border regions scene of fighting bet. India and Pakistan 1965, 1971.

Jam·na·gar \jäm-ˈnəg-ər\ *or* **Na·va·na·gar** \ˌnäv-ə-ˈnəg-ər\. City, Gujarat state, W India, on Gulf of Kutch 310 m. NW of Bombay; pop. (1970e) 207,199; cement, pottery, textiles, salt; dyeing, and gold embroidery; founded 1540; was ✻ of the former Navanagar state.

Jam·rud \jəm-ˈrüd\. Fort and cantonment in North-West Frontier Province, Pakistan, 9 m. W of Peshawar; important frontier outpost at mouth of Khyber Pass; scene of military operations at various times, esp. 1836–37, 1878–79, and 1897–98; former headquarters of Khyber Rifles.

Jam·shed·pur \ˈjäm-shed-ˌpu̇(ə)r\ *or* **Ta·ta·na·gar** \ˌtət-ə-ˈnəg-ər\. City, SE Bihar, NE India, at confluence of Subarnarekha and Karkhai rivers 140 m. W of Calcutta; pop. (1970e) 414,330; center of metal industry; blast furnaces, coke ovens, steel and iron works, railroad shops, machine factories; developed around Tata steel mills 1907–11.

Jämt·land \ˈyem(p)t-ˌland\. **1** Old province of Sweden, in N cen. part bordering on Norway; ab. 20,000 sq. m.; Östersund was only important town; acquired by treaty from Norway 1645 during reign of Christina.

2 County of W Sweden. See table at SWEDEN.

Ja·mu·na \'jəm-ə-nə\. River, Bangla Desh; main stream of Brahmaputra river from the Tista to the Ganges.

Jamundá. See NHAMUNDA.

Ja·mur·sba, Cape \-jä-'mu̇rs-bä\ *or formerly* **Cape of Good Hope.** Most northerly point of Doberai Penin., NW Irian Barat, Indonesia.

Ja·nau·cu \zhə-'nau̇-(ˌ)'kü\. Island in the mouth of the Amazon river, N of Caviana I., off NE coast of Pará state, Brazil.

Janes·ville \ˈjānz-ˌvil\. Industrial city, ⊗ of Rock co., S Wisconsin, 12 m. N of Beloit; pop. (1970c) 46,426; automobiles, fountain pens, electrical equipment, textiles, church furniture; settled 1835, incorporated 1853.

Janica. See GENITSA.

Ja·nic·u·lum \jə-'nik-yə-ləm\ *also* **Mons Au·re·us** \'män-'zȯr-ē-əs\. A hill on right bank of the Tiber river opp. the seven hills of Rome.

Janīn. See JENIN.

Janina. See IOANNINA 2.

Jänisjärvi. See YANISYARVI.

Ja·ni·uay \ˌhän-i-'wī\. Municipality, Iloilo prov., Panay, Phil., 19 m. NNW of City of Iloilo; pop. (1969e) 63,908; one of oldest towns on the island.

Jan·ji·ra \'jən-ji-rə\. Former Indian state, Deccan and Kolhapur States, W India, now part of Maharashtra state, on coast 50 m. S of Bombay city; 326 sq. m.; ✱ Murud.

Jankovácz. See JÁNOSHALMA.

Jan May·en Island \yän-'mī-ən-\. Norwegian volcanic island in Arctic Ocean 300 m. E of Greenland and 360 m. NNE of Iceland, 71°N, 8°W; 33 m. long and greatest width 10 m.; 144 sq. m.; highest point extinct volcano of Beerenberg 7430 ft.; meteorological station at Jameson Bay, discovered by Henry Hudson 1607; often visited by explorers; annexed to Norway May 8, 1929.

Jannabatain. See AJNADAIN.

Já·nos·hal·ma \'yän-ōsh-ˌhäl-mä\ *or* **Jan·ko·vácz** \'yän-kō-ˌväts\. Commune, Bács-Kiskun co., S Hungary, 40 m. W of Szeged; pop. (1970p) 12,476.

Jan Pie·ters·zoon Coen Peak \ˌyän-ˌpēt-ər-sən-'kün-\. Peak, E end of Maoke Mts., Irian Barat, Indonesia; named after Jan Pieterszoon Coen, governor-general of Dutch possessions in the East 1618–23, 1627–29.

Ja·nu·á·ria \zhan-'wär-ē-ə\. Municipality, Minas Gerais state, E Brazil, ab. 300 m. NNW of Belo Horizonte; pop. (1968e) 60,374.

Jao·ra \'jau̇r-ə\. **1** Former Indian state, now part of Madhya Pradesh, cen. India; 601 sq. m.; founded 1808; its ruler had title of Nawab and was descended from an Afghan from Swat.

2 Town, its ✱, 160 m. ENE of Ahmadabad; pop. (1961c) 31,140.

Ja·pan \jə-'pan, ji-, ja-\; *Jap.* **Nip·pon** *also* **Nip·hon** \nip-'än\ *or* **Ni·hon** \'nē-'hȯn\. Independent state, consisting of an island chain in W Pacific Ocean, off E coast of Asia; 143,619 sq. m.; pop. (1970c) 104,665,171; ✱ Tokyo. *Physical features:* Comprises four main islands (Honshū, Shikoku, Kyūshū, and Hokkaidō). All islands mountainous, including many high peaks (7000 to 10,000 ft.) and volcanoes; highest peak Fuji 12,388 ft., on S Honshū; lies in earthquake belt of W Pacific and has suffered from many destructive shocks, esp. Sept. 1923 and Dec. 1946; islands indented with many bays, affording fine harbors; most important water area Inland Sea (*q.v.*); off shores of large islands are many smaller islands (Sado, Awaji, Tsushima) and groups (Oki, Gotō, Izu Shichitō, Bonin, Volcano); rivers short and rapid and only a few partly navigable; many beautiful lakes (Biwa, Chuzenji, Inawashiro). *Chief products:* Rice, vegetables, tea; coal, sulfur, copper, zinc; manufacturing: steel, chemicals, textiles, motor vehicles, electrical machinery, electronic equipment, optical and scientific instruments; shipbuilding, oil refining. *Chief cities:* Tokyo, Ōsaka, Yokohama, Nagoya, Kyōto, Kōbe, Kitakyūshū, Sapporo, Kawasaki, Fukuoka, Sakai, Hiroshima. Administratively divided into the following prefectures (listed by island; for pronunciation of their names, see their individual entries):

NAME	AREA[1] (sq. m.)	POP. (1970c)	CAPITAL
Hokkaidō			
Hokkaidō	30,313	5,184,287	Sapporo
Honshū			
Aichi	1,955	5,386,163	Nagoya
Akita	4,482	1,241,376	Akita
Aomori	3,712	1,427,520	Aomori
Chiba	1,950	3,366,624	Chiba
Fukui	1,617	744,230	Fukui
Fukushima	5,321	1,946,077	Fukushima
Gifu	4,092	1,758,954	Gifu
Gumma	2,452	1,658,909	Maebashi
Hiroshima	3,258	2,436,135	Hiroshima
Hyōgo	3,221	4,667,928	Kōbe
Ibaraki	2,351	2,143,551	Mito
Ishikawa	1,620	1,002,420	Kanazawa
Iwate	5,898	1,371,383	Morioka
Kanagawa	917	5,472,247	Yokohama
Kyōto	1,781	2,250,087	Kyōto
Mie	2,227	1,543,083	Tsu
Miyagi	2,813	1,819,223	Sendai
Nagano	5,244	1,956,917	Nagano
Nara	1,425	930,160	Nara
Niigata	4,855	2,360,982	Niigata
Okayama	2,727	1,707,026	Okayama
Ōsaka	710	7,620,480	Ōsaka
Saitama	1,467	3,866,472	Urawa
Shiga	1,550	889,768	Ōtsu
Shimane	2,559	773,575	Matsue
Shizuoka	300	3,089,895	Shizuoka
Tochigi	2,479	1,580,021	Utsunomiya
Tokyo	783	11,408,071	Tokyo
Tottori	1,347	568,777	Tottori
Toyama	1,642	1,029,695	Toyama
Wakayama	1,821	1,042,736	Wakayama
Yamagata	3,600	1,225,618	Yamagata
Yamaguchi	2,347	1,511,448	Yamaguchi
Yamanashi	1,723	762,029	Kōfu
Kyūshū			
Fukuoka	1,896	4,027,416	Fukuoka
Kagoshima	3,530	1,729,150	Kagoshima
Kumamoto	2,848	1,700,229	Kumamoto
Miyazaki	2,986	1,051,105	Miyazaki
Nagasaki	1,579	1,570,245	Nagasaki
Ōita	2,437	1,155,566	Ōita
Saga	929	838,468	Saga
Ryukyu Is.[2]			
Okinawa	848	945,111	Naha
Shikoku			
Ehime	2,183	1,418,124	Matsuyama
Kagawa	719	907,897	Takamatsu
Kōchi	2,743	786,882	Kōchi
Tokushima	1,600	791,111	Tokushima

[1]Area = land area.

[2]S and central part under U.S. control 1945–72; N part under U.S. control 1945–53.

History: Earlier inhabitants, the Ainu, were driven northward by invaders, probably of Manchu-Korean and Malayan stock; traditional history dates from 660 B.C., accession of Jimmu Tenno, ruler of Yamato (*q.v.*) and founder of the imperial line; written history began in 5th cent. A.D. when Japan entered contact with highly developed Chinese culture from which it adopted handwriting; Buddhism introduced 552; closely imitated Chinese institutions 6th–9th cents.; in 794, imperial capital moved to Heian-kyo (modern Kyōto) where it remained until 1869; from 9th–12th cents., court dominated by Fujiwara family; in 1192, Minamoto Yoritomo became shogun (military dictator) and founded first of the shogunates which controlled emperor 1192–1867; in Kamakura period 1192–1333, military feudalism, evolved since 9th cent., reached full development; invaded by Mongols 1274, 1281; in 15th cent. (Ashikaga shoguns 1338–1568), general breakdown of feudalism.

First visited by Europeans (Portuguese) 1542–43; Christianity introduced by St. Francis Xavier 1549–51; in late 16th cent. Japanese Empire united and outlying provinces conquered by Hideyoshi and Iyeyasu (first of Tokugawa shoguns 1603–1867); edicts of successors of Iyeyasu cut off Japanese contact with foreigners, including European traders and missionaries, except at Nagasaki (*q.v.*); in 1854, Commodore Perry, an American, secured first commercial treaty; Meiji era 1868–1912 began with emperor's resumption of direct rule 1868; rapidly adopted Occidental civilization, modified government (constitution of 1889) and extended foreign contacts; fought war with China over Korea (*q.v.*) 1894–95 (see SHIMONOSEKI); allied with Great Britain 1902; victorious in Russo-Japanese war 1904–05; annexed Korea 1910; made twenty-one demands on China 1915; for participation in World War I, secured former German possessions in Pacific, N of equator.

Occupied Manchuria (*q.v.*) 1931–32, Shanghai 1932, and began war with China gradually taking over all large coastal cities and many interior areas 1937–45. Signed military alliance with Germany and Italy 1940; entered World War II Dec. 7, 1941 by surprise attack on Pearl Harbor, Hawaii; attacked Philippines Dec. 8, 1941; occupied Manila Jan 2, 1942 and after long and severe fighting on Bataan Penin. overwhelmed smaller American and Filipino force Apr. 9, 1942 and took Corregidor May 6. Seized Hong Kong Dec. 25, 1941; invaded Malay Penin. Dec. 8–9, 1941, and forced surrender of Singapore Feb. 15, 1942; invaded Siam (Thailand) Dec. 1941 and Burma Feb. 8, 1942, cutting Burma Road (*q.v.*). Seized Ambon, E coast of Borneo, and Sumatra, and Java Jan.–Mar. 1942. Received first setback in naval and air battles of Midway June 3–6, 1942 and Coral Sea May 7–8; defeated on land and sea at Guadalcanal Aug. 1942–Feb. 1943; driven out of SE New Guinea (Territory of Papua) Dec. 1942–Jan. 1943 and out of Aleutians Aug. 1943; defeated at Tarawa Nov. 21–24, 1943; lost Kwajalein Jan. 30–Feb. 6, 1944 and Eniwetok Feb. 17–22 in the Marshall Is. Driven back in N Burma, Feb.–May 1944 and defeated in Manipur Mar.–June 1944; lost Admiralty Is. Mar. 18, 1944, Saipan June 15–July 9, Tinian July 23–Aug. 1, and Guam July 20–Aug. 10, 1944; lost Manila Jan. 9–Feb. 23, 1945. Partly successful in China 1944–45 but with great losses of ships, planes, and material sources, unable to hold Iwo Jima Feb.–Mar. 1945 and Okinawa Apr.–June; many large cities devastated by carrier planes; Hiroshima Aug. 6 and Nagasaki Aug. 9 practically destroyed by atomic bombs; attacked by U.S.S.R. Aug. 8 in Manchuria; surrendered Aug. 14; mainland (first in Tokyo area) occupied by Allied troops in Sept.; adopted new constitution 1947; signed mutual security treaty with U.S. 1951; regained control over N Ryukyu Is. 1953; member of UN 1956; regained control over Bonin Islands 1968; 1960's marked by strong economic growth, giving Japan third highest gross national product in the world; reversion of S Ryukyu Is. to Japanese control 1972.

Japan, Sea of. Branch of W Pacific Ocean lying bet. Japan on E, and Primorski Krai, Russian S.F.S.R., U.S.S.R., and Korean penin. on W; 389,100 sq. m.; max. depth 12,276 ft.; on N connects by Tatar Strait with Sea of Ōkhotsk; on NE by Sōya Strait bet. Sakhalin and Hokkaidō with Sea of Ōkhotsk; on E by Tsugaru Strait bet. Hokkaidō and Honshū with the Pacific; and on SW by Korea Strait bet. Korean penin. and Japan with East China Sea. For naval battle fought here 1905, see TSUSHIMA STRAIT.

Japan Current *or* **Black Stream** *or Jap.* **Ku·ro·shio** \ˌkůr-ō-ˈshē-ˌō\. A branch of the equatorial current of the Pacific Ocean, flowing along the E coast of Taiwan, thence NE along E coast of Honshū, Japan, and merging into the easterly drift of the North Pacific Ocean S of the Aleutian Is.; noticeable for its deep blue color (hence the name *Black Stream*); has influence on climate similar to that of the Gulf Stream (*q.v.*).

Japan Trench. Any of several deeps of the Pacific Ocean off the E coast of Japan; several have been measured more than 30,000 ft. deep.

Japara. See DJEPARA.

Japara–Rembang. See DJAPARA-REMBANG.

Ja·pen *or* **Jap·pen** \ˈyäp-ən\. Island in Sarera Bay, on N coast of Irian Barat, Indonesia, S of Schouten Is.; 936 sq. m.; has elevated central ridge; highest point 4907 ft.; chief settlements Seroei in cen. part of S coast, and Ansoes on S coast near W end.

Ja·pu·rá \ˌzhäp-ə-ˈrä\ *also* **Ya·pu·rá** \ˌyä-pü-\. River, NW South America; ab. 1750 m. long; rises in SW Colombia, where it is known as the **Ca·que·tá** \ˌkäk-ə-ˈtä\, and flows SE across Brazilian border into Amazon river.

Jap·vo, Mount \-ˈjəp-(ˌ)vō\. Mountain in S part of Naga Hills, NE India, on N boundary of Manipur; 9890 ft.; highest mountain in Naga Hills.

Jaquemel. See JACMEL.

Jarābius. See JERABLUS.

Ja·ra·ma \hə-ˈräm-ə\. River, cen. Spain; 120 m. long; joins Henares river 10 m. ESE of Madrid and empties into Tagus river a little below Aranjuez.

Jarash. See JERASH.

Jar·di·nes de la Rei·na \här-ˈdēn-əs-ˌdel-ə-ˈrā-nə\. Chain of small islands in West Indies, extending NW to SE in Caribbean Sea S of cen. Cuba; belong to Cuba.

Jar·geau \zhär-ˈzhō\. Town, Loiret dept., N cen. France, on the Loire 10 m. E of Orléans; pop. (1962c) 2378; scene of victory of Joan of Arc over the English 1429.

Ja·ri *or* **Ja·rí** *or* **Ja·ry** \zhə-ˈrē\. River, NE Brazil; 360 m. long; rises in Tumuc-Humac Mts. and flows SSE from SW Surinam border into Amazon river near its mouth.

Jarlsberg. See VESTFOLD.

Jar·maq National Park \ˈjär-mäk-\. National park, Israel; 35 sq. m.; ancient ruins; established 1955.

Jar·nac \zhär-ˈnak\. Commune, Charente dept., W France, on the Charente 18 m. W of Angoulême; pop. (1962c) 4574; scene of battle Mar. 13, 1569 in which Catholics under duke of Anjou (later Henry III) defeated the Huguenots under Prince of Condé and in which Condé was killed.

Ja·ro \ˈhär-ˌō\. Municipality, Leyte prov., Leyte, Phil., on E slope of mountains 15 m. W of Tacloban; pop. (1969e) 44,300; taken by Americans Oct. 31, 1944.

Ja·ro·sław \yä-ˈrȯ-ˌsläf\ *or Ger.* **Ja·ro·slau** \ˈyär-ə-ˌslau̇\ *or Russ.* **Ya·ro·slav** \ˈyär-ə-ˌsläf, -ˌsläv\. City, Rzeszów prov., SE Poland, on San river 28 m. E of Rzeszów; pop. (1970e) 29,100; agricultural center; scene of German defeat by Russians Oct. 1914; occupied by Germans and Austrians May 1915 and by Germans June 1941.

Jar·rā·hī \ˌjar-ə-ˈhē\. River, SW cen. Iran; ab. 165 m. long; flows generally SW into head of Persian Gulf; seaport of Bandar-e Shāhpūr is at its mouth.

Jar·row \ˈjar-(ˌ)ō\. Municipal borough, Durham, N England, 6 m. E of Newcastle upon Tyne; pop. (1971p) 28,779; paper mills, shipbuilding yards, iron and steel foundries and mills; ships coal; ruins of 7th cent. monastery where the Venerable Bede spent most of his life.

Ja·ru·co \hä-ˈrü-(ˌ)kō\. Municipality, La Habana prov., W Cuba, 23 m. ESE of Havana; pop. (1967e) 20,080.

Jar·vis Island *also* **Jer·vis Island** \ˈjär-vəs-\. One of the Line Is. (*q.v.*) just S of the equator in cen. Pacific Ocean, 190 m. SW of Christmas I.; 1.6 sq. m.; worked by an American company for its guano 1857–79; annexed by Great Britain 1889; claimed by United States 1935.

Jary. See JARI.

Jash·pur \ˈjəsh-ˌpu̇(ə)r\. Former Indian state in Eastern States, NE India; now in Madhya Pradesh; 1955 sq. m.; ✱ **Jash·pur·na·gar** \-ˈnəg-ər\.

Jasiołda. See YASELDA.

Jāsk \ˈjäsk\. Seaport, S Iran, on Gulf of Oman 140 m. SE of Bandar ʻAbbās; was capital of former Makran prov.; formerly a British station.

Ja·sło \ˈyäs-(ˌ)lō\. Commune, Rzeszów prov., Poland, 30 m. SE of Tarnów; pop. (1968e) 13,900; oil; pilgrimage chapel; battle 1914.

Jas·mund \ˈyäs-ˌmu̇nt\. Peninsula, NE Rügen I., East Germany; in waters of Baltic Sea nearby occurred battle May

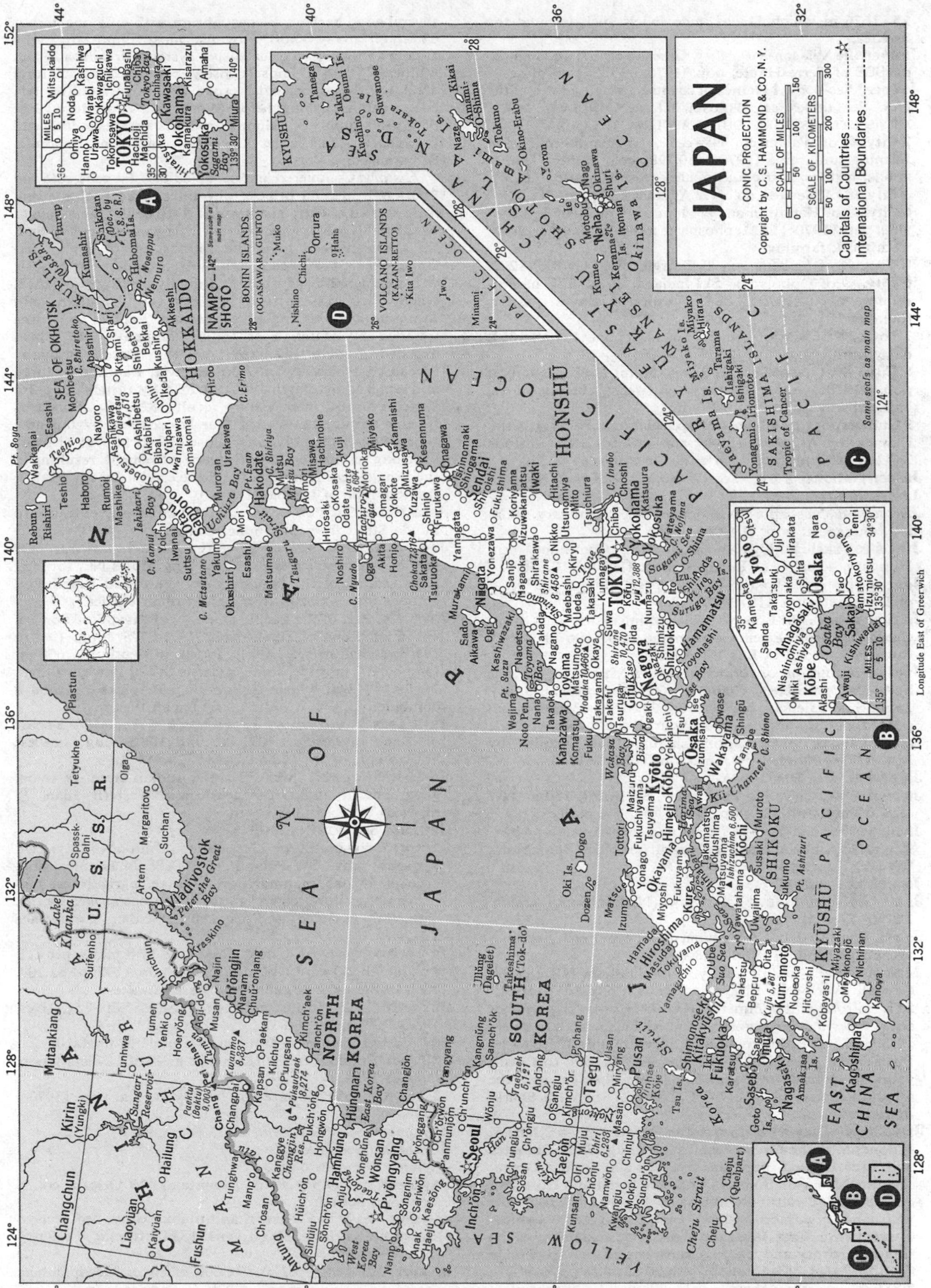
JAPAN
CONIC PROJECTION
Copyright by C. S. HAMMOND & CO., N. Y.
SCALE OF MILES
SCALE OF KILOMETERS
Capitals of Countries
International Boundaries
SEA OF JAPAN
SEA OF OKHOTSK
PACIFIC OCEAN
EAST CHINA SEA
YELLOW SEA
HONSHŪ
HOKKAIDO
SHIKOKU
KYŪSHŪ
NORTH KOREA
SOUTH KOREA
U. S. S. R.
MANCHURIA
CHINA
NAMPO-SHOTO
BONIN ISLANDS (OGASAWARA GUNTO)
VOLCANO ISLANDS (KAZAN-RETTO)
NANSEI SHOTO
SAKISHIMA ISLANDS
TOKYO
Longitude East of Greerwich

25, 1676 in which Danes under Niels Juel defeated the Swedes.

Ja·son·ville \'jā-sən-ˌvil\. City, Greene co., SW Indiana, 23 m. SSE of Terre Haute; pop. (1970c) 2335; coal mine.

Jas·per \'jas-pər\. **1** Names of counties in eight states of the U.S. See tables at GEORGIA, ILLINOIS, INDIANA, IOWA, MISSISSIPPI, MISSOURI, SOUTH CAROLINA, TEXAS.

2 City, ⊗ of Walker co., NW cen. Alabama, 38 m. NW of Birmingham; pop. (1970c) 10,798; coal mines; leather goods, textiles; cattle and poultry raising; settled 1815.

3 City, ⊗ of Newton co., NW Arkansas; pop. (1970c) 394.

4 City, ⊗ of Hamilton co., N Florida, 79 m. W of Jacksonville; pop. (1970c) 2221; phosphate mine; lumber, fertilizer, feed; truck farming.

5 City, ⊗ of Pickens co., N Georgia; pop. (1970c) 1202.

6 City, ⊗ of Dubois co., SW Indiana, 36 m. ESE of Vincennes; pop. (1970c) 8641; furniture, gloves, veneer; founded 1818.

7 Town, ⊗ of Marion co., S Tennessee; pop. (1970c) 1811; dairy farming.

8 City, ⊗ of Jasper co., E Texas, 58 m. N of Beaumont; pop. (1970c) 6251; cannery, oil wells; chairs, crates, baskets; truck and poultry farming.

9 Unincorporated village in Jasper National Park, Alberta, Canada, on Athabaska river; pop. (1966c) 2505; altitude 3472 ft.; starting point for park excursions.

Jasper National Park. See CANADA, *National Parks.*

Jassy. See IAȘI.

Jász·a·pá·ti \'yäs-ˌäp-ə-tē\. Commune, cen. Hungary, 50 m. E of Budapest; pop. (1970p) 10,485.

Jász·á·rok·szál·lás \'yäs-ä-rōk-ˌsäl-äsh\. Commune, cen. Hungary, 42 m. E of Budapest; pop. (1970p) 10,256.

Jász·be·rény \'yäs-bə-ˌrān-yə\. City, cen. Hungary, 37 m. E of Budapest; pop. (1970p) 29,785.

Ja·ti·bo·ni·co \ˌhät-i-bə-'nē-(ˌ)kō\. Municipality and town, Camagüey prov., E cen. Cuba; munic. pop. (1967e) 30,230; town on railroad at Las Villas border.

Já·ti·va *or* **Já·ti·ba** *or formerly* **Xá·ti·va** \'hät-i-ˌvä\ *or anc.* **Se·ta·bis** \'set-ə-bəs\. Commune, Valencia prov., E Spain, 35 m. S of Valencia; pop. (1970p) 21,578; agriculture; paper, oil, pottery, leather, soap, flour. Roman colony; made episcopal see under Goths; captured and fortified by Moors; reconquered by James I of Aragon 1244.

Jatiwangi. See DJATIWANGI.

Jaú \zhə-'ü\. City, São Paulo state, SE Brazil, 150 m. NW of São Paulo; munic. pop. (1968e) 63,947; coffee.

Jau·a·pe·ri \ˌzhaù-ə-pə-'rē\ *also* **Yau·a·pe·ry** \ˌyaù-ə-pə-'rē\. River, NE Amazonas state, N Brazil; ab. 240 m. long; flows SW and S into the Rio Negro.

Jauer. See JAWOR.

Jauf \'jaùf\ *or* **Al–Jawf** \al-\. Town, N Nejd, Saudi Arabia, 250 m. E of Ma'an.

Jau·ja \'haù-(ˌ)hä\. Town, Junín dept., cen. Peru, just N of Huancayo; pop. (1961c) 12,800.

Jaun·pur \'jaùn-ˌpù(ə)r\. City, Uttar Pradesh, N India, on Gomati river 60 m. ENE of Allahabad; pop. (1961c) 61,851; railroad and commercial center; known for perfumes and papier-mâché articles; founded by Gaharwar rulers 11th cent.; after destruction by floods rebuilt 1359–64 by Firuz Shah III, King of Delhi; has an old fort with gateway, notable mosques, and a fine bridge over the Gomati; capital 1394–1479 of princes of so-called Sharki dynasty.

Ja·va \'jäv-ə, 'jav-ə\ *or Indonesian* **Dja·wa** \'jäv-ə\. Island, Indonesia, in the Greater Sunda Is. group, SE of Sumatra and S of Borneo, between Java Sea and Indian Ocean; separated from SE Sumatra by Sunda Strait and from Bali on E by Bali Strait; 661 m. long by 124 m. at widest part; with smaller adjacent islands comprises three provinces **Central Java, East Java,** and **West Java;** also contains the capital territory and the Jogjakarta special dist. (see table at INDONESIA). Mountainous with 20 or more peaks above 8000 ft., mostly volcanic with about 13 active today; highest Semeru 12,060 ft.; N coast land generally low with several good harbors; S coast abrupt with only one harbor Tjilatjap; many short streams, most important Solo, Brantas, Liwung; has extensive system of railroads and highways. One of most densely populated agricultural areas on the globe; chief crops rice, sugar, coffee, tea, cocoa, rubber; fishing; before World War II produced 90% of world's supply of quinine; produces also teak, coal, and petroleum. Chief cities Djakarta, Surabaja, Bandung, Semarang, Surakarta.

History: Conquered and occupied bet. 1st cent. A.D. and 700 A.D. by Hindu princes who introduced Brahmanism; little known of early history until 14th cent. when state of Madjapahit in E Java conquered Srivijaya empire of Sumatra and expanded to include almost all of Malay Archipelago 1335–80; Madjapahit lost its colonies by c. 1478, was conquered by Muslims and finally destroyed by 1518; when Europeans arrived in 16th cent., Bantam and Mataram were leading Muslim states; Batavia (*q.v.*) was founded by Dutch East India Company 1619 which expelled English 1623 (see AMBON); Dutch gradually spread control eastward from Batavia; Bantam captured and annexed by Dutch 1808–09; held by British 1811–16; Dutch control, menaced by revolt 1825–30, afterwards became stronger; in World War II occupied by Japanese Mar. 1942–Sept. 1945; after close of World War II scene of strong Indonesian independence movement, resulting in the Linggadjati Agreement and the establishment 1947 of the Republic of Indonesia (*q.v.*).

Java Head. Cape on extreme W end of Java at entrance to Sunda Strait from the Indian Ocean.

Ja·va·ri \ˌzhäv-ə-'rē\ *or* **Ya·va·ri** \ˌyä-və-'rē\. River, NW cen. South America; ab. 600 m. long; flows NE, forming large section of the boundary bet. Peru and Brazil, and empties into Amazon river on Brazilian border.

Java Sea. Part of the Pacific Ocean N of Java, S of Borneo, and E of S end of Sumatra; lat. 3° to 7°S, long. 106° to 116°E; a shallow sea, 300 ft. or less in depth; ab. 600 m. long by 200 m. wide; scene of battle SW of Bawean I. Feb. 26–28, 1942 in which Japanese naval forces defeated a combined U.S.-U.K.-Australian-Dutch fleet.

Java Trench *or formerly* **Java Trough.** Trench, off S coast of island of Java, in 10°S lat. and 108°E long.; deepest known part of the Indian Ocean; 25,344 ft.

Ja·whar \jə-'hwär, -'wär\. Former Indian state, W India; geographically in NW Maharashtra in Western Ghats, 75 m. N of Bombay; 308 sq. m.

Jawlan. See GOLAN HEIGHTS.

Ja·wor \'yäv-ˌò(ə)r\ *or Ger.* **Jau·er** \'yaù-ər\. City, cen. Wrocław prov., SW Poland, 11 m. SSE of Legnica; pop. (1968e) 15,700; manufactures sausage, agricultural machinery, furniture, cigars; raises sugar beets; late Gothic cathedral; assigned to Poland by Potsdam Conference 1945.

Ja·worz·no \yə-'vòzh-(ˌ)nò\. Commune, W Kraków prov., S Poland, ab. 30 m. WNW of Kraków; pop. (1970p) 63,300; coal, calomine; zinc refineries, glass furnaces.

Jax·ar·tes \jak-'särt-ēz\ *or* **Iax·ar·tes** \ˌī-ak-'särt-ēz\. River, U.S.S.R. See SYR DARYA.

Jay \'jā\. **1** County in Indiana. See table at INDIANA.

2 Town, Franklin co., W Maine, 28 m. N of Lewiston; pop. (1970c) 3954.

3 Town, ⊗ of Delaware co., NE Oklahoma; pop. (1970c) 1594.

Jayabum. See CHAIYAPHUM.

Jayanath. See CHAINAT.

Jayhun. See AMU DARYA.

Jay Peak *or* **Big Jay Peak.** Mountain, NW Orleans co., N Vermont; 3861 ft.

Ja·yu·ya \hä-'yü-yə\. Town and municipality, cen. Puerto Rico; pop. (1970c) 3800 (town), 13,603 (munic.); town is 15 m. N of Ponce.

Ja·zi·ra, Al– \ˌal-jə-'zir-ə\. Region of upper Mesopotamia; the Tigris-Euphrates valley NW of Baghdad, Iraq.

Jazirah, Al–. See GEZIRA.

Jean·er·ette \ˌjen-ə-ˈret\. Town, Iberia parish, S Louisiana, 32 m. SE of Lafayette; pop. (1970c) 6322; sugar, pecans, rice.

Jean·nette \jə-ˈnet\. Industrial city, Westmoreland co., SW Pennsylvania, 22 m. ESE of Pittsburgh; pop. (1970c) 15,209; coal mines; plastics, glassware, truck bodies, generators, sheet metal; settled 1888.

Jebeil. See JUBAYL.

Jeb·el \ˈjeb-əl\; *Arab.* **Ja·bal** \ˈjab-ˌal\ *also* **Ge·bel** \ˈjeb-əl, ˈgab-ˌal\ *or French* **Dje·bel** \jā-bel\. Forms from the Arabic word meaning "mountain, hill"; often used in place names in North Africa and SW Asia. For names of mountains containing this word, see the second element, as **Djebel Chélia, Jebel Sham,** etc., see at CHÉLIA, SHAM, etc.

Jebel Au·lia \-ˈau̇-lē-ə\ *also* **Khaz·zān Ja·bal Al–Aw·li·yā** \kə-ˈzan-ˌjab-əl-al-ˈȯl-ē-(y)ə\. Site of storage dam across the White Nile, 27 m. S of Khartoum in Sudan; completed 1937; holds back Nile flood waters July–October.

Jebel ed Druz \-ed-ˈdrüz\ *or* **Jebel Druze** *or* **Djeb·el Druze** \ˌjeb-əl-ˈdrüz\. 1 Former subdivision of the Republic of Syria, SW Asia, E of the Sea of Galilee and bordering on N Jordan; 2700 sq. m.; ✻ Es Suweida. Plateau and mountainous region; highest point Jebel Druze 5907 ft.; inhabited by Druses, survivors of Muslim sect founded in 10th cent. A.D.; recognized 1921 as autonomous state within French mandate of Syria; led nationalist revolt in Syria against French 1925; incorporated in the Republic of Syria Jan. 12, 1942.

2 Mountain in this area. See DRUZE, JEBEL.

Jed·burgh \ˈjed-b(ə-)rə\. Burgh, ⊗ of Roxburgh co., SE Scotland; pop. (1969e) 3714; ruins of noted 12th cent. abbey; the proverbial Jedburgh justice (punishing first and trying afterwards) is so called from an early 17th cent. summary execution of a band of malefactors here.

Jedda. See JIDDA.

Ję·drze·jów \ye^{n}(n)-ˈjā-ˌyüf\. Commune, Kielce prov., SE cen. Poland, 27 m. SSW of Kielce; pop. (1968e) 13,500.

Jeff Da·vis \ˈjef-ˈdāv-əs\. Name of counties in two states of the U.S. See tables at GEORGIA and TEXAS.

Jef·fer·son \ˈjef-ər-sən\. 1 River, SW Montana; 217 m. long; formed by confluence of branches in NW Madison co., flows N and E to unite with Madison and Gallatin rivers and form Missouri river.

2 Name of parish in Louisiana and of counties in twenty-five states of the U.S. See tables at ALABAMA, ARKANSAS, COLORADO, FLORIDA, GEORGIA, IDAHO, ILLINOIS, INDIANA, IOWA, KANSAS, KENTUCKY, LOUISIANA, MISSISSIPPI, MISSOURI, MONTANA, NEBRASKA, NEW YORK, OHIO, OKLAHOMA, OREGON, PENNSYLVANIA, TENNESSEE, TEXAS, WASHINGTON, WEST VIRGINIA, WISCONSIN.

3 City, ⊗ of Jackson co., NE Georgia; pop. (1970c) 1647; cotton mills; dairy farming.

4 City, ⊗ of Greene co., W cen. Iowa, 33 m. SSW of Fort Dodge; pop. (1970c) 4735; market center; soybean processing; concrete blocks, farm machinery, sporting goods.

5 Town, Coos co., N New Hampshire, in White Mts.; pop. (1970c) 714; summer resort.

6 Town, ⊗ of Ashe co., NW North Carolina; pop. (1970c) 943.

7 Village, ⊗ of Ashtabula co., NE corner of Ohio, 8 m. S of Ashtabula; pop. (1970c) 2472; chemicals; dairy farming.

8 Village, Madison co., SW cen. Ohio, 16 m. W of Columbus; pop. (1970c) 3664.

9 Borough, Allegheny co., SW Pennsylvania, S of Pittsburgh; pop. (1970c) 8512.

10 City, ⊗ of Marion co., NE Texas, near W end of Caddo Lake 15 m. N of Marshall; pop. (1970c) 2866; oil wells; lumbering; strawberries; founded 1836 on route followed by Sam Houston, and, later, by David Crockett.

11 City, ⊗ of Jefferson co., SE Wisconsin, 13 m. S of Watertown; pop. (1970c) 5429; furniture, sausage; diversified agriculture; settled 1836.

Jefferson, Mount. 1 Peak in Presidential Range of White Mts., in S Coos co., N New Hampshire; 5715 ft.

2 Peak, W Jefferson co., N cen. Oregon; 10,495 ft.

Jefferson City. 1 City, ✻ of Missouri and ⊗ of Cole co., cen. Missouri; pop. (1970c) 32,407; commercial center; bookbinding; shoes, clothing, electrical appliances; Lincoln Univ. (1866). Selected as capital 1821 and occupied as such 1826; incorp. as town 1825, as city 1839; occupied by Union troops June, 1861.

2 Town, Jefferson co., E Tennessee, WSW of Morristown; pop. (1970c) 5124; Carson-Newman Coll. (1851).

Jefferson Da·vis \-ˈdāv-əs\. Name of a parish in Louisiana and of a county in Mississippi. See tables at LOUISIANA and MISSISSIPPI.

Jefferson Heights. Urban community (unincorporated), Jefferson parish, SE Louisiana, W of New Orleans; pop. (1970c) 16,489.

Jef·fer·son·ville \ˈjef-ər-sən-ˌvil\. 1 City, ⊗ of Twiggs co., cen. Georgia; pop. (1970c) 1302; dairy farming.

2 City, ⊗ of Clark co., S Indiana, on Ohio river across from Louisville, Kentucky; pop. (1970c) 20,008; U.S. army quartermaster depot; shipyard, oil refinery.

Jehlam. See JHELUM.

Je·hol \jə-ˈhōl, ˈrō-ˈhō\. 1 Region, NE China, N of the Great Wall; 74,278 sq. m.; long considered a part of Inner Mongolia; later, the N part of Chihli prov., China Proper, from which it was separated 1928 to become a province of SW Manchuria; from 1933 to 1945 with reduced area a province of the newly established Japanese state of Manchukuo (*q.v.*) with capital at Ch'eng-te (Jehol); later a province of China; in 1955 divided among Inner Mongolia, Hopeh, and Liaoning.

2 City, its ✻. See CH'ENG-TE.

Je·hosh·a·phat, Valley of \-ji-ˈhäs(h)-ə-ˌfat, -fət\. A common name of the valley of the Kidron (*Joel* iii. 2, 12).

Je·jui Gua·zú \he-ˌhwē-gwä-ˈsü\. River in E cen. Paraguay, flowing W into Paraguay river.

Jek·yll Island \ˌjek-əl-\. Island in Atlantic Ocean, off mainland of Glynn co., SE Georgia; 10 sq. m.; formerly owned by the Jekyll Island Club, a group of wealthy men who maintained summer homes here; now a state park.

Je·lai \ˈjā-ˌlī\. River, W headstream of the Pahang, NW Pahang state, Malaysia; joins the Tembeling to form the Pahang at 4°03′N.

Jelalabad. See JALĀLĀBĀD.

Je·le·nia Gó·ra \yā-ˌlen-yə-ˈgu̇r-ə\; *Ger.* **Hirsch·berg** \ˈhərsh-ˌbərg, ˈhi(ə)rsh-ˌbe(ə)rg\ *also* **Hirschberg in Schle·si·en** \-in-ˈshlā-zē-ən\ *or* **Hirschberg im Rie·sen·ge·bir·ge** \im-ˈrēz-^{ə}n-gə-ˌbi(ə)r-gə\. Manufacturing city, W Wrocław prov., SW Poland, ab. 60 m. WSW of Wrocław; pop. (1970p) 55,700; manufactures paper, iron, glass, textiles; assigned to Poland by Potsdam Conference 1945.

Je·lep–la \ˈjel-əp-ˌlä\ *or Chin.* **Chih–lieh–p'u** \ˈjir-lē-e-ˈpü\. Pass (*la*), on border of Sikkim, leading into Tibet, China, ab. 45 m. NE of Darjeeling, India; alt. 14,390 ft.

Jel·ga·va *also* **Yel·ga·va** \ˈyel-gə-və\ *or Ger.* **Mi·tau** \ˈmē-ˌtau̇\. City, S Latvian S.S.R., U.S.S.R., on Lielupe river; pop. (1969e) 51,000.

History: Founded 1266 by Teutonic Knights; became capital of duchy of Kurland 1561; fell under Russian rule 1795; headquarters Oct. 1919 of Bolshevik troops, who were expelled from the city by a combined Latvian and Lithuanian army; in World War II held by German forces 1941–44.

Jel·li·co \ˈjel-ə-ˌkō\. City, Campbell co., N Tennessee, on Kentucky border; pop. (1970c) 2235; coal mines; lumber.

Jem, Al–. See AL-JEM.

Je·mappes \zhə-'map\. Commune, Hainaut prov., SW Belgium, just W of Mons; pop. (1969e) 12,548; steel; battlefield where the French under Dumouriez defeated the Austrians Nov. 6, 1792.

Jember. See DJEMBER.

Je·meppe \zhə-'mep\. Commune, Liège prov., E Belgium, W suburb of Liège on Meuse river; pop. (1969e) 12,475.

Je·mez Springs \ˌhā-məs-\. Village, Sandoval co., NW cen. New Mexico; pop. (1970c) 356; S of it is the Jemez Indian Pueblo, established ab. 1700, on the **Jemez River** (tributary of the Rio Grande, ab. 50 m. long); N of it is the **Jemez State Monument** with ruins of early mission.

Je·na \'jēn-ə\. Town, ⊗ of La Salle parish, cen. Louisiana; pop. (1970c) 2239; oil wells, lumber.

Jena \'yā-nə\. City, Gera dist., East Germany, on Saale river 25 m. E of Erfurt; pop. (1970e) 88,346; chemicals, glass products, optical instruments (formerly a world center for lens-making); univ. (1588); remains of old fortifications; 11th cent. church; 14th cent. town hall; first planetarium built here; first mentioned bet. 881 and 899; became city 1284; scene of famous victory of Napoleon over Prussian and Saxon armies Oct. 14, 1806; original *Burschenschaft* organized here 1815; severely damaged in World War II.

Jenil. See GENIL.

Je·nin \je-'nēn\ *or* **Ja·nīn** \ja-\ *or anc.* **En·gan·nim** \en-'gan-əm, eŋ-\. Town at S end of Plain of Esdraelon, Jordan, in area occupied by Israel 1967; pop. (1968e) 13,400.

Jen·kins \'jenk-ənz\. 1 County in Georgia. See table at GEORGIA.
2 City, Letcher co., SE Kentucky, 22 m. SSW of Pikeville; pop. (1970c) 2552; coal mines.

Jen·kin·town \'jeŋ-kən-ˌtau̇n\. Residential borough, Montgomery co., SE Pennsylvania, 10 m. N of Philadelphia; pop. (1970c) 5990; steel and paper products; Manor Junior Coll. (1947).

Jenné. See DJENNÉ.

Jen·nings \'jen-iŋz\. 1 County in Indiana. See table at INDIANA.
2 City, ⊗ of Jefferson Davis parish, SW Louisiana, 36 m. E of Lake Charles; pop. (1970c) 11,783; cotton gin, bottling plant; rice, truck crops.
3 City, St. Louis co., E Missouri, 4 m. N of St. Louis; pop. (1970c) 19,379; residential suburb of St. Louis.

Je·quié \zhə-'kyā\. City, SE cen. Bahia state, E Brazil, 125 m. SW of Salvador; munic. pop. (1968e) 84,430.

Je·qui·ti·nho·nha \zhə-ˌkēt-ən-'yōn-yə\. River, E Brazil; ab. 500 m. long; rises in cen. Minas Gerais state, flows NE and E through Bahia state into Atlantic Ocean.

Je·ra·blus *or* **Ja·rā·blus** \ˌjer-ə-'blüs\ *or Fr.* **Dje·ra·blous** \jer-ä-blüs\. Town, N Syria, on the Euphrates.

Je·rash *or* **Ja·rash** \'jer-ˌäsh\ *or anc.* **Ger·a·sa** \'jer-ə-sə\. Town, N Jordan, ab. 20 m. N of Amman; ancient Gerasa a city of the Decapolis; ruins.

Je·rauld \jə-'rȯld\. County in South Dakota. See table at SOUTH DAKOTA.

Jer·ba *or* **Djer·ba** \'jər-bə, 'je(ə)r-\ *or anc.* **Me·ninx** \'mē-niŋks\. Island in cen. Mediterranean Sea, off SE coast of Tunisia, at S side of entrance to the Gulf of Gabès; 197 sq. m.; pop. (1966c) 62,445; a fertile island producing much fruit; exports olive oil and dates; contains remains of ancient Roman civilization.

Je·ré·cua·ro \he-'rā-kwär-ˌō\. Municipality, Guanajuato state, Mexico, 35 m. SE of Celaya; pop. (1970p) 37,589; diversified agriculture.

Jé·ré·mie \ˌzher-ə-'mē\. Seaport on NW Tiburon Penin., Haiti, 120 m. W of Port-au-Prince.

Je·rez \hə-'rās\ *or in full* **Jerez de la Fron·te·ra** \hə-'rez-də-lə-ˌfrən-'ter-ə\ *or formerly* **Xe·res** \'sher-ēz\. City, Cádiz prov., SW Spain, 13 m. NE of Cádiz; pop. (1970p) 149,867; commercial center; noted esp. for its sherry (named for the town); raises horses; Roman colony; believed by some to be scene of famous battle of Moors under Tariq with West Goths under Roderick 711 (see BARBATE, RÍO); recaptured but lost by Ferdinand III and finally taken 1264 by Alfonso X.

Jerez de Gar·cía Sa·li·nas \-də-gär-ˌsē-ə-sə-'lēn-əs\. Town, Zacatecas state, cen. Mexico, W of Zacatecas; munic. pop. (1970p) 49,202.

Jerez de los Ca·ba·lle·ros \he-ˌrez-də-lōs-ˌkab-ə-'le(ə)r-(ˌ)ōs, -ə(ˌ)-'ye(ə)r-\. Manufacturing commune, Badajoz prov., SW Spain, 37 m. SSE of Badajoz; pop. (1970p) 11,598; agricultural trade center; marble quarries; Moorish walls, gates, and fortress; birthplace of Balboa; thought to have been founded by Phoenicians; reconquered from Moors 1229; enlarged and given to Knights Templar 1232.

Jer·i·cho \'jer-i-ˌkō\. 1 Urban community (unincorp.), Nassau co., SE New York, on Long I.; pop. (1970c) 14,010; beverages; residential.
2 *Arab.* **Arī·hā** \ə-'rē-hə\. Village, Jordan, ab. 14 m. ENE of Jerusalem, in area occupied by Israel 1967; 825 ft. below sea level. Site of an important ancient city, a stronghold commanding the valley of the lower Jordan; captured c. 1400 B.C. by Joshua (*Josh.* vi). Later several times destroyed and rebuilt on a site at or near the modern village of Arīhā; captured by British Feb. 21, 1918 in World War I.

Jerid, Shatt al–. See DJERID, CHOTT.

Jer·i·moth Hill \ˌjer-i-ˌmäth-, -ˌmȯth-\. Elevation, Providence co., Rhode Island, W of Providence on Connecticut border; 812 ft.; highest point in the state.

Jer·myn \'jər-mən\. Borough, Lackawanna co., NE Pennsylvania, NE of Scranton; pop. (1970c) 2435; coal.

Je·rome \jə-'rōm\. 1 County in Idaho. See table at IDAHO.
2 Town, Yavapai co., cen. Arizona; pop. (1970c) 290.
3 City, ⊗ of Jerome co., S Idaho, 14 m. N of Twin Falls; pop. (1970c) 4183; creamery; diversified agriculture.

Jer·sey \'jər-zē\. 1 Colloquial for NEW JERSEY.
2 County in Illinois. See table at ILLINOIS.
3 One of the Channel Is., in the English Channel; 44.87 sq. m.; pop. (1971p) 72,629; ✱ St. Helier; constitutes a bailiwick; resort; dairy and truck farming.

Jersey Bay. Bay, SE end of St. Thomas I., Virgin Is., West Indies.

Jersey City. City and port, ⊗ of Hudson co., NE New Jersey, on Hudson river and Upper New York Bay, across from New York City; pop. (1970c) 260,545; railroad center; chemicals, paper products, locomotives, clothing, toys; St. Peter's Coll. (1872), Jersey City State Coll. (1929), New Jersey Coll. of Medicine and Dentistry (1955). Purchased from Indians c. 1630 and settled by 1650; taken by British 1664; chartered as town 1668; scene of defeat of British by "Light Horse Harry" Lee 1779; chartered as City of Jersey 1820, as Jersey City 1838; became ⊗ 1840; important station on Underground Railroad; scene of Black Tom explosion 1916.

Jersey Shore. Borough, Lycoming co., N cen. Pennsylvania, on West Susquehanna river 13 m. W of Williamsport; pop. (1970c) 5322; mobile homes, structural steel.

Jer·sey·ville \'jər-zē-ˌvil\. Village, ⊗ of Jersey co., W Illinois, 60 m. SW of Springfield; pop. (1970c) 7446.

Je·ru·sa·lem \jə-'rü-s(ə-)ləm, -'rüz-(ə-)ləm\. 1 District of E cen. Israel. See table at ISRAEL.
2 *or Arab.* **Al–Quds** \al-'küts\ *or Heb.* **Ye·ru·sha·lay·im** \ye-ˌrü-shə-'lī-əm\ *or anc.* **Hi·er·o·sol·y·ma** \ˌhī-ə-rō-'säl-ə-mə\. City, ✱ of Israel and ✱ of district of Jerusalem; pop. (Arab and Israeli sectors; [1970e]) 291,700; situated on two rocky hills at altitude of 2500 ft., 35 m. from the Mediterranean and ab. 13 m. W of N end of Dead Sea; connected by railroad with Tel Aviv-Jaffa on the coast and center of ancient highways N, E, S, and W; tourism. Holy City of Jews, Christians, and Muslims; called "City of David" and "City of the Great King" (*Ps.* xlviii. 2): see ZION 2; Hebrew Univ. (1925); numerous churches, synagogues, and mosques (3d Holy City of Islam).

History: First mentioned in Tell al-'Amarna letters c. 1370 B.C.; fortress of Jebusites captured by David c. 1000 B.C. and made the capital of kingdom of Israel, and later, of Judah (*qq.v.*); walls of city were built and the Temple founded by Solomon c. 970 B.C.; destroyed by Nebuchadnezzar of Babylon 586 B.C.; restored to Jews by Cyrus (see IRAN) 538 B.C.; in mid-5th cent. B.C., Nehemiah rebuilt its walls; as city of Palestine (*q.v.*) ruled by Alexander the Great, Ptolemies, Seleucids, and by Romans who ruled it during Christ's lifetime; partly destroyed by Titus 70 A.D. and by Hadrian in 135; rebuilt as Roman city, **Ae·lia Cap·i·to·li·na** \'ē-lē-ə-ˌ'kap-ət-ᵊl-'īnə\; held by Persians 614–629; taken by Muslim Arabs 638; its capture in 1077 by Seljuks who mistreated Christian pilgrims was immediate cause of Crusades; captured by Crusaders who erected Latin kingdom of Jerusalem (1099–1187); after its fall into hands of Saladin 1187, its recovery was goal of several Crusades; held continuously by Muslims 1244–1917; occupied by British in campaign against Turks Dec. 9, 1917; old city taken over by Transjordan Arabs 1948; new city captured by Israeli forces 1948, on Feb. 1, 1949 declared by the provisional government of Israel to be part of the new state, and in 1950 made ✱; Jordanian part of city occupied by Israel 1967 and integrated with Israeli sector.

Jer·vaulx \'jər-(ˌ)vō\. Hamlet, North Riding, Yorkshire, N England; noted for ruins of its abbey, ab. 4 m. SW, dating from 1156.

Jer·vis Bay \ˌjär-vəs-\. Inlet of South Pacific, on E coast of New South Wales, SE Australia; equidistant (ab. 90 m.) SSW from Sydney and ENE from Canberra; 10 to 12 m. long; 28 sq. m., including the harbor on S side of bay; a part of Australian Capital Territory (*q.v.*).

Jervis Island. See JARVIS ISLAND.

Jesi. See IESI.

Jes·sa·mine \'jes-(ə-)mən\. County in Kentucky. See table at KENTUCKY.

Jesselton. See KOTA KINABALU.

Jes·sore \je-'sō(ə)r, -'sȯ(ə)r\. **1** Former district, SE Bengal, India; 2925 sq. m.; divided 1947 so that ab. 6/7 of it was assigned to East Pakistan (now Bangla Desh), the remainder to West Bengal, India.

2 Town, Bangla Desh, 90 m. SW of Dacca; pop. (1961c) 46,366.

Jes·sup \'jes-əp\. Locality, Lackawanna co., NE Pennsylvania, ab. 8 m. NE of Scranton; pop. (1970c) 4948.

Jes·up \'jes-əp\. City, ⊗ of Wayne co., SE Georgia, 40 m. NE of Waycross; pop. (1970c) 9091; textiles, lumber, furniture; diversified agriculture.

Je·sus Island \ˌjē-zəs-, -zəz-\ *or Fr.* **Île Jé·sus** \ēl-zhā-zue\. Island in St. Lawrence river just W of Montreal I., Canada; 84 sq. m.; separated from Montreal I. by Rivière des Prairies and from mainland by Rivière des Mille Îles; chief city Laval.

Je·thou \zhə-'tü\. One of the Channel Is., in Guernsey bailiwick, S of Herm; 44 acres; uninhabited.

Jet·more \'jet-ˌmō(ə)r, -ˌmȯ(ə)r\. City, ⊗ of Hodgeman co., SW cen. Kansas; pop. (1970c) 936; livestock raising; rye.

Jet·pur \'jet-ˌpu̇(ə)r\. Town, Gujarat state, W India, in cen. Kathiawar penin., 240 m. NW of Bombay; pop. (1961c) 31,186.

Jette \'zhet\. Manufacturing commune, Brabant prov., cen. Belgium, a suburb of Brussels; pop. (1969e) 38,970.

Jeu·mont \zhər-'mōⁿ\. Commune, Nord dept., N France, near Belgian frontier; pop. (1962c) 9660; French customs station; manufactures esp. glass; partly destroyed in World War I.

Jew·el Cave National Monument \ˌjü-əl-\. See UNITED STATES, *National Monuments.*

Jew·ell \'jü-əl\. County in Kansas. See table at KANSAS.

Jew·ett City \ˌjü-ət-\. Manufacturing borough in town of Griswold, Connecticut; pop. (1970c) 3372; synthetic fabrics. See GRISWOLD.

Jewish Autonomous Oblast \-'ȯ-bləst, -ˌblast\ *also* **Bi·ro·bi·dzhan** *or* **Bi·ro–Bi·djan** \ˌbir-ō-bi-'jän\. Autonomous subdivision of the Russian S.F.S.R., U.S.S.R.; on Amur river; 13,900 sq. m.; pop. (1970p) 173,000; ✱ Birobidzhan; tin and iron mining, lumbering; marble and limestone quarries; agriculture; territory set aside 1928 by Soviet government for colonization by Jews; made autonomous region 1934; majority of population non-Jewish.

Jeypore. See JAIPUR.

Jezairi–Bahri–Sefid. See ARCHIPELAGO.

Je·zio·rak \ye-'zhȯ-(ˌ)räk\ *or formerly* **Lake Ge·se·rich** \-'gā-zə-rik\. Lake, Olsztyn prov., N Poland; 12 sq. m.; formerly in East Prussia, Germany.

Jeziret ibn Omar. See CİZRE.

Jez·re·el \'jez-rē-ˌel, -ˌrē(ə)l\ *or* **Yiz·ré·el** \ˌyiz-rē-'el\. Town, Samaria, ancient Palestine, NW of Mt. Gilboa; a capital of Ahab (*1 Kings* xviii. 45); scene of death of Jezebel (*2 Kings* ix. 30–35).

Jezreel, Valley of. See ESDRAELON, PLAIN OF.

Jha·bua \'jäb-ə-wə\. Former Indian state, N cen. India, 80 m. W of Indore; now part of Madhya Pradesh; 1265 sq. m.; ✱ Jhabua.

Jha·la·war \'jäl-ə-ˌwär\. Former princely state, now a district of Rajasthan, NW India; 2405 sq. m.; pop. (1961c) 490,609.

Jhal·ra·pa·tan \ˌjäl-rə-'pät-ᵊn\ *or* **Jhalrapatan Chhao·ni** \-'chau̇-nē\. Town, ✱ of former Jhalawar state, SE Rajputana, India, 160 m. S of Jaipur; pop. (1961c) 9100.

Jhang \'jəŋ\. District, Punjab, Pakistan; 3401 sq. m.; pop. (1961c) 1,078,747; ✱ Jhang-Maghiana; Jhelum and Chenab rivers unite within its borders.

Jhang–Ma·ghi·a·na \-ˌməg-ē-'än-ə\. Town, Punjab, Pakistan, near left bank of Chenab river 120 m. WSW of Lahore; pop. (1961c) 94,971; a joint municipality of which Maghiana is newer and more important part; trades in grain and cloth.

Jhan·si \'jän(t)-sē\. **1** Division, Uttar Pradesh, India; 11,374 sq. m.; pop. (1961c) 3,498,827; ✱ Jhansi.

2 City, its ✱, 130 m. S of Agra; pop. (1970e) 181,904; has military cantonment; rail point with large railroad workshops; walled community with ancient Mogul fort, constructed 1613; city founded by Marathas 1732; capital of independent Maratha principality 1770–1853 when the last prince died without issue and sovereignty of British followed; scene of massacre during Sepoy Mutiny.

Jhe·lum *also* **Jeh·lam** \'jā-ləm\ *or anc.* **Hy·das·pes** \hī-'das-(ˌ)pēz\. **1** River, India and Pakistan; ab. 450 m. long; one of the "Five Rivers" of the Punjab; rises in Himalayas in Jammu and Kashmir, India, flows NW through Vale of Kashmir, passing through Srinagar, then SW out of India through Pir Panjal Range into Punjab, Pakistan, flowing S and uniting with the Chenab; source of canals and irrigation systems in the Punjab; navigable except through the mountains.

2 District, Rawalpindi division, Punjab, Pakistan; 2772 sq. m.; pop. (1961c) 749,229.

3 Town, its ✱, on Jhelum river 105 m. NNW of Lahore; pop. (1961c) 52,585.

Jhind. See JIND.

Jibuti. See DJIBOUTI.

Ji·ca·rón \ˌhē-kə-'rōn\. Island in Pacific Ocean off SW coast of Panama.

Ji·čín \'yich-ˌēn\ *or Ger.* **Gi·tschin** \gich-'ēn\. Town, Czech S.R., W Czechoslovakia, ab. 45 m. NE of Prague; pop. (1968e) 12,906; market center; founded 1302 by Wenceslaus II.

Ji·co \'hē-(ˌ)kō\. Town, Veracruz state, E Mexico; munic. pop. (1970p) 14,153.

Jid·da \'jid-ə\ *or* **Jed·da** \'jed-ə\ *or* **Jud·dah** \'jəd-ə\ *or* **Djed·dah** *also* **Ged·da** \'jed-ə\. Port on Red Sea, Hejaz, W Saudi Arabia, 46 m. W of Mecca and its seaport; pop.

(1965e) 194,000; import center; walled city, ab. 300 years old; chief port for pilgrims to Mecca; resisted Wahabi attacks in early 19th cent.; Turkish until June 1916 when it yielded to British and became part of the Hejaz; after yearlong siege surrendered Dec. 23, 1925 to ibn-Saud.

Ji·gua·ní \ˌhē-gwə-ˈnē\. Municipality and town, Oriente prov., E Cuba, 48 m. NW of Santiago de Cuba; munic. pop. (1967e) 136,370.

Jigüero, Point. See HIGÜERO, POINT.

Ji·güey Bay \hē-ˈgwā-\. Bay on NW coast of Camagüey prov., E cen. Cuba, SW of Romano Cay.

Jih–k'a–tse \ˈjē-ˈkä-ˈtse\ *or* **Shi·ga·tse** \shi-ˈgät-se\. Town, SE Tibet, W China, on S bank of Tsangpo (Brahmaputra) river ab. 140 m. W of Lhasa; about 1 m. SW is the walled and fortified monastery (**Te·shi Lum·po** \ˌtā-shē-ˈlùm-(ˌ)pō\ *or* **Tashilumpo** \ˌtä-\); prior to the Chinese occupation of Tibet (1950), ab. 3500 priests lived in the monastery.

Ji·hla·va \ˈyil-ə-ˌvä, ˈyēl-\ *or Ger.* **Iglau** \ˈē-(ˌ)glaù\. City, W Czech S.R., cen. Czechoslovakia; pop. (1968e) 39,313; mining community, silver mines nearby having been worked since the Middle Ages; textiles and tobacco products.

Jihun. See CEYHAN 1.

Jijelli. See DJIDJELLI.

Ji·ji·ga \ˈjē-ji-gə\. Town, Harer prov., E Ethiopia, ab. 50 m. E of Harer; pop. (1970e) 7500; taken by British Mar. 1941.

Ji·lo·te·pec de Aba·so·lo \hē-ˌlōt-ə-ˈpek-dā-ˌäb-ə-ˈsōl-ō\. Municipality, México state, Mexico, 40 m. NW of Mexico City; pop. (1970p) 34,566; lumber; agriculture.

Ji·ma \ˈjē-mə\ *or* **Jim·ma** *also* **Gim·ma** \ˈjim-ə\. Town, ✻ of Kefa prov., SW Ethiopia, ab. 170 m. SW of Addis Ababa; pop. (1970e) 41,848.

Ji·ma·ní \ˌhē-mə-ˈnē\. Town, ✻ of Independencia prov., SW Dominican Republic; pop. (1970p) 5522.

Jim·bo·lia \zhim-ˈbòl-yə\ *also* **Zsom·bo·lya** \ˈzhōm-bōl-yä\ *or Ger.* **Hatz·feld** \ˈhäts-ˌfelt\. Town, Timiş co., Romania, W of Timişoara near border of Yugoslavia; munic. pop. (1966c) 13,633; formerly belonged to Hungary; to Yugoslavia 1920; part of Romania since 1923.

Ji·me·nez \hi-ˈmen-əs, -ˈmān-\. Municipality, W Misamis Occidental prov., Mindanao, Phil., on W shore of Iligan Bay, 57 m. W of Cagayan de Oro; pop. (1968e) 28,400.

Ji·mé·nez \hi-ˈmen-əs, -ˈmān-\. Town, Chihuahua state, N Mexico, on railroad 120 m. SE of Chihuahua; munic. pop. (1970p) 27,044.

Jim Hogg \ˈjim-ˈhòg, -ˈhäg\. County in Texas. See table at TEXAS.

Jimma. See JIMA.

Jim Thorpe \ˈjim-ˈthò(ə)rp\. Borough, Carbon co., E Pennsylvania, SSE of Wilkes-Barre; pop. (1970c) 5456; mountain resort; coal mines; formed 1954 from former boroughs of Mauch Chunk and East Mauch Chunk.

Jim Wells \ˈjim-ˈwelz\. County in Texas. See table at TEXAS.

Jind *or* **Jhind** \ˈjind\. **1** Former Indian state, one of the three Phulkian States, now in S Punjab and N Haryana states, India; 1299 sq. m., in three separate tracts; ✻ Sangrur; founded by a Sikh raja 1763, recognized by Mogul emperor 1768; loyal to British in Mutiny of 1857; rendered service to British government in other wars, esp. World War I.

2 Town, Haryana, N India, 72 m. NW of Delhi; pop. (1961c) 24,216.

Jin·dři·chův Hra·dec \ˈyin-dər-zhi-ˌküf-ˈhräd-ˌets\ *or Ger.* **Neu·haus** \ˈnòi-ˌhaùs\. Town, Czech S.R., W Czechoslovakia, 70 m. SSE of Prague; pop. (1968e) 12,243.

Jin·ja \ˈjin-jə\. Town, Uganda, E Africa, on Lake Victoria just above Owen Falls Dam at beginning of Victoria Nile; pop. (1969p) 47,298.

Ji·no·te·ga \ˌhē-nə-ˈteg-ə\. **1** Department of W cen. Nicaragua. See table at NICARAGUA.

2 Town, its ✻, NNW of Matagalpa; pop. (1967e) 8636.

Ji·no·te·pe \ˌhē-nə-ˈtep-ā\. Town, ✻ of Carazo dept., SW Nicaragua, 20 m. S of Managua; munic. pop. (1970e) 23,903.

Jinsen. See INCH'ŎN.

Jin·to·to·lo Channel \ˌhin-tə-ˈtō-(ˌ)lō-\. Passage bet. SW Masbate I. and NE Panay I., Phil., connecting Visayan Sea with Sibuyan Sea; 20 m. wide.

Ji·pa·ra·ná *or formerly* **Gy–Pa·ra·ná** \ˌzhē-ˌpar-ə-ˈnä\. River, W cen. Brazil; ab. 500 m. long (with longest headstream); rises in W Mato Grosso state, flows N and NW into Madeira river.

Ji·pi·ja·pa \ˌhē-pē-ˈhäp-ə\. City, Manabí prov., W Ecuador, ab. 75 m. NW of Guayaquil; pop. (1962c) 13,367; manufactures Panama hats made of toquilla straw from the leaves of the jipijapa (*Carludovica palmata*).

Ji·quil·pán de Juá·rez \ˌhē-kēl-ˌpän-də-ˈ(h)wär-ˌez, -ˌes, -əs\. Town, Michoacán state, SW Mexico; munic. pop. (1970p) 26,451.

Jiquipilco. See SAN JUAN JIQUIPILCO.

Jisera. See ISER.

Jitomir. See ZHITOMIR.

Ji·ul \ˈzhē-(ˌ)ül\ *or* **Schyl** \ˈshēl\. River, S Romania; ab. 200 m. long; flows SSE past Craiova into the Danube.

Ji·wa·ni, Cape \-ji-ˈwän-ē\ *or* **Cape Ji·un·ri** \-jē-ˈün-rē\. Cape, SW Pakistan, extending into Arabian Sea.

Jo \ˈjō\ *or* **Hwei** \ˈ(h)wā\. River, N China; ab. 200 m. long.

Jo·a·ça·ba \ˌzhō-ə-ˈsäb-ə\ *or formerly* **Cru·zei·ro** \krü-ˈze(ə)r-(ˌ)ü\. City, Santa Catarina state, S Brazil, on tributary of Uruguay river.

Joachimsthal. See JÁCHYMOV.

João Pes·soa \ˌzhwaù^{n}(m)-pə-ˈsō-ə\ *or formerly* **Pa·ra·í·ba** \ˌpar-ə-ˈē-bə\. City, ✻ of Paraíba state, E Brazil; munic. pop. (1970p) 221,484; ships cotton; cement, cigars, footwear; univ. (1955); founded 1585.

Joazeiro. See JUÀZEIRO.

Job Peak \ˈjōb-\. Mountain in cen. Churchill co., W Nevada; 8799 ft.

Jo·cas·see Dam and **Jocassee Reservoir** \jō-ˌkas-ē-\. See UNITED STATES, *Dams and Reservoirs.*

Jó·dar \ˈhō-(ˌ)där, -thär\. Commune, Jaén prov., S Spain, 22 m. E of Jaén; pop. (1970p) 12,020.

Jo Da·viess \ˈjō-ˈdā-vəs\. County in Illinois. See table at ILLINOIS.

Jodh·pur \ˈjäd-pər, -ˌpù(ə)r\. **1** *or* **Mar·war** \ˈmär-ˌwär\. Former Indian state, now part of Rajasthan state, NW India; 36,120 sq. m.; ✻ Jodhpur; region borders on Thar Desert on W, touches Great Rann of Kutch on SW; traversed by Luni river flowing SW; irrigated sections produce wheat and cotton; breeds best camels in India.

2 City, Rajasthan, India, 235 m. N of Ahmadabad; pop. (1967e) 252,657; ivory carvings, lacquer ware, vegetable dyes, brass and iron utensils, bicycles, textiles; univ. (1962); ruins of Mandor, former capital of princes of Marwar, 5 m. N; a walled city, with large fort containing the maharaja's palace, founded 1459 by Rao Jodha; recognized English sovereignty 1818.

Jod·rell Bank \ˌjäd-rəl-\. Locality, NE Cheshire, England, ab. 15 m. SSW of Manchester; site of radio telescope maintained by Univ. of Manchester.

Jo·en·suu \ˈyò-ən-ˌsü\. Commercial city, ✻ of Pohjois-Karjala prov., S Finland; pop. (1970p) 36,576; copper mining; founded 1848.

Jœuf \ˈzhə(r)f\. Commune, Meurthe-et-Moselle dept., NE France, 37 m. N of Nancy; pop. (1968e) 12,305; a principal metallurgical center of Lorraine.

Jof·fre, Mount \-ˈzhäf-ər\. Peak, SE British Columbia, Canada, on Alberta border SW of Calgary; 11,313 ft.

Jog Falls. See GERSOPPA, FALLS OF.

Jog·gins \ˈjäg-ənz\. Unincorporated mining town, Cumberland co., N Nova Scotia, Canada, on Chignecto Bay 17 m. WSW of Amherst; pop. (1966c) 799; coal; widely known source of fossils.

Jog·ja·kar·ta \ˌjäg-yə-ˈkärt-ə\ *or* **Djok·ja·kar·ta** \ˌjäk-\ *or* **Jok·ya·kar·ta** \ˌjäk-\. **1** Special autonomous district, Java,

Indonesia; 1193 sq. m.; pop. (1970e) 2,779,000; a former sultanate; incl. city of Jogjakarta; led revolt against Dutch 1825–30; occupied by Japanese 1942; center of activities of Republic of Indonesia from 1945.

2 City, its ✻, at foot of Mt. Merapi 175 m. WSW of Surabaja; several colleges; destroyed by earthquake 1867 and rebuilt.

Johanna. See ANJOUAN.

Jo·han·nes·burg \jō-ˈhan-əs-ˌbərg, -ˈhän-\. City, S Transvaal, NE Rep. of South Africa, 300 m. NW of Durban; pop. (1970p) 654,682, met. area pop. 1,432,643; the republic's largest city and leading industrial center; chemicals, textiles, leather products; engineering industries; gold mines; Univ. of Witwatersrand (1922), Rand Afrikaans Univ. (1966); has own observatory and also branch observatory of Leiden Univ.; founded 1886 after discovery of gold; occupied by British during Boer War 1900; created a city 1928.

Jo·han·nis·berg \yō-ˈhän-əs-ˌbe(ə)rg\. Village, Hesse, West Germany, in the Rheingau on Rhine river; to the S lies its castle, built 1759 and given to Prince Metternich 1816; surrounded by vineyards yielding the famous Johannisberger wine.

John Day \ˈjän-ˈdā\. River, N Oregon; 281 m. long; rises in E Grant co. in E cen. part of state and flows W and N into Columbia river on boundary bet. Sherman and Gilliam cos.; principal tributaries the **South Fork** rising in N Harney co. and flowing N, and **Middle Fork** and **North Fork** which join in N Grant co. and flow SW; basin notable for fossil beds.

John o'Groat's House \ˌjän-ə-ˈgrōts-\. Point on N coast of Caithness, N Scotland; popularly considered most northerly point of Great Britain (see DUNNET HEAD); the usual terminus of races the length of Great Britain from Land's End.

John·son \ˈjän(t)-sən\. 1 River, Alaska; 215 m. long; tributary of the Kuskokwim (*q.v.*).

2 Name of counties in twelve states of the U.S. See tables at ARKANSAS, GEORGIA, ILLINOIS, INDIANA, IOWA, KANSAS, KENTUCKY, MISSOURI, NEBRASKA, TENNESSEE, TEXAS, WYOMING.

3 *or* **Johnson City.** City, ⊗ of Stanton co., SW Kansas; pop. (1970c) 1038; wheat.

John·son·burg \ˈjan(t)-sən-ˌbərg\. Industrial borough, Elk co., NW cen. Pennsylvania, 25 m. N of Du Bois; pop. (1970c) 4304; paper, electronic components.

Johnson City. 1 Village, Broome co., S New York, 3 m. W of Binghamton; pop. (1970c) 18,025; with Endicott and Binghamton, one of so-called Triple Cities; tanneries; shoes, felt, photographic supplies.

2 City, Washington co., NE Tennessee, 20 m. S of Virginia border; pop. (1970c) 33,770; furniture, tobacco, electrical equipment, plastics, bricks, tools; limestone quarries; tourist center; East Tennessee State Univ. (1909); first settled in 1760's; incorp. 1869.

3 City, ⊗ of Blanco co., cen. Texas; pop. (1970c) 767.

John·ston \ˈjän(t)-stən, -sən\. 1 Name of counties in two states of the U.S. See tables at NORTH CAROLINA and OKLAHOMA.

2 Town, Providence co., N Rhode Island, ab. 5 m. SW of Providence; pop. (1970c) 22,037; granite quarries; settled 1650; originally part of Providence; became separate town 1759.

3 Town, Edgefield co., W South Carolina, 47 m. SW of Columbia; pop. (1970c) 2552; cotton clothing; diversified agriculture.

4 Coral atoll, with two small islets **(Johnston and Sand** \-ˈsand\) and reef, cen. Pacific Ocean; ab. 700 m. SW of Honolulu, 16°45′N, 169°32′W; ab. 9 m. long, 4 m. wide; belongs to the United States; not included in Hawaii statehood bill; discovered 1807 by British sea captain; claimed by the U.S. 1858; worked for guano; made part of U.S. defense system 1934.

Johnston City \ˌjän(t)-sən-\. City, Williamson co., S Illinois, 8 m. N of Marion; pop. (1970c) 3928; coal; wheat.

John·stone \ˈjän-s(t)ən\. Manufacturing burgh, Renfrew co., SW Scotland; pop. (1971p) 22,629; engineering works; paper.

Johnstone, Lake. Lake, S Saskatchewan, Canada, ab. 20 m. SW of Moose Jaw; 131 sq. m.

Johnstone Strait. Narrow passage, along N coast of Vancouver I., SW British Columbia, Canada, connecting Queen Charlotte Strait with Strait of Georgia; ab. 60 m. long.

Johns·town \ˈjän-ˌstau̇n\. 1 City, ⊗ of Fulton co., E New York, 11 m. WNW of Amsterdam; pop. (1970c) 10,045; tanneries; gloves, hosiery, blankets; diversified agriculture; Fulton-Montgomery Community Coll. (1963); founded by Sir William Johnson 1762.

2 Village, Licking co., cen. Ohio, 21 m. NE of Columbus; pop. (1970c) 3208; diversified agriculture.

3 Industrial city, Cambria co., SW cen. Pennsylvania, on Conemaugh river 60 m. E of Pittsburgh; pop. (1970c) 42,476; coal-mining center; iron and steel, mining and railroad equipment, fertilizers, electrical supplies; Christ the Saviour Seminary of Johnstown. Incorporated as village 1800, as borough 1831, as city 1889; scene of many disastrous floods (esp. May 31, 1889, when Conemaugh Dam above city burst after heavy rains and more than 2200 were drowned).

4 Town, Ontario, Canada. See PRESCOTT 4.

Jo·hore *or* **Jo·hor** \jə-ˈhō(ə)r, -ˈhȯ(ə)r\. 1 Short stream of SE Johore state, Malaysia, S Malay Penin., SE Asia; long and wide estuary.

2 A state of Malaysia, Malay Penin., SE Asia, lying between South China Sea and Strait of Malacca; 7360 sq. m.; pop. (1970p) 1,273,990; ✻ Johore Bahru; two-thirds covered with jungle; mountainous in E cen. part (3300 ft.) but highest point, Mount Ophir 4186 ft., is in NW near Malacca border; principal streams the Muar, Endau, and Johore; coastline ab. 250 m. long with numerous small islands; separated from it to the S by Johore Strait is island of Singapore; rubber, fruit, bauxite, iron ore; fishing.

History: A Muslim-ruled state founded after 1511 by former sultan of Malacca (*q.v.*); came under British influence in 19th cent.; ceded Singapore 1819; its relations with Great Britian established by treaties 1885 and 1914; occupied by Japanese Jan. 1942; became part of the independent Federation of Malaya 1957; became a state of Malaysia 1963.

Johore Bah·ru \-ˈbär-(ˌ)ü\ *or* **Johor Ba·ha·ru** \-bə-ˈhär-(ˌ)ü\. Town, ✻ of Johore state, in S part on Johore Strait opp. Singapore I., Malaysia; pop. (1970p) 135,936; residence of sultan.

Johore Strait *or Malay* **Se·lat Te·brau** \ˌslät-tə-ˈbrau̇\. Channel bet. Singapore I. and the mainland of Johore state, S Malay Penin.; crossed by causeway from Woodlands to Johore Bahru; ab. 3/4 m. wide and 32 m. long; large naval base at E end; scene of heavy fighting Feb. 1942.

Joi·gny \zhwan-ˈyē\ *or anc.* **Jo·vi·ni·a·cum** \ˌjō-və-ˈnī-ə-kəm\. Commune, Yonne dept., NE cen. France, on Yonne river 15 m. NNW of Auxerre; pop. (1965e) 9465; probably of Roman origin; seat of a countship in 10th cent.; unsuccessfully besieged by English 1429.

Join·vi·le \zhóin-ˈvē-lē\ *or formerly* **Join·vi·lle** \-ˈvē-lē\. City, Santa Catarina state, S Brazil, 25 m. inland from port of São Francisco do Sul; munic. pop. (1968e) 88,647.

Join·ville Island \ˌjȯin-vil-\. Island in West Antarctica off tip of Antarctic Penin., British Antarctic Terr., at NW point of Weddell Sea, 63°15′S, 55°45′W; ab. 40 m. wide by 20 m. long.

Joinville–le–Pont \zhwa^{n}-ˌvēl-lə-ˈpō^{n}\. Commune, Val-de-Marne dept., N France, ESE suburb of Paris; pop. (1968c) 17,467; photographic and cinematographic supplies; military school.

Jo·ju·tla \hō-ˈhü-tlä\. Municipality, Morelos state, Mexico, 60 m. S of Mexico City; pop. (1970p) 31,196; thermal springs; center for saddle making; rice, sugar.

Jö·kulsá á Brú \ˈyək-əls-ˌaù-aù-ˈbrü\. River, E Iceland, flowing NE into Norwegian Sea.

Jökulsá á Fjöl·lum \-aù-ˈfyət-(ˌ)lüm\. River, NE Iceland, flowing N into Arctic Ocean; 128 m. long; 2d longest river in Iceland.

Jokyakarta. See JOGJAKARTA.

Joliba. See NIGER 2.

Jo·li·et \ˌjō-lē-ˈet, *chiefly by outsiders* ˌjäl-ē-\. City, ⊗ of Will co., NE Illinois, 35 m. SW of Chicago; pop. (1970c) 78,887; railroad shops, oil refineries, coal mines, limestone quarries; wire, machinery, clothing; state penitentiary; Coll. of St. Francis (1874); Joliet Junior Coll. (1902).

Jo·liette \ˌzhō-lē-ˈet\. 1 County, Quebec, Canada. See table at QUEBEC.

2 Manufacturing city, its ⊗, 35 m. N of Montreal; pop. (1971p) 19,497; railroad junction; steel plate, beverages, clothing; diversified agriculture; founded 1841 by descendant of the explorer Jolliet, incorporated 1863.

Jolla, La. See LA JOLLA.

Jo·lo \ˈhō-(ˌ)lō\ *or* **Su·lu** \ˈsü-(ˌ)lü\. 1 Chief island, Sulu Archipelago, Sulu prov., Phil., SW of Basilan I.; 345 sq. m.; pop., with adjacent small islands, (1960c) 165,607; chief town Jolo; lies bet. Sulu Sea and Celebes Sea; of volcanic origin, crossed by three parallel mountain chains with several peaks, highest 2664 ft.; good climate, fertile soil, agriculture well developed; thickly wooded. Inhabitants converted to Islam in 14th cent. See SULU 1.

2 Municipality, ✱ of Sulu prov., on NW coast of Jolo I.; pop. (1969e) 46,800; port of entry with considerable trade with Zamboanga, Manila, and Singapore; headquarters for pearl fishing; ancient residence of Sulu sultans but most traces of Moro town now gone; present town begun by Spaniards 1878; taken by American troops Apr. 9, 1945.

Jo·ma·lig *or* **Ho·ma·lig** \hō-ˈmäl-ig\. Island, E Polillo group, Phil., at NE corner of Lamon Bay E of Luzon; 20 sq. m.; belongs to Quezon prov.

Jomanes. See YAMUNA.

Jomonjol. See HOMONHON.

Joms·borg \ˈyȯmz-ˌbȯrg\. Viking fortified settlement built c. 970 near Julin on Wolin I. at mouth of the Oder, Germany; destroyed by Danes 1098.

Jones \ˈjōnz\. Name of counties in six states of the U.S. See tables at GEORGIA, IOWA, MISSISSIPPI, NORTH CAROLINA, SOUTH DAKOTA, TEXAS.

Jones, Mount. Mountain, Antarctica, 77°14′S, 142°11′W; 12,040 ft.

Jones·boro \ˈjōnz-ˌbər-ə, -ˌbə-rə\. 1 City, a ⊗ of Craighead co., NE Arkansas, 67 m. NNW of Memphis, Tennessee; pop. (1970c) 27,050; trading center; cotton gins, rice mill; lumber, shoes, brick, flour; cotton, rice; Arkansas State Univ. (1909); founded 1859; incorporated 1883.

2 City, ⊗ of Clayton co., NW cen. Georgia; pop. (1970c) 4105.

3 City, ⊗ of Union co., SW Illinois, 30 m. SW of Marion; pop. (1970c) 1676.

4 Town, Grant co., N cen. Indiana, 5 m. S of Marion; pop. (1970c) 2466; insulated wire and cable, glassware.

5 Town, ⊗ of Jackson parish, N Louisiana, 41 m. WSW of Monroe; pop. (1970c) 5072; diversified agriculture.

6 Town, ⊗ of Washington co., NE Tennessee, 7 m. W of Johnson City; pop. (1970c) 1510; meeting place of constitutional convention and first legislative sessions of State of Franklin until 1785.

Jones Mountain. Peak, Hinsdale and San Juan cos., SW Colorado; 13,851 ft.

Jones·port \ˈjōnz-ˌpō(ə)rt, -ˌpȯ(ə)rt\. Town, Washington co., SE Maine, on Atlantic Ocean bet. Englishman and Pleasant bays; pop. (1970c) 1326; fishing and sardine packing; summer resort.

Jones Sound. Channel, N Franklin dist., Northwest Territories, Canada, bet. S Ellesmere I. and N Devon I.; ab. 40 m. wide; opens into Baffin Bay.

Jones·ville \ˈjōnz-ˌvil\. 1 Town, Catahoula parish, cen. Louisiana, 45 m. ENE of Alexandria; pop. (1970c) 2761.

2 Town, Yadkin co., NW cen. North Carolina, 36 m. W of Winston-Salem; pop. (1970c) 1659.

3 Town, ⊗ of Lee co., SW tip of Virginia; pop. (1970c) 700.

Jong·song \ˈjäŋ-ˈsäŋ\. Peak on Nepal-Sikkim boundary; 24,472 ft.

Jön·kö·ping \ˈyə(r)n-ˌchə(r)p-iŋ\. 1 County of S Sweden. See table at SWEDEN.

2 City, its ⊗, at S end of Lake Vättern; pop. (1970e) 55,-372; matches, airplanes, paper, machinery; an old town, chartered 1284, important in early history of Sweden; destroyed 1612 but soon rebuilt; place where treaty was signed 1809 bet. Sweden and Denmark.

Jon·quière \ˌzhō^{n}-kē-ˈe(ə)r\. Town, Chicoutimi co., S Quebec, Canada, 8 m. W of Chicoutimi, bet. the Saguenay and Lake Kenogami; pop. (1971p) 28,080; pulp mills; founded 1847.

Jop·lin \ˈjäp-lən\. City, Jasper and Newton cos., SW Missouri, 72 m. W of Springfield; pop. (1970c) 39,256; leather goods, alcohol, fertilizer, missiles; Missouri Southern Coll. (1937); Ozark Bible Coll. (1942); founded 1839; chartered 1874.

Joppa. See JAFFA.

Jor·dan \ˈjȯrd-ᵊn\. 1 *or officially* **Ha·shem·ite Kingdom of Jordan** \ˈhash-ə-ˌmīt-\ *or formerly* **Trans·jor·dan** \(ˈ)trants-, (ˈ)tranz-\. Kingdom, SW Asia, bounded on N by Syria, on NE by Iraq, on E and S by Saudi Arabia, and on W by Israel; 37,737 sq. m.; pop. (1970e) 2,348,000 (figures include Jordanian territory on W bank of Jordan river); ✱ Amman; largely desert; region on W side of Jordan river is mountainous; has port on Gulf of ʻAqaba. *Chief products:* Wheat, phosphates, citrus fruits, olives. *Chief towns:* Amman, Zarqa, Nablus, Irbid.

History: Created 1921 out of former Turkish territory and proclaimed an independent state 1923 under Emir Abdullah ibn-Husein, but a mandate under British protection; first legislative council assembled 1929; mandate revoked 1946 and by treaty of Mar. 22, 1946 became an independent kingdom; engaged in war with Israel 1948–49; at signing of armistice agreement with Israel Apr. 1949 held the cen. part of Palestine and adopted name of Jordan; formally annexed Arab Palestine (area on W side of Jordan river) 1950; terminated special treaty relations with Great Britain 1957; participated in Arab-Israel War 1967, as a result of which its territory W of Jordan river came under Israeli military occupation.

2 River, N cen. Utah, flows from Utah Lake N into Great Salt Lake; 60 m. long.

3 Town, ⊗ of Garfield co., Montana; pop. (1970c) 529.

4 River, SW Asia; ab. 200 m. long; rises in Syria, flows S through the Waters of Merom and Sea of Galilee to N end of the Dead Sea; narrow and sluggish at its mouth; most of it S of Sea of Galilee forms boundary bet. Israel and Jordan and lies in the great depression of the Ghor (ab. 65 m. long); not navigable; noted for associations with Old Testament and New Testament history.

Jordan \hȯr-ˈdän\. Municipality, N coast of Guimaras I., Iloilo prov., Phil., on Iloilo Strait opp. City of Iloilo; pop. (1969e) 28,300.

Jordan, Mount \-ˈjȯrd-ᵊn\. Peak in Sierra Nevada, N Tulare co., S cen. California; 13,316 ft.

Jor·ge Montt \ˌhȯr-hā-ˈmȯnt\. Island off SW coast of Chile, S of Hanover I.

Jos \ˈjȯs\. Town, ✱ of Benue-Plateau State, Nigeria, ab. 143 m. S of Kano; pop. (1969e) 104,838; tin mines.

Jo·se Pañg·a·ni·ban \hō-ˌsā-ˌpäŋ-ə-nē-ˈbän\. Municipality on N coast of Camarines Norte prov., Luzon, Phil., W of Paracale; pop. (1969e) 37,200.

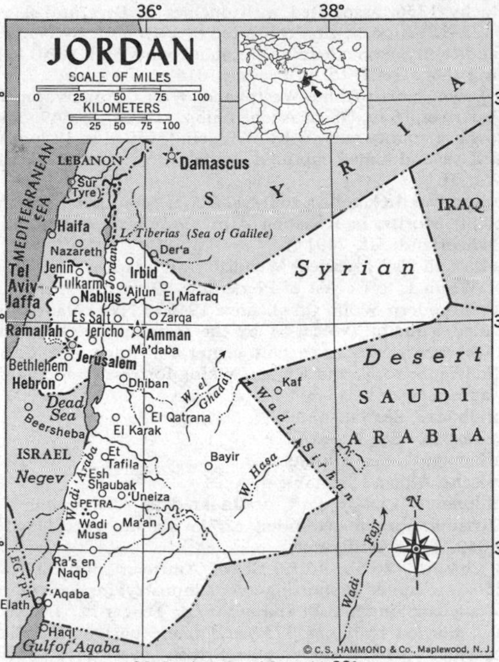

36° Longitude East of Greenwich 38°

Jo·seph \ˈjō-zef *also* -səf\. One of the Safety Is. (*q.v.*).

Joseph, Lake. Lake, NW Muskoka dist., SE Ontario, Canada, in the Muskoka Lake region, connected with lakes Muskoka (*q.v.*) and Rosseau; summer vacation land.

Joseph Bo·na·parte Gulf \-ˌbō-nə-ˌpärt-\. Inlet of Timor Sea in NE corner of Western Australia; 225 m. long E–W and 100 m. long N–S; divides into Cambridge Gulf and Queens Channel.

Jo·se·phine \ˈjō-zə-ˌfēn, ˈjō-sə-\. 1 County in Oregon. See table at OREGON.
2 Locality, Indiana co., W cen. Pennsylvania, ab. 18 m. NW of Johnstown.

Joseph Peak. Mountain in Yellowstone National Park, NW Wyoming; 10,300 ft.

Joshin. See KIMCH'AEK.

Josh·ua Tree National Monument \ˈjäsh-(ə-)wə-ˌtrē-\. See UNITED STATES, *National Monuments.*

Jos·se·lin \zhȯ-ˈslaⁿ\. Town, Morbihan dept., NW France, W of Ploërmel; pop. (1962c) 2098; once seat of countship held 13th cent. by Lusignan family; 16th cent. castle.

Jos·te·dals·bre·en \ˈyüs-tə-ˌdälz-ˌbrā-ən\. Plateau in Sogn og Fjordane co., W Norway; bet. 400 and 500 sq. m.; highest point 6396 ft.; contains largest ice field in Europe.

Jost Van Dyke \ˌyōst-van-ˈdīk\. One of the British Virgin Is., West Indies, W of Tortola; ab. 3 sq. m.; pop. (1967e) 200; mountainous.

Jo·tap·a·ta \jō-ˈtäp-ət-ə\. Ancient fortress, Galilee, N Palestine, N of Sepphoris, commanded by Josephus 67 A.D. when it was taken by Vespasian after siege of 47 days.

Jo·tun·hei·men \ˈyōt-ᵊn-ˌhā-mən\ *or* **Jo·tun·fjell** \-ˌfyel\. Mountain region in Oppland co., S cen. Norway, containing Galdhøpiggen (8100 ft.) and Glittertind (8110 ft.) peaks.

Jour·dan·ton \ˈjərd-ᵊn-tən\. City, ⊗ of Atascosa co., S Texas; pop. (1970c) 1841; oil wells.

Joux \ˈzhü\. Lake, Vaud canton, SW Switzerland, N of Lake of Geneva; 6 m. long and ⅔ m. wide.

Jouy–en–Jo·sas \ˈzhwē-ˌäⁿ-zhō-ˈzäs\. Commune, Yvelines dept., N France, SE of Versailles; pop. (1966e) 5733; site of workshop set up 1759 by Christophe Oberkampf which later became textile factory noted for manufacture of printed cloth (Jouy print).

Jo·ve·lla·nos \ˌhō-və-ˈyän-(ˌ)ōs\. Town and municipality, Matanzas prov., W cen. Cuba; munic. pop. (1967e) 20,610; transportation center 16 m. S of Cárdenas.

Joviniacum. See JOIGNY.

Jowz·jan \ˈju̇z-ˌjän\. Province of N Afghanistan. See table at AFGHANISTAN.

Ju·ab \ˈjü-(ˌ)ab\. County in Utah. See table at UTAH.

Jua·na \ˈ(h)wän-ə\. An early name of Cuba island, Greater Antilles, West Indies. See CUBA 1.

Jua·na·ca·tlán \ˌ(h)wän-ə-kə-ˈtlän\. Falls in Santiago river, Jalisco state, W cen. Mexico, near Guadalajara; 72 ft. high; used for waterpower.

Juana Dí·az \ˌ(h)wän-ə-ˈdē-ˌäs\. Town and municipality, S Puerto Rico; pop. (1970c) 8729 (town), 36,041 (munic.); town 7 m. ENE of Ponce.

Juan Al·da·ma \ˌ(h)wän-äl-ˈdäm-ə\. Town, Zacatecas state, cen. Mexico, 115 m. N of Zacatecas; munic. pop. (1970p) 13,661.

Juan de Fu·ca Strait \ˌ(h)wän-də-ˈfyü-kə-\. Strait bet. Vancouver I., Canada, and Clallam co., NW Washington; 100 m. long and 15 to 20 m. wide.

Juan de No·va \ˌ(h)wän-də-ˈnō-və\. Small island in N cen. Mozambique Channel bet. NE cen. Mozambique and NW cen. Malagasy Republic; belongs to Malagasy Republic.

Juan Fer·nán·dez \ˌ(h)wän-fər-ˈnan-dəs\. Group of 3 islands, Más Afuera, Más a Tierra and Santa Clara or Goat I., belonging to Chile, in S Pacific Ocean ab. 400 m. W of Chile; 70 sq. m.; Alexander Selkirk, the original of Defoe's hero Robinson Crusoe, lived on Más a Tierra Oct. 1704 to Feb. 1709.

Juan Gual·ber·to Go·mez \ˌ(h)wän-gwäl-ˌber-tō-ˈgō-ˌmäs, -ˌmez\; *formerly* **Sa·ba·ni·lla** \ˌsäb-ə-ˈnē-(y)ə\ *or in full* **Sabanilla del En·co·men·da·dor** \-ˌdel-eŋ-kō-ˌmen-ə-ˈdȯr\. Municipality, Matanzas prov., W cen. Cuba, 12 m. S of Matanzas; pop. (1967e) 9080.

Juan–les–Pins \ˌzhwäⁿ-lā-ˈpaⁿ\. Village, Alpes-Maritimes dept., SE France, on Cap d'Antibes SW of Antibes; coastal resort.

Juárez. See CIUDAD JUÁREZ.

Juà·zei·ro *or formerly* **Joa·zei·ro** \zhwə-ˈze(ə)r-(ˌ)ü\. City, N border of Bahia state, E Brazil, 275 m. NW of Salvador; munic. pop. (1968e) 45,770.

Juàzeiro do Nor·te \-dü-ˈnȯrt-ə\. City, Ceará state, NE Brazil; munic. pop. (1968e) 72,600.

Ju·ba \ˈjü-bə\. 1 *or Ital.* **Giu·ba** \ˈjü-bə\. River, E Africa; ab. 1000 m. long; rises in several headstreams (Dawa, Genale, and Weyib) in mountains of S cen. Ethiopia, flows S across SW Somalia into Indian Ocean; the port of Kismayu is just S of its mouth.
2 Town, ✱ of Equatoria prov., S Sudan, on Bahr al-Jebel (Nile) river.

Ju·bail \ju̇-ˈbā(ə)l\. Town, port of al-Hasa, E Nejd, Saudi Arabia, on Persian Gulf.

Ju·ba·land \ˈjü-bə-ˌland\ *or* **Trans–Ju·ba** \ˈtran(t)s-, ˈtranz-\ *or Ital.* **Ol·tre Giu·ba** \ˌōl-trā-ˈjü-bə\. Region, SW Somalia, E Africa, bet. Kenya border and the Juba river; formerly a province of Kenya, ceded by Britain to Italy 1925; administered as separate colony until July 1, 1926 when it became part of Italian Somaliland.

Ju·bayl \ju̇-ˈbā(ə)l\; *Fr.* **Dje·beil** *or* **Je·beil** \jə-bā(ə)l\ *or anc.* **Byb·los** \ˈbib-ləs\. Coast village, Lebanon, 20 m. N of Beirut; as Byblos, a very old city of Phoenicia (the **Ge·bal** \ˈgē-bəl\ of the Bible, *Ezek.* xxvii. 9), seat of the worship of Adonis; an early Phoenician inscription has been found here and excavations have uncovered remains of temple, citadel, tombs, etc.; exported papyrus to Egypt, hence the Greek *biblos* book, papyrus, and Eng. *Bible.*

Jubbulpore. See JABALPUR.

Ju·by, Cape *or* **Cape Yu·bi** \-'yü-bē\. Cape, SW coast of Morocco, NW Africa, E of Canary Is. See TARFAYA.

Jú·car \'hü-ˌkär\. River, E Spain; 309 m. long; rises in N Cuenca prov., flows S, then turns E in N Albacete prov., and flows through cen. Valencia prov. into Mediterranean Sea 26 m. S of Valencia.

Ju·chi·tán \ˌhü-chi-'tän\ *or officially* **Juchitán de Za·ra·go·za** \-dā-ˌzar-ə-'gō-zə\. Town, Oaxaca state, SE Mexico; pop. (1960c) 19,797; port on S side of Isthmus of Tehuantepec on Gulf of Tehuantepec; supply depot for agricultural region.

Ju·daea *or* **Ju·dea** \jü-'dē-ə\. The southern division of Palestine under Persian, Greek, and Roman rule, succeeding the kingdom of Judah (*q.v.*); bounded on N by Samaria, its N boundary extending approximately from N of Joppa to the Jordan ab. 13 m. above the Dead Sea; on E bounded by the Jordan and Dead Sea, on SW by Sinai (Egypt), and on W by the Mediterranean; became Roman province after conquests of Pompey; in late Roman years included Idumaea.

Ju·dah \'jüd-ə\. Ancient kingdom in S Palestine, bet. the Mediterranean and the Dead Sea; ✻ Jerusalem; the southern kingdom of the Jews after N part of Israel (*q.v.*) had broken away c. 933 B.C.; passed under Babylonian rule 605 B.C.; kingdom came to an end with destruction of Jerusalem (*q.v.*) by Nebuchadnezzar 586 B.C. See JUDAEA.

Juddah. See JIDDA.

Ju·dith \'jüd-əth\. River, cen. Montana; ab. 100 m. long; flows NE and N through Judith Basin and Fergus cos. into the Missouri river.

Judith, Point \-'jüd-əth, -'jüd-ē\. Southeast point, Washington co., Rhode Island, at W side of entrance to Narragansett Bay.

Judith Basin. County in Montana. See table at MONTANA.

Juf, Al–. See AL-JUF.

Juggernaut. See PURI.

Jugoslavia *or* **Jugoslavija.** See YUGOSLAVIA.

Juhaynah. See GIHEINA.

Jui·gal·pa \hwē-'gäl-pə\. Town, ✻ of Chontales dept., S cen. Nicaragua, ab. 15 m. from NE shore of Lake Nicaragua; munic. pop. (1970e) 25,349.

Juist \'yüst\. Narrow island, East Frisian Is., off NW coast of West Germany, NE of Borkum; 9 m. long.

Juiz de Fo·ra \zhə-ˌwēzh-də-'fōr-ə, -'fór-\. Manufacturing city, S Minas Gerais state, E Brazil, on railroad ab. 80 m. N of Rio de Janeiro; munic. pop. (1968e) 194,135; textiles; univ. (1960).

Ju·juy \hü-'hwē\. 1 Province of NW Argentina. See table at ARGENTINA.

2 *or in full* **San Sal·va·dor de Jujuy** \san-ˌsal-və-ˌdó(ə)r-də-\. Town, its ✻; pop. (1960c) 44,188; altitude ab. 4000 ft.

Jules·burg \'jü(ə)lz-ˌbərg\. Town, ⊗ of Sedgwick co., NE corner of Colorado, on South Platte river; pop. (1970c) 1578; railroad division point, founded 1881; the fourth and only remaining town of that name in vicinity.

Julfa. See DZHULFA.

Ju·lia·ca \hül-'yäk-ə\. Town, Puno dept., SE Peru, 189 m. by rail NE of Arequipa; pop. (1969e) 33,600; altitude 12,-550 ft.; railroad junction for Cuzco and Lake Titicaca; wool, hides.

Julia Joza. See TARIFA.

Julian Alps. See table at ALPS.

Juliana Top. See MANDALA.

Ju·li·a·ne·håb \ˌyü-lē-'an-ə-ˌhóp\. Settlement near S end of Greenland; pop. (1968e) 3086; radio station; center for seal hunting.

Jul·ian March \ˌjül-yən-'märch\. The borderland region bet. NW Yugoslavia and NE Italy traversed by Julian Alps and Isonzo river; Trieste and Istrian Penin. lie to the S.

Julia Traducta. See TARIFA.

Jü·lich \'yü-lik\. 1 Region of West Germany bet. Cologne on the Rhine and Aachen (Aix-la-Chapelle); ab. 1600 sq. m.; chief town Jülich; county 11th to 14th cent.; became duchy 1356, associated with duchies of Berg and Cleve 1423–1592; possession contested in 17th cent. by Netherlands and Saxony; held by German counts until 1801; held by France 1801–15; to Prussia 1815.

2 Town, North Rhine-Westphalia, West Germany, on the Rur river 16 m. NE of Aachen; pop. (1968e) 19,649; chief town of county and duchy of Jülich; fortified in 17th cent. and several times captured; largely destroyed in World War II.

Ju·lier, Col du \ˌkól-də-zhül-'yā, ˌkəl-\. Mountain pass, SW of St. Moritz, in Rhaetian Alps, Graubünden canton, E Switzerland; alt. 7491 ft.

Ju·lin \yü-'lēn\. Ancient Wendish trading town on S coast of Wolin I., off coast of Pomerania, Germany, identified with modern Wolin (*q.v.*), since 1945 in NW Poland, and called **Vi·ne·ta** \vi-'nāt-ə\ by the Germans; in 10th and 11th cents. was important center for trade bet. Scandinavia, Saxony, and Russia; Viking fortress of Jomsborg was nearby.

Juliobona. See LILLEBONNE.

Juliobriga. See LOGROÑO 2.

Juliomagus. See ANGERS.

Julische Alpen. See table at ALPS.

Jul·lun·dur \'jəl-ən-dər\ *or* **Ja·lan·dhar** \'jəl-ən-dər\. 1 Division, Punjab, N India; 12,719 sq. m.; pop. (1961c) 9,052,154; ✻ Jullundur.

2 City, its ✻, ab. 46 m. SE of Amritsar; pop. (1967e) 256,611; center of sporting-goods industry; former capital of ancient kingdom of Jullundur (*or* **Tri·gar·ta** \tri-'gärt-ə\); burned by Sikhs 1757 and made part of the Sikh jurisdiction 1811; came under British sovereignty 1846.

Ju·met \zhü-'mā\. Commune, Hainaut prov., SW Belgium, 25 m. S of Brussels; pop. (1969e) 27,977; mining, smelting, glass-manufacturing center.

Jumhūrīyat as–Sūdān ad–Dīmuqratīyah. See SUDAN 2.

Ju·mi·lla \hü-'mē(l)-yə\. Commune, Murcia prov., SE Spain, 38 m. NNW of Murcia; pop. (1970p) 20,103; vineyards, orchards; brandy, soap, oil; 15th cent. church; castle.

Jummoo. See JAMMU.

Jumna. See YAMUNA.

Jump \'jəmp\. River, NW cen. Wisconsin; ab. 100 m. long; rises in Price co., flows SW into Chippewa river in N Chippewa co.

Jump·off \'jəm-ˌpóf\. Mountain, Sevier co., E Tennessee, in Great Smoky Mts; 6100 ft.

Jumporn. See CHUMPHON.

Ju·na·gadh \jü-'näg-əd\ *or* **Ju·na·garh** \-'näg-ər\. 1 Former Indian state, now part of Gujarat state, S cen. Kathiawar, W India; 3337 sq. m.; ruined temple of Somnath; entered into relations with British 1807.

2 Town, its ✻, 240 m. NW of Bombay; pop. (1961c) 74,298; produces gold and silver embroideries and brass- and copperware; located at foot of sacred Girnar Hills (highest 3664 ft.); has an old fort, cave dwellings, temples, and other remains of early Hindu and Muslim times; seat of college of arts.

Jun·cal \hüŋ-'käl\. Peak in Andes Mts. on boundary bet. Chile and Argentina just S of Mt. Aconcagua; 19,877 ft.

Jun·cos \'hüŋ-(ˌ)kōs\. Town and municipality, E Puerto Rico, SE of San Juan; pop. (1970c) 7911 (town), 21,762 (munic.).

Junc·tion \ˌjəŋ(k)-shən\. 1 City, ⊗ of Kimble co., W cen. Texas, on Llano river 113 m. W of Austin; pop. (1970c) 2654; ships livestock, wool, pecans.

2 Town, ⊗ of Piute co., S cen. Utah; pop. (1970c) 135.

Junction City. City, ⊗ of Geary co., NE cen. Kansas, 18 m. SW of Manhattan at junction of Republican and Smoky Hill rivers; pop. (1970c) 19,018; in grain, stock, and dairy farming area.

Junction Peak. Mountain in Sierra Nevada, NE Tulare co., S cen. California; 13,625 ft.

Jun·diaí \ˌzhün-dyə-'ē\. City, SE São Paulo state, SE Brazil; munic. pop. (1968e) 124,368; railroad junction point 25 m. NNW of São Paulo; textiles.

Ju·neau \'jü-(,)nō\. 1 County in Wisconsin. See table at WISCONSIN.

2 Seaport city, ✻ of Alaska, on Gastineau Channel, ab. 90 m. NE of Sitka; pop. (1970c) 13,556; has steamer and air-line connections with Seattle and Vancouver; trading center of mining and lumbering region; salmon-canning industry; plywood mill. Founded 1880; became seat of administration (transferred from Sitka) 1906; continued as capital of organized territory 1912 and of state 1959; municipal boundaries enlarged 1970, making it largest city in area (3108 sq. m.) in U.S.

3 City, ⊗ of Dodge co., SE cen. Wisconsin; pop. (1970c) 2003; cheese, fertilizer; peas.

Jungbunzlau. See MLADÁ BOLESLAV.

Jung·frau \'yůŋ-,fraů\. Peak, SW cen. Switzerland, in Bernese Alps; 13,642 ft.; on border bet. Bern and Valais cantons S of Interlaken which is famous for its view of the Jungfrau.

Ju·ni·ata \,jü-nē-'at-ə\. 1 River, S cen. Pennsylvania; ab. 150 m. long; formed by two branches in Huntingdon co., flows E through Mifflin, Juniata, and Perry cos. into Susquehanna river.

2 County in Pennsylvania. See table at PENNSYLVANIA.

Ju·nín \hü-'nēn\. 1 Town, Buenos Aires prov., E Argentina, on railroad 150 m. W of Buenos Aires; pop. (1960c) 53,489; grain, cattle.

2 *or* **Chin·chay·co·cha** \,chin-chī-'kō-chə\. Lake, Junín dept., cen. Peru; altitude 12,225 ft.; ab. 25 m. long and 8–10 m. wide.

3 Department of cen. Peru. See table at PERU.

4 Town, Junín dept., Peru, 10 m. SE of the S end of Junín lake ab. 100 m. NE of Lima; pop. (1961c) 5000; in wars of independence, scene of a decisive battle Aug. 6, 1824 in which Spaniards under the viceroy La Serna and Gen. Canterac were defeated by Bolívar and Sucre.

Junkseylon. See PHUKET 1.

Ju·pi·ter \'jü-pət-ər\. Town, Palm Beach co., SE Florida, 15 m. N of Palm Beach; pop. (1970c) 3136; tomatoes.

Jupiter, Mount. Peak, Jefferson co., W Washington; 5650 ft.

Jupiter Inlet. Narrow strait leading from Atlantic Ocean through barrier reefs off NE coast of Palm Beach co., SE Florida.

Jupiter Island. Island in Atlantic Ocean, off coast of Martin co., SE Florida.

Jupiter Peak. Mountain, La Plata co., SW Colorado; 13,837 ft.

Ju·qui·la \hü-'kē-lə\. Municipality, Oaxaca state, Mexico, 70 m. SW of Oaxaca; pop. (1970p) 54,831.

Jur \'jů(ə)r\. River, SW Sudan; ab. 300 m. long; flows N and NE in Equatoria prov. to join with the Bahr al-Arab in Upper Nile prov. to form the Bahr al-Ghazal.

Ju·ra \'jůr-ə\. 1 Mountain range extending 143 m. along boundary bet. France and Switzerland; highest peak Crête de la Neige 5652 ft. in Ain dept., France; the W slopes are source of the Doubs and Ain rivers of France.

2 Department of E France. See table at FRANCE.

3 Island of the Inner Hebrides, off W coast of Scotland; 24 m. long; pop. (1961c) 946; nearly cut in two by Loch Tarbert (*q.v.*); in S are the Paps of Jura, highest point 2571 ft.; administratively a part of Argyll co.; fishing, agriculture, granite quarrying.

Jura, Sound of. Body of water off W coast of Scotland bet. island of Jura and Scottish mainland.

Jurjura. See DJURDJURA.

Ju·ruá \,zhůr-(ə-)'wä\. River, NW cen. South America; ab. 900 m. long; navigable length ab. 600 m.; rises in Andes Mts. in E cen. Peru, flows NE and empties into the Solimões, upper course of the Amazon, in NW Brazil.

Ju·rue·na \,zhůr-(ə-)'wā-nə\. River, W cen. Brazil; ab. 600 m. long; flows N in Mato Grosso state, receives the Arinos river from the E; forms part of boundary bet. Mato Grosso and Amazonas states; on border bet. Amazonas and Pará states is joined by the Teles Pires to form the Tapajós.

Ju·ru·pa·ri \,zhůr-ə-pə-'rē\. Small island in mouth of Amazon river, off NE coast of Pará state, Brazil.

Jus·tice \'jəs-təs\. Village, Cook co., NE Illinois, 14 m. SW of Chicago; pop. (1970c) 9473.

Justinianopolis. See KIRŞEHİR 2.

Justinopolis. See KOPER.

Ju·taí *or formerly* **Ju·ta·hy** \,zhüt-ə-'ē\. River, a S tributary of the Amazon in W Amazonas state, NW Brazil; 400 m. long; flows NE and joins the Amazon above the Juruá.

Ju·tia·pa \,hüt-ē-'äp-ə\. 1 Department of SE Guatemala. See table at GUATEMALA.

2 Town, its ✻, 45 m. SE of Guatemala City; munic. pop. (1964p) 43,775; sugarcane, corn, rice.

Ju·ti·cal·pa \,hüt-ə-'käl-pə\. Town, ✻ of Olancho dept., E cen. Honduras, 70 m. NE of Tegucigalpa; pop. (1961c) 7210; agriculture.

Jut·land \'jət-lənd\ *or Dan.* **Jyl·land** \'yü-(,)lan\. Peninsula projecting N from West Germany and extending bet. the North Sea and the Kattegat, comprising Danish mainland and N part of Schleswig-Holstein state, West Germany. Politically the name applies only to the mainland of Denmark; including islands N of Lim Fjord, 11,436 sq. m.; has given its name to major naval battle fought off its W coast in North Sea May 31–June 1, 1916, bet. British and German fleets; although British losses were greater, the battle in its results was a British victory.

Juvavum. See SALZBURG 2.

Ju·vi·sy \,zhü-və-'zē\ *or in full* **Juvisy–sur–Orge** \-sü(ə)r-'ȯ(ə)rzh\. Commune, Essone dept., N France, S of Paris; pop. (1968c) 12,507; important railroad junction; observatory founded by Flammarion 1882.

Jux·tla·hua·ca \,hüs-tlä-'wäk-ə\. Municipality, Oaxaca state, Mexico, 90 m. WNW of Oaxaca; pop. (1970p) 37,095.

Jylland. See JUTLAND.

Jy·väs·ky·lä \'yü-və-,sk(y)ü-lə\. City, ✻ of Keski-Suomi prov., S cen. Finland, at N end of Lake Päijänne; pop. (1970p) 57,148; paper mills; univ. (1966); founded 1837.

K2. See GODWIN AUSTEN.

Ka·a·la \kə-ˈäl-ə\. Peak, Waianae Range, W Oahu I., Hawaii; 4040 ft.; highest peak on Oahu.

Kaapprovinsie. See CAPE PROVINCE.

Kaapstad. See CAPE TOWN.

Kaa·ters·kill Creek \ˌkät-ərz-ˌkil-, ˌkȯt-\. Creek in Catskill Mts., New York; has waterfalls in its upper course; in lower course goes through a steep-sided, narrow ravine, **Kaaterskill Clove** \-ˈklōv\.

Ka·ba·can \ˌkäb-ə-ˈkän\. Municipality, NE cen. Cotabato prov., Mindanao, Phil., N of marsh region on left bank of Pulangi river; pop. (1969e) 28,300; communications center of S Mindanao, taken by American forces from Japanese Apr. 1945.

Ka·ba·e·na \ˌkäb-ə-ˈā-nə\. Island in N part of Flores Sea, off SE coast of Celebes I., Malay Archipelago, Indonesia; part of South-East Sulawesi prov.

Ka·ba·lo \kə-ˈbäl-(ˌ)ō\. Town on Lualaba river (upper Congo), SE Zaire; terminus of railroad running 170 m. to Kalemi on Lake Tanganyika.

Ka·ban·ka·lan \ˌkäb-äŋ-ˈkäl-ən\. Municipality, S Negros Occidental, Negros, Phil., on Ilog river 50 m. S of City of Bacolod; pop. (1969e) 81,100.

Kab·ar·di·no–Bal·kar·i·an Autonomous Soviet Socialist Republic \ˌkab-ər-ˈdē-(ˌ)nō-ˌbȯl-ˈkar-ē-ən-, -ˌbal-, -ˈker-\. Autonomous republic in cen. part of N slopes of Caucasus Mts., SE Russian S.F.S.R., U.S.S.R., bounded on N by Stavropol Krai, on E and SE by North Ossetian A.S.S.R., on S and W by Georgian S.S.R.; 4826 sq. m.; pop. (1970p) 589,000; ✻ Nalchik. Its component areas are **Ka·bar·dia** \kə-ˈbärd-ē-ə\, mainly the N level part, and **Bal·kar·ia** \bȯl-ˈkar-ē-ə, bal-, -ˈker-\, the mountain area in the S. Chief river the Terek with many headstreams, all flowing NE. Chief mountains include some of the highest peaks of the Caucasus, such as Dykh Tau 17,070 ft., Shkhara 17,063 ft., and Koshtan Tau 16,899 ft. Chief occupations agriculture (maize, millet, vegetables, and the vine), raising of horses (in Kabardia), and raising of cattle, sheep, and goats; has extensive forests; tungsten, chromium, and nickel mining; food processing. Area penetrated by Russians early 19th cent.; part of Terek government under the tsars; after the Revolution became part of the Mountain Republic; two areas combined 1922 as one autonomous area; made a republic 1936.

Ka·bin·da \kə-ˈbin-də\. **1** Portuguese territory and seaport, Angola. See CABINDA.

2 Town, Kasai Oriental prov., S Zaire.

Ka·bou·dia, Cape \-kə-ˈbüd-ē-ə\. Cape on E coast of Tunisia.

Ka·bul \ˈkäb-əl, kə-ˈbül\. **1** River, E Afghanistan and Pakistan; 435 m. long; rises on S slopes of Koh-i-Baba range W of Kabul; has several important tributaries including the Kunar from the N and the Swat in Pakistan; passes through gorges of Mohmand Hills N of Khyber Pass to the Indus near Campbellpore, Punjab, Pakistan.

2 A province of E Afghanistan. See table at AFGHANISTAN.

3 City, ✻ of Afghanistan and ✻ of Kabul prov., on Kabul river at W end of its valley; met. area pop. (1970e) 488,844; largest city in Afghanistan; alt. above 1 m.; textiles, leather goods; univ. (1931), technical coll. (1967); commands strategic routes through mountain passes into Pakistan from the W; for centuries has been in path of great invasions of the peninsula—as of Alexander the Great, Mahmud of Ghazni, Genghis Khan, Babur, Nadir Shah, and Ahmad Shah. For two centuries (1526–1738) included in the Muslim empire of Delhi; with Kandahār one of the two capitals under Ahmad Shah (1747–73) and made only capital 1774 under his successor; in First Afghan War occupied 1842 by British, who partially destroyed it; again occupied by Lord Roberts 1879; after 1880 rebuilt and modernized by the emir Abd-er-Rahman Khan; ruler's palace just outside the city.

Ka·bu·ru·ang \ˌkä-bü-ˈrü-ˌäŋ\. See TALAUD ISLANDS.

Kabūshīyah. See MEROË.

Ka·bwe \ˈkäb-ˌwā\ *or formerly* **Bro·ken Hill** \ˌbrō-kən-\. Town, cen. Zambia, on railroad ab. 70 m. N of Lusaka; pop. (1967e) 49,000; mining (lead, zinc, vanadium); nearby was discovered (1921) the Broken Hill skull, a prehistoric human skull (Rhodesian man), proto-Australoid in type.

Ka·by·lia, Great *and* **Little Kabylia** \-kə-ˈbī-lē-ə, -ˈbil-ē-\. Two regions in N Algeria inhabited by Kabyles.

Kach·hi \ˈkäch-ē\ *or* **Kach Gan·da·va** \ˌkäch-gən-ˈdäv-ə\. Arid region, NE Baluchistan, Pakistan, a flat area E of mountains of N Kalat; ab. 5300 sq. m.; outlet is through Jacobabad in Sind.

Ka·chin State \kə-ˈchin-\. State of N Burma. See table at BURMA.

Ka·cza·wa \kä-ˈchä-və\ *or Ger.* **Katz·bach** \ˈkäts-ˌbäk\ *also* **Ko·ca·ba** \kȯt-ˈsä-bə\. River, SW Poland, flowing NE past Lignica into the Oder; scene of battle of Katzbach Aug. 26, 1813 in which one of Napoleon's armies was defeated by Germans under Blücher.

Ka·dan Island \kə-ˈdän-\ *or formerly* **King Island** \ˈkiŋ-\. Island, N Mergui Archipelago (*q.v.*), Burma.

Kadavu. See KANDAVU.

Ka·desh \ˈkā-ˌdesh\. **1** Ancient city in W Syria, on Orontes river ab. 15 m. SW of modern Homs; in early times a kingdom, probably a survival of Hyksos power; seized by the Egyptian king Thutmose III, after Megiddo, c. 1471 B.C.; scene of indecisive battle bet. the Hittites and Ramses II of Egypt 1288 B.C.

2 City, ancient Palestine. See KADESH-BARNEA.

Kadesh–bar·nea \ˌkā-desh-ˈbär-nē-ə\ *or* **Kadesh.** City, ancient Palestine, in the country of the Amalekites SW of the Dead Sea and on W edge of Wilderness of Zin; its location not exactly known; twice scene of encampments of Israelites (*Num. xiii.* 26; *xx.* 1; *xxxiii.* 36).

Kadesia. See KADISIYA.

Ka·dhi·main \ˌkät͟h-ə-ˈmān\ *or* **Al–Kadhimain** \al-\ *or* **Al–Ka·zī·mī·yah** \al-ˌkäz-ə-ˈmē-(y)ə\. City, cen. Iraq, a N suburb of Baghdad; one of the three holy Shiite cities of Iraq.

Ka·di \ˈkəd-ē\. Division of former Baroda state, W India, now in Gujarat state, N of Ahmadabad.

Ka·dı·köy \ˌkäd-i-ˈkȯi\ *or anc.* **Chal·ce·don** \ˈkal-sə-ˌdän, kal-ˈsēd-ᵊn\. City, İstanbul prov., Turkey, a suburb and district of the city of İstanbul, opp. the city on E side of entrance to Bosporus and S of Üsküdar. Ancient Chalcedon founded 685 B.C. by Greeks of Megaris; later a city of Bithynia, then of Pergamum; became Roman 133 B.C.; under Byzantine Empire seat of Fourth Ecumenical Council 451 A.D. which condemned the Eutychian heresy; suffered much in attacks by barbarians, Persians, and Turks.

Ka·di·si·ya \ˌkäd-ə-ˈsē-(y)ə\ *or* **Ka·de·sia** *or Arab.* **al–Qā·di·sī·yah** \ˌal-ˌkäd-ə-ˈsē-(y)ə\. Locality in medieval Persia (now in Iraq), on the Euphrates near Hilla and S of Baghdad; scene of battle 637 A.D. in which the caliph Omar I defeated the Persian forces of Yazdegerd III, last of the Sassanids.

Ka·di·yev·ka \kə-ˈdē-(y)əf-kə\ *or from 1937 to 1943* **Ser·go** \ˈse(ə)r-gə\. Industrial town, W Voroshilovgrad Oblast, E Ukrainian S.S.R., U.S.S.R., 32 m. E of Artemovsk; pop. (1970p) 137,000; metallurgical industries; coal mining.

Ka·do·ka \kə-ˈdōk-ə\. City, ⊗ of Jackson co., SW cen. South Dakota; pop. (1970c) 815; livestock.

Ka·do·ma \kä-ˈdōm-ə\. City, Ōsaka prefecture, Honshū, Japan; pop. (1969e) 124,000.

Ka·du·na \kə-ˈdü-nə\. Town, ✻ of North-Central State, Nigeria, ab. 140 m. SW of Kano; pop. (1969e) 173,849; cotton mills.

Ka·é·di \kä-'äd-ē\. Town, S Mauritania, on Senegal river; pop. (1971e) 13,000.

Ka·e·na Point \kä-ˌā-nə-\. 1 Cape on NW coast of Lanai I., Hawaii.
2 Cape on extreme NW point of Oahu I., Hawaii.

Ka–erh \'kä-'e(ə)r\ *or formerly* **Gar·tok** \'gär-ˌtäk\. Town, SW Tibet, China, on upper Indus at W end of Kailas Range; alt. 15,200 ft.; trading center opened by British 1904.

Kae·sŏng \'kā-ˌsȯŋ\ *or Jap.* **Kai·jo** \'kī-(ˌ)jō\. Town, North Korea; 2072 sq. m.; pop. (1966e) 265,000; has special administrative status.

Kaewieng. See KAVIENG.

Kafa *or* **Kaffa.** See KEFA.

Kaffa. See FEODOSIYA.

Kaf·frar·ia \kə-'frar-ē-ə, ka-, -frer-\. Region of Cape Province, Rep. of South Africa, from Great Kei river on S to Natal on N bet. the Drakensberg Mts. and the coast; inhabited by the Kaffirs, South African natives of Bantu race, who fought serious wars with British 1846–47, 1850–53, and 1877–78; British Kaffraria is the region to the SW bet. the Great Kei and Fish rivers.

Kafirévs. See CAPHAREUS.

Kafiristan. See NURISTAN.

Ka·fir·ni·gan \ˌkäf-ər-ni-'hän, -'gän\. River, a N tributary of the Amu Darya, in SW Tadzhik S.S.R., U.S.S.R.; flows SW near Uzbek border.

Kafr al–Sheikh \ˌkaf-ər-al-'shāk\. Governorate of Egypt. See table at EGYPT.

Ka·fue \kə-'fü-ē\. River, Zambia; ab. 600 m. long; flows in winding course S, W, and E to the Zambezi river.

Kafue National Park. National park, S cen. Zambia; 8650 sq. m.; wide variety of wildlife, incl. antelope, elephant, rhinoceros, zebra; established 1950.

Ka·ga \'kä-gə\. City, Ishikawa prefecture, Honshū, Japan, 30 m. SW of Kanazawa; pop. (1970c) 56,154.

Ka·ga·wa \kä-'gä-wə, 'käg-ə-ˌwä\. Prefecture, Shikoku, Japan; 719 sq. m.; pop. (1970c) 907,897; ✱ Takamatsu; barley, rice, salt.

Ka·ge·ra \kə-'ger-ə\. River, NW Tanzania, E Africa; ab. 429 m. long; flows N, along boundary of Rwanda; turns E along boundary of Uganda and empties into Lake Victoria; known as the longest headstream of the Nile.

Kagera National Park. National park, E Rwanda; 965 sq. m.; antelope, zebra; established 1934.

Kâ·gi·tha·ne \ˌkä-yi-'tän-ā\. Town, İstanbul prov., NW Turkey; pop. (1965c) 55,157.

Ka·go·shi·ma \ˌkäg-ə-'shē-mə, kä-'gō-shə-\. 1 Prefecture, Kyūshū, Japan; 3530 sq. m.; pop. (1970c) 1,729,150; ✱ Kagoshima; forestry; coastal fishing.
2 Seaport city, its ✱, on W coast of **Kagoshima Bay,** a deep inlet on S coast of Kyūshū, Japan; pop. (1970c) 403,340; well-protected harbor; center of manufacture of Satsuma ware; univ. (1949). An ancient place, long the castle city of a powerful daimyo of the Satsuma clan, esp. important at time of Restoration; bombarded by British warships 1863; destroyed by fire 1877; severely damaged by eruption of On-take (on island in bay) 1914; in World War II severely bombed by Allies June–Aug. 1945.

Ka·gul \kə-'gül\ *or Rom.* **Ca·hul** \kä-'hül\. Town, Moldavian S.S.R., U.S.S.R.; pop. (1967e) 20,000; before 1945 in Romania.

Ka·ha·jan \kə-'hä-ˌyän\ *or* **Great Da·yak** \-'dī-ˌak\. River, S Borneo, Indonesia; ab. 225 m. long; rises in E end of Schwaner Mts. and flows S to Java Sea.

Ka·ha·ku·loa Head \kə-ˌhäk-ə-ˌlō-ə-\. Cape on NW coast of Maui I., Hawaii, on W side of Kahului Bay.

Ka·ha·la Point \kə-ˌhäl-ə-\. Cape on NE coast of Kauai I., Hawaii.

Ka·ha·na Bay \kə-ˌhän-ə-\. Bay on NE coast of Oahu I., Hawaii.

Ka·hilt·na Glacier \kə-ˌhilt-nə-\. Glacier in the Alaska Range, S Alaska, just S of Mount McKinley National Park; 47 m. long, ab. 4 m. wide near its terminus.

Kahlamba. See DRAKENSBERG MOUNTAINS.

Kah·len·berg \'käl-ən-ˌbe(ə)rg\. Eminence ab. 5½ m. NW of Vienna, Austria, in the Wienerwald; 1587 ft.

Kahlur. See BILASPUR.

Ka·ho·ka \kə-'hōk-ə\. City, ⊗ of Clark co., NE corner of Missouri, 54 m. NNW of Hannibal; pop. (1970c) 2207; limestone quarry; diversified agriculture.

Ka·ho·o·la·we \kä-ˌhō-ə-'lä-vē, -wē\. Island in S cen. Hawaii, W of S Maui I.; 45 sq. m.; a part of Maui co.

Ka·hu·ku \kä-'hü-kü\. Village, Honolulu co., Hawaii, near **Kahuku Point,** the N point of Oahu I.; pop. (1970c) 917.

Ka·hu·lui \ˌkä-hü-'lü-ē\. City, Maui co., Hawaii, on **Kahului Bay** on N coast of Maui I.; pop. (1970c) 8280.

Kai·a·ka Bay \ˌkī-ə-ˌkä-\. Bay on N coast of Oahu I., Hawaii, at base of Kaena Point.

Kai·a·poi \ˌkī-ə-'pȯi\. Borough, E South I., New Zealand, N of Christchurch at mouth of Waimakariri river; pop. (1970e) 3730.

Kai·bab Plateau \'kī-ˌbab-\. Tableland in N Arizona, on N rim of Grand Canyon (*q.v.*); forests set aside as **Kaibab National Forest.**

Kai Besar. See KAI ISLANDS.

Kai·bi·to Plateau \kī-ˌbēt-ō-\. Tableland in NE Coconino co., N cen. Arizona.

Kaieiewaho. See KAUAI 1.

Kai·e·teur Falls \ˌkī-ə-ˌtu̇(ə)r-\. Waterfall in Potaro river, cen. Guyana; 741 ft. high, ab. 350 ft. wide.

Kaieteur National Park. National park in Pakaraima Mts. on Potaro river, Guyana; 45 sq. m.; savanna; established 1930.

K'ai–feng \'kī-'feŋ\. City, N Honan province, E cen. China, ab. 340 m. NW of Nanking; pop. (1970e) 330,000; in Yellow river valley and often menaced by floods. One of most historic cities of China, an early settlement site and junction point of routes to the east and south; capital of the empire in period of the Five Dynasties (907–960 A.D.) and, as **Pien–ching** \'byen-'jiŋ\, under Northern Sung dynasty (960–1127); site of a Jewish colony which flourished esp. 12th–15th cents., as recorded on an inscription stone still in existence.

Kaiffa. See HAIFA.

Kai Islands *or* **Kei Islands** \'kī-\. Island group of SE Moluccas, Indonesia, Malay Archipelago, SE of Ceram I. and W of Aru Is.; 572 sq. m.; pop. (1957e) 39,660. Comprises **Kai Be·sar** \-be-'sär\ *or* **Great Kai Island,** 290 sq. m., 50 m. long, mountainous (volcanic), **Kai Ke·tjil** \-kā-'chēl\ *or* **Little Kai,** and many small islets scattered over E end of Banda Sea. Inhabitants are skilled boatbuilders.

Kaijo. See KAESŎNG.

Kai·kou·ra Range \kī-ˌkōr-ə-, -ˌkȯr-\. Mountain range in NE South I., New Zealand, N of Clarence river; elev. from 4000 ft. to highest peak Tapuaenuku 9463 ft.

Kai·las \kī-'läs\ *or Chin.* **Kang–ti–ssu** \'käŋ-'tē-'sü\. 1 Mountain range, SW Tibet, China; highest peak Kailas; contains sources of the Indus and Sutlej rivers and headstreams of the Brahmaputra.
2 Peak in cen. part of Kailas range, 31°04′N, 81°19′E, N of Lake Manasarowar and SE of Ka-erh; 22,027 ft.; sacred to Hindus and before 1962 an important pilgrimage resort; famous in Sanskrit literature as Siva's paradise.

Kai·lua \kī-'lü-ə\. 1 City, Honolulu co., Hawaii, on Kailua Bay; pop. (1970c, with Lanikai) 33,783.
2 *or* **Kailua–Ko·na** \-'kō-nə\. Village, Hawaii co., Hawaii, on W coast of Hawaii I. N of Kealakekua; pop. (1970c) 365; residence of early kings of the islands; landing place of first missionaries to Hawaii 1820.

Kailua Bay. Bay on E coast of Oahu I., Hawaii, N of Makapuu Point.

Kai·lu·ka National Park \kī-'lü-kə-\. National park, N Bulgaria, near Pleven (town); ab. 3 sq. m.; river valley; established 1939.

Kai·ma·na \kī-'män-ə\. Town, S coast of Irian Barat, Indonesia, 125 m. SE of Fakfak; important trading post.

Kai·ma·na·wa Mountains \kī-'män-ə-wə-\. Mountain range in cen. North I., New Zealand; highest peak 7534 ft.

Kai·nan \kī-'nän\. City, Wakayama prefecture, Honshū, Japan, 6 m. SE of Wakayama; pop. (1970c) 53,370.

Kai·pa·ra Harbor \ˌkī-p(ə-)rə-\. Inlet of Pacific Ocean on W coast of N extension of North I., New Zealand, forming an excellent harbor.

Kai·ra \'kīr-ə\. Town, SE Gujarat, W India, 20 m. S of Ahmadabad; pop. (1961c) 9641; dates back to 5th cent.

Kair·ouan \ker-'wän\ *or* **Kair·wan** \kī(ə)r-'wän\ *or Arab.* **Qair·wan** \kīr-'wän\. City, NE Tunisia, ab. 32 m. WSW of Sousse; pop. (1966c) 46,199; trades in leather goods and carpets; a Holy City of the Muslims, has several mosques; founded 670 A.D. by the Arab general, Okba, to whom one of the mosques is dedicated; capital of the Aghlabite dynasty 800–909. In World War II occupied by Allies Apr. 1943.

Kais. See QEYS.

Kaisargarh. See TAKHT-I-SULAIMAN 1.

Kaisaria. See KAYSERİ.

Kaiserin Augusta. See SEPIK.

Kai·sers·lau·tern \ˌkī-zərz-'lau̇t-ərn\. Industrial city, Rhineland-Palatinate, West Germany, 43 m. NW of Karlsruhe; pop. (1969e) 99,917; machinery, electrical equipment, textiles, beer, automobiles; first mentioned 882; became city 1276; scene of French victory over Prussians 1793; capital of French department of Donnersberg 1797–1814; passed to Bavaria 1816.

Kai·ser·stuhl \'kī-zər-ˌs(h)tül\. Mountain group, SW Baden-Württemberg, West Germany, NW of Freiburg; highest peak 1827 ft.

Kai·sers·werth \'kī-zərz-ˌve(ə)rt\. Former town, West Germany, 6 m. below Düsseldorf on Rhine river; since 1929 a part of Düsseldorf; grew up around a Benedictine monastery built 710; scene of activities of Theodor Fliedner, who became pastor here 1821 and opened refuge for discharged female convicts 1833 and later several other charitable institutions.

Kaiser Wilhelm Canal. See NORD-OSTSEE KANAL.

Kaiser Wilhelm II Land. See WILHELM II COAST.

Kaiser–Wilhelmsland. See NORTH-EAST NEW GUINEA.

Kaishu. See HAEJU.

Kai·thal \'kīt-ᵊl\. Town, Haryana state, NW India, 90 m. NNW of Delhi; pop. (1961c) 34,890; an old town; connected with Hindu legends, esp. with the monkey god Hanuman. Held by Sikhs 1767 to 1843 when it became British.

Kai·wi \'kī-wē\. Channel bet. Oahu I. and Molokai I., Hawaii; 23 m. wide.

K'ai–yüan \'kī-yu̇-'än\. Town, E Liaoning prov., China, ab. halfway bet. Mukden and Ch'ang-ch'un; consists of walled town and new town around railroad station; distribution center for soybeans.

Kai·zu·ka \kī-'zü-kə\. City, Ōsaka prefecture, Honshū, Japan, 20 m. SW of Ōsaka; pop. (1970c) 73,366.

Ka·jaa·ni \'kä-ˌyän-ē\. City, Oulu prov., cen. Finland; pop. (1970e) 19,677; on rapids just SE of Oulujärvi; trade and transportation center; sawmills, paper mills; manufactures cellulose; founded 1651.

Ka·jan \'kä-ˌyän\. River, E Borneo, Indonesia; ab. 250 m. long; rises in mountains of N cen. Borneo and flows E to Celebes Sea.

Ka·jang \'kä-ˌyäŋ\. Town, E cen. Selangor, Malaysia, on W coast railroad line 10 m. S of Kuala Lumpur; center for rubber plantations.

Ka·je·li \kä-'yā-lē\. Village on bay on E coast of Buru I., Moluccas, Indonesia.

Ka·kam·bo·na \ˌkä-kəm-'bōn-ə\ *also* **Ko·kum·bo·na** \ˌkō-\. Coastal village, NW Guadalcanal I., SE Solomon Is., W Pacific Ocean, W of the Mataniko river; scene of severe fighting Aug. and Oct. 1942; not captured by Americans until Jan. 25, 1943.

Ka·ka·me·ga \ˌkäk-ə-'meg-ə\. Town, ✱ of Western province, W Kenya; pop. (1962c) 3939.

Ka·ke·ga·wa \ˌkäk-ə-'gä-wə, kä-'keg-ə-ˌwä\. City, Shizuoka prefecture, Honshū, Japan, 18 m. E of Hamamatsu; pop. (1970c) 59,153.

Ka·ki·na·da *or formerly* **Coc·a·na·da** \ˌkäk-ə-'näd-ə\. City, NE Andhra Pradesh, E India, on Bay of Bengal at N side of Godavari delta, 300 m. NNE of Madras; pop. (1970e) 149,146; harbor facilities maintained with difficulty because of alluvial soil; chief exports rice, cotton, oil seeds.

Käkisalmi. See PRIOZERSK.

Ka·ko·ga·wa \ˌkäk-ə-'gä-wə\. City, Hyōgo prefecture, Honshū, Japan; pop. (1970c) 127,112.

Kala, El. See EL KALA.

Kalaat Saman. See QAL 'AT SAMAN.

Ka·la·ba·hi \ˌkäl-ə-'bä-(ˌ)hē\. Chief town on Alor I., Lesser Sunda Is., Indonesia, at head of **Kalabahi Bay** at W end of island; excellent anchorage.

Ka·lach–na–Do·nu \kə-ˌläch-nə-'dō-nü\. Town, W cen. Volgograd Oblast, SE Russian S.F.S.R., U.S.S.R., on E bank of the Don at its nearest point to the Volga; pop. (1967e) 21,000; head of navigation of the Don and W terminus of Volga-Don canal; an important bridgehead in World War II with heavy fighting in July and Nov. 1942.

Ka·la·dan \ˌkəl-ə-'dən\. River, NE India and W Burma; ab. 300 m. long; flows S from Chin Hills to Bay of Bengal at Sittwe, Burma; known as **Boi·nu** \'boi-(ˌ)nü\ river in its upper course; one upper tributary rises in the Lushai Hills in Mizoram, India; its valley scene of much fighting 1943–44.

Ka Lae \kä-'lä-ä\ *or* **South Cape** *or* **South Point.** Cape on S extremity of Hawaii I.; missile-tracking station.

Kalaeloa Point. See BARBERS POINT.

Ka·la·han·di \ˌkäl-ə-'hän-dē\ *or formerly* **Ka·rond** \kə-'rönd\. Former Indian state, NE India, now part of Kalahandi district, Orissa state; 3559 sq. m.; dist. pop. (1961c) 14,300; ✱ Bhawanipatna.

Ka·la·ha·ri Desert \ˌkal-ə-ˌhär-ē-\. Plateau and partly desert region, Botswana, W cen. Rep. of South Africa, and part of South-West Africa, N of the Orange river and S of Lake Ngami; area exceeds 100,000 sq. m.; S portion traversed by dry river beds, as the Molopo and the Kuruman; average elevation ab. 3000 ft.; vegetation mostly grass, dense scrub in W and N; big game; first crossed by David Livingstone and William C. Oswell 1849; **Kalahari Gems·bok National Park** \-'gemz-ˌbäk-\ in SW part.

K'a–la–k'a–shih \'kä-'lä-'kä-'shē\ *or* **Qa·ra Qash** *or* **Ka·ra·kash** \ˌkär-ə-'käsh\. River, SW Sinkiang Uighur, W China; rises in Karakoram range on Kashmir border, flows N and NE through E end of Kunlun Mts. to join the Ho-t'ien below Khotan city.

K'a–la–k'un–lun Shan K'ou. See KARAKORAM PASS.

Kalámai. See KALAMATA.

Kalamas. See THÍAMIS.

Kal·a·ma·ta \ˌkal-ə-'mät-ə\ *or* **Ka·lá·mai** \kə-'läm-ē\. Commercial seaport city, ✱ of Messenia dept., SW Peloponnesus, S Greece, at head of Gulf of Messenia; pop. (1971p) 39,346; nearby is site of ancient Pharae; sacked by Ibrahim Pasha 1825.

Kalamata, Gulf of. See MESSENIA, GULF OF.

Kal·a·ma·zoo \ˌkal-ə-mə-'zü\. 1 River, SW Michigan; 200 m. long; rises in Hillsdale co., flows N, then W into Lake Michigan in Allegan co.

2 County in Michigan. See table at MICHIGAN.

3 City, its ⊗, 47 m. S of Grand Rapids; pop. (1970c) 85,555; manufactures paper, drugs, musical instruments, gas heaters, machine tools, clothing; Kalamazoo Coll. (1833), Nazareth Coll. (1897), Western Michigan Univ. (1903), Kalamazoo Valley Community Coll. (1966); first settlement 1829; incorporated as city 1884.

Ka·lam·bo Falls \kə-ˌläm-bō-\. Falls in short river flowing into S part of Lake Tanganyika, on Tanzania-Zambia border; 726 ft. high.

Ka·lan \kə-ˈlän\. Town, ✻ of Tunceli prov., E cen. Turkey; pop. (1965c) 5825.

Ka·lat *or* **Khe·lat** *also* **Ke·lat** \kə-ˈlät\. 1 Former Indian state, now part of Baluchistan, Pakistan; 72,503 sq. m.; has rugged and barren mountains, but also wide, fertile valleys; in 1947 remained independent of newly formed Pakistan but joined the new state 1948.

2 Walled town with citadel, its ✻; 88 m. SSW of Quetta; pop. (1961c) 5321; altitude 6780 ft.; occupied by British 1839; made site of British garrison 1854.

Ka·la·u·pa·pa \kə-ˌlä-ü-ˈpäp-ə\. Village and leper settlement, Kalawao div., Maui co., Hawaii, on N coast of Molokai I. on Kalaupapa Penin.; leper settlement one of best equipped in the world, covering 8575.8 acres. See KALAWAO.

Kalaupapa Peninsula *also* **Ma·ka·na·lua Peninsula** \mə-ˌkän-ᵊl-ˈü-ə-\. Promontory in center of N coast of Molokai I., Hawaii, in Kalawao div. (*q.v.*).

Ka·la·wao \ˌkäl-ə-ˈwau̇\. 1 Division, Maui co., N Molokai I., Hawaii; 14 sq. m.; called **Kalawao County** but area consists only of the Kalaupapa leper settlement and has no local government; represented in state legislature as part of Maui county.

2 Village, N Molokai, site of original leper settlement, where Father Damien began his work 1873.

Kal·bar·ri National Park \kal-ˈbär-ē-\. National park, Western Australia; 560 sq. m.; rocky gorges; established 1963.

Ka·le·mi \kə-ˈlā-mē\ *or formerly* **Al·bert·ville** \ˌal-ber-ˈvē(ə)l, ˈal-bərt-ˌvil\. Port, Shaba prov., Zaire, on W shore of Lake Tanganyika; pop. (1967e) 86,687.

Kale Sultanie. See ÇANAKKALE 2.

Ka·le·wa \kä-ˈlā-wə\. Town, W Upper Burma, on Chindwin river 150 m. NW of Mandalay; scene of fighting in World War II Japanese campaign against India; taken by Allies Dec. 2, 1944.

Kal·gan \ˈkal-ˈgan\ *also* **Ch'ang–chia–k'ou** \ˈjäŋ-jē-ˈä-ˈkō\ *or formerly* **Wan–ch'uan** \ˈwän-chü-ˈän\. City, Hopeh prov., N China; pop. (1970e) 1,000,000; textiles; under Ming and Manchu dynasties was a city of military and commercial importance; occupied by Japanese 1937–1945; taken over by Communist forces Dec. 1948.

Kal·goor·lie \kal-ˈgu̇(ə)r-lē\. Municipality, S Western Australia, 335 m. ENE of Perth; pop. (1968e) 9400; in mining area; Western Australia School of Mines; gold discovered in region 1887–88, nickel 1966.

Kalhu. See CALAH.

Ka·li \ˈkäl-ē\. Upper course of Sarda river (*q.v.*), N India.

Ka·lia·kra, Cape *also* **Cape Ca·lia·cra** \-käl-ˈyäk-rə\. Cape, NE Bulgaria, on the Black Sea, 43°21′N, 28°27′E.

Kalian Point. See CALIAN POINT.

Kali Bay \ˌkäl-ē-\. Inlet, W end of Manus I., Admiralty Is., W Pacific Ocean.

Ka·li·bo \kə-ˈlē-(ˌ)bō\ *or formerly* **Ca·li·vo** \-(ˌ)vō\. Municipality, ✻ of Aklan prov., N Panay, Phil., near coast 28 m. WNW of Roxas; pop. (1969e) 29,000.

Kalimantan. See BORNEO.

Ka·li·man·tan, Central \-ˌkal-ə-ˈman-ˌtan, -ˌkäl-ə-ˈmän-ˌtän\ *or* **Central Borneo** \-ˈbȯr-nē-ˌō\. Indonesian province on island of Borneo; 60,445 sq. m.; pop. (1970e) 626,000; ✻ Palangkaraja; mountainous in N; rivers include the Barito and Kahajan.

Kalimantan, East *or* **East Borneo.** Indonesian province on island of Borneo; 78,231 sq. m.; pop. (1970e) 695,000; ✻ Samarinda; mountainous in W; chief river Mahakam; produces oil.

Kalimantan, South *or* **South Borneo.** Indonesian province on island of Borneo; 13,144 sq. m.; pop. (1970e) 1,857,000; ✻ Bandjarmasin.

Kalimantan, West *or* **West Borneo.** Indonesian province on island of Borneo; 60,643 sq. m.; pop. (1970e) 1,994,000; ✻ Pontianak; mountainous in N and NE; chief river the Kapuas.

Kali Mas \ˌkäl-ē-ˈmäs\. River, E Java, Indonesia; ab. 35 m. long; leaves the Brantas river (*q.v.*) near Modjokerto and flows NE and N through city of Surabaja to Surabaja Strait; a branch of the Brantas.

Ka·lim·pong \ˈkäl-im-ˌpȯŋ\. Town, N West Bengal, NE India, ab. 8 m. ENE of Darjeeling; pop. (1961c) 25,100; alt. 3933 ft.; hill sanatorium.

Ka·lin·ga–Apa·yao \kä-ˈliŋ-gə-ə-ˈpä-ˌyau̇\. Province, N Luzon, Phil.; 2721 sq. m.; pop. (1970p) 143,850; ✻ Tabuk; S part incl. valley of Chico river; W and SW mountainous, with peaks ranging from 5000 to 8400 ft.; has forests and much grass area; not well suited to agriculture but raises some rice, corn, and sweet potatoes.

Ka·li·nin \kə-ˈlē-nən\ *or before 1932* **Tver** \tə-ˈve(ə)r\. City, ✻ of Kalinin Oblast, Russian S.F.S.R., U.S.S.R., 100 m. NW of Moscow, on both banks of the Volga; pop. (1970p) 345,000; on Moscow-Leningrad railroad; machinery, rolling stock, textiles, rubber.

History: An old city, begun c. 1180 as a fort in W part of Suzdal principality; for two centuries capital of Tver principality; long a rival of Moscow for supremacy in Russia, but annexed to it 1485 under Ivan III; suffered 1570 a great massacre of its citizens under Ivan the Terrible; briefly occupied by Germans in autumn of 1941.

Ka·li·nin·grad \kə-ˈlē-nən-ˌgrad\ *or Ger.* **Kö·nigs·berg** \ˈkā-nigz-ˌberg, ˈkə(r)n-igz-, -ˌbe(ə)rg, -ˌbe(ə)rk\. 1 Industrial and commercial seaport, ✻ of Kaliningrad Oblast, Russian S.F.S.R., U.S.S.R., on Pregolya river near the Vislinski Zaliv 80 m. ENE of Gdánsk, Poland; pop. (1970p) 297,000; connected with Gulf of Danzig by ship canal; paper, rolling stock, machinery, electrical equipment, chemicals; naval base; base for fishing fleet; 14th cent. Gothic cathedral, palace, 17th cent. citadel; university (1544; destroyed in World War II); birthplace of Immanuel Kant. Founded 1255; joined Hanseatic League 1340; fortified 1626; in World War I invested by Russians 1914; in World War II occupied by Soviet armies Apr. 9, 1945 after long siege, assigned to U.S.S.R. by Potsdam Conference 1945; named Kaliningrad by U.S.S.R. 1946.

2 Town, Moscow Oblast, Russian S.F.S.R., U.S.S.R., ab. 15 m. NNE of Moscow; pop. (1970p) 106,000; lumber.

Kaliningrad Oblast \-ˈō-bləst, -ˌblast\. Subdivision of the Russian S.F.S.R., U.S.S.R., comprising the area around Kaliningrad (see KALININGRAD 1); 5830 sq. m.; pop. (1970p) 732,000; ✻ Kaliningrad; includes cities of Sovetsk (Tilsit) and Chernyakhovsk (Insterburg); smallest oblast in the U.S.S.R.

Kalinin Oblast \-ˈō-bləst, -blast\. Subdivision of the Russian S.F.S.R., U.S.S.R., hilly country at source of Volga; 32,471 sq. m.; pop. (1970p) 1,718,000; ✻ Kalinin; well drained by the upper Volga and its tributaries, esp. the Mologa; crossed by canal system connecting the Baltic with the Volga; has some agriculture (esp. grain) and dairying; textiles; light engineering; chief cities Kalinin, Vyshni Volochek, and Rzhev.

Kalininsk. See PETROZAVODSK.

Kal·i·spell \ˈkal-ə-ˌspel, ˌkal-ə-ˈ\. City, ⊗ of Flathead co., NW Montana, 8 m. NW of N end of Flathead Lake; pop. (1970c) 10,256; lumber mill, aluminum plant; market center, tourist resort.

Ka·lisz \ˈkäl-ēsh\ *or Ger.* **Ka·lisch** \ˈkäl-ish\. Commune, Poznań prov. W cen. Poland, on Prosna river ab. 65 m. SE of Poznań; pop. (1970p) 81,200; railroad junction; manufactures textiles and leather products.

History: Mentioned by Ptolemy 2d cent. A.D.; received town rights 1282; scene of Swedish defeat by combined army of Russians and Poles 1706; place where Prussia and Russia formed coalition against Napoleon Feb. 28, 1813; occupied by Germans Aug. 1914 and greater part destroyed; again under Germans in World War II.

Ka·li·wun·gu *or Du.* **Ka·li·woen·goe** \ˌkäl-ə-ˈwüŋ-(ˌ)gü\. Town, Central Java prov., Indonesia, just W of Semarang.

Ka·lix \ˈkäl-iks\. River, N Sweden; 267 m. long; flows SE and S into head of Gulf of Bothnia; many rapids.

Kal·ka \ˈkal-kə\ *or mod.* **Kal·mi·us** \ˈkal-mē-əs\. Short river, SE Ukrainian S.S.R., U.S.S.R., flows S into the Gulf of Taganrog; scene of victory of the Mongols over Russians 1223.

Kalka \ˈkäl-kə, ˈkal-\. Village, on border bet. Haryana and Himachal Pradesh, NW India; pop. (1961c) 18,100; border station on railroad from Ambala to Simla.

Kalkandelen. See TETOVO.

Kal·kas·ka \kal-ˈkas-kə\. 1 County in Michigan. See table at MICHIGAN.

2 Village, ⊗ of Kalkaska co., N Michigan; pop. (1970c) 1475.

Kal·la·ve·si \ˈkal-ə-ˌves-ē\. Lake in S cen. Finland, 100 m. E of Vaasa; W shore site of city of Kuopio.

Kal·li·théa *or* **Cal·li·thea** \ˌkäl-ə-ˈthā-ə\. Commune, Greece, S suburb of Athens; pop. (1961e) 54,720.

Kal·lo·ní, Gulf of \-ˌkäl-ə-ˈnē\ *or Gk.* **Kól·pos Kal·lo·nís** \ˌkȯl-pȯs-ˌkäl-ə-ˈnēs\. Long inlet of Aegean Sea in S Lesbos I., Aegean Is., widening out in center of island; town of **Kalloní** lies at head of it.

Kal·mar *also* **Cal·mar** \ˈkäl-ˌmär, ˈkal-\. 1 County of SE Sweden. See table at SWEDEN.

2 Seaport, its ⊗, on Kalmarsund opp. Öland I.; pop. (1970e) 38,912; shipbuilding yards; machinery, matches, railroad cars; ships timber; tourism; place where Union of Kalmar was formed 1397, uniting Denmark, Sweden, and Norway into a single monarchy (1397–1523).

Kal·mar·sund \ˈkal-mər-ˌsənd\. Body of water separating Öland I. in Baltic Sea from Swedish mainland.

Kalmius. See KALKA.

Kal·myk Autonomous Soviet Socialist Republic \(ˌ)kal-ˌmik-\ *also* **Kal·myk·ia** \kal-ˈmik-ē-ə\. Autonomous republic, SE Russian S.F.S.R., U.S.S.R., on NW shore of Caspian Sea and W of lower Volga; 29,305 sq. m.; pop. (1970p) 268,000; ✱ Elista; largely steppe land, dry desert with hills along W border; no railroad except from Astrakhan S along the Caspian shore; chief occupations livestock raising and fishing (at Volga mouth).

History: Region settled early 17th cent. by Kalmucks, or Kalmyks, a nomadic, Buddhist people, western Mongols from cen. China, who became subject to Russia 1646 and later furnished fighting men for some of Peter the Great's armies; its present inhabitants descended from the western Kalmucks who were left behind when 300,000 of their people, fearing oppression, suddenly left Jan. 5, 1771 to return to China, undertaking a journey of great privations (see De Quincey's *The Revolt of the Tartars*) from both cold and heat and from attacks by Kirghiz and Bashkirs, barely a third of their number reaching the destination; suffered heavily during civil war and famine after the Revolution 1917; established as an autonomous oblast 1920; made a republic 1935; after recapture of Volgograd (formerly Stalingrad) by Russians 1943, republic liquidated and its territory partitioned among Stavropol Krai, Volgograd and Rostov oblasts, and the newly formed Astrakhan Oblast, which received most of it; reestablished as an autonomous oblast within Stavropol Krai 1957, regaining status of autonomous republic 1958.

Ka·lo·csa \ˈkäl-ə-(ˌ)chä\. City, S Hungary, near Danube river 70 m. S of Budapest; pop. (1970p) 16,004; in an agricultural region; archbishopric, founded c. 1135; cathedral; frequently attacked by Turks in 16th cent.

Ka·lo·hi \kə-ˈlō-(h)ē\. Channel bet. Molokai I. on N and Lanai I. on S, Hawaii; ab. 9 m. wide.

Kal·pi \ˈkäl-pē\. Town, SW Uttar Pradesh, N India, on Yamuna river 45 m. SW of Kanpur; pop. (1961c) 17,300; founded 4th cent. A.D.; important in early wars; captured by British 1803; scene of Sir Hugh Rose's defeat of rebels of Jhansi 1858.

Ka·lu·ga \kə-ˈlü-gə\. City, E Kaluga Oblast, Russian S.F.S.R., U.S.S.R., ab. 90 m. SW of Moscow; pop. (1970p) 211,000; on left bank of Oka river and on several railroad lines; smelting works, sawmills; manufactures machinery, railroad equipment. Dates back to 14th cent.; included in Moscow principality 1518; in early 17th cent. devastated by Cossacks, plague, and fire; in World War II held by Germans winter 1941.

Kaluga Oblast \-ˈȯ-bləst, -ˌblast\. Subdivision of the Russian S.F.S.R., U.S.S.R., in black earth area N of the Ukrainian S.S.R.; 11,544 sq. m.; pop. (1970p) 995,000; ✱ Kaluga; crossed by Oka river; flax, potatoes; livestock; iron ore; region formerly part of Tula Oblast; estab. 1944.

Ka·lush \ˌkə-ˈlu̇sh\ *or Pol.* **Ka·łusz** \ˈkä-(ˌ)lüsh\. Town, Ivano-Frankovsk Oblast, SW Ukrainian S.S.R., U.S.S.R., on a tributary of the Dniester 18 m. WNW of Ivano-Frankovsk (formerly in Poland); pop. (1967e) 34,000; potassium and salt mines; manufactures beer, liquors, leather; scene of battles bet. Russians and Germans July 1917.

Ka·lu·ta·ra \ˌkäl-ə-ˈtär-ə\. Town, SW Western province, Ceylon, on Indian Ocean 26 m. S of Colombo; pop. (1968e) 27,000.

Kaluwawa. See FERGUSSON.

Kal·yan \kəl-ˈyän\. Town, W Maharashtra, W India, 33 m. NE of Bombay; pop. (1961c) 73,500; important railroad junction point; silk, nylon, bricks and tiles; a commercial center in 17th cent.

Kal·ya·ni \kəl-ˈyä-nē\. Town, N Mysore state, India, ab. 40 m. N of Gulbarga; pop. (1961c) 17,600; formerly (10th to 12th cent.) seat of powerful Chalukya dynasty.

Ka·lym·nos \ˈkäl-əm-ˌnȯs\; *Ital.* **Ca·li·no** \kə-ˈlē-(ˌ)nō\ *or* **Ca·lim·no** \kə-ˈlēm-(ˌ)nō\; *anc.* **Ca·lym·na** \kə-ˈlim-nə\ *or* **Ca·lym·nos** \kə-ˈlim-nəs\. 1 An island of the Dodecanese (*q.v.*), off end of Bodrum Penin. N of Kos I.; 49 sq. m.

2 *or* **Po·thea** \pȯ-ˈthē-ə\. Town, its ✱, on the S coast.

Kalyub. See QALYUB.

Kalyubīya. See QALYUBĪYA.

Ka·ma \ˈkäm-ə\. River in E Russian S.F.S.R., U.S.S.R.; 1261 m. long; drainage basin 201,544 sq. m.; rises in N border of Udmurt A.S.S.R., flows N in Kirov Oblast, then E and S in Perm Oblast along W slope of Middle Urals, then S in SE Udmurt A.S.S.R. and WSW in Tatar A.S.S.R. to the Volga ab. 40 m. below Kazan; largest tributary of the Volga; navigable for ab. 1000 m.; important part of Soviet water transportation system; chief tributaries Belaya, Vyatka, and Chusovaya.

Ka·mai·ki Point \kə-ˌmī-kē-\. Cape on SE coast of Lanai I., Hawaii.

Ka·maing \ˈkäm-ˌīŋ\. Town, N Burma, 20 m. NW of Mogaung; taken by Chinese June 18, 1944.

Ka·ma·i·shi \kə-ˈmī-shē\. Town, Iwate prefecture, N Honshū, Japan; pop. (1970c) 72,923; site of large ironworks largely destroyed in July 1945.

Ka·ma·kou \ˌkäm-ə-ˈkō\. Mountain, E Molokai I., Hawaii; 4970 ft.

Ka·ma·ku·ra \ˌkäm-ə-ˈku̇r-ə, ˌkam-\. Town, Kanagawa prefecture, SE Honshū, Japan, on Sagami Sea ab. 10 m. S of Yokohama; pop. (1970c) 139,249; railroad junction and residential area; Museum of National Treasures, Museum of Modern Art.

History: Historically one of most important towns of Japan; probably founded in 7th cent. A.D.; selected by Minamoto Yoritomo as his residence and on his assumption of the shogunate 1192 became seat of government of Japan to remain so until downfall of Hojo rulers 1333 when it was nearly destroyed; during Minamoto shogunate perhaps had population of 800,000 to 1,000,000; with rise of Tokyo to power 1603 declined to a fishing village. Since the Restoration 1868 has become a favorite resort; site of

Daibutsu, the great bronze image of Buddha, cast in 1252, 50 ft. in height and 96 ft. in circumference; has a shrine of Hachiman (founded 1063) and several temples.

Ka·ma·ran *or* **Qa·ma·ran** \ˌkam-ə-ˈrän\. Island in S Red Sea, off coast of Yemen (✱ San'a), 45 m. N of Hodeida, SW Asia; 70 sq. m.; pop. (1965e) 1000; fishing; formerly administered as part of British colony of Aden; since 1967 part of Yemen (✱ Aden).

Kamar Bay. See QAMR BAY.

Ka·mar·ha·ti \ˌkäm-ər-ˈhät-ē\. Town, West Bengal, NE India, on left bank of Hooghly river 12 m. N of Calcutta; pop. (1970e) 198,523.

Kambaeng Petch. See KAMPHAENG PHET.

Kam·bo·dja \käm-ˈbō-jə\. Town on coast of South Vietnam, S of Saigon; former capital of Khmer kingdom of Cambodia (*q.v.*); founded c. 435 A.D.

Kambryk. See CAMBRAI.

Kam·chat·ka \kam-ˈchat-kə\. 1 Peninsula, NE Russian S.F.S.R., U.S.S.R.; 750 m. long, extending S bet. Sea of Okhotsk and Bering Sea to a point (Cape Lopatka) 7 m. from Shumshu, northernmost of Kuril Is.; 104,260 sq. m., width varies from 80 to 300 m.; constitutes major portion of Kamchatka Oblast, within which is Koryak National Okrug; chief occupations hunting of fur-bearing animals and fishing; timber. Its mountain system, the **Kamchatka Mountains,** consists of two main ranges: the Eastern Range, the shorter, along E coast, having many high volcanic peaks, including Klyuchevskaya Sopka 15,584 ft., highest in Siberia; the Central Range extending length of the peninsula, average height 3000 ft. First visited by Russians 1696; explored in 18th cent.; developed slowly since 1850.

2 Chief river of the peninsula; 478 m. long; rises in Central Range, flows N and E to Bering Sea.

Kamchatka Oblast \-ˈó-bləst, -ˌblast\. A subdivision of the Russian S.F.S.R., U.S.S.R.; 182,355 sq. m.; pop. (1970p) 287,000; approx. coterminous with the peninsula (see KAMCHATKA 1); established 1956.

Kam·chi·ya \ˈkäm-chē-ˌ(y)ä\. River in E Bulgaria; ab. 110 m. long; flows E into Black Sea S of Varna.

Ka·men \ˈkäm-ən\. 1 Industrial city, North Rhine-Westphalia, West Germany, 9 m. NE of Dortmund; pop. (1969e) 41,049; coal mining, metalworking; electrical and optical equipment; received civic rights mid-13th cent.

2 City, U.S.S.R. See KAMEN-NA-OBI.

Ka·me·nets–Po·dol·ski \ˌkäm-ə-ˌnets-pə-ˈdól-skē\. City, Ukrainian S.S.R., U.S.S.R.; on a bluff on a small tributary of the Dniester 12 m. N of Khotin; pop. (1969e) 56,000; textiles, machinery.

History: First mentioned 1196; destroyed by Mongols 1240; a major church city with cathedrals and monasteries dating from 14th cent.; became chief town of Podolia 1434; suffered much in 15th and 16th cents. from invasions of Tatars, Moldavians, and Turks; came under Turks 1672, restored to Poland 1699, and annexed to Russia 1795. In World War II held by Germans July 1941 to Mar. 1944.

Ka·me·nic·ký Še·nov \ˌkäm-ə-ˌnit-skē-ˈshen-ˌóf\ *or Ger.* **Stein·schö·nau** \s(h)tīn-ˈshər-ˌnaů\. Commune, N Czech S.R., W Czechoslovakia, E of the Labe (Elbe) and ab. 20 m. NE of Litoměřice; makes crystal glass.

Ka·me·njak, Cape \-ˈkäm-ən-ˌyäk\ *or Ital.* **Cape Pro·mon·to·re** \-ˌprō-mən-ˈtór-ē\. Southern tip of Istria Penin., NW Yugoslavia.

Ka·men–na–Obi \ˌkäm-ən-nə-ˈōb-ē\ *or formerly* **Kamen.** Town, Altai Krai, Russian S.F.S.R., U.S.S.R., on Ob river, ab. 110 m. SW of Novosibirsk.

Kamenskoye. See DNEPRODZERZHINSK.

Ka·mensk Shakh·tin·ski \ˈkäm-ən(t)sk-shäk-ˈtin(t)-skē\ *or formerly* **Kamensk.** Town, W Rostov Oblast, Russian S.F.S.R., U.S.S.R., on Donets river; pop. (1969e) 73,000; coal mines; machinery, synthetic textiles; on trunk railroad line; in World War II within German lines July 1942–Feb. 1943.

Kamensk–Ural·ski \-ů-ˈral-skē\ *or formerly* **Kamensk.** Town, N Sverdlovsk Oblast, Russian S.F.S.R., U.S.S.R., ab. 50 m. SE of Sverdlovsk; pop. (1970p) 169,000; aluminum, rolled steel, electrical equipment.

Ka·menz \ˈkäm-ˌen(t)s\. City, Dresden dist., East Germany, on the Schwarze Elster river 17 m. WNW of Bautzen; pop. (1970e) 16,653; manufactures ceramics, glass, machinery; birthplace of Lessing; founded c. 1200.

Kamerun. See CAMEROONS.

Ka·met \ˈkəm-āt\. Peak in the Himalayas, Uttar Pradesh, N India, on India-China border; 25,447 ft.; ascended June 1931, at that time the highest peak ever climbed.

Ka·mien·na Gó·ra \kä-ˌm(y)en-ə-ˈgůr-ə\; *Ger.* **Lan·des·hut** \ˈlän-dəs-ˌhüt\ *also* **Landeshut in Schle·si·en** \-in-ˈshlā-zē-ən\. City, S Wrocław prov., SW Poland, on Bóbr river 52 m. WSW of Wrocław; pop. (1970p) 21,100; manufactures textiles, shoes. Scene of Prussian victory over Austrians 1745 and of Austrian victory over Prussians 1760; assigned to Poland by Potsdam Conference 1945.

Ka·mi·na \kə-ˈmēn-ə\. Town, Shaba prov., Zaire, 190 m. NW of Likasi; pop. (1967e) 114,804.

Ka·mi·ri \kə-ˈmir-ē\. See NUMFOOR.

Kam·loops \ˈkam-ˌlüps\. City, S British Columbia, Canada, at confluence of N and S branches of Thompson river 160 m. NE of Vancouver; pop. (1971p) 25,599; railroad divisional point; center of supply for large mining (gold and copper) and lumbering region; fruit canneries; resort area; founded 1810 as Fort Thompson.

Kammer, Lake. See ATTER, LAKE.

Kammersee. See ATTER, LAKE.

Kam·ou·ras·ka \ˌkam-ů-ˈras-kə\. County, Quebec, Canada. See table at QUEBEC.

Kam·pa·la \käm-ˈpäl-ə\. City, ✱ of Uganda, E Africa, 21 m. NNE of Entebbe; pop. (1969p) 331,889; textiles; food processing; univ. (1963).

Kam·par \ˈkäm-ˌpär\. 1 Town, S cen. Perak state, Malaysia, 20 m. SE of Ipoh; pop. (1957c) 24,602; on E coast trunk line railroad in Kinta Valley tin region.

2 River, cen. Sumatra, Indonesia; ab. 200 m. long; rises in Barisan Mts. N of Bukittingi, flows E into S end of Strait of Malacca.

Kam·pen \ˈkäm-pən\. Commercial commune, Overijssel prov., E Netherlands, on IJssel river; pop. (1970e) 28,902; formerly a member of Hanseatic League; town hall; church of St. Nicholas.

Kam·phaeng Phet *or* **Kam·baeng Petch** \käm-ˌpaŋ-ˈpet\. 1 Province, W Thailand; 3457 sq. m.; pop. (1960c) 173,346. 2 Town, its ✱, on left bank of Ping river 65 m. NW of Nakhon Sawan; pop. (1960c) 7137.

Kam·pi·nos National Park \ˈkäm-pə-ˌnós-\. National park, Poland, near Warsaw; 84 sq. m.; prehistoric dwellings; established 1959.

Kamp–Lint·fort \kämp-ˈlint-fərt, (ˌ)fórt\ *or formerly* **Lintfort.** Commune, North Rhine-Westphalia, West Germany, WNW of Oberhausen; pop. (1968e) 38,183; electronic equipment; coal mines.

Kampo. See CAMPO.

Kam·pong Cham \ˌkäm-póŋ-ˈchäm\. Town, SE Cambodia, ab. 39 m. NE of Pnompenh, near Mekong river; pop. (1962p) 27,977.

Kampong Chhnang \-chə-ˈnäŋ\. Town, cen. Cambodia, ab. 52 m. NNW of Pnompenh; pop. (1962p) 12,949.

Kâmpóng Saôm. See KOMPONG SOM.

Kam·pot \ˈkäm-ˈpōt\. Seaport town, S Cambodia, 75 m. SSW of Pnompenh; pop. (1962p) 12,558; center of pepper culture.

Kamp·tee *or* **Kam·thi** \ˈkäm(p)-tē\. Town, NE Maharashtra state, India, on Wainganga river 10 m. NNE of Nagpur;

pop. (1961c) 40,800, with cantonment 46,700; founded 1821 as military cantonment; a trade center of decreasing importance.

Kamranh Bay. See CAMRANH BAY.

Kam·sack \'kam-ˌsak\. Town, SE Saskatchewan, Canada, on Assiniboine river 35 m. NE of Yorkton; pop. (1971p) 2779; creamery; grain, dairy farming.

Kamthi. See KAMPTEE.

Ka·mui, Cape \-'käm-ə-wē\. Cape on W coast of Hokkaidō, Japan, W of entrance to Ishikari Bay.

Ka·my·shin \kə-'mish-ən\. Town, N Volgograd Oblast, Russian S.F.S.R., U.S.S.R., on the Volga opp. Nikolayevski ab. 110 m. NNE of Volgograd; pop. (1969e) 82,000; river port; terminus of railroad from Tambov; textiles, paint, canning.

Kan \'gän\. 1 River in Kiangsi prov., SE China; 537 m. long; flows N through P'o-yang Hu (lake) into the Yangtze.

2 River, South Korea. See HAN 3.

Ka·nab \kə-'nab\. City, ⊗ of Kane co., S Utah; pop. (1970c) 1381; lumber mill; livestock farming.

Ka·na·bec \kə-'nā-bek, -'nò-\. County in Minnesota. See table at MINNESOTA.

Kanab Plateau. Tableland, N Mohave co., NW Arizona, on NW border of Grand Canyon National Monument; 6000 ft. high.

Ka·na·ga \kə-'näg-ə\. One of the Andreanof Is. in Aleutian Is., W of Adak I., SW Alaska.

Ka·na·ga·wa \kə-'näg-ə-wə\. 1 Prefecture, Honshū, Japan; 917 sq. m.; pop. (1970c) 5,472,247; ✱ Yokohama; rice; fishing, horticulture.

2 Town, Kanagawa prefecture, Honshū, Japan, N suburb of Yokohama; pop. (1970c) 207,362; formerly an important port, now incorporated with Yokohama; treaty signed here Mar. 31, 1854 bet. U.S. and Japan, opening two ports to trade. See URAGA.

Kanalit Mts. See ACROCERAUNIA.

Ka·nan·ga \kə-'näŋ-gə\ *or formerly* **Lu·lu·a·bourg** \lü-'lü-ə-(ˌ)bü(ə)r\. Town, ✱ of Kasai-Occidental prov., Zaire, on Lulua river 475 m. ESE of Kinshasa; met. area pop. (1971e) 483,438.

Kananur. See CANNANORE.

Ka·na·ra \'kän-ə-rə\ *formerly* **North Kanara.** Former district, now part of Mysore state, W India; 3961 sq. m.; ✱ Karwar.

Kanara, South. See SOUTH KANARA.

Kan·ash \kə-'näsh\. Town, Chuvash A.S.S.R., Russian S.F.S.R., U.S.S.R., ab. 45 m. SSE of Cheboksary; pop. (1967e) 41,000; brickworks; machinery; founded 1893.

Ka·na·wha \kə-'nò-(w)ə, -'nò-ē, -'nòi\. 1 *or* **Great Kanawha.** Navigable river, W West Virginia; 97 m. long; formed by junction of New and Gauley rivers in Fayette co., flows NW into the Ohio river.

2 County in West Virginia. See table at WEST VIRGINIA.

Ka·na·za·wa \kə-'näz-ə-wə, ˌkan-ə-'zä-wə\. Seaport city, ✱ of Ishikawa prefecture, W Honshū, Japan, near coast of Sea of Japan; pop. (1970c) 361,379; silk and other textiles, lacquer ware, porcelain; univ. (1949); during 300 years of feudalism the seat of one of the most powerful of daimyos; scene of victory of Nobunaga over rebellious priests 1575.

Kan·cha·na·bu·ri \ˌkän-bu-'rē—*sic*\. 1 Province, SW Thailand; 7524 sq. m.; pop. (1960c) 233,341; ✱ Kanchanaburi.

2 Town, its ✱, WNW of Bangkok on Klong river; pop. (1960c) 12,957; sapphire mines.

Kan·chen·jun·ga \ˌkan-chən-'jəŋ-gə, -'juŋ-\ *also* **Kun·chin·jun·ga** \ˌkən-chin-\ *or* **Kin·chin·jun·ga** \ˌkin-chən-\. Peak in the Himalayas, on boundary bet. Nepal and Sikkim; 28,146 ft.; 3d highest mountain in the world; visible from Darjeeling, India; first climbed May 1955.

Kan·chi·pu·ram \kän-'chē-pə-rəm\ *also* **Con·jee·ve·ram** \kən-'jē-və-rəm\. Town, NE Tamil Nadu, S India, 40 m. WSW of Madras; pop. (1961c) 92,714; noted for silk and cotton fabrics and saris; very ancient city with numerous temples and shrines—for Hindus, one of India's seven most sacred cities. Capital of Pallava dynasty in early cents. A.D.; under sovereignty of Delhi 1310 and in realm of the Great Mogul 1646; captured by Clive 1752.

Kan–chou \'gän-'jō\ *or formerly* **Kan·hsien** \'gän-shē-'en\. Town, S Kiangsi prov., SE China, on upper Kan river ab. 200 m. NNE of Canton; in World War II site of American air base; taken by Japanese 1945, retaken by Chinese July 15, 1945.

Kan·chra·pa·ra \ˌkänch-rə-'pär-ə\. Town, West Bengal, NE India; pop. (1961c) 68,966.

Kan·da·hār \'kan-də-ˌhär\. 1 Province of S Afghanistan. See table at AFGHANISTAN.

2 *or anc.* **Al·ex·an·dria Ar·a·cho·si·o·rum** \ˌal-ig-'zan-drē-ə-ˌar-ə-ˌkō-zē-'ōr-əm, ˌel-, -'òr-əm\. Commercial city, its ✱, 300 m. SW of Kabul; pop. (1970e) 130,212; second city in size in the country; at elevation of 3300 ft., connected with Quetta over the Chaman Pass; has long been a trading center both for imports and exports; ships wool and fruit; technical coll.

History: Held by Mogul Empire of India (*q.v.*) after its capture by Babur; captured 1625 by Shah Abbas I of Persia; center of successful Afghan rising against Persia 1706–08; independent until 1737; under Ahmad Shah (1747–73), one of the capitals of Afghanistan (*q.v.*); held by British 1839–42 and 1879–81, during the latter period its garrison relieved 1880 by memorable march of Gen. Frederick Roberts. See ARACHOSIA.

Kan·da·lak·sha \ˌkan-də-'lak-shə\. Coast town, SW Murmansk Oblast, Russian S.F.S.R., U.S.S.R., at head of Kandalaksha Gulf and on Leningrad-Murmansk railroad; pop. (1967e) 40,000; chief occupation fishing; aluminum works; military base in attack on Finland 1939–40.

Kandalaksha Gulf *or* **Kandalaksha Bay** *or Russ.* **Kan·da·laksh·ski Za·liv** \ˌkan-də-ˌlaksh-(s)kē-'zä-l(y)əf\. Inlet of NW White Sea on NW coast of Russian S.F.S.R., U.S.S.R., S and SW of Kola Penin., Murmansk Oblast.

Kan·da·vu \kän-'dä-(ˌ)vü\ *or* **Ka·da·vu** \kä-'dä-(ˌ)vü, kə-'dä-\. Island, Fiji, in SW part of group, in SW Pacific Ocean; 32 m. long, area 165 sq. m.; almost cut in two by narrow isthmus at center; mountainous and fertile, but undeveloped.

Kandavu Passage. Channel, Fiji, bet. Viti Levu I. on N and Kandavu I. on S; ab. 38 m. wide.

Kan·der·steg \'kän-dər-ˌshtäk\. Town, S Bern canton, Switzerland, ab 35 m. SSE of Bern; pop. (1970c) 957; health resort, winter sports center.

Kan·dı·ra \ˌkän-də-'rä\. Town, Kocaeli prov., NW Turkey, near Black Sea coast 25 m. NW of Adapazarı.

Kan·di·yo·hi \ˌkan-də-yō-'hī\. County in Minnesota. See table at MINNESOTA.

Kan·dy \'kan-dē\. Town, Ceylon, on Mahaweli river 60 m. ENE of Colombo; pop. (1968e) 78,000; in midst of noted mountain and lake scenery; last capital of ancient kings of Ceylon; contains Buddhist temples, including Dalada Maligawa, the world's most sacred Buddhist temple; palaces of ancient kingdoms, crypts and tombs of ancient rulers and heroes; famous botanical gardens at Peradeniya, 3 m. SW. Held briefly by Dutch 1763; taken over 1802 by British who gained permanent control 1814–15.

Kane \'kān\. 1 Name of counties in two states of the U.S. See tables at ILLINOIS and UTAH.

2 Borough and health resort, McKean co., N Pennsylvania, 23 m. SSW of Bradford; pop. (1970c) 5001; electronic components, wood products; oil and gas wells; Christmas trees.

Kanea. See CANEA.

Kane Basin. Section of the channel bet. E Ellesmere I. and NW Greenland, N of Baffin Bay.

Ka·nem \'kän-ˌem\. Former protected state of French Equatorial Africa, NE of Lake Chad, now a prefecture of Chad; (prefecture) 44,216 sq. m.; pop. (1970e) 187,000; chief town Mao; a native state founded 9th cent.; became Muslim 11th cent. and reached height of its power 300 years later; became subject to Bornu 13th cent. forming with it a strong native empire until 19th cent.; for a time subject to Ouadaï; since 1958 part of Chad.

Ka·ne·o·he \ˌkän-ē-ˈō-ē, -ˈō-(ˌ)hā\. City, Honolulu co., Hawaii, on **Kaneohe Bay,** wide inlet on E coast of Oahu I., N of Honolulu; pop. (1970c) 29,903; missile-tracking station.

Kanesh. See KANISH.

Kan·gar \ˈkäŋ-ˌgär\. Town, ✱ of Perlis state, Malaysia, near coast; pop. (1970p) 8757.

Kan·ga·roo Island \ˌkaŋ-gə-ˌrü-\. Island, S of Yorke Penin. at entrance to Gulf of St. Vincent, South Australia; 90 m. long; 1970 sq. m.; pop. (1961c) 3285.

Kan·gā·var \ˌkaŋ-gə-ˈvär\. Town, W Iran, ab. 40 m. SW of Hamadān; pop. (1966c) 9414; on a main highway; in a fertile region at altitude of 6000 ft.

Kang·e·an \ˈkäŋ-ē-ˌän\. 1 Island group of Indonesia, in Java Sea 80 m. E of Madura; 258 sq. m.

2 Largest island of the group; 188 sq. m.

Kang·gye \ˌkäŋ-ˈgyā\. Town, ✱ of Chagang prov., North Korea.

Kang·nŭng \ˈkäŋ-ˈnəŋ\. Town, Kangwŏn prov., South Korea, ab. 105 m. ENE of Seoul; pop. (1970e) 74,489.

Kan·gra \ˈkäŋ-grə\. Town, Himachal Pradesh, NW India, ab. 40 m. ESE of Pathankot; pop. (1961c) 5800; important in early Indian history.

Kang–shan \ˈkäŋ-ˈshän\ *or formerly* **Oka·ya·ma** \ˌō-kə-ˈyäm-ə\. Town, near SW coast of Taiwan, just N of Kaohsiung; in World War II a Japanese air base.

K'ang–ting \ˈkäŋ-ˈdiŋ\ *or formerly* **Ta·tsien·lu** \ˈdä-jē-ˈen-ˈlü\. City, Szechwan prov., S China, 260 m. W of Chungking; altitude 8500 ft.; formerly a Chinese administrative center for Tibetan affairs; became capital of former province of Sikang ab. 1928.

Kang–ti–ssu. See KAILAS.

Kang·to \ˈkäŋ-ˈtō\. Mountain peak, E Himalayas, China, on border bet. Arunachal Pradesh, India and SE Tibet; 23,620 ft.

Kang·wŏn \ˈkäŋ-ˌwən\. 1 Province of North Korea. See table at KOREA, NORTH.

2 Province of South Korea. See table at KOREA, SOUTH.

Kanha National Park \ˈkän-ə-\. National park, Madhya Pradesh, India; 98 sq. m.; noted for its wildlife; established 1956.

Kanhsien. See KAN-CHOU.

Kaniapiskau. See CANIAPISCAU.

Ka·ni·gu·ram \ˌkən-i-ˈgu̇r-əm\. Chief town of the Wazirs, cen. South Waziristan, North-West Frontier Province, Pakistan, NE of Wana and ab. 80 m. NW of Dera Ismail Khan.

Ka·nin Peninsula \ˌkan-ən-\. Peninsula projecting into Barents Sea on N coast of Nenets National Okrug, Russian S.F.S.R., U.S.S.R., having Cheshskaya Bay on E and entrance to White Sea on W; its NW extremity is **Kanin Point.**

Ka·nish \ˈkän-ish\ *or* **Ka·nesh** \-ˌesh\. Ancient city of E cen. Asia Minor, home of a branch (Kaneshite) of the Hittites; now the village of **Kul·te·pe** \ˌku̇l-tə-ˈpā\, an archaeological site SW of Kayseri and W of Erciyas Daği; mines of area supplied silver to Assyria 1900 B.C.

Kan·jut Sar \ˌkän-ju̇t-ˈsär\. Mountain in the Karakoram Range, in region of Jammu and Kashmir under Pakistani control; 25,461 ft.

Kan·ka·kee \ˌkaŋ-kə-ˈkē\. 1 River, Indiana and Illinois; 225 m. long; rises in N Indiana and flows SW and W to unite with the Des Plaines in NE Illinois and form the Illinois river.

2 County in Illinois. See table at ILLINOIS.

3 City, ⊗ of Kankakee co., NE Illinois, 32 m. SSE of Joliet; pop. (1970c) 30,944; home appliances, furniture, farm machinery; ships grain and livestock; Olivet Nazarene Coll. (1907), Kankakee Community Coll. (1966).

Kan·kan \käⁿ-ˈkäⁿ\. Town, E Guinea, W Africa; pop. (1965e) 20,000; terminus of railroad from Conakry; highway junction point.

Kan·ker \ˈkäŋ-kər\. Former Indian state, now part of Madhya Pradesh, NE India; 1413 sq. m.; pop. (1961c) 6500; ✱ Kanker.

Kanko. See HAMHŬNG.

Kan·maw Kyun \ˌkän-ˌmä-ˈkyün\ *or formerly* **Kis·se·raing** \ˈkis-ə-ˌrīŋ\ *or* **Ki·tha·reng** \ˈkith-ə-ˌreŋ\. Island in E cen. Mergui Archipelago (*q.v.*), Burma.

Kan·nap·o·lis \kə-ˈnap-(ə-)ləs\. Unincorporated town, Cabarrus and Rowan cos., S cen. North Carolina, ab. 7 m. N of Concord; pop. (1970c) 36,293; manufactures towels, blankets, sheets, pillowcases.

Kan·nauj \kə-ˈnau̇j\. Town, SW cen. Uttar Pradesh, N India, on Ganges river 50 m. NW of Kanpur; pop. (1961c) 24,646; noted for perfumes. An ancient city, famous in early times; mentioned by Ptolemy; in 7th cent. reached height of its magnificence as capital of Harsha's kingdom; captured by Mahmud of Ghazni 1019 and came under Muslim sovereignty 1194; memorials of the Hindu age have completely disappeared.

Kannstatt. See CANNSTATT.

Ka·no \ˈkän-(ˌ)ō\. 1 State of N Nigeria. See table at NIGERIA.

2 Commercial city, its ✱, on railroad in N cen. Nigeria 500 m. NE of Lagos; pop. (1971e) 357,098; ships peanuts, leather and hides; oil refinery; textiles, canned meat, concrete block, steel furniture; center of caravan routes; inhabitants chiefly Hausa, with a considerable number of Fulahs. Known to Arab geographers in 12th cent.; figured prominently as center of Hausa state in Negro wars in 15th–16th cents.; early converted to Islam; conquered by Fulahs c. 1800; visited by H. Barth 1851 and 1854; became British 1903.

Ka·no·ya \kə-ˈnȯi-ə, ˈkän-ə-(ˌ)yä\. City, Kagoshima prefecture, S Kyūshū, Japan, on E side of Kagoshima Bay 22 m. SE of Kagoshima; pop. (1970c) 66,995.

Kan·pur \ˈkän-ˌpu̇(ə)r\ *or Eng.* **Cawn·pore** \ˈkȯn-ˌpō(ə)r, -ˌpȯ(ə)r\. City, S cen. Uttar Pradesh, N India, on right bank of Ganges river 245 m. SE of Delhi; pop. (1970e) 1,197,255; important rail junction; most important industrial center of the state; leather, cotton, wool, and sugar industries; Indian Institute of Technology (1960). Garrisoned by British troops in 1778. Known for the massacre by Nana Sahib of British soldiers and European families during Sepoy Mutiny July 15, 1857.

Kanra. See HALLA.

Kan·san·shi \kän-ˈsän-shē\. Town, NW Zambia, S cen. Africa, 260 m. NW of Lusaka near Zaire border; extensive copper deposits.

Kan·sas \ˈkan-zəs *also* ˈkan(t)-səs\. 1 *in Kansas usu. called* **Kaw** \ˈkȯ\. River, formed by confluence of Republican and Smoky Hill rivers at Junction City, Geary co., E Kansas, flows E into Missouri river at Kansas City.

2 A central state of U.S.A., bounded on N by Nebraska, on E by Missouri, on S by Oklahoma, on W by Colorado; 14th state in area, 82,264 sq. m. (land area 82,056 sq. m.); 28th state in population, (1970c) 2,249,071; ✱ Topeka; 34th state admitted to Union (1861).

Nicknames: Sunflower State; Jayhawker State. *State flower:* Sunflower. *Motto:* Ad Astra per Aspera (To the Stars through Difficulties). *Rivers:* In S the Arkansas, flowing from W border E to cen. area and then S across border into Oklahoma; in N, also flowing W to E, the Saline and Solomon rivers, tributaries of the Smoky Hill river which joins the Republican river from the N to form Kansas river (see 1, above). *Highest point:* Mt. Sunflower, 4039 ft., on W border in Wallace co. *Chief products:* Wheat, sorghums, corn, oats; dairy products; oil, salt; manufacturing: aerospace equipment, machinery, chemicals. *Chief cities:* Wichita, Kansas City, Topeka, Overland Park,

Lawrence. See *Table of States* at UNITED STATES. Divided into the following 105 counties (for pronunciation of their names, see their individual entries):

NAME	LOCATION	AREA* (sq. m.)	POP. (1970c)	CO. SEAT
Allen	SE	505	15,043	Iola
Anderson	E	577	8,501	Garnett
Atchison	NE	427	19,165	Atchison
Barber	S	1,146	7,016	Medicine Lodge
Barton	cen.	894	30,663	Great Bend
Bourbon	SE	639	15,215	Fort Scott
Brown	NE	577	11,685	Hiawatha
Butler	S	1,442	38,658	El Dorado
Chase	E cen.	774	3,408	Cottonwood Falls
Chautauqua	SE	647	4,642	Sedan
Cherokee	SE corner	587	21,549	Columbus
Cheyenne	NW corner	1,027	4,256	Saint Francis
Clark	S	984	2,896	Ashland
Clay	NE cen.	658	9,890	Clay Center
Cloud	N	711	13,466	Concordia
Coffey	E	656	7,397	Burlington
Comanche	S	800	2,702	Coldwater
Cowley	S	1,136	35,012	Winfield
Crawford	SE	598	37,850	Girard
Decatur	NW	899	4,988	Oberlin
Dickinson	E cen.	855	19,993	Abilene
Doniphan	NE corner	388	9,107	Troy
Douglas	E	471	57,932	Lawrence
Edwards	SW cen.	617	4,581	Kinsley
Elk	SE	647	3,858	Howard
Ellis	cen.	900	24,730	Hays
Ellsworth	cen.	717	6,146	Ellsworth
Finney	W	1,301	19,029	Garden City
Ford	S	1,091	22,587	Dodge City
Franklin	E	577	20,007	Ottawa
Geary	NE cen.	400	28,111	Junction City
Gove	W	1,070	3,940	Gove
Graham	NW cen.	891	4,751	Hill City
Grant	SW	571	5,961	Ulysses
Gray	SW	872	4,516	Cimarron
Greeley	W	783	1,819	Tribune
Greenwood	SE	1,142	9,141	Eureka
Hamilton	W	992	2,747	Syracuse
Harper	S	801	7,871	Anthony
Harvey	SE cen.	540	27,236	Newton
Haskell	SW	580	3,672	Sublette
Hodgeman	SW cen.	860	2,662	Jetmore
Jackson	NE	656	10,342	Holton
Jefferson	NE	550	11,945	Oskaloosa
Jewell	N	910	6,099	Mankato
Johnson	E	476	220,073	Olathe
Kearny	W	855	3,047	Lakin
Kingman	S cen.	865	8,886	Kingman
Kiowa	S	720	4,088	Greensburg
Labette	SE	654	25,775	Oswego
Lane	W	720	2,707	Dighton
Leavenworth	NE	466	53,340	Leavenworth
Lincoln	cen.	726	4,582	Lincoln
Linn	E	606	7,770	Mound City
Logan	W	1,073	3,814	Russell Springs
Lyon	E	852	32,071	Emporia
McPherson	cen.	896	24,778	McPherson
Marion	E cen.	959	13,935	Marion
Marshall	NE	883	13,139	Marysville
Meade	SW	979	4,912	Meade
Miami	E	592	19,254	Paola
Mitchell	N cen.	716	8,010	Beloit
Montgomery	SE	649	39,949	Independence
Morris	E cen.	706	6,432	Council Grove
Morton	SW corner	728	3,576	Richfield
Nemaha	NE	708	11,825	Seneca
Neosho	SE	587	18,812	Erie
Ness	W cen.	1,081	4,791	Ness City
Norton	N	880	7,279	Norton
Osage	E	720	13,352	Lyndon
Osborne	N cen.	898	6,416	Osborne
Ottawa	NE cen.	723	6,183	Minneapolis
Pawnee	cen.	755	8,484	Larned
Phillips	N	897	7,888	Phillipsburg
Pottawatomie	NE	820	11,755	Westmoreland
Pratt	S cen.	729	10,056	Pratt
Rawlins	NW	1,078	4,393	Atwood
Reno	cen.	1,262	60,765	Hutchinson
Republic	N	718	8,498	Belleville
Rice	cen.	725	12,320	Lyons
Riley	NE cen.	597	56,788	Manhattan
Rooks	N	886	7,628	Stockton
Rush	cen.	724	5,117	La Crosse
Russell	cen.	897	9,428	Russell
Saline	cen.	720	46,592	Salina
Scott	W	724	5,606	Scott City
Sedgwick	S cen.	1,007	350,694	Wichita
Seward	SW	646	15,744	Liberal
Shawnee	NE	548	155,322	Topeka
Sheridan	NW	893	3,859	Hoxie
Sherman	NW	1,055	7,792	Goodland
Smith	N	893	6,757	Smith Center
Stafford	cen.	795	5,943	Saint John
Stanton	SW	676	2,287	Johnson
Stevens	SW	731	4,198	Hugoton
Sumner	S	1,186	23,553	Wellington
Thomas	NW	1,070	7,501	Colby
Trego	W cen.	901	4,436	Wakeeney
Wabaunsee	E	792	6,397	Alma
Wallace	W	911	2,215	Sharon Springs
Washington	N	891	9,249	Washington
Wichita	W	724	3,274	Leoti
Wilson	SE	574	11,317	Fredonia
Woodson	SE	504	4,789	Yates Center
Wyandotte	NE	152	186,845	Kansas City

*Area = land area.

History: Probably entered by Coronado's expedition 1540; the greater part came to U.S. as part of Louisiana Purchase (*q.v.*) 1803; by Kansas-Nebraska Act 1854, organized as territory which was to become free or slave state on basis of popular sovereignty (repeal of Missouri Compromise of 1820); scene of virtual civil war bet. rival slave and free interests 1854–56; adopted constitution 1859; admitted to Union as free state Jan. 29, 1861.

Kansas City. 1 Industrial city, ⊗ of Wyandotte co., NE Kansas, at confluence of Kansas and Missouri rivers, separated from Kansas City, Missouri, by state line; 2d largest city in state; pop. (1970c) 168,213; railroad center; stockyards, packinghouses, and large grain-storage facilities, soap factories, flour mills, automobiles, paper products, chemicals; ships corn, wheat, sorghum, oats; Kansas City Kansas Community Coll. (1923); Donnelley Coll. (1949). First settled by Wyandot Indians 1843; sold to federal government 1855; settled by whites 1857; modern city formed 1886 by consolidation of a number of adjoining towns.

2 City, Clay, Platte, and Jackson cos., W Missouri, on S bank of Missouri river on Kansas-Missouri state line adjoining Kansas City, Kansas; pop. (1970c) 507,330; 2d largest city in state; railroad, industrial, and commercial center; stockyards and packinghouses; hay, grain, horse, and mule market; food processing; aerospace equipment, chemicals, petroleum products, salt; Avila Coll. (1866), Rockhurst Coll. (1910), Metropolitan Junior Coll. (1915), Univ. of Missouri at Kansas City (1929), Calvary Bible Coll. (1932), Kansas City Art Inst.

History: Permanent settlement dates from 1821 when trading post established within present boundaries of city by the Chouteaus, fur traders; city grew out of settlements of Westport, founded 1833, and Westport Landing (on the river 4 m. N), which became busy port for river traffic; **Town of Kansas,** laid out 1838, developed after 1846; name changed to **City of Kansas** 1853 and to Kansas City 1889.

Kansk \'kän(t)sk\. Industrial city, S Krasnoyarsk Krai, Russian S.F.S.R., U.S.S.R., on a tributary of the Yenisei and on Trans-Siberian R.R. 110 m. E of Krasnoyarsk; pop. (1969e) 90,000; near lignite and iron ore deposits; cotton, timber, food processing; founded 1628.

Kan·su \'kan-'sü, 'gän-\. Province of N cen. China, forming a long narrow wedge bet. Ningsia Hui on N and Tsinghai on S, touching Shensi on E, Szechwan on SE, and Sinkiang Uighur on W; 137,104 sq. m.; pop. (1968e) 13,000,000; ✱ Lan-chou. Crossed by the upper Yellow river from SW to NE, whose tributaries and the Jo (in N cen. part) afford valleys for highways. Mountainous, includes N ranges of Nan Shan in W (20,000 ft.) and E extension (Min Shan) of Kunlun Mts. in S (17,000 ft.); at lower levels characterized by sandy plains and (esp. in the E) by rich loess terraces. Great part of it traversed by W end of Great Wall, with its branches. Produces wheat, cotton, tobacco, oil. Chief towns Lan-chou, Chiu-ch'üan, Yü-men, T'ien-shui, P'ing-liang. Served as corridor for great highway to the W, the old Silk Road (*q.v.*)—to Turkistan, India, Persia; for several centuries a part of the kingdom of Wei; came under Kublai Khan in 13th cent.; under the Mings a part of

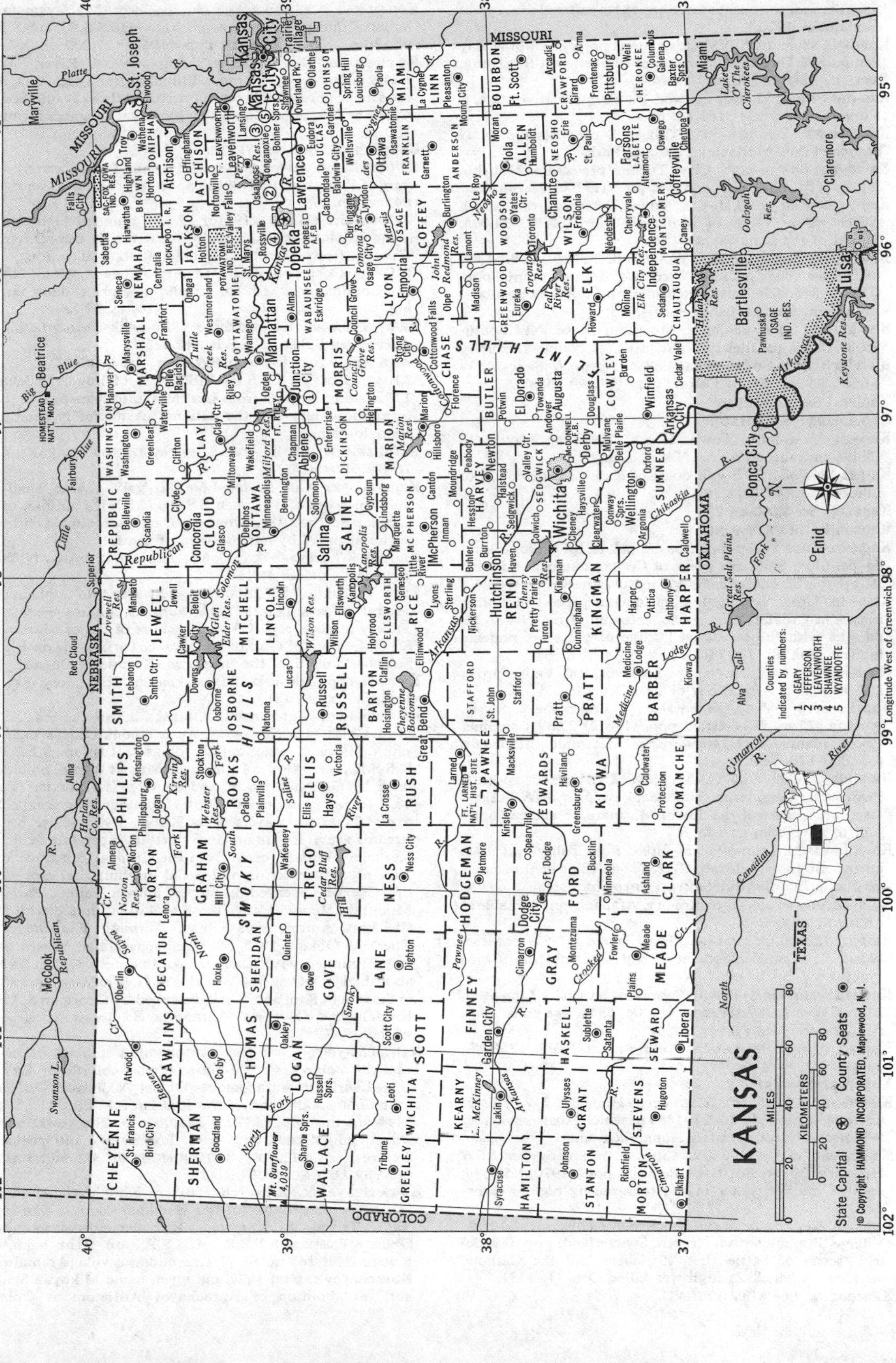
KANSAS
NEBRASKA
MISSOURI
OKLAHOMA
COLORADO
TEXAS
CHEYENNE
RAWLINS
DECATUR
NORTON
PHILLIPS
SMITH
JEWELL
REPUBLIC
WASHINGTON
MARSHALL
NEMAHA
BROWN
DONIPHAN
SHERMAN
THOMAS
SHERIDAN
GRAHAM
ROOKS
OSBORNE
MITCHELL
CLOUD
CLAY
RILEY
POTTAWATOMIE
JACKSON
ATCHISON
JEFFERSON
LEAVENWORTH
WALLACE
LOGAN
GOVE
TREGO
ELLIS
RUSSELL
LINCOLN
OTTAWA
DICKINSON
GEARY
WABAUNSEE
SHAWNEE
DOUGLAS
JOHNSON
WYANDOTTE
GREELEY
WICHITA
SCOTT
LANE
NESS
RUSH
BARTON
ELLSWORTH
SALINE
McPHERSON
MARION
MORRIS
LYON
OSAGE
FRANKLIN
MIAMI
HAMILTON
KEARNY
FINNEY
HODGEMAN
PAWNEE
STAFFORD
RICE
RENO
HARVEY
BUTLER
CHASE
GREENWOOD
COFFEY
ANDERSON
LINN
BOURBON
ALLEN
WOODSON
STANTON
GRANT
HASKELL
GRAY
FORD
EDWARDS
KIOWA
PRATT
KINGMAN
SEDGWICK
COWLEY
ELK
WILSON
NEOSHO
CRAWFORD
MORTON
STEVENS
SEWARD
MEADE
CLARK
COMANCHE
BARBER
HARPER
SUMNER
CHAUTAUQUA
MONTGOMERY
LABETTE
CHEROKEE
SMOKY HILLS
FLINT HILLS
Topeka
Wichita
Kansas City
Counties indicated by numbers:
1 GEARY
2 JEFFERSON
3 LEAVENWORTH
4 SHAWNEE
5 WYANDOTTE
MILES
KILOMETERS
State Capital
County Seats
Longitude West of Greenwich
© Copyright HAMMOND INCORPORATED, Maplewood, N.J.

Shensi; made a separate province 1911; suffered from great earthquake 1920.

Kan·tang \'kän-'täŋ\. Village and port on W coast of Malay Penin., SW Thailand, 85 m. SE of Phuket; port for Trang.

Kantara, Al–. See AL-KANTARA.

Kan·ta·ra·wa·di \ˌkän-tə-rə-'wäd-ē\. Former native state, E Karenni, E Burma; 3161 sq. m.

Kan·tish·na \kan-'tish-nə\. Village, S cen. Alaska, on N border of Mt. McKinley National Park.

Ka·nu·ma \kə-'nü-mə\. City, Tochigi prefecture, Honshū, Japan, 8 m. W of Utsunomiya; pop. (1970c) 77,746.

Kan·ye *or* **Kan·ya** \'kän-yə\. Town, Botswana, cen. South Africa, 70 m. NNW of Mafeking; pop. (1969e) 34,045; capital of the Bangwaketsi tribe.

Kao–hsiung \'kau̇-shē-'u̇ŋ, 'gau̇-\; *Jap.* **Ta·kao** \tä-'kä-(ˌ)ō\ *or* **Ta·kow** \-'kau̇\. City, SW coast of Taiwan; munic. pop. (1971e) 845,905; Taiwan's leading port; petrochemicals, aluminum, textiles; fisheries.

Kao·ko·veld \'kau̇-kō-ˌfelt\. Mountain range, NW South-West Africa, parallel to coast just E of Namib Desert.

Ka·o·lack *or* **Ka·o·lak** \'kau̇-ˌlak\. Town, W Senegal, W Africa, 95 m. ESE of Dakar; pop. (1969e) 95,000.

Kaolan. See LAN-CHOW.

Kao Luang. See KHAO LUANG.

Kao–mi \'kau̇-mē\. Town, E cen. Shantung prov., NE China, on railroad 40 m. NW of Tsingtao.

Ka·paa \kä-'pä-ə\. City, E coast of Kauai I., Hawaii, N of Lihue; pop. (1970c) 3794.

Kapaau. See KOHALA 2.

Kapaonik. See KOPAONIK.

Ká·pe·la, Cape \-'käp-ə-ˌlä\ *or Gk.* **Ák·ra Ka·pél·lo** \ˌäk-rə-kə-'pel-(ˌ)ō\. Southern point of Cerigo, one of the Ionian Is. off the SE coast of Peloponnesus, Greece.

Ka·pe·la, Great *and* **Little Kapela** \-kə-'pel-ə\. Mountain ranges in Croatia, Yugoslavia, extending from NW to SE parallel with the coast; on E edge of the Kras plateau; highest peak ab. 4600 ft.

Ka·pen·gu·ria \ˌkäp-ən-'gu̇r-ē-ə\. Town, Rift Valley prov., NW Kenya, E Africa, SW of Lake Rudolf.

Kap·fen·berg \'käp-fən-ˌbe(ə)rg\. Commune, Styria, Austria, 25 m. N of Graz; pop. (1961c) 23,894; summer resort; manufactures steel, paper, electronic equipment; founded 12th cent.

Ka·pı·da·ğı \ˌkäp-ē-dä-'(g)ē\ *or anc.* **Cyz·i·cus** \'siz-i-kəs\. Peninsula, triangular in shape, Balıkesir prov., NW Turkey, Asia, on S coast of the Sea of Marmara; in ancient times said to have been an island.

Ka·pi·la·vas·tu \ˌkap-ə-lə-'vəs-(ˌ)tü\. Principality and town in ancient India; site ab. 27°28′N, 83°18′E; birthplace of Gautama Buddha, the Sakya Prince Siddhartha.

Kā·pī·sā \kə-'pē-sə\. Province of E Afghanistan. See table at AFGHANISTAN.

Ka·pi·ti Island \ˌkäp-ət-ē-\. Small island off SW coast of North I., New Zealand, at N end of Cook Strait; bird sanctuary.

Kap·lan \'kap-lən\. Town, Vermilion parish, S Louisiana, 23 m. SW of Lafayette; pop. (1970c) 5540; rice mills; ships rice, cotton, poultry, eggs.

Kaplan, Mount. Mountain, Antarctica, 84°33′S, 175°18′E; 13,878 ft.

Kapoeas. See KAPUAS.

Ká·pol·na \'käp-əl-ˌnȯ\. Town, cen. Hungary, SW of Eger; scene of battle Feb. 26–27, 1849 in which Austrians under Windisch-Graetz defeated Hungarians under Dembiński.

Ka·pos·vár \'kȯ-pōsh-ˌvär\. City, ⊗ of Somogy co., SW Hungary, 30 m. S of Lake Balaton; pop. (1970p) 58,099; textiles; market center in livestock-raising region; cathedral.

Kap·pel \'käp-əl\ *or in full* **Kappel am Al·bis** \-äm-'äl-bis\. Village, Zurich canton, NE cen. Switzerland; pop. (1970c) 636; scene of battle (bet. Zurichers and the Catholic cantons) in which Zwingli was killed Oct. 11, 1531.

Kaproncza. See KOPRIVNICA.

Kap·su·kas \'käp-sə-kəs\ *or formerly* **Ma·ri·yam·po·lė** \ˌmär-i-'yäm-pō-(ˌ)lā\. Town, Lithuanian S.S.R., U.S.S.R., ab. 30 m. SW of Kaunas; pop. (1967e) 27,000.

Ka·pu·as *or Du.* **Ka·poe·as** \'käp-ə-ˌwäs\. River, West Kalimantan prov., Borneo, Indonesia; ab. 450 m. long; rises in mountains of N cen. Borneo and flows W into South China at Pontianak; navigable for small steamers for over 300 m.

Kapudzhikh. See KAPYDZHIK.

Ka·pur·tha·la \kə-'pu̇rt-ᵊl-ə\. **1** Former Indian state, now part of Punjab state, NW India, on left bank of Beas river; 645 sq. m.
2 Town, its ✱; pop. (1961c) 29,334; founded 11th cent.

Kap·us·ka·sing \ˌkap-ə-'skā-siŋ\. **1** River, N cen. Ontario, Canada; flows N to the Mattagami; ab. 180 m. long.
2 Town, Cochrane dist., E Ontario, Canada, 80 m. NNW of Timmins; pop. (1971p) 12,789; newsprint; dairy farming.

Ka·py·dzhik *also* **Ka·pu·dzhikh** \ˌkäp-ə-'jik\. Mountain, SW Azerbaijan S.S.R., U.S.S.R.; 12,815 ft.

Ka·ra \'kär-ə\. **1** River in NW Iran. See QAREH SŪ.
2 River, Russian S.F.S.R., U.S.S.R., E of Yugorski Penin.; 130 m. long; flows N from Ural Mts. into Kara Sea; in part forms boundary bet. the national okrugs of Nenets and Yamalo-Nenets.

Karabakh Mountain Area. See NAGORNO-KARABAKH AUTONOMOUS OBLAST.

Kara–Bo·gaz Gol \ˌkär-ə-bō-ˌ(g)äz-'gəl\. Large shallow gulf, on coast of Turkmen S.S.R., U.S.S.R., an inlet of E Caspian Sea; ab. 100 m. long by 85 m. wide; almost entirely enclosed on W by narrow strip of sand.

Ka·ra·bük \ˌkär-ə-'bük\. Town, Zonguldak prov., N Turkey; pop. (1965c) 46,169.

Kara Bu·run *or* **Ka·ra·bu·run** \ˌkär-ə-bə-'rün\. Name of several capes or points (Turk. *burun* cape) on the coast of Turkey in Asia, esp.: (1) on SW shore of Sea of Marmara; (2) on E shore of Gulf of Antalya, S Turkey; (3) on Black Sea coast just E of the Bosporus (Karadeniz Boğazı).

Ka·ra·ca·dağ \ˌkär-ə-jə-'dä(g)\. Peak in SE Turkey, SW of Diyarbakır; 6070 ft.

Ka·ra·cha·yev Autonomous Oblast \ˌkär-ə-'chä-yəf . . . 'ō-bləst, -ˌblast\ *or* **Ka·ra·chai Autonomous Oblast** \ˌkär-ə-'chī-\. Former autonomous oblast, Russian S.F.S.R., U.S.S.R., on N slope of Caucasus Mts. at W end, bounded on S by Georgian S.S.R. and on W by Krasnodar Krai; 3821 sq. m.; mountainous, along S boundary several peaks over 10,000 ft.; traversed by Kuban river whose headstreams are in mountains in S part; its inhabitants chiefly Karachayevs, who came from the Crimea 15th cent. and after much wandering and racial intermixture, esp. with the Cherkess, settled in upper Kuban valley. Part of Mountain Republic after the Revolution; united with the Cherkess Autonomous Oblast (forming Karachayevo-Cherkess Oblast) 1922–26; given separate administration 1926; reunited with Cherkess Autonomous Oblast 1936; abolished (1944) during World War II, N half incorporated in Stavropol Krai and S half absorbed by Georgian S.S.R.; Karachayevo-Cherkess Autonomous Oblast (*q.v.*) restored 1957.

Ka·ra·cha·ye·vo–Cher·kess Autonomous Oblast \ˌkär-ə-'chä-yev-ə-chir-'kes . . . 'ō-bləst; -cher-, -ˌblast\ *or* **Ka·ra·chai–Cherkess Autonomous Oblast** \ˌkär-ə-'chī-\. Autonomous subdivision of the Russian S.F.S.R., U.S.S.R.; 5444 sq. m.; pop. (1970p) 345,000; ✱ Cherkessk; corn, wheat, millet; coal, zinc, lead. For history and physical features, see CHERKESS AUTONOMOUS OBLAST and KARACHAYEV AUTONOMOUS OBLAST.

Ka·ra·cha·yevsk \ˌkär-ə-'chī-efsk\ *or* **Klu·kho·ri** \klü-'kȯr-(y)i\ *or formerly* **Mi·ko·yan Sha·khar** \ˌmik-ə-ˌyän-shə-'kär\. Town, ✱ of former Karachayev Autonomous Oblast, Russian S.F.S.R., U.S.S.R., on right bank of Kuban river 165 m. SE of Krasnodar; a village rebuilt as Karachayev capital 1927 and given name Mikoyan Shakhar; on abolition of Karachayev Autonomous Oblast (*q.v.*), renamed Klukhori and relocated in Georgian S.S.R. From it the **Klu·khor Pass** \klů-'kȯ(ə)r-\ (8400 ft.) leads through the Caucasus Mts. W of Mt. Elbrus to Sukhumi.

Ka·ra·chi \kə-'räch-ē\. City and seaport, ✱ of Sind, Pakistan, former ✱ of Pakistan, on arm of Arabian Sea just NW of the mouths of the Indus, ab. 92 m. SW of Hyderabad; met. area pop. (1971e) 3,442,000; principal seaport of Pakistan; trade and distribution center for extensive hinterland; exports grain, raw cotton, hides, skins, and raw wool; manufactures chemicals, textiles, plastics; shipbuilding; univ. (1951); founded early 18th cent.; became British 1843 and development of city has taken place almost entirely since then.

Ka·ra·dag *or* **Ka·ra Dağ**\ˌkär-ə-'dä(g)\. Name of several mountains (Turk. *dağ* mountain) in Turkey, esp.: (1) In S, peak near W end of Taurus Mts. and SE of Konya; 7451 ft. (2) In SE, peak in mountains of Kurdistan, SE of Lake Van; 11,910 ft.

Karadeniz Boğazı. See BOSPORUS.

Karaferieh. See VEROIA.

Ka·ra·fu·to \ˌkär-ə-'füt-(ˌ)ō\. 1 Japanese name of Sakhalin I. 2 Former Japanese possession comprising S half of Sakhalin I., S of 50°N lat.; ab. 13,931 sq. m.; since 1946 belongs to U.S.S.R. See SAKHALIN.

Ka·ra·gan·da \ˌkar-ə-gən-'dä\. City, ✱ of Karaganda Oblast, Kazakh S.S.R., U.S.S.R., on railroad 135 m. SSE of Tselinograd; pop. (1970p) 522,000; large coal beds in vicinity; iron and steel foundries.

Karaganda Oblast \-'ō-bləst, -ˌblast\. Subdivision of the Kazakh S.S.R., U.S.S.R., NW of Lake Balkhash; 153,977 sq. m.; pop. (1970p) 1,522,000; ✱ Karaganda; extensive steppe region; wheat; livestock; coal, copper, lead, zinc, iron ore.

Ka·ra·gin \kə-'räg-ən, -'rag-\. Island, W Bering Sea, Russian S.F.S.R., U.S.S.R., ab. 30 m. off E coast of N Kamchatka Penin.; highest point 3140 ft.; formerly in Khabarovsk Krai, now attached to Koryak National Okrug.

Karahissar. See ŞEBINKARAHISAR.

Ka·rai·ku·di *or* **Ka·raik·ku·di** \kə-'rī-kəd-ē\. Town, Tamil Nadu, S India, 38 m. ESE of Madurai; pop. (1961c) 43,698.

Ka·raj \kə-'räj\. Town, N Iran, ab. 22 m. NW of Tehran; pop. (1971e) 48,000.

Ka·ra·kal·pak Autonomous Soviet Socialist Republic *or* **Kara–Kalpak Autonomous Soviet Socialist Republic** \ˌkar-ə-kal-'pak-\. An autonomous region in NW part of Uzbek S.S.R., U.S.S.R., SE of Aral Sea and N of the Khiva oasis along right bank of the Amu Darya and in the delta; 63,938 sq. m.; pop. (1970p) 702,000; ✱ Nukus; much of it desert (SW part of the Kyzyl Kum); cotton; cattle, karakul sheep. Chief towns Nukus, Khodzheili, Chimbai, Turtkul; first became Russian 1867 as a part of Turkistan; made autonomous 1932.

Karakash. See K'A-LA-K'A-SHIH.

Ka·ra·ke·long \ˌkär-ə-'kā-ˌlȯŋ\. Chief island of the Talaud Is., NE of Celebes, Indonesia; ab. 41 m. long by 15 m. wide; chief town Beo on W coast.

Karakhoto. See KHARA KHOTO.

Karaklis. See KIROVAKAN.

Karakol. See PRZHEVALSK.

Kar·a·ko·ram Pass \ˌkar-ə-'kōr-əm-, -'kȯr-\ *or Chin.* **K'a–la–k'un–lun Shan K'ou** \'kä-'lä-'kün-'lün-'shän-'kaů\. Pass through Karakoram Range, Jammu and Kashmir, in region under Pakistani control, SE of Mount Godwin Austen; alt. 18,290 ft.; traditionally the chief route over the Himalayas bet. Jammu and Kashmir and China.

Karakoram Range *or* **Karakorum Range.** Mountain range, N Jammu and Kashmir, India and Pakistan; highest peak Godwin Austen 28,250 ft.; has approximately 60 peaks at ab. 22,000 ft.

Kar·a·ko·rum *also* **Qa·ra·qo·rum** \ˌkar-ə-'kōr-əm, -'kȯr-\ *or Mongolian* **Har Ho·rin** \'här-hə-'rin\. 1 Ruins of ancient ✱ of Mongolia, on right bank of upper Orhon, 47°14′N, 102°50′E, 200 m. WSW of Ulan Bator.

History: At first a Mongol camp, established by Genghis Khan as his capital early in 13th cent.; rebuilt and palace erected by Ogadai, his son and successor (1229–41); deserted by Kublai Khan for new capital at Khanbalik (Marco Polo's Cambaluc, *mod.* Peking) 1267; visited by Marco Polo c. 1275; later destroyed and by 16th cent. abandoned.

2 Ruins of earlier city, ✱ of Uighur kingdom 8th to 12th cent., 15 to 20 m. NW on left bank of the Orhon.

Ka·ra·kul *or* **Ka·ra Kul** *or* **Qa·ra Kul** \ˌkär-ə-'kəl\. Lake, Pamir plateau, NE Gorno-Badakhshan Autonomous Oblast, E Tadzhik S.S.R., U.S.S.R.; 140 sq. m.; alt. 12,890 ft.

Ka·ra Kum *or* **Qa·ra Qum** \ˌkär-ə-'küm\ *or* **Ka·ra·ku·my** \-'küm-ē\. Desert area, S of Aral Sea; 115,830 sq. m.; ab. 600 m. long and 250 m. wide; including most of Turkmen S.S.R., U.S.S.R., stretching from the Caspian to the Amu Darya on the E, Asia.

Ka·ra·man \ˌkär-ə-'män\ *or anc.* **La·ran·da** \lə-'ran-də\. Town, SE Konya prov., SW cen. Turkey, on railroad 62 m. SE of Konya; pop. (1965c) 26,051; renowned for its castle and mosques; early history obscure; became seat of Isaurian pirates; in 13th cent. made capital of an independent Armenian state, **Karaman** or **Kar·a·ma·nia (Ca·ra·man** *or* **Ca·ra·ma·nia)** \ˌkar-ə-'mā-nē-ə\, long at war with various Asiatic states, overcome by Ottoman Turks under Mohammed II 1473.

Ka·ra·mea Bight \ˌkär-ə-ˌmā-ə-\. Wide gulf on NW coast of South I., New Zealand, bet. Kahurangi Point and Cape Foulwind.

Ka·rang \'kär-äŋ\. Mountain, W Java, Indonesia, near Sunda Strait; 5833 ft.

Ka·ran·ja \kə-'rən-jə\. Island on E side of entrance to Bombay Harbor, on W coast of India.

Ka·ra·pa·che·ta *also* **Ca·ra·pa·che·ta** \ˌkär-ə-pə-'chā-tə\. Peak, cen. Cochabamba dept., cen. Bolivia; 16,400 ft.

Ka·ra Sea \ˌkär-ə-\ *or Russ.* **Kar·skoye Mo·re** \ˌkär-skō-yə-'mōr-ə\. Arm of Arctic Ocean extending E of Novaya Zemlya and off coasts of Taimyr, Yamolo-Nenets, and Nenets national okrugs, Russian S.F.S.R., U.S.S.R.; has many small islands; frozen much of the year.

Ka·ra·shahr *also* **Qa·ra Shahr** \ˌkär-ə-'shä(-ə)r\ *or* **Yen·ki** \'yen-'jē\. Town, cen. Sinkiang Uighur, W China.

Kara Strait *or Russ.* **Pro·liv Kar·skiye Vo·rota** \ˌprōl-if-ˌkär-skē-yə-və-'nō-tə\. Strait connecting Kara Sea with Barents Sea, bet. Novaya Zemlya and Vaigach I., Nenets National Okrug, Russian S.F.S.R., U.S.S.R.; ab. 35 m. wide.

Kara Su \ˌkär-ə-'sü\. 1 River in SW Bulgaria and NW Greece. See MESTA.

2 *also* **Western Eu·phra·tes** \-yů-'frāt-(ˌ)ēz\. River in E Turkey, the main headstream of the Euphrates; rises N of Erzurum and flows W and S to unite with the Murat Nehri (or Eastern Euphrates) and continue as the Euphrates river (*q.v.*).

Karasubazar. See BELOGURSK.

Karatala. See KARTHALA.

Ka·ra·tsu \kə-'rät-(ˌ)sü\. Seaport city, Saga prefecture, NW Kyūshū, Japan; pop. (1970c) 74,233; coalfields.

Ka·rau·li \kə-'raů-lē\. 1 Former Indian state, now part of Rajasthan state, India; bordered on Jaipur on NW and was separated from Gwalior on SE by Chambal river; 1227 sq. m. Founded in 11th cent.; for a time under Mogul emperors and Marathas; taken under British protection 1817.

2 Town, its ✱, Rajasthan, 85 m. SE of Jaipur; pop. (1961c) 23,696.

Kara Usu Nur. See HAR US NUUR.

Karawanken. See table at ALPS.

Kar·ba·la \'kär-bə-lə\ *or* **Ker·be·la** \'kər-bə-lə\. Town, cen. Iraq, 55 m. SSW of Baghdad, on edge of the desert W of Hindiya river; pop. (1965c) 83,301; Holy City for Muslims of the Shiite branch, containing the shrine of Husain, slain here in 680 A.D. and commemorated in the Muharram; active trade center.

Kar·cag \'kórt-ˌsóg\. City, E Hungary, 35 m. WSW of Debrecen; pop. (1970p) 24,631; brick works.

Karchi. See KHALKÊ.

Kar·di·tsa *or Gk.* **Kar·dí·tsa** \kär-'dēt-sə\. 1 Department of Greece. See table at GREECE.

2 Town, its ✱, W Thessaly, Greece; pop. (1971p) 25,523.

Ka·re·li·an Autonomous Soviet Socialist Republic \kə-'rē-lē-ən-, -'rēl-yən-\ *or formerly* **Ka·re·lo–Finn·ish Soviet Socialist Republic** \kə-ˌrē-lō-'fin-ish-\; *historically* **Ka·re·lia** \kə-'rē-lē-ə, -'rēl-yə\. An autonomous republic of the Russian S.F.S.R., U.S.S.R., in NW part of U.S.S.R., bounded on N by Murmansk Oblast, on E by White Sea and Arkhangelsk Oblast, on S by Vologda and Leningrad oblasts, and on W by Finland; 66,564 sq. m.; pop. (1970p) 714,000; ✱ Petrozavodsk; geologically similar to Finland with its low hills (highest ab. 1000 ft.) and numerous lakes, marshes, and streams; includes practically all of Lake Onega and N part of Lake Ladoga, also other smaller lakes as Seg, Kunto, and Top. Forests its chief wealth; agriculture much restricted by cold climate and poor soil; hunting and fishing important; iron and copper mining. Chief towns Petrozavodsk, Segezha, Kem, Sortalava.

History: Karelians, one of the chief divisions of the Finns, first mentioned in history in 9th cent.; their folk tales and songs the source of the Finnish epic *Kalevala;* they formed in medieval times a strong independent state which in 17th cent. came under Swedish dominion and in 1721 was annexed by Russia; region constituted as the Karelian A.S.S.R. 1923; territory much affected by Russian-Finnish War of 1939–40; after treaty of Mar. 15, 1940 by which certain border areas of Finland (ab. 13,500 sq. m.) were transferred to the U.S.S.R., the Karelo-Finnish S.S.R. was constituted Mar. 31, incorporating the new territory; part of this new union republic occupied 1941–43 by Germans and Finns; abolished 1956 and Karelian A.S.S.R. reconstituted.

Karelian Isthmus. The strip of land bet. W shore of Lake Ladoga and the Gulf of Finland, Russian S.F.S.R., U.S.S.R.; ab. 65 m. wide; including region around Vyborg which was formerly part of Finland; in World War II scene of fighting 1939–40 and again in 1944; taken by U.S.S.R. at end of war and added to Leningrad Oblast.

Karelo–Finnish Soviet Socialist Republic. See KARELIAN AUTONOMOUS SOVIET SOCIALIST REPUBLIC.

Ka·ren·ni \kə-'ren-ē\. Former district in E Burma; 4519 sq. m.; ✱ Loikaw; comprised a group of three feudatory states, Kantarawadi, Bawlake, and Kyebogyi; country of the Karens, a group of Indo-Chinese tribes; was not part of British Burma but administered by own chiefs under advice of Commissioner of Federated Shan States. Proclaimed a state 1947; its area enlarged and name changed to Kayah State 1952.

Ka·ren State \kə-'ren-\. State, S Burma, including parts of former Toungoo, Thaton, and Amherst districts; Karens in a state of sporadic rebellion against Burmese government.

Karfreit. See KOBARID.

Kar·gha·lik *also* **Qar·gha·liq** \ˌkär-gə-'lik\ *or* **Yeh·cheng** \'ye-'chəŋ\. Town, SW Sinkiang Uighur, W China.

Kar·hu·la \'kär-hu̇-lə\. Town, Kymi prov., S Finland; pop. (1970e) 22,093; glass, steel; estab. 1951.

Ka·ri·ba Dam \kə-'rē-bə-\. Dam in Kariba Gorge of Zambezi river, bet. SE Zambia and N Rhodesia, SE of Lusaka; maximum height 420 ft.; completed Dec. 1958; forms **Kariba Lake** (175 m. long; 2050 sq. m.; max. depth 390 ft.).

Kar·i·bib \ˌkar-ə-'bib\. Town, W cen. South-West Africa, 90 m. WNW of Windhoek; pop. (1960c) 1395; tin mines.

Ka·ri·kal \ˌkar-ə-'käl\. 1 Province of former French India, on Coromandel Coast E of Thanjavur 150 m. S of Madras; 52 sq. m.; received by French 1739 from raja of Tanjore (now Thanjavur); changed hands several times but was established as French 1817; reorganized 1947 as one of the five free cities of French India within the French Union; transferred to India 1954.

2 Seaport town, its ✱, 90 m. S of Pondicherry, on one of mouths of Cauvery river; pop. (1961c) 22,252.

Ka·ri·ma·ta Islands \ˌkär-ə-ˌmät-ə-\. Group of islands of Indonesia, in South China Sea W of island of Borneo, on NE side of Karimata Strait; 86 sq. m.; chief island **Karimata,** or **Great Karimata,** 70 sq. m.; a part of West Kalimantan province.

Karimata Strait. Passage bet. SW Borneo and Belitung I., connecting South China Sea and Java Sea; ab. 125 m. wide.

Ka·rim·na·gar \kə-'rim-nə-gər\. Town, N Andhra Pradesh, S cen. India, 87 m. NE of Hyderabad; pop. (1961c) 31,554.

Ka·ri·mun·dja·wa *or Du.* **Ka·ri·moen·djo·wo** \ˌkär-i-mün-'jō-vō\. Group of 27 islands in Java Sea, ab. 55 m. N of Djepara, Java, Indonesia; 19 sq. m.

Kariot. See IKARIA.

Kar·i·sim·bi \ˌkar-ə-'sim-bē\. Peak on boundary bet. Rwanda and E Zaire, NE of Lake Kiva; 14,787 ft.; a quiescent volcano; highest peak in the Virunga Mts.

Káristos. See CARYSTUS.

Ka·ri·ya \kə-'rē-(y)ə\. City, Aichi prefecture, Honshū, Japan, 14 m. SSE of Nagoya; pop. (1970c) 87,671.

Kar·kar \'kär-ˌkär\. 1 Small island in Bismarck Archipelago, W Pacific Ocean, off E coast of Papua New Guinea, New Guinea I., N of Madang; occupied by Allies June 1944.

2 *or* **Qar·qar** \'kär-ˌkär\. Unidentified place in W part of ancient Syria, perhaps Apamea on the Orontes river; scene of indecisive battle 854 (or 853) B.C. bet. Shalmaneser III, King of Assyria, and Ahab of Israel and his ally, Benhadad of Damascus.

Kar·kheh *or* **Ker·kheh** \kər-'kä\ *or anc.* **Cho·as·pes** \kō-'as-(ˌ)pēz\. River, W Iran; 200 m. long; rises S of Mt. Alwand, flows SW to marshlands E of the Tigris in SE Iraq.

Kar·ki·nit Bay \kər-ˌkē-nət-\. Inlet of Black Sea on NW coast of the Crimean Oblast, Ukrainian S.S.R., U.S.S.R.; indents the Perekop isthmus.

Kar·ko·nos·ki National Park \ˌkär-kə-'nós-kē-\. National park, SE Poland; 22 sq. m.; mountainous region; established 1959.

Kar·li \'kär-lē\. Village, W Maharashtra state, W India, ab. 32 m. NW of Poona; celebrated caves containing Buddhist temples, some of the oldest and best preserved in India.

Karl–Marx–Stadt \kärl-'märk-ˌs(h)tät\. 1 District of East Germany. See table at GERMANY, EAST.

2 *or formerly* **Chem·nitz** \'kem-ˌnits, -nəts\. City, its ✱, on Chemnitz river at foot of Erzgebirge 43 m. SE of Leipzig; pop. (1970e) 299,312; transportation center; textiles, clothing, machinery, chemicals; made free imperial city 1125; given monopoly of bleaching 1357, making it an early center of textile industry; heavily damaged in World War II; name changed from Chemnitz to Karl-Marx-Stadt 1953.

Karlö \'kär-ˌlə\. Island, N Gulf of Bothnia, W of Oulu, Finland.

Karlócza. See SREMSKI KARLOVCI.

Kar·lo·vac \'kär-lə-ˌväts\ *or Ger.* **Karl·stadt** \'kär(-ə)l-ˌs(h)tät\. Industrial city, Croatia, NW Yugoslavia, 30 m. SW of Zagreb; pop. (1965e) 38,000; hydroelectric power plants; founded 1579.

Kar·lo·vo \'kär-lō-(ˌ)vō\. Town, Plovdiv prov., cen. Bulgaria, ab. 35 m. N of Plovdiv; pop. (1968e) 22,099; silk.

Kar·lo·vy Va·ry \ˌkär-lə-vē-'vär-ē\; *Ger.* **Karls·bad** *or* **Carls·bad** \'kär(ə)lz-ˌbad, -ˌbät\. Town, NW Czech S.R., W Czechoslovakia, on the Ohře, an Elbe tributary ab. 70 m. W of Prague; pop. (1968e) 45,310; health resort; sulfur springs; scene of drawing up of the Carlsbad Decrees 1819 by ministers of the German states led by Prince Metternich, designed to suppress liberalism in German universities.

Karlowitz. See SREMSKI KARLOVCI.

Karlsburg. See ALBA IULIA.

Karls·hamn \kärls-'häm-ᵊn\. Town, Blekinge co., S Sweden, on Baltic coast just W of Karlskrona; pop. (1970e) 31,610; received city charter 1664.

Karl·sko·ga \kär(ə)l-'skü-gə\. Industrial city, Örebro co., S cen. Sweden, 23 m. W of Örebro; pop. (1970e) 38,981; guns and explosives, clothing.

Karls·kro·na \kärl-'skrü-nə\. City, ✱ of Blekinge co., S Sweden; pop. (1970e) 36,236; built on the mainland and five nearby islands in Baltic Sea; excellent fortified harbor, principal Swedish naval base; dry docks; fishing port; manufactures naval equipment, porcelain; granite quarries; founded 1679.

Karls·ru·he *also* **Carls·ru·he** \'kärlz-ˌrü-ə\. City, NW Baden-Württemberg, West Germany, on the Rhine 35 m. S of Mannheim; pop. (1969e) 256,238; machinery, building equipment, bicycles and motorcycles, electrical and radio equipment; technical coll. (1825), univ. (1865); ✱ of former state of Baden. Founded and laid out 1715 by Margrave Karl Wilhelm von Baden-Durlach; heavily damaged in World War II; since 1956 a nuclear research center of West Germany.

Karl·stad \'kär(ə)l-ˌstä(d)\. City, ✱ of Värmland co., SW Sweden, on Lake Vänern; pop. (1970e) 54,072; wood products, heavy wood-processing machinery; founded 1584; destroyed by fire 1865; scene of signing of treaty 1905 ending union of Sweden and Norway.

Karlstadt. See KARLOVAC.

Karm·øy \'kär-ˌmöi\. Island in North Sea, a part of Rogaland co., SW Norway; 67 sq. m.; 18 m. long; pop. (1969e) 26,653; aluminum smelting plant.

Kar·nak \'kär-ˌnak\. Village on the right (E) bank of the Nile in Upper Egypt; N part (Luxor is S part) of site of ancient Thebes (*q.v.*); site of early temple of Amen, perhaps prehistoric; later temple of Middle Kingdom replaced by great structure of Amenhotep III, which with additions by kings of Diospolite dynasties, esp. by Seti I and Ramses II, with its great hall, pylons, statues, obelisks, etc., is still well preserved.

Kar·nal \kər-'näl\. Town, Punjab state, NW India, on Yamuna canal 7 m. from Yamuna river, 75 m. N of New Delhi; pop. (1961c) 72,109; said to have been founded by Raja Karna, mythical champion of the Kauravas.

Karnali. See GHĀGHARA.

Kar·na·phu·li \ˌkär-nə-'pü-lē\. River, Bangla Desh, flowing W into Bay of Bengal; navigable to Chittagong.

Karnatik. See CARNATIC.

Karnes \'kärnz\. County in Texas. See table at TEXAS.

Karnes City. Town, ⊗ of Karnes co., S Texas, 52 m. SSE of San Antonio; pop. (1970c) 2926; oil and gas wells.

Kar Nicobar. See CAR NICOBAR.

Karnische Alpen. See table at ALPS.

Kärnten. See CARINTHIA.

Karnul. See KURNOOL.

Karolinen. See CAROLINE ISLANDS.

Karond. See KALAHANDI.

Ka·ron·ga \kə-'räŋ-gə, -'röŋ-\. Town, Malawi, SE Africa, at N end of Lake Nyasa on W side; pop. (1966c) 979; lake trading port; important in World War I as military headquarters.

Karoo. See KARROO.

Kar·pa·thos \'kär-pə-ˌthäs\ *or Ital.* **Scar·pan·to** \'skär-pən-ˌtō\ *or Gk.* **Kár·pa·thos** \'kär-pə-ˌthȯs\; *anc.* **Car·pa·thus** \-thəs\ *or* **Car·pa·thos** \-ˌthäs\. An island of the Dodecanese (*q.v.*), bet. Rhodes and the E end of Crete; 117 sq. m.; pop. (1961c) 6689; largest of the Dodecanese proper and next in size to Rhodes with which its history has long been closely connected; under Venetian rule 1306 to 1540 when it passed to the Turks; ceded to Italy 1912; returned to Greece Mar. 31, 1947.

Karpathos Strait *or* **Scarpanto Strait** *or Gk.* **Ste·nón Kar·pa·thon** \ste-'nȯn-'kär-pə-ˌthȯn\. Channel in S Dodecanese, separating islands of Rhodes and Karpathos; ab. 30 m. wide.

Kar·pe·ni·sion \ˌkär-pə-'nē-sē-ˌȯn\ *also* **Car·pe·ni·si** \ˌkär-pə-'nē-sē\ *or Gk.* **Kar·pe·ní·si·on** \ˌkär-pə-'nē-sē-ˌȯn\. Town, ✱ of Eurytania dept., W Greece, at S end of Pindus Mts. and NE of Agrinion; pop. (1971p) 4643; battle nearby Aug. 20, 1823 with Turks, in which the Greek leader, Marco Bozzaris, was killed.

Kar·pinsk \kär-'pin(t)sk\. Town, Sverdlovsk Oblast, Russian S.F.S.R., U.S.S.R., ab. 20 m. NW of Serov; pop. (1967e) 41,000; coal mining; brickworks.

Kar·roo *also* **Ka·roo** \kə-'rü\. An arid tableland region of Cape Province, Rep. of South Africa; area in excess of 100,000 sq. m.; divided into three parts: **(1) Great Karroo** *or* **Central Karroo,** in S cen. part, ab. 300 m. from E to W and from 2000 to 7000 ft. above sea level, characterized by dry air and little rain, no grass, only vegetation being karroo bush (*Acacia horrida*); chief towns Beaufort West, Graaff Reinet, Aberdeen. **(2) Little Karroo** *or* **Southern Karroo,** in S along coast, ab. 200 m. long, 1000 to 2000 ft. altitude; separated from Great Karroo by Swartberg Mts.; some fertile sections; chief towns Worcester, Oudtshoorn, Robertson. **(3) North Karroo** in N part along Orange river; largely desert.

Kars *also* **Qars** \'kärs\. **1** Province, NE Turkey; 7165 sq. m.; pop. (1969e) 657,100; ✱ Kars; a mountainous region; after Middle Ages occupied or invaded by Turks, Kurds, Kabardians, Circassians, and others; as a result of Russo-Turkish War 1877–78 transferred to Russia; returned to Turkey by treaty 1921.

2 City, its ✱, 110 m. NE of Erzurum; pop. (1965c) 41,376; woolen textiles, felt; built on a mountain spur, its citadel (built in 16th cent.) long a strong military post. Capital of an independent Armenian principality in 9th and 10th cents.; captured by Seljuk Turks in 11th cent., by Mongols in 13th cent., and by Tamerlane in 1387; stormed and captured by Russians 1828, 1855, and 1878.

Kar·shi \'kär-shē\ *or formerly* **Bek–Bu·di** \bek-'büd-ē\. Town, Kashka-Darya Oblast, SE Uzbek S.S.R., U.S.S.R., ab. 90 m. SE of Bukhara; pop. (1970p) 71,000; transportation center; mosque; residence of Tamerlane.

Karskiye Vorota, Proliv. See KARA STRAIT.

Karskoye More. See KARA SEA.

Karst. See KRAS.

Kar·ta·bo \kär-'täb-(ˌ)ō\. Village, Guyana, ab. 40 m. SW of Georgetown on lower Essequibo river.

Kar·ta·ly \kər-'täl-ē\. Town, Chelyabinsk Oblast, Russian S.F.S.R., U.S.S.R., ab. 70 m. ESE of Magnitogorsk; pop. (1967e) 40,000.

Kar·tha·la \kär-'täl-ə\ *or* **Ka·ra·ta·la** \ˌkär-ə-'täl-ə\. Volcano, S Great Comoro I., Comoro Is., N Mozambique Channel, NW of Malagasy Republic; 7874 ft.; eruptions 1830, 1855, 1858, 1904.

Kā·rūn \kə-'rün\. River, W Iran; 528 m. long; flows W and S in Khūzestān prov. and empties into the Shatt-al-Arab at Khorramshahr at N end of Ābādān I.; has winding course through mountains, navigable in its lower course; chief tributary the Ab-i-Dez from the N.

Kar·vi·ná \'kär-və-ˌnä\ *or Ger. and Pol.* **Kar·win** \'kär-ˌvēn\. City, Czech. S.R., cen. Czechoslovakia, just E of Ostrava; pop. (1968e) 75,884; in a lumbering and coal-mining area; held by Poland 1938–45.

Kar·war \'kär-ˌwär\. Town, W Mysore state, W India, on coast 50 m. S of Panaji; pop. (1961c) 23,096.

Kasaba. **1** Town, Cyprus. See KTIMA.

2 City, Turkey. See TURGUTLU.

Ka·sai *also* **Kas·sai** *or Port.* **Cas·sai** \kə-'sī\. River, SW Africa; 1338 m. long; rises in cen. Angola, flows E, then N, forming section of Angola-Zaire boundary; continues N and NW through S cen. and W Zaire to empty into Congo river on border of Congo; chief S tributary of the Congo. See KWAMOUTH.

Kasai–Oc·ci·den·tal \-ˌōk-si-dä^{n}-'täl\. Province of cen. Zaire. See table at ZAIRE 1.

Kasai–Ori·en·tal \-ˌȯr-ē-ä^{n}-'täl\. Province of cen. Zaire. See table at ZAIRE 1.

Ka·sa·ma \kə-'säm-ə\. Town, NE Zambia, 100 m. S of S end of Lake Tanganyika; pop. (1963c) 6384.

Kasamansa. See CASAMANCE.

Kasan. Former government and city, U.S.S.R. See KAZAN.

Ka·san·ga \kə-'säŋ-gə\ *or formerly* **Bis·marck·burg** \'biz-ˌmärk-ˌbu̇(ə)rg\. Port at S end of Lake Tanganyika, SW Tanzania, E Africa.

Ka·sa·o·ka \ˌkä-sə-'ō-kə\. City, Okayama prefecture, Honshū, Japan, 30 m. WSW of Okayama; pop. (1970c) 62,405.

Ka·sar, Cape \-kə-'sär\. Cape on NE coast of Africa, extending into the Red Sea; marks N limit of Ethiopia.

Ka·sa·ri \'käs-ə-rē\. River, W Estonian S.S.R., U.S.S.R.; ab. 60 m. long; flows SW to an inlet of Baltic Sea.

Kasbek. See KAZBEK.

Kaschau. See KOŠICE.

Kas·ganj \'käs-ˌgənj\. Town, W Uttar Pradesh, N India, on affluent of Ganges river 100 m. SE of Delhi; pop. (1961c) 37,559.

Kā·shān \kä-'shän\. City, cen. Iran, N of Eşfahān, on railroad 65 m. from Qom; pop. (1971e) 62,000; an old town formerly famous for its velvets and brocades and for its faïence; now produces woolen and silk carpets.

Kash·gar \'kash-ˌgär\ *or* **K'a–shih–ka** \'kä-'shē-'kä\. 1 River, W Sinkiang Uighur, W China; ab. 200 m. long; flows E toward Yarkand river.

2 *or Chin.* **K'o–shih** \'kō-'shē\. Chief commercial town of W Sinkiang Uighur, W China, on Kashgar river; pop. (1970e) 175,000; in fertile region but dependent on irrigation; alt. ab. 4000 ft.; chief exports raw wool, cotton and cotton goods, tea, sheep, and dyes.

History: Occupied in 3d cent. B.C. by the Yuechi; later held by Chinese, Turkish tribes, and Mongols; conquered by Genghis Khan and Tamerlane; visited and described by Marco Polo c. 1275; from 14th cent. to 1759 suffered many changes (completely destroyed 1514); Chinese since 1755 but at times under Russian influence; chief city of Chinese Turkistan (Kashgaria).

Kashgaria. See CHINESE TURKISTAN.

Ka·shi·ha·ra \kä-'shē-här-ə, ˌkä-shē-'här-ə\. City, Nara prefecture, Honshū, Japan, 20 m. SE of Ōsaka; pop. (1970c) 75,508.

Kashing. See CHIAHSING.

Ka·shi·ra \kə-'shir-ə\. Town, Moscow Oblast, Russian S.F.S.R., U.S.S.R., on Oka river 48 m. NNE of Tula; severe fighting Dec. 1941.

Ka·shi·wa·za·ki \ˌkäsh-ē-'wä-zä-kē\. City, Niigata prefecture, Honshū, Japan, 47 m. SW of Niigata; pop. (1970c) 73,569.

Kash·ka–Dar·ya Oblast \ˌkäsh-kə-dər-'yä-'ō-bləst, -ˌblast\. Subdivision of the Uzbek S.S.R., U.S.S.R.; 10,965 sq. m.; pop. (1970p) 802,000.

Kash·mir \'kash-ˌmi(ə)r, 'kazh-, kash-', kazh-'\. Former princely state, now part of Jammu and Kashmir. See JAMMU AND KASHMIR.

Kashmir North. See BARAMULLA 1.

Kashmir South. See SRINAGAR.

Ka–shun–no–erh \'kä-'shün-'nō-'e(ə)r\ *also* **Ga·shiun Nor** \'gä-ˌshün-'nō(ə)r\. Large salt lake, W Gobi desert, NW Ningsia Hui, N China; receives O-chi-na river.

Kasi. See VARANASI 2.

Ka·si·mov \kə-'sē-məf\. Town, Ryazan Oblast, Russian S.F.S.R., U.S.S.R., on Oka river 70 m. ENE of Ryazan; pop. (1967e) 34,000; founded 1152 and an important Tatar city from 15th cent. to 1667.

Ka·si·ru·ta \ˌkäs-ə-'rüt-ə\. See BATJAN.

Kas·kas·kia \ka-'skas-kē-ə\. 1 River, SW Illinois; ab. 320 m. long; partly navigable, rises in Champaign co., flows SW into Mississippi river in SW cen. Randolph co.

2 Village, Randolph co., SW Illinois, near junction of the Kaskaskia river with the Mississippi; pop. (1970c) 79; near site of oldest town in the West, founded 1703 as an Indian village, passed to the British 1765, made capital of territory of Illinois 1809, capital of state of Illinois 1818–20; by 1910 town completely destroyed as result of flood 1844 and further encroachments of the Mississippi 1881 and later.

Kas·ka·wulsh Glacier \ˌkas-kə-ˌwu̇lsh-\. Glacier in the St. Elias Mountains, SW Yukon, Canada; 40 m. long, ab. 4 m. wide near its terminus.

Kas·ki·nen \'käs-kə-nən\ *or Swed.* **Kaskö** \'käs-ˌkə\. Seaport town, Vaasa prov., SW Finland, on small coastal island ab. 50 m. S of Vaasa; pop. (1970e) 1435; founded 1785.

Ka·sos *or Gk.* **Ká·sos** \'käs-ˌos\ *or Ital.* **Ca·so** \'käs-(ˌ)ō\ *also* **Ca·sus** \'kā-səs\. An island of the Dodecanese (*q.v.*), SW of Karpathos and NE of E end of Crete; 27 sq. m.

Kasr, Al–. See AL-QASR.

Kasr al–Kebir. See ALCÁZARQUIVIR.

Kassa. See KOŠICE.

Kassai. See KASAI.

Kas·sa·la \'kas-ə-lə\. 1 Province of NE Sudan. See table at SUDAN.

2 Town, its ✻, 250 m. E of Khartoum near border of Ethiopia; pop. (1969e) 81,230; fruit gardens; transportation center; built on a plain at ab. 1700 ft.; founded by Egyptians as a fort 1840; held by Mahdists 1885–94; retaken by Italian force after battle of July 17, 1894 and restored to Egypt 1897; in World War II held briefly by Italians 1940–41.

Kas·sán·dra \kə-'sän-drə\ *or anc.* **Pal·le·ne** \pə-'lē-nē\. Southwest peninsula of Chalcidice, projecting into Aegean Sea on NE coast of Greece, and forming part of E side of the Gulf of Salonika; on narrow isthmus at its base is Potidaea.

Kassandra, Gulf of. See TORONAIC GULF.

Kas·sel *also* **Cas·sel** \'kas-əl, 'käs-\. City, Hesse, West Germany, on Fulda river 71 m. WNW of Erfurt; pop. (1969e) 213,118; transportation center; railroad rolling stock and locomotives, optical instruments, synthetic fabrics; palace of former elector of Hesse-Cassel, 14th cent. church; ✻ of the former Hesse-Nassau prov.

History: Founded before 913 A.D.; became city in 12th cent.; captured by French in Seven Years' War; supplied mercenaries to aid British against American colonies; capital of kingdom of Westphalia 1807–13; passed to Prussia 1866; in World War II frequently bombed 1943–45, taken by Americans Apr. 4, 1945; scene of discussions between Chancellor Brandt of West Germany and Premier Stoph of East Germany, May 1970.

Kasserine. See AL-QASRAYN.

Kas·ta·mo·nu \ˌkäs-tə-mō-'nü\ *or* **Kas·ta·mu·ni** \-mü-'nē\. 1 Province of N Turkey. See table at TURKEY.

2 Town, its ✻, on a tributary of the Kızıl Irmak 110 m. NNE of Ankara; pop. (1965c) 23,485; near copper mines, noted for its manufacture of copper utensils; became Turkish 1393.

Kas·tav \'käs-ˌtäv\ *or Ital.* **Ca·stua** \'käs-(ˌ)twä\. Commune, SW Slovenia, Yugoslavia, ab. 6 m. W of Rijeka (Fiume) on the coast; Roman remains; on 1946 Italian border.

Kas·tel·lor·i·zon \ˌkäs-tə-'lȯr-ə-ˌzän\ *or angl.* **Ca·stel·lo·ri·zo** \ˌkäs-tə-'lȯr-ə-ˌzō\ *or Ital.* **Ca·stel·ros·so** \ˌkäs-tel-'rȯs-(ˌ)ō\ *or Gk.* **Kas·tel·lór·i·zon** \ˌkäs-tə-'lȯr-ə-ˌzȯn\; *anc.* **Me·gis·te** \mi-'jis-tē\. Island in E Mediterranean Sea, 80 m. E of Rhodes and 2 m. off SW coast of Turkey in Asia; 9 sq. m.; pop. (1961c) 476; included in the Dodecanese, ceded by Turkey to Italy 1923; population entirely Greek; retroceded to Greece 1947.

Ka·sto·ria \ˌkäs-tə-ˈrē-ə\. 1 Department of Greece. See table at GREECE.

2 Commune, ✱ of Kastoria dept., W Macedonia, N Greece, 20 m. SSW of Florina on **Lake Kastoria** (20 sq. m.); pop. (1971p) 15,990.

Kastro. 1 Seaport, Greece. See KÁSTRON.

2 City, Greece. See MYTILENE 2.

Kastron. See CHIOS 2.

Ká·stron *also* **Cas·tron** \ˈkäs-ˌtrȯn\ *or* **Ka·stro** *also* **Cas·tro** \ˈkäs-(ˌ)trō\. Seaport commune on W coast of Lemnos I., Aegean Sea; pop. (1961c) 3460; ✱ of the island; in Lesbos dept., Greece.

Kastrop–Rauxel. See CASTROP-RAUXEL.

Ka·su·mi·ga·u·ra *or* **Ka·su·mi·ga Ura** \ˌkäs-ə-ˌmē-gä-ˈu̇r-ə\. Lagoon, Ibaraki prefecture, SE Honshū, Japan, on lower course of the Tone river ab. 50 m. NE of Tokyo; ab. 18 m. long and 17 m. wide at its broadest part; 73 sq. m.; resort.

Ka·sur \kə-ˈsu̇(ə)r\. Town, Punjab, Pakistan, near Sutlej river 34 m. SSE of Lahore; pop. (1969e) 86,300; settled comparatively late by a Pathan colony from beyond the Indus.

Kasvin. See QAZVIN.

Ka·ta·gum \kə-ˈtäg-əm\. Region, N Nigeria, W Africa; formerly an independent emirate, taken over by British 1903; chief town Hadejia.

Ka·tah·din, Mount *also* **Mount Ktaa·dn** \-kə-ˈtäd-ᵊn\. Peak, E Piscataquis co., N cen. Maine; 5268 ft.; highest point in the state.

Katanga. See SHABA.

Ka·tang·lad Mountains \kə-ˈtäŋ-ˌläd-\. Mountain group in W cen. Bukidnon prov., N cen. Mindanao, Phil.; highest point ab. 9000 ft.

Katar. See QATAR.

Katch·all \ˈkach-əl\. One of the Nicobar Is. (*q.v.*).

Ka·te·na \kə-ˈtā-nə\. Village on W coast of Okinawa, near S end ab. 12 m. N of Naha, Ryukyu Is., Japan; airport, taken by American forces Apr. 1, 1945.

Ka·te·rí·nē \ˌkät-ə-ˈrē-nē\. Town, ✱ of Pieria dept., W cen. Macedonia, Greece, on W shore of Gulf of Salonika, SSW of Salonika; pop. (1971p) 29,151; market town; flour mills.

Kates Needle \ˈkāts-\. Mountain on boundary bet. SE Alaska and W British Columbia, Canada; 10,002 ft.

Ka·tha \kə-ˈthä\. 1 District, Sagaing state, Burma; 5229 sq. m.; pop. (1962e) 326,940.

2 Town, its ✱, on right bank of the upper Irrawaddy 155 m. N of Mandalay; port for river steamers; railroad terminus.

Katharinenstadt. See MARKS.

Kath·er·i·na, Geb·el \ˌjeb-əl-ˌkath-ə-ˈrē-nə\ *or* **Mount Cath·er·ine** \-ˈkath-(ə-)rən\. Mountain, highest part of Gebel Musa mountain group, Sinai Penin.; 8652 ft.

Kath·er·ine \ˈkath-(ə-)rən\. 1 River, Northern Territory, Australia; 150 m. long; seasonal; upper course of the Daly river.

2 Post station, N Northern Territory, Australia, on Katherine river and on railroad ab. 170 m. SE of Darwin.

Katherine Gorge National Park. National park, Northern Territory, Australia; 88 sq. m.; varied wildlife; established 1963.

Ka·thi·a·war \ˌkät-ē-ə-ˈwär\. Peninsula, W Gujarat state, W coast of India; 23,432 sq. m.; bounded on N by Rann of Kutch, on E by Ahmadabad dist., and on S and W by Arabian Sea; formerly included two British agencies—Eastern Kathiawar and Western Kathiawar—later subdivisions of the Western India States Agency; comprised also 188 Indian states, including 16 larger and independent states, formerly under a resident at Rajkot, but after 1947 semi-independent or associated with India; also parts of Baroda (Amreli and Okhamandal) and part of Ahmadabad dist. Home of many important old Hindu races, with notable antiquities. The states of Jetpur, Wankaner, Morvi, Palitana, Gondal, Wadhwan, Porbandar, and Navanagar joined a new confederation July 7, 1947.

Kathmandu. See KATMANDU.

Katia. See QATIA.

Katif. See QATIF.

Ka·ti·har \ˈkət-ə-ˌhär\. Town, Bihar, NE India; pop. (1961c) 59,344.

Ka·ti·pu·nan \ˌkät-ə-pü-ˈnän\ *or formerly* **Lu·bung·an** \lü-ˈbüŋ-än\. Municipality, N Zamboanga del Norte prov., Mindanao, Phil.; pop. (1969e) 40,600; port on S side of passage bet. Sulu Sea and Mindanao Sea.

Kat·mai, Mount \-ˈkat-ˌmī\. Volcano in **Katmai National Monument** (see UNITED STATES, *National Monuments*), at N end of Alaska Penin. on Shelikof Strait, S Alaska; 6715 ft.; main crater one of largest in world; top of mountain blown off by great eruption of June 1912; region of importance to volcanologists because phenomena exist on scale of great magnitude. See VALLEY OF TEN THOUSAND SMOKES.

Kat·man·du *also* **Kath·man·du** *or* **Khat·man·du** \ˌkat-man-ˈdü, ˌkät-, -mən-\. City, ✱ of Nepal, in valley of Himalayas ab. 75 m. from Indian frontier; pop. (1971p) 153,405; commercial and transportation center of Nepal; univ. (1958); founded 723 A.D.; captured by Gurkha kings 1768 and made capital; severely damaged by earthquake 1934.

Ka·to·wi·ce \ˌkät-ə-ˈvēt-sə\ *or Ger.* **Kat·to·witz** \ˈkät-ə-ˌvits\. 1 Province of S Poland. See table at POLAND.

2 Industrial city, its ✱, 45 m. WNW of Kraków; pop. (1970p) 303,300; Roman Catholic episcopal see; major railroad center; coal mining, metalworking; iron, zinc, chemicals, heavy machinery; univ. (1968). Founded in 16th cent.; became city 1865; to Poland 1921; in World War II occupied by Germans Sept. 1939–Jan. 1945.

Kat·rine, Loch \-ˈka-trən\. Lake in SW Perth co., cen. Scotland, 5 m. E of Loch Lomond; ab. 9½ m. long, 2 m. wide; maximum depth 495 ft.; scene of Scott's *Lady of the Lake.* See ELLEN'S ISLE.

Ka·tri·ne·holm \ˌkat-ˌrēn-ə-ˈhōlm\. Town, Södermanland co., SE Sweden, 70 m. WSW of Stockholm; pop. (1970e) 21,790.

Ka·tsi·na \ˈkät-si-nə\. Town, North-Central State, Nigeria, 85 m. NW of Kano; pop. (1969e) 104,996; commercial center; exports hides, leather, cotton, peanuts; ✱ of ancient kingdom of **Katsina,** one of earliest of the Hausa states; ancient seat of learning; probably had population of ab. 100,000 in 17th and 18th cents.; seized by the Fulahs in early 19th cent.; taken over by British 1904; Muslim teachers college; hospital.

Ka·tsu·ta \kät-ˈsüt-ə\. City, Ibaraki prefecture, Honshū, Japan, 65 m. NE of Tokyo; pop. (1970c) 66,754.

Kat·ta·kur·gan \kə-ˌtä-ku̇r-ˈgän\. Town, Samarkand Oblast, Uzbek S.S.R., U.S.S.R., ab. 40 m. WNW of Samarkand; pop. (1967e) 44,000.

Kat·te·gat *also* **Cat·te·gat** \ˈkat-i-ˌgat\. Broad arm of North Sea, bet. Sweden on E and Jutland, Denmark, on W; max. width 88 m.; connected with North Sea through the Skagerrak and with Baltic Sea through Øresund, the Great Belt, and the Little Belt.

Kattowitz. See KATOWICE.

Ka·tun \kə-ˈtün\. River, W and S Gorno-Altai Autonomous Oblast, Russian S.F.S.R., U.S.S.R.; 386 m. long; flows N, joins the Biya to form the Ob.

Kat·wijk \ˈkät-ˌvīk\ *or* **Katwijk aan Zee** \-än-ˈzā\. Commune, South Holland prov., SW Netherlands, at mouth of the Oude Rijn; pop. (1970c) 36,236; fishing town and seaside resort 5 m. NW of Leiden.

Ka·ty \ˈkāt-ē\. City, Fort Bend, Harris, and Waller cos., SE Texas, 30 m. W of Houston; pop. (1970c) 2923.

Katzbach. See KACZAWA.

Kat·zen·buck·el \ˈkät-sən-ˌbu̇k-əl\. Mountain, N Baden-Württemberg, West Germany; 2054 ft.; highest point in the Odenwald.

Kau \kä-ˈü\. Division, Hawaii co., Hawaii, S part of Hawaii I.; chief village Pahala.

Kau·ai \ˈkau̇-ˌī\. 1 *or formerly* **Ka·i·e·i·e·wa·ho** \kä-ˌē-ä-ˌē-ä-ˈwä-(ˌ)hō\. Channel bet. the islands of Oahu and Kauai, Hawaii; 63 m. wide.

2 Island in NW Hawaii, WNW of Oahu; 555 sq. m.; with Niihau forms Kauai co.; mountainous, its two chief peaks, Kawaikini and Waialeale, in the center; has several short streams, being the only island of the Hawaiian group that may be said to have rivers; its more important anchorages Nawiliwili, Hanalei, and Hanapepe Bays; chief town Lihue; principal industry raising sugar.

3 County, NW Hawaii. See table at HAWAII.

Kauf·beu·ren \kau̇f-ˈbȯi-rən\. City, Bavaria, West Germany; pop. (1969e) 39,542; precision and electronic instruments; breweries, glassworks; to Bavaria 1803.

Kauf·man \ˈkȯf-mən\. 1 County in NE Texas. See table at TEXAS.

2 City, its ⊗, 30 m. ESE of Dallas; pop. (1970c) 4012; cotton gins, oil wells; meat-packing.

Kaufmann Peak. See LENIN PEAK.

Kau·i·ki Head \kau̇-ˌē-kē-\. Cape and promontory on E end of Maui I., Hawaii.

Kau Kau Bay \ˌkau̇-ˌkau̇-\. Bay on N side of E end of Guadalcanal I., SE Solomon Is., W Pacific Ocean.

Kau·kau·na \kȯ-ˈkȯ-nə\. City, Outagamie co., E Wisconsin; pop. (1970c) 11,292; precision tools, paper, cheese; stone quarries; dairy products; Outagamie County Teachers Coll. (1912).

Kau·kau Veld \ˌkau̇-ˌkau̇-ˈfelt, -ˈvelt\. Barren region NW of the Kalahari Desert, S Africa, extending over NE South-West Africa and NW Botswana W of the Okavango Swamp.

Ka·u·la \kä-ˈü-lə\ *or* **Ta·hu·ra** \tə-ˈhu̇r-ə\. Small barren uninhabited rock in Pacific Ocean 23 m. WSW of Niihau I., Hawaii; alt. 550 ft.

Kau·la·ka·hi \ˌkau̇-lə-ˈkä-(ˌ)hē\. Strait bet. islands of Niihau and Kauai, Hawaii.

Kaulun *or* **Kaulung.** See KOWLOON.

Kau·ma·la·pau \ˌkau̇-mə-ˈlä-ˌpau̇\. Village, Maui co., Hawaii, on W coast of Lanai I.

Kau·na·ka·kai \ˌkau̇-nə-ˈkä-ˌkī\. Village, Maui co., Hawaii, on S coast of Molokai I.; pop. (1970c) 1070.

Kau·nas \ˈkau̇-nəs, -ˌnäs\ *or Russ.* **Kov·no** \ˈkȯv-(ˌ)nō\ *or Pol.* **Kow·no** \ˈkȯv-ˌnȯ\. City, Lithuanian S.S.R., NW U.S.S.R., at confluence of Neris with Neman river; pop. (1967e) 284,000; transportation center; metal goods, paper, textiles, electrical machinery; several old buildings, esp. the Lithuanian-Gothic church of Vytautas (15th cent.).

History: Founded in 11th cent.; in medieval times often attacked and partially destroyed; to Russia at third partition of Poland 1795; in World War I captured by Germans 1915; capital of Lithuania 1920–40 after Poland's second seizure of the former capital, Vilnius, Oct. 9, 1920; in World War II occupied by U.S.S.R. 1940 and by Germans 1941–44.

Kau·ra Na·mo·da \ˌkau̇-rə-nə-ˈmōd-ə\. Town, North-Western State, N Nigeria, 100 m. SE of Sokoto; pop. (1963c) 29,039.

Kauriala. See GHĀGHARA.

Ka·va·jë \kə-ˈvä-yə\. Town, Durrës province, W Albania, on coast ab. 10 m. S of Durrës; pop. (1967e) 18,800; tobacco.

Ka·val·la *also* **Ca·val·la** \kə-ˈval-ə\ *or Gk.* **Ka·vál·la** \-ˈväl-\. 1 Department of Greece. See table at GREECE.

2 Seaport city, ✱ of Kavalla dept., NE Macedonia, NE Greece, at head of **Gulf of Kavalla** *or Gk.* **Kól·pos Ka·vál·las** \ˌkȯl-pȯs-kə-ˈväl-əs\ opp. Thasos I.; pop. (1971p) 46,679; exports tobacco; near site of ancient Neapolis where St. Paul landed on way to Philippi; center of revolution 1935. Birthplace of Mehemet Ali.

Kavalli. See CAVALLY.

Ka·va·rat·ti Island \ˌkəv-ə-ˈrət-ē-\. One of the Laccadive Is., ab. 230 m. off the coast of Kerala, S India; its only town, **Kavaratti,** is the administrative center of the Indian territory of Laccadive, Minicoy, and Amindivi Is.

Kaveri. See CAUVERY.

Ka·vi·eng *or* **Kae·wi·eng** \ˌkav-ē-ˈeŋ\. Town with good harbor on North Cape, NW tip of New Ireland, Bismarck Archipelago, Papua New Guinea, ab. 162 m. NW of Rabaul; pop. (1966p) 2142; chief port on the island and ✱ of New Ireland administrative district; shipping point of many coconut plantations; in World War II occupied by Japanese 1942–45; bypassed in Allied advance.

Kavkazki Khrebet. See CAUCASUS MOUNTAINS.

Ka·vo Mountains \ˌkäv-ō-\. Range extending lengthwise of the island of Guadalcanal, British Solomon Is., W Pacific Ocean; highest peak Popomanasiu 7648 ft.

Kaw. See KANSAS 1.

Ka·wa·goe \kə-ˈwäg-ˌȯi\. City, Saitama prefecture, SE cen. Honshū, Japan, ab. 20 m. NW of Tokyo; pop. (1969e) 152,000.

Ka·wa·gu·chi \ˌkä-wə-ˈgü-chē\. 1 Lake in S Honshū, Japan, near Fuji; ab. 10 m. in circumference; altitude 2700 ft.

2 City, Saitama prefecture, SE Honshū, Japan, just N of Tokyo; pop. (1970c) 305,886.

Ka·wai·hae \ˌkä-wə-ˈhī\. Village, Hawaii co., Hawaii, on **Kawaihae Bay** on NW coast of Hawaii I.; interisland steamer landing.

Ka·wai·hau \ˌkä-wī-ˈhau̇\. Division, NE Kauai I., Kauai co., Hawaii; chief town Kapaa.

Ka·wai·hoa, Cape \-ˌkä-wī-ˈhō-ə\ *or* **Kawaihoa Point.** Cape on S end of Niihau I., Hawaii.

Kawaihoa Point. Promontory, Oahu, Hawaii. See KOKO HEAD.

Ka·wai·ki·ni \ˌkä-wī-ˈkē-nē\. Mountain, cen. Kauai I., Hawaii; 5170 ft.

Ka·wa·ni·shi \kä-ˈwän-i-shē, ˌkä-wə-ˈnē-shē\. City, Hyōgo prefecture, Honshū, Japan, 12 m. NW of Ōsaka; pop. (1970c) 87,127.

Ka·war·dha \kə-ˈwärd-ə\. 1 Former Indian state, now part of Madhya Pradesh, cen. India; 794 sq. m.

2 Town, its ✱, 140 m. NE of Nagpur; pop. (1961c) 10,100.

Ka·war·tha Lakes \kə-ˌwȯr-thə-\. A series of lakes in Peterborough and Victoria cos., SE Ontario, Canada, forming a chain E and W in region N of Peterborough and Lindsay; traversed by Trent Canal system.

Ka·wa·sa·ki \ˌkä-wə-ˈsäk-ē\. City, Kanagawa prefecture, Honshū, Japan, a S suburb of Tokyo on W coast of Tokyo Bay; pop. (1970c) 973,486; major industrial center; shipbuilding, heavy machinery, and chemicals; 12th cent. temple; almost completely destroyed in World War II, but since rebuilt.

Ka·we·ah Peaks \kə-ˈwē-ə-\. Four mountains in Sierra Nevada, in Tulare co., S cen. California: **Black Kaweah** 13,752 ft., **Red Kaweah** 13,754 ft., **Gray Kaweah** 13,728 ft., and **Big Kaweah** 13,816 ft.

Ka·we·li·koa Point \kə-ˌwā-li-ˈkō-ə-\. Cape on SE coast of Kauai I., Hawaii.

Ka·whia Harbor \ˌkä(f)-wē-ə-\. Inlet of Pacific Ocean on NW cen. coast of North I., New Zealand.

Ka·wi \ˈkä-wē\. Mountain group, E Java, Indonesia; highest point 9968 ft.; includes Mt. Kelud and adjoins Mt. Ardjuno on the N.

Ka·wich Range \ˌkä-wich-\. Range in S cen. Nye co., S Nevada; highest point **Kawich Peak** 9404 ft.

Kaw·thu·le State \kä-ˈthü-lā-\. State of S cen. Burma. See table at BURMA.

Kay \ˈkā\. County in Oklahoma. See table at OKLAHOMA.

Ka·yah State \ˈkī-ə-\. State of E cen. Burma. See table at BURMA; see also KARENNI.

Kay·ak \ˈkī-ˌak\. Island off coast of SE Alaska, E of Prince William Sound; islet at its S end is Cape St. Elias.

Kayan. See KEN.

Kayes \'kāz\. Town, SW Mali, W Africa, on Senegal river; munic. pop. (1970e) 147,805; on railroad from Dakar and Thiès in Senegal to Bamako and Koulikoro.

Kay·nar·dzha \ˌkī-när-'jə\ *or formerly* **Ku·chuk Kai·nar·ji** \kü-'chük-ˌkī-nər-'jē\ *or Rom.* **Cai·nar·ge·a·va–Mi·că** \kī-ˌnär-jə-və-'mē-kə\. Village, Bulgaria, a few miles SE of Silistra; scene of treaty July 21, 1774, terminating Russo-Turkish War, by which Russia gained: (1) territory on the Bug and Kuban rivers and Kerch on the Crimea (see CRIMEAN OBLAST); (2) freedom for Russian shipping on Black Sea; (3) right of intervention in Danubian Principalities; (4) protection of Orthodox Christians in Ottoman Empire.

Ka·yo Bay \ˌkī-ō-\ *or formerly* **Hum·boldt Bay** \ˌhəm-bōlt-\. Bay, NE coast of Irian Barat, Indonesia; scene of Allied landing Apr. 1944.

Kay·ser \'kī-zər\. Peak in SW Surinam; 3020 ft.

Kay·ser·ge·berg·te National Park \'kī-zər-gə-ˌbe(ə)rg-tə-\. National park, Surinam; 618 sq. m.; established 1966.

Kay·se·ri \ˌkī-zə-'rē\ *or* **Kai·sa·ria** \ˌkī-sə-rē-'(y)ə\. 1 Province of cen. Turkey, Asia. See table at TURKEY.

2 *or anc.* **Cae·sa·rea Maz·a·ca** \ˌsē-zə-ˌrē-ə-'maz-ə-kə, ˌsēz-ə-, ˌses-ə-\ *or* **Mazaca.** City, its ✱, at foot of Erciyas Dağı; pop. (1965c) 126,635; for centuries an important trade center. Caesarea Mazaca was chief city of ancient Cappadocia; destroyed by Persians 260 A.D.; modern city founded 4th cent.

Kays·ville \'kāz-ˌvil\. City, Davis co., N Utah, 18 m. S of Ogden; pop. (1970c) 6192; diversified agriculture; flour mills.

Ka·zakh Soviet Socialist Republic \kə-'zak-, -'zäk-\ *or* **Ka·zakh·stan** *or* **Ka·zak·stan** \-'stan, -'stän\. A constituent republic of the U.S.S.R., bounded on N by Russian S.F.S.R., on E by China, on S by Kirgiz, Uzbek, and Turkmen Soviet Socialist Republics, on W by the Caspian Sea, and on NW by Russian S.F.S.R.; 1,048,300 sq. m.; pop. (1970p) 12,850,000; ✱ Alma-Ata; occupied in cen. part by great Kirgiz Steppe and in S by desert regions: in SW the Ustyurt and in SE the Moinkum. Includes N half of Aral Sea, all of Lake Balkhash, and the smaller lakes Zaisan, Tengiz, and Chelkar Tengiz. Chief rivers the Syr Darya in S, upper Irtysh in NE, the lower Ural in W; other important streams the Ishim, Tobol, Ili, and Emba. In E, N of Lake Balkhash, plateau lands rise to the lofty Tien Shan and W Altai Mts. on Chinese boundary. *Chief products:* Wheat, fruit, tobacco; livestock; coal, tungsten, copper, zinc; oil refining, leatherworking; chemicals, textiles. *Chief towns:* Alma-Ata, Karaganda, Chimkent.

History: Region came under the Mongols in 13th cent. and fragments of the Golden Horde long settled here; gradually 1730–1853 came under Russian rule and formed large part of Russian Turkistan; an autonomous republic erected by the Kazakh Kirghiz 1920; admitted to U.S.S.R. as constituent republic 1936.

Ka·zan \kə-'zan\. River, cen. Canada; 455 m. long; rises in SE Mackenzie dist., Northwest Territories, flows NNE through Yathkyed and other lakes to enter Baker Lake in Keewatin dist.; one of main streams of the Barren Grounds.

Kazan \kə-'zan, -'zän(-yə)\ *also* **Ka·san** \-'sän\. 1 Former government in E Russia in Europe, now included in Mari, Chuvash, and Tatar A.S.S.Rs., Russian S.F.S.R., U.S.S.R.

2 City, ✱ of Tatar A.S.S.R., Russian S.F.S.R., U.S.S.R., on short tributary 3 m. from the Volga where it turns S 200 m. E of Gorki; pop. (1970p) 869,000; on Moscow-Sverdlovsk railroad ab. 40 m. above the junction of the Kama with the Volga; a key city, commercially and industrially, of the Middle Volga Area; oil refining; linen, leather goods, felts, soap, hides, furs, chemicals, electrical equipment; many of its old buildings—kremlin, cathedral, tower, monastery, etc.—are still standing, although some were damaged during the Revolution; university (founded ab. 1804), many technical schools; original Kazan, not far from present city, under Black Bulgarian empire; converted to Islam in 10th cent.; conquered by Tatars in 13th cent.; new city founded 1437 and made capital of kingdom 1438 by khan of the Golden Horde; captured by Ivan the Terrible 1552; in 18th cent. main base for Russian expansion to S; burned by Pugachev 1773; center of Tatar national movement Oct. 1917; captured by Czechs Aug. 1918; suffered during Revolution and subsequent famine 1921–22.

Ka·zan·lŭk \ˌkä-zän-'lək\ *or* **Ka·zan·lik** \-'lik\. Town, Stara Zagora prov., cen. Bulgaria, ab. 17 m. NW of Stara Zagora; pop. (1968e) 48,816; center of attar of roses industry; taken by Russians Jan. 7, 1878 in war with Turkey.

Kazan Retto. See VOLCANO ISLANDS.

Kaz·bek *also* **Kas·bek** \kəz-'byek\. Peak, cen. Caucasus Mts., U.S.S.R., bet. the South Ossetian Autonomous Oblast, Georgian S.S.R., and the North Ossetian A.S.S.R., Russian S.F.S.R.; 16,558 ft.; an extinct volcano with steep slopes, towering above Daryal Pass; eight glaciers; first climbed 1868; subject of many legends.

Kazdağı. See IDA.

Kā·ze·rūn \ˌkäz-ə-'rün\. Town, Fārs prov., SW Iran, ab. 70 m. W of Shīrāz; pop. (1971e) 42,000; orange and date groves; produces cotton, rice, and almonds.

Kazīmīyah, Al–. See KADHIMAIN.

Kazvin. See QAZVĪR.

Kéa. See KEOS.

Ke·a·au \ˌkā-ə-'ä-(ˌ)ü\. Town, Hawaii co., Hawaii, E Hawaii I., S of Hilo; pop. (1970c) 951.

Ke·a·ho·le Point \ˌkä-ə-ˌhō-lē-\. Cape on W coast of Hawaii I.

Ke·a·lai·ka·hi·ki \kā-ˌäl-ˌī-kə-'hē-kē\. Channel bet. Lanai and Kahoolawe Is., Hawaii; ab. 20 m. wide.

Ke·a·la·ke·kua \kā-ˌäl-ə-kə-'kü-ə\. Village, Hawaii co., Hawaii, on **Kealakekua Bay** on W coast of Hawaii I.; pop. (1970c) 740; landing place of Capt. James Cook on his second visit to Hawaiian Is. Jan. 1779 and place where he was killed in quarrel with natives Feb. 14; a favorite place of anchorage for visiting foreign vessels in early years of kingdom; has monument to Cook erected 1874 by Lord Byron.

Keans·burg \'kēnz-ˌbərg\. Borough, Monmouth co., E cen. New Jersey, on Raritan Bay; pop. (1970c) 9720; resort and port of call for pleasure and fishing craft.

Kear·ney \'kär-nē\. 1 County in Nebraska. See table at NEBRASKA.

2 City, ⊗ of Buffalo co., S cen. Nebraska, on Platte river 45 m. WSW of Grand Island; pop. (1970c) 19,181; feed mills; diversified agriculture; Kearney State Coll. (1905).

Kearn Peak \'kərn-\. Mountain in Sierra Nevada, E Tulare co., S cen. California; 11,493 ft.

Kearns \'kərnz\. Urban community (unincorporated), Salt Lake co., N Utah, SW of Salt Lake City; pop. (1970c) 17,071; dairy products, sugar beets.

Kear·ny \'kär-nē\. 1 County in Kansas. See table at KANSAS.

2 Town, Pinal co., S Arizona, 50 m. N of Tucson; pop. (1970c) 2829; agriculture.

3 Town, Hudson co., NE New Jersey, bet. Passaic and Hackensack rivers at head of Newark Bay, 2 m. N of Newark; pop. (1970c) 37,585; brick and tile; plastics, chemicals, furniture, electronic equipment, textiles; truck farming.

Kearsarge. See PEQUAWKET.

Kear·sarge, Mount \-'ki(ə)r-ˌsärj\. Peak, Merrimack co., S cen. New Hampshire; 2937 ft.

Kears·ley \'ki(ə)rz-lē\. Urban district, Lancashire, NW England, 8 m. NW of Manchester; pop. (1971p) 11,243.

Ke·a·wai·ki Bay \ˌkā-ə-ˌwī-kē-\. Bay on NW coast of Hawaii I., bet. Kiholo Bay and Honokaope Bay.

Ke·bil·li \kə-'bil-ē\. Town, S cen. Tunisia, on SE corner of Chott Djerid; pop. (1966c) 4500.

Ké·bir, Oued al– \ˌwed-al-kā-'bi(ə)r\ *or* **Wa·di al–Ke·bir** \ˌwäd-ē-\. River, NE Algeria, flowing NNE through city of Constantine into Mediterranean Sea near Skikda; not navigable; in its upper course sometimes known as the **Rum·mel** \'rủm-əl\ river.

Kebir, Wadi al–. See GUADALQUIVIR.

Keb·ne·kai·se \ˌkeb-nə-'kī-sə\. Peak in the Kjølen Mts., N Sweden; 6965 ft.; highest peak in Sweden.

Ke·bu·men *or Du.* **Ke·boe·men** \kā-'bü-mən\. Town, Central Java prov., Indonesia, on railroad near S coast 50 m. W of Jogjakarta; pop. (1961c) 25,125.

Kecs·ke·mét \'kech-kə-ˌmāt\. City, ⊗ of Bács-Kiskun co., cen. Hungary, 52 m. SE of Budapest; pop. (1970p) 77,484; market center for agricultural, fruit-growing, and livestock-raising region; distilleries; leatherworking.

Ke·dah \'ked-ə\. A state of Malaysia, Malay Penin., SE Asia, bounded on NE by Thailand, on SE and S by Perak state, on SW by Penang state, on W by Andaman Sea, and on NW by Perlis state; 3660 sq. m.; pop. (1970p) 955,374; ✱ Alor Setar; includes large island of Langkawi off NW coast; generally level with short streams; has mountain range on E border (3000 to 6100 ft.); rice, rubber; fishing.

History: Goes back to 400 A.D. according to Sanskrit and Arab records; converted to Islam in 15th cent.; held captive by king of Atjeh in 17th cent.; leased Penang to British East India Company 1786; subject to Siam 1821–1909, transferred to Great Britain 1909; overrun by Japanese Dec. 1941; became part of the independent Federation of Malaya 1957; became a state of Malaysia 1963.

Ke·dar·nath \kā-'där-ˌnät\. Peak in the Himalayas, Uttar Pradesh, N India, W of Badrinath; 22,770 ft.; place of pilgrimage.

Ke·da·wung *or Du.* **Ke·da·woeng** \kā-'dä-ˌwủŋ\. Town, West Java prov., Indonesia; suburb of Tjirebon.

Ke·desh \'kē-ˌdesh\ *or* **Kedesh–naph·ta·li** \-'naf-tə-ˌlī\. Archaeological site, N Israel, ab. 23 m. N of Tiberias; was a city of refuge, frequently mentioned in the Bible.

Kedg·es Straits \ˌkej-əz-\. Strait in Chesapeake Bay, Maryland, bet. South Marsh I. and Smith I., connecting Tangier Sound with Chesapeake Bay.

Ke·di·ri \kā-'di(ə)r-ē\. 1 River in Java. See BRANTAS.

2 Former residency of the Neth. Indies, now part of the Indonesian prov. of East Java; 2718 sq. m.; ✱ Kediri; fertile plain region in valley of the Brantas bet. the Wilis and Kelut mountain groups; center of sugar industry; rice, cotton, coffee; in 11th–13th cents. part of a Hindu kingdom.

3 City, its ✱, East Java prov., Indonesia, on Brantas river 65 m. SW of Surabaja; pop. (1961c) 158,918; center of sugar industry.

Ked·le·ston \'ked-ᵊl-stən\. Parish, Derbyshire, N cen. England, 3½ m. NW of Derby; home of Lord Curzon.

Kedron. See KIDRON.

Ke·du *or Du.* **Ke·doe** \'kā-ˌdü\. Former residency of the Neth. Indies, now part of Indonesian prov. of Central Java; 1799 sq. m.; ✱ Magelang; bordered Banjumas on W, Semarang on N, and Jogjakarta and Surakarta principalities on E; area includes or is bordered by some of the highest mountains of Java; has no harbors on S coast; one of most densely populated areas on the globe; agriculturally highly developed.

Ke·dung·wu·ni *or Du.* **Ke·doeng·woe·ni** \ˌkā-ˌdủŋ-'wü-nē\. Town, Central Java prov., Indonesia, just S of Pekalongan.

Kee·go Harbor \ˌkē-gō-\. City, Oakland co., SE Michigan, 25 m. NW of Detroit; pop. (1970c) 3092; residential; diversified agriculture.

Keele \'kēl\. River, Northwest Territories, Canada; 230 m. long; flows E from Mackenzie Mts. to Mackenzie river above Fort Norman.

Keele Peak. Peak in Selwyn Mts., NW Canada, Yukon Territory near boundary with Mackenzie dist., Northwest Territories; 9750 ft.

Kee·ler, Cape \-'kē-lər\. Promontory on E coast of Antarctic Penin., Antarctica, 68°51′S, 63°13′W; 1700 ft. high; discovered 1928.

Keeling Islands. See COCOS ISLANDS.

Keelung. See CHI-LUNG.

Keene \'kēn\. 1 City, ⊗ of Cheshire co., SW corner of New Hampshire, on Ashuelot river 40 m. W of Manchester; pop. (1970c) 20,467; market center in farming area; mica quarries; machine tools, toys, lumber; summer resort; Keene State Coll. (1909); first permanent settlement 1750, incorporated as city 1873.

2 Town, New York. See KEENE VALLEY.

3 Resort village, New York. See KEENE VALLEY.

Keene Valley. Village and resort, Essex co., NE New York, ab. 39 m. SSW of Plattsburgh; summer home of landscape painters and scholars; ab. 3 m. S of resort village of **Keene,** and with it included in **Keene** town (pop. [1970c] 763).

Keese·ville \'kēz-(ˌ)vil\. Village, Clinton and Essex cos., NE New York, 12 m. S of Plattsburgh; pop. (1970c) 2128; shirts; dairy and fruit farming.

Keet·mans·hoop \'kāt-män(t)s-ˌhōp\. Town, S South-West Africa, 270 m. SSE of Windhoek; pop. (1970p) 10,297; in sheep country; railroad engineering shops.

Kee·wa·tin \kē-'wāt-ᵊn\. 1 District, SE Northwest Territories, Canada; area including water 228,160 sq. m.; pop. (1961c) 2345; includes E part of mainland of N Canada NW of Hudson Bay and the islands in Hudson and James bays; administered from Ottawa. Created 1876 when it included a much larger area (ab. 516,000 sq. m.); has several times been reorganized with parts of it added to Manitoba and Ontario provs.

2 Town, Kenora dist., W Ontario, Canada, on N shore of Lake of the Woods at source of Winnipeg river across from Kenora; pop. (1971p) 2099; large power plant, flour mills, and sawmills.

Kef, Le. See LE KEF.

Ke·fa \'kēf-ə, kə-'fä\ *also* **Ka·fa** \'kaf-ə, 'käf-ə, kə-'fä\ *or* **Kaf·fa** \'kaf-ə, 'käf-ə, kə-'fä\. Province, SW Ethiopia; 21,081 sq. m.; pop. (1970e) 663,200; ✱ Jima; coffee; conquered by Muslims 16th cent., by Ethiopians 1897.

Kefallinía. See CEPHALONIA.

Kefe. See FEODOSIYA.

Kef·la·vík \kyep-lə-ˌvēk\. Town, SW Iceland, ab. 22 m. WSW of Reykjavík on SW shore of Faxa Bay; pop. (1970c) 5663; fishing; location of **Keflavík Field,** international airport. See MEEKS FIELD.

Ke·gon–no–ta·ki \ˌkeg-ōn-nō-'täk-ē\. Waterfall in Tochigi prefecture, cen. Honshū, Japan, near Nikkō; ab. 330 ft. high and 18 ft. wide.

Ke·gon·sa, Lake \-ki-'gän(t)-sə\. See FOUR LAKES.

Kehl \'kāl\. Commune, Baden-Württemberg, West Germany, on the Rhine opp. Strasbourg, France; pop. (1968e) 15,602; steel; first mentioned 1299.

Kei, Great. See GREAT KEI.

Keigh·ley \'kēth-lē\. Municipal borough, West Riding, Yorkshire, N England, in the Aire valley 17 m. WNW of Leeds; pop. (1971p) 55,263; manufactures woolen goods, spinning machinery, machine tools.

Kei·hin Port \'kā-'hēn-\ *also* **Kei·shin Port** \-'shēn-\. Name given 1941 to the amalgamated Tokyo-Yokohama harbor after completion of extensive improvements.

Kei Islands. See KAI ISLANDS.

Keijo. See SEOUL.

Keilberg. See KLÍNOVEC.

Keishin Port. See KEIHIN PORT.

Kei·te·le \'kāt-ᵊl-ˌā\. Lake, S cen. Finland; 174 sq. m.

Keith \'kēth\. County in Nebraska. See table at NEBRASKA.

Kei·zer \'kī-zər\. Urban community (unincorporated), Marion co., NW Oregon, N of Salem; pop. (1970c) 11,045.

Kej·im·ku·jik National Park \ˌkej-ə-mə-'kü-jē-\. See CANADA, *National Parks.*

Kejser Franz Josephs Fjord. See FRANZ JOSEF FJORD.

Ke·ka·ha \kā-ˈkä-(ˌ)hä\. Town, on SW coast of Kauai I., Hawaii, W of Waimea; pop. (1970c) 2408.

Ke·kri \ˈkā-krē\. Town, SE Rajasthan, NW India, 50 m. SE of Ajmer; pop. (1961c) 12,400.

Keksgolm. See PRIOZERSK.

Ke·lang \kə-ˈläŋ\ *or* **Klang** \ˈkläŋ\. Town, Selangor state, Malaysia, near coast; pop. (1967e) 75,649.

Ke·la·ni \ˈkā-lə-nē\ *or* **Kelani Gan·ga** \-ˈgəŋ-gə\. River (*ganga*), W Ceylon; ab. 90 m. long; flows W to Indian Ocean near Colombo.

Ke·lan·tan \kə-ˈlan-ˌtan\. **1** River in Kelantan state, Malaysia; ab. 150 m. long; rises in the mountains on the SW border, flows NNE into the South China Sea; navigable for much of its course; has many tributaries.

2 A state of Malaysia, bounded on N by Thailand, on NE by South China Sea, on E by Trengganu state, on S by Pahang, on W by Perak; 5780 sq. m.; pop. (1970p) 680,626; ✱ Kota Bharu; level and fertile in N, hilly in S, with mountains on Pahang border (see TAHAN, GUNONG); almost entirely in basin of Kelantan river; rice, rubber, coconuts; fishing.

History: In 14th cent. under Java, later under Malacca, and at end of 19th cent. under Siam; became a British dependency 1909; overrun by Japanese Dec. 1941; became part of the independent Federation of Malaya 1957; became a state of Malaysia 1963.

Ke·la·sa Strait \ke-ˈläs-ə-\ *or formerly* **Gas·par Strait** \ˌgas-pər-\. Channel bet. Bangka and Belitung islands, Indonesia, E of S Sumatra; ab. 45 m. wide.

Kelat. See KALAT.

Kel·heim \ˈkäl-ˌhīm\. Town, E Bavaria, West Germany, on the Danube where the Altmühl joins it ab. 12 m. SW of Regensburg; pop. (1968e) 11,750; founded c. 1200.

Ke·li·bia \kā-ˈlēb-ē-ə\. Town, NE Tunisia, on E coast of Cape Bon Penin. S of Cape Bon; pop. (1966c) 14,000.

Kel·kit \kel-ˈkēt\. River in NE Turkey; 232 m. long; flows generally W into the Yesil Irmak near its mouth.

Kel·ler·wand \ˈkel-ər-ˌvänt\ *or Ital.* **Mon·te Co·gli·ans** \ˌmōⁿ-tē-kōl-ˈyäns\. Mountain on border bet. Austria and Italy; 9217 ft.; highest peak in Carnic Alps.

Kel·leys Island \ˌkel-ēz-\. Island in Lake Erie, off NE coast of Ottawa co., N Ohio; a part of Erie co., Ohio.

Kel·logg \ˈkel-ˌȯg, -ˌäg\. City, Shoshone co., NE Idaho, 35 m. ESE of Coeur d'Alene; pop. (1970c) 3811; gold, zinc, lead mining; pine timber.

Kellogg, Mount. Peak, NE Pima co., S Arizona; 8385 ft.

Kells \ˈkelz\ *or anc.* **Ce·a·nan·nus** \ˌsē-ə-ˈnan-əs\. Town, W co. Meath, E Eire, 25 m. W of Drogheda; pop. of urban district (1971p) 2274; site of monastery, founded c. 550 by Saint Columba, dissolved 1551, where the Book of Kells was produced, an elaborately illuminated manuscript of the Gospels in Latin, with certain local records, in the Irish Celtic style of the 7th to 9th cents., preserved in library of Trinity College, Dublin.

Kel·ly Field \ˌkel-ē-\. U.S. Air Force base, Bexar co., S Texas, 5 m. SW of San Antonio; established May 1917; Air Corps Advanced Flying School (until 1942); air matériel depot.

Keloet. See KELUD.

Ke·low·na \ki-ˈlō-nə\. City, S British Columbia, Canada, on E shore of Okanagan Lake 60 m. N of U.S. border; pop. (1971p) 19,089; wine; sawmills, canneries; fruits and vegetables, dairy products.

Kel·so \ˈkel-(ˌ)sō\. **1** City, ⊗ of Cowlitz co., SW Washington, on Cowlitz river just NE of Longview; pop. (1970c) 10,296; fishing, lumbering, dairy farming.

2 Burgh, Roxburgh co., SE Scotland, on the Tweed; pop. (1971p) 4854; ruined abbey; place where Sir Walter Scott attended school.

Keltsy. See KIELCE.

Ke·lud \kə-ˈlüd\ *also* **Ke·lut** \kə-ˈlüt, ˈklüt\ *or Du.* **Ke·loet** \kə-ˈlüt, ˈklüt\. Volcano, East Java prov., Java, Indonesia; 5679 ft.

Kem \ˈkem\. **1** River, Karelian A.S.S.R., Russian S.F.S.R., U.S.S.R.; ab. 250 m. long; flows E to White Sea opp. Solovetski Is.; outlet of Lake Kunto and other lakes of N cen. Karelian A.S.S.R.

2 Seaport town, NE Karelian A.S.S.R., Russian S.F.S.R., U.S.S.R., on Kem river ab. 10 m. above its mouth, 185 m. W of Arkhangelsk; pop. (1967e) 20,000; lumbering, fishing; station on Murmansk R.R.

Kemarat. See KHEMMARAT.

Ke·me·ro·vo \ˈkem-ə-rə-və, -rō-və, -rə-ˌvō\. City, ✱ of Kemerovo Oblast, Russian S.F.S.R., U.S.S.R., in Kuznetsk Basin 125 m. E of Novosibirsk; pop. (1970p) 382,000; industrial city on the Tom river, a tributary of the Ob, above Tomsk; sawmills, coal mines; coke, chemicals, fertilizers, mining machinery, plastics.

Kemerovo Oblast \-ˈȯ-bləst, -ˌblast\. Subdivision of the Russian S.F.S.R., U.S.S.R.; 36,873 sq. m.; pop. (1970p) 2,918,000; ✱ Kemerovo; Kuznetsk Basin in cen. part; mountainous in S; watered by Tom and Chulym rivers and their tributaries; coal, lead, zinc; iron and steel, chemicals; estab. 1943.

Ke·mi \ˈkem-ē\. **1** River in Oulu prov., N Finland; ab. 300 m. long; flows S into head of Gulf of Bothnia.

2 Seaport, Lappi prov., N Finland, on Gulf of Bothnia; pop. (1970e) 29,671; sawmills; rail connections to the NE through Kemijärvi to Kandalaksha in Murmansk Oblast, Russian S.F.S.R., U.S.S.R., and to the SE with Oulu; founded 1869.

Ke·mi·jär·vi \ˈkem-ē-ˌyar-vē\. Lake in N cen. Finland, formed by expansion of Kemi river.

Kemiö. See KIMITO.

Kem·mel, Mont \ˌmōⁿ-ke-ˌmel\. Height, 5 m. SW of Ieper (Ypres), Belgium; scene of heavy fighting in 1918, taken by Germans Apr. 24–27 and recaptured by British Aug. 31.

Kem·merer \ˈkem-ər\. Town, ⊗ of Lincoln co., SW Wyoming, 45 m. NNE of Evanston; pop. (1970c) 2292; ships coal, livestock; phosphate mines.

Kemp, Lake. See BIG WICHITA DAM.

Kemp Coast *or formerly* **Kemp Land** \ˈkemp-\. Section of coast of Antarctica W of Mac Robertson Land, on shore of Indian Ocean.

Kem·pen \ˈkemp-ən\. Commune, North Rhine-Westphalia, West Germany, 40 m. NW of Cologne; pop. (1968e) 11,278; steel; birthplace of Thomas a Kempis; first mentioned c. 890.

Kem·per \ˈkem-pər\. County in Mississippi. See table at MISSISSIPPI.

Kemp Land. See KEMP COAST.

Kemp·ston \ˈkem(p)-stən\. Urban district, Bedfordshire, SE cen. England, suburb of Bedford on the Ouse; pop. (1971p) 12,790.

Kemp·ten \ˈkem(p)-tən\. City, Bavaria, West Germany, on Iller river 65 m. WSW of Munich; pop. (1969e) 44,057; railroad center; dairy products, textiles, paper, beer; dates from Roman times; town made imperial city 1289; to Bavaria 1803.

Kemp·ton Park \ˌkem(p)-tən-\. Town, Transvaal, Rep. of South Africa, suburb of Johannesburg; pop. (1967e) 56,200.

Ken \ˈkān, ˈken\ *or* **Ka·yan** \ˈkä-yən\. River, N cen. India; ab. 235 m. long; flows N into S Uttar Pradesh to the Yamuna W of Allahabad.

Kena. See QENA.

Ke·nai \ˈkē-ˌnī\. City, S Alaska, on Cook Inlet on NW coast of Kenai Penin.; pop. (1970c) 3533; airfield.

Kenai Mountains. Mountain range on Kenai Penin., S Alaska; highest peak Cooper Mt. 5269 ft.

Kenai Peninsula. 1 Peninsula, S Alaska, bet. Cook Inlet on W and Prince William Sound on E; ab. 160 m. long by 130 m. wide; location of Seward and Seldovia.

2 Borough in Alaska. See table at ALASKA.

Ke·nans·ville \'kēn-ənz-ˌvil\. Town, ⊗ of Duplin co., SE North Carolina.

Ken·dal \'ken-dᵊl\. Municipal borough, Westmorland, NW England, on the Kent 62 m. NNW of Manchester; pop. (1971p) 21,572; has manufactured woolen goods since 14th cent.; also manufactures boots and shoes, paper, laundry machinery. Ruins of a castle which was birthplace of Catherine Parr, 6th wife of Henry VIII.

Ken·dall \'ken-dᵊl\. Counties in two states of the U.S. See tables at ILLINOIS and TEXAS.

Ken·dall·ville \'ken-dᵊl-ˌvil\. City, Noble co., NE Indiana, 27 m. N of Fort Wayne; pop. (1970c) 6838; refrigerators, pumps, boats, furniture.

Ken·da·ri \ken-'där-ē\. Town and port, ✱ of South-East Sulawesi prov., Celebes I., Indonesia, on E coast of the SE peninsula 240 m. ENE of Makasar; pop. (1961c) 29,765; exports rattans, varnish resins, and native silverware; in World War II occupied by Japanese Feb. 1, 1942, and used as naval and air base.

Ken·drick Peak \'ken-drik-\. Mountain, cen. Coconino co., N cen. Arizona; 10,418 ft.

Ken·e·dy \'ken-ə-dē\. 1 County in Texas. See table at TEXAS.

2 City and health resort, Karnes co., S Texas, 49 m. W of Victoria; pop. (1970c) 4156; oil wells; cattle, flax, corn.

Kenesaw Mountain. See KENNESAW MOUNTAIN.

Keng·tung \'keŋ-'tu̇ŋ\. 1 Former state, E Burma, was largest of Southern Shan States; 12,405 sq. m.; ✱ Kengtung; since 1947 part of Shan State; **Kengtung Hills** in cen. part rise to above 6500 ft.

2 Town, its ✱, on a tributary of the Mekong river and on main highway to Thailand 230 m. ESE of Mandalay.

Ken·horst \'ken-ˌhȯrst\. Borough, Berks co., SE Pennsylvania; pop. (1970c) 3482.

Kenia. See KENYA.

Ken·il·worth \'ken-ᵊl-ˌwərth\. 1 Village, Cook co., NE Illinois, 17 m. N of Chicago; pop. (1970c) 2980.

2 Borough, Union co., NE New Jersey, 4 m. W of Elizabeth; pop. (1970c) 9165.

3 Urban district, Warwickshire, cen. England; pop. (1971p) 20,121; ruins of major castle (celebrated by Sir Walter Scott in his novel *Kenilworth*) founded by Geoffrey de Clinton c. 1120, and the property of Simon de Montfort in 13th cent. and of John of Gaunt in middle 14th cent., presented by Queen Elizabeth to Robert Dudley, Earl of Leicester, who entertained the queen there in 1575 (as described in Scott's novel), abandoned 17th cent.

Ke·ni·tra \kə-'nē-trə\ *or formerly* **Port Ly·au·tey** \ˌpȯr-lē-ˌō-'tā\. River port, NW Morocco, 10 m. from the Atlantic Ocean, ab. 30 m. NE of Rabat; pop. (1966e) 112,000; exports agricultural products and ores; landing here by American forces Nov. 1942.

Ken·mare. 1 \'ken-ˌma(ə)r, -ˌme(ə)r\. City, Ward co., NW cen. North Dakota, 50 m. NW of Minot; pop. (1970c) 1515; coal mines; dairy farming; potatoes.

2 \ken-'ma(ə)r, -'me(ə)r\. Village and summer resort, co. Kerry, SW Eire; pop. (1961c) 2739; at head of **Kenmare River,** a deep narrow inlet of Atlantic Ocean N of Bantry Bay, 5 m. wide at mouth.

Ken·more. 1 \'ken-ˌmō(ə)r, -ˌmȯ(ə)r\. Residential village, in town of Tonawanda, Erie co., W New York, on Niagara river 7 m. N of Buffalo; pop. (1970c) 20,980; Sulpician Sem. of the Northwest (1930).

2 \ken-'mō(ə)r, -'mȯ(ə)r\. Village and parish, Perth co., cen. Scotland, at NE end of Loch Tay near where river Tay flows out of it; pop. (1961c) 1009.

Ken·ne·bec \ˌken-ə-'bek, 'ken-ə-ˌ\. 1 River, W cen. and S Maine; flows S from Moosehead Lake to Atlantic Ocean; ab. 150 m. long; navigable for large vessels to Bath.

2 County in Maine. See table at MAINE.

3 Town, ⊗ of Lyman co., S cen. South Dakota; pop. (1970c) 372.

Ken·ne·bunk \'ken-ə-ˌbəŋk, ˌken-ə-'bəŋk, -ē-\. Town, York co., SW Maine, 8 m. S of Biddeford; pop. (1970c) 5646; lumber, shoes; summer resort; poultry farming.

Ken·ne·bunk·port \ˌken-ə-'bəŋk-ˌpō(ə)rt, -ē-, -pȯ(ə)rt\. Town, York co., SW Maine, on Atlantic Ocean 9 m. S of Biddeford; pop. (1970c) 2160; summer resort.

Ken·ne·dale \'ken-ə-ˌdāl\. Town, Tarrant co., N Texas, 10 m. SE of Fort Worth; pop. (1970c) 3076; furniture, feed, printing machinery; diversified agriculture.

Ken·ne·dy, Cape \-'ken-əd-ē\ *or formerly* **Cape Ca·nav·er·al** \-kə-'nav-(ə-)rəl\. Cape in Brevard co., Florida, on E coast of Canaveral Penin., E of Merrit I.; Patrick Air Force base; John F. Kennedy Space Center, site of launching of U.S. manned space flights from 1961 incl. 1st manned lunar landing 1969. See UNITED STATES, *Manned Space Flights.*

Kennedy, Mount. Peak in Saint Elias Mountains, SW Yukon, Canada; 13,905 ft.

Kennedy Channel. Channel, NW coast of Greenland, bet. Washington Land and NE coast of Ellesmere I.; connects Kane and Hall basins; ab. 110 m. long.

Ken·ner \'ken-ər\. City, Jefferson parish, SE Louisiana, on Mississippi river 12 m. W of New Orleans; pop. (1970c) 29,858.

Ken·ne·saw \'ken-ə-ˌsȯ\. City, Cobb co., NW Georgia, 20 m. NW of Atlanta; pop. (1970c) 3548.

Kennesaw Mountain *or* **Kenesaw Mountain.** Isolated peak in Cobb co., NW Georgia, near Atlanta; 1809 ft.; scene of battle June 27, 1864 in which Sherman made an unsuccessful frontal attack on Confederate troops in his campaign against Atlanta; set aside 1917 as Kennesaw Mountain Battlefield Site (648 acres), battlefield site abolished 1947; now part of **Kennesaw Mountain National Battlefield Park.** See UNITED STATES, *National Historical Parks.*

Ken·net \'ken-ət\. River, S England; 44 m. long; flows ENE through Wiltshire and Berkshire into the Thames at Reading.

Ken·neth City \ˌken-əth-\. Town, Pinellas co., W Florida; pop. (1970c) 3862.

Ken·nett \'ken-ət\. City, ⊗ of Dunklin co., SE Missouri, 22 m. W of Caruthersville; pop. (1970c) 9852; lumber; cotton gins; agriculture.

Kennett Square. Borough, Chester co., SE Pennsylvania, 33 m. WSW of Philadelphia; pop. (1970c) 4876; plumbing supplies, canned foods; grows mushrooms.

Ken·ne·wick \'ken-ə-ˌwik\. City, Benton co., S Washington, on Columbia river 5 m. W of its confluence with Snake river; pop. (1970c) 15,212; fruit orchards; dairy farming.

Ke·nog·a·mi \kə-'näg-ə-mē\. 1 River, cen. Ontario, Canada; ab. 200 m. long; flows NE and N from its chief source, Long Lake, just N of Lake Superior, to the Albany.

2 Lake, Lake St. John and Chicoutimi cos., S Quebec, Canada; receives the Chicoutimi river, which flows out of it NE into Saguenay river.

3 City, Chicoutimi co., S Quebec, Canada, on Saguenay river 8 m. W of Chicoutimi and near Jonquière; pop. (1971p) 10,955; pulp and paper mills.

Ke·no·ra \kə-'nōr-ə, -'nȯr-\. 1 District, Ontario, Canada. See table at ONTARIO.

2 Town, administrative center of Kenora dist., W Ontario, Canada, on Winnipeg river just N of Lake of the Woods; pop. (1971p) 10,889; flour, lumber, and paper mills; hay, potatoes; summer resort; railroad divisional point and commercial airfield. Founded 1879 as **Rat Portage** \'rat-'pōrt-ij, -'pȯrt-; 'rä-pȯr-'täzh\; contested in boundary dispute bet. Manitoba and Ontario, with serious riots, July 1883; name changed 1904 to Kenora.

Ke·no·sha \kə-'nō-shə\. 1 County in Wisconsin. See table at WISCONSIN.

2 Industrial city, ⊗ of Kenosha co., SE corner of Wisconsin, on Lake Michigan 10 m. S of Racine; pop. (1970c) 78,805; automobiles, furniture, tools, brass and copper

products, hosiery; Carthage Coll. (1846; moved to Kenosha 1964); founded 1835.

Ke·no·va \kə-ˈnō-və\. City, Wayne co., SW West Virginia, at mouth of Big Sandy river 8 m. W of Huntington; pop. (1970c) 4860; railroad center; petroleum products, chemicals, electrical equipment.

Ken·sing·ton \ˈken-siŋ-tən, -ziŋ-\. Subdivision of town of Berlin, Connecticut; metal and paper goods. See BERLIN 1.

Kensington and Chel·sea \ˈken-ziŋ-tən . . . ˈchel-sē\. A borough of Greater London, SE England. See table at LONDON 4.

Kensington and Nor·wood \-ˈnō(ə)r-wu̇d, -ˈnȯ(ə)r-\. Joint municipality, SE South Australia, E suburb of Adelaide; pop. (1966c) 11,900.

Kent \ˈkent\. **1** Counties in five states of the U.S. See tables at DELAWARE, MARYLAND, MICHIGAN, RHODE ISLAND, TEXAS.

2 Town, W Litchfield co., NW Connecticut, on New York border; pop. (1970c) 1990; aircraft seats; dairy farming; resort and art colony; Kent School (preparatory school for boys); incorporated 1739.

3 Manufacturing city, Portage co., NE Ohio, on Cuyahoga river 8 m. ENE of Akron; pop. (1970c) 28,183; meat-packing; plastics, air compressors, machine parts, flour; fruit and dairy farming; Kent State Univ. (1910).

4 City, King co., W cen. Washington, 16 m. S of Seattle; pop. (1970c) 16,275; residential; canned and frozen foods, furniture, fishing tackle, plastics; diversified agriculture.

5 Counties in two provinces of Canada. See tables at NEW BRUNSWICK and ONTARIO.

6 River, Westmorland, NW England; ab. 20 m. long; flows S into Morecambe Bay.

7 County, SE England; area 1443 sq. m.; pop. (1971p) 1,396,030; ⊗ Maidstone; agriculture (orchards, hops, barley, potatoes, truck farming, sheep grazing, dairying), fisheries, manufacturing (paper, pottery, iron products), shipbuilding; towns incl. Canterbury, Maidstone, Dover, Folkestone, Chatham, Ramsgate, Sheerness.

History: Territory occupied by the Cantii, a people of Britain, when Caesar arrived; settled by Anglo-Saxons, probably by Jutes, 5th cent. A.D.; first kingdom of Anglo-Saxon Heptarchy (*q.v.*) to attain under Ethelbert (560–616) supremacy S of the Humber; converted to Roman Christianity in 597 by Augustine, first archbishop of Canterbury; maintained its identity as subkingdom until 9th cent. although it was soon ruled by Mercia (*q.v.*) and later by Wessex (*q.v.*).

Ken·tau \ˈken-(ˌ)tau̇\. Town, Chimkent Oblast, Kazakh S.S.R., U.S.S.R., ab. 100 m. NW of Chimkent; pop. (1969e) 55,000; lead and zinc mining; formed 1955.

Kentei Shan. See HENTIYN NURUU.

Kent Island. Island in upper Chesapeake Bay, W Queen Annes co., E Maryland; 15 m. long; largest island in the bay; site of trading station established 1631 by William Claiborne.

Kent·land \ˈkent-lənd\. Town, ⊗ of Newton co., NW Indiana, 37 m. NW of Lafayette; pop. (1970c) 1864; fertilizer, feed; stone quarry; grain and dairy farming.

Ken·ton \ˈkent-ᵊn\. **1** County in Kentucky. See table at KENTUCKY.

2 City, ⊗ of Hardin co., NW cen. Ohio, on the Scioto river 26 m. E of Lima; pop. (1970c) 8315; mining machinery, toys; limestone quarries; onions.

Kent Point. South tip of Kent I., Chesapeake Bay, Maryland.

Ken·tucky \kən-ˈtək-ē\. **1** Navigable river, N cen. Kentucky; 259 m. long; formed by confluence of forks in Lee co., flows NW into Ohio river in N Carroll co.

2 An east central state of U.S.A., bounded on N by Illinois, Indiana, and Ohio, on E by West Virginia and Virginia, on S by Tennessee, and on W by Missouri; 37th state in area, 40,395 sq. m. (land area 39,851 sq. m.); 23d state in population, (1970c) 3,219,311; ✱ Frankfort; 15th state admitted to Union (1792).

Nickname: Bluegrass State. *State flower:* Goldenrod. *Motto:* United We Stand, Divided We Fall. *Rivers:* Ohio, forming N boundary of the state, and receiving in W the waters of the Tennessee and the Cumberland, and in N cen. region the waters of the Kentucky and the Licking. *Highest point:* Black Mountain, 4145 ft., in Harlan co. *Chief products:* Tobacco, corn, wheat; livestock; oil, natural gas, coal; manufacturing: cigarettes, farm equipment, chemicals. *Chief cities:* Louisville, Lexington, Covington, Owensboro, Bowling Green, Paducah. See *Table of States* at UNITED STATES. Divided into the following 120 counties (for pronunciation of their names, see their individual entries):

NAME	LOCATION	AREA[1] (sq. m.)	POP. (1970c)	CO. SEAT
Adair	S cen.	393	13,037	Columbia
Allen	S	364	12,598	Scottsville
Anderson	cen.	206	9,358	Lawrenceburg
Ballard	W	259	8,276	Wickliffe
Barren	S	486	28,677	Glasgow
Bath	NE	287	9,235	Owingsville
Bell	SE	370	31,121	Pineville
Boone	N	249	32,812	Burlington
Bourbon[2]	NE	300	18,476	Paris
Boyd	NE	160	52,376	Catlettsburg
Boyle	cen.	183	21,090	Danville
Bracken	NE	204	7,227	Brooksville
Breathitt	E	494	14,221	Jackson
Breckinridge	NW cen.	564	14,789	Hardinsburg
Bullitt	cen.	300	26,090	Shepherdsville
Butler	W cen.	443	9,723	Morgantown
Caldwell	W	357	13,179	Princeton
Calloway	SW	384	27,692	Murray
Campbell	N	149	88,561	Alexandria & Newport
Carlisle	SW	195	5,354	Bardwell
Carroll	N	130	8,523	Carrollton
Carter	NE	402	19,850	Grayson
Casey	cen.	435	12,930	Liberty
Christian	SW	725	56,224	Hopkinsville
Clark	E cen.	259	24,090	Winchester
Clay	SE	474	18,481	Manchester
Clinton	S	190	8,174	Albany
Crittenden	W	365	8,493	Marion
Cumberland	S	310	6,850	Burkesville
Daviess	NW	462	79,486	Owensboro
Edmonson[3]	SW cen.	304	8,751	Brownsville
Elliott	NE	240	5,933	Sandy Hook
Estill	E	260	12,752	Irvine
Fayette[4]	NE cen.	280	174,323	Lexington
Fleming	NE	350	11,366	Flemingsburg
Floyd	E	399	35,889	Prestonsburg
Franklin	N cen.	211	34,481	Frankfort
Fulton	SW corner	203	10,183	Hickman
Gallatin	N	100	4,134	Warsaw
Garrard	E cen.	236	9,457	Lancaster
Grant	N	249	9,999	Williamstown
Graves	SW	560	30,939	Mayfield
Grayson	W cen.	512	16,445	Leitchfield
Green	cen.	282	10,350	Greensburg
Greenup	NE	351	33,192	Greenup
Hancock	NW cen.	187	7,080	Hawesville
Hardin	cen.	616	78,421	Elizabethtown
Harlan	SE	469	37,370	Harlan
Harrison	N	308	14,158	Cynthiana
Hart[3]	cen.	425	13,980	Munfordville
Henderson	NW	433	36,031	Henderson
Henry	N	289	10,910	New Castle
Hickman	SW	246	6,264	Clinton
Hopkins	W	553	38,167	Madisonville
Jackson	SE	337	10,005	McKee
Jefferson	N cen.	375	695,055	Louisville
Jessamine	E cen.	177	17,430	Nicholasville
Johnson	E	264	17,539	Paintsville
Kenton	N	165	129,440	Independence
Knott	SE	356	14,698	Hindman
Knox	SE	373	23,689	Barbourville
Larue[5]	cen.	260	10,672	Hodgenville
Laurel	SE	446	27,386	London
Lawrence	E	425	10,726	Louisa
Lee	E	210	6,587	Beattyville
Leslie	SE	412	11,623	Hyden
Letcher	SE	339	23,165	Whitesburg
Lewis	NE	486	12,355	Vanceburg
Lincoln	E cen.	340	16,663	Stanford

NAME	LOCATION	AREA[1] (sq. m.)	POP. (1970c)	CO. SEAT
Livingston	W	312	7,596	Smithland
Logan	S	563	21,793	Russellville
Lyon	W	253	5,562	Eddyville
McCracken	W	250	58,281	Paducah
McCreary	SE	408	12,548	Whitely City
McLean	W	257	9,062	Calhoun
Madison	E cen.	446	42,730	Richmond
Magoffin	E	303	10,443	Salyersville
Marion	cen.	343	16,714	Lebanon
Marshall	W	303	20,381	Benton
Martin	E	231	9,377	Inez
Mason	NE	238	17,273	Maysville
Meade	NW cen.	305	18,796	Brandenburg
Menifee	E	210	4,050	Frenchburg
Mercer	cen.	256	15,960	Harrodsburg
Metcalfe	S	296	8,177	Edmonton
Monroe	S	334	11,642	Tompkinsville
Montgomery	E	204	15,364	Mount Sterling
Morgan	E	369	10,019	West Liberty
Muhlenberg	W	481	27,537	Greenville
Nelson	cen.	437	23,477	Bardstown
Nicholas	NE	204	6,508	Carlisle
Ohio	W cen.	596	18,790	Hartford
Oldham	N	184	14,687	La Grange
Owen	N	351	7,470	Owenton
Owsley	E	197	5,023	Booneville
Pendleton	N	279	9,949	Falmouth
Perry	SE	343	26,259	Hazard
Pike	E	786	61,059	Pikeville
Powell	E	173	7,704	Stanton
Pulaski	SE cen.	654	35,234	Somerset
Robertson	NE	101	2,163	Mount Olivet
Rockcastle	SE cen.	311	12,305	Mount Vernon[4]
Rowan	NE	290	17,010	Morehead
Russell	S	238	10,542	Jamestown
Scott	N cen.	284	17,948	Georgetown
Shelby	N cen.	383	18,999	Shelbyville
Simpson	S	239	13,054	Franklin
Spencer	cen.	193	5,488	Taylorsville
Taylor	cen.	284	17,138	Campbellsville
Todd	SW	376	10,823	Elkton
Trigg	SW	459	8,620	Cadiz
Trimble	N	146	5,349	Bedford
Union	W	340	15,882	Morganfield
Warren	S	546	57,432	Bowling Green
Washington	cen.	307	10,728	Springfield
Wayne	S	440	14,268	Monticello
Webster	W	339	13,282	Dixon
Whitley	SE	459	24,145	Williamsburg
Wolfe	E	227	5,669	Campton
Woodford	E cen.	193	14,434	Versailles

[1]Area = land area.
[2]The term *Bourbon whisky* was originally applied to corn whisky made in this county.
[3]Mammoth Cave National Park in Edmonson co. (E cen. and E; major portion of park, including Mammoth Cave itself) and Hart co. (W).
[4]Center of the "Bluegrass" region and of race-horse breeding.
[5]Central portion contains Abraham Lincoln National Historical Park.

History: First entered by English 1750; included in territory ceded by French 1763; explored by expeditions under Daniel Boone from 1769; first permanent English settlement at Boonesborough made by Transylvania Company 1775; because of its many Indian wars known as the "Dark and Bloody Ground"; organized as county of Virginia 1776; included in territory of U.S. by Treaty of Paris 1783; received consent of Virginia to statehood 1789; admitted to Union June 1, 1792; despite an attempt to be neutral in American Civil War, invaded by Confederate troops 1862.

Kentucky Dam. See table at TENNESSEE VALLEY AUTHORITY.

Kent·ville \'kent-(ˌ)vil\. Agricultural town, ⊗ of Kings co., W Nova Scotia, Canada, 55 m. NW of Halifax; pop. (1971p) 5129; cannery; fruit and dairy farming; settled 1760; near site of early Acadian settlements.

Kent·wood \'kent-ˌwu̇d\. 1 Town, Tangipahoa parish, SE Louisiana, 54 m. NE of Baton Rouge; pop. (1970c) 2736; lumber mill, cotton gin; dairy farming.
2 City, Kent co., W Michigan, 8 m. S of Grand Rapids; pop. (1970c) 20,310.

Ken·ya *also* **Ken·ia** \'ken-yə, 'kēn-\ *or formerly* **East Africa Protectorate.** Republic, E Africa, bounded on NW by Sudan, on N by Ethiopia, on E by Somalia, on SE by the Indian Ocean, on S by Tanzania, and on W by Uganda; 224,960 sq. m.; pop. (1971e) 11,694,000, (1969p) 10,890,500; ✱ Nairobi. *Physical features:* Mountainous in W half, having two N–S ranges with the Great Rift Valley bet. them; highest peaks Mt. Kenya 17,058 ft. in center, and Mt. Elgon 14,178 ft. on Uganda border. Lowland strip along coast extends gradually up into wide level plain which in the N is high and arid. Noted for its abundance of big game. Rivers are Tana and Ewaso Ng'iro in the E and many short streams in the W flowing into lakes Victoria on SW and Rudolf, a large long lake in NW; many small lakes in Great Rift Valley (*q.v.*). *Chief products:* Coffee, cotton, wheat, sisal, corn, tea, fruit; livestock raising; tourism. *Chief towns:* Nairobi, Mombasa, Nakuru, Kisumu. Administratively divided into the Nairobi Area and seven provinces:

NAME	AREA (sq. m.)	POP. (1969p)	CAPITAL
Central	5,093	1,663,100	Nyeri
Coast	32,279	936,000	Mombasa
Eastern	61,734	1,899,200	Embu
Nairobi Area	264	477,600	Nairobi
North-Eastern	48,997	244,200	Wajir
Nyanza	6,240	2,115,900	Kisumu
Rift Valley	67,125	2,219,400	Nakuru
Western	3,228	1,335,100	Kakamega

History: East African coast frequented by British traders from early 19th cent.; coastal strip belonging to ruler of Zanzibar (*q.v.*) leased 1887 to British East Africa Company which soon extended its holdings into the interior; boundaries with German East Africa (see TANZANIA) fixed 1886, 1890; region organized as British East Africa Protectorate 1895; except for the coastal strip (ab. 10 m. wide, extending from S boundary to Tana river), which together with its islands was named Kenya Protectorate, region made British colony 1920; became independent member of Commonwealth of Nations 1963; established a republic 1964; formed, with Tanzania and Uganda, the East African Community 1967.

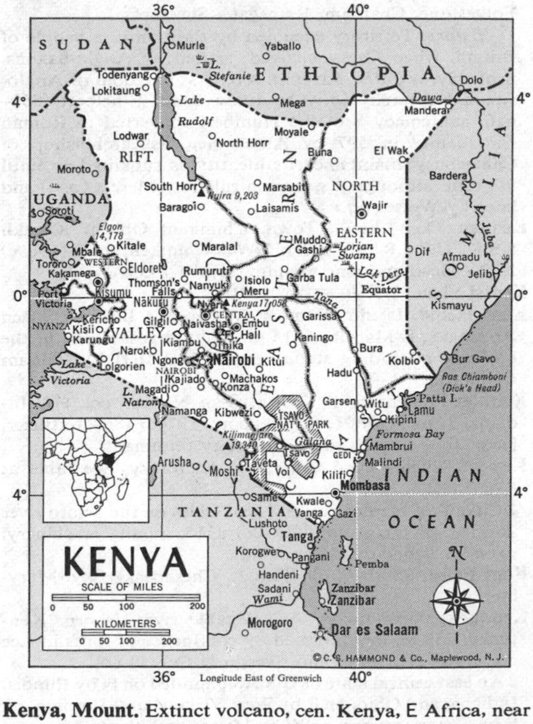

Kenya, Mount. Extinct volcano, cen. Kenya, E Africa, near the equator; 17,058 ft.

Ken–zan–fu. See SIAN.

Ke·o·kuk \'kē-ə-ˌkək\. 1 County in Iowa. See table at IOWA.

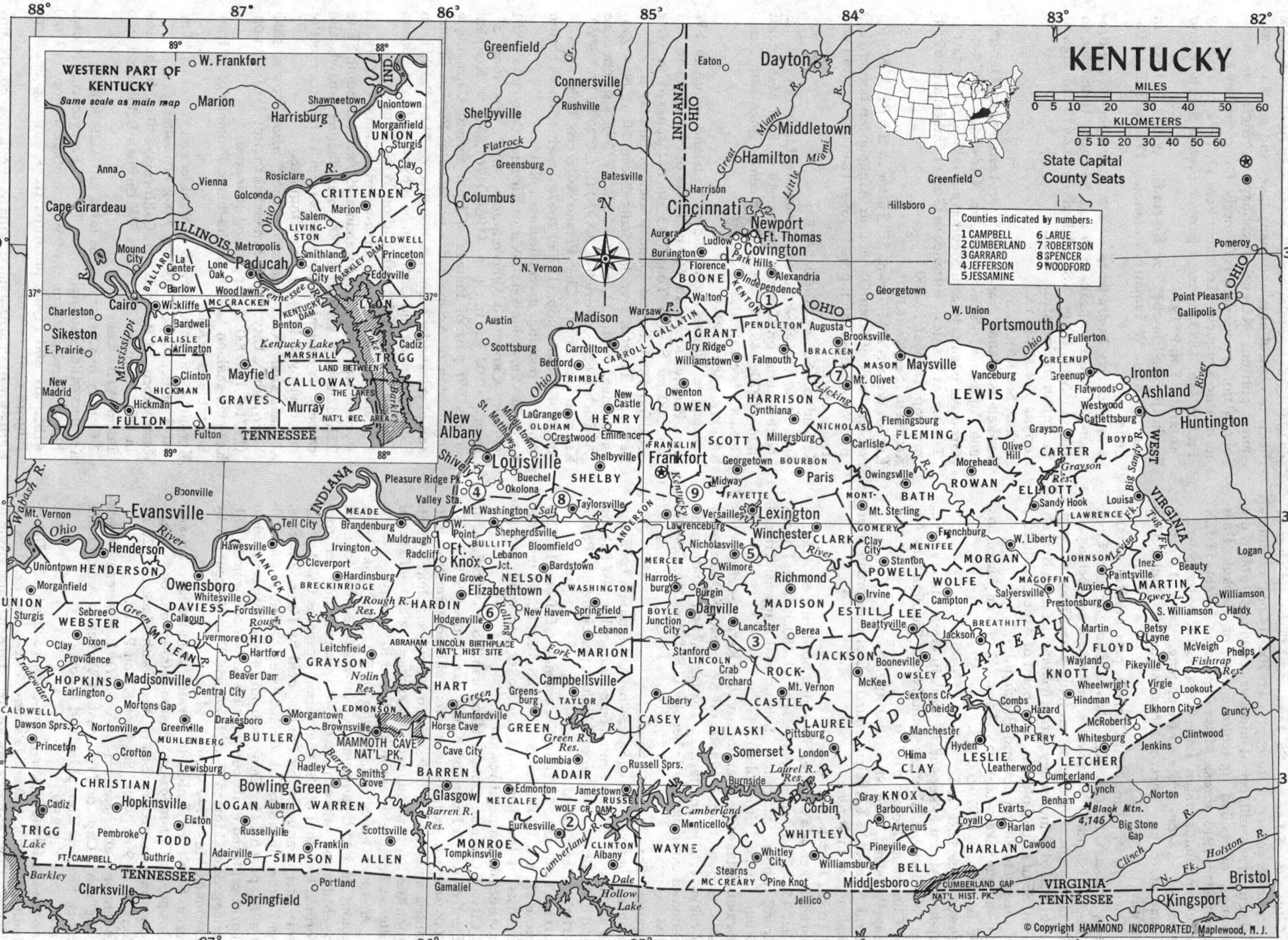
KENTUCKY
MILES
0 5 10 20 30 40 50 60
KILOMETERS
0 5 10 20 30 40 50 60
State Capital
County Seats
Counties indicated by numbers:
1 CAMPBELL
2 CUMBERLAND
3 GARRARD
4 JEFFERSON
5 JESSAMINE
6 LARUE
7 ROBERTSON
8 SPENCER
9 WOODFORD
WESTERN PART OF KENTUCKY
Same scale as main map
INDIANA
OHIO
ILLINOIS
WEST VIRGINIA
VIRGINIA
TENNESSEE
CUMBERLAND PLATEAU
Frankfort
Louisville
Lexington
Covington
Newport
Cincinnati
Paducah
Owensboro
Bowling Green
Evansville
Ashland
Huntington
MAMMOTH CAVE NAT'L PK.
CUMBERLAND GAP NAT'L HIST. PK.
ABRAHAM LINCOLN BIRTHPLACE NAT'L HIST SITE
LAND BETWEEN THE LAKES NAT'L REC. AREA
Kentucky Lake
Lake Barkley
Black Mtn. 4,145
Longitude West of Greenwich
© Copyright HAMMOND INCORPORATED, Maplewood, N.J.

2 City, a ⊗ of Lee co., SE Iowa, on Mississippi river at extreme SE corner of state; pop. (1970c) 14,631; commercial center; sawmill; cereal and dairy products, rubber, die castings; diversified agriculture; site of **Keokuk Dam** (completed 1913 across Mississippi river, height 53 ft.), which impounds water, **Lake Keokuk,** for water power.

Ke·on·jhar \kā-ˈōn-jər\ *also* **Ke·un·jhar** \-ˈən-\. 1 Former Indian state, now part of Orissa state, NE India; 3206 sq. m.

2 Town, its ✱, 83 m. N of Cuttack; pop. (1961c) 12,600.

Ke·os \ˈkē-ˌäs\ *or Gk.* **Kéa** \ˈkē-ə, ˈkā-ə\ *or anc.* **Ce·os** \ˈsē-ˌäs\. Island, NW Cyclades, in Aegean Sea; belongs to Cyclades dept., Greece; 12 m. long, area 67 sq. m.; pop. (1961c) 2361; wine, honey, citrus fruits; chief town **Kéa;** ab. 13 m. SE of Cape Colonna, the S point of Attica; birthplace of the poets Simonides and Bacchylides.

Ke·o·sau·qua \ˌkē-ə-ˈsȯ-kwə\. Town, ⊗ of Van Buren co., SE Iowa; pop. (1970c) 1018.

Keowee. See SENECA 2.

Kep·hart, Mount \-ˈkep-ˌhärt\. Peak in Great Smoky Mts., on boundary bet. Tennessee and North Carolina 8 m. NE of Clingmans Dome; 6100 ft.

Keppel's Island. See NIUATOPUTAPU.

Ke·rak \ˈker-ək\. 1 Ancient emirate, E of the Jordan river; region now in Jordan.

2 Town, Jordan. See AL-KARAK.

Ke·ra·la \ˈker-ə-lə\. State, SW India, bordering on Arabian Sea; 15,007 sq. m.; pop. (1971p) 21,280,397; ✱ Trivandrum; rubber, tea, timber; fishing; major towns: Trivandrum, Calicut, Ernakulam.

Ke·ra·ma Islands \kə-ˈräm-ə-\ *or Jap.* **Kerama–rettō** \-ˈret-(ˌ)ō\. Group of small islands off SW coast of Okinawa I., Ryukyu Is., Japan; largest Tokashiki; first landings in Okinawa campaign made here by U.S. forces Mar. 26–27, 1945.

Kerasun. See GİRESUN.

Ker·bau, Gu·nong \ˌgü-ˌnȯŋ-kər-ˈbaů\. Mountain (*gunong*) in Malaysia, S Malay Penin., on boundary bet. NW Pahang and E Perak; 7159 ft.; second highest peak in Malay Penin.

Kerbela. See KARBALA.

Kerch \ˈke(ə)rch\. 1 Peninsula, extending E from the Crimean Oblast, Ukrainian S.S.R., U.S.S.R.; ab. 70 m. long; consists of low land with salt lakes and mud springs; considerable mineral resources.

2 City, E Crimean Oblast, Ukrainian S.S.R., U.S.S.R., at E end of Kerch Penin. on Kerch Strait; pop. (1970p) 128,000; seaport; exports iron ore; railroad terminus; iron mines, limestone quarries; fishing; fertilizer; church of St. John the Baptist, founded 717; archaeologically of special interest because of antiquities found in vicinity.

History: One of oldest cities of S U.S.S.R.; as Greek colony of **Pan·ti·ca·pae·um** \ˌpant-ə-kə-ˈpē-əm\, founded by Milesians 6th cent. B.C.; with surrounding territory formed kingdom of the Cimmerian Bosporus (*q.v.*) which was later conquered by Pontus; held by Huns, Khazars, and other invaders of Crimea (see CRIMEAN OBLAST); trading port held by Genoese from 14th to 15th cent. when Turks captured it; its conquest by Russia confirmed 1774; damaged in Crimean War. In World War II occupied by Germans May 1942–Apr. 1944.

Kerch Strait *or* **Eni·ka·le Strait** \ˌā-ni-kä-ˈlā-\ *or anc.* **Bos·por·us Cim·me·ri·us** \ˌbäs-pə-rə(s)-sə-ˈmir-ē-əs\. Shallow strait connecting Sea of Azov with Black Sea; 25 m. long, 2 to 9 m. wide; lies E of Kerch Penin.

Ke·rem·pe Cape \ˌker-əm-ˈpā-\ *or Turk.* **Kerempe Bu·run** \-bů-ˈrün\. Cape on NW coast of Turkey in Asia, on the Black Sea bet. Zonguldak and Sinop.

Keren. See CHEREN.

Ker·gue·len Islands \ˈkər-gə-lən-, ˌkər-gə-ˈlən-\ *also* **Des·o·la·tion Islands** \ˌdes-ə-ˌlā-shən-, ˌdez-\ *or Fr.* **Îles de Dé·so·la·tion** \ēl-də-dā-zō-lä-syȯ^{n}\. French island group in S Indian Ocean, consisting of one major island, **Kerguelen** (2239 sq. m.) and ab. 300 other islets (total area 2394 sq. m.). Main island mountainous (highest point Mt. Ross 6430 ft.), has irregular coastline and deep fjords with snow fields in central area and many lakes and pools in lower outer portion; Kerguelen cabbage (*Pringlea antiscorbutica*) not so abundant as formerly. Discovered by French navigator Kerguélen-Trémarec Feb. 13, 1772; annexed by France Jan. 1893; became part of French Southern and Antarctic Lands 1955.

Ke·rin·tji \kə-ˈrin-chē\ *or* **Ko·rin·tji** \kȯ-\. 1 Lake in Barisan Mts., W Sumatra, Indonesia, 115 m. SSE of Padang.

2 *or formerly* **In·dra·pu·ra** *or Du.* **In·dra·poe·ra** \ˌin-drə-ˈpůr-ə\. Volcanic peak, in W cen. Sumatra, Indonesia, in Barisan Mts. 80 m. SSE of Padang; 12,483 ft.; highest mountain in Sumatra.

Keriya. See K'O-LI-YA.

Kerka. See KRKA.

Ker·ken·na Islands \kər-ˈken-ə-\ *or Arab.* **Ju·zur Qar·qan·nah** \ˌjəz-ər-kär-ˈkan-ə\ *or anc.* **Cer·ci·na** \sər-ˈsī-nə\. Group of islands in cen. Mediterranean Sea, off E coast of Tunisia, at N side of entrance to Gulf of Gabès; area 69 sq. m.; pop. (1966c) 12,600.

Kerkheh. See KARKHEH.

Ker·ki \ke(ə)r-ˈkē\. Town, SE Turkmen S.S.R., U.S.S.R., on left bank of Amu Darya near Afghanistan border, 170 m. SW of Samarkand; pop. (1969e) 18,000; a caravan and trade center.

Kerkinitis. See AKHINOU, LAKE.

Kerk·ra·de \ˈke(ə)r-ˌkräd-ə\. Commune, Limburg prov., SE Netherlands, on German frontier 18 m. E of Maastricht; pop. (1970e) 48,150; coal-mining center since 12th cent.

Kerkuk. See KIRKUK.

Kérkyra. See CORFU.

Ker·mad·ec Islands \kər-ˈmad-ək-\. Island group in SW cen. Pacific Ocean, ab. 600 m. NNW of New Zealand and ab. 500 m. S of S Tonga; 13 sq. m.; annexed to New Zealand 1887; largest island Raoul, or Sunday I.

Kermadec Trench. Trench, Pacific Ocean, NE of New Zealand; max. depth 32,964 ft. (30°S, 177°W); also contains **Al·drich Deep** \ˌȯl-drich-\, 30,930 ft. (30°27′S, 176°39′W).

Ker·man \ˈkər-mən\. City, Fresno co., S cen. California, 14 m. W of Fresno; pop. (1970c) 2667; slaughterhouse, cotton gin; fruit packing; diversified agriculture.

Ker·mān \kər-ˈmän, ke(ə)r-\ *also* **Kir·man** \kər-, ki(ə)r-\. 1 *or anc.* **Car·ma·nia** \kär-ˈmā-nē-ə, -nyə\. Province, SE Iran; 74,508 sq. m.; pop. (1966c) 761,851; ✱ Kermān; covers SW part of Plateau of Iran; ancient Carmania a subdivision of Ariana and a province of Persian Empire and of Alexander's Empire, bounded on N by Parthia, on E by Drangiana and Gedrosia, on S by water (*mod.* Persian Gulf and Gulf of Oman), and on W by Persis.

2 *or anc.* **Car·ma·na** \kär-ˈmān-ə, -ˈman-, -ˈmän-\. City, its ✱, on motor road from Eşfahān and Yazd extending SE to Zāhedān; pop. (1971e) 88,000; manufactures shawls and carpets; its ancient mosque dates from 11th cent.; most of city destroyed 1794 by an earthquake.

Ker·mān·shāh \ˌker-män-ˈshä, -ˈshȯ\ *also* **Kir·man·shah** \ˌker-, ˌkir-\. City, ✱ of Kermānshāhan prov., W Iran; pop. (1971e) 190,000; sugar and oil refineries.

Ker·mān·shāh·an \ˌker-män-shä-ˈhän\. Province of W Iran. See table at IRAN.

Ker·mit \ˈkər-mət\. City, ⊗ of Winkler co., W Texas, 43 m. NNE of Pecos; pop. (1970c) 7884; oil wells.

Kern \ˈkərn\. 1 River, S cen. California; 150 m. long; rises in NE Tulare co., and flows SW through Bakersfield into Buena Vista Lake.

2 County in California. See table at CALIFORNIA.

Ker·ners·ville \ˈkər-nərz-ˌvil\. Town, Forsyth co., N cen. North Carolina, 9 m. E of Winston-Salem; pop. (1970c) 4185; silk and rayon, furniture; truck farming; Southern Pilgrim Coll. (1946).

Kerns·town \ˈkərnz-ˌtaůn\. Village, Frederick co., N Virginia, 4 m. S of Winchester; battle Mar. 23, 1862 in which Union forces under Gen. Nathan Kimball defeated Gen. Jackson's Confederate troops.

Ké·ro·man \kā-rò-'mä^{n}\. Village and fishing port of Brittany, NW France, adjacent to Lorient; after 1920 developed by French government as port for trawlers and during World War II by Germans as U-boat base.

Kerr \'kər\. County in Texas. See table at TEXAS.

Kerr·ville \'kər-ˌvil, -vəl\. City, ⊗ of Kerr co., SW cen. Texas, 55 m. NNW of San Antonio; pop. (1970c) 12,672; airplanes; mohair market; summer resort; livestock farming; Schreiner Inst. (1923).

Ker·ry \'ker-ē\. County in Munster prov., SW Eire; 1815 sq. m.; pop. (1971p) 112,941; ⊗ Tralee; mountainous area, with many lakes (Lakes of Killarney, etc.); agriculture, dairy farming, fishing, quarrying (limestone, slate); exploitation of extensive peat bogs.

Kerry Head. Cape on SW coast of Ireland, on S side of mouth of Shannon river.

Ker·shaw \kə(r)-'shò\. County in South Carolina. See table at SOUTH CAROLINA.

Ker·u·len \'ker-ə-ˌlen\. 1 *or Chin.* **K'o–lu–lun Ho** \'kō-'lü-'lùn-'hō\ *or Mongol.* **Her·len Gol** \'he(ə)r-'len-'gəl, 'ke(ə)r-\. River, NE Mongolian People's Republic; 785 m. long; rises in Hentiyn Nuruu, flows S then E to Hu-lun in NW Manchuria; a headstream of the Amur.

2 Town, Mongolian People's Republic. See CHOYBALSAN.

Ke·sen·nu·ma \kā-'sen-ù-mə, ˌkā-se-'nü-mə\. City, Miyagi prefecture, Honshū, Japan, 60 m. NE of Sendai; pop. (1970c) 63,265.

Ke·she·na \kə-'shēn-ə\. Unincorporated village, ⊗ of Menominee co., E cen. Wisconsin; pop. (1971e) 950.

Kes·ki–Suo·mi \ˌkes-kē-'swò-mē\. Province of S cen. Finland. See table at FINLAND.

Kes·sel–lo \ˌkes-ə(l)-'lō\. Commune, Brabant prov., cen. Belgium, adjacent to Louvain 7 m. E of Brussels; pop. (1969c) 22,789.

Kes·te·ven, The Parts of \-ke-'stē-vən\. See LINCOLNSHIRE 2.

Kes·wick \'kez-ik\. Urban district, Cumberland, NW England, near N end of Derwent Water; pop. (1971p) 5169; lead pencils from locally mined graphite; tourist center; village is 3½ m. S of Skiddaw and is cen. point for various expeditions in the Lake District; home of Coleridge 1800–09 and of Southey 1803–43. Scene of first Keswick Convention 1875 and headquarters of Keswick Movement.

Keszt·hely \'kest-(ˌ)hā\. Commune, Veszprem co., W Hungary, at W end of Lake Balaton; pop. (1970p) 16,731.

Ket \'ket\. Navigable river, Russian S.F.S.R., U.S.S.R.; 842 m. long; rises N of Krasnoyarsk in SW Krasnoyarsk Krai, flows W into Ob river at Kolpashevo.

Ke·ta *or* **Ki·ta** \'kēt-ə\ *or* **Kwit·ta** \'kwit-ə\. Seaport, E Ghana, W Africa, on **Keta Lagoon;** pop. (1970p) 16,100.

Ke·ta·pang \kə-'täp-ˌäŋ\. Seaport town, West Kalimantan prov., SW Borneo, Indonesia; pop. (1961c) 3279; on Karimata Strait and only port of importance on Borneo coast bet. Pontianak and Bandjarmasin.

Ketch·i·kan \'kech-i-ˌkan\. Town and seaport on SW coast of Revillagigedo I., SE Alaska; pop. (1970c) 6994; pulp mill; salmon fishing; gold, copper, uranium mining; fur raising; timber.

Ketch·um \'kech-əm\. Village, Blaine co., cen. Idaho, SE of Sawtooth Range; pop. (1970c) 1454; just N of it is Sun Valley (*q.v.*).

Ke·toi \ke-'tòi\. One of the Kuril Is. (*q.v.*).

Kęt·rzyn \'kent-ˌchin\ *or Ger.* **Ra·sten·burg** \'räs-tən-ˌbù(ə)rg\. City, NE Olsztyn prov., N Poland, W of Lake Mamry; pop. (1968e) 18,200.

Ket·ter·ing \'ket-ə-riŋ\. 1 City, Montgomery co., SW Ohio, S of Dayton; pop. (1970c) 71,864; Kettering Coll. of Medical Arts (1967).

2 Urban district, Northamptonshire, cen. England, 50 m. E of Birmingham; pop. (1971p) 42,628; iron mining; boots and shoes.

Ket·tle \'ket-^{ə}l\. River, British Columbia, Canada, and NE Washington; ab. 160 m. long; rises in British Columbia, flows S across Washington border, bends NE and enters British Columbia for a short distance, then turns S across border and joins Columbia river in E Ferry co., Washington.

Kettle Dome. Peak in Sierra Nevada, E Fresno co., S cen. California; 9452 ft.

Kettle Peak. Mountain in Sierra Nevada, N Tulare co., S cen. California; 10,038 ft.

Kettle River Range. Range in N Ferry co., NE Washington, extending N into British Columbia, Canada.

Keu·ka Lake \'kyü-kə-, kā-'yü-\ *or* **Crook·ed Lake** \'krùk-əd-\. Lake in W New York; 17½ sq. m.; extends across boundary bet. Yates and Steuben cos.; one of the Finger Lakes; ab. 18 m. long and 1½ m. average width; outlet from N end into Seneca Lake; vineyards along its shores.

Keuka Park. Village, Yates co., W New York, on Keuka Lake; Keuka Coll. (1890).

Keunjhar. See KEONJHAR.

Ke·ve·laer \'kā-və-ˌlär\. Town, North Rhine-Westphalia, West Germany, NW of Düsseldorf; pop. (1968e) 20,178; bookbinding; area to S scene Mar. 3, 1945 of contact bet. American and Canadian forces.

Kew \'kyü\. 1 Municipality, S Victoria, SE Australia, NE suburb of Melbourne; pop. (1966c) 32,816.

2 Parish, Greater London borough of Richmond upon Thames, SE England; Royal Botanic Gardens, originating in 1759 and became a national establishment 1841; Gardens have 25,000 varieties, area with adjoining pleasure grounds 288 acres.

Ke·wa·nee \ki-'wän-ē\. City, Henry co., NW Illinois, 38 m. ESE of Rock Island; pop. (1970c) 15,762; coal mines; boilers, gloves, truck bodies, agricultural and mining machinery.

Ke·wau·nee \ki-'wän-e\. 1 County in E Wisconsin. See table at WISCONSIN.

2 City, its ⊗, on Lake Michigan 25 m. E of Green Bay (city); pop. (1970c) 2901; furniture, cheese, butter; dairy farming, potatoes.

Ke·wee·naw \'kē-wi-ˌnò\. County in Michigan. See table at MICHIGAN.

Keweenaw Bay. Inlet of Lake Superior, SE of Keweenaw and upper Houghton cos. and extending S into Baraga co., NW Michigan penin.

Keweenaw Peninsula. Peninsula, NW part of Michigan penin., including Keweenaw co. and part of Houghton co., extending into Lake Superior; tip end is called **Keweenaw Point.** The **Keweenaw Waterway** crosses the peninsula from Keweenaw Bay, through Portage Lake to Lake Superior, shortening the route to Duluth, Minnesota.

Kew Gardens. Residential community in Queens borough of New York City, Queens co., SE New York, on Long I.

Kexholm. See PRIOZERSK.

Keya Pa·ha \'kē-ə-'pä-(ˌ)hä\. 1 River in Nebraska and South Dakota; 101 m. long; tributary of the Niobrara.

2 County in Nebraska. See table at NEBRASKA.

Key Bis·cayne \'kē-bis-'kān\. Island off coast of Dade co., SE Florida, bet. N Biscayne Bay and Atlantic Ocean; site of vacation home of U.S. President Richard M. Nixon.

Key Lar·go \-'lär-(ˌ)gō\. One of the larger of the Florida Keys, 30 m. long, less than 2 m. wide; traversed by the first island link of the Overseas Highway (see FLORIDA KEYS).

Keyn·sham \'kān-shəm\. Urban district, Somersetshire, England; pop. (1971p) 19,007.

Key·port \'kē-ˌpō(ə)rt, -ˌpò(ə)rt\. 1 Borough, Monmouth co., E cen. New Jersey, on Raritan Bay 7 m. SSE of Perth

Amboy; pop. (1970c) 7205; tile, soft drinks, boats, women's coats and suits; truck and dairy farming.

2 Village, Kitsap co., W Washington, on arm of Puget Sound N of Bremerton; site of a naval torpedo station.

Key·ser \'kī-zər\. City, ⊗ of Mineral co., NE West Virginia, on North Branch of the Potomac river 58 m. W of Martinsburg; pop. (1970c) 6586; paper and pulp mill; diversified agriculture; Potomac State Coll. of West Virginia (1901); supply point and battleground in Civil War.

Key·stone \'kē-ˌstōn\. City, McDowell co., S West Virginia, 8 m. E of Welch; pop. (1970c) 1008.

Keytes·ville \'kēts-ˌvil\. City, ⊗ of Chariton co., N cen. Missouri; pop. (1970c) 730.

Key Vaca \-'vak-ə\. See FLORIDA KEYS.

Key West \-'west\. City, ⊗ of Monroe co., SW corner of Florida, on Key West island (less than 4 m. long by 2 m. wide at SW extremity of Florida Keys) 60 m. SW of S tip of Florida; pop. (1970c) 29,312; southernmost city of mainland U.S.; commercial fishing (incl. shrimp, crab, turtle); cigar making; Florida Keys Junior Coll. (1965); U.S. naval station and fort (Fort Taylor); winter and fishing resort; naval station established 1822; city incorporated 1828; suffered extensive damage from hurricane 1935.

Kha·ba·rovsk \kə-'bär-əfsk\ *or* **Ha·bar·ovsk** \hə-'bär-əfsk\. City, ✱ of Khabarovsk Krai, Russian S.F.S.R., U.S.S.R., on right bank of Amur river 29 m. below Ussuri tributary; pop. (1970p) 437,000; junction station on Trans-Siberian R.R.; market for products of the Ussuri valley; center in the fur trade; oil refining, shipbuilding; machinery, lumber, furniture; site of fort established 1652; settled by Russian colonists under Count N. Muraviëv-Amurski 1858.

Khabarovsk Krai \-'krī\. A territory of the Russian S.F.S.R., U.S.S.R., along Pacific coast of Siberia from Amur river to Bering Strait, bounded on W and NW by Yakutsk A.S.S.R., on NE by Koryak National Okrug, on E by Pacific Ocean, on SE by Primorski Krai, on S by China, and on SW by Chita Oblast; 318,378 sq. m.; pop. (1970p) 1,346,000; ✱ Khabarovsk; almost entirely encloses the Sea of Okhotsk; includes the Jewish Autonomous Oblast. *Rivers:* S part lies in basin of the lower Amur, which forms for ab. 700 m. the boundary with China; other rivers are the Zeya and Amgun, tributaries of the Amur, and the upper courses of the Maya and Kolyma. *Mountains:* Traversed by numerous ranges, running generally NE and SW, esp. E end of the Stanovoi Mts. and the Kolyma Mountains; in Kamchatka are the highest peaks in Siberia and the only active volcanoes. *Chief products:* Potatoes, wheat, oats, corn; has great mineral resources, esp. in coal and iron, also manganese, molybdenum; steel industry at Komsomolsk-na-Amure and other cities; many new power plants, oil refineries, mills and factories; fishing and agriculture. *Chief cities:* Khabarovsk, Komsomolsk-na-Amure, Sovietskaya Gavan, Birobidzhan.

History: First settlements were forts at Okhotsk and on Kamchatka, established by Cossacks in latter half of 17th cent.; settlements along the Amur began in 19th cent. and Amur made the boundary by Treaty of Aigun 1858; Trans-Siberian R.R. completed 1915; much disorder in region 1917–20 but independent Far Eastern Republic set up 1920; established 1938. See FAR EASTERN REGION.

Kha·bur *or* **Kha·bour** \kä-'bu̇(ə)r\ *or anc.* **Ha·bor** \'hā-ˌbȯ(ə)r\. River, SE Turkey and NE Syria; ab. 200 m. long; rises in S slopes of Karacadağ mountain and flows S into the Euphrates river just below the town of Deir-ez-Zor.

Kha·bu·ra \kə-'bu̇r-ə\ *or* **Al–Khā·bū·rah** \al-\. Coastal town, Oman, SE Arabian Penin., on Gulf of Oman ab. 100 m. WNW of Masqat.

Khaf. See KHUĀF.

Kha·fa·je \'käf-ə-ˌyā\. Site of ancient Sumerian city, Mesopotamia, on E bank of Diyala river just E of Baghdad, E Iraq; has revealed archaeological objects, esp. Sumerian stone statuettes dating ab. 3000 B.C.

Khaibar. See KHYBER.

Khaifa. See HAIFA.

Khai·ra·garh \'kī-rə-ˌgär\. 1 Former Indian state, now part of Madhya Pradesh, India; 931 sq. m.

2 Town, its ✱, 107 m. E of Nagpur; pop. (1961c) 6600.

Khair·pur \'kī(ə)r-ˌpu̇(ə)r\. 1 Former Indian state, now part of Sind, Pakistan, E of the Indus river; 5989 sq. m.; loyal to British in Afghan campaigns of 19th cent.

2 Town, its ✱, 15 m. S of Sukkur; pop. (1961c) 56,500; textiles.

Kha·kass Autonomous Oblast \kə-'kas . . . 'ȯ-bləst, -ˌblast\. Autonomous subdivision of the Russian S.F.S.R., U.S.S.R., in SW Krasnoyarsk Krai; 23,900 sq. m.; pop. (1970p) 446,000; ✱ Abakan; mountainous; corn, wheat; lumbering; copper, coal, gold, and iron mines; formed 1930.

Khalépa. See HALEPA.

Kha·li·fat \'kəl-i-fət\. Peak, N Baluchistan, Pakistan, E of Quetta; 11,434 ft.

Khalīj aṭ–Ṭīnah. See PELUSIUM.

Khalīj Surt. See SIDRA, GULF OF.

Khalīl, Al–. See HEBRON 4.

Khalka. See HA-LO-HSIN.

Khal·kē \'käl-kē\ *also* **Kar·chi** \'kär-kē\ *or Ital.* **Cal·chi** \'käl-kē\. An island of the Dodecanese (*q.v.*), W of Rhodes; 12 sq. m.

Khalkidhikí. See CHALCIDICE.

Khalkís. See CHALCIS.

Kham·gaon \'käm-ˌgau̇n\. Town, N Maharashtra, cen. India, 166 m. W of Nagpur; pop. (1961c) 44,432; cotton market.

Kham·seh *or* **Kham·se** \käm-'sā\. Former province, NW Iran; 10,825 sq. m.; ✱ Zanjān.

Kha·na·qin \ˌkän-ə-'kēn\. Town on E frontier of Iraq, 90 m. NE of Baghdad on a tributary of the Diyala; pop. (1965c) 23,527; in oil-producing region.

Khan Bagh·da·di \ˌkän-bəg-'dad-ē\ *or* **Khān al–Bagh·da·dī** \-al-\. Town, W cen. Iraq, on W bank of Euphrates 20 m. NW of Hit; battle Mar. 26–27, 1918 in World War I in which Turks were defeated by British.

Khan·ba·lik *or* **Khan·ba·liq** \ˌkän-bə-'lēk\. Mongol name of Kublai Khan's capital of China, rebuilt by him 1264–67 on the site of the earlier Yen, corresponding to the modern Peking (*q.v.*); called **Cam·ba·luc** \'kam-bə-ˌlək\by Marco Polo who described it as a magnificent city; its Chinese name was **Ta–tu** \'dä-'dü\("great capital").

Khand·pa·ra \kən(d)-'pär-ə\. 1 Former Indian state, now part of Orissa state, NE India; 229 sq. m.

2 Town, its ✱, S of the Mahanadi and 50 m. W of Cuttack.

Khand·wa \'kən-(ˌ)dwä\. Town, S Madhya Pradesh, India, 185 m. WNW of Nagpur; pop. (1961c) 65,505; rail junction and cotton center.

Khanhhoa. See DIEN KHANH.

Khaniá. See CANEA.

Khan·ka \'kaŋ-kə\ *or* **Han·ka** \'haŋ-kə\ *or Chin.* **Hsing–k'ai Hu** \'shiŋ-'kī-'hü\. Lake, on boundary bet. China and Primorski Krai, Russian S.F.S.R., U.S.S.R., N of Vladivostok; ab. S three quarters lies in Soviet territory; 1700 sq. m.; 55 m. long; max. depth 33 ft.; unnavigable for large vessels; well stocked with fish; outlet is a W tributary of the Ussuri.

Khan·lar \kän-'lär\ *or formerly* **Bi·bi Ei·bat** \bē-ˌbē-ā-'bät\. Locality, Apsheron Penin., Azerbaijan S.S.R., U.S.S.R., 5 m. W of Baku; has one of oldest and richest oil fields in Europe.

Khan–Ten·gri \'kän-'teŋ-(g)rē\ *also* **Tengri Khan** \ˌteŋ-(g)rē-'kän\. Mountain in the cen. Tien Shan, on boundary bet. Kirgiz S.S.R., U.S.S.R., and Sinkiang Uighur, China; 23,620 ft.

Khan·ty–Man·si National Okrug \ˌkant-ē-'man(t)-sē . . . 'ȯ-ˌkrük\ *or from 1930 to 1940* **Ostyak–Vo·gul National Okrug** \ˌəs-ˌtyak-və-'gül-\. National district, Tyumen Oblast, Russian S.F.S.R., U.S.S.R.; 201,969 sq. m.; pop. (1970p) 272,000; ✱ **Khanty–Man·sisk** \-'man-ˌsisk\, town at junction of the Ob and Irtysh; a large area of marshland traversed by Ob and Irtysh rivers; fishing, hunting; established 1930.

Khan Yun·is \kän-'yü-nəs\. Frontier town, Gaza Strip (see GAZA 1), on coast at Egyptian border 5 m. NE of Rafa and ab. 15 m. SW of Gaza.

Khanzi. See GHANSI.

Khao Lu·ang *or* **Kao Luang** \kaù-'lü-ˌäŋ\. Isolated peak, SW Thailand; in cen. Malay Penin. W of Nakhon Si Thammarat; 5860 ft.

Khao Sam Roi Yord National Park \'kaù-'säm-'ròi-'yòrd-\. National park, Thailand; 23 sq. m.; caves; established 1966.

Kha·rag·pur \'kər-əg-ˌpù(ə)r\ *or* **Kha·rak·pur** \-ək-\. City, West Bengal, NE India, on Kasai river 65 m. W of Calcutta; pop. (1970e) 165,925; Indian Institute of Technology (1951).

Kha·ra Kho·to \ˌkär-ə-'kōt-ō\ *or* **Ka·ra·kho·to** \ˌkär-ə-\. Ruined town, Inner Mongolia, N China, on E edge of O-chi-na river valley and on S edge of Gobi desert; discovered 1909, with its valuable library of 2500 volumes, by Russian scientist Pëtr Kozlov; formerly a great trade center, possibly the Etzina of Marco Polo.

Khara Nur. See HAR NUUR.

Khara Usu Nur. See HAR US NUUR.

Kharbin. See HARBIN.

Kharg. See KHĀRK.

Khār·ga \'kär-gə\. Valley and oasis in Egypt, 25°30'N, 30°35'E; chief town Al-Khārga.

Khārga, Al–. See AL-KHĀRGA.

Kha·rim·ko·tan \kə-ˌrēm-kə-'tän\ *or Jap.* **Ha·ri·mu·ko·tan** \ˌhär-i-mü-'kō-ˌtän\. Small island of the Kuril Is., S of Onekotan; transferred to U.S.S.R. 1946.

Khārk \'kärk\ *or* **Kharg** \'karg\. Small island in NE Persian Gulf, off SW coast of Iran, NW of Būshehr; site of major oil-export terminal; important as last Dutch foothold in Persian Gulf, given up 1766 after destruction of factory by Persians.

Khar·kov \'kär-ˌkòf, -ˌkòv, -kəf\ *or Ukrainian* **Khar·kiv** \-kif\. City, ✻ of Kharkov Oblast, Ukrainian S.S.R., U.S.S.R., on small tributaries of the Donets, 400 m. S of Moscow; pop. (1970p) 1,223,000; sixth largest city in U.S.S.R.; one of the major railroad and industrial centers of the U.S.S.R.; its proximity to the coal of the Donets Basin and the iron of Krivoi Rog has made it a center for manufacture of heavy metal products, including agricultural machinery, electrical equipment, turbines, locomotives, machine tools, diesel engines; paint, footwear, flour; university (founded 1805), now the Institute of People's Education.

History: Founded 1656 as an outpost fortress of Moscow; kept by Cossacks in allegiance to Russian tsars during 17th cent. and made capital of the Ukraine 1765; increased rapidly with development of the Donbas (Donets Basin); in World War I seized by Germans Apr. 1918; suffered considerably in civil war period until 1920; capital of new Ukrainian S.S.R., U.S.S.R. 1921–34; in World War II held by Germans Oct. 1941–Aug. 1943.

Kharkov Oblast \-'ò-bləst, -ˌblast\. Subdivision of the Ukrainian S.S.R., U.S.S.R.; 12,124 sq. m.; pop. (1970p) 2,826,000; ✻ Kharkov; crossed by Donets river; wheat, corn, sugar beet, hemp.

Kharput. See HARPUT.

Khar·ta·phu \'kärt-ə-ˌpü\. Peak in the Himalayas, NE of Mt. Everest; 23,800 ft.

Khar·ti·chang·ri \ˌkärt-ə-'chäŋ-rē\. Peak in the Himalayas, NE of Mt. Everest; 23,420 ft.

Khar·toum *or* **Khar·tum** \kär-'tüm\. 1 Province of NE cen. Sudan. See table at SUDAN.
2 City, ✻ of the Sudan and of Khartoum prov., at junction of White Nile and Blue Nile; pop. (1969e) 230,600; transportation and trade center; tanning, gum processing; textiles, glass; printing; univ. (1956), Industrial Research Institute (1965); founded under Mehemet Ali 1823; abandoned after its seizure by the Mahdi 1885; reoccupied by British 1898 and rebuilt.

Khartoum, North *or* **North Khartum.** Suburb of the city of Khartoum, Sudan; textile mills; agricultural coll. (1954); under siege by the Mahdi's army 1885; Gordon killed and city captured; recovered by Anglo-Egyptian army 1898.

Khart·syzsk \kərt-'sisk\. Town, Donetsk Oblast, Ukrainian S.S.R., U.S.S.R., ab. 17 m. E of Donetsk; pop. (1967e) 42,000.

Kha·ruf, Je·bel \ˌjeb-əl-kä-'rüf\. Mountain, on boundary bet. SW Israel and NE Sinai Penin.; 3301 ft.

Kha·sav·yurt \ˌkäs-äv-'yù(ə)rt\. Town, NW Dagestan A.S.S.R., Russian S.F.S.R., U.S.S.R., 45 m. WNW of Makhachkala; pop. (1969e) 50,000; on railroad in hilly region; practically destroyed during civil war 1917–21.

Khashm al–Gir·ba \ˌkäsh-əm-al-'gir-bə\. Town, Sudan, ab. 230 m. ESE of Khartoum; resettlement area for evacuees from Wadi Halfa (*q.v.*); sugar refinery.

Khasi and Jaintia Hills. See UNITED KHASI AND JAINTIA HILLS.

Khasi Hills \'käs-ē-\. Hill region, Meghalaya and Assam, NE India, bet. the Brahmaputra and Surma rivers; highest peak 6433 ft.

Khasi States. Group of 25 former Indian states in Khasi Hills, now part of Assam and Meghalaya states, NE India; 3788 sq. m.; chief town Shillong; largest were Khyrim and Mylliem.

Khas·ko·vo \'käs-kə-ˌvō\ *or* **Has·ko·vo** \'häs-kə-ˌvō\. 1 Province of S Bulgaria. See table at BULGARIA.
2 City, its ✻, 35 m. S of Stara Zagora; pop. (1968e) 63,840; agriculture, rose growing, tobacco.

Kha·tan·ga \kə-'täŋ-gə, -'taŋ-\. 1 River, E Taimyr National Okrug, Russian S.F.S.R., U.S.S.R.; rises in highlands N of Arctic Circle in NE Krasnoyarsk Krai, flows SE and N through broad estuary (**Khatanga Bay**) to Laptev Sea.
2 Town on right bank of Khatanga river ab. 150 m. from its mouth.

Khatmandu. See KATMANDU.

Kha·wak Pass \kä-'wäk-\. Pass in E Hindu Kush Mts., Afghanistan; altitude 11,640 ft.

Kha·zar·ia \kə-'zar-ē-ə, -'zer-\. Ancient region of SE Russia, inhabited 6th–10th cents. A.D. by the Khazars or Chozars, probably of Turkish origin. At first their home was in the Caucasus but later they controlled the lands bet. the Caucasus Mts. and the Volga and Don rivers and even beyond to the Dnieper and the Crimea (now Crimean Oblast) and organized the trade routes bet. the Black Sea and the Caspian; in 8th cent. the majority embraced Judaism; conquered by Russians in 10th and 11th cents.

Khazzān Jabal Al–Awliyā. See JEBEL AULIA.

Khelat. See KALAT.

Khem–Belder. See KYZYL.

Khem·ma·rat *or* **Ke·ma·rat** \'kem-ə-ˌrät\. Town on Mekong river, E Thailand.

Khe·ri \'ke(ə)r-ē\. Town, Uttar Pradesh, N India, 73 m. N of Lucknow; pop. (1961c) 10,200.

Kher·son \ke(ə)r-'sòn\. Seaport city, ✻ of Kherson Oblast, Ukrainian S.S.R., U.S.S.R., on the Dnieper ab. 19 m. from its mouth; pop. (1970p) 261,000; shipyards; jams and preserves; has rail connection with Nikolayev 35 m. to the NW; harbor closed by ice Dec. to early March; named from the probable site of an early Greek colony, the Chersonesus Heracleotica; founded 1778 by Potëmkin as a naval station and fortress; in World War II held by Germans 1941 to Mar. 1944.

Kherson Oblast \-'ò-bləst, -ˌblast\. Subdivision of the S Ukrainian S.S.R., U.S.S.R.; borders on Black Sea and Sea of Azov and connects on S with Crimean Oblast; 10,927 sq. m.; pop. (1970p) 1,031,000; ✱ Kherson; crossed by lower Dnieper river; corn, wheat.

Khe·ta \'ket-ə\. River, chief tributary of the Khatanga in Taimyr National Okrug, Russian S.F.S.R., U.S.S.R.; ab. 500 m. long; flows N and NE.

Khil·chi·pur \'kil-chi-ˌpu̇(ə)r\. Former state, central India, now part of Madhya Pradesh; 274 sq. m.; pop. (1961c) 7000; ✱ Khilchipur.

Khi·lok \kil-'ȯk\. River, SW Chita Oblast and S Buryat A.S.S.R., Russian S.F.S.R., U.S.S.R.; 380 m. long; rises in Yablonovy Mts., flows SW into Selenga river above Ulan Ude.

Khim·ki \'kēm-kē\. Town, Moscow Oblast, Russian S.F.S.R., U.S.S.R., ab. 10 m. NW of Moscow; pop. (1969e) 75,000.

Khing·an \'shiŋ-'än\. Two mountain ranges of E Asia: **Greater Khingan Range** *or* **Ta–hsing–an–ling Shan–mo** \'tä-'shiŋ-'än-'liŋ-'shän-'mō\, range running N and S in Inner Mongolia, China, averaging 3000 to 5000 ft.; forms a barrier bet. Mongolia and Manchuria; **Lesser Khingan Mountains** *or* **Hsiao–hsing–an–ling Shan–mo** \'shau̇-\, in E Heilungkiang prov., NE China, W of Amur river, separating it from the Sungari valley; highest point ab. 3600 ft.

Khíos. See CHIOS.

Khir·bat Qum·ran \kir-ˌbät-ku̇m-'rän\. Locality, NW Jordan near NW shore of the Dead Sea, in region occupied by Israel 1967; site of an ancient religious community (c. 100 B.C.–A.D. 68) of a Jewish sect, probably Essenes. Nearby is a series of caves in which since 1947 have been found manuscripts left by this group and known as the Dead Sea scrolls.

Khirbat Saylūn. See SHILOH.

Khirgis Nur. See HYARGAS NUUR.

Khi·tai \ki-'tī\. Persian name of China. See CATHAY.

Khiuma. See HIIUMAA.

Khi·va \'kē-və\. **1** *or anc.* **Cho·ras·mia** \kȯ-'raz-mē-ə\ *or later* **Khwa·rizm** \kwə-'raz-əm\. Former khanate, W Asia, on left bank of the lower Oxus (Amu Darya); after its conquest by the Russians 1873 incorporated as subject territory in the empire; declared a republic 1920 and included in Uzbek S.S.R., U.S.S.R., 1924, now constituting Khorezm Oblast; lies S of Aral Sea and except for region along the Amu Darya and oases is chiefly desert.
2 Town in oasis region W of lower Amu Darya, NW Uzbek S.S.R., U.S.S.R.; pop. (1967e) 22,000; former ✱ of Khiva khanate and of Khoresm exclave (now Khorezm Oblast); a flourishing city 7th–12th cents., but later suffered much from invasions; has a citadel and many mosques and Muslim schools.

Khmel·nit·ski \kə-mel-'nit-skē\ *or formerly* **Pros·ku·rov** \prə-'sku̇r-əf\. Town, ✱ of Khmelnitski Oblast, Ukrainian S.S.R., U.S.S.R., 150 m. WSW of Kiev; pop. (1970p) 113,000; food processing; machine tools; founded 15th cent.

Khmelnitski Oblast \-'ȯ-bləst, -ˌblast\. Subdivision of the Ukrainian S.S.R., U.S.S.R.; 7954 sq. m.; pop. (1970p) 1,616,000; ✱ Khmelnitski; wheat, corn, tobacco; sugar refineries; formed 1937.

Khmer Republic. See CAMBODIA.

Khoa Yai National Park \'kō-ə-'yī-\. National park, Thailand; 837 sq. m.; big game animals; established 1963.

Khobdo. See HOVD.

Khodzhent. See LENINABAD.

Khoi. See KHVOY.

Kho·jak Pass \ˌkō-jək-\. Pass in a W ridge of the Sulaiman Mts., N Baluchistan, Pakistan, 30°51′N, 66°34′E; altitude ab. 7400 ft.

Khojend. See LENINABAD.

Khokand. See KOKAND.

Kholm \'kȯlm, 'hȯlm\. **1** Commune, Poland. See CHELM.
2 Town, NW Kalinin Oblast, Russian S.F.S.R., U.S.S.R., on left bank of Lovat river 60 m. NE of Velikiye Luki; in World War II held by Germans from Aug. 1941 to spring of 1943.

Khol·mo·go·ry \ˌkəl-mə-'gȯr-ē\. Town, Arkhangelsk Oblast, NW Russian S.F.S.R., U.S.S.R., on left bank of Northern Dvina river 50 m. SE of Arkhangelsk city; important, esp. in time of Peter the Great, as center for cattle raising and for shipping.

Kholmsk \'kȯlmsk\ *or formerly* **Ma·o·ka** \mä-'ō-kə\. Town, W coast of Sakhalin I., Sakhalin Oblast, Russian S.F.S.R., U.S.S.R., on Tatar Strait; pop. (1967e) 39,000; connects with Yuzhno-Sakhalinsk by railroad and highway; Japanese until 1945.

Khoms. See HOMS.

Khong \'kȯŋ\. Town and island in the Mekong river, S Laos, on the Cambodia boundary.

Khon Kaen \'kȯn-'kan\. **1** Province, E cen. Thailand; 5175 sq. m.; pop. (1960c) 844,075; ✱ Khon Kaen.
2 Town, its ✱, on railroad 100 m. N of Nakhon Ratchasima; pop. (1960c) 19,548; univ. (1964).

Kho·per \kə-'pyȯ(ə)r\. River, SE Russian S.F.S.R., U.S.S.R.; 626 m. long; rises in Penza Oblast and flows generally S through Saratov, Voronezh, and Volgograd oblasts into the Don; navigable most of the year to Borisoglebsk.

Khoqand. See KOKAND.

Kho·rā·sān \ˌkȯr-ə-'sän, ˌkär-\ *also* **Khu·ra·san** \ˌku̇r-\ *or* **Kho·ras·san** \ˌkȯr-, ˌkär-\. Province, NE Iran; 120,980 sq. m.; pop. (1966c) 2,497,381; ✱ Mashhad.

History: In early times under Arab rulers covered more area; forms part of Plateau of Iran; its population comprises many different races; overrun by Muslims c. 650; scene of widespread unrest and revolts in 8th cent.; rise of the Veiled Prophet (al-Mokanna) c. 774–780; conquered 1220 by Genghis Khan and 1380 by Tamerlane.

Khorat. See NAKHON RATCHASIMA.

Kho·rezm Oblast *or* **Kho·resm Oblast** \kə-'rez-əm-'ȯ-bləst, -ˌblast\. Subdivision of the Uzbek S.S.R., U.S.S.R.; 1737 sq. m.; pop. (1970p) 554,000; chief towns Urgench (its ✱) and Khiva. See KHWARIZM.

Kho·rog \kə-'rōg\. Town, ✱ of Gorno-Badakhshan Autonomous Oblast, SE Tadzhik S.S.R., U.S.S.R.; pop. (1970p) 12,000.

Khor·ra·mā·bād \kȯ-'ram-ə-ˌbäd\ *or* **Khur·ra·ma·bad** \kə-\. Town, ✱ of Lorestān gov., W Iran; pop. (1971e) 62,000; distributing center on highway running N from Persian Gulf ports through Ahvāz and Dezfūl to Arāk and Hamadān.

Khor·ram·shahr \ˌkȯr-əm-'shär, ˌkär-\ *or formerly* **Mo·ham·me·rah** \mə-'ham-ə-ˌrä\. Town, ✱ of Khūzestān prov., W Iran, on the Kārūn at its junction with the Shatt-al-Arab, NNW of Ābādān; pop. (1971e) 90,000; date orchards; during World War II developed considerably as a trading port and oil-refining center.

Khors·a·bad \'kȯr-sə-ˌbäd\. Village, N Iraq, ab. 12 m. N of Mosul E of the Tigris; extensive ruins uncovered here are believed to be the ancient city Dur Sharrukin, with palace and temple, of Sargon II, King of Assyria, 722–705 B.C.

Kho·tan \'kō-'tän\. **1** River, China. See HO-T'IEN.
2 *or Chin.* **Ho–t'ien** \'hō-'tyen\. Town and oasis on Ho-t'ien river, SW Sinkiang Uighur, W China, 160 m. SE of So-ch'e; pop. (1958e) 50,000; at foot of Kunlun Mts. and on S caravan and motor highway across Sinkiang Uighur; agricultural center, raising cereal crops, cotton, fruits; gold mining; silk, carpets; has been from earliest times on the Silk Road and the largest and most important oasis supply base on S edge of Takla Makan Desert; through it Buddhist culture introduced from India; has experienced many political changes; Chinese since 1878.

Kho·tin \kə-'t(y)ēn\ *or Rom.* **Ho·tin** \hȯ-'tēn\ *also* **Cho·cim** \'kȯt-sēm\ *or* **Cho·tin** \kə-'t(y)ēn\. Town, SW Ukrainian S.S.R., U.S.S.R., on right bank of the Dniester 30 m. NE of Chernovtsy; pop. (1959c) 10,319; formerly in Bessarabia; has some manufacturing and local trading activity but more important for its location, a former military post at a much-used crossing of the Dniester. In medieval times a Genoese colony; belonged successively to Moldavians,

Poles, Russians, Turks, and Romanians; scene of Turkish defeat 1621 by Poles under Chodkiewicz and Stanisław Lubomirski and again in 1673 by John III Sobieski; seized by Russia 1739 and with Bessarabia incorporated in Russian Empire 1812; under Romania 1918–40; held by Germans 1941–44.

Khroub, El. See EL KHROUB.

Khuāf \ˈkwäf\ *or* **Ru–i–Khaf** \ˌrü-ē-ˈkäf\ *or* **Khaf** \ˈkäf\. Town, Khorāsān prov., NE Iran, ab. 40 m. from the Afghanistan border and 120 m. S of Mashhad; pop. (1966c) 5001.

Khua Kem \ˌkü-ə-ˈkem\. See YENISEI.

Khulm \ˈku̇lm\. See TASHKURGHAN.

Khul·na \ˈku̇l-nə\. 1 District, Bangla Desh; 4652 sq. m.; pop. (1961c) 2,448,720; forms large part of swampy forested islands (Sundarbans) of Ganges Delta.
2 Town, its ✱, 77 m. NE of Calcutta, India; pop. (1961c) 127,970; exports timber and forest products; shipbuilding.

Khunsar. See KHVONSĀR.

Khūrān Strait. See CLARENCE STRAIT 3.

Khurasan. See KHORĀSĀN.

Khur·ja \ˈku̇(ə)r-jə\. Town, W Uttar Pradesh, N India, on Kali Nadi river 50 m. SE of Delhi; pop. (1961c) 41,491; trades in grain, indigo, sugar, and ghee; has a modern Jain temple.

Khurramabad. See KHORRAMĀBĀD.

Khust \ˈküst\ *or Czech* **Chust** \ˈküst\ *or Hung.* **Huszt** \ˈhu̇st\. Town, Transcarpathian Oblast, Ukrainian S.S.R., U.S.S.R., in foothills of E Carpathian Mts.; pop. (1967e) 24,000; before 1945 in Carpathian Ruthenia, E Czechoslovakia.

Khuwarizm. See KHWARIZM.

Khū·ze·stān \ˌkü-zi-ˈstän, -ˈstan\ *or formerly* **Ara·bi·stan** \ˌar-ə-bē-ˈstän, -ˈstan\ *or anc.* **Su·si·ana** \ˌsü-zē-ˈan-ə, -ˈän-ə, -ˈā-nə\. Province, SW Iran; 24,962 sq. m.; pop. (1966c) 1,578,079; ✱ Ahvāz; a fertile region, raising dates, melons, cotton, sorghum, vegetables; rich oil fields; its extent closely corresponds to the ancient country of Elam (*q.v.*) and to the later Susiana, a province of the Persian and Alexandrian empires, at the head of the gulf and bordered by Media on N, Persis on E, and Babylonia on W.

Khva·lynsk \kə-və-ˈlinsk\. Town and river port, N Saratov Oblast, Russian S.F.S.R., U.S.S.R., on the Volga ab. 110 m. NE of Saratov; pop. (1967e) 17,000; grain trade.

Khvon·sār \kvän-ˈsär\ *or* **Khun·sar** \kün-ˈsär\. Town, W cen. Iran, ab. 80 m. NW of Eşfahān and on highway from Eşfahān to Iraq (Sultanabad); pop. (1966c) 10,947; fruit.

Khvoy \kə-ˈvȯi\ *or* **Khoi** \ˈkō-ē\. Town, West Azerbaijan prov., NW Iran; pop. (1971e) 50,000; important trade and communications center in mountains N of Lake Urmia on highway from Tabrīz to Erzurum, Turkey; because of its nearness to Turkish and Russian boundaries, strongly fortified, esp. since ab. 1800; has several times been object of fighting.

Khwa·rizm \kwä-ˈriz-əm\ *also* **Khwa·rezm** \-ˈrez-əm\ *or* **Khu·wa·rizm** \kwä-\ *or* **Khwa·razm** \-ˈraz-əm\. The region corresponding roughly with Chorasmia, a N province of ancient Persia; covered valley of lower Oxus and extended across steppes W to Caspian Sea and E to Bukhara. In 12th cent. an empire, founded by a slave in service of Seljuk sultan Malik Shah; extended conquests in Transoxiana, making Samarkand its capital; overwhelmed 1220 by Mongols under Genghis Khan and again by Tamerlane 1378. First Russian contact in 17th cent., but all military incursions repulsed until 19th cent. Under U.S.S.R. approximately same region known as Khorezm Oblast (*q.v.*). See KHIVA.

Khy·ber \ˈkī-bər\ *also* **Khai·bar** \ˈkī-bər\. Former agency, North-West Frontier Province, India, now part of Peshawar div., Pakistan; 995 sq. m.; pop. (1961c) 301,319.

Khyber Pass. Pass in Safed Koh range and S of Mohmand Hills on border bet. Afghanistan and Pakistan, 10 ½ m. W of Peshawar (see JAMRUD); ab. 33 m. long; ravine and watercourse, from 50 to 450 ft. wide, in places bet. cliffs (600 to 1000 ft. high) and mountains (1400 to 3000 ft. high); former British forts **Ali Mas·jid** \ˌəl-ē-ˈməs-jəd\, in center of pass, and **Lan·di Ko·tal** \ˌlən-dē-ˈkō-ˌtəl\, at Afghan border (the highest point, ab. 3518 ft.); probably not used by Alexander the Great, but has been traversed for centuries by armies and peoples invading India; scene of sharp fighting in Afghan Wars 1839–42 and 1878–80 and with Afridis; now a strategic military road.

Khy·rim \ˈkī-ˌrim\. See KHASI STATES.

Kia \ˈkē-ə\. Settlement, NW end of Santa Isabel I., British Solomon Is., W Pacific Ocean.

Kiachta. See ALTANBULAG.

Kialing. See CHIA-LING.

Ki·a·ma \kī-ˈam-ə\. Town, E New South Wales, Australia, on Pacific Ocean 50 m. SSW of Sydney; pop. (1966c) 5865; agriculture, coal mining; has artificial port.

Kiambone, Ras. See DICKS HEAD.

Ki·a·michi \ˌkī-ə-ˈmish-ē\. River, SE Oklahoma; ab. 100 m. long; rises in E Le Flore co., flows SW into Red river in SE Choctaw co.

Kiamusze. See CHIA-MU-SSU.

Kian. See CHI-AN.

Kiang·an \kē-ˈäŋ-ˈän\ *or formerly* **Quiang·an** \kē-ˈäŋ-\. Name under Spanish rule of Ifugao subprovince (now a full province), N cen. Luzon, Phil.

Kiangling. See CHIANG-LING.

Kiangmai. See CHIANG MAI.

Kiang–nan \jē-ˈäŋ-ˈnän\. Province of China in Ming period. See ANHWEI.

Kiang–ning. See NANKING.

Kiang·si \jē-ˈäŋ-ˈsē\. Province, SE China, bounded on N by Hupeh and Anhwei provs., on E by Chekiang and Fukien, on S by Kwangtung, and on W by Hunan; 63,629 sq. m.; pop. (1968e) 22,000,000; ✱ Nan-ch'ang; for the most part coincides with basin of Kan river; watered by many tributaries of the Kan, has very fertile soil; chief crops rice, wheat, beans, sweet potatoes; tobacco, cotton, peanuts, citrus fruits; exports bamboo, varnish, turpentine, fish. Hilly, esp. in S half; bordered by mountain ranges, highest Tachin Shan on E; has mineral wealth, esp. coal in P'ing-hsiang mines in W, most of which is shipped to industrial Wuhan cities, also produces wolfram and tungsten; for centuries has produced at Fowliang (Ching-te-chen) some of finest porcelain of China; chief cities Nan-ch'ang, Ching-te-chen, Kan-chou, Chiu-chang, Chi-an, Shang-jao. In early times a N and S corridor for migrations and communication; for varying periods a part of Wei kingdom and under the Western Chin, Southern Sung, and T'ang dynasties; under the Mongol dynasty (1206–1368) included W half of Kwangtung.

Kiang·su \jē-ˈäŋ-ˈsü\. Province, E China, bounded on N by Shantung prov., on E by Yellow Sea and East China Sea, on S by Chekiang, and on W by Anhwei; 40,927 sq. m.; pop. (1968e) 47,000,000; ✱ Nanking; one of smallest and most densely populated provinces of China, constituting for most part a deltaic plain, the mouth of the Yangtze; traversed also since 1938 by the Yellow river following in part its old course of 1852 and by the Grand Canal; covered with numerous lakes, largest T'ai Hu; S part rich agriculturally; chief products rice, cotton, wheat, barley, mulberry, peanuts, and melons; fishing, pig and poultry raising; the leading industrial province; chief cities Nanking, Süchow, Wu-hsi, Ch'ang-chou, Nan-t'ung. Under Ming dynasty (1368–1644) a part of Nanking prov.; under Manchus E part of Kiang-nan; set up as separate province in 18th cent.; headquarters 1853–54 during Taiping Rebellion; with growth of Shanghai (*q.v.*, now an independent municipality) increased rapidly in importance.

Kiangtu. See YANG-CHOU.

Kiangyin. See CHIANG-YIN.

Kiaochow. 1 Territory, China. See CHIAO HSIEN.

2 Town, China. See CHIAO-HSIEN.

Kiaohsien. See CHIAO-HSIEN.

Kiating. See LO-SHAN.

Ki·awah Island \ˌkē-(ˌ)wȯ-\. Island in Atlantic Ocean, in Charleston co., South Carolina, ab. 15 m. SW of Charleston.

Ki·a·yu·kwan \jē-ˌä-yü-ˈgwän\. See GREAT WALL.

Ki·ba·we \kē-ˈbä-wā\. Municipality, Bukidnon prov., Mindanao, Phil., 60 m. ENE of Cotabato; pop. (1969e) 52,500.

Ki·bo \ˈkē-(ˌ)bō\. Highest peak of Mt. Kilimanjaro, Tanzania, E Africa; the highest point in Africa; 19,340 ft.

Kibris. See CYPRUS.

Kick·a·poo \ˈkik-ə-ˌpü\. River, SW Wisconsin; ab. 100 m. long; rises in Monroe co., flows S into Wisconsin river in S Crawford co.

Kick·ing Horse Pass \ˈkik-iŋ-ˌhȯ(ə)rs-\. Mountain pass, Canadian Rockies, on boundary bet. SE British Columbia and Banff National Park in Alberta.

Ki·da·pa·wan \ˌkē-də-ˈpä-(ˌ)wän\. Municipality, Cotabato prov., Mindanao, Phil., 55 m. ESE of Cotabato; pop. (1969e) 84,400.

Kid·der \ˈkid-ər\. County in North Dakota. See table at NORTH DAKOTA.

Kid·der·min·ster \ˈkid-ər-ˌmin(t)-stər\. Municipal borough, Worcestershire, W cen. England, on the Stour 18 m. WSW of Birmingham; pop. (1971p) 47,255; worsteds, metalware; Kidderminster carpets (manufactured since 1735).

Kid·nap·pers, Cape \-ˈkid-ˌnap-ərz\. Cape on SE cen. coast of North I., New Zealand, forming S side of Hawke Bay.

Kid·ron \ˈkid-rən, ˈkī-drən\ *or* **Ked·ron** \ˈked-rən, ˈkē-drən\. Valley, Jordan, in region occupied by Israel 1967; source of stream **(Kidron)** rising on E side of Jerusalem, separating it from Mount of Olives and flowing E to Dead Sea.

Kids·grove \ˈkidz-ˌgrōv\. Urban district, Staffordshire, W cen. England; pop. (1971p) 22,036.

Kid·wel·ly \kid-ˈwel-ē\. Town, Carmarthenshire, S Wales, near coast of Carmarthen Bay; pop. (1971p) 3076; 13th cent. church and castle (original structure built late 11th cent.).

Kiel \ˈkē(ə)l\. 1 City, Calumet and Manitowoc cos., E Wisconsin, 18 m. NW of Sheboygan; pop. (1970c) 2848.

2 Seaport city, ✱ of Schleswig-Holstein, West Germany, at head of Kiel Harbor 40 m. NW of Lübeck; pop. (1970c) 271,719; good harbor, 7 m. long; shipbuilding, printing, fish curing, brewing; machinery; exports coal, timber, fish, machinery; univ. (1665).

History: Became city 1242; joined Hanseatic League 1284; part of kingdom of Denmark 1773; Peace of Kiel signed here 1814; passed to Prussia 1866; main base of German Imperial fleet in World War I; scene of mutiny of German sailors which preceded German revolution of 1918; in World War II many times bombed and much damaged 1943–45.

Kiel Bay *or Ger.* **Kie·ler Bucht** \ˈkē-lər-ˌbu̇kt\. Part of the Baltic Sea on the E coast of Schleswig-Holstein, West Germany, extending E to Fehmarn I.; in SW is **Kiel Harbor** *or Ger.* **Kieler För·de** \-ˌfərd-ə\, the inlet at the head of which is the port of Kiel.

Kiel Canal. See NORD-OSTSEE KANAL.

Kiel·ce \kē-ˈelt-(ˌ)sā\ *or Russ.* **Kel·tsy** \ˈkelt-sē\. 1 Province of SE Poland. See table at POLAND.

2 City, its ✱, 90 m. S of Warsaw; pop. (1970p) 126,000; railroad junction; episcopal see; agricultural center; copper mines; marble quarries; founded 1173; scene of battles bet. Russians and Germans 1914, 1915 in World War I; occupied by Germans in World War II; recaptured by U.S.S.R. Jan. 1945.

Kienow *or* **Kienning.** See CHIEN-OU.

Ki·e·ta \kē-ˈāt-ə\. 1 District, Papua New Guinea. See BOUGAINVILLE 2.

2 Chief town of the Solomon Is., on E coast of Bougainville I. on Arawa Bay, W Pacific Ocean; trading center; has radio station and airfield; taken by Japanese Jan. 23, 1942.

Ki·ev *or Russ.* **Kiyev** \ˈkē-ˌ(y)ef, -ˌ(y)ev, -(y)əf\ *or Ukrainian* **Ki·yiv** \ˈkē-yif\. City, ✱ of Kiev Oblast, Ukrainian S.S.R., U.S.S.R., on right bank of the Dnieper 470 m. SW of Moscow; pop. (1970p) 1,632,000; third largest city in U.S.S.R.; important communications center; smelting works, flour mills, refineries, machinery, glass, and leather factories; chemicals, textiles, footwear, furniture; shipbuilding, wood processing; distributing point for a wide area, its trading activity having grown out of its former annual fair, the Kiev Contract Fair; univ. (1834); in its Old Town were many old buildings famous in its long history, among them: the cathedral of St. Sophia (completed 1037), oldest in U.S.S.R.; monastery of St. Michael (1108); church of St. Andrew (1753), built by Rastrelli; and the Kiev-Pechersky Monastery, an ancient (founded in 11th cent.) and sacred place of pilgrimage.

History: One of the oldest cities in U.S.S.R. and so long prominent that it is known to Russians as "the Mother of Cities." As the town of Kiev, 9th cent. A.D., became capital of a Varangian principality, which, under Prince Oleg (c. 880–912), was chief of a number of small Russian states; center for trade down the Dnieper to Black Sea and on the route from Scandinavia to Constantinople; became seat of the metropolitan of Russian Christianity 988; its power and wealth declined in 12th cent.; became object of rivalry among other princes, captured by prince of Suzdal 1169; overrun and ruined by Mongol invasion 1240; became part of Lithuania in 14th cent. and of Poland in 16th cent.; finally incorporated by Russia 1686. Capital of independent Ukrainian republic 1917–19, when it was fought over by Bolsheviks and German expeditionary force; again made capital of the Ukrainian S.S.R. 1934; in World War II occupied by Germans Sept. 1941–Nov. 1943, suffering extensive damage.

Kiev Oblast \-ˈō-bləst, -ˌblast\. Subdivision of the Ukrainian S.S.R., U.S.S.R.; 11,197 sq. m.; pop. (1970p) 1,826,000; ✱ Kiev; crossed by Dnieper river; sugar beet, flax, potatoes; dairying.

Kifisós. See CEPHISUS.

Kifissós Voiotikós. See CEPHISUS 2.

Ki·ga·li \ki-ˈgäl-ē\. Town, ✱ of Rwanda, in cen. part E of Lake Kivu; pop. (1970e) 60,000.

Ki·go·ma \ki-ˈgō-mə\. 1 Administrative region of W Tanzania. See table at TANZANIA.

2 Port, its ✱, on Lake Tanganyika 4 m. N of Ujiji; pop. (1967e) 21,639; terminus of railroad from Dar es Salaam; ships timber, cotton, tobacco.

Ki·ho·lo Bay \kē-ˌhō-lō-\. Bay on NW coast of Hawaii I., S of Keawaiki Bay.

Kii \ˈkē(-ˌē)\. Old province, cen. part of S coast of Honshū, Japan; now Wakayama prefecture and part of Mie prefecture.

Kii Channel. Strait bet. E coast of Shikoku I. and S coast of Honshū I., Japan, and connecting Harima Sea and Ōsaka Bay (through Kitan Strait) with the Pacific Ocean; ab. 25 m. wide.

Ki·kai·ga–shi·ma \kē-ˌkī-gə-ˈshē-mə\ *or* **Ki·kai Shi·ma** \ˌkē-kī-ˈshē-mə\ *or* **Kikai Ji·ma** \-ˈjē-mə\. Island, NE Amami Is., N Ryukyu Is., Japan; 23 sq. m.

Ki·ke·pa Point \ki-ˌkā-pə-\. Point, N end of Niihau I., Hawaii.

Ki·kin·da \ˈkē-kin-də\. Town, Serbia, NE Yugoslavia, ab. 70 m. N of Belgrade; pop. (1965e) 33,000; brickworks.

Kikládhes. See CYCLADES.

Ki·koa Point \ki-ˌkō-ə-\. Point on SE coast of Lanai I., Hawaii, on Kealaikahiki Channel.

Ki·ko·ri \ki-ˈkōr-ē, -ˈkȯr-\. 1 River, New Guinea I., Papua New Guinea; ab. 200 m. long; flows SE to Gulf of Papua.

2 Settlement in delta of Kikori river, 7°35′S, 144°16′E at head of Gulf of Papua; has rainfall of ab. 230 inches annually.

Ki·ku·yu \kē-ˈkü-(ˌ)yü\. Village in Central province, Kenya, E Africa, near Nairobi.

Ki·lau·ea \ˌkē-lau̇-ˈā-ə\. Crater, on E side of Mauna Loa, in Hawaii Volcanoes National Park, S cen. Hawaii I., Hawaii; 2 m. wide and at an altitude of 4090 ft.; largest active crater in the world; erupted 1968. See HALEMAUMAU.

Kilauea Point. Point on N coast of Kauai I., Hawaii, 22°14′N, 159°24′W.

Kil·bren·nan Sound \kil-ˈbren-ən-\ *or* **Kil·bran·nan Sound** \-ˈbran-\. Channel bet. Kintyre Penin. and Arran I., off SW coast of Scotland; ab. 14 m. long and 4 m. wide.

Kil·col·man \kil-ˈkəl-mən\. Castle N of Mallow, N co. Cork, SW Eire; home of Edmund Spenser; ruins.

Kil·dare \kil-ˈda(ə)r, -ˈde(ə)r\. 1 County, Leinster prov., E Eire; 654 sq. m.; pop. (1971p) 71,522; ⊗ Naas; rivers Liffey, Boyne, Barrow; sheep and cattle raising, textile manufacture, brewing and distilling; agricultural machinery.

2 Town, co. Kildare, E Eire, 30 m. SW of Dublin; pop. (1971p) 5280; Protestant cathedral; remains of 13th cent. castle; the Curragh is just E of it.

Kil·gore \ˈkil-ˌgō(ə)r, -ˌgȯ(ə)r\. City in Gregg and Rusk cos., NE Texas, 25 m. E of Tyler; pop. (1970c) 9495; large oil fields; cattle; Kilgore Coll. (1935).

Ki·lid Bahr \ki-ˈlēd-ˈbär\ *or Turk.* **Ki·lit·i·ba·hir** \ki-ˌlēt-ē-bä-ˈhi(ə)r\. Fortified town on Gallipoli Penin., Turkey in Europe, on W bank of Dardanelles nearly opp. Çanakkale.

Ki·li·fi \kə-ˈlē-fē\. Coastal town, E Kenya, E Africa, ab. 40 m. N of Mombasa.

Ki·lik Pass \ˌkil-ik-\. Pass in range bet. E Hindu Kush and W Karakoram Range, Jammu and Kashmir, in area controlled by Pakistan, near Afghan border; alt. 15,600 ft.

Kilimane. See QUELIMANE.

Kil·i·man·ja·ro \ˌkil-ə-mən-ˈjär-(ˌ)ō, -ˈjar-\. Administrative region of NE Tanzania. See table at TANZANIA.

Kilimanjaro, Mount. Mountain in NE Tanzania, near Kenya border, E Africa; highest peak Kibo 19,340 ft., the highest point in Africa, first climbed 1889; next highest peak Mawenzi 16,896 ft., first climbed 1912.

Ki·li·na·i·lau Islands \ˌkē-li-ˌnī-ˌlau̇-\. Group of islets N of Bougainville I., NW Solomon Is., W Pacific Ocean; part of Papua New Guinea.

Kil·in·di·ni \ˌkil-ən-ˈdē-nē\. Town on SW side of Mombasa I., off S coast of Kenya, E Africa; **Kilindini Harbor,** the finest landlocked and sheltered harbor on E African coast, forms modern part of Mombasa harbor.

Ki·lis *or* **Kil·lis** \ki-ˈlēs\. Town, Gaziantep prov., S Turkey, 36 m. N of Aleppo, Syria; pop. (1965c) 38,095; center of olive cultivation; silk and cotton.

Kilitibahir. See KILID BAHR.

Ki·li·ya \ˈkē-lē-(y)ə\ *or Rom.* **Chi·lia** \ˈkēl-(ˌ)yä\. 1 River, the N branch of the Danube delta, E Romania; ab. 65 m. long; borders Letea I. on N and marks boundary bet. Romania and U.S.S.R.

2 *or Rom.* **Chilia–Nouă**\-ˈnau̇-ə\. Town, Odessa Oblast, S Ukrainian S.S.R., U.S.S.R., on the Kiliya branch of the Danube delta; pop. (1967e) 24,000.

Kil·ken·ny \kil-ˈken-ē\. 1 County, Leinster prov., SE Eire; 796 sq. m.; pop. (1971p) 61,811; ⊗ Kilkenny; rivers Suir, Nore, Barrow; coal mining, brewing and distilling; agriculture.

2 Municipal borough, its ⊗; pop. (1971p) 10,292; coal mining, brewing; College of St. John (founded in 16th cent.) which had as students Swift, Congreve, Farquhar, Bishop Berkeley; noted 12th cent. castle and 13th cent. cathedral.

History: Site of convention 1342 at which Anglo-Irish drew up a remonstrance to Edward III protesting a discriminatory proclamation; scene of parliament 1367 which passed statute to curb the growing lawlessness of the Anglo-Irish; scene of a synod of Irish Catholic bishops and clergy, 1642, which tried to overcome the hostility bet. the old Irish and Anglo-Irish.

Kil·kís \kil-ˈkēs\. 1 Department of Greece. See table at GREECE.

2 Town, its ✱, W cen. Macedonia, N Greece, ab. 24 m. N of Salonika; pop. (1971p) 12,425.

Kil·lala Bay \kil-ˌal-ə-\. Inlet of Atlantic Ocean on NW coast of Ireland, bet. cos. Sligo and Mayo, Eire; Moy river flows into it at its head.

Kil·lar·ney \kil-ˈär-nē\. 1 Town, SW Manitoba, Canada, 47 m. SSE of Brandon; pop. (1971p) 2056; feed mill, creamery; summer resort; stock farming.

2 Urban district, co. Kerry, SW Eire, near Lakes of Killarney; pop. (1971p) 7179; tourist center; ruins of an ancient castle and two ancient abbeys nearby.

Killarney, Lakes of. Three lakes, co. Kerry, SW Eire; lowest and largest (ab. 8 sq. m.) is Lough Leane; all are studded with islands and noted for their scenery; on Ross I. in Lough Leane is Ross Castle; other ruins nearby (see MUCKROSS).

Kil·la·ry Harbour \ˌkil-ə-rē-\. Inlet of Atlantic Ocean on W coast of Ireland, S of Clew Bay.

Kill Devil Hill. See KITTY HAWK.

Kil·leen \kil-ˈēn\. City, Bell co., cen. Texas, N of Austin; pop. (1970c) 35,507; concrete products; Central Texas Coll. (1967).

Kil·lie·cran·kie \ˌkil-ē-ˈkraŋ-kē\. Mountain pass, Perth co., cen. Scotland, in SE part of the Grampians; nearby occurred battle July 17, 1689 in which John Graham of Claverhouse, 1st Viscount Dundee, defeated the Scots at the cost of his own life.

Kil·li·nek \ˈkil-ə-ˌnek\ *or formerly* **Kil·li·nik** \-ˌnik\. Small island off N tip of Labrador, Canada, S of E entrance to Hudson Strait; Port Burwell is on it and Cape Chidley is its N point; separated from mainland by McLelan Strait.

Kil·ling·ly \ˈkil-iŋ-lē\. Town, E Windham co., NE corner of Connecticut, on Quinebaug river and Rhode Island border; pop. (1970c) 13,573; includes borough of Danielson (*q.v.*); settled 1693, incorp. 1708.

Kil·ling·ton Peak \ˌkil-iŋ-tən-\. Mountain, E cen. Rutland co., W Vermont; 4241 ft.

Kil·ling·worth \ˈkil-iŋ-ˌwərth\. Village, Northumberland, England, 6 m. NE of Newcastle upon Tyne; place where George Stephenson tried his first locomotive 1814.

Killíni. See CYLLENE.

Killinik. See KILLINEK.

Killis. See KİLİS.

Kill van Kull \ˌkil-van-ˈkəl, -vən-\. Channel bet. New Jersey and Staten I., New York; connects Newark Bay with Upper New York Bay.

Kilmain. See QUELIMANE.

Kil·mar·nock \kil-ˈmär-nək\. Burgh, Ayr co., SW Scotland, 12 m. NE of Ayr; pop. (1971p) 48,785; carpets, woolens, locomotives, pumps, whiskey, dairy products.

Ki·lo·sa \ˈkē-lə-ˌsä\. Town, E cen. Tanzania, E Africa, 150 m. W of Dar es Salaam; pop. (1967c) 4500.

Kil·ro·nan \kil-ˈrōn-ən\. Chief town in Aran Is., co. Galway, W Eire, on Inishmore; pop. (1961c) 459; region noteworthy for ancient remains.

Kil·rush \kil-ˈrəsh\. Urban district on Shannon estuary, SW coast of co. Clare, W Eire; pop. (1971p) 2671; fishing, flagstone quarrying; on nearby Scattery I. are remains of 6th cent. monastery.

Kil·syth \kil-ˈsīth\. Burgh, Stirling co., cen. Scotland; pop. (1971p) 10,168; coal mining, ironworking, stone quarrying; scene of victory of Montrose and his Cavaliers over the Covenanters under Baillie Aug. 15, 1645.

Kil·wa \ˈkil-(ˌ)wä\ *or in full* **Kilwa Ki·vin·je** \-ki-ˈvin-(ˌ)jā\. Coastal town, SE Tanzania, E Africa; poor harbor.

History: Probably founded 1830 by people from **Kilwa** *or* **Kilwa Ki·si·wa·ni** \-ˌkē-sə-ˈwän-ē\ 25 m. to the S; an ancient town with an excellent harbor, on a small island off the coast; founded 975 A.D. by a Persian prince; many remains of its early times; capital of Zanguebar (*q.v.*); occupied by Portuguese 1505–12; became center of the slave trade; Germans, ruling from 1885, laid out modern town.

Kil·win·ning \kil-ˈwin-iŋ\. Burgh, Ayr co., SW Scotland; pop. (1971p) 8291; ruined abbey (founded c. 1140); according to tradition, birthplace of freemasonry (said to have been brought in by foreign craftsmen who built the abbey) in Scotland.

Kim·ball \ˈkim-bəl\. **1** County in W Nebraska. See table at NEBRASKA.

2 City, its ⊗, 43 m. S of Scottsbluff; pop. (1970c) 3680; ships potatoes and beans; oil wells; dairy farming.

Kimball, Mount. Mountain, N Wrangell Mts., SE Alaska, S of the Alaska Highway and E of the Richardson Highway; 10,351 ft.

Kim·be \ˈkim-bē\. Township, ✱ of West New Britain dist., New Britain I., Papua New Guinea; became ✱ 1969.

Kimbe Bay. Large inlet of Bismarck Sea on N coast of New Britain, Bismarck Archipelago; bordered on W by Willaumez Penin.

Kim·ber·ley \ˈkim-bər-lē\. **1** Town, British Columbia, Canada, 60 m. ENE of Nelson; pop. (1971p) 7441; zinc and silver mining; diversified agriculture.

2 Town, N Cape Province, Rep. of South Africa, 86 m. WNW of Bloemfontein, near Orange Free State border; pop. (1968e) 96,200; world's diamond center with Kimberley, De Beers, and other famous mines nearby; commercial center; horse breeding. Founded 1871 shortly after discovery of diamonds in region; capital 1873–80 of Griqualand West before it became part of Cape Colony; besieged by Boers for four months during Boer War Oct. 14, 1899–Feb. 15, 1900. Scenery marked by immense pits and heaps of earth, the aftermath of mining operations. See BEACONSFIELD.

Kim·ber·leys \ˈkim-bər-lēz\. Plateau region, N Western Australia; includes all territory N of 19°30′S lat.; ab. 144,000 sq. m.; chief town Wyndham; goldfields.

Kim·ber·ly \ˈkim-bər-lē\. Village, Outagamie co., E Wisconsin, 4 m. E of Appleton; pop. (1970c) 6131.

Kim·ble \ˈkim-bəl\. County in Texas. See table at TEXAS.

Kim·ch'aek \kēm-ˈchak\; *formerly* **Jo·shin** \jō-ˈshēn\ *also* **Song·jin** \səŋ-ˈjēn\. Seaport town, North Hamgyŏng prov., North Korea.

Kími. See KÝMĒ.

Ki·mi·to \ˈchim-i-ˌtō\ *or* **Ke·miö** \ˈkem-ē-ˌər\. **1** Finnish island in Gulf of Bothnia off SW Finland.

2 Town, Turku ja Pori prov., SW Finland, on Kimito I.; pop. (1970e) 4354.

Kímolos. See CIMOLUS.

Ki·movsk \kē-ˈmȯfsk\. Town, Tula Oblast, Russian S.F.S.R., U.S.S.R., ab. 40 m. ESE of Tula; pop. (1967e) 42,000.

Kimpolung. See CÎMPULUNG.

Kim·ry \ˈkēm-rē\. Town, SE Kalinin Oblast, Russian S.F.S.R., U.S.S.R., at NE end of reservoir, E of Kalinin and 75 m. N of Moscow; pop. (1969e) 52,000; a center of Soviet shoe and leather industry.

Kin. See KŬM.

Kin·a·ba·lu *or* **Kin·a·bu·lu** \ˌkin-ə-bə-ˈlü\ *or formerly* **Kin·i·ba·lu** \ˌkin-i-\. Mountain in N cen. Sabah, East Malaysia; 13,455 ft.; highest peak on island of Borneo.

Kinabalu National Park. National park, Sabah, Malaysia; 275 sq. m.; incl. Mt. Kinabalu; established 1964.

Kin·a·ba·tang·an \ˌkin-ə-bə-ˈtäŋ-ˌän\. River, Sabah, East Malaysia; ab. 350 m. long; flows E into the Sulu Sea; navigable for ab. 200 m.

Kinabulu. See KINABALU.

Kin·caid \kin-ˈkād\. Village, Christian co., cen. Illinois, 22 m. SE of Springfield; pop. (1970c) 1424.

Kin·car·dine \kin-ˈkärd-ᵊn\. **1** Resort town, Bruce co., SE Ontario, Canada, on E shore of Lake Huron 47 m. SW of Owen Sound; pop. (1971p) 3200; furniture, butter, cheese; fisheries; dairy and stock farming.

2 *or* **Kin·car·dine·shire** \-ˌshi(ə)r, -shər\ *or formerly* **The Mearns** \-ˈmərnz\. County, E Scotland; 382 sq. m.; pop. (1971p) 25,050; ⊗ Stonehaven; agriculture (esp. oats and potatoes), livestock raising, fishing, distilling; tourism.

Kin·che·loe Point \ˌkin-chə-ˌlō-\. Point on W coast of Tillamook co., NW Oregon.

Kinchinjunga. See KANCHENJUNGA.

Kinchow. See CHIN-CHOU 1.

Kin·der·hook \ˈkin-dər-ˌhu̇k\. Village, Columbia co., SE New York, E of Hudson river; pop. (1970c) 1223; birthplace of Martin Van Buren, 8th president of the U.S.

Kinder Scout. See PEAK DISTRICT.

Kin·ders·ley \ˈkin-dərz-lē\. Town, Saskatchewan, Canada, 115 m. SW of Saskatoon; pop. (1971p) 3402; agriculture.

Kin·dia \ˈkin-dē-ə\. Town, W Guinea, W Africa, on railroad 60 m. NE of Conakry.

Kin·du \ˈkin-(ˌ)dü\. Town, W Kivu prov., E Zaire, on upper Congo river.

Kin·eo, Mount \-ˈkin-ē-ˌō\. Peak on E shore of Moosehead Lake, NW cen. Maine; 1788 ft.; composed of flint.

Ki·nesh·ma \ˈkē-nish-mə\. Industrial city on right bank of the Volga, N Ivanovo Oblast, Russian S.F.S.R., U.S.S.R., on railroad 50 m. NE of Ivanovo; pop. (1969e) 94,000; chief river port of the region; grain elevators; textiles and chemicals.

King \ˈkiŋ\. **1** Name of counties in two states of the U.S. See tables at TEXAS and WASHINGTON.

2 Name of several islands. See KING ISLAND.

3 Town, South Africa. See KINGWILLIAMSTOWN.

King. See CHING.

King and Queen \-ˈkwēn\. County in Virginia. See table at VIRGINIA.

King and Queen Courthouse. Village, ⊗ of King and Queen co., E Virginia, 34 m. ENE of Richmond.

King·bor·ough \ˈkiŋ-ˌbər-ə, -ˌbə-rə, -b(ə-)rə\. Municipality, Tasmania, Australia; pop. (1970e) 10,610.

Kingchow. See CHIANG-LING.

King City. City, Monterey co., W California, on Salinas river 90 m. SE of San Jose; pop. (1970c) 3717; ships vegetables; asbestos products; diversified agriculture.

King Ed·ward VIII Falls \-ˌed-wərd-t͟hə-ˈātth-\. Waterfall in a tributary of the Mazaruni river, W Guyana, in Serra Pacaraima; 840 ft.; NW of Kaieteur Falls.

King Edward VII Land. See EDWARD VII PENINSULA.

King·fish·er \ˈkiŋ-ˌfish-ər\. **1** County in cen. Oklahoma. See table at OKLAHOMA.

2 City, its ⊗, 36 m. NW of Oklahoma City; pop. (1970c) 4042; feed; oil refining; grain and stock farming.

Kingfisher Peak. Mountain, SW Park co., NW Wyoming; 11,100 ft.

King Fred·er·ik VIII Land \-ˌfred-(ə-)rik-t͟hə-ˈātth-\. Coastal region in NE Greenland.

King George \-ˈjȯ(ə)rj\. **1** County in E Virginia. See table at VIRGINIA.

2 Village, its ⊗.

King George, Mount. 1 Peak, SE British Columbia, Canada, near Alberta border; 11,226 ft.

2 Peak in St. Elias Mountains, SW Yukon, Canada, E of Mt. Logan; 12,300 ft.

King George V Land. See GEORGE V COAST.

King George Island. See SOUTH SHETLAND ISLANDS.

King George Sound. Inlet of Indian Ocean, S coast of Western Australia, 35°03′S, 117°57′E; forms outer harbor of Albany.

Kin·gi·sepp \ˌkiŋ-gi-ˈsep\; *formerly* **Yamburg** \ˈyäm-ˌbu̇(ə)rg\ *or* **Ya·ma** \ˈyäm-ə\. Railroad town, NW Leningrad Oblast, Russian S.F.S.R., U.S.S.R., 20 m. E of Narva; one of oldest towns in U.S.S.R.; founded as Yama in 9th cent. and important later in 14th cent. in Baltic wars; a Bolshevik base in 1917 for Yudenich's army; in 1944 after being under German control for 3 years retaken by U.S.S.R.; name changed in 1922 from Yamburg to Kingisepp in honor of revolutionary leader V. E. Kingisepp.

King Island. 1 Steep rocky island at S end of Bering Strait off W coast of Seward Penin., Alaska, and ab. 65 m. SE of the Diomede Is.; discovered by Capt. Cook 1778; center for walrus hunting.

2 Island at W end of Bass Strait, 50 m. NW of Tasmania, Australia; ab. 42 m. long; 424 sq. m.

3 Island, Burma. See KADAN ISLAND.

4 Island off coast of British Columbia, Canada; 324 sq. m.

King·man \ˈkiŋ-mən\. 1 County in Kansas. See table at KANSAS.

2 City, ⊗ of Mohave co., NW corner of Arizona, 65 m. ESE of Boulder Dam; pop. (1970c) 7312; gold, zinc, lead, feldspar mining; livestock raising.

3 City, ⊗ of Kingman co., S cen. Kansas, 30 m. SSW of Hutchinson; pop. (1970c) 3622; grain and livestock farming.

Kingman Reef. Reef in cen. Pacific at N end of Line Is., 920 m. S of Honolulu; triangular in shape, 9 m. by 5 m., enclosing a deep lagoon; discovered 1798; annexed by U.S. May 1922; bet. 1934 and 1938 used as an experimental aviation station.

King Peak. Peak in St. Elias Mountains, Yukon Territory, Canada; 17,130 ft.

Kings \ˈkiŋz\. 1 River, NW Arkansas and SW Missouri; ab. 75 m. long; rises in SE Madison co., flows N across Missouri boundary and empties into White river.

2 River, S cen. California; rises in E Fresno co., flows W and disappears in region formerly covered by Tulare Lake; upper canyon forms part of Kings Canyon National Park.

3 Name of counties in two states of the U.S. See tables at CALIFORNIA and NEW YORK.

4 Name of counties in three provinces of Canada. See tables at NEW BRUNSWICK, NOVA SCOTIA, PRINCE EDWARD ISLAND.

King's. See OFFALY.

Kings Bay. Inlet on NW coast of Spitsbergen I., Norway, S of Cross Bay.

Kings·burg \ˈkiŋz-bərg\. City, Fresno co., S cen. California, 20 m. SE of Fresno; pop. (1970c) 3843; poultry farming; wineries; grapes, peaches, cotton.

Kings·bury \ˈkiŋz-ˌber-ē\. County in South Dakota. See table at SOUTH DAKOTA.

Kings Canyon National Park. See UNITED STATES, *National Parks.*

Kings·ford \ˈkiŋz-fərd\. City, Dickinson co., S Michigan penin., 3 m. W of Iron Mountain; pop. (1970c) 5276; hydroelectric power plant; lumber, chemicals.

King's Lynn \ˈkiŋz-ˈlin\ *or* **Lynn Re·gis** \-ˈrē-jəs\ *or* **Lynn.** Municipal borough, Norfolk, E England, on the Ouse near the Wash 90 m. NNE of London; pop. (1971p) 30,102; formerly one of chief ports in England; imports timber; sugar refining, fruit canning; fertilizers.

Kings·mill \ˈkiŋz-ˌmil\. 1 Early name of Gilbert Is., W Pacific Ocean.

2 Island group comprising 7 islands in S part of Gilbert Is. group S of the equator.

King's Mill. See MOLINO DEL REY.

Kings Mountain. 1 Ridge in NW York co., N South Carolina, and SE Cleveland co., S North Carolina; the part in South Carolina is scene of an American victory over the British Oct. 7, 1780 and has been set aside as **Kings Mountain National Military Park** (see UNITED STATES, *National Historical Parks*).

2 City in Kings Mountain township, Gaston and Cleveland cos., SW North Carolina, at foot of Kings Mt. 11 m. W of Gastonia; pop. (1970c) 8465; textile mills.

King Sound. Inlet, N Western Australia, SE of Cape Leveque; connected by Sunday Strait with Timor Sea; receives Fitzroy river.

Kings Peak. Peak in the Uinta Mts., Duchesne co., NE Utah; 13,528 ft.; highest point in Utah.

Kings Point. Village, Nassau co., near Great Neck, Long Island, New York; pop. (1970c) 5614; United States Merchant Marine Academy (1938).

Kings·port \ˈkiŋz-ˌpō(ə)rt, -ˌpȯ(ə)rt\. Industrial city, Hawkins and Sullivan cos., NE Tennessee, on Holston river 22 m. NW of Johnson City; pop. (1970c) 31,938; books, paper, chemicals, plastics, glass, leather; settled 1761, chartered 1915.

Kings·ton \ˈkiŋ(k)-stən\. 1 Town, Plymouth co., SE Massachusetts, on Plymouth Bay 16 m. ESE of Brockton; pop. (1970c) 5999; concrete products; cranberries.

2 City, ⊗ of Caldwell co., NW Missouri; pop. (1970c) 291.

3 City, Rockingham co., SE New Hampshire, 19 m. E of Manchester; pop. (1970c) 2882.

4 City, ⊗ of Ulster co., SE New York, on Hudson river 15 m. N of Poughkeepsie; pop. (1970c) 25,544; resort in Catskill Mts. region; boatbuilding; computers, cigars, clothing, iron casting, road and farm machinery; apples, mushrooms. Established as Dutch trading post c. 1615; passed into English hands 1667; played important role in Revolution; meeting place of first state government, court, and legislature 1777; burned by British 1777; rebuilt, and incorporated as village 1805; chartered as city 1872.

5 Borough, Luzerne co., E Pennsylvania, 3 m. N of Wilkes-Barre; pop. (1970c) 18,325; coal mining; railroad repair shops; hosiery, tobacco products, aircraft parts; figured in Wyoming Valley Indian massacre of 1778; incorporated 1857.

6 Unincorporated village in South Kingstown town (*q.v.*), Washington co., S Rhode Island, 17 m. NE of Westerly; pop. (1970c) 5601; ⊗ 1752–1900; University of Rhode Island (1892).

7 Village, ⊗ of Roane co., E Tennessee; pop. (1970c) 4142; agriculture.

8 Seaport town, SE South Australia, 145 m. SSE of Adelaide; pop. (1966c) 1065.

9 City, ⊗ of Frontenac co., SE Ontario, Canada, on NE shore of Lake Ontario near head of St. Lawrence river; pop. (1971p) 61,870; important transshipment point for Welland Ship Canal and outlet for traffic on Rideau Canal; has locomotive works, grain elevators; shipbuilding; manufactures aluminum sheeting, diesel engines, synthetic fibers, ceramics, leather; Queen's Univ. (1841) and Royal Military Coll. of Canada (1876). Fort Frontenac erected here by French 1673 and shortly thereafter destroyed by Iroquois Indians; restored 1695, it became key to Upper St. Lawrence; present city founded 1783 by Loyalist refugees; used as base for British naval force on Lake Ontario during War of 1812; capital of Canada 1841–44.

10 Commercial seaport, ✱ of Jamaica, West Indies; met. area pop. (1970e) 506,200; built on an excellent harbor; commercial center; oil refining, food processing; clothing and shoes; Univ. of the West Indies (1946, royal charter 1962); has numerous old buildings. Founded in 1692 after earthquake had destroyed Port Royal; became seat of government in 1872; has suffered much from fires and earthquakes, almost destroyed by earthquake 1907.

Kingston upon Hull. See HULL 4.

Kingston upon Thames \-ˈtemz\. A borough of Greater London, SE England. See table at LONDON 4.

Kings·town \ˈkiŋ-ˌstau̇n\. 1 City, Eire. See DUN LAOGHAIRE.

2 Seaport, ✱ of St. Vincent, Windward Is., West Indies; pop. (1968e) 4994; on SW coast at head of **Kingstown Bay**

at foot of the mountains; has government buildings, cathedral church, and a botanic garden (estab. 1763), oldest institution of its kind in Western Hemisphere. It was to obtain breadfruit plants for this garden that Capt. Wm. Bligh made his famous voyage 1787 on the *Bounty* to Tahiti.

King's Town. See NEWCASTLE 2.

Kings·tree \ˈkiŋz-(ˌ)trē\. Town and winter resort, ⊗ of Williamsburg co., E South Carolina, on Black river 35 m. S of Florence; pop. (1970c) 3381; lumber; dairy and truck farming; tobacco.

Kings·ville \ˈkiŋz-ˌvil, -vəl\. 1 City, ⊗ of Kleberg co., S Texas, 34 m. SW of Corpus Christi; pop. (1970c) 28,915; headquarters of King Ranch (ab. 2000 sq. m.); natural gas; ships dairy cattle, cotton, winter vegetables; manufactures cottonseed oil, butter, brooms; Texas Arts and Industries Univ. (1917).

2 Town, Essex co., SE Ontario, Canada, on Lake Erie 25 m. SE of Windsor; pop. (1971p) 4078; summer resort.

Kings·wood \ˈkiŋz-ˌwu̇d\. Urban district, Gloucestershire, SW cen. England, NE suburb of Bristol; pop. (1971p) 30,-269.

Kingtehchen. See CHING-TE-CHEN.

King·us·sie \kiŋ-ˈyüs-ē\. Burgh, E Inverness co., N cen. Scotland, on the Spey; pop. (1971p) 1076; health resort; across the river is **Ruth·ven** \ˈrəth-vən\, birthplace of James Macpherson, self-alleged translator of *The Poems of Ossian.*

King Wil·helms Land \-ˈvil-helmz-\. Coastal region, NE Greenland.

King Wil·liam \-ˈwil-yəm\. 1 County in E Virginia. See table at VIRGINIA.

2 Village, its ⊗.

King William Island. Island, S Franklin dist., Northwest Territories, Canada, SW of Boothia Penin; 4955 sq. m.

King·wil·liams·town \kiŋ-ˈwil-yəmz-ˌtau̇n\ *or* **King Wil·liams Town** *also* **King William's Town** *or locally* **King.** Town, SE Cape Province, S Rep. of South Africa, on Buffalo river 130 m. ENE of Port Elizabeth; pop. (1967e) 15,000; trade center for farming and lumbering region; cotton textiles; in vicinity is one of republic's largest Kaffir farming communities. Founded 1835 and named after William IV; abandoned 1836–46 during unsettled conditions; after first Kaffir War made capital of British Kaffraria 1847–65.

King·wood \ˈkiŋ-ˌwu̇d\. Town, ⊗ of Preston co., N West Virginia, 19 m. SE of Morgantown; pop. (1970c) 2550; coal mines, limestone quarries.

Kinhwa. See CHIN-HUA.

Kinibalu. See KINABALU.

Kin·loch \ˈkin-ˌläk\. City, St. Louis co., E Missouri, NW of St. Louis; pop. (1970c) 5629.

Kin·naird \kən-ˈne(ə)rd\. Village, British Columbia, Canada; pop. (1971p) 2838.

Kin·nairds Head \kin-ˌa(ə)rdz-, -ˌe(ə)rdz-\. Headland projecting into North Sea on NE coast of Scotland, NE Aberdeen co.; lighthouse.

Kin·ne·lon \ˈkin-ᵊl-ən\. Borough, Morris co., N New Jersey, 13 m. NW of Paterson; pop. (1970c) 7600.

Kin·ney \ˈkin-ē\. County in Texas. See table at TEXAS.

Kin·ross \kin-ˈrȯs\. 1 *or* **Kin·ross–shire** \-ˈrȯs(h)-ˌshi(ə)r, -shər\. County, E cen. Scotland; 82 sq. m.; pop. (1971p) 6422; sheep raising; woolens and linen.

2 Burgh, its ⊗, 12 m. NW of Kirkcaldy; pop. (1971p) 2418.

Kinsai. See HANGCHOW.

Kin·sale \kin-ˈsāl\. Urban district and seaport, S co. Cork, SW Eire, at head of **Kinsale Harbour;** pop. (1971p) 1628; tourist center; fisheries; scene of short-lived landing of Spanish expeditionary force to assist Irish insurrectionaries 1601 and of James II and his French auxiliaries 1690.

Kinsale, Old Head of. Cape on S coast of Eire, S of Kinsale; lighthouse.

Kin·sha \ˈjin-ˈshä\ *or* **Kinsha–kiang** \-jē-ˈäŋ\. Chinese name for the upper course of Yangtze river down to I-pin, junction point with the Min.

Kin·sha·sa \kin-ˈshäs-ə\ *or formerly* **Lé·o·pold·ville** \ˈlē-ə-ˌpōld-ˌvil, ˈlā-\. City, ✻ of Zaire, on W border, at outlet of the Stanley Pool in the Congo river; constitutes a federal district; 763 sq. m.; pop. (1969e) 1,052,520; commercial center of the republic; major river port; food processing, brewing, tanning; chemical and textile plants; univ. (1954); became capital of Belgian colony (see ZAIRE 1) in 1920's and of independent republic 1960; renamed and placed under military administration 1966.

Kins·ley \ˈkinz-lē\. City, ⊗ of Edwards co., SW cen. Kansas, 38 m. ENE of Dodge City; pop. (1970c) 2212; flour mills; grain and stock farming.

Kins·man Mountain \ˌkinz-mən-\. Two peaks in Grafton co., New Hampshire, W of Franconia Notch; (north) 4275 ft., (south) 4363 ft.

Kin·ston \ˈkin(t)-stən\. City, ⊗ of Lenoir co., E North Carolina 25 m. ESE of Goldsboro; pop. (1970c) 23,020; lumber, yarn, fertilizer; cotton and truck farming; Lenoir County Coll. (1960).

Kin·ta Valley \ˌkin-(ˌ)tä-\. Area in SE Perak state, Malaysia; center of tin-producing region, one of the richest in the world; formed by the **Kinta River,** an E tributary of the Perak.

Kint·la Lake \ˌkint-lə-\. Lake, Flathead co., NW Montana, in Glacier National Park; 6 m. long; alt. 4000 ft.

Kintla Peak. Mountain, Flathead co., NW Montana, in Glacier National Park; 10,110 ft.

Kin·tyre \kin-ˈtī(ə)r\ *or* **Can·tyre** \kan-\. Peninsula in Argyll co., extending S on coast of SW cen. Scotland, with the North Channel and the Atlantic Ocean on W and Kilbrennan Sound (an arm of the Firth of Clyde) on E; ab. 40 m. long and 6½ m. average width.

Kintyre, Mull of *or* **Mull of Cantyre.** Cape on S extremity of Kintyre Penin., off SW Scotland, projecting into North Channel; lighthouse.

Kin·yang Chhish \ˌkin-yäŋ-ˈchish\. Mountain in the Karakoram Range, in part of Jammu and Kashmir controlled by Pakistan; 25,762 ft.

Kin·zua Dam \kin-ˌzü-ə-\ *or* **Al·le·ghe·ny Dam** \ˌal-ə-ˈgān-ē-\. Dam across Allegheny river, Warren co., N Pennsylvania; 234 ft. high; completed 1965; forms reservoir 27 m. long extending into S New York.

Kioga. See KYOGA.

Ki·on·ga \ˈkyȯŋ-gə\. District, known as the **Kionga Triangle,** NE Mozambique, SE Africa, S of Rovuma river; 400 sq. m.; formerly a part of German East Africa, transferred to Portugual 1919.

Kiōto. See KYŌTO.

Ki·o·wa \ˈkī-ə-ˌwä\. 1 Name of counties in three states of the U.S. See tables at COLORADO, KANSAS, OKLAHOMA.

2 Town, ⊗ of Elbert co., E cen. Colorado; pop. (1970c) 235.

Kip·a·wa \ˈkip-ə-ˌwä\. Lake, SE of Lake Timiskaming in Timiskaming co., SW Quebec, Canada; 117 sq. m.

Kipp, Mount \-ˈkip\. Peak in Glacier National Park, NW Montana; 8800 ft.

Kip·pure \kip-ˈyu̇(ə)r\. Mountain range on boundary bet. cos. Dublin and Wicklow, E Eire; highest peak 2473 ft.

Ki·ra Ki·ra \ˌkir-ə-ˈkir-ə\. Settlement on N cen. coast of San Cristóbal I., SE Solomon Is., W Pacific Ocean.

Kir·by \ˈkər-bē\. City, Bexar co., S cen. Texas, 4 m. W of San Antonio; pop. (1970c) 2558.

Kirch·heim un·ter Teck \ˈki(ə)r-ˌkīm-ˌu̇n-tər-ˈtek\. City, cen. Baden-Württemberg, West Germany, 16 m. ESE of Stuttgart; pop. (1969e) 28,599; steel; first mentioned 960.

Ki·rensk \ki-ˈren(t)sk\. Town, E cen. Irkutsk Oblast, Russian S.F.S.R., U.S.S.R., on right bank of Lena river 425 m. NE of Irkutsk; a commercial and trading center.

Kir·ghiz *or* **Qir·ghiz** \ki(ə)r-ˈgēz\. Former name of Kazakh S.S.R., U.S.S.R.— so called because the Kazakhs are an important branch of the Kirghiz people.

Kir·giz Range *or* **Kir·ghiz Range** \ki(ə)r-ˈgēz-\; *formerly* **Ale·ksan·dr Range** *or* **Alexander Range** \ˌal-ik-ˈsan-dər-, -ig-ˈzan-\. Mountain range, N Kirgiz S.S.R., U.S.S.R., extends W from Issyk-Kul; its highest peak is at E end, Mt. Semenov 15,994 ft.; crossed by passes 6550 to 11,825 ft.

Kirgiz Soviet Socialist Republic *or* **Kirghiz Soviet Socialist Republic** *also* **Kir·gi·zia** \kir-ˈgē-z(h)ē-ə, -zhə\. A constituent republic of the U.S.S.R., bounded on N by Kazakh S.S.R., on E and SE by China, on SW by Tadzhik S.S.R., and on W by Uzbek and Kazakh Soviet Socialist Republics; 76,641 sq. m.; pop. (1970p) 2,933,000; ✻ Frunze; entirely mountainous with Tien Shan range along Chinese boundary and Alai Mts. in SW part, high peaks ranging from 16,000 to 23,620 (Khan-Tengri) ft.; many glaciers and lakes at high altitudes (largest Issyk-Kul); its chief river, the Naryn, a tributary of the Syr Darya, runs W in a high valley. *Chief products:* Wheat, tobacco, rice; livestock; coal, oil, mercury; textiles, agricultural machinery. *Chief towns:* Frunze, Osh, Dzhalal Abad, Przhevalsk. Region inhabited, probably earlier than 13th cent., by the Kirghiz, a people of Turkic speech and Mongolian race; annexed to Russia 1864 as part of Russian Turkistan; after 1917 nominally a Kara-Kirghiz autonomous area, which was reorganized 1926 and made a constituent republic of the U.S.S.R. 1936.

Kirgiz Steppe *or* **the Steppes.** Steppe region of cen. Kazakh S.S.R., U.S.S.R.

Kiria. See K'O-LI-YA.

Kı·rık·ka·le \kə-ˈrik-ə-ˌlä\. Town, Ankara prov., W cen. Turkey, ab. 36 m. ESE of Ankara; pop. (1965c) 57,668.

Ki·rin \ˈkē-ˈrin\ *also* **Gi·rin** \ˈjē-ˈrin\. 1 Province, NE China; 72,201 sq. m.; pop. (1968e) 17,000,000; ✻ Ch'ang-ch'un; corn, wheat, sugar, tobacco, coal; chief cities Ch'ang-ch'un, Kirin, Ssu-p'ing, Liao-yüan; formed 1945.

2 One of the three original provinces of Manchuria, China, in cen. and E part; 109,384 sq. m.; ✻ Kirin. Within its borders under Japanese control 1932–45 it included the following provinces of Manchukuo: Kirin, Mutankiang (now Mu-tan-chiang), parts of Sankiang, Pinkiang, and Chientao; much of its territory now part of Kirin prov. (1 above).

3 Former province 1932–45, SE cen. Manchukuo; 34,284 sq. m.; ✻ Kirin.

4 *or* **Chi–lin** \ˈjir-ˈlin\ *or formerly* **Yung·ki** \ˈyůŋ-ˈjē\. City, Kirin prov., China; pop. (1970e) 1,200,000; chemicals, plastics; founded 1673; seat of a Chinese military government 1750–1911; capital of Kirin prov. (see 1 above) until 1954.

Ki·ri·shi·ma \ˌkir-ə-ˈshē-mə, kə-ˈrē-shə-mə\. Mountain in **Kirishima Range,** NE Kagoshima prefecture, S Kyūshū I., Japan; 5574 ft.; regarded as sacred because, according to legend, the god Ninigi descended on its E summit (Takachihodake) as the forerunner of Jimmu, the first Japanese sovereign.

Ki·ri·wi·na \ˌkir-ə-ˈwē-nə\. 1 Largest of the Trobriand Is., W Solomon Sea, 50 m. N of Fergusson I.; ab. 25 m. long and bet. 3 and 6 m. wide, chief town Losuia, near N end. Occupied by Americans and Australians July 2, 1943 and used as air base.

2 Former name of Trobriand Is. group.

Kirjath–Arba. See HEBRON 4.

Kirk·bur·ton \kərk-ˈbərt-ᵊn\. Urban district, West Riding, Yorkshire, England; pop. (1971p) 19,520.

Kirk·by \ˈkər-bē\. Urban district, Lancashire, NW England; pop. (1971p) 59,759.

Kirkby in Ash·field \-ˈash-fēld\. Urban district, Nottinghamshire, N cen. England, 12 m. NNW of Nottingham; pop. (1971p) 23,638.

Kirk·cal·dy \kər-ˈkȯ(l)d-ē, -ˈkad-, -ˈkäd-\. Seaport burgh, Fife co., E Scotland, on the Firth of Forth 26 m. N of Edinburgh; pop. (1969e) 52,097; linoleum and oilcloth, linen, malt, rope and twine, furniture; birthplace of Adam Smith.

Kirk·cud·bright \kər-ˈkü-brē\. 1 *or* **Kirk·cud·bright·shire** \-ˌshi(ə)r, -shər\. County, S Scotland; 897 sq. m.; pop. (1971p) 27,450; agriculture, livestock and dairy farming; hydroelectric power stations.

2 Burgh, its ⊗, at head of Dee estuary 30 m. SW of Dumfries; pop. (1971p) 2506; creamery; oil storage depot; 16th cent. ruined castle; ruins of Dundrennan Abbey nearby; at St. Mary's Isle Burns first said the well-known grace "Some hae meat . . . "

Kir·kee \ˈkər-kē\. Town, suburb of Poona (*q.v.*), Maharashtra state, W India; pop. (1961c) 58,500; scene of British victory 1817 over Baji Rao, the last peshwa of the Marathas.

Kir·ke·nes \ˈkir-kə-ˌnās\. Seaport town, Finnmark co., N Norway, at head of inlet on S side of Varanger Fjord near Finland border; developed as tourist resort before World War II; held by Germans as base during the war.

Kirk·in·til·loch \ˌkər-kən-ˈtil-ək\. Burgh, Dunbarton co., W cen. Scotland, on Forth and Clyde Canal 8 m. NE of Glasgow; pop. (1971p) 25,185; valves, mining machinery, concrete products.

Kirk·land \ˈkər-klənd\. City, King co., W cen. Washington, on inlet of Puget Sound 8 m. NE of Seattle; pop. (1970c) 15,249; residential; feed mill; furniture, paint; vegetables; Northwest Coll. (1934).

Kırk·lar·e·li \ˈkərk-ˌlär-ə-ˈlē\. 1 Province of NE Turkey, bordering on Black Sea on the E. See table at TURKEY.

2 *or formerly* **Kirk–Ki·lis·sa** \ˈkirk-ˌkil-ə-ˈsä\. Town, its ✻, on highway and branch railroad 35 m. E of Edirne; pop. (1965c) 24,790; commercial center in agricultural region; has many mosques and Greek churches, large proportion of its inhabitants are Bulgarians and Jews; has considerable trade with İstanbul. Scene of defeat of Turks by Bulgarians Oct. 25, 1912.

Kirk·pat·rick, Mount \-ˌkərk-ˈpa-trik\. Mountain, S Victoria Land, Antarctica, S of Mt. Markham, long. 166°19′E, lat. 84°20′S; 14,855 ft.; the highest peak in Queen Alexandra Range.

Kirks·ville \ˈkərks-ˌvil\. City, ⊗ of Adair co., N Missouri, 55 m. N of Moberly; pop. (1970c) 15,860; coal mines; shoes, electrical appliances; dairy farming; Northeast Missouri State Coll. (1867).

Kir·kuk \ki(ə)r-ˈkük\ *also* **Ker·kuk** \kər-\. Town, NE Iraq, 90 m. SE of Mosul; pop. (1965c) 167,413; agricultural and market center; sheep raising; oil fields; inhabitants mainly Turkmeni; terminus of railroad from Baghdad; seized by Arab forces Apr. 1941 but retaken by British before June 1, 1941.

Kirk·wall \ˈkər-ˌkwȯl, -kwəl\. Burgh, ⊗ of Orkney co., NE Scotland; on Pomona I. in the Orkney Is.; pop. (1971p) 4618; good harbor; exports beef cattle and dairy products; fisheries, boat building; cathedral.

Kirk·wood \ˈkər-ˌkwůd\. City, St. Louis co., E Missouri, 13 m. W of St. Louis; pop. (1970c) 31,769; commercial and residential suburb of St. Louis.

Kirman. See KERMĀN.

Kirmanshah. See KERMĀNSHĀH.

Kirmasti. See MUSTAFA KEMAL PAŞA.

Kir Moab *or* **Kir of Moab.** See AL-KARAK.

Ki·rov \ˈkē-ˌrȯf, -ˌrȯv, -rəf\ *or formerly* **Vyat·ka** \vē-ˈat-kə, -ˈät-\. City, ✻ of Kirov Oblast, Russian S.F.S.R., U.S.S.R., on left bank of Vyatka river 265 m. NE of Gorki; pop. (1970p) 332,000; metalworking; heavy machinery, agricultural equipment, lumber, artificial leather; a cultural center with research and technical institutes. Founded 1181 as a colony of Novgorod; capital of a medieval principality; plundered twice by Tatars in 14th and 15th cents.; came under Moscow 1489; name changed from Vyatka to Kirov 1934.

Ki·ro·va·bad \ki-ˈrō-və-ˌbad\; *formerly* **Gan·dzha** *also* **Gan·dja** \ˈgän-jə\; *from 1813 to 1920* **Eli·sa·vet·pol** \i-ˌliz-ə-ˈvet-ˌpōl\ *also* **Ye·li·za·vet·pol** \yi-\. City, W Azerbaijan S.S.R., U.S.S.R., S of Kura river, on railroad 110 m. SE of Tbilisi; pop. (1970p) 190,000; on N spur of Armenian plateau at altitude of ab. 1440 ft.; textiles, cottonseed oil, soap, flour, agricultural machinery. An old Armenian town, its inhabitants now represent many races; controlled variously in medieval times; annexed by Russia 1804; scene of Persian defeat by Russians 1826; name changed from Gandzha 1935. Birthplace 1141 of Persian poet Nizami.

Ki·rov·a·kan \ki-ˌrōv-ə-ˈkän\ *or formerly* **Ka·rak·lis** \kə-ˈräk-lis\. Town, Armenian S.S.R., U.S.S.R., ab. 40 m. N of Yerevan; pop. (1970p) 107,000; chemicals, machinery.

Kirov Oblast \-ˈō-bləst, -ˌblast\. Subdivision of the Russian S.F.S.R., U.S.S.R., plateau country W of the Ural Mts.; 46,641 sq. m.; pop. (1970p) 1,726,000; ✱ Kirov; occupies large part of Vyatka river basin; thickly forested, extensive peat beds; oats, rye, potatoes; lumbering; iron ore.

Ki·ro·vo–Che·petsk \ˌkir-ə-(ˌ)vō-chə-ˈpetsk\ *or formerly* **Kirovo–Che·pet·ski** \-ˈpet-skē\. Town, Kirov Oblast, Russian S.F.S.R., U.S.S.R., ab. 20 m. ESE of Kirov; pop. (1967e) 43,000.

Ki·ro·vo·grad \ki-ˈrō-və-ˌgrad\; *formerly* **Zi·nov·ievsk** \zə-ˈnōv-ˌyefsk, -yevsk\ *also* **Eli·sa·vet·grad** \i-ˌliz-ə-ˈvet-ˌgrad\ *or* **Ye·li·za·vet·grad** \yi-\. City, ✱ of Kirovograd Oblast, Ukrainian S.S.R., U.S.S.R., on E bank of Ingul river 155 m. SE of Kiev; pop. (1970p) 189,000; primarily an agricultural center in the black-earth region of the S Ukrainian S.S.R., producing wheat, corn, sunflowers, and sugar beets; large agricultural machinery plants; founded as a fortress 1754 and named after Empress Elizabeth; in 1917, after the Revolution, Elisavetgrad renamed in honor of the Bolshevik leader G. E. Zinoviev, who was born here; again renamed 1935 after Sergei Kirov; in World War II held by Germans 1941–44.

Kirovograd Oblast \-ˈō-bləst, -ˌblast\. Subdivision of the Ukrainian S.S.R., U.S.S.R., S of the Dnieper; 9498 sq. m.; pop. (1970p) 1,260,000; ✱ Kirovograd; wheat, corn, sugar beets, sunflowers; livestock.

Ki·rovsk \ˈkē-ˌrōfsk, -rəfsk\. Town, W cen. Murmansk Oblast, Russian S.F.S.R., U.S.S.R., at base of Kola Penin.; pop. (1967e) 46,000; commercial town on railroad 85 m. S of Murmansk and E of Lake Imandra; uranium deposits nearby.

Kir·rie·muir \ˌkir-ē-ˈmyu̇(ə)r\. Burgh, Angus co., E Scotland; pop. (1971p) 4137; linen weaving; birthplace ("Thrums") of Sir James M. Barrie.

Kir·sa·nov \kir-ˈsän-əf, -ˈsan-\. Town, E Tambov Oblast, Russian S.F.S.R., U.S.S.R., on Tambov-Saratov R.R.; pop. (1967e) 21,000; in iron-mining area; important smelting works; flour mills.

Kır·şe·hir \ˌkər-shə-ˈhi(ə)r\. **1** Province of cen. Turkey. See table at TURKEY.
2 *or anc.* **Jus·tin·i·an·op·o·lis** \jə-ˌstin-ē-ə-ˈnäp-ə-ləs\. Town, its ✱, on highway N of the Kızıl Irmak and ab. 85 m. SE of Ankara; pop. (1965c) 24,681; noted for its carpets; important in Byzantine period; enlarged and renamed by Emperor Justinian.

Kir·te \ˈkir-tä\ *also* **Kri·thia** \krē-ˈthyä\. Village near tip of Gallipoli Penin., Turkey; early objective of Anzac troops in Gallipoli campaign Apr.–June 1915.

Kir·thar Range \ki(ə)r-ˈtär-\ *or* **Ha·la Mountains** \ˌhäl-ə-\. Mountain range bet. Baluchistan and Sind, NW Pakistan; highest peak ab. 7000 ft.

Kirt·land \ˈkərt-lənd\. Village, Lake co., NE Ohio; pop. (1970c) 5530.

Kirun. See CHI-LUNG.

Ki·ru·na \ˈkir-u̇-ˌnä\. Town, Norrbotten co., N Sweden, SE of Torne Träsk, on railroad bet. Narvik, Norway, and Luleå, Sweden; pop. (1970e) 28,942; a mining town near rich deposits of high iron content; geophysical institute.

Kir·yū \ˈki(ə)r-(ˌ)yü\. Town, Gumma prefecture, Honshū, Japan, ab. 55 m. NNW of Tokyo; pop. (1970c) 133,141; a center of the textile industry.

Kis–Alföld. See ALFÖLD.

Ki·san·ga·ni \ˌkē-sən-ˈgän-ē\ *or formerly* **Stan·ley·ville** \ˈstan-lē-ˌvil\. City, ✱ of Haut-Zaïre prov., Zaire, on Congo river 750 m. NE of Kinshasa; pop. (1966e) 149,900; river port and commercial center; textiles; univ. (1963).

Ki·sar \ki-ˈsär\. Small island ab. 15 m. N of E tip of Timor, S Malay Archipelago; 51 sq. m.; belongs to Indonesia.

Ki·sa·ra·zu \ˌkē-sə-ˈrä-(ˌ)zü\. City, Chiba prefecture, Honshū, Japan, on Tokyo Bay 22 m. SW of Tokyo; pop. (1970c) 73,319.

Ki·se·levsk \ki-ˈsel-(ˌ)yōfsk\. Town, Kemerovo Oblast, Russian S.F.S.R., U.S.S.R., ab. 90 m. SSE of Kemerovo; pop. (1970p) 126,000.

Kish \ˈkish\. One of most important of the ancient cities of Sumer and Akkad; its ruins lie ab. 8 m. E of site of Babylon (*q.v.*) and in early times was on the Euphrates whose course changed later; ruins are very extensive and different strata give valuable archaeological information of different eras: near the surface were found ruins of great temple of the time of Nebuchadnezzar II and Nabonidus 605–539 B.C., below it the palace of Sargon I c. 2600 B.C., and at lowest level remains of Sumerian culture of 4th millennium B.C.; according to legend the ruling city after the Flood.

Ki·shan·garh *or* **Ki·shen·garh** \ˈkish-ən-ˌgär\. **1** Former Indian state, now part of Rajasthan, NW India; 837 sq. m.; made treaty with British government 1818; became member of Union of Rajasthan June 26, 1947.
2 Town, its ✱; pop. (1961c) 25,244; founded 1611.

Ki·shi·nev \ˈkish-ə-ˌnef, -ˌnev\ *or Rom.* **Chi·şi·nău** \ˌkē-shi-ˈnau̇\. City, ✱ of Moldavian S.S.R., U.S.S.R., on a tributary of the Dniester 90 m. NW of Odessa; pop. (1970p) 357,000; commercial town on railroad from Iaşi to Odessa; exports fruit, leather, flour, tobacco, and wine; univ. (1945), cathedral. Founded before 1420; attacked by Turks; acquired 1812 by Russia from Moldavia; scene of massacre of Jews Apr. 1903 instigated by Russian officials; as part of Bessarabia was under Romanians 1918–40; made capital of Moldavian S.S.R. 1940; held by Axis powers 1941–44; entered by U.S.S.R. Aug. 24, 1944.

Ki·shi·wa·da \ˌkē-shi-ˈwäd-ə\. City, Ōsaka prefecture, Honshū, Japan; suburb of Ōsaka; pop. (1970c) 162,022; textiles.

Kishm. See QESHM.

Kishon. See QISHON.

Kis·ka \ˈkis-kə\. Island, most westerly and largest of Rat Is. group, W Aleutian Is., SW Alaska; 110 sq. m.; mountainous, highest point above 4000 ft.; Kiska Harbor is on E coast; seized by Japanese June 1942; reoccupied by American and Canadian forces Aug. 15, 1943.

Kis·ki·min·e·tas \ˌkis-ki-ˈmin-ət-əs\. River, SW Pennsylvania; ab. 20 m. long; formed by confluence of Conemaugh river and Loyalhanna Creek in SW Indiana co.; flows NW into Allegheny river.

Kis·kö·rös \ˈkish-kə-(ˌ)rəsh\. Commune, S Hungary, 65 m. S of Budapest; pop. (1970p) 13,824.

Kis·kun·do·rozs·ma \ˈkish-ku̇n-ˌdō-rōzh-ˌmō\ *or* **Do·rozs·ma** \ˈdō-rōzh-ˌmō\. Commune, S Hungary, just NW of Szeged; pop. (1970p) 10,087.

Kis·kun·fé·legy·há·za \ˈkish-ku̇n-ˈfā-lij-ˌhäz-(ˌ)ō\ *or* **Fé·legy·há·za** \ˈfā-lij-ˌhäz-(ˌ)ō\. City, cen. Hungary, 66 m. SE of Budapest; pop. (1970p) 34,127; market center for livestock, tobacco, fruits, and wines; present town dates from ab. 1743.

Kis·kun·ha·las \ˌkish-ku̇n-ˈhō-ˌlōsh\ *or* **Ha·las** \ˈhō-ˌlōsh\. City, S Hungary, 35 m. NW of Szeged; pop. (1970p) 28,447; poultry, wine.

Kis·kun·maj·sa \ˈkish-ku̇n-ˌmōi-shō\. Commune, S Hungary, 25 m. NW of Szeged; pop. (1970p) 12,446.

Kis·lo·vodsk \ˌkis-lə-ˈvōtsk\. City, S Stavropol Krai, Russian S.F.S.R., U.S.S.R., on a tributary of the Kuma; pop. (1969e) 85,000; in foothills of N Caucasus Mts. (alt. 2690 ft.) at end of branch railroad ab. 15 m. SW of Pyatigorsk; health resort; mineral springs; founded 1803.

Kis·ma·yu \kis-'mī-(,)ü\ *or formerly* **Chi·si·ma·io** \,kē-zē-'mä-(,)yō\. Seaport, S Somalia; pop. (1968e) 17,872.

Ki·so \'kē-(,)sō\. River, SW cen. Honshū, Japan; 144 m. long; rises in Nagano prefecture and flows SW into the head of Ise Bay.

Kisseraing. See KANMAW KYUN.

Kis·sim·mee \kis-'im-ē\. 1 River, S cen. Florida; 140 m. long; flows S from Tohopekaliga Lake through **Lake Kissimmee** (ab. 12 m. long) into Lake Okeechobee.
2 City, ⊗ of Osceola co., cen. Florida penin., on Tohopekaliga Lake 18 m. S of Orlando; pop. (1970c) 7119; boatbuilding, fruit packing; plastics; diversified agriculture.

Kis·sing·en \'kis-iŋ-ən\ *or* **Bad Kissingen** \'bät-\. Town, Bavaria, West Germany, on Fränkische Saale river ab. 62 m. E of Frankfurt; pop. (1968e) 12,175; mineral waters.

Kistna. See KRISHNA.

Kis·új·szál·lás \'kish-ü-,sä-läsh\. City, Szolnok co., E Hungary, 12 m. SW of Karcag; pop. (1970p) 13,391.

Ki·su·mu \ki-'sü-(,)mü\ *or formerly* **Port Flor·ence** \-'flȯr-ən(t)s, -'flär-\. Town, ✱ of Nyanza prov., Kenya, E Africa; pop. (1969p) 30,700; port on Homa Gulf, NE Lake Victoria.

Kis·vár·da \'kish-,vär-də\. Commune, Szabolcs-Szatmár co., NE Hungary, 60 m. NE of Miskolc; pop. (1970p) 13,-759.

Ki·ta \'kēt-ə\. 1 Seaport, Ghana. See KETA.
2 Town, W Mali, W Africa, on Bamako-Dakar railroad 100 m. W of Bamako.

Ki·tai \ki-'tī\. See CATHAY.

Ki·ta·iba·ra·ki \,kē-tä-,ē-bə-'räk-ē, -ē-'bär-ə-kē\. City, Ibaraki prefecture, Honshū, Japan, on Pacific coast 95 m. NE of Tokyo; pop. (1970c) 48,323.

Kita Iwo. See VOLCANO ISLANDS.

Ki·ta·ka·mi \kē-'tä-'käm-ē\. River, Iwate and Miyagi prefectures, N Honshū, Japan; 152 m. long; flows S into Ishinomaki Bay at Ishinomaki.

Ki·ta·kyū·shū \kē-'tä-'kyü-(,)shü\. City, Fukuoka prefecture, N Kyūshū, Japan; pop. (1970c) 1,042,321; formed 1963 by amalgamation of Kokura, Moji, Tobata, Wakamatsu, and Yawata; a major center of heavy industry; ships coal; shipbuilding, fishing; iron, steel, glass, textiles, chemicals, machinery, cement; technical institute (1921).

Ki·ta·le \ki-'täl-ē\. Town, W Kenya, E Africa, near Uganda border and just E of Mt. Elgon; pop. (1969p) 11,500.

Ki·ta·mi \kē-'täm-ē\. City, Hokkaidō, Japan, 145 m. NE of Sapporo; pop. (1970c) 82,727.

Ki·tan Strait \ki-'tän-\ *or formerly* **Yu·ra Strait** \yü-'rä-\. Strait bet. S Honshū I., Japan, and SE Awaji I., connecting Ōsaka Bay (a branch of the Inland Sea) with Kii Channel and the Pacific Ocean.

Kit Car·son \'kit-'kär-sən\. County in Colorado. See table at COLORADO.

Kit Carson Mountain. Mountain, Saguache co., S Colorado; 14,165 ft.

Kitch·e·ner \'kich-(ə-)nər\ *or formerly* **Ber·lin** \bər-'lin\. Industrial city, ⊗ of Waterloo co., SE Ontario, Canada, 62 m. WSW of Toronto; pop. (1971p) 109,954, met. area pop. 224,390; rubber goods, furniture; meat packing, distilling; St. Jerome's Coll. (1864). First settled 1806 by Pennsylvania Dutch, then by Germans 1825 who named it Berlin; name changed 1916 in honor of Lord Kitchener.

Kithairón. See CITHAERON.

Kithareng. See KANMAW KYUN.

Kíthira. See CERIGO.

Kithnos. See KYTHNOS.

Kit·i·mat \'kit-ə-,mat\. Seaport, W British Columbia, Canada, at head of Douglas Channel; pop. (1966c) 9782; aluminum plant.

Kit·sap \'kit-səp\. County in Washington. See table at WASHINGTON.

Kit·tan·ning \kə-'tan-iŋ\. Borough, ⊗ of Armstrong co., W Pennsylvania, on Allegheny river 37 m. NE of Pittsburgh; pop. (1970c) 6231; gas and oil wells; brick and cement products; castings; limestone; diversified agriculture.

Kit·ta·tin·ny Mountain \,kit-ə-,tin-ē-\. Ridge of the Appalachian Mts., extending from Ulster co., SE New York, SW through Sussex and Warren cos. in NW New Jersey, and into Pennsylvania where it forms boundary bet. Monroe, Carbon, and Schuylkill cos. on the NW and Northampton, Lehigh, and Berks cos. on the SE, and continuing SW to the Maryland border; average height ab. 2000 ft.; known as Shawangunk in New York and Blue Mts. in Pennsylvania.

Kit·tery \,kit-ə-rē\. Town, York co., SW Maine, across bay from Portsmouth, New Hampshire; pop. (1970c) 11,028; site of Portsmouth Navy Yard (established 1806). See PORTSMOUTH 1.

Kittery Point. Extreme S point, York co., SW Maine.

Kittim. See CITIUM.

Kit·ti·tas \'kit-i-təs\. County in Washington. See table at WASHINGTON.

Kitt·son \'kit-sən\. County in Minnesota. See table at MINNESOTA.

Kit·ty Hawk \'kit-ē-,hȯk\. Small village, Dare co., E North Carolina, on narrow sand barrier opp. Albemarle Sound; nearby is Kill Devil Hill (now a national memorial) where Wright brothers performed experiments, making first airplane flight in U.S. Dec. 17, 1903.

Kit·we \'kē-,twā\. Town, Zambia, 180 m. N of Lusaka; pop. (1967e) 160,000; copper mines.

Kitz·bühel \'kits-(,)byü(-ə)l\. Resort town, Tirol, W Austria, 48 m. ENE of Innsbruck; pop. (1961c) 7744; received charter 1271.

Kit·zing·en \'kit-siŋ-ən\. City, Bavaria, West Germany, on Main River; pop. (1968e) 18,400.

Kiuchuan. See CHIU-CH'ÜAN.

Kiukiang. See CHIU-CHIANG.

Kiungshan. See CH'IUNG-SHAN.

Kiūshū. See KYŪSHŪ.

Ki·vi·jär·vi \'kiv-ē-,ya(ə)r-vē\. Lake in Vaasa prov., SW cen. Finland.

Ki·vu \'kē-(,)vü\ *or formerly* **Cos·ter·mans·ville** \'käs-tər-mənz-,vil\. Province of E Zaire. See table at ZAIRE 1.

Kivu, Lake. Lake on E border of Zaire in cen. Africa, bet. Kivu, Zaire, and Rwanda, N of Lake Tanganyika and S of Lake Edward; 1042 sq. m.; alt. 4790 ft.; max. depth 1558 ft.; chief town on its shores Bukavu at S end; center of volcanic region: Karisimbi, Mikeno, Nyamlagira, and Nyiragongo, all above 10,000 ft., nearby.

Kiyang. See CH'I-YANG.

Kiyev *or* **Kiyiv.** See KIEV.

Ki·zel \ki-'zel, kiz-'yel\. Town, Perm Oblast, Russian S.F.S.R., U.S.S.R., ab. 90 m. NE of Perm; pop. (1969e) 54,000.

Kizil. See KYZYL.

Kızıl Adalar. See KIZIL ISLANDS.

Kizil Arvat. See KIZYL-ARVAT.

Kı·zıl Ir·mak \kə-,zil-i(ə)r-'mäk\ *or anc.* **Ha·lys** \'hā-ləs\. River, cen. and N cen. Turkey; ab. 715 m. long; rises in the mountains E of Sıvas and flows in a great curve SW, W, N, and NE into the Black Sea bet. Samsun and Sinop; the largest river of Asia Minor; its main tributaries are the Delice from the E and the Gök from the W.

Kı·zıl Islands \kə-'zil-\ *or Turk.* **Kızıl Ada·lar** \-,äd-ə-'lär\ *or Eng.* **Princ·es Islands** \,prin-səz-\ *or anc.* **De·mo·ne·si In·su·lae** \,dē-mə-,nē-sī-'in-s(y)u̇-lē\. Nine small islands in E part of the Sea of Marmara, near coast of Asia Minor ab. 15 m. S of İstanbul and constituting a district of İstanbul prov., Turkey; ab. 5½ sq. m.; pop. (1965e) 15,246; summer resort; in Byzantine times used as place of banishment and have extensive Byzantine remains, including monasteries, convents, tombs, villas, etc.

Kizil Kum. See KYZYL KUM.

Kizil Uzen. See QIZIL UZUN.

Kiz·lyar \ˌkiz-lē-ˈär\. Town, E Dagestan A.S.S.R., Russian S.F.S.R., U.S.S.R., at head of Terek delta ab. 40 m. from the Caspian Sea; pop. (1967e) 27,000; on the Astrakhan-Makhachkala railroad ab. 75 m. NNW of the latter. Surrounded by gardens and vineyards; noted for its wines; has active trade in wheat, corn, and fruits; fishing an important industry. An old town; now has Georgian, Tatar, Armenian, and Persian inhabitants; first became prominent 1715; its citadel or fortress dates from 1736.

Ki·zu \ˈkē-(ˌ)zü\ *or* **Ki·zu·ga·wa** \ˌkē-zu̇-ˈgä-wə\. River, S Honshū, Japan, rising in Mie prefecture; a tributary of the Yodo, joining it S of Kyōto.

Kizugawa. 1 River, Japan. See KIZU.
2 River mouth, Japan. See YODO 2.

Ki·zyl–Ar·vat *also* **Ki·zil Arvat** \kə-ˌzil-är-ˈvät\. Town, SW Turkmen S.S.R., U.S.S.R., on railroad; pop. (1967e) 20,000.

Kjøge Bight. See KØGE BIGHT.

Kjø·len Mountains \ˈchəl-ən-\ *or Swed.* **Kö·len** \ˈchəl-ən\. Range along boundary bet. NE Norway and NW Sweden; highest peak Kebnekaise 6965 ft.

Kla·bat \ˈkläb-ˌät\. Volcanic peak, on NE tip of Celebes I., Indonesia, just E of Manado; 6632 ft.

Klabat Bay. Inlet of South China Sea, N coast of Bangka I., Indonesia.

Klad·no \ˈkläd-(ˌ)nō\. Industrial city, NW Czech S.R., W Czechoslovakia, 15 m. W of Prague; pop. (1968e) 56,529; coal and iron mines; blast furnaces, rolling mills.

Kla·gen·furt \ˈkläg-ən-ˌfu̇(ə)rt\. City, ✱ of Carinthia, Austria, near Yugoslav border just N of Karawanken Mts. and 62 m. WSW of Graz; pop. (1969e) 73,156; iron and woodworking plants; matches, leather, confectionary; 16th cent. provincial assembly hall; became city 1279; at height of commercial importance in 18th cent.; occupied by Yugoslav troops 1919; center of plebiscite area in 1920.

Klai·pė·da \ˈklī-pəd-ə\. 1 *or Ger.* **Me·mel·ge·biet** \ˈmām-əl-gə-ˌbēt\ *or* **Me·mel·land** \-ˌland, -ˌlänt\. Former German territory, E coast of Baltic Sea, now part of Lithuanian S.S.R., U.S.S.R.; 1092 sq. m. For history, see 2 below.
2 *or Ger.* **Me·mel** \ˈmām-əl\. Commercial and manufacturing seaport city, Lithuanian S.S.R., U.S.S.R., on the Baltic Sea at the mouth of Neman river; pop. (1970p) 140,000; exports lumber, agricultural products, fish; manufactures chemicals, soap, wood pulp, textiles, fertilizer.

History: Founded as a fort 1252; later, as **Me·mel·burg** \ˈmā-məl-ˌbu̇(ə)rg\, acquired by the Teutonic Knights; an important trading town in Hanseatic League; in 17th cent. held by Sweden and occupied by Russian troops 1757 and 1813, but Prussian possession since 17th cent.; treaty bet. England and Prussia signed here 1807. Taken by Russia in World War I; after 1919 administered by France under the League of Nations; seized by Lithuanians Jan. 15, 1923 as their only good port; made part of autonomous Memel territory, created by Memel Statute of May 8, 1924; seized by Germany early in 1939 and held until taken by Soviet armies Jan. 1945; made part of Lithuanian S.S.R., under Soviet control.

Klam·ath \ˈklam-əth\. 1 River, S Oregon and NW California; 250 m. long; rises in Lake Ewauna, Klamath co., S Oregon, flows SW across NW extremity of California into the Pacific Ocean.
2 County in Oregon. See table at OREGON.

Klamath Falls. Industrial city, ⊗ of Klamath co., S Oregon, at S end of Upper Klamath Lake and on E slope of Cascade Range, 15 m. N of California border; pop. (1970c) 15,775; saw mills; lumber, crates and boxes; dairy, grain, and livestock farming; Oregon Polytechnic State Coll. (1947); settled c. 1867.

Klamath Lakes. Two connected lakes, **Upper Klamath Lake** in SW Klamath co., S Oregon, and **Lower Klamath Lake** (now dry) extending into Siskiyou co., N California; length of combined lakes ab. 44 m.

Klamath Mountains. Mountain range of the Coast Ranges in NW California, extending from Siskiyou co. N into Oregon; includes, in N part, the Siskiyou Mountains.

Klang. See KELANG.

Klar \ˈklär\. River, SE cen. Norway and W Sweden; ab. 215 m. long; rises in SE cen. Norway, flows S across Swedish border into Lake Vänern.

Kla·ten \ˈklät-ən\. Town, cen. Java prov., Indonesia, 20 m. SW of Surakarta; pop. (1961c) 33,400.

Kla·to·vy \ˈklät-ə-vē\ *or Ger.* **Klat·tau** \ˈklä-ˌtau̇\. Town, Czech S.R., W Czechoslovakia, ab. 70 m. SW of Prague; pop. (1968e) 16,493; chemicals, beer; 16th cent. town hall; founded 13th cent.

Klausenburg. See CLUJ 2.

Klau·sen Pass \ˌklau̇z-ᵊn-\. Alpine pass, Uri canton, cen. Switzerland, E of Altdorf; 6390 ft.

Klausthal–Zellerfeld. See CLAUSTHAL-ZELLERFELD.

Kle·berg \ˈklā-(ˌ)bərg\. 1 County in Texas. See table at TEXAS.
2 City, Dallas co., NE Texas, 14 m. SE of Dallas; pop. (1970c) 4768.

Kleine Mythe. See MYTHEN.

Kleine Scheidegg. See SCHEIDEGG.

Kleinrosseln. See PETITE-ROSSELLE.

Klerks·dorp \ˈkle(ə)rks-ˌdȯ(ə)rp\. Town, S Transvaal, NE Rep. of South Africa, 10 m. N of Vaal river and 100 m. WSW of Johannesburg; pop. (1967e) 60,400; gold and uranium mining; lumber; beverages, machinery, cereals; founded 1838, first Boer settlement in Transvaal.

Kle·ve *also* **Cle·ve** \ˈklā-və\ *or Eng.* **Cleves** \ˈklēvz\ *or Fr.* **Clèves** \klev\. Manufacturing and resort city, North Rhine-Westphalia, West Germany, near the Rhine river 66 m. WSW of Münster; pop. (1969e) 22,423; footwear; old ducal castle (Schwanenburg). Seat of old duchy of same name whose Duke John, a leader of German Protestantism, was father of Anne of Cleves (1515–57) fourth wife of Henry VIII; passed to Elector of Brandenburg by treaty 1614 and later to Prussia; to France 1805; reverted to Prussia 1814; after World War I occupied by Belgians to 1925; in World War II N anchor of German Westwall, taken by Canadians Feb. 12, 1945.

Klick·i·tat \ˈklik-ə-ˌtat\. 1 River, S Washington; flows S in Yakima co. and through Klickitat co. into Columbia river.
2 County in Washington. See table at WASHINGTON.

Klin \ˈklēn, ˈklin\. Town, Moscow Oblast, Russian S.F.S.R., U.S.S.R., on Moscow-Leningrad R.R. 31 m. NW of Moscow; pop. (1969e) 74,000; farthest point E in German drive on Moscow reached Nov. 25, 1941.

Klí·no·vec \ˈklēn-ō-ˌvets\ *or Ger.* **Keil·berg** \ˈkīl-ˌbe(ə)rg\. Highest peak in the Erzgebirge, Czech S.R., Czechoslovakia; 4080 ft.

Klin·tsy \ˈklin(t)-ˈsē\. Town, W Bryansk Oblast, Russian S.F.S.R., U.S.S.R., on railroad ab. 85 m. WSW of Bryansk; pop. (1969e) 55,000; founded in 18th cent.

Klip·heu·vel \ˈklip-ˌhə(r)-vəl\. Town, SW Cape Province, S Rep. of South Africa, 22 m. NE of Cape Town.

Kłodz·ko \ˈklȯt-(ˌ)skō\ *or Ger.* **Glatz** \ˈgläts\. Manufacturing city, S Wrocław prov., SW Poland, 52 m. SSW of Wrocław; pop. (1970p) 26,100; tourist center; iron foundries; varied manufactures. Assigned to Poland by Potsdam Conference 1945.

Klofajökull. See VATNAJÖKULL.

Klon·dike \ˈklän-ˌdīk\. District, cen. Yukon Territory, Canada, in Yukon river basin S of Ogilvie Mountains; ab. 800 sq. m.; lies on both sides of **Klondike River,** ab. 90 m. long, a tributary of the Yukon flowing W to join it near Dawson; has very severe winter climate. Rich gold-bearing gravel occurs along the small creeks; gold discovered Aug. 16, 1896 on Bonanza Creek, ab. 3 m. from Dawson; news reached U.S. Jan. 1897 and was followed by rush 1897–99 of 30,000 persons by way of Lynn Canal, Chilkoot and White Passes, and the Yukon; peak of production reached in 1900 ($22,000,000); total production 1885 to 1929 was more than $175,000,000.

Klong \'klôŋ\ *or* **Me·klong** \'mā-\. River, W Thailand; 250 m. long; rises at S end of Dawna Range, flows S and SSE to head of Gulf of Siam; Samut Songkhram is the port at its mouth.

Klo·ster·neu·burg \ˌklō-stər-'nȯi-ˌbu̇(ə)rg\. City, Lower Austria, on Danube river 17 m. NW of Vienna; pop. (1968e) 23,000; pharmaceuticals, leather goods, wine; tourism.

Klos·ter–Ze·ven \ˌklōs-tər-'zā-vən, -'tsā-vən\. See ZEVEN.

Klu·ane Lake \klü-ˌän-\. Lake, largest in Yukon Territory, Canada, in SW part along N slope of St. Elias Mountains; 184 sq. m.; its outlet is **Kluane River,** ultimately discharging into White and Yukon rivers; the Alaska Highway extends along its S and W shores through the station of Burwash Landing.

Klu·ang \klu̇-'äŋ\. Town on railroad, N Johore state, Malaysia; pop. (1961e) 31,200; airfield.

Klucz·bo·rk \klüch-bȯr-ek\; *Ger.* **Kreuz·burg** \'krȯits-ˌbu̇(ə)rg\ *also* **Kreuzburg in Ober·schle·si·en** \-in-'ō-bər-ˌshlā-zē-ən\. Town, Opole prov., S Poland, 30 m. NNE of Opole; pop. (1968e) 16,900; formerly in Germany, assigned to Poland by Potsdam Conference 1945.

Klukhori. See KARACHAYEVSK.

Klut·lan Glacier \ˌklüt-ˌlan-\. Glacier in SW Yukon, Canada; 55 m. long, ab. 4 m. wide near its terminus.

Kly·až·ma \klē-'az-mə\. River, W cen. Russian S.F.S.R., U.S.S.R.; ab. 390 m. long; rises just N of Moscow, flows E to join the Oka of Gorki.

Klyu·chev·ska·ya Sop·ka \klē-u̇-'chef-skə-yə-'sȯp-kə\. Volcano (*sopka*) in Eastern Range, Kamchatka Penin., Khabarovsk Krai, Russian S.F.S.R., U.S.S.R.; 15,580 ft.; highest mountain in Siberia.

Knä·red \kə-'nar-ed\. Town, Halland co., S Sweden, SE of Halmstad; pop. (1970e) 2005; scene of signing of peace bet. Sweden and Denmark Jan. 28, 1613.

Knares·bor·ough \'na(ə)rz-b(ə-)rə, 'ne(ə)rz-\. Urban district, West Riding, Yorkshire, N England; pop. (1971p) 11,863; market town; limestone quarries; ruins of ancient castle.

Kne·za \kə-'nez-ə\. Town, Vratsa dept., NW Bulgaria, 28 m. WNW of Pleven.

Knife \'nīf\. River, W North Dakota; 165 m. long; rises in N Billings co., flows E into Missouri river at Stanton, in E Mercer co.

Knight Inlet \'nīt-\. Narrow inlet, SW British Columbia, Canada; ab. 70 m. long; opens into Queen Charlotte Strait.

Knin \kə-'nēn\. Town, E Croatia, W Yugoslavia, 28 m. NNE of Šibenik; pop. (1965e) 3000.

Knit·tel·feld \kə-'nit-ᵊl-ˌfelt\. Industrial city, Styria, Austria, on Mur river 30 m. WNW of Graz; pop. (1961c) 14,259; founded c. 1224.

Knock·a·doon Head \ˌnäk-ə-ˌdün-\. Cape on S coast of Eire, S of entrance to Youghal Bay.

Knockanaffrin. See COMERAGH MOUNTAINS.

Knock·meal·down \näk-'mēl-ˌdau̇n\. Mountain range in S Eire, on boundary bet. cos. Tipperary and Waterford; highest peak Knockmealdown 2609 ft.

Knos·sos *or* **Cnos·sus** *or* **Gnos·sus** \'näs-əs\. Royal city of ancient Crete, near the N coast of the island; ruins of its great palace are a few miles SE of Candia. Center of Cretan Bronze Age culture; probably flourished c. 2000–1400 B.C. Seat of legendary King Minos (or line of kings of that name) and site of the labyrinth of Daedalus.

Knott \'nät\. County in Kentucky. See table at KENTUCKY.

Knot·ting·ley \'nät-iŋ-lē\. Urban district, West Riding, Yorkshire, N England; pop. (1971p) 16,360.

Knowl·ton \'nōlt-ᵊn\. Village, ⊗ of Brome co., S Quebec, Canada, on Brome Lake 32 m. SW of Sherbrooke; pop. (1966c) 1486; summer resort.

Knox \'näks\. 1 Name of counties in nine states of U.S. See tables at ILLINOIS, INDIANA, KENTUCKY, MAINE, MISSOURI, NEBRASKA, OHIO, TENNESSEE, TEXAS.

2 City, ⊗ of Starke co., NW Indiana, 33 m. SW of South Bend; pop. (1970c) 3519; dairy and truck farming.

Knox Coast. Section of coast of Wilkes Land, Antarctica, on Indian Ocean, 66°30'S and 104°E to 109°E.

Knox·ville \'näks-ˌvil, -vəl\. 1 Town, ⊗ of Crawford co., cen. Georgia.

2 City, Knox co., W Illinois, 5 m. ESE of Galesburg; pop. (1970c) 2930; diversified agriculture.

3 City, ⊗ of Marion co., S cen. Iowa, 32 m. ESE of Des Moines; pop. (1970c) 7755; ships livestock; poultry and dairy farming.

4 Commercial and industrial city, ⊗ of Knox co., E Tennessee, on Tennessee river ab. 105 m. NE of Chattanooga; pop. (1970c) 174,587; manufactures textiles, furniture, chemicals, plastics, aluminum, foundry products, flour and feed; marble quarries; timber; tobacco warehouses; tourism; administrative center of Tennessee Valley Authority (1933 ff.); Univ. of Tennessee (1794), Knoxville Coll. (1863). Settled 1786; became ⊗ 1792; served as 1st capital of Tennessee 1796–1812, again 1817–19; incorp. as city 1815; occupied by Union troops of Gen. Burnside 1863, besieged by Confederate army under Longstreet 1863.

Knud Ras·mus·sen Land \(kə-)'nüd-'räs-ˌmu̇s-ᵊn-, -'ras-mə-sən-\. Region, N and NW Greenland, between Baffin Bay and Lincoln Sea.

Knu·rów \kə-'nu̇r-(ˌ)üf\. Town, Katowice prov., S Poland, ab. 14 m. W of Katowice; pop. (1970p) 28,500.

Knuts·ford \'nəts-fərd\. Urban district, Cheshire, NW England, near the Birken 13 m. SSW of Manchester; pop. (1971p) 13,765; residential; the *Cranford* of Elizabeth Cleghorn Gaskell.

Knys·na \kə-'nis-nə\. Town, S Cape Province, S Rep. of South Africa, 160 m. W of Port Elizabeth; pop. (1967e) 13,900; in forest region.

Ko \'kō, 'kō\ *also* **Koh.** Siamese word for "island." For names beginning with this word, see the second element, as **Ko Kut,** see KUT 2.

Ko·ba·rid \'kō-bə-ˌrēd\ *or Ger.* **Kar·freit** \'kär-ˌfrīt\ *or Ital.* **Ca·po·ret·to** \ˌkap-ə-'ret-(ˌ)ō\. Village, Slovenia, NW Yugoslavia; in World War I campaign from Oct. 24 to Dec. 26, 1917, scene of a major defeat of Italian forces under Gen. Cadorna who were driven back to the Piave by Austro-German forces under Gen. Otto von Below.

Kobdo. 1 River, Mongolian People's Republic. See HOBDO GOL.

2 Town, Mongolian People's Republic. See HOVD.

Kō·be \'ko-be, -ˌba\. Seaport and commercial city, ❋ of Hyōgo prefecture, S coast of W Honshū, Japan; pop. (1970c) 1,288,937; built partly along the N shore of Ōsaka Bay and partly on the hillsides; has close connections with city of Ōsaka ab. 20 m. to the E; extensive port facilities; Japan's principal port (in value of trade); shipbuilding, manufacture of steel, rubber, electrical equipment, textiles, books; Kōbe Univ. of Economics (1948); Kōbe Univ. (1949). Until the Restoration 1868 only a fishing village; has absorbed the old town of Hyōgo; in World War II severely bombed by Allied forces; but entirely rebuilt since 1945.

Köbenhavn. See COPENHAGEN.

Ko·blenz *or* **Co·blenz** \'kō-ˌblen(t)s\ *or anc.* **Con·flu·en·tes** \ˌkän-flu̇-'en-(ˌ)tēz\. Commercial and manufacturing city, North Rhine-Westphalia, West Germany, at confluence of Moselle and Rhine rivers 50 m. SSE of Cologne; pop.

(1969e) 105,648; trades in wine; furniture, aluminum; tourism.

History: Originally a Roman station; became city 1254; besieged by French 1688; principal place of refuge for French émigrés during Revolution; occupied by French 1794; became capital 1801 (Treaty of Lunéville) of French department of Rhin-et-Moselle; to Prussia 1815; capital of Rhine Province (Prussia) 1822; fortified; occupied by American troops 1919–23 and by French troops 1923–29; in World War II scene of battle Mar. 16, 1945 in which it was taken by Americans.

Kob·rin \'kò-brən\ *or Pol.* **Kob·ryń** \-brən(-yə)\. Town, SW Belorussian S.S.R., U.S.S.R., 28 m. ENE of Brest; formerly in Poland; pop. (1969e) 19,000.

Ko·bro·or *or* **Ko·bro·ör** \'kō-brə-ˌwər\. Island, forming the central section of Tanahbesar, Aru Is., Indonesia.

Ko·buk \kō-'bùk\. River, NW Alaska, S of Baird Mts.; ab. 300 m. long; flows W to Kotzebue Sound.

Koca. See XANTHUS 1.

Kocaba. See KACZAWA.

Kocabaş. See GRANICUS.

Ko·ca·e·li \ˌkò-ˌjä-e-'lē\. 1 Province of NW Turkey, Asia. See table at TURKEY.

2 Town, Turkey. See İZMIT.

Ko·čev·je \'kō-chev-yə\ *or Ger.* **Gott·schee** \'gòt-ˌshā\. Town, Slovenia, NW Yugoslavia, in mountains NE of Rijeka.

Ko·cher \'kòk-ər\. River, Baden-Württemberg, West Germany; ab. 100 m. long; flows into Neckar river 6 m. N of Heilbronn.

Kō·chi \'kō-chē\. 1 Prefecture, Shikoku, Japan; 2743 sq. m.; pop. (1970c) 786,882; ✻ Kōchi; agricultural machinery, paper, raw silk.

2 Seaport city, its ✻, on S coast of Shikoku I. on inlet of Tosa Bay; pop. (1970c) 240,481; fish processing.

Koch Peak \'käch-\. Mountain, E Madison co., SW Montana; 11,293 ft.

Kocs \'kōch\. Village, NW Hungary, SSE of Komárom; the coach (English word derived from name of the village) said to have originated here.

Ko·dai·ka·nal \kō-'dī-kə-ˌnal\. Sanatorium, Tamil Nadu, India, 50 m. NW of Madurai; pop. (1961c) 12,900; government meteorological observatory, alt. ab. 7000 ft.

Ko·dai·ra \kō-'dīr-ə\. City, Honshū, Japan, E suburb of Tokyo; pop. (1970c) 137,373.

Ko·di·ak \'kōd-ē-ˌak\. 1 Island in Gulf of Alaska SE of Alaska Penin., S Alaska; 5363 sq. m.; constitutes, with adjacent islands, an organized borough of Alaska; chief industry fishing, esp. for salmon, which is more abundant here than anywhere else in Alaska; fur raising. Habitat of Kodiak bear. Site of first Russian colony in America (founded 1784); headquarters of Russian Trading Company until 1805.

2 Borough, Alaska. See 1 above and table at ALASKA.

3 City, ⊗ of Kodiak borough, on NE coast of Kodiak island; pop. (1970c) 3798; incorporated 1940.

Ko·dok \'kōd-ˌäk\ *or formerly* **Fa·sho·da** \fə-'shōd-ə\. Town, N Upper Nile prov., SE Sudan, NE of Malakal; its seizure by a French force created serious international crisis 1898 almost causing war bet. Great Britain and France.

Koedoes. See KUDUS.

Koe·kel·berg \'kü-kəl-ˌbe(ə)rg\. Commune, Brabant prov., Belgium, suburb of Brussels; pop. (1969e) 17,655.

Koepang. See KUPANG.

K'o–erh–ch'in–yu–i–ch'ien–ch'i \'kùr-chin-'yü-ē-'chen-(ˌ)chē\ *or* **Wang·yeh·miao** \'wäŋ-'ye-mē-'aù\. Town, Inner Mongolia, NE China, on a tributary of the Nen river 200 m. NW of Ch'ang-ch'un.

Koesfeld. See COESFELD.

Koetai. See MAHAKAM.

Koetaradja. See BANDA ATJEH.

Koetoardjo. See KUTOARDJO.

Koett·litz Glacier \ˌket-lits-\. Glacier in the Royal Society Range, Antarctica; ab. 53 m. long, 8 m. wide near its terminus.

Ko·fo·ri·dua \ˌkō-ˌfōr-i-'dü-ə\. Town, ✻ of Eastern Region, S Ghana, W Africa, on railroad ab. 38 m. N of Accra; pop. (1970p) 44,768.

Kō·fu \'kō-(ˌ)fü\. City, ✻ of Yamanashi prefecture, S cen. Honshū, Japan, 65 m. W of Tokyo; pop. (1970c) 182,669; formerly center of silk industry; tourism; grapes; in feudal era a seat of several powerful lords.

Ko·ga \'kō-gə\. City, Ibaraki prefecture, Honshū, Japan, 37 m. N of Tokyo; pop. (1970c) 54,173.

Ko·ga·nei \ˌkō-gä-'nā\. City, Tokyo prefecture, Honshū, Japan, 18 m. W of Tokyo; pop. (1970c) 94,448.

Kog·a·rah \'käg-(ə-)rə\. Municipality, E New South Wales, SE Australia, S suburb of Sydney, W of Botany Bay; pop. (1966c) 47,654.

Kø·ge Bight *or* **Kjø·ge Bight** \ˌkər-gə-\. Bay on E cen. coast of Sjælland I., Denmark; scene of battle June 30, 1677 in which Danes under Niels Juel defeated superior Swedish naval force under Evert Horn.

Ko·gur·yu \ˌkō-gùr-'yü\. See history at KOREA.

Koh. 1 \'kō(h)\ *also* **Kuh** \'kü\. Persian word for "mountain." For names beginning with this word, see the second element.

2 Siamese word. See KO.

Ko·ha·la \kō-'häl-ə\. 1 Divisions, Hawaii. See NORTH KOHALA, SOUTH KOHALA.

2 *or* **Kapa·au** \kə-'pä-ˌaù\. Village, Hawaii co., Hawaii, near coast at N end of Hawaii I.; pop. (1970c) 237. Birthplace and burial place of Kamehameha I, first Hawaiian king, and his headquarters during the struggle for control of the islands.

Kohala Mountains. Range in N end of Hawaii I., Hawaii; highest peak 5505 ft.

Ko·hat \kō-'hät\. Town on affluent of Indus river 37 m. S of Peshawar; pop., incl. cantonment, (1961c) 49,854; in Pathan country; former military base for southern Afridi frontier. Connected with Peshawar by **Kohat Pass** (ab. 13 m. long and 400 yd. to 1¼ m. wide).

Ko·hi·ma \'kō-hē-mə\. Town, ✻ of Nagaland state, NE India; near N Manipur border and 30 m. SE of the railroad at Dimapur; pop. (1961c) 7746; taken by Japanese in Manipur campaign Mar.–June 1944; recaptured by Anglo-Indian troops in important battle June 30, 1944.

Koh–i–nuh. See ARARAT 3.

Koh·ler \'kōl-ər\. Residential village, Sheboygan co., E Wisconsin, 5 m. W of Sheboygan; pop. (1970c) 1738.

Kohl·scheid \'kōl-(ˌ)shīt\. Commune, North Rhine-Westphalia, West Germany, N suburb of Aachen; pop. (1968e) 15,614; coal mining; metal founding.

Koht·la–Jär·ve *or Russ.* **Kokht·la–Yar·ve** \ˌkōt-lə-'yär-vā\. Town, Estonian S.S.R., U.S.S.R., ab. 30 m. W of Narva; pop. (1969e) 67,000.

Ko Hu. See HO HU.

Koil *or* **Koil–Aligarh.** See ALIGARH 2.

Koivisto. See PRIMORSK.

Kŏ·je–do \ˌkəj-ā-'dō\. Island in Korea Strait, off SE coast of South Korea near Pusan.

Ko·kand *or* **Kho·kand** *or* **Kho·qand** \kō-'kand\. 1 Region around towns of Kokand and Fergana, E Uzbek S.S.R., U.S.S.R.; became powerful khanate in 18th cent.; ab. 1760 recognized Chinese sovereignty; after 1800 came into conflict with other Turkic peoples of Turkistan and finally with the Russians; last Central Asian khanate to be conquered by Russia 1875–76; made a province of Turkistan under ancient name of Fergana; became part of newly formed Uzbek S.S.R., U.S.S.R., 1924.

2 City, Fergana Oblast, E Uzbek S.S.R., U.S.S.R., ab. 100 m. SE of Tashkent; pop. (1967e) 131,000; important rail and trade center in a fertile oasis region; center for cotton industry. Its early history obscure; town founded 1732, chief town of Kokand khanate.

Kok·che·tav \ˌkäk-chə-ˌtäf, -ˈtäv-\. Town, ✻ of Kokchetav Oblast, Kazakh S.S.R., U.S.S.R., on railroad 115 m. S of Petropavlovsk; pop. (1970p) 81,000; railroad junction; food processing.

Kokchetav Oblast \-ˈó-bləst, -ˌblast\. Subdivision of Kazakh S.S.R., U.S.S.R., in N bet. North Kazakhstan and Tselinograd oblasts; 30,154 sq. m.; pop. (1970p) 590,000; ✻ Kokchetav; dairying; salt, iron ore, gold; established 1944.

Kokhtla–Yarve. See KOHTLA-JÄRVE.

Kok·ko·la \ˈkó-kó-lə\. Seaport, Vaasa prov., W Finland, on Gulf of Bothnia 70 m. NNE of Vaasa; pop. (1970e) 20,748; exports timber; founded 1620.

Ko·ko·da \kə-ˈkōd-ə\. Settlement, New Guinea I., Papua New Guinea, WSW of Buna on E side of Owen Stanley Range; connected with Port Moresby by highway ab. 100 m. long over the mountains; used by Japanese as base for attacks Sept.–Oct. 1942; occupied by Australians Nov. 3, 1942.

Ko·ko Head \ˌkō-(ˌ)kō-\ *or* **Ka·wai·hoa Point** \ˌkä-wī-ˌhō-ə-\. Promontory on SE coast of Oahu I., Hawaii, on E side of Maunalua Bay; 642 ft. high.

Ko·ko·le Point \kə-ˌkō-lē-\. Cape on W coast of Kauai I., Hawaii.

Ko·ko·mo \ˈkō-kə-ˌmō\. Industrial city, ⊗ of Howard co., N cen. Indiana, 50 m. N of Indianapolis; pop. (1970c) 44,042; automobile parts, plastics, glass, tool steel, canned goods; founded ab. 1843; home of inventor Elwood Haynes.

Koko Nor. 1 Lake, China. See TSING HAI.
2 Province, China. See TSINGHAI.

Ko·ko·po \ˈkō-kə-ˌpō\. Town, NE New Britain I., Bismarck Archipelago, W Pacific Ocean, 14 m. SE of Rabaul; formerly **Her·berts·hö·he** \ˈher-berts-ˌhə-(r)ə\, and former German capital of New Britain (Neu-Pommern).

Kok·so·ak \ˈkäk-sə-ˌwak\. River, N Quebec, Canada; 110 m. long; formed by confluence of Caniapiscau and Larch rivers, flows NE into S Ungava Bay.

Kok·stad \ˈkäk-ˌstad\. Town, NE Cape Province, S Rep. of South Africa, 110 m. SW of Durban; pop. (1967e) 10,000; the chief town of Griqualand East (*q.v.*) in the Transkeian Territories; center of farming area, esp. for sheep and cattle raising; important cheese industry; good climate and high altitude (4500 ft.), health resort.

Ko·ku·bun·ji \ˌkō-kü-ˈbün-jē\. City, Tokyo prefecture, Honshū, Japan, 15 m. W of Tokyo; pop. (1970c) 81,259.

Kokumbona. See KAKAMBONA.

Ko·ku·ra \ˈkō-kə-ˌrä, kō-ˈkür-ə\. See KITAKYŪSHŪ.

Kol. See ALIGARH 2.

Ko·la \ˈkō-lə\. 1 South tributary of the Tuloma river, W Murmansk Oblast, Russian S.F.S.R., U.S.S.R., joining it at Kola.
2 Town, Murmansk Oblast, Russian S.F.S.R., U.S.S.R., ab. 12 m. S of Murmansk and at junction of Kola river with the Tuloma; one of oldest towns in extreme N of U.S.S.R.; several times destroyed by Swedes and British.

Ko·la·ba \kə-ˈläb-ə\. District, SW Maharashtra, W India; 2723 sq. m.; pop. (1961c) 1,058,855; ✻ Alibag.

Kola Bay \ˌkō-lə-\. Inlet of Barents Sea, NW Murmansk Oblast, Russian S.F.S.R., U.S.S.R.; ab. 22 m. long; Murmansk is at its head; receives Tuloma river.

Kola Peninsula *or Russ.* **Kol·ski Po·lu·o·strov** \ˌkól-skē-ˌpól-ə-ˈó-strəf\. Peninsula projecting E on NW coast of Russian S.F.S.R., U.S.S.R., bet. the White Sea and the Arctic Ocean (Barents Sea); forms Murmansk Oblast (*q.v.*).

Ko·lar \kō-ˈlär, ˈkō-ˌ\. Town, E Mysore, S India, 140 m. W of Madras; pop. (1961c) 32,600; textiles.

Kolar Gold Fields. City, E Mysore, S India, 145 m. W of Madras; pop. (1967e) 167,610; gold mines.

Kolberg. See KOŁOBRZEG.

Kolchugino. See LENINSK-KUZNETSKI.

Kold·ing \ˈkəl-iŋ\. Seaport, Vejle co., SE Jutland, Denmark, on inlet of Little Belt; pop. (1970e) 39,609; exports cattle, fish, grain. Dates back to 10th cent.; scene of two battles in Danish history: (1) 1644 victory over Swedes; (2) Danish defeat in Schleswig-Holstein conflict Apr. 22, 1849; has oldest stone church in Denmark (13th cent.).

Kol·gu·yev \kəl-ˈgü-yəf\. Island in Barents Sea, 50 m. off the mainland, NE of Kanin Penin., Nenets National Okrug, N Russian S.F.S.R., U.S.S.R.; 2300 sq. m.; chiefly tundra; reindeer herding.

Kol·ha·pur \ˈkō-lə-ˌpü(ə)r\. 1 Former Indian state, chief state of the Deccan and Kolhapur States, now part of SW Maharashtra, W India; 3219 sq. m.; in Western Ghats with E part sloping into plain of the Deccan; former ruling family traced descent from younger son Sivaji, founder of Maratha power; invaded by British expeditions 1765 and 1792; came under control of British in 1812.
2 City, Maharashtra, W India, 180 m. SSE of Bombay; pop. (1970e) 259,109; trade center; univ. (1962); many old Buddhist temples.

Kolhapur and Deccan States. See DECCAN AND KOLHAPUR STATES.

Kolima. See KOLYMA.

Kolima Mountains. See KOLYMA MOUNTAINS.

Kolimski Khrebet. See KOLYMA MOUNTAINS.

Ko·lín \ˈkō-ˌlēn\ *or Ger.* **Ko·lin** \kō-ˈlēn\. Town, Czech S.R., W Czechoslovakia, on Labe (Elbe) river E of Prague; pop. (1968e) 26,300; pharmaceuticals, chemicals; nearby is battlefield where Frederick the Great was defeated June 18, 1757 by Austrian marshal Daun.

Ko·li Point \ˌkō-lē-\. Point on N coast of Guadalcanal I., British Solomon Is., W Pacific Ocean, ab. 3 m. E of Lunga Point; American base for fighting along the Metapona river Nov. 1942.

K'o–li–ya \ˈkə-ˈlē-ˈyä\ *or* **Ke·ri·ya** *also* **Ki·ria** \ˈkə-ˈlē-ˈyä—*sic*\. River, SW Sinkiang Uighur, W China; rises in A-erh-chin Shan-mo and flows N into Takla Makan (desert).

Kol·kas·rags \ˈkōl-kəs-ˌrägs\ *or formerly* **Cape Do·mes·nes** \-ˈdüm-əs-ˌnes\. Cape on NW coast of Latvian S.S.R., U.S.S.R., on S side of entrance to Gulf of Riga.

Kollam. See QUILON.

Kölln \ˈkəln\. A 13th cent. Wendish village which with village of Berlin united under name Berlin. See history at BERLIN.

Kolmar. See COLMAR.

Köln. See COLOGNE.

Ko·ło \ˈkó-(ˌ)lō\. Commune, Poznań prov., Poland, on Warta river 44 m. WNW of Łódź; pop. (1968e) 11,900.

Ko·loa \kō-ˈlō-ə\. 1 Division, S Kauai I., Kauai co., Hawaii.
2 Village in division, near S coast of Kauai I. SW of Lihue; pop. (1970c) 1368; had first sugar plantation in Hawaii (estab. 1835).

Koloa Bay. Bay on S coast of Kauai I., Hawaii, E of Lawai Bay.

Ko·łob·rzeg \kə-ˈlób-ˌzhek\ *or Ger.* **Kol·berg** \ˈkól-ˌbe(ə)rg\. City and port on Gulf of Pomerania, N Koszalin prov., NW Poland, 25 m. W of Koszalin; pop. (1970p) 25,400; health and beach resort; fishing, ship repairing. Polish from 10th cent.; to Prussia 1648; member of Hanseatic League; captured by U.S.S.R. Mar. 19, 1945; assigned to Poland by the Potsdam Conference 1945.

Ko·lom·bang·a·ra \ˌkō-läm-ˈbaŋ-ə-rə\. Island off W end of New Georgia I., British Solomon Is., W Pacific Ocean; circular shaped, ab. 17 m. in diameter, with volcanic cone 5799 ft.; bet. it and New Georgia is Kula Gulf (naval battles July 1943); on S shore Japanese had airfield at Vila (*q.v.*); object of air attacks, but bypassed in Allied advance northward (see VELLA LAVELLA).

Kolomea. See KOLOMYYA.

Ko·lom·na \kə-ˈlóm-nə\. City, Moscow Oblast, Russian S.F.S.R., U.S.S.R., on railroad near confluence of Moskva and Oka rivers, 65 m. SE of Moscow; pop. (1970p) 136,-000; diesel engines, machine tools, rubber; first mentioned 1177; to Moscow 1305; sacked four times by Tatars.

Ko·lo·my·ya *or Pol.* **Ko·ło·my·ja** \ˌkäl-ə-ˈmē-(y)ə\ *or Ger.* **Ko·lo·mea** \ˌkō-lə-ˈmā-ə\. City, SW Ukrainian S.S.R., U.S.S.R., on Prut river 30 m. SSE of Ivano-Frankovsk; pop. (1967e) 39,000; at E end of gateway through E Carpathian Mts. via Jablonica Pass and in rail communication with Ivano-Frankovsk and Chernovtsy; agricultural trade center; manufactures chemicals, textiles. Captured Feb. 1915 by Germans; held by both Russians and Germans in World War II.

Ko·lon·jë\kə-ˈlȯn-yə\. 1 *or formerly* **Er·se·ke** \er-ˈsek-ē\. Province of SE Albania. See table at ALBANIA.

2 Town, its ✱; pop. (1967e) 2570.

Ko–lo–shan \ˈkō-ˈlō-ˈshän\. Suburb of Chungking, Szechwan prov., S cen. China; contained several government offices during air raids of 1938–45.

Kolozsvár. See CLUJ 2.

Kol·pa·she·vo \ˌkäl-pə-ˈshȯ-və\. Town, cen. Tomsk Oblast, Russian S.F.S.R., U.S.S.R., on right bank of the Ob where the Ket joins it; pop. (1969e) 62,000.

Kolski Poluostrov. See KOLA PENINSULA.

K'o–lu–lun Ho. See KERULEN.

Kol·we·zi \kōl-ˈwā-zē\. Town, Shaba prov., Zaire, 90 m. WNW of Likasi; pop. (1968e) 70,558.

Ko·ly·ma *or* **Ko·li·ma** \kə-ˈlē-mə\. River, Russian S.F.S.R., U.S.S.R.; 1110 m. long; rises in Kolyma Mountains in Khabarovsk Krai, flows generally N and NE into Arctic Ocean; navigable to Verkhne-Kolymsk; gold diggings worked along its course; its chief tributaries the Omolon and Anyui.

Kolyma Mountains *or* **Kolima Mountains** *or Russ.* **Ko·lym·ski Khre·bet** *also* **Ko·lim·ski Khrebet** \kə-ˌlim(p)-skē-kri-ˈbyet\. Mountain range in NE Khabarovsk Krai, Russian S.F.S.R., U.S.S.R., N of the Sea of Okhotsk and nearly parallel to coastline.

Ko·ma·ga·ta·ke \kō-ˌmäg-ə-ˈtäk-ē\. Name of several mountain peaks in Japan: (1) Active volcano, SW shore of Uchiura Bay, SW Hokkaidō I.; 1183 ft. (2) Volcanic peak, W Kanagawa prefecture, SE Honshū, near Hakone; 4349 ft. (3) Peak, S cen. Nagano prefecture, cen. Honshū; 9666 ft. (4) Peak, W Yamanashi prefecture, S cen. Honshū; 2966 ft.

Ko·ma·ki \kō-ˈmäk-ē\. City, Aichi prefecture, Honshū, Japan, 8 m. N of Nagoya; pop. (1970c) 77,996.

Ko·man·dor·ski·ye Islands \ˌkäm-ən-ˈdȯr-skē-ə-\ *or Eng.* **Com·mand·er Islands** \kə-ˈman-dər-\. Island group E of Kamchatka Penin., in SW Bering Sea; 850 sq. m.; administered as part of Khabarovsk Krai, U.S.S.R.; chief islands Bering or Beringa (on which the explorer Vitus Bering died 1741) and Medny; chief settlement Nikolskoye; former hunting ground for the fur seal, but by 1911 practically all animals slaughtered; now a radio and naval station; nearby waters scene of U.S. naval victory over Japanese, March, 1943.

Ko·már·no \ˈkȯ-mär-ˌnȯ\ *or Ger.* **Ko·morn** \ˈkō-ˌmȯrn\ *or Hung.* **Ko·má·rom** \ˈkō-mə-ˌrōm\. Town, S Slovak S.R., E cen. Czechoslovakia, at confluence of the Váh with the Danube opp. Komárom; pop. (1968e) 26,800; commercial and shipping center; builds river craft; transferred from Hungary to Czechoslovakia 1920 by Treaty of Grand Trianon; birthplace of the Hungarian novelist Jókai.

Ko·má·rom \ˈkō-mə-ˌrōm\. 1 Town, Czechoslovakia. See KOMÁRNO.

2 County of N Hungary. See table at HUNGARY.

3 *or Ger.* **Ko·morn** \ˈkō-ˌmȯrn\. City, NW Hungary, on Danube river 48 m. WNW of Budapest; pop. (1970p) 11,-271.

Ko·ma·ti \kə-ˈmät-ē\. River, S Africa; ab. 500 m. long; rises in N Drakensberg Mts., SE Transvaal, N Rep. of South Africa, flows E, curves through N Swaziland, turns N; joined by Crocodile river; ab. a mile below junction flows through a cleft 600 ft. deep at Komatipoort; crosses boundary bet. Rep. of South Africa and Mozambique and flows in a wide curve N then S, into Delagoa Bay.

Ko·ma·ti·poort \kō-ˈmät-ē-ˌpu̇(ə)rt\. Frontier railroad town, E Transvaal, NE Rep. of South Africa, ab. 48 m. NW of Lourenço Marques, Mozambique, on Komati river.

Ko·mat·su \kō-ˈmät-(ˌ)sü\. City, Ishikawa prefecture, Honshū, Japan, 15 m. SW of Kanazawa; pop. (1970c) 95,684.

Komba. River, Africa. See GRANDE, RIO 1.

Komi Autonomous Soviet Socialist Republic *or formerly* **Zyr·i·an Autonomous Area** \ˈzir-ē-ən-\. Autonomous republic, NE Russian S.F.S.R., U.S.S.R., W of the Northern Urals; 160,579 sq. m.; pop. (1970p) 965,000; ✱ Syktyvkar. Mostly level country, with tundra in N, mountain slopes of Urals in E, and the Timan height of land in NW; lies chiefly in the basins of the Pechora and upper Vychegda rivers. Two thirds of area is covered by forests (largely spruce, pine, birch); has some agriculture: potatoes, rye, oats; livestock (cattle, reindeer); fur trapping; many industries connected with lumbering; no railroads until 1943 when 700 m. of Northern Pechora R.R. completed NE from Kotlas; major branch of economy is now mining: alabaster, limestone, coal, oil, natural gas. Predominant ethnic strain is Finno-Ugrian. An autonomous area created 1921; N strip along the Arctic transferred 1929 to Nenets National Okrug; reorganized 1936 as a republic.

Ko·mi–Perm·iak National Okrug \ˌkō-mē-ˈperm-yak . . . ˈō-ˌkrük\ *or* **Komi–Perm National Okrug** \-ˈpe(ə)rm-\. National district, Russian S.F.S.R., U.S.S.R., W of the Ural Mts.; 12,703 sq. m.; pop. (1970p) 212,000; ✱ Kudymkar; in basin of upper Kama river; lumbering; formed 1925 from area S of Komi A.S.S.R.

Kom·mu·narsk \ˌkə-mü-ˈnärsk\; *formerly* **Vo·ro·shi·lovsk** \ˌvȯr-ə-ˈshē-ˌlȯvsk\ *or* **Al·chevsk** \al-ˈchefsk\. City, SW Voroshilovgrad Oblast, Ukrainian S.S.R., U.S.S.R., ab. 30 m. W of Voroshilovgrad; pop. (1970p) 123,000; industrial city in the Donets Basin.

Kommunizma, Pik. See COMMUNISM PEAK.

Ko·mo·do \kə-ˈmōd-(ˌ)ō\. Small island, E of Sumbawa I. and W of Flores I., in the Lesser Sunda Is., Indonesia; ab. 25 m. long by 12 m. wide; wild and rugged and little known until giant lizards (dragon lizard, *Varanus komodoensis*) were discovered on it in 1912.

Komorn. 1 Town, Czechoslovakia. See KOMÁRNO.

2 City, Hungary. See KOMÁROM 3.

Komotau. See CHOMUTOV.

Ko·mo·ti·nē *or* **Ko·mo·ti·ní** \ˌkȯ-mə-ti-ˈnē\ *or Turk.* **Gü·mül·ji·na** \ˌgyü-məl-yi-ˈnä\. City, ✱ of Rhodope dept., Western Thrace, NE Greece, E of Xanthe; pop. (1971p) 32,123; market town; dates from Byzantine times.

Kom·pong Som \ˈkäm-ˈpȯŋ-ˈsȯm\ *or* **Kompong Son** \-ˈsȯn\ *also* **Kâm·póng Saôm** \ˈkäm-ˈpȯŋ-ˈsau̇m\ *or formerly* **Si·ha·nouk·ville** \sē-ˈhän-u̇k-ˌvil\. Port, S Cambodia; pop. (1962p) 6578; Cambodia's principal port.

Kom·so·mo·lets \ˌkäm(p)-sə-ˈmȯ-ləts\. Northernmost of the large islands of the Severnaya Zemlya group, in Arctic Ocean, Taimyr National Okrug, Russian S.F.S.R., U.S.S.R.; 80°30′N, 95°E.

Kom·so·molsk–na–Amure \ˌkäm(p)-sə-ˌmȯlsk-nə-ə-ˈmu̇r-ə\. City, S Khabarovsk Krai, Russian S.F.S.R., U.S.S.R., on left bank of Amur river 165 m. NNE of Khabarovsk; pop. (1970p) 218,000; an entirely new city, begun 1932 by 4000 volunteers of the Young Communist League (Russ. *Komsomol*—hence the name); has had very rapid growth, being now third largest city in Soviet Far East; on Trans-Siberian R.R. extension from Khabarovsk to Nikolayevsk-na-Amure and terminal of N transcontinental line (the BAM —Baikal-Amur-Magistral; *Eng.* Main Baikal-Amur Line); has major steelworks and one of largest shipyards in the Far East; oil refineries, pulp and paper mills; heavy machinery; fishing.

Kŏ·mun–do \ˌkō-mən-ˈdō\ *or formerly* **Port Ham·il·ton** \-ˈham-əl-tən\. Island group off South Korea; good harbor, occupied by Great Britain 1885–87.

Ko·na \ˈkō-nə\. Divisions, Hawaii. See NORTH KONA, SOUTH KONA.

Ko·na·hu·a·nui \ˌkō-nə-ˌhü-ə-ˈnü-ē\. Peak in Koolau Range, E Oahu I., Hawaii; 3105 ft.

Konakri. See CONAKRY.

Ko·nan \ˈkō-ˌnän, kō-ˈnän\. City, Aichi prefecture, Honshū, Japan, 11 m. N of Nagoya; pop. (1970c) 77,996.

Kon·arhā \kə-ˈnär-ə\. Province of NE Afghanistan. See table at AFGHANISTAN.

Kon·a·wa \ˈkän-ə-ˌwä\. Town, Seminole co., cen. Oklahoma, 14 m. N of Ada; pop. (1970c) 1719; oil wells; feed; corn, alfalfa, peanuts.

Kon·doa \kän-ˈdō-ə\. Town, N Tanzania, E Africa, 250 m. NW of Dar es Salaam; pop. (1967c) 4500.

Kong \ˈkȯŋ\. 1 Region, E cen. Ivory Coast, W Africa; home of a tribe of the Mandingo, formerly a native kingdom of some importance.

2 Town, Ivory Coast, on highway 100 m. N of Bouaké; pop. (1963c) 2200.

Kön·gä·mä \ˈkə(r)n-gə-ˌmä\ *or* **Kön·kä·mä** \-kə-\. River in N extremity of Sweden, forming its extreme N boundary with Finland; flows SE to join the Muonio river.

Kong·ju \ˈgȯŋ-ˈjü\ *or Jap.* **Ko·shu** \ˈkō-(ˌ)shü\. Town, South Ch'ungch'ŏng prov., South Korea; important in early Korean history.

Kongmoon *or* **Kongmoonfow.** See CHIANG-MEN.

Kongo–Central. See BAS-ZAÏRE.

Kon·go·lo \käŋ-ˈgō-(ˌ)lō\. Town on Lualaba river, N Shaba prov., Zaire.

Kongo River. See CONGO 4.

Kongosan. See KŬMGANG MOUNTAINS.

Kongs·berg \ˈkȯŋz-(ˌ)be(ə)r\. Town, Buskerud co., S Norway, WSW of Oslo; pop. (1969e) 18,061; hydroelectric power plant, arms and munitions factory; formerly a silver-mining center.

Kongs·weg·en \ˈkȯŋz-ˌvā-gən\. Glacier, Spitsbergen, Norway; 17 m. long, ab. 2 m. wide near its terminus.

Konia *or* **Konieh.** See KONYA.

Königgrätz. See HRADEC KRALOVÉ.

Königinhof. See DVŮR KRÁLOVÉ NAD LABEM.

Kö·nigs·berg \ˈkā-nigz-ˌbərg, ˈkə(r)n-igz-, ˈkā-niks-, ˈkə(r)n-iks-, -ˌbe(ə)rg, -ˌbe(ə)rk\. 1 Former district, NW East Prussia prov., Prussia, Germany; 5076 sq. m.; since 1946 the greater part of it has formed Kaliningrad Oblast, Russian S.F.S.R., U.S.S.R.

2 City, U.S.S.R. See KALININGRAD.

Kö·nigs·see \ˈkā-niks-ˌzā, ˈkə(r)n-iks-\. Small lake located in E end of Bavarian Alps, S of Berchtesgaden in extreme SE corner of Bavaria, West Germany; 5 m. long by ab. 1 m. wide.

Kö·nigs·win·ter \ˈkā-niks-ˌvin-tər, ˈkə(r)n-iks-\. Town, S North Rhine-Westphalia, West Germany, on the Rhine SE of Bonn; pop. (1968e) 31,201; summer resort.

Ko·nin \ˈkō-nēn\. Commune, Poznań prov., cen. Poland, on Warta river ab. 55 m. ESE of Poznań; pop. (1970p) 40,700; aluminum; coal mines.

Koninginne Bay. See BAJUR BAY.

Kó·ni·tsa \ˈkȯ n(y)it-ˌsä\. Commune, Ioannina dept., N Epirus, NW Greece, near Albanian border ab. 27 m. N of Ioannina.

Konitz. See CHOJNICE.

Kö·niz \ˈkā-nəts, ˈkə(r)n-əts\. Commune, Bern canton, W cen. Switzerland, SW suburb of Bern; pop. (1970c) 32,505; furniture, beer; old church and castle.

Könkämä. See KÖNGÄMÄ.

Kon·kan \ˈkäŋ-kən\. Coast region of Maharashtra state, W India; a humid, fertile plain; lacking in good harbors and made dangerous for shipping by violence of monsoon winds; coastal region marked by sand dunes.

Kon·kou·ré \ˌkäŋ-kü-ˈrā\. River, Guinea, W Africa; 160 m. long; rises in Fouta Djallon, flows SW into Atlantic Ocean N of Conakry.

Ko·no·top \ˌkän-ə-ˈtäp\. City, W Sumy Oblast, NE Ukrainian S.S.R., U.S.S.R., 125 m. NE of Kiev; pop. (1969e) 62,000; railroad junction point in rich farming area, on main line from Kiev to Moscow; raises and exports grain; flour mills; manufactures farm machinery. In World War II taken by Germans 1941; retaken by U.S.S.R. Aug. 26, 1943.

Końs·kie \ˈkȯn(t)-skē-ˌā\. Commune, Kielce prov., SE cen. Poland, 18 m. NNW of Kielce; pop. (1968e) 12,100; iron ore deposits nearby.

Kon·stan·ti·nov·ka \ˌkän(t)-stən-ˈtē-nəf-kə\. City, Donetsk Oblast, E Ukrainian S.S.R., U.S.S.R., SW of Artemovsk, in the Dnieper bend; pop. (1970p) 106,000; large steel mills.

Kon·stanz \ˈkȯn-ˌstän(t)s\; *Eng.* **Con·stance** \ˈkän(t)-stən(t)s\ *or less commonly* **Con·stanz** \ˈkȯn-ˌstän(t)s\; *anc.* **Con·stan·tia** \kən-ˈstan-ch(ē-)ə\ *or in Middle Ages sometimes called* **Kost·nitz** \ˈkȯst-(ˌ)nits\. Lake port, Baden-Württemberg, West Germany, on Lake Constance 75 m. S of Stuttgart; pop. (1969e) 60,821; electronic equipment, textiles, chemicals; univ. (1966); cathedral, grand-ducal residence, and the Kaufhaus (in which Council of Constance met). Thought to have been founded by Constantius Chlorus c. 300 A.D.; seat of famous Council of Constance (partly ecumenical) 1414–18 in which three antipopes were deposed and the doctrines of Huss, Wycliffe, and Jerome of Prague were condemned as heretical; annexed to Austria 1548, to Baden 1805.

Kon·ya *also* **Kon·ieh** *or* **Kon·ia** \kȯn-ˈyä\. 1 Province of SW cen. Turkey, Asia. See table at TURKEY.

2 *or anc.* **Ico·ni·um** \ī-ˈkō-nē-əm\. City, its ✱, on SW edge of cen. Turkish plateau; pop. (1965c) 157,934; fruit orchards; grain, sugar, flax; teacher training coll. (1962); declined in prosperity in 19th cent., but has grown rapidly since coming of the railroad 1896; contains mosque of the dancing dervishes.

History: Ancient Iconium in Phrygia later became capital of Lycaonia; visited by Paul on his first missionary journey; in 1099 became capital of Seljuk sultans of Rum, later seized by Crusaders; in 13th cent. a cultural center under Ala-ad-Din I; in 15th cent. a secondary city of Karaman; became part of Ottoman Empire 1472.

Koo·chi·ching \ˈkü-chə-chiŋ\. County in Minnesota. See table at MINNESOTA.

Koochiching Falls. Falls in the Rainy river, S Ontario, Canada, near Fort Frances and International Falls.

Ko·o·la·u·loa \ˌkō-ō-ˌlä-ü-ˈlō-ə\. Division, Honolulu co., NE Oahu I., Hawaii; chief locality Kahuku village.

Ko·o·la·u·po·ko \ˌkō-ō-ˌlä-ü-ˈpō-kō\. Division, Honolulu co., SE Oahu I., Hawaii; chief locality Kaneohe village.

Ko·o·lau Range \ˌkō-ō-ˌlä-ü-\. Mountain range extending along E side of Oahu I., Hawaii; highest peak 3150 ft.

Kooringa. See BURRA.

Koo·te·nai \ˈküt-ᵊn-ˌā, -ᵊn-ē\. 1 County in Idaho. See table at IDAHO.

2 River, Canada and U.S. See KOOTENAY.

Kootenai Mountain. Peak in Glacier National Park, NW Montana; 8300 ft.

Koo·te·nay *also* **Ku·te·nai** *or in U.S. known as the* **Koo·te·nai** \ˈküt-ᵊn-ˌā, -ᵊn-ē\. River, SW Canada and NW U.S.; 407 m. long (of which 276 m. in Canada); rises on W slopes of Rocky Mts. N of Kootenay National Park, SE British Columbia, flows S through the park into NW Montana where it turns W and N through Idaho; again crosses border into British Columbia and enters **Kootenay Lake** (65 m. long, 168 sq. m.) at its S end; issues from W side of lake to flow W past Nelson to the Columbia river. Explored by David Thompson in 1807; 25 m. section between Kootenay Lake and Columbia river utilized for hydroelectric power production.

Kootenay National Park. See CANADA, *National Parks.*

Kopaïs. See COPAIS.

Ko·pa·o·nik \'kō-ˌpau̇-ˌnēk\ *or* **Ka·pao·nik** \'kä-\. Mountain range, S cen. Yugoslavia, in cen. Serbia E of the Ibar river; highest peak Pančičev 6617 ft.

Kopar. See KOPER.

Kó·pa·vo·gur \'kōp-ə-və-ˌgu̇r\. Town, SW Iceland, S of Reykjavík; pop. (1970c) 11,165.

Ko·pe·isk \kō-'pāsk\. Town, Chelyabinsk Oblast, Russian S.F.S.R., U.S.S.R., just SE of Chelyabinsk; pop. (1970p) 156,000; coal mining.

Köpenick. See CÖPENICK.

Ko·per \'kō-ˌpe(ə)r\ *or* **Ko·par** \'kō-ˌpär\ *or Ital.* **Ca·po·di·stria** \ˌkap-ə-'dis-trē-ə, ˌkäp-ə-'dēs-\; *anc.* **Ægi·dia** \ē-'jid-ē-ə\ *or later* **Jus·tin·op·o·lis** \ˌjəs-tə-'näp-ə-ləs\. Seaport, Istria penin., Slovenia, Yugoslavia, on Gulf of Trieste just SSW of Trieste; pop. (1965e) 14,000; cathedral; old fort. Before achieving independence 1478, belonged alternately to Venice and Genoa from 10th cent.; became capital of Istria; fell to Austria 1797–1805, 1814–1918, and to Italy 1918–47.

Ko·pet–Dag \ˌkȯ-pet-'dä(g)\ *or* **Kop·peh Dāgh** \ˌkȯ-pe-'dä(g)\. Mountain range bet. NE Iran and the Turkmen S.S.R., U.S.S.R., extending ab. 400 m. NW to SE along border, E of S end of Caspian Sea; highest point 9650 ft.

Kö·ping \'chə(r)p-(ˌ)iŋ\. Town, Västmanland co., E Sweden, at W end of Lake Mälaren; pop. (1970e) 21,887; textiles.

Kop·par·berg \'kȯp-ar-ˌba(ə)r\ *or formerly* **Dal·e·car·lia** \ˌdal-ə-'kär-lē-ə\. County of cen. Sweden. See table at SWEDEN.

Koppeh Dāgh. See KOPET-DAG.

Köprili. See TITOV VELES.

Ko·priv·ni·ca \'kō-ˌprēv-nit-ˌsä\ *or Hung.* **Ka·pron·cza** \'kō-prōn(t)-ˌsȯ\ *or Ger.* **Ko·prei·nitz** \kō-'prī-nəts\. Town, Croatia, N Yugoslavia, S of the Drava and ab. 50 m. NE of Zagreb; pop. (1965e) 13,000.

Kor \'kȯr\. River, SW cen. Iran; ab. 175 m. long; flows SW into Lake Bakhtegān.

Korat. See NAKHON RATCHASIMA.

Kor·çë *or formerly* **Korr·çë** \'kȯr-chə\ *or Gk.* **Ko·ry·tsa** \ˌkȯr-ət-'sä\ *or Ital.* **Co·riz·za** \kə-'rēt-sə\. **1** Province of SE Albania. See table at ALBANIA.

2 Town, its ✻, near Greek border; pop. (1967e) 45,858; industrial and commercial center in agricultural region; textiles, leather products, bricks. In World War II used in 1940 as advanced base by Italians in operations against Greece; captured by Greeks Nov. 22, 1940.

Kor·ču·la \'kȯr-chu̇-ˌlä\ *or Ital.* **Cur·zo·la** \'ku̇rt-sə-ˌlä\. **1** *or anc.* **Cor·cy·ra Ni·gra** \kȯr-ˌsī-rə-'nī-grə, -'nig-rə\. Yugoslav island in Adriatic Sea off Dalmatian coast; 105 sq. m.; pop. (1961c) 10,223; olives, grapes, fishing; administratively part of Croatia.

2 Town on E end of the island; 15th cent. monastery; originally settled by Greeks; under Austrian rule 1815–1918; passed to newly organized Yugoslavia 1918.

Kor·de·stān \ˌkȯrd-ə-'stän, -'stan\. Province of NW Iran. See table at IRAN.

Kor·do·fan \ˌkȯrd-ə-'fan\. Province of cen. Sudan, NE Africa. See table at SUDAN.

Ko·rea \ˌkȯr-ē-'ä\. Former Indian state, now part of Madhya Pradesh, India; 1647 sq. m.; ✻ Sonhat.

Korea \kə-'rē-ə\; *Korean* **Cho·sŏn** \'chō-'sȯn\ *or* **Tae Han** \'ta-'hän\; *Jap.* **Cho·sen** \'chō-'sen\. Former kingdom, a peninsula on E coast of Asia, since 1948 partitioned (along the 38th parallel) into two republics. See KOREA, NORTH and KOREA, SOUTH.

History: Kingdom of Chosŏn established in N part of peninsula by Chinese perhaps as early as 12th cent. B.C.; in 3d cent. B.C. a vassal of Yen; N kingdom conquered and annexed by Chinese 108 B.C.; by 1st cent. B.C., had developed into three independent kingdoms of Silla, Koguryu, and Pakche; introduced to Buddhism 4th cent. A.D. which Koreans later carried to Japan (*q.v.*); in period of predominance of kingdom of Silla 670–935, Chinese culture flourished; under Koryo (from 935), a state founded in W cen. Korea, most of Korea united as one kingdom under Chinese suzerainty; invaded by Mongols 1231; kingdom of Chosŏn with capital at Seoul (Keijo) ruled by Li dynasty 1392–1910; invaded by Japanese under Hideyoshi 1592–98; from c. 1637, shut out foreign contacts; forced to grant treaty opening ports to Japan 1876 which recognized Korean independence; in period of internal disorder, forced to unite with Japan in resisting Chinese interference (Korea considered Chinese vassal), thus bringing on Chinese-Japanese war 1894–95; Russo-Japanese rivalry over Korea a cause of war 1904–05; became Japanese protectorate 1907; formally annexed to Japan as province 1910; freed from Japanese control on defeat of Japan Aug. 1945; after the war divided at 38th parallel into two zones of occupation, Russian in N and American in S, in which were established (1948) respectively, North Korea (Democratic People's Republic of Korea; ✻ P'yŏngyang) and South Korea (Republic of Korea; ✻ Seoul); scene of warfare between North Korea and allied forces of the United Nations 1950–53.

Korea, North; *officially* **Democratic People's Republic of Korea** *or Korean* **Cho·sŏn Min·ju·juŭi In'·min Kong·hwa·guk** \'chō-sȯn-'min-jü-'jü-ē-'in-min-'kȯŋ-hwä-'gük\. Republic, on E coast of Asia, bounded on N by China, on NE by the U.S.S.R., on E by the Sea of Japan, on S by South Korea, and on W by the Yellow Sea and Korea Bay; 46,609 sq. m.; pop. (1971e) 14,000,000; ✻ P'yŏngyang. *Physical features:* Generally a mountainous region, especially in N, with several peaks over 8000 ft.; relief less pronounced in W and SW; W coast has numerous estuaries and tidal flats. *Chief products:* Rice, wheat, corn, potatoes; fishing; iron ore, coal, copper, graphite, lead, zinc; manufacturing: iron and steel, chemicals, textiles, agricultural implements. *Chief cities:* P'yŏngyang, Wŏnsan, Hŭngnam, Sinŭiju, Kaesŏng, Hamhŭng. Administrative divisions shown in the table below (for pronunciation of their names, see their individual entries):

NAME	AREA (sq. m.)	POP. (1966e)	CAPITAL
Special cities			
Kaesŏng[1]	2,072	265,000	
P'yŏngyang	77	1,364,000	
Provinces[2]			
Chagang	6,178	739,000	Kanggye
Kangwŏn	4,151	1,050,000	Wŏnsan
North Hamgyong	6,178	1,333,000	Ch'ŏngjin
North Hwanghae	3,243	993,000	Sariwŏn
North P'yŏngan	4,633	1,599,000	Sinŭiju
South Hamgyŏng	6,757	1,699,000	Hamhŭng
South Hwanghae	2,896	1,301,000	Haeju
South P'yŏngan	5,019	1,875,000	Sain-ni
Yanggang	5,405	422,000	Hyesan

[1]Includes district.
[2]Exclusive of the special cities Kaesŏng and P'yŏngyang.

History: For history prior to 1948, see KOREA. Communist republic established 1948 N of 38th parallel; invaded South Korea 1950, precipitating the Korean War (1950–53; armistice was signed July 26, 1953); withdrawal of Chinese forces (allied with North Koreans during war) completed 1958; during the 1960's provoked numerous border incidents along the 38th parallel, and repeatedly called for the establishment of a unified, Communist-controlled Korea.

Korea, South; *officially* **Republic of Korea** *or Korean* **Tae Han Min'·guk** \ta-'hän-min-'gük\. Republic, E Asia, bounded on N by North Korea, on E by the Sea of Japan, on S by the Korea Strait, and on W by the Yellow Sea; 38,022 sq. m.; pop. (1966c) 29,207,856; ✻ Seoul. *Physical features:* Mountainous in E and S cen. regions; S and SW coastlines characterized by numerous islands; best ports located on W coast, along which are found a number of alluvial plains. *Chief products:* Rice, barley, wheat, cotton, tobacco; coal, tungsten; livestock raising, fishing; manufacturing: textiles, plywood, footwear, chemicals, cement. *Chief cities:* Seoul, Pusan, Inch'ŏn, Suwŏn, Ch'unch'ŏn, Wŏnju. Administrative divisions shown in the table below (for pronunciation of their names, see their individual entries):

NAME	AREA (sq. m.)	POP. (1970e)	CAPITAL
Special cities			
Pusan	144	1,880,710	
Seoul	237	5,536,377	
Provinces			
Cheju	706	365,522	Cheju
Kangwŏn	6,453	1,866,928	Ch'unch'ŏn
Kyŏnggi[1]	4,231	3,358,105	Seoul
North Chŏlla	3,108	2,434,522	Chŏnju
North Ch'ungch'ŏng	2,871	1,481,566	Ch'ŏngju
North Kyŏngsang	7,644	4,559,584	Taegu
South Chŏlla	4,656	4,005,735	Kwangju
South Ch'ungch'ŏng	3,359	2,860,690	Taejŏn
South Kyŏngsang[2]	4,613	3,119,393	Pusan

[1]Excludes Seoul city.
[2]Excludes Pusan city.

History: For history prior to 1948, see KOREA. Established as an independent republic 1948; fought Korean War (with aid of U.N. forces) 1950–53; government overthrown by military junta 1961.

Korea Bay. Northeast arm of Yellow Sea bet. Liao-tung Penin. and North Korea; receives the Yalu river.

Korea Strait. Channel bet. South Korea and SW Japan; ab. 120 m. wide; divided into Western Channel on NW and Tsushima Strait on SE by the island of Tsushima in its center; connects SW Sea of Japan with East China Sea.

Kor·hogo \kȯ-'rō-(ˌ)gō\. Town, N Ivory Coast, W Africa, ab. 310 m. NNW of Abidjan; pop. (1963e) 23,766.

Koriak National Okrug. See KORYAK NATIONAL OKRUG.

Korinthiakós Kólpos. See CORINTH, GULF OF.

Kórinthos. See CORINTH 3.

Korinthou, Isthmos. See CORINTH, ISTHMUS OF.

Korintji. See KERINTJI.

Kō·ri·ya·ma \ˌkōr-ē-'(y)äm-ə, ˌkȯr-\. City, Fukushima prefecture, N cen. Honshū, Japan, 25 m. S of Fukushima; pop. (1970c) 241,673; produces textiles, chemicals, and machinery; in World War II bombed in Apr. 1945.

Kor·ki·no \'kȯr-ki-nə\. Town, Chelyabinsk Oblast, Russian S.F.S.R., U.S.S.R., ab. 20 m. S of Chelyabinsk; pop. (1969e) 79,000; glass; coal mining.

Kor·ma·kí·tis, Cape \-ˌkȯr-mə-'kēt-is\. Cape near cen. part of N coast of Cyprus, in E Mediterranean Sea.

Kor·man·tine *or* **Cor·man·tyne** \'kȯr-mən-ˌtīn\. Coastal village and remains of Dutch fort ab. 3 m. W of Saltpond, Ghana, W Africa; first slaves for British West Indies were taken from this port.

Körmöczbánya. See KREMNICA.

Korn·west·heim \kȯrn-'vest-ˌhīm\. City, Baden-Württemberg, West Germany; pop. (1969e) 28,277, footwear; church (1516).

Ko·ro \'kōr-(ˌ)ō, 'kȯr-\. Island of the Lomai Viti group, Fiji (*q.v.*), SW Pacific Ocean, in cen. part S of Vanua Levu on NW border of Koro Sea; 58 sq. m.; cotton, copra, arrowroot, tortoise shell.

Ko·ro·li Desert \kə-ˌrō-lē-\. Desert area in N Kenya, SE Africa, E of S end of Lake Rudolf.

Ko·rom·ba, Mount *or* **Mount Ku·ram·ba** \-kə-'räm-bə\. Peak, W Viti Levu I., Fiji, SW Pacific Ocean; 3526 ft.

Ko·ro·na·dal \ˌkȯr-ō-nə-'däl\. Municipality, ✱ of Cotabato del Sur, Mindanao, Phil.; pop. (1969e) 44,800.

Korónē, Gulf of. See MESSENIA, GULF OF.

Ko·ró·nia, Lake \-kȯ-'rō-nē-ə\ *or formerly* **Lake Lan·ka·da** \-ˌläŋ-gä-'t͟hä\. Lake, N Chalcidice, Macedonia, NE Greece, W of Lake Bolbē and ENE of Salonika.

Ko·ror *or* **Kor·ror** \'kȯr-ˌȯ(ə)r\. Town on small island of same name off S tip of Babelthuap I. in Palau Is., W Pacific Ocean; has good harbor and was trading center under German regime; from 1921 to 1945 administrative capital of all Japanese mandated islands (called **Nan·yo** \'nän-(ˌ)yō\ by the Japanese) in the Pacific.

Kö·rös \'kər-ˌəsh\. River in E Hungary; ab. 120 m. long; formed by confluence of streams which rise in W Romania, flows SW into Tisza river at Csongrád.

Ko·ro Sea \ˌkōr-(ˌ)ō-, ˌkȯr-\. Open sea in cen. area of Fiji, SW Pacific Ocean; Nanuku Passage on NE is steamship lane to the NE.

Ko·ro·sten \ˌkōr-ə-'sten, ˌkȯr-\. Town, NE Zhitomir Oblast, W Ukrainian S.S.R., U.S.S.R., in steppe region 90 m. WNW of Kiev; pop. (1967e) 46,000; a key railroad junction on the N to S line from the Belorussian S.S.R. to Berdichev and on the E to W line from Kiev to Kovel and Lublin; scene of severe fighting Nov.–Dec. 1943 during Soviet advance W of Kiev; taken by Soviets Dec. 29, 1943.

Ko·ro·vin \kə-'rō-vən\. **1** Volcano, N part of Atka I., Aleutians, SW Alaska; 4852 ft.

2 Bay, inlet on N coast of Atka I.

Korrçë. See KORÇË.

Korror. See KOROR.

Kor·sa·kov \'kȯr-sə-ˌkəf, -ˌkəv\ *or Jap.* **Oto·ma·ri** \ˌōt-ō-'mär-ē\ *or* **Odo·ma·ri** \ˌōd-ō-\. Seaport, S Sakhalin I., Russian S.F.S.R., U.S.S.R., on Aniva Bay; pop. (1967e) 34,000; formerly Japanese.

Kor·sør \kȯr-'sər\. Seaport, Vestsjælland co., SW Sjælland, Denmark, 62 m. WSW of Copenhagen; pop. (1970e) 13,-674; trading center; fisheries.

Kor·sun–Shev·chen·kov·ski \kər-ˌsün-shef-chen-'kȯf-skē\. Town, Cherkassy Oblast, N Ukrainian S.S.R., U.S.S.R., 80 m. SSE of Kiev; pop. (1967e) 67,000; on main railroad line of cen. Ukraine; scene of battle 1648 in which Bogdan Chmielnicki, Cossack hetman, defeated the Poles; in World War II held by Germans 1941–44; taken by U.S.S.R. Feb. 1944.

Kort·rijk \'kȯ(ə)rt-ˌrīk\ *or Fr.* **Cour·trai** \ku̇r-trā\. Commune, West Flanders prov., NW Belgium, on Leie (Lys) river 15 m. NNE of Lille; pop. (1969e) 45,138; linens and lace. In Middle Ages a populous commercial city of Flanders; scene of battle of the Golden Spurs July 11, 1302 in which Flemish burghers defeated French barons and knights; also a battleground in later wars.

Ko·ryak National Okrug *or* **Ko·riak National Okrug** \kər-'yak . . . 'ō-ˌkrük\. District, Russian S.F.S.R., U.S.S.R., borders Chukot National Okrug on N and Khabarovsk Krai on SW; 116,409 sq. m.; pop. (1969e) 31,000; ✱ Palana; comprises chiefly the mountainous region on coast of Bering Sea at the base, in the isthmus, and the NW third of Kamchatka Penin. and the region of the Penzhina basin NE of the Sea of Okhotsk; includes also Karagin I.; inhabitants are Koryaks, a Palaeo-Asiatic people; their chief industry is fishing. Originally a part of the Far Eastern Region; established 1930 as a national district but for many years considered as part of Khabarovsk Krai; important in recent years in air communications routes of E Siberia.

Ko·ryak·ska·ya Sop·ka \kər-ˌyak-skə-yə-'sȯp-kə\. Volcano (*sopka*), at S end of Eastern Range, Kamchatka Penin., Khabarovsk Krai, Russian S.F.S.R., U.S.S.R.; 11,342 ft.

Korytsa. See KORÇË.

Kos \'käs\ *or* **Cos** *or Ital.* **Coo** \'kō-ˌō\. **1** An island of the Dodecanese (*q.v.*), off end of Bodrum Penin., SW Turkey; 111 sq. m.; pop. (1961c) 19,987; settled in very early times by Dorians; celebrated temple of Aesculapius, and belonged to the Pentapolis of Asia Minor; birthplace of Hippocrates.

2 Town on NE coast of the island; pop. (1961c) 8138.

KOREA
POLYCONIC PROJECTION
SCALE OF MILES
0 20 40 60 80
KILOMETERS
0 20 40 60 80
Capitals of Countries
International Boundaries
© C. S. HAMMOND & Co., Maplewood, N. J.
124°
126°
128°
130°
132°
42°
40°
38°
36°
34°
24°
Longitude East of Greenwich
MANCHURIA
CHINA
U. S. S. R.
NORTH KOREA
SOUTH KOREA
YELLOW SEA
SEA OF JAPAN
JAPAN
HONSHU
KYUSHU
Liaoyüan
Sifeng
Kaiyüan
Hailung
Hweinan
Sungari
Antu
Yenki
Tumen
Onsong
Hunchun
Chongsŏng
Kyŏnghŭng
Peter the Great Bay
Holung
Hoeryŏng
Aoji-dong
Unggi
Sŏsura
Najin
Tsingyüan
Liuho
Fusung
Paektu-san (Baktu) 9,003
Pai Shan
Musan
Fushun
Sinpin
Tunghwa
Linkiang
Chang Pai
Yalu
Saji-dong
Nanam
Kwanmo-bong 8,337
Ch'ŏngjin
Kyŏngsŏng
Chuŭronjang
Ŏdaejin
Chasŏng
Huch'ang
Changpai
Hyesan
Pongdu-ri
Myŏngch'ŏn
Ip'yŏng-dong
Kasan-dong
Changjin
Tuun-bong 8,130
Hochon
Paekam
Hwanjen
Manp'o
Tsian
Saimachi
Kosanjin
Kanggye
Kapsan
Kŏmdŏk-san 7,054
P'oha-dong
Wiwŏn
Sang-ni
P'ungsan
Kilchu
Kwantien
Sup'ung Res.
Ch'osan
Puksubaek-san 8,274
Obŏk-tong
Musu-dan
Pyŏktong
Mup'yŏng-ni
Pujŏn Res.
Kosŏng-ni
Susang-ni
Kimch'aek
Fencheng
Ai
P'anp'yong-ni
Yudam-ni
Changjin Res.
Changhŭng-ni
Iwŏn
Tanch'ŏn
Sakchu
Antung
Ŭiju
Taean-dong
Hŭich'ŏn
Kot'o-ri
Pukch'ŏng
Ch'aho
Sinŭiju
Pukchin
Myohyang-san 6,263
Hongwŏn
Sinp'o
Sinch'ang
Kusŏng
Hamhŭng
Mayang-do
Pihyŏn
Namsi
Sŏnch'ŏn
Ch'ŏngch'ŏn
Kujang
Chŏngp'yŏng
Hŭngnam
Yongampo
Ch'ŏlsan
Pakch'ŏn
Anju
Aech'ang
Yŏnp'o
Tŏkch'ŏn
Yongsap'o
Kaech'ŏn
Sinanju
Taedong
Yŏnghŭng
East Korea Bay
Sinmi-do
West Korea Bay
Sunch'ŏn
Sinch'ang-ni
Kowŏn
Hanch'ŏn
Sunan
Unsan
Munch'ŏn
Taegang-got
Yŏnghŭng-man
Chŭngsan
Yangdŏk
Wŏnsan
Hŭpkok
Hamjong-ni
Kang-dong
Anbyŏn
Nan
T'ongch'ŏn
P'yŏngyang
Kangsŏ
Hwach'ŏn-ni
Nam'p'o
Sŏngnim
Suan
Sin'gosan
Changjŏn
Kosŏng
Hoeyang
Kŭmgang-san 5,374
Ch'o-do
Hwangju
Sariwŏn
Kŏksan
Imjin
Pukhan
Changnyŏn
Anak
Cease-fire line 1953
Chaeryŏng
Kŭmsŏng
Kansŏng
Changyŏn
P'yŏnggang
Sinch'ŏn
P'yŏngsan
Yesŏng
Kŭmhwa
Changsan-got
Sinwŏn-ni
Ch'ŏrwŏn
Hwach'ŏn Res.
Sŏrak-san 5,604
Haeju
Ch'ŏngdan
Kaesŏng
Yangmun-ni
Yangyang
Paengnyŏng-do
Ongjin
Yŏnan
Taebaek-sanmaek
Panmunjŏm
Kap'yŏng
Ch'unch'ŏn
Chumunjin
Kangnŭng
Haeju-man
Kanghwa
Kebang-san 5,174
Tŭngsan-got
Kanghwa-do
Ŭijŏngbu
Hongch'ŏn
Mukhojin-ni
Kanghwa Bay
Sosa
Han
Yangp'yŏng
Hoengsŏng
Inch'ŏn
SEOUL
Chŏngsŏn
Samch'ŏk
Ullŭng-do (Dagelet I.)
Tok-do (Takeshima) (claimed by S.Korea & Japan)
Tŏkchŏk-kundo
Anyang
Suwŏn
Ich'ŏn
Wŏnju
P'yŏngch'ang
Osan
Yŏngwŏl
Taebaek-san 5,121
Chech'ŏn
Changhowŏn
P'yŏngt'aek
Ansŏng
Ch'ungju
Ch'unyang
Ulchin
Sŏnghwan
Bonghwa
Sŏsan
Chinch'ŏn
P'unggi
T'aean
Onyang
Ch'ŏnan
Yŏngju
Yean
P'yonghae
Haemi
Yesan
Mun'gyŏng
Yech'ŏn
Hongsŏng
Choch'iwŏn
Ch'ŏngju
Poŭn
Hamch'ang
Andong
Yonghae
Kwangch'ŏn
Kum
Ŭisŏng
Kongju
Sangju
Yŏngdŏk
Taech'ŏn
Puyŏ
Taejŏn
Ch'ŏngsan
Naktong
Ch'ŏngha
Okch'ŏn
Sŏnsan
Kunwi
Yongil-man
Kanggyŏng
Nonsan
Yŏngdong
Sinnyŏng
Kigye
Changyŏng-gap
Kŭmsan
Kimch'ŏn
Kuryongp'o
Kunsan
Iri
Kosan
Muju
Sŏngju
Waegwan
P'ohang
Kogunsan-kundo
Kŭmje
Chŏnju
Koch'ang
Taegu
Yŏngch'ŏn
Kyŏngju
Kamp'o
Ch'ulp'o
Puan
Chinan
Kyŏngsan
Ch'ŏngdo
Wi-do
Anŭi
Ulsan
Ansan
Chŏngup
Taein
Hamyang
Ch'angnyŏng
Miryang
Pangŏ-ri
Pŏpsŏngp'o
Koch'ang
Namwŏn
Samga
Samnangjin
Yŏnggwang
Koksŏng
Chiri-san 6,283
Kimhae
Kijang
Changsŏng
Kurye
Chinhae
Naju
Tamyang
Sŭnggu
Chinju
Masan
Chido
Kwangju
Hadong
PUSAN
Hwasun
Kosŏng
Korea Strait
Hamp'yŏng
Yŏnsan'p'o
Sŭngju
Changsŭngp'o
Hong-do
Pigŭm-do
Mokp'o
Yŏsu
Kwangyang
Samch'ŏnp'o
Ch'ungmu
Kŏje-do
Taehŭksan-do
Yŏngam
Posŏng
Ch'anghŭng
Kohŭng
Tolsan-do
Kŭmo-do
Tsu Is.
Chin-do
Haenam
Wando
Kogŭm-do
Sohŭksan-do
Soan-kundo
Sŏ-do (Port Hamilton)
Cheju Strait
Tsushima Strait
Cheju
Kŭmnyŏng
Taejong
Cheju (Quelpart I.)
Iki
Karatsu
Hamada
Masuda
Hagi
Yamaguchi
Tokuyama
Shimonoseki
Ube
Suo Sea
Kitakyushu
Nakatsu
Fukuoka
Saga
Kurume
Beppu
Oita

Ko·sa·la \'kō-sə-lə\. An Aryan kingdom in N India (modern Oudh) c. 550–320 B.C.; ✱ Ajodhya (*q.v.*); now in Uttar Pradesh; the chief state in time of Buddha.

Ko·ścian \'kȯsh-ˌchän\ *or Ger.* **Ko·sten** \'kȯ-stən\. Commune, Poznań prov., W cen. Poland, 22 m. SSW of Poznań; pop. (1968e) 17,500.

Kos·ci·us·ko \ˌkäs-ē-'əs-ˌkō\. 1 County in Indiana. See table at INDIANA.

2 City, ⊗ of Attala co., cen. Mississippi, 46 m. SE of Greenwood; pop. (1970c) 7266; lamps, furniture, flour; pine and hickory timber; diversified agriculture.

Kosciusko, Mount \-ˌkäz-ē-'əs-(ˌ)kō\. Mountain of Australian Alps, SE New South Wales; 7316 ft.; highest peak in Australia; winter sports.

Kosel. See KOŹLE.

Ko·shi·ga·ya \kō-'shē-gä-yə, ˌkō-shi-'gä-yə, -'gī-ə\. Town, Saitama prefecture, Honshū, Japan, 16 m. N of Tokyo; pop. (1970c) 139,368.

K'o–shih. See KASHGAR 2.

Ko·shi·ki Archipelago \'kō-shə-ˌkē-\ *or Jap.* **Koshiki Ret·tō** \-'re-(ˌ)tō\. Group of small islands off SW coast of Kyūshū, Japan.

Kosh·ko·nong, Lake \-'käs(h)-kə-ˌnäŋ\. Lake, SW Jefferson co., SE Wisconsin; ab. 8 m. long, 4 m. wide; an expansion of Rock river.

Kosh·tan Tau \ˌkȯsh-tän-'tau̇\. Mountain (*tau*) in Caucasus Mts. near Dykh Tau, in S Kabardino-Balkarian A.S.S.R., Russian S.F.S.R., U.S.S.R.; 16,875 ft.

Ko·shu \'kō-ˌshü\. 1 Town, South Chōlla prov., South Korea. See KWANGJU.

2 Town, South Ch'ungch'ŏng prov., South Korea. See KONGJU.

Ko·si \'kō-sē\ *or* **Ku·si** \'kü-\. River, E Nepal and N India; ab. 304 m. long; formed by confluence of three streams in E Nepal, flows S across border into India and through N Bihar prov. into the Ganges E of Bhagalpur.

Ko·ši·ce \'kȯ-shət-ˌsä\ *or Hung.* **Kas·sa** \'kȯ-(ˌ)shȯ\ *or Ger.* **Ka·schau** \'käsh-ˌau̇\. City, SE Slovak S.R., Czechoslovakia, on the Hernád river 135 m. NE of Budapest; pop. (1968e) 136,397; commercial and market center; wine; univ. (1959); 14th cent. Gothic cathedral. Originally a city of N Hungary; became part of Czechoslovakia 1918; held by Hungary 1938–45 but returned to Czechoslovakia.

Kosi Lake \ˌkō-sē-\. Lake, N Natal, NE Rep. of South Africa, near coast, just S of border of Mozambique; in NE corner has an outlet by way of a short river, **Kosi River,** which flows NE into the Indian Ocean at **Kosi Bay.**

Köslin. See KOSZALIN.

Koso Gol. See HÖVSGÖL.

Ko·so·vo *or* **Kos·so·vo** \'kȯ-sə-ˌvō\ *or* **Kosovo Po·lje** \-'pȯl-(ˌ)yä\. Elevated plain, S Yugoslavia, W of Priština, (since 1946) in Kosovo-Methohija autonomous region. Site of important battle in Balkan history June 20, 1389 in which Serbs, Albanians, and Bosnians were defeated by Turks under Murad I; as a result Serbian Empire was crushed, and Serbia (*q.v.*) became vassal of Ottoman Empire; in a second battle Oct. 17, 1448 John Hunyadi was defeated by Sultan Murad II; on Nov. 20–25, 1915 the scene of final defeat of Serbians by Bulgarian army in World War I.

Kosovo–Me·to·hi·ja \-me-'tō-hē-ˌ(y)ä\. Autonomous region, S Yugoslavia, in W part of republic of Serbia; 4203 sq. m.; pop. (1971p) 1,244,755; subdivision formed under constitution of 1946.

Ko·sov·ska Mi·tro·vi·ca \ˌkō-sȯv-skə-'mē-trə-ˌvēt-sə\ *or formerly* **Mitrovica.** Town, Serbia, S Yugoslavia, 65 m. NW of Skopje; pop. (1965e) 31,000.

Kosseir. See AL-QUSEIR.

Kosso–gol. See HÖVSGÖL.

Kossovo. See KOSOVO.

Kos·suth \kə-'süth\. County in Iowa. See table at IOWA.

Kosten. See KOŚCIAN.

Köstendil. See KYUSTENDIL.

Kos·ti \'kȯs-tē\ *or* **Kūs·tī**\'ku̇s-\. Town, Blue Nile prov., E Sudan, S of Ed Dueim.

Kostnitz. See KONSTANZ.

Ko·stro·ma \ˌkäs-trə-'mä\. 1 River, N cen. Russian S.F.S.R., U.S.S.R.; rises in NE corner of Kostroma Oblast, flows SSW to the Volga at Kostroma; 250 m. long; navigable for 200 m.

2 City, SW Kostroma Oblast, Russian S.F.S.R., U.S.S.R., on left bank of Volga where it is joined by the Kostroma, ab. 45 m. ENE of Yaroslavl; pop. (1970p) 223,000; flax-processing center; linen, textile machinery, river craft; 13th cent. cathedral; has suburbs on opp. side of Volga. One of oldest towns in Russia, founded 1152; in 13th cent. in Rostov-Suzdal principality, later, in 15th cent., absorbed by Moscow principality; frequently plundered by Tatars.

Kostroma Oblast \-'ō-bləst, -ˌblast\. Subdivision of the Russian S.F.S.R., U.S.S.R.; 23,243 sq. m.; pop. (1970p) 871,000; ✱ Kostroma; rye, oats, flax; lumbering; created for economic reasons during World War II out of E half of Yaroslavl Oblast.

Kos·trzyn \'kȯs-chin\; *Ger.* **Kü·strin** *also* **Cü·strin** \kyü-'strēn\. Industrial city, NW Zielona Góra prov., W Poland, on the Oder at its confluence with the Warta; pop. (1968e) 10,300; paper, cellulose; 16th cent. castle in which Frederick the Great was held prisoner Sept.–Nov. 1730.

History: First mentioned 1232; passed to Brandenburg 1262; made seat of margravate 1535 and fortified; held by French 1806–14; fortifications expanded and improved in 19th cent.; in World War II an important German defense post in campaign of U.S.S.R. for Berlin 1945; taken by Soviet troops Mar. 29; assigned to Poland by Potsdam Conference 1945.

Koswig. See COSWIG.

Ko·sza·lin \kȯ-'shäl-ˌēn\ *or Ger.* **Kös·lin** \ˌkər-'slēn\. 1 Province of N Poland. See table at POLAND.

2 City, its ✱, NW Poland, near Baltic Sea 88 m. NE of Szczecin; pop. (1970p) 64,400; food processing; lumber, agricultural machinery. Founded at end of 12th cent.; became city 1266; to Brandenburg 1648; in World War II taken by U.S.S.R. Feb. 14, 1945; assigned to Poland by Potsdam Conference 1945.

Kö·szeg \'kə-(ˌ)seg\ *or* **Ko·szeg·szer·da·he·ly** \-ˌser-dä-'hā\. Town, W Hungary, N of Szombathely near Austrian border; pop. (1970p) 1902; in fruit and wine-producing region.

Kotabaru. See DJAJAPURA.

Ko·ta Bha·ru \ˌkōt-ə-'bär-(ˌ)ü\ *or* **Kota Ba·ha·ru** \-bə-'här-(ˌ)ü\. Town, ✱ of Kelantan state, Malaysia, near coast at head of delta of Kelantan river; pop. (1970p) 55,052; one of the first places seized (Dec. 10, 1941) by Japanese in campaign against Singapore.

Ko·tah \'kōt-ə\. 1 Former Indian state, now part of Rajasthan state, NW India; 5714 sq. m.; drained by the Chambal and its tributaries; formed from Bundi state ab. 1625.

2 District, part of the former state, Rajasthan, NW India; 4794 sq. m.; pop. (1961c) 848,389; ✱ Kotah.

3 Town, its ✱, on right bank of Chambal river 120 m. S of Jaipur; pop. (1970e) 215,634; muslins and carpets; includes old city walls, palaces of the maharao, and temples.

Kota Ki·na·ba·lu \'kōt-ə-ˌkin-ə-bə-'lü\ *or formerly* **Jes·sel·ton** \'jes-əl-tən\. Seaport town, ✱ of Sabah, Malaysia, on island of Borneo; pop. (1970p) 41,830.

Kota Kota \ˌkōt-ə-'kōt-ə\. Town on W shore of Lake Nyasa, Malawi, SE Africa.

Ko·tel·nich \kō-'tel-nich\. Railroad and commercial town, W Kirov Oblast, Russian S.F.S.R., U.S.S.R., on Vyatka river 50 m. SW of Kirov; pop. (1967e) 29,000.

Ko·tel·ni·kovo \kō-'tel-ni-ˌkȯ-və\. Town, Volgograd Oblast, Russian S.F.S.R., U.S.S.R., ab. 90 m. SSW of Volgograd;

pop. (1967e) 19,000; in World War II taken by Germany Aug. 1942; retaken by U.S.S.R. Dec. 29, 1942.

Ko·tel·ny *or* **Ko·tel·ni** \kō-'tel-nē\. Island, largest of the New Siberian Is., in W part of group; 110 m. long; belongs to Yakutsk A.S.S.R., Russian S.F.S.R., U.S.S.R.

Kö·then *also* **Cö·then** \'kərt-ᵊn\. City, Halle dist., East Germany, 12 m. SW of Dessau; pop. (1970e) 36,587; railroad junction; boilers, heavy machinery; sugar beets; first mentioned 1115; was granted charter 1200.

Kot·ka \'kȯt-kə\. Seaport, Kymi prov., SE Finland, on a small island in the Gulf of Finland E of Helsinki; pop. (1970e) 34,218; ships lumber; hydroelectric power plant; manufactures paper, cellulose, prefabricated houses; founded 1879.

Kot·las \kət-'las\. Town, SE Arkhangelsk Oblast, Russian S.F.S.R., U.S.S.R., on right bank of Northern Dvina; pop. (1969e) 61,000; a river and railroad junction point at head of Northern Dvina navigation; ships coal and lumber; sawmills, pulp and paper plants.

Kot·lik \'kät-lik\. Village on the W coast of Alaska, on S shore of Norton Sound and at N end of the Yukon delta; pop. (1970c) 228.

Kot·lin \'kät-lən\. Russian island, E end of Gulf of Finland. See KRONSHLOT.

Kotonu. See COTONOU.

Ko·tor \'kō-ˌtȯ(ə)r\ *or* **Cat·ta·ro** \'kät-ə-ˌrō\. Seaport and commercial center, formerly in Zetska co., S Yugoslavia, on the **Gulf of Kotor,** an inlet of the Adriatic Sea; pop. (1961c) 8572; since 1946 in Montenegro republic, Yugoslavia; excellent harbor, formerly a base of Austro-Hungarian navy; under Venetian rule 1420–1797; passed to Austria 1797, to France 1807–14, back to Austria 1814–1918, to Yugoslavia 1918.

Kotosho. See HUNG-T'OU.

Ko·tovsk \kə-'tȯfsk\. Industrial city, Odessa Oblast, Russian S.F.S.R., U.S.S.R.; pop. (1967e) 34,000; formerly a part of Tambov, made a separate city 1944.

Ko·tri \'kō-trē\. Town, S Sind, Pakistan, on right bank of the Indus opp. Hyderabad; pop. (1961c) 52,685; important railroad and river transportation center.

Kot·ta·gu·dem \ˌkät-ə-'güd-əm\. Town, Andhra Pradesh, India, 139 m. E of Hyderabad; pop. (1961c) 69,728.

Kot·ta·yam \'kät-ə-yəm\. Town, W Kerala, S India, on inlet of Arabian Sea; pop. (1961c) 52,685; market center; cement factory; noted as site of an old Syrian Christian community.

Kottbus. See COTTBUS.

Kot·te \'kō-(ˌ)tā\. Town, Ceylon, ab. 7 m. SE of Colombo; pop. (1968e) 83,000.

Kot·to \'kät-(ˌ)ō\. River, cen. Africa; 400 m. long; flows S through E Central African Republic, N cen. Africa, into Ubangi river on the border of Zaire.

Kot·ze·bue \ˌkät-sə-ˌbyü\. City, NW Alaska, at tip of long neck of land (Baldwin Penin.) in Kotzebue Sound; pop. (1970c) 1696; U.S. air base.

Kotzebue Sound. Large inlet, Chukchi Sea, NW Alaska, just NE of Bering Strait; 40 to 65 m. wide; receives Noatak and Kobuk rivers.

Kouang–Tchéou–Wan. See KWANGCHOWAN.

Kou·dou·gou \kü-'dü-(ˌ)gü\. Town, cen. Upper Volta, ab. 55 m. W of Ouagadougou; pop. (1965e) 25,394.

Kou·li·ko·ro \ˌkü-li-'kōr-(ˌ)ō, -'kȯr-\. Town, Mali, W Africa, on the Niger just NE of Bamako; founded 1884.

Koulouri. See SALAMIS 2 and 3.

Koun·rad·ski \kün-'rat-skē\. Town, SE Karaganda Oblast, Kazakh S.S.R., U.S.S.R.; railroad terminus just N of Balkhash and N shore of Lake Balkhash; copper-mining center.

Kountze \'kün(t)s\. City, ⊗ of Hardin co., E Texas; pop. (1970c) 1703; diversified agriculture.

Kou·rous·sa \kü-'rü-sə\. Town, E cen. Guinea, W Africa, on railroad from Conakry to Kankan and on left bank of upper Niger.

Kou·vo·la \'kō-və-ˌlä\. Town, ✻ of Kymi prov., S Finland; pop. (1970p) 26,505; cellulose; railroad junction point; formed 1921.

Ko·vel \'kō-vəl, 'kȯ-vəl(-yə)\ *or Pol.* **Ko·wel** \'kȯ-vel\. City, Volyn Oblast, NW Ukrainian S.S.R., U.S.S.R., 43 m. NW of Lutsk; pop. (1967e) 31,000; formerly in Poland; important railroad junction and agricultural center; captured by Austrians Aug. 17, 1915; held by Germans in World War II until July 1944.

Kovno. See KAUNAS.

Kov·rov \kəv-'rȯf, -'rȯv\. Town, Vladimir Oblast, Russian S.F.S.R., U.S.S.R., on Klyazma river, 150 m. E of Moscow; pop. (1970p) 123,000; railroad junction; textiles, machinery.

Kov·zha \'kȯv-zhə\. Stream, Russian S.F.S.R., U.S.S.R.; ab. 50 m. long; flows SSE to Lake Beloye; forms part of the Volga-Baltic Waterway.

Koweit. See KUWAIT.

Kowel. See KOVEL.

Ko·wie \kō-'vē\. Short river, Cape Province, S Rep. of South Africa; flows into Indian Ocean at Port Alfred.

Kow·loon \'kaů-'lün\ *also* **Kau·lun** \'kaů-'lün\ *or* **Kau·lung** \ji-'ō-'lůŋ\. 1 Peninsula. See HONG KONG.

2 Town on W shore of Kowloon Penin., SE China, separated from Victoria on Hong Kong I. by Hong Kong harbor, 1 m. wide at narrowest point; pop. (1971p) 715,440; extends N into leased New Territories (see HONG KONG) and includes Kowloon, **New Kowloon,** and **Kowloon City;** much of area is modern development; connected by rail with Canton; important commercial center. Ceded to British 1860.

Kowno. See KAUNAS.

Koy·u·kuk \'kī-ə-ˌkək\. River, W Alaska; ab. 500 m. long; flows SW from Brooks Range to Yukon river.

Ko·zá·nē *or* **Ko·zá·ni** \kȯ-'zän-ē\. 1 Department of Greece. See table at GREECE.

2 City, its ✻, ab. 67 m. SW of Salonika; pop. (1971p) 23,884; held by Germans Apr. 1941 to Oct. 1944.

Kozhikode. See CALICUT.

Koźle \'kȯzh-(ˌ)lā\; *Ger.* **Co·sel** *or* **Ko·sel** \'kō-zəl\. Town, W Opole prov., SW Poland, on the Odra (Oder) W of Zabrze; pop. (1968e) 13,300; formerly in Germany.

Kozlov. See MICHURINSK.

Kra, Isthmus of \-'krä\. Narrow section in N cen. Malay Penin., in SW Thailand, 10°20′N, 99°E; ab. 40 m. wide at its narrowest part; Pakchan river flows S in the isthmus forming S end of boundary bet. Lower Burma and Thailand; Ranong is Thai port at its mouth; range of hills at narrowest part ab. 2000 ft. high.

Kra·bi \'kräb-ē\. 1 Province, SW Thailand; 1785 sq. m.; pop. (1960c) 93,895; ✻ Krabi.

2 Town, its ✻, a port on W coast of Malay Penin. 40 m. ENE of Phuket; pop. (1960c) 2685.

Krâchéh. See KRATIÉ.

Kra·gerø \'kräg-ə-ˌrər\. Seaport town, Telemark co., S Norway, 40 m. NE of Arendal; pop. (1970e) 10,121; lumber.

Kra·gu·je·vac *or* **Kra·gu·ye·vats** \'kräg-ů-yə-ˌväts\. Town, Serbia, NE Yugoslavia, 60 m. SE of Belgrade; pop. (1965e) 59,000; automobile assembly plant; capital of Serbia 1818–39, and a residence of Serbian princes to 1842; usual meeting place of Serbian legislature 1868–80; captured by Bulgarians and Germans Nov. 1, 1915 in World War I; had iron foundry and ammunition factory and formerly chief arsenal and garrison town of Serbia.

Krain. See CARNIOLA.

Kra·ka·tau \ˌkrak-ə-'taů\ *or* **Kra·ka·toa** \-'tō-ə\ *also* **Kra·ka·tao** \-'taů\; *local Malay name* **Ra·ka·ta** \rə-'kät-ə\. Island volcano in center of Sunda Strait, between Sumatra and Java, Indonesia. Its eruption Aug. 26–28, 1883 was the most violent of modern times. Before the eruption ab. 2620 ft. high; its top blown off by an explosion, which caused tidal wave ab. 50 ft. high, killing 36,000 people in W Java; dust, ashes, and smoke rose to height of ab. 17 m. and the sound of the explosion was heard in İstanbul, Australia,

Philippines, and Japan; atmospherical effects encircling the globe caused strange sunrise and sunset conditions for months afterward; active during 1960's.

Kra·ków *or Eng.* **Cra·cow** \'kräk-ˌaù, 'krak-, 'krāk-, -(ˌ)ō, *Pol.* 'krä-ˌküf\ *or Ger.* **Kra·kau** \'kräk-ˌaù\. 1 Province of S Poland. See table at POLAND.

2 City, its ✻, on Vistula river 156 m. SSW of Warsaw; pop. (1970p) 583,000; metallurgical industries; chemicals, building materials; seat of Polish Academy of Science; univ. (1364), technical univ. (1945), several museums; 14th cent. Gothic cathedral.

History: Polish town, in 10th cent. part of territory under Boleslav I of Bohemia (*q.v.*); captured by Boleslav I of Poland 999; established as capital of Polish kingdom and an hereditary principality by Boleslav III (1102–38); invaded by Mongols 1241; received municipal rights (Magdeburg rights) 1257; made Polish capital by Ladislas I Lokietek 1305 and remained capital to 1609 (see WARSAW3); captured by Swedes 1655, 1702; coronation and burial place of Polish kings to 1764; taken by Austria in Third Partition of Poland 1795; included in Napoleon's grand duchy of Warsaw 1809–15; independent buffer state; republic of Kraków erected 1815; restored to Austria 1846; belonged to independent Poland after World War I; held by Germans in both World War I and II; taken by Russians Jan. 19, 1945.

Kra·len·dijk \'kräl-ən-ˌdīk\. Chief town on Bonaire I., Netherlands Antilles, on W coast; pop. (1960c) 839.

Krá·lic·ká \'kräl-ət-ˌskä\ *or Ger.* **Kra·litz** \'kräl-əts\. Town, Czechoslovakia, just E of Prostějov; here was printed 1579–93 the Kralitz or Brothers' Bible, the most important Bohemian version.

Kraljevina Srba, Hrvata i Slovenaca. See YUGOSLAVIA.

Kra·lje·vo \'kräl yə-ˌvō\. Town, Serbia, E Yugoslavia, at junction of the Ibar with Western Morava river; pop. (1965e) 27,000; railway coaches; 12th cent. Zica and Studenica monasteries; Zica monastery medieval site of coronation of Serbian kings.

Kra·ma·torsk \ˌkräm-ə-'tò(ə)rsk\. City, N Donets Oblast, E Ukrainian S.S.R., U.S.S.R., in cen. Donets Basin on a tributary of the Donets ab. 25 m. W of Artemovsk; pop. (1970p) 151,000; diversified heavy industry, incl. iron, steel, coke, cement, machinery; developed late 19th cent.; held by Germans from 1941 to Sept. 1943.

Kranj \'krīn-yə\. Town, Slovenia, NW Yugoslavia; pop. (1965e) 24,000; optical instruments, footwear.

Krapotkin. See KROPOTKIN.

Kras \'kräs\ *or Ger.* **Karst** \'kärst\ *or Ital.* **Car·so** \'kär-(ˌ)sō\. Mountain plateau, Italy and Yugoslavia, N of Trieste and E of the Isonzo river; battles in World War I: (1) May 1916, and (2) May 1917 in which the Italians were victors over the Austrians (but lost their gains Oct. 1917); since treaty of 1947 greater part in NW Yugoslavia.

Kras·li·ce \'kräs-lət-ˌsä\ *or Ger.* **Gras·litz** \'gräs-ləts\. Town, NW Czech S.R., W Czechoslovakia, ab. 20 m. NNE of Cheb; manufactures musical instruments.

Kraś·nik \'kräsh-nik\. Commune, Lublin prov., E Poland, 28 m. SSW of Lublin; pop. (1968e) 13,900; agriculture; scene of Austrian defeat by Russians Aug. 1914.

Kras·no·ar·meisk \ˌkras-nō-ər-'m(y)āsk\. Town, Donetsk Oblast, Ukrainian S.S.R., U.S.S.R., ab. 30 m. NW of Donetsk; pop. (1969e) 54,000; coal mining.

Kras·no·dar \'kras-nə-ˌdär\ *or formerly* **Eka·te·ri·no·dar** \i-ˌkat-ə-'rē-nə-ˌdär\ *also* **Ye·ka·te·ri·no·dar** \yi-\. City, ✻ of Krasnodar Krai, Russian S.F.S.R., U.S.S.R., 160 m. S of Rostov-na-Donu; pop. (1970p) 465,000; on right bank of Kuban river and on railroad from Rostov-na-Donu to Novorossisk; food processing, oil refining; machine tools; Workers' Scientific Institute, museum, and art gallery. Founded 1794 as a small fort by Empress Catherine II; occupied by Germans Aug. 9, 1942 and retaken Feb. 12, 1943.

Krasnodar Krai \-'krī\. Territory of the Russian S.F.S.R., U.S.S.R., bounded on N by Rostov Oblast, on E by Stavropol Krai and Karachayevo-Cherkess Autonomous Oblast, on SE by Abkhazia A.S.S.R. (in Georgian S.S.R.), on S and SW by Black Sea, and on W by Sea of Azov; 32,278 sq. m.; pop. (1970p) 4,511,000; ✻ Krasnodar; separated from E Crimean Oblast (Kerch Penin.) by Kerch Strait; includes the Adygei Autonomous Oblast and the lower and middle course of the Kuban river. In S contains mountains and foothills of W Caucasus; constituted W part of the former North Caucasus region; much of it is fertile plain with marshland along the Azov shore; crossed by several railroad lines; essentially an agricultural region producing wheat, barley, rice, tobacco, sunflowers, vegetables, and sugar beets; has oil fields, and forests in S; cattle raising also important. Chief towns Sochi, Armavir, Novorossisk. In medieval period under Tatar khanates; came under Russian control for the most part in 19th cent. See NORTH CAUCASUS. Territory created 1937; largely overrun by German armies 1942–43.

Kras·no·don \ˌkras-nə-'dòn\. Town, Voroshilovgrad Oblast, Ukrainian S.S.R., U.S.S.R., ab. 30 m. SE of Voroshilovgrad; pop. (1969e) 67,000; coal.

Kras·no·gorsk \'kras-nō-ˌgòrsk\. Town, Moscow Oblast, Russian S.F.S.R., U.S.S.R., ab. 12 m. W of Moscow; pop. (1969e) 55,000.

Kras·no·grad \'kras-nə-ˌgrad\. Town, Kharkov Oblast, NE Ukrainian S.S.R., U.S.S.R., 55 m. SW of Kharkov; pop. (1967e) 16,000; railroad and highway junction point; recaptured by Russians Feb. 1943.

Krasnogvardeisk. See GATCHINA.

Kras·no·kamsk \'kras-nō-ˌkäm(p)sk\. Town, Perm Oblast, Russian S.F.S.R., U.S.S.R., ab. 20 m. WNW of Perm; pop. (1969e) 54,000; cellulose; formed 1929.

Krasnostav. See KRASNYSTAW.

Kras·no·tu·rinsk \ˌkras-nō-tùr-'insk, -'ēnsk\. Town, Sverdlovsk Oblast, Russian S.F.S.R., U.S.S.R., ab. 15 m. NW of Serov; pop. (1969e) 61,000; aluminum.

Kras·nou·fimsk \ˌkras-nō-ü-'fēm(p)sk\. Town, Sverdlovsk Oblast, Russian S.F.S.R., U.S.S.R., ab. 110 m. WSW of Sverdlovsk; pop. (1967e) 40,000; machinery; food processing.

Kras·no·u·ralsk \ˌkras-nō-yù-'ralsk\. Town, W Sverdlovsk Oblast, Russian S.F.S.R., U.S.S.R., 45 m. N of Sverdlovsk; pop. (1967e) 40,000; industrial town on E slope of Ural Mts.

Kras·no·vodsk \ˌkras-nə-'vòtsk\. Seaport town on **Krasnovodsk Gulf,** NW Turkmen S.S.R., U.S.S.R.; pop. (1970p) 64,800; across Caspian Sea from Baku; railroad terminus; exports cotton, fish, and petroleum products; dates from a fort built in 1717.

Kras·no·yarsk \ˌkras-nə-'yärsk\. Town, ✻ of Krasnoyarsk Krai, Russian S.F.S.R., U.S.S.R., on left bank of upper Yenisei river and on Trans-Siberian R.R., 420 m. E of Novosibirsk; pop. (1967e) 576,000; commercial and hydroelectric power center; metalworking, shipbuilding; heavy machinery, cement, lumber. Founded as a fort by Cossacks 1628; in later 17th cent. frequently attacked by Tatars and Kirghiz.

Krasnoyarsk Krai \-'krī\. A territory of the Russian S.F.S.R., U.S.S.R., bounded on N by Arctic Ocean (Laptev and Kara seas), on E by Yakutsk A.S.S.R. and Irkutsk Oblast, on S by Tuva A.S.S.R., and on W by Kemerovo and Tomsk oblasts and the Khanty-Mansi and Yamalo-Nenets national okrugs; 927,258 sq. m.; pop. (1970p) 2,962,000; ✻ Krasnoyarsk. Includes Taimyr and Evenki national okrugs and Taimyr peninsula. In SW includes Khakass Autonomous Oblast which is politically independent; includes Yenisei river and the greater part of the valleys of its tributaries (see TUNGUSKA), and also the Khatanga (in Taimyr National Okrug); largely tundra in the Taimyr and lower Yenisei region, hilly in cen. part, and quite mountainous in S, containing foothills of Sayan Mts. Crossed by the Trans-Siberian R.R., passing through Achinsk and Krasnoyarsk, also by a parallel trunk line farther S, reaching the rich mining and agricultural lands about Minusinsk. Great mineral wealth (gold, nickel, copper, iron ore, uranium, antimony, and bauxite); timber working. Chief towns Krasnoyarsk, Norilsk, Kansk, Chernogorsk. Colonized by Russians from middle of 17th cent. but developed slowly; long a place of exile; after completion of Trans-Siberian R.R. (1891–98) from Moscow to Vladivostok, marked by rapid growth; originally part of West Siberia Region, made subdivision of Russian S.F.S.R. 1934.

Kras·no·ye Se·lo \ˈkras-nə-yə-shə-ˈlō\. Town, Leningrad Oblast, Russian S.F.S.R., U.S.S.R., just SSW of Leningrad and N of Gatchina; pop. (1967e) 22,000; taken by Germans in assault on Leningrad Sept. 4, 1941.

Krasny. See KYZYL.

Kras·ny Luch \ˌkras-nē-ˈlüch\. City, Voroshilovgrad Oblast, Ukrainian S.S.R., U.S.S.R., in the Donets Basin; pop. (1970p) 102,000; coal mining.

Kras·ny·staw \kräs-ˈnis-ˌtäf\ *or Russ.* **Kras·no·stav** \ˌkräs-nə-ˈstäf, -ˈstäv\. Commune, Lublin dept., Poland, 32 m. SE of Lublin; pop. (1968e) 12,100; captured by Russians in battle, July 18, 1915.

Krasny Su·lin \ˌkras-nē-sül-ˈēn\. Town, Rostov Oblast, Russian S.F.S.R., U.S.S.R., ab. 15 m. NNW of Shakhty; pop. (1967e) 41,000.

Kra·tie \krä-ˈtyā\ *or* **Krâ·chéh** \krä-ˈchā\. Commercial town on the Mekong, E Cambodia, SE Asia, 105 m. NE of Pnompenh; pop. (1962p) 11,908.

Kra·wang \krä-ˈwäŋ\. Town, West Java prov., Indonesia, on railroad 35 m. ESE of Djakarta; pop. (1958e) 66,596.

Kre·feld \ˈkrā-ˌfelt\ *or formerly* **Krefeld–Uer·ding·en** \-ˈu̇rd-iŋ-ən\. City, W North Rhine-Westphalia, West Germany, on Rhine river 19 m. WSW of Essen; pop. (1969e) 226,795; machinery, clothing, textiles, silk, railway equipment; printing, dyeing; 13th cent. castle; granted city charter 1373; to Prussia 1702; bombed in World War II.

Kre·men·chug \ˌkrem-ən-ˈchük, -ˈchüg\. City, S Poltava Oblast, E cen. Ukrainian S.S.R., U.S.S.R., on the Dnieper 160 m. SE of Kiev; pop. (1970p) 148,000; hydroelectric power station; steel castings, agricultural machinery, flour, tobacco products; has rail connections N to Moscow and Kharkov and S across the Dnieper with Kirovograd by a long tubular bridge; many churches. Founded 1571; capital of New Russia 1765–89; in the Revolution and succeeding civil war 1917–21, suffered much damage; in World War II seized by Germans Sept. 1941 but retaken in great Soviet drive Sept.–Dec. 1943.

Kre·me·nets \ˌkrem-ə-ˈnets\ *or Pol.* **Krze·mie·niec** \kə-shem-ˈyen-yets\. City, W Ukrainian S.S.R., U.S.S.R., 47 m. SSE of Lutsk; pop. (1967e) 20,000; formerly in Poland; trades in grain. Formerly site of a famous lyceum (transferred 1833 to Kiev and combined with university there).

Krem·lin–Bi·cê·tre \krem-ˌlaⁿ-bē-ˈsetrᵊ\. Commune, Val-de-Marne dept., N France, S suburb of Paris; pop. (1968c) 20,798.

Krem·ni·ca \ˈkrem-nət-ˌsä\ *or Ger.* **Krem·nitz** \ˈkrem-nəts\ *or Hung.* **Kör·mōcz·bá·nya** \ˌkər-mərts-ˈbän-(ˌ)yȯ\. Commune, Slovak S.R., E cen. Czechoslovakia, NW of Zvolen; pop. (1961e) 5300; leather goods; formerly produced much gold and silver; belonged to Hungary until 1920.

Krems \ˈkrem(p)s, ˈkremz\ *or* **Krems an der Do·nau** \-än-dər-ˈdō-ˌnau̇\. City, Lower Austria, on Danube river 38 m. WNW of Vienna; pop. (1961c) 21,408; machinery, metal goods; active trade in wine and fruit; first mentioned 995.

Kremsier. See KROMĚŘÍŽ.

Krētikòn Pélagos. See CRETE, SEA OF.

Kreuzburg *or* **Kreuzburg in Oberschlesien.** See KLUCZBORK.

Kreuz·ling·en \ˈkrȯit-sliŋ-ən\. Commune, Thurgau canton, NE Switzerland, near W end of Lake Constance, adjoining Konstanz; pop. (1970c) 15,760; church (1650–53; destroyed by fire 1962, since rebuilt).

Kreuz·nach \ˈkrȯits-ˌnäk\ *or* **Bad Kreuznach** \ˈbät-\. City, Rhineland-Palatinate, West Germany, on Nahe river; pop. (1969e) 44,139; mineral springs; health resort; trades in wine.

Kreuz·tal \ˈkrȯit-stäl\. City, North Rhine-Westphalia, West Germany, 41 m. E of Cologne; pop. (1969e) 27,444; made city 1969.

Kri·bi \ˈkrē-bē\. Port, Cameroon, W Africa, on the Bight of Biafra 80 m. S of Douala.

Kri·lov, Cape \-ˈkrē-ləf, -ˌlȯv, -ˌlȯf\ *or Jap.* **Cape Ni·shi No·to·ro** \-ˌnish-ē-ˈnō-tə-ˌrō\. Cape on SW extremity of Karafuto, Sakhalin I., Russian S.F.S.R., U.S.S.R., opp. N tip of Hokkaidō, Japan.

Krimmitschau. See CRIMMITSCHAU.

Krimm·ler Falls \ˌkrim-lər-\. Falls in **Krimmler River,** an upper tributary of the Salzach flowing N from the Hohe Tauern, SW Austria; in three parts with total drop of 1250 ft.

Krio, Cape \-krē-ˈō\. 1 *or* **Cape Kri·ós** \-krē-ˈós\ *or Gk.* **Kri·oú Me·to·pon** \krē-ˈü-ˈmet-ə-ˌpȯn\. Southwest point of the island of Crete, E Mediterranean Sea.

2 Cape at W end of long narrow peninsula on SW coast of Turkey in Asia, S of Bodrum Penin.; site of ancient Cnidus.

Krish·na \ˈkrish-nə\ *or formerly* **Kist·na** \ˈkis(t)-nə\. River of the Deccan, S India; ab. 800 m. long; rises near Mahabaleshwar in Maharashtra in the Western Ghats within 40 m. of the Arabian Sea, flows SSE into Mysore, continues E, flowing into Andhra Pradesh, then flows NE and SE into Bay of Bengal through several mouths S of Maghilipatnam.

Krish·na·gar \ˈkrish-nə-gər\. Town, West Bengal, NE India, on Hooghly river 58 m. N of Calcutta; pop. (1961c) 70,440; horticultural research station; contains former residence of the maharajas of Nabadwip.

Kristiania. See OSLO.

Kris·tian·sand *or* **Chris·tian·sand** \ˈkris(h)-chən-ˌsan(d)\. Seaport, ⊗ of Vest-Agder co., SW Norway, on the Skagerrak SW of Oslo; pop. (1970e) 56,152; large ice-free port; shipbuilding, metalworking; lumber, wood pulp, chemicals; 11th cent. church; 17th cent. Gothic cathedral; has resort beaches. Founded 1641; in World War II captured by Germans Apr. 9, 1940 after brief resistance in which German cruiser *Karlsruhe* was sunk.

Kris·tian·stad \ˈkris(h)-chən-ˌstad, kri-ˈshan-(ˌ)stä\. 1 County of S Sweden. See table at SWEDEN.

2 Seaport, its ⊗; pop. (1970e) 42,819; trade center in agricultural region; flour mills, slaughterhouses; food processing; textiles; 17th cent. church. Founded 1614 by Christian IV of Denmark; ceded to Sweden 1658; captured by Danes 1676, recaptured by Swedes 1678.

Kris·tian·sund *or* **Chris·tian·sund** \ˈkris(h)-chən-ˌsu̇n(d)\. Seaport, Møre og Romsdal co., W Norway, WSW of Trondheim; pop. (1970e) 18,621; built on three small islands enclosing a harbor; base of large trawler fleet; exports fish; shipbuilding yards; inhabited in prehistoric times; incorporated 1742.

Kris·ti·ne·hamn \ˌkris-tēn-ə-ˈham-ən\. Lake port, Värmland co., SW Sweden, on Lake Vänern; pop. (1970e) 22,018; machine factories; founded 1642.

Krithia. See KIRTE.

Kríti. See CRETE 3.

Kri·voi Rog \ˌkriv-ȯi-ˈrōg, -ˈrȯk\. City, W Dnepropetrovsk Oblast, SE cen. Ukrainian S.S.R., U.S.S.R., 80 m. SW of Dnepropetrovsk; pop. (1970p) 573,000; railroad and industrial city, located in midst of rich iron mines and on W edge of the Donets Basin, a major coal-producing region; metallurgical plants, foundries, mills, and chemical works; coke, cement, mining and drilling machinery. Village founded 17th cent.; rapid expansion followed exploitation of high-grade iron ore deposits beginning 1881–1884; city and mines seized by Germans 1941; retaken by U.S.S.R. Feb. 22, 1944.

Krk \'kərk\ *or Ital.* **Ve·glia** \'vel-(ˌ)yä\. **1** Island at head of the Adriatic Sea, Croatia, NW Yugoslavia; 157 sq. m.; pop. (1961c) 14,548; highly fertile; producing wine, olives, and figs.

2 Town on S coast of island; pop. (1961c) 1280; 11th cent. cathedral; settled by Greeks, and successively under rule of Rome, Croatia, Venice, Austria 1797–1809, France 1809–13, Austria again 1813–1918; to Yugoslavia 1920.

Kr·ka \'kər-kə\ *or* **Ker·ka** \'ker-, 'kər-\ *or anc.* **Ti·ti·us** \'tish-əs, -ē-əs\. River, Bosnia and Herzegovina, W Yugoslavia; 46 m. long; flows S into Adriatic Sea a little below Šibenik; has a long, wide estuary and is noted for several waterfalls bet. Knin and Šibenik.

Krknoše. See RIESENGEBIRGE.

Kr·nov \'kər-ˌnȯf\ *or Ger.* **Jä·gern·dorf** \'yā-gərn-ˌdȯrf\. Town, Czech S.R., N cen. Czechoslovakia, 30 m. NW of Ostrava; pop. (1968e) 22,854; textile mills.

Kroja. See KRUJË.

Kro·le·vets \krə-'lā-vəts\. Town, Sumy Oblast, Ukrainian S.S.R., U.S.S.R., ab. 23 m. N of Konotop; pop. (1967e) 16,000.

Kro·mě·říž \'krȯ-myər-ˌzhēsh\ *or Ger.* **Krem·sier** \'krem-ˌzi(ə)r\. Town, Czech S.R., cen. Czechoslovakia, on Morava river 35 m. E of Brno; pop. (1968e) 21,724; industrial and commercial center; meeting place of Austrian Reichstag 1848–49.

Kro·no·berg \'krü-nü-ˌbar\. County of S Sweden. See table at SWEDEN.

Kro·nots·ka·ya Sop·ka \krə-ˌnȯt-skə-yə-'sȯp-kə\. Volcano (*sopka*), in Eastern Range, Kamchatka Penin., Khabarovsk Krai, Russian S.F.S.R., U.S.S.R.; 15,580 ft.

Kro·nots·ki, Cape \-krə-'nȯt-skē\. Point extending into Bering Sea, E coast of Kamchatka Penin., Russian S.F.S.R., U.S.S.R., at 54°45′N, 162°07′E.

Kron·shlot \'krȯn-ˌshlət\; *formerly* **Kron·stadt** *or* **Cron·stadt** \'krōn-ˌstat, krän-'s(h)tät\. Fortress on Kotlin I., E end of Gulf of Finland, NW Leningrad Oblast, Russian S.F.S.R., U.S.S.R., ab. 25 m. W of Leningrad. Island seized by Peter the Great 1703 and fortress founded 1710; has large harbor but blocked by ice for ab. 5 months yearly; was strong defense point for Russian Empire and is now most important Soviet naval station; important commercial harbor before deep channel to Leningrad constructed 1875–85; scene of mutinies 1825, 1882, 1905; took active part in Revolution of 1917; in 1921 navy mutiny against Soviets was vigorously suppressed; its fortifications played important role during siege of Leningrad 1941–44.

Kronstadt. **1** City, Romania. See BRAŞOV 2.

2 Fortress, U.S.S.R. See KRONSHLOT.

Kroon·stad \'krōn-ˌstat\. Town, N Orange Free State, E cen. Rep. of South Africa, 120 m. NE of Bloemfontein; pop. (1967e) 50,700; center of rich farm district; railroad junction; clothing factory; popular resort.

Kro·pot·kin *or formerly* **Kra·pot·kin** \krə-'pät-kən\. Town, E Krasnodar Krai, Russian S.F.S.R., U.S.S.R., on Kuban river 80 m. ENE of Krasnodar; pop. (1970p) 64,000; railroad junction; a center for grain trade; flour mills, elevators, machine factories.

Kros·no \'krȯs-(ˌ)nō\. Commune, Rzeszów prov., SE Poland; pop. (1970p) 26,600; glass; petroleum and natural-gas industries.

Kro·to·szyn *or Ger.* **Kro·to·schin** \krə-'tȯ-shən\. Commune, Poznań prov., W cen. Poland, 50 m. SSE of Poznań; pop. (1970p) 22,000; machinery, cement. Legendary residence of first Piast ruler.

Kroub, El. See EL KHROUB.

Kru Coast \'krü-\. That section of the SE coast of Liberia NW of Cape Palmas inhabited by Krumen.

Kru·ger National Park \'krü-gər-\. Park and game reserve, E Transvaal, NE Rep. of South Africa, on Mozambique frontier; crossed by Olifants river; 200 m. long by 40 m. wide, 8000 sq. m.; has large numbers of wild animals native to South Africa. Established 1926 by Act of Parliament; had its origin in President Kruger's game sanctuary established 1898, then known as the Sabi reserve and including country bet. Limpopo and Sabi rivers.

Kru·gers·dorp \'krü-gərz-ˌdȯrp\. Town, S Transvaal, NE Rep. of South Africa, 20 m. W of Johannesburg; pop. (1967e) 100,500; in manganese and gold mine region. Founded 1887; separated from Randfontein 1929. The Pardekraal monument, commemorative of victory of Boers over Zulu chieftain Dingaan, Dec. 16, 1838, is object of annual pilgrimage.

Kru·jë *also* **Kro·ja** \'krü-yə\ *or Ital.* **Cro·ia** \'krȯ-(ˌ)yä\.
1 Province of W Albania. See table at ALBANIA.

2 Town, its ✱; pop. (1967e) 7195; brick, cement.

Krung Thep. See BANGKOK.

Kru·še·vac \'krü-shə-ˌväts\. Town, Serbia, E Yugoslavia, on Western Morava river ab. 95 m. SE of Belgrade; pop. (1965e) 33,000; market town in agricultural and cattle-raising region. Capital of Serbia 1839–42; occupied by Germans 1941.

Krušnéhory. See ERZGEBIRGE.

Kru·zof \'krü-ˌzȯf\. Small island in Alexander Archipelago, SE Alaska, W of Baranof I. and opp. Sitka; Mt. Edgecumbe at its S end.

Krym. See CRIMEAN OBLAST.

Krymsk \'krim(p)sk\ *or formerly* **Krym·ska·ya Sta·nit·sa** \'krim(p)-skī-ə-'stän-it-sə\. Town, Krasnodar Krai, Russian S.F.S.R., U.S.S.R., ab. 50 m. WSW of Krasnodar; pop. (1967e) 40,000.

Krzemieniec. See KREMENETS.

Ksour Mountains \'(k)sü(ə)r-\. Range of the Atlas Mts. in N Saoura dept., NW Algeria.

Ksto·vo \kə-'stȯ-və\. Town, Gorki Oblast, Russian S.F.S.R., U.S.S.R., ab. 10 m. SE of Gorki; pop. (1967e) 43,000.

Ktaadn, Mount. See KATAHDIN, MOUNT.

Kti·ma \kə-'tē-mə\ *or Turk.* **Ka·sa·ba** \kə-'säb-ə, ˌkä-sə-'bä\ *or Gk.* **Ktē·ma** \kə-'tā-mə\. Town, W Cyprus, near the coast and just N of site of ancient Paphos.

K2. See GODWIN AUSTEN.

Kua·la Kang·sar \ˌkwäl-ə-'kaŋ-sər, kü-'äl-\. Town, N cen. Perak state, Malaysia, on Perak river and W coast railroad.

Kuala Ku·bu Bha·ru \-ˌkü-bü-'bär-(ˌ)ü\ *or* **Kuala Kubu Ba·ha·ru** \-bə-'här-(ˌ)ü\. Town, NE Selangor state, W Malaysia, on main railroad line 25 m. N of Kuala Lumpur; starting point of highway NE to Pahang state.

Kuala Li·pis \-'lē-pəs\. Town, ✱ of Pahang state, in NW cen. Malaysia, on the central and E coast railroad of Malay Penin. ab. 75 m. N of Kuala Lumpur; pop. (1957c) 8753.

Kuala Lum·pur \-'lüm-ˌpü(ə)r, -'ləm-\. City, ✱ of Malaysia, on main W coast railroad line ab. 200 m. NW of Singapore (246 m. by rail); pop. (1970p) 451,728; the most important Malay city on the peninsula; commercial center; tin mines and rubber plantations in surrounding districts; univ. (1959). Founded as tin-mining camp 1857; became capital of Selangor 1880; underwent rebuilding and rapid expansion after 1882; capital of Federated Malay States 1895; occupied by Japanese in World War II 1942–45; made capital of Malaya 1957 and of Malaysia 1963.

Kua–la–man–ta–t'a \'kwä-lä-män-'tä-tä\ *or* **Gur·la Man·dha·ta** \ˌgür-lə-mänd-'hät-ə\. Peak in the Himalayas, in SW Tibet, China, near border of Nepal; 25,355 ft.

Kuala Pi·lah \-'pē-(ˌ)lä\. Town, cen. Negri Sembilan state, Malaysia.

Kuala Se·lang·or \-sə-'läŋ-ˌȯ(ə)r\. Coastal town on Strait of Malacca, NW Selangor state, Malaysia; fishing center.

Kuala Treng·ga·nu \-treŋ-'gän-(ˌ)ü\ *or* **Kuala Te·reng·ga·nu** \-tə-reŋ-'gän-(ˌ)ü\. Town, ✱ of Trengganu state, Malaysia, in NE part, at mouth of Trengganu river; pop. (1970p) 53,353.

Kuang–chou. See CANTON.

Kuang–hua \'kwäŋ-'wä\ *or* **Lao·ho·kow** \'lau̇-'hō-'kō\. City, N Hupeh prov., E cen. China, ab. 200 m. NW of Hankow; in World War II American air base, scene of considerable fighting in 1945.

Kuang–te *also* **Kwang·teh** \'gwäŋ-'də\. Town, SE Anhwei prov., E China, ab. 65 m. NW of Hangchow; an important transportation center and scene of considerable fighting in World War II, esp. in 1943.

Kuan·tan \'kwän-ˌtän\. Coastal town, ✱ of Pahang state, Malaysia, N of the mouth of the Pahang river; pop. (1970p) 43,391; harbor at river mouth and was a key point on E coast seized by Japanese in their invasion of Malay Penin. Dec. 1941–Jan. 1942. British warships *Prince of Wales* and *Repulse* lost in naval battle Dec. 10, 1941 off this coast.

Ku·ba \ku̇-'bä\. Town, NE Azerbaijan S.S.R., U.S.S.R., on E slopes of Caucasus Mts. 95 m. NW of Baku; pop. (1967e) 18,000; silk goods, carpets.

Ku·ban \kü-'ban, -'bän\. 1 *or anc.* **Hyp·a·nis** \'hip-ə-nəs\. River in region NW of Caucasus Mts., SE Russian S.F.S.R., U.S.S.R.; 584 m. long; rises in the Caucasus in Georgian S.S.R., flows N and NW into a wide marshy delta with three mouths—two on the Sea of Azov and one on the Black Sea; navigable for less than 150 m.; its main headstream rises on slopes of Mt. Elbrus.

2 Former government of SE Russia, NE of the Black Sea; since the Revolution has been reorganized into Krasnodar Krai and several autonomous oblasts.

Kubango. See OKAVANGO.

Ku·ben·sko·ye, Lake \-ˌkü-bən-skə-yə\. Lake, W cen. Vologda Oblast, Russian S.F.S.R., U.S.S.R.; ab. 40 m. long; outlet the Sukhona river, a tributary of the Northern Dvina.

Ku·cha *or Chin.* **K'u–ch'e** \'kü-'chə\. Town and oasis, W cen. Sinkiang Uighur, W China, S of Tien Shan range on early Silk Road (*q.v.*) and midway bet. Aksu and Karashahr on modern caravan and motor highway; an old city, apparently an early Aryan colony; praised by travelers for its wealth and productiveness; in medieval times under the Uigurs.

Kuchan. See QUCHAN.

Kuchengtze. See CH'I-T'AI.

Ku·ching \'kü-chiŋ\ *or formerly* **Sa·ra·wak** \sə-'rä-(ˌ)wä(k), -ˌwak\. Seaport, ✱ of Sarawak, East Malaysia, on Sarawak river ab. 10 m. from its mouth; pop. (1970p) 63,491; trade center; founded 1839.

Kuchuk Kainarji. See KAYNARDZHA.

Küçük Menderes. See MENDERES 2.

Ku·da·ma·tsu \ˌku̇d-ə-'mät-(ˌ)sü\. City, Yamaguchi prefecture, SW Honshū, Japan, 53 m. E of Shimonosek on N shore of Inland Sea; pop. (1970c) 49,627.

Ku·dat \'kü-ˌdät\. Town, N Sabah, East Malaysia, on W side of Marudu Bay near N tip of island of Borneo.

Ku·dus *or Du.* **Koe·does** \'kü-ˌdüs\. Town, Central Java prov., Indonesia; pop. (1961c) 74,911.

Ku·dym·kar *or* **Ku·dim·kar** \kü-'dim-kər\. Town, ✱ of Komi-Permiak National Okrug, Russian S.F.S.R., U.S.S.R., on a tributary of the Kama river 100 m. NW of Perm; pop. (1967e) 70,000.

Kuei *or* **Kwei** \'gwā\ *or* **Kuei Chiang** \-chē-'äŋ\. River, E Kwangsi Chuang, S China; ab. 200 m. long; flows S to join the Hsi at Wu-chou.

Kuei–lin *or* **Kwei·lin** \'gwā-'lin\. City, NE Kwangsi Chuang, SE China, on right bank of Kuei river 235 m. NW of Canton; pop. (1970e) 235,000; former capital of Kwangsi Chuang; an old city dating back to Sui dynasty (c. 589 A.D.); has trade connections by river with Wu-chou and Canton; exports silk, skins. In World War II again made capital and developed 1944 – 45 as American air base; attacked by Japanese Sept. 1944; abandoned by U.S. Air Force Sept. 17 and destroyed Oct. 28; retaken July 27, 1945 after a six-week battle.

Kuei–p'ing *or* **Kwei·ping** \'gwā-'piŋ\. Town, E Kwangsi Chuang, SE China, 23°24′N, 110°05′E; here the Hung-shui and the Hsiang rivers unite to form the Hsi.

Kuei–yang *or* **Kwei·yang** \'gwā-'yäŋ\ *or formerly* **Kwei·chu** \-'jü\. City, ✱ of Kweichow prov., S China, 220 m. S of Chungking ab. halfway on highway bet. K'un-ming and Chungking; pop. (1970e) 1,500,000; on plateau at 3400 ft. elevation; administrative and transportation center of the province. In World War II developed as an American air base.

Kuenlun Shan. See KUNLUN SHAN.

K'u–erh–lo \'kü-'er-'lō\ *also* **Kur·la** \'ku̇r-lə\. Town, cen. Sinkiang Uighur, W China.

Kufa, Al–. See AL-KUFA.

Kufara. See AL-KUFRAH.

Kufow. See CH'Ü-FOU.

Kufra. See AL-KUFRAH.

Kuft. See QIFT.

Kuh. See KOH 1.

Kūh–e Taftān *or* **Kuh–i–Taftan.** See TAFTĀN, KŪH-E-.

Kuh–i–Alwand. See ALWAND, MOUNT.

Kui·by·shev *or* **Kuy·by·shev** \'kwē-bə-ˌshef, 'kü-ē-bə-, -ˌshev\. 1 Town, W Novosibirsk Oblast, Russian S.F.S.R., U.S.S.R., just N of the Trans-Siberian R.R. 190 m. W of Novosibirsk; pop. (1967e) 40,000.

2 *or before 1935* **Sa·mara** \sə-'mär-ə\. City and river port, ✱ of Kuibyshev Oblast, Russian S.F.S.R., U.S.S.R., on left bank of Volga at loop where it reaches farthest point E and where Samara river joins it, 550 m. SE of Moscow; pop. (1970p) 1,047,000; machine tools, cables, bearings, railway equipment; flour milling, shipbuilding, oil refining, food processing, brewing; univ. (1919); a trading center since end of 18th cent. with the Kirgiz Steppe region and cities of Turkistan. Established 1586; scene of Pugachev's rebellion against Catherine II 1773–74; in World War II became temporary capital of U.S.S.R. Oct. 16, 1941 when Moscow was threatened by German advance.

Kuibyshevka. See BELOGORSK.

Kuibyshev Oblast \-'ō-bləst, -ˌblast\. Subdivision of the Russian S.F.S.R., U.S.S.R., at bend of middle Volga; 20,695 sq. m.; pop. (1970p) 2,752,000; ✱ Kuibyshev; traversed by the Volga which here makes great bend to the E; tableland region W of river, flat steppes to E; wheat, corn, sunflowers; oil and natural gas, sulfur, phosphorite; engineering and petrochemical industries; chief cities Kuibyshev, Syzran, and Chapayevsk.

Ku·iu \'kü-(ˌ)yü\. Island, SE Alaska, W of Kupreanof I. and separated from Baranof I. by Chatham Strait.

Ku·jū \'kü-ˌjü\ *or* **Ku·ju·san** \-'sän\. Mountain, Ōita prefecture, NE Kyūshū, Japan; 5861 ft.

Ku·kës \'kük-əs\ *also* **Kuk·si** \'ku̇k-sē\. 1 Province of NE Albania. See table at ALBANIA.

2 Town, its ✱, on Drin river 25 m. E of Pukë; pop. (1967e) 4795.

Kukong. See SHAO-KUAN.

Kukukhoto. See HUHEHOT.

Ku·kum \'kü-kəm\. Village on NW coast of Guadalcanal I., SE Solomon Is., W Pacific, just W of Lunga Point; used 1942 by Japanese as landing base, then by Americans as naval operating base.

Ku·la \ku̇-'lä\. Town, Manisa prov., W Turkey, ab. 15 m. N of Alaşehir; rugmaking.

Kula Gulf \ˌkü-lə-\. Body of water, bet. NW New Georgia I. and Kolombangara I. in the Solomon Is.; 17 m. long, ab. 10 m. wide; closed by small Arundel I. at SW. Scene of two Japanese-American naval engagements July 5 and 13, 1943, both victories for Americans.

Kula Kan·gri \kü-ˌlä-kän-'grē\. Mountain in the Himalayas, on Bhutan-Tibet boundary; 24,784 ft.

Ku·la·ma·dau \ˌkül-ə-ˈmä-(ˌ)dau̇\. Village, port of Bonagai and chief settlement on Woodlark I. (*q.v.*) in Solomon Sea.
Ku–lang \ˈkü-ˈläŋ\. See AMOY.
Kul·dja *or* **Kul·ja** \ˈku̇l-jə\ *or Chin.* **I–ning** \ˈē-ˈniŋ\ *or formerly* **Ning·yuan** \ˈnīŋ-yə-ˈwän\. Town, NW Sinkiang Uighur, W China, 320 m. W of Urumchi; pop. (1970e) 160,000; in mountain region bet. the Tien Shan and the Ala Tau ranges; chief crops cereals; formerly an important trade center and still connected by routes to Issyk-Kul and Alma Ata in U.S.S.R. Seized by Russia in 1871, but restored by treaty 1881.
Ku·le·ba·ki \ˌkül-(y)ə-ˈbäk-ē\. Town, Gorki Oblast, Russian S.F.S.R., U.S.S.R., ab. 85 m. SW of Gorki; pop. (1967e) 46,000; furniture.
Külek Boğazi. See CILICIAN GATES.
Ku·li·ko·vo \ˌku̇l-i-ˈkȯ-və\. Plain in E Tula Oblast, Russian S.F.S.R., U.S.S.R., near source of the Don; battle Sept. 8, 1380 in which Dimitri Donskoi and Russian princes decisively defeated the Tatars.
Kulja. See KULDJA.
Kulm. See CHEŁMNO.
Kulm·bach \ˈku̇lm-ˌbäk\. City, Bavaria, West Germany, on Main river 13 m. NNW of Bayreuth; pop. (1969e) 22,774; brewing; 15th cent. Gothic church, 17th cent. Baroque monastery; 13th cent. Plassenburg (Hohenzollern fort) overlooks city; first mentioned 966 A.D.; passed to Prussia 1791, to Bavaria 1810.
Kulmsee. See CHEŁMŻA.
Kulpa. See KUPA.
Kulp·mont \ˈkəlp-ˌmänt\. Borough, Northumberland co., E cen. Pennsylvania, 17 m. WNW of Pottsville; pop. (1970c) 4026; coal mining.
Kultepe. See KANISH.
Ku·lu \ˈkü-(ˌ)lü\. Valley, Himachal Pradesh, N India, in Himalayas SE of Chamba; forms mountain basin of upper Beas river; chief town Sultanpur (alt. 4584 ft.); higher villages at 9000 ft.; in ancient times a Rajput principality.
Kulun. See ULAN BATOR.
Ku·lyab \ku̇l-ˈyab\. Town, SW Tadzhik S.S.R., U.S.S.R., in mountains N of the Amu Darya; pop. (1967e) 33,000.
Kum. Province and city, Iran. See QOM.
Kŭm \ˈku̇m\ *or formerly* **Kin** \ˈkēn\. River, South Korea; 247 m. long; flows SW into the Yellow Sea.
Ku·ma \ku̇-ˈmä\. River, rises in Caucasus Mts., SE Russian S.F.S.R., U.S.S.R.; ab. 360 m. long; flows E to the Caspian Sea, reaching the sea only in flood season.
Ku·ma·ga·ya \ku̇-ˈmäg-ə-yə, ˌku̇m-ə-ˈgī-ə\. Town, Saitama prefecture, SE cen. Honshū, Japan, 35 m. NW of Tokyo; pop. (1970c) 120,841.
Ku·ma·mo·to \ˌküm-ə-ˈmōt-(ˌ)ō\. **1** Prefecture, Kyūshū, Japan; 2848 sq. m.; pop. (1970c) 1,700,229; ✻ Kumamoto; rice, tobacco; forestry, fishing.
2 City, its ✻, on Shira river near its mouth on the W coast and in an extensive plain; pop. (1970c) 440,020; market center for agricultural region; food processing; textiles, chemicals; founded in late 16th cent. at time of building of its great castle; confiscated 1632 and given to the daimio Hosokawa, whose family retained town and castle until 1868. During feudal period the castle was one of strongest in all Japan; partly destroyed 1877. Town has a Buddhist temple that attracts many pilgrims.
Ku·ma·no Sea \ku-ˌmän-ō-\. Inlet of W Pacific Ocean on S coast of Honshū, Japan, SW of Enshu Bight.
Ku·ma·no·vo \ˈkü-mə-nə-ˌvō\. Town, Macedonia, S Yugoslavia, 15 m. NE of Skopje; pop. (1965e) 38,000; trade center, esp. in fruits, liquor, and cattle; battlefield 1912 where Serbians defeated the Turks; occupied 1941 by Bulgarians.
Kumara. See HU-MA-ERH HO.
Ku·ma·si \kü-ˈmäs-ē, -ˈmas-\ *or formerly* **Coo·mas·sie** \-ˈmas-\. City, ✻ of Ashanti Region, Ghana, W Africa, ab. 115 m. NW of Accra; pop. (1970p) 234,274; connected by rail with Accra and Takoradi; commercial center; market town for cocoa-producing region; diversified handicrafts; univ. (1961). Capital of tribe which in 18th cent. became leading Ashanti people and established Ashanti confederation or kingdom (see ASHANTI); entered by British under Wolseley 1874 during Second Ashanti War; captured by Sir Francis Scott 1896 in Fourth Ashanti War; as capital of British protectorate, besieged by natives in rising Apr.–July 1900.
Kum·ba·ko·nam \ˌku̇m-bə-ˈkō-nəm\ *or* **Com·ba·co·num** \ˌkäm-bə-ˈkō-nəm\. City, SE Tamil Nadu, S India, 190 m. SE of Madras; pop. (1961c) 92,600; has brass and silk industries; a stronghold of Brahmanism, one of southern India's most famed temple cities with splendid pagodas, gopuras, and tanks; every twelve years scene of Mahamakan festival held in the temple lake, attended by thousands of pilgrims. Once a capital of the Chola kingdom.
Ku·me \ˈku̇m-(ˌ)ā\. Small island of Okinawa group, S Ryukyu Is., Japan, ab. 55 m. W of Naha; seized by U.S. forces June 1945 in Okinawa campaign.
Kŭm·gang Mountains \ˌku̇m-ˌgäŋ-\ *also* **Di·a·mond Mountains** \ˌdī-(ə-)mənd-\ *or Jap.* **Kon·go·san** \ˌkōn-gō-ˈsän\. Group of mountain peaks along cen. part of E coast of North Korea, S of Wŏnsan, covering area of ab. 75 sq. m.; highest point 5373 ft.; remarkable for geological formation with many beautiful scenic wonders; even more notable as center of Buddhist religion for centuries, with temples, cloisters, colossal Buddha images, etc. In early Korean legend, the land of "twelve thousand peaks"; probably first visited by Buddhist priests in 4th cent. A.D. but after 16th cent. declined under persecution.
Kumilla. See COMILLA.
Kum Ka·le \ˌküm-kä-ˈlā\. Turkish fort on S side of Dardanelles at its W end, Turkey in Asia; scene of action in World War I when its guns were silenced by British fleet and landings made by French Apr. 1915.
Ku·mo \ˈkü-(ˌ)mō\. Town, North-Eastern State, Nigeria; pop. (1969e) 75,238.
Ku·mon Range \ˌkü-ˌmōn-\. Mountain range in N Burma; source of Chindwin river.
Ku·mu·ka·hi, Cape \-ˌkü-mü-ˈkä-(ˌ)hē\. Cape on E extremity of Hawaii I., Hawaii.
Ku·na Peak \ˌkü-nə-\. Mountain in Sierra Nevada, cen. California in Yosemite National Park; 12,951 ft.
Ku·nar \kü-ˈnär\. The lower course of the Chitral river in E Afghanistan.
Ku·na·shir \ˌkü-nə-ˈshi(ə)r\ *or Jap.* **Ku·na·shi·ri** \ku̇-ˈnäsh-ə-rē\. One of the Kuril Is. (*q.v.*); the second in size and the one nearest Hokkaidō, Japan.
Kunchinjunga. See KANCHENJUNGA.
Kun·dar \ˈku̇n-ˌdär\. River, Pakistan; flows NE into Gumal river, in its lower course forming a section of the Pakistan-Afghanistan boundary.
Kun·dūz \ku̇n-ˈdu̇z\. **1** River, NE Afghanistan; ab. 250 m. long; flows N from Hindu Kush to Amu Darya and forms in part W boundary of Badakshān.
2 Province of NE Afghanistan. See table at AFGHANISTAN.
3 Town, its ✻; pop. (1969e) 80,143; cotton, soap.
Kuneitra, Al–. See AL-KUNEITRA.
Kunene. See CUNENE.
Kunersdorf. See KUNOWICE.
Kung·hit Island \ˌkəŋ-ˌhit-\. Southern island of the Queen Charlotte Is. off W British Columbia, W Canada.
Kung–ko–erh \ˈku̇ŋ-ˈkō-ˈe(ə)r\ *or* **Kun·gur** *or* **Qun·gur** \ˈku̇n-ˈgu̇(ə)r\. Mountain, W Sinkiang Uighur, China, SW of Kashgar; 25,325 ft.; highest point in Mu-ssu-t'a-ko-a-t'e range.
Kun·gur \ku̇n-ˈgu̇(ə)r\. Town, SE Perm Oblast, Russian S.F.S.R., U.S.S.R., at foot of W slope of Ural Mts. on railroad ab. 50 m. SSE of Perm; pop. (1969e) 72,000; ma-

chinery, building materials, leather goods; founded in 1648; scene of much tribal conflict; because of its favorable location early became important in trade with Far East.

Kun·he·gyes \'kůn-ˌhed-yesh\. Commune, Szolnok co., E Hungary, ab. 10 m. NW of Karcag; pop. (1970p) 10,124.

Kunie. See ÎLE DES PINS.

Kun·lun Shan *or* **Kuen·lun Shan** *or* **K'un–lun Shan** *or* **Kwen·lun Shan** \'kün-'lün-'shän\. Mountain ranges (*shan*), W China; highest peak Wu-lu-k'o-mu-shih 25,348 ft.; on N edge of Tibetan plateau, extending from Pamirs and Karakoram Range into Tsinghai; has many subsidiary ranges.

K'un–ming \'kůn-'miŋ\ *or formerly* **Yun·nan** \yü-'nän\. City, ✻ of Yunnan prov., S China, in E part of province 380 m. SW of Chungking; pop. (1970e) 1,700,000; chief city of SW China, advantageously situated on fertile plain at elevation of 6400 ft. on N shore of a large lake (Tien); trade and transportation center, linked by narrow-gauge railroad (opened 1910) to Hanoi, North Vietnam; metalworking; electrical equipment, textiles, copper; univ. (1934). In World War II of great importance as transportation center, American air base, and Chinese military headquarters; frequently bombed by Japanese.

Ku·no·wi·ce \ˌkü-nə-'vēt-sə\ *or Ger.* **Ku·ners·dorf** \'kü-nərz-ˌdȯrf\. Village, Zielona Góra prov., W Poland; battle of Kunersdorf fought here Aug. 12, 1759, during Seven Years' War, in which Frederick the Great was badly defeated by Russians and Austrians.

Kun·san \'kůn-'sän\; *formerly* **Gun·zan** \'gůn-'zän\ *or* **Gun·san** \-'sän\. Seaport, North Chŏlla prov., South Korea; pop. (1970e) 112,453; salt, cotton cloth.

Kun·szent·már·ton \'kůn-sent-ˌmär-tōn\. Commune, SE Hungary, on Körös river N of Csongrád; pop. (1970p) 11,097.

Kuo·la·yar·vi \'kwȯ-lə-ˌyär-vē\ *or Finnish* **Kuo·la·jär·vi** \-ˌya(ə)r-vē\. Town, NW Karelian A.S.S.R., Russian S.F.S.R., U.S.S.R., in region ceded by Finland to U.S.S.R. 1940.

Kuo·pio \'kwȯ-pē-ˌō\. 1 Province of S cen. Finland. See table at FINLAND.
2 City, its ✻, on W shore of Lake Kallavesi; pop. (1970p) 64,398; lumber center; sawmills, match factories; winter sports center; chartered 1782.

Ku·pa \'kü-pə\ *or* **Kul·pa** \'kůl-pə\. River, Croatia, NW Yugoslavia; 184 m. long; flows E into Sava river.

Ku·pang *or Du.* **Koe·pang** \'kü-ˌpäŋ\. Town, ✻ of East Nusa Tenggara prov., Indonesia, SW end of Timor I. on **Kupang Bay;** pop. (1961c) 123,373; founded by Dutch 1618.

Ku·pre·a·nof \ˌkü-prē-'an-ˌȯf\. Island, E Alexander Archipelago, SE Alaska; chief town Kake.

Ku·pyansk \kůp-'yan(t)sk\. Town, E Kharkov Oblast, NE Ukrainian S.S.R., U.S.S.R., on Oskol river 60 m. E of Kharkov; railroad junction point.

Ku·ra \kə-'rä, 'kůr-ə\ *or anc.* **Cy·rus** \'sī-rəs\. River, U.S.S.R. and Turkey; 941 m. long; rises in NE Turkey (where it is called **Ku·ru·çay** \ˌkůr-ů-'chī\) in mountains NW of Kars, flows N into Georgian S.S.R., U.S.S.R., then ESE through Azerbaijan S.S.R. to the Caspian Sea S of Baku. Has large delta, just above which it is joined by its largest tributary the Araks from the S; fed by many mountain streams and has rapid current in upper course; furnishes hydroelectric power at Tbilisi.

Kuramba, Mount. See KOROMBA, MOUNT.

Ku·ra·shi·ki \ků-'rä-shē-kē, ˌkůr-ə-'shēk-ē\. City, Okayama prefecture, Honshū, Japan, ab. 10 m. WSW of Okayama; pop. (1970c) 339,799.

Ku·ra·yo·shi \ˌkůr-ə-'yō-shē\. City, Tottori prefecture, Honshū, Japan, 24 m. W of Tottori; pop. (1970c) 49,629.

Kur·di·stan \ˌkůrd-ə-'stan, ˌkərd-\. Mountainous region with indefinite boundaries forming a nonpolitical region in SE Turkey in Asia, and in adjoining areas of NW Iran, NE Iraq, and NE Syria; ab. 74,000 sq. m.; inhabited by Kurds; lies chiefly in Turkey S of Armenia and N of the Tigris, extending from the Euphrates on W to the mountains of Iran W of Hamadān and including Lake Van; chief towns Diyarbakır, Bitlis, and Van in Turkey, Mosul and Kirkuk in Iraq, and Kermānshāh in Iran. There are also many Kurds in Armenian S.S.R., U.S.S.R. A Kurdish autonomous state was provided for in Treaty of Sèvres 1920 but terms never carried out.

Kŭrd·zha·li \'kůrd-zhä-lē\. 1 Province of S Bulgaria. See table at BULGARIA.
2 Town, its ✻; pop. (1968e) 38,921.

Ku·re \'k(y)ů(ə)r-ē, 'kü-(ˌ)rā\. City, Hiroshima prefecture, SW Honshū, Japan, on N shore of Inland Sea at its W end, 12 m. SE of Hiroshima; pop. (1970c) 235,193; excellent natural harbor; shipbuilding; before World War II major Japanese naval dockyard and site of naval academy; heavily bombed during 1945.

Kure Island \ˌkü-(ˌ)rā-\ *or* **Ocean Island** \ˌō-shən-\. Uninhabited islet of Leeward Is., Hawaiian Is., in cen. Pacific Ocean ab. 1500 m. NW of Niihau, 28°25′N, 178°25′W; 500 acres; included in state of Hawaii and in Hawaiian Islands Bird Reservation.

Ku·res·saa·re *or Russ.* **Ku·res·sa·re** \'kůr-ə-ˌsär-ē\ *or Ger.* **Arens·burg** \'är-ənz-ˌbů(ə)rg\. Seaport on S shore of Saaremaa I., W Estonian S.S.R., U.S.S.R.; seaside resort; in World War I held by Germans 1917–18 and by Bolsheviks 1918–19; in World War II held by Germans.

Kurg. See COORG.

Kur·gan \ků(ə)r-'gan, -'gän\. City, ✻ of Kurgan Oblast, Russian S.F.S.R., U.S.S.R., on Trans-Siberian R.R. 140 m. E of Chelyabinsk; pop. (1970p) 244,000; on the Tobol river in a rich agricultural plain E of the Urals; trade center for farm products, esp. butter, cattle, and grain; machine shops, mills, and factories; produces agricultural machinery and electrical equipment. In a region long settled; its name means "tumulus " or "barrow " and it is so called from the many ancient burial mounds in the vicinity.

Kurgan Oblast \-'ō-bləst, -ˌblast\. Subdivision of the Russian S.F.S.R., U.S.S.R.; 27,413 sq. m.; pop. (1970p) 1,085,000; ✻ Kurgan; barley, wheat, oats, rye; dairying; established 1943 out of E half of Chelyabinsk Oblast; bounded on E and S by Kazakh S.S.R.

Kurgan Tyube \-tyü-'bā\. Town, SW Tadzhik S.S.R., U.S.S.R.; 40 m. S of Dushanbe; pop. (1967e) 31,000.

Ku·ria Mu·ria Islands \ˌk(y)ůr-ē-ə-'m(y)ůr-ē-ə-\. Group of five rocky islets in the Arabian Sea off SW coast of Oman, bet. capes Nus and Sharbatat, SE Arabian Penin.; 28 sq. m.; pop. (1967e) 85. Largest is Hallaniya. Ceded by the sultan of Masqat to Great Britain 1854 for a cable station; ceded by British to Oman 1967.

Ku·ri·ha·ma \ˌkůr-ē-'häm-ə\. Small coastal town, Kanagawa prefecture, SE Honshū, Japan, ab. 1 m. S of Uraga; place where Commodore Perry landed to meet the representative of the shogunate 1853.

Ku·ril Islands *or* **Ku·rile Islands** \'kyů(ə)r-ˌēl-, kyů-'rē(ə)l-\ *also* **Ku·rils** *or* **Ku·riles** \'kyů(ə)r-ˌēlz, kyů-'rē(ə)lz\ *or Russ.* **Ku·ril·'ski·ye Ostro·va** \ků-ˌrēl-ski-yə-'os-trə-və\ *or Jap.* **Chi·shi·ma Ret·tō** \ˌchē-shē-mä-'re-(ˌ)tō\. Group of 56 islands off E coast of Asia, extending 750 m. N and S bet. S tip of Kamchatka Penin., U.S.S.R., to NE coast of island of Hokkaidō, Japan; 6023 sq. m.; administratively part of Sakhalin Oblast, Russian S.F.S.R., U.S.S.R.; a former province of Hokkaidō prefecture, Japan; fishing (esp. crab), whaling; vegetables. The 9 most important islands, named from N to S , are Shumshu, Paramushir, Onekotan, Shiashkhotan, Shimushir, Urup, Iturup, Shikotan-tō (SE of Kunashir), and Kunashir. All islands of volcanic origin, some having active volcanoes today; highest point on Atlasova I. 7674 ft.; many peaks bet. 3000 and 6000 ft.; no really good harbors; only a few islands inhabited, some aboriginal Ainus still found. Islands discovered 1634 by Dutch navigator Martin de Vries; N part of chain occupied by Russians in 18th cent.; given to Japan 1875 in exchange for N Sakhalin I.; after end of World War II, returned to U.S.S.R. Sept. 1945.

Kuril Strait *or* **Kurile Strait** *or Jap.* **Chi·shi·ma Kai·kyo** \'chē-shē-(,)mä-'kī-kyō\. Channel, separating Kuril Is. from S end of Kamchatka Penin. and connecting the Sea of Okhotsk with Bering Sea; ab. 7 m. wide.

Ku–ring–gai \kə-'riŋ-,gī\. Municipality, E New South Wales, SE Australia, N suburb of Sydney; pop. (1966c) 86,876.

Kurische Nehrung. See KURSKAYA KOSA.

Kurisches Haff. See KURSKI ZALIV.

Kurla. See K'U-ERH-LO.

Kur·land *or* **Cour·land** \'kü(ə)r-lənd\. Former Russian government on E Baltic shore, area now in Latvian S.S.R., U.S.S.R.; included Kurzeme (*q.v.*). See BALTIC PROVINCES. In 1237 duchy, inhabited by Lettish people, Cours or Kurs, conquered by Teutonic Knights; given up to Poland and Lithuania and transformed into duchy under Polish suzerainty 1561; after 1737 its duke a client ruler of Russian throne; placed self under Russian rule 1795; scene of severe fighting between Germans and Russians 1914–15; became part of Latvia 1918 (see LATVIAN SOVIET SOCIALIST REPUBLIC).

Kurna. See AL-QURNA.

Kur·nool \kər-'nül\ *also* **Kar·nul** \kər-, kär-\. Town, W Andhra Pradesh, S India, on Tungabhadra river 240 m. NW of Madras; pop. (1970e) 164,248; trade center; cottonseed oil; has remains of old Hindu fort.

Kuroshio. See JAPAN CURRENT.

Kur·ram \'kür-əm\. **1** River, Pakistan; ab. 200 m. long; rises in the Safed Koh, flows E and SE to the Indus river W of Mianwali.

2 Former agency, Pakistan, W of Kohat; 739 sq. m.; comprises valley of Kurram river S of the Safed Koh, inhabited chiefly by Turi.

Kursk \'kü(ə)rsk\. City, ✱ of Kursk Oblast, Russian S.F.S.R., U.S.S.R., in cen. part, on N bank of Seim river; pop. (1970p) 284,000; main railroad center of the region; food processing, distilling; mining machinery, electrical equipment, pig iron; first mentioned 1095; destroyed by Tatars 1240; rebuilt as frontier post 1586; in World War II occupied by Germans 1941–43.

Kur·ska·ya Ko·sa \'kür-skī-(y)ə-'kò-sə\ *or Ger.* **Kur·ische Nehr·ung** \,kür-ish-ə-'ner-(,)üŋ\. Long spit of land separating the Kurski Zaliv from the Baltic Sea; 61 m. long; formerly part of East Prussia, Germany, now in U.S.S.R.

Kur·ski Za·liv \,kür-skē-'zäl-if\ *or Ger.* **Kur·isch·es Haff** \,kür-ish-əs-'häf\. Inlet of the Baltic Sea, U.S.S.R.; S part in Kaliningrad Oblast, Russian S.F.S.R., N part in Lithuanian S.S.R.; ab. 625 sq. m.; formerly in East Prussia, Germany.

Kursk Oblast \-'ò-bləst, -,blast\. Subdivision of the Russian S.F.S.R., U.S.S.R., in cen. Russian plateau; 11,506 sq. m.; pop. (1970p) 1,474,000; ✱ Kursk; crossed by Seim river; is source of Donets and tributaries of Donets and Dnieper. In N part of black-earth (chernozem) area, produces rye and oats, also sugar beets, wheat, millet, potatoes; has forests in N; large-scale exploitation of extensive iron ore deposits begun during 1950's. Lack of educational facilities, poor transportation, World War I, and famine of 1921 retarded its progress; in World War II area scene of last major German offensive on Eastern Front, July 1943.

Kuruçay. See KURA.

Ku·ru·man \'kür-ə-,män\. Town, N Cape Province, S Rep. of South Africa, just SE of the Kalahari Desert, ab. 120 m. NW of Kimberley; pop. (1967e) 7000; mission station of Robert Moffat 1825 ff.; nearby in a dolomite cave is a spring yielding 5 million gallons of water a day; it is the source of the **Kuruman River** which formerly flowed W into the Molopo river but has disappeared over most of its lower course in S part of the Kalahari Desert (see also MOLOPO).

Ku·ru·me \'kür-ə-,mā, kə-'rü-(,)mā\. City, Fukuoka prefecture, N Kyūshū, Japan, 55 m. NE of Nagasaki; pop. (1970c) 194,178; textiles (including Kurume-Gasuri, a blue-figured cotton fabric).

Ku·ru·ne·ga·la \,kür-ə-'neg-ə-lə\. Town, W Ceylon, 52 m. NE of Colombo; pop. (1968e) 23,000; trade and distribution center for important agricultural region growing rice, coconuts, and rubber.

Kur·ze·me \'kür-zə-,mā\ *or* **Kur·land** \'kü(ə)r-lənd\. Former province, W Latvian S.S.R., U.S.S.R., along coast of Baltic Sea and SW shore of Gulf of Riga; 5099 sq. m. Often a battlefield in World War I; ceded to Germany by Treaty of Brest Litovsk 1918; became a part of newly organized Latvia 1918; Bolshevik forces driven out Oct. 1919. See KURLAND.

Kuş·a·da·sı *or* **Kush Ada·si** \,küsh-,äd-ə-'sē\. Seaport on Kuşadası Gulf, İzmir prov., W Turkey, 40 m. S of İzmir and near ruins of Ephesus; pop. (1965c) 7388.

Kuşadası Gulf. Inlet of E Aegean Sea on W coast of Turkey, NE of island of Samos; extends inland ab. 45 m., average width 20 m.

Ku·saie \kü-'sī-,ə\. Island, in E part of the Caroline Is., part of the U.S. Trust Territory of the Pacific Islands, W Pacific Ocean, 330 m. ESE of Ponape I.; ab. 9 m. long and 6 m. wide; has several mountains (highest 2064 ft.) and two good harbors, esp. Lele on E coast. Bombed by Americans but left in Japanese control 1942–44.

Kush. See CUSH.

Ku·shi·ro \'küsh-i-,rō, kü-'shi(ə)r-,ō\. Seaport, SE coast of Hokkaidō, Japan; pop. (1970c) 191,948; exports sulfur and lumber.

Kushk \'küshk\. Town, NW Afghanistan, 40 m. N of Herāt and N of Paropamisus mountain range; on the Kushka river ab. 30 m. from the Soviet frontier post of Kushka.

Kush·ka \'küsh-kə, küsh-\. Soviet military post and railhead, SE Turkmen S.S.R., U.S.S.R., on Afghan border 66 m. N of Herāt; on the **Kushka River** (Koshk in Afghanistan), 150 m. long, a tributary of the Murgab.

Kush·va \'küsh-və, 'küsh-\. Town, Sverdlovsk Oblast, Russian S.F.S.R., U.S.S.R., ab. 100 m. NNW of Sverdlovsk; pop. (1967e) 47,000.

Kusi. See KOSI.

Kus·ko·kwim \'kəs-kə-,kwim\. River, SW Alaska, S of the Yukon; ab. 600 m. long; flows SW to **Kuskokwim Bay,** an inlet of Bering Sea; its two upper tributaries North Fork and South Fork rise in Alaska Range near Mt. McKinley National Park.

Küs·nacht \'kyüs-,näkt\. Commune, Zurich canton, Switzerland, on Lake of Zurich just SSE of Zurich; pop. (1970c) 12,193.

Küss·nacht \'kyüs-,näkt\ *or in full* **Küssnacht am Rigi** \-äm-'rē-gē\. Village, Schwyz canton, Switzerland, at NE corner of Lake of Lucerne just E of Lucerne; pop. (1970c) 7956; nearby is scene, according to legend, of William Tell's shooting of Gessler.

Ku·sta·nai \,küs-tə-'nī\. Town, ✱ of Kustanai Oblast, Kazakh S.S.R., U.S.S.R., in N part on left bank of Tobol river 170 m. E of Magnitogorsk; pop. (1970p) 123,000; market for grains of surrounding fertile black-earth area; gold mining; flour, leather, electrical equipment; founded 1879.

Kustanai Oblast \-'ò-bləst, -'blast\. Subdivision of Kazakh S.S.R., U.S.S.R.; 75,367 sq. m.; pop. (1970p) 985,000; ✱ Kustani; millet, oats, wheat; cattle, sheep; gold.

Küstendil. See KYUSTENDIL.

Küstenja. See CONSTANȚA 2.

Kü·sten·land \'kyüs-tən-,länt\ *or Eng.* **Coast·land** \'kōst-,land\. Former administrative district (province) of Austria, including the crownlands Istria and Görz and Gradisca, now largely in NW Yugoslavia.

Kūstī. See KOSTI.

Küstrin. See KOSTRZYN.

Kut \'küt\. **1** *or* **Al–Kūt** \al-\. City, Iraq, on the Tigris 100 m. SE of Baghdad; pop. (1965c) 42,116; grain market. Captured by British after battle of Sept. 28, 1915; besieged by Turks from Dec. 8, 1915 until they finally forced British surrender Apr. 29, 1916; recaptured by new British expeditionary force under Gen. Maude Feb. 23, 1917.

2 *or* **Ko Kut** \kō-\. Island (Thai *ko*) in NE Gulf of Siam off SE coast of Thailand.

Kü·tah·ya *or* **Ku·ta·iah** \kü-'tä-yə\. **1** Province of W Turkey, Asia. See table at TURKEY.

2 Commerical town, its ❋, on railroad 65 m. SE of Bursa; pop. (1965e) 49,301.

Kutai. See MAHAKAM.

Ku·ta·i·si \kü-'tī-sē\ *or* **Ku·ta·is** \-'tīs\. City, W Georgian S.S.R., U.S.S.R., on both banks of Rioni river ab. 65 m. NE of Batumi; pop. (1970p) 161,000; major industrial center of W Georgian S.S.R. and an important trading center; motor vehicles, mining machinery, textiles, clothing, furniture, processed foods; coal mining. Chief town, under the name **Aea** \'ē-ə\, of ancient Colchis; later capital of Imeritia; occupied by Russians 1773; suffered much in wars bet. Persians, Mongols, Turks, and Russians.

Kutaraja. See BANDA ATJEH.

Kutch *or* **Cutch** \'kəch\. District, Gujarat, NW India; 17,060 sq. m.; pop. (1961c) 696,440; ❋ Bhuj; a former state; in N and E is the Rann of Kutch.

Kutch, Gulf of *or* **Gulf of Cutch.** Inlet of Arabian Sea, Gujarat, W India; at its head adjoins the Little Rann of Kutch.

Kutch, Rann of *or* **Rann of Cutch** \'rən-\. Large salt marsh, NW Gujarat, W India; the N section is the **Great Rann of Kutch,** and the E section is the **Little Rann of Kutch;** scene of military clash between India and Pakistan 1965 (ab. 300 sq. m. awarded to Pakistan 1968) and 1971.

Kutenai. See KOOTENAY.

Kut·ná Ho·ra \ˌkút-nə-'hȯr-ə\ *or* *Ger.* **Kut·ten·berg** \'kút-ᵊn-ˌbe(ə)rg\. Town, W Czechoslovakia, 45 m. E of Prague; pop. (1968e) 17,574; 14th cent. Gothic cathedral; built up near silver mines, worked from 13th cent.; suffered during severe fighting of the Hussite struggles 1420–33 and the Thirty Years' War 1618–48; the flooding of the mines aided its decline.

Kut·no \'küt-(ˌ)nō\. Commune, Łódź prov., cen. Poland, ab. 35 m. NNW of Łódź; pop. (1970p) 30,300; railroad junction; manufactures textiles, sugar; produces grain. Scene of German defeat of Russians Nov. 1914, in the battle for control of Łódź; in World War II scene of capture of Polish army by Germans Sept. 15, 1939.

Ku·to·ar·djo *or* *Du.* **Koe·to·ar·djo** \ˌküt-ō-'är-ˌjō\. Town, Central Java prov., Indonesia, 30 m. W of Jogjakarta.

Kuttenberg. See KUTNÁ HORA.

Kutz·town \'kúts-ˌtaún\. Borough, Berks co., SE Pennsylvania, 15 m. NE of Reading; pop. (1970c) 4166; clothing, shoes; limestone quarries; dairy farming; potatoes; Kutztown State Coll. (1860); settled 1771.

Kuu·san·kos·ki \'kü-sən-ˌkōs-kē\. Town, Kymi prov., S Finland; pop. (1967e) 22,433.

Ku·wait *or* **Ku·weit** *also* **Ko·weit** \kə-'wāt\. **1** Independent state, NW coast of Persian Gulf, forming wedge of desert territory bet. Iraq and Saudi Arabia; 6200 sq. m.; pop. (1970c) 738,663; ❋ Al-Kuwait; an important oil producing state; fisheries; chemicals, construction materials. Ruled by descendants of a dynasty founded in 18th cent.; independence under British protection recognized by Great Britain 1914; oil discovered 1938; became fully independent of Great Britain June 1961; joined U.N. 1963. See BŪBIYĀN and BAHRAIN.

2 Seaport. See AL-KUWAIT.

Ku·wa·na \kú-'wän-ə\. Coastal city, Mie prefecture, S Honshū, Japan, ab. 15 m. SW of Nagoya near mouth of Kiso river; pop. (1970c) 81,015; in rice-growing area.

Kuweit. See KUWAIT.

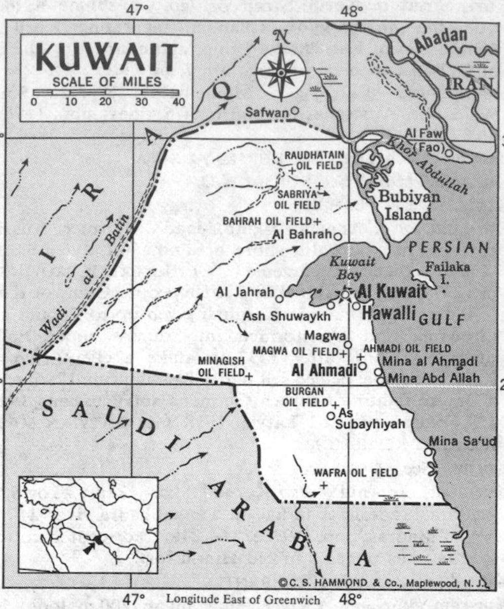

Ku·yun·jik \ˌkü-yən-'jik\. Mound on E bank of the Tigris, N Iraq, the site of ancient Nineveh (*q.v.*); discovered 1820, excavations begun by Layard 1845.

Kuz·bas *or* **Kuz·bass** \kúz-'bas\. Short for Kuznetsk Basin (*q.v.*).

Kuz·netsk \kúz-'netsk\. City, E Penza Oblast, Russian S.F.S.R., U.S.S.R., ab. 65 m. E of Penza; pop. (1969e) 79,000; important trade center.

Kuznetsk Basin. Basin of Tom river, cen. Kemerovo Oblast, Russian S.F.S.R., U.S.S.R., extending from Tomsk to Novokuznetsk; immense coal deposits around and S of Kemerovo; has been converted into major independent industrial area based on discovery of rich iron ore deposits at Temirtau, S of Novokuznetsk.

Kuznetsk Sibirski. See NOVOKUZNETSK.

Kvae·nang·en Fjord \kə-ˌvā-näŋ-ən-, ˌkfä-\. Inlet of Arctic Ocean on NW coast of Norway.

Kval·øy \kə-'väl-ˌòi, 'kfä-\. Name of two islands in Arctic Ocean off N coast of Norway: **North Kvaløy,** in Finnmark co., 127 sq. m., chief town Hammerfest; **South Kvaløy,** in Troms co., 284 sq. m. Tromsø is on islet bet. South Kvaløy and mainland.

Kvar·ner \'kvär-nər\. **1** *or* **Ve·li·ki Kvarner** \ˌvel-i-kē-\ *or* *Ital.* **Quar·ne·ro** \kwər-'ne(ə)r-(ˌ)ō\. Inlet of N Adriatic Sea, E side of Istria Penin., NW Yugoslavia; Cres I. is to the E and Rijeka at its head.

2 Gulf, NE Adriatic Sea. See MALI KVARNER.

Kvi·tø·ya \'kvēt-ə-yə\ *or* **White Island** *or* **Gil·lis Island** \ˌgil-əs-\. Island of the Spitsbergen archipelago (Svalbard), bet. NE Spitsbergen and Franz Josef Land; 102 sq. m.

Kwa·ja·lein \'kwäj-ə-lən, -ˌlān\. Island (atoll) in cen. part of Ralik Chain, W Marshall Is., W Pacific, 2415 m. SW of Pearl Harbor, 9°05′N, 167°20′E; ab. 78 m. long, with 18 islets and large anchorage in the lagoon; chief islets Kwajalein at SE and Roi and Namur at N. Strongly fortified by Japanese; taken Jan. 30–Feb. 6, 1944 by Americans; site of missile tracking and testing facility.

Kwa·koe·gron \'kwäk-ə-ˌgrón\. Town, N Surinam, 50 m. SSW of Paramaribo on the Saramacca river.

Kwa·mouth \'kwä-ˌmaúth\. River port on Congo river, Zaire, at mouth of Kasai river, the confluence being called the **Kwa** mouth.

Kwan·do \'kwän-(ˌ)dō\ *or* *Port.* **Cuan·do** \'kwän-(ˌ)dō\. River, S Africa; ab. 500 m. long; rises in cen. Angola, flows

SE, forming S section of boundary bet. Angola and Zambia, continues E along NE boundary of Botswana, and empties into Zambezi river just above Victoria Falls.

Kwang·cho·wan \'gwäŋ-'jō-'wän, 'kwäŋ-\ *or* **Kwang·chow** \'gwäŋ-'jō\ *or Fr.* **Kouang–Tché·ou–Wan** \kwäŋ-cheü-'wän\. Former French leased territory, SW coast of Kwangtung prov., SE China, on E side of Luichow Penin. ab. 270 m. W of Hong Kong; 325 sq. m.; ✱ Fort Bayard (now called Chan-chiang). Narrow coastal area, two large islands and many small ones, and adjacent waters acquired by France 1898 by lease for 99 years; was attached to French Indochina but during World War II was held by Japanese 1942–45; returned to China by France 1946.

Kwang·ju \'gwȯŋ-'jü\ *or formerly* **Ko·shu** \'kō-'shü\. Town, ✱ of South Chŏlla prov., South Korea; pop. (1970e) 502,753; rice, cotton; two colleges.

Kwan·go \'kwäŋ-(ˌ)gō\ *or Port.* **Cuan·go** \'kwäŋ-(ˌ)gō\. River, S cen. Africa; ab. 300 m. long; rises in cen. Angola, flows N, forming a section of Angola-Zaire boundary, and empties into Kasai river in W Zaire ab. 100 m. above its junction with the Congo river.

Kwang·si Chu·ang \'gwäŋ-'sē-chə-'wäŋ, 'kwän-\. Autonomous region, SE China, bounded on N by Kweichow and Hunan provs., on E and S by Kwangtung, on SW by North Vietnam, and on W by Yunnan; 85,096 sq. m.; pop. (1968e) 24,000,000; ✱ Nan-ning; hilly; traversed by the Yu, Hung-shui, and Kuei rivers, all tributaries of the Hsi; produces much rice in the river valleys and also has valuable forest products, including cassia, camphor, cinnamon, and wood oil. Chief cities Nan-ning, Kuei-lin, and Liu-chou.

Kwangteh. See KUANG-TE.

Kwang·tung \'gwäŋ-'du̇ŋ, 'kwäŋ-, -'tu̇ŋ\. Province, SE China, bounded on N by Hunan and Kiangsi provs., on NE by Fukien, on E and S by South China Sea, and on W by Kwangsi Chuang; 89,344 sq. m.; pop. (1968e) 40,000,000; ✱ Canton. Lies largely in the tropics and has both mountain and plain regions, with four large rivers, Hsi, Pei, Tung, and Han; varied agricultural products, esp. rice, tea, sugar, tobacco, and fruit; also trades in silk, salt, fish; industrial development severely limited by lack of fuel and mineral resources. Coastline almost 800 m. long, provides several excellent harbors; has many islands, esp. Hainan (*q.v.*) and those in the Hsi delta. Chief cities Canton, Swatow, Fo-shan, Ch'ao-an.

History: In early centuries was too far from ruling dynasties in the north to have any marked influence; created under Ming dynasty (1368–1644); after 1757 was center of Chinese contact with foreign countries, esp. through Canton (*q.v.*) which was for nearly a century the only port opened to trade. Illicit importation of Indian opium into it brought on first war with Great Britain 1841–42 with resulting cession of Hong Kong and Treaty of Nanking 1842 providing for establishment of five treaty ports; ceded Kowloon to British 1860 and 1898, and Macao to Portugal 1887; Kwangchowan (*q.v.*) leased to France 1898 (restored 1946). The province most disaffected with imperial rule; marked by much unrest at time of revolution 1911 and the formation of the Kuomintang under Sun Yat-sen 1912; occupied by Japanese 1938; in World War II in 1944 and 1945 had several important American air bases and was scene of much fighting.

Kwan·tung \'gwän-'du̇ŋ, 'kwän-, -'tu̇ŋ\ *or* **Kwantung Leased Territory** *also* **Kwan·to** \-'dȯ, -'tȯ\. Former territory, S part of Liaotung Penin., Liaoning prov., NE China; 1444 sq. m.; ✱ Dairen. Mountainous peninsula with two ports, Dairen and Port Arthur. Leased to Russia by China 1898 under pressure; taken over by Japan 1905 by Treaty of Portsmouth and lease extended in 1915 to 99 years; again leased to U.S.S.R. by treaty 1945; returned to China 1950 and Soviet forces withdrawn 1955.

Kwanza. See CUANZA.

Kwa·ra \'kwär-ə\. State of W Nigeria. See table at NIGERIA.

Kwathlamba. See DRAKENSBERG MOUNTAINS.

Kwei. See KUEI.

Kwei·chow \'gwā-'jō, 'kwā-\. 1 Province, S China, bounded on N by Szechwan prov., on E by Hunan, on S by Kwangsi Chuang, and on W by Yunnan; 67,181 sq. m.; pop. (1968e) 17,000,000; ✱ Kuei-yang; a plateau region bet. the tributaries of the Yangtze and Hsi rivers; contains many aboriginal peoples, chiefly the Miao; wheat, beans, corn, potatoes; has rich mercury deposits. Chief towns Kuei-yang, Tsun-i, An-shun, Tu-yün; has not played a significant part in Chinese history but in World War II was important as Chinese and Allied base.

2 City, S Szechwan, China. See FENG-CHIEH.

Kweichu. See KUEI-YANG.

Kweilin. See KUEI-LIN.

Kweiping. See KUEI-P'ING.

Kweisui. See HUHEHOT.

Kweiyang. See KUEI-YANG.

Kwenlun Shan. See KUNLUN SHAN.

Kwi·dzyn \kə-'vē-ˌjin (-yə), 'kfē-\ *or Ger.* **Ma·ri·en·wer·der** \mä-'rē-ən-ˌve(ə)rd-ər\. Manufacturing town, Gdańsk prov., N Poland, ab. 45 m. SSE of Gdańsk; pop. (1970p) 23,100; dyeworks; clay products, tobacco, preserved foodstuffs; trades in agricultural products. Founded 1233 by the Teutonic Order; center of plebiscite 1920 by which people of town and vicinity voted to remain in East Prussia; in section of East Prussia assigned to Poland by Potsdam Conference, 1945.

Kwitta. See KETA.

Kwo·ka \'kwō-kə\. Mountain, Arfak range, NW Irian Barat, Indonesia; 8042 ft.; highest point in the range.

Kworra. See NIGER 2.

Kyakhta. See ALTANBULAG.

Kyaring Tso. See CHA-LIN.

Kyauk·pyu \'chau̇k-'pyü\. 1 District, Arakan division, Lower Burma; 4793 sq. m.; pop. (1962e) 335,386; ✱ Kyaukpyu.

2 Town, its ✱, on Combermere Bay at N end of Ramree I.; pop. (1953c) 7335.

Kyauk·se \'chau̇k-(ˌ)sā\. 1 District, Mandalay division, Upper Burma; 1601 sq. m.; pop. (1962e) 242,892; ✱ Kyaukse.

2 Town, its ✱, on railroad 25 m. S of Mandalay; pop. (1953c) 8659.

Kyauk·taw \'chau̇k-(ˌ)tȯ\. Town, Arakan division, W Burma, on the Kaladan river N of Sittwe; in region of severe fighting 1943–44; taken by British Feb. 25, 1944.

Kyi *or* **Kyichu.** See LA-SA.

Kyle \'kī(ə)l\. District, cen. Ayrshire, SW Scotland; celebrated in poetry of Robert Burns.

Kyle Dam Game Reserve. Wildlife reserve, SE cen. Rhodesia; 35 sq. m.; contains **Lake Kyle;** large reedbuck population, eland, white rhinoceros; established 1964.

Kyl·lē·nē \kə-'lē-nē\. Commune, Elis dept., NW Peloponnesus, S Greece.

Ký·mē *or* **Kími** \'kē-mē\. Seaport commune, Euboea dept., Greece, on E coast of Euboea I.

Ky·mi \'kü-mē\. Province of SE Finland. See table at FINLAND.

Ky·nance Cove \ˌkī-ˌnan(t)s-\. Inlet of Atlantic Ocean off SW coast of England, 1½ m. W of Lizard Head.

Kynosura. See CYNOSURA.

Kyo·ga *or* **Kio·ga** \kē-'ō-gə\. Lake, S cen. Uganda, E Africa; 1710 sq. m.; 50 m. long; max. depth 25 ft.; Victoria Nile flows through it.

Kyō·ga, Cape \-kē-'ō-gə\. Cape on N coast of W extension of Honshū I., Japan; W of Wakasa Bay.

Kyŏng·gi \kē-'ŏŋ-'gē\. Province of South Korea. See table at KOREA, SOUTH.

Kyongsong. See SEOUL.

Kyŏng·ju \kē-'ȯŋ-'jü\. Town, North Kyŏngsang prov., South Korea, ab. 37 m. E of Taegu; pop. (1970e) 92,093.

Kyō·to *also* **Kiō·to** \kē-'ōt-(,)ō\. 1 Prefecture, Honshū, Japan; 1781 sq. m.; pop. (1970c) 2,250,087; ✻ Kyōto; numerous historic sites.

2 Manufacturing city, its ✻, W cen. Honshū; pop. (1970c) 1,419,165; on a plain with mountain ranges on all sides except the S, 6 m. W of S end of Lake Biwa and ab. 26 m. NNE of Ōsaka; center of Japanese art, having many factories producing porcelain, lacquer ware, embroidery, brocades, bronzes, etc.; part of the Ōsaka-Kōbe industrial area, manufacturing electrical equipment, chemicals, textiles; Kyōto Univ. (1897); Kyōto Univ. of Industrial Arts and Textiles (1949).

History: Residence for more than 1000 years of the imperial family; some palace buildings remain and there are many fine Buddhist and Shinto temples, shrines, and other structures. City founded as **Hei·an–kyo** \,hā-än-'kyō\ and established as capital of Japan in 794 by Emperor Kwammu; at times superseded as actual seat of government (see KAMAKURA, capital of shogunate 1192–1333), but remained the classical capital till 1869, when government was removed to Tokyo.

Kypros. See CYPRUS.

Ky·ra Pé·la·gos \kē-rä-'pā-lə-,gȯs\. Island, in Euboea dept., Greece; Northern Sporades, NW Aegean Sea, NE of Alonēsos.

Ky·re·nia \ki-'rē-nyə, -nē-ə\. 1 District, N Cyprus, E Mediterranean Sea; 247 sq. m.; pop. (1968e) 32,500.

2 Seaport, its ✻, in cen. part of N coast; pop. (1968e) 5000.

Kyth·nos \'kith-nəs\ *or* **Cyth·nos** \'sith-\ *or Gk.* **Kith·nos** \'kith-\ *also* **Ther·mia** \ther-'myä\. Island, NW Cyclades, Aegean Sea; part of Cyclades dept., Greece; ab. 8 m. SSE of Keos; ab. 18 sq. m.; chief town **Ký́th·nos** \'kyēth-,nȯs\ on NE coast; level and fertile; has thermal springs.

Kyū·shū *also* **Kiū·shū** \kē-'ü-(,)shü\. Southernmost of the four main islands of Japan, in Pacific Ocean off E coast of Asia, separated on N from SW Honshū by Shimonoseki Strait and on E from Shikoku by Bungo Strait; 16,205 sq. m.; pop. (1970c) 12,072,179; a mountainous island with several famous peaks, ranging from 5000 to 6500 ft.: Aso, Kujū, Kirishima, On-take. Its coastline irregular with good harbors; chief cities Kitakyūshū, Fukuoka, Nagasaki, Kumamoto, Kagoshima; was first part of Japanese Empire opened to foreigners (see DESHIMA, HIRADO).

Kyu·sten·dil *or* **Kü·sten·dil** *also* **Kö·sten·dil** \'kyü-stən-,dil\. 1 Province of W Bulgaria. See table at BULGARIA.

2 City, its ✻, 43 m. SW of Sofia; pop. (1968e) 41,762; hot mineral springs; trades in wine, fruit, tobacco. Dates from Roman times; in 14th cent. was seat of independent Macedonian principality.

Ky·zyl *or* **Ki·zil** \kə-'zil\ *or Russ.* **Kras·ny** \'kras-nē\ *or formerly* **Khem–Bel·der** \'kem-'bel-dər\. Town, ✻ of Tuva A.S.S.R., Russian S.F.S.R., U.S.S.R., in cen. part at junction of the Bei Kem and Khua Kem (Mongol *kem* river); pop. (1970p) 52,000.

Kyzyl Kum *also* **Kiz·il Kum** *or* **Qi·zil Qum** \kə-'zil-'küm\. Desert, Uzbek and Kazakh S.S.Rs., U.S.S.R., SE of Aral Sea; covers 115,000 sq. m. bet. Amu Darya and the Syr Darya rivers.

Kzyl–Or·da *also* **Qi·zil Orda** \kə-'zil-ȯr-'dä\ *or formerly* **Pe·rovsk** \pə-'rȯfsk\. Town, ✻ of Kzyl-Orda Oblast, S Kazakh S.S.R., U.S.S.R., 315 m. NW of Tashkent on N bank of Syr Darya; pop. (1970p) 123,000; brickmaking and brewing.

Kzyl–Orda Oblast \-'ȯ-bləst, -,blast\. Subdivision of the Kazakh S.S.R., Russian S.F.S.R., U.S.S.R., in S part E of Aral Sea; traversed by lower course of the Syr Darya; 85,135 sq. m.; pop. (1970p) 492,000; ✻ Kzyl-Orda; grain, cotton, melon; deposits of saltpeter, phosphorite, and magnesium sulfate; chief cities Kyzl-Orda, Aralsk.

Laagen. See LÅGEN.

La Al·bue·ra \läl-ˈbwer-ə\. Commune, Badajoz prov., SW Spain, 15 m. SE of Badajoz; pop. (1970p) 1814; scene of defeat May 16, 1811 of French under Marshal Soult by British, Portuguese, and Spanish under Viscount Beresford in Peninsular War.

La Al·ta·gra·cia \lə-ˌäl-tə-ˈgräs-ē-ə\. Province, E Dominican Republic. See table at DOMINICAN REPUBLIC.

La Asun·ción \lä-ˌsün(t)-sē-ˈōn\. Town, ✱ of Nueva Esparta state, Venezuela, located on E Margarita I., in Caribbean Sea off N coast of Venezuela; pop. (1961c) 5517.

Laatokka. See LADOGA.

La·au Point \lä-ˈau̇-\. Cape on SW extremity of Molokai I., Hawaii.

La·ba·le·kang \lä-ˌbäl-ə-ˈkäŋ\. Volcano, S end of Lomblen I., Indonesia; 5394 ft.

La Ban·da \lə-ˈbän-də\. Town, Santiago del Estero prov., N Argentina; pop. (1960c) 23,772; NE suburb of Santiago del Estero.

La Bar·ca \lə-ˈbär-kə\. Town, Jalisco state, W cen. Mexico, near E end of Lake Chapala; munic. pop. (1970p) 40,331; center of region producing grain and sugar; founded 1529.

La Bas·sée \lä-ba-ˈsā\. Commune, Nord dept., N France, 13 m. SW of Lille; pop. (1962c) 5573; in World War I captured by Germans Sept. 1914; subjected to many attacks by British but not retaken until Oct. 3, 1918.

La Baule–Es·cou·blac \lä-ˌbōl-ˌes-ku̇-ˈbläk\. Joint municipality, Loire-Atlantique dept., NW France; pop. (1968c) 13,336; beach resort.

Labe. See ELBE.

La·bé \la-ˈbā\. Town, W cen. Guinea, W Africa, 170 m. NE of Conakry; chief town of the Fulah in the Fouta Djallon.

La·belle \lə-ˈbel\. County, Quebec, Canada. See table at QUEBEC.

La Belle \lə-ˈbel\. City, ⊗ of Hendry co., S Florida; pop. (1970c) 1823; oil wells; cotton, citrus fruits.

La Belle–Al·liance \lä-ˌbel-äl-ˈyäⁿs\. Hamlet in Belgium; battlefield of Waterloo.

La·berge \lə-ˈbe(ə)rzh\. Lake, S Yukon, NW Canada, N of Whitehorse; 87 sq. m.; Yukon river flows through it.

La·bette \lə-ˈbet\. County in Kansas. See table at KANSAS.

La Biche, Lac \ˌläk-lə-ˈbish\. Lake, E Alberta, Canada; 94 sq. m.; outlet is short stream, **La Biche River,** a tributary of the Athabaska.

La·bin \ˈläb-ˌēn\ *or Ital.* **Al·bo·na** \äl-ˈbōn-ə\. Commune, W Croatia, NW Yugoslavia, on Istria Penin. 21 m. NE of Pula.

La·binsk \lə-ˈb(y)in(t)sk\ *or formerly* **La·bin·ska·ya** \ˈlab-ən-skə-yə\. Town, SE Krasnodar Krai, Russian S.F.S.R., U.S.S.R., ab. 40 m. ENE of Maikop; pop. (1969e) 53,000; manganese and coal deposits in vicinity.

La·bo \lä-ˈbō\. Mountain, S Camarines Norte, Luzon, Phil., at point where boundary bet. Quezon and Camarines Sur joins Camarines Norte border; 5066 ft.

La Bo·ca \lə-ˈbō-kə\. Pacific coast seaport, Balboa dist., Canal Zone.

Lab·ra·dor \ˈlab-rə-ˌdȯ(ə)r\. 1 Large peninsula, Canada, divided bet. Newfoundland and Quebec provs.; 625,000 sq. m. See NEW QUEBEC, UNGAVA.

2 Mainland section of Newfoundland prov., Canada, ab. 1/5 of Labrador Penin.; 112,826 sq. m. (land area 102,631 sq. m.); pop. (1966c) 21,157. Borders on Atlantic on E and on Quebec prov. on S and W; its N point, Cape Chidley on Killinek I. is at entrance to Hudson Strait. Only large river is the Churchill in the S, which enters Lake Melville; in it are Churchill Falls; the river and its tributaries drain several large lakes in SW part (Ashuanipi, Dyke, Lobstick, Michikamau). A plateau region, little explored, but its highest mountains are above 5000 ft.; along its S border (1000–2000 ft.) rise several streams of E Quebec flowing into the Gulf of St. Lawrence. Coast much indented with long fjords and lined with many small islands. Has good harbors: Battle Harbour, Cartwright, Hopedale, Nain; important iron ore deposits. Coast known to Norsemen as early as 10th cent.; visited by John Cabot (1498), Corte-Real (1500), and Jacques Cartier. Boundary with Canada, under dispute since 1809, settled by decision of Committee of British Privy Council Mar. 1927; became part of Canada 1949.

Labrador Current *also* **Arc·tic Current** \ˈärk-tik-, ˈärt-ik-\. Ocean current flowing S along W Greenland and Labrador coasts and E of Newfoundland, Canada, uniting with Gulf Stream in the area of the Grand Bank; its cold waters meeting with the warm waters of the Gulf Stream cause the frequent fogs of this part of the N Atlantic.

Lá·brea \ˈlab-rē-ə\. Town and municipality, Amazonas state, W Brazil, on right bank of Purus river, ab. 380 m. SSW of Manaus; munic. pop. (1968e) 20,354.

La Brea \lə-ˈbrā-ə\. Village and port on S shore of Gulf of Paria, W Trinidad; location of Brighton Pier whence the pitch from Pitch Lake just S of the port is exported.

Lab·ro·foss \ˈläb-rə-ˌfȯs\. Waterfall in Lågen river, S Norway, 3 m. below Kongsberg; 140 ft. high.

La·bu·an \lə-ˈbü-ən\. Island on N side of Brunei Bay, off NW coast of Borneo, 725 m. NE of Singapore; 38 sq. m.; pop. (1960c) 14,904; constitutes with adjacent small islands a settlement attached to Sabah, Malaysia; chief town Victoria, which has excellent harbor and is shipping and distributing point for parts of N Borneo; well cultivated; chief products coconuts, rubber, rice, fruits.

History: At suggestion of James Brooke ceded 1846 to Great Britain by Sultan of Brunei; made crown colony 1848 and for a time (1889–1905) administered by British North Borneo; transferred to Straits Settlements 1906 with which it was incorporated 1907 as part of Singapore; constituted a separate settlement 1912 under governor of Straits Settlements; seized by Japanese Dec. 1941; made part of colony of North Borneo (now Sabah) 1946; became part of Malaysia 1963.

La·buk \lä-ˈbu̇k\. River, E Sabah, Malaysia; 210 m. long; flows ENE to **Labuk Bay,** large inlet of Sulu Sea.

Lab·y·rinth, The \-ˈlab-ə-ˌrin(t)th\. Fortified position in Pas-de-Calais dept., N France, S of Neuville-Saint-Vaast and near Vimy Ridge, scene of series of battles May 30–June 19, 1915.

La Calamine. See MORESNET.

La Calle. See EL KALA.

La Ca·margue \ˌläk-ə-ˈmärg\. Marshy island in delta of the Rhone river, S France.

La Ca·na·da–Flint·ridge \ˌlä-kən-ˈyäd-ə-ˈflint-rij\. Urban community (unincorporated), Los Angeles co., SW California, NW of Pasadena; pop. (1970c) 20,652; residential; Descanso Gardens.

La Car·lo·ta \ˌlä-kär-ˈlōt-ə\. Chartered city, W cen. Negros Occidental prov., Negros, Phil., 18 m. S of City of Bacolod; pop. (1970e) 79,300.

La Ca·ro·li·na \lə-ˌkär-ə-ˈlēn-ə\. Commune, Jaén prov., S Spain, on S slope of the Sierra Morena 32 m. N of Jaén; pop. (1970p) 15,771; trades in minerals, oil, wine; lead mining; silk factories. Settled by Swabian colonists 1769 through efforts of Charles III to encourage exploitation of the Sierra Morena.

La Cas·tel·la·na \lä-ˌkäs-tə-ˈyän-ə\. Municipality, cen. Negros Occidental prov., Negros, Phil., 24 m. S of City of Bacolod; pop. (1969e) 48,600.

Lac·ca·dive Islands \ˈlak-ə-ˌdiv-\. Group of islands and coral reefs in Arabian Sea, Madras prov. of British India, lat. 10°–12°20′N and long. 72°–74°E, 200 m. off SW coast of India; the S group being assigned to the Malabar dist. and the N group (sometimes called the **Amin·di·vi Islands** \ˌəm-ən-ˈdē-vē-\) to the South Kanara dist.; since 1956 part of **Laccadive, Min·i·coy, and Amindivi Islands** \-ˈmin-i-ˌkȯi-\ territory of India. Territory comprises ab. 20 islands, and has area of ab. 11 sq. m. and pop. (1971p) 31,798; territorial ✱ Kavaratti.

Lac du Flam·beau \ˌläk-də-ˈflam-(ˌ)bō\. Lake in Vilas co., N Wisconsin; a source of Flambeau river.

Lacedaemon. See SPARTA 7.

La Cei·ba \lä-ˈsā-bə\. Caribbean seaport, ✱ of Atlántida dept., N Honduras; pop. (1961c) 24,863; bananas.

La·cey \ˈlā-sē\. City, Thurston co., W Washington, 7 m. E of Olympia; pop. (1970c) 9696; livestock raising; dairy farming.

La·cha, Lake \-ˈläch-ə\. Lake, SW Arkhangelsk Oblast, Russian S.F.S.R., U.S.S.R.; ab. 141 sq. m.; one of the sources of Onega river.

La Chaux–de–Fonds \lä-ˌshōd-ə-ˈfō^{n}\. Industrial commune, Neuchâtel canton, W Switzerland, in Jura Mts. 31 m. WNW of Bern; pop. (1970c) 42,347; watchmaking.

Lach Dera. See EWASO NG'IRO.

La·chine \lə-ˈshēn\. Manufacturing city, Montreal I., S Quebec, Canada, on St. Lawrence river 8 m. SW of Montreal; pop. (1971p) 44,345; electrical appliances, machinery; active as port, upper terminus of **Lachine Canal** (Lachine to Montreal, $8\frac{3}{4}$ m., 5 locks, constructed 1821–24; opened 1825) around the **Lachine Rapids** (ab. 3 m.) of the St. Lawrence, below Lake St. Louis and S of Montreal I. (now largely supplanted by 18 m. long canal of Saint Lawrence Seaway). First settled as estate of Robert La Salle 1668 and named (Fr. *La Chine* China) in mockery of his dream that it was a westward passage to China; later settled as town 1675; destroyed by Iroquois 1689 and nearly all inhabitants massacred.

La·chish \ˈlā-kish\. Ancient fortified city, W Judah, Palestine, W of Hebron; its ruins now marked by a mound, Tell ed-Duweir, ab. 16 m. E of Gaza. An inhabited place probably as early as 3200 B.C.; at time of Israelite conquest of Canaan overcome by Joshua; later besieged by Sennacherib 701 B.C., and by Nebuchadnezzar c. 586 B.C.

Lach·lan \ˈläk-lən\. River, tributary of Murrumbidgee, cen. New South Wales, SE Australia; 922 m. long; first river of Australian interior to be explored (1815–17); flows W from Blue Mts. but volume small in dry seasons.

La Cho·rre·ra \ˌläch-ə-ˈrer-ə\. Town, cen. Panama, 19 m. W of Panama; pop. (1970p) 26,026.

La·chute \lə-ˈshüt\. City, ⊗ of Argenteuil co., SW Quebec, Canada, 40 m. WNW of Montreal; pop. (1971p) 11,789; shipping center for farm and dairy products; receives water-power from falls (Fr. *chute*) in North river and has cotton, lumber, paper, and felt mills.

Lacinium Promontorium. See COLONNE, CAPE.

La Cio·tat \ˌläs-yə-ˈtä\ *or anc.* **Cith·a·ris·ta** \ˌsith-ə-ˈris-tə\. Commune, Bouches-du-Rhône dept., SE France, on Mediterranean 12 m. SE of Marseilles; pop. (1968c) 23,916; shipbuilding.

La Cisa Pass. See table at APENNINES.

Lack·a·wan·na \ˌlak-ə-ˈwän-ə\. 1 County in Pennsylvania. See table at PENNSYLVANIA.

2 Industrial city, Erie co., W New York, on Lake Erie 5 m. S of Buffalo; pop. (1970c) 28,657; shipbuilding; steel, abrasives, refractories.

La·clede \lə-ˈklēd\. County in Missouri. See table at MISSOURI.

Lac–Mégantic. See MEGANTIC 3.

Lacobriga. Seaport commune, S Portugal. See LAGOS.

La·combe \lə-ˈkōm\. Town, S cen. Alberta, Canada, 74 m. S of Edmonton; pop. (1971p) 3407; creamery; summer resort; diversified agriculture.

La·con \ˈlā-kən\. City, ⊗ of Marshall co., N cen. Illinois, on Illinois river 25 m. N of Peoria; pop. (1970c) 2147; brickyard, gravel pits; livestock farming.

La Con·cep·ción \ˌläk-ən-ˌsep-sē-ˈōn\. Town, Chiriquí prov., W Panama, W of David; pop. (1970p) 9179.

La Con·da·mine \lä-ˌkō^{n}(n)d-ə-ˈmēn\. Commune, Monaco; pop. (1961c) 11,007; seaside resort.

La·co·nia \lə-ˈkō-nē-ə, -nyə\. 1 Manufacturing city, ⊗ of Belknap co., cen. New Hampshire, 22 m. N of Concord; pop. (1970c) 14,888; lakes Paugus, Winnisquam, and Opechee S of city; summer and winter resort; trading center; knitting machinery, skis, shoes, plywood. Settled 1761 (long known as **Mer·e·dith Bridge** \ˌmer-ə-dəth-\); incorporated as town 1855, as city 1893.

2 Tract of land of indefinite limits around Lake Champlain, extending N to the St. Lawrence; granted 1629 to John Mason and Sir F. Gorges.

3 *or* **La·con·i·ca** \lə-ˈkän-i-kə\. Ancient country occupying SE Peloponnesus, Greece; ✱ Sparta. Bounded on N by Arcadia and Argolis, on E by Aegean Sea, on S by Mediterranean (Gulf of Laconia) and on W by Gulf of Messenia and Messenia. Lofty Taygetus Mts. are along its W coast and border, containing highest peak in the Peloponnesus (7887 ft.); Parnon range is in the E. Drained by Eurotas river. Its two peninsulas on the S enclosing Gulf of Laconia are long rugged promontories terminating in capes Malea and Taínaron. Off Cape Malea is Cerigo I., administered as one of the Ionian Is. Central part of river valley is fertile and productive but agriculture is restricted by general mountainous character. Chief towns Sparta, Gythium, Monemvasía. Its history is that of Sparta. See SPARTA 7.

4 *also* **La·ko·nia** \ˌläk-ə-ˈnē-ə\. Department of Greece. See table at GREECE.

Laconia, Gulf of *or Gk.* **La·ko·ni·kós Kól·pos** \lə-ˌkȯn-ə-ˈkȯs-kȯl-ˌpȯs\. Inlet of the Mediterranean Sea on the S coast of Peloponnesus, S Greece, bet. capes Taínaron and Malea; 30 m. long.

La Co·ru·ña \ˌläk-ə-ˈrün-yə\. 1 Province of NW Spain. See table at SPAIN.

2 *or Eng.* **Co·run·na** \kə-ˈrən-ə\ *or anc.* **Ca·ro·ni·um** \kə-ˈrō-nē-əm\. Seaport commune, its ✱, on Atlantic Ocean 127 m. W of Oviedo; pop. (1970p) 189,654; trades in livestock, fruits, vegetables, wine, hams, sardines, leather; manufactures cigars, cordage, paper, linen goods, barrels; lighthouse (Torre de Hércules) thought to have been built by Carthaginians.

History: Believed to antedate Roman times; reached height of prosperity in Middle Ages; part of caliphate of Córdoba; captured by Portugal 1370; point of departure for Spanish Armada 1588; sacked by Drake 1589; scene of English naval victories over French 1747 and 1805; noted esp. for victory of English under Sir John Moore over French under Marshal Soult 1809; captured by French 1823 and by Carlists 1836.

La·cos·ta Island \lə-ˌkäs-tə-, -ˌkȯs-\. Island in Gulf of Mexico, off W coast of Lee co., SW Florida, at S entrance to Charlotte Harbor.

La Cour·neuve \ˌläk-ər-ˈnərv\. Commune, Seine-St-Denis dept., N France; NNE suburb of Paris; pop. (1968c) 43,318; manufactures chemicals, railroad supplies.

Lac qui Parle \ˌlak-ē-ˈpärl\. 1 Small lake, W Minnesota, an expansion of the Minnesota river; forms part of boundary bet. Lac qui Parle and Chippewa cos.

2 County in Minnesota. See table at MINNESOTA.

La Cres·cent \lə-ˈkres-ᵊnt\. Village, Houston co., Minnesota, 57 m. ESE of Rochester; pop. (1970c) 3296.

La Crosse \lə-ˈkrȯs\. 1 County in Wisconsin. See table at WISCONSIN.

2 City, ⊗ of Rush co., cen. Kansas; pop. (1970c) 1583.

3 City, ⊗ of La Crosse co., W Wisconsin, at junction of Black and Mississippi rivers; pop. (1970c) 51,153; trade and shipping center of agricultural region; agricultural implements, rubber footwear, sheet metal, lumber, beer, heating and air-conditioning equipment; Wisconsin State Univ. (1909); Viterbo Coll. (1931); settled 1841; chartered as city 1856.

Lac–Saint–Jean. See SAINT JOHN, LAKE.

Lac–Saint–Jean–Est. See LAKE SAINT JOHN, EAST.

Lac–Saint–Jean–Ouest. See LAKE SAINT JOHN, WEST.

La Cumbre. See ANDES.

Lacus Asphaltites. See DEAD SEA.

Lac Vieux De·sert \läk-ˌvyüd-ə-ˈza(ə)r, -ˈze(ə)r\. Lake on boundary bet. Vilas co., N Wisconsin, and Gogebic co., NW corner of Michigan penin.; source of the Wisconsin river.

La·cy–Lake·view \ˈlā-sē-ˈlāk-ˌvyü\. City, McLennan co., cen. Texas, 7 m. NW of Waco; pop. (1970c) 2558.

La·da Bay \ˌläd-ə-\ *or formerly* **Pe·per Bay** \ˌpā-pər-\. Inlet of Sunda Strait at W end of island of Java, Indonesia.

La·dakh *or* **La·dak** \lə-ˈdäk\. District, Jammu and Kashmir (*q.v.*); 45,762 sq. m.; ✱ Leh; region contains W Himalayas (Ladakh Range) and Karakoram Range, also valley of upper Indus river. After cease-fire agreement 1949 S Ladakh to India, remainder to Pakistan; part of Indian sector occupied by Chinese (1959) who ceded ab. 750 sq. m. to Pakistan 1963.

Ladakh Range *or* **Ladak Range.** Mountain range in N India and N Pakistan, NE of Indus river; average height 19,000 ft.

La Digue \lə-ˈdēg\. See SEYCHELLES.

La·do Enclave \ˌläd-ō-\. A territory on the W bank of the Nile river N of Lake Albert, now in N Uganda and in SE Sudan; 15,000 sq. m.; explored by British 1870 and later, and claimed for Great Britain 1894; leased to Belgium 1894–1910. Chief town was Lado, on the Nile just S of Mongalla, Sudan.

Lad·o·ga \ˈlad-ə-gə, ˈläd-\ *or Russ.* **La·dozh·sko·ye Oze·ro** \ˈlad-əsh-(s)kə-yə-ˈō-zə-rə\ *or Finnish* **Laa·tok·ka** \ˈlät-ə-ˌkä\. Lake, U.S.S.R.; 6835 sq. m.; 124 m. long, 75 m. wide; max. depth 738 ft.; largest in Europe and 2d largest in U.S.S.R.; formerly divided bet. U.S.S.R. and Finland; now entirely in U.S.S.R., divided bet. Karelian A.S.S.R. and Leningrad Oblast; fed by ab. 70 streams mostly in Finland and Karelian A.S.S.R. on N and W; on the S in U.S.S.R. by the Volkhov and Syas, on the E by the Svir, the outlet of Lake Onega; its outlet is the Neva, from the SW corner through Leningrad to the Gulf of Finland; frozen from October to April; has abundance of fish and has canal system along its S and E shores. Chief towns on its shores are Petrokrepost and Novaya Ladoga in Leningrad Oblast and Serdobol (Sortavala) and Priozersk (Käkisalmi) in Karelian A.S.S.R. (formerly in Finland). Approximately northwestern two thirds and adjacent lands taken by U.S.S.R. as result of treaty of 1940; S part held by Germans 1941–44 in World War II but regained 1944; during siege of Leningrad road built across ice of lake brought supplies to city in the winter.

La Dôle \lä-ˈdōl\. See DÔLE 2.

La Do·ra·da \ˌlä-də-ˈräd-ə\. River port, Caldas dept., W cen. Colombia, on Magdalena river 613 m. from Barranquilla and 109 m. from Puerto Berrio; munic. pop. (1968e) 35,703.

La·dri·lle·ro Gulf \ˌläd-rē-ˌ(y)e(ə)r-ō-\. Inlet of Pacific Ocean W of Wellington I., off SW coast of Chile.

Ladrone Islands. 1 Islands, China Sea. See WAN-SHAN ISLANDS.

2 Islands, Pacific Ocean. See MARIANA ISLANDS.

La·drones \lə-ˈdrōnz, -ˈdrō(ˌ)nās\. Group of small islands in Pacific Ocean off extreme SW coast of Chiriquí prov., Panama.

La·due \lə-ˈd(y)ü\. City, St. Louis co., E Missouri, 10 m. W of St. Louis; pop. (1970c) 10,594.

La·dy·brand \ˈlā-dē-ˌbrand\. Town, E Orange Free State, E cen. Rep. of South Africa, on Caledon river 80 m. E of Bloemfontein; pop. (1967e) 8000.

La·dy·smith \ˈlād-ē-ˌsmith\. 1 City, ⊗ of Rusk co., NW Wisconsin, at falls of Flambeau river 30 m. E of Rice Lake (city); pop. (1970c) 3674; lake resort; creamery, paper mill; dairy farming; Mount Senario Coll. (1962).

2 Town, SE Vancouver I., British Columbia, Canada, on Strait of Georgia 43 m. NNW of Victoria; pop. (1966c) 3410; terminus of ferry from mainland and shipping port for adjacent mining region; center of extensive logging industry; oyster fishery. Incorporated 1904 and named after Ladysmith (3 below).

3 Town, W Natal, E Rep. of South Africa, on a tributary of the Tugela river 115 m. NW of Durban; pop. (1967e) 27,900; active center of trade with N Natal, Orange Free State, and Transvaal; railroad junction; food processing; textiles. Scene of most famous siege of Boer War; occupied by British troops and invested by Boers Oct. 1899–Feb. 28, 1900. See COLENSO.

Lae \ˈlä-ˌā\. Town on New Guinea I., Papua New Guinea, 6°45′S, 147°E, ab. 200 m. N of Port Moresby; pop. (1970e) 24,339. After partial destruction of Rabaul by volcanoes, made capital of Trust Territory of New Guinea 1941. Seized by Japanese Feb. 1942 and used as major supply base; frequently bombed by Allies 1942–43; occupied by Australians Sept. 16, 1943.

Lae·ken \ˈlak-ə(n)\. Former commune in Brabant prov., cen. Belgium, now part of Brussels; site of royal palace.

Læsø *also* **Lä·sø** *or* **Lessø** \ˈles-ˌər\. Island forming a part of Denmark, lying in the upper Kattegat off NE coast of Jutland Penin.; 43 sq. m.; pop. (1965) 2851.

La Es·pe·ran·za \lä-ˌes-pə-ˈrän-sə\. Town, ✱ of Intibucá dept., SW Honduras; pop. (1961c) 1764.

La Es·tra·da \ˌlä-es-ˈträd-ə\. City, Pontevedra prov., NW Spain, 20 m. NNE of Pontevedra; pop. (1970p) 27,550; in rich agricultural and stock-raising region; mineral springs.

La Es·tre·lle·ta \lä-ˌes-tre-ˈlāt-ə, -ˈyāt-ə\. Province, Dominican Republic. See table at DOMINICAN REPUBLIC.

La·fay·ette \ˌläf-ē-ˈet, ˌlā-fē-, ˌlaf-ē-, lə-ˈfā(-ə)t\. 1 Name of a parish in Louisiana and of counties in five states of the U.S. See tables at ARKANSAS, FLORIDA, LOUISIANA, MISSISSIPPI, MISSOURI, WISCONSIN.

2 City, ⊗ of Chambers co., E Alabama; pop. (1970c) 3530; pulpwood mills; clothing; potatoes.

3 City, Contra Costa co., W California, 20 m. NE of San Francisco; pop. (1970c) 20,484; residential; walnuts, horses.

4 City, Boulder co., N cen. Colorado, 18 m. NNW of Denver; pop. (1970c) 3498; coal mining; sugar beets, alfalfa.

5 City, ⊗ of Tippecanoe co., W cen. Indiana, on Wabash river 58 m. NW of Indianapolis; pop. (1970c) 44,955; in agricultural region; market center for grain and livestock; manufactures flour, lumber, electrical appliances, rubber and aluminum products, automobile parts, pharmaceuticals; Purdue Univ. (1865). The battlefield of Tippecanoe, in which General William Henry Harrison defeated the Indians 1811, is on the edge of the city.

6 City, ⊗ of Lafayette parish, S Louisiana, 55 m. WSW of Baton Rouge; pop. (1970c) 68,908; market and distributing center for cotton, cottonseed oil, sugar, lumber, livestock; supply center for S Louisiana oil and natural gas industry; Univ. of Southwestern Louisiana (1900); settled 1824; before World War II a predominantly French-speaking city.

7 City, ⊗ of Macon co., N Tennessee; pop. (1970c) 2583.

La Fay·ette \lə-ˈfet\. City, ⊗ of Walker co., NW Georgia, 18 m. WSW of Dalton; pop. (1970c) 6044; agricultural trading center; textile mills; scene of local engagements (1864) in the Civil War.

Lafayette, Mount \-ˌläf-ē-ˈet\. Peak in Franconia Mts., in N Grafton co., N cen. New Hampshire; 5249 ft.

Lafayette National Park. Former name (1919–29) of *Acadia National Park.* See UNITED STATES, *National Parks.*

La Fère \lə-'fe(ə)r\. Commune, Aisne dept., N France; pop. (1962c) 3917; important point on Hindenburg Line during World War I, occupied by Germans Sept. 3, 1914–Oct. 10, 1918.

La Fe·ria \lə-'fer-e-ə\. City, Cameron co., S Texas, 25 m. NW of Brownsville; pop. (1970c) 2642; packs and ships fruits and vegetables; cotton gins.

La Fer·té–Ber·nard \läf-er-'tā-ber-'när\. Commune, Sarthe dept., NW France, 27 m. NE of Le Mans; pop. (1962c) 6235; captured by English 1424 after siege of 4 months; belonged to Guise family in 16th cent.

La Ferté–Mi·lon \-mē-'lō^{n}\. Commune, Aisne dept., N France, 47 m. SW of Reims; pop. (1962c) 1778; birthplace of Jean Racine; partially destroyed in World War I.

La·fia \lə-'fē-ə\. Town, Benue-Plateau State, Nigeria; pop. (1969e) 62,237.

La·flèche \lə-'flesh\. City, Chambly co., S Quebec, Canada; pop. (1971p) 15,036; residential suburb of Montreal.

La Flèche \lə-'flesh\. Commune, Sarthe dept., NW France, on Loir river 24 m. SSW of Le Mans; pop. (1968c) 13,768; manufactures gloves and hats; 16th cent. castle (once a Jesuit college in which Descartes studied).

La Fol·lette \lə-'fäl-ət\. City, Campbell co., N Tennessee, 31 m. NNW of Knoxville; pop. (1970c) 6902; coal mines; lake resort; diversified agriculture.

La·fourche \lə-'füsh\. 1 Bayou, SE Louisiana; an outlet of Mississippi river; ab. 150 m. long; navigable by steamboats.
2 Parish in Louisiana. See table at LOUISIANA.

La Futa Pass. See table at APENNINES.

Lag·an \'lag-ən\. River, NE Ireland; ab. 35 m. long; rises in co. Down, SE Northern Ireland; flows NNE into Belfast Lough at Belfast.

La·gan \'läg-ˌän\. River, S Sweden; 180 m. long; flows S and W into the Kattegat S of Halmstad.

La Ga·renne–Co·lombes \ˌläg-ə-'ren-kə-'lōm, -'lō^{n}b\. Commune, Hauts-de-Seine dept., N France; NW suburb of Paris; pop. (1968c) 26,562; chemicals.

La·ga·ri·na \ˌläg-ə-'rē-nə\. Valley of the Adige river in Trentino-Alto Adige, NE Italy, E of Lake Garda; ab. 50 m. long.

La·gar·to \lə-'gärt-(ˌ)ō\. 1 Municipality, Sergipe state, E Brazil, ab. 45 m. W of Aracaju; pop. (1968e) 50,998.
2 River in cen. Panama, W of the Canal Zone; flows NW into the Caribbean Sea.

La·gash \'lā-ˌgash\ *or* **Shir·pur·la** \shi(ə)r-'pür-lə\. Sumerian city and city-state in S Babylonia (its site now in Iraq), bet. the Euphrates and Tigris rivers ab. lat. 31°30′N and long. 46°09′E. Flourished c. 2700 B.C. to c. 2400 B.C.; its classical period, esp. in sculpture and literature was under its ruler Gudea, c. 2150 B.C.; excavations have revealed ruins of palace and temple and many inscribed tablets.

La·ga·we \lə-'gä-(ˌ)wā\. Municipality, ❋ of Ifugao prov., Luzon, Phil.; pop. (1970e) 19,300.

Lå·gen *or* **Laa·gen** \'lō-gən\ *or* **Nu·me·dals·lå·gen** \'nü-mə-ˌdäls-ˌlō-gən\. River, S Norway; 212 m. long; flows S into Skagerrak at Larvik.

La·ges \'lä-zhish\. Municipality, Santa Catarina state, S Brazil; pop. (1968e) 96,889.

Lag·gan, Loch \-'lag-ən\. Lake in Perth co., cen. Scotland.

Laggan Bay. Inlet of Atlantic Ocean on S coast of Islay I., off W coast of Scotland.

Lagh·mān \läg-'män\. Province of NE Afghanistan. See table at AFGHANISTAN.

La·ghou·at \lä-'gwät\. Oasis and commune, Oasis dept., Algeria, in the Atlas Mts.; pop. (1966c) 26,553.

La Giudecca. See GIUDECCA.

La·go *Span.* 'läg-(ˌ)ō, *Port.* 'läg-(ˌ)ü\. Spanish and Portuguese for "lake"; in such names as **Lago Puyehue, Lago Rupanco,** etc., see PUYEHUE, LAGO; RUPANCO, LAGO.

La·goa \lə-'gō-ə\. Portuguese for "lagoon" or "lake"; in such names as **Lagoa dos Patos,** etc., see PATOS, LAGOA DOS.

La Goajira *or* **La Goagira.** See LA GUAJIRA.

La·go·noy \'lä-gō-ˌnȯi\. Municipality, E Camarines Sur prov., Luzon, Phil., NE of Mt. Isarog and near head of Lagonoy Gulf; pop. (1969e) 43,300.

Lagonoy Gulf. Large inlet of the Pacific Ocean in SE Luzon, Phil.; its N and W shores formed by Camarines Sur prov. and its S shore by Albay prov. and the chain of four islands: San Miguel, Cagraray, Batan, and Rapu-Rapu; on the NE is Catanduanes I.

Lagoon Islands. See ELLICE ISLANDS.

La·gos \'lā-ˌgäs, 'läg-əs\. 1 Island off low and marshy coast of SW Nigeria, W Africa; 5 sq. m.; named in 15th cent. by Portuguese explorers because of its many lagoons or lakes (Port. *lagos*).
2 State of SW Nigeria. See table at NIGERIA.
3 Seaport, ❋ of Nigeria and ❋ of Lagos State, on Lagos I. (with section on mainland), at W end of a large lagoon, SW Nigeria; met. area pop. (1971e) 1,112,463; connected by rail with Kano in N; chief port of Nigeria; international airport; major trade and industrial center; brewing, food processing, ship repairing, printing; steel, textiles, soap, tires, furniture, paper; univ. (1962). Ceded to Britain 1861; governed from Sierra Leone 1866–74 and as part of Gold Coast to 1886, then separate colony; joined to protectorate of Southern Nigeria 1906; city confirmed as federal capital 1960.

Lagos \'lag-(ˌ)üsh\ *or anc.* **Lac·o·bri·ga** \ˌlak-ə-'brī-gə\. Seaport commune, Faro dist., S Portugal, on Atlantic Ocean 41 m. WNW of Faro; munic. pop. (1970p) 16,610; sardine and tunny fisheries; naval battle in **Lagos Bay** Aug. 18, 1759, in which French fleet was defeated by English under Admiral Boscawen.

Lagos de Mo·re·no \'läg-(ˌ)ōs-də-mə-'ren-(ˌ)ō\. Municipality, Jalisco state, Mexico, 25 m. NW of León; pop. (1970p) 66,273; vegetable oils, dairy products, preserves; diversified agriculture.

Lagosta. See LASTOVO.

La Goulette. See HALQ AL-WADI.

La Grand'·Combe \lə-'grä^{n}-'kō^{n}b\. Mining and manufacturing commune, Gard dept., S France, on Gardon d'Alès river 31 m. NNW of Nîmes; pop. (1968c) 13,240; coal.

La Grande \lə-'grand\. City, ⊗ of Union co., NE Oregon, on Grande Ronde river at foot of Blue Mts. 40 m. N of Baker; pop. (1970c) 9645; lumber, flour, beverages; diversified agriculture; Eastern Oregon Coll. (1929); first settled on old Oregon Trail 1861.

La·grange \lə-'grānj\. 1 County in N Indiana. See table at INDIANA.
2 Town, its ⊗, 40 m. E of South Bend; pop. (1970c) 2053; livestock and dairy farming.

La Grange \lə-'grānj\. 1 City, ⊗ of Troup co., W Georgia, 40 m. N of Columbus; pop. (1970c) 23,301; textiles, lumber; La Grange Coll. (1831); incorporated 1828.
2 Village, Cook co., NE Illinois, 13 m. W of Chicago; pop. (1970c) 16,773; suburb of Chicago; prehistoric Indian burial mounds nearby.
3 City, ⊗ of Oldham co., N Kentucky; pop. (1970c) 1713.
4 Town, Lenoir co., E North Carolina, 13 m. ESE of Goldsboro; pop. (1970c) 2558; lumber, tobacco.
5 City, ⊗ of Fayette co., SE cen. Texas, on Colorado river 32 m. WSW of Brenham; pop. (1970c) 3092; in section growing cotton and corn.

La Grange Park. Village, Cook co., NE Illinois; pop. (1970c) 15,626; a W suburb of Chicago.

La Granja. See SAN ILDEFONSO 2.

La Gran Pie·dra \lä-ˌgrän-pē-'ā-drə\. Peak near Santiago de Cuba, Cuba; 4100 ft.

La Guai·ra \lə-'gwī-rə\. Seaport town in the Federal District, N Venezuela; pop. (1961c) 20,497; port for Caracas; the leading seaport of Venezuela with good harbor, dry dock, and shipbuilding plant; in direct line 8 m. N of Caracas but 23 m. by railroad in winding line up the mountains to the capital at 3020 ft.; also connected by 10 m. road opened during 1950's. Founded 1577; destroyed by earthquake of 1812 and damaged during war for independence.

La Gua·ji·ra *also* **La Goa·ji·ra** *or* **La Goa·gi·ra** \lä-gwä-'hir-ə\. Department of NE Colombia; forms a peninsula ab. 80 m. long by 30 to 60 m. wide bet. Gulf of Venezuela and the Caribbean; its N point is Point Gallinas. See table at COLOMBIA.

La·guna \lə-'gü-nə\. Spanish and Portuguese for "lake" or "lagoon"; in such names as **Laguna Blanca, Laguna del Perro, Laguna Madre,** etc. See BLANCA, LAGUNA; PERRO, LAGUNA DEL; MADRE, LAGUNA.

Laguna. 1 Indian village and pueblo, Valencia co., W New Mexico, in Laguna Indian Reservation, ab. 42 m. W of Albuquerque.

2 Seaport city, Santa Catarina state, S Brazil, 60 m. S of Florianópolis; munic. pop. (1968e) 37,146.

3 Province of irregular shape, S cen. Luzon, Phil.; 679 sq. m.; pop. (1970p) 718,518; ❋ Santa Cruz; on N and NE borders on Laguna de Bay and its NE portion N of the lake borders on Rizal prov.; bounded on E and SE by Quezon prov., on SW by Batangas, and on W by Cavite; mountainous in the NE and S parts; highest points Maquiling 3650 ft., and San Cristobal on the Quezon border ab. 4900 ft.; well watered by many short streams from the mountain ranges to the lake, some of which are remarkable for waterfall (see PAGSANJAN), grottoes, or mineral springs. Its most notable physical feature the Lake of Bay (Laguna de Bay), which abounds in fish. Has fertile soil and produces coconuts, rice, sugarcane, abacá, and corn chiefly for Manila markets; varied and important industries. Inhabitants mostly Tagalogs. Chief towns San Pablo, Calamba, Biñan, Santa Cruz, and Santa Rosa.

History: Region well populated when visited by Spaniards 1571; scene of uprising of Chinese 1639; invaded by British 1763; scene of revolt 1840; boundaries changed several times in latter part of 19th cent.; active in 1896 revolt; civil government established July 1902.

Laguna, La. See LA LAGUNA.

Laguna Beach. City, Orange co., SW California, 27 m. SE of Long Beach; pop. (1970c) 14,550; resort and artists' colony in rugged coastal area.

Laguna Dam. Dam across Colorado river on S California-Arizona boundary N of Yuma, Arizona; forms **Laguna Reservoir** S of and adjoining Imperial Reservoir.

Laguna de Bay. See BAY, LAGUNA DE.

Laguna de Flores. See PETÉN ITZA.

La Ha·ba·na \ˌlä-(ä-)'vän-ə\. 1 Province of W Cuba. See table at CUBA.

2 Seaport, Cuba. See HAVANA 2.

La Ha·bra \lə-'häb-rə\. City, Orange co., SW California, 19 m. NE of Long Beach; pop. (1970c) 41,350; electronic components; citrus fruit.

La Hague, Cape \-lə-'häg\ *or Fr.* **Cap de la Hague** \käp-də-lä-äg\. Headland on the coast of Manche dept., NW France, W of Cherbourg, projecting into the English Channel.

La·hai·na \lə-'hī-nə\. 1 Division, Maui co., Hawaii, W end of Maui I.

2 City in division, on NW coast of Maui on Auau Channel; pop. (1970c) 3718; the channel at this point being known as **Lahaina Roadstead,** formerly an important anchorage of U.S. Pacific fleet; long a place of residence of Hawaiian kings and an early mission station; in 1840 rival of Honolulu as a leading town; importance decreased after 1875.

La Haye–du–Puits \lä-ˌā-dü-pü-'ē\. Commune, Manche dept., NW France, on W side of Cotentin Penin. S of Cherbourg; pop. (1962c) 1704; captured by Americans July 5–6, 1944.

Lahej *or* **Lahij.** See AL-HOUTA.

La Hi·gue·ra \ˌlä-ē-'ger-ə\. Commune, cen. Chile. See CRUZ GRANDE.

La·hi·la·hi Point \ˌlä-hē-'lä-hē-\. Cape on W cen. coast of Oahu I., Hawaii.

Lahn \'län\. River, Hesse, West Germany; 152 m. long; flows S and SW into Rhine river 4 m. SE of Koblenz; navigable to Giessen.

La Hogue \lə-'hōg\ *or* **La Hougue** \-'hüg\. Roadstead off Point Barfleur on the E coast of Cotentin Penin., Manche dept., NW France; naval battle May 19–23, 1692 in which French under de Tourville were defeated by the combined English and Dutch fleets under Adm. Edward Russell.

La·hore \lə-'hō(ə)r, -'hȯ(ə)r\. 1 Former division of the Punjab, NW Brit. India; 12,203 sq. m.; in 1947 divided: Gujranwala, Sheikhupura, and Sialkot dists. and parts of Gurdaspur and Lahore dists. assigned to Pakistan; Ambala and Jullundur dists. and remainders of Gurdaspur and Lahore assigned to India.

2 District of division, Pakistan; 2216 sq. m.

3 City, ❋ of Punjab prov., Pakistan, near Ravi river; met. area pop. (1971e) 1,985,800; military cantonment; important rail junction and trade center; large railroad workshops; iron, steel, rubber, textiles, shoes, gold and silver lace and ornaments; Univ. of the Punjab (1882); West Pakistan Univ. of Engineering and Technology (1961). The modern city includes the old walled city, the former European quarter, several suburbs, and the large cantonment of Mian Mir; especially notable among the fine architectural remains are the Fort and the mosque of Wazir Khan, the tomb of Emperor Jahangir in nearby Shahdara (across the Ravi), the famous suburban Shalamar Gardens of Shah Jahan with magnificent terraces and fountains, and the tomb of Sikh prince Ranjit Singh.

History: An ancient city, but not prominent until the time of the Moguls; capital of Ghazni and Ghuri sultans in 11th and 12th cents. and often the residence of the Great Mogul—1584–98 under Akbar and 1622–27 under Jahangir; became part of Sikh kingdom in 1767 and flourished anew under Ranjit Singh; conquered by British troops 1846, placed under British sovereignty 1849.

Lahr \'lär\. Manufacturing city, Baden-Württemberg, West Germany, 22 m. N of Freiburg; pop. (1969e) 24,838; cigars, leather, lumber; 13th cent. church. First mentioned 1250; made city 1366; passed to Baden by Peace of Lunéville 1801.

Lah·ti \'lät-ē\. City, Häme prov., S Finland, NNE of Helsinki; pop. (1970e) 89,360; center of Finnish furniture industry; beer, clothing; received charter 1878.

Lahu, Grand. See GRAND LAHOU.

Laibach. See LJUBLJANA.

Laichow. See I-HSIEN.

Laie \'lī-ā\. Town, Honolulu co., Hawaii, 25 m. NW of Honolulu; pop. (1970c) 3009.

Laigue, Fo·rêt de \fō-ˌräd-ᵊl-'āg\. Woods near Compiègne, N France. See RETHONDES.

Laing's Nek. See LANG'S NEK.

Lainsitz. See LUŽNICE.

Lai–yang \'lī-'yäŋ\. City, E Shantung prov., NE China, 50 m. SW of Chefoo; silk trade.

La·ja \'lä-(ˌ)hä\. 1 A lake in cen. Chile, in the Andes Mts.

2 River, S cen. Chile; ab. 150 m. long; flows W from Laja lake into Bío-Bío river; **Laja Falls** are a short distance from the city of Concepción.

La·jas \'lä-(ˌ)häs\. Town and municipality, SW Puerto Rico; pop. (1970c) 3364 (town), 16,437 (munic.); town in railroad junction point ab. 12 m. SE of Mayagüez.

La·je·a·do \lə-zhē-'äd-(ˌ)ü\. Municipality, Rio Grande do Sul, S Brazil, ab. 70 m. NW of Pôrto Alegre; pop. (1968e) 56,065.

La·jes do Pi·co \ˌlä-zhēs-də-'pē-kü\. See PICO 3.

La Jol·la \lə-ˈhȯi-ə\. A NW section of San Diego, California; site of University of California, San Diego.

La·jos·mi·zse \ˈlä-yōsh-ˌmizh-ə\. Commune, Bács-Kiskun co., cen. Hungary, 40 m. SE of Budapest; pop. (1970p) 12,789.

Lajta. See LEITHA.

La Jun·ta \lə-ˈhənt-ə\. City, ⊗ of Otero co., SE Colorado, on Arkansas river 63 m. ESE of Pueblo; pop. (1970c) 7938; cannery, meat-packing plant; sugar beets, melons; Otero Junior Coll. (1941); founded 1875.

Lake \ˈlāk\. **1** Name of counties in twelve states of the U.S. See tables at CALIFORNIA, COLORADO, FLORIDA, ILLINOIS, INDIANA, MICHIGAN, MINNESOTA, MONTANA, OHIO, OREGON, SOUTH DAKOTA, TENNESSEE.
2 River, E cen. Tasmania, Australia; ab. 35 m. long; flows N to join the South Esk at Longford.

Lake Al·fred \-ˈal-frəd, -fərd\. City, Polk co., cen. Florida, 15 m. E of Lakeland; pop. (1970c) 2847.

Lake An·des \-ˈan-(ˌ)dēz\. City, ⊗ of Charles Mix co., S South Dakota; pop. (1970c) 948.

Lake Ar·thur \-ˈär-thər\. Town, Jefferson Davis parish, SW Louisiana, 37 m. ESE of Lake Charles; pop. (1970c) 3551; resort; rice, sugar.

Lake Bluff \-ˈbləf\. Village, Lake co., NE corner of Illinois, on Lake Michigan 8 m. S of Waukegan; pop. (1970c) 4979; summer resort.

Lake But·ler \-ˈbət-lər\. City, ⊗ of Union co., NE Florida; pop. (1970c) 1598; truck farming.

Lake Charles \-ˈchär(ə)lz\. Commercial and industrial city, ⊗ of Calcasieu parish, SW Louisiana, 13 m. NNE of Calcasieu Lake; pop. (1970c) 77,998; ships cotton, sugar, rice; sulfur and oil deposits nearby; oil refineries; chemicals, rubber; McNeese State Coll. (1939); founded 1852.

Lake City. 1 Town, a ⊗ of Craighead co., NE Arkansas; pop. (1970c) 948.
2 Town, ⊗ of Hinsdale co., Colorado, 43 m. SE of Montrose; pop. (1970c) 91.
3 City, ⊗ of Columbia co., N Florida, 44 m. NNW of Gainesville; pop. (1970c) 10,575; resort; lumber, turpentine; poultry farming; Lake City Junior Coll. and Forest Ranger School (1947); headquarters for Ocala National Forest.
4 City, Calhoun co., NW cen. Iowa; pop. (1970c) 1910.
5 City, ⊗ of Missaukee co., NW cen. Michigan; pop. (1970c) 704.
6 City, Wabasha co., SE Minnesota, on Mississippi river 31 m. NNE of Rochester; pop. (1970c) 3594; resort; precision tools; diversified agriculture.
7 Town, Florence co., E South Carolina, 22 m. S of Florence; pop. (1970c) 6247; stock and truck farms.
8 Town, Anderson co., E Tennessee, 9 m. W of Norris Dam; pop. (1970c) 1923.

Lake Dallas Dam. See GARZA DAM.

Lake District. Mountainous region in NW England, comprised within Cumberland, Westmorland, and Furness dist., Lancashire, containing many well-known lakes and peaks. Among the lakes are Bassenthwaite, Buttermere, Coniston Water, Crummock Water, Derwent Water, Ennerdale Water, Grasmere, Hawes Water, Loweswater, Rydal Water, Thirlmere, Ullswater, Wast Water, Windermere. A favorite resort of English poets, especially since Wordsworth's long residence here and his association with the other Lake Poets Southey and Coleridge; now a major center for tourism.

Lake For·est \-ˈfȯr-əst, -ˈfär-\. City, Lake co., NE corner of Illinois, on Lake Michigan 10 m. S of Waukegan; pop. (1970c) 15,642; residential; Lake Forest Coll. (1857), Barat Coll. of the Sacred Heart (1857).

Lake Forest Park. City, King co., W cen. Washington; pop. (1970c) 2530.

Lake Ge·ne·va \-jə-ˈnē-və\. **1** City and resort, Walworth co., S Wisconsin, on shore of Lake Geneva 30 m. W of Kenosha; pop. (1970c) 4890; Yerkes Observatory nearby.
2 Lake, Switzerland and France. See GENEVA, LAKE OF.

Lake George \-ˈjȯ(ə)rj\. Village, ⊗ of Warren co., E New York, on S end of Lake George 40 m. NE of Amsterdam; pop. (1970c) 1046; year-round sports center.

Lake Grove. Village, Suffolk co., SE New York, 7 m. NE of Islip; pop. (1970c) 8133.

Lake·hurst \ˈlāk-(ˌ)hərst\. Borough, Ocean co., E New Jersey, 8 m. NW of Toms River; pop. (1970c) 2641; U.S. Naval Air Station; estab. 1919; here *Graf Zeppelin* started and finished 21-day around-the-world trip 1929 and the *Hindenburg* was destroyed by fire May 6, 1937.

Lake in the Hills. Village, McHenry co., N Illinois, 10 m. N of Elgin; pop. (1970c) 3240.

Lake Jack·son \-ˈjak-sən\. City, Brazoria co., SE Texas, S of Houston; pop. (1970c) 13,376; metalworking; dairy and fruit farms.

Lake·land \ˈlā-klənd\. **1** City, Polk co., cen. Florida penin., 30 m. E of Tampa; pop. (1970c) 41,550; phosphate mining; citrus fruits; winter resort; Florida Southern Coll. (1886), South-Eastern Bible Coll. (1935).
2 City, ⊗ of Lanier co., S Georgia, 20 m. NE of Valdosta; pop. (1970c) 2569; agricultural market.

Lake Man·ya·ra National Park \-mən-ˈyär-ə-\. National park, NE Tanzania; 123 sq. m.; incl. most of **Lake Manyara;** wide variety of wildlife; established 1960.

La·kem·ba \lə-ˈkem-bə\. **1** Island group, ab. 33 islands, S end of Lau group, SE Fiji, SW Pacific Ocean.
2 Chief island of the Lakemba group, 18°10′S, 178°47′W; 12 sq. m.; long a meeting place bet. Fijians and Tonga islanders; produces copra and tropical fruits. Here first Wesleyan missionaries settled 1835.

Lake Mills \-ˈmilz\. **1** Town, Winnebago co., N Iowa, 26 m. NW of Mason City; pop. (1970c) 2124; livestock.
2 City, Jefferson co., SE Wisconsin, 23 m. E of Madison; pop. (1970c) 3556; summer resort; dairy equipment; dairy and poultry farms.

Lake·more \ˈlāk-ˌmō(ə)r, -mȯ(ə)r\. Village, Summit co., NE Ohio, 8 m. SE of Akron; pop. (1970c) 2708.

Lake Na·ku·ru National Park \-nä-ˈkü(ə)r-(ˌ)ü-\. National park, Kenya, ab. 81 m. NW of Nairobi; 18 sq. m.; habitat for ab. 380 species of birds; established 1961.

La·ken·heath \ˈlā-kən-ˌhēth\. Village, NW Suffolk, E England, 9 m. W of Thetford; pop. (1961c) 1713; U.S. air base.

Lake of the Cherokees. See PENSACOLA DAM.

Lake of the Ozarks. See OZARKS, LAKE OF THE.

Lake of the Woods. 1 Lake in N Minnesota and extending into Canadian provinces of Manitoba (on the W) and Ontario (on the E); 72 m. long and from 10 to 60 m. wide; area 1695 sq. m., of which 642 sq. m. are in U.S. territory; max. depth 69 ft.; elevation 1060 ft.; receives Rainy river from the SE and drains N into Lake Winnipeg.
2 County in Minnesota. See table at MINNESOTA.

Lake Ori·on \-ˈōr-ē-ən, -ˈȯr-\. Village, Oakland co., SE Michigan, 10 m. NNE of Pontiac; pop. (1970c) 2921; summer resort; aircraft parts; diversified agriculture.

Lake Os·wego \-ä-ˈswē-(ˌ)gō\. City, Clackamas, Multnomah, and Washington cos., NW Oregon, 8 m. S of Portland; pop. (1970c) 14,573; residential suburb of Portland.

Lake Park. Town, Palm Beach co., SE Florida, 5 m. N of Palm Beach; pop. (1970c) 6993.

Lake Plac·id \-ˈplas-əd\. Village, Essex co., NE New York, in Adirondack Mts. on Mirror Lake, near Lake Placid (*q.v.*), 40 m. SW of Plattsburg; pop. (1970c) 2731; summer and winter resort, scene of Winter Olympic Games 1932; site of Lake Placid Club, founded 1895 by Melvil Dewey.

Lake Pleas·ant \-ˈplez-ənt\. Village and resort, ⊗ of Hamilton co., NE cen. New York, 50 m. ENE of Utica.

Lake Pleasant Dam. Dam across Agua Fria river on boundary of Yavapai and Maricopa cos., W cen. Arizona; height 256 ft.; completed 1927; impounds water for irrigation and waterpower.

Lake·port \ˈlāk-ˌpō(ə)rt, -ˌpȯ(ə)rt\. City, ⊗ of Lake co., W California, on W side of Clear Lake; pop. (1970c) 3005; summer resort; beans, pears, walnuts.

Lake Prov·i·dence \-ˈpräv-əd-ən(t)s, -ə-den(t)s\. Town, ⊗ of East Carroll parish, NE corner of Louisiana, on Mississippi river 60 m. ENE of Monroe; pop. (1970c) 6183; fishing; wood products; diversified agriculture.

Lake Saint John. See SAINT JOHN, LAKE.

Lake Saint John, East \-sānt-ˈjän\ *or Fr.* **Lac–Saint–Jean–Est** \lák-saⁿ-zhäⁿ-est\. County, Quebec, Canada. See table at QUEBEC.

Lake Saint John, West *or Fr.* **Lac–Saint–Jean–Ouest** \-west\. County, Quebec, Canada. See table at QUEBEC.

Lake·side Park \ˈlāk-ˌsīd-\. City, Kenton co., N Kentucky, 5 m. S of Cincinnati, Ohio; pop. (1970c) 2511.

Lake Spaul·ding Dam \-ˈspȯl-diŋ-\. Dam across S Yuba river, N cen. California; height 275 ft.; completed 1913; impounds water for waterpower.

Lake Suc·cess \-sək-ˈses\. Unincorporated village, Nassau co., SE New York, W Long Island, near N shore E of Flushing and ab. 4½ m. NW of Mineola; pop. (1970c) 3254; headquarters of United Nations Security Council 1946–51.

Lake·view \ˈlāk-ˌvyü\. 1 Unincorporated urban area, Calhoun co., S Michigan, SW of Battle Creek; pop. (1970c) 11,391.

2 Town, ⊗ of Lake co., S Oregon, 6 m. N of Goose Lake; pop. (1970c) 2705; lumber; livestock raising.

3 Town, Jefferson co., SE Texas, 17 m. SE of Beaumont; pop. (1970c) 3567.

Lake Village. City, ⊗ of Chicot co., SE corner of Arkansas, 80 m. SSE of Pine Bluff; pop. (1970c) 3310; resort on Lake Chicot; clothing; cotton, soybeans.

Lake·ville \ˈlāk-(ˌ)vil\. 1 Subdivision of town of Salisbury, Connecticut; trade center. See SALISBURY 1.

2 Town, Plymouth co., SE Massachusetts, 15 m. S of Brockton; pop. (1970c) 4736; in agricultural region.

3 Village, Dakota co., SE Minnesota, 26 m. SE of Minneapolis; pop. (1970c) 7556.

Lake Wales \-ˈwā(ə)lz\. City, Polk co., cen. Florida penin., 25 m. ESE of Lakeland; pop. (1970c) 8240; winter resort; ships citrus fruits; Edward W. Bok's Mountain Lake bird sanctuary with Singing Tower nearby. See MOUNTAIN LAKE.

Lake Washington Ship Canal. See WASHINGTON, LAKE.

Lake·wood \ˈlā-ˌkwu̇d\. 1 City, Los Angeles co., SW coastal California, NE of Long Beach; pop. (1970c) 82,993.

2 City, Jefferson co., cen. Colorado, W of Denver; pop. (1970c) 92,787; residential.

3 Unincorporated community, Ocean co., E New Jersey, 14 m. SW of Asbury Park; pop. (1970c) 17,874; electronic components; poultry farming; health resort in pine forest and lake region; Georgian Court Coll. (1908).

4 Village, Chautauqua co., SW corner of New York, on Chautauqua Lake 5 m. W of Jamestown; pop. (1970c) 3864.

5 City, Cuyahoga co., N Ohio, on Lake Erie 5 m. W of Cleveland; pop. (1970c) 70,173; residential suburb of Cleveland.

Lake Worth \-ˈwərth\. 1 Lagoon, SE Florida. See WORTH, LAKE.

2 City, Palm Beach co., SE Florida, on Lake Worth 6 m. S of West Palm Beach; pop. (1970c) 23,714; winter resort; Palm Beach Junior Coll. (1933); incorporated 1923.

Lake Worth Village. City, Tarrant co., N Texas, 13 m. NW of Fort Worth; pop. (1970c) 4958.

Lake Zu·rich \-ˈzu̇(ə)r-ik\. Village, Lake co., NE Illinois, 18 m. SW of Waukegan; pop. (1970c) 4082; lake resort; concrete products, tools.

La·khim·pur \ˈlək-əm-ˌpu̇(ə)r\. Town, E Uttar Pradesh, India, 75 m. N of Lucknow; pop. (1961c) 32,285.

Lakhnauti. See GAUR.

Lakhon. See NAKHON PHANOM.

La·kin \ˈlā-kən\. City, ⊗ of Kearny co., W Kansas; pop. (1970c) 1570; gas and oil wells.

Lakonia. See LACONIA 4.

Lakonikós Kólpos. See LACONIA, GULF OF.

La·kor \ˈläk-ˌȯ(ə)r\. Small island in E part of Leti Is., Indonesia; 10 m. by 6 m.

La·ko·ta \lə-ˈkōt-ə\. City, ⊗ of Nelson co., E North Dakota; pop. (1970c) 964; dairy and grain farming.

Lak·se Fjord \ˌläk-sə-\. Inlet of Arctic Ocean on NE coast of Norway, bet. Porsanger Fjord and Tana Fjord.

Lak·se·våg \ˌläk-sə-ˈvȯg\. Commune, Hordaland co., Norway; pop. (1970e) 22,060.

La La·gu·na \ˌläl-ə-ˈgü-nə\. Commune, Santa Cruz de Tenerife prov. (W Canary Is.), Spain, NE Tenerife I., 2 m. NNW of Santa Cruz de Tenerife; pop. (1970p) 79,963; former capital; univ. (founded 18th cent., reorganized 1927); 16th cent. cathedral; brandy, tobacco, leather.

Lā·leh Zār, Kūh–e \ˌkü-(h)ə-ˌläl-ə-ˈzär\. Peak in Kermān prov., SE Iran, S of Kermān; 14,347 ft.

La Li·ber·tad \ˌläl-ˌib-ər-ˈtä(th)\. 1 Department of SW El Salvador. See table at EL SALVADOR.

2 Seaport, its ✱, 23 m. SSW of San Salvador; pop. (1961c) 4943; beach resort; coffee, sugar.

3 Department of NW Peru. See table at PERU.

4 Municipality, NE Negros Oriental prov., Negros, Phil., on Tanon Strait, 51 m. N of Dumaguete; pop. (1969e) 34,700.

La·lin \ˈlä-ˈlin\. River, Kirin prov., China; ab. 200 m. long; flows NW and W into Sungari river.

La·lín \lä-ˈlēn\. Commune, Pontevedra prov., NW Spain, 28 m. NE of Pontevedra; pop. (1970p) 52,452; agriculture; tanneries; paper mills.

La Lí·nea \lä-ˈlē-nē-ə\. Commune, Cádiz prov., SW Spain, on Bay of Gibraltar and Gibraltar frontier 56 m. SE of Cádiz; pop. (1970p) 52,127; military garrison.

La·lit·pur \lə-ˈlit-ˌpu̇(ə)r\ *also* **Pa·tan** \ˈpät-ᵊn\. Town, E cen. Nepal, adjoining Katmandu on the S; pop. (1968e) 53,930; gold and silver smithing; palace, Buddhist temples.

La Loche \lə-ˈlōsh\. Small lake, NW Saskatchewan, Canada; its immediate outlet a short stream to Churchill Lake. At its N end is **La Loche Portage,** ab. 12 m. long, to Clearwater river, a headstream of the Athabaska and Mackenzie river system; much used by trappers and hunters.

La·lo Point \ˌläl-(ˌ)ō-\. Cape at S end of Tinian I., Mariana Is., W Pacific, 14°55′N, 140°38′E; last stand of Japanese on the island Aug. 1, 1944.

La Lou·vière \ˌläl-ü-ˈvye(ə)r\. Manufacturing commune, Hainaut prov., SW Belgium, 27 m. S of Brussels; pop. (1969e) 23,644.

Lama. See POK LIU CHAU.

La Mad·da·le·na \lä-ˌmad-ᵊl-ˈā-nə\. Seaport, Sassari prov., NW Sardinia, Italy, on Maddalena I. in Strait of Bonifacio 54 m. NE of Sassari; pop. (1968e) 10,988.

La Ma·de·leine \lə-ˌmad-ᵊl-ˈān\. 1 Rock shelter on the Vézère river above Les Eyzies (see EYZIES, LES), Dordogne dept., SW France; type station, from primitive implements and carvings found here, of the Magdalenian period representing the highest Paleolithic culture in Europe.

2 Commune, Nord dept., N France, NE suburb of Lille; pop. (1968c) 23,203; metalworks, spinning mills, potteries.

La Mag·da·le·na Con·tre·ras \lä-ˌmäg-də-ˈlā-nə-kən-ˈtrer-əs\. Town, N Federal District, cen. Mexico; munic. pop. (1970p) 74,776.

La Mal·baie \lä-mal-ˈbā\. Resort town, ⊗ of East Charlevoix co., S Quebec, Canada, at confluence of Malbaie and St. Lawrence rivers; pop. (1971p) 4032; summer resort. Visited 1608 by Champlain who gave it its name because of poor anchorage; settled chiefly by Scots; American war prisoners confined here during American Revolution.

La Man·cha \lə-'män-chə\. Region, S cen. Spain; comprises Ciudad Real, S Toledo, NW Albacete, and SW Cuenca provs.; formerly the southernmost division of New Castile; high (ab. 2000 ft.), level, arid, treeless plateau, producing chiefly esparto grass and, in lesser quantity, grain and wine; celebrated in Cervantes' novel *Don Quijote de la Mancha*.

La Manche. See ENGLISH CHANNEL.

La·mar \lə-'mär\. 1 Name of counties in four states of the U.S. See tables at ALABAMA, GEORGIA, MISSISSIPPI, TEXAS.
2 City, ⊗ of Prowers co., SE Colorado, on Arkansas river 50 m. E of La Junta; pop. (1970c) 7767; feed mills; agriculture; Lamar Junior Coll. (1937).
3 City, ⊗ of Barton co., SW Missouri, 32 m. NNE of Joplin; pop. (1970c) 3760. Birthplace of Harry S. Truman, 33d president of the U.S.

La·marck, Mount \-lə-'märk\. Peak in Sierra Nevada, in E Fresno co., S cen. California; 13,302 ft.

La Marque \lə-'märk\. City, Galveston co., SE coastal Texas, SE of Houston; pop. (1970c) 16,131; oil refining.

La·mas \'läm-əs\. Town, San Martín dept., N Peru, 45 m. SE of Moyobamba; pop. (1961c) 7100.

Lamb \'lam\. County in Texas. See table at TEXAS.

Lambaesis. See TAZOULT.

Lam·balle \läⁿ-'bal\. Commune, Côtes-du-Nord dept., NW France, ESE of St-Brieuc; pop. (1962c) 6114; capital of the counts of Penthièvre 1134–1420.

Lam·ba·ré·né \,läm-bə-'rā-nē, -nə\. Town, W Gabon, W Africa, on lower Ogooué river; pop. (1970e) 17,770; hospital and medical settlement.

Lam·ba·ye·que \läm-bə-'yā-kē\. 1 Department of Peru. See table at PERU.
2 Town, Lambayeque dept., NW Peru, near the coast just N of Chiclayo; pop. (1961c) 10,600.

Lambayong. See SULTAN SA BARONGIS.

Lam·ber·sart \,läⁿ-,ber-'sär\. Commune, Nord dept., N France, NW suburb of Lille; pop. (1968c) 26,833; spinning mills.

Lam·bert·ville \'lam-bərt-,vil\. City, Hunterdon co., NW cen. New Jersey, on Delaware river 14 m. NNW of Trenton; pop. (1970c) 4359; lace, clothing, hosiery; poultry and truck farms.

Lambèse *or* **Lambessa.** See TAZOULT.

Lam·beth \'lam-bəth\. A borough of Greater London, SE England. See table at LONDON 4.

Lamb·ton \'lam(p)-tən\. County, Ontario, Canada. See table at ONTARIO.

Lam·bu·nao \läm-'bü-(,)naů\. Municipality, Iloilo prov., Panay, Phil., in foothills of W range 26 m. NNW of City of Iloilo; pop. (1969e) 43,200.

La Meije. See MEIJE.

La–meng \'lä-'meŋ\. Town, W Yunnan, S China, on Burma Road just W of the Salween and NE of Lung-ling; fighting June 1944.

La·me·sa \lə-'mē-sə\. City, ⊗ of Dawson co., NW Texas, 43 m. NNW of Big Spring; pop. (1970c) 11,559; oil wells; diversified agriculture.

La Me·sa \lə-'mā-sə\. Residential city, San Diego co., SW corner of California, 8 m. NE of San Diego; pop. (1970c) 39,178; residential; truck farming; citrus fruits.

La·mia \lə-'mē-ə\; *formerly* **La·mía** \lä-'mē-ə\ *or* **Zi·tu·ni** \zē-'tü-nē\. Inland town, ✱ of Phthiotis dept., Greece, near head of Gulf of Maliakós; in ancient times in Malis and nearer the shoreline; pop. (1971p) 38,495. Antipater besieged here by confederate Greeks under Leosthenes for several months (Lamian War, 4th cent. B.C.).

Lamia, Gulf of. See MALIAKÓS, GULF OF.

La Mi·ra·da \,läm-ə-'räd-ə\. City, Los Angeles co., SW California, 17 m. SE of Los Angeles; pop. (1970c) 30,808.

Lam·jung \läm-'jůŋ\. Mountain in the Himalayas, Nepal, ab. 90 m. NW of Katmandu; 26,041 ft.

Lam·lash \lam-'lash\. Village, E coast of Arran I., Bute co., SW Scotland; on **Lamlash Bay,** an inlet of the Firth of Clyde; fine harbor.

Lamma. See POK LIU CHAU.

Lam·me Fjord \,läm-ə-\. W extension of Ise Fjord on N coast of Sjælland, Denmark.

Lam·mer·muir Hills \,lam-ər-,myů(ə)r-\ *or* **Lam·mer·moor Hills** \-,mů(ə)r-\. Range of hills in East Lothian and Berwick cos., SE Scotland; highest point Lammer Law 1733 ft.

La·moille \lə-'mȯi(ə)l\. 1 River, NW Vermont; ab. 75 m. long; flows W through Lamoille and S Franklin cos., S and W into Lake Champlain in NW Chittenden co.
2 County in Vermont. See table at VERMONT.

La·mon Bay \lə-,mȯn-\. Large landlocked bay, an inlet of the Pacific on E coast of Luzon, Phil.; ab. 60 m. each way, N to S and E to W; chiefly in Quezon prov., its SE shore in Camarines Norte; protected on N by the islands of Polillo, Patnanongan, and Jomalig and contains the large island of Alabat in the S; Japanese landed here Dec. 22–28, 1941.

La·mong·an \lä-'mȯŋ-(,)än\. Town, East Java prov., Indonesia, on railroad 25 m. WNW of Surabaja; pop. (1961c) 17,986.

La·mo·ni \lə-'mōn-(,)ī\. Town, ⊗ of Decatur co., S Iowa, 68 m. SSW of Des Moines; pop. (1970c) 2540; Graceland Coll. (1895).

La Mon·ja \lə-'mȯŋ-(,)hä\. Rocky islet, outer part of entrance to Manila Bay, part of Corregidor Is., Phil., nearly 3 m. W of Corregidor I.

La·motte Peak \lə-,mät-\. Mountain, cen. Summit co., NE Utah; 12,723 ft.

La Moure \lə-'mů(ə)r\. 1 County in SE North Dakota. See table at NORTH DAKOTA.
2 City, its ⊗; pop. (1970c) 951.

Lam·pang \'läm-,päŋ\. 1 Province, NW Thailand; 4833 sq. m.; pop. (1960c) 471,699; ✱ Lampang.
2 Town, its ✱, on left bank of Wang river and on railroad 45 m. SE of Chiang Mai; connected by highway with Chiang Rai; pop. (1960c) 36,486; commercial center; sugar refining.

Lam·pas·as \lam-'pas-əs\. 1 County in cen. Texas. See table at TEXAS.
2 City, its ⊗, 45 m. W of Temple; pop. (1970c) 5922; shipping point for livestock, pecans, wool, mohair; tourist resort, with mineral springs nearby; poultry and livestock farming.

Lam·pe·du·sa \,lam-pə-'dü-sə, -zə\ *or anc.* **Lop·a·du·sa** \,läp-ə-'d(y)ü-sə\. One of the Pelagian Is. in Mediterranean Sea, midway bet. Malta and Tunisia; 8 sq. m.; pop. (1968e; including Linosa) 4620; politically attached to Agrigento prov., SW Sicily, Italy; has one village, the port of Il Porto. Modern settlement dates from 18th cent.; in World War II bombarded for one day by Allied fleet June 12, 1943; taken June 13; according to peace treaty of 1947 its fortifications destroyed.

Lam·pert·heim \'läm-pərt-,hīm\. Commune, Hesse, West Germany, near Rhine river 22 m. SSW of Darmstadt; pop. (1969e) 23,882; manufactures furniture; electrical works.

Lam·phun *or* **Lam·pun** \läm-'pün\. 1 Province, NW Thailand; 1702 sq. m.; pop. (1960c) 249,820; ✱ Lamphun; produces rice and tobacco.
2 Town, its ✱, on railroad 15 m. S of Chiang Mai; pop. (1960c) 10,600.

Lam·pio·ne \läm-'pyō-nē\. See PELAGIAN ISLANDS.

Lamp·sa·cus \'lam(p)-sə-kəs\ *or mod.* **Lap·se·ki** \,läp-sə-'kē\. Ancient Greek colony in Mysia on the Hellespont opp. Gelibolu; famous for its wine. Under Persia early in 5th cent. B.C.; ally of Athens 479 B.C., later of Rome. Home of Strato of Lampsacus, Greek peripatetic philosopher.

Lam·pung Bay \'läm-,půŋ-\ *or* **Lam·pong Bay** \-,pȯŋ-\ *or Du.* **Lam·poeng Bay** \-,půŋ-\. Bay at the S end of the island of Sumatra, Indonesia, opening into Sunda Strait. Port of Telukbetung is at its head.

Lamta. See LEPTIS MINOR.

La·mu \'läm-(,)ü\. 1 Island off the E coast of Kenya, E Africa, SW of Dicks Head and 150 m. N of Mombasa.

2 Seaport on the island of Lamu; pop. (1962c) 5828.

3 Town, Arakan division, W Lower Burma, near coast opp. Ramree I.

La·nai \lə-'nī\. Island in cen. Hawaii, W of Maui I.; 141 sq. m.; a division of Maui co., state of Hawaii; separated from Molokai on the N by Kalohi Channel, from Maui on the E by Auau Channel, and from Kahoolawe on the SE by Kealaikahiki Channel. A single mountain, highest point 3369 ft.; pineapple plantations.

Lanai City. Town in Lanai div., Hawaii, in center of Lanai I.; pop. (1970c) 2122.

La·nal·hue, Lake \-lä-'näl-(,)wā\. Lake in S Chile, 23 m. SE of the port of Lebu on the Pacific Ocean.

La·nao, Lake \-lə-'naů\. Lake in W Lanao del Sur prov., Mindanao, Phil.; 131 sq. m.; 22 m. long, max. width ab. 16 m.; largest lake on Mindanao; in plateau region N of range of active volcanoes; outlet is Agus river, flowing N to Iligan Bay.

Lanao del Nor·te \-del-'nȯrt-ē\. Province, Mindanao, Phil.; 1194 sq. m.; pop. (1970p) 383,096; ✱ Iligan; bounded on N by Iligan Bay; established 1959.

Lanao del Sur \-del-'sů(ə)r\. Province, Mindanao, Phil.; 1495 sq. m.; pop. (1970p) 714,231; ✱ Marawi; contains Lake Lanao; established 1959.

Lan·ark \'lan-ərk\. 1 County, Ontario, Canada. See table at ONTARIO.

2 *or* **Lan·ark·shire** \-,shi(ə)r-, -shər\. County, S cen. Scotland; area 897 sq. m.; pop. (1971p) 1,524,848; ⊗ Hamilton; chief river Clyde; shipbuilding (esp. at Glasgow), textile and machinery manufacture, iron and steel founding, engineering, livestock raising, and agriculture; main towns incl. Glasgow, Airdrie, Coatbridge, East Kilbride, Hamilton.

3 Burgh, Lanark co., S cen. Scotland, on the river Clyde 30 m. SE of Glasgow; pop. (1971p) 8701. **New Lanark,** founded (1784) by David Dale and Richard Arkwright 1 m. SW, was the scene of some of Robert Owen's social and industrial experiments.

Lan·bi Island \län-,bē-\ *or formerly* **Sul·li·van Island** \,səl-ə-vən-\. Island, S cen. Mergui Archipelago (*q.v.*), Burma.

Lan·ca·shire \'laŋ-kə-,shi(ə)r, -shər\ *or* **Lan·cas·ter** \'laŋ-kə-stər\. Maritime, manufacturing, and mining county, NW England; 1878 sq. m.; pop. (1971p) 5,106,123; ⊗ Lancaster; rivers include the Mersey and Ribble; deposits of coal, iron, lead, limestone; mining, manufacturing of textiles (esp. cotton), chemicals, machinery, glass, motor vehicles, aircraft, electrical equipment, and rubber; shipbuilding, printing, dyeing; agriculture (esp. vegetables and dairy farming); industrial centers Liverpool, Manchester; seaside resorts Blackpool, Fleetwood, Morecambe and Heysham, Southport.

History: Region part of Anglo-Saxon kingdom of Northumbria and of the Danelaw; honor of Lancaster an important medieval fief which in late 14th cent. became a county palatine; Lancastrian line of English kings the heirs of John of Gaunt, Duke of Lancaster; esp. in Industrial Revolution in 18th cent. Lancashire became noted manufacturing center (see MANCHESTER 11, LIVERPOOL 4, etc.).

Lan·cas·ter \'laŋ-kə-stər, 'lan-,kas-tər, 'laŋ-\. 1 Name of counties in four states of the U.S. See tables at NEBRASKA, PENNSYLVANIA, SOUTH CAROLINA, VIRGINIA.

2 Unincorporated urban area, Los Angeles co., SW coastal California, NE of Los Angeles; pop. (1970c) 30,948; Antelope Valley Coll. (1929).

3 City, ⊗ of Garrard co., E cen. Kentucky, 13 m. E of Danville; pop. (1970c) 3230; diversified agriculture.

4 Town, Worcester co., cen. Massachusetts, 10 m. SE of Fitchburg; pop. (1970c) 6095; Atlantic Union Coll. (1882) at South Lancaster.

5 City, ⊗ of Schuyler co., N Missouri; pop. (1970c) 821.

6 Industrial town, ⊗ of Coos co., N New Hampshire, on Connecticut river 18 m. W of Berlin; pop. (1970c) 3166; summer resort and skiing center.

7 Village, Erie co., W New York, 11 m. E of Buffalo; pop. (1970c) 13,365; residential suburb of Buffalo.

8 City, ⊗ of Fairfield co., S cen. Ohio, 27 m. SE of Columbus; pop. (1970c) 32,911; trade center of dairying and livestock region; glass, shoes, machinery; founded 1800, incorporated 1831. Birthplace of William T. Sherman.

9 City, ⊗ of Lancaster co., SE Pennsylvania, 35 m. ESE of Harrisburg; pop. (1970c) 57,690; trade center in region of diversified agriculture; cattle market; industrial products include watches, television tubes, linoleum, electrical appliances; Franklin and Marshall Coll. (1787), Lancaster School of the Bible (1933). Founded 1730; became gunmaking center; played important part in French and Indian War, and, later, in Revolution; capital of U.S. briefly in 1777 and capital of Pennsylvania for 13 years before 1812; became W terminus of Philadelphia and Lancaster turnpike 1794.

10 Town, ⊗ of Lancaster co., N South Carolina, 21 m. SE of Rock Hill; pop. (1970c) 9186; manufactures textiles, cottonseed oil, fertilizer.

11 City, Dallas co., NE Texas, S of Dallas; pop. (1970c) 10,552; clothing; truck farming.

12 Village, ⊗ of Lancaster co., E Virginia.

13 City, ⊗ of Grant co., SW corner of Wisconsin, 13 m. WNW of Platteville; pop. (1970c) 3756; dairy farming.

14 City, St. John co., S New Brunswick, Canada, 6 m. SW of St. John; pop. (1966c) 15,836.

15 County, England. See LANCASHIRE.

16 Municipal borough, ⊗ of Lancashire, England, on the Lune 46 m. N of Liverpool; pop. (1971p) 49,525; textiles, linoleum, furniture, shoes; printing, dyeing, brewing; Univ. of Lancaster (1964); ancient castle. Norman with traces of Roman and Saxon construction; received first town charter 1193, made a city 1937.

Lancaster Sound. Channel, bet. Devon I. and N Baffin I., E Franklin dist., Northwest Territories, N Canada; ab. 50 m. wide; opens into NW Baffin Bay.

Lan–ch'i \'län-'chē\. City, cen. Chekiang prov., E China, on railroad a few miles NW of Chin-hua.

Lan–chou *or* **Lan–chow** \'län-'jō\ *or* **Kao-lan** \'kaů-'län\. City, ✱ of Kansu prov., N cen. China, on right bank of Yellow river and near Great Wall; pop. (1970e) 1,500,000; connected by highway with Sian to the ESE (310 m. by air); food processing, oil refining; cement, textiles, leather goods; univ. (1946).

Lan·cia·no \län-'chän-(,)ō\. Commune, Chieti prov., Abruzzi, cen. Italy, 14 m. ESE of Chieti; pop. (1968e) 29,789; cathedral; remains of 11th cent. walls.

Lan·dau \'län-,daů\ *also* **Landau in der Pfalz** \-in-dərp-'fälts\. City, Bavaria, West Germany, 18 m. NW of Karlsruhe; pop. (1969e) 32,094; machinery, cigars, shoes, hats; ships grain, wine, timber, cattle; 13th and 15th cent. churches; founded 13th cent., made city 1291; French 1680–1815.

Lan·deck \'län-dek\. Town, W Tirol, SW Austria, on the Inn river ab. 40 m. W of Innsbruck; pop. (1961c) 6154; E terminal of the Arlberg pass and tunnel route to Vorarlberg.

Land·er \'lan-dər\. 1 County in Nevada. See table at NEVADA.

2 Town, ⊗ of Fremont co., cen. Wyoming, at SE corner of Shoshone Indian Reservation; pop. (1970c) 7125; oil wells; gold and uranium mines; livestock raising.

Lan·der·neau \,läⁿ-der-'nō\. Commune, Finistère dept., NW France, ENE of Brest; pop. (1970c) 12,781.

Landes \'läⁿ(n)d\. Department of SW France. See table at FRANCE.

Landes, Les. See LES LANDES.

Landes de Lan·vaux \-də-lä^n-'vō\. Strip of rocky, desolate land, S Morbihan dept., Brittany, France, near coast; studded with megalithic monuments. See CARNAC.

Landeshut *or* **Landeshut in Schlesien.** See KAMIENNA GÓRA.

Landi Kotal. See KHYBER PASS.

Lands·berg \'län(t)s-ˌbe(ə)rg\. 1 *also* **Landsberg am Lech** \-äm-'lek\. Commune, Bavaria, West Germany, on Lech river ab. 20 m. S of Augsburg; pop. (1968e) 14,432. 2 *also* **Landsberg an der Warthe.** City, Poland. See GORZÓW WIELKOPOLSKI.

Lands End *or* **Land's End** \'lan(d)-'zend\ *or anc.* **Bo·le·ri·um** \bə-'lir-ē-əm\. Cape, SW coast of Cornwall, SW England; westernmost land of England.

Lands·hut \'län(t)s-ˌhüt\. City, Bavaria, West Germany, on Isar river NE of Munich; pop. (1969e) 51,182; machinery, electronic components, furniture, chocolate, beer, paint, tobacco products; 13th–16th cent. castle, 14th cent. town hall. Became city 1279; residence of dukes of Bavaria-Landshut 1255–1340, 1392–1503; site of a university 1800–26; scene of Napoleon's defeat of Archduke Charles 1809.

Lands·kro·na \lan(t)s-'krü-nə\. Seaport, Malmöhus co., SW Sweden; pop. (1970e) 33,898; shipbuilding, metalworking, tanning, food processing; machinery, fertilizers; first mentioned 1412; Swedes won naval victory off this port 1677 over the Danes.

Lane \'lān\. Name of counties in two states of the U.S. See tables at KANSAS and OREGON.

Lanes·bor·ough \'lānz-ˌbər-ə, -ˌbə-rə\. Town, Berkshire co., W Massachusetts, 6 m. N of Pittsfield; pop. (1970c) 2972.

La·nett \lə-'net\. City, Chambers co., E Alabama, on Georgia border 40 m. E of Martin Lake; pop. (1970c) 6908; textiles.

Lan·ga·nes, Cape \-'laůŋ-gə-ˌnās\. Cape on NE extremity of Iceland.

Lan·ga·no, Lake \-läŋ-'gän-(ˌ)ō\. Lake in cen. Ethiopia, bet. lakes Ziway and Shala, S of Addis Ababa.

Lang–chung \'läŋ-'jůŋ\ *or formerly* **Pao·ning** \'baů-'niŋ\. City, N Szechwan prov., S cen. China, on right bank of Chia-ling river ab. 135 m. N of Chungking.

Lang·dale Pikes \ˌlaŋ-ˌdāl-\. Two mountain peaks, **Har·ri·son Stick·le** \ˌhar-ə-sən-'stik-əl\ 2401 ft. and **Pike o' Stickle** \ˌpīk-ə-\ 2323 ft., in NW Westmorland, NW England, in the Lake District.

Lang·don \'laŋ-dən\. City, ⊗ of Cavalier co., NE North Dakota, 49 m. NNE of Devils Lake (city); pop. (1970c) 2182; ships wheat and cattle.

Lang·e·land \'läŋ-ə-ˌlän\. Island, forming a part of Denmark, in Baltic Sea off SE coast of Fyn I. and bet. Fyn and Lolland; ab. 33 m. long and 3 m. wide; 110 sq. m.; pop. (1965c) 17,745; chief town Rudkøbing.

Langeland Belt. Strait in the Baltic Sea, S of the Great Belt, and bet. Langeland I. and Lolland I., Denmark.

Lang·e·marck \'läŋ-ə-ˌmärk\. Commune, West Flanders prov., NW Belgium, 5 m. NE of Ieper (Ypres); pop. (1970c) 4782; destroyed during World War I and rebuilt since that time. First successful poison gas attack said to have been made here Apr. 22, 1915; lost to Allies but recovered Aug. 16, 1917.

Lang·en \'läŋ-ən\. City, Hesse, West Germany; pop. (1969e) 30,111; metalworking; became city 1883.

Langenbielau. See BIELAWA.

Lang·en·feld \'läŋ-ən-ˌfelt\. City, North Rhine-Westphalia, West Germany; pop. (1969e) 44,281; textiles.

Lang·en·ha·gen \ˌläŋ-ən-ˌhäg-ən\. City, Lower Saxony, West Germany; pop. (1969e) 36,629; electronic equipment; metalworking; became city 1959.

Lang·en·sal·za \ˌläŋ-ən-'zält-sə\. City, Erfurt dist., East Germany, 19 m. WNW of Erfurt; pop. (1970e) 16,951; sulfur spring; health resort. Scene of battles in Seven Years' War 1761 and in Seven Weeks' War 1866, when the Prussians defeated the Hanoverians; joined to Prussia 1815.

Lang·en·thal \'läŋ-ən-ˌtäl\. Commune, Bern canton, Switzerland, E of Solothurn; pop. (1970c) 13,007; textiles.

Lang·e·oog \'läŋ-ə-ˌōk\. Narrow island in cen. part of East Frisian Is., off NW coast of West Germany, W of Spiekeroog; 9 m. long.

Lang·ford, Mount \-'laŋ-fərd\. Peak in Yellowstone National Park, NW Wyoming; 10,600 ft.

Lang·ka·wi, Pu·lau \'pü-ˌlaů-läŋ-'kä-wē\. Island (*pulau*) in Andaman Sea off NW coast of Kedah state, Malaysia; has peak 2890 ft.

Lan·glade \'laŋ-ˌlād\. County in Wisconsin. See table at WISCONSIN.

Langlade. See MIQUELON ISLAND.

Langlade, Isthmus of \-lä^n-'gläd\. Isthmus connecting the former islands of Great Miquelon and Little Miquelon (Langlade); 7 m. long; has been created by the accumulation of sand on the reef bet. the two islands which were very close together and now comprise a single island (see MIQUELON ISLAND).

Lang·ley \ˌlaŋ-lē\. City, British Columbia, Canada, 25 m. ESE of Vancouver; pop. (1971p) 4634; diversified agriculture.

Langley, Mount. Peak in Sierra Nevada, in E Tulare co., S cen. California; 14,028 ft.

Langley Field. U.S. Air Force base, Elizabeth City co., SE Virginia, 3 m. N of Hampton; Headquarters Tactical Air Command; research station of the National Aeronautics and Space Administration; founded 1916.

Lang·øy \'läŋ-ˌöi\. Westernmost island of the Vesterålen, in the Norwegian Sea off NW coast of Norway; 332 sq. m.

Langreo. See SAMA DE LANGREO.

Lan·gres \'la^{n}gr^ə\; *anc.* **An·de·ma·tun·num** \ˌan-di-mə-'tən-əm\ *or later* **Lin·go·nes** \'liŋ-gə-ˌnēz\. Commune, Haute-Marne dept., NE France, ab. 38 m. NNE of Dijon on a high part (ab. 1550 ft.) of **Langres Plateau;** pop. (1968c) 10,846; road and railroad junction; electrical equipment, cheese, cutlery. In earlier times was important point strategically; 11th–12th cent. cathedral and 14th cent. Church of St. Martin; remains of Roman town.

Lang·side \'laŋ-ˌsīd\. South suburb of Glasgow, Scotland; scene of the defeat of Mary, Queen of Scots, May 13, 1568.

Lang's Nek *or* **Laing's Nek** \'laŋz-'nek\. Mountain pass, cen. Drakensberg Mts., E Rep. of South Africa; railroad bet. Durban and Pretoria goes through a tunnel here; scene Jan. 28, 1881 of Boers' defeat of a British force which attempted to enter the Transvaal.

Lang Son *or* **Lang·son** \'laŋ-'sän\. Town, North Vietnam, near Chinese frontier, 85 m. NE of Hanoi; most important town on NE frontier; connected by rail with Hanoi. Occupied by French 1885.

Langs Point \'laŋz-\. Elevation in Cheyenne co., W Nebraska; 4460 ft.

Lang·ston \'laŋ(k)-stən\. Town, Logan co., cen. Oklahoma; pop. (1970c) 486; Langston Univ. (1897); founded 1890.

Lang Su·an *or* **Lang·su·an** \läŋ-'sü-ˌän\. Town, SW Thailand, on railroad along E coast of Malay Penin. (on Isthmus of Kra) 55 m. N of Surat Thani.

Lan·gue·doc \ˌlaŋ-gə-'däk, lä^{n}ŋ-'dȯk, läŋg-'dȯk\. Historical region of S cen. France; bounded anciently on N by Auvergne and Lyonnais, E by Dauphiné, Comtat Venaissin, and Provence, SE by Mediterranean Sea, S by Roussillon, SW by Countship of Foix, W by Gascony, NW by Guienne; capitals Toulouse and Montpellier; Cévennes Mts. in E.

History: Region without unity except that based on a common language (*Fr.* langue d'oc) and culture (oriented towards Provence, Italy, and Muslim Spain) until 13th cent. when it was brought under influence of the counts of Toulouse; home of the Albigenses, exterminated in wars of religion in 13th cent.; region from Carcassonne to the Rhone passed to Louis IX of France 1229; western part left to counts of Toulouse until seized 1271 by Philip III; from 16th to 18th cents. scene of persecution of Protestants terminating in War of the Camisards 1702–05.

La·nier \lə-'ni(ə)r\. County in Georgia. See table at GEORGIA.

La·nín \lä-'nēn\. Volcanic peak on Argentina-Chile border, bet. SW Neuquén prov., W Argentina, and NE Valdivia prov., S cen. Chile; 12,388 ft.

Lanka. See CEYLON.

Lankada, Lake. See KORÓNIA, LAKE.

Lan·nion \la-'nyō^n\. Town, Côtes-du-Nord dept., NW France, NW of St-Brieuc; pop. (1968c) 12,535; active port on a river that flows into the English Channel; ruins of 15th cent. castle of Tonguédec ab. 6 m. to the SE.

Lans·dale \'lanz-ˌdāl\. Borough, Montgomery co., SE Pennsylvania, 21 m. N of Philadelphia; pop. (1970c) 18,541; boilers, radiators, castings, aircraft parts, hosiery.

Lans·downe \'lanz-ˌdaun\. 1 Residential borough, Delaware co., SE Pennsylvania, 5 m. W of Philadelphia; pop. (1970c) 14,090; residential suburb of Philadelphia.

2 Cantonment and hill station, N Uttar Pradesh, N India, 120 m. NE of Delhi; pop. (1961c) 6400.

L'Anse \'lans\. Village, ⊗ of Baraga co., NW Michigan penin., on Lake Superior 52 m. WNW of Marquette; pop. (1970c) 2538; summer resort; lumber mill.

Lans·ford \'lan(t)s-fərd, 'lanz-\. Borough, Carbon co., E Pennsylvania, 28 m. S of Wilkes-Barre; pop. (1970c) 5168; coal mines; clothing.

Lan·sing \'lan(t)-siŋ\. 1 Village, Cook co., NE Illinois, on Indiana border 24 m. S of Chicago; pop. (1970c) 25,805.

2 City, Leavenworth co., NE Kansas, 40 m. NW of Topeka; pop. (1970c) 3797.

3 City, ✻ of Michigan, in Clinton, Eaton, and Ingham cos., S Michigan, 50 m. WSW of Flint; pop. (1970c) 131,546; automobile manufacturing center and trading point for agricultural region; manufactures also agricultural implements, diesel engines, boilers, pumps, tents, automobile and aircraft accessories, tools; Lansing Community Coll. (1957); settled c. 1840, made capital of Michigan 1847; site of first agricultural college in U.S., Michigan State Univ. (1857; now in East Lansing).

Lan·tana \lan-'tan-ə\. Town, Palm Beach co., SE Florida, S of Lake Worth; pop. (1970c) 7126.

Lan Tao *or* **Lan·tao** \'län-'dau\. Island, SW part of New Territories, Hong Kong, across E part of mouth of Pearl river W of Hong Kong I.; 58 sq. m.; 16 m. long.

Lan–ts'ang. See MEKONG.

La·nús \lə-'nüs\. City, Buenos Aires prov., E Argentina, S suburb of Buenos Aires; pop. (1960c) 375,428; part of Greater Buenos Aires.

La·nu·vi·um \lə-'n(y)ü-vē-əm\ *or modern* **La·nu·vio** \lə-'nü-(ˌ)vyō\ *or formerly* **Ci·vi·ta La·vi·nia** \ˌchē-vi-tä-lä-'vēn-yä\. City in ancient Latium, Italy, near Albanus Mons, 20 m. SE of Rome.

La·nu·za Bay \lə-ˌnü-zə-\. Inlet of Pacific on E coast of Surigao del Sur prov., Mindanao, Phil., ab. 13 m. wide at entrance; Cauit Point marks its SE corner.

Lan·za·ro·te \ˌlan-zə-'rōt-ē\. One of the Canary Is. (*q.v.*), in Las Palmas prov., Spain; 109 m. NE of Grand Canary I. and easternmost island of the group; 323 sq. m.; pop. (1970p) 41,912; wine, vegetables; bold and precipitous coast; basaltic cliffs; volcanic in origin; chief town Arrecife.

La·oag \lə-'wäg\. 1 River, largest of Ilocos Norte prov., Luzon, Phil.; ab. 60 m. long; has many tributaries in upper course spreading out fanwise in mountains to N and S; lower course flows W to South China Sea.

2 Chartered city, ✻ of Ilocos Norte prov., Luzon, Phil., on right bank of Laoag river; pop. (1970e) 69,300; center of local commerce.

La·oang \lə-'wäŋ\. Municipality, NE coast of Samar del Norte prov., on **Laoang Island** (12 sq. m.), Phil., 57 m. NNE of Catbalogan; pop. (1969e) 56,900.

Lao Cai *or* **Lao·kay** \'lau-'kī\. Border town, North Vietnam, on Red river 155 m. NW of Hanoi, on railroad leading from Hanoi into Yunnan prov., China. Only large town in region; strategically important, long subject to conflict bet. Chinese and Vietnamese; came under French control 1886.

Lao–chün–miao. See YÜ-MEN.

Laodicea. See DENİZLİ 2 and LATAKIA 2.

Laoet. See LAUT.

Laohokow. See KUANG-HUA.

Laoigh, Ben. See BEN LUI.

Laoighis \'lāsh, 'lēsh\ *or* **Leix** \'lāsh, 'lēsh\ *or formerly* **Queen's** \'kwēnz\. County, Leinster prov., cen. Eire; 664 sq. m.; pop. (1971p) 45,349; ⊗ Maryborough; rivers Barrow, Nore; agriculture, dairy farming, textile manufacture.

Laokay. See LAO CAI.

Laon \'lä^n\ *or anc.* **Lau·du·num** \lȯ-'d(y)ün-əm\. Commercial commune, ✻ of Aisne dept., N France, 77 m. NE of Paris; pop. (1968c) 26,316; railroad center; sugar refining, metal founding; plastics; ships grain and wine; 12th cent. Gothic cathedral, old episcopal palace (now the palace of justice), 12th cent. church, 13th cent. gates; to the SW is the Abbey of Prémontré, founded 1119.

History: Probably the *Bibrax* of the Gauls; fortified by Romans; episcopal see 5th–18th cents.; checked invasions of Franks, Vandals, Huns, etc.; gained charter 1239; held successively by Burgundians, English, French in Hundred Years' War; scene of Napoleon's defeat by Blücher 1814; occupied by Germans in Franco-Prussian War and both World Wars; taken by Americans Aug. 1944.

La Oro·ta·va \lä-ˌȯr-ə-'täv-ə\. Commune, N cen. Tenerife I., W Canary Is.; pop. (1970p) 26,840; part of Santa Cruz de Tenerife prov., Spain; includes **Puer·to Orotava** \ˌpwert-ō-\, N cen. Tenerife I., 20 m. WSW of Santa Cruz de Tenerife, and **Vil·la Orotava** \ˌvēl-yə-, ˌvē-(y)ə-\, 4 m. SE of Puerto Orotava; health resort.

La Oro·ya \lä-ō-'rō-yä\. Town, Junín dept., cen. Peru, 80 m. ESE of Lima; pop. (1969e) 31,700; altitude 12,180 ft.; lead refinery, large copper smelter.

Laos \'laus, 'lä-ōs, 'lā-ˌäs, 'lā-əs, 'lauz\. Kingdom, SE Asia, bounded on N by China and North Vietnam, on E by North Vietnam and South Vietnam, on S by Cambodia, on W by Thailand, and on NW by Thailand and Burma; 91,428 sq. m.; pop. (1971e) 3,033,000; administrative ✻ Vientiane, royal ✻ Luang Prabang. *Physical features:* In the NW occupies the valley of the Mekong but most of its N and S extent lies E of that river which forms large part of boundary with Thailand; mountainous, with peaks in the N above 9000 ft. and in the S ab. 5000 ft.; thickly forested. *Chief products:* Rice, corn, tobacco, tea; fishing, tin mining. *Chief towns:* Vientiane, Savannakhet, Pakse, Luang Prabang.

History: Much of area now known as Laos united as one kingdom 1353; administrative seat moved from Luang Prabang to Vientiane 1563 due to hostilities with Burmese and Thais; disintegration of kingdom into several states (early 18th cent.) which gradually came under Thai control (Vientiane captured by Thais 1778, destroyed 1827); latter part of 19th cent. marked by Franco-Thai border clashes, resulting in establishment of French protectorate over Laos 1899; occupied by Japanese 1945, French control restored 1946; founding of Pathet Lao (a Communist organization) 1951; achieved total independence 1954; became a member of the U.N. 1955; 1960's marked by civil strife involving Communist, neutralist, and rightist forces; Communist-controlled areas bombed by U.S. 1965–69 during fighting in Vietnam War.

Lao–shan Bay \'lau-'shän-\. Bay overlooked by hills **(Lao Shan),** E Shantung, NE China, ab. 20 m. NE of Tsingtao.

La·pac \lə-'päk\. Island in Tapul group, cen. Sulu Archipelago, Phil., just W of Siasi I.; 16 sq. m.; forms part of Siasi municipality.

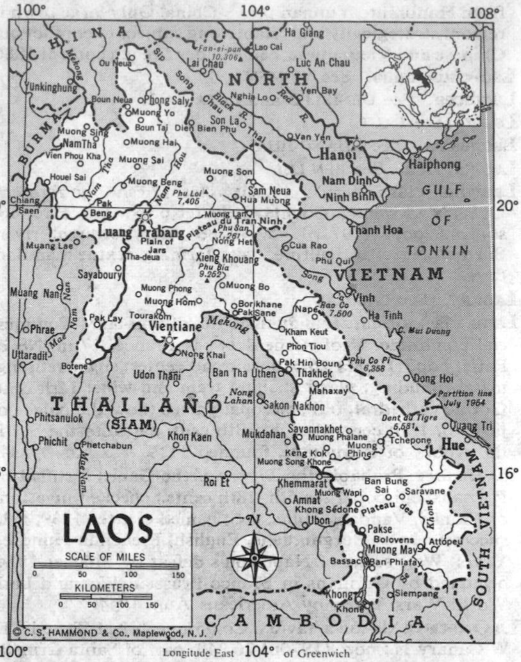

La Pal·lice \lä-pə-'lēs\. Port, NW Charente-Maritime dept., W France, ab. 3 m. W of La Rochelle; built to accommodate large vessels which cannot get into the harbor of La Rochelle; German submarine base during World War II.

La Pal·ma \lə-'päl-mə\. 1 City, Orange co., SW California, 18 m. SE of Los Angeles; pop. (1970c) 9687.

2 Town and port, ✻ of Darién prov., E Panama; pop. (1970p) 1845; on an inlet of Gulf of Panama 100 m. SE of Panama.

3 *or originally* **San Mi·guel de la Pal·ma** \ˌsan-mi-'gel-dā-lə-'päl-mə\. One of the Canary Is. (*q.v.*), in Santa Cruz de Tenerife prov., Spain, 53 m. WNW of Tenerife I.; 280 sq. m.; pop. (1970p) 65,291; mountainous; chief town Santa Cruz de la Palma. Occupied by Alonzo de Lugo 1491.

La Pam·pa \lä-'päm-pə\. Province of cen. Argentina. See table at ARGENTINA.

La Parida. See BOLÍVAR, CERRO.

La Paz \lə-'paz, -'päz, -'päs\. 1 Town, Entre Ríos prov., E Argentina, on left bank of the Paraná ab. 85 m. NNE of Paraná; pop. (1960c) 11,028.

2 Department of W Bolivia. See table at BOLIVIA.

3 *or in full* **La Paz de Aya·cu·cho** \-dā-ī-ə-'kü-(ˌ)chō\. City, administrative ✻ of Bolivia and ✻ of La Paz dept., E of Lake Titicaca; met. area pop. (1971e) 850,000; altitude 12,001 ft.; highest capital in the world, located in valley at foot of Illimani; principal industrial and distributing center of Bolivia; manufactures chemicals, textiles, glass, furniture, electrical appliances; exports bar tin, quinine bark, wolfram, antimony, lead, and silver; cathedral, univ. (1830), National Institute of Bacteriology.

History: Founded 1548 by Alonso de Mendoza as Pueblo Nuevo de Nuestra Señora de la Paz; twice besieged by Indians in revolt 1781–82; joined Chuquisaca (Sucre) in revolt against Spanish (July 1809) which was later suppressed; became part of independent Bolivia 1825 and name changed to La Paz de Ayacucho (literally, The Peace of Ayacucho) to commemorate the battle of Ayacucho; made administrative capital of republic 1898.

4 Department of S El Salvador. See table at EL SALVADOR.

5 Department of SW Honduras. See table at HONDURAS.

6 Town, ✻ of La Paz dept., SW Honduras, 33 m. W of Tegucigalpa; pop. (1961c) 4705; agricultural center.

7 Town, SE Baja California Sur territory, NW Mexico, on S shore of **La Paz Bay;** has trade connections with chief Pacific ports of North America; center for pearl fishing and silver mining.

La·peer \lə-'pi(ə)r\. 1 County in E Michigan. See table at MICHIGAN.

2 City, its ⊗, 20 m. E of Flint; pop. (1970c) 6314; lake resort; furniture; dairy farming.

La Pe·rouse Bay \ˌläp-ə-ˌrüz-\. Bay on S coast of Maui I., Hawaii.

La Pérouse Island. See VANIKORO.

La Pérouse Strait. See SŌYA STRAIT.

La Pie·dad \ˌlä-pyā-'t͟hät͟h\ *or in full* **La Piedad Ca·va·das** \ˌläp-yā-ˌt͟häk-ə-'vä-t͟həs\. Municipality, Michoacán state, SW Mexico, on Lerma river and on railroad 110 m. W of Querétaro; pop. (1970p) 51,484.

Lapin. See LAPPI 2.

La·pi·nin \ˌlä-pi-'nēn\. Long flat island off NE Bohol on W side of Canigao Channel, Phil.; 20 sq. m.; mangrove-covered.

Lap·land \'lap-ˌland, -lənd\ *or Norw.* **Lap·land** \'läp-län\ *or Swed.* **Lapp·land** \'lap-land\ *or Finnish* **Lap·pi** \'lap-ē\. A region extending over N Norway, N Sweden, N Finland, and the Kola Penin. in NW Russian S.F.S.R., U.S.S.R., all above the Arctic Circle; total area ab. 150,000 sq. m., with larger parts in Sweden and U.S.S.R.; pop. (1968e) 36,500; Lapps (two thirds in Norway), a Mongoloid race; mountains, tundra, swamps, forests, and many lakes (Torne, Inari, Imandra) and rivers; chief industries fishing and reindeer herding; has several mining towns, esp. Kiruna and Gällivare in Sweden; increasing exploitation of timber resources. Lapps known from earliest times but have usually been held subject by stronger peoples (Swedes, Norwegians, Finns, or Russians); since 19th cent. they have been treated with somewhat more consideration by the controlling governments.

La Pla·ta \lə-'plat-ə\. Town, ⊗ of Charles co., S Maryland; pop. (1970c) 1561; Charles County Community Coll. (1958).

La Plata \lə-'plat-ə, -'plät-\. County in Colorado. See table at COLORADO.

La Plata \lə-'plät-ə\. 1 Seaport, ✻ of Buenos Aires prov., E Argentina, 35 m. ESE of Buenos Aires; pop. (1960c) 337,060; large artificial harbor; meat-packing, oil refining; chemical and electrical industries; univ. (1890); founded 1882 as the new capital of the province at village of Ensenada, now part of it; laid out like Washington, D.C.

2 River in E cen. Puerto Rico; ab. 35 m. long; flows N into Atlantic Ocean.

3 *or* **Bue·nos Ai·res** \ˌbwā-nə-'sa(ə)r-ēz, ˌbō-nə-, -'se(ə)r-, -'sī(ə)r-\. Viceroyalty in Spanish South America, established 1776, including modern Argentina, Uruguay, Paraguay, and Bolivia (then known as Upper Peru); ✻ Buenos Aires; unsuccessfully attacked by British 1806, 1807; divided into self-governing units during wars for independence of Latin American states c. 1812–28.

la Plata, Río de. See PLATA, RÍO DE LA.

La Plata Mountains \lə-'plat-ə-, -'plät-\. A range of the Rocky Mts. in SW Colorado; highest peak Hesperus Peak 13,225 ft.

La Plata Peak. Mountain in Chaffee co., cen. Colorado; 14,336 ft.

La Po·ca·tière \lä-ˌpōk-ə-'tye(ə)r\. Town, Kamouraska co., S Quebec, Canada, on St. Lawrence river 65 m. NE of Quebec City; pop. (1971p) 4246.

La Pointe \lə-'pȯint\. Settlement on Madeline I., one of the Apostle Is. (*q.v.*), Wisconsin.

La·porte \lə-'pō(ə)rt\. Borough and mountain resort, ⊗ of Sullivan co., NE Pennsylvania; pop. (1970c) 207.

La Porte \lə-'pō(ə)rt\. 1 County in Indiana. See table at INDIANA.

2 Industrial city, ⊗ of La Porte co., N Indiana, 25 m. W of South Bend; pop. (1970c) 22,140; agricultural machinery, radiators, steel castings; settled 1832; chartered 1852.

3 City, Harris co., SE Texas, on Galveston Bay 20 m. ESE of Houston; pop. (1970c) 7149; oil wells; summer resort.

La Porte City. Town, Black Hawk co., NE cen. Iowa, 16 m. SE of Waterloo; pop. (1970c) 2256; agriculture.

Lap·peen·ran·ta \ˈlap-ān-ˌran-tə\ *or Swed.* **Vill·man·strand** \ˈvil-mən-ˌstrand\. Town, Kymi prov., SE Finland, near border of Karelian A.S.S.R., Russian S.F.S.R., U.S.S.R.; pop. (1970e) 50,958; cement, machinery; founded 1649.

Lap·pi \ˈlap-ē\. 1 Region, Arctic. See LAPLAND.

2 *or* **La·pin** \ˈlap-ən\. Province of N Finland; the Finnish part of the region of Lapland. See table at FINLAND.

Lappland. See LAPLAND.

Lapp·mark \ˈlap-ˌmärk\. General name for the N districts of Sweden (see LAPLAND), inhabited by Lapps.

La·prai·rie *or* **La Prai·rie** \lə-ˈpre(ə)r-ē\. 1 County, Quebec, Canada. See table at QUEBEC.

2 Town, its ⊗, on St. Lawrence river ab. 8 m. SSE of Montreal across the river; pop. (1971p) 8310; summer resort; has an old fort which was attacked 1691 by New England troops; starting point of first railroad in British North America 1832.

La Pro·vi·dence \lä-ˌprō-vi-ˈdäns, -ˈdäⁿs\. Village, St. Hyacinthe co., S Quebec, Canada, 25 m. E of Montreal; pop. (1971p) 4671.

Lapseki. See LAMPSACUS.

Lapteva Strait. See DMITRI LAPTEV STRAIT.

Lap·tev Sea \ˈlap-ˌtef-, -ˌtev-\ *or Russ.* **Mo·re Lap·te·vykh** \ˌmȯr-ə-ˈläp-tə-ˌvik\ *or formerly* **Nor·den·skjöld Sea** \ˈnȯrd-ᵊn-ˌshəld-, -ˌshu̇ld-, -ˌshēld-\. Part of Arctic Ocean along N coast of Russian S.F.S.R., U.S.S.R., bet. Severnaya Zemlya on W and New Siberian Is.

La·puan \ˈlap-ˌwän\. River, Vaasa prov., W Finland; ab. 100 m. long; flows N into Gulf of Bothnia.

La Puen·te \ˌläp-u̇-ˈent-ē\. City, Los Angeles co., SW California, NNE of Long Beach; pop. (1970c) 31,092; residential; incorporated 1956.

La·pu–La·pu \ˌläp-ü-ˈläp-ü\ *or formerly* **Opon** \ˈō-ˌpȯn\. Chartered city on NW coast of Mactan I., Cebu prov., Phil.; pop. (1970e) 67,800.

La Pun·ti·lla \ˌläp-ün-ˈtē-(y)ə\. Cape on SW coast of Ecuador, the tip of Santa Elena Penin.

Lapurdum. Town, France. See BAYONNE.

Lap·wai \ˈlap-(ˌ)wī\. Village, Nez Perce co., W Idaho, ab. 12 m. E of Lewiston on S tributary of the Clearwater river; pop. (1970c) 400; first white settlement in Idaho 1836; abandoned 1847 after Whitman massacre; reopened 1871. Site of U.S. Indian agency.

La Quia·ca \lä-ˈkyä-kə\. Town, N Jujuy prov., NW Argentina, on border of Bolivia ab. 140 m. N of Jujuy; pop. (1960c) 6290; altitude over 10,000 ft.; railroad terminus; on the Pan American Highway.

L'Aquila. See AQUILA.

La·quin·horn \ˌläk-ˈvēn-ˌhȯ(ə)rn\. Peak in the Pennine Alps, S Switzerland, S of Simplon Pass; 13,140 ft.

Lār \ˈlär\. Town, Persian Gulf prov., S Iran, on caravan route 125 m. WNW of Bandar 'Abbās; pop. (1966c) 21,576.

La·ra \ˈlär-ə\. State of NW Venezuela. See table at VENEZUELA.

La·ra·cha \lə-ˈräch-ə\. Commune, La Coruña prov., NW Spain, 11 m. WSW of La Coruña; pop. (1970p) 10,898.

La·rache \lə-ˈrash, lə-ˈräch-(ˌ)ā\ *or Arab.* **Al–Araish** \ˌal-ə-ˈrīsh\ *or anc.* **Lix·us** \ˈlik-səs\. Seaport on Atlantic coast, N Morocco; pop. (1960c) 30,763; fishing; exports cork, timber, beans, fruit, wool; ancient city of importance under the Phoenicians and as a Roman colony; belonged to Spain 1610–89 and from 1912 to 1956.

Lar·a·mie \ˈlar-ə-mē\. 1 River, N Colorado and SE Wyoming; 216 m. long; rises in N Colorado, flows N across Wyoming border, turns NE and empties into North Platte river.

2 County in Wyoming. See table at WYOMING.

3 City, ⊗ of Albany co., SE Wyoming, 45 m. WNW of Cheyenne; pop. (1970c) 23,143; trade center in livestock-raising region; sawmills, railroad shops; cement, lumber, brick; tourist center; Univ. of Wyoming (1886); settled 1868, incorporated 1873.

Laramie Range *or formerly* **Laramie Mountains.** Range in SE Wyoming and N Colorado; highest point **Laramie Peak,** in Wyoming, 10,272 ft.

Laranda. See KARAMAN.

La·ran·tu·ka *or Du.* **La·ran·toe·ka** \ˌlär-ən-ˈtü-kə\. Town and port on NE coast of Flores I., Lesser Sunda Is., Indonesia; seat of important native state in early times.

La·rat \ˈlär-ˌät\. Island in N part of Tanimbar Is., E Malay Archipelago, Indonesia; 20 m. long by 7 m. wide.

L'Arba. See AL-ARBA.

L'Ar·baa Na·ït Ira·then \ˌlär-bə-ˌnä-it-i-ˈräth-ən\ *or formerly* **Fort–Na·tio·nal** \ˌfȯr-ˌnäs-yō-ˈnäl\. Commune, Tizi-Ouzou dept., N Algeria, in hilly region ab. 64 m. E of Algiers; pop. (1966c) 2353.

Larch \ˈlärch\. River, N Quebec, Canada; 270 m. long; flows NE to unite with the Caniapiscau river and form the Koksoak river.

Larch·mont \ˈlärch-ˌmänt\. Residential village, Westchester co., SE New York, on Long Island Sound 20 m. NE of New York City; pop. (1970c) 7203.

La·re·do \lə-ˈrād-(ˌ)ō\. City and port of entry, ⊗ of Webb co., S Texas, on Rio Grande opp. Nuevo Laredo, Mexico; pop. (1970c) 69,024; ships livestock, fruits and vegetables, coal; oil and gas wells; brick, glassware, clothing, machine tools, electronic components; oil refining; tourism; Laredo Junior Coll. (1947). Established by Spanish settlers 1755; occupied by Texas Rangers 1846 and by forces of Gen. Lamar 1847; chartered as city 1852.

Laredo, Nuevo. See NUEVO LAREDO.

La·res \ˈlär-(ˌ)ās\. Town and municipality, W cen. Puerto Rico; pop. (1970p) 4505 (town), 24,896 (munic.).

Lar·go \ˈlär-(ˌ)gō\. City, Pinellas co., W cen. Florida, S of Clearwater; pop. (1970c) 22,031; citrus fruit; dairy farming.

Largo Cay \-ˈkē, -ˈkā\. Island in N Caribbean Sea, E of Isle of Pines and S of W Cuba.

Largs \ˈlärgz\. Seaport burgh, Ayr co., SW Scotland; pop. (1971p) 9775; seaside resort; scene of victory of King Alexander III over Haakon IV of Norway 1263.

La Ri·ca·ma·rie \ˌlä-ri-ˈkäm-ə-ˈrē\. Commune, Loire dept., SE cen. France, 2 m. SSE of Saint-Étienne; pop. (1968c) 11,539; coal mining.

La Riège. See ARIÈGE.

Lar·i·mer \ˈlar-ə-mər\. County in Colorado. See table at COLORADO.

Lar·i·more \ˈlar-ə-ˌmō(ə)r, -ˌmȯ(ə)r\. City, Grand Forks co., E North Dakota, 28 m. W of Grand Forks; pop. (1970c) 1469; livestock; wheat.

La Rio·ja \ˌlär-ē-ˈō-(ˌ)hä\. 1 Province of NW Argentina. See table at ARGENTINA.

2 Town, ✱ of La Rioja prov., NW Argentina, in Andine region 90 m. SW of Catamarca; pop. (1960c) 35,431; founded 1591.

3 A region of N Spain, chiefly in Logroño prov.; ab. 1690 sq. m.; a wine-growing district along the upper Ebro.

La·ris·sa \lə-ˈris-ə\ *or Gk.* **La·ri·sa** \ˈlär-ĭ-sə\. 1 Department of Greece. See table at GREECE.

2 City, ✱ of Larissa dept., E Thessaly, Greece, on Piniós river ENE of Trikkala; pop. (1971p) 72,762; railroad and agricultural trading center. Anciently capital of the Pelasgians; supported Athens in Peloponnesian War; headquarters of Ali Pasha in Greek War of Independence; scene of severe fighting bet. Germans and army of Greeks and British Apr. 1941.

La·ri·stan \ˌlar-ə-ˈstan\. Former province, S Iran, on the Persian Gulf, now part of Fārs and Persian Gulf provinces;

21,020 sq. m.; ✱ Bandar 'Abbās; mountains, arid upland, and swampy coastal strip.

Larius, Lacus. See COMO, LAKE.

Lark *or* **Larke** \'lärk\. River, Suffolk and Cambridge, E England; ab. 26 m. long; flows ENE into the Ouse near Ely.

Lar·ka·na *or* **Lar·kha·na** \lär-'kän-ə\. Town, Sind, Pakistan, near W bank of Indus river 200 m. NNE of Karachi; pop. (1961c) 48,008; manufactures cotton, silk, leather, metalware.

Lark·spur \'lärk-ˌspər\. City, Marin co., W California, ab. 10 m. NW of San Francisco; pop. (1970c) 10,487.

Larks·ville \'lärks-ˌvil\. Borough, Luzerne co., E Pennsylvania, 3 m. W of Wilkes-Barre; pop. (1970c) 3937.

Lar·na·ca \'lär-nə-kə\. **1** District, SE Cyprus, E Mediterranean Sea; 436 sq. m.; pop. (1968e) 61,000; ✱ Larnaca.
2 Seaport, its ✱, 23 m. SE of Nicosia; pop. (1970e) 21,400; tannery; cheese, commercial salt; on part of site of ancient Citium (*q.v.*).

Larne \'lärn\. Municipal borough, co. Antrim, NE Northern Ireland, seaport at head of Lough Larne; pop. (1971p) 18,219; trade center and seaside resort; linen, paper, cement; port facilities. Edward Bruce landed nearby 1315 on his journey to accept Irish throne.

Lar·ned \'lär-nəd\. City, ⊗ of Pawnee co., cen. Kansas, at confluence of Arkansas and Pawnee rivers 24 m. SW of Great Bend; pop. (1970c) 4567; flour, feed; diversified agriculture.

La Ro·chelle \ˌlär-ə-'shel\ *or anc.* **Ru·pel·la** \rü-'pel-ə\. Seaport, ✱ of Charente-Maritime dept., W France, on Bay of Biscay 124 m. SW of Tours; pop. (1968c) 73,347; aircraft, automobiles, chemicals; oil refining; fishing. Anciently capital of Aunis; made commune 1199; became chief Huguenot stronghold in 16th cent.; besieged by Richelieu 1627–28 and forced through famine to capitulate. See LA PALLICE.

La Roche–sur–Yon \lə-ˌrósh-ˌsü(ə)r-'yōⁿ\. Commune, ✱ of Vendée dept., W France, 37 m. S of Nantes; pop. (1968c) 36,067; agricultural trade center; horse breeding. Founded by Napoleon 1804 to serve as capital of Vendée dept.; called **Na·po·lé·on–Ven·dée** \na-ˌpō-lā-'ōⁿ-väⁿ-'dā\ 1804–14, 1848–70, and **Bour·bon–Vendée** \ˌbu̇(ə)r-ˌbōⁿ-\ 1814–48.

La Ro·da \lä-'rōd-ə\. Commune, Albacete prov., SE Spain, 21 m. NW of Albacete; pop. (1970p) 11,663; agricultural products.

La Ro·ma·na \ˌlär-ə-'män-ə\. **1** Province, E Dominican Republic. See table at DOMINICAN REPUBLIC.
2 Seaport, its ✱, 23 m. E of San Pedro de Macorís; pop. (1970e) 31,297; sugar refining; ships livestock.

la Ronge, Lac. See RONGE, LAC LA.

Lar·rey Point \ˌlar-ē-\. Cape on NW coast of Western Australia at 19°58′S, 119°07′E.

Lar·sa \'lar-sə\ *or Bib.* **El·la·sar** \el-'lā-ˌsär\. Ancient city of S Babylonia, on left bank of the Euphrates river bet. Erech and Ur. Known in time of Abraham (*Gen.* xiv. 1) and flourished in period of Sumerian decline c. 2000 to c. 1760 B.C.

Lars Chris·ten·sen Coast \ˌlärz-'kris-tən-sən-\. Section of coast of Antarctica, E of Mac Robertson Land on the Indian Ocean; 69°30′S, 68°E; discovered by Norwegian whalers Jan. 1931.

Lar·sen Ice Shelf \'lärs-ᵊn-\. Ice shelf in NW Weddell Sea, along E coast of Antarctic Penin., Antarctica, 68°30′S, 62°30′W; explored and named 1893.

La·rue \lə-'rü\. County in Kentucky. See table at KENTUCKY.

Lar·vik \'lär-vik, -ˌvēk\. Seaport, Vestfold co., SE Norway, at head of **Larvik Fjord;** pop. (1970e) 10,376; lumber, granite quarries, distilleries.

La–sa \'lä-'sä\ *also* **Kyi** \'kyē\ *or* **Kyi·chu** \'kyē-'chü\. River, SE Tibet, China; ab. 200 m. long; N tributary of the Upper Brahmaputra; Lhasa is on its right bank.

La Sa·gra \lə-'säg-rə\. Mountain in E Andalusia, Granada prov., S Spain; 7813 ft.

La Salle \lə-'sal\. **1** Name of a parish in Louisiana and of counties in two states of the U.S. See tables at ILLINOIS, LOUISIANA, and TEXAS.
2 City, La Salle co., N Illinois, 13 m. W of Ottawa; pop. (1970c) 10,736; steel mills, brewery; coal mines; clocks, motors, electrical equipment; Illinois Valley Community Coll. (1924).
3 City on S shore of Montreal I., S Quebec, Canada; part of Greater Montreal; pop. (1971p) 72,916; N terminus of railroad bridge.

La Sal Mountains \lə-ˌsal-\. Mountain group, Grand and San Juan cos., E Utah; highest peak Mt. Peale 13,089 ft.

La Sa·lud \ˌläs-ə-lü(th)\. Municipality, La Habana prov., W Cuba, 18 m. S of Havana; pop. (1967e) 7260.

Las An·i·mas \la-'san-ə-məs\. **1** County in Colorado. See table at COLORADO.
2 City, ⊗ of Bent co., SE Colorado, on Arkansas river 20 m. E of La Junta; pop. (1970c) 3148; oil and gas wells; grain elevator; agriculture.

La Sarre \lə-'sär\. Town, Abitibi co., SW Quebec, Canada; pop. (1971p) 5095; soft drinks, electrical equipment.

Las Be·la \ləs-'bāl-ə\. Former state, SE Baluchistan States, now part of Pakistan; 7043 sq. m.; ✱ Bela; formerly under suzerainty of Kalat; Hab river formed most of E boundary with Sind; valley and delta of Porali river occupy cen. and W part.

La·scar \lə-'skär\. Volcano, Antofagasta prov., Chile; 19,652 ft.; erupted 1951.

Las Cas·ca·das \ˌlä-skäs-'käd-əs\. Village, Balboa dist., SE Canal Zone, on W side of Panama Canal just NW of Gaillard Cut.

Las·caux Cave \la-'sko-\. See MONTIGNAC.

Las Charcas. See CHARCAS 2.

Las Conchas. See TIGRE 1.

Las Cru·ces \lä-'skrü-səs\. Town, ⊗ of Dona Ana co., S New Mexico, near the Rio Grande 42 m. NNW of El Paso, Texas; pop. (1970c) 37,857; in irrigated agricultural region (cotton, sugar beets, melons, alfalfa); livestock; cottonseed oil. New Mexico State Univ. (1888) in nearby University Park.

La Selle \lə-'sel\. Mountain group in SE Haiti, Hispaniola I., West Indies; highest peak La Selle 8793 ft.

La·sem \'läs-əm\. Town, Central Java prov., Indonesia, near coast just E of Rembang.

La Se·re·na \ˌläs-ə-'rā-nə\. City, ✱ of Coquimbo prov., cen. Chile, ab. 220 m. N of Valparaíso; pop. (1966e) 48,647; beach resort; bishopric; court of appeals. Founded 1543; destroyed by Indians; rebuilt 1549; sacked by English pirates 1680; scene of Chilean Declaration of Independence Feb. 12, 1818; heavily damaged by earthquake 1922.

Lasēthion. See LASITHION.

La Seyne–sur–Mer \lə-ˌsān-su̇(ə)r-'me(ə)r, -ˌsen-\. Seaport commune, Var dept., SE France, on Mediterranean Sea 4 m. SW of Toulon; pop. (1968c) 43,783; major shipbuilding center.

Las Flo·res \läs-'flōr-əs\. Town, Buenos Aires prov., E Argentina, 110 m. S of Buenos Aires; pop. (1960c) 14,838.

Las Guá·si·mas \läs-'gwäs-ə-məs\. Locality in S Oriente prov., E Cuba, ESE of Santiago de Cuba; scene of engagement June 24, 1898, won by Americans, which was preliminary to battle of El Caney and taking of Santiago.

Las He·ras \läs-'e(ə)r-əs\. Town, Mendoza prov., W cen. Argentina, ab. 10 m. N of Mendoza; pop. (1960c) 36,494.

Lash·kar \'ləsh-kər\. City, Madhya Pradesh, N cen. India; formerly ✱ of Gwalior state; trade center; constitutes the new part of Gwalior town (see GWALIOR 3) and lies a few miles S of the old city; originally the camp site (Hindustani *lashkar* the camp) of the maharaja's army.

Lashkar Gah \ˌləsh-kər-'gär\. Town, ✱ of Helmand prov., S Afghanistan; pop. (1969e) 28,388.

La Sila. See table at APENNINES.

La·si·thi·on *or* **La·sē·thi·on** \lə-'sē-thē-ˌón\ *also* **Las·si·thi** \lə-'sē-thē\. Department of Greece. See table at GREECE.

Las Mar·ga·ri·tas \läs-ˌmär-gə-ˈrēt-əs\. Municipality, Chiapas state, Mexico, 90 m. SE of Tuxtla Gutiérrez; pop. (1970p) 31,296; lumber; sugarcane, corn, fruit.

Las Ma·rí·as \ˌlä-smə-ˈrē-əs\. Municipality, W Puerto Rico, ENE of Mayagüez; pop. (1970p) 7904.

Las Na·vas de To·lo·sa \lä-ˈsnäv-əs-ˌdāt-ᵊl-ˈō-sə\. Village, Jaén prov., NE Andalusia, S Spain; scene of battle July 16, 1212 in which Alfonso VIII defeated the Moors.

Läsø. See LÆSØ.

La So·la·na \ˌläs-ə-ˈlän-ə\. Commune, Ciudad Real prov., S cen. Spain, 39 m. E by S of Ciudad Real; pop. (1970p) 13,894; agricultural products.

La Soufrière. See SOUFRIÈRE 4.

Las Pal·mas \lä-ˈspäl-məs\. 1 Province of Spain. See table at SPAIN.

2 *or* **Las Palmas de Gran Ca·na·ria** \-də-ˌgrän-kä-ˈnär-yə\. Seaport city, ✱ of Las Palmas prov., Spain, in NE Grand Canary I., 57 m. SE of Santa Cruz de Tenerife; pop. (1970p) 287,038; largest city and chief port of Canary Is.; exports sugar, tomatoes, almonds, bananas; manufactures glass, leather, hats, woolen goods; commercial fishing; boatbuilding; governor's palace, an 18th cent. cathedral, town hall; year-round seaside resort; founded late 15th cent.; major growth since opening of port 1883.

La Spe·zia \lä-ˈspet-sē-ə\. 1 Province of Liguria, NW Italy. See table at ITALY.

2 Fortified seaport, its ✱, on **Gulf of La Spezia** 51 m. ESE of Genoa; pop. (1968e) 129,219; naval arsenal; largest harbor in Italy; became chief naval station of Italy 1861; shipbuilding works; summer and winter resort. In World War II surrendered by Germans Apr. 23, 1945.

Las Pie·dras \ˌläs-pē-ˈā-drəs\. 1 Town and municipality, E Puerto Rico; pop. (1970p) 4625 (town), 18,048 (munic.); town is inland just NW of Humacao.

2 Town, Canelones dept., S Uruguay; pop. (1963c) 41,509.

Las Ro·sas \läs-ˈrō-səs\. Town, Chiapas state, SE Mexico; pop. (1960c) 7836.

Lassa. See LHASA.

Las·sen \ˈlas-ᵊn\. County in California. See table at CALIFORNIA.

Lassen Peak. Volcano, NE California, at S end of Cascade Range, in Shasta co., near border of Plumas co.; 10,457 ft.; only active volcano in conterminous U.S.; cinder cone 6913 ft.; sudden spectacular eruption 1914–16 after 200 years' quiescence; principal feature in **Lassen Volcanic National Park:** see UNITED STATES, *National Parks.*

Las·si·gny \la-sēn-ˈyē\. Village, Oise dept., N France, near Compiègne; pop. (1962c) 769; fighting 1914 and Mar. 1917; captured by French Aug. 21, 1918.

Lassithi. See LASITHION.

L'As·somp·tion \lə-səm(p)-shən, lə-ˌsō^{n}(m)p-sē-ˈō^{n}\. 1 River, chiefly in Joliette and L'Assomption cos., S Quebec, Canada; ab. 100 m. long; flows generally S; empties in St. Lawrence river opp. N end of Montreal I.

2 County, Quebec, Canada. See table at QUEBEC.

3 Town, its ⊗, 23 m. NNE of Montreal on L'Assomption river; pop. (1971p) 4885.

Lass·wade \la-ˈswād\. Village, Midlothian co., SE Scotland, SE of Edinburgh; residence 1798–1804 of Sir Walter Scott; De Quincey established his daughters here 1840 and lived with them at intervals until his death 1859.

Las Ta·blas \lä-ˈstäb-ləs\. Town, ✱ of Los Santos prov., S Panama; pop. (1970p) 3571; near coast on W side of Gulf of Panama.

Last Mountain Lake \ˈlast-\. Long narrow lake, S cen. Saskatchewan, Canada; S end ab. 20 m. NW of Regina; 89 sq. m.; discharges into Qu'Appelle river.

La·sto·vo \ˈläs-tə-ˌvō\ *or Ital.* **La·go·sta** \lə-ˈgäs-tə\. Island in Adriatic Sea off Dalmatian coast; administratively a part of Bosnia and Herzegovina, W Yugoslavia; 24 sq. m.; formerly Italian; as commune includes nearby small island of Sušac.

La·stra a Si·gna \ˌläs-trə-ä-ˈsēn-yə\. Commune, Firenze prov., Tuscany, cen. Italy, on Arno river 8 m. W of Florence; pop. (1968e) 16,521; church with 14th cent. frescoes; 14th cent. walls.

Las Tres Vír·ge·nes \ˌläs-ˈtrās-ˈvi(ə)r-hə-ˌnās\. Mountain, E cen. Baja California, NW Mexico; 6547 ft.

Las Ve·gas \läs-ˈvā-gəs\. 1 City, ⊗ of Clark co., SE corner of Nevada, 22 m. NW of Boulder Dam; pop. (1970c) 125,787; altitude 2030 ft.; distributing center for mining and stock-raising region; major tourist resort; Univ. of Nevada (1957); hot springs NW of city; housed offices for Hoover Dam (Boulder Dam) project until 1932. Occupied by Mormons 1855–57; bought by railroad for townsite and division point 1903; became ⊗ 1909; created City of Las Vegas 1911.

2 Urban community, San Miguel co., NE cen. New Mexico, ab. 40 m. E of Santa Fe; total pop. (1970c) 13,835; constitutes two municipalities separated from each other by Gallinas river: **City of Las Vegas,** *sometimes called* **East Las Vegas** *or* **New Town** (pop. 7528), ⊗ of San Miguel co.; and **Town of Las Vegas,** *sometimes called* **West Las Vegas** *or* **Old Town** (pop. 6307); shipping point and supply depot in cattle and sheep country; manufactures lumber, dairy products, flour; diversified agriculture; New Mexico Highlands Univ. (1893); health resort and hot springs nearby; Conchas Dam (1939) to the E. Old Town settled on Santa Fe Trail by Spaniards 1823–33; taken for U.S. by Gen. Stephen W. Kearny 1846; became seat of military operations 1851 following establishment of military post.

Las Vi·llas \läs-ˈvē-(y)əs\ *or formerly* **San·ta Clara** \ˌsant-ə-ˈklar-ə, ˈkler-ə\. Province of W cen. Cuba. See table at CUBA.

Las·wa·ri \lə-ˈswär-ē\. Village, Rajasthan, NW India, in former Alwar state, 12 m. E of Alwar and ab. 78 m. SSW of Delhi; scene of Lord Lake's defeat of Marathas Nov. 1, 1803 in Second Maratha War.

La Syrie. See SYRIA 2.

La·ta·cun·ga \ˌlät-ə-ˈküŋ-gə\. City, ✱ of Cotopaxi prov., cen. Ecuador, 50 m. S of Quito; pop. (1970e) 17,300; on plateau ab. 9150 ft. above sea level; ab. 25 m. S of the great volcano Cotopaxi; has suffered repeatedly from eruptions and earthquakes; founded by Spanish 1534.

La·tah \ˈlā-ˌtä, lə-ˈtä\. County in Idaho. See table at IDAHO.

Lat·a·kia \ˌlat-ə-ˈkē-ə\. 1 Former republic, originally a territory, now a governorate of Syria; 1671 sq. m.; pop. (1960c) 526,551; ✱ Latakia; coastal region bet. N extension of Lebanon Mts. (Djebel Ansariya) and the Mediterranean Sea and opp. island of Cyprus; the Orontes forms part of its E boundary. Chief towns Latakia, Tartūs, and Baniyas. Before World War I a part of Turkey; became a territory of the French mandate of Syria 1920, known as **Ala·wi·ya** \ˌal-ə-ˈwē-(y)ə\ or the **Territory of the Alaou·ites** \ˈal-au̇-ˌwītz\; made a state 1922 and in 1926 an autonomous part of Syria; made an integral part of Syria 1946.

2 *or Fr.* **Lat·ta·quié** \lat-ə-kyā\; *anc.* **La·od·i·cea** \ˌlā-ˌäd-ə-ˈsē-ə\ **Laodicea ad Ma·re** \-ad-ˈmā-(ˌ)rē, ˈmär-(ˌ)ē\. Seaport, ✱ of Latakia, W Syria; pop. (1960c) 67,799; center of rich agricultural region; exports asphalt, eggs, cereals, pottery, tobacco; sponge fishing; in antiquity had several other names; captured by Tancred 1103; became an important and wealthy city during the Crusades; taken by Saladin 1188; declined in importance but revived in 17th cent. by its cultivation of and trade in (Latakia) tobacco, which is still a major export.

La Tène \lä-ˈten, -ˈtān\. Shallows at E end of Lake of Neuchâtel, Switzerland; site of discovery of Iron-Age remains; name now applied to a period of the Iron Age assumed to date from 500 B.C. to 200 A.D.

La·ter·za \lə-ˈtert-sə\. Commune, Taranto prov., Apulia, SE Italy, 27 m. NW of Taranto; pop. (1968e) 12,224.

La Teste \lə-ˈtest\ *or formerly* **La Teste–de–Buch** \lə-ˌtes-təd-ə-ˈbyüsh\. Town, Gironde dept., SW France, SSE of Arcachon; pop. (1968e) 17,287; ancient capital of the **Pays de Buch** \ˌpād-ə-\.

La·thom and Burs·cough \ˈlā-t͟həm . . . ˈbər-(ˌ)skō\. Former urban district, Lancashire, NW England, NE of Liverpool; site of **Lathom House,** formerly seat of the Stanley family (earls of Derby) and object of siege by Parliamentarians Feb.–May 1644 when it was defended by the Countess of Derby, Charlotte de la Trémoille.

La·thrup Village \ˈlā-thrəp-\. City, Oakland co., SE Michigan; pop. (1970c) 4676.

La Thuile \lə-ˈtwē(ə)l\. Town, Aosta prov., Valle d'Aosta, NW Italy; terminal of Little Saint Bernard Pass; pop. (1968e) 694.

La·tia·no \lä-ˈtyä-(ˌ)nō\. Commune, Brindisi prov., Apulia, SE Italy, 13 m. SW of Brindisi; pop. (1968e) 14,322.

Lat·i·mer \ˈlat-ə-mər\. County in Oklahoma. See table at OKLAHOMA.

La·ti·na \lə-ˈtē-nə\ *or formerly* **Lit·to·ria** \li-ˈtōr-ē-ə, -ˈtȯr-\. 1 Province of Latium, cen. Italy. See table at ITALY.

2 Commune, its ✱, 35 m. SE of Rome; pop. (1968e) 68,781.

Latin America. Spanish America (*q.v.*) and Brazil.

Latin Empire. Part of the Byzantine Empire ruled by the Crusaders 1204–61; ✱ Constantinople; included lands on W, N, and NE shores of the Aegean Sea (except Euboea) and around the Sea of Marmara. See BYZANTINE EMPIRE.

Latin Way *or Lat.* **Via La·ti·na** \ˌvī-ə-lə-ˈtī-nə\. Ancient Roman road running SE from Rome past Tusculum and joining the Appian Way near Capua, or, as some state, at Beneventum.

La·ti·um \ˈlā-sh(ē-)əm\. 1 Ancient country of Italy in cen. part of W coast on Tyrrhenian Sea, bounded by Etruria on NW and by Campania on SE; inhabited by Latins whose cities (Ardea, Lavinium, Tusculum, Laurentum, Alba Longa, etc.) had formed Latin League by 500 B.C.; dominated by Rome from 4th cent. B.C.; Latins revolted and Latin League dissolved after its defeat in Latin War 340–338 B.C.; after Social War 90–88 B.C. Latin cities received rights of Roman citizenship.

2 *or Ital.* **La·zio** \ˈlät-sē-ˌō\. Autonomous region, cen. Italy; 6642 sq. m.; pop. (1968e) 4,565,448; ✱ Rome; lies bet. Tyrrhenian Sea and Apennines and bet. Tuscany and Campania; includes the Campagna di Roma (*q.v.*) and the Pontine Marshes (see PONTINO, AGRO); watered chiefly by Tiber river. Established 1948; received limited autonomy 1970.

La Tor·tu·ga \ˌlä-tȯr-ˈtü-gə\. Venezuelan island in the Caribbean Sea off N cen. coast of Venezuela, 55 m. W of the island of Margarita; 85 sq. m.

La Trappe. See SOLIGNY-LA-TRAPPE.

La Tri·ni·dad \lä-ˌtrē-nə-ˈt͟hä(t͟h)\. Municipality, ✱ of Benguet prov., Luzon, Phil., ab. 3 m. N of Baguio; pop. (1969e) 17,000; at elevation of ab. 8000 ft.; has cool climate; fruits and vegetables of temperate zone raised in surrounding gardens.

La Tri·ni·ta·ria \lä-ˌtrē-nə-ˈtär-ē-ə\. Municipality, Chiapas state, Mexico, 95 m. SE of Tuxtla Gutiérrez; pop. (1970p) 28,028.

La Tri·ni·té \lä-ˌtrē-nə-ˈtā\. Commune, E coast of Martinique, West Indies.

La·trobe \lə-ˈtrōb\. 1 Borough, Westmoreland co., SW Pennsylvania, 26 m. W of Johnstown; pop. (1970c) 11,749; coal mining; ceramics, plastics, tool steel; St. Vincent Coll. (1840).

2 Town, N Tasmania, Australia, near mouth of Mersey river 5 m. S of Devonport; pop. (1970e) 5190.

La·trun \lə-ˈtrün\. Village in Israeli-occupied zone of Jordan, on highway 15 m. W of Jerusalem; site of British detention camp 1946.

Lattaquié. See LATAKIA 2.

Lat·ti·mer Mines \ˌlat-ə-mər-\. Locality, Luzerne co., E Pennsylvania, near Hazleton.

La·tu·kan, Mount \-ˌlät-ə-ˈkän\. Active volcano, Lanao del Sur prov., Mindanao, Phil., on Cotabato boundary; 7078 ft.

La Tuque \lə-ˈtyük\. Town, Champlain co., S Quebec, Canada, on Saint-Maurice river 77 m. N of Three Rivers; pop. (1971p) 13,071; resort; paper, shoes; hydroelectric power station.

La·tur \lä-ˈtu̇(ə)r\. Town, SE Maharashtra, S cen. India, 140 m. NW of Hyderabad; pop. (1961c) 40,913.

Lat·vi·an Soviet Socialist Republic \ˈlät-vē-ən-\ *or* **Lat·via** \ˈlat-ve-ə\ *or Lettish and Lithuanian* **Lat·vi·ja** \ˈlät-vē-ˌ(y)ä\ *or Fr.* **Let·to·nie** \let-ō-nē\ *or Ger.* **Lett·land** \ˈlet-ˌlänt\. A constituent republic of the U.S.S.R., bounded on N by the Estonian S.S.R., on E by the Russian S.F.S.R., on SE by the Belorussian S.S.R. and Poland, on S by the Lithuanian S.S.R., and on W by the Baltic Sea; 24,595 sq. m.; pop. (1970p) 2,365,000; ✱ Riga. Northern half of its W coast indented by Gulf of Riga, large inlet of Baltic Sea. A low-lying plain, with no part above 1000 ft. Chief river the Western Dvina, flowing from SE to Gulf of Riga near Riga; other streams the Venta, Lielupe, and Gauja. *Chief products:* Flax, barley, rye; livestock; paper, textiles, chemicals, transportation equipment. *Chief towns:* Riga, Liepāja, Daugavpils.

History: See BALTIC PROVINCES, KURLAND, LIVONIA, and BALTIC STATES. Proclaimed an independent republic Nov. 1918; chiefly from the former Russian governments of Kurland and southern Livonia; recognized by U.S.S.R. 1920; joined League of Nations 1921; ratified nonaggression treaty with U.S.S.R. 1932; established nationalist dictatorship 1934; signed mutual assistance treaty with U.S.S.R. and met German problem by repatriation 1939; annexed by U.S.S.R. Aug. 3, 1940; overrun by German army 1941, but retaken 1944–45; incorporation in U.S.S.R. not recognized by United States.

Lauban. See LUBAN.

Lauch·ham·mer \ˈlau̇k-ˌhäm-ər\. City, Cottbus dist., East Germany, 30 m. SW of Cottbus; pop. (1970e) 27,458; mining, machinery, coke, plastics; founded 1721.

Lau·der·dale \ˈlȯd-ər-ˌdāl\. 1 Name of counties in three states of the U.S. See tables at ALABAMA, MISSISSIPPI, TENNESSEE.

2 Village, Ramsey co., E Minnesota; pop. (1970c) 2571.

Lauderdale–by–the–Sea. Town, Broward co., SE Florida; pop. (1970c) 2879.

Lauderdale Lakes. City, Broward co., SE Florida; pop. (1970c) 10,577; residential suburb of Fort Lauderdale.

Lau·der·hill \ˈlȯd-ər-ˌhil\. City, Broward co., SE Florida; pop. (1970c) 9071; residential suburb of Fort Lauderdale.

Laudunum. See LAON.

Laudus. See SAINT-LÔ.

Lau·en·burg \ˈlau̇-ən-ˌbu̇(ə)rg\. 1 Region, SE Schleswig-Holstein, West Germany, E of Hamburg; formerly a duchy; 453 sq. m.; under German rulers 1260–1689; during next two cents. to 1864 belonged for varying periods to France, Hannover, Prussia, and Denmark; became part of Prussia 1865 but retained its constitution and special privileges; entered North German Confederation 1866 and German Empire 1870; incorporated in Prussia 1876; ceased to be duchy 1918.

2 *also* **Lauenburg in Pom·mern** \-in-ˈpȯm-ərn\. City, Poland. See LĘBORK.

Lauf·feld *or* **Lauf·feldt** \ˈlau̇-ˌfelt\ *also* **Law·feld** \ˈlō-ˌfeld\. Village in NE Belgium, just W of Maastricht, Netherlands; scene of victory of Marshal Saxe over Allies July 2, 1747.

Lau Group \ˈlau̇-\ *or* **Eastern Group.** Group of many small islands in E part of Fiji, SW Pacific Ocean; ab. 45 sq. m.; comprises two main groups, Exploring Is. in N and Lakemba Is. in S.

Lauis. See LUGANO.

Laun. See LOUNY.

Laun·ces·ton \'lȯn(t)-sə-stən, 'län(t)-\ *or orig.* **Pat·er·so·nia** \ˌpat-ər-'sō-nyə\. City, NE Tasmania, Australia, at confluence of North and South Esk rivers 40 m. from Bass Strait; pop. (1970e) 36,620; hydroelectric power plant; seaport; exports agricultural produce and timber; textiles, pottery, aluminum, flour.

Launces·ton \'lȯn(t)-stən, 'län(t)-\ *or anc.* **Dun·he·ved** \'dün-ˌhev-əd\. Municipal borough, Cornwall, SW England, 52 m. WSW of Exeter near the Tamar river; pop. (1971p) 4725; ruins (chiefly the circular keep) of old Norman castle, seat of the earls of Cornwall.

La Union \ˌlä-ü-'nyȯn\. Narrow coastal province, NW Luzon, Phil., along South China Sea; 576 sq. m.; pop. (1970p) 374,659; ✱ San Fernando. Well watered by many short streams. Has several good ports, esp. San Fernando. Produces sugar, coconuts, tobacco, rice, sisal hemp; makes cloth, pottery, baskets, hats, mats, embroidery. Inhabitants mainly Ilokanos. Chief towns San Fernando, Bauang, Agoo, Naguilian, Luna.

History: Province created 1854 from the "union" of towns and districts formerly parts of Pangasinan and Ilocos Sur—hence the name. Region explored by Spanish as early as 1572; experienced a short-lived successful rebellion 1661; joined the Filipino revolutionary movement of 1896; civil government established Aug. 1901; invaded by Japanese Dec. 1941.

La Unión \ˌlä-ü-'nyȯn\. 1 City, Valdivia prov., S cen. Chile; pop. (1960c) 11,558.

2 Department of E El Salvador. See table at EL SALVADOR.

3 Town, its ✱, on Gulf of Fonseca; pop. (1968e) 15,189; major seaport of El Salvador, exporting cotton and livestock.

4 Commune, Murcia prov., SE Spain, 28 m. SE of Murcia; pop. (1960c) 11,687; iron, sulfur, manganese mines nearby.

La·u·pa·ho·e·hoe \ˌlä-ü-pä-ˌhō-ə-'hō-ə\. Village, Hawaii co., Hawaii, on E coast of Hawaii I. ab. 22 m. NNW of Hilo; pop. (1970c) 452.

Lau·rel \'lȯr-əl, 'lär-\. 1 County in Kentucky. See table at KENTUCKY.

2 Town, Sussex co., S Delaware, 15 m. SW of Georgetown; pop. (1970c) 2408; ships fruits and vegetables; lumber, hosiery; diversified agriculture.

3 Town, Prince Georges co., S cen. Maryland, 18 m. NNE of Washington; pop. (1970c) 10,525; poultry and dairy farms.

4 City, a ⊗ of Jones co., SE Mississippi, 53 m. SW of Meridian; pop. (1970c) 24,125; oil refining; lumber, building board, clothing; Southeastern Baptist Coll. (1948); founded 1882, incorporated 1890.

5 City, Yellowstone co., S cen. Montana, on Yellowstone river 17 m. SW of Billings; pop. (1970c) 4454; wheat.

Lau·rel·dale \'lȯr-əl-ˌdāl, 'lär-\. Borough, Berks co., SE Pennsylvania, 5 m. N of Reading; pop. (1970c) 4519.

Laurel Hill. Ridge in SW Pennsylvania, extending along boundary bet. Somerset co. on E and Fayette and Westmoreland cos. on W, and N into Cambria and Indiana cos.; coal deposits.

Laurel Mountain. Peak in E Preston co., N West Virginia; 2603 ft.

Laurel Springs. Borough, Camden co., SW New Jersey, 14 m. SE of Camden; pop. (1970c) 2566.

Lau·rens \'lȯr-ənz, 'lär-\. 1 Name of counties in two states of the U.S. See tables at GEORGIA and SOUTH CAROLINA.

2 City, ⊗ of Laurens co., NW South Carolina, 23 m. NNE of Greenwood; pop. (1970c) 10,298; textiles, carpets, glass; cotton, peaches.

Lau·ren·tian Highlands \lȯ-'ren-chən-\ *or* **Canadian Shield.** Plateau region, E Canada and NE U.S., extending E from the Mackenzie basin to Davis Strait and S to S Quebec, S Ontario, NE Minnesota, N Wisconsin, NW Michigan, and NE New York including the Adirondack Mts.

Laurentian Hills *or* **Laurentian Mountains** *also* **Lau·ren·tide Hills** \'lȯr-ən-ˌtīd-, 'lär-, -ˌtēd-\ *or* **Laurentide Mountains.** Range in Quebec prov., Canada, N of the St. Lawrence river on S edge of the Laurentian Highlands; highest point 3905 ft.

Lau·ren·tides Park \'lȯr-ən-ˌtīdz-, 'lär-, -tēdz-, -tēd-\. Canadian provincial park, N of Quebec city, SE Quebec prov.; in Laurentian Highlands S of Lake St. John; 3613 sq. m.; contains many lakes and streams with fine fishing; game preserve.

Lau·ren·tum \lȯ-'rent-əm\. Ancient city of Latium, cen. Italy, near coast NW of Lavinium with which it became united.

Lau·ria \laů-'rē-ə\. Commune, Potenza prov., Basilicata, S Italy, 42 m. S of Potenza; pop. (1968e) 13,343.

Lau·rin·burg \'lȯr-ən-ˌbərg, 'lär-\. City, ⊗ of Scotland co., S North Carolina, 39 m. WSW of Fayetteville; pop. (1970c) 8859; textiles, watches, furniture; diversified agriculture; St. Andrews Presbyterian Coll. (1857).

Lau·ri·um \'lȯr-ē-əm, 'lär-\. Residential village, Houghton co., NW Michigan penin., 70 m. NW of Marquette; pop. (1970c) 2868; potatoes, strawberries.

Laurium *or* **Lau·ri·on** \'lȯr-ē-ən, 'lär-\ *or Gk.* **Lá·vri·on** \ˌlä-vrē-'ȯn\. Seaport, Greece, ab. 26 m. SE of Athens; pop. (1961c) 6553; near **Mount Laurium,** famous in ancient Greece for its silver mines, worked 6th–2d cents. B.C.

Lau·sanne \lō-'zän, -'zan\. Commune, ✱ of Vaud canton, W Switzerland, on N shore of Lake of Geneva 32 m. NE of Geneva; pop. (1970c) 137,883; railroad junction; metalworking; precision instruments, leather products, clothing, beer, chocolate; 13th cent. cathedral, 13th cent. castle (former episcopal palace), univ. (1537). Made episcopal see in late 6th cent. (bishopric removed to Fribourg 1663); Reformation introduced 1536 after conquest by Bernese, who occupied city until 1798; made capital of Vaud canton 1803; treaties concluded here 1912, 1923; Lausanne Pact concluded here 1932 reducing German war reparations about 90 percent.

Lausitz. See LUSATIA.

Lausitzer Neisse. See NEISSE.

Laut *or Du.* **Laoet** \'laůt\. Island in the Java Sea, off SE coast of Borneo, Indonesia; 796 sq. m.

Lau·ta·ro \laů-'tär-(ˌ)ō\. City, Cautín prov., S cen. Chile, 150 m. W of Valdivia; pop. (1960c) 10,448.

Lau·ter·brun·nen \'laůt-ər-ˌbrůn-ən\. Valley in Bern canton, SW cen. Switzerland, S of Interlaken and NW of the Jungfrau; pop. (1970c) 3431; lace making; numerous waterfalls.

Lau·to·ka \laů-'tō-kə\. Seaport, W coast of Viti Levu, Fiji, SW Pacific Ocean; pop. (1969e) 11,287; center of sugar industry.

Lau·wers Zee \'laů-vər(s)-ˌzā\. Inlet of North Sea on N coast of Netherlands, on border bet. Friesland and Groningen provs.

Lau·zon \lō-zōⁿ\. City, Levis co., S Quebec, Canada, on right bank of St. Lawrence river opp. Quebec city; pop. (1966c) 12,877; shipbuilding.

La·va \'lav-ə\ *or Ger.* **Al·le** \'äl-ə\ *or Pol.* **Ły·na** \'lin-(ˌ)ä\. Tributary of Pregolya river, NE Poland and Kaliningrad Oblast, Russian S.F.S.R., U.S.S.R.; 137 m. long.

Lava, Mount \-'läv-ə, -'lav-\. Peak, Uinta co., SW Wyoming; 10,400 ft.

Lava Beds National Monument. See UNITED STATES, *National Monuments.*

La·vaca \lə-'vak-ə\. 1 River, SE Texas; ab. 100 m. long; rises in Lavaca co., flows S into **Lavaca Bay** in Calhoun co., an arm of Matagorda Bay.

2 County in Texas. See table at TEXAS.

Lava Hot Springs. City, Bannock co., SE Idaho, 25 m. SE of Pocatello; pop. (1970c) 516; hot mineral springs; interesting rock formations.

La·val \lə-'val\. 1 *or in full* **Ville de Laval** \ˌvēl-də-\. City, Canada. See JESUS ISLAND.
2 Commune, ✻ of Mayenne dept., NW France, 44 m. E of Rennes; pop. (1968c) 45,674; center of agricultural region; textiles, machinery; lignite mining; castle with 12th cent. donjon; 15th cent. gate; 16th cent. castle (housing law courts). Founded before 9th cent. A.D.; Vendeans defeated Republicans here 1793.

La·va·lle·ja \ˌlä-vä(l)-'yā-ə\ *or formerly* **Mi·nas** \'mēn-əs\. Department of S Uruguay. See table at URUGUAY.

La·van·saa·ri \'läv-an-ˌsär-ē\. Small island in Gulf of Finland, E of Hogland.

La·va·pié, Point \-ˌläv-ə-'pyā\. Cape on coast of Bío-Bío prov., S cen. Chile, S of Gulf of Arauco.

La·vaur \lá-'vȯr\. Commune, SW Tarn dept., S France; pop. (1962c) 6622; an old town of Languedoc, taken by Simon de Montfort 1211 during his campaign against the Albigenses; seat of bishopric until the Revolution.

La Ve·ga \lə-'veg-ə\. 1 Province, cen. Dominican Republic. See table at DOMINICAN REPUBLIC.
2 *or formerly* **Con·cep·ción de la Vega** \kən-ˌsep-sē-'ōn-ˌdel-ə-'veg-ə\. Commune, its ✻; pop. (1970e) 23,759.

La·vel·lo \lə-'vel-(ˌ)ō\. Commune, Potenza prov., Basilicata, S Italy, 29 m. N of Potenza; pop. (1968e) 12,729.

La Ven·ta \lə-'vent-ə\. Village, W Tabasco state, SE Mexico, near Tonalá river; on an island ab. 4 m. wide in mangrove swamps on the coast; site of excavations by the National Geographic Society and the Smithsonian Institution; among the finds were some excellent jade and five huge heads carved of basalt, representing "La Venta culture" of a people flourishing c. 450 to 800 A.D.

La Vé·ren·drye Provincial Park \lə-ˌver-ən-'drē-\. Canadian provincial park in SW Quebec, NW of Ottawa; 4953 sq. m.; numerous lakes and rivers.

La Verne \lə-'vərn\. City, Los Angeles co., SW California, 25 m. E of Los Angeles; pop. (1970c) 12,965; citrus fruit; La Verne Coll. (1891).

La Ve·ta Pass \lə-ˌvēt-ə-\. Mountain pass, Costilla co., S Colorado, in Sangre de Cristo Range of the Rocky Mts.; 9413 ft.; westernmost branch of the Santa Fe Trail passed through it; highway.

La·via·na \lä-'vyä-nə\. Commune, Oviedo prov., NW Spain, 15 m. ESE of Oviedo; pop. (1970p) 14,883.

La Vic·to·ria \ˌläv-ik-'tōr-ē-ə, -'tȯr-\. Town, Aragua state, N Venezuela; pop. (1970e) 32,553.

Lavinia, Civita. See LANUVIUM.

La·vin·i·um \lə-'vin-ē-əm\. Ancient town in NW Latium, cen. Italy, near the coast 19 m. S of Rome; sacred to the Penates and to Vesta; said to have been founded by Aeneas and named for his wife Lavinia.

La Vis·ta \lə-'vis-tə\. City, Sarpy co., E Nebraska; pop. (1970c) 4807.

Lavongai. See NEW HANOVER 2.

La·vo·nia \lə-'vōn-ē-ə, -'vōn-yə\. City, Franklin co., NE Georgia, 37 m. NNE of Athens; pop. (1970c) 2044; lumber; cotton.

La·vras \'lav-rəs\. City, S cen. Minas Gerais state, E Brazil, 150 m. NW of Rio de Janeiro; munic. pop. (1968e) 39,586.

Lávrion. See LAURIUM.

La·wai Bay \lə-'wī-\. Bay on S coast of Kauai I., Hawaii, bet. Koloa Bay and Wahiawa Bay.

Lawers, Ben. See BEN LAWERS.

Lawfeld. See LAUFFELD.

Lawk·sawk \'lȯk-ˌsȯk\. Former state, W Southern Shan States, now part of Shan State, E cen. Burma; 2365 sq. m.; chief town Lawksawk, 30 m. N of Taunggyi.

Lawn·dale \'lȯn-ˌdāl, 'län-\. City, Los Angeles co., SW California, E of Manhattan Beach; pop. (1970c) 24,825.

Lawn·side \'lȯn-ˌsīd, 'län-\. Borough, Camden co., SW New Jersey, 7 m. SSE of Camden; pop. (1970c) 2757; incorporated 1926.

Lawoe. See LAWU.

Law·ra \'lȯr-ə\. Town, NW Ghana, W Africa, near Upper Volta border 160 m. NW of Tamale.

Law·rence \'lȯr-ən(t)s, 'lär-\. 1 Name of counties in eleven states of the U.S. See tables at ALABAMA, ARKANSAS, ILLINOIS, INDIANA, KENTUCKY, MISSISSIPPI, MISSOURI, OHIO, PENNSYLVANIA, SOUTH DAKOTA, TENNESSEE.
2 Town, Marion co., cen. Indiana, NE of Indianapolis; pop. (1970c) 16,646; residential; grows mushrooms.
3 City, ⊗ of Douglas co., E Kansas, on Kansas river 25 m. E of Topeka; pop. (1970c) 45,698; a residential and food-processing center; Univ. of Kansas (1863). Founded 1854 by New England Emigrant Aid Company; center of Free State activities in pre-Civil War years; scene of massacre by Quantrill's guerrillas Aug. 21, 1863.
4 Industrial city, a ⊗ of Essex co., NE corner of Massachusetts, on Merrimack river 9 m. ENE of Lowell; pop. (1970c) 66,915; textiles (esp. worsted cloth), textile machinery, paper, leather goods, electrical equipment, clothing; has many parks and playgrounds, and an athletic stadium; incorporated as a city 1853.
5 Residential village, Nassau co., SE New York, on Long I., 16 m. ESE of New York; pop. (1970c) 6566.

Law·rence·burg \'lȯr-ən(t)s-ˌbərg, 'lär-\. 1 City, ⊗ of Dearborn co., SE Indiana, on Ohio river 55 m. SE of Shelbyville; pop. (1970c) 4636; feed, lumber; distilleries; dairy farming.
2 City, ⊗ of Anderson co., cen. Kentucky, 12 m. S of Frankfort; pop. (1970c) 3579; distillery; cheese; diversified agriculture.
3 City, ⊗ of Lawrence co., S Tennessee, 31 m. SSW of Columbia; pop. (1970c) 8889; clothing, bicycles, concrete products; dairy and poultry farming.

Law·rence·ville \'lȯr-ən(t)s-ˌvil, 'lär-, -vəl\. 1 City, ⊗ of Gwinnett co., N Georgia, 26 m. ENE of Atlanta; pop. (1970c) 5115; aluminum products, boats; corn; became ⊗ 1821.
2 City, ⊗ of Lawrence co., SE Illinois, 55 m. N of Evansville, Indiana; pop. (1970c) 5863; oil and gas wells; oil refining; chemicals, asphalt, metal furniture.
3 Town, Mercer co., W cen. New Jersey, ab. 6 m. N of Trenton; named in honor of Capt. James Lawrence; Lawrenceville School (1810).
4 Town, ⊗ of Brunswick co., S Virginia, SW of Petersburg; pop. (1970c) 4636; St. Paul's Coll. (1888).

Law·ton \'lȯt-ᵊn\. City, ⊗ of Comanche co., SW Oklahoma, 80 m. SW of Oklahoma City; pop. (1970c) 74,470; farming (esp. cotton); manufactures clothing, cement products, flour, dairy products; hematite, granite, limestone quarries nearby; oil wells; Cameron State Agricultural Coll. (1908); founded 1901. Wichita National Forest and Game Preserve in vicinity, Fort Sill (*q.v.*) 4 m. N.

Law·ton·ka, Lake \-lȯ-'täŋ-kə\. Lake, Comanche co., SW Oklahoma; 2 sq. m.; formed by dam (60 ft. high, 375 ft. long) across Medicine Bluff creek; water supply for Fort Sill and Lawton to the S.

La·wu *or Du.* **La·woe** \'lä-(ˌ)wü\. Mountain, E cen. Java, Indonesia; 10,712 ft.

Lay·san \'lī-ˌsän\. Islet of the Leeward Is., Hawaiian Is., cen. Pacific Ocean, ab. 750 m. NW of Niihau I., 25°50′N, 171°50′W; included in Hawaiian Islands Bird Reservation.

Lay·ton \'lāt-ᵊn\. City, Davis co., N Utah, N of Salt Lake City; pop. (1970c) 13,603; sugar refining; feed mill; potatoes, sugar beets.

La·zi \'lä-sē\. Municipality, S coast of Siquijor I., Negros Oriental prov., Negros, Phil.; pop. (1969e) 18,000; has good harbor.

Lazio. See LATIUM 2.

Lea \'lē\. 1 County in New Mexico. See table at NEW MEXICO.
2 River, SE England; 46 m. long; rises in Bedfordshire, flows SE through Hertfordshire and S bet. Essex and Greater London cos. into the Thames.

Lead \'lēd\. City, Lawrence co., W South Dakota, 33 m. WNW of Rapid City; pop. (1970c) 5420; gold mining; tourist resort.

Lead·bet·ter Point \ˌled-ˌbet-ər-\. Point on NW coast of Pacific co., SW Washington, at S entrance to Willapa Bay.

Lead·ville \'led-ˌvil\. Mining city, ⊗ of Lake co., cen. Colorado, in Rocky Mts. 75 m. WSW of Denver; pop. (1970c) 4314; alt. 10,190 ft.; one of principal centers of 19th cent. American mining history; mines gold, silver, lead, zinc, copper, bismuth, manganese, and molybdenum; founded 1860 as gold camp.

Leaf \'lēf\. 1 River, SE Mississippi; ab. 180 m. long; rises in S Scott co., flows SE to unite with Chickasawhay river in N George co. and form the Pascagoula river.

2 River, N Quebec prov., Canada; 300 m. long; flows NE from Lake Minto into Ungava Bay.

League City \'lēg-\. City, Galveston co., SE Texas, 25 m. NW of Galveston; pop. (1970c) 10,818; brooms; truck and dairy farming.

League Island. District, S Philadelphia city, Pennsylvania; U.S. Navy Yard.

Leake \'lēk\. County in Mississippi. See table at MISSISSIPPI.

Leakes·ville \'lēks-ˌvil, -vəl\. Town, ⊗ of Greene co., SE Mississippi; pop. (1970c) 1090; lumber.

Lea·key \'lēk-ē\. City, ⊗ of Real co., SW cen. Texas; pop. (1970c) 393.

Le·a·lui \ˌlē-ə-'lü-ē\. Town, Zambia, on E bank of Zambezi river.

Leam *or* **Leame** \'lēm\. River, cen. England; 25 m. long; flows into the Avon near Warwick.

Lea·ming·ton \'lē-miŋ-tən\. Town, Essex co., SE Ontario, Canada, 30 m. ESE of Windsor, near Lake Erie shore; pop. (1971p) 10,589; resort; truck farming; tobacco.

Leam·ing·ton \'lem-iŋ-tən\ *or officially* **Royal Leamington Spa.** Municipal borough, Warwickshire, cen. England, on the Leam river 2 m. NE of Warwick; pop. (1971p) 44,989; health resort, with mineral springs.

Leane, Lough \'läk-'lān\. Largest of the Lakes of Killarney (*q.v.*).

Lea·side \'lē-ˌsīd\. Residential town, York co., SE Ontario, Canada, N suburb of Toronto; pop. (1966c) 21,250.

Leath·er·head \'leth-ər-ˌhed\. Urban district, Surrey, S England; pop. (1971p) 40,112.

Leav·en·worth \'lev-ən-ˌwərth\. 1 County in NE Kansas. See table at KANSAS.

2 City, its ⊗, on Missouri river 22 m. NW of Kansas City; pop. (1970c) 25,147; railroad, trading, and industrial center; manufactures iron and steel, flour, furniture, stoves, mining machinery, washing machines; Saint Mary Coll. (1923) in S suburb of Xavier. Settled 1854 by proslavery emigrants from Missouri; oldest city in Kansas. See FORT LEAVENWORTH.

3 City, Chelan co., cen. Washington, on Wenatchee river 20 m. NW of Wenatchee; pop. (1970c) 1322; sawmill; diversified agriculture.

Leav·itt Peak \ˌlev-ət-\. Mountain in Sierra Nevada, on boundary bet. Mono and Tuolumne cos., E cen. California; 11,570 ft.

Lea·wood \'lē-ˌwu̇d\. City, Johnson co., E Kansas, S of Kansas City; pop. (1970c) 10,349; dairy and truck farms.

Leb·a·dea \ˌleb-ə-'dē-ə\ *also* **Li·vad·ca** \li-'vad-ē-ə\ *or Gk.* **Le·vá·dhia** \le-'väth-yə\. Commune, ✱ of Boeotia dept., E Central Greece and Euboea region, Greece, ab. 60 m. NW of Athens; pop. (1961c) 12,609.

Lebanese Republic. See LEBANON 1.

Leb·a·non \'leb-(ə-)nən\. 1 *or Fr.* **Li·ban** \lē-bäⁿ\. Republic, at E end of Mediterranean Sea, bounded on N and E by Syria, on S by Israel, and on W by Mediterranean Sea; 3949 sq. m.; pop. (1970e) 2,800,000; ✱ Beirut. *Physical features:* Largely mountainous, Lebanon Mountains in cen. part; bounded on E by Anti-Lebanon range; valley bet. the two ranges, known as Al-Bika (*anc.* Coele-Syria), watered by the Litani river in S and by the upper Orontes in N; Mt. Hermon on SE border. *Chief products:* Citrus fruit, vegetables, tobacco, olives, iron ore; manufacturing: textiles, building materials, leather goods; food processing, oil refining; tourism. *Chief towns:* Beirut, Tripoli, Zahle, Sidon.

History: Inhabited by Maronites, members of a Syrian Christian sect established in 7th cent. A.D. and subject to Rome from 12th cent.; in 1841 and 1860, Maronites massacred by the Druses (see JEBEL ED DRUZ); under pressure of European powers especially France, **Great Lebanon** (*Fr.* **Grand Liban** \gräⁿ-\) established as autonomous government under Christian governor appointed by the Porte 1861–1914; declared autonomous under French mandate 1920; reorganized as **Lebanese Republic** 1926 (see SYRIA 2); after treaty with France 1936, its constitution, previously suspended, was restored 1937; under control of Vichy authorities 1940; passed under control of the British and Free French July 1941; declared independent 1941, but evacuation of French troops not completed until 1946; participated in Arab-Israeli War 1948–49; U.S. troops sent to Lebanon July 1958 (withdrawn Oct. 1958) following government's request for U.S. assistance during period of internal strife; disrupted oil shipments to Western nations during Arab-Israeli War 1967.

2 County in Pennsylvania. See table at PENNSYLVANIA.

3 Agricultural town, N New London co., SE corner of Connecticut, 5 m. S of Willimantic; pop. (1970c) 3804.

4 City, St. Clair co., SW Illinois, 20 m. E of East St. Louis; pop. (1970c) 3564; grain farming; McKendree Coll. (1828).

5 City, ⊗ of Boone co., cen. Indiana, 25 m. NW of Indianapolis; pop. (1970c) 9766; tools, automobile parts; dairy and livestock farming.

6 City, E Smith co., N Kansas; pop. (1970c) 517; former geographical center of U.S. (until admission of Alaska) ab. 4 m. NW, at 39°49′N, 98°33′W.

7 City, ⊗ of Marion co., cen. Kentucky, 28 m. W of Danville; pop. (1970c) 5528; distillery; meat-packing; tobacco.

8 City, ⊗ of Laclede co., S cen. Missouri, 25 m. S of E end of Lake of the Ozarks; pop. (1970c) 8616; boats, cheese, tools and dies; lake resort.

9 Industrial city, Grafton co., W New Hampshire, 19 m. N of Claremont; pop. (1970c) 9725; lake resort; sports gear and clothing, ball bearings, electrical equipment.

10 Village, ⊗ of Warren co., SW Ohio, 18 m. E of Hamilton; pop. (1970c) 7934; fabricated steel; grain farming; prehistoric mounds and earthworks nearby.
11 City, Linn co., W Oregon, 20 m. E of Corvallis; pop. (1970c) 6636; sawmills; lumber; fruit and berry farming.
12 Industrial city, ⊗ of Lebanon co., SE cen. Pennsylvania, 25 m. E of Harrisburg; pop. (1970c) 28,572; iron and steel, textiles, chemicals, clothing, electrical equipment. Laid out 1756, incorp. as city 1868.
13 City, ⊗ of Wilson co., N cen. Tennessee, 31 m. E of Nashville; pop. (1970c) 12,492; flour, clocks, woolen blankets, barrel staves; Coll. of Cumberland (1842).
14 Town, ⊗ of Russell co., SW Virginia, NNE of Bristol; pop. (1970c) 2272; diversified agriculture.

Lebanon Mountains *or Arab.* **Ja·bal Lub·nān** \ˌjab-əl-ˌlüb-ˈnän\ *or anc.* **Lib·a·nus** \ˈlib-ə-nəs\. Mountain range in Lebanon, parallel with the Mediterranean coast; ab. 100 m. long; highest peak Qurnet as Sauda 10,131 ft. near N end.

Lebanon Springs. Village and health resort, Columbia co., SE New York, near Massachusetts border ab. 22 m. SE of Albany; mineral springs.

Le Bar·do \le-ˈbär-dō\ *or* **Bār·daw** \ˈbär-ˌdä\. Town, Tunisia, ab. 2 m. NW of Tunis; pop. (1966c) 40,714.

Leb·be·ke \ˈleb-ə-kə\. Commune, East Flanders prov., W cen. Belgium, ab. 15 m. NW of Brussels; pop. (1969e) 13,097.

Lebda. See LEPTIS MAGNA.

Le Bec–Hel·louin \lə-ˈbek-el-ˈwaⁿ\. Commune, Eure dept., N France, ab. 25 m. NW of Évreux; pop. (1962c) 465; remains of the Benedictine Abbey of Bec, founded 1034, which became famous under Lanfranc (prior 1045–62) and Anselm (prior 1063–78, abbot 1078–93).

Leb·e·dos \ˈleb-ə-ˌdäs\. Ancient city, one of the 12 Ionian Cities, situated on coast of Asia Minor bet. Teos and Ephesus.

Le Blanc–Mes·nil \lə-ˌbläⁿ-mā-ˈnēl\. Commune, Seine-St-Denis dept., N France, NE suburb of Paris; pop. (1968e) 48,487.

Le·bong \lə-ˈbȯŋ\. See DARJEELING.

Lę·bork \lem-ˈbȯ(ə)rk\; *Ger.* **Lau·en·burg** \ˈlaů-ən-ˌbů(ə)rg\ *also* **Lauenburg in Pom·mern** \-in-ˈpȯm-ərn\. City, N Gdańsk prov., N Poland, ab. 40 m. WNW of Gdańsk; pop. (1970p) 25,000; railroad junction; lumber, machinery; brewing and distilling; founded 1341; in World War II taken by U.S.S.R. Mar. 11, 1945; assigned to Poland by Potsdam Conference 1945.

Le Bour·get \lə-bůr-ˈzhā\. Commune, Seine-St-Denis dept., N France, 6 m. NE of Paris; formerly site of major airport (closed 1969), where Charles A. Lindbergh landed May 21, 1927 after first nonstop solo transatlantic flight.

Le Bous·cat \lə-bü-ˈskä\. Commune, Gironde dept., SW France, NNW suburb of Bordeaux; pop. (1968e) 22,550.

Le·bri·ja \lā-ˈbrē-(ˌ)hä\; *older* **Le·bri·xa** \lā-ˈbrē-(ˌ)shä\ *or* **Ne·bri·ja** \nā-ˈbrē-(ˌ)hä\ *or* **Ne·bri·xa** \-(ˌ)shä\; *anc.* **Na·bris·sa** \nə-ˈbris-ə\ *or* **Ne·bris·sa** \nə-\. Commune, Sevilla prov., SW Spain, on Guadalquivir river 33 m. S of Seville; pop. (1970p) 21,712; agricultural trading center; clay deposits; manufactures aluminum products; cathedral. Settled by Greeks; reconquered from Moors by Ferdinand III 1248 and Andrew the Wise 1264. Birthplace of Elio Antonio de Nebrija (1444–1532), leader of the revival of learning in Spain.

Le·bu \ˈlā-(ˌ)bü\. Seaport and coal-mining center, ✱ of Arauco prov., S cen. Chile, ab. 60 m. SW of Concepción; pop. (1960c) 6248.

Le Can·net \lə-ka-ˈnā\. Commune, Alpes-Maritimes dept., SE France, NNE suburb of Cannes; pop. (1968c) 23,231; tourist resort; produces flowers and perfume essences.

Le Cap. See CAP HAITIEN.

Le Ca·teau \lə-ka-ˈtō\ *or formerly* **Le Cateau–Cam·bré·sis** \-ˌkäⁿ-brā-ˈzē\. Commune, Nord dept., N France, 13 m. ESE of Cambrai; pop. (1962c) 9444; treaty (Cateau-Cambrésis) Apr. 2–3, 1559, bet. France, England, and Spain, confirmed French possession of Calais and surrendered French conquests in Italy; suffered much during religious conflicts of 16th cent. (1562–98), again during the Revolution, and in World War I; battle Aug. 26, 1914 when British suffered severe losses during retirement from Mons; captured by British Oct. 10, 1918 and suffered heavy bombardment.

Le Ca·te·let \lə-ka-ˈtlā\. Village, Aisne dept., N France, 11 m. N of St-Quentin; pop. (1962c) 249; battle Sept. 29, 1918 when small force of U.S. troops was cut off; has American cemetery.

Lec·ce \ˈlā-chē, ˈlech-ē\. 1 Province of Apulia, SE Italy. See table at ITALY.
2 Commune, its ✱, near Adriatic Sea 207 m. E by S of Naples; pop. (1968e) 81,048; textiles, pottery, canned foods; processes wine and oil; 12th cent. cathedral and Roman amphitheater; univ. (1959); made diocese 6th cent.; fortified by Aragonese.

Lec·co \ˈlā-(ˌ)kō, ˈlek-(ˌ)ō\. Manufacturing commune, Como prov., Lombardy, N Italy, at S end of SE branch (**Lake Lecco**) of Lake Como at mouth of Adda river, 16 m. E by N of Como; pop. (1968e) 51,991; metalworking.

Le Cen·ter \lə-ˈsent-ər\. Village, ⊗ of Le Sueur co., S Minnesota, 20 m. NNE of Mankato; pop. (1970c) 1890.

Lech \ˈlek\ *or anc.* **Li·cus** \ˈlī-kəs\. River, in Austria, and Bavaria, West Germany; 155 m. long; rises in Vorarlberg, SW Austria, flows N through Tirol and S cen. Bavaria past Augsburg into the Danube river.

Le Cham·bon–Feu·ge·rolles \lə-shäⁿ-ˈbōⁿ-fərzh-(ə-)ˈrȯl\. Commune, Loire dept., SE cen. France, 4 m. SW of St-Étienne; pop. (1968c) 21,937; metalworks.

Le Châ·te·lard \lə-shät-ˈlär\. Commune, Vaud canton, W Switzerland, near E shore of Lake of Geneva 15 m. ESE of Lausanne; pop. (1960c) 12,222. See MONTREUX.

Lech·feld \ˈlek-ˌfelt\. Field or plain on Lech river, Bavaria, West Germany, S of Augsburg; scene of battle 955 in which Otto I defeated the Magyars.

Lech·lade \ˈlech-ˌlād\. Parish, Gloucestershire, SW cen. England, on the Thames; terminus of Thames and Severn Canal.

Le·comp·ton \li-ˈkäm(p)-tən\. City, Douglas co., E Kansas; pop. (1970c) 434; scene of framing of the Lecompton Constitution Oct.–Nov. 1857, a proslavery constitution for the state of Kansas which was overwhelmingly defeated by the voters.

Le Conte, Mount \-lə-ˈkänt\. 1 Mountain, Tulare co., S cen. California, on E boundary of Sequoia National Park; 13,960 ft.
2 Peak, Sevier co., E Tennessee, in Great Smoky Mts.; 6593 ft.

Le Crac. See AL-KARAK.

Le Creu·sot \lə-krə(r)-ˈzō\. Commune, Saône-et-Loire dept., E cen. France, 39 m. NNW of Mâcon; pop. (1968c) 34,102; coal and iron mining; steel, mining machinery, locomotives, and turbines; its modern development dates from 1837.

Lec·toure \lek-ˈtů(ə)r\. Commune, N Gers dept., SW France; pop. (1962c) 4251; dates from pre-Roman times; capital of Armagnac from 1325; bishopric suppressed 1790; church (15th–17th cents.), formerly the cathedral.

Lectum, Cape. See BABA, CAPE.

Łę·czy·ca \leⁿ(n)-ˈchit-sə\ *or Russ.* **Len·chi·tsa** \lin-ˈchēt-sə\ *or Ger.* **Len·tschi·za** \len-ˈchēt-sə\. Commune, Łódź prov., cen. Poland, on Bzura river 20 m. NNW of Łódź; pop. (1968e) 13,800; sugar refining; agricultural products.

Ledang, Gunong. See OPHIR, MOUNT.

Le·de·berg \ˈlād-ə-ˌbərg, -ˌbe(ə)rg\. Commune, East Flanders prov., NW cen. Belgium, just SE of Gent; pop. (1969e) 10,339.

Ledi, Ben. See BEN LEDI.

Ledja. See AL-LEDJA.

Le·do \ˈlēd-(ˌ)ō, ˈlād-\. Town, Arunachal Pradesh, NE India, ab. 35 m. S of Sadiya; branch railhead of Bengal-Assam railroad and starting point of **Ledo Road,** strategic military highway begun in Dec. 1942 by U.S. Army engineers to connect with Burma Road (*q.v.*); road built under great difficulties across Patkai Range through Hukawng valley to Mogaung, Myitkyina (Ledo to Myitkyina 262 m.), and Bhamo in N Burma; name changed to Stilwell Road (*q.v.*) Jan. 1945.

Ledo Salinarius. See LONS-LE-SAUNIER.

Le·duc \lə-'dük\. Town, Alberta, Canada, 20 m. S of Edmonton; pop. (1971p) 3994; diversified agriculture; flour and grist mills.

Led·yard \'led-yərd, 'lej-ərd\. Agricultural town, New London co., SE Connecticut, E of Thames river 7 m. NE of New London; pop. (1970c) 14,837; incorporated 1836.

Lee \'lē\. 1 Name of counties in twelve states of the U.S. See tables at ALABAMA, ARKANSAS, FLORIDA, GEORGIA, ILLINOIS, IOWA, KENTUCKY, MISSISSIPPI, NORTH CAROLINA, SOUTH CAROLINA, TEXAS, VIRGINIA.

2 Town, Berkshire co., W Massachusetts, 9 m. S of Pittsfield; pop. (1970c) 6426; paper mills.

3 River, SW Eire; ab. 50 m. long; flows from W to E across co. Cork into Cork Harbour.

Leech·burg \'lēch-ˌbərg\. Industrial borough, Armstrong co., W Pennsylvania, 25 m. ENE of Pittsburgh; pop. (1970c) 2999; foundry; radioactive isotopes.

Leech Lake \'lēch-\. Lake in N Cass co., N cen. Minnesota; 176 sq. m.; ab. 20 m. long and from 4 to 15 m. wide; altitude 1297 ft.; outlet E into Mississippi river.

Leeds \'lēdz\. 1 City, Jefferson, Shelby, and St. Clair cos., cen. Alabama, 15 m. ENE of Birmingham; pop. (1970c) 6991; lumber, steel wire; cotton, hay.

2 County, Ontario, Canada. See table at ONTARIO.

3 City and county borough, West Riding, Yorkshire, N England, on the Aire 36 m. ENE of Manchester; pop. (1971p) 494,971; major transportation, commercial, and industrial center; produces clothing, textiles, heavy machinery, electrical equipment, paper, metalware, leather goods, chemicals; Univ. of Leeds (1904); incorporated 1626; early center of woolen industry but principal development took place from late 18th cent.; became city 1893.

Leeds and Liverpool Canal. See BARROWFORD.

Leek \'lēk\. Urban district, Staffordshire, W cen. England; pop. (1971p) 19,368; market town; ruins of 13th cent. Cistercian abbey.

Lee·la·nau \'lē-lə-ˌnȯ\. County in Michigan. See table at MICHIGAN.

Leer \'le(ə)r\ *also* **Leer in Ost·fries·land** \-in-'ōst-'frē-ˌslänt\. Commercial and manufacturing city, Lower Saxony, West Germany, near right bank of lower Ems river 34 m. WNW of Oldenburg; pop. (1969e) 29,964; manufactures paper, machinery. In World War II taken by Allies Apr. 23, 1945.

Leer·dam \le(ə)r-'däm\. Commune, South Holland prov., SW Netherlands; pop. (1970e) 13,282; glass manufactures.

Lees·burg \'lēz-ˌbərg\. 1 City, Lake co., cen. Florida penin., 36 m. WNW of Orlando; pop. (1970c) 11,869; concrete products; packs citrus fruit; truck and citrus farms; fishing resort; Lake-Sumter Junior Coll. (1962).

2 City, ⊗ of Lee co., SW Georgia; pop. (1970c) 996; cotton, peanuts.

3 Town, ⊗ of Loudoun co., N Virginia, 38 m. NW of Alexandria; pop. (1970c) 4821; meat-packing; wheat.

Lees Ferry \'lēz-\. Locality, N Coconino co., N Arizona, on Colorado river at head of Marble Canyon; ferry established 1872, only crossing of the Colorado river for many miles until construction of Navajo Bridge 5 m. downstream; 467 ft. above the river; 616 ft. long; completed 1929.

Lee's Summit \'lēz-\. City, Jackson co., W Missouri, 18 m. SE of Kansas City; pop. (1970c) 16,230; meat products.

Lees·ville \'lēz-ˌvil\. Town, ⊗ of Vernon parish, W Louisiana, 53 m. W of Alexandria; pop. (1970c) 8928; lumber mills; hardwood timber; corn, sweet potatoes.

Leeu·war·den \'lā-ˌvärd-ᵊn\. Commercial and industrial commune, ✱ of Friesland prov., N Netherlands, on the Ee river; pop. (1970e) 88,668; steel, textiles, paper, dairy products; in 16th–18th cent. noted for its manufactures in gold and silver; Groote Kerk (built ab. 1480), Frisian Museum, stadhouse, Kanselarij (chancellery).

Leeu·win, Cape \-'lü-ən\. The extreme SW point of Australia.

Lee·ward Islands \'lē-wərd-, 'lü-ərd-\. 1 The chain of small islets, rocks, and shoals, some composed of lava rock, some of coral and sand, extending 1250 m. WNW from main islands of the Hawaiian Is., ab. 162°W to 178°25′W; all except Midway are uninhabited and seldom visited, and constitute the **Hawaiian Islands Bird Reservation,** set aside 1909 by U.S. government as a bird sanctuary; islets include Nihoa, Necker, Gardner Pinnacles, Laysan, Lisianski, Pearl and Hermes Reef and Kure, or Ocean. Since discovery 1859 considered as belonging to the Hawaiian Is.; under the jurisdiction of Honolulu co.

2 *or Fr.* **Îles sous le Vent** \ēl-sü-lə-väⁿ\. Western group of the Society Is., French Polynesia, S Pacific Ocean; 154 sq. m.; pop. (1967e) 15,274; chief islands Huahiné, Raïatéa, and Tahaa.

3 Geographically, the northern chain of islands in the Lesser Antilles, E West Indies—so called because of their more sheltered position than the Windward Is. from the prevailing northeasterly winds. The chain extends from Dominica on the S to Virgin Is. on the N; administratively divided bet. the U.S. (St. Thomas, St. Croix, and St. John in the Virgin Is.), Netherlands (Saba, St. Eustatius, and S part of St. Martin), France (Guadeloupe, Marie Galante, Désirade, Les Saintes, St. Barthélemy, and N part of St. Martin) and Great Britain (for geographical descriptions and history, see 4, below, entries for individual islands, and VIRGIN ISLANDS).

4 Former division of the West Indies Federation (formed 1958, dissolved 1962), consisting of: Anguilla, Antigua, Barbuda, British Virgin Is., Montserrat, Nevis, Redonda, St. Christopher, Sombrero.

History: First British settlement, on St. Christopher 1625, followed by period of conflict with Spanish (17th cent.) and French (17th and 18th cents.); islands united under a common legislature early in 18th cent. and, after a lapse of this form of government, reunited under a common council 1871. For further details, see entries for individual islands.

Leeward Passage. Channel bet. Hans Lollik I. and N St. Thomas I., Virgin Is., West Indies.

Le·flore \lə-'flō(ə)r, -'flȯ(ə)r\. County in Mississippi. See table at MISSISSIPPI.

Le Flore \'lə-'flō(ə)r, -'flȯ(ə)r\. County in Oklahoma. See table at OKLAHOMA.

Le·froy, Lake \-lə-'frȯi\. Lake, S Western Australia, N of Lake Cowan and near Boulder.

Le·gas·pi *or* **Le·gaz·pi** \lə-'gas-pē, -'gäs-\. Chartered city, ✱ of Albay prov., Phil., at head of Albay Gulf, near S base of Mt. Mayon; pop. (1970c) 84,700; deepwater port; exports copra and Manila hemp; comprises original municipalities of Legaspi on the coast, Albay ab. 2 m. inland, and 18 barrios; two municipalities merged in 1907 and name of Albay changed to Legaspi 1925. Founded ab. 1636; partly destroyed by eruption of Mayon 1815; occupied by Japanese in World War II, Dec. 1941–Apr. 1945.

Leg·horn \'leg-ˌ(h)ȯ(ə)rn\ *or Ital.* **Li·vor·no** \lē-'vȯr-(ˌ)nō\. Seaport commune, ✱ of Livorno prov., Tuscany, cen. Italy, on Tyrrhenian Sea 160 m. NW of Rome; pop. (1968e) 172,794; major transportation and industrial center; shipbuilding, oil refining; precision tools, chemicals, electrical equipment, glass; exports processed foods, mineral oils, marble, copper products; Italian naval academy; 16th cent. cathedral. Under Florentine rule 1421; made free port by Cosimo I; for three centuries most important harbor of Tuscany; under Napoleon, capital of French department of La Méditerranée; joined Italy 1860; in World War II occupied by U.S. troops July 1944; heavily damaged but rebuilt since 1945.

Le·gio·no·wo \ˌleg-yȯ-ˈnȯ-vȯ\. Town, Warzawa prov., E cen. Poland; pop. (1970p) 20,800.

Le·gna·go \lā-ˈnyäg-(ˌ)ō\. Commune, Verona prov., Veneto, NE Italy, on Adige river 23 m. SE of Venice; pop. (1968e) 25,809; connected by canal with Po river. Venetian and Austrian fortified stronghold.

Le·gna·no \lā-ˈnyän-(ˌ)ō\. Commune, Milano prov., Lombardy, N Italy, 11 m. NNW of Milan; pop. (1968e) 46,438; metalworking; machine tools; candles, soap; Frederick Barbarossa defeated here 1176 by Lombard League.

Leg·ni·ca \leg-ˈnēt-sə\ *or Ger.* **Lieg·nitz** \ˈlēg-nəts\. City, cen. Wrocław prov., SW Poland, 39 m. WNW of Wrocław; pop. (1970p) 75,800; railroad junction; textile manufacturing, food processing, metalworking; 12th cent. castle. Received civic rights 1252; capital of duchy 1249–1675; to Prussia 1742; scene of victory of Frederick the Great over Austrians Aug. 15, 1760; in World War II taken by U.S.S.R. Feb. 10, 1945; assigned to Poland by Potsdam Conference 1945.

Leg·nic·kie Po·le \leg-ˌnēts-kyə-ˈpō-lə\ *or formerly* **Wahlstatt** \ˈväl-ˌs(h)tät, ˈwäl-\. Village, Wrocław prov., SW Poland, suburb of Legnica; formerly in Prussia, Germany; scene of battle Apr. 9, 1241 in which Batu Khan defeated Henry, Duke of Silesia.

Le Grand Andely. See LES ANDELYS.

Le Grand–Montrouge. See MONTROUGE.

Le·guan \ˈlā-ˌgwän\. Island at mouth of the Essequibo river, off NE coast of Guyana.

Leh \ˈlā\. Town, ✱ of Ladakh frontier dist., E Jammu and Kashmir, N India; pop. (1961c) 3700; on N bank of Indus at altitude of 11,500 ft., 160 m. E of Srinagar.

Le Ha·vre \lə-ˈhävrᵊ, -ˈhäv\ *or Eng.* **Havre** \ˈhävrᵊ, ˈhäv-ər, ˈhav-ər\ *or formerly* **Le Havre–de–Grâce** \lə-ˌhäv-rəd-ə-ˈgräs, -ˌhäv-də-ˈ-\. Commercial seaport, Seine-Maritime dept., N France, on English Channel on N side of Seine estuary 110 m. WNW of Paris; pop. (1968c) 199,509; principal French port for transatlantic passenger liners; major port for exports from Paris region and NW France; important industrial center; sugar and oil refining, shipbuilding; heavy machinery, electrical equipment; church of Notre Dame, town hall (former gubernatorial palace), round tower of Francis I, arsenal, barracks, exchange, and theater; seaside resort adjacent on NW. Developed as port from 16th cent.; naval base under Napoleon I; major Allied base in World War I; in World War II occupied by Germans June 1940–Sept. 1944.

Le·hi \ˈlē-ˌhī\. City, Utah co., N cen. Utah, on Utah Lake 16 m. NNW of Provo; pop. (1970c) 4659; farming (sugar beets, fruit); canning and sugar-refining industries.

Le·high \ˈlē-ˌhī\. 1 River, E Pennsylvania; ab. 100 m. long; rises in S extremity of Wayne co., flows SW, then turns SE to empty into the Delaware river at Easton.

2 County in Pennsylvania. See table at PENNSYLVANIA.

Le·high·ton \lē-ˈhīt-ᵊn\. Borough, Carbon co., E Pennsylvania, on Lehigh river 21 m. NW of Allentown; pop. (1970c) 6095; hosiery, furniture, silk; diversified agriculture. Settled by Moravians 1746; destroyed by Indians 1755; resettled 1794; incorporated as borough 1866.

Leh·man Caves National Monument \ˌlē-mən-\. See UNITED STATES, *National Monuments.*

Lehr·te \ˈle(ə)rt-ə\. City, Lower Saxony, West Germany, 10 m. E of Hannover; pop. (1969e) 21,828; chemicals, sugar.

Le·hua Island \lā-ˌhü-ə-\ *or* **Egg Island** \ˈeg-, ˈāg-\. Small barren uninhabited rock off tip of Niihau I., NW Hawaii; lighthouse, 702 ft. above the sea.

Lei \ˈlā\. River, E Hunan, SE cen. China; ab. 200 m. long; flows W and N to the Hsiang.

Leices·ter \ˈles-tər\. 1 Town, Worcester co., cen. Massachusetts, 6 m. W of Worcester; pop. (1970c) 9140; textiles; Leicester Junior Coll. (1784).

2 County of England. See LEICESTERSHIRE.

3 City and county borough, ⊗ of Leicestershire, cen. England, on the Soar 35 m. ENE of Birmingham; pop. (1971p) 283,549; railroad junction; hosiery, knitwear, footwear; Univ. of Leicester (1957); ruins of an ancient Norman castle, and of an abbey founded in 1143. Place where Richard III spent the night before he was killed in the battle of Bosworth Field, and to which his body was brought for burial.

Leices·ter·shire \ˈles-tər-ˌshi(ə)r, -shər\ *or* **Leices·ter** \ˈles-tər\. County, cen. England; 834 sq. m.; pop. (1971p) 771,213; ⊗ Leicester; rivers include the Soar and Wreak; grazing (esp. sheep), agriculture, quarrying (limestone, slate), textiles, woolen hosiery; main towns incl. Leicester, Loughborough, Wigston.

Leich·hardt \ˈlī-ˌkärt\. River, Queensland, Australia; ab. 300 m. long; flows N to Gulf of Carpentaria.

Lei–chou pan–tao. See LUICHOW PENINSULA.

Lei·den *or* **Ley·den** \ˈlīd-ᵊn, *Du. usu.* ˈlā-yə\ *or anc.* **Lug·du·num Bat·a·vo·rum** \ˌləg-ˈd(y)ü-nəm-ˌbat-ə-ˈvōr-əm, -ˈvȯr-\. Commune, South Holland prov., SW Netherlands, on Oude Rijn river; pop. (1970e) 101,221; metalworking, printing, food processing; Univ. of Leiden (1575); birthplace of Rembrandt and of John of Leiden; residence of the Pilgrims for 11 years before they sailed 1620 for America; famous for its heroic defense May–Oct. 1574 against Spanish siege; home of the Elzevir family of printers.

Leid·schen·dam \ˌlīd-shən-ˈdäm, ˌlād-\. Commune, South Holland prov., Netherlands; pop. (1970e) 29,265.

Lei·dy, Mount \-ˈlīd-ē\. Peak, E cen. Teton co., NW Wyoming; 10,317 ft.

Leidy Peak. Mountain, N Uintah co., E Utah; 12,013 ft.

Leie. See LYS.

Leigh \ˈlē\. Municipal borough, Lancashire, NW England, 11 m. W of Manchester; pop. (1971p) 46,117; coal mining; textiles, electric cables.

Leigh·ton–Lins·lade \ˈlāt-ᵊn-ˈlin-ˌslād\. Urban district, Bedfordshire, England; pop. (1971p) 20,326.

Lei·ne \ˈlī-nə\. River, largely in West Germany; 119 m. long; rises in the Eichsfeld, East Germany, and flows W and N past Göttingen and Hannover to the Aller SE of Verden.

Lein·ster \ˈlen(t)-stər\. Province, E Eire; 7581 sq. m.; pop. (1971p) 1,494,544; includes cos. Carlow, Dublin, Kildare, Kilkenny, Laoighis, Longford, Louth, Meath, Offaly, Westmeath, Wexford, Wicklow. One of the early provinces of Ireland; its N part, Meath, made a separate kingdom in 2d cent. A.D.; remainder independent in 12th and 13th cents., and cos. Carlow and Wexford independent until 16th cent.

Leinster, Mount. Peak on boundary bet. cos. Carlow and Wexford, SE Eire; 2610 ft.

Leip·sic \ˈlīp-sik\. Village, Putnam co., NW Ohio, 17 m. WNW of Findlay; pop. (1970c) 2072.

Leip·zig \ˈlīp-sig, -sik\. 1 District, East Germany. See table at GERMANY, EAST.

2 *also* **Leip·sic** \-sik\ *or Latin* **Lip·sia** \ˈlip-sē-ə\. City, its ✱, at confluence of Weisse Elster, Pleisse, and Parthe rivers; pop. (1970e) 584,365; railroad junction; iron and steel, chemicals, plastics, paper, electrical and agricultural machinery, textiles; Karl Marx Univ. (1409, present name 1952), largest in East Germany; St. Thomas Church (16th cent.; burial place of J. S. Bach); 18th cent. palace; before World War II center of German publishing industry; scene of annual trade fairs founded c. 1170.

History: First mentioned c. 11th cent.; chartered in 12th cent., scene of famous debate bet. Luther, Karlstadt, and Eck 1519; accepted Reformation 1539; in Thirty Years' War, two battles (sometimes called battles of Breitenfeld) won by Swedes nearby, 1631 and 1642; in 17th cent., supplanted Frankfurt as center of German book trade; scene of "Battle of the Nations" (*Ger.* Völkerschlacht) Oct. 16–19, 1813, when Napoleon's power in Germany was broken by the Allies. In World War II taken by U.S. forces, Apr. 20, 1945; heavily damaged, with most of 17th cent. buildings destroyed.

Lei·ria \lā-'rē-ə\. 1 District of W cen. Portugal. See table at PORTUGAL.
2 Commune, its ✻, on Liz river 73 m. N by E of Lisbon; pop. (1970p) 10,286; cathedral (1571); first Portuguese printing press 1466.

Leitch·field \'lich-ˌfēld\. City, ⊗ of Grayson co., W cen. Kentucky; pop. (1970c) 2983; agriculture.

Leith \'lēth\. Former burgh, Midlothian co., SE Scotland, now united to Edinburgh; a great seaport and shipbuilding center, with many industries.

Lei·tha *or Hung.* **Laj·ta** \'lī-(ˌ)tä\. River, E Austria; 112 m. long; flows NE across Hungarian border and enters the Rába near its junction with the Danube; historically, formed section of boundary bet. Austria and Hungary until transfer of Burgenland to Austria 1922. See CISLEITHANIA.

Leith Hill. See NORTH DOWNS.

Leitmeritz. See LITOMĚŘICE.

Lei·trim \'lē-trəm\. County, N Eire, in Connacht prov.; 589 sq. m.; pop. (1971p) 28,313; ⊗ Carrick on Shannon; livestock grazing; oats, potatoes.

Lei U Mun Pass *also* **Ly·e·mun Pass** *or* **Ly·ee·moon Pass** \'lē-'yü-'mün-\. Strait bet. NE Hong Kong I. and mainland; ¼ m. wide.

Leix \'lāsh, 'lēsh\. County, Leinster prov., Eire. See LAOIGHIS.

Lei·xõ·es \ˌlā-i-'shō^{n}-esh\. Seaport, NW Portugal, in parish of Matozinhos; artificial harbor, main port of Pôrto.

Lek \'lek\. The northern branch of the Lower Rhine in Netherlands, a continuation W of the Neder Rijn; unites with Merwede river to form the Nieuwe Maas; scene of heavy fighting in World War II esp. Sept. 17–25, 1944, during Allied airborne attack near Arnhem.

Le Kef \lə-'kef\ *or* **Al–Kef** \al-\ *or anc.* **Sic·ca Ve·ne·ria** \ˌsik-ə-və-'nir-ē-ə\. Town, N Tunisia, ab. 90 m. SSW of Tunis; pop. (1966c) 23,244; built on a steep rock at a junction of main highways; made a Roman colony by Augustus; remains of Roman temple and baths.

Le·land \'lē-lənd\. 1 Village, ⊗ of Leelanau co., NW Michigan.
2 City, Washington co., W Mississippi, 10 m. E of Greenville; pop. (1970c) 6000; cottonseed oil, soybean meal, furniture; cotton, rice.

Le·le \lə-'lā\. Village and harbor on E coast of Kusaie I., E Caroline Is., W Pacific Ocean; has ruins nearby; formerly a rendezvous for whaling vessels.

Le·le·i·wi Point \ˌlā-lā-ˌē-wē-\. Point on E coast of Hawaii I., Hawaii, S of Hilo Bay.

Le Lo·cle \lə-'lo-kl^{ə}\. Commune, Neuchâtel canton, W Switzerland, on French border 5 m. SW of La Chaux-de-Fonds; pop. (1970c) 14,452; watch-making center.

Lelupe. See LIELUPE.

Le Madonie. See MADONIE MOUNTAINS.

Le·ma·ha·bang \ˌlem-ə-'häb-äŋ\. Town, West Java prov., Indonesia, just SSE of Tjirebon.

Le Maine. See MAINE.

Le Maire Strait \lə-'ma(ə)r-, -'me(ə)r-\. Strait, Isla de los Estados and SE Tierra del Fuego I., S Argentina; ab. 20 m. wide.

Le·man \'lē-mən, 'lem-ən, lə-'man\. Name of Vaud canton, W Switzerland, under the Helvetic Republic 1798–1803.

Leman, Lake; *anc.* **Lemannus** *or* **Lemanus.** See GENEVA, LAKE OF.

Le Mans \lə-'mä^{n}\. Commercial and manufacturing city, ✻ of Sarthe dept., NW France, on Sarthe river 117 m. SW of Paris; pop. (1968c) 143,246; railroad center; railroad shops; electrical equipment, tobacco products, textiles, plastics, automobile parts; agricultural trade center; 11th–12th cent. church; 11th–15th cent. cathedral; 18th cent. town hall; French defeated here by Prussians during Franco-Prussian War 1870–71. Birthplace of Henry II, the first Plantagenet.

Le Marche. See MARCHES.

Le Mars \lə-'märz\. City, ⊗ of Plymouth co., NW Iowa, 25 m. NNE of Sioux City; pop. (1970c) 8159; meat-packing; dairy products; ships livestock; Westmar Coll. (1900).

Le Mas d'Azil \lə-ˌmas-də-'zē(ə)l\. Commune, N Ariège dept., S France, ab. 40 m. SW of Toulouse; pop. (1962c) 1643; in 1887 nearby cave scene of discovery of prehistoric human remains representative of culture now called *Azilian* belonging to a period of the Stone Age immediately preceding the Neolithic.

Lem·bang \'lem-ˌbäŋ\. Village, W Java, Indonesia, N of Bandung at foot of Tangkubanperahu; alt. 4000 ft.; health resort.

Lemberg. See LVOV.

Le·me·ry \ˌlā-mə-'rē\. Municipality, Batangas prov., Luzon, Phil., near E shore of Balayan Bay; pop. (1969e) 32,-500.

Lemessus. See LIMASSOL 2.

Lem·go \'lem-(ˌ)gō\. City, North Rhine-Westphalia, West Germany, 44 m. SW of Hannover; pop. (1969e) 36,693; furniture; metalworking; founded c. 1200.

Lem·hi \'lem-ˌhī\. 1 River, E cen. Idaho; 75 m. long; rises in SE Lemhi co., flows N into Salmon river at Salmon.
2 County in Idaho. See table at IDAHO.

Lemhi Range. Range in E cen. Idaho, chiefly in Lemhi and Butte cos.; highest point 11,300 ft.

Lem·men·jo·ki National Park \'lem-ən-ˌyō-kē-\. National park, Finland; 149 sq. m.; lakes; established 1956.

Lem·mon \'lem-ən\. City, Perkins co., NW South Dakota, on North Dakota border 14 m. N of Grand river; pop. (1970c) 1992; coal mines; stock and grain farming.

Lemmon, Mount *also* **Mount Lem·on** \-'lem-ən\. Mountain, highest peak in Santa Catalina Mts., in NE corner of Pima co., S Arizona; 9157 ft.

Lem·nos \'lem-ˌnäs, -nəs\ *or Gk.* **Lím·nos** \'lēm-ˌnōs\. Island in N Aegean Sea off W coast of Turkey in Asia; 177 sq. m.; pop. (1961c) 21,808; administratively part of Lesbos dept., Greece; ✻ Kástron; mountainous and fertile; grazing and fruit growing; harbor at Moudros on S coast; produces a medicinal earth (Lemnian bole or earth) long sold in Europe as an astringent. Important in Greek mythology, esp. as sacred to Hephaestus.
History: Occupied by ancient Greeks; held by Persians at beginning of 5th cent. B.C.; in Delian League and important part of Athenian Empire; in Roman, Byzantine, and Ottoman Empires; taken from Ottoman Empire by Greece 1913; base of British fleet in Dardanelles campaign of World War I.

Lem·on Grove \'lem-ən-\. Urban community (unincorporated), San Diego co., S California, E of San Diego; pop. (1970c) 19,690; residential.

Lemon Rock. See SKELLIGS.

Le·mont \lə-'mänt\. Village, Cook co., NE Illinois, on Illinois river 25 m. SW of Chicago; pop. (1970c) 5080.

Le·moore \lə-'mō(ə)r, -'mȯ(ə)r\. City, Kings co., SW cen. California, 29 m. S of Fresno; pop. (1970c) 4219; dairy, fruit, poultry, truck farming.

Le Mort Homme \lə-mȯr-'tȯm\ *or* **Hill 295** *or* **Dead Man's Hill.** Height ab. 6 m. NW of Verdun, NE France; scene of violent battle when captured by Germans May 29, 1916; recaptured by French Aug. 20, 1917.

ə abut; ^{ə} kitten, Fr. table; ər further; a back; ā bake; ä cot, cart; ȧ Fr. bac; aù out; ch chin; e less; ē easy; g gift
i trip; ī life; j joke; k̲ Ger. ich, Buch; ^{n} Fr. vin; ŋ sing; ō flow; ȯ flaw; œ Fr. bœuf; œ̄ Fr. feu; ȯi coin; th thin
t̲h̲ this; ü loot; u̇ foot; ue Ger. füllen; ue̅ Fr. rue; y yet; ^{y} Fr. digne \dēn^{y}\, nuit \nw^{y}ē\; yü few; yu̇ furious; zh vision

Le Moule \lə-'mül\. Seaport, Grande Terre I., E part of island of Guadeloupe, West Indies; pop. (1967e) 8184.

Le Mous·tier \lə-mü-'styā\. Cave, Dordogne dept., SW France, on right bank of the Vézère above Les Eyzies; (see EYZIES, LES); from important archaeological finds here, including a human skeleton and flint points, gives its name to the *Mousterian* period of Paleolithic culture marking culmination of Neanderthal race.

Lemovices. See LIMOGES.

Le·moyne \lə-'mȯin\. 1 Residential borough, Cumberland co., S Pennsylvania, on Susquehanna river across from Harrisburg; pop. (1970c) 4625; building materials; grain farming.

2 *also* lə-'mwän\. Town, Quebec, Canada, ab. 3 m. E of Montreal; pop. (1966c) 8888.

Lem·pa \'lem-pə\. River, El Salvador; ab. 200 m. long; flows through Lake Guija E and S into the Pacific Ocean.

Lem·pi·ra \lem-'pir-ə\ *or formerly* **Gra·cias** \'gräs-ē-əs\. Department of W Honduras. See table at HONDURAS.

Lem·ro \'lem-'rō\. River, Arakan division, W Lower Burma; 180 m. long; rises in Chin Hills and flows S into Hunter's Bay, inlet of Bay of Bengal, E of Sittwe.

Le·na \'lē-nə, 'lā-\. River, E cen. Russian S.F.S.R., U.S.S.R.; 2653 m. long, with drainage basin estimated at 936,000 sq. m.; rises on W slopes of Baikal Mts. W of Lake Baikal, flows NE in Irkutsk Oblast through wooded mountain ranges, then E forming part of S boundary of Yakutsk A.S.S.R.; from ab. 117°E flows in great bend E and N entirely within the Yakutsk A.S.S.R. to enter Laptev Sea in delta 250 m. wide at ab. 72°N. Has many tributaries (estimated by some at 1000), chief of which on right are Vitim, Olekma, and Aldan, on left Vilyui; land along upper course and on tributaries rich in minerals, including gold, salt, and diamonds. In lower 1200 m. of course fall is slight and width is 4 to 20 m.; Yakutsk is only large town on its entire course. Delta first reached 1637; scene of death 1881 of members of expedition of American explorer, George W. DeLong.

Lena \'lā-nə\. Commune, Oviedo prov., NW Spain, 13 m. S of Oviedo; pop. (1970p) 14,921; iron, and coal mining; meat-packing plants.

Len·a·wee \'len-ə-,wē\. County in Michigan. See table at MICHIGAN.

Lenchitsa. See ŁĘCZYCA.

Len·di·na·ra \,len-di-'när-ə\. Commune, Rovigo prov., Veneto, NE Italy, 10 m. W of Rovigo; pop. (1968e) 13,395; manufactures silk.

Lendum. See LENS.

Le·nexa \lə-'nek-sə\. City, Johnson co., E Kansas, 10 m. SW of Kansas City; pop. (1970c) 5242.

Len·ge·rich \'leŋ-ə-,rik\. City, North Rhine-Westphalia, West Germany, 27 m. N of Münster; pop. (1969e) 21,402; machine tools, cement, lime, packing materials.

Len·gua de Va·ca, Point \-,leŋ-gwəd-ə-'väk-ə\. Cape on W coast of Coquimbo prov., cen. Chile, S of city of Coquimbo.

Len·in·a·bad \'len-ə-nə-,bäd, 'lān-\; *formerly* **Kho·jend** \kō-'jend\ *or Russ.* **Kho·dzhent** \kō-'jent\. Town, NW Tadzhik S.S.R., U.S.S.R., on left bank of Syr Darya river 90 m. S of Tashkent; pop. (1970p) 103,000; meat-packing; silk, textiles; one of oldest towns in central Asia; became Russian 1866; renamed 1936; ✻ of former Leninabad Oblast.

Le·nin·a·kan \,len-ə-nä-'kän, ,lān-\; *formerly* **Ale·ksan·dro·pol** *or* **Al·ex·an·dro·pol** \,al-ik-san-'drȯ-pəl(-yə), -ig-zan-\ *or* **Gum·ry** \gu̇m-'rē\. City, NW Armenian S.S.R., U.S.S.R., on a tributary of the Araks 55 m. NW of Yerevan; pop. (1970p) 164,000; industrial center producing textiles, machinery, soap, copper products; remains of Turkish fortress.

Len·in·grad \'len-ən-,grad\. City, ✻ of Leningrad Oblast and (as **St. Pe·ters·burg** \sānt-'pēt-ərz-,bərg, sənt-\) ✻ of Russian Empire 1712–1917; second largest city in U.S.S.R., at E end of Gulf of Finland, built on the Neva delta; pop. (1970p) 3,950,000; an industrial center with shipbuilding, heavy engineering, electrical, chemical, textile, brewing, printing, and food-processing industries; A. A. Zhdanov State Univ. (1819) and numerous other educational institutions; libraries incl. the Saltykov-Shchedrin public library (1795; contains ab. 12 million volumes); major cultural center, incl. publishing, theatre, and music; intersected by many canals, crossed by more than 600 bridges; many fine buildings (Academy of Sciences, Winter Palace [1754–62], Palace of Art, St. Isaac's Cathedral [1819–58], Peter and Paul fortress, and museums), making it a major center for Western tourism.

History: Town of St. Petersburg founded in 1703 by Peter the Great as "a window into Europe" and in 1712 made capital of Russia; a scene of Decembrist revolt 1825 and of incident known as Red Sunday in 1905 revolution; renamed **Pet·ro·grad** \'pe-trə-,grad\ 1914; original center of Russian Revolution of 1917 (Kerenski government and Petrograd Soviet), but capital of Soviet Russia moved to Moscow March 1918; renamed Leningrad 1924; during World War II underwent siege by Germans Sept. 1941–Jan. 1944 during which ab. 1,000,000 persons died and city suffered extensive damage; largely rebuilt since 1945.

Leningrad Area. Former subdivision of Russian S.F.S.R., U.S.S.R., in NW part; 127,473 sq. m.; ✻ Leningrad; included several provinces whose centers were Leningrad, Novgorod, Pskov, Cherepovets, and the exclave of the Murmansk dist. and Kola Penin.

Leningrad Oblast \-'ō-bləst, -,blast\. Subdivision of the Russian S.F.S.R., U.S.S.R., bounded on N by Karelian A.S.S.R. and on W by Estonian S.S.R.; 33,166 sq. m.; pop. (1970p) 5,386,000; ✻ Leningrad; approximately two thirds of Lake Ladoga lies within its borders. Its principal streams are the Neva (outlet of Lake Ladoga), Svir (outlet of Lake Onega), and Volkhov (outlet of Lake Ilmen). Level country with forests and some marsh lands; has considerable agricultural development; mining, esp. peat, bauxite, clay, limestone; timber working in E; exploitation of oil shales and natural gas. Its manufacturing industries highly developed and varied, esp. in Leningrad. Chief cities Leningrad, Vyborg, Gatchina, Volkhov, Slantsy. Region early settled by Finnish tribes; for several centuries nominally subject to Novgorod but contended for by Swedes; part included in Ingria (*q.v.*) 1617–1703 but with capture of Swedish fort on the Neva by Peter the Great 1703, history of region centers on St. Petersburg (see LENINGRAD). After World War II extended to include all of Karelian Isthmus, N part of which was formerly in Finland.

Len·in Peak \,len-ən-, ,lān-, -,ēn-\ *or formerly* **Kauf·mann Peak** \,kau̇f-mən-\. Mountain in Trans Alai range, bet. Kirgiz S.S.R. and the Gorno-Badakhshan Autonomous Oblast, NE Tadzhik S.S.R., U.S.S.R.; 23,405 ft.; second highest peak in the U.S.S.R.

Le·nin·o·gorsk \'len-ən-ə-,gȯrsk, 'lān-\. 1 Town, East Kazakhstan Oblast, Kazakh S.S.R., U.S.S.R., ab. 50 m. NE of Ust-Kamenogorsk; pop. (1969e) 68,000; lead and zinc mining.

2 *or formerly* **No·va·ya Pi·smyan·ka** \,nō-və-yə-pēs-'myäŋ-kə\. Town, Tatar A.S.S.R., Russian S.F.S.R., U.S.S.R., ab. 15 m. WNW of Bugulma; pop. (1967e) 42,000.

Len·insk \'len-in(t)sk, 'lā-\. 1 Town, Leningrad Oblast, U.S.S.R. See PETRODVORETS.

2 *or formerly* **Pri·shib** \pri-'shib\. City, E Volgograd Oblast, Russian S.F.S.R., U.S.S.R., 35 m. E of Volgograd on an E arm of the lower Volga; near site of Sarai (*q.v.*).

3 Town, E Turkmen S.S.R., U.S.S.R. See CHARDZHOU.

Leninsk–Kuz·nets·ki \-ku̇s-'n(y)et-skē\ *or formerly* **Kol·chu·gi·no** \,kəl-'chü-gə-nə\. Mining town in center of Kuznetsk Basin, W Kemerovo Oblast, Russian S.F.S.R., U.S.S.R., on Tom river 75 m. NW of Novokuznetsk; pop. (1970p) 128,000; coal mining; mining machinery, chemicals, electric lights; coal mining begun on site 1912.

Len·ko·ran \ˌleŋ-kə-ˈrän\. Seaport town, SE Azerbaijan S.S.R., U.S.S.R., on SW shore of Caspian Sea near the Iranian border; pop. (1967e) 31,000; livestock raising; rice, citrus fruit, bamboo; first mentioned 17th cent.; passed to Russia 1813.

Len·nox \ˈlen-əks, -iks\. 1 Urban area, Los Angeles co., SW California, SE of Santa Monica; pop. (1970c) 16,121.

2 City, Lincoln co., SE South Dakota, 18 m. SSW of Sioux Falls; pop. (1970c) 1487; stock and grain farms.

Lennox and Ad·ding·ton \-ˈad-iŋ-tən\. County, Ontario, Canada. See table at ONTARIO.

Lennox Hills. Range of hills in Dunbarton and Stirling cos., SW cen. Scotland; highest point **Earl's Seat** \ˈərlz-\ 1894 ft.

Len·nox·ville \ˈlen-əks-ˌvil, -iks-\. Town, Sherbrooke co., S Quebec, Canada, 4 m. SSE of Sherbrooke; pop. (1971p) 3867; Bishop's Univ. (1843).

Le·noir \lə-ˈnō(ə)r, -ˈnȯ(ə)r\. 1 County in North Carolina. See table at NORTH CAROLINA.

2 Town, ⊗ of Caldwell co., W North Carolina, near Blue Ridge Mts. 38 m. W of Statesville; pop. (1970c) 14,705; summer resort; lumber and furniture, veneers, hosiery; agriculture.

Lenoir City. City, Loudon co., E Tennessee, on Tennessee river; pop. (1970c) 5324; lumber, foundry products; diversified agriculture.

Le·nore Lake \lə-ˌnō(ə)r-, -ˌnȯ(ə)r-\. Lake, NW Grant co., cen. Washington; 8 m. long.

Len·ox \ˈlen-əks\. Town, Berkshire co., W Massachusetts, 7 m. S of Pittsfield; pop. (1970c) 5804; summer resort; Berkshire Christian Coll. (1897); estate including site of Hawthorne's cottage and Tanglewood where summer concerts of Boston Symphony Orchestra are given.

Lens \ˈläⁿs\; *anc.* **Len·ti·um** \ˈlen-ch(ē-)əm\ *or* **Len·dum** \ˈlen-dəm\. Industrial city, Pas-de-Calais dept., N France, 11 m. NNE of Arras; pop. (1968c) 41,874; coal mining; coke, chemicals, machinery. Scene of French victory over Spaniards Aug. 2, 1648; in World War I occupied by Germans 1914–18, scene of battle Aug. 15, 1917 in which Canadians attacked successfully, and again on Oct. 3, 1918 when it was retaken by Allies; largely destroyed during both World Wars.

Lentia. See LINZ.

Len·ti·ni \len-ˈtē-nē\ *or anc.* **Le·on·ti·ni** \ˌlē-ən-ˈtī-ˌnī\. Commune, Siracusa prov., SE Sicily, Italy, 22 m. NW of Syracuse; pop. (1968e) 32,590; oldest Greek settlement in Sicily, founded 729 B.C.

Lentium. See LENS.

Lentschiza. See ŁĘCZYCA.

Le·o·ben \lā-ˈō-bən\. City, Styria, Austria, on Mur river 27 m. NW of Graz; pop. (1961c) 36,259; railroad junction; manufactures metal goods; lignite mining; coll. of mining and metallurgy (1840); preliminary peace treaty bet. France and Austria signed here Apr. 18, 1797.

Leobschütz. See GŁUBCZYCE.

Le·o·la \lē-ˈō-lə\. City, ⊗ of McPherson co., N South Dakota; pop. (1970c) 787.

Leom·in·ster. 1 \ˈlem-ən-stər\. Industrial city, Worcester co., cen. Massachusetts, 5 m. SSE of Fitchburg; pop. (1970c) 32,939; plastics, furniture, paper products. Part of Lancaster until 1740; chartered as city 1915.

2 \ˈlem(p)-stər, ˈlem-ən-stər\. Municipal borough, Herefordshire, W England, on the Lugg 40 m. WSW of Birmingham; pop. (1971p) 7071; market town.

Le·on. 1 \ˈlē-ən\. River, Texas; 185 m. long; rises in Eastland co.

2 \ˈlē-ən, ˈlē-ˌän\. Name of counties in two states of the U.S. See tables at FLORIDA and TEXAS.

3 \ˈlē-ən, ˈlē-ˌän\. City, ⊗ of Decatur co., S Iowa, 60 m. S of Des Moines; pop. (1970c) 2142; ships livestock and dairy products.

4 \lā-ˈōn\. Municipality, SW Iloilo prov., Panay, Phil., 14 m. WNW of City of Iloilo; pop. (1969e) 34,300.

Le·ón \lā-ˈōn\. 1 Former name of Cotopaxi prov., Ecuador. See COTOPAXI 2.

2 Municipality, Guanajuato state, cen. Mexico, 32 m. WNW of Guanajuato; pop. (1970p) 453,976; tanneries, flour mills; leather and woolen goods, soap, gold and silver embroidery; founded 1576, made city 1836.

3 Department of W Nicaragua. See table at NICARAGUA.

4 City, ✱ of León dept. and 2d largest city in Nicaragua, on railroad near Pacific coast ab. 50 m. NW of Managua; munic. pop. (1970e) 90,897; cotton gins; cigars, leather products; exports sugar and cotton; founded by Córdoba 1524 on the shore of Lake Managua; destroyed 1609 by violent eruption of Momotombo and earthquake, and rebuilt on its present site 1610; former capital of Nicaragua; has had long political and commercial rivalry with city of Granada.

5 Region and ancient kingdom, NW Spain; 14,884 sq. m.; bounded on N by Asturias, E by Old Castile, S by Estremadura, SW by Portugal, NW by Galicia; comprises modern provinces of León, Salamanca, Zamora; traversed by Duero river and its affluents, the Esla and Tormes; central subtropical valley rises to severely cold mountain ranges on N and S borders; produces citrus fruits, hops; olives, wheat, flax, cereals; beech and chestnut timber; coal, iron mines; stock raising; manufactures flour, textiles, iron products.

History: Independent Christian kingdom, ruled 909–914 by Garcia, son of Alfonso III of Asturias, after Asturian reconquest of town of León from Moors in 8th cent.; ruled 999–1027 by Alfonso V, the Restorer of León; reconquest of León from Moors completed in 11th cent.; united with Castile 1037–1157, independent kingdom 1157–1230, and permanently reunited with Castile 1230; its chief city after union with Castile was Burgos.

6 Province of NW Spain. See table at SPAIN.

7 City, ✱ of León prov., NW Spain, 82 m. NW of Valladolid; pop. (1970p) 105,235; tourist center; leather goods, iron, lumber; 13th cent. Gothic cathedral, 12th cent. convent, and the 11th cent. church of San Isidoro containing burial place of the early kings and queens of León and Castile. Ancient Roman military station; capital of medieval kingdom of León.

León, Is·la de \ˈez-lə-ˌdā-lē-ˈōn\. 1 Island, Cádiz prov., SW Spain; 10 m. long and 2 m. wide.

2 Seaport, Spain. See SAN FERNANDO 8.

Leon·ard Mur·ray, Mount \-ˌlen-ərd-ˈmər-ē, -ˈmə-rē\. Mountain, Papua New Guinea, cen. New Guinea I., E of Strickland river basin and NW of Kikori; 7808 ft.; source of several rivers.

Leon·ard·town \ˈlen-ərd-ˌtau̇n\. Town, ⊗ of Saint Marys co., S Maryland, on an inlet of the Potomac river estuary; pop. (1970c) 1406; tobacco, wheat.

Le·on·berg \ˈla-an-ˌbe(ə)rg\. City, Baden-Wurttemberg, West Germany, 8 m. WNW of Stuttgart; pop. (1969e) 25,-413; machine shops, rubber; 14th cent. church; became city 1248; to Württemberg 1318.

Le·o·ne, Mon·te \ˌmänt-ē-lā-ˈō-nē\. Highest peak of the Lepontine Alps, bet. Switzerland and Italy, on SW side of Simplon Pass; 11,654 ft.

Le·on·for·te \ˌlā-ən-ˈfȯ(ə)r-(ˌ)tā\. Commune, Enna prov., cen. Sicily, Italy, 7 m. NNE of Enna; pop. (1968e) 16,573; in agricultural region.

Le·o·nia \lē-ˈō-nyə, -nē-ə\. Residential borough, Bergen co., NE New Jersey, 10 m. N of Jersey City; pop. (1970c) 8847; X-ray instruments.

Le·o·nine City \ˌlē-ə-ˌnīn-\. Section of Rome, Italy, W of the Tiber river; includes the Vatican.

Leontini. See LENTINI.

Le·on·top·o·lis \ˌlē-ən-'täp-ə-ləs\. City of ancient Egypt, in Nile delta 17 m. N of Cairo; site of the Temple of Onias supposed to have been built during 2d cent. B.C. by the Jewish high priest Onias III; residence of Hieracas and the Hieracites 4th cent. A.D.

Le·o·pold and As·trid Coast \ˌlē-ə-ˌpōld . . . 'as-trəd-\. Section of Antarctica coast on Indian Ocean, W of Wilkes Land, 67°10'S, 84°10'E; discovered 1934.

Leopold Coast. See LUITPOLD COAST.

Le·o·polds·berg \'lē-ə-ˌpōl(d)z-ˌbərg, 'lā-ə-ˌpolts-ˌbe(ə)rg\. Elevation, Austria, ab. 5½ m. NW of Vienna, in the Wienerwald; 1388 ft.

Leopold II, Lake *or Fr.* **Léopold II, Lac.** See MAI-NDOMDE, LAKE.

Léopoldville. See KINSHASA.

Le·o·ti \lē-'ō-ˌtī\. City, ⊗ of Wichita co., W Kansas; pop. (1970c) 1916; dairy and grain farms.

Le·pan·to \li-'pan-(ˌ)tō\. See NÁVPAKTOS.

Lepanto, Gulf of. See CORINTH, GULF OF.

Lepanto Strait. Narrow channel connecting Gulfs of Patras and Corinth and separating N Peloponnesus from cen. mainland of Greece. For battle of Lepanto see NÁVPAKTOS.

Le Per·reux–sur–Marne \lə-pe-'rər-sü(ə)r-'märn\. Commune, Val de Marne dept., N France, ESE suburb of Paris on Marne river; pop. (1968c) 29,099; shipbuilding.

Le Petit Andely. See LES ANDELYS.

Le Pe·tit–Que·vil·ly \ləp-(ə-)ˌtē-kə-vē-'yē\. Industrial commune, Seine-Maritime dept., N France, WSW suburb of Rouen on Seine river; pop. (1968c) 22,876.

Le·pi·ni Mountains \lā-ˌpē-nē-\ *or Ital.* **Mon·ti Lepini** \ˌmon-tē-lā-'pē-nē\. Mountain range in SE Roma prov., Latium, cen. Italy; highest peak 5039 ft.; in ancient times known as Volscian Mts.

L'Épi·pha·nie \lā-ˌpē-fə-'nē\. Village, L'Assomption co., S Quebec, Canada, 27 m. N of Montreal; pop. (1971p) 2757.

Le Ples·sis–Rob·in·son \lə-ple-'sē-rō-baⁿ-'sōⁿ\. Commune, Hauts-de-Seine dept., France; pop. (1968c) 22,590.

Lepontine Alps. See table at ALPS.

Le Port \lə-'pȯr\ *or formerly* **Port–des–Ga·lets** \ˌpȯr-dā-ga-'lā\. Seaport on NW coast of the French island of Réunion in the Indian Ocean E of the Malagasy Republic; pop. (1967c) 17,280; good harbor; railroad terminus.

Le Pré–Saint–Ger·vais \lə-'prā-ˌsaⁿ-zher-'vā\. Industrial commune, Seine-St-Denis dept., N France, NE suburb of Paris; pop. (1968c) 14,772; foundries; paints, varnishes.

Lep·tis Mag·na \lep-tə-'smag-nə\ *or mod.* **Leb·da** \'leb-də\. Ancient seaport in Roman Africa, a suburb of Homs, Libya; founded by Phoenicians from Sidon; one of three chief cities of Tripolis (see TRIPOLI 1); under Masinissa after Second Punic War, from 202; made a Roman colony by Trajan; birthplace of L. Septimius Severus who was largely responsible for present plan of the city; ruins of the forum, baths, and a basilica.

Leptis Mi·nor \lep-tə-'smī-nər\ *or* **Leptis Par·va** \-tə-'spär-və\ *or mod.* **Lam·ta** \'lam(p)-tə\. Ancient town, Byzacium, N Africa, SE of Hadrumetum (*mod.* Sousse, Tunisia); loyal to Rome from end of Second Punic War, prosperous under the empire; ruins of docks along the coast; amphitheater, Byzantine fort.

Le Puglie. See APULIA.

Le Puy \lə-'pwē\ *or formerly* **Le Puy–en–Ve·lay** \-äⁿv-(ə-)'lā\ *or medieval* **Ani·ci·um** \ə-'nish-(ē-)əm\ *or* **Po·di·um An·i·cen·sis** \'pōd-ē-ə-ˌman-ə-'sen(t)-səs\. Manufacturing city, ✱ of Haute-Loire dept., S cen. France, 65 m. SE of Clermont-Ferrand; pop. (1968c) 26,389; in a mountainous volcanic region; has 12th cent. Romanesque cathedral and 10th cent. Gothic church.

Le Ques·noy \lə-kē-'nwä\. Commune, Nord dept., N France, 9 m. SE of Valenciennes; pop. (1962c) 4763; many times besieged, esp. by Austrians 1793; in World War I captured by New Zealand troops Nov. 5, 1918.

Lera. See LÉRINS, ÎLES DE.

Le Rain·cy \lə-raⁿ-'sē\. Manufacturing commune, Seine-St-Denis dept., N France, NNE suburb of Paris; pop. (1968c) 14,224; made commune 1869.

Ler·ca·ra Frid·di \ler-ˌkär-ə-'frē-dē\. Commune, Palermo prov., NW cen. Sicily, Italy, 29 m. ESE of Palermo; pop. (1968e) 11,294; sulfur mining.

Ler·do \'le(ə)rd-(ˌ)ō\. Town, Durango state, NW cen. Mexico, just S of Gómez Palacio; munic. pop. (1970p) 53,551.

Le·ri·ci \'ler-i-ˌchē\. Seaport, La Spezia prov., Liguria, NW Italy, on Gulf of La Spezia 6 m. SE of La Spezia; pop. (1968e) 14,444; 12th cent. castle; sea bathing.

Lé·ri·da \'lā-rəd-ə, 'ler-əd-\. **1** Province of NE Spain. See table at SPAIN.
2 *or anc.* **Iler·da** \il-'ərd-ə\. Commune, its ✱, on Segre river 77 m. E of Saragossa; pop. (1970p) 90,884; trades in wine, wool, leather, cattle, and fruit; two cathedrals, palaces, convents. Scene of defeat of Pompey's generals by Caesar 49 B.C.; made episcopal see during Visigoth occupation; seat of medieval university; captured by Ramón Berenguer IV 1149 and by French 1707 and 1808.

Lerin. See FLORINA 2.

Lé·rins, Îles de \ēl-də-lā-raⁿs\. Two islands, **Sainte–Mar·gue·rite** \sānt-ˌmär-gə-'rēt, sent-\ (*or anc.* **Le·ra** \'lir-ə\) and **Saint–Ho·no·rat** \saⁿ-ˌtän-ə-'rä\ (*or anc.* **Le·ri·na** \lə-'rī-nə\), in the Mediterranean Sea off Cannes, Alpes-Maritimes dept., SE France.

Ler·ma \'le(ə)r-mə\. The upper course of the Santiago river, SW Mexico. See SANTIAGO 10.

Ler·na \'lər-nə\ *or* **Ler·ne** \-(ˌ)nē\. Marsh and stream in ancient Argolis, E Peloponnesus, S Greece, near Argos; celebrated in Greek legend as the place where Hercules killed the Lernaean Hydra.

Le Roncole. See RONCOLE.

Le·ros \'li(ə)r-äs\ *or Ital.* **Le·ro** \'le(ə)r-(ˌ)ō\. An island of the Dodecanese (*q.v.*), N of Kalymnos; 28 sq. m.

Le·roy \li-'rȯi, 'lē-ˌrȯi\. City, McLean co., cen. Illinois, 15 m. SE of Bloomington; pop. (1970c) 2435; soybeans, corn.

Le Roy \li-'rȯi, 'lē-ˌrȯi\. Village, Genesee co., W New York, 24 m. WSW of Rochester; pop. (1970c) 5118; automobile parts, crushed stone; fruit and dairy farms.

Ler·wick \'lər-wik\. Burgh, ⊗ of Zetland co., Shetland Is., N Scotland; pop. (1971p) 6107; fishing; knitwear; most northerly town in British Isles.

Les An·de·lys \ˌlā-zäⁿ-'dlē\. Commune, Eure dept., N France, on right bank of Seine river 20 m. NE of Évreux; pop. (1962c) 6640; formed from two small settlements, **Le Grand An·de·ly** \lə-ˌgräⁿ-täⁿ-'dlē\ and **Le Pe·tit Andely** \ləp-tē-täⁿ-dlē\, the former dating from 526 A.D., the latter from 1196; 13th cent. cathedral; site of Château Gaillard built by Richard Cœur de Lion; manufactures textiles and imitation pearls.

Le Sars \lə-'sär\. Village, Pas-de-Calais dept., N France, just SW of Bapaume; pop. (1962c) 235; battle Sept.–Oct. 1916, a phase of the battle of the Somme.

Le·sa·ti·ma \ˌle-sə-'tēm-ə\ *or* **Sat·ti·ma** \sə-'tēm-ə\. Peak, cen. Kenya, E Africa, N of Nairobi; 13,104 ft.

Les Baux–de–Pro·vence \lā-ˌbō-də-prə-'väⁿs\ *or formerly* **Les Beaux** \lā-'bō\. Commune, Bouches-du-Rhône dept., SE France, 9 m. NE of Arles; pop. (1962c) 253; important in Middle Ages, now has many ruins; bauxite first discovered here 1821.

Les·bos \'lez-ˌbäs, -bəs\ *or* **Myt·i·le·ne** *or Gk.* **Mi·ti·lí·ni** \ˌmit-ᵊl-'ē-nē\. Island in E Aegean Sea off NW coast of Turkey in Asia, by some included among the Southern Sporades (see SPORADES); 630 sq. m.; pop. (1961c) 117,371; exports olives; fishing, livestock raising; wine, oil, grain, marble, soap, hides and skins; with Lemnos and Hagios Evstrátios, forms Lesbos dept., Aegean Is. division, Greece (see table at GREECE). Hilly, with highest point 3080 ft.; cut from S into center by Gulf of Kalloni. Chief town Mytilene.

History: Peopled by Aeolians and became chief Aeolian settlement on Asiatic coast; active in commerce; in 7th cent. B.C. famous for its lyric poets, esp. Alcaeus and

Sappho; declined in influence in 6th cent. B.C.; yielded to Persians; member of Delian League; off its shores 406 B.C. the Athenian Conon defeated in naval battle; frequently involved in wars before beginning of Christian Era. Held by Byzantines, Seljuks, Venetians, and after 1462 by Turks; annexed by Greece 1913; held by Germans Apr. 1941 to Oct. 1944. See AEGEAN ISLANDS.

Les Éparges \lā-zā-ˈpärzh\. Village, Meuse dept., NE France, 7 m. SE of Verdun; pop. (1962c) 69; scene of bitter fighting bet. French and Germans June 1915.

Les Eyzies. See EYZIES, LES.

Les Gonaïves. See GONAÏVES.

Lesh \ˈlesh\ *or Ital.* **Ales·sio** \ə-ˈles-ē-ˌō\. 1 Province of NW Albania. See table at ALBANIA.

2 *or anc.* **Lis·sus** \ˈlis-əs\. Town, its ✱, at mouth of Drin river; pop. (1967e) 3540; founded by Dionysius of Syracuse 385 B.C.

Lesina. See HVAR.

Le·si·na, Lake \-lā-ˈzē-nə\. Small lake on N coast of Mount Gargano, SE Italy.

Les·ko·vac *or* **Les·ko·vats** \ˈles-kə-ˌväts\. Town, Serbia, SE Yugoslavia, on the Southern Morava river ab. 75 m. NE of Skopje; pop. (1965e) 40,000; manufactures furniture, soap; brick kilns; thermal springs; in a region growing flax and hemp. Occupied by Germans 1941.

Les Landes \lā-ˈlä^{n}d\. Sandy coastal region, Gironde and Landes depts., SW France, bet. the Gironde and the Adour; lagoons near the seashore; pine forests inland.

Les·lie \ˈles-lē\. County in Kentucky. See table at KENTUCKY.

Les Li·las \ˌlā-lē-ˈlä\. Industrial commune, Seine-St-Denis dept., N France, NW suburb of Paris; pop. (1968c) 15,187; produces metal goods, glassware.

Les Martigues. See MARTIGUES.

Les Mu·reaux \ˌlā-mu̇r-ˈō\. Commune, Yvelines dept., N France; pop. (1968c) 21,733.

Le·so·tho \lə-ˈsō-(ˌ)tō\ *or formerly* **Ba·su·to·land** \bə-ˈsüt-ō-ˌland\. Kingdom, S Africa, an enclave lying within the Rep. of South Africa; 11,716 sq. m.; pop. (1972e) 1,080,857; ✱ Maseru. *Physical features:* Mountainous, with ab. 80 percent of land between 6000 and 11,000 ft. above sea level; has Drakensberg Mts. along E border; highest point Thabana Ntlenyana 11,425 ft.; main rivers Orange and Caledon, the latter constituting country's W border. *Chief products:* Corn, wheat, peas, sorghum; mohair; diamonds. *Chief towns:* Maseru, Mohales Hoek, Mafeteng.

History: Before 1800 mostly uninhabited; in early 19th cent. many disputes with Boers; first received British protection 1843; annexed 1868 and made part of Cape Colony 1871; separated from Cape Colony and made a British colony 1884; achieved independence 1966.

Les Pa·vil·lons–sous–Bois \lā-ˌpav-ē-ˌ(y)ō^{n}-sü-ˈbwä\. Commune, Hauts-de-Seine dept., N France, ENE suburb of Paris; pop. (1968c) 19,084.

Les Planches \lā-ˈplä^{n}sh\. 1 Town, Canada. See AMHERST 8.

2 Commune, Vaud canton, W Switzerland, at E end of Lake of Geneva. See MONTREUX.

Les Sa·bles–d'Olonne \lā-ˌsäb-lə-dō-ˈlȯn\. Commune, Vendée dept., W France, on Bay of Biscay 21 m. SW of La Roche-sur-Yon; pop. (1968c) 18,093; fishing port; shipbuilding; produces canned sardines and anchovies.

Les Saintes \lā-ˈsa^{n}(n)t\. Island group in the French overseas dept. of Guadeloupe, West Indies, S of Guadeloupe I.; 5$\frac{1}{2}$ sq. m.; pop. (1960c) 2800.

Les Saules \lā-ˈsōl\. Town, Quebec co., S Quebec, Canada, 5 m. W of Quebec city; pop. (1966c) 6242.

Les·say \le-ˈsā\. Village, Normandy, Manche dept., NW France, 12 m. NNW of Coutances; pop. (1962c) 1336; occupied by U.S. troops July 16, 1944 in advance on St-Lô.

Les·se \ˈles, ˈles-ə\. River, SE Belgium; 50 m. long; flows W through rocky gorges, partly underground, into Meuse river.

Lesse et Lomme National Park \ˈles-ā-ˈlȯm-\. National park, Belgium; 4 sq. m.; unusual geological formations; established 1954.

Lesser An·til·les \-an-ˈtil-ēz\. One of the three divisions of the West Indies (*q.v.*) comprising the islands stretching in an arc from Puerto Rico to the NE coast of South America and the islands N of Venezuela; includes Virgin Is., Leeward Is., Windward Is., and the islands of the Netherlands Antilles, and is generally considered to include Barbados, Trinidad, and Tobago.

Lesser Ar·me·nia \-är-ˈmē-nē-ə, -nyə\. 1 Region of E Pontus, Asia Minor, 1st cent. B.C., on W border of Armenia.

2 Kingdom, Cilicia. See LITTLE ARMENIA.

3 Region, Turkey. See CILICIA.

Lesser Khingan Mountains. See KHINGAN.

Lesser Slave Lake \-ˈsläv-\. Lake, cen. Alberta, Canada; 461 sq. m.; its outlet is **Lesser Slave River,** a tributary of the Athabaska.

Lesser Sunda Islands. See SUNDA ISLES.

Lesser Tunb. See TUNB.

Lesser Walachia. See OLTENIA.

Les·sines \le-ˈsēn\. Manufacturing commune, Hainaut prov., SW Belgium, on Dender river 25 m. SW of Brussels; pop. (1969e) 8984; porphyry quarries.

Les·si·ni Mountains \lə-ˌsē-nē-\ *or Ital.* **Mon·ti Lessini** \ˌmȯn-tē- lə-ˈsē-nē\. Mountain group, SW Dolomites, NE Italy, E of Lake Garda; highest peak 5485 ft.

Lessø. See LÆSØ.

Les Trois–Évê·chés \lā-ˈtrwä-zā-ve-ˈshā, ˌlā-trə-ˈwä-\. Ancient district in duchy of Lorraine; comprised the three bishoprics of Verdun, Toul, and Metz (the cities and some surrounding territory) which belonged to Germany in Middle Ages; taken by Henry II of France 1552; now included in Meuse, Moselle, and Meurthe-et-Moselle depts., NE France.

Le Sueur \lə-ˈsu̇(ə)r\. 1 County in Minnesota. See table at MINNESOTA.

2 City, Le Sueur co., S Minnesota, on Minnesota river 20 m. N of Mankato; pop. (1970c) 3745; canned foods, aluminum; poultry and dairy farms.

Lesz·no \ˈlesh-(ˌ)nō\ *or Ger.* **Lis·sa** \ˈlis-ə\. Commune, Poznań prov., W Poland, 41 m. SSW of Poznań; pop. (1970p) 33,900; food processing, sawmilling; cattle and grain market; machinery. Settled by Moravians 16th cent.; became city 1547; center of Moravians in Poland in 17th cent.; residence of Comenius; burned by Poles 1656 in war with Sweden; ceded to Prussia 1793; returned to Poland 1919.

Letch·er \'lech-ər\. County in Kentucky. See table at KENTUCKY.

Letch·worth \'lech-(,)wərth\. Urban district, Hertfordshire, SE England, 34 m. N of London; pop. (1971p) 30,884; machinery, apparel; printing and publishing; first British "garden city" (1903).

Le·tea \'le-(,)tyä\ *also* **Lu·tea** \'lü-\. Marshy region, E Romania, on Black Sea coast forming an island bet. the Kiliya (on N) and Sulina branches of the Danube.

Le Teil \lə-'tāʸ\. Town, Ardèche dept., SE France, on the Rhone 42 m. NNW of Avignon; pop. (1962c) 8344; limestone quarries.

Leth·bridge \'leth-(,)brij\. City, S Alberta, Canada, on Oldman river 110 m. SSE of Calgary; pop. (1971p) 40,706; center of irrigated farming region; canning and freezing plants, sugar refinery; Lethbridge Junior Coll. (1957), Univ. of Lethbridge (1967); founded 1885.

Le·ti *or* **Let·ti** \'let-ē\. **1** Island group, Moluccas, Indonesia, in S part NE of Timor; ab. 290 sq. m.; comprises Leti, Moa, and Lakor Is. and a few adjacent islets.

2 Westernmost island of Leti group ab. 25 m. E of E point of Timor; 9 m. long by 3 to 5 m. wide.

Le·ti·cia \lə-'tē-sē-ə\. Town, ✱ of Amazonas commissary, SE Colombia, on the Amazon river; pop. (1968e) 4605; border town claimed by Peru and Colombia until Peru ceded it by treaty 1922; seized by Peruvian forces 1932; restored to Colombia 1933 by League of Nations, decision finally accepted by both countries 1934.

Let·mathe \'lät-,mät-ə\. City, North Rhine-Westphalia, West Germany, 27 m. ESE of Essen; pop. (1969e) 27,605; metalworking.

Let·pa·dan \,let-pə-'dän\. Town, Pegu div., Burma, on railroad 75 m. NW of Rangoon.

Le Tré·port \lə-'trā-'pō(ə)r\. Town, N Seine-Maritime dept., N France, on the English Channel 19 m. NE of Dieppe; pop. (1962c) 6136; seaside resort; 16th cent. church; important port in Middle Ages.

Let·sôk–aw Island \,lät-sō-'kō-\ *or formerly* **Do·mel Island** \'dō-,mel-\. Island, cen. Mergui Archipelago (*q.v.*), Burma.

Let·ter·ken·ny \,let-ər-'ken-ē\. Urban district, cen. co. Donegal, N Eire, near S end of Lough Swilly; pop. (1971p) 4825; market town.

Letti. See LETI.

Lettland. See LATVIAN SOVIET SOCIALIST REPUBLIC.

Lettonie. See LATVIAN SOVIET SOCIALIST REPUBLIC.

Leucadia. See LEUKAS.

Leucates. See DOUKATO, CAPE.

Leu·ca·yec \,leü-kä-'yek\. Island in N section of Chonos Archipelago, in Pacific Ocean off SW coast of Chile.

Leucosia. See NICOSIA 2.

Leuc·tra \'lük-trə\. Ancient village in Boeotia, E cen. Greece, 10 m. SW of Thebes; scene of battle 371 B.C. in which Thebans under Epaminondas defeated Spartans under Cleombrotus I, breaking Spartan supremacy.

Leuk \'lòik\. Town, Valais canton, SW cen. Switzerland, on the Rhone NE of Sion; pop. (1970c) 2796; hot mineral springs.

Leu·kas \'lü-kəs\ *or* **Lev·kás** \lef-'käs\ *or anc.* **Leu·ca·dia** \lü-'kād-ē-ə\ *or Ital.* **San·ta Mau·ra** \,sant-ə-'maů-rə, ,sänt-\. One of the Ionian Is., in the Ionian Sea off W coast of Greece, S of the entrance to the Ambracian Gulf; 125 sq. m.; pop. (1971p) 24,599; chief town Leukas; constitutes a department, Greece. Mountainous (highest ab. 3000 ft.), with little level ground; produces much olive oil, currants, and wine. Southern point is Cape Doukato (*q.v.*). Early settled by Corinthians; has ancient cyclopean walls and remains of temple to Apollo Leukates, and several Turkish forts; by some scholars thought to be the Ithaca of the *Odyssey*, rather than nearby Ithaca itself.

Leu·ser, Mount \-'lü-sər\ *also* **Mount Lo·ser** \-'lō-sər\. Mountain, ab. 200 m. from NW end of Sumatra, Indonesia, near coast; 11,090 ft.

Leuthen. See LUTYNIA.

Leuven. See LOUVAIN.

Leuze \'lə(r)z\. Manufacturing commune, Hainaut prov., SW Belgium, 11 m. E of Tournai; pop. (1969e) 7267; scene of battle Sept. 20, 1691 in which forces of Louis XIV under the Duc de Luxembourg defeated the army of the Grand Alliance under Prince of Waldeck.

Léva. See LEVICE.

Le·vack \lə-'vak\. Town, Sudbury district, SE Ontario, Canada, 20 m. NW of Sudbury; pop. (1971p) 2943.

Levádhia. See LEBADEA.

Le Val d'Ajol \lə-,väl-dä-'zhōl\. Commune, Vosges dept., NE France, comprising many hamlets in the Vosges Mts.; pop. (1962c) 6224.

Le·val·lois–Per·ret \lə-,väl-,wä-pə-'rā\. Industrial commune, Hauts-de-Seine dept., N France, NW suburb of Paris on Seine river; pop. (1968e) 59,941; automobiles, radar and optical equipment, perfume; foundries, distilleries; developed after 1820; became commune 1867.

Le·vang·er \lə-'väŋ-ər\. Town, Nord-Trøndelag co., N cen. Norway, at head of Trondheim Fjord; pop. (1970e) 14,810.

Le·vant \lə-'vant\. Name given to the E shores of the Mediterranean Sea, W Greece to W Egypt.

Levante, Riviera di. See RIVIERA.

Levant States. See SYRIA 2.

Le Vauclin. See VAUCLIN.

Lev·el·land \'lev-ə(l)-,land\. City, ⊗ of Hockley co., NW Texas, 26 m. W of Lubbock; pop. (1970c) 11,445; oil refinery; livestock and fruit farming; South Plains Coll. (1958).

Le·ven \'lē-vən\. **1** River, Dunbarton co., W Scotland; ab. 7 m. long; flows out of S end of Loch Lomond into Clyde river at Dumbarton.

2 River, Kinross and Fife cos., E Scotland; 16 m. long; flows E out of Loch Leven into Firth of Forth.

3 Seaport burgh, Fife co., E Scotland, on Firth of Forth at mouth of the Leven; pop. (1971p) 9454; iron and steel, paper, jute, lumber; seaside resort. Nearby is Largo, birthplace of Alexander Selkirk.

Leven, Loch \'läk-, 'läk-\. **1** Arm of Loch Linnhe, W Scotland, extending along boundary bet. Argyll and Inverness cos.; 11 m. long.

2 Lake in Kinross co., E cen. Scotland; max. depth 83 ft.; has island on which are ruins of Lochleven Castle.

Le·veque, Cape \-lə-'vek\. Cape at N tip of Dampier Land on N coast of Western Australia.

Le·ver·ku·sen \,lā-vər-'küz-ᵊn\. Industrial city, North Rhine-Westphalia, West Germany, on Rhine river 16 m. SE of Düsseldorf; pop. (1969e) 110,767; chemicals, textiles; formed 1930.

Le·ver·ock \'lē-vər-,äk, 'lev-ər-\. See SABA.

Le Vé·si·net \lə-,vā-zi-'nā\. Commune, Yvelines dept., N France, WNW suburb of Paris; pop. (1968c) 18,549.

Le·vi·a·than Peak \li-'vī-ə-thən-\. Mountain, San Juan co., SW Colorado; 13,528 ft.

Le·vi·ce \'lev-ət-,sä\ *or Hung.* **Lé·va** \'lā-,vò\ *or Ger.* **Le·wenz** \'lā-,ven(t)s\. Town, Slovak S.R., E cen. Czechoslovakia, 75 m. E of Bratislava; pop. (1968e) 16,148.

Le·vi·co \'lā-vi-,kō\. Commune, S Trento prov., Trentino-Alto Adige, NE Italy, in the Dolomites just E of Trent; pop. (1968e) 5525; mineral springs.

Le·vin \lə-'vēn\. Borough, SW North I., New Zealand; pop. (1970e) 12,300.

Le·vis \'lē-vəs\ *or Fr.* **Lé·vis** \lā-vē\. **1** County, Quebec, Canada. See table at QUEBEC.

2 *or formerly* **Pointe Le·vi** \,pwaⁿ(n)t-lā-'vē\. City, Levis co., S Quebec, Canada, on St. Lawrence river opp. Quebec; pop. (1971p) 16,566; railroad terminus and landing place for transatlantic passengers; has large dry dock, shipyards, sawmills, foundries; Coll. de Lévis (1853); overlooked by heights occupied by four large forts. Founded 1679; incorporated as a city 1916.

Le·vi·sa Bay \lā-ˌvē-sə-\. Bay in N coast of Oriente prov., E Cuba, E of and adjoining Nipe Bay.

Levisa Fork \lə-ˌvī-sə-\. River, E Kentucky; ab. 160 m. long; rises in NW Buchanan co., SW Virginia, flows N into Kentucky and unites with Tug Fork to form the Big Sandy river (*q.v.*).

Lev·it·town \ˈlev-ət-ˌtau̇n\. 1 Urban community (unincorporated), Nassau co., SE New York, on Long I. E of New York; pop. (1970c) 65,440.

2 Urban township. See WILLINGBORO.

Lev·ka \ˈlef-(ˌ)kä\. Mountain, W cen. Crete, Greece, S of Canea; 8045 ft.; second highest peak in the island.

Levkás. See LEUKAS.

Levkosia. See NICOSIA 2.

Lé·vri·er Bay \ˌlāv-rē-ˌā-\. Inlet of Atlantic Ocean on W coast of Mauritania, W Africa, E of Cape Blanc.

Le·vu·ka \lə-ˈvü-kə\. Town, E coast of Ovalau I., W cen. Fiji, SW Pacific Ocean; pop. (1969e) 1685; important trade center in early days and ✱ of Fiji under British 1874–82.

Le·vy \ˈlē-vē\. County in Florida. See table at FLORIDA.

Lewenz. See LEVICE.

Lew·es \ˈlü-əs\. 1 Seaport town, Sussex co., S Delaware, on S end of Delaware Bay 15 m. NW of Georgetown; pop. (1970c) 2563; settled 1631 by Dutch; bombarded by British 1813. Delaware Breakwater (built 1818–90).

2 *or* **Upper Yukon.** River, considered the upper course of the Yukon, S cen. Yukon, Canada; 338 m. long; rises in Tagish and Atlin lakes on S border and flows NW through Lake Laberge to unite with Pelly river and form the Yukon river; dammed for power production 1958.

3 Municipal borough, ⊗ of East Sussex, S England, on the Ouse 6 m. N of English Channel and 43 m. S of London; pop. (1971p) 14,015; agricultural implements, cement, soap, beer, ruins of 11th cent. castle; scene of battle May 14, 1264 in which Simon de Montfort defeated Henry III.

Lew·ey, Mount \-ˈlü-ē\. Peak, Adirondack Mts., Hamilton co., NE cen. New York; 3740 ft.

Lewey Lake Mountain. Peak in the Adirondack Mts., NE New York; 3903 ft.

Lew·is \ˈlü-əs\. 1 Early name of Snake river, Idaho.

2 River, SW Washington; ab. 80 m. long; rises in NE Skamania co., flows WSW into Columbia river forming boundary bet. Cowlitz and Clark cos.

3 Name of counties in seven states of the U.S. See tables at IDAHO, KENTUCKY, MISSOURI, NEW YORK, TENNESSEE, WASHINGTON, WEST VIRGINIA.

4 *or* **The Lews** \-ˈlüz\. North section of the island of Lewis with Harris, in the Outer Hebrides off NW coast of Scotland; belongs to Ross and Cromarty co.

Lewis, Butt of \ˌbət-\. Headland on N tip of island of Lewis with Harris, in the Outer Hebrides off NW coast of Scotland; lighthouse.

Lewis and Clark \-ˈklärk\. County in Montana. See table at MONTANA.

Lewis and Clark Cavern *also* **Mor·ri·son Cave** \ˌmȯr-ə-sən-, ˌmär-\. Limestone cave in SE Jefferson co., cen. Montana; forms Lewis and Clark Caverns State Park.

Lewis Bay. Inlet of Nantucket Sound on S coast of Barnstable co., Massachusetts.

Lew·is·burg \ˈlü-əs-ˌbərg\. 1 Borough, ⊗ of Union co., cen. Pennsylvania, 21 m. SSE of Williamsport; pop. (1970c) 6736; furniture, feed, lumber; dairy farming; Bucknell Univ. (1846).

2 Town, ⊗ of Marshall co., S cen. Tennessee, 18 m. SE of Columbia; pop. (1970c) 7207; stoves, shoes; sawmills, limestone quarry; dairy farming. Home of James K. Polk.

3 Town, ⊗ of Greenbrier co., SE West Virginia; pop. (1970c) 2407; Greenbrier Coll. (1808).

Lew·i·sham \ˈlü-ə-shəm\. A borough of Greater London, SE England. See table at LONDON 4.

Lewis Lake. Lake in Yellowstone National Park, NW Wyoming, SW of Yellowstone Lake.

Lew·is·porte \ˈlü-əs-ˌpō(ə)rt, -ˌpȯ(ə)rt\. Town, Newfoundland, Canada, 160 m. NW of St. John's; pop. (1971p) 3166; paint; sawmill, seafood packing plant.

Lewis Range. A range of the Rocky Mts., W Montana, along E side of Glacier National Park N into Canada; highest peak Mt. Cleveland 10,448 ft.; according to some authorities extends SE through Flathead and Lewis and Clark cos.

Lew·is·ton \ˈlü-ə-stən\. 1 City, ⊗ of Nez Perce co., W Idaho, at confluence of Clearwater and Snake rivers across from Washington, 95 m. SSE of Spokane; pop. (1970c) 26,068; pulp and paper mills, canning and freezing plants; fruit and grain farms; Lewis-Clark Normal School (1955); first incorporated town in Idaho Territory, and first capital of the Territory (1863).

2 Commercial and industrial city, Androscoggin co., SW Maine, on Androscoggin river 30 m. N of Portland; pop. (1970c) 41,799; textiles, footwear, lumber, machinery, leather products, transistors, glass; Bates Coll. (1864); settled 1770, became city 1861.

3 Village, Niagara co., W New York, on Niagara river 7 m. N of Niagara Falls; pop. (1970c) 3292; first white settlement c. 1800; burned by British and Indians 1813.

4 City, Cache co., N Utah, on Idaho border 16 m. N of Logan; pop. (1970c) 1244; grain and dairy farms.

Lew·is·town \ˈlü-ə-ˌstau̇n\. 1 City, ⊗ of Fulton co., W cen. Illinois, 37 m. SW of Peoria; pop. (1970c) 2706; coal mines; prehistoric Indian burial mounds; home of Edgar Lee Masters.

2 City, ⊗ of Fergus co., cen. Montana, ESE of Great Falls; pop. (1970c) 6437; building materials; oil refinery, gold mine; livestock raising.

3 Industrial borough, ⊗ of Mifflin co., cen. Pennsylvania, 45 m. WNW of Harrisburg; pop. (1970c) 11,098; synthetic yarns, locomotive parts, clothing, electronic equipment; sand pits; diversified agriculture; settled 1790.

Lew·is·ville \ˈlü-əs-ˌvil\. 1 City, ⊗ of Lafayette co., SW Arkansas; pop. (1970c) 1653.

2 City, Denton co., N Texas, 15 m. SSE of Denton; pop. (1970c) 9264; feed mills; boats, aluminum windows, toys; diversified agriculture.

Lewis with Har·ris \ˌlü-ə-swət͟h-ˈhar-əs, -swəth-\. Most northerly island of the Outer Hebrides, off NW coast of Scotland; 770 sq. m.; the larger N section (see LEWIS 4) is administratively part of Ross and Cromarty co.; the smaller S section (see HARRIS 2) a part of Inverness co.

Lews, The. See LEWIS 4.

Lex·ing·ton \ˈlek-siŋ-tən\. 1 County in South Carolina. See table at SOUTH CAROLINA.

2 Town, ⊗ of Oglethorpe co., NE Georgia; pop. (1970c) 322; pine timber; poultry farms.

3 City, ⊗ of Fayette co., NE cen. Kentucky, 23 m. ESE of Frankfort; pop. (1970c) 108,137; tobacco market; raises thoroughbred horses; automobile parts, electrical machinery, furniture; distilleries; Transylvania Coll. (1780), oldest educational institution W of the Alleghenies, Univ. of Kentucky (1865); home of Henry Clay 1797–1852; settled 1779, incorporated 1832.

4 Residential town, Middlesex co., NE Massachusetts, 10 m. NW of Boston; pop. (1970c) 31,886; scene of battle Apr. 19, 1775 in which a force of minutemen resisted a British contingent marching to seize stores at Concord (see CONCORD 3), the opening engagement of the American Revolution.

5 City, ⊗ of Holmes co., W cen. Mississippi, 29 m. S of Greenwood; pop. (1970c) 2756; cotton; truck farming; Saints Junior Coll. (1918).

6 City, ⊗ of Lafayette co., W Missouri, on Missouri river 33 m. E of Independence; pop. (1970c) 5388; coal mines,

rock quarry; Wentworth Military Acad. (1880); scene of Confederate victory Sept. 18–20, 1861.
7 City, ⊗ of Dawson co., S cen. Nebraska, on Platte river 37 m. W of Kearney; pop. (1970c) 5618; flour mills; diversified agriculture.
8 Manufacturing city, ⊗ of Davidson co., cen. North Carolina, 19 m. WSW of High Point; pop. (1970c) 17,205; textiles, clothing, furniture; grain and dairy farming; Davidson County Community Coll. (1961).
9 Village, Richland co., N cen. Ohio, 8 m. SW of Mansfield; pop. (1970c) 2972.
10 Town, ⊗ of Lexington co., cen. South Carolina; pop. (1970c) 969; resort; cannery; peaches.
11 City, ⊗ of Henderson co., W Tennessee, 26 m. E of Jackson; pop. (1970c) 5024; truck farming; battle of Parker's Crossroads fought nearby 1863.
12 Town, ⊗ of Rockbridge co. but politically independent, W cen. Virginia, 30 m. NW of Lynchburg; 2 sq. m.; pop. (1970c) 7597; tourist center; market town in agricultural region; Washington and Lee Univ. (1749); Virginia Military Inst. (1839); burial place of Stonewall Jackson and Robert E. Lee; became town 1777; rebuilt after fire 1796; bombarded during Civil War.

Leyden. See LEIDEN.

Ley·land \ˈlā-lənd\. Urban district, Lancashire, NW England, 22 m. NNE of Liverpool; pop. (1971p) 723,391.

Ley·te \ˈlāt-ē\. Island, one of the Visayan Is., E Phil.; 2785 sq. m.; constitutes with adjacent islands two provinces: **Leyte** (2420 sq. m.; pop. [1970p] 1,091,887; ✱ Tacloban) and **Southern Leyte** (670 sq. m.; pop. [1970p] 248,128; ✱ Maasin) . Of irregular shape, having many bays, some of which form good harbors; 121 m. long from NW to SE, varies in width from 14 m. at center to ab. 45 m. in the N. Separated from Samar on NE by very narrow San Juanico Strait; off its N end is Biliran I. and off S end Panaon I. Mountainous, with long range N to S through the center, highest peak 4426 ft.; many peaks are extinct volcanoes; has many streams but few large ones. Raises hemp, rice, cotton, corn, sugar, and tobacco; also produces timber, coal, sulfur, and iron. Chief towns Ormoc, Tacloban, Baybay, Maasin, Abuyog, Burauen, and San Isidro.

History: Discovered Mar. 1521 by Magellan, who celebrated Mar. 31 first Mass in the Philippines on Limasawa, at S end; visited by Villalobos 1543 and by Legaspi 1565; in early years of Spanish government under jurisdiction of Cebu; scene of revolts 1622, 1649; its administration separated from that of Samar 1768; civil government established by Americans Apr. 22, 1901. In World War II occupied by Japanese 1942 but scene of continued opposition by guerrilla forces; invaded Oct. 20, 1944 by Americans, who defeated Japanese fleet Oct. 21–26 in Leyte Gulf (*q.v.*) and completely conquered the island by Dec. 1944 after severe fighting around Ormoc; divided into two provinces 1959.

Leyte Gulf. Inlet of Pacific Ocean, E Phil., E of Leyte and S of Samar; on S connects by Surigao Strait with Mindanao Sea. Offers good anchorage for large fleet; partially shut off from Pacific on E by Homonhon I.; entered Oct. 19, 1944 by American invasion fleet under Gen. MacArthur which protected landings on E Leyte shore; scene of major air-sea battle, in which Japanese were decisively defeated, Oct. 25–26, 1944.

Lha·sa *also* **Las·sa** \ˈläs-ə, ˈlas-\. City, ✱ of Tibet, China, in SE part ab. 250 m. NE of Darjeeling, India; pop. (1970e) 175,000; alt. 11,830 ft.; located in a level plain on a tributary (La-sa) of the Brahmaputra, surrounded by hills, on one of which is the **Po·ta·la** \ˈpōt-ᵊl-ä\, the great palace (oldest part built ab. 12 cents. ago) of the Dalai Lama, former religious and political head of the country. Has many temples, monasteries, convents, esp. the Jokhang temple (said to have been founded 652), formerly the religious center of Tibet; nearby are several other great monasteries (Sera, Debung, Galdan); formerly the center of national pilgrimages and great festivities, esp. at New Year's; numerous monastic institutions closed or destroyed by the Chinese following Tibetan revolt against Chinese rule 1959; was for centuries the seat of Tibetan rulers. Because of its inaccessibility and the religious exclusiveness and hostility of the lamas, long closed to all foreign visitors, hence its name, the "Forbidden City." First visited by Europeans (except for a few pilgrims) by the British expedition 1904 of Col. Francis E. Younghusband; had a considerable trade with India and Nepal (over Himalayan passes) before sealing of borders after Tibetan revolt of 1959.

L'Hay–les–Roses \ˌlā-lā-ˈrōz\. Commune, Val-de-Marne dept., N France; pop. (1968c) 24,352.

Lho·tse I *and* **Lhotse II** \ˈ(h)lōt-ˈsā\. Name of two peaks in the Himalayas, on Nepal-Tibet boundary; 27,923 ft. and 27,560 ft.

Li \ˈlē\ *or formerly* **Wu** \ˈwü\. 1 *or* **Lin** \ˈlin\. River, N Hunan prov., SE cen. China; 251 m. long; flows E to Tungting lake; crosses cen. part of China's "rice bowl"; scene of much fighting during Chinese-Japanese War 1937–45.
2 River, SE China, a S tributary of the Yu in Kwangsi Chuang, which it joins just W of Nan-ning; ab. 150 m. long.

Liakhov Islands. See LYAKHOV ISLANDS.

Li·an·ga Bay \lē-ˌäŋ-ˈä-\. Inlet of Pacific on SE coast of Surigao del Sur prov., Mindanao, Phil.; ab. 20 m. wide at its mouth; at its head is **Lianga,** pop. (1969e) 23,900.

Liao \lē-ˈau̇\. River, NE China, chiefly in Liaoning prov. and Inner Mongolia; ab. 700 m. long; rises in S Inner Mongolia, flows NE, then turns SW to the Gulf of Liaotung just below Ying-k'ou; navigable for ab. 400 m.

Liao·ning \lē-ˈau̇-ˈniŋ\; *formerly* **Feng·tien** \ˈfəŋ-tē-ˈen\ *also* **Sheng·king** \ˈshəŋ-ˈjiŋ\. Province, NE China, 58,301 sq. m.; pop. (1968e) 28,000,000; ✱ Mukden; soybeans, corn, cotton; coal, iron ore; under Japanese control 1932–45; contains important industrial areas.

Liao·peh \lē-ˈau̇-ˈbā\. Former prov., China; 40,498 sq. m.; ✱ Szepingkai.

Liao·tung, Gulf of \-lē-ˈau̇-ˈdu̇ŋ\. North part of the Gulf of Chihli, W of Liaotung Penin., NE China.

Liaotung Peninsula. Peninsula, S part of Liaoning prov., NE China.

Liao–yang \lē-ˈau̇-ˈyäŋ\. City, S Liaoning prov., NE China, on a tributary of the Hun river 35 m. S of Mukden; pop. (1970e) 250,000; trade and market center for agricultural region producing soybeans, millet, cotton, and fruit; an ancient town, important as a district center under early dynasties; site of great battle, a victory of the Japanese under Oyama over the Russian armies under Kuropatkin Aug. 25–Sept. 4, 1904.

Liaoyuan. See SHUANG-LIAO.

Li·ard \ˈlē-ˌärd\. 1 River, W Canada; 755 m. long; rises in Stikine Mts. in SE Yukon, flows E across N British Columbia and turns N and NE to empty into Mackenzie river in SW Mackenzie dist., Northwest Territories. The Alaska Highway follows its N bank for many miles in N British Columbia.
2 Trading post on the Liard. See FORT LIARD.

Li·ba·cao \ˌlē-bə-ˈkau̇\. Municipality, Aklan prov., Panay, Phil., on river at foot of the mountains 32 m. WSW of Roxas; pop. (1969e) 20,200.

Liban. See LEBANON 1.

Lí·ba·no \ˈlē-və-ˌnō\. Town, Tolima dept., W cen. Colombia, 33 m. ESE of Manizales; munic. pop. (1968e) 56,-245.

Libanus. See LEBANON MOUNTAINS.

Libau. See LIEPĀJA.

Lib·by \ˈlib-ē\. City, ⊗ of Lincoln co., NW corner of Montana, on Kootenai river 60 m. WNW of Kalispell; pop. (1970c) 3286; lead and silver mines; dairy farming.

Libby Dam and **Libby Reservoir.** See UNITED STATES, *Dams and Reservoirs.*

Li·benge \lē-ˈbä^{n}zh\. Town, NW Zaire, S cen. Africa, on the Ubangi river ab. 50 m. S of Bangui, Central African Republic.

Lib·e·ral \ˈlib-(ə-)rəl\. City, ⊗ of Seward co., SW Kansas, on Oklahoma border 73 m. SW of Dodge City; pop. (1970c) 13,789; oil refineries, flour mills; Seward Community Junior Coll. (1967).

Liberalitis Julia. See ÉVORA 2.

Li·be·rec \ˈlib-ə-ˌrets\ *or Ger.* **Rei·chen·berg** \ˈrī-kən-ˌbe(ə)rg\. City, Czech S.R., W Czechoslovakia; pop. (1968e) 72,640; woolen and cotton manufactures; cloth industry here dates from 16th cent.; a center of the German Sudeten movement 1938.

Li·be·ria \lī-ˈbir-ē-ə\. 1 Republic, W Africa, bounded on N by Guinea, on E by Ivory Coast, on S by the Atlantic Ocean, and on NW by Sierra Leone; 43,000 sq. m.; pop. (1970e) 1,200,000; ✱ Monrovia. *Physical features:* Coastline is marked by lagoons; its coast is known as the Grain Coast (*q.v.*) and the SE section is called the Kru Coast; its SE point on Ivory Coast border is marked by Cape Palmas; has no good natural harbors. A plateau country well watered and densely forested; highest point Mt. Wutivi 4528 ft., in N; chief rivers Mano, St. Paul, St. John, Cestos, and Cavally. *Chief products:* Rubber, palm products, mangoes, rice, coffee, timber; iron ore, diamonds; manufacturing: building materials, furniture, footwear; food processing. *Chief towns:* Monrovia, Buchanan, Harper.

History: Project for settlement of freed American Negroes begun by American Colonization Society 1817; settled at Monrovia 1822; named by Robert G. Harper from the Latin *liber* "free"; established as Free and Independent Republic of Liberia 1847; separate republic of Maryland, founded 1833, united with Liberia 1857; because of bankruptcy and internal disorder 1909 placed virtually under U.S. protection 1911; declared war on Germany 1917; Firestone Company of U.S. granted 1926 concession of one million acres for rubber plantation; declared war on Germany and Japan 1944; became a member of Organization of African Unity 1963.

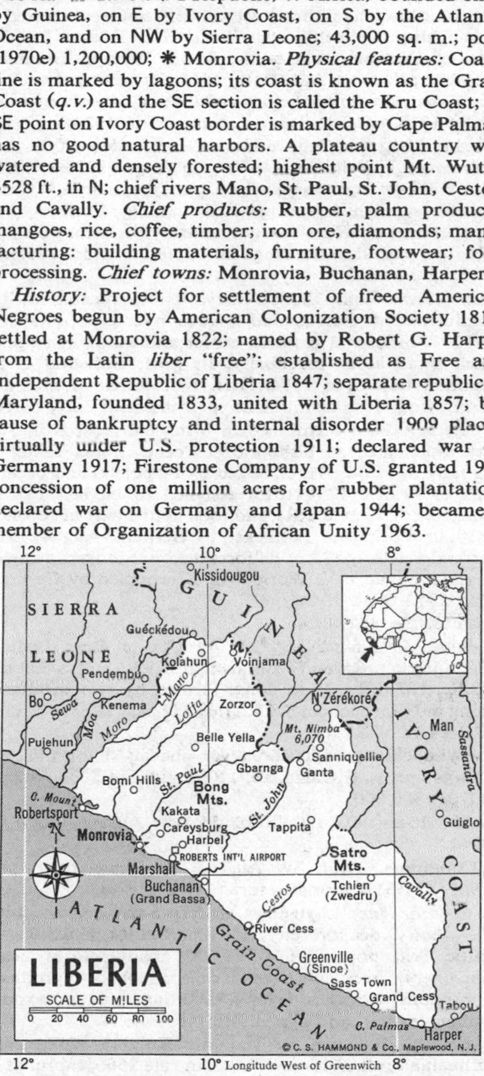

2 Town, ✱ of Guanacaste prov., NW Costa Rica; pop. (1968e) 8484.

Libertad, La. See LA LIBERTAD.

Lib·er·ty \ˈlib-ərt-ē\. 1 Name of counties in four states of the U.S. See tables at FLORIDA, GEORGIA, MONTANA, TEXAS.
2 Town, ⊗ of Union co., E Indiana, 13 m. S of Richmond; pop. (1970c) 1831.
3 City, ⊗ of Casey co., cen. Kentucky; pop. (1970c) 1765.
4 Town, ⊗ of Amite co., SW Mississippi; pop. (1970c) 612.
5 City, ⊗ of Clay co., NW Missouri, 13 m. NNE of Kansas City; pop. (1970c) 13,704; William Jewell Coll. (1849).
6 Village, Sullivan co., SE New York, 45 m. W of Poughkeepsie; pop. (1970c) 4293; year-round resort.
7 Borough, Allegheny co., SW Pennsylvania, 11 m. SE of Pittsburgh; pop. (1970c) 3594.
8 Town, Pickens co., NW South Carolina, in Blue Ridge foothills 18 m. W of Greenville; pop. (1970c) 2860.
9 City, ⊗ of Liberty co., E Texas, on Trinity river 39 m. ENE of Houston; pop. (1970c) 5591; in farming and ranching region; oil wells nearby.

Liberty, Mount. Peak in Grafton co., New Hampshire; 4460 ft.

Liberty Cap. Mountain in Mount Ranier National Park, Washington; 14,112 ft.

Liberty Island; *formerly* **Bed·loe's Island** \ˌbed-lōz-\ *or* **Bed·loe Island** \-lō-\. Small island in Upper New York Bay; purchased by City of New York 1758 and c. 1800 ceded to U.S. government; location of Bartholdi's statue Liberty Enlightening the World.

Lib·er·ty·ville \ˈlib-ərt-ē-ˌvil\. Village, Lake co., NE corner of Illinois, 10 m. SW of Waukegan; pop. (1970c) 11,684.

Libia. See LIBYA 2.

Libian Desert. See LIBYAN DESERT.

Lib·i·an Sa·ha·ra \ˌlib-ē-ən-sə-ˈhar-ə, -ˈher-, -ˈhär-\. Former (Italian) administrative and military territory, cen. and S Libya; 465,362 sq. m.

Lib·ma·nan \lēb-ˈmän-än\. Municipality, W cen. Camarines Sur prov., Luzon, Phil., on tributary of lower Bicol river 11 m. NW of Naga; pop. (1969e) 71,800; has hemp and rice industries.

Li·bourne \lē-ˈbu̇(ə)rn\. Commune, Gironde dept., SW France, on Dordogne river 17 m. ENE of Bordeaux; pop. (1968c) 22,123; shipbuilding; preserved foods, wines.

Li·brary \ˈlī-ˌbrer-ē\. Locality, Allegheny co., SW Pennsylvania, ab. 10 m. S of Pittsburgh.

Li·brazhd \li-ˈbräzhd\. 1 Province of E Albania. See table at ALBANIA.
2 Town, its ✱; pop. (1967e) 1230.

Li·bre·ville \ˈlē-brə-ˌvil\. Seaport town, ✱ of Gabon, W equatorial Africa; pop. (1970e) 105,080; exports timber.

Li·bur·nia \lī-ˈbər-nē-ə, -nyə\. District on the coast of the Adriatic Sea in ancient Illyria; included in modern Croatia, Yugoslavia; its inhabitants, the Liburni, inventors of the Liburnian galley, noted for their skill in navigation.

Lib·ya \ˈlib-ē-ə\. 1 Ancient Greek name for N Africa, outside of Egypt; later, for that part of Africa immediately W of Egypt which was afterwards divided into Marmarica and Cyrenaica and became part of the Roman colony of Africa.
2 *also* **Lib·ia** \ˈlēb-yə\ *or officially* **Lib·yan Arab Republic** \ˈlib-ē-ən-\. Republic, N Africa, bounded on N by the Mediterranean Sea, on E by Egypt, on SE by Sudan, on S by Chad and Niger, on W by Algeria, and on NW by Tunisia; 679,358 sq. m.; pop. (1971e) 2,010,000; ✱ Tripoli. *Physical features:* Largely desert, forming NE section of Sahara; agricultural areas developed along the coast, in the Barka Plateau, and in the oases; highland areas in N cen. part and along S border; in the interior are the Hammada al-Hamra (desert in NW), Fezzan (desert and oases region in SW), Murzuch (dunes in SW), and the oases of Giofra, Fezzan, Al-Kufrah, and Giarabub; coast is marked by wide indentation of Gulf of Sidra. *Chief export:* Oil; other products: barley, wheat, dates, olives; gypsum, limestone. *Chief towns:* Tripoli, Benghazi, Derna, Barka, Tobruk.

History: For early history, see TRIPOLI 1, CYRENAICA, and FEZZAN. Occupied by Italians 1914; provinces of Cyrenaica and Tripolitania united 1934, Fezzan being governed as part of military territory of South Tripolitania;

formally incorporated into Italy 1939; scene of several extended campaigns bet. British and Italian-German forces in World War II; Axis forces expelled spring 1943; administered by British and French military governors 1943–51; achieved independence as the **Kingdom of Libya** 1951; began exporting oil 1961; monarchy overthrown by military junta 1969; formed confederation with Egypt and Syria 1971.

Lib·y·an Desert *or* **Lib·i·an Desert** \ˈlib-ē-ən-\. Desert area of the eastern Sahara W of the Nile in N Africa, in Libya, Egypt, and Sudan.

Li·can·cá·bur \ˌlē-käŋ-ˈkäb-ər\ *or* **Li·can·caur** \ˌlē-käŋ-ˈkaů(ə)r\. Volcano in N Chile, NE of Antofagasta and near SW Bolivian border; 19,455 ft.

Li·ca·ta \li-ˈkät-ə\ *or anc.* **Phin·ti·as** \ˈfint-ē-əs\. Seaport commune, SW Sicily, Italy, on Mediterranean 26 m. SE of Agrigento; pop. (1968e) 40,422; exports asphalt and sulfur; in World War II a beachhead for the landing of U.S. forces July 11, 1943.

Lich·field \ˈlich-ˌfēld\. Municipal borough, Staffordshire, W cen. England, 15 m. NNE of Birmingham; pop. (1971p) 22,672; brewing; cathedral, dating in part from 13th cent.; grammar school, founded 1495, numbers among its pupils Samuel Johnson, Joseph Addison, David Garrick.

Li–chiang *or* **Li·kiang** \ˈlē-jē-ˈäŋ\. Town, NW Yunnan prov., S China, near the Yangtze 80 m. N of Ta-li.

Lich·ten·burg. 1 \ˈlik-tən-ˌbů(ə)rg\. Village, Cottbus dist., East Germany, on the Elbe just N of Torgau; Nazi concentration camp in World War II.

2 \ˈlik-tən-ˌbərg\. Town, SW Transvaal, NE Rep. of South Africa, 120 m. W of Johannesburg; pop. (1967e) 15,800; diamonds in vicinity; experimental dry farming.

Lich·ten·stein \ˈlik-tən-ˌs(h)tīn\ *or formerly* **Lichtenstein–Calln·berg** \-ˈkäln-ˌbe(ə)rg\. City, Karl-Marx-Stadt dist., East Germany, 14 m. WSW of Karl-Marx-Stadt; pop. (1970e) 15,099; clothing; 16th cent. castle.

Lick·ing \ˈlik-iŋ\. 1 River, NE Kentucky; 320 m. long; rises in Magoffin co., flows NW into Ohio river at Covington. 2 County in Ohio. See table at OHIO.

Li·co·sa, Cape \-li-ˈkō-sə\. Promontory on S end of Gulf of Salerno, Campania, S Italy.

Licus. See LECH.

Li·da \ˈlē-də\. City, Grodno Oblast, W Belorussian S.S.R., U.S.S.R., 25 m. NW of Novogrudok (formerly in Poland); pop. (1967e) 39,000; railroad junction; tobacco factories.

Lidg·er·wood \ˈlij-ər-ˌwůd\. City, Richland co., SE corner of North Dakota, ab. 30 m. WSW of Wahpeton; pop. (1970c) 1000; wheat, barley.

Li·di·ce \ˈlid-ə(t)-sē, -ˌsā\. 1 Village, Will co., NE Illinois, just N of Joliet; formerly **Stern Park Gardens** \ˈstərn-\, a small Czech-American community, renamed July 12, 1942 in ceremonies in memory of Lidice, Czechoslovakia.

2 Village, Czech S.R., Czechoslovakia, 3½ m. E of Kladno and ab. 10 m. WNW of Prague; its male inhabitants (ab. 200) killed, its women sent to concentration camps, its children placed in German institutions, and all buildings completely destroyed June 9–10, 1942 by Nazi Gestapo in revenge for killing of Reinhard Heydrich, German Deputy Reich Protector in Bohemia and Moravia.

Li·dingö \ˈlēd-iŋ-ˌər\. City, Stockholm co., SE Sweden, residential suburb NE of Stockholm; pop. (1970e) 36,334; made city 1926.

Lid·kö·ping \ˈlēd-ˌchə(r)-piŋ\. City, Skaraborg co., Sweden, on Lake Vänern; pop. (1970e) 34,871; porcelain, matches.

Li·do \ˈlēd-(ˌ)ō\ *or in full* **Lido di Ma·la·moc·co** \-di-ˌmäl-ə-ˈmò-(ˌ)kō\. Island reef outside the Lagoon of Venice, Venezia prov., NE Italy, separating the lagoon from the Gulf of Venice; esp., **the Lido,** town at N end of island, formerly a fashionable sea-bathing resort, with many hotels, villas, etc.

Lidz·bark War·miń·ski \ˈlits-ˌbärk-vär-ˈmin(t)-skē, ˈlēts-\ *or Ger.* **Heils·berg** \ˈhīls-ˌbe(ə)rg\. Town, N cen. Olsztyn prov., N Poland, 25 m. N of Olsztyn on the Łyna river; pop. (1968e) 12,500; railroad junction; grain and cattle market; 13th cent. castle; founded 1240; received town rights 1308; to Prussia 1772; assigned to Poland by Potsdam Conference 1945.

Liech·ten·stein \ˈlik-tən-ˌs(h)tīn\; *officially* **Principality of Liechtenstein** *or Ger.* **Fürst·en·tum Liechtenstein** \ˈfyůr-stən-ˌtüm-\. Independent principality on E bank of the Rhine bet. Saint Gallen and Graubünden cantons in NE Switzerland and province of Vorarlberg in W Austria; 62 sq. m.; pop. (1970c) 21,350; ✱ Vaduz. Narrow strip of lowland along the Rhine; peaks of spur of Rhaetian Alps in S are above 8400 ft. Chief products corn, wine, fruit; dairy products; manufacturing: textiles, pharmaceutical products, precision instruments; tourism.

History: In 1719, counties of Schellenberg and Vaduz, in hands of branch of house of Liechtenstein, were erected as principality of Liechtenstein in the Holy Roman Empire; part of Confederation of the Rhine 1806; in Germanic Confederation (see GERMANY) 1815–66; belonged to Austrian customs union before collapse of Hapsburg monarchy 1918; entered Swiss customs union 1924.

Li·ège *or* **Li·ége** \lē-ˈāzh, -ˈezh\ *or Ger.* **Lüt·tich** \ˈl(y)ü-tik\. 1 Province, E Belgium; 1497 sq. m.; pop. (1970e) 1,019,-309; ✱ Liège; sugar beets, wheat, oats, rye; dairying; varied industries, manufacturing, coal mining. Formerly, an independent church state, governed by the prince-bishops of Liège; passed to the kingdom of Netherlands 1815, and to Belgium 1830.

2 *or Flem.* **Luik** \ˈlòik\. City, its ✱, located at the confluence of Ourthe and Meuse rivers; pop. (1970e) 147,277; industrial research center and major river port; steel, small arms, machinery. Its great cathedral of St. Lambert destroyed 1794; later, the church of St. Paul, dating from 10th cent., made the cathedral; univ. (1816).

History: First mentioned in historical records in 558; city established as bishopric 8th cent.; noted center of learning in Middle Ages; seized by Napoleon and became part of France 1794–1815; assigned to Netherlands by Congress of Vienna 1815 and took active part in revolt of 1830; in World War I attacked by Germans Aug. 4, 1914, surrendered Aug. 7 but its forts held out longer, delaying German advance; in World War II occupied by Germans May 1940–Sept. 1944.

Liegnitz. See LEGNICA.

Lie·lu·pe \lē-ˈel-ə-ˌpā\ *or Ger.* **Aa** \ˈä\ *or Russ.* **Le·lu·pe** \ˈlel-ə-p(y)ə\. River, N Lithuanian S.S.R. and S Latvian S.S.R., U.S.S.R.; 74 m. long; formed by two tributaries rising in N Lithuanian S.S.R., flows N past Jelgava to Gulf of Riga W of Riga.

Lien–yün–chiang–shih \lē-ˈen-ˈyůn-chē-ˈäŋ-ˈshi(ə)r\. Town, Kiangsu prov., E China, ab. 120 m. ENE of Süchow; pop. (1970e) 300,000.

Li·enz \ˈlē-en(t)s\. 1 Political district, Austria. See EAST TIROL.

2 Commune, Tirol, SW Austria, on Drava river; pop. (1961c) 11,312; tourist resort.

Lie·pā·ja *or Russ.* **Li·ye·pa·ya** \lə-ˈyep-ə-yə\ *or Ger.* **Li·bau** \ˈlē-(ˌ)baů\. Seaport city, Latvian S.S.R., U.S.S.R., on Baltic Sea; pop. (1969e) 88,000; manufactures heavy machinery, iron and steel, veneers, tobacco products, paints and varnishes; fishing, distilling, tanning; exports timber, leather, and agricultural produce.

History: Founded by Teutonic Knights 1263; under Lithuanian rule 1418, and Prussian rule 1560; captured by Charles XII of Sweden 1701, and in 1795 by the Russians, who developed its port 1893–1906. In World War I became a German base; provisional Latvian government established here Dec. 1918 when Bolshevik army attacked Riga; under German occupation from Apr. to June 1919 and in World War II 1941–44.

Lier \ˈli(ə)r\ *or* **Lierre** \lē-ˈe(ə)r\. Commune, Antwerp prov., N Belgium, ab. 8 m. SE of Antwerp; pop. (1969e) 28,370; lace, clothing; 15th cent. High Gothic church. In World War I captured by the Germans Oct. 5, 1914.

Lies·tal \ˈlē-ˌstäl\. Commune, ✱ of Basel-Land demicanton, Basel canton, NW Switzerland, 8 m. SE of Basel; pop. (1970c) 12,500; textiles, chemicals, iron goods; printing; produces wine; 15th cent. town hall; made city in latter half of 13th cent.

Lietuva. See LITHUANIAN SOVIET SOCIALIST REPUBLIC.

Lié·vin \lē-ā-ˈvaⁿ\. Commune, Pas-de-Calais dept., N France, 9 m. N of Arras; pop. (1968c) 35,853; coal; completely destroyed in World War I.

Liè·vre \lē-ˈevrᵊ\. River, SW Quebec, Canada; 205 m. long; flows S through Labelle and Papineau cos. into the Ottawa river below Hull; outlet of many lakes.

Lif·fey \ˈlif-ē\. River, E Eire; 50 m. long; rises among the Wicklow Mts. in co. Wicklow, curves NW and NE into Dublin Bay (an inlet of the Irish Sea) at Dublin.

Lif·ford \ˈlif-ərd\. Town, ⊗ of co. Donegal, N Eire; on Foyle river opp. Strabane in Northern Ireland.

Li·fou *or* **Li·fu** \lē-ˈfü\. Largest and most important island of the Loyalty Is., New Caledonia territory (French), SW Pacific Ocean, ab. 60 m. E of New Caledonia; 50 m. long and 10 to 15 m. wide; 650 sq. m.; pop. (1971e) 7097; irregular in shape and flat, with no hills or rivers; very fertile.

Li·fu·ka \li-ˈfü-kə\. Island in NW part of Haapai group, Tonga, SW cen. Pacific Ocean; contains the only considerable village (Pangai) in the group.

Li·gao \li-ˈgau̇\. Municipality, cen. Albay prov., Luzon, Phil., on railroad 16 m. NW of Legaspi; pop. (1969e) 73,200; in fine hemp-growing district, W of Mt. Mayon.

Liger. See LOIRE.

Light·house Point \ˈlīt-ˌhau̇s-\. 1 E tip of Franklin co., NW Florida, at W entrance to Apalachee Bay.

2 City, Broward co., SE Florida; pop. (1970c) 9071; residential suburb of Fort Lauderdale.

Li·gny \lē-ˈnyē\. Commune, Namur prov., S Belgium, 14 m. NW of Namur; pop. (1969e) 1995; battlefield where Napoleon defeated the Prussians June 16, 1815 just before the battle of Waterloo.

Ligny–en–Bar·rois \-äⁿ-bär-ˈwä\. Commune, S Meuse dept., NE France, SE of Bar-le-Duc; pop. (1962c) 5522; 13th–17th cent. church; ancestral castle of Marshal Luxembourg.

Lig·o·nier \ˌlig-ə-ˈni(ə)r\. 1 City, Noble co., NE Indiana, 35 m. NW of Fort Wayne; pop. (1970c) 3034; flour; grain farms.

2 Borough and mountain resort, Westmoreland co., SW Pennsylvania, 19 m. WSW of Johnstown; pop. (1970c) 2258; summer and winter resort; dairy and poultry farms.

Li·gu·ria \lə-ˈgyu̇r-ē-ə\. 1 Ancient geographical region inhabited by Ligurians, people of pre-Indo-European stock, who lived in SW Europe; the Ligurians E of Rhone river were gradually subdued by Romans during 2d cent. B.C.; an Augustan region in Roman Empire; in 1797 a strip of coast surrounding Genoa was erected as Ligurian Republic which France annexed 1805.

2 Autonomous region of NW Italy, on Ligurian Sea bet. France and Tuscany; 2089 sq. m.; pop. (1968e) 1,866,186; ✱ Genoa; consists of extremely fertile coastal strip—the Italian Riviera—a major tourist center, and an inland mountainous region; produces citrus fruit, wine, olives, nuts; shipbuilding, iron, and machine-making works; chemicals, textiles. Established 1948; received limited autonomy 1970.

Ligurian Alps. See table at ALPS.

Ligurian Apennines *or Ital.* **Ligure, Appennino.** See table at APENNINES.

Li·gur·i·an Sea \lə-ˈgyu̇r-ē-ən-\ *or anc.* **Si·nus Li·gus·ti·cus** \ˌsī-nə-slə-ˈgəs-ti-kəs\. Branch of Mediterranean Sea enclosed by the Italian autonomous regions of Liguria and Tuscany on N and E, and the French island of Corsica on the S; includes the Gulf of Genoa.

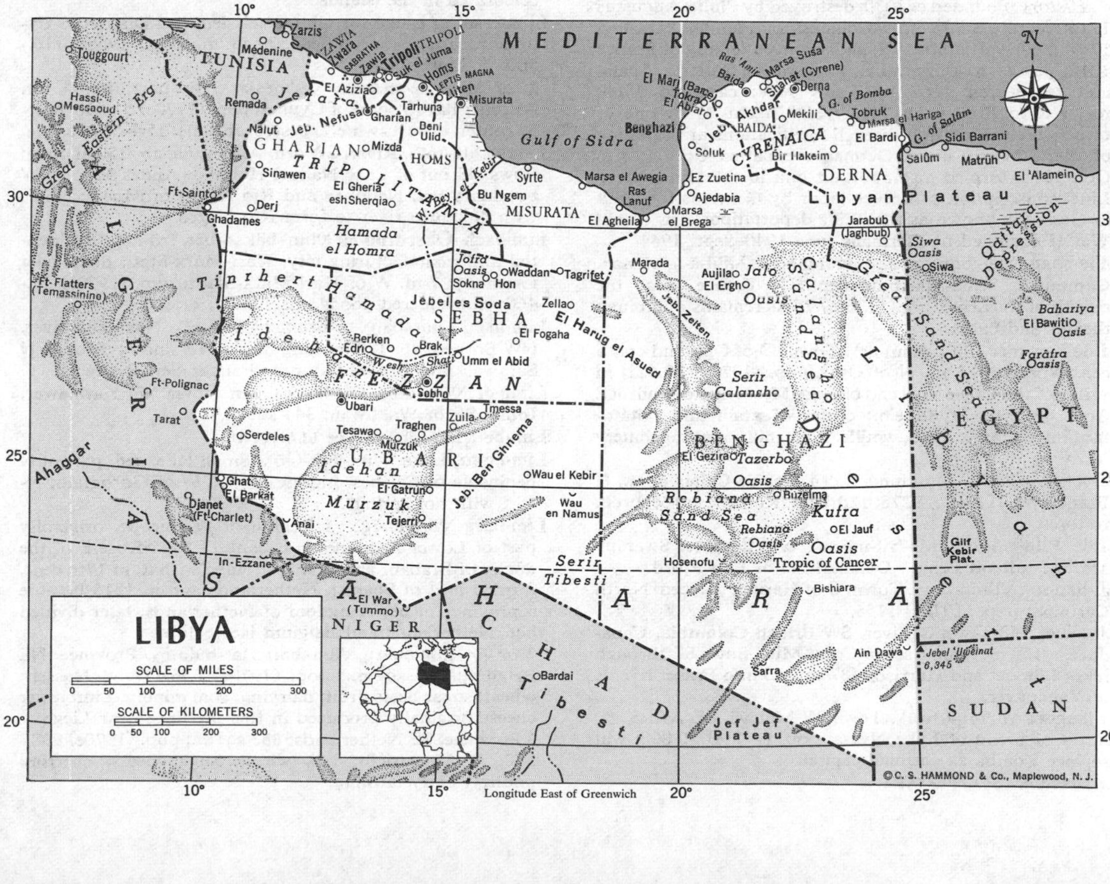

Li·hir \'lē-ˌhi(ə)r\. Small island in the Bismarck Archipelago, W Pacific Ocean, off NE coast of New Ireland.

Li·hou \'lē-ˌhü\. One of the Channel Is., just W of Guernsey; 38 acres.

Lihou Reefs and Cays \'lē-hō-\. Coral reefs in SW Coral Sea off NE Queensland, Australia; mark E limit of Great Barrier Reef formations.

Li–hsien. See BLACK 9.

Li·hue \li-'hü-ē\. 1 Division, SE Kauai I., Kauai co., Hawaii.

2 City, Lihue div., ⊗ of Kauai co., SE Kauai I.; pop. (1970c) 3124; has steamer connection with Honolulu via Nawiliwili Bay.

Liim Fjord. See LIM FJORD.

Li·ka·si \li-'käs-ē\ *or formerly* **Ja·dot·ville** \ˌzhä-dō-'vē\. City, SE Shaba prov., Zaire; pop. (1968e) 113,217; copper-mining center.

Likhvin. See CHEKALIN.

Likiang. See LI-CHIANG.

Li·ki·ep \'lē-kē-ˌep\. Island (atoll), cen. part of Ratak Chain, N cen. Marshall Is., W Pacific Ocean; has 44 islets.

Li·ko·ma \li-'kō-mə\. Island in E cen. Lake Nyasa, Malawi; SE Africa; site of a cathedral, built by native Christians.

Lilas, Les. See LES LILAS.

L'Île Rousse \lēl-'rüs\ *or* **Île Rousse** \ēl-'rüs\. Seaport, NW Corsica, France; pop. (1962c) 1867; exports citron; founded 1758 by Pasquale di Paoli, the Corsican patriot.

Lilibeo, Cape. See BOÈO, CAPE.

Lille \'lē(ə)l\; *formerly* **Lisle** \'lē(ə)l, 'lī(ə)l\ *or sometimes* **L'Isle** \'lēl\; *Lat.* **In·su·la** \'in(t)-sə-lə\ *or Flem.* **Rys·sel** \'ri-səl\. Manufacturing and commercial city, ✱ of Nord dept., N France, 130 m. NNE of Paris; pop. (1968c) 190,-546; arsenal; textiles, iron, steel, machinery, chemicals; brewing, distilling, sugar refining; two 15th cent. churches, a 16th cent. church, and the 17th cent. exchange; univ. (1560).

History: Founded c. 1030; destroyed by Philip Augustus 1214; rebuilt by Joanna, Countess of Flanders; retaken 1297; medieval capital of Flanders; given to king of France 1312; passed to Burgundian possessions, Austria, Spain, and recaptured 1667 by Louis XIV; captured 1708; restored to France by Treaty of Utrecht 1713; one of principal elements in N French fortifications at beginning of World War I; under German occupation Oct. 1914 to Oct. 1918, formed an important link in the Hindenburg Line; conscription of French labor by Germans for work in Germany known as the "Lille deportations"; in World War II occupied by Germans June 1940–Sept. 1944.

Lille·bonne \lēl-'bȯn\ *or anc.* **Ju·li·o·bo·na** \ˌjül-ē-ə-'bō-nə\. Commune, Seine-Maritime dept., N France, near the mouth of the Seine; pop. (1968c) 7870; remains of Roman theater and baths.

Lil·le·ham·mer \'lil-ə-ˌhäm-ər\. Town, ⊗ of Oppland co., S cen. Norway, 85 m. N of Oslo; pop. (1970e) 20,522; in valley of the Lågen at N end of Lake Mjøsa and on railroad from Oslo to Trondheim; center of grain and potato-farming country; has sawmills, flour mills, and machinery factories.

Lil·lers \lē-'lär\. Commune, E cen. Pas-de-Calais dept., N France; pop. (1962c) 9278; 12th cent. Romanesque church, restored.

Lil·le Vild·mo·se \'li-lə-'vil-mō-sə\ *or* **Vildmose.** Swampy area, N Jutland Penin., Denmark, N of Lim Fjord.

Lil·ling·ton \'lil-iŋ-tən\. Town, ⊗ of Harnett co., cen. North Carolina; pop. (1970c) 1155.

Lil·loo·et \'lil-ə-ˌwet\. River, SW British Columbia, Canada; ab. 150 m. long; rises in Coast Mts., flows SE through lakes Lillooet and Harrison (87 sq. m.) into Fraser river E of Vancouver.

Li·long·we \li-'lȯŋ-(ˌ)wā\. Town, W Malawi, SE Africa, 50 m. W of S end of Lake Nyasa; pop. (1971e) 40,000; will replace Zomba as national capital.

Lilybaeum. See MARSALA.

Lim \'lim, 'lēm\. River, Montenegro and Bosnia, S cen. Yugoslavia; 136 m. long; rises in North Albanian Alps and flows N into Drina river.

Li·ma \'lī-mə\. Industrial city, ⊗ of Allen co., NW Ohio, 68 m. SSW of Toledo; pop. (1970c) 53,734; motor vehicles, steel castings, aircraft parts, machine tools, building machinery; center of diversified agricultural region; founded 1831, incorporated 1841; in late 19th cent. center of N Ohio oil fields.

Lima \'lē-ma\. 1 Department of cen. Peru. See table at PERU.

2 City, ✱ of Peru, also ✱ of Lima dept., on Rímac river ab. 8 m. E from its port Callao; pop. (1970e) 2,541,300; altitude 512 ft.; economic and cultural center of Peru; diversified industries, including textiles, cement, leather goods, processed foods, clothing, furniture; foundries, oil refineries. Called "City of the Kings" because its site was chosen on Jan. 6, the feast of the Wise Men or the Three Kings; 16th cent. cathedral, government palace, and the University of San Marcos (founded 1551, the oldest university in South America). Founded by Pizarro 1535; audiencia established 1542; capital of viceroyalty of Peru (*q.v.*); largely destroyed by earthquake 1746; occupied by Chilean forces during War of the Pacific 1881–83.

Lima, Point \-'lē-mə\. Cape on E coast of Puerto Rico.

Li·ma·che \li-'mä-chē\ *or* **San Fran·cis·co de Limache** \ˌsan-frən-'sis-(ˌ)kō-dā-\. City, Valparaíso prov., cen. Chile; pop. (1960c) 14,488.

Li·man \'lē-ˌmän\. Mountain, highest point of Wilis mountain group, E cen. Java, Indonesia, SE of Madiun; 8409 ft.

Lima Reservoir \ˌlī-mə-\. Reservoir in Red Rock Creek, SE Beaverhead co., SW Montana.

Li·ma·sa·wa \ˌlē-mə-'sä-wə\. Long, narrow island ab. 2 m. off S end of Leyte I., Phil.; 3 sq. m.; has two small barrios. Site of Magellan's second landing in the Philippines Mar. 25, 1521; here on Easter Sunday, Mar. 31, first Mass celebrated in the islands.

Li·mas·sol *or* **Li·ma·sol** \ˌlim-ə-'sȯl, ˌlēm-\. 1 District, S Cyprus, E Mediterranean Sea; 539 sq. m.; pop. (1968e) 116,-500; ✱ Limassol.

2 *or anc.* **Le·mes·sus** \li-'mes-əs\. Seaport, its ✱, on Akrotiri Bay, S coast of Cyprus; pop. (1970e) 51,500; tourist center; exports wine, asbestos, chrome; 15th cent. castle.

Li·may \lē-'mī\. River, SW cen. Argentina; ab. 250 m. long; flows NE out of Lake Nahuel Huapí in Andes Mts. on W boundary bet. Neuquén and Río Negro provinces; unites with Neuquén river to form Río Negro.

Lim·bach–Ober·froh·na \'lim-ˌbäk-ˌō-bər-'frō-nə\. Residential and manufacturing city, Karl-Marx-Stadt dist., East Germany, 7 m. W of Karl-Marx-Stadt; pop. (1970e) 25,-460; embroidered goods, machinery; bricks.

Lim·bang \'lim-ˌbäŋ\ *or* **Bru·nei** \'brü-ˌnī\. Navigable river, NW Borneo; ab. 120 m. long; flows NW and N through N Sarawak into Brunei Bay near Bandar Seri Begawan.

Limb·di \'lim-dē\. Former Indian state, NE Kathiawar, India, SE of Wadhwan; 344 sq. m.

Lim·be \'lim-(ˌ)bā\. See BLANTYRE.

Lim·bo·to, Lake \-lim-'bōt-(ˌ)ō\. Small lake, cen. part of N peninsula of Celebes, Indonesia, just W of Gorontalo; resort with hot springs.

Lim·burg \'lim-ˌbərg\. 1 Region of W Europe, originally part of Lower Lorraine on E bank of the Meuse E of the duchy of Brabant and at times joined with it; in 17th cent. formed part of Spanish Netherlands and in 1815 became a province of new kingdom of Netherlands; later divided bet. Netherlands and Belgium (see below).

2 *or Fr.* **Lim·bourg** \'lim-ˌbərg, laⁿ-bu̇(ə)r\. Province, NE Belgium; 935 sq. m.; pop. (1970e) 656,477; ✱ Hasselt; wheat, sugar beets, fruit; dairying; coal mining. Limburger cheese originally produced in this province near Liège.

3 Province, SE Netherlands; 853 sq. m.; pop. (1970e) 998,-570; ✱ Maastricht; rye, wheat, sugar beets, cherries; poultry; dairy farming.

Limburg an der Lahn \-än-dər-'län\. City, Hesse, West Germany, on Lahn river 23 m. NNW of Wiesbaden; pop. (1968e) 14,708; railroad junction; manufactures machinery, metal and paper goods, soap, brewery products; cattle market; 13th cent. cathedral and castle. Became city in 13th cent.

Li·mei·ra \lə-'mer-ə\. Town, São Paulo state, SE Brazil, 80 m. NW of São Paulo; munic. pop. (1968e) 71,690; center of orange cultivation and silkworm culture.

Lim·er·ick \'lim-(ə-)rik\ *or Gaelic* **Luim·neach** \'lim-nək\. 1 County in Munster prov., SW Eire; 1037 sq. m.; pop. (1971p) 140,370; ⊗ Limerick; chief river Shannon; agriculture, livestock raising, dairy farming, salmon fishing.

2 County borough, its ⊗, seaport on the Shannon; pop. (1971p) 57,137; exports fish and farm products; flour mills, creameries, breweries; lace-making, salmon fishing; castle erected under King John; 12th cent. cathedral. Important Norse settlement in 9th and 10th cents.; received charter 1197; object of many sieges, notably by Oliver Cromwell 1651 and, as the last important stronghold of the Jacobites, by William of Orange 1691.

Li·mes Ger·man·i·cus \'lī(,)mēz-jər-'man-i-kəs\. A part of the Roman defense system against the tribes of the N, E of the Rhine and along NE border of Germania Superior; built c. 74 A.D.

Lime·stone \'līm-,stōn\. 1 Name of counties in two states of the U.S. See tables at ALABAMA and TEXAS.

2 Town, Aroostook co., N Maine, 18 m. NNE of Presque Isle; pop. (1970c) 10,360.

Lim Fjord *also* **Lym Fjord** *or* **Liim Fjord** \'lēm-, 'lim-\. Fjord in N section of Jutland, Denmark, extending from North Sea ENE across the peninsula to the Kattegat, and cutting off Vendsyssel-Thy; wide section (ab. 13 m.) in center of fjord known as Løgstør Bredning.

Lim·it, Point \-'lim-ət\. Point of land, Cavite prov., S Luzon, Phil., S of entrance to Manila Bay.

Lim·mat \'lim-ät\. River, Zurich and Aargau cantons, Switzerland; ab. 87 m. long; flows NW from NW end of Lake of Zurich to Aare river; the city of Zurich is on the lake and on both sides of the river. See LINTH.

Lim·men Bight \,lim-ən-\. Shallow inlet in W part of Gulf of Carpentaria on E coast of Northern Territory, NE Australia, to the SW of Groote Eylandt.

Limnos. See LEMNOS.

Li·mo·ei·ro \lim-'we(ə)r-(,)ü\. City, NE Pernambuco state, E Brazil; on railroad 40 m. NW of Recife; munic. pop. (1968e) 52,814.

Li·moges \lē-'mōzh\; *anc.* **Au·gus·to·ri·tum Lem·o·vi·cen·si·um** \(,)ò-,gəs-tə-'rit-əm-,lem-ə-vī-'sen-ch(ē-)əm\ *or later* **Lem·o·vi·ces** \,lem-ə-'vī-(,)sēz\. Manufacturing and commercial city, ✻ of Haute-Vienne dept., W cen. France, on Vienne river 110 m. NE of Bordeaux; pop. (1968c) 132,935; chief seat of porcelain industry in France (begun 1736); also produces leather goods, paper, furniture, precision tools, textiles; printing and meat-packing; as important center of enamel art work, which flourished here in 12th cent., produced series of artists noted for paintings in enamel; univ. (1808, suppressed 1840; reopened 1965); 13th cent. Romanesque-Gothic cathedral; old fortified city walls converted into promenades; meteorological observatory. Gallic tribal capital; destroyed 5th cent. A.D., and two separate towns developed by 9th century (merged 1792); stormed and sacked by English 1370.

Li·mon \'li-'mōn\. Village near N coast of Leyte I., Phil., ab 31 m. W of Tacloban; scene of severe fighting during American invasion, captured by Americans Nov. 23, 1944.

Li·món \li-'mòn\. 1 Province of E cen. Costa Rica. See table at COSTA RICA.

2 City. See PUERTO LIMÓN.

Limon Bay \li-'mòn-\ *or Span.* **Ba·hía de Limón** \bə-,hē-ə-,dā-\. Inlet of the Caribbean Sea, at the N end of the Panama Canal, in the Canal Zone.

Limonum. See POITIERS.

Li·mou·sin \,lē-mə-'zaⁿ, ,lim-ə-'zēn\. Historical region of cen. France; a plateau bounded anciently on N by Marche, E by Auvergne, S by Guienne, W by Angoumois, NW by Poitou; ✻ Limoges.

History: Inhabited by ancient Gallic tribe of Lemovices; conquered by Romans; devastated by Normans 9th cent. A.D.; part of Aquitaine and included in dowry given by Eleanor of Aquitaine to Henry II of England on her marriage to him 1152; captured by Philip Augustus 1208; given 1259 to Henry III of England who renounced claims to Normandy, Maine, and Poitou; in Hundred Years' War ceded to English by Treaty of Brétigny 1360 but regained by French 1370–74; viscountship passed to Albret family in 15th cent.; returned to the French crown under Henry IV and was province of France until Revolution.

Li·moux \lē-'mü\. Commune, Aude dept., S France; pop. (1968c) 10,824; produces wine.

Lim·pio \'lim-pē-,ō\. Town, a suburb of Asunción, in Central dept., S Paraguay; pop. (1970e) 11,918.

Lim·po·po \lim-'pō-(,)pō\ *or* **Croc·o·dile** \'kräk-ə-,dīl\. River, SE Africa; ab. 1100 m. long; rises near Johannesburg in Transvaal prov., Rep. of South Africa, flows N and NE, forming the NW and N boundary of the Transvaal, turns SE across S Mozambique and empties into Indian Ocean. Both its entire course and its headstream sometimes called the Crocodile.

Lin. See LI 1.

Li·na·pa·can \,lē-nə-'päk-än\. Island, Palawan prov., Phil., N of Palawan I. in the channel connecting Sulu Sea with South China Sea; 40 sq. m.; chief barrio San Miguel on NE coast.

Linard, Piz. See SILVRETTA.

Li·na·res \li-'när-əs\. 1 Province of S cen. Chile. See table at CHILE.

2 City, its ✻, ab. 173 m. S of Santiago; pop. (1966c) 31,878; trading and distributing center in agricultural region.

3 Town, Nuevo León state, NE Mexico, on railroad 75 m. SE of Monterrey; munic. pop. (1970p) 49,397.

4 Mining commune, Jaén prov., S Spain, 24 m. N of Jaén; pop. (1970p) 50,516; center of lead mining; produces mining equipment and explosives. Carthaginians defeated nearby by Scipio Africanus 208 B.C.

Lin–ch'ing *also* **Lin–tsing** \'lin-'chiŋ\. City, W Shantung prov., NE China, on the Grand Canal NW of Tsinan.

Lin–ch'uan *or* **Lin·chwan** \'lin-chə-'wän, 'linch-'wän\. City, E cen. Kiangsi prov., SE China, S of P'o-yang lake and ab. 55 m. SE of Nan-ch'ang.

Lin·coln \'liŋ-kən\. 1 Name of a parish in Louisiana and of counties in twenty-three states of the U.S. See tables at ARKANSAS, COLORADO, GEORGIA, IDAHO, KANSAS, KENTUCKY, LOUISIANA, MAINE, MINNESOTA, MISSISSIPPI, MISSOURI, MONTANA, NEBRASKA, NEVADA, NEW MEXICO, NORTH CAROLINA, OKLAHOMA, OREGON, SOUTH DAKOTA, TENNESSEE, WASHINGTON, WEST VIRGINIA, WISCONSIN, WYOMING.

2 City, Placer co., E California, 25 m. N of Sacramento; pop. (1970c) 3176; fruit canning; clay pits; dairy and fruit farms.

3 City, ⊗ of Logan co., cen. Illinois, 30 m. NNE of Springfield; pop. (1970c) 17,582; in agricultural and coal-mining region; ships dairy products; glassware, clothing, electrical equipment; Lincoln Coll. (1865), Lincoln Christian Coll. (1944); founded 1853.

4 *or* **Lincoln Center.** City, ⊗ of Lincoln co., cen. Kansas, on Saline river 32 m. WNW of Salina; pop. (1970c) 1582; flour mill; stock and dairy farms.

5 Town, Penobscot co., E cen. Maine, 42 m. N of Bangor; pop. (1970c) 4759; paper; truck farms.

6 Town, Middlesex co., NE Massachusetts, 13 m. WNW of Boston; pop. (1970c) 7567; agriculture.
7 City, ✱ of Nebraska and ✱ of Lancaster co., SE Nebraska, 52 m. WSW of Omaha; pop. (1970c) 149,518; railroad junction and commercial center; produces plumbing supplies, agricultural machinery, office equipment, pharmaceuticals, dairy and meat products; flour mills, grain elevators, railroad shops; Univ. of Nebraska (1867), Nebraska Wesleyan Univ. (1887), Union Coll. (1891). Originally called Lancaster; chosen state capital 1867 and renamed after Abraham Lincoln; incorporated 1869; home of William Jennings Bryan 1887–1921.
8 Town, Grafton co., W New Hampshire, 18 m. SSE of Littleton; pop. (1970c) 1341; summer resort.
9 Town, Providence co., N Rhode Island, ab. 9 m. SE of Woonsocket; pop. (1970c) 16,182; administrative center Lonsdale village (*q.v.*); taken from Smithfield and incorporated 1871; includes several villages; limestone quarries.
10 County, Ontario, Canada. See table at ONTARIO.
11 County in England. See LINCOLNSHIRE 2.
12 *or anc.* **Lin·dum** \ˈlin-dəm\. City and county borough, ⊗ of Parts of Lindsey, Lincolnshire, E England, on the Witham 39 m. ESE of Sheffield; pop. (1971p) 74,207; market for agricultural area; diesel engines, automobile parts, pumps, agricultural machinery; cathedral, built bet. 1075 and 1501; site of Roman, Saxon, Danish settlements, and of castle built by William the Conqueror in 1068; received first charter 1157.

Lincoln, Mount. 1 Peak, Park co., cen. Colorado; 14,286 ft.; highest peak of Park Range of the Rocky Mts.
2 Peak in the Franconia Mts., N Grafton co., N cen. New Hampshire; 5018 ft.
3 Peak in E Addison co., W Vermont; 4013 ft.

Lincoln Heights. City, Hamilton co., SW Ohio, N of Cincinnati; pop. (1970c) 6099.

Lincoln Highway. Former highway from New York City to San Francisco, California; 3332 m. long; laid out 1913, completed 1927; now a local name for sections of the route still in use.

Lincoln Park. 1 Residential city, Wayne co., SE Michigan, 9 m. SW of Detroit; pop. (1970c) 52,984; became city 1925.
2 Borough, Morris co., N New Jersey, 7 m. W of Paterson; pop. (1970c) 9034.

Lincoln Sea. Part of Arctic Ocean N of Ellesmere I. and Greenland, 82° to 85°N; connects by Robeson and Kennedy channels with Kane Basin and Baffin Bay.

Lin·coln·shire \ˈliŋ-kən-ˌshi(ə)r, -shər\. 1 Village, Lake co., NE Illinois, 25 m. NW of Chicago; pop. (1970c) 2531.
2 *or* **Lincoln.** Maritime county, E England; area 2662 sq. m.; pop. (1971p) 808,384; comprising three administrative counties: the Parts of Holland, 418 sq. m., pop. 105,643, ⊗ Boston; the Parts of Kesteven, 734 sq. m., pop. 232,215, ⊗ Sleaford; the Parts of Lindsey, 1510 sq. m., pop. 470,526, ⊗ Lincoln; chief rivers Trent and Witham; fisheries along the coast, agriculture (esp. barley, wheat, oats, potatoes, cattle and pigs) inland; industries include iron and steel, chemicals, fertilizer, building materials, and agricultural machinery; main towns incl. Grimsby, Lincoln, Grantham, Louth, Stamford.

Lin·coln·ton \ˈliŋ-kən-tən\. 1 Town, ⊗ of Lincoln co., E Georgia; pop. (1970c) 1442; clothing; agriculture.
2 Town, ⊗ of Lincoln co., SW cen. North Carolina, 15 m. NNW of Gastonia; pop. (1970c) 5293; flour, cotton yarn, furniture; agriculture.

Lincoln Tunnel. Vehicular tunnel under the Hudson river from Manhattan I., New York City, to Weehawken, New Jersey; 8216 ft. long; south tube opened 1937, north tube 1945.

Lin·coln·wood \ˈliŋ-kən-ˌwu̇d\. Village, Cook co., NE Illinois, N of Chicago; pop. (1970c) 12,929.

l'Incudine, Mont. See INCUDINE, MONT L'.

Lin·dau \ˈlin-ˌdau̇\ *also* **Lindau im Bo·den·see** \-im-ˈbōd-ᵊn-ˌzā\. City, Bavaria, West Germany, partly on island in Lake Constance 25 m. ESE of Konstanz; pop. (1969e) 26,283; Renaissance town hall, 10th cent. church; resort; trade center for agricultural and dairy products.

Lin·den \ˈlin-dən\. 1 Town, ⊗ of Marengo co., W Alabama; pop. (1970c) 2697; sawmills; agriculture.
2 Industrial city, Union co., NE New Jersey, 4 m. SSW of and adjoining Elizabeth; pop. (1970c) 41,409; chemicals, paints, machine tools, automobiles, petroleum products, beverages; site settled early 18th century; four villages consolidated into township 1861; became city 1924.
3 Town, ⊗ of Perry co., W Tennessee; pop. (1970c) 1062.
4 Town, ⊗ of Cass co., NE Texas; pop. (1970c) 2264.

Linden Harbour. Inlet of Solomon Sea on S coast of New Britain I., Bismarck Archipelago, W Pacific Ocean, E of Gasmata; good harbor.

Lin·den·hurst \ˈlin-dən-ˌhərst\. 1 Village, Lake co., NE Illinois, 10 m. W of Waukegan; pop. (1970c) 3141.
2 Industrial village, Suffolk co., SE New York, on Long I., on Great South Bay 35 m. E of New York City; pop. (1970c) 28,338; lumber, paper, chemicals, electrical equipment.

Lin·den·wold \ˈlin-dən-ˌwōld\. Borough, Camden co., SW New Jersey, 12 m. SSE of Camden; pop. (1970c) 12,199; plastics, plumbing fixtures; meat-packing plant.

Lin·des·nes \ˈlin-də-ˌsnās\ *or* **The Naze** \-ˈnāz\. Cape on S extremity of Norway, projecting into the North Sea, 58°N, 7°02′E.

Lin·di \ˈlin-dē\. 1 River, NE Zaire; ab. 375 m. long; rises W of Lake Edward, flows NW and then curves toward the S; enters the Congo at Kisangani.
2 Seaport, Tanzania, at mouth of Lukuledi river; pop. (1967e) 13,352.

Lindisfarne. See HOLY ISLAND.

Lind Lakes \ˈlind-\. Village, Anoka co., E Minnesota, 12 m. N of St. Paul; pop. (1970c) 3692.

Lin·dos \ˈlin-ˌdäs, -dəs\ *or anc.* **Lin·dus** \ˈlin-dəs\. Town on E coast of Rhodes off SW Turkey; ancient city, one of the Pentapolis of Asia Minor.

Lind·say \ˈlin-zē\. 1 City, Tulare co., S cen. California, 52 m. SE of Fresno; pop. (1970c) 5206; fruit and vegetable packing; grows citrus fruit and olives.
2 City, Garvin co., S cen. Oklahoma, on Washita river 27 m. SE of Chickasha; pop. (1970c) 3705; oil wells.
3 Town, ⊗ of Victoria co., SE Ontario, Canada, on Scugog river 24 m. W of Peterborough; pop. (1971p) 12,705; market center in grain and livestock region; summer resort; textiles, boats, patent medicines, lumber.

Lindsay, Mount. Mountain in Macpherson Range bet. Queensland and New South Wales, Australia, near coast; 4064 ft.

Linds·borg \ˈlinz-ˌbərg\. City, McPherson co., cen. Kansas, on Smoky Hill river 20 m. S of Salina; pop. (1970c) 2764; trade center in grain and stock farming area; Bethany Coll. (1881).

Lind·sey, Mount \-ˈlin-zē\ *or formerly* **Old Baldy Peak** \-ˈbȯl-dē-\. Mountain, Costilla co., Colorado; 14,125 ft.

Lindsey, The Parts of. See LINCOLNSHIRE 2.

Lindum. See LINCOLN 12.

Lindus. See LINDOS.

Línea, La. See LA LÍNEA.

Line Islands \ˈlīn-\. Group of islands in cen. Pacific Ocean S of the Hawaiian Is., N and S of the equator, extending from Kingman Reef at 6°24′N, 162°22′W to Flint I., 11°26′S, 151°48′W; Jarvis, Kingman Reef, and Palmyra I. belong to U.S.; Washington I., Fanning I., and Christmas I., N of the equator, 158 sq. m., pop. (1968p) 1180, are attached to British colony of Gilbert and Ellice Islands; S of the equator Malden, Starbuck, Caroline, Vostok, and Flint, 40 sq. m., are in area claimed by both Great Britain and United States.

Lin–fen \ˈlin-ˈfən\. Town, S cen. Shansi prov., NE China, 140 m. SSW of T'ai-yüan.

Lin·ga·yen \ˌliŋ-gä-ˈyen\. Municipality, ✱ of Pangasinan prov., Luzon, Phil., in N part, on S shore of Lingayen Gulf W of Dagupan (terminus of railroad to Manila); pop.

(1969e) 62,200; one of chief cities of Luzon and important since early times; situated on an island in the Agno delta. Landing place of the Japanese forces in their invasion of Dec. 1941 and also of American forces in Jan. 1945.

Lingayen Gulf. Large inlet of South China Sea on NW coast of Luzon, Phil.; ab. 35 m. long and 23 m. across its entrance from Santiago I. to San Fernando Point; affords good anchorage for large number of vessels. Borders on La Union prov. on E and on Pangasinan on S and W and receives Agno river. Lingayen, Dagupan, San Fabian, and Sual are chief ports of Pangasinan on its shores. Scene of major naval and landing operations by Japanese Dec. 1941 and by Americans Jan. 1945.

Lingeh. See BANDAR-E LENGEH.

Ling·en \'liŋ-ən\ *also* **Lingen an der Ems** \-ˌän-də-'remz, -'rem(p)s\. City, Lower Saxony, West Germany, on Ems river 42 m. NNW of Münster; pop. (1969e) 26,013; textiles, sausage; cattle market; oil refining; founded 13th cent.

Ling·ga \'liŋ-gə\. Chief island of the Lingga Archipelago, Indonesia; 40 m. long; 360 sq. m.

Lingga Archipelago. Island group off the E coast of Sumatra, in Indonesia, S of Riau Archipelago; 841 sq. m. Comprises Lingga I. and Singkep I. and many small islands, mainly of coral growth and in shallow water; separated from Sumatra by Berhala Strait.

Ling·ga·dja·ti \ˌliŋ-gə-'jät-ē\. Town, N coast of Java, a suburb of Tjirebon; agreement bet. Dutch and representatives of Republic of Indonesia initialed here Nov. 15, 1946.

Ling–ling \'liŋ-'liŋ\. Town, S Hunan prov., SE cen. China, on Hsiang river and on the Kue-lin to Heng-yang highway; in World War II American air base, seized by Japanese Sept. 7, 1944.

Ling·mell \'liŋ-ˌmel\. Mountain, Cumberland co., NW England, 9 m. SW of Keswick, in the Lake District; 2649 ft.

Lingones. See LANGRES.

Lin·gua·glos·sa \ˌlēŋ-gwä-'glȯs-ə\. Commune, Catania prov., E Sicily, Italy, just N of Mt. Etna; pop. (1968e) 6084.

Linguetta, Cape. See GJUHËZËS, CAPE.

Li·nha·res \lēn-'yär-ish\. Municipality, Espírito Santo state, E Brazil, ab. 70 m. NNE of Vitória; pop. (1968e) 88,305.

Lin–i \'lin-'ē\ *or formerly* **Ichow** \'ē-'jō\. Town, SW Shantung prov., NE China, on small stream E of the Grand Canal.

Lin·kö·ping \'lin-ˌchə(r)p-iŋ\. City, ⊗ of Östergötland co., SE Sweden, near S shore of Lake Roxen 110 m. SW of Stockholm; pop. (1970e) 80,767; railroad junction; aircraft, automobiles, tobacco, textiles, rope; college (1967); 12th–15th cent. cathedral; 13th cent. castle; bishop's see established c. 1100; in 1598 scene of victory of Vasas over Sigismund III of Poland, assuring Vasa and Protestant succession in Sweden.

Lin·lith·gow \lin-'lith-(ˌ)gō\. 1 County in Scotland. See WEST LOTHIAN.

2 Burgh, ⊗ of West Lothian co., SE Scotland; pop. (1971p) 4412; market town; ruins of palace, residence of Scottish kings and birthplace of James V of Scotland and Mary, Queen of Scots.

Linlithgowshire. See WEST LOTHIAN.

Linn \'lin\. 1 Name of counties in four states of the U.S. See tables at IOWA, KANSAS, MISSOURI, OREGON.

2 City, ⊗ of Osage co., cen. Missouri, ESE of Jefferson City; pop. (1970c) 1289; diversified agriculture.

Lin·nan·saa·ri National Park \'lin-ən-ˌsär-ē-\. National park, SE Finland; ab. 3 sq. m.; consists of about 20 islands in Lake Haukivesi; rare plants; established 1956.

Lin·ne·us \'lin-ē-əs\. City, ⊗ of Linn co., N Missouri; pop. (1970c) 400.

Linn·he, Loch \'läk-'lin-ē, 'läk-\. Inlet of Atlantic Ocean on W coast of Scotland, extending NE 20 m. from the head of the Firth of Lorn, in Argyll co.

Li·no·sa \li-'nō-sə\ *or anc.* **Ae·gu·sa** \i-'gyü-sə\. One of the Pelagian Is. (*q.v.*), N of Lampedusa; taken by Allies June 13, 1943.

Lins \'lēⁿs\. City, W cen. São Paulo state, SE Brazil, on railroad 230 m. WNW of São Paulo; munic. pop. (1968c) 56,601; coffee, lumber.

Lintfort. See KAMP-LINTFORT.

Linth \'lint\. River, E cen. Switzerland; ab. 26 m. long; rises in S Glarus canton, flows N into W end of Lake Wallen; as the **Linth Canal** it connects Lake Wallen with the Lake of Zurich; the Limmat, flowing from the Lake of Zurich to the Aare, is sometimes considered as the lower course of the Linth.

Lin·ton \'lint-ᵊn\. 1 City, Greene co., SW Indiana, 32 m. SSE of Terre Haute; pop. (1970c) 5450; machine shops, coal mines; agriculture.

2 City, ⊗ of Emmons co., S North Dakota, 46 m. SSE of Bismarck; pop. (1970c) 1695; grain and dairy farming.

Lin–tsing. See LIN-CH'ING.

Lin·wood \'lin-ˌwu̇d\. City, Atlantic co., SE New Jersey, 8 m. W of Atlantic City; pop. (1970c) 6159.

Linyu. See SHAN-HAI-KUAN.

Linz \'lin(t)s, 'linz\ *or anc.* **Len·tia** \'len-ch(ē-)ə\. Commercial and manufacturing city, ✱ of Upper Austria, on Danube river 95 m. W of Vienna; pop. (1971p) 204,600; railroad junction; river port; steel, nitrates, machinery, electrical equipment, tobacco products; school of social sciences and economics (1962); cultural center, with two cathedrals, episcopal palace, town hall. Developed from Roman camp 1st cent. A.D.; important trade center by 13th cent. but without civic rights; suffered considerable damage in World War II; occupied by U.S. troops May 6, 1945.

Li·ons, Gulf of \-'lī-ənz\ *or Fr.* **Golfe du Lion** \gȯlf-dūē-lyōⁿ\ *or anc.* **Si·nus Gal·li·cus** \ˌsī-nəs-'gal-i-kəs\. Inlet of Mediterranean Sea on S coast of France, extending from peninsula of Giens, near Hyères, E of Marseilles, to Cape Creus on NE coast of Spain.

Li·pa \li-'pä\. Chartered city, E cen. Batangas prov., Luzon, Phil., E of Lake Taal, 15 m. N of Batangas; pop. (1970e) 96,500; second largest town in province, an active inland trade center.

Lípa, Česká. See ČESKÁ LÍPA.

Lip·a·ri Islands \ˌlip-ə-rē-\ *or Ital.* **Iso·le Eo·lie** \'ē-zə-ˌlā-ā-'ō-lē-ˌā\ *or anc.* **Ae·o·li·ae In·su·lae** \ē-'ō-lē-ˌē-'in(t)-sə-ˌlē\. Group of small volcanic islands in the SE Tyrrhenian Sea off N coast of Messina prov., Sicily, Italy; 44 sq. m.; pop. (1961c) 13,774; includes the islands Salina, Vulcano, Stromboli, and the chief island **Lipari** (*or anc.* **Lip·a·ra** \'lip-ə-rə\), 13 sq. m., on which is located the town of **Lipari.** According to legend, the island on which Aeolus kept the winds confined in caves was one of this group. Inhabited since Neolithic times; held successively by Greeks, Carthaginians, Romans, Saracens, Normans, and Aragonese.

Li·petsk \'lē-ˌpetsk\. Town, ✱ of Lipetsk Oblast, Russian S.F.S.R., U.S.S.R., 65 m. N of Voronezh; pop. (1970p) 290,000; food processing; iron pipe and castings, tractors, chemicals, cement; founded by Peter the Great as iron-working center 1707.

Lipetsk Oblast \-'ō-bləst, -ˌblast\. Subdivision of the Russian S.F.S.R., U.S.S.R.; 9305 sq. m.; pop. (1970p) 1,224,000; ✱ Lipetsk; rye, wheat; iron ore; formed 1954.

Lip·no \'lēp-(ˌ)nō, 'lip-\. Commune, Bydgoszcz prov., N cen. Poland, 87 m. NW of Warsaw; pop. (1968e) 11,100; agriculture.

Lip·pe \'lip-ə\. 1 River, West Germany; 147 m. long; rises in the Teutoburger Wald and flows W in North Rhine-Westphalia into Rhine river at Wesel.

2 Former German state, now part of North Rhine-Westphalia, West Germany, bet. Teutoburger Wald and Weser river; 469 sq. m.; ✱ Detmold. Originally settled by

the Cherusci, a German tribe, whose leader Arminius defeated the Romans at Teutoburger Wald in 9 A.D.; appeared as separate state in 12th cent.; became principality of Holy Roman Empire 1720; in Confederation of Rhine 1807, Germanic Confederation 1815–66; joined North German Confederation 1867; became republic 1918; lost sovereign rights to Reich 1933–35; incorporated 1947 in North Rhine-Westphalia state.

Lipp·stadt \ˈlip-ˌs(h)tät\. Industrial city, North Rhine-Westphalia, West Germany, on Lippe river 38 m. SE of Münster; pop. (1969e) 41,860; furniture, textiles; 12th and 13th cent. churches; founded 1168; member of Hanseatic League; sold to Prussia 1850.

Lips·comb \ˈlip-skəm\. 1 County in Texas. See table at TEXAS.

2 City, Jefferson co., cen. Alabama, 8 m. SW of Birmingham; pop. (1970c) 3223.

3 Village, ⊗ of Lipscomb co., NW Texas.

Lipsia. See LEIPZIG 2.

Lip·sos \ˈlip-ˌsäs\ *or Gk.* **Lip·sós** \ˌlēp-ˈsȯs\; *Ital.* **Lis·so** \ˈlē-(ˌ)sō\ *or* **Lip·so** \ˈlēp-(ˌ)sō\. An island of the Dodecanese (*q.v.*) N of Leros and E of Patmos; 7 sq. m.

Lip·tov·ský Mi·ku·láš \ˌlip-tȯf-skē-ˈmik-u̇-ˌläsh\ *or Hung.* **Lip·tó·szent·mi·klós** \ˈlip-(ˌ)tō-sent-ˈmik-ˌlōsh\. Town, Slovak S.R., E cen. Czechoslovakia, on the Váh river E of Ružomberok; pop. (1968e) 15,280.

Li·ra \ˈlir-ə\. Town, N Uganda, E Africa, N of Lake Kyoga.

Li·ri \ˈlir-ē\ *or anc.* **Li·ris** \ˈlī-rəs\. River, cen. Italy; ab. 100 m. long; rises near Avezzano E of Rome, flows SE bet. parallel ranges of cen. Apennine Mts. and forms valley of the Liri; joined by the Sacco near Frosinone and farther E near Cassino by the Rapido after which it turns S to enter Gulf of Gaeta (Tyrrhenian Sea) near Minturno; its lower course also known as the Garigliano. In World War II its valley invaded by Allies May 1944 after fighting Feb.–Mar. in effort to take Cassino (*q.v.*), key point on the Gustav Line, which barred Allied advance on Rome.

Lis. See LIZ.

Lis·boa \lēzh-ˈvō-ə\. 1 District of W Portugal. See table at PORTUGAL.

2 City, Portugal. See LISBON 6.

Lis·bon \ˈliz-bən\. 1 Town, New London co., SE Connecticut; pop. (1970c) 2808.

2 Town, Androscoggin co., SW Maine, 8 m. SE of Lewiston; pop. (1970c) 6544.

3 Manufacturing town, Grafton co., W New Hampshire, 9 m. SW of Littleton; pop. (1970c) 1480; summer and winter sports; township includes **Sug·ar Hill** \ˌshu̇g-ər-\, a hilltop settlement, center of Millerism in 19th cent.

4 City, ⊗ of Ransom co., SE North Dakota, 38 m. SSE of Valley City; pop. (1970c) 2090; grain and dairy farms.

5 Village, ⊗ of Columbiana co., E Ohio, 23 m. S of Youngstown; pop. (1970c) 3521; leather goods; clay pits; agriculture. Site of Morgan's surrender 1863 nearby.

6 *or Port.* **Lis·boa** \lēzh-ˈvō-ə\; *anc.* **Olis·i·po** \ō-ˈlis-ə-ˌpō\ *also* **Fe·lic·i·tas Ju·lia** \fə-ˌlis-ə-tas-ˈjül-yə\. Seaport city, ✱ of Portugal and of Lisboa dist., W Portugal; pop. (1970p) 782,266; Portugal's leading seaport; exports olive oil, timber, wine, and fish; manufactures textiles, soap, flour, steel; sugar refining, shipbuilding; oil refining; Univ. of Lisbon (1911), Technical Univ. of Lisbon (1930); built on terraced hills; ancient fortress, cathedral (former Moorish mosque), two aqueducts, Ajuda palace, castle of St. George; birthplace of Camões.

History: Ancient Iberian settlement; held by Phoenicians and Carthaginians; became Roman municipium; captured by Visigoths and 716 by Moors; reconquered 1147 by Portuguese; sacked by Castile in 14th cent. wars; during period of Portuguese voyages and colonial expansion, flourished as a leading European commercial center; began to lose prosperity at end of 16th cent.; held by Spain 1580–1640; devastated by earthquake 1755 with loss of life exceeding 50,000; occupied by French 1807–08. See PORTUGAL.

Lis·burn \ˈliz-bərn\. Municipal borough, co. Antrim, NE Northern Ireland, on Lagan river 8 m. SW of Belfast; pop. (1971p) 28,904; market town; a center of linen industry; 17th cent. Protestant cathedral.

Lis·burne, Cape \-ˈliz-bərn\. Cape on NW coast of Alaska, on Chukchi Sea.

Lis·can·nor Bay \lis-ˌkan-ər-\. Inlet of Atlantic Ocean on W coast of Eire, S of Galway Bay.

Li–shui \ˈlē-ˈshwā\ *or formerly* **Chu·chow** \ˈchü-ˈjō\. City, S cen. Chekiang prov., E China, ab. 55 m. WNW of Wenchou. Scene of fighting bet. Chinese and Japanese 1942.

Lis·i·an·ski \ˌlis-ē-ˈan(t)-skē\. Islet of Leeward Is., Hawaiian Is., in cen. Pacific Ocean 860 m. NW of Niihau I.; included in Hawaiian Islands Bird Reservation. Discovered 1805.

Li·si·chansk \ˌlis-i-ˈchänsk\. Town, Voroshilovgrad Oblast, Ukrainian S.S.R., U.S.S.R., ab. 45 m. WNW of Voroshilovgrad, on the Donets river; pop. (1970p) 117,000.

Li·sieux \lēz-ˈyə(r)\ *or anc.* **No·vi·om·a·gus** \ˌnō-vē-ˈäm-ə-gəs\. City, Calvados dept., NW France, 27 m. E of Caen; pop. (1968c) 23,830; cattle market, breweries; machinery, plywood; 12th–16th cent. cathedral. Named for its ancient inhabitants, the Lexovii; captured by Caesar; taken subsequently by Normans 877 A.D., Bretons 1130, Geoffrey Plantagenet 1141; episcopal see until Revolution; heavily damaged in World War II. St. Thérèse, the Little Flower, lived in Carmelite convent here.

Lis·kamm \ˈlis-ˌkäm\. Mountain in Alps, on Swiss-Italian border; 14,852 ft.

Lis·keard \lis-ˈkärd\. Town and municipal borough, Cornwall, SW England, WNW of Plymouth; pop. (1971p) 5255; nearby are the hurlers, prehistoric stone circles. An important manor in 11th cent., made a free borough 1240.

Liski. See GEORGIU-DEZH.

Lisle \ˈlīl\. 1 Village, Du Page co., NE Illinois, ab. 5 m. S of Wheaton; pop. (1970c) 5329; diversified agriculture; St. Procopius Coll. (1887).

2 *or* **L'Isle** \ˈlēl, ˈlīl\. City, France. See LILLE.

L'Is·let \lē-ˈlā, -ˈle\. County, Quebec, Canada. See table at QUEBEC.

Lis·more \ˈliz-ˌmō(ə)r, -ˌmȯ(ə)r\. Town and river port, NE New South Wales, SE Australia, 100 m. S of Brisbane; pop. (1968e) 20,040; dairying; sugarcane.

Lismore \liz-ˈmō(ə)r, -ˈmȯ(ə)r\. Island at entrance to Loch Linnhe, Argyll co., W Scotland; 9½ m. long; site of remains of a castle and a cathedral.

Lissa. 1 Commune, Poland. See LESZNO.

2 Island, Yugoslavia. See VIS.

Lisso. See LIPSOS.

Lis·so·ne \lē-ˈsō-nē\. Commune, Milano prov., Lombardy, N Italy, 7 m. N of Milan; pop. (1968e) 28,716.

Lissus. See LESH 2.

Lis·ter, Mount \-ˈlis-tər\. Mountain, Antarctica, 78°04′S, 162°41′E; 13,205 ft.

Lister og Mandals. See VEST-AGDER.

List Land \ˈlist-ˌlänt\. Northern part of the island of Sylt, off W coast of Schleswig-Holstein, West Germany.

Lis·tow·el \lis-ˈtō-əl\. 1 Industrial town, Perth co., SE Ontario, Canada, 26 m. N of Stratford; pop. (1971p) 4677; woolen mills; dairy farming.

2 Market town and urban district, N co. Kerry, SW Eire; pop. (1971p) 3019; remains of old castle.

Li·su·land \ˈlē-sü-ˌland\. Name given to region of NW Yunnan in S China, inhabited in part by the Chinese tribe Lisu; lies in the very mountainous country (peaks 12,000 to 25,000 ft.) cut by the four great rivers of SE Asia—the Yangtze, Mekong, Salween, and Irrawady.

Li·ta·ni \li-ˈtän-ē\ *or Arab.* **Nahr al–Lī·ta·nī** \ˌnär-al-li-ˈtän-ē\. River, S Lebanon; 90 m. long; rises near Baalbek, flows S bet. the Lebanon and Anti-Lebanon mountain ranges, turns SW and empties into Mediterranean Sea 6 m. N of Tyre.

Litch·field \ˈlich-ˌfēld\. 1 County in Connecticut. See table at CONNECTICUT.

2 Town, cen. Litchfield co., NW Connecticut; pop. (1970c) 7399; summer resort; agriculture; manufactures electrical devices; Wisdom Coll. (1958); incorporated 1719; important trading center and strategic military depot in Colonial and Revolutionary times; site of first law school in America (1782); birthplace of Ethan Allen, Henry Ward Beecher, and Harriet Beecher Stowe. Includes borough of Litchfield.

3 City, Montgomery co., S cen. Illinois, 45 m. S of Springfield; pop. (1970c) 7190; clothing, paper products; dairy farming.

4 City, ⊗ of Meeker co., S cen. Minnesota, 35 m. SSW of St. Cloud; pop. (1970c) 5262; summer resort; butter, sausage, woolens; dairy and poultry farms.

Lith·er·land \'lith-ər-lənd\. Urban district, Lancashire, NW England, 4½ m. N of Liverpool; pop. (1971p) 23,670.

Lith·gow \'lith-(ˌ)gō\. Town, E New South Wales, SE Australia, 65 m. WNW of Sydney; pop. (1968e) 12,710; industrial community in extensive coal region; iron and steel foundries and mills, small-arms factory, pipe works, chemical and textile factories; first steelworks established 1875.

Li·tho·nia \li-'thō-nē-ə\. City, De Kalb co., NW cen. Georgia, 16 m. E of Atlanta; pop. (1970c) 2270; clothing; dairy and poultry farms.

Lith·u·a·ni·an Soviet Socialist Republic \ˌlith-(y)ə-'wā-nē-ən-, -nyən-\ *also* **Lith·u·a·nia** \-nē-ə, -nyə\ *or Lith.* **Lie·tu·va** \lye-'tü-və\ *or Russ.* **Lit·va** \'l(y)ēt-vä\. A constituent republic of the U.S.S.R., bounded on N by Latvian S.S.R., on E and SE by Belorussian S.S.R., on SW by Poland and Kaliningrad Oblast, Russian S.F.S.R., and on W by Baltic Sea; 25,174 sq. m.; pop. (1970p) 3,129,000; ✱ Vilnius. Mostly low-lying land with many lakes and swamps; highest point is not above 1000 ft.; crossed in S part by Neman river (*Lithuanian,* Nemunas); also drained in N by upper courses of Venta and Lielupe; has only ab. 15 m. of coast on the Baltic; lacks good port. *Chief products:* Rye, barley; livestock; food processing; textiles, machine tools, agricultural machinery. *Chief towns:* Vilnius, Kaunas, Klaipėda.

History: Region occupied before 12th cent. by pagan Lithuanians; their attack on Poles caused latter to seek aid of Teutonic Knights; united as grand duchy to oppose the Teutonic Order ab. 1250; expanded 1316–40 by Gediminas into large state including Polotsk, Minsk, and region W of mid-Dnieper; under Algirdas (d. 1377) domain extended along Dnieper to Black Sea; by marriage of Jagello to Jadwiga of Poland formed personal union 1386 with Poland (*q.v.*); became predominantly Roman Catholic; merged with Poland by Union of Lublin 1569; acquired by Russia in three partitions of Poland 1772, 1793, 1795; administered by Russia separately from Poland; joined Polish revolt 1863; demanded self-government 1905; occupied by Germans during World War I; proclaimed independent republic Feb. 16, 1918; recognized by U.S.S.R. 1920; seizure of Vilnius (*q.v.*) by Poland 1920 caused rupture of relations which lasted 1922–38; joined League of Nations 1921; invaded Memel (Klaipėda) 1923; military coup d'état 1926; forced by Polish ultimatum to reestablish relations 1938; Memel taken by Germany and Vilnius by U.S.S.R. 1939; signed mutual assistance pact with U.S.S.R. which prepared way for annexation Aug. 3, 1940 as Lithuanian S.S.R.; overrun by German army 1941; recovered by U.S.S.R. 1944; incorporation in U.S.S.R. not recognized by United States.

Lit·itz \'lit-əts\. Industrial borough, Lancaster co., SE Pennsylvania, 8 m. N of Lancaster; pop. (1970c) 7072; shoes, clothing, chocolate, cigars, paper products; founded by Moravians 1757.

Li·to·mě·ři·ce \'lit-ə-ˌmyer-zhət-ˌsä\ *or Ger.* **Leit·me·ritz** \'līt-mə-ˌrits\. Town, Czech S.R., W Czechoslovakia, on the Labe (Elbe) river at head of steamer navigation, 35 m. NNW of Prague; pop. (1968e) 18,894; manufacturing and commercial center in agricultural region; 17th cent. cathedral.

Lit·tle \'lit-ᵊl\. 1 River, E North Carolina; 80 m. long; rises in Wake co., flows SE into Neuse river near Goldsboro.

2 River, Oklahoma and Arkansas; ab. 150 m. long; rises in Le Flore co., SE Oklahoma, flows S, then E across Arkansas border to empty into Red river on SW boundary of Hempstead co., SW Arkansas.

Little Abaco. See ABACO.

Little Alföld. See ALFÖLD.

Little America. Settlement of the Byrd Antarctic Expedition (1928–30) near the outer edge of Ross Ice Shelf on Bay of Whales, Ross Sea, Antarctica; used also as base of Byrd's second expedition (1933–35), by later explorers, and by Byrd's expedition of 1946–47.

Little Andaman. One of the Andaman Is. (*q.v.*).

Little Ar·me·nia \-är-'mē-nē-ə, -nyə\ *or* **Lesser Armenia.** Medieval feudal kingdom, 13th and 14th cents., of Armenians in Cilicia (*q.v.*); few Armenians survived Turkish massacres.

Little Atlas. See ATLAS MOUNTAINS.

Little Bahama Bank. See BAHAMA BANKS.

Little Bald \-'bȯld\. Peak in Unicoi co., NE Tennessee; 5000 ft.

Little Barrier Island. Small island off E coast of N extension of North I., New Zealand, in entrance to Hauraki Gulf.

Little Bear Peak \-'ba(ə)r-, -'be(ə)r-\. Mountain, Costilla co., S Colorado; 14,037 ft.

Little Belt. Strait bet. Fyn I. and the mainland of Denmark, connecting the Kattegat with the Baltic Sea; 30 m. long, varies from ab. 700 yds. to 18 m. in width. See GREAT BELT.

Little Belt Mountains. A range of the Rocky Mts. in cen. Montana, chiefly in Cascade and Judith Basin cos.

Little Big·horn \-'big-ˌhȯ(ə)rn\ *also* **Little Horn.** River, S Montana; ab. 90 m. long; rises in N Wyoming, flows N through Big Horn co., S Montana, into Bighorn river; on its banks Gen. Custer and his command were defeated and slain by Indians June 25, 1876; site of battle now Custer Battlefield National Monument (see UNITED STATES, *National Monuments*).

Little Bitter Lake. See BITTER LAKES.

Little Blue. River, Nebraska and Kansas; rises in S Nebraska and flows SE across Kansas border into Big Blue river below Marysville, Marshall co., NE Kansas.

Lit·tle·bor·ough \'lit-ᵊl-ˌbər-ə, -ˌbə-rə, -b(ə-)rə\. Urban district, Lancashire, NW England, on the Roch 13 m. NE of Manchester; pop. (1969e) 11,100.

Little Bras d'Or. See BRAS D'OR.

Little Car·pa·thi·an Mountains \-kär-'pāth-ē-ən-\ *also* **Little Carpathians** \-ənz\ *or Czech* **Ma·lé Kar·paty** \ˌmäl-ā-kär-'pät-ē\. Mountain range, a SW extension of the Carpathian Mts., Slovak S.R., Czechoslovakia, N of Bratislava; highest point ab. 2500 ft.

Little Cayman. See CAYMAN ISLANDS.

Little Chief Mountain \-'chēf-\. Peak in Glacier National Park, NW Montana; 9552 ft.

Little Chute \-ˌshüt\. Village, Outagamie co., E Wisconsin, on rapids in Fox river 8 m. E of Appleton; pop. (1970c) 5365; dairying.

Little Co·co \-'kō-(ˌ)kō\. Small island of the Andaman Is., separated from North Andaman I. by Coco Channel.

Little Col·o·ra·do \-ˌkäl-ə-'rad-(ˌ)ō, -'räd-\. River, NE Arizona; 315 m. long; rises in S Apache co., flows NW into the Colorado river on E edge of Grand Canyon National Park.

Little Comp·ton \-'käm(p)-tən\. Town, Newport co., SE Rhode Island, 8 m. E of Newport; pop. (1970c) 2385; agriculture.

Little Corn Island. See CORN ISLANDS.

Little Creek Peak. Mountain, E Iron co., SW Utah; 10,142 ft.
Little Cumbrae Island. See CUMBRAES, THE.
Little Current. Town, Manitoulin dist., S Ontario, Canada, on N Manitoulin I. bet. Georgian Bay and North Channel; pop. (1971p) 1559; summer resort; fisheries; poultry farms.
Little Cuyahoga River. See CUYAHOGA 1.
Little Diomede. See DIOMEDE ISLANDS.
Little Dunmow. See DUNMOW.
Little Egg Harbor. Inlet of Barnegat Bay, on SE coast of Ocean co., E New Jersey.
Little Egg Inlet. Narrow strait, on extreme S tip of Ocean co., E New Jersey, leading from Atlantic Ocean into Great Bay.
Little Elobey. See ELOBEY.
Little Exuma. See EXUMA.
Little Falls. 1 City, ⊗ of Morrison co., cen. Minnesota, on Mississippi river 25 m. S of Brainerd; pop. (1970c) 7467; market and trade center in agricultural region.
2 Township, Passaic co., N New Jersey, on Passaic river 5 m. SW of Paterson; pop. (1970c) 11,727.
3 City, Herkimer co., NE cen. New York, 20 m. E of Utica; pop. (1970c) 7629; knit goods, textiles, paper products, dairy machinery; dairy farms. Settled c. 1725; burned by Tories and Indians 1782; incorporated as city 1895. The Mohawk river near here passes through **Little Falls Gorge** and falls ab. 45 ft. in one mile of its course.
Little Ferry. Borough, Bergen co., NE New Jersey, on Hackensack river 9 m. N of Jersey City; pop. (1970c) 9042; carpets, ornamental iron products.
Lit·tle·field \ˈlit-ᵊl-ˌfēld\. City, ⊗ of Lamb co., NW Texas, in the panhandle, 33 m. NW of Lubbock; pop. (1970c) 6738; cotton gins; ships livestock, grain, vegetables.
Little Fork. River, N Minnesota; ab. 132 m. long; rises in N cen. St. Louis co., flows NW into Rainy river on United States-Canada boundary.
Lit·tle·hamp·ton \ˈlit-ᵊl-ˌham(p)-tən\. Urban district, West Sussex, S England, on the coast at the mouth of the Arun river; pop. (1971p) 18,621; seaside resort.
Little Hay·stack Mountain \-ˈhā-ˌstak-\. Peak in the Adirondack Mts., Essex co., NE New York; 4700 ft.
Little Horn. See LITTLE BIGHORN.
Little Inagua. See INAGUA.
Little Jay Peak \-ˈjā-\. Mountain, NW Orleans co., N Vermont; 3202 ft.
Little Kai Island. See KAI ISLANDS.
Little Ka·na·wha \-kə-ˈnȯ-(w)ə, -ˈnȯ-ē\. River, cen. and W West Virginia; ab. 160 m. long; rises in S Upshur co., flows W and NW into Ohio river at Parkersburgh; navigable by small boats for 48 m.
Little Kapela. See KAPELA, GREAT and LITTLE KAPELA.
Little Karroo. See KARROO.
Little Lake. Lake on boundary bet. Jefferson and Lafourche parishes, SE Louisiana.
Little Le·ver \-ˈlē-vər\. Urban district, Lancashire, NW England, 3 m. SE of Bolton; pop. (1971p) 9124.
Little Loch Broom. See BROOM, LOCH.
Little Lyakhov. See LYAKHOV ISLANDS.
Little Mi·ami \-mī-ˈam-ē\. River, Ohio; ab. 140 m. long; rises in Clark co., flows S to Ohio river just E of Cincinnati.
Little Minch \-ˈminch\. Strait off NW coast of Scotland, extending bet. Skye I. of the Inner Hebrides and the cen. islands of the Outer Hebrides; varies in width bet. 14 and 20 m.
Little Miquelon. See MIQUELON ISLAND.
Little Mis·sou·ri \-mə-ˈzu̇(ə)r-ē, -ˈzu̇r-ə\. 1 River, Arkansas; ab. 150 m. long; rises in Pike co. and flows SE into the Ouachita river.
2 River, NW United States; 560 m. long; flows from NE Wyoming NE across SE corner of Montana and NW corner of South Dakota into North Dakota, and continuing N into McKenzie co., where it turns E to empty into Missouri river in NE Dunn co., W North Dakota.
Little Monadnock. See MONADNOCK, MOUNT.
Little Moose Mountain \-ˈmüs-\. Peak in Adirondack Mts., Hamilton co., NE cen. New York; 3630 ft.
Little Namaqualand. See NAMAQUALAND.
Little Neck Bay. Inlet of Long Island Sound, Queens borough, W Long I.; formerly source of saddle-rock oysters and littleneck clams, beds condemned 1909 because of pollution of the water.
Little Nemaha. See NEMAHA.
Little Nethe. See NETHE.
Little Nicobar. One of the Nicobar Is. (*q.v.*).
Little Paternosters. See BALABALAGAN ISLANDS.
Little Peconic Bay. See PECONIC BAY.
Little Pee Dee \-ˈpē-ˌdē\. River, North Carolina and South Carolina; 145 m. long; flows from Scotland co., S North Carolina, S across South Carolina border into Pee Dee river near its mouth.
Little Pow·der \-ˈpau̇d-ər\. River, Wyoming and Montana; 100 m. long; flows from cen. Campbell co., NE Wyoming, N into Powder river in Powder River co., SE Montana.
Little Quemoy. See QUEMOY.
Little Rann of Kutch. See KUTCH, RANN OF.
Little Red. River, Arkansas; ab. 120 m. long; formed by two branches in Van Buren co., flows SE into the White river on E boundary of White co., E Arkansas.
Little River. 1 Rivers, United States. See LITTLE.
2 County in Arkansas. See table at ARKANSAS.
Lit·tle Rock \ˈlit-ᵊl-ˌräk\. City, ✱ of Arkansas and ⊗ of Pulaski co., cen. Arkansas, on S bank of the Arkansas river; pop. (1970c) 132,483; largest city in the state; clothing, electrical equipment, furniture, lumber, paper products, plastic pipe, cottonseed products; sawmills, railroad shop; bauxite mines, marble quarries; center of cotton and grain-farming region; Arkansas Baptist Coll. (1884); Philander Smith Coll. (1868). Founded 1821 and made territorial capital same year; state capital on admission of Arkansas to the Union 1836; incorporated as city 1835; in Civil War occupied by Union forces September, 1863; in 1957 federal troops sent to city to prevent interference by state authorities with school desegregation.
Little Ross \-ˈrȯs\. Small island off S coast of Kirkcudbright co., S Scotland; E of entrance to Wigtown Bay; lighthouse.
Little Russia. Former area with indefinite boundaries including Carpathian Ruthenia (see TRANSCARPATHIAN OBLAST), E Poland, Ukraine (now Ukrainian S.S.R.), and W shores of Black Sea; inhabited chiefly by Ukrainians, who were also called Little Russians or Ruthenians.
Little Sa·ble Point \-ˈsā-bəl-\. Point on W coast of Oceana co., W Michigan, extending into Lake Michigan.
Little Saint Bernard. Alpine pass. See ALPS.
Little Sal·ke·hatch·ie \-ˌsȯl-kə-ˈhach-ē\. River, South Carolina; ab. 50 m. long; rises in Bamberg co., flows SE to unite with Salkehatchie river and form Combahee river.
Little Sandy. River, NE Kentucky; 45 m. long; rises in S Elliott co., flows NE into the Ohio river in NE Greenup co.
Little Sark. See SARK 1.
Little Sa·tilla \-sə-ˈtil-ə\. River, SE Georgia; ab. 60 m. long; rises in Jeff Davis co., flows SE into Satilla river in Brantley co.
Little Scheidegg. See SCHEIDEGG.
Little Schütt. See SZIGETKÖZ.
Little Sil·ver \-ˈsil-vər\. Borough, Monmouth co., E cen. New Jersey, SE of Perth Amboy; pop. (1970c) 6010.
Little Sioux \-ˈsü\. River, Minnesota and Iowa; 221 m. long; flows from Jackson co., S Minnesota, S into Missouri river in W Harrison co., W Iowa.
Little Skel·lig \-ˈskel-ig\. See SKELLIGS.
Lit·tles·town \ˈlitᵊlz-ˌtau̇n\. Borough, Adams co., S Pennsylvania, near Maryland border 25 m. SW of York; pop. (1970c) 3026.
Little Ten·nes·see \-ˌten-ə-ˈsē, -ˈten-ə-ˌsē\. River, S United States; ab. 150 m. long; rises near N boundary of Georgia and flows N through Macon co., SW North Carolina, N and W across Tennessee border, and into Tennessee river

in Loudon co., E Tennessee. In its course in North Carolina near Tennessee border is Fontana Dam, one of the dams of the Tennessee Valley Authority (*q.v.*).

Little Tibet. See BALTISTAN.

Little To·ba·go \-tə-ˈbā-(ˌ)gō\. Island in Atlantic Ocean off NE coast of Tobago; 1 sq. m.

Lit·tle·ton \ˈlit-ᵊl-tən\. 1 Town, ⊗ of Arapahoe co., NE cen. Colorado, 8 m. S of Denver; pop. (1970c) 26,466; residential; trucks, explosives, electronic equipment, precision instruments; Arapahoe Junior Coll. (1965).

2 Town, Middlesex co., NE Massachusetts, 12 m. SW of Lowell; pop. (1970c) 6380; dairy and poultry farms.

3 Town, Grafton co., W New Hampshire, 30 m. WSW of Berlin; pop. (1970c) 5290; summer and winter resort; shoes; dairy farms; active in antislavery movement.

Little Tra·verse Bay \-ˈtrav-ərs-\. Inlet of Lake Michigan on SW coast of Emmet co., N Michigan.

Little Tupper Lake. See TUPPER LAKES.

Little Valley. Village, ⊗ of Cattaraugus co., SW New York; pop. (1970c) 1340.

Little Wa·bash \-ˈwȯ-ˌbash\. River, Illinois; ab. 200 m. long; rises in Coles co., flows SE into the Wabash river 8 m. from its mouth.

Little Walachia. See OLTENIA.

Little Zab. See ZAB.

Little Zimbabwe. See ZIMBABWE.

Littoria. See LATINA.

Litva. See LITHUANIAN SOVIET SOCIALIST REPUBLIC.

Lit·ví·nov \lit-ˈvē-nȯf\. Town, Czech S.R., W Czechoslovakia, ab. 50 m. NW of Prague; pop. (1968e) 23,129.

Litz·mann·stadt \ˈlits-män-ˌs(h)tät\. German name of ŁÓDŹ during World War II. See ŁÓDŹ 2.

Liu–Kung \lē-ˈü-ˈgu̇ŋ\. See WEI-HAI.

Li·vad·ia \li-ˈvad-ē-ə\. 1 Commune, Greece. See LEBADEA.

2 Suburb of Yalta, Crimean Oblast, Ukrainian S.S.R., U.S.S.R.; residence of former emperors; buildings now used as Soviet sanitariums, hotels, etc.

Live·ly \ˈlīv-lē\. Town, Ontario, Canada, ab. 10 m. SW of Sudbury; pop. (1971p) 2988.

Li·ven·za \li-ˈven(t)-sə\. River, Veneto, NE Italy, N of Piave river; 70 m. long; flows from the Alps SE into Adriatic Sea.

Live Oak \ˈlīv-ˌōk\. 1 County in Texas. See table at TEXAS.

2 City, Sutter co., N cen. California, 45 m. N of Sacramento; pop. (1970c) 2645; machine shops; diversified agriculture.

3 City, ⊗ of Suwannee co., N Florida, 62 m. NW of Gainesville; pop. (1970c) 6830; pulpwood, fertilizer; livestock, tobacco, watermelons.

4 City, Bexar co., S cen. Texas; pop. (1970c) 2779.

Liv·er·more \ˈliv-ər-ˌmō(ə)r, -ˌmȯ(ə)r\. 1 City, Alameda co., W California, 23 m. E of San Francisco Bay; pop. (1970c) 37,703; steel pipe; wineries.

2 City, McLean co., W Kentucky, 18 m. S of Owensboro; pop. (1970c) 1594; furniture.

Livermore, Mount *or* **Baldy Peak** \ˌbȯl-dē-\. Mountain, Jeff Davis co., W Texas, one of Davis Mts.; 8382 ft.

Livermore Falls. Town, Androscoggin co., SW Maine, 26 m. N of Lewiston; pop. (1970c) 3450; paper, gloves; dairy and poultry farms.

Liv·er·pool \ˈliv-ər-ˌpül\. 1 Village, Onondaga co., cen. New York, 5 m. N of Syracuse; pop. (1970c) 3307; dairy and truck farms.

2 Municipality within the Sydney met. area, E New South Wales, SE Australia; pop. (1966c) 60,552.

3 Town, ⊗ of Queens co., SW Nova Scotia, Canada, on Atlantic Ocean 74 m. SW of Halifax; pop. (1971p) 3610; paper, lumber, iron castings; fisheries; truck farms. Founded 1759 by New England settlers; base of operations for British privateers during American Revolution and War of 1812.

4 County borough and city, Lancashire, NW England, on the Mersey river estuary; pop. (1971p) 606,834; port, second only to London in commercial importance; extensive docks; manufactures diesel and jet engines, electronic equipment, rubber, chemicals, soap, vegetable oils; oil and sugar refining, shipbuilding and repairing; the cathedral (begun 1904) is the largest in England; town hall (opened 1754), University of Liverpool (1903). First colonized by Norsemen late 8th cent.; received first charter 1207; developed rapidly as major Atlantic port from mid-18th cent.; suffered heavy damage from German bombing in World War II.

Liverpool Range. Mountains, NE New South Wales, SE Australia; highest point Oxleys Peak 4500 ft.; extends W from Great Dividing Range, SW of New England Plateau.

Liv·ing·ston \ˈliv-iŋ-stən\. 1 Name of a parish in Louisiana and of counties in five states of the U.S. See tables at ILLINOIS, KENTUCKY, LOUISIANA, MICHIGAN, MISSOURI, NEW YORK.

2 Town, ⊗ of Sumter co., W Alabama; pop. (1970c) 2358; beans, cotton; Livingston Univ. (1840).

3 City, Merced co., cen. California, 14 m. NW of Merced; pop. (1970c) 2588; grapes, peaches, almonds.

4 Village, ⊗ of Livingston parish, SE Louisiana, 27 m. E of Baton Rouge; pop. (1970c) 1398.

5 City, ⊗ of Park co., S Montana, 95 m. SE of Helena; pop. (1970c) 6883; tourist center; marble and granite quarries; livestock raising.

6 Township, Essex co., NE New Jersey, 9 m. NW of Newark; pop. (1970c) 30,127; in dairy, poultry, and truck-farming region.

7 Town, ⊗ of Overton co., N Tennessee, 20 m. NNE of Cookeville; pop. (1970c) 3050; flour, lumber; tobacco.

8 Town, ⊗ of Polk co., E Texas, 45 m. SSW of Lufkin; pop. (1970c) 3965; truck and poultry farms.

Li·ving·ston \ˈliv-iŋ-stən\. Port, Izabal dept., E Guatemala, on Amatique Bay 14 m. NW of Puerto Barrios; munic. pop. (1964p) 11,592; bananas, coffee.

Liv·ing·stone \ˈliv-iŋ-stən\. 1 Island in center of Victoria Falls, Zambezi river, bet. Zambia and Rhodesia.

2 Town, S Zambia, near Victoria Falls on Zambezi river 250 m. WNW of Bulawayo; pop. (1967e) 41,000; marketing and distribution center; established 1905; capital of Northern Rhodesia 1907–35.

Livingstone Falls. Name of a number of rapids in Congo (*q.v.*) river between Matadi and Kinshasa; total drop 876 ft.

Livingstone Mountains. Range on NE border of Lake Nyasa, S Tanzania, E Africa; highest point ab. 7000 ft.

Livingston Island. Island, W end of South Shetland Is., British Antarctic Territory, on S side of Drake Passage, 62°36′S, 60°30′W; 37 m. long by 5 to 19 m. wide; discovered 1819.

Liv·ny \ˈliv-nē\. Town, SE Orel Oblast, Russian S.F.S.R., U.S.S.R., 28 m. SW of Yelets; pop. (1967e) 34,000.

Li·vo·nia \lə-ˈvō-nē-ə, -nyə\. City, Wayne co., SE Michigan, W of Detroit; pop. (1970c) 110,109; automobile parts, tools and dies, paint; Madonna Coll. (1937), Schoolcraft Coll. (1961).

Livonia *or* **Liv·land** \ˈliv-ˌland, -lənd\ *or Russ.* **Li·vo·ni·ya** \liv-ˈȯ-nē-(y)ə\. Former government in Russia's Baltic Provinces in region E of the Baltic Sea, now included in Latvian and Estonian S.S.Rs., U.S.S.R. Inhabited originally by Livs, a Finnish people, neighbors of the Letts and Esths; in 13th cent. conquered and converted to Christianity by Livonian Brothers of the Sword, who in 1237 united with Teutonic Knights; eastern expansion and Christianization continued through 14th and 15th cents.; region disputed by Poland, Sweden, and Russia in Livonian War 1557–82; except for Tartu, which Russia took, became Polish 1561 and grand master of former order became duke of Kurland (*q.v.*); conquered by Gustavus Adolphus of Sweden 1629 and cession confirmed by Treaty of Oliva 1660. Ceded to Russia 1721 (as result of Great Northern War); freed from Russia, N part became part of Estonia and S part joined to Latvia 1918.

Li·vor·no \lē-'vȯr-(,)nō\. 1 Province of Tuscany, Italy. See table at ITALY.
2 Seaport commune, Italy. See LEGHORN.

Livramento. See SANTANA DO LIVRAMENTO.

Li·vry–Gar·gan \lēv-'rē-gär-'gäⁿ\. Commune, Seine-Saint-Denis dept., N France, ENE suburb of Paris; pop. (1968c) 32,063; agricultural machinery.

Li·wung \'lē-,wu̇ŋ\ *or Du.* **Tji·li·wong** \'chi-lē-,vȯŋ\. River, W Java, Indonesia; ab. 50 m. long; rises on N slopes of Mt. Pangrango and flows N to Djakarta Bay at Djakarta.

Lixus. See LARACHE.

Liyepaya. See LIEPĀJA.

Liz *or* **Lis** \'lēsh\. River, cen. Portugal; flows N near Leira, then W into Atlantic Ocean.

Liz·ard, The \-'liz-ərd\. Peninsula, S Cornwall, SE England, extending S from Helston and Helford river; its S end is extreme S point of Great Britain, **Lizard Point** or **Lizard Head,** 49°56'N, 5°13'W (186 ft. high); lighthouses and signal station for ships.

Ljubelj. See LOIBL.

Lju·blja·na *also* **Lyu·blya·na** \lē-,ü-blē-'än-ə, lē-'ü-blē-ə-,nä\ *or Ger.* **Lai·bach** \'lī-,bäk\ *or anc.* **Emo·na** \i-mō-nə\. City, ✱ of Slovenia, NW Yugoslavia, on Sava river ab. 75 m. WNW of Zagreb; pop. (1971p) 173,530; railroad, industrial, and commercial center; manufactures machinery, textiles, footwear, soap, furniture, bricks, tobacco products; univ. (1595), cathedral, museum, art gallery.

History: Ancient city of Emona founded by Augustus 34 B.C.; besieged by Alaric 400 A.D. and left in ruins by the Huns 451. Became part of Carinthia 12th cent.; came under rule of Hapsburgs 1277; received civic rights 1320; capital of Illyrian Provinces 1809–13; capital of kingdom of Illyria 1816–49; meeting place 1821 of a congress of European powers (Congress of Laibach) which authorized Austria to use force to crush liberal revolutionary movements in Italy; to Yugoslavia 1918.

Ljung·an \'yəŋ-,än\. River, Västernorrland co., E Sweden; 217 m. long; flows SE to the Gulf of Bothnia near Sundsvall.

Ljus·nan \'yüs-,nän\. River, cen. Sweden; 267 m. long; rises on Norway border and flows SE into the Gulf of Bothnia S of Söderhamn.

Llan·ber·is \(h)lan-'ber-əs\. Village and parish, Caernarvonshire, NW Wales, S of Bangor near the foot of Mt. Snowdon; pop. (1961c) 2373; at entrance to the **Pass of Llanberis,** 1169 ft., narrow, rocky defile.

Llan·daff \'(h)lan-,daf, (h)lan-'dav\. Suburb of Cardiff, Glamorganshire, SE Wales; cathedral.

Llan·do·ve·ry \(h)lan-'dəv-rē\. Municipal borough, Carmarthenshire, S Wales, NE of Carmarthen; pop. (1971p) 1999; sawmills; tourist center; remains of 12th cent. Norman castle; school, founded 1848; noted for printing press in early 19th cent.

Llan·drin·dod Wells \(h)lan-,drin-,däd-'welz\. Urban district, Radnorshire, E Wales; pop. (1971p) 3379; mineral springs; health resort.

Llan·dud·no \(h)lan-'did-(,)nō, -'dəd-\. Urban district, NE Caernarvonshire, NW Wales; pop. (1971p) 19,009; on the small peninsula terminating in Great Ormes Head; seaside resort.

Lla·nel·ly \(h)la-'nel-ē\. Municipal borough and commercial seaport, Carmarthenshire, S Wales; pop. (1971p) 26,320; steel and tin-plate mills, chemical plants, potteries; incorporated 1913.

Lla·ne·ra \lä-'nār-ə, yä-\. Commune, Oviedo prov., NW Spain, 6 m. from Oviedo; pop. (1970p) 10,099; fruits, vegetables, coal.

Lla·nes \'lä-nās, 'yä-\. Seaport commune, Oviedo prov., NW Spain, on Bay of Biscay 58 m. ENE of Oviedo; pop. (1970p) 15,509; large coastal trade; fish-salting works; 14th cent. Gothic cathedral.

Llan·fair \'(h)lan-,fa(ə)r, -,fe(ə)r\ *or* **Llan·fair·pwll·gwyn·gyll** \-pül-'gwin-gəl\. Village, SE Anglesey I., NW Wales, on Menai Strait; pop. (1961c) 992; its full name (variously spelled) has 54 to 58 letters.

Llan·gef·ni \(h)lan-'gev-nē\. Urban district, Anglesey, NW Wales; pop. (1971p) 3949.

Llan·gol·len \(h)lan-'gäl-ən\. Town and urban district, SE Denbighshire, N Wales; dist. pop. (1971p) 3108; summer resort; manufactures flannel; since 1946 home of the international musical Eisteddfod.

Llan·id·loes \(h)lan-'id-,lȯis\. Town and municipal borough, Montgomeryshire, cen. Wales, on the Severn; pop. (1971p) 2333; market center for an agricultural region; was center for lead-mining district (esp. 1860–80), and manufactured shawls and tweeds until 1918.

Llano \'lan-(,)ō\. 1 River, cen. Texas; 100 m. long; formed in Kimble co. by union of North and South Llano rivers; flows E into Colorado river on E boundary of Llano co.
2 County in Texas. See table at TEXAS.
3 City, ⊗ of Llano co., cen. Texas, on Llano river 62 m. NW of Austin; pop. (1970c) 2608; resort; chemical plant; livestock raising.

Lla·no de la Mag·da·le·na \'lan-ō-,del-ə-,mäg-də-'len-ə, 'län-, 'yän-\. Extensive plain in SW Baja California, NW Mexico.

Llano Es·ta·ca·do \,lan-(,)ō-,es-tə-'käd-(,)ō, län-\ *or* **Staked Plain** \'stākt-\. Extensive plateau, SE New Mexico, W Texas, and NW Oklahoma; ab. 35,000 sq. m.; grazing; wheat; oil and natural gas.

Lla·nos \'lan-(,)ōz, 'län-; 'yän-(,)ōs\. Vast plains in N South America; drained by the Orinoco river and its tributaries; ab. 225,000 sq. m. (approx. 125,000 sq. m. in Venezuela, 100,000 in Colombia); cattle raising; sparsely populated.

Llan·qui·hue \läŋ-'kē-(,)wā, yäŋ-\. Province of S cen. Chile. See table at CHILE.

Llanquihue, Lake. Lake, Llanquihue prov., S cen. Chile, just N of Puerto Montt; 22 m. long by 15 m. wide; ab. 240 sq. m.

Llan·twit Ma·jor \,lan-twit-'mā-jər\. Village and parish, S Glamorganshire, SE Wales, on Bristol Channel; parish pop. (1961c) 1504; site of monastery, famous as a school, estab. 6th cent. by St. Illtyd, a native of Brittany; church of St. Illtyd, with remains of early Celtic Christianity; ruins of a Roman villa.

Llerena, Point. See LLORONA, POINT.

Llew·el·lyn Park \lü-,el-ən-\. Suburb of West Orange, New Jersey.

Lleyn Peninsula *or* **Lleyn Promontory** \'(h)līn-\. Headland extending SW into St. George's Channel from NW coast of Wales; 28 m. long, average width 6½ m.; encloses Cardigan Bay on N.

Llo·bre·gat \,(l)yō-bri-'gät\. River, NE Spain; 98 m. long; flows S into Mediterranean Sea 3 m. S of Barcelona.

Llo·ro·na, Point \-(l)yȯr-'ōn-ə\ *or formerly* **Point Lle·re·na** \-(l)yer-\. Cape on W coast of Osa Penin., S Costa Rica.

Lloyd Harbor \,lȯid-\. Village, Suffolk co., SE New York, 6 m. E of Northport; pop. (1970c) 3371.

Lloyd·min·ster \'lȯid-,min(t)-stər\. City, Canada, on Alberta-Saskatchewan border 82 m. WNW of North Battleford; pop. (1971p) 8542; feed mill, gas and oil wells; grain and livestock farms; headquarters of "all-British" colony established 1903.

Lloyd Shoals Reservoir \'lȯid-'shōlz-\. Reservoir in NW Jasper co., cen. Georgia; ab. 4½ sq. m.; formed by dam (built 1910) in Ocmulgee river.

Llu·llai·lla·co \,yü-,yī-'yäk-(,)ō\. Volcano in Andes Mts., N Chile, just W of Argentina boundary; 22,057 ft.

Llw·chwr \'lü-kər\ *or* **Lou·ghor** \'lək-ər\. Urban district, Glamorganshire, SE Wales; pop. (1971p) 26,845; steel and tin-plate works.

Lo. See MUSTANG.

Loa \'lō-ə\. 1 Town, ⊗ of Wayne co., S cen. Utah; pop. (1970c) 324.

2 River, Antofagasta prov., N Chile; ab. 275 m. long; flows into the Pacific Ocean.

Loanda. See LUANDA.

Lo·an·ge \lō-'aŋ-gə\ *or Port.* **Lu·an·gue** \lü-'aŋ-gə\. River in the Congo basin, S cen. Africa; ab. 425 m. long; rises in NE cen. Angola, flows N into Kasai river in SW Zaire; forms boundary bet. Bandundu and Kasai-Occidental provs.

Lo·an·go \lō-'aŋ-(,)gō\. 1 Former African kingdom N of Congo river, part of the ancient kingdom of Congo.

2 Seaport, S Congo, equatorial Africa, ab. 100 m. N of the mouth of the Congo river.

Loangwa. See LUANGWA.

Lo·a·no \lō-'än-(,)ō\. Commune, Savona prov., Liguria, NW Italy, on Italian Riviera 17 m. SW of Savona; pop. (1968e) 11,605; scene of victory of French over Austrians Nov. 23–24, 1795.

Lö·bau \'lər-,baù\. Industrial city, Dresden dist., East Germany, 40 m. E of Dresden; pop. (1970e) 17,820; textiles, shoes, rubber goods, sugar.

Lo·bi·to \lō-'bēt-(,)ō\. Seaport on **Lobito Bay,** W cen. Angola; pop. (1969e) 97,758; road and railway center; airport; shipbuilding, metalworking, food processing; grain, fruit, sisal, coconuts, peanuts; founded 1843.

Lo·bos \'lō-,bōs, -,bōz, -bəs\. Island in Gulf of Mexico off coast of N Veracruz state, Mexico.

Lobos, Cape. Cape on coast of W cen. Sonora state, Mexico, extending into the Gulf of California.

Lobos, Cay *or* **Lobos Cay.** Small island of S Bahama Is., separated by Old Bahama Channel from NE cen. Cuba; lighthouse (estab. 1860).

Lobos, Point. 1 Point, San Francisco, California, on S side of entrance to Golden Gate.

2 Promontory, Monterey co., California, on Carmel Bay SW of Carmel; state park.

Lobos Islands *also* **Seal Islands** \'sē(ə)l-\. Two groups of small islands in Pacific Ocean off N coast of Peru, including **Lobos de Tie·rra** \-də-'tyer-ə\ and **Lobos de Afue·ra** \-,dā-ə-'fwer-ə\; guano deposits.

Lobositz. See LOVOSICE.

Lob·stick Lake \,läb-stik-\. Large lake of irregular shape, W Labrador, Canada, SE of Dyke Lake; forms part of course of Churchill river.

Loburi. See LOP BURI.

Lo·car·no \lō-'kär-(,)nō\ *or Ger.* **Lug·ga·rus** \lə-'gär-əs\. Commune, Ticino canton, SE cen. Switzerland, on N shore of Lake Maggiore 11 m. W of Bellinzona; pop. (1970c) 14,143; winter and health resort; site of old castle of dukes of Milan (now government buildings).

History: First mentioned 749 A.D.; passed to dukes of Milan 1342; taken by Swiss 1512; part of former Swiss canton of Lugano 1798–1803; scene of signing Dec. 1, 1925 of Locarno Pact, a series of five treaties and arbitration conventions bet. Germany, on the one hand, and Belgium, France, Great Britain, Italy, Poland, and Czechoslovakia on the other, designed to guarantee the continuation of peace and existing territorial boundaries.

Loch·a·ber \lä-'käb-ər, -'kab-\. Mountainous district in S Inverness co., NW Scotland, at W end of the Grampians and NE of Loch Linnhe; includes Ben Nevis.

Loch·ar Moss \,läk-ər-'mòs\. Tract of moorland, Dumfries co., S Scotland; ab. 10 m. long.

Loches \'lōsh\. Town, Indre-et-Loire dept., W cen. France, 25 m. SE of Tours; pop. (1962c) 4526; numerous medieval buildings including castle of counts of Anjou.

Loch·gel·ly \läk-'gel-e\. Burgh, Fife co., E Scotland, W of Kirkcaldy; pop. (1971p) 7982; ironworks, collieries.

Loch·gilp·head \läk-'gilp-(,)hed\. Burgh, ⊗ of Argyll co., W Scotland, at head of arm of Firth of Clyde 15 m. N of Greenock; parish pop. (1971p) 1184; herring fishing.

Loch·ma·ben \läk-'māb-ən\. Royal burgh and parish, Dumfries co., S Scotland, 8 m. NE of Dumfries; pop. (1971p) 1262; several lakes in district; resort; ruins of castle; associated with Robert Bruce.

Lochy, Loch \-'läk-ē\. Lake, Inverness co., N cen. Scotland; 10 m. long; forms part of Caledonian Canal.

Locke, Mount \-'läk\. Peak in Davis Mts., Jeff Davis co., W Texas; 6791 ft.; on its top McDonald Observatory, opened May 5, 1939.

Lock·hart \'läk-,(h)ärt\. City, ⊗ of Caldwell co., S cen. Texas, 29 m. S of Austin; pop. (1970c) 6489; clothing, furniture; corn, watermelons.

Lock Ha·ven \läk-'hā-vən\. City, ⊗ of Clinton co., cen. Pennsylvania, on West Branch of Susquehanna river 25 m. WSW of Williamsport; pop. (1970c) 11,427; light aircraft, paper, silk, brick; diversified agriculture; Lock Haven State Coll. (1870); settled 1769; lumber center in 19th cent.

Lock·land \'läk-lənd\. City, Hamilton co., SW corner of Ohio, 9 m. N of Cincinnati; pop. (1970c) 5288; paper products, jet engines, soap, machine tools.

Lock·port \'läk-pō(ə)rt, -pò(ə)rt\. 1 City, Will co., NE Illinois, 30 m. SW of Chicago; pop. (1970c) 9985; site of a lock and dam marking the end of the Chicago Sanitary and Ship Canal in the Illinois Waterway system; oil refinery, grain elevator; Lewis Coll. (1930).

2 Manufacturing city, ⊗ of Niagara co., W New York, 20 m. ENE of Niagara Falls; pop. (1970c) 25,399; on N.Y. State Barge Canal; automobile parts, flour, pulp and paper, textiles, glass, brass and bronze products; in Niagara fruit-growing region; settled 1816, incorporated 1865.

Locle, Le. See LE LOCLE.

Lo·cri \'lō-,krī, 'läk-,rī\. Ancient city in Magna Graecia, on E coast of SW extremity of Italy; founded ab. 680 B.C.; the Locrian code, framed by Zaleucus, said to be earliest written system of Greek legislation.

Lo·cris \'lō-krəs, 'läk-rəs\. Region in cen. part of ancient Greece, comprising: **Eastern Locris,** divided into two parts: **Locris Ep·ic·ne·mid·ia** \-,ep-i(k)-nə-'mid-ē-ə\ along S shore of Gulf of Maliakós extending E from Pass of Thermopylae and bordering on Malis, Doris, and Phocis; separated by narrow strip of Phocis from **Locris Opun·tia** \-ō-'pən-ch(ē-)ə\ on Euboean Sea (*mod.* Atalante channel) opp. Euboea, E of Phocis and N of Boeotia; chief town Opus. **Western Locris,** *or* **Locris Oz·o·lis** \-'äz-ə-ləs\, mountainous region along N shore of strait joining Gulfs of Calydon (*mod.* Gulf of Patras) and Corinth, S of Aetolia and W of Phocis; chief town Amphissa. Locrians were probably early inhabitants of Greece, long subject to Phocians.

Loc·sin \lōk-'sin\. Municipality, E Albay prov., Luzon, Phil., on railroad 2 m. W of Legaspi; pop. (1969e) 57,500.

Lo·cust Grove \,lō-kəst-\. Urban community (unincorporated), Nassau co., SE New York, on Long I.; pop. (1970c) 11,626.

Locust Mountain. Ridge in Schuylkill co., E cen. Pennsylvania; contains rich coal deposits.

Lod \'lōd\ *also* **Lyd·da** \'lid-ə\. City, Israel, 23 m. NW of Jerusalem; pop. (1970e) 29,300; aircraft, electronic equipment. The ancient city, (*1 Chron.* viii. 12), in Judaea in the Plain of Sharon, had long history; visited by Peter (*Acts* ix. 32); destroyed by Romans 66 and 68 A.D.; rebuilt and became a bishopric; by some supposed to be birthplace of St. George, patron saint of England; destroyed by Saladin 1191 and rebuilt by Richard of England.

Lo·de·lin·sart \,lōd-lan-'sär\. Commune, Hainaut prov., SW Belgium, N suburb of Charleroi; pop. (1969e) 10,656.

Lo·dève \lō-'dev\ *or anc.* **Lu·te·va** \lü-'tē-və\. Commune, N Hérault dept., S France, in S Cévennes; pop. (1962c) 7234; cathedral, founded 950. Dates from pre-Roman times.

Lodge·pole Creek \ˌläj-pōl-\. River, SE Wyoming and W Nebraska; 212 m. long; flows E into South Platte river near Nebraska-Colorado boundary.

Lo·di \ˈlō-ˌdī\. 1 City, San Joaquin co., cen. California, 12 m. N of Stockton; pop. (1970c) 28,691; packs and ships fruit; wine, olive oil, canned fruits and vegetables; vineyards and fruit orchards.

2 Industrial borough, Bergen co., NE corner of New Jersey, 5 m. SE of Paterson; pop. (1970c) 25,213; chemicals, dyes, plastics; Immaculate Conception Junior Coll. (1923).

Lodi \ˈlȯd-(ˌ)ē\. Manufacturing commune, Milano prov., Lombardy, N Italy, on Adda river 20 m. SE of Milan; pop. (1968e) 42,757; center of dairy industry; ceramics, wrought iron; 12th cent. cathedral; episcopal palace. Built 1158 by Barbarossa 4 m. from the ancient Lodi destroyed by the Milanese in 1111; scene of defeat of Austrians by Napoleon May 10, 1796.

Lod·o·me·ria \ˌläd-ə-ˈmir-ē-ə\. Principality of 12th and 13th cents. in Volhynia—also known as **Vlad·i·mir in Vol·hyn·ia** \ˈvlad-ə-ˌmi(ə)r . . . väl-ˈ(h)in-ē-ə, vlə-ˈdē-ˌmi(ə)r-\; joined with Halicz in 13th cent. to become part of Poland and later (1772) a division of Galicia. See VLADIMIR-VOLYNSK 1.

Lo·dore \lə-ˈdō(ə)r, -ˈdȯ(ə)r\. Waterfall in the Lake District, Cumberland, NW England, near head of Derwent Water.

Łódź \ˈlüj, ˈlädz\ *or Russ.* **Lodz** \ˈlȯts(-yə)\. 1 Province of cen. Poland. See table at POLAND.

2 Industrial city, its ✱, ab. 75 m. WSW of Warsaw; 83 sq. m.; pop. (1970p) 762,000; textile center (esp. cotton); episcopal see; univ. (1945), technical univ. (1945). Before World War I belonged to Russians, who in 19th cent. developed it from small village into large industrial city; occupied by Germans Nov. 11–25, 1914 after severe fighting; became part of Poland 1918; in World War II occupied by Germans Sept. 1939.

Loei *or* **Loey** \ˈlȯi\. 1 Province, N Thailand; 4222 sq. m.; pop. (1960c) 210,335; ✱ Loei.

2 Town, its ✱, 20 m. S of the Mekong 90 m. E of Uttaradit; pop. (1960c) 7278.

Loemadjang. See LUMADJANG.

Lo·fo·ten \ˈlō-ˌfōt-ᵊn\. Island group in Norwegian Sea, in Nordland co., off NW coast of Norway, SW of Vesterålen; 475 sq. m.; principal islands Austvågøy, Vestvågøy, Moskenes; valuable fisheries.

Lof·tus \ˈlȯf-təs\. Urban district, North Riding, Yorkshire, N England; pop. (1971p) 7706.

Lo·gan \ˈlō-gən\. 1 Counties in ten states of the U.S. See tables at ARKANSAS, COLORADO, ILLINOIS, KANSAS, KENTUCKY, NEBRASKA, NORTH DAKOTA, OHIO, OKLAHOMA, WEST VIRGINIA.

2 Town, ⊗ of Harrison co., W Iowa, 25 m. N of Council Bluffs; pop. (1970c) 1526; diversified agriculture.

3 City, ⊗ of Hocking co., S cen. Ohio, 16 m. SE of Lancaster; pop. (1970c) 6269; oil and gas wells; furniture, pottery, lumber, automobile parts; founded 1816.

4 City, ⊗ of Cache co., N Utah, 36 m. N of Ogden; pop. (1970c) 22,333; grain, sugar beets; dairy and livestock farming; Mormon Tabernacle and Mormon Temple; Utah State Univ. of Agriculture and Applied Science (1888); settled by Mormons c. 1855, incorp. 1886.

5 City, ⊗ of Logan co., SW West Virginia, 20 m. NE of Williamson; pop. (1970c) 3311; coal mines, bottling works.

Logan, Mount. 1 Peak in N Mohave co., NW Arizona; 7700 ft.

2 Peak in St. Elias Mountains, SW Yukon Territory, Canada, near Alaska boundary; 19,850 ft.; highest mountain in Canada.

Logan Mountain. Peak in Glacier National Park, NW Montana; 9252 ft.

Lo·gans·port \ˈlō-gənz-ˌpō(ə)rt, -ˌpȯ(ə)rt\. City, ⊗ of Cass co., N cen. Indiana, 22 m. NNW of Kokomo; pop. (1970c) 19,255; electrical equipment, die castings, airplane parts, lumber, rubber goods; ships livestock and grain; founded 1828; incorporated as city 1838.

Lo·gar \ˈlō-gər\. Province of E Afghanistan. See table at AFGHANISTAN.

Lo·gone \lə-ˈgōn\. River in NW equatorial Africa, bet. Chad and Cameroon; 240 m. long; flows N into Chari river.

Lo·gro·ño \lə-ˈgrōn-(ˌ)yō\. 1 Province of N Spain. See table at SPAIN.

2 *or anc.* **Ju·li·ob·ri·ga** \ˌjü-lē-ˈäb-ri-gə\. Commune, its ✱, on Ebro river 155 m. NNE of Madrid; pop. (1970p) 84,456; trade center for agricultural region; lumber, wine, textiles; ancient city walls, bridge (built 1138). Captured by Moors 8th cent.; unsuccessfully besieged by French 1521; occupied by French 1808–13.

Løg·stør Bred·ning \ˌlərg-stər-ˈbred-niŋ\. Wide section (ab. 13 m.) in cen. part of Lim Fjord, N Jutland, Denmark.

Lo·ha·ru \lō-ˈhär-(ˌ)ü\. Former Indian state, now part of Haryana, NW India; 226 sq. m.; ✱ Loharu.

Loheiya. See LUHAIYA.

Löh·ne \ˈlə(r)-nə\. City, North Rhine-Westphalia, West Germany; pop. (1969e) 36,944; metalworking; made city 1969.

Loibl \ˈlȯi-bəl\ *or* **Lju·belj** \ˈlyü-bəl-yə\. Pass over the Karawanken Alps, connecting with highway Klagenfurt in Carinthia, Austria, and Ljubljana in NW Yugoslavia; elev. 4487 ft.

Loi·kaw \ˈlȯi-ˈkȯ\. Town, Kayah State, E cen. Burma, on a tributary of the Salween ab. 70 m. NE of Toungoo.

Loi·pyet Hills \ˌlȯi-ˌpyet-\. Range of hills in N Burma, S of Kumon Range and W of upper Irrawaddy.

Loir \lə-ˈwär\. River, NW cen. France; 193 m. long; rises in Eure-et-Loir dept., flows W into Sarthe river 5 m. N of Angers.

Loire \lə-ˈwär\ *or anc.* **Li·ger** \ˈlī-jər\. 1 Longest river in France; 634 m. long; rises in Ardèche dept., SE France, flows N and NW to Orléans, then turns W and flows through Blois, Tours, and Nantes and empties into Bay of Biscay by a wide estuary below Saint-Nazaire; navigable.

2 Department of France. See table at FRANCE.

Loire–At·lan·tique \-at-läⁿ-ˈtēk\. Department of France. See table at FRANCE.

Loi·ret \lə-wä-ˈrā\. Department of N cen. France. See table at FRANCE.

Loir–et–Cher \-ā-ˈshe(ə)r\. Department of N cen. France. See table at FRANCE.

Lo·í·za \lō-ˈē-sə\ *or formerly* **Ca·nó·va·nas** \kə-ˈnō-və-nəs\. Town and municipality, NE Puerto Rico; town is on railroad ab. 17 m. ESE of San Juan; pop. (1970p) 2709 (town), 38,351 (munic.).

Loíza Al·dea \-äl-ˈdā-ə\. Village in Loíza municipality, NE Puerto Rico; pop. (1970p) 3360.

Lo·ja \ˈlō-(ˌ)hä\. 1 Province of SW Ecuador. See table at ECUADOR.

2 City, its ✱, on Zamora river ab. 133 m. SSE of Guayaquil; pop. (1970e) 38,300; in corn and dairy-farming region; univ. (1943); founded 1546.

3 *or earlier* **Lo·xa** \ˈlō-(ˌ)hä\. Commune, Granada prov., S Spain, on Genil river 21 m. W of Granada; pop. (1970p) 21,656; manufactures textiles, leather, pottery, paper; ancient churches, ducal palace, Moorish citadel. As important strategic point in defense of Granada, strongly fortified by Moors; reconquered by Ferdinand III 1226 and by Ferdinand and Isabella 1486.

Lo·ke·ren \ˈlō-kə-rən\. Commune, East Flanders prov., NW cen. Belgium, 23 m. NW of Brussels; pop. (1969e) 26,651; textiles, rope, plastics; scene of fighting Oct. 9, 1914, resulting in forced withdrawal of the British across Dutch frontier.

Lo·ko·ja \lə-ˈkō-jə\. Town, Kwara State, Nigeria, on Niger river at mouth of Benue river; pop. (1963c) 25,001; founded 1860; formerly capital of Northern Nigeria.

Lok·tak Lake \ˌläk-ˌtäk-\. Marshy lake, S Manipur state, NE India; ab. 25 sq. m.; its outlet is the Manipur river.

Lol·land \ˈläl-ənd\. Island of Denmark, lying in Baltic Sea S of Sjælland and W of Falster; 477 sq. m.; pop. (1965c) 81,760; sugar beet; forms part of Storstrøm co.

Lo·lo·bau \'lō-lə-ˌbau̇\. Small island in Bismarck Sea off N coast of E end of New Britain I., Bismarck Archipelago; part of Trust Territory of New Guinea.

Lom \'lȯm\ *or* **Lom–Pa·lan·ka** \-pə-'läŋ-kə\. Town, Mikhaylovgrad prov., NW Bulgaria, on Danube river; pop. (1968e) 28,492.

Lo·ma·lo·ma \ˌlō-mə-'lō-mə\. Chief town of the Exploring Is., E Fiji, SW Pacific Ocean, on S shore of Vanua Mbalavu I.; has good harbor.

Lo·ma·mi \lō-'mäm-ē\. River, Zaire; ab. 800 m. long; rises in S cen. part, flows N parallel with and W of the Lualaba and the upper Congo and empties into the Congo below Kisangani.

Lo·mas de Za·mo·ra \'lō-ˌmäz-də-zə-'mōr-ə, -'mȯr-\. City, Buenos Aires prov., E Argentina, part of Greater Buenos Aires; pop. (1960c) 272,116; chemical, electrical, and cement industries.

Lom·bard \'läm-ˌbärd\. Residential village, Du Page co., NE Illinois, 20 m. W of Chicago; pop. (1970c) 36,194; plastics; dairy farms.

Lom·bard·sij·de *also* **Lom·bart·zy·de** \'lȯm-bärt-ˌzī-də\. Commune, West Flanders prov., NW Belgium, near Nieuwpoort; pop. (1969e) 1814; scene of battles Oct. and Nov. 1914 and July 10, 1917 during World War I.

Lom·bar·dy \'läm-ˌbärd-ē, -bərd-\ *or Ital.* **Lom·bar·dia** \ˌläm-bər-'dē-ə\. Autonomous region, N Italy, in Italian Alps bet. Piedmont and Trentino-Alto Adige and Veneto; for provincial divisions, see table at ITALY; 9202 sq. m.; pop. (1968e) 8,231,667; ✱ Milan; contains numerous Alpine peaks, glaciers, and lakes; descends to fertile valley of Po river; important both agriculturally (wheat, rice, fruit; livestock; honey) and industrially (automobiles, steel, chemicals, machine tools, textiles).

History: Center of kingdom founded in Po valley by Lombards, a German people who invaded Italy in 6th cent. A.D.; kingdom extended rule over almost all of Italy (except south) until it was crushed by Charlemagne 773–774; became part of Carolingian empire and of Holy Roman Empire; cities of Lombard plain formed 1167 Lombard League against Emperor Frederick I whom they defeated 1176 at Legnano; cities received independence by peace signed 1183; Lombard territory came to be scene of rise of duchy of Milan (*q.v.*) which became Spanish 1535; ceded to Austria 1713; became part of Napoleon's Cisalpine Republic 1797 and kingdom of Italy 1805; restored to Austria as part of Lombardo-Venetian kingdom 1815; ceded to Napoleon III of France who turned it over to Piedmont 1859 (see ITALY); received limited autonomy 1970.

Lom·blen \'läm-'blen\. Island of the Lesser Sunda Is., Indonesia, E of Flores I. and separated from Pantar I. by Alor Strait; 468 sq. m.; ab. 50 m. long by 22 m. wide, of irregular shape. Has numerous mountains, highest Labalekang 5394 ft., an active volcano.

Lom·bok \'läm-ˌbäk\. Island of the Lesser Sunda Is., West Nusa Tenggara prov., Indonesia, E of Bali I.; ab. 70 m. long by 50 m. at widest point; 1826 sq. m.; pop. (1961c) 1,300,234. Separated on W from Bali by Lombok Strait, and on E from Sumbawa by Alas Strait. Has two mountain ranges, one along N coast and the other along the S, with wide valley between; in N range is the volcano Rindjani 12,224 ft., one of highest mountains in Indonesia. Mountain regions forest-clad and undeveloped, lowlands highly cultivated, producing rice and coffee; industry includes weaving of clothes and mats and work in gold, silver, and iron. Its fauna and flora of great interest because the island, situated on Wallace's line, marks a meeting point of Asian and Australian forms. In early times under Sultan of Makasar; suffered from piracy in 17th cent. and later subject to Bali; began relations with Dutch 1843 and came entirely under their control by 1894; occupied by Japanese in World War II 1942–45.

Lombok Strait. Channel bet. E Bali I. and W Lombok I., Indonesia, connecting W Flores Sea with the Indian Ocean; ab. 22 m. wide; of interest to scientists as an important part of Wallace's line.

Lo·mé \lō-'mā\. Seaport town, ✱ of Republic of Togo, W Africa; pop. (1970p) 83,845; ✱ of former French Togo and of German protectorate of Togo; connected by rail with inland towns and with other coast towns.

Lo·me·la \lō-'mā-lə\. **1** River, cen. Zaire; 290 m. long; flows NW into Tshuapa river.

2 Town, Kasai-Oriental prov., S cen. Zaire, on the Lomela river ab. 180 m. N of Lusambo; airport.

Lo·mié \lō-'myā\. Town, SE Cameroon.

Lo·mi·ta \lō-'mēt-ə\. City, Los Angeles co., SW California, SE of Torrance; pop. (1970c) 19,784; residential.

Lomme \'ləm\. Commune, Nord dept., N France, WNW suburb of Lille; pop. (1968c) 29,315; spinning mills; clothing, hats; partially destroyed in World War I.

Lom·mel \'lȯ-məl\. Commune, N Limburg prov., Belgium; pop. (1969e) 21,498.

Lomond, Ben. See BEN LOMOND.

Lo·mond, Loch \läk-'lō-mənd, läk̲-\. Lake in Stirling and Dunbarton cos., S cen. Scotland; $27\frac{1}{4}$ sq. m., 24 m. long by $\frac{3}{4}$ to 5 m. wide; largest lake in Scotland; surrounded by many mountains (Ben Lomond, Ben Vorlich); S part expands and contains many islets; Luss on W side and Balloch at S end are chief towns on its shores; on its E shore near Ben Lomond is the region made famous by Rob Roy, 18th cent. outlaw of the clan Macgregor.

Lo·mo·no·sov \lə-'mȯn-ə-ˌsȯv, -ˌsȯf, -səf\; *formerly* **Ora·ni·en·baum** *also* **Ora·niy·en·baum** \ȯ-'rän-ē-ən-ˌbau̇m, ə-'rən-yin-\. Town, NW Leningrad Oblast, Russian S.F.S.R., U.S.S.R., on the Gulf of Finland opp. Kronshlot; pop. (1967e) 32,000; has palace which was imperial residence 1727–1914; bricks; founded 1711.

Lom–Palanka. See LOM.

Lom·po·ba·tang \ˌlȯm-pō-'bä-ˌtäŋ\ *or formerly* **Bon·thain** \bȯn-'tīn\. Peak, SW Celebes, Indonesia, E of Makasar; 9419 ft.

Lom·poc \'läm-ˌpäk\. City, Santa Barbara co., SW California, near Pacific Ocean 45 m. WNW of Santa Barbara; pop. (1970c) 25,484; oil wells; truck farms; founded 1874; Vandenberg Air Force Base (to the W).

Łom·ża \'lȯm-ˌzhä\ *or Russ.* **Lom·zha** \-zhə\. City, W Białystok prov., NE Poland, on the Narew river 80 m. NE of Warsaw; pop. (1970p) 25,500; founded before the 9th cent.; long a prosperous commercial town, esp in 16th cent.; later suffered in wars; in partition of Poland 1795 came under Prussian rule, then Russian 1807 to 1918. In World War II taken by Russians 1939, and by Germans 1941; retaken and included in Belorussian S.S.R. 1944 but ceded back to Poland Aug. 1945.

Lo·na·to \lə-'nät-(ˌ)ō\. Commune, Brescia prov., Lombardy, N Italy, ab. 15 m. W of Brescia near S end of Lake Garda; pop. (1968e) 9731; scene of an early victory of Napoleon over the Austrians Aug. 3, 1796.

Lon·co·che \lȯŋ-'kō-chē\. City, Cautín prov., S cen. Chile; pop. (1960c) 6619.

Lon·don \'lən-dən\. **1** City, ⊗ of Laurel co., SE Kentucky, 43 m. NW of Middlesborough; pop. (1970c) 4337; Sue Bennett Coll. (1896).

2 Manufacturing and agricultural city, ⊗ of Madison co., SW cen. Ohio, 23 m. W of Columbus; pop. (1970c) 6481; metal products, tile, automobile parts; stock and dairy farms.

3 Industrial city, ⊗ of Middlesex co., SE Ontario, Canada, on Thames river 23 m. N of Lake Erie; pop. (1971p) 221,-430, met. area pop. 284,469; railroad center; food and paper products, diesel locomotives, beverages, textiles, refrigerators, hosiery; Huron Coll. (1863), Univ. of Western Ontario (1878), King's Coll. (1912), Brescia Coll. (1919), London Coll. of Bible and Missions (1935), Philatea Coll. (1946). First settled 1826; incorporated as village 1840, town 1848, city 1855; its port is Port Stanley on Lake Erie.

4 City, ✱ of the United Kingdom, lying on both sides of the Thames ab. 40 m. from its mouth; 621.8 sq. m.; pop. (1971p) 8,196,807; since 1965 comprises the **City of London,** *anc.* **Lon·din·i·um** \län-'din-ē-əm, ˌlən-\, known as **The City** (the older part, now included in its financial district), and 32 boroughs, which together are referred to as **Greater London;** a major political, industrial, cultural, financial, and transportation center (for further details, see table page 683).

History: From 43 to 409 A.D. a Roman town, Londinium; scene of revolt of Boadicea, Queen of Iceni (see GREAT BRITAIN, *History*) 60 A.D.; its fortifications, which had been destroyed by Danes 851, restored by Alfred the Great; from Anglo-Saxon times, grew as trade center of England; received charter privileges from 11th cent.; one of the Hanse Towns; city proper, governed by Lord Mayor and Aldermen of trade guilds, came to be the commercial center; Westminster the seat of English government; scene of Wat Tyler's rebellion 1381; in Wars of the Roses generally supported Yorkists; in Civil War (17th cent.) opposed to king and later to the Army; after the setbacks of severe plague 1665 and great fire 1666, grew to be the most populous city and most important trade center of the world; violently opposed James II; in 18th cent. Whig headquarters; scene of Gordon Riots 1780; by act of 1888 London area placed under London County Council; in World War I raided by German planes and dirigibles 1915–18; in World War II suffered esp. 1940–41 from bombings by German planes and June–Sept. 1944 from robot bombs; adopted new administrative structure 1963 (effective 1965).

Treaties, etc.: Conference 1827–32 on establishment of kingdom of Greece; Treaty May 1852 determined succession to Danish crown; Treaty May 11, 1867, establishing neutrality of Luxembourg; declaration Feb. 1909 attempted to determine maritime law in time of war; Treaty May 30, 1913 ended First Balkan War; Pact Sept. 1914 by which France, Russia, and Great Britain agreed not to make a separate peace; Treaty Apr. 26, 1915, secret agreement of Allies with Italy; Declaration 1922 on reparations; Conference 1930 on naval affairs (unsuccessful); Conference 1933 on World Monetary and Economic affairs (unsuccessful); site of meeting of first part of first session of the United Nations 1946; conference 1954 on termination of occupation regime in West Germany; during 1950's and 1960's site of numerous conferences relating to constitutional developments in British dependencies.

Lon·don·der·ry \ˌlən-dən-'der-ē, 'lən-dən-ˌder-ē\ *or* **Der·ry** \'der-ē\. 1 County, NW Northern Ireland; 814 sq. m.; pop. (1971p) 182,173 (including Londonderry county borough); ✱ Londonderry; oats, potatoes; fishing, brewing, manufacturing (esp. clothing, rubber products, and fertilizers).

2 County borough and seaport, its ⊗, on Foyle river near head of Lough Foyle 95 m. NW of Belfast; pop. (1971p) 51,617; good harbor; shipbuilding yards; trading center for agricultural products; fisheries, tanneries, breweries; manufactures flour, textiles (linens, woolens). Began with an abbey founded by St. Columba mid-6th cent.; an ecclesiastical settlement until 16th cent.; scene of defeat 1566 of earl of Tyrone in rebellion against the English; burned in 1608; unsuccessfully besieged and blockaded for 105 days in 1689 by army of James II; has two cathedrals (Anglican and Roman Catholic); Magee University Coll. (1865). In World War II a U.S. convoy supply base.

Londonderry, Cape. Northernmost point of Western Australia, on Timor Sea; 13°45′S, 126°55′E.

Lon·dri·na \lō(^{n})n-'drē-nə\. Town, Paraná state, S Brazil; munic. pop. (1968e) 226,332.

Lone Mountain \'lōn-\. 1 Peak, SW Gallatin co., S Montana; 11,194 ft.

2 Peak in E Esmeralda co., SW Nevada; 9114 ft.

Lone Pine Peak \'lōn-ˌpīn-\. Mountain in cen. Custer co., cen. Idaho; 9652 ft.

Long \'lȯŋ\. County in Georgia. See table at GEORGIA.

Long, Loch. Inlet in Argyll co., W coast of Scotland, a N extension of Firth of Clyde; ab. 16 m. long.

Lon·ga·ví \ˌlȯŋ-gə-'vē\. Peak, E Linares prov., S cen. Chile; 10,597 ft.

Long Bay. 1 Bay off S coast of North Carolina and NE coast of South Carolina, extending SW from Cape Fear.

2 Bay on W end of island of Jamaica, West Indies.

Long Beach. 1 Narrow sandy island, SE Ocean co., E New Jersey.

2 Industrial and resort city, Los Angeles co., SW California, on San Pedro Bay 20 m. S of Los Angeles; pop. (1970c) 358,633; artificial harbor with modern facilities; shipbuilding, fishing; paper, glass, aircraft, chemicals, paint, soap, plastics; oil and gas wells; Long Beach City Coll. (1913), Pacific Christian Coll. (1928), California State Coll. at Long Beach (1949); incorporated 1897; major development took place after discovery of oil 1921; suffered substantial damage from earthquake 1933.

3 City, Harrison co., SE Mississippi, 5 m. W of Gulfport; pop. (1970c) 6170.

4 City, Nassau co., SE New York, on an island in Atlantic Ocean off S shore of Long I. 21 m. ESE of New York City; pop. (1970c) 33,127; residential; seaside resort.

Long·ben·ton \lȯŋ-'bent-ᵊn\. Urban district, Northumberland, N England, 3 m. NE of Newcastle upon Tyne; pop. (1971p) 48,970; coal mining.

Long·boat Key \ˌlȯŋ-bōt-\. City, Manatee and Sarasota cos., W cen. Florida, on Gulf of Mexico 20 m. NW of Sarasota; pop. (1970c) 2850.

Long Branch. 1 City, Monmouth co., E cen. New Jersey, on Atlantic Ocean 21 m. SE of Perth Amboy; pop. (1970c) 31,774; summer resort; clothing, boats, electronic equipment; truck farms.

2 Village, York co., SE Ontario, Canada, on Lake Ontario 9 m. W of Toronto; pop. (1966c) 12,980.

Long Cay. One of the SE Bahama Is., SW of Crooked I.; 8 sq. m.; pop. (1963c) 22; lighthouse; as a former rendezvous of wreckers, known also as **Fortune Island.**

Long·champ \lō^n-'shä^n\. See BOIS DE BOULOGNE.

Long·den·dale \'lȯŋ-dən-ˌdāl\. Urban district, Cheshire, NW England; pop. (1971p) 10,351.

Long Ea·ton \-'ēt-ᵊn\. Urban district, Derbyshire, N cen. England, 7 m. WSW of Nottingham; pop. (1971p) 33,694; railway yards; market town.

Long·fel·low Peak \'lȯŋ-ˌfel-(ˌ)ō-, -ˌfel-ə(-w)-\. Mountain in Glacier National Park, NW Montana; 8900 ft.

Long·ford \'lȯŋ-fərd\. 1 Town, N Tasmania, Australia, 15 m. S of Launceston; pop. (1970e) 5210; one of earliest settlements in Tasmania; dairying and farming.

2 County, E cen. Eire; 403 sq. m.; pop. (1971p) 28,227; ⊗ Longford; chief river Shannon; potatoes, oats; livestock raising, dairying.

3 Urban district, ⊗ of co. Longford, Eire; pop. (1971p) 3875; processes bacon, butter; leather tanning; 19th cent. cathedral.

Long Ga·bles \'lȯŋ-'gā-bəlz\. Mountain, Antarctica, 78°11′S, 86°14′W; 13,620 ft.

Long Island. 1 Islands, Florida. See FLORIDA KEYS.

2 Island in Atlantic Ocean in Hancock co., SE coast of Maine.

3 Island along SE approach to harbor of Boston, Massachusetts.

4 Island, SE of New York and S of Connecticut, lying bet. Long Island Sound on N and Atlantic Ocean on S; 118½ m. long, 23 m. at greatest width; 1401 sq. m. (including water, 1723 sq. m.); comprises Suffolk, Nassau, Queens, and Kings cos. of New York state; borough of Brooklyn (Kings co.) at its SW extremity. At W end separated from

NAME	AREA (sq. m.)	POP. (1971p)	BUILDINGS, LANDMARKS, ETC.
City of London	1.0	5,324	Bank of England, Royal Exchange, Stock Exchange; financial center; City Univ. (1966).
Boroughs			
Barking	13.9	189,430	Ruins of Barking Abbey (c. 666 A.D.), Valence Manor House (1600); automobile manufacturing.
Barnet	34.5	320,438	Chipping Barnet Church (1250); mainly residential; aircraft parts, electrical components.
Bexley	24.9	205,400	Ruins of Lessness Abbey (f. 1178), St. Mary's Church (13th cent.), Hall Place (c. 1540); oil refineries, chemical and engineering works.
Brent	17.1	311,530	Oxgate Farm House (16th–17th cents.), The Grange (c. 1700); Empire Stadium; engineering works; food processing; electrical and photographic equipment.
Bromley	61.3	267,771	Camden Place (1609), National Recreation Center, Bromley Technical College (1959); electrical and scientific equipment, paper.
Camden	8.4	258,318	British Museum, John Keats House and Museum, University Coll. (1826), Gray's Inn, Lincoln's Inn, Post Office Tower (1964); railway terminals: Euston (1849); King's Cross (1852), St. Pancras (1874).
Croydon	37.2	310,433	St. Michael and All Angels (1871), Fairfield Halls; mainly residential; electrical and scientific equipment.
Ealing	21.4	310,690	An important industrial center; engineering works; chemicals, glass, motor vehicles, plastics.
Enfield	31.3	208,112	St. Andrew's Church (14th cent.), Enfield Grammar School (c. 1590), Salisbury House (16th–17th cents.); engineering and gas works; electronic equipment, textiles.
Greenwich	19.0	235,549	Royal Navy College, National Maritime Museum, Rotunda Museum, Charlton House (1607–12), Morden Coll. (c. 1695), Ranger's House (c. 1750).
Hackney	7.5	265,349	London College of Furniture, Geffrye Museum; parks include: Clissold Park, Springfield Park, Victoria Park.
Hammersmith	6.2	241,431	St. Paul's School (1509), Wormwood Scrubs Prison (1874), White City Stadium; television studios.
Haringey	11.7	277,316	Civic Center; Alexandra Park, Finsbury Park; mainly residential; footwear, furniture.
Harrow	19.6	219,484	St. Mary's Church (consecrated 1094), Harrow School (1571); mainly residential; optical and photographic equipment.
Havering	46.3	192,094	Mainly residential; beer, chemicals, clothing.
Hillingdon	42.6	210,312	St. Dunstan's Church (14th cent.); Ruislip Lido; London Airport; Brunell Univ. (1966); aircraft, electrical equipment; motion-picture production.
Hounslow	22.8	211,075	Hogarth House (17th cent.), Chiswick House (designed 1725); precision instruments, soap.
Islington	5.8	271,002	Canonbury Tower, Charterhouse, Armoury House (1735); Sadler's Wells; beer, furniture, scientific and surgical instruments.
Kensington and Chelsea	4.6	219,117	Kensington Palace, Chelsea Royal Hospital (1682–92), Baden Powell House, Central Library (1960), Commonwealth Institute (1962).
Kingston upon Thames	14.5	146,615	Mainly residential; aircraft, electronic equipment, plastics.
Lambeth	10.5	346,964	Lambeth Palace, Royal Festival Hall, Queen Elizabeth Hall, National Theatre; Oval Cricket Ground.
Lewisham	13.4	303,071	Mainly residential; light engineering.
Merton	14.6	200,140	Mitcham Common, Wimbledon Common; milk-bottling; radar, toys.
Newham	14.5	294,017	West Ham College of Technology (1898), Passmore Edwards Museum; Royal Docks, railway yards.
Redbridge	21.8	258,902	Epping Forest (part of); mainly residential; chemicals, radio components.
Richmond upon Thames	21.8	188,100	Hampton Court Palace, Orleans House, Ham House; Royal Botanic Gardens; film and television studios.
Southwark	11.5	337,638	Dulwich College (1619), Guy's Hospital (1725), Imperial War Museum; commercial docks.
Sutton	16.7	176,151	All Saints Church (12th cent., restored 1893); mainly residential; chemicals, paper and plastic products.
Tower Hamlets	7.8	230,790	Christ Church (1723–29), Bethnal Green Museum (1872), Queen Mary College (1907); industrial and commercial center; extensive docks.
Waltham Forest	15.3	275,468	Chingford Old Church; largely residential.
Wandsworth	13.9	330,883	Battersea Park, Putney Heath; Battersea College of Technology, Wandsworth Technical Coll.; brewing, light engineering.
Westminster, City of	8.3	300,332	Buckingham Palace, Houses of Parliament, Imperial College of Science and Technology (1907), National and Tate galleries, Royal Albert Hall, Westminster Abbey.

the Bronx and Manhattan by East river and from Staten I. by the Narrows. Has 280 m. of coastline indented by numerous inlets and bays, esp. Peconic and Gardiners Bays at E end and Great South and Jamaica Bays on S shore. Hilly along N shore; has many beaches along the S (Rockaway, Jones, Fire Island, Coney Island). At its E end is Montauk Point with several large islands in adjacent waters (Shelter, Gardiners, Plum, etc.). Has grown to be major residential district for New York City; most important industry outside New York metropolitan area is aircraft manufacturing.

History: Included in grant to Plymouth Company by James I 1620; conveyed to William Alexander, Earl of Stirling, 1635; became part of British colony of New York by treaty 1674; earliest settlement by Dutch 1623, and by English ab. 1640; scene of battle of Long Island (at Brooklyn Heights) in Revolutionary War Aug. 27, 1776 in which Lord Howe defeated Americans under Washington, who, however, successfully withdrew his forces across the river.

5 Island in S end of Willapa Bay, Pacific co., SW Washington; 8 sq. m.

6 Island in SW Lake Superior, Wisconsin. See APOSTLE ISLANDS.

7 One of the SE Bahama Is., SW of San Salvador; 230 sq. m.; pop. (1963c) 4176.

8 British islands, North Atlantic Ocean. See BERMUDA.

9 Islands, Atlantic Ocean. See HEBRIDES.

10 Island in Bismarck Archipelago off NE coast of New Guinea, WNW of Umboi I. and separated from mainland by Vitiaz Strait; highest point 4278 ft.; part of Papua New Guinea.

Long Island City. Former city, since 1898 part of Queens borough of New York City, on Long I. and East river, SE New York; settled by Dutch c. 1640; industrial center; manufactures foods, machinery, furniture, cut stone, footwear. Former village of Astoria now a part of it.

Long Island Sound. Body of water bet. S shore of Connecticut and N shore of Long I., New York, connecting with East river on W and with Block Island Sound on E; 1299 sq. m.; 110 m. long, from 10 to 25 m. wide.

Long·ju·meau \ˌlō^n-zhü-ˈmō\. Commune, Essonne dept., N France, ab. 11 m. S of Paris; pop. (1965e) 8780; short-lived truce in wars of religion signed here Mar. 23, 1568 bet. Charles IX and Protestant leaders.

Long Key. See FLORIDA KEYS.

Long Lake. **1** Lake in NE Hamilton co., NE cen. New York; ab. 14 m. long and 1 m. wide; elevation 1615 ft.; receives water from Raquette Lake to the SW and drains through Raquette river flowing N.

2 Lake extending across S boundary bet. Kidder and Burleigh cos., S cen. North Dakota.

Long·mead·ow \ˈlȯŋ-ˈmed-ō\. Residential town, Hampden co., SW Massachusetts, on Connecticut river S of and adjoining Springfield; pop. (1970c) 15,630; Bay Path Junior Coll. (1897).

Long·mont \ˈlȯŋ-ˌmänt\. City, Boulder co., N cen. Colorado, 30 m. N of Denver; pop. (1970c) 23,209; agricultural equipment; coal mines; sugar beets; founded 1870.

Long Point. **1** Cape on S side of tip of Cape Cod, Massachusetts.

2 Cape, S Norfolk co., SE Ontario, Canada, extending E into Lake Erie S of **Long Point Bay.**

Long Prairie. Village, ⊗ of Todd co., cen. Minnesota, 23 m. ENE of Alexandria; pop. (1970c) 2416.

Long Range Mountains. Range of hills, W Newfoundland I., Canada; incl. highest peak on island, 2672 ft.

Long·ships \ˈlȯŋ-ˌships\. Rocky islets, Cornwall, SW England, 1¼ m. W of Lands End; lighthouse, 117 ft. high, visible 16 m.

Longs Peak \ˈlȯŋz-\. Mountain, Boulder co., N cen. Colorado, in Front Range; 14,256 ft.; highest peak in Rocky Mountain National Park. Named in honor of Stephen H. Long, American army officer and explorer, who discovered it 1820.

Long·ton \ˈlȯŋ-tən\. See POTTERIES, THE.

Lon·gueuil \lȯŋ-ˈgāl\. Residential city, ⊗ of Chambly co., S Quebec, Canada, on St. Lawrence river across from Montreal; pop. (1971p) 97,483; part of Greater Montreal; industrial center producing food products, furniture, men's clothing, agricultural machinery; iron foundries.

Longue·val \lō^{n}g-ˈväl\. Village, Somme dept., N France, 7 m. ENE of Albert; pop. (1962c) 263; in center of territory gained by the British in the battle of the Somme July–Nov. 1916.

Long·view \ˈlȯŋ-ˌvyü\. **1** Town, Burke and Catawba cos., W North Carolina, 41 m. NW of Charlotte; pop. (1970c) 3360.

2 City, ⊗ of Gregg co., NE Texas, 20 m. W of Marshall; pop. (1970c) 45,547; steel, chemicals, plastics, paper, oil-drilling machinery; oil and gas wells, iron mines, oil refineries; Le Tourneau Coll. (1946).

3 City, Cowlitz co., SW Washington, at confluence of Cowlitz and Columbia rivers 37 m. N of Vancouver; pop. (1970c) 28,373; center of lumber and pulp industry; seaport; Lower Columbia Coll. (1934); founded as model city on site of old Monticello 1922; incorp. 1924; connected with Oregon by large cantilever bridge 1930.

Longvilliers. See NOAILLES 2.

Long·wood \ˈlȯŋ-ˌwu̇d\. City, Seminole co., cen. Florida, 10 m. N of Orlando; pop. (1970c) 3203.

Long·wy \lō^n-ˈwē\. Commune, Meurthe-et-Moselle dept., NE France, 60 m. N of Nancy; pop. (1968c) 21,087; iron mines; steel mills. Fortified by Vauban; battles 1815 and 1870; destroyed and taken by Germans 1914; recaptured by American forces 1918.

Long Xuyen *or* **Long·xuyen** \ˌlau̇ŋ-ˈswē-ən\. Town, South Vietnam, on S side of Mekong delta 100 m. W of Saigon; pop. (1968p) 47,401; market town in agricultural region.

Long·year City \ˌlȯŋ-ˌyi(ə)r-\ *or Norw.* **Long·year·by·en** \-ˈbü-ən\. Village on Advent Bay, Ice Fjord, Spitsbergen I.; coal mines.

Lo·ni·go \lō-ˈnē-gō\. Commune, Vicenza prov., Veneto, NE Italy, 13 m. SSW of Vicenza; pop. (1968e) 11,518.

Lon·ne·ker \ˈlȯn-ə-kər\. Commune, Overijssel prov., E Netherlands, suburb of Enschede 3 m. to NE, near German border.

Lo·noke \ˈlō-ˌnōk\. **1** County in cen. Arkansas. See table at ARKANSAS.

2 City, its ⊗, ab. 22 m. ENE of Little Rock; pop. (1970c) 3140; rice, cotton.

Lons·dale \ˈlänz-ˌdāl\. Village, Providence co., N Rhode Island, ab. 7 m. SE of Woonsocket; seat of government for town of Lincoln.

Lons–le–Sau·nier \ˌlō^n-lə-sō-ˈnyā\ *or anc.* **Le·do Sal·i·nar·i·us** \ˈlēd-(ˌ)ō-ˌsal-ə-ˈnar-ē-əs, -ˈnər-\. Commune, ✱ of Jura dept., E France, 44 m. NW of Geneva, Switzerland; pop. (1968c) 18,769; produces wines; warm saline springs; salt mines in a W suburb; 12th–15th cent. church.

Lontor. See GREAT BANDA.

Loochoo Islands. See RYUKYU ISLANDS.

Loo·goo·tee \lə-ˈgō-tē\. Residential city, Martin co., SW Indiana, 33 m. E of Vincennes; pop. (1970c) 2953.

Look·out, Cape \-ˈlu̇k-ˌau̇t\. **1** Cape, S tip of Core Bank off Carteret co., SE North Carolina; lighthouse.

2 Cape in Tillamook co., NW Oregon, S of Netarts Bay.

Lookout, Point. Point, SE tip of St. Marys co., S Maryland, on N side of mouth of Potomac river; lighthouse.

Lookout Mountain. **1** Peak, W Custer co., cen. Idaho; 9893 ft.

2 Ridge in SE Tennessee, extending into Georgia and Alabama; highest point 2126 ft., near Chattanooga, where battle was won by Union army Nov. 24, 1863 in which Hooker, in command of Grant's right wing, forced the withdrawal of Longstreet's corps.

3 Residential and resort town, Hamilton co., SE Tennessee, on Lookout Mt. on Georgia border SW of Chattanooga; pop. (1970c) 1741; Covenant Coll. (1955).

Lookout Peak. 1 Mountain in the Sierra Nevada, W Inyo co., S cen. California; 10,144 ft.
2 Mountain, San Juan and San Miguel cos., SW Colorado; 13,660 ft.
3 Mountain, Lawrence co., W South Dakota; 4887 ft.

Lo·on \lō-'ōn\. Municipality, W coast of Bohol I., Phil., NNW of Tagbilaran; pop. (1969e) 41,300; important trade center with good harbor.

Loon op Zand \ˌlō-nōp-'zänt\. Commune, North Brabant prov., S Netherlands, 4 m. N of Tilburg; pop. (1970e) 16,437.

Loop Head \'lüp-\. Cape on W coast of Eire, on N shore of mouth of the Shannon; lighthouse.

Lo·os \lō-'ōs\. 1 Manufacturing commune, Nord dept., N France, 4 m. W of Lille; pop. (1968c) 20,000.
2 *or* **Loos–en–Go·helle** \-äⁿ-gō-'el\. Commune, Pas-de-Calais dept., N France, ab. 3 m. NNW of Lens; pop. (1962c) 7944; in battle Sept. 15 to Oct. 13, 1915, part of Marshal Joffre's offensive in Champagne, village captured by British with heavy losses. Nearby are 14 British cemeteries.

Loos, Îles de. See LOS ISLANDS.

Lopadusa. See LAMPEDUSA.

Lopatino. See VOLZHSK.

Lo·pat·ka, Cape \-lō-'pat-kə\. Cape on S extremity of Kamchatka Penin., Khabarovsk Krai, Russian S.F.S.R., U.S.S.R., projecting into Kuril Strait opp. Shumshu I.

Lop Bu·ri *or* **Lo·bu·ri** \ləp-'bu̇-'rē\. 1 Province, SW cen. Thailand; 2544 sq. m.; pop. (1960c) 335,661; ✱ Lop Buri.
2 City, its ✱, 30 m. N of Phra Nakhon Si Ayutthaya; pop. (1960c) 21,232.

Lo·pe·vi \lō-'pā-vē\. Volcano on island of same name, S cen. New Hebrides group, SW Pacific Ocean; 4755 ft.

Lo·pez, Cape \-'lō-ˌpez\. Cape extending into Gulf of Guinea on W coast of Gabon, equatorial Africa.

Lopez Island. See SAN JUAN ISLANDS.

Lop Nor \'lōp-'nȯ(ə)r\ *or Chin.* **Lo–pu–no–erh** \'lō-'pü-'nō-'e(ə)r\. Salt, marshy depression at E end of Tarim basin, Sinkiang Uighur, W China, N of the A-erh-chin Shan-mo, 40°30'N, 90°30'E; divided into two lake basins which receive the Tarim river but have no outflow; river has shifted channels at intervals, leading to changes in location of lake. In region is major Chinese nuclear research and testing facility and probable site of first Chinese nuclear detonation 1964.

Lo·po·ri \lō-'pōr-ē, -'pȯr-\. River, NW cen. Zaire; ab. 380 m. long; flows NW and W nearly parallel with the Congo to join the Maringa and form the Lulonga.

Lora, Hamun–i–. See HAMUN-I-LORA.

Lo·ra del Río \'lōr-ə-del-'rē-(ˌ)ō, 'lȯr-\. Commune, Sevilla prov., SW Spain, 29 m. NE of Seville; pop. (1970p) 18,163; agriculture and mining.

Lo·rain \lə-'rān, lō-\. 1 County in Ohio. See table at OHIO.
2 City and lake port, Lorain co., N Ohio, on Lake Erie 25 m. W of Cleveland; pop. (1970c) 78,185; shipbuilding; steel, construction equipment; railroad shops, motor vehicle assembly plants; settled 1807; incorporated 1874.

Lo·ra·lai \'lȯr-ə-ˌlī\. Town, Baluchistan, Pakistan, 100 m. E of Quetta; pop. (1961c) 5519.

Lor·ca \'lȯr-kə\ *or anc.* **Eli·o·cro·ca** \ˌē-lē-ə-'krō-kə\. Commune, Murcia prov., SE Spain, 34 m. SW of Murcia; pop. (1970p) 60,609; in grain and livestock farming region; manufactures hemp sandals; Moorish castle.

Lorch \'lȯ(ə)rk\. Town, E cen. Baden-Württemberg, West Germany, 6 m. N of Göppingen; pop. (1961c) 5935; 12th cent. church containing tombs of the Hohenstaufens.

Lord Howe Island \-'hau̇-\. 1 Island of volcanic origin in SW Pacific Ocean, off E coast of New South Wales 436 m. ENE of Sydney, Australia, 31°33'S, 159°05'E; 5 sq. m.; belongs to New South Wales. Highest point 2840 ft.
2 Small island off S coast of Ndeni I., Santa Cruz Is., SW Pacific Ocean, part of British Solomon Islands.

Lord Howe Islands. See ONTONG JAVA.

Lords·burg \'lȯrdz-ˌbərg\. Mining city, ⊗ of Hidalgo co., SW corner of New Mexico, 38 m. SW of Silver City; pop. (1970c) 3429; copper and silver mines; diversified agriculture.

Lo·re·lei \'lōr-ə-ˌlī, 'lȯr-\ *or* **Lur·lei** \'lu̇(ə)r-ˌlī\. Rock on right bank of Rhine, near Sankt Goarshausen bet. Bingen and Koblenz, West Germany; ab. 440 ft. above river; in German legend, said to be haunted by a siren (Lorelei or Lurlei) who by her beauty and singing enticed sailors to destruction on the reef below.

Lo·re·na \lə-'rā-nə\. City, São Paulo state, SE Brazil, 115 m. NE of São Paulo; munic. pop. (1968p) 39,263.

Lo·reng·au *also* **Lo·rung·au** \ˌlōr-əŋ-'au̇\. Seaport on E tip of Manus I., Admiralty Is., Bismarck Archipelago, W Pacific Ocean; ✱ of Manus administrative dist., Papua New Guinea; occupied by Japanese Apr. 8, 1942, retaken by Americans Mar. 18, 1944.

Lo·re·stān \ˌlȯr-ə-'stän, 'lȯr-ə-ˌstan\ *also* **Lu·ri·stan** \'lu̇r-ə-ˌstan, -ˌstän\. Governorship, W Iran; 12,116 sq. m.; pop. (1966c) 686,307; ✱ Khorramābād; mountainous region, including the Zagros Mts.; watered by the Karkheh and Kārūn. Independent 12th–15th cents.; its inhabitants chiefly Bakhtiaris.

Lo·re·to \lə-'rāt-(ˌ)ō, -'ret-\. 1 Commune, Ancona prov., Marches, cen. Italy, near the coast 15 m. S of Ancona; pop. (1968e) 9143; place of pilgrimage, famous for its Holy House (Santa Casa), said to be that in which Jesus lived, brought by angels from Nazareth. The Loretto, or Loreto, nuns, or Ladies of Loretto, though named after it, were founded near Dublin, Ireland, 1822. See LORETTO 1.
2 Town, Concepción dept., E Paraguay; pop. (1970e) 11,-642.
3 Department, NE Peru; includes territory N of Marañón river which was in dispute, claimed by both Peru and Equador (*qq.v.*), until settlement of 1942; 184,685 sq. m.; pop. (1969e) 485,700; ✱ Iquitos; forested region, watered by tributaries of the Amazon; separated from coastal departments by Andes Mts.; chief products rubber, Brazil nuts, skins and hides, hardwoods, tobacco.

Lo·rette·ville \lə-'ret-ˌvil\. City, ⊗ of Quebec co., S Quebec, Canada, on St. Charles river 7 m. WNW of Quebec; pop. (1971p) 11,646; suburb of Quebec, formerly site of Huron village (**Lo·rette** \lə-'ret\), established 1697; church, erected c. 1750, a reproduction of Santa Casa of Loreto, Italy. Nearby in St. Charles river are **Falls of Lorette,** ab. 100 ft. high.

Lo·ret·to \lə-'ret-ō\. 1 City, Marion co., cen. Kentucky, 8 m. NW of Lebanon; pop. (1970c) 985; place where the Lorettine order of nuns (or Sisters of Loretto) was founded 1812. See LORETO 1.
2 Borough, Cambria co., SW cen. Pennsylvania, ab. 20 m. NE of Johnstown; pop. (1970c) 1661; St. Francis Coll. (1847).

Lo·ri·an Swamp \ˌlōr-ē-ən-, ˌlȯr-\. Swamp, E Kenya, E Africa; traversed by the Vasa Nyira river.

Lo·ri·ca \lə-'rēk-ə\. Seaport town, Córdoba dept., N Colombia, at mouth of Sinú river; munic. pop. (1968e) 67,119.

Lo·rient *or formerly* **L'Ori·ent** \ˌlȯr-ē-'äⁿ\. Fortified seaport commune, Morbihan dept., NW France, on the Bay of Biscay 29 m. WNW of Vannes; pop. (1968c) 66,444; harbor 4 m. from the sea formed by junction of Blavet and Scorff rivers; naval station and arsenal; shipbuilding, fishing and fish canning. Founded 1664 by French East India Company (Compagnie de l'Orient); became military fort 1690. Used as submarine base by Germans in World War II; frequently bombed and heavily damaged by Allied airplanes 1943–44; taken by Allies May 1945. See KÉROMAN.

L'Ori·gnal \lȯr-'nel, lȯr-in-'yäl\. Village, ⊗ of Prescott and Russell cos., in Prescott co., SE Ontario, Canada, on Ottawa river 50 m. ENE of Ottawa; pop. (1971p) 1297; has sawmills and port facilities.

Lorn, Firth of \-'lȯ(ə)rn\. Strait bet. Mull I. and mainland (Argyll co.) of W Scotland.

Lör·rach \'lər-ˌäk\. City, SW Baden-Württemberg, West Germany, near Black Forest, 28 m. SSW of Freiburg and on Swiss border near Basel; pop. (1969e) 32,671; textiles, wine, fruit, timber; received civic rights 1682.

Lor·raine \lə-'rān, lȯ-\ *or anc.* **Lo·tha·rin·gia** \ˌlō-thə-'rin-j(ē-)ə\ *or Ger.* **Lo·thring·en** \'lōt-riŋ-ən\. 1 Medieval kingdom, originally part of Austrasia (*q.v.*); by Treaty of Verdun 843 became part of realm (sometimes known as Middle Kingdom) of Emperor Lothair I; inherited by his son Lothair II 855–869, from whom it received name Lotharingia (Lat. *Lotharii regnum*); controlled by Germany, esp. King Louis the Child, until 911.

2 Duchy, formed by division of kingdom of Lorraine 959 into 2 duchies: **Lower Lorraine,** bet. Rhine and Schelde (later developing into separate duchies of Brabant, Limburg, etc.) and **Upper Lorraine,** commonly called **Lorraine,** region of upper Meuse and Moselle; French claim to it relinquished by Hugh Capet 987; ruled from 11th cent. continuously by a ducal family until its union with Hapsburgs; gradually reduced in size as French kingdom expanded; bishoprics (Les Trois-Évêchés) of Metz, Toul, and Verdun seized 1552 by Henry II of France; at times entirely held by French sovereigns; ruled 1737–66 by Stanislas I Leszczyński, dethroned king of Poland and father-in-law of Louis XV; permanently French from 1766; its chief cities Metz and Nancy; a province in revolutionary France, divided later into departments of Meuse, Moselle, Meurthe-et-Moselle, and Vosges; after Franco-Prussian War 1871 ceded to Germany as part of Alsace-Lorraine (*q.v.*).

Lorungau. See LORENGAU.

Los Ala·mi·tos \lȯ-ˌsal-ə-'mē-təs\. City, Orange co., SW California, 9 m. NE of Long Beach; pop. (1970c) 11,346.

Los Al·a·mos \lȯ-'sal-ə-ˌmōs\. 1 County of New Mexico. See table at NEW MEXICO.

2 Unincorporated community, Los Alamos co., New Mexico, ab. 35 m. NW of Santa Fe, on a mesa in Jemez Mts.; pop. (1970c) 11,310; alt. ab. 7400 ft.; chosen 1942 as site for research and development of nuclear weapons, place where U-235 and plutonium were first assembled into bombs; remains site of a major nuclear research facility.

Los Al·tos \lȯ-'sal-təs\. City, Santa Clara co., W California, SSE of Palo Alto; pop. (1970c) 24,726; residential; fruit packing; truck farms.

Los An·des \lȯ-'sän-(ˌ)dās\. 1 See ANDES.

2 Former territory, NW Argentina, in the Andes Mts.; practically coextensive with the Puna de Atacama region.

3 City, Aconcagua prov., cen. Chile, ab. 40 m. N of Santiago; pop. (1966e) 23,847; on Transandine R.R. 65 m. E of Valparaíso (83 m. by rail); alt. 2675 ft.

Los An·ge·les \lȯ-'san-jə-ləs, -'saŋ-g(ə-)ləs, -ˌlēz\. 1 County in SW California. See table at CALIFORNIA.

2 City, its ⊗, at its center ab. 15 m. from the Pacific Ocean although extending to the coast in several places; pop. (1970c) 2,809,596, making it the largest city in the state and 3d largest in the U.S.; excellent harbor at San Pedro Bay ab. 25 m. S of center of city; a major industrial center, producing military and civil aircraft and accessories, machinery, fabricated metal products, women's clothing, petroleum products, electronic equipment, glass, chemicals, cement, paint; oil refining, printing; fish canning and distributing; ships oranges, truck crops, and dairy products; Hollywood, a district of Los Angeles, is a major center of the American motion-picture and television industry; tourist center. City area has absorbed many towns and villages and now completely surrounds independent cities of Santa Monica, Beverly Hills, Culver City, Redondo Beach, etc. Has numerous parks, recreational areas, and cultural facilities; several small structures of the early Spanish period. Water supply brought from Colorado river by aqueduct (completed 1939) 300 m. long; suffers from increasingly serious water shortages and from chronic air-pollution problem. An important educational center: Loyola Univ. of Los Angeles (1865), Univ. of Southern California (1879), Univ. of California at Los Angeles (1881), Woodbury Coll. (1884), Occidental Coll. (1887), Los Angeles Coll. of Optometry (1904), West Coast Univ. (1909), Southwestern Univ. (1913), Immaculate Heart Coll. (1916), Mount St. Mary's Coll. (1925), Los Angeles City Coll. (1929), Marymount Coll. at Loyola Univ. (1933), Pepperdine Coll. (1937), East Los Angeles Coll. (1945), Univ. of Judaism (1947), California State Coll. at Los Angeles (1947), Los Angeles Trade-Technical Coll. (1949), Center for Early Education (1963). Founded 1781 on a Spanish grant and named Nuestra Señora Reina de los Angeles; captured by Commodore Stockton, U.S. Navy, 1846; incorporated 1850; growth accelerated by arrival of Southern Pacific R.R., discovery of nearby petroleum deposits 1894, and improvement of the harbor 1912.

Los Ángeles \lȯ-'säŋ-hə-ˌlās\. City, ✱ of Bío-Bío prov., S cen. Chile, 58 m. SE of Concepción in valley of Bío-Bío river; pop. (1966e) 41,719.

Los Ara·bos \lȯs-ə-'räb-əs\. Municipality, Matanzas prov., W cen. Cuba, on railroad 38 m. SE of Cárdenas; pop. (1967e) 15,690.

Los Ba·nos \lȯs-'ban-əs\. City, Merced co., cen. California, 60 m. WNW of Fresno; pop. (1970c) 9188; diversified agriculture.

Los Ba·ños \lȯs-'bän-yəs\. Municipality, cen. Laguna prov., Luzon, Phil., on S shore of Laguna de Bay 15 m. SW of Santa Cruz; pop. (1969e) 29,500; on provincial highway 34 m. SE of Manila; mineral springs; seat of College of Agriculture of the Univ. of the Philippines. American air base 1941; Japanese concentration camp captured Feb. 23, 1945.

Los Cho·rros National Park \lȯs-'chȯr-əs-\. National park in La Libertad dept., SW El Salvador; waterfalls; established 1958.

Loser, Mount. See LEUSER, MOUNT.

Los Estados, Isla de. See ESTADOS, ISLA DE LOS.

Los Gat·os \lȯs-'gat-əs\. City, Santa Clara co., W California, 8 m. SW of San Jose; pop. (1970c) 23,735; health resort; radar equipment; oil wells; fruit and poultry farms.

Lo–shan \'lō-'shän\ *or formerly* **Kia·ting** \jē-'ä-'diŋ\. City, SW Szechwan prov., S cen. China, on right bank of Min river 77 m. S of Ch'eng-tu; starting point for pilgrimage to traditionally sacred mountain, O-mei, ab. 30 m. to the W.

Los Her·ma·nos \ˌlȯ-ser-'män-əs\. Group of small Venezuelan islands in Caribbean Sea off NE cen. coast 50 m. NNW of Margarita I.

Lo·šinj \'lō-ˌshēn-yə\ *or Ital.* **Lus·si·no** \lu̇-'sē-(ˌ)nō\. Small island in the Kvarner Gulf, S of Cres I., NW Yugoslavia; 24 m. long; 29 sq. m.; administratively a part of Croatia; formerly Italian.

Losinoostrovsk. See BABUSHKIN.

Los Islands \'lȯs-\ *or* **Îles de Lo·os** \ˌēl-də-lō-'ȯs\. Group of small islands off Conakry, part of Guinea, W Africa; 6 sq. m.; largest Tamara, with good harbor. Came into British possession 1818; ceded to France 1904.

Los Lu·nas \lȯs-'lün-əs\. Village, ⊗ of Valencia co., W New Mexico, on the Rio Grande 18 m. S of Albuquerque; pop. (1970c) 973; sawmills; dairy farming.

Losoncz. See LUČENEC.

Los Pa·la·cios \ˌlȯs-pə-'läs-yəs\. Municipality, Pinar del Río prov., W Cuba; pop. (1967e) 28,480.

Los Pa·tos \lȯ-'spät-əs\ *or* **Por·ti·llo de los Patos** \pōr-'tē-yō-ˌdel-ō-'spät-əs\. Mountain pass in the Andes Mts., W Argentina, ab. 100 m. N of Aconcagua; 11,700 ft.

Los Re·yes \lȯ(s)-'rā-əs\. Town, Michoacán state, SW Mexico, 30 m. WNW of Uruapan; munic. pop. (1970p) 33,879.

Los Rí·os \lȯ(s)-'rē-əs\. Province of W cen. Ecuador. See table at ECUADOR.

Los Ro·ques \lȯ(s)-ˈrō-kəs\. Group of small Venezuelan islands in Caribbean Sea off N cen. coast of Venezuela; produces salt and phosphates.

Los San·tos \lȯ(s)-ˈsänt-əs\. Province of S cen. Panama. See table at PANAMA.

Los·ser \ˈlȯ-sər\. Commune, Overijssel prov., E Netherlands, 6 m. NE of Enschede on West German border; pop. (1970e) 18,713.

Los·sie·mouth and Bran·der·burgh \ˈlȯ-sē-ˌmau̇th . . . ˈbran-dər-ˌbər-ə, -ˌbə-rə, -b(ə-)rə\. Burgh, Moray co., NE Scotland, on North Sea at mouth of the Lossie, 5½ m. N of Elgin; pop. (1971p) 5681; port and seaside resort.

Lost City. See OVERTON 2.

Los Te·ques \lȯ-ˈstek-əs\. Town, ✻ of Miranda state, N Venezuela, ab. 15 m. SW of Caracas; pop. (1970e) 54,253.

Los Tes·ti·gos \ˌlȯ-stə-ˈtē-gəs\. Group of small Venezuelan islands, in Caribbean Sea N of NE Venezuela, ab. 50 m. NE of Margarita I.

Lost Mine Peak \ˌlȯst-ˌmīn-\. Mountain, S Brewster co., W Texas; 7750 ft.

Lost River Range. Range in E cen. Idaho, chiefly in Custer and Butte cos.

Lost·with·i·el \lȯs-ˈtwith-ē-əl\. Town and municipal borough, Cornwall, SW England, 30 m. W of Plymouth; borough pop. (1961c) 1904; railroad workshops; castle of Restormel nearby; scene of battle Sept. 2, 1644 in which Charles I defeated earl of Essex.

Lo·su·ia \lə-ˈsü-yə\. Chief town of Trobriand Is. off SE New Guinea I., on W coast of Kiriwina I. near N end.

Lot \ˈlät, ˈlȯt\. 1 *or anc.* **Ol·tis** \ˈäl-təs, ˈȯl-\. Navigable river in S France; ab. 300 m. long; rises in Lozère dept. on slopes of the Lozère Mts.; flows W into Garonne river W of Agen.

2 Department of S cen. France. See table at FRANCE.

Lo·ta \ˈlōt-ə\. Seaport, Concepción prov., S cen. Chile, 21 m. S of Concepción; pop. (1966e) 57,773; coal-mining center from 1852; copper smelters; nearby is Cousiño Park, containing plants and trees from all over the world; founded 1662.

Lota Al·to \ˌlōt-ə-ˈäl-(ˌ)tō\. Mining town, Chile, just NE of Lota (*q.v.*); pop. (1960c) 20,954.

Lot·bi·nière \ˌlō-bi-ˈnye(ə)r\. County, Quebec, Canada. See table at QUEBEC.

Lot–et–Ga·ronne \ˈlät-ā-gə-ˈrän, ˈlȯt-, -ˈrōn\. Department of SW France. See table at FRANCE.

Lotharingia. See LORRAINE.

Lo·thi·an \ˈlō-thē-ən\. Region of S Scotland; in early times, c. 547 to 1018, a district of N Northumberland extending from the Tweed to the Firth of Forth; later divided into 3 counties, **The Lo·thi·ans** \-ənz\, East Lothian, Midlothian, and West Lothian.

Lothringen. See LORRAINE.

Löt·schen Pass \ˌlər-chən-\. Mountain pass in the Bernese Alps bet. Bern and Valais cantons, SW cen. Switzerland; 8823 ft.; under it is the **Lötsch·berg** \ˈlərch-ˌbərg, -ˌbe(ə)rg\ railroad tunnel, 9 m. long, at an altitude of 4080 ft.

Lötzen. See GIŻYCKO.

Loualaba. See LUALABA.

Lou·don \ˈlau̇d-ᵊn\. 1 County in E Tennessee. See table at TENNESSEE.

2 Town, its ⊗, on Tennessee river 30 m. SW of Knoxville; pop. (1970c) 3728; hosiery, furniture, plastics; diversified agriculture.

Loudon Hill. Locality, Ayr co. SW Scotland, E of Kilmarnock; scene of victory of Robert Bruce over the English 1307.

Lou·don·ville \ˈlau̇d-ᵊn-ˌvil\. Village, Ashland and Holmes cos., N cen. Ohio, 15 m. SE of Mansfield; pop. (1970c) 2865; motor vehicle bodies, dairy products.

Lou·doun \ˈlau̇d-ᵊn\. County in Virginia. See table at VIRGINIA.

Lou·dun \lü-ˈdəⁿ\. Commune, NW Vienne dept., W cen. France, 40 m. SW of Tours; pop. (1962c) 6434; a Protestant community, suffered much after revocation of the Edict of Nantes; has traces of Roman times.

Lough·bor·ough \ˈləf-ˌbər-ə, -ˌbə-rə, -b(ə-)rə\. Municipal borough, Leicestershire, cen. England, 13 m. SSW of Nottingham; pop. (1971p) 45,863; market center; electrical equipment, hosiery, pharmaceuticals, bell founding; Loughborough Univ. of Technology (1966); formerly a lacemaking center.

Loughor. See LLWCHWR.

Lough·rea \läk-ˈrā, läk-\. Market town, SE co. Galway, W Eire, on N shore of Lough Rea 18 m. SW of Ballinasloe; pop. (1961c) 2890; remains of Norman castle and Carmelite friary; a cromlech is nearby.

Lou·i·sa \lü-ˈēz-ə, *Iowa* -ˈīz-\. 1 Name of counties in two states of the U.S. See tables at IOWA and VIRGINIA.

2 City, ⊗ of Lawrence co., E Kentucky, on Big Sandy river 25 m. S of Ashland; pop. (1970c) 1781; flour; oil and gas wells, coal mines; diversified agriculture.

3 Town, ⊗ of Louisa co., cen. Virginia; pop. (1970c) 633.

Louis·burg \ˈlü-is-ˌbərg\. 1 Town, ⊗ of Franklin co., N North Carolina, 30 m. NE of Raleigh; pop. (1970c) 2941; lumber; tobacco, cotton; Louisburg Coll. (1787).

2 *or* **Lou·is·bourg** \-ˌbərg\. Town, Cape Breton co., E Nova Scotia, Canada, on Atlantic Ocean 18 m. SE of Sydney; pop. (1971p) 1578; coal-shipping port and anchorage for fishing fleet.

History: Founded by French 1713; strongly fortified (1720–40) to maintain its strategic control of entrance to the Gulf of St. Lawrence; besieged and captured by American colonials under Sir William Pepperell 1745; returned to the French by Treaty of Aix-la-Chapelle 1748; again taken by the English under Gen. Jeffrey Amherst and Admiral Boscawen 1758 and its fortifications destroyed. Site of the fort and its remains now preserved as a national historic park (**Fortress of Louisbourg:** see CANADA, *National Historic Parks*).

Lou·ise, Lake \-lu̇-ˈēz\. Lake near Banff, SW Alberta, Canada; 1½ m. by ¾ m.; altitude 5670 ft.; in Banff National Park, at foot of high peaks; its outlet is short stream flowing into Bow river; region noted for its scenery.

Louise Island. Island, cen. Queen Charlotte Is. off W British Columbia, Canada, on Hecate Strait.

Lou·ise·ville \lu̇-ˈēz-ˌvil\. Town, ⊗ of Maskinongé co., S Quebec, Canada, on Lake St. Peter 20 m. WSW of Three Rivers; pop. (1971p) 4015; textiles, clothing, furniture.

Louis Gentil. See YOUSSOUFIA.

Lou·i·si·ade Archipelago \lu̇-ˌē-zē-ˈäd-, -ˈad-\. Island group in Solomon Sea SE of E end of New Guinea; ab. 600 sq. m.; pop. ab. 3000; administratively part of Papua New Guinea; chief village, Bwagaoia, on E end of Misima I.; comprises large islands of Misima, Tagula, and Rossel, and many small islands and reefs; gold mines on Tagula I. Discovered by de Torres 1606; used early in 1942 by Japanese as seaplane base but given up after battle of Coral Sea May 1942.

Lou·i·si·ana \lu̇-ˌē-zē-ˈan-ə, ˌlü-ə-zē-, ˌlü-zē-\. 1 A southern state of U.S.A., bounded on N by Arkansas, on E and SE by Mississippi and the Gulf of Mexico, on S by the Gulf of Mexico, and on W by Texas; 31st state in area, 48,523 sq. m. (land area 45,155 sq. m.); 20th state in population (1970c) 3,643,180; ✻ Baton Rouge; 18th state admitted to Union (1812).

Nicknames: Pelican State; Creole State. *State flower:* Magnolia. *Motto:* Union, Justice, Confidence. *Rivers:* Mississippi, forming NE and E cen. boundary and flowing SE into Gulf of Mexico; Sabine, forming W cen. and SW boundary, and flowing into Gulf of Mexico; Red, flowing from NW diagonally SE across state and into the Mississippi. *Highest point:* Driskill Mountain 535 ft., in Bienville parish. *Chief products:* Rice, soybeans, cotton lint, sugarcane; oil, natural gas, sulfur, salt; manufacturing: chemicals, transportation equipment, lumber. *Chief cities:* New Orleans, Shreveport, Baton Rouge, Lake Charles, Monroe. See *Table of States* at UNITED STATES. Divided into the following 64 parishes (for pronunciation of their names, see their individual entries):

NAME	LOCATION	AREA[1] (sq. m.)	POP. (1970c)	PAR. SEAT
Acadia	S	663	52,109	Crowley
Allen	SW	774	20,794	Oberlin
Ascension	SE	301	37,086	Donaldsonville
Assumption	SE	356	19,654	Napoleonville
Avoyelles	cen.	832	37,751	Marksville
Beauregard	SW	1,184	22,888	De Ridder
Bienville	NW	832	16,024	Arcadia
Bossier	NW	849	64,519	Benton
Caddo	NW corner	899	230,184	Shreveport
Calcasieu	SW	1,105	145,415	Lake Charles
Caldwell	N cen.	551	9,354	Columbia
Cameron	SW corner[2]	1,441	8,194	Cameron
Catahoula	cen.	742	11,769	Harrisonburg
Claiborne	N	763	17,024	Homer
Concordia	E cen.	718	22,578	Vidalia
De Soto	NW	904	22,764	Mansfield
East Baton Rouge	SE cen.	459	285,167	Baton Rouge
East Carroll	NE corner	436	12,884	Lake Providence
East Feliciana	E	454	17,657	Clinton
Evangeline	S cen.	669	31,932	Ville Platte
Franklin	NE	648	23,946	Winnsboro
Grant	cen.	670	13,671	Colfax
Iberia	S[2]	589	57,397	New Iberia
Iberville	S	627	30,746	Plaquemine
Jackson	N	582	15,963	Jonesboro
Jefferson	SE[2]	331	338,229	Gretna
Jefferson Davis	SW	658	29,554	Jennings
Lafayette	S	283	111,745	Lafayette
Lafourche	SE[2]	1,141	68,941	Thibodaux
La Salle	cen.	643	13,295	Jena
Lincoln	N	469	33,800	Ruston
Livingston	SE	654	36,511	Livingston
Madison	NE	661	15,065	Tallulah
Morehouse	N	804	32,463	Bastrop
Natchitoches	NW cen.	1,295	35,219	Natchitoches
Orleans	SE[2]	205	593,471	New Orleans
Ouachita	N	638	115,387	Monroe
Plaquemines	SE[2,3]	1,030	25,225	Pointe a la Hache
Pointe Coupee	SE cen.	563	22,002	New Roads
Rapides	cen.	1,318	118,078	Alexandria
Red River	NW	406	9,226	Coushatta
Richland	NE	576	21,774	Rayville
Sabine	W	1,029	18,638	Many
Saint Bernard	SE[2]	514	51,185	Chalmette
Saint Charles	SE	288	29,550	Hahnville
Saint Helena	E	420	9,937	Greensburg
Saint James	SE	253	19,733	Convent
Saint John the Baptist	SE	250	23,813	Edgard
Saint Landry	S cen.	932	80,364	Opelousas
Saint Martin[4]	S	736	32,453	Saint Martinville
Saint Mary	S[2]	624	60,752	Franklin
Saint Tammany	SE	925	63,585	Covington
Tangipahoa	SE	807	65,875	Amite City
Tensas	NE	626	9,732	St. Joseph
Terrebonne	SE[2]	1,368	76,049	Houma
Union	N	906	18,447	Farmerville
Vermilion	S[2]	1,205	43,071	Abbeville
Vernon	W	1,357	53,794	Leesville
Washington	E	665	41,987	Franklinton
Webster	NW	615	39,939	Minden
West Baton Rouge	SE cen.	203	16,864	Port Allen
West Carroll	NE	356	13,028	Oak Grove
West Feliciana	E cen.	405	11,376	St. Francisville
Winn	N cen.	950	16,369	Winnfield

[1] Area = land area.
[2] Parishes in extreme S and SE of state, bordering Gulf of Mexico, are largely composed of swampland intersected by bayous.
[3] Forms peninsula in extreme SE of state; bisected by Mississippi river whose delta is at SE end of parish.
[4] Area in SE separated from rest of parish by cen. part of Grand Lake and part of Iberia parish.

History: Name originally applied to entire Mississippi river basin, claimed for France by La Salle 1682; first settlement in region at Biloxi, Mississippi, 1699, there being no successful settlement within area of present state until foundation of New Orleans (*q.v.*) 1718; region E of Mississippi river ceded by France to Great Britain 1763 and, except West Florida (see FLORIDA), by British to U.S. 1783; region W of Mississippi river sold by France to U.S. 1803 (see LOUISIANA PURCHASE) and out of this region Territory of Orleans organized 1804, admitted to Union Apr. 30, 1812 as state of Louisiana, the first to be carved out of Louisiana Purchase; part of state E of Mississippi river N of Lake Pontchartrain acquired with occupation of West Florida by U.S. 1813; passed ordinance of secession Jan. 26, 1861; repealed ordinance of secession, abolished slavery 1864; readmitted to Union July 18, 1868; present constitution adopted 1921.

2 City, Pike co., E Missouri, on Mississippi river 25 m. SE of Hannibal; pop. (1970c) 4533; dairy products, plastics; apples.

Louisiana Point. Point at SW extremity of Louisiana, on E side of entrance to Sabine Pass.

Louisiana Purchase. The territory purchased Apr. 30, 1803 for $15,000,000 by the United States from France; extended from the Mississippi to the Rocky Mts. and from Gulf of Mexico to British America (Canada), including the basin of the Missouri river and the major part of the Great Plains drained by western tributaries of the Mississippi; 885,000 sq. m.; out of it were later formed four states (Arkansas, Iowa, Missouri, and Nebraska) and parts of nine others (Louisiana, Minnesota, Oklahoma, Kansas, Colorado, Wyoming, Montana, North Dakota, and South Dakota); with ill-defined boundaries, had been acquired by Spain from France 1762 in compensation for Spanish losses as French ally in the Seven Years' War; and was retroceded to France by Treaty of San Ildefonso Oct. 1, 1800.

Lou·is Trich·ardt \lü-i(s)-ˈtrich-ərt\. Town, N Transvaal, NE Rep. of South Africa, 225 m. NE of Pretoria; pop. (1967e) 14,800; on S slope of Squtpansberg Mts.; in agricultural region (esp. cotton).

Lou·is·ville \ˈlü-ē-ˌvil, ˈlü-əs-\. 1 Town, Boulder co., N cen. Colorado, 18 m. NW of Denver; pop. (1970c) 2409; residential.

2 City, ⊗ of Jefferson co., E cen. Georgia, 40 m. SW of Augusta; pop. (1970c) 2691; lumber; peanuts; capital of Georgia 1796–1805.

3 Village, ⊗ of Clay co., SE cen. Illinois; pop. (1970c) 1020; oil wells; diversified agriculture.

4 City, ⊗ of Jefferson co., N cen. Kentucky, on Ohio river; largest city in the state; pop. (1970c) 361,958; market and trade center; produces food products, tobacco, chemicals, clothing, aluminum products, automobiles, rubber goods, electrical machinery; printing, brewing, distilling. Univ. of Louisville (1798; oldest municipal university in U.S.), Catherine Spalding Coll. (1829), Simons Univ. (1879), Bellarmine Ursuline Coll. (1950), Kentucky Southern Coll. (1960), Jefferson Community Coll. (1967). Settled 1778; chartered as city 1828; grew rapidly as major river port from 1820; heavily damaged by tornado 1890.

5 City, ⊗ of Winston co., E cen. Mississippi, 45 m. SW of Columbus; pop. (1970c) 6626; bricks; sawmill; poultry and dairy farms.

6 Village, Stark co., NE Ohio, 7 m. ENE of Canton; pop. (1970c) 6298; structural steel, women's clothing; foundry; dairy farms.

Lou·lé \lō-ˈlā\. Commune, Faro dist., S Portugal, 10 m. NNW of Faro; manufactures leather, porcelain, esparto-grass and palm products; silver and copper mines.

Lou·ny \ˈlō-nē\ *or Ger.* **Laun** \ˈlau̇n\. Town, Czech S.R., NW Czechoslovakia, 35 m. NW of Prague on the Ohře river; pop. (1968e) 13,574.

Loup \ˈlüp\. 1 River, E cen. Nebraska; including North Loup ab. 280 m. long; rises in three branches, North Loup, Middle Loup, and South Loup rivers, and flows E into Platte river at Columbus in SE Platte co.

2 County in Nebraska. See table at NEBRASKA.

Loup City. City, ⊗ of Sherman co., cen. Nebraska, 42 m. NW of Grand Island; pop. (1970c) 1456.

Lourdes \ˈlu̇(ə)rd(z)\. Commune, Hautes-Pyrénées dept., SW France, on the Gave de Pau 11 m. SSW of Tarbes; pop.

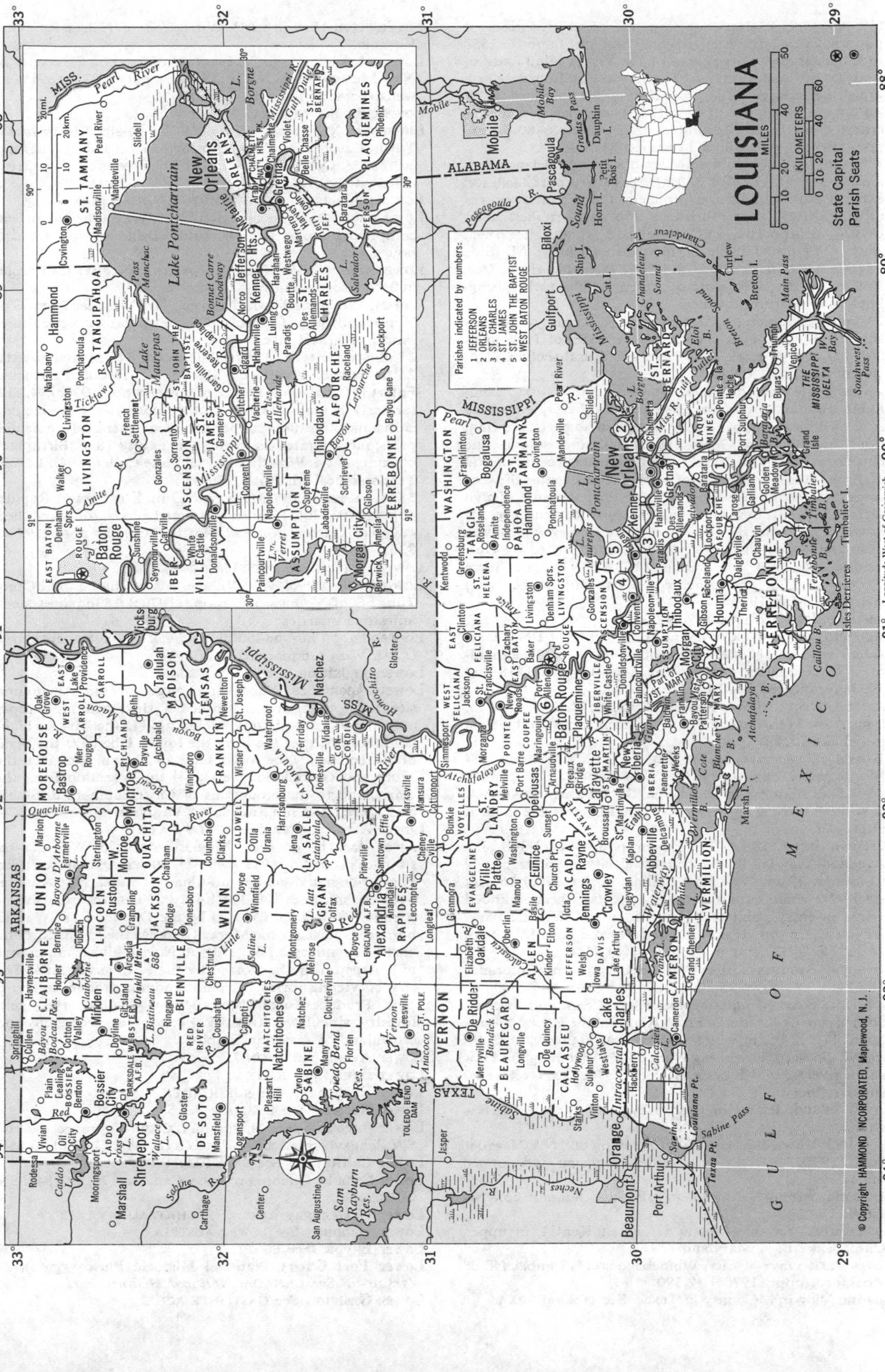

LOUISIANA
MILES
KILOMETERS
State Capital
Parish Seats
Parishes indicated by numbers:
1 JEFFERSON
2 ORLEANS
3 ST. CHARLES
4 ST. JAMES
5 ST. JOHN THE BAPTIST
6 WEST BATON ROUGE
GULF OF MEXICO
Longitude West of Greenwich
© Copyright HAMMOND INCORPORATED, Maplewood, N.J.
ARKANSAS
MISSISSIPPI
TEXAS
ALABAMA
Baton Rouge
New Orleans
Shreveport
Lake Charles
Lafayette
Monroe
Alexandria
Lake Pontchartrain

(1968c) 17,939; slate quarries; one of chief shrines of pilgrimage in Europe, having become famous 1858 through reputed apparitions of the Virgin (Our Lady of Lourdes) to a peasant girl (Bernadette of Lourdes) in a grotto here; large underground basilica completed 1958.

Lou·ren·ço Mar·ques \lə-ˌren(t)-(ˌ)sō-ˌmär-ˈkes\. 1 Southernmost district of Mozambique, SE Africa; 6480 sq. m.; pop. (1970p) 799,358; ✱ Lourenço Marques.
2 Seaport, its ✱, also ✱ of Mozambique, on Delagoa Bay; met. area pop. (1970p) 383,775; extensive port facilities; exports coal, agricultural products, timber; produces cement, pottery, soap, furniture, footwear, rubber; univ. (1962); incorporated 1887; developed rapidly after 1895.

Louth. 1 \ˈlau̇th, ˈlau̇t͟h\. County, Leinster prov., NE Eire; 317 sq. m.; pop. (1971p) 74,899; ⊗ Dundalk; rivers Dee, Boyne, Glyde; oats, potatoes, turnips; livestock raising, linen manufacture, tourism.
2 \ˈlau̇th\. Municipal borough, Parts of Lindsey, Lincolnshire, E England, on the Lud 28 m. SSE of Hull; pop. (1971p) 11,746; trade center in agricultural section.

Loutro. See PHOENIX 4.

Lou·vain \lü-ˈva^{n}\ *or Flem.* **Leu·ven** \ˈlə(r)v-ə(n)\. Commune, Brabant prov., cen. Belgium, on the Djile river 15 m. E of Brussels; pop. (1969e) 32,419; radio parts; brewing, flour milling; has Gothic town hall and several fine churches. Residence of dukes of Brabant 11th cent.; capital of Brabant and at height of prosperity as center of wool trade 14th cent.; decreased in importance because of civil wars 1379–83, but later became seat of learning; its university (founded 1425) had great library which was destroyed when town was captured and sacked by Germans Aug. 1914, and rebuilt (1921–28) by gifts from citizens of U.S. and other countries, only to be again destroyed May 1940.

Louvière, La. See LA LOUVIÈRE.

Lou·viers \lü-ˈvyā\. Commune, Eure dept., N France, on Eure river 14 m. N of Évreux; pop. (1968c) 15,326; agricultural trade center; textiles. Taken by English 1418 and 1431; recaptured 1440 by French.

Lo·vat \lə-ˈvat\. River, Russian S.F.S.R., U.S.S.R.; 320 m. long; flows N through Velikiye Luki and Novgorod Oblast into Lake Ilmen.

Lov·ćen \ˈlōv-ˌchen\ *or* **Lov·chen** \-ˌchen\. Mountain, SW Montenegro, Yugoslavia, just W of Cetinje; 5735 ft.

Love \ˈləv\. County in Oklahoma. See table at OKLAHOMA.

Lo·vech \ˈlō-ˌvech\. 1 Province of cen. Bulgaria. See table at BULGARIA.
2 Town, its ✱, 18 m. S of Pleven; pop. (1968e) 36,138.

Love·land \ˈləv-lənd\. 1 Commercial city, Larimer co., N Colorado, 12 m. S of Fort Collins; pop. (1970c) 16,220; steel, electronic equipment; sugar beets, wheat; founded 1877; an entry point to Rocky Mountain National Park.
2 City, Clermont, Hamilton, and Warren cos., SW Ohio, 16 m. NE of Cincinnati; pop. (1970c) 7144.

Loveland Mountain. Peak in Park co., cen. Colorado; 13,624 ft.

Loveland Pass. Mountain pass, Clear Creek and Summit cos., N cen. Colorado, in Front Range of the Rocky Mountains; 11,992 ft.; in winter sports area; highway.

Lov·ell \ˈləv-əl\. Town, Big Horn co., N Wyoming, on Shoshone river 43 m. NE of Cody; pop. (1970c) 2371; oil wells, sugar refinery.

Lovell Island. Island in Boston Bay, off Boston, Massachusetts.

Love·lock \ˈləv-ˌläk\. City, ⊗ of Pershing co., NW Nevada; pop. (1970c) 1571; tourist center; tungsten and copper mines.

Lo·ve·nia, Mount \-lō-ˈvē-nē-ə\. Peak, E Summit co., NE Utah; 13,227 ft.

Love Point \ˈləv-\. Point at N end of Kent I. in upper Chesapeake Bay, Maryland.

Loves Park \ˈləvz-\. City, Winnebago co., N Illinois, NE of Rockford; pop. (1970c) 12,390.

Lov·ing \ˈləv-iŋ\. County in Texas. See table at TEXAS.

Lov·ing·ston \ˈləv-iŋ-stən\. Village, ⊗ of Nelson co., cen. Virginia.

Lov·ing·ton \ˈləv-iŋ-tən\. Town, ⊗ of Lea co., SE corner of New Mexico, 23 m. NNW of Hobbs; pop. (1970c) 8915; oil wells, potash mines; agriculture.

Lovongai. See NEW HANOVER 2.

Lo·vo·si·ce \ˈlō-və-ˌsit-sə\ *or Ger.* **Lo·bo·sitz** \ˈlō-bə-ˌzits\. Town, Czech S.R., W Czechoslovakia, on Labe (Elbe) river; battle Oct. 1, 1756 in which Frederick the Great defeated the Austrians.

Low Archipelago. See TUAMOTU ARCHIPELAGO.

Low Countries. Name of region bordering on the North Sea, comprising modern Netherlands, Belgium, and Luxembourg.

Lowe, Mount \-ˈlō\. Peak, Los Angeles co., SW California; 5601 ft.; scenic railway; tourist resort.

Low·ell \ˈlō-əl\. 1 Town, Lake co., NW Indiana, 20 m. S of Hammond; pop. (1970c) 3839; septic tanks; agriculture; sand and gravel pits.
2 Industrial city, a ⊗ of Middlesex co., NE Massachusetts, 23 m. NW of Boston on Merrimack river at Pawtucket Falls (32 ft.), its chief source of power; pop. (1970c) 94,239; formerly a major textile center; industries now include electronics, plastics, rubber products, chemicals, machine parts; incorporated as town 1826, as city 1836. Birthplace of James A.M. Whistler. Lowell State Coll. (1894); Lowell Technological Institute (1895).
3 City, Kent co., W Michigan, 17 m. E of Grand Rapids; pop. (1970c) 3068; furniture, canned goods, tools and dies.
4 Town, Gaston co., SW North Carolina; pop. (1970c) 3307.

Lowell, Lake. See DEER FLAT DAM.

Low·ell·ville \ˈlō-əl-ˌvil\. Village, Mahoning co., NE Ohio, 7 m. SE of Youngstown; pop. (1970c) 1836; sheet steel; limestone quarries.

Lö·wen·burg \ˈlər-vən-ˌbu̇(ə)rg\. Peak of the Siebengebirge (*q.v.*), West Germany; 1506 ft.

Lower Andalusia. See ANDALUSIA 2.

Lower Apennines. Subsidiary ranges of the Apennines, situated in the triangular space bet. the Apennines proper and the W coast of Italy, including: (1) the Tuscan highland, bounded on the S by the lower Tiber; (2) the plain of Maremma; (3) the Alban Hills and Lepini Mts. (bet. the Tiber and Garigliano rivers); (4) the S section from the Garigliano to the mountains of Castellammare di Stabia and Sorrento Penin., including Vesuvius.

Lower Arrow Lake. See ARROW LAKE.

Lower Austria *or Ger.* **Nie·der·ö·ster·reich** \ˌnē-dər-ˈœ-stə(r)-ˌrīk\; *from 1938 to 1945* **Lower Danube** *or Ger.* **Nie·der·do·nau** \ˌnē-dər-ˈdō-(ˌ)nau̇\. State, NE Austria; 7402 sq. m.; pop. (1971p) 1,411,000 (figures exclusive of Vienna); ✱ Vienna. Crossed by the Danube from W to E; bordered on NE by the Morava and has the Leitha forming part of boundary on SE. Hilly in N with higher mountains of E Alps on the S, crossed by the Semmering Pass. The city of Vienna forms a separate administrative unit in E part. Produces sugar beet, potatoes, wheat, rye, fruit; forestry, viticulture; livestock. Formerly an archduchy and crownland of Austrian Empire.

Lower Avon. See AVON 7.

Lower Bann. See BANN.

Lower Burgundy. See BURGUNDY.

Lower Burma. See BURMA.

Lower Bur·rell \-ˈbər-əl, -ˈbə-rəl\. City, Westmoreland co., SW Pennsylvania, NE of Pittsburgh; pop. (1970c) 13,654.

Lower California. See BAJA CALIFORNIA.

Lower Canada. Quebec province, Canada, 1791 to 1841. See QUEBEC.

Lower Chateaugay Lake. See CHATEAUGAY LAKES.

Lower Danube. See LOWER AUSTRIA.

Lower Egypt. See EGYPT.

Lower Fort Gar·ry National Historic Park \-ˈga(ə)r-ē-, -ˈge(ə)r-\. See CANADA, *National Historic Parks.*

Lower Gastein. See GASTEINER ACHE.

Lower Guinea. See GUINEA 1.

Lower Hell Hole Dam and **Lower Hell Hole Reservoir.** See UNITED STATES, *Dams and Reservoirs.*

Lower Hutt \-'hət\. City, suburb of Wellington, S North I., New Zealand; pop. (1970e) 59,400.

Lower Klamath Lake. See KLAMATH LAKES.

Lower Lorraine. See LORRAINE 2.

Lower Mat·e·cum·be Key \-ˌmat-ə-'kəm-bē-\. See FLORIDA KEYS.

Lower Mer·i·on \-'mer-ē-ən, -'mar-\. Urban township, Montgomery co., SE Pennsylvania, NW of Philadelphia; pop. (1970c) 63,470.

Lower New York Bay. See NEW YORK BAY.

Lower Palatinate. See PALATINATE.

Lower Peninsula. Southern part of Michigan, S of Straits of Mackinac.

Lower Red Lake. See RED LAKE 1.

Lower Rhine *or Ger.* **Nie·der·rhein** \ˌnēd-ə(r)-'rīn\ *or Du.* **Ne·der Rijn** \ˌnād-ə(r)-'rīn\. The section of the Rhine river bet. Bonn, West Germany, and the North Sea; in Netherlands the general name for its various sections.

Lower Saranac Lake. See SARANAC LAKES.

Lower Sax·o·ny \-'sak-sə-nē\ *or Ger.* **Nie·der·sach·sen** \'nēd-ər-ˌzäk-sən\. A state of West Germany; 18,305 sq. m.; pop. (1969e) 7,067,200; ✻ Hannover; wheat, livestock; iron ore, petroleum; established 1946.

Lower Silesia. See SILESIA.

Lower South·amp·ton \-sau̇th-'(h)am(p)-tən\. Urban township, Bucks co., SE Pennsylvania, NE of Philadelphia; pop. (1970c) 17,578.

Lower Tunguska. See TUNGUSKA.

Lowes·toft \'lō-stəf(t), -ˌstȯft\. Municipal borough, East Suffolk, E England, on North Sea 23 m. ESE of Norwich; pop. (1971p) 52,182; shipbuilding; fisheries; manufactures electrical equipment, footwear, television sets; yachting center and seaside resort.

Lowes·water Lake \'lōz-ˌwȯt-ər-, -ˌwät-\. Lake, Cumberland, NW England, 6 m. SSE of Cockermouth; 1¼ m. long.

Ło·wicz \'lȯ-vich\. Commune, Łódź prov., cen. Poland, 47 m. WSW of Warsaw; pop. (1970p) 20,500; manufactures leather, clay goods; cattle market. In World War I taken by Germans Nov.–Dec. 1914 after fall of Łódź.

Lowlands, The. See HIGHLANDS, THE.

Lowndes \'lau̇n(d)z\. Counties in three states of the U.S. See tables at ALABAMA, GEORGIA, MISSISSIPPI.

Low·ther Hill \ˌlau̇-t͟hər-\. Mountain in the Lowthers, S Scotland; 2377 ft.

Low·thers, The \-'lau̇-t͟hərz\ *or* **Lead·hills** \'led-ˌhilz\. Mountain range in S Scotland, along boundary bet. Lanark and Dumfries cos.; highest peak **Green Lowther** 2403 ft.

Low·ville \'lau̇-ˌvil\. Village, ⊗ of Lewis co., N cen. New York, 26 m. ESE of Watertown; pop. (1970c) 3671; lumber; dairy farms.

Loxa. See LOJA 3.

Loy·al·han·na Creek \ˌlȯi(-ə)l-'han-ə-\. River, SW Pennsylvania; ab. 40 m. long; flows NW through Westmoreland co. to unite with Conemaugh river in SW Indiana co. and form Kiskiminetas river.

Loy·all \'lȯi(-ə)l\. City, Harlan co., SE Kentucky, 28 m. NE of Middlesborough; pop. (1970c) 1212.

Loy·al·ty Islands \'lȯi(ə)l-tē-\ *or* **Loy·al·ties** \-tēz\ *or* **Îles Loy·au·té** \ˌēl-lwȧ-yō-'tā\. Island group in E part of New Caledonia overseas territory, forming a chain 60 m. E of New Caledonia and ab. 160 m. SW of the S end of the New Hebrides group; 755 sq. m.; pop. (1956c) 11,409. Chief islands Lifou, Maré, and Uvéa. Mostly low coral upheavals; exports copra and rubber.

Lo–yang \'lō-'yäŋ\ *also* **Ho·nan** \'hō-'nan, 'hə-'nän\. City, N Honan prov., E cen. China, ab. 120 m. W of K'ai-feng S of the Yellow river; pop. (1970e) 750,000; trade center; coal mining, food processing; agricultural machinery; in early history of China successively the capital of the Eastern Han, Chin, Northern Wei, and Sui dynasties; also the east capital under the T'ang dynasty and the west capital under the Sung dynasty.

Lo·zère \lō-'ze(ə)r\. 1 Range in Cévennes Mts., S France; highest peak Pic de Finiels 5585 ft.

2 Department of S France. See table at FRANCE.

Lu. See TO.

Lu·a·la·ba \ˌlü-ə-'läb-ə\ *or Fr.* **Lou·a·la·ba** \lwȧ-lȧ-bȧ\. River, SE Zaire; flows N and joins the Luapula to form the Congo river; ab. 400 m. long to confluence with Luapula; from this point to Stanley Falls, 1000 m., the upper Congo often called the Lualaba.

Lu·an *or* **Lwan** \lə-'wän\. River, Hopeh prov., NE China; ab. 400 m. long; rises in E Inner Mongolia, flows N, then E, then SE to Gulf of Chihli. Ch'eng-te on its N bank.

Lu·an·da \lu̇-'an-də\ *or* **Lo·an·da** \lō-\. 1 District, NW Angola; 13,046 sq. m.; pop. (1970p) 302,538.

2 *also* **São Pau·lo de Loanda** \sau̇ⁿm-'pau̇-lü-ˌdel-u̇-'an-də\. Commercial city and seaport, ✻ of Angola and ✻ of Luanda dist., on Bay of Bengo; pop. (1970p) 475,328; exports ores and agricultural produce; oil refining; univ. (1962); founded by Paulo Dias de Novais 1576; made administrative center of Angola 1627.

Luang Pra·bang *or* **Luang·pra·bang** \lu̇-ˌäŋ-prə-'bäŋ\. 1 Former native Lao state (kingdom), N Laos, SE Asia; formerly under French protection, declared its independence of the French Apr. 1945; amalgamated with rest of Laos 1946.

2 Town, N Laos, on the left bank of the Mekong river; pop. (1970e) 25,000; trade and market center; connected by highway with Vientiane; limit of navigation on the Mekong. Has large pagoda on hill above the town; residence of king of Laos.

Luangue. See LOANGE.

Lu·ang·wa \lü-'äŋ-(ˌ)wä\ *also* **Lo·ang·wa** \lō-'äŋ-wä\. River, E Zambia; ab. 500 m. long; flows SSW into Zambezi river, in its lower course forming a section of the W boundary of Mozambique.

Lu·an·shya \lü-'än-(ˌ)shä\. Town, cen. Zambia; pop. (1967e) 73,000; copper mining; metalworking and clothing industries.

Lu·a·pu·la \ˌlü-ə-'pü-lə\. River, cen. Africa; outlet of Lake Bangweulu through the large swamp S of the lake, actually a continuation of the Chambezi; flows N along boundary bet. NW Zambia and SE Zaire through Lake Mweru and joins Lualaba to form Congo river.

Luar·ca \lu̇-'är-kə\. Seaport, Oviedo prov., NW Spain, on Bay of Biscay 37 m. WNW of Oviedo; pop. (1970p) 19,599; metal products, paper; meat-salting plants.

Lu·ba·an·tun \ˌlü-bə-'än-ˌtün\. Site, S British Honduras, 15 m. NW of Punta Gorda; Mayan ruins, discovered 1924.

Lu·bań \'lü-ˌbän (-yə)\ *or Ger.* **Lau·ban** \'lau̇-ˌbän\. City, W Wrocław prov., SW Poland, 38 m. WSW of Legnica; pop. (1968e) 16,800; town hall (1539–43); made city in 13th cent.; formerly in Germany, assigned to Poland by Potsdam Conference 1945.

Lu·bang \lü-'bäŋ\. 1 Group of islands, Phil., off NW coast of Mindoro I. 46 m. SW of entrance to Manila Bay and separated from Luzon by Verde Island Passage; 95 sq. m.; chief town Lubang. Comprises Lubang I. and the small islands of Ambil, Golo, and Cabra. Inhabitants are Tagalogs. Occupied by U.S. forces Mar. 1945.

2 Largest island of group; 74 sq. m.; 17 m. long.

3 Municipality on N coast of the island; pop. (1969e) 16,200.

Lu·bao \lü-ˈbä-ō\. Municipality, S Pampanga prov., Luzon, Phil., on NW edge of Pampanga delta 9 m. SW of San Fernando; pop. (1969e) 60,700.

Lüb·be·nau \ˈlü-bə-ˌnau̇\. City, Cottbus dist., East Germany, on the Spree river 18 m. NW of Cottbus; pop. (1970e) 21,035; vegetable packing.

Lub·bock \ˈləb-ək\. 1 County in NW Texas. See table at TEXAS.

2 Industrial city, its ⊗; pop. (1970c) 149,101; major cotton market; cottonseed oil, dairy products, feed; oil wells; dairy and poultry farms; Texas Technological Coll. (1923); Lubbock Christian Univ. (1957); town laid out 1891, incorporated as city 1907.

Lu·bec \lü-ˈbek\. Town, Washington co., SE corner of Maine, on Passamaquoddy Bay across from Campobello I.; pop. (1970c) 1949; fishing.

Lü·beck \ˈlü-ˌbek\. Commercial and manufacturing city, Schleswig-Holstein, West Germany, on two small streams connecting with Lübeck Bay 35 m. NE of Hamburg; pop. (1969e) 242,855; West Germany's most important Baltic port, exporting salt, iron, coal, chemicals; shipbuilding, fish processing, iron and steel founding; five 13–14th cent. Gothic churches, Gothic town hall, 13th cent. hospital.

History: Founded 1143 by count of Holstein; taken by Henry the Lion (see SAXONY) 1158, secured final privileges of imperial city 1226; became leading center for medieval German trade in Baltic region and "Queen of the Hanse" (see HANSE TOWNS); declined from 16th cent.; by Treaty of Lübeck 1629, Denmark withdrew from Thirty Years' War; captured by French 1810; its autonomy restored 1815, joined (*Ger.*) Zollverein and North German Confederation; lost its status as autonomous free state 1937 (see GERMANY). In World War II suffered major damage from Allied bombing and was taken by Allied forces May 4, 1945.

Lübeck Bay. Inlet of SW Bay of Mecklenburg; lies bet. Schleswig-Holstein, West Germany and Rostock dist., East Germany.

Lu·be·fu \lu̇-ˈbā-(ˌ)fü\. River in the Congo basin; ab. 200 m. long; flows W in cen. Zaire into the Sankuru river shortly before its junction with Kasai river.

Lu·bi·lash \lü-ˈbē-ˌlash\. River, the upper course of the Sankuru, S cen. Zaire.

Lu·bin \ˈlü-bən\ *or Ger.* **Lü·ben** \ˈlü-bən\. Town, N cen. Wrocław prov., SW Poland, ab. 40 m. WNW of Wrocław; pop. (1970p) 28,400; first mentioned 1267.

Lub·lin \ˈlü-blən, -ˌblēn\ *or Russ.* **Lyu·blin** \lē-ˈü-blən\. 1 Province of E Poland. See table at POLAND.

2 City, its ✱, 95 m. SE of Warsaw; pop. (1970p) 236,000; automobiles, agricultural implements, meat, sugar, and tobacco products; brewing, hop-drying; Catholic Univ. of Lublin (1918), Marie Curie-Sklodowska Univ. (1944), coll. of agriculture (1955). Once seat of several Polish diets, and later of High Polish Law Courts; received town rights 1317; captured by Austrians Aug. 1914 and July 1915; seat of Austrian-Hungarian military government in Poland during World War I. In World War II taken by Germans Sept. 1939 and retaken by Soviet forces July 25, 1944.

Lubnān, Jabal. See LEBANON MOUNTAINS.

Lub·ny \ˈlüb-nē\. Town, N Poltava Oblast, N cen. Ukrainian S.S.R., U.S.S.R., 110 m. E of Kiev; pop. (1967e) 36,000.

Lub·sko \ˈlüp-(ˌ)skȯ\ *or Ger.* **Som·mer·feld** \ˈzȯm-ər-ˌfelt\. Town, S Zielona Góra prov., W Poland, SE of Gubin; pop. (1968e) 12,700.

Lu·bua·gan \lü-ˈbwäg-än\. Municipality, ✱ of Kalinga-Apayao prov., Luzon, Phil.; pop. (1969e) 14,200.

Lu·bum·bashi \ˌlü-büm-ˈbäsh-ē\ *or formerly* **Eli·sa·beth·ville** \i-ˈliz-ə-bəth-ˌvil\. City, ✱ of Shaba prov., Zaire; pop. (1971e) 334,857; copper mining and smelting; food processing; bricks, soap; univ. (1955); founded 1910; center of the province's secession movement during initial years of republic's independence.

Lubungan. See KATIPUNAN.

Luca. See LUCCA 2.

Lu·ca·la \lu̇-ˈkäl-ə\. River, N Angola; ab. 130 m. long.

Lu·ca·nia \lü-ˈkān-yə, -ˈkän-\. 1 Ancient district of S Italy including modern Basilicata and part of Salerno prov. in S Campania.

2 Autonomous region, Italy. See BASILICATA.

Lucania Mountain \lü-ˈkā-nē-ə-, -nyə-\. Peak in St. Elias Mountains, SW Yukon Territory, Canada, N of Mt. Logan near Alaska border; 17,147 ft.

Lucanian Apennines *or Ital.* **Lucano, Appennino.** See table at APENNINES.

Lu·cas \ˈlü-kəs\. Name of counties in two states of the U.S. See tables at IOWA and OHIO.

Lu·ca·yas \lu̇-ˈkī-əs\. Early Spanish name of the BAHAMA ISLANDS.

Luc·ban \lük-ˈbän\. Municipality, Quezon prov., Luzon, Phil., near Laguna border 15 m. NNW of Lucena; pop. (1969e) 23,700; in mountainous region; center of rice growing.

Luc·ca \ˈlü-kə\. 1 Province of Tuscany, cen. Italy. See table at ITALY.

2 *or anc.* **Lu·ca** \ˈlü-kə\. Commune, its ✱, 38 m. W by N of Florence; pop. (1968e) 91,401; road and rail center; market town in olive-growing region; silk, flour, paper, jute; 11th–14th cent. cathedral; 8th cent. church of San Frediano; ducal palace; aqueduct; ancient Roman remains.

History: Ancient town founded as Roman colony in territory conquered from Ligurians before 180 B.C.; on ancient Cassian Way; chief town in Tuscany before rise of Florence (*q.v.*); early in 14th cent. lost freedom and came to be ruled as duchy by Castruccio Castracani 1327; sold to Florence 1341 but achieved independence by mid-15th cent. as republic ruled by an oligarchy; occupied by French 1799 and given as a principality to Napoleon's sister 1805; awarded to member of Spanish Bourbon family 1815; reunited with Tuscany 1847 and thus became part of kingdom of Italy 1860.

Luce \ˈlüs\. 1 County in Michigan. See table at MICHIGAN.

2 Small river in N France, an E tributary of Avre river, ab. 10 m. SE of Amiens; battles 1918.

Luce Bay. Inlet of Irish Sea on extreme SW coast of Scotland; enclosed by Mull of Galloway on W; 16 m. long; 18 1/2 m. wide at the mouth.

Luce·dale \ˈlüs-ˌdāl\. Town, ⊗ of George co., SE Mississippi; pop. (1970c) 2083.

Lu·ce·na \lü-ˈsā-nə\. 1 Chartered city, ✱ of Quezon prov., Luzon, Phil., on N shore of Tayabas Bay 63 m. SE of Manila; pop. (1970e) 68,500; made capital 1901.

2 Commune, Córdoba prov., S Spain, 39 m. SE of Córdoba; pop. (1970p) 27,920; horse breeding; mineral waters; manufactures copper and zinc products, glassware, shoes, iron products, chemicals.

Lu·če·nec \ˈlüch-ə-ˌnets\ *or Hung.* **Lo·soncz** \ˈlō-ˌshōn(t)s\. Town, Slovak S.R., Czechoslovakia, on the Ipel' 65 m. NE of Budapest; pop. (1968e) 20,156; textiles.

Lucentum. See ALICANTE 2.

Lu·ce·ra \lü-ˈcher-ə\. Commune, Foggia prov., Apulia, SE Italy, 12 m. WNW of Foggia; pop. (1968e) 29,523; building materials, wool, dairy products; oil refineries; early 14th cent. cathedral; ruins of castle built by Frederick II.

Lu·cerne \lü-ˈsərn\ *or Ger.* **Lu·zern** \lüt-ˈse(ə)rn\. 1 Swiss canton; see history and table at SWITZERLAND.

2 Commune, its ✱, cen. Switzerland, on W shore of Lake of Lucerne 25 m. SSW of Zurich; pop. (1970c) 69,879; rail and steamer connections; textiles; a major tourist center; medieval circular walls and watch towers, 14th cent. Kapellbrücke, 15th cent. Mühlenbrücke (covered bridges with notable paintings, including a *Danse macabre*), Renaissance town hall, 17th cent. cathedral, Jesuit church, and many monuments, including esp. the famous Lion of Lucerne carved in rock. Developed around monastery of St. Leodegar (8th cent.); joined Swiss Confederation 1332; stronghold of Catholicism during Reformation; took part in Sonderbund War (see SWITZERLAND); occupied by Federals 1847.

Lucerne, Lake of *or* **Lake of the Four Forest Cantons** *or Ger.* **Vier·wald·stät·ter See** \fi(ə)r-'vält-ˌs(h)tet-ər-ˌzā\. Lake in cen. Switzerland, enclosed by Schwyz, Uri, Unterwalden, and Lucerne cantons; 24 m. long and bet. 1/2 m. and 2 m. wide; 44 sq. m.; max. depth 702 ft.

Lucerne Mines. Unincorporated locality, Indiana co., W cen. Pennsylvania, ab. 4 m. S of Indiana (borough); pop. (1970c) 1380.

Lu–chou *or* **Lu·chow** \'lü-'jō\ *or formerly* **Lu·hsien** \'lü-shē-'en\. City, S Szechwan prov., S cen. China, on N bank of the Yangtze ENE of I-pin, 146 m. SSE of Ch'eng-tu; pop. (1970e) 225,000; chief market in W China in salt trade.

Lu·chow \'lü-'jō\. 1 City, Anhwei, E China. See HO-FEI.

2 City, Szechwan, S cen. China. See LU-CHOU.

Luchu Islands. See RYUKYU ISLANDS.

Łuck. See ŁUTSK.

Luck·au \'lu̇k-ˌau̇\. Commune, Cottbus dist., East Germany, in Lower Lusatia 45 m. SSE of Berlin; pop. (1965e) 6300; scene of defeat of Oudinot by Count von Bülow 1813.

Luck·en·wal·de \ˌlu̇k-ən-'väl-də\. City, Potsdam dist., East Germany, 31 m. SSW of Berlin; pop. (1970e) 28,984; clothing, furniture, paper; brewing, metalworking. Site of Cistercian monastery in 12th cent.; received charter 1442; became important mid-18th cent.

Luck·now \'lək-ˌnau̇\. City, ✱ of Uttar Pradesh, N India, on Gomati river 270 m. ESE of Delhi; pop. (1970e) 783,718; important rail center with railroad workshops; paper and metal factories, a distillery, printing presses, and native handicrafts; univ. (1921). Has many fine old buildings including the white marble Imambara, Pearl Palace with its famed collection of Oriental manuscripts, palaces of Chhattar Manzil, spacious Kaisar Bagh, unfinished great mosque with the mausoleum of Mohammed Ali Shah, and the suburban palace of Bibiapur; also the residency where in the Mutiny the British were besieged from June 1857 till relieved by Gen. Campbell in Nov.; forced to abandon the city, the British retook it Mar. 1858. After capture in 1528 gained prominence under the Moguls and in 18th cent. as capital of Oudh, a position held until Oudh and Agra were joined as United Provinces 1902.

Lu·çon \lü-'sōⁿ\. Commune, S Vendée dept., W France; pop. (1962c) 8332; connected with sea by canal ab. 8 m. long; bishopric; had among its bishops Richelieu 1607–14.

Lu·cre·cia, Point \-lü-'krā-sē-ə\. Cape on N coast of Oriente prov., E Cuba.

Lucronius. See LOGROÑO.

Lucus Augusti. See LUGO 3.

Lü·den·scheid \'lüd-ᵊn-ˌshīt\. Industrial city, North Rhine-Westphalia, West Germany, 37 m. E of Düsseldorf; pop. (1969e) 79,107; manufactures aluminum, metal goods, plastics; tourist resort; settled 9th cent.; chartered 13th cent.; member of Hanseatic League; to Brandenburg in 17th cent.

Lü·de·ritz \'lüd-ə-rəts\ *or formerly* **An·gra Pe·que·na** \ˌaŋ-grə-pə-'kwē-nə\. Town, SW South-West Africa, on Atlantic Ocean 520 m. NNW of Cape Town; pop. (1960c) 3604; well-sheltered harbor which is seaboard terminus for rail line; health resort; founded 1883. See SOUTH-WEST AFRICA.

Lu·dhi·a·na \ˌlüd-ē-'än-ə\. Town, Punjab, NW India, near Sutlej river; pop. (1970e) 377,664; railroad junction; trade center; hosiery, textiles; women's medical school, agricultural univ. (1962); founded 1840.

Lud·ing·ton \'ləd-iŋ-tən\. City, ⊗ of Mason co., W Michigan, on Lake Michigan 51 m. N of Muskegon; pop. (1970c) 9021; diversified light industry, resort center and lake port.

Lud·low \'ləd-(ˌ)lō\. 1 Industrial city, Kenton co., N Kentucky, NW suburb of Covington; pop. (1970c) 5815; electrical equipment; agriculture.

2 Town, Hampden co., SW Massachusetts, 7 m. NE of Springfield; pop. (1970c) 17,580; part of Springfield until 1775.

3 Village in Ludlow town (pop. [1970c] 2463), Windsor co., E Vermont, on Black river 13 m. WNW of Springfield; pop. (1970c) 1508.

4 Market town, Shropshire, W England, on the Teme 37 m. WSW of Birmingham; rural dist. pop. (1971p) 23,481; tourist center; chartered 1189; here Samuel Butler wrote *Hudibras,* and in the 11th cent. Norman castle Milton's *Comus* was first performed (1634).

Ludlow, Mount. Peak, S cen. Vermont, on boundary bet. Windsor and Rutland cos.; 3372 ft.

Lu·do·wici \ˌlüd-ə-'wis-ē\. City, ⊗ of Long co., SE Georgia; pop. (1970c) 1419; lumber; agriculture.

Lud·vi·ka \'lüd-vik-ə\. Town, Kopparberg co., Sweden; pop. (1970e) 21,689; iron foundry.

Lud·wigs·burg \'lüd-vigz-ˌbu̇(ə)rg\. City, Baden-Württemberg, West Germany, W of the Neckar and 8 m. N of Stuttgart; pop. (1969e) 78,812; machinery, iron and wire products, musical instruments, textiles; 18th cent. baroque church; two 18th cent. castles; founded early 18th cent.; a famous porcelain center 1758–1824.

Lud·wigs·ha·fen am Rhein \ˌlüd-vigz-'häf-ən-äm-'rīn\. Commercial and manufacturing city, SE Rhineland-Palatinate, West Germany, on W bank of Rhine river opp. Mannheim; pop. (1969e) 174,024; important railroad junction and river port; tourist center; large chemical industry; steel, glass; founded early 17th cent.; named by Louis I of Bavaria 1843; made city 1859; in World War II heavily damaged by Allied bombing.

Lu·e·bo \lu̇-'ā-(ˌ)bō\. Town, Kasai-Occidental prov., S cen. Zaire, on the Lulua river.

Lu·em·be \lu̇-'em-bē\. River in the Congo basin, S cen. Africa; ab. 350 m. long; rises in NE Angola, flows N into Kasai river.

Lu–feng \'lü-'feŋ\. Town, cen. Yunnan, S China, 65 m. W of K'un-ming.

Luf·kin \'ləf-kən\. Commercial and industrial city, ⊗ of Angelina co., E Texas, 115 m. NE of Houston; pop. (1970c) 23,049; paper, vehicle bodies, iron and steel, lumber; diversified agriculture.

Lug. See LUGG.

Lu·ga \'lü-gə\. Town, W Leningrad Oblast, Russian S.F.S.R., U.S.S.R., 80 m. S of Leningrad on railroad to Pskov; pop. (1967e) 29,000; held by Germans 1941–44; retaken by U.S.S.R. Feb. 13, 1944.

Lu·ga·no \lü-'gän-(ˌ)ō\ *or Ger.* **Lau·is** \lau̇-əs\. Commune, Ticino canton, SE cen. Switzerland, on N shore of Lake Lugano 13 m. S of Bellinzona; pop. (1970c) 22,280; episcopal see; tourist and health resort; manufactures chocolate, tobacco; banking. First mentioned in 6th cent.; taken from duke of Milan by Swiss Confederation 1512; capital of former Swiss canton of Lugano, became part of Ticino canton 1803.

Lugano, Lake; *Ital.* **La·go di Lugano** \'läg-ō-dē-\ *or* **Lago Ce·re·sio** \-chə-'res-ē-ˌō\; *anc.* **La·cus Ce·re·si·us** \ˌlā-kə(s)-sə-'rē-zh(ē-)əs\. Lake in S Ticino canton, S Switzerland and N Italy, bet. Lakes Maggiore and Como; ab. 19 sq. m.; max. depth 945 ft.

Lugansk. See VOROSHILOVGRAD.

Luganville. See SANTO.

Lu·gau \'lü-ˌgau̇\. Industrial city, Karl-Marx-Stadt dist., East Germany, at N foot of Erzgebirge 10 m. SW of Karl-Marx-Stadt; pop. (1970e) 10,194; coal mining; iron founding; manufactures gloves, chemicals.

Lug·du·nen·sis \ˌləg-d(y)ə-'nen(t)-səs\. One of the five administrative divisions of Gaul established by Augustus 27 B.C. comprising the cen. and N part and named from its capital, Lugdunum (Lyons); later Armorica formed its NW part; in 5th cent. A.D. most of it passed to the Franks.

Lugdunum. See LYONS.

Lugdunum Batavorum. See LEIDEN.

Lu·gen·da \lü-'jen-də\. River, N Mozambique, SE Africa; flows out of Lake Chiuta NE into Ruvuma river.

Lugg *or* **Lug** \'ləg\. River, E Wales and W England; over 40 m. long; rises in Radnorshire, Wales, flows SE across English border into the Wye 5 m. below Hereford.

Luggarus. See LOCARNO.

Lugnaquilla. See WICKLOW MOUNTAINS.

Lu·go \'lü-(ˌ)gō\. 1 Commercial commune, Ravenna prov., Emilia-Romagna, N Italy, 15 m. W of Ravenna; pop. (1968e) 34,822; trade center, esp. for cattle and silk cocoons.

2 Province of NW Spain. See table at SPAIN.

3 *or anc.* **Lu·cus Au·gus·ti** \ˌlük-əs-ó-'gəs-(ˌ)tī, -ə-'gəs-\. Commune, ✱ of Lugo prov., NW Spain, on Miño river 48 m. SE of La Coruña; pop. (1970p) 63,830; trade center, esp. in cattle and preserved meats; manufactures leather, hats; sulfur spring; ancient Roman walls; 12th cent. cathedral; a former capital of Galicia; several times captured and destroyed.

Lu·goj \'lü-gȯzh\. Commercial city, Timiş co., W Romania, ab. 35 m. ESE of Timişoara on Timiş river; munic. pop. (1970e) 39,052; textiles.

Luguvallium *or* **Luguvallum.** See CARLISLE 6.

Lu·hai·ya *or* **Lo·hei·ya** \lü-'hī-ə, -'hā-\ *or* **Al–Lu·hay·yah** \ˌal-lü-'hī-ə, -'hā-ə\. Seaport, NW Yemen (✱ San'a), on Red Sea coast ab. 100 m. NW of San'a.

Lu·hit \'lü-ˌhit\ *or Chin.* **Lu–hei–t'e** \'lü-'hī-'tā\. River rising in SW China, and flowing SW into the Brahmaputra at the great bend in Arunachal Pradesh, NE India; Sadiya on its N bank near its mouth.

Lu–hsi \'lü-'shē\ *or formerly* **Mang·shih** \'mäŋ-'shi(ə)r\. Town, SW Yunnan prov., S China, ab. 270 m. NE of Mandalay, Burma; alt. 3500 ft.

Luhsien. See LU-CHOU.

Lui, Ben. See BEN LUI.

Lui·chow Peninsula \'lā-'jō-\ *or Chin.* **Lei–chou pan–tao** \'lā-'jō-'pän-'taù\. Peninsula of SW Kwangtung prov., SE China, separated from Hainan I. by Hainan Strait; on its E coast is Kwangchowan, a former French leased territory.

Luik. See LIÈGE 2.

Luimneach. See LIMERICK.

Lui·no \lə-'wē-(ˌ)nō\. Commune, Varese prov., Lombardy, N Italy, on E shore of Lake Maggiore 14 m. NNW of Varese; pop. (1968e) 13,525; scene of battle bet. Garibaldi and Austrians Aug. 14, 1848.

Lu·it·pold Coast \ˌlü-ət-ˌpȯlt-\ *or formerly* **Le·o·pold Coast** \ˌlē-ə-ˌpōld-\. Section of coast of Antarctica, ab. 78°38'S, 32°W, on SE coast of Weddell Sea, a part of Coats Land.

Lu·ján \lü-'hän\. 1 Short river in NE Buenos Aires prov., E cen. Argentina; flows E into Río de la Plata 23 m. NW of the city of Buenos Aires.

2 Town, Buenos Aires prov., E cen. Argentina, ab. 40 m. W of Buenos Aires; pop. (1960c) 28,976.

Lu·kan·ga Swamp \lü-ˌkäŋ-gə-\. Large marsh area in cen. Zambia, S cen. Africa.

Lukchun. See TURFAN 1.

Lu·ke·nie \lü-'kā-nyē\. River, cen. Zaire; ab. 450 m. long; flows W into Kasai river shortly before it joins the Congo; in its lower course, after being joined by waters from Lake Mai-Ndomde, known as Fimi river.

Lu–kou–ch'iao \'lü-'gō-chē-'aù\. City, Peking municipality, NE China, on E bank of the Yung-ting 9 m. SW of Peking; river crossed here by the Marco Polo Bridge (*q.v.*); scene July 7, 1937 of the clash bet. Chinese and Japanese troops which precipitated the Chinese-Japanese War (1937–45); after several demands by both governments China rejected the Japanese ultimatum of July 26, and Peiping (Peking) surrendered July 28.

Łu·ków \'lü-ˌküf\. Commune, Lublin prov., E Poland, 49 m. N of Lublin; pop. (1968e) 14,100; leather, oil.

Lu·ku·ga \lù-'kü-gə\. River, E Zaire; 200 m. long; flows W from Lake Tanganyika into the Lualaba (upper course of the Congo).

Lule. See LULEÄLV.

Lu·leå \'lü-lə-ˌō, -lē-ˌō\. Seaport, ⊗ of Norrbotten co., N Sweden, on Gulf of Bothnia at mouth of Luleälv river; pop. (1970e) 57,838; exports iron ore, timber, wood pulp; founded 1621; moved to present site 1649.

Lu·le·älv \'lü-lə-ˌelv\ *also* **Lu·le** \'lü-lə\. River in Norrbotten co., Sweden; 280 m. long; flows SE into the Gulf of Bothnia.

Lü·le·bur·gaz *or* **Lü·le Bur·gas** \ˌlü-lə-bùr-'gäz\. Town, S Kirklareli prov., Turkey, Europe, 86 m. WNW of İstanbul; pop. (1965c) 25,667; scene of decisive battle of the First Balkan War Oct. 28–30, 1912 in which Turks were defeated, causing their retirement to Constantinople.

Lu·ling \'lü-'liŋ\. See CHI-AN.

Luling \'lü-liŋ\. City, Caldwell co., S cen. Texas, 42 m. S of Austin; pop. (1970c) 4719; oil wells; diversified agriculture.

Lu·lon·ga \lü-'lȯŋ-gə\. River in NW Zaire; formed by junction of the Maringa and Lopori rivers, flows W into the Congo.

Lu·lua \lù-'lü-ə\. River, S Zaire; ab. 550 m. long; flows N into Kasai river.

Luluabourg. See KANANGA.

Lu·ma·djang *or Du.* **Loe·ma·djang** \ˌlü-mə-'jäŋ\. Town, East Java prov., Indonesia, in plain E of Mt. Semeru and S of Probolinggo; pop. (1961c) 39,536.

Lum·ber \'ləm-bər\. River, rising near boundary bet. Montgomery and Moore cos., cen. North Carolina, and flowing SE across South Carolina border, then S into Little Pee Dee river; 125 m. long.

Lum·ber·ton \'ləm-bərt-ᵊn\. City, ⊗ of Robeson co., S North Carolina, 32 m. S of Fayetteville; pop. (1970c) 16,191; cottonseed oil, fertilizer; bottling plant; agriculture.

Lump·kin \'ləm(p)-kən\. 1 County in Georgia. See table at GEORGIA.

2 City, ⊗ of Stewart co., W Georgia; pop. (1970c) 1431.

Lu·na \'lü-nə\. 1 County in New Mexico. See table at NEW MEXICO.

2 *or mod.* **Lu·ni** \'lü-nē\. Ancient town, Etruria, N Italy, on boundary bet. Etruria and Liguria; modern town site is W of Carrara, Tuscany; near the famous Carrara marble quarries. Destroyed by Saracens 1016. Gave its name to the district, **Lu·nig·i·a·na** \lù-ˌnij-ē-'än-ə\.

Lund \'lənd\. City, Malmöhus co., SW Sweden; pop. (1970e) 54,410; packaging materials, textiles; printing; educational center with univ. (1666) and technical institute (1961). Made bishopric 11th cent., archbishopric 1103, its archbishop becoming primate of Scandinavia 1163; reduced to bishopric 1536; scene of signing of a treaty 1679 bet. Sweden and Denmark.

Lundenburg. See BŘECLAV.

Lundi. See SAVE.

Lun·dy Island \ˌlən-dē-\. Island in Bristol Channel, 12 m. off coast of NW Devonshire, SW England; ab. 3½ m. long by ½ m. wide; ab. 2 sq. m.; lighthouse; once a pirate stronghold. Prehistoric remains; also ruins of chapel and castle.

Lun·dy's Lane \ˌlən-dēz-\. Roadway near Niagara Falls, Ontario, Canada; indecisive battle July 25, 1814 in which Americans and British both lost heavily.

Lü·ne·burg \'lü-nə-ˌbù(ə)rg\. City, Lower Saxony, West Germany, SE of Hamburg; pop. (1969e) 59,728; railroad junction and trade center; textiles, wax, building materials; salt works (operating since 10th cent.). Became city before 1200; member of Hanseatic League from 2d half of 13th cent.; to Hanover 1705, to Prussia 1866; in World War II taken by Allies Apr. 1945.

Lü·ne·bur·ger Hei·de \ˌlü-nə-ˌbùr-gər-'hīd-ə\. Heath bet. the Elbe and Aller rivers, West Germany; ab. 55 m. long.

Lu·nel \lü-'nel\. Commune, E Hérault dept., S France, SW of Nîmes; pop. (1968c) 9821; wine.

Lü·nen \ˈlü-nən\ *also* **Lünen an der Lip·pe** \-ˌän-dər-ˈlip-ə\. Industrial city, N cen. North Rhine-Westphalia, West Germany, on Lippe river 25 m. S of Münster; pop. (1969e) 72,207; coal mining; aluminum, copper, iron; 18th cent. palace.

Lu·nen·burg \ˈlü-nən-ˌbərg\. 1 County in Virginia. See table at VIRGINIA.

2 Town, Worcester co., cen. Massachusetts, 4 m. E of Fitchburg; pop. (1970c) 7419.

3 County, Nova Scotia, Canada. See table at NOVA SCOTIA.

4 Fishing town, ⊗ of Lunenburg co., S Nova Scotia, Canada, on Atlantic Ocean 37 m. SW of Halifax; pop. (1971p) 3201; home port of an important fishing fleet. Founded 1753 by Germans (from Lüneburg, Hannover) and Swiss on site of old French village; seized by privateers 1782 and plundered.

Lu·né·ville \ˈlü-nə-ˌvil\. Manufacturing city, Meurthe-et-Moselle dept., NE France, on Meurthe river 18 m. SE of Nancy; pop. (1968c) 23,177; railway rolling stock, machinery, textiles, pottery. Capital of 10th cent. countship; fell to dukes of Lorraine 1344; residence 1735 ff. of Stanislas Leszczyński, former king of Poland and last reigning duke of Lorraine; Peace of Lunéville signed 1801 bet. Germany and French Republic; suffered during German invasion 1914–18.

Lun·ga \ˈlùŋ-gə\. Village at mouth of **Lunga River** on NW coast of Guadalcanal, SE Solomon Is., W Pacific Ocean, ab. 25 m. E of Cape Esperance on **Lunga Point.** The point was the landing place of U.S. Marines Aug. 7, 1942; just E of the river is a ridge of hills, **Lunga Ridge,** scene of a severe battle Sept. 12–13, 1942, which the Americans finally won; off Lunga Point a naval battle won by the Americans Nov. 30, 1942.

Lunga, Iso·la \ˌē-zò-lə-ˈlüŋ-gə\. See DUGI OTOK.

Lungchingtsun. See YEN-CHI-HSIEN.

Lung–chou \ˈlùŋ-ˈjō\. Town and port, SW Kwangsi Chuang, SE China, on left bank of the Li, tributary of the Hsiang on North Vietnam border; in direct connection with Lang Son in North Vietnam; made a treaty port 1889; during late 1930's a major trade center because of Japanese blockade of other Chinese ports.

Lung·ern, Lake of \-ˈlùŋ-ərn\. Small lake in cen. Switzerland, S of Lake of Sarnen; traversed by Aa river.

Lungki. See CHANG-CHOU.

Lung·kiang \ˈlùŋ-jē-ˈäŋ\. 1 Former province (1932–45), N cen. Manchukuo; 25,904 sq. m.

2 City, China. See CH'I-CH'I-HA-ERH.

Lung–k'ou \ˈlùŋ-ˈkō\. Port, Shantung prov., NE China, on N coast of Shantung Penin. W of Chefoo.

Lung–ling \ˈlùŋ-ˈliŋ\. Town, W Yunnan prov., S China, bet. the Salween and Shweli rivers 85 m. NE of Wan-t'ing; alt. ab. 4500 ft.; 523 m. by road from K'un-ming. Taken by Japanese May 1942 and made into air base; recaptured by Chinese Nov. 1944.

Lu·ni \ˈlü-nē\. 1 River, NW India; ab. 330 m. long; rises on W slopes of Aravalli Range, flows SW in cen. and SW Rajputana to the Great Rann of Kutch.

2 Town in Italy. See LUNA 2.

Lunigiana. See LUNA 2.

Lupatia. See ALTAMURA.

Lupin. See MAN-CHOU-LI.

Lup·ków \ˈlüp-ˌküf\. Pass in the East Beskids, Carpathian Mts., on highway from Sanok, Poland, to E Czechoslovakia; 2135 ft.; used by Russian and German armies in winter fighting of 1915–16.

Lu·que \ˈlü-(ˌ)kā\. City, Central dept., S Paraguay, 9 m. E of Asunción; munic. pop. (1970e) 35,790; founded 1635; 2d capital of the republic during war against the Triple Alliance 1865–70.

Lu·qui·llo \lü-ˈkē-(ˌ)(y)ō\. Town and municipality, NE Puerto Rico; town on coast and on railroad 27 m. E of San Juan; pop. (1970p) 2412 (town), 10,270 (munic.).

Luquillo Mountains *or Span.* **Si·e·rra de Luquillo** \sē-ˌer-ə-dā-\. Range in E Puerto Rico; highest peak El Yunque 3496 ft.

Lu·ray \ˈlü-(ˌ)rā\. Town, ⊗ of Page co., N Virginia, in Blue Ridge Mts. 30 m. NE of Harrisonburg; pop. (1970c) 3612; clothing; creamery, tannery; diversified agriculture; **Luray Caverns** (discovered 1878) nearby are a major tourist attraction.

Lure \ˈlür\. Commune, E Haute-Saône dept., E France; pop. (1962c) 7924; abbey founded c. 610 by a disciple of St. Columban.

Lur·gan \ˈlər-gən\. Municipal borough, co. Armagh, S Northern Ireland, 20 m. SW of Belfast; pop. (1971p) 23,853; market town; linen manufacturing.

Luristan. See LORESTĀN.

Lurlei. See LORELEI.

Lu·sa·ka \lü-ˈsäk-ə\. City, ✱ of Zambia; pop. (1967e) 176,000; center of a farming region; cement; univ. (1965).

Lu·sa·tia \lü-ˈsā-sh(ē-)ə\ *or Ger.* **Lau·sitz** \ˈlaù-ˌzits\. Region of East Germany bet. the Elbe and Oder; in 10th cent. became a margravate of the Holy Roman Empire, in 1303 part of Brandenburg, and in 1368 part of Bohemia; in 15th cent. divided into Upper and Lower Lusatia; annexed to Saxony 1635; partitioned between Saxony and Prussia by Treaty of Vienna 1815. Its inhabitants, Lusatians, originally a Slavic tribe (the Wends).

Lu·shai Hills \ˌlü-ˌshī-\. Hilly region, Mizoram, NE India; highest point ab. 7000 ft.; part of N Arakan Yoma system. Inhabited by Lushais, an Indo-Chinese tribe, whose predatory raids 1840–90 made them troublesome in the region; came under British control 1895.

Lush·nje \ˈlüsh-nyə\. 1 Province of W Albania. See table at ALBANIA.

2 Town, its ✱; pop. (1967e) 17,545.

Lüshun. See PORT ARTHUR 4.

Lu·si·gnan \ˌlü-zi-ˈnyäⁿ\. Commune, Vienne dept., W cen. France, 15 m. SW of Poitiers; pop. (1962c) 2310; ancient town, original seat of Lusignan family, rulers of Cyprus 1192–1474, and of Jerusalem and Armenia.

Lu·si·ta·nia \ˌlü-sə-ˈtā-nē-ə, -nyə\. 1 Region of W Hispania, corresponding approximately to the greater part of modern Portugal and the Spanish provinces of Salamanca and Cáceres; from 27 B.C. until end of 4th cent. A.D. a province of the Roman Empire.

2 Country, Europe. See PORTUGAL.

Lusk \ˈləsk\. Town, ⊗ of Niobrara co., E Wyoming, 50 m. N of Torrington; pop. (1970c) 1495; oil refinery; livestock raising.

Lu·so \ˈlü-zü\. Town, E cen. Angola, 440 m. E of Lobito; met. area pop. (1960c) 40,048.

Lussino. See LOŠINJ.

Lü–ta. See DAIREN.

Lutch·er \ˈləch-ər\. Town, St. James parish, SE Louisiana, on Mississippi river 40 m. W of New Orleans; pop. (1970c) 3911; sawmill; rice, sugarcane.

Lutea. See LETEA.

Lutetia *or* **Lutetia Parisiorum.** See PARIS 10.

Luteva. See LODÈVE.

Lu·ther·ville–Ti·mo·ni·um \ˈlü-thər-ˌvil-tə-ˈmōn-ē-əm\. Unincorporated urban area, Baltimore co., Maryland; pop. (1970c) 24,055; vehicle bodies; residential.

Lu·ton \ˈlüt-ᵊn\. County borough, Bedfordshire, SE cen. England, on the Lea 28 m. NNW of London; pop. (1971p) 36,213; hats, motor vehicles, ball bearings, electrical equipment; 15th cent. church; became borough 1876.

Lutsk \ˈlütsk\ *or Pol.* **Łuck** \ˈlütsk\. City, Volyn Oblast, NW Ukrainian S.S.R., U.S.S.R., on Styr river 125 m. ESE of Lublin; pop. (1970p) 94,000; textiles, leather goods. An important town of medieval Volhynia, esp. wealthy in 15th cent.; declined in wars bet. Russia and Poland 1557–82; taken by Russia 1791. In World War I center of Brusilov's offensive operations June–Aug. 1916; became part of Poland 1918. In World War II occupied by U.S.S.R. 1939 and by Germany 1941–44.

Lut·ter am Ba·ren·ber·ge \ˈlu̇t-ər-äm-ˈbär-ən-ˌbe(ə)r-gə\. Town, Lower Saxony, West Germany, 23 m. SW of Brunswick; pop. (1968e) 1950; during Thirty Years' War scene of battle Aug. 17–27, 1626 in which the forces of the Catholic League under Field Marshal Tilly defeated the Protestants under King Christian IV of Denmark and Norway.

Lüttich. See LIÈGE.

Lu·ty·nia \lü-ˈtin-yə\ *or Ger.* **Leu·then** \ˈlȯit-ən\. Village, SW Poland, near Wrocław; pop. (1968e) 1200; scene of battle Dec. 5, 1757 in which Frederick the Great defeated the Austrians.

Lüt·zel·burg \ˈlu̇t-səl-ˌbu̇(ə)rg\. Former German name of LUXEMBOURG.

Lüt·zen \ˈlüt-sən\. Commune, Halle dist., East Germany, SW of Leipzig; pop. (1965e) 4800; scene of two battles: (1) Nov. 16, 1632 in which the Swedes under Gustavus Adolphus defeated the Imperialists led by Wallenstein and in which Gustavus Adolphus was killed and (2) May 2, 1813 in which Napoleon overcame the Russians and Prussians (also called battle of Grossgörschen).

Lu·uk \lü-ˈük\. Municipality, E Jolo I., Phil., 22 m. ESE of Jolo; pop. (1969e) 25,400.

Lu·verne. 1 \lü-ˈvərn\. Town, ⊗ of Crenshaw co., S Alabama; pop. (1970c) 2440; agricultural trade center.

2 \lə-ˈvərn\. City, ⊗ of Rock co., SW corner of Minnesota, 30 m. W of Worthington; pop. (1970c) 4703; livestock, creamery, and grain cooperatives; granite quarries.

Lu·vua \lu̇-ˈvü-ə\. Name given to the Luapula river, cen. Africa, from where it leaves Lake Mweru to its junction with the Lualaba (upper Congo river) in E Zaire.

Lux·em·bourg *or* **Lux·em·burg** \ˈlu̇k-səm-ˌbu̇(ə)rg, ˈlək-səm-ˌbərg\. **1** Medieval county and duchy, now largely in the Grand Duchy of Luxembourg and the Belgian province of Luxembourg.

2 *or officially* **Grand Duchy of Luxembourg** *or Fr.* **Grand–Du·ché de Luxembourg** \gräⁿ-dü-shā-də-lük-säⁿ-bu̇rg\ *or Ger.* **Gross·herz·og·tum Lux·em·burg** \grōs-ˈhert-sə-ˌtüm-\. Grand duchy, W Europe, bounded on N and W by Belgium, on E by West Germany, and on S by France; 999 sq. m.; pop. (1972e) 343,000; ✱ Luxembourg. *Physical features:* Forms part of plateau of Ardennes; hilly and well-forested; watered by Sauer and Alzette rivers of the Moselle basin. *Chief products:* Iron ore, wheat, rye, potatoes; wine; livestock; manufacturing: iron and steel, chemicals, textiles. *Chief towns:* Luxembourg, Esch-sur-Alzette, Dudelange, Differdange.

History: County of Luxembourg (in Holy Roman Empire) emerged in 10th cent. A.D.; beginning with Henry VII (1308–13), house of Luxembourg produced four German emperors (see also BOHEMIA); raised to rank of duchy 1354; through Burgundian house which secured it 1451, duchy passed to Spanish and later, to Austrian Hapsburgs as part of the Netherlands (*q.v.*); occupied by French 1794; Grand Duchy of Luxembourg, estab. by Congress of Vienna, part of kingdom of the Netherlands 1815–30; after Belgian revolt, W half given to Belgium, but rest remained Grand Duchy of Luxembourg in personal union with the Netherlands 1839; joined German *Zollverein* 1842; neutrality and independence of Luxembourg guaranteed and Prussian garrison of town of Luxembourg withdrawn after Franco-German crisis 1867; with accession of Adolph of Nassau as grand duke 1890, broke connection with the Netherlands; occupied by Germany in World War I; concluded economic union with Belgium 1922; occupied by Germans May 1940 to Sept. 1944; formed customs union with Belgium and the Netherlands 1947; became a member of NATO 1949, and of the European Economic Community 1958.

3 Province, SE Belgium; 1706 sq. m.; pop. (1970e) 219,186; ✱ Arlon; rivers Ourthe, Semois; crossed by Ardennes forest; oats, rye, potatoes, wheat, tobacco; livestock; iron mining and quarrying (slate) formerly important.

4 Manufacturing and commercial city, ✱ of Grand Duchy of Luxembourg; pop. (1970e) 77,500; on a rocky height with steep cliffs on three sides on the Alzette in S part; steel, textiles; brewing; univ. (1958); tourism; scene of discussions 1971 relating to British entry into the European Economic Community.

Lu·xeuil \lük-ˈsəʸ\ *or in full* **Luxeuil–les–Bains** \-lā-ˈbaⁿ\. Commune, Haute-Saône dept., E France; pop. (1962c) 9015; thermal springs. Dates from pre-Roman times; often devastated, esp. by Attila 451, by Saracens in 8th cent., and by Normans in 9th cent.; noted for its abbey, founded 590 by St. Columban, suppressed during the Revolution.

Lux·or \ˈlək-ˌsȯ(ə)r, ˈlu̇k-\; *Arab.* **Al–Uq·sor** *or* **Al–Aq·sur** \al-ˈu̇k-su̇r\ *or* **Al–Qu·sur** \al-ˈku̇-su̇r\. Town on E bank of the Nile, Upper Egypt; pop. (1970e) 84,600; S part of site of ancient Thebes; tombs of kings; ruins of ancient temple built by Amenhotep III (reigned c. 1411–1375 B.C.) and of other structures by Ikhnaton and Ramses II. See KARNAK.

Luzern. See LUCERNE.

Lu·zerne \lu̇-ˈzərn\. **1** County in Pennsylvania. See table at PENNSYLVANIA.

2 Borough, Luzerne co., E Pennsylvania, 3 m. NNW of Wilkes-Barre; pop. (1970c) 4504; coal mining.

Luž·ni·ce \ˈlu̇zh-nət-sə\ *or Ger.* **Lain·sitz** \ˈlīn-ˌzits\. River, W Czech S.R., Czechoslovakia; 129 m. long; rises in Austria, flows N to Tabor, then turns abruptly SW and empties into the Vltava.

Lu·zon \lü-ˈzän\. Chief island of the Philippines, in N part; 41,765 sq. m.; pop. (1970p) 16,669,724; for administrative divisions, see table at PHILIPPINES. Of irregular shape, coastline much indented forming many good anchorages, esp. Manila Bay, Lingayen Gulf, Lamon Bay, and Lagonoy Gulf. Has many islands and islets off its shores, esp. Babuyan Is. to the N, Catanduanes and Polillo off E coast. Principal mountain group, Cordillera Central, in NW; Sierra Madre range along NE coast; highest peak Pulog 9606 ft.; in S are active volcanoes Taal and Mayon. Chief rivers Pampanga, Cagayan, Agno, Pasig; only large lakes Laguna de Bay and Taal. Products incl. rice, sugar, coconuts, tobacco, and hemp (abacá); gold, copper, manganese. For history, see PHILIPPINES.

Luzon Strait. Name sometimes given to wide passage bet. N Luzon, Phil., and S Taiwan; connects the Pacific Ocean with the South China Sea and includes Bashi Channel, Balintang Channel, Babuyan Channel.

Luz–Saint–Sau·veur \'lüz-ˌsaⁿ-sō-'vər\. Village, SW Hautes-Pyrénées dept., SW France; pop. (1962c) 1249; thermal springs; has church of 12th and 13th cents. built by the Knights of St. John of Jerusalem.

Luz·za·ra \lüt-'sär-ə\. Commune, Reggio nell'Emilia prov., Emilia-Romagna, N Italy, 18 m. N of Reggio nell'Emilia; pop. (1968e) 8337; scene of victory of Prince Eugene over Spanish and French army 1702.

Lvov \lə-'vȯf, -'vȯv\ *or Pol.* **Lwów** \lə-'vüf, -'vüv\ *or Ger.* **Lem·berg** \'lem-bərg, -be(ə)rg\ *or Ukrainian* **Lwiw** \lə-'vēf\. Commercial city, ✱ of Lvov Oblast, Ukrainian S.S.R., U.S.S.R., 115 m. SW of Lutsk; pop. (1970p) 553,000; railroad junction; industrial center producing motor vehicles, electrical equipment, agricultural machinery, glass, textiles, foodstuffs, paint, furniture; Ivan Franko univ. (1661; renamed 1945); a center of Ukrainian culture.

History: Founded 1256 by Ukrainian prince; captured by Poles 1340; became city 1352, Roman Catholic episcopal see 1412; one of the great trading towns of medieval Europe; passed to Austria after first partition of Poland 1772 and made capital of Austrian province of Galicia. In World War I center of two great battles bet. U.S.S.R. and German allies: Aug. 26 to Sept. 1, 1914, and June 3 to 22, 1915; occupied by Ukrainians 1918 who set up republic (Western Ukrainia); Ukrainians subdued by Poles Nov. 1918. Occupied in World War II by Soviet troops 1939, by German armies July 1941; retaken by U.S.S.R. July 27, 1944.

Lvov Oblast \-'ō-bləst, -ˌblast\. Subdivision of the Ukrainian S.S.R., U.S.S.R.; 8417 sq. m.; pop. (1970p) 2,428,000; ✱ Lvov; rye, wheat, sugar beet, corn, timber; oil and natural gas; formerly in Poland.

Lwan. See LUAN.

Lwiw. See LVOV.

Lwów \lə-'vüf, -'vüv\. 1 Former Polish department; 10,960 sq. m. After World War II greater part (E and cen.) transferred to Ukrainian S.S.R., U.S.S.R. Smaller W part now in Rzeszów prov., SE Poland.
2 City, Ukrainian S.S.R., U.S.S.R. See LVOV.

Lya·khov Islands *also* **Lia·khov Islands** \lē-'äk-əf-\. Two islands, **Bol·shoi Lyakhov** \bōl-'shȯi-, bȯl-\ (Great Lyakhov) and **Ma·ly Lyakhov** \'mäl-ē-\ (Little Lyakhov), S of New Siberian Is., Russian S.F.S.R., U.S.S.R., E of Laptev Sea, belonging to Yakutsk A.S.S.R.; Bolshoi Lyakhov separated from mainland by Dmitri Laptev Strait. The group considered by some to be a part of New Siberian Is. Has great deposits of animal and vegetable remains of Ice Age. Discovered and described 1770 by a Russian merchant, Lyakhov.

Ly·all·pur \'lī-əl-ˌpu̇(ə)r\. Town, Punjab, Pakistan, 75 m. W of Lahore; pop. (1969e) 853,700; market for cloth and grain; center of textile, hosiery, and flour milling industries; also produces vegetable oils and sugar; univ. (1961); founded 1892.

Lyc·a·bet·tus \ˌlik-ə-'bet-əs, ˌlī-kə-\ *or Gk.* **Ly·ka·bet·tos** \ˌl(y)ēk-ə-ve-'tȯs\. Mountain in NE part of Athens, Greece; 909 ft.

Ly·cae·us \lī-'sē-əs\. Mountain in ancient Arcadia, Greece, NW of Megalopolis; on border bet. present departments of Arcadia and Messenia; sacred to Zeus.

Lyc·a·o·nia \ˌlik-ā-'ō-nē-ə, ˌlī-kā-, -nyə\. Ancient district and Roman province, S Asia Minor (Turkey), interior elevated region, in Biblical times bounded on N by Galatia, on E by Cappadocia, on S by Cilicia, and on W by Pisidia and Phrygia, but its boundaries varied greatly; successively under Persia, Syria, and Rome, becoming a separate province 371 A.D. Its cities of Lystra, Iconium, and Derbe visited by Paul (*Acts* xiv).

Ly·ce·um \lī-'sē-əm\. A locality on the Ilissus in E part of ancient Athens, Greece, comprising an enclosure dedicated to Apollo and adorned with fountains and buildings erected by Pisistratus, Pericles, and Lycurgus; frequented by Athenian youths for exercise and by philosophers for teaching, esp. Aristotle and his followers (Peripatetics).

Lychnidus. See OHRID.

Lychnitis. 1 Lake, Yugoslavia and Albania. See OHRID 1.
2 Lake, U.S.S.R. See SEVAN.

Ly·cia \'lish-(ē-)ə\. Ancient district in S Asia Minor (Turkey), a mountainous coastal region watered by the Xanthus; bounded on NW by Caria and on NE by Pamphylia; chief towns Myra and Patara. Settled in early times, came under Persia and Syria and in 1st cent. A.D. annexed by Rome; as a Roman province ultimately united with Pamphylia, Pisidia, etc. (**Lycia et Pam·phyl·ia** \-et-pam-'fil-ē-ə, -'fil-yə\).

Lyck. See EŁK.

Ly·com·ing \lī-'kōm-iŋ\. County in Pennsylvania. See table at PENNSYLVANIA.

Lycoming Creek. River, N cen. Pennsylvania; ab. 35 m. long; rises in N Lycoming co., flows S and SW into the West Branch of Susquehanna river in S Lycoming co. near Williamsport.

Lycopolis. See ASYŪT 2.

Lyc·o·rea \ˌlik-ə-'rē-ə, ˌlīk-\. 1 Southernmost peak of Mount Parnassus, Phocis, cen. Greece.
2 Ancient town at its foot.

Lyc·o·su·ra \ˌlik-ə-'su̇r-ə, ˌlīk-\. Ancient city of S Arcadia, cen. Peloponnesus, Greece, WSW of Megalopolis, said by Pausanias to be the oldest city of Greece; some ruins remain.

Lydd \'lid\. Municipal borough, SE Kent, SE England, NW of Dunge Ness on coast of Strait of Dover; pop. (1971p) 4301; military camp nearby where the explosive *lyddite* was first developed; received rights of Cinque Ports (*q.v.*) 1155.

Lydda. See LOD.

Ly·den·burg \'līd-ᵊn-ˌbərg\. Town, E cen. Transvaal, NE Rep. of South Africa, 145 m. ENE of Pretoria; pop. (1967e) 8000; agriculture, sheep farming; platinum mined in vicinity. Founded 1846 by Boers and made center of a district which they proclaimed a republic; became part of Utrecht dist. 1858 but remained in Transvaal when Utrecht (*q.v.*) was ceded to Natal 1903.

Lyd·ia \'lid-ē-ə\. Ancient country in W part of Asia Minor, (Turkey); bounded on N by Mysia, on E by Phrygia, on S by Caria, and on W by the Aegean; ✱ Sardis; included the valleys of the Hermus and Caÿster; important towns Magnesia, Philadelphia, and Thyatira. Its early dynasties legendary, but under the Mermnadae (685–546 B.C.) it became a powerful and cultured kingdom, contributing notably to ancient economic progress, esp. in coinage; conquered by Persians under Cyrus 546 B.C., later passed to Syria and Pergamum, and under the Romans became a part of the province of Asia.

Lyeemoon Pass *or* **Lyemun Pass.** See LEI U MUN PASS.

Ly·ell, Mount \-'lī-əl\. Peak in Sierra Nevada, near junction point of Madera, Mariposa, and Tuolumne cos., E cen. California; 13,110 ft.

Lyell Island. Island, cen. Queen Charlotte Is., off W British Columbia, Canada, on Hecate Strait.

Lykabettos. See LYCABETTUS.

Ly·kens \'lī-kənz\. Borough, Dauphin co., SE cen. Pennsylvania, 23 m. NNE of Harrisburg; pop. (1970c) 2506; clothing, dies, paper boxes; diversified agriculture.

Ly·man \'lī-mən\. 1 County in South Dakota. See table at SOUTH DAKOTA.

2 Town, Spartanburg co., NW South Carolina, ab. 11 m. W of Spartanburg; pop. (1970c) 1159.

Lyme Bay \'līm-\. Widemouthed inlet of the English Channel on S coast of Somersetshire, SW England.

Lyme Re·gis \-'rē-jəs\. Municipal borough, Dorsetshire, S England; pop. (1971p) 3394; seaside resort; Monmouth landed here with some of his rebels 1685.

Lym Fjord. See LIM FJORD.

Lym·ing·ton \'lim-iŋ-tən\. Municipal borough and seaport, Hampshire, S England, on the Lymington near English Channel 6 m. SW of city of Southampton; pop. (1971p) 35,644; yachtbuilding yards; received charter 1150; had important salt works until mid-19th cent.

Lymm \'lim\. Urban district, Cheshire, NW England, 12 m. SW of Manchester; pop. (1971p) 10,458.

Lympne \'lim\ *or anc.* **Por·tus Le·ma·nis** \ˌpōrt-əs-li-'mān-əs, ˌpȯrt-\. Village, Kent, SE England, 2 m. W of Hythe; parish pop. (1961c) 592; 15th cent. castle, now a modern mansion.

Łyna. See LAVA.

Lyn·brook \'lin-(ˌ)bru̇k\. Village, Nassau co., SE New York, on S shore of Long I. 18 m. E of New York City; pop. (1970c) 23,776; residential; sheet metal products, furniture; truck farms.

Lynch·burg \'linch-ˌbərg\. 1 Town, ⊗ of Moore co., S Tennessee; pop. (1970c) 361; tobacco, wheat.

2 City, S cen. Virginia, in Campbell co. but politically independent, on James river in foothills of Blue Ridge Mts., 48 m. ENE of Roanoke; 23 sq. m.; pop. (1970c) 54,083; textiles, hosiery, clothing, footwear, pharmaceuticals, steel products; Virginia Seminary and Coll. (1888); Randolph-Macon Women's Coll. (1891); Lynchburg Coll. (1903); settled by Quakers 1757; incorp. as town 1805, as city 1852; Confederate supply base in Civil War.

Lynch·es \'lin-chəz\. River, North Carolina and South Carolina; 140 m. long; rises in S North Carolina and flows SE into Pee Dee river on SE boundary of Florence co., South Carolina.

Lyn·den \'lin-dən\. City, Whatcom co., NW Washington, 14 m. N of Bellingham; pop. (1970c) 2808; dairy products; diversified agriculture.

Lynd·hurst \'lind-ˌhərst\. City, Cuyahoga co., N Ohio, 11 m. E of Cleveland; pop. (1970c) 19,749; residential.

Lyn·don \'lin-dən\. 1 City, ⊗ of Osage co., E Kansas; pop. (1970c) 958; dairy and grain farms.

2 Town in Vermont. See LYNDON CENTER.

Lyndon Center. Village in Lyndon town, Caledonia co., NE Vermont, ab. 8 m. N of St. Johnsbury; pop. (1970c) 246 (village), 3705 (town); Lyndon State Coll. (1911).

Lyng·en \'leŋ-ən, ˌlu̇ŋ-\. Inlet of Arctic Ocean on NW coast of Norway, E of Tromsø.

Lynmouth. See LYNTON.

Lynn \'lin\. 1 County in Texas. See table at TEXAS.

2 City, Essex co., NE corner of Massachusetts, on Lynn Harbor 10 m. NE of Boston; pop. (1970c) 90,294; transportation equipment, electrical machinery; formerly the leading shoe-manufacturing center of the U.S. Originally known as **Sau·gus** \'sȯ-gəs\, settled 1629, incorp. as town 1631, renamed 1637; incorp. as city 1850; manufacture of shoes began 1635, reached its height in 19th cent.

3 Municipal borough, England. See KING'S LYNN.

Lynn Canal. Deep fjord, SE Alaska, leading N from Juneau; 80 m. long, 6 m. wide; near its head divides into Chilkat Inlet on W and Chilkoot Inlet on E; Taiya Inlet, at entrance to which is Skagway, is an upper arm of Chilkoot Inlet. Important S gateway to Klondike region.

Lynn·field \'lin-ˌfēld\. Town, Essex co., NE corner of Massachusetts, 10 m. NNE of Boston; pop. (1970c) 10,826.

Lynn Harbor. Inlet of Massachusetts Bay on S shore of Essex co., NE corner of Massachusetts; the city of Lynn is at its N end.

Lynn Haven. City, Bay co., NW Florida; pop. (1970c) 4044.

Lynn Regis. See KING'S LYNN.

Lynn·wood \'lin-ˌwu̇d\. City, Snohomish co., NW cen. Washington, on Puget Sound 15 m. N of Seattle; pop. (1970c) 16,919; prefabricated homes and paneling; diversified agriculture; hatcheries.

Lyn·ton \'lint-ᵊn\. Urban district, N Devonshire, SW England, NE of Barnstaple; pop. (1971p) 1981; on a cliff ab. 430 ft. high above **Lyn·mouth** \'lin-məth\, village on shore of Bristol Channel; both popular resorts; nearby is Doone Valley (*q.v.*).

Lyn·wood \'lin-ˌwu̇d\. Industrial city, Los Angeles co., SW California, 8 m. S of Los Angeles; pop. (1970c) 43,353; residential; chemicals, printing presses, scientific instruments.

Ly·on \'lī-ən\. 1 Counties in five states of the U.S. See tables at IOWA, KANSAS, KENTUCKY, MINNESOTA, NEVADA.

2 River in Perth co., cen. Scotland; flows into the Tay river; 34 m. long.

Lyon. City, France. See LYONS.

Lyonais. See LYONNAIS.

Lyon Mountain \ˌlī-ən-\. Peak in the Adirondack Mts., Clinton co., NE corner of New York; 3880 ft.

Ly·on·nais *or* **Ly·o·nais** \ˌlē-ə-'nā\. Historical region of SE France; bounded anciently on N by Burgundy, SE by Dauphiné, S by Languedoc, SW by Auvergne, NW by Bourbonnais; equivalent to modern departments of Rhône and Loire; ✱ Lyons. Ancient territory of the Segusiavi; ruled by counts of Forez 11th–13th cents. A.D., later by the count-archbishops of Lyons; passed to house of Bourbon 1371; confiscated by French crown 1527; made province of France and appanage of crown under the Valois.

Ly·ons \'lī-ənz\. 1 City, ⊗ of Toombs co., SE cen. Georgia, 72 m. W of Savannah; pop. (1970c) 3739; lumber; diversified agriculture.

2 Residential village, Cook co., NE Illinois, 8 m. W of Chicago; pop. (1970c) 11,124; located at an old portage bet. the Des Plaines river and the Chicago river, which was used by Marquette and other early French explorers and by the Indians.

3 City, ⊗ of Rice co., cen. Kansas, 27 m. NNW of Hutchinson; pop. (1970c) 4355; flour and feed mills; grain farms.

4 Village, ⊗ of Wayne co., W New York, 24 m. WNW of Auburn; pop. (1970c) 4496; fertilizer; machine shops, canning plant; fruit orchards.

Lyons \lē-'ōⁿ, 'lī-ənz\ *or Fr.* **Ly·on** \lyōⁿ\ *or anc.* **Lug·du·num** \lu̇g-'dü-nəm, ˌləg-\. Manufacturing and commercial city, ✱ of Rhône dept., E cen. France, at confluence of Rhone and Saône rivers 58 m. NW of Grenoble; pop. (1968c) 527,890; railroad center; 13 bridges over Saône river, 11 bridges over Rhone river, extensive quays; major river port; important center of the silk industry; produces chemicals, dyes, fertilizer, glue, pharmaceuticals, plastics, machinery, electrical cables, sheet iron, wire; 12th–15th cent. Gothic cathedral (with four towers), 17th cent. *hôtel de ville;* 15th cent. archiepiscopal palace, univ. (1809, university status 1896), a free Catholic univ. (1875).

History: Founded 43 B.C.; sometime residence of Roman emperors; made episcopal see 2d cent. A.D. (Irenaeus bishop of Lyons 177); sacked by Huns and Visigoths; held by Saracens 8th cent.; became capital of kingdom of Provence on dissolution of Charlemagne's empire; incorporated into Holy Roman Empire 1032; site of ecumenical church councils 1245, 1274; united to French crown 1312; received municipal charter 1320; attained great prosperity during 16th cent., but declined during wars of religion; suffered during French Revolution; site of revolts 1831, 1834, 1849, 1871. Birthplace of Caracalla, St. Irenaeus, Ampère. In World War II a center of the resistance movement; occupied by Free French forces Sept. 3, 1944.

Lys \'lēs\ *or Flemish* **Leie** \'lā-ə, 'lī-ə\. River in France and Belgium; ab. 120 m. long; flows NE, forming a section of the French-Belgian boundary, and joins the Schelde river at Gent; navigable for ab. 100 m.

Ly·saght, Mount \-'lē-ˌsäkt\. Peak, Antarctica, 82°49′S, 161°19′E; 12,326 ft.

Ły·sa Go·ra \ˌlis-ə-ˈgȯr-ə\. Elevation, S cen. Poland, E of Kielce; 2005 ft.

Ly·se Fjord \ˌlē-sə-, ˌlü-\. Inlet of North Sea on SW coast of Norway, E of Stavanger.

Lys·tra \ˈlis-trə\. Town in ancient Lycaonia, Asia Minor; its site is ab. 20 m. SSW of Konya; visited by Paul (*Acts* xiv. 6–21).

Lys·va \ˈlis-və\. City, Perm Oblast, Russian S.F.S.R., U.S.S.R., on railroad 50 m. E of Perm; pop. (1969e) 79,000.

Lyth·am St. Anne's \ˈlith-əm . . . ˈanz\. Municipal borough, Lancashire, NW England, on Irish Sea at mouth of the Ribble 22 m. N of Liverpool; pop. (1971p) 40,089; seaside resort.

Lyt·tel·ton \ˈlit-ᵊl-tən\ *or formerly* **Port Coo·per** \-ˈküp-ər, -ˈku̇p-\. Borough, port and suburb of Christchurch, E South I., New Zealand; pop. (1970e) 3550; exports wool, meat, wheat.

Lyu·ber·tsy \ˈl(y)ü-b(y)ert-sē\. Town, Moscow Oblast, Russian S.F.S.R., U.S.S.R., ab. 13 m. ESE of Moscow; pop. (1970p) 139,000.

Lyublin. See LUBLIN.

Lyublyana. See LJUBLJANA.

M'-, Mc-. Abbreviated forms of MAC-. Names beginning with this prefix are all alphabetized as if spelled MAC-. M' is sometimes written M', esp. in British references.

Maa·la·ea Bay \m(ə-)ˌäl-ə-ˌā-ə-\. Bay on SW side of Maui I., Hawaii.

Ma·'an \mə-'an\. Town, SW Jordan, ab. 60 m. SSE of the Dead Sea; pop. (1961c) 6643; on railroad S from Amman and on highway S to 'Aqaba; trade center.

Maa·rian·ha·mi·na \'mär-yan-ˌham-ə-ˌnä\ *or Swed.* **Ma·rie·hamn** \mə-ˌrē-'ham-ən\. Seaport on Ahvenanmaa I., ✱ of Ahvenanmaa prov., Finland, in the Gulf of Bothnia; pop. (1970p) 8461; founded 1861.

Maas. See MEUSE.

Maas·bree \'mäs-(ˌ)brā\. Commune, Limburg prov., SE Netherlands, W of the Meuse near Venlo; pop. (1969e) 7510.

Maas·eik *also* **Maes·eyck** \'mäs-ˌīk\. Commune, Limburg prov., NE Belgium, on the Meuse river; pop. (1970e) 7676; reputed birthplace of Hubert and Jan van Eyck.

Ma·a·sin \mə-'äs-ᵊn\. Municipality, Southern Leyte prov., SW coast of Leyte I., Phil., 78 m. SSW of Tacloban; pop. (1969e) 53,700; a hemp port and has active coastwise trade.

Maas·sluis \mä-'slȯis\. Commune, South Holland prov., SW Netherlands; W of Rotterdam on the Nieuwe Maas; pop. (1970e) 25,878; chemicals; fishing.

Maas·tricht *or* **Maes·tricht** \mä-'strikt\. Commune, ✱ of Limburg prov., SE Netherlands, on Maas (Meuse) river near the Belgian frontier; pop. (1970e) 98,927; steel, chemicals, cement, paper, glass, pottery, cigars; grain and butter market; church of St. Servatius, dating from 6th cent., oldest church in Netherlands; a Romanesque church dating from 12th cent. Founded on site of Roman town; its location as a border town has subjected it frequently to siege or capture in various wars, esp. in 1579 when 8000 of its inhabitants were massacred by Spaniards, and in 1673, 1748, and 1794; withstood siege in 1830; occupied by Germans 1940; retaken by Americans Sept. 15, 1944.

Ma·ba·la·cat \ˌmäb-ə-'läk-ət\. Municipality, Pampanga prov., Luzon, Phil., on Manila-Dagupan R.R. 15 m. NNW of San Fernando; pop. (1969e) 43,100.

Ma·bi·ri, Cape \-mə-'bi(ə)r-ē\. Cape on E cen. Bougainville I., NW Solomon Is., W Pacific Ocean.

Ma·cá, Mon·te \ˌmänt-ē-mə-'kä\. Peak, S Chile, E of Melchor I. and NW of Puerto Aysén; 9710 ft.

Ma·ca·be·be \ˌmäk-ə-'bā-bē\. Municipality, Pampanga prov., Luzon, Phil., on edge of Pampanga delta 8 m. S of San Fernando; pop. (1969e) 38,300.

Mc·Adoo \'mak-ə-ˌdü\. Borough, Schuylkill co., E cen. Pennsylvania, 18 m. NE of Pottsville; pop. (1970c) 3326; coal mining; textiles.

Ma·caé \ˌmak-ə-'ā\. Coastal city, Rio de Janeiro state, SE Brazil, 95 m. ENE of Rio de Janeiro; munic. pop. (1968e) 78,270.

Ma·ca·ja·lar Bay \ˌmak-ə-hə-ˌlär-\. Inlet of S Mindanao Sea in Misamis Oriental prov., N Mindanao, Phil., Cagayan de Oro at its head; ab. 19 m. across its mouth.

Mc·Al·es·ter \mə-'kal-ə-stər\. City, ⊗ of Pittsburg co., SE Oklahoma, 50 m. S of Okmulgee; pop. (1970c) 18,802; clothing, feed, vegetable oils; coal mines, gas wells; grain and cattle farming.

Mc·Al·len \mə-'kal-ən\. City, Hidalgo co., S Texas, 50 m. WNW of Brownsville; pop. (1970c) 37,636; ships citrus fruits and vegetables; canneries; founded 1905, incorporated 1911.

Ma·cao *or Port.* **Ma·cau** \mə-'kau̇\. 1 Portuguese overseas province, consisting of Macao peninsula (see 2, below), and the two small islands of Taipa and Colôane, ab. 40 m. W of Hong Kong; 6 sq. m.; pop. (1970e) 314,000; administrative center Macao (3 below); exports salt fish, fireworks, textiles.

2 Peninsula on the coast of SE China, W of mouth of Pearl river; ab. 2 sq. m.; contains almost entire population of the Portuguese overseas province of Macao.

3 Town, administrative center of Macao (see 1 above), approx. coextensive with Macao penin.; its harbor somewhat silted up; tourism.

History: Settled by Portuguese 1557; from 1717 until 19th cent., Macao and Canton were the only Chinese ports open to European trade; its independence declared by Portuguese 1849 but not recognized by China as Portuguese territory until 1887; for many years a haven for missionaries and traders; Portuguese administration faced considerable opposition from leftist Chinese 1967. Burial place of Robert Morrison and nearby is place where St. Francis Xavier died and was buried; residence c. 1558–59 of the Portuguese poet Camoëns, who wrote part of *The Lusiad* here.

Ma·ca·pá \ˌmak-ə-'pä\. City, ✱ of Amapá terr., N Brazil; port, N of Amazon delta; pop. (1970p) 87,755.

Ma·ca·rá \ˌmäk-ə-'rä\. Town, Loja prov., SW Ecuador, on Peruvian border; pop. (1962c) 5027.

Ma·ca·re·na Mountains \ˌmäk-ə-ˌrā-nə-\ *or Span.* **Se·rra·nía de la Macarena** \ˌser-ə-'nē-ə-ˌdel-ə-ˌmäk-ə-'\. Mountain range, SE Colombia, ab. 200 m. SE of Bogotá; ab. 150 m. long; highest peak ab. 10,000 ft.

Mc·Ar·thur \mə-'kär-thər\. Village, ⊗ of Vinton co., S Ohio, 26 m. E of Chillicothe; pop. (1970c) 1543; oil and gas wells; limestone quarries.

MacArthur. See ORMOC.

Ma·cas \'mäk-äs\. Town, ✱ of Morona-Santiago prov., E Ecuador, on Santiago river 123 m. E of Guayaquil; pop. (1970e) 2100.

Macassar. See MAKASAR.

Macau. See MACAO.

Mac·bride Head \mək-ˌbrīd-\. Promontory extending into South Atlantic Ocean from NE coast of East Falkland I., Falkland Is.

Maccaluba. See ARAGONA.

Mc·Ca·mey \mə-'kā-mē\. City, Upton co., W Texas, 38 m. ENE of Fort Stockton; pop. (1970c) 2647; oil refinery; cattle and truck farms.

Mc·Cau·ley Peak \mə-ˌkȯ-lē-\. Mountain, La Plata co., SW Colorado; 13,558 ft.

Mc·Clain \mə-'klān\. County in Oklahoma. See table at OKLAHOMA.

McClellan–Kerr Arkansas River Navigation System. See ARKANSAS RIVER NAVIGATION SYSTEM.

Mac·clen·ny \mə-'klen-ē\. Town, ⊗ of Baker co., NE Florida; pop. (1970c) 2733; lumber; truck farms.

Mac·cles·field \'mak-əlz-ˌfēld\. Municipal borough, Cheshire, NW England, on the Bollin 17 m. S of Manchester; pop. (1971p) 44,240; center of silk manufacture in England; also produces cork, shoes, electrical appliances; Jodrell Bank Experimental Station (radio telescope) nearby (to W).

M'Clin·tock Channel \mə-ˌklint-ək-\. Passage, Franklin dist., Northwest Territories, Canada, bet. E Victoria I. and W Prince of Wales I.; 170 m. long; 65 to 130 m. wide.

McCluer Gulf. See BERAU BAY.

M'Clure Strait *or* **Mc·Clure Strait** \mə-'klu̇(ə)r-\. Channel bet. Banks I. and Melville I., Franklin dist., Northwest Territories, Canada; opens on W into Arctic Ocean and on E into Viscount Melville Sound.

Mc·Clus·ky \mə-'kləs-kē\. City, ⊗ of Sheridan co., cen. North Dakota; pop. (1970c) 664; dairy farms.

Mc·Coll \mə-'käl\. Town, Marlboro co., NE South Carolina, 10 m. ENE of Bennettsville; pop. (1970c) 2524; clothing, lumber; fruit, truck, and livestock farms.

Mc·Comb \mə-'kōm\. City, Pike co., S Mississippi, 60 m. ESE of Natchez; pop. (1970c) 11,969; clothing; sawmill; dairy and truck farms.

Mc·Cone \mə-ˈkōn\. County in Montana. See table at MONTANA.

Mc·Con·nells·burg \mə-ˈkän-ᵊlz-ˌbərg\. Borough, ⊗ of Fulton co., S Pennsylvania; pop. (1970c) 1228; resort.

Mc·Con·nels·ville \mə-ˈkän-ᵊlz-ˌvil\. Village, ⊗ of Morgan co., SE Ohio, on Muskingum river 21 m. SSE of Zanesville; pop. (1970c) 2107; tools, bearings, furniture; oil and gas wells.

Mc·Cook \mə-ˈku̇k\. **1** County in South Dakota. See table at SOUTH DAKOTA.

2 City, ⊗ of Red Willow co., S Nebraska, 65 m. S of North Platte; pop. (1970c) 8285; railroad shops; bottling and packing plants; grain and livestock farms; McCook Coll. (1926).

Mc·Cor·mick \mə-ˈkȯr-mik\. **1** County in W South Carolina. See table at SOUTH CAROLINA.

2 Town, its ⊗; pop. (1970c) 1864.

Mc·Crack·en \mə-ˈkrak-ən\. County in Kentucky. See table at KENTUCKY.

Mc·Crea·ry \mə-ˈkri(ə)r-ē\. County in Kentucky. See table at KENTUCKY.

Mc·Cro·ry \mə-ˈkrōr-ē, -ˈkrȯr-\. City, Woodruff co., NE cen. Arkansas; pop. (1970c) 1378; shoes; cotton gin.

Mc·Cul·loch \mə-ˈkəl-ə\. County in Texas. See table at TEXAS.

Mc·Cur·tain \mə-ˈkərt-ᵊn\. County in Oklahoma. See table at OKLAHOMA.

Macdhui, Ben. See BEN MACDHUI.

Mc·Don·ald \mək-ˈdän-ᵊld\. **1** County in Missouri. See table at MISSOURI.

2 Village, Trumbull co., NE Ohio, 6 m. NW of Youngstown; pop. (1970c) 3177.

3 Borough, Allegheny and Washington cos., SW Pennsylvania; pop. (1970c) 2879; coal mines; dairy farms.

Mac·don·ald, Lake \-mək-ˈdän-ᵊld\. Lake in desert region of cen. Australia, on Tropic of Capricorn, on boundary bet. Western Australia and Northern Territory.

McDonald Islands. See HEARD ISLAND.

Mac·don·nell Ranges \mək-ˌdän-ᵊl-\. A series of parallel ridges and valleys of hard folded Paleozoic rocks, running east and west, S Northern Territory, Australia; highest Mt. Ziel 4953 ft.

Mc·Don·ough \mək-ˈdän-ə\. **1** County in Illinois. See table at ILLINOIS.

2 City, ⊗ of Henry co., NW cen. Georgia; pop. (1970c) 2675; clothing, tools.

Mac·dou·gall \mək-ˈdü-gəl\. Lake, NW Keewatin dist., Northwest Territories, Canada; 318 sq. m.; its outlet is Back river.

Mc·Dow·ell \mək-ˈdau̇(-ə)l\. **1** Name of counties in two states of the U.S. See tables at NORTH CAROLINA and WEST VIRGINIA.

2 Town, Highland co., W Virginia; scene of Confederate victory May 8, 1862, Confederate leaders Gens. Jackson and Edward Johnson.

Mc·Duf·fie \mək-ˈdəf-ē\. County in Georgia. See table at GEORGIA.

Mac·e·do·nia \ˌmas-ə-ˈdō-nyə, -nē-ə\. **1** Village, Summit co., NE Ohio, 18 m. N of Akron; pop. (1970c) 6735.

2 A region in cen. Balkan Penin., NW of the Aegean Sea, with somewhat indefinite boundaries but including Macedonia region of Greece, most of middle Vardar valley in SE Yugoslavia, and SW Bulgaria W of Mesta river; ab. 25,700 sq. m.

3 *or* **Mac·e·don** \ˈmas-əd-ən, -ə-ˌdän\. Ancient country and kingdom in the Macedonia region; ✱ Pella. Ancient kingdom originally located N of Thessaly and NW of Aegean Sea; under Philip II (359–336 B.C.), who developed the Macedonian phalanx, it came to include Thrace, Chalcidice, Thessaly, and Epirus; attained final hegemony over Greece in battle of Chaeronea 338 B.C.; Macedonian Empire, comprising Macedonia and countries conquered by Alexander III (the Great) 336–323 B.C., reached from Macedon beyond eastern boundaries of former Persian Empire into upper India; empire soon broke up (see IPSUS), and Macedon sought to retain its power in Greece and Aegean Sea; decisively defeated 197 B.C. at Cynoscephalae by Rome after a series of wars; opposition to Rome finally suppressed and the empire ended when Perseus, last king of the Macedonians, was defeated at Pydna 168 B.C.; made a Roman province 148 B.C., division of Byzantine Empire, lying W of Mesta river, when invaded by Slavic peoples 6th cent. A.D.; included successively in medieval Bulgarian and Serbian empires; gradually came under Ottoman Empire (Salonika held out to 1430) which held it until 1912; with rise of Bulgarian nationalism after 1878, "Macedonian question," i.e. independence of Macedonia from Turkey and rival Bulgarian, Serb, and Greek claims to Macedonia, finally led to Balkan Wars 1912–13; as result of Second Balkan War 1913 and of Bulgarian participation in World War I on side of Central Powers, Macedonia was partitioned bet. Yugoslavia and Greece, to exclusion of Bulgaria 1919; during 1920's and 1930's, revolutionary activity in Macedonia threatened relations of Bulgaria with other Balkan powers; after World War II status of Macedonia an issue in Greek-Yugoslavian relations.

4 *or Gk.* **Ma·ke·do·nia** \ˌmäk-ə-t͟h-ˈnē-ə\. Administrative region of modern Greece; includes all of N Greece except Western Thrace; 12,304 sq. m.; pop. (1971p) 1,883,156; forms departments of Chalcidice, Drama, Florina, Hematheia, Kastoria, Kavalla, Kilkís, Kozánē, Pella, Pieria, Serrai, and Thessalonike (see table at GREECE). Mountainous in W where it is drained by Vistritsa river; in E crossed by Vardar and Struma rivers; includes peninsula of Chalcidice. Chief towns Salonika, Kavalla, Serrai, and Drama.

5 A constituent republic of Yugoslavia, comprising the Yugoslav section of the region of Macedonia; 9928 sq. m.; pop. (1971p) 1,647,104; ✱ Skopje; wheat, barley, corn; chief towns: Skopje, Bitola, Prilep; made a constituent republic in 1946 constitution.

Ma·ceió \ˌmas-ā-ˈō\. City, ✱ of Alagoas state, E Brazil, 130 m. SSW of Recife; munic. pop. (1970p) 269,415; seaport, exporting sugar, cotton, and rum; univ. (1961); founded 1815; became city and ✱ of state 1839.

Macequece. See VILA DE MANICA.

Ma·ce·ra·ta \ˌmäch-ə-ˈrät-ə\. **1** Province of Marches, Italy. See table at ITALY.

2 Commune, its ✱, 110 m. NNW of Rome; pop. (1968e) 42,602; brewing; bricks, musical instruments; univ. (1290); founded 11th cent.

Mc·Far·land \mək-ˈfär-lənd\. City, Kern co., S California, 23 m. N of Bakersfield; pop. (1970c) 4177; fruit packing; diversified agriculture.

Mc·Gehee \mə-ˈgē\. Commercial city, Desha co., SE Arkansas, near Mississippi river 56 m. SE of Pine Bluff; pop. (1970c) 4683; food processing; gloves; agriculture.

Mc·Gill \mə-ˈgil\. Unincorporated community, White Pine co., E Nevada, ab. 13 m. NNE of Ely; pop. (1970c) 2164; owned by Nevada Consolidated Copper Company; smelter (1906).

Mac·gil·li·cud·dy's Reeks \mə-ˌgil-ə-ˌkəd-ēz-\. Mountain range, co. Kerry, SW Eire; highest peak Carrantuohill 3414 ft., highest mountain in Ireland.

Mc·Grath \mə-ˈgrath\. Unincorporated community, SW cen. Alaska, on upper Kuskokwim river W of Mt. McKinley; pop. (1970c) 279.

Mc·Greg·or \mə-ˈgreg-ər\. City, McLennan co., cen. Texas, 13 m. SSW of Waco; pop. (1970c) 4365; furniture; cotton and grain farms.

Mc·Guire, Mount \-mə-ˈgwī(ə)r\. Peak, NW Lemhi co., E cen. Idaho; 10,079 ft.

Ma·cha·chi \mə-ˈchäch-ē\. Resort town, Pichincha prov., N cen. Ecuador, in Andes Mts. at alt. 10,118 ft., just S of Quito; mineral-water springs.

Machaerus. See MUKĀWIR.

Ma·cha·la \mə-ˈchäl-ə\. Town, ✱ of El Oro prov., SW Ecuador, 75 m. S of Guayaquil; pop. (1970e) 63,300; produces cacao, coffee, hides; gold mining in vicinity; its port is Puerto Bolívar.

Mc·Hen·ry \mə-ˈken-rē\. 1 Name of counties in two states of the U.S. See tables at ILLINOIS and NORTH DAKOTA.

2 City, McHenry co., N Illinois, 23 m. W of Waukegan; pop. (1970c) 6772; in lake region, summer resort.

Ma·chi·as \mə-ˈchī-əs\. 1 River, SE Maine; ab. 70 m. long; rises in NE Hancock co., flows SE across Washington co. into Machias Bay.

2 Town, ⊗ of Washington co., SE corner of Maine, adjacent to Machias Bay 33 m. S of Calais; pop. (1970c) 2441; synthetic fibers; granite quarries; truck farms; Washington State Coll. of the Univ. of Maine (1909).

Machias Bay. Inlet of Atlantic Ocean on S coast of Washington co., SE Maine; receives Machias river on N.

Ma·chi·cha·co, Cape \-ˌmäch-i-ˈchäk-(ˌ)ō\. Cape extending into Bay of Biscay from Vizcaya prov., N coast of Spain, NE of Bilbao.

Ma·chi·da \mə-ˈchē-də, ˈmäch-i-ˌdä\. City, Tokyo prefecture, Honshū, Japan; pop. (1970c) 202,801.

Ma·chi·li·pat·nam \ˌməsh-ə-lē-ˈpət-nəm\ *or* **Ma·su·li·pat·nam** \ˌməs-ə-\ *or* **Ban·dar** \ˈbən-dər\. Seaport city, NE Andhra Pradesh, India, on Bay of Bengal on one of the mouths of Krishna river, 215 m. NNE of Madras; pop. (1967e) 116,275; manufactures scientific instruments, carpets; educational center. British agency established here 1611, earliest British settlement on Coromandel Coast; British expelled by French in wars of the Carnatic; retaken by British 1759; destroyed by a cyclone and flood 1864 with loss of 30,000 lives.

Machpelah, Cave of. See HEBRON 4.

Ma·chu Pic·chu \ˌmäch-(ˌ)ü-ˈpēk-(ˌ)chü\. Site of ancient Inca city on a mountain in the Andes, NW of Cuzco, Peru; fairly extensive ruins include a temple; citadel was surrounded by terraced gardens; discovered by Hiram Bingham 1911.

Ma·chyn·lleth \mə-ˈkin-ˌleth\. Urban district, W Montgomeryshire, Wales, on the Dyfi (Dovey) river; pop. (1971p) 1766; tourist resort; fishing (salmon).

Ma·cie·jo·wi·ce \ˌmät-sə-yȯ-ˈvēt-sə, ˌmäch-ə-\. Commune, E Poland, near E bank of the Vistula 43 m. SE of Warsaw; scene, Oct. 10, 1794, of Russian victory over rebelling Polish forces under Kosciusko who was wounded and captured.

Ma·ciel \ˌmäs-ē-ˈel\. Town, Caazapá dept., SE Paraguay; pop. (1970e) 5043.

Mc·In·tosh \ˈmak-ən-ˌtäsh\. 1 Name of counties in three states of the U.S. See tables at GEORGIA, NORTH DAKOTA, OKLAHOMA.

2 City, ⊗ of Corson co., N South Dakota; pop. (1970c) 563; coal mines; grain and livestock farms.

Mac·kay \mə-ˈkī\. Town, E Queensland, Australia, on Pacific Ocean within Great Barrier Reef 180 m. NNW of Rockhampton; pop. (1968e) 19,100; port facilities; in fertile agricultural region devoted largely to sugar and fruits, also to grazing and mining.

Mackay, Lake. Lake in desert region, cen. Australia, on boundary bet. Western Australia and Northern Territory.

Mc·Kay Dam \mə-ˈkā-\. Dam across **McKay Creek** (tributary of Umatilla river), S of Pendleton, Umatilla co., NE Oregon; height 165 ft.; completed 1927; impounds water for irrigation.

Mac·Kay Lake \mə-ˈkī-, -ˈkā-\. Lake, E cen. Mackenzie dist., Northwest Territories, Canada; 250 sq. m.; connected with Lake Aylmer.

Mc·Kean \mə-ˈkēn\. 1 County in Pennsylvania. See table at PENNSYLVANIA.

2 One of the smaller islands of the Phoenix Is. (*q.v.*) group, in W part, WSW of Canton I., cen. Pacific Ocean, 3°36′S lat., 174°08′W long.; 1 sq. m.

Mc·Kee \mə-ˈkē\. City, ⊗ of Jackson co., SE Kentucky; pop. (1970c) 255.

Mc·Kees·port \mə-ˈkēz-ˌpō(ə)rt, -ˌpȯ(ə)rt\. Industrial city, Allegheny co., SW Pennsylvania, at confluence of Youghiogheny and Monongahela rivers 10 m. ESE of Pittsburgh; pop. (1970c) 37,977; coal mines, gas fields; manufactures steel pipes and tubes, sheet steel and tin plate, boilers and radiators, river barges, steel castings. Settled 1755; center of conflict during Whisky Insurrection 1794; chartered as city 1890.

Mc·Kees Rocks \mə-ˈkēz-\. Borough, Allegheny co., SW Pennsylvania, near Ohio river 4 m. WNW of Pittsburgh; pop. (1970c) 11,901; steel, railroad cars, paint, castings; shipyards, coal mines. Settled 1764, incorporated 1892.

Mac·kel·lar, Mount \-mə-ˈkel-ər\. Mountain, Antarctica; 83°59′S, 166°39′E; 14,098 ft.

Mc·Ken·zie \mə-ˈken-zē\. 1 River, W Oregon; 80 m. long; rises in SE Linn co., flows W into Willamette river near Eugene.

2 County in North Dakota. See table at NORTH DAKOTA.

3 City, Carroll and Weakley cos., W Tennessee, 17 m. SSW of Paris; pop. (1970c) 4873; furniture, clothing, shoes, boats; agriculture; Bethel Coll. (1842).

Mac·ken·zie \mə-ˈken-zē\. 1 River, W Mackenzie dist., Northwest Territories, Canada; ab. 1120 m. long; when considered as including Slave river, Peace river, and Finlay river, ab. 2635 m. long, second longest river in North America; flows NNW into Mackenzie Bay; navigable for greater part of its length (rapids in Slave river); its valley is rich in forests and mineral resources. Discovered and descended by Alexander Mackenzie 1789. Trading posts of Hudson's Bay Company established along its course; these forts are now settlements, esp. Fort McPherson, Fort Good Hope, Fort Norman, Fort Simpson, and Fort Providence. Aklavik is chief settlement in delta and Fort Resolution on Great Slave Lake.

2 District, cen. and W Northwest Territories, Canada; area including water 527,490 sq. m.; pop. (1961c) 14,895; includes the greater part of N mainland of Canada bet. Yukon Territory and Keewatin dist. and also most of the Mackenzie river valley, Great Bear Lake, Great Slave Lake, the Yellowknife Preserve, and many other lakes. Administered from Edmonton. Created 1895; boundaries redefined 1918. Extensive oil fields and uranium deposits.

McKenzie, Mount. Peak in the Adirondack Mts., Essex co., NE New York; 3872 ft.

Mackenzie Bay. Widemouthed inlet of Beaufort Sea, N of Yukon Terr. and NW Mackenzie dist., Northwest Territories, Canada; 100 m. long, 120 m. wide; receives Mackenzie river.

Mackenzie Mountains. Range in E Yukon Territory and W Mackenzie dist., Northwest Territories, Canada; highest point Keele Peak 9750 ft. Watershed of tributaries of Mackenzie and Yukon rivers.

Mack·i·nac \ˈmak-ə-ˌnȯ\ *or formerly* **Mich·i·li·mack·i·nac** \ˌmish-ə-lē-ˈmak-ə-ˌnak, -ˌnȯ\. County in Michigan. See table at MICHIGAN.

Mackinac, Straits of \-ˈmak-ə-ˌnak, -ˌnȯ\. Straits connecting Lake Huron and Lake Michigan; 4 m. wide at narrowest point; site of Mackinac Bridge, completed 1957 (3800-ft. span), connecting upper and lower Michigan peninsulas.

Mackinac Island \ˈmak-ə-ˌnak-, -ˌnȯ-\. Island in Straits of Mackinac, in Mackinac co., SE Michigan penin.; coextensive with Mackinac Island city; 3 m. long; pop. (1970c) 517; state park; resort; Mackinac Coll. (1965).

Mack·i·naw \ˈmak-ə-ˌnȯ\. River, cen. Illinois; ab. 100 m. long; flows W, from E McLean co. into the Illinois river a few miles below Pekin.

Mc·Kin·ley \mə-ˈkin-lē\. County in New Mexico. See table at NEW MEXICO.

McKinley, Mount; *Russ.* **Bol·sha·ya** \bəl-'shī-ə\ *also* **Bulshaia** \bu̇l-\; *former Indian name* **De·na·li** \də-'näl-ē\. Mountain in Mount McKinley National Park, S cen. Alaska; 20,320 ft.; highest mountain in North America. See UNITED STATES, *National Parks,* and CHURCHILL PEAKS.

McKinley Park. Station for Mount McKinley National Park on railroad SSW of Fairbanks, E cen. Alaska, at NE end of Alaska Range.

Mc·Kin·ney \mə-'kin-ē\. City, ⊗ of Collin co., NE Texas, 30 m. N of Dallas; pop. (1970c) 15,193; dairy products, feed, clothing; dairy and livestock farms.

Mc·Lean \mə-'klān\. Name of counties in three states of the U.S. See tables at ILLINOIS, KENTUCKY, NORTH DAKOTA.

Mc·Leans·boro \mə-'klānz-ˌbər-ə, -ˌbə-rə\. City, ⊗ of Hamilton co., SE Illinois, SE of Mount Vernon; pop. (1970c) 2630; clothing; horse breeding; diversified agriculture.

Mc·Lel·an Strait \mə-ˌklel-ən-\. Strait separating Killinek I. from the mainland of Labrador, Canada.

Mc·Len·nan \mə-'klen-ən\. County in Texas. See table at TEXAS.

Mc·Leod \mə-'klau̇d\. County in Minnesota. See table at MINNESOTA.

Macleod. See FORT MACLEOD.

Mc·Lough·lin, Mount \-mə-'gläk-lən\ *or formerly* **Mount Pitt** \-'pit\. Peak, E Jackson co., SW Oregon; 9510 ft.

Mc·Mech·en \mək-'mek-ən\. Residential city, Marshall co., N West Virginia, on Ohio river 5 m. N of Moundsville; pop. (1970c) 2808.

McMillan Dam *and* **McMillan Lake.** See CARLSBAD 2.

Mc·Minn \mək-'min\. County in Tennessee. See table at TENNESSEE.

Mc·Minn·ville \mək-'min-ˌvil\. **1** City, ⊗ of Yamhill co., NW Oregon, 21 m. NNW of Salem; pop. (1970c) 10,125; mobile homes, paint, electronic components; livestock and hop farms; Linfield Coll. (1857); settled 1844.

2 \-ˌvil, -vəl\. Town, ⊗ of Warren co., cen. Tennessee, 53 m. NW of Chattanooga; pop. (1970c) 10,662; wood products, clothing, dairy products; foundry, marble quarries; diversified agriculture; settled c. 1800.

Mc·Mul·len \mək-'məl-ən\. County in Texas. See table at TEXAS.

Mc·Mur·do Sound \mək-ˌmərd-ō-\. Inlet of SW Ross Sea, bet. James Ross I. and the coast of Victoria Land, Antarctica, 77°30'S, 165°E; site of a major U.S. research and exploration base.

McMurray. See FORT MCMURRAY.

Mc·Nairy \mək-'ne(ə)r-ē\. County in Tennessee. See table at TENNESSEE.

Mac·Naugh·ton, Mount \-mək-'nȯt-ᵊn\. Peak in Adirondack Mts., Essex co., NE New York; 3976 ft.

Mc·Neill Peak \mək-'nē(ə)l-\. Mountain, Yakima co., S Washington; 6788 ft.

Ma·comb \mə-'kōm\. **1** County in Michigan. See table at MICHIGAN.

2 City, ⊗ of McDonough co., W Illinois, 37 m. SSW of Galesburg; pop. (1970c) 19,643; pottery, clay and steel products; coal mines; agriculture; Western Illinois Univ. (1899).

Macomb Mountain. Peak in the Adirondack Mts., Essex co., NE New York; 4371 ft.

Ma·con \'mās-ᵊn\ *or originally* **Ma·çon** \mä-'sōⁿ\. Bayou, NE Louisiana; 150 m. long; rises near the Arkansas boundary and flows S to the Tensas river in SE Franklin parish; part of its course forms boundary bet. Madison and Richland parishes; navigable.

Macon \'mā-kən\. **1** Name of counties in six states of U.S. See tables at ALABAMA, GEORGIA, ILLINOIS, MISSOURI, NORTH CAROLINA, TENNESSEE.

2 City, ⊗ of Bibb co., cen. Georgia, on Ocmulgee river 78 m. SE of Atlanta; pop. (1970c) 122,423; processing and distributing center in an agricultural region producing grain, cotton, pulpwood, fruit, and nuts; clay, limestone, automobile accessories, drugs, clothing, aircraft parts; Mercer Univ. (1833), Wesleyan Coll. (1836), Macon Junior Coll. (1968); Robins Air Force Base. Settled 1821; chartered 1832; captured by Union forces in Civil War April 20, 1865.

3 City, ⊗ of Noxubee co., E Mississippi, 28 m. SSW of Columbus; pop. (1970c) 2612; wood products, building materials; dairy and livestock farming.

4 City, ⊗ of Macon co., N Missouri 23 m. N of Moberly; pop. (1970c) 5301; coal mines; ships livestock; diversified agriculture.

Mâ·con \mä-'kōⁿ\ *or anc.* **Ma·tis·co Ædu·o·rum** \mə-'tis-(ˌ)kō-ˌēj-ə-'wōr-əm, -'wȯr-\. Manufacturing city, ✱ of Saône-et-Loire dept., E cen. France, on Saône river 22 m. WNW of Bourg; pop. (1968c) 33,445; railroad center; ships wine; copper founding, printing, rope making; remains of 12th cent. cathedral. Episcopal see, 6th cent. until Revolution; Huguenot stronghold in 16th cent.

Macoraba. See MECCA.

Macorís. Short form of SAN PEDRO DE MACORÍS.

Ma·cou·pin \mə-'kü-pən\. County in Illinois. See table at ILLINOIS.

Mc·Part·land Mountain \mək-ˌpärt-lən(d)-\. Peak in Glacier National Park, NW Montana; 8400 ft.

Mc·Pher·son \mək-'fərs-ᵊn\. **1** Name of counties in three states of the U.S. See tables at KANSAS, NEBRASKA, SOUTH DAKOTA.

2 City, ⊗ of McPherson co., cen. Kansas, 27 m. NE of Hutchinson; pop. (1970c) 10,851; oil refining; dairy, grain, and stock farms; McPherson Coll. (1887), Central Coll. (1914).

3 Trading station, Canada. See FORT MCPHERSON.

Mac·pher·son Range \mək-ˌfərs-ᵊn-\. Short range of mountains forming E end of boundary bet. New South Wales and SE Queensland, Australia; highest peak 4449 ft.

Mac·quar·ie \mə-'kwär-ē\. **1** River, E cen. New South Wales, Australia; 590 m. long; flows NNW from Blue Mts. to Darling river.

2 River, an E tributary of Lake river, E Tasmania, Australia; ab. 65 m. long.

Macquarie Harbour. Large inlet of Indian Ocean on W coast of Tasmania, Australia; ab. 20 m. long; receives Gordon river at S end. Cape Sorell is at W of entrance and town of Strahan is situated at N end.

Macquarie Island. Island in S Pacific Ocean, 850 m. SE of Tasmania, Australia, 54°36'S, 158°55'E; administered by Tasmania; 89 sq. m.; crest of submarine mountain. Discovered 1810; nature reserve; home of seals, sea elephants, penguins, etc., but seals now practically exterminated. Base of Mawson polar expedition 1911–14; Australian research station established on island 1948.

Mc·Rae \mə-'krā\. City, ⊗ of Telfair co., S cen. Georgia, 78 m. NE of Albany; pop. (1970c) 3151; lumber, clothing; fruit farms.

Mac Rob·ert·son Land \mə-'kräb-ərt-sən-\. Section of Antarctica coast on Indian Ocean, 70°S lat., 59°40' to 69°30'E long.; E of Enderby Land.

Mc·Sher·rys·town \mək-'sher-ēz-ˌtau̇n\. Borough, Adams co., S Pennsylvania, 12 m. E of Gettysburg; pop. (1970c) 2773.

Mac·tan \mäk-'tän\. Island off E coast of Cebu prov., Phil.; 24 sq. m.; pop. (1960c) 57,844; separated from Cebu I. by channel 1 m. wide. Has mangrove swamps, coconut groves, and some cultivated area; chief town Lapu-Lapu. Here on Apr. 27, 1521, Ferdinand Magellan was killed in an expedition on behalf of a native sovereign.

Mactaris. See MAKTAR.

Ma·cu·ri·jes, Point \-ˌmäk-ə-ˈrē-(ˌ)hās\. Cape extending W from S coast of Camagüey prov., E cen. Cuba, S of the mouth of the San Pedro river.

Ma·cus·pa·na \ˌmäk-ü-ˈspän-ə\. Municipality, Tabasco state, Mexico, 28 m. SE of Villahermosa; pop. (1970p) 75,013; wheat, rice, beans, coffee, sugarcane.

Ma·cu·to \mä-ˈküt-(ˌ)ō\. Seaside resort on N coast of Venezuela, adjoining La Guaira; pop. (1961c) 7041.

Mad \ˈmad\. River, W cen. Ohio; 100 m. long; flows S and SE, from Logan co., to Miami river at Dayton.

Ma'dabā. See MADEBA.

Mad·a·gas·car \ˌmad-ə-ˈgas-kər\. Island, constituting with minor adjacent islands the Malagasy Republic (*q.v.*).

Ma·dame Island \mə-ˌdam-, ma-\. Island off S coast of Cape Breton I., Nova Scotia, Canada; belongs to Richmond co., Nova Scotia; Arichat is on its S shore.

Ma·dang \ˈmäd-ˌäŋ\. 1 Administrative district, E New Guinea I., Papua New Guinea; 10,800 sq. m.; pop. (1969e) 162,717.

2 *or formerly* **Frie·drich–Wil·helms·ha·fen** \ˌfrē-drik-ˈvil-ˌhelmz-ˌhäf-ən, -ˈvil-əmz-\. Seaport town, its ✻, on Astrolabe Bay; pop. (1970e) 11,151; good harbor; object of Australian drive along the coast Sept. 1943 to Feb. 1944; captured by Australian and U.S. forces Apr. 24, 1944.

Ma·da·ri·pur \mə-ˈdär-ē-ˌpu̇(ə)r\. Town, Bangla Desh, on Ganges Delta; pop. (1961c) 25,328.

Ma·dau·ros \mə-ˈdȯr-əs\. Ancient city, Numidia, N Africa; near modern **Mdaou·rouch** \em-ˈdau̇-ˌrüsh\, commune pop. (1961c) 16,000; ab. 50 m. NNW of Tebessa, Algeria; celebrated for its schools; birthplace of Apuleius; ruins of Roman baths and mausoleum, and of Byzantine basilica and fortress.

Mad·a·was·ka \ˌmad-ə-ˈwäs-kə\. 1 Town, Aroostook co., N Maine, on St. John river 17 m. ENE of Fort Kent; pop. (1970c) 5585; paper mill; truck and dairy farms.

2 River, SE Ontario, Canada; 130 m. long; rises in lakes in Haliburton co. and flows SE and NE in Renfrew co. into the Ottawa river at Arnprior above Ottawa.

3 County, New Brunswick, Canada. See table at NEW BRUNSWICK.

Mad·da·le·na \ˌmad-ᵊl-ˈā-nə, ˌmäd-\. Island in Tyrrhenian Sea off extreme NE coast of Sardinia; pop. (1961c) 12,360; administratively, a commune in Sassari prov., Sardinia, Italy.

Maddalena, La. See LA MADDALENA.

Mad·da·lo·ni \ˌmad-ᵊl-ˈō-nē\. Commune, Caserta prov., Campania, S Italy, 15 m. NNE of Naples; pop. (1968e) 33,679; castle, ancient towers; Ponti della Valle aqueduct (built by Vanvitelli 1753–64) nearby.

Mad·e·ba *or* **Ma'da·bā** \ˈmad-ə-bə\ *or anc.* **Med·e·ba** \ˈmed-ə-bə\. Town, N cen. Jordan, SSW of Amman; pop. (1961c) 11,224; wheat and barley; ancient Moabite town; fighting here during Wars of the Maccabees.

Ma·dei·ra \mə-ˈdir-ə\. Village, Hamilton co., SW corner of Ohio, NE suburb of Cincinnati; pop. (1970c) 6713.

Madeira \mə-ˈdir-ə, -ˈder-ə\. 1 River, W Brazil, most important tributary of Amazon river; 2013 m. long (with the Mamoré); formed by confluence of Bolivian rivers Mamoré and Beni at the Brazilian border; flows NE into Amazon below Manaus.

2 Island group in E Atlantic Ocean off coast of Morocco, N of the Canary Is. and SE of the Azores, 32°30′N lat. to 33°07′ and 16°13′W long. to 17°30′; 308 sq. m.; pop. (1970e) 268,700; comprises two inhabited islands, Madeira and Porto Santo, and two groups of barren islets, the Desertas and Selvagens; constitutes the Funchal dist. of Portugal; ✻ Funchal on Madeira I.

History: Possibly known to Genoese by mid-14th cent.; Porto Santo sighted by João Goncalves Zarco 1418; Madeira discovered 1420 by Zarco who founded Funchal 1421; British occupied Madeira for a short time in 1801 and again 1807–14.

3 Largest island of the group ab. 440 m. W of Morocco; ab. 34 m. long and ab. 12 m. wide; ✻ Funchal; has deep ravines and rugged mountains, with highest Pico Ruivo 6106 ft. in center of island; N coast is steep and very wild. Produces wine (*madeira*), sugar, bananas, tropical fruits, potatoes; fishing; handicrafts; tourism.

Madeira Beach \mə-ˌdir-ə-\. City, Pinellas co., W cen. Florida, on Boca Ciega Bay 5 m. W of St. Petersburg; pop. (1970c) 4342.

Madeira Falls \mə-ˌdir-ə-, -ˌder-ə-\. Waterfall in the Madeira river, W Brazil, near junction of Mamoré and Beni rivers on the Bolivian border.

Mä·de·le·ga·bel \ˈmād-ᵊl-ə-ˌgäb-əl\. Peak in the Algäu Alps, on the border bet. Bavaria and the Tirol; 8689 ft.; 2d highest peak in West Germany.

Madeleine, Îles de la. See MAGDALEN ISLANDS.

Madeleine, La. See LA MADELEINE.

Ma·de·leine, Ri·vière de la \ˌriv-ē-ˈe(ə)rd-ᵊl-ä-ˌmad-ᵊl-ˈān\. River, Gaspé Penin., SE Quebec, Canada; ab. 70 m. long; flows NE and N into St. Lawrence river.

Ma·de·lia \mə-ˈdēl-yə\. Village, Watonwan co., S Minnesota, 21 m. WSW of Mankato; pop. (1970c) 2316; poultry, stock and truck farms.

Mad·e·line Island \ˌmad-ᵊl-ən-\. See APOSTLE ISLANDS.

Ma·de·ra \mə-ˈder-ə\. 1 County in California. See table at CALIFORNIA.

2 City, ⊗ of Madera co., cen. California, 20 m. NW of Fresno; pop. (1970c) 16,044; vegetable oils, sheet metal; granite quarry; founded 1876.

3 Municipality, Chihuahua state, Mexico, 140 m. WNW of Chihuahua; pop. (1970p) 32,367; cattle, goats; wheat, barley, potatoes.

4 Volcano, Nicaragua; 4572 ft.; one of two peaks (see CONCEPCIÓN 4) on the island of Ometepe in Lake Nicaragua.

Madhumati. See GANGES DELTA.

Ma·dhya Bha·rat \ˌmäd-yə-ˈbär-ət\. Former state, cen. India; union of 20 princely states, including Gwalior and Indore, formed 1948; became part of Madhya Pradesh 1956.

Madhya Pra·desh \-prə-ˈdāsh, -ˈdesh\ *or formerly* **Central Provinces and Be·rar** \-bā-ˈrär\. State, cen. India; 171,220 sq. m.; pop. (1971p) 41,449,729; ✻ Bhopal; rice, wheat, corn, sugarcane, cotton; manganese, iron ore; chief cities: Indore, Jabalpur, Gwalior, Bhopal.

History: Territory in Central Provinces conquered by Marathas in 18th cent. and ruled from Nagpur (*q.v.*); taken for British by Dalhousie under doctrine of lapse 1853; Berar (*q.v.*) transferred to Central Provinces 1903; constituted an autonomous province 1937; adopted present name 1950, present boundaries 1956.

Ma·di·di \mə-ˈdēd-ē\. River, NW Bolivia; ab. 190 m. long; flows NE into the Beni river.

Ma·dill \mə-ˈdil\. City, ⊗ of Marshall co., S Oklahoma, 22 m. ESE of Ardmore; pop. (1970c) 2875; oil wells.

Madinah, Al–. See MEDINA 6.

Ma·di·nat ash Sha'b \mə-ˈdē-ˌnət-ash-ˈshab\ *or formerly* **Al–It·ta·had** \ˌal-ˌit-ə-ˈhad\. Town, administrative ✻ of Yemen, ab. 10 m. W of Aden; pop. (1967e) 20,000.

Madioen. See MADIUN.

Mad·i·son \ˈmad-ə-sən\. 1 River, SW Montana; ab. 180 m. long; rises in S Gallatin co., flows W and N through Madison co. to unite with Jefferson and Gallatin rivers and form the Missouri river.

2 Name of a parish in Louisiana and of counties in nineteen states of the U.S. See tables at ALABAMA, ARKANSAS, FLORIDA, GEORGIA, IDAHO, ILLINOIS, INDIANA, IOWA, KENTUCKY, LOUISIANA, MISSISSIPPI, MISSOURI, MONTANA, NEBRASKA, NEW YORK, NORTH CAROLINA, OHIO, TENNESSEE, TEXAS, VIRGINIA.

3 Town, Madison co., N Alabama, 7 m. W of Huntsville; pop. (1970c) 3086.

4 Town, SE New Haven co., S Connecticut, on Long Island Sound and Hammonasset river; pop. (1970c) 9768; beach resort.

5 City, ⊗ of Madison co., N Florida, 52 m. E of Tallahassee; pop. (1970c) 3737; sawmills; in region producing corn, tobacco, melons; livestock.

6 City, ⊗ of Morgan co., N cen. Georgia, 25 m. S of Athens; pop. (1970c) 2890; lumber, dairy farms, peach orchards.

7 City, Madison co., SW Illinois, 5 m. N of East St. Louis; pop. (1970c) 7042.

8 City, ⊗ of Jefferson co., SE Indiana, on Ohio river 38 m. NE of New Albany; pop. (1970c) 13,081; canvas products, furniture; diversified agriculture.

9 Town, Somerset co., W Maine, on Kennebec river 20 m. NW of Waterville; pop. (1970c) 4278; pulp and paper mills.

10 City, ⊗ of Lac qui Parle co., W Minnesota, 22 m. W of Montevideo; pop. (1970c) 2242; dairy products, fertilizer, grain, poultry, and livestock farms.

11 City, ⊗ of Madison co., NE Nebraska, 14 m. S of Norfolk; pop. (1970c) 1595; butter; grain farms.

12 Borough, Morris co., N New Jersey, 4 m. SE of Morristown; pop. (1970c) 16,710; residential suburb; Drew Univ. (1866); headquarters of Anthony Wayne during American Revolution.

13 Town, Rockingham co., N North Carolina, 25 m. NNE of Winston-Salem; pop. (1970c) 2018; textiles.

14 City, ⊗ of Lake co., E South Dakota, 38 m. NNW of Sioux Falls; pop. (1970c) 6315; summer resort; grain elevators; livestock and grain farms; Dakota State Coll. (1881).

15 Town, ⊗ of Madison co., N Virginia; pop. (1970c) 229.

16 Town, ⊗ of Boone co., SW West Virginia; pop. (1970c) 2342; coal mines, gas wells; truck farms.

17 City, ❋ of Wisconsin and ⊗ of Dane co., S Wisconsin, on isthmus between Lake Monona and Lake Mendota; pop. (1970c) 172,007; wholesale and retail trade center; produces farm machinery, automobile parts, hospital equipment, and machine tools; meat-packing; Univ. of Wisconsin (1836), Edgewood Coll. of the Sacred Heart (1927); site chosen for capital of Wisconsin Territory 1836; incorporated as village 1846, as city 1856.

Madison, Mount. Peak in the Presidential Range, White Mts., in S Coos co., N of Mt. Adams, N New Hampshire; 5362 ft.

Madison Heights. City, Oakland co., SE Michigan, N suburb of Detroit; pop. (1970c) 38,599.

Mad·i·son·ville \ˈmad-ə-sən-ˌvil\. 1 City, ⊗ of Hopkins co., W Kentucky, 33 m. N of Hopkinsville; pop. (1970c) 15,332; clothing, dairy products; coal mines, oil wells; agriculture.

2 Town, ⊗ of Monroe co., SE Tennessee; pop. (1970c) 2614; sawmills; Hiawassee Coll. (1849).

3 City, ⊗ of Madison co., E cen. Texas, 33 m. NE of Bryan; pop. (1970c) 2881; hardwood timber; oil and gas wells.

Ma·di·un *or Du.* **Ma·di·oen** \ˌmad-ē-ˈün\. 1 Subdivision of the Indonesian province of East Java, Java; 2348 sq. m.; pop. (1961c) 509,428; ❋ Madiun. Region extends to S coast of island but has no port. Has fertile and well-watered plains in the N and lies bet. Mts. Lawu and Wilis. Raises esp. rice and sugar; produces teak; a residency of the former Neth. Indies.

2 City, its ❋, on railroad in cen. plain 90 m. WSW of Surabaja; pop. (1961c) 123,373; site of principal repair shops of state railroads; also produces textiles, lumber; cigarettes; scene of considerable fighting during Indonesian revolution 1948.

Ma·dja·pa·hit \ˌmäj-ə-ˈpä-ˌhit\. Malay kingdom in the East Indies 1293–1518 with its center in E Java and controlling most of Sumatra, coastal regions of Borneo and Celebes, and the Lesser Sunda Is.; finally overcome by Muslims.

Madoera. See MADURA.

Madoera Strait. See MADURA STRAIT.

Ma·do·nie Mountains \ˌmäd-ə-ˌnē-ˌā-\; *Ital.* **Le Madonie** \lā-\ *or* **Mon·ti Madonie** \ˌmȯn-tē-\. Mountain range in Palermo prov., NW cen. Sicily, Italy; highest peak 6491 ft.

Mad·ra·ka, Cape \-ˈmad-rə-kə\ *or Arab.* **Ras al–Mad·ra·kah** \ˌräs-al-\. Cape on E coast of Oman, SE Arabian Penin., extending into the Arabian Sea at 19°N, 57°52′E.

Mad·ras \ˈmad-rəs\. City, ⊗ of Jefferson co., N cen. Oregon; pop. (1970c) 1689; diversified agriculture.

Ma·dras \mə-ˈdras, -ˈdräs\. 1 State, India. See TAMIL NADU.

2 City, ❋ of Tamil Nadu state, India, on Coromandel Coast; pop. (1970e) 2,086,036; the main port on India's SE coast although harbor is wholly artificial; rail center; exports hides and skins, oilseeds, cotton, chrome, magnesite, produces cotton textiles, railroad rolling stock, bicycles; motion-picture production, printing, automobile and motorcycle assembly; univ. (1857); technical institute (1959).

History: Founded 1639 by Francis Day of the British East India Company; grew by process of accretion to original fort (**Fort St. George** \-sānt-ˈjȯ(ə)rj, -sənt-\); blockaded by Daud Khan 1702; unsuccessfully attacked by Marathas 1741; captured by French 1746 but returned by Treaty of Aix-la-Chapelle 1748; besieged by French 1758 and relieved by English fleet; successfully defended against Haidar Ali 1769 and 1780; harbor constructed 1862–1901. St. Thomé, now part of city, founded by Portuguese 1504, ceded to English 1749; held by French 1672–74. Traditional burial place of the apostle Thomas.

Madras States. Former agency, S India, including 5 Indian states: Travancore, Cochin, Pudukkottai, Banganapalle, and Sandur; 10,757 sq. m.

Mad·re, La·gu·na \lə-ˌgü-nə-ˈmäd-rē\. 1 Long inlet of Gulf of Mexico bet. Padre I. and the mainland of S Texas, S of Corpus Christi.

2 Long narrow inlet of the Gulf of Mexico on coast of NE cen. Mexico, state of Tamaulipas.

Madre, María. See MARÍA MADRE.

Ma·dre de Dios \ˌmäd-rē-ˌdād-ē-ˈōs\. 1 River in Peru and Bolivia; 600 m. long; rises in SE Peru, flows E across Bolivian border into Beni river in N Bolivia.

2 Department of SE Peru. See table at PERU.

Madre de Dios Archipelago. Group of islands in S Pacific Ocean, off SW coast of Chile, N of Archipelago of Reina Adelaida, and S of Wellington I.; 50°25′S, 75°05′W.

Mad·rid \ˈmad-rəd\. City, Boone co., cen. Iowa, 22 m. NNW of Des Moines; pop. (1970c) 2448; coal mines; agriculture.

Ma·drid \mə-ˈdrid\. 1 Province of cen. Spain. See table at SPAIN.

2 City, ❋ of Spain and of Madrid prov., cen. Spain, on Manzanares river 40 m. NNE of Toledo and 34 m. WSW of Guadalajara; pop. (1970p) 3,146,071; principal transportation center of Spain; archiepiscopal see; commercial center for interior provinces; cultural center; important industrial city producing aircraft, trucks, optical and electrical equipment, radios, rubber, plastics, leather goods, pharmaceuticals, furniture; univ. (founded 1499 at Alcalá de Henares; transferred to Madrid 1836); formerly surrounded by 20-foot wall, three of the gates of which still remain; 18th cent. royal palace on site of old Moorish alcazar; numerous art galleries including esp. the Prado museum; national library; numerous parks, among them the famous Buen Retiro gardens; several notable 17th and 18th cent. churches; bullring; the Escorial, often associated with Madrid, is 27 m. NW of the city.

History: Moorish fortress captured in 932 A.D. by Ramiro II of León; again taken from Moors by Alfonso VI of Castile c. 1083; made capital of Spain by Philip II 1561; occupied by French 1808–12 during Peninsular War; in Spanish Civil War held by Loyalists 1936–39; surrendered to Insurgents Mar. 29, 1939.

Mad River. See MAD.

Ma·driz \mə-'driz\. Department of NW cen. Nicaragua. See table at NICARAGUA.

Ma·dru·ga \mə-'drü-gə\. Municipality, La Habana prov., W Cuba, 20 m. WSW of Matanzas; pop. (1967e) 12,300.

Ma·du·ra *or Du.* **Ma·doe·ra** \mə-'du̇r-ə\. Island off NE coast of Java, Indonesia; a part of East Java prov.; 2113 sq. m.; pop. (1957e) 1,883,401; ✻ Pamekasan. Hilly, highest point 1545 ft. Chief industries cattle breeding, fishing, and salt production; raises esp. maize, cassava, and rice. Chief towns Pamekasan, Sumenep, Sampang, and Bangkalan. Under Mataram 1624–74; Dutch influence established at end of 17th cent.; attached to Java as a residency 1885.

Ma·du·rai \ˌmäd-ə-'rī\ *or* **Mad·u·ra** \'maj-ə-rə\. City, S Tamil Nadu, S India, 270 m. SSW of Madras; pop. (1970e) 493,842; cotton-manufacturing center; tourism; univ. (1966). Noted for its great temple with colonnades and nine massive gate towers or gopuras adorned with elaborate carving and enclosing a quadrangle, the "Tank of the Golden Lilies"; also has several fine palaces; government industrial school. Capital of old Pandya dynasty from 5th cent. B.C. to end of 11th cent. A.D.; came under Vijayanagar in 14th cent.; under Nayak dynasty from middle 16th cent. to c. 1736 when taken by Nawab of Carnatic; taken over by British East India Company 1801.

Ma·du·ra Strait *or Du.* **Ma·doe·ra Strait** \mə-'du̇r-ə-\. Arm of the Java Sea, extending S of Madura I. and NE end of Java I., Indonesia; connects with Java Sea to the N by narrow Surabaja Strait W of Madura. Naval battle here Feb. 4, 1942 in which U.S.S. *Marblehead* participated.

Maeander. See MENDERES 1.

Mae·ba·shi *also* **Ma·ye·bash·i** \ˌmä-yə-'bäsh-ē, mī-'bäsh-\. City, ✻ of Gumma prefecture, cen. Honshū, Japan; pop. (1970c) 233,632; in mountainous region with soil of volcanic origin favorable to the mulberry, hence remains one of the leading centers in growing silkworms and producing silk; univ. (1949).

Mae Hong Son *or* **Mae·hong·son** \ˌma-ˌhȯŋ-'sȯn\ *also* **Mu·ai To** \ˌmü-ˌī-'tō\. 1 Province, NW Thailand; 5105 sq. m.; pop. (1960c) 80,807; ✻ Mae Hong Son.

2 Town, its ✻, near Burma border 75 m. NW of Chiang Mai.

Mae Klong. See MEKLONG.

Mael·strom \'mā(ə)l-strəm, -ˌsträm\ *or Norwegian* **Mal·strøm** \'mäl-ˌstrœm\. Strong current in the Norwegian Sea, off the NW coast of Norway just S of Moskenes I.; under certain conditions of wind and tide forms a whirlpool; formerly supposed to suck in all vessels within a long radius.

Mae Nam Khong. See SALWEEN.

Mae·o·nia \mē-'ō-nē-ə\. Earlier name of Lydia, Asia Minor; later, a small district in NE Lydia.

Maeotis, Palus. See AZOV, SEA OF.

Maeseyck. See MAASEIK.

Maes·teg \mī-'steg\. Urban district, Glamorganshire, S Wales, 12 m. E of Swansea; pop. (1971p) 20,970; coal mining.

Maestra, Sierra. See SIERRA MAESTRA.

Maestricht. See MAASTRICHT.

Ma·e·wo \'mī-(ˌ)wō\ *or* **Au·ro·ra** \ə-'rōr-ə, ȯ-, -'rȯr-\. One of the New Hebrides Is., SW Pacific Ocean, in NE part of the group 65 m. E of Espíritu Santo I.; 29 m. long and 4 m. wide; 104 sq. m.; pop. (1967c) 1196. Has long central range of mountains, thickly wooded.

Maf·e·king \'maf-ə-kiŋ\. Town, N Cape Province, S Rep. of South Africa, 160 m. W of Pretoria, near W Transvaal border; pop. (1967e) 6200; until 1965 seat of administration of Bechuanaland Protectorate (now Botswana). Trade and business center for region devoted to dairy and livestock farming. Founded 1885. Starting point for the Jameson Raid 1895; scene of famous siege during Boer War lasting 217 days, Oct. 12, 1899 to May 17, 1900.

Ma·fe·teng \'maf-ə-ˌteŋ\. Town, W Lesotho, ab. 38 m. SSW of Maseru; pop. (1966c) 3222.

Ma·fia \'mäf-ē-ə, 'maf-\. Island in the Indian Ocean off E coast of Tanzania, opp. mouth of Rufiji river, E Africa, ab. 90 m. S of the N tip of Zanzibar; 170 sq. m.; administratively a part of Tanzania.

Ma·fra \'maf-rə\. 1 City, Santa Catarina state, S Brazil, on a headstream of the Iguaçu river 130 m. NW of Florianópolis; munic. pop. (1968e) 37,526.

2 Commune, Lisboa dist., W Portugal, near Atlantic Ocean 16 m. NNW of Lisbon; pop. (1970p) 7149; monastery containing a church and over 800 rooms, built in imitation of the Escorial, 1717–32.

Ma·ga·dan \ˌmäg-ə-'dan, -'dän\. Port, ✻ of Magadan Oblast, Russian S.F.S.R., U.S.S.R., on N shore of Sea of Okhotsk; pop. (1970p) 92,000; mining and industrial town; fish canning; starting point of highways northward to head of navigation on the Kolyma.

Magadan Oblast \-'ō-bləst, -ˌblast\. Subdivision of the Russian S.F.S.R., U.S.S.R.; 462,973 sq. m.; pop. (1970p) 352,000; ✻ Magadan; mountainous region; reindeer herding; gold mining; formed 1953.

Ma·ga·dha \'məg-əd-ə, 'mäg-\. Ancient kingdom, India, including Bihar S of the Ganges; ✻ Pataliputra (*mod.* Patna); scene of many incidents in life of Gautama Buddha; especially powerful under the Maurya dynasty (c. 322–185 B.C.) founded by Chandragupta and extended by Asoka (273–232 B.C.) and by the later Gupta dynasty; declined ab. 5th cent. A.D.

Ma·ga·di \mə-'gäd-ē\. Town, S cen. Kenya, E Africa, 50 m. SSW of Nairobi; terminus of railroad branch line.

Magadi, Lake. Lake, S Kenya, E Africa, near Tanzania border; 240 sq. m.; ab. 30 m. long; has large soda deposits. See NATRON, LAKE.

Ma·ga·lla·nes \ˌmä-gə-'yän-(ˌ)ās\. 1 Province of S Chile. See table at CHILE.

2 City, Chile. See PUNTA ARENAS.

Magallanes, Estrecho de. See MAGELLAN, STRAIT OF.

Ma·gan·gué \mə-ˌgäŋ-'gā\. Town, Bolívar dept., N Colombia, at the junction of the Cauca and Magdalena rivers 90 m. SE of Cartagena; munic. pop. (1968c) 73,868.

Ma·gat \mä-'gät, mə-\. River, an important left tributary of the upper Cagayan river, NE Luzon, Phil.; ab. 90 m. long; rises in Caraballo Mts. and flows generally NE to the Cagayan above Ilagan.

Mag·a·zine Mountain \ˌmag-ə-ˌzēn-\. Peak, Logan co., NW cen. Arkansas, in Ouachita Mts.; 2753 ft.; highest point in state.

Mag·da·la \'mag-də-lə\ *or Heb.* **Mig·dal** \mig-'däl\ *or Arab.* **Al–Maj·dal** \al-'maj-ˌdal\ *also* **Mej·del** \'mej-ˌdel\. Ancient town on the W shore of the Sea of Galilee; now an archaeological site just N of Tiberias, Israel. Supposed home of Mary Magdalene (*Luke* viii. 2).

Mag·da·le·na \ˌmag-də-'lē-nə\. Village, Socorro co., cen. New Mexico, 74 m. SSW of Albuquerque; pop. (1970c) 652.

Magdalena \ˌmag-də-'lā-nə\. 1 Island off SW coast of Chile, NE of Chonos Archipelago.

2 River, S cen. and N Colombia; 956 m. long; rises on E slopes of Andes in S Colombia, flows N into the Caribbean Sea near Barranquilla (*q.v.*); navigable for over 930 m.; with its many tributaries provides ab. 2500 m. of navigable waterways.

3 Department of N Colombia. See table at COLOMBIA.

4 Island, Marquesas Is. See FATU HIVA.

Magdalena, María. See MARÍA MAGDALENA.

Magdalena Bay \ˌmag-də-ˌlā-nə-\. Inlet of Pacific Ocean on SW coast of Baja California.

Mag·da·len Islands \ˌmag-də-lən-\ *or Fr.* **Îles de la Ma·de·leine** \ēl-də-lá-má-d(ə-)len\. Island group constituting a county of Quebec, S cen. part of the Gulf of St. Lawrence, E Quebec, Canada; 102 sq. m.; pop. (1969e) 13,151; comprises 13 islands (largest are Coffin, Amherst, Grindstone). About 50 m. N of East Point, Prince Edward Island and ab. 100 m. SW of Newfoundland. Most of inhabitants are Acadians; chief occupation fishing; formerly mined gypsum.

Mag·de·burg \ˈmäg-də-ˌbu̇(ə)rg, ˈmag-də-ˌbərg\. 1 District, East Germany. See table at GERMANY, EAST.

2 Manufacturing and commercial city, its ✻, on Elbe river 82 m. WSW of Berlin; pop. (1970e) 270,692; most important inland port of East Germany; railroad junction; iron and steel, chemicals, textiles; sugar refineries; technical coll. (1953); 13th–16th cent. cathedral; 11th cent. church. First mentioned 805 A.D.; made archiepiscopal see 962; member of Hanseatic League for nearly 200 years; sacked and burned during Thirty Years' War 1631; captured by French 1806; to Prussia 1814. In World War II a major industrial center in the war effort; repeatedly bombed by Allies and taken Apr. 18–19, 1945.

Ma·ge·lang \ˌmäg-ə-ˈläŋ\. City, Central Java prov., Indonesia, 37 m. SSW of Semarang; pop. (1961c) 94,089; center for tourists visiting Borobudur temple (*q.v.*); almost in exact geographical center of Java on railroad bet. Semarang on the N and Jogjakarta on the S; in fertile plain (alt. 1100 ft.) with high mountains on E and W.

Ma·gel·lan, Strait of \-mə-ˈjel-ən, *chiefly Brit.* -ˈgel-\ *or Span.* **Es·tre·cho de Ma·ga·lla·nes** \e-ˈstrech-ō-dā-ˌmäg-ä-ˈyän-es\. Strait at S extremity of South America, passing in a winding course bet. the mainland (Magallanes prov., Chile) and Tierra del Fuego Archipelago (*q.v.*); 350 m. long; it connects S Atlantic with S Pacific Ocean, both its entrance and exit being 52°30′S. Dungeness Point (on N) and Cape Espíritu Santo (on S) mark entrance from the Atlantic; Cape Pilar at NW extremity of Desolación I. marks entrance from the Pacific. Punta Arenas (formerly Magallanes) is only town of importance on its course. Discovered Oct.–Nov. 1520 by Ferdinand Magellan.

Ma·gens Bay \ˌmā-gənz-\. Bay in N coast of St. Thomas I., Virgin Is., West Indies.

Ma·gen·ta \mə-ˈjent-ə\. Commune, Milano prov., Lombardy, N Italy, 14 m. W of Milan; pop. (1968e) 22,059; produces matches; scene of victory of French and Sardinian army over Austrian forces June 4, 1859; magenta dye named in honor of battle.

Ma·ger·øy \ˌmäg-ə-ˈrəi\. Island in Arctic Ocean off extreme N coast of Norway; 111 sq. m.; its N tip is North Cape (*q.v.*).

Ma·gers·fon·tein \ˈmäg-ərz-ˌfän-ˌtān\. Battlefield, W Orange Free State, E cen. Rep. of South Africa; here Cronje checked British in their advance to relief of Kimberly Dec. 1899.

Ma·ge·tan \mä-ˈge-ˌtän\. Town, East Java prov., Indonesia, a few miles W of Madiun at foot of Mt. Lawu; pop. (1961c) 26,818.

Mag·gia \ˈmäj-ə\. River, Ticino canton, SE cen. Switzerland; ab. 35 m. long; rises in Lepontine Alps, flows SE into N end of Lake Maggiore near Locarno; hydroelectric power stations.

Maggiorasca Monte. See BUE, MONTE.

Mag·gio·re, Lake \-mə-ˈjōr-ē, -ˈjȯr-\; *anc.* **Ver·ba·nus Lacus** \(ˌ)vər-ˌbā-nə-ˈslā-kəs\. Lake, N Italy and S Switzerland; 40 m. long and ab. 2 m. wide; 81 sq. m.; max. depth 1220 ft.; traversed (N to S) by Ticino river; Locarno, Ticino canton, Switzerland, is at N end. Has many resorts on its shores and is nearly surrounded by mountains of S Lepontine Alps. See BORROMEAN ISLANDS.

Maghiana. See JHANG-MAGHIANA.

Ma·ghrib *or* **Ma·ghreb** \ˈməg-rəb\. Arabic name for NW Africa and, during the Moorish occupation, Spain; now used to include Morocco, Algeria, Tunisia, and, sometimes, Libya.

Ma·gi·cienne Bay \mə-ˌzhē-sē-ˌen-\. Inlet on SE coast of Saipan I., Mariana Is.

Ma·gil·li·gan Point \mə-ˌgil-i-gən-\. Cape on N coast of Ireland, on E side of entrance to Lough Foyle.

Ma·gi·not Line \ˌmazh-ə-ˌnō-, ˌmaj-\. A system of defensive fortifications built 1930–34 by France to protect its eastern border—named after André Maginot (1877–1932), French minister of war; extended nearly 200 m. from S of Belfort to the Belgian border; was position of major part of French army during first few months of World War II but yielded with little fighting after German invasion of Low Countries and collapse of French armies in May 1940.

Ma·gio·ne \mä-ˈjō-(ˌ)nā\. Commune, Perugia prov., Umbria, cen. Italy, 11 m. WNW of Perugia; pop. (1968e) 10,750.

Mag·le·mo·se \ˈma(g)-lə-ˌmō-sə, -ˈmau̇-\. Locality on W coast of Sjælland, Denmark, NW of Slagelse; archaeological site yielding bone and stone implements.

Ma·glie \ˈmäl-(ˌ)yā\. Commune, Lecce prov., Apulia, SE Italy, 15 m. SSE of Lecce; pop. (1968e) 13,751.

Mag·na \ˈmag-nə\. Unincorporated community, Salt Lake co., N Utah, ab. 12 m. WSW of Salt Lake City; pop. (1970c) 5509; copper mill; diversified agriculture.

Magna Char·ta Island \ˌmag-nə-ˌkärt-ə-\. See RUNNYMEDE.

Magna Grae·cia \ˌmag-nə-ˈgrē-shə\. Collective name for the ancient Greek seaport colonies in S Italy; chief cities Tarentum (*mod.* Taranto), Sybaris (the oldest, founded c. 720 B.C.), Crotona (*mod.* Crotone), Heraclea (*qq.v.*).

Mag·ne·sia \mag-ˈnē-zhə, -shə\. 1 Narrow coastal district in ancient Thessaly, Greece, extending along the Aegean Sea from Peneus river S to and including the peninsula enclosing the Sinus Pagasaeus (Gulf of Volos) on the E; according to tradition its inhabitants founded both cities of the same name in Asia Minor.

2 Department of Greece, approx. coextensive with anc. district. See table at GREECE.

3 *or* **Magnesia ad Mae·an·drum** \-ˌad-mē-ˈan-drəm\. Ancient city on the Menderes near its mouth, SE of Ephesus and just NE of modern Turkish town of Söke, W Asia Minor. Destroyed by Cimmerians c. 650 B.C. but rebuilt by Ionian colonists; site of temple to Artemis.

4 *or* **Magnesia ad Sipylum.** City, Turkey. See MANISA 2.

Magnetic Pole. Either of two spots on the earth's surface toward which the compass needle points from any direction throughout adjacent regions (except in their immediate vicinity where the horizontal intensity is so small that the compass cannot be used to determine direction) and at which the needle dips vertically. The **North Magnetic Pole** was formerly located on W shore of Boothia Penin., Canada, at approximately 71°N lat., 96°W long. (British Admiralty charts 70°40′N, 96°50′W), this location differing by nearly a degree from that found by Sir James C. Ross in 1831; according to calculations made in 1970 it was located at 76°20′N, 101°W; according to scientists cannot be exactly fixed because of variations due to several causes. The location of the **South Magnetic Pole** was calculated (1970) to be at 66°S, 139°06′E.

Mag·ni·to·gorsk \mag-ˈnēt-ə-ˌgȯrsk\. City, SW Chelyabinsk Oblast, Russian S.F.S.R., U.S.S.R., on the left bank of the Ural river 160 m. SSW of Chelyabinsk; pop. (1970p) 364,-000; site of one of the world's largest integrated metallurgical plants; produces mining and transportation equipment, cement, and glass. For centuries a village on steppe E of the Urals, inhabited by Bashkirs and Kirghiz engaged in cattle raising; named **Mag·nit·na·ya** \mag-ˈnēt-nə-yə\ in early 18th cent. after discovery that two small mountains (Aider-Ly and Atach) nearby consisted of magnetized iron; began to be developed 1930 by the Soviet government; by 1933 a large city, with plants built largely by American engineers and workers; during World War II and since, a major producer of military equipment, esp. armored vehicles and artillery.

Mag·no·lia \mag-'nōl-yə\. 1 City, ⊗ of Columbia co., SW Arkansas, 35 m. W of El Dorado; pop. (1970c) 11,303; clothing, lumber; oil wells and refinery; corn, hogs; Southern State Coll. (1909).

2 City, ⊗ of Pike co., S Mississippi, 7 m. S of McComb; pop. (1970c) 2973.

3 Borough, Camden co., SW New Jersey, 8 m. SSE of Camden; pop. (1970c) 5893.

Ma·gof·fin \mə-'gäf-ən\. County in Kentucky. See table at KENTUCKY.

Ma·gog \'mā-ˌgäg\. Industrial city, Stanstead co., S Quebec, Canada, on N end of Lake Memphremagog 17 m. SW of Sherbrooke; pop. (1971p) 13,280; textiles, dairy products; resort; dairy and truck farms; founded 1776 by Loyalist emigrants from U.S.

Ma·gra \'mäg-rə\. River, NW Italy; ab. 40 m. long; rises near the Cisa Pass and marks approximately the line bet. the Ligurian and Tuscan Apennines; flows S into Ligurian Sea near La Spezia.

Ma·gua·ri·nho, Cape \-ˌməg-wə-'rēn-(ˌ)yü, -(ˌ)yō\ *or formerly* **Cape Ma·gua·rí** \-'rē\. Cape on NE extremity of Marajó I. at the mouth of the Amazon river, NE Brazil.

Maguntiacum. See MAINZ.

Ma·gwe \mə-'gwā\. 1 Division of W cen. Burma. See table at BURMA.

2 District of Magwe division; 3724 sq. m.; pop. (1962e) 711,449; ✱ Magwe; includes Yenangyaung oil field.

3 Town, ✱ of district, on left bank of Irrawaddy 145 m. SW of Mandalay; pop. (1953c) 13,270.

Magyarország. See HUNGARY.

Magyaróvár. See MOSONMAGYARÓVÁR.

Mah·ā·bād \ˌmä-hə-'bäd\ *or formerly* **Sa·uj·bu·lagh** \sä-ˌüj-bü-'läg\. Town, West Azerbaijan prov., NW Iran; 20 m. S of Lake Urmia; pop. (1971e) 30,000.

Ma·ha·ba·lesh·war \mə-ˌhäb-ə-'lesh-wər\. Village and hill station, cen. Maharashtra, W India, ab. 90 m. SE of Bombay; pop. (1961c) 6000; on summit of a ridge of Western Ghats, alt. 4500 ft.; rainfall excessive, often 300 to 400 in. per year; site of sanatorium established 1828 by Sir John Malcolm; near source of the Krishna river, sacred to the Hindus.

Maha Chai. See SAMUT SAKHON.

Ma·ha·jam·ba Bay \ˌmä-hə-ˌjäm-bə-\. Inlet of Mozambique Channel, on NW coast of the Malagasy Republic.

Ma·ha·kam \mə-'häk-əm\ *or* **Ku·tai** *or* **Koe·tai** \kü-'tī\. River, East Kalimantan prov., E Borneo, Indonesia; ab. 400 m. long; rises in mountains of cen. Borneo and flows ESE to Makasar Strait in wide delta ab. 1°S of the equator; navigable for most of its course; ab. 100 m. from its mouth joined in a region of marsh and lakes by the Belajan and Telen. Samarinda is the port near its mouth.

Ma·hal·la al–Ku·bra \mə-ˌhal-ə-al-'kü-brə\. City, Gharbīya gov., Egypt, in Nile delta W of Damietta branch 16 m. NE of Tanta; pop. (1970e) 225,800; center of Egyptian textile industry; cotton gins, rice and flour mills.

Ma·ha·na·di *also* **Ma·ha·nud·dy** \mə-'hän-əd-ē\. River, SE India; ab. 560 m. long; rises in mountains of S Madhya Pradesh, flows N, turns E, and flows S and E through Orissa to the Bay of Bengal through several mouths E of Cuttack; its chief tributary is the Seonath. Has great volume in flood season; its waters source of irrigation system.

Ma·ha·noy City \ˌmä-(h)ə-ˌnȯi-\. Borough, Schuylkill co., E cen. Pennsylvania, 12 m. NE of Pottsville; pop. (1970c) 7257; clothing, cigars; coal mines.

Mahanoy Mountain. Ridge in Schuylkill and Northumberland cos., E cen. Pennsylvania; highest point 1745 ft.; forms N boundary of Mahanoy coal basin and contains rich deposits of anthracite.

Mahanuddy. See MAHANADI.

Ma·ha·rash·tra \ˌmä-hə-'räsh-trə\. 1 Region of W cen. India marking the original land of the Marathas; it lay S of the Narmada and extended from E of Nagpur westward to the coast bet. Daman and Goa; its chief cities were Poona and Satara.

2 State, W cen. India; 118,637 sq. m.; pop. (1971p) 50,295,-081; ✱ Bombay; comprises the Marathi-speaking SE portion of former Bombay state; bounded on W by the Arabian Sea; rice, wheat, cotton, manganese; textiles, electrical engineering; largest cities: Bombay, Nagpur, Poona, Sholapur. Formed 1960. See GUJARAT 3.

Ma·ha·rès \ˌmä-hə-'res\. Coastal town, E Tunisia, N Africa, on Gulf of Gabès SW of Sfax; pop. (1966c) 6700.

Ma·ha Sa·ra·kham *or* **Ma·ha·sa·ra·gam** \mə-ˌhäs-ə-'räk-ˌäm\ *also* **Ta·lat** \tä-'lät\. 1 Province, E cen. Thailand; 2224 sq. m.; pop. (1960c) 499,373; ✱ Maha Sarakham.

2 Town, its ✱, 16 m. NW of Roi Et; pop. (1960c) 15,673.

Ma·has·ka \mə-'has-kə\. County in Iowa. See table at IOWA.

Ma·ha·we·li \ˌma-hä-'wā-lē\ *or* **Ma·ha·ve·li–gan·ga** \ˌma-hä-ˌvā-lē-'gəŋ-(ˌ)gä\. Chief river (*ganga*) of Ceylon; 206 m. long; flows N from Central Province to Bay of Bengal S of Trincomalee.

Mah·bub·na·gar \mə-'büb-nə-gər\. Town, S Andhra Pradesh, S cen. India, 55 m. SSW of Hyderabad; pop. (1961c) 35,588; cotton gins and presses.

Mah·dia *or* **Meh·dia** \mə-'dē-ə\. Seaport town, E Tunisia, N Africa, SE of Sousse; pop. (1966c) 15,900; fishing, olive growing; handicrafts; founded 912.

Ma·hé \mä-'hā\. 1 Chief island, Seychelles, Indian Ocean; 59 sq. m.; pop. (1969e) 41,294; chief town Victoria; mountainous, highest point 2993 ft.

2 *or formerly* **May·ya·li** \mī-'yäl-ē\. Town, SW India, on Malabar Coast ab. 40 m. N of Calicut; 23 sq. m.; pop. (1960e) 18,298; grows rice; formerly only French settlement on W coast of India. Occupied by French 1726; changed hands several times in French-English wars, restored to France 1817, administration reorganized 1947; transferred to India 1954 and made part of territory of Pondicherry.

Ma·he·bourg \ˌmä-hə-'bü(ə)r\. Town on the SE coast of the island of Mauritius; pop. (1962c) 13,005.

Ma·hen·ge \mə-'heŋ-(ˌ)gä\. Town, Morogoro region, E cen. Tanzania, on a tributary of the Rufiji 220 m. SW of Dar es Salaam; pop. (1967c) 2000.

Ma·hi \'mä-hē\. River, W India; 350 m. long; rises in NW Madhya Pradesh, flows NW and SW through S Rajputana and Gujarat into a wide estuary at the head of the Gulf of Cambay, E of the mouth of the Sabarmati river.

Ma·hia Peninsula \'mä-hē-ə-\. Peninsula projecting S from E cen. coast of North I., New Zealand, forming E side of Hawke Bay, 39°10'S, 177°54'E.

Mah·no·men \mȯ-'nō-mən\. 1 County in NW Minnesota. See table at MINNESOTA.

2 Village, its ⊗, 47 m. NE of Moorhead; pop. (1970c) 1313.

Ma·hón \mə-'(h)ōn\ *or Eng.* **Port Ma·hon** \-mə-'hōn\ *or anc.* **Por·tus Ma·go·nis** \ˌpōrt-ə-smə-'gō-nəs, ˌpȯrt-\. Seaport, ✱ of Minorca I., Baleares prov., Spain, 89 m. ENE of Palma; pop. (1970p) 19,279; good natural harbor, formerly of strategic importance; exports wine, brandy, cheese, and agricultural produce; manufactures shoes and jewelry. Believed to have been founded by Carthaginian general Mago; held by Moors 8th–13th cents.; sacked by Barbarossa II 1535; occupied by English 1708–56 and 1763–82; by French 1756–62; captured by Spain 1782 and 1798; restored to Spain by Treaty of Amiens 1802.

Ma·hone Bay \mə-ˌhōn-\. Inlet of Atlantic Ocean in Lunenburg co., S Nova Scotia, Canada; the city of Lunenburg is located at its S entrance.

Ma·ho·ning \mə-'hō-niŋ\. 1 River, NE Ohio and Pennsylvania; ab. 95 m. long; rises in Columbiana co., E Ohio, flows NE then SE through Youngstown into Pennsylvania and joins Shenango river 4 m. SW of New Castle to form Beaver river.

2 County in Ohio. See table at OHIO.

Ma·ho·pac \'mā-ə-ˌpak\. Village, Putnam co., SE New York, on **Lake Mahopac,** ab. 12 m. NE of Peekskill; pop. (1970c) 5265; center of a resort region.

Mah·ra \ˈmär-ə\. Former sultanate in E Hadhramaut on S coast of Arabian Penin., now part of Yemen (✱ Aden); mainly desert; chief town port of Qishn, 200 m. ENE of Mukalla.

Mahratta States, Southern. See SOUTHERN MARATHA STATES.

Mähren. See MORAVIA.

Mährisch–Ostrau. See OSTRAVA.

Mährisch–Schönberg. See ŠUMPERK.

Mährisch–Weisskirchen. See HRANICE.

Mah·to·me·di \ˌmät-ə-ˈmē-(ˌ)dī\. Village, Washington co., E Minnesota; pop. (1970c) 2640.

Ma·hu·ko·na \ˌmä-hu̇-ˈkō-nə\. Village, Hawaii co., Hawaii, on NW coast of Hawaii I. S of Upolu Point; its harbor port of call for interisland steamers.

Maiao. See TUBUAI MANU.

Mai·dan \mī-ˈdan, mā-\. **1** Town, ✱ of Wardak prov., E cen. Afghanistan; pop. (1969e) 54,299.

2 *or* **May·dān.** Town, NE Iraq, on upper Diyala near Iranian border, NNE of Baghdad.

Maid·en \ˈmād-ᵊn\. Manufacturing town, Catawba co., W cen. North Carolina, 22 m. N of Gastonia; pop. (1970c) 2146; furniture, textiles; agriculture.

Maid·en·head \ˈmād-ᵊn-ˌhed\. Municipal borough, Berkshire, S England, on the Thames 27 m. W of London; pop. (1971p) 45,306; residential region and summer resort; chartered 1582.

Maid·ens \ˈmād-ᵊnz\. Group of rocks in the Irish Sea off E coast of co. Antrim, NE Northern Ireland; lighthouse.

Maid·stone \ˈmād-stən, -ˌstōn\. Municipal borough, ⊗ of Kent, SE England, on the Medway 30 m. ESE of London; pop. (1971p) 70,918; papermaking, brewing and malting; received first charter 1549.

Maidstone Lake \ˌmād-ˌstōn-\. Lake in E Essex co., NE corner of Vermont.

Mai·du·gu·ri \mī-ˈdü-gə-rē\. Town, ✱ of North-Eastern State, Nigeria; in Lake Chad region ab. 315 m. E of Kano; pop. (1969; incl. Yerwa) 162,316.

Mai·har \ˈmī-hər\. **1** Former Indian state, now part of Madhya Pradesh, E cen. India, 412 sq. m.

2 Town, its ✱, NE Madhya Pradesh, ab. 95 m. NNE of Jabalpur; pop. (1961c) 12,100.

Mai·ka·la Range \ˌmī-kə-lə-\. Mountain range in cen. India, extending NE to SW chiefly in NE Madhya Pradesh; highest point 3185 ft.

Mai·kop \mī-ˈkȯp\. City, Adygei Autonomous Oblast, Russian S.F.S.R., U.S.S.R., 65 m. SE of Krasnodar; pop. (1970p) 111,000; has mineral springs and is center of oil fields and region rich in minerals; has grown rapidly in recent years as industrial city. Occupied by the Germans from Aug. 1942 to Feb. 1943.

Mai·li \ˈmī-lē\. City, Honolulu co., Hawaii, 20 m. WNW of Honolulu; pop. (1970c) 4397.

Maimachin. See ALTANBULAG.

Mai·mā·na \mī-ˈmän-ə\. Town, ✱ of Faryab prov., N Afghanistan; pop. (1969e) 55,489.

Maimansingh. See MYMENSINGH.

Main \ˈmīn, ˈmān\ *or anc.* **Moe·nus** \ˈmē-nəs\. **1** River, West Germany; 325 m. long; rises in the Fichtelgebirge in N Bavaria, flows W into the Rhine opp. Mainz, passing through Wurzburg, Aschaffenburg, and Frankfurt in its course; navigable for ab. 240 m.

2 River in co. Antrim, NE Northern Ireland; ab. 30 m. long; flows into Lough Neagh.

Main \ˈmān-\ **Barrier Range** *also* **Stan·ley Range** \ˈstan-lē-\. Mountain range, W New South Wales, SE Australia; highest point ab. 2000 ft.; rich in lead, silver, and zinc ores. See BROKEN HILL 1.

Mai–Ndom·de, Lake \-ˌmī-en-ˈdȯm-dē\; *formerly* **Lake Leo·pold II** \-ˈlē-ə-ˌpōld-t̲h̲ə-ˈsek-ənd\ *or Fr.* **Lac Lé·o·pold II** \lȧk-lā-ō-pȯl-dœ̄\. Lake, W Zaire; 900 to 3200 sq. m. according to the season; drains S into Fimi river and on into the Congo.

Maine \ˈmān\. A northeast state of U.S.A., bounded on N and E by Canadian province of New Brunswick, on S by Atlantic Ocean, on W by New Hampshire and Canadian province of Quebec; 39th state in area, 33,215 sq. m. (land area 30,933 sq. m.); 38th state in population, (1970c) 993,663; ✱ Augusta; 23d state admitted to Union (1820).

Nicknames: Pine Tree State; Lumber State. *State flower:* White pine cone and tassel. *Motto:* Dirigo (I Direct). *Rivers:* St. Croix, forming lower section of E boundary; Penobscot, flowing from cen. area S to Atlantic Ocean; Kennebec, flowing from W cen. region S to Atlantic Ocean; Salmon Falls forming section of extreme SW boundary. *Lakes:* Has ab. 1600; the largest Moosehead, Sebago, Chesuncook, Chamberlain, Grand, and the Rangeley lakes. *Highest point:* Mt. Katahdin, 5268 ft., in Piscataquis co. *Chief products:* Potatoes, corn, barley; poultry; gravel; lumbering, fishing; *manufacturing:* food processing; leather goods, paper products. *Chief cities:* Portland, Lewiston, Bangor, Auburn, South Portland, Augusta. See *Table of States* at UNITED STATES. Divided into the following 16 counties (for pronunciation of their names, see their individual entries):

NAME	LOCATION	AREA[1] (sq. m.)	POP. (1970c)	CO. SEAT
Androscoggin	SW	474	91,279	Auburn
Aroostook	N[2]	6,821	94,078	Houlton
Cumberland	SW; coastal	879	192,528	Portland
Franklin	W	1,709	22,444	Farmington
Hancock[3]	SE; coastal	1,537	34,590	Ellsworth
Kennebec	SW	872	95,247	Augusta
Knox	S; coastal	369	29,013	Rockland
Lincoln	S; coastal	454	20,537	Wiscasset
Oxford	W	2,082	43,457	South Paris
Penobscot	E cen.	3,390	125,393	Bangor
Piscataquis[4]	N cen.	3,903	16,285	Dover-Foxcroft
Sagadahoc	S; coastal	257	23,452	Bath
Somerset[4]	W	3,894	40,597	Skowhegan
Waldo	S; coastal	737	23,328	Belfast
Washington	SE corner; coastal	2,554	29,859	Machias
York	SW; coastal	1,001	111,576	Alfred

[1]Area = land area.
[2]Northernmost point of E U.S.A.
[3]Includes Mount Desert Island, containing Acadia National Park.
[4]Includes part of Moosehead Lake.

History: Coast visited by Gosnold 1602 and other Englishmen just before it was included in grant to Plymouth Company 1606; first settlement by English at mouth of the Sagadahoc (Kennebec) 1607 failed, but Saco and Monhegan I. were settled c. 1622; through series of grants, beginning in 1622 and 1628, claimed by Massachusetts colony and Gorges; annexed to Massachusetts (1652) which bought out Gorges's claim 1678; N parts frequently attacked by French who ceased active claims after 1713; a district of Massachusetts until 1820; admitted to Union as free state Mar. 15, 1820; boundary with Canada settled by treaty with Great Britain 1842.

Maine \ˈmān, ˈmen\. **1** River, NW cen. France; 8 m. long; formed by confluence of Sarthe and Mayenne rivers near Angers, flows S into Loire river.

2 *or* **Le Maine** \lə-\. Historical region of NW France; bounded anciently on N by Normandy, E by Orléanais, S by Touraine and Anjou, W by Brittany; ✱ Le Mans.

History: Inhabited by Aulerci Cenomani; became countship in 10th cent. A.D.; united with countship of Anjou through marriage of heiress with count of Anjou 1126; became English when Henry Plantagenet became king of England 1154; taken by Philip Augustus 1204; passed to house of Anjou; reverted to French crown 1481; made duchy under Louis XIV.

Maine–et–Loire \-ˌā-lə-ˈwär, -ˌāl-ˈwär\. Department of W France. See table at FRANCE.

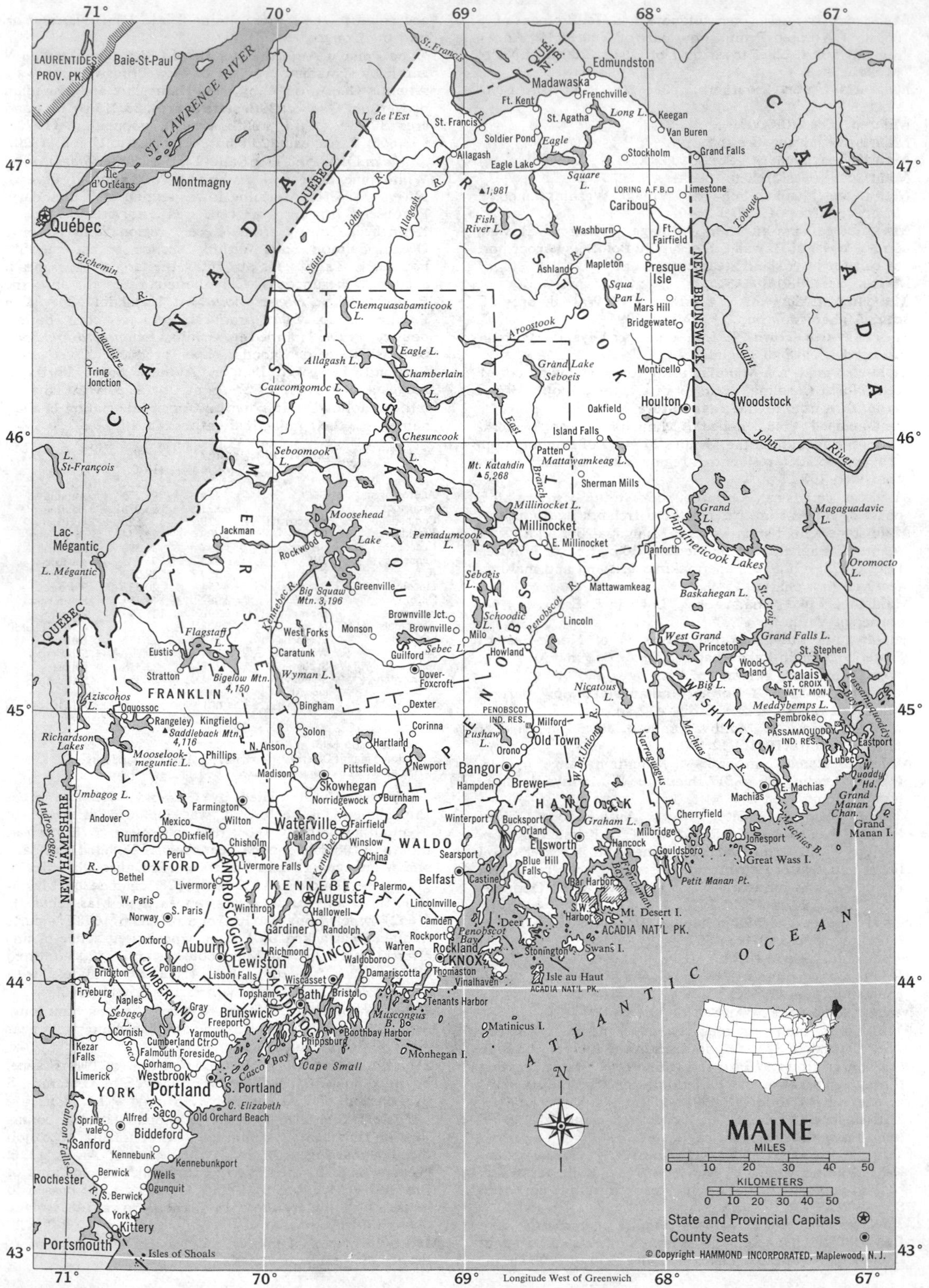
MAINE
71° 70° 69° 68° 67°
47° 46° 45° 44° 43°
LAURENTIDES PROV. PK.
Baie-St-Paul
ST. LAWRENCE RIVER
Île d'Orléans
Montmagny
Québec
Etchemin R.
Chaudière R.
Tring Jonction
L. St-François
Lac-Mégantic
L. Mégantic
QUÉBEC
CANADA
QUE. N.B.
Edmundston
Madawaska
Frenchville
Ft. Kent
St. Agatha
Long L.
Keegan
Van Buren
St. Francis
St. Francis R.
L. de l'Est
Soldier Pond
Eagle L.
Allagash
Eagle Lake
Stockholm
Grand Falls
Square L.
Limestone
LORING A.F.B.
Caribou
▲1,981
Fish River L.
Washburn
Ft. Fairfield
Ashland
Mapleton
Presque Isle
Squa Pan L.
Mars Hill
Bridgewater
Tobique R.
NEW BRUNSWICK
Saint John R.
Allagash R.
Chemquasabamticook L.
Eagle L.
Allagash L.
Chamberlain L.
Caucomgomoc L.
Aroostook
AROOSTOOK
Grand Lake Seboeis
Monticello
Houlton
Woodstock
Oakfield
Island Falls
Patten
Mattawamkeag L.
Chesuncook L.
Seboomook L.
Mt. Katahdin ▲5,268
East Branch
Sherman Mills
Millinocket L.
Millinocket
E. Millinocket
Pemadumcook L.
Moosehead Lake
Jackman
Rockwood
Big Squaw Mtn. 3,196
Greenville
Kennebec R.
Danforth
Chiputneticook Lakes
Grand L.
Magaguadavic L.
Oromocto L.
Seboeis L.
Mattawamkeag
Baskahegan L.
Penobscot
Schoodic L.
Lincoln
Brownville Jct.
Brownville
Milo
Monson
West Forks
Caratunk
Guilford
Sebec L.
Howland
West Grand L.
Princeton
Grand Falls L.
St. Croix
St. Stephen
Woodland
Calais
ST. CROIX I. NAT'L MON.
PISCATAQUIS
SOMERSET
PENOBSCOT
Eustis
Flagstaff L.
Stratton
Bigelow Mtn. 4,150
Wyman L.
Dover-Foxcroft
FRANKLIN
Bingham
Dexter
PENOBSCOT IND. RES.
Nicatous L.
Big L.
Meddybemps L.
Aziscohos L.
Oquossoc
Rangeley
Kingfield
Saddleback Mtn. 4,116
Solon
Corinna
Milford
Pushaw L.
Old Town
WASHINGTON
Pembroke
PASSAMAQUODDY IND. RES.
Eastport
Passamaquoddy B.
Richardson Lakes
Mooselookmeguntic L.
Phillips
N. Anson
Hartland
Orono
W. Br. Union R.
Narraguagus R.
Machias R.
Lubec
W. Quoddy Hd.
Madison
Pittsfield
Newport
Bangor
Hampden
Brewer
Skowhegan
Umbagog L.
Norridgewock
Burnham
HANCOCK
E. Machias
Machias
Grand Manan Chan.
Grand Manan I.
Androscoggin R.
Farmington
Andover
Mexico
Wilton
Waterville
Fairfield
Winterport
Bucksport
Orland
Graham L.
Cherryfield
Rumford
Dixfield
Chisholm
Oakland
Winslow
WALDO
Ellsworth
Hancock
Milbridge
Jonesport
Machias B.
Peru
OXFORD
Livermore Falls
China
Searsport
Blue Hill Falls
Frenchman Bay
Gouldsboro
Great Wass I.
NEW HAMPSHIRE
R.
Bethel
Livermore
ANDROSCOGGIN
KENNEBEC
Belfast
Castine
Bar Harbor
Petit Manan Pt.
W. Paris
Augusta
Palermo
Lincolnville
Norway
S. Paris
Winthrop
Hallowell
Camden
S.W. Harbor
Mt. Desert I.
Gardiner
Randolph
Rockport
Penobscot Bay
Deer I.
ACADIA NAT'L PK.
Oxford
Auburn
Richmond
LINCOLN
Warren
Rockland
Stonington
Swans I.
Lewiston
Waldoboro
Thomaston
KNOX
Isle au Haut
ACADIA NAT'L PK.
Bridgton
Poland
CUMBERLAND
Lisbon Falls
SAGADAHOC
Wiscasset
Damariscotta
Vinalhaven
Fryeburg
Naples
Gray
Topsham
Bath
Bristol
Tenants Harbor
Sebago L.
Brunswick
Freeport
Muscongus B.
Matinicus I.
Cornish
Yarmouth
Boothbay Harbor
Phippsburg
Kezar Falls
Cumberland Ctr.
Falmouth Foreside
Gorham
Saco R.
Casco Bay
Cape Small
Monhegan I.
Limerick
Westbrook
YORK
Portland
S. Portland
C. Elizabeth
Saco
Old Orchard Beach
Alfred
Springvale
Biddeford
Sanford
Salmon Falls R.
Kennebunk
Kennebunkport
Berwick
Wells
Rochester
Ogunquit
S. Berwick
York
Kittery
Portsmouth
Isles of Shoals
ATLANTIC OCEAN
N
MILES
0 10 20 30 40 50
KILOMETERS
0 10 20 30 40 50
State and Provincial Capitals
County Seats
© Copyright HAMMOND INCORPORATED, Maplewood, N.J.
Longitude West of Greenwich

Maing·kwan \'miŋ-'kwän\. Town, N Burma, on upper Chindwin river, in Hukawng valley; amber mines; taken by Chinese from Japanese Mar. 4, 1944.

Ma·i·nit, Lake \-mä-'ē-nət\. Lake, NE Mindanao, Phil.; 67 sq. m.; ab. 14 m. long.

Main·land \'mān-ˌland, -lənd\. 1 Chief island of Japan. See HONSHŪ.

2 Island, Orkney Is. See POMONA 2.

3 Chief island of the Shetland Is., NE of N Scotland; ab. 225 sq. m.; pop. (1961c) 18,268; chief town Lerwick.

Main Pass \'mān-\. One of the channels at the mouth of the Mississippi river (*q.v.*).

Main·pu·ri \'mīn-pə-(ˌ)rē\. Town, W Uttar Pradesh, N India, 63 m. E of Agra; pop. (1961c) 33,610; tobacco, carved wood articles; cotton gins, glass works.

Main·ti·ra·no \ˌmīn-ti-'rän-(ˌ)ō\. Coastal town, W Malagasy Republic, in cen. part on Mozambique Channel.

Mainz \'mīn(t)s\ *or Fr.* **Ma·yence** \mȧ-yäⁿs\. Manufacturing and commercial city, ✱ of Rhineland-Palatinate, West Germany, on Rhine at mouth of Main river 20 m. WSW of Frankfurt am Main; pop. (1970c) 172,195; river port; center of Rhenish wine industry; chemicals, glassware, cement, machinery, brandy, paper, optical instruments, cosmetics; univ. (1476, closed 1816, reopened 1946); 11th cent. Romanesque cathedral; 17th cent. electoral palace; old citadel on site of Roman camp (see below); residence of Gutenberg; famous pedagogical institute.

History: Settled near Roman fort **Mo·gon·ti·a·cum** \ˌmō-gän-'tī-ə-kəm\, *also* **Ma·gun·ti·a·cum** \ˌmā-gən-\, founded by Drusus 1st cent. B.C.; destroyed several times during barbarian invasions; made seat of archbishop c. 780 A.D.; attained self-government and became in 13th cent. head of Rhenish League; archbishop made an imperial elector 1356; city lost privileges after civil war 1462; occupied by French and Swedes during Thirty Years' War; held by French 1792–93 and 1798–1814; Hesse, Nassau, and Prussia received some of former territory 1814; headquarters of French army of occupation 1918–30; in World War II was largely destroyed but has been extensively rebuilt.

Ma·io *or* **Ma·yo** \'mī-(ˌ)ü\. One of the Cape Verde Is.; 104 sq. m.; pop. (1960c) 2718; occupied by British until end of 18th cent.

Mai·po \'mī-(ˌ)pō\ *or* **Mai·pú** \mī-'pü\. 1 River in Santiago prov., cen. Chile; flows W into Pacific Ocean. On its banks a few miles S of Santiago, in a battle Apr. 5, 1818, San Martín gained a victory over the Spanish forces that had been sent to regain Chile after its independence had been proclaimed (Feb. 12, 1818).

2 Volcano on Chile-Argentina boundary SE of Santiago, Chile; 17,459 ft.

Maipo, Pa·so de *or* **Paso de Maipú** \ˌpäs-ō-ˌdā-mī-'pü\. Andean mountain pass on Argentina-Chile border, bet. W Mendoza prov., W Argentina, and E Santiago prov., cen. Chile; altitude 11,230 ft.

Mai·que·tía \ˌmī-kə-'tē-ə\. Coastal town and resort in Federal District, N Venezuela; pop. (1961c) 75,687.

Maire Strait, Le. See LE MAIRE STRAIT.

Mai·sí, Cape *or* **Cape May·sí** \-mī-'sē\. Cape at E extremity of Cuba, projecting into Windward Passage.

Mais·khal Island \ˌmī-skäl-\. Island, Bangla Desh, ab. 80 m. S of Chittagong, separated from the mainland by **Maiskhal Channel.**

Mai·son·neuve \ˌmā-zə-'nə(r)v\. Eastern suburban residential section of the city of Montreal, S Quebec, Canada.

Mai·sons–Al·fort \mā-ˌzōⁿ-al-'fȯ(ə)r\. Commune, Val-de-Marne dept., N France, SE suburb of Paris on Marne river; pop. (1968c) 53,149.

Maisons–La·fitte \mā-ˌzōⁿ-lə-'fēt\. Commune, Yvelines dept., N France, on Seine river 7 m. NW of Paris; pop. (1968c) 24,223; racecourse.

Maisur. See MYSORE.

Mait·land \'māt-lənd\. 1 City, Orange co., cen. Florida, 8 m. N of Orlando; pop. (1970c) 7157; citrus fruit.

2 City, E New South Wales, SE Australia, on Hunter river 20 m. NW of Newcastle; pop. (1966c) 28,428; market town in agricultural and dairying region; produces textiles, rayon, bricks, and clothing; coal mines in vicinity.

Mai·zu·ru \'mī-zə-ˌrü\. City and seaport, Kyōto prefecture, N coast of SW Honshū, Japan, NNW of Kyōto; pop. (1970c) 95,895; formerly an important Japanese naval base.

Ma·ja \'mī-ə\. Island, Indonesia, off SW coast of Borneo; part of West Kalimantan prov.

Ma·ja·gua Bay \mə-ˌhäg-wə-\. Bay in NE coast of Humacao municipality, E Puerto Rico.

Ma·jāz al–Bāb \mə-ˌjaz-al-'bab\ *also* **Me·djez–el–Bab** \mə-ˌjez-el-'bab\. Town and road junction, N Tunisia, N Africa, ab. 40 m. WSW of the city of Tunis; in front line of fighting in Tunisian campaign Nov. 1942–Apr. 1943.

Majdal, Al–. See MAGDALA.

Maj·ma'a *or* **Maj·ma·'ah** \'maj-mə-ˌa\. Town at N end of Jabal Tuwaiq, E Nejd, Saudi Arabia, ab. 90 m. ESE of Anaiza.

Ma·jor \'mā-jər\. County in Oklahoma. See table at OKLAHOMA.

Ma·jor·ca \mə-'jȯr-kə\ *or Span.* **Mal·lor·ca** \mə(l)-'yȯr-kə\ *or anc.* **Bal·e·ar·is Ma·jor** \ˌbal-ē-ˌar-ə-'smā-jər, -ˌer-\. Largest island of the Balearic group, Baleares prov., Spain, in W Mediterranean 145 m. E of Spanish coast; 1405 sq. m.; pop. (1970p) 460,030; ✱ Palma; irregularly shaped with deeply indented coastline, esp. in NE; extremely mountainous in NW, gently rolling and fertile in S and E; important tourist center; economy primarily agricultural, cereals, olives, apricots, oranges, figs, almonds, grapes; wine and brandy; sheep raising; marble quarries.

History: See also BALEARIC ISLANDS; kingdom of Mallorca erected by James I of Aragon (1213–76), included Minorca, Ibiza, Roussillon, and Cerdagne; united to Aragon in mid-14th cent.; with Palma as port, was most prosperous of Balearic Is. until civil disorders and rise of Italian cities brought decline in trade in 15th cent.; its peasants rose in revolt 1521–23; in Spanish Civil War 1936–39, joined Insurgents and was a base of Italian aid against Loyalists.

Ma·ju·ba Hill \mə-ˌjü-bə-\. Height in NW Natal, Rep. of South Africa, ab. 75 m. N of Ladysmith; scene of Boer victory over the British Feb. 27, 1881.

Ma·ju·li Island \ˌmäj-ə-lē-\. Island, formed by two channels of the Brahmaputra river in NE Assam, NE India; 485 sq. m.

Ma·jun·ga \mə-'jəŋ-gə\. Seaport town on Bombetoka Bay, NW coast of Malagasy Republic; pop. (1970e) 53,993; important port for transshipment; food processing; soap, sugar, cement; base for French expeditionary force 1895.

Ma·ju·ro \mə-'jü(ə)r-(ˌ)ō\. Island (atoll) in S part of Ratak chain, SE Marshall Is., W Pacific, 7°09′N, 171°12′E; has 33 islets. In World War II occupied by Allies Jan. 31, 1944.

Ma·ka·ha \mə-'kä-hə\. City, Honolulu co., Hawaii, 25 m. NW of Honolulu; pop. (1970c) 4644.

Ma·ka·hu·e·na Point \mä-ˌkä-hü-ˌā-nə-\. Cape on S coast of Kauai I., Hawaii.

Ma·ka·ki·lo City \ˌmäk-ə-'kē-(ˌ)lō-\. Town, Honolulu co., Hawaii; pop. (1970c) 3499.

Makalakari. See MAKARIKARI.

Makale. See MEKELE.

Ma·ka·lu \'mək-ə-ˌlü\ *or Chin.* **Ma–k'a–lu Feng** \-'fəŋ\ *also* **Cho·mo Lon·zo** \ˌchō-mō-'lōn-(ˌ)zō\. Peak in the Himalayas in NE Nepal; 27,824 ft.; first scaled 1955.

Makanalua Peninsula. See KALAUPAPA PENINSULA.

Ma·ka·ri·ka·ri \mə-ˌkär-i-ˈkär-ē\ *or* **Ma·ka·la·ka·ri** \-ˌkäl-ə-\ *also* **Soa Salt Pan** \ˈsō-ə-\. Large salt basin, NE Botswana, S Africa.

Ma·kar·ska \ˈmäk-ə-ˌskä\. Town, W Yugoslavia, on Dalmatian coast ab. 35 m. SE of Split. Prosperous under Romans (**Moc·rum** \ˈmäk-rəm\); destroyed by Avars 639 A.D.

Ma·kas·ar *or* **Ma·kas·sar** *or* **Ma·cas·sar** \mə-ˌkas-ər\. Seaport city, ✱ of South Sulawesi prov., SW Celebes I., Indonesia; pop. (1961c) 384,159; harbor improved by extensive construction since 1925; exports copra, gums and resins, rubber, coffee, spices, hides and skins; univ. (1956).

History: First visited by Portuguese 1512 who erected a fort; settled by Dutch 1607; its inhabitants massacred 1618; town and fort seized by the Dutch 1667, when fort was named Rotterdam; developed by the Dutch as important trading center, made free port 1848; in World War II occupied by the Japanese 1942–45; in 1946 made capital of Dutch-sponsored state of East Indonesia; to Rep. of Indonesia 1949.

Makasar Strait *or* **Makassar Strait** *or Indonesian* **Se·lat Makasar** \se-ˈlät-\. Passage bet. E Borneo and W Celebes, Indonesia, connecting Celebes Sea on the N with Java Sea on the S; average width 155 m., narrowest (at N end) ab. 65 m.; length ab. 450 m. Contains Balabalagan Is. in W cen. part and the large island of Laut at its SW corner. Forms a part of Wallace's line, separating fauna and flora of Oriental and Australian regions. Scene of naval and air battles bet. Japanese and Allied Nations Jan. 23–25, 1942.

Ma·ka·téa \ˌmäk-ə-ˈtā-ə\. One of the more important islands of the Tuamotu Archipelago, French Polynesia, 140 m. NNE of Tahiti, in the S Pacific; 8 sq. m.; 5 m. long by 3 m. wide; pop. (1967e) 55; 15°50′S, 148°15′W; large phosphate deposits (see also OCEAN ISLAND); developed by British and French since 1908.

Ma·ka·ti \ˌmä-kə-ˈtē\. Municipality, Rizal prov., Luzon, Phil., on S bank of the Pasig 1 m. E of E boundary of Manila; pop. (1969e) 158,900.

Ma·ka·tu·ring, Mount \-ˌmäk-ə-tü-ˈriŋ\. Active volcano, Mindanao, Phil., S of Lake Lanao; 5720 ft.; eruption 1872.

Ma·ka·wao \ˌmä-kə-ˈwä-ō\. Division, Maui co., Hawaii, cen. part of Maui I.; chief town Paia.

Makeevka. See MAKEYEVKA.

Ma·ke·mo \mə-ˈkā-(ˌ)mō\. Island (atoll), NW cen. Tuamotu Archipelago, 125 m. E of Fakarava, 16°35′S, 143°40′W.

Ma·ke·yev·ka *also* **Ma·ke·ev·ka** \mə-ˈkā-əf-kə\. City, cen. Donetsk Oblast, Ukrainian S.S.R., U.S.S.R., ab. 12 m. NE of Donetsk; pop. (1970p) 393,000; a major industrial center, one of the most important in the Donets Basin, esp. in steel production; also important coal-mining center; produces machinery, shoes, chemicals.

Ma·khach·ka·la \mə-ˌkäch-kə-ˈlä\ *or formerly* **Pe·trovsk** \pə-ˈtrȯfsk\. City, ✱ of Dagestan A.S.S.R., Russian S.F.S.R., U.S.S.R., on W coast of Caspian Sea; pop. (1970p) 186,000; on railroad from Astrakhan to Baku; transshipment point of oil from Grozny to the Volga; fishing, oil refining, textile and shoe manufacturing, brewing; univ. (1957); founded 1844; renamed 1921.

Makīlī, Al-. See AL-MECHILI.

Ma·kin \ˈmäk-en, ˈmäk-\ *or* **Bu·ta·ri·ta·ri** \bü-ˌtär-ē-ˈtär-ē\. Island (atoll) at N end of Gilbert Is. ab. 100 m. N of Tarawa, W Pacific Ocean; 11 m. at greatest width; lagoon and good anchorage; occupied by Japanese 1942; taken by U.S. army Nov. 20–24, 1943.

Makira. See SAN CRISTÓBAL 7.

Ma·ki·ra Bay \mə-ˌkir-ə-\. Widemouthed inlet on S coast of San Cristóbal I., at W end, SE Solomon Is., W Pacific Ocean.

Makkah. See MECCA.

Mak Khaeng, Ban. See UDON THANI.

Mak·nas·sy \mak-ˈnas-ē\. Town, cen. Tunisia, N Africa, ab. 65 m. WSW of Sfax; pop. (1966c) 2700; battles Mar.–Apr. 1943.

Mako. See P'ENG-HU 3.

Ma·kó \ˈmȯ-(ˌ)kō\. City, SE Hungary, on Mureşul river near Romanian border; pop. (1970p) 30,097; market town in agricultural and livestock-raising region; textiles. Birthplace of Joseph Pulitzer, American journalist.

Ma·kran *or* **Me·kran** \mə-ˈkrän\ *or Persian* **Mo·krān** \mō-ˈkrän\. 1 Southwest division of former Kalat state, Baluchistan; region now in Pakistan; ab. 26,000 sq. m.; mountainous and arid; chief cultivated area is in Kej river (upper tributary of Dasht) valley in cen. part, producing esp. dates; Gwadar, its seaport, belonged to Oman until 1958.

2 Coastal region, formerly a province, SE Iran, now part of Balūchestān va Sīstān prov.; as province its capital was Jāsk; adjoins Makran region of Pakistan.

Mak·tar \ˈmak-tər\ *or anc.* **Mac·ta·ris** \ˈmak-tə-ris\. Town, N Tunisia, W of Ousseltia; pop. (1966c) 5400; became Roman colony 200 A.D.; has triumphal arch of Trajan, a temple, and part of an old aqueduct.

Makua. See UBANGI.

Makumma. See MORONA.

Makun *or* **Makung.** See P'ENG-HU 3.

Ma·kur·di \mä-ˈku̇rd-ē\. Town, Benue-Plateau State, Nigeria, on Benue river and on railroad ab. 170 m. N of Calabar; pop. (1969e) 62,585.

Ma·ku·shin \mə-ˈkü-shən\. Volcano, NE Unalaska I., near Dutch Harbor, SW Alaska; 6678 ft.

Mak·war \ma-ˈkwär\. Village on Blue Nile, Blue Nile prov., Sudan. See SENNAR 2.

Ma·la, Point \-ˈmäl-ə\. Cape, on E extremity of Azuero Penin. on S cen. Panama coast, at W entrance to the Gulf of Panama.

Mal·a·bar \ˈmal-ə-ˌbär\. Former district, now part of Kerala, India; 5790 sq. m.; ✱ Calicut; abolished 1956.

Malabar Coast. Region of the SW coast of India, Mysore and Kerala states, bet. Western Ghats and Arabian Sea.

Mal·a·ba·ta, Point \-ˌmal-ə-ˌbät-ə\. Point, N Morocco, NW Africa, E of Tangier.

Ma·la·bon \ˌmä-lə-ˈbȯn\. Municipality, NW Rizal prov., Luzon, Phil., just N of Manila; pop. (1969e) 104,000.

Malaca. See MÁLAGA 3.

Ma·lac·ca \mə-ˈlak-ə\ *or* **Me·la·ka** \mə-ˈläk-ə\. 1 State of Malaysia, on W coast of S Malay Penin., SE Asia, bounded on N by Negri Sembilan, on E by Johore, on S and W by Strait of Malacca; 640 sq. m.; pop. (1970p) 403,722; ✱ Malacca; rice, rubber. British colony 1824; part of independent Federation of Malaya 1957; became a state of Malaysia 1963.

2 Seaport municipality, its ✱, on Strait of Malacca 118 m. by sea from Singapore; pop. (1970p) 86,357; coastal trade.

History: Founded in 14th cent. by Srivijaya refugees from Sumatra; in process of developing a Muslim empire when it was taken for Portuguese by Albuquerque 1511; early center of East Indian spice trade; its capture by Dutch (1641) secured Dutch predominance in Indies; held by British 1795–1802 and 1811–18; ceded to Great Britain in exchange for Bengkulu 1824; under Japanese control 1942–45.

Malacca, Strait of *or sometimes* **Straits of Malacca.** Channel bet. the S Malay Penin. and the island of Sumatra, connecting the Indian Ocean with the South China Sea; ab. 500 m. long and varies in width from 40 m. in the S to ab. 300 m. in the N.

Ma·lad City \mə-ˈlad-\. City, ⊗ of Oneida co., S Idaho; pop. (1970c) 1848.

Ma·la·de·ta \ˌmäl-ə-ˈdet-ə\. Mountain range in the Pyrenees, in NE Spain near the French border; incl. Pico de Aneto, 11,168 ft., highest in the Pyrenees.

Má·la·ga \ˈmal-ə-gə\. 1 Town, Santander dept., N cen. Colombia, ab. 45 m. SE of Bucaramanga; munic. pop. (1968e) 16,421.

2 Province of S Spain. See table at SPAIN.

3 *or anc.* **Mal·a·ca** \ˈmal-ə-kə\. Commercial, manufacturing, and seaport city, ✱ of Málaga prov., S Spain, on Mediterranean 66 m. NE of Gibraltar; pop. (1971p) 374,-

452; important Spanish Mediterranean port; exports fruit, nuts, olive oil, canned fish, wine, iron; produces building materials, foodstuffs, beer, fertilizer, textiles; 13th cent. citadel, called the Gibralfaro; cathedral begun 16th cent. on site of old Moorish mosque. Founded by Phoenicians 12th cent. B.C.; held by Romans and Visigoths; taken by Moors 711; reconquered by Ferdinand and Isabella 1487; occupied by the French 1810–12.

Ma·la·ga·ra·si \mə-ˌläg-ə-ˈräs-ē\. River, W Tanzania, E Africa; 250 m. long; flows S and W into Lake Tanganyika.

Mal·a·gasy Republic \ˌmal-ə-ˌgas-ē-\ *or* **Mal·gache Repub·lic** \ˌmal-ˈgash-\ *or Fr.* **Ré·pu·blique Malgache** \rā-pūē-blēk-mȧl-gȧsh\ *also* **Mad·a·gas·car** \ˌmad-ə-ˈgas-kər\. Republic occupying island of Madagascar, Indian Ocean, separated from SE Africa by the Mozambique Channel; 226,657 sq. m.; pop. (1970e) 7,423,864; ✱ Tananarive. *Physical features:* Excluding Australia, the fourth largest island in the world; max. length 995 m., max. width 360 m.; plateau and mountainous regions cover practically the entire island; Ankaratra group (volcanic) in the center, and Tsaratanana Massif in the N (highest point 9449 ft.). Has many short streams, most of them flowing E to W; among the more important are the Betsiboka and the Mangoky. Only large inlet is Antongil Bay on NE coast; numerous small islands along the coast, notably Sainte-Marie on the E and Nossi-Bé on NW. *Chief products:* Rice, cassava, manioc, coffee, sugar, cloves, vanilla; livestock; graphite, mica; manufacturing: cement, soap, textiles; food processing. *Chief towns:* Tananarive, Tamatave, Majunga, Fianarantsoa, Diégo-Suarez.

History: Discovered by Portuguese 1500; short-lived French stations established in 17th cent., reopened in 18th cent.; French posts held by British 1810–11; tribes of Madagascar in 19th cent. came to be ruled by Hovas, a native group, who had almost expelled Europeans before accession of a Christian ruler 1861; concluded treaty with France 1868; declared a French protectorate 1882, but resisted in war in 1883 and 1894–96; made French colony 1896 and gradually subdued; monarchy abolished by French 1897; administrative system reorganized 1924; occupied by British 1942; became a territory within the French Union 1946; establishment of the Malagasy Republic with membership in the French Community 1958; achieved independence 1960.

Ma·lai·ta \mə-ˈlāt-ə\. Long, narrow island in SE Solomon Is. in the SW Pacific Ocean, 50 m. SE of Santa Isabel I. and NE of Guadalcanal; ab. 100 m. long; area 1870 sq. m.; pop. (1970p) 50,661; chief village Auki. Part of British Solomon Is. protectorate; has many coastal villages. Interior largely unexplored; no good harbors; highest point 4275 ft.

Ma·la·ka \mə-ˈläk-ə\. Malay and Dutch forms of MALACCA.

Ma·la·kal \ˈmäl-ə-ˌkäl\. Town, ✱ of Upper Nile prov., SE Sudan, on right bank of White Nile 410 m. S of Khartoum.

Ma·la·kand \ˈmäl-ə-ˌkənd\. Division, N North-West Frontier Province, Pakistan; 12,344 sq. m.; pop. (1961c) 1,536,766; includes former princely states of Dir, Swat, and Chitral.

Ma·la·khov *also* **Ma·la·koff** \mə-ˈlak-əf\. Fortification, SE part of Sevastopol, Crimean Oblast, Ukrainian S.S.R., U.S.S.R.; captured by the French Sept 8, 1855 after a long siege; in World War II captured by the Germans July 1942.

Mal·a·koff \ˌmal-ə-ˈkȯf\. 1 City, Henderson co., NE Texas, ab. 42 m. SW of Tyler; pop. (1970c) 2045; lignite mines; diversified agriculture.

2 *also* **Malakoff–la–Tour** \-lə-ˈtu̇(ə)r\. Commune, Hauts-de-Seine dept., N France, S suburb of Paris; pop. (1968c) 36,198; manufactures chemicals, metal goods, precision instruments.

Ma·la·lag \mə-ˈläl-əg\. Municipality, Davao del Sur prov., Mindanao, Phil., ab. 40 m. SSW of Davao; pop. (1969e) 55,300.

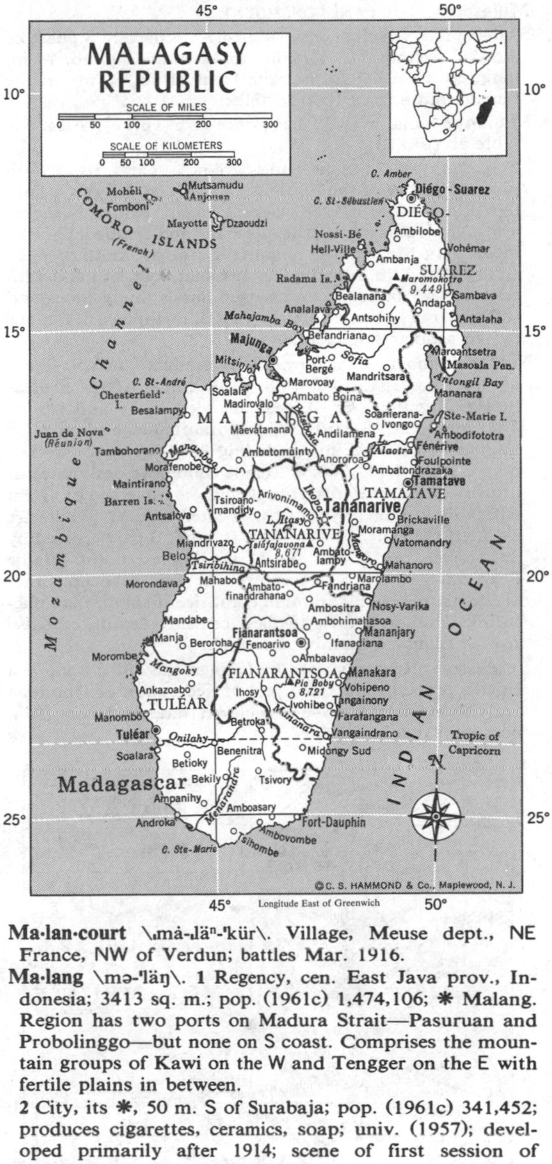

Ma·lan·court \ˌmȧ-ˌläⁿ-ˈkür\. Village, Meuse dept., NE France, NW of Verdun; battles Mar. 1916.

Ma·lang \mə-ˈläŋ\. 1 Regency, cen. East Java prov., Indonesia; 3413 sq. m.; pop. (1961c) 1,474,106; ✱ Malang. Region has two ports on Madura Strait—Pasuruan and Probolinggo—but none on S coast. Comprises the mountain groups of Kawi on the W and Tengger on the E with fertile plains in between.

2 City, its ✱, 50 m. S of Surabaja; pop. (1961c) 341,452; produces cigarettes, ceramics, soap; univ. (1957); developed primarily after 1914; scene of first session of Indonesian parliament Feb. 1947.

Ma·lan·je *or* **Ma·lan·ge** \mə-ˈlan-jə\. Inland town, N cen. Angola; munic. pop. (1960c) 35,817; railroad terminus E of Luanda.

Ma·la Pas·cua, Point \-ˌmäl-ə-ˈpäs-kwə\. Cape on SE extremity of Puerto Rico.

Mä·lar·en \ˈmā-ˌlar-ən\. Lake, SE Sweden; extends from the Baltic Sea 70 m. inland; 440 sq. m.; the city of Stockholm is situated on both sides of the strait connecting the lake with the Baltic Sea.

Ma·lar·tic \ˌmal-är-ˈtēk\. Town, Abitibi co., SW Quebec, Canada; pop. (1971p) 5357.

Ma·la·si·qui \ˌmä-lə-ˈsē-kē\. Municipality, Pangasinan prov., Luzon, Phil., on Manila-Dagupan R.R. 14 m. SE of Lingayen; pop. (1969e) 69,600; on a branch of the Agno river.

Malaskirt. See MALAZGIRT.

ə abut; ᵊ kitten, Fr. table; ər further; a back; ā bake; ä cot, cart; ȧ Fr. bac; au̇ out; ch chin; e less; ē easy; g gift
i trip; ī life; j joke; k̲ Ger. ich, Buch; ⁿ Fr. vin; ŋ sing; ō flow; ȯ flaw; œ Fr. bœuf; œ̄ Fr. feu; ȯi coin; th thin
t̲h̲ this; ü loot; u̇ foot; ue Ger. füllen; ūē Fr. rue; y yet; ʸ Fr. digne \dēnʸ\, nuit \nwʸē\; yü few; yu̇ furious; zh vision

Malaspina. See CANLAON, MOUNT.

Mal·a·spi·na Glacier \ˌmal-ə-'spē-nə-\. Glacier, S coast of Alaska, S from Mt. St. Elias to Yakutat Bay; ab. 90 m. long; covers 1500 sq. m. with front of ab. 60 m. on the Pacific; more than 1000 ft. thick.

Ma·la·tya \ˌmäl-ə-'tyä\. 1 Province of E Turkey, Asia. See table at TURKEY.

2 *or anc.* **Mel·i·te·ne** \ˌmel-ə-'tē-nē\. City, its ✱, on railroad just W of the Euphrates ab. 112 m. NE of Gaziantep; pop. (1965c) 104,428; cement, sugar, textiles; in region are many ruins of Hittite, Roman, and medieval settlements. As Melitene an important Roman military post, enlarged and improved under Justinian; bet. 6th and 12th cents. as a frontier town changed hands many times and suffered much; became Turkish 1102. Birthplace of famous Syrian scholar Bar-Hebraeus 1226.

Ma·la·wi \mə-'lä-wē\; *formerly* **Ny·asa·land** \nī-'as-ə-ˌland, nē-\ *or from 1893 to 1907* **British Central Africa Protectorate.** Republic, SE Africa, bounded on N and NE by Tanzania, on E, S, and SW by Mozambique, and on W by Zambia; 45,193 sq. m. (including 8868 sq. m. of water); pop. (1971e) 4,552,000; ✱ Zomba (Lilongwe designated as future ✱). *Physical features:* Country is traversed by Great Rift Valley; Lake Nyasa (*q.v.*) located in E; W of lake are elevated plateaus, 5000 to 8000 ft. high; S part crossed by Shire river, outlet of Lake Nyasa; highest point Mlanje Peak 9848 ft., in S. *Chief exports:* Tea, tobacco; other products: peanuts, sorghum, corn, rice; fishing; manufacturing: leather goods, textiles, cement, furniture. *Chief towns:* Blantyre, Zomba, Lilongwe.

History: Region visited by Livingstone 1859; became a British protectorate 1891; part of Federation of Rhodesia and Nyasaland 1953–63; achieved independence 1964; became a republic 1966.

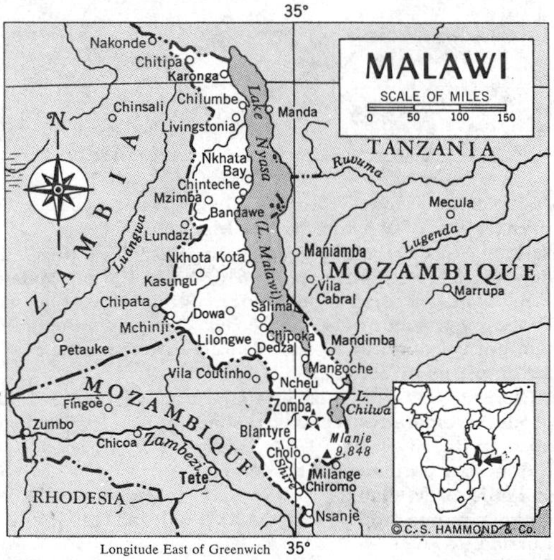

Longitude East of Greenwich 35°

Malawi, Lake. See NYASA, LAKE.

Malaya. See MALAY PENINSULA and MALAYA, FEDERATION OF.

Ma·laya, Federation of \-mə-'lā-ə, -mā-\. A former federation of the nine Malay States of the Malay Penin. (the former Federated Malay States of Negri Sembilan, Pahang, Perak, and Selangor and the former Unfederated Malay States of Johore, Kedah, Kelantan, Perlis, and Trengganu) and two of the Straits Settlements (Malacca and Penang); ab. 60,000 sq. m.; ✱ Kuala Lumpur. Comprised the larger part of British Malaya; set up Apr. 1, 1946 as **Union of Malaya;** reorganized and established Feb. 1, 1948 as the Federation of Malaya; achieved independence 1957; became part of Federation of Malaysia Sept. 16, 1963. For physical features, see MALAY PENINSULA, MALACCA, PENANG, and the names of the various states.

Ma·lay Archipelago \mə-'lā-, 'mā-(ˌ)lā-\ *or formerly* **Ma·lay·sia** \mə-'lā-zh(ē-)ə, -sh(ē-)ə\. The largest island group in the world, off SE coast of Asia bet. the Pacific and Indian Oceans. Major islands include: Borneo, Celebes, Java, Luzon, Mindanao, New Guinea, Sumatra.

History: Southern Malay Penin., Sumatra, cen. Java, and E Borneo were colonized from c. 1st cent. B.C. by Hindu Pallavas from SE India; later influenced by Buddhism; Sumatra, united under ruler of Srivijaya, by 12th cent. ruled empire including Philippines, Moluccas, Borneo, W Java, Ceylon, and S Malay Penin.; Srivijaya empire conquered by kingdom of Singosari and state of Madjapahit in Java (*q.v.*) 13th–14th cents.; in early 15th cent., Malay states came under Chinese influence, but later, Muslim traders gained ascendancy in several states (see MALACCA); after 1511, dominated by Portuguese who were succeeded by Dutch (see INDONESIA) and, on mainland, by British (see MALAYA, FEDERATION OF; MALAYSIA 1; SABAH; and SARAWAK). During World War II most of archipelago under Japanese control. Independence: Philippines 1946, Indonesia 1949, Federation of Malaya 1957.

Ma·lay·ba·lay \ˌmäl-ī-'bäl-ī\. Municipality, ✱ of Bukidnon prov., Mindanao, Phil.; pop. (1969e) 45,200.

Malay Peninsula *also* **Ma·laya** \mə-'lā-ə, mā-\; *anc.* **Cher·so·ne·sus Aurea** \ˌkər-sə-ˌnē-sə-'sōr-ē-ə\ *or Eng.* **Golden Cher·so·nese** \-'kər-sə-ˌnēz, -ˌnēs\. Peninsula, SE Asia, comprising West Malaysia and SW part of Thailand; ab. 70,000 sq. m. Has range of mountains extending its entire length, dividing it on E and W unequally; highest peak Tahan 7186 ft. on border bet. Kelantan and Pahang. Noted for wealth of its tin mines.

Ma·lay·sia \mə-'lā-zh(ē-)ə, -sh(ē-)ə\. 1 *or officially* **Federation of Malaysia.** Independent federation, SE Asia, consisting of eleven states (**West Malaysia**) on the Malay Peninsula and two states (**East Malaysia**) on the island of Borneo; 128,727 sq. m.; pop. (1970p) 10,424,325; ✱ Kuala Lumpur. *Chief products:* Rubber, rice, timber, coconuts, palm oil; tin, iron ore, bauxite. *Chief cities:* Kuala Lumpur, Penang, Ipoh, Johore Bahru, Kelang, and Malacca. Constituent states shown in table below (for further details see their individual entries).

NAME	AREA (sq. m.)	POP. (1970p)	CAPITAL
East Malaysia			
Sabah	29,545	655,622	Kota Kinabalu
Sarawak	48,342	977,013	Kuching
West Malaysia			
Johore	7,360	1,273,990	Johore Bahru
Kedah	3,660	955,374	Alor Setar
Kelantan	5,780	680,626	Kota Bharu
Malacca	640	403,722	Malacca
Negri Sembilan	2,590	479,312	Seremban
Pahang	13,920	503,131	Kuantan
Penang	400	776,770	Penang
Perak	8,030	1,562,566	Ipoh
Perlis	310	121,062	Kangar
Selangor	3,150	1,629,386	Shah Alam
Trengganu	5,000	405,751	Kuala Trengganu

History: For history prior to 1963, see entries of individual states; see also MALAYA, FEDERATION OF and STRAITS SETTLEMENTS. Federation (consisting of Federation of Malaya, Sabah, Sarawak, and Singapore) established Sept. 16, 1963; period 1963–66 marked by hostilities with Indonesia; secession of Singapore from federation 1965; suspended constitution 1969–71.

2 Island group, Asia. See MALAY ARCHIPELAGO.

Malay States. The native states of the Malay Penin., esp. those formerly under British protection; formerly included, in cen. and N part of the peninsula, a group of semi-independent states inhabited chiefly by Malays and governed by Malay rulers; these states, now part of Thailand, have been reorganized into provinces, esp. Pattani, Satun, and Yala (*qq.v.*); S states now part of Malaysia (*q.v.*).

Ma·laz·girt \ˌmäl-ˌäz-'ki(ə)rt\ *also* **Ma·las·kirt** \ˌmäl-ə-'skirt\ *or formerly* **Man·zi·kert** \'man-zə-ˌkərt\. Ancient village, E Turkey, ab. 25 m. NW of Lake Van. Scene of defeat and capture of Emperor Romanus IV Diogenes by Seljuk Turks under Alp Arslan who thus crushed power of Byzantine Empire (*q.v.*) in Asia Minor 1071.

Mal·baie \mal-ˈbā\. River, Charlevoix co., S Quebec, Canada; ab. 80 m. long; flows in wide curve, finally to the SE into the St. Lawrence river at La Malbaie.

Malbaie, La. See LA MALBAIE.

Mal·bork \ˈmäl-ˌbȯ(ə)rk\; *Ger.* **Ma·ri·en·burg** \mə-ˈrē-ən-ˌbu̇(ə)rg\ *also* **Marienburg in West·preus·sen** \-in-vest-ˈprȯis-ᵊn\. City, Gdańsk prov., N Poland, on Nogat river 25 m. SE of Gdańsk; pop. (1970p) 30,900; flax milling, sugar processing, dairy products; 13th cent. castle; received town rights 1276; seat of Grand Master of Teutonic Knights 1309–1457; to Poland 1466; to Prussia 1772; assigned to Poland by Potsdam Conference 1945.

Mal·da \ˈmäl-də\. District, West Bengal, NE India; 1436 sq. m.; pop. (1961c) 1,221,923.

Mal·de·gem \ˈmäl-də-k̲əm\. Commune, East Flanders prov., NW cen. Belgium, just E of Brugge; pop. (1969e) 14,462.

Mal·den \ˈmȯl-dən\. 1 City, Middlesex co., NE Massachusetts, 5 m. N of Boston; pop. (1970c) 56,127; residential suburb; manufactures clothing, paint, food products, aircraft parts, pharmaceuticals; founded 1640; incorporated 1649; chartered as city 1881.

2 City, Dunklin co., SE Missouri, 28 m. ESE of Poplar Bluff; pop. (1970c) 5734.

3 Island of the Line Is. in cen. Pacific Ocean S of Hawaii and 275 m. SE of Jarvis I., 4°03′S, 154°59′W; 35 sq. m.; yields guano; stone structures of unknown origin, now believed to be of comparatively recent Polynesian origin. In area claimed by Great Britain and U.S.

Mal·dives \ˈmal-ˌdīvz, ˈmȯl-\ *or formerly* **Mal·dive Islands** \ˈmal-ˌdīv-, ˈmȯl-\. Republic, group of 19 clusters of coral islands (atolls) in Indian Ocean ab. 400 m. SW of Ceylon; land area 115 sq. m.; pop. (1970c) 114,469; chief island and ✱ Male; principal industry is fishing; came under British protection in 19th cent.; became independent 1965; proclaimed itself a republic 1968.

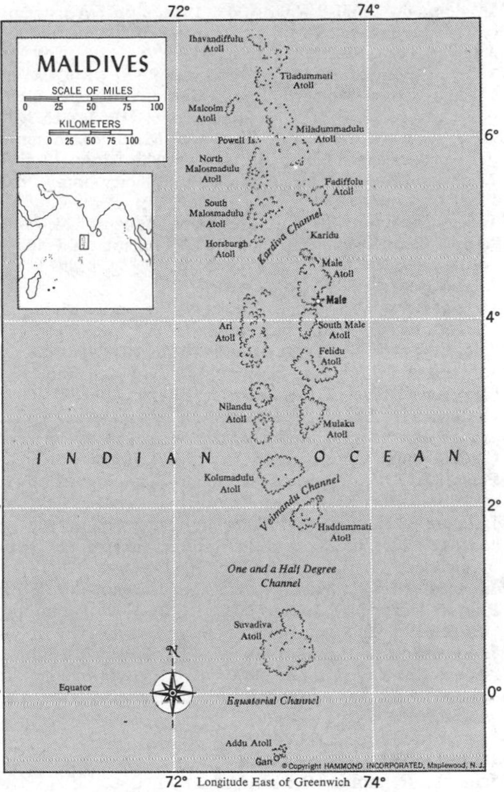

Mal·don \ˈmȯl-dən\. Municipal borough, Essex, SE England, on Blackwater estuary 38 m. ENE of London; pop. (1971p) 13,840; scene of battle 991 A.D. bet. the East Saxons and the Danes, and celebrated in an Old English poem.

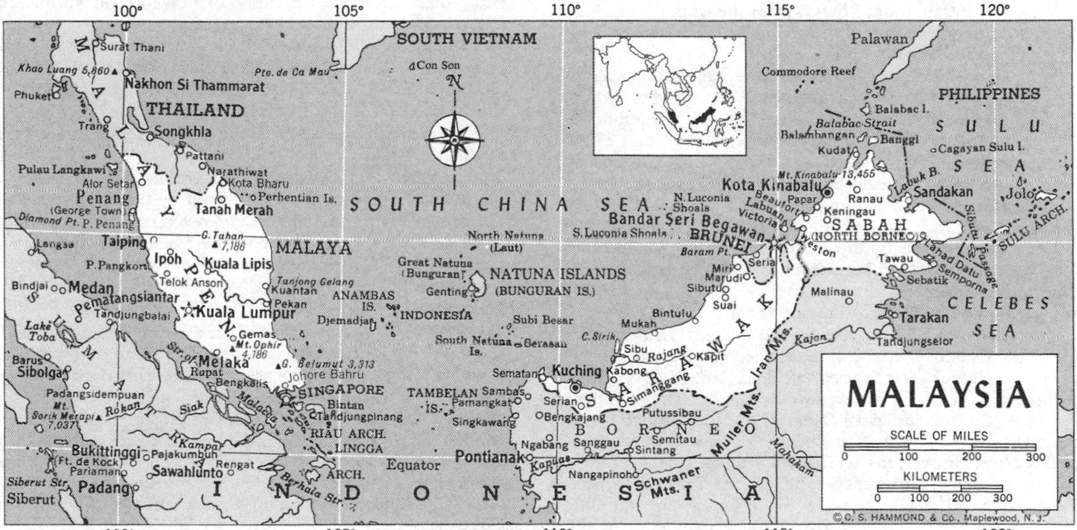

Mal·do·na·do \ˌmäl-də-ˈnäd-(ˌ)ō\. 1 Cape on SW extremity of Guerrero state, S Mexico.
2 Town, Peru. See PUERTO MALDONADO.
3 Department of SE Uruguay. See table at URUGUAY.
4 Seaport town and resort, ✱ of Maldonado dept., S Uruguay, ab. 65 m. E of Montevideo; pop. (1963c) 15,361.

Ma·le \ˈmäl-ē\. Chief atoll and ✱ of Maldives, in central part; actually two groups of islets: **North Male,** 32 m. by 23 m., and **South Male,** 20 m. by 12 m.; city pop. (1970c) 13,610.

Ma·lea, Cape \-mə-ˈlē-ə\ *or Gk.* **Ák·ra Ma·lé·as** \ˌäk-rə-mə-ˈlā-əs\. Cape at extremity of the E peninsula of Peloponnesus, S Greece.

Malebo Pool. See STANLEY POOL.

Ma·le·gaon \ˌmäl-ə-ˈgau̇n\. Town, NW India, in Maharashtra 160 m. NE of Bombay; pop. (1970e) 258,126.

Malé Karpaty. See LITTLE CARPATHIAN MOUNTAINS.

Mal·e·ku·la \ˌmal-ə-ˈkü-lə\ *or* **Mal·li·co·lo** \ˌmal-ə-ˈkō-(ˌ)lō\. An island of the New Hebrides in the SW Pacific Ocean 25 m. SE of Espíritu Santo; second in size of the group, ab. 50 m. long by 23 m. wide; 781 sq. m.; pop. (1967e) 7866. Mountainous in cen. part, highest point Mt. Penot 2922 ft.; several good harbors, esp. Port Sandwich in SE and Port Stanley in NE.

Má·le·me \ˈmäl-ə-mā\. Village and large airport on NW coast of Crete, in Canea dept., Greece; taken from British by airborne German force May 20–25, 1941.

Ma·ler Kot·la *or* **Ma·ler·kot·la** \ˌmäl-ər-ˈkōt-lə\. Town, Punjab state, NW India, 155 m. NNW of Delhi; pop. (1961c) 39,543.

Ma·le·tsun·ya·ne \ˌmäl-ət-su̇-ˈnyän-ē\. River, Lesotho, S Africa; flows S into the Sinqu river, headstream of the Orange river; has notable waterfall **Maletsunyane Falls** which drops 630 ft.

Maleventum. See BENEVENTO 2.

Mal·fa \ˈmäl-fə\. See SALINA.

Malgache Republic. See MALAGASY REPUBLIC.

Mal·heur \mal-ˈhu̇(ə)r\. 1 River, E Oregon; rises in S Grant co., flows S, then turns NE into Snake river on NE boundary of Malheur co.
2 County in Oregon. See table at OREGON.

Malheur Lake. Lake in cen. Harney co., SE Oregon.

Malhon. See HOMONHON.

Ma·li \ˈmäl-ē\ *or* **Mali Kha** \-ˈkä\. River (*kha*), Upper Burma; ab. 200 m. long; flows S from the slopes of the hills on N boundary and unites with Nmai to form the Irrawaddy river above Myitkyina.

Mali *or from 1958 to 1960* **Su·da·nese Republic** \ˌsüd-^{ə}n-ˈēz-, -ˈēs-\; *prior to 1958* **French Su·dan** \-sü-ˈdan, -ˈdän\ *or Fr.* **Sou·dan fran·çais** \sü-dä^{n}-frä^{n}-sā, -se\. Republic, W Africa, bounded on N and NE by Algeria, on E and SE by Niger, on S by Upper Volta and Ivory Coast, on SW by Guinea, on W by Senegal and Mauritania, and on NW by Mauritania; 478,652 sq. m.; pop. (1970e) 5,031,500; ✱ Bamako. *Physical features:* Generally flat; N region part of Sahara; crossed in S by Upper Niger which flows through marshy region SW of Tombouctou; *Chief products:* Sorghum, rice, millet, cotton, peanuts; livestock; fishing. *Chief towns:* Bamako, Kayes, Sikasso, Ségou.

History: By 1899 agreement with Great Britain after Fashoda (Kodok) crisis, E Sudan region recognized as open to French; territories of Senegambia and Niger formed into colony 1904, known as **Upper Senegal–Niger** until 1920; frontier with Anglo-Egyptian Sudan (now Sudan) settled 1924; had status of a colony until reorganized as French overseas territory 1946; became a republic within French Community 1958; joined Senegal in Mali Federation 1959–60; became an independent republic 1960; government, which had adopted a socialist program, overthrown by army 1968.

Maliacus Sinus. See MALIAKÓS, GULF OF.

Ma·li·a·kós, Gulf of \-ˌmä-lē-ə-ˈkȯs\ *or formerly* **Gulf of La·mia** \-lə-ˈmē-ə\ *or anc.* **Ma·li·a·cus Si·nus** \mə-ˌlī-ə-kə(s)-ˈsī-nəs\. Inlet of Aegean Sea on E coast of Greece; a W extension of the Atalante channel; on its S shore is the Pass of Thermopylae (*q.v.*).

Mali Federation. Federation of Senegal and Sudanese Republic (now Mali) 1959–60; ✱ Dakar.

Ma·ligne \mə-ˈlēn\. Lake in E cen. part of Jasper National Park, SW Alberta, Canada; 18 sq. m.; altitude ab. 5500 ft.; its outlet is **Maligne River,** tributary of the Athabaska. Largest glacier-fed lake in Canadian Rockies.

Maligne, Isle. See SAINT JOSEPH D'ALMA.

Mali Island *or formerly* **Ta·voy Island** \tə-ˈvȯi-\. Island in Andaman Sea off W coast of Lower Burma, S of Tavoy Point; northernmost island of the Mergui Archipelago.

Ma·lik, Wa·di al– \ˌwäd-ē-al-ˈmal-ik\. Riverbed, cen. Sudan; extends W from Kordofan prov. NE to Nile river.

Ma·lik–Si·ah, Kuh–i– \ˌkü-(h)ē-ˌmäl-lēk-sē-ˈyä\ *or* **Kūh–e Ma·lek Sī·āh** \-ˌmäl-ək-\. Peak at junction of Iran-Afghanistan-Pakistan boundaries; 5390 ft.

Ma·li Kvar·ner \ˌmäl-ēk-ˈvär-nər\ *or Ital.* **Quar·ne·ro·lo** \ˌkwär-nə-ˈrȯ-(ˌ)lō\. Gulf or channel, NE Adriatic Sea, bet. Cres I. and Lošinj I. on W and Pag I. and Rab I. on E.

Ma·li·nao \mə-ˈlē-nau̇\. Municipality on NE coast of Albay prov., Luzon, Phil., at entrance to Tabaco Bay 17 m. N of Legaspi; pop. (1969e) 23,100; in hemp region.

Ma·lin·che *or* **Ma·lin·tzi** \mə-ˈlin-chē\. Mountain on Puebla-Tlaxcala border, Mexico; 14,636 ft.; native name is **Ma·tlal·cue·yatl** \ˈmä-ˌtläl-ˈkwā-ˌyät-^{ə}l\.

Ma·lin·dang, Mount *or* **Gran Malindang** \-ˌmäl-ən-ˈdäŋ\. Mountain, S Misamis Occidental prov., Mindanao, Phil., 16 m. WNW of Ozamiz; 7954 ft.; highest point in province.

Ma·lin·di \mə-ˈlin-dē\. Seaport town, SE Kenya, E Africa; pop. (1962c) 5818; early capital of Portuguese East Africa; reached 1498 by Vasco da Gama who erected a monument, still standing. Nearby are ruins of ancient Gedi (possibly of Persian origin) with mosque, tombs, palace, and encircling wall (ab. 6 m.).

Malines. See MECHELEN.

Mal·in Head \ˌmal-ən-\. Cape on N coast of co. Donegal, N Eire; 55°23′N, 7°24′W, the northernmost point of Ireland.

Malintzi. See MALINCHE.

Ma·lis \ˈmā-ləs\. District of ancient Greece, S of Thessaly and Othrys Mts. and extending along N and W shores of Gulf of Maliakós. Its inhabitants were Dorians.

Ma·li·ta \mə-ˈlē-tə\. Municipality, Davao del Sur prov., Mindanao, Phil., on SW coast of Davao Gulf 46 m. S of City of Davao; pop. (1969e) 38,100.

Ma·lit·bog \mä-ˈlēt-bȯg\. Municipality, Southern Leyte prov., on W shore of Sogod Bay, Phil.; pop. (1969e) 31,300.

Mal·la·wī \mə-ˈla-wē, -ˈlä-\. Town, Minya gov., Egypt, on the Nile 43 m. NNW of Asyūt; pop. (1970e) 65,600.

Ma·lle·co \mä-ˈyā-ˌkō\. Province of S cen. Chile. See table at CHILE.

Mal·lee \ˈmal-ē\. Regions in Australia covered with the dense brushwood or thicket formed by the eucalypts (esp. *Eucalyptus dumosa* and *E. oleosa*); esp. an area (**The Mallee**) in NW Victoria along the Murray river, formerly covering 14,000,000 acres, now under farms.

Mallicolo. See MALEKULA.

Mallorca. See MAJORCA.

Mal·low \ˈmal-(ˌ)ō, -ə(-w)\. Urban district, N cen. co. Cork, SW Eire, on Blackwater river; pop. (1971p) 5894; market town; tanning, sugar processing; mineral waters; tourism.

Mal·lus *or* **Mal·los** \ˈmal-əs\. Town, ancient Cilicia, near coast of modern Gulf of İskenderun; home of Crates of Mallus, Stoic philosopher of 2d cent. B.C.

Mal·mai·son \ˌmal-mā-ˈzō^{n}\. Château ab. 7 m. W of Paris, France; residence (1809–14) of Empress Josephine and later of Maria Christina of Spain, and of the Empress Eugénie.

Malmasia. See MONEMVASÍA.

Mal·mé·dy \ˌmal-mā-ˈdē\. Commune, E Liège prov., E Belgium; pop. (1969e) 6559; in World War II scene of "Malmédy Massacre," Dec. 17, 1944, in which ab. 100 U.S. prisoners were shot by Germans. See EUPEN.

Mal·mes·bury \ˈmämz-b(ə-)rē, ˈmälmz-\. **1** Municipal borough, Wiltshire, S England; pop. (1971p) 2526; William of Malmesbury was a monk at the ancient abbey here, and Aldhelm was the first abbot (c. 673).

2 Town, SW Cape Province, S Rep. of South Africa, 35 m. NNE of Cape Town; pop. (1967e) 8000.

Malmö \ˈmal-ˌmə(r)\. Fortified seaport, ⊗ of Malmöhus co., SW Sweden, on Øresund opp. Copenhagen, Denmark; pop. (1970e) 258,311; 3d largest city in Sweden; important port; exports grain, sugar, cement, clay; shipbuilding and food processing industries; produces textiles, railway cars, clothing; 16th cent. town hall; 14th cent. church; mentioned 12th cent.; under Danish rule until 1658; conquered and made a part of Sweden by Charles X.

Malm·ö·hus \ˈmäl-mə-ˌhüs\. County of S Sweden. See table at SWEDEN.

Ma·lo·e·lap \ˌmäl-ō-ā-ˈläp\. Island (atoll), cen. part of Ratak chain, E Marshall Is., W Pacific Ocean, 8°45′N, 171°03′E; has 64 islets. One of the 5 Japanese air bases in the Marshalls; raided by U.S. Navy fleet 1942; bypassed in advance toward Japan.

Ma·lo–les–Bains \ma-ˌlō-lā-ˈbaⁿ\. Commune, Nord dept., N France, NE suburb of Dunkerque on North Sea; pop. (1968c) 15,223; seaside resort.

Ma·lo·los \mə-ˈlō-ləs\. Municipality, ✱ of Bulacan prov., Luzon, Phil.; pop. (1969e) 67,100; trade center in rice and vegetable-growing region. Chosen as capital of Philippine Republic 1898; meeting place of the revolutionary congress. Constitution of the republic framed here in the Barasoain Church Sept.–Nov. 1898 and proclaimed on Jan. 23, 1899.

Ma·lone \mə-ˈlōn\. Village, ⊗ of Franklin co., NE New York, 45 m. WNW of Plattsburg; pop. (1970c) 8048; port of entry near boundary bet. U.S. and Canada; dairy products, footwear, clothing, paper, concrete products; truck farms; selected by Irish-American Fenians as base for invasion of Canada 1866.

Ma·lo·ya·ro·sla·vets \ˌmal-ə-ˌyar-ə-ˈslav-əts\. Town, Kaluga Oblast, Russian S.F.S.R., U.S.S.R., N of Kaluga; pop. (1967e) 20,000; scene of battle Oct. 24, 1812 in which the Russians prevented Napoleon's army from retreating southward. In World War II, an outer defense of Moscow, taken by Germans Oct. 17, 1941; retaken in 1942.

Mal·pe·lo Island \mäl-ˌpā-lō-\. Island, E Pacific Ocean, W of Buenaventura, Colombia, 3°59′N, 81°35′W; belongs to Colombia.

Mal·peque Bay \ˌmȯl-pek-\ *or formerly* **Rich·mond Bay** \ˈrich-mən(d)-\. Inlet of Gulf of St. Lawrence, in NE Prince Edward Island, SE Canada.

Mal·pla·quet \ˌmal-plə-ˈkā\. Hamlet in Nord dept., N France; scene of Marlborough's victory over the French under Villar Sept. 11, 1709.

Malstrøm. See MAELSTROM.

Mal·ta \ˈmȯl-tə\. **1** *also* **Mal·tese Islands** \mȯl-ˈtēz-\ *or officially* **Sovereign State of Malta.** Independent state, consisting of three islands in the Mediterranean Sea, ab. 58 m. S of Sicily, Italy; 122 sq. m.; pop. (1970e) 330,000; ✱ Valletta; major island is Malta (*anc.* **Mel·i·ta** \me-ˈlē-tə\), 95 sq. m.; smaller islands are Comino and Gozo. *Chief products:* Potatoes, tomatoes, citrus fruit; textiles; brewing; tourism. *Chief towns:* Sliema, Birkirkara, Qormi, Valletta.

History: Phoenician and Carthaginian colony; captured by Romans 218 B.C.; part of Byzantine holdings when overrun by Saracens 870 A.D.; taken by Norman kingdom of Sicily (*q.v.*) 1090; given to Knights of St. John by Emperor Charles V 1530; held out against Turkish siege 1565; held by Napoleon 1798–1800; captured by British

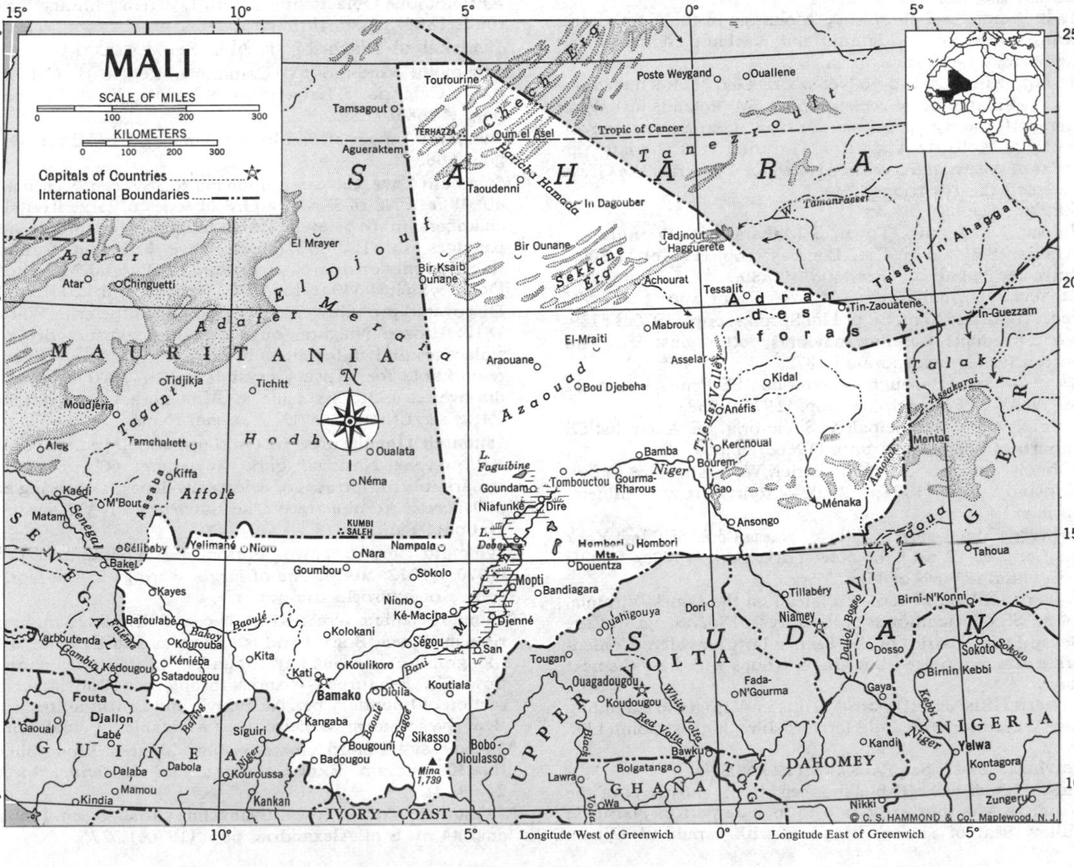

1800 and retained by them 1814; received dominion government 1921; its status reverted to that of crown colony 1933, after the church-state controversy of 1930–32. In 19th cent. developed as powerful naval base; in World War II became world's most bombed spot, undergoing more than 1200 air raids; achieved independence 1964; 1960's and early 1970's marked by economic difficulties in part attributable to Great Britain's abandonment of naval facilities on Malta.

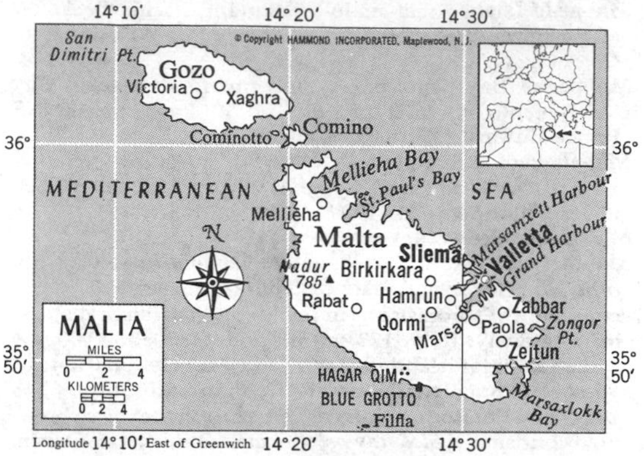

2 City, ⊗ of Phillips co., N Montana, 62 m. WNW of Glasgow; pop. (1970c) 2195.

Malta Channel. Part of Mediterranean Sea constituting the passage bet. SE Sicily and Malta; ab. 58 m. wide.

Malt·by \ˈmölt-bē\. Urban district, West Riding, Yorkshire, N England; pop. (1971p) 14,050.

Maltese Islands. See MALTA 1.

Ma·lu·bi·ting \mä-ˌlü-bi-ˈtiŋ\. Mountain in the Karakoram Range, in region of Jammu and Kashmir controlled by Pakistan; 24,470 ft.

Ma·łu·jo·wi·ce \ˌmäl-ə-yō-ˈvēt-sə\ *or Ger.* **Moll·witz** \ˈmöl-ˌvits\. Village, SE Wrocław prov., SW Poland, just W of Brzeg; formerly in Silesia, Prussia, Germany; scene of battle of Mollwitz Apr. 10, 1741 during First Silesian War (War of Austrian Succession) in which Frederick the Great defeated the Austrians.

Maluku. See MOLUCCAS.

Mal·van \ˈmäl-vən\. Town, S Maharashtra, W India, on Arabian Sea 200 m. S of Bombay; pop. (1961c) 17,800.

Malvasia, Napoli di. See MONEMVASÍA.

Mal·vern. 1 \ˈmal-vərn\. City, ⊗ of Hot Spring co., SW cen. Arkansas, 15 m. SE of Hot Springs; pop. (1970c) 8739; wood products, building materials; cotton gins; dairy and cotton farms; incorporated 1872.

2 \ˈmal-vərn\. Borough, Chester co., SE Pennsylvania, 22 m. WNW of Philadelphia; pop. (1970c) 2583.

3 \ˈmöl-vərn\. Municipality, S Victoria, SE Australia; SE suburb of Melbourne; pop. (1966c) 50,059.

4 \ˈmöl-vərn, ˈmö-\. Urban district, Worcestershire, W cen. England; pop. (1971p) 29,004; tourist resort; mineral springs.

Mal·verne \ˈmal-vərn\. Village, Nassau co., SE New York on Long I., 17 m. E of New York; pop. (1970c) 10,036; residential suburb of New York.

Malvern Hill \ˌmal-vərn-\. Plateau on the James, Virginia, 14 m. SE of Richmond; battle July 1, 1862, the last of the Seven Days' Battles of the Peninsular Campaign; Confederate attack repulsed but Union troops withdrew the next day.

Malvern Hills \ˌmȯ(l)-vərn-\. Hills in W England extending bet. Worcestershire and Herefordshire; highest point 1395 ft.

Malvinas, Islas. See FALKLAND ISLANDS.

Mal·wa \ˈmäl-wə\. Tableland, cen. India, mostly N of the Vindhya Mts. but extends S to include part of Narmada valley. Seat of ancient kingdom with capital at Ujjain; invaded by Muslims 1235; an independent kingdom 1401–1531; annexed to Mogul Empire 1561; in 18th and 19th cents. battleground of rival Maratha powers.

Maly Lyakhov. See LYAKHOV ISLANDS.

Ma·ly Ye·ni·sei \ˌmäl-ē-ˌyen-ə-ˈsā\. See YENISEI.

Mamai Kurgan. See HILL 102.

Ma·mar·o·neck \mə-ˈmar-ə-ˌnek, -nik\. Residential village, Westchester co., SE New York, on Long Island Sound 22 m. NE of New York; pop. (1970c) 18,909; yachting center; produces lighting fixtures, electronic components, water tanks; incorporated 1895. See RYE 2.

Mam·ba·jao \mam-ˈbä-hau̇\. Municipality, ❋ of Camiguin prov., on N coast of Camiguin I., Phil.; pop. (1969e) 20,-200.

Mam·be·ra·mo \ˌmam-bə-ˈräm-(ˌ)ō\ *or* **Ta·ri·kai·kea** \ˌtär-ə-ˈkī-kē-ə\. Largest river of Irian Barat, Indonesia; ab. 500 m. long; flows NW into Pacific Ocean near Cape Perkam; formed by junction of two large streams, the Tariku from the W and the Taritatu from the E. Navigable for 100 m. by large vessels; junction point of two tributaries is in extensive marshy region S of mountain range, but sources of streams are on N slopes of the Maoke Mts.

Mam·bu·rao \mäm-ˈbu̇r-au̇\. Municipality, ❋ of Mindoro, Occidental prov., Mindoro I., Phil.; pop. (1969e) 8100.

Mam·bu·sao \mäm-ˈbü-sau̇\. Municipality, cen. Capiz prov., Panay, Phil., on W tributary of Panay river, 17 m. SW of Roxas; pop. (1969e) 26,500; founded c. 1605.

Ma·metz \ˌmä-ˈmets\. Village, Somme dept., N France, 4 m. SSE of Albert; pop. (1962c) 150; battle July 1, 1916 in which British were victors.

Ma·mi·son Pass \ˌmam-ə-ˌzȯn-\. Mountain pass over cen. Caucasus Mts., U.S.S.R., just S of Uilpata and on boundary bet. North Ossetian A.S.S.R. and South Ossetian Autonomous Oblast; alt. 9279 ft. Ossetian Military Road (built 1889) passes through it.

Mamlakah al-Maghribīyah, Al-. See MOROCCO 1.

Mam·mo·la \ˈmä-mō-lə\. Commune, Reggio di Calabria prov., Calabria, S Italy, 38 m. NE of Reggio di Calabria; pop. (1968e) 8059.

Mam·moth \ˈmam-əth\. Mountain in Grant co., E cen. Oregon; 6885 ft.

Mammoth Cave. Cave in Edmonson co., SW cen. Kentucky, ab. 28 m. ENE of Bowling Green; series of large irregular chambers in five levels (total length of chambers and passages ab. 150 m.); shafts have been cut forming so-called pits or domes, as Bottomless Pit and Mammoth Dome which is 540 ft. long, 200 ft. wide, and 120 ft. high. Discovered probably c. 1799; source of saltpeter in War of 1812; Frozen Niagara (onyx cascades, gypsum flowers, stalactites and stalagmites) discovered 1923; new caverns remarkable for gypsum crystals and a 7000 ft. avenue discovered 1938; set aside as **Mammoth Cave National Park:** see UNITED STATES, *National Parks.*

Mammoth Hot Springs. Hot springs, ab. 70 in number, in Yellowstone National Park, Wyoming; 60° to 175°F.; remarkable for terraces of calcareous deposits covering ab. 200 acres. Administrative headquarters of Yellowstone National Park.

Mammoth Spring. Town, Fulton co., N Arkansas; pop. (1970c) 1072; site of one of largest springs in the world, source of hydroelectric power.

Ma·mo·ré \ˌmäm-ə-ˈrā\. River, N cen. Bolivia; 930 m. long; rises in W cen. Bolivia and is known as **Río Gran·de** \ˌrē-(ˌ)ō-ˈgrand-ē\ *or* **Gua·pay** \guä-ˈpī\ in its upper course; flows SE, then turns NW and N through cen. Bolivia; forms section of boundary bet. NE Bolivia and Brazil; unites with Beni river to form Madeira river; navigable for small craft.

Ma·mo·stang Kan·gri \ˌmäm-ō-ˌstäŋ-ˈkäŋ-grē\. Mountain in the Karakoram Range, Jammu and Kashmir, India; 24,693 ft.

Ma·mou \mə-ˈmü\. Town, Evangeline parish, S cen. Louisiana, 44 m. S of Alexandria; pop. (1970c) 3275.

Mam·ry \'mäm-rē\ *or Ger.* **Mau·er** \'mau̇(-ə)r\. Lake, NE Olsztyn prov., N Poland, NE of Olsztyn; ab. 40 sq. m.; Węgorzewo is at its N end.

Mam Soul \mam-'sau̇l\. Peak, Ross and Cromarty co., N Scotland; 3862 ft.

Man \'män\. Town, Ivory Coast, 280 m. NW of Abidjan; pop. (1963e) 34,633.

Man, Calf of \ˌkaf . . . 'man, ˌkȧf-\. Small island in the Irish Sea off SW coast of the Isle of Man.

Man, Isle of *or anc.* **Mo·na·pia** \mə-'nā-pē-ə\ *or* **Mo·na** \'mō-nə\. Island in the Irish Sea off NW coast of England; 221 sq. m.; pop. (1971p) 56,248; ✻ Douglas; a crown possession; held by Norse (9th–13th cents.), Scots (13th–14th cents.), English (from 14th cent.); its language, Manx, now virtually extinct; has own legislature and laws; tourist center.

Ma·na \mə-'nä\. 1 River, cen. and N French Guiana; 170 m. long; flows N into Atlantic Ocean near the Surinam boundary.

2 Coastal town, N French Guiana, at mouth of Mana river.

Mana, Web·be \ˌweb-ā-'män-ə\. River, S Ethiopia; ab. 140 m. long; flows SE; a tributary of the Genale.

Ma·na·bí \ˌmä-nä-'bē\. Province of W Ecuador. See table at ECUADOR.

Ma·na·cor \ˌmän-ə-'kȯ(ə)r\. Commune, Baleares prov., Spain, E Majorca I., 30 m. E of Palma; pop. (1970p) 23,278; agricultural produce; manufactures brandy, tile, pottery; 13th cent. palace; resort, noted esp. for the underground lakes and caves nearby.

Ma·na·do \mə-'nä-(ˌ)dō\ *or* **Me·na·do** \mā-\. 1 A residency of the former Neth. Indies, now part of the Indonesian province of North Sulawesi, Celebes I.; 34,191 sq. m.; comprised the E peninsula, N half of cen. part of island, the long N peninsula (Minahasa), and adjacent island groups, esp. Banggai, Penju, Sangihe, and Talaud. Encloses on three sides the Gulf of Tomini. Mountainous, many peaks above 5000 ft.; highest Nokilalaki 10,860 ft., in SW part (N cen. part of island); volcanic (Mt. Klabat) in extreme NE; no rivers of importance.

2 Commercial seaport, ✻ of North Sulawesi prov., Indonesia, at the NE end of Celebes I. (on Minahasa Penin.), on W slopes of Mt. Klabat; pop. (1961c) 129,912; good harbor; directly on sea routes from Hong Kong and Manila to Australia. Established by Dutch 1657; held by Japanese 1942–45.

Ma·na·ga·sha National Park \ˌmän-ə-'gä-shə-\. National park, cen. Ethiopia; 12 sq. m.; experimental forestry; established 1958.

Ma·na·gua \mə-'näg-wə\. 1 Department of W Nicaragua. See table at NICARAGUA.

2 City, ✻ of Nicaragua, also ✻ of Managua dept., located on S shore of Lake Managua; munic. pop. (1970e) 374,178; alt. 200 ft.; largest city and chief commercial center of Nicaragua; univ. college (1960); of minor importance during the Spanish era; made capital 1857; largely rebuilt after devastation by earthquake and fire 1931.

Managua, Lake. Lake, W Nicaragua; drains S through Tipitapa river into Lake Nicaragua; 38 m. long by 16 m. wide; area 575 sq. m.

Ma·na·hi·ki *or* **Ma·ni·hi·ki** \ˌmä-nə-'hē-kē\ *or formerly* **Hum·phrey** \'həm(p)-frē\. Chief island (atoll) of the Northern Cook Is., 650 m. N of Rarotonga; 2 sq. m.; pop. (1968e) 619; chief villages Tuko on N end, and Tauhunu on W coast; produces copra and pearl shell.

Ma·na·ka·ra \ˌmän-ə-'kär-ə\. Coastal town, SE Malagasy Republic; pop. (1966e) 15,829; railroad terminus.

Ma·na·kha \mə-'näk-ə\. Town, cen. Yemen (✻ San'a), SW Arabian Penin., SW of San'a.

Ma·na·ma \mə-'nam-ə\ *or* **Al–Ma·na·mah** \ˌal-\. Town, ✻ of Bahrain, Persian Gulf, on N coast of Bahrain I.; pop. (1971p) 89,728; connected by causeway with Muharraq on adjacent island.

Manam Island. See VULCAN, MOUNT.

Ma·nan·ja·ry \ˌmän-än-'zhär-ē\. Coastal town, E Malagasy Republic, E of Fianarantsoa; pop. (1966e) 10,970.

Ma·na·oag \mə-'nä-wäg\. Municipality, Pangasinan prov., Luzon, Phil., 17 m. E of Lingayen; pop. (1969e) 56,400.

Manáos. See MANAUS.

Ma·na·pia·ri \ˌmän-ə-pē-'är-ē\. River, S cen. Venezuela; ab. 100 m. long; flows S into Ventuari river.

Ma·na·pi·re \ˌmän-ə-'pi(ə)r-ē\. River, N Venezuela; 130 m. long; flows S into Orinoco river.

Ma·na·pla \mə-'nä-plə\. Municipality, NW Negros Occidental prov., Negros, Phil., on Guimaras Strait 24 m. NNE of City of Bacolod; pop. (1969e) 64,100.

Ma·na·pou·ri Lake \ˌmän-ə-ˌpu̇(ə)r-ē-\. Lake, SW South I., New Zealand; 48 sq. m.; a source of the Waiau river.

Manar. See MANNAR.

Ma·nas \mə-'näs\. River, E Bhutan; flows S across Indian border and into the Brahmaputra near Goalpara.

Man·a·sa·ro·war \ˌman-ə-sə-'rō-ər\ *or Chin.* **Ma–na–sa–lo–wu** \'mä-'nä-'säl-ō-'wü\. Lake in Himalayas, SW Tibet, China, S of Kailas Peak; at 15,000 ft. elevation; former place of pilgrimage for Hindus.

Man·a·squan \'man-ə-ˌskwän\. Borough, Monmouth co., E cen. New Jersey, on Atlantic Ocean 8 m. S of Asbury Park; pop. (1970c) 4971; summer resort.

Ma·nas·sas \mə-'nas-əs\. Town, ⊗ of Prince William co., NE Virginia, 25 m. W of Alexandria; pop. (1970c) 9164; agriculture; battles of Bull Run (called Manassas by Confederates) fought here July 21, 1861 and Aug. 29 and 30, 1862.

Manassas National Battlefield Park. See UNITED STATES, *National Historical Parks.*

Manassas Park. Town, Prince William co., NE Virginia, SW of Alexandria; pop. (1970c) 6814.

Ma·ná–Ta·rá, Ce·rro \'ser-(ˌ)ō-mə-ˌnä-tə-'rä\. Peak, NW Venezuela, W of Lake Maracaibo; 12,240 ft.

Man·a·tee \ˌman-ə-'tē, 'man-ə-ˌtē\. County in Florida. See table at FLORIDA.

Ma·na·tí \ˌmän-ə-'tē\. 1 Town, Atlántico dept., N Colombia; munic. pop. (1968e) 8618.

2 River, cen. and N cen. Puerto Rico; 25 m. long; flows N into Atlantic Ocean.

3 Town and municipality, N Puerto Rico; pop. (1970p) 13,433 (town), 30,724 (munic.); town is on Manatí river and on railroad 25 m. W of San Juan.

Manatí, Point. Cape on SE coast of Las Villas prov., W cen. Cuba.

Ma·naus \mə-'nau̇s\ *or* **Ma·ná·os** \mə-'nau̇s\. City, ✻ of Amazonas state, W Brazil, on left bank of Rio Negro 12 m. above its junction with the Amazon; munic. pop. (1970p) 303,155; trading port for products of the Amazon basin (cacao, rubber, Brazil nuts, lumber, fruits); thermoelectric power plant, oil refinery; 1000 m. from the mouth of the Amazon but accessible to ocean steamers; univ. (1965); museum, notable botanical gardens; founded 1660; made provincial capital 1850.

Ma·na·wa·tu \ˌmän-ə-'wä-(ˌ)tü\. River, SW North I., New Zealand; 113 m. long; flows SW and W into Cook Strait.

Mancha, La. See LA MANCHA.

Manche \'mänsh\. Department of NW France. See table at FRANCE.

Manche, La. See ENGLISH CHANNEL.

Man·ches·ter \'man-ˌches-tər, -chə-stər\. 1 Manufacturing town, E Hartford co., N Connecticut; pop. (1970c) 47,994; automobile parts, soap, tools, paper products, parachutes; dairy farms; Manchester Community Coll. (1963); settled 1672; incorporated 1823.

2 Industrial city, Meriwether and Talbot cos., W Georgia, 32 m. NE of Columbus; pop. (1970c) 4779; lumber mills; agriculture.
3 City, ⊗ of Delaware co., E Iowa, 35 m. NNE of Cedar Rapids; pop. (1970c) 4641; dairy products, veneers, brass castings; meat-packing plant; diversified agriculture.
4 City, ⊗ of Clay co., SE Kentucky, 38 m. N of Middlesborough; pop. (1970c) 1664; coal mines.
5 Town, Essex co., NE Massachusetts, on Atlantic Ocean 21 m. NE of Boston; pop. (1970c) 5151; boatbuilding; furniture; summer resort.
6 Village, St. Louis co., E Missouri, 16 m. W of St. Louis; pop. (1970c) 5301.
7 Industrial city, Hillsborough co., S New Hampshire, on Merrimack river 18 m. N of Massachusetts border; pop. (1970c) 87,754; largest city in the state; supplied with power by Amoskeag Falls; produces textiles, rubber and leather goods, automobile accessories, electrical equipment, dairy products; state industrial school; St. Anselm's Coll. (1889), New Hampshire Coll. of Accounting and Commerce (1932), Notre Dame Coll. (1950). Settled c. 1722; incorporated as **Der·ry·field** \ˈder-ē-ˌfēld\ 1751; renamed 1810; chartered as city 1846; became major center of textile industry but was forced to diversify local industry after 1935.
8 Village, Ontario co., W New York, 24 m. ESE of Rochester; pop. (1970c) 1305; in Finger Lakes resort region.
9 Village, Adams co., S Ohio, on Ohio river 32 m. W of Portsmouth; pop. (1970c) 2195; men's clothing; sawmill.
10 Village in Manchester town, a ⊗ of Bennington co., SW corner of Vermont, 21 m. N of Bennington; pop. (1970c) 435 (village), 2919 (town); summer resort (Equinox Mt. nearby); manufactures fishing rods and tackle.
11 County borough and city, Lancashire, NW England, on the Irwell 30 m. ENE of Liverpool; pop. (1971p) 541,468; a major commercial and transportation center; produces textiles, machinery, clothes, dyes, chemicals, plastics, and electronic equipment; food processing, oil refining; important seaport, made accessible to ocean steamers by the Manchester Ship Canal (*q.v.*); cathedral (originally a parish church, bishopric estab. 1847); Victoria Univ. of Manchester (1880); several technical institutes.

History: Woolen and linen manufacture introduced 14th cent., first cotton mill opened 1781; strong center of Puritanism 17th cent., in 18th cent. strongly Jacobite; at beginning of 19th cent. without representation in Parliament despite its growing size and importance as industrial city, became center of reform agitation initiated by the Peterloo Massacre Aug. 16, 1819, when a crowd, gathered on St. Peter's Fields to voice their grievances, was dispersed by cavalrymen, with several killed and many injured; became a city 1853; severely affected by cotton famine during American Civil War; frequently bombed by Germans in spring of 1941. Birthplace of David Lloyd George.

Manchester Ship Canal. Canal by which Manchester was made a port accessible to large ocean steamers; from Eastham, NW Cheshire, NW England, to Manchester; 35½ m. long; 28 ft. minimum depth; 120 ft. wide at the bottom; commenced in 1887 and formally opened in 1894; rise of 60½ ft. divided among 5 sets of locks; water supply provided from the Mersey and Irwell rivers.

Man–chou–li \ˈmän-ˈjō-ˈlē\ *or formerly* **Lu·pin** \ˈlü-ˈpin\. Town, Inner Mongolia, N China.

Manchow. See MANCHURIA.

Man·chu·kuo *or* **Man·chou·kuo** \ˈman-ˈchü-ˈkwō, man-ˈchü-(ˌ)kwō\ *also* **Man·chu·ti·kuo** \ˈmän-ˈchü-ˈtē-ˈkwō\. A former state of E Asia, 1932–45, set up under Japanese influence, comprising the 3 provinces of Manchuria (*q.v.*) and Jehol; approx. 482,440 sq. m.; ✻ Hsinking (now Ch'angch'un); traditional provinces subdivided and reorganized 1934 into 18 provinces and the special municipality of Hsinking, but their boundaries were changed several times. (For physical features, etc., see MANCHURIA and JEHOL.) Set up as independent republic Feb. 1932 after Japanese occupation of Manchuria 1931; created an empire 1934 with puppet Manchu emperor K'ang Tê as nominal ruler; Jehol occupied by Japanese and added to it 1933; its boundary with Mongolian People's Republic subject to dispute with U.S.S.R. from 1931; dissolved 1945 at end of World War II.

Man·chu·ria \man-ˈchu̇r-ē-ə\ *or Chin.* **Man·chow** \ˈmän-ˈjō\. Region, comprising the 3 provinces of Liaoning, Kirin, and Heilungkiang (see table at CHINA), NE China, bounded on NW, N, and E by the U.S.S.R. (separated from it by the Amur and its tributaries, the Argun and Ussuri), on the S by Hopeh prov. (China), North Korea, and inlets of the Yellow Sea, and on the W by Inner Mongolia. Its N two thirds is watered by the tributaries of the Amur, esp. the Sungari which covers with its tributaries all the central and N area; in the S is the Liao and on the North Korean border the Yalu. Much of its area is mountainous, of especial importance being the Greater Khingan Range in the NW and the Ch'ang-pai Shan on the North Korean border. In the S the wide Liaotung Penin. projects into the Gulf of Chihli, separating the Gulf of Liaotung on the W from Korea Bay. The most important industrial region of China: iron and steel, machine tools, chemicals, textiles; food processing, shipbuilding; coal, iron ore, manganese, molybdenum, zinc; soybeans, spring wheat, barley, oats, cotton.

History: Included at various times in Chinese Empire; under Khitans and other Mongol peoples to N and W of Manchuria; original home of Manchus, of Mongol stock, who built a strong state under Nurhachu (d. 1627); conquered China and began Chinese Manchu dynasty (1644–1912); from 17th cent., when Russia began eastward advance, its N boundary came to be established at the Amur (*q.v.*); under loose Chinese control, coveted by Russia and Japan, the rivalry bet. these two countries over Manchuria being a partial cause of Russo-Japanese War 1904–05; Chinese civil administration set up 1907; increasingly the destination of Chinese immigration; adhered to Chinese Nationalist government 1928; annexed Jehol as a province 1928; after Mukden (*q.v.*) incident 1931, occupied by Japanese troops; despite action of League of Nations in Manchurian affair, set up by Japan as puppet state of Manchukuo (*q.v.*) 1932, dissolved 1945 at end of World War II; scene of fighting bet. Chinese Nationalist and Communist troops 1946–48; came under complete control of Communists with their occupation of Mukden Nov. 1, 1948; region utilized as a staging area for Chinese troops during Korean War 1950–53; administratively reorganized (incl. loss of Jehol) 1955–56.

Manchutikuo. See MANCHUKUO.

Man·cos \ˈmaŋ-kəs\. 1 River, Montezuma co., SW Colorado; ab. 60 m. long; flows S and SE into San Juan river in NW New Mexico; Mesa Verde National Park on W bank.
2 Town, Montezuma co., SW Colorado; pop. (1970c) 709; near Mesa Verde National Park.

Mand \ˈmänd\ *or* **Mund** \ˈmünd\. River, in SW Iran; ab. 300 m. long; flows W and SW into E cen. Persian Gulf S of Büshehr.

Man·da \ˈman-də\. Town, S Tanzania, East Africa, on good harbor on NE shore of Lake Nyasa.

Man·da·la \män-ˈdä-lə\ *or formerly* **Ju·li·a·na Top** \ˌyü-lē-ˌän-ə-ˈtȯp\. Peak, E end of Maoke Mts., Irian Barat, Indonesia; 15,416 ft.

Man·da·lay \ˌman-də-ˈlā\. 1 Division of N Burma. See table at BURMA.
2 District, Mandalay division; 2113 sq. m.; pop. (1962e) 499,865; ✻ Mandalay.
3 City, ✻ of division and of district, ab. 365 m. N of Rangoon; met. area pop. (1962e) 667,000; a trade center with railroad and steamer connections; many bazaars; religious center for Burmese Buddhists; at foot of Mandalay Hill are the 730 pagodas (*Kuthodaw*); univ. (1958). Its cantonment, a moated citadel known as Fort Dufferin,

was old city built 1857–59 and containing palace, halls, and other buildings of King Thebaw; capital of kingdom of Burma 1860–85. In World War II occupied by Japanese May 1942–Mar. 1945; largely destroyed.

Man·da·lu·yong \ˌmän-də-lü-ˈyȯŋ\. Municipality, Rizal prov., Luzon I., Phil.; pop. (1969e) 99,300.

Man·dan \ˈman-dən, -ˌdan\. City, ⊗ of Morton co., SW cen. North Dakota, across Missouri river from Bismarck; pop. (1970c) 11,093; iron and brass fixtures, butter, flour, tile; diversified agriculture; incorporated 1883.

Manda National Park \ˈman-də-\. National park, Chad; 417 sq. m.; wildlife refuge (buffalo, elephant, giraffe, hippopotamus, hyena); established 1965.

Man·dar, Gulf of \-ˈmän-ˌdär\. Inlet of Makasar Strait on SW coast of Celebes I., Indonesia, N of Makasar; its NW point is **Tan·djung Ran·ga·sa** \ˈtän-ˌjuŋ-räŋ-ˈgäs-ə\ *or Du.* **Hoek van Mandar** \ˌhük-vän-\.

Man·da·vi \ˈmən-də-vē\. See GOA 1.

Man·da·we \män-ˈdä-(ˌ)wē\. Chartered city, Cebu I., Phil.; pop. (1970e) 40,700.

Man·deure \mäⁿ-ˈdər\. Commune, NE Doubs dept., E France; pop. (1962c) 5186; Roman remains.

Man·de·ville \ˈman-də-ˌvil\. Town, St. Tammany parish, SE Louisiana; pop. (1970c) 2282; boats; strawberries.

Man·di \ˈmən-dē\. 1 District, Himachal Pradesh state, N India; 1523 sq. m.; pop. (1961c) 384,529; ✱ Mandi.
2 Town, its ✱, 45 m. NNW of Simla; pop. (1961c) 13,034; trade center.

Man·din·ga \män-ˈdiŋ-gə\. Port, NE cen. Panama, on N shore of Gulf of San Blas.

Man·di·o·li \ˌmän-dē-ˈō-lē\. See BATJAN.

Mand·la \ˈmən-dlə\. Town, cen. Madhya Pradesh, India, ab. 40 m. SE of Jabalpur; pop. (1961c) 19,416; road junction.

Man·dø \ˈmän-də(r)\. Island, North Frisian Is., Denmark, S of Esbjerg; pop. (1965c) 151.

Man·dor \ˈmən-ˌdȯ(ə)r\. See JODHPUR.

Man·du·ria \män-ˈdu̇r-ē-ə\. Commune, Taranto prov., Apulia, SE Italy, ESE of Taranto; pop. (1968e) 27,832; cathedral; pre-Roman remains of walls.

Mand·vi \ˈmäŋ-dvē\. Seaport town, S coast of Kutch, Gujarat state, W India, on Gulf of Kutch 210 m. W of Ahmadabad; pop. (1961c) 26,609.

Man·fre·do·nia \ˌman-frə-ˈdō-nē-ə\. Seaport, Foggia prov., Apulia, SE Italy, on Gulf of Manfredonia 22 m. NE of Foggia; pop. (1968e) 44,998; tourism; cathedral; 13th cent. church; castle; built 1263 by King Manfred, destroyed by Turks 1620.

Manfredonia, Gulf of. Inlet of Adriatic Sea, in NE Apulia region, on SE coast of Italy.

Mang·a·ia \mäŋ-ˈ(g)ī-ə\. Island in SE part of the Cook Is., in S Pacific Ocean 110 m. ESE of Rarotonga, 21°55′S, 157°55′W; 20 sq. m.; pop. (1968e) 2139; chief village Oneroa, on W side of island. Remarkable geologically as a fine example of "makatea" formation—a circular island with broad coastal strip of coral limestone and completely encircled by a reef.

Man·gal·dan \ˌmäŋ-gəl-ˈdän\. Municipality, Pangasinan prov., Luzon, Phil., near coast on Dagupan-San Fernando R.R.; pop. (1969e) 46,000.

Man·ga·lore \ˈmäŋ-gə-ˌlōr\. City, SW Mysore state, S India, on Malabar Coast 190 m. W of Bangalore; pop. (1970e) 171,759; seaport, exporting coffee, sandalwood, nuts, coir, and fish; manufactures textiles and roofing tiles; four colleges. Site of Portuguese factory erected 1596; conquered by Haidar Ali of Mysore 1763; captured by British 1783 but the British garrison forced by Tipu Sahib to capitulate 1784; restored to British authority 1799.

Mang·a·re·va \mäŋ-ä-ˈrā-vä\. Chief island of the Gambier Is., French Polynesia, S Pacific Ocean; 5 m. long; ab. 7 sq. m.; pop. (1967e) 516; has high central ridge covered with much vegetation.

Man·ga·rin Bay \ˌmäŋ-gə-ˈrēn-\. Inlet on SW coast of Mindoro I., Phil.; San Jose is on its N shore. Occupied by Americans Dec. 15, 1944.

Man·ga·ta·rem \ˌmäŋ-gə-ˈtä-rem\. Municipality, S Pangasinan prov., Luzon, Phil., near left bank of the Agno 16 m. S of Lingayen; pop. (1969e) 39,900.

Man·ger·ton \ˈmaŋ-gərt-ᵊn\. Mountain, cen. co. Kerry, SW Eire; 2756 ft.

Mangishlak. See MANGYSHLAK.

Mang·ka·li·hat, Cape \-ˌmäŋ-kə-lē-ˈhät\. Cape on E coast of the island of Borneo, East Kalimantan prov., Indonesia; projects into Celebes Sea at N entrance to Makasar Strait.

Man·gla·res, Cape \-mäŋ-ˈglä-rās\ *or* **Cape Man·gles** \-ˈmäŋ-glās\. Cape extending into Pacific Ocean at SW extremity of Colombia.

Mango \ˈmäŋ-(ˌ)ō\. Island, Fiji, SW Pacific Ocean, SW of Vanua Mbalavu I. in the Exploring Is., ab. 3 m. in diameter.

Man·go·che \mäŋ-ˈgō-chē\ *or formerly* **Fort John·ston** \-ˈjän(t)-stən\. Town, S Malawi, SE Africa, 6 m. from S end of Lake Nyasa, ab. 65 m. N of Zomba; pop. (1966c) 1467.

Man·go·ky \man-ˈgō-kē\. River, S cen. Malagasy Republic; ab. 350 m. long; flows W into Mozambique Channel.

Mang·o·le \mäŋ-ˈō-lē\. One of the Sula Is., Indonesia, E of Taliabu I. and N of Sanana; 63 m. long by ab. 13 m. wide; borders on Molucca Sea to the N.

Mang·o·nui \ˌmäŋ-ə-ˈnü-ē\. Village, on E coast of N extension of North I., New Zealand.

Man·gots·field \ˈmaŋ-gəts-ˌfēld\. Urban district, Gloucestershire, SW cen. England; pop. (1971p) 23,269.

Man·grove Lagoon \ˈman-ˌgrōv-, ˈmaŋ-\. Inlet of Jersey Bay in SE St. Thomas I., Virgin Is. of the U.S., West Indies.

Mangshih. See LU-HSI.

Man·guei·ra, La·goa da \lə-ˈgō-ə-də-mä(ⁿ)ŋ-ˈgā-(ə-)rə\. Lake, S Rio Grande do Sul, S Brazil, along coast in strip of land bet. Lake Mirim and the Atlantic Ocean; 62 m. long.

Man·gue·ni, Plateau of \-ˌmäŋ-gə-ˈnē\. Elevated region, NE Niger, W Africa, on Libyan border; 500 m. E to W by 400 m. N to S.

Man·gui·to \maŋ-ˈgēt-(ˌ)ō\. Municipality and town, Matanzas prov., W cen. Cuba, 35 m. SE of Cárdenas; munic. pop. (1967e) 25,450.

Man·gum \ˈmaŋ-gəm\. City, ⊗ of Greer co., SW Oklahoma, 20 m. NNW of Altus; pop. (1970c) 4066; feed mills, machine shops; agriculture.

Man·gun·ça \maŋ-ˈgün(t)-sə\. Island in Atlantic Ocean off N coast of Maranhão state, Brazil, at the entrance to Cabelo da Velha Bay.

Man·gysh·lak *also* **Man·gish·lak** \ˌmäŋ-gish-ˈläk\. Peninsula on the E coast of N Caspian Sea, SW Kazakh S.S.R., U.S.S.R.; oil-producing region.

Man·has·set Bay \man-ˌhas-ət-\. Inlet of Long Island Sound on coast of Nassau co., Long I., New York.

Man·hat·tan \man-ˈhat-ᵊn, mən-\. 1 Island at N end of New York Bay, bounded on N and NE by Spuyten Duyvil Creek and Harlem river, on E by East river, on S by New York Bay, and on W by Hudson river; 13½ m. long and 2¼ m. wide; 22 sq. m.; forms New York co. of New York state, and Manhattan borough (see below) of New York City. See history of NEW YORK 1 and 3.
2 Borough, SE New York, coextensive with New York co. (area 22 sq. m.) and Manhattan I., part of New York City bet. Hudson and East rivers; pop. (1970c) 1,524,541; separated from Long I. by East river and from mainland by Harlem river and Spuyten Duyvil Creek; includes islands: Welfare (Blackwells), Randall's, and Ward's, all in East river; chartered as one of 5 boroughs comprising city

of New York Jan. 1, 1898; contains main financial and commercial and important residential sections of the city. Columbia Univ. (chartered 1754 as King's College), New York Univ. (1831), City Univ. of New York (f. as the Free Academy 1848), Manhattan Coll. (1853), Barnard Coll. (1889; affiliated with Columbia Univ.), Cooper Union (1859), Juilliard School of Music (1926), Manhattan Bible Coll. (1927); New York Public Library, Metropolitan Museum of Art, American Museum of Natural History, Museum of Modern Art, Rockefeller Center (including Radio City), Lincoln Center for the Performing Arts, United Nations headquarters. Governed as part of New York City by a mayor and city council; has a borough president, with local and county functions conducted independently of central municipal government. See also NEW YORK 3.

3 City, ⊗ of Riley co., NE cen. Kansas, on Kansas river 50 m. W of Topeka; pop. (1970c) 27,575; agricultural machinery; food processing; truck farms; Kansas State Univ. of Agriculture and Applied Science (1863); settled 1854; incorporated 1857.

Manhattan Beach. 1 City, Los Angeles co., SW California, on Pacific Ocean 13 m. SW of Los Angeles; pop. (1970c) 35,352; residential; electronic components, furniture.

2 Bathing beach and amusement resort, E end of Coney I., Brooklyn borough, New York City.

Man·heim \'man-ˌhīm\. Borough, Lancaster co., SE Pennsylvania, 10 m. NNW of Lancaster; pop. (1970c) 5434; men's clothing, asbestos products; diversified agriculture.

Ma·ni·ca \mə-'nē-kə\. Former district, W cen. Mozambique, SE Africa, now part of Manica and Sofala dist.; Portuguese part of **Ma·ni·ca·land** \-ˌland\, territory in E Rhodesia and W Mozambique; region has valuable goldfields. With Sofala, district formerly administered by Mozambique Company (see MOZAMBIQUE).

Manica and So·fa·la \-sə-'fäl-ə\. District, W and S cen. Mozambique, SE Africa; 50,137 sq. m.; pop. (1970p) 1,085,209; ✱ Beira.

Manich. See MANYCH.

Man·i·coua·gan \ˌman-ə-'kwäg-ən\. River, SE Quebec, Canada; 285 m. long; flows S into St. Lawrence river near its mouth; one branch flows through **Lake Manicouagan** (ab. 87 sq. m.); river dammed in two places.

Manihiki. See MANAHIKI.

Manihiki Islands. See NORTHERN COOK ISLANDS.

Ma·nila \mə-'nil-ə\. 1 Town, ⊗ of Daggett co., NE Utah; pop. (1970c) 226.

2 Chartered city, SW Luzon, Phil., on E shore of Manila Bay; pop. (1970p) 1,330,788; principal port and commercial, cultural, and industrial center of the Philippines; diversified industries include shipbuilding, food processing, fish canning; produces textiles, chemicals, lumber, clothing, vegetable oils; Far Eastern Univ. (1934) and other educational institutions; practically divided into two parts by the Pasig river; Intramuros or Walled City, the original Spanish fortified settlement, surrounded until World War II by a thick stone wall 25 ft. high and ab. 2½ m. in circumference.

History: Founded by Legaspi 1571; under early Spanish rule, became important commercial center; occupied by British 1762–63; captured by U.S. forces Aug. 13, 1898 during Spanish-American War, after Admiral Dewey's defeat of the Spanish fleet (see MANILA BAY). In World War II captured by Japanese Jan. 2, 1942; retaken by U.S. forces Feb. 1945; much of Intramuros and many buildings in other sections destroyed during the conflict; much of damage repaired during post-war expansion and modernization. See QUEZON CITY.

Manila Bay. Large inlet of South China Sea in W Luzon, Phil.; forms a landlocked sea of 770 sq. m., 120 m. in circumference, 30 m. across from Manila to Corregidor I. and 36 m. from the NW corner to Cavite shore. Its entrance is through North and South channels on either side of Corregidor I. Scene of a decisive naval battle of the Spanish-American War on May 1, 1898, when U.S. Admiral George Dewey's fleet destroyed the Spanish fleet off Cavite, with no U.S. losses. In World War II U.S. shipping bombed and destroyed Dec. 1941–Jan. 1942; Japanese vessels similarly attacked and destroyed by U.S. aircraft 1944–45. Came again under complete U.S. control Feb.–Mar. 1945.

Ma·nin·djau \mə-'nin-ˌjau̇\. Crater lake in Barisan Mountains, W Sumatra, Indonesia, W of Bukittinggi, ab. 11 m. long by 6 m. wide.

Ma·ni·pa Strait \mə-ˌnē-pə-\. Channel bet. Buru and Ceram islands in the Moluccas, E Malay Archipelago; connects Ceram Sea with Banda Sea.

Ma·ni·pur \ˌman-ə-'pu̇(ə)r, ˌmən-\. 1 River, W Upper Burma; flows S out of Loktak Lake, S Manipur state, NE India; crosses border into W Upper Burma; bends E and N to empty into Chindwin river.

2 State, NE India, on Burma border; 8628 sq. m.; pop. (1971p) 1,069,555; ✱ Imphal. Consists of wide valley with surrounding hills and mountains. Inhabited chiefly by Manipuris and Meithei. Had first relations with British 1762; scene of serious uprising 1890; government reorganized 1907; invaded Mar.–June 1944 by Japanese, who were driven out by Aug. 1944; territory 1947–72; estab. as a state 1972.

Ma·ni·sa *or* **Ma·nis·sa** \ˌmän-ə-'sä\. 1 Province of W Turkey, Asia. See table at TURKEY.

2 *or anc.* **Mag·ne·sia** \mag-'nē-zhə, -zhē-ə\. City, its ✱, 20 m. NE of İzmir; pop. (1965c) 69,711; commercial center; on main railroad line E to Afyonkarahisar; has buildings from Seljuk and early Osmanli period. Made seat of Byzantine government 1204 under Nicaean emperors and later (1313) the capital of a Turkoman emirate; conquered by Bajazet I 1398. Nearby are ruins of **Magnesia (ad Sip·y·lum** \-ad-'sip-i-ləm\) where in 190 B.C. the Romans defeated Antiochus the Great.

Man·is·tee \ˌman-ə-'stē\. 1 River, NW Michigan; 150 m. long; rises in W Crawford co., flows SW into Lake Michigan at Manistee, in Manistee co.; navigable for a short distance.

2 County in Michigan. See table at MICHIGAN.

3 City, ⊗ of Manistee co., NW Michigan, on Lake Michigan at mouth of Manistee river 20 m. N of Ludington; pop. (1970c) 7723; summer resort; manufactures boats, footwear, iron forgings and castings; dairy and fruit farms.

Man·is·tique \ˌman-ə-'stēk\. 1 River, S Michigan penin.; flows from Manistique Lake in SW Luce co. SW into N Lake Michigan at Manistique.

2 City, ⊗ of Schoolcraft co., S Michigan penin., on Lake Michigan at mouth of Manistique river, 43 m. ENE of Escanaba; pop. (1970c) 4324; summer resort; pulp and paper products; former lumbering center.

Manistique Lake. Lake in Luce and Mackinac cos., E Michigan penin.; outlet, Manistique river.

Man·i·to·ba \ˌman-ə-'tō-bə\. Province, easternmost of the Prairie Provinces, cen. Canada, bounded on N by Keewatin dist., on NE by Hudson Bay, on E by Ontario, on S by U.S.A. (Minnesota and North Dakota), and on W by Saskatchewan; 251,000 sq. m. (incl. 39,225 sq. m. of water); pop. (1970e) 981,000; ✱ Winnipeg. *Physical features:* Level country with many lakes and rivers, most draining to Hudson Bay. Has three large lakes—Winnipeg (larger than Lake Ontario), Winnipegosis, and Manitoba—in cen. part; these are fed by Red, Winnipeg, and Saskatchewan rivers and have the Nelson as their outlet; the Churchill and Seal are farther N. The port of Churchill at mouth of Churchill river has direct connection in summer months with Liverpool, England. Has one large national park (Riding Mountain), 9 provincial parks. *Chief products:* Wheat, oats, barley; livestock raising; nickel, copper, gold, zinc, oil; manufacturing: food processing, iron and steel products, electrical goods, chemicals. *Chief cities:* Winnipeg, St. Boniface, St. James, Brandon.

History: Region first visited along the shore of Hudson Bay in early 17th cent.; Hudson's Bay Company post established at Port Nelson 1670; S part explored by La Vérendrye and site of Winnipeg reached 1738; title to region surrendered by French 1763; Red River Settlement (*q.v.*) founded by Lord Selkirk 1811; became part of Assiniboia region; scene of Riel's Rebellion 1869–70; nucleus of province established 1870; enlarged 1881 and 1912; its growth accelerated by completion of railroads 1878–86.

Manitoba, Lake. Lake, S Manitoba, Canada, SW of Lake Winnipeg; 1817 sq. m.; ab. 140 m. long; outlet through Dauphin river to Lake Winnipeg.

Man·i·tou Island \ˈman-ə-ˌtü-\. Island in Lake Superior, the NE extremity of Keweenaw co., N tip of Michigan penin.

Manitou Island, North. Island in N Lake Michigan, in Leelanau co., NW Michigan.

Manitou Island, South. Island in N Lake Michigan, in Leelanau co., NW Michigan.

Man·i·tou·lin \ˌman-ə-ˈtü-lən\. District, Ontario, Canada. See table at ONTARIO.

Manitoulin Island *also* **Grand Manitoulin.** Island, N Lake Huron, S Ontario, Canada; 80 m. long; separated from the mainland by North Channel; with Cockburn and other small adjacent islands forms Manitoulin dist.

Manitou Springs \ˈman-ə-tü-\. Town, El Paso co., E cen. Colorado, at foot of Pikes Peak 3 m. NW of Colorado Springs; pop. (1970c) 4278; tourist and health resort; mineral springs; Garden of the Gods and Cave of the Winds in vicinity.

Man·i·to·woc \ˈman-ət-ə-ˌwäk\. **1** County in Wisconsin. See table at WISCONSIN.

2 Commercial and industrial city and port of entry, its ⊗, E Wisconsin, on Lake Michigan 25 m. N of Sheboygan; pop. (1970c) 33,430; electrical appliances, processed foods, machine tools, concrete products, metal furniture; shipyards, aluminum and iron foundries; Holy Family Coll. (1869); Manitowoc County Teachers Coll. (1901); fur-trading post 1795; settled 1835.

Man·i·wa·ki \ˌman-ə-ˈwȯ-kē\. Town, ⊗ of Gatineau co., SW Quebec, Canada, on Gatineau river 67 m. N of Hull; pop. (1971p) 6457; sawmills; dairy farming.

Man·i·za·les \ˌman-ə-ˈzäl-əs, -ˈzal-\. City, ✱ of Caldas dept., W cen. Colombia, 110 m. W of Bogotá; pop. (1968e) 219,-496; important coffee center in the Cordillera Central of the Andes, alt. 7064 ft.; has direct rail connection with Buenaventura; univ. (1943).

Manj·ra \ˈmənj-(ˌ)rä\. River, cen. SE Maharashtra, S cen. India; ab. 385 m. long; rises on W border, flows SE, then turns N at border of Andhra Pradesh to join the Godavari NW of Nizamabad.

Man·ju·yod \mäŋ-ˈhü-yȯd\. Municipality, E Negros Oriental, Negros, Phil., on Tanon Strait near its S end, 28 m. NNW of Dumaguete; pop. (1969e) 25,400.

Man·ka·to \man-ˈkāt-(ˌ)ō\. **1** City, ⊗ of Jewell co., N Kansas; pop. (1970c) 1287.

2 City, ⊗ of Blue Earth co., S Minnesota, on Minnesota river 65 m. SSW of Minneapolis; pop. (1970c) 30,895; flour, building materials, dairy products, farm machinery; oil refinery; breweries; livestock and dairy farms; Mankato State Coll. (1866); Bethany Lutheran Coll. (1911).

Man·li·us \ˈman-lē-əs\. Village, Onondaga co., cen. New York, 10 m. E of Syracuse; pop. (1970c) 4295; military academy (1869).

Man·ly \ˈman-lē\. City, E New South Wales, SE Australia, NE suburb of Sydney on Port Jackson; pop. (1966c) 38,-141; beach noted for surf bathing.

Man·ma·noc, Mount \-män-ˈmän-ək\. Peak in Cordillera Central, N Luzon, Phil., on E border of Abra prov.; 6334 ft.

Man·nar *or* **Ma·nar** \mə-ˈnär\. **1** Island in W Northern Province, Ceylon, at the E end of Adam's Bridge.

2 Town on island; pop. (1968e) 10,000.

Mannar, Gulf of. Part of Indian Ocean W of Ceylon and SE of the S point of India; extends NE to Adam's Bridge; pearl fisheries.

Man·nar·gu·di \mə-ˈnär-gəd-ˌē\. Town, E Tamil Nadu, India, ab. 100 m. NE of Madurai; pop. (1961c) 33,558.

Man·ner·heim Line \ˌmän-ər-ˌhām-, ˌman-, -ˌhīm-\. Finnish fortified line across Karelian isthmus, extending from the Gulf of Finland to Lake Ladoga, ab. 80 m. long and with deep defenses reaching back nearly to Vyborg (now in U.S.S.R.); forts on Koivisto I. marked its W end. Begun 1939, never completely finished; penetrated by Soviet forces Feb. 1940; retaken 1941 by Finns and Germans but taken a second time by Soviet forces June 18, 1944. Area now entirely in U.S.S.R.

Mann·heim \ˈman-ˌhīm, ˈmän-\. Commercial and manufacturing city, Baden-Württemberg, West Germany, on Rhine at confluence of Neckar river, 44 m. S by W of Frankfurt am Main; pop. (1969e) 327,992; river port, manufactures chemicals, cellulose, steel, electrical equipment, tobacco; 18th cent. electoral palace, univ. (1967). First mentioned 766; received municipal charter 1607; taken by Tilly 1622 (Thirty Years' War); completely destroyed by French 1689; rebuilt 1697; seat of Rhine Palatinate 1719–77; captured by French 1795, by Austrians 1799; to Baden 1803. In World War II heavily damaged by Allied air raids; captured by U.S. forces ab. Mar. 30, 1945.

Man·ning \ˈman-iŋ\. **1** Town, Carroll co., W cen. Iowa, 62 m. NE of Council Bluffs; pop. (1970c) 1656.

2 Town, ⊗ of Clarendon co., E cen. South Carolina, 17 m. SSE of Sumter; pop. (1970c) 4025; women's clothing, canned foods; grain and tobacco farms.

3 River, New South Wales, Australia; 139 m. long.

Manning Provincial Park. Canadian provincial park in S British Columbia, in Cascade Mts. E of Vancouver; 276 sq. m.

Manning Strait. Channel bet. SE Choiseul and NW Santa Isabel Is., cen. Solomon Is., W Pacific Ocean; ab. 35 m. wide; contains many small islands.

Man·ning·ton \ˈman-iŋ-tən\. City, Marion co., N West Virginia, 12 m. W of Fairmont; pop. (1970c) 2747; oil and gas wells.

Ma·no \ˈmän-(ˌ)ō\. River, W Africa; ab. 200 m. long; flows SW through N and NW Liberia, forming in its lower course a section of the boundary bet. Liberia and Sierra Leone.

Ma·no·kin \mə-ˌnō-kən\. River, W shore of Somerset co., SE Maryland; flows into Tangier Sound.

Ma·nok·wa·ri \ˌmän-ə-ˈkwär-ē\. Town, on NE coast of Doberai Penin., Irian Barat, Indonesia, forming NW point of entrance to Sarera Bay; has good harbor; bypassed by Allies in World War II.

Ma·nom·bo \mə-ˈnäm-(ˌ)bō\. Coastal town, SW Malagasy Republic, N of Tuléar.

Man·or·bier \ˌman-ər-ˈbi(ə)r\. Village, Pembrokeshire, SW Wales, on coast of Bristol Channel; ruins of castle, birthplace of Giraldus de Barri, Welsh ecclesiastical geographer and historian.

Man·or·ha·ven \ˈman-ər-ˌhāv-ən\. Village, Nassau co., SE New York; pop. (1970c) 5488.

Man·re·sa \män-ˈrā-sə\. Manufacturing commune, Barcelona prov., NE Spain, 30 m. NNW of Barcelona; pop. (1970p) 57,846; metalworking; tires, textiles, glass; 13th and 17th cent. churches; important during the Middle Ages.

Mans, Le. See LE MANS.

Man·sa \ˈmän-sə\ *or formerly* **Fort Rose·bery** \-ˈrōz-ˌber-ē, -b(ə-)rē\. Town, N Zambia; pop. (1963c) 4928.

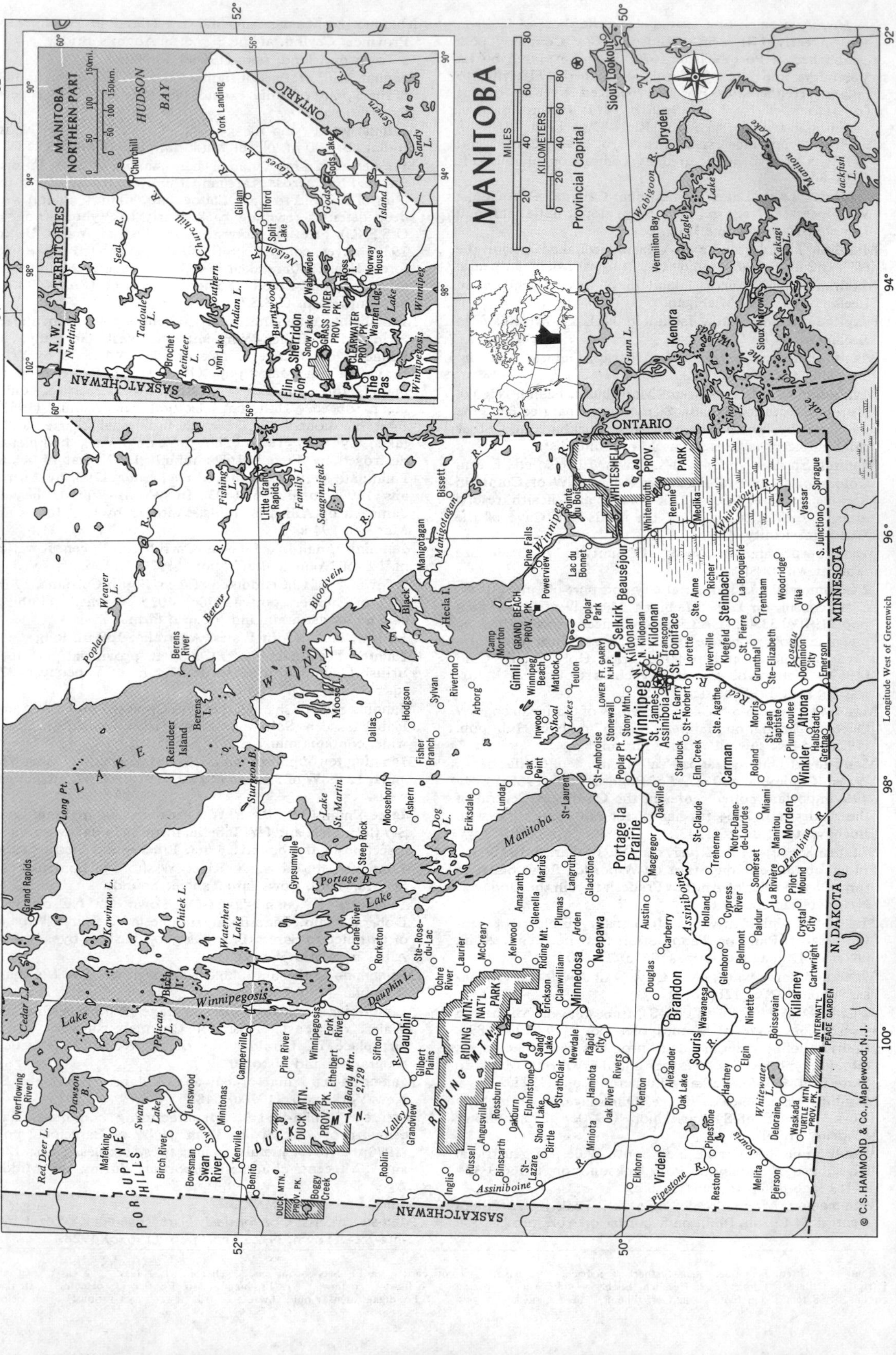
MANITOBA
MANITOBA NORTHERN PART
HUDSON BAY
MILES
KILOMETERS
Provincial Capital
SASKATCHEWAN
ONTARIO
N. DAKOTA
MINNESOTA
N. W. TERRITORIES
PORCUPINE HILLS
LAKE WINNIPEG
Lake Winnipegosis
Lake Manitoba
Winnipeg
St. James
Assiniboia
St. Boniface
Kildonan
Brandon
Portage la Prairie
Selkirk
Dauphin
Flin Flon
The Pas
Sherridon
Churchill
York Landing
Gillam
Norway House
Split Lake
Kenora
Dryden
Sioux Lookout
Swan River
Virden
Souris
Neepawa
Minnedosa
Morden
Winkler
Altona
Carman
Steinbach
Killarney
Gimli
Beausejour
RIDING MTN. NAT'L PARK
DUCK MTN. PROV. PK.
WHITESHELL PROV. PARK
GRAND BEACH PROV. PK.
TURTLE MTN. PROV. PK.
INTERNAT'L PEACE GARDEN
Baldy Mtn. 2,729
Assiniboine R.
Red R.
Souris R.
Pembina R.
Nelson R.
Churchill R.
Hayes R.
Lake of the Woods
Longitude West of Greenwich
© C.S. HAMMOND & Co., Maplewood, N.J.

Man·sel Island \ˌman(t)-səl-\. Island, NE Hudson Bay, Keewatin dist., Northwest Territories, Canada; crossed by 62°N, 80°W; 70 m. long.

Mans·field \ˈmanz-ˌfēld, ˈman(t)s-\. 1 Agricultural and manufacturing town, E Tolland co., N Connecticut, on Willimantic river; pop. (1970c) 19,994; incorporated 1703.

2 City, ⊗ of De Soto parish, NW Louisiana, 33 m. S of Shreveport; pop. (1970c) 6432; lumber, clothing, radio parts, oil wells; nearby, at Sabine Crossroads, Union forces under Gen. Banks were defeated Apr. 8, 1864 by Confederate forces under Gen. Kirby-Smith and Gen. Taylor.

3 Industrial town, Bristol co., SE Massachusetts, WSW of Brockton; pop. (1970c) 9939; chemicals, writing implements, dies, chocolate.

4 Industrial city, ⊗ of Richland co., N cen. Ohio, 54 m. WSW of Akron; pop. (1970c) 55,047; electrical appliances, rubber products, automobile bodies, sheet steel, plumbing fixtures, thermostats; first surveyed 1808.

5 Borough, Tioga co., N Pennsylvania, on Tioga river 39 m. N of Williamsport; pop. (1970c) 4114; coal mines, gas wells; dairy farms; Mansfield State Coll. (1858).

6 City, Johnson and Tarrant cos., N Texas, 18 m. SE of Fort Worth; pop. (1970c) 3658; diversified agriculture.

7 Municipal borough, Nottinghamshire, N cen. England, on the Maun 15 m. N of Nottingham; pop. (1971p) 57,598; coal mining; produces textiles, plastics, nylon, radio and electronics parts, footwear; 12th cent. church.

Mansfield, Mount. Peak, Lamoille co., N Vermont; 4393 ft.; highest point in Vermont and Green Mts.

Mansfield Wood·house \-ˈwu̇d-ˌhau̇s\. Urban district, Nottinghamshire, N cen. England; N suburb of Mansfield; pop. (1971p) 24,787.

Man·so, Point \-ˈmän-(ˌ)sō\ *or formerly* **Point Ca·rre·ta** \-kä-ˈrāt-ə\. Cape, S Uruguay, extending into the Rio de la Plata near Montevideo.

Man·şūr, Jeb·el \ˌjeb-əl-man-ˈsu̇(ə)r\. Mountain, N cen. Tunisia, WSW of Zaghouan; 2224 ft.; scene of fighting in World War II.

Mansūra, Al–. See AL-MANSŪRA.

Man·ta \ˈmän-tä\. Seaport on S shore of Manta Bay, Manabí prov., W Ecuador, 100 m. NW of Guayaquil; pop. (1969e) 44,386; port for Montecristi, Portoviejo, and Jipijapa.

Manta Bay. Inlet of Pacific Ocean on W coast of Ecuador, NW of Guayaquil.

Man·ta·ling·a·jan, Mount \-ˌmant-ᵊl-iŋ-ˈä-ˌhän\. Highest point on Palawan I., Phil., at S end, in **Mantalingajan Range;** 6839 ft.

Man·ta·ro \män-ˈtär-(ˌ)ō\. River, S cen. Peru; ab. 360 m. long; flows E to Apurímac river.

Man·te·ca \man-ˈtē-kə\. City, San Joaquin co., cen. California, 10 m. S of Stockton; pop. (1970c) 13,845; wineries, sugar refinery; diversified agriculture.

Man·te·na \man-ˈten-ə\. Municipality, Minas Gerais state, E Brazil; pop. (1968e) 77,486.

Man·te·no \man-ˈtē-nō\. Village, Kankakee co., NE Illinois, 10 m. N of Kankakee; pop. (1970c) 2864.

Man·teo \ˈman-tē-ˌō\. Town and resort, ⊗ of Dare co., E North Carolina, on Roanoke I. bet. Albemarle and Pamlico sounds; pop. (1970c) 547.

Mantes–la–Jo·lie \ˌmäⁿ(n)t-ˌläzh-ə-ˈlē\; *formerly* **Mantes–Gas·si·court** \-ˌgas-ē-ˈku̇(ə)r\ *or* **Mantes–sur–Seine** \-su̇(ə)r-ˈsān, -ˈsen\ *or Lat.* **Me·dun·ta** \me-ˈdən-tä\. Commune, Yvelines dept., N France, on Seine river 32 m. WNW of Paris; pop. (1968c) 26,058.

Man·ti \ˈman-ˌtī\. City, ⊗ of Sanpete co., cen. Utah, 48 m. WSW of Price; pop. (1970c) 1803; flour mill; poultry and livestock farms; Mormon Temple.

Man·ti·nea \ˌmant-ᵊn-ˈē-ə\ *or* **Man·ti·neia** \-ᵊn-ˈī-ə\. Ancient village in E Arcadia, near Argolis border, E Peloponnesus, S Greece; scene of three battles: 418 B.C. in the Peloponnesian War in which Agis, King of Sparta, defeated the Argives and Mantineans; 362 B.C. in which Epaminondas was killed; and 207 B.C. in which Spartans were defeated by Philopoemen, Greek general of the Achean League.

Mantiqueira, Serra da. See SERRA DA MANTIQUEIRA.

Man·tor·ville \ˈman-tər-ˌvil\. Village, ⊗ of Dodge co., SE Minnesota, 13 m. WNW of Rochester; pop. (1970c) 479.

Man·to·va \ˈmänt-ə-və\. 1 Province of Lombardy, Italy. See table at ITALY.

2 Commune, Italy. See MANTUA.

Man·tua \ˈmän-twə\. Municipality, Pinar del Río prov., W Cuba, 37 m. W of Pinar del Río; pop. (1967e) 20,340.

Mantua \ˈmanch-(ə-)wə, ˈmant-ə-wə\ *or Ital.* **Man·to·va** \ˈmänt-ə-və\. Manufacturing commune, ✱ of Mantova prov., Lombardy, N Italy, on Mincio river 80 m. WSW of Venice; pop. (1968e) 66,089; processing and shipping of agricultural products; tourism; buildings include cathedral (interior designed by Giulio Romano), several notable churches, ducal palace and castle of Gonzaga family, home of Giulio Romano, Vergilian Academy of Sciences and Fine Arts.

History: Ancient town probably of Etruscan origin; Roman municipium, near which Vergil was born; taken by Lombards (see LOMBARDY) 6th cent. A.D.; in 11th cent. belonged to margrave of Canossa, but became independent 1115; member of Lombard League; ruled by Gonzaga family 1328–1708; became duchy in 16th cent.; in War of Mantuan Succession 1627–31, France and German emperor backed rival claimants to duchy; ceded to Austria 1714; taken in 1797 by Napoleon after a siege; duchy belonged to Cisalpine Republic 1797 and to Italian kingdom 1805; restored to Austria 1814; one of the forts of the famous Quadrilateral by which Austria controlled N Italy; ceded to Italian kingdom 1866.

Ma·nua Islands \mə-ˌnü-ə-\. Group of 3 islands, Tau (area 17 sq. m.; pop. [1970p] 1317), Ofu, and Olosega, in American Samoa, SW Pacific Ocean, 65 m. E of the island of Tutuila; total area 22 sq. m.; pop. 2138; group constitutes an administrative district of American Samoa (*q.v.*).

Ma·nu·kau \ˈmän-ə-ˌkau̇\. City, North I., New Zealand, ab. 12 m. SE of Auckland; pop. (1970e) 96,000.

Manukau Harbor. Inlet of Tasman Sea on NW coast of North I., New Zealand, forming an excellent harbor; suburbs of Auckland on its N shore.

Ma·nus \ˈmän-(ˌ)üs\. 1 Administrative district of Papua New Guinea, comprising the Admiralty Is. and adjacent islands; 800 sq. m.; pop. (1969e) 21,588; ✱ Lorengau.

2 *or* **Great Ad·mi·ral·ty Island** \-ˈad-m(ə-)rəl-tē-\. Largest of the Admiralty Is. and chief part of Manus administrative district; ab. 50 m. long and 17 m. wide; area 600 sq. m.; terrain mountainous, and interior largely unexplored; has large harbor at Lorengau at its E tip; coconut plantations. Seized by Japanese Apr. 1942; occupied by Allies and Lorengau captured Mar. 18, 1944; made into a major fleet repair station. Taken over by Australia Dec. 1947.

Man·ville \ˈman-ˌvil\. 1 Borough, Somerset co., N cen. New Jersey, 9 m. WNW of New Brunswick; pop. (1970c) 13,029; asbestos, building materials, plastics, clothing; truck farms.

2 Village in Lincoln town, Providence co., N Rhode Island, ab. 3 m. SE of Woonsocket; manufactures cotton, rayon, silk.

Many \ˈman-ē\. Town, ⊗ of Sabine parish, W Louisiana; pop. (1970c) 3112; lumber.

Manyara, Lake. See LAKE MANYARA NATIONAL PARK.

Man·yas Lake \män-ˈyäs-\ *or Turk.* **Manyas Gö·lü** \-gəl-ˈyü\. Lake, NW Turkey, Asia, near S shore of Sea of Marmara, S of Bandırma; 69 sq. m.

Ma·nych *also* **Ma·nich** \mə-ˈnich\. 1 Valley or depression extending SE and NW from the lower Don to the lower Kuma river, Russian S.F.S.R., U.S.S.R.; 330 m. long; crosses S Rostov Oblast and forms S boundary of Astrakhan Oblast; usually a series of salt lakes but when flooded in spring season, two rivers are formed flowing in opposite directions from a high point ab. long. 44°E. The Kalaus river (ab. 160 m. long) flows from the S to join the Eastern Manych river.

2 A lake in Manych valley, SW Astrakhan Oblast, Russian S.F.S.R., U.S.S.R.

3 *or* **Western Manych.** River in Manych valley, Russian S.F.S.R., U.S.S.R.; 162 m. long; a tributary of the lower Don, entering it near its mouth; receives the waters of Manych lake during spring seasons. Another stream, the **Eastern Manych,** flows E at high water to the Kuma.

Man·zala, Lake \-man-ˈzäl-ə\ *also* **Lake Men·za·la** \-mən-\ *or Arab.* **Bu·ḥay·rat Al–Man·zi·lah** \bu̇-ˈhā-rät-al-ˈman-zi-lə\. Large lagoon, Egypt, SE of Damietta; N part of Suez Canal passes along its E edge. See TANIS.

Man·za·nar \ˈman-zə-ˌnär\. Station, Inyo co., E California, ab. 12 m. N of Owens Lake; during World War II a Japanese relocation center.

Man·za·na·res \ˌman-zə-ˈnär-əs\. 1 River, Madrid prov., cen. Spain; 50 m. long; flows past Madrid into Jarama river, a tributary of the Tagus river.

2 Manufacturing commune, Ciudad Real prov., S cen. Spain, on Manzanares river 30 m. E of Ciudad Real; pop. (1970p) 15,692; textiles, oil, wine; medieval castle.

Man·za·ni·llo \ˌman-zə-ˈnē-(ˌ)(y)ō\. 1 Municipality and seaport on SW coast of Oriente prov., E Cuba, on Guacanayabo Bay; munic. pop. (1967e) 183,900; exports sugar, molasses, tobacco, hardwood; mangrove swamps; founded 1784.

2 Seaport, Colima state, SW Mexico, on Manzanillo Bay 38 m. WSW of Colima; pop. (1969e) 29,347; exports coffee, hides.

Manzanillo, Point. N extremity of Panama, extending into the Caribbean Sea NE of Colón.

Manzanillo Bay. 1 Inlet of Caribbean Sea, Panama; separated from Limón Bay, N Canal Zone, to the W by peninsula on which Colón is located.

2 Bay in N coast of the island of Hispaniola, West Indies, on boundary bet. Haiti and the Dominican Republic.

Man·zano Peak \man-ˌzan-ō-, -ˌzän-\. Mountain, W Torrance co., cen. New Mexico; 10,086 ft.; highest point in the **Manzano Mountains.**

Manzikert. See MALAZGIRT.

Manzilah, Buḥayrat Al–. See MANZALA, LAKE.

Man·zi·ni \män-ˈzē-nē\ *or formerly* **Bre·mers·dorp** \ˈbrā-mərz-ˌdȯrp\. Town, cen. Swaziland, SE Africa; pop. (1966c) 6081; before 1902 capital of Swaziland.

Mao \ˈmau̇\. 1 Town, W Chad, N cen. Africa, NE of Lake Chad; pop. (1968c) 3983; chief town of Kanem.

2 Town, ✻ of Valverde prov., Dominican Republic, ab. 42 m. SE of Montecristi; pop. (1970p) 27,111.

Maoka. See KHOLMSK.

Mao·ke Mountains \ˌmau̇-kā-\; *formerly* **Snow Mountains** *or Du.* **Sneeuw Ge·berg·te** \ˌsnā-ü-kə-ˈberk-tə\. Range of mountains, cen. Irian Barat, Indonesia, running E and W from boundary of Papua New Guinea (141°E) to the narrow isthmus S of Sarera Bay, ab. 425 m. long; comprises the subordinate ranges of Sudirman and Djajawidjaja (*qq.v.*). Highest point is Mt. Djaja 16,535 ft. in Sudirman Range; has many peaks above 13,000 ft.; not known until 20th cent.

Ma·pia \ˈmäp-ē-ə\ *or* **Saint Da·vid** \-ˈdā-vəd\. Group of three small islands and several islets in Pacific Ocean 150 m. N of Numfoor I. off N coast of Irian Barat, Indonesia, 134°20′E, 0°50′N; occupied by U.S. forces Nov. 15, 1944.

Ma·pi·mí, Bol·són de \bȯl-ˈsȯn-də-ˌmäp-ə-ˈmē\. Rocky depression, N cen. Mexican plateau region, in Coahuila and Chihuahua states; ab. 50,000 sq. m.

Ma·ple Creek \ˈmā-pəl-\. Town, SW Saskatchewan, Canada, 80 m. WSW of Swift Current; pop. (1971p) 2268; ships cattle; livestock and grain farms.

Maple Grove. Village, Hennepin co., SE cen. Minnesota, 14 m. NW of Minneapolis; pop. (1970c) 6275.

Maple Heights. City, Cuyahoga co., N Ohio, 10 m. SE of Cleveland; pop. (1970c) 34,093; residential suburb of Cleveland.

Maple Peak. Mountain, N Greenlee co., E Arizona; 8302 ft.

Maple Shade. Urban township, Burlington co., S cen. New Jersey, ab. 7 m. E of Camden; pop. (1970c) 16,464; manufacturing; truck and grain farms.

Ma·ple·wood \ˈmā-pəl-ˌwu̇d\. 1 Village, Ramsey co., E Minnesota, N suburb of St. Paul; pop. (1970c) 25,222.

2 Residential city, St. Louis co., E Missouri, 7 m. W of St. Louis; pop. (1970c) 12,785.

3 Township, Essex co., NE New Jersey, S of South Orange and 6 m. W of Newark; pop. (1970c) 24,932; residential suburb of New York and Newark.

Ma·po·cho \mä-ˈpō-ˌchō\. River, cen. Chile; ab. 75 m. long; flows into Maipo river 32 m. SW of Santiago.

Ma·pue·ra \mə-ˈpwer-ə\. River, N Brazil; 270 m. long; rises near S border of Guyana; flows SE into Trombetas river NW of Lake Erepecu.

Ma·pu·to \mə-ˈpüt-(ˌ)ō\. Navigable river, S Mozambique, SE Africa; 50 m. long; formed by the Usutu and Pongolo rivers; flows E to Delagoa Bay.

Ma·que·da Bay \mə-ˌkād-ə-\. Inlet on W coast of Samar, Phil., partly enclosed on W by Buad I.

Ma·qui·ling, Mount \-mə-ˈkē-liŋ\. Mountain, S Laguna prov., Luzon, Phil., on Batangas border; 3650 ft.

Ma·quo·ke·ta \mə-ˈkō-kət-ə\. 1 River, E cen. Iowa; ab. 150 m. long; rises in S Fayette co., NE Iowa, flows SE into Mississippi river in E Jackson co., E Iowa.

2 City, ⊗ of Jackson co., E Iowa, 30 m. S of Dubuque; pop. (1970c) 5677; beverages; limestone quarries; dairy farms.

Mar, Serra do. See SERRA DO MAR.

Ma·ra \ˈmär-ə\. Administrative region of N Tanzania. See table at TANZANIA.

Ma·ra·cá \ˌmar-ə-ˈkä\. Island in Atlantic Ocean off NE coast of Pará state, Brazil.

Mar·a·cai·bo \ˌmar-ə-ˈkī-(ˌ)bō, ˌmär-\. City, ✻ of Zulia state, NW Venezuela, on W side of channel bet. Lake Maracaibo and the Gulf of Venezuela; pop. (1970e) 665,578; one of largest cities in Venezuela; exports oil; chemicals, building materials, textiles, soap, rope and twine. Founded 1571; after 1668 a center for inland trade; major expansion took place entirely after discovery of oil 1917.

Maracaibo, Gulf of. See VENEZUELA, GULF OF.

Maracaibo, Lake. South extension of Gulf of Venezuela, in NW Venezuela; 5217 sq. m.; 133 m. long, 72 m. wide; max. depth 115 ft.; receives Catatumbo river from SW; in region of rich oil fields, some wells having been sunk on the bottom of the lake through 50 ft. of water.

Maracanda. See SAMARKAND 2.

Ma·ra·cay \ˌmär-ə-ˈkī\. City, ✻ of Aragua state, N Venezuela, on highway 50 m. WSW of Caracas; pop. (1970e) 192,863; alt. 1500 ft.; center of Venezuelan cattle industry; produces meat products, paper, textiles, chemicals, building materials; gas wells, sugar refineries; developed under dictatorship of Juan Vicente Gómez (1908–35), when it was the effective capital of Venezuela.

Ma·ra·dals·fos \ˈmär-ə-ˌdäls-ˌfȯs\. Waterfall, cen. Norway, just W of the Dovrefjell plateau; 650 ft.

Ma·ra·di \mə-ˈrä-dē\. Town, S Niger; pop. (1969e) 27,670.

Ma·rā·gheh \ˌmar-ə-ˈgā\ *or* **Ma·ra·gha** \-ˈgä\. Town, East Azerbaijan prov., NW Iran, ab. 18 m. E of Lake Urmia; pop. (1971p) 56,000; center of fruit-growing region. Seat of government of Hulagu, Mongol ruler who conquered the region in 13th cent.

Ma·rah \ˈmar-ə, ˈmer-ə\. Locality on E coast of Gulf of Suez, Sinai Penin., NE Egypt, in region occupied by Israel 1967; first halting place of the Israelites after passing through the Red Sea and entering the wilderness; the waters were bitter (*Exod.* xv. 23–25).

Ma·rais \ma-'rā\. Marshy district in S Vendée dept., W France; once partly covered by the sea.

Mar·ais des Cygnes \'merd-ə-ˌzēn\. River, E Kansas and Missouri; ab. 150 m. long; flows from S Wabaunsee co., Kansas E and SE to Osage river on boundary bet. Bates and Vernon cos., Missouri. See OSAGE 1.

Ma·ra·jó \ˌmar-ə-'zhō\. Island in the Amazon delta, NE Brazil, bet. the Amazon and Pará rivers; 15,444 sq. m.; W part low-lying and often flooded; E part higher, largely savanna; cattle raising in E part.

Marakesh. See MARRAKECH.

Ma·ra·mag \ˌmar-ə-'mag\. Municipality, Bukidnon prov., Mindanao, Phil., ab. 60 m. SSE of Cagayan de Oro; pop. (1969e) 46,400.

Máramarossziget. See SIGHET MARMAŢIEI.

Ma·ra·ma·si·ke \ˌmär-ə-mə-'sē-kə\. Narrow island off SE coast of Malaita I., SE Solomon Is., W Pacific Ocean; ab. 32 m. long.

Ma·ra·mureş \ˌmä-rä-'mür-esh\. County of N Romania. See table at ROMANIA.

Ma·ra·nhão \ˌmar-ən-'yaüⁿ\. 1 *or* **São Lu·ís** \ˌsaüⁿ-lü-'ēs\ *or* **São Luís do Maranhão** \-dü-\. Island off N coast of Maranhão state, NE Brazil, bet. São Marcos Bay on the W and São José Bay on the E; 28 m. long; site of the state capital, São Luís.

2 State, NE Brazil; 126,897 sq. m.; pop. (1970p) 2,883,211; ✻ São Luís; sugarcane, coffee, rice, cotton; oil.

Mar·a·noa \ˌmar-ə-'nō-ə\. River, SE Queensland, Australia; 200 m. long; flows S and joins the Condamine to form the Culgoa.

Ma·ra·no di Na·po·li \mə-ˌrän-ō-di-'näp-ə-lē\. Commune, Napoli prov., Campania, S Italy, 9 m. NW of Naples; pop. (1968e) 23,118.

Ma·ra·ñón \ˌmär-ən-'yōn\. River, Peru; ab. 1000 m. long; rises in the Andes Mts. in W cen. Peru, flows NW to N Peru, bends E and joins the Ucayali river to form the Amazon river (*q.v.*); navigable by shallow-draft steamers for ab. 500 m.

Ma·ra·pi \ˌmar-ə-'pē\. River, N Brazil; rises in Tumuc-Humac Mts.; flows S to unite with Paru de Oeste.

Ma·raş *or* **Ma·rash** \mə-'räsh\. 1 Province of S cen. Turkey, Asia. See table at TURKEY.

2 City, its ✻, at foot of E Taurus Mts. and near Ceyhan river 96 m. NE of Adana; pop. (1965c) 63,284; commercial center; exports carpets and embroideries. In very early times a Hittite town; under Muslim control c. 700–1097, when it was captured by Crusaders. Became Turkish in 16th cent.; held for a short time by Egyptians 1832.

Mă·ră·şeş·ti \ˌmər-ə-'shest(-ē)\. Commune, Vrancea co., Romania, N of Focşani; pop. (1966c) 8059; battle Aug. 1917.

Mar·a·thon \'mar-ə-ˌthän, -thən\. 1 County in Wisconsin. See table at WISCONSIN.

2 Plain in E Attica dept., Greece, ab. 24 m. NE of Athens; 5 m. long, 2 m. wide; borders on **Bay of Marathon** (*Gk.* **Ór·mos Ma·ra·thó·nos** \'ör-ˌmös-ˌmär-ə-'thön-ˌös\), inlet of Aegean Sea, and ends in marsh at N.

3 Ancient town on this plain, probably located S of the modern town of **Ma·ra·thón** \ˌmär-ə-'thön\; scene of battle in Sept. 490 B.C., in which Miltiades and 10,000 Greeks (mostly Athenians) completely defeated Datis and Artaphernes with a larger army of Persians.

Marathus. See 'AMRIT.

Ma·ra·va·tío \ˌmär-ə-və-'tē-(ˌ)ō\. Municipality, Michoacán state, Mexico, 50 m. NE of Morelia; pop. (1970p) 35,383; livestock raising; agriculture.

Ma·ra·wi \mə-'rä-wē\ *or formerly* **Dan·sa·lan** \ˌdän-sə-'län\. Municipality, ✻ of Lanao del Sur prov., Mindanao I., Phil.; pop. (1970e) 38,500.

Ma·ra·wī \mə-'rä-wē\ *also* **Mer·o·we** \mə-'rä-wā\. Town, Northern Province, N Sudan, on the Nile river near the Fourth Cataract.

Mar·be·lla \mär-'bā-(l)yä\. Commune, Málaga prov., S cen. Spain, on Mediterranean SW of Málaga; pop. (1970p) 33,203.

Mar·ble Canyon \'mär-bəl-\. Gorge along the Colorado river, N Arizona, extending from Lees Ferry (*q.v.*) S to the Little Colorado; often considered the upper part of Grand Canyon; established as national monument 1969. See UNITED STATES, *National Monuments.*

Mar·ble·head \'mär-bəl-ˌhed, ˌmär-bəl-'hed\. Town, Essex co., NE Massachusetts, on Atlantic Ocean 15 m. NE of Boston; pop. (1970c) 21,295; built on a rocky promontory (**Marblehead Neck**); noted as a resort and yachting center; boatbuilding, fishing. Founded ab. 1629, until 1649 a part of Salem; important in early history of American navy, declining in importance after War of 1812.

Marble Hill. 1 City, ⊗ of Bollinger co., SE Missouri; pop. (1970c) 589.

2 Small section of Manhattan borough, New York City, on mainland N of Spuyten Duyvil Creek, bounded on N, W, and E by the Bronx.

Marble Point. Peak, Baker co., E Oregon; 6672 ft.

Mar·burg \'mär-ˌbü(ə)rg, -ˌbərg\. 1 *also* **Marburg an der Lahn** \-än-dər-'län\. City, Hesse, West Germany, on Lahn river 46 m. N of Frankfurt; pop. (1969e) 51,070; pottery; tourism; univ. (1527, Europe's first Protestant university); 12th and 14th cent. churches; 13th–15th cent. castle; associated with St. Elizabeth and Luther (Colloquy of Marburg 1529); founded in 12th cent.; passed to Prussia 1866.

2 City, Yugoslavia. See MARIBOR.

Mar·ca·ria \ˌmär-kə-'rē-ə\. Commune, Mantova prov., Lombardy, N Italy, 13 m. W of Mantua; pop. (1968e) 8504.

Mar·ce·line \ˌmär-sə-'lēn\. City, Linn co., N Missouri, 35 m. NW of Moberly; pop. (1970c) 2622; coal mines.

March \'märch\. 1 River, Czechoslovakia. See MORAVA 1.

2 Urban district, Cambridgeshire and Isle of Ely co., E England, on the Nene 52 m. E of Leicester; pop. (1971p) 14,268.

Marche \'märsh\ *or Lat.* **Mar·chia** \'mär-kē-ə\. Historical region of cen. France; bounded anciently on N by Touraine, NE by Berry and Bourbonnais, SE by Auvergne, S by Limousin, W by Poitou. Became countship in 10th cent.; in possession of Lusignan family in 13th cent.; acquired by dukes of Bourbon, later confiscated by Francis I; province of France until Revolution.

Mar·che·na \mär-'cha-nə\. Commune, Sevilla prov., SW Spain, 32 m. E of Seville; pop. (1970p) 20,918; woolens, pottery; stock raising, esp. for the bullring; sulfur baths.

Mar·che·na Island \mär-ˌchā-nə-\ *or* **Bind·loe Island** \ˌbin-(ˌ)dlō-\. One of the Galápagos Is. (*q.v.*).

March·es \'mär-chəz\ *or Ital.* **Le Mar·che** \lā-'mär-(ˌ)kā\. Autonomous region of cen. Italy; 3742 sq. m.; pop. (1968e) 1,358,089; ✻ Ancona; for provincial divisions see table at ITALY; lies bet. Adriatic Sea and Umbria, and bet. Emilia-Romagna and Abruzzi; produces grain, wine, tobacco. Formerly part of States of the Church (*q.v.*) against whom they voted in favor of union with Italy 1860; established as administrative region 1948; received limited autonomy 1970.

March·feld \'märk-ˌfelt\. Plain lying N of the Danube at Vienna, Austria, and W of the Morava; ab. 328 sq. m.; scene of battle Aug. 1278 bet. Ottokar II, King of Bohemia, and Rudolf of Hapsburg, in which Ottokar was killed; in Napoleonic Wars scene of battles of Aspern (*q.v.*), Essling, and Wagram (*q.v.*).

Marchia. See MARCHE.

Mar·chienne–au–Pont \ˌmär-shē-ˌen-ō-ˈpō^{n}\. Commune, Hainaut prov., SW Belgium, on the Sambre near Charleroi; pop. (1969e) 19,455; foundries and machine works.

Mar Chi·qui·ta \ˌmär-chi-ˈkēt-ə\. Salt lake, Córdoba prov., N cen. Argentina; 580 sq. m., 45 m. long.

Mar·cia·ni·se \ˌmär-chə-ˈnē(ˌ)zā\. Commune, Caserta prov., Campania, S Italy, N of Naples; pop. (1968e) 27,873.

Mar·ci·nelle \ˌmär-sə-ˈnel\. Commune, Hainaut prov., SW Belgium; suburb of S Charleroi; pop. (1969e) 27,627; cable.

Marcodurum. See DÜREN.

Mar·coing \mär-ˈkwa^{n}\. Commune, Nord dept., N France, on the Schelde canal near Cambrai; pop. (1962c) 2165; in World War I destroyed during fighting around Cambrai Nov. 20–Dec. 7, 1917.

Mar·co Po·lo Bridge \ˌmär-kō-ˌpō-lō-\. A marble bridge, with many arches, pillars, and sculptured lions, across the Yung-ting at Lu-kou-ch'iao (*q.v.*), NE China, 9 m. SW of Peking; 900 ft. long; so named from Marco Polo's description of it in his chronicle.

Mar·cos Paz \ˌmär-kəs-ˈpäs\. Town, Buenos Aires prov., E Argentina, 26 m. W of Buenos Aires; pop. (1960c) 7697.

Marcq–en–Ba·rœul \ˌmär-ˌkä^{n}-bə-ˈrər(-ə)l\. Commune, Nord dept., N France, NNE suburb of Lille; pop. (1968c) 35,136; textiles; iron foundries.

Mar·cus Hook \ˈmär-kəs-\. Industrial borough and port, Delaware co., SE Pennsylvania, on Delaware river 18 m. WSW of Philadelphia; pop. (1970c) 3041; rayon; oil refineries, shipyards.

Marcus Island *or Jap.* **Mi·na·mi–To·ri–Shi·ma** \mi-ˌnäm-ē-ˌtȯr-ē-ˈshē-mə, -ˈtȯr-ēsh-(ə-)ˌmä\. Small, triangular-shaped island in W Pacific Ocean, NE of the Marianas and ab. 725 m. NW of Wake I., 24°18′N lat., 153°58′E long.; settlement on S coast. In World War II a Japanese air base; frequently bombed by U.S. forces; administered by U.S. from 1945; returned to Japan 1968.

Mar·cy, Mount \-ˈmär-sē\. Peak in the Adirondack Mts., NE New York; 5344 ft.; highest peak in the Adirondacks, and in New York state.

Mar·dan \ˈmär-ˌdan\. Town, Pakistan, 30 m. NE of Peshawar; met. area pop. (1969e) 113,400.

Mar del Pla·ta \ˌmär-del-ˈplät-ə\. Coastal city, Buenos Aires prov., E Argentina, S of Buenos Aires; pop. (1960c) 211,365; seaside resort; major fishing port; fish canneries.

Mar·din \mär-ˈdēn\. **1** Province of SE Turkey, Asia. See table at TURKEY.
2 Town, its ✱, on branch railroad near Syrian border 53 m. SE of Diyarbakır; pop. (1965c) 30,974; local trading center.

Ma·re \ˈmā-(ˌ)rē, ˈmär-(ˌ)ā\. Latin meaning "sea"; used in classical names of bodies of water, as **Mare Adriaticum, Mare Ionium,** etc. See the second element of these names, or its anglicized form.

Ma·ré \mä-ˈrā\. One of the Loyalty Is., at SE end of chain; 248 sq. m.; ab. 22 m. long and 10 m. wide; pop. (1969c) 3410; low coral formation.

Ma·reb \mä-ˈreb\. River, E Africa; ab. 300 m. long; rises in N Ethiopia; flows NW, crosses W Eritrea into E Sudan, and during high-water seasons empties into the Atbara river; known as the **Gash** \ˈgash\ in its lower course.

Mare Cantabricum. See BISCAY, BAY OF.

Ma·ree, Loch \ˌläk-mə-ˈrē, läk-\. Lake, Ross and Cromarty co., N Scotland; 12½ m. long; max. depth 367 ft.; connected with Loch Ewe by a short river.

Mare Germanicum. See NORTH SEA.

Mare Internum. See MEDITERRANEAN SEA.

Mare Island \ˈma(ə)r-, ˈme(ə)r-\. Island in E San Pablo Bay, W cen. California; separated from Vallejo by narrow **Mare Island Strait.** U.S. Navy Yard, estab. 1853; now a major naval building and repair facility.

Ma·rem·ma \mə-ˈrem-ə\. Marshy region in W Italy, chiefly in Grosseto prov., SW Tuscany.

Ma·ren·go \mə-ˈreŋ-(ˌ)gō\. **1** County in Alabama. See table at ALABAMA.
2 City, McHenry co., N Illinois, 25 m. E of Rockford; pop. (1970c) 4235; electronic components, iron castings; dairy and poultry farms.
3 Town, Crawford co., S Indiana; pop. (1970c) 767; nearby is **Marengo Cave,** a stalactite cave.
4 City, ⊗ of Iowa co., E cen. Iowa, 25 m. WSW of Cedar Rapids; pop. (1970c) 2235; diversified agriculture.
5 Village, Alessandria prov., SE Piedmont, NW Italy; scene of battle June 14, 1800 in which Napoleon defeated the Austrians.

Mar·e·o·tis, Lake \-ˌmar-ē-ˈō-tis\ *or Arab.* **Buḥ·ra·yat Mar·yūt** \ˈbu̇-rī-ˌyät-mər-ˈyüt\. Lake in the Nile delta, N Egypt, W of Rosetta mouth of the Nile; Alexandria is situated on narrow strip of land bet. it and the Mediterranean Sea.

Mare Rubrum. See ERYTHRAEAN SEA.

Ma·res·cot, Mount \-mə-ˈres-kət\. Peak, SE Santa Isabel I., E cen. Solomon Is., W Pacific Ocean; ab. 3900 ft.; highest point on the island.

Mare Suevicum. See BALTIC SEA.

Mar·eth \ˈmar-əth\. Town, SE Tunisia, N Africa, SSE of Gabès; pop. (1966c) 1400; anchor point at N end of French defense line (**Mareth Line**); held by Germans 1942–43; penetrated by the British Mar. 27, 1943.

Mare Tirreno. See TYRRHENIAN SEA.

Ma·ret·ti·mo \mə-ˈret-i-(ˌ)mō\. One of the Egadi Is. (*q.v.*).

Mar·fa \ˈmär-fə\. City, ⊗ of Presidio co., W Texas, 40 m. E of the Rio Grande; pop. (1970c) 2628; summer resort; livestock and truck farms.

Mar·ga·nets \ˌmär-gə-ˈnets\. Town, Dnepropetrovsk Oblast, Ukrainian S.S.R., U.S.S.R., ab. 60 m. SSW of Dnepropetrovsk; pop. (1967e) 44,000.

Mar·ga·ri·ta \ˌmär-gə-ˈrēt-ə\. Venezuelan island in the Caribbean Sea; 414 sq. m.; pop. (1961e) 75,000; chief town Porlamar; produces tiles and ceramics, footwear, hats; fishing, boatbuilding, tourism; forms major part of the Venezuelan state of Nueva Esparta (island group); discovered by Columbus 1498; settled as center of pearl fishing; frequently raided by pirates; played prominent role in the wars of independence; after 1969 developed as free port with extensive tourist facilities.

Mar·gate \ˈmär-ˌgāt\. City, Broward co., SE Florida; pop. (1970c) 8867.

Margate \ˈmär-ˌgāt, -gət\ *or formerly* **Mer·gate** \ˈmər-gət\. Municipal borough, Kent, SE England, on coast of Isle of Thanet 65 m. E of London; pop. (1971p) 50,145; popular seaside resort; incorporated 1857; suffered considerable damage in World War II.

Margate City \ˌmär-gāt-\. City, Atlantic co., SE New Jersey, on Atlantic Ocean 5 m. WSW of Atlantic City; pop. (1970c) 10,576.

Margelan. See MARGILAN.

Margherita, Mount. See RUWENZORI, MOUNT.

Mar·ghe·ri·ta di Sa·vo·ia \ˌmär-gā-ˈrē-tə-dē-sä-ˈvō-yə\ *or before 1879* **Sa·li·ne di Bar·let·ta** \sə-ˈlē-nā-dē-bär-ˈlāt-tə\. Commune, Foggia prov., Apulia, SE Italy, on Adriatic Sea 31 m. ESE of Foggia; pop. (1968e) 13,445; important sea-salt works.

Mar·gi·lan *also* **Mar·ge·lan** \ˌmär-gə-ˈlän\. Town, Fergana Oblast, E Uzbek S.S.R., U.S.S.R., E of Kokand and adjoining Fergana; pop. (1969e) 75,000; an old city; mosques and bazaars; an agricultural center; most important silk weaving center of the U.S.S.R. Known as **Old Margelan** 1876–1907 to distinguish it from **New Margelan,** now Fergana (*q.v.*).

Mar·go·sa·tu·big \ˌmär-gō-sə-ˈtü-big\. Municipality, SE Zamboanga del Sur prov., Mindanao, Phil., on an inlet of Moro Gulf 87 m. NE of City of Zamboanga.

Mar·gra·ten \ˈmär-ˌgrät-ə(n)\. Locality, Netherlands; largest temporary war cemetery in Europe for U.S. soldiers killed in World War II.

Mar·gum \ˈmär-gəm\ *or* **Mar·gus** \-gəs\. Ancient town, Moesia Superior, at mouth of the Margus (*mod.* Morava) on the Danubius (Danube); scene of battle 285 A.D. in which Carinus defeated Diocletian.

Margus. 1 River, Yugoslavia. See MORAVA 3.
2 Ancient town, Moesia. See MARGUM.

Ma·ría Cle·o·fás \mə-ˌrē-ə-ˌklā-ə-ˈfäs\. Island of the Tres Marías group (*q.v.*) in the Pacific Ocean off W coast of cen. Mexico.

María Ele·na \mə-ˈrē-ə-ā-ˈlā-nə\. Town, Antofagasta prov., N Chile, ab. 100 m. NNE of Antofagasta; pop. (1960c) 9572; nitrate-processing plant.

Ma·ria Island \mə-ˌrī-ə-\. 1 Small island, W Gulf of Carpentaria, Australia, in Limmen Bight; 13 sq. m.
2 Island off SE coast of Tasmania, Australia, N of Tasman Penin.; ab. 37 sq. m.; cement industry.
3 *or* **Hull Island** \ˈhəl-\. Island, NW Tubuai Is., French Polynesia, S Pacific Ocean.

María Ma·dre \mə-ˌrē-ə-ˈmäd-rē\. Island of the Tres Marías group (*q.v.*) in Pacific Ocean off W coast of cen. Mexico.

María Mag·da·le·na \-ˌmäg-də-ˈlen-ə\. Island of the Tres Marías group (*q.v.*) in Pacific Ocean off W coast of cen. Mexico.

Ma·ri·ana Islands \ˌmar-ē-ˈan-ə-, ˌmer-\ *or commonly* **Marianas** \-əz\ *or formerly* **La·drone Islands** \lə-ˈdrōn-\. Island group in W Pacific Ocean, ab. 1500 m. E of the Philippines and 1350 m. S of Honshū I., Japan; lat. 12° to 21°N and long. 144° to 146°E; comprises 15 islands; area 184 sq. m. (including Guam, 393 sq. m.); pop. (1970e; excl. Guam) 12,256; Guam is an unincorporated U.S. territory, the remaining islands constitute part of the U.S. Trust Territory of the Pacific Islands; major islands incl.: Saipan, Tinian, Rota, Pagan, Guguan, Agrihan, Aguijan.

History: Discovered by Magellan 1521; called *Islas de los Ladrones* by ship's crew because natives pilfered articles from the boat; named *Las Marianas* 1668 in honor of Mariana of Austria, widow of Philip IV of Spain; sold (except for Guam) by Spain to Germany 1899 and assigned as Japanese mandate 1919 after World War I; under Japanese developed large sugar production and before 1941 were fortified to become "stationary island aircraft carriers." Saipan and Tinian (see also GUAM) attacked and seized by American forces June 15–Aug. 9, 1944; became part of Trust Territory of the Pacific Islands, assigned to U.S. 1947.

Ma·ria·nao \ˌmär-ē-ə-ˈnaù\. Municipality and city, La Habana prov., W Cuba; munic. pop (1967e) 350,260; residential; army base; produces textiles, paper products, tobacco, pharmaceuticals; founded 1726; developed rapidly after 1900 as suburb of Havana.

Mariana Trench. Ocean trench, W Pacific Ocean, extending from SE of Guam to NW of the Mariana Is.; max. depth (11°21′N, 142°12′E) 36,198 ft.

Mar·i·an·na \ˈmər-ē-ˈān-ə\. 1 City, ⊗ of Lee co., E Arkansas, 12 m. W of Mississippi river SW of Memphis, Tennessee; pop. (1970c) 6196; lumber, clothing; agriculture.
2 City, ⊗ of Jackson co., NW Florida, 62 m. WNW of Tallahassee; pop. (1970c) 6741; limestone quarries, meat-packing plant; peanuts, oranges, corn, sweet potatoes; Chipola Junior Coll. (1947).

Ma·rián·ské Láz·ně \ˌmär-ē-ˌän(t)-skə-ˈläz-nə\ *or Ger.* **Ma·ri·en·bad** \mə-ˈrē-ən-ˌbad, -ˌbät\. Town, Czech S.R., W Czechoslovakia, ab. 20 m. SSW of Karlovy Vary; pop. (1968e) 13,496; mineral springs; ab. 7 m. E is the abbey of Tepl, founded 1193.

Ma·ri·as \mə-ˈrī-əs\. River, NW Montana; 210 m. long; rises in Glacier co., NW Montana, flows E and SE into Missouri river in cen. Chouteau co., N cen. Montana.

Marías, Las. See LAS MARÍAS.

Marias Pass. Mountain pass, NW Montana, in Lewis Range of Continental Divide at SE corner of Glacier National Park; 5215 ft.; discovered 1889; railroad, highway.

Maria–Theresiopel. See SUBOTICA.

Ma·ria·to, Point \-ˌmär-ē-ˈät-(ˌ)ō\. Cape on SW extremity of Azuero Penin., S Panama.

Ma·ría Tri·ni·dad Sán·chez \mə-ˈrē-ə-ˈtri-nə-ˌdad-ˈsän-chez\. Province, Dominican Republic. See table at DOMINICAN REPUBLIC.

Ma·ri Autonomous Soviet Socialist Republic \ˌmär-ē-, *Russ.* ˈmä-ryȯ-\. Autonomous republic, E cen. Russian S.F.S.R., U.S.S.R.; 8958 sq. m.; pop. (1970p) 685,000; ✱ Yoshkar-Ola; level country N of the Volga with lakes and peat bogs and large forest area. Few roads and only one railroad (branch from Kazan to Yoshkar-Ola). Major economic activity is cutting and processing timber; wooden barges, turpentine, and alcohol also produced; flax, potatoes, corn, rye. Predominant ethnic strain is Finno-Ugrian. The Mari speak a Finnish dialect and are akin to the Mordvinians and Permiaks; the Russians call them the Cheremiss. Region annexed in 16th cent., but people were not assimilated. Created an autonomous area 1920 and made a republic 1936.

Ma·ria van Die·men, Cape \-mə-ˌrē-ə-van-ˈdē-mən\. Cape on NW extremity of North I., New Zealand.

Ma·rib \ˈmar-əb\ *or Arab.* **Maʻ·rib** \ˈma-rib\. Ruins of ancient city of the Sabaeans, Yemen (✱ Sanʻa), Arabian Penin., 60 m. ENE of Sanʻa; a chief city of ancient Sheba; a major trading center; esp. famous for its great dam, constructed c. 7th cent. B.C. and destroyed in 6th cent. A.D., an event of importance in early Arab chronicles.

Ma·ri·bo \ˈmär-i-ˌbō\. Town, Storstrøm co., Denmark, located on Lolland I.; pop. (1970e) 5235; sugar refineries.

Ma·ri·bor \ˈmär-i-ˌbȯ(ə)r\ *or Ger.* **Mar·burg** \ˈmär-ˌbù(ə)rg, -ˌbərg\. City, Slovenia, NW Yugoslavia, on Drava river near Austrian border ab. 65 m. NE of Ljubljana; pop. (1971p) 97,167; major industrial city, producing iron and tinware, automobiles, railroad cars; hydroelectric power station; 12th cent. cathedral, 15th cent. castle; present town dates from 10th cent.

Ma·ri·ca·ban \ˌmär-i-kä-ˈbän\. Island off S Batangas prov., Luzon, Phil.; 12 sq. m., ab. 7 m. long; in Verde Island Passage off the point that separates Balayan Bay from Batangas Bay. Its barrios belong to Bauan municipality.

Ma·ri·cao \ˌmär-i-ˈkaù\. Town and municipality, W Puerto Rico; pop. (1970c) 1479 (town), 5936 (munic.); town is inland on highway 11 m. E of Mayagüez.

Ma·ri·co \mə-ˈrē-(ˌ)kō\. River, a headstream of the Limpopo, W Transvaal, Rep. of South Africa; ab. 130 m. long; flows N through fertile Marico valley, producing citrus fruits, wheat, oats, and cotton; chief town Zeerust.

Mar·i·co·pa \ˌmar-ə-ˈkō-pə\. County in Arizona. See table at ARIZONA.

Maricopa Mountains. Small range in SE Maricopa co., SW cen. Arizona.

Ma·rie Byrd Land \mə-ˌrē-ˈbərd-\. Large section of Antarctica E of Ross Ice Shelf and Ross Sea and extending E to Ellsworth Land; lat. ab. 73° to 85°S and long. 100° to 150°W; claimed for the U.S. by Richard E. Byrd 1929.

Marie Ga·lante *or* **Marie–Galante** \-gə-ˈlänt\. Island in E West Indies, a dependency of the French overseas territory of Guadeloupe 16 m. SE of Guadeloupe; 58 sq. m.; pop. (1961c) 16,341; ✱ Grand Bourg; sugar; discovered by Columbus Nov. 3, 1493.

Mariehamn. See MAARIANHAMINA.

Ma·riel \ˌmär-ē-ˈel\. Municipality, Pinar del Río prov., W Cuba; pop. (1967e) 17,800.

Ma·rie·mont \mə-ˈrē-ˌmänt\. Village, Hamilton co., SW Ohio, 8 m. NE of Cincinnati; pop. (1970c) 4550.

Marienbad. See MARIÁNSKÉ LÁZNĚ.

Marienburg *or* **Marienburg in Westpreussen.** See MALBORK.

Ma·ri·en·tal \mä-ˈrē-ən-ˌtäl\. Town, S cen. South-West Africa, on railroad S of Windhoek; pop. (1960c) 3456.

Marienwerder. See KWIDZYŃ.

Mar·ies \'mar-ēz\. County in Missouri. See table at MISSOURI.

Ma·rie·stad \mə-'rē-ˌstäd\. Town, ⊗ of Skaraborg co., S Sweden, on Lake Vänern; pop. (1970e) 16,810.

Mar·i·et·ta \ˌmar-ē-'et-ə, ˌmer-\. 1 Residential city, ⊗ of Cobb co., NW Georgia, 20 m. NW of Atlanta; pop. (1970c) 27,216; major center of aircraft industry; Kennesaw Junior Coll. (1965); U.S. Air Force base; incorporated 1834; in Civil War held by Confederates for a time against Sherman's advance on Atlanta; at Kennesaw Mt. nearby Union forces repulsed in major battle June 27, 1864; has large national cemetery.
2 City, ⊗ of Washington co., SE Ohio, on Ohio river 45 m. SE of Zanesville; pop. (1970c) 16,681; chemicals, plastics, metal alloys, office equipment; oil and gas wells; truck farms; Marietta Coll. (1797); pioneer city in Northwest Territory and oldest permanent settlement in Ohio (1788); developed as river port and shipbuilding center.
3 City, ⊗ of Love co., S Oklahoma, 17 m. S of Ardmore; pop. (1970c) 2013; oil and gas wells.
4 Borough, Lancaster co., SE Pennsylvania, on Susquehanna river 15 m. W of Lancaster; pop. (1970c) 2838.

Ma·rie·ville \mə-'rē-ˌvil\. Town, ⊗ of Rouville co., S Quebec, Canada, 23 m. ESE of Montreal; pop. (1971p) 4521.

Ma·ri·glia·no \ˌmär-ēl-'yän-(ˌ)ō\. Commune, Napoli prov., Campania, S Italy, 11 m. NE of Naples; pop. (1968e) 20,853; castle; damaged by eruptions of Vesuvius 1631 and 1793.

Ma·ri·gnane \ˌmä-rē-'nyän\. Town, Bouches-du-Rhône dept., SE France, ab. 12 m. NW of Marseille; pop. (1968c) 20,044.

Marignano. See MELEGNANO.

Mariguana. See MAYAGUANA.

Mariinsk Waterway. See VOLGA-BALTIC WATERWAY.

Ma·ri·ki·na *also* **Ma·ri·qui·na** \ˌmär-ə-'kē-nə\. 1 River, Rizal prov., Luzon, Phil.; ab. 30 m. long; rises in Montalban reservoir system; flows into Pasig river near Pasig.
2 Municipality, Rizal prov., Luzon, Phil., on Marikina river 5 m. N of Pasig; pop. (1969e) 55,200.

Ma·rí·lia \mə-'rēl-yə\. City, W cen. São Paulo state, SE Brazil, 230 m. NW of São Paulo; munic. pop. (1968e) 107,305.

Ma·rin \mə-'rin\. County in California. See table at CALIFORNIA.

Ma·rín \mä-'rēn\. Seaport commune, Pontevedra prov., NW Spain, on inlet of Atlantic Ocean 6 m. SSW of Pontevedra; pop. (1970p) 19,816; fish-salting works; manufactures textiles.

Ma·ri·na \mə-'rē-nə\. 1 Waterfall in a tributary of the Essequibo river, W Guyana, in the Serra Pacaraima NW of Kaieteur Falls; 500 ft.
2 Island, New Hebrides Is. See ESPÍRITU SANTO 1.

Ma·rin·du·que \ˌmar-ən-'dü-(ˌ)kā, ˌmär-\. Island and province, cen. Phil., separated from S coast of Quezon prov. by Mompog Pass; 370 sq. m.; pop. (1970p) 143,777; ✱ Boac. NW coast borders on Tayabas Bay and S coast on Sibuyan Sea. Covered with hills; hemp (abacá) and coconuts; exports iron ore; chief town in addition to Boac is Santa Cruz. Occupied by Americans Jan. 1945.

Ma·rine City \mə-'rēn-\. City, St. Clair co., SE Michigan, on St. Clair river 16 m. S of Port Huron; pop. (1970c) 4567; summer resort; boatbuilding.

Mar·i·nette \ˌmar-ə-'net, ˌmer-\. 1 County in NE Wisconsin. See table at WISCONSIN.
2 City, its ⊗, on Green Bay 44 m. NNE of Green Bay (city); pop. (1970c) 12,696; summer resort; paper, gloves, aluminum castings, boats, automobile parts, dairy products.

Ma·rin·ga \mə-'riŋ-gə\. River, S cen. Africa; 270 m. long; flows WNW in NW Zaire and joins the Lopori river to form the Lulonga river.

Ma·rin·gá \ˌmar-ən-'gä\. Municipality, Paraná state, S Brazil, 220 m. NW of Curitiba; pop. (1968e) 111,773.

Ma·ri·no \mə-'rē-(ˌ)nō\. Commune, Roma prov., Latium, cen. Italy, 12 m. SE of Rome; pop. (1968e) 41,201.

Mar·i·on \'mer-ē-ən, 'mar-\. 1 Name of counties in seventeen states of the U.S. See tables at ALABAMA, ARKANSAS, FLORIDA, GEORGIA, ILLINOIS, INDIANA, IOWA, KANSAS, KENTUCKY, MISSISSIPPI, MISSOURI, OHIO, OREGON, SOUTH CAROLINA, TENNESSEE, TEXAS, WEST VIRGINIA.
2 City, ⊗ of Perry co., W cen. Alabama, 45 m. SSE of Tuscaloosa; pop. (1970c) 4289; agriculture; Judson Coll. (1838), Marion Institute (1842).
3 City, ⊗ of Crittenden co., E Arkansas; pop. (1970c) 1634.
4 City, ⊗ of Williamson co., S Illinois, 45 m. S of Mt. Vernon; pop. (1970c) 11,724; explosives, batteries; coal mines; fruit farms.
5 City, ⊗ of Grant co., N cen. Indiana, 28 m. NW of Muncie; pop. (1970c) 39,607; automobile parts, plastics, glassware, paper, wire and cable, dairy products; Marion Coll. (1920).
6 City, Linn co., E Iowa, 7 m. ENE of Cedar Rapids; pop. (1970c) 18,028; farm machinery, concrete products, flour; dairy farms.
7 City, ⊗ of Marion co., E cen. Kansas, 48 m. NNE of Wichita; pop. (1970c) 2052; diversified agriculture.
8 City, ⊗ of Crittenden co., W Kentucky, 35 m. ENE of Paducah; pop. (1970c) 3008; fluorspar mines.
9 Town, Plymouth co., SE Massachusetts, on Buzzards Bay 9 m. ENE of New Bedford; pop. (1970c) 3466; summer resort; boatbuilding.
10 Town, ⊗ of McDowell co., W North Carolina, 32 m. E of Asheville; pop. (1970c) 3335; lake resort; cotton textiles, furniture.
11 Industrial city, ⊗ of Marion co., cen. Ohio, 43 m. N of Columbus; pop. (1970c) 38,646; road-building and excavating equipment, home appliances, automobile parts, industrial rubber products, flour; limestone quarries; settled c. 1821; incorporated as village 1830, as city 1890; home of Warren G. Harding, 29th President of the United States.
12 Town, ⊗ of Marion co., E South Carolina, 24 m. E of Florence; pop. (1970c) 7435; clothing, brick; diversified agriculture.
13 Town, ⊗ of Smyth co., SW Virginia, 42 m. ENE of Bristol; pop. (1970c) 8158; furniture, bricks, lumber, flour; limestone quarries; Marion Coll. (1873).

Marion, Lake. See SANTEE DAM.

Marion Reef. Circular coral atoll in Pacific off cen. part of Great Barrier Reef, Queensland, Australia, 19°10′S, 152°17′E.

Mar·i·po·sa \ˌmar-ə-'po-sa, -za\. 1 County in California. See table at CALIFORNIA.
2 Village, its ⊗.

Mariquina. See MARIKINA.

Ma·ris·cal Es·ti·ga·rri·bia \ˌmär-ə-'skäl-ˌes-tə-gär-'ē-bē-ə\. Town, ✱ of Boquerón dept., NW Paraguay, in the Chaco; dist. pop. (1970e) 36,788.

Mariscal Mountain \ˌmar-ə-ˌskäl-\. Peak in Big Bend National Park, S Brewster co., W Texas; 3940 ft.

Ma·rí·ti·ma, Cor·di·lle·ra \ˌkȯrd-ᵊl-'(y)er-ə-mə-'rēt-ə-mə, ˌkȯrd-ē-'er-\. The Cordillera Occidental in Peru. See ANDES.

Maritima Avaticorum. See MARTIGUES.

Maritime Alps. See table at ALPS.

Maritime Atlas. See ATLAS MOUNTAINS.

Maritime Krai. See PRIMORSKI KRAI.

Mar·i·time Province \ˌmar-ə-ˌtīm-\. Former province of the U.S.S.R., comprising the coastal region of Siberia from Bering Strait to Vladivostok, with coastline of ab. 2300 m.; the Russian Far East; organized after region became Russian by Peking Convention 1860; became a part of the Far Eastern Region (*q.v.*) 1920. See PRIMORSKI KRAI.

Maritime Provinces *or often* **The Mar·i·times** \-'mar-ə-ˌtīmz\. The Canadian provinces of New Brunswick, Nova Scotia, and Prince Edward Island.

Ma·ri·tsa \mə-'rēt-sə\ *or Turk.* **Me·riç** \mə-'rēch\ *or Gk.* **Év·ros** \'ev-ˌrȯs\ *or anc.* **He·brus** \'hē-brəs\. River, SE Europe; ab. 300 m. long; flows E in S Bulgaria, then turning S at Edirne, flows as the Meriç bet. Turkey in Europe and Greece to empty into the Aegean Sea; receives the Tundzha at Edirne.

Mariupol. See ZHDANOV.

Ma·ri·ve·les \ˌmär-ə-ˈvā-ləs\. Municipality at S end of Bataan, Luzon, Phil., WNW of Corregidor I., on **Mariveles Bay** (inlet of North Channel); pop. (1969e) 12,500; scene of severe fighting in Bataan campaign Apr. 1942; retaken by American forces Feb. 15, 1945.

Mariveles, Mount. Mountain, an extinct volcano, at S end of Zambales Mts. at S end of Bataan Penin., Luzon, Phil.; 4444 ft.; highest peak on Bataan.

Mariyampole. See KAPSUKAS.

Mark \ˈmärk\. Medieval county, now part of North Rhine-Westphalia, West Germany; belonged to Brandenburg in 17th cent.

Mar·ka·gunt Plateau \ˈmär-kə-ˌgənt-\. Elevated region, SW Utah, in which is located Cedar Breaks National Monument (see UNITED STATES, *National Monuments).*

Marked Tree \ˈmärk(t)-ˈtrē\. City, Poinsett co., NE Arkansas, at confluence of St. Francis and Little rivers, 26 m. SE of Jonesboro; pop. (1970c) 3208; agriculture.

Mar·ken \ˈmär-kə(n)\. Commune, North Holland prov., W Netherlands, in SW part of IJsselmeer off Monnikendam and ab. 10 m. NE of Amsterdam; pop. (1970e) 1865; will eventually be in reclaimed SW polder; has 7 small hamlets frequently visited by tourists; connected since 1959 with mainland by dike carrying a highway.

Mar·ket Har·bor·ough \ˌmär-ket-ˈhär-b(ə-)rə\. Urban district, Leicestershire, cen. England, on the Welland 15 m. SE of Leicester; pop. (1971p) 14,527; textiles, farm implements, rubber goods.

Mark·ham \ˈmär kəm\. 1 Village, Cook co., NE Illinois, S suburb of Chicago; pop. (1970c) 15,987.

2 Town, York co., SE Ontario, Canada, 17 m. NE of Toronto; pop. (1971p) 36,636; diversified agriculture; flour and feed mills.

3 River, E New Guinea I., Papua New Guinea; rises in mountains in NE, flows S and SE to Huon Gulf at Lae; an upper tributary is the Bulolo (*q.v.*); its valley scene of fighting during campaign for Lae 1943.

Markham, Mount. Peak in Victoria Land, Antarctica, bet. Mt. Albert Markham and Mt. Kirkpatrick, 82°51′S, 161°21′E; 14,275 ft.

Markirch. See SAINTE-MARIE-AUX-MINES.

Mark·klee·berg \ˈmärk-lā-ˌbərg, -ˌbu̇(ə)rg\. City, Leipzig dist., East Germany, 5 m. S of Leipzig; pop. (1970e) 22,-220; metalworking, candy, textiles, food processing.

Mark·lee·ville \ˈmärk-lē-ˌvil\. Town, ⊗ of Alpine co., E California.

Marks \ˈmärks\. Town, ⊗ of Quitman co., NW Mississippi; pop. (1970c) 2609; chemicals; agriculture.

Marks \ˈmärks\ *or Ger.* **Marx·stadt** \ˌmärk(s)-ˌs(h)tät\ *or formerly* **Eka·te·ri·nen·stadt** \i-ˌkat-ə-ˌrē-nən-ˈs(h)tät\ *also* **Ka·tha·ri·nen·stadt** \ˌkät-\ *or* **Ye·ka·te·ri·nen·shtadt** \yi-ˌkat-\. Town, Saratov Oblast, Russian S.F.S.R., U.S.S.R., on left bank of Volga 35 m. NNE of Saratov; pop. (1967e) 16,000; center of agricultural area; formerly in N Volga German Autonomous Socialist Republic. Founded 1795; originally named after Empress Catherine II, renamed 1922 in honor of Karl Marx.

Marks·ville \ˈmärks-ˌvil\. Town, ⊗ of Avoyelles parish, cen. Louisiana; pop. (1970c) 4519; cotton.

Marl \ˈmär(ə)l\. City, North Rhine-Westphalia, West Germany, N of Gelsenkirchen; pop. (1969e) 75,905; coal and zinc mines; chemicals; made city 1936.

Marl·boro \ˈmärl-ˌbər-ə, -ˌbə-rə\. 1 County in South Carolina. See table at SOUTH CAROLINA.

2 City, Massachusetts. See MARLBOROUGH 2.

Marl·bor·ough \ˈmärl-ˌbər-ə, -ˌbə-rə\. 1 Town, Hartford co., N Connecticut, 13 m. SE of Hartford; pop. (1970c) 2991.

2 *also* **Marl·boro.** City, Middlesex co., NE Massachusetts, 13 m. ENE of Worcester; pop. (1970c) 27,936; footwear, paper, wire and foundry products; dairy farms.

Marles–les–Mines \ˌmär-lā-ˈmēn\. Commune, Pas-de-Calais dept., N France, 19 m. NW of Arras; pop. (1962c) 11,119; coal mines.

Mar·lin \ˈmar-lən\. City and health resort, ⊗ of Falls co., cen. Texas, 20 m. SSE of Waco; pop. (1970c) 6351; health resort; agriculture.

Mar·lin·ton \ˈmär-lən-tən\. Town, ⊗ of Pocahontas co., E cen. West Virginia; pop. (1970c) 1286.

Mar·low \ˈmär-(ˌ)lō\. 1 City, Stephens co., S Oklahoma, 26 m. E of Lawton; pop. (1970c) 3995; feed mill; watermelons.

2 Urban district, Buckinghamshire, SE cen. England, on the Thames 30 m. W of London; pop. (1971p) 11,706.

Mar·ly–le–Roi \(ˌ)mär-ˌlē-lə-ˈrwä\. Suburb of Versailles, Yvelines dept., N France; pop. (1969e) 11,925; castle ruins.

Mar·mande \mär-ˈmäⁿd\ *or anc.* **Mar·man·da** \mär-ˈman-də\. Commune, Lot-et-Garonne dept., SW France, on Garonne river 32 m. NW of Agen; pop. (1968c) 15,559.

Mar·ma·ra \ˈmär-mə-rə\ *or* **Mar·mo·ra** \ˈmär-mə-rə\ *or anc.* **Proc·on·ne·sus** \ˌpräk-ə-ˈnē-səs\. Island in the Sea of Marmara; 11 m. long; area 50 sq. m.

Marmara, Sea of *or Turk.* **Marmara De·ni·zi** \ˈmär-mə-ˌrä-ˌden-i-ˈzē\ *or anc.* **Pro·pon·tis** \prō-ˈpän-təs\. Sea in NW Turkey, bet. Europe and Asia; 175 m. long; area 4429 sq. m.; max. depth over 4000 ft.; connected with the Black Sea through the Bosporus, and with the Aegean Sea through the Dardanelles. Has several islands, esp. Marmara in the W and Kızıl Is. near İstanbul, a large promontory, Kapıdağı (Cyzicus), on the S coast, and two long inlets on the E.

Mar·mar·i·ca \mär-ˈmar-i-kə\. Desert plateau region of N Africa along the Mediterranean Sea bet. ancient Cyrenaica and Egypt; by some authorities extended into NW Egypt nearly to Alexandria; in ancient times scene of conflict in many wars by Romans, Egyptians, Libyans, Arabs. In modern times the name was given by Italians to the NE section of Cyrenaica; scene in World War II of much fighting 1942–43.

Mar Me·nor *or* **Mar·me·nor** \ˌmär-mə-ˈnȯ(ə)r\. Lagoon on SE coast of Spain, extending N from Cape of Palos ab. 14 m.; greatest width ab. 6 m.

Mar·mo·la·da \ˌmär-mə-ˈläd-ə\. Highest peak in the Dolomites, NE Italy, bet. Veneto and Trentino-Alto Adige; 10,-965 ft.

Marmora. See MARMARA.

Marmore, Cascata delle. See VELINO.

Marne \ˈmärn\ *or anc.* **Mat·ro·na** \ˈma-trə-nə\. River, NE France; 326 m. long; rises in NE cen. France, flows NW and W into Seine river at Charenton-le-Pont, near Paris; navigable for ab. 220 m.; scene of battles in World War I: Sept. 6–9, 1914 in which the Allies were victorious; and July 15–Aug. 4, 1918 in which after successes of Germans around Reims, the French and Americans made a successful counterattack at Château-Thierry under Foch, resulting in German defeat. In World War II reached by Americans Aug. 27–28, 1944.

Marne. Departments of NE France: **Haute–Marne** and **Marne.** See table at FRANCE.

Maroc. See MOROCCO 1.

Ma·ro·ni \mə-ˈrō-nē\ *or Du.* **Ma·ro·wij·ne** \ˌmär-ə-ˈvī-nə\. River, N South America; ab. 450 m. long; with its tributary, the Itany, forms boundary bet. Surinam and French Guiana; empties into Atlantic Ocean.

Ma·roon Peak \mə-ˈrün-\. Mountain, Pitkin co., W cen. Colorado; 14,156 ft.

Maros. See MUREŞUL.

Maros–Vásárhely. See TÎRGU-MUREŞ.

Ma·roua \mə-ˈrü-ə\. Town, N Cameroon; pop. (1970e) 31,-000.

Ma·ro·vo \mə-ˈrō-(ˌ)vō\. Lagoon, Solomon Islands. See NEW GEORGIA.

Marowijne. See MARONI.

Mar·pi Point \ˌmär-pē-\. Northern point of Saipan I., Mariana Is., W Pacific Ocean.

Mar·ple \ˈmär-pəl\. **1** Urban township, Delaware co., SE Pennsylvania, W suburb of Chester; pop. (1970c) 25,040.
2 Urban district, Cheshire, NW England, on the Goyt 9 m. SE of Manchester; pop. (1971p) 23,217.

Mar·que·sas Islands \mär-ˈkā-səz-\ *also* **Mar·que·zas** \-zəz\ *or Fr.* **Îles Mar·quises** \ēl-mär-ˈkēz\. Group of ten islands of French Polynesia, S Pacific Ocean, bet. ab. lat. 8° to 11°S and long. 140°W, N of Tuamotu Archipelago and 2000 m. SSE of Honolulu; 480 sq. m.; ✱ Hakapehi on Nuku Hiva I. The more important islands are in three groups: Nuku Hiva, Ua Pu, and Ua Huka in the center; Hiva Oa, Tahuata, and Fatu Hiva in the SE, and the small islands of Eïao and Hatutu in the NW. Rocky and mountainous islands of volcanic origin; highest point on Hiva Oa 4134 ft.; have fertile and well-watered valleys. First discovered by Âlvaro de Mendaña in 1595; rediscovered by Capt. Cook 1774; taken by France 1842; French settlement not complete until after 1870.

Marquesas Keys \mär-ˌkēz-əz-\. Small group of islands W of the SW end of Florida Keys, N of entrance to Gulf of Mexico, a part of Monroe co., Florida.

Mar·quette \mär-ˈket\. **1** Counties in two states of the U.S. See tables at MICHIGAN and WISCONSIN.
2 City, ⊗ of Marquette co., N Michigan penin., on Lake Superior; pop. (1970c) 21,967; ships iron ore; chemicals, foundry products, mining machinery; Northern Michigan Univ. (1899); founded 1849; incorporated as village 1859, city 1871.

Mar·ra·kech *or* **Mar·ra·kesh** *also* **Ma·ra·kesh** \mə-ˈräk-ish, ˌmar-ə-ˈkesh\ *or formerly* **Mo·roc·co** \mə-ˈräk-(ˌ)ō\. City, W cen. Morocco, NW Africa; pop. (1970e) 305,000; popular tourist resort; situated in N foothills of W end of the Grand Atlas; many mosques, fountains; palace; modern European town founded 1913. Founded 1062 by Yusuf ibn-Tashfin as African capital of Almoravides dynasty; later (1147) also capital of the Almohades; in medieval period one of great cities of Islam; taken by French Sept. 7, 1912.

Mar·rick·ville \ˈmar-ik-ˌvil\. Municipality, E New South Wales, SE Australia, S suburb of Sydney; pop. (1966c) 76,763.

Marruecos. See MOROCCO 1.

Mar·sa·la \mär-ˈsäl-ə\ *or anc.* **Lil·y·bae·um** \ˌlil-i-ˈbē-əm\. Seaport, Trapani prov., Sicily, Italy, on Mediterranean 18 m. S of Trapani; pop. (1968e) 82,724; exports wine, grain, salt; cathedral, theater, walls, catacombs; Garibaldi and volunteer forces landed here 1860.

Marsan. See MONT-DE-MARSAN.

Mar·scia·no \mär-ˈshän-(ˌ)ō\. Commune, Perugia prov., Umbria, cen. Italy, 15 m. S of Perugia; pop. (1968e) 15,825.

Mars Diep \ˈmärz-ˈdēp\. Strait separating island of Texel from mainland of N North Holland prov., W Netherlands; ab. 2 m. wide; outlet of Wadden Zee to North Sea.

Mar·seilles \mär-ˈsālz\. **1** City, La Salle co., N Illinois, on Illinois river 8 m. E of Ottawa; pop. (1970c) 4320; paper products; foundry; grain and livestock farms.
2 *or Fr.* **Mar·seille** \mȧr-ˈsaʸ\ *or anc.* **Mas·si·lia** \mə-ˈsil-ē-ə\. Seaport, ✱ of Bouches-du-Rhône dept., SE France, on NE shore of Gulf of Lions 98 m. WSW of Nice; pop. (1968c) 889,028; archiepiscopal see; military and naval station; major commercial seaport, exporting oil, construction materials, food products, automobiles, wine, metalwork; manufactures soap, sugar, building materials, glass, chemicals, oil refining, shipbuilding, fishing; modern Byzantine cathedral (1893), Romanesque church of Notre Dame de la Garde, Renaissance-style Palais des Arts de Longchamps, mint.

History: Ancient Massilia colonized by Phocaeans (Ionian Greeks) c. 600 B.C.; developed trade up the Rhone valley and in the Mediterranean; planted several colonies on Gallic and Spanish coasts; aided by Rome in conflict with Carthage; deprived of its colonies when Caesar took it 49 B.C.; early seat of Christian bishopric; overrun by Visigoths, Ostrogoths, and Franks, 5th and 6th cents.; in 879 belonged to kingdom of Arles, and in 10th cent. to Provence; became independent 13th cent.; passed to French crown 1481; became important again in 19th cent. with development of French colonial empire and opening of Suez Canal. In World War II occupied by Germans Nov. 1942–Aug. 1944.

Mar·shall \ˈmär-shəl\. **1** Counties in twelve states of U.S. See tables at ALABAMA, ILLINOIS, INDIANA, IOWA, KANSAS, KENTUCKY, MINNESOTA, MISSISSIPPI, OKLAHOMA, SOUTH DAKOTA, TENNESSEE, WEST VIRGINIA.
2 City, ⊗ of Searcy co., N Arkansas; pop. (1970c) 1397.
3 City, ⊗ of Clark co., E Illinois, 53 m. S of Danville; pop. (1970c) 3468; oil refinery.
4 City, ⊗ of Calhoun co., S Michigan, 12 m. ESE of Battle Creek; pop. (1970c) 7253; paint, feed, automobile parts; onions, livestock.
5 City, ⊗ of Lyon co., SW Minnesota, 35 m. S of Montevideo; pop. (1970c) 9886; dairy products; diversified agriculture; Southwest Minnesota State Coll. (1963).
6 City, ⊗ of Saline co., W cen. Missouri, 28 m. N of Sedalia; pop. (1970c) 12,051; shoes, dairy products; Missouri Valley Coll. (1888).
7 Town, ⊗ of Madison co., W North Carolina, 15 m. NNW of Asheville; pop. (1970c) 982; pine, oak timber.
8 City, ⊗ of Harrison co., NE Texas, 54 m. ENE of Tyler; pop. (1970c) 22,937; manufactures wood pulp, car wheels, foundry products, brick and tile, pottery; oil, gas, lignite, clay deposits nearby; in resort region. Wiley Coll. (1873), East Texas Baptist Coll. (1914). Settled 1841; incorp. as city 1848; served (in Texas) as temporary active capital of Missouri in administration of Confederate affairs during the Civil War.
9 Coastal town, W Liberia, W Africa, 30 m. SE of Monrovia; port for shipping rubber.

Marshall Islands. Group of 32 atolls and more than 867 reefs in W Pacific Ocean, E of the Caroline Is. and NNW of the Gilbert Is., 5°30′ to 15°N lat. and 161° to 172°E long.; comprise the Ratak and Ralik chains of islands; land area 69 sq. m., including lagoons 4500 sq. m.; pop. (1970e) 20,206.

History: Probably first sighted by Spanish navigator 1529; explored by English captains Gilbert and Marshall 1788; for next century uncontrolled; claimed by Germany 1885 and all rights to islands purchased by her from Spain 1899; invaded and seized by Japan 1914 and granted to Japan as mandate 1920; held with absolute sovereignty by Japan from 1935; invaded Jan.–Feb. 1944 by Americans, who seized Kwajalein and Eniwetok; became part of U.S. Trust Territory of the Pacific Islands 1947.

Mar·shall·town \ˈmär-shəl-ˌtau̇n\. City, ⊗ of Marshall co., cen. Iowa, 48 m. NE of Des Moines; pop. (1970c) 26,219; wholesale trade center; furnaces, valves, die castings, canned goods; Marshalltown Community Coll. (1927); settled 1851; incorporated 1863.

Marsh·field \ˈmärsh-ˌfēld\. **1** Town, Plymouth co., SE Massachusetts, 15 m. E of Brockton; pop. (1970c) 15,223; residence of Daniel Webster during latter part of his life.
2 City, ⊗ of Webster co., S Missouri, 24 m. ENE of Springfield; pop. (1970c) 2961; dairy products; diversified agriculture.
3 City, Oregon. See COOS BAY 2.
4 City, Marathon and Wood cos., cen. Wisconsin, 25 m. NW of Wisconsin Rapids; pop. (1970c) 15,619; shoes, cheese, mobile homes, veneers; brewery; dairy and poultry farms.

Mars Hill \ˈmärz-\. Isolated mountain, Aroostook co., N Maine, near E Maine boundary; 1660 ft.

Mars' Hill. See AREOPAGUS.

Marsh Island \ˈmärsh-\. Island off S coast of Louisiana, at entrance to Vermilion Bay; a game preserve.

Marsh Peak. Mountain in N Uintah co., E Utah; 12,219 ft.

Marsivan. See MERZIFON.

Mars–la–Tour \ˌmärs-lə-ˈtu̇(ə)r\. Village, Meurthe-et-Moselle dept., NE France, SW of Metz; pop. (1962c) 780; with Vionville scene of battle Aug. 16, 1870 in which French under Marshal Bazaine were defeated by the Prussians.

Mars·ton Moor \ˌmär-stən-\. Moor, N England, 7 m. W of York, in English Civil War scene of battle July 2, 1644 in which Parliamentarians under Fairfax, Cromwell, and Leslie defeated Royalists under Prince Rupert and Goring.

Mart \ˈmärt\. City, McLennan co., cen. Texas, 12 m. E of Waco; pop. (1970c) 2183; cannery, grain elevators; cotton.

Mar·ta \ˈmär-(ˌ)tä\. River, W cen. Italy; ab. 25 m. long; flows from Lake Bolsena into the N Tyrrhenian Sea.

Mar·ta·ban \ˌmärt-ə-ˈbän, -ˈban\. Town, SE Lower Burma, at mouth of the Salween river opp. Moulmein.

Martaban, Gulf of. Inlet of Bay of Bengal on coast of Lower Burma, bet. 16° and 17°N lat. and 96° and 98°E long.; receives waters of the Salween river and the Sittang river.

Mar·ta·pu·ra *or Du.* **Mar·ta·poe·ra** \ˌmärt-ə-ˈpu̇r-ə\. River, SE Borneo, Indonesia; ab. 100 m. long; an E tributary of the Barito, joining it just below Bandjarmasin.

Marthasville. See ATLANTA 1.

Mar·tha's Vine·yard \ˌmär-thəz-ˈvin-yərd\. Island in Atlantic Ocean off SW coast of Cape Cod, SE Massachusetts, bet. Elizabeth Is. to the W and Nantucket to the E; part of Dukes co., Mass.; 108 sq. m.; ab. 20 m. long, 2 to 10 m. wide; summer resort; chief town Edgartown, on E coast.

Mar·tí \mär-ˈtē\. Municipality and town, Matanzas prov., W cen. Cuba, near N coast 19 m. E of Cárdenas; munic. pop. (1967e) 17,520.

Mar·tigues \ˌmär-ˈtēg\ *or* **Les Martigues** \lā-\ *or anc.* **Ma·rit·i·ma Avat·i·co·rum** \mə-ˈrit-ə-mə-ə-ˌvat-ə-ˈkōr-ˈəm\. Commune, Bouches-du-Rhône dept., SE France, on Mediterranean 18 m. NW of Marseilles; pop. (1968c) 27,-945; manufactures chemicals. Important during Middle Ages; formerly important fishing port.

Mar·tin \ˈmärt-ᵊn\. **1** Name of counties in six states of the U.S. See tables at FLORIDA, INDIANA, KENTUCKY, MINNESOTA, NORTH CAROLINA, TEXAS.

2 City, ⊗ of Bennett co., S South Dakota; pop. (1970c) 1248; flax, livestock.

3 City, Weakley co., NW Tennessee, 31 m. W of Paris; pop. (1970c) 7781; clothing, flour, preservatives, dairy products; strawberries.

4 Town, Slovak S.R., E cen. Czechoslovakia; pop. (1968e) 31,585.

Martinach. See MARTIGNY.

Mar·ti·na Fran·ca \mär-ˌtē-nə-ˈfräŋ-kə\. Commune, Taranto prov., Apulia, SE Italy, 17 m. NNE of Taranto; pop. (1968e) 38,771; 17th cent. baroque palace.

Martin Dam. Dam across Tallapoosa river, E cen. Alabama; height 168 ft.; completed 1926; impounds water for power, forming **Martin Lake** in Elmore, Tallapoosa, and Coosa cos.

Mar·ti·nez \mär-ˈtē-nəs\. Industrial city, ⊗ of Contra Costa co., W California, on Suisun Bay 18 m. NE of Oakland; pop. (1970c) 16,506; copper smelters, oil refinery, wineries; John F. Kennedy Univ. (1964); vertical lift bridge across Suisan Bay (horizontal clearance 291.5 ft.); settled 1849.

Mar·tí·nez de la To·rre \mär-ˈtē-nəs-də-lä-ˈtōr-rē\. Municipality, Veracruz state, Mexico, 87 m. NW of Veracruz; pop. (1970p) 62,707; sugar processing; livestock raising; corn, sugarcane, mangoes, coffee.

Martin Gar·cía \mär-ˌtēn-gär-ˈsē-ə\. Island in the mouth of the Río de la Plata, off SW coast of Uruguay; claimed by both Argentina and Uruguay.

Mar·ti·nique \ˌmärt-ᵊn-ˈēk\. Island, Windward Is., E West Indies; 425 sq. m.; pop. (1961e) 292,062; ✱ Fort-de-France; constitutes a department of France; mountainous, volcano of Mt. Pelée (*q.v.*) in N and Carbet (3929 ft.) in NW cen. part; has many rivers; large inlet, Fort-de-France Bay, on N shore of which is the capital Fort-de-France. Exports sugar (chief industry), rum, bananas. Discovered by Columbus 1502; settled by French 1635; passed to French crown 1674; attacked by Dutch and British in 17th cent.; captured by Rodney 1762 but restored; again occupied by British 1794–1802 and 1809–1814; by French constitution of 1946 made an overseas department of France. Birthplace of Empress Josephine.

Mar·tin·puich \ˌmȧr-taⁿ-ˈpwēsh\. Village, Pas-de-Calais dept., N France, 6 m. NE of Albert; pop. (1962c) 289; battle Sept. 15, 1916.

Mar·tins·burg \ˈmärt-ᵊnz-ˌbərg\. Industrial city, ⊗ of Berkeley co., NE West Virginia, in E panhandle; pop. (1970c) 14,626; hosiery, building materials, cement, dynamite; ships fruit. Chartered as town 1778, as city c. 1859; important base in Shenandoah valley military operations (1861–63) during Civil War.

Mar·tins Ferry \ˌmärt-ᵊnz-\. City, Belmont co., E Ohio, on Ohio river 19 m. S of Steubenville; pop. (1970c) 10,757; steel products, glass, furniture; coal mines.

Mar·tins·ville \ˈmärt-ᵊnz-ˌvil\. **1** City, ⊗ of Morgan co., cen. Indiana, 28 m. SW of Indianapolis; pop. (1970c) 9273; health resort; furniture, aircraft parts; grain farms.

2 Industrial city, ⊗ of Henry co., S Virginia, but politically independent, 32 m. W of Danville; 10 sq. m.; pop. (1970c) 19,653; furniture, clothing, lumber; diversified agriculture; founded 1793.

Mar·ton \ˈmärt-ᵊn\. Borough, S North I., New Zealand, 90 m. NNE of Wellington; pop. (1970e) 4860.

Mar·tos \ˈmärt-əs\. Commune, Jaén prov., S Spain, 14 m. SW of Jaén; pop. (1970p) 21,493; mineral baths; manufactures textiles, flour, pottery; stock raising.

Mar·tre, Lac la \ˌläk-lə-ˈmär-trə\. Lake, S cen. Mackenzie dist., Northwest Territories, Canada; 685 sq. m.; its outlet flows SE to Great Slave Lake.

Ma·ru·du Bay \mə-ˌrüd-ü-\. Inlet, N Sabah, Malaysia, S of Balabac Strait.

Ma·ru·ga·me \ˌmär-ü-ˈgäm-(ˌ)ā\. City, Kagawa prefecture, Shikoku I., Japan, on N coast on Inland Sea WSW of Takamatsu; pop. (1970c) 59,214.

Ma·ru·téa \ˌmär-ü-ˈtā-ə\. Large atoll of the Tuamotu Archipelago, French Polynesia, S Pacific Ocean, ab. 125 m. E of Fakarava.

Mar·vine, Mount \-ˈmär-vən\. Peak, Sevier co., cen. Utah; 11,600 ft.

Marwar. See JODHPUR.

Marxstadt. See MARKS.

Ma·ry \mä-ˈrē\ *or formerly* **Merv** \ˈme(ə)rv\. Town, Turkmen S.S.R., U.S.S.R., in an oasis on Murghab river 180 m. E of Ashkhabad; pop. (1969e) 61,000; center of rich cotton-producing region.

History: A town of great antiquity, in Hindu, Parsi, and Arab tradition believed to be the ancient Paradise, hence the original home (Mouru) of the Aryan families and hence of the human race; center of a province (Margiana) of ancient kingdoms; under Arabs (646–874); overrun by Turks 1040, and conquered by Mongols 1221; occupied by Russians 1883.

Mar·y·bor·ough \ˈmer-ē-ˌbər-ə, ˈmar-, -ˌbə-rə, -b(ə-)rə\. **1** Town, SE Queensland, Australia, on Mary river 140 m. N of Brisbane; pop. (1968e) 19,850; markets coal, cattle, sheep, grains, and sugar; foundries, railroad shops.

2 *or* **Port Laoigh·i·se** \-ˈlā-ə-shə\. Town, ⊗ of co. Laoighis, cen. Eire, on Triogue river; pop. (1966c) 3434; remnant of old castle.

Mary Es·ther \ˌmer-ē-ˈes-tər, ˌmar-ē-\. Town, Okaloosa co., NW Florida, 27 m. E of Pensacola; pop. (1970c) 3192.

Mary Island. See CANTON ISLAND.

Mar·y·land \ˈmer-ə-lənd\. **1** A middle Atlantic state of U.S.A., bounded on N by Pennsylvania, on E by Delaware and the Atlantic Ocean, on S by Virginia and West Virginia, and on W by West Virginia; 42d state in area, 10,577 sq. m. (land area 9881 sq. m.); 18th state in population, (1970c) 3,922,399; ✱ Annapolis; one of the original states of the Union, the 7th to ratify the Federal Constitution (Apr. 28, 1788).

Nicknames: Old Line State; Cockade State. *State flower:* Black-eyed Susan. *Motto:* Fatti Maschii, Parole Femine (Manly Deeds, Feminine Words). *Rivers:* Potomac, forming S boundary; Patuxent, flowing SE into Chesapeake Bay; Susquehanna, flowing across NE corner into headwaters of Chesapeake Bay. *Highest point:* Backbone Mt., 3360 ft., in Garrett co. *Chief products:* Dairy products, tobacco; livestock; fishing; manufacturing: primary metals, transportation equipment, chemicals, apparel. *Chief cities:* Baltimore, Rockville, Hagerstown, Bowie, Cumberland. See *Table of States* at UNITED STATES. Divided into the following 23 counties (for pronunciation of their names, see their individual entries):

NAME	LOCATION	AREA[1] (sq. m.)	POP. (1970c)	CO. SEAT
Allegany	NW	428	84,044	Cumberland
Anne Arundel	cen.	423	297,539	Annapolis
Baltimore	N	598[2]	621,871	Towson
Baltimore city[3]		75	905,759	
Calvert	S	217	20,682	Prince Frederick
Caroline	E	321	19,781	Denton
Carroll	N	456	69,006	Westminster
Cecil	NE corner	362	53,291	Elkton
Charles	S	459	47,678	La Plata
Dorchester	SE	594	29,405	Cambridge
Frederick	N	665	84,927	Frederick
Garrett	NW corner	659	21,476	Oakland
Harford	NE	453	115,378	Bel Air
Howard	cen.	251	62,394	Ellicott City
Kent	NE	281	16,146	Chestertown
Montgomery	cen.	496	522,809	Rockville
Prince Georges	S cen.	484	661,192	Upper Marlboro
Queen Annes	E	375	18,422	Centreville
Saint Marys	S	373	47,388	Leonardtown
Somerset	SE	339	18,924	Princess Anne
Talbot	E	261	23,682	Easton
Washington	N	459	103,829	Hagerstown
Wicomico	SE	381	54,236	Salisbury
Worcester	SE; coastal	479	24,442	Snow Hill

[1] Area = land area.
[2] Exclusive of city of Baltimore which is administratively independent of the county.
[3] Administratively independent of Baltimore co. and has itself the status of a county.

History: Granted to George Calvert (Lord Baltimore) as proprietary colony 1632; first American colony to achieve religious freedom; first settled at St. Marys 1634, which was its capital 1634–94; a royal colony 1689–1715; its boundary with Pennsylvania, in dispute from 1681, settled by drawing of Mason and Dixon's Line 1763–69; first constitutional convention Aug. 14–Nov. 11, 1776; adopted Articles of Confederation 1781; ceded territory for District of Columbia (*q.v.*); invaded by Confederate forces 1862; abolished slavery 1864; adopted present constitution 1867. See BALTIMORE.

2 The southernmost county of Liberia, W Africa; 1675 sq. m.; pop. (1967e) 67,809; set up as an independent African state 1833 by Negroes from the United States; annexed to Liberia 1857.

Mar·y·port \ˈme(ə)r-ē-ˌpō(ə)rt, ˈma(ə)r-ē-, -ˌpȯ(ə)rt\. Urban district, Cumberland, NW England, on Solway Firth at mouth of the Ellen, 28 m. SW of Carlisle; pop. (1971p) 11,615.

Mar·ys·vale Peak \ˌme(ə)r-ēz-ˌvāl-, ˌma(ə)r-ēz-\. Mountain, Piute co., S cen. Utah; 10,943 ft.

Mar·ys·ville \ˈme(ə)r-ēz-ˌvil, ˈma(ə)r-ēz-\. **1** City, ⊗ of Yuba co., N cen. California, 42 m. N of Sacramento; pop. (1970c) 9353; fruit canning; fruit, dairy, and livestock farms; Yuba Coll. (1927).

2 City, ⊗ of Marshall co., NE Kansas, 45 m. N of Manhattan on Big Blue river; pop. (1970c) 3588; radar equipment; poultry-packing plant; diversified agriculture.

3 City, St. Clair co., SE Michigan, on St. Clair river 5 m. S of Port Huron; pop. (1970c) 5610.

4 Village, ⊗ of Union co., Ohio, 27 m. NW of Columbus; pop. (1970c) 5744; brass goods, plastics, lumber; dairy and grain farms.

5 Borough, Perry co., S cen. Pennsylvania, on Susquehanna river 8 m. N of Harrisburg; pop. (1970c) 2328.

6 Town, Snohomish co., NW cen. Washington, on Puget Sound 5 m. N of Everett; pop. (1970c) 4343; boats, shingles, leather goods; dairy farms.

7 Town, York co., SW New Brunswick, Canada, 5 m. N of Fredericton; pop. (1966c) 3572.

Maryūt, Buḥrayat. See MAREOTIS, LAKE.

Mar·y·ville \ˈmar-i-vəl, ˈmer-, -ˌvil\. **1** City, ⊗ of Nodaway co., NW Missouri, 42 m. N of St. Joseph; pop. (1970c) 9970; tools, cement blocks; diversified agriculture; Northwest Missouri State Coll. (1905).

2 City, ⊗ of Blount co., E Tennessee, near Great Smoky Mts. National Park 15 m. S of Knoxville; pop. (1970c) 13,808; lumber, electronic components, fabricated aluminum; limestone quarries; tobacco, corn; Maryville Coll. (1819).

Ma·sa·da \mə-ˈsäd-ə\. Fortified hill on W shore of Dead Sea at S end, SE Israel; fortifications constructed 1st cent. B.C.; in 72–73 A.D. scene of final stand of Jews against Romans (defenders killed themselves rather than surrender).

Más Afue·ra \ˌmäs-ə-ˈfwer-ə\ *or* **Ale·jan·dro Sel·kirk** \ˌäl-i-k̲än-drō-ˈsel-ˌkirk\. An island of the Juan Fernández group. See JUAN FERNÁNDEZ.

Ma·san \ˈmäs-ˌän\ *or formerly* **Ma·sam·po** \mə-ˈsäm-(ˌ)pō\. Seaport city, South Kyŏngsang prov., South Korea, at head of an inlet of Western Channel 26 m. W of Pusan; pop. (1970e) 190,992; a commercial and industrial center; opened to foreign trade 1899.

Masandam, Ras. See MUSANDAM, CAPE.

Masanutton Mountain. See MASSANUTTEN MOUNTAIN.

Más a Tier·ra \ˌmäs-ə-tē-ˈer-ə\ *or* **Ro·bin·son Cru·soe Island** \ˌräb-ən-sən-ˈkrü-ˌsō-\. An island of the Juan Fernández group. See JUAN FERNÁNDEZ.

Ma·sa·ya \mə-ˈsä-yə, -ˈsī-ə\. **1** Department of SW Nicaragua. See table at NICARAGUA.

2 Town, its ✱; pop. (1970e) 49,691; 5th largest city in Nicaragua; center of rich agricultural region; produces cigars, soap, leather goods, footwear, hats.

Mas·ba·te \mäs-ˈbät-ē\. **1** Island and province in Visayan Is., cen. Phil., S of SE Luzon; 1563 sq. m.; pop. (1970p) 492,868; ✱ Masbate. Formerly a subprovince of Sorsogon from which it is separated by Ticao Pass and Ticao I.; on the E borders on Samar Sea, on the S on Visayan Sea, and on the W on Sibuyan Sea; separated from NE Panay by Jintotolo Channel. Covered with mountains ranging from 1200 to 2000 ft. As province includes Burias I. and Ticao I. Produces sugarcane, cotton, hemp, and some rice; noted for its cattle and horses. Chief towns Masbate, Cataingan, Aroroy, Milagros, Dimasalang.

History: Explored by Spaniards in latter half of 16th cent.; long a part of Albay prov.; made separate comandancia 1846; under Americans received civil government Mar. 1901 and made subprovince of Sorsogon; created a province 1939; invaded by Americans Apr. 1945.

2 Municipality, ✱ of Masbate prov., Phil., on NE coast of Masbate I. opp. Ticao I.; pop. (1969e) 43,700; port of entry.

Mas·ca·ra \ˈmas-kə-rə\. Commune, SW Mostaganem dept., NW Algeria, 60 m. SE of Oran; pop. (1966c) 43,000; built on a mountain slope at alt. 1800 ft.; exports red and white wine, olive oil, grain. Importance increased when it became headquarters of Abd-el-Kader 1832; captured twice by French, 1835 and 1841, and considerably damaged.

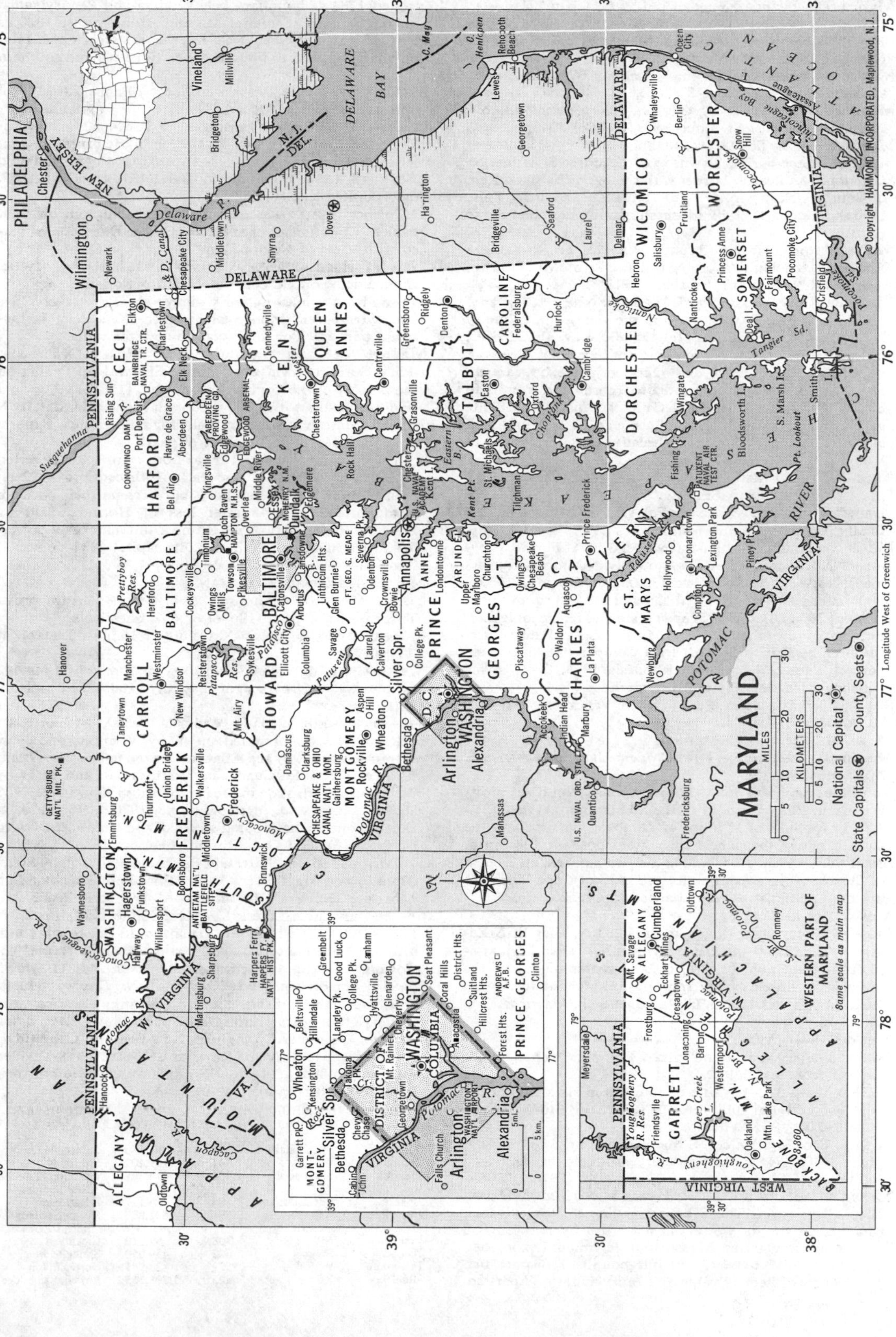
MARYLAND
PENNSYLVANIA
DELAWARE
NEW JERSEY
VIRGINIA
W. VIRGINIA
PHILADELPHIA
Wilmington
Chester
Newark
Chesapeake City
Middletown
Smyrna
Dover
Harrington
Bridgeville
Seaford
Laurel
Delmar
Georgetown
Lewes
Rehoboth Beach
Ocean City
Bridgeton
Vineland
Millville
DELAWARE BAY
C. May
C. Henlopen
Delaware R.
C. & D. Canal
N.J.
DEL.
ATLANTIC OCEAN
Assateague Bay
Chincoteague Bay
CECIL
Elkton
Charlestown
Elk Neck
Rising Sun
Port Deposit
BAINBRIDGE NAVAL TR. CTR.
CONOWINGO DAM
Susquehanna
HARFORD
Havre de Grace
Aberdeen
ABERDEEN PROVING GD.
EDGEWOOD ARSENAL
Edgewood
Bel Air
BALTIMORE
Kingsville
Middle River
Essex
Dundalk
FT. McHENRY N.M.
Edgemere
Loch Raven
HAMPTON N.H.S.
Overlea
Towson
Timonium
Cockeysville
Owings Mills
Pikesville
Catonsville
Arbutus
Lansdowne
Linthicum Hts.
Hereford
Prettyboy Res.
KENT
Chestertown
Kennedyville
Rock Hall
QUEEN ANNES
Centreville
Chester R.
Grasonville
Chester
Kent I.
Greensboro
Ridgely
Denton
CAROLINE
Federalsburg
Hurlock
TALBOT
Easton
St. Michaels
Oxford
Tilghman
Choptank R.
Eastern B.
Kent Pt.
Cambridge
DORCHESTER
Wingate
Fishing
WICOMICO
Salisbury
Hebron
Fruitland
Nanticoke
Whaleysville
Berlin
WORCESTER
Snow Hill
Pocomoke
SOMERSET
Princess Anne
Deal I.
Fairmount
Crisfield
Pocomoke City
Pocomoke Sd.
Tangier Sd.
Smith I.
S. Marsh I.
Bloodsworth I.
CHESAPEAKE BAY
Pt. Lookout
Annapolis
U.S. NAVAL ACADEMY
Severna Pk.
FT. GEO. G. MEADE
Glen Burnie
Odenton
Crownsville
ANNE ARUNDEL
Londontowne
Bowie
Upper Marlboro
Churchton
Owings
Chesapeake Beach
Prince Frederick
CALVERT
Patuxent R.
PATUXENT NAVAL AIR TEST CTR.
Lexington Park
Leonardtown
Hollywood
ST. MARYS
Compton
Piney Pt.
POTOMAC RIVER
Newburg
CHARLES
La Plata
Waldorf
Aquasco
Piscataway
PRINCE GEORGES
Indian Head
Marbury
Accokeek
U.S. NAVAL ORD. STA.
Quantico
Fredericksburg
Mahassas
Alexandria
Arlington
WASHINGTON
D.C.
Bethesda
Silver Spr.
College Pk.
Laurel
Calverton
Savage
Columbia
Ellicott City
HOWARD
Sykesville
Patapsco
Reisterstown
Westminster
CARROLL
Manchester
Hanover
Taneytown
New Windsor
Mt. Airy
MONTGOMERY
Rockville
Wheaton
Aspen Hill
Gaithersburg
Clarksburg
Damascus
CHESAPEAKE & OHIO CANAL NAT'L MON.
FREDERICK
Frederick
Union Bridge
Walkersville
Thurmont
Emmitsburg
Middletown
Brunswick
Monocacy
GETTYSBURG NAT'L MIL. PK.
WASHINGTON
Hagerstown
Funkstown
Boonsboro
Williamsport
Halfway
ANTIETAM NAT'L BATTLEFIELD SITE
Sharpsburg
Harpers Ferry
HARPERS FY. NAT'L HIST. PK.
Martinsburg
Waynesboro
Hancock
ALLEGANY
Oldtown
Potomac R.
Conococheague
Cacapon
SOUTH MTN.
CATOCTIN MTN.
APPALACHIAN MTS.
VA.
Garrett Pk.
Kensington
Chevy Chase
Takoma Pk.
Cabin John
Georgetown
DISTRICT OF COLUMBIA
Mt. Rainier
Hyattsville
Langley Pk.
Hillandale
Beltsville
College Pk.
Greenbelt
Good Luck
Lanham
Glenarden
Cheverly
Seat Pleasant
Coral Hills
District Hts.
Suitland
Hillcrest Hts.
Anacostia
Forest Hts.
ANDREWS A.F.B.
Clinton
Falls Church
WASHINGTON NAT'L AIRPORT
5 mi.
5 km.
WESTERN PART OF MARYLAND
Same scale as main map
GARRETT
Oakland
Mtn. Lake Park
Friendsville
Youghiogheny R. Res.
Deep Creek
Meyersdale
Frostburg
Lonaconing
Barton
Westernport
Cresaptown
Eckhart Mines
Mt. Savage
Cumberland
Oldtown
Romney
BACKBONE MTN.
WEST VIRGINIA
MILES
KILOMETERS
State Capitals
County Seats
National Capital
Longitude West of Greenwich
© Copyright HAMMOND INCORPORATED, Maplewood, N.J.

Mas·ca·rene Islands \ˌmas-kə-'rēn-\. Group of islands in the Indian Ocean, bet. 400 and 500 m. E of the Malagasy Republic, comprising Réunion, Mauritius, and Rodriguez (*qq.v.*).

Mas·co·ma Lake \ˌmas-kə-mə-\. Lake in SW Grafton co., W New Hampshire.

Mas·cou·tah \mas-'küt-ə\. City, St. Clair co., SW Illinois, 23 m. ESE of East St. Louis; pop. (1970c) 5045.

Mas d'Azil, Le. See LE MAS D'AZIL.

Ma·se·ru \'maz-ə-ˌrü\. Town, ✱ of Lesotho, S Africa, on Caledon river near W border with Orange Free State, Rep. of South Africa; pop. (1971e) 16,000; alt. 4950 ft.; univ. (1964); founded 1869 by Moshesh, paramount chief of the Basuto.

Ma·sher·brum \'məsh-ər-ˌbrüm\. Peak in the Karakoram Range of the Himalayas, N India, SW of Mt. Godwin Austen (K2); 25,660 ft.; scaled 1960.

Mash·had \mə-'shad\ *also* **Me·shed** \mə-'shed\. City, ✱ of Khorāsān prov., Iran; situated in the valley of a tributary of the Hari Rud; pop. (1971e) 425,000; elev. ab. 3200 ft.; in rich agricultural region; has for centuries been an important trade center and junction point on caravan routes and highways from India to Tehran and from N to S bet. Turkistan towns and Gulf of Oman. Has Shiite shrine and is place of annual pilgrimage. In 19th and 20th cents. important strategically because of its proximity to Russian and Afghan borders.

Mash·kel \mash-'kel\ *or Pers.* **Rūd–e Māsh·kid** \'rü-dē-mäsh-'kēd\. River in SE Iran and Pakistan; rises in SE Iran, flows in a curve E across Pakistan boundary, NE, and finally NW into Hamun-i-Mashkel.

Ma·sho·na·land \mə-'shän-ə-ˌland, -'shō-nə-\. Former province, NE Rhodesia, S Africa, now divided into two provinces: **Northern Mashonaland** (30,032 sq. m.; pop. [1969p] 600,420) and **Southern Mashonaland** (20,983 sq. m.; pop. [1969p] 366,660); region is open plain and fertile tableland, rich in gold, inhabited by Mashonas, a Bantu race; acquired by British South Africa Company 1890; became part of colony of Southern Rhodesia 1923. Chief towns Salisbury, Hartley, Gatooma, Umtali.

Ma·sia·ti \ˌmäs-ē-'ät-ē\. Peak in S cen. Venezuela, near Brazil border; ab. 4900 ft.

Masikesi. See VILA DE MANICA.

Ma·sin·di \mə-'sin-dē\. Town, W cen. Uganda, E Africa, E of Lake Albert.

Ma·sin·loc \ˌmäs-ən-'lȯk\. Town on coast, Zambales prov., W Luzon, Phil., 16 m. N of Iba; munic. pop. (1969e) 21,-100; in foothills of W slope of Zambales Mts. behind the town is one of the richest chromite deposits in the world.

Ma·si·rah \mə-'sir-ə\. Island in the Arabian Sea, off E coast of Oman, SE Arabian Penin., 150 m. S of Cape Hadd; 44 m. long; administratively attached to Oman.

Masis. See ARARAT 3.

Mas·jed So·ley·mān \mas-ˌjid-ˌsü-lā-'män\. City in S Zagros Mts. ab. 60 m. NE of Ahvāz and near Maidan-i-Naftun, Iran; pop. (1971e) 66,000; center of one of the important oil fields of W Iran; has oil pipeline to Ahvāz.

Mask, Lough \läk-'mask, läk-\. Lake, S co. Mayo, W Eire; 32 sq. m.

Maskat. See MASQAT.

Mas·ki·non·gé \ˌmäs-kē-nōⁿ-'zhā\. County, Quebec, Canada. See table at QUEBEC.

Ma·son \'mās-ᵊn\. **1** Name of counties in six states of the U.S. See tables at ILLINOIS, KENTUCKY, MICHIGAN, TEXAS, WASHINGTON, WEST VIRGINIA.

2 City, ⊗ of Ingham co., S Michigan, 12 m. S of Lansing; pop. (1970c) 5468; plastics, dairy products; beans.

3 City, ⊗ of Mason co., cen. Texas; pop. (1970c) 1806.

Mason and Dix·on's Line \-'dik-sənz-\ *also* **Mason–Dix·on Line** \-'dik-sən-\. The S boundary line of Pennsylvania, run (except for its westernmost 36 m.) by two English astronomers, Charles Mason and Jeremiah Dixon, bet. 1763 and 1767 to settle an old boundary dispute bet. proprietors of Pennsylvania and Maryland; its W part accepted 1784 as boundary bet. Virginia and Pennsylvania; became famous at time of Missouri Compromise 1820 as part of boundary bet. free and slave states; name later popularly applied to boundary bet. northern and southern states.

Mason City. 1 City, Mason co., cen. Illinois, 28 m. N of Springfield; pop. (1970c) 2611; diversified agriculture.

2 City, ⊗ of Cerro Gordo co., N Iowa, 62 m. NW of Waterloo; pop. (1970c) 30,379; in agricultural region; fertilizer, cement, brick; meat-packing, sugar refining; Northern Iowa Community Coll. (1918); settled 1853, incorporated as city 1881.

3 Former town, Okanogan co., N Washington, on right bank of Columbia river at Grand Coulee Dam; consolidated with town of Coulee Dam 1943.

Ma·sons Island \ˌmās-ᵊnz-\. Island in the harbor of Mystic, Connecticut, off SE coast of New London co.

Ma·son·town \'mās-ᵊn-ˌtaün\. Borough, Fayette co., SW Pennsylvania, on Monongahela river 11 m. W of Uniontown; pop. (1970c) 4226; coal mines; gas wells.

Mas·qat *or* **Mas·kat** \'məs-ˌkat\ *or* **Mus·cat** \'məs-ˌkat, -kət\. Seaport town, ✱ of Oman, SE Arabian Penin., on the S coast of the Gulf of Oman; pop. (1969e) 9973; on a small peninsula with steep mountain range behind it; its N suburb Matrah is starting point for land routes. Exports dates, dried fish, and mother-of-pearl.

History: Came under Persians 6th cent. B.C.; converted to Islam c. 630 A.D.; from early 16th cent. to 1622 an unimportant Portuguese port, but became their Arabian headquarters 1622–48 after loss of Hormuz; held by Persians 1650–1741; then became a sultanate, esp. powerful during middle of 19th cent.; its capital 1832–56 was at Zanzibar.

Masqat and Oman. see OMAN.

Mas·sa \'mäs-ə\. Commune, ✱ of Massa-Carrara prov., Tuscany, Italy; pop. (1968e) 62,447; chemicals.

Mas·sac \'mas-ˌak, 'mas-ək\. County in Illinois. See table at ILLINOIS.

Massa–Car·ra·ra \ˌmäs-ə-kə-'rär-ə\ *or formerly* **Ap·ua·nia** \ə-'pwän-yə\. Province of Tuscany, Italy. See table at ITALY.

Mas·sa·chu·setts \ˌmas-(ə-)'chü-səts, -zəts\. A northeast state of U.S.A., bounded on N by Vermont and New Hampshire, on E by the Atlantic Ocean, on S by the Atlantic Ocean, Rhode Island, and Connecticut, and on W by New York; 45th state in area, 8257 sq. m. (land area 7833 sq. m.); 10th state in population, (1970c) 5,689,170; ✱ Boston; one of the original states of the Union, the 6th to ratify the Federal Constitution (Feb. 6, 1788).

Nicknames: Bay State; Old Bay State; Old Colony State. *State flower:* Mayflower. *Motto:* Ense Petit Placidam Sub Libertate Quietem (By the Sword We Seek Peace, but Peace Only under Liberty). *Rivers:* Connecticut, flowing N to S across W part of state; Taunton, in SE, flowing into arm of Narragansett Bay; Merrimack, in extreme NE, flowing into Atlantic Ocean. *Highest point:* Mt. Greylock, 3491 ft., in Berkshire co. *Chief products:* Dairy products, fruit, vegetables; fishing; manufacturing: electrical machinery, footwear; printing and publishing. *Chief cities:* Boston, Worcester, Springfield, New Bedford, Cambridge, Fall River. See *Table of States* at UNITED STATES. Divided into the following 14 counties (for pronunciation of their names, see their individual entries):

NAME	LOCATION	AREA[1] (sq. m.)	POP. (1970c)	CO. SEAT
Barnstable[2]	SE; coastal	393	96,656	Barnstable
Berkshire	W	941	149,402	Pittsfield
Bristol	SE; coastal	554	444,301	Fall River, Taunton, New Bedford
Dukes[3]	SE; insular	104	6,117	Edgartown
Essex	NE corner; coastal	594	637,887	Salem, Newburyport, Lawrence
Franklin	NW	708	59,210	Greenfield
Hampden	SW	622	459,050	Springfield
Hampshire	W	529	123,981	Northampton
Middlesex	NE	825	1,398,355	Lowell, Cambridge

NAME	LOCATION	AREA[1] (sq. m.)	POP. (1970c)	CO. SEAT
Nantucket[4]	SE; insular	46	3,774	Nantucket
Norfolk[5]	E; coastal	394	604,854	Dedham
Plymouth	SE; coastal	654	333,314	Plymouth
Suffolk	E; coastal	56	735,190	Boston
Worcester	cen.	1,513	637,079	Worcester, Fitchburg

[1]Area = land area.
[2]Coextensive with Cape Cod (*q.v.*).
[3]Comprises Martha's Vineyard, Elizabeth Is., and other islands.
[4]Comprises Nantucket I. and a few islets.
[5]Comprises a main area whose NE corner borders Boston Bay and two smaller areas separated from main area: one on Massachusetts Bay and surrounded on landward side by Plymouth co., the other enclosed by Middlesex and Suffolk cos.

History: Coast skirted by Verrazano 1524; Cape Cod discovered by Gosnold 1602 who made first (temporary) settlement within present limits of state; Plymouth (see PLYMOUTH 4) settled by Pilgrims 1620; a charter colony, founded and governed by Massachusetts Bay Company 1629–84; Harvard College founded 1636; joined New England Confederation 1643; acquired province of Maine 1652; after loss of first charter 1684, governed as part of Dominion of New England 1686; by its second charter 1691, received confirmation to Maine and to Plymouth colonies; in 18th cent., gradually became a center of resistance to imperial colonial policy (see BOSTON 1); evacuated by British troops after Lexington and Concord 1775; battle of Bunker Hill 1775; gave up claims to western lands 1785–86; western Massachusetts scene of Shays' Rebellion 1786–87; eastern Massachusetts early center of American cotton manufacture (see WALTHAM). Maine became separate state 1820.

Massachusetts Bay. Inlet of Atlantic Ocean on E coast of Massachusetts, extending from Cape Ann on the N to Cape Cod on the S; ab. 60 m. long by 25 m. wide; the city of Boston is situated at its W end.

Mas·sa·cre Bay \ˌmas-i-kər-\. Inlet on SE coast of Attu I. in the Aleutians, Alaska; landing here of American troops led to defeat of Japanese May–June 1943.

Mas·sa·fra \mə-ˈsäf-rə\. Commune, Taranto prov., Apulia, SE Italy, 9 m. NW of Taranto; pop. (1968e) 22,493.

Massa Ma·rit·ti·ma \-mə-ˈrēt-tē-mə\. Commune, Grosseto prov., Tuscany, cen. Italy, 24 m. NNW of Grosseto; pop. (1968e) 11,054; 13th cent. cathedral and town hall; in mining region (copper, iron, lead, and silver).

Mas·sa·nut·ten Mountain *or* **Mas·a·nut·ton Mountain** \ˌmas-ə-ˈnət-ᵊn-\. Mountain ridge, N Virginia, in Blue Ridge, bet. north and south forks of Shenandoah river.

Mas·sa·pe·qua \ˌmas-ə-ˈpē-kwə\. Unincorporated community, Nassau co., SE New York, on S shore of Long I., ab. 10 m. SE of Mineola; pop. (1970c) 26,951; resort and residential section.

Massapequa Park. Village, Nassau co., SE New York, on Long I.; pop. (1970c) 22,112.

Mas·sa·ro·sa \ˌmäs-ə-ˈrō-zə\. Commune, Lucca prov., Tuscany, cen. Italy, 9 m. W of Lucca; pop. (1968e) 16,327.

Massaua *or* **Massawa.** See MESEWA.

Mas·se·na \mə-ˈsē-nə\. Manufacturing village, St. Lawrence co., N New York, in town of Massena near St. Lawrence river 31 m. W of Malone; pop. (1970c) 14,042; aluminum products, automobile parts; dairy farms.

Mas·sén·ya \mə-ˈsā-nyə\. Town, SW Chad, N cen. Africa, on a tributary of the Chari.

Mas·si·cault \ˌmȧ-sē-ˈkō\. Town, N Tunisia, N Africa, ab. 12 m. SW of Tunis on the road bet. Tunis and Majāz al-Bāb; taken by British May 6, 1943.

Mas·si·cus \ˈmas-i-kəs\ *or Ital.* **Mas·si·co** \ˈmäs-i-ˌkō\. Mountain ridge, Caserta prov., Campania, Italy, NW of Capua near shore of Gulf of Gaeta; noted for wine (*Massic*).

Mas·sif Cen·tral \ma-ˌsēf-sen-ˈträl, -säⁿ-\. Plateau region, SE cen. France; 32,819 sq. m.; highest point Puy de Sancy 6186 ft. of the Monts Dore; centers in departments of Cantal, Haute-Loire, and Aveyron; source of many streams, esp. Loire, Allier, Cher, and Creuse.

Massilia. See MARSEILLES 2.

Mas·sil·lon \ˈmas-ə-lən, -ˌlän\. City, Stark co., NE Ohio, 8 m. W of Canton; pop. (1970c) 32,539; alloys and stainless steels, household wares, automobile parts, aluminum, farm implements; printing; founded 1826, incorporated 1853.

Mas·sive, Mount \-ˈmas-iv\. Mountain, Lake co., cen. Colorado, in Sawatch Range; 14,421 ft.; 2d highest mountain in Colorado.

Massowa. See MESEWA.

Mas·sy \mä-ˈsē\. Commune, Essonne dept., N France, ab. 10 m. SSE of Paris; pop. (1968c) 37,055.

Mas·ter·ton \ˈmas-tərt-ᵊn\. Borough, S North I., New Zealand, 50 m. ENE of Wellington; pop. (1970e) 18,650.

Ma·su·da \mə-ˈsü-də\. City, Shimane prefecture, Honshū, Japan, 40 m. NW of Hiroshima; pop. (1970c) 50,071.

Masulipatnam. See MACHILIPATNAM.

Ma·su·ria *also* **Ma·zu·ria** \mə-ˈzu̇r-ē-ə, -ˈsu̇r-\ *or Ger.* **Ma·su·ren** \mə-ˈzu̇r-ən\. Region, NE Poland; includes **Ma·su·ri·an Lakes** \-ˈzu̇r-ē-ən-, -ˈsu̇r-\, scene of battles in World War I resulting in defeats for the Russian armies: Sept. 6–12, 1914, and (Suwałki) Feb. 7–14, 1915. Formerly part of East Prussia, Germany; lake region under control of U.S.S.R. Jan. 1945; assigned to Poland by Potsdam Conference 1945.

Maṣ·yāf \ˌmas-ē-ˈaf\. Mountain stronghold, E Latakia, Syria, at S end of Djebel Ansariya; in 12th cent. became chief seat of Syrian branch of the Assassins; taken 1272 by the Mameluke sultan Baybars.

Mat \ˈmät\. Province of N cen. Albania. See table at ALBANIA.

Mat·a·be·le·land \ˌmat-ə-ˈbē-lē-ˌland\. Former province, SW Rhodesia, S Africa, now divided into two provinces: **Northern Matabeleland** (30,032 sq. m.; pop. [1969e] 600,420) and **Southern Matabeleland** (20,983 sq. m.; pop. 366,660); region lies bet. the Limpopo and Zambezi rivers; rich in gold. Inhabited by Matabele, a Zulu race of the Bantu nation driven out of Natal 1827 and from Transvaal 1837; came under British South Africa Company 1889; became part of Southern Rhodesia 1923. Chief towns Bulawayo, Gwelo, Selukwe.

Mata Bia \ˌmat-ə-ˈbē-ə\. Mountain, E Portuguese Timor, Malay Archipelago; 7710 ft.

Ma·ta·di \mə-ˈtäd-ē\. River port, ✱ of Bas-Zaïre prov., W Zaire, ab. 80 m. from Atlantic coast; pop. (1968e) 75,834; the major port of the republic.

Mat·a·dor \ˈmat-ə-ˌdō(ə)r, -ˌdȯ(ə)r\. Town, ⊗ of Motley co., NW Texas; pop. (1970c) 1091; cattle ranches.

Ma·ta·fao, Mount \-ˌmät-ə-ˈfau̇\. Highest point on Tutuila I., American Samoa, SW cen. Pacific; 2141 ft.

Mat·a·gal·pa \ˌmat-ə-ˈgal-pə\. **1** Department of cen. Nicaragua. See table at NICARAGUA.
2 Town, its ✱, ab. 60 m. NNE of Managua; pop. (1967e) 20,718; alt. 3000 ft.; trade center in coffee-raising region.

Mat·a·gam·on Lake \ˌmat-ə-ˌgam-ən-\. Lake on upper E boundary of Piscataquis co., N cen. Maine.

Mat·a·gor·da \ˌmat-ə-ˈgȯrd-ə\. County in Texas. See table at TEXAS.

Matagorda Bay. Inlet of Gulf of Mexico, S Matagorda co. and E Calhoun co., SE Texas; 30 m. long; receives the Colorado river (of Texas) on the NE.

Matagorda Island. Island in Calhoun co., S Texas, lying bet. San Antonio Bay and the Gulf of Mexico.

Matagorda Peninsula. Narrow spit of land lying bet. Matagorda Bay and the Gulf of Mexico in Matagorda co., SE Texas.

Ma·ta·le \ˈmət-ᵊl-ˌā\. Town, Ceylon, 14 m. N of Kandy; pop. (1968e) 28,000; Buddhist monastery and temple of Alu Vihara 2 m. distant.

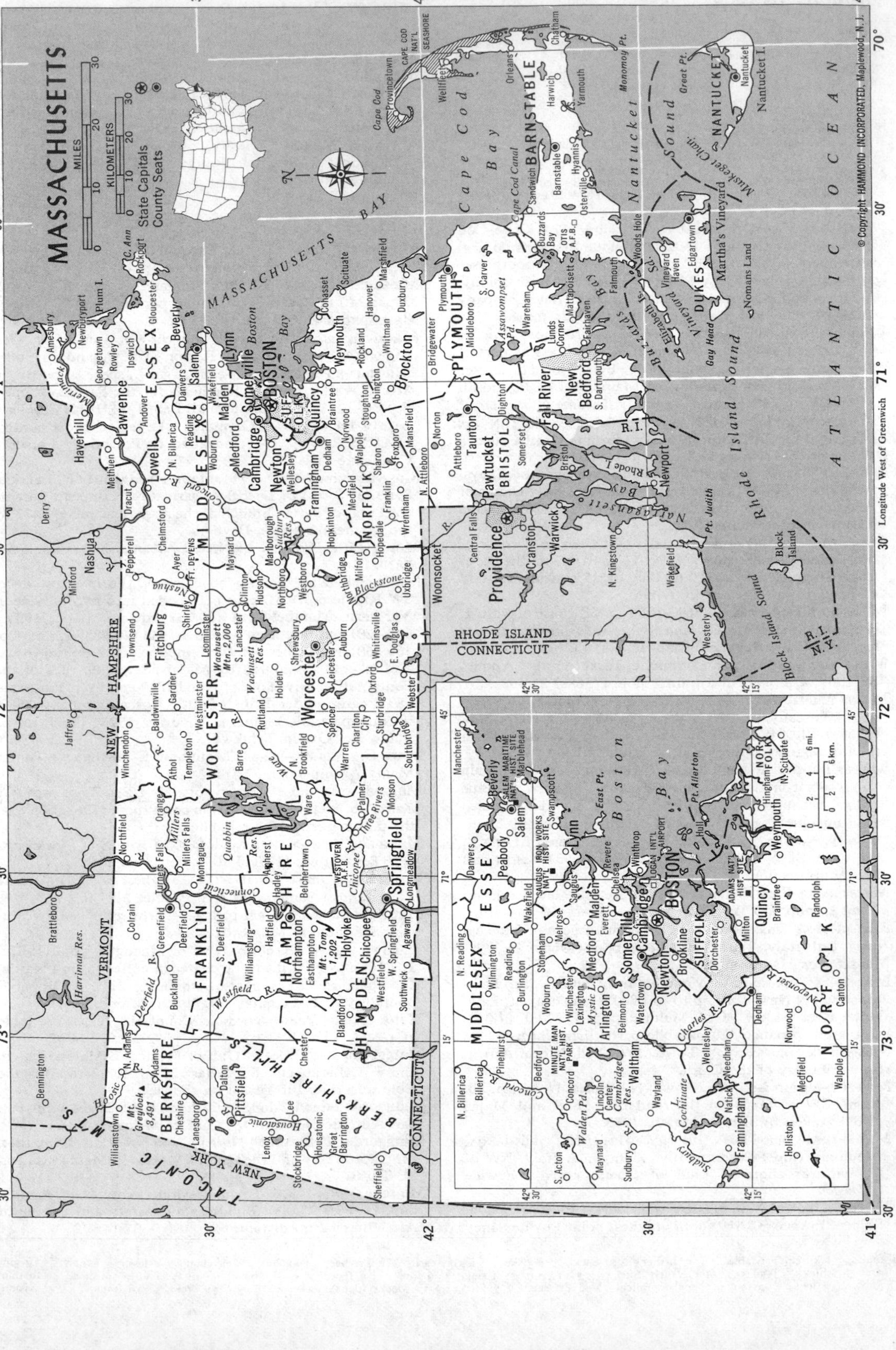

MASSACHUSETTS
MILES
0 10 20 30
KILOMETERS
0 10 20 30
State Capitals
County Seats
BERKSHIRE
FRANKLIN
HAMPSHIRE
HAMPDEN
WORCESTER
MIDDLESEX
ESSEX
SUFFOLK
NORFOLK
BRISTOL
PLYMOUTH
BARNSTABLE
DUKES
NANTUCKET
BOSTON
Springfield
Worcester
Pittsfield
Lowell
Lawrence
Haverhill
Fitchburg
Holyoke
Chicopee
Cambridge
Newton
Quincy
Brockton
Lynn
Fall River
New Bedford
Taunton
Providence
Pawtucket
Nashua
VERMONT
NEW HAMPSHIRE
NEW YORK
CONNECTICUT
RHODE ISLAND
MASSACHUSETTS BAY
Cape Cod Bay
Nantucket Sound
Vineyard Sound
Buzzards Bay
Rhode Island Sound
Block Island Sound
ATLANTIC OCEAN
TACONIC MTS.
BERKSHIRE HILLS
Mt. Greylock 3,491
Wachusett Mtn. 2,006
Mt. Tom 1,202
Quabbin Res.
Wachusett Res.
CAPE COD NAT'L SEASHORE
Martha's Vineyard
Nantucket I.
Block Island
Longitude West of Greenwich
© Copyright HAMMOND INCORPORATED, Maplewood, N.J.

Mat·a·mo·ros \ˌmat-ə-ˈmōr-əs, -ˈmȯr-\. 1 Town, Coahuila state, NE Mexico, just E of Torreón; munic. pop. (1970p) 44,103.

2 *or in full* **Izú·car de Matamoros** \i-ˈzü-kərd-ə-\. Town, Puebla state, SE cen. Mexico; munic. pop. (1970p) 44,074.

3 Town, Tamaulipas state, E Mexico, on the Rio Grande 25 m. from its mouth and opp. Brownsville, Texas; munic. pop. (1970p) 182,887; center of irrigated agricultural region; port of entry for tourists; exports coffee and hides. Founded ab. 1810; taken by Americans May 18, 1846 in Mexican War.

Ma·ta·na, Lake \-mə-ˈtän-ə\. Lake in mountainous region of cen. Celebes, Indonesia, near Lake Towuti; has been sounded to a depth of 1500 ft.

Ma·tane \mə-ˈtan\. 1 County, Quebec, Canada. See table at QUEBEC.

2 Town, its ⊗, on Gaspé Penin. on St. Lawrence river; pop. (1971p) 11,826; paper, wood pulp, plywood; agriculture.

Ma·ta·ni·ko \mə-ˈtan-i-ˌkō\. Short stream, NW coast of Guadalcanal I., SE Solomon Is., W Pacific Ocean; flows N to a point just E of Point Cruz and ab. 3 m. W of Lunga Point. Scene of severe battles Oct. 8–10 and Oct. 21, 1942.

Mat·a·nus·ka \ˌmat-ə-ˈnüs-kə\. Village, S Alaska, on railroad ab. 30 m. NE of Anchorage at foot of valley of **Matanuska River** (ab. 90 m. long). See PALMER 1.

Matanuska–Su·sit·na \-sü-ˈsit-nə\. Borough in Alaska. See table at ALASKA.

Ma·tan·za \mə-ˈtan-zə\. River in NE Buenos Aires prov., E Argentina; flows NE into Río de la Plata on S side of the city of Buenos Aires.

Ma·tan·zas \mə-ˈtan-zəs\. 1 Province of W cen. Cuba. See table at CUBA.

2 Municipality and city, its ✱, in NW part ab. 60 m. E of Havana; munic. pop. (1967e) 84,100; major seaport, exporting sugar and henequen fiber; produces rayon, shoes, fertilizer; founded 1693.

Matanzas Inlet. Passage connecting the Atlantic Ocean with the **Matanzas River** (a lagoon, NE Florida, S of St. Augustine) at S end of Anastasia I.; the lagoon, separating Anastasia I. from the mainland, contains a small island on which is located Fort Matanzas, built of coquina ab. 1736 by the Spaniards, and forming part of Fort Matanzas National Monument (see UNITED STATES, *National Monuments*).

Ma·ta·pa·lo, Cape \-ˌmät-ə-ˈpäl-(ˌ)ō\. Cape on S tip of Osa Penin., S Costa Rica, W of Gulf of Dulce.

Matapan, Cape. See TAÍNARON, CAPE.

Ma·ta·pé·dia \ˌmat-ə-ˈpēd-ē-ə, -ˈpād-\. 1 River in Matapédia and Bonaventure cos., W Gaspé Penin., SE Canada; ab. 60 m. long; flows SE out of **Lake Matapédia** into Restigouche river.

2 County, Quebec, Canada. See table at QUEBEC.

Ma·ta·ra \ˈmät-ə-rə\. Town, Ceylon, on Indian Ocean 24 m. E of Galle; pop. (1968c) 36,000; commercial center in district rich in coconut palms and cinnamon trees; has old Portuguese fort.

Ma·ta·ram \mə-ˈtär-əm\. 1 Town, ✱ of West Nusa Tenggaru, Indonesia, on the W coast of Lombok I.; pop. (1961c) 81,949.

2 Muslim sultanate in Malay Archipelago, founded 1582 and at height of its power in 17th cent., controlling all of Java except Bantam and E tip, and SE Borneo. Overcome by Dutch by 1755 and divided bet. principalities of Surakarta and Jogjakarta.

Ma·ta·ra·ni \ˌma-tə-ˈran-ē\. Seaport town, Arequipa dept., S Peru, ab. 8 m. NW of Mollendo.

Matarīya, Al–. See AL-MATARĪYA.

Ma·ta·ró \ˌmät-ə-ˈrō\. Manufacturing commune and seaport, Barcelona prov., NE Spain, on Mediterranean 15 m. NE of Barcelona; pop. (1970p) 73,129; exports wine; produces soap, clothing, chemicals, vehicle bodies.

Ma·ta·ta \mə-ˈtät-ə\. Village on Bay of Plenty, N North I., New Zealand, W of mouth of Rangitaiki river.

Ma·ta·tie·le \ˌmät-ə-ˈtyā-lā\. Town, NE Cape Province, S Rep. of South Africa, 138 m. WSW of Durban.

Ma·tau·ra \mə-ˈtaů-rə\. 1 River, S South I., New Zealand; 149 m. long; flows S into Foveaux Strait E of Invercargill.

2 Borough, S South I., New Zealand, on Mataura river 27 m. NE of Invercargill; pop. (1970e) 2760.

Ma·ta–Uta \ˌmät-ə-ˈüt-ə\. See UVÉA 2.

Mat·a·wan \ˈmat-ə-ˌwän\. Borough, Monmouth co., E cen. New Jersey, 7 m. S of Perth Amboy; pop. (1970c) 9136; pottery, electroplating supplies; truck farms.

Ma·te·hua·la \ˌmät-ə-ˈwäl-ə\. Town, San Luis Potosí state, cen. Mexico, 100 m. N of San Luis Potosí; munic. pop. (1970p) 48,368; in mining region.

Ma·te·ra \mə-ˈter-ə\. 1 Province of Basilicata, S Italy. See table at ITALY.

2 Commune, its ✱, 126 m. E by S of Naples; pop. (1968e) 44,254; 13th cent. cathedral; castle; museum of antiquities; prehistoric artifacts found nearby.

Matesian Mountains *or Ital.* **Matese.** Plateau region of the Neapolitan Apennines. See table at APENNINES.

Má·té·szal·ka \ˈmät-ā-ˌsäl-kä\. Commune, Szabolcs-Szatmár co., NE Hungary, 43 m. NE of Debrecen; pop. (1970p) 12,325.

Ma·teur \ˌmä-ˈtər\. Town, N Tunisia, N Africa, ab. 10 m. SSW of Menzel Bourguiba; pop. (1966c) 16,900; occupied by Germans Dec. 1942; taken by Americans May 3, 1943 in battle for Bizerte. See HILL 609.

Ma·the·ran \ˌmät-ə-ˈrän\. Sanatorium, cen. Maharashtra, W India, 30 m. E of Bombay; pop. (1961c) 2800.

Math·ews \ˈmath-(ˌ)yüz\. 1 County in E Virginia. See table at VIRGINIA.

2 Village, its ⊗.

Math·ew Town \ˈmath-yü-\. Town on SW coast of Great Inagua I., Bahama Is.

Ma·thi·as Point \mə-ˌthī-əs-\. Point at NE tip of King George co., E Virginia, extending into Potomac river.

Math·is \ˈmath-əs\. City, San Patricio co., S Texas, 33 m. NW of Corpus Christi; pop. (1970c) 5351.

Ma·thu·ra \ˈmət-ə-rə\ *or* **Mut·tra** \ˈmət-rə\. City, W Uttar Pradesh, N India, on the right bank of the Yamuna river 30 m. NW of Agra; pop. (1970e) 137,720; ancient city, one of the most important centers of Indian art (the Mathura school, sculptures in red sandstone, 3d cent. B.C. to 6th cent. A.D.), and revered by Hindus as birthplace of Krishna; in early Christian era a center of Buddhism and Jainism; has a mosque built by Aurangzeb and a museum of antiquities. Plundered by Mahmud of Ghazni c. 1018 and destroyed by the Lodi sultan Sikandar II c. 1500; the great temple demolished by Aurangzeb in 1667; sacked by Ahmad Shah in 1756; under British sovereignty 1803.

Ma·ti \ˈmät-ē\. Municipality, ✱ of Davao Oriental prov., Mindanao, Phil.; pop. (1970c) 32,700.

Matianus. See URMIA, LAKE.

Ma·tin·i·cus \mə-ˈtin-i-kəs\. Island in Atlantic Ocean off S cen. coast of Maine.

Matisco Æduorum. See MÂCON.

Matlalcueyatl. See MALINCHE.

Mat·lock \ˈmat-ˌläk\. Urban district, Derbyshire, N cen. England, on the Derwent 19 m. S of Sheffield; pop. (1971p) 19,575; tourist resort; stone quarrying and flour milling.

Mat·ma·ta \mat-ˈmät-ə\. Town, SE Tunisia, ab. 27 m. S of Gabès. Nearby **Matmata Hills** (highest 2000 ft.), noted for centuries for their cave dwellers; formed German defense in World War II; taken by British Indian troops Mar. 1943.

Ma·toch·kin Shar \ˌmat-əch-kən-ˈshär\. Channel bet. the two islands of Novaya Zemlya (*q.v.*); 3 m. wide.

Ma·to Gros·so \ˌmat-ə-ˈgrō-(ˌ)sō\ *or formerly* **Mat·to Gros·so.** 1 State, SW Brazil; 745,501 sq. m.; pop. (1970p) 1,475,117; ✻ Cuiabá; livestock raising; coffee, cotton, sugar.
2 Town on Guaporé river, Mato Grosso state, SW Brazil; munic. pop. (1968e) 4134.

Mato Grosso, Plateau of. Highland in E cen. Mato Grosso state, SW Brazil; source of the Araguaia, Xingu, and Paraguay rivers, of headstreams of the Tapajós, and of many tributaries of the Alto Paraná.

Ma·to·po Hills *or* **Ma·top·po Hills** \me-ˌtō-pō-\. Mountain group, S Rhodesia, S of Bulawayo; tomb of Cecil Rhodes (see WORLD'S VIEW).

Ma·to·pos National Park \mə-ˈtō-pəs-\. National park, S Rhodesia; 153 sq. m.; Bushmen's cave paintings; established 1953.

Ma·to·zi·nhos \ˌmat-ə-ˈzē-(ˌ)nyüsh\. Parish, NW Portugal, NW of Pôrto on the coast; includes port of Leixões (*q.v.*).

Ma·trah \ˈmät-rə\. Seaport town, N Oman, SE Arabian Penin., on the Gulf of Oman; N suburb of Masqat; pop. (1960c) 14,119; trade center for land routes into the interior.

Matrona. See MARNE.

Ma·trūh \mə-ˈtrü\. 1 Governorate of NW Egypt. See table at EGYPT.
2 *or* **Mer·sa Matrūh** \mər-ˌsä-\ *or anc.* **Par·ae·to·ni·um** \ˌpar-ē-ˈtō-nē-əm\. Town, its ✻, on coastal road, NW Egypt, E of Sīdī Barrāni and W of Fūka, 150 m. W of Alexandria; pop. (1970e) 11,800; site of old Roman town; in World War II taken and retaken several times 1942–43.

Matsang. See BRAHMAPUTRA.

Ma–tsu \ˈmät-(ˌ)sü\. Island, SE China, on coast ENE of Foochow; administered by Taiwan. See also QUEMOY.

Ma·tsu·ba·ra \ˌmät-sü-ˈbär-ə\. City, Ōsaka prefecture, Honshū, Japan, 12 m. S of Ōsaka; pop. (1970c) 111,562.

Mat·su·do \mät-ˈsü-(ˌ)dō\. City, Chiba prefecture, Japan, suburb of Tokyo; pop. (1970c) 253,591.

Ma·tsue *or* **Ma·tsu·ye** \ˈmät-sə-ˌwä, -sü-ˌyä\. City, ✻ of Shimane prefecture, N coast of W Honshū, Japan; pop. (1970c) 118,005; tourist center.

Ma·tsu·mae \ˌmät-sə-ˈmä-(ˌ)yä, -ˈmī\ *or formerly* **Fu·ku·ya·ma** \ˌfük-ə-ˈyäm-ə\. Town at SW tip of Hokkaidō, Japan, on Tsugaru Strait; pop. (1970c) 18,624; oldest town on Hokkaidō I.; has citadel as monument of feudal days.

Ma·tsu·mo·to \ˌmät-sə-ˈmōt-(ˌ)ō\. City, Nagano prefecture, cen. Honshū, Japan, 95 m. NE of Nagoya; pop. (1970c) 162,931; chief commercial city of the prefecture; univ. (1949); prominent in feudal days.

Mat·su·sa·ka \ˌmät-sə-ˈsäk-ə\ *or* **Ma·tsu·za·ka** \-ˈzäk-\. Town, Mie prefecture, S Honshū, Japan, ab. 50 m. SSW of Nagoya; pop. (1970c) 102,138.

Ma·tsu·shi·ma \ˌmät-sü-ˈshē-mə, mät-ˈsü-shi-mə\. Group of more than 800 small islands of soft, porous, volcanic rock worn by waves into fantastic shapes, in **Matsushima Wan** \-ˈwän\ (bay), Miyagi prefecture, N Honshū, Japan, ab. 10 m. NE of Sendai.

Matsuwa. See MATUA.

Ma·tsu·ya·ma \ˌmät-sə-ˈyäm-ə\. City, ✻ of Ehime prefecture, W Shikoku I., Japan, near Inland Sea; pop. (1970c) 322,902; cotton and synthetic textiles, paper, chemicals, machinery.

Matsuye. See MATSUE.

Matsuzaka. See MATSUSAKA.

Mat·ta·gami \mə-ˈtag-ə-mē\. River, E Ontario, Canada; 275 m. long; rises in Mattagami Lake and other lakes in Cochrane dist., flows N to join the Missinaibi and form the Moose river.

Mattagami Lake. 1 Lake in Cochrane dist., Ontario, Canada; a source of the Mattagami river.
2 Lake, Abitibi co., SW Quebec, Canada; ab. 91 sq. m.; with outlet N through Nottaway river into James Bay.

Mat·ta·mus·keet Lake \ˌmat-ə-mə-ˈskēt-\. Lake in SE Hyde co., E North Carolina.

Mat·tan·che·ri \mə-ˈtän-chə-rē\. Town, cen. Kerala state, S India, on Malabar Coast just S of Calicut; pop. (1961c) 83,896; commercial center; 16th cent. Portuguese palace; ancient Jewish community with 16th cent. synagogue.

Mat·ta·poi·sett \ˌmat-ə-ˈpȯi-sət\. Town, Plymouth co., SE Massachusetts, on Buzzards Bay 6 m. E of New Bedford; pop. (1970c) 4500; summer resort.

Mat·ta·po·ni \ˌmat-ə-pə-ˈnī\. River, E Virginia; ab. 125 m. long; rises in Spotsylvania co., flows SE to unite with Pamunkey river at West Point and form York river.

Mat·ta·wa \ˈmat-ə-ˌwä, -ˌwȯ\. 1 River, SE Ontario, Canada; ab. 45 m. long; flows E out of Trout Lake into the Ottawa river.
2 Town, Nipissing dist., SE Ontario, Canada, at confluence of Mattawa and Ottawa rivers 38 m. E of North Bay; pop. (1971p) 2878; formerly a fur-trading post of the Hudson's Bay Company.

Mat·ta·wam·keag \ˌmat-ə-ˈwäm-ˌkeg\. River, E Maine; ab. 50 m. long; formed by confluence of forks in S Aroostook co., flows SW into Penobscot river in E cen. Penobscot co.

Mat·ta·win \ˈmat-ə-wən\. River, S Quebec, Canada; 100 m. long; flows E into the Saint-Maurice river.

Mat·tea·wan \ˈmat-ə-ˌwän\. Former village, Dutchess co., SE New York; part of Beacon since 1913.

Mat·ter·horn \ˈmat-ər-ˌhȯ(ə)rn, ˈmät-\ *or* **Mont Cer·vin** \ˌmōⁿ-sər-ˈvaⁿ\. Peak in the Pennine Alps on the Swiss-Italian border; 14,690 ft.; first scaled 1865.

Matterhorn Peak \ˌmat-ər-ˌhȯ(ə)rn-\. Mountain, Hinsdale co., SW Colorado; 13,585 ft.

Mat·te·son \ˈmat-sən\. Village, Cook co., NE Illinois, 26 m. S of Chicago; pop. (1970c) 4741.

Matto Grosso. See MATO GROSSO.

Mat·toon \mə-ˈtün, ma-\. City, Coles co., E cen. Illinois, 40 m. SE of Decatur; pop. (1970c) 19,681; road-building machinery, electrical equipment, cement block, shoes, metal hose; diversified agriculture; Lake Land Coll. (1966); incorporated 1855.

Ma·tua \ˈmät-wä\ *or Jap.* **Ma·tsu·wa** \ˈmät-sə-ˌwä\. One of the Kuril Is. in cen. part of chain N of Rasshua; formerly under Japanese control, now part of Russian S.F.S.R., U.S.S.R.

Matupi, Mount. See TAVURVUR, MOUNT.

Ma·tu·rín \ˌmät-ə-ˈrēn\. Town, ✻ of Monagas state, NE Venezuela; pop. (1970e) 97,257.

Ma·tu·tum, Mount \-mə-ˈtüt-əm\. Mountain, NE Cotabato del Sur prov., Mindanao, Phil.; 7521 ft.; highest peak in the province.

Mauá \maů-ˈä\. Municipality, just SE of São Paulo, SE Brazil; pop. (1968e) 34,150.

Ma·u·ban \ˌmä-ü-ˈbän\. Municipality, S Quezon prov., Luzon, Phil., near E coast of Lamon Bay 19 m. NNE of Lucena; pop. (1969e) 24,200; important in coastal trade. Here Japanese landed Dec. 23, 1941.

Mau·beuge \mō-ˈbərzh\. Industrial city, Nord dept., N France, on Sambre river near Belgian border 49 m. SE of Lille; pop. (1968c) 32,028; manufactures firearms, iron and steel goods, leather. Built around monastery founded in 7th cent.; fell to France 1678; captured by Germans 1914 after siege in which it suffered heavy damages; recaptured 1918.

Ma·u·bin \ˈmä-ˈü-bən\. 1 District, Irrawaddy division, Lower Burma; 1651 sq. m.; pop. (1962c) 576,546; ✻ Maubin.
2 Town, its ✻, on the Irrawaddy 40 m. W of Rangoon.

Mauch·berg \ˈmaůk-ˌbe(ə)rg\. Peak, E cen. Transvaal, Rep. of South Africa; 8725 ft.

Mauch Chunk \mȯ-ˈchəŋk\. Former borough, E Pennsylvania. See JIM THORPE.

Mauch·line \ˈmȯk-lən\. Town, Ayr co., SW Scotland, 8 m. ESE of Kilmarnock; pop. (1966e) 4460; ab. 1 m. N is **Moss·giel** \mȯs-ˈgē(ə)l\, the farm where Robert Burns lived with his brother 1784–88.

Mau·er \ˈmaů(-ə)r\. 1 Village, Baden-Württemberg, West Germany, SE of Heidelberg; pop. (1969e) 2400; Heidelberg jaw found here 1907.
2 Lake, Poland. See MAMRY.

Maug \ˈmau̇g\. Small island, N Mariana Is., 140 m. N of Pagan, 20°01′N, 145°13′E; taken by U.S. troops Aug. 1945.

Mau·ga Si·li, Mount \-ˌmau̇-gə-ˈsē-lē\. Peak, center of Savai'i I., Western Samoa; 3503 ft.

Maui \ˈmau̇-ē\. **1** Island of S cen. state of Hawaii; 728 sq. m.; a part of the county of Maui; 2d largest island of the Hawaiian group; its E and W ends are high mountains with flat isthmus in center connecting them. In E is Haleakala National Park including Red Hill 10,023 ft. and in W Puu Kukui 5787 ft. and Eke Crater 4480 ft. Maalaea Bay is large inlet on S coast and Lahaina Roadstead in Auau Channel on NW is anchorage. Chief town Wailuku city; large sugar plantations.

2 County, Hawaii. See table at HAWAII.

Ma·u·ke \ˌmau̇-ˈkā\ *also* **Par·ry Island** \ˈpar-ē-\. One of the Cook Is. in S Pacific Ocean, 150 m. NE of Rarotonga; 7 sq. m.; pop. (1968e) 718.

Maul·din \ˈmȯl-dən\. Town, Greenville co., NW South Carolina, 7 m. SE of Greenville; pop. (1970c) 3797.

Mau·le \ˈmau̇-(ˌ)lā\. **1** River, Maule prov., S cen. Chile; ab. 140 m. long; flows into Pacific Ocean near the town of Constitución, S of Valparaíso.

2 Province of S cen. Chile. See table at CHILE.

Mau·llín \mau̇-ˈyēn\. River, Chiloé prov., S cen. Chile; flows out of Llanquihue Lake into the Pacific Ocean; waterfalls.

Maulmain. See MOULMEIN.

Mau·mee \mȯ-ˈmē, ˈmȯ-mē\. **1** River, Indiana and Ohio; ab. 175 m. long; formed by confluence of St. Joseph and St. Marys rivers at Fort Wayne, Allen co., NE Indiana, flows E and NE into Lake Erie at Toledo, NW Ohio. Navigable for 12 m. from mouth.

2 Residential city, Lucas co., NW Ohio, 8 m. SW of Toledo; pop. (1970c) 15,937; settled 1817 on site of Fort Miami (1764), where Wayne defeated the Indians Aug. 20, 1794 at battle of Fallen Timbers.

Maumee Bay. Inlet of Lake Erie in NE Lucas co., NW Ohio, N of Toledo.

Ma·un \mä-ˈu̇n\. Town, N Botswana, S Africa, NE of Lake Ngami; pop. (1970e) 6000.

Mau·na·bo \mau̇-ˈnäb-(ˌ)ō\. Town and municipality, SE Puerto Rico, on coast 14 m. E of Guayama; pop. (1970p) 1819 (town), 10,817 (munic.).

Mau·na Kea \ˌmau̇-nə-ˈkā-ə\. Extinct volcano, N cen. Hawaii I., Hawaii; 13,796 ft.; highest peak in the state.

Mauna Loa \-ˈlō-ə\. **1** Mountain, W Molokai I., Hawaii; 1382 ft.

2 Volcano, on S cen. Hawaii I., Hawaii, in Hawaii National Park; 13,680 ft.; largest mountain in the world in cubic content; central crater pit is sometimes active, but there has been no eruption from it in historic times; many great lava flows in recent years have burst from the sides at elevations from 7000 to 13,000 ft. See KILAUEA and MOKUAWEOWEO.

Mau·na·lua Bay \ˌmau̇-nə-ˈlü-ə-\. Bay on SE coast of Oahu I., Hawaii, W of Koko Head.

Mau·nath Bhan·jan \ˌmau̇-nät-ˈbən-jən\. Town, E Uttar Pradesh, N India, on tributary of Ganges river 55 m. NE of Varanasi; pop. (1961c) 48,785.

Maung·daw \ˈmau̇ŋ-ˈdȯ\. Town, W Lower Burma, on coast near India border 60 m. NW of Sittwe; scene of fighting in World War II.

Mau·per·tuis \ˌmō-pər-ˈtwē\. Battlefield 7 m. SE of Poitiers, France; where the Black Prince defeated the French 1356. See POITOU.

Mau·pi·ti \mau̇-ˈpēt-ē\. One of the Leeward Is., Society Is., S Pacific Ocean, ab. 30 m. W of Bora Bora; 5 sq. m.; ab. 6 m. in circumference enclosing wide lagoon; pop. (1967e) 635.

Mau·re·pas, Lake \-ˌmȯr-ə-ˈpä, -ˌmȯr-\. Lake in SE Louisiana; connected on the E, through a river ab. 2 m. long, with Lake Pontchartrain.

Maures, Monts des \-ˌmōⁿd-ā-ˈmō(ə)r, -ˈmȯ(ə)r\. Mountain massif, Var dept., SE France, on the Mediterranean coast at W end of the Riviera; highest point 2558 ft.

Mau·re·ta·nia \ˌmȯr-ə-ˈtā-nē-ə, ˌmär-, -nyə\ *or* **Mau·ri·ta·nia** \ˌmȯr-ə-ˈtā-nē-ə, ˌmar-, -nyə\. Ancient country in N Africa, W of Numidia; included modern Morocco and part of Algeria.

History: Ancient region of North Africa, part of Carthaginian empire; Mauretanian kingdom received W part of Numidia (*q.v.*) after fall of Jugurtha 106 B.C.; c. 25 B.C. Roman provinces of **Mauretania Cae·sar·i·en·sis** \-si-ˌzar-ē-ˈen(t)-səs, -ˌzer-\ (eastern) and **Mauretania Tin·gi·ta·na** \-ˌtin-jə-ˈtā-nə, -ˈtan-ə\ (western) were erected; in 5th cent. A.D. overrun by Vandals and later by Muslim Arabs; for later history, see BARBARY and MOROCCO.

Mau·rice \ˈmȯr-əs, ˈmär-\. River, SW New Jersey; ab. 40 m. long; flows S into **Maurice River Cove** of Delaware Bay.

Mau·ri·ta·nia \ˌmȯr-ə-ˈtā-nē-ə, ˌmär-, -nyə\. **1** *or Fr.* **Mau·ri·ta·nie** \mȯ-rē-tȧ-nē\ *or officially* **Islamic Republic of Mauritania.** Republic, W Africa, bounded on NW by Spanish Sahara, on N by Spanish Sahara and Algeria, on E and S by Mali, on SW by Senegal, and on W by the Atlantic Ocean; 397,955 sq. m.; pop. (1971e) 1,160,000; ✻ Nouakchott. *Physical features:* W extremity of Sahara covers most of territory; rich alluvial soils occur along Senegal river on SW boundary; mountainous plateaus in N and cen. have max. elev. of ab. 1500 ft. *Chief exports:* Iron ore, copper, gum arabic; other products: millet, rice; livestock raising, fish processing. *Chief towns:* Nouakchott, Kaédi, Atar.

History: Coast opened by Portuguese who discovered Arguin in 15th cent.; coastal territory disputed by traders of different European nations; although recognized as in French sphere from 1817 Senegal treaty, it was not occupied until after 1900; made protectorate 1903 and part of French West Africa 1904, but conquered only gradually; made colony 1921; became an overseas territory 1946 and an autonomous republic of the French Community 1958; achieved independence 1960; period 1963–66 marked by development of important mineral deposits; claims to Mauritanian territory withdrawn by Morocco 1969.

2 Ancient country, N Africa. See MAURETANIA.

Mau·ri·ti·us \mȯ-ˈrish-(ē-)əs\ *or formerly* **Île de France** \ˌēl-də-ˈfräⁿs\. Island of the Mascarene Is., in the Indian Ocean ab. 450 m. E of the Malagasy Republic; 720 sq. m.; pop. (1970e) 830,700; with dependencies (island of Rodriguez and Agalega Is.) constitutes an independent state; ❋ Port Louis; mountainous, with fertile valleys and coastal plains; highest point Piton de la Rivière Noire in SW 2711 ft.; chief industry is growing sugarcane; other products are rice, vanilla, coconut oil, spice.

History: Discovered by Portuguese 1505; occupied by Dutch 1598–1710; held by French 1715–1810 when British captured it; formally ceded to British 1814; became independent Mar. 12, 1968.

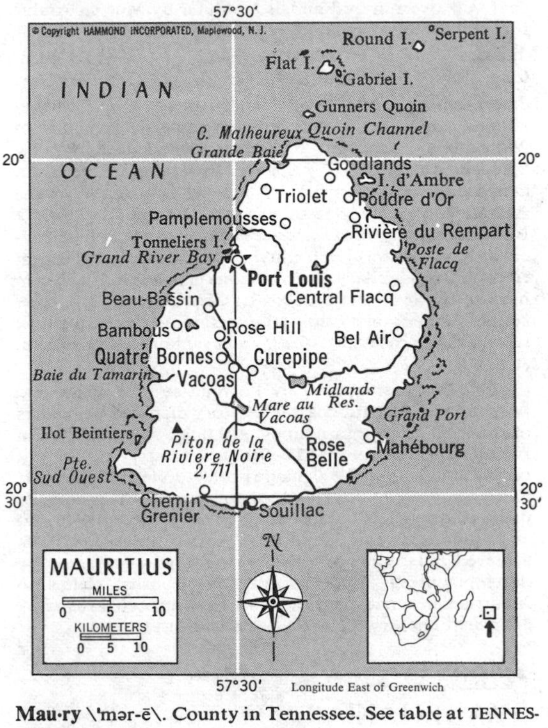

Mau·ry \ˈmər-ē\. County in Tennessee. See table at TENNESSEE.

Maus·ton \ˈmȯs-tən\. City, ⊗ of Juneau co., cen. Wisconsin, 35 m. WNW of Portage; pop. (1970c) 3466.

Maut·hau·sen \ˈmau̇t-ˌhau̇-zən\. Village, Upper Austria, on the Danube opp. the mouth of the Enns; pop. (1969e) 4200; site of concentration camp during World War II.

Mauvaises Terres. See BAD LANDS.

Mav·er·ick \ˈmav-(ə-)rik\. County in Texas. See table at TEXAS.

Maverick, Mount. Peak in Brewster co., W Texas; 3495 ft.

Ma·wen·zi \mə-ˈwen-zē\. Second highest peak of Mount Kilimanjaro, Tanzania, E Africa; 16,896 ft.

Maw·jib, Wa·di al– \ˌwäd-ē-al-ˈmau̇-jib\ *also* **Wadi al–Mo·jib** \-ˈmō-jib\ *or anc.* **Ar·non** \ˈär-(ˌ)nän\. River, W Jordan, flowing W into Dead Sea; in ancient times boundary (*Num.* xxi. 14) bet. Moab on S and country of Amorites on N; later, boundary bet. Moab and Palestine.

Maw·laik \ˈmȯ-ˌlīk\. Town, Sagaing division, Upper Burma, on the Chindwin NE of Tiddim and 165 m. NW of Mandalay.

Mawsil, Al–. See MOSUL.

Má·xi·mo Gó·mez \ˌmäk-si-(ˌ)mō-ˈgō-ˌmez\. Town, Matanzas prov., W cen. Cuba, on railroad 15 m. SE of Cárdenas; munic. pop (1967e) 12,140.

May, Cape \-ˈmā\. **1** Cape, S tip of Cape May co., at extreme S point of New Jersey, at entrance to Delaware Bay.
2 City, New Jersey. See CAPE MAY 3.

Ma·ya \ˈmī-ə\. River, chiefly in cen. Khabarovsk Krai, Russian S.F.S.R., U.S.S.R.; ab. 660 m. long; rises on NW slopes of the Stanovoi Mts. and flows SW and NW to the Aldan river in SE Yakutsk A.S.S.R.

Maya, Point \-ˈmī-ə\. Cape on NW coast of Matanzas prov., W cen. Cuba.

May·a·gua·na \ˌmā-ə-ˈgwän-ə\ *or* **Mar·i·gua·na** \ˌmar-ə-\. One of the Bahama Is. in Atlantic Ocean E of Acklins I.; ab. 25 m. long and bet. 3 and 5 m. wide; 110 sq. m.; pop. (1963c) 707.

Mayaguana Passage. Channel in the Bahama Is., ESE of Crooked I. and Acklins I. and NW of Mayaguana I.

Ma·ya·güez \ˌmī-ə-ˈgwās\. Municipality and seaport city, W Puerto Rico; pop. (1970p) 69,485, munic. pop. 86,267; exports sugar, coffee, tropical fruits; electronic components, canned foods, beverages; seat of a college of the University of Puerto Rico (Agriculture and Mechanics); founded 1763.

Ma·ya Mountains \ˈmī-ə-\. Mountain range in S British Honduras; its highest point, Victoria Peak 3681 ft., is the highest mountain in British Honduras.

Ma·ya·rí \ˌmī-ə-ˈrē\. Municipality, Oriente prov., E Cuba, near Nipe Bay on N coast 45 m. N of Santiago de Cuba; pop. (1967e) 127,190.

May·bole \mā-ˈbōl\. Burgh, Ayrshire, SW Scotland, 8 m. S of Ayr; pop. (1971p) 4523; Culzean Castle.

Maydān. See MAIDAN 2.

Mayebashi. See MAEBASHI.

May·en \ˈmī-ən\. Manufacturing city, N Rhineland-Palatinate, West Germany, in the Eifel 44 m. SSE of Cologne; pop. (1968e) 18,156.

Mayence. See MAINZ.

Ma·yenne \mä-ˈyen\. **1** River, NW France; ab. 125 m. long; rises in Orne dept., flows S to unite with Sarthe river near Angers and form Maine river; navigable for ab. 75 m.
2 Department of NW France. See table at FRANCE.
3 Commune, N Mayenne dept., NW France; pop. (1968c) 11,382; market town in agricultural region; cider-making; center of conflict in 11th cent. campaigns of William the Conqueror, in wars of religion 16th cent. (it belonged to Guise family), and in wars of the Vendée 18th cent.

Mayes \ˈmāz\. County in Oklahoma. See table at OKLAHOMA.

May·fair \ˈmā-ˌfa(ə)r, -ˌfe(ə)r\. A fashionable district in West End, London, England, in Westminster borough E of Hyde Park—so called from an annual fair (abolished 1708) held there in May.

May·field \ˈmā-ˌfēld\. **1** City, ⊗ of Graves co., SW Kentucky, 22 m. S of Paducah; pop. (1970c) 10,724; clothing, flour, furniture; tobacco, corn.
2 Borough, Lackawanna co., NE Pennsylvania, 11 m. NE of Scranton; pop. (1970c) 2176; coal mining.

Mayfield Heights. City, Cuyahoga co., N Ohio, 13 m. E of Cleveland; pop. (1970c) 22,139; residential suburb.

May·myo \ˈmā-(ˌ)myō\. Town, Mandalay dist., Lower Burma, on railroad 30 m. ENE of Mandalay; pop. (1962e) 55,954; at an alt. of ab. 3500 ft.; in region producing fruit and coffee.

May·nard \ˈmā-nərd\. Town, Middlesex co., NE Massachusetts, 16 m. SSW of Lowell; pop. (1970c) 9710; woolens.

May·nard·ville \ˈmā-nərd-ˌvil\. City, ⊗ of Union co., NE Tennessee; pop. (1970c) 702.

May·nooth \mā-ˈnüth\. Town, NE co. Kildare, E Eire; pop. (1961c) 886; St. Patrick's Coll. (1795), noted Irish Roman Catholic seminary.

Mayo \ˈmā-(ˌ)ō\. **1** Town, ⊗ of Lafayette co., NW Florida penin.; pop. (1970c) 793.
2 County, Connacht prov., NW Eire; 2084 sq. m.; pop. (1971p) 109,497; ⊗ Castlebar; livestock raising; strawberries; fishing, tourism.

Ma·yo \ˈmī-(ˌ)ō\. **1** Peak, S Chile, on the Argentina border W of Lake Argentino; 7810 ft.

2 River in Chihuahua and Sonora states, Mexico; ab. 250 m. long; flows into the Gulf of California.

Mayo. See MAIO.

May·o·dan \mā-'ō-dan\. Town, Rockingham co., N North Carolina, 27 m. NNE of Winston-Salem; pop. (1970c) 2875.

Ma·yon, Mount \-mä-'yōn\. Active volcano, E Albay prov., SE Luzon, Phil.; 8284 ft., the most perfect volcanic cone known; crowned almost continuously with a halo of vapor which at night becomes a fiery glow; has had destructive eruptions, esp. 1814, 1897, and 1928.

Ma·yor, Is·la \ˌēz-lä-mä-'yȯ(ə)r\. Island, W of Guadalquivir river in a swamp S of Seville, Spain; 25 m. long.

Ma·yotte \mä-'yȯt\. One of the Comoro Is. (*q.v.*), in SE part; 144 sq. m.; pop. (1970e) 48,000; chief town Mamoutzu; highest point 2165 ft.

Mayoumba. See MAYUMBA.

May Pen \'mā-ˌpen\. Town, Jamaica, 23 m. W of Kingston; pop. (1970e) 26,200.

May·ra·i·ra Point \ˌmī-rə-ˌir-ə-\. Most northerly point of Ilocos Norte prov., Luzon, Phil. and of the island of Luzon, 18°40′N, 120°50′E; marks W point of Pasaleng Bay.

Maysí, Cape. See MAISÍ, CAPE.

Mays Landing \māz-\. Town (unincorporated), ⊗ of Atlantic co., SE New Jersey, on Great Egg river 17 m. WNW of Atlantic City; pop. (1970c) 1272; resort; Atlantic Christian Coll. (1964).

Mays·ville \'māz-ˌvil\. 1 City, ⊗ of Mason co., NE Kentucky, on Ohio river 53 m. SE of Covington; pop. (1970c) 7411.

2 City, ⊗ of De Kalb co., NW Missouri; pop. (1970c) 1045; diversified agriculture.

Ma·yu \mə-'yü\. River, Lower Burma; ab. 70 m. long; flows S into Bay of Bengal just N of Sittwe; the narrow tongue of land extending S bet. it and the Bay of Bengal forms **Mayu Point** where there was fighting 1943–44 in Japanese attack on India.

Ma·yum·ba *or formerly* **Ma·youm·ba** \mə-'yüm-bə\. Seaport, S Gabon, W equatorial Africa.

Mayu Range. Coastal range of the Arakan Yoma system, Burma, W of Mayu river and extending along Mayu Point; scene of severe fighting Feb. 1944.

Ma·yur·bhanj \mə-'yu̇(ə)r-ˌbanj\. District, Orissa, E India; 4022 sq. m.; pop. (1961c) 204,043.

May·ville \'mā-ˌvil\. 1 Village and resort, ⊗ of Chautauqua co., SW corner of New York; pop. (1970c) 1567.

2 City, Traill co., E North Dakota; pop. (1970c) 2554; grain and dairy farms; Mayville State Coll. (1889).

3 City, Dodge co., SE cen. Wisconsin, 22 m. S of Fond du Lac; pop. (1970c) 4139; dairy products, sheet metal; summer resort; Dodge County Teachers Coll. (1925).

May·wood \'mā-ˌwu̇d\. 1 Residential city, Los Angeles co., SW California, 5 m. SE of Los Angeles; pop. (1970c) 16,996; furniture, automobiles.

2 Residential village, Cook co., NE Illinois, 12 m. W of Chicago; pop. (1970c) 30,036; incorporated 1881.

3 Borough, Bergen co., NE corner of New Jersey, 6 m. ESE of Paterson; pop. (1970c) 11,087; chemicals.

Mayyali. See MAHÉ 2.

Mazaca. See KAYSERİ 2.

Mazagan. See AL-JADIDA.

Ma·za·ma, Mount \-mə-'zäm-ə\. Prehistoric volcanic mountain of Cascade Mts., W Klamath co., S Oregon; its caldera now occupied by Crater Lake (*q.v.*).

Ma·za·met \ˌmä-zä-'mā\. Commune, Tarn dept., S France, 35 m. SSE of Albi; pop. (1968c) 16,171; manufactures textiles and clothing; foundries, tanneries.

Mā·zan·da·rān \ˌmäz-ˌän-də-'rän\. Province of N Iran. See table at IRAN.

Ma·za·ra del Val·lo \mät-ˌsär-ə-del-'väl-(ˌ)ō\. Seaport, Trapani prov., NW Sicily, Italy; pop. (1968e) 39,951; cathedral.

Ma·zār–i–Sha·rīf \ma-ˌzar-ē-shə-'rēf\. City, ✻ of Balkh prov., N Afghanistan, 190 m. NW of Kabul; pop. (1969e) 43,197; trade center; ships lambskins and carpets; chief town of Afghan Turkistan, just E of ancient Balkh; mosque venerated by Shiite Mussulmans as the tomb of Ali, son-in-law of Mohammed.

Ma·za·rrón \ˌmä-thär-'rōn, -sär-\. Commune, Murcia prov., SE Spain, 3 m. from Mediterranean and 27 m. S of Murcia; pop. (1970p) 9096; copper, lead, and iron mines (once worked by Romans and Phoenicians).

Maz·a·ru·ni \ˌmaz-ə-'rü-nē\. River, Guyana; ab. 350 m. long; flows in wide curve SE to NE into the Essequibo river near its mouth; just before entering the Essequibo joins the Cuyuni river; diamond fields.

Ma·za·ru·ni–Po·ta·ro \ˌmaz-ə-ˌrü-nē-pō-'tär-(ˌ)ō, ˌmäz-\. See ESSEQUIBO 2.

Ma·za·te·nan·go \ˌmäz-ə-tə-'naŋ-(ˌ)gō\. Town, ✻ of Suchitepéquez dept., SW Guatemala; pop. (1971e) 23,932; in area producing coffee, sugar, cocoa, and fruits.

Ma·za·tlán \ˌmäs-ə-'tlän\. Seaport, Sinaloa state, W Mexico; munic. pop. (1970p) 171,835; largest Mexican seaport on the Pacific coast; chief exports metal ores, hides, tobacco, istle, shrimp; tourist resort.

Ma·za·tzal Peak \ˌmäz-ət-ˌsäl-\. Mountain in **Mazatzal Mountains,** on boundary bet. Gila and Yavapai cos., cen. Arizona; 7888 ft.

Ma·zin·garbe \ma-za^{n}(ŋ)-'gärb\. Commune, Pas-de-Calais dept., N France, near Béthune; pop. (1968c) 10,060; coal mines.

Ma·zoe \mä-'zü\. Town, NE cen. Rhodesia, S Africa, 20 m. N of Salisbury; pop. (1969c) 3510; mining and agricultural center in fertile valley.

Ma·zo·via \mə-'zō-vē-ə\. Ancient principality, Poland, E of the Vistula; long semi-independent; in 14th–16th cents. sent many colonists into Masuria; completely united to Poland by 1529; from 16th cent. its capital was Warsaw, succeeding Płock; became the province of Warsaw; after 1945 divided between Warsaw and Białystok provinces.

Mazuria. See MASURIA.

Maz·za·ri·no \ˌmät-sə-'rē-(ˌ)nō\. Commune, Caltanissetta prov., cen. Sicily, Italy, 16 m. SE of Caltanissetta; pop. (1968e) 16,563.

Mba \em-'bä\ *or* **Ba** \'bä\. River, NW Viti Levu I., Fiji, SW Pacific Ocean.

Mba·bane \ˌem-bə-'bän\. Town, ✻ of Swaziland, SE Africa, 93 m. WSW of Lourenço Marques, Mozambique; pop. (1966c) 13,803.

Mba·la \em-'bäl-ə\ *or formerly* **Ab·er·corn** \'ab-ər-ˌkȯ(ə)rn\. Town, NE Zambia, 15 m. SE of S end of Lake Tanganyika; alt. 5700 ft.; scene of surrender of last of German African forces Nov. 14, 1918.

Mba·le \em-'bäl-ē\. Town, Uganda, ab. 120 m. NE of Kampala; pop. (1969p) 23,593.

Mban·da·ka \ˌem-bän-'dak-ə\ *or formerly* **Co·quil·hat·ville** \kō-kē-'at-ˌvil, kō-'kē-ə-vil\. Town, ✻ of Équateur prov., Zaire, on the Congo river where it is joined by the Ruki; pop. (1967e) 86,672.

Mbau \em-'bau̇\. Town, former native ✻ of Viti Levu, Fiji, on small island off E coast N of the Rewa delta.

Mbe·ya \em-'bā-ə\. 1 Administrative region of SW Tanzania. See table at TANZANIA.

2 Town, its ✻; pop. (1967c) 12,479.

Mbo·ca·ya·ty \(ˌ)em-ˌbō-kə-'yät-ē\. Town, Guairá dept., S cen. Paraguay; dist. pop (1970e) 5865.

Mbomu. See BOMU.

Mbu·ji–Ma·yi \em-'bü-jē-'mī-(y)ē\ *or formerly* **Ba·kwan·ga** \bə-'kwäŋ-gə\. Town, ✻ of Kasai-Oriental prov., Zaire; pop. (1971e) 305,818; diamond mining.

Mbu·ya·pey \em-bü-'yäp-(ˌ)ā\. Town, Paraguarí dept., S Paraguay; dist. pop. (1970e) 10,056.

Mdaourouch. See MADAUROS.

Mead, Lake \-ˈmēd\. Reservoir in Colorado river in Mohave co., NW Arizona, and Clark co., SE Nevada, formed by Boulder Dam (see UNITED STATES, *Dams and Reservoirs*); area 227 sq. m., length 115 m., depth over 500 ft. near the dam; has capacity of over 31,250,000 acre-feet of water, used for flood control, irrigation, and power.

Meade \ˈmēd\. 1 Name of counties in three states of the U.S. See tables at KANSAS, KENTUCKY, SOUTH DAKOTA.
2 City, ⊗ of Meade co., SW Kansas, 37 m. SSW of Dodge City; pop. (1970c) 1899; silica mines; livestock.

Meade Peak. Mountain, Bear Lake co., SE Idaho; 9953 ft.

Mead·ow \ˈmed-(ˌ)ō, -ə\. River, S cen. West Virginia; ab. 50 m. long; flows NW from Greenbrier co. and forms boundary bet. Nicholas and Fayette cos. until it joins the Gauley river.

Meadow Lake. Town, Saskatchewan, Canada, 135 m. NW of Prince Albert; pop. (1971p) 3426; timber; agriculture; summer resort.

Mead·ow·lands–Mc·Gov·ern \ˈmed-ō-ˌlan(d)z-mə-ˈgəv-ərn\. Unincorporated community, Washington co., SW Pennsylvania, ab. 4 m. N of Washington; pop. (1970c) 3609.

Mead·ville \ˈmēd-ˌvil\. 1 Town, ⊗ of Franklin co., SW Mississippi; pop. (1970c) 594.
2 City, ⊗ of Crawford co., NW Pennsylvania, 33 m. S of Erie; pop. (1970c) 16,572; rayon, machine tools, iron castings, electrical equipment; Allegheny Coll. (1815); settled 1788.

Mea·ford \ˈmē-fərd\. Town, Grey co., SE Ontario, Canada, on Nottawasaga Bay 20 m. E of Owen Sound; pop. (1971p) 4055; hardwood products; lake port; agriculture.

Mea·gher \ˈmär\. County in Montana. See table at MONTANA.

Me·a·rim \ˌmā-ə-ˈrim\. River, Maranhão state, SE Brazil; flows N to São Marcos Bay; chief tributaries the Pindaré and the Grajaú.

Mearns, The. See KINCARDINE 2.

Meath \ˈmēth, ˈmēt͟h\. County, Leinster prov., E Eire; 903 sq. m.; pop. (1971p) 71,616; ⊗ Trim; rivers Boyne, Blackwater; principal economic activity is livestock raising. Kingdom set up in 2d cent. B.C. more extensive than present county; made county 1296 but status and boundaries not definitely established until early 17th cent.

Meaux \ˈmō\. Manufacturing commune, Seine-et-Marne dept., N France, 32 m. NNE of Melun; pop. (1968c) 30,167; paper, metal stamping, copper, printing industries; ships wheat and sugar beets; chief town of Brie; episcopal see since 375 A.D.; 13th to 16th cent. cathedral; episcopal palace; chartered 1170; prominent in 16th cent. Wars of Religion.

Meb·ane \ˈmeb-ən\. Town, Alamance and Orange cos., N cen. North Carolina, 24 m. WNW of Durham; pop. (1970c) 2433; furniture, cotton yarn, bricks, flour.

Mec·a·ti·na, Cape *or* **Cape Mec·ca·ti·na** \-ˌmek-ə-ˈtē-nə\. Point, SE Quebec, Canada, on Strait of Belle Isle.

Mec·ca *also* **Mek·ka** \ˈmek-ə\ *or Arab.* **Mak·kah** \ˈmak-ə\ *or anc.* **Mac·o·ra·ba** \ˌmak-ə-ˈrā-bə\. City, ✱ of Hejaz, W Saudi Arabia; in a valley surrounded by low hills ab. 50 m. from the coast; pop. (1965e) 185,000; Institute for Higher Education (1962); Holy City of Islam; birthplace of Mohammed 570 A.D.; contains the Great Mosque with the Kaaba and sacred Black Stone; its Red Sea port is Jidda; has large bazaars.
History: A place of religious pilgrimage before Mohammed whose home it was until 622, when he was forced to flee to Medina (see MEDINA 6); sacked by Karmathians early 10th cent.; came under Ottoman Turks 1517; early in 19th cent. seized by Wahabis whom Mehemet Ali defeated; seat of Grand Sherif of Mecca who, in 1908, was Husein ibn-Ali; under Husein, declared independence of Turkey 1916 and became capital of kingdom of Hejaz (*q.v.*); in 1924 occupied by Wahabis under ibn-Saud who later erected kingdom of Saudi Arabia (*q.v.*).

Me·chan·ic Falls \mi-ˌkan-ik-\. Town, Androscoggin co., SW Maine, 10 m. W of Lewiston; pop. (1970c) 2193.

Me·chan·ics·burg \mi-ˈkan-iks-ˌbərg\. Borough, Cumberland co., S Pennsylvania, 9 m. WSW of Harrisburg; pop. (1970c) 9385; structural steel, forgings, clothing, flour; settled 1790.

Me·chan·ics·ville \mi-ˈkan-iks-ˌvil\. Locality in Hanover co., Virginia, ab. 7 m. NE of Richmond; pop. (1970c) 5189; battle June 26, 1862 in which Confederates under Hill and Longstreet were repulsed with severe loss by Union forces; also known as the battle of **Beaver Dam Creek.**

Me·chan·ic·ville \mi-ˈkan-ik-ˌvil\. City, Saratoga co., E New York, on Hudson river 17 m. N of Albany; pop. (1970c) 6247.

Me·chant, Lake \-mi-ˈshän\. Lake in S Terrebonne parish, SE Louisiana; connected through Caillou Lake with Gulf of Mexico.

Me·che·len \ˈmek-ə-lə(n)\ *or Fr.* **Ma·lines** \mȧ-lēn\ *or Eng.* **Mech·lin** \ˈmek-lən\. Commune, Antwerp prov., N Belgium; pop. (1969e) 65,823; large vegetable market; furniture, tapestries, beer; formerly noted lace-making center; 13th–15th cent. cathedral; enjoyed great prosperity in 15th and early 16th cents.

Mechili, Al–. See AL-MECHILI.

Me·chum \ˈmē-chəm\. River, cen. Virginia; ab. 30 m. long; flows NE and SE in Albemarle co. to empty into Rivanna river.

Meck·len·burg \ˈmek-lən-ˌbərg\. 1 Name of counties in two states of the U.S. See tables at NORTH CAROLINA and VIRGINIA.
2 *also* -ˌbu̇(ə)rg\. Former German state, now part of East Germany; 6068 sq. m.; ✱ Schwerin; included also cities of Rostock and Neustrelitz.
History: Originally Germanic territory which was occupied c. 600 A.D. by Slavic peoples who were gradually driven back by German colonization carried out under Henry the Lion; ruled briefly in 13th cent. by Waldemar II of Denmark; became duchy 1348; because of participation (in first part of Thirty Years' War) on Danish side, lost lands to Wallenstein 1629; received bishoprics of Schwerin and Ratzeburg 1648; in 1701 divided into duchies of **Mecklenburg–Schwe·rin** \-shfā-ˈrēn\ and **Mecklenburg–Stre·litz** \-ˈs(h)trā-ləts\; both became grand duchies 1815 and joined North German Confederation 1867; republics in 1918; reunited in 1934; lost sovereign rights 1933–35; divided into the districts of Rostock, Schwerin, and Neubrandenburg 1952. See GERMANY.

Mecklenburg, Bay of. Inlet of SW Baltic Sea, bounded on W by West Germany and on S and E by East Germany; includes Lübeck Bay.

Me·cos·ta \mi-ˈkäs-tə, -ˈkȯs-\. County in Michigan. See table at MICHIGAN.

Me·dan \mā-ˈdän\. Commercial city, ✱ of North Sumatra prov., NE Sumatra, Indonesia; pop. (1961c) 479,098; largest city of Sumatra; on small Deli river ab. 15 m. from its mouth and from the port of Belawan; center of a rich agricultural region, shipping rubber, tobacco, coffee, and sisal; Islamic Univ. of North Sumatra (1952), Univ. of North Sumatra (1957).

Me·da·no·sa, Point \-ˌmed-ᵊn-ˈō-sə\. Cape on N cen. coast of Santa Cruz prov., S Argentina.

Med·dy·bemps Lake \ˈmed-ē-ˌbem(p)s-\. Lake in E cen. Washington co., E Maine.

Mé·déa \ˌmā-dā-ˈä\. 1 Department of N Algeria. See table at ALGERIA.
2 Town, its ✱, S of Algiers; pop. (1966c) 54,000.

Medeba. See MADEBA.

Me·del·lin \ˌmed-ᵊl-ēn, ˌmā-t͟hə-ˈyēn\. Municipality on extreme NW coast of Cebu I., Phil., at N end of Tanon Strait opp. Bantayan I.; pop. (1969e) 28,800.

Me·del·lín. 1 \ˌmed-ᵊl-ˈēn, ˌmā-t͟hə-ˈyēn\. City, ✱ of Antioquia dept., NW Colombia, NW of Bogotá; pop. (1971e) 1,039,800; 2d largest city in Colombia; coffee market; glassware, ceramics, chemicals, foodstuffs, textiles, steel;

educational center, with two universities and various colleges; founded 1675.

2 \ˌmā-t͟hə-ˈyēn\. Village, Badajoz prov., Spain, on the Guadiana river; pop. (1970p) 2625; in ancient Estremadura; birthplace of Hernando Cortes; ruined castle.

Mé·de·nine \mād-ˈnēn\. Town, SE Tunisia, near Mareth 45 m. SSE of Gabès; pop. (1966c) 8000.

Med·field \ˈmed-ˌfēld\. Town, Norfolk co., E Massachusetts, 17 m. SW of Boston; pop. (1970c) 9821; burned in King Philip's War 1675.

Med·ford \ˈmed-fərd\. 1 City, Middlesex co., NE Massachusetts, 5 m. N of Boston; pop. (1970c) 64,397; residential suburb of Boston; vehicle bodies, valves, wax, leather products, batteries, concrete blocks; Tufts Univ. (1852).

2 Town, ⊗ of Grant co., N Oklahoma; pop. (1970c) 1304; oil wells; livestock farms.

3 City, ⊗ of Jackson co., SW Oregon, 60 m. W of Klamath Falls; pop. (1970c) 28,454; summer resort; canned fruit, lumber; diversified agriculture; point of entry to Crater Lake National Park.

4 City, ⊗ of Taylor co., N Wisconsin, 32 m. W of Merrill; pop. (1970c) 3454; dairy products; poultry farms; Taylor County Teachers Coll. (1912).

Medford Lakes. Borough, Burlington co., S cen. New Jersey, 18 m. ESE of Camden; pop. (1970c) 4792.

Med·gi·dia \me-ˈjē-dē-ə, -dyə\. Town, Constanța co., SE Romania, ab. 20 m. WNW of Constanța; pop. (1970e) 33,-629.

Me·dia \ˈmēd-ē-ə\. 1 Borough, ⊗ of Delaware co., SE Pennsylvania, 15 m. W of Philadelphia; pop. (1970c) 6444; plastics, pork products; peaches.

2 Ancient country, S Asia, originally the plateau region corresponding to NW part of modern Iran which was occupied by Medes, an Iranian people; in 8th cent. B.C. divided into small principalities; part of Assyrian Empire to 626 B.C.; independent kingdom under Cyaxares, aided Babylon in bringing about downfall of Assyria 612 B.C.; expanded territory to include part of Assyria, Armenia, and Cappadocia on W, to the Oxus river on NE, and Persia in S, capital Rhages; conquered by Cyrus, founder of Persian Empire 550 B.C. As a province of Persia it was bounded on N by the Elburz Mts., on NE by Hyrcania, on E by Parthia, on S by Persis and Susiana, on SW by Babylonia, on W by Assyria, and on NW by Armenia. After the conquest of Persia by Alexander it was divided into **Media At·ro·pa·te·ne** \-ˌa-trə-pə-ˈtē-nē\ in the N (capital Gazaca) and **Media Mag·na** \-ˈmag-nə\ in the S (capital Ecbatana, *mod.* Hamadān). See AZERBAIJAN 1.

Me·di·aş \med-ˈyäsh\. Town, Sibiu co., cen. Romania; munic. pop. (1970e) 55,924; glass, leather goods; gas wells.

Med·i·cal Lake \ˌmed-ə-kəl-\. Town, Spokane co., E Washington, 15 m. WSW of Spokane; pop. (1970c) 3529.

Me·di·ci·na \ˌmā-dē-ˈchē-nä\. Commune, Bologna prov., Emilia-Romagna, N Italy, 15 m. E of Bologna; pop. (1970c) 12,842.

Med·i·cine Bow \ˈmed-ə-sən-ˌbō\. River, S Wyoming; ab. 120 m. long; formed by confluence of branches in E Carbon co., flows N and W into North Platte river.

Medicine Bow Mountains. A range of the Rocky Mts., extending N and S in Colorado and Wyoming; highest peaks Medicine Bow Peak 12,013 ft. and Elk Mountain 11,156 ft. in S cen. Wyoming.

Medicine Bow Peak. Mountain, S cen. Wyoming; 12,013 ft.; highest point in Medicine Bow Range.

Medicine Creek. River, S cen. South Dakota; ab. 60 m. long; rises in E Jones co., flows E, then N into Missouri river on N boundary of Lyman co.

Medicine Hat. City, SE Alberta, Canada, on South Saskatchewan river 94 m. ENE of Lethbridge; pop. (1971p) 26,058; railroad divisional point; river port; flour mills, grain elevators, foundries, planing and lumber mills, machine shops; coal mines, natural-gas wells; Medicine Hat Junior Coll. (1965); founded 1883.

Medicine Lake. Lake in S Sheridan co., NE Montana.

Medicine Lodge. City, ⊗ of Barber co., S Kansas, 64 m. SW of Hutchinson; pop. (1970c) 2545; oil and gas wells; dairy and grain farms.

Me·di·na \mə-ˈdē-nə\. 1 River, S cen. Texas; 116 m. long; flows through Bandera and Medina cos. to join the San Antonio river below San Antonio. See MEDINA DAM.

2 Name of counties in two states of the United States. See tables at OHIO and TEXAS.

3 Village, Orleans co., W New York, 41 m. W of Rochester on N.Y. State Barge Canal; pop. (1970c) 6415; pipes and fittings, canned goods, men's clothing, aircraft parts; fruit and truck farms.

4 City, ⊗ of Medina co., N Ohio, 18 m. WNW of Akron; pop. (1970c) 10,913; aluminum castings, lumber; pickles; beekeeping.

5 City, King co., W cen. Washington, 6 m. E of Seattle; pop. (1970c) 3455.

6 *or Arab.* **Al–Ma·dī·nah** \ˌal-ma-ˈdē-nə\ *or earlier* **Yath·rib** \ˈyath-rəb\. Inland city, E cen. Hejaz, W Saudi Arabia, 210 m. N of Mecca; ab. 120 m. from the Red Sea coast; pop. (1965e) 100,000; pottery; fruit, grain; Islamic Univ. (1962); its port is Yenbo'. Second most important holy city of Islam, containing the tomb of Mohammed; noted for its mosque enclosing the tomb and its palaces and fountains; the refuge of Mohammed after his flight (hegira) from Mecca; date of his arrival Sept. 20, 622, later adopted as beginning of Muslim calendar. Capital of the caliphate 622–661; after its sack by Ommiads 683 declined in influence; later came under Turks, Egyptians, and Wahabis; city of the new kingdom of Hejaz 1919–24 when after a long siege it fell to ibn-Saud.

Medina–Arkosh. See ARCOS DE LA FRONTERA.

Medina Dam. Dam across Medina river, bet. Bandera and Medina cos., S cen. Texas; height 178 ft.; completed 1913; impounds water, **Medina Lake,** for irrigation.

Medina del Cam·po \mā-ˈt͟hē-nə-t͟hel-ˈkäm-pō\. Commune, Valladolid prov., NW cen. Spain, 25 m. SSW of Valladolid; pop. (1970p) 16,528; manufactures brandy, flour; stock raising.

Medina–Si·do·nia \-sē-ˈt͟hō-nyə\. Commune, Cádiz prov., SW Spain, 19 m. ESE of Cádiz; pop. (1970p) 13,651; cattle raising; Gothic church; ancestral palace of dukes of Medina-Sidonia.

Mediolanum. 1 Ancient city, France. See SAINTES.

2 Ancient city, Italy. See MILAN.

Mediomatrica. See METZ.

Med·i·ter·ra·ne·an Sea \ˌmed-ə-tə-ˈrā-nē-ən-, -nyən-\ *or anc.* **Ma·re In·ter·num** \ˌmā-(ˌ)rē-in-ˈter-nəm, ˌmär-(ˌ)ā-\. Inland sea, enclosed by Europe on the W and N, Asia on the E, and Africa on the S; 969,100 sq. m.; max. E-W extent 2300 m.; max. depth 16,896 ft.; connected on W with the Atlantic Ocean by the Strait of Gibraltar, on SE with the Red Sea by the Suez Canal, and on NE with the Black Sea by the Dardanelles, Sea of Marmara, and Bosporus. Its main subdivisions are the Adriatic Sea, Aegean Sea, Tyrrhenian Sea, Ionian Sea, and Ligurian Sea; its chief islands Sicily, Sardinia, Corsica, Crete, Cyprus, Balearic Is., Dodecanese, Cyclades, Sporades, Ionian Is., Malta.

Me·di·um Lake \ˈmēd-ē-əm-\. Lake in Palo Alto co., N Iowa; ab. 4 m. long.

Me·djer·da *or* **Me·jer·da** \mə-ˈjerd-ə\ *or anc.* **Bag·ra·das** \ˈbag-rə-ˌdas\. River, N Africa; 230 m. long; rises in NE Algeria, flows E across N Tunisia into the Gulf of Tunis; fighting along its course Apr.–May 1943.

Medjerda Mountains. Range of the Little Atlas Mts. in NE Annaba dept., NE Algeria, extending across border into NW Tunisia; highest point ab. 3300 ft.

Medjez–el–Bab. See MAJĀZ AL-BĀB.

Med·men·ham \'med-nəm\. Village, S Buckinghamshire, SE cen. England; site of ruined Cistercian abbey, scene of revels of the Hell-fire Club or the secret society of the "Mad Monks of Medmenham" founded c. 1755 by Sir Francis Dashwood.

Med·ny \'med-nē\. Island, Bering Sea. See KOMANDORSKIYE ISLANDS.

Medoacus Major. See BRENTA.

Mé·doc \mā-'däk\. District, NW Gironde dept., SW France, N of Bordeaux; ab. 50 m. long, 6 to 7 m. wide; vineyards.

Me·do·ra \mi-'dōr-ə\. Village, ⊗ of Billings co., W North Dakota; pop. (1970c) 129.

Me·dūm \me-'düm\. Locality, Egypt, bet. Memphis and Al-Faiyūm, ab. 40 m. S of Cairo; site of step pyramid built by Snefru, last king of Memphite dynasty.

Medunta. See MANTES-LA-JOLIE.

Med·ve·di·tsa \med-'ved-ət-sə\. Unnavigable river, SE Russian S.F.S.R., U.S.S.R.; ab. 425 m. long; flows SSW to the Don river in Volgograd Oblast.

Med·ve·zhe·gorsk \med-ˌvezh-ə-'gȯ(ə)rsk\. Town, S cen. Karelian A.S.S.R., Russian S.F.S.R., U.S.S.R., at N end of Lake Onega; pop. (1967e) 17,000; on Murmansk railroad 80 m. N of Petrozavodsk.

Medvezhi Ostrova. See BEAR ISLANDS.

Med·way \'med-ˌwā\. 1 Town, Norfolk co., E Massachusetts, 22 m. SW of Boston; pop. (1970c) 7938.

2 River, SE England; 70 m. long; formed by confluence of branches in Kent, flows N into the Thames at Sheerness; its estuary extends W to Rochester.

Meeanee. See MIANI.

Mee·ker \'mē-kər\. 1 County in Minnesota. See table at MINNESOTA.

2 Town, ⊗ of Rio Blanco co., NW Colorado; pop. (1970c) 1597; resort; coal and uranium mines.

Meeks Field \'mēks-\. United States Army air base at Keflavík, SW Iceland; built during World War II, turned over to Iceland Oct. 1946 and renamed **Kef·la·vík Field** \'kyep-lə-ˌvēk-\; now an international airport.

Meenen. See MENEN.

Mee·ra·ne \mā-'rän-ə\. Industrial city, Karl-Marx-Stadt dist., East Germany, 21 m. W of Karl-Marx-Stadt; pop. (1970e) 24,933; textiles, machinery, boilers, vehicle bodies.

Meers·sen *or* **Mer·sen** \'me(ə)r-sən\. Commune, Limburg prov., SE Netherlands, just NNE of Maastricht; pop. (1970e) 8800. Treaty signed here Aug. 8, 870 bet. Charles the Bald, Holy Roman emperor, and Louis the German, king of Germany, divided the kingdom of their nephew, Lothair II.

Mee·rut \'mā-rət, 'mir-ət\. 1 Division, Uttar Pradesh, N India; 9225 sq. m.; pop. (1961c) 7,939,770.

2 District; 2322 sq. m.; pop. (1961c) 2,712,960.

3 City, ✱ of district and of division, on a tributary of the Ganges river 40 m. NE of Delhi; pop. (1970e) 250,126; industrial center, producing textiles, chemicals, paint, varnish, sugar, leather goods, hosiery, sports goods, and musical instruments; important military cantonment; established 1806 by British; scene of first uprising of the Mutiny 1857 (see BARRACKPORE).

Me·ga \mə-'gä\. Town, Sidamo, S Ethiopia, on highway from Addis Ababa to Nairobi, Kenya; pop. (1967e) 1428.

Meg·a·lóp·o·lis \ˌmeg-ə-'läp-ə-ləs\. City, S Arcadia dept., cen. Peloponnesus, Greece, just E of the Alpheus river. Founded 370 B.C. as Arcadian federal capital at suggestion of Epaminondas after the battle of Leuctra; its inhabitants made up of persons taken from ab. 40 Arcadian towns; intended to be a defense against Sparta; usually an ally of Thebes and Macedon; joined Achaean League 234 B.C.; destroyed by Cleomenes III 222 B.C.

Me·gan·tic \mə-'gant-ik\ *or Fr.* **Mé·gan·tic** \mā-gäⁿ-tēk\. 1 Lake, S Frontenac co., S Quebec, Canada; 14 sq. m.; its outlet is the Chaudière.

2 County, Quebec, Canada. See table at QUEBEC.

3 *or* **Lac–Mégantic** \ˌläk-\. Town, ⊗ of Frontenac co., S Quebec, Canada, on NE shore of Lake Megantic; pop. (1966c) 6958; dairy products, plywood.

Meg·a·ra \'meg-ə-rə\. 1 Ancient city and state, N Africa. See CARTHAGE 8.

2 *or* **Mé·ga·ra** \'meg-ə-rə\. Seaport city, Attica dept., Greece, on N coast of Saronic Gulf W of Athens; pop. (1961c) 15,450. Anciently capital of Megaris; flourished as maritime city under Dorians, establishing colonies on shores of Propontis and Euxine; ruined commercially in Peloponnesian War. Birthplace of Euclid, founder of the Megarian school of philosophy.

Megara Hy·blaea \-hī-'blē-ə\. Ruins of town on E coast of Sicily, Italy, near Augusta and just NW of Syracuse; founded 728 B.C. by Dorians from Megara; came under control of Gelon in 5th cent. B.C.

Meg·a·ris \'meg-ə-rəs\. District in ancient Greece, bet. the Saronic Gulf and Gulf of Corinth; ab. 143 sq. m.; ✱ Megara; formed E part of Isthmus of Corinth.

Me·gha·la·ya \ˌmā-gə-'lā-ə\. State, NE India; 8665 sq. m.; pop. (1971p) 983,336; ✱ Shillong; was created a union territory 1970, a state 1972.

Megh·na \'māg-nə\. River, Bangla Desh; ab. 125 m. long; formed by the Surma and its tributaries, flows S and is joined by the Padma (the merged Brahmaputra and Ganges) SE of Dacca; its wide lower course is the E mouth of the Ganges Delta (*q.v.*); navigable but dangerous at certain seasons because of the high bore.

Me·gid·do \mi-'gid-(ˌ)ō\ *or* **Tel Megiddo** \ˌtel-\. City, anc. Palestine, now an archaeological site in Israel, on S side of Plain of Esdraelon ab. 15 m. S of Haifa; modern excavations have shown that it was settled ab. 3500 B.C. A great battlefield of ancient history (see ARMAGEDDON): in 1468 B.C. Thutmose III of Egypt defeated here a Syrian army; in 13th cent. B.C. Deborah and Barak near the site overcame Sisera (*Judges* iv); ab. 609 B.C. Josiah was killed by Necho II of Egypt. In World War I Gen. Allenby began here his major offensive against the Turks Sept. 18, 1918.

Megiste. See KASTELLORIZON.

Mehdia. See MAHDIA.

Me·he·dinți \ˌmā-hā-'dēnts, -'dēn-tsē\. County of SW Romania. See table at ROMANIA.

Me·her·rin \mə-'her-ən\. River, S Virginia and NE North Carolina; 160 m. long; flows E and SE from Virginia across state border to the Chowan river.

Meh Klong. See MEKLONG.

Meh·sa·na \mā-'sän-ə\. 1 District, Gujarat, W India; 4324 sq. m.; pop. (1961c) 1,689,963; ✱ Mehsana; cotton, wheat, pulses.

2 Town, its ✱, N of Ahmadabad; pop. (1961c) 32,577; cotton gins.

Me·hun–sur–Yè·vre \mə-ˌəⁿ-sü(ə)r-'yevrᵊ\. Town, Cher dept., cen. France, NW of Bourges; pop. (1962c) 5700; ruins of 14th cent. castle where Charles VII was crowned 1422 and died 1461.

Meiggs \'megz\. Peak, Lima dept., cen. Peru, NE of the city of Lima; 15,518 ft.

Meigs \'megz\. Name of counties in two states of the U.S. See tables at OHIO and TENNESSEE.

Meije \'mezh\ *or* **La Meije** \lä-\. Mountain in the Dauphiné Alps, SE France, bet. Isère and Hautes-Alpes depts.; 13,081 ft.

Meik·ti·la \'mek-tə-lə\. 1 District, Mandalay division, S Upper Burma; 2232 sq. m.; pop. (1962e) 428,130; ✱ Meiktila; rice, peanuts, corn, peas.

2 Town, its ✱, on railroad 75 m. S of Mandalay; pop. (1953c) 25,180; a Buddhist center.

Mei·ning·en \'mīn-iŋ-ən\. City, Suhl dist., East Germany, near Werra river 40 m. SW of Erfurt; pop. (1970e) 25,357; paper, machinery; 17th cent. castle; first mentioned 982; became city 1344; until 1918 capital of dukes of Saxe-Meiningen.

Meis·sen \'mīs-ᵊn\. Manufacturing city, Dresden dist., East Germany, on the Elbe river 14 m. NW of Dresden; pop.

(1970e) 45,571; center of porcelain and ceramics manufacturing since early 18th cent.; leather; metalworking; 15th cent. castle; 13th–14th cent. Gothic cathedral.

Mejdel. See MAGDALA.

Mejerda. See MEDJERDA.

Me·ji·ca·nos \ˌme-hē-ˈkän-(ˌ)ōs\. Town, San Salvador dept., S El Salvador; pop. (1961c) 14,731.

Méjico. See MEXICO.

Me·ji·llo·nes \ˌme-hē-ˈyō-nəs\. Small port, Antofagasta prov., N Chile, ab. 40 m. N of Antofagasta; pop. (1960c) 3663; exports nitrate, borax, copper, tin.

Mejillones del Sur, Bay of \-del-ˈsu̇(ə)r\. Inlet on N coast of Chile, 38 m. N of Antofagasta.

Me·ke·le \ˈmāk-ə-ˌlā\ *also* **Ma·ka·le** \ˈmäk-ə-ˌlā\. Town, ✱ of Tigre prov., N Ethiopia, NE of Lake Tana; pop. (1970e) 27,895.

Mekka. See MECCA.

Me·klong *also* **Mae Klong** *or* **Meh Klong** \ˈmā-ˈklȯŋ\. 1 River, Thailand. See KLONG.

2 Seaport, Thailand. See SAMUT SONGKHRAM.

Mek·nes \mek-ˈnes\ *or Fr.* **Mek·nès** \mek-nes\ *or Span.* **Me·qui·nez** \ˌmā-kə-ˈnās\. City, N Morocco, NW Africa, 36 m. WSW of Fès; a former ✱ of Morocco; pop. (1966e) 195,000; textiles, canned foods, cement, vegetable oils. Founded 10th cent.; in Middle Ages an Almohade citadel; for many years from 17th cent. was the residence of the Moroccan sultan; has large palace, mosques, gateway.

Me·kong \ˈmā-ˈkȯŋ, -ˈkäŋ\ *or Tibetan* **Dza–chu** \ˈ(d)zä-ˈchü\ *or Chin.* **Lan–ts'ang** \ˈlän-ˈ(t)säŋ\. River, SE Asia; ab. 2600 m. long; rises in T'ang-ku-la Range of E Tibet, China, flows SE through Yunnan prov., S China, and through E Indochina, forming the boundary bet. Laos and Burma and a large part of the boundary bet. Laos and Thailand; continues S through Cambodia and South Vietnam, where it empties into the South China Sea through several mouths; receives the Yang-p'i from the E in cen. Yunnan. Navigable to Luang Prabang; its wide delta forms a fertile rice-producing area. In Yunnan passes through deep gorges and lies between and close to the upper courses of the Salween and the Yangtze.

Mekran. See MAKRAN.

Melaka. See MALACCA.

Me·la·lap \mə-ˈläl-əp\. Town, SW cen. Sabah, Malaysia, on island of Borneo.

Mel·a·ne·sia \ˌmel-ə-ˈnē-zhə, -shə\. Collective name for the islands in the Pacific Ocean NE of Australia, including New Caledonia, New Hebrides, Solomon Is., Admiralty Is., Bismarck Archipelago, Fiji, etc.; a subdivision of Oceania.

Mel·bourne \ˈmel-bərn\. 1 City, ⊗ of Izard co., N Arkansas; pop. (1970c) 1043; livestock raising.

2 City, Brevard co., E Florida, on Indian river 58 m. SE of Orlando; pop. (1970c) 40,236; winter resort; electronic components; Florida Institute of Technology (1958); incorporated 1923.

3 City, ✱ of Victoria, SE Australia, at N end of Port Phillip Bay at mouth of the Yarra river; pop. (1970e) 76,900, met. area pop. 2,425,300; good natural harbor; financial center; exports flour, wool, meat, fruit, and dairy products; industrial center, producing motor vehicles, railway rolling stock, machine tools, agricultural machinery, radio and television sets, textiles, clothes, glass, and rubber; Melbourne Univ. (1855), Monash Univ. (1958), La Trobe Univ. (1964). Founded 1835 by settlers from Tasmania; made capital of Victoria when state established 1851; a center of the gold rush during the 1850's; temporary capital of Australia 1901–27; site of Summer Olympic Games 1956.

Mel·chor \mel-ˈchȯ(ə)r\. Island in Chonos Archipelago, in Pacific Ocean off SW coast of Chile.

Melchor Múz·quiz \mel-ˈchȯr-ˈmüs-kēs\. Municipality, Coahuila state, Mexico, 175 m. NNW of Monterrey; pop. (1970p) 45,945; cattle and goat raising; wheat.

Meleda. See MLJET.

Me·le·gna·no \ˌmā-lā-ˈnyä-nō\ *or formerly* **Ma·ri·gna·no** \ˌmä-rē-ˈnyä-nō\. Commune, Milano prov., Lombardy, N Italy, 10 m. SE of Milan; pop. (1968c) 17,906. Destroyed by Frederick II 1239; victory of King Francis I over Swiss troops of duke of Milan 1515; French victory over Austrians June 8, 1859.

Me·le·kess \ˌmel-ə-ˈk(y)es\. Town, Ulyanovsk Oblast, Russian S.F.S.R., U.S.S.R., ab. 55 m. E of Ulyanovsk; pop. (1969e) 79,000; textiles; food processing; nuclear research institute.

Me·le·na del Sur \me-ˌlān-ə-del-ˈsu̇(ə)r\. Municipality, N cen. La Habana prov., W Cuba; pop. (1967e) 13,990.

Mel·fi \ˈmel-fē\. Commune, Potenza prov., Basilicata, S Italy, 26 m. NNW of Potenza; pop. (1968e) 16,612; tourism; produces cereals, wine, oil, apples; 12th cent. cathedral, 13th cent. castle; a Roman foundation; to Italy 1861; destructive earthquakes 1851 and 1930.

Mel·fort \ˈmel-fərt\. Town, S cen. Saskatchewan, Canada, 55 m. ESE of Prince Albert; pop. (1971p) 4740; ships hogs; grain farms.

Melghir, Shatt al–. See MELRHIR, CHOTT.

Mel·i·boea \ˌmel-ə-ˈbē-ə\. Ancient town near the coast of Magnesia, Greece, bet. Mt. Pelion and Mt. Ossa.

Me·li·lla \mə-ˈlē-(y)ə\ *or anc.* **Rus·ad·dir** \ˌrəs-ə-ˈdi(ə)r\. Spanish presidio and commercial city, N coast of Morocco, NW Africa; pop. (1970p) 60,843; ships iron ore; on SE coast of Cape Tres Forcas in Er Rif region. Conquered by Spain 1497; many times under siege; hinterland secured 1909; scene of Riffian revolt 1921 under Abd-al-Krim; reoccupied 1926; scene of revolt of army chiefs which led to Spanish Civil War 1936.

Me·li·mo·yu \ˌmel-i-ˈmō-(ˌ)yü\. Peak, S Chile, E of Moraleda Channel; 7872 ft.

Me·li·pi·lla \ˌmel-i-ˈpē-(y)ə\. City, Santiago prov., cen. Chile, 38 m. SW of Santiago; pop. (1960c) 15,593.

Melita. 1 Independent state, Mediterranean Sea. See MALTA 1.

2 Island, Adriatic Sea. See MLJET.

Melitene. See MALATYA 2.

Me·li·to·pol \ˌmel-ə-ˈtȯ-pəl\. Town, S Zaporozhye Oblast, Ukrainian S.S.R., U.S.S.R., near NW shore of Sea of Azov 70 m. S of Zaporozhye; pop. (1970p) 130,000; center of agricultural region; diesel engines, compressors, clothing; settled late 18th cent.; in World War II occupied by Germans 1941–43.

Mel·la·ha \mə-ˈlä-hə\. Village, an E suburb of Tripoli, Libya.

Mel·len \ˈmel-ən\. City, Ashland co., N Wisconsin; pop. (1970c) 1168; summer resort; dairy products.

Mel·lette \mə-ˈlet\. County in South Dakota. See table at SOUTH DAKOTA.

Mĕl·ník \ˈmyel-ˌnyēk\ *or Ger.* **Mel·nik** \ˈmel-nik\. Town, Czech S.R., W Czechoslovakia, 18 m. N of Prague at junction of Elbe and Vltava rivers; pop. (1968e) 14,902; chemicals; 14th cent. town hall.

Me·lo \ˈmel-(ˌ)ō, ˈmā-(ˌ)lō\. City, ✱ of Cerro Largo dept., E Uruguay, 205 m. NE of Montevideo; pop. (1963c) 33,378; distributing center for NE Uruguay.

Melodunum. See MELUN.

Me·lo·nes Dam \mə-ˈlō-nēz-\. Dam across Stanislaus river, Tuolumne and Calaveras cos., N cen. California; height 225 ft.; completed 1926; impounds water for irrigation.

Me·lo·ria \mə-ˈlōr-ē-ə, -ˈlȯr-\. Small island 4 m. off Leghorn, Italy; naval battles 1241 in which Sardinian king defeated Genoese and 1284 in which Genoese destroyed Pisan fleet.

Me·los \ˈmē-ˌläs\ *or Gk.* **Mí·los** \ˈmē-ˌlȯs\ *or Ital.* **Mi·lo** \ˈmē-(ˌ)lō\. 1 An island of the Cyclades, Cyclades dept., Greece; 58 sq. m.; 14 m. long; pop. (1961c) 4910; chief town Melos; exports salt and gypsum. Of volcanic origin, highest point 1854 ft.; has large harbor on N which nearly divides the island. In early period occupied by Dorians; attacked and conquered 416 B.C. by Athenians and its people either killed or enslaved.
2 Ruined city on Melos; here the famous statue of Venus (Venus of Milo) was discovered 1820 and is now in the Louvre museum in Paris.
3 *or formerly* **Pla·ka** \ˈpläk-ə\. Chief town of island of Melos, Cyclades dept., Greece.

Me·lou·sa *also* **Me·lu·sa** \mā-ˈlü-sə\. Town, N Morocco, NW Africa.

Mel·rhir, Chott \ˌshät-mel-ˈri(ə)r\ *or Arab.* **Shatt Al-Mel·ghir** \ˌshät-al-mel-ˈgi(ə)r\ *also* **Shott Melghir** \ˌshät-\. Marshy saline lake, N of Touggourt, NE Algeria; 80–100 m. long.

Mel·rose \ˈmel-ˌrōz\. 1 Residential city, Middlesex co., NE Massachusetts, 7 m. N of Boston; pop. (1970c) 33,810.
2 City, Stearns co., cen. Minnesota, 30 m. WNW of St. Cloud; pop. (1970c) 2273.
3 Burgh, N Roxburgh co., SE Scotland; pop. (1969e) 2242; the "Kennaquhair" of Scott's *Abbot* and *Monastery.* Ruins of a Cistercian abbey, founded 1136 by David I.

Melrose Park. Village, Cook co., NE Illinois, 15 m. W of Chicago; pop. (1970c) 22,716; steel mills, railroad yards.

Mel·tham \ˈmel-thəm\. Urban district, West Riding, Yorkshire, N England; pop. (1971p) 6595.

Mel·ton Hill Dam \ˈmelt-ᵊn-\. See table at TENNESSEE VALLEY AUTHORITY.

Melton Mow·bray \-ˈmō-brā, -brē\. Urban district, Leicestershire, cen. England, 15 m. NE of Leicester; pop. (1971p) 19,932; food products; iron foundry.

Me·lun \mə-ˈlœⁿ\ *or anc.* **Mel·o·du·num** \ˌmel-ə-ˈd(y)ü-nəm\. Manufacturing city, ✱ of Seine-et-Marne dept., N France, on Seine river 27 m. SSE of Paris; pop. (1968c) 34,518; pharmaceuticals; 11th cent. Romanesque church; fine château nearby. Conquered by Romans 53 B.C.; taken by Normans; royal residence under Capetians; taken by English 1420 and retaken by Joan of Arc 1430.

Melusa. See MELOUSA.

Mel·ville \ˈmel-ˌvil\. 1 Town, St. Landry parish, S cen. Louisiana, 37 m. NNE of Lafayette; pop. (1970c) 2706.
2 City, SE Saskatchewan, Canada, 26 m. SW of Yorkton; pop. (1966c) 5690; dairy and stock farms.

Melville, Cape. 1 Cape, NE Queensland, Australia, on E coast of Cape York Penin., 14°11′S, 144°30′E.
2 Cape, S Balabac I., Palawan prov., SW Phil.

Melville, Lake. Lake, SE Labrador, Canada; 1133 sq. m.; constitutes inner basin of Hamilton Inlet; at its SW corner receives the Churchill river.

Melville Bay. Large inlet of NE Baffin Bay on NW coast of Greenland, E of Cape York.

Melville Island. 1 Island off NW coast of Northern Territory, Australia; 2400 sq. m.; separated from mainland by Clarence Strait.
2 Island in Queen Elizabeth Is., W Franklin dist., Northwest Territories, Canada, N Victoria I.; 16,369 sq. m.; 200 m. long by 130 m. wide.

Melville Peninsula. Peninsula, S Franklin dist., Northwest Territories, Canada, bet. Committee Bay on the W and Foxe Basin on the E.

Melville Sound. See VISCOUNT MELVILLE SOUND.

Mel·vin·dale \ˈmel-vən-ˌdāl\. Residential city, Wayne co., SE Michigan, 8 m. WSW of Detroit; pop. (1970c) 13,862.

Me Ma·o·ya, Mount \-ˌmä-mä-ˈō-yə\. Peak, cen. New Caledonia, SW Pacific Ocean; 4728 ft.

Mem·ba Bay \ˌmem-bə-\. Inlet of Mozambique Channel on NE coast of Mozambique, N of Cape Loguno.

Memel. 1 River, U.S.S.R. See NEMAN.
2 City, U.S.S.R. See KLAIPĖDA 2.

Memelburg. See KLAIPĖDA 2.

Memelgebiet *or* **Memelland.** See KLAIPĖDA 1.

Mem·ming·en \ˈmem-iŋ-ən\. Industrial city, Bavaria, West Germany, 42 m. SW of Augsburg; pop. (1969c) 35,142; textiles, chemicals, electrical equipment, beer; 16th cent. town hall. First mentioned 1010; became city 1286; took part in Tetrapolitan Confession; Austrians defeated by Moreau nearby 1800; passed to Bavaria 1802.

Mem·phis \ˈmem(p)-fəs\. 1 City, ⊗ of Scotland co., NE Missouri, 28 m. NE of Kirksville; pop. (1970c) 2081; dairy and poultry farms.
2 Commercial and industrial city, ⊗ of Shelby co., SW corner of Tennessee, on Mississippi river 10 m. N of Mississippi border; pop. (1970c) 623,530; cotton and hardwood lumber market; produces chemicals, agricultural machinery, pharmaceuticals, rubber products, textiles, paper, furniture. Southwestern at Memphis (1848), Le Moyne-Owen Coll. (1870), Christian Brothers Coll. (1871), Memphis State Univ. (1909), Siena Coll. (1921), Southern Coll. of Optometry (1932), Memphis Academy of Arts (1936), Mid-South Bible Coll. (1944).
History: Forts erected by French, later by Spanish, and by U.S. in 1797; platted and settled in 1819 by colony sent by Andrew Jackson, John Overton, and James Winchester; incorp. as town 1826, as city 1840; made port of customs 1850; became Confederate military center at beginning of Civil War 1861; temporary state capital 1862; captured by Union forces after battle of Memphis 1862, and remained in Union control until after the war; suffered from yellow fever epidemics 1867, 1873, and, esp., 1878; became impoverished and surrendered charter to state 1879; rechartered as city 1893.
3 City, ⊗ of Hall co., NW Texas, in the panhandle 75 m. SE of Amarillo; pop. (1970c) 3227; cotton gins.
4 Ancient city in Lower Egypt, its site now partly covered by village of **Mit Ra·hi·na** \ˌmēt-rə-ˈhē-nə\, ab. 14 m. S of Cairo; traditionally the capital of Menes (c. 3100 B.C.) and of most of the rulers of the Old Kingdom and of the Middle Kingdom down to the XVIIIth dynasty; superseded by Heracleopolis during IXth and Xth dynasties and later by Thebes at beginning of New Kingdom; lost its importance after the conquest of Egypt by Alexander. Sacred to the worship of Ptah. In its ruins are the great temple of Ptah, royal palaces, an extensive necropolis. Pyramids of Saqqara nearby and Pyramids of Giza just to the N; in the Old Testament called **Noph** \ˈnäf\ (*Isaiah* xix. 13; *Jer.* ii. 16, and elsewhere).

Mem·phre·ma·gog, Lake \-ˌmem(p)-fri-ˈmā-ˌgäg\. Lake, extending across U.S.-Canada border from N Vermont into S Quebec; ab. 30 m. long (7 in Vermont) and from 1 to 4 m. wide; its outlet flows into the St. Francis river, Quebec.

Me·na \ˈmē-nə\. City, ⊗ of Polk co., W Arkansas, in Ouachita Mts. 70 m. W of Hot Springs; pop. (1970c) 4530; clothing, leather products; sawmills; diversified agriculture.

Menado. See MANADO.

Menaeum. See MINEO.

Men·ai Strait \ˈmen-ˌī-\. Channel bet. Anglesey I. and the mainland, off NW coast of Wales; 14 m. long, from 200 yards to 2 m. wide; spanned by two bridges, tubular and suspension.

Me·nal·du·ma·deel \mā-ˈnäl-dü-mä-ˌdāl\. Commune, Friesland prov., N Netherlands, just W of Leeuwarden; pop. (1970e) 10,234.

Me Nam *or* **Menam.** See CHAO PHRAYA.

Me·nands \mə-ˈnan(d)z\. Village, Albany co., E New York, on Hudson river 2 m. N of Albany; pop. (1970c) 3449.

Me·nang·ka·bau \ˌmā-näŋ-ˈkäb-ˌau̇\. Former empire of cen. and W Sumatra, regarded as the original home of the Malay race; migrations to Malay Penin. and other parts of the Malay Archipelago began probably in middle of 12th cent. A.D. Partial conversion to Islam in 15th cent.; overcome by Dutch in 18th cent.

Me·nard \mə-ˈnärd\. 1 Name of counties in two states of the U.S. See tables at ILLINOIS and TEXAS.

2 Town, ⊗ of Menard co., W cen. Texas, 52 m. SE of San Angelo; pop. (1970c) 1740; resort; ships wool and livestock; ruins of old Spanish mission (1757) nearby.

Me·nasha \mə-ˈnash-ə\. City, Winnebago co., E Wisconsin, on Lake Winnebago and Fox river 5 m. S of Appleton; pop. (1970c) 14,905; summer resort; paper, wire weaving machinery; printing; dairy farms; forms a continuous community with twin city of Neenah (*q.v.*); settled 1843.

Mende \ˈmäⁿd\ *or anc.* **Mi·ma·tum** \mī-ˈmā-təm\. Commune, ✱ of Lozère dept., S France, 76 m. NW of Avignon; pop. (1968c) 9713; tourism; cathedral (15th cent.; rebuilt early 17th cent.). See CÉVENNES.

Men·den \ˈmen-dən\. City, cen. North Rhine-Westphalia, West Germany, ESE of Dortmund; pop. (1969e) 30,626; manufactures metal and electrical goods.

Men·den·hall \ˈmen-dən-ˌhȯl\. Town, ⊗ of Simpson co., S cen. Mississippi; pop. (1970c) 2402.

Men·de·res \ˌmen-də-ˈres\. 1 *or* **Bü·yük Menderes Neh·ri** \bu̇-ˈyuk . . . ˈner-ē\ *or anc.* **Mae·an·der** \mē-ˈan-dər\. River, W Turkey; ab. 240 m. long; rises in mountains W of Afyonkarahisar and flows SW and W into Aegean Sea S of the island of Samos; notable in ancient legend for its wanderings. Near the mouth of the modern stream is the large Lake Bafa; its fertile valley noted for production of olives. The ancient Maeander flowed across N Caria and on or near its banks were the ancient cities of Laodicea, Magnesia, and Miletus.

2 *or* **Kü·çük Menderes** \ku̇-ˈchu̇k-\ *or anc.* **Sca·man·der** \skə-ˈman-dər\. River, NW Turkey; 60 m. long; rises in Kazdağı (Mt. Ida) and flows W and NW into the Dardanelles across the plain of ancient Troy. The ancient Scamander, flowing past Troy, in its lower course is supposed to have been E of the modern stream.

Men·des \ˈmen-(ˌ)dēz\. Archaeological site in Nile delta, N Egypt, E of Damietta branch and just SE of Al-Mansūra; seat of veneration of Osiris. Near here c. 378 B.C. Egyptians under Nectanebo I defeated the Persians.

Mend·ham \ˈmen-dəm\. Borough, Morris co., N New Jersey, 8 m. W of Morristown; pop. (1970c) 3729; dairy farming.

Men·dip Hills \ˈmen-ˌdip-\. Range of hills, NE Somersetshire, SW England; ab. 18 m. long; highest elevation **Black Down** 1068 ft.

Men·do·ci·no \ˌmen-də-ˈsē-(ˌ)nō\. County in California. See table at CALIFORNIA.

Mendocino, Cape. Cape on W coast of Humboldt co., NW California; extreme W point of California, 40°75′N, 124°25′W.

Men·don \ˈmen-dən\. Town, Worcester co., cen. Massachusetts, 17 m. SE of Worcester; pop. (1970c) 2524.

Men·do·ta \men-ˈdōt-ə\. 1 City, Fresno co., S cen. California, 34 m. W of Fresno; pop. (1970c) 2705.

2 City, La Salle co., N Illinois, 20 m. NW of Ottawa; pop. (1970c) 6902; farm machinery, building materials, feed; livestock farms.

Mendota, Lake. See FOUR LAKES.

Mendota Heights. Village, Dakota co., SE Minnesota, S suburb of St. Paul; pop. (1970c) 6165.

Men·do·za \men-ˈdō-zə\. 1 River, W Argentina; ab. 200 m. long; rises on slopes of Aconcagua Mt., flows E and N into Guanacache Marshes.

2 Province of W Argentina. See table at ARGENTINA.

3 City, its ✱, ab. 60 m. SE of Aconcagua; pop. (1960c) 109,122; center of grape culture; alt. 2320 ft.; univ. (1939). Founded c. 1560; came under viceroyalty of La Plata 1776; headquarters of San Martin in preparing for march across Andes to Chile 1817; destroyed by earthquake and fire 1861; rebuilt 1863 ff.

Me·ne·men \ˌmen-ə-ˈmen\. Town, İzmir prov., W Turkey, 14 m. NNW of İzmir; pop. (1965c) 16,588.

Me·nen *also* **Mee·nen** \ˈmān-ən\ *or Fr.* **Me·nin** \mə-ˈnaⁿ\. Industrial commune, West Flanders prov., NW Belgium, on Lys river at French border; pop. (1969e) 22,195; textiles; tobacco.

Ménerville. See THENIA.

Menevia. See SAINT DAVID'S.

Men·fi \ˈmen-fē\. Commune, Agrigento prov., SW Sicily, Italy, 40 m. NW of Agrigento; pop. (1968e) 7903.

Mêng Chiang \ˈməŋ-jē-ˈäŋ\. Former Japanese buffer state bet. Manchukuo and Outer Mongolia; comprising approximately the provinces of Chahar and Suiyuan of Inner Mongolia; ab. 220,000 sq. m.; ✱ Hu-ho-hao-t'e; estab. 1937, collapsed with defeat of Japan 1945.

Meng·ku \ˈməŋ-ˈkü\. Chinese name of Mongolia.

Meng–ting \ˈməŋ-ˈdiŋ\. Town, SW Yunnan prov., S China, near Burma border SE of Lung-ling; held by Japanese 1942–43.

Meng–tzu *or Fr.* **Mong–tseu** *also* **Meng·tseu** *or* **Meng·tze** \ˈməŋ-ˈ(d)zə\. City and former treaty port, S Yunnan, S China, near North Vietnam border SSE of K'un-ming; on fertile plateau (alt. 4300 ft.).

Men·i·fee \ˈmen-ə-fē\. County in Kentucky. See table at KENTUCKY.

Menin. See MENEN.

Meninx. See JERBA.

Men·lo Park \ˌmen-lō-\. 1 Residential city, San Mateo co., W California, 23 m. SE of San Francisco; pop. (1970c) 26,906; Menlo Coll. (1915); settled c. 1861, incorporated 1930.

2 Unincorporated community, Middlesex co., cen. New Jersey, ab. 6 m. SE of Plainfield; 129 ft. Memorial Tower (topped by huge electric light bulb) on site of Edison's laboratory where he invented incandescent light 1879. See WEST ORANGE 1.

Me·nom·i·nee \mə-ˈnäm-ə-nē\. 1 River, NE Wisconsin; 125 m. long; formed by confluence of Michigamme and Brule rivers, flows SE on Wisconsin-Michigan boundary and empties into Green Bay; provides water power.

2 County in Michigan. See table at MICHIGAN.

3 County in Wisconsin. See table at WISCONSIN.

4 City, Menominee co., Wisconsin, S tip of Michigan penin., on Green Bay; pop. (1970c) 10,748; summer resort; sawmills, brewery; dairy farms.

Menominee Range. Low range in upper Michigan penin. and NE Wisconsin; noted for iron-ore production.

Me·nom·o·nee Falls \mə-ˌnäm-ə-nē-\. Village, Waukesha co., SE Wisconsin, NNW of Milwaukee; pop. (1970c) 31,697.

Me·nom·o·nie \mə-ˈnäm-ə-nē\. City, ⊗ of Dunn co., W Wisconsin, 21 m. W of Eau Claire; pop. (1970c) 11,275; dairy products; poultry farms; Stout State Coll. (1893).

Menorca. See MINORCA.

Men·ta·na \mān-ˈtä-nə\. Commune, Roma prov., W Latium, cen. Italy, NE of Rome; pop. (1968e) 14,459; scene of battle Nov. 3, 1867 in which Garibaldi was defeated by combined papal and French troops.

Men·ta·wai \men-ˈtä-ˌwī\. Island group of ab. 70 islands in the Indian Ocean off the W cen. coast of Sumatra, Indonesia; 2354 sq. m.; includes large islands of Siberut, Sipura, North Pagai, and South Pagai. Of volcanic origin and surrounded by reefs; inhabitants belong to very early indigenous peoples of Sumatra.

Men·teith, Loch \-men-ˈtēth\. Small lake in Perth co., cen. Scotland, near border of Stirling co.

Men·ton \mäⁿ-ˈtōⁿ\ *or Ital.* **Men·to·ne** \mān-ˈtō-nē\. Commune, Alpes-Maritimes dept., SE France, on Mediterranean Sea 12 m. ENE of Nice; pop. (1968c) 25,040; famous health and winter resort. Founded in 10th cent.; under princes of Monaco from 14th cent. to 1848; independent republic 1848–60; to France 1860. Grimaldi (*q.v.*) caves nearby.

Men·tone \'men-ˌtōn\. Village, ⊗ of Loving co., W Texas; pop. (1970c) 44.

Men·tor \'men-tər\. Village, Lake co., NE Ohio, on Lake Erie 22 m. NE of Cleveland; pop. (1970c) 36,912; residential suburb of Cleveland; Lakeland Community Coll. (1967).

Mentor–on–the–Lake. Village, Lake co., NE Ohio, on Lake Erie 24 m. NE of Cleveland; pop. (1970c) 6517.

Menufieh. See MINŪFIYA.

Menzala, Lake. See MANZALA, LAKE.

Men·zel Bour·gui·ba \men-ˌzel-bu̇r-'gē-bə\ *or formerly* **Fer·ry·ville** \'fer-ē-ˌvil\. Town, N Tunisia, N Africa, on S shore of Lake Bizerte; pop. (1966c) 33,800; occupied by U.S. troops May 7, 1943.

Me·o·qui \mā-'ō-kē\. Municipality, Chihuahua state, Mexico, 48 m. SE of Chihuahua; pop. (1970p) 27,000; livestock raising; diversified agriculture.

Meping. See PING.

Mep·pel \'mep-əl\. Commune, Drenthe prov., NE Netherlands, 14 m. NNE of Zwolle; pop. (1970e) 19,864.

Mequinez. See MEKNES.

Meq·uon \'mē-ˌkwän\. City, Ozaukee co., E Wisconsin, S of Sheboygan; pop. (1970c) 12,150.

Merabéllou, Kólpos. See MIRABELLA BAY.

Mer·a·mec \'mer-ə-ˌmak\. River, SE cen. Missouri; 174 m. long; rises in Dent co., flows NE into Mississippi river below St. Louis.

Me·ra·no \mə-'rän-(ˌ)ō\ *or Ger.* **Me·ran** \mā-'rän\. Commune, Bolzano prov., Trentino-Alto Adige, NE Italy, on S slope of the Alps 17 m. NW of Bolzano; pop. (1968e) 33,594; tourist and health resort; 15th cent. castle, 14th cent. church. Near site of 1st cent. (A.D.) *Castrum Maiense;* first mentioned 857 A.D.; received city rights 1305; capital of the Tirol 12th cent. to c. 1420; under Austrian rule until ceded to Italy 1919 by treaty of St-Germain.

Me·ra·pi \mə-'räp-ē\. 1 Volcano, cen. Java, Indonesia, just N of Jogjakarta; 9551 ft.

2 Crater, Java, Indonesia. See IDJEN.

3 Volcanic peak in the Padang Highlands, W Sumatra, Indonesia, 40 m. NE of Padang and near Bukittinggi; 9485 ft.; a peak of the Barisan Mts.; violent eruptions 1867, 1876.

Me·rau·ke \mə-'rau̇-kə\. Seaport and chief town on S coast of Irian Barat, Indonesia, at mouth of **Merauke River** (ab. 125 m. long) 60 m. from Papua New Guinea border; chief product copra.

Mer·ba·bu *or Du.* **Mer·ba·boe** \mər-'bäb-(ˌ)ü\. Volcano, cen. Java, Indonesia, N of Jogjakarta; 10,308 ft.

Mer·can Dağ·la·rı \mer-'jän-ˌdä(g)-lə-'rē\. Mountain group, E cen. Turkey, S of Erzincan; highest peak 11,359 ft.

Mer·ca·ra \mer-'kär-ə\. Town, S Mysore, India; pop. (1960c) 14,500.

Mercatino Marecchia. See NOVAFELTRIA.

Mer·ca·to San Se·ve·ri·no \mer-'kät-(ˌ)ō-ˌsän-ˌsev-ə-'rē-(ˌ)nō\. Commune, Salerno prov., Campania, S Italy, 7 m. N of Salerno; pop. (1968e) 17,855.

Mercato Sa·ra·ce·no \-ˌsär-ə-'chā-nō\. Commune, Forlì prov., Emilia-Romagna, N Italy, 20 m. SSE of Forlì; pop. (1968e) 6477.

Mer·ced \mər-'sed\. 1 River, cen. California; ab. 150 m. long; rises in S Yosemite National Park, flows W through the 6-mile long Yosemite Valley (*q.v.*) and into the San Joaquin river.

2 County in cen. California. See table at CALIFORNIA.

3 City, its ⊗, in valley of the San Joaquin and S of the Merced river 55 m. NW of Fresno; pop. (1970c) 22,670; fruit packing, dairy products; diversified agriculture; Merced Coll. (1963); Castle Air Force Base (7 m. NW).

Mer·ce·da·rio \ˌmer-sə-'där-ē-ˌō\. Peak, San Juan prov., W Argentina, near Chilean border; 22,211 ft.

Mer·ce·des \mər-'sād-(ˌ)ēz\. City, Hidalgo co., S Texas, 20 m. E of McAllen; pop. (1970c) 9355; oil and gas wells; fruit and vegetable packing.

Mercedes \mer-'sād-əs\. 1 Town, Buenos Aires prov., E Argentina, 55 m. W of Buenos Aires; pop. (1960c) 25,778.

2 Town, cen. Corrientes prov., NE Argentina, 120 m. SE of Corrientes; pop. (1960c) 13,368.

3 City, San Luis prov., cen. Argentina, ab. 60 m. E of San Luis; pop. (1960c) 35,449.

4 City and river port, ✱ of Soriano dept., SW Uruguay, on Río Negro 155 m. NW of Montevideo; pop. (1963c) 31,352; commercial center; tourism.

Mer·ced Peak \mər-'sed-\. Mountain on S boundary of Yosemite National Park, E cen. California; 11,726 ft.

Mer·cer \'mər-sər\. 1 Name of counties in eight states of the U.S. See tables at ILLINOIS, KENTUCKY, MISSOURI, NEW JERSEY, NORTH DAKOTA, OHIO, PENNSYLVANIA, WEST VIRGINIA.

2 Borough, ⊗ of Mercer co., W Pennsylvania, 17 m. NNE of New Castle; pop. (1970c) 2773.

3 Village, N North I., New Zealand, on Waikato river 32 m. SSE of Auckland. Near here was old frontier bet. Maori and colonist; adjacent terrain scene of numerous encounters bet. Maoris and British troops 1863–64. Seat of St. Stephen's Maori Boys Coll. for Maori youths.

Mercer Island. City, King co., W cen. Washington, in Lake Washington 4 m. E of Seattle; pop. (1970c) 19,047; residential suburb of Seattle.

Mer·cers·burg \'mər-sərz-ˌbərg\. Borough, Franklin co., S Pennsylvania, 17 m. WSW of Chambersburg; pop. (1970c) 1727; leather products, hardwood timber; limestone quarries; Mercersburg Academy (1836); home 1796–1809 of James Buchanan, 15th president of the United States.

Mer·chant·ville \'mər-chənt-ˌvil\. Borough, Camden co., SW New Jersey, 3 m. E of Camden; pop. (1970c) 4425.

Mer·cia \'mər-sh(ē-)ə\. Ancient Anglian kingdom in cen. England, one of a group of seven Anglo-Saxon kingdoms, sometimes known as the Heptarchy (*q.v.*); in 632 A.D. its pagan ruler overthrew Christian king of Northumbria (*q.v.*); leading member of Heptarchy in 8th cent.; conquered 829 by Egbert, ruler of Wessex (*q.v.*) 802–839; in 9th cent. English Mercia separated by Watling Street from Danish Mercia to the NE in Danelaw; Danelaw reconquered in 10th cent.

Mer·e·dith \'mer-ə-dith\. Town, Belknap co., cen. New Hampshire, on Lakes Winnipesaukee and Waukewan 9 m. N of Laconia; pop. (1970c) 2904; lake resort; lumber; dairy farms.

Meredith Bridge. See LACONIA 1.

Me·re·va·ri \ˌmer-ə-'vär-ē\. River in SE cen. Venezuela; flows N into Caura river.

Mergate. See MARGATE.

Mer·gui \ˌmər-'gwē\. 1 District, S Tenasserim division, Lower Burma; 11,325 sq. m.; pop. (1967e) 227,833; ✱ Mergui; includes Mergui Archipelago; tin mines; rubber.

2 Seaport town, its ✱, on a coastal island; pop. (1953c) 33,697.

Mergui Archipelago. Group of more than 200 islands in Andaman Sea off coast of Mergui dist. in S Lower Burma; bet. ab. lat. 9° and 13°N; largest is Mali I. at N end; among the other large islands (N to S) are Kadan, Thayawthadangyi, Daung, Saganthit, Bentinck, Kanmaw Kyun, Letsôkaw, and Lanbi. Sparsely inhabited, chiefly by Selungs and Burmans; pearl fishing.

Meriç. See MARITSA.

Mé·ri·court \ˌmār-i-'ku̇(ə)r\. Commune, Pas-de-Calais dept., N France, 9 m. from Arras; pop. (1968c) 13,416; coal mines; destroyed in World War I.

Me·ri·da \'mer-əd-ə\. Municipality on W side of Ormoc Bay, Leyte prov., NW coast of Leyte I., Phil., SW of Ormoc and 42 m. SW of Tacloban; pop. (1969e) 21,600.

Mé·ri·da \'mer-əd-ə\. 1 City, ✱ of Yucatán state, SE Mexico; munic. pop. (1970p) 253,856; sisal industry; exports sisal, chicle, hides, and farm products; handicrafts; tourism; 16th cent. cathedral; univ. (1624, univ. status 1922); port is Progreso. Founded 1542 on a site within the ancient Maya Empire.

2 *or anc.* **Au·gus·ta Emer·i·ta** \ó-ˌgəs-tə-i-ˈmer-ət-ə, ə-ˌgəs-\. Commune, Badajoz prov., SW Spain, on Guadiana river 33 m. ENE of Badajoz; pop. (1970p) 40,059; textiles, leather, soap, cork, hats; noted esp. for its Roman ruins, including an amphitheater, bridge, aqueduct, circus, temple, arch by Trajan, and colonnaded theater. Founded 25 B.C. by Augustus; became Visigothic episcopal see; taken by Moors 712 A.D.; reconquered 1228 by Alfonso IX.

3 State of Venezuela. See table at VENEZUELA.

4 Town, * of Mérida state, W Venezuela, in the Cordillera Mérida ab. 30 m. S of the S end of Lake Maracaibo on highway to Colombia; pop. (1970e) 75,634; center of coffee-growing region; textiles, cordage, tobacco products, vegetable oils; cathedral; univ. (1785, univ. status 1810); founded 1558; destroyed by earthquakes 1812 and 1894.

Mérida, Cordillera. See CORDILLERA MÉRIDA.

Mérida, Sierra Nevada de. See CORDILLERA MÉRIDA.

Mer·i·den \ˈmer-əd-ᵊn\. 1 Manufacturing city, New Haven co., S Connecticut, 17 m. NE of New Haven; pop. (1970c) 55,959; plated ware, ball bearings, cut glass, hardware, electrical equipment, cutlery. Settled 1661; incorporated 1867; consolidated 1922 with town (incorporated 1806) with which it is coextensive.

2 Village, Sullivan co., SW New Hampshire, ab. 12 m. N of Claremont; bird sanctuary (estab. 1910).

Me·rid·i·an \mə-ˈrid-ē-ən\. 1 City, Ada co., SW Idaho, 10 m. W of Boise; pop. (1970c) 2616; diversified agriculture.

2 City, ⊗ of Lauderdale co., E Mississippi, 16 m. W of Alabama border; pop. (1970c) 45,083; clothing, truck bodies, fertilizer, building materials, furniture; lumber and cottonseed oil mills, stockyards; Meridian Junior Coll. (1937), T. J. Harris Junior Coll. (1956); founded 1854; incorporated 1860; burned during Civil War 1864 but afterwards rebuilt.

3 City, ⊗ of Bosque co., cen. Texas; pop. (1970c) 1162.

Mé·ri·gnac \ˌmār-i-ˈnyäk\. Commune, Gironde dept., SW France; suburb of Bordeaux; pop. (1968c) 45,951; footwear; 13th cent. dungeon (Tour de Veyrines).

Me·ri·kar·via \ˈmer-i-ˌkär-vē-ə\. Coastal town, Turku ja Pori prov., SW Finland, S of Kristiina; pop. (1970e) 4979.

Merín. See MIRIM, LAKE.

Mer·i·on·eth·shire \ˌmer-ē-ˈän-əth-ˌshi(ə)r, -shər\ *or* **Mer·i·on·eth** \ˌmer-ē-ˈän-əth\. County, W Wales; area 660 sq. m.; pop. (1971p) 35,277; ⊗ Dolgellau; hilly region; rivers Dyfi, Dee, Mawddach; livestock raising (esp. sheep and cattle); oats, potatoes, turnip; forestry. In ancient times when a center of resistance to the English, Harlech (*q.v.*) was its capital; slate industry became important in 18th cent., declined since 1914.

Mer·i·on Station \ˌmer-ē-ən-\. Unincorporated community, Montgomery co., SE Pennsylvania; pop. (1970c) 5686.

Mer·i·weth·er \ˈmer-ē-ˌweth-ər\. County in Georgia. See table at GEORGIA.

Me·ri·zo \mə-ˈrē-(ˌ)zō\. Electoral district, SW coast of Guam, Mariana Is.; pop. (1970p) 1532.

Merk·sem \ˈme(ə)rk-səm\. Commune, Antwerp prov., N Belgium; N suburb of Antwerp; pop. (1969e) 40,019; metalworking.

Mer·kus, Cape \-ˈmər-kəs\. Cape on SW coast of New Britain, Bismarck Archipelago; near Arawe, landing place of American invasion forces Dec. 1943.

Mer·lo \ˈme(ə)r-(ˌ)lō\. Town, Buenos Aires prov., E Argentina, ab. 20 m. W of Buenos Aires; part of Greater Buenos Aires; pop. (1960c) 100,146.

Mer·oë \ˈmer-ə-ˌwē\ *also* **Mer·o·we** \mə-ˈrä-wā\. Ancient city on E bank of the Nile, lat. 17°N; capital of Ethiopian kings from c. 750 B.C., of Nubia 500 to 300 B.C., and of the later kingdom of Meroë (Meroitic kingdom) lasting until ab. 350 A.D.; its extensive ruins (temples, palaces, necropolis) are near modern **Ka·bū·shī·yah** \kə-ˈbü-shē-ə\, Northern Province, Sudan. The kingdom included the **Isle of Meroë** (*anc.* **Meroe In·su·la** \-ˈin(t)-sə-lə\), the region bet. the Nile, the Blue Nile, and the Atbara rivers, notable as a great center of commerce and caravan trade and also for the language (Meroitic) of its inhabitants, written in hieroglyphics, and about which little is known.

Me·ron, Mount \-mā-ˈrōn\. Mountain, N Israel; 3692 ft.; highest mountain in Israel.

Merowe. 1 Ancient city, Egypt. See MEROË.

2 Town, Sudan. See MARAWI.

Mer·ri·am \ˈmer-ē-əm\. City, Johnson co., E Kansas, suburb SSW of Kansas City; pop. (1970c) 10,851.

Mer·rick \ˈmer-ik\. 1 County in Nebraska. See table at NEBRASKA.

2 Urban community (unincorporated), Nassau co., SE New York, on Long I.; pop. (1970c) 25,904.

3 Peak, Kirkcudbright co., S Scotland; 2764 ft.

Mer·rill \ˈmer-əl\. City, ⊗ of Lincoln co., N Wisconsin, on Wisconsin river 15 m. N of Wausau; pop. (1970c) 9502; Lincoln County Teachers Coll. (1907).

Mer·ri·mac \ˈmer-ə-ˌmak\. Town, Essex co., NE Massachusetts, on Merrimack river NE of Lowell; pop. (1970c) 4245; boats; truck farms.

Mer·ri·mack \ˈmer-ə-ˌmak\. 1 River, S New Hampshire and NE Massachusetts; 110 m. long; formed by junction of Pemigewasset and Winnipesaukee rivers at Franklin, New Hampshire, flows S across Massachusetts border, then turns NE and empties into the Atlantic Ocean at Newburyport, NE Massachusetts.

2 County in New Hampshire. See table at NEW HAMPSHIRE.

3 Town, Hillsborough co., S New Hampshire; pop. (1970c) 8595.

Mer·ri·man Dam \ˌmer-ə-mən-\. See UNITED STATES, *Dams and Reservoirs.*

Mer·ritt, Mount \-ˈmer-ət\. Peak in Glacier National Park, NW Montana; 9954 ft.

Merritt Island. Island off E coast of Brevard co., E cen. Florida; ab. 40 m. long and 6 m. wide at N end; 93 sq. m.; separated from the mainland by the Indian river and from Canaveral Penin. by Banana river.

Mers–al–Kabir. See MERS EL-KÉBIR.

Mersa Matrūh. See MATRŪH 2.

Mer·se·burg \ˈmer-zə-ˌbu̇(ə)rg\. Manufacturing city, Halle dist., East Germany, on Saale river 18 m. W of Leipzig; pop. (1970e) 55,986; a center of the chemical industry; also produces leather, beer, cellulose; 13th cent. cathedral, 15th cent. castle. Important frontier fortification in Carolingian times; made episcopal see 968; made city 1188; residence 1656–1738 of dukes of Sachsen-Merseburg; passed to Prussia through Congress of Vienna; in World War II bombed 1944–45; taken by Allied armies Apr. 1945.

Mers el–Ké·bir \ˌme(ə)r-sel-kə-ˈbi(ə)r\ *or* **Mers–al–Ka·bir** \-al-\. Town, NW Algeria, on coast just W of Oran; formerly a French naval base; in naval battle here July 3, 1940 several French warships were destroyed by the British; seized by Allies Nov. 10, 1942.

Mersen. See MEERSSEN.

Mer·sey \ˈmər-zē\. 1 River, N Tasmania, Australia; ab. 65 m. long; flows generally N to Bass Strait at Devonport.

2 River, NW England; 70 m. long; rises in N Derbyshire, flows NW and W bet. Cheshire and Lancashire into the Irish Sea through a large estuary that forms the harbor of Liverpool. See MANCHESTER SHIP CANAL. Mersey Railway Tunnel, constructed 1925–30, 2¹/₇ m. long, passes under the river from Birkenhead to Liverpool.

Mer·sin \mer-ˈsēn\ *also* **İçel** \ē-ˈchel\. Seaport city, * of İçel prov., S Turkey, 40 m. WSW of Adana; pop. (1965c) 86,692; exports minerals and agricultural produce.

Mer·thyr Tyd·fil \ˌmər-thər-ˈtid-ˌvil\. County borough, Glamorganshire, S Wales; pop. (1971p) 55,215; chemicals, hosiery, machinery, household appliances; coal mines; Richard Trevithick's steam locomotive, the first to be tried on rails, successfully hauled a train of ten tons of iron and seventy men on the Merthyr Tydfil-Pontypridd tramway 1804.

Mer·ton \ˌmərt-ᵊn\. A borough of Greater London, SE England. See table at LONDON 4. Ruins of an Augustinian priory founded in 1115, and scene 1236 of meeting of barons who passed the Statute of Merton amending the law about conflicting rights of the lords and their tenants to make profit of lands, wastes, woods, and pastures.

Mert·zon \ˈmər-tsən\. Town, ⊗ of Irion co., W cen. Texas; pop. (1970c) 513.

Me·ru, Mount \-ˈmā-(ˌ)rü\. Peak, N Tanzania, E Africa, W of Mount Kilimanjaro; 14,954 ft.

Meru National Park. National park, cen. Kenya; 380 sq. m.; grassland and rain forest.

Merv. See MARY.

Mer·ville \mer-ˈvēl\. Industrial town, Nord dept., N France, on the Lys 18 m. W of Lille; pop. (1962c) 6779.

Mer·we·de \ˈme(ə)r-ˌvād-ə\. The lower Meuse river below the Waal, in Netherlands, until its junction with the Lek to form as its right branch the Nieuwe Maas river. The section of the Merwede from Dordrecht to the Lek is sometimes called the Noord. See OUDE MAAS.

Mer·zi·fon \ˌmer-zi-ˈfōn\ *or* **Mar·si·van** \ˌmär-sə-ˈvän\. Town, Amasya prov., N Turkey, 25 m. NW of Amasya; pop. (1965c) 23,410; cotton textiles; 15th cent. mosque.

Mer·zig \ˈme(ə)rt-sik\. Commercial commune, Saarland, West Germany, on the Saar 21 m. NW of Saarbrücken; pop. (1968c) 23,410; blast furnaces; bombed by Allies 1944.

Me·sa \ˈmā-sə\. 1 County in Colorado. See table at COLORADO.

2 City, Maricopa co., SW cen. Arizona, 15 m. E of Phoenix; pop. (1970c) 62,853; electronic components, aircraft parts; ships citrus fruit; winter resort; diversified agriculture; Mesa Community Coll. (1963); founded 1878 by Mormons.

Me·sa·bi Range \mə-ˈsäb-ē-\. Range in St. Louis and Itasca cos., NE Minnesota, ab. 100 m. long; average height 200–500 ft.; highest point ab. 2000 ft.; contains vast deposits of iron ore.

Me·sa·gne \mā-ˈsän-(ˌ)yā\. Commune, Brindisi prov., Apulia, SE Italy, 8 m. SW of Brindisi; pop. (1968e) 25,580.

Mesarás, Kólpos. See MESSARA, BAY OF.

Mesa Verde National Park \ˌmā-sə-ˈvərd-, -ˈve(ə)rd-ē-\. See UNITED STATES, *National Parks.*

Mes·ca·le·ro Ridge \ˌmes-kə-ˌle(ə)r-ō-\. Ridge in SE New Mexico, extending from cen. Lea co. NW along the Lea-Chaves cos. boundary.

Mesen. See MESSINES.

Me·se·wa \mə-ˈsä-wə\ *or* **Mas·sa·ua** *or* **Mas·so·wa** \mə-ˈsä-wə, -ˈsaů-ə\ *or* **Mas·sa·wa** \mə-ˈsä-we\. Seaport, Eritrea prov., Ethiopia, on the **Mesewa Channel** (inlet of the Red Sea); pop. (1970e) 18,490; situated partly on an island, partly on the mainland; shipyards, cement and saltworks, glue factory; pearl fishing; Ethiopian naval academy.

Meshed. See MASHHAD.

Me·sil·la \mā-ˈsē-yə\. Unincorporated town, Dona Ana co., S New Mexico, on the Rio Grande near Las Cruces; founded after end of Mexican War, it was in Mexican territory until Gadsden Purchase 1853 made it part of U.S.

Me·so·la \mā-ˈzō-lə\. Commune, Ferrara prov., Emilia-Romagna, N Italy, in Po delta 34 m. ENE of Ferrara; pop. (1968e) 8326.

Me·so·lón·gi·on \ˌmes-ə-ˈlȯŋ-gē-ˌȯn\ *or* **Mis·so·lon·ghi** \ˌmis-ə-ˈlȯŋ-gē\. Commercial city, ✱ of Aetolia and Acarnania dept., W Central Greece and Euboea region, Greece, on N shore of Gulf of Patras; pop. (1971p) 12,368; ships fish and wine. Withstood first Turkish siege 1822–23, but fell in the second 1825–26. The poet Byron died here 1824.

Mes·o·po·ta·mia \ˌmes-(ə-)pə-ˈtā-mē-ə, -myə\. The region in SW Asia bet. the Tigris and Euphrates rivers, extending from the mountains of Asia Minor on the N to the Persian Gulf on the S. First so called after the time of Alexander the Great; in the Bible known as Paddan-Aram (*Gen.* xxv. 20). Its N part called by Arabs Al-Jazira (see JAZIRA, AL-); in modern usage region includes ʻIraq ʻArabi and whole Tigris-Euphrates valley.

History: The fertility and location of the region made it seat of early civilizations of Babylonia and Assyria (*qq.v.*) c. 3000–625 B.C.; Upper Mesopotamia the home of kingdom of the Mitanni c. 1475–1360 B.C.; part of Persian Empire from 538 B.C. until conquered by Alexander of Macedon c. 331 B.C.; prior to Arab conquest in mid-7th cent. A.D., formed part of Parthian, Roman, and Neo-Persian (Sassanid) empires; Basra, Al-Kufa, and later, Baghdad the centers of Arab control; after Mongol invasion 1258, importance of region as political and commercial center declined; taken by Ottoman Turks 1638; regained strategic value for Great Britain in 19th cent., esp. after Germans proposed Berlin-Baghdad R.R. and after discovery of petroleum deposits; scene of British Mesopotamian campaign against Turks 1914–18; became British mandate 1920; kingdom of Iraq (*q.v.*) established 1921.

Mes·quite \mə-ˈskēt, me-\. City, Dallas co., NE Texas, E of Dallas; pop. (1970c) 55,131; pharmaceuticals, paint, building materials; rock quarries.

Messana. See MESSINA 2.

Mes·sa·pia \mə-ˈsā-pē-ə\. In ancient geography, that part of SE Italy inhabited by the Messapii; later applied also to Calabria.

Mes·sa·ra, Bay of \-ˌmes-ə-ˈrä\ *or Gk.* **Kól·pos Me·sa·rás** \ˈkȯl-pȯs-ˌmes-ə-ˈrȯs\. Inlet of Mediterranean Sea on S coast of Crete, near cen. part.

Mes·se·ne \mə-ˈsē-nē\. 1 *or Gk.* **Mes·sí·ní** \mə-ˈsē-nē\. Commune, Messenia dept., SW Peloponnesus, Greece. Ancient city founded c. 369 B.C. on site chosen by Epaminondas as new capital of Messenia and as a check against Sparta. Its acropolis was the peak **Itho·me** \ith-ˈō-mē\ 2630 ft., and on it was a temple of Zeus.

2 Seaport, Sicily, Italy. See MESSINA 2.

Mes·se·nia \mə-ˈsē-nē-ə, -nyə\. 1 A division of ancient Greece in SW Peloponnesus; bounded on N by Elis, on N and NE by Arcadia, on E by Laconia and Gulf of Messenia, and on S and W by Ionian Sea. Its S part forms westernmost point of peninsulas of Peloponnesus, terminating in Cape Akritas. One of the most fertile districts of Greece.

History: Dorians, first colonizers, united with original inhabitants to form strong people, but unable to resist Sparta; overcome by Spartans in First Messenian War c. 736–716 B.C., and reduced to helots; completely subjugated after revolt led by Aristomenes in Second Messenian War c. 650–630 B.C.; revolted again in 464 B.C. (Third Messenian War) but many Messenians forced to leave their land c. 460 B.C.; after the battle of Leuctra 371 B.C. city of Messene (*q.v.*) founded; later, a member of the Achaean League and after 146 B.C. under Romans.

2 Department of Greece. See table at GREECE.

Messenia, Gulf of *or* **Gulf of Ko·ró·nē** \-kə-ˈrō-nē\ *or* **Mes·si·nia·kós Kól·pos** \mə-ˌsē-nē-ä-ˈkȯs-ˈkȯl-pȯs\ *also* **Gulf of Kal·a·ma·ta** \ˌkal-ə-ˈmät-ə\. Inlet of the Mediterranean Sea on SW coast of Peloponnesus, S Greece; its E shore formed by Laconia.

Mes·si·na \mə-ˈsē-nə\. 1 Province of Sicily, Italy. See table at ITALY.

2 *or anc.* **Zan·cle** \ˈzaŋ-ˌklē\; *later* **Mes·sa·na** \mə-ˈsän-ə\ *also* **Mes·se·ne** \mə-ˈsē-nē\. Seaport, ✱ of Messina prov., NE Sicily, Italy, on Strait of Messina; pop. (1968e) 270,246; trade and transportation center; exports agricultural products, chemicals, building materials; produces chemicals, pharmaceuticals, preserved foods, citrus fruit products; viceregal and archiepiscopal palaces, cathedral (possibly Byzantine, rebuilt 12th cent. and restored after 1908); univ. (1548).

History: Founded c. 730 B.C. by Greeks from Chalcis; destroyed by Carthaginians 397 B.C.; Roman free city 241 B.C.; captured by Saracens 831 A.D.; occupied by Crusaders under Richard I of England 1190; under Spanish rule 1282–1676 and 1678–1713; suffered from plague 1743; destroyed by earthquakes 1783 and 1908; to Italy 1860; in World War II suffered heavy damage; occupied by Allied forces Aug. 1943.

3 Town, N Transvaal, NE Rep. of South Africa; near S bank of Limpopo river and on one of main railroad lines to Rhodesia; pop. (1967e) 12,500; site of large copper mines.

Messina, Strait of *or anc.* **Sic·u·lum Fre·tum** \ˌsik-yə-ləm-ˈfrēt-əm\. Channel bet. S Italy and NE island of Sicily; 2½ to 12 m. wide.

Mes·sines \me-ˈsen\ *or* **Me·sen** \ˈmā-zən\. Commune in West Flanders prov., NW Belgium, near Ieper (Ypres); pop. (1969e) 1122. **Messines Ridge** dominates the surrounding terrain; battles Nov. 1, 1914, in which Germans seized the ridge, and June 7–14, 1917, in which it was retaken by the British.

Messíní. See MESSENE 1.

Messiniakós Kólpos. See MESSENIA, GULF OF.

Mes·ta \me-ˈstä\ *or Turk.* **Ka·ra Su** \ˌkär-ə-ˈsü\ *or in Greece* **Nes·tos** \ˈnes-ˌtäs\. River, SW Bulgaria and NE Greece; ab. 150 m. long; flows from W end of Rhodope Mts. SE into N Aegean Sea opp. the island of Thasos.

Mes·u·ra·do, Cape \-ˌmes-ə-ˈräd-(ˌ)ō\. Cape on the W coast of Liberia, W Africa, near Monrovia.

Me·ta \ˈmāt-ə\. 1 River, Colombia; ab. 621 m. long; rises in W cen. Colombia, flows NE and E forming a section of Colombia-Venezuela boundary, and empties into Orinoco river on the Colombia-Venezuela boundary.

2 Department of cen. Colombia. See table at COLOMBIA.

Meta In·cog·ni·ta \ˌmēt-ə-in-ˈkäg-nət-ə\. Name given by Sir Martin Frobisher to S part of Baffin I.

Met·a·po·na \ˌmet-ə-ˈpō-nə\. Short stream E of Koli Point on N coast of Guadalcanal I., SE Solomon Is., W Pacific Ocean; fighting here Nov. 8–10, 1942.

Met·a·pon·tum \ˌmet-ə-ˈpänt-əm\. Ancient Greek city, Lucania, S Italy, on NW shore of Gulf of Tarentum; founded by colonists from Crotona and Sybaris c. 700 B.C.; Pythagoras died here 497 B.C.; location of Hannibal's headquarters after Cannae. Ruins include two temples and some of the walls.

Mét·a·scou·ac \ˌmet-ə-ˈskwak, -skü-ˈyak\ *also* **Grand Lake Métascouac.** Lake, S Quebec, Canada, in NW Laurentides Park.

Me·tau·ro \mə-ˈtau̇(ə)r-(ˌ)ō\ *or anc.* **Me·tau·rus** \-ˈtȯr-əs\. Small river in E cen. Italy; flows E into Adriatic Sea N of Ancona; battle of Metaurus in Second Punic War 207 B.C. in which Roman consuls completely defeated the Carthaginians under Hasdrubal, ending Hannibal's hope of conquest of Rome.

Met·calfe \ˈmet-ˌkaf, -kəf\. County in Kentucky. See table at KENTUCKY.

Meteor Crater. See CRATER MOUND.

Me·te·pec \ˌmā-tā-ˈpek\. Municipality, México state, Mexico, 30 m. W of Mexico City; pop. (1970p) 31,435; pottery.

Met·how \ˈmet-ˌhau̇\. River, N Washington; ab. 60 m. long; flows S in Okanogan co. into Columbia River.

Me·thu·en \mə-ˈth(y)ü-ən\. Industrial town, Essex co., NE corner of Massachusetts, 9 m. NE of Lowell; pop. (1970c) 35,456; settled ab. 1642; was part of Haverhill until 1725.

Meth·ven \ˈmeth-vən\. Village, Perth co., Scotland, ab. 7 m. NW of Perth; pop. (1961c) 673; castle 1 m. E; scene of battle 1306 in which English defeated Robert Bruce.

Me·tin·ic \mə-ˈtin-ik\. Island in Atlantic Ocean off S cen. Maine coast.

Metis. See METZ.

Met·la·kat·la *or* **Met·la·kaht·la** \ˌmet-lə-ˈkat-lə\. Village on Annette I., S of Ketchikan, Revillagigedo I., SE Alaska; pop. (1970c) 1050; formerly had U.S. Air Force base. Settled 1887 by refugee Indians.

Me·to·hi·ja \me-ˈtō-hē-yə\. District, SW Yugoslavia, forming part of autonomous province Kosovo-Metohija.

Me·trop·o·lis \mə-ˈträp-(ə-)ləs\. City, ⊗ of Massac co., S Illinois, on Ohio river NW of Paducah, Kentucky; pop. (1970c) 6940; chemicals, gloves; diversified agriculture.

Met·ter \ˈmet-ər\. City, ⊗ of Candler co., E cen. Georgia, 16 m. W of Statesboro; pop. (1970c) 2912; tobacco.

Mett·mann \ˈmet-ˌmän\. City, North Rhine-Westphalia, West Germany, E of Düsseldorf; pop. (1969e) 29,848; foundries; rubber goods.

Met·tray \me-ˈtrā\. Village, Indre-et-Loire dept., NW cen. France, ab. 5 m. NW of Tours; pop. (1962c) 137; reformatory, founded 1839.

Me·tuch·en \mə-ˈtəch-ən\. Borough, Middlesex co., cen. New Jersey, 5 m. WNW of Perth Amboy; pop. (1970c) 16,031; paper products, tools, chemicals, electrical appliances.

Metz \ˈmets, *Fr.* mes\; *anc.* **Di·vo·du·rum** \ˌdī-və-ˈd(y)u̇r-əm\ *or* **Divodurum Me·di·o·mat·ri·cum** \-ˌmēd-ē-ō-ˈma-tri-kəm\; *later* **Me·di·o·mat·ri·ca** \-tri-kə\ *also* **Me·tis** \mēt-əs\. City, ✱ of Moselle dept., NE France, on Moselle river 178 m. ENE of Paris; pop. (1968c) 107,537; center of iron-mining region; shoes, metal goods, canned fruits and vegetables, tobacco; brewing, printing; 13th–16th cent. cathedral; 4th cent. church of St. Pierre-aux-Nonnains, oldest church in France.

History: Pre-Roman foundation; fortified by Romans; sacked by Attila in 5th cent. A.D.; under Franks became capital of Austrasia; at height of prosperity as free imperial city in 13th cent.; with Toul and Verdun (Les Trois-Évêchés, the three bishoprics) taken by French 1552; formally ceded to France 1648 under Treaty of Westphalia; surrendered to Germans after major siege 1870; under German rule 1871–1918; reverted to France after World War I; in World War II heavily damaged in severe fighting Sept.–Oct. 1944; captured by Allies Nov. 20.

Meu·don \mər-ˈdōⁿ\. Commune, Hauts-de-Seine dept., N France; SW suburb of Paris on Seine river; pop. (1968c) 50,623; residential; astronomical observatory. The Forest of Meudon (*Fr.* Forêt de Meudon) formerly surrounded a famous château built by Louis XIV; later the wood became a holiday resort for Parisians.

Meu·le·be·ke \ˈmə-lə-ˌbā-kə\. Commune, West Flanders prov., NW Belgium, 9 m. E of Roeselare; pop. (1969e) 10,525.

Meurthe \ˈmərt\. River, Vosges and Meurthe-et-Moselle depts., NE France; 105 m. long; rises in Vosges Mts., flows NW into the Moselle near Nancy.

Meurthe–et–Mo·selle \-ā-mō-ˈzel\. Department of NE France. See table at FRANCE.

Meuse \ˈmyüz, ˈmə(r)z\ *or Du.* **Maas** \ˈmäs\ *or anc.* **Mo·sa** \ˈmō-zə\. 1 River, W Europe; 580 m. long; rises in Haute-Marne dept., NE France, flows N across E Belgium, forming a section of the NE boundary of Belgium; enters Netherlands and as the Maas curves W uniting at Gorinchem with the Waal, entering the North Sea through Hollandsch Diep. It receives the tributaries Sambre and Ourthe in Belgium and in the Netherlands the Rur from West Germany. The chief towns on its banks are Verdun, Sedan, and Mézières in France, Namur and Liège in Belgium, and Maastricht in Netherlands; Rotterdam is on the Nieuwe Maas in the Rhine delta. Its valley, esp. in NE France, was scene of much severe fighting in World War I; held by Germans until 1918; in World War II overrun by German armies in May and June 1940 and in Jan. 1945 its course SW of Liège was almost reached by Germans in Battle of the Bulge.

2 Department of NE France. See table at FRANCE.

Meu·sel·witz \ˈmȯi-zəl-ˌvits\. Industrial city, Leipzig dist., East Germany, 22 m. S of Leipzig; pop. (1970e) 10,308;

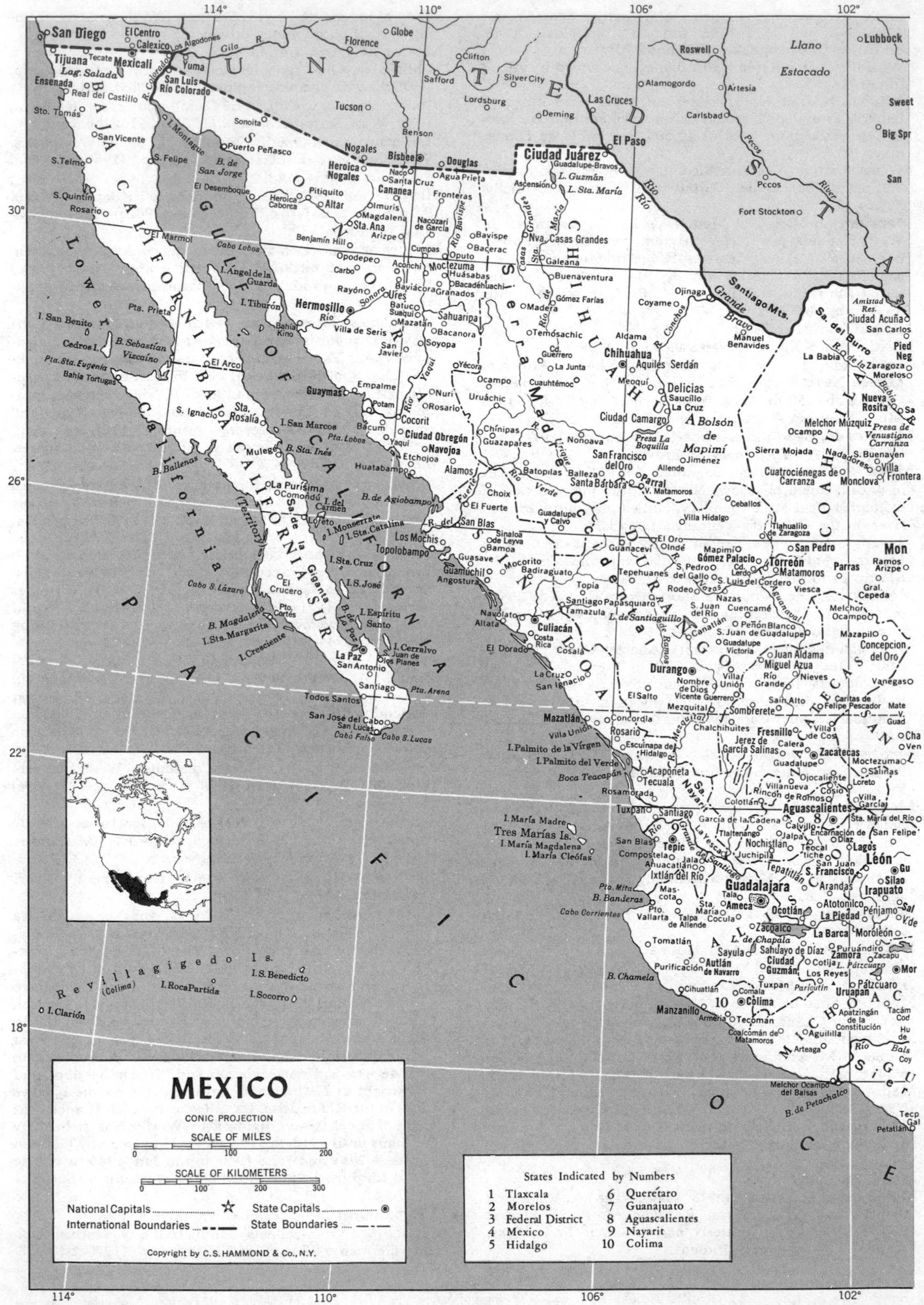
MEXICO
CONIC PROJECTION
SCALE OF MILES
0
100
200
SCALE OF KILOMETERS
0
100
200
300
National Capitals
State Capitals
International Boundaries
State Boundaries
Copyright by C. S. HAMMOND & Co., N.Y.
States Indicated by Numbers
1 Tlaxcala
2 Morelos
3 Federal District
4 Mexico
5 Hidalgo
6 Querétaro
7 Guanajuato
8 Aguascalientes
9 Nayarit
10 Colima
114°
110°
106°
102°
30°
26°
22°
18°
U N I T E D S T A T E S
B A J A C A L I F O R N I A
Lower California
BAJA CALIFORNIA SUR
(Territory)
GULF OF CALIFORNIA
S O N O R A
C H I H U A H U A
S I N A L O A
D U R A N G O
C O A H U I L A
Z A C A T E C A S
J A L I S C O
M I C H O A C Á N
P A C I F I C
O C E A N
Sierra Madre Occidental
San Diego
El Centro
Calexico
Los Algodones
Tijuana
Tecate
Mexicali
Yuma
Lag. Salada
Ensenada
Real del Castillo
San Luis Río Colorado
Sto. Tomás
San Vicente
S. Telmo
S. Quintín
Rosario
El Marmol
Pta. Prieta
I. San Benito
Cedros I.
B. Sebastián Vizcaíno
Pta. Sta. Eugenia
Bahía Tortugas
El Arco
S. Ignacio
Sta. Rosalía
Mulegé
B. Sta. Inés
B. Ballenas
La Purísima
Comondú
Loreto
I. del Carmen
I. Monserrate
I. Sta. Catalina
I. Sta. Cruz
I. S. José
El Crucero
Cabo S. Lázaro
B. Magdalena
I. Sta. Margarita
I. Creciente
Pto. Cortés
I. Espíritu Santo
I. Cerralvo
La Paz
San Antonio
San Juan de los Planes
Santiago
Pta. Arena
Todos Santos
San José del Cabo
San Lucas
Cabo Falso
Cabo S. Lucas
Sa. de la Giganta
Revillagigedo Is.
(Colima)
I. S. Benedicto
I. Roca Partida
I. Socorro
I. Clarión
Gila R.
Florence
Globe
Clifton
Safford
Silver City
Tucson
Lordsburg
Deming
Sonoita
Benson
Nogales
Bisbee
Douglas
Heroica Nogales
Naco
Santa Cruz
Agua Prieta
Cananea
Fronteras
Puerto Peñasco
I. Montague
B. de San Jorge
El Desemboque
Pitiquito
Heroica Caborca
Altar
Imuris
Magdalena
Sta. Ana
Arizpe
Nacozari de García
Benjamín Hill
Cumpas
Bavispe
Bacerac
Opodepe
Oputo
Carbo
Aconchi
Moctezuma
Huásabas
Bacadéhuachi
Baviácora
Granados
Rayón
Ures
I. Angel de la Guarda
Cabo Lobos
I. Tiburón
Hermosillo
Río Sonora
Batuco
Suaqui
Sahuaripa
Bahía Kino
Villa de Seris
Mazatán
Bacanora
San Javier
Soyopa
Yécora
Guaymas
Empalme
Potam
Nuri
Rosario
Río Yaqui
Cocorit
Bácum
I. San Marcos
Pta. Lobos
Ciudad Obregón
Navojoa
Yaqui
Etchojoa
Huatabampo
Alamos
B. de Agiobampo
Río Fuerte
El Fuerte
Choix
San Blas
Los Mochis
Topolobampo
Sinaloa de Leyva
Bamoa
Guasave
Guamúchil
Angostura
Mocorito
Badiraguato
Navolato
Altata
Culiacán
Costa Rica
Cosalá
El Dorado
La Cruz
San Ignacio
Mazatlán
Villa Unión
Concordia
Rosario
Escuinapa de Hidalgo
I. Palmito de la Virgen
I. Palmito del Verde
Boca Teacapán
Acaponeta
Tecuala
Rosamorada
Tuxpan
Santiago
I. María Madre
Tres Marías Is.
I. María Magdalena
I. María Cleófas
San Blas
Tepic
Compostela
Jala
Ahuacatlán
Ixtlán del Río
Pta. Mita
B. Banderas
Cabo Corrientes
Mascota
Pto. Vallarta
Talpa de Allende
Tomatlán
B. Chamela
Purificación
Autlán de Navarro
Cihuatlán
Manzanillo
Armería
Comala
Colima
Tecomán
Coalcomán de Matamoros
Arteaga
Melchor Ocampo del Balsas
B. de Petacalco
Petatlán
Ciudad Juárez
Guadalupe-Bravos
L. Guzmán
L. Sta. María
Ascensión
Nva. Casas Grandes
Galeana
Buenaventura
Gómez Farías
Madera
Temósachic
Cd. Guerrero
La Junta
Cuauhtémoc
Ocampo
Uruáchic
Chínipas
Guazapares
Batopilas
Nonoava
Chihuahua
Aquiles Serdán
Aldama
Meoquí
Delicias
Saucillo
La Cruz
Ciudad Camargo
Presa La Boquilla
San Francisco del Oro
Parral
Santa Bárbara
Balleza
V. Matamoros
Allende
Jiménez
Bolsón de Mapimí
Ojinaga
Coyame
Santiago Mts.
Manuel Benavides
Sierra Mojada
Ceballos
Villa Hidalgo
Guadalupe y Calvo
Tlahualilo de Zaragoza
El Oro
Indé
Guanaceví
Mapimí
Gómez Palacio
Cd. Lerdo
Torreón
Matamoros
S. Pedro del Gallo
Tepehuanes
S. Luis del Cordero
Rodeo
Nazas
Topia
Santiago Papasquiaro
Tamazula
L. de Santiaguillo
S. Juan del Río
Cuencamé
Peñón Blanco
Canatlán
S. Juan de Guadalupe
Guadalupe Victoria
Durango
Nombre de Dios
Villa Unión
Vicente Guerrero
Juan Aldama
Miguel Azua
Nieves
Río Grande
El Salto
Mezquital
Sombrerete
Sain Alto
Chalchihuites
Fresnillo
Villa de Cos
Jerez de García Salinas
Calera
Zacatecas
Guadalupe
Ojocaliente
Villanueva
Rincón de Romos
Cosío
Colotlán
García de la Cadena
Aguascalientes
Tlaltenango
Jalpa
Calvillo
Nochistlán
Juchipila
Teocaltiche
Tepatitlán
Guadalajara
Tala
Ameca
Ocotlán
Cocula
L. de Chapala
Sayula
Sahuayo de Díaz
Ciudad Guzmán
Zacoalco
La Barca
Jiquilpan
Cotija
Zamora
Los Reyes
Tuxpan
Paricutín
Uruapan
Pátzcuaro
Apatzingán de la Constitución
Aguililla
Río Balsas
Sa. Madre del Sur
León
Lagos
S. Francisco
Arandas
Irapuato
Silao
Atotonilco
La Piedad
Pénjamo
Moroleón
Purúandiro
Zacapu
L. Pátzcuaro
Parras
Viesca
Ramos Arizpe
Gral. Cepeda
Melchor Ocampo
Mazapil
Concepción del Oro
Vanegas
Caritas de Felipe Pescador
Moctezuma
Salinas
Loreto
Villa García
Sta. María del Río
San Felipe
Encarnación de Díaz
San Juan
San Pedro
Cuatrociénegas de Carranza
Monclova
Frontera
Nadadores
S. Buenaventura
Ocampo
Melchor Múzquiz
Presa de Venustiano Carranza
Nueva Rosita
Sabinas
La Babia
Zaragoza
Morelos
Pied Neg
Ciudad Acuña
San Carlos
Amistad Res.
Sa. del Burro
Río Grande
Bravo
Las Cruces
El Paso
Alamogordo
Roswell
Artesia
Carlsbad
Pecos
Fort Stockton
Llano Estacado
Lubbock
Big Spr
Sweet
Mon
Tecp Gal

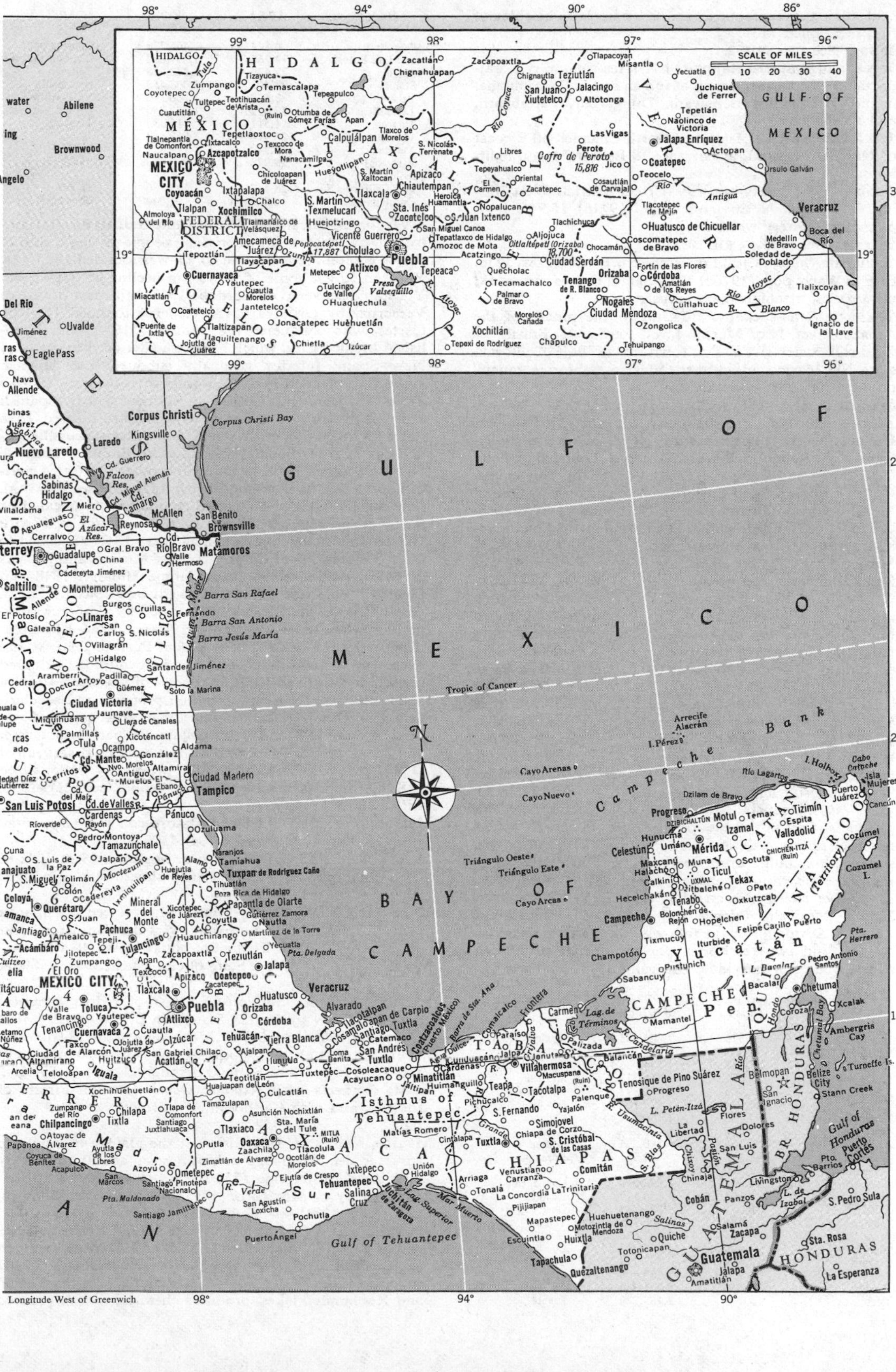
98°
94°
90°
86°
99°
98°
97°
96°
SCALE OF MILES
0 10 20 30 40
HIDALGO
H I D A L G O
MÉXICO
MEXICO CITY
FEDERAL DISTRICT
M O R E L O S
T L A X C A L A
P U E B L A
V E R A C R U Z
GULF OF MEXICO
Tula
Zumpango
Tizayuca
Temascalapa
Tepeapulco
Coyotepec
Tultepec
Teotihuacán de Arista
(Ruin)
Otumba de Gómez Farías
Apan
Cuautitlán
Tepetlaoxtoc
Tlalnepantla de Comonfort
Ixtacalco
Texcoco de Mora
Naucalpan
Azcapotzalco
Nanacamilpa
Chicoloapan de Juárez
Coyoacán
Ixtapalapa
Chalco
Tlalpan
Xochimilco
Almoloya del Río
Tlalmanalco de Velásquez
Amecameca de Juárez
Tepoztlán
Tlayacapan
Ozumba
Cuernavaca
Yautepec
Cuautla Morelos
Miacatlán
Coatetelco
Jantetelco
Puente de Ixtla
Tlaltizapan
Tlaquiltenango
Jojutla de Juárez
Jonacatepec
Huehuetlán
Chietla
Izúcar
Zacatlán
Chignahuapan
Zacapoaxtla
Calpulalpan
Tlaxco de Morelos
Hueyotlipan
S. Martín Xaltocan
Apizaco
Chiautempan
Tlaxcala
S. Martín Texmelucan
Huejotzingo
Vicente Guerrero
Popocatépetl 17,887
Cholula
Puebla
Atlixco
Metepec
Tulcingo de Valle
Huaquechula
Presa Valsequillo
Atoyac
Sta. Inés Zocotelco
S. Juan Ixtenco
San Miguel Canoa
Tepatlaxco de Hidalgo
Amozoc de Mota
Acatzingo
Tepeaca
Quecholac
Tecamachalco
Palmar de Bravo
Morelos Cañada
Xochitlán
Tepexi de Rodríguez
Chapulco
S. Nicolás Terrenate
Libres
Tepeyahualco
El Carmen
Oriental
Heroica Huamantla
Zacatepec
Nopalucan
Río Coyuca
Chignautla
Teziutlán
San Juan Xiutetelco
Jalacingo
Altotonga
Tlapacoyan
Misantla
Las Vigas
Perote
Cofre de Perote 15,816
Jico
Cosautlán de Carvajal
Tlachichuca
Aljojuca
Citlaltépetl (Orizaba) 18,700
Chocamán
Ciudad Serdán
Tenango de R. Blanco
Orizaba
Nogales
Ciudad Mendoza
Zongolica
Tehuipango
Yecuatla
Juchique de Ferrer
Tepetlán
Naolinco de Victoria
Jalapa Enríquez
Actopan
Coatepec
Teocelo
Úrsulo Galván
Río Antigua
Tlacotepec de Mejía
Huatusco de Chicuellar
Coscomatepec de Bravo
Fortín de las Flores
Córdoba
Amatlán de los Reyes
Cuitlahuac
R. Blanco
Río Atoyac
Medellín de Bravo
Soledad de Doblado
Veracruz
Boca del Río
Tlalixcoyan
Ignacio de la Llave
30°
19°
26°
22°
18°
G U L F O F M E X I C O
BAY OF CAMPECHE
Tropic of Cancer
Campeche Bank
N
Abilene
Brownwood
Angelo
Del Rio
Uvalde
Eagle Pass
Jiménez
Nava
Allende
Corpus Christi
Corpus Christi Bay
Kingsville
Laredo
Nuevo Laredo
Cd. Guerrero
Falcon Res.
Nva. Cd. Guerrero
Cd. Miguel Alemán
Cd. Camargo
Candela
Sabinas Hidalgo
Villaldama
Mier
El Azúcar Res.
Reynosa
McAllen
San Benito
Brownsville
Cerralvo
Aguaeguas
Gral. Bravo
Río Bravo
Valle Hermoso
Matamoros
Guadalupe
China
Cadereyta Jiménez
Saltillo
Montemorelos
Allende
Barra San Rafael
Burgos
Cruillas
San Fernando
Barra San Antonio
Barra Jesús María
Linares
Galeana
San Carlos
S. Nicolás
Villagrán
Hidalgo
Aramberri
Padilla
Santander Jiménez
Güémez
Soto la Marina
Ciudad Victoria
Jaumave
Llera de Canales
Palmillas
Tula
Xicoténcatl
Ocampo
Aldama
González
Cd. Mante
Nvo. Morelos
Antiguo Morelos
Altamira
Ebano
Ciudad Madero
Tampico
Cd. de Valles
San Luis Potosí
Cardenas
Rayón
Pánuco
Ozuluama
Naranjos
Tamiahua
Tamazunchale
Jalpan
Tuxpan de Rodríguez Caño
Tihuatlán
Poza Rica de Hidalgo
Papantla de Olarte
Gutiérrez Zamora
Nautla
Martínez de la Torre
Yecuatla
Pta. Delgada
Querétaro
S. Juan
Pachuca
Tulancingo
Mineral del Monte
Huauchinango
Xicotepec de Juárez
Coyutla
Zacapoaxtla
Teziutlán
Jalapa
Coatepec
Huatusco
Orizaba
Córdoba
Veracruz
Alvarado
Tlacotalpan
Cosamaloapan de Carpio
Santiago Tuxtla
Catemaco
San Andrés Tuxtla
Coatzacoalcos (Puerto México)
Cosoleacaque
Acayucan
Minatitlán
Isthmus of Tehuantepec
Acámbaro
El Oro
MEXICO CITY
Toluca
Cuernavaca
Tlaxcala
Puebla
Atlixco
Apizaco
Texcoco
Zacatepec
Tehuacán
Tierra Blanca
Izúcar
Acatlán
Iguala
Taxco
Teloloapan
Huajuapan de León
Cuicatlán
Tlaxiaco
Oaxaca
Tlacolula
Mitla (Ruin)
Zimatlán de Alvarez
Ocotlán de Morelos
Ejutla de Crespo
Putla
Tehuantepec
Juchitán de Zaragoza
Salina Cruz
Ixtepec
Unión Hidalgo
Matías Romero
Pochutla
Puerto Angel
Pinotepa Nacional
Santiago Jamiltepec
Pta. Maldonado
Gulf of Tehuantepec
Lag. Superior
Mar Muerto
Chilpancingo
Chilapa
Tixtla
Acapulco
Ayutla de los Libres
Ometepec
Zumpango del Río
Xochihuehuetlán
San Marcos
Sierra Madre del Sur
G U E R R E R O
O A X A C A
C H I A P A S
T A B A S C O
Cárdenas
Villahermosa
Teapa
Tacotalpa
Macuspana
Jalpa
Paraíso
Frontera
Comalcalco
Huimanguillo
Pichucalco
Palenque
Tenosique de Pino Suárez
Balancán
Carmen
Lag. de Términos
Palizada
R. Candelaria
R. Usumacinta
Simojovel
Chiapa de Corzo
Tuxtla
S. Cristóbal de las Casas
Comitán
Yajalón
Cintalapa
Arriaga
Tonalá
Venustiano Carranza
La Concordia
La Trinitaria
Pijijiapan
Mapastepec
Escuintla
Huixtla
Motozintla de Mendoza
Tapachula
Quezaltenango
Huehuetenango
Quiche
Totonicapan
Guatemala
Amatitlán
Jalapa
Zacapa
Salamá
Cobán
Panzos
Chinaja
San Luis
Dolores
Flores
La Libertad
L. Petén-Itzá
San Ignacio
Belmopan
Belize City
Stann Creek
Turneffe Is.
Ambergris Cay
BR. HONDURAS
G U A T E M A L A
Livingston
L. de Izabal
Pto. Barrios
Puerto Cortés
Gulf of Honduras
S. Pedro Sula
Sta. Rosa
HONDURAS
La Esperanza
Chetumal
Chetumal Bay
Corozal
Xcalak
Bacalar
L. Bacalar
Río Hondo
Pedro Antonio Santos
Felipe Carillo Puerto
Q U I N T A N A R O O (Territory)
Y U C A T Á N
Yucatán Pen.
C A M P E C H E
Campeche
Champotón
Sabancuy
Mamantel
Pustunich
Tixmucuy
Iturbide
Hopelchen
Bolonchén de Rejón
Tenabo
Hecelchakán
Calkiní
Halachó
Maxcanú
Muna
Uxmal
Ticul
Tekax
Oxkutzcab
Peto
Sotuta
Chichén-Itzá (Ruin)
Valladolid
Espita
Tizimín
Izamal
Mérida
Umán
Hunucmá
Celestún
Progreso
Dzibichaltún
Motul
Temax
Dzilam de Bravo
Río Lagartos
I. Holbox
Cabo Catoche
Isla Mujeres
Puerto Juárez
Cancún
Cozumel
Cozumel I.
Pta. Herrero
Arrecife Alacrán
I. Pérez
Cayo Arenas
Cayo Nuevo
Triángulo Oeste
Triángulo Este
Cayo Arcas
Longitude West of Greenwich

coal mining; manufactures textiles, porcelain, machinery; first mentioned 1139.

Mewar. See UDAIPUR 2.

Me·war and Southern Raj·pu·ta·na States \mā-ˈwär . . . ˌräj-pə-ˈtän-ə-\. A former group of Indian states, S Rajputana, including Udaipur, Banswara, Dungarpur, Partabgarh, and Kushalgarh.

Mew Island \ˈmyü-\. Island in North Channel, off E coast of Northern Ireland, at entrance to Belfast Lough; lighthouse.

Mex·bor·ough \ˈmeks-b(ə-)rə\. Urban district, West Riding, Yorkshire, N England; pop. (1971p) 15,946; iron, glass, and pottery works.

Mexcala. See BALSAS, RÍO DE LAS.

Me·xia \mə-ˈhā-ə\. City, Limestone co., E cen. Texas, 37 m. ENE of Waco; pop. (1970c) 5943; manufactures cottonseed oil, textiles, machinery; oil industries.

Me·xi·a·na \ˌmā-shē-ˈan-ə\. Island in the mouth of the Amazon river, N of Marajó I., off Pará state, Brazil.

Mex·i·cali \ˌmek-si-ˈkal-ē\. Town, ✱ of Baja California state, NW Mexico, adjacent to Calexico, California; munic. pop. (1970p) 390,411; univ. (1957).

Mex·i·co \ˈmek-si-ˌkō\ *or Span.* **Mé·ji·co** \ˈme-hē-(ˌ)kō\; *in Mexico* **Mé·xi·co** \ˈme-hē-(ˌ)kō\ *or officially* **Es·ta·dos Uni·dos Me·xi·ca·nos** \ā-ˌstäth-(ˌ)ō-sü-ˌnē-(ˌ)thōz-ˌme-hē-ˈkän-(ˌ)ōs\. Republic, S North America, bounded on N by U.S., on W and S by the Pacific, on SE by Guatemala, British Honduras, and Caribbean Sea, and on E by Gulf of Mexico; separated from U.S. on NE boundary by the Río Bravo (Rio Grande in U.S.); 759,530 sq. m. (incl. uninhabited islands 761,600 sq. m.); pop. (1970p) 48,313,438; ✱ Mexico City. *Physical features:* NW part (peninsula of Baja California) separated from rest of Mexico by Gulf of California; in SE is peninsula of Yucatán. Narrowest part, Isthmus of Tehuantepec 130 m. *Chief mountains:* Sierra Madre (S extension of Rocky Mts. system) dividing into mountain chains on E (Oriental) and W (Occidental) sides of central plateau (see ANÁHUAC), which has average altitude of 6000 ft. and occupies over 50 percent of country; highest point Citlaltépetl (volcano) 18,700 ft. in cen. Veracruz state; other peaks Popocatépetl (volcano) 17,887 ft., Iztaccíhuatl 17,343 ft., Nevado de Toluca (volcano) 14,406 ft., Malinche 14,636 ft., and Colima (volcano) 13,993 ft. *Chief rivers:* Pánuco, Grijalva, Balsas, Santiago, Usumacinta, Conchos, Río Bravo (Rio Grande). *Chief lakes:* Chapala, Cuitzeo, Pátzcuaro, Texcoco. *Chief products:* Cotton, wheat, corn, beans, tomatoes, coffee; livestock raising, fishing; silver, lead, zinc, copper, iron ore, sulfur, oil; manufacturing: textiles, chemicals, steel, building materials, motor vehicles, electrical apparatus; tourism. *Chief cities:* Mexico City, Guadalajara, Monterrey, Juarez, Mexicali, Puebla, Tijuana, León, Chihuahua, Torreón. Divided into the following 29 states, one federal district, and two territories (for pronunciation of their names, see their individual entries):

NAME	AREA (sq. m.)	POP. (1970p)	CAPITAL
Federal District	579	7,005,855	Mexico City
States			
Aguascalientes	2,158	334,936	Aguascalientes
Baja California	27,071	856,773	Mexicali
Campeche	21,666	250,391	Campeche
Chiapas	28,528	1,578,180	San Andrés Tuxtla
Chihuahua	95,400	1,730,012	Chihuahua
Coahuila	58,522	1,140,989	Saltillo
Colima	2,106	240,235	Colima
Durango	46,196	919,381	Durango
Guanajuato	11,810	2,285,249	Guanajuato
Guerrero	24,631	1,573,098	Chilpancingo
Hidalgo	8,103	1,156,177	Pachuca
Jalisco	30,941	3,322,750	Guadalajara
México	8,286	3,797,861	Toluca
Michoacán	23,114	2,341,556	Morelia
Morelos	1,908	620,392	Cuernavaca
Nayarit	10,664	547,992	Tepic
Nuevo León	24,925	1,653,808	Monterrey
Oaxaca	36,820	2,011,946	Oaxaca
Puebla	13,096	2,483,770	Puebla
Querétaro	4,544	464,226	Querétaro
San Luis Potosí	24,266	1,257,028	San Luis Potosí
Sinaloa	22,429	1,273,228	Culiacán
Sonora	71,403	1,092,458	Hermosillo
Tabasco	9,522	766,346	Villahermosa
Tamaulipas	30,822	1,438,350	Ciudad Victoria
Tlaxcala	1,511	418,334	Tlaxcala
Veracruz	28,114	3,813,613	Jalapa
Yucatán	16,749	774,011	Mérida
Zacatecas	28,973	949,663	Zacatecas
Territories			
Baja California Sur	28,447	123,786	La Paz
Quintana Roo	16,228	91,044	Chetumal

History: Central and S part, from Gulf to Pacific, controlled by Aztecs, an aboriginal people of high culture whose capital, Tenochtitlán (*q.v.*), was founded 1325 A.D.; Yucatán (*q.v.*), home of Mayas, in decline by 15th cent.; Yucatán discovered by Córdoba 1517, and coast (to site of Veracruz) by Grijalva 1518; Veracruz founded 1519 by Cortes, who conquered the country 1519–21 and established Mexico City, which became center of viceroyalty of New Spain; interior gradually subdued and Spanish authority extended N to California in 16th cent., though Texas and California not effectively occupied by Spanish until 18th cent.; audiencia of Guadalajara created 1548 (later included SW of present U.S.). After successful second revolt from Spain 1821, ruled by Emperor Iturbide 1822–23; joined by Guatemala and other Central American states for brief period during 1822–23 (see CENTRAL AMERICA); established a federal republic 1824; defeated by independent republic of Texas 1836; fought war with United States over annexation of Texas 1846–48; ceded to United States Upper California, New Mexico, and N parts of Mexico by Treaty of Guadalupe Hidalgo 1848 and Gadsden Purchase 1853; underwent invasions by Spain, Great Britain, and France 1861; ruled by Emperor Maximilian who was supported by France 1864–67; under dictatorship 1877–1911 of President Porfirio Díaz, whose overthrow inaugurated period of revolution; adopted revised constitution 1917; in policies of nationalization of resources, expropriation of church property and secularization of education, and subdivision of great estates, faced opposition of U.S. and Great Britain, Roman Catholicism, and Mexican Conservatives, respectively; final settlement (1947) made by government for previously nationalized U.S. oil interests; resolved border dispute (see CHAMIZAL) with U.S. 1963.

Mexico \ˈmek-si-ˌkō\. **1** Town, Oxford co., W Maine, 36 m. NNW of Lewiston; pop. (1970c) 4309.

2 City, ⊗ of Audrain co., NE cen. Missouri, 29 m. ENE of Columbia; pop. (1970c) 11,807; shoes, clay products; wheat, soybeans.

3 *or Span.* \ˈme-hē-ˌkō\. Municipality, E cen. Pampanga prov., Luzon, Phil., on a tributary of the Pampanga river ab. 3 m. NE of San Fernando; pop. (1969e) 40,400.

Mé·xi·co \ˈme-hē-(ˌ)kō\. State of cen. Mexico. See table at MEXICO.

Mexico, Gulf of. Gulf on SE coast of North America; bounded on N by United States, on E by United States, Cuba, and Mexico, on S by Mexico, on W by Mexico and United States; ab. 615 sq. m.; extends ab. 1000 m. E to W and ab. 775 m. N to S; max. depth 12,245 ft. in SW cen. part; connects with Atlantic Ocean through Straits of Florida, and with Caribbean Sea through Strait of Yucatán.

Mexico, Valley of. Subdivision of the plateau of Anáhuac (*q.v.*) in cen. Mexico; a vast oval basin ab. 50 m. long by 40 m. wide; total area 1758 sq. m.; mean elev. 7470 ft.

Mexico City *or* **Mexico** *or officially* **Ciu·dad de Mé·xi·co, D.F.** \syü-ˈthäth-də-ˈme-hē-(ˌ)kō-\. City, ✱ of Mexico and of the Federal District (Distrito Federal), located near S end of great cen. plateau and ab. 200 m. WNW of Veracruz on the Gulf of Mexico; pop. (1970p) 3,025,564; alt. 7347 ft.; a few miles W of Lake Texcoco and NW of the Chalco and Xochimilco lakes; produces chemicals, steel, tobacco products, cement; tourism. Regularly laid out with cathedral, national palace, and municipal building around a large square (Plaza Mayor) forming the political and commercial center. Has many churches, monasteries, museums; several universities and colleges including National Autonomous Univ. of Mexico (1551).

History: Before Spanish invasion, Mexico City was the site of the Aztec capital (Tenochtitlán); captured by Cortés 1521; seat of the viceroyalty of New Spain 1521–1821; captured by Mexican revolutionists under Gen. Iturbide 1821; captured by Gen. Winfield Scott 1847 in the Mexican War; held by the French 1863–67; greatly improved in modern times, esp. during the presidency of Porfirio Díaz 1876–80, 1884–1911; site of Summer Olympic Games 1968.

Mey·ca·ua·yan \ˌme-ē-ˌkä-wə-'yän\. Municipality, Bulacan prov., Luzon, Phil., on Manila-Dagupan R.R. 10 m. N of Manila; pop. (1969e) 44,400.

Mey·ers·dale \'mī(-ə)rz-ˌdāl\. Borough, Somerset co., S Pennsylvania, 35 m. S of Johnstown; pop. (1970c) 2648; clothing; coal mines; agriculture.

Mèze \'mez\. Seaport, Hérault dept., S France; pop. (1962c) 4546; near shore of the Étang de Thau opposite Sète.

Me·zen \'māz-ᵊn\. 1 River, N Russian S.F.S.R., U.S.S.R.; ab. 533 m. long; rises in W Komi A.S.S.R. and flows generally NW through cen. Arkhangelsk Oblast into **Gulf of Mezen,** an arm (ab. 50 m. long) of the E White Sea.

2 Town, Arkhangelsk Oblast, Russian S.F.S.R., U.S.S.R., on right bank of Mezen river near its mouth, ab. 130 m. NE of Arkhangelsk; a fishing and trading port.

Mé·zenc, Mount \-mā-'zaŋk\. Volcanic peak in the Cévennes Mts., S France, in Haute-Loire dept. near Ardèche border; 5755 ft.

Mezh·du·re·chensk \ˌmezh-dùr-ə-'chensk\. Town, Kemerovo Oblast, Russian S.F.S.R., U.S.S.R., ab. 140 m. SE of Kemerovo; pop. (1969e) 81,000.

Mézières. See CHARLEVILLE-MÉZIÈRES.

Me·ző·be·rény \'mez-ər-ˌber-ān-yə\. Commune, 60 m. SW of Debrecen, SE Hungary; pop. (1970p) 12,666.

Me·ző·kö·vesd \'mez-ər-ˌkər-vesht\. Commune, NE cen. Hungary, 72 m. NE of Budapest; pop. (1970p) 18,045; produces embroideries.

Me·ző·túr \'mez-ˌər-ˌtü(ə)r\. City, E cen. Hungary, 60 m. NE of Szeged; pop. (1970p) 21,788; textiles.

Mfini. See FIMI.

Mfumbiro Mountains. See VIRUNGA MOUNTAINS.

Mge·ni \em-'gā-nē\ *or* **Um·ge·ni** \ùm-\. River, S Natal, E Rep. of South Africa; ab. 100 m. long; flows SE to Indian Ocean just N of Durban; noted for its waterfall 311 ft. high at Howick, NW of Pietermaritzburg.

Mhow \'maù\. Town, Madhya Pradesh, cen. India, 13 m. SSW of Indore; pop. with cantonment (1961c) 48,000.

Mia·gao \myä-'gaù\. Municipality, Iloilo prov., Panay, Phil., on Iloilo Strait 22 m. WSW of City of Iloilo; pop. (1969e) 43,600; nearby was traditional settlement of Bornean datos in pre-Spanish times.

Mi·a·haut·lán de Por·fi·rio Díaz \ˌmyä-wä-'tlän-dē-pòr-ˌfir-ē-ō-'dē-äs\. Municipality, Oaxaca state, Mexico, 60 m. S of Oaxaca; pop. (1970p) 79,140; livestock and poultry raising; coffee, sugarcane.

Mi·ami \mī-'am-ē, -'am-ə\. 1 *or formerly* **Great Miami.** River, W Ohio; 160 m. long; rises in Indian Lake, Logan co., and flows S into the Ohio river at the SW extremity of Ohio.

2 Name of counties in three states of the U.S. See tables at INDIANA, KANSAS, OHIO.

3 Town, Gila co., E cen. Arizona, 68 m. E of Phoenix; pop. (1970c) 3394; copper and asbestos mining.

4 City, ⊗ of Dade co., SE Florida, on Biscayne Bay; pop. (1970c) 334,859; southernmost large city in the U.S. at lat. 25°46'S (see KEY WEST); alt. 11 ft.; center of a major winter resort area, including Miami Beach, Coral Gables, Hialeah; transportation center; produces cement, plastics, electronic components; boatbuilding; has a bathing beach 7 m. long; Barry Coll. (1940), Miami Bible Coll. (1946), Miami-Dade Junior Coll. (1960). Permanent settlement began around Army post 1836 ff.; incorporated 1896; development retarded by hurricane 1926; major development as resort and residential city after World War II.

5 City, ⊗ of Ottawa co., NE corner of Oklahoma, 66 m. E of Bartlesville; pop. (1970c) 13,880; aluminum products, tires, cheese, clothing; railroad shops, lead and zinc mines; Northeastern Oklahoma Agricultural and Mechanical Coll. (1919).

6 City, ⊗ of Roberts co., NW Texas; pop. (1970c) 611.

Miami Beach. City, Dade co., SE Florida, on island across Biscayne Bay from Miami; pop. (1970c) 87,702; popular resort and tourist center, connected with Miami by four causeways.

Mi·am·is·burg \mī-'am-ēz-ˌbərg\. Industrial city, Montgomery co., SW Ohio, on Miami river 10 m. S of Dayton; pop. (1970c) 14,797; tobacco market; diversified agriculture; large Indian mound outside city.

Miami Shores. Village, Dade co., SE Florida, on Biscayne Bay 9 m. N of Miami; pop. (1970c) 9425.

Miami Springs. Town, Dade co., SE Florida, NW suburb of Miami; pop. (1970c) 13,279.

Mī·ā·neh \ˌmē-ə-'nā\. Town, East Azerbaijan, NW Iran, on main highway 90 m. SE of Tabrīz.

Mi·ang·as \mē-'äŋ-əs\ *or* **Pal·mas** \'päl-məs\. Small island in the Malay Archipelago, in the Pacific Ocean ab. 60 m. SE of Cape San Agustin, Mindanao; N of Talaud Is. and nearest point of Indonesia to Philippines.

Mi·a·ni *also* **Mee·a·nee** \mē-'än-ē\. 1 Village, cen. Sind, Pakistan, 6 m. N of Hyderabad; scene of victory Feb. 17, 1843 of Sir Charles Napier with small British force over mirs of Sind, which led to conquest and annexation of Sind.

2 Town, Punjab, Pakistan, 100 m. NW of Lahore; pop. (1961c) 6387; large salt mines.

Mi·an·us \mī-'an-əs\. Subdivision of town of Greenwich, Connecticut. See GREENWICH.

Mi·an·wa·li \mē-'än-'wäl-ē\. Town, Punjab, Pakistan, on the Indus 105 m. S of Peshawar; pop. (1961c) 31,398.

Mi·ca Peak \ˌmī-kə-\. Mountain in Kootenai co., N Idaho; 5250 ft.

Mi Chai. See NONG KHAI.

Mi·cha·lov·ce \'mik-ə-ˌlòft-sə\ *or Hung.* **Nagy·mi·hály** \'näj-'mē-ˌhī\. Town, E cen. Czechoslovakia, 29 m. E of Košice; pop. (1968e) 18,845.

Mi·chel·son, Mount \-'mī-kəl-sən\. Highest peak in Brooks Range, Alaska; 9239 ft.

Mich·i·gam·me \ˌmish-ə-'gäm-ē, -'gam-\. River, W Michigan penin.; rises in Baraga co., flows E and S until it joins the Brule to form the Menominee river on the Wisconsin-Michigan boundary.

Mich·i·gan \'mish-i-gən\. A north central state of U.S.A.; the upper peninsula is bounded on N by Lake Superior, on E by Whitefish Bay and St. Marys river, on S by Lake Huron and Lake Michigan, and on SW and W by Wisconsin; the lower peninsula is bounded on N by Lake Michigan and Lake Huron, on E by Lake Huron, Canadian province of Ontario, Lake St. Clair, and Lake Erie, on S by Ohio and Indiana, and on W by Lake Michigan; 23d state in area, 58,216 sq. m. (land area 56,817 sq. m.); in addition to this area has also 38,575 sq. m. of water of the Great Lakes; 7th state in population, (1970c) 8,875,083; ✱ Lansing; 26th state admitted to Union (1837).

Nicknames: Wolverine State; Lake State. *State flower:* Apple blossom. *Motto:* Si Quaeris Peninsulam Amoenam, Circumspice (If You Seek a Beautiful Peninsula, Look

Around You). *Rivers:* Montreal, Brule, and Menominee, forming W and SW boundary of upper peninsula; St. Clair, separating Michigan from Ontario bet. Lake Huron and Lake St. Clair; Detroit, separating Michigan from Ontario bet. Lake St. Clair and Lake Erie. *Highest point:* Mt. Curwood 1980 ft., in Baraga co. *Chief products:* Dairy products, fruit; iron ore, limestone, copper, gypsum, salt, natural gas; manufacturing: motor vehicles, machine tools, industrial patterns. *Chief cities:* Detroit, Grand Rapids, Flint, Warren, Lansing, Livonia. See *Table of States* at UNITED STATES. Divided into the following 83 counties (for pronunciation of their names, see their individual entries):

NAME	LOCATION[1]	AREA[2] (sq. m.)	POP. (1970c)	CO. SEAT
Alcona	NE	670	7,113	Harrisville
Alger	N penin.	905	8,568	Munising
Allegan	SW	826	66,575	Allegan
Alpena	NE	565	30,708	Alpena
Antrim	NW	476	12,612	Bellaire
Arenac	E	367	11,149	Standish
Baraga	NW penin.	901	7,789	L'Anse
Barry	SW	554	38,166	Hastings
Bay	E	447	117,339	Bay City
Benzie	NW	316	8,593	Beulah
Berrien	SW corner	580	163,875	St. Joseph
Branch	S	506	37,906	Coldwater
Calhoun	S	709	141,963	Marshall
Cass	SW	491	43,312	Cassopolis
Charlevoix[3]	NW	414	16,541	Charlevoix
Cheboygan	N	721	16,573	Cheboygan
Chippewa[3]	E and NE penin.	1,590	32,412	Sault Ste. Marie
Clare	cen.	571	16,695	Harrison
Clinton	S cen.	572	48,492	St. Johns
Crawford	N	561	6,482	Grayling
Delta[3]	S penin.	1,177	35,924	Escanaba
Dickinson	S penin.	757	23,753	Iron Mountain
Eaton	S	577	68,892	Charlotte
Emmet	N	461	18,331	Petoskey
Genesee	SE cen.	642	445,589	Flint
Gladwin	cen.	503	13,471	Gladwin
Gogebic	NW corner of penin.	1,107	20,676	Bessemer
Grand Traverse	NW	462	39,175	Traverse City
Gratiot	cen.	566	39,246	Ithaca
Hillsdale	S	600	37,171	Hillsdale
Houghton	NW penin.	1,017	34,652	Houghton
Huron	E	819	34,083	Bad Axe
Ingham	S	559	261,039	Mason
Ionia	S cen.	575	45,848	Ionia
Iosco	NE	544	24,905	Tawas City
Iron	SW penin.	1,171	13,813	Crystal Falls
Isabella	cen.	572	44,594	Mount Pleasant
Jackson	S	698	143,274	Jackson
Kalamazoo	SW	562	201,550	Kalamazoo
Kalkaska	N	566	5,272	Kalkaska
Kent	W	857	411,044	Grand Rapids
Keweenaw[4]	N tip of penin.	528	2,264	Eagle River
Lake	W	571	5,661	Baldwin
Lapeer	E	658	52,361	Lapeer
Leelanau[3]	NW	345	10,872	Leland
Lenawee	S	753	81,951	Adrian
Livingston	SE	572	58,967	Howell
Luce	NE penin.	906	6,789	Newberry
Mackinac[3]	SE penin.	1,014	9,660	St. Ignace
Macomb	SE	480	625,309	Mount Clemens
Manistee	NW	552	20,094	Manistee
Marquette	N penin.	1,829	64,686	Marquette
Mason	W	490	22,612	Ludington
Mecosta	cen.	560	27,992	Big Rapids
Menominee	S tip of penin.	1,038	24,587	Menominee
Midland	cen.	520	63,769	Midland
Missaukee	NW cen.	565	7,126	Lake City
Monroe	SE corner	557	118,479	Monroe
Montcalm	cen.	712	39,660	Stanton
Montmorency	NE	555	5,247	Atlanta
Muskegon	W	501	157,426	Muskegon
Newaygo	W	849	27,992	White Cloud
Oakland	SE	867	907,871	Pontiac
Oceana	W	536	17,984	Hart
Ogemaw	NE	571	11,903	West Branch
Ontonagon	NW penin.	1,316	10,548	Ontonagon
Osceola	cen.	581	14,838	Reed City
Oscoda	NE	563	4,726	Mio
Otsego	N	527	10,422	Gaylord
Ottawa	W	563	128,181	Grand Haven
Presque Isle	NE	648	12,836	Rogers City
Roscommon	N cen.	521	9,892	Roscommon
Saginaw	cen.	814	219,743	Saginaw
Saint Clair	SE	723	120,175	Port Huron
Saint Joseph	S	506	47,392	Centerville
Sanilac	E	961	35,181	Sandusky
Schoolcraft	S penin.	1,181	8,226	Manistique
Shiawassee	S cen.	540	63,075	Corunna
Tuscola	E	815	48,603	Caro
Van Buren	SW	603	56,173	Paw Paw
Washtenaw	SE	711	234,103	Ann Arbor
Wayne	SE	605	2,669,604	Detroit
Wexford	NW	559	19,717	Cadillac

[1]Counties in the upper peninsula (extending eastwards from Wisconsin boundary, bet. Lake Superior on N and Lakes Michigan and Huron on S and SE) are indicated by the addition of "penin." Counties in the lower peninsula are located with reference only to that part of the state, and are given no additional distinguishing term.
[2]Area = land area.
[3]Includes islands.
[4]Includes Isle Royale, off Canadian shore NW of county proper.

History: Shores of Lake Michigan explored by French from 1634; first settled at Sault Sainte Marie by Marquette 1668; military post of Detroit (*q.v.*) founded 1701; ceded to England 1763 and to U.S. 1783; nominally included in Northwest Territory 1787, but British retained control until 1796; became part of Indiana Territory (1800, 1803) until organized as Michigan Territory 1805; boundaries of Michigan Territory were extended 1818 and 1834; admitted as free state after settled boundary dispute with Ohio Jan. 26, 1837; Lansing became capital 1847; adopted present constitution 1963.

Michigan, Lake. Lake in NE cen. U.S., 3d in size of the 5 Great Lakes (*q.v.*) and the only one wholly within the U.S.; bounded on N and E by Michigan, on S by Indiana, on SW by Illinois, on W by Wisconsin; ab. 307 m. long; 22,400 sq. m.; area of drainage basin 67,900 sq. m.; max. depth 923 ft.; elevation 579 ft.; at N end connected through Straits of Mackinac with Lake Huron; at its SW end is the city of Chicago; connected by means of the Chicago and Illinois rivers and connecting canals (see ILLINOIS WATERWAY) with the Mississippi river. See GREEN BAY.

Michigan City. City, La Porte co., N Indiana, on Lake Michigan; pop. (1970c) 39,369; railroad cars, electronic equipment, building materials, clothing, furniture, chemicals, mining machinery; lake port and yachting center; founded 1832.

Michigan Island. See APOSTLE ISLANDS.

Mich·i·ka·mau Lake \ˌmish-i-kə-ˌmȯ-\. Lake, W Labrador, Canada; 566 sq. m.

Michilimackinac. See MACKINAC.

Mi·chin·má·hui·da \ˌmich-ən-ˈmä-wəd-ə\. Peak, S cen. Chile, E of Corcovado Gulf; 8104 ft.

Mich·i·pi·co·ten Bay \ˌmish-ə-pə-ˌkōt-ᵊn-\. Port, SE Ontario, Canada, on NE shore of Lake Superior; ships ore.

Michipicoten Island. Island in NE Lake Superior off SW coast of Algoma co., S Ontario, Canada.

Mich·mash \ˈmik-ˌmash\ *or Arab.* **Mukh·mas** \mu̇k-ˈmas\. Locality, W Jordan, in region occupied by Israel 1967; scene of Jonathan's victory over the Philistines (*1 Samuel* xiv).

Mi·cho·a·cán \ˌmē-chə-wä-ˈkän\. State, SW Mexico. See table at MEXICO.

Mi·chu·rinsk \mə-ˈchu̇r-ən(t)sk\ *or formerly* **Koz·lov** \käz-ˈlȯf, -ˈlȯv\. City, W Tambov Oblast, Russian S.F.S.R., U.S.S.R., 35 m. WNW of Tambov and ab. 115 m. S of Ryazan; pop. (1969e) 93,000; important industrial town and railroad junction point; trades in grain, cattle, and farm products. Began as a small monastery (founded 1627) in the forest; later became a frontier fort against the Tatars.

Mi·cro·ne·sia \ˌmī-krə-ˈnē-zhə, -shə\. Islands of the W Pacific Ocean E of Phil., widely scattered bet. 1° and 20°32′N lat. and 131° and 177°E long.; a subdivision of Oceania; total area 1055 sq. m. Includes the Mariana, the Palau, Caroline, Marshall, and Gilbert Is.; the Marianas, Palaus, and many of the Caroline Is. are of volcanic origin, some with peaks of 1000 to 2500 ft.; others of the Carolines and all of the Marshall and Gilbert Is. are low coral atolls. Political divisions: Gilbert and Ellice Is., Guam, Nauru, and the Trust Territory of the Pacific Is. The Micronesians

Longitude West of Greenwich

are a mixed race of Melanesian, Polynesian and some Malaysian stock; their language is a subdivision of the Melanesian branch of Austronesian languages. All the island groups were placed under Japanese mandate 1919, except Guam, Wake, Nauru, and the Gilbert Is., which were taken over by the Japanese 1941–42 in World War II but for the most part retaken by American forces 1943–45.

Midbar Zin. See ZIN, WILDERNESS OF.

Mid·del·burg \ˈmid-ᵊl-ˌbərg\. 1 Commune, ✱ of Zeeland prov., SW Netherlands, on Walcheren I. just N of Vlissingen; pop. (1970e) 30,211; market town; textiles; tourism; 16th cent. town hall; in Middle Ages a Hanse town.

2 Town, cen. Cape Province, S Rep. of South Africa, 170 m. N of Port Elizabeth; pop. (1967e) 11,700; cattle, sheep, and ostrich farming.

3 Town, S cen. Transvaal, NE Rep. of South Africa, 75 m. E of Pretoria; pop. (1967e) 25,100; a coal-mining community; copper, iron, and cobalt also found.

Middle America. Region including Mexico and Central America; name sometimes used to incl. the islands of the Caribbean.

Middle Andaman. One of the Andaman Is. (*q.v.*).

Middle Atlas. See ATLAS MOUNTAINS.

Middle Bass Island. See BASS ISLAND.

Mid·dle·bor·ough \ˈmid-ᵊl-ˌbər-ə, -ˌbə-rə\. Town, Plymouth co., SE Massachusetts, 14 m. S of Brockton; pop. (1970c) 13,607; shoes, varnishes, fire fighting equipment; dairy farms.

Mid·dle·bourne \ˈmid-ᵊl-ˌbȯrn\. Town, ⊗ of Tyler co., NW West Virginia; pop. (1970c) 814.

Mid·dle·burg \ˈmid-ᵊl-ˌbərg\. Borough, ⊗ of Snyder co., cen. Pennsylvania; pop. (1970c) 1369; silk.

Middleburg Heights. City, Cuyahoga co., N Ohio, suburb S of Cleveland; pop. (1970c) 12,367.

Mid·dle·bury \ˈmid-ᵊl-ˌber-ē\. 1 Town, NW New Haven co., S Connecticut, near Naugatuck river; pop. (1970c) 5542.

2 Village in Middlebury town, ⊗ of Addison co., W Vermont, 30 m. NNW of Rutland; pop. (1970c) 6532; clothing, plastics; fruit and dairy farms; Middlebury Coll. (1800). Chartered 1761 as New Hampshire grant; became part of New York 1764; settled 1773; abandoned 1778–83; organized in state of Vermont 1786; incorporated 1832.

Middle Cascade. Waterfall in Yosemite Valley, California, in a tributary of the Merced river; total drop ab. 910 ft.

Middle Concho. River, Texas; 66 m. long; rises in E Upton co. and flows E.

Middle Congo. See CONGO 3.

Middle East. An extensive region comprising the countries of SW Asia and NE Africa; term formerly also included Afghanistan, Pakistan, India, and Burma; an indefinite and unofficial term; the U.S. Department of State does not officially employ it.

Middle Europe. See CENTRAL EUROPE.

Mid·dle·field \ˈmid-ᵊl-ˌfēld\. Town, Middlesex co., S Connecticut, 3 m. E of Meriden; pop. (1970c) 4132.

Middle Island. Island, New Zealand. See SOUTH ISLAND 2.

Middle Kingdom. See CHINA.

Middle Loup \-ˈlüp\. River, cen. Nebraska; ab. 220 m. long; rises in S Cherry co., flows E and SE to unite with North Loup and South Loup rivers and form Loup river.

Middle Park. Plateau in Grand co., N Colorado; bet. 60 and 70 m. long; crossed by the Colorado river; with North Park, South Park, and San Luis Park (*qq.v.*) forms a N–S chain of high, level, grassy areas enclosed by snow-capped mountains.

Mid·dle·port \ˈmid-ᵊl-ˌpō(ə)rt, -ˌpȯ(ə)rt\. 1 Village, Niagara co., W New York, 30 m. ENE of Niagara Falls; pop. (1970c) 2132.

2 Village, Meigs co., SE Ohio, on Ohio river 40 m. SW of Marietta; pop. (1970c) 2784.

Middle Rhine. The English name sometimes used for the section of the Rhine river bet. Mainz and Bonn, West Germany.

Middle River. Urban area, Baltimore co., N Maryland, E suburb of Baltimore; pop. (1970c) 19,935.

Middle Saranac Lake. See SARANAC LAKES.

Mid·dles·bor·ough *or* **Mid·dles·boro** \ˈmid-ᵊlz-ˌbər-ə, -ˌbə-rə\. City, Bell co., SE Kentucky, at Cumberland Gap on Tennessee border; pop. (1970c) 11,878; railroad division point; coal mines.

Mid·dle·sex \ˈmid-ᵊl-ˌseks\. 1 Name of counties in four states of the U.S. See tables at CONNECTICUT, MASSACHUSETTS, NEW JERSEY, VIRGINIA.

2 Borough, Middlesex co., cen. New Jersey, 6 m. N of New Brunswick; pop. (1970c) 15,038; paint, chemicals, perfumes.

3 County, Ontario, Canada. See table at ONTARIO.

4 Former county, SE England; since 1965 part of Greater London.

Middle Te·ton \-ˈtē-ˌtän\. Peak in cen. Grand Teton National Park, NW Wyoming; 12,798 ft.

Mid·dle·ton \ˈmid-ᵊl-tən\. 1 Town, Essex co., NE corner of Massachusetts, 15 m. ESE of Lowell; pop. (1970c) 4044.

2 City, Dane co., S Wisconsin, 7 m. W of Madison; pop. (1970c) 8286; condensed milk; diversified agriculture.

3 Town, Annapolis co., W Nova Scotia, Canada, 32 m. WSW of Kentville; pop. (1971p) 1813.

4 Municipal borough, Lancashire, NW England, on the Irk 6 m. NNE of Manchester; pop. (1971p) 53,419; chemicals; engineering industries.

Mid·dle·town \ˈmid-ᵊl-ˌtau̇n\. 1 City, Middlesex co., S Connecticut, on Connecticut river 14 m. S of Hartford; pop. (1970c) 36,244; marine hardware, automobile parts, paper products, textiles, rubber footwear; Wesleyan Univ. (1831), Middlesex Community Coll. (1966); settled 1650; town incorporated 1651, city 1784; town and city consolidated 1923; formerly ⊗ of Middlesex co.

2 Town, New Castle co., N Delaware, 23 m. SW of Wilmington; pop. (1970c) 2644; flour mills.

3 Town, Henry co., E cen. Indiana; pop. (1970c) 2046.

4 City, Orange co., SE New York, 23 m. W of Newburgh; pop. (1970c) 22,607; summer resort; cosmetics, valves, leather goods, clothing; Orange County Community Coll. (1950).

5 Industrial city, Butler co., SW Ohio, 11 m. NE of Hamilton; pop. (1970c) 48,767; aircraft parts, steel, paper products; founded 1802, incorporated as city 1883.

6 Borough, Dauphin co., SE cen. Pennsylvania, on Susquehanna river 9 m. SE of Harrisburg; pop. (1970c) 9080; shoes, clothing, boilers.

7 Town and summer resort, Newport co., SE Rhode Island, on Narragansett Bay 5 m. N of Newport; pop. (1970c) 29,290; dairy farms; center Middletown village; set off from Newport and incorporated as separate town 1743; pillaged by British fleet 1776.

Middle Urals. See URAL MOUNTAINS.

Middle Vol·ga Area \-ˈväl-gə-, -ˈvȯl-, -ˈvōl-\. Former administrative region, Russian S.F.S.R., U.S.S.R., along the middle course of the Volga including part or most of Kuibyshev Oblast and the Tatar, Mari, Chuvash, and Mordovian A.S.S.Rs; ab. 92,000 sq. m.; ✱ Samara (now Kuibyshev).

Mid·dle·wich \ˈmid-ᵊl-ˌwich\. Urban district, Cheshire, NW England, 21 m. SSW of Manchester; pop. (1971p) 7783.

Mid·field \ˈmid-ˌfēld\. City, Jefferson co., cen. Alabama, 3 m. SW of Birmingham; pop. (1970c) 6340.

Mi·di \mē-ˈdē\. The south, esp. of France.

Midi, Dent du. See DENT DU MIDI.

Mid·i·an \ˈmid-ē-ən\. Ancient region of NW Arabian Penin., E of the Gulf of ʻAqaba and bordered by Edom on the NW; the Midianites of Old Testament times were frequently at war with the Israelites.

Mid·land \ˈmid-lənd\. 1 Name of counties in two states of the U.S. See tables at MICHIGAN and TEXAS.

2 City, ⊗ of Midland co., cen. Michigan, 18 m. W of Bay City; pop. (1970c) 35,176; chemicals, concrete, plastics, dairy products; oil and gas wells.

3 Borough, Beaver co., W Pennsylvania, on Ohio river 29 m. WNW of Pittsburgh; pop. (1970c) 5271; steel, steel mill equipment, titanium alloys.
4 City, ⊗ of Midland co., W Texas, 120 m. SSW of Lubbock; pop. (1970c) 59,463; center of major oil-producing and cattle-raising region; chemicals, machine tools, potash; founded 1884; incorporated 1906.
5 *or formerly* **Midland Junction.** Town, SW Western Australia, suburb of Perth on Swan river; pop. (1966c) 9335; railway workshops.
6 Industrial town, Simcoe co., SE Ontario, Canada, on Georgian Bay 27 m. NNW of Barrie; pop. (1966c) 10,129; fiberglass, wood products, flour; shipyards; summer resort.

Midland Junction. See MIDLAND 5.

Midland Park. Manufacturing borough, Bergen co., NE corner of New Jersey, 5 m. N of Paterson; pop. (1970c) 8159.

Mid·lands, The \-ˈmid-lən(d)z\. The central counties of England, esp. Derbyshire, Nottinghamshire, Leicestershire, Rutlandshire, Northamptonshire, Warwickshire, and Staffordshire; contains many of the large industrial cities: Birmingham, Coventry, Leicester, Derby, Walsall, Burton on Trent, Stoke-on-Trent; suffered severely from German air raids Nov. 1940 to Dec. 1941.

Mid·lo·thi·an. 1 \mid-ˈlō-thē-ən\. Village, Cook co., NE Illinois, 18 m. S of Chicago; pop. (1970c) 15,939.
2 \mid-ˈlō-t͟hē-ən\; *formerly* **Ed·in·burgh** \ˈed-ᵊn-ˌbər-ə, -ˌbə-rə, -b(ə-)rə\ *or* **Ed·in·burgh·shire** \-ˌshi(ə)r, -sher\. County, SE Scotland; 366 sq. m.; pop. (1971p) 595,631; ⊗ Edinburgh; rivers Esk, Almond, Tyne; barley, oats, potatoes, wheat; livestock raising, dairying, fisheries, shipbuilding, manufacturing (paper, machinery, carpets, foodstuffs), distilling.

Mid·na·pore \ˈmid-nə-ˌpō(ə)r, -ˌpȯ(ə)r\ *or* **Mid·na·pur** \ˈmid-nə-pu̇(ə)r\. Town, West Bengal, NE India, 68 m. W of Calcutta; pop. (1961c) 59,532.

Mid·sa·yap \ˌmid-sə-ˈyäp\. Municipality, Cotabato prov., Mindanao, Phil., on a N tributary of Mindanao river 20 m. E of Cotabato; pop. (1969e) 61,200.

Mid·vale \ˈmid-ˌvāl\. City, Salt Lake co., N Utah, 11 m. S of Salt Lake City; pop. (1970c) 7840; sugar processing, ore smelting; poultry farms.

Mid·way \ˈmid-ˌwā\. Two small islands, Eastern I. and Sand I., parts of a low coral atoll in cen. Pacific Ocean, 1304 statute m. (1134 naut. m.) WNW of Honolulu, 28°13′N, 177°26′W; 2 sq. m.; under administration of the U.S. Navy; not incorporated in state of Hawaii. Discovered and claimed by U.S. 1859; formally occupied for U.S. 1867; Sand I. made a submarine cable station 1905; transpacific commercial air station 1936. In World War II attacked unsuccessfully by Japanese Dec. 1941 and Jan. 1942; another Japanese attacking force defeated by U.S. naval aircraft in one of the decisive naval battles of World War II; has U.S. naval air base, no commercial air service.

Midway–Hard·wick \-ˈhärd-(ˌ)wik\. Urban area, Baldwin co., cen. Georgia; pop. (1970c) 14,047.

Mid·west City \ˌmid-west-\. City, Oklahoma co., cen. Oklahoma, E suburb of Oklahoma City; pop. (1970c) 48,-212.

Mid–Western. State of S Nigeria. See table at NIGERIA.

Mid·ye \mid-ˈyā\. Town, Kırklareli prov., NE Turkey, port on the Black Sea 64 m. NW of İstanbul.

Mie *also* **Mi·ye** \ˈmē-(ˌ)yā\. Prefecture, Honshū, Japan; 2227 sq. m.; pop. (1970c) 1,543,083; ✱ Tsu; cotton, lumber; cement; lobster and shrimp fishing; tourism.

Mi·e·lec \ˈmye-lets\. Town, Rzeszów prov., SE Poland, ab. 35 m. NW of Rzeszów; pop. (1970p) 26,900.

Mier·cu·rea–Ciuc \myer-ˌkür-yä-ˈchük\. Town, ⊗ of Harghita co., NE cen. Romania, ab. 50 m. NNE of Braşov; pop. (1966c) 15,329.

Mie·res \mē-ˈer-əs\. Commune, Oviedo prov., NW Spain, 9 m. SSE of Oviedo; pop. (1970p) 64,552; iron, coal, and sulfur mines nearby.

Mierzeja Wiślana. See VISLINSKI ZALIV.

Miff·lin \ˈmif-lən\. County in Pennsylvania. See table at PENNSYLVANIA.

Miff·lin·burg \ˈmif-lən-ˌbərg\. Borough, Union co., cen. Pennsylvania, 24 m. S of Williamsport; pop. (1970c) 2607; clothing; fruit farms.

Miff·lin·town \ˈmif-lən-ˌtau̇n\. Borough, ⊗ of Juniata co., S cen. Pennsylvania; pop. (1970c) 828.

Mifraz Shlomo. See SHARM AL-SHEIKH.

Migdal. See MAGDALA.

Migiurtinia. See MIJERTINS.

Mi·glia·ri·no \ˌmē-lyä-ˈrē-nō\. Commune, Ferrara prov., Emilia-Romagna, N Italy, 19 m. ESE of Ferrara; pop. (1968e) 4453.

Mi·ha·ra \mi-ˈhär-ə\. City, Hiroshima prefecture, Honshū, Japan, 40 m. E of Hiroshima; pop. (1970c) 82,621.

Mi·ja·res \mi-ˈhär-əs\ *or* **Mi·lla·res** \mēl-ˈyär-əs\. River, E Spain; 97 m. long; flows SE, empties into Mediterranean Sea S of Castellón de la Plana.

Mij·er·tins \ˈmij-ərt-ᵊnz\ *or* **Mij·jar·ten** \ˈmij-ərt-ən\ *or Ital.* **Mi·giur·ti·nia** \ˌmē-jər-ˈtēn-yə\. Region, NE Somalia, E Africa; includes Cape Asir; formerly a sultanate.

Mi·ke·no \mi-ˈkā-(ˌ)nō\. Quiescent volcano, Rwanda, cen. Africa, E of Lake Kivu; above 12,000 ft.

Mi·khai·lov·ka \mi-ˈkī-ləf-kə, -əv-\. Town, Volgograd Oblast, Russian S.F.S.R., U.S.S.R., ab. 110 m. NW of Volgograd; pop. (1967e) 47,000.

Mi·khay·lov·grad \mi-ˈhī-ləv-ˌgrad, -ˈkī-\. 1 Province of N Bulgaria. See table at BULGARIA.
2 Town, its ✱, ab. 50 m. N of Sofia; pop. (1968e) 32,062.

Mik·ke·li \ˈmik-ə-lē\. 1 Province of S Finland. See table at FINLAND.
2 *or Swed.* **Sankt Mi·chel** \säŋ(k)t-ˈmē-kəl\. City, its ✱; pop. (1970e) 25,188; commercial center in livestock-raising and lumbering region; founded 1838.

Mi·ko·łów \mi-ˈkȯ-(ˌ)lüf\. Commune, Katowice prov., SW Poland, 7 m. SSW of Katowice; pop. (1970p) 21,400; near pre-World War II Polish boundary.

Mikoyan Shakhar. See KARACHAYEVSK.

Mikrí Prespa. See PRESPA, LAKE.

Mi·ku·lov \ˈmik-ü-ˌlȯf\ *or Ger.* **Ni·kols·burg** \ˈnē-kōls-ˌbu̇(ə)rg\. Commune, Czechoslovakia, ab. 30 m. S of Brno; treaty of peace signed here Dec. 31, 1621, bet. Emperor Ferdinand II and Gabriel Bethlen, Prince of Transylvania; truce signed here July 26, 1866 bet. Austria and Prussia.

Mi·ku·mi National Park \mi-ˈkü-mē-\. National park, E cen. Tanzania; 650 sq. m.; large variety of wildlife, incl. elephant, giraffe, hippopotamus, impala, lion, zebra; established 1964.

Mi·la \ˈmē-lə\. Commune, Constantine dept., NE Algeria, just NW of Constantine; pop. (1966c) 33,000.

Mi·laca \mə-ˈlak-ə\. Village, ⊗ of Mille Lacs co., E cen. Minnesota, 28 m. ENE of St. Cloud; pop. (1970c) 1940; dairy farms; potatoes.

Mi·la·gro \mi-ˈläg-(ˌ)rō\. Town, Guayas prov., W Ecuador, 25 m. E of Guayaquil; pop. (1962c) 28,148; in agricultural district.

Mi·la·gros \mi-ˈläg-rōs\. Municipality, Masbate prov., S Masbate I. on Asid Gulf, Phil.; pop. (1969e) 23,700.

Mi·lam \ˈmī-ləm\. County, Texas. See table at TEXAS.

Mi·lan \ˈmī-lən\. 1 Village, Rock Island co., NW Illinois, 4 m. S of Rock Island; pop. (1970c) 4873; quarries, gravel pits; industrial pumps; diversified agriculture.
2 Village, Monroe and Washtenaw cos., SE Michigan, 13 m. S of Ann Arbor; pop. (1970c) 4533.
3 City, ⊗ of Sullivan co., N Missouri; pop. (1970c) 1794; cheese; livestock farms.

4 Town, Gibson co., NW Tennessee, 21 m. N of Jackson; pop. (1970c) 7313; ships vegetables; diversified agriculture.

Milan \mə-'lan, -'län\ *or Ital.* **Mi·la·no** \mē-'län-(,)ō\ *or anc.* **Me·di·o·la·num** \,mĕd-ē-ō-'län-əm, ,med-\. Commercial and industrial commune, ✱ of Lombardy and of Milano prov., N Italy, 76 m. NE of Genoa in a fertile plain between Adda and Ticino rivers; pop. (1970e) 1,713,539, met. area pop. 3,817,873; archepiscopal see; principal financial center of Italy; produces machinery, textiles (esp. silk), chemicals, motor vehicles, clothing; numerous notable buildings, including white-marble cathedral (begun 1387, completed 1858), 3d largest in Europe; castle, amphitheater, triumphal arch, basilica of St. Ambrose (4th cent., restored), royal and archepiscopal palaces, Brera palace (incl. Brera art gallery), Ambrosian library (earliest public library in Europe), La Scala theater, Ospedale Maggiore (1456, first municipal hospital); Univ. of Milan (1924), technical institute (1863).

History: Ancient Gallic city captured by Romans 222 B.C.; in 4th cent. A.D. a chief city of Western Roman Empire from which Constantine issued Edict of Milan 313; seat of Archbishop Ambrose (d. 397); overrun by Huns, by Odoacer, and by Ostrogoths (539); under strong episcopal authority, it became semi-independent of the empire and took lead in opposition to Emperor Frederick I in his struggle with Lombard League (see LOMBARDY); rebuilt after its destruction by Frederick 1162; ruled by the Visconti as dukes of Milan 1349–1447 and under them expanded until the **Duchy of Milan** *or Ital.* **Du·ca·to di Milano** \dü-,kät-ō-dē-\ *also* **The Mil·a·nese** \-,mil-ə-'nēz, -'nēs\ at its height included territory on both sides of middle Po and shared with Venice control of N Italy including Genoa; under Sforza family 1447–1535 duchy became pawn in Hapsburg-French rivalry in Italian wars of 16th cent.; duchy became Spanish 1535, ceded to Austria 1713; under Napoleon 1796–1814 city became capital of his Cisalpine Republic and kingdom of Italy (1805); as part of Lombardy 1815–59 duchy belonged to Austria again and was included in cession of Lombardy to Piedmont 1859; became part of Italy 1860; nucleus of the duchy now the province of Milano; in World War II city heavily damaged by bombing; reached by Allied forces Apr. 29, 1945.

Mi·la·no \mē-'län-(,)ō\. 1 Province of Lombardy, Italy. See table at ITALY.
2 Commune, Italy. See MILAN.

Mi·las \mi-'läs\ *or anc.* **My·la·sa** \mī-'lā-sə\. Town, Muğla prov., SW Turkey, near coast; pop. (1965c) 12,987; fruit-growing center; formerly famous for its rugs (Melas rugs); ancient Mylasa was a flourishing city of Caria.

Mi·laz·zo \mi-'lät-(,)sō\ *or anc.* **My·lae** \'mī-(,)lē\. Seaport, Messina prov., NE Sicily, Italy, on Tyrrhenian Sea 17 m. W of Messina; commune pop. (1968e) 25,651; tourism; center of wine and fruit producing area; Spanish castle (now a prison); 17th cent. cathedral. Scene of victory of Garibaldi over Bourbon forces 1860; waters off ancient Mylae scene of naval victory of Gaius Duilius over the Carthaginians 260 B.C. in First Punic War.

Milazzo, Gulf of. Inlet of the Mediterranean Sea on N coast of Sicily, Italy; 16 m. long.

Mil·bank \'mil-,baŋk\. City, ⊗ of Grant co., NE South Dakota, 34 m. NE of Watertown; pop. (1970c) 3727; granite quarries; wheat, livestock.

Mil·den·hall \'mil-dən-,hȯl\. Town, West Suffolk, E England, 8 m. NE of Newmarket; pop. (1961c) 7132; 15th cent. market cross, 17th cent. manor house.

Mil·du·ra \mil-'d(y)u̇r-ə\. Town, NW Victoria, SE Australia, on Murray river 15 m. above its junction with the Darling and ab. 300 m. NW of Melbourne; pop. (1968e) 13,120.

Mile 26. See EIELSON FIELD.

Miles City \'mīlz-\. City, ⊗ of Custer co., SE Montana, on Yellowstone river 140 m. ENE of Billings; pop. (1970c) 9023; ships wool, livestock; leather products; agriculture; Miles Community Coll. (1939).

Mile·stone Mountain \'mīl-,stōn-\. Peak in Sierra Nevada, N Tulare co., S cen. California; 13,641 ft.

Mi·let·to, Mon·te \,mȯn-tē-mə-'let-(,)ō\. Mountain, highest in Neapolitan Apennines (see table at APENNINES).

Mi·le·tus \mī-'lēt-əs, mə-\. Ruined city (archaeological site), Turkey, near the mouth of the Menderes in the modern province of Aydın; one of the great cities of Asia Minor, on the coast of Caria and the southernmost and most important of the 12 Ionian Cities; had four harbors and a large trade, founded colonies on the Black Sea and in Egypt and Italy, and for a time was the rival of Lydia; led Ionian revolt 500 B.C. but was overcome by Persia; later taken by Alexander; in Roman times yielded in influence to Ephesus; distinguished as a literary center.

Mil·ford \'mil-fərd\. 1 City, SW New Haven co., S Connecticut, on Long Island Sound and Housatonic river; pop. (1970c) 50,858; residential; brass goods, electronic equipment, electric motors; founded 1639; shipbuilding center until early 19th cent.; incorporated as city 1959.
2 Industrial city, Kent and Sussex cos., cen. Delaware, 18 m. S of Dover; pop. (1970c) 5314; clothing, canned foods, bricks; truck farms.
3 Village, Iroquois co., E Illinois; pop. (1970c) 1656.
4 Town, Worcester co., cen. Massachusetts, 16 m. ESE of Worcester; pop. (1970c) 19,532; rubber goods, tools and dies, footwear.
5 Village, Oakland co., SE Michigan, 17 m. W of Pontiac; pop. (1970c) 4699; summer resort; diversified agriculture.
6 Manufacturing and fruit-growing town, Hillsborough co., S New Hampshire, 11 m. WNW of Nashua; pop. (1970c) 6622; granite quarries; apples, peaches.
7 Village, Clermont and Hamilton cos., SW Ohio, 12 m. ENE of Cincinnati; pop. (1970c) 4828; agriculture.
8 Borough, ⊗ of Pike co., NE Pennsylvania, on Delaware river 47 m. E of Scranton; pop. (1970c) 1190.

Milford Haven. Urban district and seaport, Pembrokeshire, SW Wales; pop. (1971p) 13,745; major oil port, with three refineries and extensive dock facilities for tankers; excellent harbor on **Milford Haven** (large inlet of St. George's Channel); Henry Tudor (afterwards Henry VII) landed here from France 1485 to conduct his successful campaign for English throne.

Milford Sound. Inlet of Tasman Sea on SW coast of South I., New Zealand; noted for its scenery.

Milh, Cape \-'mil\ *or Arab.* **R'as al–Milh** \,räs-,al-\. Cape, NE Libya, near Egyptian border.

Milhau. See MILLAU.

Mi·li \'mē-lē\. Atoll at S end of Ratak Chain, SE Marshall Is., W Pacific Ocean; has 30 islets enclosing lagoon 23 m. long, 6°08′N, 171°55′E; often bombed by Americans 1942–44.

Mil·ia·na \mil-'yän-ə\. Commune, N Al-Asnam dept., N Algeria, on railroad 60 m. WSW of Algiers; pop. (1966c) 28,000.

Mi·li·ane \mēl-'yän\. Small river flowing NE across N cen. Tunisia, N Africa, and emptying into Mediterranean Sea just below and E of Tunis.

Mi·li·tel·lo in Val di Ca·ta·nia \,mēl-i-'tel-(,)ō-in-,väl-dē-kə-'tän-yə\. Commune, Catania prov., E Sicily, Italy, 23 m. SW of Catania; pop. (1968e) 10,764.

Milk \'milk\. River, S Alberta, Canada, and N Montana; 625 m. long; rises in Glacier co., NW Montana, flows NE across Canadian border and E along S Alberta, turns SE across Montana border and E along N Montana into Missouri river in S Valley co., NE Montana.

Mil·lard \'mil-ərd\. 1 County in Utah. See table at UTAH.
2 City, Douglas and Sarpy cos., E Nebraska, 11 m. SW of Omaha; pop. (1970c) 7460.

Millares. See MIJARES.

Mil·lau *also* **Mi·lhau** \mē-'yō\ *or anc.* **Æmil·i·a·num** \i-,mil-ē-ā-nəm, -'an-əm\. Commune, Aveyron dept., S France, 30

m. SE of Rodez; pop. (1968c) 22,595; gloves, textiles; tanneries, coal mines.

Mill·brae \ˈmil-(ˌ)brā\. City, San Mateo co., W California, NW of San Mateo; pop. (1970c) 20,920; chemicals, steam turbines; residential.

Mill·brook \ˈmil-(ˌ)bru̇k\. Residential village and summer resort, Dutchess co., SE New York, 13 m. ENE of Poughkeepsie; pop. (1970c) 1735; Bennett Coll. (1891).

Mill·bury \ˈmil-ˌber-ē, -bə-rē\. Town, Worcester co., cen. Massachusetts, 5 m. S of Worcester; pop. (1970c) 11,987; felt, wire, weaving machinery.

Mil·ledge·ville \ˈmil-ij-ˌvil\. City, ⊗ of Baldwin co., cen. Georgia, 30 m. NE of Macon; pop. (1970c) 11,601; building materials, mobile homes, textiles; agriculture; Georgia Military Coll. (1879), Georgia Coll. at Milledgeville (1889); settled 1803.

Mille Îles, Ri·vière des \rē-ˌvyer-dā-mēl-ˈēl\. River, a part of the course of the St. Lawrence river, NW and N of Jesus I., S Quebec, Canada; ab. 24 m. long; separates Jesus I. from the mainland; flows NE from Lake of Two Mountains to junction with Rivière des Prairies.

Mille Lacs \mil-ˈ(l)ak(s)\. **1** Lake on boundary bet. Aitkin and Mille Lacs cos., E cen. Minnesota; ab. 16 m. in diameter; 207 sq. m.

2 County in Minnesota. See table at MINNESOTA.

3 Lake, W Ontario, Canada, NW of Thunder Bay; 103 sq. m.

Mil·len \ˈmil-ən\. City, ⊗ of Jenkins co., E Georgia, 47 m. S of Augusta; pop. (1970c) 3713; clothing, aluminum products, poultry.

Mil·ler \ˈmil-ər\. **1** Name of counties in three states of the U.S. See tables at ARKANSAS, GEORGIA, MISSOURI.

2 City, ⊗ of Hand co., E cen. South Dakota; pop. (1970c) 2148; grain and livestock farms.

Miller, Mount. Mountain, Antarctica, 83°20′S, 165°48′E; 13,648 ft.

Mil·le·ro·vo \ˌmil-ə-ˈrō-və\. Town, W Rostov Oblast, Russian S.F.S.R., U.S.S.R., on railroad N of Kamensk Shakhtinski, ab. 60 m. ENE of Voroshilovgrad; pop. (1967e) 35,000; furniture.

Miller Peak. Mountain in SW Cochise co., SE Arizona; 9445 ft.

Mil·lers \ˈmil-ərz\. River, N Massachusetts; ab. 60 m. long; rises in S New Hampshire, flows S across Massachusetts border, then W into Connecticut river in cen. Franklin co., NW Massachusetts.

Mil·lers·burg \ˈmil-ərz-ˌbərg\. **1** Village, ⊗ of Holmes co., NE cen. Ohio, 20 m. SE of Mansfield; pop. (1970c) 2979; plastic and rubber products; oil and gas wells, coal mines.

2 Borough, Dauphin co., SE cen. Pennsylvania, on Susquehanna river 20 m. N of Harrisburg; pop. (1970c) 1838; footwear; tools; dairy farms.

Mil·lers·ville \ˈmil-ərz-ˌvil\. Borough, Lancaster co., SE Pennsylvania, 4 m. SW of Lancaster; pop. (1970c) 6396; Millersville State Coll. (1854).

Mill Hall \ˌmil-\. Borough, Clinton co., cen. Pennsylvania, 28 m. WSW of Williamsport; pop. (1970c) 1838.

Mil·li·gan College \ˈmil-i-gən-\. Village (unincorp.), Carter co., NE Tennessee, ab. 6 m. SW of Elizabethton; Milligan Coll. (1882).

Mil·ling·ton \ˈmil-iŋ-tən\. Town, Shelby co., SW corner of Tennessee, N of Memphis; pop. (1970c) 21,177; hats, wire; livestock farms.

Mil·li·nock·et \ˌmil-ə-ˈnäk-ət\. Town, Penobscot co., E cen. Maine, 54 m. SW of Houlton; pop. (1970c) 7742.

Millinocket Lake. **1** Lake on W boundary of Penobscot co., E cen. Maine, SE of Mt. Katahdin and just NE of Pemadumcook Lake with which it is connected by a short stream.

2 Small lake, NE Piscataquis co., N cen. Maine.

Mil·lis \ˈmil-əs\. Town, Norfolk co., E Massachusetts, 20 m. SW of Boston; pop. (1970c) 5686.

Mill·port \ˈmil-ˌpō(ə)rt, -ˌpȯ(ə)rt\. Burgh, Bute co., SW Scotland, at S end of Great Cumbrae I.; pop. (1969e) 1159; resort.

Mills \ˈmilz\. Name of counties in two states of the U.S. See tables at IOWA and TEXAS.

Mills, Fort. See FORT MILLS.

Mill Springs \ˈmil-\. Village in Wayne co., S Kentucky, on Cumberland river; scene of battle Jan. 19, 1862 in which Confederates were defeated.

Mill·stät·ter Lake \ˈmil-ˌs(h)tet-ər-\ *or Ger.* **Millstätter See** \-ˌzā\. Lake (*see*), in cen. Carinthia, S Austria, in Drau (Drava) valley ab. 33 m. W of Klagenfurt; 5 sq. m.; ab. 7½ m. long; max. depth 462 ft.; resort area.

Mill·town \ˈmil-ˌtau̇n\. Borough, Middlesex co., cen. New Jersey, 3 m. S of New Brunswick; pop. (1970c) 6470; rayon; sand pits; truck farms.

Mill·vale \ˈmil-ˌvāl\. Borough, Allegheny co., SW Pennsylvania, on Allegheny river 3 m. N of Pittsburgh; pop. (1970c) 5815; metal stampings; agriculture.

Mill Valley. Residential city, Marin co., W California, NW of San Francisco; pop. (1970c) 12,942; near Mt. Tamalpais and Muir Woods National Monument.

Mill·ville \ˈmil-ˌvil\. **1** Town, Worcester co., cen. Massachusetts, SE of Worcester; pop. (1970c) 1764.

2 Manufacturing city, Cumberland co., SW New Jersey, 10 m. ESE of Bridgeton on Maurice river; pop. (1970c) 21,366; lake resort; glass, garments, hosiery; diversified agriculture; settled 1720.

Milne Bay \ˈmil(n)-\. Bay at SE extremity of New Guinea I., Papua New Guinea; Samarai is near its SE point; occupied by Japanese Aug. 1942 but they were driven out by Australians Sept.–Oct. 1942.

Mil·ner·ton \ˈmil-nər-tən\. Town, S Cape Province, S Rep. of South Africa, on coast 5 m. N of Cape Town of which it is a suburb; pop. (1967e) 6400.

Miln·ga·vie \mil-ˈgī\. Burgh, Dunbarton co., W cen. Scotland; pop. (1971p) 10,742; residential suburb of Glasgow.

Miln·row \ˈmil(n)-ˌrō\. Urban district, Lancashire, NW England, SE suburb of Rochdale; pop. (1971p) 10,329.

Mi·lo \ˈmī-(ˌ)lō\. **1** Town, Piscataquis co., N cen. Maine, 35 m. NNW of Bangor; pop. (1970c) 2572.

2 Island and city, Greece. See MELOS.

Mil·pa Al·ta \ˌmēl-pə-ˈäl-tə\. Municipality, Federal District, Mexico, 18 m. SE of Mexico City; pop. (1970p) 33,557; lumber; dairy farming; diversified agriculture.

Mil·pi·tas \mil-ˈpēt-əs\. City, Santa Clara co., W California, S of Palo Alto; pop. (1970c) 27,149; paints; automobile assembly plant; citrus fruits.

Mil·ton \ˈmilt-ᵊn\. **1** Town, ⊗ of Santa Rosa co., NW Florida, 18 m. NE of Pensacola; pop. (1970c) 5360.

2 Town, Norfolk co., E Massachusetts, 6 m. S of Boston; pop. (1970c) 27,190; residential suburb of Boston; Curry Coll. (1879), St. Columban's Coll. and Seminary (1923); settled 1636, incorporated 1662.

3 Borough, Northumberland co., E cen. Pennsylvania, 19 m. SSE of Williamsport; pop. (1970c) 7723; steel products, clothing; agriculture.

4 Town, Chittenden co., Vermont, 10 m. NNE of Burlington; pop. (1970c) 4495.

5 Town, King and Pierce cos., W cen. Washington, 7 m. E of Tacoma; pop. (1970c) 2607.

6 Town, Cabell co., W West Virginia, 18 m. E of Huntington; pop. (1970c) 1567; glass; truck farms.

7 Village, Rock co., S Wisconsin, 8 m. NNE of Janesville; pop. (1970c) 3699; Milton Coll. (1844).

8 Town, ⊗ of Halton co., SE Ontario, Canada, 29 m. WSW of Toronto; pop. (1966c) 6601; flour, bronze and steel products; fruit farms.

ə abut; ᵊ kitten, Fr. table; ər further; a back; ā bake; ä cot, cart; à Fr. bac; au̇ out; ch chin; e less; ē easy; g gift
i trip; ī life; j joke; k̲ Ger. ich, Buch; ⁿ Fr. vin; ŋ sing; ō flow; ȯ flaw; œ Fr. bœuf; œ̄ Fr. feu; ȯi coin; th thin
t̲h̲ this; ü loot; u̇ foot; ue Ger. füllen; ue̅ Fr. rue; y yet; ʸ Fr. digne \dēnʸ\, nuit \nwʸē\; yü few; yu̇ furious; zh vision

Mil·ton–Free·water \-'frē-ˌwȯ-tər, -ˌwä-\. City, Umatilla co., NE Oregon, 28 m. NE of Pendleton; pop. (1970c) 4105; ships fruits and vegetables.

Milvian Bridge. See SAXA RUBRA.

Mil·wau·kee \mil-'wȯ-kē\. 1 River, SE Wisconsin; 100 m. long; rises in Fond du Lac co., flows into Lake Michigan at Milwaukee.

2 County in SE Wisconsin. See table at WISCONSIN.

3 Commercial and industrial city and lake port, its ⊗, on Lake Michigan; largest city in the state; pop. (1970c) 717,372; major lake port, shipping coal and grain; produces electrical machinery, castings and forgings, machine tools, automobile parts, motorcycles, footwear, meat products, beer. De Sales Preparatory Seminary (1856), Saint Francis Seminary (1856), Marquette Univ. (1857), Mount Mary Coll. (1872), Alverno Coll. (1887), Wisconsin Coll. Conservatory (1899), Milwaukee School of Engineering (1903), Univ. of Wisconsin at Milwaukee (1908), Layton School of Art (1920), Milwaukee Technical Coll. (1923), Cardinal Stritch Coll. (1932). Platted 1835; settled 1836 ff.; incorporated 1846; major center of German immigration 1840 –1900.

Mil·wau·kie \mil-'wȯ-kē\. City, Clackamas and Multnomah cos., NW Oregon, on Willamette river 7 m. S of Portland; pop. (1970c) 16,379; batteries, plywood.

Mimatum. See MENDE.

Mim·bres \ˌmim-brəs\. Village, Grant co., SW New Mexico, on the Mimbres river, W of Mimbres Mts.; hot springs; pueblo ruins nearby.

Mimbres Mountains. Range in SW New Mexico, extending along boundary bet. Grant and Sierra cos.

Mim·i·co \'mim-i-ˌkō\. Residential town, York co., SE Ontario, Canada, on Lake Ontario 6 m. W of Toronto; pop. (1966c) 19,341.

Min \'min\. 1 *or* **Min Chiang** \'min-jē-'äŋ\. River (*chiang*), Szechwan prov., S cen. China; ab. 350 m. long; flows SE through the Red Basin into Yangtze river at I-pin; navigable for most of its course.

2 *or* **Min–Kong** \-'kȯŋ\. Navigable river (*kong*), N cen. Fukien prov., SE China; ab. 250 m. long; flows SE into East China Sea near Foochow.

Mī·nāb \mē-'näb\. Town, S Iran, 50 m. E of Bandar 'Abbās; pop. (1966c) 5310; fruit orchards.

Mi·na·ha·sa *also* **Mi·na·has·sa** \ˌmē-nə-'häs-ə\. Peninsula forming NE end of Celebes I., Indonesia.

Minami, Cape. See O-LUAN, CAPE.

Mi·na·mi–Alps National Park \mi-ˌnäm-ē-\. National Park, Honshū, Japan; 138 sq. m.; mountainous area; established 1964.

Minami Iwo. See VOLCANO ISLANDS.

Minami–Tori–Shima. See MARCUS ISLAND.

Mi·nas \'mēn-əs\. 1 Dept., Uruguay. See LAVALLEJA.

2 Town, ✱ of Lavalleja dept., SE Uruguay; pop. (1963c) 31,388; tourism, brewing.

Minas Basin \ˌmī-nəs-\. Northeast extension of the Bay of Fundy, in cen. Nova Scotia, Canada; connected by **Minas Channel** with the Bay of Fundy.

Minas de Rí·o·tin·to \'mēn-əs-dā-ˌrē-ō-'tēn-tō\. Commune, Huelva prov., SW Spain, on Tinto river 36 m. NE of Huelva; pop. (1970p) 7903; copper mines.

Minas Ge·rais \ˌmē-nəs-zhə-'rīs\. State, E Brazil; 226,707 sq. m.; pop. (1970p) 11,279,872; ✱ Belo Horizonte; iron ore, manganese, diamonds, bauxite, nickel; cattle.

Mi·na·ti·tlán \ˌmē-nə-ti-'tlän\. Town, Veracruz state, E Mexico, head of navigation on the Coatzacoalcos river 24 m. from its mouth; munic. pop. (1970p) 89,412; petroleum refinery.

Min·bu \'min-'bü\. 1 District, Magwe division, Upper Burma; 3602 sq. m.; pop. (1962e) 361,071; ✱ Minbu; peanuts, fishing; oil fields.

2 Town, its ✱, on right bank of Irrawaddy opp. Magwe, ab. 145 m. SW of Mandalay; pop. (1962e) 85,273.

Minch *also* **Minsh** \'minch\. Channel bet. the Outer Hebrides and the NW coast of Scotland; includes the North Minch and Little Minch (*qq.v.*).

Min Chiang. See MIN 1.

Min·cio \'mēn-(ˌ)chō, 'min-chē-ˌō\ *or anc.* **Min·ci·us** \'min-sh(ē-)əs, 'min(t)-sē-əs\. River, N Italy; 115 m. long; issues from Lake Garda, flows S and E past Mantua and empties into Po river SE of Mantua; navigable up to Mantua.

Min·da·nao \ˌmin-də-'nä-ˌō, -'naů\. 1 Island, S Phil.; including small adjacent islands, 38,254 sq. m.; pop. (1970p) 7,292,691; for administrative subdivisions, see table at PHILIPPINES. Of irregular triangular shape, indented with many gulfs or bays. Basilan I. in SW is largest island attached to it (Zamboanga del Sur prov.) politically; other important islands are Dinagat, Siargao, Camiguin, Samal, and Bucas Grande. Separated from Visayan Is. to N by Mindanao Sea and bordered on E by Philippine Sea (part of Pacific), on S by Celebes Sea, and on W by Sulu Sea. Mountainous with many peaks above 5000 ft.; highest Apo 9690 ft. (highest in the archipelago). Has two great river systems, the Agusan in E and the Mindanao (with the Pulangi) in S and cen. parts. Products include corn, rice, coconuts, timber, coffee, abacá.

2 *or* **Rio Gran·de de Mindanao** \ˌrē-ō-'gran-dē-də-\ *or formerly* **Co·ta·ba·to** \ˌkōt-ə-'bät-(ˌ)ō\. River, cen. Mindanao, Phil.; ab. 200 m. long; known in its upper course as the Pulangi; rises in NE Bukidnon prov., flows S and SW to form the main stream in cen. Cotabato prov., whence it flows WNW to Illana Bay; navigable; with its many tributaries forms a wide fertile basin. Municipality of Cotabato is on N side of delta.

Mindanao Sea. Large interisland body of water, S Phil., bordered on N by islands of Negros, Cebu, Bohol, and Leyte, and on S by Mindanao; ab. 70 m. from N to S and 180 m. from E to W; at W end opens into Sulu Sea and connects on NE with the Pacific by Surigao Strait and on N with Visayan Sea by Tanon Strait and with Camotes Sea by Bohol Strait and Canigao Channel. Contains the islands of Camiguin and Siquijor.

Mindello. See PORTO GRANDE.

Min·den \'min-dən\. 1 City, ⊗ of Webster parish, NW Louisiana, 28 m. E of Shreveport; pop. (1970c) 13,996; oil wells, cottonseed oil mills.

2 City, ⊗ of Kearney co., S Nebraska, 16 m. SSE of Kearney; pop. (1970c) 2669; butter; diversified agriculture.

3 Village, ⊗ of Douglas co., W Nevada, 14 m. S of Carson City.

4 Village, ⊗ of Haliburton co., SE Ontario, Canada, 30 m. ESE of Bracebridge; pop. (1966c) 625.

5 *or anc.* **Min·thun** \'min-thən\. Manufacturing city, North Rhine-Westphalia, West Germany, on Weser river 58 m. ENE of Münster; pop. (1969e) 51,236; textiles, glass, ceramics, furniture, machinery; 12th cent. churches, town hall with 13th cent. façade, 13th cent. early Gothic cathedral.

History: Founded in Roman times; bishopric founded here by Charlemagne in 8th cent.; member of Hanseatic League; besieged several times during Thirty Years' War; to Brandenburg 1648 by Peace of Westphalia; French decisively defeated near here by Duke Ferdinand of Brunswick Aug. 1, 1759; to kingdom of Westphalia 1807; to Prussia 1814; in World War II entered by Allied troops Apr. 6, 1945.

Min·do·ro \min-'dōr-(ˌ)ō, -'dȯr-\. Island, cen. Phil., SW of Luzon; 3759 sq. m.; divided into two provinces, **Mindoro Oc·ci·den·tal** \-ˌȯk-si-den-'täl\ (incl. Lubang Is.; 2270 sq. m.; pop [1970p] 145,689; ✱ Mamburao) and **Mindoro Ori·en·tal** \-ˌōr-ē-en-'täl\ (1685 sq. m.; pop. [1970p] 328,251; ✱ Calapan). Roughly of oval shape with long axis NW to SE, ab. 80 m. long by ab. 50 m. wide. Touches South China Sea on W and Sulu Sea on S, separated from Luzon on N by Verde Island Passage, from Tablas and other islands on E by Tablas Strait, and from Calamian Is. on SW by Mindoro Strait. Has fairly regular coastline with several good harbors; most important adjacent islands are Lubang Is. to NW, Semirara Is. to S, and Ilin I. off SW coast. Mountain range, with several high peaks, runs through center; highest are Halcon in N 8469 ft. and Baco in the center 8163 ft.; coastal plains on E and W sides are wide and fertile. Numerous rivers with falls and rapids. Main products rice, copra, abacá, corn, sugar, and fruits; lumbering and fishing.

History: Known to Chinese before coming of Spaniards; first visited by Spaniards 1570; at first administered from Batangas; suffered from Moro raids in 17th and 18th cents.; came under American control 1901 and organized into a province 1902; held by Japanese through World War II; invaded by Americans who landed near San Jose Dec. 15, 1944; divided into two provinces 1950.

Mindoro Strait. Passage connecting South China Sea and N Sulu Sea, bet. SW Mindoro and Calamian Is.; ab. 50 m. wide; much traveled by ships bet. Manila, Hong Kong, and other Asiatic ports on N and ports of S Philippines and Netherlands Indies on S.

Mind·szent \'mind-sent\. Commune, Csongrád co., S Hungary, on Tisza river 20 m. N of Szeged; pop. (1970p) 8762.

Mine·head \'mīn-ˌhed\. Urban district, Somersetshire, SW England, on Bristol Channel 43 m. WSW of Bristol; pop. (1971p) 8063; seaside resort; chartered 1558.

Mi·neo \mē-'nā-ō\ *or anc.* **Me·nae·um** \me-'nē-əm\. Commune, Catania prov., E Sicily, Italy, 27 m. SW of Catania; pop. (1968e) 8574; geophysical observatory, medieval crypts; terra-cotta; mineral springs.

Min·e·o·la \ˌmin-ē-'ō-lə\. 1 Village, ⊗ of Nassau co., SE New York, on Long I. 20 m. E of New York; pop. (1971e) 21,744; suburb of New York City.

2 City, Wood co., NE Texas, 23 m. N of Tyler; pop. (1970c) 3926; fruit and truck farms.

Mi·ner \'mī-nər\. County in South Dakota. See table at SOUTH DAKOTA.

Min·er·al \'min-ər-əl\. Name of counties in four states of the U.S. See tables at COLORADO, MONTANA, NEVADA, WEST VIRGINIA.

Mi·ne·ral·ny·ye Vo·dy \ˌmin-ə-'räl-nē-ə-'vȯd-ē\. Town, Stavropol Krai, Russian S.F.S.R., U.S.S.R., ab. 80 m. SE of Stavropol; pop. (1967e) 47,000.

Mineral Point. City, Iowa co., SW Wisconsin, 17 m. ENE of Platteville; pop. (1970c) 2305; dairy products; lead and zinc mines.

Mineral Wells. City, Palo Pinto and Parker cos., N cen. Texas, 42 m. W of Fort Worth; pop. (1970c) 18,411; aluminum products; health resort; truck farms.

Min·ers·ville \'mī-nərz-ˌvil\. Borough, Schuylkill co., E cen. Pennsylvania, 4 m. WNW of Pottsville; pop. (1970c) 6012.

Mi·ner·va \mə-'nər-və\. Village, Carroll and Stark cos., E Ohio, 15 m. ESE of Canton; pop. (1970c) 4359; electrical equipment, dairy products, tools and dies; diversified agriculture.

Mi·ner·vi·no Mur·ge \ˌme-nər-ˌvē-nō-'mu̇(ə)r-(ˌ)jā\. Commune, Bari prov., Apulia, SE Italy, 40 m. W of Bari; pop. (1968e) 15,578.

Min·gan Islands \ˌmiŋ-gən-\. Group of islands in Gulf of St. Lawrence, Canada, N of Anticosti I., near mouth of Romaine river.

Min·go \'miŋ-(ˌ)gō\. County in West Virginia. See table at WEST VIRGINIA.

Mingo Junction. City, Jefferson co., E Ohio, on Ohio river 3 m. S of Steubenville; pop. (1970c) 5278.

Min·gre·lia \min-'grē-lē-ə, miŋ-\. Region and former principality now included in NW Georgian S.S.R., U.S.S.R.; lies within borders of ancient Colchis, partly in Caucasus Mts. and partly along Black Sea coast. Declared its independence early in 15th cent. but was subject to some extent to Persia and Turkey; came under Russian control 1803 and incorporated permanently 1867. The Mingrelians are a Georgian people of Caucasian race.

Min·gu·lay \'miŋ-ə-ˌlā\. See BARRA.

Mi·nho \'mē-(ˌ)nyü\ *or Span.* **Mi·ño** \'mē-(ˌ)nyō\ *or anc.* **Min·i·us** \'min-ē-əs\. River, Spain and Portugal; 171 m. long; rises in N Lugo prov., NW Spain, flows S and SW, forming boundary bet. Portugal and Spain, and empties into Atlantic Ocean on the boundary S of Vigo.

Minhow. See FOOCHOW.

Min·i·coy \'min-i-ˌkȯi\. Small island, S Laccadive Is., off SW coast of India; administratively part of the Indian territory of Laccadive, Minicoy, and Amindivi Is.

Min·i·do·ka \ˌmin-ə-'dō-kə\. County in Idaho. See table at IDAHO.

Minieh. See MINYA.

Minius. See MINHO.

Min–Kong. See MIN 2.

Min·na \'min-ə\. Town, North-Western State, Nigeria, on railroad ab. 65 m. N of the Niger river; pop. (1969e) 69,567.

Min·ne·ap·o·lis \ˌmin-ē-'ap-(ə-)ləs\. 1 City, ⊗ of Ottawa co., NE cen. Kansas, on Solomon river 20 m. N of Salina; pop. (1970c) 1971; in agricultural and livestock-raising section.

2 City, ⊗ of Hennepin co., SE cen. Minnesota, on Mississippi river at the Falls of Saint Anthony (*q.v.*); largest city in the state; pop. (1970c) 434,400; twin city with Saint Paul (*q.v.*); railroad center and grain market; produces agricultural machinery, precision instruments, metal and paper products, linseed oil, electrical equipment; food processing, printing and publishing, flour milling. Univ. of Minnesota (1851), Augsburg Coll. (1869), Minneapolis School of Art (1886), Minnesota Bible Coll. (1913), North Central Bible Coll. (1930), Saint Mary's Junior Coll. (1964), Metropolitan State Junior Coll. (1965). Site visited by Hennepin 1680; included in area of Fort Snelling military reservation 1819; developed as center of lumber industry and later as center of flour milling; incorporated 1867.

Min·ne·do·sa \ˌmin-ə-'dō-sə\. Town, SW Manitoba, Canada, 29 m. N of Brandon; pop. (1971p) 2629; lake resort; farm equipment.

Min·ne·ha·ha \ˌmin-ē-'hä-hä\. County in South Dakota. See table at SOUTH DAKOTA.

Minnehaha Creek. Small stream, Hennepin co., SE cen. Minnesota; outlet of Lake Minnetonka; flows through S part of Minneapolis (area set aside as a park); the falls, ab. 50 ft. high, celebrated by Longfellow's use in his poem *Hiawatha,* occur just before the creek reaches the Mississippi river; natural flow of water small.

Min·nei Peak \'min-(ˌ)ā-\. Volcano, Ambrim I., New Hebrides, SW Pacific Ocean; 4380 ft.; eruption 1913.

Min·ne·so·ta \ˌmin-ə-'sōt-ə\. 1 River, S Minnesota; 332 m. long; flows out of Big Stone Lake on South Dakota-Minnesota boundary, bends SE, then NE to join the Mississippi river at St. Paul.

2 A north central state of U.S.A., bounded on N by Canadian provinces of Manitoba and Ontario, on E by Lake Superior and Wisconsin, on S by Iowa, and on W by South Dakota and North Dakota; 12th state in area, 84,068 sq. m. (land area 79,278 sq. m.), in addition to this area Minnesota has also 2212 sq. m. of water of the Great Lakes; 19th state in population, (1970c) 3,805,069; ✱ St. Paul; 32d state admitted to Union (1858).

Nicknames: Gopher State; New England of the West; North Star State. *State flower:* Pink and white moccasin flower. *Motto:* L'étoile du Nord (Star of the North). *Rivers:* Mississippi, rising in N cen. region, flowing SE, and forming SE boundary of state; St. Croix, forming E cen. boundary and flowing into the Mississippi; Minnesota (see 1, above). *Highest point:* Eagle Mt. 2301 ft. in Cook co. *Chief products:* Oats, corn, soybeans, sugar beets; dairy products; iron ore, granite, limestone; manufacturing:

machinery, pulp and paper products; food processing. *Chief cities:* Minneapolis, St. Paul, Duluth, Bloomington, Rochester. See *Table of States* at UNITED STATES. Divided into the following 87 counties (for pronunciation of their names, see their individual entries):

NAME	LOCATION	AREA[1] (sq. m.)	POP. (1970c)	CO. SEAT
Aitkin[2]	E cen.	1,831	11,403	Aitkin
Anoka	E	424	154,595	Anoka
Becker	NW cen.	1,297	24,372	Detroit Lakes
Beltrami	N	2,507	26,373	Bemidji
Benton	cen.	402	20,841	Foley
Big Stone	W	490	7,941	Ortonville
Blue Earth	S	737	52,322	Mankato
Brown	S	610	28,887	New Ulm
Carlton	E	862	28,072	Carlton
Carver	SE cen.	359	28,331	Chaska
Cass[3]	N cen.	1,998	17,323	Walker
Chippewa	SW cen.	582	15,109	Montevideo
Chisago	E	419	17,492	Center City
Clay	W	1,045	46,608	Moorhead
Clearwater[4]	NW	1,000	8,013	Bagley
Cook	NE corner	1,346	3,423	Grand Marais
Cottonwood	SW	636	14,887	Windom
Crow Wing	cen.	995	34,826	Brainerd
Dakota	SE	576	139,808	Hastings
Dodge	SE	435	13,037	Mantorville
Douglas	W cen.	647	22,910	Alexandria
Faribault	S	711	20,896	Blue Earth
Fillmore	SE	859	21,916	Preston
Freeborn	S	700	38,064	Albert Lea
Goodhue	SE	753	34,763	Red Wing
Grant	W	546	7,462	Elbow Lake
Hennepin	SE cen.	567	960,080	Minneapolis
Houston	SE corner	555	17,556	Caledonia
Hubbard	N cen.	932	10,583	Park Rapids
Isanti	E	438	16,560	Cambridge
Itasca	N	2,633	35,530	Grand Rapids
Jackson	S	696	14,352	Jackson
Kanabec	E	524	9,775	Mora
Kandiyohi	SW cen.	783	30,548	Willmar
Kittson	NW corner	1,123	6,853	Hallock
Koochiching	N	3,127	17,131	International Falls
Lac qui Parle	W	768	11,164	Madison
Lake	NE	2,062	13,351	Two Harbors
Lake of the Woods[5]	N	1,311	3,987	Baudette
Le Sueur	S	440	21,332	Le Center
Lincoln	SW	531	8,143	Ivanhoe
Lyon	SW	709	24,273	Marshall
McLeod	S cen.	488	27,662	Glencoe
Mahnomen	NW	563	5,638	Mahnomen
Marshall	NW	1,789	13,060	Warren
Martin	S	703	24,316	Fairmont
Meeker	S cen.	619	18,349	Litchfield
Mille Lacs[2]	E cen.	571	15,703	Milaca
Morrison	cen.	1,127	26,949	Little Falls
Mower	S	703	43,783	Austin
Murray	SW	703	12,508	Slayton
Nicollet	S	432	24,518	St. Peter
Nobles	SW	712	23,208	Worthington
Norman	NW	885	10,008	Ada
Olmsted	SE	656	84,104	Rochester
Otter Tail[6]	W cen.	1,962	46,097	Fergus Falls
Pennington	NW	622	13,266	Thief River Falls
Pine	E	1,414	16,821	Pine City
Pipestone	SW	464	12,791	Pipestone
Polk	NW	2,013	34,435	Crookston
Pope	W cen.	669	11,107	Glenwood
Ramsey	E	155	476,350	St. Paul
Red Lake	NW	432	5,388	Red Lake Falls
Redwood	SW	874	20,024	Redwood Falls
Renville	SW cen.	979	21,139	Olivia
Rice	S	496	41,582	Faribault
Rock	SW corner	485	11,346	Luverne
Roseau	NW	1,676	11,569	Roseau
Saint Louis	NE	6,092	220,693	Duluth
Scott	SE	353	32,423	Shakopee
Sherburne	cen.	430	18,344	Elk River
Sibley	S cen.	583	15,845	Gaylord
Stearns	cen.	1,342	95,400	St. Cloud
Steele	S	425	26,931	Owatonna
Stevens	W	558	11,218	Morris
Swift	W	739	13,177	Benson
Todd	cen.	942	22,114	Long Prairie
Traverse	W	568	6,254	Wheaton
Wabasha	SE	522	17,224	Wabasha
Wadena	cen.	536	12,412	Wadena
Waseca	S	415	16,663	Waseca
Washington	E	386	82,948	Stillwater
Watonwan	S	433	13,298	St. James
Wilkin	W	752	9,389	Breckenridge
Winona	SE	620	44,409	Winona
Wright	S cen.	674	38,933	Buffalo
Yellow Medicine	SW	753	14,523	Granite Falls

[1]Area = land area.
[2]Upper half of Mille Lacs Lake in Aitkin co., lower half in Mille Lacs co.
[3]Contains many lakes including Leech Lake.
[4]Includes Lake Itasca, source of Mississippi river.
[5]Includes part of Lake of the Woods and a section of land on W shore of the lake N of the 49th parallel.
[6]Contains many lakes, including Otter Tail Lake.

History: Probably visited by Radisson and Groseilliers 1654–60; Upper Mississippi valley explored by La Salle and Hennepin 1680; region W of Mississippi was part of Louisiana Purchase 1803; part E of Mississippi, ceded to British 1763 and to U.S. 1783, in part included in Northwest Territory 1787 and later in Indiana Territory 1800; Fort Snelling established 1820; N boundary settled by Ashburton Treaty 1842; included in various territories before erection of Minnesota Territory 1849 (included region W from Wisconsin to the Missouri and N from Iowa to Canada); admitted to Union as state May 11, 1858; Sioux uprising occurred in S Minnesota 1862.

Min·ne·ton·ka \ˌmin-ə-ˈtäŋ-kə\. Village, Hennepin co., SE Minnesota, W suburb of Minneapolis; pop. (1970c) 35,737.

Minnetonka, Lake. Lake, Hennepin co., SE cen. Minnesota, ab. 10 m. W of Minneapolis; ab. 12 m. long; outlet is Minnehaha Creek (*q.v.*).

Min·ne·tris·ta \ˌmin-ə-ˈtris-tə\. Village, Hennepin co., SE cen. Minnesota; pop. (1970c) 2878.

Min·ne·was·ka, Lake \-ˌmin-ə-ˈwäs-kə\. Lake, Pope co., W cen. Minnesota; ab. 7 m. long.

Min·ne·wau·kan \ˌmin-ə-ˈwȯ-kən\. City, ⊗ of Benson co., N cen. North Dakota; pop. (1970c) 496.

Minni. See ARMENIA 1.

Miño. See MINHO.

Mi·nonk \mi-ˈnäŋk, -ˈnəŋk\. City, Woodford co., N cen. Illinois, 33 m. ENE of Peoria; pop. (1970c) 2267; dairy products; grain and livestock farms.

Mi·nor·ca \mə-ˈnȯr-kə\ *or Span.* **Me·nor·ca** \mā-ˈnȯr-kə\. Second largest island of the Balearic group, Baleares prov., Spain, in W Mediterranean ab. 25 m. NE of Majorca; 271 sq. m.; pop. (1970p) 50,217; ✱ Mahón; rugged and irregular coast with numerous bays; hilly and generally arid in N, fertile plateau in S; tourism; produces cheese, leather footwear; livestock raising; principal crops are cereals, potatoes, almonds, melons, and pomegranates.

History: See also BALEARIC ISLANDS; part of kingdom of Majorca; in 1709 captured by British during War of Spanish Succession and retained by Treaty of Utrecht 1713; taken by France 1756 in Seven Years' War; ceded by French to British 1763; recovered by Spain by treaty terminating War of American Independence 1783; in Spanish Civil War 1936–39, remained Loyalist until forced to surrender Feb. 1939.

Mi·not \ˈmī-ˌnät\. City, ⊗ of Ward co., NW cen. North Dakota, on Souris river 100 m. N of Bismarck; pop. (1970c) 32,390; dairy and meat products, farm machinery, building materials, petroleum compounds; Minot State Coll. (1913).

Mi·nots Ledge \ˌmī-nəts-\ *or* **Co·has·set Rocks** \kō-ˌhas-ət-\. Reef in Cohasset harbor, 15 m. SE of Boston, Massachusetts; lighthouse.

Minsh. See MINCH.

Min Shan \ˈmin-ˈshän\. Mountain range in Kansu prov., cen. China, along N boundary of Szechwan prov.; peaks ab. 14,000 ft.; E extension of Kunlun Mts.

Min·si, Mount \-ˈmin(t)-sē\. Peak, E Monroe co., E Pennsylvania, forming part of the W side of Delaware Water Gap; ab. 1500 ft.

Minsk \ˈmin(t)sk\. City, ✱ of the Belorussian S.S.R., U.S.S.R., also ✱ of Minsk Oblast, on a tributary of Berezina river near Polish border; pop. (1970p) 916,000; largest city in U.S.S.R. on the main railroad line from Warsaw to Moscow and an important commercial and industrial city; produces motor vehicles, machine tools, television and radio sets, foodstuffs, leather goods, cloth-

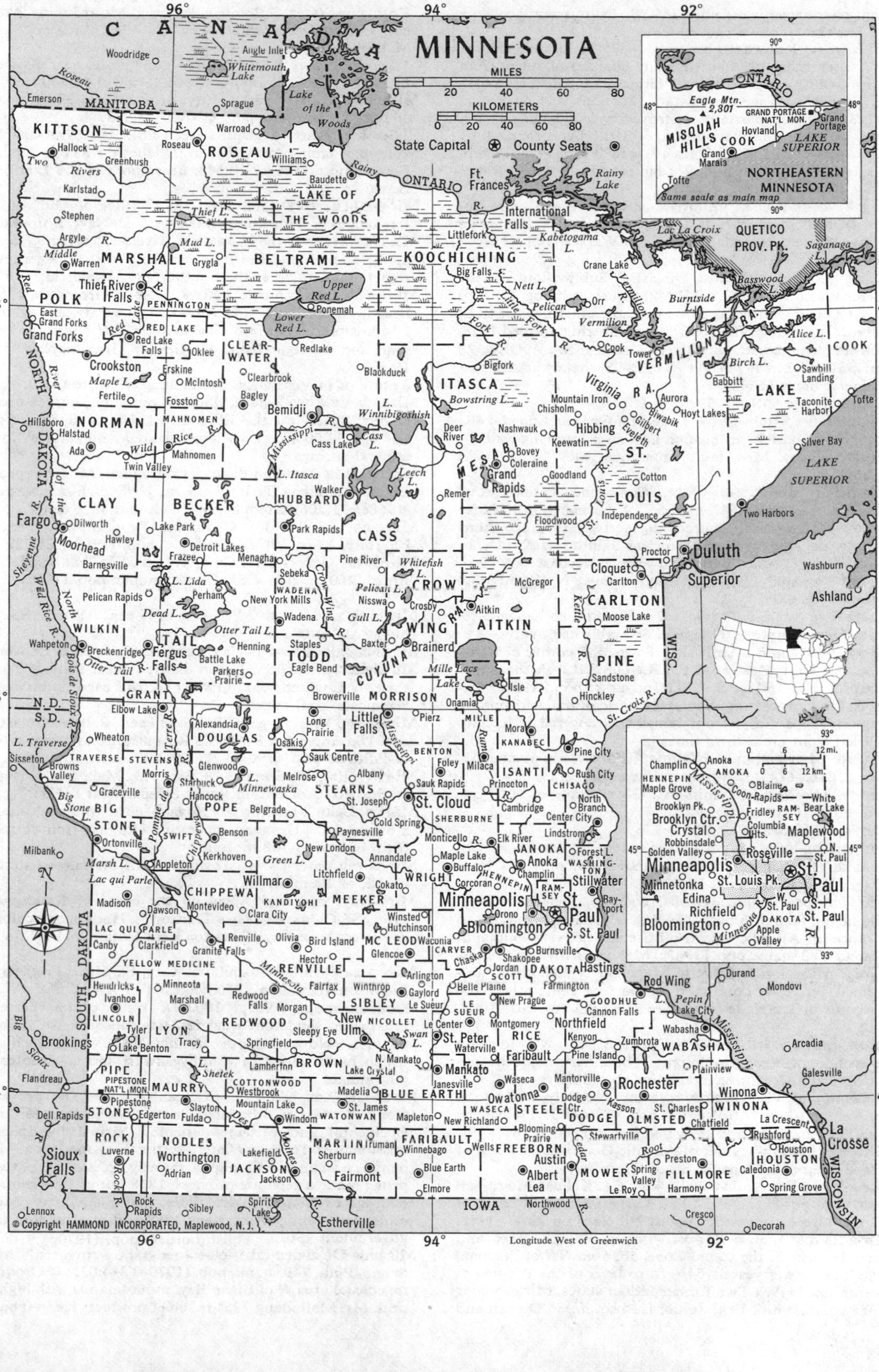
MINNESOTA
MILES
0 20 40 60 80
KILOMETERS
0 20 40 60 80
State Capital
County Seats
CANADA
MANITOBA
ONTARIO
NORTH DAKOTA
SOUTH DAKOTA
IOWA
WISCONSIN
N.D.
S.D.
WISC.
Lake of the Woods
Rainy Lake
Upper Red L.
Lower Red L.
Mille Lacs Lake
LAKE SUPERIOR
L. Winnibigoshish
Leech L.
Mississippi R.
Minnesota R.
Red R.
St. Croix R.
Des Moines R.
KITTSON
ROSEAU
LAKE OF THE WOODS
MARSHALL
BELTRAMI
KOOCHICHING
POLK
PENNINGTON
RED LAKE
CLEARWATER
ITASCA
NORMAN
MAHNOMEN
CLAY
BECKER
HUBBARD
CASS
ST. LOUIS
LAKE
COOK
WILKIN
OTTER TAIL
WADENA
CROW WING
AITKIN
CARLTON
PINE
TODD
GRANT
DOUGLAS
MORRISON
MILLE LACS
KANABEC
TRAVERSE
STEVENS
POPE
STEARNS
BENTON
ISANTI
CHISAGO
BIG STONE
SWIFT
SHERBURNE
ANOKA
WASHINGTON
CHIPPEWA
KANDIYOHI
MEEKER
WRIGHT
HENNEPIN
RAMSEY
LAC QUI PARLE
YELLOW MEDICINE
RENVILLE
MC LEOD
CARVER
SCOTT
DAKOTA
LINCOLN
LYON
REDWOOD
SIBLEY
NICOLLET
LE SUEUR
RICE
GOODHUE
WABASHA
PIPESTONE
MURRAY
COTTONWOOD
BROWN
BLUE EARTH
WASECA
STEELE
DODGE
OLMSTED
WINONA
ROCK
NOBLES
JACKSON
MARTIN
WATONWAN
FARIBAULT
FREEBORN
MOWER
FILLMORE
HOUSTON
Duluth
Superior
Minneapolis
St. Paul
St. Cloud
Rochester
Bloomington
Mankato
Moorhead
Fargo
Grand Forks
International Falls
Bemidji
Brainerd
Hibbing
Winona
La Crosse
Sioux Falls
NORTHEASTERN MINNESOTA
Same scale as main map
Eagle Mtn. 2,301
MISQUAH HILLS
GRAND PORTAGE NAT'L MON.
Grand Portage
Grand Marais
QUETICO PROV. PK.
VERMILION RA.
MESABI RA.
CUYUNA RA.
© Copyright HAMMOND INCORPORATED, Maplewood, N.J.
Longitude West of Greenwich
96°
94°
92°
48°
46°
44°

ing, pharmaceuticals; univ. (1921), Belorussian Academy of Sciences.

History: Known as early as 1067, its location on the western border has caused many changes of rulers from 13th to 18th cents.—at times Lithuanian, Russian, Polish, or Swedish; ravaged by Tatars 1505; annexed by Russia 1793 but again partially destroyed by Napoleon 1812; a key point in the Revolution of 1917 but occupied by Germans 1918 and by Poles 1919; in World War II again seized by Germans July 1941 but retaken by Soviet forces July 3, 1944.

Mińsk Ma·zo·wiec·ki \ˈmin(t)sk-ˌmäz-ə-ˈvyet-skē\ *also* **No·wo–Mińsk** \ˌnó-vó-ˈmin(t)sk\. Commune, Warszawa prov., NE cen. Poland, 23 m. ESE of Warsaw; pop. (1970p) 24,200.

Minsk Oblast \-ˈó-bləst, -ˌblast\. Subdivision of the Belorussian S.S.R., U.S.S.R.; 40,800 sq. m.; pop. (1970p) 2,456,000; ✻ Minsk; swamps widespread, esp. in S and E; wheat, rye, barley, flax; dairying, lumbering; formed 1938.

Min·ster \ˈmin(t)-stər\. Village, Auglaize co., W Ohio, 28 m. SSW of Lima; pop. (1970c) 2405; metalworking machinery; dairy farms.

Minthun. See MINDEN 5.

Min·to, Lake \-ˈmin-(ˌ)tō\. Lake, NW Quebec, Canada; 485 sq. m.; has outlet NE through Leaf river into Ungava Bay.

Minto, Mount. Mountain, Antarctica, 71°47′S, 168°45′E; 13,658 ft.

Min·tur·no \min-ˈtu̇(ə)r-(ˌ)nō\. Commune, Latina prov., Latium, cen. Italy, 47 m. ESE of Latina; pop. (1968e) 16,699; 12th cent. church (formerly cathedral); ruins nearby on Appian Way of ancient **Min·tur·nae** \-nē\. In World War II Allied base in advance from coast May 1944.

Mi·nūf \mi-ˈnüf\. Town, Minūfīya gov., N Egypt; pop. (1966c) 48,300.

Mi·nū·fī·ya \ˌmin-ü-ˈfē-(y)ə\ *also* **Me·nu·fi·eh** \ˌmən-ü-ˈfē-yə\. Governorate of N Egypt. See table at EGYPT.

Mi·nu·sinsk \ˌmin-ü-ˈsin(t)sk\. Town, SW corner of Krasnoyarsk Krai, Russian S.F.S.R., U.S.S.R., on the upper Yenisei river 160 m. S of Krasnoyarsk; pop. (1967e) 42,000; food processing; center of agricultural and mining region. Apparently, from remains discovered, a locality settled from prehistoric times.

Min·ute Man National Historical Park \ˈmin-ət-ˌman-\. See UNITED STATES, *National Historical Parks.*

Min·ya *also* **Min·ieh** \ˈmin-yə\. Governorate of N Egypt. See table at EGYPT.

Minya, Al–. See AL-MINYA.

Minya Kon·ka \ˌmin-yə-ˈkäŋ-kə\ *also* **Bo·kun·ka** *or* **Bo·kon·ka** \ˈbó-ˌkəŋ-kä\. Mountain, Szechwan prov., S China, 30 m. S of K'ang-ting; 24,900 ft.

Mio \ˈmī-(ˌ)ō\. Village, ⊗ of Oscoda co., NE Michigan.

Miq·ue·lon Island \ˈmik-ə-ˌlän-\. Small island, belonging to France, in Atlantic Ocean off S coast of Newfoundland, Canada; 83 sq. m.; pop. (1962c) 628; originally two islands, **Great Miquelon** and **Little Miquelon** *or* **Lan·glade** \läⁿ-ˈglad\, but now connected by narrow shingle bar, the Isthmus of Langlade (*q.v.*). See SAINT PIERRE AND MIQUELON.

Mi·ra \ˈmir-ə\. 1 River in N Ecuador; flows NW, forming a section of Ecuador-Colombia boundary, and empties into Pacific Ocean; navigable for ab. 30 m.

2 Commune, Venezia prov., Veneto, NE Italy, on Lagoon of Venice 10 m. W of Venice; pop. (1968e) 31,196; site of the Palazzo Foscarino in which Byron resided 1817–19.

Mira Bay \ˌmī-rə-\. Inlet of Atlantic Ocean on NE coast of Cape Breton I., Canada, SE of Glace Bay.

Mir·a·bel·la Bay \ˌmir-ə-ˌbel-ə-\ *or Gk.* **Kól·pos Me·ra·bél·lou** \ˈkól-pós-ˌmer-ə-ˈbel-(ˌ)ü\. Large inlet on N coast of Crete, Greece; town of Hagios Nikólaos on its W shore.

Mir·a·flo·res \ˌmir-ə-ˈflōr-əs, -ˈflór-\. Village, lake, and double locks in the Canal Zone, ab. 5 m. NW of Panama; the locks lower vessels 54⅔ ft. to level of the Pacific.

Mi·raj \mi-ˈrəj\. 1 Two former Indian states: **Miraj Senior** (368 sq. m.) and **Miraj Junior** (194 sq. m.) in Deccan and Kolhapur States, S Bombay, W India. Miraj Junior joined new United Deccan State Aug. 26, 1947. Area now in S Maharashtra state.

2 Town, former ✻ of Miraj (Senior) state, near Krishna river 194 m. SE of Bombay; pop. (1961c) 53,300.

Mi·ra·mar \ˈmir-ə-ˌmär\. 1 City, Broward co., SE Florida S of Fort Lauderdale; pop. (1970c) 23,973.

2 Seaside resort, Argentina. See GENERAL ALVARADO.

Mi·ra·mas \ˌmir-ə-ˈmä\. Town, Bouches-du-Rhône dept., S France; pop. (1968c) 10,544; near shore of the Étang de Berre.

Mir·a·mi·chi Bay \ˌmir-ə-mə-ˌshē-\. Inlet of Gulf of St. Lawrence, E Northumberland co., E New Brunswick, Canada; receives the **Miramichi River,** 135 m. long, rising in Victoria co. and flowing from the SW, the main stream sometimes known as the **South West Miramichi.**

Mi·ran·da \mə-ˈran-də\. 1 River, S Mato Grosso state, SW Brazil; 225 m. long; flows NW into the Paraguay river.

2 Municipality, S Mato Grosso state, SW Brazil, on railroad and on right bank of Miranda river; pop. (1968e) 19,394.

3 State of N Venezuela. See table at VENEZUELA.

Miranda de Ebro \-dē-ˈā-(ˌ)brō\. Commune, Burgos prov., N cen. Spain, on the Ebro 36 m. NE of Burgos; pop. (1970p) 33,905; cereals, wine, fruit; manufactures flour; mineral springs.

Mi·ran·do·la \mi-ˈrän-də-lə\. Commune, Modena prov., Emilia-Romagna, N Italy, 19 m. NNE of Modena; pop. (1968e) 21,706; sarcophagi of 14th and 15th cents.

Mi·ra·no \mi-ˈrän-(ˌ)ō\. Commune, Venezia prov., Veneto, NE Italy, 12 m. WNW of Venice; pop. (1968e) 21,222.

Mi·ras·sol \ˌmir-ə-ˈsól\. City, NW cen. São Paulo state, SE Brazil, 260 m. NW of São Paulo; munic. pop. (1968e) 23,851.

Mir·di·të \mēr-ˈdē-tə\. Province of N cen. Albania. See table at ALBANIA.

Mi·re·ba·lais \ˌmir-ə-bə-ˈlā\. Town, E Haiti, SE of St. Marc.

Mir·field \ˈmər-ˌfēld\. Urban district, West Riding, Yorkshire, N England; pop. (1969e) 16,070; carpets, blankets, chemicals; coal mines.

Mir·go·rod \ˈmi(ə)r-gə-ˌräd\. Town, cen. Poltava Oblast, E cen. Ukrainian S.S.R., U.S.S.R., on railroad 50 m. WNW of Poltava; pop. (1967e) 27,000.

Mi·ri \ˈmi(ə)r-ē\. Seaport, NE Sarawak, Malaysia, on island of Borneo, S of Baram Point; extensive oil fields.

Mi·rim, Lake \-mə-ˈrim\ *or Span.* **Me·rín** \mā-ˈrēn\. Lake, E boundary of Uruguay, separating Uruguay from extreme S tip of Brazil; 108 m. long.

Mīr·jā·veh \ˌmēr-jə-ˈve\. Town, SE Iran, on railroad ab. 120 m. NE of Bampur.

Mirs Bay \ˈmi(ə)rz-\. Bay on the coast of Kwangtung prov., SE China, E of New Territories, Hong Kong colony; its waters leased by China to Great Britain in 1898 for 99 years.

Mir·za·pur \ˈmi(ə)r-zə-ˌpu̇(ə)r\. City, SE Uttar Pradesh, N India, on right bank of Ganges river 45 m. ESE of Allahabad; pop. (1961c) 100,097; trade center; carpets, brassware; sandstone quarries; has mosques and Hindu temples. Now includes **Bin·dha·chal** \ˈbind-ˌhäch-əl\, which has a shrine of Vindhyeshwari and is a center of pilgrimage.

Mi·sa·mis \mi-ˈsäm-əs\. In Spanish times the province along N coast of Mindanao, now divided into Misamis Occidental and Misamis Oriental. Visited by Spanish missionaries 1622 and later; settlements made on Mindanao coast and on Camiguin; in early times a part of Cebu prov.; made a separate province 1818 but in 19th cent. its boundaries changed several times; also suffered from Moro raids; came under Americans 1899 and was granted civil government 1901.

Misamis Oc·ci·den·tal \-ˌók-sə-den-ˈtäl\. Province, N Mindanao, Phil.; 749 sq. m.; pop. (1970p) 344,025; ✻ Oroquieta; coastal area W of Iligan Bay; mountainous with highest peak Mt. Malindang 7954 ft.; chief products hemp (abacá) and coconuts. Chief towns Ozamiz, Oroquieta, Tangub, Jimenez, and Plaridel. For history, see MISAMIS.

Misamis Orien·tal \-ˌȯr-ē-en-ˈtäl\. Province, N Mindanao, Phil.; 1378 sq. m.; pop. (1970p) 477,282; ✱ Cagayan de Oro; long coastal strip E of Iligan Bay and Camiguin I. in S cen. Mindanao Sea; contains two inlets Macajalar Bay and Gingoog Bay; has volcanic cone Hibokhibok 5620 ft. on Camiguin I.; has fertile soil; chief products hemp (abacá) and coconuts. Chief towns Cagayan de Oro, Mambajao, Balingasag, and Initao. For history, see MISAMIS.

Mi·sant·la \mi-ˈsänt-lə\. City, Veracruz state, Mexico, 70 m. NW of Veracruz; munic. pop. (1970p) 44,268; commercial center; coffee, sugarcane, oranges, vanilla; scene of Spanish victory 1817 in Mexican War of Independence.

Mi·sa·wa \mi-ˈsä-wə\. Town, Aomori prefecture, N Honshū, Japan, near coast ab. 14 m. N of Hachinohe; pop. (1970c) 35,343.

Misch·a·bel·hör·ner \ˈmish-ˌäb-əl-ˌhər-nər\. Mountain group in the Pennine Alps, Valais canton, SW cen. Switzerland; highest peak the Dom 14,913 ft.

Mis·cou Island \ˌmis-(ˌ)kü-\. Island off NE tip of New Brunswick, Canada, S of entrance to Chaleur Bay; its N tip is **Point Miscou.**

Mi–sen \ˈmē-ˈsen\. See ITSUKU-SHIMA.

Mi·se·no \mi-ˈzā-(ˌ)nō, -ˈzen-(ˌ)ō\. Promontory, NW of the Bay of Naples and S of ruins of Cumae, Italy; at its base to the N is Porto di Miseno, site of ancient town of **Mi·se·num** \mī-ˈsē-nəm\, a naval base under Augustus, constructed by Agrippa 31 B.C.

Mis·ery, Mount \-ˈmiz-(ə)rē\. Peak on the island of St. Christopher, West Indies; 3792 ft.

Mish, Slieve. See SLIEVE MISH.

Mi·shāb, Kūh–e \ˌkü-ə-mə-ˈshab\. Mountain range in NW Iran, N of Lake Urmia; highest point 10,430 ft.

Mi·shaum Point \mə-ˌshȯm-\. Southern point of Bristol co., SE Massachusetts; extends into Buzzards Bay.

Mish·a·wa·ka \ˌmish-ə-ˈwȯ-kə, -ˈwäk-ə\. Industrial city, St. Joseph co., N Indiana, SE of South Bend; pop. (1970c) 35,517; guided missiles, rubber goods, plastics, tools and dies; Bethel Coll. (1947).

Mi·shi·ma \mə-ˈshē-mə\. City, Shizuoka prefecture, Honshū, Japan, 31 m. NE of Shizuoka; pop. (1970c) 78,-141.

Mi·sil·me·ri \ˌmē-sil-ˈmer-e\. Commune, Palermo prov., Sicily, Italy, 8 m. SE of Palermo; pop. (1968e) 15,193; castle.

Mi·si·ma \mi-ˈsē-mə\ *or* **Saint Ai·gnan** \ˌsaⁿ-tā-ˈnyäⁿ\. Island in Louisiade Archipelago, administratively part of Papua New Guinea, 140 m. E of Milne Bay; ab. 100 sq. m.; ab. 25 m. long and bet. 1 and 4 m. wide; at E end is Bwagaoia, chief village of the group; mountainous, with some peaks above 3000 ft.; formerly important gold producer.

Mi·sio·nes \ˌmis-ē-ˈō-nəs\. 1 Province of N cen. Argentina. See table at ARGENTINA.

2 Department of S Paraguay. See table at PARAGUAY.

Misiones, Sierra de. See SIERRA DE MISIONES.

Misis. See MOPSUESTIA.

Misithra. See MISTRA.

Miskish, Slieve. See SLIEVE MISKISH.

Miskito Coast. See MOSQUITO COAST.

Mis·kolc \ˈmish-ˌkōlts\. City, ⊗ of Borsod-Abaúj-Zemplén co., NE Hungary, 85 m. NE of Budapest; pop. (1970p) 172,952; major industrial center, producing iron and steel, flour, textiles, leather goods, wine; 13th cent. church. Nearly destroyed by Mongols 1241–43.

Mi·so·ol \ˈmē-sə-ˌwȯl\ *or* **Mi·sol** \ˈmē-ˌsȯl\. Island, Indonesia, N of Ceram and just W of Doberai Penin. of W Irian Barat; ab. 50 m. long by 23 m. wide; 672 sq. m.

Misore Islands. See SCHOUTEN ISLANDS 1.

Mis·quah Hills \ˌmis-ˌkwȯ-\. Elevation, Cook co., NE corner of Minnesota; 2246 ft.

Miṣr. See EGYPT.

Misrātah. See MISURATA.

Mis·sau·kee \mi-ˈsȯ-kē\. County in Michigan. See table at MICHIGAN.

Mis·si·nai·bi \ˌmis-ə-ˈnī-bē\. River, E cen. Ontario, Canada; 265 m. long; rises in **Missinaibi Lake** and flows N and NE to join the Mattagami and form the Moose river.

Mis·sion \ˈmish-ən\. 1 City, Johnson co., E Kansas, 4 m. W of Kansas City; pop. (1970c) 8376; residential suburb of Kansas City.

2 City, Hidalgo co., S Texas, near the Rio Grande 5 m. W of McAllen; pop. (1970c) 13,043; oil wells; packs and ships citrus fruits and vegetables; diversified agriculture.

Mis·sion·ary Ridge \ˌmish-ə-ˌner-ē-\. Ridge extending NE to SW in Hamilton co., Tennessee, and Dade co., Georgia; a section of this ridge near Chattanooga was the site of a Union victory Nov. 25, 1863 in the Civil War.

Mission City. Town, SW British Columbia, Canada, on right bank of Fraser river and on railroad 38 m. E of Vancouver; pop. (1966c) 3412; Seminary of Christ the King (1932).

Mission Hills. City, Johnson co., E Kansas; pop. (1970c) 4177.

Mission Range. A range of the Rocky Mts. chiefly in Lake and Missoula cos., W Montana; highest point 9900 ft.

Mis·sis·quoi \mə-ˈsis-ˌkwȯi\. 1 River, United States and Canada; ab. 90 m. long; rises in Orleans co., NW Vermont, flows N into Canada, then S into Franklin co., Vermont, and W into Lake Champlain.

2 County, Quebec, Canada. See table at QUEBEC.

Mis·sis·sa·gi \ˌmis-ə-ˈsäg-ē\. River, SE Ontario, Canada; ab. 130 m. long; flows SW and S into North Channel.

Mississagi, Strait of. Strait bet. W Manitoulin I. and Cockburn I. in NE Lake Huron, SE Ontario, S Canada.

Mis·sis·sip·pi \ˌmis-(ə-)ˈsip-ē\. 1 Navigable river, cen. United States; 2348 m. long to head of the Passes, or, if measured from headwaters of Missouri river, 3860 m. long; head of the Passes to Gulf of Mexico 17 m.; drainage area 1,234,700 sq. m.; rises in Lake Itasca, NW Minnesota, flows SE to form lower section of Minnesota-Wisconsin boundary, and the Iowa-Wisconsin and Iowa-Illinois boundaries, the Missouri-Illinois, Missouri-Kentucky, and Missouri-Tennessee boundaries, the Arkansas-Tennessee and Arkansas-Mississippi boundaries, and the N section of Louisiana-Mississippi boundary, then continuing SE into the Mississippi river delta and into the Gulf of Mexico through several mouths, known locally as the Passes—Main Pass, North Pass, South Pass, Southwest Pass.

History: Crossed by De Soto 1541; upper reaches explored by Marquette and Jolliet 1673; lower part traced by La Salle who laid claim for French to entire Mississippi valley (see LOUISIANA) 1682; after French cessions of 1762 and 1763, was boundary bet. Spanish on W and British on E; became W boundary of U.S. 1783, but its mouth was controlled by Spain which finally granted free navigation by treaty 1795; U.S. obtained control of W part of valley by Louisiana Purchase 1803; upper reaches explored by Pike 1805–06; after c. 1820, navigated by steamboats; during American Civil War, gradually opened by Union forces until capture of Vicksburg 1863 destroyed Confederate hold upon the river.

2 Southeastern state of U.S.A., bounded on N by Tennessee, on E by Alabama, on S by the Gulf of Mexico and Louisiana, and on W by Louisiana and Arkansas; 32d state in area, 47,716 sq. m. (land area 47,358 sq. m.); 29th state in population, (1970c) 2,216,912; ✱ Jackson; 20th state admitted to Union (1817).

Nicknames: Magnolia State; Bayou State. *State flower:* Magnolia. *Motto:* Virtute et Armis (By Valor and Arms).

Rivers: Mississippi, forming W boundary; Pearl, flowing SW and S and forming SW boundary bet. Mississippi and Louisiana; Big Black, flowing from N cen. area SW into the Mississippi; Tennessee, forming boundary in extreme NE area. *Highest point:* Woodall Mt. 806 ft., in Tishomingo co. *Chief products:* Cotton, soybeans, corn; livestock; petroleum, natural gas; manufacturing: chemicals, apparel, wood products. *Chief cities:* Jackson, Biloxi, Meridian, Gulfport, Greenville. See *Table of States* at UNITED STATES. Divided into the following 82 counties (for pronunciation of their names, see their individual entries):

NAME	LOCATION	AREA[1] (sq. m.)	POP. (1970c)	CO. SEAT
Adams	SW	449	37,293	Natchez
Alcorn	NE	405	27,179	Corinth
Amite	SW	729	13,763	Liberty
Attala	cen.	724	19,570	Kosciusko
Benton	N	412	7,505	Ashland
Bolivar	NW	923	49,409	Cleveland and Rosedale
Calhoun	N cen.	575	14,623	Pittsboro
Carroll	cen.	637	9,397	Vaiden and Carrollton
Chickasaw	NE	506	16,805	Houston and Okolona
Choctaw	cen.	417	8,440	Ackerman
Claiborne	SW	489	10,086	Port Gibson
Clarke	E	697	15,049	Quitman
Clay	E	414	18,840	West Point
Coahoma	NW	569	40,447	Clarksdale
Copiah	SW	780	24,764	Hazlehurst
Covington	S	416	14,002	Collins
De Soto	NW corner	476	35,885	Hernando
Forrest	SE	468	57,849	Hattiesburg
Franklin	SW	568	8,011	Meadville
George	SE	481	12,459	Lucedale
Greene	SE	728	8,545	Leakesville
Grenada	N cen.	431	19,854	Grenada
Hancock	S; coastal	482	17,387	Bay St. Louis
Harrison	SE; coastal	585	134,582	Gulfport
Hinds	SW cen.	876	214,973	Jackson and Raymond
Holmes	W cen.	769	23,120	Lexington
Humphreys	W	421	14,601	Belzoni
Issaquena	W	414	2,737	Mayersville
Itawamba	NE	541	16,847	Fulton
Jackson	SE corner; coastal	736	87,975	Pascagoula
Jasper	SE cen.	683	15,994	Bay Springs and Paulding
Jefferson	SW	521	9,295	Fayette
Jefferson Davis	S	414	12,936	Prentiss
Jones	SE	702	56,357	Ellisville and Laurel
Kemper	E	757	10,233	De Kalb
Lafayette	N	668	24,181	Oxford
Lamar	S	500	15,209	Purvis
Lauderdale	E	721	67,087	Meridian
Lawrence	S	433	11,137	Monticello
Leake	cen.	586	17,085	Carthage
Lee	NE	455	46,148	Tupelo
Leflore	W	592	42,111	Greenwood
Lincoln	SW	586	26,198	Brookhaven
Lowndes	E	548	49,700	Columbus
Madison	cen.	751	29,737	Canton
Marion	S	550	22,871	Columbia
Marshall	N	710	24,027	Holly Springs
Monroe	NE	769	34,043	Aberdeen
Montgomery	N cen.	403	12,918	Winona
Neshoba	E cen.	568	20,802	Philadelphia
Newton	E cen.	580	18,983	Decatur
Noxubee	E	695	14,288	Macon
Oktibbeha	NE cen.	454	28,752	Starkville
Panola	NW	693	26,829	Sardis and Batesville
Pearl River	S	828	27,802	Poplarville
Perry	SE	653	9,065	New Augusta
Pike	S	409	31,813	Magnolia
Pontotoc	N	501	17,363	Pontotoc
Prentiss	NE	418	20,133	Booneville
Quitman	NW	412	15,888	Marks
Rankin	S cen.	800	43,933	Brandon
Scott	cen.	615	21,369	Forest
Sharkey	W	436	8,937	Rolling Fork
Simpson	S cen.	587	19,947	Mendenhall
Smith	S cen.	642	13,561	Raleigh
Stone	SE	448	8,101	Wiggins
Sunflower	W	694	37,047	Indianola
Tallahatchie	NW	644	19,338	Charleston and Sumner
Tate	NW	405	18,544	Senatobia
Tippah	N	464	15,852	Ripley
Tishomingo	NE corner	443	14,940	Iuka
Tunica	NW	458	11,854	Tunica
Union	N	422	19,096	New Albany
Walthall	S	403	12,500	Tylertown
Warren	W	581	44,981	Vicksburg
Washington	W	734	70,581	Greenville
Wayne	SE	827	16,650	Waynesboro
Webster	N cen.	416	10,047	Walthall
Wilkinson	SW corner	674	11,099	Woodville
Winston	E cen.	606	18,406	Louisville
Yalobusha	N	488	11,915	Coffeeville and Water Valley
Yazoo	W cen.	938	27,314	Yazoo City

[1]Area = land area.

History: Part of French Louisiana (*q.v.*); Biloxi settled by Iberville 1699; except for S part (British West Florida), region ceded to U.S. 1783; organized as territory 1798 comprising S half of present states of Mississippi and Alabama; enlarged 1804 and 1813 to include all of present states of Alabama and Mississippi; W part of this territory admitted to Union Dec. 10, 1817 as state of Mississippi; seceded Jan. 9, 1861; scene of important battles during Civil War; readmitted to Union Feb. 23, 1870; adopted present constitution 1890.

3 Name of counties in two states of the U.S. See tables at ARKANSAS and MISSOURI.

4 River, SE Ontario, Canada; 105 m. long; rises in Frontenac co. and flows NE and N through **Mississippi Lake** in Lanark co. into the Ottawa river.

Mississippi Sound. Inlet of Gulf of Mexico bet. mainland of S Mississippi and SW Alabama and an island chain off the coast; receives the Pascagoula river.

Missolonghi. See MESOLÓNGION.

Mis·sou·la \mə-ˈzü-lə\. 1 County in W Montana. See table at MONTANA.

2 City, its ⊗, near confluence of Bitterroot river and Clark Fork; pop. (1970c) 29,497; lumber, paper pulp, dairy products; sugar refining; Univ. of Montana (1893).

Mis·sou·ri \mə-ˈzu̇(ə)r-ē, -ˈzu̇r-ə\. 1 River, cen. and NW cen. United States; 2466 m. long (or 2683 m. including longest tributaries to ultimate source) to its junction with the Mississippi river; formed by confluence of Jefferson, Madison, and Gallatin rivers in Gallatin co., S Montana; flows E to cen. North Dakota, then S across South Dakota to form E section of South Dakota-Nebraska boundary, and the Nebraska-Iowa and Nebraska-Missouri boundaries, and the N section of the Kansas-Missouri boundary, turns E across cen. Missouri and joins the Mississippi river ab. 10 m. N of St. Louis. During high water, navigable by flat-bottomed boats nearly to Great Falls, Montana (*q.v.*). First explored by French traders; traced to its sources by Lewis and Clark 1804–06.

2 Central state of U.S.A., bounded on N by Iowa, on E by Illinois, Kentucky, and Tennessee, on S by Arkansas, on W by Oklahoma, Kansas, and Nebraska; 19th state in area, 69,686 sq. m. (land area 69,046 sq. m.); 13th state in population, (1970c) 4,677,399; ✱ Jefferson City; 24th state admitted to Union (1821).

Nicknames: Show Me State; Bullion State. *State flower:* Hawthorn. *Motto:* Salus Populi Suprema Lex Esto (Let the Welfare of the People Be the Supreme Law). *Rivers:* Missouri (see 1 above); Mississippi, forming E boundary; Des Moines, forming boundary at extreme NE tip of state and emptying into the Mississippi. *Highest point:* Taum Sauk Mt. 1772 ft., in Iron co. *Chief products:* Soybeans, corn, wheat, cotton; livestock; cement, lead, iron ore, coal; manufacturing: transportation equipment, chemicals, fabricated metal products. *Chief cities:* St. Louis, Kansas City, Springfield, Independence, St. Joseph. See *Table of States* at UNITED STATES. Divided into the following 114 counties (for pronunciation, see their individual entries):

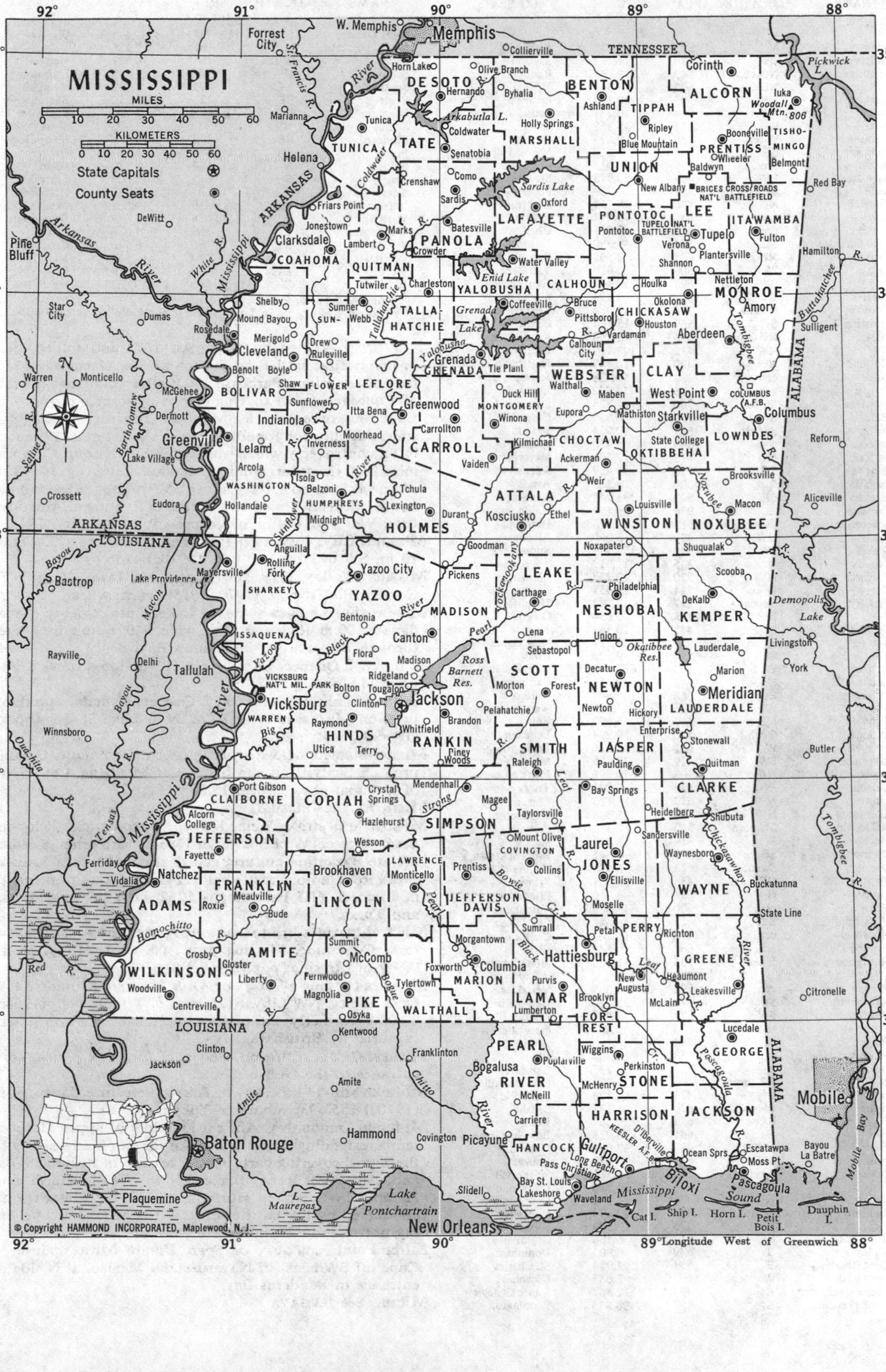

© Copyright HAMMOND INCORPORATED, Maplewood, N.J.

NAME	LOCATION	AREA[1] (sq. m.)	POP. (1970c)	CO. SEAT
Adair	N	572	22,472	Kirksville
Andrew	NW	436	11,913	Savannah
Atchison	NW corner	549	9,240	Rockport
Audrain	NE cen.	692	25,362	Mexico
Barry	SW	783	19,597	Cassville
Barton	SW	594	10,431	Lamar
Bates	W	841	15,468	Butler
Benton	W cen.	735	9,695	Warsaw
Bollinger	SE	621	8,820	Marble Hill
Boone	cen.	685	80,911	Columbia
Buchanan	NW	404	86,915	St. Joseph
Butler	SE	715	33,529	Poplar Bluff
Caldwell	NW	430	8,351	Kingston
Callaway	cen.	835	25,991	Fulton
Camden	S cen.	640	13,315	Camdenton
Cape Girardeau	SE	574	49,350	Jackson
Carroll	NW cen.	697	12,565	Carrollton
Carter	SE	506	3,878	Van Buren
Cass	W	698	39,448	Harrisonville
Cedar	W	496	9,424	Stockton
Chariton	N cen.	754	11,084	Keytesville
Christian	SW	567	15,124	Ozark
Clark	NE corner	506	8,260	Kahoka
Clay	NW	412	123,702	Liberty
Clinton	NW	420	12,462	Plattsburg
Cole	cen.	384	46,228	Jefferson City
Cooper	cen.	566	14,732	Boonville
Crawford	SE cen.	760	14,828	Steelville
Dade	SW	504	6,850	Greenfield
Dallas	SW cen.	537	10,054	Buffalo
Daviess	NW	563	8,420	Gallatin
De Kalb	NW	423	7,305	Maysville
Dent	SE cen.	756	11,457	Salem
Douglas	S	809	9,268	Ava
Dunklin	SE	543	33,742	Kennett
Franklin	E	934	55,127	Union
Gasconade	E cen.	519	11,878	Hermann
Gentry	NW	488	8,060	Albany
Greene	SW	677	152,929	Springfield
Grundy	N	435	11,819	Trenton
Harrison	N	720	10,257	Bethany
Henry	W	734	18,451	Clinton
Hickory	SW cen.	397	4,481	Hermitage
Holt	NW	458	6,654	Oregon
Howard	N cen.	472	10,561	Fayette
Howell	S	920	23,521	West Plains
Iron	SE	554	9,529	Ironton
Jackson	W	603	654,178	Independence
Jasper	SW	642	79,852	Carthage
Jefferson	E	668	105,647	Hillsboro
Johnson	W	826	34,172	Warrensburg
Knox	NE	512	5,692	Edina
Laclede	S cen.	770	19,944	Lebanon
Lafayette	W	632	26,626	Lexington
Lawrence	SW	619	24,585	Mount Vernon
Lewis	NE	508	10,993	Monticello
Lincoln	E	625	18,041	Troy
Linn	N	622	15,125	Linneus
Livingston	N	530	15,368	Chillicothe
McDonald	SW corner	540	12,357	Pineville
Macon	N	814	15,432	Macon
Madison	SE	496	8,641	Fredericktown
Maries	S cen.	525	6,851	Vienna
Marion	NE	438	28,121	Palmyra
Mercer	N	455	4,910	Princeton
Miller	cen.	600	15,026	Tuscumbia
Mississippi	SE	415	16,647	Charleston
Moniteau	cen.	419	10,742	California
Monroe	NE	669	9,542	Paris
Montgomery	E cen.	534	11,000	Montgomery City
Morgan	cen.	592	10,068	Versailles
New Madrid	SE	679	23,420	New Madrid
Newton	SW	629	32,981	Neosho
Nodaway	NW	877	22,467	Maryville
Oregon	S	784	9,180	Alton
Osage	cen.	608	10,994	Linn
Ozark	S	732	6,226	Gainesville
Pemiscot	SE corner	493	26,373	Caruthersville
Perry	E	471	14,393	Perryville
Pettis	W cen.	679	34,137	Sedalia
Phelps	S cen.	677	29,567	Rolla
Pike	E	681	16,928	Bowling Green
Platte	NW	427	32,081	Platte City
Polk	SW	642	15,415	Bolivar
Pulaski	S cen.	551	53,781	Waynesville
Putnam	N	518	5,916	Unionville
Ralls	NE	478	7,764	New London
Randolph	N cen.	484	22,434	Huntsville
Ray	NW	573	17,599	Richmond
Reynolds	SE	817	6,106	Centerville
Ripley	S	639	9,803	Doniphan
Saint Charles	E	551	92,954	St. Charles
Saint Clair	W	697	7,667	Osceola
Sainte Genevieve	E	499	12,867	Sainte Genevieve
Saint Francois	E	457	36,875	Farmington
Saint Louis[2]	E	499	951,671	Clayton
Saint Louis city		61	622,236	
Saline	W cen.	757	24,837	Marshall
Schuyler	N	306	4,665	Lancaster
Scotland	NE	441	5,499	Memphis
Scott	SE	421	33,250	Benton
Shannon	S	999	7,196	Eminence
Shelby	NE	501	7,906	Shelbyville
Stoddard	SE	823	25,771	Bloomfield
Stone	SW	449	9,921	Galena
Sullivan	N	654	7,572	Milan
Taney	S	615	13,023	Forsyth
Texas	S	1,183	18,320	Houston
Vernon	W	838	19,065	Nevada
Warren	E	426	9,699	Warrenton
Washington	E	760	15,086	Potosi
Wayne	SE	766	8,546	Greenville
Webster	S	590	15,562	Marshfield
Worth	NW	267	3,359	Grant City
Wright	S	684	13,667	Hartville

[1]Area = land area.
[2]Exclusive of city of St. Louis, which is politically independent of the county.

History: Visited by Marquette 1673 and Jolliet 1683; probably first settled by French at Ste. Genevieve 1735; part of Louisiana Purchase 1803; after admission of state of Louisiana (*q.v.*) to Union, rest of former territory of Louisiana organized as Missouri Territory 1812; Missouri's application for admission as slave state 1817 caused bitter controversy which was settled by Missouri Compromise 1820 (Missouri admitted as slave state Aug. 10, 1821, Maine as free, no slavery above 36°30′–later repealed); did not secede from Union 1861; scene of fighting in American Civil War 1861–64; adopted present constitution 1945.

Missouri City. City, Fort Bend and Harris cos., SE Texas, 15 m. SW of Houston; pop. (1970c) 4136.

Missouri Valley. City, Harrison co., W Iowa, 20 m. N of Council Bluffs; pop. (1970c) 3159; corn, wheat.

Mis·tas·si·ni \ˌmis-tə-ˈsē-nē\. **1** Lake, S cen. Quebec, Canada; ab. 100 m. long and 12 m. wide; 840 sq. m.; discharges through Rupert river into James Bay.

2 River, S Quebec, Canada; ab. 185 m. long; flows S into Lake St. John.

3 Town, Lake St. John co., S Quebec, Canada, opp. Dolbeau on Mistassini river 10 m. N of Lake St. John; pop. (1966c) 3884.

Mi·ster·bian·co \ˌmē-ster-bē-ˈäŋ-(ˌ)kō\. Commune, Catania prov., E Sicily, Italy, on S slope of Mt. Etna 4 m. WNW of Catania; pop. (1968e) 15,958.

Misti, El. See EL MISTI.

Mi·stra \mi-ˈsträ\. Ruined town, Laconia, SE Peloponnesus, Greece, W of Sparta; in 13th to 15th cents. a center of late-Byzantine culture; called also **Mi·si·thra** \ˌmis-ə-thrä\ from famous castle built 1249; capital of principality of Michael VIII Palaeologus 1262; later held by Greeks and Turks.

Mi·stret·ta \mēs-ˈtrā-tə\ *or anc.* **Ames·tra·tus** \ə-ˈmes-trə-təs\. Commune, Messina prov., NE Sicily, Italy, 68 m. WSW of Messina; pop. (1968e) 8167; castle.

Mi·su·ra·ta \ˌmis-ə-ˈrät-ə\ *or Arab.* **Mis·rā·tah** \mis-ˈrā-tə\. Coastal city, NW Libya, 125 m. E of Tripoli; pop. (1964c) 37,000; formerly an important Italian garrison town; captured by British Jan. 1943.

Misurata, Cape. Cape on N coast of Libya, N Africa, W of entrance to the Gulf of Sidra.

Mi·ta·ka \mi-ˈtä-kə\. Town, Tokyo prefecture, Japan; pop. (1970c) 155,693; suburb of Tokyo.

Mi·tan·ni \mi-ˈtan-ē\. Ancient kingdom of upper Mesopotamia, extending from the bend of the Euphrates nearly to the Tigris, covering parts of later regions of Assyria, Syria, and Armenia; among its cities were Carchemish and Aleppo. Founded by Hurrians c. 1475 B.C.; lasted until conquered by the Hittites c. 1275 B.C. Mitannians probably not of Indo-European stock.

Mi·ta Point \ˌmēt-ə-\ *or Span.* **Pun·ta Mita** \ˌpün-tə-\. Cape off SW coast of Nayarit state, Mexico, at N side of entrance to Banderas Bay.

Mitau. See JELGAVA.

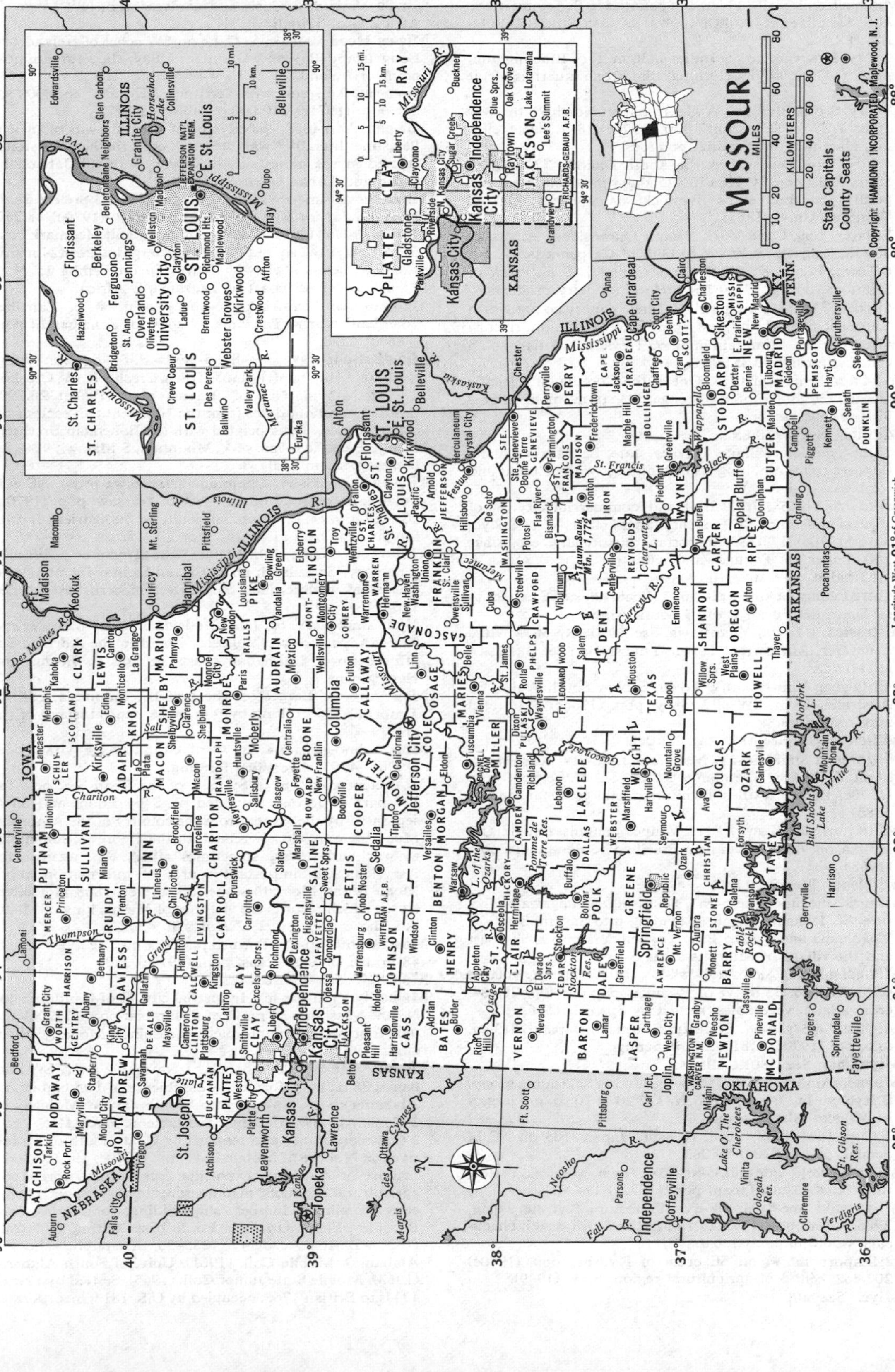

MISSOURI
MILES
KILOMETERS
State Capitals
County Seats
© Copyright HAMMOND INCORPORATED, Maplewood, N.J.
Longitude West 91° of Greenwich
ST. LOUIS
KANSAS CITY
Jefferson City
IOWA
ILLINOIS
KANSAS
NEBRASKA
OKLAHOMA
ARKANSAS
KY.
TENN.

Mitch·ell \'mich-əl\. 1 Name of counties in five states of the U.S. See tables at GEORGIA, IOWA, KANSAS, NORTH CAROLINA, TEXAS.

2 City, Lawrence co., S Indiana, 30 m. S of Bloomington; pop. (1970c) 4092; clothing; limestone quarries; fruit growing.

3 City, Scotts Bluff co., W Nebraska, on North Platte river 10 m. WSW of Scottsbluff; pop. (1970c) 1842; sugar refining, aluminum fabricating; potatoes.

4 City, ⊗ of Davison co., SE South Dakota, 72 m. W of Sioux Falls; pop. (1970c) 13,425; dairy products; meat and poultry packing; ships livestock; dairy farms; Dakota Wesleyan Univ. (1883).

5 River, cen. Cape York Penin., Queensland, Australia; 300 m. long; flows WNW to Gulf of Carpentaria.

6 Town, Perth co., SE Ontario, Canada, 13 m. WNW of Stratford; pop. (1971p) 2549; clothing, dairy products.

Mitchell, Mount. Peak in Black Mts., Yancey co., W North Carolina; 6684 ft.; highest point E of Mississippi river.

Mitchell Peak. Mountain in Sierra Nevada, N Tulare co., S cen. California; 10,351 ft.

Mit·i·a·ro \ˌmit-ē-'är-(ˌ)ō\. One of the Cook Is. in S Pacific Ocean, 150 m. NE of Rarotonga; 8½ sq. m.; pop. (1968e) 321; produces copra.

Mitilíni. See MYTILENE.

Mi·tla \'mit-lə\. Village, Oaxaca state, SE Mexico; many Zapotec ruins, esp. long stone buildings with columns and frescoes.

Mi·to \'mē-(ˌ)tō\. Industrial and commercial city, ✱ of Ibaraki prefecture, SE Honshū, Japan, 60 m. NE of Tokyo; pop. (1970c) 173,789; important historically, esp. since 1600 under the Tokugawa shogunate.

Mit Rahina. See MEMPHIS 4.

Mi·tre Peninsula \mē-ˌtrā-, 'mi-\. Peninsula at SE extremity of Tierra del Fuego I. off S South America.

Mitrovica. 1 Town, Yugoslavia. See KOSOVSKA MITROVICA.

2 *or Ger.* **Mitrowitz.** Town, Yugoslavia. See SREMSKA MITROVICA.

Mit·ta·gong \'mit-ə-ˌgäŋ\. Town, E New South Wales, SE Australia, 60 m. SW of Sydney; pop. (1966c) 5910; coal and iron mines.

Mitteleuropa. See CENTRAL EUROPE.

Mitt·wei·da \mit-'vīd-ə\. Manufacturing city, Karl-Marx-Stadt dist., East Germany, 34 m. SE of Leipzig; pop. (1970e) 19,600; textiles, furniture, metal goods; made city 1286.

Mi·tú \mi-'tü\. Town, ✱ of Vaupés commissary, SE Colombia, on Vaupés river near Brazilian border; munic. pop. (1968e) 7311.

Mitylene. See MYTILENE.

Mi·u·ra \mē-'ür-ə, 'mē-ə-ˌrä\. Peninsula, Kanagawa prefecture, SE Honshū, Japan, extending into Sagami Sea S of Yokohama and Tokyo Bay; Yokosuka is on its NE coast and the village of Miura is at its S tip.

Mix·qui·a·hua·la \ˌmēs-kyä-'wä-lə\. Municipality, Hidalgo state, Mexico, 35 m. W of Pachuca; pop. (1970p) 26,484; corn, alfalfa, vegetables; settled by Spanish 1546.

Mi·ya·gi \mē-'yäg-ē\. Prefecture, Honshū, Japan; 2813 sq. m.; pop. (1970c) 1,819,223; ✱ Sendai.

Miyajima. See ITSUKU-SHIMA.

Mi·ya·ko \mē-'yäk-(ˌ)ō\. 1 Small island in Sakishima group, S Ryukyu Is., Japan, 24°47′N, 125°20′E; 70 sq. m.; largest in **Miyako Islands** group.

2 City, Iwate prefecture, Honshū, Japan, 105 m. NE of Sendai; pop. (1970c) 59,063.

Mi·ya·ko·no·jō \mē-ˌyäk-ə-nō-'jō\. Town, Miyazaki prefecture, SE Kyūshū, Japan; pop. (1970c) 114,802.

Mi·ya·za·ki \mē-'(y)äz-ˌäk-ē\. 1 Prefecture, Kyūshū, Japan; 2986 sq. m.; pop. (1970c) 1,051,105; ✱ Miyazaki; chemicals, wood pulp, charcoal.

2 Seaport, its ✱, on SE coast of Kyūshū; pop. (1970c) 202,862; center of agricultural region; univ. (1949).

Miye. See MIE.

Miz·da \'miz-də\. Oasis and caravan stop, NW Libya, N Africa, S of Tripoli.

Miz·en Head \ˌmiz-ᵊn-\. Cape on SW coast of Ireland bet. Long Island Bay and Dunmanus Bay; the southernmost point of Ireland, 51°27′N, 9°49′W.

Mi·zo·ram \mi-'zȯr-əm\. Territory, NE India; ab. 8000 sq. m.; pop. (1971e) 310,000; established 1972.

Miz·pah \'miz-(ˌ)pä, -pə\. Name of several towns of ancient Palestine; literally "watchtower"; esp., the heap of stones erected in the mountains of Gilead N of the Jabbok by Jacob and Laban (*Gen.* xxxi. 44–49).

Mi·zu·sa·wa \ˌmē-zə-'sä-wə\. Town, S Iwate prefecture, N Honshū, Japan, 60 m. N of Sendai; pop. (1970c) 48,267.

Mjø·sa \'myər-(ˌ)sä\. Lake in Oppland and Hedmark cos., SE Norway; 142 sq. m.; 62 m. long; largest lake in Norway.

Mko·a·ni \ˌem-kə-'wän-ē\. Township on Pemba I., N of Zanzibar, off NE coast of Tanzania, E Africa.

Mko·ko·to·ni \em-ˌkō-kə-'tō-nē\. Town, ✱ of Zanzibar Shambani North, Tanzania, N coast of Zanzibar I.; pop. (1967c) 2220.

Mla·dá Bo·le·slav \əm-ˌläd-ä-'bȯ-lə-ˌsläf\ *or Ger.* **Jung·bunz·lau** \yu̇ŋ-'bu̇n(t)-ˌslau̇\. Town, Czech S.R., W Czechoslovakia, 32 m. NE of Prague; pop. (1968e) 28,790; railroad junction; dates from the 10th cent.; an ecclesiastical center closely associated with the Bohemian Brethren.

Mlan·je Peak \em-'lan-yē-\. Mountain, S Malawi; 9848 ft.; highest peak in Malawi.

Mła·wa \əm-'läv-ə\. Commune, Warszawa prov., NE cen. Poland, on railroad 65 m. NNW of Warsaw; pop. (1970p) 20,000; trades in grain; agricultural industries. Battles fought near here in World War I 1915.

Mlil·wa·ne Game Sanctuary \ˌem-lil-'wän-ē-\. Wildlife sanctuary, Swaziland; ab. 2 sq. m.; habitat for numerous species of wildlife, incl. the white rhinoceros; established 1964.

Mljet \məl-'yet\ *or Ital.* **Me·le·da** \'mel-ə-ˌdä\ *or anc.* **Mel·i·ta** \'mel-ət-ə\. Yugoslav island in the Adriatic Sea off the lower Dalmatian coast; belongs to Bosnia and Herzegovina.

Moa \'mō-ə\. Largest of the Leti Is., Indonesia, ENE of Timor; ab. 25 m. long by 9 m. wide; central island of the group.

Mo·ab \'mō-ˌab\. 1 City, ⊗ of Grand co., E Utah; pop. (1970c) 4793; diversified farming.

2 Ancient kingdom in Syria, E of the Dead Sea, now the SW part of Jordan; bounded on S by Edom and on N separated by the Arnon from the country of the Amorites. Moabites were closely related to the Hebrews; sometimes at war with them, sometimes allied, esp. against the Assyrians. An important source of information about Moab is the Moabite stone, discovered 1868 at Dhiban (*q.v.*), which records the victories of Mesha, king of Moab, esp. those over Israel (*2 Kings* iii. 4,5,27).

Mo·apa \mō-'ap-ə\. Township, Clark co., SE Nevada, ab. 48 m. NE of Las Vegas; pop. (1970c) 353.

Mobangi. See UBANGI.

Mo·ber·ly \'mō-bər-lē\. Industrial city, ⊗ of Randolph co., N cen. Missouri, 34 m. N of Columbia; pop. (1970c) 12,988; footwear, dairy products; coal mines; Moberly Junior Coll. (1927).

Mo·bile \mō-'bē(ə)l, 'mō-ˌbēl\. 1 Navigable river, SW Alabama; 38 m. long; formed by confluence of Tombigbee and Alabama rivers, flows S into Mobile Bay at Mobile.

2 County in SW Alabama. See table at ALABAMA.

3 Commercial city and seaport, its ⊗, at mouth of Mobile river on N shore of Mobile Bay; pop. (1970c) 190,026; only seaport of Alabama, exporting cotton, coal, forest and agricultural products; manufactures textiles, paper, chemicals, aluminum, lumber; shipbuilding, food processing; Brookley Field, U.S. Air Force base. Spring Hill Coll. (1830), Barton Academy (1835–36, first public school in Alabama), Mobile Coll. (1961), Univ. of South Alabama (1963), Mobile State Junior Coll. (1965). Settled by French 1711; to Britian 1763; occupied by U.S. 1813; incorporated

as town 1814, as city 1819; battle of Mobile Bay (*q.v.*) 1864; taken by Union troops 1865.

Mobile Bay. Inlet of Gulf of Mexico, forming boundary bet. Baldwin co. on E and Mobile co. on W, SW Alabama; 30 m. long, 10 to 12 m. wide; receives the Mobile river on the N; scene of Civil War naval battle Aug. 5–23, 1864 in which Admiral Farragut ran a blockade of torpedoes (i.e., mines), dispersed the Confederate fleet, and secured surrender of the forts defending the bay (Aug. 7 and 23).

Mobile Point. Point at SW extremity of Baldwin co., Alabama, at S entrance to Mobile Bay.

Mo·bridge \'mō-ˌbrij\. City, Walworth co., N South Dakota, on Missouri river 30 m. S of North Dakota border; pop. (1970c) 4545; market town; coal mines.

Mo·ca \'mō-kə\. 1 Town and municipality, ✱ of Espaillat prov., N cen. Dominican Republic; pop. (1970p) 18,965 (town), 94,709 (munic.); cacao raising.

2 Town and municipality, NW Puerto Rico; pop. (1970p) 2323 (town), 22,266 (munic.); town is on highway near Aguadilla.

Moçambique. See MOZAMBIQUE.

Mo·çâ·me·des \mō-'sam-ə-ˌdēz\. Seaport, SW Angola, SW Africa; pop. (1960c) 7963; has rail connections with interior towns and steamer lines to Pôrto.

Mo·ca·pra \mō-'käp-rə\. River, N Venezuela; ab. 100 m. long; flows S into Guárico river.

Mo·cha \'mō-kə\. 1 Island in Pacific Ocean off cen. Chile; administratively part of Cautín prov.; 8 m. long.

2 *or* **Mo·kha** \'mō-kə\ *or Arab.* **Mu·khā** \mü-'kä\. Seaport, SW Yemen (✱ San'a), SW Arabian Penin.; formerly noted for its export of coffee.

Moch·los \'mäk-ˌläs\. Ruins, E Crete, Greece, on N coast on Mirabella Bay; tombs; jewels and pottery found here.

Mo·cho Mountains \ˌmō-(ˌ)chō-\. Range in S cen. Jamaica, West Indies.

Mo·chu·di \mō-'chüd-ē\. Town, SE Botswana, S Africa, on railroad ab. 25 m. NE of Gaborone; pop. (1969e) 15,995.

Mocks·ville \'mäks-(ˌ)vil\. Manufacturing town, ⊗ of Davie co., cen. North Carolina; pop. (1970c) 2529; furniture, plastics, clothing.

Mo·co, Mount \-'mō-(ˌ)kō\. Mountain, W Angola; 8397 ft.; highest mountain in Angola.

Mo·coa \mō-'kō-ə\. Town, ✱ of Putumayo commissary, S Colombia, 45 m. E of Pasto; munic. pop. (1968e) 15,995.

Mo·co·ri·to \ˌmō-kə-'rē-tō\. Municipality, Sinaloa state, Mexico, 60 m. NE of Culiacán; pop. (1970p) 49,957; sugarcane, potatoes, maguey.

Mocrum. See MAKARSKA.

Mo·dane \mō-'dän\. Town, SE Savoie dept., E France; pop. (1962c) 5137; terminus of Mont Cenis Pass and Tunnel (see ALPS).

Mod·der \'mäd-ər\. River, Orange Free State, Rep. of South Africa, a tributary of the Riet; ab. 180 m. long; battle Nov. 28, 1899 in which British forces under Paul Methuen defeated Boers under Cronje. See also PAARDEBERG.

Mo·de·na \'mȯd-^{ə}n-ə, -ˌä\. 1 Province of Emilia-Romagna, N Italy. See table at ITALY.

2 *or anc.* **Mu·ti·na** \'myüt-^{ə}n-ə\. Manufacturing commune, its ✱, 207 m. NNW of Rome; pop. (1968e) 164,811; archiepiscopal see; automobiles, machine tools, agricultural machinery, light alloys; metalworking, iron founding, tanning; 11th cent. Romanesque cathedral, 13th cent. campanile, 17th cent. ducal palace (now a military school), Palazzo dei Musei (art gallery; Estense library), univ. (1175).

History: Ancient Etruscan city; made Roman colony 183 B.C.; successfully defended against siege by Mark Antony 44–43 B.C.; destroyed and rebuilt under Constantine; to Este family 1288; made a duchy 1452; taken by French 1796 and made part of the Cisalpine Republic 1797 and of the Napoleonic kingdom of Italy 1805; lost by Este family on extinction of male line 1803 but reverted to descendant, Francis IV, 1815; to kingdom of Italy 1860.

Mo·des·to \mə-'des-(ˌ)tō\. City, ⊗ of Stanislaus co., cen. California, on Tuolumne river 25 m. SE of Stockton; pop. (1970c) 61,712; canning and freezing plants, wineries; ships meat and dairy products, olive oil; fruit and nut orchards; Modesto Junior Coll. (1921); founded 1870.

Mo·di·ca \'mȯd-i-kə\ *or anc.* **Mo·ty·ca** \'mōt-i-kə\. Commune, Ragusa prov., SE Sicily, Italy, 5 m. SSE of Ragusa; pop. (1968e) 44,574; center of agricultural region; 15th cent. convent (now a prison); castle, destroyed by earthquake 1693.

Mo·djo·ker·to *or* **Mo·jo·ker·to** \ˌmō-jə-'ke(ə)rt-(ˌ)ō\. Town, East Java prov., Indonesia, on Brantas river; pop. (1961c) 51,732; railroad junction point 20 m. SW of Surabaja; center of sugar industry. Near here very early remains of fossil man were found 1934 and named *Homo modjokertensis;* probably much older than *Pithecanthropus erectus* (Java man).

Mo·dlin \'mȯd-ˌlēn\; *Russ.* **No·vo·geor·gievsk** \ˌnȯ-və-gē-'ȯr-gē-əfsk\. Fortified commune, Warszawa dept., Poland, 20 m. NW of Warsaw; founded as a fort built by Napoleon 1807; became important Russian military post in World War I; captured by Germans Aug. 12, 1915.

Mödl·ing \'mərd-liŋ\. Manufacturing city, Austria, 8 m. SSW of Vienna; pop. (1961c) 17,274; metal goods, machinery, shoes; first mentioned 903, made city 1897.

Mo·doc \'mōd-ˌäk\. County in California. See table at CALIFORNIA.

Mo·du·gno \mō-'dün-yō\. Commune, Bari prov., Apulia, SE Italy, 5 m. SW of Bari; pop. (1968e) 15,228; Renaissance church.

Moe \'mō-ē\. Town, Victoria, Australia; pop. (1968e) 16,690; textiles.

Moearatewe. See MUARATEWE.

Moehne. See MÖHNE.

Moel Sych \'mȯil-'sik\. Peak, highest in the Berwyn Mts., N Wales; 2713 ft.

Mo·en \'mō-ən\ *or* **Ha·ru** \'här-(ˌ)ü\. Island in NE part of Truk Is. (*q.v.*); ab. 5 m. long by 4 m. wide.

Möen. See MØN.

Moena. See MUNA.

Moengo \'müŋ-(ˌ)ō\. Town, NE Surinam, ab. 55 m. ESE of Paramaribo; bauxite deposits.

Mo·en·ko·pi Plateau \ˌmō-ən-ˌkō-pē-\. Tableland in E Coconino co., N cen. Arizona, along E boundary of the Painted Desert.

Moenus. See MAIN.

Moer·dijk \mü(ə)r-'dīk\. Village, North Brabant prov., S Netherlands, NW of Breda, on S bank of the Hollandsch Diep, here crossed by one of longest railroad bridges in Europe, partly destroyed by Germans May 1940.

Moe·ris, Lake \-'mir-əs\. Large ancient lake occupying Faiyūm depression in Faiyūm gov., N Upper Egypt. See BIRKET QĀRŪN.

Moers. See MÖRS.

Moesi. See MUSI 2.

Moe·sia \'mē-sh(ē-)ə\. Ancient country of SE Europe S of Danube river and extending from Drinus river to the Euxine (Black Sea), inhabited by a Thracian people and including part of early Thrace. Invaded by Romans 75 B.C. but not conquered until c. 30 B.C.; made Roman province 15 A.D. and later divided into two provinces: **Moesia Superior** (Upper Moesia, i.e., Serbia) and **Moesia Inferior** (Lower Moesia, i.e., N Bulgaria); occupied by Goths in 4th cent. A.D. and by Slavs and Bulgarians in 7th cent.

Moes·kroen \'mü-ˌskrün\ *or Fr.* **Mous·cron** \mü-skrō^{n}\. Commune, West Flanders prov., NW Belgium, just S of Kortrijk; pop. (1968e) 37,552.

Mof·fat \'mäf-ət\. County in Colorado. See table at COLORADO.

Moffat Tunnel. Railroad tunnel through James Peak, Gilpin and Grand cos., N cen. Colorado, ab. 50 m. NW of Denver; 6 m. long.

Mof·fett Field \ˌmäf-ət-\. Air base, W California, at S end of San Francisco Bay; laboratory of the National Aeronautics and Space Administration.

Mog·a·disho \ˌmäg-ə-'dish-(ˌ)ü, -'dēsh-\ *or* **Mog·a·di·scio** \-'dish-(ˌ)ō, -'dēsh-, -ē-ˌō\. Seaport, ✱ of Somalia, E Africa; pop. (1969e) 200,000; the republic's principal port; univ. (1959).

Mogador. See ESSAOUIRA.

Mog·a·dore \'mäg-ə-ˌdō(ə)r\. Village, Portage and Summit cos., NE Ohio, 7 m. ESE of Akron; pop. (1970c) 4825.

Mog·a·la·kwe·na \ˌmōg-ə-lə-'kwē-nə\. River, N Transvaal, NE Rep. of South Africa; 130 m. long; flows N into Limpopo river.

Mo·ga·mi \mō-'gäm-ē\. River, Yamagata prefecture, N Honshū, Japan; 134 m. long; flows N and NW into the Sea of Japan at Sakata.

Mo·gaung \'mō-'gau̇ŋ\. Town, N Upper Burma, on railroad 30 m. W of Myitkyina, on **Mogaung River,** a tributary of the upper Irrawaddy; valley scene of fighting bet. Japanese and Allied forces Apr.–June 1944.

Mo·gi das Cru·zes \mü-ˌzhēd-əs-'krü-zēs\. City, São Paulo state, SE Brazil, on coast 30 m. E of São Paulo; munic. pop. (1968e) 111,554.

Mo·gi·lev \'mäg-ə-ˌlef, -ˌlev\ *or* **Mogilev on the Dnie·per** \-'nēp-ər\. City, ✱ of Mogilev Oblast, Belorussian S.S.R., U.S.S.R., on both banks of the Dnieper 112 m. E of Minsk; pop. (1970p) 202,000; produces construction machinery, synthetic fibers, leather goods; brickmaking, brewing, food processing; has several old churches and an ancient tower built by the Tatars. Founded probably in 13th cent.; often changed in ownership—Russian, Polish, or Swedish; suffered from church persecution and in 1708 was partly destroyed by Peter the Great; annexed to Russia 1772; near here Russian army under Bagration was defeated July 1812 by French; scene of much disorder in civil war period 1917–20; in World War II occupied by Germans Aug. 1941–June 1944.

Mogilev Oblast \-'o-bləst, -ˌblast\. Subdivision of the Belorussian S.S.R., U.S.S.R., in E part; 11,197 sq. m.; pop. (1970p) 1,222,000; ✱ Mogilev; flax; dairying, timber processing.

Mogilev Po·dol·ski \-ˌpə-'dȯl-skē\ *or* **Mogilev on the Dnies·ter** \-'nēs-tər\. Town, SW Vinnitsa Oblast, W Ukrainian S.S.R., U.S.S.R., on the Dniester 60 m. S of Vinnitsa; pop. (1967e) 24,000; connected by rail with Zhmerinka; food processing; formerly more important as a trading center at a much used crossing of the Dniester on a main highway from Moldavia to Ukraine. Founded at end of 16th cent.; scene of much fighting bet. Cossacks, Poles, and Turks; suffered severely in World War I and the civil war that followed; in World War II held by Axis powers 1941–Mar. 1944.

Mo·gi Mi·rim \mü-ˌzhē-mə-'rēm\. City, E São Paulo state, SE Brazil, 80 m. N of São Paulo; munic. pop. (1968e) 32,803.

Mo·glia·no Ve·ne·to \mōl-ˌyän-ō-'ven-ə-ˌtō, -'vā-nə-\. Commune, Treviso prov., Veneto, NE Italy 8 m. S of Treviso; pop. (1968e) 19,173.

Mog·mog \'mäg-ˌmäg\. See ULITHI.

Mo·gok \'mō-ˌgōk\. Town, Upper Burma, on highway E of the Irrawaddy 70 m. NNE of Mandalay; formerly a major ruby-mining center.

Mo·gol·lon Mountains *or* **Mogollon Range** \ˌməg-ē-'ōn-, ˌmō-gə-'yōn-\. Range in S Catron co., W New Mexico, extending across county boundary into Grant co.; highest point Whitewater Baldy 10,892 ft.; also includes **Mogollon Peak** 10,778 ft.

Mogollon Rim. Escarpment in S Coconino co., Arizona.

Mogontiacum. See MAINZ.

Mo·guer \mō-'ger\. Commune, S Huelva prov., SW Spain, E of Huelva; pop. (1960c) 7222; Columbus obtained some members of his crew from here.

Mo·hács \'mō-ˌhach, -ˌhäch\. City, Baranya co., S Hungary, on Danube river; pop. (1970p) 19,583; commercial center; battlefield Aug. 29–30, 1526 where Turks completely defeated Hungarians; the "Second battle of Mohács" Aug. 12, 1687, in which Charles of Lorraine defeated the Turks, occurred at nearby Harkány (*q.v.*).

Mo·ha·les Hoek \mō-ˌhäl-əs-'hu̇k\. Town, SW Lesotho; pop. (1966c) 3538.

Mo·hall \'mō-ˌhȯl\. City, ⊗ of Renville co., N North Dakota; pop. (1970c) 950; stock and dairy farms.

Mo·ham·ma·dia \mō-ˌham-ə-'dyä\ *or formerly* **Per·ré·gaux** \ˌper-ā-'gō\. Commune, Oran dept., NW Algeria, 40 m. ESE of Oran; pop. (1966c) 38,000.

Mo·ham·me·dia \mō-ˌham-ə-'dyä\ *or formerly* **Fe·da·la** \fə-'däl-ə\. Town, Morocco, N Africa, on coast 14 m. NE of Casablanca; pop. (1960c) 35,010; one of landing places of American troops Nov. 7, 1942.

Mohammerah. See KHORRAMSHAHR.

Moharek. See MUHARRAQ.

Mo·ha·ve \mə-'häv-ē\. County in Arizona. See table at ARIZONA.

Mohave Desert. See MOJAVE DESERT.

Mo·hawk \'mō-ˌhȯk\. **1** River, largest tributary of the Hudson river, E cen. New York; 148 m. long; formed by junction of east and west branches in Oneida co., flows S and E into Hudson river at Cohoes, above Troy; parallels the N.Y. State Barge Canal. See LITTLE FALLS 3. **2** Village, Herkimer co., NE cen. New York, on Mohawk river 12 m. ESE of Utica; pop. (1970c) 3301; forms single community with Frankfort, Ilion, and Herkimer; originally settled by Palatines; ravaged during French and Indian and Revolutionary Wars.

Mo·hé·li \mȯ-'ā-lē\ *also* **Mo·hil·la** \mō-'hil-ə\. One of the Comoro Is.; 112 sq. m.; pop. (1970e) 12,000; chief town Fomboni.

Mo·hen·jo–Da·ro \mō-ˌhen-jō-'där-(ˌ)ō\. Prehistoric city, S Sind, Pakistan, a site of the Chalcolithic epoch of Indus valley culture, c. 3000 –2000 B.C., ab. 140 m. NE of Karachi; excavations of recent years have disclosed a large, well-planned city. See HARAPPA.

Mo·hi·can \mō-'hē-kən\. River, cen. Ohio; ab. 40 m. long; flows S to the Walhonding river.

Mohilla. See MOHÉLI.

Mohl, Mount \-'mōl\. Mountain, Antarctica, 78°33'S, 85°05'W; 12,172 ft.

Moh·mand Hills \mō-'mand-\. Spur of Hindu Kush on border bet. Pakistan and E Afghanistan, just N of Khyber Pass in the Safed Koh; through gorges in the range passes the Kabul river.

Möh·ne *also* **Moeh·ne** \'mər-nə\. River in North Rhine-Westphalia, West Germany; ab. 35 m. long; flows W to the Ruhr at Neheim. In its lower course is great reservoir dam, bombed and broken by the Royal Air Force May 16, 1943; restored 1946.

Moin·kum \'mȯin-'ku̇m\ *also* **Mo·yun–Kum** \mō-'yu̇n-'ku̇m\. Sandy desert region, SE Kazakh S.S.R., U.S.S.R., N of the Syr Darya river.

Moi·sie \mwä-'zē\. River, cen. Saguenay co., SE Quebec, Canada; 210 m. long; flows S from border of SW Labrador to the St. Lawrence at its mouth.

Mois·sac \mwa-'säk\. Town, Tarn-et-Garonne dept., S France, on Tarn river; pop. (1968c) 11,856; 15th cent. church with 12th cent. porch; cloisters adjoining the church.

Mois·son \mwa-'sōⁿ\. Village, Yvelines dept., N France, on the Seine 6 m. N of Mantes-la-Jolie; pop. (1962c) 350; Boy Scout World Jamboree 1947.

Mo·ja·ve Desert *or* **Mo·ha·ve Desert** \mə-'häv-ē-\. Arid basin in S California, including parts of San Bernardino, Kern, and Los Angeles cos.; ab. 15,000 sq. m.

Mo·ji \'mō-(ˌ)jē\. See KITAKYŪSHŪ.

Mojib, Wadi al–. See MAWJIB, WADI AL-.

Mojokerto. See MODJOKERTO.

Mo·kai \ˈmō-ˌkī\. Village, N cen. North I., New Zealand, just N of Lake Taupo.

Mo·ka·pu \mō-ˈkä-pü\. City, Honolulu co., Hawaii; pop. (1970c) 7860.

Mo·kau \ˈmō-ˌkau̇\. River, W North I., New Zealand; 98 m. long; flows SW to North Taranaki Bight.

Mo·kel·um·ne \mō-ˈkel-ə-mē, -ˈkäl-\. River, cen. California; ab. 140 m. long; rises in the Sierra Nevada and flows into San Joaquin river ab. 20 m. NW of Stockton.

Mokha. See MOCHA 2.

Mok·mer \ˈmäk-mər\. Airfield on Biak I., Irian Barat, Indonesia; captured by Americans June 17, 1944. See BOSNIK.

Mok·ni·ne \ˈmȯk-nē-nē\. Coastal town, E Tunisia, N Africa, SSE of Sousse; pop. (1966c) 20,500.

Mok·p'o \ˈmäk-(ˌ)pō\. Seaport, South Chŏlla prov., South Korea; pop. (1970e) 177,801; textiles; fishing; opened to foreign trade 1897.

Mokrān. See MAKRAN.

Mok·sha \ˈmȯk-shə\. River, E cen. Russian S.F.S.R., U.S.S.R.; 430 m. long; rises near Penza and flows N and W through Mordovian A.S.S.R. to the Oka above Murom; navigable for much of its course.

Mo·ku·a·we·o·weo \mō-ˈkü-ə-ˌwā-ō-ˈwā-(ˌ)ō\. The summit crater of Mauna Loa in S cen. Hawaii I., Hawaii; 3.7 m. in circumference, 13,500 ft. high.

Mol *or formerly* **Moll** \ˈmȯl\. Commune, Antwerp prov., N Belgium, 30 m. E of Antwerp; pop. (1969e) 28,440; furniture, glass; nuclear research.

Mo·la di Ba·ri \ˌmȯ-ləd-ē-ˈbär-ē\. Commune, Bari prov., Apulia, SE Italy, on Adriatic 12 m. ESE of Bari; pop. (1968e) 23,867; small harbor; 13th cent. castle and cathedral.

Mola di Gaeta. See FORMIA.

Mold \ˈmōld\. Urban district, ⊗ of Flintshire, NE Wales; pop. (1971p) 8239; in farming and coal-mining section; site of victory of native Christians under St. Germain over pagan Picts and Scots 430.

Moldau. 1 River, Czechoslovakia. See VLTAVA.

2 Region, Romania. See MOLDAVIA.

Mol·da·via \mäl-ˈdā-vē-ə, -vyə\ *or Rom.* **Mol·do·va** \mȯl-ˈdȯ-və\ *or Ger.* **Mol·dau** \ˈmȯl-ˌdau̇, ˈmōl-\. Former principality, E of Transylvania and N of E Walachia; included Bessarabia and Bukovina; later a province of Romania, area 14,690 sq. m. Founded in 14th cent. of Vlach and Hungarian elements; ruled by voivodes who were, from 1372, dependent upon Hungarian or Polish control; came under rule of Ottoman Turks in 16th cent.; united briefly to Walachia by Michael the Bold (d. 1601); from early 18th cent. governed for Turks by Greek Phanariots; Bukovina annexed to Austria 1774 and Bessarabia (*q.v.*) to Russia; for history after 1774, see DANUBIAN PRINCIPALITIES.

Mol·da·vi·an Car·pa·thi·an Mountains \mäl-ˈdā-vē-ən-kär-ˈpā-thē-ən-, -vyən-\. Southeast end of the Carpathians in Romania, forming boundary bet. Moldavia and Transylvania.

Moldavian Republic. 1 Independent Bessarabia 1917. See BESSARABIA 2.

2 *or officially* **Moldavian Autonomous Soviet Socialist Republic.** Former autonomous republic, U.S.S.R.; 3200 sq. m.; ✱ Balta, later Tiraspol; a part of Ukrainian S.S.R. organized in 1924 from several districts of former Podolsk government (Podolia) of the U.S.S.R. Plain country along E bank of Dniester, with black soil; raises grains, fruit, and vegetables; produces sugar and wine. In 1940 merged with most of Bessarabia (*q.v.*) to form Moldavian S.S.R. (*q.v.*).

Moldavian Soviet Socialist Republic *also* **Mol·da·via** \mäl-ˈdā-vē-ə, -vyə\ *or formerly* **Moldavian Federal Soviet Republic.** A constituent republic of the U.S.S.R., bounded on N and NE by Ukrainian S.S.R., on SE by Black Sea, and on S and W by Romania; 13,012 sq. m.; pop. (1970p) 3,572,000; ✱ Kishinev; wheat, corn, fruit; wine; formed 1940 from Moldavian A.S.S.R. and most of Bessarabia (*q.v.*).

Mol·de \ˈmȯl-də\. Town, ⊗ of Møre og Romsdal co., W Norway, on N shore of **Molde Fjord;** pop. (1970e) 18,907; resort, fishing port.

Mol·do·va \mȯl-ˈdȯ-və\. 1 Former principality. See MOLDAVIA.

2 River, NE Romania; flows SE into the Siretul river near Roman.

Mol·do·ve·a·nul \mȯl-dȯv-ə-ˈän-u̇l\. Mountain, cen. Romania; 8343 ft.; highest peak in Transylvanian Alps.

Mo·len·beek–Saint–Jean \ˈmō-lən-ˌbāk-saⁿ-ˈzhäⁿ\. Commune, Brabant prov., cen. Belgium, a W suburb of Brussels; pop. (1969e) 68,515.

Mo·le·po·lo·le \ˌmō-lə-pə-ˈlō-lē\. Town, SE Botswana, S Africa, on SE edge of Kalahari Desert; pop. (1969e) 29,623.

Môle Saint Ni·co·las \ˌmōl-ˌsaⁿ-ˌnē-kə-ˈlä\. Town, NW Haiti, near tip of peninsula just N of Cap à Foux; Columbus landed here on first voyage.

Mo·lé·son \ˌmȯ-lā-ˈzōⁿ\ *or* **Le Moléson** \lə-\. Peak in the Alps, in Fribourg canton, W cen. Switzerland; 6567 ft.

Mol·fet·ta \mäl-ˈfet-ə\. Seaport, Bari prov., Apulia, SE Italy, on Adriatic 15 m. WNW of Bari; pop. (1968e) 65,188; fishing, boatbuilding; produces oil, cement, foodstuffs; 13th cent. cathedral.

Mo·li·na \mə-ˈlē-nə\. City, Talca prov., cen. Chile; pop. (1960c) 7621.

Molina de Se·gu·ra \-thā-sā-ˈgu̇r-ə\. Commune, Murcia prov., SE Spain, on Segura river 8 m. NNW of Murcia; pop. (1970p) 23,178; manufactures paper.

Mo·line \mō-ˈlēn\. Industrial city, Rock Island co., NW Illinois, on Mississippi river just above Rock Island; pop. (1970c) 46,237; agricultural machinery, tools, ventilators, furniture; Black Hawk Coll. (1946); settled 1847.

Moline Acres. Village, St. Louis co., E Missouri; pop. (1970c) 3722.

Mo·li·nel·la \ˌmō-lē-ˈnel-lə\. Commune, Emilia-Romagna, N Italy, 26 m. ENE of Bologna; pop. (1968e) 12,728.

Mo·li·no del Rey \mə-ˌlē-nō-del-ˈrā\ *or Eng.* **King's Mill.** Site SW of Mexico City, Mexico; scene of battle Sept. 8, 1847 in which Gen. Winfield Scott defeated superior forces of Santa Anna.

Mo·li·se \mȯ-ˈlē-ˌzā\. Autonomous region, S cen. Italy; 1713 sq. m.; pop. (1968e) 336,053; ✱ Campobasso; received limited autonomy 1970. See ABRUZZI E MOLISE.

Molise, Abruzzi e. See ABRUZZI E MOLISE.

Moll. See MOL.

Molle, Ponte. See SAXA RUBRA.

Mo·llen·do \mō-ˈyen-(ˌ)dō\. Seaport town, Arequipa dept., S Peru; pop. (1961c) 12,500; import and export center for S Peru and Bolivia; open roadstead, largely replaced as a port by that of Matarani (*q.v.*).

Mollwitz. See MAŁUJOWICE.

Möln·dal \ˈməln-ˌdäl\. City, Göteborg and Bohus co., SW Sweden; pop. (1970e) 33,296; paper mills, margarine factories.

Mo·lo·dech·no \ˌmäl-ə-ˈdech-nə\ *or Pol.* **Mo·lo·decz·no** \ˌmȯl-ə-ˈdech-(ˌ)nȯ\. Town, Minsk Oblast, NW Belorussian S.S.R., U.S.S.R., ab. 39 m. NW of Minsk; pop. (1969e) 50,000; formerly in Poland.

Mo·lo·ga \mə-ˈlȯ-gə\. River, Kalinin and Vologda oblasts, Russian S.F.S.R., U.S.S.R.; ab. 340 m. long; flows into Volga river NW of Rybinsk; lower course within the Rybinsk Reservoir.

Mo·lo·kai \ˌmäl-ə-ˈkī, ˌmō-lə-\. 1 Island, cen. Hawaii; ab. 40 m. long by 7 m. wide; 259 sq. m.; a part of Maui co. of state of Hawaii; has mountains at either end (Mauna Loa 1382 ft. at W and Kamakou 4970 ft. at E) with connecting saddle ab. 400 ft. high; on N coast is the Kalaupapa Leper Settlement. See KALAWAO.

2 Division, Maui co., Hawaii, constituting all of Molokai I. except the small Kalawao dist.

Mo·lo·po \mə-ˈlō-(ˌ)pō\. River, S Africa; usually dry; forms S boundary of Botswana, joins Orange river in S near SE border of South-West Africa; lower course through Kalahari Desert. See KURUMAN.

Mo·los·sis \mə-ˈläs-əs\ *or* **Mo·los·sia** \-ˈläsh-(ē-)ə\. District of ancient Epirus, NW Greece, extending along W bank of the Arachthus; noted for its breed of large hounds. The Molossians gradually became the most powerful people in Epirus.

Molotov. See PERM.

Molotov, Mount. See MOSKVA-PEKIN.

Molotov Oblast. See PERM OBLAST.

Molotovsk. See SEVERODVINSK.

Mol·te·no \mȯl-ˈtē-nō\. Town, E cen. Cape Province, S Rep. of South Africa, 140 m. NW of East London; pop. (1967e) 4600.

Mo·luc·cas \mə-ˈlək-əz\ *or* **Ma·lu·ku** \mə-ˈlü-(ˌ)kü\ *or* **Spice Islands** \ˈspīs-\ *or Du.* **Mo·luk·ken** \mə-ˈlək-ən\. **1** Group of islands, E Indonesia, bet. the island of Celebes and New Guinea; 32,307 sq. m.; pop. (1970e) 995,000; a province of Indonesia; province includes: three large islands: Halmahera, Ceram, Buru; several island groups, esp.: Sula, Batjan, Obi, Kai, Aru, Tanimbar, Banda, Babar, Leti; many smaller islands, as Morotai, Wetar; and the much smaller but important islands of Ambon, Ternate, and Tidore. Most of the islands are mountainous, many volcanic; dense forests with luxuriant vegetation; export sago, copra, forest products; formerly the major producers of spices (esp. nutmegs, mace, and cloves) which in 16th cent. were sought by Portuguese, Dutch, and English for world trade.

History: Discovered by Portuguese 1512; in early 17th cent., c. 1605–21, captured by Dutch who thus were aided in securing virtual monopoly of spice trade; Ambon (*q.v.*) the early seat of Dutch control; held by British 1810–14. See also entries of separate islands.

2 Residency of the former Netherlands Indies, including the Moluccas and Netherlands New Guinea (now Irian Barat); 191,632 sq. m.; ✱ Ambon.

Mo·luc·ca Sea \mə-ˈlək-ə-\ *or Indonesian* **Laut Ma·lu·ku** \ˌlau̇t-mə-ˈlü-ˌkü\ *or Du.* **Mo·luk·sche Zee** \mə-ˌlək-sə-ˈzā\. Part of Pacific Ocean bet. NE Celebes I. on W and the Moluccas on E, Malay Archipelago; connected with the Pacific; by some extended to the S to include the Banggai and Sula Is. and the waters bet. SE Celebes and Buru I.

Molukken. See MOLUCCAS.

Mom·ba·sa \mäm-ˈbäs-ə\. **1** Island off the S coast of Kenya, E Africa, 150 m. N of Zanzibar at the mouth of a deep bay; 3 m. long; 2½ m. wide; its chief harbor is Kilindini at SW end, connected by bridge with mainland.

History: Probably settled by Arabs in 11th cent.; mentioned as early as 1331 and visited by Vasco da Gama 1498; held by Portuguese 1529–1698; in 18th cent. subject to Oman whose local representative became independent ruler of Zanzibar (*q.v.*); in 1823 placed by its rulers under British protection but protectorate repudiated by British government; attached to Zanzibar until 1887; ✱ of East Africa Protectorate 1887–1907.

2 Town, ✱ of Coast prov., Kenya, on the island of Mombasa; chief port of Kenya; munic. area (incl. mainland segment) 27 sq. m.; pop. (1969p) 234,000; major agricultural market; exports coffee, fruits, grains, vegetables; produces glass, cement, beer, soap, aluminum ware, lime; remains of Portuguese buildings, esp. the fort.

Momein. See T'ENG-CH'UNG.

Mo·mence \mō-ˈmens\. City, Kankakee co., NE Illinois, 12 m. E of Kankakee; pop. (1970c) 2836.

Moming. See ZINAL ROTHORN.

Mo·mo·ste·nan·go \ˌmō-mō-stə-ˈnäŋ-(ˌ)gō\. City, Totonicapán dept., W Guatemala; munic. pop. (1964p) 30,807.

Mo·mo·tom·bo \ˌmō-mə-ˈtȯm-(ˌ)bō\. Volcano, W Nicaragua, NW of Lake Managua; 4126 ft.; had violent eruption in 1609; active in 1902 and 1905.

Mom·pog Pass \mȯm-ˈpȯg-\. Channel of interisland waters S of Luzon, Phil., bet. mainland of Quezon prov. and Marinduque I.; ab. 37 m. long by 12 m. wide.

Mom·pós \ˌmȯm-ˈpōs\. Town, N Bolívar dept., N Colombia, on the Magdalena 110 m. SE of Cartagena; munic. pop. (1968e) 43,415.

Møn \ˈmən\ *or formerly* **Mö·en** \ˈmə-ən\. Island in Sjælland group, forming a part of Denmark, lying in the Baltic Sea E of S end of island of Sjælland and NE of Falster; 84 sq. m.; pop. (1965c) 12,318; chief town Stege.

Mona. See MONA ISLAND and MAN, ISLE OF.

Mon·a·ca \ˈmän-i-kə\. Borough, Beaver co., W Pennsylvania, on Ohio river 23 m. NW of Pittsburgh; pop. (1970c) 7486; settled 1813.

Mon·a·co \ˈmän-ə-ˌkō, mə-ˈnäk-(ˌ)ō\. **1** Independent principality on the Mediterranean Sea near the French-Italian border; an enclave of SE France; ab. 370 acres; pop. (1970e) 23,614; comprises communes of Monaco, La Condamine, and Monte Carlo; tourism; has gambling casino.

History: Town of Monaco, probably of Phoenician origin, in hands of Grimaldi family from 10th cent.; became independent principality in 13th cent.; annexed to France 1793–1814; under protection of Sardinia 1815–60; sold to France rights to towns of Menton and Roquebrune 1860; its sovereignty restored by Franco-Monégasque treaty Feb. 2, 1861; granted constitution 1911; adopted new constitution 1962.

2 *or* **Monaco–Ville** \-ˈvēl\ *or anc.* **Mo·noe·cus** \mə-ˈnē-kəs\. Commune, ✱ of the principality; pop. (1961c) 1774; situated on a rocky headland projecting into the Mediterranean; contains cathedral, palace, oceanographical museum.

Mo·nadh·li·ath Mountains \ˌmō-nə-ˈlē-ə-\ *or* **Mo·nagh Lea** \ˌmō-nə-ˌlē-ə\. Range of mountains, in Inverness co., N cen. Scotland, NW of the Cairngorm Mts.; highest peak **Carn Mairg** \kärn-ˈma(ə)rg, -ˈme(ə)rg\, 3087 ft.

Mo·nad·nock, Mount \-mə-ˈnad-ˌnäk\. Peak, SE Cheshire co., SW New Hampshire; 3166 ft.; often called **Grand Monadnock** to distinguish from **Little Monadnock** 1890 ft. nearby.

Mo·na·gas \mō-ˈnäg-əs\. State of NE Venezuela. See table at VENEZUELA.

Mon·a·ghan \ˈmän-i-gən, -ə-ˌhan\. **1** County, Ulster prov., NE Eire; 498 sq. m.; pop. (1971p) 46,231; chief river Finn; flax, potatoes, oats; livestock grazing.

2 Urban district, its ⊗, NW of Dundalk; pop. (1971p) 5255; market town.

Monagh Lea. See MONADHLIATH MOUNTAINS.

Mon·a·hans \ˈmän-ə-ˌhanz\. City, ⊗ of Ward co., W Texas, 33 m. SW of Odessa; pop. (1970c) 8333; oil wells.

Mo·na Island \ˌmō-nə-\. **1** Island, West Indies; in S part of **Mona Passage** (80 m. wide), bet. Haiti on W and Puerto Rico on E; ab. 6 m. long and 4½ m. wide; 20 sq. m.; belongs to Puerto Rico.

2 Island, Wales. See ANGLESEY 1.

Monapia. See MAN, ISLE OF.

Mo·nash·ee Mountains \mə-ˌnash-ē-\. Range in SE British Columbia, Canada, W of the Selkirk Mts. and bet. the Columbia river valley on the E and Shuswap and Okanagan lakes on the W; highest peak ab. 6000 ft.

Mon·as·tir \ˌmän-ə-ˈsti(ə)r\. **1** *or anc.* **Rus·pi·na** \ˈrəs-pə-nə\. Seaport town, NE Tunisia, N Africa, SSE of Sousse; pop. (1966c) 20,400.

2 City, Yugoslavia. See BITOLA.

Mon·ca·lie·ri \ˌmȯŋ-kəl-ˈye(ə)r-ē\. Commune, Torino prov., Piedmont, NW Italy, on Po river 7 m. S by E of Turin; pop.

(1968e) 46,895; 15th cent. royal palace; meteorological observatory.

Moncay. See MONG CAI.

Mon·ca·yo \mȯŋ-'kī-(,)ō\. Peak, NE cen. Spain, ab. 55 m. W of Saragossa, on the boundary bet. Aragon and Old Castile; 7587 ft.

Mönch \'mənk\. Peak in the Bernese Alps, Bern canton, W cen. Switzerland; 13,445 ft.

Mon·che·gorsk \,män-chə-'gȯrsk\. Town, Murmansk Oblast, Russian S.F.S.R., U.S.S.R., ab. 70 m. S of Murmansk; pop. (1969e) 53,000.

Mön·chen·glad·bach \,mən-kən-'glät-,bäk\ *or before 1950* **Mün·chen–Glad·bach** \,m(y)ün-kən-'glät-,bäk\. City, North Rhine-Westphalia, West Germany, 15 m. WSW of Düsseldorf; pop. (1969e) 152,231; transportation center; major textile center; also produces machinery, iron, chemicals, paper, leather, petroleum products; 11th–13th cent. church; developed around 8th cent. monastery; chartered 1336.

Mon·chy–le–Preux \mōⁿ-,shē-lə-'prə(r)\. Village, Pas-de-Calais dept., N France, 5 m. E of Arras; pop. (1962c) 437; held by Germans 1914–Apr. 11, 1917 and Mar.–Aug. 1918.

Moncks Corner \,məŋks-\. Town, ⊗ of Berkeley co., SE South Carolina; pop. (1970c) 2314; diversified agriculture.

Mon·clo·va \mȯŋ-'klō-və\. Town, Coahuila state, NE Mexico, 110 m. N of Saltillo; munic. pop. (1970p) 80,252; altitude ab. 2000 ft.; copper, silver, zinc, and lead mines; coffee.

Mon·con·tour \,mōⁿ-kōⁿ-'tü(ə)r\. Village, Vienne dept., W cen. France, 27 m. NW of Poitiers; pop. (1962c) 582; scene of battle Oct. 3, 1569 in which Huguenots were defeated by forces of duke of Guise.

Monc·ton \'məŋ(k)-tən\. City, Westmorland co., E New Brunswick, Canada, on Petitcodiac river at head of its estuary Chignecto Bay; pop. (1971p) 47,781; transportation center; gas and oil wells; fisheries; agriculture; educational and cultural center of French Canadian population of New Brunswick: Coll. de l'Assomption (1832), Coll. Saint Joseph (1864), Coll. Notre-Dame d'Acadie (1943), Séminaire Notre-Dame du Perpétual Sécours (1956), Univ. of Moncton (1963). Originally settled by Acadian French; resettled by Germans 1763.

Mon·de·go \mōⁿ-'dā-(,)gü\. River, cen. Portugal; 130 m. long; flows SW into Atlantic Ocean at **Cape Mondego** 40°11'N, 8°55'W.

Mon·do·ñe·do \,mȯn-dō-'nyā-thō\. Commune, Lugo prov., N Spain; pop. (1970p) 6989; manufactures lace, leather, linen; 17th cent. cathedral.

Mon·do·vi \män-'dō-vē\. City, Buffalo co., W Wisconsin, 19 m. SSW of Eau Claire; pop. (1970c) 2338.

Mon·do·vì \,mȯn-də-'vē\. Manufacturing commune, Cuneo prov., Piedmont, NW Italy, 13 m. ESE of Cuneo; pop. (1968e) 21,734; ceramic products; 18th cent. cathedral; scene of French victory over Austrians 1796.

Mon·dra·go·ne \,mȯn-drə-'gō-nē\. Commune, Caserta prov., Campania, S Italy, on Tyrrhenian Sea 27 m. NW of Naples; pop. (1968e) 19,578.

Mon·em·va·sía *or* **Mon·em·ba·sia** \,mȯ-nem-və-'sē-ə\ *or Ital.* **Na·po·li di Mal·va·sia** \'näp-ə-lē-di-,mäl-və-'zē-ə\ *or medieval Latin* **Mal·ma·sia** \mal-'mā-zh(ē-)ə\. Village on small island off coast of SE Laconia dept., SE Peloponnesus, Greece; an important commercial port and fortress in Middle Ages. Valued highly by Byzantine emperors; held by Venice 1463–1540; Turkish 1540–1690, when it again became Venetian; again Turkish 1715–1821; first town of Morea to be taken by Greeks in War of Independence; made seat of first national assembly. Noted for export of a special wine, known as malmsey or malvasia.

Mo·nes·sen \mə-'nes-ᵊn\. City, Westmoreland co., SW Pennsylvania, on Monongahela river 20 m. S of Pittsburgh; pop. (1970c) 15,216; steel, cables, glass, chemicals; coal mines.

Mo·nett \'mō-,net\. City, Barry and Lawrence cos., SW Missouri, 35 m. SE of Joplin; pop. (1970c) 5937; ships fruit; dairy and truck farms.

Mon·fal·co·ne \,mȯn-fäl-'kō-nē, ,mȯm-\. Commune, Friuli-Venezia Giulia, NE Italy, near mouth of Isonzo river 17 m. NW of Trieste; pop. (1968c) 27,907; shipbuilding; manufactures chemicals; almost destroyed in World War I.

Monferrato. See MONTFERRAT.

Mon·for·te de Le·mos \mȯn-,fȯrt-ē-də-'lā-məs, mȯm-\. Commune, Lugo prov., NW Spain, 35 m. S of Lugo; pop. (1970p) 19,528; agricultural products, wine.

Mon·gala \mäŋ-'gal-ə\. River, S cen. Africa; ab. 400 m. long (incl. its headstream, the Ebola); flows SW from N Zaire and empties into Congo river.

Mong Cai *or* **Mon·cay** \'mȯŋ-'kī\. Town, North Vietnam, on Gulf of Tonkin near border of China.

Mon·ghyr \mäŋ-'gi(ə)r\. Town, NE cen. Bihar, NE India, on right bank of the Ganges river 235 m. NNW of Calcutta; pop. (1961c) 89,762; cigarettes, swords, firearms; has walls of old Mogul fort.

Mon·go·lia \män-'gōl-yə, mäŋ-, -'gō-lē-ə\. 1 Region, E cen. Asia; comprises Mongolian People's Republic (Outer Mongolia), Inner Mongolia, and Tuva A.S.S.R., U.S.S.R.; formerly considered a part of Outer China.

History: Region inhabited since early times by nomadic peoples; lacks historical clarity until 13th cent. A.D. when Genghis Khan (1167–1227), the leader of one of the tribes, the Mongols, secured supremacy and began Mongol expansion; under Genghis and his successors, Mongol Empire, with its capital first at Karakorum and later at Peking, stretched from China to the Danube in eastern Europe; chief successors of Mongol Empire after it broke up were: khanate of the Golden Horde in Russia, Il-khans in Persia, Yüan dynasty in China; in the 14th cent., the descendant of Genghis Khan, Tamerlane, established a short-lived empire in western Asia; its N border delimited in treaty bet. Russia and China 1727; modern Mongolia loosely dependent upon China until Tannu Tuva (see TUVA AUTONOMOUS SOVIET SOCIALIST REPUBLIC) became a republic 1911 and Outer Mongolia (now Mongolian People's Republic) under Russian auspices, declared its independence. (See MONGOLIAN PEOPLE'S REPUBLIC). Inner Mongolia came under Chinese control, except Jehol (a part of Manchukuo 1933–45), until 1937 when the two eastern provinces, Chahar and Suiyuan, were overrun by the Japanese, who formed them into the Federated Council of the Mongol Border Land, or Mêng Chiang, renamed 1939 the Mongolian Federated Autonomous Government; following World War II Inner Mongolia made an autonomous region of China (see MONGOLIA, INNER).

2 Republic, Asia. See MONGOLIAN PEOPLE'S REPUBLIC.

Mongolia, Inner. Autonomous region, N China, bounded on N by the Mongolian People's Republic; 454,633 sq. m.; pop. (1967e) 13,000,000; ✱ Huhehot; its N portion lies within the Gobi; its S border partly marked by the Great Wall; known as Inner Mongolia since 1644.

Mon·go·lian People's Republic \män-'gōl-yən-, mäŋ-, -'gō-lē-ən-\ *or frequently* **Mongolia** *also* **Outer Mongolia.** Republic, E cen. Asia, lying between China and the U.S.S.R.; 604,247 sq. m.; pop. (1970e) 1,290,000; ✱ Ulan Bator. *Physical features:* Mountainous in W part, with Altai Mts. (some peaks over 10,000 ft.) in SW and S, and Tannu-Ola on Tuva border in NW; in N cen. part are the Hentiyn Nuruu. The desert of Gobi (*q.v.*) covers a wide tract in cen. and SE part. Chief rivers the Selenga and its tributary, the Orhon, in N flowing into Lake Baikal, the Kerulen in E flowing into Hu-lun in NW Manchuria, and

the Hobdo Gol in extreme W flowing to the lakes Har Us Nuur and Har Nuur; other large lakes Ubsu-Nur near the Tuva border and Hövsgöl near border SW of Irkutsk. *Chief products:* Wheat, rye, oats, barley; pastoralism is an important factor in the economy; coal, oil, copper, gold, manganese. *Chief cities:* Ulan Bator, Darhan, Choybalsan.

History: For history prior to 1911, see MONGOLIA. Proclaimed itself an independent kingdom 1911, following collapse of Manchu dynasty in China; in treaties 1913 and 1915 established as an autonomous state under Chinese suzerainty; period 1919–21 marked by Chinese attempts to reassert their former sovereignty (Chinese forces expelled with aid of Soviet troops 1921, Soviet troops withdrawn 1925); became a republic 1924; signed mutual assistance pact with U.S.S.R. 1936; E border scene of fighting between Soviet-Mongol and Japanese forces 1939; republic's independence officially recognized by China 1946; admitted to UN 1961; allied itself with the U.S.S.R. during the Sino-Soviet ideological dispute of the 1960's and 1970's; concluded agreement with the U.S.S.R. (1970) on aid for its 1971–75 economic plan.

Mong–tseu. See MENG-TZU.

Mon·gu \mäŋ-ˈgü\. Town, Zambia, S cen. Africa; 7 m. SE of Lealui; pop. (1963c) 4049.

Mon·he·gan \män-ˈhē-gən\. Island in Atlantic Ocean off S coast of S Maine, in Lincoln co.; lobster fishing; settled c. 1622.

Mon·heim \ˈmōn-ˌhīm\. City, North Rhine-Westphalia, West Germany; pop. (1969e) 33,572; pharmaceuticals; oil refining.

Mönh Sarĭdag. See MUNKU-SARDYK.

Mon·i·teau \ˈmän-ə-ˌtō\. County in Missouri. See table at MISSOURI.

Mon·i·tor Peak \ˌmän-ət-ər-\. Mountain, La Plata co., SW Colorado; 13,703 ft.

Monitor Range. Range, cen. Nevada, chiefly in Nye co., extending N into Eureka co.

Monja, La. See LA MONJA.

Monk Bret·ton \ˈməŋk-ˈbret-ᵊn\. Former urban district, West Riding, Yorkshire, N England, now part of Barnsley; has Cluniac priory, founded 1157.

Mon·key Point \ˌməŋ-kē-\ *or Span.* **Pun·ta Mi·co** \ˌpün-tə-ˈmē-kō\. Cape on SE coast of Nicaragua, extending into the Caribbean Sea.

Monk·wear·mouth \məŋk-ˈwi(ə)r-məth\. Suburb of Sunderland (*q.v.*), Durham, N England; Wearmouth monastery was the birthplace of Bede.

Mon·mouth \ˈmän-məth, ˈmən-\. **1** County in New Jersey. See table at NEW JERSEY.
2 City, ⊗ of Warren co., W Illinois, 15 m. W of Galesburg; pop. (1970c) 11,022; farm implements, pottery, boats, feed; Monmouth Coll. (1853); settled 1836, incorporated 1852.
3 Town, Kennebec co., SW Maine, 12 m. NE of Lewiston; pop. (1970c) 2062.
4 Town, Polk co., NW Oregon, ab. 13 m. SW of Salem; pop. (1970c) 5237; fruit farms; Oregon Coll. of Education (1882).
5 County in Wales. See MONMOUTHSHIRE.
6 Municipal borough, ⊗ of Monmouthshire, SE Wales, near junction of Monnow, Wye, and Trothy rivers 26 m. N of Bristol; pop. (1971p) 6545; market town; tourism; ruins of a 12th cent. castle in which Henry V was born; received charter 1256.

Monmouth Court House. Now Freehold, New Jersey; scene of the battle of Monmouth June 28, 1778, and of the exploit of Molly Pitcher in taking her wounded husband's place as artilleryman in the course of the engagement. See FREEHOLD.

Mon·mouth·shire \ˈmän-məth-ˌshi(ə)r, ˈmən-, -shər\ *or* **Monmouth.** County, SE Wales, on the border of England; area 542 sq. m.; pop. (1971p) 461,459; ⊗ Monmouth; rivers Wye, Usk, Ebbw, Rhymney; livestock and dairy farming, coal mining, forestry; manufactures steel, textiles, aluminum, glass, electrical equipment; main towns incl. Newport, Abergavenny, Abetillery, Blaenavon, Caerlon. Frequently considered part of England, but for administrative purposes is part of Wales.

Mon·ni·ken·dam \ˈmōn-ē-kən-ˌdäm\. Commune, North Holland prov., W Netherlands; pop. (1970e) 6014; 17th cent. weighhouse, 14th cent. church.

Mo·no \ˈmō-(ˌ)nō\. **1** County in California. See table at CALIFORNIA.
2 River, Togo, W Africa; 250 m. long; lower course is boundary bet. Togo and Dahomey.
3 Island, largest of the Treasury Is. (*q.v.*), NW Solomon Is., W Pacific Ocean.

Mo·noc·a·cy \mə-ˈnäk-ə-sē\. **1** River, N Maryland; rises in Adams co., S Pennsylvania, crosses state boundary and flows S through Frederick co., N Maryland, into Potomac river.
2 Battlefield along river near city of Frederick, where on July 4–5, 1864 Gen. Lew Wallace and Union forces succeeded in delaying advance of Gen. Early's Confederates on Washington.

Monoecus. See MONACO 2.

Mono Lake \ˌmō-nō-\. Lake, cen. Mono co., E California; ab. 14 m. long by 9 m. wide; elevation 6425 ft.; water strongly saline; no outlet.

Mon·o·moy Point \ˌmän-ə-mȯi-\. Narrow peninsula, extending S from Chatham on Cape Cod, Massachusetts; ab. 10 m. long; at certain times becomes an island.

Mo·no·na \mə-ˈnō-nə\. **1** County in Iowa. See table at IOWA.
2 City, Dane co., S Wisconsin, SE of Madison; pop. (1970c) 10,420.

Monona, Lake. See FOUR LAKES.

Mo·non·gah \mə-ˈnäŋ-gə\. Town, Marion co., N West Virginia, 4 m. SW of Fairmont; pop. (1970c) 1194; coal mining; scene of mine disaster 1907.

Mo·non·ga·he·la \mə-ˌnän-gə-ˈhē-lə, -ˌnäŋ-gə-, -ˈhā-lə\. **1** River, N West Virginia and SW Pennsylvania; 128 m. long; formed by junction of West Fork (rises in Lewis co.) and Tygart rivers in Marion co., N West Virginia, flows N across Pennsylvania border and unites with the Allegheny river to form the Ohio river at Pittsburgh; navigable for 60 m.
2 City, Washington co., SW Pennsylvania, on Monongahela river 17 m. S of Pittsburgh; pop. (1970c) 7113; bricks, steel, chemicals; coal mines; dairy and fruit farms; settled 1792.

Mon·on·ga·lia \ˌmän-ən-ˈgā-lē-ə, -əŋ-ˈgā-, -lyə\. County in West Virginia. See table at WEST VIRGINIA.

Mono Pass \ˌmō-nō-\. Mountain pass in Sierra Nevada, Mono co., E California; altitude 10,599 ft.

Mo·no·po·li \mə-ˈnäp-ə-lē, -ˈnȯp-\. Seaport, Bari prov., Apulia, SE Italy, on Adriatic 25 m. ESE of Bari; pop. (1968e) 39,746; early 12th cent. cathedral; 11th cent. Romanesque church; castle.

Mo·nor \ˈmō-ˌnō(ə)r, -ˌnȯ(ə)r\. Commune, Pest co., cen. Hungary, ab. 20 m. SE of Budapest; pop. (1970p) 16,805.

Mon·re·a·le \ˌmōn-rē-ˈäl-ē\. Commune, Palermo prov., NW cen. Sicily, Italy, 5 m. SW of Palermo; pop. (1968e) 25,648; trade center in fruit and olive growing region; notable 12th cent. cathedral.

Mon·roe \mən-ˈrō\. **1** Name of counties in seventeen states of the U.S. See tables at ALABAMA, ARKANSAS, FLORIDA, GEORGIA, ILLINOIS, INDIANA, IOWA, KENTUCKY, MICHIGAN, MISSISSIPPI, MISSOURI, NEW YORK, OHIO, PENNSYLVANIA, TENNESSEE, WEST VIRGINIA, WISCONSIN.
2 Agricultural town, E Fairfield co., SW Connecticut, on Housatonic river; pop. (1970c) 12,047; incorporated 1923.
3 City, ⊗ of Walton co., N cen. Georgia, 23 m. SW of Athens; pop. (1970c) 8071; clothing; livestock and poultry farms.
4 Industrial city, ⊗ of Ouachita parish, N Louisiana, 100 m. E of Shreveport; pop. (1970c) 56,374; chemicals, paper and paper products, lumber, clothing, cottonseed oil; gas wells; Northeast Louisiana State Coll. (1931); founded 1785; incorporated 1820.
5 City, ⊗ of Monroe co., SE Michigan, on Lake Erie at mouth of Raisin river 35 m. SW of Detroit; pop. (1970c) 23,894; paper, office supplies, automobile parts; nurseries; Sacred Heart Novitiate (1949), Monroe County Community Coll. (1949); settled 1780; in 1813 scene of Raisin River Massacre following defeat of Americans by British-Indian force under Col. H. Proctor; chartered as city 1837.
6 Village in Monroe town, Orange co., SE New York, 15 m. SW of Newburgh; pop. (1970c) 4439.
7 City, ⊗ of Union co., S North Carolina, 24 m. SE of Charlotte; pop. (1970c) 11,282; textiles; diversified agriculture.
8 Village, Butler and Warren cos., SW Ohio, 27 m. S of Dayton; pop. (1970c) 3492.
9 Town, Snohomish co., NW cen. Washington, 15 m. ESE of Everett; pop. (1970c) 2687; truck farms.
10 City, ⊗ of Green co., S Wisconsin, 30 m. W of Beloit; pop. (1970c) 8654; cheese; Green County Teachers Coll. (1910).

Monroe, Lake. Lake on boundary bet. Volusia and Seminole cos., cen. Florida penin.

Monroe, Mount. Peak in the White Mts., S Coos co., N New Hampshire; 5385 ft.

Monroe City. City, Marion and Monroe cos., NE Missouri, 23 m. W of Hannibal; pop. (1970c) 2456; diversified farming.

Monroe Peak. Mountain in SW Sevier co., cen. Utah; 11,226 ft.

Mon·roe·ville \mən-ˈrō-ˌvil\. **1** City, ⊗ of Monroe co., SW Alabama; pop. (1970c) 4846; lumber; Patrick Henry State Junior Coll. (1965).
2 Borough, Allegheny co., SW Pennsylvania, E of Pittsburgh; pop. (1970c) 29,011; residential.

Mon·ro·via \mən-ˈrō-vē-ə\. **1** City, Los Angeles co., SW California, 14 m. ENE of Los Angeles; pop. (1970c) 30,015; hardware, dairy products, aircraft parts, electronic components; incorporated 1887.
2 Seaport, ✱ of Liberia, W Africa, near the mouth of St. Paul river; pop. (1970e) 100,000; largest city in the country and its major seaport, with modern port facilities; pharmaceuticals, cement, paint; fish processing, oil refining; univ. (estab. 1862, univ. status 1951). Founded as home for freed slaves 1822 by American Colonization Society; named after U.S. President James Monroe.

Mons \ˈmōⁿs\ *or Flem.* **Ber·gen** \ˈbe(ə)r-k̲ə(n)\. Manufacturing commune, ✱ of Hainaut prov., SW Belgium; pop. (1970e) 28,727; trades in cloth and sugar; coal mines; Late Gothic cathedral and town hall; technical coll. (1837), State Univ. Center (1965). On site of Roman camp; made capital of Hainaut 804 by Charlemagne; became trading town with cloth market in 14th cent.; often besieged in wars of 17th and 18th cents.; scene of the first engagement fought Aug. 23, 1914 by the British Expeditionary Force in World War I.

Mons Aureus. See JANICULUM.

Mons Brisiacus. See BREISACH AM RHEIN.

Mon·schau \ˈmȯn-ˌshau̇\ *or formerly* **Mont·joie** \mōⁿ-ˈzhwä\. Town, North Rhine-Westphalia, West Germany, SE of Aachen on French border; pop. (1970e) 2400; church (1649); scene of fighting during World War II Dec. 1944 and Jan. 1945.

Mon·se·li·ce \mȯn-ˈsel-i-(ˌ)chā, -ˈsāl-\. Commune, Padova prov., Veneto, NE Italy, 13 m. SSW of Padua; pop. (1968e) 17,381; 13th cent. cathedral; ancient city walls.

Mons Jo·vis \mänz-ˈjō-vəs\. See *Great Saint Bernard* Pass at ALPS.

Mons Lac·tar·i·us \ˌmänz-lak-ˈter-ē-əs\. See ANGRI.

Mon·son \ˈmən(t)-sən\. Town, Hampden co., SW Massachusetts, 14 m. E of Springfield; pop. (1970c) 7355.

Mons Rubicus. See MONTROUGE.

Mon·ster \ˈmȯn(t)-stər\. Commune, South Holland prov., SW Netherlands, on North Sea coast just S of the Hague; pop. (1970e) 17,761.

Mon·ta·gna·na \ˌmȯn-tə-ˈnyä-nə\. Commune, Padova prov., Veneto, NE Italy, 25 m. SW of Padua; pop. (1968e) 10,457; medieval city walls; 24 medieval towers; cathedral.

Mon·ta·gu \ˈmänt-ə-ˌgyü\. Town and health resort, SW Cape Province, S Rep. of South Africa, 100 m. E of Cape Town; pop. (1967e) 5800; has fine climate and thermal springs, known by early Dutch settlers and natives.

Mon·tague \män-ˈtāg\. 1 County in N Texas. See table at TEXAS.

2 Unincorporated community, its ⊗; pop. (1970c) 1265.

Mon·ta·gue \ˈmänt-ə-ˌgyü\. Town, Franklin co., NW Massachusetts, 5 m. SE of Greenfield; pop. (1970c) 8454.

Mon·ta·gue Island \ˌmänt-ə-gyü-\. Island on W side of entrance to Prince William Sound, S Alaska, E of Kenai Penin.; 50 m. long and 8 m. wide.

Mont·al·ban \ˌmȯn-täl-ˈbän\. 1 River, an upper tributary of the Marikina river, NE Rizal prov., Luzon, Phil.; it and other streams have been developed into large reservoir furnishing water supply for Manila.

2 Municipality, N Rizal, on Montalban river W of reservoir; pop. (1969e) 13,100.

Mont·al·ci·no \ˌmȯn-täl-ˈchē-nō\. Commune, Siena prov., Tuscany, cen. Italy, 22 m. SSE of Siena; pop. (1968e) 7027; 19th cent. cathedral, early 14th cent. church, 14th cent. palace and art museum.

Mont·al·to \mȯn-ˈtäl-(ˌ)tō\. Highest peak in the Aspromonte ridge, S Apennines, Italy; 6417 ft.

Montalto Uf·fu·go \-ˈüf-ü-gō\. Commune, Cosenza prov., Calabria, S Italy, 10 m. NNW of Cosenza; pop. (1968e) 10,708; settled by Waldensians in 14th cent.

Mon·tana \män-ˈtan-ə\. Northwestern state of U.S.A., bounded on N by Canadian provinces of British Columbia, Alberta, and Saskatchewan, on E by North Dakota and South Dakota, on S by Wyoming and Idaho, and on W by Idaho; 4th state in area, 147,138 sq. m. (land area 145,603 sq. m.); 43d state in population, (1970c) 694,409; ✻ Helena; 41st state admitted to Union (1889).

Nicknames: Treasure State; Mountain State. *State flower:* Bitterroot. *Motto:* Oro y Plata (Gold and Silver). *Rivers:* Missouri, rising in S area and flowing N then E across state; Yellowstone, rising in NW Wyoming and flowing through Yellowstone National Park across the boundary into Montana and then N and NE into the Missouri. *Highest point:* Granite Peak 12,799 ft. in Park co. *Chief products:* Wheat, barley, sugar beets, corn; livestock; copper, petroleum, phosphate rock; manufacturing: food processing; lumber, primary metals. *Chief cities:* Billings, Great Falls, Missoula, Butte, Helena. See *Table of States* at UNITED STATES. Divided into the following 56 counties (for pronunciation of their names, see their individual entries):

NAME	LOCATION	AREA[1] (sq. m.)	POP. (1970c)	CO. SEAT
Beaverhead	SW	5,560	8,187	Dillon
Big Horn	S	5,028	10,057	Hardin
Blaine	N	4,275	6,727	Chinook
Broadwater	SW cen.	1,193	2,526	Townsend
Carbon	S	2,067	7,080	Red Lodge
Carter	SE corner	3,313	1,956	Ekalaka
Cascade	cen.	2,661	81,804	Great Falls
Chouteau	N cen.	3,927	6,473	Fort Benton
Custer	SE	3,756	12,174	Miles City
Daniels	NE	1,443	3,083	Scobey
Dawson	E	2,370	11,269	Glendive
Deer Lodge	SW	740	15,652	Anaconda
Fallon	E	1,633	4,050	Baker
Fergus	cen.	4,242	12,611	Lewistown
Flathead[2,3]	NW	5,137	39,460	Kalispell
Gallatin	S	2,517	32,505	Bozeman
Garfield[4]	E cen.	4,455	1,796	Jordan
Glacier[2]	NW	2,964	10,783	Cut Bank
Golden Valley	cen.	1,176	931	Ryegate
Granite	W	1,733	2,737	Philipsburg
Hill	N	2,927	17,358	Havre
Jefferson	SW cen.	1,652	5,238	Boulder
Judith Basin	cen.	1,880	2,667	Stanford
Lake[3]	NW	1,494	14,445	Polson
Lewis and Clark	W cen.	3,476	33,281	Helena
Liberty	N	1,439	2,359	Chester
Lincoln	NW corner	3,714	18,063	Libby
McCone[4]	E	2,607	2,875	Circle
Madison	SW	3,528	5,014	Virginia City
Meagher	cen.	2,354	2,122	White Sulphur Springs
Mineral	W	1,222	2,958	Superior
Missoula	W	2,612	58,263	Missoula
Musselshell	cen.	1,887	3,734	Roundup
Park	S	2,626	11,197	Livingston
Petroleum	cen.	1,655	675	Winnett
Phillips	N	5,213	5,386	Malta
Pondera	NW	1,645	6,611	Conrad
Powder River	SE	3,288	2,862	Broadus
Powell	W	2,336	6,660	Deer Lodge
Prairie	E	1,730	1,752	Terry
Ravalli	W	2,382	14,409	Hamilton
Richland	E	2,079	9,837	Sidney
Roosevelt	NE	2,385	10,365	Wolf Point
Rosebud	SE	5,037	6,032	Forsyth
Sanders	NW	2,778	7,093	Thompson Falls
Sheridan	NE corner	1,694	5,779	Plentywood
Silver Bow	SW	715	41,981	Butte
Stillwater	S cen.	1,794	4,632	Columbus
Sweet Grass	S cen.	1,840	2,980	Big Timber
Teton	NW cen.	2,294	6,116	Choteau
Toole	N	1,950	5,839	Shelby
Treasure	SE cen.	985	1,069	Hysham
Valley[4]	NE	4,974	11,471	Glasgow
Wheatland	cen.	1,420	2,529	Harlowton
Wibaux	E	890	1,465	Wibaux
Yellowstone	S cen.	2,642	87,367	Billings
Yellowstone National Park (part)	S	269[5]	64	

[1]Area = land area.

[2]Glacier National Park occupies NE part of Flathead co. and NW part of Glacier co.

[3]Upper (smaller) part of Flathead Lake in Flathead co., lower part in Lake co.

[4]Fort Peck Reservoir on boundaries of Garfield co. (along both sides of its NE corner), McCone co. (upper W boundary), and Valley co. (cen. S boundary).

[5]Main part of Yellowstone National Park is within Wyoming state boundaries (3186 sq. m.), with adjacent strips in Montana (232.9 sq. m.) and Idaho (49 sq. m.). Not a county.

History: All except a small area in NW was part of Louisiana Purchase 1803; crossed by Lewis and Clark 1805–06; its boundary with Canada settled by treaties 1818 and 1846; part W of Rockies in the Oregon country, included in Washington Territory 1853 and 1859; part E of Rockies in territories of Nebraska 1854 and of Dakota 1861; part of Idaho Territory 1863; organized as Montana Territory 1864; first crossed by rail (Northern Pacific) 1883; admitted to Union Nov. 8, 1889.

Mon·ta·na \mȯn-ˈtä-nə\. Town, Valais canton, Switzerland; pop. (1970c) 1725; health resort, winter sports; nearby is **Montana–Ver·ma·la** \-ver-ˈmäl-ə\, a resort for tuberculosis patients.

Mon·ta·ña \mȯn-ˈtän-yə\. Forested region of the E slope of the Andes, esp. that of N Peru.

Mon·tar·gis \ˌmōⁿ-tär-ˈzhē\. Industrial commune, Loiret dept., N cen. France, 38 m. E of Orléans; pop. (1968c) 18,225; remains of a castle which was long a royal residence; bronze statue of the "Dog of Montargis," the dog of Aubry de Montdidier, which, according to tradition, tracked down his master's murderer and vanquished him in a sort of judicial duel arranged by Charles V 1371; unsuccessfully besieged by English 1427.

Mon·ta·taire \ˌmōⁿ-tə-ˈter\. Commune, Oise dept., N France; pop. (1962c) 9360.

Mont·au·ban \ˌmänt-ō-ˈbäⁿ\. 1 Village, Somme dept., N France, 6 m. E of Albert; scene of battle July 1, 1916, a phase of the battle of the Somme.

2 City, ✻ of Tarn-et-Garonne dept., S France, on Tarn river 31 m. N of Toulouse; pop. (1968c) 45,895; textiles, hats, furniture; food processing; cathedral, episcopal palace, town hall, and bridge. Ancient capital of Quercy; chartered 1144; as Huguenot stronghold besieged [illegible] 1621; taken by Richelieu 1629.

Mon·tauk Point \ˌmän-ˌtȯk-\. Point on E extremity of I., New York.

Mont aux Sources. See AUX SOURCES, MONT.

Mont·bé·liard \ˌmōⁿ-bāl-ˈyär\. Commune, Doubs dep France, 43 m. ENE of Besançon; pop. (1968c) 23,908; tomobiles, office machinery, electrical equipment, too. beer, sausage, cheese. Under dukes of Württemberg from 1397; occupied by French 1674–97, 1723–48; given to France by Peace of Lunéville 1801.

Mont Blanc. See BLANC, MONT.

Mont·bri·son \ˌmōⁿ-brē-ˈzōⁿ\. Town, Loire dept., SE cen. France; pop. (1962c) 9548; 13th–15th cent. church.

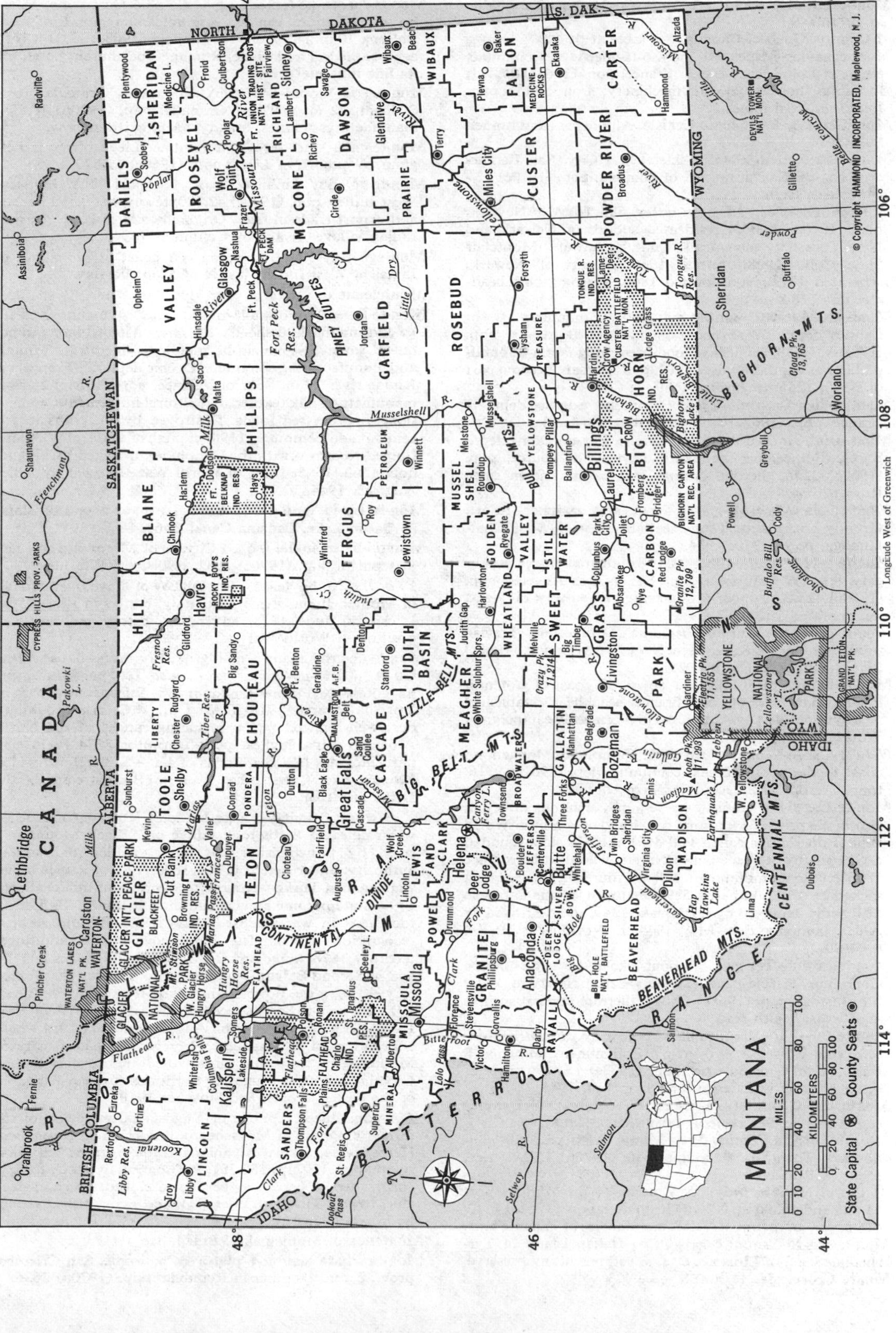
MONTANA
CANADA
BRITISH COLUMBIA
ALBERTA
SASKATCHEWAN
NORTH DAKOTA
S. DAK.
WYOMING
IDAHO
LINCOLN
FLATHEAD
GLACIER
TOOLE
LIBERTY
HILL
BLAINE
PHILLIPS
VALLEY
DANIELS
SHERIDAN
ROOSEVELT
RICHLAND
DAWSON
McCONE
GARFIELD
PRAIRIE
WIBAUX
FALLON
CARTER
CUSTER
POWDER RIVER
ROSEBUD
TREASURE
BIG HORN
YELLOWSTONE
MUSSEL SHELL
PETROLEUM
FERGUS
JUDITH BASIN
CHOUTEAU
TETON
PONDERA
CASCADE
MEAGHER
WHEATLAND
GOLDEN VALLEY
SWEET GRASS
STILL WATER
CARBON
PARK
GALLATIN
BROADWATER
JEFFERSON
LEWIS AND CLARK
POWELL
DEER LODGE
SILVER BOW
GRANITE
MISSOULA
MINERAL
SANDERS
LAKE
RAVALLI
BEAVERHEAD
MADISON
Helena
Great Falls
Billings
Butte
Missoula
Bozeman
Kalispell
Havre
Anaconda
Lewistown
Miles City
Glendive
Livingston
Sidney
Glasgow
Wolf Point
Shelby
Cut Bank
Dillon
Hamilton
Fort Peck Res.
Missouri R.
Yellowstone R.
Milk R.
Musselshell R.
YELLOWSTONE NATIONAL PARK
GLACIER NATIONAL PARK
BIGHORN MTS.
BEAVERHEAD MTS.
CENTENNIAL MTS.
BIG BELT MTS.
LITTLE BELT MTS.
BITTERROOT RANGE
ROCKY MTS.
CONTINENTAL DIVIDE
Granite Pk. 12,799
Longitude West of Greenwich
© Copyright HAMMOND INCORPORATED, Maplewood, N.J.
MILES
KILOMETERS
State Capital
County Seats

Mont·calm \mänt-ˈkäm\. 1 County in Michigan. See table at MICHIGAN.

2 County, Quebec, Canada. See table at QUEBEC.

Mont·ceau–les–Mines \mō^{n}-ˌsō-lā-ˈmen\. Commune, Saône-et-Loire dept., E cen. France; pop. (1968c) 27,421; footwear, hosiery, textile machinery; iron and copper foundries, coal mines.

Mont Cenis *or Ital.* **Monte Cenisio.** Alpine pass and tunnel. See ALPS.

Mont·clair \mänt-ˈkla(ə)r, -ˈkle(ə)r\. 1 City, San Bernardino co., SE California, NE of Pomona; pop. (1970c) 22,546; citrus fruits.

2 Town, Essex co., NE New Jersey, 6 m. NNW of Newark; pop. (1970c) 44,043; residential suburb of Newark and New York City; chemicals, paint, metalware; Montclair State Coll. (1908); settled 1666 as part of Newark; separated 1812; incorporated 1868; Washington's headquarters 1780.

Mont–de–Mar·san \ˌmō^{n}d-mär-ˈsä^{n}\. Commune, ✱ of Landes dept., SW France, 66 m. S of Bordeaux; pop. (1968c) 24,458; foundries, food-preserving factory; founded 1141 as capital of viscountship of Marsan; became part of Béarn 1256; to France 1589.

Mont·di·dier \ˌmō^{n}-dē-ˈdyā\. Commune, Somme dept., N France; pop. (1962c) 5778; devastated in battles 1918.

Mont–Dore \mō^{n}-ˈdȯ(ə)r\. Commune, Puy-de-Dôme dept., S cen. France, on the Dordogne near its source; pop. (1962c) 2256; thermal springs and baths, known since Roman times.

Mont·ea·gle \mänt-ˈē-gəl\. Town and summer resort, Grundy co., S cen. Tennessee, ab. 35 m. NW of Chattanooga; pop. (1970c) 934.

Mon·te·bel·lo \ˌmänt-ə-ˈbel-(ˌ)ō\. Residential city, Los Angeles co., SW California, 8 m. ESE of Los Angeles; pop. (1970c) 42,807; rubber products, television sets; oil wells; incorporated 1920.

Mon·te·bel·lu·na \ˌmȯnt-ē-bə-ˈlü-nə\. Commune, Treviso prov., Veneto, NE Italy, 13 m. NW of Treviso; pop. (1968e) 21,239; cathedral (built 1925).

Mon·te·bourg \mō^{n}t-ˈbü(ə)r\. Town, SE coast of Cotentin Penin., Manche dept., NW France; beachhead established nearby June 1944 by Americans in Normandy campaign of World War II.

Mon·te Car·lo \ˌmänt-i-ˈkär-(ˌ)lō\. Commune, Monaco, on coast to the N of Monaco commune; pop. (1961c) 9516; tourist resort with casino and many hotels.

Mon·te Cas·si·no \ˌmȯnt-ē-kə-ˈsē-(ˌ)nō\. Famous abbey in Frosinone prov., SE Latium, cen. Italy, on a hill (in World War II operations called Hill 516) near Cassino; founded c. 529 A.D. by St. Benedict of Nursia, who died here; since 1866 a national monument. Rebuilt four times: after being sacked by the Lombards 589, destroyed by the Saracens 884, badly damaged by earthquake 1349, and destroyed by Allied bombing Feb.–May 1944 in World War II. See CASSINO.

Mon·te·ca·ti·ni–Ter·me \ˌmȯnt-ē-kə-ˈtē-nē-ˈte(ə)r-(ˌ)mā\. Commune, Pistoia prov., Tuscany, cen. Italy, 12 m. W by S of Pistoia; pop. (1968e) 20,024; thermal mineral springs and baths; health resort.

Mon·te·cor·vi·no \ˌmȯnt-ē-kȯr-ˈvē-nō\ *or officially* **Montecorvino Ro·vel·la** \-rō-ˈvel-ə\. Commune, Campania, S Italy, 11 m. E of Salerno; pop. (1968e) 15,487; scene of bitter fighting in Salerno campaign Sept. 1943.

Mon·te·cris·ti \ˌmȯnt-ē-ˈkris-tē\. 1 Province, NW Dominican Republic. See table at DOMINICAN REPUBLIC.

2 *or in full* **San Fer·nan·do de Monte Cristi** \ˌsän-fər-ˈnän-dō-dā-\. Town, its ✱; munic. pop. (1970p) 15,141; rice, tobacco, bananas.

3 Town, Manabí prov., W Ecuador, 6 m. from its port Manta and ab. 90 m. NW of Guayaquil; pop. (1962c) 4540; center for copra industry and manufacture of Panama hats.

Mon·te·cris·to \ˌmȯnt-ē-ˈkris-(ˌ)tō\. Italian island in Tyrrhenian Sea S of Elba; ab. 6 sq. m.; state hunting preserve.

Monte Croce. See PLÖCKEN.

Mon·te·fia·sco·ne \ˌmȯnt-ē-fyä-ˈskō-nē\. Commune, Viterbo prov., Latium, cen. Italy, in volcanic region E of Lake Bolsena 10 m. NNW of Viterbo; pop. (1968e) 12,214; 16th cent. cathedral and castle; Romanesque church; noted for its fine muscatel wine.

Mon·te·frío \ˌmȯnt-ē-ˈfrē-(ˌ)ō\. Commune, Granada prov., S Spain, 22 m. WNW of Granada; pop. (1970p) 10,804; manufactures textiles, brandy, soap; cattle raising.

Mon·te·gnée \mō^{n}t-ˈnyā\. Commune, Liège prov., E Belgium, W suburb of Liège; pop. (1969e) 11,870.

Mon·te·go Bay \män-ˌtē-(ˌ)gō-\. Seaport, NW Jamaica, West Indies; pop. (1970e) 42,800; resort; has good harbor and export trade in fruit. Originally site of large Arawak Indian village, visited by Columbus 1494.

Montego Bay Point. Cape on NW coast of the island of Jamaica, West Indies, just N of Montego Bay.

Monteleone di Calabria. See VIBO VALENTIA.

Mon·té·li·mar \mō^{n}-ˌtā-lē-ˈmär\; *anc.* **Acu·num Acu·sio** \ə-ˌkyü-nə-mə-ˈkyü-shē-ˌō\ *or later* **Mon·til·i·um Ad·he·ma·ri** \män-ˈtil-ē-əm-ˌäd-hē-ˈma(ə)r-ī, -ˈme(ə)r-\. Mining and manufacturing commune, Drôme dept., SE France, on Rhone river 27 m. SSW of Valence; pop. (1968c) 26,748; manufactures silk textiles, agricultural implements, confectionery, processed foods. Destroyed by Visigoths in 5th cent.; made commune 1198; capital of state of Valdaine (joined to crown with the Dauphiné); besieged by Huguenots 1562, 1585, 1587; in World War II seized by Allies Aug. 25, 1944.

Mon·te Lir·io \ˌmȯnt-ē-ˈlir-ē-ˌō\. Town, at N end of island in Gatun Lake, Panama Canal Zone.

Mon·tel·lo \män-ˈtel-(ˌ)ō\. 1 City, ⊗ of Marquette co., cen. Wisconsin; pop. (1970c) 1082; resort; truck farms.

2 \ *or Ital.* \mōn-ˈtel-lō\. Plateau SW of Piave river and NE of Montebelluna, Veneto, NE Italy; battles in World War I, esp. in June 1918, an Italian victory; military key position in World War II.

Mon·te·ne·gro \ˌmänt-ə-ˈnē-(ˌ)grō\. 1 *or Serbo-Croat.* **Cr·na Go·ra** \ˌ(t)sər-nə-ˈgōr-ə, -ˈgȯr-\ *also* **Tser·na·go·ra** \ˌtsər-nə-ˈgȯ(ə)r-ə\. Former kingdom, SE Europe, now part of Yugoslavia; area (1918) 3733 sq. m.; ✱ Cetinje; mountainous, well-forested region including ranges of the North Albanian Alps; highest peak Durmitor 8274 ft. in cen. part; includes NW two thirds of Lake Scutari into which Morača river flows; other rivers are headstreams of the Drina and Ibar.

History: Originated after battle of Kosovo (*q.v.*) 1389, when defeated Serbs took refuge on "Black Mountain"; ruled by prince-bishops, it never yielded to Turkish authority; under Peter I (1782–1830), ally of Russia in her wars against Turkey, secured recognition of independence 1799; state became secular and modernized in 19th cent.; took part in war against Turkey 1876–78, and secured recognition of complete independence and additional territory 1878; kingdom after 1910; fought Turks in First and in Second Balkan Wars; took Shkodër but was forced to yield it to the powers who made it capital of Albania 1913; for help to Serbia, received one half of sanjak of Novi Pazar 1913; declared war on Austria-Hungary 1914 whose annexation of Bosnia and Herzegovina had frustrated Montenegrin territorial aims; voted union with Serbia, Croatia, and other Yugoslav territories to form Kingdom of the Serbs, Croats, and Slovenes 1918.

2 A constituent republic of Yugoslavia, in region of the former kingdom of Montenegro, bordering on Bosnia and Herzegovina, Serbia, Albania, and the Adriatic Sea; 5333 sq. m.; pop. (1971p) 530,361; ✱ Titograd; livestock raising; corn, wheat, tobacco; copper, bauxite, lead; iron and steel; chief towns: Titograd, Pljevlja; made a constituent republic in 1946 constitution.

Montenegro. Municipality, Brazil. See AMAPÁ 2.

Mon·te Pla·ta \ˌmȯnt-ə-ˈplät-ə\. Commune, San Cristóbal prov., E cen. Dominican Republic; pop. (1970p) 3636.

Mon·te·pul·cia·no \ˌmȯnt-ē-pül-ˈchän-(ˌ)ō\. Commune, Tuscany, cen. Italy, 29 m. SE of Siena; pop. (1968e) 14,773; 16th cent. cathedral, 13th cent. church.

Mon·te·reau–faut–Yonne \mō^{n}-ˌtrō-fō-ˈyōn\ *or anc.* **Con·da·te** \kän-ˈdāt-ē\. Manufacturing town, Seine-et-Marne dept., N France, at confluence of Yonne and Seine rivers; pop. (1968c) 19,789.

Mon·te·rey \ˌmänt-ə-ˈrā\. **1** County in California. See table at CALIFORNIA.

2 Commercial city, Monterey co., W California, at S end of Monterey Bay; pop. (1970c) 26,302; in resort area; U.S. Army facilities; U.S. Navy Postgraduate School (1909); Monterey Peninsula Coll. (1947); Monterey Institute of Foreign Studies (1955). Site of city discovered 1542 by Juan Rodríguez Cabrillo, rediscovered 1602 by Sebastián Vizcaíno; first settled 1770 through founding of Franciscan mission; became social, military, and political center of Spanish California; capital of Spanish province of California 1774–1822, of Mexican province 1822–46; to U.S. 1846; site of first California constitutional convention 1849; incorporated 1850.

3 Town, Putnam co., N cen. Tennessee, 15 m. E of Cookeville; pop. (1970c) 2351.

4 Town, ⊗ of Highland co., western Virginia; pop. (1970c) 223.

5 City, Mexico. See MONTERREY.

Monterey Bay. Inlet of Pacific Ocean in Santa Cruz and Monterey cos., W cen. California.

Monterey Park. Suburban residential city, Los Angeles co., SW California, 8 m. E of Los Angeles; pop. (1970c) 49,166.

Mon·te·ría \ˌmȯnt-ə-ˈrē-ə\. City, ✱ of Córdoba dept., N Colombia, 120 m. SSW of Cartagena; munic. pop. (1968e) 161,285; univ. (1966).

Mon·te·rrey *or sometimes angl.* **Mon·te·rey** \ˌmänt-ə-ˈrā\. City, ✱ of Nuevo León state, NE Mexico; pop. (1970p) 830,336; major industrial center, producing iron, steel, glass, textiles, cement, processed foods, beverages, plastics; univ. (1933), Technological Institute of Monterrey (1942); Topo Chico hot springs and García caves nearby. Founded 1579; scene of battle in Mexican War Sept. 21–23, 1846, in which city was taken by U.S. forces under Zachary Taylor; developed as center of metallurgical industry after 1882.

Mon·te San Gio·van·ni Cam·pa·no \ˌmȯnt-ē-sän-jō-ˈvän-ē-käm-ˈpä-nō\. Commune, Frosinone prov., Latium, cen. Italy, 9 m. E of Frosinone; pop. (1968e) 11,166.

Mon·te·sa·no \ˌmänt-ə-ˈsā-nō\. City, ⊗ of Grays Harbor co., W Washington, on Chehalis river 11 m. E of Aberdeen; pop. (1970c) 2847; lumber; dairy farming.

Mon·te Sant'An·ge·lo \ˌmȯnt-ē-sän-ˈtän-jə-ˌlō\. Commune, Foggia prov., Apulia, SE Italy, 27 m. NE of Foggia; pop. (1968e) 20,092; a center of pilgrimage; olive oil, timber; Norman castle; 13th cent. campanile.

Mon·tes Cla·ros \ˌmō(ⁿ)n-tesh-ˈklar-(ˌ)üs\. City, N cen. Minas Gerais state, E Brazil, 225 m. N of Belo Horizonte; munic. pop. (1968e) 121,428.

Mon·te Se·re·no \ˌmänt-ə-sə-ˈrē-nō\. City, Santa Clara co., W California, 12 m. SW of San Jose; pop. (1970c) 3089.

Mon·te·sper·to·li \ˌmȯnt-ē-ˈsper-tə-lē\. Commune, Firenze prov., Tuscany, cen. Italy, 10 m. SSW of Florence; pop. (1968e) 8456.

Mon·te·val·lo \ˌmänt-ə-ˈval-ō\. Town, Shelby co., cen. Alabama, 32 m. S of Birmingham; pop. (1970c) 3719; Univ. of Montevallo (1896).

Mon·te·var·chi \ˌmȯnt-ē-ˈvär-kē\. Commune, Arezzo prov., Tuscany, cen. Italy, near Arno river 17 m. WNW of Arezzo; pop. (1968e) 22,367; convent.

Mon·te·vid·eo \ˌmänt-ə-ˈvid-ē-ˌō\. City, ⊗ of Chippewa co., SW cen. Minnesota, on Minnesota river 42 m. SE of Big Stone Lake; pop. (1970c) 5661; agriculture.

Mon·te·vi·deo \ˌmänt-ə-və-ˈdā-(ˌ)ō, -ˈvid-ē-ˌō\. **1** Department of S Uruguay. See table at URUGUAY.

2 Seaport city, ✱ of Uruguay, also ✱ of Montevideo dept., in S part on N shore of La Plata estuary 135 m. E of Buenos Aires, Argentina; pop. (1967e) 1,280,000; political, industrial, commercial, and cultural center of Uruguay; exports wool, meat, and hides; produces textiles, wines, dairy products, soap, and clothing; stockyards, slaughterhouses, packing plants; tourism; Univ. of the Republic (1849).

History: Settled by Spanish 1726 to counteract Portuguese influence in area; from 1807 to 1830 alternately occupied by British, Spanish, Argentine, Portuguese, and Brazilian forces; became capital of independent Uruguay 1830; underwent siege by combined Argentine-Uruguayan forces 1843–1851, in which British and French naval forces assisted defenders.

Mon·te Vis·ta \ˌmänt-ə-ˈvis-tə\. City, Rio Grande co., S Colorado, in San Luis Park 15 m. WNW of Alamosa; pop. (1970c) 3909; ships vegetables.

Mon·te·zu·ma \ˌmänt-ə-ˈzü-mə\. **1** County in Colorado. See table at COLORADO.

2 City, Macon co., SW cen. Georgia, 45 m. SW of Macon; pop. (1970c) 4125; aluminum products; fruit and truck farms.

3 Town, ⊗ of Poweshiek co., SE cen. Iowa; pop. (1970c) 1353; livestock and grain farms.

Montezuma Castle National Monument. See UNITED STATES, *National Monuments.*

Montezuma Peak. Mountain, Archuleta co., S Colorado; 13,703 ft.

Mont·fau·con \ˌmō^{n}-fō-ˈkō^{n}\. Village, Meuse dept., NE France, 13 m. NW of Verdun; pop. (1962c) 337; held by Germans throughout World War I; taken Oct. 4, 1918 by Americans in the Meuse-Argonne offensive.

Mont·fer·rand \ˌmō^{n}-fə-ˈrä^{n}\. Ancient city, now part of the city of Clermont-Ferrand, Puy-de-Dôme dept., S cen. France.

Mont·fer·rat \ˌmō^{n}-fə-ˈrä\ *or Ital.* **Mon·fer·ra·to** \ˌmȯn-fə-ˈrät-(ˌ)ō\. Former marquisate and duchy in Italy, S of Po river, now mostly in Alessandria prov., SE Piedmont.

Mont·gom·ery \mən(t)-ˈgəm-(ə-)rē, män(t)-, -ˈgäm-\. **1** Name of counties in eighteen states of the U.S. See tables at ALABAMA, ARKANSAS, GEORGIA, ILLINOIS, INDIANA, IOWA, KANSAS, KENTUCKY, MARYLAND, MISSISSIPPI, MISSOURI, NEW YORK, NORTH CAROLINA, OHIO, PENNSYLVANIA, TENNESSEE, TEXAS, VIRGINIA.

2 Commercial city, ✱ of Alabama and ⊗ of Montgomery co., SE cen. Alabama, on Alabama river ab. 85 m. SSE of Birmingham; pop. (1970c) 133,386; cotton, livestock, and lumber market; fertilizer factories, stockyards, meat-packing plants. Alabama State Univ. (1874), Huntingdon Coll. (1909; previously founded at Tuskegee 1854 and 1872), Alabama Christian Coll. (1942); U.S. Air Force Advanced School at Maxwell Field, U.S. Air Force Special Staff School at Gunter Field. Incorporated as town 1819, as city 1837; made state capital 1847; first capital of the Confederacy 1861; taken by Union army 1865.

3 Village, Kane and Kendall cos., NE Illinois, 41 m. S of Aurora; pop. (1970c) 3278.

4 City, in Fayette and Kanawha cos., SW cen. West Virginia, on Kanawha river 22 m. ESE of Charleston; pop. (1970c) 2525; coal mining; West Virginia Institute of Technology (1895).

5 District and town, Pakistan. See SAHIWAL.

6 County in Wales. See MONTGOMERYSHIRE.

7 Municipal borough, Montgomeryshire, E Wales; pop. (1971p) 968; cattle market.

Montgomery City. City, ⊗ of Montgomery co., E cen. Missouri, 46 m. E of Columbia; pop. (1970c) 2187.

Mont·gom·er·y·shire \mən(t)-ˈgəm-(ə-)rē-ˌshi(ə)r, män(t)-, -ˈgäm-, -shər\ *or* **Montgomery.** County, E Wales; area 797 sq. m.; pop. (1971p) 42,761; ⊗ Welshpool; hilly region; rivers Dyfi, Severn, Vyrnwy; oats; sheep and cattle raising.

Mon·ti·cel·lo \ˌmänt-ə-ˈsel-(ˌ)ō\. 1 City, ⊗ of Drew co., SE Arkansas; pop. (1970c) 5085; sawmills; truck and fruit farms.

2 Town, ⊗ of Jefferson co., N Florida, 28 m. ENE of Tallahassee; pop. (1970c) 2473; pecans; hogs.

3 City, ⊗ of Jasper co., cen. Georgia, 32 m. N of Macon; pop. (1970c) 2132; peanuts, corn, peaches.

4 City, Piatt co., cen. Illinois, 25 m. NE of Decatur; pop. (1970c) 4130; agriculture.

5 City, ⊗ of White co., NW Indiana, 25 m. NNE of Lafayette on the Tippecanoe river bet. Shafer Lake and Freeman Lake (*qq.v.*); pop. (1970c) 4689; resort.

6 City, Jones co., E Iowa, 30 m. ENE of Cedar Rapids; pop. (1970c) 3509; cattle, hogs.

7 City, ⊗ of Wayne co., S Kentucky, 22 m. SW of Somerset; pop. (1970c) 3618; wheat, tobacco; oil wells.

8 Town, ⊗ of Lawrence co., S Mississippi; pop. (1970c) 1790; clothing, veneer; cotton.

9 Town, ⊗ of Lewis co., NE Missouri; pop. (1970c) 157.

10 Village, ⊗ of Sullivan co., SE New York, 42 m. W of Poughkeepsie; pop. (1970c) 5991; resort.

11 City, ⊗ of San Juan co., SE corner of Utah; pop. (1970c) 1431; uranium mines; founded by Mormons 1887; figured in San Juan river gold rush 1892.

12 Estate and residence of Thomas Jefferson, 3 m. SE of Charlottesville, Virginia.

Mon·ti·chia·ri \ˌmȯnt-ē-ˈkyä-rē\. Commune, Brescia prov., Lombardy, N Italy, SE of Brescia; pop. (1968e) 13,615.

Mon·tiel \mȯn-ˈtyel\. Town, SE Ciudad Real prov., SE cen. Spain; pop. (1970p) 2172; just NW is battlefield where Peter the Cruel was defeated 1369 by Du Guesclin and Henry of Trastamara.

Mon·ti·gnac \ˌmō^n-tē-ˈnyak\. Town, E Dordogne dept., SW cen. France; pop. (1962c) 2809; nearby is Lascaux cave with pictures of prehistoric interest.

Mon·ti·gnies–sur–Sam·bre \ˌmō^n-tē-ˈnyē-sü(ə)r-ˈsä^{n}br^ə\. Commune, Hainaut prov., SW Belgium, just E of Charleroi; pop. (1969e) 24,005; coal-mining center; manufactures ovens, machinery, and ironware.

Mon·ti·gny–en–Go·helle \ˌmō^n-tē-ˈnyē-ä^n-gō-ˈel\. Commune, Pas-de-Calais dept., N France, just E of Lens; pop. (1962c) 8884.

Montigny–lès–Metz \-ˌlā-ˈmets, -ˈmes\. Commune, Moselle dept., NE France, 5 m. SSW of Metz; pop. (1968c) 24,520; residential suburb of Metz.

Mon·ti·jo \mȯn-ˈtē-(ˌ)hō\. 1 Pacific coast port, SW cen. Panama, near the head of the Gulf of Montijo.

2 Town, Badajoz prov., W Spain, ab. 18 m. ENE of Badajoz; pop. (1970p) 12,530; scene of battle May 26, 1644 in which Portuguese under Albuquerque defeated Spanish, who opposed reign of John IV.

Montijo, Gulf of. Inlet of Pacific Ocean on the SW coast of Panama, extending NE into Panama at the W base of Azuero Penin.

Montilium Adhemari. See MONTÉLIMAR.

Mon·ti·lla \mȯn-ˈtē-(y)ə\. Commune, Córdoba prov., S Spain, 22 m. SSE of Córdoba; pop. (1970p) 22,059; agricultural products; wine, esp. amontillado; manufactures woolens, pottery, soap, tile; ducal palace; Arab mosque (now a Christian church).

Mon·ti·vil·liers \ˌmō^n-ˌtē-vēl-ˈyā\. Town, Seine-Maritime dept., N France; pop. (1962c) 8581; formerly noted for manufacture of cloth, esp. "musterdevillers," a woolen used for clothing 13th–16th cents.

Montjoie. See MONSCHAU.

Mont Jo·li \ˌmō^n-zhȯ-ˈlē\. Town, Rimouski co., S Quebec, Canada, 18 m. ENE of Rimouski; pop. (1971p) 6707; dairy products; starting point and terminal of automobile loop highway around Gaspé Penin.

Mont Lau·ri·er \mō^n-ˈlȯr-ē-ˌā\. Town, ⊗ of Labelle co., SW Quebec, Canada, on Lièvre river 77 m. N of Ottawa; pop. (1971p) 8196; terminus of branch of Canadian Pacific Railway from Montreal; Séminaire St. Joseph (1915).

Mont·lu·çon \ˌmō^n-lü-ˈsō^n\. Industrial city, Allier dept., cen. France, on Cher river 38 m. WSW of Moulins; pop. (1968c) 57,871; steel, textiles, chemicals, glass, rubber and leather goods, earthenware; founded 11th cent.; became part of royal domain 1527.

Mont·ma·gny \ˌmō^n-mä-ˈnyē\. 1 County, Quebec, Canada. See table at QUEBEC.

2 Industrial city, its ⊗, on S bank of St. Lawrence river 34 m. ENE of Quebec; pop. (1971p) 12,378; furniture, stoves, canning machinery; sawmills, foundries; incorporated as town 1885.

Mont·mar·tre \mō^n-ˈmärtr^ə\. Section in N part of Paris, France, occupying a hill above the Seine river; highest point 420 ft. Has large cemetery; an old town now within the city limits and noted for its cafés and night life; often figured in early battles and sieges.

Mont·mé·dy \ˌmō^n-mā-ˈdē\. Town, Meuse dept., NE France, near Belgian frontier 25 m. N of Verdun; pop. (1962c) 3093; has citadel and old town, built 1235; became French 1659, fortified by Louis XIV.

Mont·mo·ren·cy \ˌmänt-mə-ˈren(t)-sē\. 1 County in Michigan. See table at MICHIGAN.

2 River, Montmorency co., S Quebec, Canada; ab. 60 m. long; flows S into St. Lawrence river 6 m. below Quebec; rapid current; notable waterfalls (see 3, below).

3 Town, Quebec co., S Quebec, Canada, on N bank of the St. Lawrence at mouth of Montmorency river (see 2, above) 6 m. NE of Quebec, at **Montmorency Falls** (251 ft. in one fall) which furnish light and power for Quebec city; pop. (1971p) 4947.

4 *Fr.* mō^n-mȯ-rä^n-sē\. Commune, Val-d'Oise dept., N France, 9 m. N of Paris; pop. (1968c) 18,691; 16th cent. Gothic church. Formerly seat of Montmorency family; under Condé family (1689 ff.) and until the Revolution called **En·ghien** \ä^n-gä^n\; Rousseau resided in hermitage here 1756–57.

Montmorency No. 1 and No. 2. Counties, Quebec, Canada. See table at QUEBEC.

Mon·to·ne \mȯn-ˈtō-nē\. River, N cen. Italy; 45 m. long; flows NE into Adriatic Sea 6 m. NE of Ravenna.

Mon·to·ro \mȯn-ˈtȯr-ō\. Commune, Córdoba prov., S Spain, on Guadalquivir river 22 m. ENE of Córdoba; pop. (1970p) 11,928; produces olive oil, tropical fruit, timber.

Mon·tour \män-ˈtu̇(ə)r\. County in Pennsylvania. See table at PENNSYLVANIA.

Montour Falls. Village, Schuyler co., SW cen. New York, 16 m. N of Elmira; pop. (1970c) 1534; near head of Seneca Lake; contains Shequaga Falls, 156-ft. waterfall.

Mon·tours·ville \män-ˈtu̇(ə)rz-ˌvil\. Residential borough, Lycoming co., N cen. Pennsylvania, 5 m. E of Williamsport; pop. (1970c) 5985; settled 1807.

Mont·par·nasse \ˌmō^n-pär-ˈnäs, -ˈnas\. Quarter in S cen. Paris, since late 19th century a center of Parisian artistic, student, and bohemian life; many noted cafés. Has Montparnasse Cemetery, laid out 1824.

Mont·pe·lier \mänt-ˈpēl-yər\. 1 City, Bear Lake co., SE Idaho, 70 m. SE of Pocatello; pop. (1970c) 2604; dairy products; phosphate mines.

2 Town, Blackford co., E cen. Indiana, 20 m. E of Marion; pop. (1970c) 2093; gloves; stone quarries.

3 Village, Williams co., NW corner of Ohio, on St. Joseph river 55 m. W of Toledo; pop. (1970c) 4184; stoves, vehicle bodies, canned goods.

4 City, ✱ of Vermont and ⊗ of Washington co., N cen. Vermont, on Winooski river; pop. (1970c) 8609; granite quarries; Vermont Coll. (1834); founded 1780; became ✱ 1805; birthplace of Admiral George Dewey.

Mont·pel·lier \ˌmō^n-pe-ˈlyā\. Industrial and commercial city, ✱ of Hérault dept., S France, near Mediterranean, 77 m. WNW of Marseilles; pop. (1968c) 161,910; wine, fruit and vegetable market; produces textiles, chemicals, electronic components; notable structures include a château, citadel, 14th cent. cathedral, palace of justice, Doric triumphal arch; univ. (1220); oldest botanical garden in

France (dating from 1593). Founded in 8th cent. around Benedictine abbey; Huguenot stronghold, captured 1622 by Louis XIII. Birthplace of the philosopher Comte.

Mont·re·al \ˌmän-trē-'ȯl, ˌmən-\. 1 River, N Wisconsin; ab. 40 m. long; rises in Iron co., flows NW and forms section of Wisconsin-Michigan boundary, empties into Lake Superior.

2 *or Fr.* **Mont·ré·al** \mȯ^{n}-rā-äl\. City, ⊗ of Montreal and Jesus Islands co., on Montreal I., S Quebec, Canada, on the N bank of the St. Lawrence river; pop. (1971p) 1,197,-753, **Greater Montreal** 2,720,413. Named from Mount Royal, the hill in its center. Canada's largest city and chief port of entry; its port is active terminal for both ocean-going and inland shipping; major railroad and transportation center of E Canada; manufactures electrical apparatus, aircraft, railway rolling stock, clothing, chemicals; food processing; financial center; population predominantly Roman Catholic and of French extraction (ab. 65 percent). Contains many churches (esp. St. James Cathedral and Notre Dame), religious institutions, libraries, museums, and many public parks; Coll. de Montréal (1767), McGill Univ. (1821), Sir George Williams Univ. (1873), Univ. de Montréal (1876), Loyola Coll. (1896), Coll. Saint-Denis (1950), Univ. of Quebec (1969).

History: Occupied by Indian town of Hochelaga (*q.v.*) when visited by Jacques Cartier 1535; permanent settlement made by Sieur de Maisonneuve 1642 and given the name **Ville–Ma·rie de Montréal** \ˌvil-mə-ˌrēd-ə-\; its residents constantly embroiled with the Iroquois; the island abandoned by original company 1663 and turned over to Seminary of St. Sulpice; became center of fur trade and starting point for expeditions into the interior; last Canadian city held by the French, surrendering to the British in 1760; occupied briefly by American troops 1775–76; seat of Canadian government 1844–49; site of 1967 World's Fair.

Montreal and Je·sus Islands \-ˌje-zəs-, -zəz-\. County, S Quebec, Canada, formed from two islands on N side of the St. Lawrence river: Montreal I. and Jesus I.; 285 sq. m.; pop. (1969e) 2,412,195; ⊗ Montreal.

Montreal East *or Fr.* **Montréal–Est** \-est\. Town, Montreal I., S Quebec, Canada, on St. Lawrence river 8 m. N of Montreal; pop. (1971p) 5048.

Montreal Island. Island in St. Lawrence river, Quebec, E Canada; site of the city of Montreal and its residential suburbs.

Montreal Lake. Lake, N cen. Saskatchewan, Canada; 137 sq. m.; lower section is in Prince Albert National Park.

Montreal North *or Fr.* **Montréal–Nord** \-nȯr\. Town, Montreal I., S Quebec, Canada, on Rivière des Prairies 8 m. N of Montreal; pop. (1971p) 88,038.

Montreal West *or Fr.* **Montréal–Ouest** \-west\. Residential town, Montreal I., S Quebec, Canada, 6 m. SW of Montreal; pop. (1971p) 6364.

Mon·treuil \mō^{n}-'trə(r)\ *also* **Montreuil–sous–Bois** \-(ˌ)süb-'wä, -'trəi-\. Commune, Seine-St-Denis dept., N France, E suburb of Paris; pop. (1968c) 95,714; 12th cent. church; manufactures chemicals, porcelain, rubber goods, furniture, agricultural machinery.

Mon·treux \mō^{n}-'trə(r)\. Group of villages forming the communes of Le Châtelard and Les Planches in Vaud canton, W Switzerland; pop. (1970c) 20,421; a well-known resort at the E end of Lake of Geneva. Here in June 1936 a conference of European states met to revise the Straits Convention with Turkey.

Mon·trose \män-'trōz, 'män-ˌ\. 1 County in W Colorado. See table at COLORADO.

2 City, its ⊗, 57 m. SE of Grand Junction; pop. (1970c) 6496; trade center for irrigated agricultural region; stock raising; founded 1882.

3 Seaport burgh, Angus co., E Scotland, at mouth of the South Esk; pop. (1971p) 9963; fishing; popular resort; scene of John de Baliol's surrender 1296 to Edward I.

Mon·tross \män-'trȯs, 'män-ˌtrȯs\. Town, ⊗ of Westmoreland co., E Virginia; pop. (1970c) 419.

Mont·rouge \mō^{n}-'rüzh\ *also* **Le Grand–Montrouge** \lə-ˌgrä^{n}-\ *or anc.* **Mons Ru·bi·cus** \mänz-'rü-bi-kəs\. Commune, Hauts-de-Seine dept., N France, S suburb of Paris; pop. (1968c) 44,922; manufactures paper, perfumery, precision instruments; catacombs.

Mont Roy·al \ˌmō^{n}-rwä-'yäl\. 1 Height, Quebec, Canada. See ROYAL, MOUNT.

2 Town, Quebec, Canada. See MOUNT ROYAL.

Monts, Pointe de \ˌpwa^{n}(n)t-də-'mō^{n}\. Headland in Saguenay co., Quebec, Canada, on the St. Lawrence river; 49°19′N, 67°23′W.

Mont–Saint–Amand. See SINT AMANDSBERG.

Mont–Saint–Hi·laire \ˌmō^{n}-sa^{n}-tē-'la(ə)r, -'le(ə)r\. Town, Rouville co., S Quebec, Canada, 18 m. E of Montreal; pop. (1971p) 5966.

Mont–Saint–Jean \ˌmō^{n}-sa^{n}-'zhä^{n}\. Village in Belgium S of the village of Waterloo and N of the battlefield.

Mont–Saint–Mar·tin \ˌmō^{n}-sa^{n}-mär-'ta^{n}\. Town, Meurthe-et-Moselle dept., NE France, on the frontier near meeting point of Belgian-Luxembourg-French boundaries; pop. (1968c) 7140; steelworks.

Mont–Saint–Mi·chel \ˌmō^{n}-sa^{n}-mē-'shel\. Fortified rock in **Mont–Saint–Michel Bay,** off the SW coast of Manche dept., NW France; remarkable ancient abbey and town on the summit of the rock.

Mont·ser·rat \ˌmän(t)-sə-'rat\. 1 Mountain in Barcelona prov., NE Spain; 4054 ft.; jagged ridge, hence name (*Lat.* Mons Serratus); site of monastery dating from 9th cent.

2 Island, West Indies, 27 m. SW of Antigua; 40 sq. m.; pop. (1970c) 12,302; ✱ Plymouth. Entirely volcanic, with three groups of mountains, the highest Soufriére 3000 ft.; mountains forested and intensively cultivated.

History: Discovered by Columbus 1493; colonized by British 1632; held by French 1664–68 and 1782–84; part of Colony of Leeward Islands 1871–1956 and of West Indies Federation 1958–62.

Mont Trem·blant Park \ˌmō^{n}-trä^{n}-'blä^{n}-\. Canadian provincial park in S Quebec, N of Montreal.

Mon·tuo·sa \mȯn-'twō-sə\. Small island in Pacific Ocean, part of Veraguas prov., off SW coast of Panama; 7°28′N, 82°14′W.

Mont·vale \'mänt-ˌvāl\. Borough, Bergen co., NE New Jersey, 10 m. NW of Paterson; pop. (1970c) 7327.

Mont Valérien. See VALÉRIEN, MONT.

Mont·ville \'mänt-ˌvil\. Town, cen. New London co., SE Connecticut, on Thames river; pop. (1970c) 15,662; incorporated 1786.

Mon·u·ment Peak \'män-yə-mənt-\. Mountain, N Adams co., W Idaho; 8956 ft.

Monument Valley. Region in NE Arizona and SE Utah; a sandy plain from which rise monument-like buttes 1000 ft. high, also mesas and arches, all of red sandstone; to the W of the valley is Rainbow Bridge National Monument and to the N Natural Bridges National Monument (see UNITED STATES, *National Monuments).*

Monviso. See VISO, MOUNT.

Mon·ywa \'mōn-yə-ˌwä\. Town, Sagaing div., Burma, on left bank of lower Chindwin river 55 m. W of Mandalay; in World War II a Japanese communications center captured by British Jan. 22, 1945.

Mon·za \'mōn(t)-sə\. Commune, Milano prov., Lombardy, N Italy, 10 m. NE of Milan; pop. (1968e) 105,356; felt hats and carpets, textiles, machinery, glass, plastics, furniture; cathedral (founded 595 by Lombard queen Theodalinda; remodeled in 14th cent.); 13th cent. town hall; palace of old Lombard kings. Ancient capital of Lombardy; scene of assassination of Humbert I of Italy 1900.

Monze, Cape. See MUARI, RAS.

Moo·dy \ˈmüd-ē\. County in South Dakota. See table at SOUTH DAKOTA.

Mooltan. See MULTAN.

Moon. See MUHU.

Moon, Mountains of the. See RUWENZORI, MOUNT.

Moo·nach·ie \mü-ˈnach-ē\. Borough, Bergen co., NE corner of New Jersey, 8 m. SE of Paterson; pop. (1970c) 2951.

Moor. See MÓR.

Moore \ˈmō(ə)r, ˈmȯ(ə)r, ˈmu̇(ə)r\. 1 Name of counties in three states of the U.S. See tables at NORTH CAROLINA, TENNESSEE, TEXAS.

2 City, Cleveland co., cen. Oklahoma; pop. (1970c) 18,761.

Moore, Lake. Dry lake in SW Salt Lake Region, Western Australia, NE of Perth.

Mo·o·réa \ˌmō-ə-ˈrā-ə\ *or* **Ei·meo** \ī-ˈmā-(ˌ)ō\. One of E group (Windward Is.) of the Society Is., French Polynesia, S Pacific Ocean, 12 m. W of Papeete; 53 sq. m.; pop. (1967e) 4370; mountainous, with highest peak 3975 ft.

Moore·field \ˈmō(ə)r-ˌfēld, ˈmȯ(ə)r-, ˈmu̇(ə)r-\. 1 River, E West Virginia; 50 m. long; rises in SE Pendleton co., flows NE into South Branch of Potomac river at Moorefield in Hardy co.

2 Town, ⊗ of Hardy co., NE West Virginia; pop. (1970c) 2124; tannery; livestock farms.

Moore Haven. City, ⊗ of Glades co., S cen. Florida penin.; pop. (1970c) 974.

Moores Creek National Military Park \ˈmō(ə)rz-, ˈmȯ(ə)rz-, ˈmu̇(ə)rz-\. See UNITED STATES, *National Historical Parks.*

Moores·town \ˈmō(ə)rz-ˌtau̇n, ˈmȯ(ə)rz-, ˈmu̇(ə)rz-\. Township, Burlington co., S cen. New Jersey, 9 m. E of Camden; pop. (1970c) 15,577; Hessian headquarters 1776.

Moores·ville \ˈmō(ə)rz-ˌvil, ˈmȯ(ə)rz-, ˈmu̇(ə)rz-\. 1 Town, Morgan co., cen. Indiana, 15 m. SW of Indianapolis; pop. (1970c) 5800; paint; fruit and dairy farms.

2 Town, Iredell co., cen. North Carolina, 13 m. S of Statesville; pop. (1970c) 8808; clothing, flour, furniture.

Moor·foot Hills \ˌmō(ə)r-fu̇t-, ˌmȯ(ə)r-, ˌmu̇(ə)r-\. Range of hills in SE Midlothian co. and along the border of Peebles co., SE Scotland; highest peak **Black·hope Scar** \ˌblak-ˌhōp-\, 2136 ft.

Moor·head \ˈmō(ə)r-ˌhed, ˈmȯ(ə)r-, ˈmu̇(ə)r-\. 1 City, ⊗ of Clay co., W Minnesota, on Red river opposite Fargo, North Dakota; pop. (1970c) 29,687; trade center of region producing potatoes, grain, sugar beets; manufactures glass, sheet metal, dairy products; Moorhead State Coll. (1885), Concordia Coll. (1891); founded 1871, incorporated 1881.

2 Town, Sunflower co., W Mississippi, 19 m. W of Greenwood; pop. (1970c) 2284.

Moos·burg \ˈmōs-ˌbu̇(ə)rg\. Town, Bavaria, West Germany, on Isar river ab. 10 m. WSW of Landshut; pop. (1968e) 11,562; site of large prisoner-of-war camp in World War II, captured Apr. 29, 1945 by American forces and 110,000 prisoners liberated.

Moose \ˈmüs\. River, NE Ontario, Canada; 340 m. long (to head of Mattagami); flows NE into James Bay; a wide stream, actually the estuary of the Abitibi, Mattagami, Missinaibi, and other rivers.

Moose·head Lake \ˈmüs-ˌhed-\. Lake on boundary bet. Piscataquis and Somerset cos., NW cen. Maine; ab. 35 m. long and 10 m. wide; 117 sq. m.; max. depth 246 ft.; elevation ab. 1000 ft.; resort for fishermen and sportsmen.

Moose Jaw \ˈmüs-(ˌ)jȯ\. City, S Saskatchewan, Canada, 43 m. W of Regina; pop. (1971p) 31,284; stockyards, grain elevators, flour mills, slaughterhouses; Aldersgate Coll. (1940); founded 1882.

Moose Lake. Lake, W Manitoba, Canada; 525 sq. m.; has several outlets to Saskatchewan river and Cedar Lake.

Moose·look·me·gun·tic Lake \ˌmü-slu̇k-mi-ˈgənt-ik-\. See RANGELEY LAKES.

Moose Mountain. Peak in Adirondack Mts., Essex co., NE New York; 3921 ft.

Moose Mountain Park. Provincial park, SE Saskatchewan, Canada, SE of Regina; 154 sq. m.; fine scenery and fishing, with many lakes.

Moose Peak. Mountain in W Flathead co., NW Montana; 7521 ft.

Moo·sic \ˈmü-sik\. Borough, Lackawanna co., NE Pennsylvania, 5 m. SW of Scranton; pop. (1970c) 4273.

Moo·si·lauke, Mount \-ˈmü-sə-ˌlȯk\. Peak, cen. Grafton co., W New Hampshire; 4810 ft.

Moo·sup \ˈmüs-əp\. Subdivision of town of Plainfield, Connecticut; pop. (1970c) 3376; manufacturing. See PLAINFIELD 1.

Mop·su·es·tia \ˌmäp-su̇-ˈes-ch(ē-)ə\ *or mod.* **Mi·sis** \mi-ˈsēs\. Ancient city in Cilicia, Asia Minor, on the Pyramus (Ceyhan) river, now a village in Seyhan prov., S Turkey. Birthplace of Theodore of Mopsuestia.

Mop·ti \ˈmȯp-tē\. Town on Niger river, Mali, W cen. Africa, on E edge of Niger depression area ab. 275 m. NE of Bamako; pop. (1970e) 158,935.

Mo·que·gua \mō-ˈkeg-wə\. 1 Department of S Peru. See table at PERU.

2 Town, its ✱, ab. 530 m. SE of Lima; pop. (1961c) 7795; grapes, olives; founded 1626; destroyed by earthquake 1868.

Mór \ˈmō(ə)r\ *or Ger.* **Moor** \ˈmō(ə)r\. Commune, Fejér co., W Hungary, 43 m. W of Budapest; pop. (1970p) 12,136.

Mo·ra \ˈmōr-ə, ˈmȯr-\. 1 County in New Mexico. See table at NEW MEXICO.

2 Village, ⊗ of Kanabec co., E Minnesota, 47 m. ENE of St. Cloud; pop. (1970c) 2582.

3 Village, ⊗ of Mora co., NE New Mexico, 40 m. NE of Sante Fe.

4 Commune, Toledo prov., cen. Spain, 18 m. SE of Toledo; pop. (1960c) 10,657; olive oil, wine.

Mora Bay. Bay in SW coast of Oriente prov., E Cuba.

Mo·ra·ča \ˈmōr-ə-ˌchä, ˈmȯr-\. Small river in S Yugoslavia, flowing S into Lake Scutari.

Mo·rad·a·bad \mə-ˈräd-ə-ˌbäd, -ˈrad-ə-ˌbad\. City, Uttar Pradesh, N India, 90 m. ENE of Delhi; pop. (1970e) 208,556; metalware, cotton textiles; 17th cent. fort and mosque; founded 1625 by Rustum Khan.

Mo·raine \mə-ˈrān\. City, Montgomery co., SW Ohio, 5 m. S of Dayton; pop. (1970c) 4898.

Mo·ra·le·da Channel \ˌmōr-ə-ˌled-ə-, ˌmȯr-\. Passage bet. Chonos Archipelago off SW coast of Chile and the Chilean mainland.

Mo·ra·man·ga \ˌmōr-ə-ˈmäŋ-gə, ˌmȯr-\. Town, E cen. Malagasy Republic; railroad junction 45 m. E of Tananarive.

Mo·ran, Mount \-mə-ˈran\. Peak in N Grand Teton National Park, NW Wyoming; 12,694 ft.

Mo·rant Bay \mə-ˈrant-\. Town and bay, SE coast of island of Jamaica, West Indies; pop. (1960c) 5054.

Morant Cays. Three small guano islands 33 m. SE of Morant Bay, off SE coast of Jamaica; a dependency of Jamaica since 1882.

Morant Point. Cape at E end of Jamaica, West Indies.

Mor·ar, Loch \läk-ˈmȯr-ər, läk̲-\. Lake in W Inverness co., on coast of W cen. Scotland, 1½ m. S of Lake Nevis; max. depth 1017 ft.; deepest lake in Scotland.

Mo·rat \mȯ-ˈrä\ *or Ger.* **Mur·ten** \ˈmu̇(ə)rt-ᵊn\. Commune, Fribourg canton, Switzerland, on E shore of Lake of Morat; pop. (1970c) 4256; scene of Swiss victory over Charles the Bold of Burgundy June 22, 1476.

Morat, Lake of *or Ger.* **Mur·ten·see** \ˈmu̇(ə)rt-ᵊn-ˌzā\. Lake, Switzerland, 2 m. SE of the Lake of Neuchâtel; ab. 9 sq. m.

Morata. See GOODENOUGH.

Mo·ra·ta·lla \ˌmōr-ə-ˈtī-ə, -ˈtä-yə\. Commune, Murcia prov., SE Spain, 39 m. WNW of Murcia; pop. (1970p) 10,549; manufactures brandy, soap, flour, textiles.

Mo·ra·tu·wa \mə-ˈrət-ə-wə\. Town, W Ceylon, on Indian Ocean 12 m. S of Colombo; pop. (1968e) 86,000.

Mo·ra·va \ˈmȯr-ə-və\. 1 *or Ger.* **March** \ˈmärk\. River, Slovak S.R., Czechoslovakia; 218 m. long; flows SW and S, forming a section of the boundary bet. Slovak S.R. and Lower Austria; empties into Danube river 8 m. W of Bratislava; navigable for 78 m.
2 Former province, Czechoslovakia. See MORAVIA.
3 *or anc.* **Mar·gus** \ˈmär-gəs\. River in E Yugoslavia, formed by confluence of **Southern Morava** and **Western Morava** at a point 33 m. NW of Niš; flows NNW into Danube river near Smederevo; 100 m. long from point of confluence to the Danube; the Western Morava receives the Ibar from the S.

Mo·ra·via \mə-ˈrā-vē-ə\ *or Czech* **Mo·ra·va** \ˈmȯr-ə-və\ *or Ger.* **Mäh·ren** \ˈmā-rən, ˈme(ə)r-ən\. Region, Czech S.R., cen. Czechoslovakia.
History: Settled by a Slavic people, Moravians, from end of 6th cent. A.D.; became tributary to empire of Charlemagne (d. 843); introduced to Christianity by Cyril and Methodius; under Svatopluk, Great Moravia (including Bohemia and other territories in cen. Europe) revolted against German emperor and became independent kingdom 870; defeated by Magyars who settled in Tisza valley 893; conquered by Magyars (see HUNGARY) 906; in 10th cent., made part of Bohemian, and briefly, of Polish kingdoms; in 1029 reconquered by Bohemia (*q.v.*); in 1849 became a separate crownland of Austria, with capital at Brno, and in 1918 organized as a province of Czechoslovakia; united with Silesia 1927 forming province of **Moravia and Silesia** \-sī-ˈlē-zh(ē-)ə, sə-, -sh(ē-)ə\; all of Silesia and some areas in N and S Moravia became parts of German Sudetenland 1938, remainder of Moravia joined with Bohemia as German protectorate (1939–45) of Bohemia-Moravia (*q.v.*); restored to Czechoslovakia 1945.

Mo·ra·vi·an Gap *or* **Moravian Gate** \mə-ˈrā-vē-ən-\. Mountain pass and ancient trade (amber) route in cen. Europe along upper courses of Oder and Vistula rivers bet. SE Sudetic and W Carpathian Mts. where former German Silesia, Poland, and Czechoslovakia meet. In modern history a strategic communications line bet. N and S.

Mo·rav·ska \ˈmȯr-äv-ˌskä\. Former county (1929–45), E Yugoslavia; 10,120 sq. m.; ⊗ Niš; since 1945 part of the federated republic of Serbia.

Moravská Ostrava. See OSTRAVA.

Mor·a·whan·na \ˌmȯr-ə-ˈ(h)wan-ə, ˌmär-\. Town and small port, extreme N Guyana, 150 m. NW of Georgetown, on the Barima river near Venezuela border; gold discovered in the vicinity c. 1889.

Mor·ay \ˈmər-ē, ˈmə-rē\ *or* **El·gin** \ˈel-gən\ *or* **El·gin·shire** \-ˌshi(ə)r, -shər\. County, NE Scotland; 476 sq. m.; pop. (1971p) 51,485; ⊗ Elgin; rivers Lossie, Spey, Findhorn; barley, oats, wheat, potatoes; livestock grazing, fishing, whisky distilling, lumbering.

Moray Firth. Deep inlet of the North Sea on NE coast of Scotland; extends inland 39 m.; the city of Inverness is near its head.

Mo·ra·zán \ˌmȯr-ə-ˈzän, -ˈsän\. Department of NE El Salvador. See table at EL SALVADOR.

Mor·bi·han \ˌmȯr-bē-ˈäⁿ\. Department of NW France. See table at FRANCE.

Mor·den \ˈmȯrd-ᵊn\. Town, Manitoba, Canada, 70 m. SW of Winnipeg; pop. (1971p) 3276; dairy products, pumps; diversified agriculture; grain elevators.

Mor·di·al·loc \ˌmȯr-dē-ˈal-ək\. Urban center, S Victoria, SE Australia, SE suburb of Melbourne on E shore of Port Phillip Bay; pop. (1966c) 28,076.

Mor·do·vi·an Autonomous Soviet Socialist Republic \mȯr-ˌdō-vē-ən-\. Autonomous republic, cen. Russian S.F.S.R., U.S.S.R.; 10,116 sq. m.; pop. (1970p) 1,030,000; ✱ Saransk. Crossed by the Moksha river; in central plateau borders on the black earth region, S and W of the Middle Volga; produces rye, wheat, millet, oats, corn, tobacco, potatoes; livestock; beekeeping; republic crossed by Moscow-Kuibyshev R.R. Principal cities: Saransk, Ruzayevka. Predominant ethnic strain Finno-Ugrian; chief nationalities Mordovian, or Mordvinian, and Russian. Formed as an autonomous oblast 1930; made an A.S.S.R. 1934.

More, Ben. See BEN MORE.

Morea. See PELOPONNESUS 1.

Mo·reau \ˈmōr-(ˌ)ō, ˈmȯr-\. River, NW South Dakota; 250 m. long; formed by confluence of north and south forks in SW Perkins co., flows E into Missouri river on E boundary of Dewey co.

More·cambe and Hey·sham \ˌmōr-kəm . . . ˈhā-shəm, ˌmȯr-\. Municipal borough, Lancashire, NW England, on Morecambe Bay 46 m. N of Liverpool; pop. (1971p) 41,863; seaside resort; oil refining.

Morecambe Bay. Inlet of Irish Sea on NW coast of England; extends inland 18 m. in N Lancashire.

Mo·ree \mō-ˈrē\. Municipality, NE New South Wales, SE Australia, on Gwydir river 315 m. N of Sydney; pop. (1965e) 7560; center of grazing and agricultural district.

More·head \ˈmō(ə)r-ˌhed, ˈmȯ(ə)r-\. City, ⊗ of Rowan co., NE Kentucky, 37 m. SSE of Maysville; pop. (1970c) 7191; agriculture; Morehead State Univ. (1922).

Morehead City. Town and ocean port, Carteret co., SE North Carolina, on Atlantic Ocean 33 m. SE of New Bern; pop. (1970c) 5233; boatbuilding; resort and fishing center; has 1000-ft. pier, the Ocean Shipping Port Terminal (erected 1935–37).

More·house \ˈmō(ə)r-ˌhau̇s, ˈmȯ(ə)r-\. Parish in Louisiana. See table at LOUISIANA.

More·land Hills \ˌmō(ə)r-lənd-, ˌmȯ(ə)r-\. Village, Cuyahoga co., N Ohio, 15 m. ESE of Cleveland; pop. (1970c) 3000.

Mo·re·lia \mə-ˈrāl-yə\. City, ✱ of Michoacán state, SW Mexico; munic. pop. (1970p) 209,507; center of agricultural region; lumber; handicraft industries; 17th cent. Baroque cathedral, 18th cent. aqueduct, univ. (1917). Founded 1541 as Valladolid; made capital 1581; renamed 1828 after revolutionary leader J. M. Morelos y Pavón.

Mo·re·los \mə-ˈrā-ləs\. State of S cen. Mexico. See table at MEXICO.

Morena, Sierra. See SIERRA MORENA.

Mo·re·na Dam \mə-ˈrē-nə-\. Dam across Cottonwood Creek, S San Diego co., SW California; height 279 ft.; completed 1932; impounds water for water supply.

Mo·re·no \mə-ˈren-(ˌ)ō\. Town, Buenos Aires prov., E Argentina, part of Greater Buenos Aires.

Moreno Bay. Inlet of Pacific Ocean in W Antofagasta prov., N Chile; location of the city of Antofagasta.

Moreno Glacier. Glacier in extreme S part of Andes, Santa Cruz prov., S Argentina; 31 m. long, ab. 2 m. wide near its terminus.

Mø·re og Roms·dal \ˌmər-ō-ˈrōmz-(ˌ)däl\. County of W Norway. See table at NORWAY.

Mores·by Island \ˌmō(ə)rz-bē-, ˌmȯ(ə)rz-\. Central island of the Queen Charlotte Is. off W British Columbia, Canada; 991 sq. m.

Mo·res·net \ˌmō-ˌrez-ˈnā\. Former neutral territory bet. Belgium and Germany, near Aachen, since 1919 part of Liège prov., Belgium; 11 sq. m.; comprises the communes of Moresnet, pop. (1969c) 1291, Neu-Moresnet, pop. 1024, and La Calamine, pop. 5566.

More·ton Bay \ˌmōrt-ᵊn-, ˌmȯrt-\. Bay, inlet of Pacific Ocean on SE coast of Queensland, Australia, at mouth of Brisbane river, enclosed on NE by **Moreton Island.**

Mo·rez \mȯ-ˈez\. Town, SE Jura dept., E France; pop. (1962c) 6101; manufactures clocks and spectacles; tourist resort, winter sports.

Mor·gan \'mȯr-gən\. 1 Name of counties in eleven states of the U.S. See tables at ALABAMA, COLORADO, GEORGIA, ILLINOIS, INDIANA, KENTUCKY, MISSOURI, OHIO, TENNESSEE, UTAH, WEST VIRGINIA.

2 City, ⊗ of Calhoun co., SW Georgia; pop. (1970c) 280.

Morgan, Mount. 1 Peak in Glacier National Park, NW Montana; 8710 ft.

2 Peak in Australian Capital Territory, Australia; 6144 ft.

Morgan City. 1 City, St. Mary parish, S Louisiana, 53 m. S of Baton Rouge; pop. (1970c) 16,586; oil and gas wells; fishing, shipbuilding; truck farms.

2 City, ⊗ of Morgan co., N Utah; pop. (1970c) 1586.

Mor·gan·field \'mȯr-gən-ˌfēld\. City, ⊗ of Union co., W Kentucky, 22 m. WSW of Henderson; pop. (1970c) 3563; coal mines; agriculture.

Morgan Hill. City, Santa Clara co., W California, 17 m. SE of San Jose; pop. (1970c) 6485; canneries, feed mills; diversified agriculture.

Mor·gan·ton \'mȯr-gən-tən\. Town, ⊗ of Burke co., W North Carolina, 15 m. SSW of Lenoir; pop. (1970c) 13,625; clothing, furniture, lumber; Western Piedmont Community Coll. (1964).

Mor·gan·town \'mȯr-gən-ˌtau̇n\. 1 City, ⊗ of Butler co., W cen. Kentucky; pop. (1970c) 1394.

2 City, ⊗ of Monongalia co., N West Virginia, on Monongahela river 15 m. NE of Fairmont; pop. (1970c) 29,341; river port, shipping coal and limestone; glass products, textiles, building materials, chemicals; coal mines, limestone quarries, sand pits; West Virginia Univ. (1867); settled 1767; chartered as town 1785, as city 1905.

Mor·gar·ten \'mō(ə)r-ˌgärt-ᵊn, 'mȯ(ə)r-\. Mountain slope in Zug canton, N cen. Switzerland, on the border of Schwyz canton, just SE of Lake of Aegeri; battle Nov. 15, 1315 in which Swiss defeated greatly superior forces of Hapsburg Duke Leopold I.

Morges \'mȯ(ə)rzh\. Commune, Vaud canton, W Switzerland, on Lake of Geneva; pop. (1970p) 11,931; view of Mont Blanc; birthplace of Fernán Caballero, Spanish novelist.

Mo·ri·ah \mə-'rī-ə\. 1 Region and hill in S part of ancient Palestine on which Abraham prepared to sacrifice Isaac (*Gen.* xxii. 2); its location is unidentified.

2 Hill in E part of Jerusalem, on which Solomon built the Temple (*2 Chron.* iii. 1).

Moriah, Mount. Peak, SE Coos co., N New Hampshire, in E White Mts. N of Carter Dome; 3750 ft.

Mo·ri·gu·chi \ˌmȯr-ə-'gü-chē\. Town, Ōsaka prefecture, Honshū, Japan; suburb of Ōsaka; pop. (1970c) 184,466; textiles.

Mo·ring·en \'mōr-iŋ-ən, 'mȯr-\. Town, SE Lower Saxony, West Germany, 12 m. N of Göttingen; pop. (1969e) 4800; Nazi concentration camp 1939.

Mo·ri·o·ka \ˌmōr-ē-'ō-kə, ˌmȯr-\. City, ✱ of Iwate prefecture, N Honshū, Japan, on the Kitakami river; pop. (1970c) 196,036; commercial and cultural center; iron kettles; Iwate Univ. (1949), Iwate Medical Univ. (1952).

Morlacca. See VELEBITSKI KANAL.

Mor·laix \mȯ(ə)r-'lā\. Commercial seaport, Finistère dept., NW France, on English Channel 42 m. NNE of Quimper; pop. (1968c) 19,919.

Mor·ley \'mȯr-lē\. Municipal borough, West Riding, Yorkshire, N England, 5 m. SW of Leeds; pop. (1971p) 44,340; woolen textiles, glass; tanneries, stone quarries, coal mines.

Mor·mal Forest \mȯr-ˌmal-\. Wooded region, Nord dept., N France, SE of Valenciennes.

Mor·mon Flat Dam \'mȯr-mən-\. Dam completed 1925 across Salt river below Horse Mesa Dam, E Maricopa co., S cen. Arizona; height 224 ft.; impounds water for power, forming **Canyon Lake** 10 m. long.

Mormon Lake. Lake, SE Coconino co., N cen. Arizona; 12 sq. m.; did not exist before 1900; formed when underground drainage channels became filled with sediment.

Mormon Mountain. Peak, NE Valley co., W cen. Idaho; 9545 ft.

Mor·ning·ton Island \ˌmȯr-niŋ-tən-\. Island in Pacific Ocean off SW coast of Chile, W of S Wellington I.

Mo·ro \'mōr-(ˌ)ō, 'mȯr-\. City, ⊗ of Sherman co., N Oregon; pop. (1970c) 290; stock and grain farms.

Mo·ro·be \mə-'rō-bē\. 1 Administrative district, Papua New Guinea, on island of New Guinea; 12,700 sq. m.; pop. (1969e) 235,886; ✱ Lae. In the interior, in the Bulolo Valley near the town of Wau, is the Morobe goldfield where in 1921 very rich gold deposits were discovered; region bet. Bulolo and the coast towns of Salamaua and Lae exceptionally mountainous and difficult so that practically all transport to and from mines is by air (ab. 46 m.) bet. Lae and Wau.

2 Seaport town in the district, on SE coast of Huon Gulf 95 m. SSE of Lae; has good harbor.

Mo·roc·co \mə-'räk-(ˌ)ō\. 1 *or Arab.* **Al–Mam·la·kah al–Ma·ghri·bī·yah** \al-məm-'läk-ə-al-mə-'grib-ē-(y)ə\ *or Fr.* **Ma·roc** \må-rȯk\ *or Span.* **Mar·rue·cos** \ˌmär-ů-'ā-(ˌ)kōs\. Kingdom, NW Africa, bounded on N by the Mediterranean Sea, on E and S by Algeria, on SW by Spanish Sahara, and on W by the Atlantic Ocean; 172,413 sq. m.; pop. (1970e) 15,530,000; ✱ Rabat. *Physical features:* Characterized by the great mountain range of Grand Atlas and its smaller subsidiary ranges (see ATLAS MOUNTAINS) stretching from SW to NE, the mountainous Er Rif belt along the Mediterranean, the wide fertile plain along the Atlantic, and the plain, partly desert, in the SE beyond the Atlas range; highest point Toubkal 13,671 ft. Rivers of the Atlantic plain are numerous but short; chief are the Moulouya in N and the Tensift; many short streams on SE slopes of the Atlas are lost in the Sahara. *Chief products:* Wheat, corn, barley, citrus fruit, grapes, olives; livestock raising, fishing; phosphates, iron ore, lead; manufacturing: cement, paper, textiles; tourism. *Chief cities:* Casablanca, Rabat, Marrakech, Fès, Tangier, Oujda, Tétouan.

History: Roman province of Mauretania (*q.v.*) underwent Muslim invasion 7th cent. A.D.; in 11th cent., founded independent kingdom under Almoravides, a Berber dynasty which conquered Spain and Portugal but was overthrown in 1147 by the Almohades; Ceuta taken by Portuguese 1415; Morocco invaded by Portuguese who were completely defeated 1578 (see ALCAZARQUIVIR); Tangier held by England 1662–84; Mazagan, last Portuguese stronghold, abandoned 1769; as one of Barbary States (see BARBARY), engaged in piracy until early 19th cent.; engaged in hostilities with French 1844 over Algerian boundary; in war against Spain 1859–73; control of Morocco became issue of European politics after Convention of Madrid (1880); with growth of internal disorder, independence question led to agreements bet. France and England (*Entente Cordiale* 1904) and bet. France and Spain, the latter reserving the northern Mediterranean coast for itself; French rights in Morocco asserted in 1st and 2d Moroccan crises 1905 and 1911 (see TANGIER, ALGECIRAS, AGADIR); in 1912 **French Morocco** (a protectorate including most of Morocco; ab. 153,870 sq. m.; ✱ Rabat) and **Spanish Morocco** (a protectorate on the N coast; ab. 18,000 sq. m.; ✱ Tétouan) were established; Tangier internationalized 1923; in Spanish zone occurred war of Abd-al-Krim 1921–26; Ifni under effective Spanish occupation 1934–69; Melilla scene of revolt of army chiefs which lead to Spanish Civil War 1936; signed accords with both France and Spain 1956 by which it received independence; joined Arab League 1958; military clash with Algeria 1963.

2 City, one of traditional capitals of Morocco. See MARRAKECH.

Mo·ro·co·ca·la \ˌmōr-ə-kō-'käl-ə, ˌmȯr-\. Peak, W Bolivia, E of N end of Lake Poopó; 17,054 ft.

Mo·ro·go·ro \ˌmō-rō-'gō-rō\. 1 Administrative region of SE Tanzania. See table at TANZANIA.

2 Town, its ✱, 105 m. W of Dar es Salaam; pop. (1967c) 25,202; ships sisal, tobacco, kapok, sugar; mica mines.

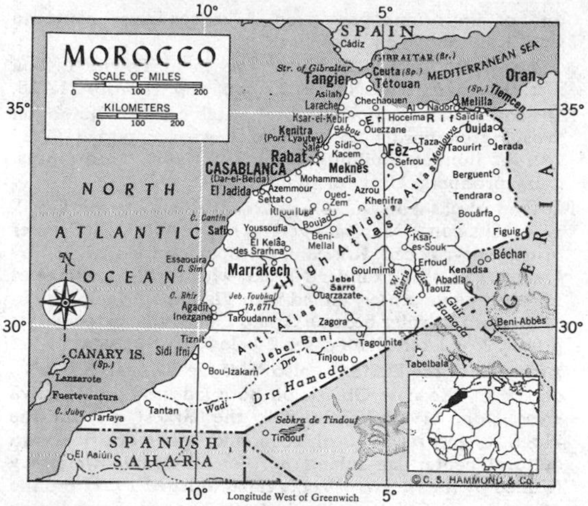

Mo·ro Gulf \ˌmōr-(ˌ)ō-, ˌmȯr-\. Large inlet in N part of Celebes Sea, SW of Mindanao, Phil.

Mo·ro·land \ˈmōr-ō-ˌland, ˈmȯr-\. Popular name sometimes given to islands in S of Phil. where the Moros live, esp. Mindanao and the Sulu Archipelago.

Mo·ro·le·ón \ˌmōr-ə-lā-ˈōn, ˌmȯr-\. Town, Guanajuato state, cen. Mexico, 60 m. S of Guanajuato; munic. pop. (1970p) 33,765.

Mo·rón \mə-ˈrōn\. 1 *or* **Seis de Sep·tiem·bre** \ˌsāz-də-se-ˈtyem-(ˌ)brā\. City, Buenos Aires prov., E Argentina, 10 m. SW of Buenos Aires; pop. (1960c) 341,920; part of Greater Buenos Aires.

2 Town, W Camagüey prov., E cen. Cuba, on railroad 68 m. NW of Camagüey; pop. (1967e) 26,600.

3 *or in full* **Morón de la Fron·te·ra** \-ˌdel-ə-ˌfrən-ˈter-ə\. Commune, Sevilla prov., SW Spain, 35 m. SE of Seville; pop. (1970p) 29,488; olive oil; red-hematite mines; marble quarries; Gothic church.

Mo·ro·na \mə-ˈrō-nə\. River, Ecuador and Peru; rises in E Ecuador where it is called the **Ma·kum·ma** \mə-ˈkü-mə\, flows S across border into Peru; ab. 260 m. long; empties into Marañón river, headstream of the Amazon.

Morona–San·ti·a·go \-ˌsant-ē-ˈäg-(ˌ)ō, -ˌsänt-\. Province of SE Ecuador. See table at ECUADOR.

Mo·ron·da·va \ˌmōr-ən-ˈdäv-ə, ˌmȯr-\. Coastal town, W Malagasy Republic.

Morón de la Frontera. See MORÓN 3.

Mo·rong \ˈmō-ˌrōŋ\. 1 Former Spanish military district, cen. Luzon, Phil.; became part of Rizal prov. 1901.

2 Municipality on W coast of Bataan prov., Luzon, Phil., 20 m. W of Balanga on SE side of entrance to Subic Bay; pop. (1969e) 7900; scene of heavy fighting in World War II during Bataan campaign.

3 Municipality, Rizal prov., Luzon, Phil., near coast of Laguna de Bay 11 m. ESE of Pasig; pop. (1969e) 18,500.

Mo·ro·ni \mō-ˈrōn-ē\. Town, ✱ of Comoro Is., on Great Comoro I.; pop. (1970e) 14,000.

Mo·ron·vil·liers \mō-ˌrōⁿ-vē-ˈlyā\. Heights ab. 13 m. E of Reims, France; held by Germans through World War I; scene of several battles 1917; taken by Allies Oct. 1918.

Mo·ro·tai \ˌmōr-ə-ˈtī, ˌmȯr-\. Island, Indonesia, in the N Moluccas N of Halmahera; ab. 50 m. long by 26 m. wide; 695 sq. m.; highest point 4101 ft. Seized by Japanese Jan. 1942 but retaken by Gen. MacArthur's force Sept. 14, 1944.

Mo·ro·vis \mə-ˈrō-vəs\. Town and municipality, N cen. Puerto Rico; pop. (1970p) 2905 (town), 19,219 (munic.); town ab. 23 m. SW of San Juan.

Mor·peth \ˈmȯr-pəth\. Municipal borough, Northumberland, N England, on the Wansbeck 12 m. N of Newcastle upon Tyne; pop. (1971p) 14,055; tanning, iron and brass founding; truck farms.

Mor·phou Bay \ˈmȯr-(ˌ)fü-\. Inlet of Mediterranean on NW coast of Cyprus; Cape Kormakítis marks its N limit.

Mor·rill \ˈmär-əl, ˈmȯr-\. County in Nebraska. See table at NEBRASKA.

Mor·ril·ton \ˈmȯr-əl-tən, ˈmär-\. City, ⊗ of Conway co., cen. Arkansas, near Arkansas river 40 m. NW of Little Rock; pop. (1970c) 6814.

Mor·ris \ˈmȯr-əs, ˈmär-\. 1 Name of counties in three states of the U.S. See tables at KANSAS, NEW JERSEY, TEXAS.

2 City, ⊗ of Grundy co., NE Illinois, 20 m. SW of Joliet; pop. (1960c) 8194; limestone quarries; dairy farms.

3 City, ⊗ of Stevens co., W Minnesota, 33 m. SW of Alexandria; pop. (1970c) 5366; butter; soybeans.

Morris, Mount. Mountain, Antarctica, 78°19′S, 86°10′W; 12,500 ft.

Mor·ris·burg \ˈmȯr-əs-ˌbərg, ˈmär-\. Village, Dundas co., SE Ontario, Canada, on St. Lawrence river 22 m. WSW of Cornwall; pop. (1971p) 2069.

Morris Dam *and* **Morris Reservoir.** See UNITED STATES, *Dams and Reservoirs.*

Morris Island. Island at S entrance to the harbor of Charleston, South Carolina.

Morris Jes·up, Cape \-ˈjes-əp\. Most northerly point of mainland of Greenland, in Peary Land on Arctic Ocean, 83°38′N, 33°52′W.

Mor·ri·son \ˈmȯr-ə-sən, ˈmär-\. 1 County in Minnesota. See table at MINNESOTA.

2 City, ⊗ of Whiteside co., NW Illinois, 40 m. NE of Rock Island; pop. (1970c) 4387; furniture; stock farms.

Morrison, Mount. See HSIN-KAO.

Morrison Cave. See LEWIS AND CLARK CAVERN.

Morris Plains. Borough, Morris co., N New Jersey, 2 m. N of Morristown; pop. (1970c) 5540.

Morris Shep·pard Dam \-ˈshep-ərd-\ *or formerly* **Pos·sum King·dom Dam** \ˌpäs-əm-ˈkiŋ-dəm-\. Dam across Brazos river, Palo Pinto co., N cen. Texas; height 190 ft.; completed 1941; impounds water for flood control and power.

Mor·ris·town \ˈmȯr-ə-ˌstau̇n, ˈmär-\. 1 Town, ⊗ of Morris co., N New Jersey, 17 m. WNW of Newark; pop. (1970c) 17,662; residential; clothing; stone quarries; Villa Walsh Coll. (1928); Morristown National Historical Park (estab. 1933). Settled 1709–10; incorporated 1865; Washington's headquarters 1776–77, 1779–80; scene of electric telegraph experiments of Morse and Vail c. 1837.

2 City, ⊗ of Hamblen co., NE Tennessee, 42 m. ENE of Knoxville; pop. (1970c) 20,318; furniture, canned goods, textiles, hosiery; diversified agriculture; Morristown Coll. (1881).

3 Town, Lamoille co., N Vermont; pop. (1970c) 4052.

Morristown National Historical Park. See UNITED STATES, *National Historical Parks.*

Mor·ris·ville \ˈmȯr-əs-ˌvil, ˈmär-\. 1 Borough, Bucks co., SE Pennsylvania, on Delaware river across from Trenton, New Jersey; pop. (1970c) 11,309.

2 Village, Lamoille co., N Vermont, on Lamoille river 20 m. N of Montpelier; pop. (1970c) 2116; veneers, dairy products.

Mor·ro \ˈmär-(ˌ)ō, ˈmȯr-\. River, Sierra Leone, W Africa, tributary of the Mano.

Morro, Point. Cape extending into Pacific Ocean on W cen. coast of Atacama prov., N cen. Chile, S of Inglesa Bay.

Morro Bay. 1 Inlet of the Pacific, San Luis Obispo co., California, NW of San Luis Obispo; only landlocked harbor between San Francisco and Los Angeles.

2 City, San Luis Obispo co., SW California, on Pacific Ocean 80 m. NW of Santa Barbara; pop. (1970c) 7109; beach resort; dairy and truck farming.

Morro Castle. 1 Ancient fortification on E side of entrance to Havana harbor, Cuba; erected 1589–97; taken by English 1762, bombarded by Americans 1898.
2 Fort forming part of defenses of Santiago de Cuba, SE Cuba, on E side of entrance to harbor.

Mo·rros·qui·llo, Gulf of \\-ˌmär-ə-ˈskē-(ˌ)(y)ō, -ˌmȯr-\\. Inlet of Caribbean Sea on NW coast of Colombia, NE of the Gulf of Urabá.

Mor·row \\ˈmär-ō, ˈmȯr-\\. 1 Name of counties in two states in the U.S. See tables at OHIO and OREGON.
2 City, Clayton co., NW cen. Georgia, 14 m. S of Atlanta; pop. (1970c) 3708.

Morrow Point Dam. See UNITED STATES, *Dams and Reservoirs.*

Mörs *or* **Moers** \\ˈmərs\\. Industrial city, North Rhine-Westphalia, West Germany, WNW of Duisburg; pop. (1969e) 44,693; market town; machinery, blankets, cement; chartered 1300; to Prussia 1702.

Mor·shansk \\mər-ˈshansk\\. Town, N Tambov Oblast, Russian S.F.S.R., U.S.S.R., 55 m. N of Tambov; pop. (1967e) 43,000; industrial town on main railroad line from Tula E to Penza and Kuibyshev; railroad shops, flour mills.

Mors Island \\ˈmȯrs-\\. Island of Denmark, in Lim Fjord in Thisted co., NW Jutland; 142 sq. m.; pop. (1965c) 25,739; chief town Nykøbing.

Mor·tagne \\mȯr-ˈtänʸ\\ *or* **Mortagne–au–Per·chey** \\-ō-per-ˈshā\\. Town, Orne dept., NW France, NE of Alençon; pop. (1962c) 4468; was capital of the Perche (*q.v.*); has church of Notre Dame (built 15th–16th cent.).

Mor·tain \\mȯr-ˈtaⁿ\\. Town, S Manche dept., NW France, E of Avranches; pop. (1962c) 2376; 13th cent. Gothic church. Scene of American breakthrough Aug. 3, 1944 and of German counterattacks Aug. 7–11.

Mor·ta·ra \\mor-ˈtär-ə\\. Commune, Pavia prov., Lombardy, N Italy, 22 m. WNW of Pavia; pop. (1968e) 15,230; 14th cent. Lombard-Gothic church; 11th cent. convent; scene of Austrian victory over Piedmontese 1849.

Mor·te·ratsch, Piz \\pēt-ˈsmȯrt-ə-ˌräch\\. Peak in the S part of the Rhaetian Alps N of Piz Bernina, Switzerland; 12,401 ft.; famous glacier.

Mort Homme, Le. See LE MORT HOMME.

Mor·ti·mer's Cross \\ˌmȯrt-ə-mərz-\\. Village, Herefordshire, W England, ab. 5 m. W of Leominster on the Lugg; scene of battle Feb. 2, 1461 in which Edward IV defeated the Lancastrians.

Mor·ton \\ˈmȯrt-ᵊn\\. 1 Name of counties in two states in the U.S. See tables at KANSAS and NORTH DAKOTA.
2 Village, Tazewell co., cen. Illinois, 10 m. SE of Peoria; pop. (1970c) 10,419; tractors, washing machines.
3 Town, Scott co., cen. Mississippi, 32 m. E of Jackson; pop. (1970c) 2672; lumbering; agriculture.
4 Borough, Delaware co., SE Pennsylvania, 9 m. W of Philadelphia; pop. (1970c) 2602.
5 Town, ⊗ of Cochran co., NW Texas; pop. (1970c) 2738; oil wells; cotton, sorghum.

Morton Grove. Village, Cook co., NE Illinois, 15 m. N of Chicago; pop. (1970c) 26,369.

Mort·sel \\mȯr-ˈsel\\. Commune, Antwerp prov., N Belgium; pop. (1969e) 28,169; S suburb of Antwerp.

Mor·van \\mȯr-ˈväⁿ\\. Mountain range in E cen. France, in departments of Nièvre, Yonne, Côte-d'Or, and Saône-et-Loire; highest peak Bois-du-Roi 2959 ft.

Mor·ven \\ˈmȯr-vən\\. 1 Peak in Aberdeen co., NE cen. Scotland; 2862 ft.
2 Peak in Caithness co., N Scotland; 2313 ft.

Mor·vi \\ˈmȯr-vē\\. 1 Former Indian state, N Kathiawar, now part of Gujarat state, W India; 822 sq. m.
2 Town, its ✱, 40 m. N of Rajkot; pop. (1961c) 50,912.

Mor·well \\ˈmȯr-(ˌ)wel, ˈmär-, -wəl\\. Town, Victoria, Australia; pop. (1966c) 16,647.

Mosa. See MEUSE.

Mos·ca Pass \\ˌmäs-kə-\\. Mountain pass, Huerfano and Saguache cos., S Colorado, in Sangre de Cristo Range of the Rocky Mts.; 9700 ft.; road and trail; used since 1850, one of important passes on Arkansas river route to California and New Mexico.

Mo·sca·vi·de \\ˌmüsh-kə-ˈvēd-ə, -ˈvē-thə\\. Town, Lisboa dist., Portugal, 5 m. NNE of Lisbon; pop. (1970p) 21,728.

Mos·cow \\ˈmäs-(ˌ)kō\\. City, ⊗ of Latah co., NW Idaho, on Washington border 25 m. N of Lewiston; pop. (1970c) 14,146; lumber, building materials, flour; wheat, peas, dairy products; Univ. of Idaho (1889).

Moscow \\ˈmäs-ˌkau̇, -(ˌ)kō\\ *or Russ.* **Mos·kva** \\mäsk-ˈvä\\ *also* **Mus·co·vy** \\mə-ˈskō-vē, ˈməs-kə-, -ˌkō-\\. 1 Former principality, W cen. Russia in Europe; founded c. 1280 by Daniel, son of Alexander Nevski, with fortified village of Moscow as its center; united with Vladimir principality in 15th cent.; its ruler became Grand Duke, who extended its power. For later history, see 2 below, and RUSSIA.
2 City, ✱ of the U.S.S.R., also ✱ of the Russian S.F.S.R., and ✱ of Moscow Oblast, on both sides of the Moskva river; pop. (1970p) 7,061,000; the largest city in the U.S.S.R. and its political, economic, transportation, and cultural center; an inland port on navigable waterway formed by the Moscow-Volga canal (opened 1937) and the Moskva river; important industrial center, producing motor vehicles, precision instruments, electrical equipment, household appliances, textiles, clothing, chemicals, paints, dyes, footwear; food processing; publishing and motion-picture making center of the U.S.S.R.; tourism. Most notable structure is the Kremlin (*Russ.* "citadel"), a large triangular fortress on the Moskva (first built in 12th cent. and built in present form c. 1367), with Red Square to the W, until 1712 the residence of the ruler; Kremlin now houses sessions of supreme soviet (in building completed 1961); Lenin Mausoleum is nearby. Numerous other notable buildings, including ab. 200 churches, several cathedrals, palaces, museums (incl. Tretyakov Gallery and Lenin Museum); Moscow Art Theater and Bolshoi Theater, the M.V. Lomonsov State Univ. (1755, the largest in the U.S.S.R.) and ab. 90 other higher educational institutions and more than 450 scientific institutes; in SW is Gorki Park.
History: Site inhabited since Neolithic times, but first mentioned as village in Russian chronicles 1147; capital of principality of Moscow (see 1 above) 1341; burned and sacked several times by the Tatars 13th–15th cents.; became seat of metropolitan of Russian church 1326; incorporated principality of Vladmir 1341; under Grand Duke Ivan III (1462–1505) overcame leading rival principality of Novgorod (*q.v.*), defeated Tatars, and invaded Lithuania. Grand Duke Ivan IV first to formally assume title of Tsar of Russia; capital of grand duchy of Russia 1547–1712 (see LENINGRAD); in 1812 occupied by French under Napoleon, being almost entirely destroyed by fire during the occupation. Became capital of U.S.S.R. 1918 and underwent major expansion as administrative center of country; in World War II the major objective of the German advance 1941; suffered considerable damage from German bombing; large-scale reconstruction and further expansion since World War II.
3 River, U.S.S.R. See MOSKVA 1.

Moscow Oblast \\-ˈȯ-bləst, -ˌblast\\. Subdivision of the Russian S.F.S.R., U.S.S.R.; 18,147 sq. m.; pop. (1970p) 12,835,000; ✱ Moscow. Traversed by the Moskva and in SE part by the Oka. Rolling country with considerable areas of forest; highly industrialized with excellent road and rail transportation; textiles, diesel locomotives, chemicals, cement; principal city is Moscow; dairying; livestock raising; flax.

Mo·selle \\mō-ˈzel\\ *or Ger.* **Mo·sel** \\ˈmō-zəl\\ *or anc.* **Mo·sel·la** \\mō-ˈzel-ə\\. 1 River, W Europe; 150 m. long; rises in Vosges dept., NE France, flows N, forming a section of the boundary bet. West Germany and the Grand Duchy of Luxembourg, turns NE and enters the Rhine at Koblenz; navigable for most of its course. Chief tributaries the Orne and Sauer from left and the Meurth and Saar from right. Passes the cities of Nancy, Metz, Thionville in France and Trier in Germany.

2 Department of NE France. See table at FRANCE.

Mo·ses Lake \ˌmō-zəz-, -zəs-\. 1 Lake, S cen. Grant co., cen. Washington; 16 m. long; its lower extension, **Pot·holes Reservoir** \ˌpät-hōlz-\, formed by O'Sullivan Dam.

2 City, Grant co., cen. Washington, on E shore of Moses Lake; pop. (1970c) 10,310; Big Bend Community Coll. (1962).

Mos·giel \ˈmȯz-gēl\. Borough, South I., New Zealand; pop. (1970e) 8340.

Mo·shi \ˈmō-shē\. Town, ✱ of Kilimanjaro region, NE Tanzania, E Africa, on S slope of Mt. Kilimanjaro; pop. (1967e) 26,864.

Mos·kal·vo \ˈmȯs-kəl-ˌvȯ\. Oil port on Gulf of Sakhalin, NW Sakhalin I., Sakhalin Oblast, Russian S.F.S.R., U.S.S.R.; rail connection with Okha on E coast of island; icebound for six months.

Mos·kva \mäsk-ˈvä\ *or* **Mos·cow** \ˈmäs-ˌkaủ, -(ˌ)kō\. 1 River, Moscow Oblast, Russian S.F.S.R., U.S.S.R.; 315 m. long; flows E through Moscow city to join the Oka river just below Kolomna; navigable from Moscow.

2 Principality and city, U.S.S.R. See MOSCOW.

Moskva–Pe·kin \-ˈpā-kin\ *or formerly* **Mount Mo·lo·tov** \-ˈmäl-ə-ˌtȯf, -ˈmȯl-, -ˈmōl-, -tȯv\. Mountain, N cen. Tadzhik S.S.R., U.S.S.R.; 22,255 ft.

Mo·son·ma·gya·ró·vár \ˈmȯ-shȯn-ˌmä-dyə-ˌrō-vär\ *or formerly* **Mag·ya·ró·vár** \ˈmä-dyə-ˌrō-vär\ *or Ger.* **Al·ten·burg** \ˈält-ən-ˌbərg, -ˌbủ(ə)rg\. Town, NW Hungary, ab. 22 m. NW of Győr; pop. (1970p) 24,452.

Mos·que·ro \mäs-ˈker-ō\. Village, ⊗ of Harding and San Miguel cos., NE New Mexico; pop. (1970c) 244.

Mos·qui·to Cays \mə-ˈskēt-(ˌ)ō-ˈkēz, -ˈkāz\. Group of small islands in Caribbean Sea off NE coast of Nicaragua.

Mosquito Coast *or* **Mi·ski·to Coast** \mi-ˌskēt-(ˌ)ō-\. Region along coast of E Nicaragua, forming Zelaya dept., Nicaragua; ab. 40 m. wide; a British protectorate 1655–1860 and later an autonomous Indian reserve; chief town Bluefields. See SAN JUAN DEL NORTE.

Mosquito Gulf *or Span.* **Gol·fo de los Mos·qui·tos** \ˈgȯl-(ˌ)fo-dā-lȯ-sməs-ˈkē-(ˌ)tōs\. Widemouthed inlet of the Caribbean Sea on the N coast of Panama, W of the Panama Canal.

Mosquito Peak. Mountain, Park and Lake cos., cen. Colorado; 13,784 ft.

Moss \ˈmȯs\. Seaport, ⊗ of Østfold co., SE Norway, on E side of Oslo Fjord; pop. (1970e) 24,580; seaside resort; shipbuilding yards, iron foundries; manufactures shoes, paper, furniture; scene of signing of agreement uniting Norway and Sweden Aug. 14, 1814.

Mos·sel Bay \ˌmȯ-səl-\ *or Afrikaans* **Mos·sel·baai** \ˌmȯs-əl-ˈbī\. Seaport on Mossel Bay (inlet of Indian Ocean), S Cape Province, S Rep. of South Africa, ab. 230 m. E of Cape Town; pop. (1967e) 15,600; harvests oysters and mussels—whence its name; summer resort. First visited by Bartholomew Dias 1488; hermitage erected here 1501 by João da Nova, first Christian place of worship in South Africa.

Mossgiel. See MAUCHLINE.

Moss·ley \ˈmȯ-slē\. Municipal borough, Lancashire, NW England, on the Tame 10 m. NE of Manchester; pop. (1971p) 10,055.

Mos·so·ró \ˌmü-sə-ˈrȯ\. City, NW Rio Grande do Norte state, NE Brazil, 150 m. WNW of Natal; munic. pop. (1968e) 53,114.

Moss Point \ˈmȯs-\. City, Jackson co., SE corner of Mississippi, 20 m. E of Biloxi; pop. (1970c) 19,321.

Mos·su·ril \ˌmȯ-sə-ˈrē(ə)l\. Coastal town, NE Mozambique, SE Africa, opp. Mozambique I.

Mos·sy·rock Dam \ˈmȯ-sē-räk-\ *and* **Mossyrock Reservoir.** See UNITED STATES, *Dams and Reservoirs.*

Most \ˈmȯst\ *or Ger.* **Brüx** \ˈbrüks\. City, Czech S.R., NW Czechoslovakia, ab. 48 m. NW of Prague; pop. (1967e) 55,383; major lignite-mining center; also produces steel, chemicals, ceramics; first mentioned 11th cent.

Mos·ta·ga·nem \mə-ˌstäg-ə-ˈnem\. 1 Department of N Algeria. See table at ALGERIA.

2 City, its ✱, 44 m. ENE of Oran; pop. (1966c) 63,297; exports wine, fruits, and vegetables; 11th cent. citadel; fell to French 1833.

Mo·star \ˈmō-ˌstär\. Town, Bosnia and Herzegovina, W Yugoslavia, on Neretva river ab. 50 m. SW of Sarajevo; pop. (1965e) 56,000; textiles, wine, and tobacco; formerly capital of Herzegovina and still its chief town; has old stone bridge.

Mo·sul \mō-ˈsül, ˈmō-səl\ *or Arab.* **Al–Maw·ṣil** \ˌal-maủ-ˈsēl\. City, N Iraq, on the W bank of the Tigris 220 m. NNW of Baghdad; pop. (1965c) 243,311; on the Turkey-Baghdad railroad and formerly an important town on caravan route from Iran across N Mesopotamia; a trading center for grain, hides, wool, livestock, fruit; produces cement, sugar, nylon, bitumen; has cosmopolitan population and numerous mosques, shrines, and churches; univ. (1967). Across the river from ruins of ancient Nineveh and other sites of ancient cities now partially excavated, as Tepe Gawra, Calah, and Dur Sharrukin. An old Arabic town taken by Muslims 636; later under Mongols, Persians, and Turks; became part of Ottoman Empire c. 1534; not included originally in mandate of Iraq but awarded to it by decision of League of Nations 1925; oil wells seized during Arab revolt Apr. 1941 but soon retaken by British.

Mo·ta·gua \mō-ˈtäg-wə\. River, S cen. Guatemala; ab. 340 m. long; flows E and NE into the Gulf of Honduras.

Mo·ta·la \ˈmü-tə-ˌlä, -ˌtal-ə\. Town, Östergötland co., SE Sweden, on NE shore of Lake Vättern 20 m. WNW of Linköping; pop. (1970e) 29,203; summer resort; hydraulic presses, diesel and electrical locomotives, radio and television sets, tape recorders; incorporated 1881.

Moth·er, Mount \-ˈmət͟h-ər\ *or* **The Mother.** Volcano at NE tip of New Britain I., Bismarck Archipelago, on a peninsula just E of and overshadowing Rabaul and Blanche Bay; its eruption and earthquakes in 1878 created Manam I. in the bay and in May 1937 Mt. Tavurvur (*q.v.*), a crater on its S slope, and Mt. Vulcan together caused great destruction at Rabaul and vicinity.

Mother Island. See HAHAJIMA.

Mother Lode. Principal belt of gold-bearing quartz along the W foothills of the Sierra Nevada, California.

Moth·er·well and Wish·aw \ˈmət͟h-ər-ˌwel . . . ˈwish-ˌȯ, -wəl-\. Burgh, Lanark co., S cen. Scotland, on right bank of the Clyde 13 m. SE of Glasgow; pop. (1971p) 73,384; iron and steel, machinery, clothing, preserves. Two burghs united 1920.

Mo·ti·ti Island \mō-ˌtēt-ē-\. Small island in the Bay of Plenty, off N cen. coast of North I., New Zealand.

Mot·ley \ˈmät-lē\. County in Texas. See table at TEXAS.

Mo·to·zin·tla \ˌmō-tō-ˈsēnt-lə\. Municipality, Chiapas state, Mexico, 120 m. SE of Tuxtla Gutiérrez; pop. (1970p) 31,158; unexploited copper, iron, titanium deposits.

Mo·tril \mō-ˈtrēl\. Commercial commune, Granada prov., S Spain, 2 m. from Mediterranean and 31 m. S of Granada; pop. (1970p) 31,716.

Mott \ˈmät\. City, ⊗ of Hettinger co., SW North Dakota; pop. (1970c) 1368; coal mines; dairy farms.

Mot·to·la \ˈmȯt-ə-lə\. Commune, Taranto prov., Apulia, SE Italy, 16 m. NW of Taranto; pop. (1968e) 15,218; 15th cent. cathedral.

Mo·tu–ari \ˌmōt-ü-ˈär-ē\. Small island of Gambier Is., S Pacific Ocean, SW of Mangareva I.

Mo·tul \mō-ˈtül\ *or in full* **Motul de Fe·li·pe Ca·rri·llo Puer·to** \-də-fə-ˈlē-pə-kär-ˌrē-yō-ˈpwer-tō\. Town, N Yucatán state, on Yucatán penin., SE Mexico, just E of Mérida; pop. (1970p) 21,087.

Mo·tu·sa \mō-'tü-sə\. Chief village of Rotuma I., Fiji, SW Pacific Ocean.

Mo·tya \'mōt-ē-ə\. Ruins of ancient Phoenician town on very small island **San Pan·ta·leo** \ˌsän-ˌpänt-ᵊl-'ā-(ˌ)ō\ *or* **San Pan·ta·le·o·ne** \-ᵊl-ā-'ō-nē\, off W coast of Sicily, Italy, just N of Marsala; destroyed 397 B.C. by Dionysius the Elder of Syracuse.

Motyca. See MODICA.

Mou·choir Bank \ˌmüsh-wär-\. Bank in Atlantic Ocean off N coast of Hispaniola in the West Indies.

Mouchoir Passage. Channel in N cen. West Indies, SE of Turks Is. and NW of Mouchoir Bank.

Mou·dros *or* **Mu·dros** *or* **Moú·dhros** \'mü-ˌdrȯs\. Town and seaport on S coast of Lemnos I. in N Aegean Sea; belongs to Lesbos dept., Greece; has fine harbor, a part of **Moudros Gulf.**

Moukden. See MUKDEN.

Moule, Le. See LE MOULE.

Mou·lins \mü-'laⁿ\. Manufacturing city, ✱ of Allier dept., cen. France, and anciently ✱ of Bourbonnais; on Allier river 58 m. SE of Bourges; pop. (1968c) 25,979; machine tools, shoes, beer, furniture; 15th cent. Gothic cathedral; 15th cent. campanile; town hall.

Moul·mein \mül-'mān, mōl-, -'mīn\ *also* **Maul·main** \mȯl-'mīn\. Commercial city, ✱ of Tenasserim division, Lower Burma, at mouth of Salween on E shore of Gulf of Martaban; pop. (1969e) 322,000; formerly a port and shipbuilding center of great importance; now has export trade in rice and teak; port for steamers up the Salween.

Mou·lou·ya *or* **Mu·lu·ya** \mu̇-'lü-yə\ *or* **Mul·wi·ya** \mül-'wē-yə\ *or anc.* **Mu·lu·cha** \'myü-lə-kə\. River, Morocco, NW Africa; 370 m. long; rises in cen. Morocco, flows NE into Mediterranean Sea E of Melilla.

Moul·ton \'mōlt-ᵊn\. Town, ⊗ of Lawrence co., N Alabama; pop. (1970c) 2470; lumber, clothing.

Moul·trie \'mōl-trē\. **1** County in Illinois. See table at ILLINOIS.

2 City, ⊗ of Colquitt co., S Georgia, 35 m. SE of Albany; pop. (1970c) 14,400; clothing, textiles, fertilizer; meatpacking.

Mound \'mau̇nd\. Village, Hennepin co., SE Minnesota, W of Minneapolis; pop. (1970c) 7572.

Mound City. 1 City, ⊗ of Pulaski co., S Illinois, on Ohio river 8 m. above its confluence with Mississippi river; pop. (1970c) 1177.

2 City, ⊗ of Lion co., E Kansas; pop. (1970c) 714.

3 City, Holt co., NW Missouri, 34 m. NW of St. Joseph; pop. (1970c) 1202; ships grain and livestock.

4 Town, ⊗ of Campbell co., N South Dakota; pop. (1970c) 164.

Mound City Group National Monument. See UNITED STATES, *National Monuments.*

Moun·dou \'mün-(ˌ)dü\. Town, S Chad, ab. 241 m. SSE of Fort-Lamy; pop. (1968c) 34,098.

Mounds \'maun(d)z\. City, Pulaski co., S Illinois, 10 m. N of confluence of Ohio and Mississippi rivers; pop. (1970c) 1718; women's clothing; diversified agriculture.

Mounds View. Village, Ramsey co., E Minnesota, N suburb of Minneapolis; pop. (1970c) 10,641.

Mounds·ville \'mau̇n(d)z-ˌvil, -vəl\. City, ⊗ of Marshall co., N West Virginia, in N panhandle on Ohio river 12 m. S of Wheeling; pop. (1970c) 13,560; chemicals, plastics, glassware; coal mines; dairy farms. Named for Grave Creek Mound, a prehistoric, conical burial mound, 320 ft. in diameter at the base and 70 ft. high, which is in center of the city.

Mount, Cape \-'mau̇nt\. Cape on SE coast of Liberia, W Africa, a promontory 1000 ft. high.

Mount Abu. See ABU, MOUNT.

Moun·tain·air \ˌmau̇nt-ᵊn-'a(ə)r, -'e(ə)r\. Town and health resort, Torrance co., cen. New Mexico, 44 m. SSE of Albuquerque; pop. (1970c) 1022; pueblo ruins in environs.

Mountain Ash. Industrial urban district, Glamorganshire, S Wales, 5 m. S of Merthyr Tydfil; pop. (1971p) 27,806; coal mining.

Mountain Brook. City, Jefferson co., cen. Alabama, E suburb of Birmingham; pop. (1970c) 19,509.

Mountain City. Town, ⊗ of Johnson co., NE corner of Tennessee; pop. (1970c) 1883; truck farms.

Mountain Grove. City, Wright co., S Missouri, 38 m. NW of West Plains; pop. (1970c) 3317; dairy products, lumber; poultry farms.

Mountain Home. 1 City, ⊗ of Baxter co., N Arkansas; pop. (1970c) 3936; cattle and dairy farms.

2 City, ⊗ of Elmore co., SW cen. Idaho; pop. (1970c) 6451; gold and copper mines; sugar beets.

Mountain Lake. 1 Bird sanctuary near Lake Wales, Polk co., cen. Florida penin.; 58 acres; established by Edward Bok; has Singing Tower (dedicated 1929), 230 ft. high with carillon of 71 bells.

2 Village, Cottonwood co., SW Minnesota, 30 m. NW of Fairmont; pop. (1970c) 1986.

Mountain Lakes. Residential borough, Morris co., N New Jersey, 7 m. N of Morristown; pop. (1970c) 4739; spread out around eight artificial lakes.

Mountain Meadows. Valley in Iron and Washington cos., SW Utah; massacre of ab. 100 emigrants occurred Sept. 1857 in Washington co., ab. 40 m. SW of Cedar City.

Mountain Province. Province, N cen. Luzon, Phil.; 810 sq. m.; pop. (1970p) 93,729; ✱ Bontoc.

History: Region but little known in 17th and 18th cents., but various expeditions carried out by Spanish bet. 1829 and 1850; later divided under Spanish rule into several politico-military comandancias; Benguet (a former subprovince, now a province) first organized 1900 under American rule and Baguio made capital; other subprovinces created 1901–08; united and organized 1908 as separate province under present name; City of Baguio incorporated 1909 and separated administratively; in 1920 former subprovinces of Lepanto and Amburayan united and boundaries of several others changed and further reorganization made before 1939; area of province greatly reduced due to creation of new provinces 1968.

Moun·tain·side \'mau̇nt-ᵊn-ˌsīd\. Borough, Union co., NE New Jersey, 11 m. SW of Newark; pop. (1970c) 7520.

Mountains of the Moon. See RUWENZORI, MOUNT.

Mountain View. 1 City, ⊗ of Stone co., N Arkansas; pop. (1970c) 1866.

2 City, Santa Clara co., W California, 11 m. NW of San Jose; pop. (1970c) 54,206; ships vegetables, fruits, and nuts; Saint Patrick's Coll. (1898); Moffett Field and Ames Laboratory of the National Aeronautics and Space Administration; settled 1852, incorp. 1902.

Mount Airy \-'a(ə)r-ē, -'e(ə)r-\. Town and summer resort, Surry co., N North Carolina, in foothills of Blue Ridge Mts. 35 m. NW of Winston-Salem; pop. (1970c) 7325; clothing; granite quarries, fruit, dairy, and tobacco farms.

Mount Al·bert \-'al-bərt\. Borough, N North I., New Zealand, SW suburb of Auckland; pop. (1970e) 25,600.

Mount An·gel \-'ān-jəl\. City, Marion co., NW Oregon, 15 m. NE of Salem; pop. (1970c) 1973; fruit, dairy products, flax; Mount Angel Coll. (1887).

Mount Apo National Park. See APO, MOUNT.

Mount Ar·ling·ton \-'är-liŋ-tən\. Borough, Morris co., N New Jersey, 13 m. NW of Morristown; pop. (1970c) 3590.

Mount Athos *or* **Ha·gi·on Oros** \ˌä-yȯn-'ȯr-ˌȯs\. See ATHOS.

Mount Ayr \-'a(ə)r, -'e(ə)r\. Town, ⊗ of Ringgold co., S Iowa, 70 m. SW of Des Moines; pop. (1970c) 1762; hogs, oats.

Mount Car·mel \-'kär-məl\. **1** City, ⊗ of Wabash co., SE Illinois, on Wabash river 30 m. SE of Olney; pop. (1970c) 8096; roofing, tools, electronic components; coal mines; Wabash Valley Coll. (1961); settled 1817.

2 Borough, Northumberland co., E cen. Pennsylvania, 15 m. WNW of Pottsville; pop. (1970c) 9317; cigars, aluminum products; coal mines.

3 Town, Hawkins co., NE Tennessee; pop. (1970c) 2821.
4 Mountain, Israel. See CARMEL, MOUNT.

Mount Car·roll \-'kar-əl\. City, ⊗ of Carroll co., NW Illinois; pop. (1970c) 2143; Shimer Coll. (1853).

Mount Clem·ens \-'klem-ənz\. City, ⊗ of Macomb co., SE Michigan, 20 m. NE of Detroit; pop. (1970c) 20,476; health resort; home appliances, boats, automobile parts; dairy farms. Selfridge Field, U.S. Air Force base.

Mount Des·ert \-də-'zərt, -'dez-ərt\. **1** Island, Hancock co., off SE Maine; 14 m. long by 8 m. wide; summer resort; damaged by forest fire 1947. Acadia National Park (see UNITED STATES, *National Parks*).
2 Town, Hancock co., SE Maine, center of Mt. Desert I.; pop. (1970c) 1659.

Mount Do·ra \-'dō(ə)r-ə, -'dȯ(ə)r-ə\. Town, Lake co., cen. Florida penin., 22 m. NNW of Orlando; pop. (1970c) 4543; resort; fruit and dairy farms.

Mount Eba \-'ē-bə\. Semiarid district, cen. South Australia, 100 m. NW of Port Augusta; Woomera range head for rockets and supersonic aircraft.

Mount Eden \-'ēd-^{ə}n\. Borough, N North I., New Zealand, S suburb of Auckland; pop. (1970e) 18,450.

Mount Edge·cumbe \-'ej-kəm\. Urban community (unincorporated), on W coast of Baranof I., SE Alaska, SW of Juneau; pop. (1970c) 885.

Mount Ephra·im \-'ē-frē-əm, -frəm\. Borough, Camden co., SW New Jersey, 5 m. S of Camden; pop. (1970c) 5625.

Mount For·est \-'fȯr-əst, -'fär-\. Industrial town, Wellington co., SE Ontario, Canada, 38 m. NW of Guelph; pop. (1971p) 3031; veneers; livestock farms.

Mount Gam·bier \-'gam-bi(ə)r\. Town, SE corner of South Australia, near Victoria border 240 m. SSE of Adelaide; pop. (1968e) 17,350.

Mount Gil·e·ad \-'gil-ē-əd\. Village, ⊗ of Morrow co., cen. Ohio, 16 m. E of Marion; pop. (1970c) 2971; hydraulic presses, pumps.

Mount Heal·thy \-'hel-thē\. City, Hamilton co., SW corner of Ohio, 9 m. N of Cincinnati; pop. (1970c) 7746.

Mount Hol·ly \-'häl-ē\. **1** Township, ⊗ of Burlington co., S cen. New Jersey, 16 m. S of Trenton; pop. (1970c) 12,713; manufactures shoes, clothing, upholstery fabrics, leather goods; site purchased by Quakers 1676; temporary capital of New Jersey 1779; occupied by British troops during Revolution; became ⊗ 1796.
2 Industrial town, Gaston co., SW North Carolina, 10 m. E of Gastonia; pop. (1970c) 5107; chemicals; woolen mills; corn, wheat.

Mount Hope Bay \-'hōp-\. Northeast arm of Narragansett Bay, E section in SE Massachusetts and W section in E Rhode Island; ab. 6 m. long and 2 m. wide; receives Taunton river at its NE extremity; city of Fall River, Mass., on its NE shore.

Mount Ida \-'īd-ə\. **1** City, ⊗ of Montgomery co., W Arkansas; pop. (1970c) 819.
2 Mountains, Asia Minor and Crete. See IDA 2 and 3.

Mount Isa \-'ī-zə\. Mining town, Queensland, Australia; pop. (1966c) 16,877; copper mines.

Mount Joy \-'jȯi\. Borough, Lancaster co., SE Pennsylvania, 12 m. WNW of Lancaster; pop. (1970c) 5041; shoes, toys, wire, aircraft parts, brooms.

Mount Ken·ya National Park \-'ken-yə-, -'kēn-\. National park, cen. Kenya; 227 sq. m.; heavily forested; contains Mt. Kenya; established 1949.

Mount Kis·co \-'kis-(ˌ)kō\. Village, Westchester co., SE New York, 36 m. NNE of New York City; pop. (1970c) 8172; residential.

Mount·lake Terrace \ˌmau̇nt-lāk-\. City, Snohomish co., NW Washington, S of Everett; pop. (1970c) 16,600.

Mount Lavinia. See DEHIWALA-MOUNT LAVINIA.

Mount Mc·Kin·ley National Park \-mə-'kin-lē-\. See UNITED STATES, *National Parks*.

Mount Mor·ris \-'mȯr-əs, -'mär-\. **1** Village, Ogle co., N Illinois, 25 m. SW of Rockford; pop. (1970c) 3173; printing and publishing center.
2 City, Genesee co., SE cen. Michigan, 8 m. N of Flint; pop. (1970c) 3778; dairy products.
3 Village in Mount Morris town, Livingston co., W New York, 34 m. SSW of Rochester; pop. (1970c) 3417; canned and frozen foods.

Mount of the Holy Cross. See HOLY CROSS, MOUNT OF THE.

Mount Ol·ive \-'äl-iv, -əv\. Town, Wayne and Duplin cos., E North Carolina, S of Goldsboro; pop. (1970c) 4914; lumber, clothing; Mount Olive Junior Coll. (1951).

Mount Ol·i·ver \-'äl-ə-vər\. Borough, Allegheny co., SW Pennsylvania, 3 m. S of Pittsburgh; pop. (1970c) 5487.

Mount Ol·i·vet \-'äl-ə-vət\. City, ⊗ of Robertson co., NE Kentucky; pop. (1970c) 442.

Mount Olym·pus National Monument \-ō-'lim-pəs-\. Former United States national monument, NW Washington; 467 sq. m.; estab. 1909, included 1938 in Olympic National Park (see UNITED STATES, *National Parks*).

Mount Pearl \-'pərl\. Town, Newfoundland, E Canada; pop. (1971p) 7110.

Mount Penn \-'pen\. Borough, Berks co., SE Pennsylvania, 3 m. E of Reading; pop. (1970c) 3465.

Mount Pleas·ant \-'plez-^{ə}nt\. **1** City, ⊗ of Henry co., SE Iowa, 28 m. WNW of Burlington; pop. (1970c) 7007; Iowa Wesleyan Coll. (1842).
2 City, ⊗ of Isabella co., cen. Michigan, 46 m. W of Bay City; pop. (1970c) 20,504; flour, gasoline, automobile parts; oil wells; Central Michigan Univ. (1892).
3 Borough, Westmoreland co., SW Pennsylvania, 21 m. NNE of Uniontown; pop. (1970c) 5895; glassware, cement, mining machinery.
4 Town, Charleston co., SE South Carolina, on Atlantic Ocean 5 m. E of Charleston; pop. (1970c) 6691; resort.
5 Town, Maury co., W cen. Tennessee, 12 m. WSW of Columbia; pop. (1970c) 3530; phosphate mines.
6 City, ⊗ of Titus co., NE Texas, 48 m. SE of Paris; pop. (1970c) 9459; asphalt; diversified agriculture.
7 City, Sanpete co., cen. Utah, 34 m. W of Price; pop. (1970c) 1516; livestock, alfalfa.

Mount Pros·pect \-'präs-ˌpekt\. Village, Cook co., NE Illinois, 21 m. NW of Chicago; pop. (1970c) 34,995.

Mount·rail \'mau̇nt-ˌrāl\. County in North Dakota. See table at NORTH DAKOTA.

Mount Rai·nier \-rə-'ni(ə)r, -rā-, -'rā-ˌ\. City, Prince Georges co., S cen. Maryland, 4 m. NE of Washington, D.C.; pop. (1970c) 8130.

Mount Rainier National Park. See UNITED STATES, *National Parks*.

Mount Rev·el·stoke National Park \-'rev-əl-ˌstōk-\. See CANADA, *National Parks*.

Mount Rob·son Park \-'räb-sən-\. Canadian provincial park, E British Columbia, W Rocky Mts.; 806 sq. m.; contains Mt. Robson.

Mount Roy·al \mau̇nt-'rȯi(-ə)l\ *or* **Mont Royal** \ˌmō^{n}-rwä-'yäl\. Town, Montreal I., S Quebec, Canada, NW of the height Mount Royal; pop. (1971p) 21,470; part of Greater Montreal.

Mounts Bay \'mau̇n(t)s-\. Inlet of Atlantic Ocean on extreme SW tip of England, bet. Lands End on the W and Lizard Head on the E.

Mount Shas·ta \-'shas-tə\. Town, Siskiyou co., N California, at foot of Mt. Shasta, ab. 100 m. NE of Eureka; pop. (1970c) 2256; resort; lumbering.

Mount Ster·ling \-'stər-liŋ\. **1** City, ⊗ of Brown co., W Illinois, 34 m. E of Quincy; pop. (1970c) 2182; cheese.
2 City, ⊗ of Montgomery co., E Kentucky, 15 m. ENE of Winchester; pop. (1970c) 5083; clothing; dairy and poultry farms; prehistoric mounds nearby.

Mount Un·ion \-'yü-nyən\. Borough, Huntingdon co., S cen. Pennsylvania, on Juniata river 24 m. SW of Lewistown; pop. (1970c) 3662; clothing, building materials.

Mount Ver·non \-'vər-nən\. 1 City, ⊗ of Montgomery co., SE cen. Georgia; pop. (1970c) 1579; Brewton Parker Coll. (1904).

2 City, ⊗ of Jefferson co., S Illinois, 20 m. SE of Centralia; pop. (1970c) 16,382; shoes, furnaces, women's clothing; diversified agriculture; settled 1819; incorporated 1872.

3 City, ⊗ of Posey co., SW corner of Indiana, on Ohio river 18 m. W of Evansville; pop. (1970c) 6770; oil wells; Mount Vernon Nazarene Coll. (1966).

4 City, Linn co., E Iowa, 13 m. E of Cedar Rapids; pop. (1970c) 3018; fruit and vegetable packing; Cornell Coll. (1852).

5 City, ⊗ of Rockcastle co., SE cen. Kentucky; pop. (1970c) 1639; coal mines.

6 City, ⊗ of Lawrence co., SW Missouri, 32 m. WSW of Springfield; pop. (1970c) 2600; diversified agriculture.

7 City, Westchester co., SE New York, on Bronx river adjacent to New York City; pop. (1970c) 72,778; residential suburb; pharmaceuticals, vehicle bodies, electronic components, cosmetics; laid out 1852 by Industrial Home Association as refuge from high rents of New York; incorporated as city 1892.

8 Manufacturing city, ⊗ of Knox co., cen. Ohio, 25 m. S of Mansfield; pop. (1970c) 13,373; diesel engines, glass, turbines, structural steel; livestock and dairy farms.

9 Town, ⊗ of Franklin co., NE Texas; pop. (1970c) 1806.

10 Home and burial place of George Washington, in Fairfax co., Virginia, on Potomac river ab. 15 m. below Washington, D.C.; acquired by Washington 1752; has been restored and is maintained by Mount Vernon Ladies' Association of the Union which bought it 1858.

11 City, ⊗ of Skagit co., NW Washington, on Skagit river 25 m. S of Bellingham; pop. (1970c) 8804; dairy products, frozen foods; Skagit Valley Coll. (1926).

Mount Wel·ling·ton \-'wel-iŋ-tən\. Borough, North I., New Zealand; pop. (1970e) 20,100.

Mourne \'mō(ə)rn, 'mȯ(ə)rn\. River, co. Tyrone, N Ireland; 10 m. long; flows NNW in W Northern Ireland to unite with the Finn on the Eire border.

Mourne Mountains. Range in SE Northern Ireland, in co. Down bet. Dundrum Bay and Carlingford Lough; highest peak Slieve Donard 2796 ft.

Mouscron. See MOESKROEN.

Mouse. See SOURIS.

Moustier, Le. See LE MOUSTIER.

Mou·vaux \mü-'vō\. Commune, Nord dept., N France; pop. (1962c) 11,140; a N suburb of Lille.

Mow·er \'mau̇(-ə)r\. County in Minnesota. See table at MINNESOTA.

Moy \'mȯi\. River, NW Eire; 40 m. long; rises in co. Sligo, curves SW, W, and N through co. Mayo into Killala Bay; navigable for a short distance.

Mo·ya·le \mō-'yäl-ē\. Town, N Kenya, E Africa, near border of Ethiopia; British base in attack on Italian East Africa 1941.

Moyen Atlas. See ATLAS MOUNTAINS.

Mo·yeu·vre–Grande \mwä-ˌyə(r)v-rə-'grän(n)d\. Commune, Moselle dept., NE France, on Orne river 11 m. NNW of Metz; pop. (1968c) 14,568; iron mines; steelworks.

Mo·yo·bam·ba \ˌmȯi-ə-'bäm-bə\. Town, ✱ of San Martín dept., N Peru, on Mayo river 420 m. N of Lima; pop. (1961c) 8400; manufactures Panama hats.

Moy·tu·ra \mȯi-'tu̇(ə)r-ə\. Two localities in Eire associated with legends of the Firbolg: **Northern Moytura,** near Sligo, Connacht, where the Firbolg met final defeat in battle; probable site now marked by a few cairns; **Southern Moytura,** near Cong bet. Lough Mask and Lough Corrib, where they had been defeated seven years earlier.

Moyun–Kum. See MOINKUM.

Mo·zam·bique \ˌmō-zəm-'bēk\ *or Port.* **Mo·çam·bi·que** \ˌmü-səm-'bē-kə\. 1 *or* **Portuguese East Africa.** Portuguese overseas province, SE Africa, bounded on N by Tanzania, on E by the Indian Ocean (Mozambique Channel), on S by Rep. of South Africa and Swaziland, and on W by Rhodesia, Zambia, and Malawi; 297,846 sq. m.; pop. (1970p) 8,233,034; ✱ Lourenço Marques. *Physical features:* Mountainous in N (highest peak 7936 ft.) and along Rhodesia border (ab. 9000 ft.). Crossed in cen. part by lower course (ab. 480 m.) of Zambezi river flowing SE into Mozambique Channel at Chinde; other important rivers the Limpopo in S, Save in S cen. part, Lugenda in N, and many shorter streams in NE; coastal plain extensive; N boundary marked by Ruvuma river and Cape Delgado. *Chief products:* Corn, sugar, peanuts, tea, copra, manioc, cotton; coal; fish; customs duties are an important source of revenue. *Chief towns:* Lourenço Marques, Nampula, Quelimane, Beira.

History: Town of Mozambique a Portuguese trading fort early in 16th cent.; in 1875, the disputed Delagoa Bay (*q.v.*) region awarded to Portugal; after efforts of Portuguese explorers to expand to interior, British secured agreement which defined its boundaries with British South and East Africa 1891; Mozambique Company chartered 1891; boundary with German East Africa determined 1894; organized as colony 1907; until 1942 was in two parts: (1) territory under direct Portuguese administration; (2) territory **(Mozambique Company's Territory)** including Manica and Sofala dists. under administration of the Mozambique Company whose charter expired 1942, the territory reverting to the Portuguese government; became an overseas province of Portugal 1951; outbreak of fighting between Portuguese forces and anti-Portuguese nationalists 1964.

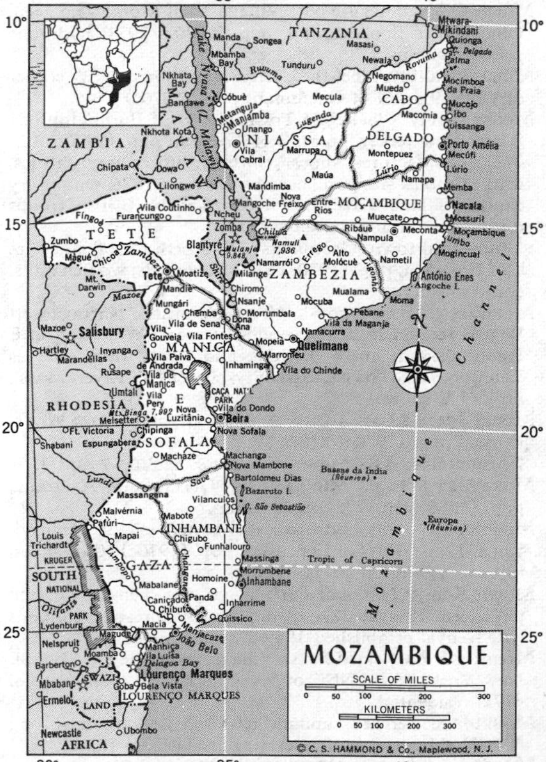

2 Seaport on small coral island **(Mozambique Island)** in Mozambique Channel, off NE coast of Mozambique, SE Africa; opp. the mainland town of Mossuril; pop. (1960c) 12,166; has good harbor; population chiefly Muslim

natives of mixed descent; exports ground nuts, oil seeds, and timber. Site of flourishing Arab town when visited by Vasco da Gama in 1498; capital of Mozambique until 1907.

Mozambique Channel. Strait bet. the Malagasy Republic and the SE African mainland (Mozambique); ab. 950 m. long; 250 m. wide at narrowest (central) part and ab. 625 m. at widest.

Mozambique Company's Territory. See MOZAMBIQUE 1.

Mozambique Current. A warm ocean current flowing from the Indian Ocean S through Mozambique Channel, past Natal (hence also called the **Na·tal Current** \nə-ˈtal-, -ˈtäl-\) and along the coast of Cape Province, S Rep. of South Africa, where it is known as the **Agul·has Current** \ə-ˈgəl-əs-\; off Cape Agulhas it is deflected to the left and flows SE toward Australia; considered to have a decided effect on the climate of Cape Province.

Mozambique Island. See MOZAMBIQUE 2.

Moz·dok \məz-ˈdȯk\. Town, North Ossetian A.S.S.R., Russian S.F.S.R., U.S.S.R., on Terek river 55 m. WNW of Grozny; pop. (1967e) 31,000; on oil pipelines.

Mo·zhaisk \mə-ˈzhīsk\. Village, Moscow Oblast, Russian S.F.S.R., U.S.S.R., on railroad 65 m. W of Moscow; pop. (1967e) 21,000. Taken by Germans Oct. 15, 1941; marks farthest advance of German armies in Nov. 1941 directly W of Moscow; regained by Soviet forces in winter drive 1941–42.

Mo·zyr \mə-ˈzi(ə)r\. Town, Gomel Oblast, Belorussian S.S.R., U.S.S.R., on Pripyat river 75 m. SW of Gomel; pop. (1967e) 43,000; in World War II held by Germans 1941–44; retaken by Soviet forces Jan. 12, 1944.

Mpon·da \em-ˈpȯn-də\. Town, S Malawi, S Africa, at S end of Lake Nyasa.

Msta \əm-ˈstä\. River, cen. Novgorod Oblast, Russian S.F.S.R., U.S.S.R.; 275 m. long; flows NW and W into N end of Lake Ilmen; navigable and connected by canals with Volga through the Tvertsa at Vyshni Volochek.

Msus \əm-ˈsüs\. Village in desert, NE Libya, 68 m. SE of Benghazi; British tank brigades destroyed here by German forces Dec. 28, 1941 and Jan 23, 1942.

Mtwa·ra \em-ˈtwär-ə\. 1 Administrative region of SE Tanzania. See table at TANZANIA.

2 Town, its ✱; pop. (1967c) 20,413.

Mu \ˈmü\. River, N cen. Burma; ab. 170 m. long; flows S through Katha and Shwebo dists. to the Irrawaddy W of Sagaing.

Muai To. See MAE HONG SON.

Muang Kham·mouan \ˈmwəŋ-kəm-ˈwän\ *or* **Thak·hek** \ˈtäk-ˈhek\. Town, Laos, SE Asia, on the Mekong, opp. Nakhon Phanom in Thailand.

Muang Thai. See THAILAND.

Mua·ni·va·tu, Mount \-ˌmwän-i-ˈvä-(ˌ)tü\. Peak, cen. Viti Levu I., Fiji, SW Pacific Ocean; 3708 ft.

Muar \ˈmwär\. 1 River, NW Johore state, Malaysia, S end of Malay Penin.; 140 m. long; its headstreams rise in Negri Sembilan and Pahang; flows SSW into the Strait of Malacca at Bandar Maharani; navigable for native boats for much of its course.

2 Seaport, Malaysia. See BANDAR MAHARANI.

Mu·a·ra·te·we *or Du.* **Moe·a·ra·te·we** \ˌmwär-ə-ˈtā-wē\. Town, South Kalimantan prov., Indonesia, on upper Barito river.

Mu·a·ri, Ras \ˌräs-mü-ˈär-ē\ *or* **Cape Mon·ze** \-ˈmȯn-(ˌ)zā\. Cape, Pakistan, 22 m. W of Karachi on the boundary bet. Sind and Baluchistan.

Much Wenlock. See WENLOCK.

Muck·ish \ˈmək-ish\. Mountain, N co. Donegal, N Eire; 2197 ft.

Muck Island \ˈmək-\. One of the Inner Hebrides, off W coast of Scotland, S of Rum I.; ab. 2 m. long; administratively a part of Argyll co.

Muck·le Flug·ga \ˌmək-əl-ˈfləg-ə\. Island, 1 m. N of Unst I. in the Shetland Is.; northernmost of the British islands.

Muck·ross \ˌmə-ˈkrȯs\. Peninsula in co. Kerry, SW Eire, bet. the upper and lower Lakes of Killarney; site of ruins of an ancient Franciscan abbey, founded 1440.

Mu·cu·ri·pe, Point \-ˌmü-kə-ˈrē-pə\. Cape extending into Atlantic Ocean on coast of Ceará state, NE Brazil, 5 m. E of Fortaleza.

Mu·dan·ya \mu̇-ˈdän-yə\. Town on Gemlik Gulf, an inlet of the Sea of Marmara, Bursa prov., NW Turkey, Asia; port of Bursa.

Mud·dus National Park \ˈmu̇t-əs-\. National park, N Sweden; 195 sq. m.; coniferous woodland, bogs; established 1942.

Mud·dy \ˈməd-ē\. River, SE Nevada; ab. 80 m. long; rises in Lincoln co., flows S into Virgin river.

Muddy Bog·gy Creek \-ˈbäg-ē-, -ˈbȯg-\. River, SE Oklahoma; ab. 100 m. long; rises in Pontotoc co., flows SE into Red river in S Choctaw co.

Muddy Pass. Mountain pass, Jackson and Grand cos., N Colorado, in Park Range of the Rocky Mts.; 8710 ft.; highway.

Mu·dhol \ˈmu̇d-ˌōl\. 1 Former Indian state, now part of Mysore state, W India; 350 sq. m.

2 Town, its ✱, 70 m. SE of Kolhapur; pop. (1961c) 12,100.

Mud·ki \ˈmu̇d-kē\. Village, Punjab state, NW India, 18 m. SE of Firozpur; scene of British victory Dec. 11, 1845 by Sir Hugh Gough over Sikhs.

Mud Lake \ˈməd-\. Intermittent lake, E Washoe co., Nevada.

Mud Mountain Dam. See UNITED STATES, *Dams and Reservoirs.*

Mudros. See MOUDROS.

Mu·fu·li·ra \ˌmü-fə-ˈlir-ə\. Town, Zambia, 21 m. NNE of Kitwe; pop. (1967e) 78,000.

Mufumbiro Mountains. See VIRUNGA MOUNTAINS.

Mug·gia \ˈmü-ˌjə\. Seaport, Trieste prov., Fruili-Venezia Giulia, NE Italy, on bay in Gulf of Trieste at N end of Adriatic Sea 4 m. SW of Trieste; pop. (1969e) 13,001; 15th cent. cathedral; 9th cent. basilica.

Muğ·la *or* **Mugh·la** \mü(g)-ˈlä\. 1 Province of SW Turkey. See table at TURKEY.

2 Town, its ✱, near coast; pop. (1965c) 16,048; center of medieval emirate noted for piracy.

Mu·gu, Point \-mə-ˈgü\. Cape, Ventura co., SW California, SE of Oxnard; site of Point Mugu Naval Air Missile Test Center.

Mu·ham·mad, Ra's \ˌräs-mə-ˈham-əd\. Cape, S end of Sinai Penin., NE Egypt, extending S into Red Sea; Sinai Penin. occupied by Israel 1967.

Mu·har·raq \mu̇-ˈhär-ək\ *also* **Mo·ha·rek** \mō-\. 1 Island in Bahrain, Persian Gulf, ab. 1½ m. NE of Bahrain I.; 4 m. long by 1 m. wide.

2 Town, on Muharraq I.; pop. (1971c) 37,732. See MANAMA.

Mühl·berg \ˈm(y)ül-ˌbe(ə)rg\. Town, East Germany, on the Elbe ab. 37 m. E of Leipzig; scene of battle Apr. 24, 1547 in which the Elector John Frederick of Saxony was defeated by Emperor Charles V; in World War II taken by U.S.S.R. Apr. 23, 1945.

Mühl·dorf \ˈm(y)ül-ˌdȯrf\. Town, Bavaria, West Germany, on the Inn river 45 m. E of Munich; pop. (1968e) 11,031; in World War II had subterranean jet plane factory built 1944 by 5000 slave laborers.

Muh·len·berg \ˈmyü-lən-ˌbərg\. County in Kentucky. See table at KENTUCKY.

Muh·len·fels Point \ˈmyü-lən-ˌfelz-\. Cape on S coast of St. Thomas I., Virgin Is. of U.S., West Indies.

Mühl·hau·sen in Thü·ring·en \m(y)ül-ˈhau̇z-ᵊn-in-ˈtu̇r-iŋ-ən\. Industrial city, Erfurt dist., East Germany, 29 m. NW of Erfurt; pop. (1970e) 45,385; textiles, leather, wood and metal products; 13th cent. town hall. First mentioned 775 A.D.; became city c. 1200; to Prussia 1802, to kingdom of Westphalia 1807, again to Prussia 1815.

Mühl·heim am Main \'m(y)ül-ˌhīm-äm-'mīn\. City, Hesse, West Germany, 8 m. E of Frankfurt am Main; pop. (1969e) 21,598; metalworking, leather, rubber, concrete products.

Mu·hu \'mü-(ˌ)hü\ *or Ger.* **Moon** \'mōn\ *or Russ.* **Mu·khu** \'mü-(ˌ)kü\. Island in Baltic Sea bet. Saaremaa I. and the mainland; 80 sq. m.; attached to Estonian S.S.R., U.S.S.R.

Muichdhui, Ben. See BEN MACDHUI.

Muil·rea *or* **Mweel·rea** \mwēl-'rā\. Mountain in SW co. Mayo, W Eire; highest point 2688 ft.

Muir, Mount \-'myu̇(ə)r\. Peak in Sierra Nevada, E Tulare co., S cen. California; 14,015 ft.

Muir Glacier. Glacier in Glacier Bay National Monument, SE Alaska; covers ab. 350 sq. m.; crossed by 59°N, 136°W. See UNITED STATES, *National Monuments.*

Muir Pass. Mountain pass, Fresno co., S cen. California; in N part of Kings Canyon National Park on the John Muir Trail which extends from Yosemite National Park to Sequoia National Park; 12,059 ft.

Muir Woods National Monument. See UNITED STATES, *National Monuments.*

Mui·zen·berg \'māz-ᵊn-ˌbərg, 'mȯi-zən-\. Town, SW Cape Province, S Rep. of South Africa, on NW shore of False Bay 14 m. SSE of Cape Town; now included in municipality of Cape Town; summer resort; cottage in which Cecil Rhodes died 1902.

Mu·je·res \mü-'her-əs\. An island belonging to Mexico in the Caribbean Sea off NE coast of Yucatán penin.

Mu·ka·che·vo *or Czech* **Mu·ka·če·vo** \'mu̇k-ə-ˌchev-(ˌ)ȯ\ *or Hung.* **Mun·kács** \'mu̇ŋ-käch\. Town, Transcarpathian Oblast, W Ukrainian S.S.R., U.S.S.R., formerly in Carpathian Ruthenia, E Czechoslovakia; pop. (1969e) 61,000; tobacco, beer and spirits, furniture; flour mills. Transferred to Hungary 1938, to U.S.S.R. July 29, 1945.

Mu·kah \'mü-(ˌ)kä\. Coastal town, W Sarawak, Malaysia, on island of Borneo, just NE of the Rajang delta.

Mu·kal·la \mu̇-'kal-ə\. Seaport and chief town of Hadhramaut, Yemen (✱ Aden), S Arabian Penin., 320 m. NE of Aden; pop. (1970e) 65,000; exports gums, hides, and coffee.

Mu·kā·wir \mü-'kä-wir\. Town, Jordan, E of Dead Sea; site of fortified village (**Ma·chae·rus** \mə-'kir-əs\) of anc. Moab, place where John the Baptist was beheaded.

Muk·den *also* **Mouk·den** \'mu̇k-dən, 'mək-; mu̇k-'den\ *or Chin.* **Shen–yang** \'shən-'yäŋ\ *or formerly* **Feng·tien** \'fəŋ-tē-'en\. Industrial city, Liaoning prov., NE China; pop. (1970e) 3,750,000; strategically located on the Hun for control over N to S routes in S Manchurian plain; one of China's leading industrial cities, producing machinery, transformers, wires and cables, machine tools, flour, textiles, soap, paper, and chemicals; trades in agricultural and forest products. Divided into three major parts: old walled city, ab. 4 m. in circumference; new town, orig. Japanese concession; Teihsi district, center of modern heavy industries. Educational and cultural center; has notable palaces, mausoleums, and monuments.

History: Capital of Kin Tatars in 12th cent.; base for Manchu conquest of China in 17th cent. and site of royal tombs and treasury during rule of Manchu dynasty 1644–1912; in Russo-Japanese War scene of major battle Feb. 19–Mar 10, 1945 when it fell to Japanese; seat of important warlord Chang Tso-Lin during civil war 1924–1928; occupied by Japanese 1931–1945; scene of heavy fighting in Chinese civil war 1947–48; occupied by Communist forces Nov. 1, 1948.

Mukhā. See MOCHA 2.

Mukhmas. See MICHMASH.

Mukhu. See MUHU.

Mu·ko–shi·ma \mu̇k-ə-'shē-mə\. One of the Bonin Is., Japan.

Mu·la \'mü-lə\. Commune, Murcia prov., SE Spain, 18 m. WNW of Murcia; pop. (1970p) 13,922; thermal springs and baths; ruins of ancient castle.

Mulahacen. See MULHACÉN.

Mul·ber·ry \'məl-ˌber-ē\. City, Polk co., cen. Florida penin., 12 m. S of Lakeland; pop. (1970c) 2701; phosphate mines; fruit and truck farms.

Mul·chén \mül-'chān\. Town, Bío-Bío prov., S cen. Chile, 80 m. SE of Concepción; pop. (1960c) 10,729.

Mul·de \'mu̇l-də\. River, East Germany; ab. 156 m. long; rises in the Erzgebirge and flows N past Karl-Marx-Stadt into Elbe river near Dessau.

Mule Ear Peaks. Mountain, S Brewster co., W Texas; 3880 ft.

Mu–leng \'mü-'ləŋ\ *or* **Mu·ling** \-'liŋ\. River, Heilungkiang prov., NE China; 260 m. long; flows NE into Ussuri river.

Mule·shoe \'myül-ˌshü\. Town, ⊗ of Bailey co., NW Texas; pop. (1970c) 4525; truck farms.

Mul·grave \'məl-ˌgrāv\. Island in Torres Strait, N of Queensland, Australia, adjacent to Banks I. and N of Thursday I.

Mul·ha·cén \ˌmü-lä-'sān, -'sen\ *also* **Mu·la·ha·cen** \mü-ˌlä-ä-\ *or* **Mu·ley–Ha·cén** \mü-ˌlā-ä-\. Peak in the Sierra Nevada, Granada prov., S Spain; 11,407 ft.; highest peak in Europe outside of the Alps and Caucasus.

Mül·heim an der Ruhr \'m(y)ül-ˌhī-ˌmän-də(r)-'ru̇(ə)r\. Commercial and manufacturing city, North Rhine-Westphalia, West Germany, on Ruhr river near its mouth 7 m. WSW of Essen; pop. (1969e) 190,408; ships coal; electrical machinery, steel wire, turbines; iron and steel foundries, tube and rolling mills, machine shops, breweries; 11th cent. church; first mentioned 1093; to Prussia 1815; bombed by Allies 1943–45; taken with other cities that fell with surrender of the Ruhr April 1945.

Mul·house \mə-'lüz\ *or Ger.* **Mül·hau·sen** \myül-'hau̇z-ᵊn\. Industrial and commercial commune, Haut-Rhin dept., NE France, on Ill river 22 m. S of Colmar; pop. (1968c) 116,336; fertilizers, chemicals, textiles, machinery; 15th cent. town hall. First mentioned 803 A.D.; imperial free city 1308; allied with Swiss 15th–18th cents.; became French 1798; model workingmen's colony founded here 1853; under German rule 1871–1918; reverted to France 1918.

Mu·li·a·ma \ˌmü-lē-'ä-mə\. Village on E coast of New Ireland, Bismarck Archipelago, W Pacific Ocean; has good harbor.

Muling. See MU-LENG.

Mull \'məl\. Largest island of the Inner Hebrides, off W coast of Scotland; ab. 27 m. long by 20 m. wide max.; pop. (1961c) 3185; chief town Tobermory; stock farms, granite quarries; highest point 3185 ft.; administratively a part of Argyll co.

Mull, Ross of \'rȯs-\. Long SW peninsula of the island of Mull, off W coast of Scotland.

Mull, Sound of. Body of water bet. the NE coast of island of Mull and the Scottish mainland.

Mul·lagh·more \ˌməl-ə-'mō(ə)r, -'mȯ(ə)r\. Promontory extending N into Donegal Bay, NW Eire, 13 m. N of Sligo.

Mul·lan Trail \ˌməl-ən-\. Wagon trail, NW United States, from Fort Benton, Montana, at head of navigation of Missouri river, across Bitterroot Range to Walla Walla, Washington; built 1859–62 under direction of Lt. John Mullan; helped to open rich mining region.

Mul·len \'məl-ən\. Village, ⊗ of Hooker co., W cen. Nebraska; pop. (1970c) 667.

Mul·lens \'məl-ənz\. City, Wyoming co., S West Virginia, 18 m. SSW of Beckley; pop. (1970c) 2967; railroad shop; ships coal; dairy farms.

Mul·ler Mountains \ˌməl-ər-\. Range in cen. island of Borneo, Indonesia, running N and S bet. provinces of West, South, and East Kalimantan; average height 4000 to 5000 ft.; highest point 7349 ft.; source of many of the streams of the island.

Mul·let \ˈməl-ət\. Peninsula in co. Mayo, on W coast of Eire, S of Erris Head, enclosing Blacksod Bay on the W, and connected with the mainland by a narrow isthmus at the NE.

Mul·lett Lake \ˈməl-ət-\. Lake in N Cheboygan co., N Michigan; outlet N into Straits of Mackinac.

Mul·li·ca \ˈməl-i-kə\. River, S New Jersey; ab. 40 m. long; flows from W Burlington co. SE into Great Bay.

Mul·lin·gar \ˌməl-ən-ˈgär\. Town, ⊗ of co. Westmeath, N cen. Eire; pop. (1966c) 6471; trade center in agricultural district; furniture; trout fishing.

Mul·lins \ˈməl-ənz\. Town, Marion co., E South Carolina, 32 m. E of Florence; pop. (1970c) 6006; lumber.

Mull of Galloway. See GALLOWAY, MULL OF.

Mull of Kintyre. See KINTYRE, MULL OF.

Mull of Oa. See OA, MULL OF.

Mul·roy Bay \məl-ˈrȯi-\. Inlet of Atlantic Ocean on N coast of co. Donegal, N Eire, W of Lough Swilly.

Mul·tan *also* **Mool·tan** \mu̇l-ˈtän\. 1 Division, Punjab, Pakistan; 24,826 sq. m.; pop. (1961c) 6,602,924.
2 City, its ✱, near Chenab river 200 m. WSW of Lahore; pop. (1969e) 596,000; major industrial center, with cotton gins, textile mills, foundries, glass factory, flour mills, and various cottage industries incl. pottery, camelskin work, and lacquerware. An ancient city, possibly one of the Indian cities taken by Alexander; seized by Mahmud of Ghazni 1006; under emperors of Delhi 1526–1779 and Afghans till 1818, when it was taken by the Sikhs under Ranjit Singh; under British sovereignty 1849. Includes surrounding wall and fort enclosing shrines of two Muslim saints and an ancient Hindu temple; large military cantonment.

Mult·no·mah \məlt ˈnō mə\. County in Oregon. See table at OREGON.

Multnomah Falls. Waterfall, Multnomah co., NW Oregon, E of Portland, in a small tributary of the Columbia river which rises near summit of Larch Mt., 4095 ft. high; height of falls 620 ft.

Mulucha *or* **Muluya.** See MOULOUYA.

Mul·vane \məl-ˈvan\. City, Sedgwick and Sumner cos., S Kansas, 16 m. SSE of Wichita; pop. (1970c) 3185; stock farms.

Mulvius, Pons. See SAXA RUBRA.

Mulwiya. See MOULOUYA.

Mun \ˈmün\. River, E Thailand; ab. 350 m. long; rises in hills NE of Bangkok, flows E into the Mekong river on the border of Laos; receives large tributary, the Chi, ab. 50 m. from its mouth. Largest town on its banks is Nakhon Ratchasima; navigable in wet season.

Mu·na *or Du.* **Moe·na** \ˈmü-nə\. Island off SE coast of Celebes I., Indonesia; 63 m. long by 35 m. wide; 1124 sq. m.

München. See MUNICH.

München-Gladbach. See MÖNCHENGLADBACH.

Mun·cie \ˈmən(t)-sē\. Industrial city, ⊗ of Delaware co., E cen. Indiana, 50 m. ENE of Indianapolis; pop. (1970c) 69,082; trade center; aircraft, automobile parts, wire, structural steel, lawn furniture, electrical equipment; Ball State Univ. (1918); founded 1824; incorporated as town 1854, as city 1865.

Mun·cy \ˈmən(t)-sē\. Borough, Lycoming co., N cen. Pennsylvania, 13 m. E of Williamsport; pop. (1970c) 2872; machinery, wire rope.

Mund. See MAND.

Mun·da. 1 \ˈmün-də, ˈmən-\. Settlement on S side of NW end of New Georgia I., cen. Solomon Is., W Pacific Ocean. Site of Japanese air base 1942–43; taken by American forces Aug. 5, 1943.
2 \ˈmən-də\. Ancient town, S Baetica, S Spain; scene of Caesar's victory over Pompey's sons 45 B.C.

Mun·de·lein \ˈmən-də-ˌlīn\. Village, Lake co., NE Illinois, NW of Chicago; pop. (1970c) 16,128.

Mün·den \ˈm(y)ün-dən, ˈmin-\ *also* **Han·no·versch–Mün·den** \hä-ˌnō-vərsh-\. City, S Lower Saxony, West Germany, at confluence of Werra and Fulda rivers 10 m. NE of Kassel; pop. (1968e) 19,236; summer resort; river port; 11th cent. castle; 14th cent. stone bridge; 17th cent. Renaissance town hall.

Mun·ford·ville \ˈmən(t)-fərd-ˌvil\. City, ⊗ of Hart co., cen. Kentucky; pop. (1970c) 1233.

Mun·hall \ˈmən-ˌhȯl\. Industrial borough, Allegheny co., SW Pennsylvania, on Monongahela river 7 m. E of Pittsburgh; pop. (1970c) 16,574; steel products.

Mu·ni \ˈmü-nē\. River, Equatorial Guinea, W Africa; 50 m. long; empties into Corisco Bay.

Mu·nich \ˈmyü-nik\ *or Ger.* **Mün·chen** \ˈm(y)ün-kən\. Industrial city, ✱ of Bavaria, West Germany, on Isar river; pop. (1970c) 1,293,590; trade, cultural, and industrial center; manufactures precision instruments, optical equipment, motor vehicles, chemicals, cigarettes; slaughterhouse, stockyards, wholesale vegetable market; noted center of brewing industry. Numerous notable buildings, including 12th cent. Peterskirche (restored), three 14th cent. town gates, 15th cent. cathedral, 15th cent. town hall, 16th cent. Michaelkirche (Renaissance), 17th cent. palace, 19th cent. Glyptothek museum, many 18th cent. palaces and town houses; noted univ. (founded at Ingolstadt 1472; transferred to Landshut, then to Munich 1826), technical univ. (1868).
History: Founded 1158; became capital of Bavaria under Wittelsbachs 1255; occupied by Swedes 1632; by Austria 1705 and 1742; site of attempted revolt by Hitler ("Beer Hall Putsch") Nov. 8–9, 1923 and of early activities of Nazi party; scene Sept. 29, 1938 of four-power conference (Germany, Italy, Great Britain, France) leading to partition of Czechoslovakia; in World War II suffered considerable damage from Allied bombing; occupied by Allied forces May 1, 1945; extensively rebuilt since war; site of Summer Olympic Games 1972.

Mu·ni·sing \ˈmyü-nə-ˌsiŋ\. City, ⊗ of Alger co., N Michigan penin., on Lake Superior 37 m. E of Marquette; pop. (1970c) 3677; paper; fruit and dairy farms.

Munkács. See MUKACHEVO.

Mun·ku–Sar·dyk \ˌmu̇ŋ-kü-ˈsär-dik\ *or* **Mönh Sa·rī·dag** \ˈməŋ-ˌsär-i-ˈdäg\. Highest peak in the Sayan Mts., on boundary bet. Buryat A.S.S.R., Russian S.F.S.R., U.S.S.R. and Mongolian People's Republic, at the N end of Hövsgöl; 11,451 ft.

Mu·ñoz \mü-ˈnyōs\. Municipality, Nueva Ecija prov., Luzon, Phil., ab. 16 m. N of Cabanatuan; pop. (1969e) 37,500.

Mun·roe Falls \mən-ˈrō-, ˈmən-rō-\. Village, Summit co., Ohio, 7 m. NE of Akron; pop. (1970c) 3794.

Mun·sey Park \ˈmən(t)-sē-\. Village, Nassau co., SE New York; pop. (1970c) 2980.

Mun·ster \ˈmən(t)-stər\. 1 Town, Lake co., NW corner of Indiana, 10 m. S of Lake Michigan; pop. (1970c) 16,514.
2 Province, S Eire; 9315 sq. m.; pop. (1971p) 880,018; includes cos. Clare, Cork, Kerry, Limerick, Tipperary (North Riding and South Riding), Waterford.

Mün·ster \ˈmin(t)-stər, ˈm(y)ün(t)-, ˈmu̇n(t)-, ˈmən(t)-\ *also* **Münster in West·fa·len** \-in-vest-ˈfäl-ən\. Manufacturing and commercial city, North Rhine-Westphalia, West Germany, near the Dortmund-Ems canal 78 m. NNE of Cologne; pop. (1969e) 203,324; railroad junction; machinery, textiles, building materials; restored 13th cent. cathedral, 14th cent. Liebfrauenkirche, 14th cent. town hall, 18th cent. castle; univ. (1780, received univ. status 1902). Grew up in 12th cent. around a monastery or minster (Ger. *münster*); fell to Anabaptists 1532–35; Treaty of Westphalia signed here Oct. 24, 1648, ending Thirty Years'

War; in World War II suffered heavy damage; taken by Allies Apr. 3, 1945.

Mun·te·nia \ˌmən-ˈtē-nē-ə\ *or* **Greater Wa·la·chia** \-wə-ˈlāk-ē-ə\. Region, S Romania, E part of Walachia; 20,267 sq. m.; formerly a province.

Mun·tok \ˈmün-ˌtu̇k\. Seaport, NW Bangka I., Indonesia; chief export center for tin mined in the island.

Muong·sing \ˈmwȯŋ-ˈsiŋ\. Town, NW Laos, SE Asia, near China border just E of the Mekong.

Muo·nio \ˈmwō-nē-ˌō\. River, NW Finland; ab. 200 m. long; flows S into Torne river, forming a section of the boundary bet. Finland and Sweden.

Mu·pa National Park \ˈmü-pə-\. National park, S Angola; 2548 sq. m.; wildlife refuge (antelope, black rhinoceros, elephant, zebra); established 1964.

Muqaiyir. See UR.

Mur \ˈmu̇(ə)r\ *or Serbo-Croat.* **Mu·ra** \ˈmu̇r-ə\. River, Austria and N Yugoslavia; 279 m. long; rises in E end of Hohe Tauern and flows E in Salzburg, E and NE across Styria, turns S and SE across Yugoslav border into Drava river 25 m. E of Varaždin.

Mu·ra·no \mü-ˈrän-(ˌ)ō\. North suburb of Venice, Italy, on five small islands in the lagoon of Venice; noted for its cathedral and for the manufacture of Venetian glass.

Mu·rat·daği \mu̇-ˌrät-dä-ˈ(g)ē\. Peak, W Turkey, W of Afyonkarahisar; 7583 ft.

Mu·rat Neh·ri \mu̇-ˌrät-nā-ˈrē\ *also* **Eastern Eu·phra·tes** \-yu̇-ˈfrāt-(ˌ)ēz\ *or anc.* **Ar·sa·ni·as** \är-ˈsā-nē-əs\. One of the two headstreams of the Euphrates river; rises in NE Turkey in Asia in the mountains SW of Mt. Ararat, and flows W to unite with the Kara Su and form the Euphrates river.

Mur·chi·son \ˈmər-chə-sən\. River, W Western Australia; 440 m. long; flows W to Indian Ocean.

Murchison Falls. 1 Waterfall in the Victoria Nile, just above Lake Albert, in Uganda; 130 ft. high. See NILE.

2 Waterfall in the Shire river, Malawi, SE Africa, 15°54′S, 34°44′E.

Murchison Falls National Park. National park, NW Uganda; 1504 sq. m.; contains Murchison Falls; established 1952.

Mur·cia \ˈmər-sh(ē-)ə\. 1 Region and ancient kingdom, SE Spain; 10,106 sq. m.; bounded N and NW by New Castile, SW by Andalusia, S by Mediterranean, and E by Valencia; comprises modern provinces of Albacete and Murcia; watered by the Segura and its affluents; climate varies from subtropical to temperate and its arid regions require irrigation for agricultural exploitation; produces principally citrus fruit, esparto, hemp, cotton, and olives; zinc, lead, sulfur, copper, and tin mines; fishing.

History: Center of Carthaginian colonization in Spain; conquered by Moors in 8th cent.; made province of Caliphate of Córdoba; became independent Moorish kingdom in early 11th cent.; conquered by Castile 1266.

2 Province of SE Spain. See table at SPAIN.

3 Commune, ✱ of Murcia prov., SE Spain, on Segura river 47 m. SW of Alicante; pop. (1970p) 243,759; ships cereals, almonds, citrus fruit; manufactures silk, textiles, flour, aluminum products, leather goods, hats; univ. (1915); 14th–16th cent. Gothic-Romanesque cathedral, 18th cent. episcopal palace; Moorish granary; city walls. First settled by Romans; reconquered from Moors in 13th cent.; capital of ancient kingdom of Murcia.

Mur·cié·la·gos, Gulf of \-ˌmu̇r-sē-ˈel-ə-gəs\ *or formerly* **Cu·le·bra Gulf** \k(y)u̇-ˌlā-brə-, -ˌleb-rə-\. Inlet of Pacific Ocean on NW coast of Costa Rica.

Mur·do \ˈmər-(ˌ)dō\. City, ⊗ of Jones co., S cen. South Dakota; pop. (1970c) 865.

Mur·doch·ville \ˈmər-ˌdäk-ˌvil\. Town, Gaspé-Ouest co., SE Quebec, Canada, 75 m. NE of Dalhousie, New Brunswick; pop. (1971p) 2858.

Mu·reş \ˈmu̇(ə)r-ˌesh\. County of N cen. Romania. See table at ROMANIA.

Mu·re·şul \ˌmü-rə-ˈsül\ *or* **Mu·resh** \ˈmü-resh\ *or Hung.* **Ma·ros** \ˈmär-ōsh\. River, Hungary and Romania; 550 m. long; rises in the Carpathian Mts., flows W across N Romania, continues W across Hungarian border and into Tisza river opp. Szeged; navigable for small boats for over 200 m.

Mur·frees·boro \ˈmər-f(r)ēz-ˌbər-ə, -ˌbə-rə\. 1 City, ⊗ of Pike co., SW Arkansas; pop. (1970c) 1350.

2 Town, Hertford co., NE North Carolina, 50 m. WNW of Elizabeth City; pop. (1970c) 3508; peanuts; Chowan Coll. (1848).

3 Commercial city, ⊗ of Rutherford co., cen. Tennessee, on West Fork of Stone River 33 m. SE of Nashville; pop. (1970c) 26,630; silk and rayon, flour, lumber, dairy products; Middle Tennessee State Univ. (1909). Made county seat 1811, capital of Tennessee 1819–25; during Civil War site of battle (also called battle of Stones River, *q.v.*) Dec. 31, 1862–Jan. 2, 1863 in which Union forces under Rosecrans won a strategic victory over Confederates under Bragg.

Mur·gab \mu̇r-ˈgäb\. 1 River, Afghanistan and U.S.S.R. See MURGHAB 1.

2 *or* **Mur·ghak** \mu̇r-ˈgäk-\. River, Tadzhik S.S.R., U.S.S.R.; flows W in Pamirs.

Murgh \ˈmu̇(ə)rg\. Pass, NE Afghanistan, N of Kabul, in the Hindu Kush; 7480 ft.

Murgh·ab \mu̇r-ˈgäb\. 1 *or Russ.* **Mur·gab** \mu̇r-ˈgap\. River, NW Afghanistan and SE Turkmen S.S.R., U.S.S.R.; ab. 500 m. long; rises in W slopes of the Hindu Kush and flows W and NW until lost in the sands of the Kara Kum Desert beyond Mary.

2 Plain, ancient Persia. See PASARGADAE.

Murghak. See MURGAB 2.

Mu·riaé \ˌmu̇r-yə-ˈā\. City, SE Minas Gerais state, E Brazil, 75 m. NE of Juiz de Fora; munic. pop. (1968e) 60,539.

Mü·ritz, Lake \-ˈm(y)u̇r-əts\. Lake, Neubrandenburg dist., East Germany, W of Neustrelitz; 44 sq. m.; largest natural lake in East Germany.

Mur·man Coast \mu̇r-ˈman-, -ˈmän-\ *or* **Mur·mansk Coast** \mu̇r-ˈman(t)sk-, -ˈmän(t)sk-\ *also earlier* **Nor·man Coast** \ˌnȯr-mən-\. The N coast of Kola Penin., Murmansk Oblast, NW Russian S.F.S.R., U.S.S.R.; ab. 165 m. long from 36°E to 41°E; generally ice-free because of warm easterly ocean current; has many inlets and good harbors and in many places cliffs 300 to 1000 ft.

Mur·mansk \mu̇r-ˈman(t)sk, -ˈmän(t)sk\. City, ✱ of Murmansk Oblast, NW Russian S.F.S.R., U.S.S.R.; in NW part on Kola Bay, ab. 22 m. from the ocean; pop. (1970p) 309,000; largest city in the world N of the Arctic Circle; ice-free port; naval base; shipyards, breweries, fish canneries, sawmills; base for large fishing fleet. Founded 1916 as supply port; occupied by British, French, and American expeditionary forces during intervention against Communists 1918; in World War II a major supply base, the main port for the Anglo-American convoys.

Murmansk Oblast \-ˈō-bləst, -ˌblast\. Subdivision of the Russian S.F.S.R., U.S.S.R., nearly coextensive with Kola Penin.; 55,946 sq. m.; pop. (1970p) 799,000; ✱ Murmansk. A plateau with average elevation of 600 to 700 ft., highest point 3906 ft.; a tundra region of many lakes (largest Imandra), small rivers, morasses; chief river the Tuloma, in the NW. Chief cities: Murmansk, Monchegorsk, Kirovsk. Chief inhabitants Lapp, with some Russians and Finns; main occupations fishing, hunting, lumbering, and reindeer raising; its shore controlled 1918–19 by British fleet; since 1944 has included in the NW Petsamo (Pechenga) and surrounding territory acquired from Finland (see PECHENGA).

Mu·ro Lu·ca·no \ˌmu̇r-ō-lü-ˈkä-nō\. Commune, Potenza prov., W Basilicata, S Italy; pop. (1968e) 8683; castle, scene of death of Joanna I, Queen of Naples.

Mu·rom \ˈmu̇r-əm\. Town, SE Vladimir Oblast, E cen. Russian S.F.S.R., U.S.S.R., on the Oka 90 m. SW of Gorki; pop. (1969e) 100,000; machinery, textiles, lumber; locomotive repair shops; one of oldest Russian cities, first mentioned 862; to Moscow 1393.

Mu·ro·ran \mu̇r-ə-ˈrän\. Seaport, SW Hokkaidō, Japan, on N side of Uchiura Bay; pop. (1970c) 162,059; ships coal, wood pulp, lumber; iron and steel center of N Japan; oil refining.

Mu·ros \ˈmu̇r-ōs\. Commune, La Coruña prov., NW Spain, on inlet of Atlantic Ocean 49 m. SW of La Coruña; pop. (1970p) 21,491; agricultural products; flour, soap, textiles; commercial fisheries.

Mu·ro·to, Cape \-mu̇-ˈrōt-(ˌ)ō\. Cape on SE coast of Shikoku I., Japan; lighthouse.

Mur·phy \ˈmər-fē\. 1 Town, ⊗ of Owyhee co., SW corner of Idaho; shipping point for livestock.

2 Town and mountain resort, ⊗ of Cherokee co., W tip of North Carolina, 5 m. W of Georgia border and 16 m. E of Tennessee border; pop. (1970c) 2082; textiles, lumber; fruit and dairy farms.

Mur·phys·boro \ˈmər-fēz-ˌbər-ə, -ˌbə-rə\. City, ⊗ of Jackson co., SW Illinois, 24 m. W of Marion; pop. (1970c) 10,013; shoes, feed, fertilizer; settled 1850.

Mur·ray \ˈmər-ē, ˈmə-rē\. 1 Counties of three states of the U.S. See tables at GEORGIA, MINNESOTA, OKLAHOMA.

2 City, ⊗ of Calloway co., SW Kentucky, 22 m. ESE of Mayfield; pop. (1970c) 13,537; lumber, tobacco, dairy products; Murray State Univ. (1922).

3 City, Salt Lake co., N Utah, on Jordan river 8 m. S of Salt Lake City; pop. (1970c) 21,206; suburb of Salt Lake City; textiles; diversified agriculture.

4 Major river of Australia; 1609 m. long; to the source of the Darling (*q.v.*) 2310 m. Rises in Kosciusko Plateau, E Victoria, flows NW as boundary bet. Victoria and New South Wales into SE South Australia where it turns S and flows into Encounter Bay through Lake Alexandrina (*q.v.*); at ab. 142°E it receives the Darling from the N and farther E at 143°13′E the Murrumbidgee. In the dry season often shallow; in the wet season navigable to Albury for smaller vessels; sandbars at its mouth prevent entrance of large vessels.

Murray, Lake. 1 Lake extending across boundary bet. Carter and Love cos., S Oklahoma.

2 Large lake in swamp and lake region bet. Fly and Strickland rivers, Papua New Guinea, New Guinea I.

Murray Bridge. Town, SE South Australia, on Murray river near its mouth 40 m. WSW of Adelaide; pop. (1966c) 5957.

Mur·rum·bidg·ee \ˌmər-əm-ˈbij-ē, ˌmə-rəm-\. River, S New South Wales, SE Australia; 981 m. long; flows W from Great Dividing Range near Canberra to join Murray river at ab. 143°E; navigable for small vessels for ab. 500 m. in rainy season.

Mur·shid·a·bad \ˈmu̇r-shəd-ə-ˌbäd\. Town, West Bengal, NE India, on left bank of the Bhagirathi (old channel of the Ganges); pop. (1961c) 17,000; founded 1704 by Murshid Kuli Khan as Muslim capital of Bengal; a populous city in 18th cent. and headquarters of Siraj-ud-daula at the time of Plassey 1757; contains fine palace of the Nawab of Bengal.

Murtana. See PERGA.

Murten. See MORAT.

Murtensee. See MORAT, LAKE OF.

Murua. See WOODLARK.

Mu·rud \mə-ˈru̇d\. Seaport town, E Maharashtra, W India, 45 m. S of Bombay; pop. (1961c) 10,100.

Murviedro. See SAGUNTO.

Mur·wa·ra \mu̇r-ˈwar-ə\. Town, cen. Madhya Pradesh, India, on the Son river ab. 200 m. NNE of Nagpur; pop. (1961c) 46,200.

Mürz \ˈm(y)u̇(ə)rts\. River, Styria, SE Austria; ab. 45 m. long; rises in N Styria and flows SW to the Mur at Bruck.

Mur·zuch \ˈmu̇(ə)r-ˌzu̇k\. *or Arab.* **Mur·zuq** \ˈmu̇r-ˌzu̇k\. Oasis, Fezzan, SW Libya.

Muş *or* **Mush** \ˈmüsh\. 1 Province of E Turkey. See table at TURKEY.

2 Town, its ✱, 45 m. W of Lake Van; pop. (1965c) 15,687.

Mu·sa, Geb·el \ˌjeb-əl-ˈmü-sə\. Mountain group, S Sinai Penin., Egypt; name applied by some only to N peak 7497 ft.; highest in the group Gebel Katherina 8652 ft. On its N slope is St. Catherine's Monastery of Mt. Sinai which has fine library; in it Tischendorf 1844–45 found one of oldest Greek Biblical MSS. known, the *Codex Sinaiticus,* which became property of the tsar, then of U.S.S.R., and was sold to British Museum 1933 for £100,000. See SINAI, MOUNT.

Musa, Jeb·el \ˌjeb-əl-ˈmü-sə\; *anc.* **Ab·i·la** *or* **Ab·y·la** \ˈab-ə-lə\. Mountain, Ceuta, N Morocco, opp. Gibraltar; 2775 ft. See PILLARS OF HERCULES.

Mu·sa·la \ˌmü-sə-ˈlä\. Highest peak in the Rhodope Mts., in the Rila Dagh, SW Bulgaria, SSE of Sofia; 9596 ft.

Mu·san·dam, Cape \-mə-ˈsan-dəm\ *or Arab.* **Ras Ma·san·dam** \ˌräs-mə-ˈsan-dəm\. Cape, N Oman, SE Arabian Penin., extending N into the Strait of Hormuz.

Mu·sa·shi·no \mu̇-ˈsä-shē-ˌnō\. City, Tokyo prefecture, Honshū, Japan; pop. (1970c) 136,959; suburb of Tokyo.

Muscat. See MASQAT.

Muscat and Oman. See OMAN.

Mus·ca·tine \ˌməs-kə-ˈtēn\. 1 County in E Iowa. See table at IOWA.

2 City, its ⊗, on Mississippi river 25 m. W of Davenport; pop. (1970c) 22,405; buttons, feeds, canned foods, steel cabinets, pumps; founded 1833, incorporated 1851.

Mus·cle Shoals \ˌməs-əl-\. 1 Rapids extending ab. 37 m. in Tennessee river, in Lauderdale co., N Alabama; now submerged under at least 9 ft. of water by completion of Wilson Dam at W end and Wheeler Dam at E end. See TENNESSEE 1.

2 Town, Colbert co., NW Alabama, near Wilson Dam 3 m. S of Tennessee river; pop. (1970c) 6907.

Mus·co·gee \məs-ˈkō-gē\. County in Georgia. See table at GEORGIA.

Mus·co·net·cong \ˌməs-kə-ˈnet-ˌkäŋ\. River, N New Jersey; 50 m. long; flows from Lake Hopatcong SW to Delaware river at SW extremity of Warren co.

Mus·con·gus Bay \mə-ˌskäŋ-gəs-\. Inlet of Atlantic Ocean on SW coast of Knox co., S Maine.

Muscovy. See MOSCOW.

Mus·grave Ranges \ˌməs-grāv-\. Mountain ranges along boundary bet. South Australia and Northern Territory; highest point Mt. Woodroffe 4724 ft.

Mush. See MUŞ.

Mu·shin \ˈmü-ˌshin\. Town, Lagos state, SW Nigeria; pop. (1969e) 169,287; textiles; metalworking.

Mu·sho·zu \mu̇-ˈshō-(ˌ)zü\. See IKI.

Mu·si \ˈmü-sē\. 1 River, Andhra Pradesh, S cen. India; flows E and then S into Krishna river.

2 *or Du.* **Moe·si** \ˈmü-sē\. River, S Sumatra, Indonesia; ab. 325 m. long; rises in Barisan Mts. NE of Bengkulu, flows E and NE to Bangka Strait; has many tributaries; Palembang on it 56 m. from its mouth.

Mu·sic Pass \ˌmyü-zik-\. Mountain pass, Huerfano and Saguache cos., S Colorado, in the Sangre de Cristo Range of the Rocky Mts.; 11,800 ft.; was used by travelers on Arkansas river route to California and New Mexico in late 19th century; trail.

Musigny. See CHAMBOLLE-MUSIGNY.

Mus·keg Bay \ˌməs-keg-\. Inlet of Lake of the Woods, in NE Roseau co., N Minnesota.

Mus·ke·get Channel \mə-ˌskē-gət-\. Strait bet. Martha's Vineyard on the W and Muskeget I., Tuckernuck I., and Nantucket on the E, in SE Massachusetts; connects Nantucket Sound with the Atlantic Ocean.

Muskeget Island. Island in Atlantic Ocean at E entrance of Muskeget Channel S of Cape Cod, SE Massachusetts; a part of Nantucket co.

Mus·ke·go \məs-ˈkē-(ˌ)gō\. City, Waukesha co., SE Wisconsin, 16 m. SW of Milwaukee; pop. (1970c) 11,573.

Mus·ke·gon \mə-ˈskē-gən\. 1 River, W cen. Michigan; 200 m. long; rises in Houghton Lake, Roscommon co., flows SW into Lake Michigan at Muskegon, in Muskegon co.; navigable for a short distance.

2 County in W Michigan. See table at MICHIGAN.

3 City, its ⊗, on Lake Michigan at mouth of Muskegon river 35 m. WNW of Grand Rapids; pop. (1970c) 44,631; lake port and railroad center; automobile parts and engines, office furniture, steel, brass, and aluminum castings, boats, electric cranes, wire products; Muskegon Business Coll. (1885), Muskegon County Community Coll. (1926); trading post on site founded 1812; city incorporated 1869; in late 19th cent. a major lumbering and lumber-shipping center.

Muskegon Heights. City, Muskegon co., W Michigan, S suburb of Muskegon; pop. (1970c) 17,304.

Mus·kin·gum \mə-ˈskiŋ-(g)əm\. 1 River, E Ohio; 120 m. long; formed by confluence of Tuscarawas and Walhonding rivers in Coshocton co., E cen. Ohio, flows S and SE into Ohio river at Marietta, Washington co.; navigable for 90 m.

2 County in Ohio. See table at OHIO.

Mus·ko·gee \mə-ˈskō-gē\. 1 County in E Oklahoma. See table at OKLAHOMA.

2 City, its ⊗, on Arkansas river 47 m. SE of Tulsa; pop. (1970c) 37,331; dairy products, iron and steel, rare metals, glass, clothing, rocket and missile fuel; oil wells and refineries, canning plants, railroad yard; founded 1872, incorporated 1898.

Mus·ko·ka \mə-ˈskō-kə\. District, SE Ontario, Canada. See table at ONTARIO.

Muskoka, Lake. Lake, Muskoka dist., SE Ontario, Canada; 54 sq. m.; with Lakes Rosseau and Joseph and several hundred small lakes forms **Muskoka Lake Region,** noted for its scenery, its hunting and fishing, and as a summer resort. Outlet is **Muskoka River,** ab. 100 m. long, with two headstreams rising in lakes of Haliburton co. and Muskoka dist. and flowing SW through Lake Muskoka to Georgian Bay. Bracebridge is on it.

Mus·li·mi·ya *or* **Mus·li·mī·yah** \ˌmu̇s-lə-ˈmē-(y)ə\. Town, NW Syria, ab. 8 m. N of Aleppo; junction on railroads NW to Adana in Turkey and NE to Nusaybin in Turkey.

Mu·so·ma \mü-ˈsō-mə\. Town, ✱ of Mara region, N Tanzania; pop. (1967c) 15,412.

Mus·sau \mü-ˈsau̇\. Island, W Pacific Ocean, N Bismarck Archipelago, in Saint Mathias group NNW of New Hanover; ab. 20 m. long by 10 m. wide; largest island in the group.

Mus·sel·shell \ˈməs-əl-ˌshel\. 1 River, cen. Montana; 300 m. long; rises in Meagher co., flows E, then N into Missouri river in NW Garfield co.

2 County in Montana. See table at MONTANA.

Mus·so·me·li \ˌmü-sə-ˈmel-ē\. Commune, Caltanissetta prov., cen. Sicily, Italy, 18 m. WNW of Caltanissetta; pop. (1968e) 12,849; castle; sulfur mining.

Mus·soo·rie \mə-ˈsu̇r-ē\. Hill station and sanitarium, N Uttar Pradesh, N India, 135 m. NNE of Delhi; pop. (1961c) 9900; formerly one of chief summer resorts of Europeans of N India; alt. 6600 ft.

Mu–ssu–t'a–ko–a–t'e \ˈmü-ˈsü-ˈtä-ˈkō-ˈä-ˈtə\. 1 *also* **Muztagh Ata Range** \müs-ˈtä(g)-ə-ˈtä-\. Mountain range running N and S along border of E Tadzhik S.S.R., U.S.S.R., in W Sinkiang Uighur, W China; by some considered part of the Pamirs; highest point Kung-ko-erh, in N part of range, 25,325 ft.; many peaks above 20,000 ft.

2 *also* **Muztagh Ata.** Mountain, W Sinkiang Uighur, W China, near the border of the Tadzhik S.S.R., U.S.S.R., and ab. 75 m. SW of Kashgar; 24,757 ft.

Mus·ta·fa Ke·mal Pa·şa \ˌmu̇s-tə-ˌfä-kə-ˈmäl-pə-ˈshä\ *or formerly* **Kir·mas·ti** \ˌkir-mə-ˈstē\. Town, W Bursa prov., NW Turkey, 37 m. WSW of Bursa; pop. (1965c) 23,179.

Mus·tagh Range \mü-ˌstä(g)-\. Former name of Karakoram Range (*q.v.*).

Mu·stang \mu̇-ˈstäŋ\ *also* **Lo** \ˈlō\. Region, N Nepal, bounded on N, W, and E by Tibet; largest town is Mustang.

Mus·tang Island \ˌməs-taŋ-\. Island in Nueces co., S Texas, bet. Corpus Christi Bay and the Gulf of Mexico; one of the chain of islands along the Texas coast including St. Joseph I. and Padre I. (*qq.v.*).

Mus·ters, Lake \-ˈməs-tərz, -ˈmü-ˌste(ə)rz\. Lake in S Chubut prov., S cen. Argentina, W of Gulf of San Jorge.

Mu·su–dan \ˈmü-ˈsu̇-ˈdän\ *or formerly* **Bu·sui·tan** \ˌbu̇-swā-ˈtän\. Cape on E coast of North Korea extending into the Sea of Japan, 40°50′N, 129°43′E.

Mu·su·la, Mount \-mu̇-ˈsü-lə\. See BULGARIA.

Mu–tan \ˈmü-ˈdän\. River, E Kirin prov., NE China; ab. 310 m. long; flows NE and N to join the Sungari at I-lan.

Mu–tan–chiang \ˈmü-ˈdän-jē-ˈäŋ\. City, Heilungkiang prov., NE China, on Mu-tan river ab. 160 m. SE of Harbin; pop. (1970e) 400,000.

Mutina. See MODENA 2.

Mu·tsu Bay \ˈmüt-(ˌ)sü-\. Large bay in Aomori prefecture, N extremity of Honshū, Japan.

Mut·tenz \ˈmu̇t-ˌen(t)s\. Commune, Basel-Land demicanton, Switzerland, SE of Basel; pop. (1970c) 15,518; ruined castle.

Muttra. See MATHURA.

Mu·zaf·fa·ra·bad \mu̇-ˌzəf-ər-ə-ˈbäd\. Town, ✱ of Pakistani-controlled section of Jammu and Kashmir (see JAMMU AND KASHMIR), ab. 50 m. NNE of Islamabad.

Mu·zaf·far·na·gar \mu̇-ˈzəf-ər-ˌnəg-ər\. Town, NW Uttar Pradesh, N India, 63 m. NNE of Delhi; pop. (1961c) 87,-622; trades in wheat and sugar.

Mu·zaf·far·pur \mə-ˈzäf-ər-ˌpu̇(ə)r\. 1 District, Tirhut division, NW Bihar, NE India; 3018 sq. m.; pop. (1961c) 4,118,-398.

2 Town, its ✱, and ✱ of Tirhut division, 35 m. N of Patna; pop. (1970e) 158,087; Muslim religious center; univ. (1952).

Mu·zo \ˈmü-(ˌ)zō\. Municipality, Boyacá dept., cen. Colombia, SW of Chiquinquirá; pop. (1968e) 11,216; emerald mines.

Mu·zon, Cape \-ˈmü-ˌzän\. Southern point of Dall I. on Dixon Entrance, SE Alaska.

Muztagh Ata. See MU-SSU-T'A-KO-A-T'E 2.

Muztagh Ata Range. See MU-SSU-T'A-KO-A-T'E 1.

Muz·tagh Tow·er \müs-ˈtä(g)-ˈtau̇(-ə)r\. Mountain in the Karakoram Range, in region of Jammu and Kashmir controlled by Pakistan; 23,882 ft.

Mwan·za \ˈmwän-zə\. 1 Administrative region of N Tanzania. See table at TANZANIA.

2 Town, its ✱, on S shore of Lake Victoria; pop. (1967c) 34,186; lake port and railroad terminus.

Mweelrea. See MUILREA.

Mwe·ru \mə-ˈwe(ə)r-(ˌ)ü\. Lake, cen. Africa, on boundary bet. SE Zaire and Zambia, W of S tip of Lake Tanganyika; 76 m. long; 1770 sq. m.; max. depth 84 ft.; the Luapula, a headstream of the Congo river, flows through it.

Mya, Wa·di \ˌwäd-ē-mē-ˈa\. Dry river course in NE cen. Algeria, S of Chott Melrhir.

Myaung·mya \ˈmyau̇ŋ-mē-ˈä\. 1 District, Irrawaddy division, SW Lower Burma, in Irrawaddy delta; 2835 sq. m.; pop. (1962c) 593,025.

2 Town, its ✱, 22 m. SE of Vasi.

Myc·a·le \ˈmik-ə-(ˌ)lē\. Ancient name of promontory in the S of Ionia (NW Caria) on the coast of Asia Minor; a religious center with temple to Poseidon on N shore. Battle fought 479 B.C. on the shore of this promontory was a contest for the Persian ships and was a Greek victory.

My·ce·nae \mī-ˈsē-(ˌ)nē\. Ruined city, NE Peloponnesus, Greece, ab. 7 m. N of Argos. One of the most ancient cities of Greece; a natural rock citadel on N edge of Argive plain.

History: Flourished during Bronze Age; on basis of Minoan or Cretan culture (see CRETE), built a distinctive art and civilization known as Mycenaean (more accurately

Late Helladic c. 1600–1100 B.C., corresponding to Late Minoan); at height of its supremacy in Aegean area c. 1400 B.C.; declined c. 1100 B.C. before invasion of Greeks from north; scene of Schliemann's great archaeological discoveries 1874, 1876, including "Treasury of Atreus," which revealed existence of Bronze Age civilization in Aegean; ruins include famous Lion Gate, beehive tombs, shaft grave tombs, etc. Legendary capital of King Agamemnon.

My·ers·town \ˈmī(-ə)rz-ˌtau̇n\. Borough, Lebanon co., SE cen. Pennsylvania, 22 m. W of Reading; pop. (1970c) 3645; chemicals, clothing, medicine.

Myin·gyan \ˈmyin-ˌjän\. 1 District, Mandalay division, Upper Burma; 3078 sq. m.; pop. (1964e) 83,000.

2 Town, its ✱, on the left bank of the Irrawaddy river at its confluence with the Chindwin 60 m. WSW of Mandalay; pop. (1964e) 40,000; river port.

Myit·kyi·na \ˌmē-chē-ˈnō\. 1 District, N Sagaing division, Kachin State, N Burma; 22,317 sq. m.; pop. (1964e) 18,000.

2 Town, ✱ of Kachin State, N Burma, on left bank of upper Irrawaddy near China border 260 m. NNE of Mandalay; pop. (1964e) 14,000; most important town in N Burma N of Bhamo with which it is connected by small steamers through the upper defile of the Irrawaddy; on the Stilwell Road; terminus of railroad from Rangoon; ships teak. Captured by the Japanese Apr. 1942 but after severe fighting was retaken by Allied forces Aug. 1944.

Myit·nge \ˈmyit-(ˌ)ŋgā\. River, NE Burma; ab. 250 m. long; flows SW and W to the Irrawaddy river just S of Mandalay.

Myk·o·nos \ˈmik-ə-ˌnäs, -nəs\ *or Gk.* **Mý·ko·nos** \ˈmē-kə-ˌnȯs\. Island, NE Cyclades, Aegean Sea, in Cyclades dept., Greece, SE of Tenos; 35 sq. m.; chief village Mykonos; island of Delos is off its SW coast.

Mylae. See MILAZZO.

Mylasa. See MILAS.

Myl·liem \mil-ˈlēm\. See KHASI STATES.

My·men·singh *also* **Mai·man·singh** \ˌmī-mən-ˈsiŋ\ *or formerly* **Na·sir·a·bad** \nə-ˈsir-ə-ˌbäd\. Town, Bangla Desh, ab. 67 m. N of Dacca; pop. (1961c) 53,256; agricultural coll. (1961).

My·nydd·is·lw·yn \mə-ˌnith-ˈis-lə-wən\. Urban district, Monmouthshire, SE Wales, 28 m. WNW of Bristol, England; pop. (1971p) 15,369.

My·nydd Ta·rw \mə-ˌnith-ˈtär-(ˌ)ü\. Peak in the Berwyn Mts., N Wales; 2230 ft.

My·ra \ˈmī-rə\. One of the chief cities of ancient Lycia, S Asia Minor, on the coast; site of ancient ruins and rock tombs.

Mýr·dals·jö·kull \ˈmi(ə)r-ˌdäls-ˌyər-ˌkyütᵊl\. Glacier in S Iceland.

My·ri·na \mə-ˈrī-nə\. Ancient town of Aeolis, NW Asia Minor, on the coast 5 m. W of Gryneion; excavations here have uncovered many small terra-cotta figures.

Myr·tle Beach \ˌmərt-ᵊl-\. City, Horry co., E South Carolina, on Atlantic Ocean 13 m. SE of Conway; pop. (1970c) 9035; seaside resort; fishing, agriculture.

Myrtle Creek. City, Douglas co., SW Oregon, 67 m. S of Eugene; pop. (1970c) 2733; lumber; stock raising.

Myrtle Point. City, Coos co., SW Oregon, 41 m. SW of Roseburg; pop. (1970c) 2511; timber.

My·sia \ˈmish-ē-ə\. Ancient country in NW Asia Minor; bounded on N by Propontis, on E by Bithynia and Phrygia (E boundary varied with the fortunes of the kingdoms on that side), on S by Lydia, and on W by the Aegean; included regions of the Troad in the NW and Aeolis along SW coast; chief cities Pergamum and Cyzicus. Became subject to Croesus of Lydia, then of Persia and Syria; assigned to Pergamum by Rome 190 B.C.; became part of Roman province of Asia 129 B.C.

Mys·ki \ˈmis-kē\. Town, Kemerovo Oblast, Russian S.F.S.R., U.S.S.R., ab. 30 m. E of Novokuznetsk; pop. (1967e) 40,000.

Mys·ło·wi·ce \ˌmis-lō-ˈvēt-sə\ *or Ger.* **Mys·lo·witz** \ˈmis-lə-ˌvits\. Industrial commune, Katowice prov., S Poland, 8 m. ESE of Katowice; pop. (1970p) 44,700; metalworking; chemicals; coal mines; first mentioned in 14th cent.; to Poland 1922.

My·sore \mī-ˈsō(ə)r, -ˈsȯ(ə)r\ *or* **Mai·sur** \mī-ˈsu̇(ə)r\. 1 State, S India; 74,037 sq. m.; pop. (1971p) 29,224,046; ✱ Bangalore; occupies plateau region of Southern Deccan with hills in W; has many rivers, including Krishna and Tungabhadra; rice, peanuts, cotton, timber, gold; largest cities: Bangalore, Mysore, Hubli-Dharwar.

History: From early times to c. 1400 for the most part ruled by Hindu dynasties (Cholas, Cheras, etc.); succeeded by Hindu rajas of Vijayanagar, who were overwhelmed 1565 by Muslims from the N; throne usurped by Haidar Ali 1761, who with his son Tipu Sultan ruled until 1799; period of Mysore Wars; administration taken over by British 1831; returned to native rule 1881; became part of India 1947; boundaries altered 1953 and 1956.

2 City, S Mysore state, S India, S of Cauvery river 85 m. SW of Bangalore; pop. (1970e) 263,131; important industrial city, producing textiles, rice, sandalwood oil, chemicals, leather goods, coffee, and cigarettes; numerous notable buildings, including former maharaja's palace; univ. (1916). Site occupied before 3d cent. B.C.; one of the capitals of Muslim state which emerged late 16th cent.; occupied by British 1831.

Mys·tic \ˈmis-tik\. 1 Short river rising in **Mystic Lakes** (2 connected lakes), Middlesex co., NE Massachusetts; flows SE into Boston Harbor N of Charlestown; navigable as far as Medford.

2 Subdivision of town of Stonington, Connecticut, at mouth of Mystic river (short stream flowing S to Long Island Sound); pop. (1970c) 2568; notable maritime museum. See STONINGTON.

My·then \ˈmēt-ᵊn\. Twin peaks, Schwyz canton, E cen. Switzerland, near Schwyz; **Gros·se My·the** \ˈgrō-sə-ˌmēt-ə\, 6229 ft., and **Klei·ne Mythe** \ˈklī-nə-\, 5955 ft.

My Tho \ˈmē-ˈtō\. Town, South Vietnam, in the Mekong delta 45 m. SSW of Saigon; terminus of railroad from Saigon; former French naval base.

Myt·i·le·ne *also* **Mi·ty·lene** \ˌmit-ᵊl-ˈē-nē\ *or Gk.* **Mi·ti·lí·ni** \ˌmit-ᵊl-ˈē-nē\. 1 Island. See LESBOS.

2 *or formerly* **Ka·stro** \ˈkäs-(ˌ)trō\. City, ✱ of Lesbos dept., Aegean Is., Greece; pop. (1971p) 24,157; two harbors; chief town on Lesbos I.

My·tish·chi \mi-ˈt(y)ē-shē\. Town, Moscow Oblast, Russian S.F.S.R., U.S.S.R., ab. 10 m. NNE of Moscow; pop. (1970p) 119,000; chemicals, transportation equipment.

Mýto Vysoké. See VYSOKÉ MÝTO.

My·us \ˈmī-əs\. Ancient city, one of the 12 Ionian Cities, near the mouth of the Maeander and just ENE of Miletus, Asia Minor.

Mzu·zu \em-ˈzu-ˌzü\. Town, N Malawi; pop. (1970e) 9000.

N

Naab *or* **Nab** \ˈnäp\. River, West Germany; 90 m. long; rises in the Fichtelgebirge and flows S in E Bavaria to join the Danube above Regensburg.

Naald·wijk \ˈnält-ˌvīk\. Commune, South Holland prov., SW Netherlands, near mouth of the Meuse 9 m. SSW of The Hague; pop. (1970e) 22,306.

Na·a·le·hu \ˌnä-ə-ˈlā-(ˌ)hü\. Village, Hawaii co., Hawaii, on S coast of Hawaii I. NE of Ka Lae; pop. (1970c) 1014.

Naar·den \ˈnärd-ᵊn\. Commune, North Holland prov., W Netherlands, ab. 12 m. ESE of Amsterdam on S shore of Zuider Zee; pop. (1970e) 17,447; chemicals.

Naas \ˈnās\. Urban district, ⊗ of co. Kildare, E Eire; pop. (1971p) 5080; notable fox-hunting center; once seat of kings of Leinster; sacked and burned by Owen McRory O'More 1597.

Nab. See NAAB.

Na·bad·wip \ˌnə-bəd-ˈwip\ *or formerly* **Na·dia** \ˈnəd-ē-ˌä\. Town, West Bengal, India, on Bhagirathi river ab. 60 m. N of Calcutta; pop. (1961c) 72,861; founded 1063; notable Hindu educational center.

Naband. See NĀY BAND.

Nab·be·ru, Lake \-ˌnab-ə-ˈrü\. Lake on W edge of Gibson Desert, cen. Western Australia.

Na·bes·na Glacier \nə-ˈbes-nə-\. Glacier in the Wrangell Mountains, S Alaska; 54 m. long, ab. 2 m. wide near its terminus.

Na·beul \na-ˈbə(r)l\ *or Arab.* **Na·bul** \ˈnab-əl\ *or anc.* **Ne·ap·o·lis** \nē-ˈap-ə-ləs\. Coastal town, NE Tunisia, at S end of base of Cape Bon Penin.; pop. (1966c) 34,134; ancient Phoenician ruins on the shore.

Na·bha \ˈnäb-hə\. 1 Former Indian state, now part of Punjab state, NW India; 947 sq. m.; one of the Sikh states of the Phulkian group; established its independence c. 1763.
2 Town, its ✱, 37 m. W of Ambala; pop. (1961c) 30,603.

Nab·lus \ˈnab-ləs, ˈnäb-\ *or Arab.* **Nāb·u·lus** \ˈnab-ü-ˌlüs\. 1 Governorate, W Jordan; 969 sq. m.; pop. (1968e) 427,000; occupied by Israel 1967.
2 *or anc.* **She·chem** \ˈshē-kəm, -ˌkem\ *or later* **Ne·ap·o·lis** \nē-ˈap-ə-ləs\. Town, its ✱, 30 m. N of Jerusalem in a valley bet. Mts. Ebal and Gerizim; pop. (1967e) 44,223. Ancient Shechem in hill country of Ephraim important in early Biblical period; home of Jacob; Jacob's well and tomb of Joseph; scene of Jeroboam's rebellion and, as chief city of Samaria, became his capital of Israel; fell into decay; rebuilt and renamed Neapolis by Emperor Vespasian; suffered damage in Crusades and from Ibrahim Pasha 1834.

Nabrissa. See LEBRIJA.

Na·bua \ˈnäb-wä\. Municipality, Camarines Sur prov., Luzon, Phil., 5 m. W of Iriga; pop. (1969e) 92,900.

Nabul. See NABEUL.

Nābulus. See NABLUS.

Na·ca·o·me \ˌnäk-ə-ˈōm-ē\. Town, ✱ of Valle dept., S Honduras, 22 m. NNE of Amapala; pop. (1961c) 3724.

Nacham. See NA SAM.

Nach·es \ˈnach-ˌēz\. River, S cen. Washington; ab. 60 m. long; flows SE through N Yakima co. into Yakima river at Yakima.

Ná·chod \ˈnäk-ˌȯt\. Town, Czech S.R., W Czechoslovakia, on Polish border ab. 75 m. NE of Prague; pop. (1968e) 19,027; battlefield June 1866 where Prussians defeated Austrians in Austro-Prussian War.

Na·ci·mien·to Peak \ˌnäs-ə-mē-ˌent-ō-\. Mountain, S Rio Arriba co., N New Mexico; 10,045 ft.

Nacka \ˈnäk-ə\. Town, Sweden, suburb of Stockholm; pop. (1970e) 26,865.

Nac·og·do·ches \ˌnak-ə-ˈdō-chəz\. 1 County in E Texas. See table at TEXAS.
2 Industrial and commercial city, its ⊗, 20 m. N of Lufkin; pop. (1970c) 22,544; clothing, furniture, fertilizer, brass goods; watermelons; Stephen F. Austin State Coll. (1917); developed from Spanish mission established 1716; figured in Texas revolution 1819 ff.; battle 1832.

Nadezhdinsk. See SEROV.

Nadi. See NANDI.

Na·dia \ˈnəd-ē-ə\. 1 District, formerly in Presidency division, Bengal, NE India; 2879 sq. m.; ✱ Krishnagar; divided 1947, ab. half of it being assigned to West Bengal, India, remainder to East Pakistan (now Bangla Desh).
2 Town, West Bengal, India. See NABADWIP.

Na·di·ad \ˌnəd-ē-ˈäd\. Town, N Gujarat state, India, on tributary of Sabarmati river 30 m. SE of Ahmadabad; pop. (1961c) 72,861.

Na·dor \nə-ˈdȯ(ə)r\. Town, N Morocco, on coast ab. 10 m. S of Melilla; pop. (1960c) 17,583; center of sheep-herding region.

Nad·vor·na·ya \nad-ˈvȯr-nə-yə\ *or Pol.* **Nad·wór·na** \näd-ˈvür-nə\. Commune, S cen. Ivano-Frankovsk Oblast, Ukrainian S.S.R., U.S.S.R., battle Feb. 15–21, 1915 bet. Austrians and Russians.

Nad·zab \ˈnäd-(ˌ)zäb\. Village, Papua New Guinea, New Guinea I., 19 m. NW of Lae; Japanese airdrome in World War II seized by American paratroopers Sept. 1943.

Næst·ved \ˈnest-ˌveth\. City, Storstrøm co., SE Sjælland, Denmark; pop. (1970e) 24,831; railroad center.

Nafa. See NAHA.

Na·fa·da \nə-ˈfäd-ə\. Town, North-Eastern State, Nigeria, NE of Bauchi; pop. (1963c) 22,164.

Nä·fels \ˈnā-ˌfels\. Village, Glarus canton, Switzerland; pop. (1970c) 3739; scene of battle Apr. 9, 1388 in which Swiss defeated Austrians.

Naft–e–Shāh \ˌnaf-tē-ˈshä\. Oil field, W Iran, at border W of Kermānshāh; adjoins Naft Khaneh oil field of E Iraq.

Naft Kha·neh \ˌnaft-kä-ˈnā\. Oil field, E Iraq, on Iranian border NE of Baghdad.

Na·ga \ˈnäg-ə\. 1 Municipality, Cebu prov., on E coast of Cebu I., Phil., 11 m. SW of City of Cebu; pop. (1969e) 44,300; has coastwise trade.
2 *or formerly* **Nue·va Ca·ce·res** \nü-ˌā-və-ˈkäs-ə-ˌrās\. Chartered city, Camarines Sur, Luzon, Phil., on Bicol river ab. 5 m. S of San Miguel Bay; pop. (1970e) 76,700; univ. (1954); visited by Spaniards as early as 1573; Spanish town of Nueva Caceres founded on its site.

Naga Hills \ˌnäg-ə-, nə-ˈgä-\. Hill region, India and Burma, including Naga and Patkai hills; part of N Arakan Yoma system. See BARAIL RANGE. Highest point 9890 ft. Inhabited by Nagas, formerly headhunters; subdued by British 1865–80.

Na·ga·land \ˈnäg-ə-ˌland\. State, NE India; 6366 sq. m.; pop. (1971p) 515,561; ✱ Kohima; rice; established 1961.

Na·ga·no \nä-ˈgän-(ˌ)ō\. 1 Prefecture, Honshū, Japan; 5244 sq. m.; pop. (1970c) 1,956,917; ✱ Nagano; sericulture; hydroelectric power.
2 City, its ✱, ab. 100 m. NW of Tokyo; pop. (1970c) 285,355; commercial center; silk; site of Buddhist temple and monastery; founded in 7th cent. A.D. and developed as major shrine.

Na·ga·o·ka \ˌnä-gə-ˈō-kə, nä-ˈgä-ō-(ˌ)kä\. City, Niigata prefecture, NW Honshū, Japan, 35 m. S of Niigata; pop. (1970c) 162,262; chemicals; important in feudal times; declined on downfall of the Tokugawa; later regained prosperity with discovery of oil fields in vicinity.

Na·ga·pat·ti·nam \ˌnag-ə-ˈpət-ə-nəm\ *or* **Ne·ga·pa·tam** \ˌneg-ə-ˈpət-nəm\ *or* **Ne·ga·pat·ti·nam** \ˌneg-ə-ˈpət-ə-nəm\. Seaport town, SE Tamil Nadu, S India, on Coromandel Coast 160 m. S of Madras; pop. (1961c) 61,305. Site of Portuguese factory at beginning of 16th cent.; occupied by Dutch 1660–71, by British 1799. Since 1866 forms joint municipality with **Na·gore** \nə-ˈgō(ə)r\, a port ab. 5 m. N.

Na·gar \ˈnəg-ər\. See HUNZA 2.

Na·ga·ra \nä-ˈgär-ə\. Tributary of the Kiso river in SW cen. Honshū, Japan; flows past Gifu.

Nagara. For towns in Thailand having Nagara or Nagor as first element, see those beginning NAKHON (meaning "town").

Na·ga·sa·ki \ˌnäg-ə-ˈsäk-ē, ˌnag-; ˌnag-ə-ˈsak-ē\. 1 Prefecture, Kyūshū, Japan; 1579 sq. m.; pop. (1970c) 1,570,245; ✻ Nagasaki; coal mining, fishing.

2 Seaport and commercial city, its ✻, at head of inlet ab. 3 m. long; pop. (1970c) 421,114; major economic activity is shipbuilding; fishing port.

History: Unimportant before arrival of first Portuguese ships 1571; thereafter principal center of contact with foreigners and of Japanese Christianity; made an imperial city by Hideyoshi 1587; a port of call for Spanish, Dutch, and Portuguese ships; after measures taken by Iyemitsu to exclude foreigners 1636 ff., the only port in Japan kept open to foreign trade (see DESHIMA); reopened to foreign trade 1859; important into 20th cent. as industrial center and coaling station but later declined; in World War II inner city destroyed by atomic bomb Aug. 9, 1945, with ab. 40,000 persons killed; rebuilt since 1945.

Na·ga·to \nä-ˈgät-(ˌ)ō\. Old province at SW tip of Honshū, Japan, now part of Yamaguchi prefecture.

Nag·car·lan \ˌnäg-kär-ˈlän\. Municipality, SE cen. Laguna prov., Luzon, Phil., 45 m. SE of Manila; pop. (1969e) 24,800.

Na·ger·coil \ˈnäg-ər-ˌkȯi(ə)l\. City, S Tamil Nadu, India, 10 m. N of Cape Comorin, extreme S tip of India; pop. (1970e) 139,875; lace, coir.

Na·gi·na \ˈnäg-i-nə\. Town, Uttar Pradesh, N India, on tributary of Ramganga river 95 m. NE of Delhi; pop. (1961c) 30,427; trades in sugar.

Na·god \nə-ˈgōd\. 1 Former Indian state, now part of Madhya Pradesh state, cen. India; 532 sq. m.

2 Town, its ✻, 100 m. SW of Allahabad; pop. (1961c) 5800.

Nagore. See NAGAPATTINAM.

Na·gor·no–Ka·ra·bakh Autonomous Oblast \nə-ˌgȯr-(ˌ)nō-ˈkär-ə-ˌbäk- . . . ˈō-bləst, -ˌblast\ *or formerly* **Karabakh Mountain Area.** Autonomous subdivision within the Azerbaijan S.S.R., U.S.S.R.; 1699 sq. m.; pop. (1970p) 149,000; ✻ Stepanakert; chief nationalities Armenian and Turkic; a mountainous forested area, well watered by short tributaries of the Kura; wheat, corn, barley, millet; livestock; taken from Persia by Russia 1813.

Na·go·ya \nə-ˈgȯi-ə\. City, ✻ of Aichi prefecture, S Honshū, Japan, ab. 75 m. E of Kyōto at head of Ise Bay; pop. (1970c) 2,036,053; industrial center, producing textiles, lumber, motor vehicles, aircraft, synthetic fibers, machine tools, chemicals, and ceramics; univ. (1939), technical institute (1949); 17th cent. castle; Buddhist temple. Modern rise dates from construction of castle 1610; port facilities opened 1907; heavily bombed in World War II 1944–45 but entirely reconstructed since.

Nag·pur \ˈnäg-ˌpu̇(ə)r\. 1 Division, Maharashtra, India; 37,346 sq. m.; pop. (1961c) 9,233,742.

2 District in the division; 3842 sq. m.; pop. (1961c) 1,512,807.

3 City, ✻ of district and of division, 265 m. N of Hyderabad; pop. (1970e) 903,826; major commercial and industrial center; textiles, pottery, glass, leather and iron goods, pharmaceuticals, brassware, cigarettes; printing, dyeing, flour milling, fruit canning. Founded 18th cent. by Gond prince; passed to Marathas after 1743; to British 1853.

Na·gua \ˈnäg-wə\. Town, ✻ of María Trinidad Sánchez prov., Dominican Republic; pop. (1970p) 13,937.

Na·gua·bo \nə-ˈgwäb-(ˌ)ō\. Town and municipality, E Puerto Rico; pop. (1970c) 4136 (town), 17,862 (munic.); town near coast 7 m. NE of Humacao.

Na·gui·li·an \ˌnäg-i-ˈlē-(ˌ)än\. Municipality, La Union prov., Luzon, Phil., 9 m. SE of San Fernando; pop. (1969e) 26,-700.

Nagybánya. See BAIA-MARE.

Nagybecskerek. See ZRENJANIN.

Nagyenyed. See AIUD.

Nagy·ka·ni·zsa \ˈnäj-ˈkȯ-ni-ˌzhȯ\. Industrial and commercial city, SW Hungary, ab. 65 m. WNW of Pécs; pop. (1970p) 39,411; oil and natural gas wells nearby; held by Turks 1600–90.

Nagykároly. See CAREI.

Nagy·kő·rös \ˈnäj-ˈkər-ˌəsh\. City, cen. Hungary, 47 m. SE of Budapest; pop. (1970p) 25,785; market center in grape-growing section.

Nagymihály. See MICHALOVCE.

Nagyszalonta. See SALONTA.

Nagyszentmiklós. See SÎNNICOLAU MARE.

Nagyszombat. See TRNAVA.

Nagyvárad. See ORADEA.

Na·ha \ˈnä-(ˌ)hä\ *or* **Na·wa** \ˈnä-(ˌ)wä\ *also* **Na·fa** \ˈnä-(ˌ)fä\. Seaport, ✻ of Okinawa prefecture, Ryukyu Is., Japan, on W coast of S Okinawa I.; pop. (1970c) 276,380; commercial center of the Ryukyu Is.; two universities; scene of severe fighting in battle for the city May 17–June 7, 1945.

Na·han \ˈnä-hən\. 1 State, India. See SIRMUR.

2 Town, Himachal Pradesh, N India, 35 m. ENE of Ambala; pop. (1961c) 12,400; ✻ of former Sirmur state.

Nahanni, South. See SOUTH NAHANNI.

Na·hant \nə-ˈhant\. Town, Essex co., NE corner of Massachusetts, 9 m. ENE of Boston on a long narrow peninsula extending S from Lynn into Massachusetts Bay; pop. (1970c) 4119; summer resort.

Nahant Bay. Inlet of Massachusetts Bay on S shore of Essex co., NE corner of Massachusetts, separated from Lynn Harbor by the peninsula on which Nahant is situated.

Na·hā·vand \ˌnä-hə-ˈvand\ *also* **Ne·ha·vend** \ˌnē-hə-ˈvend\. Town, W Iran, 42 m. S of Hamadān; pop. (1966c) 23,922; battle 641 A.D. in which the Persians under Yazdegerd III were completely defeated by the Arabs.

Nahawend. See NEHAVEND.

Na·he \ˈnä-ə\. River, Saarland and Rhineland-Palatinate, West Germany; 72 m. long; flows NE into Rhine river at Bingen on SE border of the Hunsrück.

Nahr. Arabic word meaing "river"; for names including this word, see the second element.

Nahr·wan \när-ˈwän\. Ancient canal, E of the Tigris river near Baghdad, E Iraq; ab. 60 m. long.

Nahud, En. See EN NAHUD.

Na·huel Hau·pí, Lake \-nä-ˌwel-wä-ˈpē\. Lake in Andes Mts., in S Neuquén prov., SW Argentina, on boundary of Río Negro prov., near Chilean border; alt. 2516 ft.; area 212 sq. m.; depth nearly 1000 ft. in places; source of Limay river; surrounded by mountains, Monte Tronador to SW; one of best-known of Argentine resorts; in **Nahuel Huapí National Park.**

Na·hui·zal·co \ˌnä-wi-ˈsäl-ˌkō\. Town, Sonsonate dept., SW El Salvador, 5 m. from Sonsonate.

Na·hun·ta \nā-ˈhənt-ə\. City, ⊗ of Brantley co., SE Georgia; pop. (1970c) 974; corn, tobacco.

Na·ic \ˈnä-ēk\. Municipality, N coast of Cavite prov., Luzon, Phil., ab. 25 m. SW of Manila; pop. (1969e) 38,200.

Nai·ha·ti \nī-ˈhät-ē\. Town, West Bengal, NE India, on Hooghly river 23 m. N of Calcutta; pop. (1961c) 58,457.

Nā'īn *or* **Nain** \ˈnīn\. Town, cen. Iran, 75 m. E of Eṣfahān; pop. (1966c) 5925; highway junction point; makes fine earthenware.

Na·in \ˈnā(-ə)n\ *or* **Nein** \ˈnān, ˈnen\. Village, Galilee (*q.v.*), 5 m. SSE of Nazareth (*Luke* vii. 11–17).

Nai·ni·tal \ˌnī-nē-ˈtal\. Town and hill station, ✻ of Kumaun division, NE Uttar Pradesh, N India, 148 m. NE of Delhi;

pop. (1961c) 16,400 (incl. cantonment); alt. 6400 ft.; popular resort and sanatorium; summer capital of Uttar Pradesh; suffered from severe landslide Sept. 1880.

Nairn \'na(ə)rn, 'ne(ə)rn\. 1 Small river in Nairn co., NE Scotland; 38 m. long; flows NE into Moray Firth.

2 *or* **Nairn·shire** \-shi(ə)r, -shər\. County, NE Scotland, S of Moray Firth; area 163 sq. m.; pop. (1971p) 11,049; ⊗ Nairn; rivers Nairn, Findhorn; barley, oats, potatoes; livestock grazing, distilling, quarrying.

3 Burgh, ⊗ of Nairn co., on Moray Firth at mouth of the Nairn; pop. (1971p) 8038; fishing; seaside resort.

Nai·ro·bi \nī-'rō-bē\. City, ✱ of Kenya, forming an extra-provincial division (Nairobi Area; 264 sq. m.), S cen. Kenya, E Africa; pop. (1969p) 478,000; the republic's principal commercial and industrial city; ships coffee and timber; food products, building materials, tobacco, furniture, hides and skins; railway repair shops; Univ. of Kenya (founded as Royal College, Univ. of East Africa; received new status 1970); Nairobi National Park game reserve nearby. Founded 1899 as site of railroad workshops; became seat of government 1905; was made municipality 1919, city 1950; its area greatly expanded by constitution of 1963.

Nairobi National Park. National park, Kenya, ab. 15 m. S of Nairobi; 44 sq. m.; noted for its wildlife, incl. cheetah, leopard, lion, giraffe; established 1948.

Nais·saar \'nī-ˌsär\ *or Russ.* **Nais·sar** \-sər\. Island in Gulf of Finland, ab. 12 m. off Tallinn, N Estonian S.S.R., U.S.S.R.; ab. 5 m. long.

Naissus *or* **Naïssus.** See NIŠ.

Nai·va·sha \nī-'väsh-ə\. Town on Lake Naivasha, SW cen. Kenya, E Africa, ab. 40 m. NW of Nairobi.

Naivasha, Lake. Lake, SW cen. Kenya, E Africa, in the Great Rift Valley (*q.v.*); 12 m. long by 9 m. wide; 108 sq. m.; altitude 6135 ft.; has no known outlet.

Najaf, An. See AN NAJAF.

Na·ja·fā·bād \nə-ˌjäf-ə-'bäd\. Town, Eşfahān prov., W cen. Iran, ab. 15 m. W of Eşfahān; pop. (1971e) 46,000.

Na·ja·sa \nə-'häs-ə\. River, SE Camagüey prov., E cen. Cuba; ab. 50 m. long; flows S into Caribbean Sea.

Najd. See NEJD.

Ná·je·ra \'nä-her-ə\. Commune, Logroño prov., N Spain, W of Logroño; pop. (1970p) 5034; scene of victory of Black Prince over Henry II (of Trastamara) 1367 in his campaign for Peter the Cruel; also called battle of Navarrete.

Na·jib·a·bad \nə-'jēb-ə-ˌbäd\. Town, NW Uttar Pradesh, N India, E of Ganges river 98 m. NE of Delhi; pop. (1961c) 34,310; trades in timber, sugar, grain; founded in middle of 18th cent. by Rohilla chief and has several fine Rohilla architectural monuments.

Na·ka·dō·ri \nä-'käd-ə-rē; ˌnäk-ə-'dōr-ē, -'dȯr-\. Island in Gotō Archipelago (*q.v.*), Japan.

Na·ka·gu·su·ku Bay \nä-ˌkä-gə-'sü-kü-, ˌnäk-ə-gə-\ *also* **Buck·ner Bay** \ˌbək-nər-\. Inlet of the Pacific Ocean in SE coast of Okinawa I., Ryukyu Is., Japan; U.S. fleet anchorage in Okinawa campaign Apr.–June 1945.

Naka Iwo. See IWO JIMA.

Na·ka·le·le Point \ˌnäk-ə-ˌlā-lē-\. Point on N coast of Maui I., Hawaii, near W end on Pailolo Channel.

Na·ka·no Shi·ma \nä-ˌkän-ō-'shē-mə, ˌnäk-ə-'nō-shə-mə\. Volcanic island, Tokara Is., in N Ryukyu Is., Japan; 3125 ft. high.

Na·ka·tsu \nä-'kät-(ˌ)sü\. Seaport town, Ōita prefecture, NE Kyūshū, Japan, 27 m. SSE of Kitakyūshū on S shore of Suō Sea; pop. (1970c) 57,461; birthplace of Yukichi Fukuzawa.

Nakel. See NAKŁO NAD NOTECIA.

Na·khi·che·van \ˌnäk-i-chə-'vän\ *or anc.* **Nax·u·a·na** \ˌnak-shü-'ān-ə\. Town, ✱ of Nakhichevan A.S.S.R., on Araks river 85 m. SE of Yerevan; pop. (1970p) 33,000; wine, dairy products, furniture; according to Armenian tradition founded by Noah. Ancient trading center; often plundered by Persians, Mongols, Armenians; ceded to Russia 1828.

Nakhichevan Autonomous Soviet Socialist Republic. Autonomous republic, Azerbaijan S.S.R., U.S.S.R., in SW mountainous part in bend of Araks river; 2124 sq. m.; pop. (1970p) 202,000; ✱ Nakhichevan. An agricultural area on a high plateau; produces wheat and cotton; vineyards, fruit orchards; silkworm breeding, cattle raising. Predominant ethnic strain Turko-Tatar; chief nationalities Turkic and Armenian. Chief towns Nakhichevan, Dzhulfa; republic established 1924.

Na·khod·ka \nə-'kȯt-kə\. Seaport town, S Primorski Krai, Russian S.F.S.R., U.S.S.R., 55 m. ESE of Vladivostok; pop. (1970p) 105,000; railroad terminus, fishing port; naval base.

Na·khon Na·yok \ˌnä-ˌkȯn-'nä-ˌyək\ *also* **Na·ga·ra Nayok** \ˌnä-ˌkon-'nä-ˌyək—*sic*\. 1 Province, S Thailand; 932 sq. m.; pop. (1960c) 153,683.

2 Town, its ✱, on a tributary of the Chao Phraya and on highway to Cambodia 60 m. NE of Bangkok; pop. (1964e) 8043.

Nakhon Pa·thom \ˌnä-ˌkȯn-pä-'təm\ *or* **Na·ga·ra Pathom** \ˌnä-ˌkȯn-pä-'təm—*sic*\. 1 Province, SW Thailand; 841 sq. m.; pop. (1960c) 340,481.

2 Town, its ✱, ab. 38 m. WNW of Bangkok; pop. (1964e) 31,746; large temple.

Nakhon Pha·nom \ˌnä-ˌkȯn-pä-'nəm\ *also* **Na·ga·ra Pa·nom** \ˌnä-ˌkȯn-pä-'nəm—*sic*\ *and* **La·khon** \'lä-ˌkȯn\. 1 Province, NE Thailand; 3764 sq. m.; pop. (1960c) 436,482.

2 Town, its ✱, on Mekong river; pop. (1964e) 13,257; site of major U.S. Air Force base during Vietnam War 1965 ff.

Nakhon Rat·cha·si·ma \ˌnä-ˌkȯn-rä-'chä-si-ˌmä\ *or* **Khorat** *also* **Ko·rat** \kō-'rät\. 1 Province, S Thailand; 7564 sq. m.; pop. (1960c) 1,094,774.

2 Town, its ✱, on Mun river 110 m. E of Phra Nakhon Si Ayutthaya; pop. (1965e) 54,310; railroad junction point; distributing and trading center for E part of Thailand; an ancient walled town, formerly subject to Cambodia.

Nakhon Sa·wan \ˌnä-ˌkȯn-sä-'wän\ *also* **Na·ga·ra Svar·ga** \ˌnä-ˌkȯn-sä-'wän—*sic*\. 1 Province, W Thailand; 3736 sq. m.; pop. (1960c) 647,602.

2 Commercial town, its ✱, on the Chao Phraya where it is formed by confluence of Nan and Ping rivers; pop. (1965e) 46,081.

Nakhon Si Tham·ma·rat \'nä-ˌkȯn-ˌsē-ˌtäm-ə-'rät\ *also* **Na·ga·ra Sri·dhar·ma·raj** \'nä-ˌkȯn-ˌsē-ˌtäm-ə-'rät—*sic*\. 1 Province, SW Thailand; 3926 sq. m.; pop. (1960c) 730,402.

2 Seaport town, its ✱, on E coast of Malay penin. 100 m. N of Songkhla; pop. (1964e) 29,237; railroad terminus; a very old town; noted for its niello work in silver.

Na·kło nad No·te·cią \'näk-(ˌ)lȯ-näd-nȯ-'tech-ȯ\ *or Ger.* **Na·kel** \'näk-əl\. Commune, SW Bydgoszcz prov., N cen. Poland, 20 m. W of Bydgoszcz on Noteć river; pop. (1968e) 16,600; agricultural industries.

Nak·nek Lake \'nak-ˌnek-\ *or formerly* **Lake Co·ville** \-'kō-ˌvil\. Lake, SW Alaska, near base of Alaska Penin.; almost entirely within Katmai National Monument.

Naksh–i–Rus·tam \ˌnäk-shē-rü-'stäm\. See PERSEPOLIS.

Nak·skov \'näk-ˌskau̇\. Seaport, Storstrøm co., on W coast of Lolland I., Denmark; pop. (1970e) 15,994; sugar refineries, shipbuilding yards; St. Nicholas church, dating from the 15th cent.

Na·ku·ru \nä-'ku̇(ə)r-(ˌ)ü\. Town, ✱ of Rift Valley prov., W cen. Kenya, E Africa; pop. (1969p) 47,800.

Nal. See HINGOL.

Na·la·garh \'näl-ə-ˌgär\ *or* **Hin·dur** \'hin-dər\. Former Indian state, now part of Himachal Pradesh state, NW India, W of Simla; 276 sq. m.; ✱ Nalagarh.

Nal·chik \'näl-chik\. Town, ✱ of Kabardino-Balkarian A.S.S.R., Russian S.F.S.R., U.S.S.R., 63 m. NW of Ordzhonikidze; pop. (1970p) 146,000; railroad terminus; health resort situated in a mountain valley; footwear, clothing, furniture, processed foods; founded as fortress 1818; in World War II taken by Germans Oct. 29, 1942; retaken by U.S.S.R. early in 1943.

Nal·gon·da \nəl-ˈgän-də\. Town, cen. Andhra Pradesh, India, 55 m. ESE of Hyderabad; pop. (1961c) 24,383.

Na·mak, Dar·yā·cheh–ye \där-ˈyäch-ə-yə-nə-ˈmäk\. Salt lake and swamp (*darya*), NW cen. Iran, S of Tehran.

Namakagon. See NAMEKAGON.

Na·mak·zār \ˌnäm-äk-ˈzär\. Swampy lake in Khorāsān prov., E cen. Iran.

Namaland. See NAMAQUALAND.

Na·man·gan \ˌnäm-äŋ-ˈgän\. Town, ✱ of Namangan Oblast, NE Uzbek S.S.R., U.S.S.R., in the Fergana valley NE of Kokand; pop. (1970p) 175,000; textiles, foodstuffs.

Namangan Oblast \-ˈō-bləst, -ˌblast\. Subdivision of the Uzbek S.S.R., U.S.S.R.; 3012 sq. m.; pop. (1970p) 847,000; ✱ Namangan; established 1941, abolished 1960, reestablished 1967.

Na·ma·qua·land \nə-ˈmäk-wə-ˌland\ *or* **Na·ma·land** \ˈnäm-ə-ˌland\. 1 Coastal region, SW Africa, extending from ab. 23°S to 31°S and from 80 to 350 m. inland; divided by Orange river into **Great Namaqualand** to the N (in South-West Africa) and **Little Namaqualand** to the S (in Cape Province, Rep. of South Africa); sandy plains and bare hills; rich in copper.

2 Administrative district of Little Namaqualand, Rep. of South Africa; ✱ Springbok.

Na·ma·ta·nai \ˌnäm-ə-tə-ˈnī\. Village on NE coast of New Ireland, Bismarck Archipelago, W Pacific Ocean; good harbor.

Nam·ber \ˈnäm-bər\. See NUMFOOR.

Nam·cha Bar·wa \ˌnäm-chə-ˈbär-(ˌ)wä\. Peak at E end of the Himalayas, SE Tibet, China, in the bend of the Brahmaputra; 25,445 ft.

Nam Dinh \ˈnäm-ˈdēn(-yə)\. Town, North Vietnam, in Red river delta 45 m. SE of Hanoi; a trade center; connected by rail with Hanoi; came under French control 1883.

Nam·e·ka·gon *or* **Nam·a·ka·gon** \ˌnam-ə-ˈkäg-ən\. River, NW Wisconsin; ab. 75 m. long; flows out of **Namekagon Lake,** S Bayfield co., SW and W into St. Croix river in Burnett co.

Namen. See NAMUR.

Namh·kam \ˈnäm-ˌkäm\. Town, Shan State, Burma, on Shweli river near China border 60 m. N of Lashio. Held by Japanese 1942–45 but retaken Jan. 15, 1945 by Chinese troops.

Namhoi. See FO-SHAN.

Na·mib Desert \ˌnäm-ib-\. Arid region, along coast of South-West Africa; 800 m. long by 30–100 m. wide.

Namibia. See SOUTH-WEST AFRICA.

Nam·lea \ˈnäm-lā-ˌä\. Village on bay on E coast of Buru I., Indonesia; port of call for steamers.

Namnetes. See NANTES.

Nam·ni Pass \ˌnäm-nē-\. Mountain pass on N border of Burma; 15,300 ft.; leads from upper valley of Nmai river to China.

Nam·oi \ˈnam-ˌȯi\. River, NW New South Wales, SE Australia; 526 m. long; flows into Darling river.

Na·mo·nu·i·to \ˌnäm-ə-nü-ˈēt-(ˌ)ō\. Atoll group in cen. Caroline Is. in W Pacific Ocean, 8°46′N, 150°02′E, NW of Truk.

Namosi Peak. See VUIMASIA.

Nam·pa \ˈnam-pə\. City, Canyon co., SW Idaho, 18 m. W of Boise; pop. (1970c) 20,768; railroad center; sugar refining, milk processing, vegetable seed production; Northwest Nazarene Coll. (1913); founded 1886.

Nam Pawn \ˈnäm-ˌpȯn\. River, Burma; ab. 160 m. long; flows S out of Shan State and empties into Salween river.

Nam·p'o \ˈnäm-ˈpō\ *or formerly* **Chin·nam·po** \ˈchēn-ˈnäm-ˈpō\. City, North Korea, on the W coast 25 m. SW of P'yŏngyang; former treaty port, opened to foreign trade 1897.

Nam·pu·la \nam-ˈpü-lə\. Town, N Mozambique, SE Africa; met. area pop. (1960p) 103,985; on automobile highway and railroad.

Nam–quan. See NA SAM.

Nam·sen \ˈnäm-sən\. River, N cen. Norway; 130 m. long; flows SSW and W past Namsos into **Namsen Fjord,** an inlet of Norwegian Sea on W coast of Norway.

Nams·os \ˈnäm-ˌsōs\. Seaport, Nord-Trøndelag co., N cen. Norway, on N shore at head of Namsen Fjord; pop. (1970e) 11,223; lumbering, fishing; textile mills; cannery; copper deposits. Occupied by British troops Apr. 14 to May 3, 1940 in expedition to aid Norway.

Nam Teng \ˈnäm-ˈteŋ\ *or* **Teng.** River (*nam*), tributary of Salween river, E cen. Burma; ab. 225 m. long; flows S in Shan State and enters Salween river just N of Karenni dist. border.

Nam Tso. See NA-MU LAKE.

Nam·tu \ˈnäm-(ˌ)tü\ *or* **Namtu–Pang·hai** \-ˈpäŋ-ˌhī\. Town, Shan State, E Burma, 25 m. WNW of Lashio.

Na·mu \ˈnäm-(ˌ)ü\. Islet in Bikini atoll, 8°N, 168°10′E.

Na–mu Lake \ˈnä-ˈmü-\ *or* **Nam Tso** \ˈnäm-ˈtsō\ *or* **Teng·ri Nor** \ˌteŋ-ˌ(g)rē-ˈnȯ(ə)r\. Salt lake, E Tibet, W China, 30°42′N, 90°30′E; 50 m. long and 25 m. wide at its greatest extent; alt. 15,186 ft.; hot springs nearby on the NW.

Na·mu·li \nə-ˈmü-lē\. Mountain, N Mozambique, SE Africa, E of Lake Chilwa; 7936 ft.

Na·mur \nä-ˈmu̇(ə)r\ *or Flem.* **Na·men** \ˈnäm-ən\. 1 Province, S Belgium; 1413 sq. m.; pop. (1970e) 384,689; ✱ Namur; rivers Meuse, Sambre; rye, potatoes, oats, sugar beets; livestock; metalworking and glass industries.

2 Fortified manufacturing commune, its ✱, at confluence of Sambre and Meuse rivers; pop. (1970e) 32,507; glass, leather, soap, metal goods, cement; tourism; 18th cent. cathedral; medieval citadel. Often scene of conflict: besieged by Louis XIV 1692 and retaken 1695 by William of Orange; fortifications reduced by German artillery Aug. 20–25, 1914 and city captured by the Germans; scene of fighting again in World War II.

Namur \ˈnə-ˈm(y)u̇(ə)r\. Islet of Kwajalein atoll (*q.v.*), Marshall Is.; taken by Allies Feb. 1–3, 1944.

Namyung. See NAN-HSIUNG.

Nan \ˈnän\. 1 River, one of main tributaries of the Chao Phraya river, W Thailand; 390 m. long; flows S from Laos border to unite with Ping river to form the Chao Phraya near Nakhon Sawan.

2 Province, N Thailand; 4515 sq. m.; pop. (1960c) 240,471.

3 Town, its ✱, on upper Nan river 90 m. NNE of Uttaradit; pop. (1964e) 15,282.

Na·nai·mo \nə-ˈnī-(ˌ)mō\. City, SE Vancouver I., British Columbia, Canada, on Strait of Georgia 38 m. W of Vancouver; pop. (1971p) 14,762; harbor; center of coal-mining and lumbering region; sawmills, brickyards, lumber mills; home port of salmon and cod fleet. Site of blockhouse erected by Hudson's Bay Company 1833; founded 1853.

Na·na·ku·li \ˌnän-ə-ˈkü-lē\. City, Honolulu co., Hawaii, 18 m. W of Honolulu; pop. (1970c) 6506.

Na·nam \ˈnä-ˈnäm\ *or formerly* **Ra·nan** \ˈrä-ˈnän\. Coastal town, North Hamgyŏng prov., North Korea, WSW of port of Ch'ongjin.

Na·nao \ˈnän-ˌau̇\. Town, Ishikawa prefecture, W coast of Honshū, Japan, on E side of Noto Penin.; pop. (1970c) 47,855; seaport.

Nance \ˈnans\. County in Nebraska. See table at NEBRASKA.

Nan–ch'ang \ˈnän-ˈchäŋ\. Old walled city, ✱ of Kiangsi prov., SE China, on right bank of Kan river just SW of P'o-yang Lake; pop. (1970e) 900,000; trades in rice, tea, cotton, hemp; vegetable oils, textiles, paper, agricultural machinery; in World War II occupied by Japanese 1939–45.

Nancheng. See HAN-CHUNG.

Nan·cow·ry *or* **Nan·kau·ri** \nan-'kaů(ə)r-ē\. 1 Island, cen. group of Nicobar Is., Bay of Bengal, India; 19 sq. m.
2 Town at S end of island; good harbor.

Nan·cy \'nan(t)-sē, nänⁿ-'sē\. Manufacturing city, ✱ of Meurthe-et-Moselle dept., NE France, on Meurthe river 178 m. E of Paris; pop. (1968c) 123,428; transportation center; episcopal see; center of coal and iron mining region; produces salt, glass, clothing, velvet, beverages and foodstuffs, lumber, ironware; 18th cent. cathedral, Gothic church of St. Épyre, 15th cent. church of the Cordeliers, 17th cent. town hall, ducal palace; univ. (founded 1572 at Pont-à-Mousson; removed here 1768).

History: Capital of ancient Lorraine; scene of battle in which Charles the Bold, Duke of Burgundy, was defeated and slain by René II, Duke of Lorraine, 1477; residence (1737 ff.) of Stanislas Leszczyński, Duke of Lorraine and Bar, former king of Poland; passed to French crown 1766; occupied by Germans 1870–73; important railroad center in World War I; unsuccessfully attacked by Germans 1914, suffered under heavy bombardment; in World War II reached by American forces Sept. 5, 1944 and taken Sept. 15.

Nan·da De·vi \ˌnən-də-'dā-vē\. Peak in the Himalayas, Uttar Pradesh, N India, on border of Garhwal; 25,645 ft.

Nan·da·rua \nan-də-'rü-ə\. Peak, cen. Kenya, E Africa; ab. 12,900 ft.

Nan·der \'nän-ˌde(ə)r\ *or* **Nan·ded** \-ˌded\. Town, SE Maharashtra, S cen. India, on Godavari river 140 m. NNW of Hyderabad; pop. (1961c) 81,087; market town; cotton processing.

Nand·gaon \'nän(d)-ˌgaůn\. Former Indian state, Eastern States Agency, NE India, N of Bastar; 872 sq. m.; ✱ Raj-Nandgaon.

Nan·di *or* **Na·di** \'nän-dē\. 1 Small river on Viti Levu I., Fiji, W Pacific Ocean; flows W into **Nandi Bay,** inlet of Pacific Ocean. Coast near its mouth developed 1943–44 as American base in World War II.
2 Village, Fiji, on W Viti Levu I. at mouth of Nandi river; international airport.

Nandi Drug *or* **Nan·di·droog** \'nən-di-ˌdrůg\. Fortified hill, E Mysore, S India, 31 m. N of Bangalore; 4813 ft.; fort constructed by Haidar Ali and Tipu Sultan; taken by storm 1791 by British under Lord Cornwallis.

Nan·dyal \nən-'dyäl\. Town, W Andhra Pradesh, S India, on tributary of Penner river 125 m. S of Hyderabad; pop. (1961c) 42,927.

Nangal Dam. See BHAKRA DAM.

Nan·ga Par·bat \ˌnəŋ-gə-'pər-bət\. Peak in the W Himalayas, in region of Jammu and Kashmir under Pakistani control; 26,660 ft.; first scaled 1953.

Nan·gar·hār \ˌnäŋ-gər-'här\. Province of E Afghanistan. See table at AFGHANISTAN.

Nang·tud, Mount \-näŋ-'tüd\. Mountain, W Panay, Phil., in cen. part of range bet. Antique and Capiz provs.; 6724 ft.

Nan–hsiung \'nän-shē-'ůŋ\ *or* **Nam·yung** \'näm-'yůŋ\. Town, N Kwangtung prov., SE China, ab. 150 m. NE of Canton; in important wolfram-mining district. In World War II American air base; captured by Japanese Feb. 1945, retaken by Chinese July 25, 1945.

Naniwa. See ŌSAKA 2.

Nan·kai \'nän-'kī\. Island in Western Channel, off S coast of South Korea.

Nan·kai·do \nän-'kīd-(ˌ)ō\. Former division of Japan including Shikoku and Awaji islands and Kii prov. on Honshū.

Nankauri. See NANCOWRY.

Nan·king \'nan-'kiŋ, 'nän-\; *formerly* **Chian–ning** \jē-'äŋ-'niŋ\ *or* **Kiang–ning** \jē-'äŋ-'niŋ\. Commercial city, ✱ of Kiangsu prov., E China, on S bank of Yangtze, 150 m. NW of Shanghai and ab. 200 m. above it by river; pop. (1970e) 2,000,000; ✱ of China 1928–37 and 1946–49; fertilizers, steel, textiles, motor vehicles, cement, optical instruments; univ. (1902) and several colleges.

History: Founded 1368 in Ming dynasty although built on site of important cities known by various names for more than 2000 years; capital of empire under Mings 1368–1403; taken by British 1842; scene of treaty signed Aug. 29, 1842 which ceded Hong Kong to Great Britain and opened five treaty ports; covered wide extent and was surrounded by high walls; contained imperial tombs and notable buildings, esp. the porcelain tower (begun 1413); largely destroyed by Taiping rebels who held city as their headquarters 1853–64; declared a treaty port 1858 but not opened until 1899; chosen 1928 by the Kuomintang as capital; capital removed to Chungking 1937 after the occupation of the city by the Japanese; became capital again 1946; occupied by Communist forces 1949; became ✱ of Kiangsu prov. 1952.

Nan–k'ou *or* **Nan·kow** \'nän-'kō\. Town, Peking municipality, NE China, ab. 25 m. NW of Peking; nearby to the E in valley 6 m. long are Ming Tombs (or Thirteen Tombs, a semicircle of tombs of 13 of the 16 rulers of the Ming dynasty) reached by an avenue (Holy Way) under a great arch (*pailou*) and bordered by large stone animals. **Nan–k'ou Pass** is 5 to 12 m. NW of Nan–k'ou through hills and gate in Great Wall; highest point ab. 1900 ft.; four railroad tunnels.

Nan Ling \'nän-'liŋ\ *or* **Nan Shan** \'nän-'shän\. Mountain system in S China, roughly separating Kwangtung prov. and Kwangsi Chuang from Hunan and Kweichow provs.

Nan–ning \'nän-'niŋ\ *or from 1913 to 1945* **Yung–ning** \'yůŋ-'niŋ\. City, ✱ of Kwangsi Chuang, SE China, ab. 330 m. W of Canton; pop. (1970e) 375,000; in region producing sugarcane, fruits, aniseed; a former treaty port, opened 1907; supply base for Communist forces during anti-French campaign in Indochina (ending 1954).

Nan–p'ing \'nän-'piŋ\ *or formerly* **Yen·ping** \'yen-'piŋ\. City on Min river, N cen. Fukien prov., SE China, 85 m. WNW of Foochow.

Nansei Islands. See RYUKYU ISLANDS.

Nan·se·mond \'nan(t)-s(ə-)mənd\. 1 Short stream in Nansemond co., SE Virginia; flows NNE into Hampton Roads.
2 County in Virginia. See table at VIRGINIA.

Nan·sen Sound \ˌnan-sən-\. Strait bet. W Grant Land, Ellesmere I. and Axel Heiberg I., Canada.

Nan Shan *or* **Nan·shan** \'nän-'shän\. 1 Mountain range on border bet. Tsinghai and Kansu provs., cen. China, running NW to SE; forms NE rampart of Tibetan plateau; peaks 18,000 to more than 20,000 ft.; traversed by passes 12,000–14,000 ft.; long valleys 12,000–14,000 ft. high; has lake, Tsing Hai, at E end.
2 Mountain range, China. See NAN LING.

Nan·ta·ha·la \ˌnant-ə-'hā-lə, -lē\. River, W North Carolina; rises near Georgia-North Carolina boundary and flows N through Nantahala National Forest into Little Tennessee river in Swain co.; noted for scenery and the deep Nantahala Gorge.

Nan–t'ai. See FOOCHOW.

Nan·tai \'nän-'tī\ *or* **Nan·tai–zan** \-'zän\. Peak, N cen. Honshū, Japan, NNE of Lake Chuzenji; 8150 ft.; has extinct crater 1000 ft. in diameter.

Nan·tas·ket Beach \nan-ˌtas-kət-\. Summer resort in Plymouth co., Massachusetts, on Massachusetts Bay, 10 m. SE of Boston.

Nan·terre \näⁿ-'te(ə)r\. Commune, ✱ of Hauts-de-Seine dept., N France, W suburb of Paris; pop. (1968c) 90,332; automobiles, machine tools, electrical equipment, perfume; birthplace of the Revolutionary hero Hanriot.

Nantes \'nan(t)s, 'näⁿt\ *or Breton* **Naoned;** *anc.* **Con·di·vin·cum** \ˌkän-di-'viŋ-kəm\ *or later* **Nam·ne·tes** \nam-'nēt-(ˌ)ēz\. Manufacturing and commercial city, ✱ of Loire-Atlantique dept., NW France, on Loire river 107 m. W of Tours; pop. (1968c) 259,208; connected by ship canal with St-Nazaire; seaport; major industrial center, producing locomotives, motor vehicles, aircraft parts, household appliances, machine tools, fertilizers, glass, soap, paint; oil refining, shipbuilding and repairing, sugar processing, food canning; univ. (1962); cathedral, 13th cent. Gothic church, ducal castle, palace of justice, town hall.

History: Capital of ancient Namnetes before Roman conquest of Gaul; passed to Romans; unsuccessfully besieged by Huns 445 A.D.; captured by Normans in 9th cent.; ravaged by fire 1118; held by dukes of Brittany; passed to France 1499 on marriage of Anne of Brittany to Louis XII; famous Edict of Nantes issued by Henry IV Apr. 30, 1598; scene of Noyades (mass drownings) during French Revolution; in World War II heavily damaged by Allied bombing; reached by Americans Aug. 10, 1944.

Nan·ti·coke \'nant-i-ˌkōk\. 1 River, SE Maryland; 63 m. long; rises in S cen. Delaware, flows SW into Chesapeake Bay, SE Maryland.

2 City, Luzerne co., E Pennsylvania, on Susquehanna river 8 m. W of Wilkes-Barre; pop. (1970c) 14,632; silk and rayon; coal mines.

Nan·tuck·et \nan-'tək-ət\. 1 Island, Atlantic Ocean S of Cape Cod, Massachusetts, constituting with adjoining islands Nantucket co., SE Massachusetts; area 57 sq. m.; summer resort.

2 County in Massachusetts. See table at MASSACHUSETTS.

3 Town, ⊗ of Nantucket co., SE Massachusetts, on Nantucket Sound in N cen. Nantucket I.; pop. (1970c) 3774; former whaling center.

Nantucket Sound. Body of water bet. S coast of Cape Cod and Nantucket I., SE Massachusetts, connecting with Atlantic Ocean on the E and Vineyard Sound on the W.

Nan–t'ung \'nän-'tu̇ŋ\ *or formerly* **Tung·chow** \'tu̇ŋ-'jō\. Seaport city, SE Kiangsu prov., E China, on N side of Yangtze estuary 65 m. NW of Shanghai; pop. (1970e) 300,-000.

Nant·wich \'nant-(ˌ)wich\. Urban district, Cheshire, NW England, on the Weaver 30 m. SE of Liverpool; pop. (1971p) 11,666; clothing, leather; health resort; 14th cent. church.

Nan·ty–Glo \'nant-ē-'glō\. Borough, Cambria co., SW cen. Pennsylvania, 11 m. NNE of Johnstown; pop. (1970c) 4298; coal mines; agriculture.

Nan·ty·glo and Blai·na \ˌnant-ē-ˌglō . . . 'blī-nə\. Urban district, Monmouthshire, SE Wales, 34 m. NW of Bristol, England; pop. (1971p) 10,609; trade center in coal-mining and ironworking section.

Na·nu·ku Passage \nə-'nü-kü-\. Channel bet. Taveuni I. on the W and islets of N Lau group on the E, NE Fiji, SW Pacific Ocean; ab. 30 m. wide; leads out of Koro Sea and at its NE end is Welangilala islet to guide ships going from Suva NE to Samoa and U.S.

Na·nu·mea \ˌnän-ə-'mā-ə\. Island (atoll), N end of Ellice Is., W Pacific Ocean; 6 m. long; two islets with no sheltered anchorage; taken over by U.S. Marines Sept. 1943 and developed as a base.

Na·nu·sa Islands \nə-'nü-sə-\. See TALAUD ISLANDS.

Nan–yang \'nän-'yäŋ\. City, SW Honan prov., E cen. China, ab. 150 m. SW of K'ai-feng.

Nan·yo \'nän-'yō\. 1 Japanese name of the South Sea Mandated Territories (see JAPAN), the islands in the Pacific that were under Japanese mandate 1919–45; ✽ Koror, in the Palau Is.

2 Town, its ✽. See KOROR.

Nan·yu·ki \nän-'yü-ke\. Town, cen. Kenya, E Africa, ab. 90 m. NNE of Nairobi; pop. (1969p) 11,200.

Nao, Cape \-'nau̇\ *or Span.* **Ca·bo de la Nao** \ˌkäb-ō-ˌdā-lə-\. Cape on E coast of Spain, 47 m. NE of Alicante, 38°44′N, 0°14′E.

Naoned. See NANTES.

Na·os \'nau̇s\. Small island in the Bay of Panama, just off SE end of Panama Canal.

Naoua. See NAWA.

Napa \'nap-ə\. 1 County in W cen. California. See table at CALIFORNIA.

2 City, its ⊗, on Napa river 10 m. N of San Pablo Bay; pop. (1970c) 35,978; clothing, leather, dairy products, wine; citrus orchards, vineyards; Napa Coll. (1941); settled 1847–48, incorp. 1863.

Nap·a·nee \'nap-ə-ˌnē\. Town, ⊗ of Lennox and Addington co., SE Ontario, Canada, 25 m. W of Kingston at E end of Bay of Quinte; pop. (1971p) 4600.

Nap·a·ta \'nap-ət-ə\. Town, ancient Egypt, below the Fourth Cataract near modern Marawī; capital 750 B.C. of the kingdom of Nubia.

Nap·a·tree Point \ˌnap-ə-ˌtrē-\. Southwest extremity of Washington co., S Rhode Island, on the Connecticut border.

Na·per·ville \'nā-pər-ˌvil\. City, Du Page co., NE Illinois, 28 m. W of Chicago; pop. (1970c) 23,885; North Central Coll. (1861), Coll. of Du Page (1966).

Na·pi·er \'nā-pē-ər\. City, E North I., New Zealand, on Hawke Bay 170 m. NE of Wellington; pop. (1970e) 38,200; exports fruit, wool, frozen meats, dairy products.

Na·pi·er·ville \'nā-pē-ər-ˌvil\. 1 County, S Quebec, Canada. See table at QUEBEC.

2 Village, its ⊗, 24 m. SSE of Montreal near New York state border; pop. (1971p) 1993.

Na·pi·li Bay \nä-ˌpē-lē-\. Inlet of Pailolo Channel on W coast of Maui I., Hawaii.

Na·ples \'nā-pəlz\. 1 City, Collier co., SW Florida, on Gulf of Mexico 35 m. S of Fort Myers; pop. (1970c) 12,042; resort; shrimp fisheries.

2 Village, Ontario co., W New York, 24 m. NNE of Hornell; pop. (1970c) 1324; vineyards.

3 *or Ital.* **Na·po·li** \'näp-ə-lē\ *or anc.* **Ne·ap·o·lis** \nē-'ap-ə-ləs\. Seaport and industrial commune, ✽ of Campania, also ✽ of Napoli prov., S Italy, on N side of Bay of Naples 117 m. SE of Rome; pop. (1970e) 1,278,051; commercial and cultural center of S Italy; archiepiscopal see; major seaport; diversified industries, including textiles, steel, ship, locomotive and aircraft parts, electrical machinery; shipbuilding, food processing, oil refining, handicrafts; near heights of Posilipo and Vesuvius; five medieval castles (among them Saint Elmo), Virgil's tomb, 13th cent. Gothic cathedral, church of the Holy Apostles (said to have been founded by Constantine the Great), church of St. Paul (1817–31; in imitation of Pantheon at Rome), and numerous other notable churches; the royal palace, the Galleria Umberto I, and a national museum containing artifacts of ancient Pompeii and Herculaneum; university (1224); zoological station, and marine aquarium and laboratory; naval and military station, arsenal.

History: Founded on site of ancient Parthenope (hence its ancient name *Neapolis,* i.e. "new city") c. 600 B.C. by refugees from Cumae, an ancient Greek colony; conquered by Romans in 4th cent. B.C.; included successively in kingdoms of Ostrogoths, Byzantines, and Muslims; conquered by Norman ruler of Sicily and became part of Kingdom of The Two Sicilies (see SICILY); after 1282, when Sicily became Aragonese, kingdom of Naples (included Italy south of Papal States) remained under Angevin house 1268–1435; crown of Naples reunited with that of Sicily under Alfonso of Aragon 1442; in late 15th cent., succession to Neapolitan throne claimed by French (Valois) kings and thus was precipitated Hapsburg-Valois struggle in Italy; conquered by Spanish 1503; ceded to Austria 1713; with Sicily, retroceded to Spain which refounded Kingdom of Two Sicilies under house of Bourbon 1735; capital of Napoleon's Parthenopean Republic 1799 and Sicilian kingdom 1806; scene of revolt 1820 which was suppressed by Austrian intervention; as result of Garibaldi's expedition 1860, joined Italian kingdom. In World War II heavily damaged by Allied and German bombing; occupied by Allies Oct. 7, 1943; extensive reconstruction since 1945.

Naples, Bay of. Inlet of Tyrrhenian Sea on SW coast of Italy, S of Gulf of Gaeta and N of Gulf of Salerno; 22 m. long.

Na·po \ˈnäp-(ˌ)ō\. 1 Province of NE Ecuador. See table at ECUADOR.
2 River, NW South America; ab. 700 m. long; rises near Cotopaxi Mt. in N cen. Ecuador, flows E and SE across Peruvian border, and empties into Amazon river.

Na·po·le·on \nə-ˈpōl-yən, -ˈpō-lē-ən\. 1 City, ⊗ of Logan co., S North Dakota; pop. (1970c) 1036.
2 City, ⊗ of Henry co., NW Ohio, 35 m. WSW of Toledo; pop. (1970c) 7791; automobile parts; diversified agriculture.

Napoléon–Vendée. See LA ROCHE-SUR-YON.

Na·po·le·on·ville \nə-ˈpōl-yən-ˌvil, -ˈpōl-ē-ən-\. Town, ⊗ of Assumption parish, SE Louisiana; pop. (1970c) 1008.

Napoletano, Appennino. See table at APENNINES.

Na·po·li \ˈnäp-ə-lē\. 1 Province of Campania, Italy. See table at ITALY.
2 City, Italy. See NAPLES 3.

Napoli di Malvasia. See MONEMVASÍA.

Na·po–Pas·ta·za \ˌnäp-ō-pä-ˈstäz-ə\. Former province, E Ecuador, E of the Andes and N of the Pastaza river; ✻ Tena; formed 1925; with the province of Santiago-Zamora, constituted the Eastern Region of Ecuador; 33,237 sq. m.; divided into Napo and Pastaza provs. 1960.

Nap·pa·nee \ˈnap-ə-ˌnē\. City, Kosciusko and Elkhart cos., N Indiana, 20 m. SE of South Bend; pop. (1970c) 4159; canned goods, lumber, flour.

Na·qa·da \nə-ˈkäd-ə\. Village, archaeological site on left bank of the Nile, cen. Egypt, just N of Karnak; excavations by Petrie 1895.

Naqura, En. See EN NAQURA.

Nar. See NERA.

Na·ra \ˈnär-ə\. 1 Prefecture, W cen. Honshū, Japan; 1425 sq. m.; pop. (1970c) 930,160; ✻ Nara.
2 City, its ✻, 26 m. E of Ōsaka, on the slope of a range of hills; pop. (1970c) 208,266; major tourist center; univ. (1949); has extensive park, the largest in Japan, in which are temples, shrines, a museum, and a great image of Buddha (*daibutsu*) slightly larger than that at Kamakura (*q.v.*). The oldest permanent capital of Japan 710–784; chief Buddhist center of early Japan and when capital several times larger than today; suffered rapid decline after Emperor Kwammu removed the court to Nagaoka (784).
3 Water channel, E Sind, Pakistan, probably a former bed of the Indus; ab. 250 m. long; has been transformed into an irrigation canal system with 631 m. of canals; main channel is E of the Indus and flows N across the desert, crossing Khaipur and entering the Indus at Sukkur.

Na·rada Falls \nə-ˌrad-ə-\. Waterfall, Mount Rainier National Park, W cen. Washington; 168 ft. high.

Naradhivas. See NARATHIWAT.

Narainganj. See NARAYANGANJ.

Na·ran·ji·to \ˌnär-ˌäŋ-ˈhēt-(ˌ)ō\. Town and municipality, NE cen. Puerto Rico; pop. (1970c) 3285 (town), 19,784 (munic.); town on highway 14 m. SW of San Juan.

Na·ran·jo \nä-ˈräŋ-(ˌ)hō\. Site of early Maya city near Tikal, N Guatemala.

Na·ra·shi·no \ˌnär-ə-ˈshē-(ˌ)nō, nə-ˈräsh-i-ˌnō\. City, Chiba prefecture, Honshū, Japan, 16 m. E of Tokyo; pop. (1970c) 99,951.

Na·ra·thi·wat \ˌnär-ə-tē-ˈwät\ *or* **Na·ra·dhi·vas** \ˌnär-ə-tē-ˈwät—*sic*\. 1 Province, SW Thailand; 1632 sq. m.; pop. (1960c) 266,038.
2 Town, its ✻, seaport on Gulf of Siam on E coast of Malay Penin. 100 m. SE of Pattani; pop. (1964e) 19,067.

Na·ra·yan·ganj \nə-ˈrä-yən-ˌgənj\ *also* **Na·rain·ganj** \nä-ˈrīn-\. Town, SE Bangla Desh, on Meghna river 12 m. E of Dacca; met. area pop. (1969e) 326,500; jute and hide market; river port; textiles, glass, leather goods.

Narbada. See NARMADA.

Nar·berth \ˈnär-bərth\. Residential borough, Montgomery co., SE Pennsylvania, 7 m. WNW of Philadelphia; pop. (1970c) 5151; perfumes, metalware.

Narbo Martius. See NARBONNE.

Nar·bo·nen·sis \ˌnär-bə-ˈnen(t)-səs\ *or* **Gal·lia Narbonensis** \ˈgal-ē-ə-\. Part of ancient Gallia (see GAUL); under Augustus and Tiberius made one of 5 administrative areas into which Gaul was divided; in SE part bet. the Alps and Cévennes, extending up the Rhone as far as Vienna (Vienne) and W as far as Tolosa (Toulouse); chief town Narbo Martius.

Nar·bonne \när-ˈbän, -ˈbən\ *or anc.* **Nar·bo Mar·ti·us** \ˌnär-bō-ˈmär-sh(ē-)əs\. Commune, Aude dept., S France, near Mediterranean 31 m. E of Carcassonne; pop. (1968c) 38,441; trades in wine and salt; honey; sulfur refining, distilling, barrel-making; 11th–14th cent. church, 13th–14th cent. cathedral (unfinished), town hall (formerly fortified archiepiscopal palace), museums, technical coll.
History: Said to be first Roman colony beyond Alps (founded 118 B.C.); became capital of Gallia Narbonensis (see GAUL) c. 309 A.D.; taken by Visigoths 412, Saracens 719, Pepin the Short 759; prosperous manufacturing city 11th and 12th cents.; archiepiscopal see suppressed 1790; medieval fortifications replaced by boulevards by 1870.

Narborough Island. See FERNANDINA 2.

Nar·dò \när-ˈdō\. Manufacturing commune, Lecce prov., Apulia, SE Italy, on E shore of Gulf of Taranto 12 m. SW of Lecce; pop. (1968e) 30,344; 13th cent. cathedral; baroque palace and church.

Narenta. See NERETVA.

Na·rew \ˈnär-ˌef, -ˌev\ *or Russ.* **Na·rev** \nər-ˈyóf, -ˈyóv\. River, NE Poland; 296 m. long; rises SE of Białystok, flows generally W and SW into Bug river near its confluence with the Vistula; battles on its bank Mar.–Aug. 1915, resulting finally in German success; in World War II fighting on its banks Sept. 1939 and Sept. 1944.

Na·rin·da Bay \nə-ˌrin-də-\. Inlet of Mozambique Channel on NW coast of the Malagasy Republic.

Na·ri·ño \nə-ˈrē-(ˌ)nyō\. Department of S Colombia. See table at COLOMBIA.

Nar·ma·da \nər-ˈməd-ə\ *also* **Nar·ba·da** \nər-ˈbəd-ə\ *or* **Ner·bud·da** \nər-\. River, cen. India; 801 m. long; rises in the Maikala Range, Madhya Pradesh, flows W bet. the Vindhya Mts. and the Satpura Range, into the Gulf of Cambay; forms traditional boundary bet. Hindustan and the Deccan; second only to the Ganges in sacredness to the Hindus; navigable only in its lower course.

Nar·naul \nər-ˈnaủ(ə)l\. Town, Haryana state, NW India, 80 m. WSW of Delhi; pop. (1961c) 23,959.

Nar·ni \ˈnär-nē\ *or anc.* **Nar·nia** \ˈnär-nē-ə\. Commune, Terni prov., Umbria, cen. Italy, on Nera river 8 m. SW of Terni; pop. (1968e) 21,026; episcopal see; town built on a rock 787 ft. high; 12th cent. cathedral; palaces of 12th and 14th cents.

Na·ro \ˈnär-(ˌ)ō\. Commune, Agrigento prov., SW Sicily, Italy, 12 m. E of Agrigento; pop. (1968e) 14,288; ruins of castle and walls; early Christian necropolis nearby.

Naro. River, Yugoslavia. See NERETVA.

Na·roch \nə-ˈróch\ *or Pol.* **Na·rocz** \ˈnä-ˌróch\. Small lake, N Belorussian S.S.R., U.S.S.R.; 8 m. long; ab. 32 sq. m.; scene of battle on its shores in World War I, Mar. 18–Apr. 30, 1916, which resulted in disastrous defeat to Russians.

Narodna Republika Bŭlgariya. See BULGARIA.

Na·rod·na·ya, Mount \-nä-ˈród-nə-yə\. Mountain in N Ural Mts., Russian S.F.S.R., U.S.S.R.; 6214 ft.; highest peak in Ural Mts.

Naro–Fo·minsk \ˌnar-ə-ˈfō-mən(t)sk\. Industrial town, SW Moscow Oblast, Russian S.F.S.R., U.S.S.R., on railroad 40 m. SW of Moscow; pop. (1967e) 44,000; held for a few months 1941–42 by Germans.

Na·rón \när-ˈōn\. Commune, La Coruña prov., NW Spain, near Atlantic Ocean 17 m. NE of La Coruña; pop. (1970p) 21,491; produces cereals, potatoes, wine; stock raising in region.

Narova. See NARVA 1.

Nar·ra·been \'nar-ə-ˌbēn\. Coast town, New South Wales, SE Australia, NE suburb of Sydney.

Nar·ra·gan·sett \ˌnar-ə-'gan(t)-sət\. Town and summer resort, Washington co., S Rhode Island, at entrance to Narragansett Bay 9 m. WSW of Newport; pop. (1970c) 7138; includes summer resort of **Narragansett Pier** (pop. 2686). Settled 1675; scene of engagement bet. colonists and Narraganset Indians 1675; set aside 1888 as special district in South Kingstown; incorporated as separate town 1901.

Narragansett Bay. Inlet of Atlantic Ocean, in SE Rhode Island, containing a number of islands including Rhode I., Prudence I., and Conanicut I.; 28 m. long; the city of Providence is at its N extremity and the city of Newport is on Rhode I. at the E side of the entrance to the bay.

Nar·ro·gin \'nar-ə-jən\. Town, SW Western Australia, 110 m. SE of Perth; pop. (1966c) 4861.

Nar·rows, The \-'nar-(ˌ)ōz, -əz\. **1** Strait bet. W end of Long I. and Staten I., SE New York, and connecting Upper New York Bay with Lower New York Bay; min. width 1¼ m.; spanned by Verrazano-Narrows Bridge (1964), longest suspension bridge in world.

2 Narrowest part of the Dardanelles, ab. 10 m. from the Aegean Sea; ab. ¾ m. wide.

3 Narrow channel in Virgin Is., West Indies, bet. N St. John I. (U.S.) and SW Tortola (British).

Narrows Dam \ˌnar-(ˌ)ōz-, -əz-\ *or* **Yad·kin Dam** \ˌyad-kən-\. Dam across narrows of Yadkin river bet. Stanly and Montgomery cos., S cen. North Carolina; height 216 ft.; impounds water, **Ba·din Lake** \ˌbād-ən-\, for power.

Nar·sars·su·ak \ˌnär-sər-'sü-ˌak\. Village at head of a fjord on SW coast near S tip of Greenland, ab. 90 m. E of Ivigtut; airport.

Nar·singh·garh \'när-siŋ-ˌgär\. **1** Former Indian state, now part of Madhya Pradesh, India; 731 sq. m.; Rajput state, founded ab. 1681.

2 Town, its ✱, ab. 38 m. NW of Bhopal; pop. (1961c) 11,600.

Nar·singh·pur \'när-siŋ-ˌpu̇(ə)r\. **1** Former Indian state, now part of Orissa, NE India, N of Mahanadi river, W of Cuttack; 204 sq. m.

2 *or* **Nar·simh·a·pur** \-sim-ə-\. Town, cen. Madhya Pradesh, cen. India, on railroad 50 m. WSW of Jabalpur; pop. (1961c) 17,900.

Na·ru \'när-(ˌ)ü\. Island in Gotō Archipelago (*q.v.*), Japan.

Na·ru·to Strait \ˌnär-ü-ˌtō-\. Strait bet. NE Shikoku I. and Awaji I., Japan, connecting the Inland Sea with Kii Channel and the Pacific Ocean; 1 m. wide; remarkable for great velocity (7 to 11 knots an hour) of its tides, esp. in the spring.

Nar·va \'när-və\. **1** *or Russ.* **Na·ro·va** \'när-ə-və\. River, NE Estonian S.S.R., U.S.S.R.; ab. 48 m. long; the outlet of Lake Peipus, flowing N past city of Narva (8 m. from its mouth) to the Gulf of Finland; navigable to Narva but has falls just above city (20 ft.), site of hydroelectric power plant built 1955.

2 City, NE Estonian S.S.R., U.S.S.R., on Narva river ab. 8 m. from its mouth in Gulf of Finland; pop. (1969e) 53,000; chief industrial center of Estonian S.S.R.; important cotton mills, also jute, woolen, and flax mills; fisheries, lumberyards. Its port and a summer resort on the Gulf of Finland is **Narva–Jõe·suu** \-'yəi-(ˌ)sü\.

History: Founded 1223 by Danes; a seat of the Livonian Knights and the Hanseatic League; seized by Ivan the Terrible of Russia 1558; captured by Swedes 1581; scene of battle Nov. 30, 1700 in which Swedes under Charles XII defeated Peter the Great of Russia; recaptured by Russians 1704; scene of battles in World War I; occupied by Communist forces who were driven out by Latvians and Finns Jan. 1919; in World War II seized by Germans 1941 but retaken 1944.

Nar·va·can \ˌnär-və-'kän\. Municipality, Ilocos Sur prov., Luzon, Phil., on main highway 13 m. SSE of Vigan; pop. (1969e) 36,400; largest town in province.

Nar·vik \'när-vik, -ˌvēk\. Seaport, Nordland co., N Norway, on a peninsula in Ofoten Fjord opp. the Lofoten; pop. (1970e) 13,297; ice-free harbor; exports iron ore; terminus of railroad from Sweden. Occupied by Germans Apr. 9, 1940; scene of naval battles in harbor Apr. 10 and 13 in which two British destroyers and nine German ones were lost; held by British May 28–June 9, 1940.

Na·ryan–Mar \nər-'yän-'mär\. Village on right shore of Pechora delta, ✱ of Nenets National Okrug, Russian S.F.S.R., U.S.S.R., ab. 60 m. from the sea; pop. (1967e) 15,000.

Na·ryn \nə-'rin\. Town, ✱ of Naryn Oblast, SE Kirgiz S.S.R., U.S.S.R., on **Naryn River,** an upper tributary of the Syr Darya; pop. (1967e) 20,000; in mountainous region at ab. 6800 ft.

Naryn Oblast \-'ō-bləst, -ˌblast\. Subdivision of the Kirgiz S.S.R., U.S.S.R.; 19,459 sq. m.; pop. (1970p) 186,000; ✱ Naryn; sheep raising; uranium ore.

Na Sam \'nä-ˌsäm\ *also* **Na·cham** \'näch-ˌäm\ *or* **Nam–quan** \'näm-ˌkwän\. Town, North Vietnam, just NW of Lang Son, terminus of railroad from Hanoi; on Chinese frontier opp. P'ing-hsiang in Kwangsi Chuang.

Nas·ca \'näs-kə\. Town, Ica dept., SW Peru, 85 m. SE of Ica on Pan American Highway; archaeological site of early Inca culture.

Nase·by \'nāz-bē\. Parish, Northamptonshire, cen. England, 12 m. E by N of Rugby; pop. (1961c) 416; scene of battle June 14, 1645 in which Fairfax and Cromwell's Parliamentary army disastrously defeated Charles I and Prince Rupert's Royalist forces, ending all chance of success for Royalist cause.

Nash \'nash\. County in North Carolina. See table at NORTH CAROLINA.

Nash·a·we·na Island \ˌnash-ə-ˌwē-nə-\. Island in S part of Elizabeth Is., Dukes co., SE Massachusetts.

Nashborough. See NASHVILLE 6.

Nash·ua \'nash-ə-wə, -ə-ˌwā\. **1** River, NE cen. Massachusetts and SE New Hampshire; ab. 80 m. long; flows N from Wachusett Reservoir, Worcester co., cen. Massachusetts, across the state border into Merrimack river at Nashua, New Hampshire.

2 Industrial city, ⊗ of Hillsborough co., S New Hampshire, on Merrimack river 15 m. S of Manchester; pop. (1970c) 55,820; shoes, asbestos, paper products, plastics, office equipment, chemicals; Rivier Coll. (1933), New England Aeronautical Institute (1965); incorporated as city 1853.

Nash·ville \'nash-ˌvil, -vəl\. **1** City, ⊗ of Howard co., SW Arkansas, 37 m. N of Texarkana; pop. (1970c) 4016; lumber; dairy and fruit farms.

2 City, ⊗ of Berrien co., S Georgia, 26 m. N of Valdosta; pop. (1970c) 4323; tobacco, corn, peanuts.

3 City, ⊗ of Washington co., SW Illinois, 20 m. SW of Centralia; pop. (1970c) 3027; diversified agriculture.

4 Town, ⊗ of Brown co., S cen. Indiana, 17 m. W of Columbus; pop. (1970c) 527.

5 Town, ⊗ of Nash co., NE North Carolina; pop. (1970c) 1670.

6 Commercial and industrial city, ✱ of Tennessee and ⊗ of Davidson co., N cen. Tennessee, on Cumberland river; pop. (1970c) 447,877; transportation center; dacron, shoes, aircraft parts, glass and rubber products, boats and barges, structural steel, fertilizer; meat packing, railroad shops; printing and publishing; important center of recording industry. Fisk Univ. (1867), Vanderbilt Univ. (1872), George Peabody Coll. for Teachers (1875), Meharry Medical Coll. (1876), David Lipscomb Coll. (1891), Trevecca Nazarene Coll. (1901), Tennessee Agricultural and Industrial State Univ. (1909), Scarritt Coll. for Christian Workers (1924), American Baptist Coll. (1924), Free Will Baptist Bible Coll. (1942), Belmont Coll. (1951), Aquinas Junior Coll. (1961); the Hermitage (home of Andrew Jackson) nearby.

History: Founded 1779 as **Nash·bor·ough** \ˈnash-ˌbər-ə, -bə-rə\; incorporated as town 1784 and renamed Nashville; chartered as city 1806; became permanent capital of state 1843; scene of Nashville (Southern) Convention 1850; captured and held in Civil War by Union Army from Feb. 1862; scene of battle of Nashville Dec. 15–16, 1864 in which Union forces under Thomas decisively defeated Confederates under Hood.

Nä·si·jär·vi \ˈnas-ē-ˌya(ə)r-vē\. Lake, SW Finland; the city of Tampere is situated on its S shore.

Na·sik \ˈnäs-ik\. Town, cen. Maharashtra, W India, on Godavari river 100 m. NE of Bombay; pop. (1970e) 174,-039; brass and copper ware; renowned pilgrimage city of the Hindus; nearby cavern temples and cloisters of Buddhists dating from centuries just before and after the birth of Christ.

Nasira, En. See NAZARETH 2.

Na·sir·a·bad \nə-ˈsir-ə-ˌbäd\. 1 Town, Bangla Desh. See MYMENSINGH.

2 Town, cen. Rajasthan, NW India, 15 m. SSE of Ajmer; pop. (1961c) 24,128.

Nasiriya, An. See AN NASIRIYA.

Na·so Point \ˌnäs-ō-\. Southwestern point of Panay I., Phil., at S end of Antique prov.

Nasratabad. See ZĀBOL.

Nass \ˈnas\. River, W British Columbia, Canada; 236 m. long; flows SW through the Coast Mts. into Pacific Ocean (Dixon Entrance) 30 m. N of Prince Rupert.

Nas·sau \ˈnas-ˌȯ\. 1 Name of counties in two states of the U.S. See tables at FLORIDA and NEW YORK.

2 City, ✻ of Bahama Is., on NE coast of New Providence I.; pop. (1970c) 101,503; exports incl. sisal, tomatoes, sponges; good harbor; popular winter resort. Settled in 17th cent.; rendezvous of pirates until 1718; city laid out 1729; several times attacked by Spaniards, last occupation in 1782; a base for Confederate blockade runners 1861–65 and for rumrunners 1920–33.

3 *Ger.* ˈnäs-(ˌ)au̇\. Region, West Germany; former duchy, later Wiesbaden govt. dist. of Hesse-Nassau prov., Prussia, now in W Hesse and NE Rhineland-Palatinate states; chief city Wiesbaden; a thickly forested and hilly territory N and E of the Rhine, crossed by the Lahn river and Taunus Mts.

Nassau Gulf \ˌnas-ˌȯ-\. Gulf in S Tierra del Fuego Archipelago (*q.v.*), extreme S Chile, bet. Navarino I. on N and Wollaston I. on S.

Nassau Range. See SUDIRMAN RANGE.

Nas·ser, Lake \-ˈnäs-ər, -ˈnas-\. Lake, S Egypt and N Sudan; ab. 300 m. long; formed in 1960's as a result of construction of Aswan High Dam (a major hydroelectric power and irrigation project); lake has flooded a number of famous archaeological sites, including Abu Simbel.

Näss·jö \ˈnesh-ˌər\. Town, Jönköping co., S Sweden, ab. 20 m. SE of Jönköping; pop. (1970e) 20,268.

Na·su \ˈnäs-(ˌ)ü\ *or* **Na·su·da·ke** \ˌnäs-u̇-ˈdäk-(ˌ)ā\. Volcanic peak on border bet. Fukushima and Tochigi prefectures, N cen. Honshū, Japan, NE of Nikkō; 6289 ft.

Na·sug·bu \ˌnä-su̇g-ˈbü\. Municipality on W coast of Batangas prov., Luzon, Phil., on South China Sea S of entrance to Manila Bay; pop. (1969e) 47,700; American invasion forces landed here Jan. 31, 1945.

Na·tal \nə-ˈtal, -ˈtäl\. 1 Seaport city, ✻ of Rio Grande do Norte state, NE Brazil; munic. pop. (1970p) 270,124; port and naval base; ships cotton, coffee, hides, and sugar; univ. (1958); during World War II important stop on air ferry route to Africa, Europe, and Asia via Freetown, Sierra Leone (1820 m.) or Dakar, Senegal (1870 m.). Founded 1597; occupied by Dutch 1633–54.

2 Province, E Rep. of South Africa, bounded on N by Transvaal, Swaziland, and Mozambique, on E by Indian Ocean, on S and SW by Cape Province, and on W by Lesotho and Orange Free State; 33,578 sq. m.; pop. (1967e) 3,418,942; ✻ Pietermaritzburg; has sea coast ab. 375 m. long; narrow coastal plain, wide central midlands from 2000–4000 ft. above sea level, and foothills of Drakensberg Mts. along W border. *Rivers:* Pongolo along N border, Tugela in cen. part, and Umzimkulu and Umtamvuna along Cape Province border. *Chief products:* Sugar, cereals, fruit, coal; manufacturing: textiles, fertilizers, furniture, cigarettes. *Chief towns:* Durban, Pietermaritzburg, Ladysmith, Newcastle, Dundee, Vryheid.

History: Coast at Durban first sighted by Vasco da Gama on Christmas Day 1497 and named *Terra Natalis;* first visited by English 1684 but no settlement until 1824 at port of Natal (renamed Durban 1835); reached by Boers on great trek 1836–38; at war with Zulus 1838–40 and with English 1840–43; made a British colony 1843 and annexed to Cape Colony 1844; given separate government 1845 and made separate colony 1856; granted responsible government 1893; annexed Zululand 1897 and other districts in N 1903 (see UTRECHT 3 and VRYHEID); scene of battles in Boer War 1899–1900; joined Union (now Republic) of South Africa 1910.

Natal Current. See MOZAMBIQUE CURRENT.

Na·tan·ya \nə-ˈtän-yə\ *also* **Ne·tan·ya** \nə-\. Coastal city, Israel, ab. 35 m. SSW of Haifa; pop. (1970e) 65,400; diamond cutting and polishing; textiles, rubber goods; founded 1928.

Na·tash·quan *or* **Na·tash·kwan** \nə-ˈtash-kwən\. River, S Labrador and E Saguenay co., Quebec, Canada; 241 m. long; flows S to the St. Lawrence opp. E end of Anticosti I.

Nat·chaug \nə-ˈchȯg\. River, NE Connecticut; rises in NW Windham co., flows S and joins the Willimantic to form the Shetucket river at Willimantic.

Natch·ez \ˈnach-əz\. City, ⊗ of Adams co., SW Mississippi, on Mississippi river; pop. (1970c) 19,704; trade center in agricultural region; tires, wood pulp, synthetic fibers, paper products; saw and cotton mills; Natchez Junior Coll. (1885).

History: Originally site of a Natchez Indian village; visited by La Salle 1662; fortified settlement founded 1716; ceded by France to England 1763; seized by Spain 1779; yielded to U.S. 1798; capital of Territory of Mississippi 1798–1802; incorporated as city 1803; headquarters of Aaron Burr and Harman Blennerhassett in their colonization scheme; held by Union forces 1863–65.

Natchez Trace. Old road from Nashville, Tennessee, to Natchez, Mississippi; over 500 m. long; construction begun 1806; used in early 19th cent. by traders returning from Natchez after having floated produce down the Mississippi river.

Natch·i·toches \ˈnak-ə-ˌtäsh\. 1 Parish in NW cen. Louisiana. See table at LOUISIANA.

2 City, its ⊗, 52 m. NW of Alexandria; pop. (1970c) 15,-674; lumber, cottonseed oil, dairy products; poultry farms; Northwestern State Coll. of Louisiana (1884).

Na·te·wa Bay *and* **Natewa Peninsula** \nä-ˌtā-wə-\. See VANUA LEVU.

Na·thia Ga·li \ˌnät-ē-ə-ˈgäl-ē\. Town in North-West Frontier Province, Pakistan, in hills 38 m. NNE of Rawalpindi; it was the summer capital of North-West Frontier Province.

Na·tib, Mount \-nä-ˈtib\. Mountain, Zambales range, cen. Bataan prov., Luzon, Phil.; 4111 ft.

Na·tick \ˈnāt-ik\. 1 Town, Middlesex co., NE Massachusetts, 15 m. WSW of Boston; pop. (1970c) 31,057; electronic components, clocks, machine parts, sporting goods; founded 1651 by John Eliot, "Apostle of the Indians," as first of his Praying Towns.

2 Village, Kent co., cen. Rhode Island, ab. 5 m. SW of Cranston; cotton manufactures.

Na·tion·al City \ˌnash-nəl-, -ən-ᵊl-\. City, San Diego co., SW corner of California, on San Diego Bay 5 m. S of San

Diego; pop. (1970c) 43,184; residential; furniture, carpets; brass and aluminum foundries.

National Park. Borough, Gloucester co., SW New Jersey, on Delaware river 6 m. SSW of Camden; pop. (1970c) 3730.

Natoena Islands. See NATUNA ISLANDS.

Na·tron, Lake \-ˈnā-trən\. Lake, N Tanzania, near Kenya border, E Africa; ab. 35 m. long by 15 m. wide; large soda deposits. See MAGADI, LAKE and NATRON LAKES.

Na·tro·na \nə-ˈtrō-nə\. County in Wyoming. See table at WYOMING.

Natron Lakes \ˈnā-trən-\. Seven soda lakes (Arabic *natrūn* "native sodium carbonate") in **Wa·di al–Nat·run** \ˈwä-dē-al-ˈnä-trün\, a valley below sea level in N Egypt, 60 m. WNW of Cairo.

Na·tu La \ˌnä-tü-ˈlä\. Pass *(la)* over the Himalayas in SE Sikkim, E of Gangtok; alt. 14,199 ft.

Na·tu·na Islands *or Du.* **Na·toe·na Islands** \nə-ˌtü-nə-\. Island groups, **Natuna Be·sar Islands** \-be-ˈsär-\ and **Bun·gu·ran Se·la·tan Islands** \ˌbüŋ-gür-ˈän-sə-ˈlä-tən-\, of Indonesia, in the South China Sea E of S Malay Penin. and W of Borneo; area of Natuna Besar Is., including Natuna Besar *or* **Great Natoena** (40 m. by 30 m.), 727 sq. m.; area of Bunguran Selatan Is., 89 sq. m.; total area, 815 sq. m.

Natural Bridge. Village in S Rockbridge co., W cen. Virginia, 16 m. S of Lexington; site of a natural bridge (over Cedar Creek) 215 ft. high, 50–100 ft. wide, with a 90-ft. span.

Natural Bridges National Monument. See UNITED STATES, *National Monuments.*

Nat·u·ral·iste, Cape \-ˈnach-(ə-)rə-ləst\. Cape, SW Western Australia, on W side of Geographe Bay.

Nau·cal·pan de Juá·rez \naů-ˈkäl-pən-də-ˈhwär-ˌes\. City, Mexico state, Mexico, 7 m. NW of Mexico City; munic. pop. (1970p) 373,605; textiles; agriculture.

Nauchampatepetl. See COFRE DE PEROTE.

Nau·cra·tis \ˈnȯ-krət-əs\. Greek city of ancient Egypt, in the Nile delta, W of Rosetta branch.

Nau·en \ˈnaů-ən\. Commune, Potsdam dist., East Germany, 25 m. WNW of Berlin; pop. (1969e) 11,882; sugar.

Nau·ga·tuck \ˈnȯ-gə-ˌtək\. **1** River, W Connecticut; 65 m. long; rises in N Litchfield co., flows S through W New Haven co. into the Housatonic river at Derby; furnishes waterpower for industrial plants.
2 Industrial borough, New Haven co., S Connecticut, on Naugatuck river 5 m. S of Waterbury; pop. (1970c) 23,034; chemicals, iron castings; incorp. 1893.

Nau·heim \ˈnaů-ˌhīm\ *or* **Bad Nauheim** \ˌbät-\. Town, Hesse, West Germany, ab. 24 m. N of Frankfurt, NE of Taunus Mts.; pop. (1968e) 15,001; saline thermal waters.

Nau·jan \naů-ˈhän\. Municipality, NE coast of Mindoro I., Mindoro Oriental prov., Phil., just N of **Lake Naujan** 13 m. SE of Calapan; pop. (1969e) 43,600; important trade center.

Nau·lo·chus \ˈnȯ-lə-kəs\. Ancient port and Roman naval station on N coast of Sicily at its E end E of Mylae; in naval battle 36 B.C. M. Vipsanius Agrippa defeated Sextus Pompeius Magnus.

Naum·burg \ˈnaům-ˌbů(ə)rg\ *also* **Naumburg an der Saa·le** \-ˌän-dər-ˈzäl-ə\. Manufacturing city, Halle dist., East Germany, on the Saale river 28 m. SW of Halle; pop. (1970e) 37,636; 12th cent. cathedral, 16th cent. late-Gothic town hall, 16th cent. church; became episcopal see 1029; received city rights 1142; treaties signed here 1457, 1554; to Prussia 1815.

Naupactus. See NÁVPAKTOS.

Nau·plia \ˈnȯ-plē-ə\ *or Gk.* **Náv·pli·on** \ˈnäf-plē-ȯn\. Seaport city, ✱ of Argolis dept., NE Peloponnesus, Greece, on Gulf of Argolis ab. 25 m. SSW of Corinth; pop. (1971p) 9278; important commercial center in Middle Ages; changed masters several times during this period bet. Turks and Venetians; served as capital of Greece after War of Independence until 1834. One of the evacuation points of the British Apr. 24–30, 1941 in World War II.

Nauplia, Gulf of. See ARGOLIS, GULF OF.

Na·u·ru \nä-ˈü-(ˌ)rü\ *or formerly* **Pleas·ant Island** \ˈplez-ᵊnt-\. Island republic in W Pacific Ocean, W of the Gilbert Is.; area 8½ sq. m.; highest point 225 ft.; pop. (1970e) 6603; phosphate deposits.

History: Discovered 1798; annexed by Germany 1888, and made a part of Marshall Is. protectorate; island occupied by Australia 1914 and placed under mandate 1919; seized by Japanese Aug. 1942; became a joint Australian, British, and New Zealand trust territory 1947; became an independent republic 1968.

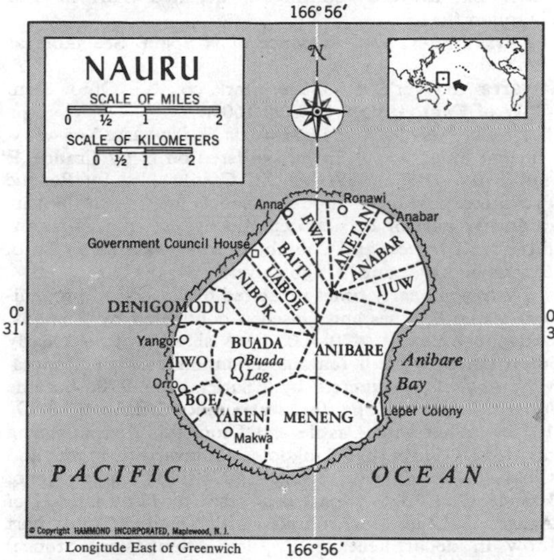

Nausari. See NAVSARI.

Nau·shon Island \nȯ-ˈshän-\. Island, largest of the Elizabeth Is., in Dukes co., SE Massachusetts; 7 m. long; summer resort.

Nau·voo \nȯ-ˈvü, ˈnȯ-(ˌ)vü\. City, Hancock co., W Illinois, on Mississippi river 45 m. N of Quincy; pop. (1970c) 1047; occupied by Mormons under Joseph Smith 1838–39; became prosperous city of 20,000 people under Smith's leadership; abandoned by Mormons who migrated to Utah 1846 after Smith was killed by a mob 1844; made site of Utopian communistic society established in 1849 by group of French Icarians under leadership of Étienne Cabet, settlement breaking up 1856 because of internal factional disagreements.

Na·va·ce·rra·da, Puer·to de \ˈpwert-ō-dā-ˌnäv-ə-sə-ˈräd-ə\. Mountain pass in the Sierra de Guadarrama, cen. Spain; 6053 ft.

Nav·a·jo \ˈnav-ə-ˌhō, ˈnäv-\. County in Arizona. See table at ARIZONA.

Navajo Dam *and* **Navajo Reservoir.** See UNITED STATES, *Dams and Reservoirs.*

Navajo Mountain. Solitary peak, San Juan co., SE Utah, near Rainbow Bridge National Monument; 10,388 ft.

Navajo National Monument. See UNITED STATES, *National Monuments.*

Navajo Peak. Mountain in Boulder and Grand cos., N cen. Colorado; 13,406 ft.

Nav·an \ˈnav-ən\ *or* **An Uaimh.** Town, cen. co. Meath, E Eire, at confluence of Blackwater and Boyne rivers 16 m. SW of Drogheda; pop. (1971p) 4607; farm implements, woolens, tanning.

ə abut; ᵊ kitten, Fr. table; ər further; a back; ā bake; ä cot, cart; à Fr. bac; aů out; ch chin; e less; ē easy; g gift
i trip; ī life; j joke; k Ger. ich, Buch; ⁿ Fr. vin; ŋ sing; ō flow; ȯ flaw; œ Fr. bœuf; œ̄ Fr. feu; ȯi coin; th thin
th this; ü loot; ů foot; ue Ger. füllen; ue̅ Fr. rue; y yet; ʸ Fr. digne \dēnʸ\, nuit \nwʸē\; yü few; yů furious; zh vision

Na·va·na·gar *or* **Na·wa·na·gar** \ˌnəv-ə-ˈnəg-ər\ *also* **Now·a·nug·gur** \ˌnau̇-ə-ˈnəg-ər\. **1** Former Indian state, now part of Gujarat state, W India; 3791 sq. m.; ✱ Jamnagar, on S shore of Gulf of Kutch.
2 City, India. See JAMNAGAR.

Nav·a·rin, Cape \-ˈnav-ə-rən\. Point, Chukot National Okrug, Magadan Oblast, Russian S.F.S.R., U.S.S.R.; extends into Bering Sea just S of Gulf of Anadyr.

Na·va·ri·no \ˌnav-ə-ˈrē-(ˌ)nō\. **1** Chilean island in Tierra del Fuego Archipelago (*q.v.*), S of E Tierra del Fuego I.
2 *or Ital.* **Py·los** \ˈpī-ˌläs\. Seaport in SW Peloponnesus, Greece; held by Athenians against Spartans in Peloponnesian War; scene of naval battle fought in nearby waters Oct. 20, 1827 in which British, French, and Russian fleets under Sir Edward Codrington defeated Turkish and Egyptian fleet.

Na·va·rra \nə-ˈvär-ə\. Province of N Spain. See table at SPAIN.

Na·varre \nə-ˈvär\. **1** Village, Stark co., NE Ohio, 8 m. WSW of Canton; pop. (1970c) 1609.
2 *or Span.* **Na·va·rra** \nə-ˈvär-ə\ *or Fr.* **Na·varre** \nȧ-vȧr\. Ancient kingdom, N Spain; bordered on N by France, E and S by Aragon, SW by Old Castile, NW by Basque Provinces; now forms modern Spanish province of Navarra and W part of French department of Pyrénées-Atlantiques; in Pyrenees and Cantabrian Mts.; watered by Ebro, Bidassoa, Arga, and Aragon rivers.
History: In early times inhabited by Vascones, progenitors of the Basques and Gascons; conquered by Romans, and subsequently, 470 A.D., by Visigoths; gained early importance through famous mountain pass of Roncesvalles (*q.v.*); conquered by Charlemagne 778; became independent kingdom 10th cent.; under Sancho III (970–1035), united with Castile and León, this domain being divided 1035 into three kingdoms of Navarre, Aragon, and Castile; reunited with Aragon 1076–1134; appanage of France 1234–1328; S part conquered by Ferdinand II of Aragon 1512 and incorporated with Castile 1515; N part (now in department of Pyrénées-Atlantiques, France) passed by inheritance 1589 to Henry IV of Bourbon, king of France.

Na·va·rre·te \ˌnäv-ə-ˈret-ē\. Commune, Logroño prov., N Spain, bet. Logroño and Nájera (*q.v.*); pop. (1970p) 2016.

Na·var·ro \nə-ˈvar-(ˌ)ō, -ˈver-\. County in Texas. See table at TEXAS.

Navas de Tolosa, Las. See LAS NAVAS DE TOLOSA.

Nav·a·so·ta \ˌnav-ə-ˈsōt-ə\. **1** River, E Texas; 125 m. long; flows S into Brazos river at point where Brazos, Grimes, and Washington cos. meet.
2 City, Grimes co., E cen. Texas, 26 m. SSE of Bryan; pop. (1970c) 5111; ships livestock and cotton; steel mills.

Na·vas·sa \nə-ˈvas-ə\. Island in Caribbean Sea bet. Jamaica and Hispaniola; 2 m. long; belongs to United States; has lighthouse.

Nav·e·sink Highlands *or* **Navesink Hills** \ˈnav-ə-ˌsiŋk-, ˈnāv-, ˈnev-\. See HIGHLANDS OF NAVESINK.

Navesink River. Estuary, NE Monmouth co., E cen. New Jersey, N of Shrewsbury river; forms an inlet about 5 m. long; barred from flowing directly into the Atlantic Ocean by the peninsula at the N end of which is Sandy Hook extending into Lower New York Bay.

Navigators Islands. See SAMOA.

Na·vo·joa \ˌnäv-ə-ˈhō-ə\. Town, S Sonora state, NW Mexico; munic. pop. (1970p) 69,792; on coastal railroad.

Na·vo·tas \nä-ˈvōt-əs\. Municipality, Rizal prov., Luzon, Phil., on coast of Manila Bay adjacent to Malabon just N of Manila; pop. (1969e) 67,200.

Na·vo·tu·vo·tu \nə-ˌvō-tə-ˈvō-ˌtü\ *or* **West Peak** *or* **Mount Se·a·tu·ro** \-ˌsä-ə-ˈtu̇(ə)r-(ˌ)ō\. Peak, SW Vanua Levu I., Fiji, SW Pacific Ocean; 2763 ft.

Náv·pak·tos \ˈnäf-ˌpäk-tȯs\ *or Ital.* **Le·pan·to** \ˈlep-ən-ˌtō, li-ˈpan-(ˌ)tō\ *or anc.* **Nau·pac·tus** \nȯ-ˈpak-təs\. Seaport in Aetolia and Acarnania dept., Greece, on the strait connecting the Gulfs of Corinth and Patras; peace treaty 217 B.C. bet. Aetolians and Philip V of Macedon; new home of Messenians after end of Third Messenian War (after 461 B.C.); in 16th cent. known as Lepanto and noted for naval battle in nearby strait Oct. 7, 1571, in which Turkish fleet was decisively defeated by combined fleets of Holy League under Don John of Austria in last major galley action.

Návplion. See NAUPLIA.

Na·vron·go \nə-ˈvrȯŋ-(ˌ)gō\. Town, N Upper Region, Ghana, W Africa, 100 m. N of Tamale.

Nav·sa·ri \nəv-ˈsär-ē\ *also* **Nau·sa·ri** \nau̇-\. Town, Gujarat, W India, near Gulf of Cambay 135 m. N of Bombay; pop. (1961c) 53,600.

Nawa. See NAHA.

Na·wa *or* **Na·oua** \ˈnä-wə\. Town, SW Syria, ab. 47 m. S of Damascus.

Na·wab·ganj \nə-ˈwäb-ˌgənj\. Town, E Uttar Pradesh, N India, 17 m. E of Lucknow; pop. (1961c) 27,080; market town; scene of victory by Sir Hope Grant June 12, 1858 during the Sepoy Mutiny.

Na·wab·shah \nə-ˈwäb-ˌshä\. Town, cen. Sind, Pakistan, ab. 60 m. N of Hyderabad; munic. pop. (1961c) 45,651.

Nawanagar. See NAVANAGAR.

Na·wi·li·wi·li Bay \nə-ˌwē-lē-ˌwē-lē-\. Bay on SE coast of Kauai I., Hawaii, S of Ninini Point.

Nax·os \ˈnak-səs, -ˌsäs\. **1** *or Gk.* **Ná·xos** \ˈnäk-ˌsȯs\. Largest island of the Cyclades, Aegean Sea, E of Paros, in Cyclades dept., Greece; ab. 22 m. long by 16 m. wide; area 165 sq. m.; pop. (1961c) 16,703; chief town Naxos (on NW coast); wine. In early times famous as a center for worship of Dionysus; seized by Persia 490 B.C.; member of Delian League, but revolted 471 and made subject to Athens; seat of a medieval duchy 1207–1566 (see AEGEAN ISLANDS) and since War of Independence has belonged to Greece.
2 Oldest Greek colony in Sicily, founded c. 735 B.C.; destroyed by Dionysius the Elder 403 B.C.; its ruins excavated in hills near Taormina on E coast 1953 ff.

Naxuana. See NAKHICHEVAN.

Na·ya·garh \nə-ˈyäg-ər\. **1** Former Indian state, now part of Orissa state, NE India; 562 sq. m.
2 Town, its ✱, 55 m. WSW of Cuttack; pop. (1961c) 5800.

Na·ya·rit \ˌnī-ə-ˈrēt\. State of W Mexico. See table at MEXICO.

Nāy Band \ˈnī-ˈbänd\ *or* **Na·band** \nä-ˈbänd\. Cape on SW coast of Iran, projecting into E cen. Persian Gulf.

Na·zan Bay \nə-ˈzan-\. Inlet, SE Atka I., Andreanof Is., Aleutian Is., SW Alaska.

Na·za·ré \ˌnaz-ə-ˈrā\ *or formerly* **Na·za·reth** \ˌnaz-ə-ˈret\. City, Bahia state, E Brazil, near coast 35 m. W of Salvador; munic. pop. (1968e) 24,307.

Naz·a·reth \ˈnaz-(ə-)rəth\. **1** Borough, Northampton co., E Pennsylvania, 13 m. NE of Allentown; pop. (1970c) 5815; cement, musical instruments, paper boxes; settled by Moravians 1740.
2 *or Heb.* **Na·ze·rat** \ˌnä-zə-ˈrät\ *or Arab.* **En Na·si·ra** \en-ˈnäs-ə-ˌrä\. Town, ✱ of Northern District, N Israel, ab. 18 m. SE of Haifa; pop. (1970e) 34,000; textiles, leather goods, cigarettes; numerous churches; junction point of highways from Haifa and Jerusalem NE to Tiberias on the Sea of Galilee and on N edge of Plain of Esdraelon. Home of Joseph and Mary and of Jesus in his childhood; site of St. Mary's Well; captured several times during the Crusades; its Christian inhabitants massacred by Baybars 1263; taken by Turks 1517 and by British cavalry Sept. 20, 1918.

Na·ze \ˈnäz-(ˌ)ā\. Chief town of Amami Is., Japan, on N coast of Amami-Ō-shima.

Naze, The \-ˈnāz\. **1** Headland on E coast of Essex, SE England, 5 m. S of Harwich.
2 Cape, Norway. See LINDESNES.

Nazerat. See NAZARETH 2.

Na·zil·li \ˌnä-zi-ˈlē\. Town, Aydın prov., SW Turkey, on railroad and on N bank of Menderes river 26 m. E of Aydın; pop. (1965c) 41,330.

Nde·ni \en-ˈdā-nē\ *or formerly* **San·ta Cruz** \ˌsant-ə-ˈkrüz\. Chief island of the Santa Cruz Is., SW Pacific Ocean, 250 m. E of S Solomon Is.; 215 sq. m.; has good harbor at Graciosa Bay.

Ndi·ke·va, Mount \-ən-də-ˈkā-və\ *or formerly* **Mount Thur·ston** \-ˈthər-stən\. Peak, E Vanua Levu I., Fiji, SW Pacific Ocean; 3134 ft.; highest point on the island.

Ndo·la \en-ˈdō-lə\. Town, N Zambia, S cen. Africa, ab. 170 m. N of Lusaka; pop. (1967e) 114,000; cement factory; center of copper-mining region.

Ndre·ke·ti \ˌen-drə-ˈket-ē\ *or* **Dre·ke·ti** \drə-ˈket-ē\. Chief river of Vanua Levu I., Fiji, SW Pacific Ocean.

Neagh, Lough \läk-ˈnā\. Lake, SW co. Antrim, Northern Ireland; 18 m. long by 15 m. wide; 153 sq. m.; largest lake in British Isles.

Ne·ah Bay \ˌnē-ə-\. Village, NW Clallam co., NW Washington, on inlet of Juan de Fuca Strait; headquarters of Makah Indian Reservation; site of earliest white settlement (by Spanish, lasted only five months, 1791) in the state of Washington.

Ne·amţ \ˈnyämts\. County of NE Romania. See table at ROMANIA.

Ne·an·der·thal \nā-ˈän-dər-ˌtäl, nē-ˈan-dər-ˌt(h)ȯl\. Valley just E of Düsseldorf, in North Rhine-Westphalia, West Germany, where parts of the skeleton of an early type of man were discovered 1856.

Ne·ap·o·lis \nē-ˈap-ə-ləs\. 1 Ancient city, Macedonia, NE Greece, the port of Philippi where St. Paul landed on his second missionary journey (*Acts* xvi. 11). Its site is near the modern Kavalla.

2 Ancient city, Italy. See NAPLES 3.

3 Town, Jordan. See NABLUS 2.

4 Town, Tunisia. See NABEUL.

Neapolitan Apennines. See table at APENNINES.

Near East. General term encompassing the countries of SW Asia (Turkey, Lebanon, Syria, Israel, Jordan, Saudi Arabia, and other countries of the Arabian Penin.); frequently extended to incl. Egypt and Sudan; as used by the U.S. Department of State, includes all of the above, Libya, and all the Middle East (*q.v.*). See also EAST, THE 1 and FAR EAST.

Near Islands \ˈni(ə)r-\. Island group, farthest W of the Aleutian Is., SW Alaska, 52°40′N, 173°30′E; E of international date line; includes Attu (*q.v.*), the chief island, and Agattu, and Semichi Is.; occupied by Japanese June 1942; retaken by Americans May–June 1943.

Neath \ˈnēth\. 1 River, S Wales; 25 m. long; flows S into Bristol Channel E of Gower Penin.

2 Municipal borough, Glamorganshire, SE Wales, on the Neath river; pop. (1971p) 28,568; iron, steel, tinplate, chemicals; coal mining, metalworking; site of ruins of Neath Abbey, founded in 1130.

Nebek. See EN NEBK.

Ne·bit–Dag \n(y)e-ˈbēt-ˈdäk\ *or formerly* **Nef·te·dag** \ˌn(y)ef-tī-ˈdäk\. Town, Turkmen S.S.R., U.S.S.R., ab. 80 m. SE of Krasnovodsk; pop. (1969e) 51,000.

Nebo. See PISGAH, MOUNT 2.

Ne·bo, Mount \-ˈnē-(ˌ)bō\. Peak, E Juab co., W Utah; 11,877 ft.

Ne·bras·ka \nə-ˈbras-kə\. A central state of U.S.A., bounded on N by South Dakota, on E by Iowa and a corner of Missouri, on S by Kansas and Colorado, and on W by Wyoming; 15th state in area, 77,227 sq. m. (land area 76,528 sq. m.); 35th state in population, (1970c) 1,483,791; ✱ Lincoln; 37th state admitted to Union (1867).

Nicknames: Cornhusker State; Blackwater State; Tree Planters State. *State flower:* Goldenrod. *Motto:* Equality Before the Law. *Rivers:* Missouri, forming E boundary; North Platte and South Platte, uniting in SW cen. area to form the Platte, flowing E into the Missouri. *Highest point:* Johnson Township, 5426 ft., in Kimball co. *Chief products:* Corn, wheat, oats; livestock; oil; manufacturing: food processing; machinery, fabricated metal products. *Chief cities:* Omaha, Lincoln, Grand Island, Hastings, Fremont. See *Table of States* at UNITED STATES. Divided into the following 93 counties (for pronunciation of their names, see their individual entries):

NAME	LOCATION	AREA[1] (sq. m.)	POP. (1970c)	CO. SEAT
Adams	S	562	30,553	Hastings
Antelope	NE	853	9,047	Neligh
Arthur	W	704	606	Arthur
Banner	W	738	1,034	Harrisburg
Blaine	cen.	710	847	Brewster
Boone	E cen.	683	8,190	Albion
Box Butte	NW	1,065	10,094	Alliance
Boyd	N	538	3,752	Butte
Brown	N	1,216	4,021	Ainsworth
Buffalo	S cen.	949	31,222	Kearney
Burt	E	483	9,247	Tekamah
Butler	E	582	9,461	David City
Cass	E	557	18,076	Plattsmouth
Cedar	NE	742	12,192	Hartington
Chase	S	890	4,129	Imperial
Cherry	N	5,971	6,846	Valentine
Cheyenne	W	1,186	10,778	Sidney
Clay	S	570	8,266	Clay Center
Colfax	E	406	9,498	Schuyler
Cuming	NE	571	12,034	West Point
Custer	cen.	2,558	14,092	Broken Bow
Dakota	NE	255	13,137	Dakota City
Dawes	NW	1,386	9,761	Chadron
Dawson	S cen.	975	19,537	Lexington
Deuel	W	436	2,717	Chappell
Dixon	NE	475	7,453	Ponca
Dodge	E	528	34,782	Fremont
Douglas	E	335	389,455	Omaha
Dundy	S	921	2,926	Benkelman
Fillmore	SE	577	8,137	Geneva
Franklin	S	578	4,566	Franklin
Frontier	S	962	3,982	Stockville
Furnas	S	722	6,897	Beaver City
Gage	SE	858	25,719	Beatrice
Garden	W	1,678	2,929	Oshkosh
Garfield	cen.	569	2,411	Burwell
Gosper	S	464	2,178	Elwood
Grant	W	764	1,019	Hyannis
Greeley	E cen.	570	4,000	Greeley
Hall	SE cen.	537	42,851	Grand Island
Hamilton	SE cen.	537	8,867	Aurora
Harlan	S	556	4,357	Alma
Hayes	S	711	1,530	Hayes Center
Hitchcock	S	712	4,051	Trenton
Holt	N	2,405	12,933	O'Neill
Hooker	W cen.	722	939	Mullen
Howard	E cen.	564	6,807	St. Paul
Jefferson	SE	577	10,436	Fairbury
Johnson	SE	377	5,743	Tecumseh
Kearney	S	512	6,707	Minden
Keith	W	1,035	8,487	Ogallala
Keya Paha	N	768	1,340	Springview
Kimball	W	953	6,009	Kimball
Knox	NE	1,107	11,723	Center
Lancaster	SE	845	167,972	Lincoln
Lincoln	SW cen.	2,522	29,538	North Platte
Logan	cen.	570	991	Stapleton
Loup	cen.	574	854	Taylor
McPherson	W cen.	856	623	Tryon
Madison	NE	572	27,402	Madison
Merrick	E cen.	480	8,751	Central City
Morrill	W	1,402	5,813	Bridgeport
Nance	E cen.	439	5,142	Fullerton
Nemaha	SE	400	8,976	Auburn
Nuckolls	S	579	7,404	Nelson
Otoe	SE	619	15,576	Nebraska City
Pawnee	SE	433	4,473	Pawnee City
Perkins	SW	885	3,423	Grant
Phelps	S	544	9,553	Holdrege
Pierce	NE	573	8,493	Pierce
Platte	E	667	26,544	Columbus
Polk	E	432	6,468	Osceola
Red Willow	S	716	12,191	McCook
Richardson	SE corner	550	12,277	Falls City
Rock	N	1,009	2,231	Bassett
Saline	SE	575	12,809	Wilber
Sarpy	E	239	66,200	Papillion
Saunders	E	759	17,018	Wahoo
Scotts Bluff	W	726	36,432	Gering
Seward	SE	571	14,460	Seward
Sheridan	NW	2,462	7,285	Rushville
Sherman	cen.	571	4,725	Loup City
Sioux	NW corner	2,063	2,034	Harrison
Stanton	NE	431	5,758	Stanton

NAME	LOCATION	AREA[1] (sq. m.)	POP. (1970c)	CO. SEAT
Thayer	S	577	7,779	Hebron
Thomas	cen.	716	954	Thedford
Thurston	NE	388	6,942	Pender
Valley	cen.	569	5,783	Ord
Washington	E	386	13,310	Blair
Wayne	NE	443	10,400	Wayne
Webster	S	575	5,396	Red Cloud
Wheeler	NE cen.	576	1,051	Bartlett
York	SE	577	13,685	York

[1] Area = land area.

History: Part of Louisiana Purchase 1803 and later of the Territory of Orleans (see LOUISIANA) and of Missouri Territory; erected as separate territory by Kansas-Nebraska Act 1854 (originally included area bet. Missouri river and the Rockies from 40°N to Canadian border); lost part of land to Dakota and Colorado territories 1861; held 1st constitutional convention 1866; admitted to Union as free state Mar. 1, 1867; established one-house legislature 1937.

Nebraska City. City, ⊗ of Otoe co., SE Nebraska, on Missouri river 41 m. S of Omaha; pop. (1970c) 7441; feed, clothing, building materials, tin cans; home of J. Sterling Morton, the originator of Arbor Day, his residence now in a state park.

Nebrija, Nebrixa, *or* **Nebrissa.** See LEBRIJA.

Ne·ca·xa \nə-ˈkä-(ˌ)hä\. River, cen. Mexico, in Puebla and Veracruz states (known as the **Te·co·lu·tla** \ˌtā-kə-ˈlü-(ˌ)tlä\ in Veracruz); has falls 540 ft. high which furnish electrical power.

Ne·chako \ni-ˈchak-(ˌ)ō\. River, cen. British Columbia, Canada; 287 m. long; flows N and E into Fraser river.

Nech·es \ˈnech-əz\. River, E Texas; 416 m. long; rises in Van Zandt co., NE Texas, runs S and SE into Sabine Lake. See SABINE-NECHES WATERWAY.

Neck·ar \ˈnek-ər, -ˌär\. River, West Germany; 228 m. long; rises in the Black Forest, S Baden-Württemberg, flows N and W into the Rhine at Mannheim; navigable up to Cannstatt, near Stuttgart.

Neck·er \ˈnek-ər\. Islet of Leeward Is. group, Hawaii, in cen. Pacific Ocean ab. 300 m. NW of Niihau I., 164°42′W, 23°35′N; included in Hawaiian Islands Bird Reservation.

Ne·co·chea \ˌnā-kə-ˈchā-ə\. Seaport town, Buenos Aires prov., E Argentina, 265 m. directly S of Buenos Aires; pop. (1960c) 29,319; one of finest sea-bathing places on Argentina coast.

Ne·der·land. 1 \ˈnād-ər-ˌlänt\. Kingdom. See NETHERLANDS.

2 \ˈnēd-ər-ˌland\. City, Jefferson co., SE Texas, near Beaumont; pop. (1970c) 16,810; chemicals; oil refinery; poultry, rice farms.

Nederlandsch–Indië. See INDONESIA 2.

Ne·der Rijn \ˌnād-ə(r)-ˈrīn\. The Lower Rhine in the Netherlands; from it the IJssel flows N into IJsselmeer, and the Lek river continues W into the Nieuwe Maas and the North Sea.

Nedjed. See NEJD.

Nee·bish Island \ˌnē-bish-\. Island in Chippewa co., E Michigan penin., in St. Marys river, S of Sault Sainte Marie.

Need·ham \ˈnēd-əm\. Town, Norfolk co., E Massachusetts, 10 m. WSW of Boston; pop. (1970c) 29,748; clothing; residential.

Nee·dle Mountain \ˌnēd-ᵊl-\. Peak, S Park co., NW Wyoming, in the Absaroka Range; 12,130 ft.

Nee·dles \ˈnēd-ᵊlz\. City, San Bernardino co., SE California, on Colorado river; pop. (1970c) 4051.

Needles, The. Three pointed rocks in the English Channel W of the Isle of Wight; lighthouse.

Ñe·em·bu·cú \ˌnā-əm-bü-ˈkü\. Department of SW Paraguay. See table at PARAGUAY.

Nee·nah \ˈnē-nə\. City, Winnebago co., E Wisconsin, on Lake Winnebago 7 m. S of Appleton; pop. (1970c) 22,892; forms one community with its twin city, Menasha (*q.v.*); paper products, cheese, clothing, lumber; machine shops, brass foundries; dairy farms; settled 1843.

Nee·pa·wa \ˈnēp-ə-ˌwȯ, -ˌwä\. Town, SW Manitoba, Canada, 35 m. NE of Brandon; pop. (1971p) 3216.

Neer·win·den \ne(ə)r-ˈvin-dən\. Village, Liège prov., E Belgium, 22 m. NW of Liège; scene of two battles: July 19, 1693, when William III of England was defeated by French under Marshall Luxembourg; Mar. 18, 1793, when General Dumouriez was defeated by Austrians.

Nef·ta \ˈnef-tə\. Town, W Tunisia, N Africa, on W shore of Chott Djerid; pop. (1966c) 10,400.

Neftedag. See NEBIT-DAG.

Nefud. See AN NAFUD.

Negapatam *or* **Negapattinam.** See NAGAPATTINAM.

Ne·gau·nee \ni-ˈgȯ-nē\. City, Marquette co., N Michigan penin., W of Marquette; pop. (1970c) 5248.

Negeri Sembilan. See NEGRI SEMBILAN.

Ne·gev \ˈneg-ˌev\ *or* **Neg·eb** \-ˌeb\. Desert region, S Israel; ab. 4700 sq. m.; max. elev. ab. 3300 ft.; largest town Beersheba; incl. several irrigated areas producing fruit and vegetables; potash, bromine, copper; assigned to Israel in partition of Palestine 1948; scene of clashes bet. Israeli and Egyptian forces 1948–49.

Ne·goi·ul \ne-ˈgȯi-ˌül\. Mountain, cen. Romania; 8317 ft.; 2d highest peak in Transylvanian Alps.

Ne·gom·bo \ni-ˈgäm-(ˌ)bō\. Seaport, Ceylon, 19 m. N of Colombo; pop. (1968e) 53,000; fishing port. Taken by Dutch from Portuguese 1640; recovered 1641; retaken by Dutch 1644; taken by English 1796.

Ne·grais, Cape \-nə-ˈgrīs\. Headland, Lower Burma, projecting into Bay of Bengal SSW of city of Vasi; lat. 16°N and long. 94°10′E.

Ne·gra Point \ˌnā-grə-, ˌneg-rə-\. Headland on NW coast of Ilocos Norte prov., Luzon, Phil., bet. Cape Bojeador on W and Mayraira Point on E; marks W side of Bangui Bay.

Ne·gri Sem·bi·lan \nə-ˌgrē-səm-ˈbē-lən\ *or* **Ne·ge·ri Sembilan** \ˌnā-gə-ˌrē-\. A state of Malaysia, SE Asia, bounded on N and NE by Pahang, on SE by Johore, on S by Malacca, on SW by the Strait of Malacca, and on W by Selangor; 2590 sq. m.; pop. (1970p) 479,312; ✱ Seremban; rubber, rice, tin.

History: Confederation of nine states (united 1889); came under British protection 1874–88; joined by two other states 1895; under Japanese control 1941–45; became part of the independent Federation of Malaya 1957; became a state of Malaysia 1963.

Ne·gro, Cape \-ˈnā-(ˌ)grō, -ˈneg-(ˌ)rō\. Point, N Morocco, N Africa, NE of Tétouan.

Negro, Mount. Peak in cen. Panama, in the Tabasara Mts.; 4429 ft.

Negro, Rio \ˌrē-ō-ˈnā-(ˌ)grō, -ˈneg-(ˌ)rō\. **1** River, Río Negro prov., S cen. Argentina; ab. 400 m. long; formed by confluence of Neuquén and Limay rivers, flows E into Atlantic Ocean N of Gulf of San Matías.

2 River, S Mato Grosso state, Brazil; flows SW and W through extensive marshland into Paraguay river.

3 *or Span.* **Río Negro** \ˌrē-ü-ˈnā-(ˌ)grü\. River, NW South America; ab. 1400 m. long; rises in E Colombia, where it is known as the **Guai·nía** \gwī-ˈnē-ə\; flows E to the Venezuela boundary, and then S forming a section of the Colombia-Venezuela boundary; crosses into Brazil and continues SE into Amazon river at Manaus; is joined also to the Orinoco river through the Casiquiare river.

4 River, cen. Uruguay; 434 m. long; rises in S Brazil, flows SW across Uruguay into the Uruguay river.

Negro Mountain. See DAVIS, MOUNT.

Negropont. 1 City, Greece. See CHALCIS.

2 *or Ital.* **Negroponte.** Island, Greece. See EUBOEA.

Ne·gros \ˈnā-(ˌ)grōs, ˈneg-(ˌ)rōs\. Island, one of the Visayan Is., cen. Phil.; 5278 sq. m.; pop. (1970p, with adjacent small islands) 2,307,493; fourth in size in the archipelago, 134 m. long; divided into two provinces, Negros Occidental and Negros Oriental (*qq.v.*).

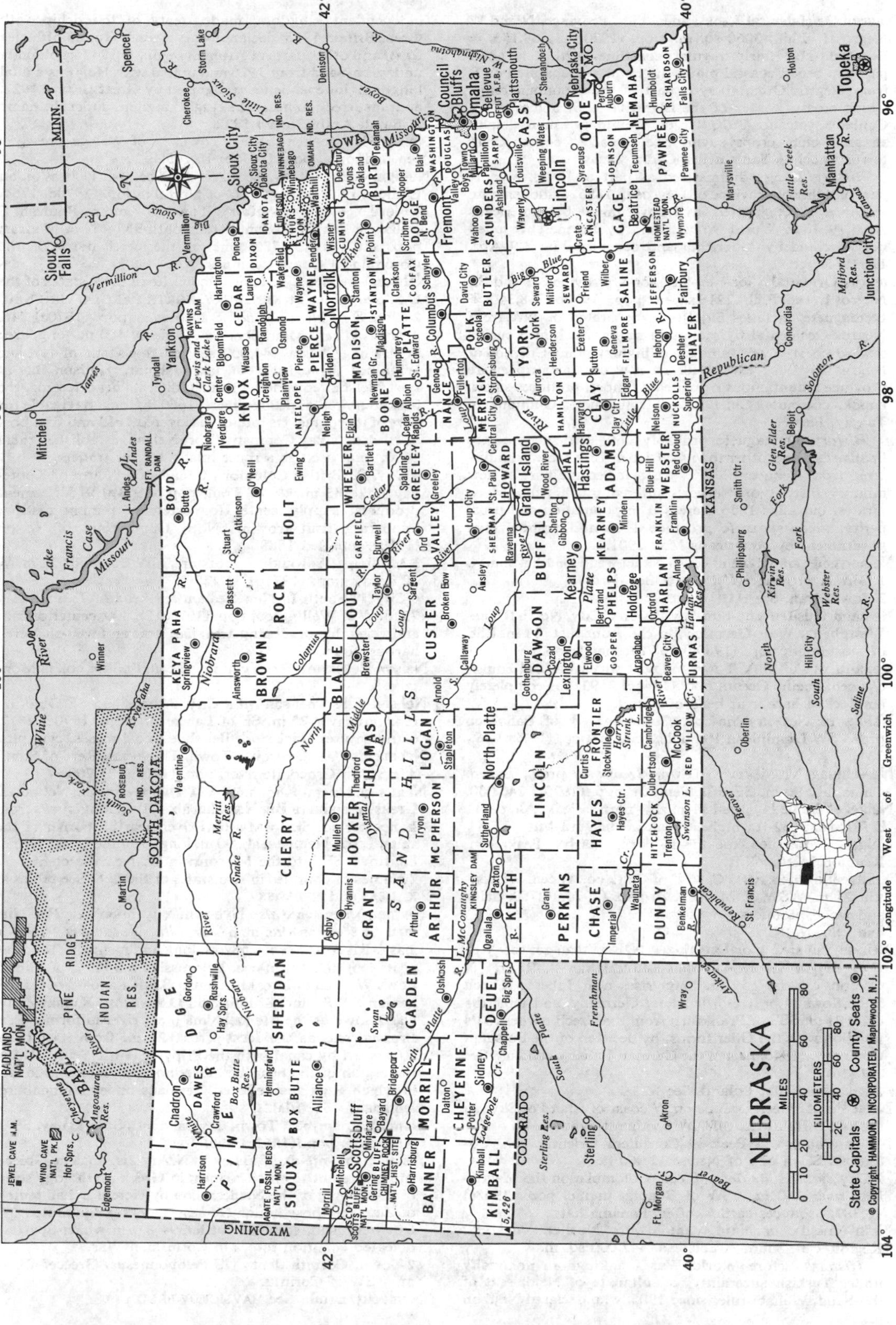
NEBRASKA
MILES
0 10 20 40 60 80
KILOMETERS
0 20 40 60 80
State Capitals
County Seats
© Copyright HAMMOND INCORPORATED, Maplewood, N.J.
102° Longitude West of Greenwich
SOUTH DAKOTA
IOWA
KANSAS
COLORADO
WYOMING
MINN.
MO.
Lincoln
Omaha
Sioux City
Topeka
North Platte
Grand Island
Kearney
Scottsbluff

Negros Oc·ci·den·tal \-ˌȯk-si-den-ˈtäl\. Province, N and W Negros I., Phil.; 3060 sq. m.; pop. (1970p) 1,589,153; ✱ Bacolod. Has fairly regular coastline, with few good harbors; broad coastal plains in N and W; separated on E from Negros Oriental by S part of the mountain range which crosses center of the island N to S; highest peak Canlaon volcano 8070 ft. on boundary; many small streams; chief crops sugar, rice, tobacco, copra. Chief towns Bacolod, San Carlos, Cadiz, Sagay.

History: Long administered as part of Iloilo; became part of military province of Negros in 1856; made separate province 1890; granted civil government by Americans Apr. 1901. In World War II held by Japanese; invaded near Bacolod by Americans and occupied Mar. 29–Apr. 12, 1945.

Negros Orien·tal \-ˌōr-ē-en-ˈtäl, -ˌȯr-\. Province, E and SE Negros I., cen. Phil.; 2218 sq. m.; pop. (1970p) 718,340; ✱ Dumaguete; includes Siquijor I. Separated on NW from Negros Occidental by mountain range which in S curves toward coast W of Dumaguete; highest point Cuernos of Negros 6101 ft.; except for narrow coastal strip entire province mountainous or plateau; timber; produces sugar, kapok, coconuts. Chief towns Dumaguete, Guihulngan, Tanjay, Bais.

History: Dumaguete probably only settlement before Spaniards came; other towns settled in 18th cent.; administered from Cebu until 1734 when it became part of new military district of Negros; suffered much from Moro pirates, but after 1856 increased in population and prosperity; made separate province 1890 and granted civil government by Americans May 1901.

Ne·ha·vend \ˌnā-hä-ˈvend\ *also* **Na·ha·wend** \ˌnā-hä-ˈvand\. 1 Former province, W Iran; ✱ Borūjerd.
2 Town, Iran. See NAHĀVAND.

Ne·heim-Hüs·ten \ˌnā-hīm-ˈh(y)ü-stən\. City, North Rhine-Westphalia, West Germany, in the Ruhr dist. 23 m. ESE of Dortmund; pop. (1969e) 36,787; metal goods.

Nei·a·fu \nā-ˈäf-(ˌ)ü\. Town and port on Vavau I., N Tonga, SW cen. Pacific Ocean; pop. (1966c) 3593; has completely landlocked harbor at head of sound.

Nei·ba *or* **Ney·ba** \ˈnā-bə\. Commune, ✱ of Bahoruco prov., SW Dominican Republic; munic. pop. (1970p) 36,-224.

Nei–chiang \ˈnā-jē-ˈäŋ\. Town, Szechwan prov., S cen. China, ab. 90 m. SE of Ch'eng-tu; pop. (1970e) 240,000.

Neige, Crête de la \ˌkred-lä-ˈnāzh, -ˈnezh\. Peak, Ain dept., E France; 5652 ft.; highest peak in the Jura Mts.

Neiges, Pi·ton des \pē-ˌtōⁿ-dā-ˈnezh, -ˈnāzh\. Peak, cen. Réunion I.; 10,069 ft.

Neills·ville \ˈnēlz-ˌvil\. City, ⊗ of Clark co., W cen. Wisconsin, 21 m. WSW of Marshfield; pop. (1970c) 2750; dairy and wood products.

Nein. See NAIN.

Neis·se \ˈnī-sə\. 1 *or* **Lau·sit·zer Neisse** \ˈlau̇-zət-sər-ˌ\ *or Pol.* **Ny·sa Łu·życ·ka** \ˌnis-ə-lu̇-ˈzhit-skə\. River, N Czechoslovakia; 159 m. long; rises near Liberec, Czech S.R., flows N past Görlitz, East Germany, and joins the Oder 21 m. SSE of Frankfurt; from the Czech border to its junction with the Oder forms, by decision of the Potsdam Conference 1945, part of the German-Polish boundary. See POLAND.
2 River and city, Poland. See NYSA.

Neist Point \ˈnēst-\. Cape on W coast of island of Skye in the Inner Hebrides, off NW Scotland; lighthouse.

Nei·va \ˈnā-və\. 1 Peak in Cordillera Oriental, cen. Colombia, SE of city of Neiva; 12,000 ft.
2 City, ✱ of Huila dept., S cen. Colombia, on the Magdalena river 150 m. SSW of Bogotá; munic. pop. (1968e) 90,387; produces cattle, coffee, Panama hats.

Nejd \ˈnejd\ *or* **Najd** \ˈnajd\ *also* **Ne·djed** \ˈnej-əd\. Region, cen. Saudi Arabia; ab. 447,000 sq. m.

History: Before World War I a kingdom nominally under Turkish suzerainty as Sultanate of Nejd; seat of ibn-Saud, Wahabi ruler since 1905, who declared Nejd an independent kingdom; made treaty of friendship with Great Britain 1915; declared wars against Husein of Hejaz (*q.v.*) and other parts of Arabian Penin. 1919–26; sultanate under ibn-Saud from 1926 and united with Hejaz as a dual kingdom; independence recognized by Great Britain 1927; after insurrection became a single kingdom under the name of Saudi Arabia (*q.v.*) 1932.

Ne·kem·te \ne-ˈkem(p)-tē\. Town, ✱ of Welega prov., W cen. Ethiopia; pop. (1970e) 16,105.

Ne·ligh \ˈnēl-ē\. City, ⊗ of Antelope co., NE Nebraska, on Elkhorn river 35 m. WNW of Norfolk; pop. (1970c) 1764.

Nel·lore \ne-ˈlō(ə)r, -ˈlȯ(ə)r\. Town, S Andhra Pradesh, S India, on Penner river near its mouth 95 m. N of Madras; pop. (1970e) 137,720; one of the chief ports of the Coromandel Coast; ceramics.

Nel·son \ˈnel-sən\. 1 Name of counties in three states of the U.S. See tables at KENTUCKY, NORTH DAKOTA, VIRGINIA.
2 City, ⊗ of Nuckolls co., S Nebraska; pop. (1970c) 746.
3 River, N cen. Manitoba, cen. Canada; 400 m. long; area of drainage basin 444,000 sq. m.; flows out of N Lake Winnipeg through several lakes NE into Hudson Bay at Port Nelson; considered as including its headstreams, the Saskatchewan and Bow rivers, 1660 m. long; navigable for part of its course. Its mouth discovered 1612 and first post of Hudson's Bay Company (Port Nelson) established there 1670; long used as a route inland for fur traders.
4 City, SE British Columbia, Canada, on W arm of Kootenay Lake 33 m. NE of Trail; pop. (1971p) 9168; cement products; supply center for extensive mining district; lumbering, fruit growing; Notre Dame Univ. of Nelson (1963); founded 1888.
5 Municipal borough, Lancashire, NW England, 28 m. W of Leeds; pop. (1971p) 31,225.
6 City, N South I., New Zealand, at head of Tasman Bay 75 m. W of Wellington; pop. (1970e) 28,300; center of fruit and vegetable producing area; has large and well-sheltered harbor; founded 1841.

Nelson Reservoir. Reservoir in NE cen. Phillips co., N Montana.

Nel·son·ville \ˈnel-sən-ˌvil\. City, Athens co., SE Ohio, on Hocking river 25 m. SE of Lancaster; pop. (1970c) 4812; manufactures brick and tile, shoes; coal mines, clay pits.

Nel·spruit \ˈnel-(ˌ)sprȯit\. Town, Transvaal, Rep. of South Africa, on Crocodile river; pop. (1967e) 21,700.

Nem·a·ha \ˈnem-ə-ˌhȯ, ˈnēm-\. 1 Two rivers, SE Nebraska: **Great Nemaha** *or* **Big Nemaha,** ab. 150 m. long, flows from Lancaster co. SE to Missouri river near SE corner of the state; **Little Nemaha,** ab. 90 m. long, N of the Great Nemaha, flows SE into the Missouri in SE Nemaha co.
2 Names of counties in two states of the U.S. See tables at KANSAS and NEBRASKA.

Ne·man \ˈnem-ən\ *also* **Nye·man** \ˈnyem-ən\ *or Pol.* **Nie·men** \nē-ˈem-ən, ˈnē-mən\ *or Lith.* **Ne·mu·nas** \ˈnam-ə-ˌnäs\. River, U.S.S.R.; 582 m. long and navigable for most of its length; rises in cen. Belorussian S.S.R., S of Minsk, flows W, then N into Lithuanian S.S.R., and W bet. Lithuanian S.S.R. and Kaliningrad Oblast into Kurski Zaliv; was known as the **Me·mel** \ˈmā-məl\ river in former East Prussia, and as the **Russ** \ˈru̇s\ 22 m. from its mouth; connected by canal with the Pripyat. Battle Sept. 1914 in the region of the bend bet. Grodno and Kaunas (Kovno) in which Russians defeated Germans under Hindenburg.

Nemausus. See NÎMES.

Nem·by \ˈnām-bē\. Town, Central dept., S Paraguay, SE of Asunción; pop. (1962c) 796.

Ne·mea \ˈnē-mē-ə\. 1 Valley in N Argolis, ancient Greece; site of present town of Nemea; in Greek mythology scene of the slaying of the Nemean lion by Hercules; had temple of Zeus in whose honor Nemean games, inaugurated 573 B.C., were held; scene of battle 394 B.C. in which Spartans defeated coalition forces in Corinthian War.
2 Town, Corinth dept., NE Peloponnesus, Greece, ab. 15 m. WSW of Corinth.

Německý Brod. See HAVLÍČKŮV BROD.

Ne·men·cha Mountains \nə-ˈmen-chə-\. Range of the Atlas Mts., NE Algeria, extending to border of Tunisia.

Nemetocenna. See ARRAS.

Ne·mi, Lake \-ˈnā-mē, -ˈnem-ē\ *or anc.* **Nem·o·ren·sis La·cus** \ˌnem-ə-ˌren(t)-sə-ˈslā-kəs\. Lake in the Alban Hills, SE of Lake Albano, Italy; ⅔ sq. m.; nearby in ancient times were a grove and temple dedicated to Diana.

Ne·mours \nə-ˈmu̇(ə)r\. Town, Seine-et-Marne dept., N France, S of Melun; pop. (1962c) 6605; seat of Nemours family, a countship created by Charles V in latter part of 14th cent.; dukedom held by Armagnac branch of the house of Orléans, by Gaston de Foix from 1505, and 1528–1659 by a branch of the house of Savoy.

Nemunas. See NEMAN.

Ne·mu·ro \ˌnem-ə-ˌrō\. Town, E Hokkaidō, Japan, at S end of Nemuro Strait; pop. (1970c) 45,381.

Nemuro Strait. Strait off E Hokkaidō, Japan, separating Kunashir I. (U.S.S.R.) from Hokkaidō.

Nen \ˈnən\ *or* **Non·ni** \ˈnən-ˈnē\. 1 River, Inner Mongolia and Heilungkiang prov., NE China; ab. 740 m. long; rises on E slopes of Greater Khingan Range in W Heilungkiang prov., flows S and joins Sungari river; waters the fertile N section of Manchurian plain.
2 River, England. See NENE.

Ne·nagh \ˈnē-nə(k)\. Urban district, co. Tipperary, S Eire, near **Nenagh River;** pop. (1971p) 4926; trade center of agricultural area; ruins of castle erected under King John; burned by Jacobites (1688).

Ne·nana \nē-ˈnan-ə\. City, E cen. Alaska, on S bank of Tanana river 50 m. WSW of Fairbanks; pop. (1970c) 362; on the Seward-Fairbanks R.R.; airport.

Nene \ˈnēn, ˈnen\ *or* **Nen** \ˈnen\. River, cen. and E England; 90 m. long; rises in N Northamptonshire, flows NE into the North Sea through the Wash.

Ne·nets National Okrug \ne-ˈnəts . . . ˈō-ˌkrük\. National district of the Samoyeds, part of Arkhangelsk Oblast, Russian S.F.S.R., U.S.S.R., the tundra coast N of Komi A.S.S.R.; 68,224 sq. m.; pop. (1970p) 39,000; ✱ Naryan-Mar; reindeer herding, fishing; established 1929.

Ne·o·de·sha \nē-ˌōd-ə-ˈshā, -ˈōd-ə-ˌshā\. City, Wilson co., SE Kansas, 13 m. N of Independence; pop. (1970c) 3295.

Ne·o·sho \nē-ˈō-(ˌ)shō, -shə\. 1 *in Oklahoma called* **Grand** \ˈgrand\. River, SE Kansas and NE Oklahoma; 460 m. long; rises in Morris co., E cen. Kansas, flows SE and S into Arkansas river in N Muskogee co., E Oklahoma.
2 County in Kansas. See table at KANSAS.
3 City, ⊗ of Newton co., SW Missouri, 16 m. SSE of Joplin; pop. (1970c) 7517; trade center in lumbering and agricultural region; lead deposit nearby.

Ne·pal \nə-ˈpȯl, -ˈpäl, -ˈpal\. Kingdom on NE border of India, bounded on N by Tibet, China, on E by Sikkim and India, and on S and W by India; 54,362 sq. m.; pop. (1971e) 11,237,616; ✱ Katmandu. *Physical features:* The S portion is level cultivated and forest land (Terai), the cen. and N parts are occupied by great Himalaya ranges; highest peaks Everest, Kanchenjunga, Dhaulagiri, Gauri Sankar, and many others above 20,000 ft.; rivers flow southward and are upper tributaries of the Ganges system. *Chief products:* Rice, corn, wheat, millet, jute, sal timber; manufacturing: textiles; food processing. *Chief cities:* Katmandu, Lalitpur, Biratnagar, Bhaktapur.

History: History goes back to a very early period; in medieval times under Rajput dynasties; first commercial treaty bet. India and Nepal signed 1792; scene of frontier attacks which led British to declare war in 1814; signed treaty (Treaty of Segauli) with Great Britain 1816. In 1923 recognized by Great Britain as entirely independent. Form of government changed from military oligarchy to constitutional monarchy 1951; signed boundary agreement with China 1961; promulgated new constitution 1962; demanded withdrawal of Indian military advisors 1969.

Ne·paug \ˈnē-ˌpȯg\. River, NW Connecticut; rises in NE Litchfield co., flows SE into Farmington river.

Nepaug Reservoir. Reservoir in Nepaug river, Litchfield and Hartford cos., N Connecticut; water supply for Hartford.

Ne·phi \ˈnē-ˌfī\. City, ⊗ of Juab co., W Utah, 38 m. S of Provo; pop. (1970c) 2699; ships livestock and grain; manufactures flour, plaster; gypsum deposits; settled 1851;

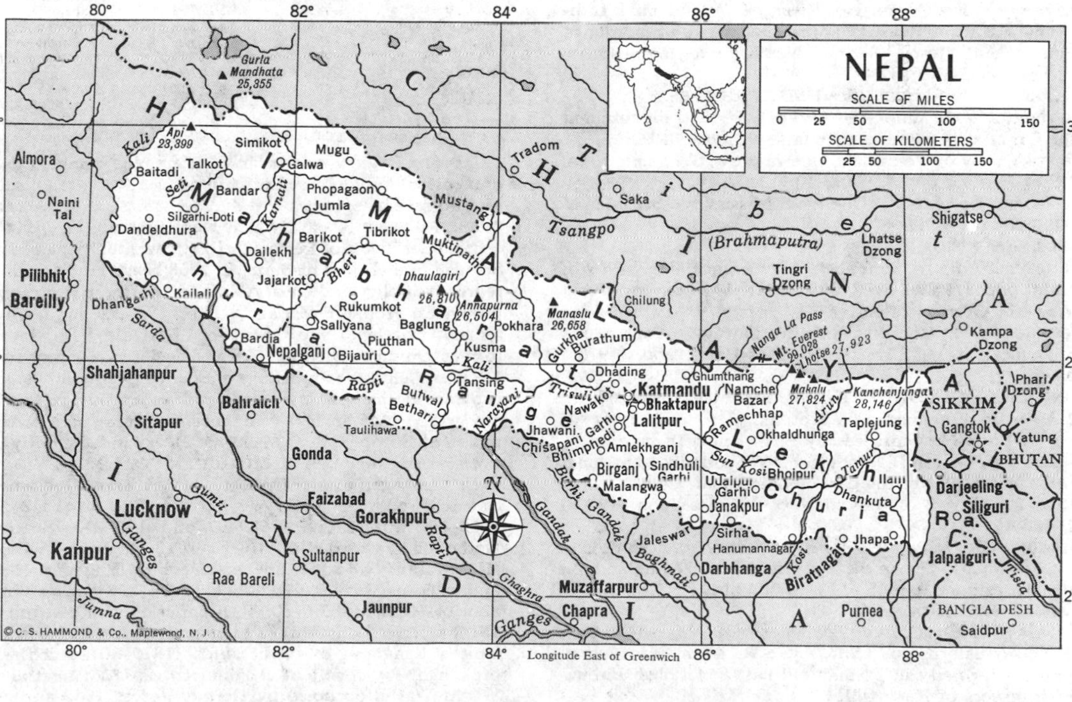

suffered in Indian raids; peace bet. Brigham Young and Chief Walker made nearby 1854.

Neph·in \'nef-ən\. Mountain, cen. co. Mayo, Connaught, NW Eire; 2646 ft.

Neph·in·beg \ˌnef-ən-'beg\. Mountain, W co. Mayo, Connaught, NW Eire; 2065 ft.

Nepigon, Lake. See NIPIGON, LAKE.

Ne·pis·i·guit Bay *or* **Ni·pis·i·guit Bay** \nə-'piz-ə-gwət-\. Southern extension of Chaleur Bay, extending into N Gloucester co., NE New Brunswick, SE Canada; receives the **Nepisiguit River** (*or* **Nipisiguit River**), ab. 75 m. long, which rises in NW Northumberland co. and flows E and N.

Nepissing, Lake. See NIPISSING, LAKE.

Nep·tune \'nep-ˌt(y)ün\. Urban township, Monmouth co., E cen. New Jersey, NW of Neptune City; pop. (1970c) 27,863.

Neptune City. Borough and ocean resort, Monmouth co., E New Jersey, SW of Asbury Park; pop. (1970c) 5502.

Ne·ra \'ner-ə\ *or anc.* **Nar** \'när\. River, cen. Italy; 80 m. long; flows out of the Apennines SW into Tiber river.

Né·rac \nā-'rak\. Town, S Lot-et-Garonne dept., SW France, on the Baïse river; pop. (1962c) 6677; center of Protestant activities during 16th cent., captured by Catholics 1562; peace bet. Catholics and Huguenots signed here 1579; headquarters of Henry IV 1580; taken by Louis XIII 1621 and subsequently ruined.

Nerbudda. See NARMADA.

Ner·chinsk \'ne(ə)r-ˌchin(t)sk\. Town, S cen. Chita Oblast, Russian S.F.S.R., U.S.S.R., near N bank of Shilka river ab. 135 m. E of Chita. Founded as a fort 1654; for two centuries one of Russian outposts in Far East; Treaty of Nerchinsk 1689 with China, the first treaty concluded with that country by any European power, delayed Russia's advance in Amur valley and was basis (as modified in 1727 and 1768) of relations with China until 1858.

Ne·ret·va \'ner-ət-ˌvä\ *or Ital.* **Na·ren·ta** \nə-'rent-ə\ *or anc.* **Na·ro** \'na(ə)r-(ˌ)ō, 'ner(ə)r-\. River, SW Yugoslavia; 135 m. long; rises E of Mostar, flows NNW, and ab. 28 m. N of Mostar turns S; flows past Mostar into Adriatic Sea; navigable for small vessels.

Ne·ris \ne-'ris\; *Russ.* nir-'yēs\ *or Pol.* **Wi·lja** \'vēl-(ˌ)yä\ *or formerly* **Vi·li·ya** \'vē-li-yə\. River, NE Poland and E Lithuanian S.S.R., U.S.S.R.; 317 m. long; rises on E border of Poland and flows W into Neman river at Kaunas, Lithuanian S.S.R.

Nerium Promontorium. See FINISTERRE, CAPE.

Ne·ro·ne, Mon·te \ˌmȯn-tē-nə-'rō-nē\. Highest mountain in the Umbrian Apennines. See table at APENNINES.

Ner·va \'ner-və\. Commune, Huelva prov., SW Spain, 37 m. NE of Huelva; pop. (1970p) 10,915.

Ne·sho·ba \nə-'shō-bə\. County in Mississippi. See table at MISSISSIPPI.

Nesis. See NISIDA.

Nesle \'nel\. Town, Somme dept., N France, 7 m. WNW of Ham; pop. (1962c) 2417; taken Mar. 1918 during World War I in German offensive.

Nes·que·hon·ing \ˌnes-kwə-'hōn-iŋ\. Borough, Carbon co., E Pennsylvania, 28 m. S of Wilkes-Barre; pop. (1970c) 3338.

Ness \'nes\. 1 County in Kansas. See table at KANSAS. 2 River, Inverness co., NW Scotland; 7 m. long; flows NE out of Loch Ness into Moray Firth below Inverness.

Ness, Loch. Lake in Inverness co., NW Scotland; 23 m. long, from NE to SW; forms part of Caledonian Canal.

Ness City. City, ⊗ of Ness co., W cen. Kansas; pop. (1970c) 1756.

Nes·ton \'nes-tən\ *or formerly* **Neston and Park·gate** \-'pärk-(ˌ)gāt\. Urban district, Cheshire, NW England, on the Dee estuary 10 m. S of Liverpool; pop. (1971p) 16,848.

Nestos. See MESTA.

Nes·vizh \'nās-vish\ *or Pol.* **Nieś·wież** \'nyesh-ˌvyesh\. Town, W Belorussian S.S.R., U.S.S.R., 44 m. SE of Novogrudok; formerly in Poland; old castle of Polish-Lithuanian princes of Radziwill.

Netanya. See NATANYA.

Ne·tarts Bay \nē-'tärts-, 'nē-ˌ\. Inlet on coast of Tillamook co., NW Oregon.

Net·cong \'net-ˌkȯŋ\. Borough, Morris co., N New Jersey, 14 m. WNW of Morristown; pop. (1970c) 2858; metallurgical machinery; center of summer resort area.

Nethe \'net\. River in Belgium; formed by the confluence of the **Great Nethe** and **Little Nethe** near Lier; flows WSW in Antwerp prov. to unite with the Dijle NW of Mechelen and form the Rupel river.

Neth·er·lands \'neth-ər-lən(d)z\ *or Du.* **Ne·der·land** \'nād-ər-ˌlänt\ *also* **Hol·land** \'häl-ənd\. Kingdom, NW Europe, bounded on the W and N by the North Sea, on E by West Germany, and on S by Belgium; 14,140 sq. m. (incl. 419 sq. m. of reclaimed land from the IJsselmeer); pop. (1970e) 12,938,836; de jure ✱ Amsterdam, court residence and de facto ✱ the Hague. *Physical features:* Part of the plain of NW Europe with nearly a quarter of its area below sea level and max. elev. ab. 1635 ft.; protected along part of the coast by dikes. All S part lies in plain and delta of the Neder Rijn and Maas (Meuse) rivers; N cen. part formerly occupied by large shallow inlet of North Sea, the Zuider Zee (*q.v.*), ab. 80 m. long, now partly reclaimed and separated from North Sea by dike from W Friesland prov. to Wieringermeer. Off N coast and enclosing large area of water is chain of West Frisian Is. (see FRISIAN ISLANDS) connecting on E with German East Frisian Is.; in SW (Zeeland prov.) are other large islands in combined delta of Schelde and Maas. Covered by many canals and canalized rivers connecting larger cities. *Chief products:* Wheat, barley, dairy products, sugar beets; horticulture; natural gas; manufacturing: chemicals, petroleum products, steel, electrical equipment; food processing, shipbuilding. *Chief cities:* Amsterdam, Rotterdam, the Hague, Utrecht, Eindhoven, Haarlem, Groningen. Divided into the following eleven provinces (for pronunciation of their names, see their individual entries):

NAME	AREA (sq. m.)	POP. (1970e)	CAPITAL
Drenthe	1,037	366,590	Assen
Friesland	1,464	521,751	Leeuwarden
Gelderland	1,981	1,505,760	Arnhem
Groningen	934	517,305	Groningen
Limburg	853	998,570	Maastricht
North Brabant	1,971	1,787,783	's Hertogenbosch
North Holland	1,124	2,244,456	Haarlem
Overijssel	1,518	920,882	Zwolle
South Holland	1,259	2,968,700	Hague, The
Utrecht	538	801,285	Utrecht
Zeeland	1,043	305,754	Middelburg

History: Region included in Charlemagne's empire; part of medieval kingdom of Lotharingia (see LORRAINE); split up into several counties and duchies (see BRABANT, FLANDERS, HOLLAND 3, etc.) which were first united in 14th cent. under dukes of Burgundy (*q.v.*); eventually passed to Spanish branch of Hapsburgs; in 1568 began revolt against repressive policy of duke of Alva; the 7 northern Protestant provinces, Holland, Zeeland, Utrecht, Gelderland, Groningen, Friesland, and Overijssel (the United Provinces) formed Union of Utrecht 1579 and declared independence 1581 (see BELGIUM for history of Spanish Netherlands, the provinces remaining loyal to Spain); independence finally recognized 1648; in 17th cent. became leading commercial nation of Europe (see AMSTERDAM 2), expanded greatly its overseas territory (see CURAÇAO, INDONESIA, NEW NETHERLAND); engaged in numerous important wars of commercial and political rivalry, with the English 1652–54, 1665–67, with France 1689–97 and 1702–13; Spanish Netherlands awarded to Austria 1713; its ruler, William III, and his wife, became co-rulers of England 1689; organized as Batavian Republic 1795–1806 and as kingdom of Holland 1806–10, both under French control; in 1814, received constitution, later revised; its ruler head of United Kingdom of Netherlands (1815–30) which was broken up by revolt of Belgium (*q.v.*) 1830; neutral in World War I; occupied by German forces 1940 and not freed until May 1945; recognized independence of Netherlands Indies 1949; became a member of NATO 1949; joined EEC 1958; in 1963 relinquished control over Irian Barat (*q.v.*).

Netherlands An·til·les \-an-'til-ēz\ *or formerly* **Cu·ra·çao** \'k(y)ůr-ə-ˌsō, -ˌsaů, ˌk(y)ůr-ə-'\. An integral part of the Netherlands realm, consisting of several islands in the West Indies: Curaçao, Bonaire and Aruba off the coast of Venezuela, and St. Martin (S section), St. Eustatius, and Saba at N end of Leeward Is.; 385 sq. m.; pop. (1969e) 220,084; ✱ Willemstad (on Curaçao); tourism; colonial status abolished by Netherlands government 1954; Curaçao scene of civil strife 1969.

Netherlands East Indies. See INDONESIA 2.

Netherlands Guiana. See SURINAM 1.

Netherlands Indies. See INDONESIA 2.

Netherlands New Guinea. See IRIAN BARAT.

Netherlands Timor. See TIMOR.

Neth·er Prov·i·dence \ˌneth-ər-'präv-əd-ən(t)s, -ə-ˌden(t)s\. Urban township, Delaware co., SE Pennsylvania; pop. (1970c) 13,644.

Nether Stow·ey \-'stō-ē\. Village, Somersetshire, SW England 7 m. WNW of Bridgwater, N of the Quantock Hills; residence 1796–98 of Samuel Taylor Coleridge who wrote *The Ancient Mariner* here.

Néthou, Pic de. See ANETO, PICO DE.

Net·ley \'net-lē\. Village, Hampshire, S England, 3 m. SE of Southampton; ruins of Cistercian abbey, founded by Henry III; military hospital.

Net·til·ling Lake \ˌnech-ə-liŋ-\. Lake in S cen. Baffin I., E Franklin district, Northwest Territories, Canada; 1956 sq. m.; 67 m. long.

Net·tu·no \nā-'tü-(ˌ)nō\. Commune, Roma prov., Latium, cen. Italy, on Tyrrhenian Sea 31 m. SSE of Rome; pop. (1968e) 22,698; Treaty of Nettuno bet. Italy and Yugoslavia signed 1925; in World War II occupied by Americans Jan 22, 1944 at same time as adjoining Anzio (*q.v.*).

Netum. See NOTO.

Ne·tza·hual·có·yotl \nā-ˌtsä-wäl-'kō-ˌyōt-ᵊl\. City, México state, Mexico, suburb of Mexico City; munic. pop. (1970p) 571,035.

Netze. See NOTEĆ.

Neu·bran·den·burg \nȯi-'brän-dən-ˌbů(ə)rg\ *or* **New Brandenburg. 1** District, East Germany. See table at GERMANY, EAST.

2 City, its ✱, 74 m. E of Schwerin; pop. (1970e) 45,685; agricultural machinery, chemicals, paper; 14th cent. city walls; founded 1248; to Mecklenburg 1292.

Neubreisach. See NEUF-BRISACH.

Neu·burg \'nȯi-ˌbů(ə)rg\. Town, Bavaria, West Germany, on the Danube ab. 11 m. W of Ingolstadt; pop. (1968e) 18,435; ceded by Bavaria to the Palatinate 1507; capital of a small principality 1557–1742; reunited with the Palatinate 1742; to Bavaria 1777.

Neu·châ·tel \ˌn(y)ü-shə-'tel, ˌnə(r)sh-ə-\. **1** Swiss canton in the Jura Mts.; 308 sq. m.; pop. (1970c) 169,173; ✱ Neuchâtel; watered by numerous tributaries of the Rhine. Independent principality 1034; under French family of Longueville 1504–1707; to Prussia 1707–1806, France 1806–14; reverted to Prussia 1814; joined Swiss Confederation 1815 as only canton with monarchical government (monarchy suppressed 1848). See table at SWITZERLAND.

2 Commune, its ✱, W Switzerland, on W shore of Lake of Neuchâtel 25 m. W of Bern; pop. (1970c) 38,784; watches, electrical appliances, jewelry; ancient castle, 12th cent. town hall, 12th cent. Gothic church; university (1838, univ. status 1909).

Neuchâtel, Lake of. Lake, W Switzerland, on S border of Neuchâtel canton; 84 sq. m.; max. depth 502 ft.; largest lake entirely within Switzerland.

Neuf–Bri·sach \ˌnə(r)-brē-'zäk\ *or Ger.* **Neu·brei·sach** \ˌnȯi-'brī-(ˌ)zäk\. Town, NE Haut-Rhin dept., NE France, near German frontier ESE of Colmar; pop. (1962c) 2127; fortress founded by Louis XIV 1699; held by Germans Nov. 10, 1870–1918.

Neuf·châ·teau \ˌnə(r)-shə-'tō\. Town, NW Vosges dept., NE France, ab. 35 m. NW of Épinal; pop. (1962c) 8120; ruins of castle of dukes of Lorraine who owned the town during Middle Ages.

Neuf·châ·tel \ˌnə(r)-shə-'tel\. **1** Town, Quebec co., S Quebec, Canada; pop. (1966c) 6618.

2 *or* **Neufchâtel en Bray** \-äⁿ-'brā\. Town, E Seine-Maritime dept., N France, ab. 25 m. NE of Rouen; pop. (1962c) 5861; chief town of Bray region; famous for its cheese.

Neu–Hannover. See NEW HANOVER 2.

Neuhaus. See JINDŘICHŮV HRADEC.

Neuhäusel. See NOVÉ ZÁMKY.

Neu·hau·sen \'nȯi-ˌhaů-zən\ *or* **Neuhausen am Rhein·fall** \-äm-'rīn-ˌfäl\. Commune, S Schaffhausen canton, N Switzerland, just SW of Schaffhausen on border of Zurich canton; pop. (1970c) 12,103.

Neu·hof \'nȯi-ˌhōf\. Name of Pestalozzi's farm in Aargau canton, Switzerland, where he established his first school for poor children c. 1776–80.

Neuil·ly–Plai·sance \nə(r)-'yē-ple-'zäⁿs\. Commune, Seine-St-Denis dept., N France, E suburb of Paris; pop. (1968c) 17,613; manufactures machinery and electrical equipment; battles 1870–71.

Neuilly–sur–Marne \-sů(ə)r-'märn\. Commune, Seine-St-Denis dept., N France, E suburb of Paris on Marne river; pop. (1968c) 22,543; manufactures rubber products, furniture.

Neuilly–sur–Seine \-ˌsů(ə)r-'sān, -'sen\. Manufacturing commune, Hauts-de-Seine dept., N France, a NW suburb of Paris near Bois de Boulogne; pop. (1968c) 70,995; automotive industry; Treaty of Neuilly signed here Nov. 27, 1919 bet. Allies and Bulgaria after World War I.

Neu–Isen·burg \nȯi-'ēz-ᵊn-ˌbů(ə)rg\. City, S Hesse, West Germany, 5 m. S of Frankfurt am Main; pop. (1969e) 35,580; manufactures leather, machinery, furniture; founded 1700; made city 1894.

Neu·kirch·en–Vluyn \'nȯi-ˌki(ə)r-kən-'flə(ə)n\. City, North Rhine-Westphalia, West Germany, 21 m. W of Essen; coal mines, sawmills; textiles.

Neu–Langenburg. See TUKUYU.

Neumarkt. See NOWY TARG.

Neu–Mecklenburg. See NEW IRELAND 1.

Neu·mün·ster \nȯi-'min(t)-stər, -'m(y)ün(t)-, -'můn(t)-, -'mən(t)-\. Commercial and manufacturing city, Schleswig-Holstein, West Germany, SSW of Kiel; pop. (1969e) 73,175; important railroad junction; manufactures leather, textiles, machinery, paper; trades in manufactured products, cattle. Founded before 1127; became city 1870.

Neun·kir·chen \'nȯin-ˌki(ə)r-kən\. **1** *or in full* **Neunkirchen am Stein·feld** \-äm-'s(h)tīn-ˌfelt\. City, Lower Austria, 35 m. SSW of Vienna; pop. (1961c) 10,860; furniture; became city 1920.

2 Industrial city, Saarland, West Germany, ab. 12 m. NE of Saarbrücken; pop. (1969e) 44,633; iron foundries; coal-mining region.

Neu–Pommern. See NEW BRITAIN 2.

Ne·u·quén \nyü-'kān\. **1** River, W cen. Argentina; 320 m. long; rises in W Neuquén prov., flows E to join Limay river on E border of Neuquén territory and form the Río Negro.

2 Province, W Argentina; 36,324 sq. m.; pop. (1970p) 154,570; on Chilean border, its W part mountainous, E part level; forests and fertile valleys in W; in S is Lake Nahuel Huapí (*q.v.*).

3 Town, its ✱, on Neuquén river; pop. (1960c) 16,738; univ. (1964).

Neurode. See NOWA RUDA.

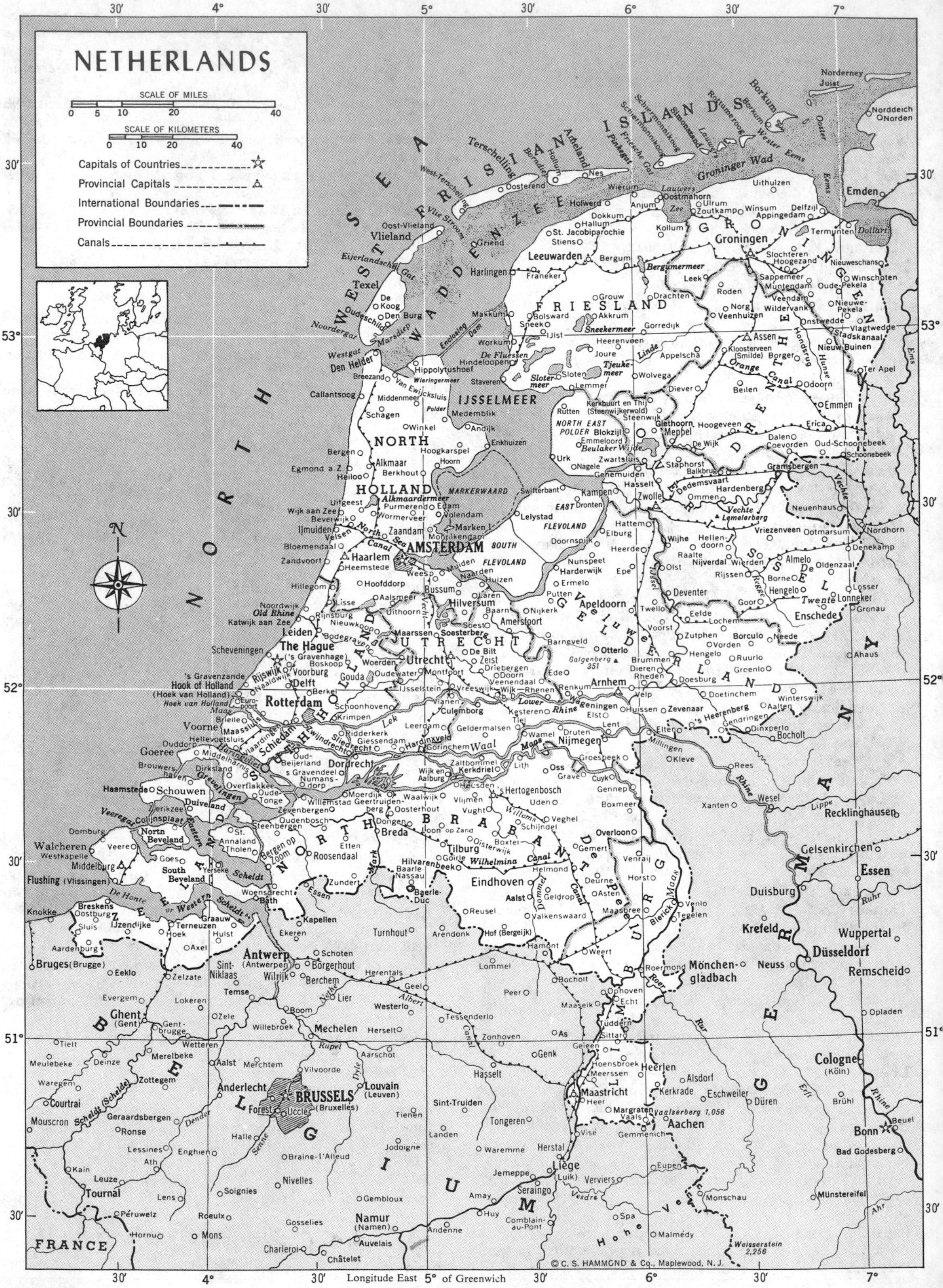
NETHERLANDS
SCALE OF MILES
0 5 10 20 40
SCALE OF KILOMETERS
0 10 20 40
Capitals of Countries
Provincial Capitals
International Boundaries
Provincial Boundaries
Canals
NORTH SEA
WEST FRISIAN ISLANDS
WADDENZEE
IJSSELMEER
NORTH HOLLAND
SOUTH HOLLAND
UTRECHT
FRIESLAND
GRONINGEN
DRENTHE
OVERIJSSEL
GELDERLAND
NORTH BRABANT
ZEELAND
LIMBURG
BELGIUM
GERMANY
FRANCE
Texel
Vlieland
Terschelling
Ameland
Schiermonnikoog
Rottumeroog
Borkum
Norderney
Juist
Groninger Wad
Den Helder
Alkmaar
Haarlem
AMSTERDAM
Zaandam
IJmuiden
Hilversum
Leiden
The Hague
('s Gravenhage)
Delft
Rotterdam
Schiedam
Dordrecht
Gouda
Utrecht
Amersfoort
Apeldoorn
Arnhem
Nijmegen
Zwolle
Kampen
Deventer
Enschede
Hengelo
Almelo
Leeuwarden
Harlingen
Groningen
Emden
Assen
Meppel
Hoogeveen
Emmen
Lelystad
FLEVOLAND
MARKERWAARD
EAST FLEVOLAND
SOUTH FLEVOLAND
NORTH EAST POLDER
's Hertogenbosch
Breda
Tilburg
Eindhoven
Roosendaal
Bergen op Zoom
Middelburg
Flushing (Vlissingen)
Walcheren
Schouwen
Duiveland
South Beveland
Nortn Beveland
Tholen
Goeree
Voorne
Hook of Holland
(Hoek van Holland)
Venlo
Roermond
Maastricht
Heerlen
Sittard
Kerkrade
Vaalserberg 1,056
Aachen
Mönchen-gladbach
Krefeld
Düsseldorf
Duisburg
Essen
Gelsenkirchen
Recklinghausen
Wuppertal
Neuss
Remscheid
Cologne
(Köln)
Bonn
Bad Godesberg
Düren
Antwerp
(Antwerpen)
Bruges (Brugge)
Ghent
(Gent)
BRUSSELS
(Bruxelles)
Louvain
(Leuven)
Mechelen
Liège
(Luik)
Namur
(Namen)
Charleroi
Mons
Tournai
Courtrai
Hasselt
Genk
Tongeren
Verviers
Spa
Malmédy
Weisserstein 2,256
Hohe Venn
Rhine
Lower Rhine
Waal
Maas
Lek
IJssel
Scheldt
De Honte or Western Scheldt
Albert Canal
Wilhelmina Canal
Galgenberg 351
Longitude East 5° of Greenwich
© C. S. HAMMOND & Co., Maplewood, N. J.

Neu·rup·pin \ˌnȯi-rü-ˈpēn\. Manufacturing city, Potsdam dist., East Germany, 40 m. NNW of West Berlin; pop. (1970e) 22,258; railroad junction; 13th cent. Gothic convent church; became city 1256; almost completely destroyed by fire 1787.

Neusalz an der Oder. See NOWA SÓL.

Neusandez. See NOWY SĄCZ.

Neusatz. See NOVI SAD.

Neuse \ˈn(y)üs\. River, E cen. North Carolina; 275 m. long; navigable to New Bern; formed by junction of streams in Durham co., NE cen. North Carolina, flows SE into Pamlico Sound, E North Carolina.

Neu·sie·dler Lake \ˈnȯi-ˌzēd-lər-\ *or Hung.* **Fer·tő tó** \ˌfer-tə-ˈtō\ *or Ger.* **Neusiedler See** \-ˌzā\. Shallow lake, E Austria and NW Hungary; 123 sq. m.; 23 m. long; formerly entirely within Hungary, but in 1922 N two thirds transferred with Burgenland to Austria.

Neusohl. See BANSKÁ BYSTRICA.

Neuss \ˈnȯis\. 1 *or anc.* **No·vae·si·um** \nō-ˈvē-zh(ē-)əm\. Industrial city, W North Rhine-Westphalia, West Germany, 5 m. W of Düsseldorf; pop. (1969e) 116,501; railroad junction; manufactures paper and iron goods, textiles, agricultural implements, machinery, chemicals. Ancient Roman camp; besieged by Charles the Bold 1474; destroyed by duke of Parma 1586; taken by French 1794 and held to 1813. In World War II taken by Allies Mar. 2, 1945.

2 Commune in Switzerland. See NYON.

Neustadt. See PRUDNIK.

Neu·stadt an der Wein·stras·se \ˈnȯi-ˌs(h)tät-än-dər-ˈvīn-ˌs(h)träs-ə\ *or formerly* **Neustadt an der Haardt** \-ˈhärt\; *anc.* **No·va Civ·i·tas** \ˌnō-və-ˈsiv-ə-təs\ *or later* **Nie·wen·stat** \ˈnēv-ən-ˌs(h)tät\. Industrial city, Rhineland-Palatinate, West Germany, 18 m. SW of Mannheim; pop. (1969e) 50,882; 14th cent. Gothic church; 18th cent. city hall; manufactures metal goods, textiles, paper, concrete; railroad junction; trades in wines. First mentioned 1235; became city 1275; during Thirty Years' War taken 1622, 1631, 1635, 1644; occupied by French 1688–97, 1793–95. Taken by Allied armies Mar. 22, 1945.

Neustadt in Oberschlesien. See PRUDNIK.

Neustettin. See SZCZECINEK.

Neu·stre·litz \nȯi-ˈs(h)trā-ləts\. City, Neubrandenburg dist., East Germany, 61 m. NNW of West Berlin; pop. (1969e) 27,992; railroad junction; printing, sawmilling, iron founding; 18th cent. grand-ducal palace; founded 1733; capital of former free state of Mecklenburg-Strelitz.

Neus·tria \ˈn(y)ü-strē-ə\. The western part of the dominions of the Franks after the conquest by Clovis in 511, comprising then the NW part of modern France bet. the Meuse, the Loire, and the Atlantic Ocean. See AUSTRASIA. After 912 the name was applied to Normandy.

Neutitschein. See NOVÝ JIČÍN.

Neutra. See NITRA.

Neutral Zone. A triangular-shaped area of desert land bet. N Saudi Arabia and SE Iraq; not included in any sovereignty due to incomplete boundary adjustments; neutral zone lying bet. SE Kuwait and NE Saudi Arabia was partitioned bet. these two states on the basis of a boundary agreement 1969.

Neu–Ulm \nȯi-ˈu̇lm\. City, Bavaria, West Germany, on right bank of Danube river 2 m. SE of Ulm; pop. (1969e) 27,435; leather goods; became city 1869.

Neuve–Cha·pelle \ˌnə(r)v-shə-ˈpel\. Town, Pas-de-Calais dept., N France, 7 m. NE of Béthune; pop. (1962c) 484; scene of battle Mar. 10–13, 1915, in which the British captured the town but failed in their objective of taking the ridge to the E; first use of artillery barrage during World War I, in which British lost 13,000 men.

Neuve–Église \ˌnə(r)-vā-ˈglēz\ *or Flem.* **Nieuw·ker·ke** \ˌnē-ü-ˈker-kə\. Village, West Flanders prov., NW Belgium, S of Ieper (Ypres); pop. (1969e) 1815; scene of heavy fighting Apr. 12–13, 1918 in World War I.

Neu·ville–Saint–Vaast \nə(r)-ˌvēl-saⁿ-ˈväst\. Commune, Pas-de-Calais dept., N France, 4 m. N of Arras; pop. (1962c) 918; battles 1915–16, esp. May 9–10, 1915.

Neu·wied \nȯi-ˈvēt\. Industrial city, North Rhine-Palatinate, West Germany, on the Rhine 7 m. NNW of Koblenz; pop. (1969e) 31,362; river port; manufactures machinery, soap, cement, rolled metal; excavations of large Roman camp nearby; founded 1653.

Neuzen. See TERNEUZEN.

Ne·va \ˈnē-və, ˈnā-\. Navigable river, NW Leningrad Oblast, Russian S.F.S.R., U.S.S.R.; ab. 40 m. long; flowing from SW corner of Lake Ladoga into the Gulf of Finland through several mouths; connected by canals and other waterways with the White Sea in the N and the Volga and Caspian Sea in the SE (see VOLGA-BALTIC WATERWAY); usually frozen Nov. to April. Leningrad (*q.v.*) is in its delta.

Ne·vada \nə-ˈvad-ə, -ˈväd-ə\. 1 A western state of U.S.A., bounded on N by Oregon and Idaho, on E by Utah and Arizona, and on SW and W by California; 7th state in area, 110,540 sq. m. (land area 109,889 sq. m.); 47th state in population, (1970c) 488,738; ✱ Carson City; 36th state admitted to Union (1864).

Nicknames: Silver State; Sagebrush State. *State flower:* Sagebrush. *Motto:* All for Our Country. *Rivers:* Humboldt, rising in NE area, flowing W then SW and emptying into Humboldt Lake; Colorado river, forming extreme SE boundary. *Chief lakes, etc.:* Pyramid and Winnemucca lakes in W, and Walker Lake in SW; many dry lakes (as Mud Lake) and marshy salt regions (Carson Sink and Humboldt Salt Marsh in W cen. part); Black Rock Desert in NW. *Highest point:* Boundary Peak, 13,140 ft. in Esmeralda co. on California-Nevada boundary. *Chief products:* Barley, wheat, oats; livestock; copper, gold, manganese, mercury; manufacturing: lumber and wood products, chemicals; mineral processing; tourism. *Chief cities:* Las Vegas, Reno, North Las Vegas, Sparks, Henderson. See *Table of States* at UNITED STATES. Divided into the following 16 counties and one independent city (for pronunciation of their names, see their individual entries):

NAME	LOCATION	AREA[1] (sq. m.)	POP. (1970c)	CO. SEAT
Churchill	W	4,883	10,513	Fallon
Clark	SE corner[2]	7,874	273,288	Las Vegas
Douglas	W	723	6,882	Minden
Elko	NE corner	17,162	13,958	Elko
Esmeralda	SW	3,570	629	Goldfield
Eureka	cen.	4,182	948	Eureka
Humboldt	NW	9,702	6,375	Winnemucca
Lander	cen.	5,621	2,666	Austin
Lincoln	E	10,649	2,557	Pioche
Lyon	W	2,010	8,221	Yerington
Mineral	SW	3,765	7,051	Hawthorne
Nye	cen. and S	18,064	5,599	Tonopah
Pershing	NW	6,001	2,670	Lovelock
Storey	W	262	695	Virginia City
Washoe	NW corner	6,375	121,068	Reno
White Pine	E	8,904	10,150	Ely
Carson City[3]	W	141	15,468	

[1]Area = land area.
[2]On SE separated from Ariz. by Colorado river, including Hoover Dam. Lake Mead in E part.
[3]Independent city.

History: Explored by John C. Frémont 1843–45; part of region ceded by Mexico to U.S. 1848; in Utah Territory 1850–61; first permanent settlement made 1851 at Mormon Station (now Genoa); received increasing number of settlers after discovery of Comstock Lode 1859 (see VIRGINIA CITY 2); organized as separate territory 1861; held first constitutional convention 1863; admitted to Union as state Oct. 31, 1864.

2 Name of counties in two states of the U.S. See tables at ARKANSAS and CALIFORNIA.

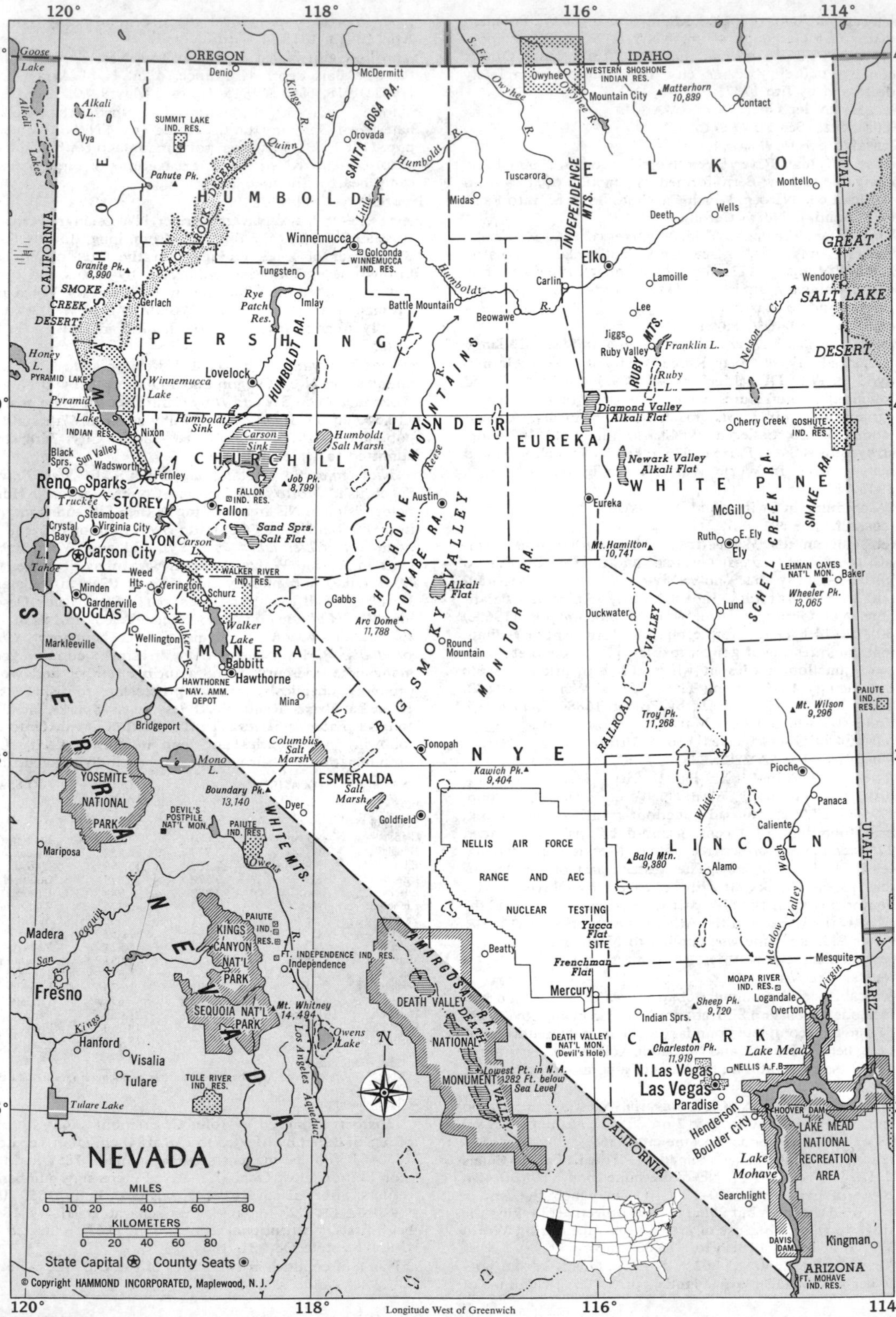

© Copyright HAMMOND INCORPORATED, Maplewood, N. J.

Longitude West of Greenwich

Ne·va·da \nə-'väd-ə\. 1 City, ⊗ of Story co., cen. Iowa, 30 m. N of Des Moines; pop. (1970c) 4952; in agricultural region; poultry-distributing point.

2 City, ⊗ of Vernon co., W Missouri, 53 m. N of Joplin; pop. (1970c) 9736; shipping point for livestock, grain, and poultry.

Ne·va·da \nə-'väd-ə\. Mountain in the Andes, on Argentina-Chile border; 20,023 ft.

Nevada, Sierra. See SIERRA NEVADA.

Ne·vada City \nə-'vad-ə-, -'väd-\. City, ⊗ of Nevada co., E California, 45 m. W of Lake Tahoe; pop. (1970c) 2314; gold mining.

Nevada de Cocuy, Sierra. See SIERRA NEVADA DE COCUY.

Nevada de Mérida, Sierra. See CORDILLERA MÉRIDA.

Nevada de Santa Marta, Sierra. See SIERRA NEVADA DE SANTA MARTA.

Nevada Falls \nə-ˌvad-ə-, -ˌväd-\. Waterfall in Yosemite National Park, E cen. California; 594 ft.

Ne·va·do \nə-'väd-(ˌ)ō\. For names of mountains beginning with this element see the distinguishing element.

Nevado de Famatina. See SIERRA DE FAMATINA.

Ne·velsk \n(y)e-'velsk\ *or Jap.* **Hon·to** \'hōn-(ˌ)tō, 'hōn-\. Town, SW coast of Sakhalin I., Russian S.F.S.R., U.S.S.R.; pop. (1967e) 22,000.

Ne·vers \nə-'ve(ə)r\ *or anc.* **No·vi·o·du·num** \ˌnō-vē-ō-'d(y)ü-nəm\. Commune, ✱ of Nièvre dept., cen. France, at confluence of Nièvre and Loire rivers 38 m. ESE of Bourges; pop. (1968c) 42,422; aeronautical engineering; episcopal see (since 506); 11th cent. Romanesque church; 13th cent. cathedral (restored 1879); 15th cent. courthouse (former ducal palace); medieval gate, 18th cent. triumphal arch; capital of former province of Nivernais.

Ne·vi·ges \'nā-vi-gəs\. City, North Rhine-Westphalia, West Germany, 21 m. NE of Düsseldorf; pop. (1969e) 22,736; machinery.

Nev·ille's Cross \ˌnev-əlz-\. Parish, Durham co., N England, near Durham; site of battle Oct. 17, 1346 in which invading Scots under King David Bruce were defeated, and the king taken prisoner, by forces of Edward III, using novel offensive tactic in which archers and spearmen successfully dislodged and defeated troops in immobile defensive formation.

Ne·vin·no·myssk \n(y)e-ˌvin-ə-'misk\. Town, Stavropol Krai, Russian S.F.S.R., U.S.S.R., ab. 30 m. S of Stavropol; pop. (1969e) 75,000.

Ne·vis \'nē-vəs, 'nev-əs\. Island in E West Indies, part of Saint Christopher-Nevis, Leeward Is.; 50 sq. m.; pop. (1965e) 14,636; chief town Charlestown; sugarcane; birthplace of Alexander Hamilton. Separated from St. Christopher on NW by narrow strait 2 m. wide; a volcanic cone, rising to height of 3232 ft. Discovered by Columbus 1493; colonized by English 1628; taken by French 1782 but restored to British after Napoleonic Wars. See SAINT CHRISTOPHER-NEVIS.

Nevis, Ben. See BEN NEVIS.

Nevis, Loch \'läk-, 'läk-\. Inlet of the Sound of Sleat on W coast of Inverness co., NW Scotland; extends inland ab. 14 m.

Nev·şe·hir \ˌnef-she-'hi(ə)r\ *or* **Nev·shehr** \nef-'she(ə)r\. 1 Province of cen. Turkey, Asia. See table at TURKEY.

2 Town, its ✱, 40 m. W of Kayseri; pop. (1965c) 21,121.

New \'n(y)ü\. 1 River, SE North Carolina; ab. 35 m. long; rises in N Onslow co., flows S into **New River Inlet** and Atlantic Ocean.

2 River, SW Virginia and S West Virginia; ab. 320 m. long; formed by junction of North and South forks in Ashe co., NW North Carolina; flows N across state of Virginia into West Virginia and joins Gauley river to form Kanawha river in N Fayette co., S cen. West Virginia.

3 Artificial stream, Hertfordshire and London, SE England; 36 m. long; commences near Ware, flows S into reservoirs at Heringey and Hackney.

New Al·ba·ny \-'ōl-bə-nē\. 1 City, ⊗ of Floyd co., S Indiana, on Ohio river across from Louisville, Kentucky; pop. (1970c) 38,402; wood products, flour, glue, machine tools; incorporated as city 1839.

2 City, ⊗ of Union co., N Mississippi, 24 m. NW of Tupelo; pop. (1970c) 6426; clothing, furniture, automobile parts; raises poultry, sorghum.

New Am·ster·dam \-'am(p)-stər-ˌdam\. 1 The Dutch city on Manhattan I. which became the city of New York; ✱ of New Netherland colony; founded 1625 by Dutch West India Co.; taken by English 1664 and renamed New York. See NEW YORK 1 and 3.

2 Town, ⊗ of East Berbice co., NE Guyana, on E bank of Berbice river near its mouth; ab. 55 m. SE of Georgetown; pop. (1970p) 18,199.

3 Island, Indian Ocean. See AMSTERDAM 3.

New Archangel. See SITKA.

New·ark \'n(y)ü-ərk, 'n(y)u̇(-ə)rk\. 1 City, Alameda co., W California, SE of San Francisco; pop. (1970c) 27,153; Fremont-Newark Junior Coll. (1966).

2 City, New Castle co., N Delaware, 12 m. WSW of Wilmington; pop. (1970c) 21,078; paper products, automobile parts; apples, wheat; Univ. of Delaware (1743); settled 1694.

3 Industrial city and port of entry, ⊗ of Essex co., NE New Jersey, on Passaic river and Newark Bay 9 m. W of New York City; pop. (1970c) 381,930; transportation center, connected to New York City by tunnel ("tube"); insurance and financial center; manufactures electrical equipment, paints, chemicals, beverages, canned goods, machinery, jewelry; distilling; Newark Coll. of Engineering (1881), Essex County Coll. (1968).

History: First settled by Puritans 1666; site of Coll. of New Jersey (later Princeton Univ.) 1748–56; Washington's supply base on retreat across state 1776; incorp. as town 1833, as city 1836; scene of major race riot 1967.

4 Village, Wayne co., W New York, 29 m. ESE of Rochester; pop. (1970c) 11,644; paper products; fruit and dairy farms.

5 City, ⊗ of Licking co., cen. Ohio, 30 m. E of Columbus; pop. (1970c) 41,836; glass, aluminum products, automobile parts, plastics, petroleum products, paper containers; oil refineries, railroad repair shops. **Newark Works,** earthworks of prehistoric mound builders in vicinity, cover ab. 4 sq. m.

6 Municipal borough, Nottinghamshire, N cen. England, 20 m. ENE of Nottingham; pop. (1971p) 24,631; market town; sugar, ball bearings; brewing, limestone quarrying. On the ancient Fosse Way; has castle of 12th–15th cents. which was besieged three times during Civil War.

Newark Bay. A bay in NE New Jersey, SE of Newark; separated from Lower New York Bay on S by Staten I. and connected with Upper New York Bay through Kill van Kull; receives on the N the Passaic and Hackensack rivers.

New Au·gus·ta \-ȯ-'gəs-tə, -ə-\. Town, ⊗ of Perry co., SE Mississippi; pop. (1970c) 511.

Ne·way·go \ni-'wā-(ˌ)gō\. County in Michigan. See table at MICHIGAN.

New Bal·ti·more \-'bȯl-tə-ˌmō(ə)r, -ˌmȯ(ə)r\. City, Macomb and St. Clair cos., SE Michigan, on Lake St. Clair 19 m. NE of Detroit; pop. (1970c) 4132; resort; truck farms.

New Bed·ford \-'bed-fərd\. City, a ⊗ of Bristol co., SE Massachusetts, on **New Bedford Harbor** on W side of Buzzards Bay, 50 m. S of Boston; pop. (1970c) 101,777; fishing port; clothing, electrical equipment, machine parts, rubber, copper, and brass goods; first settled c. 1652; separate village estab. 1760 and early became shipping and whaling center; from War of 1812 to c. 1860 leading U.S. whaling port; chartered as city 1847.

New·berg \'n(y)ü-ˌbərg\. City, Yamhill co., NW Oregon, 21 m. SW of Portland; pop. (1970c) 6507; fruit and nut packing; George Fox Coll. (1891).

New Ber·lin \-'bər-(ˌ)lin\. City, Waukesha co., SE Wisconsin, W of Milwaukee; pop. (1970c) 26,910.

New·bern \'n(y)ü-bərn\. Town, Dyer co., NW Tennessee, 10 m. NE of Dyersburg; pop. (1970c) 2124; cotton.

New Bern \'n(y)ü-(ˌ)bərn, n(y)ü-'\. City and port, ⊗ of Craven co., SE North Carolina, at confluence of Neuse and Trent rivers, 30 m. W of Pamlico Sound; pop. (1970c) 14,660; commercial center in farming and resort area; lumber, boats, chemicals. Settled by Swiss and Germans 1710; incorporated and made county seat 1723; meeting place of Colonial assembly 1745–61 (except 1752); seat of royal governors 1770–74; chosen provincial capital 1774; fortified port of the Confederacy; captured by Gen. Burnside in Civil War 1862.

New·ber·ry \'n(y)ü-ˌber-ē, -bə-rē\. 1 County in South Carolina. See table at SOUTH CAROLINA.
2 Village, ⊗ of Luce co., NE Michigan penin., 58 m. W of Sault Sainte Marie; pop. (1970c) 2334; lumber.
3 Town, ⊗ of Newberry co., NW cen. South Carolina, 32 m. ENE of Greenwood; pop. (1970c) 9218; lumber, flour, cottonseed oil; granite quarries; dairy and truck farms; Newberry Coll. (1856); settled c. 1830.

New Beth·le·hem \-'beth-li-ˌhem, -lē-(h)əm\. Borough, Clarion co., W Pennsylvania, 36 m. SE of Oil City; pop. (1970c) 1406; brick and tile; oil and gas wells.

New·big·gin by the Sea \n(y)ü-'big-ən-, 'n(y)ü-ˌbig-\. Urban district, Northumberland, N England, on the North Sea 17 m. NNE of Newcastle upon Tyne; pop. (1971p) 10,661.

New Bloom·field \-'blüm-ˌfēld\. Borough, ⊗ of Perry co., S cen. Pennsylvania.

New Bos·ton \-'bȯ-stən\. 1 City, Scioto co., S Ohio, on Ohio river 4 m. E of Portsmouth; pop. (1970c) 3325.
2 Town, Bowie co., NE Texas, 24 m. W of Texarkana; pop. (1970c) 4034; oil and gas wells, sawmills; pine timber; agriculture.

New Brandenburg. See NEUBRANDENBURG.

New Braun·fels \'-braůn-fəlz\. Industrial city, ⊗ of Comal co., S cen. Texas, on Guadalupe river 32 m. NE of San Antonio; pop. (1970c) 17,859; textiles, hosiery, gauze, flour; tannery; diversified agriculture.

Newbridge. See ABERCARN.

New Brigh·ton \-'brīt-ᵊn\. 1 Village, Ramsey co., SE cen. Minnesota, N of Minneapolis; pop. (1970c) 19,507.
2 Residential community, N Staten I., New York City, site of Sailors' Snug Harbor, a home for retired seamen, founded at bequest of Robert Richard Randall and opened Aug. 1, 1833.
3 Borough, Beaver co., W Pennsylvania, on Beaver river just S of Beaver Falls and 19 m. S of New Castle; pop. (1970c) 7637; settled 1789.

New Brit·ain \-'brit-ən\. 1 Industrial city, Hartford co., N Connecticut, 9 m. SW of Hartford; pop. (1970c) 83,441; household appliances, tools, hardware, machine tools, ball bearings; Central Connecticut State Coll. (1849). Settled 1687; incorporated 1870; consolidated 1905 with the town (incorporated 1850) with which it is coextensive.
2 *or formerly* **Neu–Pom·mern** \nȯi-'pȯm-ərn\. Largest island in the Bismarck Archipelago, administratively part of Papua New Guinea; 14,160 sq. m.; pop. (1969e) 138,689; divided into two districts: **East New Britain** (✱ Rabaul) and **West New Britain** (✱ Kimbe); crescent-shaped with several volcanoes, esp. at E end; highest peak Mt. Sinewit 7999 ft.; sudden violent eruption May 1937 (see VULCAN, MOUNT and TAVURVUR, MOUNT). Has many good harbors, esp. Blanche Bay, Talasea, Jacquinot Bay, Linden Harbour. Chief islands off coast, belonging to the two districts, are Lolobau, Vitu Is., Umboi, Long, and Duke of York Is. Rich in tropical vegetation but only coconuts and cocoa of value commercially.

History: First visited and named by William Dampier 1700 but little exploration carried on before end of 19th cent.; made part of German protectorate 1884 (see KOKOPO); after World War I a part of Australian mandate; invaded by Japanese Jan. 1942. Rabaul attacked many times 1943–45 and largely destroyed by American airmen. Landings made Dec. 15, 1943 by U.S. Marines at Arawe and Cape Gloucester and at Talasea Mar. 1944.

New Bruns·wick \-'brənz-(ˌ)wik\. 1 City, ⊗ of Middlesex co., cen. New Jersey, at head of navigation on Raritan river 9 m. W of Perth Amboy; pop. (1970c) 41,885; rubber products, footwear, hosiery, pharmaceuticals and surgical supplies, machinery, chemicals, leather goods; Rutgers, The State Univ. (1766).

History: Settled by English colonists 1681; incorporated as town 1736, as city 1784; alternately headquarters for American and British troops in War for Independence; entered by Washington's defeated army 1776; starting point for Washington's march to Yorktown 1781.

2 Province, one of the Maritime Provinces, E Canada, bounded by Quebec prov. on N, by the Gulf of St. Lawrence and Northumberland Strait (separating it from Prince Edward I.) on E, on S by Bay of Fundy, and on the W by Maine; on SE connected with Nova Scotia by isthmus of Chignecto; 28,354 sq. m.; pop. (1970e) 624,000, (1966c) 616,788; ✱ Fredericton. *Physical features:* Highest point of land Mt. Carleton 2690 ft.; larger part lies within basin of St. John river; other rivers the St. Croix (on Maine border), Miramichi, Restigouche, and Nepisiguit. *Chief products:* Potatoes, fruit, dairy products, timber; coal, gypsum, zinc. *Chief cities:* Saint John, Moncton, Fredericton, Bathurst. Divided into the following 15 counties (for pronunciation of their names, see their individual entries):

NAME	LOCATION	AREA[1] (sq. m.)	POP. (1966c)	CO. SEAT
Albert	SE	681	13,944	Hopewell Cape
Carleton	W	1,300	23,356	Woodstock
Charlotte	SW	1,243	23,543	St. Andrews
Gloucester	NE	1,854	70,301	Bathurst
Kent	E	1,734	24,736	Richibucto
Kings	S	1,374	28,548	Hampton
Madawaska	NW	1,262	37,306	Edmundston
Northumberland	E	4,671	51,711	Newcastle
Queens	S	1,373	10,940	Gagetown
Restigouche	N	3,242	41,121	Dalhousie
Saint John	S	611	92,926	Saint John
Sunbury	S cen.	1,079	25,011	Burton
Victoria	W	2,074	19,694	Andover
Westmorland	SE	1,430	95,181	Dorchester
York	SW	3,545	58,470	Fredericton

[1]Land area.

History: Down to 1784 was part of French province of Acadia (*q.v.*), then of British province of Nova Scotia. First French settlement (not permanent) made at mouth of St. Croix river 1604 by Sieur de Monts; first English settlement 1762 at Maugerville; after American Revolutionary War received great numbers of Loyalist settlers from U.S.; became separate province 1784; W boundary settled by Ashburton Treaty 1842; joined Nova Scotia, Quebec, and Ontario to form Dominion of Canada 1867; abolished county government 1966.

New Buffalo. City, Berrien co., SW Michigan, on Lake Michigan 27 m. SW of Saint Joseph; pop. (1970c) 2784; fruit growing.

New Bull·ards Dam \-'bůl-ərdz-\ *and* **New Bullards Reservoir.** See UNITED STATES, *Dams and Reservoirs.*

New·burgh \'n(y)ü-ˌbərg\. City, Orange co., SE New York, on Hudson river opp. Beacon; 15 m. S of Poughkeepsie; pop. (1970c) 26,219; ships fruit and dairy products; clothing, leather goods, aluminum castings, paints, plastic products, radio parts, bricks; Epiphany Apostolic Coll. (1888), Our Lady of Hope Seminary (1900), Mount St. Mary Coll. (1930); Steward Field, U.S. Air Force base.

History: Settled 1708–09; figured prominently in Revolution; Washington's headquarters 1782–83, where he received letter from Lewis Nicola in 1782 urging him to

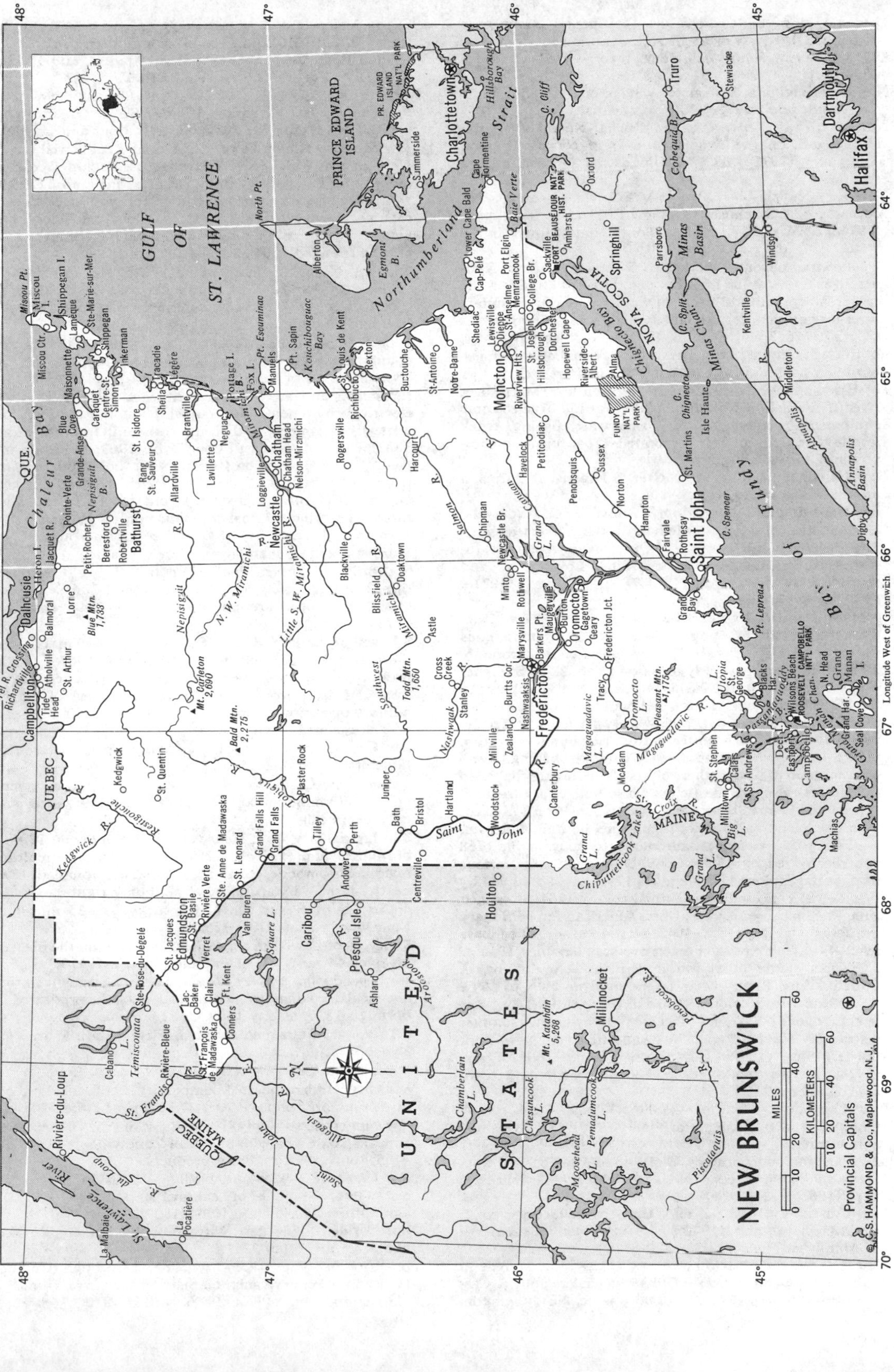
NEW BRUNSWICK
GULF OF ST. LAWRENCE
Chaleur Bay
Northumberland Strait
Bay of Fundy
PRINCE EDWARD ISLAND
NOVA SCOTIA
QUEBEC
QUE.
MAINE
UNITED STATES
Fredericton
Saint John
Moncton
Charlottetown
Halifax
Dartmouth
Campbellton
Dalhousie
Bathurst
Newcastle
Chatham
Edmundston
Grand Falls
Woodstock
Oromocto
Sackville
Amherst
Springhill
Truro
Summerside
Caribou
Presque Isle
Houlton
Millinocket
Rivière-du-Loup
Mt. Carleton 2,690
Mt. Katahdin 5,268
FUNDY NAT'L PARK
ROOSEVELT CAMPOBELLO INT'L PARK
FORT BEAUSEJOUR NAT'L HIST. PARK
PR. EDWARD ISLAND NAT'L PARK
Provincial Capitals
MILES
KILOMETERS
Longitude West of Greenwich
© C.S. HAMMOND & Co., Maplewood, N.J.

become king, and where the Continental Army was disbanded 1783; *Newburgh Addresses* issued from here 1783 by Gen. John Armstrong; incorporated as village 1800, as city 1865.

Newburgh Heights. Village, Cuyahoga co., N Ohio, SE of Cleveland; pop. (1970c) 3396; residential.

New·burn \'n(y)ü-bərn\. Urban district, Northumberland, N England, on the Tyne 5½ m. W of Newcastle upon Tyne; pop. (1971p) 39,379; in industrial and coal-mining section.

New·bury \'n(y)ü-bə-rē, 'nu̇b-ə-\. 1 Town, Essex co., NE corner of Massachusetts, 24 m. ENE of Lowell; pop. (1970c) 3804; incorp. 1635, one of the oldest towns in the state.

2 Municipal borough, Berkshire, S England, on the Kennet river 53 m. W of London; pop. (1971p) 23,696; trade center in agricultural section; woolen market; manufactures marine engines and light aircraft, scene of two battles (Sept. 20, 1643 and Oct. 26, 1644) in English Civil War, both to the slight advantage of the Parliamentary armies.

New·bur·y·port \'n(y)ü-bə-rē-ˌpō(ə)rt, -ˌpȯ(ə)rt\. City, a ⊗ of Essex co., NE Massachusetts, at mouth of Merrimack river 25 m. ENE of Lowell; pop. (1970c) 15,807; electronic equipment, textiles, footwear, silverware; fishing, truck farming; settled 1635; incorporated 1764; formerly shipbuilding and whaling center.

New Cal·a·bar \-'kal-ə-ˌbär\. River, S Nigeria, W Africa, a mouth of the Niger river.

New Cal·e·do·nia \-ˌkal-ə-'dō-nyə, -nē-ə\ *or Fr.* **Nou·velle Ca·lé·do·nie** \nü-vel-kȧ-lā-dȯ-nē\. 1 French overseas territory in SW Pacific Ocean E of Queensland, Australia; includes New Caledonia, Île des Pins, Loyalty Is., and several other islet groups; 7367 sq. m.; pop. (1971e) 113,680; ✱ Nouméa.

2 Main island of French overseas territory of New Caledonia; 6531 sq. m.; pop. (1963e) 84,000; mountainous island 248 m. long by ab. 31 m. wide, extending from ab. 20°S lat. in a southeasterly direction to ab. 22°20'S; higher peaks Mt. Panié in the NE 5314 ft. and Mt. Humboldt in the SE 5308 ft.; good rainfall and many small streams, but except for the coastal plains not particularly fertile; principal crops copra, coffee, cotton; rich in minerals, esp. nickel, iron, and chrome; livestock raising, fishing. Reefs border much of its coastline; off its NW point are the Belep Is. and off the S tip the Île des Pins. Natives are Melanesians of the Papuan type. Chief town Nouméa on SW coast, with fine harbor, also Thio, Hienghène, Bourail, and Pam.

History: Its existence made known to Bougainville 1768 and discovered by Capt. Cook 1774; visited by various navigators, explorers, and traders 1792–1840; occupied by France 1853 and set up as a penal colony 1864–94; joined Free French cause July 1940; first American Expeditionary Force arrived Mar. 10, 1942; served as an Allied base 1942–44; made part of French overseas territory 1946.

3 Former name of region in British Columbia (*q.v.*), Canada, W of Rocky Mts., extending from 52°N to 55°N.

4 Settlement and colony, Panama. See DARIÉN 1.

New Ca·naan \-'kā-nən\. Residential town and summer resort, SW Fairfield co., SW Connecticut, on New York border; pop. (1970c) 17,455; Silvermine Coll. of Art (1924); settled 1640, incorp. 1801; borough and town consolidated 1935.

New Car·lisle \-kär-'lī(ə)l, -kər-\. 1 Village, Clark co., W Ohio, 12 m. W of Springfield; pop. (1970c) 6112; diversified agriculture.

2 Village (unincorporated), ⊗ of Bonaventure co., SE Quebec, Canada, on SE coast of Gaspé Penin. on Chaleur Bay; pop. (1966c) 1213; tourism.

New Car·roll·ton \-'kar-əl-tən\. City, Prince Georges co., S cen. Maryland; pop. (1970c) 14,870; residential suburb of Washington, D.C.

New Cas·tile \-ka-'stē(ə)l\ *or Span.* **Cas·ti·lla la Nue·va** \kä-ˌstē(l)-yə-ˌlän-ù-'ā-və\. Old provincial region, S Castile, Spain; bounded on N by Old Castile, NE by Aragon, SE by Valencia and Murcia, S by Andalusia, W by Estremadura; 28,010 sq. m.; comprises modern provinces of Ciudad Real, Cuenca, Guadalajara, Madrid, and Toledo; ✱ Toledo. For its history, see CASTILE.

New·cas·tle \'n(y)ü-ˌkas-əl, -ˌkȧs-, n(y)ü-'\. 1 City, ⊗ of Weston co., NE Wyoming, 75 m. ESE of Gillette; pop. (1970c) 3432; ships livestock; oil wells, flour and sawmills.

2 *or formerly* **King's Town** \'kiŋz-ˌtau̇n\. Industrial city, E New South Wales, SE Australia, on Pacific Ocean at mouth of Hunter river 100 m. NE of Sydney; pop. (1969e) 144,860; ships coal; manufactures iron and steel, chemicals, cotton and synthetic textiles, glass, machinery, and fertilizers; shipbuilding, metalworking; Univ. of Newcastle (1965); founded 1804 as penal settlement.

3 Town, ⊗ of Northumberland co., E New Brunswick, Canada, on left bank of Miramichi river 14 m. from its mouth; pop. (1971p) 6347; summer resort; cod fisheries; lead and zinc mines.

4 *or* **Newcastle upon Tyne** \-'tīn\. Industrial city and county borough, Northumberland, N England, on the Tyne 83 m. N of Leeds; pop. (1971p) 222,153; manufactures iron and steel, coke, chemicals, salt, glass, soap, electrical equipment; important shipbuilding and repairing center; coal mines; 14th cent. cathedral (diocese estab. 1882); Univ. of Newcastle upon Tyne (1963). Station (**Pons Ae·lii** \pänz-'ē-lē-ˌī\) on Roman wall; took modern name from castle built 12th cent. by Henry II; trade in coal began 13th cent.; received first charter 1216; expanded rapidly as principal coal-shipping port of England after 16th cent.; became city 1882 and county borough 1888.

5 *or* **Newcastle–under–Lyme** \-'līm\. Municipal borough, Staffordshire, W cen. England; pop. (1971p) 76,970; textiles, clothing, brick and tile; coal mines; Univ. of Keele (1962); developed around castle built c. 1144; chartered 1173.

6 Town, W Natal, E Rep. of South Africa, 150 m. NNW of Durban at foot of Drakensberg Mts.; pop. (1967e) 16,900; produces wood, grain, hemp; center of extensive coalfields; iron and steel works; carbide factory; base of British military operations against Boers in war of 1880–81; treaty of peace signed 1881.

New Cas·tle \'n(y)ü-ˌkas-əl\. 1 County in Delaware. See table at DELAWARE.

2 City, New Castle co., N Delaware, on Delaware river 5 m. S of Wilmington; pop. (1970c) 4814; aircraft, steel castings, chemicals.

3 Industrial city, ⊗ of Henry co., E cen. Indiana, 18 m. S of Muncie; pop. (1970c) 21,215; trade center of agricultural region; automobile parts; rose nurseries; founded 1820; nearby farm was birthplace of Wilbur Wright.

4 City, ⊗ of Henry co., N Kentucky, ab. 35 m. NE of Louisville; pop. (1970c) 755.

5 City, ⊗ of Lawrence co., W Pennsylvania, on the Shenango river 44 m. NNW of Pittsburgh; pop. (1970c) 38,559; steel products, pottery, brass castings, cement, brick, chemicals; coal mines; settled c. 1798; incorporated as borough 1825, as city 1869.

6 Town, ⊗ of Craig co., western Virginia, ab. 55 m. W of Lynchburg.

Newchwang. See YING-K'OU.

New City. Unincorporated community, ⊗ of Rockland co., SE New York; pop. (1970c) 27,344; residential.

New·com·ers·town \'n(y)ü-ˌkəm-ərz-ˌtau̇n\. Village, Tuscarawas co., E Ohio, 30 m. NE of Zanesville; pop. (1970c) 4155; tools, plastics, dairy products.

New Con·cord \-'käŋ-kərd\. Village, Muskingum co., SE cen. Ohio, 14 m. E of Zanesville; pop. (1970c) 2318; agriculture; Muskingum Coll. (1837).

New Cor·dell \-kȯr-'del\. City, ⊗ of Washita co., W Oklahoma; pop. (1970c) 3261.

New Cum·ber·land \-'kəm-bər-lənd\. 1 Borough, Cumberland co., S Pennsylvania, on Susquehanna river 3 m. S of Harrisburg; pop. (1970c) 9803; settled 1810.

2 City, ⊗ of Hancock co., N tip of West Virginia panhandle, on Ohio river 31 m. NNE of Wheeling; pop. (1970c) 1865; coal mines, foundry; fruit farms.

New Del·hi \-ˈdel-ē\. City, ✱ of India, Delhi territory, N India, on Yamuna river S of Old Delhi; pop. (1970e) 371,-210. Completed in 1929 when the Viceroy took up residence there; formally opened 1931. See DELHI 2.

New Don Pe·dro Dam *and* **New Don Pedro Reservoir** \-dän-ˈpē-(ˌ)drō-, -ˈpā-\. See UNITED STATES, *Dams and Reservoirs.*

New Dorp \-ˌdörp\. Section of Richmond, borough of New York City. See RICHMOND 8.

New Ea·gle \-ˈē-gəl\. Borough, Washington co., SW Pennsylvania, on Monongahela river 16 m. S of Pittsburgh; pop. (1970c) 2497.

New Echo·ta \-i-ˈkōt-ə\. Indian town, NW Georgia; site, in Gordon co., NE of Calhoun, marked by a monument; chosen by the Cherokee as their capital 1819; by 1828 had a newspaper; given up by the Cherokee when they signed Dec. 29, 1835 the Treaty of New Echota surrendering all their lands E of the Mississippi river to the United States.

New El·len·ton \-ˈel-ən-tən\. Town, Aiken co., W South Carolina, 49 m. SW of Columbia; pop. (1970c) 2546.

New En·gland \-ˈiŋ-glənd *also* -ˈiŋ-lənd\. 1 Northeast section of the United States, comprising the states of Connecticut, Maine, Massachusetts, New Hampshire, Rhode Island, and Vermont; total area 66,608 sq. m. (land area, 63,159 sq. m.); pop. (1970c) 11,845,169.

History: Council for New England, incorporated 1620 with Sir Ferdinando Gorges as president, was granted territory from sea to sea bet. 40th and 48th parallels; its jurisdiction ignored by colonies, esp. Massachusetts Bay which was governed by Massachusetts Bay Company with powers directly from the king; Council surrendered its charter 1635. The New England Confederation (1643–84) was formed by the colonies of Massachusetts Bay, Plymouth, Connecticut, and New Haven for defense against the Indians. The Dominion of New England formed by English government in 1686 made into one province, under rule of Edmund Andros, the colonies of New Hampshire, Massachusetts, Rhode Island, and Connecticut; New York and New Jersey added in 1688 for protection against French; Andros overthrown 1689 and colonies resumed separate existences. For later history see individual states.

2 Mountain range and plateau (**New England Plateau**), NE New South Wales, SE Australia; ab. 200 m. long by 75 m. broad; part of the Great Dividing Range; highest peak Ben Lomond 4877 ft.

New·en·ham, Cape \-ˈn(y)ü-ən-ˌham\. Cape on SW coast of Alaska bet. Kuskokwim Bay and Bristol Bay, 58°37′N, 162°12′W.

New Ex·che·quer Dam \-ˈeks-ˌchek-ər-\. See UNITED STATES, *Dams and Reservoirs.*

New Fair·field \-ˈfa(ə)r-ˌfēld, -fe(ə)r-\. 1 Former name of Bridgeport, Connecticut. See BRIDGEPORT 3.

2 Town, Fairfield co., SW Connecticut, 20 m. WSW of Waterbury; pop. (1970c) 6991.

New·fane \ˈn(y)ü-ˌfān, n(y)ü-ˈfān\. Residential village, ⊗ of Windham co., SE corner of Vermont; pop. (1970c) 183.

New Forest. District in SW Hampshire, S England, bet. the Avon and Southampton Water; 130 sq. m., ab. one fourth of which, under private ownership, is cultivated, the remainder, partly bog and heath, administered as a state park; highest point Lewis Hills 2672 ft.; set apart 1079 by William the Conqueror as a hunting ground.

New Found, Lake *or* **Lake New·found** \-ˈn(y)ü-ˌfau̇nd\. Lake in SE Grafton co., cen. New Hampshire; 6 m. long by ab. 2½ m. wide.

New·found·land \ˈn(y)ü-fən-(d)lənd, -ˌ(d)land, n(y)ü-ˈfau̇n-(d)lənd\. 1 Island in Atlantic Ocean, off E coast of Canada, constituting with Labrador on the mainland a province of Canada; 43,359 sq. m.; pop. (1966c) 485,843. *Physical features:* In general a plateau (highest point in Long Range Mts., 2672 ft., ab. 25 m. WSW of Corner Brook); triangular in form with Cape Bauld at the N, Cape Race at SE, and Cape Ray at SW; coasts much indented, esp. in the E and S; separated on N from mainland (Labrador) by the Strait of Belle Isle; has many islands along coasts, esp. Belle Isle, Groais, Bell, and Fogo in the N and the French islands of St. Pierre and Miquelon off S coast; largest rivers the Exploits, Humber, and Gander; chief lakes Grand, Red Indian, and Gander. *Chief products:* Fish, lumber; copper, fluorspar, gypsum. *Chief towns:* St. John's, Corner Brook, Wabana, Grand Falls, Gander.

2 Province of Canada, consisting of island of Newfoundland (see 1 above) and Labrador (*q.v.*); 156,185 sq. m.; pop. (1971p) 518,000; ✱ St. John's.

History: Discovery 1497 by John Cabot resulted at once in visits of fishermen from countries of W Europe; ownership proclaimed formally in 1583 by Sir Humphrey Gilbert who established first colony at St. John's; site of unsuccessful settlements by John Guy 1610 and Sir George Calvert 1621–29 (see FERRYLAND); disputed by France and England; by Treaty of Utrecht 1713 became English, but fishing rights retained by France (see FRENCH SHORE); received first governor 1728; by Treaty of Versailles 1763 was granted coast of Labrador; controversies over fishing rights continued through 19th cent.; received representative government 1832 and responsible government 1855, which was withdrawn 1933; became a British colony 1934. In World War II developed great air bases near Botwood; became (with Labrador) a prov. of Canada 1949.

New France \-ˈfran(t)s\. The possessions of France in North America from the time of the discoveries of Cartier 1534–41, but esp. from 1627 (when the "Company of New France" was founded by Cardinal Richelieu) to 1763, Treaty of Paris, by which France lost to Great Britain and Spain (see QUEBEC 1). Strengthened by Colbert's new Company of the West, founded 1664; its boundaries expanded beyond the lower St. Lawrence to cover the Great Lakes and all the Mississippi Valley, the result esp. of the work of the great French missionary explorers Marquette, La Salle, Hennepin, Duluth, Jolliet, Nicolet, and others; in 1689 began the long period of rivalry in Europe bet. England and France directly affecting their possessions in the Western Hemisphere through four wars, known in America as King William's War (1689–97), Queen Anne's War (1702–13), King George's War (1744–48), and the French and Indian War (1754–63).

New Geor·gia \-ˈjȯr-jə\. 1 Group of islands, cen. Solomon Is., including New Georgia I. and Vella Lavella, Ganongga, Kolombangara, Rendova, and Vangunu Is.; administrative center on Gizo I.; part of British Solomon Is. protectorate.

2 Chief island of the group, 40 m. S of Choiseul I.; ab. 50 m. long, 10–12 m. wide; highest point 3300 ft.; in SE enclosed by Vangunu Is. and reefs is Marovo lagoon, one of largest in world; along W coast E of Munda is Roviana lagoon. Occupied by Japanese 1942 and fortified, esp. at Munda airfield on NW coast; used as base for attack on Guadalcanal Aug.–Nov. 1942; captured by Americans June–Aug. 1943. See KULA GULF.

New Glas·gow \-ˈglas-(ˌ)kō, -ˈglas-(ˌ)gō, -ˈglaz-(ˌ)gō\. Town, Pictou co., N Nova Scotia, Canada, near Pictou Harbor 37 m. NE of Truro; pop. (1971p) 10,792; heavy machinery, boilers, paint, furniture; pulp and steel mills, coal mines.

New Glouces·ter \-ˈgläs-tər, -ˈglȯs-\. Town, Cumberland co., SW Maine, 20 m. N of Portland; pop. (1970c) 2811.

New Goa. See PANAJI.

New Gra·na·da \-grə-ˈnäd-ə\ *or Span.* **Nue·va Granada** \nu̇-ˌā-və-\. 1 Name of Colombia (with Panama), 1819–30

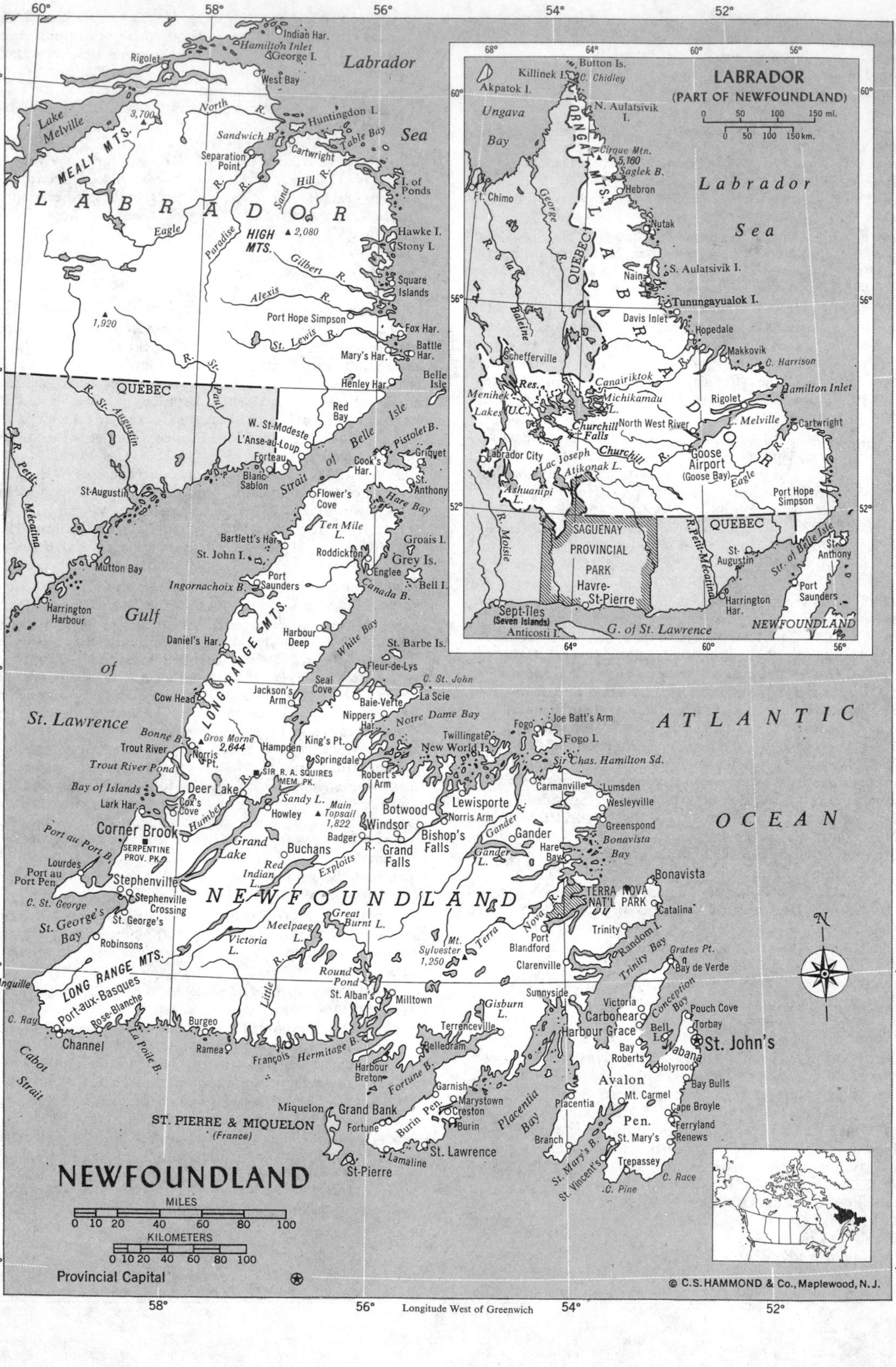
NEWFOUNDLAND
LABRADOR (PART OF NEWFOUNDLAND)
Labrador Sea
Gulf of St. Lawrence
ATLANTIC OCEAN
L A B R A D O R
N E W F O U N D L A N D
QUEBEC
MEALY MTS.
HIGH MTS.
LONG RANGE MTS.
Lake Melville
Rigolet
Indian Har.
Hamilton Inlet
George I.
West Bay
Huntingdon I.
Sandwich B.
Cartwright
Table Bay
Separation Point
I. of Ponds
Hawke I.
Stony I.
Square Islands
Port Hope Simpson
Fox Har.
Battle Har.
Mary's Har.
Henley Har.
Belle Isle
Red Bay
W. St-Modeste
L'Anse-au-Loup
Forteau
Blanc-Sablon
Strait of Belle Isle
Pistolet B.
Griquet
St. Anthony
Cook's Har.
Hare Bay
Flower's Cove
Ten Mile L.
St-Augustin
Mutton Bay
Harrington Harbour
Bartlett's Har.
St. John I.
Groais I.
Roddickton
Englee
Grey Is.
Bell I.
Canada B.
Ingornachoix B.
Port Saunders
Daniel's Har.
Harbour Deep
White Bay
St. Barbe Is.
Fleur-de-Lys
C. St. John
Cow Head
Seal Cove
Jackson's Arm
Baie-Verte
La Scie
Nippers Har.
Notre Dame Bay
Bonne B.
Gros Morne 2,644
Trout River
Norris Pt.
Trout River Pond
Hampden
King's Pt.
Springdale
Twillingate
New World I.
Fogo
Joe Batt's Arm
Fogo I.
Sir Chas. Hamilton Sd.
Bay of Islands
Deer Lake
SIR R. A. SQUIRES MEM. PK.
Robert's Arm
Carmanville
Lumsden
Wesleyville
Lark Har.
Cox's Cove
Sandy L.
Howley
Main Topsail 1,822
Botwood
Lewisporte
Norris Arm
Windsor
Greenspond
Bonavista Bay
Corner Brook
SERPENTINE PROV. PK.
Humber
Grand Lake
Badger
Buchans
Grand Falls
Bishop's Falls
Gander R.
Gander
Gander L.
Hare Bay
Port au Port B.
Lourdes
Port au Port Pen.
Stephenville
Stephenville Crossing
Red Indian L.
Exploits R.
Bonavista
TERRA NOVA NAT'L PARK
Catalina
C. St. George
St. George's
St. George's Bay
Great Burnt L.
Meelpaeg L.
Victoria L.
Robinsons
Mt. Sylvester 1,250
Terra Nova R.
Port Blandford
Trinity
Random I.
Trinity Bay
Grates Pt.
Bay de Verde
Clarenville
C. Anguille
Round Pond
Little R.
Port-aux-Basques
Rose-Blanche
St. Alban's
Milltown
Gisburn L.
Sunnyside
Victoria
Conception Bay
Pouch Cove
Carbonear
Torbay
C. Ray
Burgeo
Terrenceville
Harbour Grace
Bell I.
St. John's
Wabana
Channel
La Poile B.
Ramea
François
Hermitage B.
Belleoram
Bay Roberts
Holyrood
Cabot Strait
Harbour Breton
Fortune B.
Avalon Pen.
Bay Bulls
Garnish
Marystown
Placentia
Mt. Carmel
Miquelon
Grand Bank
Creston
Burin Pen.
Burin
Placentia Bay
Cape Broyle
Ferryland
Renews
ST. PIERRE & MIQUELON (France)
Fortune
Branch
St. Mary's
Lamaline
St. Lawrence
St. Mary's B.
Trepassey
St-Pierre
St. Vincent's
C. Race
C. Pine
MILES
0 10 20 40 60 80 100
KILOMETERS
0 10 20 40 60 80 100
Provincial Capital
© C.S. HAMMOND & Co., Maplewood, N.J.
Longitude West of Greenwich
Button Is.
Killinek I.
C. Chidley
Akpatok I.
Ungava Bay
N. Aulatsivik I.
TORNGAT MTS.
Cirque Mtn. 5,160
Saglek B.
Hebron
Ft. Chimo
George
Nutak
Nain
S. Aulatsivik I.
Tunungayualok I.
Davis Inlet
Hopedale
R. à la Baleine
Makkovik
C. Harrison
Schefferville
Canairiktok R.
Hamilton Inlet
Menihek Lakes
Res. (U.C.)
Michikamau L.
Rigolet
Churchill Falls
North West River
L. Melville
Cartwright
Labrador City
Lac Joseph
Churchill R.
Goose Airport (Goose Bay)
Atikonak L.
Ashuanipi L.
Eagle
Port Hope Simpson
SAGUENAY PROVINCIAL PARK
R. Moisie
Havre-St-Pierre
R. Petit-Mécatina
St-Augustin
Str. of Belle Isle
St. Anthony
Harrington Har.
Port Saunders
Sept-Îles (Seven Islands)
Anticosti I.
G. of St. Lawrence
NEWFOUNDLAND
0 50 100 150 mi.
0 50 100 150 km.

when it was part of Great Colombia. See *History* at COLOMBIA.

2 Spanish viceroyalty in NW South America; region conquered and named by Spaniards 1537–38 under Gonzalo Jiménez de Quesada; part of viceroyalty of Peru until 1718; as reorganized 1740 included what is now Colombia (and Panama), Venezuela, and Ecuador; freed from Spanish rule 1819. See GREAT COLOMBIA.

New·grange \n(y)ü-'grānj\. The principal tumulus of the Brugh na Boinne (*q.v.*), co. Meath, NE Eire, on N bank of the Boyne; the mound, surrounded by remains of a stone circle, has a domed chamber.

New Guin·ea \-'gin-ē\ *also* **Pap·ua** \'pap-yə-wə\ *or Indonesian* **Iri·an** \ˌir-ē-'än\ *or Du.* **Nieuw Gui·nee** \ˌn(y)ü-gi-'nā\. Island of E Malay Archipelago, in W Pacific Ocean N of Australia; second largest island in the world; 319,713 sq. m. (with politically attached islands, 344,927 sq. m.); pop. (1970e) 2,968,000; administratively divided into Irian Barat (Indonesia) and Papua New Guinea (under Australian administration).

New Guinea, British. See PAPUA, TERRITORY OF.

New Guinea, Dutch. See IRIAN BARAT.

New Guinea, Trust Territory of *or formerly* **German New Guinea.** Trust territory under Australian administration, part of Papua New Guinea, consisting of the NE section of New Guinea I. (North-East New Guinea) together with Bougainville, Buka, and adjacent small islands, and the Bismarck Archipelago; 92,160 sq. m.; pop. (1969e) 1,702,-280; ✱ Port Moresby; cocoa, coconuts, coffee, timber; in administrative union with Terr. of Papua since 1949. For description and history see NORTH-EAST NEW GUINEA and BISMARCK ARCHIPELAGO.

New Gulf *or Span.* **Gol·fo Nue·vo** \ˌgōl-fō-nü-'ā-(ˌ)vō\. Inlet, NE Chubut prov., S cen. Argentina, S of Valdés Penin.

New·ham \'n(y)ü-əm\. A borough of Greater London, SE England. See table at LONDON 4.

New Hamp·shire \-'ham(p)-shər, -ˌshi(ə)r\. A northeastern state of U.S.A., bounded on N by Canadian province of Quebec, on E by Maine and (in the extreme SE) the Atlantic Ocean, on S by Massachusetts, and on W by Vermont; 44th state in area, 9304 sq. m. (land area 9033 sq. m.); 41st state in population, (1970c) 737,681; ✱ Concord; an original state of the Union, the 9th to ratify the Federal Constitution (June 21, 1788).

Nickname: Granite State. *State flower:* Purple lilac. *Motto:* Live Free or Die. *Rivers:* Connecticut, forming W boundary; Salmon Falls and Piscataqua, forming SE boundary; Saco, flowing SE across the border into Maine; Merrimack, flowing from S cen. area S across border into Massachusetts. *Mountains:* White Mts. in N cen. part, including highest point in state Mount Washington 6288 ft., in Coos co. *Chief products:* Dairy products, apples, potatoes; poultry; gravel, mica, feldspar; manufacturing: electronic equipment, paper products, leather goods. *Chief cities:* Manchester, Nashua, Concord, Portsmouth, Dover, Keene. See *Table of States* at UNITED STATES. Divided into the following 10 counties (for pronunciation of their names, see their individual entries):

NAME	LOCATION	AREA[1] (sq. m.)	POP. (1970c)	CO. SEAT
Belknap[2]	cen.	400	32,367	Laconia
Carroll[3]	E	938	18,548	Ossipee
Cheshire	SW corner	715	52,364	Keene
Coos	N	1,820	34,291	Lancaster
Grafton	W	1,732	54,914	Woodsville
Hillsborough	S	893	223,941	Nashua
Merrimack	S cen.	930	80,925	Concord
Rockingham	SE[3]	691	138,951	Exeter
Strafford	SE	376	70,431	Dover
Sullivan	SW	539	30,949	Newport

[1]Area = land area.
[2]Includes part of Lake Winnipesaukee (larger part in Belknap co.).
[3]Only coastal county in state.

History: Coast explored by Pring 1603; included in grant to Mason and Gorges 1622 and in New Hampshire grant to Mason 1629; first settled by English near Portsmouth 1623; controlled by Massachusetts 1641–43; made a separate royal province 1679 but under same governor as Massachusetts 1699–1741; adopted 1st constitution 1776; relinquished claim to New Connecticut (Vermont) 1782; adopted present constitution 1792 which later was frequently amended; Dartmouth College case decided in U.S. Supreme Court, confirming right of private corporations 1819.

New Hamp·ton \-'ham(p)-tən\. City, ⊗ of Chickasaw co., NE Iowa, 37 m. N of Waterloo; pop. (1970c) 3621; creamery, feed mill.

New Han·o·ver \-'han-ˌō-vər, -'han-ə-\. 1 County in North Carolina. See table at NORTH CAROLINA.

2 *or* **La·von·gai** *or* **Lo·von·gai** \lə-'vȯŋ-ˌgī\ *or formerly* **Neu–Han·no·ver** \ˌnȯi-hä-'nō-vər, -'nō-fer\. Island in the Bismarck Archipelago, W Pacific Ocean, NW of New Ireland; 460 sq. m.; mountainous, with highest point 3150 ft.; coconut plantations.

New Har·mo·ny \-'här-mə-nē\. Town, Posey co., SW corner of Indiana, on Wabash river 23 m. WNW of Evansville; pop. (1970c) 921; agriculture; founded (as Harmonie) 1814 by Harmony Society under George Rapp, German religious leader; sold out 1825 to Robert Owen, who renamed it New Harmony and established a Utopian communistic colony; internal dissensions caused breakup of the community 1828.

New Hart·ford \-'härt-fərd\. Town, E Litchfield co., NW Connecticut, on Farmington river; pop. (1970c) 3970; settled 1733.

New·ha·ven \n(y)ü-'hā-vən, 'n(y)ü-ˌhā-vən\. Urban district, East Sussex, S England, on seacoast at mouth of the Ouse 55 m. S of London; pop. (1971p) 9977; boatbuilding; popular cross-channel port.

New Ha·ven \-'hā-vən\. 1 County in Connecticut. See table at CONNECTICUT.

2 Commercial and industrial city, New Haven co., S Connecticut, on New Haven Harbor 36 m. SSW of Hartford; pop. (1970c) 137,707; firearms, ammunition, aircraft parts, tools, rubber goods, clocks and watches, textiles, paper products; shipbuilding; Yale Univ. (founded 1701 at Saybrook, moved to New Haven 1716), Southern Connecticut State Coll. (1893), Albertus Magnus Coll. (1925).

History: Settled 1638 by Puritans under John Davenport and Theophilus Eaton, the latter civil governor of New Haven Colony 1639–58; at first called Quinnipiac, given present name 1640; with Hartford, joint capital of Connecticut 1701–1873; incorporated 1784; important maritime trade in late 18th and early 19th cents.; became important manufacturing center, a number of its residents, among them Eli Whitney, Charles Goodyear, and Samuel F. B. Morse, making significant contributions to industrial technology. The town (incorporated 1784) and the city were consolidated and made coextensive 1895.

3 City, Allen co., NE Indiana, 7 m. E of Fort Wayne; pop. (1970c) 5728; plastic products; dairy farms.

New Haven Harbor. Inlet of Long Island Sound, on S shore of New Haven co., Connecticut; receives Quinnipiac, Mill, and West rivers.

New Heb·ri·des \-'heb-rə-ˌdēz\ *or Fr.* **Nou·velles Hé·brides** \nü-vel-zā-brēd\. Group of islands in SW Pacific Ocean NE of New Caledonia and W of Fiji; 5700 sq. m.; pop. (1971e) 86,000; ✱ Vila; under joint British and French administration. Principal islands are Espíritu Santo, Malekula, Efate, Ambrim, Eromanga, Tana, Epi, Aneityum, Maewo, and Pentecost. Larger islands volcanic in

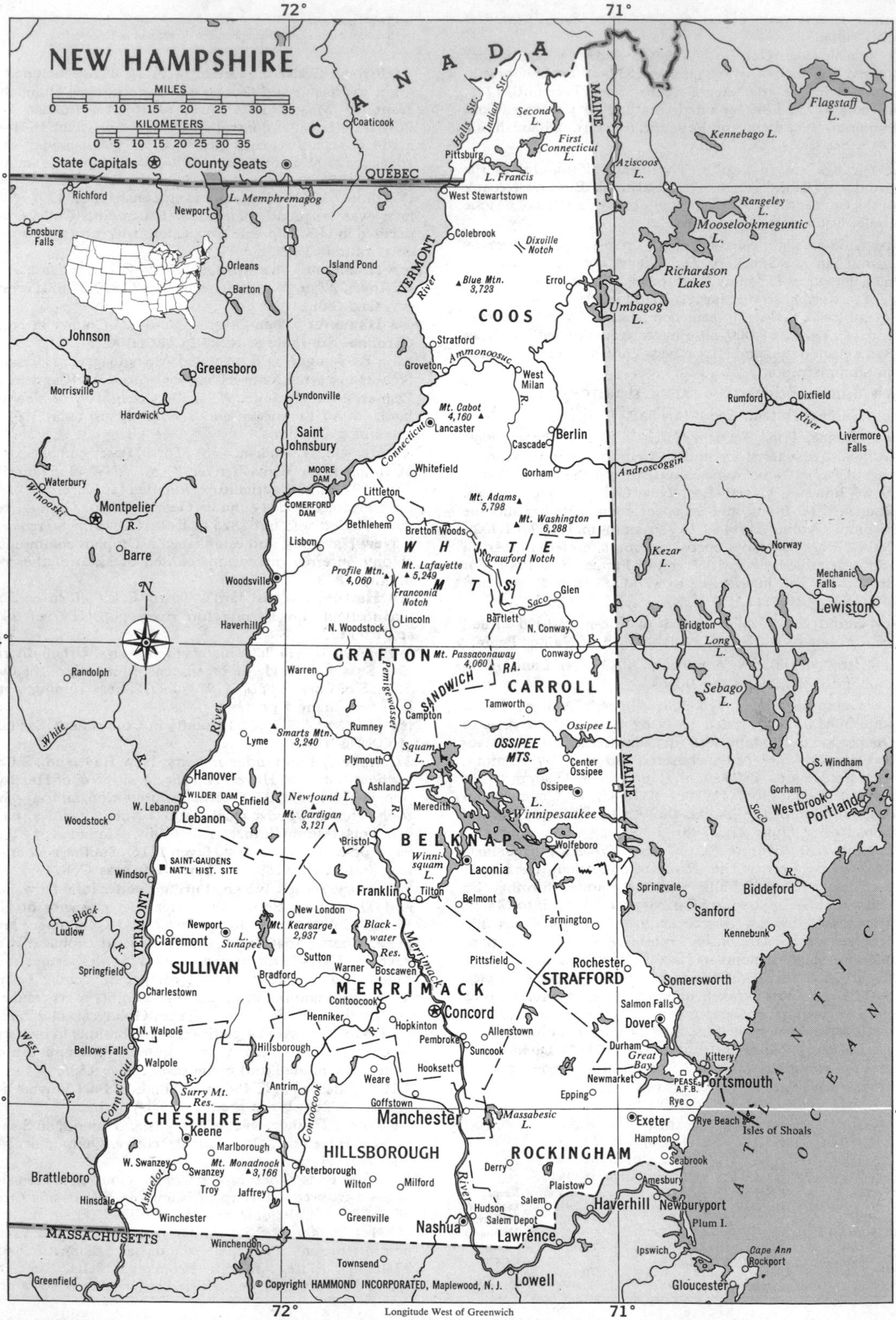

Longitude West of Greenwich

origin and mountainous; three active volcanoes; some of the islands, esp. Efate and Malekula, have good harbors. Discovered 1606 by the Portuguese navigator, Pedro de Queirós; forgotten for 160 years, then visited by Bougainville 1768 and explored by Capt. Cook 1774; visited 1788 by La Pérouse, whose expedition was lost on Vanikoro; control of group sought by both French and British who finally signed a convention Oct. 20, 1906 by which a condominium was set up; this superseded by a second protocol 1914, ratified 1922. In World War II major American naval base on Espíritu Santo I., 1942–45.

New Hol·land \-ˈhäl-ənd\. Borough, Lancaster co., SE Pennsylvania, 15 m. ENE of Lancaster; pop. (1970c) 3971; silk, dairy products, bronze castings.

New Hol·stein \-ˈhōl-ˌstēn, -ˌstīn\. City, Calumet co., E Wisconsin, 20 m. NE of Fond du Lac; pop. (1970c) 3012; agricultural machinery; dairy and truck farms.

New Hope \ˈn(y)ü-ˌhōp\. Village, Hennepin co., SE cen. Minnesota; pop. (1970c) 23,180; residential suburb of Minneapolis.

New Hyde Park \-ˈhīd-\. Village, Nassau co., SE New York, on Long Island 17 m. E of New York; pop. (1970c) 10,116; residential; truck farms.

New Ibe·ria \-ī-ˈbir-ē-ə\. City, ⊗ of Iberia parish, S Louisiana, 20 m. SSE of Lafayette; pop. (1970c) 30,147; steel, lumber, sugar; fishing, muskrat trapping; sugar and rice farming.

New·ing·ton \ˈn(y)ü-iŋ-tən\. Suburban residential town, S Hartford co., N Connecticut, SW of Hartford; pop. (1970c) 26,037; truck farms; settled 1670, incorp. 1871.

New Inlet. Narrow strait leading from Atlantic Ocean through barrier reef off SE coast of Dare co., NE North Carolina.

New Ire·land \-ˈī(ə)r-lənd\. 1 *or formerly* **Neu–Meck·len·burg** \nȯi-ˈmek-lən-ˌbərg, -ˌbu̇(ə)rg\. Island in the Bismarck Archipelago; 3340 sq. m.; ab. 200 m. long; not volcanic, terrain largely mountainous, with peaks bet. 4000 and 7000 ft.; highest Mt. Lambel 7054 ft.; chief port Kavieng, at NW end, 162 m. NW of Rabaul; harbors also at Namatanai on NE coast, and Muliama on E coast; produces copra and cocoa. Most important adjacent island is New Hanover on NW; others are Saint Matthias Group, Tabar Is., Lihir I., Dyaul I., and Tanga I. Discovered by Jacob LeMaire and William Schouten 1616, but little known of it before 1884 when it became part of German protectorate. In World War II, Kavieng occupied by Japanese Jan. 1942; often bombed, but Japanese forces bypassed.

2 Administrative district of Papua New Guinea, including the island of New Ireland and adjacent islands; 3820 sq. m.; pop. (1969e) 48,774; ✱ Kavieng.

New Jer·sey \-ˈjər-zē\. An eastern state of U.S.A., bounded on N by New York, on E by New York and the Atlantic Ocean, on S by Atlantic Ocean and Delaware Bay, on SW by Delaware Bay and Delaware, and on W by Pennsylvania; 46th state in area, 7836 sq. m. (land area 7532 sq. m.); 8th state in population, (1970c) 7,168,164; ✱ Trenton; an original state of the Union, the 3d to ratify the Federal Constitution (Dec. 18, 1787).

Nickname: Garden State. *State flower:* Violet. *Motto:* Liberty and Prosperity. *Rivers:* Hudson, forming NE boundary; Delaware, forming W boundary. *Highest point:* High Point 1803 ft., in Sussex co. *Chief products:* Corn, peppers, tomatoes; dairy products; zinc, iron ore; manufacturing: chemicals, motor vehicles, apparel, electrical machinery. *Chief cities:* Newark, Jersey City, Paterson, Elizabeth, Trenton, Camden, Clifton. See *Table of States* at UNITED STATES. Divided into the following 21 counties (for pronunciation of their names, see their individual entries):

NAME	LOCATION	AREA[1] (sq. m.)	POP. (1970c)	CO. SEAT
Atlantic	SE; coastal	569	175,043	Mays Landing
Bergen	NE corner	234	897,148	Hackensack
Burlington[2]	S cen.	819	323,132	Mount Holly
Camden	SW	221	456,291	Camden
Cape May	S; coastal	267	59,554	Cape May Court House
Cumberland	SW	500	121,374	Bridgeton
Essex	NE	130	932,299	Newark
Gloucester	SW	329	172,681	Woodbury
Hudson	NE	47	609,266	Jersey City
Hunterdon	NW cen.	434	69,718	Flemington
Mercer	W cen.	228	303,968	Trenton
Middlesex	cen.	312	583,813	New Brunswick
Monmouth	E cen.; coastal	476	461,849	Freehold
Morris	N	468	383,454	Morristown
Ocean[2,3]	E; coastal	642	208,470	Toms River
Passaic	N	193	460,782	Paterson
Salem	SW	365	60,346	Salem
Somerset	N cen.	307	198,372	Somerville
Sussex	N corner	527	77,528	Newton
Union	NE	103	543,116	Elizabeth
Warren	NW	362	73,960	Belvidere

[1] Area = land area.
[2] Fort Dix military reservation in NE Burlington co. and NW Ocean co.
[3] Includes Barnegat Bay, extending almost full length of its coastline.

History: Region first settled by Dutch and along Delaware river by Swedes; ceded to English as part of New Netherland 1664 and given the Latin name of Nova Caesarea; its E and N part (East Jersey) became a proprietary colony regranted by duke of York to Berkeley and Carteret and was sold to William Penn and associates 1682; its W and S part (West Jersey), or the lower counties on Delaware river, held by William Penn 1676–1702; became royal province 1702; scene of important battles Trenton, Princeton, and Monmouth of War of American Independence; held first constitutional convention 1776; adopted constitution 1844 (later amended); adopted new constitution 1947.

New Ken·sing·ton \-ˈken-ziŋ-tən, -ˈken(t)-siŋ-\. City, Westmoreland co., SW Pennsylvania, on Allegheny river 16 m. ENE of Pittsburgh; pop. (1970c) 20,312; aluminum products, conduits, water heaters, glass, textiles; coal mines; founded 1891.

New Kent \-ˈkent\. 1 County in E Virginia. See table at VIRGINIA.

2 Village, its ⊗.

New·kirk \ˈn(y)ü-ˌkərk\. City, ⊗ of Kay co., N Oklahoma, 14 m. N of Ponca City; pop. (1970c) 2173; gas and oil wells.

New Kowloon. See KOWLOON 2.

New Lanark. See LANARK 3.

New·land \ˈn(y)ü-lənd\. Town and resort, ⊗ of Avery co., W North Carolina; pop. (1970c) 524.

New Land. See NOVAYA ZEMLYA.

New Leb·a·non \-ˈleb-ə-nən\. Village, Montgomery co., SW Ohio, 11 m. W of Dayton; pop. (1970c) 4248.

New Len·ox \-ˈlen-əks, -iks\. Village, Will co., NE Illinois, 6 m. E of Joliet; pop. (1970c) 2855; roofing materials; diversified agriculture.

New Lex·ing·ton \-ˈlek-siŋ-tən\. Village, ⊗ of Perry co., SE cen. Ohio, 19 m. SSW of Zanesville; pop. (1970c) 2336; coal mines, gas and oil wells; agriculture.

New Lis·keard \-lis-ˈkärd\. Industrial town, Timiskaming dist., SE Ontario, Canada, 85 m. N of North Bay, near N end of Lake Timiskaming and N of Cobalt; pop. (1971p) 5487; summer resort; dairy products.

New Lon·don \-ˈlən-dən\. 1 County in Connecticut. See table at CONNECTICUT.

2 Industrial city, New London co., SE Connecticut, on Long Island Sound at mouth of Thames river 43 m. E of New Haven; pop. (1970c) 31,630; principal U.S. submarine base, with Submarine Officers' School and Underwater Sound Laboratory; manufactures clothing, printing presses, pharmaceuticals, engines, furniture, paper prod-

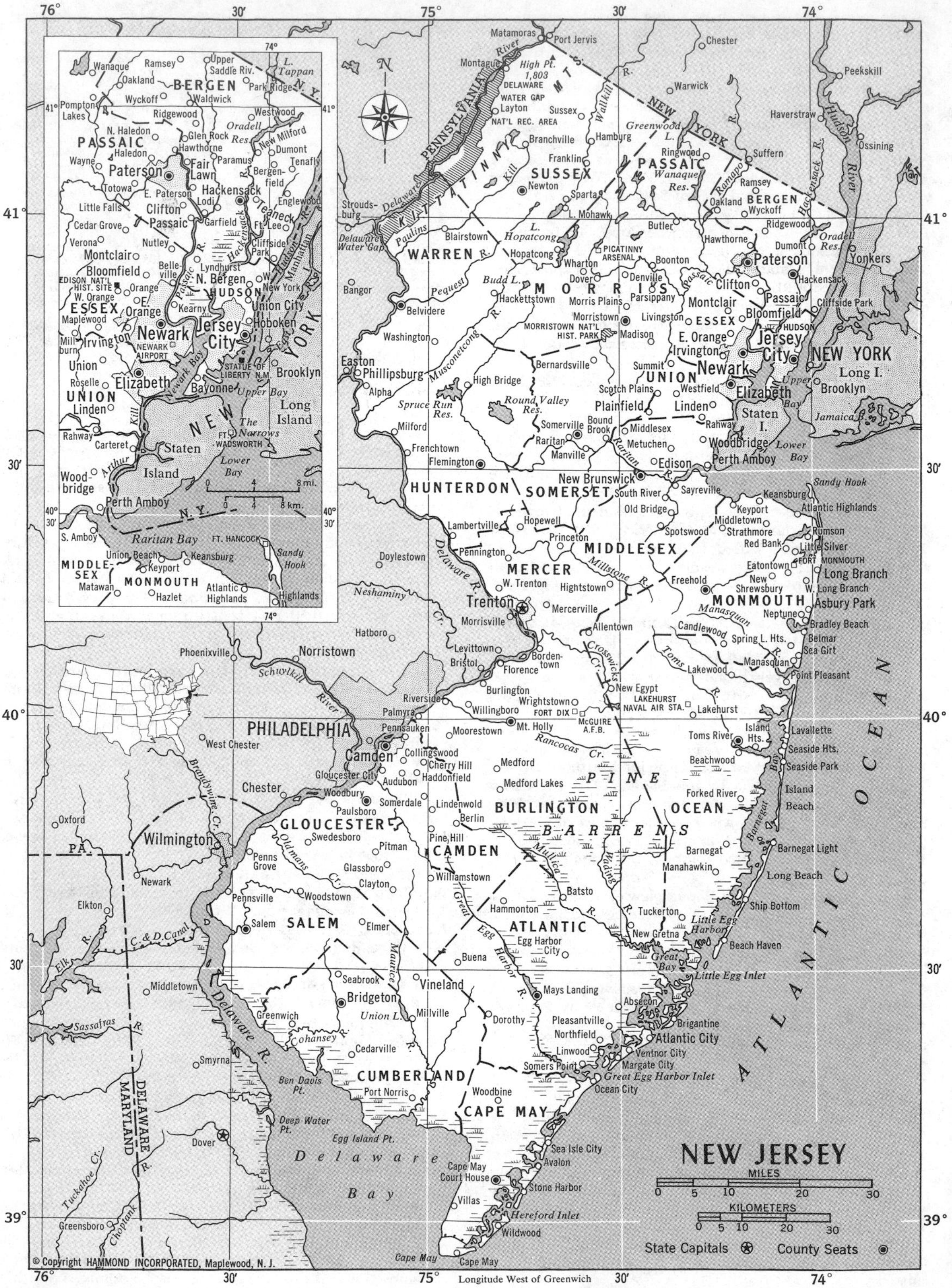
NEW JERSEY
MILES
0 5 10 20 30
KILOMETERS
0 5 10 20 30
State Capitals
County Seats
© Copyright HAMMOND INCORPORATED, Maplewood, N. J.
Longitude West of Greenwich
76°
30′
75°
74°
41°
40°
39°
ATLANTIC OCEAN
NEW YORK
PENNSYLVANIA
DELAWARE
MARYLAND
PA.
PHILADELPHIA
SUSSEX
PASSAIC
BERGEN
WARREN
MORRIS
ESSEX
HUDSON
UNION
HUNTERDON
SOMERSET
MIDDLESEX
MERCER
MONMOUTH
BURLINGTON
OCEAN
PINE BARRENS
GLOUCESTER
CAMDEN
SALEM
ATLANTIC
CUMBERLAND
CAPE MAY
KITTATINNY MTS.
Port Jervis
Matamoras
Montague
High Pt. 1,803
DELAWARE WATER GAP
Layton
NAT'L REC. AREA
Sussex
Hamburg
Branchville
Franklin
Newton
Sparta
L. Mohawk
Greenwood L.
Ringwood
Wanaque Res.
Ramsey
Oakland
Wyckoff
Ridgewood
Suffern
Chester
Warwick
Peekskill
Haverstraw
Ossining
Hudson River
Hackensack R.
Ramapo R.
Wallkill R.
Stroudsburg
Delaware Water Gap
Paulins Kill
Blairstown
L. Hopatcong
Hopatcong
PICATINNY ARSENAL
Wharton
Dover
Boonton
Denville
Morris Plains
Parsippany
Butler
Hawthorne
Paterson
Clifton
Passaic
Dumont
Oradell Res.
Yonkers
Hackensack
Cliffside Park
Montclair
Bloomfield
Livingston
Morristown
MORRISTOWN NAT'L HIST. PARK
Madison
E. Orange
Irvington
Newark
Jersey City
Elizabeth
Summit
Westfield
Linden
Rahway
Staten I.
Upper Bay
Long I.
Brooklyn
Jamaica Bay
Bangor
Belvidere
Pequest R.
Budd L.
Hackettstown
Musconetcong R.
Washington
Easton
Phillipsburg
Alpha
High Bridge
Spruce Run Res.
Round Valley Res.
Bernardsville
Somerville
Raritan
Manville
Bound Brook
Scotch Plains
Plainfield
Middlesex
Metuchen
Edison
Woodbridge
Perth Amboy
Lower Bay
Milford
Frenchtown
Flemington
New Brunswick
Raritan R.
South River
Sayreville
Old Bridge
Keansburg
Sandy Hook
Atlantic Highlands
Keyport
Middletown
Strathmore
Red Bank
Rumson
Little Silver
FORT MONMOUTH
Long Branch
W. Long Branch
Eatontown
New Shrewsbury
Asbury Park
Neptune
Bradley Beach
Belmar
Sea Girt
Spotswood
Freehold
Lambertville
Hopewell
Princeton
Pennington
Doylestown
W. Trenton
Hightstown
Millstone R.
Trenton
Mercerville
Morrisville
Neshaminy Cr.
Delaware R.
Hatboro
Allentown
Manasquan R.
Candlewood
Spring L. Hts.
Manasquan
Point Pleasant
Lakewood
Toms R.
Phoenixville
Norristown
Levittown
Bristol
Bordentown
Florence
Crosswicks Cr.
Schuylkill River
Burlington
Riverside
Palmyra
Willingboro
Wrightstown
FORT DIX
New Egypt
LAKEHURST NAVAL AIR STA.
Lakehurst
McGUIRE A.F.B.
Mt. Holly
Pennsauken
Moorestown
Rancocas Cr.
Toms River
Island Hts.
Lavallette
Seaside Hts.
Seaside Park
West Chester
Camden
Collingswood
Cherry Hill
Haddonfield
Medford
Medford Lakes
Beachwood
Island Beach
Barnegat Bay
Forked River
Gloucester City
Audubon
Woodbury
Paulsboro
Somerdale
Lindenwold
Berlin
Chester
Brandywine Cr.
Oxford
Wilmington
Swedesboro
Pitman
Pine Hill
Penns Grove
Glassboro
Clayton
Williamstown
Oldmans Cr.
Mullica R.
Wading R.
Barnegat
Barnegat Light
Manahawkin
Long Beach
Newark
Elkton
Pennsville
Woodstown
Batsto
Hammonton
Ship Bottom
Salem
Elmer
Great Egg Harbor R.
Tuckerton
Little Egg Harbor
New Gretna
Egg Harbor City
Beach Haven
Elk R.
C. & D. Canal
Buena
Great Bay
Little Egg Inlet
Seabrook
Bridgeton
Maurice R.
Vineland
Mays Landing
Middletown
Union L.
Millville
Absecon
Greenwich
Dorothy
Pleasantville
Northfield
Brigantine
Atlantic City
Sassafras R.
Cohansey R.
Cedarville
Linwood
Ventnor City
Margate City
Smyrna
Somers Point
Great Egg Harbor Inlet
Ocean City
Ben Davis Pt.
Port Norris
Woodbine
Deep Water Pt.
Egg Island Pt.
Dover
Delaware Bay
Sea Isle City
Avalon
Cape May Court House
Stone Harbor
Tuckahoe Cr.
Villas
Hereford Inlet
Wildwood
Greensboro
Choptank R.
Cape May
Wanaque
Upper Saddle Riv.
L. Tappan
N.Y.
Park Ridge
Waldwick
Pompton Lakes
Westwood
Glen Rock
N. Haledon
Haledon
Oradell Res.
New Milford
Dumont
Tenafly
Paramus
Wayne
Fair Lawn
Bergenfield
Totowa
E. Paterson
Lodi
Teaneck
Englewood
Little Falls
Garfield
Ft. Lee
Cedar Grove
Verona
Nutley
Cliffside Park
Belleville
Lyndhurst
N. Bergen
EDISON NAT'L HIST. SITE
W. Orange
Orange
Kearny
W. New York
Union City
Hoboken
Manhattan
East R.
Maplewood
Millburn
NEWARK AIRPORT
STATUE OF LIBERTY N.M.
Bayonne
Union
Roselle
Newark Bay
Kill Van Kull
NEW YORK
The Narrows
FT. WADSWORTH
Long Island
Carteret
Staten Island
Arthur Kill
Lower Bay
Wood-bridge
0 4 8 mi.
0 4 8 km.
40° 30′
S. Amboy
Raritan Bay
FT. HANCOCK
Union Beach
Keansburg
MIDDLE-SEX
MONMOUTH
Matawan
Hazlet
Atlantic Highlands
Highlands

ucts; shipbuilding (esp. submarines). Colby Junior Coll. for Women (1837), U.S. Coast Guard Academy (1876), Connecticut Coll. (1911), Mitchell Coll. (1938). Founded 1646; incorporated 1784; an early whaling port; burned by British under Benedict Arnold 1781. City and town coextensive.

3 City, ⊗ of Ralls co., NE Missouri; pop. (1970c) 967.

4 Village, Huron co., N Ohio, 23 m. N of Mansfield; pop. (1970c) 2336; clothing.

5 City, Outagamie and Waupaca cos., E Wisconsin, 18 m. NW of Appleton; pop. (1970c) 5801; lumber, dairy products; vegetables.

New Lynn \-ˈlin\. Borough, North I., New Zealand; pop. (1970e) 10,400.

New Mad·rid \-ˈmad-rəd\. 1 County in SE Missouri. See table at MISSOURI.

2 City, its ⊗, on Mississippi river 28 m. N of Caruthersville; pop. (1970c) 2719; suffered from severe earthquake 1811–12 which created Reelfoot Lake (*q.v.*) in Tennessee; during the Civil War, occupied by Confederate troops July 28, 1861 to Apr. 8, 1862.

New·man \ˈn(y)ü-mən\. City, Stanislaus co., cen. California, 21 m. S of Modesto; pop. (1970c) 2505; rose nurseries; diversified agriculture.

New Margelan. See FERGANA 2.

New·mar·ket \ˈn(y)ü-ˌmär-kət\. 1 Town, Rockingham co., SE New Hampshire, 9 m. W of Portsmouth; pop. (1970c) 3361.

2 Industrial town, York co., SE Ontario, Canada, 30 m. N of Toronto; pop. (1971p) 18,974; leather goods; dairy products; Friends' Coll.

3 Urban district, West Suffolk, England, on Cambridgeshire and Isle of Ely-West Suffolk boundary; pop. (1971p) 12,934; horse-racing center.

New Mar·ket \ˈn(y)ü-ˌmär-kət\. Town, S Shenandoah co., N Virginia; pop. (1970c) 718; victory of Confederates under Breckinridge over Union forces under Franz Sigel May 15, 1864.

New Mar·tins·ville \-ˈmärt-ᵊnz-ˌvil\. City, ⊗ of Wetzel co., N West Virginia, on Ohio river; pop. (1970c) 6528; glassware, chemicals.

New Mex·i·co \-ˈmek-si-ˌkō\. A southwestern state of U.S.A., bounded on N by Colorado, on E by Oklahoma and Texas, on S by Texas and the Mexican state of Chihuahua, on W by Arizona; 5th state in area, 121,666 sq. m. (land area 121,445 sq. m.); 37th state in population, (1970c) 1,016,000; ✱ Santa Fe; 47th state admitted to Union (1912).

Nicknames: Land of Enchantment; Sunshine State. *State flower:* Yucca. *Motto:* Crescit Eundo (It Grows as It Goes). *Rivers:* Rio Grande, bisecting state from N to S and forming for a few miles a boundary on the S with Texas; Pecos, rising in N cen. area and flowing SE across border into Texas. *Mountains:* In W crossed from N to S by Continental Divide; in S many small isolated ranges: in N the Sangre de Cristo Mts. including Wheeler Peak 13,161 ft., highest point in state. *Chief products:* Cotton, wheat, corn; livestock; oil, natural gas, potash, copper; manufacturing: food processing; chemical and petroleum products. *Chief cities:* Albuquerque, Santa Fe, Las Cruces, Roswell, Clovis. See *Table of States* at UNITED STATES. Divided into the following 32 counties (for pronunciation of their names, see their individual entries):

NAME	LOCATION	AREA[1] (sq. m.)	POP. (1970c)	CO. SEAT
Bernalillo	cen.	1,169	315,774	Albuquerque
Catron	W	6,897	2,198	Reserve
Chaves	SE	6,092	43,335	Roswell
Colfax	N	3,764	12,170	Raton
Curry	E	1,403	39,517	Clovis
De Baca	E cen.	2,356	2,547	Fort Sumner
Dona Ana	S	3,804	69,773	Las Cruces
Eddy[2]	SE	4,167	41,119	Carlsbad
Grant	SW	3,970	22,030	Silver City
Guadalupe	E cen.	2,998	4,765	Santa Rosa
Harding	NE	2,134	1,348	Mosquero
Hidalgo	SW corner	3,447	4,734	Lordsburg
Lea	SE corner	4,393	49,554	Lovington
Lincoln	cen.	4,858	7,560	Carrizozo
Los Alamos[3]	N cen.	108	15,198	Los Alamos
Luna	SW	2,957	11,706	Deming
McKinley	NW	5,454	42,391	Gallup
Mora	NE	1,940	4,673	Mora
Otero	S	6,638	41,097	Alamogordo
Quay	E	2,882	10,903	Tucumcari
Rio Arriba	N	5,853	25,170	Tierra Amarilla
Roosevelt	E	2,454	16,479	Portales
Sandoval	NW cen.	3,714	17,492	Bernalillo
San Juan	NW corner[4]	5,516	52,517	Aztec
San Miguel	NE cen.	4,741	21,951	Las Vegas
Santa Fe	N cen.	1,905	53,756	Santa Fe
Sierra	SW	4,166	7,189	Truth or Consequences
Socorro	cen.	6,603	9,763	Socorro
Taos	N	2,256	17,516	Taos
Torrance	cen.	3,346	5,290	Estancia
Union	NE corner	3,816	4,925	Clayton
Valencia	W	5,656	40,539	Los Lunas

[1]Area = land area.
[2]Carlsbad Caverns (national park) in SW part of county.
[3]Organized from parts of Sandoval and Santa Fe cos. 1949.
[4]Its NW point the only point in U.S. common to four states (New Mexico, Arizona, Utah, and Colorado).

History: Zuñi country discovered by Marcos de Niza 1539; explored by Coronado's expedition 1540 – 42; Spanish settlement begun by Oñate 1598; Santa Fe (*q.v.*) founded in 1609–10; governed by Mexico after 1821; part east of Rio Grande included in annexation of Texas 1845; rest, except for southern strip included in Gadsden Purchase 1853, ceded to U.S. by Mexico 1848 (Treaty of Guadalupe Hidalgo); organized as territory which included Arizona and part of Colorado 1850; held 1st constitutional convention 1889; admitted to Union as state Jan. 6, 1912.

New Mi·ami \-mī-ˈam-ē\. Village, Butler co., SW Ohio, 24 m. N of Cincinnati; pop. (1970c) 3273.

New Mil·ford \-ˈmil-fərd\. 1 Industrial town, Litchfield co., NW Connecticut; pop. (1970c) 14,601; summer resort; paper products, electronic components; dairy farms; settled 1707, incorporated 1712.

2 Borough, Bergen co., NE corner of New Jersey, 8 m. ENE of Paterson; pop. (1970c) 19,149.

New Mills \-ˈmilz\. Urban district, Derbyshire, N cen. England, 12 m. SE of Manchester; pop. (1971p) 9165.

New·nan \ˈn(y)ü-nən\. City, ⊗ of Coweta co., W Georgia, 35 m. SW of Atlanta; pop. (1970c) 11,205; textiles, plastics, lumber; peanuts.

New Neth·er·land \-ˈneth-ər-lənd\. Dutch colony in North America 1613–64, occupying lands bordering the Hudson river and later the lower Delaware river; conquered by English 1664 and renamed New York after its proprietor, duke of York; ✱ New Amsterdam. See NEW YORK 1.

New Nor·folk \-ˈnȯr-fək\. Town, SE Tasmania, Australia, on Derwent river 20 m. NNW of Hobart; pop. (1970e) 10,900.

New Or·ange \-ˈȯr-inj, -ˈär-\. Name given New York City 1673–74 when reconquered by the Dutch.

New Or·le·ans \-ˈȯr-lē-ənz, -ˈȯrl-(y)ənz, -ȯr-ˈlēnz\. City, ⊗ of Orleans parish, SE Louisiana, bet. the Mississippi river and Lake Pontchartrain; pop. (1970c) 593,471; largest city in the state; transportation center; major deepwater port, exporting cotton, rice, oil, sulfur, and petrochemicals; cotton and rice market; produces furniture, aluminum, clothing, fish oil and meal, paper products, soap and detergents, molasses, chemicals, plumbing supplies; shipbuilding, oil and sulfur refining. Notable tourist center, principal attractions include the annual Mardi Gras celebration. Tulane Univ. of Louisiana (1834), Loyola

NEW MEXICO
108°
106°
104°
38°
36°
34°
32°
UTAH
COLORADO
OKLA.
TEXAS
ARIZONA
MEXICO
CHIHUAHUA
SONORA
Monticello
Mt. Wilson 14,246
Silverton
SAN JUAN MTS.
Crestone Pk. 14,294
GREAT SAND DUNES NAT'L MON.
Huerfano R.
La Junta
Center
Del Norte
Monte Vista
Alamosa
Blanca Pk. 14,317
Walsenburg
Purgatoire R.
Dolores R.
Animas R.
Rio Grande
HOVENWEEP NAT'L MON.
YUCCA HOUSE N.M.
Cortez
MESA VERDE NAT'L PARK
Durango
Pagosa Sprs.
UTE MTN.
Only point in U. S. common to 4 states.
SO. UTE IND. RES.
Trinidad
Raton
CAPULIN MTN. NAT'L MON.
Dry Cimarron R.
IND. RES.
AZTEC RUINS N.M.
Aztec
Farmington
Shiprock
Bloomfield
Blanco
Navajo Res.
Dulce
Chama
Tierra Amarilla
JICARILLA IND. RES.
TAOS
Questa
Wheeler Pk. 13,161
SANGRE DE CRISTO MTS.
COLFAX
Cimarron
Eagle Nest L.
Maxwell
UNION
Clayton
NAVAJO
CHUSKA MTS.
San Juan R.
Chaco R.
SAN JUAN
Toadlena
INDIAN RESERVATION
RIO ARRIBA
Canjilon
El Rito
Arroyo Hondo
PUEBLO
Taos
Ranches of Taos
Springer
Carrizo Cr.
CHACO CANYON NAT'L MON.
DIVIDE
La Jara
Dixon
I. R.
Penasco
Velarde
San Juan Pueblo
Espanola
Truchas
MORA
Wagon Mound
FT. UNION N.M.
Mora
Roy
HARDING
Mosquero
Ute Cr.
CANYON DE CHELLY NAT'L MON.
Cuba
LOS ALAMOS
Los Alamos
BANDELIER NAT'L MON.
Chimayo
PUEBLO I. R.
Tesuque
Santa Fe
SANDOVAL
Jemez Pueblo
PUEBLO IND. RES.
San Felipe
Santo Domingo Pueblo
Glorieta
Pecos
PECOS NAT'L MON.
Watrous
Las Vegas
Rowe
SAN MIGUEL
Conchas Res.
CONCHAS DAM
Logan
Ute Res.
Canadian R.
Crownpoint
CONTINENTAL
Gamerco
Puerco R.
FT. WINGATE ARMY DEPOT
Gallup
Manuelito
Thoreau
McKINLEY
San Mateo
Mt. Taylor 11,389
Rio Puerco
Corrales
Bernalillo
SANTA FE
Tucumcari
Bluewater
Milan
Grants
Zuni R.
San Rafael
EL MORRO N. M.
Paguate
Acomita
Acoma
PUEBLO IND. RES.
Zuni
ZUNI IND. RES.
Lava Beds
BERNALILLO
KIRTLAND A.F.B.
Albuquerque
Isleta
Tijeras
Moriarty
MANZANO MTS.
PUEBLO IND. RES.
Anton Chico
Pecos
Santa Rosa
GUADALUPE
QUAY
Los Lunas
Estancia
Laguna del Perro
Encino
Alamogordo Res.
Blanco Cr.
VALENCIA
Belen
Jarales
Mountainair
Vaughn
CURRY
Melrose
Clovis
CANNON A.F.B.
Texico
Quemado
TORRANCE
Ft. Sumner
DE BACA
GRAN QUIVIRA NAT'L MON.
Corona
Portales
Salt L.
Magdalena
Lemitar
Socorro
CATRON
Fifteenmile
SOCORRO
San Antonio
Elida
ROOSEVELT
LINCOLN
Arroyo
LLANO
Reserve
San Francisco R.
Whitewater Baldy 10,892
BLACK RA.
Alamosa R.
Elephant Butte Res.
JORNADA DEL MUERTO
WHITE SANDS MISSILE RANGE
Lava Beds
Carrizozo
Capitan
Salt Cr.
Lincoln
Roswell
Sierra Blanca Pk. 12,003
SACRAMENTO MTS.
Ruidoso
Rio Hondo
MESCALERO APACHE IND. RES.
CHAVES
Tatum
GILA CLIFF DWELLINGS NAT'L MON.
Truth or Consequences
Mescalero
Dexter
Hagerman
ESTACADO
Buckhorn
GRANT
Caballo Res.
SAN ANDRES MTS.
Tularosa
TULAROSA VALLEY
Alamogordo
Lovington
Silver City
Hanover
Santa Rita
Bayard
Central
Hurley
Gila R.
SIERRA
Rincon
WHITE SANDS NAT'L MON.
HOLLOMAN A.F.B.
Artesia
Rio Penasco
Hobbs
LEA
Oil Center
L. McMillan
EDDY
Hatch
DONA ANA
Las Cruces
OTERO
L. Avalon
Carlsbad
Eunice
Lordsburg
DIVIDE
Deming
Mesilla
University Park
Loving
LUNA
La Mesa
Anthony
CARLSBAD CAVERNS NAT'L PK.
Jal
Animas
HIDALGO
CONTINENTAL
Columbus
La Union
El Paso
TEXAS
GUADALUPE MTS. NAT'L PARK
GUADALUPE MTS.
Red Bluff L.
Kermit
FT. BLISS
CHAMIZAL NAT'L MEM.
Ciudad Juárez
Salt Lakes
Delaware Cr.
Pecos R.
Fabens
Pecos
Grandes
Casas
L. Guzmán
Toyah Lake
Rio
L. Sta. María
MILES
0 20 40 60 80 100
KILOMETERS
0 20 40 60 80 100
M E X I C O
State Capital
County Seats
N
© Copyright HAMMOND INCORPORATED, Maplewood, N. J.
Longitude West of Greenwich

Univ. (1849), Dillard Univ. (1869), Newcomb Coll. (1886), Saint Mary's Dominican Coll. (1910), Our Lady of Holy Cross Coll. (1916), Delgado Coll. (1921), Notre Dame Seminary (1923), Mount Carmel Junior Coll. (1924), Louisiana State Univ. at New Orleans (1958).

History: Founded 1718 by Sieur de Bienville, and made capital of the colony a few years later; ceded to Spain, effective 1764; ceded back to France 1803 and then to U.S. 1803 by Napoleon; incorporated 1805; capital of Louisiana 1812–49; on Jan. 8, 1815, scene of victory of U.S. troops under Andrew Jackson over British; captured by Union naval force under Admiral Farragut 1862, and occupied by Union troops under Gen. Benjamin F. Butler.

New Paltz \ˈn(y)ü-ˌpȯlts\. Village, Ulster co., SE New York, 10 m. W of Poughkeepsie; pop. (1970c) 6058; State Univ. of New York Coll. at New Paltz (1828).

New Phil·a·del·phia \-ˌfil-ə-ˈdel-fyə, -fē-ə\. City, ⊗ of Tuscarawas co., E Ohio, 20 m. S of Canton; pop. (1970c) 15,184; tools, ceramics, machinery.

New Plym·outh \-ˈplim-əth\. **1** Early name (The Colony of New Plymouth) of Plymouth, Massachusetts, 1620–91. See PLYMOUTH 4.

2 City, W North I., New Zealand, on Tasman Sea 160 m. N of Wellington; pop. (1970e) 33,100; one of chief dairy centers of New Zealand; founded 1841.

New·port \ˈn(y)ü-ˌpō(ə)rt, -ˌpȯ(ə)rt, -pərt\. **1** County in Rhode Island. See table at RHODE ISLAND.

2 City, ⊗ of Jackson co., NE Arkansas, on White river 38 m. SW of Jonesboro; pop. (1970c) 7225; canneries.

3 Town, ⊗ of Vermillion co., W Indiana; pop. (1970c) 708.

4 City, a ⊗ of Campbell co., N Kentucky, on Ohio river just E of Covington; pop. (1970c) 25,998; steel; founded 1790; incorporated as city 1835.

5 Town, Penobscot co., E cen. Maine, 25 m. W of Bangor; pop. (1970c) 2260; resort.

6 Village, Washington co., E Minnesota, 6 m. SSE of St. Paul; pop. (1970c) 2922.

7 Manufacturing town, ⊗ of Sullivan co., SW New Hampshire, 8 m. E of Claremont; pop. (1970c) 5899; lumber; resort; diversified agriculture.

8 City, ⊗ of Lincoln co., W Oregon, on Pacific Ocean 41 m. W of Corvallis; pop. (1970c) 5188; salmon fisheries; seashore resort.

9 Borough, Perry co., S cen. Pennsylvania, 21 m. NW of Harrisburg; pop. (1970c) 1747; settled 1789.

10 City and port of entry, ⊗ of Newport co., SE Rhode Island, on S end of Rhode I. (island) at mouth of Narragansett Bay; pop. (1970c) 34,562; major naval base, including U.S. Naval Underwater Ordnance Station, U.S. Naval War College (1885), and numerous other maintenance and educational facilities incl. U.S. Naval Officer Candidate School; tourism. Formerly a fashionable summer resort; now has annual jazz festival. Salve Regina Coll. (1934), Vernon Court Junior Coll. (1963).

History: Settled 1639 by religious refugees from Massachusetts Bay; united with Portsmouth 1640; joined "Incorporation of Providence Plantations" (chartered 1644), separated 1651–54; haven for religious refugees (including Quakers and Jews); held by British 1776–79; headquarters of Rochambeau and troops 1780; one of capitals of Rhode Island until 1900.

11 Town, ⊗ of Cocke co., E Tennessee, 18 m. SSE of Morristown; pop. (1970c) 7328; furniture; canneries.

12 City, ⊗ of Orleans co., N Vermont, on S end of Lake Memphremagog; pop. (1970c) 4664; machine tools, furniture; lake resort.

13 Town, ⊗ of Pend Oreille co., NE corner of Washington, on Idaho border; pop. (1970c) 1418.

14 Municipal borough, S England, ⊗ of Isle of Wight in English Channel 10 m. WSW of Portsmouth; pop. (1971p) 22,286; plastics; brewing; received first charter 12th cent.

15 County borough, Monmouthshire, SE Wales, on the Usk 20 m. WNW of Bristol, England; pop. (1971p) 112,-048; large modern port, exporting metal goods; manufactures steel, aluminum, chemicals, electrical equipment; chartered in 14th cent.; Chartist riots 1839.

Newport Beach. City, Orange co., SW California, on Pacific Ocean 18 m. SE of Long Beach; pop. (1970c) 49,422; residential and resort community; electronic components, fiberglass boats, plastics; incorporated 1906.

Newport News \-ˈn(y)üz\. Independent city, SE Virginia, at mouth of James river at entrance to Hampton Roads 11 m. NNW of Norfolk; area 75 sq. m.; pop. (1970c) 138,177; with Norfolk and Portsmouth constitutes Port of Hampton Roads. Major seaport with modern facilities, handling coal, bulk liquids, and general cargo; one of the major shipbuilding and repairing centers of the U.S.; textiles, paper products, radar and electronic equipment; oil refineries, fish canneries, railroad shops; Mariner's Museum (1930). Settled c. 1621; laid out as city 1882; incorporated 1896; important embarkation point in both World Wars; absorbed city of Warwick (former Warwick co.) 1958.

New Port Rich·ey \-ˈrich-ē\. City, Pasco co., W cen. Florida, 20 m. NW of Tampa; pop. (1970c) 6098; citrus fruit.

New Prague \-ˈprāg\. City, Le Sueur and Scott cos., S Minnesota, 22 m. NW of Faribault; pop. (1970c) 2680.

New Prov·i·dence \-ˈpräv-əd-ən(t)s, -ə-ˌden(t)s\. **1** Borough, Union co., NE New Jersey, 8 m. SSE of Morristown; pop. (1970c) 13,796; diamond tools; fruit farms.

2 One of the Bahama Is., in the Atlantic Ocean bet. Andros I. on the W and Eleuthera I. on the E; dist. area 80 sq. m.; dist. pop. (1963c) 80,907; contains city of Nassau, ✱ of Bahama Is.; site of British air base in World War II.

New·quay \ˈn(y)ü-ˌkē\. Urban district, Cornwall, SW England, on Atlantic Ocean 42 m. W of Plymouth; pop. (1971p) 14,963; seaside resort.

New Quebec \-kwi-ˈbek\ *or Fr.* **Nou·veau–Qué·bec** \nü-vō-kā-bek\. District, N Saguenay co., N and E Quebec, Canada, comprising the region N of Eastmain river and bet. Hudson Bay on the W and Labrador on the E, touching Hudson Strait and Ungava Bay on the N; area about 300,000 sq. m. Organized 1912, constituting in part former region of Ungava (*q.v.*), divided 1927 bet. Quebec prov. and Labrador (Newfoundland); includes Ungava Penin. in the N.

New Quebec Crater *or Fr.* **Cra·tère du Nou·veau–Qué·bec** \krä-ter-dᵫ-nü-vō-kā-bek\ *or formerly* **Chubb Crater** \ˈchəb-\. Circular depression, N Quebec, Canada; 1300 ft. deep; has a diameter of ab. 2 m.; theories regarding its origin include (1) meteoric impact, (2) collapse of a liquid-supported dome.

New Republic *or Du.* **Nieu·we Re·pu·bliek** \ˌnē-və-ˌrā-pə-ˈblēk\. Republic (1884–88) formed by Boers from part of Zululand; capital Vryheid; now in Natal.

New Rich·mond \-ˈrich-mənd\. **1** Village, Clermont co., SW Ohio, on Ohio river SE of Cincinnati; pop. (1970c) 2650.

2 City, St. Croix co., W Wisconsin, 35 m. WNW of Menomonie; pop. (1970c) 3707; flour, cheese.

New River. **1** River, South I., New Zealand. See ORETI.

2 Name of several rivers. See NEW.

New River Inlet. See NEW 1.

New Roads. Town, ⊗ of Pointe Coupee parish, SE cen. Louisiana, on Mississippi river; pop. (1970c) 3945; fisheries.

New Ro·chelle \ˌn(y)ü-rə-ˈshel\. City, Westchester co., SE New York on Long Island Sound; pop. (1970c) 75,385; purchased 1688 by Huguenots; incorporated as city 1899;

Coll. of New Rochelle (1904), Iona Coll. (1940); Fort Slocum nearby.

New Rock·ford \-'räk-fərd\. City, ⊗ of Eddy co., E cen. North Dakota, SSW of Devils Lake (city); pop. (1970c) 1969; grain, stock, and dairy farms.

New Rom·ney \-'räm-nē\. Municipal borough, Kent, SE England, in Romney Marsh district; pop. (1971p) 3414; a seaport town, one of the Cinque Ports (*q.v.*).

New Ross \-'rȯs\. Urban district, SW co. Wexford, SE Eire, on Barrow river; pop. (1971p) 4775; salmon fisheries, brewing, tanning; site of ancient Dominican abbey.

New Russia *or Russ.* **No·vo·ros·si·ya** \ˌnȯ-və-'rȯs-ē-yə\. A former region (18th and 19th cents.) of cen. and S Ukraine (now Ukrainian S.S.R.); ab. 75,000 sq. m.; including the territory around modern Dnepropetrovsk, Kherson, Odessa, and the Crimean Oblast; its capital 1765–89 was Kremenchug; its cultural capital Odessa (*q.v.*).

New·ry \'n(y)u̇(ə)r-ē\. 1 Short canalized stream, SE Northern Ireland; flows S bet. cos. Down and Armagh into Carlingford Lough.

2 Urban district, co. Down, SE Northern Ireland, 38 m. SW of Belfast, on Newry river, part extending into co. Armagh; pop. (1971p) 11,371; has canal connections with Carlingford Lough, Bann river, and Lough Neagh; granite quarrying.

New Sa·lem \-'sā-ləm\. 1 Restored pioneer village, Sangamon co., cen. Illinois, 15 m. NW of Springfield; home of Abraham Lincoln 1831–37; in **New Salem State Park.**

2 Town, Pike co., W Illinois; pop. (1970c) 165.

New Sarum. See SALISBURY 6.

New Shore·ham \-'shō(ə)r-əm, -'shȯ(ə)r-\. Town, coextensive with Block Island (village), Washington co., SE Rhode Island; pop. (1970c) 489; legal name of Block Island, but seldom used.

New Shrews·bury \-'sh(r)üz-ˌber-ē, -b(ə-)rē\. Borough, Monmouth co., E cen. New Jersey; pop. (1970c) 8395.

New Si·be·ri·an Island \-sī-ˌbir-ē-ən-\ *or Russ.* **No·va·ya Si·bir** \ˌnȯ-və-yə-sə-'bi(ə)r\. Large island of New Siberian Is., in E part; 90 m. long by 40 m. wide.

New Siberian Islands *or Russ.* **No·vo·si·bir·ski·ye Ostro·va** \ˌnȯ-və-sə-'bir-ski-yə-ˌə-strə-'vä\. Island group in Arctic Ocean bet. Laptev Sea and East Siberian Sea, a part of Yakutsk A.S.S.R., Russian S.F.S.R., U.S.S.R.; chief islands Kotelny, Faddeyevski, and New Siberian I.; the Lyakhov Is. (*q.v.*) are by some included in the group. First visited 1712; explored 1770 ff.; site of permanent scientific stations since 1927–30.

New Smyr·na Beach \-ˌsmər-nə-\. City, Volusia co., E Florida, on Atlantic Ocean 15 m. S of Daytona Beach; pop. (1970c) 10,580; bathing, boating, and fishing resort; Spanish mission (1696); before 1930 known as New Smyrna.

New South Wales. State, SE Australia; 309,433 sq. m.; pop. (1970e) 4,567,000; ✱ Sydney. *Physical features:* Southern section of Great Dividing Range (Eastern Highlands) covers E third of state; highest point (at S end) Mt. Kosciusko 7316 ft.; nearly all of state drained by the Darling and its tributaries and the Murray (with Murrumbidgee and Lachlan rivers); Port Jackson, harbor of Sydney, one of finest in world; also good harbors at Newcastle and Jervis Bay. *Chief products:* Wheat, oats, corn, rice, grapes; coal, silver, lead, zinc; livestock raising (esp. sheep); Australia's most industrialized state: iron and steel, chemicals, textiles; food processing. *Chief cities:* Sydney, Newcastle, Wollongong, Cessnock, and Blue Mountains.

History: Discovered by Capt. Cook 1770; first settled at Botany Bay 1788 by marines and convicts, but soon transferred to Port Jackson (later Sydney); Parramatta and other towns W of Sydney founded before 1798; Newcastle and Maitland soon after. Included all of continent except Western Australia (boundary estab. 1831); interior, esp. Blue Mts. region, opened up 1840–50; South Australia (1836), Victoria (1851), Queensland (1859), and Northern Territory (1863) set up as separate colonies; became part of Commonwealth of Australia 1901; ceded 1911 Yass-Canberra (see YASS) dist. as site for Federal Capital Territory and in 1917 area on Jervis Bay; a proposed new state in N part was rejected by voters 1967.

New Spain. Former Spanish viceroyalty in North America, including SW United States, Mexico, Central America N of Panama, West Indies, and also the Philippines in the W Pacific Ocean. Mexico City was the seat of government 1521–1821.

New Sweden. Swedish colony on the Delaware river; extended from site of Trenton, New Jersey, to mouth of the river, mostly on W side of the river; founded 1638 when Fort Christina (on site of Wilmington) was built; taken by the Dutch 1655.

New Territories. See HONG KONG.

New·ton \'n(y)üt-ᵊn\. 1 Name of counties in six states of the U.S. See tables at ARKANSAS, GEORGIA, INDIANA, MISSISSIPPI, MISSOURI, TEXAS.

2 City, ⊗ of Baker co., SW Georgia; pop. (1970c) 624.

3 City, ⊗ of Jasper co., SE cen. Illinois, 20 m. N of Olney; pop. (1970c) 3024; clothing, beverages.

4 Industrial city, ⊗ of Jasper co., S cen. Iowa, 30 m. E of Des Moines; pop. (1970c) 15,619; construction machinery, dairy products.

5 City, ⊗ of Harvey co., SE cen. Kansas, 35 m. E of Hutchinson; pop. (1970c) 15,439; railroad shops, oil wells; grain, dairy, livestock farms; Bethel Coll. (1887) in North Newton.

6 Residential city, Middlesex co., NE Massachusetts, 7 m. W of Boston; pop. (1970c) 91,263; includes 14 villages, among them **Newton Corner, Newton Centre, Newton Highlands, Newton Upper Falls, Newton Lower Falls, West Newton, New·ton·ville** \'n(y)üt-ᵊn-ˌvil\; Mount Ida Junior Coll. (1889) in Newton Centre; Newton Coll. of the Sacred Heart (1946); Mount Alvernia Coll. (1959).

7 City, Newton co., E cen. Mississippi, 30 m. W of Meridian; pop. (1970c) 3556; sawmills; Clarke Memorial Coll. (1903).

8 Town, ⊗ of Sussex co., N corner of New Jersey, 23 m. NW of Morristown; pop. (1970c) 7297; slate quarries; Du Bosco Coll. (1929).

9 Town, ⊗ of Catawba co., W cen. North Carolina, 20 m. WSW of Statesville; pop. (1970c) 7857; textiles, fertilizer; dairy farms.

10 City, ⊗ of Newton co., E Texas; pop. (1970c) 1529.

Newton, Mount. Peak, E Spitsbergen, Norway; 5617 ft.; highest point on the island.

Newton Ab·bot \-'ab-ət\. Urban district, Devonshire, SW England, on Teign estuary 15 m. S of Exeter; pop. (1971p) 19,367; William of Orange proclaimed king here 1688.

Newton Centre *and* **Newton Corner.** See NEWTON 6.

Newton Falls. City, Trumbull co., NE Ohio, on Mahoning river 17 m. WNW of Youngstown; pop. (1970c) 5378.

Newton Highlands. See NEWTON 6.

Newton–le–Wil·lows \-lə-'wil-(ˌ)ōz, -əz\ *or* **Newton in Ma·ker·field** \-'mā-kər-ˌfēld\. Urban district, Lancashire, NW England, 15 m. W of Manchester; pop. (1971p) 22,380; paper, glass; iron foundries.

Newton Lower Falls, Newton Upper Falls, Newtonville. See NEWTON 6.

New·town \'n(y)ü-ˌtau̇n\. 1 Town, N cen. Fairfield co., SW Connecticut, on Housatonic river; pop. (1970c) 16,142; rubber and plastic products; dairy and fruit farms.

2 Former town, Queens co., SE New York, on Long I.; settled 1652; became part of Connecticut 1664, part of New York state 1665; since 1898 part of Queens borough in New York City.

3 City, New York. See ELMIRA 1.

4 Borough, Bucks co., SE Pennsylvania, 22 m. NE of Philadelphia; pop. (1970c) 2216; Bucks County Community Coll. (1965).

New Town. See LAS VEGAS 2.

New·town·abbey \ˌn(y)üt-ᵊn-ˈab-ē\. Urban district, co. Antrim, Northern Ireland, just N of Belfast; pop. (1971p) 57,846; textiles; was constituted 1958.

Newtown and Llan·llwch·ai·arn \-ˌ(h)lan-ˌ(h)lük-ˈhī-ˌärn\. Urban district, Montgomeryshire, E Wales; pop. (1971p) 6122; comprises parishes of Llanllwchaiarn and Newtown, Newtown being terminus of Montgomery Canal; birthplace of Robert Owen.

New·town·ards \ˌn(y)üt-ᵊn-ˈärdz\. Municipal borough, co. Down, SE Northern Ireland, 9 m. E of Belfast at N end of Strangford Lough; pop. (1971p) 15,356; linen, hosiery, sheet metal, aircraft parts; on site of Dominican priory (1244); NE of the town are ruins of an abbey said to have been founded by St. Finian c. 550.

Newtown But·ler \ˌn(y)üt-ᵊn-ˈbət-lər\. Village, co. Fermanagh, SW Northern Ireland, 16 m. SE of Enniskillen; site of a battle 1689 in which Enniskillen Protestants defeated Jacobite force.

New Towne \ˈn(y)ü-ˌtau̇n\. See CAMBRIDGE 3.

New Ulm \-ˈəlm\. City, ⊗ of Brown co., S Minnesota, on Minnesota river 24 m. WNW of Mankato; pop. (1970c) 13,051; cheese, flour, beer; twice under attack during the Sioux uprising 1862; Dr. Martin Luther Coll. (1884).

New Urgench. See URGENCH 1.

New Valley. Governorate of Egypt. See table at EGYPT.

New·ville \ˈn(y)ü-ˌvil\. Industrial borough, Cumberland co., S Pennsylvania, 21 m. NE of Chambersburg; pop. (1970c) 1631.

New Wa·ter·ford \-ˈwȯt-ər-fərd, -ˈwät-\. Town, Cape Breton co., E Nova Scotia, Canada, on Atlantic Ocean 8 m. N of Sydney; pop. (1971p) 9549; ships coal.

New West·min·ster \-ˈwes(t)-ˌmin(t)-stər\. City, SW British Columbia, Canada, on Fraser river 12 m. ESE of Vancouver and 16 m. from river's mouth; pop. (1971p) 42,083; suburb of Vancouver; ships timber, lead, zinc, fertilizer; processes lumber, vegetables, salmon; capital of British Columbia 1860–66.

New Whatcom. See BELLINGHAM 2.

New White·land \-ˈhwīt-lənd, -ˈwīt-\. Town, Johnson co., cen. Indiana, 6 m. N of Franklin; pop. (1970c) 4200.

New Wil·ming·ton \-ˈwil-miŋ-tən\. Borough, Lawrence co., W Pennsylvania, 8 m. N of New Castle; pop. (1970c) 2721; Westminster Coll. (1852).

New Windsor. See WINDSOR 11.

New World. The land of the Western Hemisphere; term first used by Peter Martyr, Italian historian, author of *De Rebus Oceanicis et Novo Orbe* (1516) giving first account of discovery of America.

New York \-ˈyȯ(ə)rk\. **1** A middle Atlantic state of U.S.A., bounded on N by Lake Ontario and the Canadian provinces of Ontario and Quebec, on E by Vermont, Massachusetts, and Connecticut, on S by Atlantic Ocean, New Jersey, and Pennsylvania, on W by Pennsylvania, Lake Erie, and the Canadian province of Ontario; 30th state in area, 49,576 sq. m. (land area 47,834 sq. m.), in addition to this area New York has also 4376 sq. m. of water of the Great Lakes; 2d state in population, (1970c) 18,241,266; ❋ Albany; an original state of the Union, the 11th to ratify the Federal Constitution (July 26, 1788).

Nicknames: Empire State; Excelsior State. *State flower:* Rose. *Motto:* Excelsior (Ever Upward). *Rivers:* Hudson, in E area, flowing into Atlantic Ocean at New York City, and in the S forming boundary bet. New York and New Jersey; St. Lawrence, forming N boundary bet. New York and Canadian province of Ontario; Delaware, forming section of S boundary bet. New York and Pennsylvania; Niagara, forming W boundary bet. New York and Canadian province of Ontario. *Mountains:* Adirondacks (in NE) and Catskills (in E). Highest point Mount Marcy 5344 ft. in Essex co. in the Adirondacks. *Chief products:* Vegetables, fruit; dairy products; cement, gypsum, zinc, iron ore; manufacturing: printing and publishing, food processing; apparel, primary and fabricated metals, electrical machinery, transportation equipment, chemicals; finance. *Chief cities:* New York City, Buffalo, Rochester, Yonkers, Syracuse, Albany. See *Table of States* at UNITED STATES. Divided into the following 62 counties (for pronunciation of their names, see their individual entries):

NAME	LOCATION	AREA[1] (sq. m.)	POP. (1970c)	CO. SEAT
Albany	E	526	285,618	Albany
Allegany	SW	1,047	46,458	Belmont
Bronx[2]	SE	41	1,472,216	Bronx or the Bronx
Broome	S	714	221,815	Binghamton
Cattaraugus	SW	1,334	81,666	Little Valley
Cayuga	cen.	698	77,439	Auburn
Chautauqua	SW corner	1,081	147,305	Mayville
Chemung	S	415	101,537	Elmira
Chenango	S cen.	909	46,368	Norwich
Clinton	NE corner	1,059	72,934	Plattsburg
Columbia	SE	645	51,519	Hudson
Cortland	cen.	502	45,894	Cortland
Delaware	S	1,458	44,718	Delhi
Dutchess	SE	814	222,295	Poughkeepsie
Erie	W[3]	1,058	1,113,491	Buffalo
Essex	NE	1,823	34,631	Elizabethtown
Franklin	NE	1,674	43,931	Malone
Fulton	E	498	52,637	Johnstown
Genesee	W	501	58,722	Batavia
Greene	SE	654	33,136	Catskill
Hamilton	NE cen.	1,735	4,714	Lake Pleasant
Herkimer	NE cen.	1,435	67,440	Herkimer
Jefferson	N	1,294	88,508	Watertown
Kings[2]	SE	70	2,601,852	Brooklyn
Lewis	N cen.	1,291	23,644	Lowville
Livingston	W	638	54,041	Geneseo
Madison	cen.	661	62,864	Wampsville
Monroe	W	675	711,917	Rochester
Montgomery	E	408	55,883	Fonda
Nassau	SE (W Long I.)	289	1,428,838	Mineola
New York[2]	SE	23	1,524,541	New York
Niagara	W[3]	532	235,720	Lockport
Oneida	cen.	1,224	273,037	Rome, Utica
Onondaga	cen.	747	472,835	Syracuse
Ontario[4]	W	651	78,849	Canandaigua
Orange	SE	833	220,558	Goshen
Orleans	W	396	37,305	Albion
Oswego	cen.	964	100,897	Oswego, Pulaski
Otsego[5]	cen.	1,013	56,181	Cooperstown
Putnam	SE	232	56,696	Carmel
Queens[2]	SE	108	1,987,174	Jamaica
Rensselaer	E	665	152,510	Troy
Richmond[2]	SE	58	295,443	Saint George
Rockland	SE	176	229,903	New City
St. Lawrence	N	2,768	111,991	Canton
Saratoga	E	818	121,764	Ballston Spa
Schenectady	E	207	161,078	Schenectady
Schoharie	E	624	24,750	Schoharie
Schuyler[6]	SW cen.	330	16,737	Watkins Glen
Seneca	W cen.	338	35,083	Ovid, Waterloo
Steuben	S	1,410	99,546	Bath
Suffolk	SE[7]	929	1,127,030	Riverhead
Sullivan	SE	980	52,580	Monticello
Tioga	S	524	46,513	Owego
Tompkins[8]	S cen.	482	77,064	Ithaca
Ulster	SE	1,141	141,241	Kingston
Warren	E[9]	887	49,402	Lake George
Washington	E[9]	836	52,725	Hudson Falls
Wayne	W	606	79,404	Lyons
Westchester	SE	443	894,406	White Plains
Wyoming	W	598	37,688	Warsaw
Yates	W	343	19,831	Penn Yan

[1]Area = land area.
[2]Each of these 5 counties is coextensive with one of the 5 boroughs of New York City and 2 of them are also coextensive with 2 islands, as follows: Bronx co. coextensive with Bronx borough, Kings co. (occupying W corner of Long I.) with Brooklyn borough, New York co. with Manhattan borough and with Manhattan I., Queens co. (on W part of Long I.) with Queens borough, Richmond co. with Richmond borough and with Staten I.
[3]Niagara river (bet. Lakes Ontario and Erie) forms W boundary of Niagara co. and NW boundary of Erie co., with American Fall (Niagara Falls) in former county.
[4]Includes most of Canandaigua Lake (cen.).
[5]Includes Otsego Lake in N cen. part.
[6]Includes lower part of Seneca Lake.
[7]Occupies E part (more than half) of Long I. and includes smaller islands off its coast.
[8]Includes lower part of Cayuga Lake.
[9]Lake George forms NE boundary of Warren co. and NW boundary of Washington co.

History: Visited by Verrazano 1524; explored by Henry Hudson who sailed up the river now bearing his name 1609; trading posts, founded by Dutch on Manhattan I. and at Fort Nassau, were taken over by Dutch West India Company; New Amsterdam founded on Manhattan 1625; New Netherland, Dutch colony, conquered by English 1664 and renamed New York after its proprietor, duke of York; became a royal province 1685; held 1st constitutional convention 1776; invaded 1777 by Burgoyne during American Revolution; in 1797 capital was moved to Albany; adopted present constitution 1894; rejected proposed new constitution 1967.

2 County in New York. See table at NEW YORK 1.

3 *or* **New York City** *or sometimes, unofficially,* **Greater New York.** City, SE New York, at mouth of the Hudson river; pop. (1970c) 7,895,563; largest city in the U.S. and 2d largest in the world; comprises five boroughs coextensive with five counties: Bronx (Bronx co.), Brooklyn (Kings co.), Manhattan (New York co.), Queens (Queens co.), and Richmond (Richmond co.); extensive harbor facilities (port has ab. 755 m. of developed frontage); the world's foremost financial center (New York Stock Exchange, American Stock Exchange, Commodity Exchange, New York Cotton Exchange, New York Cocoa Exchange, etc., are located here, as are the headquarters of many major corporations); United Nations headquarters; holds a leading position in the retail and wholesale trades, manufacturing, fashion, art, and the service industries; manufactured products include: apparel, chemicals, electrical machinery, fabricated metal products, leather goods; printing and publishing, food processing; tourism. For educational institutions, etc., see the entries of the individual boroughs.

History: Site of a trading post established at S end of Manhattan I. by Henry Hudson 1609 and Adriaen Block 1610; fortified and colonized under name New Amsterdam (*q.v.*) by Dutch West India Company; island purchased from Indians by Peter Minuit for Dutch West India Company 1626 for $24 worth of trinkets; Dutch West India Company sold tracts of land to patroons, who introduced colonists to settle and work their farms; settlements extended to Breuckelen (Brooklyn), New Harlem, Bronx, and Staaten Eylandt (Staten Island); captured by British and named New York 1664 in honor of the king's brother, the duke of York; Richard Nicolls appointed first British governor; Dutch regained control and held it for a short time 1673–74; new city charter granted 1686 which remained in force with minor changes until 1830; scene of Leisler rebellion 1689–91; after the British parliament passed the Stamp Act 1763, Stamp Act Congress met in City Hall and drew up a declaration of rights; boycott of British goods forced repeal of Stamp Act; demonstration against the British government's tax on tea 1773, provincial congress summoned and a state of war recognized by the Continental Congress; on July 4, 1776 George Washington caused the Declaration of Independence to be read to the army assembled on the common; scene of retreat of Washington after the battle of Long Island Aug. 27, 1776; city held by British to the end of the Revolutionary War; capital of state 1784–97, of U.S. 1785–90; George Washington inaugurated first president of the United States in a building (Federal Hall) on the site of the present U.S. subtreasury building on Wall Street; sharp increase in commerce and industry followed the opening of the Erie Canal (1825); suffered disastrous fire 1835; opposed the Civil War at its outbreak 1861, and was scene of serious draft riots 1863; expanded rapidly after Civil War, developing transportation and communication systems; Tweed Ring political scandal exposed 1871; by legislative act of 1896 "Greater New York" was established Jan. 1, 1898. For further details, see the boroughs of MANHATTAN 2, BRONX 3, BROOKLYN 3, QUEENS 2, and RICHMOND 8.

New York Bay. Inlet of Atlantic Ocean at mouth of Hudson river, in SE New York; it consists of **Upper New York Bay** and **Lower New York Bay,** connected by the Narrows; Manhattan I. lies at its NE end.

New York City. See NEW YORK 3.

New York Mills. Village, Oneida co., cen. New York, 5 m. E of Utica; pop. (1970c) 3805.

New York State Barge Canal. Canal system, connecting Lake Erie at Buffalo, New York, with the Hudson river at a point opp. Troy, near the mouth of the Mohawk river (*q.v.*); total length 522 m.; branches connect the main waterway, the Erie Canal (*q.v.*) with Lake Ontario (see OSWEGO CANAL) and Lake Champlain (see CHAMPLAIN CANAL); natural waterways are used to a large extent, esp. the Oswego, Seneca (see CAYUGA, LAKE and SENECA, LAKE) and Clyde rivers and Oneida Lake.

New Zea·land \-'zē-lənd\. Independent state, consisting of several islands in SW Pacific Ocean (major islands include North I., South I., Stewart I., and Chatham Is.); lat. 34°50′ to 47°S and long. 166° to 178°50′W; 103,736 sq. m.; pop. (1971p) 2,860,475; ✱ Wellington. *Chief products:* Meat, wool, dairy products; coal, gold, limestone, salt, natural gas; manufacturing: agricultural machinery, chemicals, textiles; food processing.

North Island: Mountainous, in cen. part has several ranges with volcanoes Ruapehu 9175 ft., Ngauruhoe 7515 ft., and Tongariro 6516 ft., all in Tongariro National Park; on W coast is Mt. Egmont 8260 ft.; in center is Lake Taupo in midst of remarkable hot springs country; chief rivers Waikato, Rangitaiki, Wanganui, and Rangitikei; irregular coastline, excellent harbors. *Chief cities:* Auckland, Wellington, Manukau, and Hamilton.

South Island: Mountainous, with Southern Alps (highest peak Mt. Cook 12,349 ft.) extending almost its entire length and including many glaciers and lakes; largest lakes Wakatipu, Wanaka, Te Anau; chief rivers Wairau, Rangitata, Waitaki, Clutha; coastline irregular. *Chief cities:* Christchurch, Dunedin, Nelson, and Timaru.

History: Discovered by Tasman 1642; visited by Cook 1769 who circumnavigated it; first European settlements made by whalers and missionaries; colonized in 1840 at Port Nicholson by New Zealand Company; by Treaty of Waitangi 1840 native leaders ceded lands to British who proclaimed New Zealand a crown colony under British sovereignty; first Maori War 1843–48; in new constitution 1852, organized as 6 provinces; second Maori War 1860–70; transferred capital from Auckland to Wellington 1865; provincial government abolished 1875; annexed Kermadec Is. 1887 and later Niue and other islands; colonial status formally terminated 1907; administered Western Samoa 1919–62; participated in World War I and World War II; adopted unicameral government 1950; entered into defense alliance with Australia and U.S. (ANZUS treaty) 1951; granted self-government to Cook Is. 1965.

Ne·ya·ga·wa \ˌnā-yə-'gä-wə, nā-'yäg-ə-wə\. City, Ōsaka prefecture, Honshū, Japan, suburb of Ōsaka; pop. (1970c) 206,961.

Neyba. See NEIBA.

Ney·rīz *or* **Nī·rīz** \ni-'rēz\. Town, Fārs prov., SW Iran, near SE end of Lake Bakhtegān; pop. (1966c) 16,114; on the old trade route from Kermān to Shīrāz.

Ney·shā·būr \ˌnā-shä-'bu̇(ə)r\ *or* **Ni·sha·pur** \ˌnēsh-ə-'pu̇(ə)r\. Town, Khorāsān prov., NE Iran, ab. 40 m. W of Mashhad; pop. (1966c) 33,482; market town; leather, carpets, vegetable oils; turquoise mines nearby; birthplace and burial place of the Persian poets Omar Khayyám and Farid ud-din Attar. Traditionally founded by Shapur II in 3d cent. A.D.; royal residence until middle of 5th cent.; declined but again flourished under Tahirid and Samanid dynasties (c. 820–999); destroyed three times in 13th cent.—twice by earthquakes and once by the Mongols.

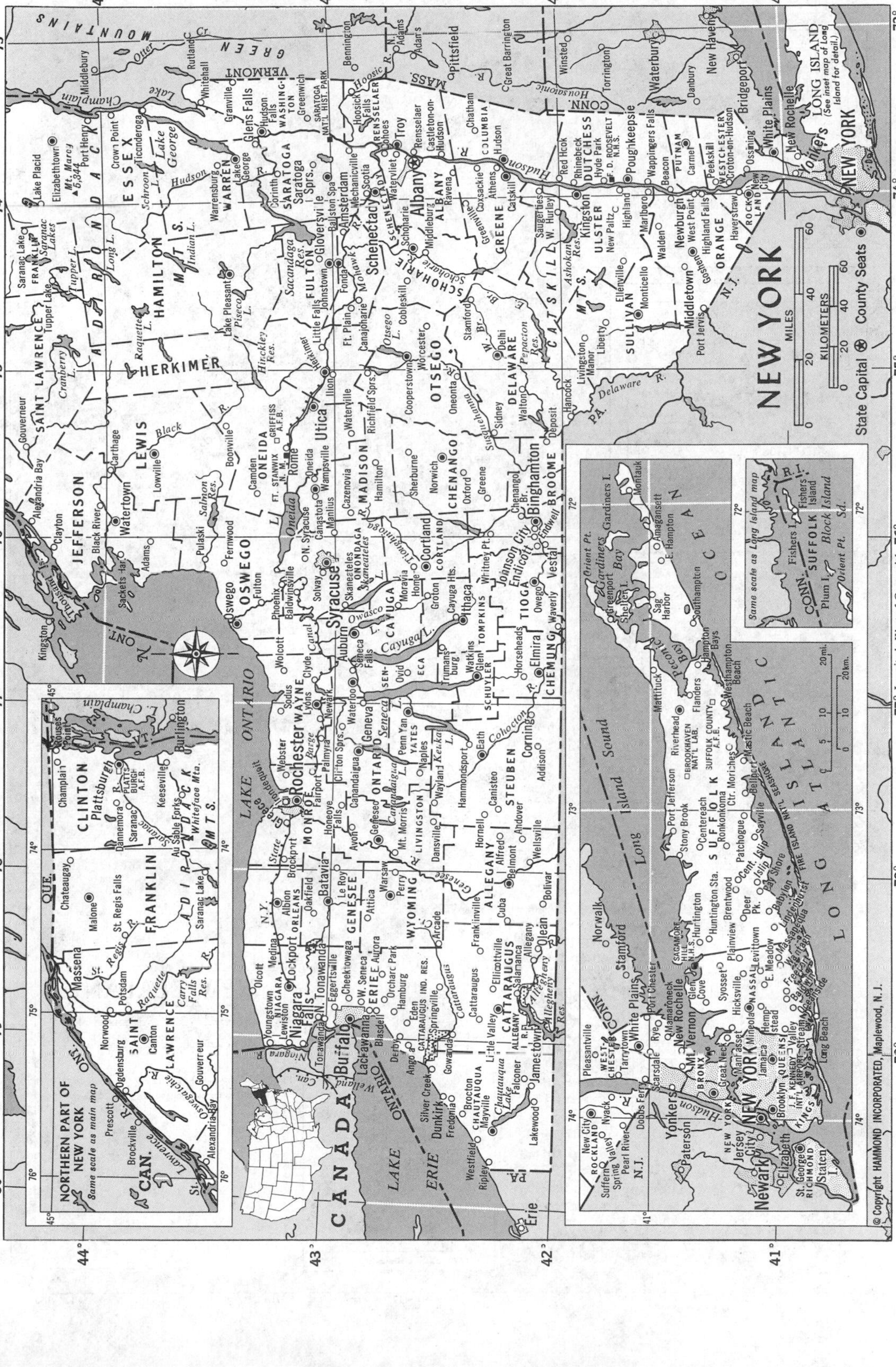
NEW YORK
MILES
0 20 40 60
KILOMETERS
0 20 40 60
State Capital County Seats
77° Longitude West of Greenwich
NORTHERN PART OF NEW YORK
Same scale as main map
LONG ISLAND
(See inset map of Long Island for detail.)
Same scale as Long Island map
LAKE ONTARIO
LAKE ERIE
CANADA
ATLANTIC OCEAN
Long Island Sound
© Copyright HAMMOND INCORPORATED, Maplewood, N.J.

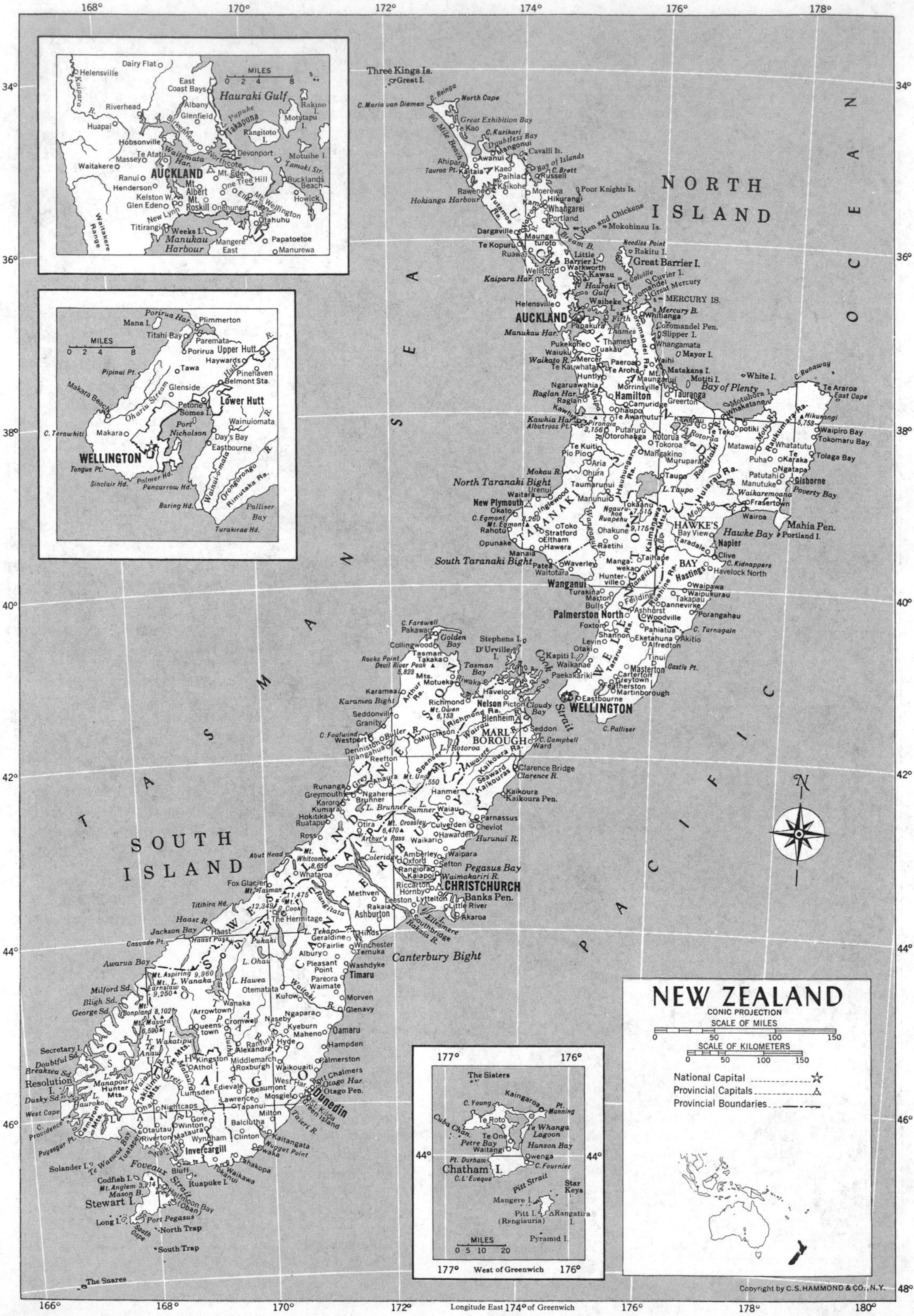
NEW ZEALAND
CONIC PROJECTION
SCALE OF MILES
0 50 100 150
SCALE OF KILOMETERS
0 50 100 150
National Capital
Provincial Capitals
Provincial Boundaries
NORTH ISLAND
SOUTH ISLAND
TASMAN SEA
PACIFIC OCEAN
AUCKLAND
WELLINGTON
CHRISTCHURCH
Dunedin
Hauraki Gulf
Manukau Harbour
Three Kings Is.
North Cape
C. Maria van Diemen
90 Mile Beach
Great Exhibition Bay
Doubtless Bay
Bay of Islands
Hokianga Harbour
Poor Knights Is.
Hen and Chickens
Mokohinau Is.
Great Barrier I.
MERCURY IS.
Kaipara Har.
Coromandel Pen.
Bay of Plenty
White I.
East Cape
Hamilton
Tauranga
Rotorua
L. Taupo
Gisborne
Poverty Bay
Mahia Pen.
Hawke Bay
Napier
Hastings
HAWKE'S BAY
New Plymouth
C. Egmont
Mt. Egmont 8,260
North Taranaki Bight
South Taranaki Bight
TARANAKI
Wanganui
Palmerston North
Masterton
C. Palliser
C. Turnagain
Cook Strait
C. Farewell
Golden Bay
Tasman Bay
Nelson
Blenheim
MARLBOROUGH
Karamea Bight
Westport
Greymouth
Hokitika
Kaikoura Pen.
Pegasus Bay
Banks Pen.
Akaroa
Ashburton
Timaru
Canterbury Bight
Mt. Cook 12,349
Mt. Tasman 11,475
WESTLAND
CANTERBURY
OTAGO
SOUTHLAND
Oamaru
Invercargill
Foveaux Strait
Stewart I.
The Snares
Mt. Aspiring 9,960
Milford Sd.
Resolution I.
Dusky Sd.
Chatham I.
Pitt I.
West of Greenwich
Longitude East 174° of Greenwich
Copyright by C.S.HAMMOND & CO., N.Y.

Ne·zhin *also* **Nye·zhin** \ˈnyā-(ˌ)zhin\. Town, cen. Chernigov Oblast, N Ukrainian S.S.R., U.S.S.R., 70 m. NE of Kiev; pop. (1969e) 58,000; rail junction point on the main Kiev-Moscow line; an old town dating from 12th cent.

Nezib. See NIZIP.

Nez·perce \ˈnez-ˈpərs\. Village, ⊗ of Lewis co., W Idaho; pop. (1970c) 555.

Nez Perce \ˈnez-ˈpərs\. **1** Mountain, cen. Grand Teton National Park, NW Wyoming; 11,900 ft.

2 County in Idaho. See table at IDAHO.

Nez Perce National Historical Park. See UNITED STATES, *National Historical Parks.*

Ngaliema, Mount. See RUWENZORI, MOUNT.

Nga·mi \eŋ-ˈgäm-ē\. Lake, NW Botswana, S Africa, N of Kalahari Desert and S of Okavango Basin; discovered by David Livingstone in 1849.

Ngan·djuk *or Du.* **Ngan·djoek** \eŋ-ˈgän-(ˌ)jük\. Town, East Java prov., Indonesia, ab. 25 m. E of Madiun; pop. (1961c) 23,499.

Nganking. See AN-CH'ING.

Ngaoun·dé·ré \eŋ-ˌgaůn-dā-ˈrā\. Town, N cen. Cameroon, W Africa; pop. (1970e) 20,000.

Nga·ru·ro·ro \eŋ-ˌgä-rə-ˈrōr-ə, -ˈrȯr-\. River, E cen. North I., New Zealand; 96 m. long; flows S and E into Hawke Bay below Napier.

Nga·tik \eŋ-ˈgät-ik\. Atoll island, Senyavin Is. group, E Caroline Is., W Pacific Ocean, ab. 90 m. SSW of Ponape, 5°51′N, 157°16′E.

Ngau·ru·hoe \eŋ-ˌgaů-rə-ˈhō-ē\. Volcano, Tongariro National Park, cen. North I., New Zealand; 7515 ft.

Nga·wi \eŋ-ˈgä-wē\. Town, East Java prov., Indonesia, ab. 17 m. NW of Madiun on the Solo river; pop. (1961c) 29,220.

N'Gela Island. See FLORIDA ISLAND.

Nge·se·bus \eŋ-ˈgā-sə-ˌbůs\. Small island just N of Peleliu, Palau Is., W Pacific Ocean; occupied by U.S. Marines Sept. 28, 1944.

Ngoenoet. See NGUNUT.

Ngong \eŋ-ˈgȯŋ\. Town, S Kenya, E Africa, just SW of Nairobi.

Ngoo Linh \eŋ-ˈgü-ˈlin\. Mountain, South Vietnam, ab. 70 m. S of Da Nang; 8521 ft.; highest mountain in South Vietnam.

Ngo·ron·go·ro Crater \eŋ-ˌgōr-ōŋ-ˈgōr-(ˌ)ō-, -ˌgȯr-ōŋ-ˈgȯr-\. Crater, N cen. Tanzania; a conservation area (established 1956) noted for its abundant wildlife.

Ngu·nut *or Du.* **Ngoe·noet** \eŋ-ˈgü-(ˌ)nüt\. Town, East Java prov., Indonesia, ab. 50 m. E of Madiun.

Ngur·do·to Crater National Park \ˌeŋ-gůr-ˌdō-tō-\. National park, Tanzania; 25 sq. m.; extinct Ngurdoto crater, rain forest, lakes; wildlife includes baboons, buffalo, warthog, waterbuck; established 1960.

Nha·mun·dá \ˌnya-mü(ⁿ)n-ˈdä\ *also* **Ja·mun·dá** \zhə-\ *or* **Ya·mun·dá** \ˌyä-\. River, N Brazil; rises near Guyana boundary, flows S into Amazon river, forming section of boundary bet. Pará and Amazonas states.

Nha Trang \ˈnyä-ˈträŋ\. Seaport town, South Vietnam, ab. 50 m. N of Phan Rang; pop. (1968e) 101,908; important fisheries; Cham temple ruins nearby.

Nhka·ta Bay \eŋ-ˌkät-ə-\. Town, W cen. shore of Lake Nyasa, Malawi, SE Africa; pop. (1966c) 1188; an administrative center with best anchorage on W side of lake.

Ni·ag·a·ra \nī-ˈag-(ə-)rə\. **1** River, W New York; connects Lake Erie with Lake Ontario and forms United States-Canada boundary. See NIAGARA FALLS.

2 County in New York. See table at NEW YORK.

3 Town, Ontario, Canada. See NIAGARA-ON-THE-LAKE.

Niagara Falls. **1** Great falls of the Niagara river, on U.S.-Canada boundary, divided by Goat I. into Horseshoe, or Canadian, Fall, 158 ft. high with crest 2600 ft. wide, and American Fall, 167 ft. high and 1000 ft. wide; ab. 6% of water passes over American Fall and remainder over the Horseshoe Fall. Boundary line bet. U.S. and Canada passes through center of Niagara river, leaving Goat I. entirely in U.S. Prospect Point on brink of ledge on American side and Queen Victoria Park on Canadian side both afford excellent views of the falls; at foot of American Fall is the Cave of the Winds, a rocky chamber 100 ft. by 75 ft., formed by erosion. River below the falls flows bet. high cliffs, forming Whirlpool Rapids; crossed by two bridges bet. the two cities of Niagara Falls; an important hydroelectrical center.

History: Falls well known to many tribes of Indians before any settlement of Europeans in U.S. or Canada; first visited and described by Father Hennepin 1678, 1683; in center of region of trading posts and frontier forts 18th cent. and in War of 1812 of several engagements (see LUNDY'S LANE, QUEENSTON, CHIPPAWA); diversion of water from American Fall undertaken 1969, permitting an examination of erosion rates.

2 City and tourist resort, Niagara co., W New York, on Niagara river 17 m. NNW of Buffalo; pop. (1970c) 85,615; extends above and below great falls of the river (Niagara Falls); opp. Niagara Falls, Ontario (bridge connection). Center of electrochemical and electrometallurgical industries: chlorine, flourine, caustic soda, aluminum products, paper, missile components, storage batteries; Niagara Reservation State Park, including Prospect Point, Luna, Goat, and other islands, and Whirlpool and Devil's Hole state parks, Cave of the Winds, and American Fall; Niagara Falls power plant (developed from 1890); Niagara Univ. (1856); Niagara County Community Coll. (1963). Site of a fort until c. 1800; formerly comprised separate villages of Niagara Falls (originally known as Manchester) and Suspension Bridge (formerly Niagara City), which were consolidated and chartered as one city of Niagara Falls 1892; annexed La Salle 1927.

3 Manufacturing city, Welland co., SE Ontario, Canada, on Niagara river just below the falls; pop. (1971p) 65,271; opp. Niagara Falls, New York, and connected with it by two bridges; from its Queen Victoria Park is finest view of the falls. Hub of large hydroelectric power development; produces chemicals, fertilizers, cereals, abrasives, silverware, sporting goods. Founded 1853; known as **Clif·ton** \ˈklif-tən\ 1856–1881; incorporated 1904.

Niagara–on–the–Lake *or* **Niagara.** Town, Lincoln co., SE Ontario, Canada, on Lake Ontario at mouth of Niagara river opp. Fort Niagara, New York; pop. (1971p) 12,501; site of Canadian lawn-tennis championship play; founded 1780; first capital of Upper Canada (to 1796); parts of Fort Massassauga still visible; town burned by American general McClure in 1813.

Niagara Peak. Mountain, Hinsdale and San Juan cos., SW Colorado; 13,800 ft.

Nia·mey \nē-ˈäm-(ˌ)ā\. City, ✻ of Niger, W Africa, on Niger river; pop. (1969e) 78,991; commercial center at intersection of trade routes; has oil mills, brick factories; consisted of several villages before being made capital 1926.

Ni·an·tic \nī-ˈant-ik\. **1** Short stream and wide inlet, in W New London co., SE Connecticut; flows S into Long Island Sound.

2 Unincorporated subdivision of town of East Lyme, Connecticut; pop. (1970c) 3422. See EAST LYME.

Ni·as \ˈnē-əs\. Island in the Indian Ocean off W coast of Sumatra, Indonesia, just N of the equator; 80 m. long by 30 m. wide; 1569 sq. m.; pop. (1961c) 314,829; chief village Gunungsitoli on NE coast. Hilly (highest point 2907 ft.) and subject to earthquakes.

Ni·as·sa *or* **Ny·as·sa** \nē-ˈas-ə, nī-\. District, NW Mozambique; 46,384 sq. m.; pop. (1970p) 297,428; from 1894 to 1929 administered by Niassa Company; united administratively with Cabo Delgado 1930–41.

Ni·caea \nī-'sē-ə\. 1 *or anglicized* **Nice** \'nīs\. Empire in Asia Minor 1204–61; extending from Black Sea coast E of Sangarius river SW across W Asia Minor to Miletus and the Maeander; ✻ Nicaea on its N border. Bordered on E and SE by sultanate of Rum or Iconium of the Seljuk Turks and on NW by the Latin Empire (1204–61). Its rulers were of the Lascaris family: Theodore I and II, John III (Ducas), John IV, and Michael VIII Palaeologus, who in 1261 restored the Byzantine emperors.
2 Ancient city, Asia Minor. See İZNİK.
3 City, France. See NICE 2.

Nic·a·ra·gua \ˌnik-ə-'räg-wə\. Republic, Central America, bounded on N by Honduras, on E by the Caribbean Sea, on S by Costa Rica, and on W by Pacific Ocean; 49,579 sq. m. (including 4061 sq. m. of water); pop. (1970c) 1,974,-924; ✻ Managua. *Physical features:* Traversed along Pacific coast by mountain range, part of the great continental axis, but in SW, near Brito, W of Lake Nicaragua cut by lowest gap from Alaska to Tierra del Fuego and hence selected as W part of possible future canal bet. Atlantic and Pacific oceans; range is volcanic and has had many eruptions in recent years; most important peaks Cosigüina Volcán, Momotombo, and the two on Ometepe I. in Lake Nicaragua (Concepción and Madera); greater part of cen. and N is hilly country. Longer coastline, ab. 300 m., is on Caribbean, known as Mosquito Coast, a swampy region; separated from Costa Rica on S by San Juan river, outlet of Lake Nicaragua; on E coast are many streams 60–210 m. long flowing E to the Caribbean, chief are Grande and Escondido; many cays off coast. *Chief products:* Coffee, cotton, sugar, rice, tobacco, corn; gold; livestock; manufacturing: chemicals, textiles; food processing. *Chief cities:* Managua, León, Granada, Chinandega, Masaya, Matagalpa. Divided into the following 16 departments (for pronunciation of their names, see their individual entries):

NAME	AREA[1] (sq. m.)	POP. (1970e)	CAPITAL
Boaco	1,924	81,841	Boaco
Carazo	398	87,272	Jinotepe
Chinandega	1,800	175,421	Chinandega
Chontales	1,910	92,914	Juigalpa
Estelí	849	86,058	Estelí
Granada	372	86,166	Granada
Jinotega	3,697	98,312	Jinotega
León	2,021	197,271	León
Madriz	679	61,238	Somoto
Managua	1,403	428,967	Managua
Masaya	210	104,748	Masaya
Matagalpa	2,623	202,830	Matagalpa
Nueva Segovia	1,290	60,219	Ocotal
Río San Juan	2,876	20,158	San Carlos
Rivas	830	85,686	Rivas
Zelaya	22,816	105,823	Bluefields

[1]Area = land area.

History: Coast discovered by Columbus 1502; Lake Nicaragua discovered by Gil González de Ávila 1522; Granada and León founded by Córdoba 1524; part of captain-generalcy of Guatemala; declared itself independent of Spain 1821; part of United Provinces of Central America 1823–38 (see SAN JUAN DEL NORTE for dispute with Great Britain); invaded by expeditions of Walker 1855–60; U.S. early began negotiations for canal across Nicaragua (became final in Bryan-Chamorro treaty 1916) and frequently intervened in political crises, notably by maintaining American forces there 1912–25, 1926–33; became a founder member of the Central American Common Market 1960; terminated Bryan-Chamorro treaty 1970.

Nicaragua, Lake. Lake in S Nicaragua; 102 m. long; area ab. 3100 sq. m.; max. depth 230 ft.; largest lake in Central America and largest body of fresh water bet. U.S. and Peru; connected with Lake Managua by Tipitapa river; source of San Juan river; discovered by Gil González de Ávila 1522.

Nicaria. See IKARIA.

Nic·a·tous Lake \ˌnik-ə-ˌtaůs-\. Lake in N Hancock co., E cen. Maine.

Nice. 1 \'nēs\. Countship, historical region of SE France, bounded anciently on N by Dauphiné, and on E and S by Savoy, and on W by Provence; equivalent to E part of modern department of Alpes-Maritimes; ✻ Nice.
2 *or Ital.* **Niz·za** \'nēt-sə\ *or anc.* **Ni·caea** \nī-'sē-ə\. Seaport, ✻ of Alpes-Maritimes dept., SE France, on Mediterranean 98 m. ENE of Marseilles; pop. (1968c) 322,442; ships olive oil, fruits, flowers; produces perfume, hats, clothing, soap, metal and rubber goods; 17th cent. cathedral, observatory, univ. (1965). The leading resort city of the French Riviera, with many theaters and two casinos.
History: Founded by colony of Phocaeans from ancient Massilia; became subject to Rome in 2d cent. B.C.; ruled by Saracens 10th cent. A.D.; became independent city; with surrounding territory (Countship of Nice) became subject to counts of Provence and, in 1388, to house of Savoy; pillaged by Turks 1543; captured several times by French; held by France 1792–1814; ceded to France by house of Savoy 1860. Birthplace of Garibaldi.
3 Empire, Asia Minor. See NICAEA.
4 Ancient city, Asia Minor. See İZNİK.

Nicephorium. See RAKKA.

Nice·ville \'nīs-ˌvil\. Town, Okaloosa co., NW Florida, 38 m. ENE of Pensacola; pop. (1970c) 4024.

Ni·chi·nan \ˌnē-chē-'nän\. City, Miyazaki prefecture, Kyūshū, Japan, 24 m. SSW of Miyazaki; pop. (1970c) 53,288.

Nich·o·las \'nik-(ə-)ləs\. Name of counties in two states of the U.S. See tables at KENTUCKY and WEST VIRGINIA.

Nicholas Channel. Channel in the W West Indies, N of W Cuba and S of Cay Sal Bank.

Nicholas II Land. See SEVERNAYA ZEMLYA.

Nich·o·las·ville \'nik-(ə-)ləs-ˌvil\. City, ⊗ of Jessamine co., E cen. Kentucky, 12 m. SSW of Lexington; pop. (1970c) 5829; diversified agriculture.

Nich·ols Hills \ˌnik-əlz-\. City, Oklahoma co., cen. Oklahoma, 4 m. N of Oklahoma City; pop. (1970c) 4478.

Nicholson Viaduct. See TUNKHANNOCK.

Nick·a·jack Dam \'nik-ə-ˌjak-\. See table at TENNESSEE VALLEY AUTHORITY.

Nick·e·rie \'nik-ə-rē\. 1 River, NW Surinam; ab. 200 m. long; flows NNW into Atlantic Ocean near border of Guyana.
2 District, W Surinam.
3 Coastal town, Surinam. See NIEUW NICKERIE.

Nic·o·bar Islands \'nik-ə-ˌbär-\ *or* **Nic·o·bars** \-ˌbärz\. Island group, Bay of Bengal, NW of Sumatra, forming S part of Andaman and Nicobar Islands territory, India; 740 sq. m.; pop. (1961c) 14,563. Comprises 3 groups of islands; chief islands Great Nicobar, Camorta with Nancowry, Car

Nicobar, Teressa, and Little Nicobar. Occupied by British Government of India 1869; joined to Andaman (*q.v.*) group for administrative purposes 1872. Held by Japanese in World War II 1942–45.

Ni·co·lás Ro·me·ro \ˌnē-kə-ˌläs-rō-ˌmer-(ˌ)ō\. Municipality, México state, Mexico, 18 m. NW of Mexico City; pop. (1970p) 55,192; textiles, paper.

Ni·co·let \ˌnēk-ə-ˈlā\. 1 County, Quebec, Canada. See table at QUEBEC.

2 Industrial town, Nicolet co., Quebec, Canada, on S shore of Lake St. Peter, 10 m. S of Three Rivers; pop. (1971p) 4716; textiles, dairy products; agriculture; cathedral; Séminaire de Nicolet (1801), Coll. Notre Dame de l'Assomption (1937), Séminaire des Vocations Tardives (1956).

Nic·ol·let \ˈnik-ə-ˌlet\. County in Minnesota. See table at MINNESOTA.

Nic·olls Town \ˈnik-əlz-\. Town, N coast of Andros I., Bahama Is.

Ni·co·ma Park \nə-ˌkōm-ə-\. Town, Oklahoma co., cen. Oklahoma, 11 m. E of Oklahoma City; pop. (1970c) 2560.

Nicomedia. See İZMİT.

Ni·cop·o·lis \nə-ˈkäp-ə-ləs, nī-\. 1 Town, Bulgaria. See NIKOPOL 1.

2 City in ancient Epirus, NW Greece; its ruins are ab. 3 m. N of Preveza on the peninsula bet. the Ionian Sea and the Ambracian Gulf. Founded 31 B.C. by Octavian (Augustus) to commemorate his victory at Actium; became capital of Epirus and Acarnania; famous for its buildings and games (Actian Games). Twice destroyed; rebuilt by Julian and Justinian. See PREVEZA.

Nic·o·sia \ˈnik-ə-ˈsē-ə\. 1 District, cen. and W cen. Cyprus, E Mediterranean Sea; 1048 sq. m.; pop. (1968e) 225,000.

2 *or* **Lev·ko·sia** \ˌlef-kō-ˈsē-ə\ *also* **Leu·co·sia** \ˌlü-kə-ˈsē-ə, ˌlef-kə-\. City, ✱ of Cyprus and ✱ of Nicosia dist., W of Famagusta (its port) in cen. part of island; pop. (1970e) 115,000; archiepiscopal see; textiles, flour, clothing, footwear, beverages; 14th cent. cathedral (now a mosque); founded before 7th cent. B.C.; capital of island from 10th cent. A.D.; fortified by Lusignan kings; sacked by Genoese, Mamelukes, and Turks; came under British 1878.

3 Commune, Enna prov., cen. Sicily, Italy, 15 m. NNE of Enna; pop. (1968e) 16,946; episcopal see; 14th cent. cathedral; medieval castle. Taken by Allies July 29, 1943.

Ni·co·ya \ni-ˈkō-yə\. Town on Nicoya Penin., NW Costa Rica; mother-of-pearl, murex.

Nicoya, Gulf of. Inlet of Pacific Ocean on NW cen. coast of Costa Rica, E of Nicoya Penin.

Nicoya Peninsula. Peninsula extending SE from NW Costa Rica, bet. Gulf of Nicoya and the Pacific Ocean.

Nictheroy. See NITERÓI.

Ni·da \ˈnēd-ə\. River, S Poland, NE of Kraków; 111 m. long; a tributary of the Vistula flowing E and S.

Nidaros. See TRONDHEIM.

Nidwalden. See UNTERWALDEN and table at SWITZERLAND.

Niederdonau. See LOWER AUSTRIA.

Nie·de·re Tau·ern \ˌnēd-ər-ə-ˈtau̇-ərn\. Mountain range in S Austria bet. valleys of the Mur and Enns; highest point 9393 ft.; a range of the Eastern Alps.

Niederösterreich. See LOWER AUSTRIA.

Niederrhein. See LOWER RHINE.

Niedersachsen. See LOWER SAXONY.

Niederschlesien. See SILESIA.

Nie·der·sel·ters \ˈnēd-ər-ˌzel-tərs\. Commune, Hesse, West Germany; pop. (1970e) 2400; mineral waters.

Niel \ˈnyel\. Commune, Antwerp prov., N Belgium, just S of Antwerp; pop. (1969e) 9874.

Niemen. See NEMAN.

Nien·burg an der We·ser \ˈnēn-ˌbu̇(ə)rg-än-dər-ˈvā-zər\. City, Lower Saxony, West Germany, on Weser river 28 m. NW of Hannover; pop. (1969e) 23,383.

Nieśwież. See NESVIZH.

Nieuport. See NIEUWPOORT.

Nieu·we Maas \ˌnē-və-ˈmäs\. A right branch of the Merwede river after it unites with the Lek river in the Netherlands; empties into North Sea at the Hook of Holland; one of the mouths of the Meuse (Maas) river.

Nieuwe Republiek. See NEW REPUBLIC.

Nieuw Guinee. See NEW GUINEA.

Nieuwkerke. See NEUVE-ÉGLISE.

Nieuw Nick·e·rie \n(y)ü-ˈnik-ə-rē\. Coastal town, ✱ of Nickerie dist., NW Surinam, on Nickerie river near its mouth 122 m. W of Paramaribo; pop. (1964c) 7400.

Nieuw·poort *or* **Nieu·port** \ˈn(y)ü-ˌpōrt\. Commune, West Flanders prov., NW Belgium, on the Yser 10 m. SW of Oostende; pop. (1969e) 7256; dates from 9th cent.; received present name 1160; scene of several battles or sieges in European wars since 14th cent.: 1488–89, 1600 (when Maurice of Nassau defeated Spaniards under Archduke Albert), and 1749; in World War I scene of almost continuous trench warfare 1914–15 and a center of fighting to end of the war.

Nieuw·veld \ˈn(y)ü-ˌfelt\. Mountain range in cen. Cape Province, Rep. of South Africa; highest point 6276 ft.

Niè·vre \ˈnyevrᵉ\. Department of cen. France. See table at FRANCE.

Niewenstat. See NEUSTADT AN DER WEINSTRASSE.

Niğ·de \nē(g)-ˈdā\. 1 Province of cen. Turkey. See table at TURKEY.

2 Town, its ✱, on railroad 75 m. NNW of Adana; pop. (1965c) 21,663; important town of Seljuk sultanate of Rum 11th–14th cents.; came under Ottomans c. 1450.

Ni·gel \ˈnī-jəl\. Town, Transvaal, Rep. of South Africa, suburb of Johannesburg; pop. (1967e) 38,400; transportation equipment.

Ni·ger \ˈnī-jər\. 1 Republic, W Africa, bounded on N by Algeria and Libya, on E by Chad, on S by Nigeria, on SW by Dahomey and Upper Volta, and on W by Mali; 459,073 sq. m.; pop. (1970e) 4,020,000; ✱ Niamey. *Physical features:* The republic is landlocked, and is characterized by savanna in S and desert in cen. and N; traversed in SW by Niger river; Aïr (*q.v.*), a mountainous region, is located in the N cen. part of the country. *Chief products:* Peanuts, cotton, rice; livestock; uranium. *Chief towns:* Niamey, Zinder, Maradi, Tahoua.

History: First explored by Europeans in late 18th cent.; became part of French sphere of influence in latter part of 19th cent.; formally constituted as part of French West Africa 1904; S boundary demarcated by Anglo-French accords of 1899 and 1904; placed under military jurisdiction 1912–22; included part of Upper Volta 1933–47; became an overseas territory of France 1946; became an autonomous republic within the French Community 1958; achieved independence 1960.

2 River, W Africa; 2600 m. long; rises in Guinea near Sierra Leone border, flows in a great curve in W Africa, first NE then E and finally SE across border into Nigeria, continues S into Gulf of Guinea; known by many native names, esp. **Jol·i·ba** \ˈjäl-ə-bə\ and **Kwor·ra** \ˈkwȯr-ə, ˈkwär-\; estimated area of basin 584,000 sq. m. Above Tombouctou, Mali, passes through swampy, treeless region with many lakes; its middle course navigable for ab. 1000 m. above Ansongo and in Nigeria but rapids and bars prevent continuous navigation; in Nigeria receives from the E its only large tributary, the Benue (*q.v.*); has very extensive delta (14,000 sq. m.) with unhealthy climate; principal mouths are the Bonny, Brass, New Calabar, Forcados (now the main channel), and Nun; chief products shipped upon it are palm kernels and oil, hence the name **Oil Rivers** for its delta region; dammed in various places (e.g., Kainji Dam, Nigeria) for power production. First explored by Mungo Park 1796–97 and 1805–06; from 1822 to end of century

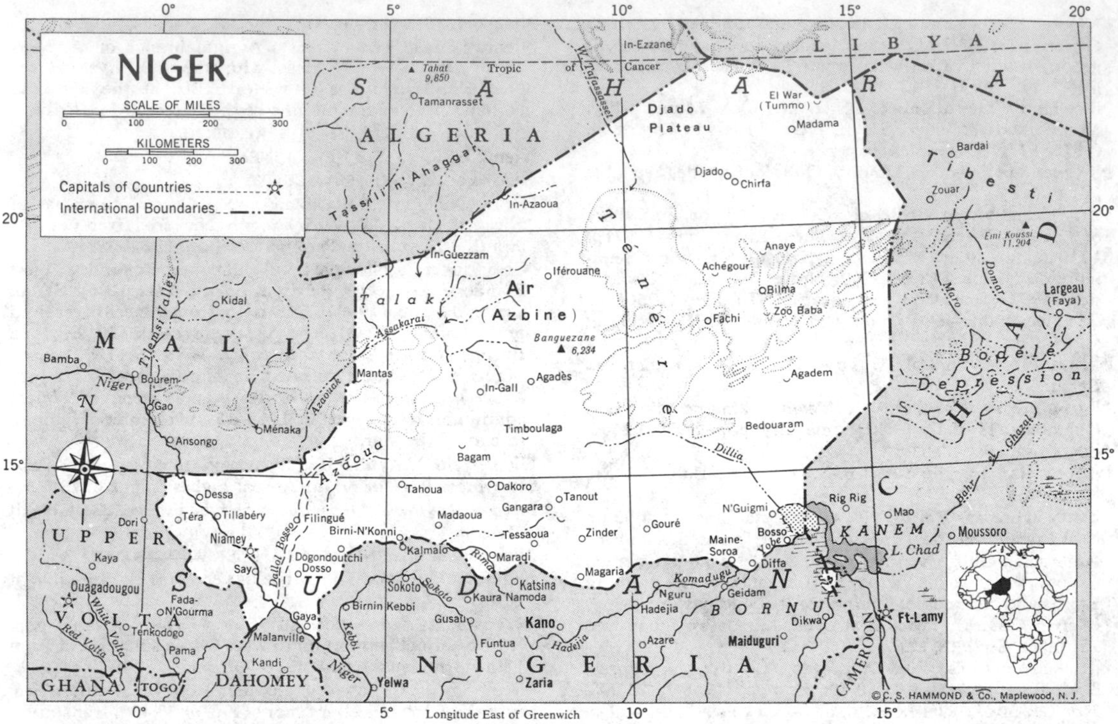

visited and explored by many British, French, and German travelers.

Ni·ge·ria \nī-ˈjir-ē-ə\ *or officially* **Federal Republic of Nigeria.** Republic, W Africa, bounded on NW and N by Niger, on NE by Lake Chad, on E by Cameroon, on S by the Gulf of Guinea (Bights of Biafra and Benin), and on W by Dahomey; 356,669 sq. m.; pop. (1971e) 67,828,000; ✱ Lagos. *Physical features:* Coastal plain varies in width from 10 to 60 m. and is characterized by mangrove swamps; in cen. is Jos Plateau (with max. elev. over 6000 ft.) and on E boundary is mountain range; extreme N is semidesert; chief rivers: Niger, Benue, Kaduna. *Chief exports:* Oil, cocoa, cotton, rubber; other products: hides, timber, tin, coal, columbite; fishing. *Chief cities:* Lagos, Ibadan, Ogbomosho, Kano, Oshogbo, Ilorin, Abeokuta. Divided into the following 12 states (for pronunciation of their names, see their individual entries):

NAME	AREA (sq. m.)	POP. (1969e)	CAPITAL
Benue-Plateau	39,204	4,649,669	Jos
East-Central	11,548	8,381,728	Enugu
Kano	16,630	6,697,024	Kano
Kwara	28,672	2,782,521	Ilorin
Lagos	1,381	1,674,091	Lagos
Mid-Western	14,922	2,940,787	Benin
North-Central	27,108	4,752,765	Kaduna
North-Eastern	105,025	9,037,979	Maiduguri
North-Western	65,143	6,648,845	Sokoto
Rivers	6,985	1,790,924	Port Harcourt
South-Eastern	10,951	4,201,084	Calabar
Western	29,100	11,002,589	Ibadan

History: For early history, see SONGHAI EMPIRE, BORNU, SOKOTO, BENIN 3. Region of the Niger (*q.v.*) visited in 18th and 19th cents. by many European explorers; Lagos, first land acquired by Great Britain, ceded by native king 1861; administered by Sierra Leone 1861–74, by Gold Coast Colony 1874 until 1886 when it was reconstituted as Colony and Protectorate of Lagos; Oil Rivers Protectorate (*q.v.*) established 1885; formed into two "Protectorates of Northern and Southern Nigeria" 1899; became "Colony and Protectorate of Nigeria" 1914; granted administration of British mandate of Cameroons (part of German Kamerun) 1922; constitution of 1954 established **Federation of Nigeria,** consisting of Lagos, the Eastern, Northern, and Western regions (Mid-West Region established 1963), and part of the British mandate of Cameroons; achieved independence 1960; in 1961 plebiscite, N part of British mandate of Cameroons voted for union with Nigeria; became a republic 1963; civilian government overthrown by army 1966; creation of twelve states in place of the former four regions 1967; civil war between central government and Eastern Region (see BIAFRA) 1967–70.

Night·in·gale \ˈnīt-ᵊn-ˌgāl, -iŋ-\. Most southerly island in Tristan da Cunha group in S Atlantic; 1 m. long.

Ni·hoa \ni-ˈhō-ə\. Islet of Hawaii, one of the Leeward Is. in cen. Pacific Ocean, ab. 125 m. NW of Niihau I.; ½ sq. m.; included in Hawaiian Islands Bird Reservation.

Nihon. See JAPAN.

Ni·i·ga·ta \nē-ˈgät-ə\. **1** Prefecture, Honshū, Japan; 4855 sq. m.; pop. (1970c) 2,360,982; ✱ Niigata; rice, oil, natural gas; coastal fishing.

2 City and seaport, its ✱, on NW coast of Honshū, 160 m. NNW of Tokyo at mouth of Shinano river; pop. (1970c) 383,919; leading port on Sea of Japan; chemicals, textiles, paper, machinery; shipbuilding; natural gas; univ. (1949).

Nii·ha·ma \ˈnē-hə-mə\. City, Ehime prefecture, Shikoku, Japan; pop. (1970c) 126,033.

Ni·i·hau \ˈnē-ˌhaů\. Island in NW Hawaii, W of Kauai I., from which it is separated by Kaulakahi Channel; 72 sq. m.; with Kauai forms Kauai co.; partly a tableland 1300 ft. high, partly low coral formation; chief village Puuwai.

Nii–shi·ma \ˈnē-shi-mə\. One of the seven islands of Izu-shichitō.

Niitakayama. See HSIN-KAO.

Ni·it·su \ˈnēt-ˌsü\. City, Niigata prefecture, Honshū, Japan, 13 m. S of Niigata; pop. (1970c) 57,089.

Ní·jar \ˈnē-ˌhär\. Commune, Almería prov., SE Spain, 18 m. ENE of Almería; pop. (1970p) 10,818; lead mines.

Nij·kerk \ˈnī-ˌke(ə)rk\. Commune, Gelderland prov., cen. Netherlands, 5 m. NE of Amersfoort; pop. (1970e) 17,718.

Nij·me·gen \ˈnī-ˌmā-gə(n)\ *or* **Nim·we·gen** \ˈnim-ˌvā-gən\ *or* **Ni·me·guen** \ˈnī-ˌmā-gən\ *or anc.* **No·vi·om·a·gus** \ˌnō-vē-'äm-ə-gəs\. Commune, Gelderland prov., E Netherlands, on Waal river 12 m. S of Arnhem; pop. (1970e) 148,790; machinery, paper, electrical equipment, synthetic fibers, footwear; 15th–16th cent. church of St. Stephen; 16th cent. town hall; univ. (1923).

History: At one time the residence of the Carlovingian emperors; later a member of the Hanseatic League; a series of six peace treaties signed here 1678–79 (France and Sweden with Holland, Spain, Austria, and Denmark), closing war of France against Holland and her allies and leaving France (under Louis XIV) at height of her power. In center of fighting Sept. 1944, suffered heavy damage.

Nijni Novgorod. See NIZHNI NOVGOROD.

Nikaria. See IKARIA.

Ni·khía \ni-'kē-ə\. Town, part of Greater Athens, Greece; pop. (1971p) 86,304.

Nik·ki \'nik-ē\. Town in NE Dahomey, West Africa, ab. 60 m. NE of Parakou.

Nik·kō \'nik-(,)ō\. City and mountain resort, Tochigi prefecture, cen. Honshū, Japan, 7 m. E of Lake Chuzenji (*q.v.*) and ab. 90 m. N of Tokyo by rail; pop. (1970c) 28,502; alt. 2000 ft. Had Shinto temple from earliest times and Buddhist temple from c. 767; esp. famous for its scenery, waterfalls, cryptomeria avenues, sacred bridge, and memorial carved shrines and temples of Iyeyasu (buried here 1617) and Iyemitsu (1651), 1st and 3d shoguns of Tokugawa dynasty.

Nikkō National Park. National park, Honshū, Japan; 543 sq. m.; volcanic area; established 1934.

Nikkō Range. Mountain range, W cen. Honshū, Japan, in which Nikkō is situated.

Nikolainkaupunki. See VAASA 2.

Nikolaevsk. See PUGACHEV.

Ni·ko·la·yev \,n(y)ik-ə-'lä-yəf\ *also* **Ver·no·le·ninsk** \,ver-nə-'len-,in(t)sk\. City and seaport, ✱ of Nikolayev Oblast, Ukrainian S.S.R., U.S.S.R., at confluence of the Bug and Ingul rivers 70 m. NE of Odessa; pop. (1970p) 331,000; major shipbuilding center; construction machinery, chemicals, clothing, pumps, footwear; naval base. Founded ab. 1789; captured by Germans Aug. 1941 and base destroyed; retaken by U.S.S.R. Mar. 13, 1944.

Nikolayev Oblast \-'ō-bləst, -,blast\. Subdivision of the Ukrainian S.S.R., U.S.S.R.; 9537 sq. m.; pop. (1970p) 1,148,000; ✱ Nikolayev; corn, wheat, sugar beet; livestock; borders on Black Sea and contains lower course of Bug river.

Ni·ko·la·yevsk–na–Amu·re \,n(y)ik-ə-'lä-yəfsk-nə-ə-'mu̇r-ə\. Seaport town, E Khabarovsk Krai, Russian S.F.S.R., U.S.S.R., near mouth of the Amur 400 m. NE of Khabarovsk; pop. (1967e) 32,000; port for transshipment from seagoing to river craft; shipbuilding and repairing, salmon fishing, brewing; iron mines; founded 1850.

Nikolsburg. See MIKULOV.

Ni·kol·sko·ye \ni-'kȯl-skə-yə\. See KOMANDORSKIYE ISLANDS.

Nikolsk–Ussuriiski. See USSURISK.

Ni·ko·pol \ni-'kȯ-pəl\. 1 *or anc.* **Ni·cop·o·lis** \nik-'äp-ə-ləs, nī-'käp-\. Commercial town, Pleven prov., N Bulgaria, on Danube river 23 m. NE of Pleven; pop. (1963e) 5817; scene of many battles, esp. 1396 in which Sigismund of Hungary, supported by French, English, and German forces, was defeated by the Turkish sultan Bajazet I; besieged by Ladislas V of Hungary 1444; scene of Turkish defeat 1595 and 1598; captured 1797, 1810, and 1829; burned by Russians 1877.

2 Town, S Dnepropetrovsk Oblast, E cen. Ukrainian S.S.R., U.S.S.R., on right bank of Dnieper 55 m. SE of Krivoi Rog; pop. (1970p) 125,000; center of manganese-mining area; steel tubes, electric cranes, beer. From early times a strategic crossing point of the Dnieper, scene of many conflicts; founded in 1630's; held by Germans Oct. 1941 to Feb. 8, 1944.

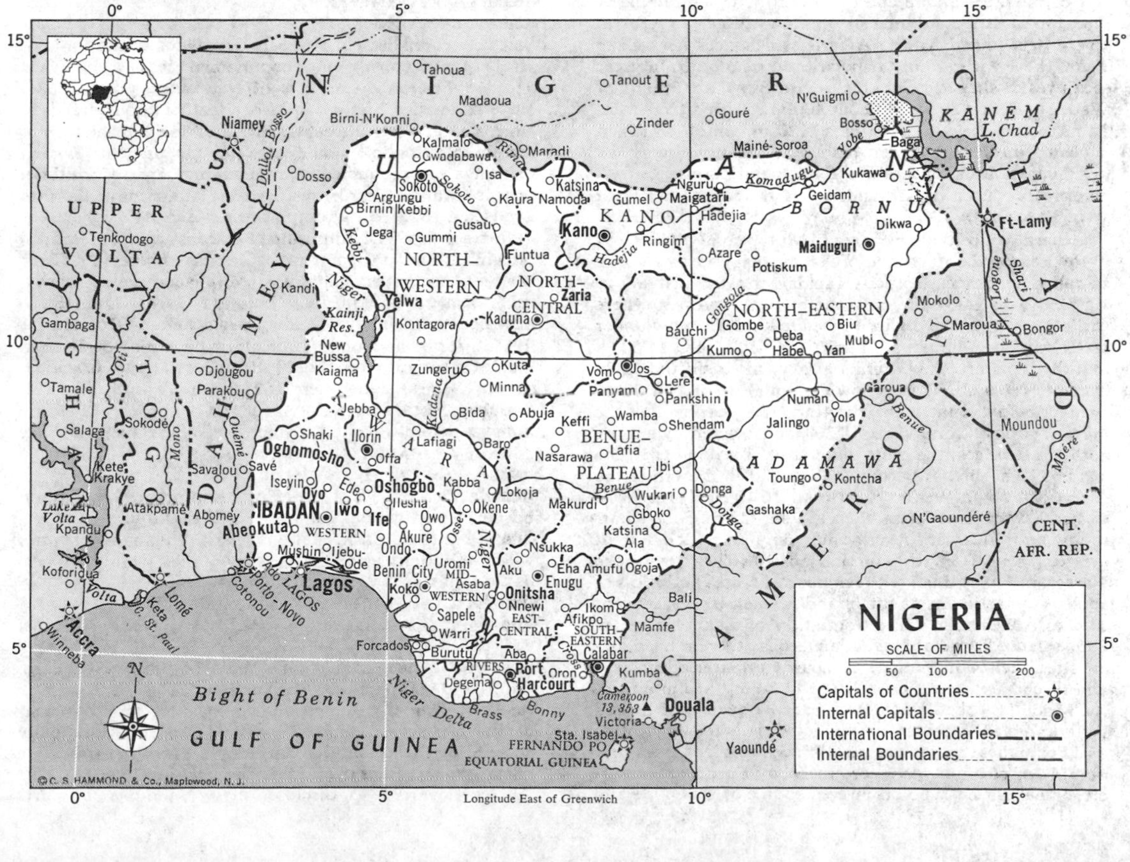

Nik·šić \'nik-ˌshich\. Town, Montenegro, S Yugoslavia, ab. 27 m. SE of Titograd; pop. (1965e) 27,000; on N–S trade route; has Byzantine cathedral, given by Russia, and ruins of old Turkish fortress.

Ni·ku·nau \'nēk-ə-ˌnau̇\ *or* **Nu·ku·nau** \'nük-\ *also* **By·ron** \'bī-rən\. Island (atoll), SE Gilbert Is., SW Pacific Ocean; 8 m. by 1½ m.; has several villages; discovered by Capt. John Byron 1765.

Nile \'nī(ə)l\ *or Lat.* **Ni·lus** \'nī-ləs\; *Arab.* **Al–Bahr** \al-'bär\ *also* **Bahr en Nīl** \-ən-'nēl\. River in E and NE Africa; the longest river in the world; in the Bible the "great river" (Shihor; *A.V.*, Sihor; *Isaiah* xxiii.3) of Egypt; 4187 m. from its remotest headstream, the Luvironza, and 3473 m. from Lake Victoria, to Mediterranean; flows generally N from E Africa through Uganda, Sudan, and Egypt; basin drained estimated at 1,107,227 sq. m. Its headwaters (longest, Kagera, *q.v.*) drain uplands of N Tanzania, SW Kenya, and country northeast of Congo basin into Lake Victoria. Nile proper, **Vic·to·ria Nile** \vik-'tōr-ē-ə-, -'tȯr-\ *or* **Som·er·set Nile** \'səm-ər-sət-, -ˌset-\, ab. 300 m., leaves N Lake Victoria (alt. ab. 3720 ft.) near Jinja (its flow controlled by the Owen Falls Dam), 30 m. N of the equator, flows N to and through Kyoga Lake, then NW over Murchison Falls (118 ft.) into NE corner of Lake Albert (*q.v.*); leaves N end (alt. c. 2200 ft.) of Lake Albert and flows N through NW Uganda (**Al·bert Nile** \'al-bərt-\); crosses into Sudan where it is called Bahr al-Jebel in the swamp (sudd) region; at Lake No (9°29′N) joined by W tributary Bahr al-Ghazal, and takes name of **White Nile** (*or Arab.* **Bahr al–Ab·yad** \ˌbär-al-'ab-yäd\); flows E to confluence, 1652 m. from Owen Falls Dam, with Sobat (from highlands of SW Ethiopia), then 520 m. N through Sudan to Khartoum; here joined by **Blue Nile** (*or Arab.* **Bahr al–Az·raq** \ˌbär-al-'az-ˌräk\), 850 m. long which rises in the mountains of Ethiopia, flows into Lake Tana, then (as the **Ab·bai** *or* **Abai** *or* **Abay** \ä-'bī \) by a wide SE to NW bend enters Sudan and flows N to join White Nile at Khartoum; then combined stream flows 200 m. to Atbara, where it is joined by the Atbara, which rises near Lake Tana; then, without any tributaries to its mouth, in great southwest S-shaped bend crosses into Egypt ab. 3 m. N of Wadi Halfa and flows N about 400 m. to Mediterranean; 12 m. below Cairo enters delta (120 m. wide), which in ancient times had seven branches but now has two principal mouths, each ab. 146 m. long: Rosetta (on W) entering sea just E of Alexandria, and Damietta (on E) just W of Port Said.

Generally navigable from sea to Murchison Falls, except in low season along stretch of 900 m. that contains its six so-called cataracts (actually rapids): the 1st just above Aswān (*q.v.*) 24°N, the only one in Egypt proper, where early Mediterranean civilization ended; the 2d (now under water) in N Sudan, just W of Wadi Halfa ab. 21°50′N, marking roughly the N limits of ancient Cush; the 3d in ancient Nubia ab. 47 m. below Dunqulah 19°50′N (700 m. by river below Khartoum); the 4th in the great bend of the Nile just above Marawī ab. 18°36′N, obstructed by granite and basalt ridges, the most difficult of all to navigate; the 5th ab. 40 m. below Berber at ab. 18°30′N; the 6th in the desert ab. 55 m. below Khartoum 16°10′N. Three large dams: Aswān High Dam, Gebel Aulia (20 m. S of Khartoum) and Makwar (near Sennar on Blue Nile). Extent between Aswān High Dam and ab. 20°40′N forms Lake Nasser; in Egypt lined with famous structures and ruins of ancient dynasties, as at Luxor and Karnak (site of ancient Thebes), Memphis, Giza (formation of Lake Nasser in 1960's caused the flooding of numerous other archaeological sites, incl. Abu Simbel). Its source a matter of mystery and legend for centuries, believed to be in "Mountains of the Moon" (probably Mt. Ruwenzori); down to 15th cent. little knowledge gained; upper regions visited by Italian and Portuguese travelers 15th–17th cents. Along its course notable discoveries have been made by European explorers: James Bruce, who discovered source of Blue Nile and traced its course 1768–73; various Egyptian expeditions bet. 1820 and 1842 that explored White Nile as far S as Gondokoro (ab. 5°N); J. H. Speke, who first determined Lake Victoria (*q.v.*) as main reservoir of Nile 1858; Speke and J. A. Grant, who further explored the lake 1860–62 by reaching Nile outlet at Ripon Falls (now flooded due to construction of Owen Falls Dam); (Sir) Samuel Baker, who in two journeys 1861–62 and 1863–65 discovered Lake Albert and Murchison Falls. Battle of the Nile fought at Abukir Bay; see ABUKIR 2.

Niles \'nī(ə)lz\. **1** Village, Cook co., NE Illinois, 14 m. N of Chicago; pop. (1970c) 31,432; residential.

2 City, Berrien co., SW Michigan, 48 m. SW of Kalamazoo; pop. (1970c) 12,988; paper products, steel cable; mushroom canning.

3 Industrial city, Trumbull co., NE Ohio, on Mahoning river 8 m. NNW of Youngstown; pop. (1970c) 21,581; sheet steel products, boilers, chemicals; railroad shops; birthplace of William McKinley, 25th president of the U.S.

Niles Center. See SKOKIE.

Nil·gi·ri \'nil-gə-rē\. **1** Former Indian state, now part of Orissa state, India, near coast of Bay of Bengal; 263 sq. m. **2** Town, its ✱, 125 m. SW of Calcutta.

Nilgiri Hills *or* **Nil·gi·ris** \'nil-gə-rēz\. Plateau, Tamil Nadu state, India; average alt. 6500 ft.; highest point Mt. Doda Betta. Chief aboriginal tribes the Kotas and Todas.

Ni·ló·po·lis \nē-'lȯ-pə-ləs\. City, Rio de Janeiro state, SE Brazil, NW of Rio de Janeiro; munic. pop. (1968e) 128,514.

Nil·sen Plateau \'nil-sᵊn-\ *or formerly* **Thor·vald Nilsen Mountains** \ˌtȯr-val(d)-\. Mountain group, Queen Maud Mountains, Ross Dependency, Antarctica, 86°20′S, 158°W; highest peaks over 13,000 ft.; discovered by Amundsen 1911.

Nilus. See NILE.

Nim·ba, Mount \-'nim-bə\. Mountain, W Ivory Coast, W Africa; 6069 ft.; highest peak in Ivory Coast.

Nimburg. See NYMBURK.

Nimeguen. See NIJMEGEN.

Nîmes *or older* **Nismes** \'nēm\ *or anc.* **Ne·mau·sus** \ni-'mȯ-səs\. Manufacturing and commercial city, ✱ of Gard dept., S France, 64 m. NW of Marseilles; pop. (1968c) 123,942; textiles, brandy, footwear, leather goods; trades in wine and grain; 11th cent. cathedral (on site of former temple of Apollo); noted esp. for its ancient Roman buildings and monuments, among which are a Corinthian temple (Maison Carrée) restored 1789 and converted into a museum 1823, a large amphitheater (Les Arènes) used as a fortress by Visigoths and Saracens against Franks, remains of an ancient tower (Turris Magna; *Fr.* Tour Magne), two gates, ruins of a nymphaeum, and, nearby, ruins of a major aqueduct (Pont du Gard). Thought to have been founded by Greek colonists; held by Romans for five centuries and one of the principal cities of Roman Gaul; Protestant stronghold in 16th cent.; treaty (Pacification of Nîmes) signed here 1629; scene of uprising 1815.

Nimfaíon, Ákra. See NYMPHAION, CAPE.

Nim·roze \'nim-(ˌ)rōz\. Province of SW Afghanistan. See table at AFGHANISTAN.

Nimrud. See CALAH.

Ni·mu·le \'nē-mu̇-ˌlā\. Town, Equatoria prov., S Sudan, on border with Uganda, ab. 90 m. SSE of Juba.

Nimule National Park. National park, Sudan; 100 sq. m.; wildlife (buffalo, elephant, hippopotamus, white rhinoceros); established 1954.

Nimwegen. See NIJMEGEN.

Nine Point Mesa. Elevation, cen. Brewster co., W Texas; 5551 ft.

Ninety Mile Beach. Straight stretch of flat coastal land, Gippsland, SE Victoria, SE Australia.

Nin·e·veh \'nin-ə-və\ *or anc.* **Ni·nus** \'nī-nəs\. Ancient capital of Assyria; its ruins on the Tigris river, originally covered by the mound Kuyunjik opp. Mosul, N Iraq. One of the greatest cities of antiquity; excavations, begun by Sir Austen Layard 1845, disclosed many buildings and parts of the walls. Greatest development took place under Sennacherib (705–681 B.C.); contained library and palace of Ashurbanipal; captured and destroyed by Nabopolassar of Babylonia and his allies 612 B.C.

Nin·fas, Cape \-ˈnim-ˌfäs\. Cape on NE coast of Chubut prov., S Argentina, at S entrance to New Gulf.

Ning–an \ˈniŋ-ˈän\ *or formerly* **Ning·u·ta** \ˈniŋ-ˈü-ˈtä\. Town, Heilungkiang prov., NE China, 150 m. ENE of Kirin.

Ning–po \ˈniŋ-ˈpō\ *or formerly* **Ning·hsien** \ˈniŋ-shē-ˈen\. City, NE Chekiang prov., E China, ab. 90 m. ESE of Hangchow on S side of Hangchow Bay and on small stream ab. 13 m. from its mouth; pop. (1970e) 350,000; textiles, electrical equipment, canned foods, soap; ships cotton, tea, and fish. Has occupied present site since 713 A.D.; first visited by Portuguese 1520; Portuguese expelled 1545; made a treaty port by Treaty of Nanking 1842.

Ning·sia *or* **Ning·hsia** \ˈniŋ-shē-ˈä\. Former province, W Inner Mongolia, N China; 106,115 sq. m.; bounded on N by Mongolian People's Republic; abolished 1954 and merged with Kansu; in 1956 most of its territory merged with Inner Mongolia, the remainder being reconstituted 1958 as Ningsia Hui (*q.v.*).

Ningsia Hui \-ˈhwē\. Autonomous region, N China; 30,039 sq. m.; pop. (1968e) 2,000,000; ✱ Yin-ch'uan; Great Wall runs along part of its NE boundary; rice, wheat; livestock; formed 1958.

Ningyuan. See KULDJA.

Ni·ni·go Group \ˈnē-ni-ˌgō-\. See NORTHWESTERN ISLANDS.

Ni·ni·ni Point \ni-ˌnē-nē-\. Point on SE coast of Kauai I., Hawaii, just N of Nawiliwili Bay.

Ni·nove \nē-ˈnòv\. Commune, East Flanders prov., NW cen. Belgium, on the Dender W of Brussels; pop. (1969e) 12,401.

Ninus. See NINEVEH.

Nio. See IOS 1.

Ni·o·brara \ˌnī-ə-ˈbrar-ə, -ˈbrer-\. 1 River, Wyoming and Nebraska; 431 m. long; flows from Niobrara co., E Wyoming, E across N Nebraska and into Missouri river in N cen. Knox co., NE Nebraska.

2 County in Wyoming. See table at WYOMING.

Ni·o·ko·lo–Ko·ba National Park \ˌnē-ə-ˌkō-lō-ˈkō-bə-\. National park, S Senegal; 965 sq. m.; antelope, elephant, hippopotamus; established 1951.

Ni·o·ro du Sa·hel \nē-ˈōr-ō-dü-sä-ˈel\. Town, Mali, W Africa, 200 m. NW of Bamako.

Niort \nē-ˈȯ(ə)r\. City, ✱ of Deux-Sèvres dept., W France, 83 m. SE of Nantes; pop. (1968c) 48,469; market town; leather goods; 15th cent. Gothic-Renaissance church; celebrated public garden and nursery gardens. Developed around castle built by Henry Plantagenet 1155; captured 1224 by Louis VIII; belonged to England 1360–73; became Protestant stronghold; suffered through Revocation of Edict of Nantes 1685.

Nip·a·win \ˈnip-ə-ˌwin\. Town, Saskatchewan, Canada, 75 m. ENE of Prince Albert; pop. (1971p) 4060; timber, fisheries; agriculture; flour mill.

Ni·pe Bay \ˌnē-pē-\. Bay on N coast of Oriente prov., E Cuba.

Niphon. See JAPAN.

Nip·i·gon, Lake \-ˈnip-i-ˌgän\ *also* **Lake Nep·i·gon** \-ˈnep-\. Lake, Thunder Bay dist., SW Ontario, Canada, ab. 35 m. N of Lake Superior; 1870 sq. m.; 72 m. long; max. depth 540 ft.; its outlet is **Nipigon River,** ab. 40 m. long, flowing S to **Nipigon Bay** in Lake Superior. Has many wooded islands and steep shores; visited by sportsmen.

Nipisiguit Bay. See NEPISIGUIT BAY.

Nip·is·sing \ˈnip-ə-ˌsiŋ\. District, Ontario, Canada. See table at ONTARIO.

Nipissing, Lake *also* **Lake Nep·is·sing** \-ˈnep-\. Lake, Nipissing dist., SE Ontario, Canada, NE of Georgian Bay; 350 sq. m.; its outlet is French river, flowing W to Georgian Bay. Contains many islands; has steamer navigation and is on projected route of canal from Ottawa river to Georgian Bay. Part of route of early French explorers to the West (1659–1743).

Nip·ple·top \ˈnip-əl-ˌtäp\. Peak in the Adirondack Mts., Essex co., NE New York; 4620 ft.

Nippon. See JAPAN.

Nip·pur \nip-ˈu̇(ə)r\. Ancient Sumerian and Babylonian city 100 m. SE of Babylon; a religious center, sacred to En-lil. Scene of archaeological excavations, in which many buildings and temple archives were uncovered.

Ni·que·ro \ni-ˈker-(ˌ)ō\. Municipality, Oriente prov., E Cuba, on S shore of Guacanayabo Bay 37 m. SW of Manzanillo; pop. (1967e) 86,820.

Niriz. 1 Town, Iran. See NEYRIZ.

2 Lake, Iran. See BAKHTIGĀN.

Niš *or* **Nish** \ˈnish\; *anc.* **Na·is·sus** *or* **Na·ïs·sus** \nā-ˈis-əs\ *or* **Nis·sa** \ˈnis-ə\. City, Serbia, E Yugoslavia, on Nišava river, ab. 125 m. SE of Belgrade; pop. (1971p) 127,178; railroad junction and commercial center; textiles, electronic equipment; food processing; railroad workshops; univ. (1965); birthplace of Constantine the Great. Held at various periods by Bulgarians, Hungarians, and Turks (for ab. 300 years); passed to Serbia 1878 and was capital of Serbia until 1901; taken by Germans 1915 and Apr. 1941; taken by U.S.S.R. Oct. 13, 1944.

Ni·saea \nī-ˈsē-ə\. Plain, ancient Media, just SW of Caspian Sea; famous for its (*Nisaean*) breed of large fine horses used by Persian kings c. 500 B.C.

Ni·ša·va *or* **Ni·sha·va** \ˈnē-shə-ˌvä\. River, Bulgaria and SE Yugoslavia; total length 135 m., of which 93 m. is in Yugoslavia; flows out of Bulgaria NW into Morava river 8 m. W of Niš.

Ni·sce·mi \ni-ˈshā-mē, -ˈshem-ē\. Commune, Caltanissetta prov., cen. Sicily, Italy, 30 m. SE of Caltanissetta; pop. (1968e) 25,351.

Nish. See NIŠ.

Nishapur. See NEYSHĀBŪR.

Nishava. See NIŠAVA.

Ni·shi·no·mi·ya \ˌnish-ə-ˈnō-mē-ˌ(y)ä\. City, Hyōgo prefecture, W Honshū, Japan, ab. 11 m. E of Kōbe on N shore of Ōsaka Bay; pop. (1970c) 377,043; chemicals, rubber, textiles, cosmetics, machinery; sake breweries.

Nishi Notoro, Cape. See KRILOV, CAPE.

Ni·shio \ni-ˈshē-(ˌ)ō, ˈnish-ē-ˌō\. City, Aichi prefecture, Honshū, Japan, 25 m. SSE of Nagoya; pop. (1970c) 75,193.

Nish·na·bot·na \ˌnish-nə-ˈbät-nə\. River, W Iowa and Missouri; 40 m. long; formed by confluence of **East Nishnabotna** (ab. 160 m. long) and **West Nishnabotna** (ab. 160 m. long), flows S across Missouri border and into Missouri river in Atchison co., NW Missouri.

Nisibin *or* **Nisibis.** See NUSAYBİN.

Ni·si·da \ˈnē-zi-ˌdä\ *or anc.* **Ne·sis** \ˈnē-səs\. Island in the Bay of Naples, S Italy, SE of Pozzuoli.

Nisiro *or* **Nísiros.** See NISYROS.

Nismes. See NÎMES.

Nísoi Aiyaíou. See AEGEAN ISLANDS 2.

Nis·qual·ly *or* **Nes·qual·ly** \nə-ˈskwäl-ē\. River, W cen. Washington; ab. 70 m. long; flows NW from **Nisqually Glacier** on S slope of Mount Rainier, forming boundary bet. Pierce and Thurston cos., and empties into **Nisqually Reach,** inlet at S end of Puget Sound.

Nissa. See NIŠ.

Nis·san \ni-ˈsän\. Main island of Green Is. group, N Solomon Is., W Pacific Ocean, E of SE New Ireland. Taken by Americans Feb. 1944.

Nissan \ˈnis-ˌan\. River, S Sweden; flows SW into the Kattegat at Halmstad.

Nistru. See DNIESTER.

Ni·sy·ros \'nē-si-ˌrȯs\ *or Gk.* **Ní·si·ros** \'nē-si-ˌrȯs\ *or Ital.* **Ni·si·ro** \'nē-zi-ˌrō\. An island of the Dodecanese (*q.v.*), S of Kos; 14 sq. m.

Ni·te·rói \ˌnēt-ə-'rȯi\ *or formerly* **Nic·the·roy** \ˌnēt-ə-'rȯi\. City, ✻ of Rio de Janeiro state, SE Brazil, on SE shore of Guanabara Bay opp. Rio de Janeiro, of which it is a suburb; pop. (1970p) 324,367; industrial center, producing textiles, glass, matches, chemicals, pharmaceuticals, cement; shipbuilding and repairing, food processing; univ. (1960). Founded 1671; became capital of state 1835; made city 1836.

Nith \'nith\. River, SW Scotland; 79 m. long; rises in Ayrshire, flows SE into Solway Firth 10 m. S of Dumfries.

Ni·tra \'n(y)i-trə\ *or Hung.* **Nyi·tra** \'nyi-(ˌ)trȯ\ *or Ger.* **Neu·tra** \'nȯit-rə\. 1 River, Slovak S.R., Czechoslovakia; ab. 110 m. long; flows S into Váh river just above Komárno on the Hungarian border.

2 Town, Slovak S.R., Czechoslovakia, on Nitra river; pop. (1968e) 42,536; in agricultural region; beer, chemicals; site of oldest church in Slovakia, estab. c. 830.

Nit·ria \'ni-trē-ə\ *or* **Nit·ri·ae** \-trē-ˌē\. Desert region of Natron Lakes, Egypt, W of Cairo; in early times seat of famous settlement of anchorites.

Ni·tro \'nī-(ˌ)trō\. City, Kanawha and Putnam cos., SW West Virginia, on Kanawha river 13 m. WNW of Charleston; pop. (1970c) 8019; grew up around powder plant erected by U.S. government 1918; incorp. 1932.

Nit·ta·ny Valley \ˌnit-ᵊn-ē-\. Fertile valley in Centre and Clinton cos., cen. Pennsylvania; ab. 30 m. long by 4 m. wide.

Ni·u·a·foo \nē-'ü-ē-ˌfō\. Island in extreme N part of Tonga, SW cen. Pacific Ocean, 400 m. N of Tongatabu; 15°34'S, 175°40'W; area 6 sq. m.; pop. (1966c) 599.

Ni·u·a·to·pu·ta·pu \nē-ˌü-ə-ˌtō-pə-'täp-(ˌ)ü\; *formerly* **Ni·u·a·to·bu·ta·bu** \-bə-'täb-\ *or* **Kep·pel's Island** \ˌkep-əlz-\. Island in N part of Tonga, SW cen. Pacific Ocean, ab. 150 m. N of Vavau group; 5 sq. m.; pop. (1966c) 1395.

Niuchwang. See YING-K'OU.

Ni·ue \nē-'ü-(ˌ)(w)ā\ *or* **Sav·age Island** \'sav-ij-\. Island in S cen. Pacific Ocean E of Tonga and 350 m. SSE of Samoa, lat. 19°02'S and long. 169°52'W; 100 sq. m.; pop. (1971e) 5128; chief village and port Alofi, on W coast; bananas, copra. A New Zealand dependency, originally part of Cook Is. administration but separate since 1922. Discovered by Capt. Cook 1774.

Nive \'nēv\. River, Pyrénées-Atlantiques dept., SW France; ab. 50 m. long; flows W to the Adour along base of W Pyrenees; several battles on its banks Dec. 1813 resulting in victory of British over French.

Ni·velles \ni-'vel\. Commune, Brabant prov., cen. Belgium; pop. (1969e) 15,903; manufactures linens, cotton goods, lace, machinery; convent dating from 7th cent.; 11th cent. Romanesque Church of Saint Gertrude.

Ni·ver·nais \ˌniv-ər-'nā\. Historical region of cen. France; bounded anciently on N, E, and SE by Burgundy, S and SW by Bourbonnais, W by Berry, NW by Orléanais; ✻ Nevers. Originally inhabited by the Ædui; part of Burgundian kingdom; comprised diocese of Nevers from beginning of 6th cent. A.D.; countship founded at end of 9th cent.; passed successively to Pierre de Courtenay 1184, Robert de Dampierre 1272, to house of Burgundy 1405; to German family of Clèves 1491; made duchy 1539; passed to Gonzaga family 1566, to Mazarin 1659; French province until Revolution.

Nivernais, Ca·nal du \kə-'nal-də-\. Canal, Yonne and Nièvre depts., cen. France; 45 m. long; connects Loire river at Decize with the Seine by way of the Seine's tributary, the Yonne river, which it follows above Auxerre.

Nix·on \'nik-sən\. City, Gonzales co., S cen. Texas, 44 m. ESE of San Antonio; pop. (1970c) 1925; peanuts.

Ni·zam·a·bad \ni-'zäm-ə-ˌbäd, nī-'zam-ə-ˌbad\. Town, NW Andhra Pradesh, S cen. India, 100 m. N of Hyderabad; pop. (1961c) 79,093; rice and sugar.

Nizam's Dominions. See HYDERABAD 1.

Nizh·ne·u·dinsk \ˌnizh-nē-ü-'dinsk\. Town, W Irkutsk Oblast, Russian S.F.S.R., U.S.S.R., on the upper Chuna river; pop. (1967e) 38,000; on the Trans-Siberian R.R.

Nizh·ni Nov·go·rod *also* **Nij·ni Novgorod** \ˌnizh-nē-'näv-gə-ˌräd\. 1 Old government and province of Russia, somewhat larger than the modern Gorki Oblast.

2 City, U.S.S.R. See GORKI.

Nizhni Ta·gil \-tə-'gil\. City, W Sverdlovsk Oblast, Russian S.F.S.R., U.S.S.R., on E slopes of Ural Mts. 80 m. N of Sverdlovsk; pop. (1970p) 378,000; blast furnaces, foundries, chemical factories; iron ore, copper, and gold mines nearby; founded 1725.

Nizhnyaya Tunguska. See TUNGUSKA.

Ni·zip \nə-'zēp\; *formerly* **Ni·zib** *or* **Ne·zib** \nə-'zēb\. Town, Gaziantep prov., S Turkey, ab. 22 m. E of Gaziantep; pop. (1965c) 22,675; scene of battle June 24, 1839, in which army of Ibrahim Pasha of Egypt completely defeated Turkish forces.

Niz·wa, Kuh–i– \ˌkü-(h)ē-nēz-'wä\. Mountain in E Elburz Mts., N Iran, ab. 55 m. SSE of Bābol; 13,051 ft.

Nizza. See NICE 2.

Niz·za Mon·fer·ra·to \ˌnēt-sə-ˌmōn-fer-'ät-(ˌ)ō\. Commune, Asti prov., SE Piedmont, NW Italy, ab. 15 m. SE of Asti; pop. (1968e) 9775.

Njommelsaska. See HARSPRÅNGET.

Nkaw·kaw \eŋ-'kō-ˌkō\. Town, Eastern Region, Ghana, ab. 60 m. ESE of Kumasi; pop. (1970p) 23,405.

Nkong·sam·ba \eŋ-kȯŋ-'säm-bə\. Town, W Cameroon, ab. 133 m. NW of Yaoundé; pop. (1970e) 71,000.

Nmai \nə-'mī\ *or* **N'mai Kha** \-ˌkä\. River (*kha*), Upper Burma; ab. 300 m. long; flows S from SE corner of Tibet, China, to unite with the Mali and form the Irrawaddy river.

No. See THEBES 1.

No, Lake \-'nō\. Lake in S cen. Sudan, E Africa, where Bahr al-Jebel and Bahr al-Ghazal join to form the White Nile (see NILE); maximum area 40 sq. m.

Noa. See NOICATTARO.

No·ailles \nō-'ī\. 1 Commune, Corrèze dept., cen. France, S of Brive-la-Gaillarde; pop. (1962c) 358; castle from which Noailles family is named.

2 Commune, cen. Oise dept., N France, SSE of Beauvais; pop. (1962c) 1267; belonged to famous Noailles family; adopted name in 17th cent. before which it was known as **Long·vil·liers** \ˌlȯⁿ-vēl-'yā\.

No·a·kha·li \ˌnō-äk-'häl-ē\ *or* **Su·dha·ram** \sü-'där-ˌäm\. Town, Bangla Desh, on E side of mouth of Ganges; pop. (1961c) 19,874.

No·a·tak \nō-'ät-ək\. 1 River, NW Alaska; ab. 400 m. long; flows W bet. Brooks Range and Baird Mts., then S to Kotzebue Sound; extensive mineral deposits in its basin. First explored 1885–86.

2 Unincorporated village and Eskimo mission station, Alaska, on right bank of the Noatak near its mouth, ab. 55 m. N of Kotzebue; pop. (1970c) 293.

No·be·o·ka \ˌnō-bē-'ō-kə\. City, Miyazaki prefecture, E coast of Kyūshū, Japan; pop. (1970c) 128,292.

Nob Hill \'näb-\. Hill in SW San Francisco, California; in early days a fashionable residential section.

No·ble \'nō-bəl\. Name of counties in three states of the U.S. See tables at INDIANA, OHIO, OKLAHOMA.

No·bles \'nō-bəlz\. County in Minnesota. See table at MINNESOTA.

No·bles·ville \'nō-bəlz-ˌvil\. City, ⊗ of Hamilton co., cen. Indiana, 20 m. NNE of Indianapolis; pop. (1970c) 7548; truck bodies, rubber products; livestock.

Noc, Big Bay de \-ˌbād-ə-'näk\. Northern extension of Green Bay on S coast of Delta co., S Michigan penin., just E of **Little Bay de Noc.**

No·ce·ra In·fe·ri·o·re \nō-'cher-ə-in-ˌfer-ē-'ōr-ē, -'ȯr-\ *or anc.* **Nu·ce·ria Al·fa·ter·na** \n(y)ü-'sir-ē-ə-ˌal-fə-'tər-nə\. Commune, Salerno prov., Campania, S Italy, 8 m. NW of Salerno; pop. (1968e) 49,167; lumber, textiles, macaroni; castle.

Nocera Su·pe·ri·o·re \-sů-ˌper-ē-ˈōr-ē, -ˈȯr-\. Commune, Salerno prov., Campania, S Italy, 5 m. NW of Salerno; pop. (1968e) 15,417; 4th cent. church.

No·ce·to \nō-ˈchā-(ˌ)tō\. Commune, Parma prov., Emilia-Romagna, N Italy, 7 m. W by S of Parma; pop. (1968e) 9005; castle.

No·chis·tlán \ˌnō-chēs-ˈtlän\. Municipality, Zacatecas state, Mexico, 105 m. S of Zacatecas; pop. (1970p) 28,463; livestock raising; wheat, barley, peanuts.

No·chix·tlán \ˌnō-chēs-ˈtlän\. Municipality, Oaxaca state, Mexico, 45 m. NW of Oaxaca; pop. (1970p) 56,998.

No·ci \ˈnō-chē\. Commune, Bari prov., Apulia, SE Italy, 27 m. SE of Bari; pop. (1968e) 17,177.

No·co·na \nə-ˈkōn-ə\. City, Montague co., N Texas, 42 m. E of Wichita Falls; pop. (1970c) 2871; leather goods; oil and gas wells.

No·da \ˈnō-də\. City, Chiba prefecture, Honshū, Japan, 22 m. N of Tokyo; pop. (1970c) 66,641.

Nod·a·way \ˈnäd-ə-ˌwā\. 1 River, Iowa and Missouri; ab. 150 m. long; rises in Cass co., SW Iowa, and flows S into Missouri river in W Andrew co., NW Missouri.
2 County in Missouri. See table at MISSOURI.

Noemfoor. See NUMFOOR.

Nœux–les–Mines \ˌnə(r)l-ā-ˈmēn\. Commune, Pas-de-Calais dept., N France, 14 m. NNW of Arras; pop. (1968c) 13,325; coal mines; destroyed in World War I.

No·fil·ia \nō-ˈfil-yə\ *also* **En Nofilia** \ˌen-\. Town, N Libya, N Africa, near S cen. coast of the Gulf of Sidra.

No·gal·es \nō-ˈgal-əs, -ˈgäl-\. 1 City, ⊗ of Santa Cruz co., S Arizona, on Mexican border 60 m. S of Tucson and immediately adjacent to Mexican town of the same name; pop. (1970c) 8946; copper, silver, and lead mines; livestock farms. Site of Spanish mission (1687); incorporated 1893; scene of skirmishes against Pancho Villa 1916.
2 Town, Sonora state, NW Mexico, on the United States frontier adjacent to Nogales, Arizona (see 1, above); munic. pop. (1970p) 52,865; port of entry; trades in cattle and minerals.
3 Town, Veracruz state, E Mexico; pop. (1970p) 19,158.

No·gal Peak \nō-ˈgal-\. Mountain in the Sierra Blanca, S cen. New Mexico; 9983 ft.

No·gat \ˈnō-ˌgät\. Eastern branch of the lower Vistula, Poland; ab. 33 m. long; flows NE out of the main stream into Vilinski Zaliv. Formerly formed boundary bet. East Prussia and Free State of Danzig.

Nō·ga·ta \nō-ˈgät-ə\. Town, Fukuoka prefecture, N Kyūshū, Japan; pop. (1970c) 55,615; coal mines.

No·gent–le–Ro·trou \nȯ-ˌzhäⁿl-rȯ-ˈtrü\. Town, W Eure-et-Loir dept., N cen. France; pop. (1968c) 11,578; the hospital contains tomb of Duc de Sully.

Nogent–sur–Marne \-sů(ə)r-ˈmärn\. Commune, Val-de-Marne dept., N France, ESE suburb of Paris on Marne river; pop. (1968c) 26,238; chemicals, hardware.

Nogent–sur–Seine \-ˈsān, -ˈsen\. Town, NW Aube dept., NE France; pop. (1965e) 4190; ab. 4 m. SE is a farm on site of the Paraclete (*Fr.* Abbaye du Paraclet), the abbey which Abélard founded for Héloïse 1123.

No·ginsk \nō-ˈgin(t)sk\ *or formerly* **Bo·go·rodsk** \ˌbäg-ə-ˈrätsk\. City, Moscow Oblast, Russian S.F.S.R., U.S.S.R., on spur of main railroad line 35 m. E of Moscow; pop. (1970p) 104,000; textiles, needles, engine parts; founded 16th cent.

No·go·yá \ˌnō-gə-ˈyä\. Town, Entre Ríos prov., E Argentina, 60 m. SE of Paraná; pop. (1960c) 10,911.

Nó·grád \ˈnō-ˌgräd\. County of N Hungary. See table at HUNGARY.

No·gue·ra Pa·lla·re·sa \nō-ˈger-ə-ˌpä(l)-yə-ˈrā-sə\. River in NE Spain; flows out of the Pyrenees into Segre river 20 m. NE of Lérida.

Noguera Ri·ba·gor·za·na \-ˌrē-bə-gȯr-ˈsän-ə\ *or* **Noguera Ri·va·go·ran·zo** \-ˌrē-və-gə-ˈrän-(ˌ)zō\. River in NE Spain; flows out of the Pyrenees into Segre river 15 m. N of Lérida.

No·hi·li Point \nō-ˌhē-lē-\. Point on W coast of Kauai I., Hawaii.

Noi·cat·ta·ro \nȯi-ˈkät-ə-(ˌ)rō\; *before 1863* **Noa** \ˈnȯ-ə\ *or* **No·ia** \ˈnȯ-yə\. Commune, Bari prov., Apulia, SE Italy, 8 m. SE of Bari; pop. (1968e) 14,103; 13th cent. Romanesque church.

Noire \ˈnwär\. French name of Black river, Indochina.

Noir·mou·tier, Île de \ˌēl-dən-ˌwär-mü-ˈtyā\. Island in Bay of Biscay off NW coast of Vendée dept., W France; ab. 12 m. long and 1 to 4 m. wide; belongs to Vendée dept.; site of monastery founded c. 680; chief town **Noirmoutier,** pop. (1962c) 3962, in NE part of the island.

Noi·sy–le–Grand \nwä-ˌzē-lə-ˈgräⁿ\. Commune, Seine-St-Denis dept., N France, ab. 9 m. E of Paris; pop. (1968c) 25,440.

Noisy–le–Sec \nwä-ˌzēl-(ə-)ˈsek\. Commune, Seine-St-Denis dept., N France, ENE suburb of Paris; pop. (1968c) 34,079; chemical and metallurgical industry.

No·ji·ma, Cape \-nō-ˈje-mə\. Cape, S tip of Chiba prefecture, SE Honshū, Japan, marking SE point of Sagami Sea.

No·ji·ri \ˈnō-jə-rē\. Lake on N border of Nagano prefecture, cen. Honshū, Japan, ab. 18 m. S of Takada; ab. 8½ m. in circumference; on a small island in the lake is a temple of Kwannon founded 730.

No·ki·la·la·ki \ˌnō-kē-lə-ˈläk-ē\. Mountain, NW cen. Celebes I., Indonesia, SE of Donggala; 10,860 ft.

No·ko·mis \nə-ˈkōm-əs\. City, Montgomery co., S cen. Illinois, 38 m. SE of Springfield; pop. (1970c) 2532.

Nokuhiva. See NUKU HIVA.

No·la \ˈnō-lə\. Commune, Napoli prov., Campania, S Italy, 16 m. ENE of Naples; pop. (1968e) 27,009; in agricultural region; cathedral (remodeled in 14th cent.); seminary; Franciscan convent. Founded before 5th cent. B.C.; passed to Rome 313 B.C.; site of battles bet. Marcellus and Hannibal 216 and 215 B.C.; place where Augustus died 14 A.D.

No·lan \ˈnō-lən\. County in Texas. See table at TEXAS.

Nol·i·chuck·ey \ˌnäl-ə-ˈchək-ē\. River, North Carolina and Tennessee; ab. 150 m. long; rises in Blue Ridge Mts., W North Carolina, and flows NW into French Broad river in Tennessee.

No Mans Land \ˈnō-ˌmanz-ˌland\. Small island in Atlantic Ocean in Dukes co., SE Massachusetts; SW of Martha's Vineyard.

Nom·bre de Dios \ˈnȯm-brē-ˌdād-ē-ˈōs\. Spanish port and early settlement on the N coast of Panama, just NE of Portobelo; founded 1510 by Nicuesa; included in Veragua region; abandoned 1597 because it was unhealthful. Until 1584 was a port of destination for cargo fleets from Spain.

Nome \ˈnōm\. City on S side of Seward Penin., W Alaska, 14 m. W of Cape Nome and ab. 100 m. E of Bering Strait; pop. (1970c) 2488; tourism, fur-trapping; formerly gold-mining center. Founded 1896 as gold mining camp and later a center of the great Alaskan gold rush 1899–1903.

Nome, Cape. Cape, W Alaska, on S side of Seward Penin., ab. 64°30′N, 165°W.

No–men–k'an \ˈnō-ˈmən-ˈkän\ *or* **No·mon·han** \-ˈmȯn-ˈhän\. Town, Inner Mongolia, NE China, on border of Mongolian People's Republic, E of Pei-erh; scene of Russian victory over Japanese 1939.

No·mo \ˈnō-(ˌ)mō\ *or Jap.* **Nomo Za·ki** \-ˈzäk-ē\. Cape (*Jap.* zaki) on S side of Nagasaki bay, W Kyūshū, Japan.

No·moi Islands \ˌnō-mȯi-\. Atoll group in S Caroline Is. in W Pacific Ocean, SE of Truk Is.; 5°27′N, 153°40′E.

Nomonhan. See NO-MEN-K'AN.

No·nan·to·la \nō-ˈnän-tə-lə\. Commune, Modena prov., Emilia-Romagna, N Italy, 6 m. NE of Modena; pop. (1968e) 9040.

Nondaburi. See NONTHA BURI.

Nong Khai \ˈnȯŋ-ˈkī\ *or* **Nong·ka·ya** \ˈnȯŋ-ˈkī—*sic*\ *also* **Mi Chai** \ˈmē-ˈchī\. 1 Province, NE Thailand; 2789 sq. m.; pop. (1960c) 256,530; ✱ Nong Khai.
2 Town, its ✱, on right bank of the Mekong; pop. (1964e) 25,173.

Nonni. See NEN.

No·no·u·ti \ˌnō-nə-ˈüt-ē\. Island (atoll) in cen. part of Gilbert Is., just S of the equator, W Pacific Ocean; 24 m. long by 10 m. wide; good anchorage.

Non·such Island \ˌnən-səch-\. Small island in the Bermuda Is., E of Castle Harbour.

Non·tha Bu·ri \ˌnən-bu̇-ˈrē—*sic*\ *or* **Non·da·bu·ri** \ˌnən-bu̇-ˈrē—*sic*\. 1 Province, S Thailand; 241 sq. m.; pop. (1960c) 196,196; ✱ Nontha Buri.
2 Town, its ✱, on left bank of the lower Chao Phraya, a N suburb of Bangkok; pop. (1964e) 18,151.

Noon·mark \ˈnün-ˌmärk\. Peak in the Adirondack Mts., Essex co., NE New York; 3552 ft.

Noord \ˈnō(ə)rt\. Name sometimes given to the Merwede (*q.v.*) bet. Dordrecht and its confluence with the Lek, W Netherlands.

Noordbrabant. See NORTH BRABANT.

Noordholland. See NORTH HOLLAND.

Noord·oost·pol·der \ˌnōrt-ˌōst-ˈpōl-dər\. Commune, Overijssel prov., Netherlands; pop. (1970e) 31,929; fruit, vegetables.

Noord·wijk \ˈnō(ə)rt-ˌvīk\. Commune, South Holland prov., SW Netherlands, on coast 12 m. N of the Hague; pop. (1970e) 20,925; seaside resort.

Noord Zee Kanaal. See NORTH SEA CANAL.

Noot·ka Sound \ˌnu̇t-kə-, ˌnüt-\. Inlet of Pacific Ocean in W Vancouver I., SW British Columbia, Canada, 49°33′N, 126°38′W; it forms a good harbor with three arms, one of which is a narrow channel separating **Nootka Island** (203 sq. m.) from Vancouver I. Visited by Capt. Cook 1778; seizure by Spanish 1789 led to breach bet. England and Spain which was settled by Nootka Convention Oct. 28, 1790.

Noph. See MEMPHIS 4.

No·ran·da \nə-ˈran-də\. Mining city, Timiskaming co., SW Quebec, Canada; pop. (1971p) 10,670; mining machinery; paper mill, copper and gold mines.

Norba Caesarea. See ALCÁNTARA.

Nor·cia \ˈnȯr-(ˌ)chä\ *also* **Nur·sia** \ˈnu̇r-sē-ə\. Commune, Perugia prov., Umbria, cen. Italy, 41 m. ESE of Perugia; pop. (1968e) 5719; 14th cent. walls; cathedral; 6th cent. church; birthplace of Saint Benedict.

Nor·co \ˈnō(ə)r-(ˌ)kō, ˈnȯ(ə)r-\. City, Riverside co., SE California, 45 m. W of Palm Springs; pop. (1970c) 14,511; diversified agriculture.

Nor·cross \ˈnȯ(ə)r-ˌkrȯs\. City, Gwinnett co., N Georgia, 15 m. NE of Atlanta; pop. (1970c) 2755.

Nord \ˈnȯr\. Department of N France. See table at FRANCE.

Nordalbingia. See DITHMARSCHEN.

Nor·den \ˈnȯrd-ᵊn\. Seaport city, NW Lower Saxony, West Germany, on North Sea 16 m. N of Emden, E of Ems estuary; pop. (1968e) 16,271; manufactures iron goods, brandy, dehydrated milk. Oldest town in Ostfriesland.

Nordenskjöld Sea. See LAPTEV SEA.

Nor·der·ney \ˌnȯrd-ər-ˈnī\. Island, Lower Saxony, West Germany, in cen. part of East Frisian Is. in the North Sea; 9 sq. m.; pop. (1961c) 7331; resort.

Nord Fjord \ˈnō(ə)r-ˈfyō(ə)r, ˈnȯ(ə)r-ˈfyȯ(ə)r\. Inlet of Norwegian Sea on SW cen. coast of Norway.

Nord·hau·sen \ˈnȯrt-ˌhau̇z-ᵊn\. Industrial city, Erfurt dist., East Germany, at S foot of Harz Mts. 36 m. NNW of Erfurt; pop. (1970e) 44,505; tractors, mining and drilling equipment, tobacco; distilling; Gothic cathedral, 17th cent. town hall. First mentioned 927 A.D.; free city 1220; to Prussia 1803, kingdom of Westphalia 1807, Prussia 1813; during World War II site of concentration camp.

Nord·horn \ˈnȯrt-ˌhȯrn\. Town, Lower Saxony, West Germany, ab. 44 m. NW of Münster; pop. (1969e) 42,706; textiles; first mentioned 890.

Nord·jyl·land \ˈnȯ(ə)rd-ˌē-lȧn\. County, N Jutland, Denmark. See table at DENMARK.

Nordkapp. See NORTH CAPE 4.

Nord·kyn, Cape \-ˈnō(ə)r-kən, -ˈnȯ(ə)r-\. Cape on NE coast of Norway, 45 m. E of North Cape (*q.v.*); northernmost point of European mainland, 70°55′N, 27°45′E.

Nord·land \ˈnō(ə)r-län\. County of W Norway. See table at NORWAY.

Nörd·ling·en \ˈnərt-liŋ-ən\. Commune, Bavaria, West Germany; pop. (1968e) 14,076; scene of two battles in Thirty Years' War: (1) in 1634, in which Swedish army under Duke Bernhard of Saxe-Weimar and Marshal Horn was defeated; (2) in 1645, in which Germans were defeated, Mercy being mortally wounded.

Nord–Ost·see Ka·nal \ˌnȯr-ˌtōst-ˌzā-kə-ˈnäl\ *or* **Kiel Canal** \ˌkē(ə)l-\ *or formerly* **Kai·ser Wil·helm Canal** \ˌkī-zər-ˈvil-ˌhelm-\. Canal extending from the Baltic Sea to the North Sea, NE to SW across Schleswig-Holstein in West Germany; 61 m. long, from city of Kiel past Rendsburg to Brunsbüttelkoog at the mouth of the Elbe; constructed 1887–95 and owned by the German government; alterations made 1914; surface width 338 ft., bottom width 144 ft., depth 37 ft.; has no locks except those at either end, necessary because of tides; frequently bombed in World War II.

Nordrhein–Westfalen. See NORTH RHINE-WESTPHALIA.

Nord Slesvig. See SOUTH JUTLAND.

Nord·strand \ˈnȯ(ə)rt-ˌs(h)tränt\. One of the Halligen Is. in S part of North Frisian Is. off W coast of Schleswig-Holstein, N West Germany; area 19 sq. m.; pop. (1969e) 3000.

Nord–Trøn·de·lag \nō(ə)r-ˈtrə(r)n-də-ˌläg, nȯ(ə)r-\. County of cen. Norway. See table at NORWAY.

Nord·vik \ˈnȯ(ə)rd-(ˌ)vik\. 1 Bay, a large inlet of Laptev Sea just E of mouth of Khatanga river, NW Yakutsk A.S.S.R., Russian S.F.S.R., U.S.S.R.
2 Village on E bank of Khatanga river at its mouth S of Nordvik Bay.

Nore \ˈnō(ə)r, ˈnȯ(ə)r\. River, SE Eire; 70 m. long; rises in N co. Tipperary, flows SE through co. Kilkenny into the Barrow river near its mouth.

Nore, The. Sandbank in center of the estuary of the Thames river in SE England, 3 m. NE of Sheerness; at its E end is **Nore Light.** Generally taken as the dividing line bet. the river and its wide estuary; 47¾ m. below London Bridge.

Nor·folk \ˈnȯr-fək, *U.S. also* -ˌfȯk\. 1 County in Massachusetts. See table at MASSACHUSETTS.
2 Residential town, N Litchfield co., NW Connecticut, on Massachusetts border; pop. (1970c) 2073.
3 Town, Norfolk co., E Massachusetts, 21 m. SW of Boston; pop. (1970c) 4656.
4 City, Madison co., NE Nebraska, 54 m. NW of Fremont; pop. (1970c) 16,607; trade center; dairy products; flour and feed mills; diversified agriculture; Norfolk Junior Coll. (1927).
5 Independent city, SE Virginia, on Elizabeth river just S of Hampton Roads; 50 sq. m.; pop. (1970c) 307,951; with Newport News and Portsmouth comprises Port of Hampton Roads; exports coal, grain, tobacco, timber, vegetables; major shipbuilding center; produces automobiles, chemicals, fertilizers, agricultural machinery, textiles, seafood, and peanut oil; Norfolk State Coll. (1935), Virginia Wesleyan Coll. (1961); major military base, with ab. 20 U.S. Navy, U.S. Marine, and NATO facilities in the city.
History: Founded 1682; incorporated as borough 1736; entirely destroyed during American Revolution, when it was a Loyalist center; incorporated as city 1845; in Civil War occupied by Union forces from May 1862.
6 County, Ontario, Canada. See table at ONTARIO.
7 Maritime county, E England; 2054 sq. m.; pop. (1971p) 616,427; ⊗ Norwich; rivers Ouse, Bure, Yare, Waveney, Nene; wheat, barley, oats, sugar beet; livestock and poultry farming; tourism; main towns incl. Norwich, Great Yarmouth, King's Lynn, Thetford.

Norfolk Broads. See BROADS, THE.

Norfolk Island. Island in S Pacific Ocean, midway bet. New Caledonia and N New Zealand, and 930 m. ENE of Sydney, Australia; an external territory of Australia; 13 sq. m.; highest point 1043 ft.; pop. (1970e) 1380; site of the Pitcairn Islanders' second home. Discovered by Capt. Cook 1774 and used as a British penal colony 1788–1813 and 1825–1855; placed under jurisdiction of New South Wales 1856; made federal territory 1913.

Norge. See NORWAY.

Noric Alps. See table at ALPS.

Nor·i·cum \'nȯr-i-kəm\. Ancient country and Roman province S of Danube river, comprising the modern Lower and Upper Austria, the greater part of Carinthia, Styria, and Salzburg, and a small part of Bavaria; to the N across the Danube was Germania, on the E Pannonia, on the S Pannonia and Italy, and on the W Raetia and Vindelicia. A mountainous country (E Alps) with rich iron mines worked by the Romans. The Celtic inhabitants were conquered by Augustus.

No·ri·ku·ra \'nō̄r-ē-ku̇-ˌrä, 'nȯr-\. Mountain peak, Gifu prefecture, W cen. Honshū, Japan; 9918 ft.

No·rilsk \nə-'rēlsk\. Town, Krasnoyarsk Krai, Russian S.F.S.R., U.S.S.R., ab. 50 m. ESE of Dudinka; pop. (1970p) 136,000; mining center (cobalt, copper, nickel).

Norische Alpen. See table at ALPS.

Nor·mal \'nȯr-məl\. 1 Village, Madison co., N Alabama, 4 m. N of Huntsville; Alabama Agricultural and Mechanical Coll. (1873).

2 Town, McLean co., cen. Illinois, 5 m. N of Bloomington; pop. (1970c) 26,396; residential; dairy and livestock farms; Illinois State Univ. (1857).

Nor·man \'nȯr-mən\. 1 County in Minnesota. See table at MINNESOTA.

2 City, ⊗ of Cleveland co., cen. Oklahoma, 18 m. S of Oklahoma City; pop. (1970c) 52,117; center of livestock and dairy farming region; oil wells; Univ. of Oklahoma (1892); settled 1889, incorporated 1902.

3 River, N Queensland, Australia; 190 m. long; flows NW into Gulf of Carpentaria.

4 Trading station, Canada. See FORT NORMAN.

5 Small island, British Virgin Is., West Indies, S of Tortola I.

Norman, Cape. Cape, N tip of Newfoundland, Canada, at NE entrance to the Strait of Belle Isle.

Nor·man·by \'nȯr-mən-bē\. One of the D'Entrecasteaux Is. off SE point of New Guinea I., 3 m. SSE of Fergusson I.; administratively part of Papua New Guinea; ab. 45 m. long and from 12 to 15 m. wide; ab. 4000 sq. m.; separated from East Cape of Papua by Goschen Strait; central mountain range (highest point 3600 ft.); good harbor; produces copra.

Norman Coast. See MURMAN COAST.

Nor·man·dy \'nȯr-mən-dē\. 1 Town, St. Louis co., E Missouri, 4 m. NW of St. Louis; pop. (1970c) 6183.

2 *or Fr* **Nor·man·die** \nȯr mäⁿ-dē\. Historical region of NW France; bounded anciently on W and N by English Channel, NE by Picardy, E by Île-de-France, S by Maine, SW by Brittany; ✱ Rouen; watered by Seine, Orne, and Eure rivers; includes Cotentin Penin.

History: Under Romans, part of Lugdunensis; part of kingdom of Neustria after Frankish invasion; invaded by Northmen (whence its name) in middle of 9th cent.; region given over to conquerors under Rollo, 1st Duke of Normandy, by Charles III of France 911; united with English kingdom after conquest of England 1066 by William, Duke of Normandy; conquered by French under Philip Augustus 1204, by English 1417, and by French 1450; province of France until Revolution. In World War II scene of "Battle of Normandy," beginning June 12, 1944 after Allied landings (June 6–12) on five beaches along a 60-mile stretch from E of Caen W to Montebourg and lasting until Allied breakthrough at St-Lô and Avranches July 31.

Normandy Park. City, King co., W cen. Washington, 10 m. S of Seattle; pop. (1970c) 4202.

Nor·man·ton \'nȯr-mən-tən\. 1 Town, N Queensland, Australia, on Norman river 23 m. from Gulf of Carpentaria; goldfields.

2 Urban district, West Riding, Yorkshire, N England; pop. (1971p) 17,656.

Norman Wells \ˌnȯr-mən-\. Station on right bank of the Mackenzie, W Mackenzie dist., Northwest Territories, Canada, 50 m. NW of Fort Norman; oil wells; opp. starting point of Canol pipeline to Skagway.

Nor·nal·up National Park \nȯr-'nal-əp-\. National park, Western Australia; 52 sq. m.; ocean beaches; established 1957.

No·ro·ton \nō-'rōt-ᵊn\ *and* **Noroton Heights.** Subdivisions of town of Darien, Connecticut. See DARIEN 1.

Norr·bot·ten \'nȯr-ˌbȯt-ᵊn\. County of N Sweden. See table at SWEDEN.

Nor·ridge \'nȯr-ij, 'när-\. Village, Cook co., NE Illinois, W suburb of Chicago; pop. (1970c) 17,020.

Nor·ridge·wock \'nȯr-ij-ˌwäk, 'när-\. Town, Somerset co., W Maine, on Kennebec river 13 m. NW of Waterville; pop. (1970c) 1964; near site of an Abnaki Indian village, destroyed by whites Aug. 1724.

Nor·ris, Mount \-'nȯr-əs, -'när-\. Peak, Yellowstone National Park, NW Wyoming; 9936 ft.

Norris Lake *or formerly* **Clinch–Pow·ell Reservoir** \'klinch-'pau̇-əl-\. Lake formed by **Norris Dam,** one of the dams of the Tennessee Valley Authority (*q.v.*). See CLINCH 1.

Nor·ris·town \'nȯr-ə-ˌstau̇n, 'när-\. Manufacturing borough, ⊗ of Montgomery co., SE Pennsylvania, on Schuylkill river 17 m. NW of Philadelphia; pop. (1970c) 38,169; machinery, leather and rubber products, chemicals, plastics, beverages, hardware; founded 1704, incorporated 1812.

Norr·kö·ping \'nȯ(ə)r-ˌchə(r)p-iŋ\. Seaport, Östergötland co., SE Sweden, SW of Stockholm, at mouth of a river (draining Lake Vättern) at head of a long inlet of **Norrköping Bay;** pop. (1970e) 95,851; major industrial center, producing textiles, paper, radio and television sets, chemicals, and rubber; founded c. 1350; chartered 1384; burned by Russians 1719.

Norr·land \'nȯ(ə)r-ˌland\. Northern division of Sweden, comprising Gävleborg, Västernorrland, Jämtland, Västerbotten, and Norrbotten; land area 93,858 sq. m.; pop. (1970e) 1,184,360.

Nor·te, Cape \-'nȯrt-ē\ *or* **Cape Ra·so** \-'ra-(ˌ)zü\. Cape, extending into Atlantic Ocean on coast of Amapá state, N Brazil, N of the mouth of the Amazon.

Nor·te de San·tan·der \'nȯ(ə)r-ˌtā-də-ˌsän-tän-'de(ə)r, -ˌsan-tan-\. Department of N Colombia. See table at COLOMBIA.

North \'nȯ(ə)rth\. River, estuary of Hudson river bet. New York and New Jersey; flows into Upper New York Bay; crossed by bridge (George Washington, at 179th St.).

North, Cape. Cape at N tip of Cape Breton I., on S side of Cabot Strait at entrance to the Gulf of St. Lawrence, SE Canada.

North Ad·ams \-'ad-əmz\. City, Berkshire co., NW Massachusetts; pop. (1970c) 19,195; electronic components, rayon, chemicals, paper products; Massachusetts State Coll. at North Adams (1894).

North Africa. A term often used to include the countries of northern Africa: Morocco, Algeria, Tunisia, and Libya; used esp. by Rome of her colonies (see AFRICA, ROMAN), and in modern times in World War II during the campaign Nov. 10, 1942 to May 12, 1943 in which the Allies defeated all German and Italian forces in Africa.

North Al·ba·nian Alps \-al-'bā-nē-ən-, -nyən-, -ȯl-\ *or Serbo-Croat.* **Pro·kle·ti·je** \prō-'klet-ē-ˌ(y)ā\ *or Albanian*

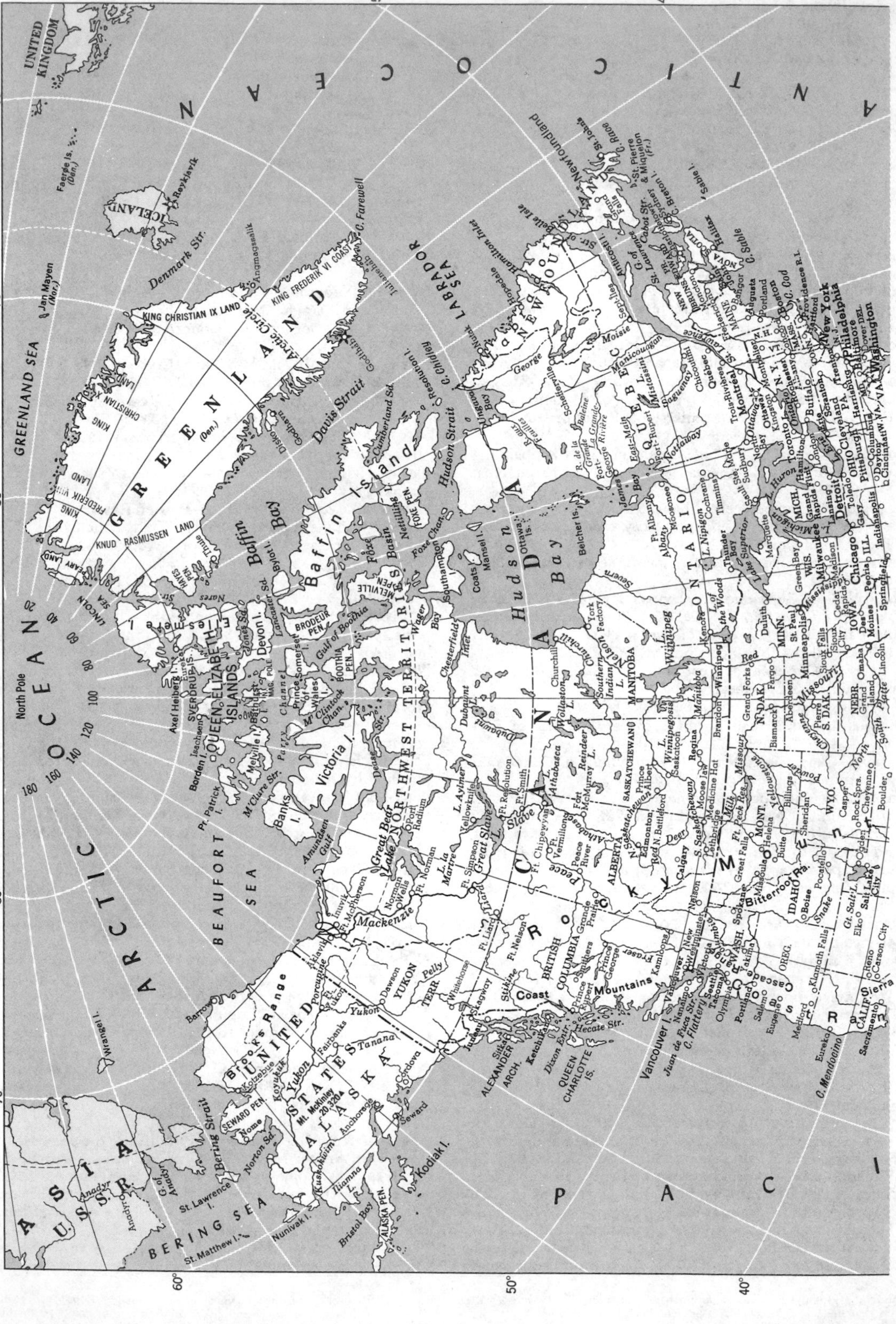
ARCTIC OCEAN
ATLANTIC OCEAN
PACIFIC
GREENLAND SEA
BEAUFORT SEA
BERING SEA
LABRADOR SEA
LINCOLN SEA
ASIA
U.S.S.R.
UNITED KINGDOM
ICELAND
Reykjavík
Faeroe Is. (Den.)
Jan Mayen (Nor.)
Denmark Str.
GREENLAND (Den.)
KING CHRISTIAN IX LAND
KING CHRISTIAN X LAND
KING FREDERIK VIII LAND
KING FREDERIK VI COAST
KNUD RASMUSSEN LAND
PEARY LAND
Arctic Circle
Angmagssalik
C. Farewell
Julianehåb
Godthåb
Godhavn
Disko I.
Thule
Davis Strait
Baffin Bay
Nares Str.
North Pole
Axel Heiberg I.
Eureka
SVERDRUP IS.
QUEEN ELIZABETH ISLANDS
Ellesmere I.
Jones Sd.
Devon I.
Lancaster Sd.
Bylot I.
Bathurst I.
Melville I.
Isachsen
Borden I.
Pt. Patrick I.
M'Clure Str.
Parry Channel
Prince of Wales I.
Somerset I.
BOOTHIA PEN.
Gulf of Boothia
BRODEUR PEN.
M'Clintock Chan.
Victoria I.
Banks I.
Amundsen Gulf
Dease Str.
Baffin Island
Cumberland Sd.
Foxe Basin
Foxe Chan.
FOXE PEN.
Nettilling L.
MELVILLE PEN.
Southampton I.
Coats I.
Mansel I.
Hudson Strait
Resolution I.
C. Chidley
Ungava Bay
Hudson Bay
Ottawa Is.
Belcher Is.
James Bay
NORTHWEST TERRITORIES
Wager Bay
Chesterfield Inlet
Dubawnt L.
Great Bear Lake
Pt. Radium
Great Slave L.
Yellowknife
Ft. Resolution
Ft. Smith
L. Aylmer
L. la Martre
Ft. Simpson
Ft. Norman
Norman Wells
Mackenzie
Inuvik
Ft. McPherson
Aklavik
Liard
Ft. Liard
Ft. Nelson
Slave
CANADA
Athabasca L.
Wollaston L.
Reindeer L.
Churchill
York Factory
Southern Indian L.
Nelson
MANITOBA
L. Winnipeg
Winnipeg
L. Winnipegosis
L. Manitoba
Brandon
SASKATCHEWAN
Saskatoon
Regina
Moose Jaw
Prince Albert
N. Saskatchewan
S. Saskatchewan
ALBERTA
Edmonton
Calgary
Red Deer
Lethbridge
Medicine Hat
N. Battleford
Ft. McMurray
Ft. Chipewyan
Ft. Vermilion
Peace River
Grande Prairie
BRITISH COLUMBIA
Prince George
Kamloops
Fraser
Vancouver
New Westminster
Victoria
Vancouver I.
Nanaimo
Juan de Fuca Str.
C. Flattery
Prince Rupert
QUEEN CHARLOTTE IS.
Hecate Str.
Dixon Entr.
Ketchikan
Sitka
ALEXANDER ARCH.
Juneau
Skagway
Stikine
Coast Mountains
YUKON TERR.
Whitehorse
Dawson
Pelly
Yukon
Porcupine
Ft. Yukon
Brooks Range
UNITED STATES
ALASKA
Barrow
Kotzebue
Koyukuk
Nome
SEWARD PEN.
Norton Sd.
Bering Strait
Wrangel I.
St. Lawrence I.
St. Matthew I.
Nunivak I.
Kuskokwim
Iliamna L.
Bristol Bay
ALASKA PEN.
Kodiak I.
Anchorage
Seward
Cordova
Fairbanks
Tanana
Mt. McKinley 20,320
Anadyr
G. of Anadyr
ONTARIO
Ft. Albany
Albany
Moosonee
Severn
Cochrane
Timmins
L. Nipigon
Thunder Bay
Lake Superior
Sault Ste. Marie
Sudbury
L. Huron
North Bay
Ottawa
Toronto
Hamilton
London
Kingston
L. of the Woods
Kenora
QUEBEC
Fort-George
La Grande Rivière
Fort-Rupert
East-Main
Mistassini L.
Nottaway
Schefferville
Manicouagan
Moisie
Saguenay
Chicoutimi
Quebec
Trois-Rivières
Montreal
St. Lawrence
Sept-Îles
Anticosti I.
Labrador
NEWFOUNDLAND
Hopedale
Hamilton Inlet
Str. of Belle Isle
Newfoundland
St. John's
C. Race
St. Pierre & Miquelon (Fr.)
Cabot Str.
G. of St. Lawrence
Cape Breton I.
Sable I.
NOVA SCOTIA
Halifax
NEW BRUNSWICK
Fredericton
Moncton
PRINCE EDWARD I.
C. Sable
MAINE
Bangor
Augusta
Portland
N.H.
VT.
Boston
MASS.
C. Cod
Providence R.I.
CONN.
Hartford
N.Y.
Albany
Rochester
Buffalo
New York
N.J.
Trenton
Philadelphia
PA.
Harrisburg
Scranton
Pittsburgh
Baltimore
MD.
DEL.
Dover
Washington
VA.
W.VA.
OHIO
Cleveland
Columbus
Dayton
Cincinnati
Toledo
Detroit
MICH.
Lansing
Flint
Grand Rapids
L. Michigan
Marquette
IND.
Indianapolis
Gary
Chicago
ILL.
Peoria
Springfield
WIS.
Green Bay
Milwaukee
Madison
MINN.
Duluth
St. Paul
Minneapolis
IOWA
Des Moines
Cedar Rapids
Sioux City
Mississippi
Missouri
N. DAK.
Fargo
Grand Forks
Bismarck
Red
S. DAK.
Aberdeen
Pierre
Sioux Falls
NEBR.
Omaha
Grand Island
Lincoln
North Platte
South Platte
MONT.
Great Falls
Helena
Butte
Billings
Missoula
Yellowstone
Ft. Peck Res.
Milk
WYO.
Casper
Sheridan
Cheyenne
Rock Spgs.
Boulder
ROCKY MTS.
IDAHO
Boise
Pocatello
Snake
Bitterroot Ra.
Gt. Salt L.
Salt Lake City
Ogden
Elko
WASH.
Spokane
Seattle
Tacoma
Olympia
Yakima
Columbia
ORE.
Portland
Salem
Eugene
Medford
Klamath Falls
Cascade Ra.
CALIF.
Eureka
Sacramento
Reno
Carson City
C. Mendocino
Sierra
60°
70°
80°
50°
40°
20
40
60
80
100
120
140
160
180

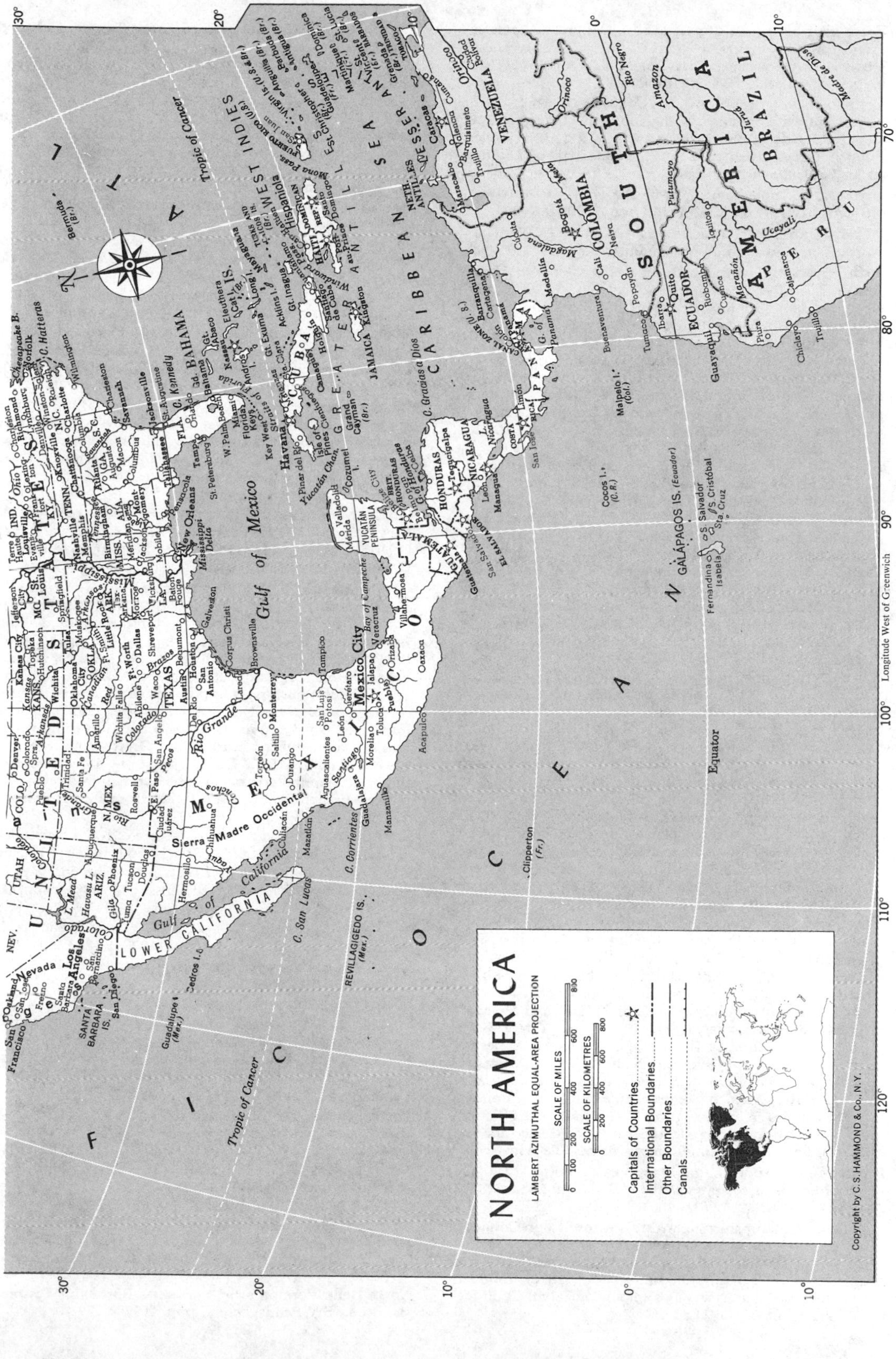
NORTH AMERICA
LAMBERT AZIMUTHAL EQUAL-AREA PROJECTION
SCALE OF MILES
0 100 200 400 600 800
SCALE OF KILOMETRES
0 200 400 600 800
Capitals of Countries
International Boundaries
Other Boundaries
Canals
Copyright by C. S. HAMMOND & Co., N.Y.
Longitude West of Greenwich
Tropic of Cancer
Equator
Gulf of Mexico
CARIBBEAN SEA
WEST INDIES
PACIFIC OCEAN
UNITED STATES
MEXICO
SOUTH AMERICA
BRAZIL
COLOMBIA
VENEZUELA
ECUADOR
PERU
CUBA
HAITI
JAMAICA
HONDURAS
NICARAGUA
GUATEMALA
EL SALVADOR
BAHAMA IS.
GALÁPAGOS IS. (Ecuador)
REVILLAGIGEDO IS. (Mex.)

Bjesh·kët e Ne·mu·na \ˌbyesh-kət-ā-nə-ˈmün-ə\. Mountain range, running generally W to E in N Albania and S Yugoslavia (Montenegro); average height 6500–8500 ft.; highest point 8835 ft. (in Albania).

North·al·ler·ton \nȯr-ˈthal-ərt-ᵊn\. Urban district, ⊗ of North Riding, Yorkshire, N England; pop. (1971p) 10,508; scene of Battle of the Standard Aug. 22, 1138 in which English forces defeated Scottish supporters of Matilda under King David, her uncle.

Nor·tham. 1 \ˈnȯr-thəm\. Town, SW Western Australia, on Avon river 47 m. E of Perth; pop. (1966c) 7400.

2 \ˈnȯr-t͟həm\. Urban district, Devonshire, SW England, on the Torridge 47 m. N of Plymouth; pop. (1971p) 8082.

North America. Continent (3d in size) in Western Hemisphere; 9,361,791 sq. m.; pop. (1970e) 320,787,000; generally considered to include island of Greenland in NE. *Boundaries:* On N, Arctic Ocean (Beaufort Sea on NW); large bodies of water in N Canada: Viscount Melville Sound, Foxe Basin, Hudson Bay and Hudson Strait; on NE, Baffin Bay and Davis Strait; most northerly point (on mainland) tip of Boothia Penin. 70°30′N, most northerly point on islands Cape Morris Jesup, N Greenland, 83°38′N; many large islands in N, belonging to Canada: Baffin, Ellesmere, Victoria, Banks, Southampton, Parry Is. On E, North Atlantic Ocean (chief inlets: Gulf of St. Lawrence, Bay of Fundy, Chesapeake Bay); most easterly point (continental) SE coast of Labrador, Canada, ab. 55°42′W; islands: Newfoundland, Anticosti, Prince Edward, Cape Breton, Long, Bermuda Is. On SE, Gulf of Mexico and Caribbean Sea; for islands see WEST INDIES. On S, Pacific Ocean (chief inlets: Gulf of Panama, Gulf of California); most southerly point SE Panama 7°15′N. On W, North Pacific Ocean (chief subdivisions: Gulf of Alaska, Bering Sea); most westerly point (continental) Cape Prince of Wales, Alaska, 168°05′W; most westerly point on islands, Attu I. in Aleutian Is. 172°30′E; separated from Asia by Bering Strait; most important islands: Vancouver, Queen Charlotte Is., islands of SE Alaska, Aleutian Is., Nunivak, and St. Lawrence. *Mountains, etc:* Greatest mountain ranges along Pacific coast (esp. Rocky Mts.) extending from Alaska into Mexico and Central America; Great Plains E of Rocky Mts. extending from Arctic Ocean to Gulf of Mexico; lowlands in center around Hudson Bay and in Mississippi Valley; highlands in E (Laurentian Highlands and Appalachian Mts.); low coastal plain along Atlantic; high ice-covered plateau in Greenland; highest point Mt. McKinley, Alaska, 20,320 ft.; lowest Badwater in Death Valley, Calif., 282 ft. below sea level. *Rivers:* Yukon (Canada and Alaska), Mackenzie, Saskatchewan and Nelson (Canada), St. Lawrence and Columbia (Canada and U.S.), Mississippi-Missouri system, Colorado (in SW), Penobscot, Connecticut, Hudson, Delaware, Susquehanna, Potomac, James, Cape Fear, Savannah (Atlantic seaboard, U.S.), Apalachicola, Mobile, Pearl, Sabine, Brazos, Colorado (Texas), to Gulf of Mexico; San Joaquin and Sacramento (W coast), Rio Grande (U.S. and Mexico), Pánuco, Balsas, Grijalva (Mexico). *Lakes:* Great Bear, Great Slave, Winnipeg (Canada); Great Lakes (Superior, Huron, Erie, Ontario—in Canada and U.S.) and Michigan (U.S.), Great Salt Lake (U.S.). *Political divisions:* Canada, United States, Mexico, Central America (*q.v.*) adjoining South America in extreme S, and West Indies off SE coast enclosing Caribbean Sea. Central America, Mexico and the West Indies are sometimes known as Middle America.

North·amp·ton \nȯr-ˈtham(p)-tən, nȯrth-ˈham(p)-\. **1** Name of counties in three states of the U.S. See tables at NORTH CAROLINA, PENNSYLVANIA, VIRGINIA.

2 City, ⊗ of Hampshire co., W Massachusetts, on Connecticut river 15 m. N of Springfield; pop. (1970c) 29,664; cutlery, wire cable, brushes, optical instruments; Smith Coll. (1871), Northampton Junior Coll. (1896); founded 1654, incorporated as city 1883; home of Calvin Coolidge, 30th President of the U.S.

3 Borough, Northampton co., E Pennsylvania, on Lehigh river 6 m. N of Allentown; pop. (1970c) 8389; furniture, paint; ammunition; agriculture; Mary Immaculate Seminary (1939).

4 County borough, ⊗ of Northamptonshire, cen. England, on the Nene 60 m. NNW of London; pop. (1971p) 126,608; footwear, leather, automobile parts, construction equipment, electronic components; first mentioned 914 A.D.; a meeting place of parliaments 12th–14th cents.; site of battle 1460 during Wars of the Roses in which Henry VI was defeated and captured by Yorkists; heavily damaged by fire 1675.

North·amp·ton·shire \nȯr-ˈtham(p)-tən-ˌshi(ə)r, nȯrth-ˈham(p)-, -shər\ *or* **Northampton.** County, cen. England; area 914 sq. m.; pop. (1971p) 467,843; ⊗ Northampton; livestock; sugar beets; iron and steel; main towns incl. Northampton, Corby, Kettering, Wellingborough.

North Andaman. One of the Andaman Is. (*q.v.*).

North An·do·ver \-ˈan-ˌdō-vər, -də-\. Industrial town, Essex co., NE Massachusetts, 10 m. ENE of Lowell; pop. (1970c) 16,284; Merrimack Coll. (1947).

North An·na \-ˈan-ə\. River, E cen. Virginia; flows SE to unite with South Anna river in N Hanover co. and form Pamunkey river; just above the junction battle occurred May 23–25, 1864 in which the Unionists under Grant failed to dislodge Lee's Confederates who were covering Richmond to the S.

North Ar·ling·ton \-ˈär-liŋ-tən\. Borough, Bergen co., NE New Jersey, on Passaic river 4 m. N of Newark; pop. (1970c) 18,096; tools and dies, clothing; truck farms.

North Atlantic Ocean. See ATLANTIC OCEAN.

North Atlantic Treaty Organization *or abbr.* **NATO.** Military alliance, consisting of Belgium, Canada, Denmark, France, West Germany, Greece, Iceland, Italy, Luxembourg, the Netherlands, Norway, Portugal, Turkey, the United Kingdom, and the United States; military headquarters Casteau, Belgium; civil headquarters Brussels, Belgium; purpose is to promote the collective security of the nations of the North Atlantic area. Has established integrated naval and military commands covering western and southern Europe; Turkey and Greece admitted 1952, West Germany 1955; France withdrew its forces from integrated command system 1966 and required removal of all non-French facilities and forces from French territory 1967.

North At·tle·boro \-ˈat-ᵊl-ˌbər-ə, -ˌbə-rə\. Town, Bristol co., SE Massachusetts; pop. (1970c) 18,665; jewelry, brushes.

North Au·gus·ta \-ȯ-ˈgəs-tə, -ə-\. City, Aiken co., W South Carolina, on Savannah river across from Augusta, Ga.; pop. (1970c) 12,883.

North Au·ro·ra \-ə-ˈrōr-ə, -ȯ-, -ˈrȯr-\. Village, Kane co., NE Illinois, 4 m. N of Aurora; pop. (1970c) 4833.

North Australia. A territory of Australia 1927–31. See NORTHERN TERRITORY.

North Bal·ti·more \-ˈbȯl-tə-ˌmō(ə)r, -ˌmȯ(ə)r\. Village, Wood co., NW Ohio, 10 m. N of Findlay; pop. (1970c) 3143; iron castings, rubber products; oil wells.

North Bar·ren \-ˈbar-ən\. Mountain, Cape Breton I., Nova Scotia, Canada; 1747 ft.; highest peak in Nova Scotia.

North Bass Island. See BASS ISLAND.

North Bat·tle·ford \-ˈbat-ᵊl-ˌfərd\. City, W Saskatchewan, Canada, on North Saskatchewan river 85 m. WNW of Saskatoon; pop. (1971p) 12,453; Saint Thomas Coll. (1932).

North Bay. 1 Village, Dade co., SE Florida, 6 m. NE of Miami; pop. (1970c) 4831.

2 City, ⊗ of Nipissing dist., SE Ontario, Canada, on NE shore of Lake Nipissing; pop. (1971p) 49,063; transportation center; dairy products, lumber, brass fittings; summer resort; military airfield and missile base; Nipissing Coll. (1967).

North Belle Ver·non \-bel-ˈvər-nən\. Borough, Westmoreland co., SW Pennsylvania; pop. (1970c) 2916.

North Bell·more \-'bel-ˌmō(ə)r, -ˌmȯ(ə)r\. Urban community (unincorporated), Nassau co., SE New York, on Long I. E of New York; pop. (1970c) 22,893.

North Bel·mont \-'bel-ˌmänt\. Urban area, Gaston co., SW North Carolina; pop. (1970c) 10,759.

North Bend. 1 Village, SW Hamilton co., SW Ohio, WSW of Cincinnati; pop. (1970c) 638; birthplace of Benjamin Harrison, 23d president of the U.S.
2 City, Coos co., SW Oregon, on inlet of Pacific Ocean 4 m. N of Marshfield; pop. (1970c) 8553; plywood; oyster packing, fishing; dairy farms.

North Ber·wick \-'ber-ik\. Royal burgh and parish, East Lothian, SE Scotland, on S shore of Firth of Forth ab. 22 m. E of Edinburgh; pop. (1971p) 4753; seaside and golfing resort.

North Beveland. See BEVELAND.

North Borneo. See SABAH.

North·bor·ough \'nȯrth-ˌbər-ə, -ˌbə-rə\. Town, Worcester co., cen. Massachusetts, 9 m. ENE of Worcester; pop. (1970c) 9218.

North Bra·bant \-brə-'bant, -'bänt\ *or Du.* **Noord·bra·bant** \ˌnōrt-brə-'bänt\. Province, S Netherlands; 1971 sq. m.; pop. (1970e) 1,787,783; ✻ 's Hertogenbosch; sheep and cattle raising. See BRABANT.

North Brad·dock \-'brad-ək\. Borough, Allegheny co., SW Pennsylvania, 9 m. E of Pittsburgh; pop. (1970c) 10,838; metalworking.

North Branch. See POTOMAC.

North Bran·ford \-'bran-fərd\. Town, New Haven co., S cen. Connecticut; pop. (1970c) 10,778.

North·bridge \'nȯrth-brij\. Town, Worcester co., cen. Massachusetts; pop. (1970c) 11,795.

North·brook \'nȯrth-ˌbru̇k\. Village, Cook co., NE Illinois, NW suburb of Chicago; pop. (1970c) 27,297.

North Brook·field \-'bru̇k-ˌfēld\. Town, Worcester co., cen. Massachusetts, 14 m. W of Worcester; pop. (1970c) 3767.

North Cald·well \-'käl-(ˌ)dwel\. Borough, Essex co., NE New Jersey, 6 m. SW of Paterson; pop. (1970c) 6425.

North Ca·naan \-'kā-nən\. Town, NW Litchfield co., NW Connecticut, on Massachusetts border; pop. (1970c) 3045.

North Ca·na·di·an \-kə-'näd-ē-ən\. River, cen. Oklahoma; 440 m. long; formed by junction of Beaver river and Wolf Creek, flows ESE through Oklahoma City to Eufaula Reservoir.

North Can·ton \-'kant-ᵊn\. Village, Stark co., NE Ohio, N of Canton; pop. (1970c) 15,228; vacuum cleaners, brick; diversified agriculture.

North Cape. 1 Cape, Iceland. See HORN.
2 Northwest point of New Ireland, Bismarck Archipelago; Kavieng is on it.
3 Cape on N extremity of North I., New Zealand.
4 *or* **Nord·kapp** \'nō(ə)r-ˌkäp, 'nȯ(ə)r-\. Cape on N Magerøy I. in Arctic Ocean off N coast of Norway; northernmost point of Europe, 71°10′20″N, 25°48′E; Cape Nordkyn (*q.v.*) is northernmost point of European mainland.

North Car·o·li·na \-ˌkar-ə-'lī-nə\. A south Atlantic state of U.S.A., bounded on N by Virginia, on E and SE by the Atlantic Ocean, on S by South Carolina and Georgia, and on W and NW by Tennessee; 28th state in area, 52,586 sq. m. (land area 49,067 sq. m.); 12th state in population, (1970c) 5,082,059; ✻ Raleigh; an original state of the Union, the 12th to ratify the Federal Constitution (Nov. 21, 1789).

Nicknames: Tar Heel State; Old North State; Turpentine State. *State flower:* Dogwood. *Motto:* To Be Rather Than to Seem. *Chief rivers:* Roanoke, entering state from S Virginia and flowing SE across NE corner of state into Albemarle Sound; Yadkin, in cen. area, flowing S to form the Pee Dee. *Mountains:* Ranges of Appalachian Mts. in W esp. Great Smoky Mts. on Tennessee border, and Blue Ridge to the E. Highest point Mount Mitchell 6684 ft. in Yancey co. *Chief products:* Tobacco, corn, cotton, peanuts; livestock; gravel, feldspar; manufacturing: textiles, cigarettes, food products, chemicals, furniture. *Chief cities:* Charlotte, Greensboro, Winston-Salem, Raleigh, Durham, High Point. See *Table of States* at UNITED STATES. Divided into the following 100 counties (for pronunciation of their names, see their individual entries):

NAME	LOCATION	AREA[1] (sq. m.)	POP. (1970c)	CO. SEAT
Alamance	N cen.	434	96,362	Graham
Alexander	W cen.	255	19,466	Taylorsville
Alleghany	N	230	8,134	Sparta
Anson	S	533	23,488	Wadesboro
Ashe	NW	427	19,571	Jefferson
Avery	W	247	12,655	Newland
Beaufort	E; coastal	831	35,980	Washington
Bertie	NE	693	20,528	Windsor
Bladen	S	879	26,477	Elizabethtown
Brunswick[2]	S; coastal	873	24,223	Southport
Buncombe[3]	W	645	145,056	Asheville
Burke	W	506	60,364	Morganton
Cabarrus	S cen.	360	74,629	Concord
Caldwell	W	476	56,699	Lenoir
Camden	NE	239	5,453	Camden
Carteret[4,5]	SE; coastal	532	31,603	Beaufort
Caswell	N	435	19,055	Yanceyville
Catawba	W cen.	406	90,873	Newton
Chatham	cen.	707	29,554	Pittsboro
Cherokee	W tip	454	16,330	Murphy
Chowan	NE	180	10,764	Edenton
Clay	SW	213	5,180	Hayesville
Cleveland	SW	466	72,556	Shelby
Columbus	S	939	46,937	Whiteville
Craven	SE	725	62,554	New Bern
Cumberland	S cen.	661	212,042	Fayetteville
Currituck	NE corner; coastal	273	6,976	Currituck
Dare[5,6]	E; coastal	388	6,995	Manteo
Davidson	cen.	546	95,627	Lexington
Davie	cen.	264	18,855	Mocksville
Duplin	SE	822	38,015	Kenansville
Durham	NE cen.	299	132,681	Durham
Edgecome	NE	511	52,341	Tarboro
Forsyth	N cen.	424	214,348	Winston-Salem
Franklin	N	494	26,820	Louisburg
Gaston	SW	358	148,415	Gastonia
Gates	NE	343	8,524	Gatesville
Graham	W	289	6,562	Robbinsville
Granville	N	542	32,762	Oxford
Greene	E	269	14,967	Snow Hill
Guilford	N cen.	651	288,645	Greensboro
Halifax	NE	722	53,884	Halifax
Harnett	cen.	606	49,667	Lillington
Haywood[7]	W	543	41,710	Waynesville
Henderson	SW	382	42,804	Hendersonville
Hertford	NE	356	23,529	Winton
Hoke	S	381	16,436	Raeford
Hyde[5]	E; coastal	634	5,571	Swan Quarter
Iredell	cen.	591	72,197	Statesville
Jackson[7]	SW	496	21,593	Sylva
Johnston	E	795	61,737	Smithfield
Jones	SE	467	9,779	Trenton
Lee	cen.	255	30,467	Sanford
Lenoir	E	391	55,204	Kinston
Lincoln	SW cen.	308	32,682	Lincolnton
McDowell	W	442	30,648	Marion
Macon	SW	517	15,788	Franklin
Madison	W	456	16,003	Marshall
Martin	E	481	24,730	Williamston
Mecklenburg	S	542	354,656	Charlotte
Mitchell	W	220	13,447	Bakersville
Montgomery	S cen.	488	19,267	Troy
Moore	cen.	705	39,048	Carthage
Nash	NE	552	59,122	Nashville
New Hanover	SE; coastal	194	82,996	Wilmington
Northampton	NE	539	24,009	Jackson
Onslow	SE; coastal	756	103,126	Jacksonville
Orange	N	398	57,707	Hillsboro
Pamlico	E; coastal	341	9,467	Bayboro
Pasquotank	NE	229	26,824	Elizabeth City
Pender	SE; coastal	857	18,149	Burgaw
Perquimans	NE	261	8,351	Hertford
Person	N	400	25,914	Roxboro
Pitt	E	656	73,900	Greenville
Polk	SW	234	11,735	Columbus
Randolph	cen.	801	76,358	Asheboro
Richmond	S	477	39,889	Rockingham
Robeson	S	944	84,842	Lumberton
Rockingham	N	572	72,402	Wentworth
Rowan	cen.	517	90,035	Salisbury
Rutherford	SW	566	47,337	Rutherfordton

NAME	LOCATION	AREA[1] (sq. m.)	POP. (1970c)	CO. SEAT
Sampson	SE	963	44,954	Clinton
Scotland	S	317	26,929	Laurinburg
Stanly	S cen.	399	42,822	Albermarle
Stokes	N	459	23,782	Danbury
Surry	N	537	51,415	Dobson
Swain[7]	W	530	7,861	Bryson City
Transylvania	SW	379	19,713	Brevard
Tyrrell	E	399	3,806	Columbia
Union	S	643	54,714	Monroe
Vance	N	249	32,691	Henderson
Wake	E cen.	864	229,006	Raleigh
Warren	N	443	15,810	Warrenton
Washington	E	336	14,038	Plymouth
Watauga	NW	320	23,404	Boone
Wayne	E	555	85,408	Goldsboro
Wilkes	NW cen.	765	49,524	Wilkesboro
Wilson	E	373	57,486	Wilson
Yadkin	NW cen.	335	24,599	Yadkinville
Yancey	W	311	12,629	Burnsville

[1]Area = land area.
[2]Includes Cape Fear, on Smith I. off SE corner.
[3]This county name is source of colloquial common noun *buncombe*.
[4]Includes offshore islands from which it is separated by Core Sound (on E) and Bogue Sound (on S).
[5]Cape Hatteras National Seashore Park comprises most of chain of islands (enclosing Pamlico Sound on ocean side) belonging to Dare, Hyde, and Carteret cos., with Cape Hatteras itself on island SE of and belonging to Dare co.
[6]Kitty Hawk (*q.v.*), scene of first airplane flight in U.S. (1903), on sand barrier NE of and belonging to Dare co.
[7]Great Smoky Mountains National Park occupies most of N and E part of Swain co., N section of Jackson co., and NW section of Haywood co. (as well as adjacent section of Tennessee).

History: Formed a part of Carolina grant given 1663 by King Charles II to eight noblemen of his court (see CAROLINA); became a royal province after the proprietors sold their rights to the crown 1729; at outbreak of American Revolution, a convention of North Carolinians met in Mecklenburg co. and drew up a statement (Mecklenburg Declaration, May 1775) containing phrases closely resembling phrases in the Declaration of Independence (1776); Provincial Congress adopted Apr. 12, 1776 the Halifax resolution that "the delegates for this colony in the Continental Congress be empowered to concur with the delegates of the other colonies in declaring independency"—the first explicit sanction of independence by an American colony; British control of colony ended with Greene's victory at Guilford Courthouse (1781); ratified Federal Constitution Nov. 21, 1789; gave up claim to western lands 1790, now part of Tennessee (see FRANKLIN, STATE OF); passed ordinance of secession May 20, 1861; secession ordinance declared null and void and slavery abolished Oct. 7, 1865; readmitted to Union July 11, 1868.

North Cas·cades National Park \-ka-'skādz-\. See UNITED STATES, *National Parks.*

North Cat·a·sau·qua \-ˌkat-ə-'sȯ-kwə\. Borough, Northampton co., E Pennsylvania, on Lehigh river N of Allentown; pop. (1970c) 2941.

North Cau·ca·sus \-'kȯ-kə-səs\. Extensive region, SE Russian S.F.S.R., U.S.S.R.; consists of Krasnodar Krai, Stavropol Krai, Rostov Oblast, and Dagestan, Kabardino-Balkarian, North Ossetian, and Checheno-Ingush A.S.S.Rs.; 137,105 sq. m.; pop. (1970p) 14,285,000; ✱ Rostov-na-Donu. Inhabitants include many different ethnic groups. Consists largely of earlier Territory of the Don Cossacks, and the Stavropol, Kuban, and Terek provs. of Tsarist Russia. Reorganized 1936.

North–Central State. State of N cen. Nigeria. See table at NIGERIA.

North Channel. 1 Strait in NE Lake Huron, SE Ontario prov., Canada, bet. Manitoulin I. and the Canadian mainland.

2 Strait of Atlantic Ocean extending bet. NE Ireland and SW Scotland; 14 m. wide at its widest part; connects with Irish Sea on the S.

3 Northern part of entrance to Manila Bay, Phil., bet. Bataan Penin. and Corregidor I.; $3^1/_2$ m. wide; called **Bo·ca Chi·ca** \ˌbō-kə-'chē-kə\ by the Spaniards.

North Chi·ca·go \-shə-'käg-(ˌ)ō, -'kȯg-\. Industrial city, Lake co., NE corner of Illinois, on Lake Michigan 5 m. S of Waukegan; pop. (1970c) 47,275; automobile parts, chemicals, generators, steel, pharmaceuticals.

North Chi·cou·ti·mi \-shi-'kü-tə-mē\ *or Fr.* **Chicoutimi–Nord** \-nȯr\. City, Chicoutimi co., S Quebec, Canada, on Saguenay river 4 m. N of Chicoutimi; pop. (1971p) 14,058.

North Chŏl·la \-'chȯ-lə\. Province of SW South Korea. See table at KOREA, SOUTH.

North Ch'ung·ch'ŏng \-'chüŋ-'chȯŋ\. Province of cen. South Korea. See table at KOREA, SOUTH.

North College Hill. City, Hamilton co., SW corner of Ohio, 9 m. N of Cincinnati; pop. (1970c) 12,363.

North Concho. River, Texas; 137 m. long; rises in Gaines co., flows SE to join Concho river.

North Con·way \-'kän-(ˌ)wā\. Unincorporated community, Carroll co., E New Hampshire, on Saco river ab. 6 m. N of Conway; pop. (1970c) 1723; summer and winter resort.

North·cote. 1 \'nȯrth-kət\. City, S Victoria, SE Australia, N suburb of Melbourne; pop. (1966c) 56,200.

2 \'nȯrth-kət, -ˌkōt\. Borough, North I., New Zealand; pop. (1970e) 8920.

North Country. An occasional name for the northern part of England.

North Da·ko·ta \-də-'kōt-ə\. A northwestern state of U.S.A., bounded on N by Canadian provinces of Saskatchewan and Manitoba, on E by Minnesota, on S by South Dakota, and on W by Montana; 17th state in area, 70,665 sq. m. (land area 69,280 sq. m.); 45th state in population, (1970c) 617,761; ✱ Bismarck; 39th state admitted to Union (1889).

Nicknames: Flickertail State; Sioux State. *State flower:* Wild prairie rose. *Motto:* Liberty and Union. *Rivers:* Missouri, entering state at upper W border and flowing E, then SE, across S border into South Dakota; Red, forming E boundary. *Highest point:* White Butte 3506 ft., in Slope co. *Chief products:* Wheat, barley, flaxseed, oats; livestock; oil, coal; manufacturing: food processing; clay and glass products. *Chief cities:* Fargo, Grand Forks, Bismarck, Minot, Jamestown. See *Table of States* at UNITED STATES. Divided into the following 53 counties (for pronunciation of their names, see their individual entries):

NAME	LOCATION	AREA[1] (sq. m.)	POP. (1970c)	CO. SEAT
Adams	SW	989	3,832	Hettinger
Barnes	E	1,479	14,669	Valley City
Benson	N cen.	1,403	8,245	Minnewaukan
Billings	W	1,139	1,198	Medora
Bottineau	N	1,677	9,496	Bottineau
Bowman	SW corner	1,170	3,901	Bowman
Burke	NW	1,119	4,739	Bowbells
Burleigh	S cen.	1,625	40,714	Bismarck
Cass	E	1,749	73,653	Fargo
Cavalier	NE	1,512	8,213	Langdon
Dickey	S	1,143	6,976	Ellendale
Divide	NW corner	1,300	4,564	Crosby
Dunn	W	2,992	4,895	Manning
Eddy	E cen.	635	4,103	New Rockford
Emmons	S	1,503	7,200	Linton
Foster	E cen.	645	4,832	Carrington
Golden Valley	W	1,014	2,611	Beach
Grand Forks	E	1,438	61,102	Grand Forks
Grant	S	1,666	5,009	Carson
Griggs	E	710	4,184	Cooperstown
Hettinger	SW	1,134	5,075	Mott
Kidder	S cen.	1,358	4,362	Steele
La Moure	SE	1,136	7,117	La Moure
Logan	S	1,001	4,245	Napoleon
McHenry	N cen.	1,871	8,977	Towner
McIntosh	S	992	5,545	Ashley
McKenzie	W	2,735	6,127	Watford City
McLean	W cen.	2,065	11,251	Washburn
Mercer	W cen.	1,042	6,175	Stanton
Morton	SW cen.	1,920	20,310	Mandan
Mountrail	NW	1,819	8,437	Stanley
Nelson	E	995	5,807	Lakota
Oliver	W cen.	721	2,322	Center
Pembina	NE corner	1,124	10,728	Cavalier
Pierce	N cen.	1,038	6,323	Rugby
Ramsey	NE	1,248	12,915	Devils Lake
Ransom	SE	861	7,102	Lisbon
Renville	N	886	3,828	Mohall
Richland	SE corner	1,449	18,089	Wahpeton
Rolette	N	913	11,549	Rolla
Sargent	SE	853	5,937	Forman

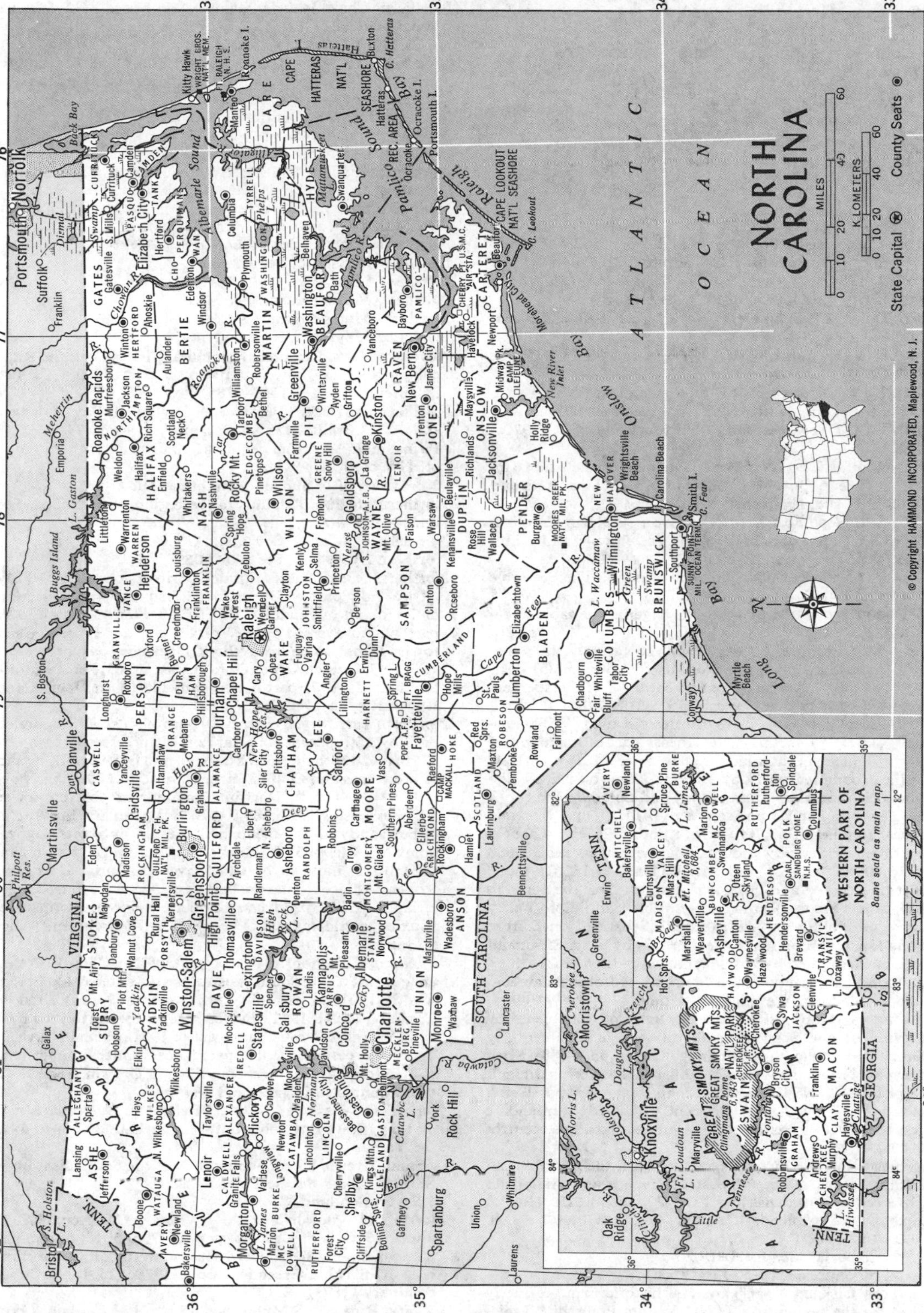
NORTH CAROLINA
MILES
0 10 20 40 60
KILOMETERS
0 10 20 40 60
State Capital
County Seats
WESTERN PART OF NORTH CAROLINA
Same scale as main map.
ATLANTIC OCEAN
VIRGINIA
SOUTH CAROLINA
GEORGIA
TENN.
© Copyright HAMMOND INCORPORATED, Maplewood, N. J.
Longitude West of Greenwich

NAME	LOCATION	AREA[1] (sq. m.)	POP. (1970c)	CO. SEAT
Sheridan	cen.	989	3,232	McClusky
Sioux	S	1,103	3,632	Fort Yates
Slope	SW	1,225	1,484	Amidon
Stark	SW	1,316	19,613	Dickinson
Steele	E	710	3,749	Finley
Stutsman	SE cen.	2,264	23,550	Jamestown
Towner	N	1,043	4,645	Cando
Traill	E	861	9,571	Hillsboro
Walsh	NE	1,286	16,251	Grafton
Ward	NW cen.	2,044	58,560	Minot
Wells	cen.	1,299	7,847	Fessenden
Williams	NW	2,064	19,301	Williston

[1]Area = land area.

History: See DAKOTA TERRITORY; N part of Dakota Territory (organized 1861); separated from South Dakota 1889; adopted constitution and admitted to Union as state Nov. 2, 1889.

North Devon Island. See DEVON ISLAND.

North Dome. 1 Peak in Sierra Nevada, E Fresno co., S cen. California; 8657 ft.

2 Peak in the Catskill Mts., Greene co., SE New York; 3593 ft.

North Downs. Range of low hills extending from W to E across S cen. England; highest point Leith Hill 965 ft.

North East. 1 Town, Cecil co., NE Maryland; pop. (1970c) 1818.

2 Borough, Erie co., NW Pennsylvania, on Lake Erie 16 m. ENE of Erie; pop. (1970c) 3846; cans and ships fruits and vegetables; summer resort; truck farms.

North East Cape Fear \-'fi(ə)r\. River, SE North Carolina; ab. 130 m. long; rises in Sampson co., flows E and S into Cape Fear river near its mouth.

North–Eastern Province. Province of NE Kenya. See table at KENYA.

North–Eastern State. State of NE Nigeria. See table at NIGERIA.

North East Frontier Agency. See ARUNACHAL PRADESH.

North East Land *or Norw.* **Nord·ost Land·et** \nō(ə)r-'ōst-ˌlän-ə, nȯ(ə)r-\. An island of Svalbard, NE of Spitsbergen, Norway; 6400 sq. m.; ice cap. See SPITSBERGEN.

North–East New Guinea *or formerly* **Kai·ser–Wil·helms·land** \ˌkī-zər-'vil-ˌhelms-\. Northeast part of mainland of New Guinea I., administratively part of Papua New Guinea; bounded on N by Pacific Ocean, on NE by Bismarck Sea, on E by Vitiaz Strait and Solomon Sea, on S by Terr. of Papua, and on W (141°E long.) by Irian Barat, Indonesia; 69,700 sq. m.; pop. (1969e) 1,420,568; entire cen. region very mountainous with many peaks 9000 to 15,000 ft.; highest peak Mt. Wilhelm 14,762 ft.; much of it unexplored and unknown. Largest river the Sepik in NW; others are the Ramu and Markham. In Bulolo Valley in SE are goldfields (see MOROBE). Separated on E from Long I. and Umboi I. and New Britain by Vitiaz Strait and on E coast marked by Huon Penin. and Huon Gulf. Along the coast are several good harbors: Morobe, Salamaua, Saidor, Madang, Wewak, and Aitape.

History: First visited in early part of 16th cent. by Portuguese and Spanish navigators and in 17th cent. by Dutch sailors; no part definitely claimed until 1884 when German protectorate was established over NE mainland and islands to NE (Bismarck Archipelago); this possession seized 1914 by Australians and included in mandate granted 1920; coastal regions under Japanese control 1942–44.

Northeast Passage. A passage by sea bet. the Atlantic and Pacific oceans along N coast of Europe and Asia; first traversed by Nordenskjöld 1878–79. See ARCTIC, THE.

North East Providence Channel. See PROVIDENCE CHANNEL, NORTH WEST.

North Emporia. See EMPORIA 2.

Northern Caucasia. See CISCAUCASIA.

Northern Cir·cars \-sər-'kärz\. A historic name formerly used for the region now in NE Andhra Pradesh, E India, along the coast bet. the Krishna river and Orissa; ✱ Eluru; ceded to Great Britain 1766.

Northern Cook Islands \-'ku̇k-\ *or* **Ma·ni·hi·ki Islands** \ˌmän-ə-'hē-kē-\. Group of seven islands in cen. Pacific Ocean N of Cook Is.; ab. 9 sq. m.; pop. (1968e) 3003; administered with Cook Is. by New Zealand; more important (inhabited) islands of the group include Manahiki, Penrhyn, and Rakahanga.

Northern District. District of N Israel. See table at ISRAEL.

Northern Donets. See DONETS.

Northern Dvina. See DVINA, NORTHERN.

Northern Highlands. Elevated plateau region of N Scotland, N part of the Highlands (see SCOTLAND) in Inverness, Ross and Cromarty, and Sutherland cos.; highest points Ben Dearg 3547 ft. and Ben More 3273 ft.

Northern Ireland. See IRELAND, NORTHERN.

Northern Kingdom. See ISRAEL 1.

Northern Land. See SEVERNAYA ZEMLYA.

Northern Mashonaland. See MASHONALAND.

Northern Matabeleland. See MATABELELAND.

Northern Moytura. See MOYTURA.

Northern Neck. Region in N colonial Virginia bet. the Rappahannock and Potomac rivers; a part of the Fairfax Proprietary estates 1649–1785.

Northern Province. 1 Province, N Ceylon, on Bay of Bengal and Palk Strait; 3429 sq. m.; pop. (1963c) 741,802; ✱ Jaffna; includes Jaffna penin., Mannar I., and other islands off NW coast.

2 Province of N Sudan. See table at SUDAN.

Northern Region. Administrative region of N Ghana. See table at GHANA.

Northern Rhodesia. See ZAMBIA.

Northern Sporades. See SPORADES.

Northern Territories. Former British protectorate, W Africa, now part of Ghana; 37,723 sq. m.; with N section of Togoland mandate, 41,063 sq. m. Plateau region in W part, plain traversed by the Volta in cen. and E parts. Chief towns Tamale, Yendi, Savelugu. Organized as a protectorate 1897; attached to Gold Coast 1901; protectorate terminated 1957; partitioned into **Northern Region** and **Upper Region** 1960.

Northern Territory. Territory, N part of Australia, bounded on S by 26th parallel of S lat., on W and E respectively by 129th and 138th meridians E long., and on N by Timor and Arafura seas and Gulf of Carpentaria; 520,280 sq. m.; pop. (1970e) 71,400; ✱ Darwin. Greater part of interior is tableland rising gradually to 1700 ft.; good grazing land in N but sandy in S; Macdonnell Ranges in S with highest point Mt. Ziel 4955 ft., Simpson Desert in SE, and region of Arnhem Land in N. Chief rivers Victoria, Daly, and Roper. Adjacent islands Bathurst, Melville, and Groote Eylandt. *Chief products:* Copper, iron ore, manganese, bauxite; cattle raising. *Major towns:* Darwin and Alice Springs.

History: Region at first a part of New South Wales; annexed 1863 to South Australia and entered Commonwealth 1901 as part of South Australia; transferred to Commonwealth 1911; divided 1927 into North Australia and Central Australia but by act of 1931 original Northern Territory reestablished; N part placed under military control following Japanese bombing of Darwin Feb. 1942; civil administration restored 1945.

North Esk \-'esk\. 1 River, NE Tasmania, Australia; ab. 45 m. long; flows E to join South Esk at Launceston to form the Tamar.

2 Small river in E cen. Scotland, N of the South Esk; flows SE into North Sea near Montrose.

3 River, Scotland. See ESK 3.

North·field \'nȯ(ə)rth-ˌfēld\. 1 Village, Cook co., NE Illinois, 15 m. N of Chicago; pop. (1970c) 5010; residential.

2 Town, Franklin co., NW Massachusetts, on Connecticut river 10 m. NE of Greenfield; pop. (1970c) 2631; Northfield Seminary (1879).

3 City, Rice co., S Minnesota, 13 m. N of Faribault; pop. (1970c) 10,235; dairy products, flour; poultry and stock farms; Concordia Coll. (1866), St. Olaf Coll. (1874).

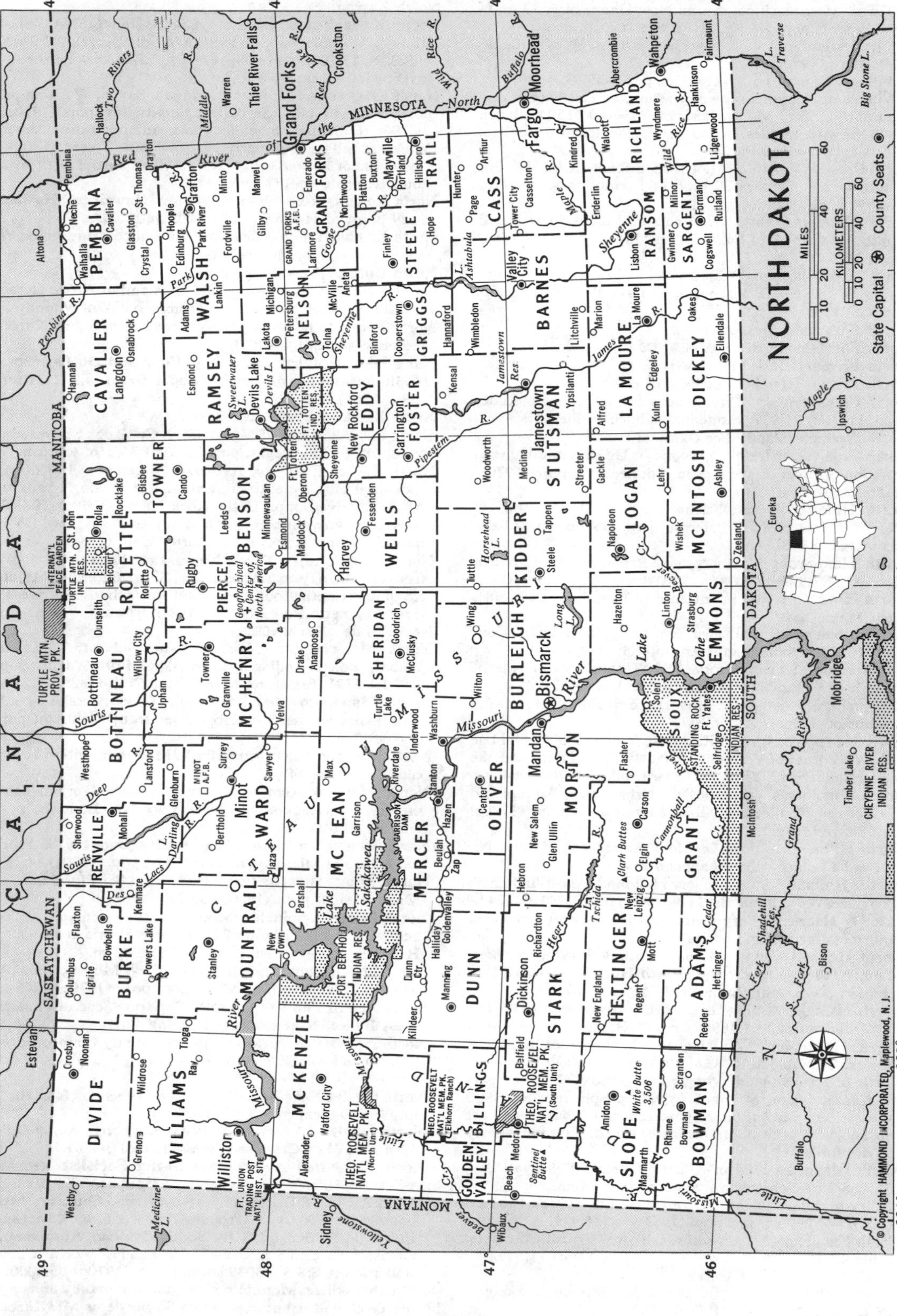
NORTH DAKOTA
MILES
0 10 20 40 60
KILOMETERS
0 10 20 40 60
State Capital
County Seats
Longitude West 100° of Greenwich
© Copyright HAMMOND INCORPORATED, Maplewood, N. J.
CANADA
SASKATCHEWAN
MANITOBA
MINNESOTA
SOUTH DAKOTA
MONTANA
DIVIDE
BURKE
RENVILLE
BOTTINEAU
ROLETTE
TOWNER
CAVALIER
PEMBINA
WILLIAMS
MOUNTRAIL
WARD
MC HENRY
PIERCE
BENSON
RAMSEY
WALSH
NELSON
GRAND FORKS
MC KENZIE
MC LEAN
SHERIDAN
WELLS
EDDY
FOSTER
GRIGGS
STEELE
TRAILL
DUNN
MERCER
OLIVER
BURLEIGH
KIDDER
STUTSMAN
BARNES
CASS
GOLDEN VALLEY
BILLINGS
STARK
MORTON
SLOPE
HETTINGER
GRANT
SIOUX
EMMONS
LOGAN
LA MOURE
RANSOM
RICHLAND
BOWMAN
ADAMS
MC INTOSH
DICKEY
SARGENT
Bismarck
Fargo
Grand Forks
Minot
Jamestown
Mandan
Williston
Dickinson
Devils Lake
Valley City
Moorhead
INTERNAT'L PEACE GARDEN
TURTLE MTN. PROV. PK.
TURTLE MTN. IND. RES.
FT. TOTTEN IND. RES.
FORT BERTHOLD INDIAN RES.
STANDING ROCK INDIAN RES.
CHEYENNE RIVER INDIAN RES.
THEO. ROOSEVELT NAT'L MEM. PK. (North Unit)
THEO. ROOSEVELT NAT'L MEM. PK. (Elkhorn Ranch)
THEO. ROOSEVELT NAT'L MEM. PK. (South Unit)
FT. UNION TRADING POST NAT'L HIST. SITE
GARRISON DAM
Lake Sakakawea
Oahe Lake
Missouri River
Geographical Center of North America
White Butte 3,506
49°
48°
47°
46°
97°
98°
99°
100°
101°
102°
103°
104°

4 Town, Merrimack co., S cen. New Hampshire, 13 m. N of Concord; pop. (1970c) 2193. See TILTON.
5 City, Atlantic co., SE New Jersey, 6 m. W of Atlantic City; pop. (1970c) 8875.
6 Village, Summit co., NE Ohio; pop. (1970c) 4283.
7 Village in Northfield town, Washington co., N cen. Vermont, 10 m. S of Montpelier; pop. (1970c) 2139 (village), 4870 (town); textiles, wood products; granite quarries; Norwich Univ. (1819).

North·fleet \'nȯ(ə)rth-ˌflēt\. Urban district, Kent, SE England, on the Thames 20 m. E of London; pop. (1971p) 26,679; dock facilities.

North Flin·ders Range \-'flin-dərz-\. Mountain range, E South Australia, E of Lake Torrens; highest peak St. Mary Peak 3825 ft.

North Fond du Lac \-'fän-dᵊl-ˌak, -'fän-jə-ˌlak\. Village, Fond du Lac co., E Wisconsin, on Lake Winnebago; pop. (1970c) 3286.

North Foreland. See FORELAND.

North Fox Island. See FOX ISLANDS 1.

North Fremantle. See FREMANTLE.

North Frisian Islands. See FRISIAN ISLANDS.

North Glenn \-'glen\. City, Adams co., NE cen. Colorado; pop. (1970c) 27,937; residential suburb of Denver.

North Graham Island. See GRAHAM LAND.

North Gros·ve·nor Dale \-'grōv-nər-\. Unincorporated subdivision of town of Thompson, Connecticut; pop. (1970c) 2156. See THOMPSON 1.

North Hale·don \-'hā(ə)l-dən\. Borough, Passaic co., N New Jersey, 4 m. N of Paterson; pop. (1970c) 7614; Salesian Coll. (1948).

North Ham·gyŏng \-'häm-'gyəŋ\. Province of NE North Korea. See table at KOREA, NORTH.

North Haven. 1 Island in entrance to Penobscot Bay, off S cen. Maine coast.
2 Suburban residential town, cen. New Haven co., S Connecticut, on Quinnipiac river; pop. (1970c) 22,194.

North Head. 1 Promontory, SW Washington, N side of mouth of Columbia river near Cape Disappointment.
2 Promontory on N side of entrance to Port Jackson, the harbor of Sydney, Australia.

North He·ro \-'hē-(ˌ)rō, -'hi(ə)r-(ˌ)ō\. Town, ⊗ of Grand Isle co., NW corner of Vermont, on **North Hero Island** in Lake Champlain 10 m. W of St. Albans; pop. (1970c) 364.

North High·lands \-'hī-lən(d)z\. Urban area, Sacramento co., N cen. California, NE of Sacramento; pop. (1970c) 31,584; residential.

North Hi·lo \-'hē-(ˌ)lō\. Division, Hawaii co., Hawaii, NE Hawaii I.; chief village Laupahoehoe.

North Holland *or Du.* **Noord·hol·land** \nōrt-'hōl-änt\. Province, W Netherlands; 1124 sq. m.; pop. (1970e) 2,244,-456; ✱ Haarlem; dairy farming, tulip growing; chemical and metallurgical industries; tourism.

North Holland Canal. Canal, extending N from Amsterdam, Netherlands, through North Holland prov. to Den Helder; 50 m. long; built 1819–25.

North Hsing·an \-'shiŋ-'än\. Former province (1932–45), NW Manchukuo; 61,489 sq. m.; ✱ Hailar.

North Hwang·hae \-'(h)wäŋ-'hī\. Province of S North Korea. See table at KOREA, NORTH.

North In·ger·man·land \-'iŋ-gər-mən-ˌland\. Northern part of former region of Ingria (*q.v.*); people revolted 1920 against new revolutionary government of Russia and set up short-lived autonomous state, quickly suppressed by Soviet forces.

North Island. 1 Island in Atlantic Ocean off Winyah Bay, SE coast of Georgetown co., South Carolina.
2 Northernmost of the three main islands of New Zealand (*q.v.*); 44,297 sq. m.; pop. (1968e) 1,956,411.

North Kam·loops \-'kam-(ˌ)lüps\. Town, British Columbia, Canada, 15 m. N of Kamloops; pop. (1966c) 11,319.

North Kanara. See KANARA.

North Kansas City. City, Clay co., NW Missouri, N suburb of Kansas City; pop. (1970c) 5183.

North Karroo. See KARROO.

North Ka·zakh·stan Oblast \-kə-ˌzak-stan-'ō-bləst, -ˌzäk-stän-, -ˌkä-, -ˌblast\. Subdivision of the Kazakh S.S.R., U.S.S.R.; 17,104 sq. m.; pop. (1970p) 557,000; ✱ Petropavlovsk; oats, wheat; livestock.

North Kings·town \-'kiŋ-stən, -ˌstau̇n\. Town, Washington co., S Rhode Island, on Narragansett Bay; pop. (1970c) 29,793; residential; machine tools; administrative center Wickford village. Formerly part of Kings Towne (Kingstown), incorporated 1674 and divided into North and South Kingstown 1723.

North Ko·ha·la \-kō-'häl-ə\. Division, Hawaii co., Hawaii, on N point of Hawaii I.; chief village Kohala.

North Ko·na \-'kō-nə\. Division, Hawaii co., Hawaii, on W side of Hawaii I.; chief village Kailua.

North Korea. See KOREA, NORTH.

North Kval·øy \-kə-'väl-ˌȯi, -'kfäl-\. Island in Arctic Ocean off NW coast of Norway, in Troms co., W of Vannøy I.

North Kyŏng·sang \-'kyəŋ-'säŋ\. Province of South Korea. See table at KOREA, SOUTH.

North·lake \'nȯ(ə)rth-ˌlāk\. City, Cook and Du Page cos., NE Illinois, suburb of Chicago; pop. (1970c) 14,212; Triton Coll. (1964).

North Land. See SEVERNAYA ZEMLYA.

North Las Vegas \-läs-'vā-gəs\. City, Clark co., SE Nevada, N suburb of Las Vegas; pop. (1970c) 36,216; tourism.

North Little Rock *or formerly* **Ar·gen·ta** \är-'jent-ə\. Industrial city, Pulaski co., cen. Arkansas, on N bank of Arkansas river opp. Little Rock; pop. (1970c) 60,040; chemicals, furniture, cotton and soybean products, flour; railroad shops, stockyards; Shorter Coll. (1884).

North Loup \-'lüp\. River, Nebraska; 212 m. long; flows from cen. Cherry co., N Nebraska, SE to unite with Middle Loup and South Loup rivers and form the Loup river.

North Magnetic Pole. See MAGNETIC POLE.

North Male. See MALE.

North Man·ches·ter \-'man-ˌches-tər, -chə-stər\. Town, Wabash co., N Indiana, 33 m. W of Fort Wayne; pop. (1970c) 5791; furniture; Manchester Coll. (1889).

North Man·ka·to \-man-'kāt-(ˌ)ō\. City, Nicollet co., S Minnesota, across Minnesota river from Mankato; pop. (1970c) 7347.

North Ma·roon Peak \-mə-'rün-\. Mountain, Pitkin co., W cen. Colorado; 14,014 ft.

North Mer·rick \-'mer-ik\. Unincorporated urban community, Nassau co., SE New York, on Long I.; pop. (1970c) 13,650.

North Mi·ami \-mī-'am-ē, -'am-ə\. City, Dade co., SE Florida; suburb of Miami on Biscayne Bay; pop. (1970c) 34,767.

North Miami Beach. City, Dade co., SE Florida, N of Miami Beach; pop. (1970c) 30,723.

North Minch \-'minch\. Strait bet. the mainland of NW Scotland and the island of Lewis with Harris in the Outer Hebrides; varies in width bet. 24 and 45 m.

North Mus·ke·gon \-mə-'skē-gən\. City, Muskegon co., W Michigan; N suburb of Muskegon; pop. (1970c) 4243.

North Ne·gril Point \-nə-'gril-\. Cape on W end of Jamaica, West Indies, N of entrance to Long Bay.

North New Hyde Park. Urban community (unincorporated), Nassau co., SE New York, on Long I. E of New York; pop. (1970c) 17,945.

North Og·den \-'ȯg-dən, -'äg-\. City, Weber co., N Utah, 14 m. N of Ogden; pop. (1970c) 5257.

North Olm·sted \-'əm-ˌsted\. City, Cuyahoga co., N Ohio, 13 m. WSW of Cleveland; pop. (1970c) 34,861.

North Os·se·tian Autonomous Soviet Socialist Republic \-ä-'sē-sh(ē-)ən-\. Autonomous republic, SE Russian S.F.S.R., U.S.S.R., on N slopes of cen. Caucasus Mts., bounded on N by Stavropol Krai, on E by Checheno-Ingush A.S.S.R., on S by South Ossetian Autonomous Oblast, Georgian S.S.R., and on W and NW by Kabardino-Balkarian A.S.S.R.; 3089 sq. m.; pop. (1970p) 553,000; ✱ Ordzhonikidze. Mountainous region watered by unnavigable Terek and tributaries; on its SE border is Mt. Kazbek, one of the highest peaks of the Caucasus; in SW Ossetian Military Road leads over mountains through Mamison Pass to Georgian S.S.R. Mineral resources incl. lead and zinc; chief occupations fruitgrowing, dairying, cattle raising. Chief towns are Ordzhonikidze and Mozdok; several health resorts. Predominant ethnic strain Iranian; chief nationalities Ossetian, Ukrainian, and Russian. Ossets are descended from the Alans, a division of the early Scythian tribes of the region, speak an Indo-Iranian language, and probably have lived in present home since 5th cent. A.D.; converted to Christianity by Queen Tamara in 15th cent.; first came in conflict with Russians 1784 and were conquered 1802. Republic first set up 1924 as part of the Mountain Republic, in 1936 as autonomous republic.

North Pacific Ocean. See PACIFIC OCEAN.

North Pagai. See PAGAI.

North Palisade. See PALISADE, NORTH.

North Palm Beach. Village, Palm Beach co., SE Florida, 7 m. N of Palm Beach; pop. (1970c) 9035.

North Park. Elevated tract, Jackson co., N Colorado, bet. Medicine Bow Mts. and Park range; contains headwaters of the North Platte. See SOUTH PARK.

North Pass. One of the channels at the mouth of the Mississippi river (*q.v.*).

North Pel·ham \-ˈpel-əm\. Residential village in Pelham town, Westchester co., SE New York; pop. (1970c) 5184.

North Plainfield. Borough, Somerset co., N cen. New Jersey, 9 m. N of New Brunswick; pop. (1970c) 21,796; Mount St. Mary Coll. (1905).

North Platte \-ˈplat\. 1 River in Colorado, Wyoming, and Nebraska; 680 m. long; rises in Jackson co., N Colorado, flows N across Wyoming border into cen. Wyoming, turns E and SE across Nebraska border through W cen. Nebraska to unite with South Platte river in Lincoln co., SW cen. Nebraska, and form the Platte river.

2 City, ⊗ of Lincoln co., Nebraska, at confluence of North Platte and South Platte rivers; pop. (1970c) 19,447; dairy products; railroad shops; diversified agriculture.

North Point. 1 Point on E coast of Alpena co., NE Michigan, at N entrance to Thunder Bay.

2 Cape at N tip of W end of Prince Edward I., SE Canada, extending into the Gulf of St. Lawrence.

North Polar Regions. See POLAR REGIONS.

North Pole. The N extremity of the earth's axis, at 90°N lat. and the N center from which start all meridians of longitude; the point from which the only direction is S. The area around it (North Polar Regions: see POLAR REGIONS) is entirely water (Arctic Ocean), usually ice-covered. First overland crossing by foot and dogsled 1968–69. See MAGNETIC POLE.

North·port \ˈnȯ(ə)rth-ˈpō(ə)rt, -ˌpȯ(ə)rt\. 1 City, Tuscaloosa co., W cen. Alabama, 3 m. N of Tuscaloosa; pop. (1970c) 9435.

2 Village in town of Huntington, Suffolk co., SE New York, on N coast of Long I.; pop. (1970c) 7494.

North Providence. Town, Providence co., N Rhode Island; NW suburb of Providence; pop. (1970c) 24,337.

North P'yŏng·an \-ˈpyəŋ-ˈän\. Province of North Korea. See table at KOREA, NORTH.

North Read·ing \-ˈred-iŋ\. Town, Middlesex co., NE Massachusetts, 13 m. ESE of Lowell; pop. (1970c) 11,264.

North Rhine–West·pha·lia \-ˌrīn-wes(t)-ˈfāl-yə, -ˈfā-lē-ə\ *or Ger.* **Nord·rhein–West·fa·len** \nōrt-ˈrīn-vest-ˈfäl-ən\. A state of West Germany; 13,142 sq. m.; pop. (1970e) 17,167,500; ✱ Düsseldorf; iron and steel; chemicals, textiles, machinery; oil refining, coal mining.

North Rich·land Hills \-ˌrich-lən(d)-\. Town, Tarrant co., N Texas, NE of Fort Worth; pop. (1970c) 16,514.

North Ridge·ville \-ˈrij-ˌvil\. Village, Lorain co., N Ohio, ab. 5 m. NE of Elyria; pop. (1970c) 13,152; residential.

North Riding. See YORKSHIRE.

North River. See NORTH.

North River Mountain. Peak in the Adirondack Mts., Essex co., NE New York; 3890 ft.

North Riv·er·side \-ˈriv-ər-ˌsīd\. Village, Cook co., NE Illinois, W suburb of Chicago; pop. (1970c) 8097.

North Ron·ald·say \-ˈrän-ᵊl(d)-ˌsā\ *or* **North Ron·ald·shay** \-ˌshā\. Northernmost of the Orkney Is. off N coast of Scotland.

North Roy·al·ton \-ˈrȯi-əl-tən\. City, Cuyahoga co., N Ohio, 13 m. S of Cleveland; pop. (1970c) 12,807.

North Saint Paul. Village, Ramsey co., E Minnesota, 7 m. NE of St. Paul; pop. (1970c) 11,950.

North Saskatchewan. See SASKATCHEWAN 1.

North Scit·u·ate \-ˈsich-(ə-)wət\. Village, Providence co., N Rhode Island, NW of Cranston; administrative center of Scituate.

Norths Coast \ˈnȯ(ə)rths-\. Section of coast of East Antarctica, 67°S, bet. 125°E and 130°E; part of Wilkes Land and Australian claim.

North Sea *also* **German Ocean** *or anc.* **Ma·re Ger·man·i·cum** \ˌmā-(ˌ)rē-jər-ˈman-i-kəm, ˌmär-(ˌ)ā-\. Arm of the Atlantic Ocean extending bet. the European continent on the S and E and Great Britain on the W; ab. 600 m. long and 350 m. wide; ab. 220 sq. m.; average depth 308 ft.; important fisheries; site of extensive oil and natural-gas fields.

North Sea Canal *or* **Amsterdam Ship Canal** *or Du.* **Noord Zee Ka·naal** \ˌnōrt-ˌzā-kə-ˈnäl\. Canal, Netherlands, from Amsterdam to North Sea at IJmuiden; 17 m. long; constructed 1865–76; restored importance of Amsterdam as commercial port.

North Sheep Mountain \-ˈshēp-\. Peak, Park and Summit cos., cen. Colorado; 13,600 ft.

North Smith·field \-ˈsmith-ˌfēld\. Town, Providence co., N Rhode Island, near Woonsocket; pop. (1970c) 9349.

North Ston·ing·ton \-ˈstōn-iŋ-tən\. Town, New London co., SE Connecticut, 14 m. NE of New London; pop. (1970c) 3748.

North Su·la·we·si \-ˌsü-lə-ˈwā-sē\. Province of Indonesia, Celebes. See CELEBES and table at INDONESIA.

North Sydney. 1 Municipality, E New South Wales, SE Australia; N suburb of Sydney on N side of Port Jackson; pop. (1966c) 51,574; connected with Sydney by noted bridge completed Mar. 1932.

2 Town, Cape Breton co., E Nova Scotia, Canada; on W side of Sydney Harbor 4 m. SW of entrance; pop. (1971p) 8498; shipping port for Sydney Mines; fishing.

North Syracuse. Village, Onondaga co., cen. New York, 8 m. NNE of Syracuse; pop. (1970c) 8687.

North Ta·ra·na·ki Bight \-ˌtär-ə-ˌnäk-ē-\. Gulf N of W bulge on W coast of North I., New Zealand.

North Tarryall Peak. See TARRYALL PEAK, NORTH.

North Tar·ry·town \-ˈtar-ē-ˌtau̇n\. Residential village, Westchester co., SE New York, on Hudson river 26 m. N of New York and adjoining Tarrytown; pop. (1970c) 8334; forms one community with Tarrytown, Irvington, and Elmsford. Nearby are Sleepy Hollow, made famous by Washington Irving's *Legend of Sleepy Hollow*, and Sleepy Hollow Cemetery.

North Thompson. See THOMPSON 2.

North To·na·wan·da \-ˌtän-ə-ˈwän-də\. Manufacturing city and port of entry, Niagara co., W New York, 10 m. E of Niagara Falls; pop. (1970c) 36,012; dies, castings, furniture, plastic, pumps, paints, chain hoists; obtains electric power from Niagara Falls. Tonawanda (*q.v.*) is its sister city.

North Truchas Peak. See TRUCHAS PEAK.

North Tyne. See TYNE 1.

North Uist \-ˈyü-əst\. Island of the Outer Hebrides, separated by Little Minch from Skye, off NW coast of

Scotland; pop. (1961c) 2579; administratively part of Inverness co.

North·um·ber·land \nȯr-'thəm-bər-lənd\. 1 Name of counties in two states of the U.S. See tables at PENNSYLVANIA and VIRGINIA.

2 Town, Coos co., N New Hampshire, on Connecticut river 18 m. WNW of Berlin; pop. (1970c) 2493.

3 Industrial borough, Northumberland co., E cen. Pennsylvania, on Susquehanna river 28 m. SSE of Williamsport; pop. (1970c) 4102. Home of Joseph Priestley 1794–1804.

4 County, New Brunswick, Canada. See table at NEW BRUNSWICK.

5 County, Ontario, Canada. See table at ONTARIO.

6 County, N England, on the border of Scotland; 2019 sq. m.; pop. (1971p) 794,975; ⊗ Newcastle upon Tyne; includes Holy I. or Lindisfarne, the Farne Is., and Coquet Isle; coal mining, shipbuilding; electrical machinery, pottery; important towns Newcastle upon Tyne, Tynemouth, Berwick-upon-Tweed, Alnwick, Morpeth, Hexham; coal deposits in SE section; chief rivers Tyne, Tweed, Till, Coquet.

Northumberland, Cape. Cape on Indian Ocean, SE corner of South Australia, 38°05′S.

Northumberland Islands. Group of islands off E coast of Queensland, Australia, enclosing Broad Sound, S of Mackay.

Northumberland Strait. Channel bet. Prince Edward I. and the SE Canadian mainland (E New Brunswick and N Nova Scotia); ab. 180 m. long and 12–30 m. wide.

North·um·bria \nȯr-'thəm-brē-ə\. Anglo-Saxon kingdom of Britain, bet. the Humber and the Firth of Forth; formed of Deira and Bernicia (*qq.v.*), traditionally, Anglian kingdoms; during most of 7th cent. A.D., the leading kingdom of the Heptarchy (*q.v.*); converted to Christianity by marriage connection with Kent (*q.v.*), and again, after subjugation by Mercia (*q.v.*), by Celtic missionaries; its ruler, Oswy, called Synod of Whitby in 664 which determined the adherence to Rome of the English Church; S part ruled by Danes from 9th cent. to 954 when first annexed to Wessex (*q.v.*).

North Ump·qua \-'əm(p)-kwə\. River, SW Oregon; ab. 85 m. long; rises in E Douglas co., flows E uniting with South Umpqua river ab. 8 m. NW of Roseburg to form Umpqua river.

North·vale \'nȯ(ə)rth-ˌvāl\. Borough, Bergen co., NE New Jersey, 12 m. NE of Paterson; pop. (1970c) 5177.

North Valley Stream. Unincorporated urban community, Nassau co., SE New York, in cen. Long I.; pop. (1970c) 14,881.

North Vancouver. Residential city, S Brit. Columbia, Canada, on Burrard Inlet across from Vancouver; pop. (1971p) 31,863; sawmills, shipyards.

North Ver·non \-'vər-nən\. City, Jennings co., SE Indiana, 36 m. S of Shelbyville; pop. (1970c) 4582; lumber, rugs, automobile parts.

North Ver·sailles \-vər-'sālz\. Urban township, Allegheny co., SW Pennsylvania, SE of Pittsburgh.

North Vietnam. See VIETNAM, NORTH.

North·ville \'nȯ(ə)rth-ˌvil\. City, Oakland and Wayne cos., SE Michigan, 23 m. WNW of Detroit; pop. (1970c) 5400; automobile parts; diversified agriculture.

North Wales \-'wālz\. Borough, Montgomery co., SE Pennsylvania, 18 m. N of Philadelphia; pop. (1970c) 3911.

North Waziristan. See WAZIRISTAN.

North West. See ESSEQUIBO 2.

Northwest Angle. The part of Lake of the Woods co., N Minnesota, which is on NW shore of Lake of the Woods N of the 49th parallel; ab. 130 sq. m.; belongs to U.S. instead of Canada because of inadequate survey at time of Treaty of 1783; boundary fixed 1908 and 1925.

North West Cape. Point, W Western Australia, at entrance to Exmouth Gulf, 21°45′S, 114°10′E.

Northwestern Islands. Widely scattered island groups N of New Guinea I. in the Admiralty Is.; forms a part of Manus dist. of Papua New Guinea; Hermit Is. and Ninigo Group are the most important.

North–Western Province. Province, W Ceylon, on Gulf of Mannar; 3016 sq. m.; pop. (1968e) 1,304,000; ✻ Kurunegala. Puttalam is an important coast town.

North–Western State. State of NW Nigeria. See table at NIGERIA.

North Western Territory. See NORTHWEST TERRITORIES.

North–West Frontier Province. Province, Pakistan, bounded on W and N by Afghanistan; 40,377 sq. m.; pop. (1969e) 10,937,000; ✻ Peshawar. Mountainous area beyond the Indus, the country of the Pathans. On its W border are Sulaiman Mts. in S, Safed Koh, and ranges of Hindu Kush; highest peaks Tirich Mir in NW Chitral 26,115 ft., Himalaya peaks in Hazara dist. 10,000–16,700 ft., Sikaram on Afghanistan border in the Safed Koh 15,619 ft., and Takht-i-Sulaiman in the Sulaiman Mts. 11,289 ft. Rivers are W tributaries of the Indus (Kabul, Kurram, Gumal). Important mountain passes are the Khyber and Gumal (*qq.v.*). Has small area under cultivation; chief crops wheat, corn, barley, rice. Chief towns Peshawar, Kohat, Mardan, Dera Ismail Khan.

History: For centuries region has been home of the Pathans, Muslims of Indo-Iranian stock, who were partially subjected by Moguls (16th–17th cents.) and later (19th cent.) by Sikhs. At end of Second Sikh War trans-Indus districts annexed by British 1849; province created and separated from Punjab 1901 under present name; hill tribes specially turbulent, causing more than 50 punitive expeditions; most serious rebellion 1919–20. Made autonomous province 1937; became part of Pakistan 1947; provincial status abolished 1955, restored 1970.

Northwest Passage. A passage by sea bet. the Atlantic and Pacific oceans along the N coast of America; long sought for by navigators; their searches led to discovery of St. Lawrence river by Jacques Cartier 1534–35, of Frobisher Sound by Martin Frobisher 1576, of Hudson Bay by Henry Hudson 1610; during 19th cent. explorations were carried on by several British naval officers including Sir John Franklin, John Ross, and Sir Robert McClure who discovered the route during his unsuccessful search (1850–54) for Franklin; the first (1903–06) to navigate the passage was the Norwegian explorer Roald Amundsen. See ARCTIC, THE.

North West Providence Channel. See PROVIDENCE CHANNEL, NORTH WEST.

North–West Provinces. Former province of British India. See AGRA 1.

North West Region. Division of Western Australia in NW part, plateau along coast extending S from Indian Ocean to Murchison river.

Northwest Territories. Federally administered division of Canada, consisting of the mainland N of 60°N bet. Yukon Terr. and Hudson Bay, the islands in Hudson, James, and Ungava Bays, and all islands N of the mainland; 1,304,903 sq. m. (incl. 51,465 sq. m. of water); pop. (1970e) 33,000; ✻ Yellowknife; divided into three districts: Franklin, Keewatin, Mackenzie. *Physical features:* A vast area including many rivers, lakes, and islands; av. elevation of peaks in Mackenzie Mts. on Yukon Terr. border is 7000 ft. (highest point Mt. Sir James MacBrien 9062 ft.), but most of the region is comparatively low. The Mackenzie river and its tributaries and the great lakes drained by them (esp. Great Bear and Great Slave Lakes) fill nearly two thirds of the mainland area; the Coppermine, Back, Dubawnt, and Kazan are other large streams. *Chief minerals:* Lead, gold, zinc, cadmium. Territory W of Prince Rupert's Land first created 1820 as **North Western Territory;** leased to Hudson's Bay Company 1821–69; transferred to Canada 1869 by acquisition of territorial rights of Hudson's Bay Company; as **North West Territory** greatly enlarged 1869–82; Ungava Penin. transferred to Quebec 1912.

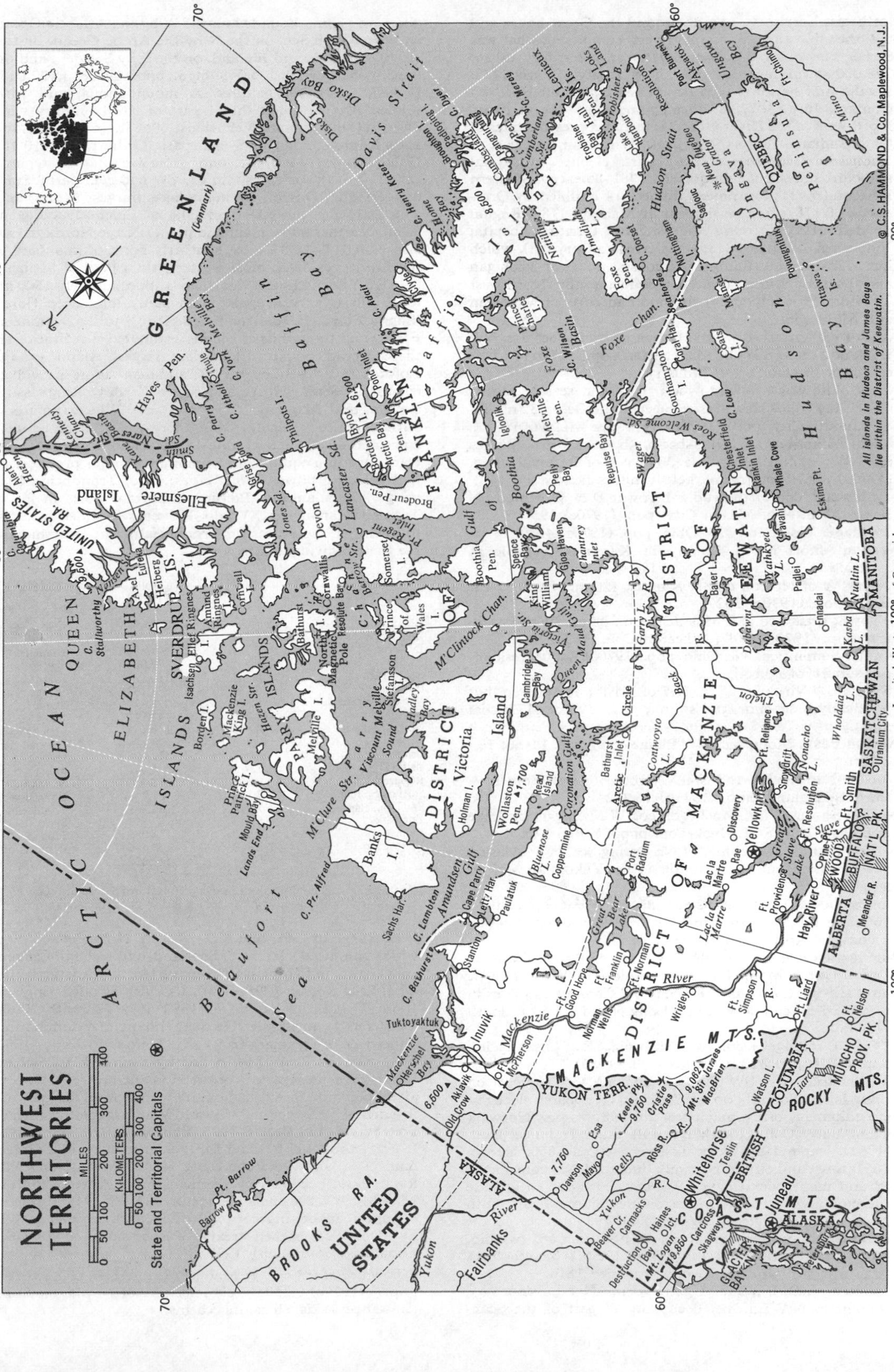
NORTHWEST TERRITORIES
MILES
0 50 100 200 300 400
KILOMETERS
0 50 100 200 300 400
State and Territorial Capitals
ARCTIC OCEAN
QUEEN ELIZABETH ISLANDS
GREENLAND
(Denmark)
Baffin Bay
Davis Strait
Beaufort Sea
Hudson Bay
Hudson Strait
Foxe Basin
Foxe Chan.
Gulf of Boothia
Lancaster Sd.
M'Clure Str.
Viscount Melville Sd.
M'Clintock Chan.
Amundsen Gulf
Coronation Gulf
Queen Maud Gulf
Victoria Island
Banks I.
Ellesmere Island
Devon I.
Baffin Island
Southampton I.
SVERDRUP IS.
PARRY ISLANDS
DISTRICT OF FRANKLIN
DISTRICT OF MACKENZIE
DISTRICT OF KEEWATIN
MACKENZIE MTS.
YUKON TERR.
BRITISH COLUMBIA
ALBERTA
SASKATCHEWAN
MANITOBA
QUEBEC
Ungava Peninsula
UNITED STATES
ALASKA
BROOKS RA.
Great Bear Lake
Great Slave Lake
Mackenzie River
Yellowknife
Whitehorse
Juneau
Inuvik
Tuktoyaktuk
Fairbanks
Dawson
Arctic Circle
Longitude West 100° of Greenwich
All Islands in Hudson and James Bays lie within the District of Keewatin.
© C.S. HAMMOND & Co., Maplewood, N.J.

Northwest Territory. Region around the Great Lakes and bet. the Ohio and Mississippi rivers, comprising what was earlier known as the *Old Northwest,* a territory of ab. 248,000 sq. m. awarded to U.S. by Treaty of Paris 1783. As the first national territory of the U.S. established by Congress July 13, 1787, officially known as "the Territory Northwest of the River Ohio," it included present states of Ohio, Indiana, Illinois, Michigan, Wisconsin, and part of Minnesota (see these entries). Parts claimed by several seaboard states but relinquished 1781–86 except Western Reserve (*q.v.*); government framework outlined by Ordinance of 1787; first settlement at Marietta 1788. Region divided 1800, forming the Indiana Territory (capital Vincennes, later, in 1813, transferred to Corydon), which included Indiana, Illinois, Wisconsin, much of Michigan and part of Minnesota, and reducing the Northwest Territory (✱ Chillicothe) to Ohio and parts of Michigan and Minnesota.

North·wich \\'nȯrth-(ˌ)wich\\. Urban district, Cheshire, NW England, 19 m. SSW of Manchester; pop. (1971p) 18,109; center of England's salt industry.

North Wild·wood \\-'wīld-ˌwu̇d\\. City and seaside resort, Cape May co., S New Jersey, on Atlantic Ocean 32 m. SW of Atlantic City; pop. (1970c) 3914. See WILDWOOD.

North Wilkes·boro \\-ˌwilks-ˌbər-ə, -ˌbə-rə\\. Town, Wilkes co., NW cen. North Carolina, 30 m. NW of Statesville; pop. (1970c) 3357; poultry market; furniture factories.

North·wood \\'nȯ(ə)rth-ˌwu̇d\\. 1 Town, ⊗ of Worth co., N Iowa, 20 m. N of Mason City; pop. (1970c) 1950.

2 Village, Wood co., NW Ohio; pop. (1970c) 4222.

Nor·ton \\'nȯrt-ᵊn\\. 1 County in Kansas. See table at KANSAS.

2 City, ⊗ of Norton co., N Kansas, 120 m. NW of Great Bend; pop. (1970c) 3627.

3 Town, Bristol co., SE Massachusetts, 11 m. SW of Brockton; pop. (1970c) 9487; Wheaton Coll. (1834).

4 City, Summit co., NE Ohio; pop. (1970c) 12,308; residential suburb of Akron.

5 City, SW Virginia, 35 m. NW of Bristol; in Wise co. but politically independent; 3 sq. m.; pop. (1970c) 4172; coal mining.

Norton Peak. Mountain, NW Blaine co., S cen. Idaho; 10,-200 ft.

Norton–Rad·stock \\-'rad-ˌstäk\\. Urban borough, Somersetshire, S England; pop. (1971p) 15,232.

Norton Shores. City, Muskegon co., W Michigan, on Lake Michigan 7 m. S of Muskegon; pop. (1970c) 22,271.

Norton Sound. Large inlet of NE Bering Sea, in W Alaska, bet. Seward Penin. and mouths of the Yukon; ab. 200 m. long.

Nor·um·be·ga \\ˌnȯr-əm-'bē-gə, ˌnär-\\. Name applied by 16th and 17th cent. map makers to undefined region along E coast of North America N of Florida.

Nor·ve·gia Cape \\nȯr-ˌvē-j(ē-)ə-\\. Cape on Princess Martha Coast, Queen Maud Land, Antarctica, 71°25′S, 12°18′W.

Nor·walk \\'nȯ(ə)r-ˌwȯk\\. 1 River, SW Connecticut; rises in cen. Fairfield co., flows S into Long Island Sound at South Norwalk.

2 City, Los Angeles co., SW California, SE of Los Angeles; pop. (1970c) 91,827; Corritos Coll. (1955).

3 Industrial city, SW Fairfield co., SW Connecticut, on Long Island Sound; pop. (1970c) 79,113; apparel, electronic equipment, office machines, air compressors; Norwalk Community Coll. (1961), Norwalk State Technical Coll. (1961); watered by Norwalk river; settled 1650, incorp. 1651; town and city of Norwalk (incorp. 1893) consolidated and made coextensive 1913 and expanded to include surrounding towns and municipalities, among them South Norwalk (*q.v.*); burned by British 1779.

4 Industrial and residential city, ⊗ of Huron co., N Ohio, 15 m. S of Sandusky; pop. (1970c) 13,386; manufactures furniture; steel and iron works; founded 1816.

Nor·way \\'nȯ(ə)r-ˌwā\\. 1 *or Norw.* **Nor·ge** \\'nȯr-gə\\. Kingdom, NW Europe, occupying W part of the Scandinavian penin., bounded on the W by the Atlantic Ocean and the North Sea, on the N by the Arctic Ocean, on the NE by U.S.S.R. and Finland, on the E by Sweden, and on the S by Skagerrak; 125,049 sq. m.; pop. (1972e) 3,922,015; ✱ Oslo. *Physical features:* A mountainous land with Kjølen Mts. forming the N part of the boundary with Sweden (highest point Kebnekaise 6965 ft., in Sweden), the Jotunheimen group in S cen. part (Glittertind 8110 ft., Galdhøpiggen 8100 ft.), and extensive plateau regions called *fjells* or *vidde,* esp. in the SW and cen. parts (Hardangervidda, Dovrefjell); many lakes (largest Mjøsa) and short streams; largest rivers Glåma, Dramselva, Lågen, Tana. Northernmost mainland point is Cape Nordkyn (see also NORTH CAPE 4), most southerly point of mainland is the Lindesnes 58°N, most westerly the island of Steinsøy 5°46′E off Sogne Fjord. Coastline is approximately 1500 m. long, but is very irregular with many long deep fjords (Sogne Fjord, Hardanger Fjord, Oslo Fjord, Trondheim Fjord) and thousands of islands; estimated shoreline of all these would be ab. 12,000 m.; largest island groups Lofoten and Vesterålen off NW and many large individual islands as Senja, North and South Kvaløy, Ringvassøy, Sørøya, and Magerøy. *Chief products:* Wheat, potatoes, barley; livestock raising, fishing; forestry; iron ore, copper, zinc; manufacturing: chemicals, pulp and paper, textiles, transportation equipment, aluminum; a major producer of hydroelectric power. *Chief cities:* Oslo, Trondheim, Stavanger, Kristiansand, Bærum; important ports in far N Tromsø, Hammerfest, Vardø, Kirkenes. Divided into the following 19 counties (for pronunciation of their names, see their individual entries):

NAME	AREA (sq. m.)	POP. (1972e)	CO.SEAT
Akershus	1,895	332,894	Oslo
Aust-Agder	3,556	81,909	Arendal
Buskerud	5,765	201,391	Drammen
Finnmark	18,783	77,060	Vadsø
Hedmark	10,557	180,175	Hamar
Hordaland[1]	6,034	377,163	Bergen
Møre og Romsdal	5,820	225,877	Molde
Nordland	14,798	241,142	Bodø
Nord-Trøndelag	8,673	119,133	Steinkjer
Oppland	9,773	174,174	Lillehammer
Oslo[2]	175	477,476	Oslo
Østfold	1,613	224,041	Moss
Rogaland	3,529	272,538	Stavanger
Sogn og Fjordane	7,168	101,740	Hermansverk
Sør-Trøndelag	7,304	235,861	Trondheim
Telemark	5,913	157,553	Skien
Troms	10,020	138,085	Tromsø
Vest-Agder	2,810	126,176	Kristiansand
Vestfold	854	177,627	Tønsberg

[1]Includes city of Bergen, which formerly constituted a separate county.
[2]Coextensive with the city of Oslo which is also ⊗ of Akershus co.

History: In 9th cent. A.D., began Norse expeditions which colonized islands off Scotland, and Ireland, Iceland, and Greenland (*qq.v.*); first converted to Christianity by Olaf Tryggvesson (995–1000); its ruler invaded England 1066; Trondheim capital to 1380; lost war with Hanse Towns and came under German commercial domination; under rule of Denmark (*q.v.*) after Union of Kalmar 1397; by Treaty of Kiel 1814, ceded by Denmark to Sweden which gave it a separate constitution and arranged personal union with Swedish monarchy; dissolved union with Sweden in 1905; neutral in World War I; formally annexed Spitsbergen and Bear I. 1925, Bouvet I. 1928, Jan Mayen I. 1929, and Peter I Island 1931; claimed coast of E Greenland 1931, and Antarctic coast bet. 20°W long. and 45°E long. 1939; occupied by German forces Apr. 9, 1940 to May 8, 1945; became a member of NATO 1949; formed a common labor market with Denmark, Finland, and Sweden 1954; signed treaty of accession to European Economic Community 1972.

2 Town, Oxford co., W Maine, 18 m. WNW of Lewiston; pop. (1970c) 3595; summer resort; manufactures snowshoes, skis, sleds, moccasins.

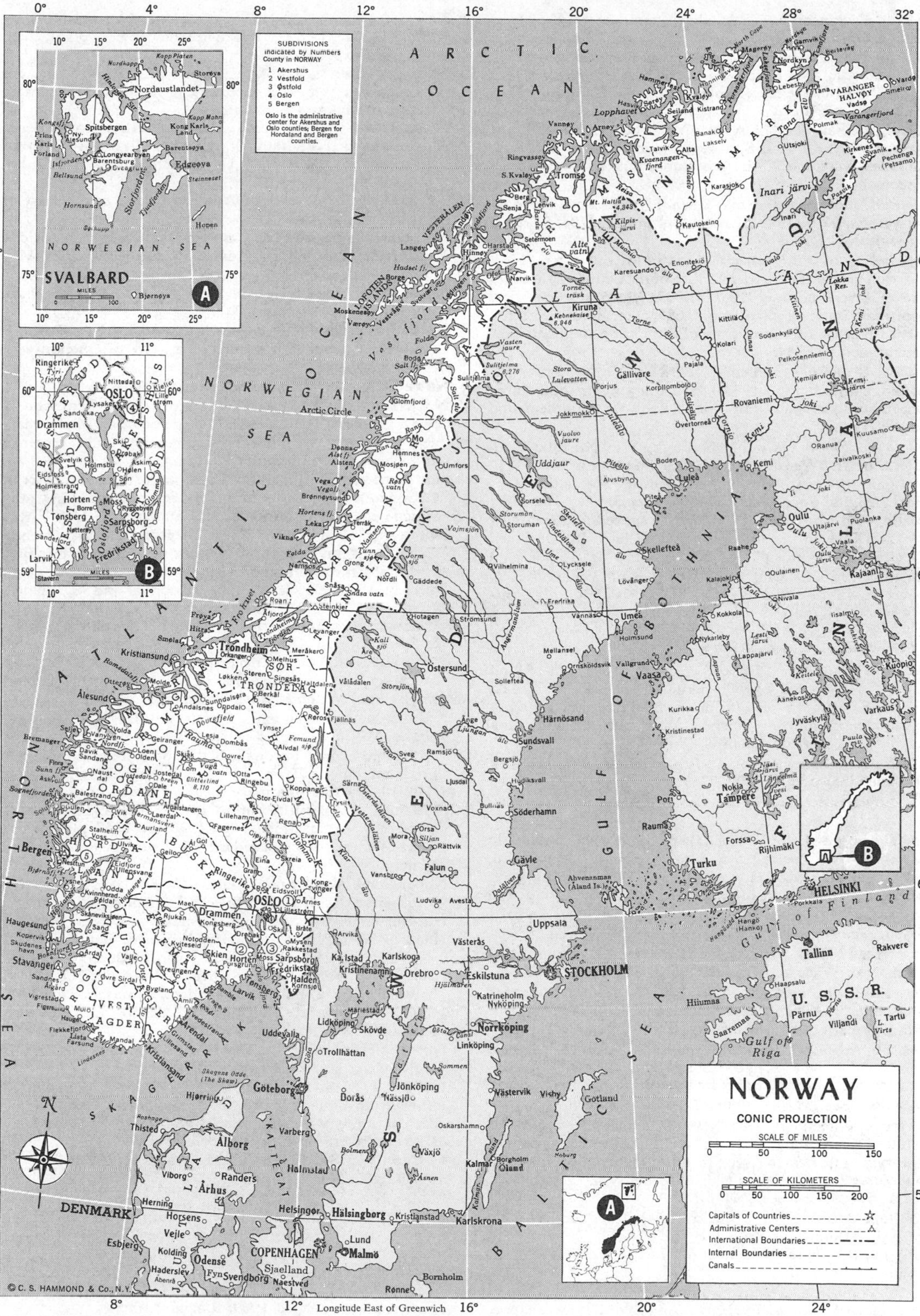
NORWAY
CONIC PROJECTION
SCALE OF MILES
0 50 100 150
SCALE OF KILOMETERS
0 50 100 150 200
Capitals of Countries
Administrative Centers
International Boundaries
Internal Boundaries
Canals
SUBDIVISIONS
indicated by Numbers
County in NORWAY
1 Akershus
2 Vestfold
3 Østfold
4 Oslo
5 Bergen
Oslo is the administrative center for Akershus and Oslo counties; Bergen for Hordaland and Bergen counties.
SVALBARD
NORWEGIAN SEA
Spitsbergen
Nordaustlandet
Edgeøya
Bjørnøya
Longyearbyen
ARCTIC OCEAN
NORWEGIAN SEA
ATLANTIC OCEAN
NORTH SEA
SKAGERRAK
KATTEGAT
GULF OF BOTHNIA
BALTIC SEA
Gulf of Finland
Gulf of Riga
Arctic Circle
LOFOTEN ISLANDS
FINNMARK
LAPLAND
FINLAND
SWEDEN
DENMARK
U. S. S. R.
OSLO
STOCKHOLM
HELSINKI
COPENHAGEN
Trondheim
Bergen
Stavanger
Tromsø
Narvik
Hammerfest
Kirkenes
Kristiansand
Drammen
Göteborg
Malmö
Uppsala
Turku
Tampere
Oulu
Tallinn
Longitude East of Greenwich
©C. S. HAMMOND & Co., N.Y.

3 City, Dickinson co., S Michigan penin., 8 m. E of Iron Mountain; pop. (1970c) 3033; former iron-mining center.

Nor·we·gian Bay \nȯr-ˌwē-jən-\. Bay in the group of islands N of Canada; Axel Heiberg is on the N, S end of Ellesmere I. on the E, NW end of Devon I. on the S, and Amund Ringnes I. on the W.

Norwegian Sea. Part of Arctic Ocean bet. Greenland and Iceland on the W and Spitsbergen and Norway on the E; includes waters off NE Greenland formerly known as Greenland Sea.

Nor·well \ˈnȯ(ə)r-ˌwel, -wəl\. Town, Plymouth co., SE Massachusetts, 12 m. ENE of Brockton; pop. (1970c) 7796; in agricultural region.

Nor·wich \ˈnȯ(ə)r-(ˌ)wich, ˈnär-\. **1** Industrial town, New London co., in N cen. part, SE Connecticut, on the Shetucket river; pop. (1970c) 41,739; chemicals, plastics, footwear. Settled 1660; incorp. 1685; coterminous with the city of Norwich; at confluence of the Yantic and Shetucket rivers; incorp. 1784.

2 City, ⊗ of Chenango co., S cen. New York, 36 m. NNE of Binghamton; pop. (1970c) 8843; dairying; manufactures pharmaceuticals and patent medicines, farm implements; settled 1788.

3 *Brit.* ˈnȯr-ich\. County borough, ⊗ of Norfolk, E England, on the Wensum 97 m. NE of London; pop. (1971p) 121,688; footwear; wire netting, electric motors; Univ. of East Anglia (incorporated 1964); remains of Norman castle; cathedral, founded 1096; city sacked and occupied by the Danes in the 11th cent. and afflicted by the Black Death in 1348 and in 17th cent.

Nor·wood \ˈnȯ(ə)r-ˌwu̇d\. **1** Town, Norfolk co., E Massachusetts, 13 m. SW of Boston; pop. (1970c) 30,815; printing works, foundries.

2 Borough, Bergen co., NE corner of New Jersey, 12 m. ENE of Paterson; pop. (1970c) 4398.

3 City, Hamilton co., SW corner of Ohio, 5 m. NE of (and almost surrounded by) Cincinnati; pop. (1970c) 30,420; residential suburb of Cincinnati; manufactures automobiles, electric motors, machine tools; printing and lithographing; The Athenaeum of Ohio (1829).

4 Borough, Delaware co., SE Pennsylvania, 9 m. WSW of Philadelphia; pop. (1970c) 7229.

5 Municipality, Australia. See KENSINGTON AND NORWOOD.

No·shi·ro \nō-shi-ˌrō, nō-ˈshi(ə)r-ō\ *or* **No·shi·ro·mi·na·to** \-mi-ˈnät-ō\. Coastal town, Akita prefecture, N Honshū, Japan, 35 m. SW of Hirosaki; pop. (1970c) 59,793; good anchorage; important in timber trade; notable production in lacquer ware and copper.

Nosop. See NOSSOB.

Noss Head \ˈnȯs-\. Rocky headland on NE coast of Scotland, N of Wick and S of Sinclair's Bay; lighthouse.

Nos·si–Bé *or* **No·sy–Bé** \ˌnȯ-sē-ˈbā\. Island, Malagasy Republic, in NE Mozambique Channel, off NW coast of Madagascar; 129 sq. m.

Nos·sob \ˈnō-ˌsäb\ *or* **No·sop** \ˈnō-ˌsäp\. River, SW Africa; ab. 500 m. long; rises in cen. South-West Africa, flows SSE into Auob river shortly before it empties into the Molopo.

Notabile. See CITTÀ VECCHIA.

No·teć \ˈnȯ-ˌtech\ *or Ger.* **Net·ze** \ˈnet-sə\. River, W Poland; 230 m. long; rises in small lakes and flows W, emptying into Warta river 6 m. E of Gorzów Wielkopolski; navigable for part of its course; formerly in Germany.

Nótiai Sporádhes. See SPORADES.

No·ti·um \ˈnō-sh(ē-)əm\. Ancient town, Ionia, on SW coast of Asia Minor S of Colophon for which it was the port; Spartan fleet under Lysander defeated Athenians 407 B.C. in nearby waters.

No·to \ˈnȯ-(ˌ)tō\ *or anc.* **Ne·tum** \ˈnēt-əm\. Commune, Siracusa prov., SE Sicily, Italy, 17 m. SW of Syracuse; pop. (1968e) 25,916; cathedral; founded 1703 SE of older town destroyed 1693 by earthquake.

Not·od·den \ˈnō-ˌtȯd-ᵊn\. Town, Telemark co., S Norway; pop. (1970e) 13,422; hydroelectric power plant, iron foundries; exports saltpeter.

Noto Peninsula \ˌnōt-ō-\. Headland projecting N into the Sea of Japan, its E coast enclosing Toyama Bay; the greater part is in Ishikawa prefecture.

No·tre Dame \ˌnōt-ər-ˈdām\. North suburb of South Bend, St. Joseph co., N Indiana; St. Mary's Coll. (1844), Univ. of Notre Dame (1842), Holy Cross Junior Coll. (1966). See SOUTH BEND.

Notre Dame Bay. Inlet of Atlantic Ocean on N coast of Newfoundland, Canada.

Notre–Dame–de–Lo·rette \ˌnȯ-trə-ˈdäm-də-lȯ-ˈret\. Ridge near Lens, Pas-de-Calais dept., N France; battles May 1915.

Notre Dame de Lorette. Village, S Quebec, Canada; pop. (1966c) 5691.

Notre Dame des Lau·ren·tides \-dā-ˌlȯr-ən-ˈtēd\. Town, S Quebec co., Quebec, Canada, 11 m. NW of Quebec; pop. (1971p) 5087.

Notre Dame des Vertus. See AUBERVILLIERS.

Notre Dame du Lac \-du̇-ˈläk\. Town, ⊗ of Témiscouata co., S Quebec, Canada, on SW shore of Lake Témiscouata near New Brunswick border; pop. (1971p) 2116; center of an extensive hunting and fishing region.

Not·ta·wa·sa·ga Bay \ˌnät-ə-wə-ˈsȯ-gə-\. Inlet in S part of Georgian Bay, Lake Huron, extending into Grey and Simcoe cos., SE Ontario prov., Canada.

Not·ta·way \ˈnät-ə-ˌwā\. River, Abitibi co., SW Quebec, Canada; 400 m. long; flows NW into SE part of James Bay; outlet of Mattagami and other lakes.

Notte·ly \ˈnät-lē\. Stream, NE Georgia and SW North Carolina; ab. 40 m. long; flows N from Blue Ridge in Union co., Ga., to join the Hiwassee in Cherokee co., N.C.; in its course in Georgia is **Nottely Dam.** See table at TENNESSEE VALLEY AUTHORITY.

Nøt·ter·øy \ˈnə(r)t-ə-ˌrȯi\. Island in Oslo Fjord, SE Norway; 17 sq. m.; chief town Tønsberg.

Not·ting·ham \ˈnät-iŋ-əm\. **1** County in England. See NOTTINGHAMSHIRE.

2 City and county borough, ⊗ of Nottinghamshire, N cen. England, on the Trent 47 m. NE of Birmingham; pop. (1971p) 299,758; pharmaceuticals, tobacco products; textile mills; lace manufacture; Univ. of Nottingham (1948); scene of three parliaments bet. 1330 and 1357; place where Charles I raised his standard 1642 and began the Civil War.

Nottingham Island. Small island at W end of Hudson Strait in SE Franklin dist., Northwest Territories, Canada.

Not·ting·ham·shire \ˈnät-iŋ-əm-ˌshi(ə)r, -shər\ *or* **Nottingham** *or* **Notts** \ˈnäts\. County, N cen. England; area 843 sq. m.; pop. (1971p) 974,640; ⊗ Nottingham; chief river the Trent; barley, oats, wheat, sugar beet, potatoes; livestock; gravel, limestone, sandstone; major towns Nottingham, Newark, Mansfield, Worksop, East Retford, Southwell.

Not·ting Hill \ˌnät-iŋ-\. District, W London, England, in Kensington and Chelsea borough.

Not·to·way \ˈnät-ə-ˌwā\. **1** River, S Virginia; 175 m. long; flows from Lunenburg co. SE across North Carolina border to unite with the Blackwater river and form the Chowan river, NE North Carolina.

2 County in S cen. Virginia. See table at VIRGINIA.

3 Village, its ⊗.

Notts. See NOTTINGHAMSHIRE.

Nouad·hi·bou \ˌnwäd-i-ˈbü\ *or formerly* **Port–Étienne** \ˈpȯr-ā-ˈtyen\. Seaport town at Cape Blanc, NW Mauritania, W Africa; pop. (1968e) 7700; fisheries.

Nouak·chott \nu̇-ˈäk-ˌshät\. Town, ✱ of Mauritania, W Africa, near coast in SW part; pop. (1971e) 35,000; desalination plant (opened 1969; first in Africa).

Nou Island \ˈnü-\. See NOUMÉA.

Noulos, Pic. See ALBÈRES, MONTS.

Nou·méa \nü-'mā-ə\. Town, ✱ of New Caledonia terr., on SW coast of New Caledonia I., SW Pacific Ocean; pop. (1971e) 57,839; has large, landlocked harbor, formed partly by Nou I., ab. 4 m. long, with seaplane base, just opp. the town; steamer connections with Australia, New Zealand, and Indonesia. Taken over as a major base by Allied forces 1942.

Noup Head \'nüp-\. Promontory on NW coast of Westray I., Orkney Is., off N coast of Scotland; lighthouse.

Nouveau–Québec. See NEW QUEBEC.

Nouveau–Québec, Cratère du. See NEW QUEBEC CRATER.

Nouvelle Calédonie. See NEW CALEDONIA 1 and 2.

Nouvelles Hébrides. See NEW HEBRIDES.

No·va Cae·sa·rea \ˌnō-və-ˌsē-zə-'rē-ə; -ˌses-ə-, -ˌsez-\. Latin name given the colony of New Jersey upon its creation in 1664.

Nova Civitas. See NEUSTADT AN DER WEINSTRASSE.

Novaesium. See NEUSS 1.

No·va·fel·tria \ˌnȯ-və-'fel-trē-ə\ *or formerly* **Mer·ca·ti·no Ma·rec·chia** \ˌmer-kə-'tē-nō-mä-'rek-yə\. Commune, Marches, cen. Italy, 33 m. W of Pesaro.

Nova Fri·bur·go \ˌnȯ-və-frē-'bu̇(ə)r-(ˌ)gō\. City, Rio de Janeiro state, SE Brazil, on railroad 65 m. NE of Rio de Janeiro; munic. pop. (1968c) 93,364.

Nova Igua·çu \-ˌē-gwə-'sü\. City, Rio de Janeiro state, SE Brazil, NW of Rio de Janeiro; munic. pop. (1968e) 478,319.

Nova Li·ma \-'lē-mə\. City, Minas Gerais state, E Brazil; S suburb of Belo Horizonte; munic. pop. (1968e) 32,336.

Nova Lis·boa \-lēzh-'vō-ə\ *or formerly* **Huam·bo** \'wäm-(ˌ)bō\. Town, in highlands of W cen. Angola, SW Africa; pop. (1969e) 49,823; alt. 5580 ft.; large railway repair shops; founded 1912.

No·va·ra \no-'var-ə\. 1 Province of Piedmont, NW Italy. See table at ITALY.

2 *or anc.* **No·var·ia** \nō-'var-ē-ə, -'ver-\. Commune, its ✱, 28 m. W of Milan; pop. (1968e) 98,941; 11th cent. cathedral, 16th cent. church of San Gaudenzio, ruins of old castle, episcopal palace; manufactures silks, cottons, linens; important trade in rice and grain. Founded by Celts; in Middle Ages second most important city of duchy of Milan; Swiss victory over French 1513; battle 1821; famous Austrian victory over Piedmontese under Charles Albert of Sardinia Mar. 23, 1849.

Nova Sco·tia \ˌno-və-'skō-shə\. Province, E Canada, one of the Maritime Provinces; 21,425 sq. m.; pop. (1970e) 766,000, (1966c) 756,129; ✱ Halifax. *Physical features:* Comprises peninsula ab. 375 m. long by 50–100 m. wide, joined to continent by isthmus of Chignecto; includes Cape Breton I. (*q.v.*) on NE, separated from it by Strait (or Gut) of Canso; separated on N from Prince Edward Island by Northumberland Strait, and on W from New Brunswick by Bay of Fundy; highest peak North Barren 1747 ft.; contains one national park (Cape Breton Highlands) and six national historic parks. *Chief products:* Coal, silver, limestone, barite; fishing. *Chief cities:* Halifax, Dartmouth, Sydney, Glace Bay, Truro. Divided into the following 18 counties (for pronunciation of their names, see their individual entries):

NAME	LOCATION	AREA[1] (sq. m.)	POP. (1966c)	CO. SEAT
Annapolis	W	1,285	21,579	Annapolis Royal
Antigonish	N	541	14,890	Antigonish
Cape Breton	E[2]	972	129,572	Sydney
Colchester	cen.	1,451	35,700	Truro
Cumberland	N	1,683	35,933	Amherst
Digby	W	970	19,827	Digby
Guysborough	E	1,611	12,830	Guysborough
Halifax	S	2,063	244,948	Halifax
Hants	cen.	1,229	26,893	Windsor
Inverness	NE[2]	1,409	18,152	Port Hood
Kings	W	842	43,249	Kentville
Lunenburg	S	1,169	36,114	Lunenburg
Pictou	N	1,124	44,490	Pictou
Queens	SW	983	12,807	Liverpool
Richmond	E[2]	489	11,218	Arichat
Shelburne	SW	979	16,284	Shelburne
Victoria	NE[2]	1,105	8,001	Baddeck
Yarmouth	SW	838	23,552	Yarmouth

[1]Land area.
[2]On Cape Breton I.

History: Coast probably explored by John Cabot 1497–98, Corte-Real 1500–02, and Verrazano 1524; first settlement 1604 by Sieur de Monts, removed 1605 to Port Royal (Annapolis Royal); granted (under name of Nova Scotia) by King James I to Sir William Alexander 1621, but settlement absorbed by French; in colonial wars Port Royal captured by English 1690, restored and again captured 1710; ceded to England by Treaty of Utrecht 1713; French fortress of Louisburg captured 1745 and 1758; Halifax founded 1749; many French Acadians deported 1755—theme of Longfellow's *Evangeline;* settled in 18th cent. by Scottish Highlanders and, after American Revolution, by Loyalists from U.S.; separated from New Brunswick 1784 and set up as a colony with name "Nova Scotia" (*Lat.,* New Scotland); entered Confederation 1867 (see CANADA).

Nova So·fa·la \ˌnȯ-və-sō-'fäl-ə\ *or formerly* **Sofala.** Seaport village, SE Mozambique, S of Beira; ancient Arab and early Portuguese port.

No·va·to \nō-'vät-(ˌ)ō\. City, Marin co., W California, N of San Francisco; pop. (1970c) 31,006.

Nová Ves Spišská. See SPIŠSKÁ NOVÁ VES.

Novaya Pismyanka. See LENINOGORSK 2.

Novaya Sibir. See NEW SIBERIAN ISLAND.

No·va·ya Zem·lya \ˌnō-və-yə-ˌzem-lē-'ä\. Two large islands in the Arctic Ocean off NE coast of Russian S.F.S.R., U.S.S.R., a part of the Arkhangelsk Oblast, bet. Barents Sea and Kara Sea; 31,382 sq. m.; islands separated by Matochkin Shar and S island separated from Vaigach I. by Kara Strait; N island permanently ice-covered; has little plant life but many animals, birds, and fish; normally visited in summer by hunters.

No·vel·la·ra \ˌnō-vā-'lär-ə\. Commune, Reggio nell'Emilia prov., Emilia-Romagna, N Italy, 10 m. N of Reggio nell'Emilia; pop (1968e) 10,310.

Novempopulana. See AQUITANIA.

No·vé Zám·ky \ˌnō-vā-'zäm(p)-kē\ *or Hung.* **Er·sek·új·vár** \ˌe(ə)r-ˌshek-'üē-ˌvär\ *or Ger.* **Neu·häu·sel** \'noi-ˌhȯi-zəl\. Town, Slovak S.R., E cen. Czechoslovakia, on Nitra river; pop. (1968e) 24,289. In early times a Hungarian town; held by Hungary 1938–45.

Nov·go·rod \'näv-gə-ˌräd\. 1 Medieval principality, 11th–15th cent., covering extensive region of all N Russia from Lake Peipus and Lithuania to the Urals. Its history centers in its capital (see 2, below).

2 City, ✱ of Novgorod Oblast, NW Russian S.F.S.R., U.S.S.R., on both sides of the Volkhov just N of Lake Ilmen; pop. (1970p) 128,000; chinaware, furniture; fish processing.

History: One of the oldest cities of Russia and of great importance 11th–15th cent. Originated as a Varangian trading town; conquered by Rurik who became its grand prince c. 862; at first dependent upon Kiev; became capital of principality and was called **Great Novgorod** *or* **Novgorod the Great;** escaped Mongol invasion 1237–40; ruled by Prince Alexander Nevski 1238–63; developed economically from its favorable location by trade with the Orient and Constantinople and with the Hanse Towns; became rival of Moscow, with many dependent towns in N Russia; its population estimated in 14th cent. at 400,000. Not subject to Tatars and fought successful wars with Germans and Swedes, but overpowered by Ivan III 1471–78 and laid waste by Ivan IV 1570; declined on the rise of St.

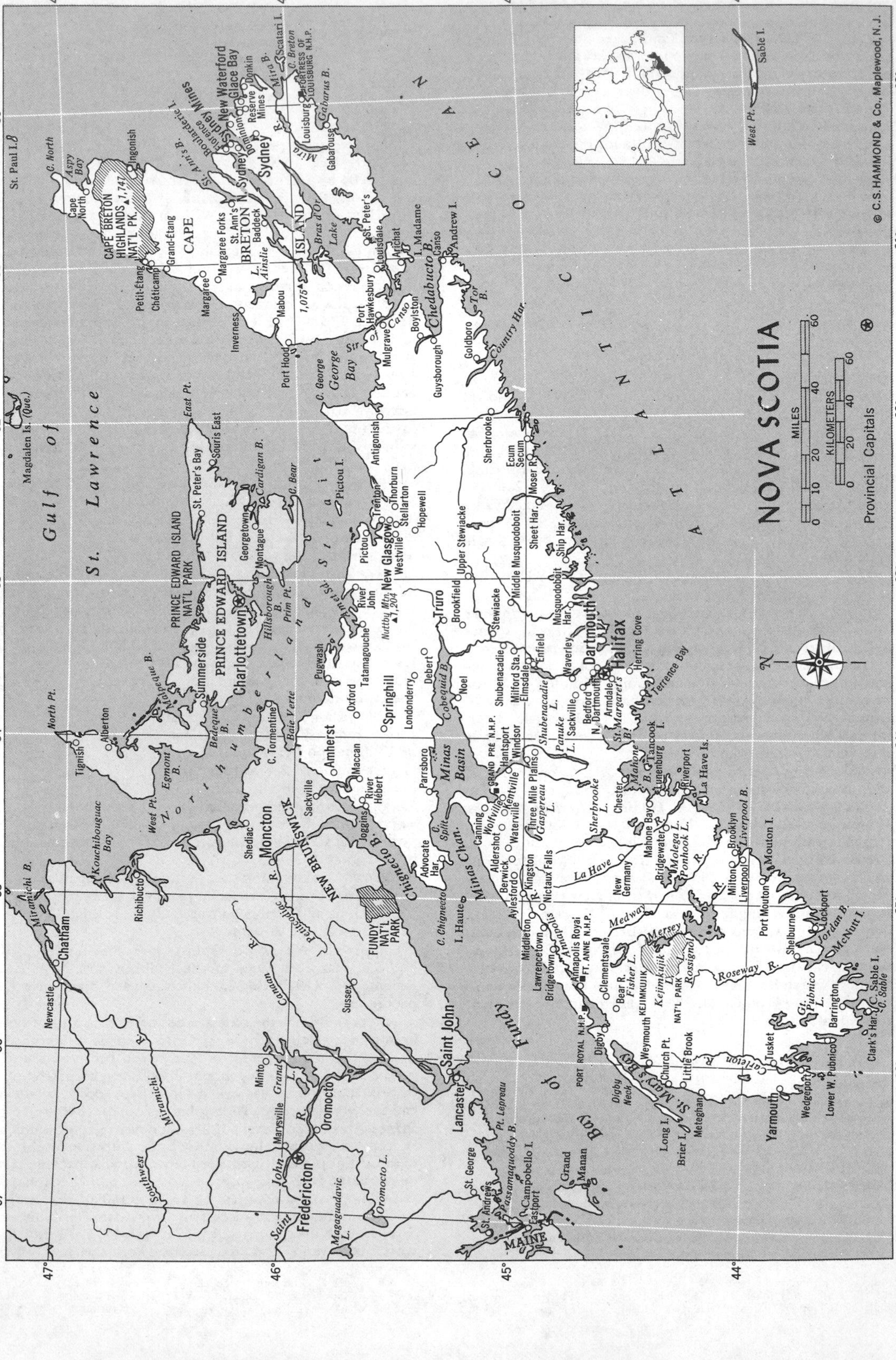
NOVA SCOTIA
MILES
0 10 20 40 60
KILOMETERS
0 20 40 60
Provincial Capitals
© C.S. HAMMOND & Co., Maplewood, N.J.
Longitude West of Greenwich
N
Gulf of St. Lawrence
ATLANTIC OCEAN
Northumberland Strait
Bay of Fundy
Magdalen Is. (Que.)
St. Paul I.
Sable I.
West Pt.
CAPE BRETON ISLAND
CAPE BRETON HIGHLANDS NAT'L PK.
1,747
C. North
Aspy Bay
Cape North
Ingonish
Petit-Étang
Chéticamp
Grand-Étang
Margaree
Margaree Forks
St. Ann's
Baddeck
Inverness
Mabou
L. Ainslie
Bras d'Or Lake
1,075
Port Hood
Sydney Mines
New Waterford
Glace Bay
Dominion
Reserve Mines
Donkin
Sydney
N. Sydney
Florence
Boularderie I.
St. Ann's B.
Mira B.
Mira
Scatari I.
C. Breton
FORTRESS OF LOUISBURG N.H.P.
Louisburg
Gabarus B.
Gabarouse
St. Peter's
Louisdale
Arichat
I. Madame
Port Hawkesbury
Mulgrave
Str. of Canso
Canso
Andrew I.
Chedabucto B.
Boylston
Guysborough
Tor B.
Goldboro
Country Har.
George Bay
C. George
Antigonish
Pictou I.
Pictou
Trenton
Thorburn
New Glasgow
Stellarton
Westville
Hopewell
Sherbrooke
Ecum Secum
Moser R.
Sheet Har.
Ship Har.
Upper Stewiacke
Middle Musquodoboit
Musquodoboit Har.
Truro
Brookfield
Stewiacke
River John
Nuttby Mtn. 1,204
Tatamagouche
Pugwash
Oxford
Springhill
Londonderry
Debert
Cobequid B.
Noel
Shubenacadie
Milford Sta.
Elmsdale
Enfield
Shubenacadie L.
Waverley
Dartmouth
Halifax
Bedford
N. Dartmouth
Armdale
Herring Cove
Terrence Bay
St. Margarets B.
Sackville
L. Sackville
Panuke L.
Mahone B.
Tancook I.
Lunenburg
Riverport
La Have Is.
Mahone Bay
Chester
Bridgewater
Molega L.
Ponhook L.
New Germany
La Have
Sherbrooke L.
Three Mile Plains
Windsor
Hantsport
GRAND PRÉ N.H.P.
Kentville
Wolfville
Waterville
Canning
Aldershot
Berwick
Aylesford
Kingston
Nictaux Falls
Gaspereau L.
Middleton
Lawrencetown
Bridgetown
Annapolis Royal
FT. ANNE N.H.P.
Annapolis
Clementsvale
Bear R.
Fisher L.
Medway
Mersey
KEJIMKUJIK NAT'L PARK
Kejimkujik L.
Rossignol L.
PORT ROYAL N.H.P.
Digby
Weymouth
Church Pt.
Little Brook
Digby Neck
St. Mary's Bay
Long I.
Brier I.
Meteghan
Yarmouth
Wedgeport
Tusket
Carleton R.
Lower W. Pubnico
Gt. Pubnico L.
Barrington
Clark's Har.
C. Sable I.
C. Sable
McNutt I.
Jordan B.
Shelburne
Lockport
Roseway R.
Port Mouton
Mouton I.
Liverpool
Liverpool B.
Milton
Brooklyn
Minas Basin
Minas Chan.
Parrsboro
Advocate Har.
C. Split
C. Chignecto
Chignecto B.
I. Haute
Amherst
Maccan
River Hébert
Joggins
Sackville
Baie Verte
C. Tormentine
PRINCE EDWARD ISLAND
PRINCE EDWARD ISLAND NAT'L PARK
Charlottetown
Summerside
Alberton
Tignish
North Pt.
West Pt.
Egmont B.
Malpeque B.
Bedeque B.
Hillsborough B.
Prim Pt.
Georgetown
Montague
Cardigan B.
St. Peter's Bay
Souris East
East Pt.
C. Bear
NEW BRUNSWICK
Moncton
Shediac
Petitcodiac R.
Kouchibouguac Bay
Richibucto
Miramichi B.
Chatham
Newcastle
Miramichi
Southwest
Canaan R.
Sussex
FUNDY NAT'L PARK
Saint John
Lancaster
Grand L.
Minto
Marysville
Oromocto
Fredericton
Saint John R.
Oromocto L.
Magaguadavic L.
St. George
Pt. Lepreau
Passamaquoddy B.
St. Andrews
Campobello I.
Eastport
Grand Manan
MAINE
47° 46° 45° 44°
67° 66° 65° 64° 63° 62° 61° 60°

Petersburg. In World War II held by Germans Aug. 1941–Jan. 20, 1944. Has Kremlin of 11th cent. and several churches, cathedrals, and monasteries dating from period of its supremacy.

3 *or* **Novgorod–Se·ver·ski** \-se-'vir-skē\. Town, NE Chernigov Oblast, N Ukrainian S.S.R., U.S.S.R., on right bank of the Desna river 95 m. ENE of Chernigov; a medieval town, formerly Lithuanian; became Russian in 1654.

Novgorod Oblast \-'ȯ-bləst, -ˌblast\. Subdivision of the Russian S.F.S.R., U.S.S.R., bounded on N by Leningrad Oblast, on NE by Vologda Oblast, on SE and S by Kalinin Oblast, and on W by Pskov Oblast; 21,351 sq. m.; pop. (1970p) 722,000; ✻ Novgorod; dairying; potatoes, oats, rye, flax, timber; includes Lake Ilmen.

No·vi \'nō-ˌvī\. Village, Oakland co., SE Michigan, NW of Detroit; pop. (1970c) 9668.

Novibazar. See NOVI PAZAR.

No·vi di Mo·de·na \ˌnȯ-vē-dē-'mȯd-ᵊn-ə, -ᵊn-ˌä\. Commune, Modena prov., Emilia-Romagna, N Italy, 17 m. N of Modena; pop. (1968e) 8966.

Novi Li·gu·re \-'lē-gu̇r-ā\. Commune, Alessandria prov., Piedmont, NW Italy, 14 m. SE of Alessandria; pop. (1968e) 32,726; manufactures silk, woolens; sericulture; scene of Austrian and Russian victory over French 1799.

Noviodunum. 1 Commune, Aisne dept., France. See SOISSONS.

2 Commune, Nièvre dept., France. See NEVERS.

3 Commune, Switzerland. See NYON.

Noviomagus. 1 City, France. See LISIEUX.

2 Commune, Netherlands. See NIJMEGEN.

Novi Pa·zar \ˌnō-vē-pə-'zär\ *or* **No·vi·ba·zar** \-bə-\. 1 Former Turkish sanjak, divided bet. Serbia and Montenegro in 1913.

2 Town, Serbia, S Yugoslavia, on a tributary of the Ibar river; pop. (1965e) 24,000; formerly an important market town. Captured by Turks in 15th cent.; became center of Turkish sanjak which separated Serbia and Montenegro; garrisoned by Austrian troops 1878–1908; evacuated in 1908 as partial compensation to Turkey for Austrian annexation of Bosnia and Herzegovina; occupied by Serbians in First Balkan War 1912; assigned to Serbia 1913; occupied by Germans in 1941.

Novi Sad \ˌnō-vē-'säd\ *or Hung.* **Új·vi·dék** \'üē-ˌvid-ˌāk\ *or Ger.* **Neu·satz** \ˌnȯi-ˌzäts\. City, chief town of Vojvodina autonomous region, Serbia, NE Yugoslavia, on Danube river; pop. (1971p) 141,712; electrochemical equipment, porcelain, soap, textiles; univ. (1960); founded in 17th cent. as seat of the Serbian patriarch; held by Hungarian troops 1941–45.

Novi Slan·ka·men \ˌnō-vē-släŋ-'kä-mən\ *or* **Slankamen** *or Hung.* **Sza·lán·ke·mén** \'sȯ-läŋ-'kam-ən\. Commune, Serbia, NE Yugoslavia, on the Danube opp. the mouth of the Tisza; scene of battle Aug. 19, 1691 in which Louis William I, Margrave of Baden-Baden, defeated the Turks.

No·vo·al·taisk \ˌnō-və-al-'tīsk\ *or formerly* **Ches·no·kov·ka** \ˌches-nə-'kȯf-kə, -'kȯv-\. Town, Altai Krai, Russian S.F.S.R., U.S.S.R., ab. 10 m. E of Barnaul; pop. (1967e) 46,000.

No·vo·cher·kassk \ˌnō-və-chər-'kask, -'käsk\. City, SW Rostov Oblast, Russian S.F.S.R., U.S.S.R., on a delta arm of the Don 25 m. NE of Rostov-na-Donu; pop. (1970p) 162,000; a commercial city on the main railroad line from Rostov-na-Donu to Voronezh; electric locomotives, iron castings, machine tools; founded by Don Cossacks in 1805; held by Germans July 1942 to Feb. 1943.

Novogeorgievsk. See MODLIN.

No·vo·gru·dok \ˌnō-və-'grüd-ək\ *or Pol.* **No·wo·gró·dek** \-'grü-ˌdek\. Town, Grodno Oblast, Belorussian S.S.R., U.S.S.R., S of Neman river and 77 m. SSE of Vilnius; pop. (1967e) 18,000; has mosque; birthplace of poet Adam Mickiewicz. Variously under Russian, Lithuanian, and Polish rule; in World War II occupied by Germans but recovered by U.S.S.R. July 1944.

No·vo Ham·bur·go \ˌnō-vü-a(ⁿ)m-'bu̇(ə)r-(ˌ)gü\. City, Rio Grande do Sul state, S Brazil, just N of Pôrto Alegre; munic. pop. (1968e) 63,113.

No·vo·ka·za·linsk \ˌnō-və-kə-'zal-ən(t)sk\. Town, S Kazakh S.S.R., U.S.S.R., on the lower Syr Darya near its mouth, NE of the Aral Sea.

No·vo·kui·by·shevsk \ˌnō-və-'kwe-bə-ˌshefsk, -'kü-ē-bə-\. Town, Kuibyshev Oblast, Russian S.F.S.R., U.S.S.R., ab. 10 m. SW of Kuibyshev; pop. (1970p) 104,000.

No·vo·kuz·netsk \ˌnō-(ˌ)vō-ku̇z-'netsk\ *or* **Kuz·netsk Si·bir·ski** \ku̇z-netsk-sə-'bi(ə)r-skē\ *or formerly* **Sta·linsk** \'stäl-(ˌ)(y)in(t)sk\. City, S Kemerovo Oblast, Russian S.F.S.R., U.S.S.R., at head of navigation of Tom river 190 m. SE of Novosibirsk; pop. (1970p) 499,000; coal mining; iron and steel, aluminum, chemicals; at S end of Kuznetsk Basin; first settled 1617 and until recently a small town.

No·vo·mos·kovsk \ˌnō-və-mə-'skȯfsk\. 1 *or formerly* **Bob·ri·ki** \'bäb-ri-kē\ *also* **Sta·li·no·gorsk** \stäl-'(y)ēn-ō-ˌgȯrsk\. City, Tula Oblast, Russian S.F.S.R., U.S.S.R., ab. 35 m. ESE of Tula; pop. (1970p) 134,000; chemicals; coal mining.

2 Town, Ukrainian S.S.R., U.S.S.R., 16 m. NE of Dnepropetrovsk, on a tributary of the Dnieper; pop. (1969e) 61,000; was a town of the Zaporogian Cossacks in 17th cent.

Novonikolaevsk. See NOVOSIBIRSK.

Novoradomsk. See RADOMSKO.

Novo Re·don·do \ˌnȯ-vō-rē-'dän-(ˌ)dō\. Coastal town, W cen. Angola, SW Africa, 100 m. NNE of Benguela; pop. (1960c) 12,708.

No·vo·ros·sisk \ˌnōv-ə-rə-'sēsk\. Seaport city, W Krasnodar Krai, Russian S.F.S.R., U.S.S.R., on Black Sea coast ab. 65 m. WSW of Krasnodar; pop. (1970p) 133,000; naval base; shipbuilding yards; cement; formerly a Turkish town, became Russian in 1829; scene of fighting in Civil War when it was held by Denikin 1919–20; in World War II captured by Germans and held for a year, Sept. 11, 1942–Sept. 16, 1943.

Novorossiya. See NEW RUSSIA.

No·vo·shakh·tinsk \ˌnō-və-shäk-'tēnsk\. Town, Rostov Oblast, Russian S.F.S.R., U.S.S.R., ab. 40 m. NNE of Rostov-na-Donu; pop. (1970p) 102,000; chemicals; coal mining.

No·vo·si·birsk \ˌnō-(ˌ)vō-sə-'bi(ə)rsk\ *or formerly* **No·vo·ni·ko·la·evsk** \-nik-ə-'lī-ˌefsk, -evsk\. City, ✻ of Novosibirsk Oblast, Russian S.F.S.R., U.S.S.R., ab. 390 m. E of Omsk, on the navigable Ob river and N terminus on the Trans-Siberian R.R. of the Turk-Sib line S to Barnaul, Semipalatinsk, and Alma-Ata; pop. (1970p) 1,161,000; important industrial center, producing mining equipment, hydraulic presses, chemicals, leather goods; steel mill; center for scientific research; univ. (1959). Founded 1896; was capital of West Siberian Region; in World War II received entire industrial plants removed bodily from war areas of W U.S.S.R.

Novosibirskiye Ostrova. See NEW SIBERIAN ISLANDS.

Novosibirsk Oblast \-'ȯ-bləst, -ˌblast\. Subdivision of the Russian S.F.S.R., U.S.S.R., bounded on N by Tomsk Oblast, on E by Kemerovo Oblast, on S by Altai Krai, on SW by Kazakh S.S.R., and on W by Omsk Oblast; 68,803 sq. m.; pop. (1970p) 2,505,000; ✻ Novosibirsk; lies in basin of middle Ob river with flat steppe and taiga land in N and cen. parts and hilly region in SE; in the SW is Lake Chany; spring wheat, oats, barley, flax; borders on the Kuznetsk Basin (*q.v.*), one of the major industrial areas of the U.S.S.R. Chief cities Novosibirsk, Berdsk, Iskitim, Kuibyshev; crossed by the Trans-Siberian R.R. Organized as new subdivision of the Russian S.F.S.R. in Asia 1936 and again reorganized and reduced in size 1946.

No·vo·troitsk \ˌnō-və-ˈtrȯ-(y)itsk\. Town, Orenburg Oblast, Russian S.F.S.R., U.S.S.R., ab. 10 m. W of Orsk; pop. (1969e) 85,000.

Novo Urgench. See URGENCH 1.

No·vo·zyb·kov \ˌnō-və-ˈzip-(ˌ)kȯf, -kəf\. Town, SW Bryansk Oblast, Russian S.F.S.R., U.S.S.R., on railroad ab. 45 m. E of Gomel; pop. (1967e) 31,000.

No·vý Ji·čín \ˌnō-vē-ˈyich-ˌēn\ *or Ger.* **Neu·tit·schein** \nȯi-ˈtich-ˌīn\. Town, Czech S.R., cen. Czechoslovakia, 21 m. SSW of Ostrava; pop. (1968e) 19,000; tobacco; brewing.

Nowanuggur. See NAVANAGAR.

No·wa Ru·da \ˌnō-və-ˈrüd-ə\ *or Ger.* **Neu·ro·de** \nȯi-ˈrōd-ə\. Town, SW Wrocław prov., SW Poland, SE of Wałbrzych; pop. (1968e) 18,500; founded 14th cent.; formerly in Silesia, Germany.

No·wa Sól *or* **No·wa·sól** \ˌnō-və-ˈsül\ *or Ger.* **Neu·salz an der Oder** \nȯi-ˈzälts-ˌän-dər-ˈōd-ər\. City, Zielona Góra prov., SW Poland, on the Odra (Oder); pop. (1970p) 33,300; railroad junction; river port; manufactures textiles, iron goods, enamel work, soap; dockyards; formerly in Germany; taken by Soviet army Feb. 15, 1945; assigned to Poland by Potsdam Conference 1945.

No·wa·ta \nō-ˈwät-ə\. **1** County in NE Oklahoma. See table at OKLAHOMA.

2 City, its ⊗, 20 m. E of Bartlesville; pop. (1970c) 3679; oil and gas wells; agriculture; manufactures oil field equipment.

Nowawes. See BABELSBERG.

Nowe Tychy. See TYCHY.

Now·gong \ˈnaů-ˌgȯŋ\. **1** Town, Assam, NE India, 56 m. E of Gauhati; pop. (1961c) 38,600.

2 Town, Madhya Pradesh, India, 175 m. W of Allahabad; pop. (1961c) 8600; ✻ of former Bundelkhand Agency.

Nowogródek. See NOVOGRUDOK.

Nowo–Mińsk. See MIŃSK MAZOWIECKI.

Now·she·ra \naů-ˈsher-ə\. Town, North-West Frontier Province, Pakistan, 20 m. E of Peshawar on the Kabul river; pop. (1961c) with cantonment 43,757.

No·wy Sącz \ˌnō-vē-ˈsȯ^{n}(n)ch\ *or Ger.* **Neu·san·dez** \nȯi-ˈzän-(ˌ)dets\. Commune, Kraków prov., S Poland, on upper Dunajec river in N foothills of Carpathian Mts. 46 m. SE of Kraków; pop. (1970p) 41,100; manufactures textiles, machinery, chemicals, leather; on highway leading S through the Carpathians and across the Slovak S.R. to Košice.

Nowy Targ \ˌnȯ-vē-ˈtärk\ *or Ger.* **Neu·markt** \ˈnȯi-ˌmärkt\. Commune, Kraków prov., Poland, on upper Dunajec river 45 m. S of Kraków; pop. (1970p) 22,900; at foot of Tatra Mts.; weaving; trade in wine.

Nox·u·bee \ˈnäk-shə-bē\. **1** *or* **Oka·nox·u·bee** \ˌō-kə-\. River, E cen. Mississippi and W cen. Alabama; ab. 140 m. long; rises in Oktibbeha co., NE cen. Mississippi, flows SE across border of Alabama into Tombigbee river, W of Eutaw, Greene co., W cen. Alabama.

2 County in Mississippi. See table at MISSISSIPPI.

No·ya \ˈnō-yə\. Seaport commune, La Coruña prov., NW Spain, 45 m. SSW of La Coruña; pop. (1970p) 11,990; agriculture and stock raising; fisheries, fish-salting plants.

Noy·elles–sous–Lens \nwä-ˈyel-sü-ˈlä^{n}s\. Commune, Pas-de-Calais dept., N France; pop. (1962c) 10,049; destroyed during World War I.

Noy·il \ˈnȯi-əl\. River, Tamil Nadu, S cen. India; ab. 95 m. long; flows E into Cauvery river.

Noy·on \nwä-ˈyō^{n}\. Manufacturing town, Oise dept., N France; pop. (1968c) 11,603; bishopric from 530; scene of crowning of Pepin the Short 752 and of Charlemagne 768, and of election of Hugh Capet 987; birthplace of John Calvin; often scene of conflict, during Hundred Years' War, in 16th cent., and during World War I when it was ruined 1917–18; of its beautiful cathedral (late 12th cent.) there remained only a tower and the walls of the nave.

Nsa·wam \en-ˌsä-ˈwäm\. Town, Eastern Region, Ghana, ab. 20 m. NNW of Accra; pop. (1970p) 25,618.

Ntem \en-ˈtem\; *formerly* **Cam·po** *or* **Kam·po** \ˈkäm-(ˌ)pō\. River, Equatorial Guinea and Cameroon, W Africa.

Ntukuyu. See TUKUYU.

Nu·ba Mountains \ˌnü-bə-\. Group of hills, S part of Kordofan prov., Sudan; highest peak 4344 ft.

Nu·bia \ˈn(y)ü-bē-ə\. Region in Nile valley, NE Africa, N of ab. lat. 16°N, extending northward to include Aswān and the First Cataract, but its boundaries indefinite; now included in Sudan and Egypt; mostly desert and includes the Nubian Desert in NE.

History: In ancient times for ab. 1800 years subject to Egypt as a part of Ethiopia; established its independence under Nubian kings and conquered Egypt (XXVth Dynasty, Ethiopian, 712–663 B.C.); capital was at Napata 750 B.C., then at Meroë 500 B.C. Under Romans desert settled by Negro tribe that became united with Hamitic stock and from 6th–14th cents. was a powerful state, with capital Dunqulah; this kingdom conquered by Arabs in 14th cent. and in 1820–22 by Mehemet Ali of Egypt; under control of the Mahdi 1885–98; construction of Aswān High Dam during the 1960's caused much of region to become flooded.

Nu·bi·an Desert \ˈn(y)ü-be-ən-\. Desert area in NE Sudan, E of the Nile river.

Ñu·ble \ˈnyü-blā\. Province of S cen. Chile. See table at CHILE.

Nuceria Alfaterna. See NOCERA INFERIORE.

Nu Chiang. See SALWEEN.

Nuck·olls \ˈnək-əlz\. County in Nebraska. See table at NEBRASKA.

Nu·e·ces \n(y)ů-ˈā-səs\. **1** River, S Texas; 315 m. long; rises near border of Edwards and Real cos., flows S and SE into **Nueces Bay,** at head of Corpus Christi Bay.

2 County in Texas. See table at TEXAS.

Nues·tra Se·ño·ra Bay \nů-ˌā-strə-sən-ˌyōr-ə-, -ˌyȯr-\. Inlet of Pacific Ocean on SW coast of Antofagasta prov., N Chile.

Nuestra Señora de la Asunción. See ASUNCIÓN.

Nueva Caceres. See NAGA 2.

Nue·va Eci·ja \nů-ˌā-və-ˈes-i-ˌhä\. Province, cen. Luzon, Phil., in central plain; 2040 sq. m.; pop. (1970p) 850,147; ✻ Palayan; W two thirds lies in level fertile country watered by the Pampanga and its many tributaries; the SE is hilly and in the NE are the foothills of the Caraballo Mts. Produces rice, also corn, fruit, sugarcane, and tobacco; chief towns Cabanatuan, Guimba, San Jose, Gapan, Cuyapo.

Nueva Es·par·ta \-es-ˈpärt-ə\. State of Venezuela, comprising an island group in the Caribbean Sea, off N coast of Venezuelan mainland; 444 sq. m.; pop. (1970e) 112,611; ✻ La Asunción; chief island Margarita.

Nueva Ge·ro·na \-he-ˈrō-nə\. Barrio in Isle of Pines municipality, La Habana prov., W Cuba; pop. (1965e) 9000.

Nueva Granada. See NEW GRANADA.

Nueva Im·pe·rial \-ˌim-per-ē-ˈäl\. Town, Cautín prov., S cen. Chile, 140 m. SSE of Concepción; pop. (1960c) 6442.

Nueva Oco·te·pe·que \-ō-ˌkō-tə-ˈpā-kē\ *or formerly* **Ocotepeque.** Town, ✻ of Ocotepeque dept., Honduras; pop. (1961c) 4120.

Nueva Pal·mi·ra \-päl-ˈmir-ə\. River port, Colonia dept., SW Uruguay, on Uruguay river ab. 150 m. NW of Montevideo; shipping point for grain and cattle.

Nueva Paz \-ˈpäs\. Municipality, E La Habana prov., W Cuba, 47 m. SE of Havana; pop. (1967e) 18,820.

Nueva Ro·si·ta \-rō-ˈsēt-ə\. Municipality, Coahuila state, NE Mexico; pop. (1970p) 37,890.

Nueva San Sal·va·dor \-san-ˈsal-və-ˌdȯ(ə)r\ *or formerly* **San·ta Tec·la** \ˌsant-ə-ˈtek-lə\. City, ✻ of La Libertad dept., SW El Salvador, 8 m. W of San Salvador; pop. (1970e) 38,063; coffee-growing center.

Nueva Se·go·via \-si-ˈgō-vē-ə\. Department of NW Nicaragua. See table at NICARAGUA.

Nueva Viz·ca·ya \-vis-ˈkī-ə\. Province, N cen. Luzon, Phil.; 2688 sq. m.; pop. (1970p) 222,438; ✻ Bayombong; a hilly and plateau province with much of it above 2000 ft.; in cen. and S parts are the Caraballo Mts. and in the E the foothills of S end of Sierra Madre; in the NE is the upper Cagayan valley and through the W and N sections flows the Magat. Contains much forested region and large areas of fertile land; chief crops rice, sugar, chocolate, tobacco, vegetables; chief towns: Bayombong and Solano.

Nue·vi·tas \nü-ˌā-ˈvē-ˌtäs\. Municipality and town, NE Camagüey prov., E cen. Cuba; munic. pop. (1967e) 62,760; on a fine harbor, **Nuevitas Bay;** chrome ore mined nearby.

Nuevo, Golfo. See NEW GULF.

Nue·vo Ca·sas Gran·des \nü-ˈā-(ˌ)vō-ˌkäs-əs-ˈgrän-dāz\. Municipality, Chihuahua state, Mexico, 140 m. SSW of Ciudad Juárez; pop. (1970p) 25,333.

Nuevo La·re·do \-lə-ˈrād-(ˌ)ō\. Municipality, Tamaulipas state, E Mexico, on the Rio Grande river opp. Laredo, Texas; pop. (1970p) 150,922; in cotton and cattle district.

Nuevo Le·ón \-lā-ˈōn\. State of NE Mexico. See table at MEXICO.

Nu·gi·ma \nü-ˈgē-mə\. Chief village of New Hanover I., Bismarck Archipelago, on NW coast.

Nûgs·su·aq \ˈnüg-sü-ˌäk\. Peninsula on W coast of Greenland in cen. part just N of Disko I.

Nuits \nü-ˈē\ *or in full* **Nuits–Saint–Georges** \-saⁿ-ˈzhȯrzh\. Town, S Côte-d'Or dept., E France, NNE of Beaune; pop. (1962c) 3979; noted for wines.

Nukahiva. See NUKU HIVA.

Nukha. See SHEKI.

Nu·ku·a·lo·fa \ˌnü-kə-wə-ˈlō-fə\. Seaport on N coast of Tongatapu I., ✱ of Tonga, SW Pacific Ocean; pop. (1966c) 15,685.

Nu·ku·fe·tau \ˌnü-kə-fə-ˈtau̇\. Island (atoll), cen. Ellice Is., W Pacific Ocean, NW of Funafuti I., comprising islets in a reef 24 m. in circuit.

Nu·ku Hi·va *also* **Nu·ka·hi·va** \ˌnü-kə-ˈhē-və\ *or* **No·ku·hi·va** \ˌnō-\. Largest of the Marquesas Is., French Polynesia, S Pacific Ocean; 127 sq. m.; has high ridge (highest point 3888 ft.) and plateau in center; coastline of 70 m. with several indentations; best harbor is Anaho Bay on N.

Nu·ku·lai·lai *or* **Nu·ku·la·e·lae** \ˌnü-kə-ˈlī-ˌlī\. Island (atoll) at S end of Ellice Is., W Pacific Ocean; ab. 6½ m. long.

Nukunau. See NIKUNAU.

Nu·ku·no·no *or* **Nu·ku No·no** \ˌnü-kə-ˈnō-(ˌ)nō\ *also* **Duke of Clar·ence** \-ˈklar-ən(t)s\. Island of the Tokelau group, cen. Pacific, N of Samoa; pop. (1970c) 408.

Nu·kus \nü-ˈküs\. Town, ✱ of Karakalpak A.S.S.R., Uzbek S.S.R., U.S.S.R., on right bank of the Amu Darya at head of delta; pop. (1970p) 74,000; furniture, apparel.

Nu·la·to \nü-ˈlät-(ˌ)ō\. City, W cen. Alaska, on right bank of Yukon 220 m. E of Nome; pop. (1970c) 308.

Null·ar·bor Plain \ˌnəl-ə-ˌbȯ(ə)r-, ˌnəl-ˌär-bər-\. Plain along SW coast of South Australia from E end of Great Australian Bight; extends inland almost to 30°S and W end extends into SE Western Australia; a major rocket research and production center.

Nu·man·tia \n(y)ü-ˈman-ch(ē-)ə\. Ancient city of Spain, on the Duero river near modern Soria; involved in war against Rome 143–133 B.C.; it resisted several sieges and was finally taken by Scipio the Younger only after a siege of 15 months.

Nu·ma·zu \nü-ˈmäz-(ˌ)ü\. Town, Shizuoka prefecture, S coast of cen. Honshū, Japan, on NE shore of Suruga Bay across from Shizuoka; pop. (1970c) 189,038; noted resort.

Numedalslågen. See LÅGEN.

Num·foor *or Du.* **Noem·foor** \ˈnüm-(ˌ)fō(ə)r, -(ˌ)fȯ(ə)r\. Island, W Schouten Is., on W side of entrance to Sarera Bay, N Irian Barat, Indonesia, 45 m. W of Biak; roughly circular; 14 m. long, 12 m. wide; generally flat; chief village Namber. Attacked July 1, 1944 by Allied forces who by July 6 gained control of important Japanese airfields at Kamiri and Namber.

Nu·mid·ia \n(y)ü-ˈmid-ē-ə\. Ancient country in North Africa; its territory approx. coextensive with modern Algeria. In Second Punic War (218–201 B.C.) its two great tribes divided, one in support of the Romans, the other of the Carthaginians; after 201 Masinissa became its king, followed by his son Micipsa (c. 148–118 B.C.); suffered under civil war and Jugurthine War 111–106 B.C.; became Roman province 46 B.C., later a part of Mauretania; its capital was Cirta and its most important city Hippo, the see of St. Augustine (see ANNABA 2); flourished until invasion by Vandals 428 A.D.

Nun \ˈnün\ *or* **Nun Entrance.** One of the mouths of the Niger river, S Nigeria, W Africa.

Nun·ea·ton \ˌnə-ˈnēt-ᵊn\. Municipal borough, Warwickshire, cen. England, 20 m. E of Birmingham; pop. (1971p) 66,979; textile mills, ironworks; coal mines nearby.

Nu·ni·vak \ˈnü-nə-ˌvak\. Second largest island in Bering Sea, in E part; 1625 sq. m.; separated from mainland of SW Alaska and Nelson I. by Etolin Strait; crossed by 167°W; usually fogbound. Inhabited by Eskimos; has been made a game and bird reservation.

Nun·kiang \ˈnün-jē-ˈäŋ\. One of the nine former provinces of Manchuria, in N cen. part; 23,912 sq. m.; created 1945.

Nuo·ro \nü-ˈōr-(ˌ)ō, -ˈȯr-\. 1 Province of E Sardinia, Italy. See table at ITALY.

2 Commune, its ✱, 75 m. N by E of Cagliari; pop. (1968e) 28,826; cathedral.

Nuremberg. See NÜRNBERG.

Nu·ri·stan \ˌnu̇r-i-ˈstan\ *or formerly* **Kaf·i·ri·stan** \ˌkaf-ə-ri-ˈstan\. Mountainous district, E Afghanistan, S of Hindu Kush; ab. 5000 sq. m.; inhabited by a small remnant of a very early Iranian people.

Nur·mes \ˈnu̇(ə)r-məs\. Town, SE cen. Finland; at N end of Pielinen lake ab. 60 m. NE of Kuopio; pop. (1970e) 2672; founded 1876.

Nur Mountains \ˈnu̇(ə)r-\ *or formerly* **Al·ma Dağ** \ˌäl-mə-ˈdä(g)\ *or anc.* **Ama·nus** \ə-ˈmān-əs\. Mountains, S Turkey, part of Taurus Mts.; S end is in Hatay prov.

Nürn·berg \ˈn(y)u̇rn-ˌbe(ə)rg\ *or angl.* **Nu·rem·berg** \ˈn(y)u̇r-əm-ˌbərg\. Commercial and manufacturing city, Bavaria, West Germany, on Pegnitz river 92 m. NNW of Munich; pop. (1969e) 474,199; metal production; business machines, electrical equipment, motor vehicles, toys, pharmaceuticals; brewing; famous for its medieval aspect; 11th cent. walls (four main gates), 11th cent. royal palace, town hall, national museum (founded 1852) in 14th cent. Carthusian monastery, old churches of St. Sebald and St. Lorenz. Founded in 11th cent.; made free imperial city 1219; became one of greatest and wealthiest of all German free imperial cities; treaty 1532; center of German culture in 16th cent.; to Bavaria 1806; after 1933 made annual meeting place of Hitler's National Socialist party; much of it destroyed in bombings of World War II; taken by Americans Apr. 21, 1945; scene of Allied trials of German war criminals 1945–46. Birthplace of Hans Sachs and Albrecht Dürer.

Nursia. See NORCIA.

Nür·ting·en \ˈn(y)u̇r-tiŋ-ən\. City, Baden-Württemberg, West Germany, 14 m. SE of Stuttgart; pop. (1969e) 21,201; textiles, metalworking, furniture, cork, cement; became city 1299.

Nur·u·hak Da·ği \ˌnu̇r-ə-ˌhäk-dä-ˈ(g)ē\. Peak in E cen. Turkey, NE of Maraş; 10,138 ft.

Nus, Cape \-ˈnüs\ *or Arab.* **Ras Nus** \ˈräs-\. Cape on S coast of Oman, SE Arabian Penin.

Nu·sa Teng·ga·ra, East \-ˌnü-sə-teŋ-ˈgär-ə\. Province of Indonesia, Lesser Sunda Islands. See table at INDONESIA 2.

Nusa Tenggara, West. Province of Indonesia, Lesser Sunda Islands. See table at INDONESIA 2.

Nu·say·bin \ˌnu̇s-ī-ˈbēn\ *or* **Ni·si·bin** \ˌnē-si-ˈbēn\ *or anc.* **Nis·i·bis** \ˈnis-ə-bəs\. Town, Mardin prov., SE Turkey, on railroad on the border of Syria; a frontier fortress, in early times important on the trade routes; residence of Armenian kings c. 150 B.C. to c. 117 A.D.; a key point for both Romans and Parthians and later a religious center; scene of Egyptian victory over the Turks 1839.

Nut·ley \ˈnət-lē\. Town, Essex co., NE New Jersey, 6 m. N of Newark; pop. (1970c) 31,913; woolen goods, paper; settled 1680; residential suburb.

Nu·u·a·nu \ˌnü-ə-ˈän-(ˌ)ü\. Valley, SE Oahu I., Hawaii, including part of Honolulu City.

Nuuanu Pa·li \-ˈpäl-ē\. Cliff and mountain pass, at head of Nuuanu valley, 6 m. from Honolulu; alt. 1207 ft.; famous as a scenic spot. Here in 1795 Kamehameha I completed his conquest of the island of Oahu.

Nu·wa·ra Eli·ya \ˌnü-wə-rə-ˈā-lē-(y)ə\. Town, S cen. Ceylon; pop. (1968e) 16,000; on elevated plateau at ab. 6000 ft. alt.; health resort.

Nu·zi \ˈnü-zē\. Archaeological site just SW of Kirkuk, NE Iraq; clay tablet with map of c. 2500 B.C. found here.

Ny·ack \ˈnī-ˌak\. Residential village, Rockland co., SE New York, on W shore of Hudson river 25 m. N of New York; pop. (1970c) 6659; boatbuilding; manufactures sewing machines, boilers; settled 1700.

Nyam·la·gi·ra \nē-ˌäm-lə-ˈgir-ə\. Volcano in the Virunga Mts., E Zaire; 10,026 ft.; erupted 1938.

Ny·an·za \nē-ˈan-zə, nī-\. Province of SW Kenya. See table at KENYA.

Ny·asa, Lake *or* **Lake Ny·as·sa** \-nī-ˈas-ə, -nē-\ *also* **Lake Ma·la·wi** \-mə-ˈlä-wē, -ˈlaů-ē\. Lake in SE Africa, bounded on W and S by Malawi, on N and NE by Tanzania, and on E by N Mozambique; ab. 360 m. long, average width 25 m.; 11,430 sq. m.; max. depth 2226 ft.; drains S into Zambezi river.

Nyasaland. See MALAWI.

Nyassa. See NIASSA.

Nyassa, Lake. See NYASA, LAKE.

Ny·borg \ˈnyü-ˌbȯ(ə)r\. Seaport, Fyn co., Denmark, on Fyn I.; pop. (1970e) 11,698; shipyards, textile mills, iron foundries, tobacco-processing works; seaside resort.

Ny·bro \ˈnyü-ˌbrü\. Town, Kalmar co., SE Sweden, ab. 16 m. WNW of Kalmar; pop. (1970e) 22,149.

Nye \ˈnī\. County in Nevada. See table at NEVADA.

Nyeman. See NEMAN.

Nyen·chen·tang·lha Range \nē-ˌen-ˌchen-ˌtäŋ-lə-\. Mountain range, S Tibet, W China, parallel with the Himalayas and N of the Brahmaputra (Tsangpo) river; ab. 600 m. long; highest point 23,250 ft. (**Nyenchentanglha Peak,** 60 m. NW of Lhasa).

Nye·ri \nē-ˈe(ə)r-ē\. Town, ✱ of Central Province, SW cen. Kenya, N of Nairobi; pop. (1969p) 9900.

Nyezhin. See NEZHIN.

Nyi·ka Plateau National Park \nə-ˈyē-kə-\. National park, N Malawi; 325 sq. m.; incl. most of **Nyika Plateau,** highest peak ab. 8000 ft.; wildlife habitat (eland, leopard, lion, zebra); established 1965.

Nyi·ra·gon·go \nē-ˌir-ə-ˈgȯŋ-(ˌ)gō, -ˈgäŋ-\. Volcano, E Zaire, at N end of Lake Kivu; 11,400 ft.

Nyí·regy·há·za \ˈnē-ˌrej-ˌhäz-ȯ\. City, ⊗ of Szabolcs-Szatmár co., NE Hungary, E of the Tisza, 30 m. N of Debrecen; pop. (1970p) 70,640; market town for tobacco, potatoes, and vegetables.

Nyi·ri Desert \ˌni(ə)r-ē-\. Desert area, S Kenya, E Africa, on border of Tanzania just NW of Mt. Kilimanjaro.

Nyitra. See NITRA.

Nyitrabánya. See HANDLOVÁ.

Ny·kø·bing \ˈnyü-ˌkər-piŋ\. 1 *or* **Nykøbing Fal·ster** \-ˈfäl(t)-stər, -ˈfȯl(t)-\. Seaport, ⊗ of Storstrøm co., on W coast of Falster I., Denmark; pop. (1970e) 17,364; sugar refineries, machine works; manufactures tobacco products, margarine.
2 Town, Viborg co., NW Jutland Penin., Denmark, on E coast of Mors I.; pop. (1970e) 8700; oyster fisheries, iron foundries, tobacco-processing works.

Ny·kö·ping \ˈnyü-ˌchər-piŋ\. Seaport, ⊗ of Södermanland co., SE Sweden, on the Baltic Sea; pop. (1970e) 32,205; textile mills, sawmills, furniture factories.

Nyland. See UUSIMAA.

Nym·burk \ˈnim-ˌbů(ə)rk\ *or Ger.* **Nim·burg** \-ˌbů(ə)rg\. Town, Czech S.R., W Czechoslovakia, on the Labe (Elbe) just E of Prague; pop. (1968e) 13,011.

Nym·phai·on, Cape \-nim-ˈfī-ən\ *or* **Cape Nym·phae·um** \-ˈfē-əm\ *or Gk.* **Ák·ra Nim·faí·on** \ˌäk-rə-nim-ˈfī-(ˌ)ȯn\. Cape at SE end of Acte Penin., Chalcidice, NE Greece, extending into Aegean Sea; in a storm off this point the fleet of Darius in an expedition against Greece was wrecked 492 B.C.

Nym·phen·burg \ˈnim-fən-ˌbů(ə)rg\. Former village, now part of Munich, Bavaria, West Germany; secret treaty signed here May 1741, forming an alliance against Austria (War of the Austrian Succession) which finally included France, Bavaria, Spain, Saxony, and Prussia.

Nyon \ˈnyōⁿ\ *or Ger.* **Neuss** \ˈnȯis\ *or anc.* **No·vi·o·du·num** \ˌnō-vē-ō-ˈd(y)ün-əm\. Commune, Vaud canton, W Switzerland, on W shore of Lake of Geneva 13 m. N of Geneva; pop. (1970c) 11,424; 16th cent. castle; produces wine; manufactures earthenware; tourism.

Nyong \nē-ˈȯŋ\. River, Cameroon, W Africa; ab. 400 m. long; flows W into Bight of Biafra.

Ny·sa \ˈnis-ə\; *Ger.* **Neis·se** \ˈnī-sə\. 1 *Ger. also* **Glat·zer Neisse** \ˈglät-sər-\. River, SW Poland; ab. 120 m. long; rises on Czechoslovak border, and flows NE joining the Odra (Oder) 15 m. NW of Opole.
2 Manufacturing city, Opole prov., S Poland, on the Nysa river 47 m. SSE of Wrocław; pop. (1970p) 31,800; bricks, lumber; formerly in Silesia, Germany; churches of 15th and 17th cents., 15th cent. tower. Founded c. 1220; withstood Hussites 1428; occupied 1621, 1632, and 1642 during Thirty Years' War; to Prussia 1742; occupied by French 1807–08; assigned to Poland by Potsdam Conference 1945.

Nysa Łużycka. See NEISSE 1.

Nys·sa \ˈnis-ə\. Town, Malheur co., SE corner of Oregon, on Snake river 12 m. S of its confluence with Malheur river; pop. (1970c) 2620; dairy products, poultry, sugar beets.

Nystad. See UUSIKAUPUNKI.

Nyu·do, Cape \-nē-ˈüd-(ˌ)ō\. Cape, Akita prefecture, NW coast of Honshū, Japan; 40°N, 139°42′E.

Oa, Mull of \ˌməl-ə-ˈvō\. Cape on S tip of Islay I. in the Inner Hebrides, off W coast of Scotland.

Oad·by \ˈōd-bē\. Urban district, Leicestershire, cen. England, ab. 4 m. SE of Leicester; pop. (1969e) 19,100.

Oa·hu \ə-ˈwä-(ˌ)hü\. Island, Hawaii, included in Honolulu co.; third in size and most important of the Hawaiian Is.; 598 sq. m. Geologically once two great volcanoes; erosion has left them as two mountain ranges—the Koolau (highest Konahuanui 3105 ft.) along NE coast parallel with the Waianae (highest Kaala 4040 ft.) along the SW coast with plateau 800–1000 ft. between; Honolulu and Pearl Harbor on S coast. Mountains very rugged (see NUUANU PALI); cen. plateau under wide cultivation. Chief towns besides Honolulu are Waipahu, Ewa, Aiea, Kahuku, Wahiawa, Waialua, Waianae. Early kings of Oahu overcome by Kamehameha 1795; royal residence and influence gradually transferred from Hawaii I. to Oahu in first half of 19th cent.

Oak \ˈōk\. One of the Apostle Is. (*q.v.*).

Oak Brook. Village, Du Page co., NE Illinois, 16 m. W of Chicago; pop. (1970c) 4164.

Oak Creek. City, Milwaukee co., SE Wisconsin, SSE of Milwaukee; pop. (1970c) 13,928; electronic components, concrete products; truck farms.

Oak·dale \ˈōk-ˌdāl\. **1** City, Stanislaus co., cen. California, 23 m. ESE of Stockton; pop. (1970c) 6594; dairy farms.
2 City, Allen parish, SW Louisiana, 37 m. SSW of Alexandria; pop. (1970c) 7301; lumber; strawberries.
3 Village, Washington co., E Minnesota; pop. (1970c) 7304; residential suburb of St. Paul.

Oak·en·gates \ˈō-kən-ˌgāts\. Urban district, Shropshire, W England, 28 m. WNW of Birmingham; pop. (1971p) 16,684.

Oakes \ˈōks\. City, Dickey co., S North Dakota, 54 m. S of Valley City; pop. (1970c) 1742; dairy farms.

Oak Forest. Village, Cook co., NE Illinois, 20 m. S of Chicago; pop. (1970c) 17,870; residential; diversified agriculture.

Oak Grove. Town, ⊗ of West Carroll parish, NE Louisiana, 52 m. ENE of Monroe; pop. (1970c) 1980; cotton.

Oak·ham \ˈō-kəm\. Urban district, ⊗ of Rutlandshire, E cen. England, 19 m. ENE of Leicester; pop. (1971p) 6411; remains of Norman castle.

Oak Harbor. **1** Village, Ottawa co., N Ohio, 20 m. ESE of Toledo; pop. (1970c) 2807; aluminum products; fruit canning.
2 City, Island co., NW Washington, 50 m. NNW of Seattle; pop. (1970c) 9167; diversified agriculture.

Oak Hill. City, Fayette co., S cen. West Virginia, 14 m. N of Beckley; pop. (1970c) 4738; coal mines.

Oak·land \ˈō-klənd\. **1** County in Michigan. See table at MICHIGAN.
2 City, ⊗ of Alameda co., W California, on E side of San Francisco Bay nearly opp. the Golden Gate; pop. (1970c) 361,561; seaport and industrial center producing automobiles, computers, electrical equipment, fabricated steel items, chemicals, pharmaceuticals; food processing, shipbuilding, oil refining; connected by Transbay Bridge (1936) with San Francisco. Mills Coll. (1852), Coll. of the Holy Name (1868), California Concordia Coll. (1906), California Coll. of Arts and Crafts (1907), Laney Coll. (1927), Peralta Junior Coll. (1927), Merritt Coll. (1953). In area settled by Spanish 1820; incorporated as city under present name 1854; grew rapidly into industrial center after 1911.
3 Town, Kennebec co., SW Maine, 5 m. W of Waterville; pop. (1970c) 3535.
4 Town, ⊗ of Garrett co., NW corner of Maryland, 52 m. WSW of Cumberland; pop. (1970c) 1786.
5 Borough, Bergen co., NE New Jersey, NNW of Paterson; pop. (1970c) 14,420.

Oakland City. Residential city, Gibson co., SW Indiana, 28 m. NNE of Evansville; pop. (1970c) 3289; coal mining; Oakland City Coll. (1885).

Oakland Park. City, Broward co., SE Florida, N of Fort Lauderdale; pop. (1970c) 16,621.

Oak Lawn. Village, Cook co., NE Illinois, 12 m. SW of Chicago; pop. (1970c) 60,305.

Oak·leigh \ˈō-(ˌ)klē\. Town, SE suburb of Melbourne, S Victoria, SE Australia; pop. (1966c) 52,706.

Oak·ley Dam \ˈō-klē-\ *or* **Goose Creek Dam** \ˈgüs-\. Dam across Goose Creek, S Cassia co., S Idaho; height 145 ft.; completed 1913; impounds water for irrigation, forming **Goose Creek Reservoir.**

Oak·lyn \ˈō-klən\. Residential borough, Camden co., SW New Jersey, 3 m. SSE of Camden; pop. (1970c) 4626.

Oak·mont \ˈōk-ˌmänt\. Borough, Allegheny co., SW Pennsylvania, on Allegheny river 11 m. ENE of Pittsburgh; pop. (1970c) 7550; pumps, gypsum products, canned fruit; dairy and truck farms.

Oak Park. **1** Residential village, Cook co., NE Illinois, 10 m. W of Chicago; pop. (1970c) 62,511; Emmaus Bible Coll. (1941); settled 1833, incorporated 1901.
2 City, Oakland co., SE Michigan, NW of Detroit; pop. (1970c) 36,762; automobile parts, tools and dies, wire, abrasives, canvas products.

Oak·ridge \ˈō-ˌkrij\. City, Lane co., W Oregon, 42 m. SE of Eugene; pop. (1970c) 3422; logging; agriculture.

Oak Ridge. City, Anderson and Roane cos., E Tennessee, 17 m. W of Knoxville; area 58,800 acres; pop. (1970c) 28,319; Oak Ridge National Laboratory, atomic research and development center (estab. 1943 as Clinton Engineer Works, later called Clinton National Laboratory until 1948) and the Oak Ridge Institute of Nuclear Studies, estab. 1948; produces radioactive isotopes and U-235.

Oak·ville \ˈōk-ˌvil\. Town, Halton co., SE Ontario, Canada, on Lake Ontario 22 m. SW of Toronto; pop. (1971p) 61,365; automobiles, plastics, aluminum ware, paper; summer resort; diversified agriculture.

Oak·wood \ˈō-ˌkwu̇d\. **1** Village, Cuyahoga co., N Ohio, 15 m. SE of Cleveland; pop. (1970c) 3127.
2 City, Montgomery co., SW Ohio, 3 m. S of Dayton; pop. (1970c) 10,095; agriculture.

Oam·a·ru \ˈäm-ə-ˌrü\. Borough, E South I., New Zealand, on Pacific Ocean 55 m. NNE of Dunedin; pop. (1970e) 13,450; has port facilities; limestone quarries.

Oaracta. See QESHM 1.

Oas \ō-ˈäs\. Municipality, N cen. Albany prov., Luzon, Phil., 18 m. NW of Legaspi; pop. (1969e) 45,900.

Oa·sis \ō-ˈā-səs, ˌō-ə-ˈzēs\. Department of Algeria. See table at ALGERIA.

Oasis Butte \ō-ˈā-səs-ˈbyüt\. Isolated peak in W Klamath co., S Oregon, NW of Crater Lake; 5685 ft.

Oates Coast \ˈōts-\. Part of Antarctica W of Victoria Land, ab. 70°S, 160°E, S of Balleny Is.; partly in Ross Dependency.

Oa·xa·ca \wə-ˈhäk-ə\. **1** State of SE Mexico. See table at MEXICO.
2 *or in full* **Oaxaca de Juá·rez** \-də-ˈ(h)wär-ˌez, -ˌes; -ˈwar-əs\. City, its ✱; munic. pop. (1970p) 116,826; altitude 5070 ft.; noted handicrafts market (glazed pottery, knives, leather goods, wool and cotton textiles) and 16th cent. buildings; univ. (1825); founded 1486 as Aztec garrison post; conquered by Spanish 1521; home of Benito Juárez and Porfirio Díaz.

Ob \ˈäb, ˈōb\. River, W Russian S.F.S.R., U.S.S.R.; 2287 m. long (with Irtysh 3461 m.); flows into the Gulf of Ob; its

OP

basin has an area of ab. 1,131,000 sq. m. Its headstreams are the Biya and Katun, rising in the Altai Mts.; its middle course is through extensive swampland, frozen much of the year; its main tributaries on the right are the Tom, Chulym, and Ket, and on the left the Irtysh; chief towns on its banks Novosibirsk, Barnaul, Kolpashevo; important source of hydroelectric power and one of the major transportation routes of Siberia.

Ob, Gulf of. Inlet of Arctic Ocean, E of Yamal Penin., N Russian S.F.S.R., U.S.S.R.; ab. 550 m. long by 50 m. wide; represents drowned lower course of the Ob.

Oba \'ō-bə\ *or* **Ao·ba** \ä-'ō-bə\. One of the New Hebrides Is., SW Pacific Ocean, ab. 30 m. E of Espíritu Santo; 152 sq. m.; 26 m. long and 9 m. wide; pop. (1967c) 5971; coconuts.

Oban \'ō-bən\. Seaport burgh, Argyll co., W Scotland, on the Firth of Lorn; pop. (1971p) 6910; tourist resort. Nearby are ruins of Dunstaffnage Castle, from which the coronation stone was removed to Scone, and which figures in Scott's *Lord of the Isles.*

Ob·bia \'ȯb-yä\. Coastal town, E Somalia, on road bet. Mogadisho and Eil.

Obeid, Al–. See AL-UBAYYID.

Ob·e·lisk \'äb-ə-ˌlisk, -ləsk\. Peak, E Fresno co., in Sierra Nevada, S cen. California; 9707 ft.

Ober·alp \'ō-bə-ˌrälp\. Small lake in the Alps, SW Uri canton, cen. Switzerland, NE of Andermatt; alt. 6654 ft. Near the lake is **Oberalp Pass,** alt. 6704 ft., on the boundary bet. Uri and Graubünden cantons.

Ober·alp·stock \ˌō-bə-'rälp-ˌs(h)tȯk\. Peak, Uri and Graubünden cantons, E cen. Switzerland; 10,915 ft.

Ober·am·mer·gau \ō-bə-'räm-ər-ˌgau̇\. Village, Bavaria, West Germany, 42 m. SSW of Munich; pop. (1961c) 4603; wood carving; a summer and winter resort, famous for its Passion play, presented every tenth year. Play first given 1634 as a result of vow by villagers because of deliverance from the plague; in 20th cent. held in 1900, 1910, 1922, 1930, 1934 (special jubilee, 300th anniversary), 1950, 1960, and 1970.

Ober·cas·sel \ˌō-bər-'käs-əl\. Town, North Rhine-Westphalia, West Germany, near Bonn; scene of discovery Feb. 1914 of two complete human skeletons of the Cro-Magnon race.

Oberdonau. See UPPER AUSTRIA.

Ober–Ga·bel·horn \ˌō-bər-'gäb-əl-ˌhȯ(ə)rn\. Peak in the Pennine Alps, Valais canton, SW Switzerland; 13,365 ft.

Ober·hau·sen \'ō-bər-ˌhau̇-zən\. Industrial city, North Rhine-Westphalia, West Germany, in the Ruhr 7 m. WNW of Essen; pop. (1969e) 249,917; railroad junction; manufactures iron and steel, wire, glass, chemicals, soap; railroad workshops, dye works, zinc smelters, sugar refineries; coal mining; 14th and 16th cent. castles; became city 1874; incorporated neighboring towns of Sterkrade and Osterfeld 1929.

Oberhollabrunn. See HOLLABRUNN.

Ober·land \'ō-bər-ˌland, -ˌlänt\. In German-speaking lands, a mountainous region; esp. in Switzerland, the **Ber·nese Oberland** \bər-ˌnēz-, -ˌnēs-\ (*Ger.* **Ber·ner Oberland** \ˌber-nər-\) including Bern canton S of Lake of Thun, and parts of Unterwalden and Uri cantons; in general usage equivalent to the Bernese Alps. See table at ALPS.

Ober·lin \'ō-bər-lən\. 1 City, ⊗ of Decatur co., NW Kansas, 75 m. ENE of Goodland; pop. (1970c) 2291; oil wells; poultry and grain farms.

2 City, ⊗ of Allen parish, SW Louisiana; pop. (1970c) 1857.

3 Residential city, Lorain co., N Ohio, 30 m. WSW of Cleveland; pop. (1970c) 8761; antislavery center before Civil War; Oberlin Coll. (1832).

Oberlin Mountain. Peak in Glacier National Park, NW Montana; 8100 ft.

Oberösterreich. See UPPER AUSTRIA.

Oberrhein. See UPPER RHINE.

Oberschlesien. See SILESIA.

Oberstein. See IDAR-OBERSTEIN.

Ober·ur·sel \ˌō-bər-'u̇r-səl\. City, Hesse, West Germany, 8 m. NW of Frankfurt am Main; pop. (1969e) 24,822; instruments, leather, glass, jewelry.

Óbi·dos \'ō-bi-ˌdüs\. Town, Pará state, N Brazil, on left bank of the Amazon where the Trombetas joins it, 500 m. above Belém; munic. pop. (1968e) 25,021; center of district producing sugar, coffee, cacao, and tobacco.

Obi·hi·ro \ˌō-bē-'hi(ə)r-ˌō\. City, Hokkaidō, Japan, ab. 95 m. E of Sapporo; pop. (1970c) 131,568.

Obi Islands \ˌō-bē-\. Island group of the N cen. Moluccas, Indonesia, in Malay Archipelago S of Batjan and Halmahera; highest point 5285 ft.; densely forested. Chief island **Obi** *or* **Obi·ra** \ō-'bir-ə\ (*formerly* **Om·bi·rah** \ȯm-\), 951 sq. m.

Obi·on \ō-'bī-ən\. 1 River, NW Tennessee; 70 m. long; formed by confluence of north and south forks in E Obion co., flows SW into Forked Deer river near its junction with the Mississippi in S Dyer co.

2 County in Tennessee. See table at TENNESSEE.

Obi·ra \ō-'bir-ə\. See OBI ISLANDS.

Obiralovka. See ZHELEZNODOROZHNY.

Obla·tos, Ba·rran·ca de \bə-ˌräŋ-kə-ˌdā-əb-'lät-əs\. Gorge of the Santiago river, W cen. Mexico, 5 m. SW of Guadalajara in Jalisco state.

Ob·ninsk \äb-'nin(t)sk\. Town, Kaluga Oblast, Russian S.F.S.R., U.S.S.R.; pop. (1967c) 38,000; atomic research center.

Obock *or* **Obok** \'ō-ˌbäk\. Seaport village, Afars and Issas, E Africa, N side of the Gulf of Tadjoura, nearly opp. Djibouti; pop. (1968e) 1000; historically important as the point of entrance of the French into this region; acquired 1862, actively occupied 1884; seat of government transferred to Djibouti 1892.

Obre·gón \ˌō-brə-'gōn\. Municipality, Federal District, Mexico, 7 m. S of Mexico City; pop. (1970p) 466,531.

O'·Bri·en \ō-'brī-ən\. County in Iowa. See table at IOWA.

Obringa. See AARE.

Observatory Peak. See OGDEN, MOUNT.

Ob·sid·ian Cliff \əb-ˌsid-ē-ən-\. Cliff of black volcanic glass in Yellowstone National Park, NW Wyoming; elevation 7350 ft.

Obua·si \ō-'bwäs-ē\. Town, S Ghana, W Africa, ab. 35 m. S of Kumasi; pop. (1970p) 31,018.

Obwalden. See UNTERWALDEN and table at SWITZERLAND.

Obydos. Older spelling of ÓBIDOS.

Ocala \ō-'kal-ə\. Commercial city, ⊗ of Marion co., N cen. Florida penin., 35 m. S of Gainesville; pop. (1970c) 22,583; packs fruit and vegetables; fertilizer; limestone and phosphate mines; citrus and truck farms; Central Florida Junior Coll. (1958); incorporated 1868.

Oca·ña \ō-'kän-yə\. City, Norte de Santander dept., N Colombia, 60 m. NW of Cúcuta; munic. pop. (1968e) 43,481; in the Cordillera Oriental at alt. of 3820 ft.; produces cacao and coffee.

Occidental Misamis. See MISAMIS OCCIDENTAL.

Occidental Negros. See NEGROS OCCIDENTAL.

Oc·cum \'äk-əm\. Subdivision of town of Norwich, Connecticut. See NORWICH 1.

Ocean \'ō-shən\. County in New Jersey. See table at NEW JERSEY.

Oce·ana \ˌō-shē-'an-ə\. County in Michigan. See table at MICHIGAN.

Ocean Cape. Cape, SE Alaska, on S side of entrance to Yakutat Bay.

Ocean City. City, Cape May co., S New Jersey, on Atlantic Ocean 10 m. SW of Atlantic City; pop. (1970c) 10,575; seaside resort; truck farms.

Ocean Grove. Summer resort, Monmouth co., E cen. New Jersey, on Atlantic coast ab. 1 m. S of and adjoining Asbury Park; founded 1869 originally for camp meetings, religious conferences, etc.; large auditorium; no industries allowed.

Oce·an·ia \ˌō-shē-'an-ē-ə, -'ä-nē-ə\ *or* **Oce·an·i·ca** \-'an-i-kə\. 1 Collective name for the lands of the cen. and S Pacific Ocean, including Micronesia, Melanesia, and Polynesia, and sometimes Australia, New Zealand, and the Malay Archipelago.
2 French overseas territory, South Pacific Ocean. See FRENCH POLYNESIA.

Ocean Island. 1 *or* **Ba·na·ba** \bə-'näb-ə\. Island in the W Pacific Ocean, ab. 57 m. S of the equator bet. the Gilbert Is. and the island of Nauru, 0°52'S, 169°35'E; ab. 2½ sq. m.; pop. (1968p) 2192; former ✱ of colony of Gilbert and Ellice Islands; large deposits of phosphate rock. Claimed by British 1900 and made part of Gilbert and Ellice Islands Colony 1916; occupied by Japanese 1942.
2 Islet, Leeward Islands. See KURE ISLAND.

Ocean Pond. See OLUSTEE.

Ocean·port \'ō-shən-ˌpō(ə)rt, -ˌpȯ(ə)rt\. Borough, Monmouth co., E cen. New Jersey, 6 m. N of Asbury Park; pop. (1970c) 7503.

Ocean·side \'ō-shən-ˌsīd\. Residential city, San Diego co., SW corner of California, on Gulf of Santa Catalina 45 m. N of San Diego; pop. (1970c) 40,494; seaside resort; rubber products; truck farms; Mira Costa Coll. (1934); Camp Pendleton, U.S. Marine Corps base, just to N. Incorporated 1888.

Ocean Springs. Town, Jackson co., SE corner of Mississippi, across inlet from Biloxi; pop. (1970c) 9580; dairy products; truck farms; seaside resort.

Oceanus Atlanticus. See ATLANTIC OCEAN.

Oceanus Britannicus. See ENGLISH CHANNEL.

Ocha·kov \ə-'chäk-əf\. Seaport town, S Ukrainian S.S.R., U.S.S.R., on the Black Sea bet. Odessa and Kherson; pop. (1959c) 8400.

Oche·ye·dan Mound \ō-ˌchēd-ᵊn-\. Hill in Osceola co., NW Iowa; 1675 ft.; highest peak in Iowa.

Ochiai. See DOLINSK.

Ochil Hills \ˌō-kəl-, ˌäk-əl-\. Range of hills in Perth co., cen. Scotland; highest peak **Ben Cleuch** \ben-'klük\ 2363 ft.

Och·il·tree \'äk-əl-ˌtrē\. County in Texas. See table at TEXAS.

O–chi–na \'ō-'chē-'nä\ *also* **Et·sin** \et-'sēn\ *or* **Ed·sin** \ed-'zēn\. River, N China; ab. 200 m. long; formed by confluence of the Jo (rises on N side of Nan Shan range) with another headstream near Ningsia Hui border; flows N to Ka-shun-no-erh, NW Ningsia Hui.

Och·lock·o·nee \äk-läk-ə-nē\. River, S Georgia and NW Florida; ab. 135 m. long; rises in Worth co., S Georgia, flows SW across NW Florida into Gulf of Mexico.

Ocho Ri·os \ˌō-chō-'rē-əs\. Seaport, N Jamaica, NW of Kingston; resort.

Ochrida. See OHRID 1.

Ocil·la \ō-'sil-ə\. 1 River, Florida. See AUCILLA.
2 City, ⊗ of Irwin co., S Georgia; pop. (1970c) 3185.

Oc·mul·gee \ōk-'məl-gē\. River, cen. Georgia; 255 m. long; formed by junction of Yellow and South rivers in Newton co., flows S and SE to join the Oconee in S Montgomery co. and form the Altamaha river.

Ocmulgee National Monument. See UNITED STATES, *National Monuments.*

Ocoa Bay \ō-ˌkō-ə-\. Bay in S coast of the Dominican Republic, Hispaniola I., West Indies.

Oco·ee \ō-'kō-ē\. 1 River, NE Georgia and SE Tennessee; ab. 70 m. long; rises in S Fannin co., Georgia, flows N and NW to Hiwassee river in Polk co., Tennessee; called **Toccoa** \tə-'kō-ə\ river in Georgia. In its course in N Georgia is the Blue Ridge Dam and in Tennessee are three dams, **Ocoee No. 1, Ocoee No. 2,** and **Ocoee No. 3.** See table at TENNESSEE VALLEY AUTHORITY.
2 City, Orange co., cen. Florida, 10 m. W of Orlando; pop. (1970c) 3937.

Oco·nee \ō-'kō-nē\. 1 River, cen. Georgia; ab. 250 m. long.; rises in Hall co., N Georgia, flows S amd SE to join the Ocmulgee and form the Altamaha river in S Montgomery co., SE cen. Georgia.
2 Name of counties in two states in the U.S. See tables at GEORGIA and SOUTH CAROLINA.

Ocon·o·mo·woc \ə-'kän-ə-mə-ˌwȯk\. City, Waukesha co., SE Wisconsin, 13 m. ESE of Watertown; pop. (1970c) 8741; summer resort; cans vegetables, honey, dairy products.

Ocon·to \ō-'kän-(ˌ)tō\. 1 River, NE Wisconsin; ab. 130 m. long; rises in SE Forest co., flows S and E into Green Bay at Oconto.
2 County in NE Wisconsin. See table at WISCONSIN.
3 City, its ⊗, on Green Bay at mouth of Oconto river 18 m. SSW of Marinette; pop. (1970c) 4667; sawmills, breweries; summer resort.

Oconto Falls. City, Oconto co., NE Wisconsin, 27 m. N of Green Bay (city); pop. (1970c) 2517; dairy products, paper.

Oco·sin·go \ˌōk-ə-'sēŋ-(ˌ)gō\. Municipality, Chiapas state, Mexico, 70 m. E of Tuxtla Gutiérrez; pop. (1970p) 50,626; cattle raising; corn, oranges, mangoes.

Oco·tal \ˌō-kə-'täl\. Town, ✱ of Nueva Segovia dept., NW Nicaragua, near Honduras border; pop. (1970e) 7377.

Oco·te·pe·que \ō-ˌkōt-ə-'pāk-ē\. 1 Department of W Honduras. See table at HONDURAS.
2 Town, Honduras. See NUEVA OCOTEPEQUE.

Oco·tlán \ˌō-kə-'tlän\. Town, Jalisco state, W cen. Mexico, at NE corner of Lake Chapala; munic. pop. (1970p) 43,394.

Ocotlán de Mo·re·los \ˌō-kə-ˌtlän-də-mə-'rā-ləs\. Municipality, Oaxaca state, Mexico, 25 m. S of Oaxaca; pop. (1970p) 45,572; distilleries; livestock raising; diversified agriculture.

Ocra·coke Island \'ō-krə-ˌkōk-\. Island off cen. North Carolina coast, in chain of narrow sandy islands lying bet. Pamlico Sound and Atlantic Ocean; 9 sq. m.; Hatteras Inlet NE of it and **Ocracoke Inlet** SW of it connect the sound with the ocean.

Ocriculum. See OTRICOLI.

October Revolution Island *or Russ.* **Ostrov Ok·tya·br·skoi Re·vo·lyu·tsi** \'ó-strəf-ək-'tyä-bər-ˌskȯi-ˌrev-əl-'yüt-sē\. Central island of the Severnaya Zemlya group, Arctic Ocean, Taimyr National Okrug, Russian S.F.S.R., U.S.S.R.

Ocu·ma·re del Tuy \ˌō-kü-ˌmär-ē-del-'twē\ *or* **Ocumare.** Town, Miranda state, N Venezuela, 30 m. S of Caracas; pop. (1961c) 15,006.

Ocus·si *or* **Oku·si** \ō-'kü-sē\. Port and military station of the Portuguese on N coast of Timor I., in the enclave of Oé-Cusse.

Ocussi Ambeno. See OÉ-CUSSE.

Oda \'ō-də\. Town, Eastern Region, Ghana, ab. 60 m. WNW of Accra; pop. (1970p) 24,770.

Ōda·te \ō-'dät-(ˌ)ā\. City, Akita prefecture, Honshū, Japan, 47 m. N of Akita; pop. (1970c) 72,958.

Oda·wa·ra \ˌōd-ə-'wär-ə\. Town, Kanagawa prefecture, SE Honshū, Japan, on Sagami Sea 50 m. SW of Tokyo; pop. (1970c) 156,654.

Öde·miş \ˌə-də-'mēsh\. Town, SE İzmir prov., W Turkey, 45 m. ESE of İzmir; pop. (1965c) 30,580.

Ödenburg. See SOPRON.

Oden·daals·rus \ˌō-dən-däls-'rəs\. Town, Orange Free State, Rep. of South Africa, 38 m. SW of Kroonstad; pop. (1960c) 15,047; largely developed after discovery of important goldfield in vicinity 1946.

Oden·se \'ōd-ᵊn-sə, *locally* 'ü-ən-zə\. City, Fyn co., N cen. Fyn I., Denmark; pop. (1970e) 102,698; third largest town of Denmark; exports agricultural produce; machinery, textiles, beer, electrical equipment; shipbuilding; 14th cent. cathedral, 18th cent. palace, univ. (1964). First mentioned c. 1000 A.D.; birthplace of Hans Christian Andersen.

Oden·wald \'ōd-ᵊn-ˌvält\. Mountainous region, S West Germany in the states of Hesse, Baden-Württemberg, and Bavaria bet. the Neckar and Main rivers; ab. 50 m. long by 25 m. wide; highest point the Katzenbuckel 2057 ft.

Oder \'ōd-ər\ *or Czech and Polish* **Odra** \'ó-drə\ *or anc.* **Vi·ad·ua** \vī-'aj-ə-wə\. River, cen. Europe; 567 m. long; rises in the mountains of Slovak S.R., Czechoslovakia; flows N through W Poland to join the Neisse 21 m. SSE of Frankfurt, East Germany, where it forms the boundary bet. Poland and East Germany, thence N into the Baltic Sea, passing through Opole, Wrocław, Frankfurt, and Szczecin in its course; navigable for most of its length; chief tributaries on the left Nysa, Kaczawa, Bóbr, and Neisse; on the right Warta. Internationalized from its confluence with the Opava at Ostrava under terms of the Treaty of Versailles 1919. In World War II much fighting along its course in early part of 1945; by Potsdam Conference 1945, its upper course, formerly in Silesia, placed in Poland, and its lower course from confluence with the Neisse made boundary bet. Germany and Poland.

Oder–Neis·se Line \ˌōd-ər-ˌnī-sə-\. Boundary line bet. East Germany and W Poland; adopted at the Potsdam Conference 1945; formed by the Neisse from the Sudetic Mts. to its junction with the Oder S of Frankfurt and the Oder thence N to the Zalew Szczeciński.

Oder·zo \ō-'dert-(ˌ)sō\ *or anc.* **Op·i·ter·gi·um** \ˌōp-ə-'tər-jē-əm\. Commune, Treviso prov., NE Veneto, NE Italy, 15 m. NE of Treviso; pop. (1968e) 13,915; 10th cent. cathedral; Roman museum.

Odes·sa \ō-'des-ə\. **1** City, Lafayette co., W Missouri, 28 m. E of Independence; pop. (1970c) 2839; shoes; livestock farms.

2 City, ⊗ of Ector co., W Texas, 56 m. WSW of Big Spring; pop. (1970c) 78,380; center of major oil field; manufactures oil-drilling equipment, chemicals, tile; potash, salt, limestone, and carbon black mining; Odessa Coll. (1946); founded 1886, incorporated 1927.

3 City, ✱ of Odessa Oblast, S Ukrainian S.S.R., U.S.S.R., 25 m. NE of the mouth of the Dniester on **Odessa Bay;** pop. (1970p) 892,000; major seaport and industrial center; base of the Soviet Antarctic whaling fleet and of a fishing fleet; produces machine tools, auto parts, agricultural machinery, gas generators, construction equipment, fertilizer, leather goods, foodstuffs; shipbuilding and repairing, oil refining; univ. (1865). Covers a series of terraced hills; port is icebound an average of three months per year.

History: Present city founded around Tatar fortress 14th cent.; passed to Turkey 1764 and to Russia 1791; made naval base and port 1794; given name Odessa 1795; rapid expansion as grain-exporting port during 19th cent.; center of revolutionary activity 1905 (incl. mutiny aboard battleship "Potemkin"); in World War II occupied by Axis forces Oct. 1941–Apr. 1944 and suffered extensive damage.

Odessa Oblast \-'ó-bləst, -ˌblast\. Subdivision of the Ukrainian S.S.R., U.S.S.R.; 12,857 sq. m.; pop. (1970p) 2,390,000; ✱ Odessa; on NW shore of Black Sea; bordered on S by lower Dniester; grain, sunflowers, and vineyards; livestock raising; industry is centered in Odessa, the only important city.

Odessus. See VARNA 2.

Odiel \ō-'dyel\. River, Huelva prov., SW Spain; ab. 60 m. long; flows S and joins the Tinto below Huelva; combined streams flow into the Mediterranean.

Odin·tso·vo \ˌə-dyin-'tsó-və\. Town, Moscow Oblast, Russian S.F.S.R., U.S.S.R., 14 m. WSW of Moscow; pop. (1967e) 43,000.

Odioñg·an \ō-'dyóŋ-än\. Municipality on W coast of Tablas I., Romblon prov., Phil., on Tablas Strait; pop. (1969e) 31,400.

Od·i·shaw, Mount \-'ōd-ə-ˌshó\. Mountain, Antarctica, 84°42′S, 174°54′E; 13,008 ft.

Odomari. See KORSAKOV.

Odon \ó-'dōⁿ\. Short stream of Normandy, NW France; a W tributary of the Orne, entering it at Caen; in World War II severe fighting on its banks in battle of Normandy June–July 1944.

Odoorn \ō-'dō(ə)rn\. Commune, Drenthe prov., NE Netherlands, 35 m. SE of Groningen near West German border; pop. (1970e) 11,730.

Odra. See ODER.

Od·za·la National Park \ōd-'zäl-ə-\. National park, W Congo; 424 sq. m.; varied wildlife; established 1940.

Oea. See TRIPOLI 4.

Oé–Cus·se \wā-'kü-sē\ *or* **Ocus·si Am·beno** \ō-ˌkü-sē-am-'bā-nō\. A wedge-shaped region on N coast of island of Timor, SE Asia, forming an exclave of Portuguese Timor; ab. 950 sq. m. Retained by Portugal in treaty of 1859 dividing Timor bet. Portuguese and Dutch.

Oedanes. See BRAHMAPUTRA.

Oeleëheuë. See ULEELHEUE.

Oels *or* **Oels in Schlesien.** See OLEŚNICA.

Oelsnitz. See ÖLSNITZ.

Oel·wein \'ōl-ˌwīn\. City, Fayette co., NE Iowa, 25 m. ENE of Waterloo; pop. (1970c) 7735; railroad shops; ships livestock; diversified agriculture.

Oe·no·tria \ē-'nō-trē-ə\. Ancient region, S Italy; comprised Bruttium (*mod.* Calabria) and Lucania (*mod.* Basilicata); noted for its vineyards; the name probably first applied by Greeks.

Oer–Er·ken·schwick \'ər-'er-kən-ˌshfik\. Town, North Rhine-Westphalia, West Germany, NE suburb of Recklinghausen; pop. (1969e) 24,096.

O–erh–ku–na. See ARGUN.

O–erh–to–ssu. See ORDOS.

Oesel. See SAAREMAA.

Oe·ta \'ēt-ə\. Mountain chain in Phthiotis and Phocis departments, cen. Greece; highest point 7060 ft. Forms an E spur of the Pindus Mts. and terminates on the E at Pass of Thermopylae on the Gulf of Maliakós; in ancient times was on E border of Aetolia. Scene of the legendary death of Hercules.

Oetztal *or* **Oetztaler Alps.** See ÖTZTALER ALPS.

O'·Fal·lon \ō-'fal-ən\. **1** City, St. Clair co., SW Illinois, 15 m. E of East St. Louis; pop. (1970c) 7268; coal mines.

2 City, St. Charles co., E Missouri, 30 m. NW of St. Louis; pop. (1970c) 7018; diversified agriculture.

Ofan·to \'ó-fən-ˌtō\ *or anc.* **Au·fi·dus** \'ó-fəd-əs\. River, SE Italy; 103 m. long; flows E through Avellino prov., Campania, into the Adriatic Sea 4 m. NW of Barletta, Apulia.

Of·fa \'äf-ə\. Town, Kwara State, SW Nigeria, ab. 30 m. SSE of Ilorin; pop. (1969e) 100,226.

Of·fa·ly \'óf-ə-lē, 'äf-\ *or formerly* **King's** \'kiŋz\. County, E cen. Eire, in W Leinster prov.; area 771 sq. m.; pop. (1971p) 51,834; ⊗ Tullamore; rivers Shannon, Brosna, Barrow, Boyne; wheat, barley; livestock raising.

Of·fa's Dyke \ˌó-fəz-\. Remains of an entrenchment extending from the Wye river to the Dee river in England and Wales; built by Offa (d. 796), king of the Mercians, along W border of Mercia as a fortification against the Welsh.

Of·fen·bach \'óf-ən-ˌbäk\ *also* **Offenbach am Main** \-äm-'mīn\. Industrial city, Hesse, West Germany, on left bank of the Main river just E of Frankfurt am Main; pop. (1969e) 117,478; center of tanning and leather goods industry; machinery, electrical equipment, chemicals, beverages, textiles; castle. First mentioned 977; to Hesse 1816; rebuilt after heavy damage in World War II.

Of·fen·burg \'óf-ən-ˌbu̇(ə)rg\. Manufacturing city, Baden-Württemberg, West Germany, at foot of the Black Forest 33 m. N of Freiburg; pop. (1969e) 32,408; structural steel, electrical equipment, chemicals, textiles; printing, tourism; became imperial city 1235.

Of·fi·da \'óf-i-də\. Commune, Ascoli Piceno prov., S Marches, cen. Italy; pop. (1970c) 6069; ruins of Sabine temple; ancient church.

Ofot·en Fjord \'ō-fə-tən-ˌfyōr, -ˌfyȯ(ə)r\ *or* **Ofot·fjord** \'ō-fōt-ˌfyō(ə)r, 'ō-fu̇t-ˌfyȯ(ə)r\. Northeast extension of Vest Fjord on NW coast of Norway; site of port of Narvik.

Ofu \'ō-(ˌ)fü\. Westernmost island of the Manua Is. (*q.v.*) in American Samoa; 3 sq. m.; separated from Olosega (2 sq. m.) on the E by so narrow a channel that the two islands appear to be one. Both islands mountainous; highest point on Ofu 1587 ft., on Olosega 2092 ft.

Oga·ki \ō-'gäk-ē\. Town, Gifu prefecture, W cen. Honshu, Japan, just W of Gifu and 20 m. NW of Nagoya; pop. (1970c) 134,942; important under the shoguns 16th–19th cents.

Ogal·la·la \ˌō-gə-'läl-ə\. City, ⊗ of Keith co., W Nebraska, on South Platte river 52 m. W of North Platte; pop. (1970c) 4976; diversified agriculture.

Ogasawara Islands *or* **Ogasawara–guntō.** See BONIN ISLANDS.

Og·bo·mo·sho \äg-bə-'mō-(ˌ)shō\. City, Western State, Nigeria, 50 m. NNE of Ibadan; pop. (1971e) 386,650; trade center and road junction; ships foodstuffs, tobacco, and livestock; founded mid-17th cent. as military camp; center of resistance to Fulani invasions of early 19th cent.

Og·den \'ȯg-dən, 'äg-\. Industrial city, ⊗ of Weber co., N Utah, 33 m. N of Salt Lake City; pop. (1970c) 69,478; altitude 4259 ft.; railroad center; dairy products, canned vegetables, clothing, electronic components, jet engines, building materials; breweries, packing plants, stockyards; tourism; Weber State Coll. (1889); Hill Air Force Base. Settled 1846 (oldest continuously settled community in Utah); incorporated 1851.

Ogden, Mount *or formerly* **Observatory Peak.** Mountain in Morgan and Weber cos., N Utah, just E of Ogden in Wasatch Range; 10,102 ft.

Og·dens·burg \'ȯg-dənz-ˌbərg, 'äg-\. Industrial city, St. Lawrence co., N New York, on St. Lawrence river 55 m. NNE of Watertown; pop. (1970c) 14,554; trades in grain and lumber; summer resort; office supplies, clothing, paint; dairy farms.

History: Site purchased in 1792 by Col. Samuel Ogden; incorporated as village 1818; chartered as city 1868; at **Heu·vel·ton** \'hyü-vəl-tən\, just SE of the city, Prime Minister Mackenzie King and President Franklin D. Roosevelt met Aug. 18, 1940 to formulate the "Ogdensburg Agreement" establishing a joint U.S.-Canadian board for studying problems of the defense of North America.

Ogee·chee \ō-'gē-chē\. River, E Georgia; ab. 250 m. long; rises in Green co., flows SE into Atlantic Ocean on border of Bryan and Chatham cos.

Oge·maw \'ō-gə-ˌmȯ\. County in Michigan. See table at MICHIGAN.

Ogi·da·ki Mountain \ˌō-gə-ˌdäk-e-\. Mountain, Ontario, Canada; 2183 ft.; highest peak in the province.

Ogil·vie Mountains \ˌō-gəl-vē-\. Range, cen. Yukon Territory, Canada; average height ab. 4000 ft.; highest point 7189 ft.

Ogle \'ō-gəl\. County in Illinois. See table at ILLINOIS.

Ogles·by \'ō-gəlz-bē\. Industrial city, La Salle co., N Illinois, 13 m. WSW of Ottawa; pop. (1970c) 4175; coal mining.

Ogle·thorpe \'ō-gəl-ˌthȯrp\. 1 County in Georgia. See table at GEORGIA.

2 City, ⊗ of Macon co., SW cen. Georgia; pop. (1970c) 1286.

Oglethorpe, Mount. Mountain, Pickens co., N Georgia; 3290 ft.; at S end of Blue Ridge Mts.

Oglio \'ȯl-(ˌ)yō\ *or anc.* **Ol·li·us** \'äl-ē-əs\. River, N Italy; 175 m. long; rises in the Rhaetian Alps, flows SE through Lake Iseo and into Po river 10 m. SW of Mantua.

Og·more and Ga·rw \'äg-ˌmō(ə)r . . . 'gär-ü, -ˌmȯ(ə)r-\. Urban district, Glamorganshire, SE Wales; pop. (1971p) 19,415; coal mining.

Ogo·ja \ō-'gō-jə\. Town, South-Eastern State, Nigeria, ab. 120 m. N of Calabar.

Ogo·ki \ō-'gō-kē\. River, a S tributary of the Albany, in cen. Ontario, Canada; ab. 300 m. long; rises in chain of lakes and flows NE and E.

Ogo·oué *or* **Ogo·we** \ˌō-gə-'wā\. River, Gabon, W equatorial Africa; 683 m. long; flows W into Atlantic Ocean S of Cape Lopez; navigable for ab. 250 m.

Ogu·lin \ō-'gü-lēn\. Commune, Croatia, NW Yugoslavia, 40 m. E of Rijeka; ancient castle of Frangipani family.

Ohau, Lake \-'ō-ˌhau̇\. Lake, S cen. South I., New Zealand; 23 sq. m.; from its S end issues the **Ohau River,** one of the headstreams of the Waitaki river.

O'·Hig·gins \ō-'hig-ənz, ō-'ē-gən(t)s\. 1 Peak, S Chile, W of Lake San Martín; 9545 ft.

2 Province of cen. Chile. See table at CHILE.

Ohio \ō-'hī-(ˌ)ō\. 1 Navigable river in Pennsylvania, Ohio, Indiana, and Illinois; 975 m. long; area of its basin 203,900 sq. m.; formed by confluence of Allegheny and Monongahela rivers at Pittsburgh, SW Pennsylvania, flows W and SW to form Ohio-West Virginia, Ohio-Kentucky, Indiana-Kentucky, and Illinois-Kentucky boundaries; empties into Mississippi river at Cairo, S extremity of Illinois.

2 A north central state of U.S.A., bounded on N by Michigan and Lake Erie, on E by Pennsylvania and Ohio river, on S by Ohio river, and on W by Indiana; 35th state in area, 41,222 sq. m. (land area 41,014 sq. m.), in addition to this area Ohio has also 3457 sq. m. of water of the Great Lakes; 6th state in population, (1970c) 10,652,017; ✱ Columbus; 17th state admitted to Union (1803).

Nickname: Buckeye State. *State flower:* Scarlet carnation. *Motto:* With God, All Things Are Possible. *Rivers:* Ohio (SE and S boundary) and its tributaries the Muskingum, Scioto, and Miami; Maumee and Sandusky flowing to Lake Erie. *Highest point:* Campbell Hill 1550 ft., in Logan co. *Chief products:* Corn, soybeans, oats; livestock; coal; manufacturing: iron and steel, rubber products, machinery, transportation equipment, primary metals. *Chief cities:* Cleveland, Columbus, Cincinnati, Toledo, Akron, Dayton. See *Table of States* at UNITED STATES. Divided into the following 88 counties (for pronunciation of their names, see their individual entries):

NAME	LOCATION	AREA[1] (sq. m.)	POP. (1970c)	CO. SEAT
Adams	S	587	18,957	West Union
Allen	NW	410	111,144	Lima
Ashland	N cen.	424	43,303	Ashland
Ashtabula	NE corner	700	98,237	Jefferson
Athens	SE	504	55,747	Athens
Auglaize	W	400	38,602	Wapakoneta
Belmont	E	534	80,917	Saint Clairsville
Brown	SW	490	26,635	Georgetown
Butler	SW	471	226,207	Hamilton
Carroll	E	390	21,579	Carrollton
Champaign	W	432	30,491	Urbana
Clark	W	402	157,115	Springfield
Clermont	SW	458	95,887	Batavia
Clinton	SW	410	31,464	Wilmington
Columbiana	E	534	108,310	Lisbon
Coshocton	E cen.	562	33,486	Coshocton
Crawford	N cen.	404	50,364	Bucyrus
Cuyahoga	N	456	1,721,300	Cleveland
Darke	W	605	49,141	Greenville
Defiance	NW	412	36,949	Defiance
Delaware	cen.	450	42,908	Delaware
Erie	N	264	75,909	Sandusky
Fairfield	S cen.	505	73,301	Lancaster
Fayette	SW cen.	406	25,461	Washington Court House
Franklin	cen.	538	833,249	Columbus
Fulton	NW	407	33,071	Wauseon
Gallia	S	471	25,239	Gallipolis
Geauga	NE	407	62,977	Chardon
Greene	SW	415	125,057	Xenia
Guernsey	E	528	37,665	Cambridge
Hamilton	SW corner	414	924,018	Cincinnati
Hancock	NW	532	61,217	Findlay
Hardin	NW cen.	467	30,813	Kenton
Harrison	E	401	17,013	Cadiz

NAME	LOCATION	AREA[1] (sq. m.)	POP. (1970c)	CO. SEAT
Henry	NW	416	27,058	Napoleon
Highland	S	549	28,996	Hillsboro
Hocking	S cen.	421	20,322	Logan
Holmes	NE cen.	424	23,024	Millersburg
Huron	N	497	49,587	Norwalk
Jackson	S	419	27,174	Jackson
Jefferson	E	411	96,193	Steubenville
Knox	cen.	531	41,795	Mount Vernon
Lake	NE	231	197,200	Painesville
Lawrence	S	456	56,868	Ironton
Licking	cen.	686	107,799	Newark
Logan	W	460	35,072	Bellefontaine
Lorain	N	495	256,843	Elyria
Lucas	NW	343	484,370	Toledo
Madison	SW cen.	464	28,318	London
Mahoning	NE	415	304,545	Youngstown
Marion	cen.	405	64,724	Marion
Medina	N	425	82,717	Medina
Meigs	SE	436	19,799	Pomeroy
Mercer	W	454	35,558	Celina
Miami	W	407	84,342	Troy
Monroe	SE	456	15,739	Woodsfield
Montgomery	SW	459	608,413	Dayton
Morgan	SE	420	12,375	McConnelsville
Morrow	cen.	403	21,348	Mount Gilead
Muskingum	SE cen.	667	77,826	Zanesville
Noble	SE	398	10,428	Caldwell
Ottawa	N	258	37,099	Port Clinton
Paulding	NW	417	19,329	Paulding
Perry	SE cen.	410	27,434	New Lexington
Pickaway	S cen.	507	40,071	Circleville
Pike	S	443	19,114	Waverly
Portage	NE	495	125,868	Ravenna
Preble	SW	428	34,719	Eaton
Putnam	NW	486	31,134	Ottawa
Richland	N cen.	496	129,997	Mansfield
Ross	S	687	61,211	Chillicothe
Sandusky	N	409	60,983	Fremont
Scioto	S	608	76,951	Portsmouth
Seneca	N	551	60,696	Tiffin
Shelby	W	408	37,748	Sidney
Stark	NE	576	372,210	Canton
Summit	NE	410	553,371	Akron
Trumbull	NE	615	232,579	Warren
Tuscarawas	E	569	77,211	New Philadelphia
Union	W cen.	434	23,786	Marysville
Van Wert	NW	409	29,194	Van Wert
Vinton	S	411	9,420	McArthur
Warren	SW	408	85,505	Lebanon
Washington	SE	641	57,160	Marietta
Wayne	NE cen.	561	87,123	Wooster
Williams	NW corner	421	33,669	Bryan
Wood	NW	619	89,722	Bowling Green
Wyandot	NW cen.	406	21,826	Upper Sandusky

[1]Area = land area.

History: Has many earthwork mounds of prehistoric mound builders; parts claimed by French and by charters of Virginia and Connecticut, and by New York 1609–1786; became part of U.S. by Treaty of Paris 1783; claims to it of other states relinquished 1784–86; included 1787 in Northwest Territory (*q.v.*); 1st settlement at Marietta 1788; W boundary with Indian lands determined by Anthony Wayne's defeat of Indians 1794 at Fallen Timbers and by Treaty of Greenville 1795; Western Reserve (*q.v.*) incorporated 1800; 1st Constitution 1802; unofficially entered Union Feb. 19, 1803. In 1953, by resolution of U.S. Congress, March 1, 1803 declared official day of admission to Union.

3 Name of counties in three states of the U.S. See tables at INDIANA, KENTUCKY, WEST VIRGINIA.

Ohi·o·ville \ō-ˈhī-ə-ˌvil\. Borough, Beaver co., W Pennsylvania, 23 m. SSW of New Castle; pop. (1970c) 3918.

Ohlau. See OŁAWA.

Ohoo·pee \ō-ˈhü-pē\. River, Georgia; 125 m. long; rises in Washington co., flows SE to Altamaha river in S Tattnall co.

Ohře \ˈȯr-zhə\ *or Ger.* **Eger** \ˈā-gər\. River, S West Germany and W Czechoslovakia; 193 m. long; rises in NE Bavaria, flows ENE across Czechoslovakia, into the Elbe river at Litoměřice.

Ohrid \ˈō-ˌkrēd\. 1 *or* **Okhri·da** \ō-ˈkrēd-ə\ *also* **Ochri·da** \-ˈkrēd-ä\; *anc.* **Lych·ni·dus** \ˈlik-nə-dəs\ *or* **Lych·ni·tis** \lik-ˈnīt-əs\. Lake, S Yugoslavia and E Albania; 25 m. long.

2 *or anc.* **Lychnidus.** Town on the lake, Macedonia, SE Yugoslavia; pop. (1965e) 19,000; tourism, fishing; cathedral.

Oich, Loch \läk-ˈȯik, läk-\. Lake, cen. Inverness co., NW cen. Scotland; 4 m. long; max. depth 154 ft.; part of the chain of lakes incorporated into the Caledonian Canal; drains NE into Loch Ness.

Oil City \ˌȯil-\. Industrial city, Venango co., NW Pennsylvania, on Allegheny river at mouth of Oil Creek, 52 m. SSE of Erie; pop. (1970c) 15,033; steel drums, tin cans, bottles, engines, pumping equipment; oil refining; founded 1860, incorporated as city 1871.

Oil Creek. River, NW Pennsylvania; ab. 50 m. long; flows S through E Crawford co. and N Venango co., enters Allegheny river at Oil City.

Oil Rivers. The delta of the Niger river, S Nigeria, W Africa, of indefinite boundaries. See NIGER 2. Protectorate over the region, **Oil Rivers Protectorate,** established by the British in 1885 and administered by the British Royal Niger Company; became Niger Coast Protectorate 1893–99.

Oi·mya·kon *also* **Oi·me·kon** \ˈȯi-myə-kən\. Town, SE Yakutsk A.S.S.R., Russian S.F.S.R., U.S.S.R., on the upper Indigirka river in mountain range S of the Cherskogo Range, 63°28′N, 142°49′E; Soviet weather station; one of the coldest places in Siberia; has had temperature of 79° below zero.

Oi·ron \wä-ˈrōⁿ\. Commune, Deux-Sèvres dept., W France, ab. 47 m. NNE of Niort; pop. (1962c) 878.

Oirot Autonomous Oblast. See GORNO-ALTAI AUTONOMOUS OBLAST.

Oirot Tura. See GORNO-ALTAISK.

Oise \ˈwäz\. 1 River, N France; 188 m. long; formed by confluence of two streams, one rising near Chimay in Belgium and the other near Rocroi in France; flows SW into Seine river at Conflans-Sainte-Honorine; navigable for ab. 80 m.

2 Department of N France. See table at FRANCE.

Ōi·ta \ˈō-i-ˌtä, ō-ˈēt-ə\. 1 Prefecture, NE Kyūshū, Japan; 2437 sq. m.; pop. (1970c) 1,155,566; ✱ Ōita; tobacco, citrus fruit; cattle.

2 Seaport city, its ✱, 65 m. SE of Moji on Beppu Bay; pop. (1970c) 260,584; ships tobacco and citrus fruit; commercial center; textiles, cement; univ. (1949). In 16th cent. a castle city that controlled nearly all Kyūshū; encouraged trade with Portuguese in period before 1600.

Ojai \ˈō-(ˌ)hī\. Residential and resort city, Ventura co., SW California, in Ojai valley of the Sierra Madre Range, 23 m. E of Santa Barbara; pop. (1970c) 5591.

Oj·cow National Park \ˈȯit-(ˌ)sōf-\. National park, Kraków prov., S Poland; 6 sq. m.; interesting geological formations; established 1956.

Ojo de Lie·bre, La·gu·na \lə-ˌgü-nə-ˈō-(ˌ)hō-ˌdā-lē-ˈeb-rē\. Inlet of Sebastián Vizcaíno Bay on coast of W cen. Baja California, Mexico.

Ojos del Sa·la·do \ˌō-(ˌ)hōz-ˌdel-sə-ˈläd-(ˌ)ō\. Mountain, NW Catamarca prov., NW Argentina, near border of Chile; 22,539 ft.

Oka \ō-ˈkä\. 1 River, cen. Irkutsk Oblast, Russian S.F.S.R., U.S.S.R.; 530 m. long; flows N from the Sayan Mts. to the Angara river.

2 River, cen. Russian S.F.S.R., U.S.S.R.; 919 m. long; rises in N part of Kursk Oblast, flows N and NE with several bends through Orel and Kaluga oblasts, to the Volga at Gorki. The largest right (W) tributary of the Volga; navigable for most of its length; important artery for lumber and grain trade; main tributaries the Klyazma, Moksha, and Moskva.

Oka–Ako·ko \ˌōk-ə-ə-ˈkō-(ˌ)kō\. Town, Western State, Nigeria; pop. (1969e) 72,783.

Oka·han·dja \ˌō-kə-ˈhän-jə\. Town, cen. South-West Africa, 43 m. N of Windhoek; pop. (1960c) 2962.

© Copyright HAMMOND INCORPORATED, Maplewood, N. J.

84° 83° Longitude West of Greenwich 82° 81°

Oka·lo·a·coo·chee Slough \ˌō-kə-ˌlō-ə-ˌkü-chē-\. The northwest section of the Everglades, S Florida, N of Big Cypress Swamp; used as pasture for cattle.

Oka·loo·sa \ˌō-kə-ˈlü-sə\. County in Florida. See table at FLORIDA.

Oka·na·gan Lake \ˌō-kə-ˈnäg-ən-\. Long narrow lake, S British Columbia, Canada; 136 sq. m.; ab. 60 m. long; its outlet is the Okanagan river, called the Okanogan (*q.v.*) in the U.S.

Oka·nog·an \ˌō-kə-ˈnäg-ən\. 1 County in N Washington. See table at WASHINGTON.

2 Town, its ⊗, on Okanogan river; pop. (1970c) 2015; in farming and lumbering section.

3 *or in Canada* **Oka·na·gan** \-ˈnäg-ən\. River, British Columbia, Canada, and N Washington; ab. 300 m. long; rises in Okanagan Lake, British Columbia, flows S across Washington border and into Columbia river on S boundary of Okanogan co.

Okanoxubee. See NOXUBEE 1.

Oka·van·go *or* **Oko·vang·go** \ˌō-kə-ˈvaŋ-(ˌ)gō\ *also* **Ku·ban·go** \kü-ˈbäŋ-(ˌ)gō\ *or Port.* **Cu·ban·go** \kü-ˈba(ⁿ)ŋ-(ˌ)gü\. River, SW cen. Africa; ab. 1000 m. long; rises in cen. Angola; flows S and then E, forming a section of the boundary bet. Angola and South-West Africa; crosses Caprivi Strip and empties into **Okavango Basin,** a large marsh N of Lake Ngami in N Botswana.

Oka·ya \ō-ˈkä-yə\. City, Nagano prefecture, Honshū, Japan, 12 m. SSE of Matsumoto; pop. (1970c) 60,350.

Oka·ya·ma \ˌō-kə-ˈyäm-ə\. 1 Prefecture, W Honshū, Japan; 2727 sq. m.; pop. (1970c) 1,707,026; ✱ Okayama; rice, grapes, peaches.

2 Seaport city, its ✱, on N side of Inland Sea 75 m. W of Kōbe; pop. (1970c) 375,106; market center; manufactures rubber products, synthetic fibers, agricultural machinery; univ. (1949); former castle town of Ikeda clan.

3 Town, Taiwan. See KANG-SHAN.

Oka·za·ki \ō-ˈkäz-ˌäk-ē, ˌō-kə-ˈzäk-ē\. Town, Aichi prefecture, S Honshū, Japan, 21 m. SE of Nagoya; pop. (1970c) 210,515; textiles; birthplace of Iyeyasu, founder of the Tokugawa shogunate.

Okee·cho·bee \ˌō-kə-ˈchō-bē\. 1 County in SE cen. Florida. See table at FLORIDA.

2 City, its ⊗, 2 m. N of Lake Okeechobee; pop. (1970c) 3715; fishing.

Okeechobee, Lake. Lake in S cen. Florida; largest lake in S United States; ab. 40 m. long by 25 m. wide; greatest depth ab. 20 ft.; elevation 19 ft. above sea level; receives Kissimmee river from N and drains to the sea through the Everglades.

Okeechobee Waterway. See CROSS-FLORIDA WATERWAY.

Oke·fe·no·kee Swamp *also* **Oke·fi·no·kee Swamp** \ˌō-kə-fə-ˈnō-kē-\. Swamp, SE Georgia, extending over the state boundary into Columbia and Baker cos., NE Florida; area 660 sq. m.

Oke·mah \ō-ˈkē-mə\. City, ⊗ of Okfuskee co., E cen. Oklahoma, 25 m. WSW of Okmulgee; pop. (1970c) 2913; wheat, corn, pecans.

Oke·ne \ō-ˈkā-nē\. Town, West Central State, Nigeria, 40 m. WSW of Lokoja.

Oker \ˈō-kər\. Stream, E cen. West Germany; ab. 65 m. long; flows N from Harz Mts. to the Aller.

Ok·fus·kee \ōk-ˈfəs-kē\. County in Oklahoma. See table at OKLAHOMA.

Okha \ə-ˈkä\. Town and port on NE coast of N Sakhalin I., Sakhalin Oblast, Russian S.F.S.R., U.S.S.R.; important port open the year round; has railroad connection with oil station on W coast of Sakhalin; oil fields nearby.

Ókhiós. See HAGIOS ELIAS, MOUNT.

Okhotsk \ō-ˈkätsk\. Town on NW coast of Sea of Okhotsk, Khabarovsk Krai, Russian S.F.S.R., U.S.S.R., 440 m. N of Nikolayevsk-na-Amure; port closed by ice for more than half the year.

Okhotsk, Sea of. Inlet of Pacific Ocean on coast of Khabarovsk Krai, Russian S.F.S.R., U.S.S.R., W of Kamchatka Penin. and the Kuril Is.; 613,838 sq. m.; average depth 3192 ft., max. depth 11,069 ft.; has Sakhalin I. in SW; main traffic outlets Tatar Strait, Sōya Strait, and Kuril Strait.

Okhrida. See OHRID 1.

Oki Archipelago \ˈō-(ˌ)kē-\ *or Jap.* **Oki Ret·to** \-ˈre-(ˌ)tō\. Group of islands in SE Sea of Japan, 44 m. off W coast of island of Honshū; 131 sq. m.; belongs to Shimane prefecture. Largest island Dōgo, on SE coast of which is Saigō, the chief port, with fine harbor.

Oki·e·ra·bu \ˌō-kē-ə-ˈräb-(ˌ)ü\. Island, S Amami Is., Ryukyu Is., Japan, just N of Okinawa.

Oki·na·wa \ˌō-kə-ˈnä-wə, -ˈnau̇-ə\. 1 Island group in center of chain of Ryukyu Is.; comprises Okinawa and small islands of Ii-shima, Iheya, Kume, and Kerama Is.; placed under U.S. control by U.S.-Japanese treaty of 1951; N part returned to Japan 1954; U.S.-Japanese agreement on restoration of Japanese sovereignty over whole group reached 1971.

2 Only large island in group, bet. East China Sea and Pacific Ocean, 26°39′N, 128°E; ab. 70 m. long; excluding adjacent islands, 454 sq. m.; pop. (1965c) 812,339; entirely of coral formation; chief town Naha at S end. Of vital importance in World War II; scene of severe fighting bet. Americans and Japanese Mar.–June 1945; bombed by U.S. carrier planes and bombarded by task force in March; center of island occupied by marines Apr. 1; island soon overrun except for S tip and area around Naha; this part not completely conquered until June 21 (see also YONABARU); campaign costly but made possible the establishment of air bases close to Japanese mainland.

3 Prefecture of Japan, comprising the S part of the Ryukyu Is. (Okinawa and Sakishima groups); 1482 sq. m.; ✱ Naha.

Oki·no–shi·ma \ˌō-kē-nō-ˈshē-mə\. Small island off SW Shikoku, Japan, on E side of Bungo Strait, 32°44′N, 132°33′E; belongs to Kōchi prefecture.

Oki Retto. See OKI ARCHIPELAGO.

Okla·ho·ma \ˌō-klə-ˈhō-mə\. 1 A southwestern state of U.S.A., bounded on N by Colorado and Kansas, on E by Missouri and Arkansas, on S by Texas, and on W by Texas and New Mexico; 18th state in area, 69,919 sq. m. (land area 68,984 sq. m.); 27th state in population, (1970c) 2,559,253; ✱ Oklahoma City; 46th state admitted to Union (1907).

Nickname: Sooner State. *State flower:* Mistletoe. *Motto:* Labor Omnia Vincit (Labor Conquers All Things). *Rivers:* Red, forming S boundary; Canadian, flowing across central region to empty into the Arkansas near E cen. border; Arkansas, flowing diagonally NW to SE across NE quarter of state. *Mountains:* Highest point Black Mesa 4973 ft. in Cimarron co. in the panhandle; Wichita Mts. in SW; W part of Ouachita Mts. in SE. *Chief products:* Wheat, cotton, oats; beef cattle; petroleum, zinc; manufacturing: food processing; textiles, petrochemicals, fabricated metal products. *Chief cities:* Oklahoma City, Tulsa, Lawton, Norman, Midwest City, Enid. See *Table of States* at UNITED STATES. Divided into the following 77 counties (for pronunciation of their names, see their individual entries):

NAME	LOCATION	AREA[1] (sq. m.)	POP. (1970c)	CO. SEAT
Adair	E	570	15,141	Stilwell
Alfalfa	N	868	7,224	Cherokee
Atoka	S	991	10,972	Atoka
Beaver	NW; in panhandle	1,790	6,282	Beaver
Beckham	W	907	15,754	Sayre
Blaine	W cen.	917	11,794	Watonga
Bryan	S	889	25,552	Durant
Caddo	W cen.	1,275	28,931	Anadarko
Canadian[3]	cen.	897	32,245	El Reno
Carter	S	830	37,349	Ardmore
Cherokee	E	756	23,174	Tahlequah
Choctaw	SE	781	15,141	Hugo
Cimarron	NW[2]	1,843	4,145	Boise City
Cleveland	cen.	541	81,839	Norman
Coal	S	526	5,525	Coalgate
Comanche[3]	SW	1,087	108,144	Lawton
Cotton	SW	651	6,832	Walters

NAME	LOCATION	AREA[1] (sq. m.)	POP. (1970c)	CO. SEAT
Craig	NE	764	14,722	Vinita
Creek	E cen.	936	45,532	Sapulpa
Custer	W	1,001	22,665	Arapaho
Delaware	NE	707	17,767	Jay
Dewey	W	1,018	5,656	Taloga
Ellis	NW	1,242	5,129	Arnett
Garfield	N	1,054	56,343	Enid
Garvin	S cen.	814	24,874	Pauls Valley
Grady	cen.	1,096	29,354	Chickasha
Grant	N	1,007	7,117	Medford
Greer	SW	633	7,979	Mangum
Harmon	SW	545	5,136	Hollis
Harper	NW	1,041	5,151	Buffalo
Haskell	E	602	9,578	Stigler
Hughes	E cen.	807	13,228	Holdenville
Jackson	SW	810	30,902	Altus
Jefferson	S	780	7,125	Waurika
Johnston	S	638	7,870	Tishomingo
Kay	N	950	48,791	Newkirk
Kingfisher	cen.	904	12,857	Kingfisher
Kiowa	SW	1,027	12,532	Hobart
Latimer	E	737	8,601	Wilburton
Le Flore	E	1,560	32,137	Poteau
Lincoln	cen.	973	19,482	Chandler
Logan	cen.	751	19,645	Guthrie
Love	S	513	5,637	Marietta
McClain	cen.	573	14,157	Purcell
McCurtain	SE corner	1,849	28,642	Idabel
McIntosh	E	608	12,472	Eufaula
Major	NW	963	7,529	Fairview
Marshall	S	366	7,682	Madill
Mayes	NE	678	23,302	Pryor Creek
Murray[4]	S	428	10,669	Sulphur
Muskogee	E	818	59,542	Muskogee
Noble	N	743	10,043	Perry
Nowata	NE	577	9,773	Nowata
Okfuskee	E cen.	637	10,683	Okemah
Oklahoma	cen.	705	527,717	Oklahoma City
Okmulgee	E cen.	700	35,358	Okmulgee
Osage	N	2,272	29,750	Pawhuska
Ottawa	NE corner	464	29,800	Miami
Pawnee	N	561	11,338	Pawnee
Payne	N cen.	694	50,654	Stillwater
Pittsburg	SE	1,241	37,521	McAlester
Pontotoc	S cen.	714	27,867	Ada
Pottawatomie	cen.	794	43,134	Shawnee
Pushmataha	SE	1,423	9,385	Antlers
Roger Mills	W	1,140	4,452	Cheyenne
Rogers	NE	712	28,425	Claremore
Seminole	cen.	630	25,144	Wewoka
Sequoyah	E	696	23,370	Sallisaw
Stephens	S	891	35,902	Duncan
Texas	NW; in panhandle	2,062	16,352	Guymon
Tillman	SW	901	12,901	Frederick
Tulsa	NE	573	399,982	Tulsa
Wagoner	NE	563	22,163	Wagoner
Washington	NE	424	42,302	Bartlesville
Washita	W	1,009	12,141	New Cordell
Woods	NW	1,298	11,920	Alva
Woodward	NW	1,251	15,537	Woodward

[1]Area = land area.
[2]W tip of panhandle; only county in U.S. to border four states (Colorado and Kansas on N, New Mexico on W, Texas on S).
[3]Contains military reservations in Canadian co. (Fort Reno, in cen. part) and Comanche co. (Fort Sill) in E cen. part.
[4]Contains Platt National Park in E cen. part.

History: Except for panhandle, formed part of Louisiana Purchase (*q.v.*) from France 1803; settled by Indians as unorganized Indian Territory 1820–40; part opened to white settlement 1889; W part organized as Oklahoma Territory 1890; rest gradually opened to whites; by Enabling Act of 1906, Indian Territory and Oklahoma Territory were merged and admitted to Union as state Nov. 16, 1907.

2 County in Oklahoma. See table at OKLAHOMA.

Oklahoma City. City, ✻ of Oklahoma and ⊗ of Oklahoma co., cen. Oklahoma; pop. (1970c) 368,856; largest city in the state and its principal commercial, financial, industrial, and transportation center; manufactures aircraft, oil drilling equipment, steel products; packinghouses, oil wells and refineries; Tinker Air Force Base. Oklahoma City Univ. (1911), Oklahoma City Southwestern Coll. (1946), Southwestern Coll. (1946), Oklahoma Christian Coll. (1950). Settled during Oklahoma land rush April 1889; incorporated 1890; made state capital 1910; rapid expansion following discovery of petroleum in region 1928.

Ok·la·wa·ha \ˌäk-lə-ˈwȯ-(ˌ)hȯ\. River, N cen. Florida penin.; ab. 60 m. long; rises in Lake co., flows N and E through Marion and Putnam cos. into St. Johns river.

Ok·mul·gee \ōk-ˈməl-gē\. 1 County in E cen. Oklahoma. See table at OKLAHOMA.

2 City, its ⊗, 37 m. S of Tulsa; pop. (1970c) 15,180; aircraft, glass, furniture; meat-packing, oil refining; oil and gas wells, coal mines; capital of the Creek Nation 1868–1907; settled 1872.

Oko·bo·ji \ˌō-kə-ˈbō-jē\. Two lakes, **East Okoboji** and **West Okoboji** (ab. 6 m. long, area ab. 6 sq. m.), in cen. Dickinson co., NW Iowa.

Oko·bo·jo Creek \ˌō-kə-ˈbō-jō-\. River, cen. South Dakota; ab. 75 m. long; rises in Potter co., flows SW into Missouri river in SW Sully co.

Oko·lo·na \ˌō-kə-ˈlōn-ə\. City, a ⊗ of Chickasaw co., NE Mississippi, 18 m. S of Tupelo; pop. (1970c) 3002.

Okovanggo. See OKAVANGO.

Ok·tib·be·ha \äk-ˈtib-ə-ˌhȯ\. County in Mississippi. See table at MISSISSIPPI.

Ok·tya·brski \ək-ˈtyä-bər-skē\. Town, Bashkir A.S.S.R., Russian S.F.S.R., U.S.S.R., ab. 100 m. WSW of Ufa; pop. (1969e) 81,000.

Oktyabrskoi Revolyutsi, Ostrov. See OCTOBER REVOLUTION ISLAND.

Oku·ji·ri \ō-ˈku̇j-ə-rē\ *or* **Oku·shi·ri** \ō-ˈku̇sh-ə-rē\. Island in the Sea of Japan off SW coast of Hokkaidō, Japan; 56 sq. m.

Okusi. See OCUSSI.

Ólafs·vík \ˈō-ləfs-ˌvēk\. Town, W Iceland, on coast of peninsula S of Breidha Fjord; pop. (1967e) 100.

Olan·cho \ō-ˈlän-(ˌ)chō\. Department of E cen. Honduras. See table at HONDURAS.

Öland \ˈər-ˌland, -lənd\. Island in Baltic Sea off SE coast of Sweden, in Kalmar co. and separated from the mainland by Kalmarsund; 85 m. long; area 519 sq. m.; pop. (1969e) 26,750; chief town Borgholm, on W coast; fishing; alum deposits. Mentioned early (8th cent.) in Scandinavian history; often a battleground in northern wars.

Ola·the \ō-ˈlā-thə\. City, ⊗ of Johnson co., E Kansas, 20 m. SW of Kansas City; pop. (1970c) 17,917; footwear, chemicals; livestock farms; Mid-America Nazarene Coll. (1966).

Ola·va·rría \ō-ˌlä-və-ˈrē-ə\. Town, Buenos Aires prov., Argentina, ab. 160 m. NNE of Bahia Blanca; pop. (1960c) 35,107.

Oła·wa \ȯ-ˈläv-ə\ *or Ger.* **Oh·lau** \ˈō-ˌlau̇\. Manufacturing city, E Wrocław prov., SW Poland, on left bank of the Oder 18 m. SE of Wrocław; pop. (1968e) 16,000; manufactures white lead, electrochemical goods, stoves; cattle market; 12th cent. church. Became city 1291; taken Feb. 7, 1945 by Soviet troops; assigned to Poland by Potsdam Conference 1945.

Öl·berg \ˈər(-ə)l-ˌbe(ə)rg\. Highest peak in the Siebengebirge (*q.v.*), West Germany; 1509 ft.

Ol·bern·hau \ˈȯl-bərn-ˌhau̇\. City, Karl-Marx-Stadt dist., East Germany, in the Erzgebirge 21 m. SE of Karl-Marx-Stadt; pop. (1969e) 13,952; manufactures furniture, toys, paper.

Ol·bia \ˈäl-bē-ə\. 1 *or formerly* **Ter·ra·no·va Pau·sa·nia** \ˌter-ə-ˈnȯ-və-pȯ-ˈsän-yə\. Commune, Sassari prov., Sardinia, Italy, on NE coast of Sardinia 50 m. E by N of Sassari; pop. (1968e) 23,818; harbor; 11th cent. church.

2 Ancient town on N coast of Black Sea, S Sarmatia, at mouth of the Hypanis.

Olcinium. See ULCINJ.

Old Ba·ha·ma Channel \-bə-ˌhäm-ə-, -ˌhā-mə-\. Channel in W West Indies, N of E cen. Cuba and SE of Santaren Channel.

Old Baldy Peak. See LINDSEY, MOUNT.

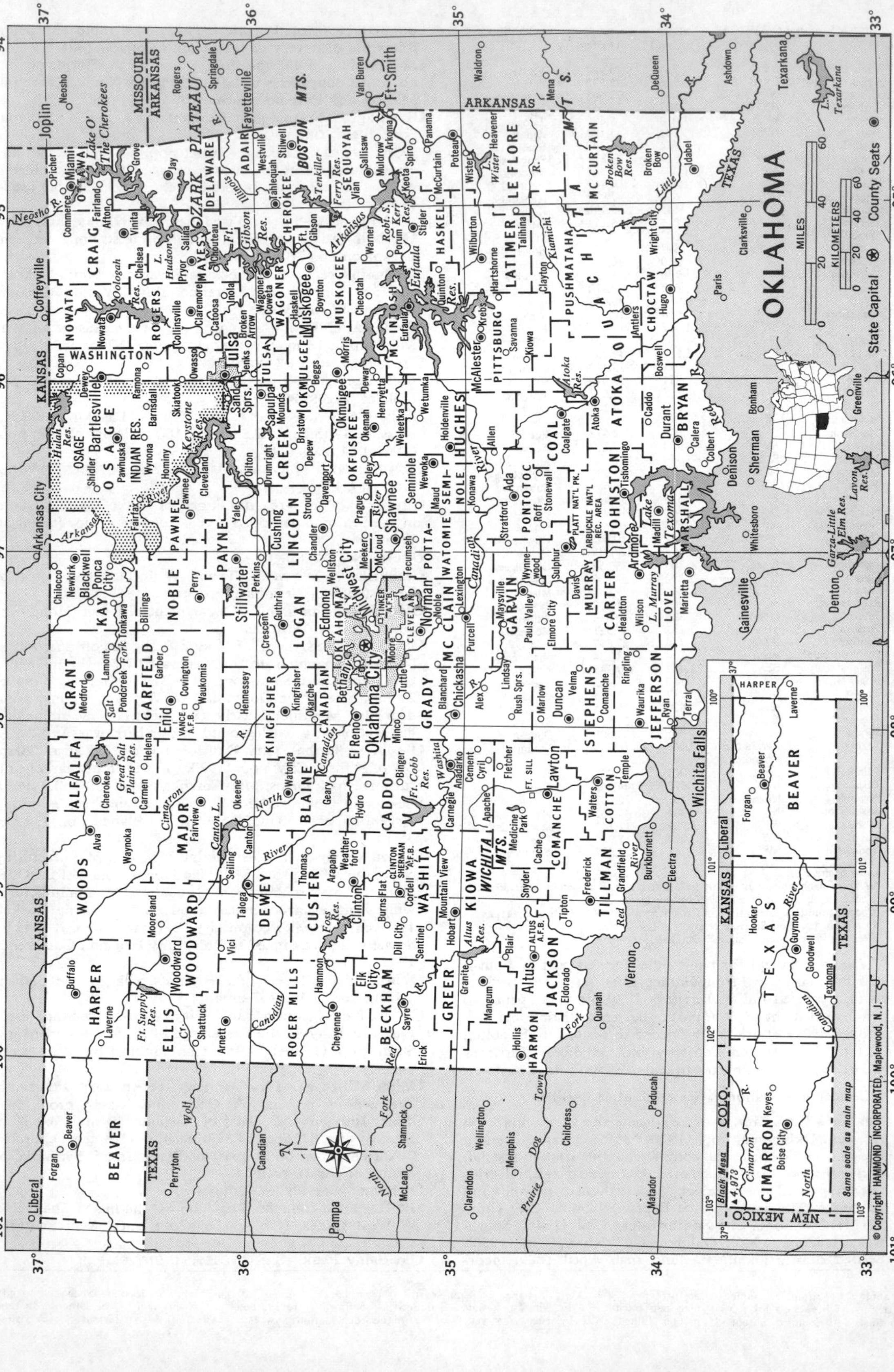
OKLAHOMA
MILES
0 20 40 60
KILOMETERS
0 20 40 60
State Capital
County Seats
Longitude West of Greenwich
© Copyright HAMMOND INCORPORATED, Maplewood, N. J.
Same scale as main map
KANSAS
MISSOURI
ARKANSAS
TEXAS
NEW MEXICO
COLO.
BEAVER
HARPER
WOODS
ALFALFA
GRANT
KAY
OSAGE
WASHINGTON
NOWATA
CRAIG
OTTAWA
DELAWARE
MAYES
ROGERS
TULSA
WAGONER
CHEROKEE
ADAIR
SEQUOYAH
MUSKOGEE
OKMULGEE
CREEK
PAWNEE
NOBLE
GARFIELD
MAJOR
WOODWARD
ELLIS
DEWEY
BLAINE
KINGFISHER
LOGAN
PAYNE
LINCOLN
OKFUSKEE
MC INTOSH
HASKELL
LE FLORE
LATIMER
PITTSBURG
HUGHES
SEMINOLE
POTTAWATOMIE
OKLAHOMA
CANADIAN
CUSTER
ROGER MILLS
BECKHAM
WASHITA
CADDO
GRADY
MC CLAIN
CLEVELAND
GARVIN
PONTOTOC
COAL
ATOKA
PUSHMATAHA
MC CURTAIN
CHOCTAW
BRYAN
JOHNSTON
MARSHALL
MURRAY
CARTER
LOVE
JEFFERSON
STEPHENS
COTTON
COMANCHE
TILLMAN
KIOWA
JACKSON
GREER
HARMON
CIMARRON
TEXAS
Oklahoma City
Tulsa
Lawton
Norman
Enid
Muskogee
Bartlesville
Ponca City
Stillwater
Shawnee
Midwest City
Ft. Smith
Wichita Falls
Joplin
Coffeyville
Arkansas City
Liberal
Amarillo
Pampa
Texarkana
Denison
Sherman
Gainesville
Vernon
WICHITA MTS.
OZARK PLATEAU
BOSTON MTS.
OSAGE INDIAN RES.
Lake Texoma
Lake O' The Cherokees
Canadian
Cimarron
Arkansas
Red
Washita
North Fork
Salt Fork
Black Mesa ▲4,973

Old Brook·ville \-'brůk-ˌvil\. Village, Nassau co., SE New York; pop. (1970c) 1785.

Old Cas·tile \-ka-'stē(ə)l\ *or Span.* **Cas·ti·lla la Vi·e·ja** \kä-'stē-lʸə-lä-'vye-k̲ə\. Old provincial region, N Castile, Spain; 25,523 sq. m.; bounded on N by Bay of Biscay, on NE by Basque Provinces and Navarre, on SE by Aragon, on S by New Castile, on W by León, and on NW by Asturias; comprises modern provinces of Ávila, Burgos, Logroño, Palencia, Santander, Segovia, Soria, and Valladolid; ❋ Burgos. For history, see CASTILE.

Old Clump Hill \-ˌkləmp-\. Mountain in Delaware co., S New York, in the Catskills near Roxbury (*q.v.*); site of "Woodchuck Lodge" where John Burroughs spent his last years.

Old Deer. See DEER, OLD.

Old Delhi. See DELHI 2.

Ol·den·burg \'ōl-dən-ˌbərg\. 1 Former German state, now part of West Germany; 2083 sq. m.; ❋ Oldenburg; became part of Lower Saxony 1946.

2 Industrial and commercial city, Lower Saxony, West Germany, on Hunte river 80 m. W of Bremen; pop. (1969e) 131,191; river port; railroad and road junction; important meat-packing center; shipbuilding, glassmaking; 13th cent. church. First mentioned 1108; made city 1345; largely destroyed by fire 1615; in World War II occupied by Allied forces May 3, 1945.

Ol·den·zaal \'öl-dən-ˌzäl\. Commune, Overijssel prov., E Netherlands, 38 m. ESE of Zwolle near West German border; pop. (1970e) 22,604.

Old Faithful. Geyser in Yellowstone National Park, NW Wyoming, erupts regularly at intervals averaging 67 minutes.

Old Flet·ton \-'flet-ən\. Urban district, Huntingdon and Peterborough co., E cen. England, S suburb of Peterborough 72 m. N of London; pop. (1971p) 13,660.

Old Forge \-'fō(ə)rj, -'fȯ(ə)rj\. Borough, Lackawanna co., NE Pennsylvania, 6 m. SW of Scranton; pop. (1970c) 9522.

Old Goa. See GOA 2.

Old Greenwich. Subdivision of town of Greenwich, Connecticut. See GREENWICH.

Old·ham \'ōl-dəm\. 1 Name of counties in two states of the U.S. See tables at KENTUCKY and TEXAS.

2 County and municipal borough, Lancashire, NW England, on the Medlock 6 m. NE of Manchester; pop. (1971p) 105,705; cotton textiles, textile machinery; incorporated 1849.

Old Harbour Bay. See PORTLAND BIGHT.

Old House Point. Cape on S coast of the island of Jamaica, West Indies, on W side of entrance to Kingston harbor.

Old Lyme \-'līm\. Residential town and summer resort, SW New London co., SE Connecticut, at mouth of Connecticut river on left bank; pop. (1970c) 4964; settled 1665, incorporated 1885; noted for numerous old homes of architectural interest.

Old·man \'ōl(d)-mən\. River, S Alberta, Canada; ab. 200 m. long; rises in Rocky Mts. near the British Columbia border and flows E to unite with the Bow and form the South Saskatchewan river; receives tributaries Belly and St. Mary from the S.

Old Man of Coniston. See CONISTON FELLS.

Old Margelan. See MARGILAN.

Old Northwest. See NORTHWEST TERRITORY.

Old Or·chard Beach \-ˌȯr-chərd-\. Town, York co., SW Maine, on Atlantic Ocean 6 m. ENE of Biddeford; pop. (1970c) 5404; summer resort.

Old Panama *or Span.* **Pa·na·má Vie·ja** \'pa-nə-ˌmä-'vye-k̲ə\. Old city on S shore of Isthmus of Panama; Pacific port of the Spaniards in 16th and 17th cents.; sacked by the pirate Morgan 1671; now in ruins; present city of Panama a few miles to the SW.

Old Point Com·fort \-'kəm(p)-fərt\. Point, Hampton, SE Virginia, on N shore of Hampton Roads.

Old Ryazan. See RYAZAN 2.

Olds \'ōl(d)z\. Town, Alberta, Canada, 50 m. N of Calgary; pop. (1971p) 3378; agriculture; feed mill, creamery, oil and gas processing.

Old Sar·um \-'sar-əm, -'ser-\ *or Latin* **Sor·bi·o·du·num** \ˌsȯr-bē-ə-'d(y)ü-nəm\. Extinct borough and city in Wiltshire, England, 2 m. N of Salisbury; extensive ruins remain: large mound and traces of the cathedral (an earlier cathedral on the site had burned down four days after its completion 1092) which was razed 1331 to furnish materials for use in Salisbury cathedral. Home of kings of Wessex; became seat of bishopric c. 1075 (*Sarum use* formulated by Osmund, bishop 1078–99); see transferred to New Sarum (Salisbury) in 13th cent.; lapsed to the crown, became one of the rotten boroughs (until 1833).

Old Saybrook. See SAYBROOK 1.

Old Scab Mountain \-ˌskab-\. Peak, Yakima co., S Washington; 6642 ft.

Old Tap·pan \-'tap-ən\. Borough, Bergen co., NE New Jersey, 11 m. NE of Paterson; pop. (1970c) 3917.

Old Town. 1 City, Penobscot co., E cen. Maine, on Penobscot river 11 m. NNE of Bangor; pop. (1970c) 9057; canoes, wood pulp; truck farms.

2 Urban community, New Mexico. See LAS VEGAS 2.

Ol·du·vai Gorge \ˌōl-də-ˌwā-, -ˌvā-\. Ravine, N Tanzania, E Africa, 150 m. WNW of Mt. Kilimanjaro; site of rich fossil beds where in 1960 an ancient fossil skull of *Zinjanthropus* was found.

Old West·bury \-'west-bər-ē, -bə-rē\. Village, Nassau co., New York, on W cen. Long I. SE of Roslyn; pop. (1970c) 2667; New York Institute of Technology (1910), State Univ. of New York at Old Westbury (1966).

Ole·an \'ō-lē-ˌan, ˌō-lē-'\. City, Cattaraugus co., SW New York, on Allegheny river; pop. (1970c) 19,169; tile, dairy products, metal specialties; railroad shops, oil wells.

O'·Lea·ry Peak \ō-ˌli(ə)r-ē-\. Mountain, cen. Coconino co., N cen. Arizona; 8925 ft.

Olek·ma \ō-'lek-mə\. River, E Russian S.F.S.R., U.S.S.R.; 794 m. long; rises in Yablonovy Mts.; flows N to the Lena river.

Ole·nek \ˌäl-ən-'yȯk\. River, NW Yakutsk A.S.S.R., Russian S.F.S.R., U.S.S.R.; ab. 1500 m. long; rises at W end of Vilyuisk Range, flows generally NE into Laptev Sea W of the Lena.

Olé·ron, Île d' \ˌēl-dȯ-lā-'rōⁿ\ *or anc.* **Uli·a·rus** \yü-'lī-ə-rəs\. Island in E Bay of Biscay, off W coast of Charente-Maritime dept., W France; 66 sq. m.; chief towns Saint-Pierre, in center of island, and Le Château, port at SE end. In early times a part of the duchy of Aquitaine; became possession of French king 1370. Noted for its Laws of Oléron, a medieval (12th cent.) code of maritime laws in use in the island and the judicial decisions connected with them, published by Eleanor, Duchess of Guienne; the code forms the basis of modern maritime law.

Oleś·ni·ca \ˌȯ-lesh-'nēt-sə\; *Ger.* **Oels** \'ər(-ə)ls\ *or* **Oels in Schle·si·en** \-in-'shlā-zē-ən\. City, E Wrocław prov., SW Poland, 17 m. ENE of Wrocław; pop. (1970p) 27,500; shoes, furniture, machinery; livestock market; 12th cent. church. Founded in late 10th cent.; became capital of independent principality 14th cent.; assigned to Poland by Potsdam Conference 1945.

Ole·vu·ga \ˌō-lə-'vü-gə\. Small island off W end of Florida I., SE Solomon Is., W Pacific Ocean.

Olhão \ül-'yaůⁿ\. Commune, Faro dist., S Portugal, on Atlantic Ocean 5 m. E by N of Faro; pop. (1970p) 10,827.

Ol·i·fants \'äl-ə-fən(t)s\. 1 River, extreme SW Africa; rises in SW Cape Province, Rep. of South Africa, flows WNW into Atlantic Ocean ab. 31°42'S, 18°12'E.

2 River, SE Africa; ab. 350 m. long; rises in S cen. Transvaal, NE Rep. of South Africa, flows NNE across Mozambique border into Limpopo river.

3 River, S Cape Province, S Rep. of South Africa; ab. 115 m. long; joins Gamka river to form the Gourits river.

4 River, South-West Africa. See ELEPHANT 2.

Oli·mar \ˌō-li-ˈmär\. River, E Uruguay; flows E into Lake Mirim.

Olím·pia \ō-ˈlim-pē-ə, -ˈli(n)m-pyə\. City, N São Paulo state, SE Brazil, 240 m. NW of São Paulo; munic. pop. (1968e) 33,707.

Olim·po \ō-ˈlēm-pō\. Department of N Paraguay. See table at PARAGUAY.

Olin·da \ō-ˈlin-də\. City, Pernambuco state, E Brazil, N suburb of Recife; munic. pop. (1968e) 119,458; sugar; notable 16th and 17th cent. buildings; founded 1537 as colonial capital; occupied by Dutch 1630–1654.

Olisipo. See LISBON 6.

Oli·va \ō-ˈlē-və\. 1 Former commune, Poland. See OLIWA.

2 Commune, Valencia prov., E Spain, on Mediterranean Sea 43 m. SSE of Valencia; pop. (1970p) 16,772; in region producing cereals, citrus fruit, olives, wine.

Oliva de la Fron·te·ra \ō-ˌlē-və-də-lä-frōn-ˈter-ə\ *or formerly* **Oliva de Je·rez** \-hə-ˈrās\. Commune, Badajoz prov., SW Spain, near Portuguese border 38 m. S of Badajoz; pop. (1970p) 8560.

Oli·va·res \ˌō-lē-ˈvär-əs\. Peak, W San Juan prov., W Argentina near Chile border; 20,512 ft.

Olive Bridge Dam. See ASHOKAN DAM.

Oli·ven·za \ˌō-lə-ˈvān-sə\. Fortified commune, Badajoz prov., SW Spain, near Portuguese border 15 m. SW of Badajoz; pop. (1970p) 9909.

Ol·i·ver \ˈäl-ə-vər\. 1 County in North Dakota. See table at NORTH DAKOTA.

2 Locality, Fayette co., SW Pennsylvania, ab. 2 m. N of Uniontown; pop. (1970c) 3091.

Oliver Springs. Town, Anderson, Morgan, and Roane cos., E Tennessee, 23 m. NW of Knoxville; pop. (1970c) 3405.

Ol·ives, Mount of \-ˈäl-ivz, -əvz\ *or* **Ol·i·vet** \ˈäl-ə-ˌvet, ˌäl-ə-ˈ\. 1 Ridge, Jordan, in region occupied by Israel 1967, running N and S on E side of Jerusalem (*Acts* i. 12); separated from the city by the valley of the Kidron. At its W foot, outside the city walls, is the Garden of Gethsemane; on its E slope the village of Al-'Ayzarīyah (Bethany).

2 A section of this ridge containing its three culminating heights; highest point 2737 ft.

Oli·vet. 1 \ˌäl-ə-ˈvet\. City, S Eaton co., S Michigan, 11 m. SW of Charlotte; pop. (1970c) 1629; Olivet Coll. (1844).

2 \ˈō-lə-(ˌ)vet\. Town, ⊗ of Hutchinson co., SE South Dakota; pop. (1970c) 103.

Ol·i·vette \ˈäl-ə-ˌvet\. City, St. Louis co., E cen. Missouri, W of St. Louis; pop. (1970c) 9238.

Oliv·ia \ō-ˈliv-ē-ə\. Village, ⊗ of Renville co., SW cen. Minnesota, 36 m. ESE of Montevideo; pop. (1970c) 2553; diversified agriculture.

Oli·wa \ò-ˈlē-(ˌ)vä\ *or Ger.* **Oli·va** \ō-ˈlē-(ˌ)vä\. Former commune, now a part of Gdańsk, Gdańsk prov., N Poland, in NW near the coast. Founded 1170; several times partially destroyed in wars of 13th to 16th cents.; peace treaty signed here May 3, 1660 by which the war with Sweden (1655–60) was ended, Livonia was ceded to Sweden, and John II Casimir of Poland relinquished claim to Swedish throne.

Ol·kusz \ˈòl-ˌküsh\. Commune, Kraków prov., S Poland, 19 m. E of Sosnowiec; pop. (1968e) 14,900; zinc and lead mining; lead mines noted in Middle Ages.

Ol·la·güe \ō-ˈyäg-(ˌ)wā\ *or* **Oya·hue** \ō-ˈyä-(ˌ)wā\. 1 Volcano, NE Antofagasta prov., N Chile, near the Bolivian border; 19,250 ft.

2 Town, NE Antofagasta prov., N Chile, at the Bolivian border N of Ollagüe peak; pop. (1960c) 333; railroad junction; on the highway from Antofagasta to Uyuni, Bolivia.

Ollius. See OGLIO.

Olm·sted \ˈäm-(ˌ)sted, ˈōm-\. County in Minnesota. See table at MINNESOTA.

Olmsted Falls. Village, Cuyahoga co., N Ohio, 12 m. SW of Cleveland; pop. (1970c) 2504; abrasives, electrical equipment.

Olmütz. See OLOMOUC.

Ol·ney \ˈäl-nē\. 1 City, ⊗ of Richland co., SE Illinois, 54 m. NE of Mount Vernon; pop. (1970c) 8974; shoes, clothing, dairy products; oil wells; Olney Community Coll. (1963).

2 City, Young co., N Texas, 40 m. S of Wichita Falls; pop. (1970c) 3624; aircraft; oil wells and refineries.

3 Town, N Buckinghamshire, SE cen. England, ab. 59 m. NNW of London; pop. (1961c) 2651; residence 1767–86 of William Cowper who assisted John Newton, curate, in composition of *Olney Hymns* 1779.

Olo·mouc \ˈò-lò-(ˌ)mōts\ *or Ger.* **Ol·mütz** \ˈòl-müts\. City, Czech S.R., Czechoslovakia, on Morava river ab. 40 m. NW of Brno; pop. (1968e) 79,545; brewing, sugar refining, malting, cheese making; univ. (1566); 14th cent. Gothic cathedral, 15th cent. town hall.

History: Possibly originated as Roman fort; made bishopric 1063; ceded to Hungary 1478 and capital of Moravia until c. 1640; besieged by Prussians 1758; scene of Conference of Olmütz 1850, at which Prussia yielded to Austrian demands that she abstain from seeking leadership among the German states.

Olo·nets \ə-ˈlò-nyəts\. 1 *or formerly* **Au·nus** \ˈaù-nùs\. Isthmus, NW Russian S.F.S.R., U.S.S.R., extending bet. Lakes Ladoga and Onega; overrun by Soviet army June 21, 1944.

2 Town, S Karelian A.S.S.R., Russian S.F.S.R., U.S.S.R., near E shore of Lake Ladoga 112 m. NE of Leningrad; Peter the Great established ironworks here.

Olon·ga·po \ō-ˌlòŋ-gə-ˈpō\. Chartered city, Zambales prov., Luzon, Phil., on NE coast of Subic Bay near Bataan border; pop. (1970e) 66,400; good harbor, formerly site of U.S. naval facility. Occupied by Japanese Dec. 1941–Feb. 1945.

Olonos. See ERYMANTHUS.

Olo·ron–Sainte–Ma·rie \ò-lò-ˌrōⁿ-saⁿt-mà-ˈrē\. City, Pyrénées-Atlantiques dept., SW France, 13 m. SW of Pau; pop. (1968c) 13,028; episcopal see to 1790; ancient city destroyed by Saracens and Normans; rebuilt 1080.

Olo·se·ga \ˌō-lə-ˈsā-gə\. One of the Manua Is. in American Samoa; pop. (1970p) 410. See OFU.

Olot \ō-ˈlòt\. Commune, Gerona prov., NE Spain, 17 m. NW of Gerona; pop. (1970p) 21,244; more than 200 prisoners of war shot here by Carlist leader Savalls.

Öls·nitz *or* **Oels·nitz** \ˈərl-snəts\. 1 *or in full* **Ölsnitz im Erz·ge·birge** \-im-ˈerts-gə-ˌbir-gə\. City, Karl-Marx-Stadt dist., East Germany, 13 m. SW of Karl-Marx-Stadt; pop. (1970e) 17,575; founded 12th cent.

2 *or in full* **Ölsnitz im Vogt·land** \-im-ˈfōkt-ˌlänt\. Industrial city, Karl-Marx-Stadt dist., East Germany, on the Weisse Elster 25 m. SSW of Zwickau; pop. (1970e) 15,590; textiles, tile, furniture, beer; 13th cent. church.

Ol·son Mountain \ˌōl-sən-\. Peak in Glacier National Park, NW Montana; 7800 ft.

Olsz·tyn \ˈòlsh-tən\. 1 Province of N Poland. See table at POLAND.

2 *or Ger.* **Al·len·stein** \ˈäl-ən-ˌs(h)tīn\. Industrial city, its ✱, on Łyna river 80 m. SE of Gdańsk; pop. (1970p) 94,100; transportation and market center in lumbering and agricultural region; 14th cent. castle. Received town rights 1353; to Poland 1466; to Prussia 1772; awarded to Germany by plebiscite 1920; assigned to Poland by Potsdam Conference 1945.

Olt \ˈòlt\. 1 *or* **Alu·ta** \ə-ˈlüt-ə\ *or Ger.* **Alt** \ˈält\. River, S Romania; 308 m. long; rises in E Transylvania, flows S, cutting through the Transylvanian Alps; enters the Danube river opp. Nikopol.

2 County of S Romania. See table at ROMANIA.

Ol·ten \ˈòlt-ᵊn\. Commune, Solothurn canton, NW Switzerland, on Aare river 7 m. WSW of Aarau; pop. (1970c)

21,209; machinery, motor vehicles, textiles, footwear; 17th cent. monastery.

Ol·te·nia \ȯl-ˈtē-nē-ə\ *or* **Little Wa·la·chia** *also* **Lesser Walachia** \-wä-ˈlā-kē-ə\. Region, S Romania, W division of Walachia; 9294 sq. m.; formerly a province.

Ol·te·ni·ța *or* **Ol·te·ni·tza** \ȯl-tə-ˌnēt-sə\ *or anc.* **Con·stan·ti·o·la** \ˌkän-stan-tē-ˈō-lə\. City, Ilfov co., S Romania, on Argeş river at its confluence with the Danube; pop. (1970e) 20,610; battle Nov. 4, 1853 in which Turks under Omer Pasha defeated the Russians.

Oltis. See LOT 1.

Ol·ton \ˈōlt-ᵊn\. City, Lamb co., NW Texas; pop. (1970c) 1782; cattle, grain farms.

Oltre Giuba. See JUBALAND.

Ol·tu \ȯl-ˈtü\ *or* **Ol·ti** \-ˈtē\. Village, NE Erzurum prov., NE Turkey; fighting bet. Russians and Turks Sept. 1915.

O–luan, Cape \-ˈō-lü-ˈän\ *or formerly* **Cape Ga·ram Bi** \-ˌgär-äm-ˈbē\ *also* **Cape Mi·na·mi** \-ˌmē-nä-ˈmē\. Cape at S end of Taiwan, on Bashi Channel.

Olus·tee \ō-ˈləs-tē\. Village, Baker co., NE Florida, 45 m. SW of Jacksonville; battle Feb. 20, 1864 in which Confederates under General Joseph Finnegan decisively defeated Union forces led by General Truman Seymour (called also battle of Ocean Pond).

Olu·tanga \ˌō-lü-ˈtäŋ-ə\. Island in N Moro Gulf, S Zamboanga del Sur prov., Mindanao, Phil.; 78 sq. m.; low island covered with mangroves.

Ol·ve·ra \ȯl-ˈver-ə\. Commune, Cádiz prov., SW Spain, 62 m. ENE of Cádiz; pop. (1970p) 11,515; agriculture and stock raising.

Olviopol. See PERVOMAISK 1.

Olym·pia \ō-ˈlim-pē-ə\. 1 City and port of entry, ✱ of Washington and ⊗ of Thurston co., W Washington, at S extremity of Puget Sound 60 m. SSW of Seattle; pop. (1970c) 23,111; ships forest products and agricultural produce; food canning; center of oyster culture; Saint Martin's Coll. (1895). Settled 1845; became first port of entry on Puget Sound 1851; capital of Territory of Washington 1853; chartered as city 1859.

2 Plain and sanctuary, ancient Elis, NW Peloponnesus, S Greece, on N bank of the Alpheus river; a center of religious worship of Greece, with notable festival (*Olympian* games) celebrated every fourth year in honor of Zeus. These began 776 B.C., the year that came to be adopted as primary date in Greek chronology (periods known as *Olympiads*); games were chiefly athletic contests. Here in the temple of Zeus was the statue of Olympian Zeus by Phidias; excavation has disclosed ruins of many temples and other buildings.

Olympia Fields. Village, Cook co., NE Illinois, 25 m. S of Chicago; pop. (1970c) 3478.

Olym·pic Mountains \ō-ˌlim-pik-\. Mountain group, part of the Coast Ranges, chiefly in Jefferson and Clallam cos., in NW Washington in the Olympic Penin.; chief peaks Mount Olympus 7965 ft. and Mount Constance 7777 ft.; part of **Olympic National Park** (see UNITED STATES, *National Parks*).

Olympic Peninsula. Peninsular part of W Washington bounded on W by Pacific Ocean, on N by Juan de Fuca Strait, and on E by Puget Sound.

Olym·pus \ō-ˈlim-pəs\. Mountain range in Thessaly, NE Greece, near coast of Gulf of Salonika; highest peak 9570 ft.; in ancient Greek mythology, the home of the gods.

Olympus, Mount. 1 Peak in Olympic Mts., Jefferson co., NW Washington; 7965 ft.

2 *or formerly* **Mount Tro·o·dos** \-ˈtrō-ə-t͟hōs\. Mountain, W cen. Cyprus; 6403 ft.; highest peak in Cyprus.

3 Mountain, Turkey. See ULU DAĞ.

Olyn·thus \ō-ˈlin(t)-thəs\. Town in ancient Macedonia, NE Greece; its site is on the Chalcidice Penin. at the head of the Toronaic Gulf and bet. Sithonia and Pallene penins. The most important of the Greek cities on the coast of Macedonia, head of a strong confederacy of Greek towns esp. after 424 B.C. At war with Sparta 382–379 B.C.; finally subdued and held subject 379–375; besieged by Philip of Macedon, and in spite of appeals to Athens and orations of Demosthenes (*Olynthiac* orations), overcome and destroyed by Philip 348 B.C. and its citizens enslaved; ruins excavated 1928–38.

Oly·phant \ˈȯl-i-fənt, ˈōl-\. Borough, Lackawanna co., NE Pennsylvania, 5 m. NE of Scranton; pop. (1970c) 5422; coal mines; resort.

Ol·yu·torsk, Cape \-ˌəl-yü-ˈtȯ(ə)rsk\. Point at NE base of Kamchatka Penin. extending into Bering Sea, in Koryak National Okrug, Russian S.F.S.R., U.S.S.R.

Om \ˈȯm\. River, W Russian S.F.S.R., U.S.S.R.; ab. 450 m. long; flows W in Novosibirsk and Omsk oblasts to join the Irtysh at Omsk.

Ōma, Cape \-ˈō-(ˌ)mä, -mə\. Cape on N extremity of Honshū, Japan, projecting into Tsugaru Strait.

Omagh \ˈō-(ˌ)mä, -mə\. Urban district, ⊗ of co. Tyrone, W cen. Northern Ireland; pop. (1971p) 11,804; dairy products; few remains of castle besieged 1509 and destroyed 1641 by Sir Phelim O'Neill.

Oma·ha \ˈō-mə-ˌhȯ, -ˌhä\. City, ⊗ of Douglas co., E Nebraska, on the Missouri river 15 m. N of its confluence with Platte river; pop. (1970c) 346,929; largest city in the state; major livestock and grain market; railroad and insurance center; produces feed, railroad equipment, agricultural machinery, ball bearings, electronic components; oil refineries, packing plants; Offutt Air Force Base, headquarters of U.S.A.F. Strategic Air Command. Creighton Univ. (1878), Univ. of Nebraska at Omaha (1908), Coll. of St. Mary (1923), Grace Bible Institute (1943).

History: Fur trading post estab. in vicinity during War of 1812; Mormon encampment 1846–47; first permanent settlement 1854; capital of Territory of Nebraska 1854–67 and eastern terminus of first transcontinental railroad; incorporated as city 1867.

Omaha Beach. West cen. part of Normandy beaches, NW France, NW of Bayeux and NE of Isigny and on either side of the Vire river at the village of Saint-Laurent-sur-Mer; landing place of part of American army in invasion of France June 6, 1944, and scene of intense fighting.

Omak \ˈō-ˌmak\. City, Okanogan co., N Washington, on Okanogan river; pop. (1970c) 4164; apples.

Omak Lake. Alkaline lake in S Okanogan co., N Washington.

Oman \ō-ˈmän, -ˈman\; *formerly* **Mus·cat and Oman** \ˈməs-ˌkat-, -kət-\ *also* **Mas·qat and Oman** \ˈməs-ˌkat-, -kət-\. Sultanate, SE Arabian Penin., bounded on N by Gulf of Oman, on E and S by the Arabian Sea, on SW by Yemen (✱ Aden), on W by Saudi Arabia, and on NW by Saudi Arabia and the United Arab Emirates; 82,000 sq. m.; pop. (1970e) 750,000; ✱ Masqat. *Physical features:* Mountainous in N, highest peak Jebel Sham, 9927 ft.; to the W borders on the Rub 'al-Khali desert; coastline ab. 1000 m. long; incl. Kuria Muria Is. and a small exclave extending into the Strait of Hormuz. *Chief products:* Oil, dates, cereals, limes; fishing. *Chief towns:* Masqat, Matrah, Sur, Salalah.

History: Ruled by independent dynasty of emirs under Abbasside caliphate at Baghdad; its capital, Masqat, captured and region controlled by Portuguese 1508–c. 1648; recovered by descendant of Yemen's imam 1741; after decline of its importance in 19th cent., became virtual political and economic dependency of British government of India; entered into close ties with Great Britain by treaty of 1939; treaty with Great Britain renewed 1951; rebellion against sultan (1954–57) suppressed with aid of British forces; ceded Gwadar (*q.v.*) to Pakistan 1958; oil in commercial quantities discovered 1964; Kuria Muria Is.

ceded by Great Britain to Oman 1967; ruling sultan deposed by his son 1970.

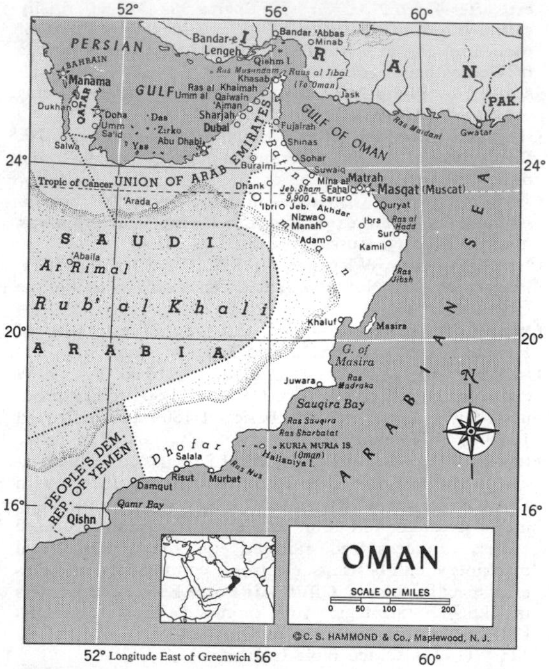

Oman, Gulf of. An arm of the Arabian Sea, extending bet. N Oman, SE Arabian Penin., and the SE coast of Iran; ab. 340 m. long by 230 m. wide at mouth.

Oma·na·go \ˌō-mə-ˈnäg-(ˌ)ō\. Peak in the Nikkō Range, N cen. Honshū, Japan, N of Lake Chuzenji; 7546 ft.

Oma·ru·ru \ˌō-mə-ˈrü-(ˌ)rü\. Town, W cen. South-West Africa, on **Omaruru River** 110 m. NW of Windhoek; pop. (1960c) 2689; railroad outlet for tin mines; dairying.

Oma·te \ō-ˈmät-ē\ *or* **Huai·na–Pu·ti·na** \ˌwī-nə-pü-ˈtē-nə\. Volcano in the Andes Mts. in Peru, SE of Arequipa; many great eruptions, esp. bet. 1582 and 1783; most disastrous eruption 1667.

Ombai. See ALOR.

Om·bai Strait \ˈȯm-ˌbī-\. Strait, extending in a curve bet. Alor I. on N and W, Timor on S, and Wetar I. on E; 17 m. wide; connects Banda Sea with E end of Savu Sea, Lesser Sunda Is., Indonesia.

Ombirah. See OBI ISLANDS.

Om·bro·ne \ȯm-ˈbrō-nē\ *or anc.* **Um·bro** \ˈəm-(ˌ)brō\. River, NW cen. Italy; ab. 100 m. long; flows S and SW through Tuscany and into the N Tyrrhenian Sea 10 m. S of Grosseto.

Om·dur·man \ˌäm-dər-ˈman\ *or Arab.* **Umm Dur·mān** \ˌu̇m-dər-ˈman\. City, NE cen. Sudan, on left bank of White Nile opp. Khartoum; pop. (1969e) 232,200; commercial center, trading in hides, textiles, and livestock; furniture, pottery, leather goods; handicrafts; univ. (1912, univ. status 1965); capital of Mohammed Ahmed 1884; scene of Anglo-Egyptian victory over Mahdi's forces Sept. 2, 1898.

Ōme \ˈō-(ˌ)mā\. City, Tokyo prefecture, Honshū, Japan, 30 m. WNW of Tokyo; pop. (1970c) 70,954.

Ome·gna \ō-ˈmān-yə\. Commune, Novara prov., Piedmont, NW Italy, at N end of Lake Orta 32 m. NNW of Novara; pop. (1970c) 15,459; manufactures textiles; has medieval gate and bridge.

O–mei \ˈō-ˈmā\ *or* **Omi** \ˈō-ˈmē\. Mountain, SW Szechwan, S cen. China, ab. 30 m. W of Lo-shan; 9957 ft.; sacred to Buddhists and formerly visited by many pilgrims. Consists of three peaks, on one of which is a great precipice several thousand feet high; top and pathway to it has many pagodas and temples.

Ome·te·pe \ˌō-mə-ˈtā-pē\. Island in Lake Nicaragua, S Nicaragua; contains the twin volcanoes Concepción and Madera.

Omi. See BIWA.

Omi. See O-MEI.

Omiš \ˈō-mēsh\ *or* **Al·mis·sa** \äl-ˈmē-sə\. Seaport, Bosnia and Herzegovina, W Yugoslavia, SE of Split.

Ōmi·ya \ō-ˈmē-ə, ˈō-mē-ˌä\. City, Saitama prefecture, Honshū, Japan, suburb of Tokyo; pop. (1970c) 268,777.

Om·me \ˈəm-ə\. River, W cen. Jutland, Denmark; flows WNW into Ringkøbing Fjord; ab. 45 m. long.

Omo \ˈō-(ˌ)mō\. River, SW Ethiopia; ab. 400 m. long; flows into N end of Lake Rudolf.

Omo·loi \ˌəm-ə-ˈlȯi\. River, N Yakutsk A.S.S.R., Russian S.F.S.R., U.S.S.R.; ab. 380 m. long; rises in Verkhoyansk Mts. and flows generally N to Buorkhaya Gulf E of the Lena.

Omo·lon \ˌəm-ə-ˈlȯn\. River, NE Khabarovsk Krai, Russian S.F.S.R., U.S.S.R.; 715 m. long; flows from the Kolyma Mountains N through Koryak and Chukot national okrugs into Kolyma river in NE Yakutsk A.S.S.R.

Omo·no \ˈō-mə-ˌnō, ō-ˈmō-(ˌ)nō\. River, N Honshū, Japan; ab. 80 m. long; flows NW into the Sea of Japan near Akita.

Om·pom·pa·noo·suc \(ˌ)äm-ˌpäm-pə-ˈnü-sək\. Small river, E Vermont; enters the Connecticut ab. 17 m. N of White River Junction.

Om·ro \ˈäm-(ˌ)rō\. City, Winnebago co., E cen. Wisconsin, W of Oshkosh; pop. (1970c) 2341.

Omsk \ˈȯm(p)sk, ˈäm(p)sk\. City, ❋ of Omsk Oblast, Russian S.F.S.R., U.S.S.R., in S part at confluence of Irtysh and Om rivers 480 m. E of Chelyabinsk; pop. (1970p) 821,000; major industrial center, producing agricultural machinery, textiles, footwear; flour mills, packing plants, sawmills and pulp mills, oil refineries and petrochemical plants; founded 1716; became town 1804; headquarters of Siberian Cossacks until late 19th cent.

Omsk Oblast \-ˈō-bləst, -ˌblast\. Subdivision of the Russian S.F.S.R., U.S.S.R.; 53,861 sq. m.; pop. (1970p) 1,824,000; ❋ Omsk. Lies in basin of middle Irtysh river; cereals, fodder crops, flax, sunflowers; livestock; crossed in cen. part by two trunk railroad lines; only major town Omsk. First part of Asia to be penetrated by Russians; developed rapidly from late 19th cent.; created an oblast of Russian S.F.S.R. 1934.

Omu·ra \ˈō-mə-ˌrä, ō-ˈmu̇(ə)r-ə\. Town, Nagasaki prefecture, NW Kyūshū, Japan, on **Omura Bay** (inlet of East China Sea) 12 m. NNE of Nagasaki; pop. (1970c) 56,538.

Omu·ram·ba Oma·ta·ko \ˌō-mə-ˈram-bə-ˌō-mə-ˈtäk-(ˌ)ō\. Riverbed, NE South-West Africa; extends from mountains in N cen. part NE to the Okavango river; dry through most of its lower course.

Omu·ta \ˈō-mə-ˌtä, ō-ˈmüt-ə\. City, Fukuoka prefecture, NW Kyūshū, Japan, on Shimabara Bay 22 m. NW of Kumamoto; pop. (1970c) 175,143; coal-mining center; zinc, alloy steel, brick, textiles, chemicals; heavily bombed 1944–45.

On. See HELIOPOLIS 1.

On·a·las·ka \ˌän-ə-ˈlas-kə\. City, La Crosse co., W Wisconsin, 5 m. N of La Crosse; pop. (1970c) 4909.

On·a·wa \ˈän-ə-ˌwä, -wə\. City, ⊗ of Monona co., W Iowa, 36 m. SSE of Sioux City; pop. (1970c) 3154; livestock and poultry farms.

On·a·way \ˈän-ə-ˌwā\. City, Presque Isle co., NE Michigan, 23 m. SSE of Cheboygan; pop. (1970c) 1262; tourist resort; Onaway State Park to the N.

On·do \ˈän-(ˌ)dō\. Town, Western State, Nigeria, 105 m. NE of Lagos; pop. (1969e) 86,215.

One·co \ō-ˈnē-ˌkō\. Urban community (unincorporated), Manatee co., Florida, SE of Bradenton; pop. (1970c) 3426.

One·ga \ō-ˈneg-ə\. 1 Bay at SW end of the White Sea extending into the coast of NW Russian S.F.S.R., U.S.S.R.; receives Onega river.

2 Lake, second in size in Europe, in S Karelian A.S.S.R., Russian S.F.S.R., U.S.S.R.; 3710 sq. m.; 145 m. long by 50 m. wide; max. depth 328 ft. Its S shore and the canal along it from the Svir to the Vytegra (see VOLGA-BALTIC WATERWAY) lie in Vologda Oblast. Its outlet is the Svir, flowing from SW corner to Lake Ladoga; main affluents Vodla, Vytegra, and Andoma, on the E; has numerous long arms or inlets and many islands along its N shore; frozen over ab. one half the year; has fisheries; timber is cut near its shores. Petrozavodsk is only large town on its shores (on W).

3 River, W part of Arkhangelsk Oblast, Russian S.F.S.R., U.S.S.R.; ab. 250 m. long; flows from Lakes Vozhe and Lacha N to Onega Bay; navigable for ab. 100 m.

4 Town at head of the bay and on right bank of Onega river at its mouth, W Arkhangelsk Oblast, 90 m. S of Arkhangelsk; chief industry lumber. Settled in 15th cent.

One·hunga \ˌōn-ə-ˈhüŋ-ə\. Borough, N North I., New Zealand, S suburb of Auckland on Manukau Harbor; pop. (1970e) 15,800.

Onei·da \ō-ˈnīd-ə\. 1 River, cen. New York; 16 m. long; flows from Oneida Lake, forming section of boundary bet. Onondaga and Oswego cos.; joins Seneca river to form Oswego river.

2 Name of counties in three states of the U.S. See tables at IDAHO, NEW YORK, WISCONSIN.

3 City, Madison co., cen. New York, 5 m. SE of Oneida Lake 13 m. WSW of Rome; pop. (1970c) 11,677; silverware, wood and paper products, cigars; founded 1829; 1848 ff. site of Utopian community, reorganized 1880 as business corporation.

4 Town, Scott co., N Tennessee, 46 m. NW of Knoxville; pop. (1970c) 2602; lumbering; diversified agriculture; coal mines.

Oneida Lake. Lake in cen. New York, bounded by Oswego, Oneida, Madison, and Onondaga cos.; 80 sq. m.; ab. 22 m. long and 6 m. wide at its greatest extent; part of N.Y. State Barge Canal system.

O'·Neill \ō-ˈnē(ə)l\. City, ⊗ of Holt co., N Nebraska, on Elkhorn river 74 m. WNW of Norfolk; pop. (1970c) 3753; dairy products; ships hogs.

On·e·ko·tan \ˌän-ə-kə-ˈtän, ˌōn-\. One of the Kuril Is. (*q.v.*), SW of Paramushir.

One·on·ta \ˌō-nē-ˈänt-ə\. 1 City, ⊗ of Blount co., N cen. Alabama; pop. (1970c) 4390; clothing, aluminum ware; truck farms.

2 City, Otsego co., cen. New York, on Susquehanna river 45 m. S of Utica; pop. (1970c) 16,030; clothing, lumber; hay and potatoes; railroad shops; State Univ. of New York Coll. at Oneonta (1889), Hartwick Coll. (1928).

One Tree Hill \ˈwən-ˌtrē-\. Borough, N North I., New Zealand, suburb of Auckland; pop. (1970e) 12,900.

Oni·da \ō-ˈnīd-ə\. City, ⊗ of Sully co., cen. South Dakota; pop. (1970c) 785.

Onion. See WINOOSKI 1.

Onit·sha \ō-ˈnich-ə\. Town, East-Central State, Nigeria, on Niger river ab. 135 m. from its mouth; pop. (1969e) 189,067; commercial and market center; ships palm products.

Ono·mi·chi \ˌō-nə-ˈmē-chē\. Industrial city on the Inland Sea, Hiroshima prefecture, SW Honshū, Japan, 45 m. W of Okayama; pop. (1970c) 101,363; several notable Buddhist temples.

Onon \ˈō-ˌnän\. River, NE Mongolian People's Republic and SW Chita Oblast, Russian S.F.S.R., U.S.S.R.; 592 m. long; flows NE to unite with Ingoda river and form the Shilka river.

On·on·da·ga \ˌän-ən-ˈdäg-ə\. County in New York. See table at NEW YORK.

Onondaga, Lake. Lake, Onondaga co., cen. New York; 5 m. long by 1 m. wide.

Ons·low \ˈänz-lō\. County in North Carolina. See table at NORTH CAROLINA.

Onslow Bay. Bay off SE coast of North Carolina bet. Cape Lookout and Cape Fear.

On·ta·ke \ōn-ˈtäk-ē\. Peak, E border of Gifu prefecture, cen. Honshū, Japan; 10,049 ft.; second to Fuji only as the most sacred peak in Japan; climbed by thousands of pilgrims every summer.

On–ta·ke \ōn-ˈtäk-ē\ *or* **Sa·ku·ra·ji·ma** \sä-ˌkür-ə-ˈjē-mə\. Volcano on a peninsula (formerly an island) in Kagoshima Bay, S Kyūshū, Japan; 3668 ft.; had destructive eruption in 1914.

On·tar·io \än-ˈter-ē-ˌō, -ˈtar-\. 1 County in New York. See table at NEW YORK.

2 Residential and industrial city, San Bernardino co., SE California, 20 m. W of San Bernardino; pop. (1970c) 64,118; aircraft and aircraft parts, wine, tile, plastics, electrical equipment; settled 1882, incorporated as city 1891.

3 Town, Wayne co., W New York, ab. 17 m. NE of Rochester; pop. (1970c) 6014.

4 Village, Richland co., N cen. Ohio, 8 m. W of Mansfield; pop. (1970c) 4345.

5 City, Malheur co., E Oregon, on Snake river just S of its confluence with Malheur river; pop. (1970c) 6523; diversified agriculture; Treasure Valley Community Coll. (1962).

6 Province, Canada, bounded on N by Hudson Bay and James Bay, on E by Quebec prov., on S by U.S., and on W by Manitoba prov.; 412,582 sq. m. (incl. 68,490 sq. m. of water); pop. (1970e) 7,637,000, (1968e) 6,904,730; ✱ Toronto. *Physical features:* Southeast part is large peninsula bet. Ottawa river on NE and St. Lawrence river and Lakes Ontario and Erie on S, Lake Huron and Georgian Bay on W. Largely a level region with generally fertile soils; highest point Ogidaki Mountain 2183 ft. Largest lakes of N and W part Lakes Nipigon, Eagle, Seul, St. Joseph, Rainy, and Abitibi; Lake of the Woods belongs in part to U.S.; in SE part Lakes Nipissing, Simcoe, Muskoka, and Kawartha chain are most important. Bordered on SE by Ottawa and St. Lawrence rivers; in most populated (SE) part chief rivers the Thames, Grand, Rideau, and Trent, and N of Lakes Huron and Superior are Moose, Albany, Attawapiskat, English, and Severn; three national parks, ab. 100 provincial parks. *Chief products:* Wheat, barley, sugar beet, tobacco, timber; livestock; nickel, gold, copper, iron ore, cobalt, salt; manufacturing: iron and steel, petroleum products, motor vehicles, aircraft, electrical equipment; food processing. *Chief cities:* Toronto, Hamilton, Ottawa, London, Windsor. Divided into the following 42 counties, 11 districts, and 1 municipal region (for pronunciation of their names, see their individual entries):

NAME	LOCATION	AREA[1] (sq. m.)	POP.[2] (1968e)	CO. SEAT
Algoma Dist.	S	19,320	103,292	Sault Sainte Marie
Brant	SE	421	88,032	Brantford
Bruce	SE	1,650	41,307	Paisley
Cochrane Dist.	E	52,237	77,963	Cochrane
Dufferin	SE	557	18,401	Orangeville
Dundas	SE	384	93,043	Cornwall[3]
Durham	SE	629	89,145	Cobourg[4]
Elgin	SE	720	59,543	Saint Thomas
Essex	SE	707	284,021	Windsor
Frontenac	SE	1,599	89,047	Kingston
Glengarry	SE	478		Cornwall[3]
Grenville	SE	463	71,570	Brockville[5]
Grey	SE	1,708	63,001	Owen Sound
Haldimand	SE	488	29,631	Cayuga
Haliburton[6]	SE	1,486	8,377	Minden
Halton	SE	363	168,786	Milton
Hastings	SE	2,323	88,301	Belleville
Huron	SE	1,295	50,010	Goderich
Kenora Dist.	W	153,220	32,290	Kenora
Kent	SE	918	95,306	Chatham
Lambton	SE	1,124	107,878	Sarnia
Lanark	SE	1,138	38,682	Perth
Leeds	SE	900		Brockville

NAME	LOCATION	AREA[1] (sq. m.)	POP. (1968e)	CO. SEAT
Lennox and Addington	SE	1,170	25,327	Napanee
Lincoln	SE	332	150,793	St. Catharines
Manitoulin Dist.	S	1,588	6,831	Gore Bay
Middlesex	SE	1,240	256,849	London
Muskoka Dist.	SE	1,585	25,703	Bracebridge
Nipissing Dist.	SE	7,560	67,999	North Bay
Norfolk	SE	634	52,058	Simcoe
Northumberland	SE	734		Cobourg
Ontario	SE	853	176,443	Whitby
Ottawa-Carleton[8]	SE	947	426,550	Ottawa
Oxford	SE	765	76,370	Woodstock
Parry Sound Dist.	SE	4,336	22,734	Parry Sound
Peel	SE	469	209,887	Brampton
Perth	SE	840	60,656	Stratford
Peterborough	SE	1,415	80,520	Peterborough
Prescott	SE	494	42,417	L'Orignal
Prince Edward	SE	390	19,543	Picton
Rainy River Dist.	SW corner	7,276	21,793	Fort Frances
Renfrew	SE	3,009	76,255	Pembroke
Russell	SE	407		L'Orignal[7]
Simcoe	SE	1,663	140,866	Barrie
Stormont	SE	412		Cornwall
Sudbury Dist.	SE	18,058	161,044	Sudbury
Thunder Bay Dist.	SW	52,471	130,287	Thunder Bay
Timiskaming Dist.	SE	5,896	40,132	Haileybury
Victoria	SE	1,348	30,683	Lindsay
Waterloo	SE	516	228,299	Kitchener
Welland	SE	387	180,650	Welland
Wellington	SE	1,019	97,755	Guelph
Wentworth	SE	458	379,277	Hamilton
York	SE	882	2,019,383	Toronto

[1]Area = land area.

[2]Several counties are united for municipal and judicial purposes:

a) Dundas, Glengarry, and Stormont.
The population given for Dundas represents the total population of the three cos.

b) Durham and Northumberland.
The population given for Durham represents the total population of the two cos.

c) Grenville and Leeds.
The population given for Grenville represents the total population of the two cos.

d) Prescott and Russell.
The population given for Prescott represents the total population of the two cos.

[3]In Stormont co.

[4]In Northumberland co.

[5]In Leeds co.

[6]A provisional county, annexed to Victoria co. for judicial purposes.

[7]In Prescott co.

[8]Municipal region.

History: In 17th cent. visited by French explorers (first by Champlain 1615) and missionaries; scene of many wars bet. French and Iroquois; passed to British 1763; in 1774 became part of province of Quebec (*q.v.* for further details); received many loyalist settlers from U.S. during American Revolution; present S boundary established 1783; at division of Quebec prov. 1791 became known as Upper Canada; scene of many battles of War of 1812; scene of unsuccessful uprising 1837; reunited with Lower Canada 1841; as Ontario became one of four provinces of the new Dominion of Canada 1867.

7 County, Ontario, Canada. See table at ONTARIO.

Ontario, Lake *or early Fr. name* **Lac Fron·te·nac** \låk-frōⁿt-nåk\. Lake, easternmost and smallest of the Great Lakes (*q.v.*), U.S. and Canada; bounded on E and S by New York, and on S, W, and N by Canadian province of Ontario; 193 m. long; area 7600 sq. m.; greatest depth 778 ft.; elevation 245 ft.; the U.S.-Canada boundary passes through the lake; connected on SW by Niagara river and Welland Ship Canal with Lake Erie; outlet on NE St. Lawrence river. See OSWEGO CANAL.

On·te·nien·te \ˌȯn-tā-ˈnyen-(ˌ)tā\. Commune, Valencia prov., E Spain, 48 m. SSW of Valencia; pop. (1970p) 23,-685.

On·to·na·gon \ˌän-tə-ˈnȯg-ən, -ˈnäg-\. 1 County in NW Michigan penin. See table at MICHIGAN.

2 Village, its ⊗, on Lake Superior 50 m. ENE of Ironwood; pop. (1970c) 2432; resort.

On·tong Ja·va \ˌän-tȯŋ-ˈjäv-ə, -ˈjav-\ *or formerly* **Lord Howe Islands** \-ˈhau̇-\. Island group comprising a coral atoll and several islets in the Solomon Is., W Pacific Ocean, 160 m. NE of Santa Isabel, 5°20′S, 159°30′E; part of British Solomon Islands protectorate.

Oodeypore. See UDAIPUR.

O'o·kiep \ō-ˈkēp\. Village, NW Cape Province, S Rep. of South Africa, connected by rail with Port Nolloth; center of rich copper mines.

Oo·len \ˈō-lə(n)\. Town, Antwerp prov., N Belgium, near Turnhout; pop. (1969e) 7947; radium extraction.

Oos–Londen. See EAST LONDON.

Oos·ta·nau·la \ˌü-stə-ˈnȯ-lə\. Navigable river, NW Georgia; formed by confluence of Conasauga and Coosawattee rivers in NW extremity of Georgia, flows S to unite with the Etowah near Rome and form the Coosa river.

Oost·en·de \ō-ˈsten-də\ *or Fr.* **Os·tende** \ȯ-stäⁿd\ *or Eng.* **Ost·end** \ä-ˈstend, ˈäs-ˌtend\. Commune, seaport, and seaside resort, West Flanders prov., NW Belgium; pop. (1969e) 56,954; leading fishing port of Belgium; lobster and oyster beds; shipbuilding; soap, tobacco. Dates from 9th cent.; developed as resort 1830 ff.; occupied by the Germans 1914 and used as submarine base; raided by British naval force May 1918 which succeeded in temporarily blocking the harbor by sinking vessels loaded with concrete across its mouth; in World War II captured by Canadians Sept. 6, 1944.

Oos·ter·hout \ˈō-stər-ˌhau̇t\. Commune, North Brabant prov., S Netherlands, just NE of Breda; pop. (1970e) 31,-826; textiles.

Oost·stel·ling·werf \ˌōst-ˌstel-iŋ-ˈve(ə)rf\. Commune, Friesland prov., N Netherlands, W of Assen; pop. (1970e) 19,-531.

Oo·ta·ca·mund *also* **Uta·ka·mand** \ˈüt-ə-kə-ˌmənd\. Town and hill station, S Tamil Nadu, S India, 280 m. WSW of Madras; on plateau (ab. 7000 ft. above sea level); pop. (1961c) 50,140; health resort.

Opa–Locka \ˌō-pə-ˈläk-ə\. City, Dade co., SE Florida, NW of Miami; pop. (1970c) 11,902; Biscayne Coll. (1962).

Opa·va \ˈȯ-pə-və\. 1 *or Ger.* **Op·pa** \ˈȯp-ə\. River, Czech S.R., Czechoslovakia; 70 m. long; flows into Oder river at Ostrava.

2 *or Ger.* **Trop·pau** \ˈtrȯp-ˌau̇\. City, Czech S.R., cen. Czechoslovakia, on a tributary of the Oder on the Polish border ab. 15 m. WNW of Ostrava; pop. (1968e) 47,334; textiles, lumber, pharmaceuticals; 15th cent. cathedral; scene of Congress of Troppau, Oct. 1820, when Russia, Prussia, and Austria adopted principle of armed intervention to suppress European liberal movements, Great Britain dissenting.

Ope·li·ka \ˌō-pə-ˈlī-kə\. City, ⊗ of Lee co., E Alabama, 57 m. ENE of Montgomery; pop. (1970c) 19,027; lumber, textiles, fertilizer, tires; dairy farms; settled c. 1840.

Op·e·lou·sas \ˌäp-ə-ˈlü-səs\. City, ⊗ of St. Landry parish, S cen. Louisiana, 22 m. N of Lafayette; pop. (1970c) 20,387; sawmills, meat-packing plants, cottonseed oil mills; diversified agriculture; became capital of the state 1862 for a short time after Union forces occupied Baton Rouge.

Opeq·uon \ō-ˈpek-ən\. Village and creek, Frederick co., N Virginia, just E of Winchester; scene of Union victory Sept. 19, 1864, more often known as the battle of Winchester. See WINCHESTER 8.

Ophir \ˈō-fər\. Ancient country of unknown location, perhaps in Arabian Penin.; rich in gold (*1 Kings* ix. 27, 28).

Ophir, Mount. 1 *or Malay* **Gu·nong Le·dang** \ˈgü-ˌnȯŋ-ˈlā-ˌdäŋ\. Mountain, NW Johore state, W Malaysia, near Malacca border; 4186 ft.; highest peak in state.

2 Peak, Sumatra, Indonesia. See TALAKMAU, MOUNT.

Ophiusa. See FORMENTERA.

Opin·a·ca *or* **Opin·a·ka** \ō-ˈpin-ə-ˌkō\. River, W and cen. Quebec, Canada; ab. 280 m. long; main tributary of the Eastmain river, entering it from the N a few miles above its mouth.

Opis \ˈō-pəs\. Ruins of ancient Assyrian city on W bank of the Tigris, E Iraq, ab. 43 m. N of Baghdad; scene of battle 539 B.C. in which Cyrus defeated the Babylonians.

Opitergium. See ODERZO.

Op·la·den \ˈȯp-ˌläd-ᵊn\. Manufacturing city, North Rhine-Westphalia, West Germany, on Wupper river just S of

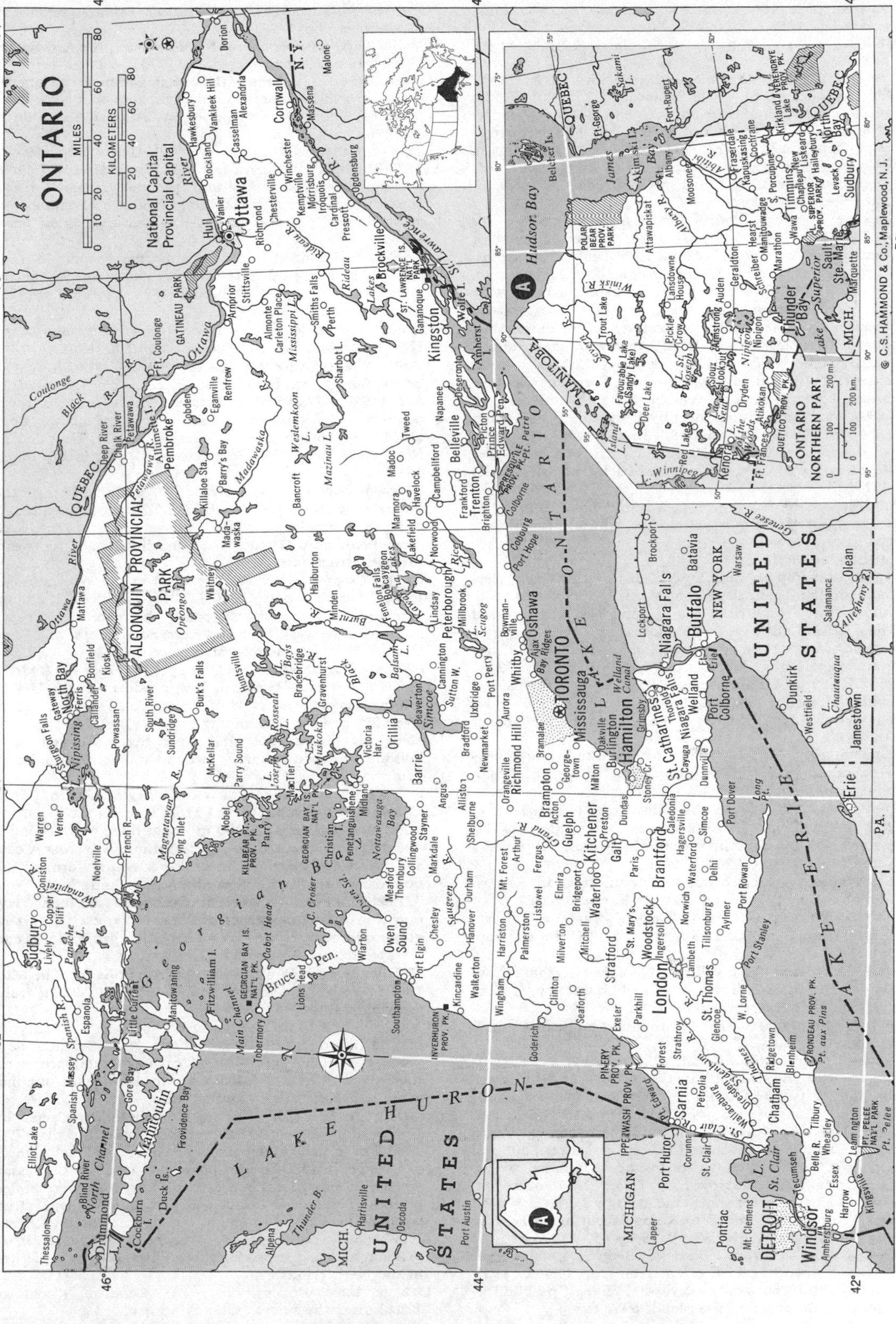

ONTARIO
MILES
KILOMETERS
National Capital
Provincial Capital
Ottawa
Hull
Vanier
Cornwall
Kingston
Brockville
Pembroke
ALGONQUIN PROVINCIAL PARK
GATINEAU PARK
North Bay
Sudbury
L. Nipissing
Manitoulin I.
Georgian Bay
Bruce Pen.
Owen Sound
Barrie
Orillia
L. Simcoe
TORONTO
Mississauga
Hamilton
Brampton
Oshawa
Peterborough
Belleville
Trenton
Kitchener
Waterloo
Guelph
Brantford
Stratford
London
St. Thomas
Woodstock
St. Catharines
Niagara Falls
Welland
Sarnia
Chatham
Windsor
DETROIT
Buffalo
LAKE HURON
LAKE ONTARIO
LAKE ERIE
L. St. Clair
UNITED STATES
QUEBEC
N.Y.
MICH.
PA.
NEW YORK
St. Lawrence R.
Ottawa River
ST. LAWRENCE IS. NAT'L PARK
GEORGIAN BAY IS. NAT'L PK.
PT. PELEE NAT'L PARK
Longitude West of Greenwich
A
Hudson Bay
James Bay
MANITOBA
ONTARIO NORTHERN PART
POLAR BEAR PROV. PARK
QUETICO PROV. PK.
Thunder Bay
Lake Superior
Sault Ste. Marie
Timmins
Kenora
L. of the Woods
L. Nipigon
© C.S. HAMMOND & Co., Maplewood, N.J.

Solingen; pop. (1969e) 43,218; chemicals; metalworking; became city 1858.

Opo·le \ó-'pȯl-ə\. 1 Province of S Poland. See table at POLAND.

2 *or Ger.* **Op·peln** \'ȯp-əln\. Industrial city, its ✱, on the Oder river 52 m. SE of Wrocław; pop. (1970p) 86,500; railroad junction and river port; cement; cast iron foundry; 14th cent. church. Capital of independent Piast principality of Oppeln 1202–1327; to Bohemia 1327 and Prussia 1742; in World War II occupied by U.S.S.R. Jan. 1945; assigned to Poland by Potsdam Conference 1945.

Opon. See LAPU-LAPU.

Opor·to \ō-'pōrt-(,)ō, -'pȯrt-\ *or Port.* **Pôr·to** \'pōr-tü\ *or anc.* **Por·tus Ca·le** \,pōrt-əs-'kā-lē\. Seaport city, ✱ of Pôrto dist., NW Portugal, on the right bank of the Douro river 2 m. from its mouth and 170 m. NE of Lisbon; pop. (1970p) 310,437; its harbor is at Leixões; exports wine (port wine, named after the city), fruit, cork, olives; produces tires, chemicals, electrical equipment, automobile parts, textiles, leather goods, silk, footwear, soap, canned goods; fishing, fish canning; restored 12th–14th cent. cathedral, 12th cent. church, 18th cent. Torre dos Clérigos, episcopal palace, and other notable buildings; univ. (1911).

History: Roman town; held by Visigoths 540–716 and by Moors 716–997; capital of N Portugal to 1174; established port wine trade 1678; scene of British victory over French under Soult May 12, 1809; besieged in civil conflict 1832–33.

Opp \'äp\. City, Covington co., S Alabama, 50 m. W of Dothan; pop. (1970c) 6493; lumber; cotton, peanuts.

Oppa. See OPAVA 1.

Oppeln. See OPOLE 2.

Op·pen·heim \'äp-ən-,hīm, 'ȯp-\. Town, Hesse, West Germany, on the Rhine 20 m. S of Mainz; pop. (1970e) 5500; wine industry. In World War II American army crossed Rhine here in advance on Frankfurt.

Op·pi·do Ma·mer·ti·na \'ȯp-ə-,dō-,mäm-ər-'tēn-ə\. Commune, Reggio di Calabria prov., Calabria, S Italy, 22 m. NE of Reggio di Calabria; pop. (1968e) 8600; episcopal see.

Oppidum Ubiorum. See COLOGNE.

Opp·land \'ȯp-,län\. County of S cen. Norway. See table at NORWAY.

Op·por·tu·ni·ty \,äp-ər-'t(y)ü-nət-ē\. Urban community (unincorporated), Spokane co., E Washington, E of Spokane; pop. (1970c) 16,604.

Op·py \ó-'pē\. Village, Pas-de-Calais dept., N France, 6 m. NE of Albert; pop. (1962c) 266; scene of fighting 1917–18.

Op·ster·land \'ȯp-stər-,länt\. Commune, Friesland prov., N Netherlands; pop. (1970e) 21,951.

Opus \'ō-pəs\. Ancient town, ✱ of Locris Opuntia (Eastern Locris), E cen. Greece, on coast of Euboean Sea.

Oqair \ō-'kīr, -'ka(ə)r\ *or* **Al-'Uqayr** \,al-ü-'kīr, -'ka(ə)r\. Coastal town, E Nejd, Saudi Arabia, NE of Hofuf and opp. Qatar.

Oquaw·ka \ō-'kwȯ-kə\. Village, ⊗ of Henderson co., W Illinois, on Mississippi river W of Galesburg; pop. (1970c) 1352; summer resort; melons.

Oquirrh Mountains \,o-kər-\. Mountain range in Utah, S of Great Salt Lake.

Ora·dea \ó-'räd-(,)yä\ *or* **Oradea Ma·re** \-'mär-ə\ *or Hung.* **Nagy·vá·rad** \'näj-,vär-äd\ *or Ger.* **Gross·war·dein** \,grōs-vär-'dīn\. City, ⊗ of Bihor co., NW Romania, on Körös river near Hungarian border; pop. (1970e) 137,662; machine tools, chemicals, mining equipment, canned foods; Greek Catholic and Roman Catholic cathedrals; cultural center. A very old town; its bishopric founded by St. Ladislas in 1080; destroyed by Tatars 1241; passed to Transylvania 1556 for short time, held by Turks 1660–92; after World War I ceded to Romania but again held by Hungary during World War II 1940–45.

Ora·dell \'ōr-ə-,del, 'ȯr-\. Borough, Bergen co., NE corner of New Jersey, 8 m. ENE of Paterson; pop. (1970c) 8903.

Örae·fa·jö·kull \'ər-,ī-və-'yər-,kyüt-l^{ə}\. Highest peak in Iceland, near SE coast of the island; 6952 ft.

Orai \ō-'rī\. Town, SW Uttar Pradesh, N India, 65 m. SW of Kanpur; pop. (1961c) 29,587.

Orai·bi \ō-'rī-bē\. Hopi pueblo, Navajo co., NE Arizona, in Hopi Indian Reservation; pop. (1970c) 600; on top of a mesa (alt. 6070 ft.), one of the oldest, and once the largest, of Hopi towns; a Spanish Franciscan mission in 17th cent.

Oran \ó-'rän\. 1 Department of NW Algeria. See table at ALGERIA.

2 Seaport city, its ✱, 210 m. WSW of Algiers; pop. (1966c) 325,481; ships wine, cereals, fruit and vegetables; produces beverages, textiles, agricultural machinery, glass, carpets, cigarettes; distilling, shipbuilding, food processing; distinguished by a great variety of architectural styles; univ. (1965).

History: Founded 10th cent.; important seaport 15–16th cent.; held by Spanish 1509–1708; devastated by earthquake 1790; occupied by French 1831; captured by U.S. forces Nov. 10, 1942.

Or·ange \'ȯr-inj, 'är-, -ənj\. 1 Counties in eight states of the U.S. See tables at CALIFORNIA, FLORIDA, INDIANA, NEW YORK, NORTH CAROLINA, TEXAS, VERMONT, VIRGINIA.

2 City, Orange co., SW California, 22 m. E of Long Beach; pop. (1970c) 77,365; ships nuts and citrus fruit; electronic components, copper wire, hose and pipe; Chapman Coll. (1861), St. Joseph Coll. of Orange (1933). Founded as **Rich·land** \'rich-lənd\ 1868; renamed 1875; incorporated 1888.

3 Town, SW New Haven co., S Connecticut, E of the Housatonic river; pop. (1970c) 13,524; market center.

4 Town, Franklin co., NW Massachusetts, 14 m. E of Greenfield; pop. (1970c) 6104; machine tools, footwear, turbines; truck farms.

5 City, Essex co., NE New Jersey, 4 m. WNW of and adjoining Newark; pop. (1970c) 32,566; residential; adding machines, clothing, aircraft parts, pharmaceuticals; separated from Newark 1806 and from East, South, and West Orange 1861–63; incorporated as city 1872.

6 Village, Cuyahoga co., N Ohio; pop. (1970c) 2112; birthplace of James A. Garfield, 20th president of the U.S.

7 City and port of entry, ⊗ of Orange co., Texas, on Sabine river 22 m. E of Beaumont; pop. (1970c) 24,459; steel, chemicals, lumber, pulp and paper; rice processing, shipbuilding, seafood canning; gas and oil wells; founded c. 1800.

8 Town, ⊗ of Orange co., N cen. Virginia, 27 m. NE of Charlottesville; pop. (1970c) 2768; dairy farms.

9 River, S Africa; ab. 1300 m. long; flows W, forming S boundary of Orange Free State; continues W across N cen. and NW Cape Province, in its lower course forming the boundary bet. Rep. of South Africa and South-West Africa; empties into Atlantic Ocean at Alexander Bay; numerous dams constructed along its course as part of major hydroelectric power and irrigation project for N and E Cape Province.

10 Town, E New South Wales, SE Australia, in Blue Mts. 130 m. WNW of Sydney; pop. (1968e) 21,970; in fruit-growing district.

Orange \ó-'rä^{n}zh\ *or anc.* **Arau·sio** \ə-'rȯ-zhē-,ō\. City, ✱ of Vaucluse dept., SE France, 17 m. N of Avignon; pop. (1968e) 24,562; vegetable and cattle market; preserves; tourist resort; extensive Roman ruins include a triumphal arch, a theater, and an amphitheater.

History: Scene of defeat of Romans under Caepio by Cimbri and Teutons 105 B.C.; episcopal see 3d cent.–1790; capital of former principality; gave name to Dutch princes of Orange; in 1530 became possession of house of Nassau whence it passed to house of princes who were styled princes of Orange-Nassau, and of whom William, afterward William III of England, was one; acquired by Louis XIV 1660; title continued to be held by the cousin of William and his descendants, who are now the royal line of the Netherlands.

Orange, Cape \-'ȯr-inj, -'är-, -ənj\. Cape on N coast of Brazil, near the French Guiana border.

Orange Bay. Bay on W end of island of Jamaica, West Indies.

Or·ange·burg \'ȯr-inj-ˌbərg, 'är-, -ənj-\. 1 County in S cen. South Carolina. See table at SOUTH CAROLINA.

2 City, its ⊗, 35 m. SSE of Columbia; pop. (1970c) 13,352; textiles, lumber, fertilizer; meat-packing plants; hogs and sweet potatoes; Claflin Univ. (1869), South Carolina State Coll. (1896).

Orange City. City, ⊗ of Sioux co., NW Iowa, 38 m. NNE of Sioux City; pop. (1970c) 3572; paint, ammunition; dairy and poultry farms.

Orange Cove. City, Fresno co., S cen. California, 27 m. SE of Fresno; pop. (1970c) 3392; fruit packing; diversified agriculture.

Orange Free State *or Afrikaans* **Oran·je Vry·staat** \ō-ˌrän-yə-'frā-ə-ˌstät, -'frī-\. Province, E cen. Rep. of South Africa, bounded on N by Transvaal, on E by Natal, on SE by Lesotho, and on S and W by Cape Province; 49,866 sq. m.; pop. (1967e) 1,661,756; ✱ Bloemfontein; forms part of inner plateau of South Africa; 4000–5000 ft. above sea level, with higher W slopes of Drakensberg Mts. along E border. Traversed along S border by Orange river, along N by the Vaal and separated for most part from Lesotho by Caledon river; crossed by tributaries of the Vaal river (Modder, Riet, Vet), flowing generally W. Wide plains afford excellent grazing; chief industry stock raising; chief agricultural products grains and fruits; gold. Chief towns Bloemfontein, Welkom, Kroonstad, Ladybrand, Bethlehem, and Ficksburg.

History: Region N of Orange river first visited by Europeans toward end of 18th cent.; a few settlements made bet. 1810–20 but occupancy began 1836 with great trek of Boers; conflicts with Zulus 1837; annexed by British 1848 but sovereignty withdrawn and independence of Boer state recognized 1854; constitution framed by Boers 1854 and country named Orange Free State; strife with Basutos ended 1869 and friendly relations established with Transvaal 1870–99; joined Transvaal in Boer War 1899–1902; overcome by British and annexed to British dominions as **Orange River Colony** May 28, 1900; granted responsible government 1907; joined Union (now Republic) of South Africa 1910. See HEILBRON.

Orange Lake. Lake, SE corner of Alachua co., N Florida penin.; ab. 14 m. long.

Orange Park. Town, Clay co., NE Florida; pop. (1970c) 7619.

Orange Range. See DJAJAWIDJAJA RANGE.

Orange River. See ORANGE 9.

Orange River Colony. See ORANGE FREE STATE.

Orange Town. Town, Saint Eustatius I., West Indies.

Or·ange·ville \'ȯr-inj-ˌvil, 'är-, -ənj-\. Industrial town, ⊗ of Dufferin co., SE Ontario, Canada, 43 m. WNW of Toronto; pop. (1971p) 8030; livestock, poultry.

Orange Walk. 1 District, NW British Honduras; 1829 sq. m.; pop. (1967e) 13,276.

2 Town, its ✱; pop. (1970p) 5413.

Oran·go \u̇-'ra(ⁿ)ŋ-ˌgü\. See BIJAGÓS, ARQUIPÉLAGO DOS.

Oranienbaum *or* **Oraniyenbaum.** See LOMONOSOV.

Ora·ni·en·burg \ō-'rän-ē-ən-ˌbu̇(ə)rg\. City, Potsdam dist., East Germany, on Havel river 19 m. NNW of East Berlin; pop. (1970e) 20,442; chemicals, steel products. Mentioned in 12th cent. under name of Bötzow; in World War II site of concentration camp.

Oran·je \ō-'rän-yə\. Peak, SE Surinam; 2428 ft.

Oranje Gebergte. See DJAJAWIDJAJA RANGE.

Oran·je·stad \ō-'rän-yə-ˌstät\. Chief town, Aruba I., Netherlands Antilles, on W coast; pop. (1965e) 14,720; oil refineries.

Oranje Vrystaat. See ORANGE FREE STATE.

Oras \ȯ-'räs\. Municipality, Samar Oriental prov., Phil., 45 m. NE of Catbalogan; pop. (1969e) 27,700; has fair harbor on **Oras Bay,** on Pacific coast.

Ora·va \'ȯr-ə-və\ *or Pol.* **Ora·wa** \ȯ-'räv-ə\. District, former county in Hungary (*Hung.* **Ar·va** \'är-(ˌ)vȯ\); divided 1920 bet. Poland and Czechoslovakia; now mostly in Czechoslovakia.

Ora·vi·ţa \ȯ-'räv-ət-ˌsä\ *or Ger.* **Ora·wi·tza** \ō-'räv-\. City, Caraş-Severin co., SW Romania, near Yugoslav border NE of Belgrade; pop. (1966c) 12,879.

Or·be·tel·lo \ˌȯr-bə-'tel-(ˌ)ō\. Commune, Grosseto prov., Tuscany, cen. Italy, on Tyrrhenian Sea 23 m. S of Grosseto; pop. (1968e) 13,624; Etruscan ruins; cathedral.

Ór·bi·go \ȯr-'bē-(ˌ)gō\. River, NW Spain; 67 m. long; rises in N León prov., flows S into Esla river.

Orcadas del Sur. See SOUTH ORKNEY ISLANDS.

Orcades. See ORKNEY ISLANDS.

Or·cas Island \'ȯr-kəs-\. See SAN JUAN ISLANDS.

Or·chard Park \ˌȯr-chərd-\. Village and resort, Erie co., W New York, 10 m. SSE of Buffalo; pop. (1970c) 3732.

Orch·ha \'ȯr-chə\ *or* **Or·cha** \'ȯr-chə\. Former Indian state, now part of Madhya Pradesh, India; 1999 sq. m.; ✱ Tikamgarh.

Or·chi·lla \ȯr-'chē-(y)ə\ *or* **Or·chi·la** \-'chē-lə\. Venezuelan island, Caribbean Sea N of N cen. Venezuela, 80 m. NW of La Tortuga; ab. 8 m. long.

Or·chom·e·nus \ȯr-'käm-ə-nəs\. 1 Ancient town, E Arcadia, cen. Peloponnesus, S Greece, ab. 9 m. NNW of Mantinea.

2 City in NW Boeotia, ancient Greece, now an archaeological site 7 m. NE of Lebadea on N bank of the Cephisus. A city of prehistoric period settled by the Minyae; in later historic times generally subject to power of Thebes; opposed to Theban hegemony and sided with Spartans against it 379 B.C.; several times destroyed and rebuilt in 4th cent. B.C.; scene of battle 85 B.C. in which Sulla destroyed an army of Mithridates VI.

Ord \'ȯ(ə)rd\. 1 City, ⊗ of Valley co., cen. Nebraska, 57 m. NNW of Grand Island; pop. (1970c) 2439.

2 River, NE Western Australia; ab. 200 m. long; flows N to Joseph Bonaparte Gulf near Wyndham.

Ord, Mount. Peak, N Brewster co., W Texas; 6800 ft.

Or·dos \'ȯrd-əs\ *or Chin.* **O–erh–to–ssu** \'ō-'er-'də-'sü\. Desert region S of the Yellow river, cen. Inner Mongolia, N China; highest point 5948 ft.

Ord Peak. Mountain, SW Apache co., E Arizona; 10,860 ft.

Or·du \ȯr-'dü\. 1 Province of N Turkey. See table at TURKEY.

2 *anc.* **Cot·y·o·ra** \ˌkät-ē-'ōr-ə, -'ȯr-ə\. Town, its ✱, on the Black Sea 80 m. E of Samsun; pop. (1965c) 27,303; ships hazelnuts. Ancient Greek Cotyora was founded c. 500 B.C.; point of embarkation for the survivors of Xenophon's "Ten Thousand."

Ord·way \'ȯrd-(ˌ)wā\. Town, ⊗ of Crowley co., E Colorado, near Arkansas river; pop. (1970c) 1017.

Or·dzho·ni·kid·ze \ˌȯr-ˌjän-ə-'kid-zə\. 1 *or formerly* **Dzau·dzhi·kau** \(d)zau̇-'jē-ˌkau̇\ *also* **Vla·di·kav·kaz** \ˌvlad-ə-ˌkaf-'kaz\. City, ✱ of North Ossetian A.S.S.R., Russian S.F.S.R., U.S.S.R., on the Terek, 70 m. WSW of Grozny; pop. (1970p) 236,000; chemicals, glass, leather goods, earthenware; univ. (1967); marked the farthest advance of German armies into Caucasus Mts. Nov. 10–19, 1942; founded 1784 as a fort, became town 1861.

2 City, U.S.S.R. See YENAKIYEVO.

Ordzhonikidzegrad. See BEZHITSA.

Ordzhonikidze Krai. See STAVROPOL KRAI.

Öre·bro \ˌər-ə-'brü\. 1 County of S cen. Sweden. See table at SWEDEN.

2 City, its ⊗, on E shore of Lake Hjälmaren 100 m. W of Stockholm; pop. (1970e) 90,930; footwear, baked goods; road junction; college (1967); 16th cent. castle (restored), 13th cent. church. Dates from 11th cent.; site of many

important diets or assemblies, incl. National Diet of 1810 at which Marshal Bernadotte was elected King of Sweden.

Or·e·gon \'ȯr-i-gən-, 'är-, *chiefly by outsiders* -ˌgän\. **1** Earlier name of Columbia river. See COLUMBIA 1.

2 A northwestern state of U.S.A., bounded on N by Washington, on E by Idaho, on S by Nevada and California, and on W by the Pacific Ocean; 10th state in area, 96,981 sq. m. (land area 96,209 sq. m.); 31st state in population, (1970c) 2,091,385; ✱ Salem; 33d state admitted to Union (1859).

Nicknames: Sunset State; Valentine State; Webfoot State; Beaver State. *State flower:* Oregon grape. *Motto:* Alis Volat Propriis (She Flies with Her Own Wings). *Rivers:* Columbia forming most of N boundary; Snake, forming upper E boundary. *Mountains:* Cascade Range, across W cen. part; highest point Mount Hood, 11,235 ft.; Blue Mts. and Wallowa Mts. in NE. *Chief products:* Wheat, fruit, vegetables; dairy products; lumbering, fishing; copper, gold, gravel; manufacturing: primary metal products, chemicals, transportation equipment. *Chief cities:* Portland, Eugene, Salem, Corvallis, Medford. See *Table of States* at UNITED STATES. Divided into the following 36 counties (for pronunciation of their names, see their individual entries):

NAME	LOCATION	AREA[1] (sq. m.)	POP. (1970c)	CO. SEAT
Baker	E	3,068	14,919	Baker
Benton	W	668	53,776	Corvallis
Clackamas	NW	1,884	166,088	Oregon City
Clatsop	NW corner; coastal	805	28,473	Astoria
Columbia	NW	640	28,790	Saint Helens
Coos	SW; coastal	1,604	56,515	Coquille
Crook	cen.	2,980	9,985	Prineville
Curry	SW corner; coastal	1,627	13,006	Gold Beach
Deschutes	cen.	3,031	30,442	Bend
Douglas	SW; coastal[2]	5,063	71,743	Roseburg
Gilliam	N	1,208	2,342	Condon
Grant	E cen.	4,531	6,996	Canyon City
Harney	SE	10,166	7,215	Burns
Hood River	N	523	13,187	Hood River
Jackson	SW	2,812	94,533	Medford
Jefferson	N cen.	1,793	8,548	Madras
Josephine	SW	1,625	35,746	Grants Pass
Klamath[3]	S	5,970	50,021	Klamath Falls
Lake	S	8,231	6,343	Lakeview
Lane	W; coastal	4,562	213,358	Eugene
Lincoln	W; coastal	986	25,755	Newport
Linn	W	2,291	71,914	Albany
Malheur	SE corner	9,861	23,169	Vale
Marion	NW	1,166	151,309	Salem
Morrow	N	2,060	4,465	Heppner
Multnomah	NW	423	554,668	Portland
Polk	NW	736	35,349	Dallas
Sherman	N	830	2,139	Moro
Tillamook	NW; coastal	1,115	18,034	Tillamook
Umatilla	NE	3,227	44,923	Pendleton
Union	NE	2,032	19,377	La Grande
Wallowa	NE corner	3,178	6,247	Enterprise
Wasco	N	2,382	20,133	The Dalles
Washington	NW	716	157,920	Hillsboro
Wheeler	N cen.	1,707	1,849	Fossil
Yamhill	NW	711	40,213	McMinnville

[1]Area = land area.
[2]NW corner borders on Pacific Ocean.
[3]Crater Lake National Park in W part.

History: Visited by Ferrelo 1543 and James Cook 1778; Columbia river discovered by Captain Robert Gray of Boston 1792, giving U.S. a claim to the region; explored by Lewis and Clark expedition 1804–06; for a time jointly occupied by England and U.S. (see OREGON COUNTRY); received white settlers with first immigration over Oregon Trail 1842; Great Britain relinquished claim to region 1846; Oregon Territory organized 1848; admitted to Union Feb. 14, 1859.

3 County in Missouri. See table at MISSOURI.

4 City, ⊗ of Ogle co., N Illinois; pop. (1970c) 3539.

5 City, ⊗ of Holt co., NW Missouri; pop. (1970c) 789.

6 City, Lucas co., NW Ohio, E of Toledo; pop. (1970c) 16,563; suburb of Toledo.

7 Village, Dane co., S Wisconsin, 11 m. S of Madison; pop. (1970c) 2533.

Oregon Caves National Monument. See UNITED STATES, *National Monuments.*

Oregon City. City, ⊗ of Clackamas co., NW Oregon, on Willamette river 11 m. S of Portland; pop. (1970c) 9176; sawmills; fruit and poultry farms; founded 1829 at terminus of Oregon Trail (*q.v.*); first capital of Oregon Territory 1849–52.

Oregon Country. Region, W North America, between the Pacific coast and the Rocky Mts. extending from the N border of California to Alaska, often so called c. 1818–46; the U.S. portion comprised all of the present states of Washington, Oregon, and Idaho and parts of W Montana and Wyoming; at beginning of the 19th century claimed by Spain, Russia, Great Britain, and the U.S.; claims withdrawn by Spain 1819 and by Russia 1825; divided at 49th parallel between Great Britain and the U.S. 1846; U.S. portion, scene of mission established by Marcus Whitman 1836, organized as a territory 1848.

Oregon Inlet. Narrow strait leading from Atlantic Ocean through barrier reef off E coast of Dare co., NE North Carolina.

Oregon Trail. An emigrant route to the Oregon Country, ab. 2000 m. long, used esp. bet. 1804 and 1860; started at Independence, W Missouri; crossed Nebraska following Platte and North Platte rivers; crossed Wyoming, traversing the Rocky Mts. through South Pass (*q.v.*) in the Wind River Range; following Snake river across Idaho to the Columbia river; terminus was Fort Vancouver; part of trail was covered by Lewis and Clark 1805; Capt. Benjamin Bonneville led his exploring party over route 1832–35; despite difficult passage through Blue Mts., wagon travel became very heavy 1842–60.

Ore·kho·vo–Zu·ye·vo \ˌȯr-ə-ˌkȯv-ə-zü-'yev-(ˌ)ō\. City, Moscow Oblast, Russian S.F.S.R., U.S.S.R., on the Moscow-Gorki railroad and the Klyazma river 58 m. E of Moscow; pop. (1970p) 120,000; a center of cotton textile industry; chemicals, plastics, machinery; peat mining; formed 1917 by consolidation of several industrial villages dating from 17th cent.

Orel \ȯ-'rel, ȯr-'yȯl\. City, ✱ of Orel Oblast, Russian S.F.S.R., U.S.S.R., on left bank of Oka river and on main railroad line 205 m. S of Moscow; pop. (1970p) 232,000; machine tools, weaving machines, glass, leather products and footwear, construction equipment, automobile parts, clocks, beer, flour; market in a grain and stock farming region. Founded 1564; occupied by Germans in World War II Oct. 1941–Aug. 1943, suffering heavy damage.

Orellana. See AMAZON.

Orel Oblast \-'ȯ-bləst, -ˌblast\. Subdivision of cen. Russian S.F.S.R., U.S.S.R., in the black-earth area N of Ukrainian S.S.R., bounded on N by Kaluga and Tula oblasts, on E by Ryazan and Voronezh oblasts, on S by Kursk Oblast, and on W by Bryansk Oblast; 9537 sq. m.; pop. (1970p) 931,000; ✱ Orel. Watered by upper course of Oka river and tributaries. Formerly a part of the Central Black Earth Region, a fertile agricultural region. Although there has been substantial exhaustion of the soil and consequent emigration, agriculture is still the main pursuit; some livestock raising; industry is concentrated in Orel, the only major town. Came under Moscow principality in 15th cent. and in 17th cent. was part of Poland; formed as oblast 1937; W two thirds of province held by German armies 1941–43 in World War II but were retaken Aug.–Sept. 1943.

Orem \'ōr-əm, 'ȯr-\. City, Utah co., N cen. Utah, 7 m. NNW of Provo; pop. (1970c) 25,729; steel; fruit farms.

Ore Mountains. See ERZGEBIRGE.

Oren·burg \ˌōr-ən-ˌbərg, ˌȯr-\ *or formerly* **Chka·lov** \chə-'käl-əf\. City, ✱ of Orenburg Oblast, Russian S.F.S.R., U.S.S.R., on Ural river; on railroad from Kuibyshev to Tashkent; pop. (1970p) 345,000; engineering industries; leather goods; first established as a fort 1735; a point of

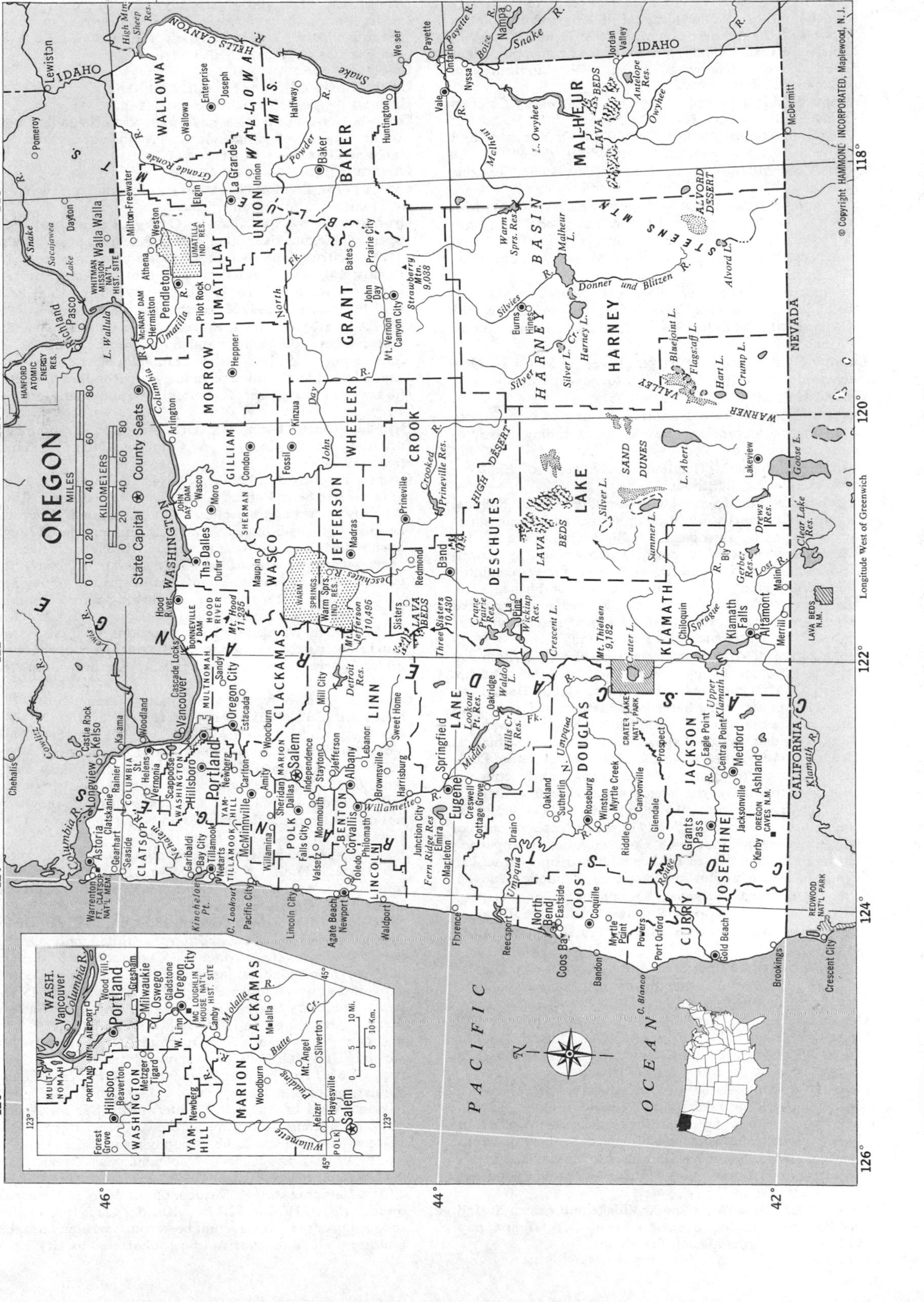
OREGON
MILES
0 10 20 40 60 80
KILOMETERS
0 20 40 60 80
State Capital ⊛ County Seats
CLATSOP
TILLAMOOK
COLUMBIA
WASHINGTON
MULTNOMAH
HOOD RIVER
WASCO
SHERMAN
GILLIAM
MORROW
UMATILLA
UNION
WALLOWA
BAKER
GRANT
WHEELER
JEFFERSON
CLACKAMAS
MARION
POLK
YAM-HILL
LINCOLN
BENTON
LINN
LANE
CROOK
DESCHUTES
HARNEY
MALHEUR
LAKE
KLAMATH
DOUGLAS
COOS
CURRY
JOSEPHINE
JACKSON
WASHINGTON
IDAHO
NEVADA
CALIFORNIA
PACIFIC
OCEAN
Astoria
Warrenton
FT. CLATSOP NAT'L MEM.
Gearhart
Seaside
Clatskanie
Rainier
St. Helens
Vernonia
Scappoose
Hillsboro
Portland
Gresham
Oregon City
Estacada
Sandy
Cascade Locks
Hood River
The Dalles
Dufur
Maupin
Moro
Wasco
Condon
Arlington
Fossil
Kinzua
Heppner
Pendleton
Hermiston
Athena
Weston
Milton-Freewater
Pilot Rock
La Grande
Union
Elgin
Enterprise
Joseph
Wallowa
Baker
Halfway
Huntington
Vale
Nyssa
Ontario
McDermitt
Jordan Valley
John Day
Canyon City
Prairie City
Mt. Vernon
Bates
Burns
Hines
Prineville
Madras
Redmond
Bend
Sisters
La Pine
Lakeview
Chiloquin
Klamath Falls
Altamont
Merrill
Malin
Bly
Medford
Ashland
Jacksonville
Central Point
Eagle Point
Prospect
Grants Pass
Kerby
OREGON CAVES N.M.
Gold Beach
Brookings
Port Orford
Bandon
Coos Bay
North Bend
Eastside
Coquille
Myrtle Point
Powers
Roseburg
Winston
Myrtle Creek
Riddle
Canyonville
Glendale
Sutherlin
Oakland
Drain
Reedsport
Florence
Cottage Grove
Creswell
Eugene
Springfield
Junction City
Harrisburg
Oakridge
Mapleton
Elmira
Corvallis
Philomath
Albany
Lebanon
Sweet Home
Brownsville
Salem
Dallas
Independence
Monmouth
Falls City
Stayton
Jefferson
Mill City
Woodburn
McMinnville
Amity
Sheridan
Willamina
Newberg
Carlton
Tillamook
Bay City
Garibaldi
Netarts
Pacific City
Lincoln City
Newport
Agate Beach
Waldport
Toledo
Valsetz
Warm Sprs.
Crater L.
CRATER LAKE NAT'L PARK
Mt. Hood 11,235
Mt. Jefferson 10,495
Three Sisters 10,430
Mt. Thielsen 9,182
Strawberry Mtn. 9,038
WALLOWA MTS.
HELLS CANYON
BLUE MTS.
STEENS MTN.
ALVORD DESERT
HIGH DESERT
HARNEY BASIN
WARNER VALLEY
SAND DUNES
LAVA BEDS
Columbia R.
Snake R.
Willamette R.
Deschutes R.
John Day R.
Klamath R.
Owyhee R.
Malheur L.
Harney L.
Goose L.
Upper Klamath L.
Summer L.
L. Abert
Silver L.
Hart L.
Crump L.
Alvord L.
Waldo L.
Crescent L.
Wickiup Res.
Crane Prairie Res.
Detroit Res.
Lookout Pt. Res.
Hills Cr. Res.
Prineville Res.
Clear Lake Res.
Gerber Res.
Drews Res.
WARM SPRINGS IND. RES.
UMATILLA IND. RES.
McNARY DAM
JOHN DAY DAM
BONNEVILLE DAM
WHITMAN MISSION NAT'L HIST. SITE
LAVA BEDS N.M.
REDWOOD NAT'L PARK
Crescent City
Longview
Kelso
Vancouver
Walla Walla
Pasco
Richland
Lewiston
Nampa
Payette
Weiser
C. Blanco
C. Lookout
Kincheloe Pt.
WASH.
Beaverton
Tigard
Milwaukie
L. Oswego
Gladstone
W. Linn
Canby
Molalla
Mt. Angel
Silverton
Keizer
Hayesville
Forest Grove
Metzger
PORTLAND INT'L AIRPORT
MC LOUGHLIN HOUSE NAT'L HIST. SITE
Longitude West of Greenwich
© Copyright HAMMOND INCORPORATED, Maplewood, N.J.

severe fighting after Revolution of 1917; suffered greatly from famine of 1920–21; capital of Kirgiz Autonomous Republic 1920–24; name changed 1938 in honor of V. P. Chkalov, Russian aviator, leader of first transpolar flight June 1937 from Moscow to Vancouver, Washington; again renamed Orenburg 1957.

Orenburg Oblast \-'ȯ-bləst, -ˌblast\ *or formerly* **Chkalov Oblast.** Subdivision of the Russian S.F.S.R., U.S.S.R.; 47,876 sq. m.; pop. (1970p) 2,050,000; ✱ Orenburg; oil and gas fields; copper, coal, salt; corn, wheat, millet.

Oren·se \ȯ-'ren(t)-(ˌ)sā\. 1 Province of NW Spain. See table at SPAIN.

2 Commune, its ✱, on Miño river 250 m. NW of Madrid; pop. (1970p) 73,379; flour, lumber, iron goods; 13th cent. cathedral, notable 13th cent. bridge; capital of the Suevi under the Visigoths; destroyed by Moors 713; rebuilt c. 884.

Øre·sund \'ər-ə-ˌsən\ *or Eng.* **The Sound.** Strait bet. Sjælland I., Denmark, and S Sweden, connecting the Kattegat with the Baltic Sea; width at its narrowest section 3½ m.

Ore·ti \ō-'rāt-ē\ *or* **New River.** River, S South I., New Zealand; 126 m. long; flows S into Foveaux Strait.

Orfani, Gulf of. See STRYMONIC GULF.

Orford, Cape \-'ȯr-fərd\. Point on S coast of New Britain I., Bismarck Archipelago, near E end, extending into Solomon Sea.

Orford Ness \-'nes\. Headland on SE coast of England, ENE of Ipswich; lighthouse.

Organization of African Unity *or abbr.* **OAU.** Political organization, consisting of all independent African states not governed by Europeans; headquarters Addis Ababa, Ethiopia; purpose is to promote cooperation in various fields among African states, and to eliminate remaining white-dominated governments in Africa; established 1963. Has supported African liberation movements; mediated Algeria-Morocco conflict 1963; adopted resolution 1968 calling for maintenance of Nigerian unity.

Organization of American States *or abbr.* **OAS.** Political organization, consisting of Argentina, Barbados, Bolivia, Brazil, Chile, Colombia, Costa Rica, Cuba, Dominican Republic, Ecuador, El Salvador, Guatemala, Haiti, Honduras, Jamaica, Mexico, Nicaragua, Panama, Paraguay, Peru, Trinidad and Tobago, United States of America, Uruguay, and Venezuela; headquarters Washington, D.C.; purpose is to promote political, social, and economic cooperation among the members; established 1948 by charter which came into effect 1951. Has acted as consultative or mediating body in several cases of conflict within the region since 1948; Cuba excluded from participation in OAS activities 1962; established Inter-American Peace Force for action in Dominican Republic 1965–66.

Organ Mountains \ˌȯr-gən-\. 1 Range in S Dona Ana co., S New Mexico, extending S across border into Texas.

2 Range in Rio de Janeiro state, SE Brazil. See SERRA DOS ORGÃOS.

Órganos, Sierra de los. See SIERRA DE LOS ÓRGANOS.

Or·gan Pipe Cactus National Monument \'ȯr-gən-ˌpīp-\. See UNITED STATES, *National Monuments.*

Orgãos, Serra dos. See SERRA DOS ORGÃOS.

Or·ge·yev \'ȯr-gē-əf\ *or Rom.* **Or·hei** \ȯr-'hā\. Town, cen. Moldavian S.S.R., U.S.S.R., on tributary of Dniester 23 m. N of Kishinev; pop. (1967e) 21,000.

Or·hon \'ȯr-ˌkȯn, -ˌhȯn\ *or* **Or·khon** \'ȯr-ˌkȯn\. River, N Mongolian People's Republic; 698 m. long; flows NE from N edge of the Gobi and joins the Selenga just W of Altanbulag at the border; ruins of Karakorum are near its banks.

Oria \'ȯr-(ˌ)yä\. Commune, Brindisi prov., Apulia, SE Italy, 16 m. SW of Brindisi; pop. (1968e) 14,784; episcopal see; 13th cent. castle.

Ori·ent \'ōr-ē-ənt, 'ȯr-, -ē-ˌent\. Village and resort, Suffolk co., SE New York, on Long I. near Orient Point; pop. (1970c) 600; Orient Beach State Park.

Orient, The. The East; generally, eastern countries. In ancient times, the countries E of the Mediterranean; today the countries of Asia generally, esp. the countries of E Asia; the Far East. See EAST, THE 1.

Orientale. See HAUT-ZAÏRE.

Oriental Misamis. See MISAMIS ORIENTAL.

Oriental Negros. See NEGROS ORIENTAL.

Orien·te \ˌōr-ē-'ent-ē, ˌȯr-\ *or formerly* **San·tia·go de Cu·ba** \ˌsant-ē-ˌäg-ōd-ə-'kyü-bə, ˌsänt-\. Province of E Cuba. See table at CUBA.

Oriente, El. See EASTERN REGION.

Orient Point. Point at NE extremity of Long I., New York, at N entrance to Gardiners Bay.

Ori·hue·la \ˌōr-ē-'wā-lə, ˌȯr-\. City, Alicante prov., SE Spain, on Segura river 30 m. SW of Alicante; pop. (1970p) 44,938; citrus fruit, potatoes, cotton, hemp, cereals, almonds; 14th cent. cathedral, 14th cent. church; formerly had a university (1516–1701). Dates from c. 1500 B.C.; held by Moors 713–1264; earthquake 1829.

Oril·lia \ō-'ril-yə\. Town, Simcoe co., SE Ontario, Canada, where lakes Couchiching and Simcoe join 21 m. NE of Barrie; pop. (1971p) 24,016; summer resort; wood and enamel products, mining machinery; boatbuilding; diversified agriculture. Site of Champlain monument erected 1925.

Orin·da Village \ə-ˌrin-də-\. Urban community (unincorporated), Contra Costa co., W California, NE of Oakland; pop. (1970c) 6790.

Ori·no·co \ˌōr-ə-'nō-(ˌ)kō, ˌȯr-\. River, Venezuela; 1281 m. long; rises in Serra Parima mountains in S Venezuela, flows W, then N, forming a section of the Colombia-Venezuela boundary; turns E in cen. Venezuela and empties through a wide delta into the Atlantic Ocean. In S Venezuela connects with Rio Negro of the Amazon system through the Casiquiare; has many tributaries, esp. the Guaviare, Vichada, and Meta, rising in and flowing E in Colombia, the Apure in W Venezuela, and the Caura and Caroní in SE Venezuela. Navigable in many sections for small vessels but is obstructed by rapids ab. 100 m. from its mouth; hydroelectric plant at lower falls of Caroní completed 1958.

Orion \ōr-'yōn, ȯr-'yȯn\. Municipality, Bataan prov., Luzon, Phil., SSE of Balanga; pop. (1969e) 20,300.

Oris·ka·ny \ȯ-'ris-kə-nē\. Village, Oneida co., cen. New York, on Mohawk river 7 m. WNW of Utica; pop. (1970c) 1627. Oriskany Battlefield, scene of Revolutionary battle Aug. 6, 1777, to W of village; an ambush by British and Indians and a defeat for the Americans although they were not driven from the field; losses on both sides severe, Gen. Herkimer killed.

Oris·sa \ȯ-'ris-ə\. State, E coast of India; 60,178 sq. m.; pop. (1971p) 21,934,827; ✱ Bhubaneswar; rice, timber; chromite, iron ore, manganese; fishing; largest cities: Cuttack, Berhampur, Bhubaneswar.

History: Conquered by British 1803; until 1912 a part of Bengal; 1912–36 a subdivision of Bihar and Orissa; constituted separate province 1936, with some additions of districts from Madras (now Tamil Nadu) and Central Provinces (now Madhya Pradesh); became a state 1950.

Orissa Feudatory States. Indian states formerly in Eastern States Agency; now in E India. See EASTERN STATES 3.

Ori·sta·no \ˌȯr-i-'stän-(ˌ)ō\. Commune, Cagliari prov., S Sardinia, Italy, on Gulf of Oristano 54 m. NW of Cagliari; pop. (1968e) 26,399; 13th cent. cathedral; Phoenician and Roman necropolis nearby.

Oristano, Gulf of. Inlet of Mediterranean Sea on W cen. coast of Sardinia; 10 m. long; receives Tirso river.

Ori·ve·si \'ō-ri-ˌve-si\. Lake, Kuopio prov., SE Finland.

Ori·za·ba \ˌōr-ə-'zäb-ə, ˌȯr-\. 1 Volcanic peak, Mexico. See CITLALTÉPETL.

2 City, Veracruz state, E Mexico, 65 m. WSW of Veracruz; munic. pop. (1970p) 92,728; altitude 4211 ft.; textiles, tobacco products, sugar, rum, beer; tourism; many notable buildings; an Aztec garrison post; chartered as city 1774.

Orkhon. See ORHON.

Ork·ney Islands \ˌȯrk-nē-\ *or* **Ork·neys** \-nēz\ *or anc.* **Or·ca·des** \'ȯr-kə-ˌdēz\. Archipelago off NE coast of Scotland, comprising **Orkney** co.; 376 sq. m.; pop. (1971p) 17,075; ✱ Kirkwall, on Pomona I.; chief islands are Pomona (or Mainland), Hoy, South Ronaldsay, North Ronaldsay, Sanday, Stronsay, Shapinsay, and Rousay; separated from Caithness co. on the mainland by Pentland Firth; islands are low (highest point 880 ft. on Pomona) and irregular in shape; in S bet. Pomona, Hoy, and South Ronaldsay is Scapa Flow; chief occupation agriculture (fertile soil produces oats, barley, turnips, and fine pasturage for cattle, sheep, and horses). A Norse dependency from 9th cent.; annexed by Scotland from Denmark 1472; major British naval base in both world wars (see SCAPA FLOW).

Or·land \'ȯr-lənd, 'ȯr-\. City, Glenn co., N California, 16 m. N of Willows; pop. (1970c) 2884; concrete blocks; fruit and nut packing; diversified agriculture.

Or·lan·do \ȯr-'lan-(ˌ)dō\. City, ⊗ of Orange co., cen. Florida penin., 78 m. NE of Tampa; pop. (1970c) 99,006; center of citrus fruit and truck farming region; boats, electronic and missile components, clothing; Florida Technological Univ. (1968); two U.S. Air Force bases; Walt Disney World (large amusement park) is ab. 16 m. to SW; settled c. 1844, incorporated as city 1875.

Orlando, Cape. Point on N coast of Sicily, Italy, near E end; in World War II landing made just E of cape Aug. 12, 1943 by U.S. forces.

Orland Park. Village, Cook co., NE Illinois, 25 m. SW of Chicago; pop. (1970c) 6391; radio appliances; diversified agriculture.

Orlau. See ORLOVÁ.

Or·lé·a·nais \ˌȯr-lē-ə-'nā\. Historical region of N cen. France, bounded anciently on N by Île-de-France, E by Champagne, Burgundy, and Nivernais, S by Berry, SW by Touraine, W by Maine; ✱ Orléans; watered by Loir, Loire, and Cher rivers; provincial appanage of younger members of ruling house of France.

Or·le·ans *La.* 'ȯr-lē-ənz, -lənz; *N.Y.* 'ȯr-(ˌ)lēnz; *Vt.* ȯr-'lēnz\. Name of a parish in Louisiana and of counties in two states of the U.S. See tables at LOUISIANA, NEW YORK, VERMONT.

Or·leans \ȯr-'lēnz\. Town, Barnstable co., SE Massachusetts, on inlet of Atlantic Ocean 18 m. ENE of Barnstable; pop. (1970c) 3055; summer resort.

Or·lé·ans \ˌȯr-lā-'äⁿ\ *or anc.* **Au·re·li·a·num** \ȯ-ˌrē-lē-'ā-nəm\. Commune, ✱ of Loiret dept., N cen. France, on Loire river 70 m. SSW of Paris; pop. (1968c) 95,828; important railroad junction; produces glass, pharmaceuticals, rubber products, textiles, automobile parts; flower nurseries; in fruit and vegetable growing region; 17th–19th cent. cathedral, 16th cent. church, 16th cent. town hall, 17th cent. prefecture, episcopal palace, museums, univ. (1962).

History: Conquered by Caesar 52 B.C.; a major cultural center in early Middle Ages; center of a royal duchy created by Philip VI in 1344; English siege relieved 1429 by Joan of Arc, also called the Maid of Orléans; heavily damaged by bombing 1940 and 1944.

Or·le·ans, Island of \-'ȯr-lē-ənz\ *or Fr.* **Île d'Or·lé·ans** \ˌēl-ˌdȯr-lā-'äⁿ\. Island in St. Lawrence river 4 m. downstream from the city of Quebec, Quebec, E Canada; 21 m. long; 72 sq. m.; part of Montmorency co.; chief town Sainte Famille.

Or·le·ans, Isle of \-'ȯr-lē-ənz, 'ȯr lənz\ *or Fr.* **Île d'Or·lé·ans** \ēl-dȯr-lā-äⁿ\. District around New Orleans, Louisiana, S of Lake Pontchartrain and E of the Mississippi; ab. 2800 sq. m.; ceded by France to Spain 1763 at time (Treaty of Paris) when she ceded rest of her Louisiana territory E of the Mississippi to Great Britain.

Orleans, Territory of. See LOUISIANA.

Or·lo·vá \'ȯr-lə-ˌvä\ *or Pol.* **Or·ło·wa** \ȯr-'lō-və\ *or Ger.* **Or·lau** \'ȯ(ə)r-ˌlau̇\. Town, Czech S.R., cen. Czechoslovakia just E of Ostrava near border with Poland; pop. (1968e) 24,234; agricultural center; coal mining. Held by Poland 1938–45.

Or·ly \ȯr-'lē\. Commune, Val-de-Marne dept., N France, SSE suburb of Paris; pop. (1968c) 30,202; **Orly Field,** principal international airport of Paris region.

Or·ma·ra \ȯr-'mär-ə\. Headland and town, S coast of Baluchistan, Pakistan, ab. 150 m. W of Karachi.

Or·moc \ȯr-'mäk, -'mȯk\ *or* **Mac·Ar·thur** \mə-'kär-thər\. Chartered city, Leyte prov., on W coast of Leyte I., Phil., on **Ormoc Bay,** an inlet of Camotes Sea; pop. (1970c) 85,900; 36 m. SW of Tacloban. In World War II developed by Japanese as military base; captured by U.S. troops Dec. 11, 1944 after severe fighting.

Or·mond Beach \ˌȯr-mən(d)-\. City, Volusia co., E Florida, on Atlantic Ocean 7 m. N of Daytona Beach; pop. (1970c) 14,063.

Ormond by-the-Sea. Community, Volusia co., E Florida; pop. (1970c) 6002.

Orms·by \'ȯrmz-bē\. Former county in Nevada; abolished 1969.

Orms·kirk \'ȯ(ə)rmz-ˌkərk\. Urban district, Lancashire, NW England, 11 m. NNE of Liverpool; pop. (1971p) 27,618; textiles.

Ormuz. See HORMUZ.

Ormuz, Strait of. See HORMUZ, STRAIT OF.

Orne \'ȯ(ə)rn\. 1 River, NW France; ab. 95 m. long; flows N in Orne and Calvados depts. past Caen into the English Channel; its bridges seized by Allies on invasion of Normandy June 6, 1944.

2 Department of NW France. See table at FRANCE.

Ornes \'ȯ(ə)rn\. Village, Meuse dept., NE France, 8 m. NE of Verdun; in World War I scene of battle Feb. 24, 1916 when it was captured by Germans.

Oro, El. See EL ORO.

Oro Bay \ˌōr-ō-, ˌȯr-\. Small inlet of Dyke Ackland Bay on New Guinea I., Papua New Guinea, 20 m. S of Buna; in 1943 site of an Allied base, often raided by Japanese.

Oro·co·vis \ˌōr-ə-'kō-vəs, ˌȯr-\. Town and municipality, cen. Puerto Rico; town is 24 m. SW of San Juan; pop. (1970p) 3783 (town), 20,321 (munic.).

Oro·fi·no \ˌȯr-ə-'fē-nō\. City, ⊗ of Clearwater co., NE Idaho, 40 m. E of Lewiston; pop. (1970c) 3883; lumbering, diversified agriculture.

Oro·he·na, Mount \-ˌōr-ə-'hā-nə, -ˌȯr-\. Peak in center of the island of Tahiti, French Polynesia, S Pacific Ocean; 7339 ft.; a double peak, steep and thickly forested.

Orolaunum. See ARLON.

Oro·moc·to \ȯr-ə-'mäk-(ˌ)tō\. Town, Sunbury co., S cen. New Brunswick, Canada, 45 m. NW of St. John; pop. (1971p) 11,518; diversified agriculture.

Oro·no \'ōr-ə-ˌnō, 'ȯr-\. 1 Town, Penobscot co., E cen. Maine, on Penobscot river 8 m. NNE of Bangor; pop. (1970c) 9989; canvas products; dairy farms; Univ. of Maine (1865).

2 Village, Hennepin co., SE cen. Minnesota, W of Minneapolis, pop. (1970c) 6787.

Oron·say \'ōr-ən-ˌzā, -ˌsā\. Small island of the Inner Hebrides near Colonsay, off W coast of Scotland; administratively a part of Argyll co.; ruins of 14th cent. priory.

Oron·tes \ō-'ränt-ēz\. 1 Mountain, Iran. See ALWAND, MOUNT.

2 *or Arab.* **Nahr Al-'Āṣī** \ˌnar-al-'as-ē\ *or Turk.* **Asi Neh·ri** \ˌas-ē-'ner-ē\. Unnavigable river, W Syria; 355 m. long; rises in the Bika valley of Lebanon near Baalbek and flows N to the W of the Anti-Lebanon Mts. past the cities of Homs and Hama, then turning W and SW through Hatay, S Turkey, past Antakya into the Mediterranean Sea at

Samandağ 40 m. N of Latakia; receives tributary Afrine from the N.

Oropeza. See COCHABAMBA 2.

Oro·pus \ò-'rō-pəs\. Ancient town of Boeotia, E cen. Greece, on the coast opp. Eretria; seized by Athenians and became part of Attica.

Oro·quie·ta \ˌōr-ə-kē-'āt-ə, ˌòr-\. Municipality, ✱ of Misamis Occidental prov., Mindanao, Phil., on NW shore of Iligan Bay; pop. (1969e) 40,100.

Oro·sei, Gulf of \-ˌōr-ə-'zā, -ˌòr-\. Widemouthed inlet of Tyrrhenian Sea on E cen. coast of the island of Sardinia.

Oros·há·za \'ō-rōsh-ˌhäz-(ˌ)ò\. Commune, SE Hungary, 32 m. NE of Szeged; pop. (1970p) 33,346; market center for grain, wine, and livestock.

Orotava, La. See LA OROTAVA.

Oro·te \ò-'rōt-ē\. Peninsula, W coast of Guam, W Pacific Ocean; ab. 4 m. long by ½ to 1 m. wide; forms S side of Apra Harbor; site of last stand of Japanese in July 1944.

Oro·ville \'ōr-ō-ˌvil, 'òr-\. 1 City, ⊗ of Butte co., N California, on Feather river 66 m. N of Sacramento; pop. (1970c) 7536; lumber, olive oil; fruit and vegetable canning.

2 Town, Okanogan co., N Washington, on Okanogan river and Osoyoos Lake 5 m. S of Canadian border; pop. (1970c) 1555; customs station.

Oroville Dam *and* **Oroville Reservoir.** See UNITED STATES, *Dams and Reservoirs.*

Oroya, La. See LA OROYA.

Or·re·fors \ˌòr-ə-'fōrz, -'fōsh\. Town, Kronoberg co., SE Sweden, ab. 26 m. NW of Kalmar; famous crystal glass factory.

Or·rell \'òr-əl\. Urban district, Lancashire, NW England, 16 m. NE of Liverpool; pop. (1971p) 12,069.

Or·ring·ton \'òr-iŋ-tən\. Town, Penobscot co., E cen. Maine, on Penobscot river 7 m. SSW of Bangor; pop. (1970c) 2702.

Orrs Island \'ò(ə)rz-, 'ō(ə)rz-\. Island in Casco Bay in Cumberland co., off E coast of SW Maine.

Orr·ville \'ò(ə)r-ˌvil, 'ō(ə)r-\. City, Wayne co., NE cen. Ohio, 20 m. SSW of Akron; pop. (1970c) 7048; preserves, fertilizer, leather goods, castings.

Or·sain·ville \òr-'san-ˌvil, -saⁿ-'vēl\. Town, Quebec co., S Quebec, Canada, 6 m. NW of Quebec; pop. (1971p) 12,561.

Orsera. See ANDERMATT.

Or·sha \'òr-shə\. Town, Vitebsk Oblast, Belorussian S.S.R., U.S.S.R., on right bank of the Dnieper 122 m. NE of Minsk; pop. (1970p) 101,000; railroad junction; textiles (esp. linen), machinery, processed foods. First mentioned 1067; a trade center in W Poland until annexed by Russia 1772; occupied by Germans in World War II July 1941–July 1944.

Orsk \'ò(ə)rsk\. Town, E Orenburg Oblast, Russian S.F.S.R., U.S.S.R., on railroad 155 m. E of Orenburg; pop. (1970p) 225,000; railroad center; produces nickel, heavy machinery, construction equipment, chemicals; oil refineries, meat-packing plants, nickel refining; founded 1735 as fortress of Orenburg (*q.v.*) which was moved downriver to present site 1743.

Orsona. See OSUNA.

Or·ta, Lake \-'ōr-tə, -'òr-\. See OMEGNA.

Orta No·va \-'nò-və\. Commune, Foggia prov., Apulia, SE Italy, 11 m. SE of Foggia; pop. (1970c) 14,837.

Or·te·gal, Cape \-ˌòrt-i-'gäl\. Cape on NW coast of Spain, projecting from N coast of La Coruña prov.

Ortelsburg. See SZCZYTNO.

Or·thez \òr-'tez\. Town, N Pyrénées-Atlantiques dept., SW France, on the Gave de Pau ab. 25 m. NW of Pau; pop. (1962c) 8829; capital of Béarn to 15th cent.; center of Protestantism during 16th cent., site of Calvinist university founded by Jeanne d'Albret and suppressed by Louis XIII. Wellington defeated Marshal Soult here Feb. 27, 1814.

Or·ti·guei·ra \ˌòrt-i-'ger-ə\. Seaport commune, La Coruña prov., NW Spain, on inlet of Bay of Biscay 35 m. NE of La Coruña; pop. (1971p) 17,559; coasting trade; agricultural products; fish-salting works.

Ort·ler \'òrt-lər\ *or Ital:* **Ort·les** \'òrt-ˌlās\. Mountain range of E Alps, bet. Trentino-Alto Adige and NE Lombardy, N Italy; highest peak the **Ortler** *or* **Ort·ler·spit·ze** \-ˌs(h)pit-sə\, 12,792 ft.

Or·tón \òr-'tōn\. River, Peru and Bolivia; ab. 340 m. long; rises in SE Peru, flows E across N Bolivia into Beni river shortly before it joins the Mamoré river.

Or·to·na \òr-'tō-nə\. Commune, Chieti prov., Abruzzi, cen. Italy, on Adriatic 13 m. E of Chieti; pop. (1968e) 22,020; fishing; ships grapes; cathedral, 15th cent. castle. A town of the Frentani; came under Rome 4th cent. B.C.; to Naples in 18th cent.; in World War II occupied by British Dec. 27, 1943.

Or·ton·ville \'òrt-ᵊn-ˌvil\. City, ⊗ of Big Stone co., W Minnesota, at S end of Big Stone Lake on South Dakota border; pop. (1970c) 2665; resort; granite quarries, dairy farms.

Or·tyg·ia \òr-'tij-ē-ə\. Name from ancient times of islands adjacent to the SE coast of Sicily and separated from the mainland by a narrow canal; a part of the city of Syracuse. See SYRACUSE 3.

Oruba. See ARUBA.

Oru·ro \ò-'rù(ə)r-(ˌ)ō\. 1 Department of W Bolivia. See table at BOLIVIA.

2 City, its ✱, 120 m. SSE of La Paz; pop. (1962e) 86,985; altitude 12,160 ft.; tin, copper; technical univ. (1892); founded 1606.

Orust \'ü-ˌrəst\. Swedish island in the Kattegat, off SW coast of Sweden SW of Lake Vänern and 28 m. NW of Göteborg; ab. 14 m. long and 10 m. wide; 133 sq. m.

Or·vie·to \ˌòr-vē-'āt-(ˌ)ō\; *anc.* **Vel·su·na** \vel-'sü-nə\ *or* **Vol·sin·ii** \väl-'sin-ē-ˌī\; *in Middle Ages* **Urbs Ve·tus** \ərbz-'vē-təs\. Commune, Terni prov., Umbria, cen. Italy, 29 m. WNW of Terni; pop. (1968e) 24,246; tourism; ceramics, wine; episcopal see (begun 1290) noted esp. for its fine façade (begun 1310) and containing art works; two 11th cent. churches, 13th cent. episcopal palace, papal palace (now a museum of antiquities); Jesuit college; Etruscan necropolis discovered here 1874; medieval mines nearby. One of twelve cities of ancient Etruria.

Or·well \'òr-ˌwel, -wəl\. River, Suffolk, E England, extending 10 m. SE from Ipswich to the Stour.

Or·wigs·burg \'òr-wigz-ˌbərg\. Borough, Schuylkill co., E cen. Pennsylvania, 7 m. ESE of Pottsville; pop. (1970c) 2661.

Oryokko. See YALU.

Or·zi·nuo·vi \ˌòrd-zi-nə-'wò-vē\. Commune, Brescia prov., Lombardy, N Italy, 17 m. WSW of Brescia; pop. (1968c) 9541.

Osage \ō-'sāj, 'ō-ˌsāj\. 1 River, W Missouri; ab. 500 m. long; largest tributary of the Missouri river; formed by junction of Marais des Cygnes and Little Osage rivers on border of Bates and Vernon cos., flows E and NE through Lake of the Ozarks formed by Bagnell Dam, and enters the Missouri river just E of Jefferson City. The Osage is sometimes considered as including the Marais des Cygnes.

2 Name of counties in three states of the U.S. See tables at KANSAS, MISSOURI, OKLAHOMA.

3 City, ⊗ of Mitchell co., N Iowa, 24 m. ENE of Mason City; pop. (1970c) 3815; limestone quarries; corn, hogs.

Osage City. City, Osage co., E Kansas, 25 m. NE of Emporia; pop. (1970c) 2600; grain farms.

Ōsa·ka \ō-'säk-ə\. 1 Prefecture, Honshū, Japan; 710 sq. m.; pop. (1970c) 7,620,480; ✱ Ōsaka; highly urbanized.

2 Seaport city, its ✱, on NE shore of Ōsaka Bay; pop. (1970c) 2,980,487; second largest city in Japan and a major commercial and industrial center; cotton textiles, steel, machinery, electrical equipment, chemicals, cement; shipbuilding; univ. (1931); castle (built 1583–85, burned 1868 and later restored). Intersected by canals and channels of the Yodo river.

History: A long-established city; formerly principal port of Kyōto and known as **Na·ni·wa** \ˈnän-i-ˌwä, nä-ˈnē-wä\; made castle town by Hideyoshi 1583; leading commercial city of Japan during feudal era; after opening of mint (1871) and port of Kōbe (*q.v.*) developed as leading industrial city of Japan; badly damaged by American bombing 1944–45; site of World's Fair 1970.

Ōsaka Bay. Inlet of Pacific Ocean on S coast of Honshū, Japan, E of Awaji I. which separates it from the Inland Sea; connected with the ocean by Kitan Strait and Kii Channel; site of ports of Ōsaka and Kōbe.

Osam. See OSŬM.

Osa Peninsula \ˌō-sə-\. Peninsula on S coast of Costa Rica bet. the Gulf of Dulce and the Pacific Ocean.

Osa·sco \ů-ˈsäs-ˌkü\. Municipality, São Paulo state, SE Brazil, 9 m. WNW of São Paulo; pop. (1968e) 135,576.

Osa·wat·o·mie \ˌō-sə-ˈwät-ə-mē\. City, Miami co., E Kansas, 45 m. SSW of Kansas City; pop. (1970c) 4294; a station on the Underground Railroad in pre-Civil War days; site of the cabin in which John Brown (known as "Old Brown of Osawatomie") lived (1856) and scene of the bloody fight (Aug. 1856) bet. Brown and his sympathizers and a group of proslavery adherents.

Os·born \ˈäz-bərn\. Former village, Greene co., SW Ohio, 10 m. NE of Dayton. See FAIRBORN.

Os·borne \ˈäz-bərn\. **1** County in N cen. Kansas. See table at KANSAS.

2 City, its ⊗, on Solomon river 59 m. W of Concordia; pop. (1970c) 1980; ships livestock.

Osca. See HUESCA 2.

Os·ce·o·la \ˌō-sē-ˈō-lə, ˌäs-ē-\. **1** Counties in three states of the U.S. See tables at FLORIDA, IOWA, MICHIGAN.

2 City, a ⊗ of Mississippi co., NE Arkansas, on Mississippi river 16 m. S of Blytheville; pop. (1970c) 7204; feed, cottonseed oil; alfalfa.

3 City, ⊗ of Clarke co., S Iowa, 39 m. SSW of Des Moines; pop. (1970c) 3124; diversified agriculture.

4 City, ⊗ of St. Clair co., W Missouri; pop. (1970c) 874; summer resort; dairy products.

5 City, ⊗ of Polk co., E Nebraska; pop. (1970c) 923.

Osceola, Mount. Mountain, N Grafton co., N cen. New Hampshire; 4326 ft.

Oschatz \ˈō-ˌshäts, ˈō-\. City, Leipzig district, East Germany, 31 m. SE of Leipzig; pop. (1970e) 16,718; manufactures shoes, felt goods, scales.

Oschers·le·ben \ˈō-shərs-ˌlā-bən\. Industrial city, Magdeburg dist., East Germany, 20 m. WSW of Magdeburg; pop. (1970e) 18,085; machinery, textiles, shoes, sugar, chemicals. Several times destroyed by fire. First mentioned 1235; bombed by Americans 1944–45.

Os·co·da \äs-ˈkōd-ə\. **1** County in Michigan. See table at MICHIGAN.

2 Village, NE Iosco co., NE Michigan, on Lake Huron at mouth of Au Sable river; pop. (1970c) 3475; resort; Wurtsmith Air Force Base.

Ose·ras \ō-ˈser-əs\. Peak in Cordillera Oriental, W cen. Colombia, S of Bogotá; 11,480 ft.

Osetia. See OSSETIA.

Osh \ˈōsh\. Town, ✱ of Osh Oblast, S Kirgiz S.S.R., U.S.S.R., on Uzbek S.S.R. border ab. 30 m. SE of Andizhan; pop. (1970p) 120,000; at E end of fertile Fergana valley; center of agricultural and mining region; silk and cotton mills; food processing. The rock Takht-i-Sulaiman, famous in Muslim legends, is just W of the town.

Osha Peak \ˌō-shə-\. Mountain, W Torrance co., cen. New Mexico; 10,223 ft.

O'·Shaugh·nes·sy Dam \ō-ˌshȯ-nə-sē-\. See UNITED STATES, *Dams and Reservoirs.*

Osh·a·wa \ˈäsh-ə-wə, -ˌwä, -ˌwȯ\. Industrial city, Ontario co., SE Ontario, Canada, on Lake Ontario 33 m. ENE of Toronto; pop. (1971p) 91,113; motor vehicles and parts, foundry products, metal stampings, glass, textiles, pharmaceuticals, plastics, furniture; founded 1795, incorporated as town 1879, as city 1924.

Oshima. See AMAMI.

Ō-shi·ma \ō-ˈshē-mə, ˈō-shə-ˌmä\ *also* **Vries Island** \ˈvrēs-\. Largest island of the Izu-shichitō island group, Japan; ab. 35 sq. m.; has active volcano Mihara 2477 ft., subject to frequent eruptions; suffered from earthquake Sept. 1, 1923.

Osh·kosh \ˈäsh-ˌkäsh\. **1** City, ⊗ of Garden co., W Nebraska; pop. (1970c) 1067; honey, corn, poultry.

2 City, ⊗ of Winnebago co., E Wisconsin, on W shore of Lake Winnebago; pop. (1970c) 53,221; clothing, automobile parts, wood products, beverages, machinery, furniture, leather goods; summer resort; Wisconsin State Univ. (1877). Settled 1836; incorporated as city 1853; a major lumbering center in latter half of 19th cent.

Osh Oblast \ˈōsh-ˈō-bləst, -ˌblast\. Subdivision of the Kirgiz S.S.R., U.S.S.R., N of the Alai Mts.; 28,533 sq. m.; pop. (1970p) 1,233,000; ✱ Osh; cotton, tobacco; coal, mercury, antimony, oil, natural gas.

Oshog·bo \ō-ˈshäg-(ˌ)bō\. City, Western State, Nigeria, on railroad ab. 50 m. NE of Ibadan; pop. (1969e) 242,336; trading center; dyeing, weaving, cotton-ginning; settled from Ibokun in pre-colonial era; from early 19th cent. to 1951 paid tribute to Ibadan.

Osi·jek \ˈō-sē-ˌ(y)ek\. City, Croatia, N Yugoslavia, on the Drava river ab. 130 m. ESE of Zagreb; pop. (1971p) 93,912; ships agricultural produce, livestock, brandy; textiles, shoes, sugar, leather goods. Settled by Romans early in Christian era; bishopric 2d cent. A.D.; scene of battle of Mursa 351 in which Constantius II defeated Magnentius; under Turks 1526–1687.

Osi·mo \ˈȯ-zi-ˌmō\. Commune, Ancona prov., Marches, cen. Italy, 9 m. S by W of Ancona; pop. (1968e) 23,738; episcopal see; ancient Roman walls; 8th cent. cathedral.

Osin·ni·ki \ə-ˈsēn-yi-kē\. Town, Kemerovo Oblast, Russian S.F.S.R., U.S.S.R., ab. 15 m. SE of Novokuznetsk; pop. (1969e) 67,000.

Osipenko. See BERDYANSK.

Os·ka·loo·sa \ˌäs-kə-ˈlü-sə\. **1** City, ⊗ of Mahaska co., SE cen. Iowa, 55 m. ESE of Des Moines; pop. (1970c) 11,224; clothing, dairy products; coal mines; livestock farms; William Penn Coll. (1873).

2 City, ⊗ of Jefferson co., NE Kansas; pop. (1970c) 955.

Os·kars·hamn \ˈȯs-kərs-ˌhäm-ən\. Coastal town, Kalmar co., SE Sweden; pop. (1970e) 25,177.

Oskol \ˌə-ˈskȯl\. River, Russian S.F.S.R., U.S.S.R.; 285 m. long; rises near Stary Oskol in Kursk Oblast and flows S into Donets river in E Ukrainian S.S.R.

Os·lo \ˈäz-(ˌ)lō, ˈäs-\. **1** County of SE Norway. See 2 below, and table at NORWAY.

2 *formerly* **Chris·ti·a·nia** *or* **Kris·ti·a·nia** \ˌkris(h)-chē-ˈan-ē-ə, ˌkris-tē-, -ˈän-\. City, ✱ of Norway, also ⊗ of Akershus co., SE Norway, at N end of **Oslo Fjord** (inlet of the Skaggerrak, extending inland 80 m.) and itself constituting a county (area 175 sq. m.); pop. (1972e) 477,476; largest city in Norway and its principal commercial, industrial, and transportation center; seaport, shipping wood products, chemicals, dairy products; produces electrical equipment, metal goods, dairy and wood products, machine tools, tobacco, chemicals, textiles; shipyards, hydroelectric power plants. Has numerous notable buildings, including royal palace (1848), national theater (1899), several museums, 17th cent. church, various government buildings, and an extensive system of parks. University (1811) and college of architecture (1965).

History: Founded by King Harald III (Haardraade) c. 1050; became capital 14th cent.; destroyed by fire 1624 and rebuilt as Christiania on present site; captured by Swedes 1716; named Oslo 1924; occupied by Germans in World War II 1940–45; site of Winter Olympics 1952.

Os·man·a·bad \ä-ˈsmän-ə-ˌbäd\. Town, SE Maharashtra, S cen. India, ab. 35 m. NNE of Sholapur; pop. (1961c) 18,900.

Os·na·brück \ˈäz-nə-ˌbru̇k\. Manufacturing city, Lower Saxony, West Germany, 30 m. NE of Münster; pop. (1969e) 140,380; road and rail junction; steel, machinery, automobile parts, paper, chemicals, textiles; 13th cent. cathedral and church, 15th cent. town hall. Episcopal see founded here 804 by Charlemagne; made city 1171; negotiations leading to Peace of Westphalia (1648) held here 1643 ff.; passed to Hannover 1803, to kingdom of Westphalia 1807; reverted to Hannover 1815. In World War II bombed by Allies 1944–45; captured Apr. 1945.

Oso, Mount \-ˈō-(ˌ)sō\. Peak, La Plata co., SW Colorado; 13,706 ft.

Osorhei. See TÎRGU-MUREŞ.

Osó·rio \u̇-ˈzȯr-(ˌ)yü\. Municipality, Rio Grande do Sul state, S Brazil, ab. 55 m. E of Pôrto Alegre; pop. (1968e) 54,887.

Osor·no \ō-ˈsȯr-(ˌ)nō\. 1 Volcanic peak, E Llanquihue prov., S cen. Chile, on E shore of Lake Llanquihue; 8730 ft.

2 Province of S cen. Chile. See table at CHILE.

3 City, its ❋, ab. 240 m. S of Concepción; pop. (1966e) 69,220; tourism; lumber, dairy products; flour mills, packing plants; ships cattle; founded 1553; destroyed by Indians 1602 and repopulated 1796; present population includes strong German element.

Oso·wiec \ȯ-ˈsȯ-vyəts\ *or Russ.* **Oso·vets** \ə-ˈsȯ-vyəts\. Village and fortress, Białystok prov., NE Poland, 32 m. NW of Białystok; for a time 1944–45 taken over by U.S.S.R. but ceded back to Poland.

Oso·yoos Lake \ə-ˌsü-yəs-\. Narrow lake, N Okanogan co., N Washington, extending N across international border into British Columbia; ab. 15 m. long.

Os·prey Reef \ˈäs-prē-, -ˌprā-\. Coral reef island in W Coral Sea, 130 m. E of Cape Melville, off NE coast of Queensland, Australia.

Os·ro·e·ne *or* **Os·rho·e·ne** \ˌäz-rə-ˈwē-nē\. Ancient kingdom, NW Mesopotamia, E of the Euphrates; ❋ Edessa; founded 2d cent. B.C.; subject for varying periods to Parthia, Armenia, and Rome; kingdom abolished by Caracalla 216 A.D.

Oss \ˈȯs\. Commune, North Brabant prov., S Netherlands, S of the Maas (Meuse) and ab. 11 m. ENE of 's Hertogenbosch; pop. (1970e) 40,085; meat products, pharmaceuticals, metalware; granted civic rights 1399.

Os·sa, Mount \-ˈäs-ə\. 1 Mountain, Tasmania, Australia; 5305 ft.; highest peak in Tasmania.

2 Peak, E Thessaly, NE Greece, NE of Larissa near the coast; 6489 ft.

Os·sa·baw Island \ˈäs-ə-ˌbȯ-\. Island in Atlantic Ocean off S mainland of Chatham co., SE Georgia.

Os·seo \ˈäs-ē-ˌō\. Village, Hennepin co., 8 m. N of Minneapolis; pop. (1970c) 2908; agriculture; feed mill.

Os·se·tia *also* **Ose·tia** \ä-ˈsē-sh(ē-)ə\. Region of the cen. Caucasus, SE U.S.S.R.; divided into the **North Os·se·tian Autonomous Soviet Socialist Republic** \-ä-ˈsē-sh(ē-)ən-\ (*q.v.*; a part of the Russian S.F.S.R.) and the **South Ossetian Autonomous Oblast** (*q.v.*; a part of the Georgian S.S.R.).

Os·sett \ˈäs-ət\. Municipal borough, West Riding, Yorkshire, N England, 9 m. S of Leeds; pop. (1970e) 17,181.

Os·si·ning \ˈȯs-ə-ˌniŋ\. Village, Westchester co., SE New York, on E bank of Hudson river overlooking Tappan Zee, 30 m. N of New York; pop. (1970c) 21,659; pharmaceuticals, furniture; residential; Sing Sing state prison (1824). Incorporated as village of **Sing Sing** \ˈsiŋ-ˌsiŋ\ 1813; name changed 1901.

Os·si·pee \ˈäs-ə-pē\. 1 River, E New Hampshire and SW Maine; flows out of Ossipee Lake E across Maine border into Saco river.

2 Town, ⊗ of Carroll co., E New Hampshire, 21 m. ENE of Laconia; pop. (1970c) 1647.

Ossipee Lake. Lake, E cen. Carroll co., E New Hampshire; ab. 8 m. long; outlet, Ossipee river, flowing E into Saco river.

Os·so·ry \ˈäs-ə-rē\. 1 Ancient kingdom, SW Leinster, Ireland; dissolved 1110.

2 Bishopric, approximately coextensive with ancient kingdom and with modern co. Kilkenny, Eire; Protestant diocese includes Ferns and Leighlin.

Os·tash·kov \əs-ˈtash-kəf\. Town, W Kalinin Oblast, Russian S.F.S.R., U.S.S.R., on S shore of Lake Seliger at source of the Volga, 100 m. WNW of Kalinin; pop. (1967e) 21,000. Under German control 1941–42.

Oste \ˈō-stə\. River, N West Germany; 99 m. long; flows N in Lower Saxony state to the Elbe river estuary 13 m. SE of Cuxhaven.

Ost·el·bi·en \ˈȯst-ˈel-bē-ən\. Literally, the region E of the Elbe in Germany, comprising before World War II the state of Mecklenburg and the Prussian provinces of Brandenburg, Pomerania, Silesia, and East Prussia.

Ostende *or* **Ostend.** See OOSTENDE.

Os·ten·so, Mount \-ˈäs-tən-ˌsō\. Mountain, Antarctica, 78°19′S, 86°14′W; 13,710 ft.

Øs·ter·dal \ˈər-stər-ˌdäl\. Valley, Norway, parallel to Swedish border and equivalent generally to the course of the Glåma river; traversed by Norway's easternmost railroad from Oslo N through Elverum, Røros, and Støren to Trondheim.

Öster Dal. See DAL.

Ös·ter·göt·land \ˌər-stər-ˈyət-ˌländ\. County of SE Sweden. See table at SWEDEN.

Øs·terø \ˈər-stər-ˌər\. Island of the Faeroes (*q.v.*), E of Strømø; 111 sq. m.; pop. (1966c) 7714.

Osterode *or* **Osterode in Ostpreussen.** See OSTRÓDA.

Os·ter·øy \ˈu̇s-tə-ˌrȯi\. Island in a fjord N of Bergen on SW coast of Norway; 127 sq. m.

Österreich. See AUSTRIA.

Ös·ter·sund \ˈər-stər-ˌsənd\. City, ⊗ of Jämtland co., W Sweden, on Lake Storsjön; pop. (1970e) 26,982; manufactures machinery and furniture.

Øst·fold \ˈərst-ˌfȯl\ *or formerly* **Smaa·le·ne·nes** \ˈsmȯ-lə-nə-ˌnās\. County of SE Norway. See table at NORWAY.

Ost·fries·land \ȯst-ˈfrē-ˌslänt\ *or* **East Fries·land** \-ˈfrēz-lənd, -ˈfrēs-ˌland\. Region on the coast of the North Sea, N West Germany, in Lower Saxony; includes the East Frisian Is. (see FRISIAN ISLANDS).

Os·tia \ˈäs-tē-ə\. Village at the mouth of the Tiber river, Latium, Italy, just E of the ancient town of same name, the port of Rome, which according to legend was founded by Ancus Marcius (641– 616 B.C.); reached height of prosperity 2d cent. A.D.; declined thereafter; abandoned mid-9th cent.; extensive ruins include dwellings, baths, temples, and a theater.

Ostia Aterni. See PESCARA 3.

Os·ti·an Way \ˌäs-tē-ən-\ *or Lat.* **Via Os·ti·en·sis** \ˌvī-ə-ˌäs-tē-ˈen(t)-səs\. Ancient road, Italy, from Rome to Ostia following the Tiber; modern road takes nearly the same course, utilizing the ancient bridges.

Ost·land \ˈȯst-ˌlänt\. Name under Nazi regime for proposed German colony in E Europe, comprising Estonian, Latvian, Lithuanian, and Belorussian S.S.Rs., U.S.S.R.

Ostmark. See history at AUSTRIA.

Ostpreussen. See EAST PRUSSIA.

Ostrasia. See AUSTRASIA.

Ostra·va \ˈȯ-strə-və\; *formerly* **Mo·rav·ská Ostrava** \ˌmȯr-əf-skə-\ *or Ger.* **Mäh·risch–Os·trau** \ˌmā-rish-ˈō-ˌstrau̇\. City, Czech S.R., cen. Czechoslovakia, near confluence of Opava and Oder rivers near Moravian Gap; pop. (1968e) 274,547; manufacturing center in coal-mining area; blast furnaces.

Os·tró·da \ȯ-ˈstrüd-ə\; *Ger.* **Oste·ro·de** \ˌō-stə-ˈrōd-ə\ *or in full* **Osterode in Ost·preus·sen** \-in-ˈōst-ˈprȯis-ᵊn\. City, Olsztyn prov., N Poland, 19 m. WSW of Olsztyn; pop. (1970p) 21,400; railroad junction; assigned to Poland by Potsdam Conference 1945.

Ostrog \ə-ˈstrȯk\ *or Pol.* **Ostróg** \ˈȯ-ˌstrük\. Town, W Ukrainian S.S.R., U.S.S.R., 59 m. SE of Lutsk on upper Goryn river; formerly in Poland; manufactures textiles, leather. Founded in 9th cent.; first complete Bible in Slavonic printed here 1581.

Os·tro·gozhsk \ˌəs-trə-ˈgȯshk\. Town, W cen. Voronezh Oblast, Russian S.F.S.R., U.S.S.R., 60 m. S of Voronezh; pop. (1967e) 33,000.

Ostro·łę·ka \ˌȯ-strə-ˈleⁿ(ŋ)-kə\ *or Russ.* **Ostro·len·ka** \ˌəs-trəl-ˈyeŋ-kə\. Commune, NE Warszawa prov., E cen. Poland, on Narew river 62 m. NNE of Warsaw; pop. (1970p) 22,000. Several battles fought here: Russians defeated by French Feb. 16, 1807; Poles defeated by Russians May 26, 1831; Russians defeated by Germans Aug. 3, 1915.

Ostrov \ˈȯs-(ˌ)trȯf\. **1** Island, Czechoslovakia. See GREAT SCHÜTT.

2 Town, Pskov Oblast, Russian S.F.S.R., U.S.S.R., ab. 30 m. S of Pskov on the Velikaya river; pop. (1967e) 18,000; railroad and commercial town on Latvian S.S.R. border.

Ostro·wiec Świę·to·krzy·ski \ȯ-ˈstrȯ-ˌvyets-shfē-eⁿ(n)t-ək-ˈshis-kē\ *or* **Ostrowiec.** Industrial commune, Kielce prov., SE cen. Poland, on a tributary of the Vistula 33 m. ENE of Kielce; pop. (1970p) 50,000; machinery, construction materials, railway rolling stock; founded in 16th or 17th cent.

Ostrów Ma·zo·wiec·ka \ˈȯ-ˌstrüf-ˌmä-zȯ-ˈvyet-skä\. Commune, E Warszawa prov., NE cen. Poland, 55 m. NE of Warsaw; pop. (1966e) 14,000; agricultural machinery.

Ostrów Wiel·ko·pol·ski \ˈȯ-ˌstrüf-vē-ˌel-kə-ˈpȯl-skē\ *or* **Ostrów** *or Ger.* **Ostro·wo** \ȯs-ˈtrō-(ˌ)vō\. Commune, Poznań prov., W cen. Poland, 62 m. SE of Poznań; pop. (1970p) 49,500; railroad junction; machine tools, lumber, clothing, ceramics; mentioned in 13th century; became town in 18th cent.; to Prussia 1793 and to Poland after World War I.

Ostsee. See BALTIC SEA.

Osttirol. See EAST TIROL.

Ostu·ni \ō-ˈstü-nē\. Commune, Brindisi prov., Apulia, SE Italy, 21 m. WNW of Brindisi; pop. (1968e) 31,425; 15th cent. cathedral; medieval towers and remains of walls.

Östvågöy. See AUSTVÅGOY.

Ostyak–Vogul National Okrug. See KHANTY-MANSI NATIONAL OKRUG.

Osŭm \ˈȯs-ŭm\ *or* **Osam** \ˈȯ-ˌsäm\. River, N Bulgaria; 195 m. long; flows N into Danube river just above Nikopol.

Osu·mi Islands \ˈō-sə-ˌmē-, ō-ˈsü-mē-\ *or Jap.* **Ōsumi Gun·tō** \-ˈgu̇n-(ˌ)tō\. Group of islands just S of Kyūshū, Japan, part of Kagoshima prefecture; chief islands Tanegashima and Yaku-shima; separated from S tip of Kyūshū by **Osumi Strait** *or* **Van Die·men Strait** \van-ˌdē-mən-\ *or Jap.* **Ōsu·mi Kai·kyō** \-ˈkī-(ˌ)kyō\.

Osu·na \ō-ˈsü-nə\ *or earlier* **Oxu·na** \ō-ˈshü-nə\; *anc.* **Ur·so** \ˈər-(ˌ)sō\ *or* **Or·so·na** \ȯr-ˈsō-nə\. Commune, Sevilla prov., SW Spain, 52 m. ESE of Seville; pop. (1970p) 21,669; flour, lime, olive oil; in agricultural region; 16th cent. Gothic church; ducal castle; university (founded 1549) suppressed 1820. Ancient Roman garrison; reconquered from Moors 1239 by Ferdinand III.

Os·wald·twis·tle \ˈäz-wəl(d)-ˌtwis-əl\. Urban district, Lancashire, NW England, on Leeds and Liverpool Canal 19 m. NNE of Manchester; pop. (1971p) 14,015; manufactures cotton goods, chemicals; coal mining.

Os·we·gatch·ie \ˌäs-wi-ˈgäch-ē\. River, N New York; ab. 150 m. long; rises in N Herkimer co., flows NW and NE into St. Lawrence river at Ogdensburg.

Os·we·go \ä-ˈswē-(ˌ)gō\. **1** River, cen. New York; 23 m. long; formed by junction of Seneca and Oneida rivers, Onondaga co., flows N into Lake Ontario at Oswego, Oswego co.; canalized (the Oswego Canal) and part of the N.Y. State Barge Canal system.

2 County in New York. See table at NEW YORK.

3 City, ⊗ of Labette co., SE Kansas, 30 m. SW of Pittsburg; pop. (1970c) 2200; coal, lead mines; diversified agriculture.

4 Industrial and commercial city, a ⊗ of Oswego co., cen. New York, on Lake Ontario at mouth of Oswego river 33 m. NNW of Syracuse; pop. (1970c) 23,844; most easterly Great Lakes port and on N.Y. State Barge Canal; center of hydroelectric power for cen. New York; boilers, malt, textiles, paper products, machinery; State Univ. of New York Coll. at Oswego (1861).

History: First English trading post on Great Lakes founded c. 1722; a contested fortress in Seven Years' War and War of 1812; incorporated 1848; became important lake port 1917 after completion of Barge Canal and international port 1959 with completion of Saint Lawrence Seaway.

5 City and lake resort, Clackamas and Multnomah cos., NW Oregon, on Willamette river 8 m. S of Portland; pop. (1970c) 14,573.

Oswego Canal. Canal connecting Lake Ontario at Oswego, New York, with the Erie Canal at Syracuse, New York; part of the N.Y. State Barge Canal system. See SYRACUSE.

Os·wes·try \ˈäz-wə-strē\. Municipal borough, Shropshire, W England, near Welsh border 55 m. WNW of Birmingham; rural dist. pop. (1971p) 30,320; market town; railroad shops, printing.

Oś·wię·cim \ȯsh-ˈvyeⁿ(n)-tsēm\ *or Ger.* **Ausch·witz** \ˈau̇sh-ˌvits\. Industrial commune, W Kraków prov., S Poland, 33 m. W of Kraków; pop. (1970p) 39,600; railroad junction; chemicals. During World War II site of the largest of the German concentration camps, in which ab. 2½ million persons were exterminated.

Ōta \ˈō-tə, -ˌtä\. City, Gumma prefecture, Honshū, Japan, 47 m. NE of Tokyo; pop. (1970c) 98,257.

Ota·go Harbor \ō-ˌtäg-ō-\. Bay, inlet of Pacific Ocean on SE coast of South I., New Zealand, ab. 11 m. long with **Otago Peninsula** on its E side, Dunedin at its head (SW), and Port Chalmers on its W shore.

Otaheite. See TAHITI.

Ota·hu·hu \ˌōt-ə-ˈhü\. Borough, N North I., New Zealand, SE suburb of Auckland; pop. (1970e) 10,150.

Ota·ru \ō-ˈtär-(ˌ)ü\. City, Hokkaidō prefecture, Japan, on W coast of Hokkaido ab. 22 m. WNW of Sapporo; pop. (1970c) 191,856; industrial and commercial center of W Hokkaidō; harbor on **Ishi·ka·ri Bay** \ˌish-ē-ˌkär-ē-\, inlet of Sea of Japan.

Ota·va·lo \ˌōt-ə-ˈväl-(ˌ)ō\. Town, Imbabura prov., N Ecuador, ab. 42 m. NNE of Quito; pop. (1962c) 8630; manufactures cotton and woolen cloth, ponchos, carpets; settled 1534; destroyed by earthquake 1868.

Ota·vi \ō-ˈtä-vē\. Town, N South-West Africa, ab. 50 m. W of Grootfontein; in copper-mining region.

Otdykh. See ZHUKOVSKI.

Otea. See GREAT BARRIER ISLAND.

Otero \ō-ˈter-(ˌ)ō\. Name of counties in two states of the U.S. See tables at COLORADO and NEW MEXICO.

Othel·lo \ō-ˈthel-(ˌ)ō\. City, Adams co., E Washington, 100 m. SW of Spokane; pop. (1970c) 4122; diversified agriculture.

Othonoí. See FANO.

Oth·rys \ˈäth-rəs, ˈō-thrəs\ *or* **Óth·ris** \ˈȯ-thris\. Mountain range in cen. Greece, extending along the N frontier of Phthiotis and Phocis dept.; highest point 5663 ft.; forms S barrier of Thessalian plain.

Oti·ra Gorge \ō-ˌtir-ə-\. Narrow cleft in Southern Alps, cen. South I., New Zealand; traversed by highway (Arthur's Pass) and railroad (through **Otira Tunnel**), connecting Christchurch with Greymouth; at W end is the village of Otira.

Otis Reservoir \ˌōt-əs-\. Reservoir on branch of Farmington river, S of Otis, SE Berkshire co., W Massachusetts.

Ot·ley \ˈät-lē\. Urban district, West Riding, Yorkshire, N England; pop. (1971p) 13,254; woolens, leather, machinery manufacture.

Otoe \ˈōt-(ˌ)ō\. County in Nebraska. See table at NEBRASKA.

Otomari. See KARSAKOV.

Oton \ō-ˈtōn\. Municipality, Iloilo prov., Panay, Phil., on Iloilo Strait 6 m. W of Iloilo; pop. (1969e) 37,400; important early settlement of the Spaniards.

Oton·a·bee \ō-ˈtän-ə-bē\. Short stream, a part of Trent river, Peterborough co., SE Ontario, Canada; forms part of Trent Canal system; Peterborough is on it.

Ot·ra \ˈü-trə\. River, S Norway; 150 m. long; flows S into the Skagerrak at Kristiansand.

Otrad·ny \ə-ˈträd-nē\. Town, Kuibyshev Oblast, Russian S.F.S.R., U.S.S.R., ab. 50 m. ENE of Kuibyshev; pop. (1967e) 43,000.

Otran·to \ō-ˈtran-(ˌ)tō, ˈō-trən-ˌtō\ *or anc.* **Hy·drun·tum** \hī-ˈdrən-təm\. Town, Lecce prov., SE tip of Apulia, S Italy; pop. (1968e) 4530; archiepiscopal see; ancient town of Calabria; destroyed by Turks 1480. During World War II an important supply base.

Otranto, Cape. Cape on SE coast of Italy, on W side of the Strait of Otranto.

Otranto, Strait of. Strait bet. SE Italy and W Albania, connecting the Adriatic Sea with the Ionian Sea; ab. 47 m. wide.

Otri·co·li \ō-ˈtrē-kə-ˌlē\. Commune, Terni prov., S Umbria, cen. Italy, on the Tiber and on the Flaminian Way; pop. (1968e) 1723; remains of ancient **Ocric·u·lum** \ō-ˈkrik-yə-ləm\.

Ot·se·go \ät-ˈsē-go\. 1 Name of counties in two states of the U.S. See tables at MICHIGAN and NEW YORK.
2 City, Allegan co., SW Michigan, 13 m. N of Kalamazoo; pop. (1970c) 3957; paper, brass, dairy products; onions.

Otsego Lake. Lake in N cen. Otsego co., cen. New York; ab. 9 m. long and an average of 1 m. wide; elevation 1193 ft.; the city of Cooperstown lies at S end; main source of Susquehanna river. Noted for its association with the novels (Leatherstocking series) of James Fenimore Cooper.

Ōtsu \ˈōt-(ˌ)sü\. City, ✻ of Shiga prefecture, W cen. Honshū, Japan, ab. 10 m. from Kyōto on SW shore of Lake Biwa; pop. (1970c) 171,777; former castle town.

Ot·ta·vi·a·no \ˌō-tä-ˈvyän-(ˌ)ō\ *or* **Ot·ta·ia·no** \ˌōt-ə-ˈyän-(ˌ)ō\. Commune, Napoli prov., Campania, S Italy, 11 m. E of Naples; pop. (1968e) 18,712.

Ot·ta·wa \ˈät-ə-wə, -ˌwä, -ˌwȯ\. 1 Name of counties in four states of the U.S. See tables at KANSAS, MICHIGAN, OHIO, OKLAHOMA.
2 City, ⊗ of La Salle co., N Illinois, on Illinois river 40 m. WSW of Joliet; pop. (1970c) 18,716; building materials, automobile parts, glass, tools; coal mines; diversified agriculture; incorporated 1837; scene of first Lincoln-Douglas debate Aug. 21, 1858.
3 City, ⊗ of Franklin co., E Kansas, 37 m. SE of Topeka; pop. (1970c) 11,036; cement, dairy products; poultry; Ottawa Univ. (1865).
4 Village, ⊗ of Putnam co., NW Ohio, 20 m. N of Lima; pop. (1970c) 3622; sugar refinery, oil wells; truck and livestock farming.
5 River, SE Ontario and S Quebec, Canada; 696 m. long; forms lower section of boundary bet. Ontario and Quebec, and continues E across S Quebec (bet. Two Mountains and Vaudreuil cos.) to empty into the St. Lawrence river (Lake of Two Mountains) at Montreal I. First explored by Champlain 1613; long a transportation route for explorers, missionaries, and traders.
6 City, ✻ of Canada, also ⊗ of Ottawa-Carleton municipal region, SE Ontario, on right bank of Ottawa river and on Rideau Canal 100 m. W of Montreal; pop. (1971p) 298,-087, met. area pop. 447,736; lumber, cement, household appliances, furniture; paper and pulp mills. Grand Séminaire d'Ottawa (1847), Univ. of Ottawa (1848), Scolasticat St-Jean (1902), Petit Séminaire d'Ottawa (1925), Bruyère Coll. (1925), St. Patrick's Coll. (1932), Carleton Univ. (1942). Numerous notable public buildings, including those of the national government (rebuilt after destruction by fire 1916) and the headquarters of several educational and cultural organizations.
History: Site reached by Champlain 1613; permanent settlement developed after construction of Rideau Canal 1827 ff.; orig. named **By·town** \ˈbī-ˌtau̇n\; incorporated as city under present name 1854; selected by Queen Victoria as capital 1858.

Ottawa–Carle·ton \-ˈkär(-ə)l-tən, -ˈkärlt-ᵊn\. Municipal region, SE Ontario, Canada. See table at ONTARIO.

Ottawa Hills. Village, Lucas co., NW Ohio, 4 m. W of Toledo; pop. (1970c) 4270.

Ottawa Islands. Group of small islands in E Hudson Bay, Keewatin dist., E Northwest Territories, Canada, off coast of N Quebec.

Ot·ter \ˈät-ər\. River, SW cen. Virginia; ab. 40 m. long; flows S through Bedford co., turns SE and empties into Roanoke river in S Campbell co.

Otter, Peaks of. Two summits in the Blue Ridge, in Bedford and Botetourt cos., W cen. Virginia; height of Southwest Peak 3875 ft., and of Flat Top 4001 ft.

Ot·ter·burn \ˈät-ər-(ˌ)bərn\. Parish, N cen. Northumberland, N England; scene of battle 1388 in which English led by Hotspur (Sir Henry Percy) were defeated by the Scots under James Douglas; Douglas was killed and Hotspur captured; celebrated by the English in the ballad *Chevy Chase* and in the old Scottish ballad *The Ballad of Otterburn.*

Otter Creek. 1 River, cen. Utah, flowing N from Piute co. into Sevier river in N Sevier co.
2 River, W Vermont; ab. 100 m. long; rises in N Bennington co., flows N into Lake Champlain in NW Addison co.

Otter Creek Reservoir. Reservoir in Otter Creek, SE Piute co., S cen. Utah.

Otter Tail. 1 River, W Minnesota; ab. 150 m. long; flows from Otter Tail Lake in cen. Otter Tail co., W cen. Minnesota, W, then S, and again W to unite with Bois de Sioux river at Breckenridge, W Minnesota, and form Red river (or Red River of the North).
2 County in Minnesota. See table at MINNESOTA.

Otter Tail Lake. Lake, cen. Otter Tail co., W cen. Minnesota; ab. 12 m. long.

Ot·tery Saint Mary \ˈät-ə-rē-\. Urban district, Devonshire, SW England; pop. (1971p) 5824; market town; notable 13th–14th cent. church; birthplace of Samuel Taylor Coleridge.

Ot·to·man Empire \ˈät-ə-mən-\ *also* **Turk·ish Empire** \ˌtər-kish-\. Former sultanate in Europe, Asia, and Africa, including at greatest extent Syria, Egypt, Iraq, Barbary States, Balkan States, and part of Russia and Hungary; ✻ Constantinople.
History: Established in 13th cent. by Turks from cen. Asia who entered Anatolia (already under Seljuks) and established small state, traditionally ruled by Osman I (1288–1326); beginning with Orkhan I (1326–62), an empire was organized on both sides of the Straits (see DARDANELLES); by end of 15th cent., it had liquidated Byzantine Empire (*q.v.*) and included Balkan region, i.e., Rumelia, Macedonia, Thessaly, Morea (Peloponnesus), Serbia, Walachia, Bosnia, Bulgaria, and Albania, most of the Aegean Is., rest of Anatolia, and Crimea; overthrew Mamelukes and secured Syria and Egypt; at its height under Suleiman the Magnificent (1520–66) who took Armenia, Azerbaijan, Mesopotamia, and Baghdad, North African coast, and, in Europe, territory from frontier of Holy Roman Empire to shores of Black Sea; although Crete, Cyprus, Arabian coasts, and Caucasus territory were later added to Ottoman holdings, the power of the empire began to decline in late 16th cent.; by series of exhausting wars with Poland, Austria, and Russia in 17th and 18th cents., Turks were expelled from Hungary and N shores of Black Sea; in 19th cent., because of internal corruption, the steady southward advance of Russia (*q.v.*),

and the successful revolts of the Balkans, the weakened Ottoman ruler came to be known as "Sick Man of Europe"; the problem of preventing too rapid a dissolution of the empire in face of Russian advance became the "Eastern Question" of European diplomacy (caused Crimean War 1854–56); after much negotiation 1888–99 and opposition from other countries, granted Nov. 25, 1899 concessions to Germany for Berlin-Baghdad R.R. (see EGYPT, TUNIS, and TRIPOLI 1 for loss of its African holdings); Macedonia, the last important European territory, lost in First Balkan War 1912–13; as one of Central Powers in World War I, was an important area of conflict (see GALLIPOLI PENINSULA, MESOPOTAMIA, etc.); sultan accepted Treaty of Sèvres (1920) by which empire gave up Cyprus, Dodecanese, Smyrna, Mesopotamia, Palestine and Syria, Arabia, Armenia, and control of Straits; meanwhile, the nationalist government at Ankara called congress 1919 and finally proclaimed republic of Turkey (*q.v.*) 1923.

Ot·tum·wa \ä-'təm-wə, ə-'təm-\. City, ⊗ of Wapello co., SE Iowa, on Des Moines river 75 m. SE of Des Moines; pop. (1970c) 29,610; brass and iron goods, dairy products, building materials, agricultural machinery, feed; railroad shops, coal mines; Ottumwa Heights Coll. (1925).

Otum·ba \ō-'tüm-bə\. Town, NE México state, cen. Mexico; pop. (1970p) 11,960; battle July 7, 1520 fought on plain of Otumba in which Cortes and Spaniards, retreating from Mexico, decisively defeated a large Aztec army.

Otvazhny. See ZHIGULEVSK.

Ot·way, Cape \-'ät-(ˌ)wā\. Cape, S Victoria, SE Australia, 70 m. SW of entrance to Port Phillip Bay.

Otway Water *or* **Otway Bay.** Wide inlet, Magallanes prov., S Chile, bet. Brunswick Penin. on the SE and Riesco I. on the NW, connecting by a narrow passage on the SW with the Strait of Magellan.

Ot·wock \'ȯt-ˌvȯtsk\. Commune, Warszawa prov., NE cen. Poland, ab. 15 m. SE of Warsaw; pop. (1970p) 39,900; summer resort.

Ötz·ta·ler Alps *also* **Oetz·ta·ler Alps** \'ərts-ˌtäl-ər-\ *or Ital.* **Al·pi Ve·nos·te** \'äl-pē-ve-'nȯs-tē\. Mountain range of the E Alps, in S Tirol, Austria, and N Trentino-Alto Adige, Italy; highest peak Wildspitze 12,382 ft.; many glaciers. Named from a valley (**Ötz·tal** *also* **Oetz·tal** \'ərts-ˌtäl\) and S tributary of the Inn in Tirol, Austria.

Ouach·i·ta *or* **Wash·i·ta** \'wäsh-ə-ˌtȯ\. 1 River, SW Arkansas and E Louisiana; 605 m. long; navigable 350 m.; rises in Polk co., W Arkansas, flows E and then SE across Louisiana border and S to the Black river in Catahoula co.
2 Name of a parish in Louisiana and of a county in Arkansas. See tables at ARKANSAS and LOUISIANA.

Ouachita Mountains. Range, W cen. Arkansas and E Oklahoma, a S continuation of Ozark Plateau; highest peak 2660 ft.

Oua·daï \ˌwä-'dī\ *also* **Wa·dai** \ˌwä-'dī\. Prefecture, E Chad; 29,436 sq. m.; pop. (1970e) 344,000; ✱ Abéché; was part of a former Muslim sultanate; came under French influence 1899, not pacified until 1912.

Oua·dane *or* **Oua·dan** \wa-'dan\ *also* **Wa·dan** \wä-'dan\. Oasis, W cen. Mauritania, W Africa.

Oua·ga·dou·gou *also* **Wa·ga·du·gu** \ˌwäg-ə-'dü-(ˌ)gü\. City, ✱ of Upper Volta, W Africa; pop. (1970e) 115,500; railroad terminus; ships peanuts; handicrafts (statuettes and carpets).

Oua·hi·gou·ya \wī-'gü-yə\. Town, Upper Volta, W Africa, 100 m. NW of Ouagadougou.

Ouarg·la *or* **Warg·la** \'wär-glə\ *also* **Warq·la** \'wȯr-klə, 'wär-\. Town and oasis, ✱ of Oasis dept., Algeria, N Africa, ab. 90 m. SW of Touggourt; pop. (1966c) 18,206.

Ouar·se·nis Mas·sif \ˌwär-sə-ˌnē-ma-'sēf\. Highland region in NE Algeria; highest peak 6512 ft.

Oubangui. See UBANGI.

Oubangui–Chari *or* **Oubangui–Chari–Tchad.** See CENTRAL AFRICAN REPUBLIC.

Ouche \'üsh\. River, Côte-d'Or dept., E France; ab. 60 m. long; flows into Saône river.

Ou·chy \ü-'shē\. Village, Vaud canton, on the Lake of Geneva in SW Switzerland; the port of Lausanne; treaty 1912.

Ou·de Maas \'aù-də-ˌmäs\. Left branch of the Merwede river in Netherlands, flowing into the North Sea just S of the Nieuwe Maas river; it leaves the Merwede near Dordrecht.

Oudenaarde. See AUDENARDE.

Oude Rijn \'aùd-ə-ˌrīn\. Branch of the Lek river in Netherlands; flows N out of the Lek and then W to the North Sea at Katwijk; passes Utrecht and Leiden in its course.

Oudh *also* **Audh** \'aùd\. A former province of Brit. India, now the NE portion of Uttar Pradesh state, India; 24,071 sq. m. Received its name from Ajodhya (*q.v.*), sacred city of the Hindus and capital of the ancient kingdom of Kosala, which was nearly coextensive with modern Oudh. Overrun by Muslim invaders 11th cent. and later; held by British as a fief of the Mogul rulers 1756–1856; annexed to British dominions; with Agra placed under one administrator 1877; made part of United Provinces 1902 under new name.

Oudjda. See OUJDA.

Oudts·hoorn \'ōts-ˌhȯ(ə)rn\. Town, S Cape Province, S Rep. of South Africa, near Olifants river 220 m. E of Cape Town; in Little Karroo; pop. (1967e) 25,800; center of once flourishing ostrich-farming industry; in fertile area watered by irrigation. Cango Caves, noted for stalactite and stalagmite formations, nearby.

Oued, Al–. See AL-OUED.

Oued–Zem \wed-'zem\. Town, W cen. Morocco, NW Africa, 110 m. E of Al-Jadida; pop. (1960c) 18,640.

Oued–Zé·na·ti \ˌwed-zā-nə-'tē\. Commune, NE Algeria, ab. 50 m. E of Constantine; pop. (1966c) 9576.

Ouessant, Île d'. See ÎLE D'OUESSANT.

Ouez·zane \we-'zan\ *or Arab.* **Waz·zan** *also* **Wa·zan** \wa-'zan\. Sacred city, N Morocco, NW Africa, 60 m. NW of Fès; pop. (1960c) 26,203.

Ou·grée \ü-'grā\. Commune, Liège prov., E Belgium, on Meuse river; S suburb of Liège; pop. (1969e) 20,801.

Oui·dah *or* **Wi·da** \'wēd-ə\ *or Eng.* **Whyd·ah** \'(h)wid-ə\. Seaport town, S Dahomey, W Africa, on lagoon 23 m. W of Cotonou; pop. (1970e) 26,000; has large orchards of orange and citron trees. Founded as a French trading port in 17th cent.

Ouj·da *or* **Oudj·da** \üj-'dä\ *or Arab.* **Uj·da** \'üj-də\. Commercial city, NE Morocco, NW Africa, near the Algerian border; pop. (1960c) 128,645; railroad junction; founded 944; to Morocco 1797.

Ou·lan·ka National Park \'ō-läŋ-kə-\. National park, Finland; 41 sq. m.; wilderness region; established 1956.

Ou·led Mous·sa \ü-ˌled-'müs-ə\ *or formerly* **Saint–Pierre–Saint–Paul** \saⁿ-ˌpyer-saⁿ-'pȯl\. Commune, N Algeria; pop. (1966c) 15,000.

Ouled–Naïl Mountains \ü-'led-'nīl-, -'nāl-\. Range of the Atlas Mts. in N cen. Algeria.

Oul·lins \ü-'laⁿ\. Commune, Rhône dept., E cen. France, SSW suburb of Lyons; pop. (1968c) 26,204.

Ou·lu \'aù-(ˌ)lü\. 1 Province of N cen. Finland. See table at FINLAND.
2 *or Swed.* **Ule·å·borg** \'ü-le-ō-ˌbȯ(ə)r\. Seaport, its ✱, on Gulf of Bothnia and at mouth of Oulu river; pop. (1970e) 87,244; pulp and flour mills, shipyards, foundries; univ. (1958); castle built 1590; founded 1605; destroyed by fire 1822.

Ou·lu·jär·vi \'aù-lù-ˌya(ə)r-vē\. Lake in cen. Finland; drains NW through **Oulu River** (65 m. long) into NE Gulf of Bothnia.

Oum er Rbia \ˌüm-er-ˌrəb-ē-'(y)ä\. River, cen. Morocco, NW Africa; 345 m. long; flows NW into Atlantic Ocean at Al-Jadida.

Ou·nas \'aù-ˌnäs\. River, NW Finland; 210 m. long; flows S into Kemi river.

Oup. See AUOB.

Our \'ù(ə)r\. River, forming section of NE boundary bet. West Germany and the Grand Duchy of Luxembourg; 50 m. long; flows S into Sauer river E of Diekirch.

Ou·ray \ü-'rā\. 1 County in SW Colorado. See table at COLORADO.
2 City, its ⊗; pop. (1970c) 741; lead, zinc, silver, uranium, and copper mining; hot springs; Ouray State Game Refuge nearby.

Ouray Peak *also* **Hunts Peak** \ˌhənts-\. Mountain, Chaffee co., cen. Colorado; 13,955 ft.

Ourcq \'ù(ə)rk\. River, Aisne dept., N France; 50 m. long; part of the water supply for Paris; battles in Sept. 1914 and in 1918.

Ou·ri·que \ō-'rē-kə\. Commune, Beja dist., S Portugal, 31 m. SSW of Beja; pop. (1970p) 3482; defeat of Moors 1139 resulting in formation of Portuguese kingdom under Alfonso I.

Ou·ro Fi·no \ˌō-rù-'fē-(ˌ)nü\. City, SW Minas Gerais state, E Brazil, 100 m. N of São Paulo; munic. pop. (1968e) 23,778.

Ouro Prê·to \-'prā-(ˌ)tü\. Town, Minas Gerais state, E Brazil, 40 m. SE of Belo Horizonte; munic. pop. (1968e) 38,-372; in agricultural district; tourism; noted for its baroque colonial architecture; national monument; founded as gold-mining settlement 1701 and a center of Brazilian gold production during 18th cent.

Ourthe \'ù(ə)rt\. River, SE Belgium; ab. 100 m. long; flows N in Luxembourg and Liège provs. into the Meuse.

Ouse \'üz\1 *or* **Great Ouse.** River, cen. and E England; 156 m. long; rises in Northamptonshire, flows in a winding course E and NE into the Wash below King's Lynn.
2 River, NE England; 45 m. long; formed by confluence of the Swale and Ure rivers in Yorkshire, flows SE to unite with the Trent river and form the Humber; navigable as far as York.
3 River, Sussex, S England; 30 m. long.

Ous·sel·tia \ü-sel-'tyä\. Town, N cen. Tunisia, 30 m. WNW of Kairouan; pop. (1966c) 2000.

Ou·ta·gam·ie \ˌaùt-ə-'gam-ē\. County in Wisconsin. See table at WISCONSIN.

Ou·tardes \ü-'tärd\. River, S cen. Quebec, Canada; 270 m. long; rises in Lake Pletipi and flows S to St. Lawrence.

Outer Hebrides. See HEBRIDES.

Outer Island. See APOSTLE ISLANDS.

Outer Mongolia. See MONGOLIAN PEOPLE'S REPUBLIC.

Outer Provinces *or Du.* **Bui·ten·ge·wes·ten** \ˌbòit-ᵊn-gə-ˌves-tən\. Those parts of the former Netherlands Indies outside of Java and Madura; comprised Sumatra, Borneo, Celebes, Moluccas, and Lesser Sunda Is.; 684,064 sq. m. See INDONESIA 2.

Outer Rhodes. See APPENZELL.

Outer San·ta Bar·ba·ra Channel \-ˌsant-ə-ˌbär-b(ə-)rə-\. Strait bet. Santa Catalina I. and San Clemente I. off NW coast of San Diego co., S California.

Ou·tes \ō-'ü-(ˌ)tās\. Commune, La Coruña prov., NW Spain, 44 m. SW of La Coruña; pop. (1970p) 9968; agriculture and stock raising; manufactures linen.

Out·jo \'ōt-(ˌ)yō\. Town, N cen. South-West Africa, 170 m. NNW of Windhoek; pop. (1960c) 2943.

Ou·tre·mont \'ü-trə-ˌmänt, *Fr.* ᵊü-trə-mōⁿ\. Residential city, an independent municipality forming part of Greater Montreal, S Quebec, Canada, lying N of Mount Royal in cen. part of Montreal I.; pop. (1971p) 28,402; Coll. Jésus-Marie d'Outremont (1933).

Ouya. See OYAK.

Ova·lau \ˌō-və-'laù\. Island, Fiji, in the Lomai Viti group, SW Pacific Ocean, ab. 12 m. off E coast of Viti Levu; 40 sq. m.; chief town Levuka, ✱ of Fiji until 1882. In early days of settlement favored by Europeans for residence.

Ova·lle \ō-'vī-ˌā, -'vä-ˌyā\. City, Coquimbo prov., cen. Chile, 200 m. N of Santiago; pop. (1966e) 29,377.

Ov·am·bo·land \ō-'vam-bō-ˌland\ *also* **Am·bo·land** \'am-bō-ˌland\. The region in the N part of South-West Africa inhabited by the Ovampo.

Ovar \ü-'vär\. Commune, Aveiro dist., NW Portugal, near Atlantic Ocean N of Aveiro; pop. (1970p) 16,004; port.

Overflakkee. See GOEREE.

Over·ijs·sel \ˌō-və-'rī-səl\. Province, E Netherlands; 1518 sq. m.; pop. (1970e) 920,882; ✱ Zwolle; livestock raising, dairy farming; industry includes textile weaving, engineering, salt and food processing.

Over·land \'ō-vər-lənd\. City, St. Louis co., E Missouri, 10 m. WNW of St. Louis; pop. (1970c) 24,949.

Overland Park. City, Johnson co., NE Kansas, S of Kansas City; pop. (1970c) 79,034.

Over·lea \'ō-vər-ˌlē\. Urban area, Baltimore co., N Maryland, NE of Baltimore; pop. (1970c) 13,086.

Overseas Highway. See FLORIDA KEYS.

Over·ton \'ō-vər-tən\. 1 County in Tennessee. See table at TENNESSEE.
2 Town, Clark co., SE Nevada, ab. 48 m. NE of Las Vegas; pop. (1970c) 900; houses relics of ancient Indian village of **Lost City** ab. 5 m. S, now covered by Lake Mead.
3 City, Rusk and Smith cos., E Texas, ESE of Tyler; pop. (1970c) 2084; oil and gas wells; fruit farms.

Ovid \'ō-vəd\. Village, a ⊗ of Seneca co., W cen. New York; pop. (1970c) 799.

Ovie·do \ˌō-vē-'ā-(ˌ)thō\. 1 Province of NW Spain. See table at SPAIN.
2 *or anc.* **As·tu·ri·as** \a-'st(y)ùr-ē-əs\. City, its ✱, 230 m. NNW of Madrid; pop. (1970p) 154,117; center of mining and agricultural region; 12th–16th cent. cathedral, two 9th cent. churches, convent; univ. (1608). Founded 8th cent.; bishopric 812; capital of Asturias until 910; sacked by French 1809 and badly damaged in Spanish Civil War 1936–39.

Ovilava. See WELS.

Ovoca. See AVOCA 3.

Owari Bay. See ISE BAY.

Owas·co Lake \ō-ˌwäs-kō-\. Lake, Cayuga co., cen. New York; ab. 11 m. long by 1 m. wide; one of the Finger Lakes (*q.v.*); N end outlet flows into Seneca river.

Owas·so \ō-'wä-sō\. Town, Tulsa co., NE Oklahoma, 8 m. N of Tulsa; pop. (1970c) 3491; diversified agriculture.

Owa·ton·na \ˌō-wə-'tän-ə\. City, ⊗ of Steele co., S Minnesota, 15 m. S of Faribault; pop. (1970c) 15,341; tools, agricultural machinery, dairy products; tannery; dairy and truck farms.

Owe·go \ō-'wē-(ˌ)gō\. Village, ⊗ of Tioga co., S New York, on Susquehanna river 20 m. W of Binghamton; pop. (1970c) 5152; summer resort; furniture; dairy farms.

Owei·nat, Jeb·el \ˌjeb-əl-ō-'wā-(ˌ)nat\ *or* **Jebel Uwei·nat** \-ü-'wā-\ *or* **Ja·bal al 'Uway·nāt** \ˌjab-əl-ˌal-ü-\. Mountain, center of Libyan Desert on NW boundary of Sudan; 6345 ft.

Ow·en \'ō-ən\. Name of counties in two states of the U.S. See tables at INDIANA and KENTUCKY.

Owen, Mount. Peak, cen. Grand Teton National Park, NW Wyoming; 12,922 ft.

Owen Falls. Former waterfall in the Victoria Nile in Uganda; 65 ft. high; submerged by **Owen Falls Dam.**

Ow·ens \'ō-ənz\. River, E California; ab. 120 m. long; rises in W Mono co., flows S, formerly into Owens Lake (*q.v.*); now by way of Los Angeles Aqueduct supplies water to city of Los Angeles.

Ow·ens·boro \'ō-ənz-ˌbər-ə, -ˌbə-rə\. City, ⊗ of Daviess co., NW Kentucky, on Ohio river 85 m. WSW of Louisville; pop. (1970c) 50,329; livestock, grain, and tobacco market; chemicals, electrical equipment, steel, whiskey, cigars; oil and gas wells; Kentucky Wesleyan Coll. (1866), Brescia Coll. (1874). Settled c. 1799; incorporated as town 1817; raided by Confederate guerrillas 1864.

Owens Lake. Dry lake bed in cen. Inyo co., E California; formerly held waters forming body ab. 18 m. long by 10 m. wide and fed by Owens river; water now taken by Los Angeles Aqueduct to Los Angeles.

Owen Sound. 1 Inlet of SW Georgian Bay, SE Ontario, Canada.

2 Industrial city, ⊗ of Grey co., SE Ontario, Canada, on Owen Sound 105 m. NW of Toronto; pop. (1971p) 18,281; port; tourist resort; furniture, boats and marine hardware, paint; dairy and fruit farms.

Owen Stan·ley Range \-ˈstan-lē-\. Mountain range extending SE and NW on New Guinea I., Papua New Guinea; ab. 600 m. long; highest peak Mount Victoria 13,363 ft. Crossed by highway through pass in cen. part from Kokoda to Port Moresby.

Ow·en·ton \ˈō-ən-tən\. City, ⊗ of Owen co., N Kentucky; pop. (1970c) 1280.

Ow·ings·ville \ˈō-iŋz-ˌvil\. City, ⊗ of Bath co., NE Kentucky; pop. (1970c) 1381; tobacco.

Owl Creek \ˈaů(ə)l-\. See BELLE FOURCHE.

Owl Creek Mountains. Range of the Rocky Mts. in NW cen. Wyoming, extending along boundary bet. Hot Springs and Fremont cos.; highest peak ab. 9600 ft.

Owls Head \ˈaů(ə)lz-\. Point of land jutting out from E mainland of Knox co., Maine, into Penobscot Bay, SE of Rockland.

Owo \ˈō-(ˌ)wō\. Town, Western State, Nigeria, 30 m. NE of Ibadan; pop. (1969e) 93,254.

Owos·so \ō-ˈwäs-(ˌ)ō\. City, Shiawassee co., S cen. Michigan, 26 m. W of Flint; pop. (1970c) 17,179; flour, electric motors; truck and livestock farms; Owosso Coll. (1909).

Ows·ley \ˈaůz-lē\. County in Kentucky. See table at KENTUCKY.

Owy·hee \ō-ˈwī-(ˌ)(h)ē\. 1 River, SE Oregon; ab. 300 m. long; formed by junction of forks in Owyhee co., SW corner of Idaho, flows NW across Oregon boundary, N through Malheur co., and empties into Snake river.

2 County in Idaho. See table at IDAHO.

Owyhee Dam *and* **Owyhee Reservoir.** See UNITED STATES, *Dams and Reservoirs.*

Ox·ford \ˈäks-fərd\. 1 County in Maine. See table at MAINE.

2 Town, New Haven co., S Connecticut, 10 m. W of New Haven; pop. (1970c) 4480.

3 Town, Worcester co., cen. Massachusetts, 10 m. SSW of Worcester; pop. (1970c) 10,345.

4 Village, Oakland co., SE Michigan, 14 m. N of Pontiac; pop. (1970c) 2536; De Lima Junior Coll. (1958).

5 City, ⊗ of Lafayette co., N Mississippi, 46 m. WNW of Tupelo; pop. (1970c) 13,846; sawmills; dairy and poultry farms; Univ. of Mississippi (1844).

6 Town, ⊗ of Granville co., N North Carolina, 30 m. NNE of Durham; pop. (1970c) 7178; clothing, lumber, tobacco.

7 Village, Butler co., SW Ohio, 12 m. NW of Hamilton; pop. (1970c) 15,868; residential; Miami Univ. (1809), Western Coll. for Women (1853).

8 Borough, Chester co., SE Pennsylvania, 25 m. SE of Lancaster; pop. (1970c) 3658; mushrooms; dairy farms.

9 County, Ontario, Canada. See table at ONTARIO.

10 County in England. See OXFORDSHIRE.

11 *or Lat.* **Ox·o·nia** \äk-ˈsō-nē-ə\. County borough, ⊗ of Oxfordshire, cen. England, on the Thames 52 m. WNW of London; pop. (1971p) 108,564; motor vehicles, steel stampings and forgings, preserves; printing and binding; cathedral (chapel of Christ Church Coll.); Univ. of Oxford (12th cent.). First mentioned 912; meeting place of several 13th cent. parliaments; chartered 1605; royalist stronghold in Civil War; made county borough 1889.

Ox·ford·shire \ˈäks-fərd-ˌshi(ə)r, -shər\ *or* **Oxford** *or* **Ox·on** \ˈäk-ˌsän, -sən\. County, cen. England; area 749 sq. m.; pop. (1971p) 380,814; ⊗ Oxford; rivers the Thames and its tributaries; grain; livestock; manufacturing (farm machinery, automobiles, aluminum, paper, leather goods); main towns Oxford, Banbury, Henley-on-Thames, Woodstock, Cowley.

Oxianus Lacus. See ARAL SEA.

Ox·leys Peak \äk-slēz-\. Highest mountain in Liverpool Range, NE New South Wales, SE Australia; 4500 ft.

Ox·nard \ˈäk-ˌsnärd\. City, Ventura co., SW California, near coast of Santa Barbara Channel 50 m. WNW of Los Angeles; pop. (1970c) 71,225; oil refining, fruit packing, vegetable canning, sugar processing; in agricultural region producing citrus fruit, truck crops, nuts, and sugar beets.

Oxon. See OXFORDSHIRE.

Oxonia. See OXFORD 11.

Oxuna. See OSUNA.

Oxus. See AMU DARYA.

Ox·y·rhyn·chus \ˌäk-si-ˈriŋ-kəs\; *Arab.* **Al–Bah·na·sā** \al-ˈban-ə-sə\ *also* **Beh·ne·sa** \ˈben-ə-sə\. Archaeological site on heights above Bahr Yusef, W bank of Nile ab. 54 m. S of Al-Faiyūm, Egypt, 28°38′N lat., 30°39′E long. Ancient papyri (*Oxyrhynchus* papyri) discovered here Jan. 1897 and in 1903; fragment contained Jesus' sayings and probably dates from 3d cent. A.D.

Oya·hue \ō-ˈyä-(ˌ)wā\. 1 Volcanic peak, SW Bolivia; 19,225 ft.

2 Volcano, Chile. See OLLAGÜE.

Oyak \ō-ˈyak\ *or* **Ou·ya** \ů-ˈyä\. River, N French Guiana; ab. 70 m. long; flows NNE into Atlantic Ocean, separating Cayenne I. from the mainland.

Oya·ma \ō-ˈyäm-ə\. 1 Peak, Japan. See DAISEN.

2 City, Tokyo prefecture, Honshū, Japan, 44 m. N of Tokyo; pop. (1968e) 90,632.

Oya·pock \ˌȯ-yə-ˈpȯk\. 1 *or* **Oya·pok** \-ˈpȯk\. River, N South America; ab. 260 m. long; rises in the Tumuc-Humac Mts. in S French Guiana, flows NE, forming boundary bet. N Brazil and French Guiana, into the Atlantic Ocean through a wide mouth, **Oyapock Bay.**

2 Port, French Guiana, on the Oyapock river N of St. Georges.

Øy·e·ren \ˈȯi-ə-rən\. Lake in SE Norway, E of Oslo; 34 sq. m.; traversed by the Glåma river.

Oyo \ˈō-(ˌ)yō\. Town, Western State, Nigeria, ab. 32 m. N of Ibadan; pop. (1969e) 130,290; in agricultural region; handicrafts; St. Andrew's Coll. (1897).

Ōyo·do \ˈō-yə-ˌdō\. River in SE Kyūshū, Japan; flows E into Pacific Ocean at Miyazaki.

Oyon·nax \ˌō-yȯ-ˈnaks\. Commune, Ain dept., E France, 12 m. E of Bourg; pop. (1968c) 19,777.

Oys·ter Bay \ˌȯi-stər-\. 1 Inlet of Long Island Sound, Nassau co., SE New York, N shore of Long I.

2 Village, Nassau co., SE New York, on Long I., on inlet of Long Island Sound; pop. (1970c) 6600; residential suburb of New York City; known as home of Theodore Roosevelt (Sagamore Hill) which is actually in nearby village of **Cove Neck** \ˈkōv-\ (pop. 344); Roosevelt Memorial Park; Roosevelt's grave in Young's Memorial Cemetery. Oyster Bay village is a part of **Oyster Bay** town (pop. 329,142), which also includes the village of **Oyster Bay Cove** (pop. 1320).

Oza·miz \ō-ˈsäm-(ˌ)ēs\. Chartered city, Misamis Occidental prov., Mindanao, Phil.; pop. (1970e) 60,000.

Ozark \ˈō-ˌzärk\. 1 County in Missouri. See table at MISSOURI.

2 City, ⊗ of Dale co., SE Alabama; pop. (1970c) 13,555; textiles, lumber; hogs, peanuts.

3 City, a ⊗ of Franklin co., NW Arkansas, on Arkansas river; pop. (1970c) 2592; coal mines.

4 City, ⊗ of Christian co., SW Missouri; pop. (1970c) 2384; summer resort; stock and dairy farms.

Ozark Plateau *also* **Ozark Mountains.** Eroded tableland, S cen. U.S., extending from SW Missouri across NW Arkansas into E Oklahoma; bet. 1500 and 2500 ft. high; approximately 50,000 sq. m.

Ozau·kee \ō-ˈzȯ-kē\. County in Wisconsin. See table at WISCONSIN.

Ózd \ˈōzd\. Town, N Hungary, ab. 25 m. WNW of Miskolc; pop. (1970p) 38,637.

Ozette, Lake \-ō-ˈzet\. Lake, W Clallam co., NW Washington.

Ozie·ri \ˌō(d)-zē-ˈe(ə)r-ē\. Commune, Sassari prov., NW Sardinia, Italy, 25 m. ESE of Sassari; pop. (1968e) 11,028; cathedral; prehistoric burial places nearby.

Ozo·na \ō-ˈzōn-ə\. Town, ⊗ of Crockett co., W Texas, 70 m. SW of San Angelo; pop. (1970c) 2864; oil wells; only town in Crockett co.

Ozor·ków \ȯ-ˈzȯ(ə)r-ˌküf\ *or Russ.* **Ozor·kov** \ˌə-zər-ˈkȯf\. Industrial commune, Łódź prov., cen. Poland, on Bzura river 14 m. NNW of Łódź; pop. (1968e) 17,700; textiles, chemicals.

Pa–an \ˈbä-än\. Town, ✻ of Kawthule state, S cen. Burma.

Paar·de·berg \ˈpärd-ə-ˌbe(ə)rg\. Battlefield, W Orange Free State, E cen. Rep. of South Africa, on the Modder river 23 m. SE of Kimberley; scene of Cronjé's surrender to Lord Roberts Feb. 28, 1900.

Paarl \ˈpär(ə)l\. Town, SW Cape Province, S Rep. of South Africa, 30 m. ENE of Cape Town on Great Berg river; pop. (1967e) 48,800; has extensive fruit orchards and vineyards; produces wine; founded 1690 by Huguenot settlers.

Pab·bay \ˈpab-(ˌ)ā\. 1 Island, Scotland, in Outer Hebrides SW of island of Lewis with Harris.

2 Island in Outer Hebrides S of Barra I.

Pab·bi·ring Archipelago \pä-ˈbir-iŋ-\ *or formerly* **Sper·mun·de Archipelago** \spər-ˈmən-də-\. Group of small low islands, SE Makasar Strait, off SW coast of Celebes Is., Malay Archipelago, Indonesia.

Pa·bia·ni·ce *or* **Pa·bja·ni·ce** \ˌpäb-yə-ˈnēt-sə\. Industrial commune, Łódź prov., cen. Poland, on railroad 10 m. SSW of Łódź; pop. (1970p) 62,300; textiles, esp. linen. Taken by Germans in 1914 and 1939.

Pab·na \ˈpəb-ˌnä\. Town, Bangla Desh, near Ganges river ab. 72 m. WNW of Dacca; munic. pop. (1961c) 40,792.

Pacaraima, Serra. See SERRA PACARAIMA.

Pac·a·rai·ma Mountains *also* **Pak·a·rai·ma Mountains** \ˌpak-ə-ˌrī-mə-\. Range in W Guyana; the NE extension of the Serra Pacaraima (*q.v.*).

Pa·cas·ma·yo \ˌpäk-əs-ˈmī-(ˌ)(y)ō\. Seaport, La Libertad dept., NW Peru, ab. 65 m. NW of Salaverry and 360 m. NW of Callao.

Pa·ca·ya \pä-ˈkī-ə\. River, a W tributary of the Ucayali river in Loreto dept., NE Peru; ab. 100 m. long.

Pa·chá·ca·mac \pə-ˈchäk-ə-ˌmäk\. Site of a pre-Incan city, ab. 20 m. SE of Lima, Peru; famous for remains of the ancient Yuncan civilization with its temple to the god Pachacamac, tombs, and city walls, and for its ruins of the later Incan temple to the sun; sacked by Pizarro 1523; site now occupied by the village of La Mamacoma, pop. (1961c) 8500.

Pa·cha·cha·ca \ˌpäch-ə-ˈchäk-ə\. Short stream, SE Peru, a tributary of the Apurimac near Abancay; in region of its headwaters was probable homeland of Aymara and Quechua Indian tribes.

Pach·aug Pond \ˈpach-ȯg-\. Lake in NE cen. New London co., SE Connecticut; outlet, **Pachaug River,** flowing NW into Quinebaug river.

Pa·chi·no \pä-ˈkē-(ˌ)nō\. Coastal commune, Siracusa prov., SE Sicily, Italy, near SE tip of Sicily 26 m. SSW of Syracuse; pop. (1968e) 23,260; tuna fishing.

Pa·chi·tea \ˌpäch-i-ˈtā-ə\. River, Peru; ab. 220 m. long; flows from the Andes Mts. into Ucayali river.

Pa·chu·ca \pə-ˈchü-kə\ *or in full* **Pachuca de So·to** \-di-ˈsōt-(ˌ)ō\. City, ✻ of Hidalgo state, cen. Mexico, 50 m. N of Mexico City; munic. pop. (1970p) 84,543; altitude 8150 ft.; silver mines, smelters, ore reduction plants; univ. (1869). Early Spanish settlement; center of silver mining since 1534.

Pachynus Promontorium. See PASSERO, CAPE.

Pa·cif·ic \pə-ˈsif-ik\. 1 County in Washington. See table at WASHINGTON.

2 City, Franklin and St. Louis cos., E Missouri, 33 m. W of St. Louis; pop. (1970c) 3247; paper products, building materials; agriculture.

Pa·cif·i·ca \pə-ˈsif-i-kə\. City, San Mateo co., W California, on Pacific coast S of San Francisco; pop. (1970c) 36,020; residential; formed 1957 by consolidation of several communities.

Pacific Grove. Residential and resort city, Monterey co., W California, at S end of Monterey Bay; pop. (1970c) 13,505; founded 1874.

Pacific Islands. The islands of the Pacific Ocean, divided into Micronesia, Melanesia, and Polynesia (including New Zealand). See OCEANIA.

Pacific Islands, Trust Territory of the. United States trust territory, comprising the Caroline Is. (with Palau Is.), Marshall Is., and Mariana Is. (except Guam); land area 699 sq. m.; pop. (1970e) 102,250; ✻ Saipan.

Pacific Ocean. Body of water extending from the Arctic circle to the equator (**North Pacific Ocean**) and from the equator to the Antarctic Regions (**South Pacific Ocean**), and from W North America and W South America to Australia, the Malay Archipelago, and E Asia; area ab. 70,000,000 sq. m.; max. depth, 11°21′N, 142°12′E (Mariana Trench) 36,198 ft.

Pacific Pal·i·sades \-ˌpal-ə-ˈsādz\. City, Honolulu co., Hawaii; pop. (1970c) 7846.

Pa·ci·jan \pä-ˈsē-ˌhän\. Island, westernmost of Camotes Is., Cebu prov., Phil.; 34 sq. m.; coextensive with San Francisco municipality.

Packhoi. See PEI-HAI.

Pa·coi·ma Dam \pə-ˌkȯi-mə-\. See UNITED STATES, *Dams and Reservoirs.*

Pacsan, Mount. See SICAPOO, MOUNT.

Pac·to·lus \pak-ˈtōl-əs\. River in Lydia, Asia Minor, yielding gold-bearing sand; a tributary of the Hermus (*mod.* Gediz) entering it near Sardis.

Padalung. See PHATTALUNG.

Pa·dang \ˈpäd-ˌäŋ\. 1 Island in Strait of Malacca, off coast of Sumatra at 1°10′N, 102°21′E.

2 Seaport city, ✻ of West Sumatra prov., Sumatra I., Indonesia, 575 m. NW of Djakarta ab. 1°S of the equator; pop. (1961c) 143,699; major port at Telukbajur 4 m. to S, shipping rubber, copra, tea, coffee, spices, cement, hides; univ. (1956). Established as Dutch factory early 17th cent.; fortified 1667; held by British 1795–1819; port constructed 1880–90; in World War II occupied by Japanese Mar. 1942–Sept. 1945.

Pa·dang·pan·djang \ˌpäd-aŋ-ˈpän-ˌjäŋ\. Town, W Sumatra, Indonesia; junction point for railroads to Padang, Bukittinggi, and Sawahlunto.

Paddan–Aram. See MESOPOTAMIA.

Pa·den City \ˌpā-dən-\. Town, NW West Virginia, in Tyler and Wetzel cos., on Ohio river 24 m. SSW of Moundsville; pop. (1970c) 3764; glass, dairy products.

Pa·der·born \ˈpäd-ər-ˌbȯ(ə)rn\. Industrial and commercial city, North Rhine-Westphalia, West Germany, 50 m. ESE of Münster; pop. (1969e) 64,576; rail and road junction; cement, lumber, iron products; 11th–13th cent. cathedral, 17th cent. town hall, restored 17th cent. Jesuit church. Meeting place of Charlemagne and Pope Leo III 799 (leading to foundation of Holy Roman Empire); came under prince bishop c. 1100; to Prussia 1802.

Pa·de·ria \pə-ˈder-ē-ə\. Town, S Nepal, near boundary of Uttar Pradesh, N India, 47 m. N of Gorakhpur.

Pad·i·ham \ˈpad-ē-əm\. Urban district, Lancashire, NW England, 24 m. N of Manchester; pop. (1971p) 10,192.

Pad·je·lan·ta National Park \ˌpäd-yə-ˈlän-tə-\. National park, N Sweden; 788 sq. m.; important botanical area; established 1962.

Padma. See GANGES DELTA.

Pa·do·va \ˈpäd-ə-və\. 1 Province of Italy. See table at ITALY.

2 Commune, Italy. See PADUA.

Pad·re Island \ˌpäd-rē-\. Uninhabited sand reef, off the mainland of Kleberg, Kenedy, Willacy, and Cameron cos.,

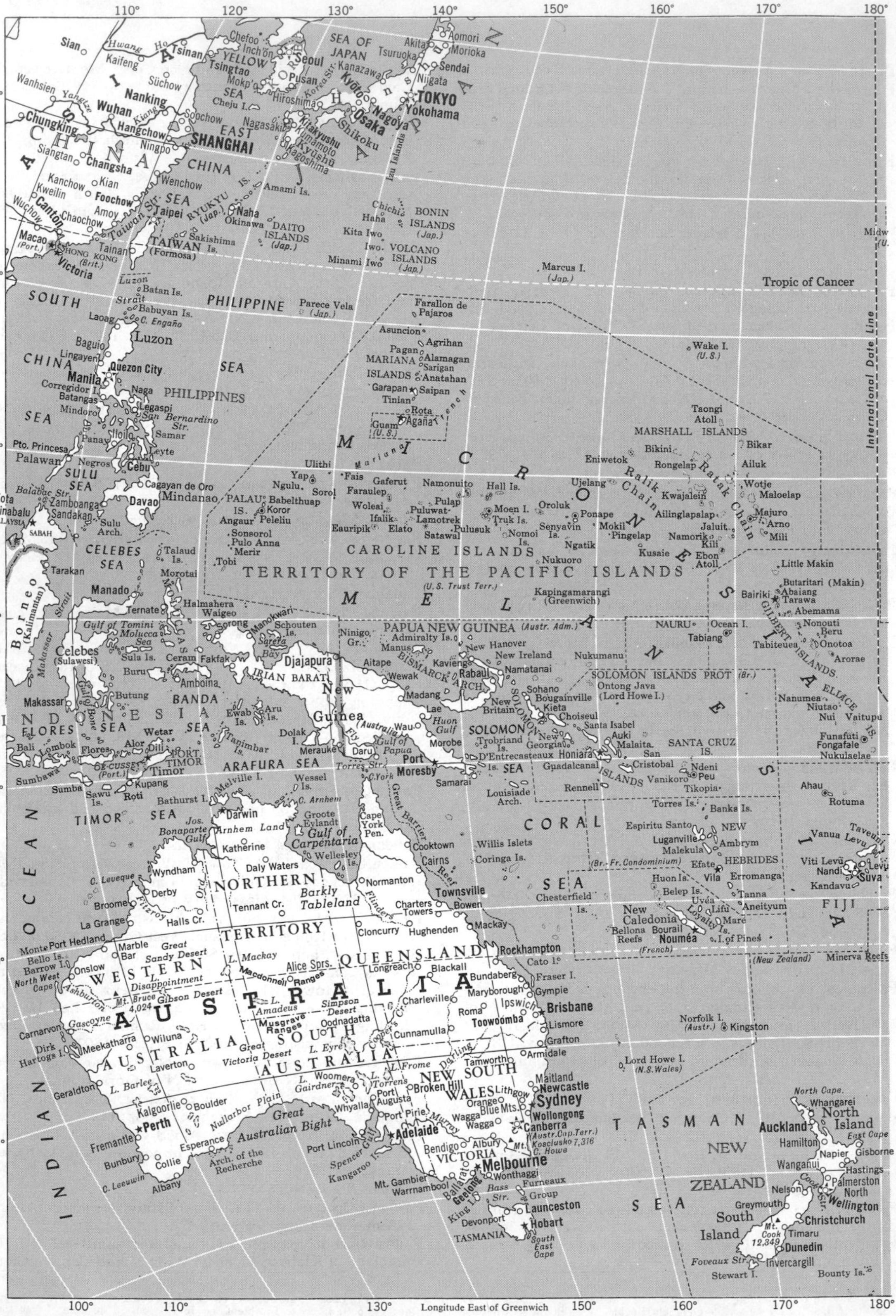

110°
120°
130°
140°
150°
160°
170°
180°
30°
20°
10°
0°
10°
20°
30°
Sian
Hwang Ho
Tsinan
Kaifeng
Süchow
Wanhsien
Yangtze
Nanking
Wuhan
Kiang
Chungking
Hangchow
Soochow
C H I N A
A S I A
Siangtan
Changsha
Ningpo
SHANGHAI
Kanchow
Kian
Kweilin
Wenchow
Foochow
Wuchow
Canton
Amoy
Chaochow
Taipei
Macao (Port.)
HONG KONG (Brit.)
Victoria
Tainan
Taiwan Str.
TAIWAN
(Formosa)
Chefoo
Inch'ŏn
YELLOW
Tsingtao
Seoul
KOREA
Pusan
Mokp'o
SEA
Cheju I.
Korea Str.
Hiroshima
Nagasaki
EAST
CHINA
SEA
Kitakyushu
Kumamoto
Kyūshū
Kagoshima
SEA OF JAPAN
Kanazawa
Kyōto
Osaka
Nagoya
Shikoku
Akita
Tsuruoka
Niigata
Aomori
Morioka
Sendai
TOKYO
Yokohama
Honshu
J A P A N
Izu Islands
Amami Is.
RYUKYU IS. (Jap.)
Naha
Okinawa
Sakishima Is.
DAITO ISLANDS (Jap.)
Chichi
Haha
BONIN ISLANDS (Jap.)
Kita Iwo
Iwo
VOLCANO ISLANDS (Jap.)
Minami Iwo
Marcus I. (Jap.)
Tropic of Cancer
Midw (U.
International Date Line
Luzon Strait
Batan Is.
Babuyan Is.
C. Engaño
SOUTH
CHINA
SEA
Laoag
Baguio
Lingayen
Luzon
Manila
Quezon City
Corregidor I.
Batangas
Mindoro
Naga
Legaspi
San Bernardino Str.
Samar
PHILIPPINES
PHILIPPINE
SEA
Parece Vela (Jap.)
Panay
Iloilo
Leyte
Negros
Cebu
Pto. Princesa
Palawan
SULU SEA
Balabac Str.
Cagayan de Oro
Mindanao
Davao
Zamboanga
Sandakan
Sulu Arch.
Kota Kinabalu
MALAYSIA
SABAH
CELEBES SEA
Talaud Is.
Morotai
Tarakan
Manado
Borneo (Kalimantan)
Makassar Strait
Ternate
Halmahera
Waigeo
Gulf of Tomini
Molucca Sea
Celebes (Sulawesi)
Sula Is.
Buru
Ceram
Fakfak
Amboina
Sorong
Manokwari
Schouten Is.
Sarera Bay
Djajapura
IRIAN BARAT
New Guinea
Makassar
Butung
BANDA SEA
I N D O N E S I A
FLORES SEA
Bali
Lombok
Sumbawa
Flores
Wetar
Alor
Dili
PORT. TIMOR
Timor
Kupang
Sumba
Sawu Is.
Roti
Aru Is.
Tanimbar Is.
Dolak I.
Merauke
ARAFURA SEA
TIMOR SEA
Farallon de Pajaros
Asuncion
Agrihan
Pagan
Alamagan
MARIANA ISLANDS
Sarigan
Anatahan
Garapan
Saipan
Tinian
Rota
Guam (U.S.)
Agaña
Trench
Mariana
M I C R O N E S I A
Ulithi
Yap
Fais
Ngulu
Sorol
Gaferut
Faraulep
Namonuito
Hall Is.
PALAU IS.
Babelthuap
Koror
Angaur
Peleliu
Woleai
Ifalik
Eauripik
Elato
Pulap
Puluwat
Lamotrek
Satawal
Pulusuk
Moen I.
Truk Is.
Nomoi Is.
Oroluk
Ponape
Senyavin Is.
Mokil
Pingelap
Ngatik
Kusaie
Nukuoro
Sonsorol
Pulo Anna
Merir
Tobi
CAROLINE ISLANDS
TERRITORY OF THE PACIFIC ISLANDS
(U.S. Trust Terr.)
Kapingamarangi (Greenwich)
Wake I. (U.S.)
Taongi Atoll
MARSHALL ISLANDS
Bikini
Bikar
Eniwetok
Rongelap
Ailuk
Ujelang
Ralik Chain
Ratak Chain
Wotje
Kwajalein
Maloelap
Ailinglapalap
Majuro
Jaluit
Arno
Namorik
Mili
Kili
Ebon Atoll
Little Makin
Butaritari (Makin)
Abaiang
Bairiki
Tarawa
Abemama
GILBERT ISLANDS
Nonouti
Beru
Tabiteuea
Onotoa
Arorae
NAURU
Ocean I.
Tabiang
M E L A N E S I A
PAPUA NEW GUINEA (Austr. Adm.)
Ninigo Gr.
Admiralty Is.
Manus
New Hanover
Kavieng
New Ireland
BISMARCK ARCH.
Rabaul
Namatanai
Aitape
Wewak
Madang
New Britain
Lae
Huon Gulf
Wau
Morobe
Fly
Gulf of Papua
Daru
Port Moresby
Samarai
Torres Str.
C. York
Nukumanu
SOLOMON ISLANDS PROT. (Br.)
Ontong Java (Lord Howe I.)
Sohano
Bougainville
Kieta
Choiseul
Santa Isabel
SOLOMON
New Georgia
Auki
Malaita
Honiara
Guadalcanal
San Cristobal
ISLANDS
Rennell
SOLOMON SEA
Trobriand Is.
D'Entrecasteaux Is.
Louisiade Arch.
SANTA CRUZ IS.
Ndeni
Peu
Vanikoro
Tikopia
Torres Is.
Banks Is.
Espiritu Santo
NEW HEBRIDES
Luganville
Malekula
Ambrym
Efate
Vila
Erromanga
Tanna
Aneityum
(Br.-Fr. Condominium)
Nanumea
Niutao
Nui
Vaitupu
ELLICE IS.
Funafuti
Fongafale
Nukulaelae
Ahau
Rotuma
Taveuni
Vanua Levu
Viti Levu
Lev
Nandi
Suva
Kandavu
FIJI
P O L Y N E S I A
Minerva Reefs
(New Zealand)
CORAL SEA
Willis Islets
Coringa Is.
Chesterfield Is.
Huon Is.
Belep Is.
New Caledonia
Bellona Reefs
Bourail
Nouméa
(French)
Uvéa
Lifu
Loyalty Is.
Maré
I. of Pines
Melville I.
Bathurst I.
Darwin
C. Arnhem
Wessel Is.
Groote Eylandt
Arnhem Land
Jos. Bonaparte Gulf
Katherine
Gulf of Carpentaria
Wellesley Is.
Cape York Pen.
Great Barrier Reef
Cooktown
Cairns
Daly Waters
Wyndham
C. Leveque
Derby
Ord
NORTHERN
TERRITORY
Barkly Tableland
Normanton
Flinders
Townsville
Bowen
Broome
Fitzroy
Tennant Cr.
Charters Towers
La Grange
Halls Cr.
Cloncurry
Hughenden
Mackay
Port Hedland
Monte Bello Is.
Barrow I.
North West Cape
Onslow
Marble Bar
Great Sandy Desert
L. Mackay
Alice Sprs.
Macdonnell Ranges
QUEENSLAND
Longreach
Blackall
Rockhampton
Cato I.
Bundaberg
Fraser I.
Maryborough
Gympie
WESTERN
L. Disappointment
Ashburton
Mt. Bruce 4,024
Gibson Desert
L. Amadeus
Simpson Desert
Charleville
Roma
Ipswich
Brisbane
Toowoomba
A U S T R A L I A
Gascoyne
Carnarvon
Musgrave Ranges
Oodnadatta
Cunnamulla
Lismore
Dirk Hartogs I.
Meekatharra
Wiluna
AUSTRALIA
SOUTH
AUSTRALIA
L. Eyre
Cooper's Cr.
Grafton
Great Victoria Desert
Laverton
Darling
Tamworth
Armidale
L. Frome
Geraldton
L. Barlee
L. Gairdner
Woomera
L. Torrens
NEW SOUTH WALES
Broken Hill
Maitland
Newcastle
Lithgow
Sydney
Kalgoorlie
Boulder
Nullarbor Plain
Port Augusta
Whyalla
Orange
Blue Mts.
Perth
Great Australian Bight
Port Pirie
Murray
Wagga Wagga
Wollongong
Canberra (Austr.Cap.Terr.)
Fremantle
Esperance
Port Lincoln
Spencer Gulf
Adelaide
Albury
Mt. Kosciusko 7,316
C. Howe
Bunbury
Collie
Arch. of the Recherche
Kangaroo I.
Bendigo
VICTORIA
Melbourne
C. Leeuwin
Albany
Mt. Gambier
Warrnambool
Ballarat
Geelong
Wonthaggi
Furneaux Group
King I.
Bass Str.
Launceston
Devonport
Hobart
TASMANIA
South East Cape
Norfolk I. (Austr.)
Kingston
Lord Howe I. (N.S.Wales)
TASMAN SEA
INDIAN OCEAN
North Cape
Whangarei
North Island
Auckland
Hamilton
East Cape
Napier
Gisborne
Wanganui
Hastings
NEW ZEALAND
Nelson
Palmerston North
Cook Str.
Wellington
Greymouth
South Island
Christchurch
Mt. Cook 12,349
Timaru
Dunedin
Foveaux Str.
Invercargill
Stewart I.
Bounty Is.
100°
110°
130°
Longitude East of Greenwich
150°
160°
170°
180°

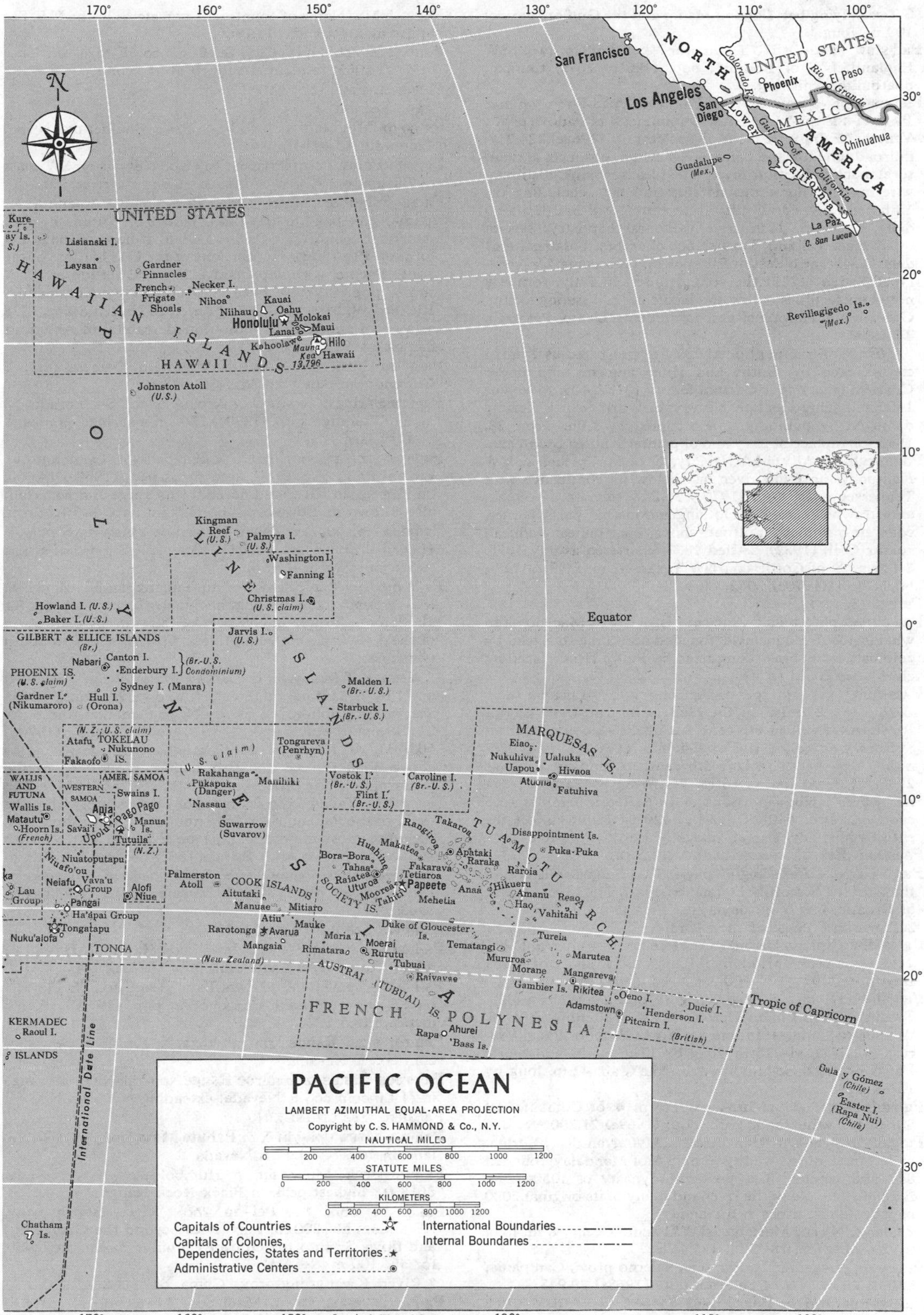
PACIFIC OCEAN
LAMBERT AZIMUTHAL EQUAL-AREA PROJECTION
Copyright by C. S. HAMMOND & Co., N.Y.
NAUTICAL MILES
0 200 400 600 800 1000 1200
STATUTE MILES
0 200 400 600 800 1000 1200
KILOMETERS
0 200 400 600 800 1000 1200
Capitals of Countries
Capitals of Colonies, Dependencies, States and Territories
Administrative Centers
International Boundaries
Internal Boundaries
Longitude West of Greenwich
NORTH AMERICA
UNITED STATES
MEXICO
San Francisco
Los Angeles
San Diego
Phoenix
El Paso
Rio Grande
Colorado R.
Chihuahua
Lower California
Gulf of California
Guadalupe (Mex.)
La Paz
C. San Lucas
Revillagigedo Is. (Mex.)
UNITED STATES
HAWAIIAN ISLANDS
HAWAII
Kure
Lisianski I.
Laysan
Gardner Pinnacles
French Frigate Shoals
Necker I.
Nihoa
Kauai
Niihau
Oahu
Honolulu
Molokai
Lanai
Maui
Kahoolawe
Mauna Kea 13,796
Hilo
Hawaii
Johnston Atoll (U.S.)
POLYNESIA
LINE ISLANDS
Kingman Reef (U.S.)
Palmyra I. (U.S.)
Washington I.
Fanning I.
Christmas I. (U.S. claim)
Howland I. (U.S.)
Baker I. (U.S.)
Jarvis I. (U.S.)
Equator
GILBERT & ELLICE ISLANDS (Br.)
Canton I.
Nabari
Enderbury I.
(Br.-U.S. Condominium)
PHOENIX IS. (U.S. claim)
Sydney I. (Manra)
Gardner I. (Nikumaroro)
Hull I. (Orona)
Malden I. (Br.-U.S.)
Starbuck I. (Br.-U.S.)
(N.Z.; U.S. claim)
Atafu
TOKELAU IS.
Nukunono
Fakaofo
Tongareva (Penrhyn)
MARQUESAS IS.
Eiao
Nukuhiva
Uahuka
Uapou
Hivaoa
Atuona
Fatuhiva
WALLIS AND FUTUNA
Wallis Is.
Matautu
Hoorn Is.
(French)
WESTERN SAMOA
AMER. SAMOA
Swains I.
Apia
Pago Pago
Savai'i
Upolu
Tutuila
Manua Is.
(U.S. claim)
Rakahanga
Pukapuka (Danger)
Manihiki
Nassau
Vostok I. (Br.-U.S.)
Caroline I. (Br.-U.S.)
Flint I. (Br.-U.S.)
Suwarrow (Suvarov)
Niuatoputapu
Niuafo'ou
(N.Z.)
Neiafu
Vava'u Group
Lau Group
Pangai
Alofi
Niue
Ha'apai Group
Tongatapu
Nuku'alofa
TONGA
Palmerston Atoll
COOK ISLANDS
Aitutaki
Manuae
Mitiaro
Atiu
Mauke
Rarotonga
Avarua
Mangaia
(New Zealand)
Rangiroa
Takaroa
TUAMOTU ARCH.
Makatea
Apataki
Raraka
Fakarava
Huahine
Bora-Bora
Tahaa
Raiatea
Uturoa
Tetiaroa
Moorea
Tahiti
Papeete
SOCIETY IS.
Mehetia
Anaa
Hikueru
Raroia
Amanu
Hao
Reao
Vahitahi
Disappointment Is.
Puka-Puka
Duke of Gloucester Is.
Tematangi
Tureia
Mururoa
Marutea
Morane
Mangareva
Gambier Is.
Rikitea
Maria I.
Moerai
Rimatara
Rurutu
Tubuai
Raivavae
AUSTRAL (TUBUAI) IS.
FRENCH POLYNESIA
Rapa
Ahurei
Bass Is.
Oeno I.
Ducie I.
Henderson I.
Adamstown
Pitcairn I.
(British)
Tropic of Capricorn
Sala y Gómez (Chile)
Easter I. (Rapa Nui) (Chile)
KERMADEC ISLANDS
Raoul I.
International Date Line
Chatham Is.
170°
160°
150°
140°
130°
120°
110°
100°
30°
20°
10°
0°
10°
20°
30°

S Texas, lying bet. Laguna Madre and the Gulf of Mexico; 100 m. long.

Pad·stow \'pad-(,)stō\. Town near N coast of Cornwall, SW England, NW of Bodmin; pop. (1961c) 2675; tourism, boatbuilding, fishing.

Pad·ua \'paj-ə-wə\ *or Ital.* **Pa·do·va** \'päd-ə-və\ *or anc.* **Pa·ta·vi·um** \pə-'tā-vē-əm\. Commune, ✱ of Padova prov., Veneto, NE Italy, 22 m. W of Venice; pop. (1968e) 224,217; railroad junction and commercial center; produces agricultural machinery, motorcycles, textiles, soap, ink; distilling, wire making; numerous notable buildings, including the 13th cent. cathedral, 13th–14th cent. town hall (Palazzo della Ragione), 12th cent. cathedral baptistry, several other medieval and Renaissance churches, botanical gardens (1545, the oldest in Europe), and museums. University of Padua (1222) the second oldest in Italy, formerly noted for faculties of law and medicine; had among faculty Galileo and Fallopius, among students Dante, Petrarch, Tasso.

History: First mentioned 302 B.C.; prospered as Roman city; sacked by Goths and Huns and restored under Charlemagne; under Carrara family 1318–1405; to Venice 1405 and shared its later history; in World War II heavily damaged by bombing and occupied by Allies Apr. 28, 1945. Birthplace of Livy and of painter Andrea Mantegna.

Pa·du·cah \pə-'d(y)ü-kə\. 1 City, ⊗ of McCracken co., W Kentucky, on Ohio river just below its confluence with Tennessee river; pop. (1970c) 31,267; tobacco, livestock, and strawberry market; clothing, automobile parts, barges, concrete products; railroad shops, coal mines; Paducah Junior Coll. (1932); settled 1827, chartered as city 1856.
2 Town, ⊗ of Cottle co., NW Texas, 87 m. ENE of Lubbock; pop. (1970c) 2052; oil wells.

Padus. See PO.

Pae·o·nia \pē-'ō-nē-ə\. Ancient district N of Macedonia in what is now S Yugoslavia; founded according to legend by colonists from Troy; conquered by Philip II of Macedon; chief town Stobi (*q.v.*).

Paes·tum \'pes-təm, 'pēs-\. Ancient city, W Lucania (now Basilicata), S Italy, on the Gulf of Salerno (*anc.* Bay of Paestum); founded 6th cent. B.C. by Greek colonists from Sybaris who called it **Pos·ei·do·nia** \,päs-ī-'dō-nē-ə, ,pō-,sī-\; taken by Lucanians 5th cent. B.C. and by Romans 273 B.C.; noted for its roses; destroyed by Saracens 871 A.D.; ruins include portions of three Doric temples (6th cent. B.C., after 540 B.C., and c. 420 B.C.) and almost the entire walls; now site of village of **Pe·sto** \'pes-tō\.

Paestum, Bay of. See SALERNO, GULF OF.

Pag \'päg\ *or Ital.* **Pa·go** \'päg-(,)ō\. 1 Yugoslav island in the Adriatic Sea off N Dalmatian coast; 111 sq. m.; a part of Croatia, NW Yugoslavia.
2 Town on E coast of the island.

Pa·ga·di·an \päg-ə-'dē-ən\. Chartered city, ✱ of Zamboanga del Sur prov., Mindanao, Phil., on NW shore of Illana Bay; pop. (1970e) 59,600.

Pa·gai *or* **Pa·gaï** *or* **Pa·gi** \'päg-,ī\ *or* **Pa·geh** \'päg-(,)ā\. Two islands in Indian Ocean, S part of Mentawai Is. off W coast of Sumatra, Indonesia; **North Pagai** *or* **Pagai Uta·ra** \-ü-'tär-ə\, ab. 25 m. long by 17 m. wide, and **South Pagai** *or* **Pagai Se·la·tan** \-,sel-ə-'tän\, ab. 42 m. long by 13 m. wide.

Pa·ga·lun·gan \,pä-gə-'lu̇ŋ-,än\. Town, ✱ of Cotabato del Sur prov., Mindanao, Phil.; pop. (1969e) 21,200.

Pa·gan \pə-'gän\. 1 Ruined town, Myingyan dist., Burma, on left bank of Irrawaddy 92 m. SW of Mandalay; founded 847 and capital of a powerful dynasty c. 1050–1298. Extends 8 m. along the river and many of its original 5000 pagodas and shrines still stand.
2 Island, N cen. Mariana Is., W Pacific Ocean; 8 m. long by 2½ m. wide; 18°17′N, 145°46′E.

Pa·ga·ni \pə-'gän-ē\. Commune, Salerno prov., Campania, S Italy, 9 m. NW of Salerno; pop. (1968e) 29,943.

Pagasaean Gulf *or* **Pagasitikós Kólpos.** See VOLOS, GULF OF.

Page \'pāj\. Name of counties of two states in the U.S. See tables at IOWA and VIRGINIA.

Page·dale \'pāj-,dāl\. City, St. Louis co., E Missouri; pop. (1970c) 5083; residential suburb of St. Louis.

Pageh *or* **Pagi.** See PAGAI.

Pago. See PAG.

Pa·go·da Mountain \pə-,gōd-ə-\. Peak, Boulder co., N cen. Colorado; 13,491 ft.

Pagoda Point. Point adjacent to Cape Negrais on SW coast of Burma, on W side of mouth of Bassein river.

Pa·go Pa·go *or formerly also* **Pango·pango** \,päŋ-(,)(g)ō-'päŋ-(,)(g)ō, ,päg-(,)ō-'päg-(,)ō\. Village on Tutuila I., ✱ of American Samoa, SW Pacific Ocean, at head of long inlet forming **Pago Pago Harbor,** one of the best harbors in the South Pacific, with important U.S. naval station on its W shore; pop. (1970p) 2491. Site chosen by Commander Richard W. Meade 1872 and ceded to United States 1878 as a naval and coaling station; made capital of American Samoa 1899.

Pa·go·sa Peak \pə-,gō-sə-\. Mountain, Mineral co., S Colorado, in San Juan Mts.; 12,674 ft.

Pagosa Springs. Town, ⊗ of Archuleta co., S Colorado, 50 m. E of Durango; pop. (1970c) 1360; hot springs; grain and poultry farms.

Pag·san·jan \,päg-saŋ-'hän\. Municipality, E Laguna prov., Luzon, Phil., 3 m. E of Santa Cruz; pop. (1969e) 14,600; on **Pagsanjan River** and noted for its gorge and waterfall, also known as **Bo·to·can** \,bō-tō-'kän\, ab. 200 ft. drop.

Pa·ha·la \pə-'hä-lə\. Town, Hawaii co., Hawaii, S part of Hawaii I. near coast; pop. (1970c) 1507; S point of access to Hawaii National Park.

Pa·hang \pə-'haŋ\. 1 River in Pahang state, Malaysia, Malay Penin.; 285 m. long; navigable for native boats for ab. 250 m.; formed in NW part of the state by confluence of the Jelai and Tembeling rivers; flows S and E to South China Sea.
2 A state of Malaysia, E coast of Malay Penin., bounded on N by Kelantan and Trengganu, on E by South China Sea, on S by Johore, on SW by Negri Sembilan, and on W by Selangor and Perak; 13,920 sq. m.; pop. (1970p) 503,131; ✱ Kuantan. Mountainous, with many peaks above 3000 ft.; has the two highest mountains of the peninsula on its border: on the NW, Kerbau 7159 ft. and on the N, Tahan 7186 ft.; most of its area lies within the basin of the Pahang river and tributaries; rice, rubber, tin; Kuantan most important port on E coast. Entered into treaty agreements with British 1887; became member of the Federated Malay States 1895, part of independent Federation of Malaya 1957; became a state of Malaysia 1963.

Pahlevī. See BANDAR-E PAHLAVĪ.

Pa·hoa \pä-'hō-ə\. Town, Hawaii co., Hawaii, E Hawaii I., inland from Cape Kumukahi; pop. (1970c) 924.

Pa·ho·kee \pə-'hō-kē\. Town, Palm Beach co., SE Florida, on SE shore of Lake Okeechobee; pop. (1970c) 15,663; incorporated 1922.

Pah·ran·a·gat Range \pə-,ran-ə-,gat-\. Range in cen. Lincoln co., E Nevada.

Pah·rock Range *or* **Pah·roc Range** \pə-'räk-\. Small range in N Lincoln co., E Nevada, extending NW into Nye co.

Pahsien. See CHUNGKING.

Pah·ute Mesa \'pä-yüt-\ *or* **Pai·ute Mesa** \'pī-yüt-\. Tableland in cen. Nye co., S Nevada.

Pahute Peak. Mountain, W Humboldt co., NW Nevada; 8618 ft.; highest peak in Black Rock Range.

Pai *or* **Pei** \'bī\. 1 *or* **Pei–ho** \-'hō\. River, Hopeh prov., NE China; ab. 300 m. long; rises beyond the Great Wall and flows SE into the Gulf of Chihli at Ta-ku; navigable for ab. 100 m. See HAI.
2 River, Kwangtung prov., China. See PEI 2.

Pa·ia \pə-'ē-ə\. Town, Maui co., Hawaii, on N coast of Maui I.; pop. (1970c) 541; Maunaolu Coll. (1861).

Päi·jan·ne \ˈpā-ˌyan-(ˌ)ä\. Lake, S Finland; 75 m. long by 14 m. wide; 411 sq. m.; max. depth 305 ft.; drains S to Gulf of Finland.

Pai Khoi. See YUGORSKI.

Pa·i·lo·lo \pī-ˈlō-(ˌ)lō\. Channel bet. Maui I. and Molokai I., Hawaii; 8 m. wide.

Paim·pol \pa^{n}-ˈpȯl\. Village, Côtes-du-Nord dept., NW France, NNW of St-Brieuc on the Gulf of St-Malo; pop. (1962c) 8044; fishing port; scene of Pierre Loti's *Pêcheurs d'Islande.*

Paine \ˈpān\. Peak, S Chile, E of Hanover I.; 8760 ft.

Paines·ville \ˈpānz-ˌvil\. City, ⊗ of Lake co., NE Ohio, 27 m. NE of Cleveland; pop. (1970c) 16,536; chemicals, machinery; railroad shops; fruit and truck farms; Lake Erie Coll. (1856).

Paint·ed Desert \ˌpānt-əd-\. Region, E Coconino co., N cen. Arizona, E of Colorado and Little Colorado rivers; ab. 150 m. long; area ab. 7500 sq. m.; erosion has worn away much of the sand, exposing many-colored rock surfaces.

Painted Post. Village, Steuben co., S New York, 16 m. W of Elmira; pop. (1970c) 2496.

Paint Rock \ˈpānt-\. Town, ⊗ of Concho co., W cen. Texas; pop. (1970c) 193.

Paints·ville \ˈpānts-ˌvil, -vəl\. City, ⊗ of Johnson co., E Kentucky, 28 m. NNW of Pikeville; pop. (1970c) 3868; coal mines, oil wells; truck farms.

Pai·sa·no Peak \pī-ˌsän-(ˌ)ō-\. Mountain, NW Brewster co., W Texas; 6050 ft.

Pais·ley \ˈpāz-lē\. 1 Village, ⊗ of Bruce co., SE Ontario, Canada; pop. (1971p) 794.

2 Burgh, ⊗ of Renfrew co., SW Scotland, 7 m. W of Glasgow; pop. (1971p) 95,344; center of thread manufacturing; produces machinery, chemicals, preserves, textiles, iron and brass goods, tobacco, flour; formerly known for Paisley shawls. Developed around abbey founded 1163; industrial center (textiles) from early 18th cent. and port from 1791.

Pa·ï·ta \pä-ˈēt-ə\. Village on the French island of New Caledonia, SW Pacific Ocean, ab. 10 m. NW of Nouméa.

Pai·ta \ˈpī-(ˌ)tä\. Seaport town, Piura dept., NW Peru, ab. 35 m. NW of Piura; pop. (1961c) 9600; harbor; shipping point for cotton, hides, and Panama hats.

Paiute Mesa. See PAHUTE MESA.

Pa·ja·res Pass \pə-ˌhär-əs-\. Mountain pass through the Cantabrian Mts., N Spain; 4524 ft.

Pa·kan·ba·ru \ˌpä-kən-ˈbär-ü\. Town, ✱ of Riau prov., Sumatra, Indonesia, 130 m. NE of Padang; pop. (1961c) 70,821.

Pakaraima Mountains. See PACARAIMA MOUNTAINS.

Pak·chan \ˈpäk-ˌchän, ˈpau̇k-\. Wide river on Isthmus of Kra, extreme S of Burma; ab. 55 m. long; flows S into Andaman Sea, forming boundary bet. S Lower Burma and Thailand.

Pak·che \ˈpäk-ˈchā\. See history at KOREA.

Pakhoi. See PEI-HAI.

Pak·i·stan \ˌpak-i-ˈstan, ˌpäk-i-ˈstän, ˈpak-i-ˌstan\ *or officially* **Is·lam·ic Republic of Pakistan** \iz-ˌlam-ik-\. Republic, S Asia, bounded on W and N by Afghanistan, on NE by China, on E and SE by India, on S by the Arabian Sea, and on SW by Iran; 312,009 sq. m.; pop. (1969e) 53,990,173; ✱ Islamabad; for physical features, see BALUCHISTAN 2, NORTH-WEST FRONTIER PROVINCE, PUNJAB, and SIND. *Chief products:* Wheat, barley, corn; coal, gypsum, natural gas; manufacturing: textiles, cement, chemicals. *Chief cities:* Karachi, Lahore, Lyallpur, Hyderabad, Multan, Rawalpindi. Formerly consisted of two parts separated by ab. 1000 m. of Indian territory: (1) **West Pakistan,** described above, and (2) **East Pakistan,** now Bangla Desh (*q.v.*). Divided into the following provinces:

NAME	AREA (sq. m.)	POP. (1969e)	CAPITAL
Baluchistan	133,107	1,483,999	Quetta
North-West Frontier	40,377	10,937,000	Peshawar
Punjab	79,542	30,427,000	Lahore
Sind	58,983	11,142,174	Karachi

History: For history prior to 1947, see BALUCHISTAN 2, INDIA 1, NORTH-WEST FRONTIER PROVINCE, PUNJAB, and SIND. Established Aug. 15, 1947 by Act (July 18, 1947) of British Parliament; military clash with India over possession of Kashmir 1947–49 (see JAMMU AND KASHMIR); became a republic 1956; concluded boundary agreement with China 1963; military clash with India (in Rann of Kutch region) 1965; declaration of independence by its E province (see BANGLA DESH) and defeat in war with India 1971.

Paknam. See SAMUT PRAKAN.

Pa·kok·ku \pə-ˈkō-(ˌ)kü\. 1 District, Magwe division, Burma; 5345 sq. m.; pop. (1962e) 711,616; ✱ Pakokku.

2 Town, its ✱, on right bank of Irrawaddy 75 m. SW of Mandalay; pop. (1962e) 156,960; trade center.

Pakokku Hill Tracts. Former district in Burma, W of Pakokku dist., now included in Chin Hills.

Paks \ˈpäksh\. Commune, Tolna co., S Hungary, on Danube river 63 m. S of Budapest; pop. (1970p) 13,963.

Pak·se *also* **Pak·sé** \ˈpäk-ˈsā\. Town, S Laos, on Mekong river; pop. (1970e) 37,000.

Pak·tīā \ˈpäk-tē-ā\. Province of E Afghanistan. See table at AFGHANISTAN.

Pala Bianca. See WEISSKUGEL.

Pa·la·cios \pə-ˈlash-əz\. Town and resort, Matagorda co., SE Texas, on Matagorda Bay 25 m. SW of Bay City; pop. (1970c) 3642; resort; fisheries; diversified agriculture.

Palacios, Los. See LOS PALACIOS.

Palaestina. See PALESTINE.

Pa·la·gru·ža Islands \ˌpäl-ə-ˈgrü-(ˌ)zhä-\ *or Ital.* **Iso·le di Pe·la·go·sa** \ˈē-zə-(ˌ)lā-di-ˌpel-ə-ˈgō-sə\ *or angl.* **Pel·a·go·sa Islands** \ˌpel-ə-ˌgō-sə-\. Group of islets, cen. Adriatic Sea, SW of Lastovo, Bosnia and Herzegovina, W Yugoslavia; before 1947 belonged to Italy.

Pa·lai·kas·tro \pä-ˈlā-kə-ˌstrō\. Archaeological site, NE coast of Crete, Greece; ruins of town of Middle and Late Minoan periods.

Pa·la·nan \pä-ˈlän-ən\. Municipality, E Isabela prov., Luzon, Phil., near **Palanan Bay** on Pacific coast; pop. (1969e) 7700; only important town on E coast of province, near mouth of Palanan river; connected with Ilagan, 37 m. to the W, by rough mountain trails. Place where Gen. Emilio Aguinaldo maintained his headquarters of the Filipino revolutionary government 1900–01 and where he was captured by Gen. Funston Mar. 23, 1901.

Pa·lan·ga \pə-ˈläŋ-gə\ *or Ger.* **Po·lang·en** \pō-ˈläŋ-ən\. Seaport town on Baltic Sea, Lithuanian S.S.R., U.S.S.R.

Pa·lang·ka·ra·ja \pa-ˈläŋ-kə-ˈrä-jə\. Town, ✱ of Central Kalimantan prov., Borneo, Indonesia; pop. (1961c) 6860.

Pa·lan·pur \ˈpäl-ən-(ˌ)pu̇(ə)r\. 1 Former Indian state, now part of Gujarat state, NW India; 1794 sq. m.; joined Union of Rajasthan June 26, 1947.

2 Town, its ✱, 77 m. N of Ahmadabad; pop. (1961c) 29,139.

Palantia. See PALENCIA 2.

Pa·la·oa Point \ˌpäl-ə-ˌō-ə-\. Southernmost point of Lanai I., Hawaii, on Kealaikahiki Channel.

Pa·la·pag \pə-ˈläp-äg\. Municipality and port, NE coast of Samar, Phil., opp. Batag I.; munic. pop. (1969e) 21,800.

Pa·lap·ye \pə-ˈlap-yē\. Town, a former ✱ of the Bamangwato tribe, E Botswana, cen. S Africa, E of Serowe on a tributary of the Limpopo river and ab. 100 m. S of Francistown; pop. (1964c) 5100.

ə abut; ə kitten, Fr. table; ər further; a back; ā bake; ä cot, cart; ȧ Fr. bac; au̇ out; ch chin; e less; ē easy; g gift
i trip; ī life; j joke; k Ger. ich, Buch; ^{n} Fr. vin; ŋ sing; ō flow; ȯ flaw; œ Fr. bœuf; œ̄ Fr. feu; ȯi coin; th thin
th this; ü loot; u̇ foot; ue Ger. füllen; ue̅ Fr. rue; y yet; ^{y} Fr. digne \dēn^{y}\, nuit \nw^{y}ē\; yü few; yu̇ furious; zh vision

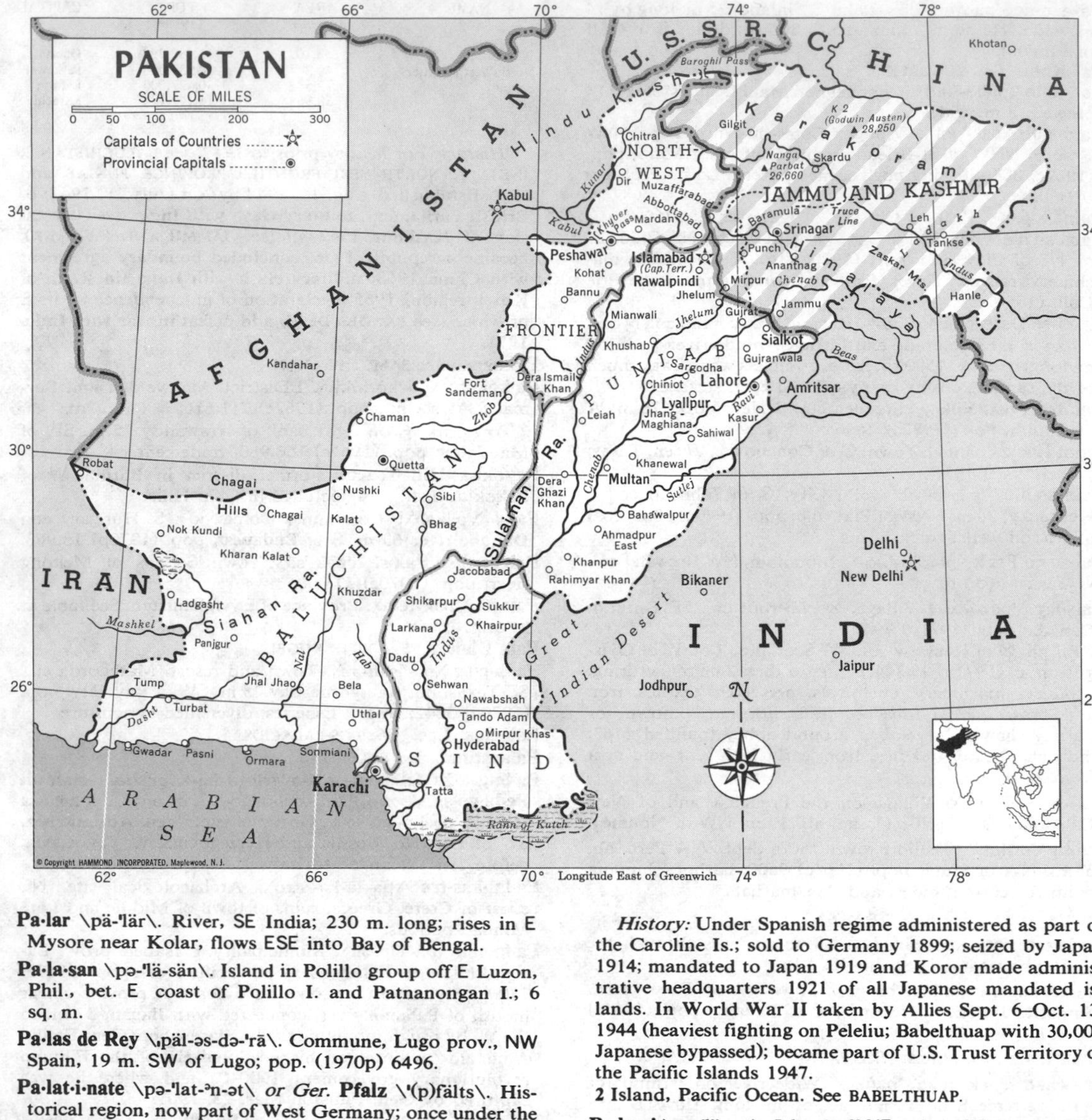

Pa·lar \pä-ˈlär\. River, SE India; 230 m. long; rises in E Mysore near Kolar, flows ESE into Bay of Bengal.

Pa·la·san \pə-ˈlä-sän\. Island in Polillo group off E Luzon, Phil., bet. E coast of Polillo I. and Patnanongan I.; 6 sq. m.

Pa·las de Rey \ˌpäl-əs-də-ˈrā\. Commune, Lugo prov., NW Spain, 19 m. SW of Lugo; pop. (1970p) 6496.

Pa·lat·i·nate \pə-ˈlat-ᵊn-ət\ *or Ger.* **Pfalz** \ˈ(p)fälts\. Historical region, now part of West Germany; once under the jurisdiction of the counts palatine, who in 14th cent. became electors of the Holy Roman Empire; in two parts: **Lower Palatinate** or **Rhine Palatinate,** on both sides of the Rhine in the area S of the Main river; the **Upper Palatinate** some distance to the east in E Bavaria around Amberg and Regensberg.

Pal·a·tine \ˈpal-ə-ˌtīn\. 1 Village, Cook co., NE Illinois, 28 m. NW of Chicago; pop. (1970c) 25,904; residential; William Rayney Harper Coll. (1965).

2 One of the seven hills of Rome. See SEVEN HILLS.

Pa·lat·ka \pə-ˈlat-kə\. City, ⊗ of Putnam co., NE Florida penin., on St. Johns river 28 m. SW of St. Augustine; pop. (1970c) 9444; lumber; fisheries; citrus fruit; Saint Johns River Junior Coll. (1958).

Pa·lau \pə-ˈlau̇\ *or formerly* **Pe·lew** \pə-ˈlü\. 1 Group of ab. 100 islands and islets, generally considered a part of the Caroline Is. (Western Carolines), W Pacific Ocean, 1060 m. SE of Manila and ab. the same distance SW of Saipan; 179 sq. m.; pop. (1970e) 12,525. Chief island Babelthuap; other islands Urukthapel, Peleliu, Angaur, Eli Malk, and Koror.

History: Under Spanish regime administered as part of the Caroline Is.; sold to Germany 1899; seized by Japan 1914; mandated to Japan 1919 and Koror made administrative headquarters 1921 of all Japanese mandated islands. In World War II taken by Allies Sept. 6–Oct. 13, 1944 (heaviest fighting on Peleliu; Babelthuap with 30,000 Japanese bypassed); became part of U.S. Trust Territory of the Pacific Islands 1947.

2 Island, Pacific Ocean. See BABELTHUAP.

Pa·la·ui \pə-ˈlä-wē\. Island off NE point of Cagayan prov., Luzon, Phil.; 10 sq. m.; its N tip is Cape Engaño; lighthouse.

Pa·la·uig \pə-ˈlä-wig\. Municipality, W Zambales prov., Luzon, Phil., on coast at **Palauig Point,** 15°26′N, 119°53′E, 10 m. N of Iba; pop. (1969e) 14,100.

Pa·la·wan \pə-ˈlä-wən\ *or formerly* **Pa·ra·gua** \pə-ˈräg-wə\. Island, SW Phil.; 4550 sq. m.; 278 m. long by 5 to 30 m. wide; with adjacent islands (Calamian, Cuyo, and Cagayan groups and Linapacan I., Dumaran I., Balabac I., and Cagayan Sulu I.) constitutes a province, 5571 sq. m., pop. (1970p) 232,322; ✱ Puerto Princesa. The province extends from Mindoro Strait SW to Balabac Strait, which separates it from N Borneo, and separates Sulu Sea from South China Sea. The island has a chain of mountains running nearly the entire length; highest Mt. Mantalingajan 6839 ft.; has lowland at N end and narrow plain along the coasts; chief products rice, corn, sweet potatoes, coconuts, and fruit; fishing. Forests provide valuable woods and island is rich in mineral resources. Inhabitants are Visayans in the N, Moros in the S, and the Bataks and Tagbanuas, primitive tribes, in the interior. There are no large towns; the most important places include Puerto Princesa, Cuyo, Culion, and Coron.

History: Earliest settlements made by Muslims; Spanish influence began in the Calamian group and in fort at Taytay in early 18th cent. Several changes in administration made by Spaniards in 19th cent.; for a time divided into three military districts. Civil government established June 1902 under name of Paragua; name changed to Palawan in 1905. In World War II occupied by American forces Mar. 1–2, 1945.

Pa·la·yan \ˌpä-ˈlä-yän\. City, ✱ of Nueva Ecija prov., Luzon, Phil.; pop. (1960c) 3887.

Pa·laz·zo·lo Acre·i·de \ˌpä-lät-ˈtsȯ-lō-ä-ˈkrā-i-də\ *or anc.* **Ac·rae** \ˈak-rē\. Commune, Siracusa prov., SE Sicily, Italy, 22 m. W of Syracuse; pop. (1968e) 10,408; ancient Greek theater and necropolis. Founded 664 B.C. by Greeks; suffered from earthquake 1693.

Palazzolo sul·l'O·glio \-sül-ˈlȯl-yō\. Commune, Brescia prov., Lombardy, N Italy, on Oglio river 19 m. WNW of Brescia; pop. (1968e) 16,728.

Pal·dis·ki \ˈpal-də-skē\ *or formerly* **Bal·tis·ki** \ˈbal-tə-skē\ *or Eng.* **Bal·tic Port** \ˈbȯl-tik-\. Seaport, NW Estonian S.S.R., U.S.S.R., at S of entrance to Gulf of Finland 26 m. W of Tallinn.

Pa·lem·bang \ˌpäl-əm-ˈbäŋ\. 1 Residency of the former Neth. Indies, now part of the Indonesian prov. of South Sumatra; 33,333 sq. m.; ✱ Palembang; was a sultanate prior to 1825.

2 City and river port, ✱ of South Sumatra prov., Indonesia, on both banks of the Musi river 56 m. from its mouth; pop. (1961c) 474,971; port for seagoing vessels, exporting rubber and oil; fertilizer, textiles, building materials; canneries, oil refinery; univ. (1960); 18th cent. mosque and several tombs of sultans. Capital of a Hindu kingdom in 7th cent. A.D.; Dutch established trading post 1617 and fort 1659; sultan expelled by British 1811 after massacre of Dutch settlers; sultanate abolished by Dutch 1825; in World War II occupied by Japanese Feb. 1942–Sept. 1945.

Pa·len·cia \pə-ˈlen-ch(ē-)ə\. 1 Province of N Spain. See table at SPAIN.

2 *or anc.* **Pa·lan·tia** \pə-ˈlan-sh(ē-)ə\. City, its ✱, on Carrión river 28 m. NE of Valladolid; pop. (1970p) 58,370; transportation center in region raising grain, flax, and sheep; produces woolen blankets and shawls; 14th cent. Gothic cathedral and two 13th cent. churches. Ancient Roman settlement; later held by Goths and Moors; recaptured by Spanish in 10th cent.; scene of the Cid's marriage to Ximena 1074; made episcopal see in 11th cent.; site of first univ. in Spain, founded by Alfonso IX 1208.

Pa·len·que \pə-ˈleŋ-(ˌ)kā\. Village in N Chiapas state, S Mexico; ruins of an ancient Maya city nearby in a forested region.

Pa·ler·mo \pə-ˈlər-(ˌ)mō, -ˈle(ə)r-\. 1 Province of Sicily, Italy. See table at ITALY.

2 *or anc.* **Pan·or·mus** *or* **Pan·hor·mus** \pan-ˈȯr-məs\. Seaport, ✱ of Sicily, also ✱ of Palermo prov., on **Bay of Palermo** 265 m. SE of Rome; pop. (1968e) 653,533; shipbuilding center; ships fruit, canned goods, glass; produces textiles; 12th–15th cent. cathedral containing tombs of Roger II and the Emperor Frederick II, 11th and 12th cent. Norman-Byzantine churches, royal palace containing notable 12th cent. Palatine Chapel, archiepiscopal palace, national museum and library, army base; univ. (founded 1779, received univ. status 1808).

History: Founded by Phoenicians 8th cent. B.C.; passed to Carthaginians and made capital of their Sicilian possessions; taken by Romans 254 B.C. as a free town, attaining great prosperity; part of Eastern Empire; ruled by Vandals; under Saracens 832–1071; taken 1072 by Roger the Norman and made capital of newly founded Norman kingdom of Sicily; revolted against French and abuses of Charles of Anjou 1282 (the famous Sicilian Vespers), passing to Savoy and later to the Bourbon house of Naples; bombarded during insurrection 1848; seized by Garibaldi 1860 and made part of the kingdom of Italy 1861; captured by Allied forces July 30, 1943.

Pal·es·tine. 1 \ˈpal-ə-ˌstīn, -ˌstēn\ *or Lat.* **Pal·aes·ti·na** \ˌpal-ə-ˈstē-nə, -ˈstī-\ *or Bib.* **Ca·naan** \ˈkā-nən\. Former British mandate, SW Asia, at E end of Mediterranean Sea; approx. coextensive with Israel and that part of Jordan lying W of the Jordan river; 10,160 sq. m.; established 1923, dissolved 1948. The Holy Land (*Zech.* ii. 12) of the Jewish and Christian religions. Ancient Palestine was somewhat larger and included Bashan and Gilead E of the Jordan.

History: From very early times, Palestine influenced by invasion from south (Egypt) and from north and west (Semites and Hittites); conquered by Egypt 1479 B.C. (see MEGGIDO); occupied by Canaanites prior to Hebrew invasion of 15th cent. B.C. (see CANAAN 3); southern coast settled by Philistines probably driven from Crete; for Hebrew kingdoms of Palestine, see ISRAEL 1, JUDAH, and JERUSALEM 2; from 8th cent. B.C., Palestine became successively part of Assyrian, Chaldean, and Persian empires; conquered by Pompey 64 B.C.; part of Roman province of Syria during lifetime of Christ c. 4 B.C.–29 A.D.; conquered by Arabs; except for Crusaders' Kingdom of Jerusalem in 12th cent. Palestine was ruled by various Muslim dynasties; under Ottoman Empire 1516–1917; conquered by British under Allenby 1917; assigned as British mandate (1920) which became effective 1923; as result of Balfour Declaration 1917, expressing British support for establishment of national home for Jews in Palestine, received many Jewish immigrants; with reversal of British policy 1939 and increase in number of Jewish immigrants in years immediately before and after World War II, became scene of increasing conflicts between Jews and Arabs and opposition of Jews to British control; British mandate abolished May 15, 1948 and territory divided into State of Israel and W portion of Kingdom of Jordan; scene of fighting between Israeli and Arab forces 1948–49 which determined boundaries 1949–67; since Arab-Israeli War of 1967 entire territory of former mandate under Israeli administration.

2 \ˈpal-ə-ˌstēn\. City, ⊗ of Anderson co., E Texas, 82 m. E of Waco; pop. (1970c) 14,525; glass, clothing, dairy products; oil and gas wells.

Pal·es·tri·na \ˌpal-ə-ˈstrē-nə\ *or anc.* **Prae·nes·te** \prē-ˈnes-tē\. Commune, Roma prov., Latium, cen. Italy, 20 m. ESE of Rome; pop. (1968e) 11,260; a very ancient city, founded before 8th cent. B.C.; allied with Rome 499 B.C.; destroyed by Sulla's forces 82 B.C.; rebuilt around a temple of fortune, Praeneste became famous for its oracle and noted as a summer resort for wealthy Romans. Modern town birthplace of Giovanni Pierluigi da Palestrina.

Pa·let·wa \pə-ˈlet-(ˌ)wä\. Town, W Burma, on the Kaladan river 85 m. N of Sittwe.

Pal·ghat \ˈpäl-ˌgät\ *also* **Pul·i·cat** \ˈpəl-i-kət\. Town, cen. Kerala, S India, on Ponnani river 112 m. WNW of Madurai; pop. (1961c) 77,620; trade center; matches, knives; Government Victoria Coll. (1898); passed to British 1790.

Pal·grave Point \ˌpal-grāv-, ˌpȯl-\. Cape on NW coast of South-West Africa.

Pali. See NUUANU PALI.

Pa·li–k'un \ˈbä-ˈlē-ˈkün\; *formerly* **Bar·kol** \ˈbär-ˈkōl\ *or* **Bar·kul** \ˈbär-ˈkül\. Town and oasis, NE Sinkiang Uighur, W China, in mountain region on SE shore of **Lake Pa–li–k'un,** off main highway ab. 60 m. NW of Ha-mi.

Pa·li·mé \pä-ˈlē-mā\. Town, SW Togo, W Africa, ab. 65 m. NW of Lomé; pop. (1970c) 20,331.

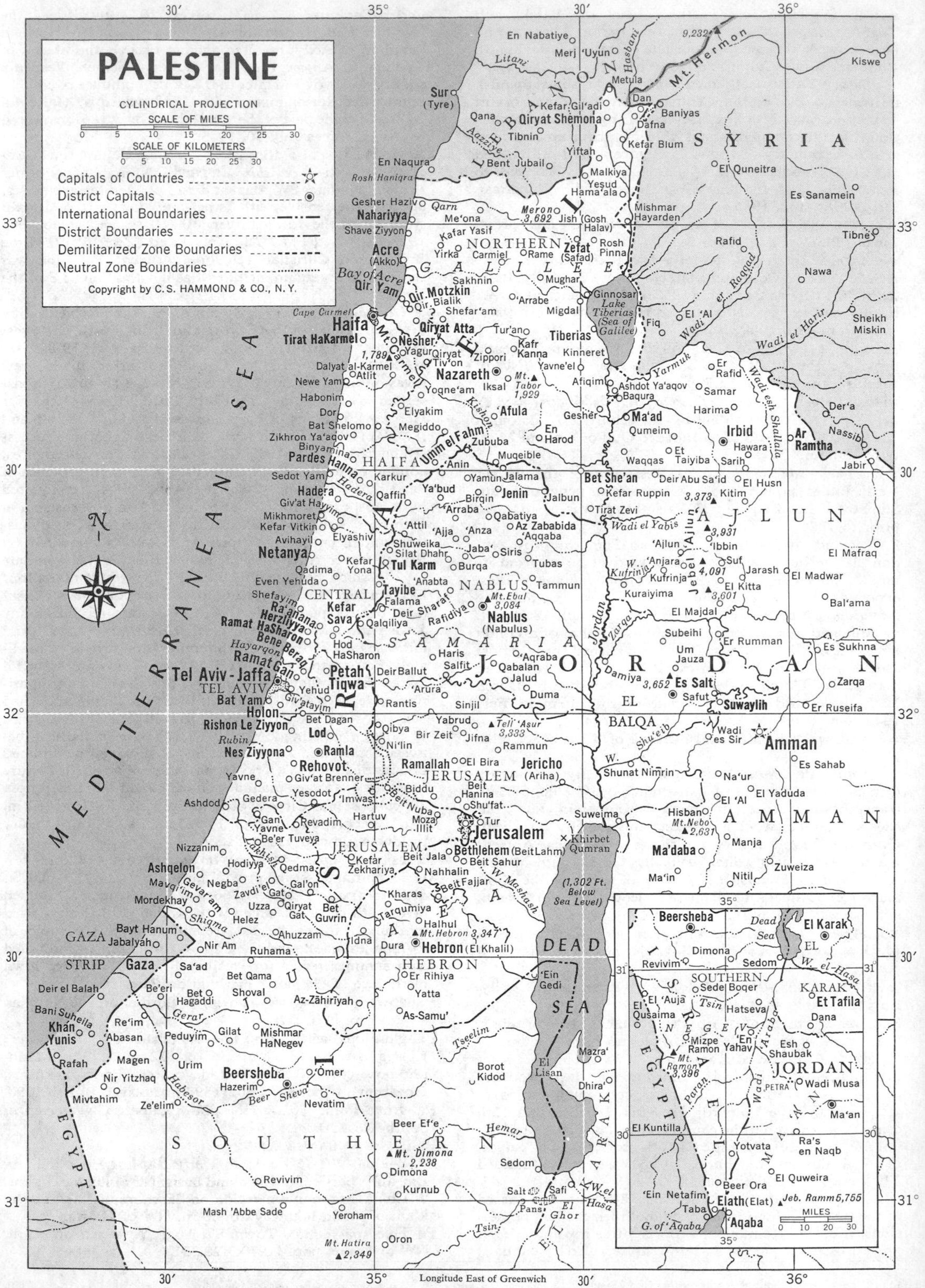
PALESTINE
CYLINDRICAL PROJECTION
SCALE OF MILES
0 5 10 15 20 25 30
SCALE OF KILOMETERS
0 5 10 15 20 25 30
Capitals of Countries
District Capitals
International Boundaries
District Boundaries
Demilitarized Zone Boundaries
Neutral Zone Boundaries
Copyright by C.S. HAMMOND & CO., N.Y.
30′
35°
30′
36°
33°
30′
32°
30′
31°
Longitude East of Greenwich
MEDITERRANEAN SEA
N
LEBANON
SYRIA
JORDAN
AJLUN
BALQA
AMMAN
ISRAEL
SAMARIA
JUDAEA
NORTHERN
GALILEE
HAIFA
CENTRAL
TEL AVIV
NABLUS
JERUSALEM
HEBRON
SOUTHERN
GAZA STRIP
EGYPT
DEAD SEA
(1,302 Ft. Below Sea Level)
En Nabatiye
Merj 'Uyun
Litani
Hasbani
9,232
Mt. Hermon
Kiswe
Metula
Dan
Sur (Tyre)
Kefar Gil'adi
Baniyas
Qana
Qiryat Shemona
Dafna
Tibnin
Kefar Blum
Yiftah
Azziye
En Naqura
Bent Jubail
Malkiya
El Quneitra
Rosh Haniqra
Yesud Hama'ala
Mishmar Hayarden
Es Sanamein
Gesher Haziv
Qarn
Merono 3,692
Jish (Gosh Halav)
Nahariyya
Me'ona
Shave Ziyyon
Kafar Yasif
Zefat (Safad)
Rosh Pinna
Rafid
Tibne
Acre (Akko)
Yirka
Carmiel
Rame
Bay of Acre
Sakhnin
Mughar
Nawa
Qir. Yam
Qir. Motzkin
Ginnosar
Qir. Bialik
Arrabe
Lake Tiberias (Sea of Galilee)
Wadi er Raqqad
Cape Carmel
Shefar'am
Migdal
Fiq
El 'Al
Haifa
Qiryat Atta
Tur'an
Tiberias
Wadi el Harir
Sheikh Miskin
Tirat HaKarmel
Nesher
Kafr Kanna
Kinneret
1,789
Yagur
Qiryat Tiv'on
Zippori
Yavne'el
Yarmuk
Er Rafid
Dalyat al-Karmel
Mt. Carmel
Atlit
Nazareth
Mt. Tabor 1,929
Afiqim
Ashdot Ya'aqov
Samar
Newe Yam
Iksal
Baqura
Wadi esh Shallala
Habonim
Yoqne'am
Dor
Elyakim
Kishon
Afula
Gesher
Ma'ad
Harima
Der'a
Bat Shelomo
Megiddo
En Harod
Qumeim
Irbid
Ar Ramtha
Nassib
Zikhron Ya'aqov
Zububa
Hawara
Binyamina
Umm el Fahm
Muqeible
Et Taiyiba
Waqqas
Sarih
Jabir
Pardes Hanna
Anin
Sedot Yam
Karkur
Yamun
Jalama
Bet She'an
Deir Abu Sa'id
El Husn
Hadera
Qaffin
Ya'bud
Jenin
Kefar Ruppin
3,373
Kitim
Giv'at Hayyim
Birqin
Jalbun
Mikhmoret
Arraba
Qabatiya
Tirat Zevi
Kefar Vitkin
'Attil
Az Zababida
Wadi el Yabis
Avihayil
Elyashiv
'Ajja
'Anza
'Aqqaba
3,931
Netanya
Shuweika
Jaba'
'Ajlun
'Ibbin
El Mafraq
Silat Dhahr
Siris
Jebel Ajlun
Kefar Yona
Tul Karm
Tubas
'Anjara
Suf
Qadima
Burqa
Kufrinja
4,091
Jarash
El Madwar
Even Yehuda
'Anabta
Tammun
El Kitta
Shefayim
Tayibe
Mt. Ebal 3,084
Kuraiyima
3,601
Bal'ama
Ra'anana
Falama
Herzliyya
Kefar Sava
Deir Sharaf
Rafidiya
Nablus (Nabulus)
El Majdal
Ramat HaSharon
Qalqiliya
Jordan
Zarqa
Subeihi
Bene Beraq
Hod HaSharon
Er Rumman
Es Sukhna
Hayarqon
Haris
'Aqraba
Um Jauza
Ramat Gan
Salfit
Qabalan
Tel Aviv-Jaffa
Petah Tiqwa
Deir Ballut
Jalud
Damiya
3,652
Es Salt
Zarqa
Yehud
'Arura
Duma
Bat Yam
Giv'atayim
Rantis
Sinjil
Safut
Suwaylih
Er Ruseifa
Holon
Bet Dagan
Yabrud
Tell 'Asur 3,333
Rishon Le Ziyyon
Qibya
Bir Zeit
Jifna
Wadi es Sir
Lod
Ni'lin
Rammun
Shu'eib
Amman
Rubin
Ramla
Nes Ziyyona
Ramallah
El Bira
Jericho (Ariha)
Es Sahab
Rehovot
W.
Yavne
Giv'at Brenner
Shunat Nimrin
Na'ur
Yesodot
'Imwas
Beit Nuba
Biddu
Beit Hanina
El 'Al
El Yaduda
Ashdod
Gedera
Shu'fat
Hartuv
Moza Illit
Tur
Suweima
Hisban
Gan Yavne
Revadim
Jerusalem
Mt. Nebo 2,631
Be'er Tuveya
Khirbet Qumran
Nizzanim
Lakhish
Bethlehem (Beit Lahm)
Ma'daba
Manja
Ashqelon
Hodiyya
Kefar Zekhariya
Beit Jala
Beit Sahur
Qedma
Nahhalin
W. Mashash
Zuweiza
Negba
Mavqi'im
Gevar'am
Gal'on
Zavdi'el
Ma'in
Nitil
Kharas
Beit Fajjar
Mordekhay
Gat
Qiryat Gat
Bet Guvrin
Tarqumiya
Uzza
Shiqma
Helez
Halhul
Bayt Hanum
Ahuzzam
Mt. Hebron 3,347
Jabalyah
Nir Am
Idna
Dura
Hebron (El Khalil)
Ruhama
Gaza
Sa'ad
Er Rihiya
Deir el Balah
Be'eri
Bet Qama
Bet Hagaddi
Shoval
Yatta
'Ein Gedi
Az-Zāhirīyah
Bani Suheila
Gerar
Re'im
As-Samu'
Khan Yunis
'Abasan
Peduyim
Gilat
Mishmar HaNegev
Tseelim
Magen
Mazra'
Rafah
Urim
Borot Kidod
Nir Yitzhaq
Beersheba
'Omer
El Lisan
Hazerim
Dhira'
Habesor
Mivtahim
Beer Sheva
Ze'elim
Nevatim
Beer Ef'e
Hemar
Mt. Dimona 2,238
Dimona
Sedom
Revivim
Kurnub
Salt Pans
Safi
W. el Hasa
Mash 'Abbe Sade
Yeroham
El Ghor
Tsin
Oron
Mt. Hatira 2,349
Beersheba
Dead Sea
El Karak
Dimona
EL
Revivim
Sedom
W. el-Hasa
SOUTHERN
KARAK
Sede Boqer
Et Tafila
El 'Auja
Tsin
El Qusaima
Hatseva
Dana
NEGEV
Mizpe Ramon
'En Yahav
'Arab
Mt. Ramon 3,396
Esh Shaubak
JORDAN
Paran
PETRA
Wadi Musa
MA'AN
Ma'an
El Kuntilla
Yotvata
Ra's en Naqb
El Quweira
Beer Ora
'Ein Netafim
Elath (Elat)
Jeb. Ramm 5,755
Taba
G. of 'Aqaba
'Aqaba
MILES
0 10 20 30

Pa·li·nu·ro \ˌpäl-ə-ˈnu̇(ə)r-(ˌ)ō\ *or anc.* **Pal·i·nu·rus** \ˌpal-ə-ˈn(y)u̇r-əs\. Cape on W coast of Italy, at 40°02′N, 15°16′E.

Pa–lin–yu–ch'i \ˈpä-ˈlin-ˈyü-ˈchē\ *or* **Ta·pan·shang** \ˈdä-ˈbän-ˈshäŋ\. Town, Inner Mongolia, NE China; in mountainous region 125 m. N of Ch'eng-te.

Pal·i·sade, Middle \-ˌpal-ə-ˈsād\. Peak in Sierra Nevada, in E Fresno co., S cen. California; 14,040 ft.

Palisade, North. Peak in Sierra Nevada, in E Fresno co., S cen. California; 14,242 ft.

Pal·i·sades \ˌpal-ə-ˈsādz\. A line of high cliffs of traprock ab. 15 m. long on W bank of Hudson river in SE New York and NE New Jersey.

Palisades Interstate Park. A chain of parks extending from Fort Lee, New Jersey, opp. New York City, to Newburgh, New York, and including Bear Mt.; total area ab. 70 sq. m.; river frontage 22 m., including 13 m. of the Palisades.

Palisades Park. Residential borough, Bergen co., NE corner of New Jersey, 9 m. N of Jersey City; pop. (1970c) 13,351; amusement park.

Pa·li·ta·na \ˌpäl-ə-ˈtän-ə\. 1 Former Indian state, SE Kathiawar Penin., now part of Gujarat state, W India; 300 sq. m.
2 Town, its ✱, 70 m. WNW of Surat; pop. (1961c) 24,581. Nearby is sacred hill of **Sa·trun·ja·ya** \sə-ˈtru̇n-jə-yə\ covered with Jain temples.

Palk Bay \ˈpȯ(l)k-\. Bay on extreme NW coast of the island of Ceylon.

Palk Strait. Channel bet. N Ceylon and SE India, N of Adam's Bridge; 40 m. wide.

Pal La·ha·ra \ˌpäl-lə-ˈhär-ə\. Former Indian state, now part of Orissa state, NE India, ab. 80 m. NW of Cuttack; 450 sq. m.; ✱ Pal Lahara.

Pal·las \ˈpal-əs\. Hamlet in co. Longford, N cen. Eire, E of Lough Ree; birthplace of Oliver Goldsmith.

Pallene. See KASSANDRA.

Pal·les–Ou·nas·tun·tu·ri National Park \ˈpal-əs-ˌōn-əs-ˈtu̇n-tə-rē-\. National park, NW Finland; 193 sq. m.; arctic region; established 1938.

Pallice, La. See LA PALLICE.

Pal·li·ser, Cape \-ˈpal-ə-sər\. Cape on S extremity of North I., New Zealand, at the E entrance to Cook Strait.

Palliser Bay. Bay on S coast of North I., New Zealand, an inlet of Cook Strait W of Cape Palliser.

Palliser Islands. Former name of TUAMOTU ARCHIPELAGO.

Pal·ma \ˈpäl-mə\ *or* **Palma de Ma·llor·ca** \-(ˌ)thā-mə(l)-ˈyȯr-kə\. Commune, ✱ of Baleares prov., Spain, and ✱ of Majorca I., on **Bay of Palma;** pop. (1970p) 234,098; chief port of Balearic Is.; trades in agricultural produce, oil, wine; manufactures flour, sugar, leather, pottery, silks and woolens, basketwork, embroidery, jewelry; tourism; Gothic cathedral, Moorish palace (the Almudaina), 16th cent. town hall, palace of Majorcan kings; birthplace and burial place of Raymond Lully; tomb of James II of Aragon. Captured from Moors by James I of Aragon 1229.

Palma, La. See LA PALMA.

Palma di Mon·te·chia·ro \ˈpäl-mə-dē-ˌmȯn-tē-kē-ˈär-(ˌ)ō\. Commune, Agrigento prov., SW Sicily, Italy, near Mediterranean Sea 14 m. SE of Agrigento; pop. (1968c) 22,567; 17th cent. cathedral.

Palmas. See MIANGAS.

Pal·mas, Cape \-ˈpäl-məs\. Cape, S Liberia, W Africa; extends into Atlantic Ocean.

Palmas, Gulf of. Gulf on SW coast of the island of Sardinia, Italy.

Palmas, Las \lä-ˈspäl-məs\. 1 Province of Spain, in Canary Is. See table at SPAIN.
2 City of Grand Canary I. See LAS PALMAS.

Palmas Al·tas \ˌpäl-mə-ˈsäl-təs\. Cape on N coast of Puerto Rico.

Palma So·ria·no \-ˌsōr-ē-ˈän-(ˌ)ō, -ˌsȯr-\. Municipality, Oriente prov., E Cuba, 18 m. NW of Santiago de Cuba; pop. (1967e) 104,430.

Palm Bay \ˈpäm-, ˈpälm-\. Town, Brevard co., E Florida, on Indian River Inlet 24 m. SSE of Cocoa; pop. (1970c) 7199.

Palm Beach. 1 County in Florida. See table at FLORIDA.
2 Resort town, Palm Beach co., SE Florida, at N end of island separating Lake Worth (lagoon) from the Atlantic; pop. (1970c) 9086.

Palm Beach Gardens. City, Palm Beach co., SE Florida; pop. (1970c) 6102.

Palm·dale \ˈpäm-ˌdāl\. City, Los Angeles co., SW California, NE of Los Angeles; pop. (1970c) 8511.

Pal·mei·ra das Mis·sões \pəl-ˈmā-rə-däs-mē-ˈsȯⁿ-əs\. Municipality, Rio Grande do Sul state, S Brazil, 190 m. NW of Pôrto Alegre; pop. (1968e) 55,128.

Pal·mei·ri·nhas Point \ˌpäl-mə-ˌrēn-yəsh-\. Cape on NW coast of Angola, S of Luanda.

Palm·er \ˈpäm-ər, ˈpäl-mər\. 1 City, ⊗ of Matanuska-Susitna borough, SE Alaska, 6 m. NE of Matanuska in the Matanuska valley; pop. (1970c) 1140.
2 Town, Hampden co., SW Massachusetts, ENE of Springfield; pop. (1970c) 11,680; wire goods, cosmetics; plastics; truck and dairy farms.

Palmer Archipelago *or formerly* **Antarctic Archipelago.** Island group bet. South America and Antarctica, 53°W to 78°W, NW of Weddell Sea; includes Anvers I., Brabant I., and other small islands off NW coast of Antarctic Penin.; part of British Antarctic Territory.

Palmer Peninsula. See ANTARCTIC PENINSULA.

Palmerston. See DARWIN.

Pal·mer·ston \ˈpä-mər-stən, ˈpäl-mər-\ *or* **Ava·rau** \ˌäv-ə-ˈrau̇\. Island (atoll) in cen. Pacific Ocean 270 m. NW of Rarotonga in the Cook Is.; 1 sq. m.; administered by New Zealand.

Palmerston, Cape. Headland, Queensland, NE Australia, SE of Mackay; 21°32′S, 149°29′E.

Palmerston North. City, S North I., New Zealand, 80 m. NE of Wellington; pop. (1970e) 51,000; knit goods, electrical equipment, pharmaceuticals; in dairy farming region; Massey Univ. (1964).

Palm·er·ton \ˈpäm-ərt-ᵊn, ˈpäl-mərt-\. Industrial borough, Carbon co., E Pennsylvania, on Lehigh river 17 m. NNW of Allentown; pop. (1970c) 5620; zinc refining.

Pal·met·to \pal-ˈmet-(ˌ)ō\. City, Manatee co., W Florida penin., at lower end of Tampa Bay; pop. (1970c) 7422; fruit packing.

Palmetto Point. Cape on NE coast of the island of Jamaica, West Indies.

Pal·mi \ˈpäl-mē\. Coastal commune, Reggio di Calabria prov., Calabria, S Italy, 21 m. NNE of Reggio di Calabria; pop. (1968e) 18,002.

Pal·mi·llas, Point \-päl-ˈmē-yəs\. Cape on SW coast of Las Villas prov., W cen. Cuba, at entrance to Cochinos Bay.

Pal·mi·ra \päl-ˈmir-ə\. 1 City, Valle dept., W Colombia, near the Cauca river; pop. (1968e) 119,152; alt. 3000 ft.; raises coffee, tobacco, cacao.
2 Town and municipality, Las Villas prov., W cen. Cuba, just N of Cienfuegos; munic. pop. (1967e) 15,460.

Pal·mi·ta de la Vir·gen \päl-ˈmēt-ə-del-ə-ˈvi(ə)r-ˌhān\. Island in Pacific Ocean off the coast of SW Sinaloa state, Mexico, N of the island of **Palmito del Ver·de** \-del-ˈve(ə)rd-ē\; the two long, narrow islands parallel the coast and appear to be a continuation of a peninsula extending N from coast of Nayarit state.

Palm Springs \ˈpäm-, ˈpälm-\. 1 Resort city, Riverside co., SE California, 44 m. SE of San Bernardino in Coachella Valley; pop. (1970c) 20,936; incorporated 1938.
2 Village, Palm Beach co., SE Florida; pop. (1970c) 4340.

Pal·my·ra \pal-ˈmī-rə\. 1 City, ⊗ of Marion co., NE Missouri, 12 m. NW of Hannibal; pop. (1970c) 3188.

2 Borough, Burlington co., S cen. New Jersey, on Delaware river 7 m. NE of Camden; pop. (1970c) 6969.

3 Village, Wayne co., W New York, 21 m. E of Rochester; pop. (1970c) 3776; near Hill Cumorah, glacial drumlin where Joseph Smith claimed to have unearthed gold plates that were source of Book of Mormon (1827).

4 Borough, Lebanon co., SE cen. Pennsylvania, 16 m. E of Harrisburg; pop. (1970c) 7615; clothing, cement products, footwear; limestone quarries.

5 Village, ⊗ of Fluvanna co., cen. Virginia.

6 *Bib.* **Tad·mor** \'tad-ˌmȯ(ə)r\ *or* **Ta·mar** \'tā-ˌmär, -mər\. Ruined city, Syria, 135 m. NE of Damascus, at an oasis on N edge of Syrian Desert; now a small village. Said to have been built by Solomon (*2 Chron.* viii. 4) but perhaps confused with Tamar in Palestine (*1 Kings* ix. 18); an ancient Aramaic town; developed at beginning of Christian Era and became prosperous because of its location on trade route from Persian Gulf to Egypt; under Roman suzerainty in 1st cent. A.D.; rose to great prominence 130 to 270 A.D.; devoted to worship of the sun. After death of Odenathus, 266 or 267, rule of kingdom succeeded to his wife Zenobia who declared her country independent. Captured and Zenobia made prisoner 272 by Emperor Aurelian; after people's revolt, city destroyed 273.

Palmyra Island. One of the Line Is. (*q.v.*), at N end of group ab. 960 m. S of Honolulu, in cen. Pacific Ocean; 1 sq. m.; formerly a part of Honolulu co., Hawaiian Is., but excluded from Hawaii when state was organized 1960. Discovered 1802 by Captain Sawle of the American ship *Palmyra;* annexed by kingdom of Hawaii 1862 and by Great Britain 1889; formally taken over by United States 1912.

Pal·my·ras Point \pal-ˌmī-rəz-\. Cape, Orissa state, NE coast of India, projecting into the Bay of Bengal N of the Mahanadi river.

Pa·lo \'pä-(ˌ)lō\. Municipality, Leyte prov., on E coast of Leyte I., Phil., on San Pedro Bay 7 m. S of Tacloban; pop. (1969e) 34,300.

Palo Al·to \ˌpal-ə-'wal-(ˌ)tō\. **1** County in Iowa. See table at IOWA.

2 City, Santa Clara co., W California, 17 m. NW of San Jose; pop. (1970c) 56,181; residential; electronic equipment; missile production and research; Stanford Univ. (1885); founded 1891.

3 Battlefield, Cameron co., S Texas, 12 m. NE of Brownsville; scene May 8, 1846 of first battle of Mexican War; Americans under Gen. Zachary Taylor defeated Mexicans under Gen. Mariano Arista.

Palo Du·ro Canyon \ˌpal-ə-ˌd(y)u̇(ə)r-ō-, -ˌdȯr-ə-\. Canyon of the Red river, in Randall and Armstrong cos., NW Texas, SE of Amarillo; contains a state park.

Pa·lo·ma·ni \ˌpal-ə-'män-ē\. Peak, W Bolivia, NE of Lake Titicaca; 18,921 ft.

Pal·o·mar Mountain \'pal-ə-ˌmär-\ *or* **Mount Palomar.** Peak, San Diego co., SW corner of California, 45 m. NNE of San Diego; 6140 ft.; astronomical observatory, erected by the Rockefeller Foundation for the Carnegie Institution and the California Institute of Technology; location of giant (200-in.) telescope.

Pa·lo·mas Mountains \pə-ˌlō-məs-\. Small range in E Yuma co., SW Arizona.

Pa·lom·pon \ˌpä-lȯm-'pȯn\. Municipality, Leyte prov., on NW coast of Leyte I., Phil., 15 m. W of Ormoc; pop. (1969e) 42,400; scene of last stand of Japanese on Leyte Dec. 1944.

Palo Pin·to \ˌpal-ō-'pin-tō, ˌpä-lō-\. **1** County in N cen. Texas. See table at TEXAS.

2 Village, its ⊗; pop. (1970c) 521; deposits of petrified wood nearby.

Pa·lo·po \pä-'lō-(ˌ)pō\. Seaport, Celebes I., Indonesia, on NW shore of Gulf of Bone; pop. (1969e) 42,400.

Pa·los \'pä-(ˌ)lōs\ *or officially* **Palos de la Fron·te·ra** \'pä-(ˌ)lōz-dā-lə-frən-'ter-ə\. Former seaport, Huelva prov., SW Spain, on Rió Tinto; pop. (1960c) 2540; Columbus sailed from here Aug. 3, 1492; harbor now silted up.

Palos, Cape of. Cape, SE coast of Spain, E of Cartagena.

Palo Se·co \ˌpal-ō-'sek-(ˌ)ō\. Leper colony, Canal Zone, on Bay of Panama on W side of canal entrance.

Palos Heights \ˌpāl-əs-\. City, Cook co., NE Illinois, 17 m. SW of Chicago; pop. (1970c) 9915.

Palos Hills. City, Cook co., NE Illinois, 15 m. SW of Chicago; pop. (1970c) 6629.

Palos Park. City, Cook co., NE Illinois, 10 m. SW of Chicago; pop. (1970c) 3297; Argonne Forest Preserve and National Laboratory (atomic energy experiments).

Palos Ver·des Estates \ˌpal-əs-ˌvərd-ēz-\. City, Los Angeles co., SW California, S of Los Angeles; pop. (1970c) 13,631; residential.

Pa·louse *or* **Pe·louse** \pə-'lüs\. **1** River, NW Idaho and SE Washington; ab. 140 m. long; rises in Latah co., NW Idaho, flows W across Washington border, turns S and empties into Snake river on E border of Franklin co.

2 *or* **Palouse Hills.** Fertile hilly region, SE Washington and NW Idaho, N of Snake and Clearwater rivers; wheat growing.

Palpana, Cerro. See CERRO PALPANA.

Palti. See YANG-CHO-YUNG.

Pa·lu \'pä-lü\. Town, ✱ of Central Sulawesi prov., Celebes, Indonesia; pop. (1961c) 52,144.

Pa·lu·an Bay \pä-ˌlü-ən-\. Inlet of South China Sea in NW coast of Mindoro, Phil.; Americans secured anchorage here and seized town of **Paluan** Jan. 8, 1945.

Pa·lus \'pā-ləs\. Latin, "marsh" or "morass," also a shallow sea, as in: (1) **Palus Maeotis.** See AZOV, SEA OF. (2) **Palus Tattaeus.** The Tuz Lake (*q.v.*) in Turkey. (3) **Palus Labeatis.** See SCUTARI, LAKE. (4) **Palus Tritonis.** See DJERID, CHOTT.

Pal·wal \'pəl-wəl\. Town, Haryana, NW India, ab. 35 m. S of Delhi; pop. (1961c) 27,863; a place of great antiquity, of importance in Aryan traditions, esp. in the Pandava kingdom.

Pam \'pam\. Town, New Caledonia, SW Pacific Ocean, on E coast of island near NW tip.

Pam·ban Channel \ˌpäm-bən-\. Shallow channel separating Rameswaram I. from the mainland of S India and connecting the Gulf of Mannar with Palk Strait.

Pa·me·ka·san \ˌpäm-i-kə-'sän\. Town, S Madura I., Indonesia, ab. 55 m. E of Surabaja; pop. (1961c) 36,321.

Pa·miers \pä-'myā\. Commune, Ariège dept., S France, on Ariège river 10 m. N of Foix; pop. (1968c) 14,564; episcopal see; manufactures paper, metal goods, lumber.

Pa·mir \pə-'mi(ə)r\. Literally, valley at foot of a mountain peak; such a glacial valley at 12,000 to 14,000 ft. altitude; usually in the plural, **The Pa·mirs** \-'mi(ə)rz\, a high altitude region of cen. Asia, mostly in Tadzhik S.S.R., U.S.S.R., partly on borders of Sinkiang Uighur, China, Jammu and Kashmir, India, and Afghanistan. Many peaks above 20,000 ft.; highest in U.S.S.R., Communism Peak in Tadzhik S.S.R. 24,590 ft.; highest in China in the Mu-ssu-t'a-ko-a-t'e, Kung-ko-erh 25,325 ft.; many glaciers. Central mountain knot from which extend great ranges: Tien Shan to N, Kunlun and Karakoram to E, and Hindu Kush to W.

Pam·li·co \'pam-li-ˌkō\. **1** River bisecting Beaufort co., E North Carolina; actually the estuary of the Tar river (*q.v.*); at its head is Washington, the county seat.

2 County in North Carolina. See table at NORTH CAROLINA.

Pamlico Sound. Sound bet. E North Carolina mainland and islands off the coast; 80 m. long and 8–30 m. wide; receives the Pamlico river on the W, and the Neuse river on the SW.

Pam·pa \'pam-pə\. Industrial city, ⊗ of Gray co., NW Texas, in the panhandle 52 m. ENE of Amarillo; pop. (1970c) 21,726; carbon black, chemicals, oil drilling equipment, clothing; oil and gas wells; livestock and grain farms.

Pampa, La. See LA PAMPA.

Pam·pan·ga \päm-ˈpäŋ-gə\. 1 *or* **Rio Gran·de de Pampanga** \ˌrē-ō-ˈgrän-dē-ˌdä-\. River, cen. Luzon, Phil.; 120 m. long; rises in Caraballo Mts. on N border of Nueva Ecija prov., flows S into Pampanga and enters N Manila Bay in a wide swampy delta in Pampanga and Bulacan provs. Navigable for smaller vessels. Has many tributaries in fertile plain; main branch is the Chico.

2 Province, cen. Luzon, Phil.; 842 sq. m.; pop. (1970p) 912,304; ✱ San Fernando. Lies in S part of cen. Luzon plain watered by lower Pampanga river and tributaries. Mountains on the W boundary are part of the Zambales range; highest Pinatubo, on the border, 5770 ft.; in the NE is isolated volcanic peak of Mt. Arayat 3867 ft., but province as a whole is level. Chief occupation agriculture; fishing also important. Entire E part is covered by Candaba swamp and the delta of the Pampanga is an extensive mangrove swamp; many streams afford easy transportation. Great majority of inhabitants are Pampangans. Chief towns San Fernando, Angeles, Lubao.

History: In pre-Spanish times home of Pampangans, a brave and progressive tribe, who had many prosperous settlements; overcome by Legaspi 1571–72 after strong resistance. Created 1571 as a province, but of much greater extent than now; its area gradually reduced, esp. in 1754, 1848, and 1860. One of first provinces to join revolution of 1896; relinquished by Americans Dec. 1941, but recovered Jan.–Feb. 1945.

Pampanga Chico. See CHICO 4.

Pam·pas \ˈpam-pəz, -pəs\. Plains of South America extending for nearly 1000 m. from the lower Paraná river to S cen. Argentina, SSW of Buenos Aires; area in Argentina ab. 294,000 sq. m.; dry in W, well watered in E; livestock raising.

Pampas del Sa·cra·men·to \-del-ˌsak-rə-ˈment-(ˌ)ō\. Plains in NE Peru, chiefly in S Loreto dept.

Pampeluna. See PAMPLONA 2.

Pam·phyl·ia \pam-ˈfil-ē-ə, -ˈfil-yə\. Ancient district and Roman province in S Asia Minor, a narrow territory on the coast S of Pisidia and bet. Lycia and Cilicia; chief town was Perga. Subject in turn to all the empires that controlled Asia Minor; became Roman 130 B.C. and then included Pisidia. See LYCIA.

Pam·plo·na \pam-ˈplō-nə\. 1 City, Norte de Santander dept., N Colombia, ab. 40 m. NE of Bucaramanga; pop. (1968e) 33,707.

2 *or formerly* **Pam·pe·lu·na** \ˌpam-pə-ˈlü-nə\ *or anc.* **Pompae·lo** \päm-ˈpē-lō\. City, ✱ of Navarra prov., N Spain, 196 m. NNE of Madrid; pop. (1970p) 147,168; center of agricultural region; manufactures kitchenware, paper, chemicals, rope, pottery, wineskins; distilling, flour milling; univ. (1952); 14th cent. cathedral. Ancient capital of the Vascones; rebuilt by Pompey 75 B.C.; taken by Goths, Franks, Moors; captured from Moors by Charlemagne 778 A.D.; became capital of kingdom of Navarre; on union 1515 of Navarre and Castile, made viceroyalty; fortified by Philip II 1571; captured by French 1808 and by British under Wellington 1813.

Pa·mun·key \pə-ˈməŋ-kē\. River, E Virginia; ab. 80 m. long; formed by confluence of North Anna and South Anna rivers in NE Hanover co., flows SE and unites with Mattaponi river at West Point to form York river.

Pa·na \ˈpā-nə\. City, Christian co., cen. Illinois, 30 m. S of Decatur; pop. (1970c) 6326; coal mines.

Pa·na·bo \pe-ˈnä-(ˌ)bō\. Municipality, Davao del Norte prov., Mindanao, Phil., ab. 15 m. NNE of Davao; pop. (1969e) 58,600.

Pa·na·du·ra \ˌpən-ə-ˈdu̇r-ə\. Seaport, W Ceylon, on Indian Ocean 16 m. S of Colombo.

Pa·nai·tan \pə-ˈnīt-ən\ *or Du.* **Prin·sen** \ˈprin(t)-sən\. Island at S end of Sunda Strait off the SW tip of Java, Indonesia; 47 sq. m.

Pa·na·ji \pän-ˈä-jē\ *or* **Pan·gim** *also* **Pan·jim** \ˈpän-ˈzhim\ *or* **New Goa** \-ˈgō-ə\. Town and seaport, ✱ of the Indian territory of Goa, Daman, and Diu, W India, on Arabian Sea at mouth of Mandavi river; ✱ of former Portuguese India; comprises the ruins of the old port (Old Goa) and the new town (New Goa) just to the W and nearer the coast; has good harbor. Became residence of the viceroy 1759; Goa annexed by India 1962.

Pan·a·ma \ˈpan-ə-ˌmä, -ˌmȯ, ˌpan-ə-ˈ\ *or Span.* **Pa·na·má** \ˌpän-ə-ˈmä\. 1 *or officially* **Re·púb·li·ca de Panamá** \rā-ˈpüb-li-kə-dā-\. Republic, S Central America, occupying the Isthmus of Panama (*q.v.*); bounded on N by the Caribbean Sea, on E by Colombia, on S by the Pacific Ocean, and on W by Costa Rica; 33,659 sq. m. (incl. 4451 sq. m. of water); pop. (1970p) 1,425,343; ✱ Panama. *Physical features:* Has coastline of ab. 760 m. on Pacific side and 470 m. on the Atlantic; traversed by two parallel ranges with valleys and plains in between; highest point is in W, near Costa Rica boundary: Chiriquí volcano 11,400 ft.; in cen. part near the Canal Zone and in the E (Serranía del Darién) average height is ab. 3000 ft. Most important rivers the Chagres, Chepo, Tuira, and only large lake is Gatun in the Canal Zone (*q.v.*). Pacific coast indented by large Gulf of Panama containing several islands (esp. Pearl Is.); on W side is Azuero Penin., and W of that is island of Coiba; on N coast are Mosquito Gulf and the Gulf of San Blas. Has fertile soil and well-forested mountain slopes. *Chief products:* Bananas, cocoa, timber, corn, rice; manufacturing: textiles, apparel, footwear, cement; food processing. *Chief cities:* Panama, Colón, David, La Chorrera, Santiago. Divided into the following nine provinces (for pronunciation of their names, see their individual entries):

NAME	AREA[1] (sq. m.)	POP. (1970p)	CAPITAL
Bocas del Toro	3,443	40,776	Bocas del Toro
Chiriquí	3,381	236,256	David
Coclé	1,944	117,949	Penonomé
Colón	2,882	134,311	Colón
Darién	6,488	22,627	La Palma
Herrera	937	72,492	Chitré
Los Santos	1,493	72,212	Las Tablas
Panama	4,360	576,866	Panama
Veraguas	4,280	151,854	Santiago

[1]Area = land area.

History: Coast skirted by Columbus 1502; settled at Darien 1510; at Isthmus of Panama, Balboa discovered Pacific Ocean 1513; city of Panama founded 1519; Portobelo the Atlantic port for important Spanish trade across the Isthmus; in viceroyalty of Peru before 18th cent.; in viceroyalty of New Granada, later part of Colombia (*q.v.*); in late 19th cent., projects for a canal across Panama were the subject of negotiations with U.S.; in 1903, Panama revolted from Colombia and was recognized by U.S. to whom it ceded Canal Zone; adopted new constitution 1946 (suspended 1968); rejected (1970) the unratified Panama-U.S. treaty of 1967 dealing with the future status of the Canal Zone.

2 Province of E cen. Panama. See table at PANAMA.

3 *or* **Panama City.** City, ✱ of the Republic of Panama and of Panama province; pop. (1970p) 418,013; commercial and transportation center of the republic; Univ. of Panama (1935), Santa Maria Univ. (1965). Old city founded 1519 and completely destroyed by Henry Morgan 1671; rebuilt on present site ab. 7 m. W; center of revolt against Colombia 1903 and made capital the same year.

Panama, Gulf of. Large inlet of Pacific Ocean on S coast of Panama; the inner part (N of the Pearl Is.) on which the city of Panama is located is called the **Bay of Panama.**

Panama, Isthmus of *or formerly* **Isthmus of Dar·i·en** \-ˌdar-ē-ˈen, -ˌder-\. The link bet. North America and South America, separating the Atlantic and Pacific oceans;

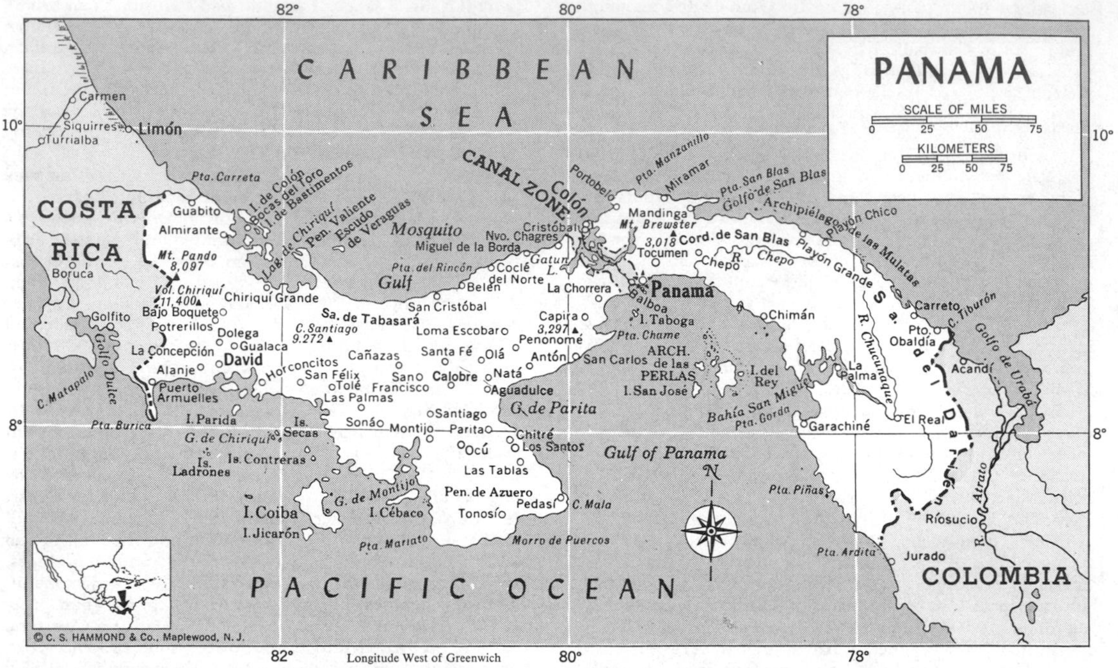

420 m. long; forms the Republic of Panama. Sometimes, in a restricted use, the name Isthmus of Panama is reserved for the crossing from Panama to Colón, the course of the Panama Canal, and the name Isthmus of Darien is reserved for the narrow crossing (46 m.) nearest the mainland of South America, and the name Isthmus of San Blas for the narrowest part (31 m.) S of the Gulf of San Blas. Isthmus also crossed by Panama R.R., in general course parallel to the canal from Colón to Panama City, built 1850–55, 46½ m. long.

Panama Canal. Ship canal across the Isthmus of Panama from Colón on the Caribbean Sea to Balboa on the Bay of Panama, the inner part of the Gulf of Panama, and the Pacific Ocean; length 40.3 m. from shore to shore and 50.7 m. from deep water to deep water; minimum width 300 ft.; minimum depth 41 ft.; highest elevation above sea level 85 ft. The Atlantic entrance to the Canal is 27 m. W of the Pacific entrance.

History: First attempt at construction of a canal undertaken by French under Ferdinand de Lesseps 1879–89; after bankruptcy of French company, U.S. investigated possibility of alternative canal routes and purchase of French concession 1899–1901; concession granted to U.S. by Panama (see CANAL ZONE) under Hay-Bunau-Varilla treaty 1903; construction of canal begun early 1904; canal opened to traffic Aug. 15, 1914; construction work to deepen and widen canal initiated 1959.

Panama Canal Zone. See CANAL ZONE.

Panama City. 1 City, ⊗ of Bay co., NW Florida, on Gulf of Mexico 30 m. W of Apalachicola river; pop. (1970c) 32,-096; fish, paper, chemicals; Gulf Coast Junior Coll. (1957); Tyndall Air Force Base (Air Tactical School) and U.S. Navy mine defense laboratory. Formed 1909 by merger of village of Panama City with adjoining villages.

2 City, Republic of Panama. See PANAMA 3.

Panamá Vieja. See OLD PANAMA.

Pan–American Highway *or* **Inter–American Highway.** International highway system, extending from the United States-Canada border to Santiago, Chile.

Pan·a·mint Mountains \ˈpan-ə-ˌmint-, -mənt-\. Mountain range, Inyo co., E California, W of Death Valley; highest peak Telescope Peak 11,049 ft.

Pa·na·on \ˌpän-ə-ˈȯn\. Island, SE of Leyte I., Phil., on W side of S end of Surigao Strait; 78 sq. m., 20 m. long by 6 m. wide; chief town Liloan at N end. Occupied by Americans Oct. 21, 1944.

Pa·nar·ea *or* **Pa·nar·ia** \pə-ˈner-ē-ə\ *or anc.* **Eu·on·y·mus** \yü-ˈän-i-məs\. One of the Lipari Is. (*q.v.*) in the Tyrrhenian Sea NE of Sicily, Italy.

Pa·na·ro \pə-ˈnär-(ˌ)ō\ *or anc.* **Scul·ten·na** \ˌskəl-ˈten-ə\. River, N Italy; 103 m. long; rises on slopes of Monte Cimone; flows N and NE into Po river.

Pa·nay \pə-ˈnī\. 1 Island, one of the Visayan Is., cen. Phil.; 4749 sq. m., 6th in size in Phil.; chief town Iloilo. Bounded on N by Sibuyan Sea, on NE by Visayan Sea, on E by Guimaras Strait, on S by Panay Gulf, and on W by Sulu Sea. Comprises four provinces of Aklan, Antique, Capiz, and Iloilo. In World War II bombed by Allies Sept. 1944; occupied Mar. 18–20, 1945.

2 River, E and cen. Capiz prov., Panay, Phil.; ab. 50 m. long; rises in mountains of SW Capiz, flows NE and N to Sibuyan Sea at Roxas. Has four large tributaries; navigable for native craft for a considerable distance.

3 Municipality, Capiz prov., Panay, Phil., 3 m. SE of Roxas; pop. (1969e) 27,300; old town, first Spanish settlement (1569) on Panay I. and second in the Philippines.

Panay Gulf. Large inlet of NE Sulu Sea, Phil., formed by S Panay I., Guimaras I., and SW Negros I.; ab. 45 m. across from Naso Point to Negros coast; connects by Guimaras Strait with Visayan Sea.

Pan·cake Range \ˈpan-ˌkāk-\. Range, SE cen. Nevada, in NE Nye co., extending N into White Pine co.

Pan·če·vo \ˈpän-chə-ˌvō\ *or Hung.* **Pan·cso·va** \ˈpȯn-chə-ˌvȯ\. City, Serbia, NE Yugoslavia, on Danube river opp. Belgrade; pop. (1965e) 52,000; transportation center; glass, chemicals, aircraft parts; first mentioned 12th cent.

Pan·či·čev \ˌpän-chē-ˈchef, -ˈchev\. See KOPAONIK.

Pan·dan \pän-ˈdän\. Municipality, Antique prov., Panay, Phil., on bend of W coast 66 m. N of San Jose de Buenavista; pop. (1969e) 27,200.

Pan de Azú·car \ˌpän-dā-ə-ˈzü-ˌkär, -ˈsü-\. 1 Small island in Pacific Ocean off NW coast of Atacama prov., Chile.

2 Peak in the cen. Andes Mts., in Venezuela, NE of Mérida; 15,978 ft.

Panderma. See BANDIRMA.

Pan·dhar·pur \ˈpən-dər-ˌpu̇(ə)r\. Town, SE Maharashtra, W India, on Bhima river 185 m. ESE of Bombay; pop. (1961c) 45,421; favorite place of pilgrimage in the Deccan, with celebrated temple to Vishnu.

Pandj, Ab–i– \ˌäb-ē-ˈpän(d)zh\ *also* **Panj** \ˈpän(d)zh\ *or* **Pyandzh** \ˈpyän(d)zh\. River on Afghanistan-U.S.S.R. boundary; ab. 400 m. long; a headstream of the Amu Darya.

Pan·do \ˈpän(ˌ)dō\. 1 *or formerly* **Colonial Territories** *or Span.* **Co·lo·nias** \kō-ˈlōn-yäs\. Department of NW Bolivia. See table at BOLIVIA.

2 Town, Canelones dept., S Uruguay, just NE of Montevideo; pop. (1963c) 12,108.

Pando, Mount. Peak in the Cordillera de Talamanca, W Panama; 8097 ft.

Pan·do·sia \pan-ˈdō-sh(ē-)ə\. Ancient town, S Italy, W of Heraclea; site of battle 326 B.C. in which Alexander I of Epirus was killed.

Paneas. See BANIYAS.

Pa·ne·vė·žys \ˌpan-ə-vā-ˈzhēs\ *or Russ.* **Pa·ne·ve·zhis** \-vā-ˈzhēs\. City, Lithuanian S.S.R., U.S.S.R., 55 m. NNE of Kaunas on Daugavpils-Šiauliai railroad; pop. (1969e) 72,000; flour milling, sugar refining, distilling, brewing; founded in 14th cent.

Pan·gae·us, Mount \-pan-ˈjē-əs\ *or Gk.* **Pan·gaí·on Óros** \päŋ-ˌgā-ə-ˈnȯr-əs\. Mountain range, NE Greece, N of Strymonic Gulf; in ancient times noted for gold and silver mines.

Pan·ga·ni \päŋ-ˈgän-ē\. 1 River, NE Tanzania, E Africa; ab. 250 m. long; flows from Mount Kilimanjaro SE into Indian Ocean opp. the island of Zanzibar. Called **Ru·vu** \ˈrü-(ˌ)vü\ in its lower course.

2 Coastal town at mouth of Pangani (or Ruvu) river, NE Tanzania, E Africa; pop. (1967c) 3000.

Pan·ga·si·nan \ˌpäŋ-gä-si-ˈnän\. Province, N cen. Luzon, Phil.; 2073 sq. m.; pop. (1970p) 1,387,632; ✱ Lingayen; bounded on N by Lingayen Gulf, and on W by South China Sea. Central part is broad level plain of the Agno river; in the E has low mountains, the foothills of the Cordillera Central, and in NW on peninsula is somewhat hilly. Chief river the Bued in the N flowing into SE corner of Lingayen Gulf, which is the notable feature of the coastline. On NW shore of the gulf are Cabarruyan I. and Santiago I.; Cape Bolinao is NW point of the peninsula and Dasol Bay is on SW coast. Agriculturally one of richest provinces of the Philippines; main products rice, corn, sugarcane, tobacco, and coconuts; important industries salt making and fishing. Inhabitants mainly Pangasinans, Ilokanos, and Sambals. Chief towns Lingayen, San Carlos, Dagupan, Malasiqui, and Urdaneta.

History: Probably a native kingdom in pre-Spanish times; explored 1572 by Spaniards and soon visited by missionaries; created a province 1611; some boundaries changed in 18th cent. Scene of two revolts, 1660 and 1765; experienced rapid economic growth during latter half of 19th cent.; civil government established Feb. 1901. In Dec. 1941 scene of early Japanese landings; in reconquest of Philippines occupied by Americans Jan. 8–31, 1945.

Pangerango. See PANGRANGO.

Pang–fou \ˈbəŋ-ˈfü\. Town, Anhwei prov., E China, ab. 80 m. N of Ho-fei; pop. (1970e) 400,000.

Panggong. See PANGONG.

Panggong Lake. See PANGONG LAKE.

Pangim. See PANAJI.

Pang·kah, Cape \-ˈpäŋ-kə\. Cape on NE coast of Java I., Indonesia, on W side of entrance to Surabaja Strait.

Pang·ka·lan·be·ran·dan \ˌpäŋ-kə-ˌlän-bə-ˈrän-dən\ *or* **Pang·ka·lan·bran·dan** \-ˈbrän-dən\. Town, N Sumatra, Indonesia, near N end of Strait of Malacca 40 m. NNW of Medan; large oil fields.

Pang·kal·pi·nang \ˌpäŋ-käl-pi-ˈnäŋ\. Town, Indonesia, on NE coast of Bangka I.; pop. (1961c) 60,283; port; highway center.

Pang·kor \ˈpäŋ-ˌkȯ(ə)r\. Small island, Malaysia, in Strait of Malacca, off W coast of S Malay Penin.; formerly belonged to Perak. Ceded to British 1826 and in 1874 became a part of the Dindings, in Penang settlement; retroceded to Perak 1935.

Pan·glao \päŋ-ˈglau̇\. Low flat island off SW Bohol I., Phil., separated from it by a narrow strait; 35 sq. m.; munic. pop. (1969e) 16,100.

Pang–nga. See PHANGNGA 2 and 3.

Pan·gong \ˈpən-ˌgȯŋ\ *or* **Pang·gong** \ˈpəŋ-ˌgȯŋ\. Mountain range SW and S of Pangong Lake; highest peak 22,060 ft.

Pangong Lake *or* **Panggong Lake.** Long narrow lake in Jammu and Kashmir, extending E across Chinese border at Tibet; elevation 14,000 ft., ab. 100 m. long; called **Pan–kung** \ˈpən-ˈku̇ŋ\ in China.

Pangopango. See PAGO PAGO.

Pang·rango \ˌpäŋ-ˈräŋ-(ˌ)ō\ *or formerly* **Pang·e·rango** \ˌpäŋ-ə-ˈräŋ-(ˌ)ō\. Extinct volcano, W Java I., Indonesia, SE of Bogor; 9882 ft.; twin peak of Mt. Gede.

Pan·guil Bay \päŋ-ˌgē(ə)l-\. Narrow inlet at SW corner of Iligan Bay, N coast of Mindanao, Phil.; ab. 23 m. long; lies bet. Misamis Occidental and Lanao del Norte provs.; Ozamiz is the port on N side of its entrance.

Pan·guitch \ˈpan-gwich\. City, ⊗ of Garfield co., S Utah, on Sevier river 34 m. ENE of Cedar City; pop. (1970c) 1318; lumber, dairy products.

Pang·u·ta·ran \ˌpäŋ-u̇-ˈtär-ən\. 1 Island group, N Sulu Archipelago, Phil., NW of Jolo; ab. 96 sq. m.; coextensive with Pangutaran municipal dist. Includes Pangutaran I., Panducan I., and ab. 12 small islands and islets. Heavily wooded; inhabitants mostly engaged in fishing.

2 Largest island of the group; 37 sq. m.

3 Town on E side of island.

Pan·han·dle \ˈpan-ˌhan-dᵊl\. 1 Any arm or projection of land like the handle of a pan; specifically: (a) NW Texas; chief town Amarillo; (b) NW Oklahoma; counties of Beaver, Texas, and Cimarron; (c) N West Virginia; counties along E bank of Ohio: Marshall, Ohio, Brooke, and Hancock; also, NE West Virginia, the "Eastern Panhandle," bet. Maryland and Virginia; hence, nickname "Panhandle State"; (d) N Idaho, bet. Washington and Montana; N Shoshone, Kootenai, Bonner, and Boundary cos.; (e) SE Alaska.

2 Town, ⊗ of Carson co., NW Texas; pop. (1970c) 2141.

Panhormus. See PALERMO 2.

Pa·nié, Mount \-pa-ˈnyā\. Highest peak on the island of New Caledonia, SW Pacific Ocean, near NE coast; 5341 ft.

Pa·ni·ha·ti \ˌpä-nə-ˈhä-tē\. Town, West Bengal, India, 10 m. N of Calcutta; pop. (1961c) 93,749.

Pa·ni·pat \ˈpän-ē-pət\. Town, Haryana, NW India, near Yamuna river 53 m. N of Delhi; pop. (1961c) 67,026; market town; cotton textiles; of great antiquity, dating back to legendary period; scene of three battles: Mogul Emperor Babur conquered Ibrahim Lodi of Delhi, Afghan sultan, 1526; Akbar the Great routed army of king of Bengal 1556; Afghan prince Ahmad Shah overcame the Marathas 1761. Came under British rule 1803.

Pa·ni·qui \pä-ˈnē-kē\. Municipality, Tarlac prov., Luzon, Phil., on a tributary of the Agno and on the Manila-Dagupan railroad 13 m. N of Tarlac; pop. (1969e) 48,600; an important transportation center; taken Jan. 1945 by Americans in advance on Manila.

Pa·ni·zos \pə-ˈnē-səs\ *or* **Pa·ni·zo** \pə-ˈnē-(ˌ)sō\. Peak, S Potosí dept., SW Bolivia; 18,025 ft.

Panj. See PANDJ, AB-I-.

Panjāb. See PUNJAB.

Panj·deh \ˈpanj-(ˌ)dā\ *or* **Penj·deh** \ˈpenj-\. Village, Turkmen S.S.R., U.S.S.R., on E bank of Kushka river near its junction with the Murghab; scene Mar. 30, 1885 of clash bet. Russian and Afghan forces over a part of boundary in dispute; Afghans defeated and boundary finally settled June 18, 1886, but incident nearly caused war bet. England and Russia.

Panjim. See PANAJI.

Panj·ko·ra \pənj-'kōr-ə, -'kȯr-\. River, North-West Frontier Province, Pakistan; rises in N Dir state and flows S to join the Swat river N of Peshawar.

Panj·nad \pənj-'näd\. Short course (ab. 50 m.) of the combined Sutlej and Chenab rivers, Pakistan, which joins the Indus at ab. 29°N. The other three streams are the Beas, Ravi, and Jhelum, rivers of the Punjab region, which join Sutlej and Chenab farther up in their courses.

Pan·kow \'päŋ-(,)kō\. District of East Berlin, East Germany; seat of East German government.

Pan–kung. See PANGONG LAKE.

Pan·na \'pən-ə\. 1 Former Indian state, now part of Madhya Pradesh, India.

2 Town, its ✱, Madhya Pradesh, N of Jabalpur; pop. (1961c) 16,700.

Pan·na·nich \'pan-ə-,nik\ *or* **Pannanich Wells.** Locality, Aberdeen co., NE Scotland, ab. 2 m. E of Ballater; chalybeate springs.

Pan·no·nia \pə-'nō-nē-ə\. Roman province including territory now mostly in Hungary and Yugoslavia; ✱ Sabaria (Szombathely); W of the Danube, E of Noricum, and N of Dalmatia. Little known before 35 B.C.; conquered by Romans 35–9 B.C. and incorporated with Illyria; at beginning of 1st cent. A.D. divided into Pannonia superior (W part) and Pannonia inferior (E part).

Pa·no·la \pə-'nō-lə\. Name of counties in two states of the U.S. See tables at MISSISSIPPI and TEXAS.

Panopolis. See AKHMÎM.

Pan·or·mos \pə-'nȯr-məs\. 1 Small seaport on Mykonos I., Cyclades, Greece; marble.

2 Seaport, Tenos I., Cyclades.

Panormus. See PALERMO 2.

Pan·si·pit \pän-'sē-pət\. Stream, Batangas prov., S Luzon, Phil.; ab. 8 m. long; flows out of Lake Taal SSW to Balayan Bay; towns of Taal and Lemery on it.

Pan·ta·nal \,pan-tə-'näl\. Region of swamps and marshland, S Mato Grosso state, SW Brazil, extending ab. 100 m. along E bank of upper Paraguay river; traversed by several tributaries of the Paraguay including the São Lourenço and the Taquari.

Pan·tar \'pan-,tär\. Island of the Alor group, Lesser Sunda Is., Indonesia, E of Lomblen I., W of Alor I., and 60 m. NW of Timor; 30 m. long by 13 m. wide. Mountainous, with rugged coast; highest point 4450 ft. Separated on W from Lomblen by Alor Strait and on E from Alor by narrow **Pantar Strait** (ab. 8 m. wide).

Pan·tel·le·ria \pan-,tel-ə-'rē-ə\; *anc.* **Co·sy·ra** *or* **Cos·sy·ra** \kə-'sī-rə\. Italian island in the Mediterranean Sea E of NE Tunisia and ab. 70 m. SW of Sicily; 32 sq. m.; pop. (1961c) 9269. In Roman times a place of banishment; in World War II a heavily fortified base, which suffered intense air and naval attack by Allies in June 1943 and surrendered June 11.

Pan·ther Mountain \,pan(t)-thər-\. 1 Peak in the Adirondack Mts., Hamilton co., NE cen. New York; 3865 ft.

2 Peak in the Catskill Mts., Ulster co., SE New York; 3760 ft.

Panther Peak. 1 Mountain in the Adirondack Mts., Essex co., NE New York; 4448 ft.

2 Mountain, S Brewster co., W Texas; 6405 ft.

Panticapaeum. See KERCH 2.

Pan·ti·co·sa \,pän-ti-'kō-sə\. Village, Huesca prov., NE Spain, in the Pyrenees near French border; pop. (1970p) 448; medicinal baths and springs.

Pan·tin \pä^{n}-'ta^{n}\. Commune, Seine-St-Denis dept., N France, NE suburb of Paris; pop. (1968c) 47,607; manufactures cotton thread, tools, foundry products; battle 1814.

Pan·tón \pän-'tȯn\. Commune, Lugo prov., NW Spain, 37 m. S of Lugo; pop. (1970p) 6954.

Pan·tu·kan \pän-'tü-,kän\. Municipality, cen. Davao del Norte, Mindanao, Phil., on NE shore of Davao Gulf opp. N end of Samal I.; pop. (1969e) 22,400.

Pá·nu·co \'pän-ə-,kō\. 1 River, cen. Mexico; ab. 100 m. long; rises in Hidalgo state, flows NE into the Gulf of Mexico 7 m. below Tampico.

2 Town, Veracruz state, E Mexico, 25 m. WSW of Tampico; munic. pop. (1970p) 49,077.

Pao–chi \'pau̇-'chē\ *or* **Pao·ki** \-'kē\. Town, W Shensi prov., NE cen. China, on Wei river ab. 100 m. W of Sian; pop. (1970e) 275,000.

Pão de Açú·car \,pau̇^{n}-dē-ə-'sü-kər\ *or Eng.* **Sug·ar·loaf Mountain** \,shu̇g-ər-,lōf-\. Rocky peak in Rio de Janeiro city on W side of entrance to Guanabara Bay, SE Brazil; 1296 ft.; aerial railroad; view of city from its summit.

Paoki. See PAO-CHI.

Paoking. See SHAO-YANG.

Pa·o·la \pā-'ō-lə\. City, ⊗ of Miami co., E Kansas, 40 m. SSW of Kansas City; pop. (1970c) 4662; dairy products; oil wells; grain farms.

Paola \'pā-'ō-lə, pä-'ȯl-ə\. Commune, Cosenza prov., Calabria, S Italy, on Tyrrhenian Sea 12 m. WNW of Cosenza; pop. (1968e) 15,018; 15th cent. chapel.

Pa·o·li \pā-'ō-lē\. 1 Town, ⊗ of Orange co., S Indiana, 22 m. S of Bedford; pop. (1970c) 3281; cannery.

2 Unincorporated urban center, Chester co., SE Pennsylvania, ab. 8 m. NE of West Chester; pop. (1970c) 5835; cement, flour, pharmaceuticals.

Paoning. See LANG-CHUNG.

Pao–shan \'bau̇-'shän\ *or formerly* **Yung·chang** \'yüŋ-'chäŋ\. Town, W Yunnan prov., S China, bet. the Salween and Mekong rivers 70 m. SW of Ta-li; alt. 5500 ft.

Pao–ting \'bau̇-'diŋ\ *or formerly* **Tsing·yuan** \'chiŋ-yü-'än\. City, cen. Hopei prov., NE China, on railroad ab. 90 m. SSW of Peking; pop. (1970e) 350,000; technical coll. (1960); surrounded by a wall built in Ming period. In civil war following World War II taken by Communists Nov. 22, 1948.

Pao–t'ou \'bau̇-'tō\. Town, cen. Inner Mongolia, N China, on left bank of the Yellow river at its great bend 90 m. W of Hu-ho-hao-t'e; pop. (1970e) 800,000; trade center; major steel plant; occupied by Japanese 1937–45.

Pá·pa \'päp-(,)ȯ\. City, Veszprém co., W Hungary, 80 m. W of Budapest; pop. (1970p) 27,775; tobacco products, textiles; truck farms; 18th cent. castle.

Pap·a·go Sa·gua·ro \'pap-ə-,gō-sə-'(g)wä-rō\. Former national monument, Maricopa co., SW cen. Arizona; 2050 acres; giant saguaros.

Pa·pa·i·kou \pä-,pä-ē-'kō-ü\. Town, Hawaii co., Hawaii, on E coast of Hawaii I. N of Hilo; pop. (1970c) 1888.

Pa·pa·ku·ra \,pap-ə-'ku̇r-ə\. Borough, North I., New Zealand; pop. (1970e) 15,150.

Papal States. See STATES OF THE CHURCH.

Pa·pan·da·jan \,pä-pän-'dä-yän\. Volcanic peak, W Java, Indonesia, ab. 12 m. SW of Garut; 8744 ft. Frequently climbed by tourists for view of Garut plain; major eruption Aug. 1772.

Pa·pan·tla de Olar·te \pä-'pän-tlä-,dā-ə-'lärt-ē\. Town, Veracruz state, E Mexico, ab. 70 m. NNW of Jalapa; munic. pop. (1970p) 94,623; nearby is an ancient pyramid, 82 ft. square at the base, 60 ft. high, covered with carvings: hieroglyphics, human figures, and reptilian creatures.

Pa·pas \'päp-(,)äs\; *anc.* **Arax·os** *or* **Arax·us** \ə-'rak-səs\. Cape on NW coast of Peloponnesus, S Greece, 20 m. W of Patras.

Pa·pa Stour \,päp-ə-'stu̇(ə)r\. One of the Shetland Is., NE of N Scotland; 2¾ m. long; pop. (1961c) 119.

Pa·pa·toe·toe \,pap-ə-toi-'toi\. City, North I., New Zealand; pop. (1970e) 22,000.

Pa·pa·wai Point \,päp-ə-,wī-, -,vī-\. Point on SW coast of Maui I., Hawaii, NW of Maalaea Bay.

Pa·pe·e·te \ˌpäp-ē-ˈät-ē, pə-ˈpēt-ē\. Seaport, ❋ of French Polynesia, also ❋ of Society Is., on NW coast of the island of Tahiti, Society Is., W Pacific Ocean; pop. (1971e) 24,000; commercial town, center for trading schooners and port for steamers to New Zealand, Australia, and San Francisco.

Papendorp. See WOODSTOCK 8.

Paph·la·go·nia \ˌpaf-lə-ˈgō-nē-ə, -nyə\. Ancient country and Roman province in N Asia Minor, on the Black Sea, and bounded on the E by Pontus, on the S by Galatia, and on the W by Bithynia. A mountainous country, one of the oldest nations of Asia Minor, but not important historically; subject much of the time to Pontus. Had several Greek colonies, esp. at Sinope.

Pa·phos \ˈpā-ˌfäs\. 1 District, W Cyprus, E Mediterranean Sea; 538 sq. m.; pop. (1968e) 62,500; ❋ Ktima.

2 Town, Paphos dist., SW coast of Cyprus, 1 m. S of Ktima; pop. (1968e) 11,000.

History: The old town of Paphos was probably founded by Phoenicians; its site is ab. 26 m. W of Limassol and 1 m. inland; long famous as the seat of worship of Aphrodite (Cypris) who is said by one legend to have landed here after her birth among the waves near Cythera (see CERIGO); hence, called the Paphian goddess; suffered greatly from earthquakes and several times rebuilt. New Paphos (the present town) was founded c. 1200 B.C., probably by Greeks, on the coast 10 m. WNW of old Paphos and after the Ptolemaic conquest of Cyprus 294 B.C. and Roman occupation 58 B.C. superseded the older town and became important Roman administrative city; its trade in olive oil was esp. flourishing. Visited by St. Paul (*Acts* xiii. 6–13). Destroyed by Saracens 960 A.D. and rebuilt in modern times; still has many Roman remains.

Pa·pil·lion \pə-ˈpil-yən\. City, ⊗ of Sarpy co., E Nebraska; pop. (1970c) 5606; diversified agriculture.

Pa·pi·neau \ˌpap-ə-ˈnō\. County, Quebec, Canada. See table at QUEBEC.

Pa·pi·neau·ville \ˌpap-ə-ˈnō-ˌvil\. Village, ⊗ of Papineau co., SW Quebec, Canada, on Ottawa river, 35 m. ENE of Ottawa; pop. (1971p) 1407.

Paps of Ju·ra \ˌpaps . . . ˈju̇r-ə\. Three mountains on Jura I., in the Inner Hebrides, off W coast of Scotland; highest peak 2571 ft.

Papua. See NEW GUINEA.

Pap·ua, Gulf of \-ˈpap-yə-wə\. Large gulf on SE coast of New Guinea I., Papua New Guinea, an inlet of the Coral Sea; Port Moresby lies at the E entrance; Kikori river enters at the N and Fly river at SW.

Papua, Territory of *or formerly* **British New Guin·ea** \-ˈgin-ē\. The southeastern section of New Guinea I., forming part of Papua New Guinea; 90,540 sq. m. (mainland 87,786 sq. m.); pop. (1968e) 598,825; ❋ Port Moresby. Includes also the D'Entrecasteaux, Trobriand, and Woodlark Is. and the Louisiade Archipelago off E coast. Has high mountain ranges in NW part and the high Owen Stanley Range in SE; highest point Mt. Victoria, 13,363 ft., NE of Port Moresby. Coastline indented at S by large Gulf of Papua, with shores low and swampy at deltas of many rivers, esp. the Fly, Kikori, and Purari; on E are several bays: Holnicote, Dyke Acland, Collingwood, Goodenough, and Milne. East Cape marks most easterly point of New Guinea at 151°E. Rich in resources but largely undeveloped; chief exports coconuts, coffee, rubber, and gold. Chief communities: Port Moresby, Daru, Samarai.

History: South coasts of New Guinea (Papua) visited in 16th and 17th cents. by Portuguese and Spanish navigators and later by French and English. Fly river discovered 1842. Region proclaimed British 1883 and 1884 but not annexed until 1888 (British New Guinea). Australian territory proclaimed Sept. 1906. Invaded July 1942 by Japanese but enemy forces confined to Milne Bay and Buna-Gona regions; all driven out by Jan. 20, 1943; administratively united with Trust Terr. of New Guinea 1949; first elections for House of Assembly 1964.

Papua New Guinea *or formerly* **Territory of Papua and New Guinea.** Australian administered territory, consisting of the Terr. of Papua and the Trust Terr. of New Guinea (*qq.v.*); 182,700 sq. m.; pop. (1968e) 2,276,632; ❋ Port Moresby.

Pa·que·tá \ˌpak-ə-ˈtä\. Island in Guanabara Bay NE of the city of Rio de Janeiro, Brazil.

Pa·rá \pə-ˈrä\. 1 Name given to the navigable E mouth of the Amazon river in Brazil; ab. 200 m. long; 40 m. wide at its mouth; flows S and E of Marajó I.; receives Tocantins river from the S.

2 State, N Brazil; 481,869 sq. m.; pop. (1970p) 1,984,785; ❋ Belém; cotton, sugarcane, rice, nuts.

3 Seaport city, Brazil. See BELÉM.

Pa·ra·bia·go \ˌpär-ə-bē-ˈäg-(ˌ)ō\. Commune, Milano prov., Lombardy, N Italy, 14 m. NW of Milan; pop. (1968e) 19,525.

Pa·ra·ca·le \ˌpär-ə-ˈkä-lə\. Municipality on an inlet of the N coast of Camarines Norte, Luzon, Phil., ab. 16 m. NW of Daet; pop. (1969e) 22,000; has gold and coal mines that were worked by the Spaniards for two centuries.

Pa·ra·cas Peninsula \pə-ˌräk-əs-\. Peninsula extending from W cen. coast of Peru, S of Lima.

Pa·ra·cel Islands \ˌpar-ə-ˈsel-\ *or Jap.* **Hi·ra·ta Gun·to** \hē-ˌrät-ə-ˈgu̇n-(ˌ)tō\. Group of small islands and reefs in the South China Sea at 16°30′N, 112°15′E. Occupied by Japan 1939; returned to China after World War II.

Pa·ra·ćin \ˈpär-ə-ˌchēn\. Commune, Serbia, E Yugoslavia, ab. 75 m. SE of Belgrade; pop. (1965e) 18,000.

Par·a·clete \ˌpar-ə-ˈklet\. See NOGENT-SUR-SEINE.

Par·a·dise \ˈpar-ə-ˌdīs, -ˌdīz\. Urban community, Butte co., N California, N of Sacramento; pop. (1970c) 14,539.

Paradise Valley. Town, Maricopa co., SW cen. Arizona; pop. (1970c) 7155.

Paraetonium. See MATRŪH 2.

Par·a·gould \ˈpar-ə-ˌgüld\. City, ⊗ of Greene co., NE Arkansas, 20 m. NE of Jonesboro; pop. (1970c) 10,639; lumber, clothing; livestock farms; Crowley's Ridge Coll. (1964).

Pa·ra·gua \pə-ˈräg-wə\. 1 *or* **Pi·ra·gua** \pə-\. River, E Bolivia; ab. 230 m. long; flows NW into Guaporé river.

2 Island, Philippines. See PALAWAN.

3 River, E Venezuela; ab. 300 m. long; a tributary of the Caroní.

Pa·ra·gua·çu *or* **Pa·ra·guas·sú** \ˌpar-ə-gwə-ˈsü\. River, Bahia state, E Brazil; ab. 300 m. long; flows E to All Saints Bay.

Pa·ra·gua·ná Peninsula \ˌpär-ə-gwə-ˈnä-\. Peninsula extending from NW coast of Venezuela, enclosing Gulf of Venezuela from the E.

Pa·ra·gua·rí \ˌpär-ə-gwä-ˈrē\. 1 Department of S cen. Paraguay. See table at PARAGUAY.

2 Town, its ❋, 35 m. SE of Asunción; pop. (1970e) 15,513; trade center in agricultural region; founded 1775; in wars of independence scene of victory over Argentine army 1811.

Paraguassú. See PARAGUAÇU.

Par·a·guay \ˈpar-ə-ˌgwī, -ˌgwā\. 1 Republic, cen. South America, bounded on N and NW by Bolivia, on NE and E by Brazil, and on SE, S, and W by Argentina; 157,043 sq. m.; pop. (1970e) 2,395,614; ❋ Asunción.

Physical features: Landlocked republic, divided by the Paraguay river into an E (Oriental) section, 61,693 sq. m., and a W (Occidental) section, 95,350 sq. m., the W section including that part of the Chaco (*q.v.*) which was added to Paraguay 1938; country is mostly low wooded plains, with much swampland; in E are densely forested low ridges;

highest point not much over 2200 ft. *Chief rivers:* Paraguay (see 2 below), the Alto Paraná on E border, and the Pilcomayo which is W tributary of the Paraguay and which forms a section of the boundary with Argentina. *Lakes:* Only large one Lake Ypoá, ab. 100 sq. m., in S near Paraguay river. *Chief exports:* Meat products, wool and hides, cotton, quebracho extract, timber; other products: corn, sugarcane, tobacco; manufacturing: textiles, footwear, cigarettes, soap. *Chief cities:* Asunción, Encarnación, Villarrica, Concepción, Pedro Juan Caballero. Divided into the federal district and 16 departments (for pronunciation of their names, see their individual entries):

NAME	AREA (sq. m.)	POP. (1970e)	CAPITAL
Federal District	77	437,136	Asunción
Alto Paraná	7,817	63,497	Hernandarias
Amambay	4,993	67,917	Pedro Juan Caballero
Boquerón	64,876	47,033	Mariscal Estigarribia
Caaguazú	8,345	226,675	Coronel Oviedo
Caazapá	3,666	105,578	Caazapá
Central	1,024	256,458	Asunción
Concepción	6,969	110,555	Concepción
Cordillera	1,910	199,621	Caacupé
Guairá	1,236	132,772	Villarrica
Itapúa	6,380	201,670	Encarnación
Misiones	3,025	74,023	San Juan Bautista
Ñeembucú	5,354	69,639	Pilar
Olimpo	7,882	4,940	Fuerte Olimpo
Paraguarí	3,187	228,192	Paraguarí
Presidente Hayes	22,579	42,141	Villa Hayes
San Pedro	7,723	127,767	San Pedro

History: Asunción, founded 1538, capital of La Plata region; field of Jesuit work among Guarani Indians 1605–1767; a part of viceroyalty of Buenos Aires (*q.v.*), it revolted from Spain 1811; governed by Francia as dictator 1814–40, by his nephew Carlos A. López as president with dictatorial powers 1844–62, and by the latter's son Francisco Solano López 1862–70, who provoked a disastrous war with Brazil, Argentina, and Uruguay 1865–70 by which Paraguay lost 55,000 sq. m. of territory and more than 1,000,000 of its people; after long dispute with Bolivia over the Chaco region, fought Chaco war 1932–35; peace treaty signed July 21, 1938; adopted new constitution 1940 which, however, was set aside on establishment of absolute rule under Higinio Morínigo Nov. 30, 1940; severed diplomatic relations with the Axis powers Jan. 1942; scene of unsuccessful rebellion against the government 1947; ousted Morínigo June 1948; scene of six revolts 1948–49; assumption of power (1954) by General Alfredo Stroessner; promulgated new constitution 1967.

2 River, S cen. South America; 1584 m. long; navigable for larger vessels to Concepción, for small craft for almost its entire length; rises in Mato Grosso state, SW Brazil, where its upper tributaries form small sections of boundary with Bolivia; flows S to form boundary bet. Brazil and NE Paraguay and, after crossing cen. Paraguay, a section of boundary bet. SW Paraguay and Argentina; empties into the Paraná at SW corner of Paraguay.

Parahiba *or* **Parahyba.** See PARAÍBA.

Pa·ra·í·ba \ˌpar-ə-ˈē-bə\; *formerly* **Pa·ra·hi·ba** *or* **Pa·ra·hy·ba** \ˌpar-ə-ˈē-bə\. **1** Either of two rivers of Brazil: (a) **Paraíba** *or* **Paraíba do Nor·te** \-də-ˈnȯrt-ē\, in Paraíba state; ab. 180 m. long; flows NE and E into Atlantic Ocean. (b) **Paraíba** *or* **Paraíba do Sul** \-ˈsül\, in E São Paulo and Rio de Janeiro states; ab. 600 m. long; flows SW, then turns NE to traverse half the length of Rio de Janeiro state and empty into Atlantic Ocean near Campos; called **Pa·ra·hi·tin·ga** \ˌpar-ə-(h)i-ˈtiŋ-gə\ in its upper course.

2 State, NE Brazil; 21,765 sq. m.; pop. (1970p) 2,383,518; ✱ João Pessoa; cotton, sisal, oiticica oil.

3 City, Brazil. See JOÃO PESSOA.

Pa·raí·so \ˌpär-ə-ˈē-sō\. Municipality, Tabasco state, Mexico, 35 m. NW of Villahermosa; pop. (1970p) 30,439; diversified agriculture.

Paraíso, El. See EL PARAÍSO.

Par·a·kou \ˌpar-ə-ˈkü\. Town, E cen. Dahomey, W Africa, ab. 200 m. N of Porto Novo; pop. (1968e) 18,000.

Par·a·mar·i·bo \ˌpar-ə-ˈmar-ə-ˌbō\. Seaport city, ✱ of Surinam, on the Suriname river ab. 13 m. from its mouth; pop. (1964c) 11,000; port limited to vessels drawing less than 20 feet of water; only large town of Surinam. Founded as French settlement 1640 on site of Indian village; made capital of English settlement, organized by Lord Willoughby of Parham; partly destroyed by fire 1821 and 1832.

Pa·ra·mé \ˌpär-ə-ˈmā\. Commune, Ille-et-Vilaine dept., NW France, E of St-Malo; pop. (1962c) 9037.

Paramithiá. See PARAMYTHIA.

Par·a·mount \ˈpar-ə-ˌmau̇nt\. City, Los Angeles co., SW California, SE of Los Angeles; pop. (1970c) 34,734; residential; plastics, resins, aluminum products; settled 1866.

Par·a·mus \pə-ˈram-əs\. Borough, Bergen co., NE corner of New Jersey, 6 m. NE of Paterson; pop. (1970c) 28,381; truck farms; Bergen Community Coll. (1965).

Pa·ra·mu·shir \ˌpär-ə-mu̇-ˈshi(ə)r\. Large island at N end of Kuril Is., Russian S.F.S.R., U.S.S.R., separated by narrow channel from Shumshu, the northernmost island of the chain; highest point 5958 ft.; chief town Severo-Kurilsk at N end. Under Japanese a strongly fortified naval base, frequently bombed by U.S. planes 1943–44; became part of U.S.S.R. 1945 (see KURIL ISLANDS).

Par·a·myth·ia \ˌpar-ə-ˈmith-ē-ə\ *or Gk.* **Pa·ra·mi·thiá** \ˌpär-ə-ˌmith-ē-ˈä\. Town, NW Epirus, Greece, ab. 20 m. SW of Ioannina.

Pa·ran, Wilderness of \-ˈpar-ən, -ˈper-\. Desert region of indefinite location; probably in NE part of Sinai Penin., Egypt, extending into S Israel; here according to the Biblical account the Israelites sojourned 38 years before entering the Promised Land (*Num.* x. 12).

Pa·ra·ná \ˌpar-ə-ˈnä\. **1** River, SE cen. South America; 1827 m. long; formed by confluence of Rio Grande and Paranaíba river in S cen. Brazil; flows S (sometimes known as **Al·to Paraná** \ˌal-(ˌ)tō-\) and forms SE and S boundary of Paraguay (Sete Quedas, *q.v.*, cataract located here); continues S through NE Argentina (as **Paraná**) and empties into Río de la Plata; its chief tributaries are: in Brazil (on left bank) Tietê, Paranapanema, Ivaí, Piquiri, Iguaçu, (on right bank) Verde, Pardo, Ivinheima; in Argentina, Salado and Gualeguay.

2 City, ✱ of Entre Ríos prov., E Argentina, on left bank of Paraná river 80 m. N of Rosario; pop. (1960c) 107,551; river port for small ocean-going vessels; in livestock and grain farming region; founded as Bajada by settlers from Santa Fé in late 16th cent.; capital of Argentina 1852–62.

3 River, E Goiás state, cen. Brazil; ab. 250 m. long; a headstream of the Tocantins.

4 State, S Brazil; 77,048 sq. m.; pop. (1970p) 6,741,520; ✱ Curitiba; coffee.

Pa·ra·na·guá \ˌpar-ə-nə-ˈgwä\. Town, chief port of Paraná state, S Brazil; munic. pop. (1968e) 65,178; chief export Paraguay tea; founded 1560.

Pa·ra·na·í·ba \ˌpär-ə-nə-ˈē-bə\ *or formerly* **Pa·ra·na·hi·ba** \ˌpär-ə-nə-ˈē-bə\. One of the headstreams of Paraná river, Brazil; 500 m. long; rises in W cen. Minas Gerais state; flows W and SW to unite with Rio Grande and form Paraná river.

Pa·ra·na·pa·ne·ma \ˌpar-ə-ˌnap-ə-ˈnā-mə\. River, SE Brazil; ab. 500 m. long; rises in SE São Paulo state, flows W, forming part of boundary bet. São Paulo and Paraná states, and empties into Paraná river.

Pa·ra·ña·que \ˌpär-ə-ˈnyä-kā\. Municipality, SW Rizal prov., Luzon, Phil., on SE shore of Manila Bay ab. 4 m. S of Manila; pop. (1969e) 85,200; residential.

Pa·ra·na·vaí \ˌpär-ə-nə-ˈvī\. Municipality, Paraná state, S Brazil, 260 m. NW of Curitiba; pop. (1968e) 67,847.

Pa·rang \ˈpär-äŋ\. **1** Municipality, SW coast of Jolo I., Sulu prov., Phil.; pop. (1969e) 33,900.

2 Municipality, Cotabato prov., SW Mindanao, Phil., on Illana Bay NNE of Cotabato; pop. (1961e) 51,500; U.S. troops landed here Apr. 19, 1945.

Parapanisus. See PAROPAMISUS 2.

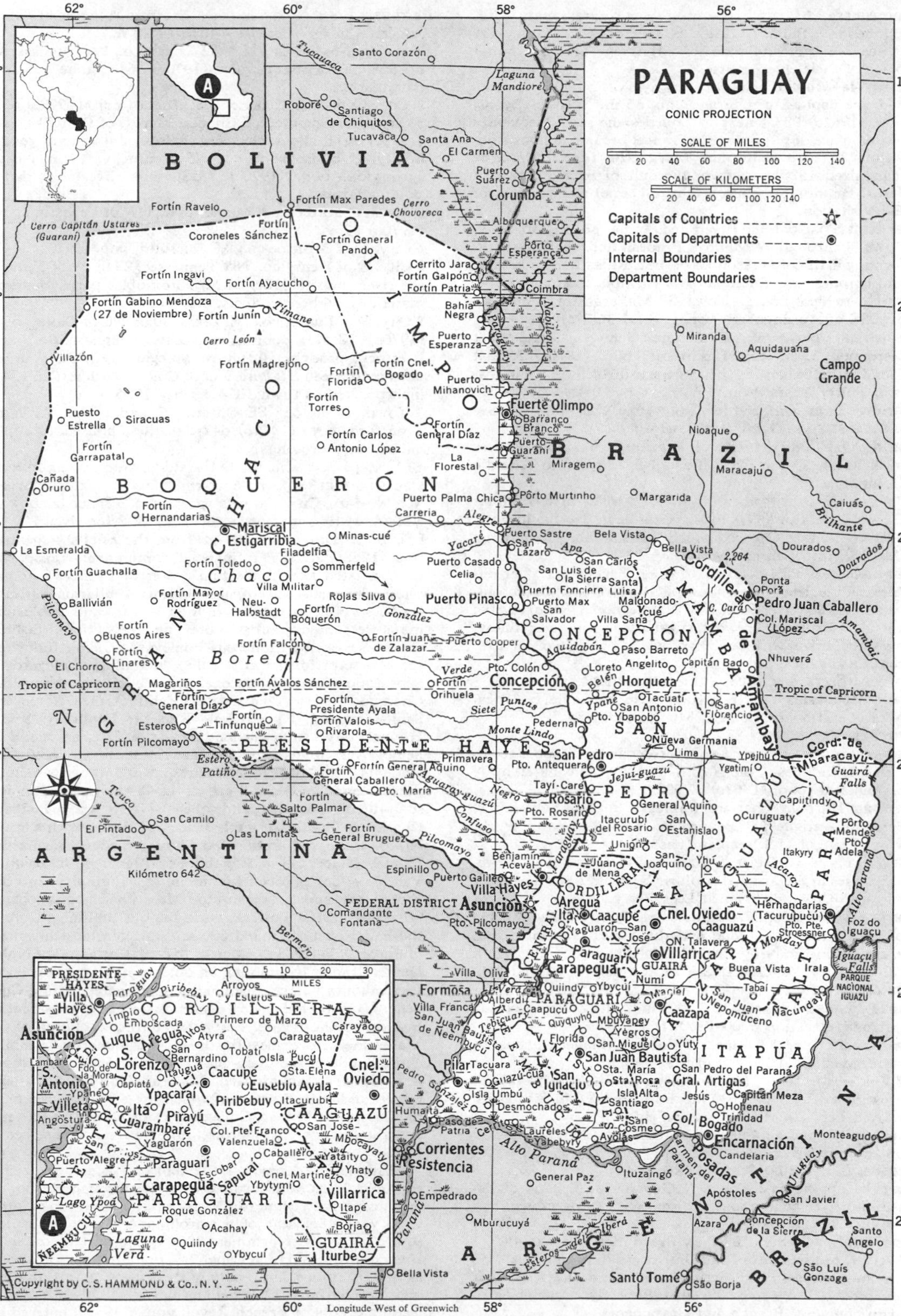

Longitude West of Greenwich

Pa·ras·nath, Mount \-pə-ˈrəs-nät\ *also* **Parasnath Hill.** Eminence, E Bihar, NE India, 50 m. E of Hazaribagh; 4481 ft.; sacred spot and place of pilgrimage of Jains; burial place of their chief saint.

Pa·ray–le–Mo·nial \pa-ˌrā-lə-mȯ-ˈnyal\. Commune, Saône-et-Loire dept., E cen. France, ab. 55 m. NNW of Lyons; pop. (1962c) 9835; next to Lourdes the most frequently visited place of pilgrimage in France; became famous from visions of 17th cent. nun, Marguerite Marie Alacoque (canonized 1920), origin of the cult of Sacred Heart of Jesus; has notable church (Notre-Dame) and convent of the Visitation.

Par·ba·ti \ˈpär-bət-ē\. River, cen. India; ab. 270 m. long; flows N through W Madhya Pradesh and SE Rajasthan, forming in its course sections of the E Rajasthan boundary, and empties into Chambal river on that boundary.

Par·bha·ni \ˈpər-bə-nē\. Town, SE Maharashtra, India, 100 m. ESE of Aurangabad; pop. (1961c) 36,795.

Par·chim \ˈpär-ˌkim\. Commune, Schwerin dist., East Germany, 23 m. SE of Schwerin; pop. (1970e) 20,534; founded 1210; had prosperous trade in 14th cent. but lost it in Thirty Years' War.

Par·dee Dam *and* **Pardee Reservoir** \ˈpär-(ˌ)dē-\. See UNITED STATES, *Dams and Reservoirs.*

Par·do \ˈpär-(ˌ)dü\. 1 River, E Brazil; ab. 400 m. long; rises in N Minas Gerais state, flows NE and E into Atlantic Ocean.

2 River, S Brazil; ab. 300 m. long; rises in SW Minas Gerais state, flows NW to Rio Grande in São Paulo state.

3 River, S Mato Grosso state, SW Brazil; ab. 230 m. long; flows SE into Paraná river.

Par·du·bi·ce \ˈpärd-ə-ˌbit-sə\ *or Ger.* **Par·du·bitz** \ˈpär-dü-ˌbits\. Industrial town, Czech S.R., NW cen. Czechoslovakia, on Elbe river 60 m. E of Prague; pop. (1968e) 69,508; chemicals, rubber; brewing, sugar processing, oil refining; historical town, with remains of walls, a church of the 13th cent., a royal castle.

Parecis, Serra dos. See SERRA DOS PARECIS.

Pa·re Mountains \ˌpär-ā-\. Range, NE Tanzania, E Africa; N of N end of the range is Mt. Kilimanjaro.

Parenzo. See POREČ.

Pa·re·pa·re *also* **Pa·re Pa·re** \ˌpär-ē-ˈpär-ē\. Seaport town, Celebes, Indonesia, on W coast of SW peninsula 80 m. N of Makasar; pop. (1961c) 67,992.

Par·ham Harbour \ˌpar-əm-\. Inlet of **Parham Sound** on N coast of Antigua I., Leeward Is., West Indies; in World War II site of U.S. seaplane base. See ANTIGUA.

Pa·ria \pə-ˈrē-ə\. River, S Utah and N Arizona; ab. 65 m. long; rises in S Garfield co., flows S across Arizona border and into Colorado river at Lees Ferry.

Paria, Gulf of. Inlet of Atlantic Ocean lying bet. the W coast of the island of Trinidad and the Venezuelan mainland; enclosed on the N by **Paria Peninsula,** extending E from NE coast of Venezuela. See DRAGON'S MOUTH and SERPENT'S MOUTH.

Paria Plateau \pə-ˌrē-ə-\. Tableland, N Coconino co., N Arizona; elevation 6000–7300 ft.

Pa·rí·cu·tin \pə-ˈrē-kə-ˌtēn\. 1 Former village, Michoacán state, Mexico, 200 m. W of Mexico City.

2 Volcano on site of former village (see 1 above); 7451 ft.; grew to a height of 1500 ft. above its base in 8 months; started Feb. 20, 1943 in a cornfield.

Pa·ri·da \pə-ˈrēd-ə\. Island at entrance to Charco Azul Bay on extreme SW Panama.

Parida, La. See BOLÍVAR, CERRO.

Pa·ri·ka \pə-ˈrē-kə\. Town, N Guyana, on E bank of Essequibo river at its mouth, 20 m. W of Georgetown.

Parikía. See PAROS 2.

Pa·ri·ma \pə-ˈrē-mə\. 1 River, Brazil. See BRANCO, RIO.

2 River, headstream of the Uraricoera, NW Brazil; ab. 50 m. long; rises in the Serra Parima and flows N; first explored 1924 by seaplane; also, formerly, name given to main course of Branco and Uraricoera.

Parima, Serra. See SERRA PARIMA.

Pa·ri·ñas, Point \-pə-ˈrēn-yəs\. Extreme W point of South America, in NW Peru at 4°40'S, 81°20'W.

Par·is \ˈpar-əs\. 1 City, a ⊗ of Logan co., W Arkansas, 42 m. SSE of Fort Smith; pop. (1970c) 3646; stone quarries; dairy farms.

2 City, ⊗ of Bear Lake co., SE Idaho; pop. (1970c) 615.

3 City, ⊗ of Edgar co., E Illinois, 38 m. S of Danville; pop. (1970c) 9971; shoes, electronic components, metal goods.

4 City, ⊗ of Bourbon co., NE Kentucky, 19 m. NE of Lexington; pop. (1970c) 7823; ships livestock; dairy, poultry farms.

5 Town, Oxford co., W Maine, 18 m. NW of Lewiston; pop. (1970c) 3739.

6 City, ⊗ of Monroe co., NE Missouri; pop. (1970c) 1442.

7 City, ⊗ of Henry co., NW Tennessee, 23 m. W of Tennessee river; pop. (1970c) 9892; automobile parts, building materials, rubber products; clay pits.

8 City, ⊗ of Lamar co., NE Texas, 90 m. NE of Dallas; pop. (1970c) 23,441; commercial center; ships cotton and livestock; produces furniture, vinegar, feed, dairy products, cottonseed oil; Paris Junior Coll. (1924); settled 1841; incorporated as town 1874, as city 1905.

9 Town, Brant co., SE Ontario, Canada, 7 m. WNW of Brantford; pop. (1971p) 6474; textiles, household appliances, dairy products.

10 *Fr.* pȧ-rē\; *anc.* **Lu·te·tia** \lü-ˈtē-sh(ē-)ə\ *or* **Lutetia Pa·ris·i·o·rum** \-pə-ˌriz-ē-ˈōr-əm, -ˈȯr-\ *or later* **Pa·ris·ii** \pə-ˈriz-ē-ˌī\. City and river port, ✱ of France, also ✱ of Ville-de-Paris dept., on both banks of Seine river 110 m. ESE of Le Havre and 107 m. from the English Channel; pop. (1968c) 2,590,771; financial, commercial, transportation, artistic, and intellectual center of France; automobiles, chemicals, electrical equipment, pharmaceuticals, leather products, jewelry; motion picture and publishing industries; major tourist center; an international fashion center; served by numerous boulevards (many following the course of former city walls), including Boulevard de Sébastopol, Rue Saint-Michel, Rue de Rivoli, Avenue des Champs-Élysées, Avenue de la Grande Armée, Boulevard Saint-Germain, Rue Royal, Rue du Faubourg Saint-Honoré; city centers around Île de la Cité, an island in Seine river; famed Latin quarter, inhabited chiefly by students, lies S of Seine; public squares and parks include the Tuileries gardens, Place de la Concorde (containing sculptured fountains and obelisk from Luxor), Place Charles de Gaulle (formerly Place de l'Étoile, with world's largest triumphal arch), Luxembourg gardens, Jardin des Plantes, Places de la République, d'Iéna, de la Bastille, Vendôme, des Innocents (containing a fountain), and des États-Unis, and the Champ de Mars (in which is located the 984 ft. Eiffel Tower); world-famous buildings include the Hôtel-Dieu (founded 600 A.D., one of oldest hospitals in Europe), Palais de Justice, 12th cent. Cathedral of Notre Dame, Louvre (containing an outstanding art collection), Luxembourg palace, Tribunal de Commerce, Sainte-Chapelle, L'Opéra, Palais de l'Élysée (residence of president of France), Bibliothèque Nationale, Panthéon, church of the Madeleine, Hôtel des Invalides, the Tuileries, Bastille, church of Saint-Germain-des-Prés, and Bourse; educational institutions include the 12th cent. University of Paris (one of oldest in Europe) of which the Sorbonne is a part, the Institut de France, Collège de France, Institut Pasteur, and the famous Observatoire; noted Père-Lachaise cemetery.

History: Pre-Roman settlement on island in Seine; captured 52 B.C. and fortified by Romans; made bishopric in 3d cent. A.D.; came to Clovis, king of the Franks, after victory of 486; seat of a Carolingian count; withstood severe siege by Northmen 885–887; after accession to French throne of Hugh Capet 987, definitely established as capital of France; University of Paris grew up in 12th cent. and was chartered 1200; held by English 1420–36; scene of leading events of French Revolution 1789–92; entered by Allies after Napoleon's defeat 1814; besieged and taken by

Germans 1870–71; the following important treaties were signed here: 1763 (concluding Seven Years' War), 1783 (War of American Independence), 1814 and 1815 (Napoleonic Wars), 1856 (Crimean War), 1898 (Spanish-American War); Declaration of Paris signed here 1856; scene of peace conference at end of World War I 1919; site of Olympic Games 1900 and 1924; occupied by Germans June 14, 1940; liberated by Allies Aug. 19–24, 1944. In 1968 scene of widespread leftist student and worker strikes and demonstrations; chosen (1969) as site of U.S.-North Vietnam peace talks on Vietnam War. See FRANCE.

Pa·ri·ta, Gulf of \-pə-ˈrēt-ə\. Inlet of the Gulf of Panama on the W, extending into W cen. Panama at the base of Azuero Penin.

Pa·rit Bun·tar \ˌpär-ət-ˈbu̇n-ˌtär\. Town, NW Perak, Malaysia, ab. 50 m. NW of Ipoh.

Par·i·um \ˈpar-ē-əm, ˈper-\ *or* **Par·i·on** \-ē-ən\. Town in ancient Mysia, Asia Minor, on the SW shore of the Propontis (Sea of Marmara).

Park. Name of counties in three states of the U.S. See tables at COLORADO, MONTANA, WYOMING.

Park City. 1 City, Lake co., NE Illinois, 5 m. W of Waukegan; pop. (1970c) 2855.

2 City, Summit co., NE Utah, 22 m. ESE of Salt Lake City; pop. (1970c) 1193; resort; lead, zinc mines.

Parke \ˈpärk\. County in Indiana. See table at INDIANA.

Parke Peak. Mountain, Glacier National Park, NW Montana; 9100 ft.

Par·ker \ˈpär-kər\. 1 County in Texas. See table at TEXAS.

2 City, Bay co., NW Florida; pop. (1970c) 4212.

3 City, ⊗ of Turner co., SE South Dakota; pop. (1970c) 1005; stock, dairy, poultry farms.

Parker Peak. 1 Mountain, Fall River co., SW corner of South Dakota; 4849 ft.

2 Mountain, Yellowstone National Park, NW Wyoming; 10,203 ft.

Par·kers·burg \ˈpär-kərz-ˌbərg\. City, ⊗ of Wood co., W West Virginia, at confluence of Ohio and Little Kanawha rivers; pop. (1970c) 44,208; river port; aluminum products, paint, synthetic textiles, insulation, plastic products; railroad shops; Ohio Valley Coll. (1960).

Parkes \ˈpärks\. Town, E cen. New South Wales, SE Australia, 180 m. WNW of Sydney; pop. (1966c) 8438; site of large radio telescope.

Parkes·burg \ˈpärks-ˌbərg\. Borough, Chester co., SE Pennsylvania, 22 m. E of Lancaster; pop. (1970c) 2701.

Park Falls. City, Price co., N Wisconsin, 50 m. SSE of Ashland; pop. (1970c) 2953; resort; lumber, paper.

Park Forest. Village, Cook and Wills cos., NE Illinois, S of Chicago; pop. (1970c) 30,638; residential.

Park Hills. City, Kenton co., N Kentucky, 3 m. SW of Covington; pop. (1970c) 3999.

Park·land \ˈpär-klənd\. Town, Pierce co., W cen. Washington, ab. 6 m. S of Tacoma; pop. (1970c) 21,012; residential; Pacific Lutheran Univ. (1890).

Park Range. A range of the Rocky Mts. in N Colorado; highest peak Mount Lincoln 14,286 ft.

Park Rapids. Village, ⊗ of Hubbard co., N cen. Minnesota, 40 m. S of Bemidji; pop. (1970c) 2722; dairy farms.

Park Ridge. 1 City, Cook co., NE Illinois, N suburb of Chicago; pop. (1970c) 42,614; residential.

2 Borough, Bergen co., NE corner of New Jersey, on New York border 12 m. NE of Paterson; pop. (1970c) 8709.

Park River. City, Walsh co., NE North Dakota, on Park river 46 m. NW of Grand Forks; pop. (1970c) 1680.

Park·side \ˈpärk-ˌsīd\. Borough, Delaware co., SE Pennsylvania, SW of Philadelphia; pop. (1970c) 2343.

Parks·ton \ˈpärk-stən\. City, Hutchinson co., SE South Dakota, 23 m. S of Mitchell; pop. (1970c) 1611.

Park·ville \ˈpärk-ˌvil\. 1 Urban community (unincorporated), Baltimore co., cen. Maryland, NE of Baltimore; pop. (with Carney; 1970c) 33,897; residential.

2 City, S Platte co., NW Missouri, 9 m. NW of Kansas City; pop. (1970c) 1253; Park Coll. (1875).

Par·la·ki·me·di \pər-ˌläk-i-ˈmād-ē\. Town, Orissa, E India, 160 m. SW of Cuttack; pop. (1961c) 22,708.

Par·ma \ˈpär-mə\. City, Cuyahoga co., N Ohio, 8 m. S of Cleveland; pop. (1970c) 100,216; residential suburb of Cleveland; automobile parts, tools and dies; incorporated as city 1932.

Parma \ˈpär-mə\. 1 Province of Emilia-Romagna, Italy. See table at ITALY.

2 Commune, its ✱, 75 m. SE of Milan; pop. (1968e) 170,267; rail and road junction; in agricultural region; produces perfume, cheese, alcohol, fertilizers, and glass; 12th cent. cathedral, 13th cent. Romanesque baptistry, late 16th cent. Palazzo della Pilotta (restored after war damage 1944), containing art gallery, museum, library; 16th cent. monastery; univ. (1064, reorganized by R. Farnese 1601).

History: Founded by Romans 183 B.C.; important Roman road junction; made bishopric 4th cent. A.D.; under successive local lords before passing as ✱ of duchy of Parma and Piacenza to Farnese, then to Austrians; after 1815 held by Marie Louise, wife of Napoleon I; became part of kingdom of Italy 1861; heavily damaged by Allied bombing 1944.

Parma Heights. City, Cuyahoga co., N Ohio, S suburb of Cleveland; pop. (1970c) 27,192.

Par·mer \ˈpär-mər\. County in Texas. See table at TEXAS.

Par·na·í·ba \ˌpär-nə-ˈē-bə\ *or formerly* **Par·na·hy·ba** \-ˈē-bə\. 1 River, NE Brazil; ab. 600 m. long; flows NE, forming boundary bet. Piauí and Maranhão states, and empties into Atlantic Ocean.

2 Port, N Piauí state, NE Brazil, 11 m. from mouth of the Parnaíba river; munic. pop. (1968e) 69,961; commercial center; exports cotton, sugar, hides; founded 1761.

Par·nas·sus \pär-ˈnas-əs\. 1 Former borough, Westmoreland co., SW Pennsylvania, on Allegheny river ab. 17 m. ENE of Pittsburgh; consolidated with New Kensington (*q.v.*) 1931.

2 *or Gk.* **Par·nas·sós** \ˌpär-nä-ˈsȯs\. Mountain, cen. Greece, N of Gulf of Corinth; 8061 ft.; in ancient times sacred to Apollo and the Muses, esp. the **Cas·ta·lian Spring** \ka-ˌstāl-yən-\, just above Delphi which lay at its foot to the S. **Co·ry·cian Cave** \kə-ˌrish-(ē-)ən-\, a stalactite grotto 350 ft. long and ab. 200 ft. wide, is bet. Delphi and the summit on a plateau.

Par·nes \ˈpär-ˌnēz\ *or Gk.* **Pár·nis** \ˈpär-nēs\. Mountain, E cen. Greece, 16 m. N of Athens; 4636 ft.; an E extension of Mt. Cithaeron.

Par·non \ˈpär-ˌnän\ *or Gk.* **Pár·non Óros** \ˌpär-nȯn-ˈȯr-əs\. Mountain range, E Laconia, SE Peloponnesus, S Greece; highest peak 6348 ft.; shuts in the valley of the Eurotas on the E.

Pär·nu *or* **Par·nu** \ˈpär-(ˌ)nü\ *or* **Pyar·nu** \ˈpyär-\ *also* **Per·nov** \ˈp(y)er-nəf\ *or Ger.* **Per·nau** \ˈpe(ə)r-ˌnau̇\. 1 Bay on SW coast of Estonian S.S.R., U.S.S.R., an inlet of the N part of the Gulf of Riga.

2 River, cen. Estonian S.S.R., U.S.S.R.; ab. 80 m. long; flows SW into Pärnu Bay.

3 Seaport, Estonian S.S.R., U.S.S.R., near mouth of Pärnu river on Pärnu Bay; pop. (1967e) 42,000; lumber, textiles, motor vehicles; fishing; seaside resort. Founded 1251; held by Sweden and Poland in 16th cent.; under Swedes again 1617–1710 and Russians 1710–1918.

Par·o·pa·mi·sus \ˌpar-ə-pə-ˈmī-səs\. 1 Mountain range, NW Afghanistan, at W end of the Hindu Kush, N of Herāt and the Hari Rud; highest point 11,772 ft.

2 *or* **Pa·ra·pa·ni·sus** \ˌpar-ə-pə-ˈnī-səs\. Ancient name of Hindu Kush (*q.v.*) range.

Par·os \'par-ˌäs, 'per-\ *or Gk.* **Pá·ros** \'pär-ˌȯs\. 1 Island, cen. Cyclades, Greece, in the Aegean Sea 6 m. W of Naxos; 75 sq. m.; pop. (1961c) 7830; ✱ Paros; formed by a mountain 2451 ft. high, from which has been obtained a fine white marble, widely used in ancient times by sculptors. Colonized by Ionians from Athens and itself founder of colonies in Thasos, Illyria, etc.; sided with Persians in Greco-Persian Wars; not historically important after 4th cent. B.C.; site of discovery 1627 of a marble tablet, known as the *Parian Chronicle,* giving an outline of Greek history from before 1000 B.C. to ab. 354 B.C., one of the Arundel marbles now at Oxford University.

2 *or* **Pa·ri·kía** \ˌpär-ə-kē-'ä\. Town, its ✱, on W coast.

Par·ot·tee Point \ˌpar-ət-ē-\. Cape on SW coast of the island of Jamaica, West Indies.

Par·o·wan \ˌpar-ə-'wan, 'par-ə-ˌwan\. City, ⊗ of Iron co., SW Utah, 17 m. NE of Cedar City; pop. (1970c) 1423; livestock farms.

Pa·rral \pə-'räl\. 1 City, Linares prov., S cen. Chile, 197 m. SSW of Santiago; pop. (1960c) 14,160.

2 *or* **Hi·dal·go del Parral** \e-'däl-(ˌ)gō-del-, -'thäl-\. City, Chihuahua state, N Mexico, 115 m. S of Chihuahua; munic. pop. (1970p) 161,729; alt. 6200 ft.; large gold, silver, lead, and zinc mines nearby.

Par·ra·mat·ta \ˌpar-ə-'mat-ə\. 1 River, E New South Wales, SE Australia; 18 m. long; actually the tidal estuary of a small creek forming W arm of Port Jackson.

2 Municipality on it, W suburb of Sydney; pop. (1966c) 106,996; textiles, machinery, automobiles, flour; founded 1790; incorporated 1861.

Par·ra·more Island \ˌpar-ə-ˌmō(ə)r-, -ˌmȯ(ə)r-\. Island in Atlantic Ocean off SE coast of Accomac co., Virginia.

Pa·rras \'pär-əs\ *or in full* **Parras de la Fuen·te** \-ˌdel-ə-fü-'en-(ˌ)tā\. Town, S Coahuila state, NE Mexico, ab. 120 m. WSW of Monterrey; munic. pop. (1970p) 32,664; in a wine-producing region.

Par·ret \'par-ət\. River, Dorsetshire and Somersetshire, SW England; 35 m. long; flows NW into Bristol Channel.

Par·ris Island \'par-əs-\. Island of the Sea Is. chain in Beaufort co., S South Carolina, S of Port Royal I.; since 1915 a U.S. Marine Corps training station.

Parrs·boro \'pärz-ˌbər-ə, -ˌbə-rə\. Town, Cumberland co., N Nova Scotia, Canada, on N shore of Minas Basin 31 m. S of Amherst; pop. (1971p) 1751; summer resort; ships coal. In a region rich for geological studies; has footprints of prehistoric animals, plant fossils, etc. (see JOGGINS).

Par·ry, Cape \-'par-ē\. Point extending from N coast of Northwest Territories, Canada, into Amundsen Gulf on E side of Franklin Bay, 70°08′N, 124°24′W.

Parry Island. See MAUKE.

Parry Islands. Group of islands in NW Franklin dist., Northwest Territories, Canada, N of Viscount Melville Sound; includes Prince Patrick I., Melville I., Bathurst I., Borden I., and Cornwallis I.

Parry Sound. 1 District, SE Ontario, Canada. See table at ONTARIO.

2 Town, its ⊗; port at center of E shore of Georgian Bay; pop. (1971p) 5840; summer resort; boatbuilding; agriculture.

Par·sip·pa·ny–Troy Hills \pär-'sip-ə-nē-'trȯi-\. Urban township, Morris co., N New Jersey, 6 m. NE of Morristown; pop. (1970c) 55,112.

Pars·nip \'pär-snəp\. River, E cen. British Columbia, Canada; 145 m. long; rises near the bend of the Fraser and flows N to unite with Finlay river and form Peace river.

Par·son Bald \ˌpärs-ᵊn-\. Peak, Blount co., E Tennessee; 4760 ft.

Par·sons \'pärs-ᵊnz\. 1 City, Labette co., SE Kansas, 33 m. W of Pittsburg; pop. (1970c) 13,105; furniture, wool and dairy products; ships poultry; Labette Community Coll. (1923).

2 City, ⊗ of Tucker co., NE West Virginia, 16 m. NNE of Elkins; pop. (1970c) 1784; coal mines.

Parsons Peak. Mountain in Sierra Nevada, near E end of boundary bet. Mariposa and Tuolumne cos., cen. California; 12,120 ft.

Parsonstown. See BIRR.

Par·tab·garh \pər-'täb-ˌgär\ *or* **Pra·tap·garh** \prə-'täp-\. 1 Former Indian state, now part of Rajasthan state, NW India; 873 sq. m.

2 Town, its ✱, ab. 78 m. SE of Udaipur; pop. (1961c) 14,600.

Par·tan·na \pär-'tän-ə\. Commune, Trapani prov., NW Sicily, Italy, 29 m. SE of Trapani; pop. (1968e) 12,851.

Partenkirchen. See GARMISCH-PARTENKIRCHEN.

Par·the·nay \ˌpär-tə-'nā\. Town, cen. Deux-Sèvres dept., W France, 27 m. NNE of Niort; pop. (1968c) 11,334; parts of 13th cent. walls, several churches (11th and 12th cents.).

Par·then·o·pe \pär-'then-ə-(ˌ)pē\. Ancient town, S Italy, on site of Naples (*q.v.*), the place where, according to legend, the Siren Parthenope was cast ashore. The **Par·then·o·pe·an Republic** \pär-ˌthen-ə-'pē-ən-\ was a short-lived republic Jan. 23–June 20, 1799 erected at Naples by Napoleon.

Par·thia \'pär-thē-ə\. Ancient country in W Asia, nearly coextensive with modern Khorāsān prov., NE Iran; a subdivision of Ariana, SE of Hyrcania; formed a province of the Assyrian and Persian empires and later of the empire of Alexander; on dissolution of Seleucid Empire c. 250 B.C., new Parthian kingdom founded by Arsaces, first of the Arsacidae, a dynasty of ab. 30 kings which ruled until overthrown by Ardashir c. 226 A.D., the first Sassanid ruler of Persia (see IRAN). Kingdom at its height, known as Parthian Empire (*Lat.* **Reg·num Par·tho·rum** \ˌreg-nəm-pär-'thōr-əm\) at beginning of 1st cent. B.C., included all regions bet. Euphrates and Indus and bet. Oxus and Indian Ocean; received its first setbacks when checked by Tigranes of Armenia 88–70 B.C. and esp. by the Romans 39–38 B.C. The Parthians were of Scythian descent and famous as horsemen and archers. Best known cities were Hecatompylos, Seleucia, and Ctesiphon whose ruins are now in Iraq.

Par·ti·ni·co \ˌpär-tə-'nē-(ˌ)kō\. Manufacturing and commercial commune, Palermo prov., Sicily, Italy, 15 m. WSW of Palermo; pop. (1968e) 27,789.

Pa·ru *or* **Pa·rú** \pə-'rü\. River, N Brazil; ab. 370 m. long; rises in the Tumuc-Humac Mts., flows SE into the Amazon.

Paru de Oes·te \-də-'wesh-tə\ *or formerly* **Ere·pe·cu·rú** \ˌer-ə-ˌpek-ə-'rü\. River, N Brazil; ab. 250 m. long; flows S into Trombetas river just before it empties into the Amazon.

Par·wān \par-'wän\. Province of E Afghanistan. See table at AFGHANISTAN.

Pa·rys \pə-'rīs\. Town, N Orange Free State, E cen. Rep. of South Africa, on Vaal river 60 m. SW of Johannesburg; pop. (1967e) 15,400; resort; jam and fruit-preserving factories.

Pas, The \thə-'pä\. Town, W Manitoba, Canada, on Saskatchewan river; pop. (1966c) 5031; lumbering.

Pa·sa·cao \ˌpäs-ə-'kau̇\. Municipality, Camarines Sur prov., Luzon, Phil., 12 m. SW of Naga and its port on Ragay Gulf; pop. (1969e) 19,800.

Pas·a·de·na \ˌpas-ə-'dē-nə\. 1 Suburban residential city, Los Angeles co., SW California, 8 m. NE of Los Angeles; pop. (1970c) 112,981; ceramics, plastics, precision instruments, pharmaceuticals; California Institute of Technology (1891), Pasadena Coll. (1902), Pasadena Playhouse Coll. of Theatre Arts (1920), Pasadena City Coll. (1924), Pacific Oaks Coll. (1945); site of Rose Bowl and of annual New Year's Day Tournament of Roses (flower festival inaugurated 1890). Founded 1874; incorporated as city 1886.

2 City, Harris co., SE Texas, 10 m. S of Houston; pop. (1970c) 89,277; chemicals; oil wells and refineries; residential; San Jacinto Coll. (1961); founded 1895, incorporated 1929; site of Santa Anna's capture after battle of San Jacinto (*q.v.*) NE of city.

Pa·sa·do, Cape \-pə-'säd-(,)ō\. Cape extending into Pacific Ocean on W cen. coast of Ecuador.

Pa·sa·je \pə-'sä-(,)hā\. Town, El Oro prov., SW Ecuador, 80 m. S of Guayaquil; pop. (1962c) 13,215.

Pa·sa·leng Bay \pə-,sä-leŋ-\. Inlet of South China Sea (Babuyan Channel), NE Ilocos Norte prov., Luzon, Phil., E of Mayraira Point; ab. 11 m. wide at mouth.

Pa·sar·ga·dae \pə-'sär-gə-,dē\. Ruined city of ancient Persia, 30 m. NE of later Persepolis; ✱ of Cyrus the Great; said to have been founded by him on the site of his victory over Astyages 550 B.C. Its ruins today are at Mashad-i-Murghab in the plain of Murghab N of Lake Bakhtegān and comprise bases of several large buildings and the tomb of Cyrus. Surrendered to Alexander 336 B.C.

Pa·say \'pä-,sī\. Chartered city, Rizal prov., Luzon, Phil., on E shore of Manila Bay 1 m. S of S boundary of Manila; pop. (1970e) 183,500. Nearly destroyed by Japanese Dec. 1941.

Pas·ca·gou·la \,pas-kə-'gü-lə\. 1 Navigable river, SE Mississippi; formed by confluence of Leaf and Chickasawhay rivers in N George co., SE Mississippi, flows S into Mississippi Sound.
2 City, ⊗ of Jackson co., SE corner of Mississippi, on Mississippi Sound 18 m. E of Biloxi; pop. (1970c) 27,264; coastal resort and fishing center; boatbuilding and shipbuilding.

Pas·co. 1 \'pas-(,)kō\. County in Florida. See table at FLORIDA.
2 \'pas-(,)kō\. City, ⊗ of Franklin co., SE Washington, on the Columbia river; pop. (1970c) 13,920; Columbia Basin Coll. (1955); developed as supply center during World War II for Richland (*q.v.*) and Hanford sites of industrial plants of the Manhattan District.
3 \'päs-(,)kō\. Department of cen. Peru. See table at PERU.

Pas·coag \'pas-,kōg\. Unincorporated community, Providence co., N Rhode Island, ab. 18 m. NW of Providence; pop. (1970c) 3132.

Pascua, Isla de. See EASTER ISLAND.

Pas–de–Ca·lais \,päd-ka-'lā\. Department of N France. See table at FRANCE.

Pas de Calais. See DOVER, STRAIT OF.

Pa·se·walk \'päz-ə-,valk\. City, Neubrandenburg dist., East Germany, 24 m. WNW of Szczecin, Poland; pop. (1970e) 14,533; iron foundries, sawmills.

Pa·sig \'päs-ig\. 1 Stream, cen. Luzon, Phil.; 14 m. long; the outlet of Laguna de Bay flowing NNW in Rizal prov. and City of Manila; navigable for small vessels.
2 Municipality, ✱ of Rizal prov., Luzon, Phil., on N bank of Pasig river near its source and 5 m. from E boundary of City of Manila; pop. (1969e) 85,100; important market town; partially destroyed at time of Revolution.

Paš·man \'päsh-,män\. Island in Adriatic Sea off coast of Yugoslavia, S of Zadar, bet. Dugi Otok I. and mainland; ab. 34 sq. m.

Pas·ni \'pəs-nē\. Seaport town, Baluchistan, Pakistan, 75 m. E of Gwadar; pop. (1961c) 7483.

Pa·so \'päs-(,)ō, 'pas-\. For names of mountain passes beginning with this element see the distinguishing element (e.g., **Paso de Maipo.** See MAIPO, PASO DE).

Paso de los To·ros \-dā-lə-'stōr-əs\. Town, Tacuarembó dept., N cen. Uruguay; pop. (1963c) 11,008.

Pasoeroean. See PASURUAN.

Paso Ro·bles \,pas-ə-'rō-bəlz\ *or officially* **El Paso de Robles** \el-,pas-əd-ə-\. City, San Luis Obispo co., SW California, on the Salinas 24 m. N of San Luis Obispo; pop. (1970c) 7168; dries and ships fruit; almond groves.

Pas·quo·tank \'pas-kwō-,taŋk\. County in North Carolina. See table at NORTH CAROLINA.

Pas·sa·con·a·way \,pas-ə-'kän-ə-,wā\. Mountain, S Grafton co., W New Hampshire; 4060 ft.; highest point in the Sandwich Range, S White Mts.

Pas·sage Island \,pas-ij-\. Small island off NE tip of Isle Royale, NW Lake Superior, a part of Keweenaw co., N tip of Michigan penin.

Pas·sa·ic \pə-'sā-ik\. 1 River, NE New Jersey; ab. 80 m. long; rises near Morristown, SE Morris co., flows S, E, and N on the Morris co. line, E across Passaic co., turns S at Paterson, where occur the **Great Falls of the Passaic** 70 ft. high; follows the line of the Essex co. boundary into Newark Bay; navigable 11 m.
2 County in New Jersey. See table at NEW JERSEY.
3 Industrial and residential city, Passaic co., N New Jersey, on Passaic river 4 m. S of Paterson; pop. (1970c) 55,124; chemicals, precision instruments, pharmaceuticals, sporting goods, clothing, plastics, electronic components, aircraft parts. Settled by Dutch 1678; incorporated as city 1873; in American Revolution, scene of Washington's crossing of Passaic river during retreat through New Jersey 1776.

Pas·sa·ma·quod·dy Bay \,pas-ə-mə-,kwäd-ē-\. Inlet of SW Bay of Fundy, SW New Brunswick, Canada, bet. SW New Brunswick and SE Maine, at the mouth of the St. Croix river; Deer I. and Campobello I. in S part of it.

Passaro, Cape. See PASSERO, CAPE.

Passarowitz. See POŽAREVAC.

Pas·sau \'päs-,aù\. City, Bavaria, West Germany, at confluence of Danube, Inn, and Ilz rivers 93 m. ENE of Munich; pop. (1969e) 31,158; railroad junction and commercial center; 17th cent. Baroque cathedral, 14th cent. town hall. Of ancient Celtic origin; treaty signed here 1552 settling religious differences bet. Emperor Charles V and German states. Captured by Allies May 2, 1945.

Pass·chen·dae·le \'päs-ᵊn-,däl-ə\. Small commune, West Flanders prov., NW Belgium; pop. (1969e) 3112; scene of heavy fighting Oct.–Nov. 1917.

Pass Chris·ti·an \'pas-'kris(h)-chən\. City, Harrison co., SE Mississippi, on Gulf of Mexico 11 m. W of Gulfport; pop. (1970c) 2979; resort; shrimp and oyster canning.

Pas·se·ro, Cape \-'päs-ə-,rō\ *also* **Cape Pas·sa·ro** \-'päs-ə-(,)rō\ *or anc.* **Pa·chy·nus Prom·on·to·ri·um** \pə-'kī-nə-,spräm-ən-'tōr-ē-əm, -'tòr-\. Cape projecting into Mediterranean Sea at SE point of the island of Sicily. Naval battle 1718 nearby in which British admiral George Byng destroyed Spanish fleet; in World War II landing place of British forces in invasion of Sicily July 10, 1943.

Passes, The. See MISSISSIPPI 1.

Pas·si \'päs-ē\. Municipality, Iloilo prov., Panay, Phil., on Jalaud river and on railroad 29 m. N of City of Iloilo; pop. (1969e) 36,900.

Pas·so Fun·do \,pas-ü-'fō(ⁿ)n-(,)dü\. City, N Rio Grande do Sul state, S Brazil, 150 m. NW of Pôrto Alegre; munic. pop. (1968e) 76,452.

Pas·sos \'pas-(,)üs\. City, SW Minas Gerais state, E Brazil, 180 m. SW of Belo Horizonte; munic. pop. (1968e) 54,523.

Pas·sump·sic \pə-'səm(p)-sik\. River, NE Vermont; rises in N Caledonia co., flows S into Connecticut river.

Pas·ta·za \pə-'stäz-ə, -'stäs-\. 1 River, Ecuador and Peru; ab. 400 m. long; rises in cen. Ecuador and flows S into Peru to empty into Marañón river, headstream of the Amazon.
2 Province of E Ecuador. See table at ECUADOR.

Pas·to \'päs-(,)tō\. 1 Volcano, Colombia. See GALERAS.
2 City, ✱ of Nariño dept., SW Colombia, on high plateau (8400 ft.) E of Galeras volcano; pop. (1968e) 87,832; commercial center; woolen textiles and hats; founded 1539.

Pas·to·ra Peak \pa-,stōr-ə-, -,stòr-\. Mountain, NE Apache co., NE Arizona; 9412 ft.

Pas·tra·na \pə-'strä-nə\. Municipality, N cen. Leyte prov., Phil., 14 m. SW of Tacloban; pop. (1969e) 11,900; severe fighting here in American invasion Oct. 1944.

Pa·su·bio \pä-'sü-bē-,ō\. Peak, Veneto, NE Italy, SE of Rovereto; 7323 ft.

Pa·su·ru·an *or Du.* **Pa·soe·roe·an** \ˌpäs-u̇-rü-ˈän\. Seaport city, East Java prov., Indonesia, at SW corner of Madura Strait; pop. (1961c) 63,408; shipbuilding, rice milling, sugar refining; ab. 30 m. S of Surabaja.

Pat·a·go·nia \ˌpat-ə-ˈgō-nyə, -nē-ə\. Region in South America S of the Limay and Río Negro rivers, or ab. 39°S, extending to the Strait of Magellan, ab. 1000 m.; ab. 311,000 sq. m.; a barren tableland bet. the Andes and Atlantic Ocean. Crossed by the Chubut, Deseado, and Chico rivers flowing E to the Atlantic; its Atlantic coastline indented by the Gulfs of San Matías and San Jorge. Practically unexplored before 1869; divided 1881 bet. Chile (Magallanes prov.) and Argentina (provs. of Río Negro, Chubut, and Santa Cruz).

Patagonia, Plateau of. Highland area in Patagonia, S Argentina, comprising esp. the W part of Chubut prov.

Pataliputra. See PATNA 3.

Patalung. See PHATTHALUNG.

Pa·tam·bán, Cer·ro de \ˌser-ōd-ə-ˌpä-täm-ˈbän\. Mountain, W Michoacán state, SW Mexico, NW of Uruapan; 12,303 ft.

Pa·tan \ˈpät-ən\. 1 *or* **Pat·tan** \ˈpät-ən\. Town, Gujarat, W India, on Saraswati river 65 m. NNW of Ahmadabad; pop. (1961c) 51,953; has numerous Jain temples with valuable Jain manuscripts. Occupies site of ancient Gujrati capital, Anhilwara, captured 1024 by Mahmud of Ghazni.
2 Town, India. See LALITPUR.

Pa·ta·ni \pä-ˈtän-ē\. Former Malay state in the Malay Penin. under Siamese protection, included among the Malay States (*q.v.*); now Pattani (*q.v.*) prov. in Thailand.

Patan Somnath. See SOMNATH.

Pa·taps·co \pə-ˈtap-(ˌ)skō\. River, N cen. Maryland; ab. 80 m. long; rises in Carroll co., N Maryland, flows SE into Chesapeake Bay; the city of Baltimore lies on a navigable estuary of this river.

Pat·a·ra \ˈpat-ə-rə\. One of the chief cities of ancient Lycia, S Asia Minor, on the coast just E of the mouth of the Xanthus.

Patavium. See PADUA.

Pa·tay \pa-ˈtā\. Town, Loiret dept., N cen. France, NW of Orléans; pop. (1962c) 1861; scene of defeat of English under Sir John Fastolf and John Talbot, Earl of Shrewsbury, by Joan of Arc June 18, 1429, just after siege of Orléans had been lifted.

Patch·ogue \ˈpach-ˌȯg\. Village and summer resort, Suffolk co., SE New York, on S shore of Long I., on Great South Bay 53 m. E of New York; pop. (1970c) 11,582.

Pa·ter·nò \ˌpät-ər-ˈnȯ\. Commune, Catania prov., E Sicily, Italy, on SW slope of Mt. Etna 12 m. WNW of Catania; pop. (1968e) 42,277; 11th cent. castle. Taken by British Aug. 1943 in Sicily campaign. See HYBLA.

Pat·er·son \ˈpat-ər-sən\. Industrial city, ⊗ of Passaic co., N New Jersey, on Passaic river 14 m. N of Newark; pop. (1970c) 144,824; manufactures clothing, chemicals, machine tools, electronic components, plastics, television sets, ribbon; formerly the principal American silk-manufacturing center. Founded 1791 as industrial settlement of Society for Establishing Useful Manufactures (S.U.M.), chartered by Alexander Hamilton as part of plan to encourage development of independent American industry; in 19th cent. a center of cotton textile and locomotive manufacturing; received city charter 1851.

Patersonia. See LAUNCESTON.

Pa·than·kot \pə-ˈtän-(ˌ)kōt\. Town, Punjab, India, ab. 65 m. NE of Amritsar; pop. (1961c) 54,810.

Path·ros \ˈpath-rəs\. Upper Egypt, a Biblical name (*Isa.* xi. 11, *Jer.* xliv. 1, 2, 15).

Pa·thum Tha·ni \pä-ˌtüm-tä-ˈnē\ *or* **Pra·thum Thani** \prä-ˌtüm-\ *or* **Pa·tum·dha·ni** \pä-ˌtüm-tä-ˈnē\. 1 Province, cen. Thailand; 578 sq. m.; pop. (1960c) 189,801; ✱ Pathum Thani.
2 Town, its ✱, on the Chao Phraya a few miles N of Bangkok; pop. (1960c) 3013.

Pa·ti \ˈpät-(ˌ)ē\. Town, Central Java prov., Indonesia, 15 m. E of Kudus; pop. (1961c) 38,246.

Pa·tía \pä-ˈtē-ə\. River, SW Colombia; ab. 200 m. long; flows WNW into Pacific Ocean.

Pa·ti·a·la \ˌpət-ē-ˈäl-ə\ *or* **Put·ti·a·la** \ˌpət-\. 1 Former Indian state, now part of Punjab state, NW India; 5942 sq. m.; chief of the three Phulkian states of the Punjab; founded by a Sikh chieftain c. 1763; came under British control 1809.
2 City, its ✱, 130 m. NNW of Delhi; pop. (1970e) 157,920; electrical equipment, vegetable oils, cotton gins, distilleries; univ. (1962).

Pa·ti·llas \pä-ˈtē-(y)əs\. Town and municipality, SE Puerto Rico; pop. (1970p) 2518 (town), 17,189 (munic.); town near coast just E of Guayama.

Pat·kai Range *or* **Patkai Hills** \ˌpät-kī-\. Hill region extending NE to SW along the border between NE India and NW Burma; commonly included with the Naga Hills on the SW. Average height 8000 to 9000 ft. Forms watershed between Brahmaputra and Chindwin rivers. See NAGA HILLS.

Pat·mos \ˈpat-məs\ *or Gk.* **Pát·mos** \ˈpät-(ˌ)mȯs\ *or Ital.* **Pat·mo** \ˈpät-(ˌ)mō\. 1 An island of the Dodecanese (*q.v.*), ab. 28 m. SSW of Samos; 13 sq. m.; pop. (1961c) 2564; scene of Saint John's exile (c. 95 A.D.) where he is supposed to have written the Apocalypse.
2 Town, S end of the island.

Pat·na \ˈpət-nə\. 1 Former Indian state, now part of Orissa state, NE India, 170 m. W of Cuttack; 2530 sq. m.; ✱ Bolangir.
2 Division of Bihar, NE India; 11,336 sq. m.; pop. (1961c) 9,812,858; ✱ Patna.
3 City, ✱ of Bihar, also ✱ of the division, on right bank of Ganges river 290 m. NW of Calcutta; pop. (1970e) 459,731; road and rail junction; univ. (1917); 15th cent. mosque. Old city extends along river for ab. 12 m.; to W lies new section, Bankipur, and to W and SW of Bankipur is modern capital area with government buildings.
History: Founded 5th century B.C. as **Pa·ta·li·pu·tra** \ˌpät-ə-li-ˈpü-trə\; capital of Mauryan empire of Asoka; fell into ruins after 4th century A.D.; revived under Moguls 16th century as viceregal capital; captured by British 1763; lost economic importance as river port with construction of railroads.

Pat·na·nong·an \ˌpät-nə-ˈnȯŋ-än\. Island in Polillo group off E Luzon, Philippines, E of Polillo; 34 sq. m.; in Quezon prov.

Pat·noñg·on \ˌpät-nȯŋ-ˈȯn\. Municipality, Antique prov., on W coast of Panay, Phil., 12 m. N of San Jose de Buenavista; pop. (1969e) 31,700.

Pa·to·ka \pə-ˈtō-kə\. River, SW Indiana; 138 m. long; rises in Orange co., flows W into Wabash river.

Pa·tos \ˈpat-üs\ *or* **Patos de Mi·nas** \-də-ˈmēn-əs\. City, W cen. Minas Gerais state, E Brazil, 190 m. NW of Belo Horizonte; munic. pop. (1968e) 83,455.

Patos \ˈpä-tōs\. Island on W side of Dragon's Mouth, strait bet. NW Trinidad and tip of Paria Penin., NE coast of Venezuela; ab. 200 acres; claim to it ceded to Venezuela by Great Britain 1942, ending 150-year dispute.

Patos, La·goa dos \lə-ˌgō-əd-ə-ˈspat-əs\. Lagoon (lake), E Rio Grande do Sul state, S Brazil; 124 m. long by 37 m. wide; has Pôrto Alegre at its N end and the port of Rio Grande at its S end where it has an outlet to the sea; separated from the Atlantic Ocean by a sandy peninsula ab. 15 m. wide.

Patos, Lago de los. See PORONGOS, LAGUNA DE.

Patos, Los. See LOS PATOS.

Patos de Minas. See PATOS.

Pa·tras \pə-ˈtras, ˈpa-trəs\ *or Gk.* **Pá·trai** \ˈpä-trā\ *or anc.* **Pa·trae** \ˈpā-(ˌ)trē\. Seaport city, ✱ of Achaea dept., NW Peloponnesus, Greece, on Gulf of Patras; pop. (1971p) 111,238; ships fruit, wine, brandy, hides, olive oil; univ. (1966); medieval castle. Important commercially by 5th cent. B.C.; chief commercial city in the Peloponnesus during

Middle Ages; occupied by Turks in 18th and 19th cents. (to 1828); place where Greek War of Independence began 1821; in World War II occupied by Axis powers Apr. 1941–Oct. 1944.

Patras, Gulf of *or* **Gulf of Cal·y·don** \-ˈkal-əd-ᵊn, -ə-ˌdän\ *or Gk.* **Pa·traï·kós Kól·pos** \ˌpät-rī-ˈkós-ˈkól-(ˌ)pós\ *or anc.* **Si·nus Cal·y·do·ni·us** \ˌsī-nə-ˌskal-ə-ˈdō-nē-əs\. Inlet of the Ionian Sea on W coast of Greece, joined by narrow strait (Lepanto Strait) to the Gulf of Corinth N of Peloponnesus.

Pa·tria, Lake \-ˈpä-trē-ə\. Small lake, 13 m. NW of Naples, Italy.

Pat·rick \ˈpat-rik\. County in Virginia. See table at VIRGINIA.

Patrimony of Saint Peter. See ROME, DUCHY OF.

Pattan. See PATAN 1.

Pat·ta·ni \pä-ˈtän-ē\ *also* **Pa·ta·ni** \pə-ˈtän-ē\. 1 Province, SW Thailand; 777 sq. m.; pop. (1960c) 281,587; ✱ Pattani. See PATANI.

2 Town, its ✱, seaport on E coast of Malay Penin. 50 m. ESE of Songkhla; pop. (1964e) 19,902; fishing; ships copra and tin.

Pat·ten \ˈpat-ən\. Town, Penobscot co., E cen. Maine, 31 m. WSW of Houlton; pop. (1970c) 1266; resort.

Pat·ter·son \ˈpat-ər-sən\. 1 City, Stanislaus co., cen. California, 12 m. SW of Modesto; pop. (1970c) 3147; boats, frozen foods; diversified agriculture.

2 Town, St. Mary parish, S Louisiana, 60 m. SE of Lafayette; pop. (1970c) 4409.

Pat·ti \ˈpät-ē\. Commune, Messina prov., NE Sicily, Italy, on N coast of Sicily 33 m. W of Messina; pop. (1968e) 11,579; episcopal see; small harbor.

Pat·ton \ˈpat-ən\. Borough, Cambria co., SW cen. Pennsylvania, 16 m. WNW of Altoona; pop. (1970c) 2762; coal mines; dairy and truck farms.

Pa·tu·ca \pə-ˈtü-kä\. River, S cen. and E Honduras; ab. 300 m. long; rises in several headstreams in mountains of cen. Honduras, flows NE into the Caribbean Sea.

Patuca Point. Cape on NE coast of Honduras, at the mouth of the Patuca river.

Patumdhani. See PATHUM THANI.

Pâ·tu·rages \ˌpä-tü-ˈräzh\. Commune, Hainaut prov., SW Belgium, just SW of Mons; pop. (1969e) 10,054.

Pa·tux·ent \pə-ˈtək-sənt\. River, cen. Maryland; ab. 100 m. long; rises in NW Howard co., flows S and SE into Chesapeake Bay in E St. Marys co., S Maryland.

Patuxent River. 1 River, Maryland. See PATUXENT.

2 U.S. Naval Air Station at Cedar Point, Maryland, on S side of mouth of Patuxent river; Naval Air Test Center; established 1943–44.

Pátz·cua·ro \ˈpäts-kwä-rō\. Town, N cen. Michoacán state, SW Mexico; munic. pop. (1970p) 44,591; on S shore of **Lake Pátzcuaro,** ab. 30 m. in circumference, alt. 6706 ft.

Pat·zi·cía \ˌpät-sē-ˈsē-ə\. Town, Chimaltenango dept., S cen. Guatemala; pop. (1964p) 8881.

Pat·zún \pät-ˈsün\. Town, Chimaltenango dept., S cen. Guatemala, E of Lake Atitlán; pop. (1964p) 14,497.

Pau \ˈpō\. Commune, ✱ of Pyrénées-Atlantiques dept., SW France, on right bank of the Gave de Pau 109 m. S of Bordeaux; pop. (1968c) 74,005; produces turbines, chemicals, footwear; oil refining; winter sports center; 12th cent. castle. Birthplace of Henry IV of France and Charles XIV (Bernadotte) of Sweden; former capital of Béarn.

Pau, Gave de \ˌgäv-də-ˈpō\. River, S France; a mountain stream (*gave*), rises in S Hautes Pyrénées dept., flows NW into the Adour on boundary bet. Pyrénées-Atlantiques and Landes depts.; Lourdes and Pau are on it. See also GAVARNIE.

Pau·car·tam·bo \ˌpau̇-kär-ˈtäm-bō\. Town, E Cuzco dept., SE Peru, on **Paucartambo River** (or **Ya·ve·ro River** \yä-ˌve(ə)r-(ˌ)ō-\, ab. 180 m. long) which flows NNW into the Urubamba; pop. (1961c) 1900.

Pauil·lac \pō-ˈyäk\. Commune, Gironde dept., SW France, on Gironde river ab. 25 m. NW of Bordeaux; pop. (1962c) 5725; in the Médoc; noted for its vineyards.

Paul·ding \ˈpȯl-diŋ\. 1 Name of counties in two states of the U.S. See tables at GEORGIA and OHIO.

2 Town, a ⊗ of Jasper co., SE cen. Mississippi.

3 Village, ⊗ of Paulding co., NW Ohio, 37 m. NW of Lima; pop. (1970c) 2983; beet sugar, brick, furniture.

Pau·lis·ta \pau̇-ˈlēsh-tə\. City, Pernambuco state, E Brazil; munic. pop. (1968e) 56,383.

Pau·lo Afon·so \ˌpau̇-lü-ə-ˈfō(ⁿ)n-(ˌ)sü\. Series of three waterfalls in the São Francisco river, Brazil, ab. 190 m. from its mouth bet. Alagoas and Bahia states; total height of falls ab. 275 ft.

Pauls·boro \ˈpȯlz-ˌbər-ə, -ˌbə-rə\. Borough, Gloucester co., SW New Jersey, 10 m. SSW of Camden; pop. (1970c) 8084; fertilizer, cigars; truck farms.

Pauls Valley \ˈpȯlz-\. City, ⊗ of Garvin co., S cen. Oklahoma; pop. (1970c) 5769; oil wells; grain, cotton.

Paumotu Archipelago. See TUAMOTU ARCHIPELAGO.

Paung·de \ˈpau̇ŋ-ˈdā\. Town, Pegu dist., S cen. Burma, ab. 30 m. SE of Prome.

Pau·ri \ˈpau̇(ə)r-ē\. See GARHWAL.

Pau·te \ˈpau̇-(ˌ)tā\. 1 River, SE Ecuador; ab. 110 m. long; unites with Zamora river to form Santiago river.

2 Town, Azuay prov., S Ecuador, in Andes Mts. just NE of Cuenca; pop. (1962c) 1511.

Pau·to \ˈpau̇-(ˌ)tō\. River, NE cen. Colombia; ab. 120 m. long; flows SE into Meta river.

Pa·via \pə-ˈvē-ə\. 1 Province of Lombardy, Italy. See table at ITALY.

2 *or anc.* **Ti·ci·num** \tə-ˈsī-nəm\. Commune, its ✱, on Ticino river 19 m. S of Milan; pop. (1968e) 85,160; manufactures sewing machines, machinery, foundry products, metalware, chemicals; 15th cent. cathedral, 12th cent. church of St. Michael, 12th cent. church of St. Peter containing the tomb of St. Augustine, 14th cent. Visconti castle, and numerous other churches and palaces; univ. (1361); 5 m. N is Certosa de Pavia, 14th cent. Carthusian monastery with notable Gothic church.

History: Originally a Roman municipality; sacked by Huns and Goths 5th cent. A.D.; came under Visconti 1361 and became a leading Italian city-state; in 1525 scene of a decisive victory of the Spanish and Imperial army over the French under Francis I, who was captured.

Pa·vil·ion Dome \pə-ˌvil-yən-\. Peak in Sierra Nevada, E Fresno co., S cen. California; 11,355 ft.

Pavillons–sous–Bois, Les. See LES PAVILLONS-SOUS-BOIS.

Pav·lo·dar \ˌpav-lə-ˈdär\. Town, ✱ of Pavlodar Oblast, NE Kazakh S.S.R., U.S.S.R., on right bank of Irtysh river 180 m. NW of Semipalatinsk; pop. (1970p) 187,000; food processing; in a rich agricultural region and on the railroad ab. halfway bet. Tselinograd and Barnaul.

Pavlodar Oblast \-ˈō-bləst, -ˌblast\. Subdivision of the Kazakh S.S.R., U.S.S.R.; 49,228 sq. m.; pop. (1970p) 697,000; ✱ Pavlodar; wheat, millet; dairying; coal, gold, salt, copper; formed 1938.

Pav·lof \ˈpav-ˌlȯf\. Volcano, SW Alaska Penin., Alaska, 55°24′N, 161°52′W; on W shore of **Pavlof Bay,** inlet ab. 50 m. long on S coast of peninsula; 8261 ft.

Pav·lo·grad \ˈpav-lə-ˌgrad\. Town, Dnepropetrovsk Oblast, E cen. Ukrainian S.S.R., U.S.S.R., ab. 37 m. E of Dnepropetrovsk; pop. (1969e) 69,000.

Pav·lo·vo \ˈpav-lə-və\. Town, Gorki Oblast, Russian S.F.S.R., U.S.S.R., ab. 40 m. SW of Gorki; pop. (1969e) 62,000.

Pa·vlovsk \ˈpav-ləfsk\ *or formerly* **Slutsk** \ˈslütsk\. Town, Leningrad Oblast, Russian S.F.S.R., U.S.S.R., near Pushkin and ab. 15 m. S of Leningrad; pop. (1961e) 17,800; former royal palace and park.

Pa·vlov·ski Po·sad \ˌpav-ləf-skē-pə-ˈsat\. Town, Moscow Oblast, Russian S.F.S.R., U.S.S.R., on the Klyazma river just E of Moscow; pop. (1969e) 66,000.

Pa·vul·lo nel Fri·gna·no \pä-ˈvü-lō-nel-frē-ˈnyä-nō\. Commune, Modena prov., Emilia-Romagna, N Italy, 21 m. S by W of Modena; pop. (1968e) 12,683.

Paw·ca·tuck \ˈpȯ-kə-ˌtək\. River, SW Rhode Island; forms S section of Rhode Island-Connecticut boundary.

Paw·hus·ka \pȯ-ˈhəs-kə\. City, ⊗ of Osage co., N Oklahoma, 22 m. W of Bartlesville; pop. (1970c) 4238; trade town of Osage Indians; diversified agriculture.

Paw·ling \ˈpȯl-iŋ\. Residential village, Dutchess co., SE New York, 20 m. SE of Poughkeepsie; pop. (1970c) 1914.

Paw·nee \pȯ-ˈnē\. 1 River, W cen. Kansas; ab. 110 m. long; rises in N Gray co., SW Kansas, flows N and E into Arkansas river at Larned, in Pawnee co., cen. Kansas.

2 Name of counties in three states of the U.S. See tables at KANSAS, NEBRASKA, OKLAHOMA.

3 City, ⊗ of Pawnee co., N Oklahoma, 30 m. SSE of Ponca City; pop. (1970c) 2443; livestock farms; site of Pawnee Agency 1876; opened for settlement 1893.

Pawnee City. City, ⊗ of Pawnee co., SE Nebraska, 35 m. ESE of Beatrice; pop. (1970c) 1267; ships livestock.

Paw Paw \ˈpȯ-ˌpȯ\. Village, ⊗ of Van Buren co., SW Michigan, 17 m. WSW of Kalamazoo; pop. (1970c) 3160; lake resort; truck farms, vineyards.

Paw·tuck·et \pə-ˈtək-ət, pȯ-\. Industrial city, Providence co., N Rhode Island, 4 m. NE of Providence on both sides of Blackstone river at Pawtucket Falls; pop. (1970c) 76,984; a center of the textile industry; also manufactures yarn, thread, wire and cable, textile machinery, and machine tools; dyeing and finishing plants. Settled 1671; site of first successful textile mill using Arkwright machinery in the U.S. 1790; incorporated as city 1885.

Pawtucket Falls. 1 City, Massachusetts. See LOWELL 2.

2 City, Rhode Island. See PAWTUCKET.

Paw·tux·et \pȯ-ˈtək-sət, pə-\. River, Rhode Island; ab. 28 m. long; flows from Scituate Reservoir E into Providence river.

Pax Augusta. See BADAJOZ 2.

Pax Julia. See BEJA 2.

Pax·os \ˈpak-səs\ *or Gk.* **Pa·xoí** \päk-ˈsē\. One of the Ionian Is., in the Ionian Sea S of Corfu, with which it forms the Corfu dept. of Greece; 7 sq. m.; pop. (1961c) 2599; chief village Gaïon.

Pax·ton \ˈpaks-tən\. 1 City, ⊗ of Ford co., NE cen. Illinois, 25 m. N of Champaign; pop. (1970c) 4373; furniture; corn, soybeans.

2 Town, Worcester co., cen. Massachusetts, 6 m. NW of Worcester; pop. (1970c) 3731.

Pa·ya·cha·ta \ˌpī-ə-ˈchät-ə\. Peak in N Tarapacá prov., N Chile; 20,767 ft.

Pay·erne \pe-ˈyern\ *or Ger.* **Pe·ter·ling·en** \ˈpā-tər-ˌliŋ-ən\. Commune, Vaud canton, Switzerland, ab. 10 m. W of Fribourg; pop. (1970c) 6899; 10th cent. abbey founded by Bertha of Burgundy, wife of Robert II of France.

Pay·ette \pā-ˈet\. 1 River, W Idaho; **North Fork** rises in NW corner of Valley co., N of the two **Payette Lakes;** flows S and in Boise co. is joined by **South Fork** which flows W across Boise co.; combined stream turns W and WNW and empties into Snake river at Payette on Oregon border; total length with North Fork is 110 m., with South Fork is ab. 70 m.

2 County in Idaho. See table at IDAHO.

3 City, ⊗ of Payette co., SW Idaho, on Snake river across from Oregon 50 m. NW of Boise; pop. (1970c) 4521; dairy products, dried fruit; diversified agriculture.

Payne \ˈpān\. County in Oklahoma. See table at OKLAHOMA.

Payne Lake. Lake, Ungava Penin., N Quebec, Canada; 230 sq. m.; has outlet **(Payne River)** E into Ungava Bay.

Pay·san·dú \ˌpī-sän-ˈdü\. 1 Department of W Uruguay. See table at URUGUAY.

2 City and port, its ✱, on E bank of Uruguay river 210 m. NW of Montevideo; pop. (1963c) 52,472; ships cereals, livestock, flax; flour mills, distilleries, breweries, tanneries; founded 1772.

Pays de Buch. See LA TESTE.

Pays de Waes. See WAES.

Pay·son \ˈpā-sən\. City, Utah co., N cen. Utah, 15 m. S of Provo; pop. (1970c) 4501; railroad shops; sugar beets, onions.

Pa·yún \pä-ˈyün, pī-ˈün\. Peak, SW Mendoza prov., W Argentina; 12,073 ft.

Paz, La. See LA PAZ.

Pa·zar·dzhik \ˌpə-zər-ˈjēk\. 1 Province of SW Bulgaria. See table at BULGARIA.

2 *or formerly* **Ta·tar Pazardzhik** \ˈtät-ər-\. City, its ✱; pop. (1968e) 59,532.

Pa·zin \ˈpäz-ˌēn\ *or Ital.* **Pi·si·no** \pi-ˈzē-(ˌ)nō\. Commune, S cen. Istria Penin., NW Yugoslavia, 27 m. NE of Pula; 13th cent. cathedral; before 1947 belonged to Italy.

Pea \ˈpē\. River, Alabama; ab. 100 m. long; rises in Bullock co., flows S and empties into the Choctawhatchee in Geneva co., near the Florida border.

Pea·body \ˈpē-ˌbäd-ē, -bəd-ē\. City, Essex co., NE corner of Massachusetts, 13 m. SE of Lowell; pop. (1970c) 48,080; leather products, plastics, resins, gelatin; originally part of Salem and then of Danvers (*qq.v.*); made town as South Danvers 1855; renamed 1868; incorporated 1916.

Peabody, Mount. Peak in Glacier National Park, NW Montana; 9200 ft.

Peace \ˈpēs\. 1 River, W cen. Florida; ab. 85 m. long; rises in Polk co., cen. Florida penin., flows S and SW into Charlotte Harbor, Charlotte co., on SW coast.

2 River, W Canada; 1195 m. long (to head of Finlay); formed by confluence of Finlay and Parsnip rivers in E cen. British Columbia, flows E across border of Alberta, turns NE and joins the Slave river just N of its outlet from Lake Athabaska.

Peace River. 1 Rivers, Florida and Canada. See PEACE.

2 Town, W Alberta, Canada, on the right bank of Peace river where it is joined by the Smoky; pop. (1971p) 4951; road and railroad center; ships grain and livestock. Began as a log fort 1793 built by Alexander Mackenzie; now the center of **Peace River Country.**

Peach \ˈpēch\. County in Georgia. See table at GEORGIA.

Peach Tree Creek. Creek in Georgia, flowing into the Chattahoochee river near Atlanta; scene of battle July 20–22, 1864 in which the Confederates failed to drive back Sherman's forces advancing on Atlanta; Gen. Hood's first engagement after replacing Gen. Johnston.

Peak District \ˈpēk-\. Plateau region in N Derbyshire, N cen. England, at S end of the Pennine Chain; highest point **Kin·der Scout** \ˈkin-dər-ˌskau̇t\ or **The Peak** 2088 ft.; region of wild moors, cultivated valleys, and hills with craggy summits.

Peak Ridge. Mountain in the Adirondack Mts., NE New York; 4375 ft.

Peale \ˈpē(ə)l\. Small island, N part of Wake I. group, bordering the lagoon on the N; airport.

Peale, Mount. Peak in N San Juan co., SE Utah; 13,089 ft.; highest in the La Sal group.

Pea Ridge \ˈpē-\. City in Benton co., NW Arkansas; pop. (1970c) 1088; scene of battle Mar. 7–8, 1862 in which Union forces under Samuel R. Curtis defeated Confederates under Van Dorn; site of **Pea Ridge National Military Park.** See UNITED STATES, *National Historical Parks.*

Pear·is·burg \ˈper-is-ˌbərg\. Town, ⊗ of Giles co., W Virginia; pop. (1970c) 2169; tannery.

Pearl \ˈpər(-ə)l\. 1 River, cen. and S cen. Mississippi; 490 m. long; rises in Neshoba co., flows SW, then S into the Gulf of Mexico, forming in the S section the Louisiana-Mississippi boundary.

2 *or Chin.* **Chu** \ˈjü\. River forming a part of the Hsi delta and flowing from the city of Canton, SE China, to the South China Sea; divided by the Bocca Tigris into the

upper and lower Pearl rivers; the lower river constitutes the bay (ab. 20 m. wide) bet. Hong Kong and Macao; below Canton the upper Pearl is joined by the Tung from the E.

Pear·land \'pa(ə)r-ˌland, 'pe(ə)r-, -lənd\. Village, Brazoria co., SE Texas, 15 m. S of Houston; pop. (1970c) 6444; machine shops; chemicals; oil refining.

Pearl and Her·mes Reef \ˌpərl . . . ˌhər-mēz-\. Reef in Hawaii consisting of 12 islets, in cen. Pacific Ocean ab. 1000 m. NW of Niihau I.; part of Leeward Is. and included in Hawaiian Islands Bird Reservation.

Pearl Cays *or* **Pearl Islands** *or Span.* **Ca·yos de Per·las** \ˌkī-ōs-dā-'per-läs\. Group of small islands in Caribbean Sea near the coast of SE cen. Nicaragua, outside of Perlas Lagoon.

Pearl City. Village, Honolulu co., S Oahu I., Hawaii, on Pearl Harbor; pop. (1970c) 19,552; suffered damage in Japanese attack on Pearl Harbor Dec. 7, 1941.

Pearl Coast. Eastern portion of N coast of Isthmus of Darien (Panama), granted 1508 to Alonso de Ojeda for settlement; earliest successful settlement was Darién (*q.v.*) 1510.

Pearl Harbor. Inlet on S coast of the island of Oahu, Hawaii, 6 m. W of Honolulu, forming a landlocked harbor used by U.S. as a naval base; connected with Pacific Ocean by Pearl Harbor entrance. By treaty of 1887 Hawaii granted U.S. exclusive right to use Pearl Harbor as coaling and repair station; not so used until 1908 when Congress authorized establishment of naval station; dry dock completed 1919; attacked without warning by Japanese Air Force Sunday morning Dec. 7, 1941.

Pearl Islands. 1 Island group, Caribbean Sea. See PEARL CAYS.

2 *or Span.* **Ar·chi·pié·la·go de las Per·las** \ˌär-chi-'pyel-ə-ˌgōd-ə-läs-'per-ləs\. Group of islands belonging to Panama in the Gulf of Panama; 450 sq. m.; pearl fisheries.

Pearl Lagoon. See PERLAS LAGOON.

Pearl Point. See PERLAS, PUNTA DE.

Pearl River. 1 River in Mississippi. See PEARL 1.

2 County in Mississippi. See table at MISSISSIPPI.

3 Unincorporated residential community, Rockland co., SE New York, near New Jersey border ab. 12 m. NE of Paterson, New Jersey; pop. (1970c) 17,146.

Pear·sall \'pi(ə)r-ˌsȯl\. City, ⊗ of Frio co., S Texas, 43 m. ESE of Uvalde; pop. (1970c) 5545; chemicals; oil wells; peanuts, melons.

Pear·son \'pi(ə)r-sən\. City, ⊗ of Atkinson co., S Georgia; pop. (1970c) 1700; lumber; agriculture.

Pea·ry Land *also* **Pea·ry·land** \'pi(ə)r-ē-\. Region of N Greenland on Arctic Ocean, forming a mountainous peninsula, 82° to 84°N; does not have the ice cap that covers most of Greenland. Its N cape, Morris Jesup, is the most northerly point of land known in the Arctic Regions; penetrated by several fjords; highest point 6300 ft. First visited by Greely and Lockwood 1881–82; explored by Peary 1892 and 1900.

Peb·ble Island \ˌpeb-əl-\. Island off N coast of West Falkland, Falkland Is.

Peć *or* **Pech** *also* **Petch** \'pech\ *or Turk.* **Ipek** \i-'pek\. Town, Serbia, S Yugoslavia, ab. 75 m. NW of Skopje; pop. (1965e) 32,000; trades in grain and fruit, in the Middle Ages, seat of the Patriarchs of the Serbian Orthodox Church.

Pe·chen·ga \pə-'cheŋ-gə\ *or Finn.* **Pet·sa·mo** \'pet-sə-ˌmō\. 1 Territory, formerly in N Finland, extending nearly to Varanger Fjord, Norway, forming a narrow strip 135 m. long from N to S bordering on W Murmansk Oblast, Russian S.F.S.R., U.S.S.R.; 3860 sq. m.; ceded by U.S.S.R. to Finland 1920; taken back by U.S.S.R. 1940 but occupied by Germans 1940–44; now part of Murmansk Oblast, U.S.S.R.

2 Village in Murmansk Oblast, Russian S.F.S.R., U.S.S.R., in extreme NW part on narrow inlet of Arctic Ocean, 60 m. W of Murmansk; center of copper-mining region and base for a fishing fleet; used by Finnish-German forces as a naval and aviation base in World War II. Belonged to Finland 1920–44.

Pechili. See POHAI, STRAIT OF.

Pe·cho·ra \pə-'chōr-ə, -'chȯr-\. River, NE U.S.S.R., chiefly in Komi A.S.S.R., Russian S.F.S.R.; 1112 m. long; rises in Middle Ural Mts. in N Perm Oblast, flows N, W, and N in great bend into Pechora Bay; its main tributaries the Tsilma and Izhma on the W and the Usa on the E; both the main stream and its tributaries are navigable for most of their courses; has extensive delta; coalfields in its basin.

Pechora Bay. Inlet of Barents Sea, NE coast of Nenets National Okrug, Russian S.F.S.R., U.S.S.R.; ab. 40 m. long; receives Pechora river from the S.

Peck·ville \'pek-ˌvil\. Community, Lackawanna co., NE Pennsylvania, NE of Scranton; post office for borough of Blakely.

Pe·con·ic Bay \pi-ˌkän-ik-\. Inlet, SW of Gardiners Bay at E end of Long I., New York, divided into **Great Peconic Bay** on the W and **Little Peconic Bay** on the E; receives the **Peconic River.**

Pe·cos \'pā-kəs\. 1 or **Rio Pecos** \ˌrē-ō-\. River, E New Mexico and W Texas; 500 m. long; rises in W Mora co., flows SE through E New Mexico across Texas border and empties into Rio Grande in S Val Verde co., SW Texas.

2 County in Texas. See table at TEXAS.

3 City, ⊗ of Reeves co., W Texas, near Pecos river 40 m. S of New Mexico border; pop. (1970c) 12,682; oil wells and refineries; alfalfa, cantaloupes.

Pecos National Monument. See UNITED STATES, *National Monuments.*

Pécs \'pāch\ *or Ger.* **Fünf·kir·chen** \'fünf-ˌki(ə)r-kən\. City, ⊗ of Baranya co. (but politically independent), S Hungary, 106 m. W of Budapest; 56 sq. m.; pop. (1970p) 145,307; wine, leather goods; center of coal-mining region; 11th cent. cathedral; univ. (1922). A settlement of Celtic tribes and Romans; made bishopric 1009; occupied by Turks 1543–1686.

Ped·docks Island \ˌped-əks-\. Island in S area of Boston Bay, E Massachusetts, off N tip of Plymouth co.

Pedee. See PEE DEE.

Ped·er·nal·es \ˌpərd-ᵊn-'al-əs\. River, cen. Texas; 106 m. long; rises in Kimble co. and flows E to Colorado river NW of Austin.

Pedernales \ˌped-ər-'näl-ās\. 1 Province, SW Dominican Republic. See table at DOMINICAN REPUBLIC.

2 Town, its ✻; pop. (1970e) 7062.

Ped·er·nal Peak \ˌped-ər-'nal-\. Mountain, S Rio Arriba co., N New Mexico; 7580 ft.

Pe·di·as \pe̅t͟h-'yäs\ *or anc.* **Ped·i·ae·us** \ˌped-ē-'ē-əs\. River on the island of Cyprus; ab. 60 m. long; flows E to Famagusta Bay.

Pedras, Point. See COQUEIROS, POINT.

Pe·dre·gal \ˌped-ri-'gäl\. 1 River, SE Mexico; ab. 50 m. long; rises in W Chiapas state, flows N to the Tonalá in Tabasco state.

2 Pacific coast port, W Panama; port for David.

Pe·dro Bank \ˌped-rō-, ˌpād-\. Shoal in NW Caribbean Sea, S of Jamaica; includes the Pedro Cays.

Pedro Be·tan·court \-ˌbe-tän-'kü(ə)rt, -ˌtäŋ-\. Town and municipality, Matanzas prov., W cen. Cuba; town 27 m. SE of Matanzas; munic. pop. (1967e) 23,240.

Pedro Cays \-'kēz, -'kāz\. Four small guano islands ab. 45 m. SW of Jamaica; a dependency of Jamaica from 1882.

Pedro Juan Ca·ba·lle·ro \-ˌ(h)wän-ˌkab-ə-'le(ə)r-(ˌ)ō, -ə(l)-'yе(ə)r-\. Town, ✻ of Amambay dept., E Paraguay, on Brazilian border 125 m. ENE of Concepción; pop. (1968e) 12,300.

Pedro Mi·guel \-mi-'gel\. Town, Balboa dist., Canal Zone, at the Pedro Miguel Locks in the Panama Canal, just NW of Miraflores; pop. (1970p) 1410.

Pedro Miguel Locks. Double locks in the Panama Canal, Canal Zone, NW of Miraflores Lake and NW of the city of Panama; lowers vessels 31 ft. to level of Miraflores Lake.

Pedro Point \ˌpē-drō-\. Cape on NW tip of the island of Jamaica, West Indies.

Pee·bles \'pē-bəlz\. 1 *or* **Pee·bles·shire** \'pē-bəl-ˌshi(ə)r, -shər\ *or* **Tweed·dale** \'twēd-ˌdāl\. County, SE Scotland; 347 sq. m.; pop. (1971p) 13,675; ⊗ Peebles; its chief river the Tweed; livestock farming, tourism.
2 Burgh, its ⊗, on the Tweed; pop. (1971p) 5881; market town; woolen textiles; tourism.

Pee Dee *also* **Pe·dee** \'pē-ˌdē\. River, North Carolina and South Carolina; 233 m. long; formed by junction of Yadkin and Uharie rivers in Montgomery co., S cen. North Carolina, flows SE into South Carolina and into Winyah Bay.

Peek·a·moose Mountain \ˌpē-kə-ˌmüs-\. Peak in the Catskill Mts., Ulster co., SE New York; 3843 ft.

Peeks·kill \'pēk-ˌskil\. City, Westchester co., SE New York, on Hudson river 39 m. N of New York; pop. (1970c) 18,891; commercial center; beverages, clothing, leather goods; diversified agriculture. In American Revolution strategically important; burned by British 1777.

Peel \'pē(ə)l\. 1 River, NW Canada; 425 m. long (to head of Ogilvie); rises in W Yukon Territory, flows E and then N into Mackenzie river in NW Mackenzie dist., Northwest Territories.
2 County, Ontario, Canada. See table at ONTARIO.
3 Coastal town, W Isle of Man, England; pop. (1971p) 3081; fishing center and seaside resort; ancient chapel dedicated to St. Patrick, who is believed to have founded first church in Isle of Man; ruins of castle and cathedral.

Peel \'pāl\. Marsh area, North Brabant and Limburg provs., S Netherlands; 60 sq. m.

Peel Sound \'pēl-\. Passage bet. Prince of Wales I. and Somerset I., Franklin dist., Northwest Territories, Canada.

Pee·ne \'pā-nə\. Navigable river, East Germany; 70 m. long; flows E into Zalew Szczeciński.

Pee·ne·mün·de \ˌpā-nə-'mün-də\. Village on small island at mouth of Peene river, East Germany, at W end of Usedom I. and NW of Zalew Szczeciński; in World War II the principal German research and testing facility for rockets and missiles; severely bombed by British Aug. 18, 1943; captured by Soviet troops Apr. 1945.

Peg·a·sus Bay \ˌpeg-ə-səs-\. Inlet of Pacific Ocean on NE cen. coast of South I., New Zealand, N of Banks Penin.; receives the Waimakariri river from the W.

Peg·nitz \'peg-nəts, 'pāg-\. River, Bavaria, West Germany; 53 m. long; flows S and W through Nürnberg to unite with the Rednitz at Fürth and form the Regnitz river.

Pe·gu \pe-'gü\. 1 River, Pegu division, Burma; ab. 150 m. long; tributary of the Rangoon river.
2 Division of Burma. See table at BURMA.
3 District in Pegu division; 4824 sq. m.; pop. (1962e) 897,395; ✱ Pegu.
4 Town, ✱ of the division, 47 m. NE of Rangoon and on railroad from Rangoon to Toungoo and to Martaban; pop. (1953c) 47,358; ships rice; has numerous pagodas, including the notable Shwemawdaw (288 ft. high), and reclining figure of Buddha (Shwethalyaung).
History: Founded c. 825 A.D. as capital of Mon kingdom; later capital of Toungoo dynasty of Pegu kingdom; Mons briefly restored 1740–57 when city destroyed by Alaungpya; annexed by British 1852; occupied by Japanese Mar. 1942–May 1944.

Pegu Yo·ma \-'yō-mə\. Mountain range, Burma, extending N and S bet. the Irrawaddy and the Sittang rivers; ab. 270 m. long; highest point Mt. Popa 4981 ft. at N end.

Peh. See PEI 2.

Pehanchen. See PEI-AN 2.

Pehpiao. See PEI-P'IAO.

Pehtaiho. See PEI-TAI-HO.

Pehtang. See PEI-T'ANG.

Pei \'bā\. 1 River, Hopeh prov., China. See PAI 1.
2 *or* **Pai** *or* **Peh** \'bā\. River, cen. Kwangtung prov., SE China; 217 m. long; rises in S Hunan and flows S to join the Hsi delta W of Canton.

Pei–an *or* **Pei·an** \'bā-'än\. 1 Former province (1932–45), N cen. Manchukuo; 27,596 sq. m.
2 *or* **Peh·an·chen** \'bā-'än-'jən\. Town, E cen. Heilungkiang prov., NE China, ab. 170 m. N of Harbin; pop. (1970e) 130,000; ✱ of former Pei-an prov.

Pei–erh \'bā-'er\ *or* **Bor Nor** \'bər-'nò(ə)r\ *or* **Buyr Nuur** \'bwēr-'nür\. Lake, NE China, on border of Mongolian People's Republic, S of Hu-lun lake.

Pei–hai \'bā-'hī\ *or* **Pak·hoi** *or earlier Fr.* **Pack·hoi** \'bäk-'hòi\. Seaport, SW Kwangtung prov., SE China, on Gulf of Tonkin ab. 350 m. W of Hong Kong; pop. (1970e) 175,000; has good anchorage and is a natural port of entry for Yunnan and Kweichow provs. and Kwangsi Chuang autonomous region. Made treaty port in 1877.

Pei–ho. See PAI 1.

Pei–lin. See SIAN.

Pei·ne \'pī-nə\. City, Lower Saxony, West Germany, 17 m. NE of Hildesheim; pop. (1969e) 30,899; iron and steel, machinery, footwear; brewing, sugar refining; founded c. 1220.

Pei–p'iao *or* **Peh·piao** \'bā-'pyaù\. Town, E Liaoning prov., NE China, 50 m. NW of Chin-chou; coal-mining region.

Peiping. See PEKING.

Pei·pus, Lake \-'pī-pəs\ *or Estonian* **Peip·si** \'pāp-sē\ *or Russ.* **Chud·sko·ye Oze·ro** \'chüt-skə-yə-'ò-z(y)ə-rə\. Lake, E Estonian S.S.R. and W Pskov Oblast, Russian S.F.S.R., U.S.S.R.; 60 m. long and 31 m. wide; 1390 sq. m. Its outlet is the Narva flowing N to Gulf of Finland; receives from the S the Velikaya and from the W the Ema. Its S extension is sometimes called Lake Pskov (*q.v.*). Estonian S.S.R.-Russian S.F.S.R. boundary line runs nearly in center except at N end, where entire N shore and Narva river are in Estonian S.S.R. Teutonic knights defeated by Alexander Nevski on ice of the lake 1242; center of much fighting in World War II, esp. in Aug. 1941 and Sept. 1944.

Peiraeus. See PIRAEUS.

Pei–tai–ho *or* **Peh·tai·ho** \'bā-'dī-'hō\. Town, NE Hopeh prov., NE China, ab. 15 m. SSW of Ch'in-huang-tao; originated 1894–95.

Pei–t'ang \'bā-'täŋ\ *or* **Peh·tang** \'bā-'täŋ\. Town, Hopeh prov., NE China, on Gulf of Chihli, at mouth of **Chi–yün River** \'chē-'yün-\ 10 m. N of Ta-ku. Treaty signed here 1859; British and French forces landed in operations against Ta-ku forts 1860.

Pei·war Pass \ˌpā-wär-\ *or* **Peiwar Ko·tal** \-'kō-ˌtəl\. Mountain pass, W end of Safed Koh range from NW Pakistan into Afghanistan, SE of Kabul, in the Kurram valley; scene of defeat of Afghans by Lord Roberts Dec. 1878.

Pe·ka·long·an \pə-ˌkä-'lòŋ-ˌän\. 1 Regency, Central Java prov., Indonesia; 2176 sq. m.; pop. (1961c) 851,224; ✱ Pekalongan; bounded on N by Java Sea; region has considerable area of flat fertile land along the coast with mountain range along S border; chief crop sugar; much rice and some coffee, cocoa, indigo, and kapok grown. Chief towns Pekalongan, Tegal, Pemalang, and Batang.
2 City, its ✱, on N coast and on railroad 55 m. W of Semarang; pop. (1961c) 102,380; exports sugar; textiles, batiks; fort built 1753.

Pe·kan \pə-'kän\. Seaport town on S side of the Pahang river near its mouth, E Pahang state, Malaysia; sultan's residence and until 1898 the capital.

Pe·kin \'pē-kən, -ˌkin\. City, ⊗ of Tazewell co., cen. Illinois, on Illinois river 10 m. S of Peoria; pop. (1970c) 31,375; river port and railroad center, shipping livestock, grain, and coal; produces aluminum and brass castings, alcohol, barrels, corn products; settled 1824, incorporated 1849.

Pe·king \'pē-'kiŋ\ *or from 1928 to 1949* **Pei·ping** \'pā-piŋ, 'bā-\. City, ✱ of China, in an extensive plain of NE China;

constitutes a special administrative unit (3386 sq. m.); pop. (1970e) 8,000,000; administrative, cultural, and educational center of China; produces flour, textiles, machine tools, printing presses, synthetic fibers, and is center of a complex of heavy-industrial and mining suburbs; numerous educational institutions, including Peking Univ. (1898), People's Univ. of China (1950), and numerous specialized technical and party (political) schools. Inner part of city consists of Inner or Tatar City in N and Outer or Chinese City in S, having a combined area of ab. 25 sq. m. and formerly surrounded by 15th cent. walls (these were partially demolished during the "Great Cultural Revolution" 1966–67, several gates remaining intact). Inner City contains old Imperial or "Forbidden City" with former imperial palace, former legations, parks, temples, hospitals, and various public buildings; extensive development in modern times of residential suburbs to N and NW and industrial suburbs to E, esp. since 1949.

History: Had various names in ancient times; a frontier town for centuries, known as Ch'i (or Yen, from the district) under Chou dynasty (1122–255 B.C.) and later. Capital of powerful monarchy, 10th to 12th cents. A.D., under the Khitan Mongols and the Kin Tatar dynasty; as Khanbalik became residence of Kublai Khan 1264–67 and capital of China 1267–1368 under Yuan dynasty; known to Europeans as Cambaluc, Marco Polo's name. Under Mings replaced as capital for a short time but in 1421 again chosen as capital and so continued under the Manchus (1644–1912). Occupied by European expeditionary forces and suffered considerable damage 1860 and during Boxer Rebellion 1900–01; in 1928 Nanking made capital and name Peking changed to Peiping. At the Marco Polo Bridge 9 m. SW (see LU-KOW-CH'IAO) on July 7, 1937 fighting broke out bet. Japanese and Chinese troops, the incident that began the Chinese-Japanese War (1937–45); surrendered to Communist forces in 1949 and again made capital; municipal area radically expanded 1953 and 1958 from 1949 figure of 300 sq. m.

Pe·la·bu·han Bay \ˌpe-lə-ˈbü-ən-\ *or Du.* **Wijn·koops–Baai** \ˌvīn-kōps-ˈbī\ *or Eng.* **Wyn·coops Bay** \ˌwīn-küps-\. Inlet of the Indian Ocean, S side of the W end of Java, Indonesia.

Pe·la·gi·an Islands \pə-ˈlā-j(ē-)ən-\ *or Ital.* **Iso·le Pe·la·gie** \ˌē-zə-(ˌ)lā-pā-ˈläj-(ˌ)ā\. Three barren Italian islands, Lampedusa, Linosa, and Lampione (uninhabited), in the Mediterranean Sea S of Sicily, Italy, and bet. Malta and Tunisia; politically attached to Agrigento prov., Italy. Taken by Allies June 12–13, 1943.

Pelagosa Islands. See PALAGRUŽA ISLANDS.

Pe·lée, Mount \-pə-ˈlā\ *or Fr.* **Mon·tagne Pelée** \mōⁿ-tan-yə-pə-lā\. Volcano, N Martinique I., West Indies; 4583 ft.; erupted 1902, destroying Saint Pierre and killing more than 30,000 persons, including all the town's inhabitants and many others that had sought refuge there.

Pe·lee, Point \-ˈpē-lē\. Headland, Essex co., SE Ontario, Canada, projecting into Lake Erie; has remarkable beaches and flora; established 1918 as a national park: see CANADA, *National Parks.* **Pelee Island,** 8 m. to the S in Lake Erie, is the most southerly point of Canada, 41°46′N, 82°39′W.

Pel·e·liu \ˌpel-ə-ˈlē-(ˌ)ü, ˈpel-ə-lē-ˌü\. Island at S end of Palau Is., W Pacific Ocean, bet. Angaur and Eil Malk; ab. 5 m. long by 2 m. wide; chief village Ngardololok. Many islets and reefs off its N shore. Bombed by U.S. naval and air forces 1944; captured by assault after severe fighting Sept. 14 to Oct. 13, 1944.

Pe·leng \ˈpā-ˌleŋ\. Largest island in the Banggai Archipelago, off the E coast of Celebes I., Indonesia, Malay Archipelago; ab. 53 m. long by 32 m. wide; 929 sq. m.

Peleng Strait. Passage bet. E peninsula of Celebes and Peleng I. of the Banggai Archipelago, connecting the Gulf of Tolo with the Molucca Sea.

Pelew. See PALAU.

Pel·ham \ˈpel-əm\. **1** City, Mitchell co., SW Georgia, 32 m. S of Albany; pop. (1970c) 4539; fertilizer, lumber; livestock, peanuts; incorporated 1881.

2 Town, Hillsborough co., S New Hampshire, 9 m. E of Nashua; pop. (1970c) 5408.

3 Village in Pelham town, Westchester co., SE New York, 17 m. NE of New York; pop. (1970c) 2076 (village), 13,933 (town).

Pelham Manor. Village in Pelham town, Westchester co., SE New York, on Long Island Sound 17 m. NE of New York; pop. (1970c) 6673; residential suburb of New York City.

Pel·i·can Island \ˌpel-i-kən-\. Island in Atlantic Ocean, off NE coast of Volusia co., E Florida.

Pelican Point. Cape on W cen. coast of South-West Africa, enclosing Walvis Bay.

Pe·li·leo \ˌpel-ə-ˈlā-(ˌ)ō\. Town, Tungurahua prov., cen. Ecuador, just N of Riobamba; pop. (1962c) 2545.

Pe·li·on \ˈpē-lē-ən\ *or Gk.* **Pí·li·on** \ˈpē-lē-ˌȯn\. Peak, S Larissa dept., E Thessaly, NE Greece, near Volos; 5089 ft. In Greek legend figured in the wars of the giants (Aloadae) and was the home of the centaurs, esp. Chiron.

Pe·lje·šac \ˈpel-yə-ˌshäts\ *or Ital.* **Sab·bion·cel·lo** \ˌsäb-yōn-ˈchel-(ˌ)ō\. Peninsula on coast of W Yugoslavia, projecting NW into the Adriatic Sea E of Korčula I.; 43 m. long.

Pel·kum \ˈpel-ˌküm\. City, North Rhine-Westphalia, West Germany, 14 m. N of Dortmund; pop. (1969e) 25,091.

Pel·la \ˈpel-ə\. **1** City, Marion co., S cen. Iowa, 17 m. WNW of Oskaloosa; pop. (1970c) 6688; dairy products, clothing, flour; coal mines; livestock farms; Central Coll. (1853).

2 Department of Macedonia, Greece. See table at GREECE.

3 Ruins of ancient city near Genitsa and 24 m. WNW of Salonika, Greece; ancient capital of Macedonia and birthplace of Alexander the Great.

Pell City \ˈpel-\. City, ⊗ of St. Clair co., NE cen. Alabama; pop. (1970c) 5602; lumber; cotton.

Pel·les·tri·na \ˌpel-əs-ˈtrē-nə\. Island in S Lagoon of Venice, Italy; 9 m. long; a part of the commune of Venice.

Pellew Islands. See SIR EDWARD PELLEW GROUP.

Pell·worm \ˈpel-ˌvȯ(ə)rm\. One of the Halligen Is., in S part of North Frisian Is. off W coast of Schleswig-Holstein, N West Germany, W of Nordstrand; area 14 sq. m.

Pel·ly \ˈpel-ē\. **1** Former city, Harris co., SE Texas, on Galveston Bay; now part of Baytown.

2 River, S cen. Yukon Territory, Canada; 330 m. long; rises in Mackenzie Mts. and flows W to unite with Lewes river and form Yukon river.

Pelly, Lake. Lake on N boundary bet. Mackenzie dist. and Keewatin dist., Northwest Territories, Canada; 331 sq. m.; connects with Lake Garry.

Pelly Bay. Bay, inlet of Gulf of Boothia, in N Keewatin dist., Northwest Territories, Canada, W of Simpson Penin.

Pe·lon·cil·lo Mountains \ˈpel-ən-ˌsē-(y)ō-\. Range, SW Hidalgo co., in extreme SW New Mexico, and extending across border into Arizona.

Pel·o·pon·nese \ˈpel-ə-pə-ˌnēz, -nēs\ *or* **Pel·o·pon·ne·sus** \ˌpel-ə-pə-ˈnē-səs\ *or* **Pel·o·pon·ne·sos** \-ses\. **1** Peninsula, forming S part of the mainland of Greece; ancient subdivisions: Achaea, Arcadia, Argolis, Corinth, Elis, Laconia, Messenia, and Sicyonia; chief cities Corinth and Sparta; under the Romans was larger part of the province Achaea 146 B.C.–c. 4th cent. A.D.; since 12th cent. when it was under the Byzantine Empire often called **Mo·rea** \mə-ˈrē-ə\ because of its resemblance in shape to a mulberry leaf (*Lat.* morus).

2 Administrative division of modern Greece, coextensive with the peninsula; 8603 sq. m.; pop. (1971p) 985,620; forms departments of Achaea, Arcadia, Argolis, Corinth, Elis, Laconia, and Messenia (see table at GREECE).

Pelorus. See FARO, CAPE.

Pe·lo·tas \pə-ˈlōt-əs\. City, SE Rio Grande do Sul state, S Brazil, at S end of Lagoa dos Patos 29 m. NNW of Rio Grande; munic. pop. (1968e) 208,672; ships meat and dairy products, rice, hides, timber; produces dried beef, flour, leather goods, footwear, soap, lard; univ. (1883, received univ. status 1960), Catholic univ. (1960); founded 1830; made city 1835.

Pelouse. See PALOUSE.

Pel·to, Lake \-ˈpel-(ˌ)tō\. Inlet of Gulf of Mexico in S Terrebonne parish, SE Louisiana.

Pe·lu·si·ac Branch \pə-ˌlü-s(h)ē-ˌak-\. Ancient E arm of the Nile river, E of the Phatnitic (Damietta) mouth, now filled up.

Pe·lu·si·um \pə-ˈlü-shē-əm\. Ancient city of Egypt, on Pelusiac Branch of the Nile; ruins are in Plain of Tina E of Suez Canal and ab. 22 m. SE of Port Said, on **Bay of Pelusium** (*or Arab.* **Kha·līj aṭ–Ṭī·nah** \kä-ˌlēj-ˌät-tē-ˈnä\), an inlet of the Mediterranean.

Pel·voux \pel-ˈvü\. Mountain group, SE France, in the Dauphiné Alps in Hautes-Alpes and Isère depts., contains Barre des Écrins 13,461 ft., highest peak of the Dauphiné Alps; **Mont Pelvoux** 12,920 ft., just SE of Barre des Écrins, was for a long time considered the highest point.

Pem·a·dum·cook Lake \ˌpem-ə-ˈdəm-ku̇k-\. Lake on boundary bet. Penobscot and Piscataquis cos., N cen. Maine; connected with Millinocket Lake on the NE; traversed NW to SE by West Branch of the Penobscot river.

Pe·ma·lang \ˌpā-mə-ˈläŋ\. Town, Central Java prov., Indonesia, on railroad near coast bet. Pekalongan and Tegal; pop. (1961c) 42,533.

Pem·a·quid Point \ˌpem-ə-kwəd-\. Point, S Lincoln co., S Maine.

Pe·ma·tang·sian·tar \pə-ˈmä-ˌtäŋ-sē-ˈän-ˌtär\. Town, NE Sumatra, Indonesia, 23 m. NE of Lake Toba; pop. (1961c) 114,870.

Pem·ba \ˈpem-bə\. Island in Indian Ocean off NE coast of Tanzania, E Africa, N of island of Zanzibar; 379 sq. m.; pop. (1967c) 164,321; ✱ Wete; included with island of Zanzibar in the former Zanzibar sultanate.

Pemba Bay. Inlet of Mozambique Channel on NE coast of Mozambique; constitutes harbor for seaport of Porto Amélia.

Pem·bi·na \ˈpem-bə-nə, -ˌnȯ\. **1** County in North Dakota. See table at NORTH DAKOTA.

2 City, Pembina co., NE North Dakota, ab. 22 m. NE of Cavalier; pop. (1970c) 741; site of earliest trading post (1797–98) and center of white settlement in North Dakota.

3 River, cen. Alberta, Canada; ab. 210 m. long; rises near E border of Jasper National Park and flows NE and N into the Athabaska.

Pem·broke \ˈpem-ˌbrōk, -ˌbru̇k\. **1** City, ⊗ of Bryan co., SE Georgia, 31 m. W of Savannah; pop. (1970c) 1361; lumber; peanuts.

2 Town, Plymouth co., SE Massachusetts, 10 m. E of Brockton; pop. (1970c) 11,193; dairy, truck farms.

3 Town, Merrimack co., S cen. New Hampshire, on Merrimack river 6 m. SE of Concord; pop. (1970c) 4261.

4 Town in Pembroke township, Robeson co., S North Carolina, ab. 12 m. NW of Lumberton; pop. (1970c) 1982; agriculture; Pembroke State Coll. (1887).

5 Town, ⊗ of Renfrew co., SE Ontario, Canada, on Allumette Lake across from Allumette I.; pop. (1966c) 16,262; fishing resort; lumber, electrical appliances, flour, butter. Probable site of limit of Champlain's exploration to the West 1613, where he was forced to turn back.

6 County in Wales. See PEMBROKESHIRE.

7 Municipal borough, ⊗ of Pembrokeshire, SW Wales; pop. (1971p) 14,092; market town and tourist center; oil refinery, woolen mill; 11th cent. castle (birthplace of Henry VII 1457); had large naval dockyard 1814–1926.

Pembroke Park. Town, Broward co., SE Florida; pop. (1970c) 2949.

Pembroke Pines. City, Broward co., SE Florida; pop. (1970c) 15,520; residential suburb of Fort Lauderdale.

Pem·broke·shire \ˈpem-bru̇k-ˌshi(ə)r, -brōk-, -shər\ *or* **Pembroke.** County, SW Wales; area 614 sq. m.; pop. (1971p) 97,295; ⊗ Pembroke; wheat, oats, potatoes; livestock and poultry farming, oil refining, tourism.

Pem·i·ge·was·set \ˌpem-i-jə-ˈwäs-ət\. River, cen. New Hampshire; 70 m. long; rises in N Grafton co., flows S through Franconia Notch, unites with Winnipesaukee river at Franklin to form the Merrimack river; the **Pemigewasset Wilderness** is the region bet. Franconia Notch and Crawford Notch (Saco river) to the E containing many peaks of the White Mts., several over 4000 ft.

Pem·i·scot \ˈpem-i-ˈskät, -ˈskō\. County in Missouri. See table at MISSOURI.

Pen \ˈpen\. Village, ancient Sussex, S England; probably Penselwood in S Somersetshire, S of Frome; scene of defeat of Canute by Edmund II 1016.

Pe·ña·la·ra, Pi·co de \ˈpē-kōd-ə-ˌpen-yə-ˈlär-ə\. Highest peak in Sierra de Guadarrama, cen. Spain; 7972 ft.

Pe·nang \pə-ˈnaŋ\ *or* **Pi·nang** \pə-\. **1** *or formerly* **Prince of Wales Island** \ˌprin(t)s-əv-ˈwālz-\. Island, 2½ m. off W coast of the Malay Penin., forming part of the Malaysian state of Penang (2 below); 108 sq. m.

2 A state of Malaysia, Malay Penin.; 400 sq. m.; pop. (1970p) 776,770; ✱ Penang; rice, rubber.

History: Penang I. the first British settlement in Malaya, acquired 1786 by cession to East India Company from sultan of Kedah; Province Wellesley (adjacent area on mainland) added 1798. Made separate presidency 1805 and was seat of government for three settlements (Penang, Malacca, Singapore) 1826–36; became part of the crown colony of Straits Settlements 1867; bombed and occupied by Japanese Dec. 1941; became part of independent Federation of Malaya 1957; became a state of Malaysia 1963.

3 *or* **Pu·lau Pi·nang** \ˌpü-ˌlau̇-pi-ˈnäŋ\ *or formerly* **George Town** \ˈjȯ(ə)rj-\. Seaport city, ✱ of Penang state; pop. (1970p) 270,019.

Pen Ar·gyl \pen-ˈär-jel\. Borough, Northampton co., E Pennsylvania, 22 m. NE of Allentown; pop. (1970c) 3668.

Pe·ña·rro·ya–Pue·blo·nue·vo \ˌpen-yə-ˈrȯi-ə-pü-ˌeb-lō-nu̇-ˈā-(ˌ)vō\. Commune, Córdoba prov., S Spain, 40 m. NW of Córdoba; pop. (1970p) 16,330; iron, lead, and coal.

Pen·arth \pe-ˈnärth\. Urban district and seaport, Glamorganshire, S Wales; pop. (1971p) 23,965; seaside resort and residential suburb of Cardiff. In World War II a U.S. naval training base.

Pe·ñas, Cape \-ˈpā-nyəs\ *or Span.* **Ca·bo de Peñas** \ˌkäb-ōd-ə-\. **1** Cape on NW coast of Spain, projecting into Bay of Biscay from Oviedo prov.

2 Cape on E cen. coast of Tierra del Fuego I., off S South America, at 53°51′S, 67°33′W.

Pe·nas, Gulf of \-ˈpā-nyəs\. Inlet of S Pacific Ocean on SW coast of Chile, S of Taitao Penin.

Pen·brook \ˈpen-bru̇k\. Borough, Dauphin co., SE cen. Pennsylvania, 3 m. NE of Harrisburg; pop. (1970c) 3379.

Pen–ch'i *or* **Pen·ki** \ˈbən-ˈchē\ *or* **Pen·hsi·hu** \ˈbən-ˈshē-ˈhü\. Town, S Liaoning prov., NE China, 30 m. E of Liaoyang; pop. (1970e) 750,000; steel producing center; cement, foundry supplies; iron and coal mines; steel industry originally developed by Japanese 1915.

Pen·co \ˈpeŋ-(ˌ)kō\. City, Concepción prov., S cen. Chile, on coast N of Concepción; pop. (1960c) 15,483.

Pen·del·i·kon \ˈpen-de-li-ˈkȯn\ *or* **Pen·tel·i·cus** \pen-ˈtel-i-kəs\. Mountain, E cen. Greece, 10 m. NE of Athens; 3639 ft.; yields excellent marble.

Pen·dem·bu \pen-ˈdem-(ˌ)bü\. Town, SE Sierra Leone, W Africa, near border of Liberia; terminus of railroad (227 m. long) from Freetown.

Pen·der \ˈpen-dər\. **1** County in North Carolina. See table at NORTH CAROLINA.

2 Village, ⊗ of Thurston co., NE Nebraska; pop. (1970c) 1229; agricultural implements.

Pen·dle·ton \ˈpen-dᵊl-tən\. **1** Name of counties in two states of the U.S. See tables at KENTUCKY and WEST VIRGINIA.

2 City, ⊗ of Umatilla co., NE Oregon, on Umatilla river ab. 42 m. NW of La Grande; pop. (1970c) 13,167; leather goods, flour, Indian blankets, canned vegetables; railroad shops; diversified agriculture; Blue Mountain Community Coll. (1962); center of E Oregon cattle country in 1870's and 1880's.

Pend Oreille \ˌpän-də-ˈrā\. 1 River, N Idaho and NE Washington, outlet of Pend Oreille Lake; ab. 100 m. long; flows W and N into Columbia river in British Columbia near Washington boundary.

2 County in Washington. See table at WASHINGTON.

Pend Oreille, Mount. Peak, Bonner co., N Idaho; 6754 ft.

Pend Oreille Lake. Lake, cen. Bonner co., N Idaho; an expansion of Clark Fork.

Pe·ne·do \pə-ˈned-(ˌ)ü\. City, Alagoas state, E Brazil, on the São Francisco near its mouth 70 m. SW of Maceió; pop. (1968e) 27,179.

Penedos de São Pedro e São Paulo. See SAINT PAUL'S ROCKS.

Pen·e·tan·gui·shene \ˌpen-ə-ˈtaŋ-gwə-ˌshēn\. Town, Simcoe co., SE Ontario, Canada, on an inlet of Georgian Bay 29 m. NNW of Barrie; pop. (1971p) 5491; summer resort; formerly Canada's naval station on the Great Lakes; has memorial church commemorating the establishment of the Jesuits on this site 1634. Visited by Champlain 1615.

Peneus. See PINIÓS.

Pen·field \ˈpen-ˌfēld\. Town, Monroe co., W New York, ab. 7 m. SE of Rochester; pop. (1970c) 23,782.

Pen·gan·ga \pen-ˈgəŋ-gə, peŋ-\. River, cen. India; ab. 200 m. long; flows E to the Wardha river.

P'eng–hu \ˈpəŋ-ˈhü\. 1 Island group, Formosa Strait. See PESCADORES.

2 Island, chief of the Pescadores group.

3 *or formerly* **Ma·ko** \ˈmä-ˈkō\ *or* **Ma·kung** *or* **Ma·kun** \ˈmä-ˈgüŋ\. Town on P'eng-hu I., Pescadores; chief town of the island group, before World War II developed by Japan as a naval base; transferred to China 1946; now administratively part of Taiwan.

P'eng–lai \ˈpəŋ-ˈlī\ *or formerly* **Teng·chow** \ˈdəŋ-ˈjō\. Town on N coast of Shantung Penin., Fukien prov., NE China, on Strait of Pohai; has good harbor.

P'eng–p'u \ˈpəŋ-ˈpü\. Town, Anhwei prov., E China, on Huai river 100 m. NW of Nanking; government base during civil war 1946 ff.; evacuated Jan. 19, 1949.

Pen·guin \ˈpen-gwən, ˈpeŋ-\. Municipality and seaport on N coast of Tasmania, Australia, 10 m. E of Burnie; munic. pop. (1970e) 5000; tourist resort.

Penhsihu. See PEN-CH'I.

Pe·nig \ˈpā-nig, -nik\. Industrial town, Karl-Marx-Stadt dist., East Germany, ab. 30 m. SE of Leipzig; site of concentration camp during World War II.

Pen·i·kese Island \ˌpen-ə-ˌkēs-\. Small island at S end of Buzzards Bay, Massachusetts, N of Cuttyhunk I.; former school of natural history, estab. 1873 by Louis Agassiz, and game sanctuary.

Peninsula, Point. Point, N New York, extending into Lake Ontario NW of Sackets Harbor.

Peninsula, The. 1 A district in SE Virginia, bet. the York and James rivers; Fort Monroe is at its SE tip; Richmond, to the NW, was Union objective in an unsuccessful campaign Apr. 4–July 1, 1862 during the Civil War; McClellan was opposed by Gen. Johnston and after Fair Oaks (*q.v.*) by Robert E. Lee who took the offensive at Mechanicsville June 26. See also GAINES' MILL and MALVERN HILL.

2 The Iberian Peninsula, including Spain and Portugal; scene of 5th phase of Napoleonic Wars, the Peninsular War 1808–14, in which the British, Portuguese, and Spanish successfully opposed Napoleon's forces and Wellington earned for himself the title of duke; chief battles at La Coruña, Talavera de la Reina, and Vitoria (*qq.v.*).

Peninsula Point. Point at S tip of peninsula forming E side of Little Bay de Noc, Delta co., S Michigan penin., jutting into Green Bay.

Pen·ja·mo \ˈpen-hə-ˌmō\. Town, SW Guanajuato state, cen. Mexico, 50 m. SW of Guanajuato; munic. pop. (1970p) 89,548.

Penjdeh. See PANJDEH.

Pen·ju Islands \pen-ˌjü-\; *formerly* **Schild·pad Islands** \ˌskilt-pät-\ *or* **Schil·pad Islands** \ˌskil-\ *also* **Tur·tle Islands** \ˌtərt-ᵊl-\. Group of islands, in E part of the Gulf of Tomini, off NE coast of Celebes I., Indonesia; extend nearly 80 m. E and W; chief islands Batudaka (largest), Talatakoh, and Togian.

Penki. See PEN-CH'I.

Pen·maen·mawr \ˌpen-mīn-ˈmau̇(ə)r\. Urban district, Caernarvonshire, NW Wales, on coast near NE entrance to Menai Strait; pop. (1971p) 3998; resort.

Pen·march \pa^{n}-ˈmär\. Village, Finistère dept., NW France, 18 m. SW of Quimper on a small peninsula which ends in **Point Penmarch;** pop. (1962c) 544; nearby are remains of the seaport which flourished 14th–16th cents.

Pen·ne \ˈpan-(ˌ)ā\ *or anc.* **Pin·na** \ˈpin-ə\. Commune, Pescara prov., Abruzzi, cen. Italy, 15 m. W of Pescara; pop. (1968e) 12,099; cathedral.

Pen·nell, Mount \-pə-ˈnel\. Peak, E Garfield co., S Utah; 11,371 ft.

Pen·ner \ˈpen-ər\. River, SE cen. India; ab. 350 m. long; rises in SE Mysore, flows N and E through S Andhra Pradesh to Bay of Bengal 15 m. N of Nellore.

Penn Hills \ˈpen-\. Urban township, Allegheny co., SW Pennsylvania, E suburb of Pittsburgh; pop. (1970c) 62,886.

Pennine Alps. See table at ALPS.

Pen·nine Chain \ˈpen-ˌīn-\. Mountain range extending S from the Scottish border to Derbyshire and Staffordshire in cen. England; highest peak **Cross Fell** \ˌkrȯs-ˈfel\ 2930 ft.

Pen·ning·ton \ˈpen-iŋ-tən\. Counties in two states of the U.S. See tables at MINNESOTA and SOUTH DAKOTA.

Penn·sau·ken \pen-ˈsȯ-kən\. Township, Camden co., SW New Jersey, just E of Camden; pop. (1970c) 36,394.

Penns Grove \ˈpenz-\. Borough, Salem co., SW New Jersey, on Delaware river opp. Wilmington, Delaware, and 24 m. SW of Camden; pop. (1970c) 5727.

Penn·syl·va·nia \ˌpen(t)-səl-ˈvā-nyə, -nē-ə, *rapid* -sə-ˈvā-\. A middle Atlantic state of U.S.A., bounded on N by New York, on E by New York and New Jersey, on S by Delaware, Maryland, and West Virginia, and on W by West Virginia and Ohio; 33d state in area, 45,333 sq. m., not including 735 sq. m. of water of the Great Lakes (land area 45,026 sq. m.); 3d state in population, (1970c) 11,793,909; ✱ Harrisburg; one of the original states of the Union, the 2d to ratify the Federal Constitution (1787).

Nickname: Keystone State. *State flower:* Mountain laurel. *Motto:* Virtue, Liberty, and Independence. *Rivers:* Delaware, forming E boundary; Susquehanna, flowing N to S through E cen. region; Monongahela in W and SW region, uniting at Pittsburgh with Allegheny river to form the Ohio river; Juniata, in S cen. region, flowing E into the Susquehanna; the Schuylkill in the SE flowing through Philadelphia to the Delaware. *Highest point:* Mt. Davis, 3213 ft., in Somerset co. *Chief products:* Corn, wheat, oats; dairy products, coal, iron ore; manufacturing: iron and steel; electrical machinery, apparel, chemicals, transportation equipment. *Chief cities:* Philadelphia, Pittsburgh, Erie, Allentown, Scranton, Reading. See *Table of States* at UNITED STATES. Divided into the following 67 counties (for pronunciation of their names, see their individual entries):

NAME	LOCATION	AREA[1] (sq. m.)	POP. (1970c)	CO. SEAT
Adams	S	526	56,937	Gettysburg
Allegheny	SW	728	1,605,133	Pittsburgh
Armstrong	W	658	75,590	Kittanning
Beaver	W	440	208,418	Beaver
Bedford	S	1,018	42,353	Bedford
Berks	SE	862	296,382	Reading
Blair	S cen.	531	133,356	Hollidaysburg
Bradford	N	1,148	57,962	Towanda
Bucks	SE	614	415,056	Doylestown
Butler	W	794	127,941	Butler
Cambria	SW cen.	695	186,785	Ebensburg
Cameron	N cen.	401	7,096	Emporium
Carbon	E	405	50,573	Jim Thorpe
Centre	cen.	1,115	99,267	Bellefonte
Chester	SE	761	278,311	West Chester
Clarion	W.	597	38,414	Clarion
Clearfield	W cen.	1,144	74,619	Clearfield
Clinton	cen.	902	37,721	Lock Haven
Columbia	E cen.	484	55,114	Bloomsburg
Crawford	NW	1,012	81,342	Meadville
Cumberland	S	555	158,177	Carlisle
Dauphin	SE cen.	518	223,834	Harrisburg
Delaware	SE	184	601,425	Media
Elk	NW cen.	807	37,770	Ridgway
Erie	NW corner	813	263,654	Erie
Fayette	SW	802	154,667	Uniontown
Forest	NW	419	4,926	Tionesta
Franklin	S	754	100,833	Chambersburg
Fulton	S	435	10,776	McConnellsburg
Greene	SW corner	578	36,090	Waynesburg
Huntingdon	S cen.	894	39,108	Huntingdon
Indiana	W cen.	825	79,451	Indiana
Jefferson	W cen.	652	43,695	Brookville
Juniata	S cen.	386	16,712	Mifflintown
Lackawanna	NE	454	234,107	Scranton
Lancaster	SE	946	320,079	Lancaster
Lawrence	W	367	107,374	New Castle
Lebanon	SE cen.	363	99,665	Lebanon
Lehigh	E	348	253,304	Allentown
Luzerne	E	888	342,301	Wilkes-Barre
Lycoming	N cen.	1,216	113,296	Williamsport
McKean	N	997	51,915	Smethport
Mercer	W	681	127,225	Mercer
Mifflin	cen.	431	45,268	Lewistown
Monroe	E	611	45,422	Stroudsburg
Montgomery	SE	496	623,921	Norristown
Montour	E cen.	130	16,508	Danville
Northampton	E	376	214,368	Easton
Northumberland	E cen.	453	99,190	Sunbury
Perry	S cen.	551	28,615	New Bloomfield
Philadelphia[2]	SE	129	1,950,098	Philadelphia
Pike	NE	542	11,818	Milford
Potter	N	1,092	16,395	Coudersport
Schuylkill	E cen.	784	160,089	Pottsville
Snyder	cen.	327	29,269	Middleburg
Somerset	S	1,085	76,037	Somerset
Sullivan	NE cen.	478	5,961	Laporte
Susquehanna	NE	835	34,344	Montrose
Tioga	N	1,150	39,691	Wellsboro
Union	cen.	318	28,603	Lewisburg
Venango	NW	678	62,353	Franklin
Warren	NW	916	47,682	Warren
Washington	SW	857	210,876	Washington
Wayne	NE corner	743	29,581	Honesdale
Westmoreland	SW	1,024	376,933	Greensburg
Wyoming	NE	398	19,082	Tunkhannock
York	S	909	272,603	York

[1]Area = land area.
[2]Coextensive with Philadelphia city since annexation by city in 1854 of remaining part of county.

History: Étienne Brulé first recorded white man to visit this area 1615–16; first settlement made by Swedes on Tinicum I. (*q.v.*) 1643; royal charter granted to William Penn, a Quaker, 1681; settlement encouraged by Penn 1682 ff.; first hospital in U.S. established in Philadelphia 1751; S boundary line determined 1763 and 1767 (see MASON AND DIXON'S LINE); Declaration of Independence pronounced in Philadelphia 1776, and 1st Constitutional Convention chosen; delegation headed by Benjamin Franklin represented Pennsylvania in Federal Constitutional Convention 1787; ratified Federal Constitution Dec. 12, 1787; Johnstown flood disaster May 31, 1889.

Penn Yan \'pen-'yan\. Village, ⊗ of Yates co., W New York, at outlet of Lake Keuka 30 m. SW of Auburn; pop. (1970c) 5293; summer resort; wineries, canneries, boatyards; diversified agriculture; site of Jemima Wilkinson's Jerusalem colony 1790–1819.

Pe·nob·scot \pə-'näb-skət, -ˌskät\. 1 River, cen. Maine; 101 m. long; navigable to Bangor (60 m.); flows S into Penobscot Bay; formed by confluence in N cen. Penobscot co. of E branch, from the N, and W branch, 112 m. long, which is formed by junction of headstreams in Somerset co., W Maine, and flows generally SE, through three lakes (Seboomook, Chesuncook, and Pemadumcook).
2 County in Maine. See table at MAINE.

Penobscot Bay. Inlet of Atlantic Ocean, SW Hancock co., SE Waldo co., and E Knox co., S Maine, receiving the Penobscot river on the N, and containing a number of islands including Deer I., North Haven I., Vinalhaven I., Isle au Haut; 30 m. long.

Pe·ñón de Vé·lez de la Go·me·ra \pā-ˌnyōn-də-'vā-ləs-ˌdel-ə-gō-'mer-ə\. Small island off N coast of Morocco, part of former Spanish Morocco, ab. 75 m. SE of Ceuta; pop. (1960c) 152; a presidio of Spain.

Pe·no·no·mé \ˌpān-ə-nō-'mä\. Town, cen. Panama, ✱ of Coclé prov.; pop. (1970p) 5067.

Pe·not, Mount \-pə-'nō\. Mountain, cen. Malekula I., New Hebrides, SW Pacific; 2922 ft.; highest point on the island.

Pen·rhyn \'pen-(ˌ)rin\. 1 *or* **Ton·ga·re·va** \ˌtäŋ-(g)ə-'rev-ə\. Island (atoll), Northern Cook Is., cen. Pacific Ocean; land area ab. 4 sq. m., with lagoon area of 108 sq. m.; pop. (1968e) 642; chief village Omoka; administratively part of Cook Is.
2 Parish, NE Caernarvonshire, NW Wales, SSE of Bangor; pop. (1961c) 1252; large slate quarries.

Pen·rith \'pen-rith\. Urban district, Cumberland, NW England, on the Eamont 16 m. SSE of Carlisle; pop. (1971p) 11,299; tourist resort on the edge of the Lake District; trade center in agricultural section; ruins of 14th cent. castle.

Pen·sa·cola \ˌpen(t)-sə-'kō-lə\. City, ⊗ of Escambia co., NW Florida, on the Gulf of Mexico 10 m. E of Alabama border; pop. (1970c) 59,507; boats, nylon, chemicals, cottonseed oil, lumber, naval stores; Pensacola Junior Coll. (1948), Univ. of West Florida (1967); U.S. Naval Air Station (principal U.S. Navy flight training school). Originally settled by Spanish 1559–61 and resettled 1596; to England 1763; reverted to Spain 1783; captured by U.S. forces under Andrew Jackson 1814 and passed to U.S. 1821; in Civil War held alternately by Union and Confederate forces.

Pensacola Bay. Inlet of Gulf of Mexico on S coast of Santa Rosa and Escambia cos., NW Florida, receiving the Escambia river on the NW and the Yellow river on the NE; the city of Pensacola is on its W shore.

Pensacola Dam *or formerly* **Grand River Dam.** Dam across Grand (Neosho) river, NE Oklahoma; height 145 ft.; completed 1940; impounds water for power; forms lake 64 sq. m. variously known as **Lake of the Cher·o·kees** \-'cher-ə-ˌkēz, -ˌcher-ə-'\, **Grand Lake,** and **Pensacola Reservoir.**

Pens·hurst \'penz-(ˌ)hərst\. Town, Kent, SE England, 4½ m. SW of Tonbridge; mansion of Sidney family, birthplace of Sir Philip Sidney.

Pen·tap·o·lis \pen-'tap-ə-ləs\. One of several ancient groups of five cities, specif.: in Italy: Rimini, Ancona, Fano, Pesaro, and Senigallia; in Asia Minor: Cnidus, Cos, Lindus, Camirus, and Ialysus; in Cyrenaica: Apollonia, Arsinoë, Berenice, Cyrene, and Ptolemaïs.

Pen·te·cost \'pent-i-ˌkȯst\. Island, NE New Hebrides Is., SW Pacific Ocean, 5 m. S of Maewo I. and ab. 60 m. SE of Espíritu Santo; 28 m. long by 7 m. wide; pop. (1967c) 6801.

Pentelicus. See PENDELIKON.

Pen·thièvre \pa^n-'tyevr^ə\. Ancient countship, Brittany, NW France, within region of present Cotes-du-Nord dept.; ✱ (1134–1420) Lamballe, later ✱ Guingamp; became duchy 1569.

Pen·tic·ton \pen-'tik-tən\. City, at S end of Okanagan Lake, S British Columbia, Canada, ab. 160 m. E of Vancouver; pop. (1971p) 17,702; lumber, sheet metal products; ships fruit; incorporated 1948.

Pent·land Firth \'pent-lən(d)-\. Channel separating the Orkney Is. from the mainland of Scotland; 14 m. long by 6½ to 8 m. wide.

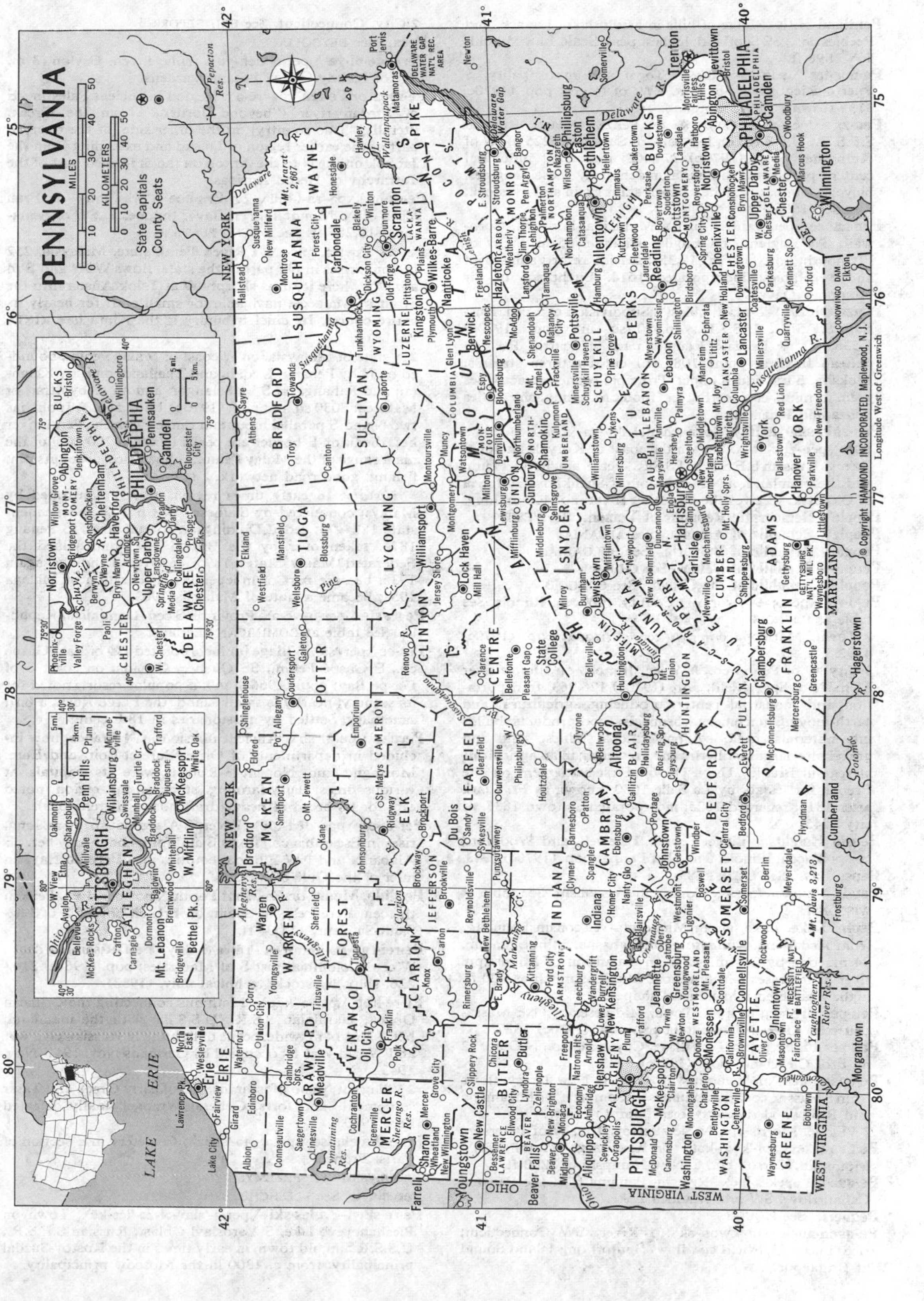
PENNSYLVANIA
MILES
0 10 20 30 40 50
KILOMETERS
0 10 20 30 40 50
State Capitals
County Seats
LAKE ERIE
NEW YORK
NEW JERSEY
OHIO
WEST VIRGINIA
MARYLAND
DELAWARE
ERIE
CRAWFORD
WARREN
MC KEAN
POTTER
TIOGA
BRADFORD
SUSQUEHANNA
WAYNE
PIKE
MERCER
VENANGO
FOREST
ELK
CAMERON
CLINTON
LYCOMING
SULLIVAN
WYOMING
LACKAWANNA
LUZERNE
MONROE
CARBON
NORTHAMPTON
LEHIGH
BUCKS
MONTGOMERY
PHILADELPHIA
DELAWARE
CHESTER
LANCASTER
BERKS
SCHUYLKILL
LEBANON
DAUPHIN
NORTHUMBERLAND
MONTOUR
COLUMBIA
UNION
SNYDER
MIFFLIN
JUNIATA
PERRY
CUMBERLAND
YORK
ADAMS
FRANKLIN
FULTON
BEDFORD
HUNTINGDON
CENTRE
BLAIR
CAMBRIA
CLEARFIELD
JEFFERSON
CLARION
INDIANA
ARMSTRONG
BUTLER
LAWRENCE
BEAVER
ALLEGHENY
WESTMORELAND
WASHINGTON
GREENE
FAYETTE
SOMERSET
Erie
Meadville
Warren
Bradford
Oil City
Franklin
Titusville
New Castle
Butler
Kittanning
Indiana
Johnstown
Altoona
State College
Lock Haven
Williamsport
Towanda
Scranton
Wilkes-Barre
Hazleton
Pottsville
Allentown
Bethlehem
Easton
Reading
Lancaster
York
Harrisburg
Carlisle
Chambersburg
Gettysburg
Norristown
Chester
Upper Darby
Camden
Trenton
Wilmington
Pittsburgh
McKeesport
Washington
Greensburg
Uniontown
Connellsville
Somerset
Bedford
Huntingdon
Lewistown
Sunbury
Shamokin
Bloomsburg
Berwick
Nanticoke
Carbondale
Honesdale
Stroudsburg
Levittown
Bristol
Hagerstown
Cumberland
Morgantown
Youngstown
Mt. Davis 3,213
Mt. Ararat 2,667
Delaware R.
Susquehanna R.
Allegheny R.
Monongahela R.
Ohio R.
Juniata R.
DELAWARE WATER GAP NAT'L REC. AREA
GETTYSBURG NAT'L MIL. PK.
FT. NECESSITY NAT'L BATTLEFIELD
CONOWINGO DAM
PITTSBURGH
ALLEGHENY
PHILADELPHIA
Longitude West of Greenwich
© Copyright HAMMOND INCORPORATED, Maplewood, N.J.

Pentland Hills. Range of hills in Midlothian, Lanark, and Peebles cos., SE Scotland; highest peak **Scald Law** \ˈskȯld-ˈlȯ\ 1898 ft.

Pe·ñue·les \ˌpān-yə-ˈwāl-əs\. Town and municipality, S Puerto Rico; town ab. 8 m. NW of Ponce; pop. (1970c) 3139 (town), 15,915 (munic.).

Pen·za \ˈpen-zə\. City, ✱ of Penza Oblast, Russian S.F.S.R., U.S.S.R.; on left bank of Sura river 225 m. W of Kuibyshev; pop. (1970p) 374,000; important industrial center, producing industrial machinery, diesel engines, bicycles, lumber, watches, paper; ships grain and livestock; founded 1666.

Pen·zance \pen-ˈzan(t)s, pən-\. Municipal borough, Cornwall, SW England, on English Channel 65 m. WSW of Plymouth; pop. (1971p) 19,352; seaside resort; ships fruit and vegetables; incorporated 1614. Birthplace of Sir Humphry Davy.

Penza Oblast \-ˈō-bləst, -ˌblast\. Subdivision of E cen. Russian S.F.S.R., U.S.S.R.; 16,680 sq. m.; pop. (1970p) 1,536,000; ✱ Penza. Occupies part of central Russian plateau (highest point 1089 ft.) cut by three streams: Moksha, Sura, and Khoper. Principal economic activities grain farming, engineering and food processing; chief cities Penza and Kuznetsk.

Pen·zhin·ska·ya Bay \ˌpen-ˌzhin(t)-skə-yə-\ *or* **Pen·zhi·na Bay** \ˌpen-zhə-nə-\. Bay on the coast of Koryak National Okrug, Russian S.F.S.R., U.S.S.R., bet. Kamchatka Penin. and the mainland, a NE extension of Shelikhov Gulf, Sea of Okhotsk; receives the **Penzhina River,** ab. 400 m. long.

People's Democratic Republic of Yemen. See YEMEN 1.

People's Republic of Albania. See ALBANIA.

People's Republic of Bulgaria. See BULGARIA.

People's Republic of China. See CHINA.

People's Republic of the Congo. See CONGO 3.

Pe·o·ria \pē-ˈōr-ē-ə, -ˈȯr-\. 1 County, NW cen. Illinois. See table at ILLINOIS.

2 Town, Maricopa co., SW cen. Arizona; pop. (1970c) 4792.

3 City, ⊗ of Peoria co., NW cen. Illinois, on Illinois river 67 m. N of Springfield; pop. (1970c) 126,963; transportation and industrial center, producing agricultural and earth-moving machinery, chemicals, food products, building materials, radio equipment; coal mines, sand and gravel pits, large distilleries and breweries; in an agricultural region; Bradley Univ. (1896). First settlement on site French fort estab. by La Salle 1680; known as Ft. Clark after 1813; renamed 1825; incorporated as town 1835, as city 1845.

Peoria Heights. Village, Peoria, Tazewell, and Woodford cos., NW cen. Illinois, 5 m. N of Peoria; pop. (1970c) 7943.

Peper Bay. See LADA BAY.

Pep·in \ˈpip-ən, ˈpep-\. County in Wisconsin. See table at WISCONSIN.

Pepin, Lake. Lake, along Minnesota-Wisconsin boundary from Red Wing, Minnesota, to Wabasha, Minnesota; ab. 34 m. long by 2–4 m. wide; an expansion of Mississippi river as it passes bet. limestone bluffs as much as 400 ft. high, weathered into unusual shapes.

Pep·per·ell \ˈpep-(ə-)rəl\. Town, Middlesex co., NE Massachusetts, 11 m. NE of Fitchburg; pop. (1970c) 5887.

Pep·per Pike \ˈpep-ər-\. Village, Cuyahoga co., N Ohio, 12 m. E of Cleveland; pop. (1970c) 5933.

Pe·quan·nock \pi-ˈkwän-ək\. 1 River, N New Jersey; flows from E Sussex co. SE and unites at Pompton with Ramapo and Ringwood rivers to form Pompton river.

2 Village, Morris co., N New Jersey, 7 m. W of Paterson.

Pe·quaw·ket \pi-ˈkwȯ-kət\ *or* **Kear·sarge** \ˈki(ə)r-ˌsärj\. Mountain, Carroll co., E New Hampshire; 3260 ft.

Pe·que·ní \ˌpek-ə-ˈnē\. River in Panama E of the Panama Canal; flows SW into Madden Lake.

Pequeri. See PIQUIRI.

Pe·quon·nock \pi-ˈkwȯn-ək\. 1 River, SW Connecticut; rises in cen. Fairfield co., flows S into Long Island Sound at Bridgeport.

2 City, Connecticut. See BRIDGEPORT 3.

Pera. See BEYOĞLU.

Per·a·de·ni·ya \ˌper-ə-ˈdēn-yə\. Village, cen. Ceylon, 3 m. SW of Kandy (*q.v.*); botanic gardens.

Pe·raea *or* **Pe·rea** \pə-ˈrē-ə\. Region in ancient Palestine, E of Jordan river ("beyond Jordan," from the Greek, literally, "[the country] on the other side [of the river]"); part of the earlier region of Gilead and extending from the Jabbok on the N to the Arnon on the S; formed part of the Tetrarchy of Herod Antipas.

Pe·ra·hu \pə-ˈrä-(ˌ)hü\ *or* **Pra·hoe** \ˈprä-(ˌ)hü\ *or* **Prau** \ˈprä-(ˌ)ü\. Mountain, cen. Java, Indonesia, SW of Semarang; 10,285 ft. See DIJENG PLATEAU.

Pe·rak \ˈper-ə, ˈpir-ə\. 1 River, Perak state, Malaysia; 252 m. long; rises in NE part of the state, flows WSW and S to ab. 4°N where it turns sharply W at Telok Anson into the Strait of Malacca; navigable for small craft for nearly its entire course. Its chief tributary is the Kinta (see KINTA VALLEY).

2 A state of Malaysia, on W coast of Malay Penin., bounded on N by Penang, Kedah, and Thailand, on E by Kelantan and Pahang, on S by Selangor, and on W by Strait of Malacca; 8030 sq. m.; pop. (1970p) 1,562,566; ✱ Ipoh; has two N and S parallel mountain ranges with the Perak river bet. them; on E border are peaks (6000 to 7000 ft.) of the main range of the Malay Penin.; rubber, rice, coconuts, tin; fishing; good road network.

History: In early times region entirely controlled by Malays; conquered by Siamese 1818 but an independent state 1824–74; ceded Dindings, a coastal strip, to Penang 1874; taken over by the British 1875 and joined the Federated Malay States 1895; received Dindings again 1935; became part of independent Federation of Malaya 1957; became a state of Malaysia 1963.

Pe·ra·via \ˌper-ə-ˈvē-ə\. Province, S cen. Dominican Republic. See table at DOMINICAN REPUBLIC.

Per·cé \per-ˈsā\. Village (unincorporated), ⊗ of East Gaspé co., E Gaspé Penin., SE Quebec, Canada, on coast S of Gaspé Bay; pop. (1966c) 569; a popular resort, noted for its scenery; nearby is small island, the **Percé Rock,** a bird sanctuary. Settled by missionaries in 18th cent.

Perche \ˈpe(ə)rsh\. Ancient division in N France, now included in departments of Orne, Eure-et-Loir, and Eure; Mortagne and Nogent-le-Rotrou were its capitals at various times; dairy-farming, stock-raising region, noted esp. for its breed of heavy draft horses (Percherons).

Per·di·do \pər-ˈdēd-(ˌ)ō\. River, S Alabama; ab. 60 m. long; rises in Escambia co., flows S and forms boundary bet. SE Alabama and NW Florida; empties into **Perdido Bay,** an inlet of the Gulf of Mexico.

Perdido, Mount *or Fr.* **Mont Per·du** \mōⁿ-per-dᵫ\. Peak in the cen. Pyrenees, NE Spain, on French border S of Luz-Saint-Sauveur; 11,004 ft.

Pe·rei·ra \pə-ˈre(ə)r-ə, -ˈrā-rə\. City, ✱ of Risaralda dept., W cen. Colombia, just S of Manizales; pop. (1968e) 216,-226; ships livestock; technical univ. (1958).

Pe·re·kop \ˌper-ə-ˈkäp\. 1 Isthmus connecting the Crimean Oblast, Ukrainian S.S.R., U.S.S.R., with the mainland; bet. 4 and 14 m. wide. Scene of fighting in Russian civil war and World War II; occupied by Germans Nov. 1941–Nov. 1943.

2 Village at N end of isthmus, site of early Greek and Tatar settlements and forts. General Wrangel finally defeated here 1920.

Père–La·chaise \ˌpe(ə)r-lə-ˈshāz\. Cemetery in E section of Paris, France.

Peremyshl. See PRZEMYŚL.

Pereslavl. See PLESHCHEYEVO.

Pe·re·slavl–Za·les·ski \ˌper-ə-ˈslav-əl-zə-ˈles-kē\. Town on Pleshcheyevo lake, S Yaroslavl Oblast, Russian S.F.S.R., U.S.S.R.; an old town, in early times in the Rostov-Suzdal principality; from c. 1300 in the Moscow principality.

Pe·re·ya·slav \ˌper-ə-yə-ˈslav\. Medieval principality on the N bank of the Dnieper E of Kiev 11th–13th cents.; chief town Pereyaslav (now Pereyaslav-Khmelnitski).

Pereyaslav–Khmel·nit·ski \-kmel-ˈnēt-skē\ *or formerly* **Pereyaslav.** Town, E Kiev Oblast, Ukrainian S.S.R., U.S.S.R., on a small tributary near the left bank of the Dnieper, 50 m. SE of Kiev; pop. (1967e) 19,000; an agricultural town that has been historically important; founded before 907 by Vladimir the Great; chief town of principality from 1054 and a Russian southern outpost for several centuries; plundered by Mongols in 1239; in 17th cent. a key town during Cossack Wars (1648–1712) and headquarters of Bogdan Chmielnicki; treaty signed here 1654; occupied by Germans in World War II 1941–44.

Pereyaslav–Ryazanski. See RYAZAN 2.

Per·ga \ˈpər-gə\. Chief town of ancient Pamphylia, Asia Minor; its ruins are at modern **Mur·ta·na** \ˌmu̇r-tə-ˈnä\, Turkey; here Paul and Barnabas began their first mission in Asia Minor (*Acts* xiii. 13).

Per·ga·mi·no \ˌper-gə-ˈmē-(ˌ)nō\. City, N Buenos Aires prov., E Argentina, 141 m. WNW of Buenos Aires; pop. (1960c) 41,612.

Per·ga·mum \ˈpər-gə-məm\ *or* **Per·ga·mus** \-məs\; *Gk.* **Per·ga·mon** \-ˌmän\ *or* **Per·ga·mos** \-məs, -ˌmäs\. Ancient Greek kingdom, at its height under Eumenes I and the Attalids, 263–133 B.C., covering most of W Asia Minor; became ally of Rome and on death of Attalus III kingdom bequeathed to Romans; divided bet. Pontus and new province of Asia; its ✱ Pergamum (now Bergama, *q.v.*).

Per·gi·ne Val·su·ga·na \ˈper-ji-nā-ˌväl-su̇-ˈgän-ə\. Commune, Trento prov., Trentino-Alto Adige, NE Italy, 5 m. E of Trento; pop. (1968e) 11,898; 16th cent. church; health resort with mineral springs.

Per·go·la \ˈper-gə-lə\. Commune, Pesaro e Urbino prov., Marches, cen. Italy, 25 m. S by W of Pesaro; pop. (1968e) 9000; cathedral.

Per·gu·sa, Lake of \-per-ˈgü-zə\. See ENNA 2.

Per·i·bon·ca \ˌper-ə-ˈbäŋ-kə\. River, S cen. Quebec, Canada; 280 m. long; rises in cen. Quebec, flows S into Lake St. John.

Pe·ri·co \pə-ˈrē-(ˌ)kō\. 1 Town and municipality, Matanzas prov., W cen. Cuba; town is on railroad 20 m. SE of Cárdenas; munic. pop. (1967e) 19,190.

2 Small fortified island, Bay of Panama, just off SE end of Panama Canal.

Pé·riers \per-ˈyā\. Town, Manche dept., NW France, 14 m. NW of Saint-Lô; pop. (1962c) 2728; taken in battle for Saint-Lô July 16–18, 1944.

Pé·ri·gord \ˌper-ə-ˈgȯ(ə)r\. Old division of N Guienne prov., SW France; ✱ Périgueux.

Pé·ri·gueux \ˌper-ə-ˈgə(r)\ *or anc.* **Ve·su·na** \vi-ˈs(y)ü-nə\. Commune, ✱ of Dordogne dept., SW cen. France, 66 m. ENE of Bordeaux; pop. (1968c) 37,450; road and rail junction, hog market; hardware, chemicals, leather goods, truffles, wine; 12th cent. cathedral, extensive Roman remains (arena, aqueducts, baths, temples, Tour de Vesonne). A settlement of the Petrocorii (whence the modern name); medieval town developed 5th–14th cents. around an abbey; suffered heavily in Wars of Religion 16th cent.

Pe·rim \pə-ˈrim\ *or Arab.* **Ba·rīm** \bə-ˈrēm\. Island in Bab al-Mandab Strait at the entrance to the Red Sea, part of Yemen (✱ Aden); 5 sq. m.; 96 m. W of Aden; under British control as part of Aden protectorate 1857–1967; formerly site of coaling station.

Pe·ri·sté·ri \ˌper-i-ˈster-ē\. Town, part of Greater Athens, E Greece; pop. (1971p) 118,765.

Pe·ri·ya·ku·lam \ˌper-i-ˈyək-ə-ləm\. Town, S Tamil Nadu, S India, 38 m. NNW of Madurai; pop. (1961c) 36,335.

Pe·ri·yar \ˌper-i-ˈyär\. River, cen. Kerala, S India; ab. 140 m. long; flows N and W to Arabian Sea N of Cochin; navigable for 60 m.; in Travancore hills has dam 176 ft. high (completed 1895) and tunnel, used for irrigation.

Per·kam, Cape \-pər-ˈkäm\ *or formerly* **Cape d'Ur·ville** \-ˈdər-ˌvil\. Cape on N coast of Irian Barat, Indonesia, just E of Sarera Bay near mouth of the Mamberamo river.

Per·ka·sie \ˈpər-kə-sē\. Borough, Bucks co., SE Pennsylvania, 18 m. SSE of Allentown; pop. (1970c) 5451; clothing, cigars, electrical switches.

Per·kins \ˈpər-kənz\. Name of counties in two states of the U.S. See tables at NEBRASKA and SOUTH DAKOTA.

Perkins, Mount. Peak in Sierra Nevada, E Fresno co., S cen. California; 12,557 ft.

Perlas, Archipélago de las. See PEARL ISLANDS 2.

Perlas, Cayos de. See PEARL CAYS.

Per·las, Pun·ta de \ˌpün-tə-dā-ˈpe(ə)r-ləs\ *or angl.* **Pearl Point** \ˌpər(-ə)l-\. Cape projecting S on E cen. coast of Nicaragua, enclosing Perlas Lagoon.

Perlas Lagoon *also* **Pearl Lagoon** \ˌpər(-ə)l-\. Inlet of the Caribbean Sea on E cen. coast of Nicaragua.

Per·le·berg \ˈper-lə-ˌbərg, -ˌbe(ə)rg\. City, Schwerin dist., East Germany, on a tributary of the Elbe 69 m. NW of Potsdam; pop. (1970e) 13,552.

Per·lis \ˈper-ləs\. A state of Malaysia, Malay Penin., bounded on NW, N, and NE by Thailand, on SE by Kedah, and on SW by Andaman Sea; 310 sq. m.; pop. (1970p) 121,062; ✱ Kangar; smallest state of Malaysia; rice, tin.

History: Until 1821 subject to Kedah; made separate state by the Siamese 1841; came under British protection by treaty of 1909, in which Siam ceded to Great Britain its rights over the state; became one of the five Unfederated Malay States of British Malaya; part of independent Federation of Malaya 1957; became a state of Malaysia 1963.

Perm \ˈpərm, ˈpe(ə)rm\ *or formerly* **Mo·lo·tov** \ˈmäl-ə-ˌtȯf, ˈmȯ-lə-, ˈmōl-ə-, -ˌtȯv\. City, ✱ of Perm Oblast, Russian S.F.S.R., U.S.S.R., in S cen. part W of Ural Mts. on Kama river; pop. (1970p) 850,000; manufactures lumber products, leather, agricultural machinery; metallurgical industries; oil refining. A village since early times; settlement added to by Russian merchant princes 1568; copper-smelting plant established here in early 18th cent.; received name of Perm 1781 when it was made district town; officially called Molotov 1942–58.

Për·met \pər-ˈmet\ *or* **Pre·met** \prə-ˈmet\. 1 Province of S Albania. See table at ALBANIA.

2 Town, its ✱, on the Vijosë river; pop. (1967e) 4310.

Perm Oblast \-ˈō-bləst, -ˌblast\ *or from 1940–57* **Molotov Oblast.** Subdivision of the Russian S.F.S.R., U.S.S.R.; 62,008 sq. m.; pop. (1970p) 3,024,000; ✱ Perm; traversed by the Kama and its tributary the Chusovaya, and along its E border by the W foothills of the Ural Mts. Important mineral reserves: potassium, salt; iron ore, copper, chromite. Chief cities Perm, Berezniki, Solikamsk. In early times occupied by a Finnic people, the Permiaks, whence the former name of the capital city and of the national district (Komi-Permiak, estab. 1925) in NW part; settled by Russian merchant princes in 16th cent.; became part of Ural Area and is now in the Ural Industrial Area (*q.v.*); organized as a subdivision of the Russian S.F.S.R. in 1936.

Per·nam·bu·co \ˌpər-nəm-ˈb(y)ü-(ˌ)kō, ˌper-nəm-ˈbü-\. 1 State, E Brazil; 37,946 sq. m.; pop. (1970p) 5,208,011; ✱ Recife; sugarcane, coffee, cotton, corn; scene of several insurrections in 19th cent.

2 City, its ✱. See RECIFE.

Pernau *or* **Pernov.** See PÄRNU.

Per·nik \ˈpe(ə)r-nik\. 1 Province of W Bulgaria. See table at BULGARIA.

2 Town, its ✱, ab. 15 m. SW of Sofia; pop. (1968e) 79,335; steel works.

Pe·ronne \pā-ˈrȯn\. Town, Somme dept., N France, ab. 35 m. N of Amiens on Somme river; pop. (1962c) 5078; because of its strategic position has been frequently occupied or besieged: by Burgundians 1465, Charles V 1536, British under Wellington 1815, Germans 1871 and in World War I.

Perouse Bay, La. See LA PEROUSE BAY.

Pérouse Island, La. See VANIKORO.

Pérouse Strait, La. See SŌYA STRAIT.

Perovsk. See KZYL-ORDA.

Per·pet·ua, Cape \-pər-ˈpech-ə-wə\. Cape on SW extremity of Lincoln co., W Oregon.

Per·pi·gnan \ˌper-pē-ˈnyä^{n}\. City, ✱ of Pyrénées-Orientales dept., S France, near Mediterranean 96 m. S of Toulouse; pop. (1968c) 102,191; major tourist resort; trades in wine, fruit, and vegetables; ceramics and various handicraft industries; 14th–15th cent. cathedral, 14th cent. univ. building, 14th cent. castle, 17th–18th cent. citadel. Said to have been founded in 10th cent.; capital of Roussillion 12th cent. ff.; chartered 1197; church council met here 1408; united to France 1659.

Per·quim·ans \pər-ˈkwim-ənz\. County of North Carolina. See table at NORTH CAROLINA.

Perrégaux. See MOHAMMADIA.

Perreux–sur–Marne, Le. See LE PERREUX-SUR-MARNE.

Per·rine \ˈpər-ˌīn\. Urban community (unincorporated), Dade co., SE Florida, SW of Miami; pop. (1970c) 10,257.

Per·ris \ˈper-əs\. City, Riverside co., SE California, 37 m. W of Palm Springs; pop. (1970c) 4228; gold and silver mining; concrete blocks, boats.

Per·ro, La·gu·na del \lə-ˌgü-nə-del-ˈper-(ˌ)ō\. Lake in cen. Torrance co., cen. New Mexico.

Perrot, Ile. See ILE PERROT.

Per·ry \ˈper-ē\. **1** Name of counties in ten states of the U.S. See tables at ALABAMA, ARKANSAS, ILLINOIS, INDIANA, KENTUCKY, MISSISSIPPI, MISSOURI, OHIO, PENNSYLVANIA, TENNESSEE.
2 Industrial city, ⊗ of Taylor co., N Florida, 48 m. ESE of Tallahassee; pop. (1970c) 7701; wood products; peanuts.
3 City, ⊗ of Houston co., cen. Georgia; pop. (1970c) 7771; carpets, veneers; peach orchards.
4 City, Dallas co., S cen. Iowa, 32 m. WNW of Des Moines; pop. (1970c) 6906; dairy products, agricultural implements; meat-packing.
5 Village, Wyoming co., W New York, 37 m. SSW of Rochester; pop. (1970c) 4538; knit goods; dairy, poultry farms.
6 City, ⊗ of Noble co., N Oklahoma, 36 m. E of Enid; pop. (1970c) 5341; diversified agriculture.

Per·rys·burg \ˈper-ēz-ˌbərg\. Village, Wood co., NW Ohio, on Maumee river 8 m. SSW of Toledo; pop. (1970c) 7693; metal stampings, cigars; corn, tomatoes.

Per·ry's Victory and International Peace Memorial National Monument \ˈper-ēz-\. See UNITED STATES, *National Monuments.*

Per·ry·ton \ˈper-ēt-ᵊn\. City, ⊗ of Ochiltree co., NW Texas, in the panhandle near the Oklahoma boundary, 58 m. N of Pampa; pop. (1970c) 7810; vehicle bodies, beverages; ships grain and livestock.

Per·ry·ville \ˈper-ē-ˌvil\. **1** City, ⊗ of Perry co., cen. Arkansas; pop. (1970c) 815.
2 City, Boyle co., E cen. Kentucky, 40 m. SW of Lexington; pop. (1970c) 730; scene of indecisive battle Oct. 8, 1862 bet. Confederates under Bragg and Union forces under Buell (Bragg withdrew his forces into Tennessee the next day).
3 City, ⊗ of Perry co., E Missouri, 35 m. NNW of Cape Girardeau; pop. (1970c) 5149; St. Mary's Seminary (1818).

Per·sa·no \pər-ˈsä-nō\. Village, Salerno prov., S Campania, S Italy, SE of Salerno; fighting Sept. 11–13, 1943.

Per·sep·o·lis \pər-ˈsep-ə-ləs\. An ancient capital of Persia, succeeding Pasargadae; its ruins lie ab. 30 m. NE of Shīrāz, SW cen. Iran, covering extensive area and comprising palaces of early Persian kings, staircases, halls, and treasuries. Partially destroyed by Alexander 330 B.C.; place remained of some importance until Arab period. Nearby at Naksh-i-Rustam are notable rock tombs of Darius and others. Below ruins excavations have disclosed remains of villages much older, perhaps of c. 4000 B.C.

Per·se·ver·ance Bay \ˌpər-sə-ˈvir-ən(t)s-\. Bay in SW coast of St. Thomas I., Virgin Is. of the United States.

Per·shing \ˈpər-shiŋ\. County in Nevada. See table at NEVADA.

Persia. See IRAN.

Persian Baluchistan. See BALUCHISTAN 1.

Per·sian Gulf \ˌpər-zhən-\. **1** *or* **Ara·bi·an Gulf** \ə-ˌrā-bē-ən-\ *or anc.* **Si·nus Per·si·cus** \ˌsī-nə-ˈspər-si-kəs\. Arm of the Arabian Sea; 550 m. long by 200 m. max. width; 88,800 sq. m.; average depth 328 ft.; connected with Gulf of Oman and Arabian Sea through Strait of Hormuz; Bahrain and Qeshm only islands of importance.
2 Province of S Iran. See table at IRAN.

Persian Gulf States. Term commonly applied to a number of states on E coast of Arabian Penin.: Bahrain (island group in Persian Gulf), Qatar, and the United Arab Emirates (*qq.v.*); sometimes expanded to include Kuwait.

Persis. See FĀRS.

Per·son \ˈpərs-ᵊn\. County in North Carolina. See table at NORTH CAROLINA.

Perth \ˈpərth\. **1** City, ✱ of Western Australia, on Swan river 10 m. from its mouth; pop. (1969e) 97,000, met. area pop. 635,500; commercial, financial, and transportation center of Western Australia; ships agricultural products and minerals; Univ. of Western Australia (1911). Founded 1829; made city 1856; developed rapidly after discovery of Coolgardie goldfields 1890 and opening of Fremantle Harbor 1897.
2 County, Ontario, Canada. See table at ONTARIO.
3 Industrial town, ⊗ of Lanark co., SE Ontario, Canada, 45 m. SW of Ottawa; pop. (1971p) 5539; shoes, lumber, textiles, dairy products.
4 *also* **Perth·shire** \-ˌshi(ə)r, -shər\. County, cen. Scotland; area 2493 sq. m.; pop. (1971p) 127,138; ⊗ Perth; rivers Forth, Tay; region has some of the finest scenery in Scotland, in the Grampian Mts. and on the shores of its many lochs; sugar beet, beans, barley, oats, wheat; livestock grazing; cotton, woolen, and linen goods; distilling, tourism; center for hydroelectric power production.
5 Burgh, ⊗ of Perth co., cen. Scotland, on the Tay river 32 m. NW of Edinburgh; pop. (1971p) 43,051; market center; distilleries, dye works, glass factories, jute mills; a Roman settlement; made a royal burgh 1210; capital of Scotland until c. 1452; at St. John's church (15th cent.) John Knox preached in 1559 his noted denunciation of idolatry.

Perth Am·boy \ˌpər-ˈtham-ˌbȯi\. Industrial city and port of entry, Middlesex co., cen. New Jersey, on Raritan Bay at mouth of Raritan river, 17 m. SSW of Newark; pop. (1970c) 38,798; steel, electrical equipment, building materials, chemicals, paints, clothing; food processing, oil refining, printing. Settled late 17th cent.; capital of East Jersey 1684–1702; incorporated as city 1718; a summer resort in first half of 19th cent.

Per·tuis \per-ˈtwē\. Town, Vaucluse dept., SE France, 38 m. SE of Avignon; pop. (1962c) 6777; ancient clock tower and 14th cent. church.

Pe·ru \pə-ˈrü\. **1** Republic, W South America, bounded on N by Ecuador and Colombia, on E by Brazil and Bolivia, on S tip by Chile, and on W by the Pacific Ocean; 496,222 sq. m. (including 1914 sq. m. of Lake Titicaca and 14 sq. m. of insular possessions); pop. (1971e) 14,014,600, (1969e) 13,171,800; ✱ Lima. *Physical features:* Greater part covered by Andes: main range, Cordillera Occidental, parallel to coast; Cordillera de Carabaya and Cordillera Oriental in SE, and Cordillera Huayhuash in cen. part; has many subsidiary ranges, esp. in S. Highest peak Huascarán 22,205 ft. in W; others Nevado Coropuna 21,079 ft., Solimana, Salcantay, Nevado Ausangate, and the volcanoes El Misti and Yucamani in S; many peaks bet. 17,000 and 20,000 ft. Coastline ab. 1400 m. long; coastal belt, 40 to 100 m. wide, bet. Pacific Ocean and coastal ranges; to the E are many valleys and plateaus shut in by the mountains and watered by streams of the Amazon system; in NE is extensive plain (chiefly Loreto dept.). *Rivers, lakes:* Marañón in N, its many tributaries, esp. Napo, Tigre, Pastaza, and Huallaga; Ucayali in E and its great headstreams Urubamba and Apurímac; sources of Purús and Madre de Dios in SE; in extreme N the Putumayo forms boundary with Colombia; many short streams in coastal belt. Includes NW half of large Lake Titicaca (*q.v.*). *Chief products:* Cotton, sugar, rice, wheat, corn; fishing; copper, lead, zinc, silver, gold, tungsten, vanadium, bismuth, oil. *Chief cities:* Lima, Callao, Arequipa, Chiclayo, Trujillo, Piura, Cuzco. Divided into one constitutional province and 23 departments (for pronunciation of their names, see their individual entries):

NAME	AREA (sq. m.)	POP. (1969e)	CAPITAL
Amazonas	15,945	165,100	Chachapoyas
Ancash	14,019	727,000	Huarás
Apurímac	7,975	327,000	Abancay
Arequipa	24,528	504,200	Arequipa
Ayacucho	17,658	468,300	Ayacucho
Cajamarca	13,675	979,300	Cajamarca
Callao[1]	29	320,700	Callao
Cuzco	29,430	742,100	Cuzco
Huancavelica	8,139	360,600	Huancavelica
Huánuco	13,635	419,500	Huánuco
Ica	8,205	349,800	Ica
Junín	16,751	678,600	Huancayo
La Libertad	8,973	762,600	Trujillo
Lambayeque	6,404	468,800	Chiclayo
Lima	13,087	3,021,000	Lima
Loreto	184,685	485,700	Iquitos
Madre de Dios	30,271	23,100	Puerto Maldonado
Moquegua	6,245	66,800	Moquegua
Pasco	8,467	182,600	Cerrc de Pasco
Piura	12,717	893,100	Piura
Puno	27,946	832,800	Puno
San Martín	20,417	221,900	Moyobamba
Tacna	5,701	90,600	Tacna
Tumbes	1,826	80,600	Tumbes

[1]Constitutional province with status of a department.

History: Seat of Inca empire, established c. 1230 with its capital at Cuzco, which ruled Quito (Ecuador) and parts of modern Bolivia and Chile; reached by Spanish 1522; finally conquered by Pizarro and Almagro 1533; Lima (*q.v.*) founded 1535; scene of strife bet. rival conquistadores 1537–54; in 1542 Spanish established viceroyalty of Peru which, up to 18th cent., included Panama and all of Spanish South America except Venezuela (see also UPPER PERU); New Granada (*q.v.*) 1718 and Buenos Aires (La Plata) 1776 were made separate viceroyalties; Peru declared its independence of Spain under San Martín 1821, but did not achieve final freedom until 1824; fought Spain 1866; defeated in War of the Pacific with Chile 1879–83, and lost Tarapacá and occupation of Tacna and Arica; received Tacna (*q.v.*) 1929 after long dispute with Chile; in dispute with Colombia over Leticia (*q.v.*) 1932–33; boundary with Ecuador under dispute for many years, subject of treaties 1860, 1887, and 1890 but not settled until 1942 when greater part of region E of Andes was assigned to Peru. In World War I broke off relations with Germany 1917 and in World War II with Axis powers in 1941; government overthrown by military junta 1968.

2 City, La Salle co., N Illinois, on Illinois river 15 m. W of Ottawa; pop. (1970c) 11,772.

3 City, ⊗ of Miami co., N cen. Indiana, 18 m. N of Kokomo; pop. (1970c) 14,139; automobile parts, furniture, canned goods, fertilizer; railroad shops.

4 Village, Nemaha co., SE Nebraska, on Missouri river 58 m. ESE of Lincoln; pop. (1970c) 1380; Peru State Coll. (1867).

Pe·ru·gia \pə-ˈrü-j(ē-)ə\. 1 Lake, Italy. See TRASIMENE.

2 Province of Umbria, Italy. See table at ITALY.

3 *or anc.* **Pe·ru·sia** \pə-ˈrü-zh(ē-)ə\. Commune, ✱ of Perugia prov., Umbria, cen. Italy, bet. Tiber river and Lake Trasimeno 85 m. N of Rome; pop. (1968e) 124,965; flour, textiles, confectionery, pasta; 13th cent. city walls, Maggiore Fountain (1278), Palazzo dei Priori (13th–16th cents.), 14th cent. cathedral, 14th cent. church of San Domenico, and several other notable churches; univ. (founded 1200, received univ. status 1308).

History: One of the 12 major cities of the Etruscans; came under Rome 310 B.C.; burned during Roman civil wars 1st cent. B.C.; became Lombard duchy 592 A.D.; in 1540 became a possession of the church; to kingdom of Italy 1860; in World War II taken by British June 1944.

Perur. See COIMBATORE.

Perusia. See PERUGIA 3.

Pe·ru·vi·an Current \pə-ˌru-vē-ən-\ *or* **Hum·boldt Current** \ˈhəm-ˌbōlt-\. A cold ocean current formed as a division of the west-wind drift of the South Pacific Ocean and directed N along the coast of Chile and Peru.

Pé·ru·welz \ˌpā-rü-ˈvelz\. Industrial commune, Hainaut prov., SW Belgium, 16 m. WNW of Mons; pop. (1969e) 7909.

Per·vo·maisk \ˌpər-və-ˈmīsk\. 1 *or formerly* **Ol·vi·o·pol** \ˌäl-vē-ˈō-ˌpōl\. Town, N Nikolayev Oblast, Ukrainian S.S.R., U.S.S.R., on Bug river 112 m. N of Odessa; pop. (1969e) 54,000.

2 Town, Voroshilovgrad Oblast, Ukrainian S.S.R., U.S.S.R., ab. 33 m. W of Voroshilovgrad; pop. (1967e) 48,000.

Per·vou·ralsk \ˌpər-vər-ˈälsk\. Town, Sverdlovsk Oblast, Russian S.F.S.R., U.S.S.R., ab. 25 m. WNW of Sverdlovsk; pop. (1970p) 117,000.

Pe·sa·ro \ˈpā-zə-ˌrō\ *or anc.* **Pi·sau·rum** \pə-ˈsȯr-əm, pī-\. Seaport, ✱ of Pesaro e Urbino prov., Marches, cen. Italy, on Adriatic 85 m. NE of Florence; pop. (1968e) 79,943; seaside resort; in agricultural region; cathedral, 15th cent. ducal palace, 15th cent. Sforza palace housing a museum, 15th cent. fortress, 15th cent. Villa Imperiale.

History: Settled by Sicilians; ruled successively by Umbrians, Etruscans, and Senonian Gauls; became Roman colony 184 B.C.; destroyed by Ostrogoths 536 A.D.; to Malatestas 1285, Sforzas 1445, and Roveres 1512; part of Papal States 1631 ff.; became part of Italy 1860.

Pesaro e Ur·bi·no \-ā-u̇r-ˈbē-nō\. Province of Marches, Italy. See table at ITALY.

Pes·ca·do·res \ˌpes-kə-ˈdōr-ēz, -ˈdȯr-, -əs\ *or Chin.* **P'eng-hu** \ˈpəŋ-ˈhü\; *Jap.* **Ho·ko Sho·to** \ˌhō-kō-shō-ˈtō\ *or* **Hoko Gun·to** \-ˈgu̇n-(ˌ)tō\. Group of ab. 48 islands in Formosa Strait bet. Taiwan and the mainland of China, separated from Taiwan by **Pescadores Channel** (30 m. wide); 49 sq. m.; largest island P'eng-hu, on which is chief town P'eng-hu, a Japanese naval base in World War II. Ceded to Japan by China 1895; retroceded 1946; since 1949 held by Taiwan government.

Pescadores, Point. Cape extending into Pacific Ocean on the coast of Arequipa dept., S Peru.

Pe·sca·ra \pe-ˈskär-ə\. 1 Lower course of the Aterno river, SE cen. Italy. See ATERNO.

2 Province of Abruzzi, Italy. See table at ITALY.

3 *or anc.* **Ater·num** \ə-ˈtər-nəm\ *or* **Os·tia Ater·ni** \ˌäs-tē-ə-ə-ˈtər-ˌnī\. Industrial and commercial seaport, ✱ of Pescara prov., Abruzzi, cen. Italy, on Adriatic at mouth of Pescara river 98 m. ENE of Rome; pop. (1968e) 113,520; textiles, machinery; tourism, fishing, shipbuilding; castle. Fortified to 1867; made provincial capital 1927; taken by Allies June 1944.

Pescara Pass. See table at APENNINES.

Pe·schie·ra del Gar·da \ˌpes-kē-ˈer-ə-del-ˈgärd-ə\; *anc.* **Aril·i·ca** \ə-ˈril-i-kə\ *or later* **Pis·car·ia** \pis-ˈkar-ē-ə, -ˈker-\. Commune, Verona prov., Veneto, NE Italy, on SE shore of Lake Garda at source of Mincio river 16 m. W of Verona;

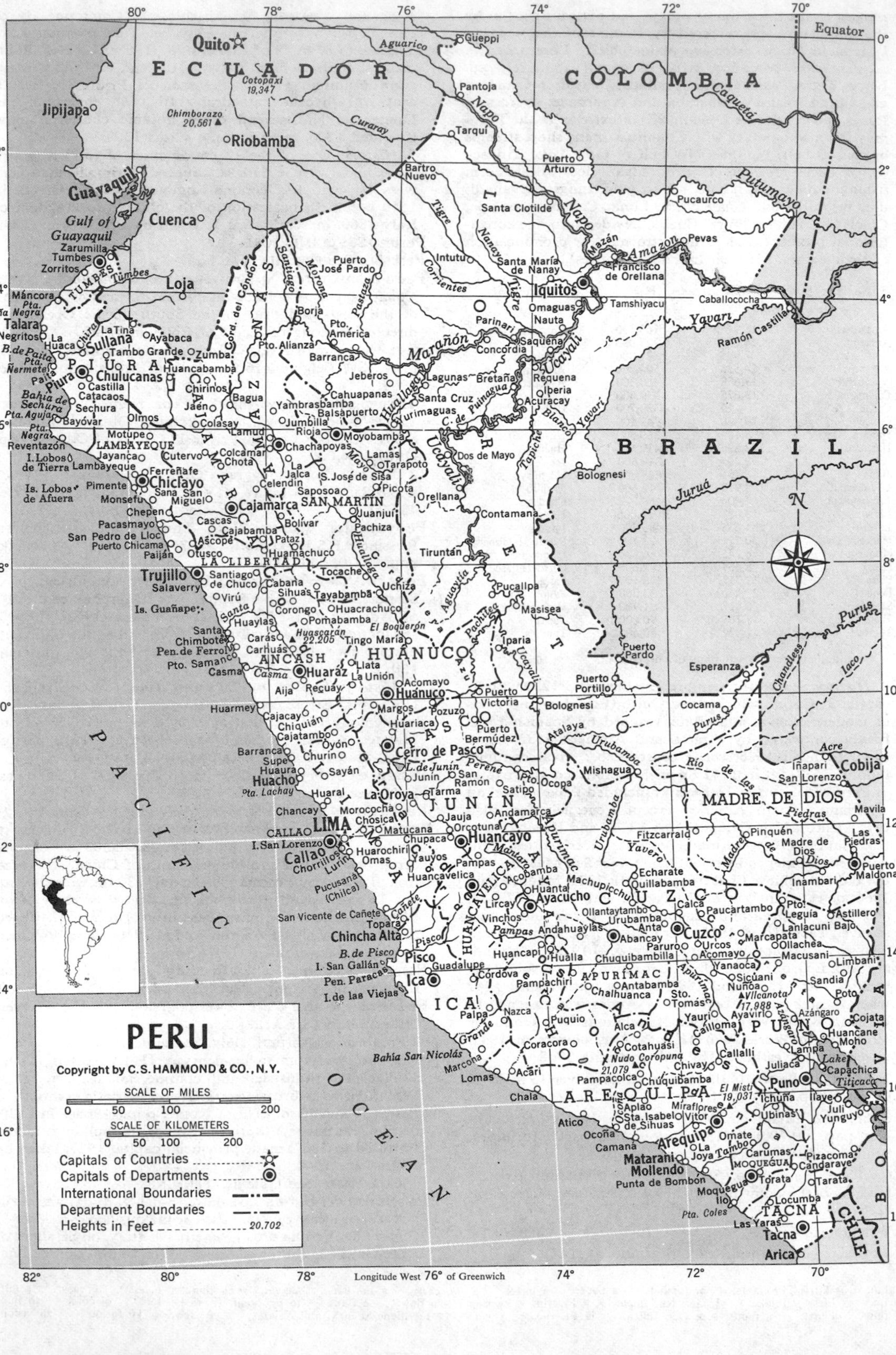
PERU
Copyright by C.S. HAMMOND & CO., N.Y.
SCALE OF MILES
0 50 100 200
SCALE OF KILOMETERS
0 50 100 200
Capitals of Countries
Capitals of Departments
International Boundaries
Department Boundaries
Heights in Feet 20,702
Longitude West 76° of Greenwich
Equator
E C U A D O R
C O L O M B I A
B R A Z I L
B O L I V I A
CHILE
P A C I F I C O C E A N
Quito
Cotopaxi 19,347
Chimborazo 20,561
Riobamba
Jipijapa
Guayaquil
Gulf of Guayaquil
Cuenca
Loja
Zarumilla
Tumbes
Zorritos
TUMBES
Máncora
Pta. Peña Negra
Talara
Negritos
La Huaca
Sullana
B. de Paita
Paita
Pta. Ñermete
Piura
P I U R A
Chulucanas
Castilla
Catacaos
Bahía de Sechura
Sechura
Pta. Aguja
Bayóvar
Pta. Negra
Reventazón
I. Lobos de Tierra
Is. Lobos de Afuera
LAMBAYEQUE
Chiclayo
Cajamarca
Trujillo
LA LIBERTAD
Is. Guañape
Chimbote
ANCASH
Huaráz
Huascarán 22,205
Casma
Huarmey
Barranca
Huacho
Pta. Lachay
Chancay
CALLAO
LIMA
Callao
I. San Lorenzo
Chorrillos
Lurín
Pucusana (Chilca)
San Vicente de Cañete
Chincha Alta
B. de Pisco
Pisco
I. San Gallán
Pen. Paracas
I. de las Viejas
Ica
ICA
Nazca
Bahía San Nicolás
Marcona
Lomas
Chala
Atico
Ocoña
Camaná
Matarani
Mollendo
Punta de Bombón
Ilo
Pta. Coles
Moquegua
MOQUEGUA
Tacna
TACNA
Arica
Las Yaras
Arequipa
AREQUIPA
El Misti 19,031
Nudo Coropuna 21,079
Puno
PUNO
Lake Titicaca
Vilcanota 17,988
Juliaca
Cuzco
CUZCO
Machupicchu
Abancay
APURIMAC
Ayacucho
AYACUCHO
Huancavelica
HUANCAVELICA
Huancayo
JUNÍN
La Oroya
L. de Junín
Cerro de Pasco
PASCO
Huánuco
HUÁNUCO
Tingo María
Pucallpa
Iquitos
LORETO
Nauta
Tamshiyacu
Caballococha
Ramón Castilla
Pevas
Francisco de Orellana
Mazán
Pucaurco
Puerto Arturo
Santa Clotilde
Pantoja
Güeppi
Tarquí
Bartro Nuevo
Moyobamba
Chachapoyas
AMAZONAS
SAN MARTÍN
Tarapoto
Yurimaguas
Contamana
Bolognesi
Puerto Portillo
Puerto Pardo
Esperanza
MADRE DE DIOS
Puerto Maldonado
Iñapari
Cobija
San Lorenzo
Mavila
Las Piedras
Inambari
Astillero
Amazon
Napo
Marañón
Ucayali
Huallaga
Urubamba
Apurímac
Mantaro
Putumayo
Caquetá
Yavarí
Juruá
Purus
Acre
Río de las Piedras
Madre de Dios
Tigre
Pastaza
Morona
Santiago
Curaray
Aguarico
Corrientes
N
80° 78° 76° 74° 72° 70°
82° 80° 78° 76° 74° 72° 70°
0° 2° 4° 6° 8° 10° 12° 14° 16° 18°

pop. (1968e) 6859; a former frontier fortress, one of Quadrilateral cities (Peschiera, Mantua, Verona, Legnago) important in the Napoleonic Wars.

Pe·schio, Mount \-'pes-(,)kyō\. Mountain in S range of Alban Hills, W Italy, just N of Velletri; 3080 ft.; taken by Americans June 1–2, 1944.

Pe·scia \'pā-(,)shä\. Commune, Pistoia prov., Tuscany, cen. Italy, 14 m. W of Pistoia; pop. (1968e) 19,711; paper, silk; remains of ancient city walls; 14th cent. cathedral.

Pe·sci·na \pā-'shē-nə\. Commune, Aquila prov., Abruzzi, cen. Italy, 27 m. SE of Aquila; pop. (1968e) 4976; 16th cent. cathedral.

Pe·sha·war \pə-'shä-wər, -'shaů(-ə)r\. 1 Division, North-West Frontier prov., Pakistan; area 28,153 sq. m.; pop. (1961c) 6,372,467.

2 District of the division; area 1646 sq. m.; pop. (1961c) 1,213,468.

3 City, ✱ of North-West Frontier prov., Pakistan, also ✱ of the division and of the district, on Bara river, tributary of the Kabul, 240 m. NW of Lahore; met. area pop. (1969e) 295,700; strategically important because of its location 9 m. from S entrance to Khyber Pass and has an important military cantonment; has cottage industries producing copper ware, leather goods, pottery, knives, and small arms; notable bazaars trading in hides, wool, carpets, and fruit; univ. (1950).

History: Capital of Indo-Scythian Kushan dynasty 1st cent. A.D.; area held by Pathan tribes 15th–16th cents.; annexed by Sikhs under Ranjit Singh 1823; to British 1849; under British rule an important military base against the Afghans and border tribes.

Pesh·ko·pi \pesh-'kō-pē\. Town, ✱ of Dibër prov., Albania, near Yugoslav border ab. 44 m. NE of Tiranë; pop. (1967e) 6075.

Pesh·ti·go \'pesh-ti-,gō\. 1 River, NE Wisconsin; ab. 150 m. long; rises in Forest co., flows SE into Green Bay S of Marinette.

2 City, Marinette co., NE Wisconsin, on Peshtigo river 6 m. WSW of Marinette; pop. (1970c) 2836; saw and paper mills, boatyards. Practically destroyed by fire Oct. 8, 1871, same day as great fire in Chicago.

Pes·quei·ra \pəsh-'ker-ə\. City, E cen. Pernambuco state, E Brazil, on railroad 115 m. W of Recife; munic. pop. (1968c) 36,986.

Pes·sac \pe-'sak\. Commune, Gironde dept., SW France, 4 m. SSW of Bordeaux; pop. (1968c) 36,986; produces wines.

Pes·si·nus \'pes-ə-nəs\. Ancient city, Galatia, Asia Minor (its site now in Turkey); site of principal shrine of Cybele, the great nature goddess of Anatolia, who was known here as Agdistis or Angdistis, from the rock Agdus on nearby Mount Dindymus, and as Dindymene, from the mountain itself.

Pest \'pest, 'pesht\. 1 County of N cen. Hungary. See table at HUNGARY.

2 Former town, Hungary. See BUDAPEST.

Pe·ta·cal·co Bay \,pe-tə-'käl-kō-\. Inlet of the Pacific Ocean on SW coast of Mexico, chiefly in NW Guerrero state.

Pe·tach Tik·va \,pet-ə(k)-'tik-və\ *or* **Pe·tah Tiq·wa** \,pet-ə-'tik-və\. Town, Israel, 7 m. NE of Tel Aviv-Jaffa; pop. (1970e) 83,200; asbestos, chemicals, textiles, agricultural machinery; incorporated as a city 1937.

Pet·al \'pet-ᵊl\. Unincorporated urban community, Forrest co., SE Mississippi, NE of Hattiesburg; pop. (1970c) 6986.

Pet·a·lu·ma \,pet-ᵊl-'ü-mə\. City, Sonoma co., W California, on Petaluma river 16 m. S of Santa Rosa; pop. (1970c) 24,870; paper and dairy products, soap; poultry farms; founded by colony of Mexicans 1833.

Pé·tange \pā-'tänzh\. Commune, Grand Duchy of Luxembourg, in SW part N of Differdange; pop. (1960c) 11,951.

Pe·ta·tlán \,pe-tət-'län\. Municipality, Guerrero state, Mexico, 100 m. NW of Acapulco; pop. (1970p) 31,088; wheat, rice, tobacco, copra.

Pet·a·wa·wa \,pet-ə-'wä-wə\. Village, Renfrew co., SE Ontario, Canada; pop. (1966c) 5574.

Petch. See PEĆ.

Petchabun. See PHETCHABUN.

Petchaburi. See PHET BURI.

Pe·tén \pe-'ten\. Department of N Guatemala. See table at GUATEMALA.

Petén It·za \-'ēt-'sä\ *or* **La·gu·na de Flo·res** \lə-,gü-nə-də-'flōr-əs, -'flȯr-\. Lake, cen. Petén dept., Guatemala; ab. 27 m. long; 38 sq. m.

Pe·ter·bor·ough \'pēt-ər-,bər-ə, -,bə-rə, -b(ə-)rə\. 1 *or* **Pe·ter·boro.** Town, Hillsborough co., S New Hampshire, 16 m. E of Keene; pop. (1970c) 3807; summer resort; apple orchards; settled 1749; place where Brigham Young was chosen leader of the Mormon Church.

2 Town, SE South Australia, 135 m. N of Adelaide; pop. (1966c) 3117.

3 County, Ontario, Canada. See table at ONTARIO.

4 Industrial city, ⊗ of Peterborough co., SE Ontario, Canada, on Otonabee river and Trent Canal 13 m. N of W end of Rice Lake; pop. (1971p) 57,498; electrical machinery, boats, marine hardware, plastics, lumber, carpets, watches; truck and dairy farms; Trent Univ. (1960); sawmills estab. on site 1821; town founded 1825, incorporated as city 1905.

5 Municipal borough, Huntingdon and Peterborough co., cen. England, on the Nene 75 m. N of London; pop. (1971p) 70,081; railroad junction; produces diesel engines, steam turbines, pumps; fruit canning, sugar refining, brickmaking; 12th–14th cent. cathedral, burial place of Catherine of Aragon.

Peterborough, Soke of. See HUNTINGDON AND PETERBOROUGH.

Pe·ter I Island \,pēt-ər-thə-'fərst-\. Island off Antarctica in Bellingshausen Sea NE of Thurston Island; 14 m. long; 68°47′S, 90°35′W; discovered and named by Bellingshausen in expedition of exploration 1819–21.

Pe·ter·head \,pēt-ər-'hed\. Seaport burgh, Aberdeen co., NE Scotland, on a peninsula 30 m. NE of Aberdeen; pop. (1971p) 14,164; woolens, canned goods; herring fisheries; founded 1593; the Old Pretender landed here on Christmas Day 1715.

Peterhof. See PETRODVORETS.

Peter Island. One of the British Virgin Is., West Indies, S of Tortola.

Peterlingen. See PAYERNE.

Pe·ter·mann Glacier \'pēt-ər-mən-\. Glacier, N Greenland; 78 m. long, 9 m. wide near its terminus.

Pe·te·roa \,pet-ə-'rō-ə\. Volcanic peak, E cen. Chile, near border of W Mendoza prov., W Argentina; 13,419 ft.

Pe·ters·burg \'pēt-ərz-,bərg\. 1 Fishing town, SE Alaska, ab. 35 m. NNW of Wrangell; pop. (1970c) 2042.

2 City, ⊗ of Menard co., cen. Illinois, 20 m. NW of Springfield; pop. (1970c) 2632; coal mines.

3 City, ⊗ of Pike co., SW Indiana, 18 m. SE of Vincennes; pop. (1970c) 2697; coal mines, oil wells; fruit and poultry farms.

4 Commercial and industrial city, SE Virginia, at head of navigation of Appomattox river 23 m. S of Richmond; an independent city; area 8 sq. m.; pop. (1970c) 36,103; manufactures tobacco products, luggage, fiberglass boats, clothing, lenses, furniture, paint; Virginia State Coll. (1882). Fort built on site 1645; town established 1748; incorporated as town 1784 and as city 1850; in Civil War besieged by Union forces under Grant and Meade June 1864–Apr. 1865 when Confederate forces were forced to withdraw to W, abandoning Petersburg and Richmond, and to surrender at Appomattox (*q.v.*); nearby is **Peters-**

burg National Battlefield Site: see UNITED STATES, *National Historical Parks.*
5 Town, ⊗ of Grant co., NE West Virginia, 32 m. S of Keyser; pop. (1970c) 2177; sawmills; agriculture.

Pe·ters·ham \'pēt-ərz-ˌham\. Town, Worcester co., cen. Massachusetts, ab. 25 m. NW of Worcester; pop. (1970c) 1014; site of Harvard Forest, 2100 acres, bird sanctuary (1000 acres) and experiment station for Harvard University's School of Forestry.

Peter the Great Bay \'pēt-ər-\ *or Russ.* **Za·liv Pet·ra Ve·li·ko·go** \ˌzä-'lēf-pə-'trä-vəl-'ē-kə-və\. Inlet of Sea of Japan at S end of Primorski Krai, Russian S.F.S.R., U.S.S.R.; its two arms, Amur Bay and Ussuri Bay, are on either side of the peninsula on which Vladivostok is situated.

Pétervárad *or* **Peterwardein.** See PETROVARADIN.

Petit Andely, Le. See LES ANDELYS.

Pet·it Bois Island \'pet-ē-ˌbwä-\. Island off coast of Alabama-Mississippi boundary, bet. Mississippi Sound and the Gulf of Mexico.

Pe·tit–Bourg \pə-'tē-'bů(ə)r\. Town on E coast of Basse-Terre, Guadeloupe, West Indies.

Petit–Ca·nal \pə-ˌtē-kə-'nal\. Commune, W coast of Grande Terre, Guadeloupe, West Indies.

Petit–Charenton. See SAINT-MAURICE.

Pet·it·co·di·ac \ˌpet-ē-'kōd-ē-ˌak\. River, SE New Brunswick, Canada; ab. 60 m. long; flows NE, E, and then S through wide estuary (20 m. long) to inlet of Chignecto Bay. Moncton is on it.

Pe·tite–Ros·selle \pə-ˌtēt-rȯ-'sel\ *or Ger.* **Klein·ros·seln** \klīn-'rȯs-əln\. Commune, Moselle dept., NE France, near the West German border; pop. (1962c) 8984.

Pe·tit Go·âve \pə-ˌtē-gȯ-'äv\. Town on N Tiburon Penin., SW Haiti.

Petitjean. See SIDI KACEM.

Pe·tit Ma·nan Point \pə-ˌtēt-mə-'nan-\. Southwest point of Washington co., SE Maine.

Petit–Quevilly, Le. See LE PETIT-QUEVILLY.

Petit–Saint–Bernard. Alpine pass. See ALPS.

Pet·it·sik·a·pau Lake \ˌpet-ē-ˌsik-ə-ˌpaů-\. Lake, W Labrador, Canada, on border of Quebec, in the NW part of the chain of lakes out of which the Churchill river flows.

Pe·to \'pā-tō\. Town, Yucatán state, on Yucatán penin., SE Mexico; munic. pop. (1970p) 11,986; railroad terminus 70 m. SE of Mérida.

Pe·to·ne \pə-'tō-nē\. Borough, S North I., New Zealand, NE suburb of Wellington on Port Nicholson; pop. (1970e) 10,250.

Pe·tos·key \pə-'täs-kē\. City, ⊗ of Emmet co., N Michigan, on Lake Michigan 31 m. SW of Cheboygan; pop. (1970c) 6342; summer resort; limestone quarries; apples; North Central Michigan Coll. (1958).

Pe·tra \'pē-trə, 'pe-\. Ruined city, SW Jordan, just W of modern **Wā·dī Mū·sa** \ˌwäd-e-'mü-sə\; usually identified with **Se·la** \'sē-lə\, ancient capital of Edom, from which the Edomites were driven c. 300 B.C. by the Nabataeans whose capital it became until 106 A.D. Notable rock city in deep gorge on NE slope of Mt. Hor (*mod.* Jebel Harun); its temples, tombs, dwellings, etc. all carved in rose, crimson, and purple limestone; was a wealthy commercial city for several centuries with important caravan trade; became chief city of Arabia Petraea. Captured by Muslims in 7th cent. and by Crusaders in 12th cent. Its ruins discovered by Burckhardt in 1812.

Petra Velikogo, Zaliv. See PETER THE GREAT BAY.

Pe·trich \'pe-trich\. Town, Blagoevgrad prov., SW Bulgaria, ab. 44 m. SSE of Blagoevgrad; pop. (1968e) 21,663.

Pet·ri·fied Forest National Park \ˌpet-rə-ˌfīd-\. See UNITED STATES, *National Parks.*

Petrikau. See PIOTRKÓW TRYBUNALSKI.

Pet·ri·la \ˌpe-'trē-lə\. Town, Hunedoara co., W cen. Romania, ab. 35 m. SE of Deva; pop. (1966c) 24,796.

Petroaleksandrovsk. See TURTKUL.

Pet·ro·dvo·rets \ˌpe-trəd-və-'rets\; *formerly* **Len·insk** \'len-ən(t)sk, 'lān-\ *also* **Pe·ter·hof** \'pēt-ər-ˌhȯf, -ˌhäf\. Coastal town, NW Leningrad Oblast, Russian S.F.S.R., U.S.S.R., 12 m. W of Leningrad; contains former imperial palaces (esp. that of Peter the Great, built 1720) and other palaces, gardens, fountains; present name adopted 1944.

Petrograd. See LENINGRAD.

Petrokov. See PIOTRKÓW TRYBUNALSKI.

Pe·tro·kre·post \ˌpe-trə-'krep-əst\; *formerly* **Shlis·sel·burg** \'shlis-əl-ˌbərg\ *or Ger.* **Schlüs·sel·burg** \'shlœs-əl-ˌbů(ə)rg\. Town, NW Leningrad Oblast, Russian S.F.S.R., U.S.S.R., on S bank of Neva river at SW corner of Lake Ladoga. A Novgorodian town founded 1323; captured 1702 by Peter the Great who erected a fortress on an island in the Neva as a key (Ger. *Schlüssel*) in his line of defense to the sea; later fortress became imperial prison in which for nearly 200 years many noted prisoners were kept; prison abolished 1917 and made a state museum. In 1941–42 defense against Germans, again a key point.

Pe·tro·le·um \pə-'trō-lē-əm\. County in Montana. See table at MONTANA.

Pe·tro·lia \pə-'trō-lē-ə\. Town, Lambton co., SE Ontario, Canada, 14 m. ESE of Sarnia; pop. (1971p) 4030; center of oil field.

Pe·tro·na Point \pə-'trō-nə-\. Cape on S coast of Puerto Rico, E of Ponce.

Pet·ro·pav·lovsk \ˌpe-trə-'pav-ˌlȯfsk\. City, ✱ of North Kazakhstan Oblast, N Kazakh S.S.R., U.S.S.R., on the Trans-Siberian R.R. 170 m. W of Omsk and on the right bank of the Ishim river; pop. (1970p) 173,000; clothing, canned goods, lumber, wood pulp, brick and tile; founded 1752.

Petropavlovsk–Kam·chat·ski \ˌpe-trə-'pav-ləfsk-kam-'chat-skē\ *or formerly* **Petropavlovsk.** Seaport town on E coast of S end of Kamchatka Penin., Kamchatka Oblast, Russian S.F.S.R., U.S.S.R.; pop. (1970p) 154,000; shipbuilding; fishing and whaling fleets; sawmills, engineering works; naval base; founded 1740.

Pe·tró·po·lis \pə-'träp-ə-ləs\. City, Rio de Janeiro state, SE Brazil, 27 m. N of Rio de Janeiro; munic. pop. (1968e) 200,052; residential and light industrial center; former imperial palace (now a museum), univ. (1961). Founded 1745; Inter-American Conference for the Maintenance of Continental Peace and Security, Aug. 15–Sept. 2, 1947, called to implement the Act of Chapultepec (*q.v.*).

Pe·tro·şe·ni *or* **Pe·tro·şa·ni** \ˌpe-trə-'shän(-ē)\ *or Hung.* **Pe·tro·zsény** \'pe-trə-ˌzhān-yə\ *or Ger.* **Pe·tro·schen** \'pā-trə-ˌshān\. Town, Hunedoara co., W Romania, ab. 40 m. SE of Deva; munic. pop. (1970e) 39,706.

Pet·ro·va·ra·din \ˌpe-trə-və-'räd-ˌēn\ *or Ger.* **Pe·ter·war·dein** \ˌpāt-ər-vär-'dīn\ *or Hung.* **Pé·ter·vá·rad** \'pāt-ər-ˌvär-ˌȯd\. Commune, NE Serbia, Yugoslavia, on S bank of the Danube opp. Novi Sad; Peter the Hermit here reviewed First Crusade 1096; scene of battle Aug. 5, 1716 in which Prince Eugene of Savoy defeated the Turks.

Petrovgrad. See ZRENJANIN.

Petrovsk. See MAKHACHKALA.

Pet·ro·za·vodsk \ˌpe-trə-zə-'vätsk\ *or* **Ka·li·ninsk** \kə-'lē-nən(t)sk\. City, ✱ of Karelian A.S.S.R., U.S.S.R., in S part on NW shore of Lake Onega, 185 m. NE of Leningrad; pop. (1970p) 185,000; metalworking, ship repairing, distilling; lumber, furniture, beer; founded by Peter the Great as ironworks 1703.

Petrozsény. See PETROŞENI.

Petsamo. See PECHENGA.

Pet·tis \'pet-əs\. County in Missouri. See table at MISSOURI.

Petuna. See FU-YÜ.

Pet·worth \'pet-(ˌ)wərth\. Village, West Sussex, England, ab. 42 m. SSW of London; Petworth house, formerly owned by Percy family.

Peu·ce \'pyü-(ˌ)sē\. Ancient name of marshy region at mouth of Danube on the Black Sea where two islands are formed by the arms of the river; birthplace of Alaric.

Pev·en·sey \ˈpev-ən-zē, -sē\. Village, SE Sussex, S England, on coast W of Hastings; pop. (1961c) 2151; site of landing of William the Conqueror 1066; 12th cent. castle.

Pe·wau·kee \pi-ˈwȯ-kē\. Village, Waukesha co., SE Wisconsin, 18 m. W of Milwaukee; pop. (1970c) 3271.

Pé·ze·nas \pāz-ˈnäs\. Manufacturing town, Hérault dept., S France, 25 m. SW of Montpellier; pop. (1962c) 7656; residence 1655–56 of Molière, who wrote *Les Précieuses Ridicules* here.

Pfäf·fi·kon \ˈ(p)fef-i-ˌkȯn\. Village, Zurich canton, Switzerland, ab. 12 m. E of Zurich; pop. (1970c) 7586; located at N end of **Lake of Pfäffikon** (*Ger.* **Pfäf·fi·ker See** \ˈ(p)fef-i-kər-ˌzā\), a marshy lake noted for many evidences of ancient lake dwellers found on its shores, esp. at Robenhausen at S end, type station for the *Robenhausian epoch,* the stage of Neolithic culture immediately preceding the Bronze Age.

Pfalz. See PALATINATE.

Pforta. See SCHULPFORTE.

Pforz·heim \ˈ(p)fȯrts-ˌhīm\. Manufacturing and commercial city, Baden-Württemberg, West Germany, on border of the Black Forest 16 m. SE of Karlsruhe; pop. (1969e) 90,022; center of jewelry and watch industry; also produces paper and radio and television sets; 13th–15th cent. castle church; made city c. 1195.

Phais·tos \ˈfīs-təs\ *or Lat.* **Phaes·tus** \ˈfes-təs, ˈfēs-\. Ancient city in S Crete, SW of Knossos, near the shore of the Bay of Messara; site of a Minoan palace.

Pha·le·ron \fə-ˈlir-ən\ *or* **Pha·le·rum** \-ˈlir-əm\. Town, an early port of Athens, in Attica, E part of ancient Greece, on **Phaleron Bay;** E of Piraeus, by which it was superseded in 5th cent. B.C.

Phal·tan \ˈpəl-tən\. 1 Former Indian state, now part of Maharashtra state, W India; 391 sq. m.; joined United Deccan State Aug. 26, 1947.

2 Town, its ✱, ab. 50 m. SE of Poona; pop. (1961c) 19,000.

Phan·a·go·ria \ˌfan-ə-ˈgōr-ē-ə\. Ancient Greek city on N shore of Pontus Euxinus at entrance to Palus Maeotis (Sea of Azov).

Phang·nga \ˈpäŋ-(ˌ)gä\. 1 *or* **Ko Phangnga** \ˈkō-\. Island (Thai *ko*) in SW Gulf of Siam, 8 m. N of Samui I.

2 *or* **Pang–nga** \ˈpäŋ-(ˌ)gä\. Province, SW Thailand; 1583 sq. m.; pop. (1960c) 93,119; ✱ Phangnga.

3 *or* **Pang–nga.** Town, ✱ of Phangnga prov., near W coast of Malay Penin. 40 m. N of Phuket; pop. (1960c) 4782.

Pha·nom Dong Rak \ˈpän-ˌəm-tōŋ-ˈräk\ *also* **Dang·rek Mountains** \ˈtōŋ-ˈrek-\. Mountain range, extending E and W along SE boundary of Thailand, separating it from N Cambodia; ab. 200 m. long; averages 1200 to 2500 ft. Its W end continues into S Thailand toward Phra Nakhon Si Ayutthaya; highest point 4167 ft.

Phanos. See FANO.

Phan Rang *or* **Phan·rang** \ˈpän-räŋ\. Coastal town, South Vietnam, 165 m. ENE of Saigon on river 7 m. from **Phan Rang Bay,** an inlet of South China Sea; pop. (1968e) 26,090; exports salt; important agricultural center.

Pha·rae \ˈfa(ə)r-ē, ˈfe(ə)r-\. Ancient town of E Messenia, SW Peloponnesus, S Greece, near modern city of Kalamata.

Pharnacia. See GİRESUN 2.

Pha·ros \ˈfar-ˌäs, ˈfer-\. Peninsula in Lower Egypt; in ancient times an island on which was located a notable lighthouse, one of the Seven Wonders of the ancient world; now part of the site of the city of Alexandria.

Phar·par \ˈfär-pər\ *or* **Phar·phar** \ˈfär-fər\. A river of Damascus (*2 Kings* v. 12); identified by many with the Awaj, a river some distance to the S of the present city of Damascus, flowing E into swamps.

Pharr \ˈfär\. City, Hidalgo co., S Texas, 2 m. E of McAllen; pop. (1970c) 15,829; packs and ships citrus fruit and vegetables; oil and gas wells.

Phar·sa·lus \fär-ˈsā-ləs\; *Gk.* **Phár·sa·los** \ˈfär-sə-ˌlȯs\ *or* **Phar·sa·la** \ˈfär-sə-lə\. Town, S Larissa dept., E Thessaly, NE Greece, near the Enipeus river; scene of Caesar's decisive defeat of Pompey 48 B.C.—called also the battle of **Phar·sa·lia** \fär-ˈsāl-yə\ from the name of the district surrounding the town.

Pharus. See HVAR.

Pha·se·lis \fə-ˈsē-ləs\. Coastal town in ancient Lycia, Asia Minor, near border of Pamphylia.

Pha·sis \ˈfā-səs\. River, W Georgian S.S.R., U.S.S.R. See RIONI.

Phatnitic. See DAMIETTA 1.

Phat·tha·lung *or* **Pa·ta·lung** *also* **Pa·da·lung** \ˈpät-ᵊl-ˌu̇ŋ\. 1 Province, SW Thailand; 1262 sq. m.; pop. (1960c) 233,844; ✱ Phatthalung.

2 Town, its ✱, on W shore of Lake Thale Luang in Malay Penin. 50 m. NW of Songkhla; pop. (1960c) 10,420.

Phazania. See FEZZAN.

Phelps \ˈfelps\. Name of counties in two states of the U.S. See tables at MISSOURI and NEBRASKA.

Phelps Lake. Lake in SE Washington co., E North Carolina, in swampland bet. Albemarle Sound and Pamlico Sound.

Phenice. See PHOENIX 4.

Phenicia. See PHOENICIA.

Phe·nix City \ˌfē-niks-\. Manufacturing city, a ⊗ of Russell co., E Alabama, on Chattahoochee river across from Columbus, Georgia; pop. (1970c) 25,281; caskets, lumber, wood products; dairy farms; incorporated 1923.

Phe·rae \ˈfi(ə)r-ē\. Ancient town in SE Thessaly, NE Greece, ab. 27 m. SE of Larissa. In mythology the home of Admetus; historically, in first half of the 4th cent. B.C., its tyrants controlled Thessaly.

Phet Bu·ri \ˈpet-bu̇-ˌrē\ *also* **Pet·cha·bu·ri** \ˈpet-bu̇-ˌrē—*sic*\ *or* **Bej·ra·bu·ri** \ˈpet-bu̇-ˌrē—*sic*\. 1 Province, cen. Thailand; 2454 sq. m.; pop. (1960c) 237,853; ✱ Phet Buri.

2 Seaport town, its ✱, on NW shore of Gulf of Siam and on railroad 60 m. SW of Bangkok; pop. (1960c) 24,654.

Phet·cha·bun \ˌpet-chä-ˈbün\ *also* **Pet·cha·bun** \ˌpet-chä-ˈbün\ *or* **Bej·ra·bu·ra·na** \ˌpet-chä-ˈbün—*sic*\. 1 Province, N Thailand; 4311 sq. m.; pop. (1960c) 319,611; ✱ Phetchabun.

2 Town, its ✱, on Sak river 70 m. SE of Phitsanulok; pop. (1960c) 5887; made capital of Thailand by Japanese 1944–45.

Phi·chit \ˈpi-ˈchit\ *also* **Pi·chit** *or* **Bi·chit·ra** \ˈpi-ˈchit—*sic*\. 1 Province, N Thailand; 1749 sq. m.; pop. (1960c) 389,122; ✱ Phichit.

2 Town, its ✱, on Nan river 55 m. N of Nakhon Sawan; pop. (1960c) 9257.

Phi·ga·lia \fi-ˈgāl-yə\. Ancient city in SW Arcadia, cen. Peloponnesus, S Greece, near N border of Messenia; ab. 5 m. to the E is **Bas·sae** \ˈbas-(ˌ)ē\, site of a temple of Apollo, still preserved, in which were the Phigalian marbles or sculptures (since 1814 in the British Museum); these form a frieze ab. 101 ft. long and 2 ft. high, representing in Parian marble in high relief battles bet. Greeks and Amazons and bet. Lapithae and Centaurs; completely preserved, probably the work of Ictinus (c. 430 B.C.).

Phil·a·del·phia \ˌfil-ə-ˈdel-fyə, -fē-ə\. 1 County in Pennsylvania. See table at PENNSYLVANIA.

2 City, ⊗ of Neshoba co., E cen. Mississippi, 38 m. NNW of Meridian; pop. (1970c) 6274; lumber; diversified agriculture.

3 City, ⊗ of and coextensive with Philadelphia co., SE Pennsylvania, at confluence of Delaware and Schuylkill rivers; pop. (1970c) 1,950,098; largest city in the state; a commercial, financial, industrial, cultural, and transportation center; major deepwater port and U.S. Navy Yard; metallurgical engineering; textile, petroleum, chemical, and food industries. Numerous educational institutions: Univ. of Pennsylvania (1740), Philadelphia Coll. of Phar-

macy and Science (1821), Saint Charles Borromeo Seminary (1832), Moore Coll. of Art (1844), Spring Garden Coll. (1850), Saint Joseph's Coll. (1851), La Salle Coll. (1863), Pierce Junior Coll. (1865), Philadelphia Musical Academy (1870), Philadelphia Coll. of Art (1876), Philadelphia Coll. of Textiles and Science (1883), Temple Univ. (1884), Comos Coll. of Music (1885), Drexel Institute of Technology (1891), Philadelphia Coll. of the Bible (1913), Pennsylvania Coll. of Optometry (1919), Curtis Institute of Music (1924), Temple Junior Coll. (1926), Holy Family Coll. (1954), Community Coll. of Philadelphia (1965); publishing center; had first daily newspaper in the U.S. (*Pennsylvania Packet,* 1784); has oldest art museum in U.S., the Academy of Fine Arts (1805), and first hospital established in U.S., Pennsylvania Hospital (1751); Veterans Stadium (1971).

History: First settlement on site made by colony of Swedes in 1640's; English settlement organized by agent of William Penn 1681, and city laid out 1682 and called Philadelphia; chartered 1701; received many immigrants from Scotland and Ireland in early 18th cent.; dominant in shaping policies of the Middle Colonies in 18th cent.; Benjamin Franklin settled in the city 1723. Prominent in opposing British policies 1763–74; First Continental Congress met in Carpenters' Hall Sept. 5, 1774; Second Continental Congress in the State House May 10, 1775; Declaration of Independence signed in Independence Hall 1776; city held by British Sept. 27, 1777–June 18, 1778; Constitutional Convention met in the city 1787 and adopted Sept. 17, 1787 the Constitution of the United States. Largest and most important city in U.S. in early 19th cent.; capital of Pennsylvania 1683–1799, and capital of U.S. 1790–1800; financial center of U.S. until 1836; leader in antislavery movement; took active part in the Civil War. Held Centennial Exposition 1876 and Sesquicentennial Exposition 1926.

4 Town, Jordan. See AMMAN.

5 City, Turkey. See ALAŞEHİR.

Phi·lae \ˈfī-(ˌ)lē\. Island in the Nile river, in Upper Egypt; site of many ancient temples and monuments; now submerged by Aswān High Dam.

Phi·li·a·tra \ˌfēl-yə-ˈträ\ *or Gk.* **Fi·li·trá** \ˌfē-lē-ˈträ\. Commune, Messenia dept., SW Peloponnesus, S Greece, on Ionian Sea.

Phil·ip \ˈfil-əp\. City, ⊗ of Haakon co., W cen. South Dakota; pop. (1970c) 983; dairy, grain farms.

Phil·ip·haugh \ˈfil-əp-ˌhȯ\. Village, S Scotland, 2 m. W of Selkirk; scene of battle Sept. 13, 1645 in which earl of Montrose was surprised and defeated by David Leslie.

Philippeville. See SKIKDA.

Phil·ip·pi \ˈfil-ə-pē\. City, ⊗ of Barbour co., N West Virginia, 19 m. ESE of Clarksburg; pop. (1970c) 3002; coal mines, oil and gas wells; scene of battle in Civil War 1861; Alderson-Broaddus Coll. (1871).

Phi·lip·pi \ˈfil-ə-ˌpī, fə-ˈlip-ˌī\ *or* **Fí·lip·poi** \ˈfē-li-ˌpē\. Ruined town in Drama dept., N cen. Macedonia, Greece, ab. 10 m. from the Aegean Sea; developed and fortified by King Philip of Macedon; scene of battle 42 B.C. in which Octavian and Antony defeated Brutus and Cassius; place where St. Paul first preached the gospel in Europe.

Phil·ip·pines \ˈfil-ə-ˌpēnz, ˌfil-ə-ˈ\; *officially* **Republic of the Philippines** *or Pilipino* **Re·pub·li·ka ng Pi·li·pi·nas** \re-ˈpüb-lē-kə-näŋ-pi-lē-ˈpē-nəs\ *or Span.* **Re·púb·li·ca de Fi·li·pi·nas** \re-ˈpüb-lē-kä-t͟hä-ˌfē-lē-ˈpē-(ˌ)näs\; *frequently* **Philippine Islands** *or Span.* **Is·las Fi·li·pi·nas** \ˈēz-läs-ˌfē-lē-ˈpē-(ˌ)näs\. Republic, an archipelago of ab. 7100 islands lying approximately 500 m. off the SE coast of Asia; 115,651 sq. m.; pop. (1970p) 37,008,419; ✱ Quezon City. *Physical features:* N–S extent of the archipelago is ab. 1152 m., E–W extent ab. 688 m.; has several sizable interisland seas—Sulu, Mindanao, Visayan, Sibuyan, Samar—and the irregular coastlines of many of the islands form many bays and fine harbors, such as Manila Bay, Lingayen Gulf, Leyte Gulf, Iligan Bay, and Davao Gulf. The San Bernardino Strait and Verde Island Passage together form the main steamship lane across the archipelago from the Pacific to Manila and farther S Surigao Strait and Mindanao Sea provide a similar route across S part. Archipelago forms part of W Pacific volcanic chain, hence all islands are mountainous with chief ranges in N Luzon; highest peak Apo 9690 ft. in SE Mindanao; ab. 20 mountains are volcanic peaks, esp. Taal and Mayon. Practically all islands are well watered but only Luzon and Mindanao have large streams (Cagayan, Pampanga, Agno, Agusan, Mindanao); Laguna de Bay and Taal on Luzon and Lanao on Mindanao are the chief lakes. Fertile volcanic soil is source of great variety of tropical products; major islands include: Bohol, Catanduanes, Cebu, Leyte, Luzon, Masbate, Mindanao, Mindoro, Negros, Palawan, Panay, Samar (for further information, see their individual entries). *Chief products:* Rice, corn, copra, fruit, sugar, timber; livestock raising, fishing; iron ore, gold, copper, manganese; manufacturing: textiles, rubber goods, pharmaceuticals, paints, paper, footwear; food processing. *Chief cities:* Manila, Quezon City, Basilan, Cebu, Bacolod, Davao, Iloilo, Cavite. Divided into the following 66 provinces (listed by island or island group; for pronunciation of their names, see their individual entries):

NAME	AREA (sq. m.)	POP. (1970p)	CAPITAL
Batan			
Batanes	81	11,425	Basco
Bohol			
Bohol	1,590	674,806	Tagbilaran
Camiguin			
Camiguin	98	56,976	Mambajao
Catanduanes			
Catanduanes	584	162,679	Virac
Cebu			
Cebu	1,965	1,632,642	Cebu
Leyte			
Leyte	2,420	1,091,887	Tacloban
Southern Leyte	670	248,128	Maasin
Luzon			
Abra	1,535	149,397	Bangued
Albay	986	672,285	Legaspi
Bataan	530	214,131	Balanga
Batangas	1,222	927,290	Batangas
Benguet	1,025	262,679	La Trinidad
Bulacan	1,032	836,714	Malolos
Cagayan	3,476	580,810	Tuguegarao
Camarines Norte	816	263,226	Daet
Camarines Sur	2,034	978,573	Pili
Cavite	497	518,483	Trece Martires
Ifugao	972	92,896	Lagawe
Ilocos Norte	1,312	343,051	Laoag
Ilocos Sur	996	385,945	Vigan
Isabela	4,118	662,891	Ilagan
Kalinga-Apayao	2,721	143,850	Tabuk
Laguna	679	718,518	Santa Cruz
La Union	576	374,659	San Fernando
Mountain Province	810	93,729	Bontoc
Nueva Ecija	2,040	850,147	Palayan
Nueva Vizcaya	2,688	222,438	Bayombong
Pampanga	842	912,304	San Fernando
Pangasinan	2,073	1,387,632	Lingayen
Quezon	4,612	971,637	Lucena
Rizal	733	2,781,081	Pasig
Sorsogon	827	426,842	Sorsogon
Tarlac	1,179	558,700	Tarlac
Zambales	1,434	339,816	Iba
Marinduque			
Marinduque	370	143,777	Boac
Masbate			
Masbate	1,563	492,868	Masbate
Mindanao			
Agusan del Norte	4,461[1]	280,100	Butuan
Agusan del Sur		175,549	Prosperidad
Bukidnon	3,202	400,307	Malaybalay
Cotabato	6,348	1,153,640	Pagalungan
Cotabato del Sur	2,840	470,527	Koronadal
Davao del Norte	3,138	438,795	Tagum
Davao del Sur	2,462	733,873	Digos
Davao Oriental	1,994	247,388	Mati
Lanao del Norte	1,194	383,096	Iligan
Lanao del Sur	1,495	714,231	Marawi
Misamis Occidental	749	344,025	Oroquieta
Misamis Oriental	1,378	477,282	Cagayan de Oro
Surigao del Norte	1,058	238,823	Surigao
Surigao del Sur	1,758	261,487	Tandag
Zamboanga del Norte	2,346	411,897	Dipolog
Zamboanga del Sur	3,831	1,032,198	Pagadian

NAME	AREA (sq. m.)	POP. (1970p)	CAPITAL
Mindoro			
Mindoro Occidental	2,270	145,689	Mamburao
Mindoro Oriental	1,685	328,251	Calapan
Negros			
Negros Occidental	3,060	1,589,153	Bacolod
Negros Oriental	2,218	718,340	Dumaguete
Palawan			
Palawan[1]	5,571	232,322	Puerto Princesa
Panay			
Aklan	702	262,690	Kalibo
Antique	974	289,627	San Jose de Buenavista
Capiz	1,017	395,774	Roxas
Iloilo	2,056	1,168,454	Iloilo
Romblon			
Romblon	524	167,665	Romblon
Samar			
Samar del Norte	1,343	305,337	Catarman
Samar Occidental	2,166	444,950	Catbalogan
Samar Oriental	1,676	274,049	Borongan
Sulu Archipelago			
Sulu	1,038	427,386	Jolo

[1]Includes Agusan del Sur.

History: Earliest inhabitants probably Negritos, followed by Indonesians; Muslims settled in S in 15th cent. Discovered by Magellan Mar. 1521 and first successful settlements made by Spanish under Legaspi 1565; Manila founded 1571. In first two centuries many conflicts with Moros in S and occasionally some trouble with Chinese. In 1762–63 Manila captured and held by British; generally in 18th and 19th cents. Spanish control strengthened and Moros finally subdued in latter half of 19th cent.; many revolts of Filipino peoples occurred, the most serious being the Revolution of 1896–99; in Spanish-American War battle of Manila Bay May 1, 1898 and treaty with Spain Dec. 10, 1898 brought archipelago under American control; conflict with Filipinos 1899–1901; civil government established 1901–03 and in 1934 independence promised for 1946. **Commonwealth of the Philippines** established Nov. 15, 1935. In World War II attacked by Japanese Dec. 8, 1941 and Manila captured Jan. 2, 1942; Bataan and Corregidor taken by Japanese Apr.–May 1942 and islands under Japanese rule until Oct. 1944, when MacArthur returned with great invasion force; naval battles of Philippine Sea, Leyte Gulf, and Surigao Strait, and land campaigns on Leyte and Luzon established practical U.S. control by Apr. 1945. Independent government established July 4, 1946; granted the United States a 99 year lease of several Philippine military facilities 1947 (treaty amended 1959); post-war Communist-dominated Huk rebellion largely suppressed by 1955; during the 1960's its relations with Malaysia strained due to the Philippine claim to Sabah.

Phil·ip·pine Sea \ˌfil-ə-ˌpēn-\. That part of W Pacific Ocean immediately E of the Phil.; touches Taiwan and Ryukyu Is. on NW, Bonin Is. on NE, Mariana Is. on E, and W Caroline Is. on S; roughly bet. 10° and 25°N and 125° and 145°E. Max. depth 34,578 ft. (10°24′N, 126°40′E; in the **Philippine Trench**); S part scene of major naval battle June 19–20, 1944, in which U.S. carrier aircraft decisively defeated Japanese fleet.

Phi·lip·po·lis \fə-ˈlip-ə-lis\. Town, SW Orange Free State, Rep. of South Africa; the oldest town in the province.

Philippopolis. See PLOVDIV.

Phil·ips·burg \ˈfil-əps-ˌbərg\. **1** City, ⊗ of Granite co., W Montana; pop. (1970c) 1128; lead, silver mines.

2 Borough, Centre co., cen. Pennsylvania, 28 m. NNE of Altoona; pop. (1970c) 3700, brick, refrigerators; coal mines; potatoes.

3 Island, West Indies. See SAINT MARTIN.

Phi·lis·tia \fə-ˈlis-tē-ə\. Country in anc. Palestine, on the coast, ab. 50 m. in length; the land of the Philistines. Its five chief towns (city-kingdoms) were Gaza, Ashkelon, Ashdod, on the coast, and Ekron and Gath inland.

Phil·lips \ˈfil-əps\. **1** Counties in four states of the U.S. See tables at ARKANSAS, COLORADO, KANSAS, MONTANA.

2 City, ⊗ of Price co., N Wisconsin, 47 m. W of Rhinelander; pop. (1970c) 1511; dairy products.

Phillips, Mount. Peak, Glacier National Park, NW Montana; 9480 ft.

Phil·lips·burg \ˈfil-əps-ˌbərg\. **1** City, ⊗ of Phillips co., N Kansas, 102 m. NNW of Great Bend; pop. (1970c) 3241; oil refining; livestock farms.

2 Industrial town, Warren co., NW New Jersey, on Delaware river opp. Easton, Pennsylvania; pop. (1970c) 17,849; drills, boilers, iron pipe, chemicals, beverages; settled 1749.

Phillips Island. Island in Atlantic Ocean off SE South Carolina coast, in Beaufort co., S of St. Helena I.

Philomelion. See AKŞEHIR.

Phintias. See LICATA.

Phit·sa·nu·lok \ˈpit-ˌsä-nü-ˈlōk\ *also* **Pit·sa·nu·lok** *or* **Bis·nu·lok** \ˈpit-ˌsä-nü-ˈlōk—*sic*\. **1** Province, N cen. Thailand; 3729 sq. m.; pop. (1960c) 351,642; ✱Phitsanulok.

2 Town, its ✱, on Nan river 75 m. N of Nakhon Sawan and on railroad N from Bangkok; pop. (1960c) 30,364; rice milling; has several interesting temples.

Phle·grae·an Fields *or* **Phlegraean Plain** \flə-ˌgrē-ən-\ *or* *Ital.* **Cam·pi Fle·grei** \ˈkäm-pē-flā-ˈgrā-ē\. Volcanic region W of Naples and E of Cumae, S Italy; has 13 low craters most recent of which was created 1538; many hot springs and fumaroles.

Phli·us \ˈflī-əs\. In ancient times chief town of a small district of NE Peloponnesus, Greece, SSW of Sicyon; usually allied with Sparta; home of the poet Timon of Phlius.

Phlórina. See FLORINA 2.

Phnom Penh. See PNOMPENH.

Pho·caea \fō-ˈsē-ə\. Ancient city on Aegean Sea, northernmost of the Ionian cities on W coast of Asia Minor; an important maritime state c. 1000–600 B.C., one of the first to engage in voyages of discovery; founded Massilia in W Mediterranean; declined under Persian rule. The modern town is Foça (*q.v.*).

Pho·cis \ˈfō-səs\. **1** Ancient territory in cen. Greece. In S cen. part is Mt. Parnassus and across N half flows Cephisus river. Chief towns Elateia, Delphi, Daulis. Early history obscure but at first controlled oracle at Delphi; after c. 590 B.C. oracle was supervised by Amphictyonic Council; in Grecian wars frequently changed sides; fought against Greeks at Plataea and was usually allied with Sparta; later opposed Thebes, Boeotia, and Thessaly and influence declined; under power of Macedonia and Aetolian League.

2 Department of Greece; includes the ancient territory. See table at GREECE.

Phoe·bus \ˈfē-bəs\. Former town, SE Virginia, in former Elizabeth City co., on Hampton Roads 8 m. E of Newport News; since 1952 part of city of Hampton.

Phoe·ni·ce \fi-ˈnī-sē\. Town of ancient Chaonia, NW Epirus, NW Greece, near the coast.

Phoe·ni·cia \fi-ˈnish-(ē-)ə, -ˈnēsh-\ *also* **Phe·ni·cia** \fi-\. Ancient maritime country in W Syria, forming a narrow strip with the Lebanon Mts. as an indefinite E boundary and stretching at its greatest extent ab. 160 m. from Dor (Tantura) just S of Mt. Carmel to Aradus I. (modern Arwad) at the N. It consisted from early times, c. 1600 B.C., of a group of city-states, as Acre, Tyre, Sidon, etc., which flourished esp. c. 1200–1000 B.C. Phoenicians were of Semitic origin and a branch of the Canaanites; they became the leading traders of ancient world and founded colonies on N African coast, including Carthage, and in W Mediterranean; introduced alphabet to Europe; under hegemony of Tyre (*q.v.*) 11th–8th cents. B.C.; conquered successively by Assyrians, Chaldeans, Persians, and by Alexander the Great; under Persians federation of three cities formed (see TRIPOLI 3); ruled by Ptolemies of Egypt 286–197 B.C. and

PHILIPPINES
POLYCONIC PROJECTION
SCALE OF MILES
0 20 40 60 80 100
SCALE OF KILOMETERS
0 25 50 75 100 150
Capital of Country
Provincial Capitals
Provincial Boundaries
Copyright by C. S. HAMMOND & Co., N. Y.
Same scale as main map
Taiwan (Formosa)
(China)
Bashi Channel
BATANES
Itbayat I.
Luzon Str.
Basco
Batan I.
BATAN IS.
Sabtang I.
PROV.
Balintang Is.
Balintang Channel
Babuyan I.
Calayan
Calayan I.
Dalupiri I.
BABUYAN IS.
Camiguin I.
Fuga I.
Claveria
Babuyan Chan.
LUZON
Aparri
C. Engaño
Gonzaga
Provinces indicated by number
1. MOUNTAIN
2. IFUGAO
3. BENGUET
4. SAMAR DEL NORTE
5. SAMAR OCCIDENTAL
6. SAMAR ORIENTAL
7. AGUSAN DEL NORTE
8. CAMIGUIN
9. DAVAO DEL NORTE
10. DAVAO DEL SUR
11. COTABATO DEL SUR
118°
120°
122°
124°
126°
18°
16°
14°
12°
10°
8°
6°
SOUTH CHINA SEA
PACIFIC OCEAN
PHILIPPINE SEA
SULU SEA
CELEBES SEA
MINDANAO SEA
VISAYAN SEA
SIBUYAN SEA
Moro Gulf
Sulu Archipelago
Manila
Quezon City
Ilocos Norte
Laoag
Vigan
Baguio
Lingayen
Tuguegarao
Ilagan
Cabanatuan
Malolos
Cavite
Batangas
Lucena
Naga
Legaspi
Sorsogon
Virac
Daet
Calapan
Mindoro
Busuanga I.
Calamian Gr.
Culion I.
Palawan
Puerto Princesa
Romblon
Masbate
Catarman
Catbalogan
Samar
Tacloban
Roxas
Iloilo
Panay
Bacolod
Negros
Cebu
Bohol
Tagbilaran
Dumaguete
Surigao
Butuan
Cagayan de Oro
Oroquieta
Iligan
Marawi
Malaybalay
Davao
Cotabato
Zamboanga
Basilan
Jolo I.
Tawitawi
Sandakan
MALAYSIA
SABAH
Tubbataha Reefs
Cagayan Sulu I.
Balabac I.
Bugsuk I.
KAWIO IS. (Indon.)
Karakelang I. (Indon.)
Pulau Miangas (Palmas)
Sarangani Is.
Mt. Apo 9,690
Mt. Pulog 9,606
Mayon Vol. 8,284
Mt. Halcon 8,469
Longitude East of Greenwich

by Seleucid kingdom of Syria 197–64 B.C.; included in Roman province of Syria (see SYRIA 1).

Phoe·nix \'fē-niks\. 1 City, ✱ of Arizona, also ⊗ of Maricopa co., on Salt river in SW cen. part of the state; pop. (1970c) 581,562; alt. 1090 ft.; largest city in the state; ships citrus fruit and vegetables; aluminum products, aircraft and aircraft parts, textiles, chemicals, clothing, alcoholic beverages, air conditioners; tourism; in cotton and truck farming region; Phoenix Coll. (1920), Grand Canyon Coll. (1949). Settled 1870; incorporated as city 1881; became territorial capital 1889 and state capital 1912 on admission of Arizona to the Union.

2 Village, Cook co., NE Illinois, 20 m. S of Chicago; pop. (1970c) 3596.

3 Village, Oswego co., cen. New York, 14 m. NNW of Syracuse; pop. (1970c) 2617; paper; dairy, fruit farms.

4 *or* **Phe·nice** \'fē-nəs\. Ancient seaport in Crete, mentioned in *Acts* xxvii. 12; probably modern **Lou·tro** \'lü-ˌtrȯ\ on the S coast, ab. long. 24°E.

5 One of the Phoenix Is. in cen. Pacific Ocean, SE of Enderbury I., 3°40′S, 170°43′W; ab. 3 sq. m.; most fertile of the group, with large coconut groves.

Phoenix Islands. Group of eight small British coral atolls in cen. Pacific Ocean, ESE of Gilbert Is.; lat. 4°S and long. 172°W; 11 sq. m. Forms part of Gilbert and Ellice Islands Colony. Group comprises Canton, Phoenix, Enderbury, Birnie, Sydney, Hull, Gardner, and McKean. Before 1930 of little commercial value, except for guano deposits; after that date, with establishment of transoceanic air routes, suddenly became of major importance because on direct line from Honolulu to New Caledonia and Fiji. Canton and Enderbury both American and British 1936–39; dispute settled amicably 1939 and the two islands placed under joint control for 50 years.

Phoe·nix·ville \'fē-niks-ˌvil\. Borough, Chester co., SE Pennsylvania, on Schuylkill river 24 m. NW of Philadelphia; pop. (1970c) 14,823; iron and steel, paint, carpets; pork packing; settled 1720.

Phour·noi *or* **Foúr·noi** \'fü(ə)r-nē\. Small island, Samos dept., Aegean Is., Greece, N part of Southern Sporades, in Aegean Sea just SW of Samos.

Phrae *or* **Prae** \'prä\. 1 Province, N Thailand; 2258 sq. m.; pop. (1960c) 299,369; ✱ Phrae.

2 Town, its ✱, on Yom river 90 m. N of Phitsanulok; pop. (1960c) 32,368.

Phra Na·khon Si Ayut·tha·ya \ˌprä-nä-'kȯn-sē-ˌä-yü-'tī-ə\; *abbr.* **Ayutthaya.** 1 Province, S Thailand; 424 sq. m.; pop. (1960c) 478,738.

2 City, S Thailand, 40 m. N of Bangkok, on an island in the lower Chao Phraya; pop. (1965e) 40,352; intersected by many canals and many of its inhabitants live on boats; chief town of one of the richest agricultural sections of the country. Founded 1350 and was Siamese capital until 1767 when it was destroyed by the Burmese; also badly damaged by Burmese 1555; site of battle bet. Dutch and English in 17th cent.

Phryg·ia \'frij-(ē-)ə\. Ancient country, W cen. Asia Minor. Settled as early as 13th cent. B.C. by population of uncertain origin which occupied extensive lands along Black Sea and Aegean coasts, esp. in Sangarius valley; gradually driven W and S, Phrygians made their home in the plateau region bounded on N by Bithynia, on E by Galatia and Lycaonia, on S by Pisidia and Lycia, and on W by Caria, Lydia, and Mysia. Conquered by Lydia 7th cent. B.C.; its art and culture reached its height c. 600 B.C. and had considerable influence on Greece. Conquered by Persia 546 B.C.; divided c. 400 B.C. into **Greater Phrygia,** the inland region, and **Phrygia Mi·nor** \-'mī-nər\ along Hellespontus. Passed into power of Alexander who seized its capital Gordium 333 B.C. and soon after 301 became a part of the new kingdom founded by Seleucus; contended for by Pergamum and Syria; fell into Roman hands 133 B.C. and its W part became part of province of Asia; c. 300 A.D. again divided by Diocletian and under Byzantine Empire name disappeared from record.

Phthia \'thī-ə\. Ancient name of the district in S Thessaly, NE Greece, later known as Phthiotis, now in Central Greece and Euboea region. In Homer Phthia was the residence of Achilles.

Phthi·o·tis \thī-'ōt-əs\. Department of Greece. See table at GREECE.

Phthiotis and Pho·cis \-'fō-səs\. Former department of Greece, now subdivided into Phthiotis and Phocis depts.

Phu Ka·dueng National Park \'pü-kä-'du̇ŋ-\. National park, Thailand; 134 sq. m.; waterfalls; established 1962.

Phu·ket *also* **Pu·ket** *or* **Bhu·ket** \'pü-'ket\. 1 *or formerly* **Sa·lang** \sä-'läŋ\ *or* **Junk·sey·lon** \ˌjəŋk-si-'län\. Island, SW Thailand, off W coast of Malay Penin. in Andaman Sea, coextensive with Phuket prov.; 309 sq. m.; pop. (1970c) 75,652; large tin mines.

2 Seaport town, ✱ of Phuket prov., at S end of island; pop. (1960c) 28,033; one of the chief Thai ports on Indian Ocean; ships tin, rubber, charcoal, and fish.

Phul·kian States \ˌpül-kyän-\. Patiala, Nabha, and Jind, former states of E and SE Punjab, now part of Punjab state, India; 8188 sq. m.; so-called from the Sikh family that established their independence in the 18th cent.

Phu·quoc \'pü-'kwu̇k\. Island in SE part of Gulf of Siam, off S shore of Cambodia S of Kampot.

Phy·le \'fī-lē\. Ruins of an ancient fortress, 11 m. NNW of Athens, Attica dept., Greece. Base used by Thrasybulus and his followers in their operations against the Thirty Tyrants 404–403 B.C.

Pia·cen·za \pyä-'chen(t)-sə, ˌpē-ə-'\. 1 Province of Emilia-Romagna, Italy. See table at ITALY.

2 *or anc.* **Pla·cen·tia** \plə-'sen-ch(ē-)ə\. Commune, its ✱, on Po river 40 m. SE of Milan; pop. (1968e) 102,785; chemicals, office furniture; in cereal farming and wine-producing region; 16th cent. walls ab. 4 m. long; 12th cent. cathedral with 14th cent. campanile, 13th cent. town hall, 16th cent. Farnese palace (uncompleted).

History: Founded by Romans 218 B.C.; destroyed by Gauls 200 B.C. and later rebuilt; made W terminus of ancient Roman Aemilian Way; became part of Lombard League 12th cent.; under Visconti family 1337, Sforza family, and popes 1512; given together with Parma to Farnese family by Pope Paul III 1545; part of duchy of Parma and Piacenza 1545–1860; became part of kingdom of Italy 1860.

Pi·ai, Cape \-pē-'ī\. Cape, Malaysia, S Malay Penin., 1°15′N; most southerly point on Asian mainland.

Piali. See TEGEA.

Pia·no·sa \ˌpē-ə-'nō-sə\. 1 *or anc.* **Pla·na·sia** \plə-'nā-zh(ē-)ə\. Small Italian island in the Mediterranean Sea SW of the island of Elba; 4 sq. m.; highest point 95 ft.; attached to Livorno prov., Italy.

2 Italian islet in cen. Adriatic Sea N of Mount Gargano and 14 m. NE of Tremiti Is.

Pia·pa·yung·an, Mount \-pē-ˌäp-ə-'yu̇ŋ-ən\. Mountain, SE Lanao del Sur prov., Mindanao, Phil., on Cotabato boundary E of Mt. Ragang; 8725 ft.

Pia·secz·no \pyä-'sech-nō\. Town, Warszawa prov., Poland, ab. 15 m. S of Warsaw; pop. (1970p) 20,600.

Piatigorsk. See PYATIGORSK.

Pi·at·ra–Ne·amț \pē-ˌä-trə-nē-'ams\. City, ⊗ of Neamț co., NE Romania, in foothills of the Carpathians and on Bistrița river, ab. 25 m. W of Roman; pop. (1970e) 53,630; textiles, chemicals, canned foods; paper mill, oil refinery; 15th cent. church.

Pi·att \'pī-ət\. County in Illinois. See table at ILLINOIS.

Pi·auí *or formerly* **Pi·au·hy** \pyau̇-ˈē\. State, NE Brazil; 96,886 sq. m.; pop. (1970p) 1,735,568; ✱ Teresina; cotton, manioc, castor beans; first settlement in region 1674.

Piauí, Serra do. See SERRA DO PIAUÍ.

Pia·ve \ˈpyäv-ē, -(ˌ)ā, pē-ˈäv-\. River, NE Italy; 137 m. long; rises in the Carnic Alps S of Lienz, flows S and SE into the Adriatic Sea 22 m. ENE of Venice; scene of battles 1917–18, when it became the line of defense of the Italians after their retreat from Caporetto; the Austrians made several unsuccessful attempts to cross the river.

Piaz·za Ar·me·ri·na \pē-ˌät-sə-ˌär-mə-ˈrē-nə\; *Sicilian* **Chiaz·za** \kē-ˈät-sə\. Commune, Enna prov., cen. Sicily, Italy, 13 m. SSE of Enna; pop. (1968e) 23,120; cathedral.

Pi·bor \ˈpē-ˌbȯ(ə)r\. River, SE Sudan; ab. 200 m. long; flows N and unites with Baro river on border of W Ethiopia to form Sobat river.

Pic \ˈpēk\. French term meaning "peak" or "mountain"; for some entries beginning with *Pic*, see the distinguishing element.

Pi·ca·ra Point \pi-ˌkär-ə-\. Tip of long narrow peninsula on N coast of St. Thomas I., Virgin Is. of the United States, West Indies, which forms E side of Magens Bay.

Pic·ar·dy \ˈpik-ərd-ē\ *or Fr.* **Pi·car·die** \pē-kȧr-dē\. Historical region of N France; bounded before 1790 on N by Strait of Dover, Artois, and Flanders, E by Champagne, S by Île-de-France, SW by Normandy, W by English Channel; ✱ Amiens (to 1790); watered by Somme river.

History: Name first recorded in 13th cent.; military government organized c. 1350 by Valois family; joined to Burgundy 1435; province of France 1477 until Revolution; region scene of heavy fighting in World War I (battle of Picardy Mar. 21, 1918 ff.).

Pic·a·yune \ˌpik-ē-ˈ(y)ün, -ə-ˈyün\. City, Pearl River co., S Mississippi, 35 m. WNW of Gulfport; pop. (1970c) 10,467; tung oil, clothing, lumber; dairy, livestock farms.

Pi·ce·num \pī-ˈsē-nəm\. Ancient Roman province in E Italy, on the Adriatic Sea; chief towns Ancona and Asculum Picenum (Ascoli Piceno), the capital.

Pi·chin·cha \pə-ˈchin-chə\. 1 Volcano, Ecuador, NW of the city of Quito; 15,173 ft.; scene of battle May 24, 1822. See ECUADOR.

2 Province of N cen. Ecuador. See table at ECUADOR.

Pichit. See PHICHIT.

Pichones, Cayos. See PIGEON CAYS.

Pick·a·way \ˈpik-ə-ˌwā\. County of Ohio. See table at OHIO.

Pick·ens \ˈpik-ənz\. 1 Counties in three states of the U.S. See tables at ALABAMA, GEORGIA, SOUTH CAROLINA.

2 Town, ⊗ of Pickens co., NW South Carolina, 19 m. W of Greenville; pop. (1970c) 2954; resort; lumber, textiles, electronic components.

Pick·ett \ˈpik-ət\. County in Tennessee. See table at TENNESSEE.

Pick·wick Landing Dam \ˌpik-wik-\. Dam in Tennessee river, Hardin co., SW Tennessee, at village of **Pickwick Dam,** Tennessee, forming **Pickwick Landing Reservoir** extending along the Alabama-Mississippi boundary and into Lauderdale co., NW Alabama. See table at TENNESSEE VALLEY AUTHORITY.

Pi·co. 1 *Span.* ˈpē-(ˌ)kō, *Port.* -(ˌ)kü\. Spanish and Portuguese name for "mountain" or "peak"; for names beginning with *Pico*, see the distinguishing element.

2 \ˈpē-(ˌ)kō\. Town, Argentina. See GENERAL PICO.

3 \ˈpē-(ˌ)kü\. Island, cen. Azores, in the district of Horta; 167 sq. m.; pop. (1960c) 21,626; chief town Lajes do Pico; highest point 7711 ft. (see ALTO, PICO).

Pico Ri·ve·ra \ˌpē-(ˌ)kō-rə-ˈvir-ə\. City, Los Angeles co., SW California, SE of Los Angeles; pop. (1970c) 54,170; plastics, cement, dairy products, lumber, pharmaceuticals.

Pic·qui·gny \ˌpē-kē-ˈnyē\. Commune, Somme dept., N France, 8 m. NW of Amiens; pop. (1962c) 1195; treaty signed here Aug. 19, 1475 bet. Edward IV of England and Louis XI of France.

Pic·ton \ˈpik-tən\. 1 Town, ⊗ of Prince Edward co., SE Ontario, Canada, on inlet of Lake Ontario 16 m. SE of Belleville; pop. (1971p) 4860.

2 Borough and port on inlet of Cook Strait, NE South I., New Zealand; pop. (1970e) 2700.

Picton Channel. Strait, W of Wellington I., off SW coast of Chile, connecting Trinidad Gulf with the Pacific.

Pic·tou \ˈpik-(ˌ)tü\. 1 County, N Nova Scotia, Canada. See table at NOVA SCOTIA.

2 Town, its ⊗, on Pictou Harbor, an inlet of Northumberland Strait; pop. (1971p) 4247; summer resort, coastal port, and trawler fleet base; shipyards, lobster fisheries; Pictou Academy (1818); founded 1763.

Pic·tured Rocks \ˌpik-chərd-\. Cliffs on S shore of Lake Superior, in Alger co., N Michigan penin.; erosion features.

Pi·du·ru·ta·la·ga·la \ˌpid-ə-ˌrüt-ᵊl-ˈäg-ə-lə\. Mountain, highest peak in Ceylon, ab. 60 m. E of Colombo; 8281 ft.

Piedad, La. See LA PIEDAD.

Pie·de·cues·ta \pē-ˌād-ə-ˈkwes-tə\. Town, Santander dept., N cen. Colombia, S of Bucaramanga; munic. pop. (1968e) 24,812.

Pied·mont \ˈpēd-ˌmänt\. 1 City, Calhoun co., NE Alabama, 20 m. E of Gadsden; pop. (1970c) 5063; sawmills, iron mines; diversified agriculture.

2 Residential city, Alameda co., W California, suburb of Oakland 5 m. E of San Francisco Bay; pop. (1970c) 10,917.

3 *or Ital.* **Pie·mon·te** \pyā-ˈmōn-(ˌ)tā\. Autonomous region, NW Italy; 9807 sq. m.; pop. (1968e) 4,316,466; ✱ Turin; (for provincial divisions, see table at ITALY); borders on France and Switzerland; almost entirely surrounded by mountains; slopes to fertile plain producing grains, olives, wine, chestnuts, dairy products; industries include automobiles, textiles, glass. In ancient times part of Transpadane Gaul; held from 11th cent. by house of Savoy (*q.v.*) one of whose rulers took title of Prince of Piedmont; administrative region established 1948; received limited autonomy 1970.

Piedmont Region *or* **Piedmont Plateau.** An upland belt, that part of the Atlantic plain of E United States lying E of the Blue Ridge and Appalachian Mts., extending from the Hudson river to cen. Alabama.

Piedras, Las. See LAS PIEDRAS.

Pi·e·dras Blan·cas Point \pē-ˌā-drəs-ˈblaŋ-kəs-\. Point on NW coast of San Luis Obispo co., SW California.

Pie·dras Ne·gras \pē-ā-drə-ˈsnā-grəs\. 1 Archaeological site on right bank of the Usumacinta river, NW Guatemala; Mayan sculptural art.

2 *or formerly* **Ciu·dad Por·fi·rio Dí·az** \ˌsē-ü-ˌthä-pȯr-ˈfir-ē-ˌō-ˈdē-ˌäs, -ü-ˌdad-\. City, Coahuila state, NE Mexico, on the Rio Grande river opp. Eagle Pass, Texas, with which it is connected by an international bridge; munic. pop. (1970p) 65,883; northern terminus of Mexican National Railways; in agricultural and mining region.

Pie·dras Point \pē-ˌā-drəs-\. Cape on E cen. coast of Argentina, SE of Buenos Aires, extending into the Río de la Plata opp. Brava Point in Uruguay. See BRAVA POINT.

Pie·gan, Mount \-pē-ˈgan\. Peak, Glacier National Park, NW Montana; 9230 ft.

Pie·ka·ry Śląs·kie \ˌpye-ˈkä-rē-ˈshləs-kē\. Town, Katowice prov., S Poland, ab. 12 m. NNW of Katowice; pop. (1970p) 36,300.

Piek·sä·mä·ki \pē-ˈek-sə-ˌmak-ē\. Town, Mikkeli prov., S Finland, ab. 45 m. N of Mikkeli; pop. (1970e) 12,790; formed 1930.

Pie·li·nen \ˈpyel-ən-ən\ *or* **Pie·lis·jär·vi** \pē-ˈel-əs-ˌya(ə)r-vē\. Lake, Kuopio prov., SE Finland; 56 m. long, 422 sq. m.

Pie·man \ˈpī-mən\. River, NW Tasmania, Australia; ab. 70 m. long; rises on W edge of central highlands and flows W to Indian Ocean.

Piemonte. See PIEDMONT 3.

Pien–ching. See K'AI-FENG.

Pie·ni·ny National Park \pye-ˈnē-nē-\. National park, Poland; 10 sq. m.; mountain range; deer, lynx, rare insects.

Pierce \'pi(ə)rs\. 1 Name of counties in five states of the U.S. See tables at GEORGIA, NEBRASKA, NORTH DAKOTA, WASHINGTON, WISCONSIN.

2 City, ⊗ of Pierce co., NE Nebraska; pop. (1970c) 1360; diversified agriculture.

Pi·e·ria \pī-'ir-ē-ə\. 1 Department of Macedonia, Greece. See table at GREECE.

2 A region of ancient Macedonia, W of the Gulf of Salonika; seat of worship of the Muses; location of the Pierian Spring, a fountain believed sacred to the Muses.

Pier·mont \'pi(ə)r-ˌmänt\. Residential village, Rockland co., SE New York, on Hudson river 22 m. N of New York; pop. (1970c) 2386.

Pierre \'pi(ə)r\. City, ✱ of South Dakota, also ⊗ of Hughes co., cen. South Dakota, on the Missouri river; pop. (1970c) 9699; in grain and dairy farming region. Founded as railroad terminus 1880; named state capital 1889.

Pierre·fitte–sur–Seine \pyer-'fēt-sər-'sān, -'sen\. Commune, Seine-St-Denis dept., N France, N suburb of Paris; pop. (1968c) 19,017; electrical equipment.

Pierre·fonds \pyer-'fōⁿ\. 1 City, Montreal and Jesus Islands co., S Quebec, Canada; pop. (1971p) 33,046.

2 Town, E Oise dept., N France, SE of Compiègne; pop. (1962c) 1295; mineral springs; château, built 1390–1405, destroyed by Louis XIII, restored by Viollet-le-Duc 1858 ff.

Pi·e·rus \'pī-ə-rəs\. Mountain in ancient Pieria, Macedonia, Greece, N of Mt. Olympus.

Pieš·t'a·ny \'pyesh-tə-nē\ *or Hung.* **Pös·tyén** \'pərsh-ˌtyān\ *or Ger.* **Pis·tyan** \'pis-ˌtyän\. Town, Slovak S.R., E cen. Czechoslovakia, on the Váh ab. 45 m. NE of Bratislava; pop. (1968e) 22,170.

Pie·tar·saa·ri \pē-'et-ər-ˌsär-ē\ *or Swed.* **Ja·kob·stad** \'yäk-əp-ˌstä(d)\. Seaport, Vaasa prov., W Finland, on the Baltic Sea; pop. (1970e) 18,725; trade center; exports lumber; birthplace of the national poet Johan Ludvig Runeberg; formed 1653.

Pietas Julia. See PULA.

Pie·ter·mar·itz·burg \ˌpēt-ər-'mar-əts-ˌbərg\. Town, ✱ of Natal, E Rep. of South Africa, in S part of Natal, 40 m. W of Durban; pop. (1968e) 112,693; footwear, aluminum and rubber products, furniture, candy; rice mill; in area growing wattle trees, whose bark furnishes mimosa extract for tanning. Founded 1839 and named after two Boer leaders, Pieter Retief and Gert Maritz; incorporated 1853; made capital 1856.

Pie·ters·burg \'pēt-ərz-ˌbərg\. Town, N cen. Transvaal, NE Rep. of South Africa, 150 m. NNE of Pretoria; pop. (1967e) 35,700; in rich agricultural region; center of a district in which gold, silver, asbestos, iron, and corundum are found. For a time headquarters of Dutch forces during Boer War.

Pietola. See VIRGILIO.

Pie·tra·per·zia \pē-ˌe-trə-'per-tsē-ə\. Commune, Enna prov., cen. Sicily, Italy, 13 m. SW of Enna; pop. (1968c) 12,076.

Pie·tra·san·ta \pē-ˌe-trə-'sänt-ə\. Commune, Lucca prov., Tuscany, cen. Italy, 16 m. NW of Lucca; pop. (1968e) 25,375; 14th cent. cathedral; marble works.

Piet Re·tief \'pēt-rə-'tēf\. Town, SE Transvaal, NE Rep. of South Africa, near Swaziland border; pop. (1967e) 8100.

Pi·geon \'pij-ən\. 1 River, extreme NE Minnesota; 40 m. long; flows into N Lake Superior, forms section of United States-Canada boundary.

2 River, E Tennessee; 75 m. long; rises in W North Carolina, flows NW across Tennessee border and into French Broad river in W Cocke co.

Pigeon Cays \-'kīz, -'kāz\ *or Span.* **Ca·yos Pi·cho·nes** \ˌkī-ōs-pē-'chō-nəs\. Group of small islands in Caribbean Sea off E coast of Honduras.

Pigeon Cove. Unincorporated community, Essex co., NE Massachusetts, 33 m. NNE of Boston and ab. 2 m. N of Rockport; pop. (1970c) 1466; summer resort.

Pigeon Peak. Mountain, La Plata co., SW Colorado; 13,961 ft.

Pig·gott \'pig-ət\. City, a ⊗ of Clay co., NE corner of Arkansas, 49 m. NE of Jonesboro; pop. (1970c) 3087; lumber, shoes; ships hogs.

Pignerol. See PINEROLO.

Pigs, Bay of. See COCHINOS BAY.

Pihkva. See PSKOV and PSKOV, LAKE.

Pike \'pīk\. Name of counties in ten states of the U.S. See tables at ALABAMA, ARKANSAS, GEORGIA, ILLINOIS, INDIANA, KENTUCKY, MISSISSIPPI, MISSOURI, OHIO, PENNSYLVANIA.

Pike o'Stickle. See LANGDALE PIKES.

Pikes Peak \'pīks-\. Mountain, El Paso co., E cen. Colorado, near Colorado Springs; 14,110 ft.; tourist resort, noted for view from its summit; has mountain railroad and automobile highway to summit. Discovered 1806 by Zebulon M. Pike.

Pikes·ville \'pīks-'vil\. Urban community (unincorporated), Baltimore co., cen. Maryland, NW of Baltimore; pop. (1970c) 25,395.

Pike·ville \'pīk-ˌvil\. 1 City, ⊗ of Pike co., E Kentucky, 42 m. ENE of Hazard; pop. (1970c) 4899; coal mines, gas wells; Pikeville Coll. (1859).

2 Town, ⊗ of Bledsoe co., SE cen. Tennessee; pop. (1970c) 1454; clothing; poultry, strawberries.

Pi·ła \'pē-lə\ *or Ger.* **Schnei·de·mühl** \'shnīd-ə-ˌmyül\. City, Poznań prov., W cen. Poland, ab. 55 m. N of Poznań; pop. (1970p) 43,800; railroad junction; ships potatoes; foundries, machine shops, sawmills, railroad shops. First mentioned 15th cent.; made city 1513; to Prussia 1772; in World War II occupied by U.S.S.R. Feb. 14, 1945; assigned to Poland by Potsdam Conference 1945.

Pi·lar \pi-'lär\. 1 Town, Buenos Aires prov., E cen. Argentina, ab. 28 m. NW of Buenos Aires; pop. (1960c) 10,375.

2 *or* **Vi·lla del Pilar** \ˌvē-(y)ə-del-\. Town and river port, ✱ of Neembucú dept., SW cen. Paraguay, on Paraguay river opp. the mouth of the Bermejo, 120 m. SW of Asunción; pop. (1970e) 15,324; ships agricultural produce; sawmills, distilleries; founded 1778.

3 Municipality, Sorsogon prov., Luzon, Phil., on inlet W of Sorsogon Bay 22 m. W of Sorsogon; pop. (1969e) 40,700.

4 Municipality, Capiz prov., Panay, Phil., on S shore of Pilar Bay 18 m. ESE of Roxas; pop. (1969e) 11,900.

5 Municipality, Cebu prov., Phil. See PONSON.

Pilar, Cape *or* **Cape Pil·lar** \-'pil-ər\. Cape on Desolación I. at W entrance into Strait of Magellan, off S coast of South America.

Pilar Bay. Inlet of SE Sibuyan Sea in NE Capiz prov., Panay, Phil.

Pi·lat \pe-'lä\. Peak in the Cévennes range, Loire dept., SE cen. France; 4704 ft.

Pi·la·tus \pi-'lät-əs\. Peak, Unterwalden canton, cen. Switzerland, near border of Lucerne canton; 6983 ft.; railway.

Pil·co·ma·yo \ˌpil-kə-'mī-(ˌ)ō\. River, S cen. South America; ab. 1000 m. long; rises in E Andes Mts., W cen. Bolivia, flows SE and forms boundary bet. Argentina and the Chaco region of Paraguay; empties into Paraguay river at Asunción. See CONFUSO.

Pi·li \'pē-lē\. 1 Peak, E Antofagasta prov., N Chile; 19,849 ft.

2 Municipality, Camarines Sur prov., Luzon, Phil., on railroad 8 m. SE of Naga; pop. (1969e) 31,400.

Pi·li·bhit \ˌpē-li-'bēt\. Town, N Uttar Pradesh, N India, ab. 50 m. N of Shahjahanpur; pop. (1961c) 57,527; sugar refining; 18th cent. mosque.

Pi·li·ca \pi-ˈlēt-sə\ *or* **Pi·li·tsa** \pi-ˈlēt-sə\. River, Poland; 195 m. long; rises in SW Poland, flows N and NE into Vistula river above Warsaw.

Pi·lim·sit \ˌpi-lim-ˈsit\ *or formerly* **Iden·burg** \ˈī-dən-ˌbərg\. Peaks in Sudirman Range, W Irian Barat, Indonesia; highest point 15,784 ft.

Pílion. See PELION.

Pilipinas, Republika ng. See PHILIPPINES.

Pilitsa. See PILICA.

Pil·lar, Cape \-ˈpil-ər\. 1 Southeast point of Tasmania, Australia, at S end of Tasman Penin., extending into Tasman Sea.

2 Cape, Strait of Magellan. See PILAR, CAPE.

Pillar Mountain. Peak, Cumberland co., NW England, in the Lake District; 2927 ft.

Pí·lla·ro \ˈpē-yə-ˌrō\. Town, Tungurahua prov., cen. Ecuador, N of Riobamba; pop. (1962c) 2714.

Pil·lars of Her·cu·les \ˌpil-ərz . . . ˈhər-kyə-ˌlēz\. The two promontories at E end of Strait of Gibraltar: Rock of Gibraltar in Europe, and Jebel Musa at Ceuta in Africa. Of various explanations for origin of term, most probable is fable that before existence of strait they formed one mountain range which Hercules wrenched apart to join the seas, or that in his travels to find the oxen of Geryon he set them there as a memorial.

Pillau. See BALTISK.

Pill·nitz \ˈpil-nəts\. Castle on the Elbe just SE of Dresden, East Germany; scene of conference Aug. 1791 at which Emperor Leopold II and Frederick William II, king of Prussia, agreed to form an alliance against France.

Pills·bury Sound \ˌpilz-ber-ē-, -b(ə-)rē-\. Body of water off N coast of E end of St. Thomas I., Virgin Is. of the United States, West Indies.

Pi·lo·ña \pi-ˈlō-nyə\. Commune, Oviedo prov., NW Spain, 24 m. E of Oviedo; pop. (1970p) 12,194; mineral baths; marble quarries; mining; stock raising.

Pílos. See PYLOS.

Pi·lot Knob \ˌpī-lət-\. 1 Peak, San Juan and San Miguel cos., SW Colorado; 13,750 ft.

2 Peak, cen. Idaho co., N cen. Idaho; 7134 ft.

3 Hill, Iron co., SE Missouri; contains iron ore.

Pilot Peak. 1 Mountain on S boundary of Plumas co., NE California, in Sierra Nevada Mts.; 7508 ft.

2 Mountain, cen. Boise co., W cen. Idaho; 8560 ft.

3 Mountain, N Valley co., W cen. Idaho; 8061 ft.

4 Mountain, S Mineral co., SW Nevada; highest in Excelsior Mts.; 9187 ft.

5 Mountain, NW Park co., in the Absaroka Range, NW Wyoming; 11,500 ft.

Pilt·down *or* **Pilt Down** \ˈpilt-ˌdau̇n\. Locality in East Sussex, S England, ab. 7 m. N of Lewes; site of discovery 1911–15 of skull and jawbone fragments originally held to derive from a distinctive early Pleistocene hominoid but later shown to be the product of a deliberate hoax.

Pi·ma \ˈpē-mə\. County in Arizona. See table at ARIZONA.

Pi·men·tel \ˌpē-mən-ˈtel\. Seaport, Lambayeque dept., NW Peru, 8 m. from Chiclayo; pop. (1961c) 6300; trade center of Lambayeque dept.

Pim·li·co \ˈpim-li-ˌkō\. Southwest district of London, England, bet. Westminster and Chelsea; includes Belgravia. In Elizabethan times, a resort famous for its ale.

Pi·ná·cu·lo \pi-ˈnäk-ə-ˌlō\. Peak, SW Santa Cruz prov., S Argentina, near Chile border; 7090 ft.

Pi·nal \pə-ˈnal\. County in Arizona. See table at ARIZONA.

Pin·a·le·no Mountains \ˌpin-əl-ˈā-nō-\. Mountain range, including Graham Peak (*q.v.*), in Graham co., SE Arizona.

Pinal Peak. Mountain in SW Gila co., SE cen. Arizona; 7850 ft.

Pi·na·ma·la·yan \ˌpin-ə-mə-ˈlä-ˌyän\. Municipality, Mindoro Oriental prov., in center of E coast of Mindoro I., Phil., on coastal highway 33 m. SE of Calapan; pop. (1969e) 54,500.

Pi·na·mung·a·jan \ˌpin-ə-ˌmu̇ŋ-ˈä-ˌhän\. Municipality, Cebu prov., on W coast of Cebu I., Phil., in cen. part on Tanon Strait 22 m. WSW of City of Cebu; pop. (1969e) 29,800.

Pinang. See PENANG.

Pinang, Pulau. See PENANG 3.

Pi·nar del Río \pi-ˌnär-del-ˈrē-(ˌ)ō\. 1 Province of W Cuba. See table at CUBA.

2 City, its ✻, in S cen. part; pop. (1967e) 67,600.

Pi·ñas \ˈpē-nyəs\. Town, El Oro prov., SW Ecuador; pop. (1962c) 3344.

Pi·na·tu·bo, Mount \-ˌpin-ə-ˈtü-(ˌ)bō\. Mountain on boundary bet. E Zambales and W Pampanga provs., Luzon, Phil.; 5770 ft.

Pin·cher Creek \ˌpin-chər-\. Town, Alberta, Canada, 57 m. W of Lethbridge; pop. (1971p) 3231; natural gas; ranching.

Pin·chot, Mount \-ˈpin-(ˌ)shō\. 1 Peak in Sierra Nevada, in E Fresno co., S cen. California; 13,495 ft.

2 Peak in Glacier National Park, NW Montana; 9375 ft.

Pinciacum. See POISSY.

Pinck·ney·ville \ˈpiŋk-nē-ˌvil\. City, ⊗ of Perry co., SW Illinois, 34 m. SW of Mount Vernon; pop. (1970c) 3377; agriculture.

Pin·court \ˈpin-ˌkō(ə)rt, -ˌkȯ(ə)rt\. Town, S Quebec, Canada; pop. (1966c) 5656.

Pin·da·ré \ˌpēn-də-ˈrā\. River, Maranhão state, NE Brazil; ab. 200 m. long; flows NE into Mearim river just before it enters São Marcos Bay.

Pin·dus Mountains \ˈpin-dəs-\ *or Gk.* **Pín·dhos Óros** \ˈpin-dȯs-ˈȯ-rȯs\. 1 In modern times, range of mountains in NW Greece, extending into Albania; ab. 68 m. long; average width 20 m.; highest point 8136 ft.

2 In classical times, the mountains forming the boundary between Epirus and Thessaly.

Pine \ˈpīn\. 1 County of Minnesota. See table at MINNESOTA.

2 River, E British Columbia, Canada; ab. 125 m. long; flows E and N into Peace river near Fort St. John.

Pine, Cape. Cape, SE Newfoundland, Canada, W of Cape Race.

Pine Bluff. Commercial city, ⊗ of Jefferson co., SE cen. Arkansas, on Arkansas river 43 m. SE of Little Rock; pop. (1970c) 57,389; cotton market; electrical transformers, lumber and wood products, textiles, chemicals, cottonseed oil, food products; Agricultural, Mechanical, and Normal Coll. (1873). Founded c. 1820 as Mount Marie; renamed 1832; chartered 1835; defended by Union forces against Confederate attack Oct. 25, 1863.

Pine City. Village, ⊗ of Pine co., E Minnesota, 60 m. N of Minneapolis; pop. (1970c) 2143; dairy products; poultry, grain, stock farms.

Pine Creek. River, N cen. Pennsylvania; ab. 100 m. long; rises in Potter co., N Pennsylvania, flows E and S into West Branch of Susquehanna river in S Lycoming co.

Pine·dale \ˈpīn-ˌdāl\. Town, ⊗ of Sublette co., W Wyoming; pop. (1970c) 948.

Pine Flat Dam. See UNITED STATES, *Dams and Reservoirs*.

Pine Forest Range. Range in Humboldt co., NW Nevada; includes Duffer Peak 9458 ft.

Pi·neg·ska·ya Yen·ta·la \ˌpē-ˈneg-skə-yə-ˌyen-ˌtä-lə\. River, Arkhangelsk Oblast, N Russian S.F.S.R., U.S.S.R.; 407 m. long; flows into the Northern Dvina near its mouth.

Pine Hill. Borough, Camden co., SW New Jersey, 13 m. SSE of Camden; pop. (1970c) 5132.

Pine·hurst \ˈpīn-ˌhərst\. Unincorporated winter resort, Moore co., cen. North Carolina, ab. 63 m. SW of Raleigh; pop. (1970c) 1056; established 1895.

Pine Island. Island off W coast of Lee co., SW Florida, S of Charlotte Harbor; 31 sq. m.

Pine Island Sound. Sound W of Pine I. and E of outer island chain off coast of Lee co., SW Florida.

Pine Lawn. City, St. Louis co., E Missouri, NW suburb of St. Louis; pop. (1970c) 5773.

Pi·nel·las \pī-ˈnel-əs\. County in Florida. See table at FLORIDA.

Pinellas Park. City, Pinellas co., W cen. Florida, N of St. Petersburg; pop. (1970c) 22,287; air conditioners, medical equipment, plastics.

Pinellas Peninsula. Peninsula, Pinellas co., W cen. Florida, W of Tampa Bay; St. Petersburg is situated at its S end.

Pine Mountain. Range extending along N section of Kentucky-Virginia boundary.

Pine Point. 1 Cape on W shore of Dixie co., NW Florida penin., extending into the Gulf of Mexico.

2 Extreme S point, Cumberland co., SW Maine.

Pi·ne·ro·lo \ˌpē-nə-ˈrō-(ˌ)lō\ *or Fr.* **Pi·gne·rol** \pē-nyə-rȯl\. Industrial commune, Torino prov., Piedmont, NW Italy, at foot of Alps 22 m. SW of Turin; pop. (1970c) 35,724; textile mills, iron foundries, printing plants; 15th–16th cent. cathedral; palaces. First mentioned 996; center of cloth industry in 14th cent.; successively under Savoy and France; episcopal see 1748.

Pines, Isle of \-ˈpīnz\. 1 Island in Caribbean Sea. See ISLE OF PINES.

2 Island, Pacific Ocean. See ÎLE DES PINS.

Pine·town \ˈpīn-ˌtau̇n\. Town, Natal, Rep. of South Africa, ab. 10 m. WNW of Durban; pop. (1967e) 21,100.

Pine View Dam. Dam across Ogden river E of Ogden, Utah; height 132 ft.; completed 1937; impounds water, **Pine View Reservoir,** for irrigation.

Pine·ville \ˈpīn-ˌvil, -vəl\. 1 City, ⊗ of Bell co., SE Kentucky; pop. (1970c) 2817; summer resort.

2 City, Rapides parish, cen. Louisiana, 5 m. NE of Alexandria; pop. (1970c) 8951; fishing, diversified agriculture; Louisiana Coll. (1906).

3 Town, ⊗ of McDonald co., SW Missouri; pop. (1970c) 444; resort; flour; truck farms.

4 Town, Mecklenburg co., S North Carolina, on South Carolina border 11 m. S of Charlotte; pop. (1970c) 1948; birthplace of James Knox Polk, 11th president of U.S., nearby.

5 Town, ⊗ of Wyoming co., S West Virginia; pop. (1970c) 1187; coal mines.

Pin·ey Point Village \ˈpī-nē-ˌpȯint-\. City, Harris co., SE Texas, 11 m. W of Houston; pop. (1970c) 2548.

Ping \ˈpiŋ\ *or* **Me·ping** \ˈmā-\. River, W Thailand; ab. 300 m. long; rises N of Chiang Mai, flows SSE to join with the Nan at Nakhon Sawan to form Chao Phraya.

Ping·e·lap \ˈpiŋ-ə-ˌlap\. Island group of three small islands halfway bet. Ponape and Kusaie, E Caroline Is., W Pacific.

P'ing–hsiang \ˈpiŋ-shē-ˈäŋ\ *or formerly* **Ping·siang** \ˈpiŋ-shē-ˈäŋ\. 1 Town, W Kiangsi prov., SE China, SE of Ch'ang-sha.

2 Town, SW Kwangsi Chuang, S China, on North Vietnam border.

Pingkiang. See PINKIANG 2.

P'ing–liang \ˈpiŋ-lē-ˈäŋ\. Town, E Kansu prov., N cen. China, 170 m. E of Lan-chou near Shensi border.

Pingsiang. See P'ING-HSIANG.

Pi·nhei·ro \pi-ˈnye(ə)r-(ˌ)ü\. City, Maranhão state, NE Brazil, ab. 50 m. W of São Luís; munic. pop. (1968e) 68,918.

Pi·ni \ˈpē-nē\. See BATU.

Pi·ni·ós \ˌpēn-ē-ˈȯs\ *or* **Sa·lam·bria** \sə-ˈlam-brē-ə\ *or anc.* **Pe·ne·us** \pə-ˈnē-əs\. River, Thessaly, N cen. Greece; ab. 125 m. long; rises in Pindus Mts., flows SE and ENE through plain of Thessaly and Vale of Tempe into the Gulf of Salonika.

Pin·kiang \ˈbin-jē-ˈäŋ, ˈbiŋ-\. 1 Former province (1932–45), E cen. Manchukuo; 24,651 sq. m.; ✱ Harbin.

2 *or* **Pingkiang.** City, China. See HARBIN.

Pink·ie \ˈpiŋ-kē\. Battlefield near Edinburgh, Scotland; scene of victory of duke of Somerset over the Scots Sept. 10, 1547.

Pinna. See PENNE.

Pin·na·cles National Monument \ˈpin-ə-kəlz-\. See UNITED STATES, *National Monuments.*

Pin·ne·berg \ˈpin-ə-ˌbe(ə)rg\. Town, Schleswig-Holstein, West Germany, on Pinnau river 12 m. NW of Hamburg; pop. (1969e) 36,101; rose nurseries.

Pi·nole \pi-ˈnōl\. City, Contra Costa co., W California, N of Oakland; pop. (1970c) 13,266; chemicals.

Pin·op·o·lis Dam \ˈpīn-ˈäp-(ə-)ləs-\. Dam across Cooper river, cen. Berkeley co., SE South Carolina; height 140 ft.; completed 1941; impounds water, **Pinopolis Reservoir,** for water power.

Pi·nos \ˈpē-nōs\. Municipality, Zacatecas state, Mexico, 70 m. SE of Zacatecas; pop. (1970p) 35,994.

Pinos, Mount \-ˈpē-ˌnōs\. Peak, N Ventura co., SW California, in the Coast Ranges (*q.v.*); 8831 ft.

Pinos–Puen·te \ˈpē-nōs-ˈpwen-tā\. Commune, Granada prov., S Spain, 11 m. NW of Granada; pop. (1970p) 12,734.

Pinsk *or Pol.* **Pińsk** \ˈpin(t)sk\. Town, Brest Oblast, Belorussian S.S.R., U.S.S.R., 103 m. E of Brest at confluence of the Pina and Pripet rivers; pop. (1969e) 62,000; lumber, veneer, furniture; shipbuilding and repairing. First mentioned 1097; capital of an early Russian principality of the same name; to Lithuania in 13th cent. and then to Poland; to Russia under second partition 1793; returned to Poland 1918 but again ceded to U.S.S.R. 1945.

Pinsk Marshes. See POLESYE.

Pinsk Oblast \-ˈō-bləst, -ˌblast\. Former subdivision of the Belorussian S.S.R., U.S.S.R.; ✱ Pinsk; abolished 1954.

Pin·ta Island \ˌpint-ə-, ˌpēnt-\ *or* **Ab·ing·don Island** \ˌab-iŋ-dən-\. One of the Galápagos Is. (*q.v.*).

Pintuaria. See TENERIFE.

Pint·wa·ter Range \ˈpīnt-ˌwȯt-ər-, -ˌwät-\. Small range in N Clark co., SE Nevada, extending N into Lincoln co.; highest peak 6370 ft.

Pin·yon Peak \ˈpin-yən-\. Mountain, NW Custer co., cen. Idaho; 9945 ft.

Pi·oche \pē-ˈōch\. Village, ⊗ of Lincoln co., E Nevada; pop. (1969e) 600.

Piom·bi·no \pyōm-ˈbē-(ˌ)nō\. Commune, Livorno prov., Tuscany, cen. Italy, on Ligurian Sea 43 m. S of Leghorn; pop. (1968e) 39,618; seaport with iron and steel works; under Pisan rule in the Middle Ages; as a principality, under the Viscontis 1399 ff.; to Spain 1603; to Ludovisi family 1634; passed to Buoncompagni family 1700; to French 1801; to Tuscany 1815.

Pio·tr·ków Try·bu·nal·ski \ˈpyȯt-ər-ˌküf-ˌtrib-ü-ˈnäl-skē, pē-ˈȯt-, -ˌku̇v-\ *or Russ.* **Pe·tro·kov** \ˈpet-rə-ˌkȯf, -ˌkȯv\ *or Ger.* **Pe·tri·kau** \ˈpā-tri-ˌkau̇\. Commune, Łódź prov., cen. Poland, 28 m. SSE of Łódź; pop. (1970p) 59,700; textiles. Under Polish kings seat of most important court of assizes—hence its name.

Pio XII \ˈpē-ü-ˌdü-ō-ˈdā-sē-ˌmō\. Municipality, Maranhão state, NE Brazil, ab. 100 m. WSW of São Luís; pop. (1968e) 51,923.

Pio·ve di Sac·co \ˌpyō-və-dē-ˈsäk-ō\. Commune, Padova prov., Veneto, NE Italy, 12 m. SE of Padua; pop. (1968e) 15,103.

Pi·per Peak \ˈpī-pər-\. Mountain, W Esmeralda co., SW Nevada; 9447 ft.

Pipe Spring National Monument \ˈpīp-\. See UNITED STATES, *National Monuments.*

Pipe·stone \ˈpīp-ˌstōn\. 1 County in SW Minnesota. See table at MINNESOTA.

2 City, its ⊗, 40 m. SW of Marshall; pop. (1970c) 5328; dairy products; agriculture; just to the N is **Pipestone National Monument:** see UNITED STATES, *National Monuments.*

Piq·ua \ˈpik-(ˌ)wä, -wə\. City, Miami co., W Ohio, 27 m. N of Dayton; pop. (1970c) 20,741; clothing, blankets, automobiles, tools, foundry products; meat-packing plant, breweries, stone quarries; settled 1797; supply base in War of 1812; important canal port in early 19th cent.

Pi·qui·ri \ˌpē-kə-'rē\ *or* **Pe·que·ri** \ˌpā-\. River, Paraná state, S Brazil; about 200 m. long; flows NW into the Paraná.

Pi·ra·ci·ca·ba \ˌpir-ə-sə-'kab-ə\. City, SE cen. São Paulo state, SE Brazil, 42 m. WNW of Campinas; munic. pop. (1968e) 137,184; ships sugar, coffee, oranges; flour, sugar, and rice mills, tanneries, distillery.

Pi·rae·us \pī-'rē-əs\ *or* **Pei·rae·us** \pī-'rē-əs\ *or Gk.* **Pi·rai·é·us** \ˌpē-re-'efs\. 1 Department of Central Greece and Euboea, Greece. See table at GREECE.
2 Seaport city, its ✻, on the Saronic Gulf 5 m. SW of Athens; pop. (1971p) 186,223; principal railroad terminus and seaport of Greece; chemical, shipbuilding, and engineering industries.
History: Planned by Themistocles c. 490 B.C.; fortifications completed after 479 and "long walls" between Athens and the port completed c. 460 B.C.; arsenal built 347–323 B.C.; burned by Romans under Sulla 86 B.C.; captured by Byzantines 1040 A.D. Hill Munychia in E part was citadel. Began modern development mid-19th cent.; heavily damaged by bombing 1941–44 in World War II.

Piragua. See PARAGUA 1.

Pi·ra·juí \ˌpir-əzh-'wē\. City, SW São Paulo state, SE Brazil, 200 m. WNW of São Paulo; munic. pop. (1968e) 32,207.

Pi·rá·mi·de \pi-'räm-ə-ˌdā\. Peak, S Chile, W of Lake San Martín; 11,090 ft.

Pi·ran \pi-'rän\ *or Ital.* **Pi·ra·no** \pi-'rän-(ˌ)ō\. Seaport, Slovenia, Yugoslavia, ab. 45 m. WNW of Rijeka; pop. (1961c) 5474; 14th cent. cathedral; scene of victory of Venetian fleet over fleet of Frederick Barbarossa and the Genoese 1177.

Pi·ra·nhas \pi-'ran-yəs\. River, NE Brazil; ab. 250 m. long; flows N through Rio Grande do Norte state into Atlantic Ocean.

Pi·ra·po·ra \ˌpir-ə-'pōr-ə, -'pȯr-\. City, Minas Gerais state, E Brazil, on the São Francisco 190 m. NNW of Belo Horizonte; munic. pop. (1968e) 16,889.

Pi·ras·su·nun·ga \ˌpir-ə-sə-'nu̇ŋ-gə\. City, São Paulo state, SE Brazil, 60 m. NNW of Campinas; munic. pop. (1968e) 32,481.

Pi·ray \pi-'rī\. River, cen. Bolivia; 150 m. long; flows N into the Río Grande.

Pi·ra·yú \ˌpir-ə-'yü\. Town, Paraguarí dept., S cen. Paraguay; pop. (1970e) 13,235.

Pírgos. See PYRGOS.

Pi·riá·po·lis \ˌpir-'yä-pə-ˌlēs\. Town, Maldonado dept., S Uruguay, on coast 50 m. E of Montevideo; seaside resort.

Pi·ri·be·buy \ˌpir-i-bə-'bwē\. Town, S Cordillera dept., cen. Paraguay; pop. (1970e) 23,869.

Pirineos. See PYRENEES.

Pir·ma·sens \ˌpi(ə)r-mə-'zen(t)s\. Manufacturing city, North Rhineland-Palatinate, West Germany, 40 m. WNW of Karlsruhe; pop. (1969e) 56,420; manufactures leather goods, esp. footwear. French defeated nearby by duke of Brunswick Sept. 14, 1793; taken by U.S. troops Mar. 22, 1945.

Pir·na \'pi(ə)r-nə\. Manufacturing city, Dresden dist., East Germany, on Elbe river 11 m. SE of Dresden; pop. (1970e) 47,468; steel castings, glass, paper, furniture, artificial silk; 16th cent. castle; founded 1240.

Piroe. See PIRU.

Pi·rot \'pē-rōt\. Town, Serbia, E Yugoslavia, on the Nišava river ab. 33 m. ESE of Niš; pop. (1965e) 21,000; cheese, handwoven carpets. Became part of Serbia 1878; occupied by Bulgarians 1885 and 1941.

Pir Pan·jal \'pēr-ˌpən-'jäl\. Mountain range, SW Jammu and Kashmir, N India; highest point over 19,000 ft.

Pi·ru *or Du.* **Pi·roe** \'pi(ə)r-ü\. Village, most important locality at W end of Ceram I., Indonesia, at head of **Piru Bay,** an inlet of Ceram Sea nearly closed by Ambon I.

Pi·sa \'pē-zə; *Ital.* -sä\. 1 Province of Tuscany, W Italy. See table at ITALY.
2 *or anc.* **Pi·sae** \'pī-(ˌ)sē\. Commune, its ✻, on Arno river 43 m. SW of Florence; pop. (1968e) 102,717; textiles, glass, machine tools, building materials; tourism; notable buildings include 11th–12th cent. cathedral, 12th–14th cent. baptistry, leaning tower (campanile of cathedral, built 1174–c. 1350, deviating 16½ ft. from the perpendicular), 14th cent. Palazzo Gambacorti, Palazzo de Medici (prefecture), Museo Civico, and numerous churches; univ. (1343).
History: One of 12 cities in Etruscan confederation; its residents granted Roman citizenship 89 B.C.; rose to prominence in Italy in 9th and 10th cents. A.D.; conquered Sardinia and Corsica 1052; defeated Saracens near Palermo 1063; pop. in 1100 estimated to have been ab. 150,000; sided with Ghibellines; defeated in long struggle with Genoa at Leghorn 1284; lost Sardinia, Corsica, and Balearic Is. 1300; subjugated by Aragon 1325; sold to Florence 1406; Council of Pisa held 1409 (Pope Gregory XII and antipope Benedict XIII deposed and Pope Alexander V elected); rebelled against Florentine rule 1494–1509; as part of grand duchy of Tuscany, became part of kingdom of Italy 1860; in World War II heavily damaged during fighting for Gothic Line July 31 to Sept. 2, 1944. Birthplace of Galileo.

Pi·sa·gua \pi-'sä-gwə\. Seaport, Tarapacá prov., N Chile, ab. 40 m. N of Iquique; pop. (1960c) 2500; in war with Peru and Bolivia (the "Nitrate War"), scene of a battle in which Chilean forces won 1879; northern-most nitrate port of the republic.

Pisaurum. See PESARO.

Piscaria. See PESCHIERA DEL GARDA.

Pis·cat·a·qua \pis-'kat-ə-ˌkwȯ\. River, Maine and New Hampshire; 12 m. long; forms part of Maine-New Hampshire boundary; tidal harbor from Portsmouth to the sea (3 m.) one of the best in United States.

Pis·cat·a·quis \pis-'kat-ə-kwis\. County in Maine. See table at MAINE.

Pis·cat·a·way \pis-'kat-ə-ˌwā\. Village, part of Piscataway township, Middlesex co., cen. New Jersey, N of Raritan river and E of New Brunswick; township pop. (1970c) 36,418.

Pis·co \'pē-(ˌ)skō\. Seaport on Pisco Bay, Ica dept., SW Peru, 130 m. S of Callao; pop. (1969e) 26,700; chief port bet. Callao and Mollendo.

Piscopi. See TELOS.

Pi·se·co Lake *or* **Piseco Inlet** \pə-ˌsē-kō-\. Lake, S Hamilton co., NE cen. New York; ab. 5 m. long; drains S through Sacandaga river into Great Sacandaga Reservoir.

Pí·sek \'pē-ˌsek\. Industrial town, Czech S.R., W Czechoslovakia, 55 m. SW of Prague on Otava river; pop. (1968e) 22,670; in cattle and grain region.

Pis·gah, Mount \-'piz-gə\. 1 Peak in the Catskill Mts., Delaware co., S New York; 3345 ft.
2 Ridge of Abarim Mts. in ancient Palestine, E of N end of the Dead Sea; highest point 2644 ft.; now in Jordan; **Ne·bo** \'nē-(ˌ)bō\ was an alternative name for it or for its top (*Deut.* xxxiv. 1).

Pi·shin \pi-'shēn\. District, N Baluchistan, Pakistan, N of Quetta; ceded to British by Afghanistan 1879.

Pishin Lo·ra \-'lōr-ə, -'lȯr-\. River, W Pakistan; ab. 300 m. long; flows SW into Hamun-i-Lora; part of course is in SE Afghanistan.

Pishpek. See FRUNZE.

Pi·sid·ia \pə-'sid-ē-ə, pī-\. Ancient country, S Asia Minor, cut off from the Mediterranean by Pamphylia; bounded on NW by Phrygia, on NE by Lycaonia, on SE by Cilicia, and on SW by Lycia. A mountainous region; its inhabitants never entirely subdued by Persians, Macedonians, or Romans; until time of Constantine was generally considered a part of Pamphylia.

Pisino. See PAZIN.

Pis·ki \'pish-kē\. Village on Mureşul river, S Transylvania, Romania, SW of Alba Iulia; scene of victory of Hungarians under Bem over Austrians Feb. 1849.

Pis·mo Beach \ˌpiz-mō-\. City, San Luis Obispo co., SW California, on Pacific Ocean 65 m. NW of Santa Barbara; pop. (1970c) 4043; beach resort; diversified agriculture.

Pisse·vache \pēs-ˈväsh\. Waterfall in Valais canton, SW cen. Switzerland; 215 ft. high.

Pi·stic·ci \pis-ˈtē-chē\. Commune, Matera prov., Basilicata, S Italy, 20 m. S by W of Matera; pop. (1968e) 15,566.

Pi·sto·ia \pi-ˈstȯi-ə, -ˈstō-yə\. 1 Province of Tuscany, W Italy. See table at ITALY.

2 *or anc.* **Pis·to·ria** \pis-ˈtōr-ē-ə, -ˈtȯr-\ *or* **Pis·to·ri·ae** \pis-ˈtōr-ē-ˌē, -ˈtȯr-\. Commune, its ✱, 17 m. NW of Florence; pop. (1968e) 90,463; railroad junction; shoes, cement, glass; tanneries, flower nurseries; 12th–13th cent. cathedral with 14th cent. baptistry, 14th cent. Ospedale del Ceppo, 13th cent. convent of San Francesco al Prato, three 12th cent. churches.

History: Settlement came under Rome c. 561 B.C.; scene of final defeat and death of Catiline 62 B.C.; became free commune 1085; important banking center c. 1200; under Florence in early 14th cent.; to Tuscany 1530 and to kingdom of Italy 1860.

Pistyan. See PIEŠT'ANY.

Pis·tyll Cain Falls \ˌpis-təl-ˌkīn-\. Falls in Prysor river, Merionethshire, Wales; 150 ft. high.

Pistyll Rhai·adr \ˈpis-təl-ˈrī-ə-dər\. Falls in **Rhaiadr River,** Denbighshire, Wales; 230 ft. high.

Pi·suer·ga \pi-ˈswer-gə\. River, N Spain; 171 m. long; rises in the Cantabrian Mts., flows SSW into Duero river 9 m. below Valladolid.

Pit \ˈpit\. River, N California; ab. 200 m. long; has source in N Modoc co., NE California, and flows S and W into the Sacramento in W cen. Shasta co.

Pi·tan·ga \pə-ˈtäŋ-gə\. Municipality, Paraná state, S Brazil, 150 m. WNW of Curitiba; pop. (1968e) 71,795.

Pit·cairn \ˈpit-ˌka(ə)rn, -ˌke(ə)rn\. Borough, Allegheny co., SW Pennsylvania, 13 m. E of Pittsburgh; pop. (1970c) 4741.

Pitcairn Island. 1 British colony, S Pacific Ocean, annexed 1839, consisting of Pitcairn I. (2, below) with the uninhabited islands of Henderson (12 sq. m.), Ducie ($2\frac{1}{2}$ sq. m.), and Oeno (2 sq. m.), annexed 1902.

2 Island in S Pacific Ocean, 25°04′S, 130°05′W, ab. 100 m. SSE of nearest island of the Tuamotus and equidistant between Tahiti and Easter I.; $2\frac{1}{2}$ m. long; area $1\frac{3}{4}$ sq. m.; pop. (1971c) 91; only village Adamstown. Of volcanic origin; highest point ab. 1000 ft.; has fertile soil.

History: Discovered by Philip Carteret 1767; uninhabited until 1790 when settled by the mutineers from the English ship *Bounty*; their settlement discovered 1808; population removed temporarily to Tahiti 1831 and to Norfolk I. 1856; some later returned to Pitcairn and their descendants constitute present population of island.

Pitch Lake \ˈpich-\. Deposit of natural asphalt in SW Trinidad, West Indies; extends over 114 acres.

Pi·te \ˈpēt-ə\. River, N Sweden; 230 m. long; rises in Pieska Lake near Norwegian border, flows SE into the head of the Gulf of Bothnia.

Pi·teå \ˈpē-tə-ˌō\. Seaport town, S Norrbotten co., N Sweden, at mouth of the Pite river on the Gulf of Bothnia; pop. (1970e) 32,365.

Pi·teş·ti \pi-ˈtesht(-ē)\. Industrial city, ⊗ of Argeş co., S cen. Romania, on Argeş river 70 m. NW of Bucharest; pop. (1970e) 74,237; produces machine tools, chemicals, building materials, textiles, footwear, food products, wine.

Pi·thi·viers \pē-tē-ˈvyā\. Town, Loiret dept., N cen. France, 25 m. NE of Orléans; pop. (1966e) 8908.

Pi·thom \ˈpī-thəm\. City of ancient Egypt, ab. 12 m. W by S of Ismailia in E Goshen, identical with or near Succoth; one of the treasure cities built for Pharaoh by the Hebrews (*Exod.* i. 11).

Pi·ti \ˈpēt-ē\. Town and port of entry on Apra Harbor, W Guam; pop. (1970p) 1289.

Pit·kin \ˈpit-kən\. County in Colorado. See table at COLORADO.

Pit·man \ˈpit-mən\. Residential borough, Gloucester co., SW New Jersey, 15 m. S of Camden; pop. (1970c) 10,257; fruit and truck farms.

Pi·ton \pē-ˈtōⁿ\. French word for "mountain peak," used esp. in the French West Indies and the Mascarene Is.; for names beginning with *Piton,* see the distinguishing element. **The Pi·tons** \-pē-ˈtōⁿ\ of Saint Lucia I. are two conical mountains (2619 ft. and 2461 ft.) forming prominent landmarks.

Pit·rea·vie \pit-ˈrē-vē\. Village on Firth of Forth, Scotland, $2\frac{3}{4}$ m. SE of Dunfermline; site of NATO naval facilities.

Pi·truf·quén \ˌpē-trüf-ˈkān\. Town, Cautín prov., S cen. Chile, 20 m. S of Temuco; pop. (1960c) 6472.

Pitsanulok. See PHITSANULOK.

Pitt \ˈpit\. County in North Carolina. See table at NORTH CAROLINA.

Pitt, Mount. See MCLOUGHLIN, MOUNT.

Pitt Island. 1 Island off W coast of British Columbia, Canada, bet. Banks I. and the mainland S of mouth of Skeena river; 537 sq. m.

2 Island, Pacific Ocean. See CHATHAM ISLANDS.

Pitt Lake. Lake, SW British Columbia, Canada; 21 sq. m.; formed by a widening of the **Pitt River** near its junction with the Fraser river E of Vancouver.

Pitts·boro \ˈpits-ˌbər-ə, -ˌbə-rə\. 1 Village, ⊗ of Calhoun co., N cen. Mississippi; pop. (1970c) 188.

2 Town, ⊗ of Chatham co., cen. North Carolina; pop. (1970c) 1447; textiles, lumber.

Pitts·burg \ˈpits-ˌbərg\. 1 County in Oklahoma. See table at OKLAHOMA.

2 Industrial city, Contra Costa co., W California, near mouth of Sacramento river at its confluence with the San Joaquin; pop. (1970c) 20,651; steel, chemicals, rubber goods, building materials, furniture; ship repairing, salmon fishing, grain farms; founded 1835, incorporated 1911.

3 Industrial and mining city, Crawford co., SE Kansas, 30 m. S of Fort Scott; pop. (1970c) 20,171; foundries, railroad shops, coal mines; diversified agriculture; Kansas State Coll. (1903).

4 City, ⊗ of Camp co., NE Texas, 42 m. NW of Marshall; pop. (1970c) 3844; furniture; oil wells; corn, sweet potatoes, poultry.

Pitts·burgh \ˈpits-ˌbərg\. Industrial city, ⊗ of Allegheny co., SW Pennsylvania, at confluence of Allegheny and Monongahela rivers where they form the Ohio; pop. (1970c) 520,117; second largest city in Pennsylvania; major inland river port and transportation center; produces steel, electrical equipment, food products, aluminum, glass, plumbing supplies; oil refining, shipbuilding; railroad shops, coal mines, oil and gas wells. Univ. of Pittsburgh (1787), Pittsburgh Theological Seminary (1794), Chatham Coll. (1869), Pennsylvania Coll. for Women (1869), Duquesne Univ. (1878), Carnegie-Mellon Univ. (1900), Robert Morris Junior Coll. (1921), Carlow Coll. (1929), Point Park Coll. (1933), Community Coll. of Allegheny County (1965); Carnegie Institute and Library (1895), Mellon Institute (1913), Buhl Planetarium (1939); Three Rivers Stadium (1970). French built Fort Duquesne on site c. 1750; fort captured by British 1758 and renamed Fort Pitt; incorporated as borough 1794 and as city 1816; in 19th cent. developed rapidly as steel-manufacturing center; since World War II scene of notable urban renewal projects. Birthplace of Stephen Collins Foster.

Pittsburg Landing. Hamlet, Hardin co., SW Tennessee, on W bank of Tennessee river; scene of battle, usually called battle of Shiloh from the name of the nearby church, Apr. 6–7, 1862 in which Confederates under Gen. Albert Sidney Johnston made successful surprise attack on Grant's Union forces who, however, with fresh reinforcements finally compelled Confederate withdrawal (Johnston was killed Apr. 6 and command taken over by Gen. Beauregard). See UNITED STATES, *National Historical Parks* (Shiloh National Military Park).

Pitts·field \ˈpits-ˌfēld\. 1 City, ⊗ of Pike co., W Illinois, 40 m. ESE of Quincy; pop. (1970c) 4244; dairy products.
2 Town, Somerset co., W Maine, 20 m. NNE of Waterville; pop. (1970c) 4274; meat packing; grain, dairy farms.
3 City, ⊗ of Berkshire co., W Massachusetts, on Housatonic river 40 m. WNW of Springfield; pop. (1970c) 57,020; alt. 1015 ft.; summer and winter resort, cultural center for music and drama; produces paper, chemicals, electrical equipment, leather goods; Berkshire Community Coll. (1960); incorporated as town 1761, as city 1890.
4 Town, Merrimack co., S cen. New Hampshire, on Suncook river 12 m. NE of Concord; pop. (1970c) 2517; summer resort; clothing, lumber; fruit farms.

Pitts·ford \ˈpits-fərd\. Village, Monroe co., W New York, 7 m. ESE of Rochester; pop. (1970c) 1755; residential suburb of Rochester.

Pitts·ton \ˈpit-stən\. City, Luzerne co., E Pennsylvania, on Susquehanna river 8 m. NE of Wilkes-Barre; pop. (1970c) 11,113; silk, textiles, stoves, paper, cigars; coal mines, railroad shops; settled 1762; incorporated as city 1894.

Pitt·syl·va·nia \ˌpit-səl-ˈvān-yə, -ˈvā-nē-ə\. County in Virginia. See table at VIRGINIA.

Pit·y·u·sae \ˌpit-ē-ˈyü-(ˌ)sē\. Ancient name (*Eng.* Pine Islands) of W group of Balearic Is., comprising the two islands Ebusus (Ibiza) and Ophiusa (Formentera).

Piu·ra \ˈpyu̇r-ə\. 1 River, N Peru; ab. 150 m. long; flows W into Pacific Ocean.
2 Department of NW Peru. See table at PERU.
3 City, its ✱, on Piura river ab. 35 m. SE of its port Paita; pop. (1969e) 106,400; cotton market with cotton gins and cottonseed oil mills; technical univ. (1961); oldest Spanish city in Peru, founded by Pizarro 1532.

Pi·ute \pī-ˈ(y)üt\. County in Utah. See table at UTAH.

Piute Dam. Dam on Sevier river, cen. Piute co., S cen. Utah; completed 1910; 98 ft. high; forms **Piute Reservoir** used for irrigation.

Piz·zo \ˈpēt-sō\ *or in full* **Pizzo di Ca·la·bria** \-dē-kä-ˈlä-brē-ə\. Seaport, Catanzaro prov., cen. Calabria, S Italy, on Tyrrhenian Sea; pop. (1968e) 8803; scene of trial and execution Oct. 13, 1815 of Joachim Murat.

Pla·cen·tia \plə-ˌsen-ch(ē-)ə\. 1 City, Orange co., SW California, 20 m. ENE of Long Beach; pop. (1970c) 21,948; oil refinery; livestock, fruit farms; incorporated 1926.
2 Commune, Italy. See PIACENZA 2.
3 Town, SE Newfoundland, Canada, on E shore of Placentia Bay 62 m. WSW of St. John's; pop. (1971p) 2174; summer resort. Founded 1660 by the French, who fortified it and held it until Treaty of Utrecht 1713.

Placentia Bay. Wide inlet of Atlantic Ocean, SE Newfoundland, Canada, W of St. John's; ab. 75 m. long; Argentia and Placentia are on its E shore. Here on the British battleship *Prince of Wales* the Atlantic Charter was signed Aug. 14, 1941 by President Roosevelt and Winston Churchill.

Plac·er \ˌplas-ər\. County in California. See table at CALIFORNIA.

Placer Mountain \ˈplas-ər-, ˈplā-sər-\. Peak, cen. Santa Fe co., N cen. New Mexico; 8928 ft.

Plac·er·ville \ˈplas-ər-ˌvil\. City, ⊗ of El Dorado co., E California, 36 m. ENE of Sacramento; pop. (1970c) 5416; building materials; gold mines; fruit orchards.

Pla·ce·tas \plä-ˈsāt-əs\. Town and municipality, Las Villas prov., W cen. Cuba; town pop. (1967e) 38,800; town is railroad junction point 20 m. SE of Santa Clara.

Plac·id, Lake \-ˈplas-əd\. 1 Lake, N Essex co., NE New York; ab. 5 m. long and 1½ m. max. width; elevation 1860 ft.
2 Village, New York. See LAKE PLACID.

Plad·da \ˈplad-ə\. Low rocky island in Firth of Clyde, S of Arran I., off SW coast of Scotland; lighthouse.

Plain·edge \ˈplā-ˌnej\. Unincorporated urban area, Nassau co., SE New York, in cen. Long I.; pop. (1970c) 10,759.

Plain·field \ˈplān-ˌfēld\. 1 Town, SE Windham co., NE Connecticut, on Quinebaug river; pop. (1970c) 11,957; settled 1689, incorporated 1699.
2 Village, Will co., NE Illinois, 8 m. NW of Joliet; pop. (1970c) 2928.
3 Town, Hendricks co., cen. Indiana, 14 m. W of Indianapolis; pop. (1970c) 8211; residential; grain, soybeans.
4 City, Union co., NE New Jersey, 11 m. WSW of Elizabeth; pop. (1970c) 46,862; residential; produces automobile parts, electronic components, printing supplies, chemicals, clothing; settled in 18th cent. as Milltown; became township 1847; incorporated as city 1869.

Plains \ˈplānz\. Town, ⊗ of Yoakum co., NW Texas; pop. (1970c) 1087; oil wells.

Plains of Abra·ham \-ˈā-brə-ˌham\. Plateau, W of old city of Quebec, Canada; battlefield Sept. 13, 1759 where the British under Gen. Wolfe defeated the French under Gen. Montcalm, decisive battle of the North American campaigns of the Seven Years' War; now National Battlefields Park within the city limits.

Plain·view \ˈplān-ˌvyü\. 1 Unincorporated urban area, Nassau co., SE New York, on Long I. E of New York; pop. (1970c) 32,195.
2 City, ⊗ of Hale co., NW Texas, 42 m. N of Lubbock; pop. (1970c) 19,076; feed, hardware, agricultural implements; canneries; diversified agriculture; Wayland Baptist Coll. (1909).

Plain·ville \ˈplān-ˌvil\. 1 Manufacturing town, SW Hartford co., N Connecticut, W of New Britain; pop. (1970c) 16,733; ball bearings, photographic equipment; truck farms.
2 City, Rooks co., N Kansas, 23 m. N of Hays; pop. (1970c) 2627; grain shipping point; livestock and poultry raising; oil wells.
3 Town, Norfolk co., E Massachusetts, 27 m. SW of Boston; pop. (1970c) 4953.

Plain·well \ˈplān-ˌwel, -wəl\. City, Allegan co., SW Michigan, 11 m. N of Kalamazoo; pop. (1970c) 3195; lake resort; paper, aluminum products; onions.

Plais·tow \ˈpla-(ˌ)stō\. Town, Rockingham co., SE New Hampshire; pop. (1970c) 4712.

Plaka. See MELOS 3.

Plá·ka, Cape \-ˈpläk-ə\ *also* **Cape Sal·mo·ne** \-sal-ˈmō-nē\. Cape at E end of island of Crete, Greece, S of Cape Sidero; mentioned in St. Paul's account of his fourth journey (*Acts.* xxvii. 7).

Planalto Central. See BRAZIL, PLATEAU OF.

Planasia. See PIANOSA 1.

Planches, Les. See LES PLANCHES.

Planka, Cape. See PLOČA, CAPE.

Plan·kin·ton \ˈplaŋ-kən-tən\. City, ⊗ of Aurora co., SE cen. South Dakota; pop. (1970c) 613.

Pla·no \ˈplā-(ˌ)nō\. 1 City, Kendall co., NE Illinois, 26 m. WNW of Joliet; pop. (1970c) 4664; plastics, hardware; dairy and livestock farms.
2 City, Collin co., NE Texas, 15 m. N of Dallas; pop. (1970c) 17,872; brass fittings; grain farms; Plano Univ. (1964).

Plan·ta·tion \plan-ˈtā-shən\. City, Broward co., SE Florida; 4 m. W of Fort Lauderdale; pop. (1970c) 23,523; residential suburb.

Plant City \ˈplant-\. City, Hillsborough co., W cen. Florida penin., 20 m. E of Tampa; pop. (1970c) 15,451; fertilizer; packs and ships citrus fruit and vegetables.

Plaque·mine \ˈplak-(ə-)mən\. Town, ⊗ of Iberville parish, S Louisiana, on Mississippi river 13 m. SSW of Baton Rouge; pop. (1970c) 7739; oil wells, sawmills, fisheries; site of Plaquemine Locks, with a lift of 55 ft., built 1909 to connect **Bayou Plaquemine** and the Intracoastal Canal with the Mississippi river; incorporated 1838.

Plaque·mines \ˈplak-(ə-)mənz\. Parish in Louisiana. See table at LOUISIANA.

Pla·ri·del \plä-ri-ˈdel\. Municipality, Misamis Occidental prov., Mindanao, Phil., on S shore of Mindanao Sea NW of Iligan Bay; pop. (1969e) 25,100.

Pla·sen·cia \plə-'sen-sh(ē-)ə\. Commune, Cáceres prov., W Spain, 43 m. NNE of Cáceres; pop. (1970p) 27,174; agricultural products, wine; manufactures leather, chinaware, cork; 15th cent. cathedral.

Plas·sey \'plas-ē\. Village, West Bengal, NE India, on E bank of Bhagirathi river ab. 80 m. N of Calcutta; site of Clive's victory June 23, 1757 with force of ab. 3000 over army of 68,000 of Siraj-ud-daula; historically the beginning of the British Empire in the East.

Plata *or* **Plata, La.** See LA PLATA.

Plata, Río de la \ˌrē-(ˌ)ō-də-lə-'plät-ə\ *or Eng.* **River Plate** \-'plāt\. Estuary of Paraná and Uruguay rivers, bet. Uruguay and Argentina; ab. 171 m. long; at mouth max. width is ab. 138 m., at Montevideo ab. 60 m., opp. Buenos Aires and above, 25 to 28 m. Discovered by Solís 1516; explored by Sebastian Cabot 1526–30; first permanent settlement in La Plata region was at Asunción 1538.

Pla·taea \plə-'tē-ə\ *or* **Pla·tae·ae** \-'tē-ˌē\. Ancient city in SE Boeotia, E cen. Greece, 9 m. S of Thebes and near Attica border. Its independence protected by Athens; sent 1000 men to aid Athenians at Marathon 490 B.C.; destroyed by Persians 480 B.C. but scene the next year 479 B.C. of the defeat of Mardonius and the Persians by Pausanias and the Greeks that assured the independence of Greece; later attacked by Thebes 431 B.C., besieged for two years 429–427 and destroyed; rebuilt but destroyed a third time by Thebans 373 B.C.; existed as an obscure town until Middle Ages.

Plate, River. See PLATA, RÍO DE LA.

Pla·teau Mountain \pla-'tō-\. Peak in the Catskill Mts., Greene co., SE New York; 3840 ft.

Pla·to \'plä-tō\. Town, Magdalena dept., N Colombia, on the Magdalena ab. 65 m. SE of Cartagena; munic. pop. (1968e) 59,281.

Platte \'plat\. 1 River, S Iowa and NW Missouri; ab. 300 m. long; rises in Union co., S Iowa, enters Missouri river in Platte co., NW Missouri, ab. 15 m. NW of Kansas City, Kansas.

2 River, cen. Nebraska; 310 m. long (with North Platte ab. 930 m.); formed by confluence of North Platte and South Platte in Lincoln co., SW cen. Nebraska, flows E into Missouri river below Omaha.

3 Name of counties in three states of the U.S. See tables at MISSOURI, NEBRASKA, WYOMING.

Platte City. City, ⊗ of Platte co., NW Missouri; pop. (1970c) 2022; diversified agriculture.

Plattensee. See BALATON.

Platte·ville \'plat-ˌvil\. City, Grant co., SW corner of Wisconsin, 60 m. WSW of Madison; pop. (1970c) 9599; dairy products; zinc mines; Wisconsin State Univ. at Platteville (1866).

Platt National Park \'plat-\. See UNITED STATES. *National Parks.*

Platts·burg \'plats-ˌbərg\. 1 City, ⊗ of Clinton co., NW Missouri, 33 m. N of Kansas City; pop. (1970c) 1832.

2 City, New York. See PLATTSBURGH.

Platts·burgh *or* **Platts·burg** \'plats-ˌbərg\. City, ⊗ of Clinton co., NE corner of New York, on W shore of Lake Champlain, 20 m. S of Canadian border; pop. (1970c) 18,715; summer resort; pulp and paper products; State Univ. of New York Coll. at Plattsburgh (1889), Clinton Community Coll. (1966); U.S. Air Force base (1956). Settled c. 1785, incorporated as city 1902; off nearby Valcour I. British defeated Americans in naval battle Oct. 11, 1776; scene of defeat of British by Americans under Commodore Macdonough in naval battle Sept. 11, 1814; site of citizens' military training camp 1916–39.

Platts·mouth \'plat-sməth, -ˌsmau̇th\. City, ⊗ of Cass co., E Nebraska, on Missouri river 17 m. S of Omaha; pop. (1970c) 6371; diversified agriculture.

Plau·en \'plau̇-ən\ *or formerly* **Plauen im Vogt·land** \-im-'fōk-ˌtlänt\. Manufacturing city, Karl-Marx-Stadt dist., East Germany, on Weisse Elster 29 m. SW of Zwickau; pop. (1970e) 81,907; manufactures lace, textiles, trucks, machinery. Probably founded by Slavs in 12th cent.; came under Bohemia 1327; to Saxony 1466. A former capital of Vogtland.

Pla·ya, Point \-'plī-ə\. Cape extending into Atlantic Ocean from E Venezuela coast, near Guyana boundary.

Pleas·ant, Lake \-'plez-ənt\. 1 Dam, Arizona. See LAKE PLEASANT DAM.

2 Lake, S cen. Hamilton co., NE cen. New York.

Pleasant, Mount. Peak, S Coos co., N New Hampshire, SW of Mt. Washington; 4775 ft.

Pleasant Bay. 1 Inlet of Atlantic Ocean, S coast of Washington co., SE Maine.

2 Inlet of Atlantic Ocean, SE coast of Cape Cod, SE Massachusetts.

Pleasant Grove. 1 Town, Jefferson co., cen. Alabama, 6 m. W of Birmingham; pop. (1970c) 5090.

2 City, Utah co., N cen. Utah, 10 m. NNW of Provo; pop. (1970c) 5327; ships fruit; silver and lead mines.

Pleasant Hill. 1 City, Contra Costa co., W California, NE of Oakland; pop. (1970c) 24,610; residential; Diablo Valley Coll. (1949).

2 Town, Sabine parish, W Louisiana, 60 m. S of Shreveport; pop. (1970c) 806; battle Apr. 9, 1864 when the Confederates under Richard Taylor made a partially successful attack on Union forces under Nathaniel Banks.

3 City, Cass co., W Missouri; pop. (1970c) 3396; corn.

Pleasant Hills. Borough, Allegheny co., SW Pennsylvania, S suburb of Pittsburgh; pop. (1970c) 10,409.

Pleasant Island. See NAURU.

Pleas·an·ton \'plez-ᵊn-tən\. 1 City, Alameda co., W California, 15 m. E of San Francisco Bay; pop. (1970c) 18,328; wine, dairy products.

2 City, Atascosa co., S Texas, 33 m. S of San Antonio; pop. (1970c) 5407; oil and gas wells; truck farms.

Pleasant Ridge. City, Oakland co., SE Michigan; pop. (1970c) 3989; residential suburb of Detroit.

Pleas·ants \'plez-ənts\. County in West Virginia. See table at WEST VIRGINIA.

Pleas·ant·ville \'plez-ᵊnt-ˌvil\. 1 City, Atlantic co., SE New Jersey, 5 m. WNW of Atlantic City; pop. (1970c) 13,778; hosiery; poultry, truck farms.

2 Residential village, Westchester co., SE New York, 30 m. NNE of New York; pop. (1970c) 7110; publishing.

Plea·sure Ridge Park \ˌplezh-ər-\. Unincorporated urban community, Jefferson co., N cen. Kentucky, S of Louisville; pop. (1970c) 28,566; residential.

Pleis·se \'plī-sə\. River, Leipzig dist., East Germany; ab. 60 m. long; flows N to the Weisse Elster at Leipzig.

Plen·ty, Bay of \-'plent-ē\. Large inlet of Pacific Ocean, NE coast of North I., New Zealand.

Plenty Coups Peak \ˌplent-ē-ˌküs-\. Mountain, W Park co., NW Wyoming, on boundary of Yellowstone National Park; 10,937 ft.

Plen·ty·wood \'plent-ē-ˌwu̇d\. City, ⊗ of Sheridan co., NE corner of Montana; pop. (1970c) 2381; coal mines; stock and grain farms.

Ple·red \'plā-ˌret\. Town, West Java prov., Indonesia, ab. 80 m. W of Tjirebon.

Plesh·che·ye·vo \plesh-'chā-ə-və\ *or formerly* **Pe·re·slavl** \ˌper-ə-'slav-əl\. Small lake, S Yaroslavl Oblast, Russian S.F.S.R., U.S.S.R.; on it the first vessels of the Russian navy were built 1691 by Peter the Great.

Pless. See PSZCZYNA.

Ples·sis·ville \'ples-ē-ˌvil\. Town, Megantic co., S Quebec, Canada, 24 m. WNW of Thetford Mines; pop. (1971p) 7224; leather goods, hosiery, furniture.

Plet·i·pi Lake \ˌplet-ə-pē-\ *or Fr.* **Lac Plé·ti·pi** \läk-plā-tē-pē\. Lake, S cen. Quebec, Canada; 138 sq. m.; outlets S through Outardes river.

Plet·ten·berg \ˈplet-ən-ˌbərg\. City, North Rhine-Westphalia, West Germany, 45 m. NE of Cologne; pop. (1969e) 30,172.

Ple·ven \ˈplev-ən\. 1 Province of N Bulgaria. See table at BULGARIA.

2 *or* **Plev·na** \ˈplev-nə\. City, its ✱, 85 m. NE of Sofia; pop. (1968e) 89,814; market center in agricultural region; produces textiles, machinery, cement, ceramics; in 1877 taken from the Turks by the Russians after a 143 day siege.

Pley·ben \plā-ˈbaⁿ\. Town, Finistère dept., NW France, ab. 16 m. N of Quimper; pop. (1962c) 1474; 16th cent. church with interesting wood carvings.

Plo·ča, Cape \-ˈplō-chə\ *or formerly* **Cape Plan·ka** \-ˈpläŋ-kə\. Cape, Croatia, W Yugoslavia, on the coast W of Split at 43°30′N, 15°58′E.

Płock *or Ger.* **Plozk** \ˈplȯtsk\. Commune, Warszawa prov., NE cen. Poland, on Vistula river 55 m. WNW of Poland; pop. (1970p) 71,700; market town; manufactures building materials; 12th cent. cathedral (containing tombs of 11th–12th cent. Polish kings and dukes). Under Prussia 1793–1806 and Russia 1815–1918; in World War II occupied by Germans 1939–45.

Plöck·en \ˈplər-kən\ *or Ital.* **Mon·te Cro·ce** \ˌmōn-tē-ˈkrō-(ˌ)chā\. Pass over the Carnic Alps bet. S Carinthia, Austria, and Friuli-Venezia Giulia, Italy; alt. 4298 ft.; connects upper valley of the Drava with N Italy. Was important in 1917 campaign of World War I.

Ploen. See PLÖN.

Plo·ër·mel \ˌplō-er-ˈmel\. Town, Morbihan dept., NW France, ab. 25 m. NNE of Vannes; pop. (1962c) 3454; 16th cent. church of St. Armel, named for the hermit who lived in the district in 6th cent. and after whom the town is named.

Plo·ieş·ti *or* **Plo·eş·ti** \plȯ-ˈyesht(-ē)\. City, ⊗ of Prahova co., SE cen. Romania, 35 m. N of Bucharest; pop. (1970e) 162,937, met. area pop. 217,341; center of important oil fields; oil refineries, petrochemical plants; in World War II bombed by Allied aircraft Aug. 1943 ff.; occupied by U.S.S.R. Aug. 31, 1944.

Plomb du Can·tal \ˌplōⁿ-dyü-käⁿ-ˈtal\. Peak in the Auvergne Mts., cen. France; 6094 ft.

Plom·bières–les–Bains \plȯⁿ-ˈbyer-lā-ˈbaⁿ\. Commune, Vosges dept., NE France, ab. 15 m. S of Épinal; pop. (1962c) 1297; hot springs.

Plön *or* **Ploen** \ˈplərn\. Commune, E Schleswig-Holstein, West Germany, SE of Kiel on **Gross·er Plö·ner See** \ˈgrōs-ər-ˈplər-nər-ˌzā\.

Płońsk \ˈplȯn(t)sk\. Commune, Warszawa prov., NE cen. Poland, 36 m. NW of Warsaw; pop. (1968e) 11,200.

Plott Bal·sam Mountain \ˌplät-ˈbȯl-səm-\. Peak, Haywood co., W North Carolina; 6200 ft.

Plou·gas·tel–Da·ou·las \ˌplü-gäs-ˈtel-dä-ü-ˈläs\. Commune, W Finistère dept., NW France, on a bay which separates it from Brest to the W; pop. (1962c) 6792.

Plov·div \ˈplȯv-ˌdif, -ˌdiv\. 1 Province of cen. Bulgaria. See table at BULGARIA.

2 *or Gk.* **Phil·ip·pop·o·lis** \ˌfil-ə-ˈpäp-ə-ləs\ *or anc.* **Eu·mol·pi·as** \yü-ˈmäl-pē-əs\. City, its ✱, on the Maritsa N of the Rhodope Mts.; pop. (1968e) 236,627; railroad junction; market town in region producing rice, fruit, wine, and tobacco; produces footwear, canned goods, textiles, cigarettes, lead and zinc; ruins of 13th cent. fortress; agricultural coll. (1950).

History: Fell to Macedonians under Philip II 341 B.C.; taken by Romans 46 B.C. and made capital of Thrace under name of Trimontium; frequently sacked and changed hands during the Middle Ages; taken by Turks 1364; to Bulgaria 1885.

Plozk. See PŁOCK.

Plum \ˈpləm\. Borough, Allegheny co., SW Pennsylvania, E suburb of Pittsburgh; pop. (1970c) 21,922.

Plu·ma·jes Point \plü-ˌmä-hās-\. Cape, W coast of Cuba, S of Guadiana Bay.

Plu·mas \ˈplü-məs\. County in California. See table at CALIFORNIA.

Plum Island. 1 Island in Atlantic Ocean off NE coast of Essex co., NE Massachusetts, just S of mouth of the Merrimack; 8½ m. long.

2 Island, E end of Long Island Sound, off NE extremity of Long I., New York; 3 m. long.

Plym·outh \ˈplim-əth\. 1 Name of counties of two states in the U.S. See tables at IOWA and MASSACHUSETTS.

2 Town, Litchfield co., NW Connecticut, N of Waterbury; pop. (1970c) 10,321; granite quarries, foundries; settled 1728, incorporated 1795.

3 City, ⊗ of Marshall co., N Indiana, 23 m. S of South Bend; pop. (1970c) 7661; automobile parts, dairy products, plastics, fertilizer.

4 Town, ⊗ of Plymouth co., SE Massachusetts, on Plymouth Bay 18 m. SE of Brockton; pop. (1970c) 18,606; cordage works, boatyards, fisheries, cranberry-packing plants; tourism; site of first permanent European settlement in New England, the **Colony of New Plymouth,** founded by the Pilgrims 1620; governed under Mayflower Compact in the absence of a royal charter until 1691 when it became part of Massachusetts Bay Colony.

5 City, Wayne co., SE Michigan, 22 m. W of Detroit; pop. (1970c) 11,758; air rifles; St. John's Provincial Seminary (1949).

6 Village, Hennepin co., SE Minnesota, NW suburb of Minneapolis; pop. (1970c) 18,077.

7 Manufacturing town, Grafton co., W New Hampshire, on Pemigewasset river 20 m. NW of Laconia; pop. (1970c) 4225; summer resort; Plymouth Teachers Coll. (1870).

8 Town, ⊗ of Washington co., E North Carolina, 10 m. S of W end of Albemarle Sound; pop. (1970c) 4774; lumber; corn, peanuts.

9 Borough, Luzerne co., E Pennsylvania, on Susquehanna river 4 m. W of Wilkes-Barre; pop. (1970c) 9536.

10 Village, Windsor co., E Vermont, ab. 14 m. SE of Rutland; pop. (1970c) 283; birthplace and grave of Calvin Coolidge, 30th president of the U.S.

11 City, Sheboygan co., E Wisconsin, 13 m. W of Sheboygan; pop. (1970c) 5810; dairy products.

12 City and county borough, Devonshire, SW England, on Plymouth Sound between Plym and Tamar estuaries 190 m. WSW of London; pop. (1971p) 239,314; manufactures machine tools, precision instruments, radio and television sets, chemicals, fertilizers, footwear; Devonport naval dockyard, a major facility of the British Navy, with naval barracks, engineering college, hospital, etc. Incorporated 1439; port from which English fleet sailed against the Spanish armada 1588; dockyard estab. 1690; made county borough 1888 and city 1928; in World War II heavily damaged by German air raids 1940–41 but reconstruction largely completed by 1962.

13 Seaport, ✱ of Montserrat, Leeward Is., West Indies, on SW coast; pop. (1968e) 3500.

Plymouth Bay. Inlet of Atlantic Ocean on E coast of Plymouth co., SE Massachusetts.

Plymouth Colony. See PLYMOUTH 4.

Plymouth Sound. Inlet of the English Channel, SW coast of England, on the boundary bet. Devonshire and Cornwall; site of the city of Plymouth.

Pl·zeň \ˈpəl-ˌzen(-yə)\. City, Czech S.R., Czechoslovakia, 52 m. WSW of Prague; pop. (1968e) 146,000; engineering industries, producing railway rolling stock, munitions, heavy industrial machinery, automobile parts; paper, pottery and tile; breweries; 14th cent. cathedral and 16th cent. town hall. First mentioned 10th cent.; chartered 1292; developed as industrial center from mid-19th cent.

Pnom·penh *or* **Pnom–Penh** *or* **Phnom Penh** \(pə-)ˈnȯm-ˈpen\. City, ✱ of Cambodia, SE Asia, at junction of Tonle Sap river with the Mekong; pop. (1970e) 468,900; transportation center and river port, shipping dried fish, rice, pepper; textiles, beverages; has palace of former dynasty (with museum) and Buddhist temples; univ. (1960) and several technical colleges. According to legend, founded 14th cent.; first chosen capital 1434; again made capital 1865; French seat of government 1886–1955; fighting in vicinity 1971 ff. between Cambodian troops and North Vietnamese forces.

Po \'pō\; *anc.* **Pa·dus** \'pā-dəs\ *also, in mythology,* **Erid·a·nus** \i-'rid-^{ə}n-əs\. River, N Italy; 405 m. long; rises on the slopes of Viso, flows NE to Turin and then E across Piedmont and Lombardy into the Adriatic Sea through several mouths; navigable to beyond Turin. Its chief tributaries in the W are the Dora Baltea, Dora Riparia, and Tanaro; others, from the N, serving as outlets of the Alpine lakes, are the Ticino, Adda, Oglio, and Mincio. Important industrial cities in its valley (Milan, Turin, Padua, Verona, Brescia).

Po·ás \'pō-ˌäs\. Volcano, Costa Rica, ab. 19 m. NW of the city of San José; 8872 ft.

Po·be·da Peak \pə-'b(y)ed-ə-\ *or Russ.* **Pik Po·be·dy** \ˌpēk-pə-'b(y)ed-ē\ *or Chin.* **Sheng–li Feng** \'sheŋ-lē-'feŋ\. Mountain, highest in Tien Shan range, on the border between Kirgiz S.S.R., U.S.S.R., and Sinkiang Uighur, China; 24,406 ft.

Po·ca·hon·tas \ˌpōk-ə-'hänt-əs\. 1 Name of counties of two states in the U.S. See tables at IOWA and WEST VIRGINIA.
2 City, ⊗ of Randolph co., NE Arkansas, on Black river 33 m. NNW of Jonesboro; pop. (1970c) 4544.
3 City, ⊗ of Pocahontas co., NW cen. Iowa, 30 m. NW of Fort Dodge; pop. (1970c) 2338; fertilizers; grain.

Po·ca·tel·lo \ˌpō-kə-'tel-(ˌ)ō, -'tel-ə\. City, ⊗ of Bannock co., SE Idaho, 60 m. N of Utah border and 70 m. W of Wyoming border; pop. (1970c) 40,036; produces chemicals, flour, cement, fertilizer, dairy products; railroad shops; Idaho State Univ. (1901); settled 1882, incorporated as city 1893.

Pochow. See POHSIEN.

Po·chu·tla \ˌpō-'chüt-lə\. Municipality, Oaxaca state, Mexico, 95 m. S of Oaxaca; pop. (1970p) 84,033; site of important discoveries of Indian sculpture.

Pock·ling·ton Reef \ˌpäk-liŋ-tən-\. Reef in S Solomon Sea, off SW Solomon Is., W Pacific Ocean.

Po·co·moke \'pō-kə-ˌmōk\. River, SE Maryland; ab. 55 m. long; rises in S Delaware, flows S across Maryland border and into Pocomoke Sound in SE Somerset co.

Pocomoke City. Town, Worcester co., SE Maryland, 22 m. S of Salisbury; pop. (1970c) 3573; lumber, fertilizer; poultry, truck farms.

Pocomoke Sound. Inlet of Chesapeake Bay, S coast of Somerset co., Maryland, and NW coast of Accomac co., Virginia, receiving Pocomoke river on NE.

Po·co·no Mountains \'pō-kə-ˌnō-\. Ridge, E Pennsylvania, chiefly in Pike, Monroe, and Carbon cos.; ab. 1600 ft. high; extends parallel with and ab. 15 m. NW of the Kittatinny Mountains.

Po·ços de Cal·das \'pō-ˌsüzh-də-'käl-dəs\. Seaside resort, Minas Gerais state, E Brazil; munic. pop. (1968e) 44,504; altitude ab. 4000 ft.; sulfur baths.

Po·co·to·paug Lake \'pō-kət-ə-ˌpȯg-\. Lake, NE Middlesex co., S Connecticut; outlet is stream flowing S into Salmon river.

Podgorica *or* **Podgoritsa.** See TITOGRAD.

Po di Pri·ma·ro \ˌpȯd-ē-pri-'mär-(ˌ)ō\. Name applied to the lower course of the Reno river, Italy.

Podium Anicensis. See LE PUY.

Podkamennaya Tunguska. See TUNGUSKA.

Podkarpatská Rus. See TRANSCARPATHIAN OBLAST.

Po·do·lia \pə-'dō-lē-ə, -'dōl-yə\ *or Russ.* **Po·dolsk** \pə-'dȯlsk\. Former region on left bank of middle Dniester; incorporated in medieval kingdom of Poland 1431; held by Turks 1672–99; divided between Russia and Austria 1772; E part was later a province of Russia; now in W Ukrainian S.S.R., U.S.S.R., nearly coextensive with Khmelnitski Oblast; chief town Kamenets-Podolski.

Po·dolsk \pə-'dȯlsk\. Industrial town, Moscow Oblast, Russian S.F.S.R., U.S.S.R., on railroad 25 m. S of Moscow; pop. (1970p) 169,000; manufactures aluminum, boilers, sewing machines, cables, cement; made town 1781.

Po·dor \'pō-ˌdȯ(ə)r\. Town on the Senegal river, N Senegal, W Africa.

Poelau. See PULAU.

Poel·ka·pel·le *or* **Poel·ca·pel·le** \ˌpu̇l-kə-'pel-ə\. Small commune, West Flanders prov., NW Belgium, NNE of Ieper (Ypres); pop. (1969e) 1921; stormed by British Oct. 4, 1917; marked the limit of British advance in the third battle of Ypres; scene of death in action Sept. 11, 1917 of the French aviation ace Capt. Guynemer.

Poerbalingga. See PURBOLINGGO.

Poerwakarta. See PURWAKARTA.

Poerwodadi. See PURWODADI.

Poerwokerto. See PURWOKERTO.

Poerworedjo. See PURWOREJO.

Poeting. See PUTING.

Poge, Cape \-'pōj\. Northeast point of Chappaquiddick I., E Martha's Vineyard, Massachusetts.

Pog·gi·bon·si \ˌpȯj-i-'bōn(t)-sē\. Commune, Siena prov., Tuscany, cen. Italy, 16 m. NW of Siena; pop. (1968e) 24,145; 13th cent. church and convent.

Pog·ra·dec \pȯ-'grä-ˌdets\. 1 Province of E Albania. See table at ALBANIA.
2 Town, its ✱, ab. 55 m. SE of Tiranë; pop. (1967e) 9702.

Po Hai. See CHIHLI, GULF OF.

Pohai, Strait of \-'bō-'hī\ *or Chin.* **Po–hai** *or formerly* **Pe·chi·li** \'bā-'ji(ə)r-'lē\. Strait bet. Liaotung Penin. and N Shantung, NE China; ab. 70 m. wide; connects Gulf of Chihli with the Yellow Sea.

P'o·hang \'pō-'häŋ\. Town, North Kyŏngsang prov., South Korea, ab. 66 m. NNE of Pusan; pop. (1970e) 79,451.

Poh·jois–Kar·ja·la \'pȯ-yȯis-'kär-yə-lə\. Province of E Finland. See table at FINLAND.

Po·hsien \'bō-shē-'en\ *or formerly* **Po·chow** \'bō-'jō\. Commercial city, NW Anhwei prov., E China, ab. 160 m. NW of Ho-fei.

Poictiers. See POITIERS.

Poin·sett \'pȯin-ˌset, -sit\. County in Arkansas. See table at ARKANSAS.

Poinsett, Lake. Lake, S Hamlin co., E South Dakota.

Point de Galle. See GALLE.

Pointe à Gatineau. See POINTE-GATINEAU.

Pointe à la Chevelure. See CROWN POINT 2.

Pointe a la Hache \'pȯint-ˌal-ə-'hash\. Village, ⊗ of Plaquemines parish, SE Louisiana; pop. (1972e) 500.

Pointe–à–Pi·tre \ˌpwant-ə-'pētr^{ə}\. Seaport, SW Grande Terre I., E Guadeloupe, West Indies; largest town in Guadeloupe; pop. (1967c) 29,757; founded mid-17th cent.

Pointe Aux Barques \ˌpȯint-ō-'bärk\. North tip of the Thumb, E Michigan. See THUMB, THE 2.

Pointe aux Trem·bles \ˌpwa^{n}(n)t-ō-'trä^{n}bl^{ə}\. City on NE shore of Montreal I., S Quebec, Canada, on St. Lawrence river 10 m. N of Montreal; pop. (1971p) 35,521.

Pointe Claire \ˌpȯint-'kla(ə)r, -'kle(ə)r\. City, Montreal I., S Quebec, Canada, on St. Lawrence river 15 m. WSW of Montreal; pop. (1971p) 27,310.

Pointe Cou·pee \'pȯint-kü-'pē\. Parish in Louisiana. See table at LOUISIANA.

Point Edward \-'ed-wərd\. Village, Lambton co., SE Ontario, Canada, on Lake Huron 3 m. N of Sarnia; pop. (1971p) 2780.

Pointe–Ga·ti·neau \ˌpwa^{n}t-ˌgat-^{ə}n-'ō\ *or* **Pointe à Gatineau** \pwa^{n}t-ə-\. Town, Hull co., SW Quebec, Canada, at confluence of Gatineau and Ottawa rivers opp. Hull and Ottawa; pop. (1971p) 15,607.

Pointe Levi. See LEVIS 2.

Pointe–Noire \ˌpwaⁿt-nə-ˈwär\. City and port, SW Congo, on the Atlantic Ocean 230 m. SW of Brazzaville; met. area pop. (1970p) 135,000; commercial center; cellulose plant; port facilities constructed 1934–39; was ✱ of Middle Congo 1950–58.

Point Hueneme. See PORT HUENEME.

Point Mountain. Peak in Glacier National Park, NW Montana; 8300 ft.

Point Pe·lee National Park \-ˈpē-lē-\. See CANADA, *National Parks.*

Point Pleas·ant \-ˈplez-ənt\. 1 Borough and seaside resort, Ocean co., E New Jersey, on Atlantic Ocean 10 m. S of Asbury Park; pop. (1970c) 15,968; truck, cranberry farms.
2 Village, S Clermont co., SW Ohio, on the Ohio river; birthplace of Ulysses S. Grant, 18th president of the United States.
3 City, ⊗ of Mason co., W West Virginia, on Ohio river 35 m. NNE of Huntington; pop. (1970c) 6122; chemicals; coal mines, iron foundries; diversified agriculture; incorporated 1833.

Point Pleasant Beach. Borough and seaside resort, Ocean co., E New Jersey, near Point Pleasant; pop. (1970c) 4882.

Point Rob·erts \-ˈräb-ərts\. 1 The tip of a peninsula, NW Washington, extending S into Strait of Georgia from British Columbia, Canada; separated from mainland of Whatcom co. by Boundary Bay.
2 Village on point.

Point Suc·cess \-sək-ˈses\. Mountain in Mt. Rainier National Park, W cen. Washington; 14,150 ft.

Pois·sy \pwa-ˈsē\ *or anc.* **Pin·ci·a·cum** \pin-ˈsī-ə-kəm\. Commune, Yvelines dept., N France, on Seine river 11 m. WNW of Paris; pop. (1968c) 33,555; distillery; church (in which Saint Louis was baptized 1215).

Poi·tiers\pwä-ˈtyā, ˌpwät-ē-ˈā\ *or formerly* **Poic·tiers** \pwä-ˈtyā, ˌpwät-ē-ˈā\ *or anc.* **Li·mo·num** \lə-ˈmō-nəm\. City, ✱ of Vienne dept., W cen. France, 100 m. ESE of Nantes; pop. (1968c) 70,681; railroad junction; market town in wheat, wine, and livestock farming region; 12th cent. cathedral, palace of former counts of Poitou (*q.v.*), several notable Romanesque churches; univ. (1431).

Poi·tou \pwä-ˈtü\. Historical region of W cen. France; bounded anciently on NW by Brittany, on N by Anjou and Saumurois, on NE by Touraine, E by Marche, SE by Limousin, S by Angoumois and Aunis, W by Atlantic Ocean; ✱ Poitiers; watered by Sèvre Nantaise and Sèvre Niortaise rivers.

History: Inhabited by ancient Pictones or Pictavi; conquered by Romans and made part of Aquitania; conquered by Visigoths 418 A.D.; Visigoths under Alaric II defeated near Poitiers by Franks under Clovis 507 A.D.; Saracens defeated by Charles Martel 732 on a site bet. Poitiers and Tours; made countship by Charlemagne 778; part of duchy of Aquitaine 990; important center of Romanesque art 11th–12th cent.; passed to Louis VII of France 1137 and later to Henry II of England; confiscated by Philip Augustus 1203; occupied 1356–69 by English after major defeat of John the Good by Edward, the Black Prince, Sept. 19, 1356 at Maupertuis, 7 m. SE of Poitiers; appanage of Jean de France Berry 1369–1416; reunited with French crown 1416; province of France until Revolution, when territory was divided into three departments, most westerly the Vendée (see VENDÉE 2) noted for the series of peasant insurrections against the Revolutionary government (Wars of the Vendée 1793–96).

Pok Liu Chau \ˈpȯk-ˈlyü-ˈjau̇\ *or* **Lam·ma** *or* **La·ma** \ˈlä-ˈmä\. Island, S part of New Territories, Hong Kong, just SW of Hong Kong I.

Po–ko–to \ˈpō-ˈkō-ˈtō\; *formerly* **Bog·do Ula** \bȯg-ˌdō-ü-ˈlä\ *or* **Bogdo–ola** \-ō-ˈlä\. Mountain range, E Tien Shan, bet. Urumchi and Pa-li-k'un, cen. Sinkiang Uighur, W China; highest peak ab. 18,000 ft., average height 14,000 ft.

Pokrovsk. See ENGELS.

Pola. See PULA.

Po·land \ˈpō-lənd\. 1 *or Pol.* **Pols·ka** \ˈpȯl-skä\; *officially* **Polish People's Republic** *or Pol.* **Polska Rze·czy·pos·po·li·ta Lu·do·wa** \ˈpȯl-skə-ˌzhe-chi-ˌpȯs-ˈpȯl-i-tä-ˈlü-dȯ-və\. Republic, cen. Europe, bounded on N by the Baltic Sea and the U.S.S.R., on E by the U.S.S.R., on S and SW by Czechoslovakia, and on W by East Germany; 120,756 sq. m.; pop. (1970p) 32,589,000; ✱ Warsaw. *Physical features:* N and cen. regions are essentially flat and characterized by morainic topography; area along S boundary is mountainous, with highest peak Rysy, 8197 ft. *Chief products:* Wheat, potatoes, rye, sugar beet, tobacco; coal, sulfur, copper, zinc, salt; manufacturing: chemicals, iron and steel, textiles; metal refining, shipbuilding, food processing. *Chief cities:* Warsaw, Łódź, Kraków, Wrocław, Poznań, Gdańsk, Szczecin, Katowice. Divided into the following administrative units (for pronunciation of their names, see their individual entries):

NAME	AREA (sq. m.)	POP. (1970p)	CAPITAL
City Provinces			
Kraków	89	583,000	
Łódź	83	762,000	
Poznań	85	469,000	
Warsaw	172	1,308,000	
Wrocław	86	523,000	
Provinces[1]			
Białystok	8,939	1,173,000	Białystok
Bydgoszcz	8,066	1,912,000	Bydgoszcz
Gdańsk	4,261	1,465,000	Gdańsk
Katowice	3,686	3,691,000	Katowice
Kielce	7,534	1,889,000	Kielce
Koszalin	6,990	793,000	Koszalin
Kraków	5,929	2,181,000	Kraków
Łódź	6,602	1,670,000	Łódź
Lublin	9,607	1,922,000	Lublin
Olsztyn	8,133	978,000	Olsztyn
Opole	3,690	1,057,000	Opole
Poznań	10,366	2,190,000	Poznań
Rzeszów	7,195	1,757,000	Rzeszów
Szczecin	4,924	897,000	Szczecin
Warszawa	11,354	2,514,000	Warsaw
Wrocław	7,306	1,973,000	Wrocław
Zielona Góra	5,628	882,000	Zielona Góra

[1] Area and population figures do not include the five cities having province rank.

History: Slavic duchy under Piast dynasty emerged in late 10th cent. in region bet. Oder and Warta rivers; under Boleslav I (992–1025), it conquered territory of the Slavs W to the Oder, Moravia, and Kraków, and was recognized as Polish kingdom; invaded by Mongols 1241; its personal union with Lithuania by marriage 1386 established Jagellon dynasty; after long struggle with Teutonic Knights, obtained West Prussia and East Prussia (*q.v.*) 1466; after 1572, Polish crown became elective, and the nobility stronger than the monarch; in 17th cent. several disastrous wars led to loss of much territory. New wars and political weakness led to three partitions: 1772, 1793, and 1795, in which Poland was completely dismembered and divided among Russia, Prussia, and Austria. Partly reestablished by Napoleon, 1807–15, as Grand Duchy of Warsaw, on part of the territory of which, following the Congress of Vienna 1815, was constituted a kingdom (frequently called **Congress Poland** *or* **Russian Poland**) under the Russian crown (ab. 49,000 sq. m.; ✱ Warsaw). Organized as autonomous kingdom of Poland in personal union with Russia 1815–30; lost autonomy after Polish Revolt 1830–31; after unsuccessful rising of Jan. 1863, became merely a Russian province; invaded by Germans and Austrians in World War I 1914–18; proclaimed independent republic 1918. West Prussia, except Danzig (see GDAŃSK), and Posen (see also POLISH CORRIDOR), ceded by Germany 1919; obtained part of Silesia, Vilna, part of Ukraine and of White Russia, and Teschen 1919–38; governed by 1921 constitution, amended after Pilsudski's coup d'état 1926; 1935 constitution formally ended democratic parliamentary rule; Danzig crisis precipitated World War II 1939; E and cen. parts completely overrun and subjugated by Germany Sept. 1939; as result of treaty bet. Germany and U.S.S.R. 1939, Pomorze, Poznań, and Upper Silesia annexed to Germany, central sector constituted into German-controlled Government-General of Poland, and eastern part incorporated in U.S.S.R.; small parts later ceded to Slovakia and Lithuania. Reoccupied by Soviet armies in 1944 and 1945. After World War II part E of Curzon Line (*q.v.*) taken by U.S.S.R. and added to Belorussian and Ukrainian S.S.Rs.; received Danzig, S two thirds of East Prussia, most of Pomerania along the Baltic, and regions of Germany E of the Oder (E Brandenburg and most of Silesia); establishment of Soviet-dominated government following controlled elections 1947; adopted new constitution 1952; became a member of the Warsaw Treaty Organization 1955; participated with U.S.S.R. in invasion of Czechoslovakia 1968; its W boundary recognized as permanent by West Germany 1970.

2 Village, Mahoning co., NE Ohio, 7 m. SW of Youngstown; pop. (1970c) 3097; automobile parts, concrete blocks; agriculture.

Polangen. See PALANGA.

Po·lan·gui \pȯ-ˈläŋ-gē\. Municipality, Albay prov., Luzon, Phil., on railroad ab. 19 m. NW of Legaspi; pop. (1969e) 52,900.

Polar Regions. Regions around the North Pole (**North Polar Regions**) and the South Pole (**South Polar Regions**); North Pole first reached by Robert E. Peary Apr. 6, 1909, by Byrd, Amundsen, Ellsworth and Nobile 1926, by Otto Schmidt 1937; South Pole first reached by Roald Amundsen Dec. 14, 1911, by Scott 1912, by Byrd 1929; both regions extensively explored since World War II; conditions of extreme cold and fields of ice are of much wider extent around the South Pole. See ARCTIC, THE, ANTARCTIC REGIONS, MAGNETIC POLE, SOUTH POLE, NORTH POLE.

Pole Mountain \ˌpōl-\. Peak, Hinsdale co., SW Colorado; 13,737 ft.

Po·le·sie \pȯ-ˈles-ē-ə\. Former Polish department; 14,169 sq. m.; ✱ Brest Litovsk; now in the U.S.S.R., divided bet. Belorussian S.S.R. and Ukrainian S.S.R.

Po·le·si·ne \pə-ˈläz-ᵊn-ˌā, -ˈlez-\. Region, NE Italy, the lowland bet. the lower Po and the lower Adige, ab. equivalent to Rovigo prov., S Veneto.

Po·les·ye \pȯ-ˈlyes-ē-ə\ *or* **Pri·pet Marshes** \ˈprip-ˌet-, -ət-\ *or* **Pri·pyat Marshes** \ˈprip-yət-\ *also* **Pinsk Marshes** \ˈpin(t)sk-\. Extensive marshlands, S Belorussian S.S.R. and NW Ukrainian S.S.R., U.S.S.R., chiefly on both sides of the Pripyat river (*q.v.*); ab. 300 m. E and W and 140 m. N and S; largest tract of swamp in Europe; formerly in E Poland. Densely wooded and nearly uninhabited, mostly impassable except in winter when frozen; formerly marked a natural boundary bet. Poland and U.S.S.R. and for centuries have greatly affected the strategy of military invasions or mass movements of peoples. In World War I scene of campaigns 1914 and 1915; in World War II bypassed by German armies 1941 and by Soviet troops 1943–44.

Po·lev·skoi \pə-ləf-ˈskȯi\. Town, Sverdlovsk Oblast, Russian S.F.S.R., U.S.S.R., ab. 30 m. SW of Sverdlovsk; pop. (1969e) 55,000.

Pol·gár \ˈpȯl-gär\ *or* **Ti·sza·pol·gár** \ˈtis-ə-ˌpȯl-gär\. Commune, Hajdú-Bihar co., E Hungary, 35 m. NW of Debrecen, E of Tisza river; pop. (1970p) 11,778.

Po·li·ca·stro, Gulf of \-pō-li-ˈkäs-(ˌ)trō\. Inlet of Tyrrhenian Sea, SW coast of Italy, S of the Gulf of Salerno.

Po·li·gna·no a Ma·re \ˌpȯ-lē-ˈnyä-nō-ä-ˈmär-ə\. Seaport commune, Bari prov., Apulia, SE Italy, on the Adriatic 21 m. ESE of Bari; pop. (1968e) 14,430; fisheries.

Po·li·llo \pȯ-ˈlē-yō\. 1 Group of islands in Pacific Ocean off E coast of Luzon, Phil., on N side of Lamon Bay; total area ab. 297 sq. m.; comprises Polillo, Jomalig, Patnanongan, Palasan, and ab. 17 islets; part of Quezon prov.

2 Largest island of the group, 14°50′N, 121°50′E, separated from Luzon mainland by **Polillo Strait** (36 m. long, 12 to 18 m. wide); 234 sq. m.

Po·lish Corridor \ˌpōl-ish-\. A strip of land in N part of Poland, bet. former German provinces of Pomerania on W and East Prussia on E, extending to Gdańsk and the Baltic Sea; ab. 90 m. long; 25 to 55 m. wide. By Treaty of Versailles 1919 taken from Germany and assigned to Poland but with the provisions 1920 of the establishment of the Free City of Danzig (see GDAŃSK 2) and after 1921 of the development of Gdynia as Polish port. After World War I caused much friction bet. Germany and Poland and in 1939 was an immediate cause of World War II; occupied by Germany 1939 but after 1945 returned with Danzig to Poland.

Polish People's Republic. See POLAND 1.

Polish Silesia. See SILESIA.

Polk \ˈpōk\. 1 Name of counties in twelve states of the U.S. See tables at ARKANSAS, FLORIDA, GEORGIA, IOWA, MINNESOTA, MISSOURI, NEBRASKA, NORTH CAROLINA, OREGON, TENNESSEE, TEXAS, WISCONSIN.

2 Residential borough and resort, Venango co., NW Pennsylvania, 13 m. WSW of Oil City; pop. (1970c) 3673.

Pol·la·chi \pō-ˈläch-ē\. Town, W Tamil Nadu, S India, 90 m. SE of Calicut; pop. (1961c) 54,369.

Pol·len·sa, Bay of \-pə-ˈlen(t)-sə\. Bay on N coast of the island of Majorca, W Mediterranean Sea.

Pol·len·za \pə-ˈlen(t)-sə, -ˈlen-zə\ *or anc.* **Pol·len·tia** \pə-ˈlen-shē-ə\. Commune, Macerata prov., S cen. Marches, cen. Italy; pop. (1968e) 5068; scene of battle 403 A.D. bet. Stilicho and Goths under Alaric who subsequently retired from Italy.

Pol·li·no, Mon·te \ˌmȯn-tē-pə-ˈlē-(ˌ)nō\. Mountain, highest in Lucanian Apennines (see table at APENNINES).

Pol·lock, Mount \-ˈpäl-ək\. Peak on Continental Divide in Glacier National Park, NW Montana; 9211 ft.

Pol·lux \ˈpäl-əks\. Peak in the Pennine Alps. See CASTOR.

Pollux Peak. Mountain in Yellowstone National Park, NW Wyoming; 11,067 ft.

Po·lo \ˈpō-lō\. City, Ogle co., N Illinois, 34 m. SW of Rockford; pop. (1970c) 2542; dairy products.

Po·lo·chic \ˌpō-lə-ˈchik\. River, S cen. Guatemala; ab. 180 m. long; flows ESE into Lake Izabal.

Po·lotsk \ˈpȯ-lətsk\. 1 Medieval principality in the region S of Lake Peipus, N Europe, bordering on the other medieval principalities of Novgorod, Smolensk, Pinsk, and Volhynia; esp. powerful 10th to 12th cents.

2 City, Vitebsk Oblast, Belorussian S.S.R., U.S.S.R., on right bank of the Western Dvina river 60 m. NW of Vitebsk; pop. (1969e) 64,000; market town; lumber, leather goods, beer, flax; oil refinery; ✱ of former Polotsk Oblast.

History: First mentioned 862; as capital of the principality (1 above) a major trade center with ab. 100,000 people; in 13th cent. came under Lithuania; became free city 1498; held by Russians 1563–79 and permanently acquired by Russians 1772, suffered severe damage in World War II.

Polotsk Oblast \-ˈȯ-bləst, -ˌblast\. Former subdivision of N Belorussian S.S.R., U.S.S.R.; ✱ Polotsk; abolished 1954.

Polska *or* **Polska Rzeczypospolita Ludowa.** See POLAND.

Pol·son \ˈpōl-sən\. City, ⊗ of Lake co., NW Montana, on S end of Flathead Lake; pop. (1970c) 2464; lake resort; lumber; dairy farms.

Pol·ta·va \pəl-ˈtäv-ə\ *also* **Pul·to·va** *or* **Pul·to·wa** \pu̇l-ˈtō-və\. City, ✱ of Poltava Oblast, Ukrainian S.S.R., U.S.S.R., on right bank of Vorskla river 85 m. WSW of Kharkov; pop. (1970p) 220,000; textiles, leather goods, canned foods, flour, clothing, machinery; railroad shops.

History: Town first mentioned 1174 but believed to date from c. 9th cent.; ceded to Tatars by Lithuania 1430; in 17th cent. a Cossack stronghold; scene of decisive battle July 8, 1709, in which Russians under Peter the Great

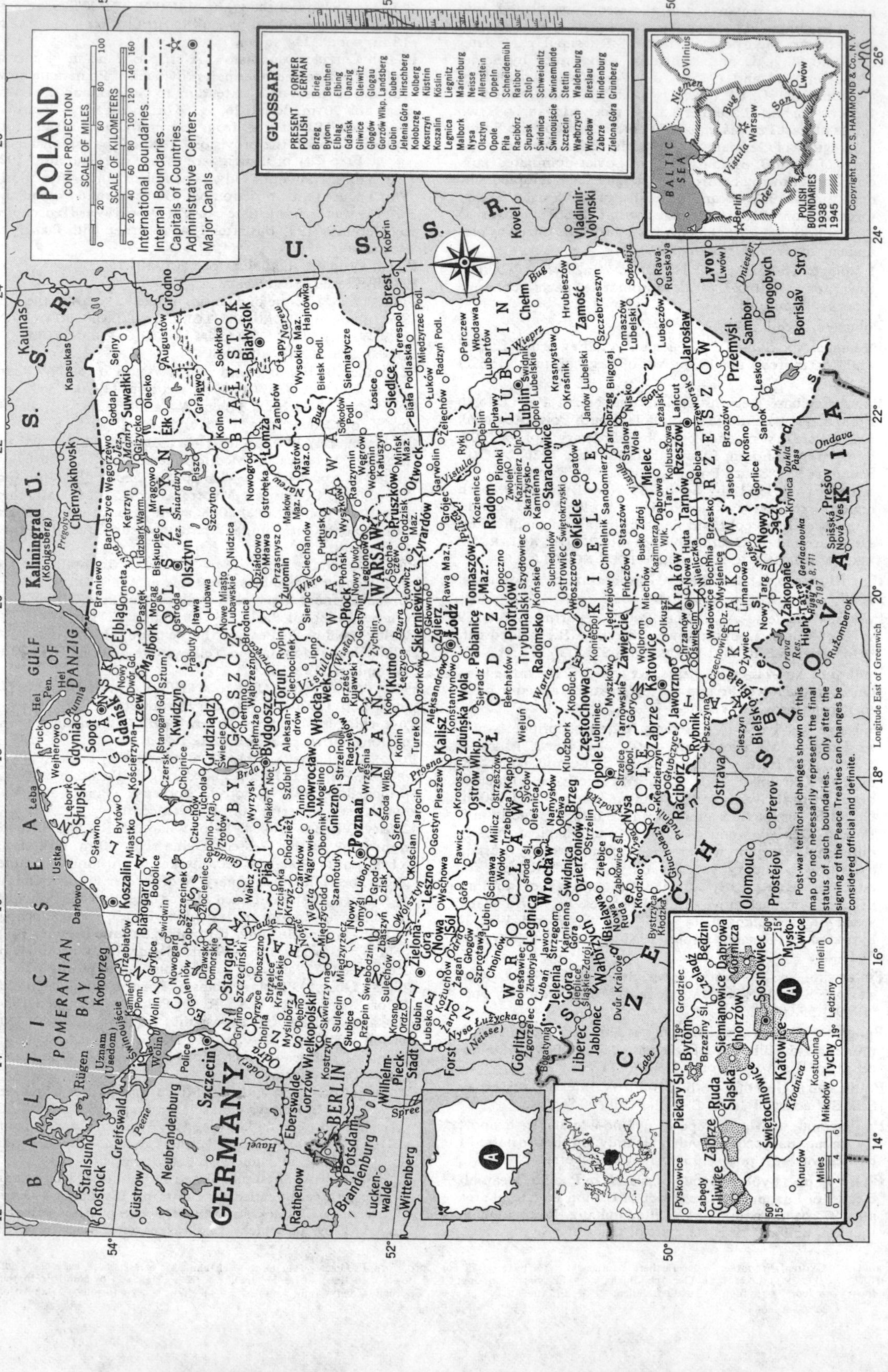
POLAND
CONIC PROJECTION
SCALE OF MILES
SCALE OF KILOMETERS
International Boundaries
Internal Boundaries
Capitals of Countries
Administrative Centers
Major Canals
GLOSSARY
PRESENT POLISH — FORMER GERMAN
Brzeg — Brieg
Bytom — Beuthen
Elbląg — Elbing
Gdańsk — Danzig
Gliwice — Gleiwitz
Głogów — Glogau
Gorzów Wlkp. — Landsberg
Gubin — Guben
Jelenia Góra — Hirschberg
Kołobrzeg — Kolberg
Kostrzyń — Küstrin
Koszalin — Köslin
Legnica — Liegnitz
Malbork — Marienburg
Nysa — Neisse
Olsztyn — Allenstein
Opole — Oppeln
Piła — Schneidemühl
Racibórz — Ratibor
Słupsk — Stolp
Świdnica — Schweidnitz
Świnoujście — Swinemünde
Szczecin — Stettin
Wałbrzych — Waldenburg
Wrocław — Breslau
Zabrze — Hindenburg
Zielona Góra — Grünberg
Post-war territorial changes shown on this map do not necessarily represent the final status of such boundaries. Only after the signing of the Peace Treaties can changes be considered official and definite.
POLISH BOUNDARIES 1938 1945
BALTIC SEA
GERMANY
U. S. S. R.
CZECHOSLOVAKIA
Longitude East of Greenwich
Copyright by C.S. HAMMOND & Co., N.Y.

defeated the Swedes under Charles XII, a battle which marked the emergence of Russia as a major European power; in World War II occupied by the Germans Sept. 1941–Sept. 1943.

Poltava Oblast \-'ō-bləst, -ˌblast\. Subdivision of the Ukrainian S.S.R., U.S.S.R.; 11,120 sq. m.; pop. (1970p) 1,706,000; ✱ Poltava; crossed by the Psel and Vorskla, tributaries of the Dnieper.

Poltoratsk. See ASHKHABAD.

Po·lyar·ny \pəl-'yär-nē\ *or formerly* **Ale·ksan·drovsk** \ə-lek-'sän-ˌdrȯfsk\. Small ice-free port at mouth of Tuloma river, NW Murmansk Oblast, Russian S.F.S.R., U.S.S.R.; now largely replaced as a port by Murmansk.

Po·lyg·y·ros \pō-'lij-ə-ˌräs\ *or Gk.* **Po·lý·gy·ros** \pȯ-'lē-yi-ˌrȯs\. Town, ✱ of Chalcidice dept., S Macedonia, NE Greece, in center of peninsula ab. 30 m. SE of Salonika; pop. (1970p) 4402.

Pol·y·ne·sia \ˌpäl-ə-'nē-zhə, -shə\. Islands of the cen. Pacific Ocean, bet. 30°N and 47°S lat.; a subdivision of Oceania. They include the large islands of New Zealand and the groups of the Hawaiian Is., Samoa, Line Is., French Polynesia, Cook Is., Phoenix Is., Ellice Is., Tonga, and Easter I. The islands are mostly small; many are coral atolls, others are of volcanic origin. The greater part of the inhabitants are Polynesians, perhaps related to the Malay, but many are of mixed origin. Their languages belong to a subfamily of the Austronesian languages. Foremost representatives are the Hawaiians, Maoris, Marquesans, Samoans, Tongans, and Tahitians.

Pom·er·a·nia \ˌpäm-ə-'rā-nē-ə, -nyə\ *or Ger.* **Pom·mern** \'pȯ-mərn\. 1 Historical region on Baltic Sea, at its greatest extent comprising the territory bet. Stralsund and the Vistula and including Rügen I. Occupied by Slavic and other peoples, entire area bet. Oder and Vistula conquered by Boleslav III of Poland 1119–23; in 12th cent. W part penetrated by Germans who erected duchy of Pomerania (included territory on both sides of the lower Oder); E part (see POMERELIA) came under Teutonic Knights and was ceded to Poland 1466 as part of West Prussia. Duchy came under Brandenburg which divided it with Sweden 1648, keeping the part E of the Oder, **Farther Pomerania** (*Ger.* **Hin·ter·pom·mern** \'hin-tər-ˌpȯ-mərn\), and giving to Sweden **Hither Pomerania** (*Ger.* **Vor·pom·mern** \'fō(ə)r-, 'fȯ(ə)r-\), including both banks of the Oder as well as territory to the W, with Rügen I. and Usedom I.; Sweden ceded S part of Hither Pomerania to Prussia 1720, keeping N part, **Swedish Pomerania** (the island of Rügen and the adjoining territory on the mainland N of the Peene river), until 1815 when it also ceded to Prussia. Occupied by U.S.S.R. Mar.–Apr. 1945; the section E of the Oder (but including Szczecin, mainly on left bank) assigned to Poland by the Potsdam Conference 1945.

2 Former department, Poland. See POMORZE.

Pom·er·an·i·an Bay \ˌpäm-ə-ˌrā-nē-ən-, -nyən-\ *or* **Bay of Pomerania** *or Ger.* **Pom·mer·sche Bucht** \'pȯ-mər-shə-ˌbu̇kt\. Widemouthed inlet of Baltic Sea bet. NE East Germany and NW Poland, N of Szczecin.

Pom·er·e·lia \ˌpäm-ə-'rē-lē-ə, -'rēl-yə\ *or Ger.* **Pom·me·rel·len** \ˌpȯ-mə-'rel-ən\. Ancient region on the Baltic Sea, W of the Vistula; originally part of Pomerania (*q.v.*) but gradually separated from it and was distinct from it when the duchy of Pomerania was created in 12th cent.; came under Teutonic Knights; ceded to Poland 1466; at partition of Poland in 18th cent. came under Prussia; to Poland again 1918 and included in former Pomorze (*q.v.*) dept.

Pom·er·oy \'päm-(ə-)ˌrȯi\. 1 Village, ⊗ of Meigs co., SE Ohio, on Ohio river 38 m. SW of Marietta; pop. (1970c) 2672; chemicals; coal mines; diversified agriculture.

2 City, ⊗ of Garfield co., SE Washington, 27 m. SW of Pullman; pop. (1970c) 1823; ships wheat.

Pom·fret \'pəm-fret, -frit\. Residential town and summer resort, N cen. Windham co., NE Connecticut, WSW of Putnam; pop. (1970c) 2529.

Po·mi·glia·no d'Ar·co \ˌpō-məl-ˌyän-ō-'där-(ˌ)kō\. Commune, Napoli prov., Campania, S Italy, at N foot of Vesuvius 8 m. NE of Naples; pop. (1968e) 25,042.

Pommerellen. 1 Ancient region on Baltic Sea. See POMERELIA.

2 Former department, Poland. See POMORZE.

Pommern. See POMERANIA.

Pommersche Bucht. See POMERANIAN BAY.

Pommersche Haff. See ZALEW SZCZECIŃSKI.

Po·mo·na \pə-'mō-nə\. 1 City, Los Angeles co., SW California, 25 m. E of Los Angeles; pop. (1970c) 87,384; residential and commercial suburb of Los Angeles; manufactures naval ordnance, missile components, paper products, building materials; citrus fruit; California State Polytechnic Coll. (1956); founded 1875, incorporated 1888.

2 *or* **Main·land** \'mān-ˌland, -lənd\. Largest of the Orkney Is., off N coast of Scotland; 190 sq. m.; pop. (1961c) 13,495; chief towns Kirkwall and Stromness.

Po·mo·rze \pȯ-'mȯ-zhā\ *or Eng.* **Pom·er·a·nia** \ˌpäm-ə-'rā-nē-ə, -nyə\ *or Ger.* **Pom·me·rel·len** \ˌpȯ-mə-'rel-ən\. Former Polish department; 9920 sq. m.; ✱ Toruń; formed 1918 from E part of Prussian province of Pomerania; after World War II most of dept. made part of Bydgoszcz province.

Pomorze Zachodnie. See SZCZECIN 1.

Pompaelo. See PAMPLONA 2.

Pom·pa·no Beach \ˌpäm-pə-nō-, ˌpəm-\. City, Broward co., SE Florida, near Atlantic Ocean 32 m. N of Miami; pop. (1970c) 39,012; resort; truck farms, citrus fruit; incorporated 1927; moved inland to present site after hurricane 1928.

Pom·pei \päm-'pā(-ˌē)\ *or before 1928* **Val·le di Pompei** \ˌväl-ā-dē-\. Commune, Napoli prov., Campania, S Italy, 14 m. ESE of Naples; pop. (1968e) 22,732; much-visited pilgrimage church (Santuario della Madonna del Rosario); geophysical observatory; mineral springs; near ancient Pompeii (*q.v.*).

Pom·pe·ii \päm-'pā, -'pā-ˌē\. Ancient city, Campania, S Italy, 15 m. SE of Naples near the foot of Mt. Vesuvius and near Herculaneum (*q.v.*); founded late 6th cent. or early 5th cent. B.C. by Oscans (though the Greeks considered its founder to be Hercules); Roman colony by 80 B.C.; became site of many villas belonging to Roman nobility and when it was destroyed by the eruption of Vesuvius 79 A.D. Pliny the Elder was one of the victims; more than three-fifths of the city has been excavated, revealing its regular plan, the forum, temples, baths, theaters, and many dwellings.

Pomp·ton \'päm(p)-tən\. River, N New Jersey; formed at Pompton just S of Pompton Lakes by confluence of Pequannock, Ramapo, and Ringwood rivers; flows S into Passaic river.

Pompton Lakes. Borough, Passaic co., N New Jersey, 9 m. NW of Paterson; pop. (1970c) 11,397; blasting equipment; settled 1682.

Po·na·pe \'pō-nə-ˌpā\ *or formerly* **As·cen·sion** \ə-'sen-chən\. Island of the Senyavin Is. group in E part of the Caroline Is., W Pacific Ocean, 410 m. E of Truk I.; 6°58′N, 158°31′E; area 176 sq. m.; pop. (1970e) 20,808. One of the largest islands of the cen. Pacific, very fertile and hilly; surrounded by a barrier reef enclosing many small islands. Settled all around the coast, but practically uninhabited in the interior. Notable for its many ruins of an earlier population. In World War II its Japanese garrison bypassed by Allies 1944.

Pon·ca \'päŋ-kə\. City, ⊗ of Dixon co., NE Nebraska; pop. (1970c) 984; livestock farms.

Ponca City. City, Kay co., N Oklahoma, on Arkansas river 52 m. ENE of Enid; pop. (1970c) 25,940; clothing, oil-drilling equipment, ceramics; oil refining, food processing; oil and gas wells; founded 1893.

Pon·ce \'pȯn(t)-(ˌ)sā\. Seaport city, S Puerto Rico, 140 m. SW of San Juan; munic. pop. (1970p) 156,498; principal city of S Puerto Rico; exports sugar; produces cement, textiles, footwear, and paper products; oil refining; Catholic Univ. of Puerto Rico (1948); founded 1692, made city 1877.

Ponce de Le·on Bay \ˌpän(t)s-də-ˌlē-ən-\. Inlet of Gulf of Mexico on SW coast of Florida, from Cape Sable to Cape Romano.

Pon·cha·tou·la \ˌpän-chə-'tü-lə\. Town, Tangipahoa parish, SE Louisiana, 41 m. NNW of New Orleans; pop. (1970c) 4545; truck and fruit farms.

Pon·dera \ˌpän-də-'rā\. County in Montana. See table at MONTANA.

Pon·di·cher·ry \ˌpän-də-'cher-ē, -'sher-\ *or Fr.* **Pon·di·ché·ry** \pȯⁿ-dē-shā-rē\. 1 Centrally administered territory of India; 183 sq. m.; pop. (1971p) 471,347; ✱ Pondicherry; composed of four former French coastal settlements (now in states of Andhra Pradesh, Kerala, Tamil Nadu); to India 1954.

2 Seaport, its ✱; pop. (1961c) 40,421; an open roadstead but with good trade; has textile industry; ✱ of former French India. Site acquired 1674 but first permanent settlement made 1683 by François Martin; held by Dutch 1693–97; several times taken by British 1761, 1778, 1793, 1803 but each time restored; French possession 1816–1954.

Pon·do·land \'pän-(ˌ)dō-ˌland\. Region, Transkei, E Cape Province, S Rep. of South Africa, on coast of Indian Ocean bet. Umtata river and Natal border (Umtamvuna river); 3906 sq. m.; ✱ Port St. Johns. Inhabited by Pondos, a Bantu race akin to the Zulus. Annexed to Cape Colony 1894.

Ponente, Riviera di. See RIVIERA.

Pon·fer·ra·da \ˌpän-fə-'räd-ə\. Commune, León prov., NW Spain, 50 m. W by S of León; pop. (1971p) 45,257.

Pon·go de Man·se·ri·che \'pȯŋ-gō-dā-ˌmän(t)-sə-'rē-(ˌ)chā\. Canyon, Peru, through which the Marañón river flows after its major curve around to the E in N Peru; ab. 2000 ft. deep; flow is very rapid and the gorge narrows to as little as 100 ft. width in places (*pongo*=narrows).

Pon·go·lo \päŋ-'gō-lə\. River, flowing bet. SE Transvaal and N Natal, Rep. of South Africa; ab. 120 m. long; unites with Usutu river to form Maputo river in Mozambique.

Pon·na·ni \pə-'nän-ē\. 1 River, W Tamil Nadu and cen. Kerala, S India; 120 m. long; flows W to Arabian Sea at Ponnani; part of its course forms N boundary of Cochin.

2 Seaport town at mouth of river, 38 m. S of Calicut, Kerala; pop. (1961c) 22,977; here Tipu Sultan was repulsed by British Nov. 1782.

Po·no·ro·go \ˌpō-nə-'rō-(ˌ)gō\. Market town, East Java prov., Indonesia, 20 m. S of Madiun; pop. (1961c) 59,552.

Pons Aelii. See NEWCASTLE 4.

Pon·son \pȯn-'sȯn\. Island, easternmost of Camotes Is., Cebu prov., Phil.; 13 sq. m.; pop. (1969e) 11,900; coextensive with municipality of Pilar.

Pons Vetus. See PONTEVEDRA 4.

Pon·ta Del·ga·da \ˌpänt-ə-del-'gäd-ə, -'gad-\. 1 District of Portugal. See table at PORTUGAL.

2 Seaport commune, its ✱, in Azores on SW coast of São Miguel I.; munic. pop. (1970p) 69,930; commercial and tourist center; exports pottery, hats, distilled liquors, and citrus fruit.

Ponta Gros·sa \ˌpō(ⁿ)nt-ə-'grȯ-sə\. City, Paraná state, S Brazil, 60 m. WNW of Curitiba; munic. pop. (1968e) 152,-581; lumber, tea, cereals, tobacco, livestock, rice.

Pont-à-Mous·son \ˌpōⁿt-ä-mü-'sōⁿ\. Industrial commune, Meurthe-et-Moselle dept., NE France, on Moselle river 12 m. NNW of Nancy; pop. (1968c) 13,406; hardware. Founded 13th cent.; university founded here 1572 (transferred to Nancy 1768); taken by Louis XIII 1632; a frontline position in World War I, held by the French from Sept. 1914; starting point of Americans in battle of St-Mihiel Sept. 12, 1918.

Pon·tar·lier \ˌpōⁿ-tär-'lyā\. Industrial commune, Doubs dept., E France, on Doubs river near Swiss border 29 m. SSE of Besançon; pop. (1968c) 16,442; manufactures distilled liquors, clocks; trades in dairy products.

Pon·tas·sie·ve \ˌpōn-tä-sē-'ā-vē, -'ev-ē\. Commune, Firenze prov., Tuscany, cen. Italy, on the Arno 10 m. E of Florence; pop. (1968e) 15,438.

Pont-Au·de·mer \ˌpōⁿ-tōd-'mer\. Commune, Eure dept., N France, ab. 39 m. NW of Évreux; pop. (1962c) 8999; a river port on the Risle, a tributary of the Seine.

Pont-Aven \pōⁿ-tə-'ven\. Village at head of estuary on coast of Bay of Biscay, Finistère dept., Brittany, NW France, ab. 18 m. WNW of Lorient; pop. (1962c) 3829.

Pont·char·train, Lake \-'pän-chər-ˌtrān, -ˌpän-chər-'\. Lake, SE Louisiana; ab. 40 m. long; 630 sq. m.; connected through Lake Borgne with Gulf of Mexico, and by canal with Mississippi river. The city of New Orleans lies bet. it and the Mississippi river.

Pont du Fahs. See QANṬARAT AL-FAHṢ.

Pon·te·cor·vo \ˌpōn-tə-'kȯr-vō\. Commune, Frosinone prov., Latium, cen. Italy, 21 m. SE of Frosinone; pop. (1968e) 11,739; a former principality; largely destroyed in World War II.

Pon·te·de·ra \ˌpōn-tā-'der-ə\. Commune, Pisa prov., Tuscany, cen. Italy, on the Arno 13 m. ESE of Pisa; pop. (1968e) 25,897.

Pon·te·fract \'pänt-i-ˌfrakt, 'pəm-frət\. Municipal borough, West Riding, Yorkshire, N England, near confluence of Aire and Calder rivers 13 m. S of Leeds; pop. (1971p) 31,335; licorice confectionary ("Pomfret cakes"), furniture, leather goods, textiles, machinery; 11th cent. castle, scene of the death of Richard II 1400. Saxon settlement which took present name before 1140; received first charter 1194; a seat of several important monastic foundations.

Pon·te No·va \ˌpōn-tə-'nȯ-və\. City, SE Minas Gerais state, E Brazil, 75 m. SE of Belo Horizonte; munic. pop. (1968e) 48,853.

Pon·te·ve·dra \ˌpänt-ə-'vā-drə\. 1 Municipality, Negros Occidental, Negros, Phil., on Guimaras Strait 20 m. S of City of Bacolod; pop. (1969e) 31,000.

2 Municipality, NE Capiz prov., Panay, Phil., just W of head of Pilar Bay 13 m. SE of Roxas; pop. (1969e) 28,700.

3 Province of NW Spain. See table at SPAIN.

4 *or anc.* **Pons Ve·tus** \pänz-'vēt-əs, -'vet-\. Commune, ✱ of Pontevedra prov., NW Spain, on inlet of Atlantic Ocean 65 m. SW of Lugo; pop. (1970p) 52,452; trades in grain and fruit; produces textiles, pottery, leather, hats, fertilizers; 16th cent. church, Roman bridge; in Middle Ages an important shipbuilding center and port.

Ponthierville. See UBUNDI.

Pon·thieu \pōⁿ-'tyər\. Ancient region in N France, in Picardy; ✱ Abbeville; became countship at end of 9th cent.; passed to Castile 1251; held by England (acquired through marriage of Eleanor of Castile to Edward I) 1272–1336, 1360–69; finally to French crown 1690.

Pon·ti·ac \'pänt-ē-ˌak\. 1 City, ⊗ of Livingston co., NE cen. Illinois, 35 m. NNE of Bloomington; pop. (1970c) 10,595; gloves, electronic components; publishing; grain farms; Winston Churchill Coll. (1965).

2 City, ⊗ of Oakland co., SE Michigan, 25 m. NNW of Detroit; pop. (1970c) 85,279; automobile-manufacturing center; rubber, paint, varnish, plastic, boats, dairy products; settled 1818; chartered as city 1861.

3 County, Quebec, Canada. See table at QUEBEC.

Pontiae. See PONZA ISLANDS.

Pon·ti·a·nak \ˌpänt-ē-'än-ək\. City, ✱ of West Kalimantan prov., W Borneo, Indonesia, at mouth of small stream on N edge of Kapuas delta; pop. (1961c) 150,220; exports rubber, sugar, and palm oil; important shipbuilding center; in region producing coconuts, pepper, rice, tobacco, and sugar. Formerly capital of a sultanate founded 1772 and supported by the Dutch; later became chief gold-exporting port of Borneo; in World War II occupied by Japanese Feb. 1942–Sept. 1945.

Pontine Islands. See PONZA ISLANDS.

Pon·ti·no, Agro \ˌä-grō-pōn-ˈtē-(ˌ)nō\ *or formerly* **Pon·tine Marshes** \ˌpän-ˌtīn-, -ˌtēn-\. District, SW Latium, cen. Italy; ab. 290 sq. m.; bounded on N by the Lepini Mts., separated from sea by low sand hills which prevent natural drainage; for many centuries an unhealthful region of malarial swamps; traversed by the Appian Way, built 312 B.C. when first attempts at drainage were made; most recent reclamation projects begun 1926 under Mussolini; has several cities, incl. Latina (*q.v.*) and **Pon·ti·nia** \pōn-ˈtē-nyə\. In SE part on a promontory which in ancient times seems to have been an island is Monte Circeo (*q.v.*); possibly the region was at one time entirely submerged.

Pontisarae. See PONTOISE.

Pon·ti·vy \ˌpō^{n}-tē-ˈvē\. Town, Morbihan dept., NW France, ab. 30 m. NNW of Vannes; pop. (1962c) 11,815; made military headquarters of Brittany by Napoleon who constructed a new town which was known as Napoléonville and which in layout remains quite distinct from the old town.

Pont–l'Ab·bé \ˌpō^{n}-lä-ˈbā\. Town, Finistère dept., NW France, ab. 12 m. SW of Quimper; pop. (1962c) 7167; Bretons of the region are called the Bigouden from the name of the distinctive headdress of the women.

Pont l'Évêque \ˌpō^{n}-lə-ˈvek\. Town, Calvados dept., NW France, 25 m. NE of Caen; pop. (1962c) 3372; noted for its cheese.

Pon·toise \pō^{n}-ˈtwäz\; *anc.* **Bri·va Is·a·rae** \ˈbrī-və-ˈis-ə-rē\ *also* **Pon·tis·a·rae** \pän-ˈtis-ə-rē\. Commune, ✱ of Val-d'Oise dept., N France, on Oise river 18 m. NNW of Paris; pop. (1968c) 17,509; market center and residential suburb of Paris; 12th cent. cathedral, 16th cent. church. Came under French crown 1064 and made capital of French Vexin; frequently besieged in 15th, 16th, and 17th cents.; meeting place of *Parlement* of Paris 1652, 1720, 1753.

Pon·tor·son \ˌpō^{n}t-ər-ˈsō^{n}\. Town, SW Manche dept., Normandy, NW France, ab. 12 m. SW of Avranches; pop. (1962c) 3687; starting point for excursions to Mont-Saint-Michel; taken by Americans Aug. 1, 1944.

Pon·to·toc \ˈpänt-ə-ˌtäk\. 1 Name of counties in two states of the U.S. See tables at MISSISSIPPI and OKLAHOMA.

2 City, ⊗ of Pontotoc co., N Mississippi, 17 m. W of Tupelo; pop. (1970c) 3543; dairy, poultry farms.

Pon·tre·mo·li \ˌpȯn-trə-ˈmȯ-lē\. Commune, Massa-Carrara prov., Tuscany, W Italy, 28 m. NNW of Carrara; pop. (1968e) 11,715; 17th cent. cathedral.

Pont Rouge \ˈpō^{n}-ˈrüzh\. Village, Portneuf co., S Quebec, Canada, on Jacques Cartier river and on railroad 25 m. W of Quebec; pop. (1971p) 3226.

Pont–Saint–Es·prit \ˈpō^{n}-ˌsa^{n}-tes-ˈprē\. Town, Gard dept., S France; pop. (1962c) 5822; on the Rhone which is here crossed by a 13th–14th cent. bridge 1000 yards long, built by friars, widened in 1860.

Pon·tus \ˈpänt-əs\. 1 Ancient country in NE Asia Minor, originally that part of Cappadocia along the shore of Pontus Euxinus (Black Sea) E of Halys river; ancient ✱ Amasia. As kingdom, bounded on E and SE by Armenia, on S by Cappadocia, and on W by Galatia and Paphlagonia. Mountainous, watered by Iris river. Kingdom established 4th cent. B.C. and continued with expanding borders until 66 B.C. when its last king, Mithridates the Great, was overcome by Pompey; annexed and partitioned as province of Roman Empire 62 B.C. Christianity introduced in first century A.D. Chief cities Trapezus (see TRABZON), Amasia, Cerasus, and Cotyora.

2 *or* **Pontus Euxinus.** See BLACK SEA.

Pon·ty·pool \ˌpänt-i-ˈpül\. Urban district, Monmouthshire, SE Wales, on the Afon Llwydd 25 m. NW of Bristol; pop. (1971p) 37,014; steel, glass, rubber, nylon products; coal mines; a center of iron and tin industry since late 16th cent.

Pon·ty·pridd \ˌpänt-i-ˈprēth\. Urban district, Glamorganshire, S Wales; pop. (1971p) 34,465; steel, electrical equipment, cables; coal mining; notable 18th cent. bridge from which community takes its name.

Pon·za Islands \ˈpȯn(t)-sə-\ *also* **Pon·tine Islands** \ˈpän-ˌtīn-, -ˌtēn-\ *or* **Pon·zia·ne Islands** \pȯn-ˈtsyä-nə-\ *or anc.* **Pon·ti·ae** \ˈpän-shē-ˌē\. Island group in Tyrrhenian Sea W of Naples; administratively a part of Napoli prov., Campania, SW Italy; chief island **Ponza** \ˈpȯnt-sə\; used as a place of banishment in ancient times and again under Mussolini.

Poole \ˈpül\. Municipal borough, Dorsetshire, S England, on English Channel 40 m. W of Portsmouth; pop. (1971p) 106,697; yachting center; manufactures pottery, chemicals, boats; chartered 1248.

Poo·na \ˈpü-nə\. 1 Division, Maharashtra, W India; 28,909 sq. m.; pop. (1961c) 10,360,282; ✱ Poona.

2 District of the division; 6033 sq. m.; pop. (1961c) 2,466,880; ✱ Poona.

3 *or* **Pu·ne** \ˈpü-nə\. City, ✱ of district and division, on tributary of the Bhima river 80 m. ESE of Bombay; pop. (1970e) 732,731; rail and road junction; textiles, paper, pharmaceuticals, machinery, munitions; numerous notable palaces and temples, including esp. the temple of Parvati, extensive public gardens and government buildings; in city and its suburbs are a number of military facilities including headquarters of southern command and National Defence Academy; univ. (1948). Given as a fief by Sultan of Ahmadnagar to Maratha chief; made capital of Maratha Empire; came under British rule 1818.

Poonch *or* **Punch** \ˈpünch\. Town, Jammu and Kashmir, N India, 45 m. SW of Srinagar; pop. (1961c) 10,200.

Po·o·pó, Lake \-ˌpō-ə-ˈpō\ *also* **Lake Au·lla·gas** \-au̇-ˈyä-gəs\. Lake in W cen. Bolivia at altitude of 12,000 ft.; 977 sq. m.; max. depth 15 ft.; receives Desaguadero river from Lake Titicaca to the N.

Pootoo. See P'U-T'O SHAN.

Po·pa, Mount \-ˈpō-pə\. Extinct volcano, cen. Burma, at N end of Pegu Yoma; 4981 ft.; highest point in the range.

Po·pa·yán \ˌpō-pə-ˈyän\. City, ✱ of Cauca dept., SW Colombia, S of Cali at foot of Mt. Puracé; pop. (1968e) 65,489; altitude 5700 ft.; primarily a cultural center with some local industry; univ. (1827). Founded 1537; during the colonial era center of a mining region and an important residential, administrative, and religious center.

Pope \ˈpōp\. Name of counties in three states of the U.S. See tables at ARKANSAS, ILLINOIS, MINNESOTA.

Popes Creek \ˈpōps-\. Small stream in Westmoreland co., Virginia, flowing into the Potomac; Wakefield, George Washington's birthplace, is on its left bank.

Pop·lar Bluff \ˌpäp-lər-\. City, ⊗ of Butler co., SE Missouri, 63 m. WSW of Cape Girardeau; pop. (1970c) 16,653; market town; flour, shoes, wood products; ships cotton and livestock; Three Rivers Junior Coll. (1966); founded 1849.

Pop·lar·ville \ˈpäp-lər-ˌvil\. Town, ⊗ of Pearl River co., S Mississippi, 37 m. SSW of Hattiesburg; pop. (1970c) 2312; turpentine, lumber; Pearl River Junior Coll. (1909).

Popo, Grand. See GRAND POPO.

Po·po Agie \pə-ˈpō-zē-ə\. River, W cen. Wyoming; rises in Wind River Range, SW Fremont co., flows NE and unites with Wind river to form Big Horn river.

Po·po·ca·té·petl \ˌpō-pə-ˈkat-ə-ˌpet-ᵊl, -ˌkat-ə-ˈ; -kə-ˈtā-ˌpet-\. Volcano, Puebla state, SE cen. Mexico, 30 m. W of Puebla; 17,887 ft.; contains crater over ½ m. in circumference and 250 ft. deep.

Po·po·ma·na·siu, Mount \-ˌpō-pə-mə-ˈnäs-ē-ˌü\. Highest peak in Kavo Mts. near S coast, Guadalcanal I., SE Solomon Is., W Pacific Ocean; 7648 ft.

Pop·pi \'päp-ē\. Commune, Arezzo prov., E Tuscany, cen. Italy, on Arno river; pop. (1968e) 6148; birthplace of the sculptor Mino da Fiesole; castle.

Pop·u·lo·ni·um \ˌpäp-yə-'lō-nē-əm\. Ancient town of Etruria, Italy, on coast of Ligurian Sea N of Piombino; had metal manufactures (iron from Elba, tin, and copper); large part of walls remain, also tombs and a water reservoir; site of a medieval castle; besieged by Sulla 82 B.C.

Po·quis \'pō-kēs\., Peak, E Antofagasta prov., N Chile, near Argentina boundary; 18,832 ft.

Po·quos·on \pə-'kwō-sən\. Town, York co., SE Virginia, 9 m. N of Newport News; pop. (1970c) 5441.

Po·ra·li \pō-'rä-lē\ *or* **Pu·ra·li** \pü-'rä-lē\. River, SE Baluchistan, Pakistan; flows S into Sonmiani Bay.

Por·ban·dar \pōr-'bən-dər\. 1 Former Indian state, now part of Gujarat state, W India, on Arabian Sea; 642 sq. m.
2 Town, its ✱, on Arabian Sea 275 m. NW of Bombay; pop. (1961c) 75,081; port with extensive coastal trade. Birthplace of Mahatma Gandhi.

Por·cher Island \'pōr-chər-\. Island off W British Columbia, Canada, N of Pitt I. and near mouth of Skeena river; 205 sq. m.

Por·cu·na \pōr-'kü-nə\. Commune, Jaén prov., S Spain, 25 m. WNW of Jaén; pop. (1970p) 8599.

Por·cu·pine \'pōr-kyə-ˌpīn\. River, N Yukon Territory, Canada, and NE Alaska; 448 m. long; flows N then W to Yukon river at Fort Yukon, Alaska.

Porcupine Mountains *or* **Porcupine Range.** Range in Gogebic and Ontonagon cos., NW extremity of upper Michigan penin.; highest point **Porcupine Mountain** 1958 ft., in Ontonagon co.

Por·de·no·ne \ˌpōrd-^{ə}n-'ō-nē\ *or Ger.* **Por·te·nau** \'pōrt-^{ə}n-ˌaù\. 1 Province of Friuli-Venezia Giulia, Italy. See table at ITALY.
2 Commune, ✱ of Pordenone prov., Friuli-Venezia Giulia, NE Italy, 37 m. SW of Udine; pop. (1968e) 44,003; textiles, wood products, ceramics; 13th cent. campanile. Destroyed in local war 1233; passed to Venice 1508; became part of Italy 1866.

Po·reč \'pō-ˌrech\ *or Ital.* **Pa·ren·zo** \pä-'ren(t)-(ˌ)sō, -'ren-zō\. Commune in NW Yugoslavia, on coast of Istria Penin. 30 m. NNW of Pula; 6th cent. basilica; before 1947 belonged to Italy.

Porfirio Díaz. See PIEDRAS NEGRAS 2.

Po·ri \'pōr-ē\ *or Swed.* **Björ·ne·borg** \'byər-nə-ˌbō(ə)r(-yə)\. Seaport, Turku ja Pori prov., SW Finland; pop. (1970e) 72,938; shipping center; manufactures machinery, textiles, paper, matches, cellulose; founded 1365. See TURKU.

Po·ri·rua \ˌpo-rə-'rü-ə\. City, North I., New Zealand; pop. (1970e) 28,500.

Pork·ka·la Peninsula \'pōr-kə-lə-, -ˌlä-\. Small tongue of land, S Finland, projecting into the Gulf of Finland ab. 19 m. W of Helsinki; ceded by Finland to U.S.S.R. in exchange for Hangö 1944; returned to Finland 1956.

Por·la·mar \ˌpōr-lə-'mär\. Port, Nueva Esparta state, Venezuela, chief town of Margarita I., in Caribbean Sea off N coast of Venezuela; pop. (1970e) 36,184.

Po·ro \'pōr-(ˌ)ō, 'pōr-\. Island, Cebu prov., Phil.; 39 sq. m.; pop. (1969e) 26,600; coextensive with municipalities of Poro and Tudela; cen. island of Camotes group.

Po·ron·gos, La·gu·na de \lə-ˌgü-nə-də-pə-'rōŋ-gəs\. Swamp region in NE Córdoba prov., N cen. Argentina, N of Mar Chiquita; no outlet. Includes **La·go de los Pa·tos** \'läg-(ˌ)ō-də-lō-'spät-əs\.

Por·que·rolles \ˌpōr-kə-'rōl\. One of the Hyères Is. (*q.v.*).

Por·ren·truy \ˌpō-rä^{n}-trə-'wē\. Commune, N Bern canton, Switzerland, ab. 27 m. SW of Basel; pop. (1970c) 7827; watch manufacturing; customs station.

Pors·ang·er Fjord \'pōrs-ˌsäŋ-ər-\. Inlet of Arctic Ocean on N coast of Norway; extends S inland 249 m.

Pors·grunn \'pōrs-ˌgrün\. Seaport, Telemark co., S Norway, near coast NW of Larvik; pop. (1970e) 31,521; noted for its manufacture of porcelain; lumber, wood products.

Por·suk \pōr-'sük\ *or* **Pur·sak** \pür-'säk\. River, W Turkey in Asia; ab. 200 m. long; rises near Murat Dağı and flows N and E into Sakarya river.

Port Ad·e·laide \-'ad-^{ə}l-ˌād\. City, SE South Australia, on Gulf of St. Vincent at mouth of Torrens river; pop. (1966c) 39,823; seaport of Adelaide.

Port·a·down \ˌpōrt-ə-'daùn, ˌpōrt-\. Municipal borough, co. Armagh, S Northern Ireland; pop. (1971p) 20,577; linen and cotton goods; agricultural center.

Portae Syriae. See BAILAN.

Por·tage \'pōrt-ij, 'pōrt-\. 1 Name of counties in two states of the U.S. See tables at OHIO and WISCONSIN.
2 Town, Porter co., NW Indiana, NW of Valparaiso; pop. (1970c) 19,127.
3 City, Kalamazoo co., SW Michigan, 8 m. S of Kalamazoo; pop. (1970c) 33,590; pharmaceuticals, paper products, mobile homes; celery.
4 Borough, Cambria co., SW cen. Pennsylvania, 15 m. ENE of Johnstown; pop. (1970c) 4151; coal mines; diversified agriculture.
5 City, ⊗ of Columbia co., S cen. Wisconsin, on Wisconsin river 34 m. N of Madison; pop. (1970c) 7821; plastics, shoes, boats; summer resort; diversified agriculture; settled 1835 on site of Fort Winnebago (1828); previously site of a 1½ m. portage between Fox and Wisconsin rivers, now connected by federally owned canal.

Portage Falls. Waterfall in the Genesee river, W New York, 45 m. SSW of Rochester; 110 ft. high.

Portage Lake. 1 Lake, N cen. Aroostook co., N Maine; drains S into Aroostook river.
2 Lake, Houghton co., NW Michigan penin., an inlet of Keweenaw Bay; Keweenaw Waterway (see KEWEENAW PENINSULA) passes through it.

Portage la Prai·rie \-lə-'pre(ə)r-ē\. City, S Manitoba, Canada, on Assiniboine river 54 m. W of Winnipeg; pop. (1971p) 12,722; railroad center; dairy products, bricks; ships grain and livestock; founded 1853 on the site of Fort La Reine (erected in 1738).

Por·tage·ville \'pōrt-ij-ˌvil, 'pōrt-\. City, New Madrid co., SE Missouri, 18 m. N of Caruthersville; pop. (1970c) 3117.

Port Al·ber·ni \-al-'bər-nē\. Resort city, E cen. Vancouver I., British Columbia, Canada, at head of Alberni Canal 75 m. W of Vancouver; pop. (1971p) 19,749; fisheries, pulp mills; diversified agriculture.

Por·ta·le·gre \ˌpōrt-^{ə}l-'eg-rē\. 1 District of E cen. Portugal. See table at PORTUGAL.
2 Fortified commune, its ✱, near Spanish frontier 100 m. ENE of Lisbon; pop. (1970p) 25,677; woolens, cork; 16th cent. cathedral.

Por·tal·es \pōr-'tal-əs\. City, ⊗ of Roosevelt co., E New Mexico, 18 m. SW of Clovis; pop. (1970c) 10,554; canneries; fruit and truck farms; Eastern New Mexico Univ. (1934).

Port Al·fred \-'al-frəd, -fərd\. 1 Town, Chicoutimi co., S Quebec, Canada, on S bank of Saguenay river 9 m. ESE of Chicoutimi; pop. (1971p) 9191.
2 Resort town, SE Cape Province, S Rep. of South Africa, at mouth of Kowie river 80 m. ENE of Port Elizabeth; pop. (1967e) 6600; founded 1825.

Port Al·le·ga·ny \-ˌal-ə-'gā-nē\. Borough, McKean co., N Pennsylvania, on Allegheny river 22 m. ESE of Bradford; pop. (1970c) 2703; glass; poultry farms.

Port Al·len \-'al-ən\. City, ⊗ of West Baton Rouge parish, SE cen. Louisiana, on Mississippi river opp. Baton Rouge; pop. (1970c) 5728; sugarcane, rice, cotton.

Port Amelia. See PORTO AMÉLIA.

Port An·ge·les \-'an-jə-ləs\. City and port of entry, ⊗ of Clallam co., NW Washington, on Juan de Fuca Strait opp. Victoria, Canada, and 65 m. WNW of Seattle; pop. (1970c) 16,637; resort; wood and paper products; commercial fisheries; dairy farms; Peninsula Coll. (1961).

Port An·to·nio \-an-ˈtō-nē-ˌō\. Seaport, NE Jamaica, West Indies, 26 m. NE of Kingston (75 m. by coastal railroad) on a bay divided in two parts by a promontory; pop. (1960c) 7830; ships bananas.

Port Apra. See APRA HARBOR.

Port Aransas. See ARANSAS PASS 2.

Port Ar·thur \-ˈär-thər\. **1** City and port of entry, Jefferson co., SE Texas, on Sabine Lake 18 m. S of Beaumont; pop. (1970c) 57,371; oil refineries and petrochemical plants, brass and iron foundries, synthetic rubber plant; deepwater channels connect it with Gulf of Mexico and make it a major petroleum-shipping port. Founded in 1890's as S terminus of Kansas Southern R.R.

2 Settlement, Tasmania, Australia. See TASMAN PENINSULA.

3 City, Ontario, Canada. See THUNDER BAY 5.

4 *or Jap.* **Ryo·jun** \rē-ˈō-jün\ *or Chin.* **Lü–shun** \ˈlü-ˈshün\. Seaport town at S end of Liaotung Penin., Liaoning prov., China, SW of Dairen (*q.v.*), on Strait of Pohai opp. N coast of Shantung; surrounded by hills on three sides, its harbor divided into two ports connected by a narrow channel; naval base.

History: Harbor used in T'ang dynasty (618–907); made a naval station by Emperor K'ang-hsi. First visited by British 1860; made chief naval base by Chinese; taken by Japanese in 1894 but returned to China; included in lease to Russia 1898, who built strong defenses around it; scene of naval engagements and protracted land siege from June 1904; captured by Japanese Jan. 2, 1905; included in Kwantung Leased Territory 1905, 1915; after 1945 by treaty made a Sino-Soviet naval base; Soviet forces withdrawn 1955.

Port Au·gus·ta \-ȯ-ˈgəs-tə, -ə-ˈgəs-\. Seaport, S South Australia, at head of Spencer Gulf 175 m. NNW of Adelaide; pop. (1968e) 10,650; trading center and shipping point for wheat-growing region and cattle and sheep raising.

Port–au–Prince \ˌpōrt-ō-ˈprin(t)s, ˌpȯrt-, -ˈpran(t)s\. Seaport, ✱ of Haiti, Hispaniola I., West Indies, on SE shore of the Gulf of Gonave; pop. (1971e) 386,250, met. area pop. 525,380; principal port and commercial center of the republic; produces sugar, flour, cottonseed oil, and textiles; Univ. of Haiti (1944), technical institute (1962). Founded by French 1749; destroyed by earthquakes 1751 and 1770 and has suffered from destructive fires on several occasions.

Port·bail \pȯr-ˈbā(ʸ)\. Town, Manche dept., NW France, near W coast of Cotentin Penin., Normandy, ab. 20 m. W of Carentan; pop. (1962c) 1490; its capture by Allies June 18, 1944 opened up corridor across the peninsula.

Port Baltic. See PALDISKI.

Port Blair \-ˈbla(ə)r, -ˈble(ə)r\. Seaport town on SE coast of South Andaman I.; ✱ of Andaman and Nicobar Is. terr., India, on one of the best harbors of S Asia, 11°39′N, 92°45′E; pop. (1961c) 14,075. First occupied by British 1789; abandoned 1796–1856; made a penal colony 1858; occupied by Japanese 1942–45; penal colony abolished 1945.

Port Bou \pōrt-ˈbō-ü, pȯrt-\. Town, Gerona prov., NE Spain, on coast and on French border; pop. (1970p) 2360; customs station.

Port–Bouët \pȯr-ˈbwā\. Seaport, Ivory Coast, W Africa, port of Abidjan on S side of lagoon opp. the capital.

Port Bur·well \-ˈbər-ˌwel, -wəl\. Harbor on SW coast of Killinek I., NE Quebec, Canada, just off N tip of Labrador.

Port Car·bon \-ˈkär-bən\. Borough, Schuylkill co., E cen. Pennsylvania, 3 m. ENE of Pottsville; pop. (1970c) 2717.

Port Car·tier \-kär-ˈtyā, -ˌkärt-ē-ˈā\. Town, Quebec, Canada; pop. (1971p) 3738.

Port Castries. See CASTRIES.

Port Chal·mers \-ˈchal-mərz, -ˈchäm-ərz\. Borough, SE South I., New Zealand, on Otago Harbor 10 m. NE of Dunedin; pop. (1970e) 2990.

Port Ches·ter \ˈpōrt-ˌches-tər, ˈpȯrt-\. Village, Westchester co., in Rye township (*q.v.*), SE New York, on Long Island Sound 25 m. NE of New York, near Connecticut boundary; pop. (1970c) 25,803; residential suburb of New York.

Port Clar·ence \-ˈklar-ən(t)s\. Inlet at W end of Seward Penin., NW of Nome, W Alaska.

Port Clin·ton \-ˈklint-ᵊn\. City, ⊗ of Ottawa co., N Ohio, on Lake Erie 30 m. ESE of Toledo; pop. (1970c) 7202; canned goods, boats; gypsum mines; fruit, truck farms.

Port Col·borne \-ˈkōl-bərn\. City, Welland co., SE Ontario, Canada, on NE shore of Lake Erie at S end of Welland Ship Canal; pop. (1971p) 21,388; shoes, flour, chemicals; steel mill, nickel refinery; dairy and poultry farms.

Port Con·way \-ˈkän-wā\. Hamlet, S King George co., NE Virginia, on the Rappahannock; birthplace of James Madison, 4th president of the U.S.

Port Cooper. See LYTTELTON.

Port Co·quit·lam \-kō-ˈkwit-ləm\. City, SW British Columbia, Canada, just N of the Fraser river 15 m. E of Vancouver; pop. (1971p) 19,570; railroad shops, stone quarries; diversified agriculture.

Port Cred·it \-ˈkred-ət\. Town, Peel co., SE Ontario, Canada, on Lake Ontario 13 m. WSW of Toronto; pop. (1971p) 9443; cans fruit.

Port Cros \pȯr-ˈkrō\. One of the Hyères Is. (*q.v.*).

Port–Cros National Park \ˌpȯr-ˌkrō-\. National park, S France; 58 sq. m.; established 1963.

Port Cyg·net \-ˈsig-nət\. Town, S Tasmania, Australia, on coast near mouth of Huon river 25 m. S of Hobart; pop. (1970e) 2390; good harbor; fruit orchards.

Port Dal·rym·ple \-ˈdal-ˌrim-pəl\. Port at mouth of Tamar river, N Tasmania, Australia; one of the earliest settlements (Oct. 1804) on the island; military post until 1846.

Port Darwin. See DARWIN.

Port–de–Paix \ˌpȯrd-ə-ˈpā\. Seaport, NW Haiti, 35 m. N of Gonaïves and opp. Tortuga I.; pop. (1961e) 9162.

Port De·pos·it \-di-ˈpäz-ət\. Town, Cecil co., NE corner of Maryland; pop. (1970c) 906; on the Susquehanna at a place where the riverbanks are 200-ft. cliffs; site of Jacob Tome Institute, founded by Jacob Tome (1810–98) businessman and philanthropist; granite quarries.

Port–des–Galets. See LE PORT.

Port Dick·son \-ˈdik-sən\. Seaport, SW coast of Negri Sembilan state, Malaysia; terminus of railroad branch line from Seremban; only good shipping point in the state; health resort.

Port Do·ver \-ˈdō-vər\. Town, Norfolk co., SE Ontario, Canada, on Long Point Bay, inlet of Lake Erie, 25 m. S of Brantford; pop. (1971p) 3403.

Port Durnford. See BUR GAVO.

Port Eads \-ˈēdz\. Station, Plaquemines parish, SE Louisiana, at mouth of middle course of Mississippi river in the delta; lighthouse, pilot's station, government engineers' quarters.

Port Eliz·a·beth \-ᵊl-ˈiz-ə-bəth, -i-ˈliz-\. Town, SE Cape Province, S Rep. of South Africa, on W side of Algoa Bay ab. 410 m. E of Cape Town; pop. (1968e) 381,227; one of the republic's major seaports, shipping citrus fruit, mineral ores, and industrial products; center of automobile industry; notable seaside resort; well-known Snake Park with ab. 2000 reptiles; Univ. of Port Elizabeth (1964). Settled 1799; developed after completion of Kimberley R.R. 1873.

Port El·len \-ˈel-ən\. Seaport village, S coast of Islay I., Inner Hebrides, Argyll co., W Scotland; pop. (1961c) 750.

Portenau. See PORDENONE.

Port–en–Bes·sin \ˌpȯr-äⁿ-be-ˈsaⁿ\. Fishing village, Calvados dept., Normandy, NW France, ab. 5 m. N of Bayeux on shore of Bay of the Seine; pop. (1962c) 1737; marked the division point bet. British and U.S. landing beaches during invasion June 1944.

Por·ter \'pōrt-ər, 'pȯrt-\. County in Indiana. See table at INDIANA.

Porter Mountain. Peak in the Adirondack Mts., Essex co., NE New York; 4070 ft.

Por·ter·ville \'pōrt-ər-ˌvil, 'pȯrt-\. City, Tulare co., S cen. California, 45 m. N of Bakersfield; pop. (1970c) 12,602; olive oil, foundry products; packs and ships citrus fruit; Porterville Coll. (1927).

Port Es·sing·ton \-'es-iŋ-tən\. Inlet of Arafura Sea, N coast of Coburg Penin., Northern Territory, Australia.

Port–Étienne. See NOUADHIBOU.

Port Florence. See KISUMU.

Port Fos·ter \-'fȯs-tər, -'fäs-\. See SOUTH SHETLAND ISLANDS.

Port Franc·qui \-fräⁿ-'kē\ *or* **Ile·bo** \i-'lā-(ˌ)bō\. Town, Kasai Occidental prov., S cen. Zaire, cen. Africa, bet. the Kasai and the Sankuru rivers at their junction.

Port Fu·ad \-fü-'äd\ *or Arab.* **Būr Fu'ād** \ˌbu̇(ə)r-fü-'äd\. Seaport, NE Egypt, at N end of Suez Canal opp. Port Said.

Port–Gen·til \ˌpȯr-zhäⁿ-'tē\. Seaport, W Gabon, W equatorial Africa, 100 m. SW of Libreville; pop. (1970e) 48,190.

Port Gib·son \-'gib-sən\. Town, ⊗ of Claiborne co., SW Mississippi, 28 m. S of Vicksburg; pop. (1970c) 2589; textiles, veneer; scene of battle Apr. 30–May 1, 1863 in Grant's Vicksburg campaign.

Port Glas·gow \-'glas-(ˌ)kō, -'glas-(ˌ)gō, -'glaz-(ˌ)gō\. Burgh, Renfrew co., SW Scotland, on the Clyde; pop. (1971p) 22,399; a seaport, with shipbuilding yards, iron and brass foundries, sawmills; adjoins Greenock.

Port Hack·ing \-'hak-iŋ\. Inlet of South Pacific Ocean, New South Wales, SE Australia, just S of Botany Bay.

Port Hamilton. See KŌMUN-DO.

Port Har·court \-'här-kərt\. Seaport, ✱ of Rivers State, S Nigeria, on the Bonny River ab. 40 m. from the sea; pop. (1969e) 208,237; railroad terminus; ships palm products, coal, tin, and peanuts; produces cement and cigarettes; first laid out 1912 and connected by rail 1916 to Enugu coalfields.

Port Hawkes·bury \-'hȯks-ˌber-ē, -b(ə-)rē\. Town, N Nova Scotia, Canada, ab. 70 m. SW of Sydney; pop. (1971p) 3427.

Porth·cawl \pōrth-'kȯl, pȯrth-\. Urban district, Glamorganshire, S Wales; pop. (1971p) 14,065; seaside resort.

Port Hed·land \-'hed-lənd\. Port, Western Australia, ab. 820 m. NNE of Perth; pop. (1966c) 1785; mineral port, exporting esp. iron ore to Japan.

Port Hood \-'hu̇d\. Town, ⊗ of Inverness co., NE Nova Scotia, Canada, port on W coast of Cape Breton I.; pop. (1966c) 472.

Port Hope \-'hōp\. Town, Durham co., SE Ontario, Canada, port on Lake Ontario 62 m. ENE of Toronto; pop. (1971p) 8747; summer resort; produces radium, chemicals, feed, dairy products; diversified agriculture.

Port Hud·son \-'həd-sən\. Village, East Baton Rouge parish, Louisiana, on Mississippi river; besieged by Union forces under Nathaniel P. Banks for six weeks 1863, surrendered July 9, after fall of Vicksburg.

Port Hue·ne·me \wī-'nē-mē\ *or* **Hueneme.** City, Ventura co., S California, on Santa Barbara Channel ab. 40 m. W of Los Angeles, near **Point Hueneme;** pop. (1970c) 14,295; in World War II a naval training base.

Port Hu·ron \-'hyu̇r-ən\. City, ⊗ of St. Clair co., SE Michigan, at Lake Huron end of St. Clair river; pop. (1970c) 35,794; paper, boats and marine hardware, copper wire, automobile parts, salt, fishing equipment; railroad shops, foundries; summer resort; Saint Clair Co. Community Coll. (1923). French fort built on site 1686; U.S. fort built 1814; town incorporated as Fort Gratiot 1840 and city, under present name, in 1857; early home of Thomas A. Edison.

Por·ti·ci \'pōrt-ə-(ˌ)chē\. Commune, Napoli prov., Campania, S Italy, on Bay of Naples 4 m. ESE of Naples; pop. (1968e) 67,888; residential and resort suburb of Naples.

Porţile de Fier. See IRON GATE.

Portillo de los Patos. See LOS PATOS.

Por·ti·mão \ˌpōr-ti-'mau̇ⁿ\ *or* **Vi·la No·va de Portimão** \ˌvē-lə-'nō-və-də-\. Commune, Faro dist., S Portugal, near Atlantic Ocean 24 m. WNW of Faro; fisheries; fish canneries, esp. for tuna, sardines.

Port Is·a·bel \-'iz-ə-ˌbel\. City and fishing resort, Cameron co., S Texas, on Gulf of Mexico 20 m. ENE of Brownsville; pop. (1970c) 3067.

Port Jack·son \-'jak-sən\. Inlet of South Pacific Ocean, New South Wales, SE Australia, forming an exceptionally good natural harbor; city of Sydney is on its S shore and N suburbs of Sydney on its N shore; has width of about 1½ m. at its mouth; ab. 8 m. long to the point where it merges with the mouth of the Parramatta river. Its shores are irregular, broken by steep points that enclose bays that form smaller harbors. Great bridge across the harbor opened Mar. 19, 1932.

Port Jef·fer·son \-'jef-ər-sən\. Village, Suffolk co., SE New York, on Long I., on Long Island Sound ab. 13 m. N of Patchogue; pop. (1970c) 5515; summer resort, yachting and boatbuilding center.

Port Jer·vis \-'jər-vəs\. City and summer resort, Orange co., SE New York, on Delaware river 38 m. W of Newburgh; pop. (1970c) 8852; silk, rayon, glass, cosmetics, knitwear; settled c. 1698, incorporated 1907.

Port Kem·bla \-'kem-blə\. Seaport town, New South Wales, Australia, ab. 55 m. S of Sydney; pop. (1961c) 7830; has steel mill (opened 1926) and copper smelting, chemical, fertilizer, and tin plate industries; artificial harbor built 1883 and expanded in 1960's.

Port Ken·ne·dy \-'ken-əd-ē\. See THURSDAY ISLAND.

Port·land \'pōrt-lənd, 'pȯrt-\. **1** Agricultural town, N Middlesex co., S Connecticut, on Connecticut river NE of Middletown; pop. (1970c) 8812; settled 1690.

2 City, ⊗ of Jay co., E Indiana, 26 m. NE of Muncie; pop. (1970c) 7115; clothing, brushes; gas and oil wells; birthplace of Elwood Haynes (1857–1925), inventor.

3 Seaport city, ⊗ of Cumberland co., SW Maine, on Casco Bay; pop. (1970c) 65,116; commercial center of SW Maine; good harbor and major oil port; produces pulp and paper, canned goods, textiles, lumber, chemicals, machinery; fishing, shipbuilding, printing; Westbrook Junior Coll. (1831), Mercy Institute (1956); founded 1632; destroyed by Indians 1676 and 1690; incorporated as town 1786; state capital 1820–1832; incorporated as city 1832; destructive fire 1866. Birthplace of Henry Wadsworth Longfellow.

4 Village, Ionia co., S cen. Michigan, 21 m. NW of Lansing; pop. (1970c) 3817; automobile parts; dairy, fruit farms.

5 Industrial city and port, ⊗ of Multnomah co., NW Oregon, on Willamette river 10 m. SE of its confluence with Columbia river; pop. (1970c) 380,620; largest city and principal port in the state; exports lumber, paper, wood pulp, fruits and vegetables; major wool market; produces canned goods, chemicals, electronic components, dairy products, paint, flour; shipyards, railroad shops, meatpacking plants. Lewis and Clark Coll. (1867), Univ. of Portland (1901), Reed Coll. (1904), Concordia Coll. (1905), Multnomah School of the Bible (1936), Warner Pacific Coll. (1937), Portland State Coll. (1946), Judson Baptist Coll. (1956), Columbia Christian Coll. (1956), Portland Community Coll. (1961). Founded 1845; incorporated 1851; developed as lumber and grain exporting port and supply center for NW gold rushes in 1860's and 1870's.

6 Town, Sumner co., N Tennessee, 33 m. NE of Nashville; pop. (1970c) 2872; lumbering; diversified agriculture.

7 City, Nueces and San Patricio cos., S Texas, on Corpus Christi Bay 12 m. NE of Corpus Christi; pop. (1970c) 7302.

8 Town, SW Victoria, SE Australia, on **Portland Bay** 185 m. WSW of Melbourne; pop. (1966c) 6690; port of call for coastal and transoceanic vessels; Portland College.
9 Urban district, Dorsetshire, S England, 4 m. S of Weymouth; pop. (1971p) 12,306; limestone quarries; 16th cent. castle; naval anchorage; on the **Isle of Portland,** a limestone peninsula, its connection with the mainland being a stretch of shingle 200 yds. wide; its tip is the **Portland Bill;** lighthouse; in nearby waters Dutch were defeated by Admiral Blake Feb. 18, 1653.

Portland, Cape. Cape on NE coast of Tasmania, Australia, on Banks Strait, 40°45′S, 147°57′E.

Portland Bay. See PORTLAND 8.

Portland Bight *or formerly* **Old Harbour Bay.** Gulf, SE coast of Jamaica, West Indies; several areas around the bight leased Sept. 2, 1940 by Great Britain to the United States as naval and air bases.

Portland Bill. See PORTLAND 9.

Portland Canal. Narrow inlet bet. SE Alaska and W British Columbia, Canada, 55°N, 130°W; ab. 80 m. long; inlet is very deep with steep sides and in some places mountains 5000 to 6000 ft. on both sides.

Portland Point. Cape projecting into the Caribbean Sea from S coast of Jamaica, on SW side of Portland Bight.

Port Laoighise. See MARYBOROUGH 2.

Port La·vaca \-lə-ˈvak-ə\. City, ⊗ of Calhoun co., S Texas, 25 m. SE of Victoria; pop. (1970c) 10,491; aluminum products; shrimp, oyster fisheries, oil and gas wells.

Port Li·món. See PUERTO LIMÓN.

Port Lin·coln \-ˈliŋ-kən\. Town, S South Australia, near mouth of Spencer Gulf on W side, 175 m. W of Adelaide; pop. (1966c) 8888; harbor.

Port Lloyd \-ˈlȯid\. Anchorage at Chichi-shima in the Bonin Is., Japan; coaling station proposed here in 1853 by Commodore Perry.

Port Lo·ko \-ˈlō-(ˌ)kō\. Town, NW Sierra Leone, W Africa, 35 m. NE of Freetown.

Port Lou·is \-ˈlü-əs, -ˈlü-ē, -lu̇-ˈē\. **1** Seaport city, ✱ of Mauritius, in Indian Ocean E of Malagasy Republic; pop. (1969e) 138,150; principal commercial center of the island, exporting sugar; has tobacco warehouse, cigarette factory, and railroad workshops; Univ. of Mauritius (1965); founded c. 1736.
2 *or* **Port–Louis** *Fr.* pȯr-lwē\. Seaport town, NW Grande Terre I., E part of island of Guadeloupe, West Indies.

Port Lyautey. See KÉNITRA.

Port Lyt·tel·ton \-ˈlit-ᵊl-tən\. Inlet of South Pacific, E coast of South I., New Zealand; ab. 9 m. long; forms harbor of Lyttelton, the shipping port of Christchurch to the N.

Port Mac·quar·ie \-mə-ˈkwär-ē\. Town, E New South Wales, SE Australia, on Pacific Ocean at mouth of Hastings river 200 m. NNW of Sydney; pop. (1966c) 6740; has active dock and is shipping port for dairying and agricultural region.

Port·mad·oc \pōrt-ˈmad-ək, pȯrt-\. Town, S Caernarvonshire, NW Wales, on NE coast of Cardigan Bay; pop. (1971p) 3665; ships slate.

Port Madryn. See PUERTO MADRYN.

Port Mahon. See MAHÓN.

Port Ma·ria \-mə-ˈrē-ə\. Seaport, N Jamaica, West Indies, 28 m. NNW of Kingston; pop. (1960c) 3998.

Port Mel·bourne \-ˈmel-bərn\. Town, S Victoria, SE Australia, SW suburb of Melbourne on Port Phillip Bay; pop. (1966c) 12,591; port for Melbourne.

Port Mol·ler \-ˈmäl-ər\. Inlet and harbor, N coast of Alaska Penin., SW Alaska; an inlet of Bering Sea.

Port Moo·dy \-ˈmü-dē\. City, SW British Columbia, Canada, at head of Burrard Inlet 12 m. E of Vancouver; pop. (1971p) 10,780; resort; sawmills, oil refineries.

Port Mores·by \-ˈmō(ə)rz-bē, -ˈmȯ(ə)rz-\. Seaport, ✱ of Papua New Guinea, on SE coast of the Gulf of Papua; pop. (1970e) 56,206; large sheltered harbor; commercial center; univ. (1965). Discovered 1873 by Capt. John Moresby; occupied by British 1883; chief settlement of the territory 1888 ff.; in World War II an Allied base and objective of Japanese advance over Owen Stanley Mountains Dec. 1942–Jan. 1943; several times bombed by Japanese aircraft.

Port Nech·es \-ˈnā-chəz\. City, Jefferson co., SE Texas, near mouth of Neches river 13 m. ESE of Beaumont; pop. (1970c) 10,894; synthetic rubber; oil refining.

Port Nel·son \-ˈnel-sən\. Trading post on N bank of **Port Nelson** (the mouth of Nelson river), NE Manitoba, Canada; first post in Manitoba, established 1670 by Hudson's Bay Company.

Port·neuf \pȯr-ˈnə(r)f\. County, Quebec, Canada. See table at QUEBEC.

Port Nich·ol·son \-ˈnik-əl-sən\ *also* **Wel·ling·ton Harbour** \ˌwel-iŋ-tən-\. Harbor, SW extremity of North I., New Zealand, an inlet of Cook Strait; the city of Wellington is located on this harbor.

Port Nol·loth \-ˈnäl-əth\. Seaport town, NW Cape Province, S Rep. of South Africa, on Atlantic Ocean 50 m. SSE of mouth of Orange river; in barren country; diamonds found in vicinity.

Pôrto \ˈpōr-(ˌ)tü\. **1** District of NW Portugal. See table at PORTUGAL.
2 City, its ✱. See OPORTO.

Pôrto Ale·gre \ˌpōrt-(ˌ)ü-ə-ˈleg-rə, ˌpȯrt-, -ˈlāg-\. Seaport city, ✱ of Rio Grande do Sul state, S Brazil, on inlet at N end of Lagoa dos Patos; munic. pop. (1968e) 932,801; most important Brazilian commercial center S of São Paulo; exports rice, tobacco, grapes, meat, and hides; produces leather and leather goods, lard, textiles and clothing, candles, flour, wine, metal goods; shipyards, meat-packing plants; Federal Univ. (1934), Catholic Univ. (1948). Founded 1742 by immigrants from the Azores; became capital of state 1807; in 19th cent. received considerable German and Italian immigrant populations.

Por·to Amé·lia \pōr-tü-ə-ˈmēl-yə\ *or* **Port Ame·lia** \-ə-ˈmēl-yə\. Seaport town on Pemba Bay, Niassa prov., NE Mozambique.

Porto Bardia. See BARDĪYAH.

Por·to·be·lo *also* **Por·to Be·llo** \ˌpōrt-ə-ˈbel-(ˌ)ō, ˌpȯrt-\ *or* **Puer·to Bello** \ˌpwert-ə-\. Seaport village on the Caribbean coast of Panama, 20 m. NE of Colón; pop. (1970p) 1779; in banana-growing area. Just W of Columbus's earlier colony of Nombre de Dios; founded 1597; became one of the two American ports yearly receiving and sending out the royal Spanish fleets; the great emporium of South American trade in 17th and 18th cents.; terminus at N end of Spanish causeway across isthmus. Sir Francis Drake died aboard ship off the town and was buried at sea (1596).

Porto d'Anzio. See ANZIO.

Porto Edda. See SARANDË 2.

Porto Em·pe·do·cle \ˌpȯrt-(ˌ)ō-em-ˈped-ə-ˌklā, ˌpȯrt-\. Seaport commune, Agrigento prov., SW Sicily, Italy, on Mediterranean 4 m. SW of Agrigento; pop. (1968e) 17,294; a point of attack in Allied invasion of Sicily July 1943.

Porto Farina. See GHĀR AL MILḤ.

Por·to·fer·ra·io \ˈpōr-tō-fe-ˈrä-yō\. Seaport commune, Livorno prov., Tuscany, Italy, on N coast of Elba I. 48 m. S of Leghorn; pop. (1968e) 10,686; chief port of Elba I. Napoleon lived here in exile 1814–15.

Por·to·fi·no \ˌpōr-tə-ˈfē-nō\. Commune, Genova prov., Liguria, NW Italy, on coast SSW of Rapallo; pop. (1968e) 954; tourist resort.

Port of Spain *or* **Port–of–Spain.** Seaport, ✱ of Trinidad and Tobago, in NW part of island of Trinidad on Gulf of Paria; pop. (1970p) 67,867; commercial center and a principal port and air transport center for the Caribbean; produces rum, beer, plastics, lumber, textiles; exports oil, sugar, citrus fruit, asphalt, and coffee; college (1960).

Porto Gran·de \'pōr-tü-'gra(ⁿ)n-də\ *or* **Min·de·llo** \mē(ⁿ)n-'dā-(,)lü\. Seaport town, NW São Vicente I., Cape Verde Is.; excellent harbor; coaling station.

Por·to·gru·a·ro \,pōrt-ō-grü-'är-(,)ō, ,pȯrt-\. Commune, Venezia prov., Veneto, NE Italy, 34 m. NE of Venice; pop. (1968e) 22,100; 14th cent. Gothic palace.

Por·to·la Valley \pȯr-'tō-lə-\. City, San Mateo co., W California, 19 m. WNW of San Jose; pop. (1970c) 4943; lumbering, dairy farming.

Por·to·mag·gio·re \,pōrt-ō-mä-'jōr-ē, -'jȯr-, ,pȯrt-\. Commune, Ferrara prov., Emilia-Romagna, N Italy, 14 m. SE of Ferrara; pop. (1968e) 13,970.

Porto–No·vo \,pōrt-ə-'nō-(,)vō\. 1 Seaport town, ✱ of Dahomey, W Africa, in SE part on coastal lagoon; pop. (1970e) 87,000; commercial center; probably founded 16th cent.; settled by Portuguese as center of slave trade; in 19th cent. seat of a native kingdom that became French protectorate 1863.

2 Seaport town, Tamil Nadu, SE India, 35 m. S of Pondicherry; pop. (1961c) 15,100. Site of Sir Eyre Coote's victory July 1781 over Haidar Ali, important to British in saving Madras presidency.

Port Orange \-'ȯr-inj, -'är-, -ənj\. City, Volusia co., E Florida, on Atlantic coast 5 m. SE of Daytona Beach; pop. (1970c) 3781.

Port Or·chard \-'ȯr-chərd\. Town, ⊗ of Kitsap co., W Washington, on Puget Sound 15 m. WSW of Seattle; pop. (1970c) 3904; resort; U.S. naval facility; fisheries; agriculture.

Porto Rico. See PUERTO RICO.

Porto San·to \,pōrt-ō-'san-(,)tō, ,pȯrt-\. One of the Madeira Is., 26 m. NE of the island of Madeira; 7 m. long; 17 sq. m.; pop. (1960c) 3554; first island of the group to be sighted by Zarco 1418; visited by Columbus c. 1479; airport.

Porto To·rres \,pōrt-ə-'tōr-əs\ *or anc.* **Tur·ris Lib·i·so·nis** \'tər-is-,lib-i-'sō-nis\. Seaport, Sassari prov., NW Sardinia, Italy; pop. (1968e) 11,103; basilica, ruins of a temple and of a Roman aqueduct.

Porto–Vec·chio \,pōrt-ō-'vek-ē-,ō, ,pȯrt-\. Seaport, SE Corsica, France, on a very shallow inlet of the Tyrrhenian Sea; pop. (1962c) 5601; cork-oak forests and salt deposits nearby.

Pôr·to Vel·ho \'pōr-tü-'vel-yü\ *also* **Velho.** Town, ✱ of Rondônia terr., W Brazil, on the Madeira river; munic. pop. (1968e) 83,178.

Por·to·vie·jo \,pōrt-ō-vē-'e-(,)hō, ,pȯrt-\ *also* **Puer·to·vie·jo** \,pwe(ə)r-(,)tō-vē-'e-(,)hō\. Town, ✱ of Manabí prov., W Ecuador, on E bank of **Portoviejo River** 90 m. NW of Guayaquil; pop. (1970e) 49,700; technical univ. (1952); founded 1534.

Port·pat·rick \pōrt-'pa-trik, pȯrt-\. Village, Wigtown co., SW Scotland; pop. (1961c) 875; nearest port of Great Britain to Ireland; summer resort.

Port Pat·te·son \-'pat-ə-sən\. See VANUA LAVA.

Port Per·ry \-'per-ē\. Village, Ontario co., SE Ontario, Canada, 34 m. NE of Toronto; pop. (1971p) 2977; diversified agriculture; flour mills; summer resort.

Port Phil·lip Bay \-'fil-əp-\ *also* **Port Phillip.** Harbor of Melbourne, S Victoria, SE Australia; 31 m. long by 20 m. wide; 800 sq. m. First entered and explored 1835.

Port Pir·ie \-'pi(ə)-rē\. Seaport, S South Australia, on E side of Spencer Gulf at its N end, 125 m. NNW of Adelaide; pop. (1968e) 13,900; ships lead, wheat; grain elevators, ore smelters; the principal outlet for the Broken Hill mines.

Port Ra·da·ma Bay \-,rad-ə-,mä-\. Inlet of Mozambique Channel, NW coast of Malagasy Republic.

Port Ra·di·um \-'rād-ē-əm\. Mining village on E shore of Great Bear Lake, Mackenzie dist., Northwest Territories, Canada, just S of Arctic Circle; site of formerly important pitchblende mine.

Port Re·pub·lic \-ri-'pəb-lik\. Village, Rockingham co., NW Virginia, in Shenandoah Valley; battle June 9, 1862 in which Stonewall Jackson defeated two brigades of Union troops.

Port Rex. See EAST LONDON.

Port Rich·mond \-'rich-mənd\. Community on N shore of Staten I. (Richmond borough), New York City; a business center for the island; residence of Aaron Burr when he died 1836.

Port Roy·al \-'rȯi(-ə)l\. 1 Town on **Port Royal Island,** one of the Sea Is., in Beaufort co., S South Carolina; pop. (1970c) 2865; tourist resort; fisheries; colony of French Huguenots founded here by Jean Ribaut 1562; in early 19th cent. a prosperous cotton-growing center; in Civil War occupied by Union forces Nov. 6–7, 1861.

2 Town, Canada. See ANNAPOLIS ROYAL.

3 Fortified town at entrance to Kingston harbor, SE Jamaica, West Indies; early capital of Jamaica; was haunt of buccaneers; destroyed by earthquakes 1692 and 1907; formerly a British naval station; use of dockyard leased to U.S. Sept. 2, 1940.

Port Royal National Historic Park. See CANADA, *National Historic Parks.*

Port Royal Sound. Inlet of Atlantic Ocean bet. islands of St. Helena and Hilton Head off SE coast of South Carolina at entrance to Broad river.

Port·rush \pōrt-'rəsh, 'pȯrt-\. Urban district, N coast of co. Antrim, NE Northern Ireland; pop. (1971p) 4746; seaside resort and seaport; nearby is Giant's Causeway (*q.v.*).

Port Said \-'sīd, -sä-'ēd\ *or Arab.* **Būr Sa'īd** \,bu̇(ə)r-sä-'ēd\. Seaport city, constituting the Port Said governorate, NE Egypt, on the Mediterranean Sea at N end of the Suez Canal, on a narrow sand strip between Mediterranean Sea and Lake Manzala; pop. (1970e) 313,000; exports rice, cotton, salt. Founded 1859 and formerly the most important coaling station in the world; landing point of French and British troops Nov. 1956 in intervention caused by Egyptian nationalization of Suez Canal; since 1967 has been shelled and bombed by Israeli forces on several occasions.

Port Saint Joe \-'jō\. City, Gulf co., NW Florida, 75 m. SW of Tallahassee on St. Joseph Bay; pop. (1970c) 4401; paper, chemicals.

Port Saint Johns \-'jänz\. Seaport town, NE Cape Province, S Rep. of South Africa, at mouth of Umzimvubu river 153 m. SW of Durban; in region producing cotton and sugar; exports marble.

Port Sand·wich \-'san-(,)(d)wich\. Port, New Hebrides. See MALEKULA.

Port·sea \'pōrt-sē, 'pȯrt-\. 1 Island off S coast of Hampshire, S England; 4 m. long and 2½–3 m. wide; site of the city of Portsmouth.

2 Ward of Portsmouth, Hampshire, S England; Portsmouth dockyards and naval station.

Port Shep·stone \-'shep-stən\. Town at mouth of Umzimkulu river, S Natal, E Rep. of South Africa, 72 m. SSW of Durban; pop. (1967e) 4200; center of a fertile farming district, but its harbor not developed.

Port Simp·son \-'sim(p)-sən\. Indian village, W British Columbia, Canada, on coast 25 m. N of Prince Rupert and on S side of entrance to Portland Canal; pop. (1966c) 102.

Ports·lade by Sea \'pōrt-,slād-, 'pȯrt-\. Urban district, East Sussex, S England, near Brighton; pop. (1971p) 18,150; manufacturing and shipping center; Roman and Anglo-Saxon remains nearby.

Ports·mouth \'pōrt-sməth, 'pȯrt-\. 1 Seaport city and port of entry, Rockingham co., SE New Hampshire, on Atlantic Ocean at mouth of Piscataqua river; pop. (1970c) 25,717; summer resort; plastics, buttons, gypsum products, machine tools; U.S. Navy Yard on Seavy's I. (part of Kittery, Maine) dates from 1790's and is principally noted for construction and repair of submarines; naval hospital and naval prison. Settled 1624; capital of provincial government until Revolution; incorporated as city 1849; site of the signing of the peace treaty ending the Russo-Japanese War 1905.

2 Industrial city, ⊗ of Scioto co., S Ohio, on Ohio river at mouth of Scioto river; pop. (1970c) 27,633; steel, chemicals, plastics, footwear, stoves; railroad shops; prehistoric Indian mounds and earthworks nearby; founded 1803.

3 Town, Newport co., SE Rhode Island, on N end of Rhode Island (island) and on the Sakonnet river 8 m. NNE of Newport; pop. (1970c) 12,521; summer resort; diversified agriculture; settled 1638; joined "Incorporation of Providence Plantations" (chartered 1644); scene of battle of Rhode Island 1778.

4 Commercial and industrial seaport city, SE Virginia, on Elizabeth river opp. Norfolk; 18 sq. m.; pop. (1970c) 110,963; politically independent; with Norfolk and Newport News comprises Port of Hampton Roads; transportation center; manufactures chemicals, fertilizer, plastics, machine tools, railroad equipment; shipyards, railroad shops, U.S. Navy Yard (estab. 1801, evacuated and burned by Union troops in Civil War 1861 but recaptured 1862); Frederick Coll. (1958). Settled 1752; suffered from yellow fever epidemic 1855; received city charter 1858.

5 Seaport and county borough, Hampshire, S England, on island of Portsea in English Channel 65 m. SW of London; pop. (1971p) 196,976; major naval base; shipyards, aircraft factories; is noted seaside resort. Founded and received first charter 1194; naval dockyard estab. 1494; became county borough 1888 and city 1928; suffered extensive damage from German bombing 1940. Birthplace of Charles Dickens and George Meredith.

6 Seaport on NW coast of Dominica I., Windward Is., West Indies.

Portsmouth Island. Island off cen. North Carolina coast, bet. S Pamlico Sound and Atlantic Ocean; 7 sq. m.

Port Stan·ley \-ˈstan-lē\. 1 Village, Elgin co., SE Ontario, Canada, on Lake Erie 8 m. S of St. Thomas; pop. (1971p) 1724; serves as port for St. Thomas and London (Ontario); summer resort.

2 Town, Falkland Is. See STANLEY 7.

3 Port, New Hebrides. See MALEKULA.

Port Ste·phens \-ˈstē-vənz\. Good harbor on E coast of New South Wales, SE Australia, ab. 90 m. NE of Sydney; lighthouse.

Port Sual. See SUAL.

Port Su·dan \-sü-ˈdan, -ˈdän\. City, E Kassala prov., NE Sudan, ab. 400 m. NE of Khartoum; pop. (1969e) 100,700; principal port of the Sudan, exporting peanuts, hides and skins, gum, cotton, and oilseeds; terminus of railroad from the Nile Valley; founded 1908 and expanded in 1950's and 1960's.

Port Sul·phur \-ˈsəl-fər\. Unincorporated settlement, Palquemines parish, SE Louisiana, on Mississippi river 20 m. SE of New Orleans; pop. (1970c) 3022; sulfur deposits.

Port Sun·light \-ˈsən-ˌlīt\. Model industrial town, Cheshire, England, on S bank of the Mersey near Liverpool; founded by Viscount Leverhulme, chairman of Lever Bros. Ltd., soap manufacturers.

Port Su·san \-ˈsüz-ᵊn\. Inlet in upper Puget Sound bet. Camano I. and Snohomish co., NW Washington.

Port Swet·ten·ham \-ˈswet-nəm, -ᵊn-əm\. Seaport town, W Selangor state, Malaysia, 27 m. SW of Kuala Lumpur; terminus of branch railroad line from Kuala Lumpur.

Port Tal·bot \-ˈtȯl-bət, -ˈtal-\. Municipal borough, W Glamorganshire, SE Wales; pop. (1971p) 50,658; port; ships coal and metal goods; large iron and steel works.

Port Tau·fiq \-tau̇-ˈfēk\ *or Arab.* **Būr Taw·fīq** \ˌbu̇(ə)r-tau̇-ˈfēk\. Town, port of Suez, Egypt, at S end of Suez Canal at head of Gulf of Suez; railroad terminus.

Port Town·send \-ˈtau̇n-zənd\. City and port of entry, ⊗ of Jefferson co., W Washington, on W side of entrance to Puget Sound 30 m. WNW of Everett; pop. (1970c) 5241; dairy and paper products; fisheries; poultry farms; settled 1851, chartered as city 1860; in late 19th cent. a major lumber port.

Por·tu·gal \ˈpōr-chi-gəl, ˈpȯr-\ *or anc.* **Lu·si·ta·nia** \ˌlü-sə-ˈtā-nē-ə, -nyə\. Republic, occupying W section of the Iberian Penin., bounded on N and E by Spain, and on S and W by the Atlantic Ocean; 35,383 sq. m.; pop. (1970e) 9,700,600; ✱ Lisbon; incl. the Azores and Madeira Is.

Physical features: Its 500-m. coastline affords good harbors only at the mouths of the principal rivers: the Tagus in cen. part, the Guadiana in S flowing into Gulf of Cádiz, the Douro and the Minho in the N; each of these rises in Spain, forms in part of its course a portion of the Portuguese-Spanish boundary, and flows through narrow gorges and restricted valleys; there are no inland lakes but there are lagoons at Aveiro and at Lisbon at the mouth of the Tagus. Mountains are parts of the E–W ranges of the Iberian Penin.: the highest, the Serra da Estrela 6532 ft., the W extension of the Sierra de Guadarrama; the mountains in the N, a SW extension of the Cantabrian Mts.; and those in the S, a SW extension of the Guadalupe Mts. *Chief products:* Wheat, corn, olives, wines; fishing; cork; iron ore, sulfur, tungsten; manufacturing: textiles, iron and steel, cement; food processing, shipbuilding; tourism. *Chief cities:* Lisbon, Oporto, Coimbra, Vila Nova de Gaia, Setúbal, Funchal, Braga. Divided into the following 22 districts (for pronunciation of their names, see their individual entries):

NAME	AREA (sq. m.)	POP. (1970e)	CAPITAL
Angra do Heroísmo[1]	274	105,800	Angra do Heroísmo
Aveiro	1,046	595,600	Aveiro
Beja	3,954	275,200	Beja
Braga	1,054	679,000	Braga
Bragança	2,527	249,600	Bragança
Castelo Branco	2,588	323,200	Castelo Branco
Coimbra	1,527	448,900	Coimbra
Évora	2,855	228,000	Évora
Faro	1,958	316,200	Faro
Funchal[2]	308	268,700	Funchal
Guarda	2,122	269,600	Guarda
Horta[3]	301	43,600	Horta
Leiria	1,357	433,500	Leiria
Lisboa	1,066	1,622,800	Lisbon
Ponta Delgada[4]	330	186,700	Ponta Delgada
Portalegre	2,274	184,000	Portalegre
Pôrto	881	1,403,200	Oporto
Santarém	2,583	485,900	Santarém
Setúbal	1,989	451,900	Setúbal
Viana do Castelo	814	289,200	Viana do Castelo
Vila Real	1,637	347,000	Vila Real
Viseu	1,938	493,000	Viseu

[1]In Azores; consists of Terceira, São Jorge, and Graciosa Is.
[2]Coextensive with Madeira Is.
[3]In Azores; consists of Pico, Faial, Flores, and Corvo Is.
[4]In Azores; consists of São Miguel and Santa Maria Is.

History: Inhabited in ancient times by Lusitanians who were subjugated by Rome from 2d cent. B.C.; conquered by Visigoths in 5th cent. A.D. and, later, by Moors; territory bet. Minho and Douro rivers reconquered in 11th cent. by ruler of León and Castile; granted to Henry of Burgundy as county of Portugal 1095; became independent kingdom under Alfonso I (1140–85); carried on war with Castile and expanded its territory southward, expelling Moors from Algarve in 13th cent.; after 1385, ruled by Aviz dynasty under whom it came to flourish as maritime and colonial power; in 15th and 16th cents., Portuguese opened African coast, found Cape route to Indies, colonized Brazil, and secured trade monopoly in India and East Indies; Lisbon (*q.v.*) became European trading center; Spanish dependency 1580–1640; lost much of empire to Dutch (see INDONESIA 2) and to English (see INDIA 1); for chief remaining overseas possessions, see ANGOLA 1, MOZAMBIQUE 1, MACAO, TIMOR, PORTUGUESE and PORTUGUESE GUINEA; in late 17th cent., became dependent ally of Great Britain; occupied by French 1807–14; its revolt 1820 inaugurated unsettled period during which it lost Brazil; proclaimed republic 1910; in war against Germany 1916–18; adopted new constitution 1933, making it an authoritarian corporative state; neutral in World War II but friendly to Allies; became a member of NATO 1949, of the United Nations 1955; Goa, a Portuguese possession, annexed by India 1962; 1960's marked by anti-Portuguese guerrilla activity in its African possessions.

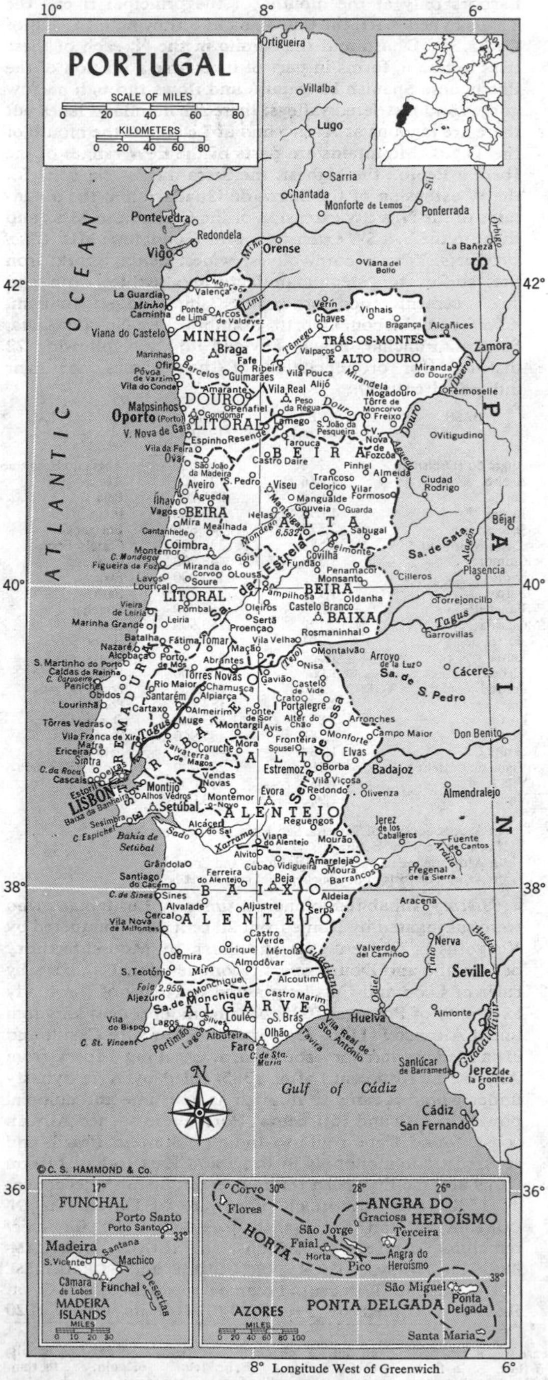

Por·tu·ga·le·te \ˌpōrt-ə-gə-ˈlāt-ē, ˌpȯrt-\. Commune, Vizcaya prov., N Spain, on Bay of Biscay 5 m. NW of Bilbao; pop. (1970p) 45,589.

Por·tu·gue·sa \ˌpōrt-ə-ˈgā-sə, ˌpȯrt-\. **1** River, W Venezuela; ab. 240 m. long; flows SE to join the Apure river 5 m. above San Fernando.

2 State of W cen. Venezuela. See table at VENEZUELA.

Por·tu·guese Con·go \ˌpōr-chi-gēz-ˈkäŋ-(ˌ)gō\. The Cabinda (*q.v.*) exclave of Angola, N of the mouth of the Congo.

Portuguese East Africa. Region formerly including most of the E coast of Africa, now limited to Mozambique. See MOZAMBIQUE 1.

Portuguese Guin·ea \-ˈgin-ē\. Portuguese overseas province, W Africa, bounded on N by Senegal, on E and SE by Guinea, and on SW and W by the Atlantic Ocean; 13,948 sq. m.; pop. (1970e) 530,000; ✱ Bissau. *Physical features:* Includes Arquipélago dos Bijagós; most of province consists of low, marshy terrain with a max. elevation of ab. 800 ft. in SE; traversed in cen. part by Gêba river. *Chief exports:* Peanuts, timber, beeswax. *Chief town:* Bissau.

History: Discovered by Portuguese 1446; in 17th and 18th cents. was active in supplying slave trade; claims of British relinquished 1870 and boundaries established by convention with France 1886 and 1902–05; outbreak of armed resistance to Portuguese rule 1962.

Portuguese India. Name formerly applied to the Portuguese possessions on the W coast of India; 1441 sq. m.; ✱ Pangim (Panaji), in Goa; annexed 1962 by India and now the Union territory of Goa, Daman, and Diu.

Portuguese Ny·as·a·land \-nī-ˈas-ə-ˌland, -nē-\. Former name of northern part of Mozambique.

Portuguese Timor. See TIMOR, PORTUGUESE.

Portuguese West Africa. See ANGOLA 1.

Portus Cale. See OPORTO.

Portus Gaditanus. See PUERTO REAL.

Portus Iulius. See AVERNUS, LAKE.

Portus Lemanis. See LYMPNE.

Portus Magnus. See ALMERÍA 2.

Portus Magonis. See MAHÓN.

Port Vue \-ˈvü\. Borough, Allegheny co., SW Pennsylvania, 10 m. SE of Pittsburgh; pop. (1970c) 5862.

Port Wash·ing·ton \-ˈwȯsh-iŋ-tən, -ˈwäsh-\. **1** Unincorporated resort, Nassau co., SE New York, on Long I., on hill overlooking Manhasset Bay, Long Island Sound, ab. 6 m. NW of Mineola; pop. (1970c) 15,923; yachting and boatbuilding center; lobster, clam fisheries.

2 Industrial city, ⊗ of Ozaukee co., E Wisconsin, on Lake Michigan 25 m. N of Milwaukee; pop. (1970c) 8752; foundry products, furniture; dairy farms; settled 1835.

Port Washington North. Village, Nassau co., SE New York; pop. (1970c) 2883.

Port Weld \-ˈweld\. Seaport, NW Perak state, Malaysia.

Port Went·worth \-ˈwent-ˌwərth\. City, Chatham co., SE Georgia, 5 m. N of Savannah; pop. (1970c) 3405.

Por·voo \ˈpȯ(ə)r-(ˌ)vō\ *or Swed.* **Bor·gå** \ˈbȯ(ə)r-(ˌ)gō\. Seaport, Uusimaa prov., S Finland, E of Helsinki on the Gulf of Finland; pop. (1970e) 16,684; exports lumber and cellulose; 15th cent. cathedral; founded 1346; place where Finnish Diet took oath of allegiance 1809 to Alexander I of Russia; home of the national poet Runeberg.

Porz am Rhein \ˌpȯrt-säm-ˈrīn\ *or formerly* **Heu·mar** \ˈhȯi-ˌmär\. Industrial commune, North Rhine-Westphalia, West Germany, ESE suburb of Cologne on the Rhine; pop. (1969e) 76,762; glass, agricultural machinery, wire cable.

Po·sa·das \pə-ˈsäd-əs\. Town, ✱ of Misiones prov., NE Argentina, on the Paraná river opp. the Paraguayan town of Encarnación; pop. (1960c) 70,691.

Poseidonia. See PAESTUM.

Po·sen *U.S.* ˈpō-zən, -sən; *Pol.* ˈpō-zən\. **1** Village, Cook co., NE Illinois, 17 m. S of Chicago; pop. (1970c) 5498.

2 Former province of Prussia (from 1793 to 1918); since 1945 part of W Poland.

3 City, Poland. See POZNAŃ 2.

Poset Bay *or* **Poseta Bay.** See POSYETA BAY.

Po·sey \'pō-zē\. County in Indiana. See table at INDIANA.

Po–shan \'pō-'shän, 'bə-'shän\. Town in mountainous district, cen. Shantung prov., NE China, 55 m. ESE of Tsinan on branch of Tsinan-Tsingtao railroad; pop. (1970e) 1,750,000; one of the chief industrial centers of Shantung; pottery, glass, dyestuffs; extensive coal mines.

Posht·kūh \,pōsht-'kü\ *or* **Pusht–i–Kuh** \,pu̇sh-tē-'kü\. Mountain range, W Iran, extending NW to SE along the boundary with Iraq; source of a headstream of the Karkheh river; highest point 5092 ft.

Po·si·li·po \pə-'zē-li-,pō\. Promontory, SW of Naples, Italy; pierced by the "Grotto," a tunnel 2264 ft. long, from 20 to 32 ft. wide, and from 23 to 71 ft. high.

Po·si·ta·no \,pō-zə-'tän-(,)ō\. Town, Salerno prov., Campania, Italy, on north coast of Gulf of Salerno 6 m. E of Sorrento; pop. (1970e) 3272; resort.

Posnania. See POZNAŃ.

Po·so \'pō-(,)sō\. Town, N Celebes I., Indonesia, on S coast of Gulf of Tomini and N of Lake Poso.

Poso, Lake. Lake, cen. Celebes I., Indonesia; has been sounded to depth of 1000 ft.

Pöss·neck \'pərs-,nek\. Manufacturing city, Gera dist., East Germany, 33 m. SE of Erfurt; pop. (1970e) 19,074; textiles, leather goods.

Possum Kingdom Dam. See MORRIS SHEPPARD DAM.

Post \'pōst\. City, ⊗ of Garza co., NW Texas, 40 m. SSE of Lubbock; pop. (1970c) 3854; textiles; oil wells.

Pos·toj·na \'pō-stòi-nə\ *or Ital.* **Pos·tu·mia** \pō-'stü-(,)myä\ *or Ger.* **Adels·berg** \'äd-ᵊls-,be(ə)rg, -ᵊlz-\. Commune, Slovenia, NW Yugoslavia, ENE of Trieste; formerly in NE Italy; stalactite caves nearby.

Pöstyén. See PIEŠT'ANY.

Po·sye·ta Bay \pȯs-,yet-ə-\ *or* **Po·se·ta Bay** \pə-'set-\ *or* **Po·set Bay** \pə-'set-\. Inlet of Sea of Japan, S tip of Primorski Krai, Russian S.F.S.R., U.S.S.R., just SW of Peter the Great Bay.

Potala. See LHASA.

Po·ta·ro \pə-'tär-(,)ō\. River, cen. Guyana; ab. 100 m. long; flows E into Essequibo river; gold deposits. See KAIETEUR FALLS.

Po·ta·to Knob \pə-'tāt-(,)ō-, pōt-'āt-, -ə(-w)-\. Peak, Yancey and Buncombe cos., W North Carolina; 6420 ft.

Potch·ef·stroom \'päch-əf-,strüm\. Town, S Transvaal, NE Rep. of South Africa, 75 m. SW of Johannesburg; pop. (1967e) 51,800; center of farm district and largest cattle-raising area in Rep. of South Africa; Potchefstroom Univ. for Christian Education (1951). Founded 1838, oldest town in Transvaal; scene of a civil war bet. opposing Boer factions 1862 and of capture of British force by Boers 1881; occupied by British during Boer War 1900.

Po·teau \'pō-,tō\. 1 River, E Oklahoma; ab. 90 m. long; flows N in Le Flore co. and empties into Arkansas river on the Arkansas border.

2 City on the river, ⊗ of Le Flore co., E Oklahoma, 9 m. W of Arkansas border; pop. (1970c) 5500; oil and gas wells; potatoes, cotton; Poteau Community Coll. (1934).

Po·teet \pō-'tēt\. City, Atascosa co., S Texas, 29 m. S of San Antonio; pop. (1970c) 3013.

Po·ten·za \pə-'ten(t)-sə, -'ten-zə\. 1 River, NE cen. Italy; ab. 60 m. long; flows ENE into Adriatic Sea 2½ m. ESE of Loreto.

2 Province of Basilicata, Italy. See table at ITALY.

3 *anc.* **Po·ten·tia** \pə-'ten-ch(ē-)ə\. Commune, ✱ of Basilicata, also ✱ of Potenza prov., S Italy, 84 m. SE of Naples; pop. (1968e) 51,481; railroad junction in an agricultural area; ships fruit and vegetables; cathedral and three medieval churches. Roman city founded 2d cent. B.C.; in Middle Ages under a succession of feudal overlords; almost completely destroyed in 13th cent.; in 1860 was first town in S Italy to expel Bourbons.

Po·ter·la, Co·llado de la \kō(l)-'yäd-ō-də-lä-pō-'ter-lə\ *or Fr.* **Pas·sage de Ta·ra·die** \pä-säzh-də-tär-ə-dē\ *or formerly* **Col de Pour·ta·let** \,kȯl-də-,pu̇rt-ᵊl-'ā\. Mountain pass in W Pyrenees on boundary bet. Spain and SW France, E of Col de Somport (*q.v.*); 5468 ft.

Pot·gie·ters·rust \'pōt-,gē-tərz-,rəst\. Town, cen. Transvaal, NE Rep. of South Africa, on branch of Limpopo river 125 m. NNE of Pretoria; pop. (1967e) 12,700; in agricultural section; lime and tin found in vicinity.

Pothea. See KALYMNOS 2.

Potholes Reservoir. See MOSES LAKE.

Po·ti \'pȯt-ē\. Seaport town, W Georgian S.S.R., U.S.S.R., on Black Sea at mouth of Batumi river, 40 m. N of Rioni; pop. (1967e) 46,000; ships manganese, cotton, citrus fruit; fishing fleet, flour mill, and meat packing plants; developed in 1880's with construction of artificial harbor and rail link to Trans-Caucasus R.R.

Pot·i·daea \,pät-ə-'dē-ə\. Ancient city of Macedonia, on the narrow isthmus joining Pallene Penin. to the Chalcidice mainland; was near Olynthus and its site is ab. 38 m. SE of Salonika. A Corinthian colony, founded 609 B.C.; its revolt from Athens 432 B.C. was one of the causes of Second Peloponnesian War; taken by Athenians 429 after siege of two years; taken again by Philip of Macedon 356 B.C. and destroyed; rebuilt c. 301 B.C. by Cassander and renamed **Cas·san·dreia** \,kas-,an-'drī-ə\.

Pot Mountain \'pät-\. Peak, E Clearwater co., NE Idaho; 6990 ft.

Po·to·mac \pə-'tō-mək, -mik\. River, West Virginia, Virginia, and Maryland; 287 m. long; formed by confluence of **North Branch** (ab. 110 m. long, flows NE from Tucker co., West Virginia, forms West Virginia-Maryland boundary) and **South Branch** (ab. 140 m. long, rises in Pendleton co., West Virginia) on N boundary of Hampshire co., NE West Virginia; flows E and SE to form West Virginia-Maryland and Virginia-Maryland boundaries and empties into Chesapeake Bay; navigable for large vessels to Washington, D.C.; above Washington are the Great Falls (*q.v.*).

Po·to·si \pə-'tō-sē\. City, ⊗ of Washington co., E Missouri, 58 m. SW of St. Louis; pop. (1970c) 2761.

Po·to·sí \,pōt-ə-'sē\. 1 Department of SW Bolivia. See table at BOLIVIA.

2 City, its ✱, situated at base of the noted silver-producing Cerro Potosí (15,380 ft.) ab. 50 m. S of Sucre; pop. (1969e) 63,590; one of the highest cities in the world, at an altitude of over 13,700 ft.; a major industrial center, producing iron, steel, footwear, furniture, electrical equipment, foodstuffs and beverages; important tin, lead, copper mines and refineries; univ. (1892). Silver discovered 1545 and city founded 1547; at height of prosperity in 1650 had ab. 160,000 residents; pop. in 1825 was only 8,000 but city has expanded in 20th cent. with diversification of mining and manufacturing industries.

Potosi Mountain \pə-,tō-sē-\. Peak in SW Clark co., SE Nevada; 8504 ft.

Potosi Peak. Mountain, in Ouray co., SW Colorado; 13,790 ft.

Po·to·tan \pō-'tō-tän\. Municipality, Iloilo prov., Panay, Phil., near right bank of Jalaud river and on railroad 17 m. N of City of Iloilo; pop. (1969e) 50,700.

Pot·re·ri·llos \,pō-trə-'rē(l)-(,)yōs\. Subdivision of Chañaral commune, N cen. Chile; pop. (1960c) 6976.

Pots·dam \'päts-,dam\. 1 Village, St. Lawrence co., N New York, 27 m. E of Ogdensburg; pop. (1970c) 9985; paper, dairy products; State Univ. of New York Coll. at Potsdam (1816), Clarkson Coll. of Technology (1896).

2 District, East Germany. See table at GERMANY, EAST.

3 Industrial city, its ✻, on Havel river 17 m. SW of West Berlin; pop. (1970e) 111,288; railroad locomotives, textiles, pharmaceuticals; several scientific and technical institutes.

History: First mentioned as Slav settlement 10th cent.; received municipal charter 14th cent.; made garrison town 1640; became summer residence of Hohenzollerns under Frederick the Great, who built the rococo Sans Souci Palace (1745–47); Peace of Potsdam, ratifying Russo-Prussian alliance against France, signed here 1805; at the end of World War II site of conference of American, British, and Soviet leaders July 17–Aug. 2, 1945, at which the preliminary details of the intended administration of Germany were determined and at which lands of E Germany (E of Oder and Neisse rivers) were assigned to Poland.

Pot·ta·wat·o·mie \ˌpät-ə-ˈwät-ə-mē\. Name of counties in two states of the U.S. See tables at KANSAS and OKLAHOMA.

Pot·ta·wat·ta·mie \ˌpät-ə-ˈwät-ə-mē\. County in Iowa. See table at IOWA.

Pot·ter \ˈpät-ər\. Counties in three states of the U.S. See tables at PENNSYLVANIA, SOUTH DAKOTA, TEXAS.

Pot·ter·ies, The \-ˈpät-ə-rēz\. District in Staffordshire, W cen. England, noted for its production of china and earthenware; the Five Towns (actually six: Stoke-on-Trent, Burslem, Fenton, Hanley, Longton, Tunstall) combined 1910 to form Stoke-on-Trent county borough; setting of Arnold Bennett's trilogy of novels *Clayhanger* (1910), *Hilda Lessways* (1911), and *These Twain* (1916).

Pot·ters Bar \ˌpät-ərz-\. Urban district, Hertfordshire, S England, 14 m. NNW of London; pop. (1971p) 24,583.

Potts·town \ˈpät-ˌstaůn\. Industrial borough, Montgomery co., SE Pennsylvania, on Schuylkill river 17 m. ESE of Reading; pop. (1970c) 25,355; manufactures steel and steel products, tires, automobile parts, iron castings, clothing, dairy products, concrete pipe; center of metallurgical industry from early 18th cent.; town laid out 1752, incorporated as borough 1815.

Potts·ville \ˈpäts-ˌvil\. City, ⊗ of Schuylkill co., E cen. Pennsylvania, on Schuylkill river 28 m. NNW of Reading; pop. (1970c) 19,715; retail trade center; aluminum products, plastics, clothing, footwear, beer; anthracite coal mines, railroad shops. Settled c. 1795; incorporated as borough 1828, as city 1911; in 1860's and 1870's a center of the activities of the Molly Maguires.

Pough·keep·sie \pə-ˈkip-sē, pō-\. City and river port, ⊗ of Dutchess co., SE New York, on E bank of Hudson river 65 m. N of New York; pop. (1970c) 32,039; railroad and highway bridges across the Hudson; computers, ball bearings, chemicals, clothing, dairy machinery; livestock and fruit farms; Vassar Coll. (1861), Marist Coll. (1946), Dutchess Community Coll. (1957). Settled by Dutch 1687; capital of New York in 1778; incorporated as city 1854.

Poult·ney \ˈpōlt-nē\. 1 River, W Vermont; ab. 35 m. long; rises in N Rutland co., flows NW, W, and SW into S end of Lake Champlain, forming for a few miles the New York-Vermont state boundary.

2 Village on river in Poultney town, Rutland co., W Vermont, 15 m. WSW of Rutland; pop. (1970c) 1914 (village), 3217 (town); Green Mountain Coll. (1834).

Poul·ton–le–Fylde \ˈpül-tən-lə-ˈfīld\. Urban district, Lancashire, NW England, 15 m. NW of Preston; pop. (1971p) 16,401.

Pour·ri, Mont \ˌmōⁿ-pů-ˈrē\. Peak in the Graian Alps, E France; 12,405 ft.

Pourtalet, Col de. See POTERLA, COLLADO DE LA.

Pou·so Ale·gre \ˈpō-zů-ə-ˈleg-rə, -ˈlāg-\. City, S Minas Gerais state, E Brazil, 180 m. WNW of Rio de Janeiro; munic. pop. (1968e) 31,809.

Pou·thi·sat \ˌpü-thi-ˈsät\ *or* **Pur·sat** \ˈpů(ə)r-ˌsät\. Town, cen. Cambodia, SE Asia, S of the Tonle Sap and on railroad 100 m. NW of Pnompenh; pop. (1962p) 14,532.

Pov·er·ty Bay \ˌpäv-ərt-ē-\. Inlet of Pacific Ocean, E coast of North I., New Zealand; Gisborne is on it.

Pó·voa de Var·zim \ˌpȯv-wə-di-vər-ˈzē(ⁿ)m\. Commune, Pôrto dist., NW Portugal, on Atlantic Ocean 20 m. NNW of Oporto; pop. (1970p) 21,165; seaside resort and fishing port. Birthplace of the novelist José Maria Eça de Queiroz (1843–1900).

Pow·der \ˈpaůd-ər\. 1 River, E Oregon; 150 m. long; rises in S Baker co., flows N and then curves SE into Snake river on E cen. boundary of Baker co.

2 River, N Wyoming and SE Montana; 375 m. long; formed by confluence of forks in Johnson co., N Wyoming, flows N across Montana border into Yellowstone river in Prairie co., E Montana.

Powder River. 1 Rivers, United States. See POWDER.

2 County in Montana. See table at MONTANA.

Powder Springs. City, Cobb co., NW Georgia, 18 m. WNW of Atlanta; pop. (1970c) 2559.

Pow·ell \ˈpaů(-ə)l\. 1 River, NE Tennessee; ab. 150 m. long; rises in Wise co., SW Virginia, flows SW across Tennessee border and into Clinch river at Norris Dam.

2 Name of counties in two states of the U.S. See tables at KENTUCKY and MONTANA.

3 City, Park co., NW Wyoming, 22 m. NNE of Cody; pop. (1970c) 4807; gas, oil wells; sugar beets; Northwest Community Coll. (1946).

Powell, Lake. Artificial lake in Glen Canyon National Recreation Area, S Utah; 252 sq. m.; altitude 3700 ft.

Powell, Mount. Peak on border bet. Eagle and Summit cos., cen. Colorado; 13,398 ft.

Powell River. 1 River in Tennessee. See POWELL 1.

2 Town, S British Columbia, Canada, on Strait of Georgia 80 m. NW of Vancouver; produces pulp and newsprint.

Pow·er \ˈpaů-ər\. County in Idaho. See table at IDAHO.

Pow·e·shiek \ˈpaů-ə-ˌshēk\. County in Iowa. See table at IOWA.

Pow·ha·tan \ˌpaů-ə-ˈtan\. 1 County in E cen. Virginia. See table at VIRGINIA.

2 Village, its ⊗.

Powhatan \paů-ˈhat-ən, ˌpaů-ə-ˈtan\. Town, a ⊗ of Lawrence co., NE Arkansas, on Black river; pop. (1970c) 84.

Powhatan Point \paů-ˈhat-ən-, ˈpaů-ə-ˌtan-\. Village, Belmont co., E Ohio, on Ohio river; pop. (1970c) 2167.

P'o–yang Hu \ˈpō-ˈyäŋ-ˈhü\. Lake (*hu*), N Kiangsi prov., SE China; 90 m. long and 20 m. wide; 1073 sq. m.; 2d largest lake in China; receives the Kan (the largest) and practically all other rivers of Kiangsi; its outlet is the Kan.

Poy·gan, Lake \-ˈpȯi-gən\. Lake, W Winnebago co., E Wisconsin; ab. 10 m. long by 3 m. wide; extends W into Waushara co.; an expansion of Wolf river.

Po·ža·re·vac \pō-ˈzhär-ə-ˌväts\ *or Ger.* **Pas·sa·ro·witz** \pä-ˈsär-ə-ˌvits\. Town, Serbia, E Yugoslavia, 35 m. ESE of Belgrade, near the Morava river and 8 m. from its port on the Danube; pop. (1965e) 25,000; market town; scene of signing of treaty July 21, 1718 bet. Turkey, Austria, and Venice; taken by Serbs 1804; occupied by Germans 1941.

Po·za Ri·ca de Hi·dal·go \ˌpō-zə-ˈrē-kə-ˌdā-(h)id-ˈal-(ˌ)gō, ˌpō-sə-, -ē-thäl-\. Municipality, Veracruz state, Mexico, 120 m. S of Tampico; munic. pop. (1970p) 121,341; oil wells; livestock raising; diversified agriculture.

Požega. See SLAVONSKA POŽEGA.

Po·zières \ˌpo-ˈzyer\. Village, Somme dept., N France, NE of Albert near Bapaume; captured by British July 1916.

Poz·nań \ˈpōz-ˌnan(-yə), ˈpȯz-, -ˌnän(-yə)\ *or Ger.* **Po·sen** \ˈpōz-ᵊn\ *also* **Pos·na·nia** \päz-ˈnā-nē-ə\. 1 Province of W cen. Poland. See table at POLAND.

2 City, its ✻, on both banks of the Warta river 167 m. W of Warsaw; pop. (1970p) 469,000; archiepiscopal see (primacy of Poland); center of metallurgical, chemical, printing, textile, and food processing industries; Gothic-style cathedral, 15th cent. church, 18th cent. archiepiscopal palace; univ. (1919), technical univ. (estab. 1919, received univ. status 1954).

History: One of the oldest cities in Poland, dating from 10th cent. A.D.; member of the Hanseatic League; reached height of prosperity 15th–17th cent. but declined due to

Northern War; to Prussia 1793; part of grand duchy of Warsaw 1807–15 and then reverted to Prussia; to Poland 1918; in World War II occupied by Germans Sept. 1939–Feb. 1945; suffered extensive damage but has been largely rebuilt; scene of strike June 1956 which precipitated nationwide demands for political liberalization.

Po·zo·blan·co \pō-sō-'blaŋ-(ˌ)kō\. Commune, Córdoba prov., S Spain, 34 m. N of Córdoba; pop. (1970p) 13,317; silver-bearing galena mines.

Pozsega. See SLAVONSKA POŽEGA.

Pozsony. See BRATISLAVA.

Poz·zal·lo \pȯt-'zä-lō\. Commune, Ragusa prov., SE Sicily, Italy, 15 m. SSE of Ragusa; pop. (1968e) 12,933.

Poz·zuo·li \pȯt-'swȯ-lē\ *or anc.* **Pu·te·o·li** \pyü-'tē-ə-ˌlī, pə-'tē-\. Commune, Napoli prov., Campania, S Italy, on **Bay of Pozzuoli** 6 m. W of Naples; pop. (1968e) 61,912; machinery, cement; fishing, food processing; cathedral (incorporating parts of ancient Roman temple) and extensive Roman remains, including a semi-submerged market, baths, amphitheater, and necropolis with painted underground chambers. Founded c. 529 B.C. by Greeks; became Roman colony 194; important commercial center under Roman Empire; declined during Middle Ages due to local volcanic activity. Nearby is Lake Avernus, the legendary mouth of hell.

Pra·chin Bu·ri *or* **Pra·chin·bu·ri** \'präch-ˌin-bü-ˌrē\. 1 Province, cen. Thailand; 4554 sq. m.; pop. (1960c) 334,895; ✱ Prachin Buri.

2 Town, its ✱, on railroad 65 m. ENE of Bangkok; pop. (1960c) 13,420.

Pra·chu·ap Khi·ri Khan *or* **Pra·chu·ab Gi·ri·khand** \'präch-ü-ˌäp-ˌkir-ē-'kän\. 1 Province, S cen. Thailand; 2461 sq. m.; pop. (1960c) 152,456; ✱ Prachuap Khiri Khan.

2 Town, its ✱, seaport on W coast of Gulf of Siam, E upper Malay Penin. 140 m. SSW of Bangkok; pop. (1960c) 6228.

Prác·ti·cos, Point \-'präk-tē-ˌkōs\. Cape on NE coast of Camagüey prov., E cen. Cuba.

Prades \'präd\. Commune, Pyrénées-Orientales dept., S France, 25 m. SW of Perpignan; pop. (1962c) 6035; scene of series of annual music festivals founded 1950 by Pablo Casals.

Prae. See PHRAE.

Praeneste. See PALESTRINA.

Prae·nes·ti·na, Via \'vī-ə-ˌprē-nes-'tī-nə\. Ancient road, Italy, from Rome to Praeneste; ab. 23 m. long.

Præstø \'pres-ˌtər\. Town, Storstrøm co., Denmark, S Sjælland I., on **Præstø Bight;** pop. (1970e) 4926.

Prague \'präg\ *or Czech* **Pra·ha** \'prä-(ˌ)hä\ *or Ger.* **Prag** \'präk\. City, ✱ of Czechoslovakia, also ✱ of the Czech S.R., on both sides of the Vltava (Moldau) river, 115 m. NW of Brno; pop. (1970p) 1,078,096; major commercial and industrial center, producing railway rolling stock, aircraft, motor vehicles, machine tools, foundry equipment, chemicals, pharmaceuticals, dairy products; food processing, printing, tanning, brewing; 14th cent. cathedral, 16th–17th cent. fortified palace (now presidential palace), 10th cent. basilica, national museum (1818), several notable churches; Charles Univ. (1348), Technical Univ. (1707), and several other educational institutions.

History: First historically recorded settlement on site in 9th cent. A.D.; by 14th cent. one of the leading cultural and trade centers of Central Europe; center of Hussite movement early 15th cent.; center of opposition to Habsburgs early 17th cent. which led to Defenestration of Prague 1618, in which several Habsburg officials were thrown from windows of palace (one of the precipitating events of the Thirty Years' War); scene of victory of Prussians under Frederick the Great over the Austrians May 6, 1757; site of Congress of Prague July 5–Oct. 11, 1813, in which Allied Powers failed to come to agreement with Napoleon; scene of signing of peace treaty between Prussia and Austria 1866 ending Seven Weeks' War. Became capital of independent Czechoslovakia 1918; under German occupation 1939–45; occupied by U.S.S.R. and other Warsaw Pact military forces Aug. 1968 in order to prevent Czech political liberalization.

Prahoe. See PERAHU.

Pra·ho·va \'prä-kə-və\. County of S cen. Romania. See table at ROMANIA.

Prah·ran \prə-'ran\. City, S Victoria, SE Australia, SE suburb of Melbourne; pop. (1966c) 54,655.

Praia \'prī-ə\. Town on São Tiago I., ✱ of Cape Verde Is.; pop. (1960c) 45,079.

Praia de Copacabana. See COPACABANA BEACH.

Prai·rie \'prer-ē\. Name of counties in two states of the U.S. See tables at ARKANSAS and MONTANA.

Prairie du Chien \ˌprer-ēd-ə-'shēn\. City, ⊗ of Crawford co., SW Wisconsin, on Mississippi river near its confluence with the Wisconsin river 53 m. S of La Crosse; pop. (1970c) 5540; butter, cement blocks, fertilizer, lumber. Settled by French c. 1781; surrendered by British to U.S. 1786; scene of battle in War of 1812; again held by British 1814–16; site of American Fur Company post 1835.

Prairie Grove. City, Washington co., NW Arkansas, 10 m. S of Fayetteville; pop. (1970c) 1582; scene of battle Dec. 7, 1862 in which Union troops under Francis J. Herron defeated Confederate forces of Thomas C. Hindman.

Prairie Provinces. The Canadian provinces of Manitoba, Saskatchewan, and Alberta—popularly so called.

Prai·ries, Ri·vière des \ˌriv-ē-'e(ə)r-ˌdā-pre-'rē\. River, part of the course of the St. Lawrence river N of Montreal I., separating it from Jesus I., S Quebec, Canada; ab. 28 m. long; flows NE.

Prairie Village. City, Johnson co., NE Kansas, S of Kansas City; pop. (1970c) 28,138.

Pralls Island \prȯlz-\. Island in Arthur Kill off NW shore of Staten I., N.Y.; part of Richmond borough.

Pram·ba·nan \präm-'bän-ˌän\ *also* **Bram·ba·nan** \bräm-\. Town, S cen. Java, Indonesia, on Jogjakarta border and on railroad ab. 12 m. ENE of Jogjakarta; on plain nearby are ruins of many Hindu (Brahmanic) temples, ab. 1100 years old.

Pran·hi·ta \'prän-i-ˌtä\. River, E Maharashtra, cen. India; ab. 80 m. long; formed by confluence of Wainganga and Wardha rivers, flows S, forming part of boundary between Maharashtra and Andhra Pradesh, to Godavari river.

Pras·lin \prä-'laⁿ\. See SEYCHELLES.

Pra·so·ne·si, Cape \-ˌpräs-ə-'nē-sē\ *or Gk.* **Cape Pra·so·ní·si** \-ˌprä-sȯ-'nē-sē\ *or* **Cape Pras·so** \-'präs-(ˌ)ō\. Cape at S extremity of the island of Rhodes, Greece.

Pratapgarh. See PARTABGARH.

Pra·tas \'prät-əs\. Cluster of reefs and islets in South China Sea bet. Hong Kong and Luzon, Phil., ab. 200 m. SE of Hong Kong.

Pra·ter, Mount \-'prāt-ər\. Peak in Sierra Nevada, E Fresno co., S cen. California; 13,501 ft.

Prathum Thani. See PATHUM THANI.

Prätigau. See PRÄTTIGAU.

Pra·to \'prät-ō\. Commune, Firenze prov., Tuscany, W Italy, 11 m. NW of Florence; pop. (1968e) 137,461; woolens, weaving machinery, cement; 12th–13th cent. cathedral, 15th cent. church, 13th cent. palace, 14th cent. city walls. Became free Italian commune in 11th cent.; came under Florence; sacked by Spanish 1512; became city 1653.

Pratt \'prat\. 1 County in S cen. Kansas. See table at KANSAS.

2 City, its ⊗, 54 m. WSW of Hutchinson; pop. (1970c) 6736; railroad shops; grain farms; Pratt Community Junior Coll. (1938).

Prät·ti·gau *or* **Prä·ti·gau** \'prāt-i-ˌgaů, 'pret-\. Highland valley in N Graubünden canton, E Switzerland, NE of Chur.

Pratt·ville \'prat-ˌvil, -vəl\. City, ⊗ of Autauga co., cen. Alabama, 12 m. NW of Montgomery; pop. (1970c) 13,116; paper, textiles, lumber; settled 1816.

Prau. See PERAHU.

Praust. See PRUSZCZ GDAŃSKI.

Prav·dinsk \'präv-(ˌ)dēn(t)sk\ *or Ger.* **Fried·land** \'frēt-ˌlänt\. Town, Kaliningrad Oblast, Russian S.F.S.R., U.S.S.R., ab. 27 m. SE of Kaliningrad; formerly in East Prussia, Germany; battle June 14, 1807 in which the Russians under Gen. Bennigsen were defeated by French under Napoleon who proceeded to occupy Königsberg (now Kaliningrad).

Pra·via \'präv-ē-ə\. Commune, Oviedo prov., NW Spain, 19 m. NW of Oviedo; pop. (1970p) 11,915.

Prebeza. See PREVEZA.

Pre·ble \'preb-əl\. County in Ohio. See table at OHIO.

Prê·cheur \pre-'shər\. Former coast town, NW Martinique I., West Indies; at foot of Mont Pelée whose eruption 1902 destroyed the town.

Pre·dap·pio \pri-'däp-ē-ˌō\. Village, Forlì prov., SE Emilia-Romagna, N Italy, ab. 10 m. SSW of Forlì; pop. (1968e) 6506; birthplace of Benito Mussolini.

Pre·daz·zo \ˌpre-'dät-sō\. Commune, Trento prov., S Trentino-Alto Adige, N Italy; pop. (1968e) 3920; resort; in Dolomites on a tributary of the Adige SE of Bolzano.

Pre·deal Pass \ˌpred-ē-'äl-\ *or Hung.* **Tö·mös Pass** \'tər-ˌmərsh-\. Chief pass in the Transylvanian Alps, Romania, 10 m. S of Braşov; 45°28′N, 25°36′E; altitude 3445 ft.

Predkavkazye. See CISCAUCASIA.

Před·most \pər-'zhed-ˌmȯst\. Village, Czech S.R., Czechoslovakia, near Přerov; site of important and extensive Paleolithic remains; excavations since 1800 have uncovered human burials, flint implements, ivory and bone carvings, mammoth remains.

Pre·gol·ya \ˌpre-'gōl-yə\ *or Ger.* **Pre·gel** \'prā-gəl\. Navigable river, Russian S.F.S.R., U.S.S.R.; ab. 80 m. long; flows W through Kaliningrad Oblast into Vislinski Zaliv; after World War II by decision of the Potsdam Conference July 17–Aug 2, 1945, its main course and part of the Angrapa assigned to U.S.S.R.

Prei·gnac \ˌpre-'nyäk\. Commune, Gironde dept., SW France; pop. (1962c) 2184; produces white wine (see SAUTERNES).

Premet. See PËRMET.

Pre·mont \'prē-ˌmänt\. City, Jim Wells co., S Texas, 20 m. SW of Kingsport; pop. (1970c) 3282; oil refining; agriculture.

Pré·mon·tré, Abbey of \-ˌprā-mōⁿ-'trā\. Abbey near Laon, Aisne dept., N France; founded 1120 by St. Norbert, founder of the Premonstratensians, a very strict order of canons regular.

Pren·tiss \'pren-təs\. 1 County in Mississippi. See table at MISSISSIPPI.

2 Town, ⊗ of Jefferson Davis co., S Mississippi; pop. (1970c) 1789; Prentiss Normal and Industrial Institute (1907).

Prenz·lau \'pren(t)s-ˌlaù\. City, Potsdam dist., East Germany, 30 m. SE of Neubrandenburg; pop. (1970e) 21,551; manufactures iron goods, machinery, dairy products, sugar. Became city 1234; to Brandenburg 1250; scene of Prussian surrender to French 1806.

Prep·a·ris Channels \ˌprep-ə-rəs-\. Passage, in E Bay of Bengal, bet. Cape Negrais, Burma, and the mouths of the Irrawaddy on the N and Great and Little Coco Is. of the Andamans on the S; 140 m. wide; the channel is divided in the center by the **Preparis Isles** into **Preparis North Channel** and **Preparis South Channel.**

Pře·rov \pər-'zher-ˌȯf\ *or Ger.* **Pre·rau** \'prā-ˌraù\. Town, Czech S.R., cen. Czechoslovakia, ab. 40 m. NE of Brno; pop. (1968e) 37,456; textile mills.

Pré–Saint–Gervais, Le. See LE PRÉ-SAINT-GERVAIS.

Pres·cot \'pres-kət\. Urban district, Lancashire, NW England, 7 m. E of Liverpool; pop. (1971p) 12,590.

Pres·cott \'pres-kət, -ˌkät\. 1 City, ⊗ of Yavapai co., cen. Arizona, 78 m. NNW of Phoenix; pop. (1970c) 13,134; altitude 5347 ft.; health resort; trade center in agricultural and mining (gold, copper, zinc, lead) region; Prescott Coll. (1966); territorial capital 1863–67, 1877–89; annual "Frontier Days" Rodeo 1888 ff.

2 Commercial city, ⊗ of Nevada co., SW Arkansas, 48 m. NE of Texarkana; pop. (1970c) 3921.

3 County, Ontario, Canada. See table at ONTARIO.

4 *or before 1860* **Johns·town** \'jänz-ˌtaùn\. Town, Grenville co., SE Ontario, Canada, on St. Lawrence river 50 m. S of Ottawa; pop. (1971p) 5178; gloves, clothing, hosiery, cement products; dairy farms; settled 1797.

Pres·i·den·cy \'prez-əd-ən-sē, 'prez-ə-ˌden(t)-\. Former division in S Bengal prov., NE British India; 16,402 sq. m.; ❋ Calcutta; in 1947 divided with 4/5 of area assigned to West Bengal, India, and 1/5 assigned to East Pakistan (now Bangla Desh).

Pre·si·den·te Hayes \ˌpres-ə-ˌdent-ē-'īs, ˌprez-, -'hāz\. Department of W cen. Paraguay. See table at PARAGUAY.

Presidente Pru·den·te \ˌprā-zi-ˌdent-ə-prü-'dent-ə\. City, SW São Paulo state, SE Brazil, on railroad near Paraná river; munic. pop. (1968e) 85,933.

Presidente Vargas. See ITABIRA.

Pres·i·den·tial Range \(ˌ)prez-(ə-)'den-chəl-\. Range of the White Mts., chiefly in S Coos co., N New Hampshire, bet. Pinkham Notch on E and Crawford Notch on W; highest peak Mount Washington 6288 ft.

Pre·sid·io \prə-'sid-ē-ˌō\. County in Texas. See table at TEXAS.

Pre·šov \'presh-ˌȯf\. Town, Slovak S.R., E cen. Czechoslovakia, 20 m. N of Kosiče; pop. (1968e) 40,495; rail and road junction; textiles, machinery; salt mines; 18th cent. Greek Catholic cathedral; founded 12th cent.; destroyed by fire 1887.

Pres·pa, Lake \-'pres-pə\ *or Serbo-Croat.* **Pres·pan·sko Je·ze·ro** \'pres-pən-ˌskō-'yez-ə-ˌrō\. Lake on the boundary bet. SW Yugoslavia, SE Albania, and N Greece, 15 m. SW of Bitola, Yugoslavia; 14 m. long by 8 m. wide; drains NW into Lake Ohrid through a subterranean channel. Near it is the smaller lake, **Mi·krí Pres·pa** \mi-'krē-'pres-pə\.

Presque Isle. 1 \pre-'skī(ə)l\. Peninsula, NW Pennsylvania, in Lake Erie, forming **Presque Isle Bay,** harbor of Erie; state park.

2 \pre-'skēl\. County in Michigan. See table at MICHIGAN.

3 \pre-'skīl\. City, Aroostook co., N Maine, 40 m. N of Houlton; pop. (1970c) 11,452; potatoes, oats; Aroostook State Coll. of Univ. of Maine (1903).

Press, Mount \-'pres\. Mountain, Antarctica, 78°05′S, 85°58′W; 12,566 ft.

Pressburg. See BRATISLAVA.

Pres·tat·yn \pres-'tat-ᵊn\. Urban district, Flintshire, NE Wales; pop. (1971p) 14,428.

Pres·teigne \pres-'tēn\. Urban district, ⊗ of Radnorshire, E Wales; pop. (1971p) 1214.

Pres·ton \'pres-tən\. 1 County in West Virginia. See table at WEST VIRGINIA.

2 Town, N cen. New London co., SE Connecticut, SE of Norwich; pop. (1970c) 3593.

3 Town, ⊗ of Webster co., W Georgia; pop. (1970c) 226.

4 City, ⊗ of Franklin co., SE Idaho, 65 m. SSE of Pocatello; pop. (1970c) 3310; sugar, flour, dairy products.

5 Village, ⊗ of Fillmore co., SE Minnesota, 30 m. SE of Rochester; pop. (1970c) 1413; poultry, dairy farms.

6 Industrial town, Waterloo co., SE Ontario, Canada, on Grand river 8 m. ESE of Kitchener; pop. (1971p) 16,530; shoes, steel, furniture; diversified agriculture.

7 County borough, Lancashire, England, on the Ribble 30 m. NNE of Liverpool; pop. (1971p) 97,365; port, market town, and important industrial center, producing aircraft, motor vehicles, chemicals, boilers, soap, paper, textiles, optical goods; shipbuilding; received first charter 1179; important royalist center during the Civil War; made county borough 1889.

Pres·ton·pans \ˈpres-tən-ˌpanz\. Burgh, East Lothian co., SE Scotland, 8 m. E of Edinburgh; pop. (1971p) 3138; coal mining, breweries; scene of a rout of troops under Sir John Cope by Prince Charles Edward and his Highlanders Sept. 21, 1745.

Pres·tons·burg \ˈpres-tənz-ˌbərg\. City, ⊗ of Floyd co., E Kentucky, 20 m. NW of Pikeville; pop. (1970c) 3422; coal mines; truck farms.

Prest·wich \ˈpres-(ˌ)twich\. Borough, Lancashire, NW England, 5 m. NNW of Manchester; pop. (1969e) 33,060; residential; cotton and rayon mills.

Prest·wick \ˈpres-(ˌ)twik\. Burgh, Ayr co., SW Scotland, ab. 3 m. N of Ayr; pop. (1969e) 13,741; tourist resort; noted golf course; international airport, built during World War II.

Pre·to·ria \pri-ˈtōr-ē-ə, -ˈtȯr-\. City, administrative ✱ of the Rep. of South Africa and ✱ of Transvaal, on small tributary of Limpopo river ab. 34 m. N of Johannesburg; pop. (1970p) 543,950; iron and steel industry; Univ. of South Africa (1873), Univ. of Pretoria (1930).

History: Founded 1855 by Marthinus W. Pretorius, first president of South African Republic, and named after his father, the Boer Voortrekker leader Andries Pretorius. Chosen capital of Boer confederation 1860 but not actually used as a seat of government until 1864; in Boer War surrendered to Lord Roberts May 1900; articles of peace ending war signed here May 31, 1902; first meeting of Parliament of Transvaal; made administrative seat of Union (now Republic) government 1910. Home and burial place of S. J. Paulus Kruger, president of South African Republic 1883–1900.

Pret·ty·boy Dam \ˌprit-ē-ˌbȯi-\. Dam across Gunpowder river, N Baltimore co., NE Maryland; height 153 ft.; completed 1934; forms **Prettyboy Reservoir,** chief reserve for water supply of Baltimore.

Preussen. See PRUSSIA.

Preussisch Eylau. See BAGRATIONOVSK.

Preussisch–Stargard. See STAROGARD GDAŃSKI.

Pre·ve·za *or* **Pre·be·za** \ˈprev-ə-ˌzä\. **1** Department of Epirus region, W Greece. See table at GREECE.

2 Seaport town, its ✱, at entrance to Ambracian Gulf; pop. (1971p) 12,816; ships dairy products, olives, hides; founded 290 B.C.; in Middle Ages superseded Nicopolis, the Roman town just to N of it; taken from Venetians by French 1797; taken from French by Ali Pasha 1798; recovered from Turks by Greeks 1912.

Prib·i·lof Islands \ˈprib-ə-ˌlȯf-\ *also* **Fur Seal Islands** \ˌfər-ˌsēl-\. Group of islands in SE Bering Sea, Alaska, ab. 180 m. N of Unalaska; pop. (1960c) 642; comprise St. Paul and St. George, and three islets. Islands are hilly with no harbors; noted as fur-seal grounds and habitat of blue and white foxes and breeding place of enormous numbers of birds. Visited annually by ab. 80% of fur seals of world (ab. 2,000,000); commercial killing operations governed by convention signed by U.S., U.S.S.R., Japan, and Canada 1957. First sighted 1767; visited 1786 by Russian explorer G. Pribilof; leased to commercial companies 1870 to 1910 whose methods nearly exterminated the seals; taken over by U.S. 1910.

Pří·bram \pər-ˈzhib-ˌram\. Town, Czech S.R., W Czechoslovakia, in mountainous region 33 m. SW of Prague; pop. (1968e) 29,689; ancient silver and lead mines.

Price \ˈprīs\. **1** River, E cen. Utah; flows through cen. Carbon and NE Emery cos. into Green river; in Carbon co., flows through a steep-walled canyon.

2 County in Wisconsin. See table at WISCONSIN.

3 City, ⊗ of Carbon co., E cen. Utah, on Price river 62 m. SE of Provo; pop. (1970c) 6218; flour, coal mines.

4 Village, Matane co., E Quebec, Canada, on Gaspé Peninsula 90 m. NW of Dalhousie; pop. (1971p) 2752.

Price Peak. Mountain in Sierra Nevada, E Tuolumne co., cen. California; 10,716 ft.

Price·ville \ˈprīs-ˌvil\. Village, Matane co., on Gaspé Penin., SE Quebec, Canada, on the St. Lawrence river 29 m. WSW of Matane; pop. (1966c) 3589.

Prich·ard \ˈprich-ərd\. Industrial city, Mobile co., SW corner of Alabama, 3 m. W of Mobile; pop. (1970c) 41,578; cotton-processing and chemical industries; incorporated 1925.

Pri·e·go de Cór·do·ba \prē-ˌā-gō-dā-ˈkȯrd-ə-bə, -və\. Commune, Córdoba prov., S Spain, 48 m. SE of Córdoba; pop. (1970p) 21,229; agricultural products; manufactures liquors, leather, pottery, cotton textiles; ancient castle; medieval church; fortified by Moors.

Pri·e·ne \prī-ˈē-nē\. Ancient Greek city in W Asia Minor, near the mouth of the Maeander river (*mod.* Menderes); scene of archaeological excavations. One of the 12 Ionian Cities, active in Ionian revolt; prosperous under Romans and Byzantine dominion; seized by Ottomans late in 13th cent.

Pries·ka \ˈprē-skə\. Town, N cen. Cape Province, S Rep. of South Africa, on Orange river 150 m. WSW of Kimberley; pop. (1967e) 7600; farmland devoted chiefly to sheep; blue asbestos, diamonds, copper, galena, and saltpeter found in vicinity.

Priest Lake \ˈprēst-\. Lake, N Bonner co., N Idaho; 24 m. long by 14 m. wide.

Prie·vid·za \ˈpr(y)e-vəd-zə\. Town, Slovak S.R., E cen. Czechoslovakia, ab. 80 m. NE of Bratislava; pop. (1968e) 27,033.

Pri·lep \ˈprē-ˌlep\. City, S Macedonia, SE Yugoslavia, ab. 47 m. S of Skopje; pop. (1965e) 44,000; ✱ of Serbian empire in medieval period; 14th cent. monastery; birthplace of Marko Kraljević; occupied by Bulgaria 1941.

Pri·lu·ki \pri-ˈlü-kē\. Town, S Chernigov Oblast, Ukrainian S.S.R., U.S.S.R., ab. 85 m. E of Kiev; pop. (1969e) 59,000; railroad town, chiefly agricultural; dates from 12th cent.

Pri·me·ro \pri-ˈme(ə)r-(ˌ)ō\. River, Córdoba prov., N cen. Argentina; ab. 130 m. long; flows NE into Mar Chiquita.

Prim·ghar \ˈprim-ˌgär\. Town, ⊗ of O'Brien co., NW Iowa; pop. (1970c) 995.

Pri·mor·je \ˈprē-mȯr-ˌyä\ *or* **Pri·mor·ska** \ˈprē-mȯr-ˌskä\. Former county, W Yugoslavia; 7476 sq. m.; ⊗ Split; now chiefly in Croatia and Herzegovina.

Pri·morsk \prē-ˈmȯrsk\ *or formerly* **Koi·vis·to** \ˈkȯi-vis-ˌtō\. Town, Leningrad Oblast, Russian S.F.S.R., U.S.S.R., formerly in SE Finland, opp. **Bol·shoi Be·re·zo·vy Island** \bōl-ˈshȯi-ˌbir-ə-ˈzȯv-ē-, bōl-\ (*or formerly* **Koivisto Island**) at E end of Gulf of Finland; port of Vyborg (formerly Viipuri) ab. 20 m. S of it on Karelian Isthmus. In war bet. U.S.S.R. and Finland 1939–40 forts on island marked W end of Mannerheim Line; scene of severe fighting; captured by U.S.S.R. Mar. 1940. See BJÖRKÖ.

Pri·mor·ski Krai \prē-ˈmȯr-skē ˈkrī\ *also* **Mar·i·time Krai** \ˈmar-ə-ˌtīm-\. Territory of the Russian S.F.S.R., U.S.S.R.; 64,054 sq. m.; pop. (1970p) 1,722,000; ✱ Vladivostok; at the extreme S along the Tumen river it touches North Korea, and along its entire coast stretch the Sikhote-Alin Mts. At its S end on Peter the Great Bay is Vladivostok, the finest Soviet seaport on the Pacific littoral; to the N along the Ussuri valley is rich agricultural country and timberland; iron ore, coal, lead, zinc; fishing. Ussurisk is an important industrial center. Part of Maritime Province (*q.v.*) 1860–1920; part of Far Eastern Region 1920–36; made a krai 1936.

Prince \ˈprin(t)s\. County, Prince Edward I., Canada. See table at PRINCE EDWARD ISLAND.

Prince Al·bert \-ˈal-bərt\. City, S cen. Saskatchewan, Canada, on North Saskatchewan river 83 m. NNE of Saskatoon; pop. (1971p) 27,613; resort; flour, dairy products, beer;

packing plants, oil refineries, sawmills; Notre Dame Coll. (1958); settled 1866.

Prince Albert National Park. See CANADA, *National Parks.*

Prince Albert Peninsula. NW section of Victoria I., W Franklin dist., Northwest Territories, Canada.

Prince Albert Sound. Inlet, W Victoria I., W Franklin dist., Northwest Territories, Canada.

Prince Charles Foreland \-'chär(ə)lz-\. Island, W of Spitsbergen I., Norway, from which it is separated by **Foreland Sound;** 60 m. long; area 241 sq. m.; has high mountain peaks.

Prince Charles Island. Island of Canadian Arctic Archipelago, E Franklin dist., Northwest Territories, in Foxe Basin; 3639 sq. m.; discovered 1948.

Prince Ed·ward \-'ed-wərd\. 1 County in Virginia. See table at VIRGINIA.

2 County, Ontario, Canada. See table at ONTARIO.

Prince Edward Island. Island in the Gulf of St. Lawrence, constituting a province of Canada; 2184 sq. m.; pop. (1970e) 110,000, (1966c) 108,535; ❋ Charlottetown. Separated from New Brunswick and Nova Scotia by Northumberland Strait; very irregular in shape with many deep inlets. Highest point ab. 465 ft.; livestock raising, fishing; vegetables; tourism. Chief towns: Charlottetown, Summerside. Divided into the following three counties:

NAME	LOCATION	AREA[1] (sq. m.)	POP. (1966c)	CO. SEAT
Kings	E	641	18,015	Georgetown
Prince	W	778	42,688	Summerside
Queens	cen.	765	47,832	Charlottetown

[1]Land area.

History: Discovered by Jacques Cartier 1534; called **Île–St–Jean** \ēl-saⁿ-zhäⁿ\ *or Eng.* **Isle St. John** \ˌīl-sānt-'jän, -sənt-\ by Champlain; renamed 1798 after Edward, Duke of Kent; colonized by French; ceded to British 1763 and became separate province 1769; resettled by Scottish immigrants at beginning of 19th cent.; entered Confederation 1873.

Prince Edward Island National Park. See CANADA, *National Parks.*

Prince Edward Islands. Two islands, S Indian Ocean, 46°35′S, 37°56′E; belong to Rep. of South Africa.

Prince Fred·er·ick \-'fred-(ə-)rik\. Town, ⊗ of Calvert co., S Maryland.

Prince George \-'jȯ(ə)rj\. 1 County in SE Virginia. See table at VIRGINIA.

2 Village, its ⊗.

3 City, cen. British Columbia, Canada, at confluence of Fraser and Nechako rivers; pop. (1971p) 32,755; summer resort; lumber, dairy products; diversified agriculture.

Prince Georg·es \-'jȯ(ə)r-jəz\. County in Maryland. See table at MARYLAND.

Prince Har·ald Coast \-ˌhar-əld-\. Section of coast, East Antarctica, on Indian Ocean, ab. 69°31′S, 36°E; part of Queen Maud Land.

Prince Island. See PRINCIPE ISLAND.

Prince of Wales, Cape \-'wā(ə)lz\. Cape on Bering Strait at W tip of Seward Penin., Alaska; most westerly point of mainland of North America, 65°40′N, 168°05′W.

Prince of Wales Island. 1 Largest island of Alexander Archipelago, in S part, SE Alaska; ab. 135 m. long by 40 m. wide; 2587 sq. m.; has valuable mineral deposits, forests, salmon fisheries. Chief towns Hydaburg and Craig.

2 Island in Torres Strait W of Cape York, Queensland, Australia, just S of Thursday I.

3 Island, cen. Franklin dist., Northwest Territories, Canada, bet. Victoria I. and Somerset I.; 12,830 sq. m.

4 Island, Malaysia. See PENANG.

Prince of Wales Strait. Narrow channel bet. Banks I. and NW Victoria I., in W Franklin dist., Northwest Territories, Canada; ab. 170 m. long.

Prince Olav Coast \-ˌō-ləf-, -ləv-\. Section of coast of Antarctica, on Indian Ocean, 68°30′S, bet. 39° and 49°30′E; a part of Queen Maud Land; discovered 1930.

Prince Pat·rick Island \-ˌpa-trik-\. Island, one of the Parry Is., NW Franklin dist., Northwest Territories, Canada; 6081 sq. m.

Prince Re·gent Inlet \-'rē-jənt-\. Channel bet. E Somerset I. and NW Baffin I., off N Canada mainland; connects with Gulf of Boothia on the S and Lancaster Sound on the N; ab. 60 m. wide.

Prince Ru·pert \-'rü-pərt\. City, W British Columbia, Canada, on Pacific Ocean at head of Dixon Entrance 10 m. N of mouth of Skeena river; pop. (1971p) 15,355; important port and W terminus of Canadian National R.R.; lumber and pulp mills, halibut fisheries, cold-storage plants.

Prince Rupert's Land ***also*** **Rupert's Land.** Historical region, N and W Canada, comprising drainage basin of Hudson Bay; granted 1670 by King Charles II to Hudson's Bay Company, purchased from it 1869 by the Dominion.

Princes Islands. See KIZIL ISLANDS.

Prin·cess Anne \ˌprin(t)-səs-'an\. Town, ⊗ of Somerset co., SE Maryland; pop. (1970c) 975; Maryland State Coll. (1886).

Princess As·trid Coast \-'as-trəd-\. Section of coast of East Antarctica, on South Atlantic Ocean, ab. 74°45′S, bet. 5° and 20°30′E; part of Queen Maud Land.

Princess Char·lotte Bay \-'shär-lət-\. Inlet of Coral Sea on NE coast of Queensland, Australia, W of Cape Melville.

Princess Mar·tha Coast \-'mär-thə-\ *or formerly* **Crown Princess Martha Land.** Section of coast of Antarctica E of Coats Land and of Weddell Sea; ab. 72°S, 7°30′W; largely ice-covered; a part of Queen Maud Land.

Princess Ragn·hild Coast \-'räŋ-ən-ˌhil-\. Section of coast of Antarctica, ab. 70°15′S, bet. 20°30′ and 34°E long.; part of Queen Maud Land.

Princess Royal Island. Island off the coast of British Columbia, Canada, 52°57′N, 128°49′W; 870 sq. m.; borders on Caamaño Sound on the W.

Prince·ton \'prin(t)-stən\. 1 City, ⊗ of Bureau co., N Illinois, 33 m. W of Ottawa; pop. (1970c) 6259; packs vegetables; fertilizer; poultry, grain farms.

2 Residential city, ⊗ of Gibson co., SW Indiana, 27 m. N of Evansville; pop. (1970c) 7431.

3 City, ⊗ of Caldwell co., W Kentucky, 42 m. E of Paducah; pop. (1970c) 6292; tobacco and livestock market; hosiery; agriculture.

4 Village, Mille Lacs co., E cen. Minnesota, 28 m. E of St. Cloud; pop. (1970c) 2531; ships dairy products.

5 City, ⊗ of Mercer co., N Missouri, 42 m. N of Chillicothe; pop. (1970c) 1328; fruit, dairy farms.

6 Borough, Mercer co., W cen. New Jersey, 11 m. NNE of Trenton; pop. (1970c) 12,311; residential and educational center; printing and publishing; Princeton Univ. (1746), Westminster Choir Coll. (1926), Saint Joseph's Coll. (1938). Founded by Quakers 1696; scene of battle of Princeton Jan. 2–3, 1777 in American Revolution; seat of Continental Congress June–Nov. 1783.

7 City, ⊗ of Mercer co., S West Virginia, 11 m. NE of Bluefield; pop. (1970c) 7523; missile components, concrete products, clothing, soap; diversified agriculture. Settled 1826; scene of engagements in Civil War May 16, 1862; burned by retreating Confederates.

Princeton, Mount. Peak in Sawatch Range, Chaffee co., cen. Colorado; 14,197 ft.

Prince·ville \'prin(t)s-ˌvil\. Town, Arthabaska co., S Quebec, Canada, 54 m. SW of Quebec; pop. (1971p) 3827.

Prince Wil·liam \-'wil-yəm\. County in Virginia. See table at VIRGINIA.

Prince William Sound. Inlet of Gulf of Alaska, S Alaska, E of Kenai Penin.; 90 to 100 m. across; Montaque I. and Hinchinbrook I. lie across its entrance.

Prin·ci·pe Island\'prin(t)-sə-ˌpā-\ *also* **Prince Island** \'prin(t)s-\. Portuguese island in the Gulf of Guinea, N of

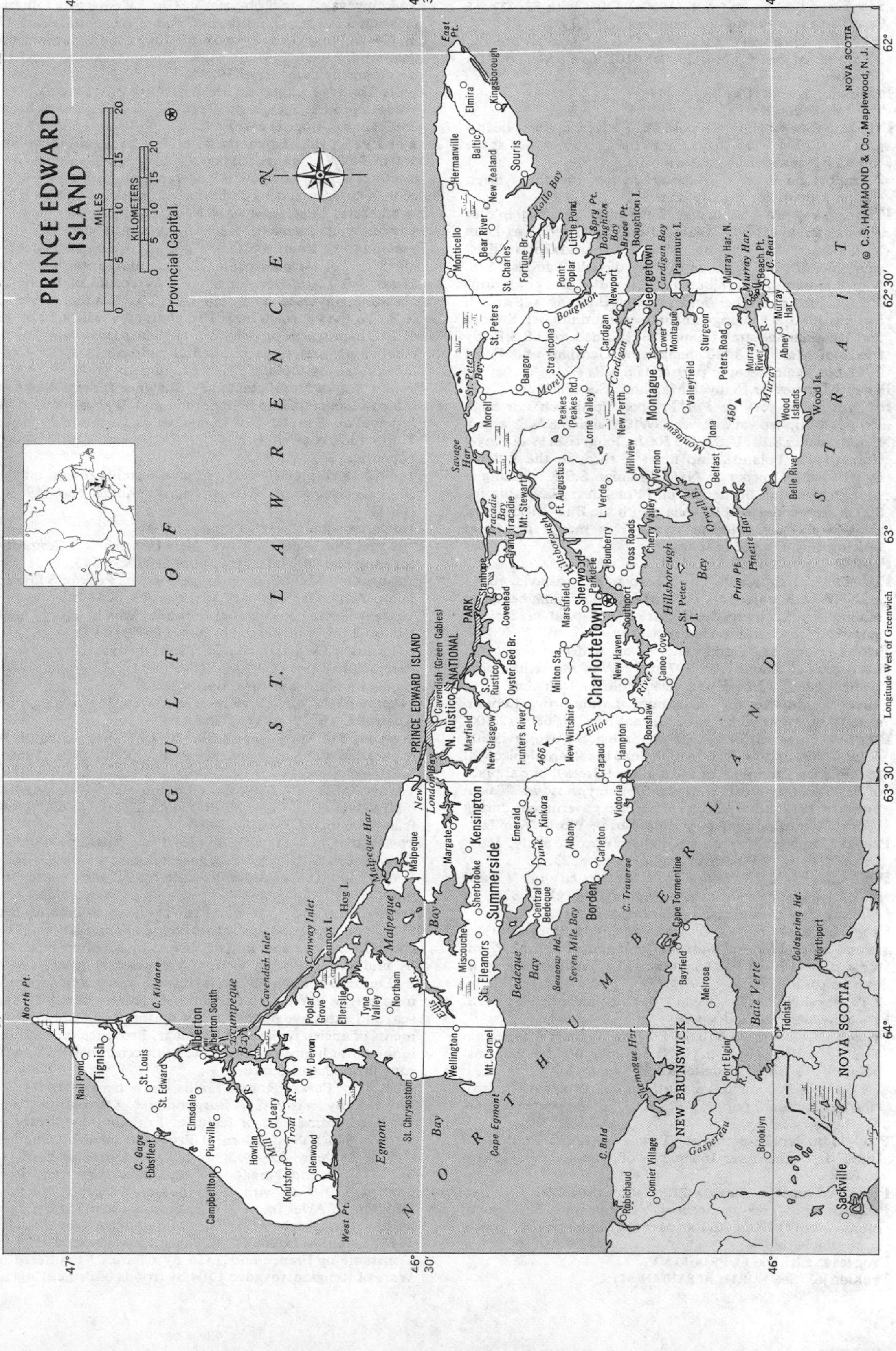
PRINCE EDWARD ISLAND
MILES
0 5 10 15 20
KILOMETERS
0 5 10 15 20
Provincial Capital
G U L F O F S T. L A W R E N C E
N O R T H U M B E R L A N D S T R A I T
PRINCE EDWARD ISLAND NATIONAL PARK
Charlottetown
Summerside
Kensington
Georgetown
Montague
Souris
Alberton
Tignish
Borden
NEW BRUNSWICK
NOVA SCOTIA
Longitude West of Greenwich
© C.S. HAMMOND & Co., Maplewood, N.J.

São Tomé ; 42 sq. m.; pop (1960c) 4305; with São Tomé (*q.v.*) forms a Portuguese overseas territory.

Prine·ville \ˈprīn-ˌvil\. City, ⊗ of Crook co., cen. Oregon, 30 m. NE of Bend; pop. (1970c) 4101; livestock, poultry, potatoes.

Prinkipo. See BÜYÜKADA.

Prinsen. See PANAITAN.

Prin·za·pol·ca \ˌprin(t)-sə-ˈpȯl-kə\. 1 River, E cen. Nicaragua; ab. 120 m. long; flows E into the Caribbean Sea at the town of Prinzapolca; gold deposits.

2 Seaport on E coast of Nicaragua, at mouth of river; shipping point for nearby mines.

Pri·o·zersk \ˌprē-ə-ˈzersk\ *or* **Keks·golm** \ˈkeks-ˌgōm\ *or Finnish* **Kä·ki·sal·mi** \ˈkäk-i-ˌsäl-mē\ *or Swed.* **Kex·holm** \ˈkeks-ˌhōm, cheks-ˈhȯlm\. Town, Leningrad Oblast, Russian S.F.S.R., U.S.S.R., on W shore of Lake Ladoga 75 m. N of Leningrad; has rail connection with Leningrad; principal trade in lumber and granite. Built as a Swedish fortress 1293–95; changed hands several times bet. Swedes and Russians; became Finnish 1811; ceded to U.S.S.R. by treaty of Mar. 12, 1940; retaken by Germans and Finns 1941 but again became part of U.S.S.R.

Pripet Marshes *or* **Pripyat Marshes.** See POLESYE.

Pri·pyat \ˈprip-yət\ *or Pol.* **Pry·peć** \ˈprip-ˌech\ *or angl.* **Pri·pet** \ˈprip-ˌet, -ət\. River, NW Ukrainian S.S.R. and S Belorussian S.S.R., U.S.S.R.; 500 m. long; rises W of Kovel (formerly in Poland), and flows E through the Polesye (*q.v.*) to the Dnieper in NW Ukrainian S.S.R., joining it near Belorussian border 50 m. N of Kiev. Navigable for 300 m. and connected by canals with the Bug (tributary of the Vistula) and Neman rivers. Has many tributaries flowing through the marshes.

Prishib. See LENINSK 2.

Priš·ti·na \ˈprish-ti-ˌnä\. Town, Serbia, S Yugoslavia, ab. 48 m. NNW of Skopje; pop. (1971p) 69,524; trading center in mining region; in medieval period a capital of Serbian empire; 14th cent. monastery nearby.

Pri·vas \prē-ˈvä\. Commune, ✱ of Ardèche dept., SE France, W of Rhone river 107 m. NNW of Marseilles; pop. (1962c) 9207; a Protestant stronghold in 16th cent.

Pri·ver·no \prē-ˈver-nō\. Commune, Latina prov., Latium, cen. Italy, 16 m. E by N of Latina; pop. (1968e) 12,300.

Priz·ren \ˈpriz-ˌren, ˈprēz-\. Town, Serbia, S Yugoslavia, ab. 40 m. WNW of Skopje; pop. (1965e) 31,000; archiepiscopal see (Roman Catholic), espiscopal see (Greek); burial place of Serbian king Dushan (d. 1355); many mosques. Taken by Serbs 1912; headquarters of Serbian government during World War I; occupied by Italy during World War II.

Priz·zi \ˈpret-sē\. Commune, Palermo prov., Sicily, Italy, 28 m. S by E of Palermo; pop. (1968e) 8523.

Pro·bo·ling·go \ˌprō-bə-ˈliŋ-(ˌ)gō\. Seaport city on N coast of East Java prov., Indonesia; pop. (1961c) 68,828; on Madura Strait 45 m. SE of Surabaja; fisheries.

Pro·ci·da \ˈprō-chi-də\ *or anc.* **Proch·y·ta** \ˈpräk-i-tə\. 1 Island in the Bay of Naples, Campania, Italy; ab. 2 m. long; pop. (1961c) 9050; highest point 250 ft.; made up of two volcanic craters.

2 Town on NE coast of island; has castle used as a prison.

Proconnesus. See MARMARA.

Proc·tor \ˈpräk-tər\. 1 Village, St. Louis co., NE Minnesota, 7 m. SW of Duluth; pop. (1970c) 3123; dairy, truck farms; before 1939 called **Proc·tor·knott** \-ˌnät\.

2 Village in Proctor town, Rutland co., W Vermont, 5 m. NNW of Rutland; pop. (1970c) 2095 (town); center of marble industry.

Prod·da·tur \ˈpräd-ə-ˌtu̇(ə)r\. Town, S Andhra Pradesh, S India, on Penner river 160 m. NW of Madras; pop. (1961c) 50,616.

Profile Mountain. See CANNON MOUNTAIN 2.

Progreso \prō-ˈgres-ō\. Seaport, Yucatán state, SE Mexico; munic. pop. (1970p) 22,100; port for Mérida; chief exports sisal, chicle, hides.

Progreso, El. See EL PROGRESO.

Prokletije. See NORTH ALBANIAN ALPS.

Pro·ko·pyevsk \prə-ˈkȯp-yəfsk\. City, Kemerovo Oblast, Russian S.F.S.R., U.S.S.R., in S end of Kuznetsk Basin 17 m. NW of Novokuznetsk; pop. (1970p) 275,000; important coal-mining center; flour mills, grain elevators; modern development dates from 1920's.

Proliv Dmitrya Lapteva. See DMITRI LAPTEV STRAIT.

Prome \ˈprōm\. 1 District, Pegu division, Lower Burma; 2593 sq. m.; pop. (1962e) 496,960; ✱ Prome.

2 *or* **Pyè** \ˈpyā\. Town, its ✱, on left bank of Irrawaddy 150 m. NNW of Rangoon; pop. (1953c) 36,997; ab. 5 m. SE is site of capital of Pyu state overcome by Burmese in 9th cent. A.D.; occupied by Japanese during World War II.

Promontore, Cape. See KAMENJAK, CAPE.

Promontorium Sacrum. See SAINT VINCENT, CAPE 2.

Prom·on·to·ry Point \ˈpräm-ən-ˌtōr-ē-, -ˌtȯr-\. Point forming S end of elevated peninsula extending into N part of Great Salt Lake, Box Elder co., NW corner of Utah; its coastline traversed by Lucin Cutoff of Southern Pacific R.R. To the N ab. 30 m. is **Promontory,** locality 30 m. W of Brigham where on May 10, 1869 last spike was driven completing first transcontinental railroad in U.S.; commemorated by Golden Spike Monument.

Proph·ets·town \ˈpräf-əts-ˌtau̇n\. Shawnee Indian village at the confluence of the Tippecanoe and Wabash rivers, W Indiana, ab. 7 m. NNE of Lafayette; destroyed in battle of Tippecanoe Nov. 7, 1811.

Propontis. See MARMARA, SEA OF.

Pro·priá \ˌprü-prē-ˈä\. City, Sergipe state, E Brazil, on the São Francisco 55 m. NNE of Aracaju; munic. pop. (1968e) 20,017.

Proskurov. See KHMELNITSKI.

Pros·pect \ˈpräs-ˌpekt\. Town, New Haven co., S Connecticut, 4 m. SE of Waterbury; pop. (1970c) 6543.

Pros·pec·tors Mountain \ˈpräs-ˌpek-terz-\. Peak in S Grand Teton National Park, NW Wyoming; 11,231 ft.

Prospect Park. 1 Residential borough, Passaic co., N New Jersey, 2 m. N of Paterson; pop. (1970c) 5176.

2 Borough, Delaware co., SE Pennsylvania, 10 m. SW of Philadelphia; pop. (1970c) 7250.

Prospect Point. See NIAGARA FALLS 2.

Prospect Reservoir. Large reservoir, New South Wales, SE Australia, ab. 12 m. W of Sydney.

Pros·pe·ri·dad \prȯ-ˌsper-i-ˈdäd, -ˈthäth\. Municipality, ✱ of Agusan del Sur prov., Mindanao, Phil.; pop. (1969e) 5200.

Pros·ser \ˈpräs-ər\. City, ⊗ of Benton co., S Washington, on Yakima river 48 m. SE of Yakima; pop. (1970c) 2964; fruit, livestock farms.

Pro·stě·jov \ˈprȯs-tə-ˌyȯf\ *or Ger.* **Pross·nitz** \ˈprȯ-snəts\. City, Czech S.R., cen. Czechoslovakia, ab. 30 m. NE of Brno; pop. (1968e) 36,965; textile mills; trade center for grain.

Pro·vence \prə-ˈväⁿs\ *or Lat.* **Pro·vin·cia** \prə-ˈvin-ch(ē-)ə\. Historical region of SE France; bounded anciently on N by Dauphiné, E by countship of Nice, S by Mediterranean, W by Languedoc, NW by Comtat Venaissin; ✱ Aix; watered by Durance and Rhone rivers; diverse topography, including plateaus in W, Alpine chains in E, ancient massifs along sea, and extensive plains; one of major provincial governments of ancien régime; its language, Provençal, important in medieval literature and, since 19th cent. revival, significant in modern literature.

History: Part of Roman Gallia Narbonensis (see GAUL); invaded by Visigoths, Burgundians, Ostrogoths, and Franks; became part of realm of Lothair I by Treaty of Verdun 843 A.D.; kingdom of Provence ruled by Charles, son of Lothair, 855–863; under the Emperor Louis II 863–875; second kingdom of Provence (Cisjurane Burgundy) 879–933; with Transjurane Burgundy became kingdom of Arles (*q.v.*) 933; made countship 1113; passed as dowry to Charles of Anjou 1246; under Angevin rule to 1481; passed to Louis XI of France 1481; invaded 1524 by Constable of France and 1536 by Charles V; suffered in Wars of Religion; invaded 1704 by troops of Prince Eugene and 1746 by duke of Savoy; province of France until Revolution.

Prov·i·dence \'präv-əd-ən(t)s, -ə-ˌden(t)s\. 1 Navigable river, a N arm of Narragansett Bay, formed by the confluence of two small rivers in the city of Providence, Rhode Island.
2 County in Rhode Island. See table at RHODE ISLAND.
3 City, Webster co., W Kentucky, 33 m. WSW of Henderson; pop. (1970c) 4270; coal mines, flour mill; tobacco.
4 Town, Maryland. See ANNAPOLIS 1.
5 Industrial city and port of entry, ❋ of Rhode Island and ⊗ of Providence co., N Rhode Island, at head of Providence river; pop. (1970c) 179,116; excellent harbor; textiles, jewelry, rubber, electronic equipment, metalware, machine tools; printing and publishing. Brown Univ. (1764), Rhode Island Coll. (1854), Bryant Coll. (1863), Rhode Island School of Design (1877), Pembroke Coll. (1891), Johnson and Wales Coll. (1914), Providence Coll. (1917), Rhode Island Junior Coll. (1964).

History: Founded by Roger Williams 1636 and became refuge for religious dissenters; joined "Incorporation of Providence Plantations" (chartered 1644); partly destroyed in King Philip's War; British revenue schooner *Gaspee* destroyed here 1772; in 18th cent. a major port in West Indies trade and in 19th cent. important center of textile industry; incorporated as city 1831.
6 Trading post, Canada. See FORT PROVIDENCE.
7 British island in the Indian Ocean, NNE of the Malagasy Republic, at 9°14′S, 51°02′E; ab. ½ sq. m.; pop. (1960c) 70; administratively part of Seychelles.

Providence Bay *or Russ.* **Pro·vi·de·ni·ya Bukh·ta** \ˌprə-vi-ˌden-ē-ə-'bük-tə\. Inlet of Bering Sea, SE of Chukotski Penin., Magadan Oblast, Russian S.F.S.R., U.S.S.R.

Providence Channel, North West *and* **North East Providence Channel.** Channels in the Bahama Is., bet. Atlantic Ocean and the Straits of Florida, S of Grand Bahama I. and Abaco I. and N of Bimini, Berry Is., and Eleuthera.

Providence Plantations. See RHODE ISLAND 2.

Pro·vi·den·cia, Is·la de \ˌēz-lä-dā-prō-və-'den(t)-sē-ə\. Small island in W Caribbean Sea off E coast of Nicaragua; belongs to Colombia and with San Andrés I. constitutes the intendancy of San Andrés y Providencia.

Prov·i·den·ci·a·les \ˌpräv-ə-ˌden(t)-sē-'äl-əs\. One of the Caicos I. See TURKS AND CAICOS ISLANDS.

Provideniya Bukhta. See PROVIDENCE BAY.

Prov·ince·town \'präv-in(t)s-ˌtaun\. Town, Barnstable co., SE Massachusetts, on N tip of Cape Cod; pop. (1970c) 2911; commercial fisheries; popular tourist resort; seat of Provincetown Players little theater group 1915–29. First landing place of Pilgrims Nov. 11 (Old Style), 1620; Mayflower Compact drawn up in harbor Nov. 21; incorporated 1727.

Province Welles·ley \-'welz-lē\. Mainland section of Penang state, Malaysia; 292 sq. m.; rice, rubber. Ceded to Great Britain by Kedah 1798; became part of Penang state 1957.

Provincia. See PROVENCE.

Provincias Vascongadas. See BASQUE PROVINCES.

Pro·vins \prō-'vaⁿ\. Town, E Seine-et-Marne dept., N France, ab. 25 m. E of Melun; pop. (1968c) 11,432; in wheat and sugar beet region; clay pits; three medieval churches. Flourished 9th–13th cents.; suffered from plague 14th cent., Hundred Years' War 14th–15th cents., and the religious wars of the 16th cent. during which it was besieged and taken by Henry IV 1592.

Pro·vo \'prō-(ˌ)vō\. 1 River, N cen. Utah; ab. 40 m. long; rises in W end of Uinta Mts., flows SW into Utah Lake; site of dam for irrigation and for Provo and Salt Lake City water supply.
2 Commercial and industrial city, ⊗ of Utah co., N cen. Utah, on Provo river 3 m. from Utah Lake 38 m. SSE of Salt Lake City; pop. (1970c) 53,131; manufactures steel and steel products, cast iron, building materials, electronic components, dairy products, canned fruit and vegetables; gold, copper, silver mines; tourist center; Brigham Young Univ. (1875); founded 1849 by Mormons; incorporated 1851.

Provo Peak. Mountain, Utah co., N cen. Utah, E of the city of Provo in the Wasatch Range; 11,068 ft.

Prow·ers \'prō-ərz\. County in Colorado. See table at COLORADO.

Proy·art \prwä-'yär\. Village, Somme dept., N France, 12 m. SW of Péronne; pop. (1962c) 469; battle Mar. 27–28, 1918.

Pru·dence Island \ˌprüd-ᵊn(t)s-\. Island in Narragansett Bay, a part of Newport co., Rhode Island, NW of Rhode I. (island).

Pru·den·tó·po·lis \ˌprü-den-'tò-pü-lēs\. Municipality, Paraná state, S Brazil, 110 m. WNW of Curitiba; pop. (1968e) 50,668.

Prud·hoe \'prəd-(ˌ)(h)ō\. Urban district, Northumberland, N England, on the Tyne 11 m. W of Newcastle upon Tyne; pop. (1971p) 11,015.

Prud·nik \'prüd-nik\; *Ger.* **Neu·stadt** \'nȯi-ˌs(h)tät\ *or* **Neustadt in Ober·schle·si·en** \-in-ˌō-bər-'shlā-zē-ən\. City, SW Śląsk prov., S Poland, W of Zabrze near Czechoslovakian border; pop. (1968e) 17,900; manufactures linen, damask, shoes, leather; formerly in Germany. Scene of battles bet. Prussians and Austrians 1745, 1760, 1779, in Silesian Wars and in War of the Bavarian Succession. Assigned to Poland by Potsdam Conference 1945.

Prusa. See BURSA 2.

Prus·sia \'prəsh-ə\ *or Ger.* **Preus·sen** \'prȯis-ᵊn\. Former German state, N and cen. Germany; 113,545 sq. m.; ❋ Berlin.

History: Early Prussians a people of Baltic stock dwelling along shore east of the Vistula; finally conquered, converted to Christianity, and colonized by Teutonic Knights 13th cent. (see EAST PRUSSIA); in 1466, W Prussia ceded by Teutonic Knights to Poland, while E Prussia became Polish fief; secularized and erected into duchy under Polish suzerainty 1525; in 17th cent., its ruler, Elector of Brandenburg, secured duchy's independence of Poland; kingdom of Prussia created from all holdings of Brandenburg (*q.v.*) 1701; as strong military state, especially under Frederick II 1740–86, Prussia expanded to include territories on Rhine, E Pomerania 1720, Silesia 1742–63, and W part of Poland (*q.v.*) 1772–95; received Rhine Province and part of Saxony 1815; provinces of West and East Prussia united 1824–78; strong German customs union (Ger. *Zollverein*) formed under Prussian leadership 1819–44; until 1918 ruled according to 1850 constitution; secured Lauenburg and administration of Schleswig (*q.v.*) 1865; after war against Austria 1866, annexed electoral Hesse, Nassau, Frankfurt, Hannover, Holstein, Austrian Silesia, and some South German territory; led North German Confederation 1867–71; German Empire (see GERMANY), of which Prussian king became Emperor William I, founded under Prussian leadership 1871; became republic 1918; annexed Waldeck 1929; after World War II by decision of Potsdam Conference 1945 lost the entire E part, portions of Silesia, Brandenburg, Pomerania, and East Prussia going to Poland and the N part of East Prussia to the U.S.S.R.; formally abolished by the Allied Control Council Mar. 1, 1947.

Prussia, East *and* **West.** See EAST PRUSSIA and WEST PRUSSIA.

Pruszcz Gdań·ski \ˌprüsh(ch)-gə-'dän(t)-skē, -'dan(t)-\ *or Ger.* **Praust** \'praust\. Commune, E cen. Gdańsk prov., N Poland, S of city of Gdańsk; pop. (1968e) 11,300.

Prusz·ków \'prüsh-(ˌ)küf\. Commune, Warszawa prov., NE cen. Poland, 7 m. WSW of Warsaw; pop. (1970p) 43,000.

Prut \'prüt\ *or Ger.* **Pruth** \'prüt\. River, E boundary of Romania; 565 m. long; rises in SW Ukrainian S.S.R., U.S.S.R., in the Carpathian Mts. and flows SSE into the Danube river at Reni, below Galaţi, 75 m. from the Black Sea. Formerly almost entirely within Romania, separating Moldavia from Bessarabia (now part of Moldavian S.S.R.). Treaty of the Pruth (July 21, 1711) signed on its banks near Iaşi by which Tsar Peter of Russia was compelled by the Turks to return Azov.

Pry·or \'prī-ər\. City, ⊗ of Mayes co., NE Oklahoma, 41 m. ENE of Tulsa; pop. (1970c) 7057; paper; diversified agriculture.

Prypeć. See PRIPYAT.

Pry·sor \'prī-zər\. River, Merionethshire, Wales. See PISTYLL CAIN FALLS.

Przas·nysz \pə-'shäs-nish, 'pshäs-\. Commune, Warszawa prov., NE cen. Poland, 53 m. N of Warsaw; pop. (1968e) 10,700; scene of battles of World War I bet. Germans and Russians Feb. and July 1915; Germans ultimately successful.

Prze·myśl \pə-'shem-ˌish(-əl), 'pshem-\ *or Russ.* **Pe·re·myshl** \ˌper-ə-'mish-əl\. City, E Rzeszów prov., SE Poland, on San river near border of Ukrainian S.S.R., U.S.S.R., and ab. 30 m. SE of Rzeszów; pop. (1970p) 53,200; metal and timber working; tourism. Founded before 10th cent.; to Poland 1340; to Austria 1772; in World War I a major Austrian fortress and twice besieged by Russians, Sept.–Oct. 1914 and Nov. 1914 to Mar. 1915, when it fell; recaptured by Austrians June 1915; to Poland 1918.

Przhe·valsk \ˌpər-zhə-'valsk\ *or formerly* **Ka·ra·kol** \ˌkär-ə-'kəl\. Town, NE Kirgiz S.S.R., U.S.S.R., at E end of Issyk-Kul; pop. (1967e) 40,000; center of agricultural region and of trade routes E and N; port for steamer traffic on the lake. Name changed in honor of the Russian explorer Nikolai M. Przhevalski, who died here 1888.

Psa·ra \(p)sə-'rä\ *or* **Ipsa·ra** \ˌēp-sə-'rä\ *or Gk.* **Psa·rá** \(p)sə-'rä\ *or anc.* **Psy·ra** \'sī-rə\. One of the Aegean Is., W of Chios; 35 sq. m.; captured by Turkey 1824; after Balkan War annexed to Greece 1914.

Psel *or* **Psiol** \(p)sē-'ōl\. River, E U.S.S.R., mostly in Ukrainian S.S.R.; 445 m. long; rises in Kursk Oblast and flows S to the Dnieper near Kremenchug; has winding course through fertile region.

Psiloriti. See IDA 3.

Pskov \pə-'skȯf, -'skȯv\ *or Estonian* **Pih·kva** \'pēk-(ˌ)vä\. City, ✱ of Pskov Oblast, Russian S.F.S.R., U.S.S.R., on Velikaya river near SE shore of Lake Pskov, 155 m. SW of Leningrad; pop. (1970p) 127,000; important railroad junction; produces linen, beer, footwear, machinery; 17th cent. cathedral.

History: One of the oldest and historically most important Russian cities; dates from 8th cent. A.D.; growth and history paralleled that of Novgorod; occupied by Teutonic Knights 1240; a dependency of Novgorod until 1348 but disputed between Russians, Germans, and Lithuanians; came under rule of Moscow 1510; besieged in 1502, 1581, and 1615; in World War II occupied by the Germans 1941–44 and suffered considerable damage.

Pskov, Lake *or Estonian* **Pihkva.** Southern arm of Lake Peipus, Russian S.F.S.R., U.S.S.R.; bet. Estonian S.S.R. and W Pskov Oblast; 274 sq. m.

Pskov Oblast \-'ō-bləst, -ˌblast\. Subdivision of NW Russian S.F.S.R., U.S.S.R.; 21,351 sq. m.; pop. (1970p) 876,000; ✱ Pskov. Occupies basins of Lovat, Shelon, and Velikaya rivers and includes part of Lake Peipus with many minor lakes and swamps; predominantly rural, with only major urban centers being Pskov and Velikiye Luki; principal economic activity agriculture (flax, dairying).

Psyra. See PSARA.

Pszczy·na \'psh(ch)in-ə\ *or Ger.* **Pless** \'ples\. Town, SE Katowice prov., SW Poland, ab. 20 m. S of Katowice; pop. (1968e) 17,600.

Ptar·mi·gan Peak \ˌtär-mi-gən-\. Mountain, Park and Lake cos., cen. Colorado; 13,736 ft.

Pteria. See BOGAZKÖY.

Ptol·e·ma·is \ˌtäl-ə-'mā-əs\. 1 Ancient town on left bank of Nile, Egypt, halfway bet. Hermopolis Magna and Thebae.
2 Seaport city, Israel. See ACRE.
3 Town, Libya. See TOLMETA.

Pu·call·pa \pü-'kī-pə\. Town, S Loreto dept., NE Peru, on the lower Ucayali river; pop. (1969e) 43,000.

Pu·cio Point \ˌpü-sē-ˌō-\. Northwestern point of Panay I. and of Antique prov., Phil.; marks boundary with Capiz.

Puck·a·way, Lake \-'pək-ə-ˌwā\. Lake in W Green Lake co., cen. Wisconsin.

Puck·le·church \'pək-əl-ˌchərch\ *or Old English* **Pu·clan Cyr·can** \ˌpü-klän-'kur-kän\. Ancient locality, Gloucestershire, SW England, ab. 10 m. NE of Bristol; Edmund I, king of the English, killed here 946.

Pu·djut, Point \-pu̇-'jüt\; *formerly* **Saint Nich·o·las Point** \-ˌnik-(ə-)ləs-\ *or Du.* **Sint Ni·co·laas Punt** \sint-ˌnē-kə-ləs-'pənt\. Cape at NW end of the island of Java, Indonesia, on Sunda Strait where the strait opens into Java Sea. Naval battle off this point Feb. 28, 1942 in which U.S.S. *Houston* and H.M.A.S. *Perth* were destroyed by Japanese.

Pud·sey \'pəd-zē\. Municipal borough, West Riding, Yorkshire, N England, 6 m. W of Leeds; pop. (1971p) 38,127; textiles; tanneries, foundries.

Pu·duk·kot·tai \ˌpu̇d-ək-'kō-ˌtī\. 1 Former Indian state, now part of Tamil Nadu state, S India, bet. Thanjavur and Madura; 1185 sq. m.
2 Town, its ✱, 38 m. SSW of Thanjavur; pop. (1961c) 50,488.

Pue·bla \pü-'eb-lə, 'pweb-, pyü-'eb-\. 1 State of SE cen. Mexico. See table at MEXICO.
2 *or in full* **Puebla de Za·ra·go·za** \-dā-ˌzar-ə-gō-zə, -ˌsär-ə-'gō-sə\. City, its ✱, ab. 75 m. SE of Mexico City; pop. (1969e) 383,879; altitude 7093 ft.; diversified light industry, including onyx, tiles, cotton, leather goods, glass, soap, pottery; two universities; notable for Spanish-style architecture; 16th cent. cathedral, 18th cent. theater.

History: Founded as **Puebla de los An·gel·es** \-dā-lȯs-'äŋ-he-lās\ by Spanish 1532; occupied by U.S. forces under Winfield Scott 1847; scene of victory of Mexicans under Ignacio Zaragoza over French May 5, 1862; occupied by French May 1863–April 1867.

Pu·eb·lo \pü-'eb-(ˌ)lō, 'pweb-, pyü-'eb-\. 1 County in SE cen. Colorado. See table at COLORADO.
2 Industrial and commercial city, its ⊗, on Arkansas river 40 m. SSE of Colorado Springs; pop. (1970c) 97,453; alt. 4690 ft.; manufactures iron, steel, and aluminum, lumber, concrete products, plumbing supplies, automobile parts, beer; center of an irrigated agricultural region producing onions, squash, canteloupe, and cucumber seed and near the major Colorado coalfields; Southern Colorado State Coll. (1933); U.S.Army ordnance depot. Founded by gold miners c. 1858; incorporated as town 1870, as city 1873; severely damaged by floods 1921.

Pueblo Bo·ni·to \-bə-'nēt-(ˌ)ō\. Largest of prehistoric pueblo ruins, Chaco Canyon National Monument, New Mexico; covers 3 acres; town flourished 10th–12th cents.

Pueblo Gran·de \-'gran-dē\. Prehistoric ruin, Maricopa co., SW cen. Arizona, 5 m. E of Phoenix; partly excavated mound is 30 ft. high, 300 ft. long, 150 ft. wide, surrounded on three sides by a wall containing a remarkable amount of stone for a pueblo ruin.

Pueblonuevo. See PEÑARROYA-PUEBLONUEVO.

Pue·blo Vie·jo, La·gu·na del \lə-'gü-nə-ˌdel . . . vē-'e-(ˌ)hō\. Inlet of Gulf of Mexico in E cen. Mexican coast, S of the mouth of the Pánuco river.

Puen·te Al·to \pu̇-ˌent-ē-'äl-(ˌ)tō\. City, Santiago prov., cen. Chile, just S of Santiago; pop. (1966e) 65,701.

Puen·te·á·re·as \pu̇-ˌent-ē-'är-ē-əs\. Commune, Pontevedra prov., NW Spain, 18 m. SSE of Pontevedra; pop. (1970p) 14,497.

Puente del In·ca \-de-'liŋ-kə\. Natural bridge in the Andes Mts., W Argentina, W of city of Mendoza; height 65 ft. over the Cuevas river; length of span 70 ft.; width 90 ft.

Puente–Ge·nil \-hā-'nē(ə)l\. Commune, Córdoba prov., S Spain, 35 m. S of Córdoba; pop. (1970p) 26,442; agricultural products; stone and lime quarries; manufactures soap, leather, flour, pottery.

Pu·eo Point \pü-'ā-(,)ō-\. Cape on E cen. coast of Niihau I., Hawaii.

Puer·co \'pwer-(,)kō\. River, NW New Mexico and E Arizona; ab. 120 m. long; rises in McKinley co., NW New Mexico, flows SW across Arizona border and joins the Little Colorado river in E cen. Arizona, in Navajo co.

Puer·ta, Point \-'pwert-ə\. Cape on E coast of Puerto Rico.

Puer·to Ar·mue·lles \,pwert-ō-är-'mwā-(y)əs\. Pacific coast port, Chiriquí prov., extreme W Panama, on Charco Azul Bay; pop. (1970p) 12,022.

Puerto Arrecife. See ARRECIFE.

Puerto Aya·cu·cho \-,ī-ə-'kü-(,)chō\. Town, ✱ of Amazonas territory, S Venezuela, on the Orinoco and on Colombia border; pop. (1961c) 5465.

Puerto Ay·sén \-ī-'sān\ *also* **Aysén.** Commune, ✱ of Aysén prov., S Chile; pop. (1960c) 5488.

Puerto Ba·rrios \-'bär-ē-,ōs\. Seaport, ✱ of Izabal dept., E Guatemala, on Gulf of Honduras ab. 150 m. NE of Guatemala City; pop. (1971e) 29,425; ships bananas.

Puerto Bello. See PORTOBELO.

Puerto Be·rrio \-'ber-ē-,ō\. River port, Antioquia dept. NW Colombia, on Magdalena river ab. 320 m. S of Barranquilla; pop. (1968e) 32,016.

Puerto Bo·lí·var \-bə-'lē-,vär\. Port on SW coast of Ecuador, 75 m. S of Guayaquil; the port of Machala (*q.v.*).

Puerto Ca·be·llo \-kə-'bā-(,) (y)ō\. Seaport, Carabobo state, N Venezuela, 70 m. W of Caracas; pop. (1970e) 70,598; the port of Valencia, exporting agricultural produce; has drydocks and naval base. During colonial period frequently sacked by pirates; heavily damaged in Wars of Independence, during which it changed hands several times.

Puerto Ca·rre·ño \-kə-'ren-(,)yō\. Town, ✱ of Vichada commissary, E Colombia, at the junction of the Meta with the Orinoco; pop. (1964p) 1449.

Puerto Cas·ti·lla \-kä-'stē-(y)ə\. Seaport on N coast of Honduras, across a bay just N of Trujillo; built and developed by the United Fruit Company; exports bananas; founded 1525 by an agent sent by Cortes.

Puerto Co·lom·bia \-kə-'lōm-bē-ə\. Coastal commune, Atlántico dept., N Colombia, 12 m. NW of Barranquilla, and formerly its port; now a seaside resort.

Puerto Cor·tés \-kȯr-'tes\. Seaport, Cortés dept., NW Honduras, on the Gulf of Honduras; pop. (1961c) 17,000; largest Atlantic port in Honduras; exports bananas; founded c. 1525.

Puerto del Ro·sa·rio \-del-rō-'sä-rē-ō\ *or formerly* **Puerto de Ca·bras** \-də-'käb-rəs\. Chief port of Fuerteventura I., Canary Is., Spain; pop. (1970p) 6680.

Puerto de San·ta Ma·ría \-də-,sänt-ə-mə-'rē-ə\ *or* **El Puerto** \el-\. Commune, Cádiz prov., SW Spain, on Bay of Cádiz at mouth of Guadalete river 8 m. NE of Cádiz; pop. (1970p) 42,111; produces and exports sherry wine; manufactures leather, soap, glass, flour; Gothic church.

Puerto De·se·a·do \-,des-ē-'äd-(,)ō\. Town and bay on E coast of Santa Cruz prov., S Argentina, at the mouth of Deseado river; pop. (1960c) 3120.

Puerto Gallegos. See GALLEGOS 2.

Puerto Ibañeta. See RONCESVALLES.

Puerto La Cruz \-lə-'krüz, -'krüs\. City and port, Anzoátegui state, N Venezuela, NE of Barcelona; pop. (1970e) 82,059; oil refineries.

Puerto Lem·pi·ra \-lem-'pir-ə\. Town, ✱ of Gracias a Dios dept., E Honduras; pop. (1961c) 104.

Puerto Li·món \-li-'mōn\ *or* **Limón** *also* **Port Limón.** Seaport, ✱ of Limón prov., E cen. Costa Rica; pop. (1968e) 22,555; chief port of Costa Rica; center of the banana trade; exporting port for coffee shipments.

Puer·to·lla·no \,pwert-ᵊl-'yän-(,)ō, ,pwert-ə-'yän-\. Commune, Ciudad Real prov., S cen. Spain, 24 m. SSW of Ciudad Real; pop. (1970p) 53,001; mineral baths; agricultural products; coal, iron, lead, manganese mines.

Puerto Ma·dryn \,pwert-ō-'mäd-rən\ *also* **Port Madryn.** Seaport, on NE coast of Chubut prov., S Argentina, on New Gulf; pop. (1960c) 5586.

Puerto Mal·do·na·do \-,mäl-də-'näd-(,)ō\. Town, ✱ of Madre de Dios dept., SE Peru, at junction of the Tambopata and Madre de Dios rivers ab. 525 m. E of Lima; pop. (1961c) 3500.

Puerto México. See COATZACOALCOS 2.

Puerto Montt \-'mȯnt\. Seaport, ✱ of Llanquihue prov., S cen. Chile, 12 m. S of Lake Llanquihue; pop. (1966e) 49,473; terminus of the southern railroad.

Puerto Mu·tis \-'müt-əs\. Pacific coast port, SW cen. Panama, at the head of the Gulf of Montijo.

Puerto Na·ta·les \-nə-'täl-əs\. Town, Magallanes prov., S Chile, N of the Strait of Magellan near Argentina border; pop. (1960c) 9399.

Puerto Orotava. See LA OROTAVA.

Puerto Pa·dre \-'päd-rē\. Town and municipality, Oriente prov., E Cuba; town on inlet on N coast 30 m. NW of Holguín; munic. pop. (1967e) 118,010.

Puerto Pi·nas·co \-pi-'näs-(,)kō\. Town, Boquerón dept., NW Paraguay, on W bank of Paraguay river ab. 178 m. N of Asunción; pop. (1970e) 10,245; makes quebracho products.

Puerto Pla·ta \-'plät-ə\. **1** Province, N Dominican Republic. See table at DOMINICAN REPUBLIC.
2 *or formerly* **San Fe·li·pe de Puerto Plata** \,sän-fə-'lē-pēd-ə-\. Commune and seaport city, its ✱; munic. pop. (1970p) 74,480; exports tobacco, sugar, hides, coffee, cacao, hardwoods.

Puerto Prin·ce·sa \-prin-'ses-ə\. Municipality, ✱ of Palawan I., Phil., on sheltered harbor in cen. part of E coast; pop. (1969e) 32,100; handles most of the trade of the island. In Spanish times a penal colony; succeeded Cuyo as capital ab. 1903; occupied by U.S. forces Feb. 28, 1945.

Puerto Príncipe. See CAMAGÜEY.

Puerto Re·al \-rā-'äl\ *or anc.* **Por·tus Gad·i·ta·nus** \,pōrt-əs-,gad-ə-'tā-nəs, pȯrt-, -'tan-əs\. Seaport, Cádiz prov., SW Spain, on Bay of Cádiz 7 m. E of Cádiz; pop. (1970p) 19,569; rebuilt 1488 by Ferdinand and Isabella.

Puerto Ri·co \,pwert-ə-'rē-(,)kō, ,pōrt-, ,pȯrt-\; *officially* **Commonwealth of Puerto Rico** *or Span.* **Esta·do Li·bre Aso·ci·a·do Puerto Rico** \e-,stä-t͟hō-'lē-brā-ä-,sō-sē-'äd-(,)ō-\ *formerly* **Por·to Rico** \,pōrt-ə-'rē-(,)kō, ,pȯrt-\. A self-governing commonwealth in union with the U.S., an island of the West Indies, 70 m. E of Hispaniola; 3435 sq. m. (land area 3423 sq. m.); pop. (1970p) 2,689,932; ✱ San Juan. *Physical features:* Has coastal plain, narrow in S, mountain ranges in interior, highest point Cerro de Punta 4389 ft.; rivers not useful for navigation; the few lakes are very small and are located in the coastal plain. *Chief products:* Sugar, tobacco, fruits; livestock raising; copper; manufacturing: textiles, metal products, petrochemicals, rum; tourism. *Chief cities:* San Juan, Ponce, Bayamon.

History: Discovered by Columbus Nov. 19, 1493; no colonization attempted until 1508 when Ponce de León set out to explore the island; Caparra founded 1509 but abandoned 1511; de León made governor 1510; after gold supply depleted, island neglected by Spain until 1533 when fortifications around San Juan were begun; first American troops landed on S coast July 25, 1898 during Spanish-American War; American occupation began Oct. 18, 1898, treaty ceding the island signed Dec. 10, 1898; name changed officially to Puerto Rico 1932; on adoption of constitution 1952 became a commonwealth with autonomy in internal affairs; its status approved by majority of electorate in 1967 plebiscite.

Puerto Rico Trench. See ATLANTIC OCEAN.

Puerto Sauce. See SAUCE.

Puerto Te·ja·da \ˌpwert-ō-tə-ˈhäd-ə\. Town, Cauca dept., SW Colombia, just S of Cali; munic. pop. (1968e) 21,250.

Puerto Va·ller·ta \-və-ˈler-tə\. Coastal town, Jalisco state, W cen. Mexico; munic. pop. (1970p) 35,542.

Puerto Va·ras \-ˈvär-əs\. City on Lake Llanquihue, Llanquihue prov., S cen. Chile, ab. 12 m. N of Puerto Montt; pop. (1960c) 10,305.

Puertoviejo. See PORTOVIEJO.

Puerto Wil·ches \-ˈwēl-(ˌ)chās\. River port, Santander dept., N cen. Colombia, on Magdalena river N of Barrancabermeja; munic. pop. (1968e) 25,272.

Pu·ga·chev \ˌpu̇g-ə-ˈchȯf\ *also* **Pu·ga·chevsk** \ˌpu̇g-ə-ˈchȯfsk\ *or formerly* **Ni·ko·la·evsk** \ˌnik-ə-ˈlī-əfsk\. Town, E Saratov Oblast, Russian S.F.S.R., U.S.S.R., 120 m. ENE of Saratov on the navigable Irgiz river; pop. (1967e) 35,000; a trading town, esp. in grain and farm products; terminus of a branch of the Saratov-Uralsk railroad. Founded 1762 by Raskolniks.

Puget Sound \ˌpyü-jət-\. Arm of Pacific Ocean extending S in W Washington from E end of Juan de Fuca Strait through Admiralty Inlet; ab. 80 m. long at its greatest extent; 561 sq. m.; important U.S. navy yard at Bremerton is on its W shore opp. Seattle. Explored by George Vancouver 1792.

Pugh, Mount \-ˈpyü\. Peak, Snohomish co., NW cen. Washington; 7150 ft.

Puglia *or* **Puglie, Le.** See APULIA.

Puig·cer·dá \ˌpwēg-sər-ˈdä\. Frontier commune, Gerona prov., NE Spain, 80 m. NNW of Barcelona; pop. (1970p) 5526. See BOURG-MADAME.

Pu·ji·lí \ˌpü-hi-ˈlē\. Town, Cotopaxi prov., cen. Ecuador, ab. 50 m. S of Quito; pop. (1962c) 2534.

Pu·ka·ki, Lake \-pu̇-ˈkäk-ē\. Lake, S cen. South I., New Zealand, near foot of Mt. Cook; 9½ m. long; 32 sq. m.

Pu·ka·pu·ka \ˌpü-kə-ˈpü-kə\. Chief island of the Danger Is., in Northern Cook Is. group, cen. Pacific Ocean, N of Cook Is.; ab. 2 sq. m.

Pu·kë \ˈpü-kə\. **1** Province of N Albania. See table at ALBANIA.
2 Town, its ✱, ab. 50 m. N of Tiranë; pop. (1967e) 1705.

Puket. See PHUKET.

P'u–k'ou *or* **Pu·kow** \ˈpü-ˈkō\. Port on N bank of the Yangtze, W Kiangsu prov., E China, opp. Nanking; railroad terminus of Tientsin-P'u-k'ou line (628 m. from Tientsin); has railroad ferry service and local river trade.

Pu·la \ˈpü-lə\ *or* **Pulj** \ˈpül-yə\ *or Ital.* **Po·la** \ˈpō-lə\ *or anc.* **Pi·e·tas Ju·lia** \ˌpī-ə-ˌtas-ˈjül-yə\. City, Croatia, NW Yugoslavia, on the Adriatic Sea ab. 45 m. SW of Rijeka; pop. (1965e) 45,000; naval base and shipbuilding center; considerable Roman remains (including temple, amphitheater, triumphal arch and city gates), Byzantine basilica.
History: Established as Roman military and naval base 178 B.C.; destroyed 39 B.C. in war against Illyrians and Dalmatians and rebuilt 35 B.C.; mere fishing village during Middle Ages; taken by Venetians 1148; scene of Genoese victory over Venetians 1379 and practically destroyed; to Austria by Peace of Campoformio 1797 and Congress of Vienna 1815; became chief Austro-Hungarian naval station; to Italy by Treaty of St-Germain 1919; in disputed region after World War II; assigned to Yugoslavia by treaty of 1947.

Pu·la·ca·yo \ˌpül-ə-ˈkī-(ˌ)ō\. Town, Potosí dept., SW Bolivia, 12 m. E of Uyuni; alt. 13,600 ft.; silver mine.

Pu·langi \pü-ˈläŋ-ē\. See MINDANAO 2.

Pu·lar \pü-ˈlär\. Peak, E Antofagasta prov., N Chile, near Argentina border; 20,423 ft.

Pu·las·ki \pə-ˈlas-kē, pyu̇-\. **1** Name of counties in seven states of the U.S. See tables at ARKANSAS, GEORGIA, ILLINOIS, INDIANA, KENTUCKY, MISSOURI, VIRGINIA.
2 Village, a ⊗ of Oswego co., cen. New York, near Lake Ontario 30 m. SSW of Watertown; pop. (1970c) 2480.
3 Town, ⊗ of Giles co., S Tennessee, 28 m. S of Columbia; pop. (1970c) 6989; lumber, clothing; phosphate mines; agriculture; Martin Coll. (1870).
4 Industrial town, ⊗ of Pulaski co., SW Virginia, in Allegheny Mts. 52 m. WSW of Roanoke; pop. (1970c) 10,279; hosiery, veneers, paper products; dairy, poultry farms.

Pu·lau \ˈpü-(ˌ)lau̇\ *also* **Poe·lau** \ˈpü-\ *or* **Pu·lo** \-(ˌ)lō\. Malay term meaning "island," often used with names of islands in the Malay Archipelago, as **Pulau Langkawi** (see LANGKAWI, PULAU).

Pu·ła·wy \pü-ˈläv-ē\. Industrial commune, Lublin prov., E Poland, on E bank of Vistula river, ab. 30 m. WNW of Lublin; pop. (1970p) 34,900; agricultural college; formerly seat of Czartoryski family.

Pul·i·cat \ˈpəl-i-kət\. **1** Town, Tamil Nadu, S India, at S end of Pulicat Lake; pop. (1961c) 4000; Dutch built fort here 1610; long their chief settlement on Coromandel Coast; several times captured, became British 1825.
2 Town, India. See PALGHAT.

Pulicat Lake. Shallow lagoon in Andhra Pradesh and Tamil Nadu, India, ab. 37 m. along coast W of Sriharikota I.

Pulj. See PULA.

Pul·ko·vo \ˈpül-kə-və, -ˌvō\. Village, cen. Leningrad Oblast, Russian S.F.S.R., U.S.S.R., 11 m. S of Leningrad; seat of national observatory 30°19'40"E, 59°46'19"N; founded 1839. Frequently used in U.S.S.R. as base for measurements instead of Greenwich.

Pul·liam Bluff \ˌpu̇l-yəm-\. Peak, S Brewster co., W Texas; 6921 ft.

Pull·man \ˈpu̇l-mən\. **1** Former industrial suburb of Chicago, Illinois, now a part of Chicago.
2 City, Whitman co., SE Washington, 65 m. S of Spokane; pop. (1970c) 20,509; dairy products; diversified agriculture; Washington State Univ. (1890).

Pulo. See PULAU.

Pu·log, Mount \-ˈpü-ˌlȯg\. Highest peak in N Luzon, Phil., at S end of Cordillera Central; 9606 ft.

Pultova *or* **Pultowa.** See POLTAVA.

Puł·tusk \ˈpül-ˌtüsk\. Industrial commune, Warszawa prov., NE cen. Poland, on Narew river 32 m. N of Warsaw; pop. (1966e) 11,800. Scene of Saxon defeat by Charles XII of Sweden Apr. 21, 1703; Russians defeated by French under Napoleon 1806; taken by Germans 1915 and 1939.

Pu·lu·wat \ˌpü-lə-ˈwät\. Atoll, cen. Caroline Is., W Pacific Ocean, 180 m. W of Truk.

Pum·mel Peak \ˈpəm-əl-\. Mountain, S Brewster co., W Texas; 6630 ft.

Pu·ná \pü-ˈnä\. Island in the Gulf of Guayaquil, SW Ecuador; 29 m. long.

Puna de Atacama. See ATACAMA, PUNA DE.

Pu·na·kha \ˈpün-ə-kə\. Town, W cen. Bhutan.

Punch. See POONCH.

Punchbowl. See HONOLULU 2.

Pune. See POONA 3.

Pún·goè *or* **Pun·gwe** \'pu̇ŋ-gwə\ *or Port.* **Pun·gue** \'pu̇ŋ-gwə\. River, S cen. Mozambique; ab. 200 m. long; flows SE into Indian Ocean at Beira.

Pun·jab \ˌpən-'jäb, -'jab, 'pən-ˌ\ *or Hind.* **Pan·jāb** \ˌpən-'jäb\. 1 Former province of British India; 99,089 sq. m.; included a number of Indian states under Punjab government, 38,146 sq. m.; total area 137,235 sq. m.; ✻ Lahore, summer ✻ Simla. Divided Aug. 1947 into East Punjab (*q.v.*), India, with ab. ⅓ the area and ½ the population of the original region, and West Punjab (see 4 below), Pakistan. Greater part occupied the valleys of the Indus and the five great tributaries (hence its name, Hind. *panj* five and *āb* waters) of the Indus: Jhelum, Chenab, Ravi, Beas, and Sutlej; these rivers now chiefly in West Punjab, the Sutlej forming part of the boundary. NE part (Kangra dist. in East Punjab) is wholly in the Himalayas. Has many evidences of prehistoric culture; was influenced by Alexander's Greek settlers 4th cent. B.C.; part of Asoka's empire 3d cent. B.C.; in succeeding centuries tributary to various rulers; from time of Mahmud of Ghazni (997–1030) to 18th cent. overrun by invading hosts (See PANIPAT); under the Sikhs 1799–1849; annexed to Brit. India 1846 and 1849; North-West Frontier Province set apart from it 1901 and Delhi prov. in 1912; constituted autonomous province 1937. See PAKISTAN.

2 Former state, India. See EAST PUNJAB.

3 *or* **Pun·jabi Su·ba** \pən-'jäb-ē-'sü-bə, -'jab-\. State, N India, formed from former Punjab state; 19,495 sq. m.; pop. (1971p) 13,472,972; ✻ Chandigarh; wheat, cotton, millets; important irrigation projects; largest cities: Amritsar, Jullundur, Ludhiana; formed 1966.

4 *formerly* **West Punjab** *or* **Western Punjab.** Province, Pakistan; 79,542 sq. m.; pop. (1969e) 30,427,000; ✻ Lahore; chief cities: Lyallpur, Multan, Rawalpindi; formed 1947 from former Punjab province; provincial status abolished 1955, reestablished 1970.

Punjab States. Group of Indian states under former Punjab government; ✻ Lahore.

Punjab States Agency. Former group of 45 Indian states and estates in the Punjab (see PUNJAB 1) in political relations with the crown representative through the resident at Lahore. The 14 most important of these (including Patiala, Bahawalpur, Khairpur, Chamba, Jind) had an area of 38,146 sq. m.; a second group, known as **Punjab Hill States** (most important Tehri Garhwal and Sirmur), had an area of 11,375 sq. m.

Pu·no \'pü-(ˌ)nō\. 1 Department of SE Peru. See table at PERU.

2 Town, its ✻, on W shore of Lake Titicaca 218 m. by rail E of Arequipa; pop. (1969e) 31,200; altitude 12,641 ft.; univ. (1962).

Pun Run, Lake \-pün-'rün\. Lake, Junín dept., cen. Peru; altitude ab. 14,200 ft.

Punt \'pu̇nt\. Ancient Egyptian name for a part of Africa not certainly identified, but probably the Somali coast. Visited by Queen Hatshepsut of the XVIIIth dynasty (reigned in 15th cent. B.C.), her voyage being depicted in reliefs in the Deir el-Bahri temple near Thebes; after this visit established trade with Egypt and for many years exported myrrh, gold, ebony, incense, also animals and fruits.

Punta, Cerro de. See CERRO DE PUNTA.

Pun·ta Al·ta \ˌpün-tə-'äl-tə\. Town, Buenos Aires prov., E cen. Argentina, ab. 20 m. SE of Bahia Blanca; pop. (1960c) 35,440.

Punta Are·nas \-ə-'rā-nəs\ *or* **Ma·ga·lla·nes** \ˌmäg-ə-'yän-əs\. Seaport city, ✻ of Magallanes prov., S Chile, on Brunswick Penin; pop. (1966e) 67,514; ships tallow, meat, wool; military and naval facilities; southernmost city in Chile (53°10′S); penal colony estab. 1843; town founded 1849.

Punta Argentera. See ARGENTERA, PUNTA.

Punta del Es·te \-del-'es-tē\. Town, Maldonado dept., S Uruguay, 70 m. E of Montevideo; seaside resort. In 1962 site of Inter-American Foreign Ministers Conference at which suspension of Cuba from active membership in the Organization of American States (*q.v.*) was agreed upon.

Punta de Pie·dras \-də-'pyā-drəs\. Town, Nueva Esparta state, Venezuela, on Margarita I. in Caribbean Sea off N coast of Venezuela.

Punta Gor·da \ˌpən-tə-'gȯr-də\. 1 City, ⊗ of Charlotte co., SW Florida, on Charlotte Harbor 20 m. in from Gulf of Mexico; pop. (1970c) 3879; yachting and fishing resort.

2 Seaport, ✻ of Toledo dist., S British Honduras; pop. (1967e) 2213; sugar, bananas, rice, and livestock.

Punta Mico. See MONKEY POINT.

Pun·ta·re·nas \ˌpün-tə-'rā-nəs\. 1 Province of W cen. Costa Rica. See table at COSTA RICA.

2 Seaport, its ✻, on Gulf of Nicoya; pop. (1970p) 31,162; exports bananas and coffee; fish processing.

Puntilla, La. See LA PUNTILLA.

Pun·to Fi·jo \ˌpün-to-'fē-(ˌ)(h)ō\. Town, Falcón state, NW Venezuela, on SW coast of Paraguaná Penin.; pop. (1970e) 53,075.

Punx·su·taw·ney \ˌpəŋk-sə-'tȯ-nē\. Borough, Jefferson co., W cen. Pennsylvania, 17 m. SW of Du Bois; pop. (1970c) 7792; textiles, beverages; foundry, coal mines; potatoes.

Pu·pa·yax \ˌpü-pə-'yäk\. Peak, W Bolivia, NE of Lake Titicaca; 19,080 ft.

Pu·quio \'pük-(ˌ)yō\. Town, Ayacucho dept., S Peru, ab. 100 m. S of Ayacucho; pop. (1961c) 8100.

Pu·ra·cé \ˌpu̇r-ə-'sā\. Active volcano, SW cen. Colombia, just SE of Popayán; 15,604 ft.; eruption during earthquake of 1827; eruption May 26, 1949.

Purali. See PORALI.

Pu·ra·ri \pu̇-'rär-ē\. River, E cen. New Guinea I., Papua New Guinea; ab. 170 m. long; flows generally SSE to Gulf of Papua.

Pur·beck, Isle of \-'pər-ˌbek\. Peninsula district in Dorsetshire, S England; 12 m. long; extends E into English Channel; harbor of Poole is on N; of geological interest; source of Purbeck marble.

Pur·bo·ling·go *or Du.* **Poer·ba·ling·ga** \ˌpu̇(ə)r-bə-'liŋ-gə\. Town, Central Java prov., Indonesia, NNE of Banjumas; pop. (1961c) 22,698.

Pur·cell \pər-'sel\. City, ⊗ of McClain co., cen. Oklahoma, on Canadian river 34 m. S of Oklahoma City; pop. (1970c) 4076; corn, alfalfa.

Purcell Mountains \'pər-səl-, pər-'sel-\. Subsidiary mountain range in SE British Columbia, Canada, bet. the Selkirk Mts. and the main range of the Rocky Mts.; highest Mt. Farnham 11,343 ft.

Pu·ré·pe·ro \pu̇-'rep-ə-ˌrō\ *or* **Purépero de Echaiz** \-dā-ā-'chīs\. Town, Michoacán state, SW Mexico, ESE of Zamora; munic. pop. (1970p) 26,477.

Pur·ga·toire \'pər-gə-ˌtwär, 'pik-ət-ˌwī(ə)r\. River, S and SE Colorado; 186 m. long; rises in W Las Animas co., flows NE into Arkansas river in Bent co.

Pur·ga·to·ry Peak \'pər-gə-ˌtōr-ē-, -ˌtȯr-\. Mountain, Costilla and Las Animas cos., S Colorado, in the Sangre de Cristo Mts.; 13,719 ft.

Pu·ri \'pu̇r-ē\ *or* **Ja·gan·nath** \'jəg-ə-ˌnät\ *or* **Jug·ger·naut** \'jəg-ər-ˌnȯt, -ˌnät\. Seaport town, E Orissa, E India, on Bay of Bengal 260 m. SSW of Calcutta; pop. (1961c) 60,815. One of the major centers of Hindu pilgrimage. Main temple (12th cent.) sacred to Krishna under the name Jagannath; scene of many festivals, including the Rathayatra, at which the image of Jagannath is carried through the streets on a huge car or *rath* with enormous wheels.

Puriramya. See BURIRAM.

ə abut; ᵊ kitten, Fr. table; ər further; a back; ā bake; ä cot, cart; ȧ Fr. bac; au̇ out; ch chin; e less, ē easy; g gift
i trip; ī life; j joke; k̲ Ger. ich, Buch; ⁿ Fr. vin; ŋ sing; ō flow; ȯ flaw; œ Fr. bœuf; œ̄ Fr. feu; ȯi coin; th thin
t͟h this; ü loot; u̇ foot; ue Ger. füllen; ue̅ Fr. rue; y yet; ʸ Fr. digne \dēnʸ\, nuit \nwʸē\; yü few; yu̇ furious; zh vision

Pur·me·rend \ˌpər-mə-ˈrent\. Commune, North Holland prov., W Netherlands, 8 m. NNE of Amsterdam; pop. (1970e) 23,288.

Pur·na \ˈpu̇(ə)r-nə\. River, cen. India; ab. 220 m. long; flows SE in NW Hyderabad to the upper Godavari river.

Pur·nea \ˈpər-nē-ə\. Town, NE Bihar, NE India, N of the Ganges ab. 50 m. NE of Bhagalpur; pop. (1961c) 40,602; trades in rice and jute.

Pursak. See PORSUK.

Pursat. See POUTHISAT.

Pu·ruán·di·ro \pu̇r-ˈwän-di-(ˌ)rō\. Town, Michoacán state, SW Mexico, just W of Lake Cuitzeo; munic. pop. (1970p) 71,523.

Pu·ru·lia \pə-ˈrü-lē-ə\. Town, West Bengal, NE India, 140 m. WNW of Calcutta; pop. (1961c) 48,134; road junction.

Pu·rus \pə-ˈrüs\. Navigable river, NW cen. South America; ab. 2100 m. long; rises in Andes Mts. in SE Peru, flows NE across Amazonas state, Brazil, and into Amazon river above Manaus.

Pur·vis \ˈpər-vəs\. Town, ⊗ of Lamar co., S Mississippi; pop. (1970c) 1860.

Pur·wa·kar·ta *or Du.* **Poer·wa·kar·ta** \ˌpu̇(ə)r-wə-ˈkärt-ə\. Town, West Java prov., Indonesia, ab. 60 m. SE of Djakarta; pop. (1961c) 45,610.

Pur·wo·da·di *or Du.* **Poer·wo·da·di** \ˌpu̇(ə)r-wə-ˈdäd-ē\. Town, Central Java prov., Indonesia; pop. (1961c) 15,811; railroad junction point 35 m. ESE of Semarang.

Pur·wo·ker·to *or Du.* **Poer·wo·ker·to** \ˌpu̇(ə)r-wə-ˈke(ə)rt-(ˌ)ō\. Town, Central Java prov., Indonesia, just NW of Banjumas; pop. (1961c) 80,556.

Pur·wo·re·jo *or Du.* **Poer·wo·red·jo** \ˌpu̇(ə)r-wə-ˈrej-(ˌ)ō\. Town, Central Java prov., Indonesia, ab. 25 m. SW of Magelang; pop. (1961c) 32,119.

Pu·san \ˈpü-ˌsän\ *or Jap.* **Fu·san** \ˈfü-ˌsän\. City, ✱ of South Kyŏngsang prov., SE South Korea, ab. 200 m. SSE of Seoul; 144 sq. m.; pop. (1970e) 1,880,710; major seaport and industrial center, with shipbuilding, textile, and metallurgical industries; railroad shops, rice mills, salt refineries; developed into major port under Japanese rule 1910–45; center of a beachhead held by UN forces during Korean War 1950.

Push·kar Lake \ˈpu̇sh-kər-\. Lake in E cen. Rajasthan, NW cen. India, 7 m. W of Ajmer; one of India's most sacred waters, it is scene of annual pilgrim fair and site of only temple in India dedicated to Brahma.

Push·kin \ˈpu̇sh-kən\; *formerly* **Tsar·sko·ye Se·lo** \ˌtsär-skə-yə-sə-ˈlō\ *also* **Det·sko·ye Selo** \ˌdet-skə-yə-sə-ˈlō\. Town, NW Leningrad Oblast, Russian S.F.S.R., U.S.S.R.; pop. (1969e) 73,000; a residential and resort suburb of Leningrad.

History: Originally a Finnish village taken by Russians under Peter the Great 1708 and presented to his wife Catherine as summer residence, Tsarskoye Selo ("The Tsar's Village"). Present palace built 1748–62 and was an important imperial residence until Revolution, when town was renamed Detskoye Selo ("Children's Village") and converted into a health resort; name later changed to Pushkin in honor of the Russian poet; palace buildings severely damaged in World War II but extensive restoration work has been undertaken since 1945.

Push·ki·no \ˈpu̇sh-kən-ə\. Town, Moscow Oblast, Russian S.F.S.R., U.S.S.R., 20 m. NE of Moscow; pop. (1967e) 41,000.

Push·ma·ta·ha \ˌpu̇sh-mə-ˈtä-(ˌ)hä, -(ˌ)hō\. County in Oklahoma. See table at OKLAHOMA.

Pusht–i–kuh. See POSHTKŪH.

Püs·pök·la·dány \ˈp(y)üsh-ˌpərk-ˈlō-ˌdän-yə\. Commune, Hajdú-Bihar co., E Hungary, 30 m. SW of Debrecen; pop. (1970p) 15,744.

Pu·ster·tal \ˈpu̇s-tər-ˌtäl\ *or* **Val Pu·ste·ria** \ˌväl-ˌpü-stə-ˈrē-ə\. Valley, N of the Carnic Alps, NE Italy and W Carinthia, Austria.

Pu·tao \pü-ˈtau̇\ *or formerly* **Fort Hertz** \-ˈərts\. Government post in extreme N of Burma, S of Namni Pass; pop. (1962e) 14,300.

Pu·teaux \pyü-ˈtō\. Industrial commune, Hauts-de-Seine dept., N France, NW suburb of Paris on Seine river; pop. (1962c) 39,640.

Puteoli. See POZZUOLI.

Pu·ti·gna·no \ˌpüt-ē-ˈnyän-(ˌ)ō\. Commune, Bari prov., Apulia, SE Italy, 23 m. SE of Bari; pop. (1968e) 21,735.

Put–in–Bay \ˌpu̇t-ˌin-\. 1 Bay in South Bass I., Lake Erie, in Ottawa co., Ohio; scene of Commodore Perry's victory over the British fleet Sept. 10, 1813.

2 Village, Ottawa co., N Ohio, on Put-in-Bay; pop. (1970c) 135; vineyards; summer resort.

Pu·ting *or Du.* **Poe·ting** \ˈpü-ˌtiŋ\ *or* **Tan·djoeng Poeting** \ˌtän-ˌju̇ŋ-\. Cape on SW coast of Borneo, Indonesia, projecting into Java Sea, 3°31′S, 111°46′E.

Pu·tla de Gue·rre·ro \ˌpüt-lə-dā-gwə-ˈrer-ˌō\. Municipality, Oaxaca state, Mexico, 85 m. W of Oaxaca; pop. (1970p) 54,874.

Put·na \ˈpu̇t-nə\. River, NE Romania; 81 m. long; flows N, E, and SE into Siretul river.

Put·nam \ˈpət-nəm\. 1 Name of counties in nine states of the U.S. See tables at FLORIDA, GEORGIA, ILLINOIS, INDIANA, MISSOURI, NEW YORK, OHIO, TENNESSEE, WEST VIRGINIA.

2 Industrial city, Windham co., NE Connecticut, on Quinebaug river at mouth of Mill river 21 m. NE of Willimantic; pop. (1970c) 6918; silk, paper, woolens, hats; dairy farms; Cargill Falls near center of city; incorporated 1895.

Put·ney \ˈpət-nē\. Ward of Wandsworth metropolitan borough, London, England.

P'u–t'o Shan *or* **Pu·to Shan** \ˈpü-ˈtō-ˈshän\ *or* **Puto** \ˈpü-ˈtō\ *also* **Poo·too** \ˈpü-ˈtü\. Small island in Chou-shan archipelago, Chekiang prov., E China, just SE of Chou-shan I.; one of the three sacred areas of Chinese Buddhism; has large monastery and is covered with temples, monuments, etc.; noted as scenic area and formerly as pilgrimage center.

Putrid Sea. See SIVASH.

Put·ta·lam \ˈpət-ᵊl-əm\. Seaport town, NW Ceylon, 80 m. N of Colombo; pop. (1968e) 15,000.

Puttiala. See PATIALA.

Pu·tu·ma·yo \ˌpüt-ə-ˈmī-(ˌ)ō\. 1 River, NW South America; ab. 980 m. long; rises in SW Colombia, flows SE, forming large section of Peru-Colombia boundary, crosses border into Brazil, where it is known as the **Içá** \ē-ˈsä\, and empties into Amazon river; flows through rubber-producing region.

2 Commissary of S Colombia. See table at COLOMBIA.

Puu Ku·kui \ˌpü-kə-ˈkü-ē\. Mountain, Maui I., at W end, Hawaii; 5787 ft.

Puu·la·ve·si \ˈpü-lə-ˌves-ē\. Lake, Mikkeli prov., S Finland; 154 sq. m.

Puu Poa Point \ˌpü-ˌpō-ə-\. Cape on N coast of Kauai I., Hawaii.

Puy. See LE PUY.

Puy·al·lup \pyü-ˈal-əp\. 1 River, W cen. Washington; ab. 50 m. long; flows NW into Puget Sound at Tacoma.

2 City, Pierce co., W cen. Washington, on Puyallup river 8 m. ESE of Tacoma; pop. (1970c) 14,742; lumber; fruit and vegetable packing; diversified agriculture.

Puy–de–Dôme \ˌpwēd-ə-ˈdōm\. Department of S cen. France. See table at FRANCE.

Puy de Dôme. See DÔME, PUY DE.

Puy de Sancy. See SANCY, PUY DE.

Pu·ye·hue, La·go \ˌläg-ō-pu̇-ˈyā-(ˌ)wā\. Lake in Osorno prov., S cen. Chile, N of Puerto Montt.

Puyehue National Park. National park, Chile; 290 sq. m.; volcanic activity; established 1941.

Puy–en–Velay, Le. See LE PUY.

Puy·mo·rens, Col de \ˌkȯl-də-ˌpwē-mō-ˈräⁿs\. Mountain pass, Pyrénées-Orientales dept., S France, in the Pyrenees just NE of Andorra; 6335 ft.

Pu·yo \'pü-yō\. Town, ❋ of Pastaza prov., cen. Ecuador; pop. (1970e) 3500.

Pwll·he·li \pül-'hel-ē\. Town, Caernarvonshire, NW Wales, on S coast of Lleyn Penin. on Cardigan Bay; pop. (1971p) 3832; market town; seaside resort.

Pyandzh. See PANDJ, AB-I-.

Pya·pon \pyä-'pōn\. 1 District, Irrawaddy division, Burma; 2136 sq. m.; pop. (1962e) 518,377; ❋ Pyapon.

2 Town, its ❋, in Irrawaddy delta 45 m. SW of Rangoon; pop. (1953c) 19,174.

Pyarnu. See PÄRNU.

Pya·si·na \'pyäs-ə-nə\. River, Krasnoyarsk Krai, Russian S.F.S.R., U.S.S.R.; 506 m. long; in W part of Taimyr Penin., flows N into the Arctic Ocean.

Pya·ti·gorsk \pē-ˌat-i-'gȯ(ə)rsk\ *also* **Pia·ti·gorsk** \pē-ˌat-i-'gȯ(ə)rsk\. Town, S Stavropol Krai, Russian S.F.S.R., U.S.S.R., on a tributary of the Kuma river 140 m. WNW of Grozny; pop. (1969e) 84,000; health resort, with mineral springs and ab. 15 sanatoria; on a plateau on the N slopes of the Caucasus.

Pyaw·bwe \'pyau̇-ˌbwā\. Town, cen. Burma, ab. 100 m. S of Mandalay; taken by British Apr. 11, 1945.

Pyd·na \'pid-nə\. Ancient town in Macedonia, N Greece; ruins on W shore of Gulf of Salonika. Scene of battle 168 B.C. in which the Romans under Aemilius Paulus defeated the Macedonians under their last king, Perseus, thus bringing to an end the independent Macedonian kingdom.

Pyè. See PROME 2.

Pyeitawinzu Myanma Naingngandaw. See BURMA.

Py·hä·häk·ki National Park \'pyü-ə-'hak-ē-\. National park, Finland; ab. 4 sq. m.; pine forest, swamp; established 1956.

Py·hä·kos·ki \'pyü-hə-ˌkȯ-skē\. Rapids in Oulu river near its mouth SE of Oulu, W Finland; known to Finns as the "Holy Rapids."

Py·hä·tun·tu·ri National Park \'pyü-ə-ˌtün-tər-ē-\. National park, N cen. Finland; ab. 12 sq. m.; most S arctic mountain in Finland; established 1938.

Pyin·ma·na \'pyin-mə-ˌnä\. Town on the Sittang river, Mandalay division, Burma; on railroad 150 m. S of Mandalay.

Py·los \'pī-ˌläs\ *or Gk.* **Pí·los** \'pē-ˌlȯs\. 1 Seaport, Greece. See NAVARINO 2.

2 Town, NW Peloponnese, Greece, on the Peneus river.

P'yŏng·yang \pē-'ȯŋ-ˌyäŋ, -'əŋ-, -ˌyaŋ\ *or Jap.* **Hei·jo** \'hā-(ˌ)jō\. City, ❋ of North Korea, on the Taedong river 30 m. from its mouth; 77 sq. m.; pop. (1966e) 1,364,000; a center of heavy industry, with cement, iron and steel, chemical, rubber, and textile plants, an arsenal, and railroad workshops; univ. (1946).

History: Site of a Chinese colony c. 108 B.C.; capital of Koguryo dynasty c. 37 B.C.–668 A.D.; made an industrial center under Japanese rule 1910–45; captured by UN forces during Korean War 1950 but retaken by Chinese Communist troops; suffered extensive damage from UN air raids but has been largely rebuilt since 1953.

Py·ote \'pī-ōt\. City, Ward co., W Texas, ab. 200 m. ESE of El Paso; pop. (1970c) 155.

Pyr·a·mid Lake \'pir-ə-ˌmid-\. Lake, S Washoe co., NW Nevada; ab. 30 m. long by 4–13 m. wide; 188 sq. m.

Pyramid Mountain. 1 Peak in Glacier National Park, NW Montana; 8100 ft.

2 Peak, Chelan co., cen. Washington; 8240 ft.

Pyramid Peak. 1 Mountain in Sierra Nevada, E cen. Eldorado co., E California; 9983 ft.

2 Mountain, Pitkin co., W cen. Colorado; 14,018 ft.

3 Mountain, NE Lemhi co., E cen. Idaho; 9594 ft.

4 Mountain, N Cascade Range, NW Washington; 7800 ft.

5 Mountain on E boundary of Yellowstone National Park, NW Wyoming; 10,047 ft.

Pyr·a·mids \'pir-ə-ˌmids\. Ancient monuments 5 m. W of Giza, near Cairo, Egypt, W of the Nile—the true pyramids, 3 in number: largest, Pyramid of Khufu (or Cheops), built by Khufu, 1st king of IVth dynasty, reigned c. 2900–2877 B.C.; second in size and age, Pyramid of Khafre (or Chephren), built by Khafre, 3d king of IVth dynasty, reigned c. 2850 B.C.; smallest and most perfect of the three, Pyramid of Menkure, built by Menkure, a king of the IVth dynasty, reigned c. 2800 B.C. Largest pyramid was originally ab. 482 ft. in height and had a base covering nearly 13 acres; built of huge limestone blocks fitted with great precision and had inner sepulchral chambers, sloping passages, etc. Other pyramids built in Egypt, esp. the Step Pyramid of Zoser at Saqqara (*q.v.*); also those (not true pyramids) erected by Assyrians and Mayas (see CHICHÉN ITZÁ, CHOLULA). The Battle of the Pyramids occurred July 21, 1798 across the Nile from Cairo and N of the Pyramids; it resulted in a victory for Napoleon over the Mamelukes and gave him control over Egypt; the victory neutralized by defeat of the French fleet Aug. 1–2, 1798 by Nelson in Battle of the Nile (see ABUKIR 2).

Pyramus. See CEYHAN 1.

Pyr·e·nees \'pir-ə-ˌnēz\ *or Fr.* **Py·ré·nées** \pē-rā-nā\ *or Span.* **Pi·ri·ne·os** \ˌpē-rē-'nā-(ˌ)ōs\ *or anc.* **Pyr·e·naei Mon·tes** \ˌpir-ə-ˌnē-ī-'män-tēz\. Mountain range extending along the French-Spanish border from the Bay of Biscay to the SW coast of the Gulf of Lions; ab. 270 m. long; highest peak Pico de Aneto 11,168 ft. in the Maladetas in cen. part; an effective barrier bet. the two countries, has principal highways only at ends near coasts; traversed by few passes, notably Somport, Poterla, and Puymorens, all over 5000 ft., and the pass at Roncesvalles 3576 ft. made famous by the *Chanson de Roland* and often used by armies; mountains noted for many streams (*gaves*) and waterfalls and for distinctive formations called *cirques*, deep, steep-walled amphitheatric recesses at upper ends of valleys.

Py·ré·nées \ˌpir-ə-'nā\. 1 Mountain range, Europe. See PYRENEES.

2 Departments of SW France: **Hautes–Pyrénées** \'ōt-\, **Pyrénées–At·lan·tiques** \ˌpir-ə-'nā-ˌzät-läⁿ-'tēk\ (formerly **Basses–Pyrénées** \'bäs-\), and **Pyrénées–Orien·tales** \-ˌzȯ-rē-aⁿ-'tal\. See table at FRANCE.

Pyr·gos \'pir-(ˌ)gȯs\ *or Gk.* **Pír·gos** \'pir-(ˌ)gȯs\. Town, ❋ of Elis dept., Peloponnese, Greece, 120 m. W of Athens; pop. (1971p) 20,380.

Py·rox·ene Peak \pə-ˌräk-sēn-\. Peak, Madison co., SW Montana; 9000 ft.

Py·sko·wi·ce \ˌpē-skȯ-'vēt-sə\. Town, Katowice prov., S Poland, ab. 20 m. WNW of Katowice; pop. (1970e) 23,100.

Pytho. See DELPHI 2.

Pyu \'pyü\. Town, cen. lower Burma, on railroad and highway W of the Sittang 30 m. S of Toungoo.

Q. For many names beginning with Q-, especially those of Arabic or Turkish origin, see the more usual forms in English beginning with K-; as, for **Qandahar, Qara Bogaz Gol,** see KANDAHĀR, KARA-BOGAZ GOL.

Qabes. See GABÈS.

Qaḍārif, Al–. See GEDAREF.

Qādisīyah, al–. See KADISIYA.

Qāhirah, al–. See CAIRO 2.

Qain. See QĀYEN.

Qairwan. See KAIROUAN.

Qais. See QEYS.

Qa·la Āhan·ga·rān \ˌkäl-ə-ə-ˌhäŋ-gə-ˈrän\. Town, ✱ of Ghor prov., cen. Afghanistan; pop. (1969e) 61,723.

Qala Nau \-ˈnau̇\. Town, ✱ of Bādghis prov., NW Afghanistan; pop. (1969e) 76,145.

Qa·lat \kə-ˈlät\. Town, ✱ of Zabul prov., SE Afghanistan; pop. (1969e) 49,743.

Qal·ʻat Sam·an *or* **Kal·aat Saman** \ˌkäl-at-sam-ˈan\. Town, NW Syria, NW of Aleppo; monastery; home of Simeon Stylites who lived 30 years on top of a pillar.

Qalunya. See EMMAUS 2.

Qal·yub *also* **Kal·yub** \käl-ˈyüb\. Town, Qalyubīya gov., Egypt, 10 m. N of Cairo, at head of Nile delta; pop. (1966c) 49,300.

Qal·yu·bi·ya *also* **Kal·yu·bi·ya** \ˌkäl-yu̇-ˈbē-(y)ə\. Governorate of N Egypt. See table at EGYPT.

Qamaran. See KAMARAN.

Qamr Bay \ˌkäm-ər-\ *or formerly* **Ka·mar Bay** \ˌkäm-ər-\. Inlet of the Arabian Sea, E Yemen (✱ Aden), S coast of Arabian Penin., E of Cape Fartak.

Qantara, Al–. See AL-QANTARA.

Qan·ṭa·rat al–Faḥṣ \ˌkän-tə-ˌrät-al-ˈfäs\ *or formerly* **Pont du Fahs** \ˌpōⁿ-dü-ˈfäs\. Town, N Tunisia, N Africa, ab. 12 m. W of Zaghouan; pop. (1966c) 4500; battles Apr.–May 1943.

Qa·ra Dagh \ˌkär-ə-ˈdä(g)\. 1 Mountain range, NW Iran, S of Araks river; highest point 9545 ft.

2 Mountain range, NE Iraq, on Iran border, SE end of mountains of Kurdistan; highest point 5923 ft.

Qara Kul. See KARAKUL.

Qara Qash. See K'A-LA-K'A-SHIH.

Qaraqorum. See KARAKORUM.

Qara Qum. See KARA KUM.

Qara Shahr. See KARASHAHR.

Qa·reh Sū \ˌkär-ə-ˈsü\ *or* **Ka·ra** \ˈkär-ə\. River, NW Iran; ab. 160 m. long; flows N into Araks river on the U.S.S.R. border.

Qarghaliq. See KARGHALIK.

Qarqannah, Juzur. See KERKENNA ISLANDS.

Qarqar. See KARKAR 2.

Qars. See KARS.

Qārūn, Birket. See BIRKET QĀRŪN.

Qa·sim \kä-ˈsēm\. District, N cen. Nejd, Saudi Arabia; pop. (1965e) 200,000; chief towns Buraida and Anaiza.

Qasr, Al–. See AL-QASR.

Qasr al–Az·raq \ˌkäs-ər-al-ˈaz-(ˌ)räk\. Town and oasis, N Jordan, 55 m. E of Amman.

Qa·tar *also* **Ka·tar** \ˈkät-ər\. Sheikhdom, occupying a peninsula projecting into SW Persian Gulf; land area 4400 sq. m.; ab. 160 m. long; pop. (1971e) 160,000; ✱ Doha; consists chiefly of low hills and sandy areas; produces oil; entered into treaty relations with Great Britain 1868; treaty renewed 1916; terminated 1971; became a member of the United Nations 1971.

Qa·tia *or* **Ka·tia** \kä-ˈtē-(y)ə\. Village, Egypt, near Mediterranean Sea, 25 m. E of the Suez Canal; battles bet. British and Turks Apr. and Aug. 1916.

Qa·tif *also* **Ka·tif** \kä-ˈtēf\. Seaport of Al-Hasa, E Nejd, Saudi Arabia, on Persian Gulf 37 m. NW of Bahrain I.; has old Karmathian fort. Taken by Wahabis from Turks 1914.

Qatrani, Al–. See AL-QATRANI.

Qat·ta·ra Depression \kə-ˌtär-ə-\. Low area in N Egypt, 130 m. W of Cairo and 40 m. S of the seacoast; ab. 7000 sq. m.; deepest point 440 ft. below sea level; because it was impassable to armies and vehicles, it formed the anchor at S end of British defense line at Al-Alamein in NW Egypt July 1942, stopping Rommel's invasion; followed by Allied success, Oct. 19 to Nov. 3, 1942, at Al-Alamein (*q.v.*).

Qā·yen *or* **Qa·in** \kä-ˈēn\. Town, Khorāsān prov., E Iran, 175 m. S of Mashhad; pop. (1966c) 6418; situated in a broad valley at 4500 ft. altitude; raises saffron as a special product and has an active industry in carpets and felts. A very old town near the Afghan border; has often changed overlords.

Qaz·vīn *or* **Kaz·vin** \kaz-ˈvēn\. 1 Former province of NW Iran; 9826 sq. m.

2 City, Tehran prov., NW Iran, ab. 90 m. NW of Tehran; pop. (1971e) 92,000; important communications center; produces grain, grapes, pistachio nuts; textile and flour mills. Founded by Shapur II in 4th cent. A.D.; favored by Harun al-Rashid, who built a mosque here; influential under Muslims, became capital of Persia under Tahmasp I in 16th cent.; capital transferred to Eşfahān by Abbas I; has suffered much from earthquakes.

Qe·na *also* **Ke·na** \ˈkē-nə, ˈkā-\ *or* **Qi·na** \ˈkē-\. 1 Governorate of Egypt. See table at EGYPT.

2 *anc.* **Cae·ne** \ˈsē-nē\ *or* **Cae·nep·o·lis** \si-ˈnep-ə-ləs\. City, its ✱, Upper Egypt, on right bank of the Nile at the bend below Luxor and 280 m. SSE of Cairo; pop. (1970e) 77,600; a trade center, noted for its manufacture of water jars and bottles.

Qena, Wa·di \ˌwäd-ē-\. Watercourse in E cen. Egypt, extending S to the Nile river at Qena.

Qeshm \ˈkesh-əm\ *or* **Qishm** *also* **Kishm** \ˈkish-\. 1 *or anc.* **Oa·rac·ta** \ˌō-ə-ˈrak-tə\. Island at SE end of Persian Gulf in Strait of Hormuz; 516 sq. m.; pop. (1960e) 15,000; administratively part of Lorestān gov., Iran; separated from mainland by Clarence Strait. Island is generally rocky and barren but has some fertile areas, producing dates and melons.

2 Chief town of Qeshm I. at its E tip.

Qeys \ˈkīs\ *also* **Qais** *or* **Kais** \ˈkīs\. Island in SE Persian Gulf, ab. 10 m. off S coast of Iran; in Middle Ages an important trade center; under Arab rule it controlled Oman and provided a market where goods of the Middle East were exchanged; declined after 14th cent.

Qe·zel Ow·zan \ˌkez-əl-au̇-ˈzan\ *also* **Qi·zil Uzun** \ˌkiz-əl-yu̇-ˈzün\ *or* **Ki·zil Uzen** \ˌkiz-əl-ü-ˈzen\. River, NW Iran; ab. 450 m. long; rises in mountains SE of Lake Urmia and flows N then SE, then turns NE through the Elburz Mts. to Caspian Sea E of Rasht; called Safīd in its lower course.

Qift \ˈkift\ *also* **Kuft** \ˈküft\ *or anc.* **Cop·tos** \ˈkäp-təs\. Village in Qena gov., Egypt, on right bank of the Nile, an ancient city N of Thebes; Coptos was starting point of 5-day caravan route from the Nile to the Red Sea.

Qirghiz. See KIRGHIZ.

Qisarya. See CAESAREA 2.

Qishm. See QESHM.

Qishn \ˈkish-ən\. Coastal town, Yemen (✱ Aden), ab. 190 m. NE of Mukalla; ✱ of former Mahra sultanate.

Qi·shon *or* **Ki·shon** \ˈkī-ˌshän, ˈkish-ˌän\. River, N Israel; 45 m. long; rises near Mt. Gilboa and flows NW through the Plain of Esdraelon to the Mediterranean just N of Haifa. On its banks Sisera was defeated by the Israelites (*Judges* v. 21) and the prophets of Baal slain by Elijah (*1 Kings* xviii. 40).

Qizil Orda. See KZYL-ORDA.

Qizil Qum. See KYZYL KUM.

Qizil Uzun. See QEZEL OWZAN.

Qom \ˈkōm\ *also* **Qum** *or* **Kum** \ˈku̇m\. Town, Tehran prov., NW cen. Iran, 75 m. SSW of Tehran; pop. (1971e) 110,000; textiles, pottery; center of grain and cotton region and important junction for several highways; has numerous mosques and, being site of shrine of Fatima, sister of Imam Riza, is a place for Shiite pilgrimages.

Qor·mi \ˈkȯr-mē\. Town, Malta, 3 m. SW of Valletta; pop. (1968e) 15,699.

Qoseir, El. See AL-QUSEIR.

Qsar al–Kbir, Al–. See ALCAZARQUIVIR.

Qua·boag \ˈkwā-ˌbäg\. River, cen. Massachusetts; rises in **Quaboag Pond** in S cen. Worcester co., flows W and joins Swift river in N Hampden co., to form Chicopee river.

Quad·rant Mountain \ˈkwäd-rənt-\. Peak in Yellowstone National Park, NW Wyoming; 10,200 ft.

Quak·er·town \ˈkwā-kər-ˌtau̇n\. Borough, Bucks co., SE Pennsylvania, 13 m. S of Allentown; pop. (1970c) 7276; manufactures hosiery, clothing, luggage, aluminum products; founded by Quakers 1715.

Qua·nah \ˈkwän-ə\. City, ⊗ of Hardeman co., N Texas, 24 m. WNW of Vernon; pop. (1970c) 3948; manufactures cottonseed oil, plaster; gypsum deposits.

Quan·da·ry Peak \ˌkwän-d(ə-)rē-\. Mountain, Summit co., cen. Colorado; 14,264 ft.

Quang Ngai *or* **Quang·ngai** \ˈkwäŋ-ˈgī\. Coastal town, South Vietnam, ab. 130 m. SE of Hue; pop. (1968e) 14,119.

Quang Tri *or* **Quang·tri** \ˈkwäŋ-ˈtrē\. Town, South Vietnam, on coastal railroad 30 m. NW of Hue; pop. (1968e) 15,581; important agricultural center.

Quan Long *or* **Quan·long** \ˈkwän-ˈlȯŋ\ *or formerly* **Ca·mau** \kə-ˈmau̇\. Town, South Vietnam, near Point Baibung; pop. (1968e) 52,404.

Quan·ti·co \ˈkwänt-ə-ˌkō\. Town, Prince William co., NE Virginia, on Potomac river 18 m. NNE of Fredericksburg; pop. (1970c) 719; U.S. Marine Corps base, first established as a naval base in Revolutionary War; made a permanent Marine Corps base 1918.

Quan·tock Hills \ˌkwänt-ək-\. Range of hills, NW Somersetshire, SW England; highest point 1262 ft.

Qu'Ap·pelle \kwä-ˈpel\. River, S Saskatchewan, Canada; ab. 270 m. long; flows E across Manitoba border and into the Assiniboine river; Moose Jaw is near its source.

Qua·raí \ˌkwär-ə-ˈē\. River, forming W section of Uruguay-Brazil boundary; ab. 160 m. long; flows W into Uruguay river.

Qua·re·gnon \ˌkar-ə-ˈnyōⁿ\. Commune, Hainaut prov., SW Belgium, just W of Mons; pop. (1969e) 18,036; coal mines.

Quarnero. See KVARNER 1.

Quarnerolo. See MALI KVARNER.

Quar·tu Sant'·Ele·na \ˈkwär-(ˌ)tü-sän-ˈtel-ə-ˌnä\. Commune, Cagliari prov., S Sardinia, Italy, 4 m. E of Cagliari; pop. (1968e) 27,520.

Quathlamba. See DRAKENSBERG MOUNTAINS.

Qua·tre Bornes \ˌka-trə-ˈbȯ(ə)rn\. Residential town, Mauritius, bet. Port Louis and Curepipe; pop. (1969e) 45,000.

Quatre Bras \-ˈbrä\. Village, Brabant prov., cen. Belgium, ab. 20 m. SSE of Brussels; battlefield where Wellington defeated the French under Ney June 16, 1815, just before the battle of Waterloo.

Quay \ˈkwā\. County in New Mexico. See table at NEW MEXICO.

Qu·chan *or* **Ku·chan** \kü-ˈchän\. Town, N Khorāsān prov., NE Iran, on highway 80 m. NW of Mashhad; pop. (1971e) 32,000; chief product grain. Suffered severely in 19th cent. from several earthquakes; in 1893 practically destroyed with great loss of life, but rebuilt.

Quds, Al–. See JERUSALEM 2.

Que, Isle of. See SELINSGROVE.

Quean·bey·an \ˈkwēn-bē-ən, kwēn-ˈ\. Town, SE New South Wales, SE Australia; pop. (1966c) 12,515; SE suburb of Canberra, outside Australian Capital Territory.

Qué·ant \kā-ˈäⁿ\. Village, Pas-de-Calais dept., N France, 11 m. W of Cambrai; pop. (1962c) 649; fortress on the Hindenburg Line during World War I. See DROCOURT.

Que·bec \kwi-ˈbek\ *or Fr.* **Qué·bec** \kā-bek\. **1** Province, E Canada, bounded on N by Hudson Strait, on E by Labrador and Gulf of St. Lawrence, on SE by New Brunswick, on S by United States and Ottawa river, and on W by Ontario prov., James Bay, and Hudson Bay; 594,861 sq. m. (incl. 71,000 sq. m. of water); pop. (1970e) 6,013,000, (1969e) 6,254,974; ✱ Quebec.

Physical features: Its general elevation is low but the Laurentian Highlands N of Quebec city average ab. 2000 ft.; the mountains of the Gaspé Penin. are the highest in the province (Mt. Jacques Cartier 4160 ft.). Has many large lakes, incl. Lake St. John, Mistassini, Minto, Bienville; in the S in the populous part is the great artery of the St. Lawrence with its many tributaries. The height of land running generally NE and SW forms the watershed for many rivers flowing W and NW into Hudson Bay and NE into Ungava Bay. Contains two national historic parks and four provincial parks. *Chief products:* Wheat, oats, dairy products; livestock raising, fishing; copper, iron ore, asbestos, gold, zinc, titanium; manufacturing: mineral processing, chemicals, pulp and paper; hydroelectric power production. *Chief cities:* Montreal, Laval, Quebec, Verdun, Sherbrooke, Hull. Divided into the following 74 counties (for pronunciation of their names, see their individual entries):

NAME	LOCATION	AREA[1] (sq. m.)	POP. (1969e)	CO. SEAT
Abitibi	SW	76,725	90,766	Amos
Argenteuil	SW	783	31,339	Lachute
Arthabaska	S	666	52,036	Arthabaska
Bagot	S	346	22,901	Saint Liboire
Beauce	S	1,131	59,900	Beauceville East
Beauharnois	S	147	53,784	Beauharnois
Bellechasse	S	645	25,094	Saint Raphaël
Berthier	S	1,816	27,286	Berthier
Bonaventure	on Gaspé Penin.	3,464	43,794	New Carlisle
Brome	S	489	15,435	Knowlton
Chambly	S	138	228,169	Longueuil
Champlain	S	8,586	112,786	Sainte Geneviève
Charlevoix-Est	S	719	17,517	La Malbaie
Charlevoix-Ouest	S	1,496	13,740	Baie Saint Paul
Châteauguay	S	265	50,015	Sainte Martine
Chicoutimi	S	17,800	169,902	Chicoutimi
Compton	S	853	18,855	Cookshire
Dorchester	S	835	38,083	Sainte Hénédine
Drummond	S	532	61,462	Drummondville
Frontenac	S	1,360	28,748	Megantic
Gaspé-Est	on Gaspé Penin.	2,348	41,568	Percé
Gaspé-Ouest	on Gaspé Penin.	2,198	18,516	Sainte Anne des Monts
Gatineau	SW	2,432	114,783	Maniwaki
Hull	SW	139	41,221	Hull
Huntingdon	S	361	14,143	Huntingdon
Iberville	S	198	19,818	Iberville
Joliette	S	2,506	50,539	Joliette
Kamouraska	S	1,038	26,851	Saint Pascal
Labelle	SW	2,491	32,436	Mont Laurier
Lake St. John, East	S	905	46,415	Saint Joseph d'Alma
Lake St. John, West	S	22,818	57,711	Roberval
Laprairie	S	170	51,861	Laprairie
L'Assomption	S	247	55,669	L'Assomption
Levis	S	272	60,603	Saint Romuald
L'Islet	S	773	23,820	Saint Jean Port Joli
Lotbinière	S	726	28,168	Sainte Croix
Magdalen Islands	E	102	13,151	Bassin
Maskinongé	S	2,378	21,198	Louiseville
Matane	on Gaspé Penin.	1,631	31,762	Matane
Matapédia	on Gaspé Penin.	1,751	30,788	Amqui
Megantic	S	783	57,085	Inverness
Missisquoi	S	375	33,447	Bedford
Montcalm	S	3,787	20,361	Sainte Julienne
Montmagny	S	638	26,822	Montmagny
Montmorency No. 1	S	2,126	20,870	Château Richer
Montmorency No. 2	S	72	5,197	Sainte Famille
Montreal and Jesus Islands	S	285	2,412,195	Montreal
Napierville	S	149	12,481	Napierville
Nicolet	S	626	31,538	Bécancour
Papineau	SW	1,581	32,714	Papineauville
Pontiac	SW	9,560	20,674	Campbell's Bay

NAME	LOCATION	AREA[1] (sq. m.)	POP. (1969e)	CO. SEAT
Portneuf	S	1,440	51,092	Cap Santé
Quebec	S	2,745	416,830	Loretteville
Richelieu	S	221	47,468	Sorel
Richmond	S	543	42,002	Richmond
Rimouski	S	2,080	65,603	Rimouski
Rivière du Loup	S	723	40,559	Rivière du Loup
Rouville	S	243	31,366	Marieville
Saguenay	SE	315,176	95,507	Tadoussac
Saint Hyacinthe	S	278	49,008	Saint Hyacinthe
Saint Johns	S	205	46,359	Saint Johns
Saint-Maurice	S	1,820	119,324	Yamachiche
Shefford	S	566	61,119	Waterloo
Sherbrooke	S	251	100,305	Sherbrooke
Soulanges	S	136	11,781	Coteau Landing
Stanstead	S	483	38,424	Ayer's Cliff
Témiscouata	S	1,160	26,197	Rivière du Loup and Notre Dame du Lac
Terrebonne	S	790	139,630	Saint Jérôme
Timiskaming	SW	8,977	59,945	Ville Marie
Two Mountains	S	279	41,395	Sainte Schloastique
Vaudreuil	S	201	37,674	Vaudreuil
Verchères	S	199	33,477	Verchères
Wolfe	S	709	16,455	Ham Sud
Yamaska	S	365	15,280	Saint François du Lac

[1]Area = land area.

History: From 1627 to 1763 this region formed the most important part of New France, claimed as result of discoveries and explorations of Jacques Cartier 1534–41 and of Samuel de Champlain 1603 and 1608–15; lower St. Lawrence site of many new settlements 1615–1763; lost to British in French and Indian War 1754–63 (see QUEBEC 3). As first set up under the British, comprised the valleys of the Ottawa and lower St. Lawrence rivers; as established by the Quebec Act 1774 the province of Quebec included additional territory W of the Ottawa river and S to the Ohio (as far W as the Mississippi); as result of American Revolution, received many loyalist settlers in region W of the Ottawa and lost to the U.S. 1783 lands now included in Minnesota, Wisconsin, Michigan, Ohio, Indiana, and Illinois (see NORTHWEST TERRITORY), the remaining territory being divided 1791 into Upper Canada (chiefly English) and Lower Canada (chiefly French); on recommendation of Durham report 1839, the two parts reunited 1841; united 1867 with New Brunswick and Nova Scotia to form the Dominion of Canada, Upper Canada then becoming the present province of Ontario (*q.v.*) and Lower Canada the present province of Quebec; boundary with Labrador determined 1825 but changed 1927 to grant more territory to Newfoundland prov. (Labrador); gained Ungava Penin. from Northwest Territories 1912.

2 County, Quebec, Canada. See table above.

3 City, ✱ of Quebec prov., Canada, on N bank of St. Lawrence river above Island of Orleans and 180 m. below Montreal; pop. (1971p) 182,418, met. area pop. 476,232; port of entry for Atlantic steamers with excellent harbor 300 m. from Gulf of St. Lawrence. Located upon a rocky promontory which rises from the edge of the St. Lawrence and St. Charles rivers in sheer cliffs; shipbuilding; textiles; exports include petroleum products, asbestos, grain, pulp and paper; consists of old Lower Town, with narrow streets and ancient houses along the shore, and Upper Town, surrounded by massive wall, part of early fortifications. Notable for its provincial government buildings, cathedrals, old Church of Notre Dame des Victoires, and the Chateau Frontenac; Laval Univ. (1852), Univ. of Quebec (1969), and several other specialized colleges and cultural institutions. Its population is predominantly French Canadian.

History: Located on site of old Indian town of **Stad·a·co·na** \ˌstad-ə-ˈkō-nə\, visited by Jacques Cartier in 1535 and 1541; first settlement made by Champlain as a trading post 1608. Captured by the British 1629 but returned to the French by Treaty of St-Germain 1632. Capital of New France 1663 to 1763. In 1690 and 1711 unsuccessfully attacked by British fleets; taken by British under Gen. Wolfe in historic battle of the Plains of Abraham 1759 in which both Wolfe and the French leader, Montcalm, met death. Besieged by French force 1760 and stormed with disastrous defeat by American troops under Benedict Arnold and Richard Montgomery 1775. Became capital of united Canada 1851–55 and 1859–67. Allied Conference held here Aug. 11–24, 1943, during World War II.

Quebec West *or* **Québec–Ouest.** See VANIER 2.

Que·bra·di·llas \ˌkeb-rə-ˈdē-(y)əs\. Town and municipality, NW Puerto Rico; town on N coast ab. 14 m. ENE of Aguadilla; pop. (1970p) 2813 (town), 15,470 (munic.).

Qued·lin·burg \ˈkfād-lən-ˌbu̇(ə)rg\. City, Halle dist., East Germany, 33 m. SSW of Magdeburg; pop. (1970e) 30,829; precision instruments, pharmaceuticals; seed-growing center; 10th cent. castle, 11th cent. church, 14th cent. town hall.

Queen Adelaide Archipelago. See REINA ADELAIDA, ARCHIPELAGO OF.

Queen Al·ex·an·dra Range \ˌkwēn-ˌal-ig-ˈzan-drə-, -ˌel-\. Mountain range, Victoria Land, Ross Dependency, Antarctica; lat. 84°S and long. 168°E; highest peak Mt. Kirpatrick 14,855 ft.; former existence of land vertebrates in Antarctica established through fossil discoveries here 1969.

Queen Annes \-ˈanz\. County in Maryland. See table at MARYLAND.

Queen Car·o·la Harbour \-ˌkar-ə-lə-, -kə-ˌrō-lə-\ *also* **Carola Haf·en** \ˌkär-ə-lə-ˈhäf-ən\. Anchorage on W coast of Buka I., NW Solomon Is., W Pacific Ocean.

Queen Char·lotte Islands \-ˈshär-lət-\. Group of islands off W British Columbia, Canada, separated from mainland by Hecate Strait and from islands of S Alaska on the N by Dixon Entrance; 3705 sq. m.; pop. (1966c) 2222. Main islands are Graham (2491 sq. m.), Moresby (991 sq. m.), Louise, Lyell, Kunghit, and several smaller islands. Chief villages are Masset, Skidegate, and Rose Harbour. Inhabitants are mainly Haida Indians; coal, copper, gold; lumbering, fishing.

Queen Charlotte Sound. Body of water off W British Columbia coast, W Canada, bet. N end of Vancouver I. and S Queen Charlotte Is.

Queen Charlotte Strait. Channel bet. N Vancouver I. and the mainland of Canada, connecting Queen Charlotte Sound with Johnstone Strait.

Queen Eliz·a·beth Islands \-ᵊl-ˈiz-ə-bəth-, -i-ˈliz-\. Islands of N Canada, N of the water passage extending from M'Clure Strait to Lancaster Sound; includes the Parry Islands, Sverdrup Islands, Devon, and Ellesmere.

Queen Elizabeth National Park. National park, SW Uganda; 764 sq. m.; varied scenery, incl. tropical forests, grassland, and volcanic craters; noted for its wildlife; established 1952.

Queen Mary Coast \-ˈme(ə)r-ē-, -ˈmā-rē-\. Region of Antarctica extending E from Cape Filchner, 91°53′E, to ab. 102°E at the Antarctic Circle W of Wilkes Land; claimed by Great Britain.

Queen Maud Gulf \-ˈmȯd-\. Gulf, NW Keewatin dist. and NE Mackenzie dist., Northwest Territories, Canada, bet. SE Victoria I. and the mainland.

Queen Maud Land. Section of Antarctica W of Enderby Land at long. 20°W to 45°E and extending S to Polar Plateau and to Coats Land on the W; claimed by Norwegian government 1939; Prince Olav Coast forms a part of its coast.

Queen Maud Mountains. Mountain range, S Ross Dependency, Antarctica, S of Ross Ice Shelf; extends 500 m. SE from lat. 84°S and from long. 175°E to 145°W, on edge of Polar Plateau.

Queen's. See LAOIGHIS.

Queens \ˈkwēnz\. 1 County in New York. See table at NEW YORK.

2 Borough of New York City, on W end of Long I., coextensive with Queens county; 108 sq. m.; pop. (1970c) 1,973,708; largest in area of five boroughs of New York

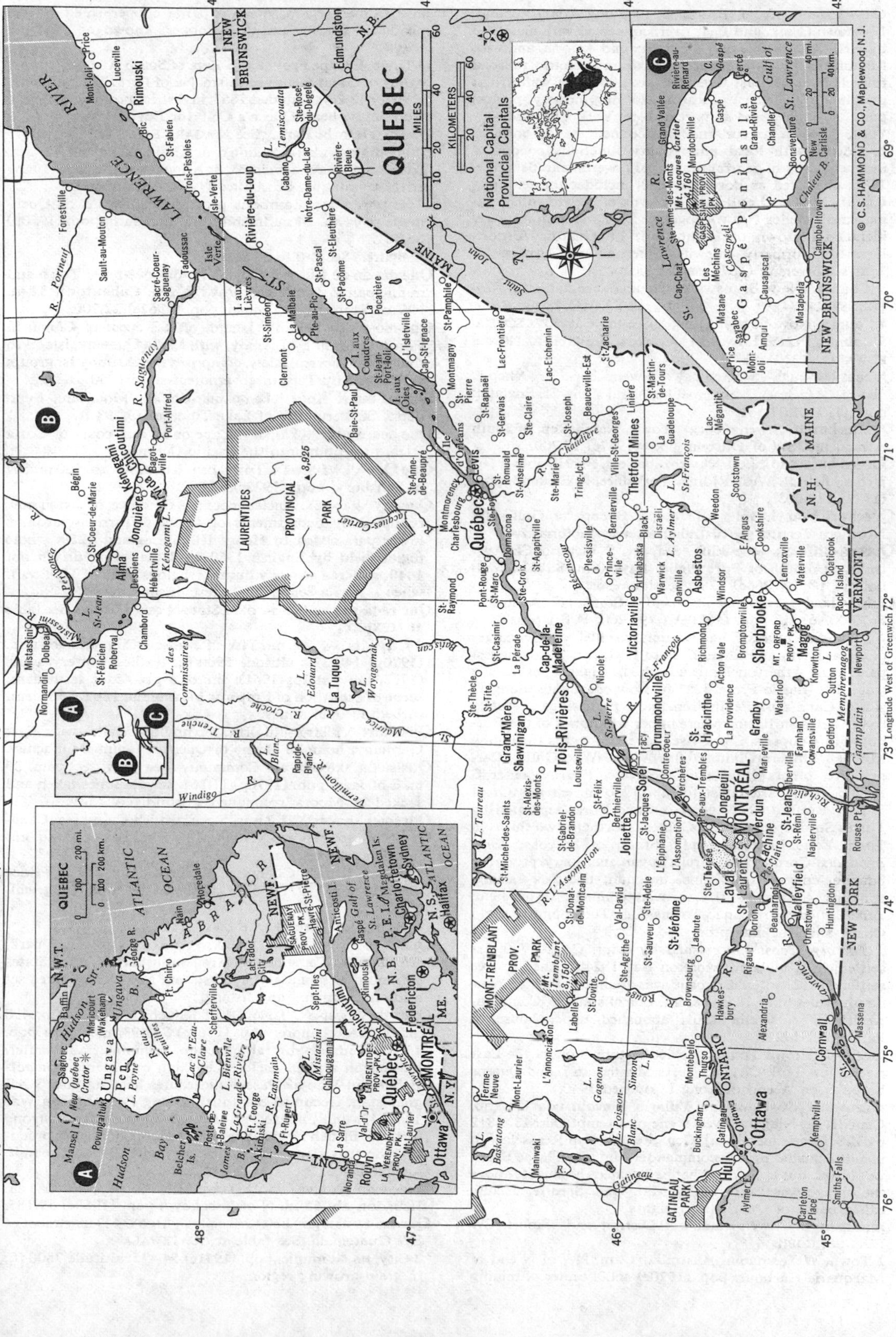
QUEBEC
MILES
KILOMETERS
National Capital
Provincial Capitals
A
B
C
QUEBEC
ATLANTIC OCEAN
Hudson Bay
Ungava Pen.
LABRADOR
N.W.T.
NEWF.
Gulf of St. Lawrence
Anticosti I.
Magdalen Is.
N.B.
N.S.
P.E.I.
Charlottetown
Halifax
Sydney
Fredericton
Québec
MONTRÉAL
Ottawa
ME.
N.Y.
ONT.
ST. LAWRENCE RIVER
NEW BRUNSWICK
MAINE
N.H.
VERMONT
NEW YORK
ONTARIO
LAURENTIDES PROVINCIAL PARK
MONT-TREMBLANT PROV. PARK
GATINEAU PARK
GASPESIAN PROV. PK.
Gaspé Peninsula
Chicoutimi
Jonquière
Kénogami
Alma
Rimouski
Rivière-du-Loup
Lévis
Trois-Rivières
Shawinigan
Grand'Mère
Cap-de-la-Madeleine
Victoriaville
Thetford Mines
Drummondville
Sherbrooke
Granby
St-Hyacinthe
Longueuil
Laval
Verdun
Lachine
St-Jean
St-Jérôme
Joliette
Sorel
Valleyfield
Hull
Cornwall
Asbestos
Magog
La Tuque
Matane
Gaspé
Percé
Mt. Jacques Cartier 4,160
Mt. Tremblant 3,150
73° Longitude West of Greenwich 72°
© C.S. HAMMOND & CO., Maplewood, N.J.

City; extends from Brooklyn to Long Island Sound, Newtown Creek, and East river; connected with mainland by Hell Gate Bridge bet. the Bronx and Astoria, and with Manhattan by Queensboro Bridge and electric railroad tunnels beneath East river; has ab. 200 m. of waterfront; manufactures bakery products, clothing, hosiery, pianos, paint, silk; governed as part of New York City (see NEW YORK 3) by a mayor and city council; has a borough president, with local and county functions conducted independently of central municipal government. Settled c. 1635; chartered as borough 1898; includes former Long Island City (*q.v.*) and former towns of Newtown, Flushing, and Jamaica (*qq.v.*), together with a section formerly included in town of Hempstead; La Guardia Airport; Kennedy (formerly Idlewild) International Airport. St. John's University (1870) in Jamaica.

3 County, New Brunswick, Canada. See table at NEW BRUNSWICK.

4 County, Nova Scotia, Canada. See table at NOVA SCOTIA.

5 County, Prince Edward I., Canada. See table at PRINCE EDWARD ISLAND.

Queens·bor·ough–in–Shep·pey \ˈkwēnz-ˌbər-ə . . . ˈshep-ē, -ˌbə-re-, -b(ə-)rə-\. Municipal borough, Kent, SE England; pop. (1971p) 31,541.

Queens·burgh \ˈkwēnz-ˌbərg\. Town, Natal, Rep. of South Africa, just SW of Durban; pop. (1967e) 17,700.

Queens·bury and Shelf \ˈkwēnz-ˌber-e . . . ˈshelf, -b(ə-)rē-\. Urban district, West Riding, Yorkshire, N England; pop. (1971p) 10,603.

Queens Channel. Inlet of Joseph Bonaparte Gulf, NW Northern Territory, Australia; receives Victoria river.

Queens·cliffe \ˈkwēnz-ˌklif\. Seaport, S Victoria, SE Australia, at mouth of Port Phillip Bay 40 m. SSW of Melbourne; pop. (1966c) 2787; seaside resort.

Queens·land \ˈkwēnz-ˌland, -lənd\. State, NE Australia; 667,000 sq. m.; pop. (1970e) 1,799,200; ✱ Brisbane.

Physical features: E half contains parallel N and S ranges of Great Dividing Range (Eastern Highlands) with highest part in the Atherton Plateau in the N; highest peak in the state, Mt. Bartle Frere 5287 ft. Low coastlands along W side of Cape York Penin.; cen. and S parts slope gradually to W (Artesian Basin) where upper tributaries of the Darling and Cooper's Creek rise. Several streams (including Mitchell, Gilbert, Flinders) flow W or NW to Gulf of Carpentaria; others (Burdekin, Brisbane, Fitzroy) enter S Pacific. Along NE coast for ab. 1250 m. extends Great Barrier Reef (*q.v.*). N point is Cape York, separated by Torres Strait from S New Guinea. Northern two thirds in Torrid Zone. Largest island is Fraser, off SE coast. *Chief products:* Corn, wheat, fruit, sugarcane, dairy products; bauxite, copper, lead, zinc, uranium; livestock raising; contains Australia's first proved commercial oil field. *Chief towns:* Brisbane, Townsville, Toowoomba, Gold Coast, and Rockhampton.

History: Coast first visited by Capt. Cook 1770; 1st settlement (penal) on Moreton Bay 1824; opened to free settlers 1842, when Brisbane was founded. Part of New South Wales until 1859; became one of states of Commonwealth of Australia 1901; abolished upper house of Parliament 1922.

Queens–Midtown Tunnel. Vehicular tunnel under the East river, New York City, connects Manhattan I. and Queens borough on W end of Long I.; opened 1940.

Queens·ton \ˈkwēn-ˌstən\. Village, Lincoln co., Ontario, Canada, on Niagara river; scene of attempt Oct. 13, 1812 by U.S. forces under Maj. Gen. Stephen Van Rensselaer to invade Canada; British commander Maj. Gen. Isaac Brock was killed, but U.S. force that had gained the heights above the village was captured by Maj. Gen. Sheaffe; usually called battle of Queenston Heights.

Queens·town \ˈkwēn-ˌstau̇n\. 1 District and seaport, SW Eire. See COBH.

2 Town, W Tasmania, Australia, 12 m. NW of N end of Macquarie Harbour; pop. (1970e) 4600; center of mining and timber region; operates large copper smelters and produces gold, silver, and copper; known as "Copper City."

3 Town, E Cape Province, S Rep. of South Africa, in upper valley of Great Kei river 160 m. NE of Port Elizabeth; pop. (1967e) 42,200; founded 1853; in district producing mainly wool and wheat. Queen's Coll. for Boys.

Queen Victoria Park. See NIAGARA FALLS 1.

Quel·i·ma·ne \ˌkel-ə-ˈmän-ə\ *or* **Quil·i·ma·ne** \ˌkil-\ *also* **Ki·li·ma·ne** \ˌkēl-ə-ˈmän-ē\ *or* **Kil·main** \kil-ˈmān\. 1 River, Mozambique, SE Africa, N of the Zambezi.

2 Seaport town, Zambézia prov., Mozambique, on Quelimane river ab. 14 m. inland from its mouth; pop. (1960p) 66,301.

Quelpart. See CHEJU 1.

Que·ma·do de Güi·nes \kā-ˌmäd-ō-dā-ˈgwē-nəs\. Town and municipality, Las Villas prov., W cen. Cuba; town 32 m. NW of Santa Clara; munic. pop. (1967e) 22,700.

Que·moy \k(w)i-ˈmȯi\. Island, off SE coast of China, in Formosa Strait E of Amoy; with **Little Quemoy,** island to the W , and several islets, comprises the Quemoy Is. group; garrisoned by Taiwan government since 1950.

Que·na·ma·ri Knot \ˌken-ə-ˌmär-ē-ˈnät\. Mountain, Puno dept., SE Peru, NW of Lake Titicaca; 19,193 ft.

Que·pos, Point \-ˈkā-pəs\. Cape on W cen. coast of Costa Rica, projecting into the Pacific Ocean.

Que Que \ˈkwā-ˈkwā\. Town, cen. Rhodesia, ab. 120 m. SW of Salisbury; pop. (1970e) 37,000.

Quer·cy \ker-ˈsē\. Ancient country, S France; in region now occupied by departments of Lot and Tarn-et-Garonne; lower part ceded to Henry III of England 1259; whole region held by English 1360 until they were driven out 1440; suffered severely during religious wars of 16th cent. when it was a center of Protestantism.

Que·ré·ta·ro \kə-ˈret-ə-ˌrō\. 1 State of cen. Mexico. See table at MEXICO.

2 City, its ✱, 160 m. NW of Mexico City; munic. pop. (1970p) 140,379; altitude 5900 ft.; textiles, pottery; univ. (1775, univ. status 1951); site of a pre-Aztec settlement; scene of execution of Emperor Maximilian 1867; 16th cent. cathedral; opal mines.

Quer·furt \ˈkfe(ə)r-ˌfü(ə)rt\. Commune, Halle dist., East Germany; home of Bruno of Querfurt (Saint Bonifacius).

Que·sa·da \kā-ˈsäd-ə\. Commune, Jaén prov., S Spain, 39 m. E of Jaén; pop. (1970p) 11,164; several times taken and sacked by Moors; reconquered definitively 1309.

Ques·nel \kə-ˈnel\. 1 River, S cen. British Columbia, Canada; 64 m. long; flows NW out of **Quesnel Lake** (100 sq. m.) into Fraser river.

2 Town, British Columbia, Canada, 60 m. S of Prince George; pop. (1971p) 6224; timber, gold mining; agriculture.

Quesnoy, Le. See LE QUESNOY.

Quet·i·co Provincial Park \ˌkwet-ə-ˌkō-\. Provincial park, SW Ontario, Canada, in lake region just N of United States (Minnesota) boundary; 1750 sq. m.; a wilderness area set aside for camping and fishing.

Quet·ta \ˈkwet-ə\. Town, ✱ of Baluchistan, Pakistan, 450 m. WSW of Lahore; pop. (1969e) 79,493, met. area pop. 130,000; important rail junction; regional trade center; located on a plain enclosed by high mountains; controls Bolan and Khojak Passes and routes heading into S Afghanistan. Occupied by British during First Afghan War 1839–42, and annexed in 1876; developed into a strong fortress; British headquarters of western command; practically destroyed in severe earthquake June 1935, but rebuilt.

Quetzalcoalco. See COATZACOALCOS.

Que·ve·do \kə-ˈvā-(ˌ)dō\. Town, Los Rios prov., W cen. Ecuador, ab. 55 m. N of Babahoyo; pop. (1969e) 39,185.

Que·zal·te·nan·go \ke(t)-ˌsäl-tə-ˈnäŋ-(ˌ)gō\. 1 Department of SW Guatemala. See table at GUATEMALA.

2 City, its ✱; munic. pop. (1971e) 54,475; altitude 7800 ft.; in grain-growing region.

Que·zal·te·pe·que \ke(t)-ˌsäl-tə-ˈpā-kē\. Town, La Libertad dept., SW El Salvador.

Que·zon \ˈkā-ˌsōn\ *or formerly* **Ta·ya·bas** \tī-ˈ(y)ä-bəs\. Province, E and S cen. Luzon, Phil.; 4612 sq. m.; pop. (1970p) 971,637; ❋ Lucena. Forms a long strip of territory of very irregular shape along the Pacific or E coast of Luzon; mountainous, with S end of Sierra Madre in the N and continuation of range, sometimes known as the Caraballo Sur, to the S; coastline includes many indentations, esp.: Baler Bay, Lamon Bay, and on S coast Ragay Gulf, Tayabas Bay, and Mompog Pass separating it from the island of Marinduque. Includes islands of Polillo group and Alabat on Pacific coast.

History: Explored by Spaniards soon after settlement of Manila; original province, of small area, created 1591; much of the present province was during Spanish rule under jurisdiction of other provinces; suffered from revolt of 1841 and often from depredations of Moro pirates; boundaries increased in 1902 and 1920.

Quezon City. City, ❋ of the Republic of the Philippines, on Luzon I., adjoining Manila on the NE; pop. (1970p) 754,452; officially became capital 1948; univ. (1908).

Quiaca, La. See LA QUIACA.

Quiangan. See KIANGAN.

Quib·dó \kib-ˈdō\. City, ❋ of Chocó dept., W Colombia, on the Atrato river 80 m. WNW of Manizales; pop. (1968e) 46,871.

Qui·be·ron \ˌkēb-(ə-)ˈrō^{n}\. Town, Morbihan dept., NW France; pop. (1962c) 4540; at tip of **Quiberon Peninsula,** a narrow, sandy peninsula, 6 m. long, forming W side of **Quiberon Bay,** site of naval battle, Nov. 20, 1759 during Seven Years' War, in which English fleets under Boscawen and Hawke defeated the French. Scene July 20–21, 1795 of defeat of French royalists who landed at base of peninsula but were driven back by forces of Gen. Hoche.

Qui·çâ·ma National Park \kē-ˈsä-mə-\. National park, Angola; 3846 sq. m.; varied wildlife; estab. 1957.

Qui·ché \kē-ˈchā\. **1** Department of W cen. Guatemala. See table at GUATEMALA.

2 Town, Guatemala. See SANTA CRUZ DEL QUICHÉ.

Quie·pe \kē-ˈā-pə\. Island in Atlantic Ocean off SE coast of Bahia state, Brazil, 70 m. SSW of Salvador.

Quié·vrain \kyā-ˈvra^{n}\. Commune, Hainaut prov., Belgium; pop. (1969e) 5703; customs station, on the French frontier bet. Mons and Valenciennes.

Quiin·dy *or* **Quiyn·dy** \kēn-ˈdē\. Town, Paraguarí dept., S Paraguay, 55 m. SE of Asunción; pop. (1970e) 18,539; formerly capital of a department of same name.

Quilimane. See QUELIMANE.

Quill Lakes \ˈkwil-\. Two connected lakes, SE cen. Saskatchewan, Canada; 236 sq. m.

Qui·llo·ta \kē-ˈ(y)ōt-ə\. Town, Valparaíso prov., cen. Chile, 30 m. NE of Valparaíso; pop. (1966e) 36,282.

Quil·mes \ˈkē(ə)l-ˌmās\. City, Buenos Aires prov., E Argentina, suburb of Buenos Aires; pop. (1960c) 317,783; industrial center; founded 1665.

Qui·lon \ˈkwē-ˌlōn\ *or* **Kol·lam** \ˈkäl-əm\. Town, SE Kerala, S India, on Malabar Coast 130 m. SW of Madurai; pop. (1961c) 91,018; seaport with extensive trade, exporting timber, coconuts, oil, pepper, tea.

Quil·pué \kil-ˈpwā\. City, Valparaíso prov., cen. Chile, ab. 10 m. E of Valparaíso; pop. (1966e) 35,232.

Quim·per \ka^{n}(m)-ˈpe(ə)r\. Manufacturing and commercial commune, ❋ of Finistère dept., NW France, near Bay of Biscay 112 m. W of Rennes; pop. (1968c) 52,496; 13th–15th cent. Gothic cathedral; sardine fisheries; manufactures pottery (called Quimper or Brittany ware); tourism. Capital of old countship of Carnouailles.

Quim·per·lé \ˌka^{n}(m)-pe(ə)r-ˈlā\. Commercial town, Finistère dept., NW France, ab. 13 m. NW of Lorient; pop. (1968c) 10,698; restoration of an 11th cent. Romanesque abbey church of Ste-Croix.

Quim·sa·cha·ta \ˌkim(p)-sə-ˈchät-ə\. Peak, N Chile, W of Lake Poopó; 19,882 ft.

Quim·sa·cruz \ˌkim(p)-sə-ˈkrüz\. Peak, W Bolivia, SE of Lake Titicaca; 19,357 ft.

Qui·na·la·sag \ˌkē-nə-lə-ˈsäg\. Island in Pacific, NE Camarines Sur prov., Luzon, Phil., off N coast of Caramoan Penin.; 13 sq. m.

Qui·na·ta \ki-ˈnät-ə\. Peak, S Venezuela, N of the Orinoco; 7415 ft.

Qui·na·uan Point \ˌkē-nə-ˌwän-\. Point, SW coast of Bataan Penin., Luzon, Phil.; extends into South China Sea WNW of Mariveles, 14°29′N, 120°23′E.

Qui·nault Lake \kwi-ˈnȯlt-\. Lake, N Grays Harbor co., W Washington, on W slope of Coast Range; traversed by **Quinault River** which rises to the NE in Jefferson co. and flows SW to the Pacific Ocean.

Quin·cy \ˈkwin(t)-sē; *in Mass.* ˈkwin-zē\. **1** Village, ⊗ of Plumas co., NE California; pop. (1970c) 3343; winter sports.

2 City, ⊗ of Gadsden co., N Florida, 20 m. WNW of Tallahassee; pop. (1970c) 8334; tobacco mart; deposits of fuller's earth in the vicinity.

3 City, ⊗ of Adams co., W Illinois, on Mississippi river across from Missouri; pop. (1970c) 45,288; truck bodies, broadcasting equipment; commercial, industrial, and distributing center in agricultural and livestock-raising area; flour mills, foundries, brick kilns; Quincy Coll. (1860); settled ab. 1822.

4 City, Norfolk co., E Massachusetts, 8 m. S of Boston; pop. (1970c) 87,966; shipyards, granite quarries; Quincy Junior Coll. (1958); birthplace of John Adams, 2d president of the U.S. and of John Quincy Adams, 6th president of the U.S.; site of settlement of Merrymount or Mt. Wollaston where Thomas Morton established his trading post c. 1625.

5 Town, Grant co., cen. Washington, 120 m. WSW of Spokane; pop. (1970c) 3237; agriculture; feed and fertilizer mills.

Quin·dío \kin-ˈdē-ō\. Department of W Colombia. See table at COLOMBIA.

Quindío Pass. Mountain pass in the Cordillera Central, in Colombia, 4°38′N, 75°32′W; alt. 11,435 ft.

Quin·e·baug \ˈkwin-ə-ˌbȯg\. River, S Massachusetts and E Connecticut; ab. 100 m. long; rises in E Hampden co., SW Massachusetts, flows SE across Connecticut border, then S across E Connecticut into the Shetucket N of Norwich.

Qui·né·ville \ˌkē-ˌnā-ˈvēl\. Commune, Manche dept., NW France, on E coast of Cotentin Penin. ab. 17 m. SE of Cherbourg; pop. (1962c) 323; at N end of Utah Beach in World War II.

Qui Nhon *or* **Qui·nhon** \kwē-ˈnyȯn\. Town on coast of South Vietnam, port of An Nhon; pop. (1968e) 116,821; has shallow harbor. A capital of the Chams in early times.

Quinn Canyon Mountains \ˌkwin-\. Small range in W Lincoln co. and E cen. Nye co., SE cen. Nevada.

Quin·ni·pi·ac \ˌkwin-ə-pē-ˈak\. River, cen. Connecticut; rises in SW Hartford co., flows S through cen. New Haven co. and empties into New Haven Harbor.

Quin·sig·a·mond, Lake \-kwin-ˈsig-ə-mənd\. Lake in cen. Worcester co., cen. Massachusetts, on E border of city of Worcester.

Quin·ta·na Roo \kēn-ˌtän-ə-ˈrō\. Territory in E Yucatán penin., SE Mexico; 16,228 sq. m.; pop. (1970p) 91,044; ❋ Chetumal; divided Dec. 1931 bet. Yucatán and Campeche states and reestablished Jan. 1935.

Quin·te, Bay of \-ˈkwint-ē\. Inlet of Lake Ontario extending N of Prince Edward co., SE Ontario, Canada, and from Trenton E to Napanee, with many inlets and islands. Favorite resort of vacationists; connected with Georgian Bay by Trent Canal (see TRENT 2).

Quin·to \'kin-(ˌ)tō\. River, Córdoba prov., N cen. Argentina; ab. 250 m. long; rises in San Luis prov.; flows ESE into a marsh.

Quiquió *or* **Quiquyo.** See QUYQUYÓ.

Qui·raing \kwi-'raŋ\. Mountain in N Skye I., off NW coast of Scotland; 1779 ft.; remarkable rock formations.

Qui·ri·guá \ˌkir-i-'gwä\. Ancient Mayan city in E Guatemala, in the Motagua valley; ruins of temple and carved monoliths.

Quir·i·nal \'kwir-ən-ᵊl\. One of the seven hills of Rome. See SEVEN HILLS.

Qui·ro·ga, Point \-ki-'rō-gə\. Cape, NE Chubut prov., S Argentina, W of entrance to Gulf of San José opp. Point Buenos Aires (*q.v.*).

Quiros. See SWAINS.

Quis·ling Cove \ˌkwiz-liŋ-\. Inlet on NW coast of Kiska I. in the Aleutians, Alaska; U.S. troops landed here Aug. 15, 1943.

Qui·ta Sue·ño Bank \ˌkēt-ə-ˌswen-yō-\. Shoal in W Caribbean Sea off NE coast of Nicaragua; controlled by U.S.A. and Colombia.

Quit·man \'kwit-mən\. **1** Name of counties in two states of the U.S. See tables at GEORGIA and MISSISSIPPI.

2 City, ⊗ of Brooks co., S Georgia, 17 m. W of Valdosta; pop. (1970c) 4818; shipping point for hams, sausages, vegetables, melons.

3 Town, ⊗ of Clarke co., E Mississippi; pop. (1970c) 2702.

4 City, ⊗ of Wood co., NE Texas; pop. (1970c) 1494; watermelon raising; oil refinery.

Qui·to \'kē-(ˌ)tō\. **1** Former Spanish presidency, now Ecuador (*q.v.*); won independence and incorporated with Great Colombia under presidency of Simón Bolívar 1822; union disrupted by constitutional assembly which proclaimed the constitution of the republic of Ecuador 1830.

2 City, ✱ of Ecuador, also ✱ of Pichincha prov., on fertile plateau, ab. 114 m. from the Pacific coast and 170 m. NE of Guayaquil; lies almost on the equator just SE of the volcano Pichincha and at an altitude of ab. 9300 ft.; pop. (1970e) 528,100; textiles, footwear, pharmaceuticals; Central Univ. (1787), technical institute (1870), Catholic Univ. (1946), observatory.

History: A pre-Columbian town, captured by the Incas 1487; taken by the Spanish under Sebastián de Belalcázar 1534; audiencia established 1563; town destroyed by eruption of Pichincha 1660; Spanish governor deposed by revolutionary junta 1809; acquired independence by victory of Gen. Sucre over the Spanish in battle of Pichincha May 24, 1822; during Spanish rule, capital of presidency of Quito; has suffered repeatedly from earthquakes, esp. in 1797, 1844, 1859, 1868, 1887.

Qui·vi·ra \ki-'vir-ə\. Mythical town of fabulous wealth sought 1541 by Coronado, generally located near Great Bend, Barton co., cen. Kansas; a site in cen. New Mexico was mistakenly identified with it and has been set aside as the Gran Quivira National Monument (see UNITED STATES, *National Monuments*).

Qui·xa·dá \ˌkē-shů-'dä\. Municipality, Ceará state, NE Brazil, ab. 100 m. S of Fortaleza; pop. (1968e) 86,759.

Qui·xe·ra·mo·bim \ki-ˌsher-ə-mō-'bē(ⁿ)m\. Municipality, Ceará state, NE Brazil, 30 m. SW of Quixadá; pop. (1968e) 55,479.

Quiyndy. See QUIINDY.

Qum. See QOM.

Qumran. See KHIRBAT QUMRAN.

Quneitra, El. See AL-KUNEITRA.

Qun·fi·dha, al– \al-'kůn-fəd-ə\. Port on the Red Sea, SW Saudi Arabia.

Qungur. See KUNG-KO-ERH.

Quoich, Loch \läk-'kȯik, lä<u>k</u>-'kȯi<u>k</u>\. Lake in W Inverness co., NW Scotland.

Qurna, Al–. See AL-QURNA.

Qur·net as Sau·da *also* **Qur·nat as Saw·dā'** \ˌků(ə)r-nət-es-'saů-də\. Mountain in the Lebanon Mts., N Lebanon; 10,131 ft.; highest peak in Lebanon.

Quseir, Al–. See AL-QUSEIR.

Qusur, Al–. See LUXOR.

Quy·quyó *also* **Qui·quió** *or* **Qui·quyo** \ˌkē-kē-'ō\. Town, Paraguarí dept., S Paraguay; pop. (1970e) 18,539; manganese and copper.

Raab. 1 River, Austria and Hungary. See RÁBA.
2 City, Hungary. See GYŐR.

Raa·he \'rä-hə\. Town, Oulu prov., W Finland, on Gulf of Bothnia 35 m. SW of Oulu; pop. (1970e) 7319; founded 1649.

Raal·te \'räl-tə\. Commune, Overijssel prov., E Netherlands, 12 m. SE of Zwolle; pop. (1970e) 19,885.

Raamses. See RAMSES.

Raa·say, Sound of \-'rä-(,)zā\. Channel bet. E Skye I. and Raasay I. in the Inner Hebrides, off NW coast of Scotland.

Raasay Island. One of the Inner Hebrides, NE of Skye I., off NW coast of Scotland; 13 m. long; pop. (1961c) 368; administratively a part of Inverness co.

Rab \'räb\ *or Ital.* **Ar·be** \'är-(,)bā\. 1 Yugoslav island off coast of Croatia, E of the Mali Kvarner at the head of the Adriatic Sea; 36 sq. m.; pop. (1961c) 8369; marble quarries, silk industry; resort.
2 Town on W coast of the island.

Ra·ba \'räb-ə\. Town on Bima Bay, NE coast of Sumbawa I., Lesser Sunda Is., Indonesia; chief town on Sumbawa.

Rá·ba \'räb-(,)ò\ *or Ger.* **Raab** \'räp\. Navigable river, SE Austria and W Hungary; 159 m. long; rises in Styria, Austria, flows E and NE across Hungarian border and into the Danube river.

Ra·bat \rə-'bät\. City, ✱ of Morocco, on Atlantic coast 57 m. NE of Casablanca, situated at the mouth of the Bou Regreg opposite Salé (*q.v.*); pop. (1970e) 325,000; textiles, carpets, asbestos; on site of a camp established 12th cent. by Abd-al-Mumin, founder of Almohade dynasty; important only since beginning of French protectorate 1912. An objective in Allied invasion of North Africa Nov. 1942.

Ra·baul \rə-'baù(ə)l\. Town and port on NE New Britain I., Bismarck Archipelago, W Pacific Ocean; ✱ of East New Britain dist. and until 1941 ✱ of the Territory of New Guinea (now Trust Terr. of New Guinea); pop. (1970e) 21,453; ships copra. On Simpson Harbour, the inner, landlocked part of Blanche Bay, and almost surrounded by active and extinct volcanoes.
History: Established as capital of German New Guinea 1910; principal town of Australian mandate 1920–41; largely destroyed by eruption of Matupi (Mount Tavurvur) and Vulcan volcanoes May 1937; seat of government moved to Lae 1941. In World War II occupied by Japanese Jan. 1942 and developed into major naval and air base, which was neutralized by Allied bombing 1943–45 and by landings at Arawe, Cape Gloucester, and Talasea Dec. 1943–Mar. 1944.

Rabbah Ammon *or* **Rabbath Ammon.** See AMMAN.

Rab·bit Ears Pass \'rab-ət-,ē(ə)rz-\. Mountain highway pass, Jackson, Routt, and Grand cos., N Colorado, in Park Range of Rocky Mts.; 9572 ft.; in a small range called the **Rabbit Ears Range** named for peculiar formation on summit of **Rabbit Ears Peak** 10,719 ft.

Ra·bun \'rā-bən\. County in Georgia. See table at GEORGIA.

Ra·cal·mu·to \,rä-kəl-'mü-(,)tō\. Commercial commune, Agrigento prov., SW Sicily, Italy, 11 m. NE of Agrigento; pop. (1968e) 10,520; sulfur and salt mining.

Rac·co·ni·gi \,räk-ə-'nē-jē\. Town, Cuneo prov., SW Piedmont, NW Italy, 24 m. S of Turin; pop. (1968e) 8994; château, former summer residence of kings of Italy from 1900.

Rac·coon \ra-'kün, rə-\. River, W cen. Iowa; 200 m. long; rises in Buena Vista co., NW Iowa, flows SE into Des Moines river at Des Moines.

Raccoon Island. Island in Atlantic Ocean, in NE Charleston co., South Carolina, NE of Charleston.

Raccoon Mountains. Ridge, NE Alabama, chiefly in De Kalb and Jackson cos.; ab. 2000 ft. high; runs from NE to SW parallel with course of Tennessee river in that area.

Raccoon Point. Point at W tip of Isles Dernieres, off S coast of Terrebonne parish, SE Louisiana.

Race, Cape \-'rās\. Southeast point of Newfoundland, Canada, extending into the Atlantic Ocean 46°40'N, 53°10'W.

Race, The. Strait S of SE Connecticut, bet. Fishers I. and islands off NE Long I., connecting Long Island Sound with Block Island Sound and the Atlantic Ocean.

Race of Al·der·ney \-'òl-dər-nē\. Dangerous channel bet. the island of Alderney and the coast of France.

Race Point. Small peninsula at tip of Cape Cod, SE Massachusetts, N of Provincetown; lighthouse.

Ra·ci·bórz \rät-'sē-,bùsh\ *or Ger.* **Ra·ti·bor** \'rät-ə-,bò(ə)r\. City, Opole prov., S Poland, 42 m. SSE of Opole on Odra (Oder) river near Czechoslovakia border; pop. (1970e) 40,400; machinery, sugar, building materials, flour, leather goods; 15th cent. Gothic church. Mentioned in 12th cent.; chartered 1235 and later capital of an independent principality which came under Bohemia 1327; to Prussia 1742; returned to Poland 1945.

Ra·cine \rə-'sēn, rā-\. 1 County in SE Wisconsin. See table at WISCONSIN.
2 City, its ⊗, on Lake Michigan 23 m. S of Milwaukee; pop. (1970c) 95,162; lake port; produces agricultural machinery, automobile parts, steel castings, electrical equipment, wax, leather goods; Dominican Coll. (1935); founded 1834, incorporated as city 1848.

Radak. See RATAK.

Ră·dă·u·ţi *or* **Ra·da·u·tsi** \,räd-ə-'üts(-ē)\ *or Ger.* **Ra·dautz** \'räd-,aùts\. Town, Suceava co., N Romania, ab. 20 m. NW of Suceava; cathedral, containing tombs of Moldavian princes.

Rad·cliff \'rad-,klif\. City, Hardin co., cen. Kentucky; pop. (1970c) 7881.

Rad·cliffe \'rad-,klif\. Municipal borough, Lancashire, NW England, on the Irwell 8 m. NNW of Manchester; pop. (1971p) 29,320; chemicals.

Ra·de·berg \'räd-ə-,be(ə)rg\. Industrial city, Dresden dist., East Germany, 8 m. NE of Dresden; pop. (1970e) 18,532; glass, ceramics, machinery, kitchenware; 16th cent. castle.

Ra·de·beul \'räd-ə-,bòil\. City, Dresden dist., East Germany, NW suburb of Dresden on Elbe river; pop. (1970e) 39,626; chemicals, machine tools, canned goods, leather products, cigars.

Ra·de·vorm·wald \'räd-ə-,förm-,vält\. Industrial city, North Rhine-Westphalia, West Germany, 25 m. E of Düsseldorf; pop. (1969e) 21,892; textiles, paper, electrical equipment.

Rad·ford \'rad-fərd\. Independent city, Montgomery co., W Virginia, 14 m. ENE of Pulaski; 5 sq. m.; pop. (1970c) 11,596; rubber, rayon, dairy products; diversified agriculture; Radford Coll. (1910).

Ra·dhan·pur \'räd-ᵊn-,pù(ə)r\. 1 Former Indian state, now part of Gujarat state, India; 1150 sq. m.
2 Town, its ✱, ab. 85 m. NW of Ahmadabad; pop. (1961c) 15,100.

Rad·lin \'räd-,lin\. Town, Katowice prov., S Poland, ab. 30 m. SW of Katowice; pop. (1970e) 20,200.

Rad·nor \'rad-nər\. Urban township, Delaware co., SE Pennsylvania, W of Philadelphia; pop. (1970p) 28,849; Cabrini Coll. (1957).

Rad·nor·shire \'rad-nər-,shi(ə)r, -shər\ *or* **Rad·nor** \'rad-nər\. County, E Wales; area 471 sq. m.; pop. (1971p) 18,262; ⊗ Presteigne; hilly area; agriculture, livestock farming; tourism.

Ra·dom \'räd-,om\. Industrial commune, Kielce prov., E cen. Poland, 37 m. NE of Kielce; pop. (1970p) 159,000; railroad junction; produces leather goods, glass, lumber, tobacco products, chemicals; first mentioned 12th cent.; received town rights 14th cent.; to Austria 1795; under grand duchy of Warsaw 1809–15; returned to Poland 1918.

Ra·dom·sko \rə-'dom(p)-(,)skō\ *or Russ.* **No·vo·ra·domsk** \,nov-ə-rə-'domsk\. Commune, Łódź prov., cen. Poland, 48 m. S of Łódź; pop. (1970e) 31,200; metal and woodworking.

Ra·do·myshl *or* **Ra·do·mysl** \,rä-də-'mish-əl\. Town, E Zhitomir Oblast, Ukrainian S.S.R., U.S.S.R., on left bank of Teterev river 55 m. W of Kiev; pop. (1959c) 11,257.

Ra·dzion·ków \,rä-jon-'kaü\. Town, Katowice prov., S Poland, ab. 10 m. NNW of Katowice; pop. (1970p) 27,800.

Rae Ba·re·li \,rī-bə-'rā-lē\. Town, S cen. Uttar Pradesh, N India, 45 m. SSE of Lucknow; pop. (1961c) 29,940; trade center; has several ancient buildings, among them a fort, palace, and several fine mosques.

Rae·ford \'rā-fərd\. Town, ⊗ of Hoke co., S North Carolina, 20 m. WSW of Fayetteville; pop. (1970c) 3180; rayon, cottonseed oil.

Rae Strait \'rā-\. Channel bet. E King William I. and N Canada mainland, N Keewatin dist.

Rae·tia *or* **Rhae·tia** \'rē-sh(ē)-ə\. Ancient Roman province S of the Danube river; included most of what are now Tirol and Vorarlberg in Austria and Graubünden in E Switzerland. Bounded on N by Vindelicia, on E by Noricum, on S by Italy, and on W by Gaul. Added to Roman Empire in reign of Augustus.

Raetia Secunda. See VINDELICIA.

Rae·va·vae \,rī-vä-'vī\. See TUBUAI ISLANDS.

Ra·fa \'räf-ə\ *or* **Ra·fi·ah** \rə-'fē-ə\ *or anc.* **Ra·phia** \rə-'fī-ə\. Town on border bet. Gaza and Egypt (Sinai Penin.), since 1967 entirely within Israeli occupied territory, ab. 2 m. S of the Mediterranean coast; pop. (1968e) 49,800; formerly consisted of two contiguous towns (Egyptian town known as **Er Rafa** \e(ə)r-\ *or* **Ra·fah** \'räf-ə\) which were amalgamated following the Arab-Israeli war 1967; scene of battle 720 B.C. when Sargon II of Assyria defeated the Philistines and Egyptians, and in 217 B.C. scene of the defeat of Antiochus the Great by Ptolemy IV Philopator of Egypt.

Ra·fa·e·la \,räf-ə-'el-ə\. City, Santa Fe prov., E cen. Argentina, 50 m. NW of Santa Fe; pop. (1960c) 35,653; important communications center.

Raf·fa·da·li \rä-'fä-də-lē\. Commune, Agrigento prov., SW Sicily, Italy, 7 m. NNW of Agrigento; pop. (1968e) 12,795.

Rafiah. See RAFA.

Ra·gang, Mount \-rä-'gäŋ\. Active volcano, SE Lanao del Sur prov., Mindanao, Phil., on Cotabato boundary; 9235 ft.

Ra·gay Gulf \rä-'gī-\. An inland water of cen. Phil., a N arm of the Sibuyan Sea in SE Luzon; ab. 60 m. long and 32 m. wide at its mouth or S end; Burias I. is S of its mouth.

Rages. See RHAGES.

Rag·ged Island \,rag-əd-\. One of the Bahama Is., in Atlantic Ocean N of E end of Cuba and W of Acklins I.; with adjacent cays, 5 sq. m.; pop. (1963c) 371.

Ragged Top, Mount. Peak, Lawrence co., W South Dakota; 6207 ft.

Rag·lan \'rag-lən\. Town, Monmouthshire, SE Wales, 6½ m. SW of Monmouth; site of castle begun c. 1465, besieged 10 weeks 1646; gave title to Field Marshal Lord Raglan (d. 1855).

Ra·gu·sa \rə-'gü-zə\. 1 Province of SE Sicily, Italy. See table at ITALY.

2 *or anc.* **Hy·bla He·raea** \,hī-blə-hə-'rē-ə\. Commune, its ✱, 113 m. SE of Palermo; pop. (1968e) 59,787; cement, plastics; oil wells, asphalt pits; 18th cent. cathedral. In World War II junction point of Americans and Canadians in occupation of Sicily July 1943.

3 Seaport, Yugoslavia. See DUBROVNIK.

Ra·ha, Har·rat ar *or* **Harrat ar–Rahā** \'här-,ät-,är-rə-'hä\. Elevated tract, N Hejaz, NW Saudi Arabia; highest point 7000 ft.

Ra·had \'rä-,had\. River, E Africa; over 300 m. long; rises in NW Ethiopia near Lake Tana, flows NW across border into the Sudan and empties into the Blue Nile (Bahr al-Azraq).

Rahaeng. See TAK.

Rahiroa. See RANGIROA.

Rah·way \'ro-,wā\. 1 Short stream, NE New Jersey; rises in Essex co., flows S through Union co., enters Arthur Kill 5 m. S of Elizabeth.

2 City, Union co., NE New Jersey, on Rahway river 5 m. SSW of Elizabeth; pop. (1970c) 29,114; chemicals, automobile parts, pharmaceuticals, soap; truck farms.

Rai. See RHAGES.

Ra·ia·téa \,rī-ə-'tā-ə\. One of the Leeward Is. group of the Society Is., French Polynesia, S Pacific Ocean, 130 m. WNW of Tahiti and just S of Tahaa; 75 sq. m.; pop. (1967e) 6187, with Tahaa 9754; highest point 3389 ft.

Rai·chur \'rī-chər\. Town, W Mysore, S cen. India, 110 m. SW of Hyderabad in the doab bet. the Krishna and Tungabhadra rivers; pop. (1961c) 63,329; contains an old fort and a palace.

Rai·dak \'rīd-,äk\ *or* **Rai·dhak** \'rīd-,(h)äk\. River, W Bhutan; flows S across Indian border to the Brahmaputra.

Raidestos. See TEKIRDAĞ 2.

Rai·garh \'rī-,gär\. 1 Former Indian state, now part of Madhya Pradesh, NE India; 1444 sq. m.

2 Town, its ✱, 185 m. NW of Cuttack; pop. (1961c) 36,933; silk.

Rain \'rīn\. Village, Bavaria, West Germany, on the Lech river near its confluence with the Danube 22 m. N of Augsburg. In battle here Apr. 15, 1632 Count Tilly was defeated by Gustavus Adolphus and mortally wounded.

Rain·bow Bridge National Monument \,rān-bō-\. See UNITED STATES, *National Monuments.*

Rainbow City. 1 Town, Etowah and St. Clair cos., NE Alabama; pop. (1970c) 3107.

2 *or formerly* **Sil·ver City** \'sil-vər-\. Town, Cristobal dist., Canal Zone, adjoining Cristobal; pop. (1970p) 2385.

Rainbow Peak. 1 Mountain, N Valley co., W cen. Idaho; 9329 ft.

2 Mountain, Glacier National Park, NW Montana; 9870 ft.

Raincy, Le. See LE RAINCY.

Rai·nier, Mount \-rə-'ni(ə)r, -rā-\. Peak, Pierce co., W cen. Washington; 14,410 ft.; highest point in Cascade Range and in the state; sometimes called **Ta·co·ma** \tə-'kō-mə\, the Indian name; in Mount Rainier National Park (see UNITED STATES, *National Parks*).

Rains \'rānz\. County in Texas. See table at TEXAS.

Rainy \'rā-nē\. River, forming part of the Canada-U.S. boundary, bet. SW Ontario prov. and N Minnesota; ab. 80 m. long; flows from Rainy Lake to Lake of the Woods, leaving Rainy Lake at Koochiching Falls.

Rainy Lake. Lake on N boundary of Minnesota, bet. Minnesota and Canadian province of Ontario; area 360 sq. m.; outlet of Rainy river.

Rainy River. District, Ontario, Canada. See table at ONTARIO.

Rai·pur \'rī-,pu̇(ə)r\. Town, SE Madhya Pradesh, India, 162 m. E of Nagpur; pop. (1970e) 212,414; univ. (1963).

Rai·ra·khol \'rī-rə-,kōl\. Former Indian state, NE India, N of the Mahanadi river; now part of NE Orissa state; 857 sq. m.; ✱ Rairakhol.

Rai·sin \'rāz-ᵊn\. River, SE Michigan; ab. 115 m. long; rises in Hillsdale co., flows NE, curves SE, and turns E into Lake Erie at Monroe, in Monroe co. See MONROE 5.

Raismes \'rām, 'rem\. Industrial commune, Nord dept., N France, 3 m. NNW of Valenciennes; pop. (1968c) 13,357; manufactures marine hardware.

Ra·ja \'rä-yə\. Peak, Schwaner Mts., W cen. Borneo, Indonesia; 7474 ft.

Rajaburi. See RAT BURI.

Ra·ja·gri·ha \ˌräj-ə-ˈgrē-ə\. Ancient city, S Bihar, NE India, in the hills SSW of Bihar; its importance indicated by extensive ruins; as capital of kingdom of Magadha under Bimbisara (d. 554? B.C.), home for many years of Gautama Buddha. Now site of modern village of **Raj·gir** \ˈräj-ˌgi(ə)r\, a place of pilgrimage.

Ra·jah·mun·dry \ˌräj-ə-ˈmu̇n-drē\. City, NE Andhra Pradesh, E India, on left bank of Godavari river 295 m. NNE of Madras; pop. (1970e) 158,498; market town; paper mill; center of timber trade. Seized from princes of Orissa by Muslims 1470; to Hindus early 16th cent., and again taken by Muslims 1572; taken by French 1753 and from latter by British 1758.

Ra·jang \ˈräj-ˌäŋ\ *or* **Re·jang** \ˈrā-ˌjäŋ\. Chief river of cen. Sarawak, Malaysia, on island of Borneo; ab. 350 m. long; flows SW and W into South China Sea; chief town on its course Sibu; navigable for ab. 80 m.; has wide delta.

Ra·ja·pa·lai·yam \ˌrä-jə-ˈpä-lī-yəm\. Town, Tamil Nadu, India, ab. 50 m. SW of Madurai; pop. (1961c) 71,203.

Ra·ja·sthan \ˈrä-jə-ˌstän\. 1 Region, India. See RAJPUTANA.

2 State, NW India; 132,149 sq. m.; pop. (1971p) 25,724,-142; ✱ Jaipur; wheat, barley, sugarcane, wool, gypsum, salt; largest cities: Jaipur, Kota, Ajmer; organized 1947 as **Union of Rajasthan;** reorganized 1956 with addition of Ajmer and other areas.

Raj·ba·ri \räj-ˈbä-rē\ *or formerly* **Go·a·lan·da** \ˌgō-ə-ˈlən-də\. Town, Bangla Desh, on right bank of Ganges at its junction with the Jamuna; munic. pop. (1961c) 16,044; often destroyed by shifting courses of the rivers.

Raj·garh \ˈräj-ˌgär\. 1 Former state, Bhopal, cen. India; now part of Madhya Pradesh state; 926 sq. m.

2 Town, its ✱, 80 m. NE of Ujjain; pop. (1961c) 9100; founded c. 1640.

Rajgir. See RAJAGRIHA.

Raj·kot \ˈräj-ˌkōt\. 1 Former state, N cen. Kathiawar, now part of Gujarat state, W India; 282 sq. m.

2 Town, its ✱, 125 m. WSW of Ahmadabad; pop. (1967e) 233,462; major railroad junction; univ. (1966).

Raj·ma·hal Hills \ˌräj-mə-ˌhäl-\. Low range of hills, E Bihar, NE India, S and W of the Ganges river; highest ab. 2000 ft.

Raj–Nand·gaon *or* **Raj·nand·gaon** \räj-ˈnän(d)-ˌgau̇n\. Town, S Madhya Pradesh, E cen. India, ✱ of former Nandgaon state, 125 m. E of Nagpur; pop. (1961c) 44,678.

Raj·pi·pla *or formerly* **Raj·pee·pla** \räj-ˈpē-plə\. 1 Former Indian state, now part of Gujarat state, W India; 1515 sq. m.; formerly in Rewa Kantha Agency.

2 Town, its ✱, NE of Surat; pop. (1961c) 21,426.

Raj·pu·ta·na \ˌräj-pə-ˈtän-ə\ *or* **Ra·ja·sthan** \ˈräj-ə-ˌstän\. Region of NW India, formerly including the Rajputana Agency (*q.v.*) and Ajmer-Merwara prov. Region now part of Gujarat, Madhya Pradesh, and Rajasthan states. The Aravalli Range crosses the S part of the region from NE to SW; the NW part is largely desert (Thar Desert or Indian Desert) but to the SE the country is generally quite fertile. Chief rivers Luni, Chambal, and Banas. The bulk of the population is Hindu. Before the coming of the Muslims, several powerful dynasties ruled the region, but by the 11th cent. A.D. these were largely overcome; in the centuries following there was much disorder under the Moguls and later under the Marathas; after 1817 the Rajput states came by treaties under British protection; in 1947 became part of India.

Rajputana Agency. Formerly the official name of a group of 21 Indian states in the Rajputana region; 132,559 sq. m. The Resident for the Crown resided at Mount Abu; he dealt directly with Bikaner and under him were four agencies: Jaipur Residency, Western Rajputana States, Eastern Rajputana States, and the Mewar and Southern Rajputana States (*qq.v.*).

Raj·sha·hi \räj-ˈshä-(ˌ)hē\. 1 Former division, N Bengal, NE British India; 19,642 sq. m.; divided Aug. 15, 1947 with ab. 2/3 of area and population in East Pakistan, (now Bangla Desh), and 1/3 in West Bengal, India. See EAST BENGAL and WEST BENGAL.

2 District in division; 2526 sq. m.; now part of Bangla Desh.

3 *or formerly* **Ram·pur Bo·a·lia** \ˈräm-ˌpu̇(ə)r-bō-ˈäl-ē-ə\. City, ✱ of district and of former division, Bangla Desh, on Ganges river 125 m. N of Calcutta; pop. (1969e) 76,000; lumber, matches, vegetable oils; univ. (1953).

Ra·ka·hanga \ˌräk-ə-ˈhäŋ-ə\. Atoll in the Northern Cook Is., cen. Pacific Ocean, N of the Cook Is. ab. 25 m. NW of Manahiki; ab. 1 1/2 sq. m.; pop. (1968e) 340; produces coconuts; administratively part of Cook Is.

Ra·ka·ia \rə-ˈkī-ə\. River, E cen. South I., New Zealand; 90 m. long; flows SE into Pacific Ocean.

Ra·ka·po·shi \ˌrək-ə-ˈpō-shē\ *or* **Ra·ka·pu·shi** \-ˈpu̇sh-ē\. Peak in the Karakoram Range, in region of Jammu and Kashmir under Pakistani control; 25,550 ft.

Rakata. See KRAKATAU.

Rak·ka \ˈräk-(ˌ)ä\ *or Arab.* **Ar Raq·qah** \ar-ˈräk-(ˌ)ä\ *or anc.* **Ni·ce·pho·ri·um** \ˌnī-si-ˈfōr-ē-əm, -ˈfȯr-\. Town, N cen. Syria, on the left bank of the Euphrates river 100 m. SE of Aleppo; pop. (1960c) 14,554; near the confluence of the Balikh with the Euphrates. Prominent under the Abbassides; a favorite residence of Harun al-Rashid and the home of the Arab astronomer al-Battani.

Ra·kov·nik \ˈräk-ȯv-ˌnik\ *or Ger.* **Ra·ko·nitz** \ˈrä-kə-ˌnits\. Town, Czech S.R., W Czechoslovakia, 33 m. W of Prague; pop. (1968e) 12,795.

Ra·ku·to \ˈräk-ə-ˌtō\. River, South Korea; ab. 270 m. long; flows S into Korea Strait at Pusan; navigable for ab. 125 m.

Ra·leigh \ˈrȯ-lē, ˈräl-ē\. 1 County in West Virginia. See table at WEST VIRGINIA.

2 Town, ⊗ of Smith co., S cen. Mississippi, ab. 45 m. SE of Jackson; pop. (1970c) 1018.

3 City, ✱ of North Carolina, also ⊗ of Wake co., E cen. North Carolina, 50 m. S of Virginia border; pop. (1970c) 123,793; retail and wholesale trade center, cotton and tobacco market; produces textiles, fabricated steel products, chemicals, flour, agricultural machinery, pharmaceuticals, paper, electronic components. Saint Mary's Junior Coll. (1842), Peace Coll. (1857), Shaw Univ. (1865), St. Augustine's Coll. (1867), North Carolina State Univ. at Raleigh (1887), Meredith Coll. (1891). Settled 1792, incorporated 1793; in Civil War occupied by Union forces under Sherman Apr. 1865.

Raleigh Bay. Bay off E coast of North Carolina bet. Cape Hatteras and Cape Lookout.

Ra·lik \ˈräl-ik\. Western chain of islands in the Marshall Is., W Pacific Ocean; includes 15 atolls and 3 coral islands in long chain of ab. 750 m. More important atolls Jaluit, Kwajalein, Wotho, and Eniwetok.

Ralls \ˈrȯlz\. County in Missouri. See table at MISSOURI.

Ral·ston \ˈrȯl-stən\. City, Douglas co., E Nebraska, 5 m. SW of Omaha; pop. (1970c) 4731; rubber products; diversified agriculture.

Ra·mac·ca *also* **Ram·mac·ca** \rə-ˈmäk-ə\. Commune, Catania prov., E Sicily, Italy, 23 m. WSW of Catania; pop. (1968e) 10,130.

Ra·ma·di \rä-ˈmad-ē\ *or Arab.* **Ar Ra·mā·ḏī** \ˈär-rə-ˈma-dē\ *also* **Ru·ma·di·ya** \ru̇m-ə-ˈdē-(y)ə\. Town, cen. Iraq, on right bank of Euphrates river 60 m. W of Baghdad; pop. (1965c) 28,723; starting point of highway across the desert to Mediterranean towns. In World War I scene of battle Sept. 28–29, 1917 in which British under Maude defeated the Turks.

Ra·mah \ˈrā-mə\. See ARIMATHEA.

Ram·a·po \'ram-ə-ˌpō\. River, S New York and N New Jersey; rises in New York N of the Ramapo Mts., flows SE traversing the range, then S and SW just S of the range to unite at Pompton (just S of Pompton Lakes) with the Pequannock and Ringwood rivers to form the Pompton river.

Ramapo Mountains. Range of the Appalachian Mts. extending NE–SW in S New York (Rockland and Orange cos.) and N New Jersey (Bergen co.); highest point 1164 ft.

Ra·mat Gan \rə-'mät-ˌgän\. Town, Israel, 2 m. E of Tel Aviv-Jaffa; pop. (1970e) 115,500; Diamond Exchange; founded 1921.

Ram·ber·vil·lers \räⁿ-ˌber-vē-'lä\. Town, Vosges dept., NE France, 15 m. NE of Épinal; pop. (1962c) 7060; noted for the time when it was defended by a force of 200 National Guardsmen against 2000 Prussians Oct. 9, 1870.

Ram·bouil·let \ˌräⁿ-bü-'yā\. Town, Yvelines dept., N France, 28 m. SW of Paris; pop. (1968c) 14,499; restored 14th cent. chateau, now summer residence of the presidents of France; Forest of Rambouillet nearby.

Ram·bu·tyo \räm-'büt-ē-ˌō\. Island in Admiralty Is., 35 m. ESE of Manus I., Bismarck Archipelago, W Pacific Ocean; 10 m. long by 8 m. wide; highest point 700 ft.

Ram·durg \'räm-ˌdu̇(ə)rg\. Former Indian state, now part of Mysore state, SW India; 166 sq. m.; ✻ Ramdurg; one of the seven states which united to form the United Deccan State Aug. 26, 1947.

Rame Head \'rām-\. Headland on the coast of Cornwall, SW England, on the W side of Plymouth Sound.

Ra·men·sko·ye \'räm-ən-skȯ-yə\. Town, Moscow Oblast, Russian S.F.S.R., U.S.S.R., 27 m. SE of Moscow; pop. (1969e) 56,000.

Ra·mes·wa·ram \rä-'mes-wə-rəm\. 1 Island, S Tamil Nadu, S India, bet. Palk Strait and the Gulf of Mannar, at the W end of Adam's Bridge.
2 Village on the island; pop. (1961c) 6800; has temple of Dravidian architecture and one of the oldest of Hindu shrines; visited annually by thousands of pilgrims.

Ram·gan·ga \räm-'gəŋ-gə\. River, Uttar Pradesh, N India; ab. 350 m. long; rises in the Himalayas, flows S into the Ganges near Kannauj; navigable for short distance only.

Ra·mil·lies–Of·fus \ˌram-(ˌ)ē-yē-ȯ-'fü\ *also* **Ramillies** \'ram-ə-lēz, ˌram-(ˌ)ē-'yē\. Village, Brabant prov., cen. Belgium, 13 m. NE of Namur; pop. (1969e) 282; scene of battle in which Marlborough defeated the French under Villeroi May 12–23, 1706.

Ram·la \'räm-lə\ *also* **Er Ram·le** \ər-'räm-lə\. Town, ✻ of Central District, Israel, 12 m. SE of Tel Aviv-Jaffa; pop. (1970e) 30,800; founded A.D. 716.

Ram·leh \'räm-lə\ *or* **Ar Ra·mal** \är-'räm-ˌəl\. City, NE suburb and seaside resort of Alexandria, Egypt.

Rammacca. See RAMACCA.

Ram·na·gar \'räm-nə-gər\. 1 Town, formerly ✻ of Benares state, SE Uttar Pradesh, N India, on S bank of Ganges opp. Varanasi; pop. (1961c) 16,100.
2 Village, Punjab, Pakistan, 55 m. NNW of Lahore; pop. (1961c) 5826; here Nov. 22, 1848, Gen. Hugh Gough won victory in Second Sikh War.

Râmnicul–Sărat. See RÎMNICU-SĂRAT.

Râmnicul–Vâlcea. See RÎMNICU-VÎLCEA.

Ra·moth Gil·e·ad \ˌrā-ˌmäth-'gil-ē-əd\. Ancient town of Gilead, E of the Jordan and N of the Zarqa; a city of refuge (*Deut.* iv. 43); a place contended for in wars bet. Israel and Syria. Its location not certainly identified.

Ram·page Mountain \ˌram-ˌpāj-\. Peak in Glacier National Park, NW Montana; 6840 ft.

Ram·part \'ram-ˌpärt, -pərt\. Village, E cen. Alaska, S of the Yukon river WNW of Fairbanks; pop. (1970c) 36.

Ram·pur \'räm-ˌpu̇(ə)r\. 1 Former Indian state, N Uttar Pradesh, N India; 894 sq. m.; level and fertile country E of the Ganges, watered by the Kosi and Ramganga rivers. State founded in 18th cent.; ruled over by a nawab, a Rohilla Pathan of the family descended from the founder.
2 City, its ✻, on Kosi river 115 m. E of Delhi; pop. (1970e) 136,463; produces sugar, sword blades, pottery, and damask.

Rampur Boalia. See RAJSHAHI 3.

Ram·ree \'räm-(ˌ)rē\. 1 Island in Bay of Bengal off W coast of Burma, in Kyaukpyu dist.; ab. 50 m. long; the town of Kyaukpyu, capital of the district, is at its N end. Occupied by Indian troops Jan. 21–Feb. 17, 1945, after withdrawal of Japanese.
2 Village on E coast of island.

Rams·bot·tom \'ramz-ˌbät-əm\. Urban district, Lancashire, NW England, on the Irwell 12 m. N of Manchester; pop. (1971p) 15,872; iron and brass goods, textiles.

Ram·ses \'ram-ˌsēz\ *also* **Ra·am·ses** \rā-'am-ˌsēz\. City of ancient Egypt, in Goshen probably near Tanis; one of the treasure cities built for Ramses II by the Hebrews (*Exod.* i. 11).

Ram·sey \'ram-zē\. 1 Name of counties in two states of the U.S. See tables at MINNESOTA and NORTH DAKOTA.
2 Residential borough, Bergen co., NE corner of New Jersey, 9 m. N of Paterson; pop. (1970c) 12,571; dairy farms.
3 Urban district, Huntingdon and Peterborough co., E cen. England, 65 m. N of London; pop. (1971p) 5646; market town. Few remains of the 10th cent. Benedictine abbey.
4 Town on NE coast of Isle of Man, England; pop. (1971p) 5048; seaside resort.
5 Island in St. George's Channel off SW coast of Wales, ab. 3 m. W of St. David's Head, N of entrance to St. Brides Bay; ab. 2 m. long.

Rams·gate \'ramz-ˌgāt, -gət\. Municipal borough, Kent, SE England, on North Sea 17 m. N of Dover; pop. (1971p) 39,482; popular seaside resort and yachting center; Hengist and Horsa and St. Augustine are believed to have landed in the vicinity.

Ram·tek \'räm-(ˌ)tāk\. Town, NE Maharashtra, India, 24 m. NNE of Nagpur; pop. (1961c) 11,800; long a sacred place for Hindus; has many old temples.

Ra·mu \'räm-(ˌ)ü\. River, New Guinea I., Papua New Guinea; ab. 400 m. long; flows NW and N. Its valley held by Japanese 1942–43 but retaken by Americans and Australians in latter part of 1943.

Ra·na \'rän-ə\. 1 River in cen. Norway; flows SW into Ranen Fjord.
2 Commune, Nordland co., N Norway; pop. (1970e) 26,109.

Ranan. See NANAM.

Ra·nau \'rän-ˌau̇\. Lake in S end of Barisan Mts., S Sumatra, Indonesia.

Ran·ca·gua \rän-'käg-wə, räŋ-\. City, ✻ of O'Higgins prov., cen. Chile, 48 m. S of Santiago; pop. (1966e) 63,116; copper mines in the vicinity; scene of a battle Oct. 1 and 2, 1814 in which Chilean revolutionists under José Carrera and Bernardo O'Higgins were overcome by the Spaniards.

Rance \'räⁿs\. River, Brittany, NW France; ab. 60 m. long; flows N into the English Channel at Saint-Malo.

Ran·chi \'rän-chē\. 1 District, Chota Nagpur division, S Bihar, NE India; 7047 sq. m.; pop. (1961c) 2,138,565.
2 Town, its ✻ and summer ✻ of Bihar, 210 m. WNW of Calcutta; pop. (1970e) 139,052; steel, coke, machine tools; univ. (1960).

Ran·cho Cor·do·va \ˌran-chō-'kȯrd-ə-və\. Urban community, Sacramento co., N cen. California; pop. (1970c) 30,451.

Rancho Ve·loz \ˌrän-chō-və-'lōs\. Municipality, Las Villas prov., W cen. Cuba, 20 m. W of Sagua la Grande; pop. (1967e) 11,820.

Ran·chue·lo \ˌrän-chə-'wā-(ˌ)lō\. Municipality, Las Villas prov., W cen. Cuba, 14 m. WSW of Santa Clara; pop. (1967e) 23,330.

Ran·co \'räŋ-(ˌ)kō\. Lake, S cen. Chile, ab. 40 m. SE of Valdivia; resort.

Rand, The. See WITWATERSRAND.

Ran·dall \'ran-dᵊl\. County in Texas. See table at TEXAS.

Ran·dall's Island \ˌran-dᵊlz-\. Island in East river, New York, part of Manhattan borough; 194 acres; site of parks, playgrounds, a municipal stadium; meeting place of three arms of the Triborough Bridge.

Ran·daz·zo \ˌrän-ˈdät-sō\. Commune, Catania prov., E Sicily, Italy, on N slope of Mt. Etna 23 m. NNW of Catania; pop. (1968e) 12,318; archaeological museum. In World War II captured by U.S. troops Aug. 13, 1943.

Ran·ders \ˈrän-ərs\. Seaport, Århus co., E Jutland Penin., Denmark, on the Gudenå river where it enters Randers Fjord 15 m. from the Kattegat; pop. (1970e) 41,253; center of agricultural region; produces dairy products, beer, rope, tiles, agricultural machinery; 15th cent. church, 18th cent. town hall.

Randers Fjord. Inlet of the Kattegat on NE cen. coast of Jutland Penin., Denmark; receives the Gudenå river.

Rand·fon·tein \ˈrant-ˌfän-ˌtān\. City, S Transvaal, NE Rep. of South Africa, 28 m. W of Johannesburg; pop. (1967e) 45,400; produces textiles and machinery; at W end of Witwatersrand goldfields; the Randfontein gold mine is one of largest in the world. See KRUGERSDORP.

Ran·dolph \ˈran-ˌdälf\. 1 Name of counties in eight states of the U.S. See tables at ALABAMA, ARKANSAS, GEORGIA, ILLINOIS, INDIANA, MISSOURI, NORTH CAROLINA, WEST VIRGINIA.
2 Residential town, Kennebec co., SW Maine, on Kennebec river 7 m. S of Augusta; pop. (1970c) 1741.
3 Town, Norfolk co., E Massachusetts, 6 m. N of Brockton; pop. (1970c) 27,035; residential.
4 Town, ⊗ of Rich co., N Utah; pop. (1970c) 500.
5 Village in Randolph town, Orange co., E Vermont, 20 m. SSW of Barre; pop. (1970c) 2115 (village), 3882 (town); furniture, plastics, gloves; dairy farms. At **Randolph Center,** to E, is Vermont Agricultural and Technical Institute (1957).

Randolph, Fort. See FORT RANDOLPH.

Randolph Field. United States Air Force base and military reservation, Bexar co., S cen. Texas, 16 m. ENE of San Antonio.

Rand·wick \ˈran-(ˌ)dwik\. City, E New South Wales, SE Australia, SE suburb of Sydney on Pacific Ocean and Botany Bay.

Ra·nen Fjord \ˈrän-ən-fē-ˌȯ(ə)rd, -ˌfyȯ(ə)rd\ *or* **Ran·fjord** \ˈrän-ˌfyü(ə)r\. Inlet of Norwegian Sea on W coast of Norway opp. Dønna I.; receives Rana river from the E.

Ran·ga·ma·ti \ˌrəŋ-ˈgäm-ət-ē\. See CHITTAGONG HILL TRACTS.

Rangasa, Tandjung. See MANDAR, GULF OF.

Rang·au·nu Bay \ˌräŋ-aů-ˌnü-\. Inlet of Pacific Ocean, NE coast of N extension of North I., New Zealand.

Range·ley Lakes \ˈrānj-lē-\. Chain of lakes in Franklin and Oxford cos., in W Maine, including Rangeley, Mooselookmeguntic, Upper Richardson, Lower Richardson, and Umbagog lakes, extending over 50 m. in length and covering an area of 80 sq. m.; elevation bet. 1200 and 1500 ft.; resort for fishermen and sportsmen.

Rang·er \ˈrān-jər\. City, Eastland co., N cen. Texas, 40 m. E of Abilene; pop. (1970c) 3094; oil wells and refineries; Ranger Coll. (1926).

Ranger Peak. Mountain, NE Idaho co., N cen. Idaho; 8810 ft.

Rang·i·o·ra \ˌräŋ-ē-ˈōr-ə, -ˈȯr-\. Borough, E South I., New Zealand, on inlet of Pegasus Bay 17 m. N of Christchurch; pop. (1970e) 4660.

Rang·i·roa \ˌräŋ-i-ˈrō-ə\ *or* **Ra·hi·roa** \ˌrä-hi-\. Atoll, largest in the Tuamotu Archipelago, French Polynesia, in S Pacific Ocean, 200 m. NNE of Tahiti; 29 sq. m.; pop. (1967e) 868; has good harbor within the lagoon.

Rang·i·tai·ki \ˌräŋ-i-ˈtī-kē\. River, cen. and N cen. North I., New Zealand; 120 m. long; flows NE and N into Bay of Plenty.

Rang·i·ta·ta \ˌräŋ-i-ˈtät-ə\. River, E cen. South I., New Zealand; 75 m. long; flows SE into Canterbury Bight.

Rang·i·tik·ei \ˌräŋ-i-ˈtik-ē\. River, SW North I., New Zealand; 150 m. long; flows S and SW into Cook Strait.

Rang·i·to·to \ˌräŋ-i-ˈtōt-(ˌ)ō\. Island on E coast of North I., New Zealand, in outer harbor of Auckland; a lava cone 854 ft. high.

Ran·goon \ran-ˈgün, raŋ-\. 1 River, S Burma; ab. 25 m. long; E outlet of the Irrawaddy in the Irrawaddy delta.
2 Division of Burma. See table at BURMA.
3 City, ✱ of Burma, also ✱ of the division, on Rangoon river 21 m. from its mouth; pop. (1969e) 1,733,000; commercial center of Burma and its principal seaport, exporting rice, lead and zinc ore, oil cake, timber, cotton, and tobacco; oil refining, timber working (esp. teak), rice milling; numerous public buildings and an extensive network of parks and gardens; notable Shwe Dagon Pagoda (368 ft. high, gold-covered); univ. (1920) and technical univ. (1963).
History: Shwe Dagon Pagoda an ancient Buddhist shrine, but no town on site until 18th cent., when Rangoon was developed as a port and commercial center by King Alaungpaya 1755 ff.; occupied by British 1824–26 and taken by them 1852 in Second Burmese War; severely damaged by earthquake and tidal wave 1930; in World War II occupied by Japanese Mar. 1942–May 1945 and suffered very heavy damage.

Rang·pur \ˈrəŋ-ˌpů(ə)r\. 1 District, formerly in N Bengal, NE British India, now in Bangla Desh; 3704 sq. m.; pop. (1961c) 3,796,043.
2 Town, its ✱, on tributary of Jamuna river; pop. (1961c) 40,364; carpets, tobacco products.

Ra·ni·ganj \ˈrän-i-ˌgənj\. Town, West Bengal, NE India, on N bank of Damodar river ab. 105 m. NW of Calcutta; pop. (1961c) 32,290.

Ra·ni·khet \ˈrän-i-ˌket\. Hill station and military sanitarium, NE Uttar Pradesh, N India, 75 m. NE of Moradabad; pop. (1961c) 10,600; alt. 6000 ft.

Ran·kin \ˈraŋ-kən\. 1 County in Mississippi. See table at MISSISSIPPI.
2 Borough, Allegheny co., SW Pennsylvania, on Monongahela river 7 m. E of Pittsburgh; pop. (1970c) 3704.
3 City, ⊗ of Upton co., W Texas; pop. (1970c) 1105.

Ran·noch, Loch \läk-ˈran-ək, läḵ-ˈran-əḵ\. Lake, Perth co., cen. Scotland; 9 m. long.

Rann of Kutch. See KUTCH, RANN OF.

Ra·nong \ˈrä-ˈnȯŋ\. 1 Province, SW Thailand; 3426 sq. m.; pop. (1960c) 37,628; ✱ Ranong.
2 Port, its ✱, on W coast of Malay Penin. at mouth of the Pakchan river, ab. 8 m. E of Victoria Point in Burma; pop. (1960c) 5993.

Ran·pur \ˈrän-ˌpů(ə)r\. Former Indian state, now in Orissa state, NE India; 204 sq. m.; ✱ Ranpur; near coast 45 m. SW of Cuttack.

Ran·sart \räⁿ-ˈsär\. Commune, Hainaut prov., SW Belgium, just N of Charleroi; pop. (1969e) 10,026.

Ran·som \ˈran(t)-səm\. County in North Dakota. See table at NORTH DAKOTA.

Ran·te·kom·bo·la \ˌrän-tə-ˈkȯm-bə-lə\. Mountain in N cen. part of the SW peninsula of Celebes I., Indonesia, near Palopo; 11,335 ft.; highest point of Celebes.

Ran·te·ma·rio \ˌränt-ə-ˈmär-ē-ˌō\. Mountain in N cen. part of the SW peninsula of Celebes I., Indonesia, near Palopo; 11,286 ft.

Ran·toul \ran-ˈtül\. Village, Champaign co., E cen. Illinois, 15 m. N of Champaign; pop. (1970c) 25,562; site of Chanute Field which has a U.S. Air Force Technical School.

Raoeng. See RAUNG.

Ra·oul, Cape \-ˈraů(ə)l\. Southern point of Tasman Penin., Tasmania, Australia, W of Cape Pillar and at E entrance to Storm Bay; extends into Tasman Sea.

Raoul Island \ˈraů(ə)l-\ *or* **Sun·day Island** \ˈsən-dē-\. Largest island of the Kermadec Is. (*q.v.*).

Ra·pa \'räp-ə\. Island at SE end of chain of Tubuai Is., French Polynesia, S Pacific Ocean, 27°36'S lat. and 144°20'W long.; ab. 20 m. in circumference; mountainous (highest 2077 ft.) and well-wooded; has harbor. Formerly had a large population of Polynesian origin. In early 19th cent. much visited by whalers; first missionaries arrived 1817.

Ra·pal·lo \rə-'päl-(,)ō\. Commercial seaport commune, Genova prov., Liguria, NW Italy, on **Gulf of Rapallo,** an inlet of Ligurian Sea, 16 m. ESE of Genoa; pop. (1968e) 25,311; tourist resort; two treaties signed here after World War I: (1) Nov. 12, 1920 bet. Italy and Yugoslavia which made Fiume an independent city; (2) Apr. 16, 1922 bet. U.S.S.R. and Germany in which both renounced claims to war indemnities.

Rapa Nui. See EASTER ISLAND.

Ra·pel \rä-'pel\. River, Chile; flows NW, enters Pacific Ocean SW of Santiago.

Raphia. See RAFA.

Rap·i·dan \,rap-ə-'dan\. River, N Virginia; ab. 70 m. long; rises in Blue Ridge Mts., flows E into Rappahannock river on boundary bet. Culpeper and Spotsylvania cos.

Rap·id City \,rap-əd-\. City, ⊗ of Pennington co., SW South Dakota, in E part of Black Hills 45 m. E of Wyoming border; pop. (1970c) 43,836; tourism; produces building materials, dairy products, flour, electronic equipment, mobile homes; gold, uranium, mica, silver, beryllium mines; livestock farms; South Dakota School of Mines and Technology (1885); Ellsworth Air Force Base; settled 1876, incorporated 1878.

Ra·pides \,rä-'pēd\. Parish in Louisiana. See table at LOUISIANA.

Ra·pi·do \'räp-i-,dō\. Short river, SE Latium, cen. Italy, flows SW past Cassino to the Liri; in World War II in campaign in Italy formed a German defense line; held against unsuccessful attempt of U.S. troops to cross Jan. 20–23, 1944; finally crossed by U.S. troops May 1944.

Rap·pa·han·nock \,rap-ə-'han-ək\. 1 River, NE Virginia; 212 m. long; navigable to Fredericksburg; rises in Blue Ridge Mts., Rappahannock co., N Virginia, flows SE forming a long estuary emptying into Chesapeake Bay; scene of Civil War campaign Nov. 1863.

2 County in Virginia. See table at VIRGINIA.

Rappoltsweiler. See RIBEAUVILLÉ.

Rap·ti \'räp-tē\. River, Nepal and N India; ab. 400 m. long; flows NW in Nepal and then SE in Uttar Pradesh, India, to the Ghāghara river; navigable in its lower course.

Ra·pu–Ra·pu \,räp-ü-'räp-(,)ü\. 1 Island, Albay prov., S Luzon, Phil.; 25 sq. m.; chief town Rapu-Rapu; coal mines; occupied by U.S. troops Apr. 13, 1945.

2 Chief town on Rapu-Rapu I., Luzon, Phil.; munic. pop. (1969e) 22,900.

Raqqah, Ar. See RAKKA.

Raq·uette \'rak-ət\. River, N New York; ab. 140 m. long; rises in Hamilton co., flows N through St. Lawrence co. into St. Lawrence river near Massena.

Raquette Lake. Lake, N Hamilton co., NE cen. New York; ab. 10 m. long; elevation 1775 ft.; drains through stream flowing NE into Long Lake; summer resort.

Rar·i·tan \'rar-ət-ᵊn\. 1 River, N cen. New Jersey; ab. 75 m. long; formed by confluence of branches in W Somerset co., flows E into Raritan Bay.

2 Borough, Somerset co., N cen. New Jersey, 11 m. WNW of New Brunswick; pop. (1970c) 6691.

Raritan Bay. Inlet of Atlantic Ocean in Middlesex co., cen. New Jersey; receives the Raritan river and Arthur Kill on the NW; city of Perth Amboy is on NW shore.

Rar·o·ton·ga \,rar-ə-'täŋ-gə\. Chief island of the Cook Is., in SW part of group, S Pacific Ocean; 21°14'S, 159°46'W; 26 sq. m.; pop. (1968e) 10,853; chief village Avarua on N coast, ✱ of Cook Is.; exports copra, oranges, bananas, tomatoes. Highest point 2140 ft. One of the most habitable of all Polynesian islands. Discovered 1820; claimed by Germany bet. 1880 and 1889, but formally annexed by Great Britain 1889; transferred to New Zealand 1901.

Ras \räs\. Arabic word meaning "cape"; for many names beginning with it, see the distinguishing element.

Ras al–Ge·nei·na \,räs-,al-gə-'nā-nə\. Mountain, S cen. Sinai Penin., NE Egypt; 5334 ft.; highest point of Egma Plateau.

Ras al–Khai·mah \,räs-al-'kī-mə\. 1 Sheikhdom, member state of the United Arab Emirates. See UNITED ARAB EMIRATES.

2 Town, its ✱; pop. (1968c) 5244.

Ras ash–Sharbatāt. See SHARBATAT, CAPE.

Ra's at Tan·nū·rah \,räs-at-tə-'nůr-ə\ *or* **Ras Ta·nu·ra** \,räs-tə-'nůr-ə\. Peninsula, cape (*ras*), and seaport just E of Qatif on W coast of Persian Gulf, al-Hasa, Saudi Arabia, ab. 35 m. NW of Bahrain; oil pipelines and refineries.

Ra's aṭ Ṭīb. See BON, CAPE.

Ras Da·shan \,räs-də-'shän\. Peak in the Simyen Mts., N Ethiopia, NE of Gonder and Lake Tana; 15,158 ft.; highest peak in Ethiopia.

Rashīd. See ROSETTA.

Rashowa. See RASSHUA.

Rasht \'rasht\ *also* **Resht** \'resht\. Industrial city, ✱ of Gīlān prov., NW Iran, near the shore of the Caspian Sea; pop. (1971p) 150,000; silk-manufacturing center; has large trade, partly through its port of Bandar-e Pahlavī; connected by motor transport road with Qazvīn and Tehran to the SE. Suffered considerably from fighting in World War I.

Ras Muari. See MUARI, RAS.

Raso, Cape. See NORTE, CAPE.

Ras Sham·ra \,räs-'sham-(,)rä\. Site of ancient city of Ugarit (*q.v.*), near coast just N of Latakia, Syria; its archaeological objects, discovered 1929, have been of very great value; they include clay tablets of second millennium B.C. bearing texts in a cuneiform alphabet (Ugaritic), objects of art and daily use of Late Bronze Age, etc.

Ras·shua *or Jap.* **Ra·sho·wa** \rə-'shü-ə\. Small island in cen. part of Kuril chain, Russian S.F.S.R., U.S.S.R., NE of Simushir.

Ras·ska·zo·vo \,rə-'skäz-ə-və\. Town, cen. Tambov Oblast, Russian S.F.S.R., U.S.S.R., ab. 20 m. E of Tambov; pop. (1967e) 37,000.

Ras Tanura. See RA'S AT TANNŪRAH.

Ra·statt *or less commonly* **Ra·stadt** \'räs(h)-,tät\. City, Baden-Württemberg, West Germany, 13 m. SW of Karlsruhe; pop. (1969e) 28,803; machinery, furniture, lumber, beer. Became city 1705; Treaty of Rastatt signed here 1714 bet. Austria and France supplementing Treaty of Utrecht (War of the Spanish Succession); insurrection 1849.

Rastenburg. See KĘTRZYN.

Ra·tak \'rä-,täk\ *or* **Ra·dak** \'räd-,äk\. Eastern chain of islands in the Marshall Is., in W Pacific Ocean; includes 14 atolls and 2 coral islands in long chain of ab. 700 m. More important atolls are Mili, Majuro, Maloelap, Wotje, Likiep, and at extreme NW, Bikini.

Rat Bu·ri *or* **Ra·ja·bu·ri** \rät-'bů-,rē\. 1 Province, SW Thailand; 1977 sq. m.; pop. (1960c) 410,573; ✱ Rat Buri.

2 Town, its ✱, on Klong river 50 m. WSW of Bangkok; pop. (1964e) 28,372.

Ra·the·daung \'räth-ə-,daůn\. Village, Arakan div., W Burma, on Mayu river 25 m. NNW of Sittwe; fighting here in 1943 and 1944.

Ra·the·now \'rät-ə-,nō\. City, Potsdam dist., East Germany, on Havel river 33 m. NW of Potsdam; pop. (1970e) 29,823; optical goods, electrical equipment, bricks; 16th cent. town hall. Became city 1295; suffered during Thirty Years' War, esp. 1631–41; occupied by the Swedes for a short time in June 1675.

Rath·lin \'rath-lən\. Island in the North Channel off the NE coast of Northern Ireland; administratively in co. Antrim

Ra·thong \rä-'tòŋ\. Mountain in the Himalayas, on the Nepal-Sikkim boundary; 24,913 ft.

Ratibor. See RACIBÓRZ.

Ra·ting·en \'rät-iŋ-ən\. City, North Rhine-Westphalia, West Germany, 6 m. N of Düsseldorf; pop. (1969e) 42,256; textiles, pottery, glass, machinery, boilers, tile; 14th cent. church; made city 1276.

Ratisbon *or* **Ratisbona.** See REGENSBURG.

Rat Island \'rat-\. Small island in center of Rat Is., Alaska; 51°55'N, 178°20'E; E of Kiska and NW of Amchitka.

Rat Islands. Group of islands, W Aleutian Is., SW Alaska, extending from 175°45'E to 179°40'E; comprises Kiska (*q.v.*), Amchitka, Semisopochnoi, Rat, and a number of islets.

Rat·lam *or* **Rut·lam** \rət-'läm\. 1 Former Indian state, now part of Madhya Pradesh state, India; 687 sq. m.

2 Town, its ✱, 60 m. NW of Indore; pop. (1961c) 87,472; textiles, pottery; railroad shops.

Rat·na·gi·ri \rət-'näg-ə-rē\. Town, SW Maharashtra, W India, on Arabian Sea 136 m. S of Bombay; pop. (1961c) 31,091; port of call for coastal steamers; 16th cent. fort.

Rat·na·pu·ra \'rət-nə-ˌpu̇r-ə\. Town, SW cen. Ceylon, 42 m. ESE of Colombo; pop. (1968e) 24,000; center of precious-stone industry. Nearby is Maha Saman Dewale, Buddhist temple.

Ra·ton \rə-'tōn, ra-, -'tün\. City, ⊗ of Colfax co., N New Mexico, 115 m. NE of Santa Fe near Colorado border; pop. (1970c) 6892; alt. 6400 ft.; flour, wood products; tourist center; coal mines, livestock farms.

Raton Pass. Mountain pass, Las Animas co., SE Colorado, on Colorado-New Mexico boundary just N of Raton, New Mexico; 7834 ft.; highway and railroad; formerly traversed by a branch of the Santa Fe Trail; used by military expeditions 1720 and 1806 and by Gen. Stephen Watts Kearny's army 1846.

Raton Range. Range in SE Colorado, extending S across border into Colfax co., N New Mexico.

Rat Portage. See KENORA 2.

Rat·tray Head \ra-ˌtrā-\. Cape on NE cen. coast of Scotland, S of Kinnairds Head; lighthouse.

Rau·far·höfn \'rōi-ˌvär-ˌhərp-ən\. Village and port on NE coast of Iceland near Cape Rifstangi; pop. (1970e) 446.

Raukawa. See COOK STRAIT.

Rau·ku·ma·ra Range \rau̇-ˌkü-mə-rə-\. Mountain range in NE North I., New Zealand.

Rau·ma \'rau̇-mə\. 1 Seaport, Turku ja Pori prov., SW Finland, on the Gulf of Bothnia 25 m. S of Pori; pop. (1970e) 25,672; exports lumber and cellulose; paper mills; formed 1442.

2 River, cen. Norway; flows NW into Romsdalsfjord SE of Molde; has several waterfalls; its valley is called Romsdal (*q.v.*).

Raung *or Du.* **Ra·oeng** \rä-'üŋ\. Mountain, E Java, Indonesia, the highest point of the Idjen volcanic plateau; 10,932 ft.

Raurkela. See ROURKELA.

Rauxel. See CASTROP-RAUXEL.

Ra·val·li \rə-'val-ē\. County in Montana. See table at MONTANA.

Ra·va·nu·sa \ˌräv-ə-'nü-zə\. Commune, Agrigento prov., SW Sicily, Italy, 23 m. E by S of Agrigento; pop. (1968e) 15,151; trades in sulfur.

Ra·vel·lo \rə-'vel-ō\. Village, Salerno prov., S Campania, S Italy, 19 m. W of Salerno; pop. (1968e) 2592; 1227 ft. above the sea; 11th cent. palace, restored 19th cent.; 12th cent. church.

Ra·ve·na \rə-'vē-nə\. Village, Albany co., E New York, on Hudson river 11 m. S of Albany; pop. (1970c) 2797.

Ra·ven·na \rə-'ven-ə\. 1 City, ⊗ of Portage co., NE Ohio, 15 m. ENE of Akron; pop. (1970c) 11,780; rubber goods, lumber, structural steel, furniture; agriculture; settled 1799.

2 Province of Emilia-Romagna, Italy. See table at ITALY.

3 Commune, ✱ of Ravenna prov., Emilia-Romagna, N Italy, 61 m. NE of Florence; pop. (1968e) 130,137; connected with the Adriatic Sea by a canal; produces wine, fertilizer, sugar, furniture, and cement; exceptionally rich collection of Roman and Byzantine architectural remains, principally churches of the 5th–8th cents., including 6th cent. San Vitale with notable mosaics, 6th cent. tomb of Theodoric, 6th cent. basilica of San Apollinaire Nuovo; 4th cent. cathedral destroyed by fire 1733 and little of original remains.

History: Said to have been founded by Sabines; made part of Roman Gallia Cisalpina 191 B.C.; important naval station under Augustus; residence of numerous emperors and of Odoacer, who was conquered by the Ostrogoth Theodoric; stronghold of the Ostrogoths 493 A.D. ff.; conquered 540 by Belisarius and made capital of Byzantine Empire in Italy (exarchate of Ravenna); passed to Lombards c. 750 and later to Franks; became independent republic in 13th cent.; under Polenta family, Venetians, and popes; part of papal dominions 1509–1859; became part of kingdom of Italy 1860. In World War II taken by Allies Dec. 5, 1944.

Ra·vens·burg \'rā-vənz-ˌbərg, 'räv-ən(t)s-ˌbu̇(ə)rg\. Manufacturing city, Baden-Württemberg, West Germany, 47 m. SSW of Ulm; pop. (1969e) 31,908; textiles, lumber, paper; 16th cent. town hall, 14th cent. church. Founded in 11th cent.; free imperial city 1276–1803; member of Swabian League in 14th cent.; to Bavaria 1803.

Ra·ven·spur \'rā-vən-ˌspər\. Former seaport town, East Riding, Yorkshire, NE England, at mouth of Humber near Spurn Head; landing place of Edward IV 1471 in Wars of Roses; swept away by sea soon after.

Ra·vens·wood \'rā-vənz-ˌwu̇d\. Town, Jackson co., W West Virginia, on Ohio river 25 m. SW of Parkersburg; pop. (1970c) 4240; chinaware, brooms; diversified agriculture; aluminum rolling mill.

Ra·vi \'räv-ē\ *or anc.* **Hy·dra·o·tes** \ˌhī-drə-'ōt-(ˌ)ēz\. River, N Pakistan; about 475 m. long; one of the "Five Rivers" of the Punjab; rises in the Himalayas, flows SW diagonally across Pakistan to the Chenab; NE of Lahore forms part of boundary bet. Pakistan and India.

Rawa Harbour. See ARAWA HARBOUR.

Ra·wal·pin·di \ˌrä-wəl-'pin-dē, rau̇l-'\. 1 Division, Punjab, Pakistan.

2 District in division; 2022 sq. m.; pop. (1961c) 1,137,085.

3 City, ✱ of division and district, 90 m. ESE of Peshawar, was temporary ✱ of Pakistan; met. area pop. (1969e) 455,100; locomotive works, iron foundry, oil refinery; textiles. Strategically located, controlling routes to Kashmir; before 1947 had India's largest military station and was headquarters of northern army. Treaty signed here Aug. 8, 1919 by which Great Britain recognized complete independence of Afghanistan.

Rawandūz. See RUWANDIZ.

Rawḍah. See RODA.

Raw·don \'rȯ-dən\. Village, Montcalm co., S Quebec, Canada, 55 m. N of Montreal; pop. (1970e) 2752; concrete products, plastics; diversified agriculture; machine shops.

Raw·hide \'rȯ-ˌhīd\. Mining camp, Mineral co., SW Nevada, ab. 35 m. NNE of Hawthorne; scene of spectacular gold rush (led by Tex Rickard and others) inspired by Goldfield boom and financial slump of 1907.

Ra·wicz \'räv-ich\ *or Ger.* **Ra·witsch** \'ra-vich\. Industrial commune, Poznań prov., W cen. Poland, 50 m. S of Poznań; pop. (1968e) 13,600.

Raw·ka \'räf-kə\. River, W Poland, a tributary of the Bzura; ab. 50 m. long; constituted Russian defense line Dec. 1914 to July 1915.

Raw·lins \'rȯ-lənz\. 1 County in Kansas. See table at KANSAS.

2 City, ⊗ of Carbon co., S Wyoming, 28 m. SW of confluence of Medicine Bow and North Platte rivers; pop. (1970c) 7855; railroad center; ships livestock, uranium ore; oil refinery; founded 1868, incorporated 1886.

Raw·marsh \'rȯ-ˌmärsh\. Urban district, West Riding, Yorkshire, N England, near Rotherham; pop. (1971p) 19,884; ironworks, potteries, coal mines.

Raw·son \'rȯs-ᵊn, 'rau̇-ˌsȯn\. Seaport, ✱ of Chubut prov., S cen. Argentina, near the mouth of Chubut river; pop. (1960c) 4109.

Raw·ten·stall \'rȯt-ᵊn-ˌstȯl\. Municipal borough, Lancashire, NW England, on the upper Irwell 17 m. N of Manchester; pop. (1971p) 21,404; footwear, chemicals, rubber, textiles.

Ray \'rā\. County in Missouri. See table at MISSOURI.

Ray, Cape. Southwest point of Newfoundland, Canada, on Cabot Strait opp. N tip of Cape Breton I.

Ray, Mount. Mountain, Antarctica, 85°07'S, 170°48'W; 12,808 ft.

Rayak. See RIYAQ.

Ray·leigh \'rā-lē\. Urban district, Essex, SE England, 32 m. ENE of London; pop. (1971p) 26,265.

Ray·mond \'rā-mənd\. 1 Town, a ⊗ of Hinds co., SW cen. Mississippi, ab. 28 m. ESE of Vicksburg; pop. (1970c) 1620; Hinds Junior Coll. (1917); in Civil War scene of battle May 12, 1863, a victory for Grant's forces.

2 Town, Rockingham co., SE New Hampshire; pop. (1970c) 3003.

3 City, Pacific co., SW corner of Washington, on Willapa Bay 21 m. S of Aberdeen; pop. (1970c) 3126; lumber, veneer; salmon and oyster fisheries.

Raymond Peak. Mountain in Sierra Nevada in E Alpine co., E California; 10,075 ft.

Ray·mond·ville \'rā-mən(d)-ˌvil\. City, ⊗ of Willacy co., S Texas, 42 m. N of Brownsville; pop. (1970c) 7987; ships cotton; diversified agriculture.

Rayne \'rān\. City, Acadia parish, S Louisiana, 16 m. W of Lafayette; pop. (1970c) 9510; rice mills, oil wells; raises sugarcane, cotton; center of Louisiana frog industry.

Rayn·ham \'rān-əm\. Town, Bristol co., SE Massachusetts, 10 m. SSW of Brockton; pop. (1970c) 6705.

Ra·yong \rä-'yȯŋ\. 1 Province, S Thailand, 1277 sq. m.; pop. (1960c) 147,713; ✱ Rayong.

2 Town, its ✱, port on NE coast of Gulf of Siam 80 m. SE of Bangkok; pop. (1964e) 13,615.

Raystown. See BEDFORD 8.

Ray·town \'rā-ˌtau̇n\. City, Jackson co., W Missouri, SE suburb of Kansas City; pop. (1970c) 33,306.

Ray·ville \'rā-ˌvil\. Town, ⊗ of Richland parish, NE Louisiana, 22 m. E of Monroe; pop. (1970c) 3962; cotton.

Raz, Pointe du \ˌpwaⁿ(n)t-də-'rä\. Headland, W Finistère dept., NW France, S of Brest; 240 ft. high.

Raz·dan \räz-'dän\ *or* **Zan·ga** \zäŋ-'gä\. River, Armenian S.S.R., U.S.S.R.; 91 m. long; the outlet of Lake Sevan, flowing from its N end to the Araks S of Yerevan.

Ra·zelm, Lake \-rä-'zelm\. Coastal lake or lagoon, Tulcea co., SE Romania, just S of mouth of the Danube.

Raz·grad \'räz-ˌgrät\. 1 Province of N Bulgaria. See table at BULGARIA.

2 Town, its ✱, ab. 25 m. N of Shumen.

Ré, Île de \ˌēl-də-'rā\. Island in E Bay of Biscay, off W coast of Charente-Maritime dept., W France, opp. La Rochelle; 16 m. long; 33 sq. m.; pop. (1962c) 9484; chief town St-Martin on NE coast.

Rea, Lough. See LOUGHREA.

Read·ing \'red-iŋ\. 1 Residential town, Middlesex co., NE Massachusetts, 11 m. N of Boston; pop. (1970c) 22,539; stoves, photographic supplies; truck, dairy farms.

2 City, Hamilton co., SW corner of Ohio, 9 m. N of Cincinnati; pop. (1970c) 14,303; chemicals.

3 Industrial and commercial city, ⊗ of Berks co., SE Pennsylvania, on Schuylkill river 50 m. WNW of Philadelphia; pop. (1970c) 87,643; textiles, hosiery, brick, optical goods, chemicals, dairy products; foundries, railroad shops, coal mines; Albright Coll. (1856), Albernia Coll. (1958). Settled 1748; incorporated as borough 1783 and as city 1847.

4 County borough, ⊗ of Berkshire, S England, on the Kennet at its confluence with the Thames 39 m. W of London; pop. (1971p) 132,023; produces baked goods, machinery, beer, iron products; brewing and malting, printing, boatbuilding; livestock and grain market; Univ. of Reading (1926); Danish encamped on site 871; town received first charter 1253; made city 1639.

Rea·gan \'rā-gən\. County in Texas. See table at TEXAS.

Reagan Dam. See *Pacoima Dam* at UNITED STATES, *Dams and Reservoirs.*

Re·al \'rē-ˌȯl\. County in Texas. See table at TEXAS.

Real, Cordillero. See ANDES.

Re·ao \rā-'au̇\ *or* **Cler·mont–Ton·nerre** \ˌkler-ˌmōⁿ-tə-'ne(ə)r\. Island in E part of the Tuamotu Archipelago, French Polynesia, S Pacific Ocean; 18°31'S, 136°23'W; 10 m. long by 1½ m. wide.

Rear·guard, Mount \-'ri(ə)r-ˌgärd\. Peak, S Carbon co., S Montana; 12,350 ft.

Reate. See RIETI 2.

Re·bun \'reb-ˌu̇n\. Small island in N Sea of Japan, off NW coast of island of Hokkaidō, Japan.

Re·ca·na·ti \ˌräk-ə-'nät-ē\. Commune, Macerata prov., Marches, cen. Italy, 9 m. NNE of Macerata; pop. (1968e) 17,782; 14th cent. Gothic cathedral; home of the poet Leopardi.

Re·cherche Archipelago \rə-'shersh-\. Group of small islands in Indian Ocean off S coast of Western Australia, at W end of Great Australian Bight.

Re·chi·tsa \rə-'chit-sə\. Town, Gomel Oblast, Belorussian S.S.R., U.S.S.R., W of Gomel; pop. (1967e) 41,000; in World War II battle Nov. 22–25, 1943 in which Germans were defeated.

Re·ci·fe \rə-'sē-fə\ *or formerly* **Per·nam·bu·co** \ˌpər-nəm-'b(y)ü-(ˌ)kō\. Seaport, ✱ of Pernambuco state, E Brazil, at mouth of Capibaribe river near Point Plata, easternmost point of South America; munic. pop. (1970p) 1,078,819; one of the leading ports of Brazil, with extensive modern facilities, exporting sugar, cotton, and agricultural produce; naval and military base; federal univ. (1946) and other educational institutions. City is built partly on the mainland, partly on a peninsula and on an island in a lagoon formed by two rivers. First settled 1535; raided and sacked by English privateers 1595; occupied by Dutch 1630–1654; in World War II U.S. naval and air base.

Recife, Cape. Cape on SE coast of Cape Province, Rep. of South Africa, on W side of Algoa Bay 6 m. SW of Port Elizabeth.

Reciţa. See REŞIŢA.

Reck·ling·hau·sen \ˌrek-liŋ-'hau̇z-ᵊn\. Industrial and commercial city, North Rhine-Westphalia, West Germany, 30 m. SW of Münster; pop. (1969e) 125,733; textiles, machinery; coal mines, iron foundries, chemical plant; 16th cent. church; originally a Saxon settlement; became city and passed under archbishop of Cologne 1236; to Prussia 1815; in World War II occupied by U.S. forces Apr. 3, 1945.

Re·co·a·ro Ter·me \ˌre-kō-ˌä-rō-'ter-mē\. Commune, NW Vicenza prov., SW cen. Veneto, NE Italy; pop. (1968e) 8719; mineral springs.

Rec·tor \'rek-tər\. City, Clay co., NE corner of Arkansas; pop. (1970c) 1990.

Re·cu·let \rə-kyü-'lā\. Peak in Ain dept., E France, in the Jura Mts.; 5633 ft.

Red \'red\. 1 Navigable river, S cen. United States; 1018 m. long; rises in high plains in E New Mexico; flows E, crossing Texas Panhandle and then becoming boundary bet. Texas and Oklahoma and for a short distance boundary bet. Texas and Arkansas; turns S in SW Arkansas and crosses border into Louisiana, flows SE across Louisiana and into the Mississippi river.

2 River, N Tennessee; rises in Sumner co., flows NW across border of Kentucky, reenters Tennessee and flows SW into Cumberland river at Clarksville.

3 *or* **Red River of the North.** River, N cen. U.S. and S cen. Canada; 355 m. long. (ab. 700 m. with longest tributary); formed by junction at Breckenridge, W Minnesota, of the Otter Tail river from the E and Bois de Sioux river from Lake Traverse to the S; flows N forming Minnesota-North Dakota boundary, crosses Canadian border and continues N to S Lake Winnipeg, S Manitoba, Canada. Chief tributaries the Sheyenne and Red Lake rivers in U.S. and the Assiniboine in Canada; drains rich wheat lands. In Canada first settled as Scottish colony known as Red River Settlement (*q.v.*).

4 *or in China* **Yüan Chiang** \ˈywän-jē-ˈäŋ\ *or in North Vietnam* **Hong** \ˈhȯŋ\ *or formerly* **Coi** \ˈkȯi\. River, SE Asia; ab. 500 m. long; rises in cen. Yunnan prov., S China, flows SE across North Vietnam, past Hanoi, into Gulf of Tonkin; has wide fertile delta E of Hanoi.

Re·dan \ri-ˈdan\. Fortification, S part of Sevastopol, Crimean Oblast, Ukrainian S.S.R., U.S.S.R.; stormed unsuccessfully June and Sept. 1855 during Crimean War by the English; evacuated Sept. 10 by Russians.

Redang. See GREAT REDANG.

Red Bank \ˈred-ˌbaŋk\. 1 Residential and resort borough, Monmouth co., E cen. New Jersey, on Navesink river ab. 6 m. inland from Atlantic Ocean, 15 m. SE of Perth Amboy; pop. (1970c) 12,847; boats, electrical equipment, wood products, beverages; yachting center; truck and dairy farms.

2 Town, Hamilton co., SE Tennessee, near Chattanooga; pop. (1970c, with White Oak) 12,715.

Red Basin. See SZECHWAN.

Red Bluff. City, ⊗ of Tehama co., N California, on Sacramento river 38 m. NW of Chico; pop. (1970c) 7676; diversified agriculture.

Red·boy \ˈred-ˌbȯi\. Mountain, Grant co., E cen. Oregon; 6021 ft.

Red·bridge \ˈred-ˌbrij\. A borough of Greater London, SE England. See table at LONDON 4.

Red Bud \ˈred-ˌbəd\. City, Randolph co., SW Illinois, 28 m. SSE of East St. Louis; pop. (1970c) 2559; tools and dies; diversified agriculture.

Red Cedar. River, W Wisconsin; ab. 85 m. long; flows from Barron co. S into Chippewa river in S Dunn co.

Red Cloud \ˈred-ˌklau̇d\. City, ⊗ of Webster co., S Nebraska, on Republican river 35 m. S of Hastings; pop. (1970c) 1531; poultry farms.

Red·cloud Peak \ˌred-klau̇d-\. Mountain, Hinsdale co., SW Colorado; 14,034 ft.

Red Cone. Mountain, W Klamath co., S Oregon, N of Crater Lake; 7372 ft.

Red Deer \ˈred-ˌdi(ə)r\. 1 River, S Alberta, Canada; 385 m. long; rises in Banff National Park, SW Alberta, flows SE and E into the South Saskatchewan river near the Alberta boundary.

2 River, S cen. Canada; ab. 140 m. long; rises in E cen. Saskatchewan, flows E across border of Manitoba prov., through **Red Deer Lake** (100 sq. m.), into Lake Winnipegosis.

3 City, S Alberta, Canada, on Red Deer river 85 m. N of Calgary; pop. (1971p) 27,428; drills, feed, dairy products; poultry, grain farms; Red Deer Junior Coll. (1964).

Red·ding \ˈred-iŋ\. 1 City, ⊗ of Shasta co., N California, on Sacramento river 67 m. NNW of Chico; pop. (1970c) 16,659; sawmills, foundries, machine shops; summer resort; agriculture; Shasta Coll. (1949).

2 Town, cen. Fairfield co., SW Connecticut; pop. (1970c) 5590; dairy, truck farms.

Red·ditch \ˈred-ich\. Urban district, Worcestershire, W cen. England, near Birmingham; pop. (1971p) 40,775; needles, fishing tackle, bicycles.

Red Eagle Mountain. Peak in Glacier National Park, NW Montana; 8800 ft.

Red·field \ˈred-ˌfēld\. City, ⊗ of Spink co., NE cen. South Dakota, 41 m. S of Aberdeen; pop. (1970c) 2943.

Redfield Mountain. Peak in the Adirondack Mts., Essex co., NE New York; 4606 ft.

Red·fish Lake \ˌred-fish-\. Lake in W Custer co., cen. Idaho.

Red Hill. See MAUI 1.

Red Indian Lake. Lake, cen. Newfoundland, Canada; 37 m. long, 64 sq. m.; Exploits river flows into the lake.

Red Kaweah. See KAWEAH PEAKS.

Red Lake. 1 Lake, Beltrami co., N Minnesota, divided into **Upper Red Lake** and **Lower Red Lake;** 38 m. long; 451 sq. m.

2 River, NW Minnesota; 196 m. long; flows W out of Lower Red Lake, turns SW to empty into Red River of the North opp. Grand Forks, North Dakota.

3 County in Minnesota. See table at MINNESOTA.

Red Lake Falls. City, ⊗ of Red Lake co., NW Minnesota, 17 m. S of Thief River Falls; pop. (1970c) 1740.

Red·lands \ˈred-lən(d)z\. Residential city, San Bernardino co., SE California, 8 m. ESE of San Bernardino; pop. (1970c) 36,355; packs and ships oranges; furniture, missiles, dairy products, hosiery; fruit, truck farms; Univ. of Redlands (1907); settled 1887, incorporated 1888.

Red Lick Mountain. Peak, Pocahontas co., E cen. West Virginia; 3533 ft.

Red Li·on \-ˈlī-ən\. Borough, York co., S Pennsylvania, 8 m. SE of York; pop. (1970c) 5645.

Red Lodge \ˈred-ˌläj\. City, ⊗ of Carbon co., S Montana, 57 m. SW of Billings; pop. (1970c) 1844; resort; coal mines.

Red·mond \ˈred-mənd\. 1 City and resort, Deschutes co., cen. Oregon, 18 m. NNE of Bend; pop. (1970c) 3721; dairy, grain farms.

2 City, King co., W cen. Washington, 10 m. NE of Seattle; pop. (1970c) 11,031.

Red Mountain. 1 Peak in Sierra Nevada, E Fresno co., S cen. California; 11,933 ft.

2 Peak, Chaffee and Pitkin cos., W cen. Colorado; 13,500 ft.

3 Peak, Glacier National Park, NW Montana; 9300 ft.

4 Peak, S Lewis and Clark co., W cen. Montana; 8802 ft.

5 Peak, Baker co., E Oregon; 8304 ft.

6 Peak, N Whatcom co., NW Washington; 7784 ft.

Red·nitz \ˈrād-nəts\. River, Bavaria, West Germany; ab. 50 m. long; flows N to unite with the Pegnitz river at Fürth and form the Regnitz river.

Red Oak \ˈred-ˌōk\. City, ⊗ of Montgomery co., SW Iowa, 37 m. SE of Council Bluffs; pop. (1970c) 6210; concrete products; printing; grain, soybean farms.

Re·don \rə-ˈdōⁿ\. Town, SW Ille-et-Vilaine dept., NW France, on the Vilaine ab. 38 m. SSW of Rennes; pop. (1968c) 9363; on site of monastery founded 9th cent.

Re·don·da \ri-ˈdän-də\. Uninhabited island in the Leeward Is., West Indies; ab. 1 sq. m.; part of Antigua; rocky, highest point 1000 ft.; source of phosphate.

Re·don·de·la \ˌre-dȯn-ˈdā-lə\. Commune, Pontevedra prov., NW Spain, 15 m. S of Pontevedra; pop. (1970p) 22,128; manufactures linen, china.

Re·don·do Beach \ri-ˌdän-dō-\. Residential and resort city, Los Angeles co., SW California, on Pacific Ocean 17 m. SE of center of Los Angeles; pop. (1970c) 57,425; incorporated 1892.

Re·doubt Volcano \ri-ˈdau̇t-\. Volcano, S Alaska, ab. 18 m. W of Cook Inlet; 10,197 ft.; erupted 1966.

Red Peak. 1 Mountain in Sierra Nevada, in E Yosemite National Park, cen. California; 11,699 ft.

2 Mountain, Costilla and Las Animas cos., S Colorado; 13,600 ft.

Red Point. Cape on SW coast of St. Thomas I., Virgin Is. of the U.S., West Indies.

Redriff. See ROTHERHITHE.

Red River. 1 Parish in Louisiana and county in Texas. See tables at LOUISIANA and TEXAS.

2 Rivers. See RED.

Red River of the North. See RED 3.

Red River Settlement. Colony established 1811–16 by Scottish leader, earl of Selkirk, in valley of Red River of the North, now in Manitoba, Canada. Destroyed 1816 in conflict with North-West Fur Company, but village of Kildonan (now part of Winnipeg) restored 1817. Two forts built 1821 and 1835; purchase of territorial rights 1869 by Canadian government caused rebellion led by Louis Riel.

Red Russia. In 18th cent. a region of S Poland bet. Volhynia and the Carpathian Mts. in the area around the upper Dniester; now a part of W Ukrainian S.S.R., U.S.S.R., and SE Poland.

Red·scar Bay \ˌred-skär-\. Small bay on S coast of New Guinea I., Papua New Guinea, N of Port Moresby.

Red Sea. 1 *or anc.* **Si·nus Arab·i·cus** \ˌsī-nəs-ə-ˈrab-i-kəs\. Inland sea bet. Arabian Penin. and NE Africa; ab. 1200 m. long; 169,100 sq. m.; on the N connects with Mediterranean Sea through the Gulf of Suez and the Suez Canal; on the S connects with Arabian Sea through the strait of Bab al-Mandab; in the Great Rift Valley (*q.v.*).

2 Part of Indian Ocean. See ERYTHRAEAN SEA.

3 Coastal governorate on the Red Sea, E Egypt. See table at EGYPT.

Red Springs. Town, Robeson co., S North Carolina, 25 m. SW of Fayetteville; pop. (1970c) 3383; rayon, fertilizer, lumber; Flora Macdonald Coll. (1896).

Red Tank. Town, Balboa dist., Canal Zone, on the Panama Canal near the Pedro Miguel Locks.

Red Volta. See VOLTA RED.

Red Willow. County in Nebraska. See table at NEBRASKA.

Red Wing \ˈred-ˌwiŋ\. City, ⊗ of Goodhue co., SE Minnesota, on Mississippi river 40 m. SE of St. Paul; pop. (1970c) 10,441; pottery, marine engines, rubber goods, footwear; dairy, grain farms.

Red·wood \ˈred-ˌwu̇d\. 1 River, SW Minnesota; ab. 90 m. long; flows NE and E in Lyon and Redwood cos. into Minnesota river.

2 County in Minnesota. See table at MINNESOTA.

Redwood City. City, ⊗ of San Mateo co., W California, 5 m. W of San Francisco Bay and ab. 18 m. SE of San Francisco; pop. (1970c) 55,686; center of electronics industry; rubber products, automobile parts, machine tools, asbestos; residential; Canada Coll. (1968); town site platted 1854; town incorporated 1867.

Redwood Falls. City, ⊗ of Redwood co., SW Minnesota, on the Redwood river 33 m. ENE of Marshall; pop. (1970c) 4774; diversified agriculture.

Redwood National Park. See UNITED STATES, *National Parks.*

Ree, Lough \-ˈrē\. Lake, cen. Ireland, E of Roscommon; 16 m. long and 1 to 7 m. wide; 39 sq. m.; the river Shannon flows S through the lake.

Reed City \ˈrēd-\. City, ⊗ of Osceola co., cen. Michigan, 26 m. SSW of Cadillac; pop. (1970c) 2286; resort.

Reed·ley \ˈrēd-lē\. City, Fresno co., S cen. California, 20 m. ESE of Fresno; pop. (1970c) 8131; canned fruits, olive oil, wine; Reedley Coll. (1926).

Reeds·burg \ˈrēdz-ˌbərg\. City, Sauk co., S cen. Wisconsin, 26 m. W of Portage; pop. (1970c) 4585; dairy products, lumber; Sauk County Teachers Coll. (1906).

Reeds·port \ˈrēdz-ˌpō(ə)rt, -ˌpȯ(ə)rt\. City, Douglas co., SW Oregon, on Pacific coast 66 m. SW of Eugene; pop. (1970c) 4039; commercial fishing; agriculture.

Reef Point \ˈrēf-\. Cape on NW coast of N extension of North I., New Zealand, forming S side of Ahipara Bay.

Reel·foot Lake \ˈrē(ə)l-ˌfu̇t-\. Shallow lake, on boundary bet. Lake and Obion cos., NW Tennessee; ab. 18 m. long; formed as result of the earthquake at New Madrid (*q.v.*) 1811–12.

Reeves \ˈrēvz\. County in Texas. See table at TEXAS.

Re·fu·gio \rə-ˈf(y)u̇r-ē-ō—*sic*\. 1 County in S Texas. See table at TEXAS.

2 Town, its ⊗, 38 m. N of Corpus Christi; pop. (1970c) 4340; oil, gas wells; grain, stock farms; founded 1790.

Re·gal·bu·to \ˌrā-gəl-ˈbü-tō\. Commune, Enna prov., cen. Sicily, Italy, 21 m. ENE of Enna; pop. (1968e) 9621.

Re·gen \ˈrā-gən\. River, Bavaria, West Germany; 114 m. long; flows W out of Bohemian Forest, then S into the Danube river at Regensburg.

Re·gens·burg \ˈrā-gənz-ˌbərg, -ˌbu̇(ə)rg\ *or formerly (Eng.)* **Rat·is·bon** \ˈrat-əs-ˌbän, -əz-\ *or medieval* **Rat·is·bo·na** \ˌrat-əs-ˈbō-nə, -əz-\; *anc.* **Re·gi·num** \ri-ˈjī-nəm\ *or* **Cas·tra Re·gi·na** \ˌkas-trə-ri-ˈjī-nə\. Commercial city, Bavaria, West Germany, on Danube river 65 m. NNE of Munich; pop. (1969e) 126,642; road and rail junction and river port; produces meat products, leather goods, electrical equipment, chemicals; notable 13th–16th cent. Gothic cathedral, 14th–15th cent. town hall, 12th cent. bridge, and numerous other notable medieval buildings; univ. (1965).

History: Of Celtic origin (c. 500 B.C.); settled by Romans 179 A.D.; made episcopal see 739; made free imperial city 1245; Catholic League intended to enforce edict of Worms against Luther formed here 1524; seven diets held here 1531–1613; seat of imperial diet 1663–1803; truce 1684; stormed by French under Napoleon 1809 (subject of a poem by Robert Browning); to Bavaria 1810; became free port 1853. In World War II often bombed by Allies 1942–44; taken by Allied armies Apr. 27, 1945.

Reg·ga·ne \ˈreg-ə-(ˌ)nē\. Town, Saoura dept., Algeria, 26°42′N, 0°10′E.

Reg·gel·lo \rə-ˈjel-(ˌ)ō\. Commune, Firenze prov., Tuscany, cen. Italy, 11 m. SE of Florence; pop. (1968e) 11,362.

Reg·gio di Ca·la·bria \ˌrej-(ē-)(ˌ)ō-ˌdē-kə-ˈläb-rē-ə\; *abbr. to* **Reggio** *or* **Reggio Calabria.** 1 Province of Calabria, S Italy. See table at ITALY.

2 *or anc. Gk.* **Rhe·gi·on** \ˈrē-jē-ˌän\; *Lat.* **Rhe·gi·um** *or* **Re·gi·um** \ˈrē-jē-əm\. Seaport and industrial commune, its ✻, on Strait of Messina 202 m. SSE of Naples; pop. (1968e) 164,819; tourist resort; exports dried herbs and essential oils for perfume and pharmaceutical industries; cathedral (rebuilt after earthquake 1908).

History: Founded by Greek colonists at end of 8th cent. B.C. as sister city to Zancle; destroyed by Dionysius (the Elder) of Syracuse 387 B.C.; allied with Rome 270 B.C.; conquered by Alaric 410 A.D., Totila 549, Saracens 918, Pisans 1005, Guiscard 1060, and the Aragonese 1282; devastated by earthquake 1783 and 1908. In World War II occupied by British Sept. 3, 1943 after Sicilian campaign.

Reggio nel·l'E·mi·lia \-ˈnel-ə-ˈmēl-yə\; *abbr.* **Reggio** *or* **Reggio Emilia.** 1 Province of Emilia-Romagna, N Italy. See table at ITALY.

2 *or anc.* **Re·gi·um Lep·i·dum** \ˌrē-jē-əm-ˈlep-əd-əm\. Commercial and industrial commune, its ✻, 71 m. NNW of Florence; pop. (1968e) 126,903; produces wine, cheese, canned meat, cement, electrical equipment, and pharmaceuticals; 9th cent. cathedral; founded by Romans 2d cent. B.C.; ruled by the Este family 1527 ff., became part of Italy 1860.

Reg·hin \rə-ˈgēn\. Town, Mureş co., N cen. Romania, ab. 15 m. NNE of Tîrgu-Mureş; pop. (1970e) 26,122.

Re·gil·lus, Lake \-ri-ˈjil-əs\. Ancient name of a small unidentified lake near Rome, Italy; scene of battle c. 496 B.C. in which Latins were defeated by the Romans.

Re·gi·na \ri-ˈjī-nə\. City, ✻ of Saskatchewan, Canada, in S part of province, 357 m. W of Winnipeg; pop. (1971p) 137,759; transportation and commercial center in livestock and grain farming region; produces steel, chemicals, electrical equipment, beer, leather, dairy products, paint; oil refineries, packing plants, railroad shops; Campion Coll. (1917), Luther Coll. (1921), Canadian Bible Coll. (1941). Founded 1822; capital of Northwest Territories of Canada 1882–1905; made capital of Saskatchewan on its formation as province 1905; headquarters of Royal Canadian Mounted Police until 1920.

Reginum. See REGENSBURG.

Regio Syrtica. See TRIPOLI 1.

Re·gi·stān \ˌrā-gi-ˈstän\. Extensive desert region, S Afghanistan.

Regium. See REGGIO DI CALABRIA 2.

Regium Lepidum. See REGGIO NELL'EMILIA 2.

Re·gla \ˈreg-lə\. Town and municipality, La Habana prov., W Cuba; munic. pop. (1967e) 39,630; an E suburb of Havana.

Reg·nitz \ˈräg-nəts\. River, Bavaria, West Germany; formed by confluence of Pegnitz and Rednitz rivers at Fürth, flows N into the Main river 3 m. NW of Bamberg.

Regnum Parthorum. See PARTHIA.

Reg·u·la·tion Peak \ˌreg-yə-ˈlā-shən-\. 1 Mountain in Sierra Nevada, in E Tuolumne co., cen. California; 10,500 ft.
2 Mountain, E Yellowstone National Park, NW Wyoming; 10,000 ft.

Re·ho·both \ri-ˈhō-bəth\. 1 *or* **Rehoboth Beach.** City, Sussex co., S Delaware, on Atlantic Ocean just S of Delaware Bay; pop. (1970c) 1614; summer beach resort.
2 Town, Bristol co., SE Massachusetts, 10 m. NNW of Fall River; pop. (1970c) 6512.
3 Town, cen. South-West Africa, on railroad 50 m. S of Windhoek; pop. (1960c) 2954.

Rehoboth Bay. Inlet of Atlantic Ocean, on E coast of Sussex co., Delaware.

Re·ho·vot *or* **Re·ho·voth** \rə-ˈhō-ˌvōt, ˈrā-hȯ-ˌvȯt\. Town, Israel, ab. 4 m. SW of Ramla; pop. (1970e) 36,600; pharmaceuticals, plastics; citrus orchards; Weizmann Institute of Science; founded 1890.

Reich \ˈrīk\. Literally "empire"; (1) originally, the Holy Roman Empire (the **First Reich**) from its founding in the 9th cent. to 1806; (2) the empire established by Bismarck (the **Second Reich**) 1871–1918; (3) following the dissolution of the Second Reich and the succeeding German Republic (1918–33), the National Socialist state (the **Third Reich**) created by Hitler and lasting from 1933 to 1945.

Rei·che·nau \ˈrī-kə-ˌnau̇\. 1 Island in W arm of Lake Constance, Baden-Württemberg, West Germany, just W of Konstanz; ab. 2 sq. m.; pop. (1961c) 4047. Site of Benedictine Abbey, founded 724, independent until 1540.
2 Village, Austria, ab. 20 m. SW of Wiener Neustadt; pop. (1961c) 4441; summer and health resort.

Rei·chen·bach \ˈrī-kən-ˌbäk\. 1 *or in full* **Reichenbach im Vogt·land** \-im-ˈfōkt-ˌlänt\. City, Karl-Marx-Stadt dist., East Germany, 10 m. SW of Zwickau; pop. (1970e) 28,818; manufactures textiles, machinery, sugar. Founded 1140; made city 1271; heavily damaged in World War II.
2 Town, Poland. See DZIERŻONIÓW.
3 River in Bern canton, Switzerland; rises in Great Scheidegg, flows NNE into Aare river; has five cascades, one over 200 ft. high.

Reichenberg. See LIBEREC.

Rei·chen·hall \ˌrī-kən-ˈhäl\ *or* **Bad Reichenhall** \bät-\. Town, Bavaria, West Germany; pop. (1968e) 14,772; salt mines; baths, health resort since 19th cent.

Reichs·land \ˈrīks-ˌlänt\. 1 Formerly, 1806–71, all German crownlands.
2 From 1871 to 1918 Alsace-Lorraine. See ALSACE-LORRAINE.

Reich·stadt \ˈrīk-ˌs(h)tät\. Village, Czech S.R., Czechoslovakia, just E of Česká Lípa; ducal castle; dukedom given to Napoleon II 1818; scene of signing of secret agreement bet. Austria-Hungary and Russia July 1876.

Reids·ville \ˈrēdz-ˌvil, -vəl\. 1 City, ⊗ of Tattnall co., SE cen. Georgia; pop. (1970c) 1806.
2 Industrial city, Rockingham co., N North Carolina, 20 m. NNE of Greensboro; pop. (1970c) 13,636; cigarettes, silk, rayon, beverages; tobacco market.

Rei·gate \ˈrī-gət\. Municipal borough, Surrey, S England, 18 m. S of London; pop. (1971p) 56,088; residential suburb of London; remnants of Norman castle; burial place of (2d) Baron Howard, commander of English fleet that defeated Spanish Armada.

Reikjavik. See REYKJAVÍK.

Reims *or* **Rheims** \ˈrēmz; *Fr.* ra^{n}s\; *anc.* **Du·ro·cor·to·rum** \ˌd(y)u̇r-ə-kȯr-ˈtōr-əm, -ˈtȯr-\ *or later* **Re·mi** \ˈrē-ˌmī\. Industrial and commercial city, Marne dept., NE France, on Vesle river 83 m. ENE of Paris; pop. (1968c) 152,967; rail and road junction and port on Aisne-Marne Canal; a major wine producing center (esp. champagne) with an extensive network of caves for storage of wine beneath city and in vicinity; textiles, machinery, glass, baked goods; 13th cent. Gothic cathedral, one of the most notable cathedrals of France; univ. (1967).

History: Ancient capital of the Remi; made archiepiscopal see from 3d cent.; sacked by Vandals 406; said to be site of baptism of Clovis and his officers 496; in 12th cent. site of one of the major European fairs; Philip Augustus crowned in cathedral 1179, and Reims cathedral thereafter the traditional coronation place of French kings until 1830; early medieval cathedral destroyed by fire early 13th cent.; present building with its western facade and four rose windows begun 1211 and completed in 14th cent.; city shelled by Germans in World War I 1914–18 and suffered extensive damage, including partial destruction of cathedral; restoration of cathedral took place 1927–38 with aid of grant from John D. Rockefeller; in World War II entered by U.S. troops Aug. 1944; scene of signature of unconditional German surrender May 7, 1945.

Rei·na Ade·lai·da, Archipelago of \-ˌrā-nə-ˌäd-ᵊl-ˈīd-ə\. Group of islands in S Pacific Ocean, off SW coast of Chile, N of W end of the Strait of Magellan.

Rein·deer Island \ˈrān-di(ə)r-\. Island in cen. Lake Winnipeg, SE Manitoba, Canada.

Reindeer Lake. Lake, cen. Canada, lying on the N section of the Saskatchewan-Manitoba boundary; 2467 sq. m.; its outlet is the **Reindeer River,** 143 m. long, flowing S to the Churchill.

Rei·no·sa \rā-ˈnō-sə\. Town, Santander prov., N Spain; on the Ebro ab. 4 m. from its source; pop. (1970p) 10,863; in the Cantabrian Mts. at 2790 ft.; resort.

Rein·stein, Mount \-ˈrīn-ˌstīn\. Peak in Sierra Nevada, in E Fresno co., S cen. California; 12,595 ft.

Re·jaf \rə-ˈjaf\. Town, Equatoria prov., S Sudan, on Bahr al-Jebel river just S of Juba.

Rejang. See RAJANG.

Re·ka·ta Bay \rə-ˌkät-ə-\. Bay on NW coast of Santa Isabel I. in the NE Solomon Is., W Pacific Ocean; used as a base by the Japanese 1942–43.

Re·ma·gen \ˈrā-ˌmäg-ən\. Town, N Rhineland-Palatinate, West Germany, on left bank of the Rhine 20 m. NW of Koblenz; pop. (1968e) 13,347. Founded as early as 11th cent.; site of the Ludendorff bridge (built 1916–18) across the Rhine, which was the only one not destroyed before Allied advance into Germany in Mar. 1945; bridge seized Mar. 8 and Rhine crossed; bridgehead on E bank opposite enlarged Mar. 8–19; bridge collapsed Mar. 17.

Rem·bang \ˈrem-ˌbäŋ\. Seaport town, Central Java prov., Indonesia, on coast 45 m. ENE of Semarang; pop. (1961c) 22,985.

Re·me·dios \rə-ˈmed-ē-ˌōs\ *or in full* **San Juan de los Remedios** \san-ˈ(h)wan-də-ˌlōs-\. Town and municipality, Las Villas prov., W cen. Cuba; munic. pop. (1967e) 31,760; town near coast, 23 m. E of Santa Clara.

Remi. See REIMS.

Re·mi·re·mont \rə-ˌmēr-ˈmō^{n}\. Commune, Vosges dept., NE France, on Moselle river 12 m. SSE of Épinal; pop. (1968c) 9312; textiles, beer, brass and iron castings; 14th–15th cent. church of abbey (founded 7th cent.).

Re·mou·champs \rə-ˌmü-'shäⁿ\. Village in Liège prov., E Belgium, on the Amblève river; location of a notable double cavern.

Rem·pang \'rem-ˌpäŋ\. Island, Riau Archipelago, Indonesia, SSE of Batam.

Rems \'rem(p)s\. River, Baden-Württemberg, West Germany; ab. 50 m. long; flows into the Neckar river just N of Stuttgart.

Rem·scheid \'rem-ˌshīt\. Manufacturing city, North Rhine-Westphalia, West Germany, near the Wupper river 25 m. ESE of Düsseldorf; pop. (1969e) 136,388; center of West German tool industry; iron products, textiles, cutlery.

Renaix. See RONSE.

Ren·dez·vous Peak \ˌrän-di-ˌvü-, -dā-\. Mountain, S of Grand Teton National Park, NW Wyoming; 10,924 ft.

Rendina, Gulf of. See STRYMONIC GULF.

Ren·do·va \ren-'dō-və\. Island off SW cen. coast of New Georgia I., cen. Solomon Is., W Pacific Ocean; separated from New Georgia by Blanche Channel. Part of British Solomon Islands protectorate. Seized by U.S. troops June 30–July 2, 1943 and used as base in operations against Munda.

Rends·burg \'ren(t)s-ˌbu̇(ə)rg\. City, Schleswig-Holstein, West Germany, on the Kiel Canal 13 m. S of Schleswig; pop. (1969e) 35,464; fertilizer, textiles; iron foundries; 13th cent. church, 16th cent. town hall. Founded before 1199; to Holstein 1252; became city 1339, fortified 1539; stronghold of Schleswig-Holstein army during German-Danish war 1848–50.

Ren·frew \'ren-(ˌ)frü\. 1 County, Ontario, Canada. See table at ONTARIO.

2 Manufacturing town, Renfrew co., SE Ontario, Canada, on Bonnechère river 32 m. SE of Pembroke; pop. (1971p) 9048; magnesium castings, radios, aircraft parts, plastics; alfalfa, dairy farms.

3 *or* **Ren·frew·shire** \-ˌshi(ə)r, -shər\. County, SW Scotland; area 225 sq. m.; pop. (1971p) 362,144; ✱ Paisley; rivers Clyde, Gryfe; livestock raising, dairying, shipbuilding, distilling, manufacturing (textiles, chemicals, machine tools, automobiles), sugar refining; towns incl. Paisley, Greenock, Port Glasgow, Johnstone.

4 Burgh, Renfrew co., SW Scotland, near S bank of the Clyde ab. 7 m. W of Glasgow; pop. (1971p) 18,589; a small section of the burgh is in Lanark co.; machinery, paint, rubber; shipbuilding.

Ren·go \'reŋ-(ˌ)gō\. City, O'Higgins prov., cen. Chile, 65 m. S of Santiago; pop. (1960c) 10,989.

Ren·kum \'reŋ-kəm\. Commune, Gelderland prov., E Netherlands, on the Neder Rijn just W of Arnhem; pop. (1970e) 33,619.

Ren·nell \'ren-ᵊl, rə-'nel\. Uplifted atoll of coral limestone, an island in NE Coral Sea, 120 m. SW of San Cristóbal I., S Solomon Is., W Pacific Ocean, 11°40′S, 160°10′W; ab. 50 m. long and 12 m. wide. Lake Te-Nggano at its E end is largest expanse of enclosed fresh water in Pacific Ocean; 50 sq. m.

Rennes \'ren\ *or anc.* **Con·da·te** \kän-'dāt-ē, -'dät-ē\ *or Breton* **Roazon.** Industrial and commercial city, ✱ of Ille-et-Vilaine dept., NW France, at junction of Ille and Vilaine rivers 193 m. WSW of Paris; pop. (1968c) 180,943; archiepiscopal see and military headquarters; railroad junction; produces automobiles, agricultural machinery, furniture, chemicals, fertilizers, textiles, honey, lace; univ. (founded at Nantes 1461, transferred to Rennes 1735); cathedral. Became capital of Brittany in 10th cent.; seat of *parlement* of Brittany 1561–1675; suffered widespread destruction from fire 1720 and in World War II 1944.

Re·no \'rē-(ˌ)nō\. 1 County in Kansas. See table at KANSAS.

2 City, ⊗ of Washoe co., NW Nevada, on Truckee river 20 m. N of Lake Tahoe; pop. (1970c) 72,863; 2d largest city in the state; alt. 4490 ft.; produces lumber, cement, electronic components; in livestock and grain farming region; important tourist center (hunting, fishing, skiing) with numerous gambling casinos; Univ. of Nevada (1874); settled 1859; developed after arrival of Union Pacific R.R. 1868; incorporated as city 1879.

Reno \'rā-(ˌ)nō, 'ren-(ˌ)ō\ *or anc.* **Re·nus** \'rē-nəs\. River, N Italy; 131 m. long; rises in the Apennines, flows N and E into the Adriatic Sea N of Ravenna.

Re·no·vo \rē-'nō-vō\. Borough, Clinton co., cen. Pennsylvania, on Susquehanna river 41 m. W of Williamsport; pop. (1970c) 2620; coal mines; truck farms.

Rens·se·laer \ˌren(t)-sə-'li(ə)r, 'ren(t)-s(ə-)lər\. 1 County in New York. See table at NEW YORK.

2 City, ⊗ of Jasper co., NW Indiana, 40 m. NNW of Lafayette; pop. (1970c) 4688; fertilizer; grain, stock farms; Saint Joseph's Coll. (1889) in Collegeville, S suburb.

3 City, Rensselaer co., E New York, across Hudson river from Albany; pop. (1970c) 10,136; suburb of Albany; chemicals, concrete products.

Ren·ton \'rent-ᵊn\. City, King co., W cen. Washington, 12 m. SSE of Seattle; pop. (1970c) 26,648; aircraft, military vehicles, steel products; coal mines, clay pits; Pacific Western Coll. (1965); incorporated 1901.

Renus. See RENO.

Ren·ville \'ren-vəl\. Name of counties in two states of the U.S. See tables at MINNESOTA and NORTH DAKOTA.

Repelen–Baerl *or* **Repeln–Baerl.** See RHEINKAMP.

Re·pen·ti·gny \rə-ˌpäⁿ-tē-'nyē\. Town, L'Assomption co., S Quebec, Canada; pop. (1971p) 19,441; residential suburb of Montreal.

Re·pub·lic \ri-'pəb-lik\. 1 County in Kansas. See table at KANSAS.

2 Town, ⊗ of Ferry co., NE Washington; pop. (1970c) 862.

República de Panamá. See PANAMA.

República Dominicana. See DOMINICAN REPUBLIC.

República Federativa do Brasil. See BRAZIL.

Re·pub·li·can \ri-'pəb-li-kən\. River, Nebraska and Kansas; 422 m. long; rises in E Colorado, flows NE and E through S Nebraska, then SE through NE cen. Kansas to unite with the Smoky Hill river at Junction City in Geary co. and form the Kansas river.

República Oriental del Uruguay. See URUGUAY.

Republic of Korea. See KOREA, SOUTH.

Republic of South Africa. See SOUTH AFRICA, REPUBLIC OF.

Republic of Vietnam. See VIETNAM, SOUTH.

République Centrafricaine. See CENTRAL AFRICAN REPUBLIC.

Re·pulse Bay \ri-'pəls-, 'rē-pəls\. 1 Inlet of Pacific Ocean, E Queensland, Australia, bet. Mackay and Bowen, 20°36′S, 148°43′E.

2 Small inlet at N end of Roes Welcome, N Hudson Bay, in S part of isthmus connecting Melville Penin. with mainland; divided bet. Keewatin and Franklin districts, Northwest Territories, Canada.

Re·que·na \rə-'kā-nə\. Commune, Valencia prov., E Spain, 36 m. W of Valencia; pop. (1970p) 17,840; mineral baths; produces silk, wine, oil, grain, fruit; conquered by the Cid, taken by Moors, reconquered by Alfonso VIII 1219.

Re·sa·ca \ri-'sak-ə\. Town, N Gordon co., NW Georgia; called **Dub·lin** \'dəb-lən\ until renamed by veterans of the battle of Resaca de la Palma; scene of Civil War battle May 15, 1864.

Resaca de la Pal·ma \ri-ˌsak-ə-ˌdā-lə-'päl-mə\. Battlefield in Cameron co., S Texas, ab. 4 m. N of Brownsville; scene of victory May 9, 1846 of Americans under Zachary Taylor over Mexicans under Mariano Arista; second encounter of the Mexican War; Mexicans driven across the Rio Grande.

Re·sen·de \rə-'zen-dē\. Municipality, Rio de Janeiro state, SE Brazil, 85 m. WNW of Rio de Janeiro; pop. (1968e) 64,950.

Res·er·va·tion Peak \ˌrez-ər-'vā-shən-\. Mountain on E boundary of Yellowstone National Park, NW Wyoming; 10,629 ft.

Re·serve \ri-'zərv\. 1 Unincorporated urban community, St. John the Baptist parish, SE Louisiana; pop. (1970c) 6381.

2 Village, ⊗ of Catron co., W New Mexico, 70 m. NNW of Silver City.

Resht. See RASHT.

Resiczabánya. See REŞIŢA.

Re·si·na \rā-ˈzē-nə\. Commune, Napoli prov., Campania, S Italy, on Bay of Naples 5 m. ESE of Naples; pop. (1968e) 51,124; starting point for ascent of Mt. Vesuvius; built over ruins of ancient Herculaneum (*q.v.*).

Re·sis·ten·cia \ˌres-i-ˈsten(t)-sē-ə\. City, ✻ of Chaco prov., N Argentina, on the bank of the Paraná river facing Corrientes; pop. (1960c) 84,036; ships cattle, quebracho wood, hides, lead.

Re·şi·ţa \ˈresh-ət-ˌsä\ *or* **Re·ci·ţa** \ˈrech-\ *or Hung.* **Re·sicza·bá·nya** \ˈresh-ət-ˌsȯ-ˈbän-ˌyȯ\. Commune, ⊗ of Caraş-Severin co., SW Romania, 65 m. SE of Arad; pop. (1970e) 67,980; center of iron and steel industry, with blast furnaces, foundries, rolling mills, and coal mines.

Resolution. See FORT RESOLUTION.

Res·o·lu·tion Island \ˌrez-ə-ˈlü-shən-\. 1 Island off SE tip of Baffin I. and on N side of entrance to Hudson Strait, SE Franklin dist., Northwest Territories, Canada; 387 sq. m.

2 Island off SW coast of South I., New Zealand.

Res·ti·gouche \ˈres-ti-ˌgüsh\. 1 River, N New Brunswick, Canada; 130 m. long; rises in NW New Brunswick, flows NW, then E in a wide estuary into Chaleur Bay; famous salmon stream.

2 County, New Brunswick, Canada. See table at NEW BRUNSWICK.

Res·ur·rec·tion Bay \ˌrez-ə-ˈrek-shən-\. Inlet of Gulf of Alaska, SE Kenai Penin., S Alaska; Seward at its head.

Re·tal·hu·leu \ˌret-ə-lü-ˈleu̇\. 1 Department of SW Guatemala. See table at GUATEMALA.

2 Town, its ✻; munic. pop. (1964e) 36,919; in coffee-growing region near the coast ab. 22 m. SSW of Quezaltenango.

Re·te·zat National Park \ˌre-tə-ˈzät-\. National park, Romania; 50 sq. m.; conifer forest; chamois, lynx; established 1935.

Re·thel \rə-ˈtel\. Commune, Ardennes dept., NE France, on the Aisne 20 m. SW of Mézières; pop. (1962c) 7856; seat of countship 10th cent. to 16th cent., made a duchy 1581, acquired by Mazarin 1663; occupied by Germans 1914–18 during World War I.

Re·thondes \rə-ˈtōⁿd\. Village, Oise dept., N France, near Compiègne in the Forêt de Laigue; pop. (1962c) 411; place where armistice of World War I was signed Nov. 11, 1918.

Re·thým·nē \re-ˈthēm-nē\. 1 Department of Crete, Greece. See table at GREECE.

2 Seaport, its ✻. See RETHYMNON.

Re·thym·non \ˈreth-ēm-ˌnȯn\ *also* **Re·thým·nē** \re-ˈthēm-nē\ *or* **Re·ti·mo** \ˈret-i-ˌmō, ˈrät-\. Seaport town, ✻ of Rethýmnē dept., on N coast of island of Crete, Greece, ab. 38 m. W of Candia; pop. (1971p) 15,367.

Ré·u·nion \rē-ˈyün-yən\; *formerly* **Bour·bon** \ˈbu̇(ə)r-bən, bu̇(ə)r-ˈbōⁿ\ *also* **Bo·na·parte** \ˈbō-nə-ˌpärt\. Island of the Mascarene Is., in the Indian Ocean 425 m. E of the Malagasy Republic; of oval shape, ab. 39 m. long by 28 m. wide; 969 sq. m.; pop. (1971e) 455,200; ✻ Saint-Denis, on N coast; principal exports sugar and rum. Mountainous, highest point Piton des Neiges 10,069 ft. in cen. part; coast has few harbors; principal harbor at Le Port at NW corner; other towns St. Paul, St. Louis, and St. Pierre. Discovered 1513; claimed by France 1638; first colonized as Isle de Bourbon 1662; renamed Réunion 1793; occupied by British July 1810–Apr. 1815; made overseas territory of France 1946.

Reus \ˈreu̇s\. Commune, Tarragona prov., NE Spain, 6 m. WNW of Tarragona; pop. (1970p) 59,095; trades in fruit, wine, and oil; manufactures textiles, machinery, chemicals, soap, leather goods; flower nurseries; Gothic church. Founded c. 13th cent.; began commercial development after establishment of English colony 1750; made city in 1840's.

Reuss \ˈrȯis\. 1 River, cen. Switzerland; 98 m. long; rises in S Uri canton, flows N through Bay of Uri and Lake of Lucerne into Aare river near its junction with the Rhine river.

2 Name of two former principalities in Thuringia: **Reuss–Greiz** \-ˈgrīts\, ✻ Greiz, and **Reuss–Schleiz–Ge·ra** \-shlīts-ˈger-ə\, ✻ Gera. Both became part of Thuringia 1918.

Reu·ter Peak \ˌrüt-ər-\. Peak, Glacier National Park, NW Montana; 8700 ft.

Reut·ling·en \ˈrȯit-liŋ-ən\. City, Baden-Württemberg, West Germany, 19 m. S of Stuttgart; pop. (1969e) 77,034; a major center of the textile industry; leather, paper, iron goods, machinery; 13th cent. Gothic church. Founded before 1090; free imperial city 1240–1802; scene of victory of Swabian League over Ulrich von Württemberg 1377; to Württemberg 1802.

Revakantha. See REWA KANTHA.

Reval. See TALLINN.

Rev·da \ˈrev-də, rē-ˈev-\. Town, Sverdlovsk Oblast, Russian S.F.S.R., U.S.S.R., ab. 10 m. WSW of Sverdlovsk; pop. (1969e) 58,000.

Rev·eille Range \ˌrev-ə-lē-\. Range in cen. Nye co., S Nevada; highest point **Reveille Peak** 8910 ft.

Revel. See TALLINN.

Rev·el·stoke \ˈrev-əl-ˌstōk\. City, SE British Columbia, Canada, on left bank of Columbia river just S of Mount Revelstoke National Park, ab. 100 m. ENE of Kamloops; pop. (1971p) 4717; trade center in mining and resort region; dairy products, lumber, beer.

Revelstoke, Mount. Mountain, SE British Columbia, Canada, just W of Selkirk Mts.; over 7000 ft.; comprises Mount Revelstoke National Park (see CANADA, *National Parks*).

Re·vere \ri-ˈvi(ə)r\. City, Suffolk co., E Massachusetts, 5 m. NE of Boston; pop. (1970c) 43,159; residential and resort community; made city 1914.

Re·ver·mont \rə-ˌver-ˈmōⁿ\. Western ridge of the Jura Mts., E Ain and E Jura depts., E France; highest point 2529 ft.

Re·vi·lla Gi·ge·do *or* **Re·vi·lla·gi·ge·do** \ri-ˌvē-(y)ə-hi-ˈhā-(ˌ)thō\. Group of islands in the Pacific Ocean ab. 450 m. W of and under administrative control of the state of Colima, Mexico, 19°N, 111°30′W; total area 320 sq. m. The largest of the group is Socorro, a rocky mountainous island 24 m. long and 9 m. wide. The westernmost island of the group is Roca Partida.

Re·vil·la·gi·ge·do Island \ri-ˌvil-ə-gə-ˈgēd-(ˌ)ō-\. Island, SE Alaska, off mainland E of Prince of Wales I.; in SE Alexander Archipelago; 50 m. long by 25 m. wide; 1145 sq. m. Ketchikan is on its SW coast.

Re·wa \ˈrā-(ˌ)wä\. Largest river on Viti Levu I., Fiji, SW Pacific Ocean; 90 m. long; flows SE across E side of the island and empties into the Pacific Ocean; navigable for ab. 40 m.

Rewa \ˈrē-wə\. 1 Former Indian state, now part of Madhya Pradesh state, cen. India; 12,830 sq. m.

2 Town, its ✻, 110 m. SSW of Allahabad; pop. (1961c) 43,065; founded 1618.

Rewa Kan·tha *or* **Re·va·kan·tha** \ˌrā-wä-ˈkän-tə\. Former British agency, now mostly in Gujarat state, W India, chiefly on banks of lower Narmada river; 978 sq. m.

Re·wa·ri \rā-ˈwär-ē\. Town, Haryana, 50 m. SW of Delhi; pop. (1961c) 36,994; produces brassware.

Rex·burg \ˈreks-ˌbərg\. City, ⊗ of Madison co., E Idaho, 25 m. NE of Idaho Falls; pop. (1970c) 8272; lumber, dairy products; sugar beets, potatoes, poultry; settled 1883.

Rey \ˈrā\. Town, Tehran prov., N Iran, just S of Tehran; pop. (1966c) 102,825.

Rey, Is·la del \ˌēz-lä-del-ˈrā\. Island, largest of the Pearl Is., in Gulf of Panama; 15 m. long; chief town San Miguel.

Reyes, Los. See LOS REYES.

Reyes, Point \-ˈrāz\. Point at S extremity of peninsula jutting out on W coast of Marin co., California, ab. 30 m. NW of Golden Gate; reputed to be windiest and foggiest place on W coast of United States S of Bering Sea, averaging 137 days of fog a year; location included in Point Reyes National Seashore (101 sq. m., estab. 1962).

Rey·kja·nes, Cape \-ˈrā-kyä-ˌnes\. Cape on SW extremity of Iceland.

Rey·kja·vík *also* **Reik·ja·vik** \ˈrāk-yə-ˌvēk, -ˌvik\. Seaport, ✻ of Iceland, on SW coast, 64°10′N, 21°58′W; pop. (1970c) 81,684; principal commercial and industrial center of the country, with food processing, metalworking, textile, and printing industries; major fishing port; univ. (1911). Region first settled c. 870; village developed in 18th cent. and received municipal rights 1786; made episcopal see 1796 and seat of Parliament (*althing*) 1843; became capital 1918; in World War II, a British and American naval and air base.

Reyn·olds \ˈren-ᵊl(d)z\. County in Missouri. See table at MISSOURI.

Reynolds, Mount. Peak in Glacier National Park, NW Montana; 9147 ft.

Reyn·olds·burg \ˈren-ᵊl(d)z-ˌbərg\. Village, Franklin and Licking cos., cen. Ohio, W of Columbus; pop. (1970c) 13,921.

Reyn·olds·ville \ˈren-ᵊl(d)z-ˌvil\. Borough, Jefferson co., W cen. Pennsylvania, 8 m. WSW of Du Bois; pop. (1970c) 2771; boats, furniture; coal mines.

Rey·no·sa \rā-ˈnō-sə\. Municipality, Tamaulipas state, E Mexico, on the Rio Grande; pop. (1970p) 143,514.

Re·zā' ī·yeh *also* **Ri·zai·yeh** \rə-ˈzī-(y)ə\ *or formerly* **Ur·mia** \ˈu̇r-mē-ə\. City, ✻ of West Azerbaijan prov., NW Iran; pop. (1971e) 120,000; in region producing fruit and tobacco; reputed birthplace of Zoroaster.

Re·zé \rə-ˈzā\. Industrial commune, Loire-Atlantique dept., NW France, on Loire river opp. Nantes; pop. (1968c) 33,509; foundries; hats, furniture, shoes, rugs.

Re·zegh \ˈrez-ˌeg\. Village, NE Libya, ab. 18 m. SSE of Tobruk; battle Nov. 1941.

Rē·zek·ne \ˈrā-zek-ˌnā\ *or formerly* **Rye·zhi·tsa** \rē-ˈā-zhət-sə\ *or Ger.* **Ro·sit·ten** \rō-ˈzit-ᵊn\. Town, E Latvian S.S.R., U.S.S.R., 55 m. NE of Daugavpils; pop. (1967e) 29,000; railroad junction on trunk line from Daugavpils to Pskov; trade center near border of U.S.S.R.

History: Founded 1285 by Teutonic Knights; under Lithuanian and Polish rule most of period 1560–1772; under Russian rule 1772 ff.; scene of battles in World War I; seized 1918–19 by Bolshevik forces which were expelled 1920 by Latvian-Polish army. In World War II seized by German armies 1941; recovered 1945.

Re·zon·ville \rə-zōⁿ-ˈvēl\. Commune, Moselle dept., NE France, just W of Metz; pop. (1962c) 226; scene of part of the battle of Mars-la-Tour Aug. 16, 1870.

Rha. See VOLGA.

Rhadames. See GADÀMES.

Rhaedestus. See TEKIRDAĞ 2.

Rhaetia. See RAETIA.

Rhaetian Alps. See table at ALPS.

Rha·ges \ˈrā-jəz\ *or anc.* **Rha·gae** \-(ˌ)jē\ *or Bib.* **Ra·ges** \ˈrā-jəz\ *or Pers.* **Rai** \ˈrī\ *or Gk.* **Eu·ro·pus** \yu̇-ˈrō-pəs\. City of ancient Media; its ruins are ab. 5 m. SE of Tehran, N Iran. According to tradition founded 3000 B.C.; excavations disclose extensive fortifications, towers, and buildings. Reckoned with Nineveh and Ecbatana (*mod.* Hamadan) as one of the great cities of antiquity. Made capital of Median Empire; flourished until Middle Ages but suffered from earthquakes and finally destroyed by Tatars in 12th cent. A.D. Under the Sassanids (226–641 A.D.) was seat of Zoroastrianism. Reputed birthplace of Harun al-Rashid.

Rhaiadr River. See PISTYLL RHAIADR.

Rham·nus \ˈram-nəs\. Locality on coast of Attica, Greece, N of Marathon and ab. 24 m. NE of Athens; ancient Temple of Nemesis, now in ruins.

Rhea \ˈrā\. County in Tennessee. See table at TENNESSEE.

Rhe·den \ˈrād-ᵊn\. Commune, Gelderland prov., E Netherlands, on IJssel just E of Arnhem; pop. (1970e) 48,713; structural steel, concrete products, enamelware; tourism.

Rhegion *or* **Rhegium.** See REGGIO DI CALABRIA 2.

Rhei·dol \ˈrī-ˌdōl\. River, cen. Wales; 22 m. long; rises NW of Plynlimmon, flows SW and S, makes sharp turn W (site of Devil's Bridge, *q.v.*) and enters Cardigan Bay at Aberystwyth.

Rheims. See REIMS.

Rhein. See RHINE.

Rhei·ne \ˈrī-nə\ *also* **Rheine in West·fa·len** \-in-vest-ˈfäl-ən\. City, North Rhine-Westphalia, West Germany, on Ems river 25 m. NNW of Münster; pop. (1969e) 51,028; textiles, hosiery, machinery, lime; 15th cent. church; 15th cent. castle.

Rheinfall. See SCHAFFHAUSEN FALLS.

Rhein·fel·den \ˈrīn-ˌfel-dən\ *or* **Rhein·feld** \-ˌfelt\. Commune, NW Aargau canton, N Switzerland, on the Rhine; pop. (1970c) 6866; scene of battle Feb. 28, 1638 during Thirty Years' War in which the Huguenot leader duc de Rohan was mortally wounded.

Rhein·hau·sen \ˈrīn-ˌhau̇z-ən\. Industrial commune, North Rhine-Westphalia, West Germany, SW suburb of Duisburg on the Rhine; pop. (1969e) 71,740; river port; ironworks and steelworks; chartered 1934.

Rhein·kamp \ˈrīn-ˌkamp\ *or formerly* **Re·pe·len–Baerl** *also* **Re·peln–Baerl** \ˌrā-p(ə-)lən-ˈbär(ə)l, ˌrā-pəln-\. City, North Rhine-Westphalia, West Germany, 22 m. NNW of Düsseldorf; pop. (1969e) 42,963.

Rheinland. See RHINELAND.

Rheinland–Pfalz. See RHINELAND-PALATINATE.

Rhein·pfalz \ˈrīn-ˌ(p)fälts\. German form of Rhine Palatinate. See PALATINATE.

Rhein·wald·horn \ˈrīn-ˌvält-ˌhȯ(ə)rn\. Highest peak in the Adula range, Lepontine Alps, SE Switzerland; 11,158 ft.

Rhe·nea \ri-ˈnē-ə\ *or Gk.* **Ri·nía** \ri-ˈnē-ə\. Small island, N Cyclades, S Aegean Sea, W of Mykonos; bet. it and Mykonos is the island of Delos.

Rhe·nen \ˈrā-nən\. Commune, Utrecht prov., cen. Netherlands, on Neder Rijn SE of Utrecht; pop. (1970e) 14,860.

Rhenus. See RHINE.

Rheydt \ˈrīt\. City, North Rhine-Westphalia, West Germany, S of Mönchengladbach; pop. (1969e) 100,329; natural and synthetic textiles, electrical equipment, machine tools, printing supplies; 16th cent. castle; received civic rights 1856.

Rhin \raⁿ\. 1 River. See RHINE.
2 Departments of France: **Bas–Rhin** \ˈbä-\ and **Haut–Rhin** \ˌō-\. See table at FRANCE.

Rhine \ˈrīn\; *Ger.* **Rhein** \ˈrīn\ *or Fr.* **Rhin** \raⁿ\ *or Du.* **Rijn** \ˈrīn\; *anc.* **Rhe·nus** \ˈrē-nəs\. River, W Europe; 820 m. long; formed by confluence of Hinterrhein and Vorderrhein in SE Switzerland; flows through Lake Constance W, N, and NW to the North Sea, forming in its course W boundary of Liechtenstein and Austria, and SW boundary of West Germany; navigable to Basel, Switzerland. The Upper Rhine (*Ger.* Oberrhein) extends from Basel to Mainz; the Lower Rhine (*Ger.* Niederrhein) begins at Bonn and leaves West Germany near Kleve; in Netherlands it curves W and divides into two branches, the Neder Rijn to the N and the Waal to the S. One branch (IJssel) of the Neder Rijn flows N into IJsselmeer; the main course of the Neder Rijn is W, where it becomes known as the Lek, which unites with the Merwede and continues to the North Sea as the Nieuwe Maas. The Waal unites with the Maas (Meuse) and in its S arm flows into the Hollandsch Diep; its N arm, known as the Merwede, divides into the Oude Maas and Nieuwe Maas (see MEUSE), both entering the North Sea close together just S of the Hook of Holland. In this wide delta are various islands of South

Holland and Zeeland provs. of Netherlands. In all its course are many canals connecting with other streams in Netherlands and with the Rhone, Marne, and Danube systems in West Germany and France. Its river trade is very extensive and both in German legend and history it has borne a prominent part. Its main tributaries on the right the Neckar, Main, Lahn, Sieg, Ruhr, and Lippe; on the left the Aare, Ill, Nahe, Moselle, and Erft. Chief cities on its banks: Konstanz, Schaffhausen, Basel, Karlsruhe, Mannheim, Ludwigshafen, Mainz, Wiesbaden, Koblenz, Bonn, Cologne, Düsseldorf, Duisburg, and Rotterdam. In World War II its course was a major line of defense Feb.–Mar. 1945; first crossed by Allies by bridge at Remagen (*q.v.*). For *Falls of the Rhine,* see SCHAFFHAUSEN FALLS.

Rhine·beck \'rīn-ˌbek\. Residential village, Dutchess co., SE New York, on Hudson river 16 m. N of Poughkeepsie; pop. (1970c) 2336; connected by ferry at **Rhine·cliff** \-ˌklif\ with Kingston.

Rhine·land \'rīn-ˌland, -lənd\ *or Ger.* **Rhein·land** \'rīn-ˌlänt\. Recently and popularly, the part of West Germany W of the Rhine river (left bank of the Rhine); ab. 9000 sq. m.; chief city Cologne.

Rhine·land·er \'rīn-ˌlan-dər, -lən-\. City, ⊗ of Oneida co., N Wisconsin, 37 m. NNW of Antigo; pop. (1970c) 8218; lumber, paper products; agriculture; center of summer resort region.

Rhineland–Pa·lat·i·nate \-pə-'lat-ᵊn-ət\ *or Ger.* **Rheinland–Pfalz** \'rīn-ˌlänt-'(p)fälts\. A state of West Germany, chiefly W of the Rhine; 7659 sq. m.; pop. (1970e) 3,677,000; ✱ Mainz; grain crops, potatoes, sugar beets; vineyards; chemicals, paper, bicycles, footwear, metalworking.

Rhine Palatinate. See PALATINATE.

Rhin–et–Mo·selle \ˌraⁿ-nā-mō-'zel\. Department of France 1801–15; ✱ Koblenz; comprised region on W bank of the Rhine which was given to France by Treaty of Lunéville 1801; to Prussia by the Congress of Vienna 1815.

Rhinns, The *or* **The Rinns** \-'rinz\. 1 Peninsula extending into Atlantic Ocean on W coast of island of Islay, Inner Hebrides, off W coast of Scotland; terminates in **Rhinns Point** or **Rinns Point;** lighthouse.

2 *also* **The Rhinns of Galloway** \-'gal-ə-ˌwā\. Peninsula on extreme SW coast of Scotland, in Wigtown co., W of Loch Ryan and Luce Bay and terminating on the N in Corsewall Point and on the S in the Mull of Galloway.

Rhinocolura. See AL-'ARISH.

Rhio. See RIOUW.

Rhir, Cape \-'ri(ə)r\ *or formerly* **Cape Guir** \-'gi(ə)r\. Cape, SW coast of Morocco.

Rho \'rō\. Commune, Milano prov., Lombardy, N Italy, 8 m. NW of Milan; pop. (1968e) 43,582; 16th cent. sanctuary.

Rhoda. See RODA.

Rhodanus. See RHONE.

Rhode Is·land \rō-'dī-lənd\. 1 *or formerly* **Aquid·neck Island** \ə-'kwid-ˌnek-\. Island in Narragansett Bay, SE Rhode Island; 15 m. long; the city of Newport is on its SW coast. Purchased by Anne Hutchinson, William Coddington, and others, and settled at Portsmouth 1638; name changed to Rhode Island 1644.

2 *or officially* **Rhode Island and Providence Plantations.** Northeastern seaboard state of U.S.A., bounded on N and E by Massachusetts, on S by the Atlantic Ocean, and on W by Connecticut; 50th state in area, 1214 sq. m. (land area 1052 sq. m.); 39th state in population, (1970c) 949,723; ✱ Providence; an original state of the Union, the 13th to ratify the Federal Constitution, May 29, 1790.

Nickname: Little Rhody. *State flower:* Violet. *Motto:* Hope. *Rivers:* Pawtuxet, Blackstone, and the Pawcatuck, forming lower SW boundary. *Highest point:* Jerimoth Hill, 812 ft., in Providence co. *Chief industries:* Textile manufacturing, foundry and machine work; jewelry making; optical instruments. *Chief cities:* Providence, Warwick, Pawtucket, Cranston. See *Table of States* at UNITED STATES. Divided into the following five counties (for pronunciation of their names, see their individual entries):

NAME	LOCATION	AREA[1] (sq. m.)	POP. (1970c)	CO. SEAT
Bristol	E	25	45,937	Bristol
Kent	cen.	173	142,382	East Greenwich
Newport	SE	108	94,228	Newport
Providence	N	416	581,470	Providence
Washington	S	331	85,706	West Kingston

[1]Area = land area.

History: Settled by religious exiles, chiefly from Massachusetts, including Roger Williams, who settled at Providence 1636, and Anne Hutchinson, who settled at Portsmouth on Aquidneck I. 1638; scattered settlements united when charter granted by Charles II to Roger Williams 1663; charter provisions continued in effect until Dorr's Rebellion 1842, when new constitution was framed, adopted, and finally declared in effect May 3, 1843.

Rhodes \'rōdz\ *or Ital.* **Ro·di** \'rȯd-ē\ *or Latin* **Rho·dus** \'rō-dəs\; *Gk.* **Ro·dos** *also* **Rho·dos** \'rȯ-ˌthȯs\. 1 Greek island in the Southern Sporades (see SPORADES), SE Aegean Sea, off SW coast of Turkey, in the Dodecanese group; 45 m. long by 22 m. at greatest width; 540 sq. m.; pop. (1961c) 68,873. Has mountain range extending length of island, highest point Mt. Attairo 3986 ft.; fine climate and fertile soil; exports fruit, vegetables, and wine. Chief island of Italian Aegean Islands 1912–45; to Greece 1947.

2 City, its ✱ and ✱ of the Dodecanese dept., Greece, at NE point of island; pop. (1971p) 32,019; commercial center and only large town of the island; two harbors; old town retains 15th cent. fortifications and is generally medieval in appearance; Palace of the Grand Masters (restored).

History: An independent kingdom as early as 1400 B.C.; in historic times settled by Dorians and established numerous colonies in Mediterranean; present city founded c. 408 B.C.; city came at various times under Sparta, Athens, Caria, and Alexander the Great; besieged 305–304 B.C. by Demetrius Poliorcetes; an ally of Rome for several centuries but destroyed as commercial center by earthquake 155 A.D. In Middle Ages conquered by Knights of St. John of Jerusalem; held against Turkish siege 1522 but finally evacuated. Occupied by Italy 1912; ceded to Italy by Turkey 1923; to Greece 1947.

Rhodes, Inner. See APPENZELL.

Rhodes, Outer. See APPENZELL.

Rho·de·sia \rō-'dē-zh(ē-)ə\. 1 Region, cen. South Africa, S of Zaire, now divided into Rhodesia and Zambia; formerly administered by British South Africa Company; named after Cecil J. Rhodes. There are evidences that man has inhabited the region since earliest times: (1) human skulls and Paleolithic hand axes; (2) many Bushman rock paintings; (3) great ruined stone buildings (see ZIMBABWE); (4) goldfields by some supposed to be source of gold of Ophir of King Solomon's times.

2 *also* **Southern Rhodesia.** Republic, S cen. Africa, bounded on NW by Zambia, on N by Zambia and Mozambique, on E and SE by Mozambique, on S by the Rep. of South Africa, and on SW and W by Botswana; 150,820 sq. m.; pop. (1970e) 5,400,000; ✱ Salisbury. *Physical features:* Forms part of great South African plateau sloping from SW to NE; cen. part at average elevation of 4000 to 5000 ft. is broad watershed bet. Zambezi (boundary with Zambia) and Limpopo and Sabi systems on SE. These large streams have many tributaries, esp. Sanyati flowing to Zambezi in NW and Lundi to Sabi in SE. In NW is Victoria Falls (*q.v.*) in the Zambezi. *Chief products:* Wheat, corn, tobacco, barley, sugar beet; livestock; asbestos, gold, chrome, coal, copper; manufacturing: textiles,

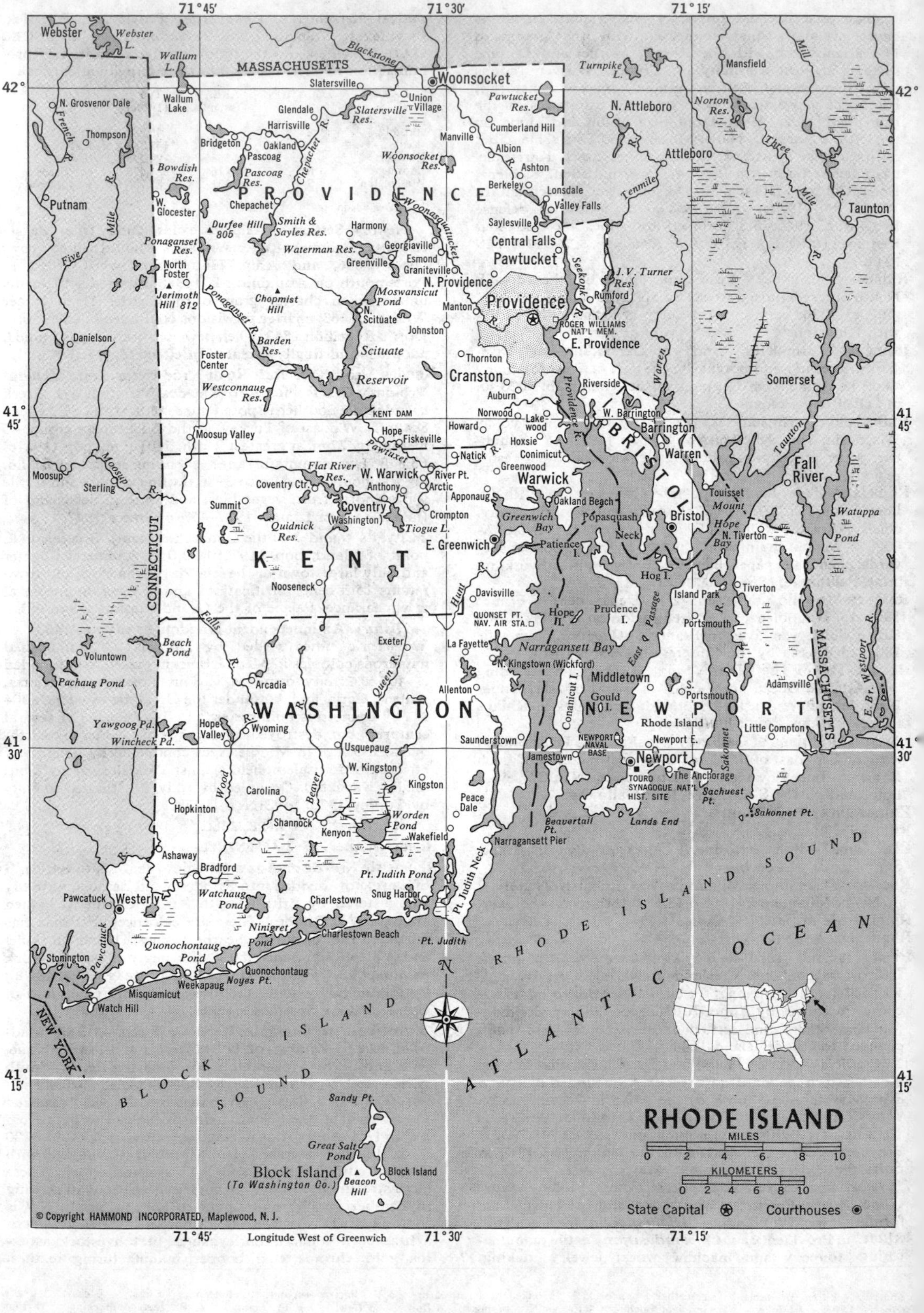
RHODE ISLAND
MILES
0 2 4 6 8 10
KILOMETERS
0 2 4 6 8 10
State Capital
Courthouses
71°45′
71°30′
71°15′
42°
41° 45′
41° 30′
41° 15′
Longitude West of Greenwich
PROVIDENCE
KENT
WASHINGTON
NEWPORT
BRISTOL
MASSACHUSETTS
CONNECTICUT
NEW YORK
RHODE ISLAND SOUND
BLOCK ISLAND SOUND
ATLANTIC OCEAN
Narragansett Bay
Providence
Pawtucket
Central Falls
Woonsocket
Cranston
Warwick
E. Providence
N. Providence
Newport
Bristol
Warren
Barrington
Westerly
E. Greenwich
Coventry
(Washington)
W. Warwick
Wakefield
Peace Dale
Kingston
W. Kingston
Narragansett Pier
Jamestown
Middletown
Portsmouth
Tiverton
Little Compton
Block Island
(To Washington Co.)
Beacon Hill
Great Salt Pond
Sandy Pt.
Scituate Reservoir
Kent Dam
Durfee Hill 805
Jerimoth Hill 812
Chopmist Hill
Prudence I.
Conanicut I.
Hope I.
Patience I.
Gould I.
Rhode Island
Point Judith
Pt. Judith Pond
Sakonnet Pt.
Beavertail Pt.
Watch Hill
Charlestown
Charlestown Beach
Quonochontaug
Misquamicut
Weekapaug
Hope Valley
Wyoming
Usquepaug
Carolina
Shannock
Kenyon
Hopkinton
Ashaway
Bradford
Exeter
Arcadia
La Fayette
Allenton
Saunderstown
N. Kingstown (Wickford)
Davisville
QUONSET PT. NAV. AIR STA.
NEWPORT NAVAL BASE
TOURO SYNAGOGUE NAT'L HIST. SITE
ROGER WILLIAMS NAT'L MEM.
Fall River
Somerset
Taunton
Attleboro
N. Attleboro
Mansfield
Webster
Putnam
Danielson
Thompson
Stonington
Pawcatuck
© Copyright HAMMOND INCORPORATED, Maplewood, N. J.

cement, iron and steel, chemicals. *Chief cities:* Salisbury, Bulawayo, Gwelo, Umtali, Fort Victoria.

History: Region under administration of British South Africa Company 1889–1923; became a self-governing British colony 1923; member of the Federation of Rhodesia and Nyasaland 1953–63; issued a unilateral declaration of independence 1965 (considered illegal by the British government); proclaimed itself a republic 1970.

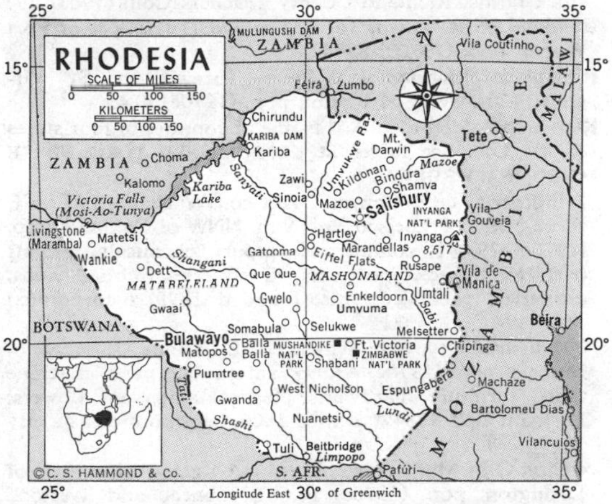

Rhodesia and Ny·as·a·land, Federation of \-nī-'as-ə-ˌland\. Former federation, S cen. Africa, consisting of Malawi (formerly Nyasaland), Rhodesia, and Zambia (formerly Northern Rhodesia); formed 1953, dissolved 1963.

Rhodes In·yan·ga National Park \'rōdz-in-'yaŋ-ə-\. National park, E Rhodesia; 133 sq. m.; mountainous region; established 1950.

Rhodes Peak. Mountain, E Clearwater co., NE Idaho; 7950 ft.

Rhodes Point. Point, Maryland, on Smith I. in lower Chesapeake Bay.

Rhod·o·pe \'räd-ə-(ˌ)pē\ *also* **Ro·do·pi** \rō-'thō-pē\ *or Turk.* **Dos·pad Dagh** \dəs-ˌpät-'dä(g)\ *or Bulg.* **Des·po·to Pla·ni·na** \'des-pə-ˌtō-ˌplän-i-'nä\. 1 Mountain range in Balkan Penin., SE Europe; ab. 180 m. long; runs SE from SW Bulgaria along border bet. Bulgaria and Macedonia, Greece; highest point Musala 9596 ft.; lies bet. Balkan Mts. and Aegean Sea; in Roman Empire marked boundary bet. Thrace and Macedonia.

2 Department of Thrace, Greece. See table at GREECE.

Rhodos *or* **Rhodus.** See RHODES.

Rhön \'rə(r)n\. Mountain range, NW Bavaria and E Hesse, West Germany, and W Suhl dist., East Germany; highest peak Wasserkuppe 3116 ft.

Rhon·dda \'rän-də, '(h)rän-thə\ *or formerly* **Ys·trad·y·fod·wg** \ˌəs-ˌtrad-ē-'väd-ˌüg\. Urban district, Glamorganshire, S Wales; pop. (1971p) 88,924; coal mining; in a valley region ab. 12 m. long, 4 m. wide, formed mainly by two rivers, the **Rhondda Fawr** \-'vaů(ə)r\ and the **Rhondda Fach** \-'vak\ separated by ridge 600–1690 ft. high.

Rhone *or Fr.* **Rhône** \'rōn\ *or anc.* **Rhod·a·nus** \'räd-ən-əs\. River, Switzerland and France; 505 m. long; rises in the Alps and flows SW to Martigny where it turns NW and flows into E end of Lake Geneva; issues from SW end of Lake Geneva, crosses French border through an opening in the Jura Mts., and continues S through Lyons, Avignon, and Tarascon to Arles; empties into the Gulf of Lions, S France, through several branches; navigable for ab. 300 m.

Rhône \'rōn\. Department of E cen. France. See table at FRANCE.

Rhudd·lan \'rith-lən\. Civil parish of St. Asaph, Flintshire, N Wales; pop. (1961c) 1701; site of Norman castle (demolished by Cromwell's troops 1646) at which Edward I enacted 1284 the statute for the government of Wales.

Rhum, Isle of. See RUM, ISLE OF.

Rhyl \'ril\. Urban district and seaport at mouth of the Clwyd, NW Flintshire, NE Wales; pop. (1971p) 21,715; seaside resort.

Rhym·ney \'rəm-nē\. 1 *or* **Rum·ney** \'rəm-nē\. River on border bet. Monmouthshire and Glamorganshire, S Wales; ab. 30 m. long; flows SE into the Bristol Channel E of Cardiff.

2 Urban district, Monmouthshire, SE Wales, on the Rhymney 38 m. NW of Bristol; pop. (1971p) 8051.

Rhyndacus. See ATRANOS.

Rhy·o·lite \'rī-ə-ˌlīt\. Former town, S Nye co., cen. and S Nevada; boom mining city (pop. 8000 from 1905–08) following Goldfield stampede; Death Valley nearby.

Ria·chos \rē-'äch-əs\. Small island in Atlantic Ocean off SE coast of Buenos Aires prov., Argentina.

Riad. See RIYADH.

Ri·al·to \rē-'al-(ˌ)tō\. 1 Residential city, San Bernardino co., SE California, 4 m. W of San Bernardino; pop. (1970c) 28,370; residential; citrus fruit.

2 Island and district on the Grand Canal, Venice, Italy; connected with San Marco I. by the **Rialto Bridge,** built ab. 1590, which has a double row of shops with a broad footway between.

Ri·au \'rē-ˌaů\. 1 Province of Sumatra, Indonesia. See table at INDONESIA.

2 Island, Indonesia. See RIOUW.

Riau Archipelago *or Du.* **Ri·ouw Archipelago** \'rē-ˌaů-\. Group of islands in Indonesia, off SE end of the Malay Penin., separated from Singapore by Singapore Strait; 2279 sq. m.; pop. (1961c) 278,966. Comprises the islands of Bintan, Batam, Rempang, the Karimun group, and smaller islands; all, including Singapore I. (*q.v.*), were once part of Johore sultanate. Occupied by Japanese 1942–45.

Riazan. See RYAZAN.

Ribachi Peninsula. See RYBACHI PENINSULA.

Rib·ble \'rib-əl\. River, NW England; rises in W Yorkshire, flows S and W through Lancashire into the Irish Sea through an estuary extending from Preston.

Rib·bon Falls \ˌrib-ən-\. Waterfall in Yosemite National Park, E cen. California; 1612 ft.

Ri·be \'rē-bə\. 1 County of SW Jutland, Denmark. See table at DENMARK.

2 Town, its ⊗, on Ribe river; pop. (1970e) 8224; iron, dairy products, leather goods; 12th cent. cathedral; first mentioned 862.

Ri·beau·vil·lé \re-ˌbō-vē-'la\ *or Ger.* **Rap·polts·wei·ler** \'räp-əlts-ˌvī-lər\. Commune, N Haut-Rhin dept., NE France; pop. (1962c) 4701; saline springs, two Gothic churches; ruins of three castles.

Ri·bei·ra \rı-'ber-ə\. 1 River, Paraná and São Paulo states, S Brazil; ab. 200 m. long; flows SW and SE into the Atlantic Ocean.

2 Commune, La Coruña prov., NW Spain, 38 m. SW of La Coruña and across the bay from Villagarcía de Arosa; pop. (1970p) 21,716.

Ribeira Gran·de \ri-ˌber-ə-'gran-də\. See SANTO ANTÃO.

Ri·bei·rão Pre·to \ˌrē-bə-'raůn-'prā-(ˌ)tü\. City, N cen. São Paulo state, SE Brazil, on railroad 180 m. NNW of São Paulo; munic. pop. (1968e) 169,845; commercial city in center of rich coffee-growing region; also produces cereals, cotton, alfalfa, and sugar.

Ri·be·ra \ri-'ber-ə\. Commune, Agrigento prov., SW Sicily, Italy, 20 m. NW of Agrigento; pop. (1968e) 19,435.

Ri·be·ral·ta \ˌrib-ə-'räl-tə\. Town, El Beni dept., N Bolivia, on Beni river at its confluence with the Madre de Dios; Bolivian customhouse; rubber and nuts.

Ricamarie, La. See LA RICAMARIE.

Ric·car·ton \'rik-ərt-ᵊn\. Borough, E South I., New Zealand, suburb of Christchurch; pop. (1970e) 7150.

Ric·cio·ne \ri-'chō-nē\. Commune, Forlì prov., SE Emilia-Romagna, N Italy, SE of Rimini on the Adriatic coast; pop. (1968e) 26,645; resort.

Rice \'rīs\. Name of counties in two states of the U.S. See tables at KANSAS and MINNESOTA.

Rice Lake. 1 City, Barron co., NW Wisconsin, 45 m. NNW of Chippewa Falls; pop. (1970c) 7278; summer resort; dairy products, beer, furniture; truck farms; Barron County Teachers Coll. (1907).

2 Lake, N Northumberland co., SE Ontario, Canada; 27 sq. m.; forms part of Trent Canal system; fishing.

Rich \'rich\. County in Utah. See table at UTAH.

Rich, Cape. Cape, SE Ontario, Canada, extending from N Grey co. into Georgian Bay.

Rich, Mount. Peak, Gilmer co., N Georgia; 4081 ft.

Rich·ards Island \ˌrich-ərdz-\. Large island in Beaufort Sea at mouth of Mackenzie river, NW Northwest Territories, Canada.

Rich·ard·son \'rich-ərd-sən\. 1 County in Nebraska. See table at NEBRASKA.

2 Village on Tanana river and Alaska Highway, 45 m. SE of Fairbanks, E Alaska.

3 City, Collin and Dallas cos., NE Texas, N of Dallas; pop. (1970c) 48,582; residential; agriculture.

Richardson Highway. Old highway N from Valdez, S Alaska, to Fairbanks; 371 m.; completed 1923; now merges with Alaska Highway at Big Delta; from it a cutoff runs from Gulkana NE to Alaska Highway at Tanacross; joined at Copper Center by Glenn Highway from Anchorage on the W.

Richardson Lakes. See RANGELEY LAKES.

Richardson Mountains. Range in N Yukon Territory, Canada; average height ab. 4000 ft.; highest point 6500 ft.; separates Porcupine river from lower Mackenzie river; forms an E extension of the Brooks Range of Alaska.

Rich·bor·ough \'rich-b(ə-)rə\. Port, Kent, SE England, on the estuary of the Stour river SW of Ramsgate; on the site of ancient **Ru·tu·pi·ae** \rü-'t(y)ü-pē-ˌē\, an important Roman port; beginning of Watling St.; ruins of castle; modern port established during World War I.

Rich·e·lieu \'rish-ə-ˌlü\. 1 River, S Quebec, Canada; 210 m. long; flows N from Lake Champlain to the head of Lake St. Peter in the St. Lawrence river at Sorel. Noted for its scenery; in early times an important travel route. Discovered by Champlain 1609.

2 County, Quebec, Canada. See table at QUEBEC.

Rich·field \'rich-ˌfēld\. 1 City, ⊗ of Morton co., SW corner of Kansas; pop. (1970c) 82.

2 Village, Hennepin co., SE cen. Minnesota, 7 m. S of Minneapolis; pop. (1970c) 47,321; suburb of Minneapolis.

3 Village, Summit co., NE Ohio, 16 m. NW of Akron; pop. (1970c) 3228.

4 City, ⊗ of Sevier co., cen. Utah, on Sevier river ab. 55 m. E of S end of Sevier Lake; pop. (1970c) 4471; dairy products, feed; uranium mines; diversified agriculture.

Richfield Springs. Village, Otsego co., cen. New York, 21 m. SSE of Utica; pop. (1970c) 1540; health and summer resort, with mineral springs; Great White Sulphur Spring in center of village.

Rich·i·buc·to \ˌrish-ə-'bək-(ˌ)tō\. Town (unincorporated), ⊗ of Kent co., E New Brunswick, Canada, on inlet of Northumberland Strait; pop. (1966c) 1668; founded 1787.

Rich·land \'rich-lənd\. 1 *or* **Richland Creek.** River, S Tennessee; 40 m. long; rises in SW Marshall co., flows S into Elk river near Alabama border.

2 Name of a parish in Louisiana and of counties in six states of the U.S. See tables at ILLINOIS, LOUISIANA, MONTANA, NORTH DAKOTA, OHIO, SOUTH CAROLINA, WISCONSIN.

3 City, California. See ORANGE 2.

4 City, Benton co., SE Washington, on the Columbia river WNW of Pasco; pop. (1970c) 26,290. Originally a farming community, it was developed 1943–45 on U.S. Atomic Energy Commission reservation as a residential community for employees of Hanford Engineer Works to NW. See HANFORD 2.

Richland Bal·sam \-'bȯl-səm\. Peak, Haywood co., W North Carolina; 6540 ft.

Richland Center. City, ⊗ of Richland co., SW Wisconsin, 53 m. WNW of Madison; pop. (1970c) 5086; dairy, livestock farms; Richland County Teachers Coll. (1903).

Richland Hills. Town, Tarrant co., NE Texas, NE of Fort Worth; pop. (1970c) 8865.

Rich·lands \'rich-lən(d)z\. Town, Tazewell co., SW Virginia, 42 m. NNE of Bristol; pop. (1970c) 4843.

Rich·mond \'rich-mənd\. 1 Name of counties in four states of the U.S. See tables at GEORGIA, NEW YORK, NORTH CAROLINA, VIRGINIA.

2 Industrial city, Contra Costa co., W California, on E shore of San Francisco Bay, 9 m. NNW of Oakland; pop. (1970c) 79,043; commercial seaport; chemicals, aircraft parts, electronic components; oil refineries, railroad shops, canneries, packing plants; founded 1899, incorporated 1905.

3 Industrial city, ⊗ of Wayne co., E Indiana, 35 m. SE of Muncie; pop. (1970c) 43,999; automobile parts, machine tools, furniture, hardware, plastics; ships cut flowers; Earlham Coll. (1847); settled 1806, incorporated as a city 1840.

4 City, ⊗ of Madison co., E cen. Kentucky, 24 m. SSE of Lexington; pop. (1970c) 16,681; tobacco and livestock market; corn; frequently scene of fighting during Civil War; Eastern Kentucky Univ. (1906).

5 Town, Sagadahoc co., S Maine, on Kennebec river 16 m. S of Augusta; pop. (1970c) 2168.

6 City, Macomb co., SE Michigan, 19 m. WSW of Port Huron; pop. (1970c) 3234; automobile parts; dairy farms.

7 City, ⊗ of Ray co., NW Missouri, 38 m. ENE of Kansas City; pop. (1970c) 4948; diversified agriculture.

8 Borough, Richmond co., SE New York, coextensive with Staten I. and Richmond co., SW part of New York City; 37 sq. m.; pop. (1970c) 295,443; includes Shooters' I., Prall's I., Meadow I., part of Buckwheat I., a few small islands to W and N, and Hoffman I. and Swinburne I. in Lower New York Bay; SW of Brooklyn, and separated from Long I. by the Narrows and from the mainland of New Jersey by Kill van Kull on N (spanned by Bayonne Bridge) and Arthur Kill on W (crossed by Goethals Bridge to Elizabeth and by Outerbridge to Perth Amboy); municipal ferry connections with Manhattan and Brooklyn. Has a free port, with large piers, and a 35-mile waterfront; beach resorts on Atlantic coast; residential sections and trade centers, including Saint George (⊗ of Richmond co.), Port Richmond, West New Brighton, Tompkinsville, Stapleton, New Dorp, Tottenville (scene 1776 of unsuccessful peace conference bet. British and Americans after battle of Long Island); shipbuilding yards, lumber mills, printing and publishing plants, oil storage tanks and refineries; manufactures soap and oil, fertilizer. Wagner Memorial Lutheran Coll. (1886; brought here from Rochester 1918); Sailors' Snug Harbor for retired sailors at New Brighton (*q.v.*). Governed as part of New York City by a mayor and city council; has a borough president, with local and county functions conducted independently of central municipal government. See also NEW YORK 3.

History: Staten I. granted to Pauw by the Dutch West India Company 1630, regranted to de Vries; passed to British 1664 and became part of the province of New Jersey; won for New York by Capt. Christopher Billopp 1668; merged as a borough of New York City 1898.

9 Town, Washington co., S Rhode Island; pop. (1970c) 2625.

10 Town, ⊗ of Fort Bend co., SE Texas, 28 m. WSW of Houston; pop. (1970c) 5777; agriculture.

11 City and port of entry, ✻ of Virginia and ⊗ of Henrico co., E cen. Virginia, on James river; 37 sq. m.; pop. (1970c) 249,430; politically independent; major tobacco market and commercial center; manufactures iron and steel, cigarettes, textiles, paper, food products; flour mills, printing and publishing plants; Virginia Commonwealth Univ. (1804), Univ. of Richmond (1832), Virginia Union Univ. (1865), Presbyterian School of Christian Education (1914).

History: Developed as trading center around Fort Charles, built at falls 1645; town laid out 1737 (subsequently occupied seven hills); incorp. 1742; scene of 2d and 3d Virginia Conventions in 1775 (at time of Patrick Henry's plea for liberty or death); made capital of Virginia 1779; figured prominently in Revolution; plundered and burned by British under Benedict Arnold 1781; incorp. as town (but called city) 1782; scene of Virginia Convention 1788 for ratification of new Federal Constitution and of Aaron Burr's trial for treason 1807; became the Confederate capital July 1861 at beginning of Civil War and remained the major objective of the Union army until its capture 1865; evacuated and burned by own people 1865, subsequently rebuilt.

12 City, S Victoria, SE Australia, E suburb of Melbourne; pop. (1966c) 32,530.

13 County, Nova Scotia, Canada. See table at NOVA SCOTIA.

14 County, Quebec, Canada. See table at QUEBEC.

15 Town, ⊗ of Richmond co., S Quebec, Canada, on St. Francis river 20 m. NNW of Sherbrooke; pop. (1971p) 4275; railroad divisional point.

16 Borough, London. See RICHMOND UPON THAMES.

17 Borough, N South I., New Zealand, at head of Tasman Bay; pop. (1970e) 5070.

Richmond Bay. See MALPEQUE BAY.

Richmond Gulf *or* **Richmond Lake.** Lake near SE coast of Hudson Bay, Quebec, Canada, opp. Belcher Is., bet. Clearwater Lake and the bay.

Richmond Heights. 1 City, St. Louis co., E Missouri, 7 m. W of St. Louis; pop. (1970c) 13,802.

2 Village, Cuyahoga co., N Ohio, NE of Cleveland; pop. (1970c) 9220.

Richmond Hill. 1 Peak in Lawrence co., W South Dakota; 6057 ft.

2 Town, York co., SE Ontario, Canada, 10 m. N of Toronto; pop. (1971p) 32,399; residential; clothing, plastics; diversified agriculture.

Richmond Lake. See RICHMOND GULF.

Richmond National Battlefield Park. See UNITED STATES, *National Historical Parks.*

Richmond upon Thames *or frequently* **Richmond.** A borough of London, SE England. See table at LONDON 4.

Rich Mountain. 1 Mountain, Arkansas. See BLUE MOUNTAIN 1.

2 Locality, Randolph co., West Virginia; scene of battle July 11, 1861 in which Union troops under Rosecrans defeated the Confederates under Col. Pegram.

Rich·ton Park \ˌrich-tən-\. Village, Cook co., NE Illinois, 30 m. S of Chicago; pop. (1970c) 2558.

Rich·wood \ˈrich-ˌwu̇d\. 1 Village, Union co., W cen. Ohio, 13 m. SSW of Marion; pop. (1970c) 2072.

2 City, Nicholas co., cen. West Virginia, 63 m. E of Charleston; pop. (1970c) 3717; lumber; coal mines.

Rick·en Tunnel \ˈrik-ən-\. Railroad tunnel, W St. Gallen canton, NE Switzerland, E of Lake of Zurich; 5.34 m. long.

Rick·mans·worth \ˈrik-mənz-ˌwərth\. Urban district, Hertfordshire, SE England, at confluence of Chess and Colne rivers 20 m. WNW of London; pop. (1971p) 29,510.

Ricomagus. See RIOM.

Rid·der·kerk \ˈrid-ər-ˌke(ə)rk\. Commune, South Holland prov., SW Netherlands, on a delta island of the Rhine just E of Rotterdam; pop. (1970e) 41,899.

Ri·deau \ri-ˈdō\. Lake on S border of Lanark co., SE Ontario, Canada; ab. 126 sq. m.; its outlet is **Rideau River** which flows from S Frontenac co. NE through Rideau Lake to the Ottawa river at Ottawa. The lake and river, with constructed section from Rideau Lake to Lake Ontario, form the **Rideau Canal,** $123\frac{1}{2}$ m. long with 47 locks, connecting Kingston on Lake Ontario with the Ottawa river below Chaudière Falls. The canal divides the city of Ottawa; it was built 1826 by British government for military purposes at suggestion of duke of Wellington. Now used commercially only; has branch $6\frac{1}{2}$ m. long from Rideau Lake to Perth.

Ridge·crest \ˈrij-ˌkrest\. Urban area, Kern co., S California, NE of Bakersfield; pop. (1970c) 7629.

Ridge·field \ˈrij-ˌfēld\. 1 Suburban residential town, W Fairfield co., SW Connecticut, on New York border; pop. (1970c) 18,188; incorp. 1709; battle Apr. 27, 1776.

2 Borough, Bergen co., NE corner of New Jersey, 8 m. N of Jersey City; pop. (1970c) 11,308.

Ridgefield Park. Village, Bergen co., NE New Jersey, 8 m. ESE of Paterson; pop. (1970c) 13,990; paper products; residential.

Ridge·land \ˈrij-lənd\. Town, ⊗ of Jasper co., S South Carolina; pop. (1970c) 1165.

Ridge·town \ˈrij-ˌtau̇n\. Town, Kent co., SE Ontario, Canada, 17 m. E of Chatham; pop. (1971p) 2836.

Ridge·wood \ˈrij-ˌwu̇d\. Residential village, Bergen co., NE corner of New Jersey, 5 m. NNE of Paterson; pop. (1970c) 27,547; concrete products; scene of American and British encampments in Revolution; fighting in locality 1780.

Ridg·way \ˈrij-ˌwā\. Borough, ⊗ of Elk co., NW cen. Pennsylvania, 20 m. N of Du Bois; pop. (1970c) 6022; tools and dies, chemicals; oil, gas wells; truck farms; settled 1817.

Riding, East. See YORKSHIRE.

Riding, North. See YORKSHIRE.

Riding, West. See YORKSHIRE.

Rid·ing Mountain National Park \ˌrīd-iŋ-\. See CANADA, *National Parks.*

Riding Mountains. Plateau, SW cen. Manitoba, Canada, W of Lake Manitoba; highest point 2411 ft.; forms main part of Riding Mountain National Park.

Rid·ley \ˈrid-lē\. Urban township, Delaware co., SE Pennsylvania, SW of Philadelphia; pop. (1970c) 39,085.

Ridley Park. Residential borough, Delaware co., SE Pennsylvania, 10 m. WSW of Philadelphia; pop. (1970c) 9025.

Riduna. See ALDERNEY.

Ried \ˈrēt\ *or* **Ried im Inn·kreis** \-im-ˈin-ˌkrīs\. Town, Upper Austria, ab. 40 m. W of Linz; pop. (1961c) 9471; treaty of alliance bet. Emperor Francis of Austria and Bavaria signed here 1813.

Riège, La. See ARIÈGE.

Rieka. See RIJEKA.

Rie·sa \ˈrē-(ˌ)zä, -zə\. City, Dresden dist., East Germany, on Elbe river 39 m. E of Leipzig; pop. (1970e) 49,746; steel, textiles, matches, rubber goods; developed around monastery 12th cent.; received first charter 1623.

Ries·co \rē-ˈes-(ˌ)kō\. Island, Magallanes prov., S Chile, N of the W end of Strait of Magellan; separated from Brunswick Penin. by Otway Water.

Rie·sen·ge·bir·ge *or* **Rie·sen Ge·bir·ge** \ˈrēz-ᵊn-gə-ˌbi(ə)r-gə\ *also* **Gi·ant Mountains** \ˈjī-ənt-\ *or Czech* **Krkno·še** \kər-kə-ˈnō-shə\. Mountain range extending along boundary between SW Poland (in region formerly included in Silesia prov., Prussia, Germany) and N Czechoslovakia; part of Sudetic Mts.; highest Sněžka 5256 ft.

Rie·si \rē-ˈā-zē, -ˈez-ē\. Commune, Caltanissetta prov., cen. Sicily, Italy, 19 m. S by E of Caltanissetta; pop. (1968e) 17,129.

Riet \ˈrēt\. River, SW Orange Free State, Rep. of South Africa; ab. 250 m. long; flows W into the Vaal.

Rie·ti \rē-ˈāt-ē, -ˈet-\. 1 Province of Latium, cen. Italy. See table at ITALY.
2 *or anc.* **Re·a·te** \rē-ˈāt-ē\. Commune, its ✱, 42 m. NNW of Rome; pop. (1968e) 38,720; synthetic textiles, olive oil, fertilizer; 12th cent. cathedral, 13th cent. papal palace. In ancient times a capital of the Sabines; birthplace of Marcus Terentius Varro 116 B.C.; Guelph free city in 12th cent. A.D.; came under States of the Church 1354.

Rif *or* **Riff.** See ER RIF.

Rifs·tan·gi, Cape \-ˈrifs-ˌtau̇ŋ-gē\. Cape, NE Iceland, W of Raufarhöfn.

Rift Valley \ˈrift-\. 1 Geological depression, Asia and Africa. See GREAT RIFT VALLEY.
2 Province of W Kenya. See table at KENYA.

Ri·ga \ˈrē-gə\ *or Lettish* **Rī·ga** \ˈrē-gə\. Industrial city and seaport, ✱ of Latvian S.S.R., U.S.S.R., at S extremity of the Gulf of Riga on the Western Dvina river 9 m. above its mouth; pop. (1970p) 733,000; one of the principal Baltic ports of the U.S.S.R.; produces diesel engines, electrical equipment, turbines, boilers, glass, chemicals, paper, cement; shipyards, fish-processing plants, sawmills; retains some medieval remains, incl. 13th cent. church, 14th cent. castle of the Livonian Order; univ. (1919).
History: Founded before 1190; established as a trading settlement 1201 by Bishop of Livonia and joined Hanseatic League 1282; fought over by Poles and Russians and burned 1558 in Livonian War (see LIVONIA); fell under Polish domination 1581; taken over by Gustavus Adolphus of Sweden 1621 and granted self-government; ceded to Peter the Great of Russia 1710 after the defeat at Poltava of Charles XII of Sweden; port closed 1915 in World War I; evacuated by Russians 1915; occupied by Germans 1917; independence of Latvia proclaimed at Riga Nov. 1918; independence recognized by U.S.S.R. in treaty signed here Aug. 11, 1920; in World War II taken by Germans June 29, 1941 and retaken by U.S.S.R. Oct. 13, 1944.

Riga, Gulf of. Inlet of NE Baltic Sea extending S into N coast of Latvian S.S.R., U.S.S.R.; ab. 100 m. long by 60 m. wide; receives the Western Dvina river.

Rig·by \ˈrig-bē\. City, ⊗ of Jefferson co., E Idaho, 15 m. NE of Idaho Falls; pop. (1970c) 2293; diversified agriculture; settled by Mormons 1884.

Ri·gi *or* **Ri·ghi** \ˈrē-gē\. Mountain mass in cen. Switzerland, bet. Lake of Lucerne and Lake of Zug; highest peaks the **Rigi–Kulm** \-ˌku̇lm\ 5905 ft. in NW, and **Rigi–Schei·degg** \-ˈshī-ˌdek\ 5462 ft. in SE.

Rig·o·let \ˌrig-ə-ˈlet\. Trading post and village at head of Hamilton Inlet on narrows leading to Lake Melville, SE Labrador, Canada.

Ri·i·shi·ri \ˈrē-shə-(ˌ)rē\. Island in N Sea of Japan, off NW coast of island of Hokkaidō, Japan.

Ri·je·ka \rē-ˈyek-ə\ *or* **Ri·eka** \rē-ˈek-ə\ *or Ital.* **Fiu·me** \ˈfyü-(ˌ)mā\ *or Ger.* **Sankt Veit am Flaum** \zäŋ(k)t-ˌfīt-äm-ˈflau̇m\. Seaport, Croatia, NW Yugoslavia, ab. 80 m. WSW of Zagreb; pop. (1971p) 132,933; ships agricultural products, lumber, tobacco, wine; shipbuilding, engineering, oil refining; naval base, episcopal see; Roman triumphal arch.
History: In Byzantine Empire; ruled by own dukes in 9th cent.; has been held by Austria, Croatia, France, and Hungary; occupied by Italy in 1918; its disposal became an issue which caused Italy to leave Peace Conference 1919; occupied by irregular troops under D'Annunzio 1919; by Treaty of Rapallo bet. Italy and Yugoslavia 1920, set up as independent free city; formally annexed to Italy 1924; transferred to Yugoslavia by Italian peace treaty 1947.

Rijn. See RHINE.

Rijs·wijk \ˈrīs-ˌvīk\ *or Eng.* **Rys·wick** \ˈriz-(ˌ)wik\. Commune, South Holland prov., NW Netherlands, suburb of the Hague; pop. (1970e) 50,172; residential; 14th cent. church. The Treaty of Ryswick, signed here Sept. 20, 1697 by France with Netherlands, England, and Spain, ended War of the Grand Alliance bet. England and France, acknowledged William III as king of England and Anne as his successor, mutually restored conquests of England and France in America, and allowed France to retain Alsace; separate treaty signed Oct. 30, 1697 by France and the Holy Roman Empire.

Ri·ker's Island \ˈrī-kərz-\. Island in the East river off S coast of the Bronx, New York City, New York; attached to Bronx borough; large penitentiary.

Ri·ku·chu \ˈrē-kə-ˌchü\. Former province, N Honshū, Japan, now Iwate prefecture.

Ri·ku·zen \ˈrē-ku̇-ˌzen\. Former province, N Honshū, Japan, now part of Miyagi prefecture.

Ri·la Dagh \ˌrē-lə-ˈdä(g)\. Range of mountains in SW Bulgaria, at W end of the Rhodope Mts.; highest point Musala 9596 ft.; contains sources of Iskŭr, Maritsa, and Mesta rivers.

Ri·ley \ˈrī-lē\. County in Kansas. See table at KANSAS.

Rí·mac \ˈrē-ˌmäk\. River, Peru; ab. 80 m. long; flows through the city of Lima into the Pacific Ocean.

Ri·ma·ta·ra \ˌrē-mə-ˈtar-ə\. See TUBUAI ISLANDS.

Ri·mav·ská So·bo·ta \ˌrim-əf-skə-ˈsȯ-bə-ˌtä\ *or Hung.* **Ri·ma·szom·bat** \ˈrim-ä-ˌsōm-ˌbät\. Town, Slovak S.R., SE Czechoslovakia, ab. 60 m. WSW of Košice near the Hungarian border; pop. (1968e) 13,343; part of Hungary 1938–45.

Ri·mi·ni \ˈrim-ə-(ˌ)nē, ˈrē-mə-\ *or anc.* **Arim·i·num** \ə-ˈrim-ə-nəm\. Seaport, Forlí prov., Emilia-Romagna, N Italy, on the Adriatic 27 m. ESE of Forlí; pop. (1968e) 114,467; railroad junction; has flour mills, wineries, and railroad shops, but is primarily a tourist center; has Roman remains including a triumphal arch and a bridge; ruins of 15th cent. Malatesta castle, 15th cent. Malatesta temple, several medieval churches.
History: Founded by Umbrians; came under Rome 268 B.C.; Roman military base in Second Punic War and during Gothic invasions; scene of Council of Rimini 359 A.D.; under the Malatestas 1239–1508; passed to Papal States until 1860 when it joined kingdom of Italy.

Rîm·ni·cu–Să·rat \ˈrəm-nē-ˌkü-sə-ˈrät\ *or* **Râm·ni·cul–Sărat** \ˈrəm-nə-ˌkül-sə-ˈrät\. Town, Buzău co., SE cen. Romania, ab. 20 m. NE of Buzău; pop. (1970e) 24,481; commercial center; has often been a battlefield: Moldavians against Wallachians, Turks against Wallachians, Austrians, and Russians; rebuilt since destructive fire 1854.

Rîmnicu–Vîl·cea \-ˈvəl-chə\ *or* **Râmnicul–Vâl·cea** \-ˈvəl-chə\. City, ⊗ of Vîlcea co., S cen. Romania, ab. 100 m. NW of Bucharest; pop. (1970e) 34,668; has cathedral and episcopal palace; in vicinity are four monasteries, thermal springs, and salt mines.

Ri·mous·ki \rim-ˈü-skē\. 1 County, Quebec, Canada. See table at QUEBEC.
2 City, its ⊗, on S bank of St. Lawrence river ab. 180 m. NE of Quebec; pop. (1971p) 26,546; lumber, dairy products; port of call for ocean steamers; tourist center; Séminaire de Rimouski (1855), Coll. des Ursulines (1906), Scolasticat Notre Dame du St. Bosaire (1957).

Rimp·fisch·horn \ˈrimp-ˌfish-ˌhȯ(ə)rn\. Peak in the Pennine Alps, in Switzerland, N of Monte Rosa; 13,776 ft.

Rin·cón \riŋ-ˈkōn\. 1 Peak, E Antofagasta prov., N Chile, on Argentina boundary; 18,353 ft.
2 Municipality, W Puerto Rico; pop. (1970p) 1534 (town), 9350 (munic.); town is on coast ab. 9 m. SW of Aguadilla.

Rincón Bay. Bay in S coast of Puerto Rico.

Rin·con Peak \ˌriŋ-kän-\. Mountain, E Pima co., S Arizona; 8465 ft.

Rin·dja·ni, Gu·nung \ˌgü-nu̇ŋ-rin-ˈjä-nē\. Volcanic peak, N part of Lombok I., Indonesia; 12,224 ft.; one of highest peaks of Malay Archipelago; erupted 1964.

Rin·ge·ri·ke \ˈriŋ-ə-ˌrē-kə\. Commune, Buskerud co., S Norway; pop. (1970e) 28,828.

Ring·gold \ˈriŋ-ˌgōld\. 1 County in Iowa. See table at IOWA.
2 City, ⊗ of Catoosa co., NW Georgia; pop. (1970c) 1381.

Ring·kø·bing \ˈriŋ-ˌkər-biŋ\. 1 County of W Jutland, Denmark. See table at DENMARK.
2 Town, its ⊗, at N end of Ringkøbing Fjord; pop. (1970e) 6536.

Ringkøbing Fjord. Lagoon, W cen. coast of Jutland, Denmark; receives Omme and Skjern rivers.

Ring·nes Islands \ˌriŋ-nes-\. The Ellef Ringnes and Amund Ringnes islands of the Sverdrup Is., N Franklin dist., Northwest Territories, Canada, W of Axel Heiberg I.

Ring·sa·ker \ˈriŋ(k)s-ä-kər\. Commune, Hedmark co., E Norway; pop. (1970e) 28,764.

Ring·vass·øy \ˈriŋ-vä-ˌsȯi\. Island in Arctic Ocean off NW coast of Norway, SW of Vannøy I., in Troms co.; 253 sq. m.

Ring·wood \ˈriŋ-ˌwu̇d\. 1 River, New York and N New Jersey; rises in Orange co., SE New York, flows S through Passaic co., New Jersey, and unites with Pequannock and Ramapo rivers to form Pompton river.
2 Borough, Passaic co., N New Jersey, 17 m. NNW of Paterson; pop. (1970c) 10,393.

Rinía. See RHENEA.

Rinns, The. See RHINNS, THE.

Rin·tja \ˈrin-(ˌ)chä\. Small island off W end of Flores I., Indonesia, ESE of Komodo I.

Rio *Span.* ˈrē-(ˌ)ō, *Port.* -(ˌ)ü\. 1 For most names of rivers beginning with Rio (Span. *Río,* Port. *Rio,* "river"), see the distinguishing element.
2 City, Brazil. See RIO DE JANEIRO 2.

Rio Al·to Peak \ˌrē-ō-ˈal-tō-\. Mountain, Custer and Saguache cos., S cen. Colorado; 13,573 ft.

Rio Ar·ri·ba \ˌrē-ō-ə-ˈrē-bə\. County in New Mexico. See table at NEW MEXICO.

Ri·o·bam·ba \ˌrē-ō-ˈbäm-bə\. City, ✱ of Chimborazo prov., cen. Ecuador, 110 m. S of Quito and ab. 20 m. SE of Chimborazo volcano; pop. (1970e) 53,700; market town; produces textiles, carpets, footwear, dairy products; original town a few miles distant destroyed by earthquake 1797; first constitution of republic of Ecuador proclaimed here Aug. 14, 1830.

Rio Blan·co \ˌrē-ō-ˈblaŋ-(ˌ)kō\. County in Colorado. See table at COLORADO.

Río Blanco \ˌrē-ō-ˈblaŋ-(ˌ)kō\. Municipality, Veracruz state, Mexico, 4 m. W of Orizaba; pop. (1970p) 27,266.

Rio Bran·co \ˌrē-ō-ˈbraŋ-(ˌ)kō\. 1 River in Brazil. See BRANCO, RIO.
2 City, ✱ of Acre state, W Brazil, on Acre river; munic. pop. (1970p) 72,835; rubber, timber.

Río Bra·vo \ˌrē-ō-ˈbräv-(ˌ)ō\. 1 *or* **Río Bravo del Nor·te** \-del-ˈnȯrt-ē\. Mexican name of the Rio Grande, bet. U.S. and Mexico. See RIO GRANDE 1.
2 Municipality, Tamaulipas state, Mexico, 40 m. W of Matamoros; pop. (1970p) 70,814; wheat, cotton.

Rio Cha·ma \ˌrē-ō-ˈchäm-ə\. River, Colorado and N New Mexico; ab. 100 m. long; rises in Conejos co., S Colorado, flows S across state border and empties into the Rio Grande in SE Rio Arriba co., N New Mexico.

Rio Cla·ro \ˌrē-ü-ˈklar-(ˌ)ō\. City, São Paulo state, SE Brazil, 90 m. NW of São Paulo; munic. pop. (1968e) 69,096.

Río Cuar·to \ˌrē-ō-ˈkwärt-(ˌ)ō\. Town, Córdoba prov., cen. Argentina, ab. 125 m. S of Córdoba; pop. (1960c) 65,569; commercial center of livestock farming region; military base and arsenal.

Rio de Ja·nei·ro \ˈre-(ˌ)ō-ˌdā-zhə-ˈne(ə)r-(ˌ)ō, -ˌdē-, -də-, -jə-, ˈni(ə)r-\. 1 State of SE Brazil. See table at BRAZIL.
2 *abbr.* **Rio** \ˈrē-(ˌ)ō\. Commercial seaport, ✱ of Guanabara state, SE Brazil, on SW shore of Guanabara Bay; pop. (1970p) 4,296,782; former ✱ of Brazil; principal port of Brazil and major transportation center; produces foodstuffs, beverages, tobacco products, clothing, soap, furniture, glass, chemicals, tires; publishing, metalworking, shipbuilding; federal univ. (1920), Catholic univ. (1960), and several other educational institutions. Located on one of the largest harbors in the world, noted for its scenery; built on an alluvial plain. The mountains come down to the shore of the bay in places, notably in Pão de Açúcar (1296 ft.) at the entrance to the bay and just W of it the Corcovado (*q.v.*) 2310 ft. Noted for its numerous wide streets, public buildings, museums, and public parks and gardens; one of the leading tourist and resort centers of South America.
History: Guanabara Bay discovered by Portuguese early 16th cent. (no proof of accuracy of traditional date 1502); first settled 1535 by French under Villegaignon; French settlement expelled by Portuguese 1567; became important in 18th cent. after discovery of gold and diamonds in Minas Gerais made it the natural outlet for mineral exports; made capital of colony of Brazil 1763, of empire 1822, and of republic 1889; scene of Pan-American Congress 1906; in 1960 was replaced as capital of Brazil by Brasilia (*q.v.*) and became capital of newly-created Guanabara state.

Rio de Janeiro Bay. See GUANABARA BAY.

Rio Dell \ˌrē-o-ˈdel\. City, Humboldt co., NW California, SE of Eureka; pop. (1970c) 2817; truck farms.

Rio del Rey \ˌrē-ō-del-ˈrā\. Seaport and estuary on the coast of Cameroon, W Africa, E of Cross river.

Río de Oro \ˌrē-ōd-ē-ˈōr-(ˌ)ō, -ˈȯr-\. Narrow bay on the coast of Río de Oro zone of Spanish Sahara, NW Africa; harbor of Villa Cisneros.

Río Dul·ce National Park \ˈrē-ō-ˈdül-sə-\. National park, NE Guatemala; 117 sq. m.; lake; wildlife; established 1955.

Río Gallegos. See GALLEGOS 2.

Rio Grande \ˌrē-(ˌ)ō-ˈgrand(-ē) *also* ˌrī-ō-ˈgrand\. 1 *in Mex.* **Río Bra·vo** \ˌrē-o-ˈbräv-(ˌ)o\ *or* **Río Bravo del Nor·te** \-del-ˈnȯrt-ē\. River, SW Colorado, cen. New Mexico, and SW and S Texas; 1885 m. long; rises in San Juan Mts. near E boundary of San Juan co., SW Colorado, flows SE, then S through San Luis Park and across cen. New Mexico, forms W and SW boundary of Texas and the Texas-Mexico boundary; the section in S part of Brewster co., Texas, includes canyons of the Big Bend National Park; empties into the Gulf of Mexico.
2 County in Colorado. See table at COLORADO.

Rio Gran·de \ˌrē-(ˌ)ü-ˈgran-də\. 1 Name of a river in Africa and two rivers in Brazil. See GRANDE, RIO.
2 *or* **São Pe·dro do Rio Grande do Sul** \sau̇(ⁿ)m-ˈpā-(ˌ)drü-də . . . də-ˈsül\. City, SE Rio Grande do Sul state, S Brazil, 150 m. SSW of Pôrto Alegre; munic. pop. (1968e) 117,500; ships meat products, wool, hides, rice; textiles, beer, canned meat and fish, cigarettes, footwear; founded 1737 as fort on site nearby; moved to present site 1745; became city 1807.

Río Gran·de \re-ō-ˈgrän-dē\. 1 Rivers in Spanish America. See GRANDE, RÍO.
2 Town, Zacatecas state, cen. Mexico, on branch railroad 80 m. NNW of Zacatecas; munic. pop. (1970p) 34,879.
3 Municipality, NE Puerto Rico; pop. (1970c) 4125 (town), 21,978 (munic.); town on railroad 19 m. ESE of San Juan.

Rio Grande City \ˌrē-ō-ˈgrand(-ē)-, ˌrī-ō-ˈgrand-\. City, ⊗ of Starr co., S Texas, on Rio Grande 38 m. W of McAllen; pop. (1970c) 5676; fertilizer; oil and gas wells; truck farms.

Rio Grande de Cagayan. See CAGAYAN 1.

Rio Grande de Mindanao. See MINDANAO 2.

Rio Grande de Pampanga. See PAMPANGA 1.

Río Grande de Santiago. See SANTIAGO 10.

Rio Gran·de do Nor·te \ˌrē-ü-ˌgrand-ē-də-ˈnȯrt-ə\. State, NE Brazil; 20,469 sq. m.; pop. (1970p) 1,603,094; ✱ Natal; interior is semiarid; livestock raising.

Rio Grande do Sul \ˌrē-ü-ˌgrand-ē-də-ˈsül\. 1 State, S Brazil; 108,951 sq. m.; pop. (1970p) 6,652,618; ✱ Pôrto Alegre; rice, corn, wheat; livestock raising.
2 City, Brazil. See RIO GRANDE 2.

Rio Grande Pyramid \ˌrē-ō-ˌgrand(-ē)-, ˌrī-ō-ˌgrand-\. Peak, Hinsdale co., SW Colorado; 13,827 ft.

Rio Grande Reservoir. Reservoir in upper course of Rio Grande river, cen. Hinsdale co., SW Colorado.

Ri·o·ha·cha *or* **Río Ha·cha** \ˌrē-ō-'(h)äch-ə\. Seaport, ✱ of La Guajira dept., N Colombia, on W side of base of La Guajira Penin. ab. 90 m. E of Santa Marta; munic. pop. (1968e) 47,732; has trade with Netherlands Antilles; one of the oldest towns in Colombia.

Rioja, La. See LA RIOJA.

Riom \rē-'ō^{n}\ *or anc.* **Ri·com·a·gus** \rī-'käm-ə-gəs\. Commune, Puy-de-Dôme dept., S cen. France, 8 m. N of Clermont-Ferrand; pop. (1968c) 15,467; ancient capital of duchy of Auvergne; site of ducal palace occupied by law courts; scene of trial Feb. 19–Apr. 2, 1942 of Édouard Daladier, Léon Blum, Maurice G. Gamelin, Pierre Jacomet, and others by the Vichy government which had set up the Supreme Court of Justice July 30, 1940 to investigate charges against leaders of the Third Republic.

Río Mu·ni \ˌrē-ō-'mü-nē\. Mainland province of Equatorial Guinea (*q.v.*), W Africa, bounded on N by Cameroon, on E and S by Gabon, and on W by the Atlantic Ocean; 10,040 sq. m.; pop. (1968e) 203,000; chief town Bata.

Rion. See RIONI.

Río Ne·gro \ˌrē-ō-'nā-(ˌ)grō, -'neg-(ˌ)rō\. 1 River, South America. See NEGRO, RÍO 3.
2 Province of cen. Argentina. See table at ARGENTINA.
3 Department of W Uruguay. See table at URUGUAY.

Ri·o·ne·ro in Vul·tu·re \ˌrē-ə-'ner-ō-ēn-'vül-tu̇r-ō\. Commune, Potenza prov., Basilicata, S Italy, 21 m. N by W of Potenza; pop. (1968e) 13,569.

Ri·oni \rē-'ó-nē, -nyē\ *or* **Ri·on** \rē-'ón\ *or anc.* **Pha·sis** \'fā-səs\. River, W Georgian S.S.R., U.S.S.R.; 179 m. long; rises in the Caucasus Mts., flows SW and W to the Black Sea at Poti. Navigable for nearly half its course; has hydroelectric station at Kutaisi. The ancient Phasis famous in Greek legends concerning Colchis, the Golden Fleece, and the Argonauts; for a time held to be boundary bet. Europe and Asia.

Rio Par·do \ˌre-ü-'pär-dü\. Municipality, Rio Grande do Sul state, S Brazil, 70 m. W of Pôrto Alegre; pop. (1968e) 56,080.

Río Pie·dras \ˌrē-ō-pē-'ā-drəs\. Former municipality and city, NE Puerto Rico; annexed to San Juan 1951, forming a SE section of that city; Univ. of Puerto Rico (1900), Puerto Rico Junior Coll. (1949).

Ríos, Los. See LOS RÍOS.

Río San Juan \ˌrē-ō-san-'(h)wän\. Department of S Nicaragua. See table at NICARAGUA.

Rí·o·su·cio \ˌrē-ō-'sü-sē-ˌō\. Town, Caldas dept., W cen. Colombia, just NW of Manizales; munic. pop. (1968e) 47,702.

Rio Tin·to \ˌrē-ü-'tēn-(ˌ)tü\. City, Paraíba state, E Brazil; munic. pop. (1968e) 29,687.

Ríotinto, Minas de. See MINAS DE RÍOTINTO.

Ri·ouw \'rē-ˌau̇\ *or* **Ri·au** \'rē-ˌau̇\ *or* **Rhio** \'rē-(ˌ)ō\. Another name for Bintan island, Indonesia. See BINTAN.

Riouw Archipelago. See RIAU ARCHIPELAGO.

Río·ver·de *or* **Río Ver·de** \ˌrē-ō-'ver-dē\. Town, San Luis Potosí state, cen. Mexico, 65 m. ESE of San Luis Potosí; munic. pop. (1970p) 57,016.

Rio Vis·ta \'rē-ō-'vis-tə\. Town, Solano co., cen. California, on Sacramento river 32 m. SSW of Sacramento; pop. (1970c) 3135; cans fruit and vegetables.

Rip·ley \'rip-lē\. 1 Name of counties in two states of the U.S. See tables at INDIANA and MISSOURI.
2 City, ⊗ of Tippah co., N Mississippi, 28 m. SW of Corinth; pop. (1970c) 3482; lumber, footwear; cotton.
3 Village, Brown co., SW Ohio, on Ohio river 42 m. SE of Cincinnati; pop. (1970c) 2745; tobacco market; corn, hogs.
4 Town, ⊗ of Lauderdale co., W Tennessee, 23 m. S of Dyersburg; pop. (1970c) 4794; dies, clothing; diversified agriculture.
5 Town, ⊗ of Jackson co., W West Virginia; pop. (1970c) 3244; aluminum plant, gas wells.
6 Urban district, Derbyshire, N cen. England, 10 m. NNE of Derby; pop. (1971p) 17,825.

Rip·on \'rip-ˌän\. 1 City, San Joaquin co., cen. California, 11 m. NW of Modesto; pop. (1970c) 2679; wineries; diversified agriculture.
2 City, Fond du Lac co., E Wisconsin, 20 m. W of Fond du Lac; pop. (1970c) 7053; home appliances; cans peas; site of a Fourieristic communistic community 1844–50; reputed birthplace of the Republican party, in a meeting Mar. 20, 1854, of Whigs, anti-Nebraska Democrats, and Free Soilers. Ripon Coll. (1851).
3 Municipal borough, West Riding, Yorkshire, N England, on the Ure 23 m. N of Leeds; pop. (1971p) 10,987; trade center in agricultural section; 12th cent. Norman cathedral with 7th cent. Saxon remnants. Fountains Abbey ruins are at Studley Royal nearby.

Ripon Falls. Former waterfall in the Victoria Nile near where it issues from Lake Victoria, Uganda, SE cen. Africa; now submerged by Owen Falls Dam.

Rip·shin Ridge \'rip-ˌshin-\. Elevation, Carter co., NE Tennessee; 4500 ft.

Ri·sa·ral·da \ˌrē-sə-'räl-də\. Department of W Colombia. See table at COLOMBIA.

Ris·ca \'ris-kə\. Urban district, Monmouthshire, SE Wales, on the Ebbw river 26 m. WNW of Bristol; pop. (1971p) 15,799.

Ris·don \'riz-dən\. Suburb of Hobart, Tasmania, Australia, ab. 4 m. above it on the left bank of the Derwent. First settled 1803 by English navy lieutenant, John Bowen, but settlement moved across the river 1804 and name changed to Hobart.

Ri·shon Le–Zi·on *or* **Rishon le Ziy·yon** \ri-'shōn-lə-tsē-'yōn\. Town, Israel, ab. 8 m. SE of Tel Aviv-Jaffa; pop. (1970e) 46,500.

Rish·ra \'rish-rə\. Town, West Bengal, NE India, on right bank of Hooghly river 12 m. N of Calcutta; pop. (1961c) 38,535; site of first power mill for spinning jute yarns set up in India 1855.

Rish·ton \'rish-tən\. Urban district, Lancashire, NW England, 22 m. NNW of Manchester; pop. (1971p) 6010.

Ris·ing Sun \ˌrīz-iŋ-'sən\. City, ⊗ of Ohio co., SE Indiana, on Ohio river 60 m. SE of Shelbyville; pop. (1970c) 2305.

Rising Wolf Mountain. Peak, Glacier National Park, NW Montana; 9505 ft.

Ri·son \'rī-zən\. Commercial city, ⊗ of Cleveland co., S Arkansas; pop. (1970c) 1214; lumber; truck farms.

Ris–Oran·gis \'rēz-ô-rä^{n}-'zhē\. Commune, Essonne dept., N France, ab. 15 m. S of Paris; pop. (1968c) 23,511.

Rist·na, Cape \-'rist-nə\. Western point of Hiiumaa I., W of Estonian S.S.R., U.S.S.R.

Ritch·ie \'rich-ē\. County in West Virginia. See table at WEST VIRGINIA.

Ritch·ie's Archipelago \'rich-ēz-\. Island group in Andaman Is., India, E of South Andaman I.; largest islands Havelock, Henry Lawrence, and Neill.

Ri·to Al·to Peak \ˌrēt-ō-'al-(ˌ)tō-\. Mountain, Saguache and Custer cos., Colorado, in the Sangre de Cristo Mts.; 13,573 ft.

Rit·ter, Mount \-'rit-ər\. Peak in Sierra Nevada, in NE Madera co., cen. California; 13,157 ft.

Ritt·man \'rit-mən\. Village, Medina and Wayne cos., NE cen. Ohio, 15 m. SW of Akron; pop. (1970c) 6308; paper and wood products; salt mines; fruit and truck farms.

Ritz·ville \'rits-ˌvil\. City, ⊗ of Adams co., E Washington, 60 m. SW of Spokane; pop. (1970c) 1876.

Riukiu Islands. See RYUKYU ISLANDS.

Ri·va \'rē-və\. Commune, Trento prov., Trentino-Alto Adige, NE Italy, at N end of Lake Garda 19 m. SW of Trent; pop. (1968e) 11,757; silk; tourism; palaces of 14th and 15th cents.

Ri·va·da·via \ˌrē-və-'dä-vē-ə\. 1 Seaport, Chubut prov., Argentina. See COMODORO RIVADAVIA.
2 Town, Mendoza prov., W Argentina, 30 m. SE of Mendoza; pop. (1960c) 14,358.

Ri·van·na \rə-'van-ə\. River, cen. Virginia; ab. 65 m. long; rises in Blue Ridge Mts., flows E and SE into James river on SE boundary of Fluvanna co.

Ri·vas \'rē-ˌväs\. 1 Department of SW Nicaragua. See table at NICARAGUA.
2 Town, its ✱, on W shore of Lake Nicaragua; pop. (1970e) 25,748.

Rive–de–Gier \ˌrēv-də-'zhā\. Industrial commune, Loire dept., SE cen. France, 13 m. NE of Saint-Étienne; pop. (1968c) 16,855; coal mines.

Ri·ve·ra \ri-'ver-ə\. 1 Department of N Uruguay. See table at URUGUAY.
2 Town, its ✱, on Brazil border opp. Santana do Livramento, ab. 270 m. N of Montevideo; pop. (1963c) 41,263; in livestock farming region.

River·bank \'riv-ər-ˌbaŋk\. City, Stanislaus co., cen. California, 11 m. NW of Modesto; pop. (1970c) 3949; dairy products, macaroni; agriculture.

River Cess \-'ses\. Coastal town, SW Liberia, W Africa, in cen. part of coast ab. 40 m. SE of Buchanan.

Riv·er·dale \'riv-ər-ˌdāl\. 1 City, Clayton co., NW cen. Georgia, 14 m. S of Atlanta; pop. (1970c) 2521.
2 Village, Cook co., NE Illinois, 14 m. S of Chicago; pop. (1970c) 15,806.
3 Town, Prince Georges co., S cen. Maryland, 8 m. NE of Washington; pop. (1970c) 5724.
4 Borough, Morris co., N New Jersey, 17 m. NW of Paterson; pop. (1970c) 2729; chemicals, concrete blocks; residential.
5 City, Weber co., N Utah, 4 m. S of Ogden; pop. (1970c) 3704.

River Edge. Borough, Bergen co., NE corner of New Jersey, 4 m. N of Hackensack; pop. (1970c) 12,850.

River Falls. City, Pierce and St. Croix cos., W Wisconsin, 12 m. NE of confluence of Mississippi and St. Croix rivers; pop. (1970c) 7238; grain elevators; poultry farms; Wisconsin State Univ. at River Falls (1875).

River Forest. Residential village, Cook co., NE Illinois, 16 m. W of Chicago; pop. (1970c) 13,402; Rosary Coll. (1901), Concordia Teachers Coll. (1864), Aquinas Institute of Philosophy and Theology (1939).

River Grove. Village, Cook co., NE Illinois, 10 m. NW of Chicago; pop. (1970c) 11,465.

Riv·er·head \'riv-ər-ˌhed\. Locality, ⊗ of Suffolk co., SE New York, at E end of Long I., on the Peconic river; pop. (1970c) 7585; manufactures aircraft; truck, poultry farms; settled 1690.

Riv·er·i·na \ˌriv-ə-'rī-nə\. District, S New South Wales, SE Australia, bounded on N by Murrumbidgee river and on S by Murray river; 26,533 sq. m.; pop. (1966c) 95,127; chief towns Albury and Wagga Wagga; flat fertile land, important for agriculture since development of irrigation; sheep and wheat in W portion; in SE grows rice, truck crops; fruit (incl. wine grapes).

River Junction. Former name of town of Chattahoochee, Florida; name changed 1941. See CHATTAHOOCHEE 3.

River Oaks. City, Tarrant co., NE Texas, NW suburb of Fort Worth; pop. (1970c) 8193.

River Point. Village, Kent co., cen. Rhode Island, ab. 7 m. SW of Cranston; governmental center of West Warwick town; textile, soap manufactures.

River Rouge \-'rüzh, -'rüj\. Industrial city, Wayne co., SE Michigan, on Detroit river 6 m. SW of Detroit; pop. (1970c) 15,947; automobiles, marine engines; shipbuilding.

Riv·ers \'riv-ərz\. State of S Nigeria. See table at NIGERIA.

Riv·ers·dale \'riv-ərz-ˌdāl\. Town, S Cape Province, S Rep. of South Africa, 165 m. E of Cape Town; pop. (1967e) 5100; in farm country.

Riv·er·side \'riv-ər-ˌsīd\. 1 County in SE California. See table at CALIFORNIA.
2 City, its ⊗, 10 m. SSW of San Bernardino; pop. (1970c) 140,019; packs and ships oranges; aircraft engines, precision instruments, paints, air conditioners; Univ. of California at Riverside (1907), Riverside City Coll. (1916), California Baptist Coll. (1950); March Field (U.S. Air Force base); settled in 1870's, incorporated 1883.
3 Subdivision of town of Greenwich, Connecticut. See GREENWICH.
4 Residential village, Cook co., NE Illinois, 8 m. W of Chicago; pop. (1970c) 10,432.
5 Township, Burlington co., S cen. New Jersey, on Delaware river 10 m. NE of Camden; pop. (1970c) 8591.

Riv·er·ton \'riv-ərt-ᵊn\. 1 Borough, Burlington co., S cen. New Jersey, on Delaware river 8 m. NE of Camden; pop. (1970c) 3412.
2 Town, Salt Lake co., Utah, 15 m. S of Salt Lake City; pop. (1970c) 2820.
3 City, Fremont co., cen. Wyoming, 25 m. NE of Lander; pop. (1970c) 7995; ships potatoes, livestock; oil wells, uranium mines; Central Wyoming Coll. (1966).

Riv·er·view \'riv-ər-ˌvyü\. 1 City, Wayne co., SE Michigan, S suburb of Detroit; pop. (1970c) 11,342.
2 Village, St. Louis co., E Missouri; pop. (1970c) 3741.

Rives·altes \rēv-'zält\. Town, Pyrénées-Orientales dept., S France, 5 m. N of Perpignan; pop. (1970c) 6262.

Ri·vi·era \ˌriv-ē-'er-ə\. Region bordering on Mediterranean Sea in SE France and NW Italy, esp. the coast extending from Cannes to La Spezia; noted for scenery and pleasant climate; one of the major tourist centers of W Europe. The Italian Riviera is divided into **Riviera di Po·nen·te** \-ˌdē-pə-'nen-(ˌ)tā\ W of Genoa, and **Riviera di Le·van·te** \-ˌdē-lə-'vän-(ˌ)tā\ E of Genoa; the French Riviera is also called **Côte d'Azur** \'kōt-də-'zu̇(ə)r\. See CORNICHE.

Riviera Beach \ri-ˌvir-ə-\. Town, Palm Beach co., SE Florida, just N of West Palm Beach; pop. (1970c) 21,401.

Ri·vière du Loup \rē-vē-ˌe(ə)r-də-'lü\. 1 County, Quebec, Canada. See table at QUEBEC.
2 *or* **Wolf River** \'wu̇lf-\. City, its ⊗, on **Rivière du Loup** just above its confluence with St. Lawrence river; pop. (1971p) 12,423; important railroad center and summer resort.

Rivière du Mou·lin \-də-mü-'laⁿ\. Town, Chicoutimi co., S Quebec, Canada, on Saguenay river just E of Chicoutimi; pop. (1971p) 4391.

Rivière Noire, Pi·ton de la \pē-'tōⁿ-də-lä-ˌrē-vē-ˌe(ə)r-nə-'wär\. Highest mountain in Mauritius, in SW part; 2711 ft.

Rivière Sa·lée \rē-vē-ˌe(ə)r-sal-'ā\. Strait, extending bet. Basse-Terre and Grande Terre, Guadeloupe, West Indies; 4 m. long.

Rivières du Sud. See GUINEA 2.

Ri·vo·li \'riv-ə-lē\. Commune, Torino prov., Piedmont, NW Italy, 8 m. W of Turin; pop. (1968e) 38,897.

Rivoli Ve·ro·ne·se \-ˌver-ə-'nā-sē, -'nā-zē\. Commune, Verona prov., Veneto, NE Italy, on Adige river 14 m. NW of Verona; pop. (1968e) 1696; scene of victory of Napoleon over Austrians Jan. 15, 1797.

Rixhöft, Cape. See ROZEWIE, CAPE.

Ri·yadh \rē-'(y)äd\ *also* **Er Ri·ad** \ˌer-rē-'äd\ *or* **Riad.** City, ✱ of Saudi Arabia, in E cen. part ab. 235 m. from Persian Gulf; pop. (1965e) 225,000; no heavy industry; formerly a walled city, but walls demolished in 1950's to make room for rapid expansion of modern quarters of the city; has royal palace and numerous mosques; univ. (1957).

Ri·yaq \ri-'yäk\ *or formerly* **Ra·yak** \ra-\. Town, E Lebanon, on railroad just E of Zahle.

Rizaiyeh. See REZĀ'ĪYEH.

Ri·zal \ri-'zäl, -'säl\. 1 Province, cen. Luzon, Phil.; 733 sq. m.; pop. (1970p) 2,781,081; ✱ Pasig; along Manila Bay and the Pasig land is low and flat; in the N part are hills and low mountain ranges. The main stream of the province is the Pasig, flowing NNW from the Laguna de Bay and through the City of Manila to Manila Bay; other streams flow S or SW to the Laguna de Bay or to the Pasig, the most important being the Marikina (and Montalban). On the S marked by two large arms of Laguna de Bay separated by peninsula ending in Tapao Point and by Talim I. Chief towns Pasig, Quezon City, Caloocan, Makati.

History: Created June 1901 out of the former Spanish military district of Morong and several towns of the former province of Manila. These regions contained some of the oldest towns in the Philippines that were prosperous settlements before the arrival of the Spaniards; their history closely connected with that of Manila. Caloocan, Pasig, and other places were scenes of first outbreaks of Revolution of 1896. See MANILA.

2 Municipality, Nueva Ecija prov., Luzon, Phil., on upper Pampanga river 18 m. NE of Cabanatuan; pop. (1969e) 26,300; univ. (1958).

Ri·ze \ri-'zā\ *or formerly* **Ço·ruh** \chȯ-rük\. 1 Province of NE Turkey. See table at TURKEY.

2 Seaport, its ✱, on the Black Sea ab. 40 m. E of Trabazon; pop. (1965c) 26,989; ships tea.

Riz·zu·to, Cape \-rit-'süt-(ˌ)ō, -rə-'züt-\. Cape on E coast of Calabria, S Italy, projecting into Ionian Sea N of Gulf of Squillace.

Rju·kan \rē-'ü-ˌkän\. 1 Waterfall in Telemark co., S Norway; 780 ft. high.

2 Town, Telemark co., S Norway, 75 m. W of Oslo; industrial center; its nitrate and hydroelectric plants destroyed 1943 during World War II; has postwar plant for making heavy water.

Road Town. Town, ✱ of British Virgin Is., on Tortola I., West Indies; pop. (1960c) 891.

Roag, Loch \läk-'rōg, läk-\. Inlet of Atlantic Ocean on W coast of island of Lewis with Harris, in the Outer Hebrides, off NW coast of Scotland.

Roane \'rōn\. Name of counties in two states of the U.S. See tables at TENNESSEE and WEST VIRGINIA.

Roan High Knob \'rōn-\. Peak, Mitchell co., W North Carolina, on the Tennessee border; 6313 ft.

Ro·anne \rō-'än\ *or anc.* **Ro·dum·na** \rō-'dəm-nə\. Manufacturing commune, Loire dept., SE cen. France, on Loire river 45 m. NNW of Saint-Étienne; pop. (1968e) 53,373; textiles, machinery, construction equipment, leather goods.

Ro·a·noke \'rō-(ə-)ˌnōk\. 1 River, S Virginia and NE North Carolina; 410 m. long; navigable for 112 m.; formed by confluence of forks in Montgomery co., western Virginia, flows E and SE across North Carolina border in NE Warren co., and continues SE into Albemarle Sound.

2 County in Virginia. See table at VIRGINIA.

3 City, Randolph co., E Alabama, 5 m. W of Georgia border and 35 m. NE of Martin Lake; pop. (1970c) 5251; automobile parts, cotton products; diversified agriculture.

4 City, Roanoke co., W Virginia, 148 m. W of Richmond; 26 sq. m.; pop. (1970c) 92,115; politically independent; railroad center; electrical equipment, clothing, building materials, varnish, textiles; tourist center; National Business Coll. (1886), Virginia Southern Coll. (1933), Virginia Western Community Coll. (1966). Settled 1740; developed after growth of railroads; incorporated as city 1884.

Roanoke Island. Island near S entrance to Albemarle Sound, Dare co., North Carolina; 12 m. long and ab. 3 m. wide; Manteo, ⊗ of Dare co., is on it; at N end is Fort Raleigh, site of first English settlement in North America 1585, established by Sir Walter Raleigh, remained only ten months; site of a second colony July 1587 with Capt. John White appointed governor by Raleigh; by 1591 all the colonists had vanished; during the Civil War island captured Feb. 8, 1862 by Union forces under Gen. Burnside.

Roanoke Rapids. Industrial city, Halifax co., NE North Carolina, 35 m. NNE of Rocky Mount; pop. (1970c) 13,508; paper, lumber; peanuts.

Roanoke Sound. Inlet of Atlantic Ocean bet. Roanoke I. and Bodie I. off NE coast of North Carolina.

Roar·ing Spring \'rōr-iŋ-, 'rȯr-\. Borough, Blair co., S cen. Pennsylvania, 13 m. S of Altoona; pop. (1970c) 2811.

Ro·a·tán \ˌrō-ə-'tän\. 1 Island, largest of the Islas de la Bahía, in the Caribbean Sea N of N cen. Honduras; 30 m. long.

2 *or* **Cox·in's Hole** \'käk-sənz-\. Town on Roatán I., ✱ of Islas de la Bahía dept., Honduras; pop. (1961c) 1629; exports coconuts and bananas.

Roazon. See RENNES.

Rob·bins \'räb-ənz\. Village, Cook co., NE Illinois, S suburb of Chicago; pop. (1970c) 9641.

Rob·bins·dale \'räb-ənz-ˌdāl\. City, Hennepin co., SE cen. Minnesota, 5 m. NW of Minneapolis; pop. (1970c) 16,845.

Rob·bins·ville \'räb-ənz-ˌvil\. Town and mountain resort, ⊗ of Graham co., W North Carolina; pop. (1970c) 777.

Rob·ert Lee \ˌräb-ərt-'lē\. City, ⊗ of Coke co., W cen. Texas; pop. (1970c) 1119; livestock farms.

Robert Moses Dam. See UNITED STATES, *Dams and Reservoirs.*

Rob·erts \'räb-ərts\. Name of counties in two states of the U.S. See tables at SOUTH DAKOTA and TEXAS.

Roberts, Point. See POINT ROBERTS.

Rob·ert·son \'räb-ərt-sən\. 1 Name of counties in three states of the U.S. See tables at KENTUCKY, TENNESSEE, TEXAS.

2 Town, SW Cape Province, S Rep. of South Africa, in the Bree river valley 85 m. E of Cape Town; pop. (1967e) 8200.

Rob·erts·port \'räb-ərts-ˌpō(ə)rt, -ˌpȯ(ə)rt\. Seaport, NW Liberia, W Africa, NW of Monrovia and SE of mouth of Mano river; pop. (1962c) 2417.

Ro·ber·val \ˌrō-bər-'val\. City, ⊗ of West Lake St. John co., Quebec, Canada, on W shore of Lake St. John; pop. (1971p) 8286; summer resort.

Rob·e·son \'räb-ə-sən\. County in North Carolina. See table at NORTH CAROLINA.

Robe·son Channel \ˌrōb-sən-\. North section of passage bet. Ellesmere I. and Greenland, extending NE to Lincoln Sea.

Rob·in·son \'räb-ən-sən\. 1 City, ⊗ of Crawford co., E Illinois, 28 m. NE of Olney; pop. (1970c) 7178; pottery; oil wells; agriculture.

2 City, McLennan co., cen. Texas, 7 m. SSE of Waco; pop. (1970c) 3807.

Robinson Crusoe Island. See MÁS A TIERRA.

Rob·ins Point \ˌräb-ənz-\. Point at S tip of Harford co., NE Maryland, extending into upper Chesapeake Bay.

Rob·son, Mount \-'räb-sən\. Peak in Mount Robson Park, E British Columbia, Canada; 12,972 ft.; highest of the Rocky Mts. in Canada.

Robs·town \'räbz-ˌtaun\. City, Nueces co., S Texas, 15 m. W of Corpus Christi; pop. (1970c) 11,217; oil refineries; livestock, truck farms.

Ro·by \'rō-bē\. City, ⊗ of Fisher co., NW cen. Texas; pop. (1970c) 984; poultry farms.

Ro·ca, Cape \-'rō-kə\ *or Port.* **Ca·bo da Roca** \ˌkȧ-vü-thə-'rō-kə\. Cape on SW cen. coast of Portugal, 9°30′W, 38°47′N; westernmost point in continental Europe.

Roca El Yunque. See EL YUNQUE 1.

Ro·ca·fuer·te \ˌrō-kə-fü-'e(ə)rt-ē\. Town, Manabí prov., W Ecuador, near coast 100 m. NW of Guayaquil; pop. (1962c) 4349.

Roca Par·ti·da \ˌrō-kə-pär-'tēd-ə\. Westernmost island of the Revilla Gigedo group (*q.v.*) in the Pacific Ocean off cen. Mexico.

Ro·cas \'rō-kəs\. Island in the Atlantic Ocean 125 m. NE of Cape São Roque, NE Brazil, 33°59′W, 3°52′S; belongs to Brazil.

Roccabruna. See ROQUEBRUNE.

Roc·ca·stra·da \ˌrō-kə-'strä-də\. Commune, Grosseto prov., Tuscany, NW Italy, 17 m. NE of Grosseto; pop. (1968e) 11,023.

Roch \'räch\. River, Lancashire, NW England; 12 m. long; rises near Yorkshire border, flows SW into the Irwell S of Bury.

Ro·cha \'rō-chə\. 1 Department of SE Uruguay. See table at URUGUAY.

2 City, its ✱, 100 m. E of Montevideo; pop. (1963c) 19,063; corn, sunflower seeds.

Roch·dale \'räch-ˌdāl\. County borough, Lancashire, NW England, on the Roch 10 m. NNE of Manchester; pop. (1971p) 91,344; cotton and synthetic textiles, rubber products, electrical equipment; asbestos; founding place of modern cooperative movement, with Rochdale Pioneers' Equitable Society (1844).

Roche·fort \rȯsh-'fō(ə)r\. 1 Town, Namur prov., SE Belgium, 15 m. SE of Dinant; pop. (1969e) 4406.

2 *or unofficially* **Rochefort–sur–Mer** \-sü(ə)r-'me(ə)r\. City, Charente-Maritime dept., W France, on Charente river 17 m. SSE of La Rochelle; pop. (1968c) 29,225; ships timber and dairy products; aircraft factory and air force base; a fortified settlement by 1047; in 17th–19th cents. a fortified town with a large naval arsenal and shipyards.

Roche–la–Mo·lière \'rȯsh-ˌläm-ōl-'ye(ə)r\. Commune, Loire dept., SE cen. France, ab. 2 m. from St-Étienne; pop. (1968c) 10,569.

Ro·chelle \rō-'shel\. City, Ogle co., N Illinois, 25 m. S of Rockford; pop. (1970c) 8594.

Rochelle, La. See LA ROCHELLE.

Rochelle Park. Urban township, Bergen co., NE corner of New Jersey, E of Paterson; pop. (1970c) 6343.

Rochers du Calvados. See CALVADOS REEF.

Roch·es·ter \'räch-ə-stər, -ˌes-tər\. 1 City, ⊗ of Fulton co., N Indiana, 40 m. S of South Bend; pop. (1970c) 4631; summer resort.

2 Residential village, Oakland co., SE Michigan, 9 m. E of Pontiac; pop. (1970c) 7054; Michigan Christian Junior Coll. (1955), Oakland Univ. (1959).

3 City, ⊗ of Olmsted co., SE Minnesota, 70 m. SSE of St. Paul; pop. (1970c) 53,776; computer accessories, dairy products, hospital supplies, canned vegetables; Rochester State Junior Coll. (1915); seat of the Mayo clinic, established 1889 by Dr. William James Mayo and his brother Dr. Charles Horace Mayo, one of the most widely known medical centers in the world.

4 Manufacturing city, Strafford co., SE New Hampshire, 9 m. NNW of Dover; pop. (1970c) 17,938; paper, woolen and rayon textiles; fruit and dairy farms.

5 Industrial city and port of entry, ⊗ of Monroe co., W New York, 70 m. ENE of Buffalo; pop. (1970c) 296,233; port on New York State Barge Canal; manufactures cameras and photographic equipment and supplies, optical goods, precision tools, dental equipment, office equipment, electronic components, machine tools; in a fruit and truck farming region. Rochester Institute of Technology (1829), Univ. of Rochester (1850), Saint Bernard's Seminary and Coll. (1893), Saint John Fisher Coll. (1952), Monroe Community Coll. (1962). First permanent settlement 1811; incorporated as village 1817, as city 1834; originating point of modern Spiritualism ("Rochester knockings" of Fox sisters in 1840's); center of abolitionist activity before Civil War; in late 19th cent. a major center of horticulture.

6 Residential borough, Beaver co., W Pennsylvania, on Ohio river 23 m. NW of Pittsburgh; pop. (1970c) 4819.

7 *or anc.* **Du·ro·bri·vae** \ˌd(y)u̇r-ə-'brī-(ˌ)vē\. Municipal borough, Kent, SE England, on the Medway 28 m. ESE of London; pop. (1971p) 55,460; seaport; cement, machinery; 12th cent. cathedral, remains of 11th cent. castle. Nearby is Gadshill (*q.v.*), the home of Charles Dickens.

Roche–sur–Yon, La. See LA ROCHE-SUR-YON.

Rock \'räk\. 1 River, S Wisconsin and N Illinois; 285 m. long; rises in Washington co., SE Wisconsin, flows S and SW across NW corner of Illinois, and empties into the Mississippi in W Rock Island co., NW Illinois.

2 Name of counties in three states of the U.S. See tables at MINNESOTA, NEBRASKA, WISCONSIN.

Rock·all \'räk-ˌȯl\. Tiny rock island in North Atlantic Ocean, ab. 250 m. NW of Ireland, at 57°35′N, 13°48′W.

Rock·a·way \'räk-ə-ˌwā\. Borough, Morris co., N New Jersey, 8 m. N of Morristown; pop. (1970c) 6383; printing and dyeing works.

Rockaway Beach. Beach on S shore of Long I., in the borough of Queens, New York City, New York; on the narrow peninsula which shelters Jamaica Bay from the Atlantic.

Rockaway Inlet. Channel on S shore at W end of Long I., New York, connecting Jamaica Bay with the Atlantic; crossed by the Marine Parkway Bridge (540-foot lift span), joining Brooklyn with Rockaway Beach.

Rock·bridge \'räk-ˌbrij\. County in Virginia. See table at VIRGINIA.

Rock·cas·tle \'räk-ˌkas-əl\. County in Kentucky. See table at KENTUCKY.

Rock·chuck, Mount \-'räk-ˌchək\. Peak in cen. Grand Teton National Park, NW Wyoming; 11,150 ft.

Rock Creek Butte. Peak in Baker co., NE Oregon; 9105 ft.; highest in Blue Mts.

Rock·dale \'räk-ˌdā(ə)l\. 1 County in Georgia. See table at GEORGIA.

2 Village, Will co., NE Illinois, suburb WSW of Joliet; pop. (1970c) 2085.

3 City, Milam co., cen. Texas, 33 m. W of Bryan; pop. (1970c) 4655; aluminum smelters, oil wells; poultry farms.

4 City, E New South Wales, SE Australia, S suburb of Sydney on W shore of Botany Bay; pop. (1966c) 81,463.

Rock·e·fel·ler Plateau \ˌräk-i-ˌfel-ər-\. Elevated region in Marie Byrd Land, E of Ross Dependency, Antarctica; at 80°S lat., 135°W long.; averages 2500 ft. to 4500 ft.; discovered 1934.

Rock Falls. City, Whiteside co., NW Illinois, 50 m. SW of Rockford; pop. (1970c) 10,287.

Rock·ford \'räk-fərd\. 1 Town, ⊗ of Coosa co., E cen. Alabama; pop. (1970c) 603; Indian relics.

2 City, ⊗ of Winnebago co., N Illinois, 80 m. NW of Chicago; pop. (1970c) 147,370; machine tools, agricultural implements, home appliances, leather goods, paint, furniture; in agricultural region; Rockford Coll. (1847), Rock Valley Coll. (1964); founded 1834; incorporated as village 1839, as city 1852.

3 City, Kent co., W Michigan, 13 m. NNE of Grand Rapids; pop. (1970c) 2428.

Rock·hamp·ton \räk-'(h)am(p)-tən\. City, E Queensland, Australia, on Fitzroy river 325 m. NNW of Brisbane; pop. (1968e) 47,000; railroad center and river port for small steamers; railroad shops, meat packing and freezing plants; center of coal mining, livestock raising, and agricultural region; made a municipality 1860.

Rock Hill. 1 City, St. Louis co., E Missouri, 9 m. W of St. Louis; pop. (1970c) 6815.

2 City, York co., N South Carolina, 64 m. N of Columbia; pop. (1970c) 33,846; textiles, paper, vehicle bodies; peaches, poultry; Winthrop Coll. (1886), Friendship Coll. (1891).

Rockies. See ROCKY MOUNTAINS.

Rock·ing·ham \'räk-iŋ-ˌham\. 1 Name of counties in three states of the U.S. See tables at NEW HAMPSHIRE, NORTH CAROLINA, VIRGINIA.

2 City, ⊗ of Richmond co., S North Carolina, 52 m. W of Fayetteville; pop. (1970c) 5582; textiles, foundry products; tobacco.

3 Town, Windham co., SE corner of Vermont; pop. (1970c) 5501.

Rock Island \'räk-'ī-lənd\. 1 County in NW Illinois. See table at ILLINOIS.
2 City, its ⊗, on the Mississippi river 78 m. NW of Peoria; pop. (1970c) 50,166; clothing, machine tools, rubber footwear, electrical equipment; foundries, railroad shops, large U.S. government arsenal; Augustana Coll. and Theological Seminary (1860); settled 1826, incorporated 1841.
3 Village, Stanstead co., S Quebec, Canada, on Vermont border 34 m. SSW of Sherbrooke; pop. (1966c) 1506; forms single community with Stanstead village and Derby Line, Vt.

Rock·land \'räk-lənd\. 1 County in New York. See table at NEW YORK.
2 City, ⊗ of Knox co., S Maine, on W shore of Penobscot Bay 37 m. ESE of Augusta; pop. (1970c) 8505; center of Penobscot Bay resort section; yachting, fishing.
3 Industrial town, Plymouth co., SE Massachusetts, 6 m. ENE of Brockton; pop. (1970c) 15,674; shoes, plastics.
4 Town, Russell co., SE Ontario, Canada, on Ottawa river 20 m. ENE of Ottawa; pop. (1971p) 3654.

Rock·ledge \'räk-(,)lej\. 1 City, Brevard co., E cen. Florida, 4 m. W of Cocoa; pop. (1970c) 10,523.
2 Borough, Montgomery co., SE Pennsylvania, 10 m. NNE of Philadelphia; pop. (1970c) 2564.

Rock·lin \'räk-lin, -lən\. City, Placer co., E California, 17 m. NE of Sacramento; pop. (1970c) 3039; sawmills; fruit growing, livestock raising.

Rock·mart \'räk-,märt\. City, Polk co., NW Georgia, 18 m. SSE of Rome; pop. (1970c) 3857; agriculture.

Rock·port \'räk-,pō(ə)rt, -,pȯ(ə)rt\. 1 City, ⊗ of Spencer co., SW Indiana, on Ohio river 28 m. E of Evansville; pop. (1970c) 2565.
2 Town, Knox co., S Maine, on W shore of Penobscot Bay 37 m. E of Augusta; pop. (1970c) 2067.
3 Town, Essex co., NE corner of Massachusetts, on Atlantic Ocean 30 m. NE of Boston; pop. (1970c) 5636; summer resort.
4 City, ⊗ of Atchison co., NW corner of Missouri; pop. (1970c) 1575; grain, livestock.
5 City and resort, ⊗ of Aransas co., S Texas, on Aransas Bay 28 m. NE of Corpus Christi; pop. (1970c) 3879; oil wells; shrimp, oyster fisheries.

Rock Rapids. City, ⊗ of Lyon co., NW corner of Iowa, 63 m. N of Sioux City; pop. (1970c) 2632; agriculture.

Rock River. See ROCK 1.

Rocks Point \'räks-\. Cape on NW coast of South I., New Zealand, at N end of Karamea Bight.

Rock·springs \räk-'spriŋz\. Town, ⊗ of Edwards co., SW cen. Texas; pop. (1970c) 1221.

Rock Springs. City, Sweetwater co., SW Wyoming, 40 m. N of Utah border; pop. (1970c) 11,657; coal and uranium mines, oil wells.

Rock·stand Knob \,räk-stan(d)-\. Peak in W North Carolina; 6002 ft.

Rock·stone \'räk-,stōn, -stən\. Town, N Guyana, on E bank of the Essequibo river 58 m. S of Georgetown.

Rock Valley. Town, Sioux co., NW Iowa, 48 m. N of Sioux City; pop. (1970c) 2205.

Rock·ville \'räk-,vil, -vəl\. 1 Former city in town of Vernon, Connecticut; merged with town of Vernon (*q.v.*) 1965.
2 Town, ⊗ of Parke co., W Indiana, 23 m. NNE of Terre Haute; pop. (1970c) 2820; coal mines.
3 City, ⊗ of Montgomery co., cen. Maryland, 15 m. NNW of Washington; pop. (1970c) 41,654.

Rockville Centre. Village, Nassau co., SE New York, on Long I. 19 m. ESE of New York; pop. (1970c) 27,444; residential suburb of New York City; Molloy Catholic Coll. for Women (1955).

Rock·wall \'räk-,wȯl\. 1 County in NE Texas. See table at TEXAS.
2 City, its ⊗; pop. (1970c) 3121.

Rock·well, Mount \-'räk-,wel\. Peak in Glacier National Park, NW Montana; 9250 ft.

Rockwell City. City, ⊗ of Calhoun co., NW cen. Iowa, 25 m. WSW of Fort Dodge; pop. (1970c) 2396; corn.

Rock·wood \'räk-,wu̇d\. 1 City, Wayne co., SE Michigan, 24 m. SW of Detroit; pop. (1970c) 3225.
2 City, Roane co., E Tennessee, 6 m. SE of Harriman; pop. (1970c) 5259; pig iron, textile machinery; coal, iron mines; agriculture.

Rocky \'räk-ē\. River, N Ohio; rises in Medina co., flows N and NE into Lake Erie on W boundary of the city of Cleveland.

Rocky Face. Peak, W North Carolina; 6031 ft.

Rocky Ford. City, Otero co., SE Colorado, on Arkansas river 12 m. WNW of La Junta; pop. (1970c) 4859; in truck and fruit (esp. melon) farming region.

Rocky Hill. 1 Town, S Hartford co., N Connecticut, on W bank of Connecticut river; pop. (1970c) 11,103; synthetic textiles; settled c. 1650.
2 Borough, Somerset co., N cen. New Jersey, ab. 4 m. NNE of Princeton; pop. (1970c) 917; Washington wrote his farewell address to the army here.

Rocky Knob. Peak, Towns co., N Georgia; 4164 ft.

Rocky Mount. 1 City, Edgecombe and Nash cos., NE North Carolina, 52 m. E of Raleigh; pop. (1970c) 34,284; tobacco market; produces cottonseed oil, textiles, lumber, electronic components, steel tanks, fertilizer; railroad shops, packing plants; North Carolina Wesleyan Coll. (1956); founded 1818; incorporated as town 1867, as city 1907.
2 Industrial town, ⊗ of Franklin co., SW cen. Virginia; pop. (1970c) 4002; textiles, furniture, plywood; poultry and fruit farms.

Rocky Mountain. Peak, Union and Towns cos., N Georgia; 4586 ft.

Rocky Mountain National Park. See UNITED STATES, *National Parks.*

Rocky Mountains *or* **Rock·ies** \'räk-ēz\. Mountain system, W North America, extending from the Mexican frontier to the Arctic, through Arizona, New Mexico, Colorado, Utah, Nevada, Wyoming, Idaho, and Montana, the Canadian provinces of Alberta and British Columbia, and Yukon Territory; highest peak in U.S. section of this range is Mount Elbert 14,433 ft. in Colorado; highest in Canadian section Mt. Robson 12,972 ft. in British Columbia.

Rocky Point. Point on SW coast of Los Angeles co., SW California, W of Long Beach, extending into Pacific Ocean.

Rocky River. City, Cuyahoga co., N Ohio, on Lake Erie 8 m. W of Cleveland; pop. (1970c) 22,958; residential suburb of Cleveland.

Rocky Trail Peak. Peak, W North Carolina; 6488 ft.

Ro·court \rȯ-'ku̇(ə)r\. Commune, Liège prov., E Belgium, just N of Liège; pop. (1969e) 4772; scene of battle Oct. 11, 1746 in which Austrian allies under Prince Charles of Lorraine were defeated by the French under Marshall Saxe.

Ro·croi *or* **Ro·croy** \rȯ-'krwä\. Town, Ardennes dept., NE France, near Belgian frontier; pop. (1962c) 2870; scene of battle May 19, 1643 in which the French under the duc d'Enghien (the Great Condé) decisively defeated the Spanish.

Ro·da *or* **Rho·da** \'rōd-ə\ *or* **Raw·ḍah** \'rō-də\ *or formerly* **Ru·da** \'rüd-ə\. Island in the Nile river near Cairo, Egypt; has an ancient Nilometer.

Roda, La. See LA RODA.

Ro·das \'rō-,thäs\. Municipality, Las Villas prov., W cen. Cuba, 15 m. NNW of Cienfuegos; pop. (1967e) 26,470.

Ro·den·kir·chen \'rō-dən-,kir-kən\. City, North Rhine-Westphalia, West Germany, on Rhine river just S of Cologne; pop. (1969e) 40,234.

Ro·de·wisch \'rōd-ə-,vish\. Industrial city, Karl-Marx-Stadt dist., East Germany, 14 m. SSW of Zwickau; pop. (1970e) 10,164.

Ro·dez \rō-'dāz, -'dez\ *or anc.* **Seg·o·du·num** \,seg-ə-'d(y)ü-nəm\. Industrial and commercial commune, ✱ of Aveyron dept., S France, on Aveyron river 78 m. NE of Toulouse;

pop. (1968c) 23,328; tourism; textiles; agricultural trade center; 13th–16th cent. Gothic cathedral. Ancient capital of the Rutheni; made seat of bishopric 401; capital of Rouergue until 1789; Catholic stronghold in Wars of Religion 16th cent.

Rodg·ers Peak \ˌräj-ərz-\. Mountain in Yosemite National Park, California, on E border of the park SSE of Mt. Lyell; 12,978 ft.

Rodi. See RHODES.

Ro·ding \'rōd-iŋ\. River, Essex co., SE England; 30 m. long; flows S and SW into the Thames 2 m. SE of East Ham.

Ro·do·ni, Cape \-rə-'dō-nē\ *or Alb.* **Kep i Ro·do·nit** \ˌkep-i-rə-'dō-nət\. Cape extending into Adriatic Sea, NW coast of Albania, N of Durrës.

Rodopi. See RHODOPE.

Rodos. See RHODES.

Rodosto. See TEKIRDAĞ 2.

Ro·dri·guez *or* **Ro·dri·gues** \rō-'drē-gəs\. Island of the Mascarene Is., in the Indian Ocean ab. 500 m. E of Malagasy Republic; 40 sq. m.; pop. (1962c) 18,335; a dependency of Mauritius; highest point 1300 ft.; many limestone caves in W part; chief town Port Mathurin. Discovered by Portuguese 1645; colonized by French from Mauritius; taken by English 1809–10.

Rodumna. See ROANNE.

Roeb·ling \'rōb-liŋ\. Town, Burlington co., S cen. New Jersey, on Delaware river ab. 7 m. S of Trenton; pop. (1970c) 3600; estab. by J. A. Roebling, founder of steel-cable factory which built Brooklyn Bridge and supplied cables for other well-known bridges.

Roe·buck Bay \ˌrō-ˌbək-\. Inlet of Indian Ocean, NW Western Australia, just SW of Dampier Land, 19°04'S, 122°17'E.

Roe·land Park \'rō-lən(d)-\. City, Johnson co., E Kansas, S suburb of Kansas City; pop. (1970c) 9974.

Roepat. See RUPAT.

Roer. See RUR.

Roer·mond \rü(ə)r-'mȯnt\. Commune, Limburg prov., SE Netherlands near West German border at confluence of the Rur and the Meuse; pop. (1970e) 35,850; chemicals, paper, cigars, electrical equipment; 13th cent. Romanesque church; 15th cent. cathedral. In medieval times the chief town of Upper Gelderland (see GELDERLAND); heavily damaged in fighting in World War II Jan.–Feb. 1945.

Roe·se·la·re \ˌrü-sə-'lär-ə\ *or Fr.* **Rou·lers** \rü-ler(s)\. Commune, West Flanders prov., NW Belgium; pop. (1969e) 40,484; 15th cent. church, 18th cent. town hall; scene of battle 1794 in which French under Pichegru and Macdonald defeated the Austrians; in World War I occupied by Germans Oct. 1914–Oct. 1918.

Roes Wel·come \'rōz-'wel-kəm\. Strait, N Keewatin dist., E Northwest Territories, Canada, bet. W Southampton I. and the mainland; 170 m. long and 50 to 115 m. wide; a part of N Hudson Bay.

Rofreit. See ROVERETO.

Ro·ga·land \'rō-gə-ˌlän\. County of SW Norway. See table at NORWAY.

Rog·er Mills \ˌräj-ər-'milz\. County in Oklahoma. See table at OKLAHOMA.

Rog·ers \'räj-ərz\. **1** County in Oklahoma. See table at OKLAHOMA.

2 Commercial city, Benton co., NW corner of Arkansas, 20 m. N of Fayetteville; pop. (1970c) 11,050; mountain resort; fruit farms.

Rogers, Mount. Peak, Grayson and Smyth cos., SW Virginia; 5927 ft.; highest point in Virginia.

Rogers City. City, ⊗ of Presque Isle co., NE Michigan, on Lake Huron 30 m. NW of Alpena; pop. (1970c) 4275; limestone quarries; apples.

Rogers Pass. Pass in Selkirk Mts., SE British Columbia, Canada, NE of Revelstoke, through which passes the Canadian Pacific Railway; 4302 ft.; discovered 1883.

Rogers Peak. Mountain in Glacier National Park, NW Montana; 7300 ft.

Rog·ers·ville \'räj-ərz-ˌvil\. Town, ⊗ of Hawkins co., NE Tennessee; pop. (1970c) 4076.

Rog·ge·veld \'räg-ə-ˌfelt\. Mountain range in W Cape Province, Rep. of South Africa, W of Nieuwveld; highest point 5249 ft.

Ro·go·a·gua·do, Lake \-ˌrōg-ō-ə-'gwäd-(ˌ)ō\. Lake, N Bolivia; drains S and E into Mamoré river.

Rogue \'rōg\. River, SW Oregon; ab. 200 m. long; rises in Crater Lake National Park, flows S and SW into Pacific Ocean in W Curry co.

Ro·hil·khand \'rō-ˌhil-ˌkənd\ *or* **Ba·reil·ly** \bə-'rā-lē\. Division of N Uttar Pradesh, N India; 11,705 sq. m.; pop. (1961c) 8,505,041; ✱ Bareilly. Practically coextensive with region of N India occupied since early part of 18th cent. by the Rohilla tribe of Afghans. An early ruler was made nawab by the Delhi emperor; the region was divided in 1749 and power of Rohillas overcome 1774 by united forces of British and Nawab of Oudh. See RAMPUR.

Rohn·ert Park \'rōn-ərt-\. City, Sonoma co., W California, 7 m. S of Santa Rosa; pop. (1970c) 6133; diversified agriculture.

Roh·tak \'rōt-ək\. **1** District, Ambala division, Haryana, NW India; 2330 sq. m.; pop. (1961c) 1,420,391; ✱ Rohtak. **2** Town, its ✱, 44 m. WNW of Delhi; pop. (1961c) 88,193; grain market; sugar refining; 12th cent. mosque.

Roi \'rȯi\. Islet of Kwajalein (*q.v.*) atoll, Marshall Is.; taken by U.S. troops Feb. 1–3, 1944.

Roi Et *or* **Roi Ed** \-'et\. **1** Province, E Thailand; 3033 sq. m.; pop. (1960c) 668,193; ✱ Roi Et.

2 Town, its ✱, near the Chi river and 70 m. SE of Khon Kaen; pop. (1964e) 12,698.

Ro·jo, Cape \-'rō-(ˌ)hō\. **1** Cape on coast of N Veracruz state, Mexico, extending into Gulf of Mexico.

2 Cape at SW end of Puerto Rico, on SE side of Mona Passage.

Ro·kan \'rō-ˌkän\. River, N cen. Sumatra, Indonesia; 175 m. long; flows NE into the Strait of Malacca.

Ro·kel *or* **Ro·kelle** \rō-'kel\ *or* **Se·li** \'sā-lē\. River, Sierra Leone, W Africa; ab. 250 m. long; flows S and W into Atlantic Ocean at Freetown; called the Sierra Leone at its estuary.

Ro·ku·gō, Cape \-'rō-kə-ˌgō\. Cape on W coast of Honshū, Japan, NW of Toyama Bay at end of Noto Penin.

Ro·lân·dia \rü-'lä(ⁿ)n-dē-ə, -dyə\. Municipality, Paraná state, S Brazil, 300 m. W of São Paulo; pop. (1968e) 74,639.

Ro·lette \ˌrō-'let\. County in North Dakota. See table at NORTH DAKOTA.

Rol·la \'räl-ə\. **1** City, ⊗ of Phelps co., S cen. Missouri; pop. (1970c) 13,245; diversified agriculture; Univ. of Missouri at Rolla.

2 City, ⊗ of Rolette co., N North Dakota; pop. (1970c) 1458; grain, poultry, dairy farms.

Roll·ing Fork \'rō-liŋ-\. Town, ⊗ of Sharkey co., W Mississippi; pop. (1970c) 2034; agriculture.

Rolling Hills Estates. City, Los Angeles co., SW California, 10 m. W of Long Beach; pop. (1970c) 6027.

Rolling Meadows. City, Cook co., NE Illinois, NW suburb of Chicago; pop. (1970c) 19,178.

Rolling Mountain. Peak, San Juan co., SW Colorado; 13,694 ft.

Rolling Thunder. Peak, N Grand Teton National Park, NW Wyoming; 10,902 ft.

Rol·lins Pass \ˌräl-ənz-\. Mountain pass, Boulder and Grand cos., N Colorado, in Front Range of Rocky Mts.; 11,680 ft.

Røm. See RØMØ.

Ro·ma \'rō-mə\. 1 Town, SE Queensland, Australia, 275 m. WNW of Brisbane; pop. (1966c) 5996.
2 Province of Latium, Italy. See table at ITALY.
3 City, Italy. See ROME 3.
4 Island, Indonesia. See ROMANG.

Ro·ma·gna \rō-'män-yə\ *or anc.* **Ro·ma·nia** \rō-'mān-yə, -'mā-nē-ə\. A former province of the States of the Church; ✱ Ravenna; under nominal papal control until ab. 1500; seized by Cesare Borgia 1501 and held by the pope until 1796; as part of Emilia incorporated 1796–1814 in Italian Republic and Napoleon's kingdom of Italy; restored to papacy 1815; revolt of 1831 put down by Austrian forces; joined Piedmont 1860. Now forms part of the autonomous region of Emilia-Romagna, N Italy.

Ro·magne–sous–Mont·fau·con \rō-'män^{y}-sü-ˌmō^{n}-fō-'kō^{n}\. Village, Meuse dept., NE France, near Montfaucon; pop. (1962c) 345; site of largest American military cemetery in France, contains graves of over 14,200 soldiers.

Ro·main, Cape \-rō-'mān\. Cape on island off mainland in Charleston co., South Carolina, extending into Atlantic Ocean.

Ro·maine \rō-'mān\. River, Saguenay co., SE Quebec, Canada; 270 m. long; rises in SW Labrador, flows S across Quebec into the Gulf of St. Lawrence opp. W end of Anticosti I.

Ro·main·ville \rȯ-ma^{n}-'vēl\. Commune, Seine-St-Denis dept., N France, NE suburb of Paris; pop. (1968c) 24,091; battle 1814.

Ro·man \'rō-ˌmän\. City, Neamţ co., NE Romania, on railroad 28 m. N of Bacău; pop. (1970e) 43,188; tube-rolling mill, chemical plants; first mentioned 1392.

Romana, La. See LA ROMANA.

Roman Africa. See AFRICA, ROMAN.

Roman Apennines. See table at APENNINES.

Roman Campagna. See CAMPAGNA DI ROMA.

Roman Empire. The empire of ancient Rome, beginning with the imperial rule of Augustus 27 B.C.; at its greatest extent (c. 117 A.D.) included all S Europe, Britannia, N Africa, Egypt, Asia Minor, N coast of Pontus Euxinus (Black Sea), Armenia and regions S of the Caucasus, Mesopotamia and adjoining regions, Syria, Palestine, and NW corner of Arabia.

History: Founded by Octavian who gained control of Italy and the west 43–35 B.C. and of east 31 B.C.; as Augustus 27 B.C.–14 A.D., Octavian annexed Egypt 30 B.C. and advanced Roman frontiers to Rhine and Danube; held Germany to Elbe 6 B.C.–13 A.D.; later major additions to territory were Dacia, Mesopotamia, and Assyria; from 3d cent. suffered decline caused partly by external factors, such as pressure of Persia and of barbarian tribes from across Danube and Germany, and partly by internal breakdown of trade and administrative system; divided for administration by line running from the Danube to Adriatic Sea S of Dalmatia; for eastern empire after 395, see BYZANTINE EMPIRE; invaded during 5th cent. by successive waves of Visigoths, Huns, Vandals, Ostrogoths, and others; end of western empire conventionally dated 476 (defeat and death of Romulus Augustulus, last Emperor of the West); for medieval "revival" of Rome's imperial authority in west, see HOLY ROMAN EMPIRE.

Ro·mang \'rō-ˌmäŋ\ *or* **Ro·ma** \'rō-mə\. Island, S Moluccas, Indonesia, E of Wetar I. and NE of Timor; ab. 15 m. long by 10 m. wide.

Ro·ma·nia *or* **Ru·ma·nia** *also* **Rou·ma·nia** \rù-'mā-nē-ə, rō-, -nyə\; *officially* **Socialist Republic of Romania** *or Rom.* **Re·pu·bli·ca So·ci·a·lis·tă Ro·mâ·nia** \re-'pü-bli-kə-ˌsō-sē-ä-ˌlēs-ta-rō-'män-yə\. Republic, SE Europe, bounded on N by the U.S.S.R., on E by the U.S.S.R. and the Black Sea, on S by Bulgaria, and on W by Yugoslavia and Hungary; 91,699 sq. m.; pop. (1970e) 20,252,541; ✱ Bucharest. *Physical features:* In the N penetrated by the SE end of the Carpathian Mts., uniting in the center of the country with the E end of the Transylvanian Alps (highest point Moldoveanul 8343 ft.). For the greater part consists of rolling and well-watered plains with fertile soil. Besides the Prut, other important tributaries of the Danube are Siretul, Ialomiţa, Argeş (with its tributary the Dîmboviţa), Olt, Jiul, and Timiş (which enters the Danube in Yugoslavia); the Transylvanian plains are watered by the Mureşul and Someşul, tributaries of the Tisza. Marshlands occur along the lower Danube and in its delta; its shoreline from Sulina at the mouth of the Danube extends ab. 125 m. to a point N of Cape Kaliakra. *Chief products:* Wheat, corn, barley, oats; livestock; oil, natural gas, bauxite, manganese; manufacturing: textiles, chemicals, iron and steel, mining equipment, leather goods, agricultural machinery. *Chief cities:* Bucharest, Cluj, Timişoara, Braşov, Ploieşti, Constanţa, Craiova, Iaşi. Divided into the following counties (for pronunciation of their names, see their individual entries):

NAME	AREA (sq. m.)	POP. (1970e)	CAPITAL
Alba	2,406	391,686	Alba Iulia
Arad	2,955	492,439	Arad
Argeş	2,626	568,854	Piteşti
Bacău	2,549	648,596	Bacau
Bihor	2,909	606,969	Oradea
Bistriţa-Năsăud	2,048	281,335	Bistriţa
Botoşani	1,917	475,240	Botoşani
Brăila	1,842	361,476	Brăila
Braşov	2,066	473,812	Braşov
Bucharest (municipality)	234	1,574,536	Bucharest
Buzău	2,344	504,942	Buzău
Caraş-Severin	3,287	366,338	Reşiţa
Cluj	2,568	666,355	Cluj
Constanţa	2,724	513,293	Constanţa
Covasna	1,431	184,407	Sfîntu-Gheorghe
Dîmboviţa	1,443	445,083	Tîrgovişte
Dolj	2,858	724,159	Craiova
Galaţi	1,708	525,135	Galaţi
Gorj	2,178	317,045	Tîrgu-Jiu
Harghita	2,552	295,386	Miercurea-Ciuc
Hunedoara	2,709	504,640	Deva
Ialomiţa	2,398	381,682	Slobozia
Iaşi	2,112	677,537	Iaşi
Ilfov[1]	3,176	797,303	Bucharest
Maramureş	2,400	458,142	Baia-Mare
Mehedinţi	1,892	317,629	Turnu-Severin
Mureş	2,585	592,427	Tîrgu Mureş
Neamţ	2,274	508,623	Piatra-Neamţ
Olt	2,130	498,863	Slatina
Prahova	1,812	752,684	Ploieşti
Sălaj	1,486	267,943	Zalău
Satu-Mare	1,701	373,933	Satu-Mare
Sibiu	2,093	440,581	Sibiu
Suceava	3,303	616,021	Suceava
Teleorman	2,267	539,605	Alexandria
Timiş	3,351	636,186	Timişoara
Tulcea	3,255	250,049	Tulcea
Vaslui	2,046	459,816	Vaslui
Vîlcea	2,203	390,036	Rîmnicu-Vîlcea
Vrancea	1,860	371,755	Focşani

[1]Excludes Bucharest (municipality).

History: For earlier history, see DACIA, MOLDAVIA, WALACHIA, and DANUBIAN PRINCIPALITIES; autonomous Danubian Principalities united and took name of Romania 1861; invaded by Russia in Russo-Turkish War 1877–78; lost Bessarabia to Russia 1878; gained Dobruja; complete independence from Turkey recognized by powers 1878; became kingdom 1881; forced Bulgaria to cede southern Dobruja 1913; entered World War I on side of Allies 1916; disastrously defeated; territory enlarged by addition of Bessarabia, Transylvania, Banat, Bukovina (*qq.v.*) 1918–20; signed treaty with Czechoslovakia, thus joining the Little Entente, Apr. 23, 1921; possession of Bessarabia tacitly recognized by U.S.S.R. in Soviet-Romanian nonaggression pact 1933; entered Balkan Pact 1934 (see BALKAN STATES); in 1940 forced to cede Bessarabia and northern Bukovina (total 21,000 sq. m.) to U.S.S.R., part of northern Transylvania (17,400 sq. m.) to Hungary, and southern Dobruja (2880 sq. m.) to Bulgaria; N Transylvania returned by treaty with Allies 1947. In World War II under authoritarian regime of Ion Antonescu forced to fight on side of Germany; overrun by U.S.S.R. in 1944 and withdrew from the conflict Aug. 23, 1944; proclaimed people's republic Dec. 1947; became a member of the

Warsaw Treaty Organization 1955; during 1960's adopted a foreign policy frequently differing from that of the U.S.S.R.; suffered large-scale economic losses (1970) due to severest floods in its history.

Romania \rō-ˈmā-nē-ə, -nyə\. **1** The Roman Empire, esp. the Byzantine Empire—so called by its neighbors.

2 The Latin Empire (*q.v.*), set up by the Crusaders 1204–61.

3 Part of region of Emilia-Romagna, Italy. See ROMAGNA.

4 European division of old Turkish empire. See RUMELIA.

Romania, Cape. See BULAT, CAPE.

Ro·ma·no, Cape \-rō-ˈmän-(ˌ)ō\. Cape on island in Gulf of Mexico off W coast of Collier co., SW Florida.

Romano Cay \rō-ˌmän-ō-ˈkē, -ˈkā\. Island off N coast of Camagüey prov., E cen. Cuba, in the Camagüey Archipelago.

Ro·mans·horn \ˈrō-mäns-ˌhȯrn\. Commune, Thurgau canton, NE Switzerland, on S shore of Lake Constance; pop. (1970c) 8329.

Ro·mans–sur–Isère \rō-ˌmäⁿ-ˌsu̇(ə)r-ē-ˈze(ə)r\. Commune, Drôme dept., SE France, on Isère river 11 m. NE of Valence; pop. (1968c) 31,545; textiles, leather goods, hats; 13th cent. church. Founded by St. Barnard 862; most important city in the Dauphiné during Middle Ages.

Roman States. See STATES OF THE CHURCH.

Ro·man·zof, Cape \-rō-ˈman-zəf\. Cape on W coast of Alaska; extends into Bering Sea, 61°47′N, 166°W.

Rom·blon \räm-ˈblän\. **1** Province, cen. Phil., island group of the Visayan Is. in Sibuyan Sea SE of Mindoro and S of Luzon; comprises three large islands—Tablas, Sibuyan, and Romblon—and ab. 30 small and dependent islands; 524 sq. m.; pop. (1970p) 167,665; ✱ Romblon. Islands generally low except Sibuyan, which has peak 6745 ft. high. Soil is fertile; chief crops abacá and copra. Chief towns Romblon on Romblon I., and Odiongan and Looc on Tablas.

History: Islands known to Spaniards from early times, visited at least as early as 1582; received first Recollect missionaries 1635; in 17th and 18th cents. often ravaged by Moros; organized into a comandancia 1853; civil government established Mar. 1901; after World War II occupied by U.S. troops Mar. 11, 1945.

2 Smallest of the three important islands of Romblon group, E of N Tablas I. and W of Sibuyan; 32 sq. m.

3 Municipality, ✱ of Romblon prov.; comprises the island of Romblon and three small adjacent islands; pop. (1969e) 23,000; on NW coast of Romblon I. is excellent harbor; active trading port on interisland passage from San Bernardino Strait to Verde Island Passage.

Rom·bo \ˈrōm-(ˌ)bü\. One of the Cape Verde Is.

Rome \ˈrōm\. **1** City, ⊗ of Floyd co., NW Georgia, 55 m. NW of Atlanta; pop. (1970c) 30,759; textiles, aluminum products, boats, furniture; in grain and livestock-farming region; Shorter Coll. (1873), Floyd Junior Coll. (1970); founded 1835; occupied by Union troops 1864.

2 Industrial city, a ⊗ of Oneida co., cen. New York, on Mohawk river 15 m. WNW of Utica; pop. (1970c) 50,148; copper products, household appliances, cables, paint, fishing tackle; packs and ships fruit; Griffiss Air Force Base. Settled 1760; played prominent role in the American Revolution as fort; township organized 1796; incorporated as village 1819, as city 1870.

3 *or Ital.* **Ro·ma** \ˈrō-mä\ *or anc.* **Roma** \ˈrō-mə\. City, ✱ of Italy, also ✱ of Roma prov., cen. Italy, on both sides of Tiber river 16 m. from its mouth and 117 m. NW of Naples; pop. (1970e) 2,778,872, met. area pop. 3,479,179; the cultural, financial, and transportation center of Italy; metallurgical industries; electrical apparatus; motion picture production; tourism; in ancient times ✱ of the Roman Empire (*q.v.*) and later ✱ of the States of the Church. Often called the "Eternal City," "City of the Seven Hills," and the "Holy City"; early city built on seven hills (see SEVEN HILLS) enclosed by Servian Wall, now extends for several miles along both banks of Tiber river and includes Vatican City, autonomous administrative center of the Roman Catholic Church (for account of papal properties in Rome, see VATICAN CITY); imperial Rome divided into 14 Augustan Regions and enclosed by the Aurelian Wall; modern city has notable public squares (Piazza del Popolo, di Venezia, di San Pietro, etc.), thoroughfares (Corso Umberto Primo, Via Venti Settembre, etc.), and city gates (Porta Pinciana, Porta Pia, Porta Maggiore, etc.); notable churches include San Giovanni in Laterno, Santa Pudenziana, and Il Gesù; Univ. of Rome (1303) and several other educational institutions; numerous libraries; noted for its palaces, as the Barberini, Colonna, Corsini, Rospigliosi, and Farnese palaces; remains of ancient city include the Colosseum, catacombs, temples, baths (esp. the Baths of Caracalla), aqueducts, arches, Forum, etc.

History: During 8th cent. B.C., early settlements on hills united to form one city (traditional date of founding of Rome 753 B.C.); predominantly Latin in population, but ruled as Etruscan city-kingdom to 6th cent. B.C.; according to tradition, republic founded 509 B.C.; by 275 B.C. Rome, having defeated Etruscan towns, Latin League, Samnites, and Greek cities in south, was supreme in Italy; began overseas expansion in Punic Wars 264–241, 218–201, 149–146 B.C. (see CARTHAGE); conquered Sicily, Sardinia, Cisalpine Gaul, Spain, and former Carthaginian islands in Mediterranean; by defeat of Macedonia (*q.v.*) 197 B.C., attained hegemony in Greece; established provinces of Illyricum, Macedonia, Africa, Achaia, and Asia; gradually acquired Balearic Is., southern Gaul, Cilicia, Bithynia, Cyrene, and Crete; Syria conquered by Pompey who captured Jerusalem 63 B.C. and reorganized eastern provinces; Gaul annexed (58–51 B.C.) by Caesar who first attempted to invade Britain 55 B.C.; after battle of Actium 31 B.C., all of Roman lands were controlled by Octavian, the first Roman emperor, 27 B.C. (for later history of Roman rule, see ROMAN EMPIRE); city of Rome the capital of Roman Empire until Constantine dedicated Constantinople 330 A.D. (see ISTANBUL); sacked by Alaric and Visigoths 410; after Ravenna (*q.v.*) became political capital of Italy, bishop of Rome, the chief defender of city, gradually obtained temporal authority and began to claim primacy among western bishops; Duchy of Rome, a Byzantine fief, 6th–8th cents.; for its theoretical position as capital of revived Roman empire, see HOLY ROMAN EMPIRE; seat of Papacy and (except 1309–77) of temporal rule of States of the Church (*q.v.*); sacked by Spanish 1527; occupied by French who erected Roman Republic 1798; annexed to French Empire 1809, but later restored to Pope; scene of republican rising 1848–49; made capital of kingdom of Italy 1870 (see VATICAN CITY for part belonging to Papacy). In World War II captured by Allies June 4, 1944; scene of signing of Treaty of Rome Mar. 25, 1957, establishing European Economic Community; site of Summer Olympic Games 1960.

Rome, Duchy of *or anc.* **Du·catus Ro·mae** \d(y)u̇-ˌkāt-əs-ˈrō-(ˌ)mē, -ˌkät-əs-ˈrō-ˌmē\. A division of the Byzantine Empire, 6th cent. to 8th cent., comprising most of modern Latium, cen. Italy; later, a province of the States of the Church, called **Patrimony of Saint Peter** \-sānt-ˈpēt-ər\.

Ro·meo \ˈrō-mē-ˌō\. Village, Macomb co., SE Michigan, 19 m. NE of Pontiac; pop. (1970c) 4012; fruit farms.

Ro·me·o·ville \ˈrō-mē-ō-ˌvil\. Village, Will co., NE Illinois, 10 m. N of Joliet; pop. (1970c) 12,674.

Ro·mil·ly–sur–Seine \ˌrȯ-mi-ˈyē-su̇(ə)r-ˈsān, -ˈsen\. Commune, Aube dept., NE France, 23 m. NW of Troyes; pop. (1968c) 17,038.

Ro·mi·ta \rō-ˈmē-tə\. Municipality, Guanajuato state, Mexico, 15 m. SSE of León; pop. (1970p) 29,042; grain.

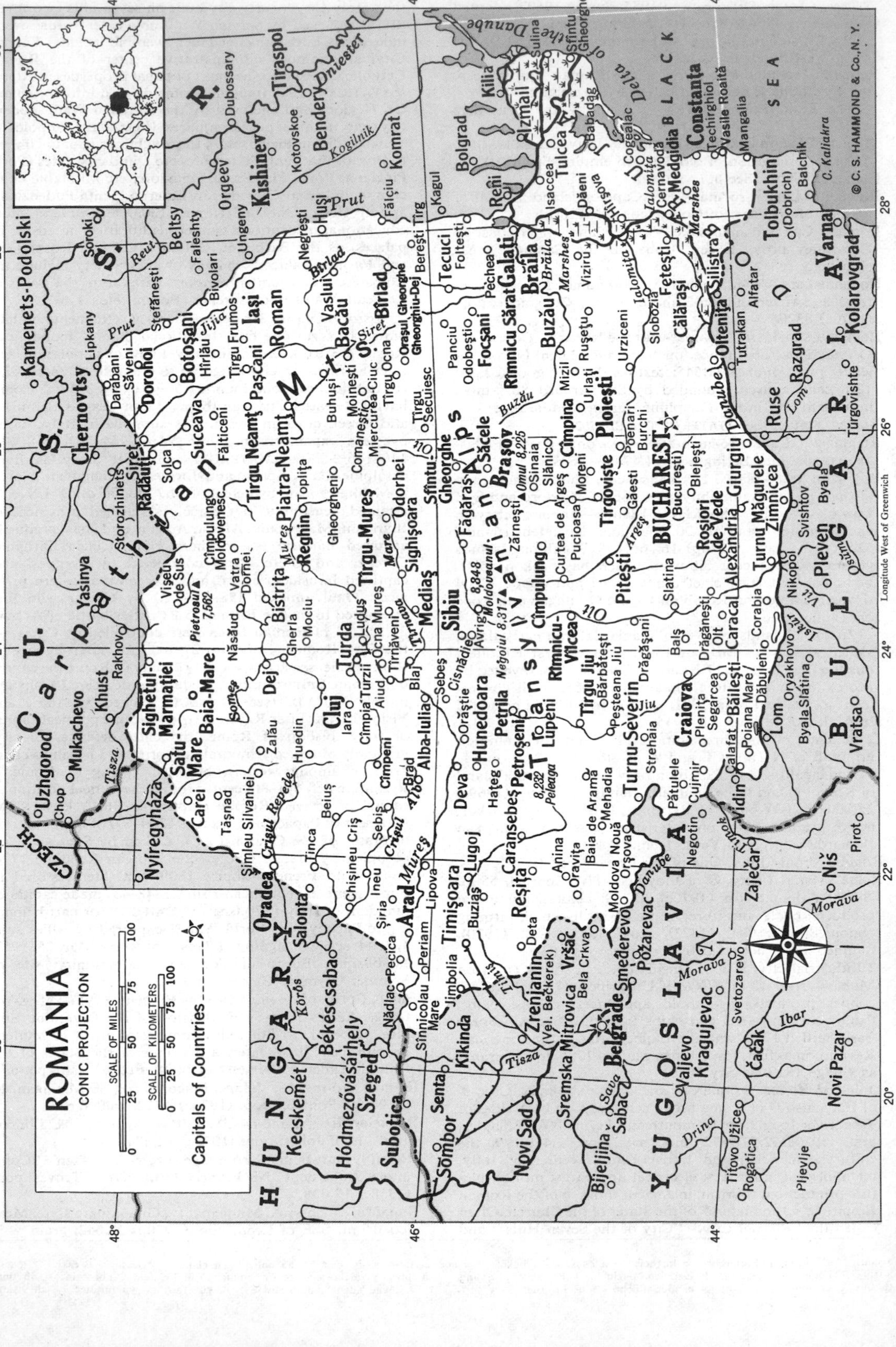
ROMANIA
CONIC PROJECTION
SCALE OF MILES
0 25 50 75 100
SCALE OF KILOMETERS
0 25 50 75 100
Capitals of Countries
© C. S. HAMMOND & Co., N. Y.
Longitude West of Greenwich
HUNGARY
YUGOSLAVIA
BULGARIA
U. S. S. R.
CZECH.
Carpathian Mts.
Transylvanian Alps
BLACK SEA
Delta of the Danube
BUCHAREST (București)
Cluj
Timișoara
Oradea
Arad
Brașov
Ploiești
Constanța
Galați
Brăila
Iași
Craiova
Sibiu
Chernovtsy
Kishinev
Belgrade
Danube
Prut
Tisza
Mureș
Olt
Siret
Dniester

Rom·ney \'räm-nē\. 1 City, ⊗ of Hampshire co., NE West Virginia, in E panhandle on South Branch Potomac river 15 m. ESE of Keyser; pop. (1970c) 2364; lumber; ships fruit; poultry, livestock farms.

2 Municipal borough, England. See NEW ROMNEY.

Romney Marsh \ˌräm-nē-, ˌrəm-\. Coastal pasture tract in Kent, SE England, NE of Rye; 68 sq. m.; before end of 13th cent. the Rother river flowed through it to the sea.

Rom·ny \'rȯm-nē\. Town, W Sumy Oblast, NE Ukrainian S.S.R., U.S.S.R., on upper Sula river 58 m. W of Sumy; pop. (1967e) 43,000; food processing.

Rø·mø \'rə(r)m-ˌə(r)\ *or* **Røm** \'rə(r)m\. One of the North Frisian Is. in the North Sea off W coast of S Jutland Penin.; 39 sq. m.; pop. (1965c) 812; belongs to Denmark.

Ro·mo·ran·tin–Lanthe·nay \ˌrō-mō-rän-'tan-ˌlänt-(ə-)'nā\ *or* **Romorantin.** Manufacturing town, Loir-et-Cher dept., N cen. France, ab. 24 m. SE of Blois; pop. (1968c) 14,096; 15th cent. castle where Francis II signed edict that prevented establishment of the Inquisition in France 1560.

Roms·dal \'rüm(p)s-däl\. Valley of the Rauma (*q.v.*), Norway; steep mountains on either side, esp. Vinjatindane (Vengetinder) 5960 ft., **Roms·dals·horn** \-däls-ˌhȯ(ə)rn\ 5105 ft., and Trolltindane (Troldtinder) 5876 ft.

Roms·dals·fjord \'rüm(p)s-ˌdäls-ˌfyō(ə)r, -ˌfyȯ(ə)r\. Fjord, long inlet of Norwegian Sea, W cen. Norway, E of Ålesund; Åndalsnes at head of it; receives Rauma river.

Rom·sey \'rəm-zē\. Municipal borough, Hampshire, S England, ab. 7 m. NW of Southampton; pop. (1971p) 10,057; brewing; truck farms; site of a Norman abbey church of 12th cent. with remains of an earlier Saxon church beneath it.

Ron·ca·de \rōŋ-'käd-ə\. Commune, Treviso prov., Veneto, NE Italy, 7 m. SE of Treviso; pop. (1968e) 10,397.

Roncador, Serra do. See SERRA DO RONCADOR.

Ron·ca·dor Cay \ˌräŋ-kə-ˌdȯ(ə)r-'kē, -'kā\. Small island in W Caribbean Sea, off E coast of Nicaragua; controlled by U.S.A. and Colombia.

Roncador Reef. Reef, Solomon Is., S of Ontong Java and N of Santa Isabel, 6°13′S, 159°22′E.

Ron·ca·glia \rōŋ-'käl-yə\. Former village, Piacenza prov., Emilia-Romagna, N Italy; now part of commune of Piacenza (*q.v.*); diets held here (1155 et al.) by Holy Roman Emperors, esp. Frederick I.

Ron·ces·va·lles \ˌrȯn(t)-səs-'vä(l)-ˌyäs\ *or Fr.* **Ron·ce·vaux** \rōⁿs-(ə-)vō\. Commune in Navarra prov., N Spain; pop. (1970p) 92; in the Pyrenees ab. 5 m. from the French boundary; mountains here crossed by the **Puer·to Iba·ñe·ta** \ˌpwert-ō-ˌē-bə-'nyāt-ə\ *often called* **Pass of Roncesvalles,** a celebrated mountain pass 3648 ft. high where Roland met his death 778. See FUENTERRABIA.

Ron·ce·verte \'rän(t)-sə-ˌvərt\. City, Greenbrier co., SE West Virginia, on Greenbrier river 26 m. E of Hinton; pop. (1970c) 1981.

Ron·co \'rōŋ-(ˌ)kō\ *or in full* **Ronco Scri·via** \-'skrē-vyə\. Commune, Genova prov., E cen. Liguria, NW Italy, N of Genoa; pop. (1968e) 5018; railroad tunnel 5.16 m. long.

Ron·co·fer·ra·ro \ˌrōŋ-kō-fər-'är-ō\. Commune, Mantova prov., Lombardy, N Italy; pop. (1968e) 7385.

Ron·co·le \'rȯŋ-kə-ˌlā\ *or* **Le Roncole** \lā-\. Village, Parma prov., NW cen. Emilia-Romagna, N Italy, near Busseto (*q.v.*) S of Cremona; birthplace of Giuseppe Verdi.

Ron·da \'rȯn-də\. Commune, Málaga prov., S Spain, 40 m. W of Málaga; pop. (1970p) 30,080; produces grain, wine, oil; manufactures flour, leather, soap, chocolates; Roman and Moorish remains; reconquered by Ferdinand the Catholic 1485; Moorish uprising 1501.

Ron·da·ne National Park \'rȯ-ˌna-nə-\. National park, Norway; 222 sq. m.; alpine region; established 1962.

Ron·deau Provincial Park \'rän-dō-\. Canadian provincial park, Kent co., SE Ontario; 8 sq. m.; comprises point of land in Lake Erie 18 m. SE of Chatham; game preserve, with forests and camping facilities.

Ron·de·bosch \'rȯn-də-ˌbȯs\. Town, Cape Province, S Rep. of South Africa, ab. 6 m. SE of Cape Town; founded 1657 by free burghers, servants of Dutch East India Company, who had obtained their freedom; residential city—site of Cecil Rhodes's home Groote Schuur, now official residence of republic's prime minister and location of Univ. of Cape Town (1918).

Ron·dô·nia \rōⁿ(n)-'dōn-yə\ *or* **Gua·po·ré** \ˌgwäp-ə-'rā\. Territory, W Brazil; 93,839 sq. m.; pop. (1970p) 95,311; ✱ Pôrto Velho; rubber; diamonds, bauxite, gypsum; established 1943.

Ron·dout \'rän-ˌdau̇t\. 1 Creek in Ulster co., SE New York; flows NE to join Wallkill river ab. 6 m. below Kingston, where the combined stream empties into Hudson river. See MERRIMAN DAM.

2 Former village in Ulster co., New York, on the Hudson river; now part of Kingston.

Ronge, Lac la \ˌlak-lə-'rōⁿzh\. Lake, N Saskatchewan, Canada; 552 sq. m.; its outlet flows N into Churchill river.

Rong·e·lap \'roŋ-ə-ˌlap\. Atoll, Marshall Is., W cen. Pacific Ocean, at NW end of Ratak Chain ab. 80 m. E of Bikini atoll.

Rong·e·rik \'rȯŋ-ə-(ˌ)rik\. Atoll, Marshall Is., W cen. Pacific Ocean, near NW end of Ratak Chain E of Bikini and Rongelap; place to which population of Bikini was removed at time of atomic-bomb tests 1946.

Ro·niu, Mount \-'rō-nē-ˌü\. Peak, on the SE peninsula (Taiarapu) of the island of Tahiti, French Polynesia, S Pacific Ocean; 4341 ft.

Røn·ne \'rə(r)n-ə\. Seaport, ⊗ of Bornholm co., on the W coast of Bornholm I., Denmark; pop. (1970e) 12,440; terra-cotta and faïence; stone quarries.

Ron·ne·by \'rȯn-ə-bē\. Town, Blekinge co., S Sweden, ab. 14 m. W of Karlskrona; pop. (1970e) 29,607.

Ron·se \'rȯn(t)-sə\ *or Fr.* **Re·naix** \rə-'nā\. Manufacturing and commercial commune, East Flanders prov., NW cen. Belgium; pop. (1969e) 25,127.

Roo·de·poort \'rüd-ə-ˌpu̇(ə)rt\. City, S Transvaal, NE Rep. of South Africa, 12 m. W of Johannesburg; pop. (1967e) 115,600; residential community in gold-mining region; has textile, cement, iron and steel, and woodworking industries; founded 1886 as gold-mining camp; declared a municipality 1904; scene of surrender of L. S. Jameson 1896.

Rood·house \'rüd-ˌhau̇s, 'rōd-\. City, Greene co., W Illinois, 45 m. WSW of Springfield; pop. (1970c) 2357.

Roof Butte \'rüf-, 'ru̇f-\. Butte, NE Apache co., NE Arizona; 9808 ft.

Rooke. See UMBOI.

Rooks \'ru̇ks\. County in Kansas. See table at KANSAS.

Roor·kee *or* **Rur·ki** \'ru̇(ə)r-kē\. Town, N Uttar Pradesh, N India, 19 m. E of Saharanpur; pop. with cantonment (1961c) 45,801; headquarters of workers and shops for Ganges canal; univ. (1949).

Roo·se·be·ke \'rō-sə-ˌbā-kə\. Village, East Flanders, Belgium, just E of Roeselare; pop. (1969e) 388; scene of battle Nov. 27, 1382 in which Charles VI of France defeated the Flemish insurgents who had revolted because of taxes imposed by the regent Louis, Duke of Anjou.

Roo·sen·daal en Nis·pen \'rōs-ᵊn-ˌdäl-ən-'nis-pən\. Commune, North Brabant prov., S Netherlands; pop. (1970e) 45,935; machinery, furniture, cigars; founded 1268.

Roo·se·velt \'rō-zə-ˌvelt, -vəlt *also* 'rü-\. 1 Counties in two states of the U.S. See tables at MONTANA and NEW MEXICO.

2 City, Jefferson co., cen. Alabama; pop. (1970c) 3663.

3 Urban community (unincorporated), Nassau co., SE New York, on Long Island SW of Hempstead; pop. (1970c) 15,008.

Roosevelt, Mount. Peak, Lawrence co., W South Dakota; 5676 ft.

Roosevelt, Rio \ˌrē-(ˌ)ü-\ *or formerly* **Rio da Dú·vi·da** \-də-ˈdü-vi-də\. River, W cen. Brazil; ab. 400 m. long; rises in W Mato Grosso state, flows N into SE Amazonas state where it joins the Aripuanã river; explored by Theodore Roosevelt 1914; lower course of the Aripuanã sometimes called Rio Roosevelt.

Roosevelt Island. 1 Island, Potomac river, U.S. See THEODORE ROOSEVELT ISLAND.
2 Ice-covered island, E Ross Ice Shelf, Ross Dependency, Antarctica, S of the Bay of Whales; ab. 90 m. long.

Roosevelt Lake. See FRANKLIN D. ROOSEVELT LAKE.

Roosevelt Park. City, Muskegon co., W Michigan, 5 m. S of Muskegon; pop. (1970c) 4176.

Ro·per \ˈrō-pər\. River, NE Northern Territory, Australia; ab. 325 m. long, navigable for ab. 90 m.; flows N and E to Limmen Bight on W side of Gulf of Carpentaria.

Ro·po·ta·mo National Park \rə-ˈpȯt-ə-ˌmō-\. National park, Bulgaria; ab. 3 sq. m.; a periodically flooded forest area; established 1962.

Ro·que·brune \ˌrȯk-(ə-)ˈbrün\ *or in full* **Roquebrune–Cap–Mar·tin** \-ˌkap-mär-ˈtaⁿ\ *or Ital.* **Roc·ca·bru·na** \ˌrȯk-ə-ˈbrü-nə\. Commune, Alpes-Maritimes dept., SE France, near coast bet. Monaco and Menton; pop. (1962c) 6605; formerly under princes of Monaco from whom it (with Menton) revolted 1848; independent 1848–60 when it became part of France.

Roque·fort–sur–Soul·zon \ˌrȯk-(ə-)ˈfō(ə)r-sù(ə)r-sül-ˈzōⁿ\. Town, SE Aveyron dept., S France; pop. (1962c) 1488; town built against limestone cliffs in which are caves where Roquefort cheeses are ripened.

Ro·que Gon·zá·lez de San·ta Cruz \ˌrȯ-kē-gən-ˈzäl-əz-dā-ˌsant-ə-ˈkrüz\. Town, Paraguarí dept., S Paraguay; pop. (1970e) 13,521.

Roques, Los. See LOS ROQUES.

Ro·rai·ma \rȯ-ˈrī-mə\. 1 Flat-topped mountain in Serra Pacaraima, at intersection of boundaries of Brazil, Venezuela, and Guyana; 9 m. long by 3 m. wide; highest point 9219 ft.; steep slopes, many waterfalls (one almost 2000 ft.), source of many rivers of Guyana, of the Amazon system to the S, and of Orinoco system to the W.
2 Territory, N Brazil; 88,843 sq. m.; pop. (1970p) 40,855; ✱ Boa Vista; cattle ranching; estab. 1943.

Rorke's Drift \ˈrȯ(ə)rks-\. Locality on a tributary of the Tugela river, N Natal, E Rep. of South Africa, 21 m. SE of Dundee; scene of successful British defense against Zulus 1879.

Rør·os \ˈrər-ˌōs\. Commune, SE Sør-Trøndelag co., cen. Norway 35 m. by road from Swedish frontier; pop. (1969e) 5256.

Ror·schach \ˈrȯ(ə)r-ˌshäk, -ˌshäk\. Commune, Saint Gallen canton, NE Switzerland, on S shore of Lake Constance 6 m. NE of Saint Gallen; pop. (1970c) 11,963; tourist resort.

Ro·sa, Mon·te \ˌmänt-ē-ˈrō-zə\. Mountain of the Pennine Alps, on the Swiss-Italian border; a mountain mass, has ten summits, the highest the Dufourspitze 15,203 ft., highest point in the Pennine Alps. At altitude of 11,500 ft. has Italian laboratory for nuclear research.

Ro·sa·les \rō-ˈsä-ləs\. Municipality, Pangasinan prov., Luzon, Phil., on left bank of the Agno 27 m. ESE of Lingayen; pop. (1969e) 33,400; captured by U.S. troops Jan. 1945.

Ro·sa·lie Peak \ˌrō-zə-(ˌ)lē-\. Mountain, Park co., cen. Colorado; 13,575 ft.

Ros·a·lind Bank \ˌräz-(ə-)lən(d)-, rō-zə-lən(d)-\. Shoal in Caribbean Sea halfway bet. W Jamaica and E Honduras.

Ro·sa·mo·ra·da \ˌrȯ-sə-mə-ˈrä-də\. Municipality, Nayarit state, Mexico, 48 m. NNW of Tepic; pop. (1970p) 28,568; mines gold, silver, lead; lumber; diversified agriculture.

Ro·sa·rio \rō-ˈzär-ē-ˌō, -ˈsär-\. 1 Commercial city, Santa Fe prov., E cen. Argentina, on the Paraná river 190 m. NW of Buenos Aires; pop. (1960c) 591,428; ships grain, hay, meat, hides, cattle, wool, and sugar; grain elevators, flour mills, tanneries, distilleries; founded 1725; began development into major city late 19th cent.
2 Town, Sinaloa state, W Mexico, 45 m. SE of Mazatlán; munic. pop. (1970p) 38,423; mining.
3 Town, San Pedro dept., cen. Paraguay, on the left bank of Paraguay river 70 m. N of Asunción; pop. (1970e) 9990.
4 Municipality, Batangas prov., Luzon, Phil., 13 m. NE of Batangas; pop. (1969e) 44,500.
5 Municipality, La Union prov., Luzon, Phil., 5 m. from E shore of Lingayen Gulf; pop. (1969e) 24,700.

Rosario, Sierra del. See SIERRA DEL ROSARIO.

Rosario Cay \-ˈkē, -ˈkā\. Island in N Caribbean Sea, E of Isle of Pines and S of W Cuba.

Rosario de la Fron·te·ra \-del-ə-ˌfrən-ˈter-ə\. Town, Salta prov., N Argentina; pop. (1960c) 7134; altitude 3200 ft.; medicinal hot springs.

Ro·sar·io Strait \rō-ˌzar-ē-(ˌ)ō-\. Strait, NW Washington, lying bet. San Juan Is. on the W and Skagit co. on the E.

Ro·sa·rio Ta·la \rō-ˌzär-ē-(ˌ)ō-ˈtäl-ə, -ˌsär-\. Town, Entre Ríos prov., E Argentina; pop. (1960c) 7350.

Ro·sar·no \rō-ˈzär-(ˌ)nō\. Commune, Reggio di Calabria prov., Calabria, S Italy, 32 m. NNE of Reggio di Calabria; pop. (1968e) 18,078.

Ro·sas, Gulf of \-ˈrō-zəs, -ˈrō-ˌsäs\. Inlet of Mediterranean Sea on NE coast of Spain, S of Cape Creus.

Roscianum. See ROSSANO.

Ros·coff \ˌrȯs-ˈkȯf\. Seaport town, N Finistère dept., NW France; pop. (1962c) 4030.

Ros·com·mon \rä-ˈskäm-ən\. 1 County in Michigan. See table at MICHIGAN.
2 Village, ⊗ of Roscommon co., N cen. Michigan; pop. (1970c) 810; Kirtland Community Coll. (1966).
3 County, N cen. Eire, in Connacht prov.; 951 sq. m.; pop. (1971p) 53,497; ⊗ Roscommon; agriculture, coal mining.
4 Town, ⊗ of co. Roscommon, N cen. Eire; pop. (1966c) 1659; ruins of 13th cent. castle; Dominican priory.

Ros·crea \räs-ˈkrā\. Town, NE co. Tipperary, S Eire; pop. (1966c) 3511; ruins of Augustinian priory founded in 7th cent.; remnants of 13th cent. castle.

Rose \ˈrōz\. Small uninhabited island in American Samoa, in SW cen. Pacific Ocean, ab. 70 m. E of Tau.

Rose, Mount. Peak, S Washoe co., NW Nevada, in Carson Range; 10,778 ft.; winter sports locale.

Ro·seau \rō-ˈzō\. 1 County in NW Minnesota. See table at MINNESOTA.
2 Village, its ⊗, 20 m. WSW of Lake of the Woods; pop. (1970c) 2552.
3 Seaport, ✱ of Dominica I., Windward Is., West Indies; pop. (1970e) 10,157.

Rose·bud \ˈrōz-ˌbəd\. 1 Creek, SE Montana; ab. 100 m. long; rises in E Big Horn co., flows NE into Yellowstone river in Rosebud co.
2 County in Montana. See table at MONTANA.

Rose·burg \ˈrōz-ˌbərg\. City, ⊗ of Douglas co., SW Oregon, 45 m. E of Coos Bay; pop. (1970c) 14,461; sawmills, nickel mine; diversified agriculture; Umpqua Community Coll. (1964).

Rose·dale \ˈrōz-ˌdāl\. 1 Former city, Wyandotte co., Kansas; annexed to Kansas City 1922.
2 City, a ⊗ of Bolivar co., NW Mississippi, on Mississippi river 31 m. N of Greenville; pop. (1970c) 2599.

Ro·seg, Piz \ˌpēts-rō-ˈzej\. Mountain in the Rhaetian Alps, Switzerland, W of Piz Bernina; 12,936 ft.

Rose Hill \ˈrōz-\. Residential town, NW Mauritius, bet. Port Louis and Curepipe; pop., with adjacent Beau Bassin, (1969e) 70,700.

Rose·land \ˈrōz-ˌland, -lənd\. Borough, Essex co., NE New Jersey, 10 m. NW of Newark; pop. (1970c) 4453.

Ro·selle \rō-ˈzel\. 1 City, Cook and Du Page cos., NE Illinois, 27 m. NW of Chicago; pop. (1970c) 6207.
2 Residential borough, Union co., NE New Jersey, 2 m. W of Elizabeth and adjoining Roselle Park; pop. (1970c) 22,585; first community in world to have streets lighted by incandescent bulbs; site of laboratory of Thomas A.

Edison in which he installed first electric lighting plant in world.

Roselle Park. Residential borough, Union co., NE New Jersey, 3 m. W of Elizabeth and adjoining Roselle; pop. (1970c) 14,277; rugs, leather goods, surgical instruments.

Rose·mead \'rōz-ˌmēd\. City, Los Angeles co., SW California, E of Alhambra; pop. (1970c) 40,972.

Ro·se·mère \ˌrōz-(ə-)'mer, -'mi(ə)r\. Town, Terrebonne co., S Quebec, Canada, 15 m. NW of Montreal; pop. (1971p) 6727.

Rose·mont \'rōz-ˌmänt\. 1 Village, Cook co., NE Illinois, 14 m. NW of Chicago; pop. (1970c) 4360.

2 Locality, Montgomery co., SE Pennsylvania, ab. 6 m. S of Norristown; Rosemont Coll. (1921).

Ro·sen·berg \'rōz-ᵊn-ˌbərg\. 1 City, Fort Bend co., SE Texas, 31 m. WSW of Houston; pop. (1970c) 12,098; oil wells; agriculture.

2 Town, Czechoslovakia. See RUŽOMBEROK.

Ro·sen·daël \ˌrō-zäⁿ-'däl\. Commune, Nord dept., N France, E suburb of Dunkerque; pop. (1968c) 19,591; seaside resort; shipbuilding, jute weaving; breweries.

Rose·neath \'rōz-ˌnēth\. Parish, Dunbarton co., W cen. Scotland, on Gare Loch ab. 23 m. NW of Glasgow; U.S. naval base in World War II.

Ro·sen·heim \'rōz-ᵊn-ˌhīm\. Industrial city, Bavaria, West Germany, at foot of Alps on Inn river 34 m. SE of Munich; pop. (1969e) 35,957; machinery, lumber; salt.

Rose Peak \'rōz-\. Mountain, N Greenlee co., E Arizona; 8789 ft.

Rose Point. Cape, NE Graham I., N Queen Charlotte Is., off W British Columbia, Canada.

Ro·se·to de·gli Abruz·zi \rō-'zāt-ō-ˌdel-yē-ä-'brüt-sē, -ə-'brüt-\. Commune, Teramo prov., Abruzzi, cen. Italy, on Adriatic Sea 17 m. E of Teramo; pop. (1968e) 17,765.

Rose·town \'rōz-ˌtaun\. Town, Saskatchewan, Canada, 72 m. SW of Saskatoon; pop. (1971p) 2543; oil refining; agriculture.

Ro·set·ta \rō-'zet-ə\ *or Arab.* **Ra·shīd** \rä-'shēd\ *or anc.* **Bol·bi·ti·ne** \ˌbäl-bə-'tī-nē\. 1 Name given to W branch of Nile river in the Nile delta, Egypt; ab. 146 m. long; its mouth is the **Rosetta Mouth** (*anc.* **Bol·bi·tin·ic Mouth** \ˌbäl-bə-'tin-ik-\).

2 City, Beheira gov., Egypt, on left bank of Rosetta, ab. 9 m. SSE of its mouth; pop. (1966c) 36,700. The Rosetta stone, a piece of black basalt, was found near here 1799; it bore a trilingual inscription (in hieroglyphics, demotic characters, and Greek) and furnished the clue to Jean F. Champollion, French Egyptologist, toward deciphering Egyptian hieroglyphics.

Rose·ville \'rōz-ˌvil\. 1 City, Placer co., E California, 18 m. NE of Sacramento; pop. (1970c) 18,221; fruit, wine.

2 Residential city, Macomb co., SE Michigan, 13 m. NE of Detroit; pop. (1970c) 60,529.

3 Village, Ramsey co., E Minnesota, N suburb of St. Paul; pop. (1970c) 34,518.

Ro·si·clare \'rōz-ə-ˌkla(ə)r, -ˌkle(ə)r\. City, Hardin co., SE Illinois, on Ohio river across from Kentucky; pop. (1970c) 1421.

Ro·si·gna·no Ma·rit·ti·mo \ˌrō-zi-'nyän-(ˌ)ō-mə-'rēt-ə-ˌmō\. Commune, Livorno prov., Tuscany, W Italy, near Ligurian Sea 10 m. ESE of Leghorn; pop. (1968e) 29,153.

Ros·ig·nol \ˌräs-ig-'näl\. Town, NE Guyana, situated on W bank of Berbice river opp. New Amsterdam.

Ro·sil·los Mountains \rō-ˌsē-(y)əs-\. Range, S Brewster co., W Texas; 5420 ft.

Ro·şio·ri–de–Ve·de \rō-ˌshō-rē-de-'ved-ə\. Commune, Teleorman co., S Romania, ab. 58 m. SW of Bucharest; pop. (1970e) 24,598.

Rositten. See RĒZEKNE.

Ros·kil·de \'rəs-ˌkil-ə\. 1 County of Denmark, E Sjælland I. See table at DENMARK.

2 City, Roskilde co., at head of Roskilde Fjord, W of Copenhagen; pop. (1970e) 39,984; residential suburb of Copenhagen; capital of Denmark from 10th cent. to 1443; cathedral, dating from 12th cent. and containing Danish royal mausoleum; scene of the signing of the Peace of Roskilde 1658 bet. Denmark and Sweden.

Roskilde Fjord. Eastern extension of Ise Fjord on N coast of Sjælland, Denmark; extends S inland for ab. 25 m.

Ro·slavl \rə-'släv-ᵊl\. Town, S Smolensk Oblast, Russian S.F.S.R., U.S.S.R., ab. 65 m. SE of Smolensk; pop. (1967e) 46,000; railroad junction and market town; in World War II occupied by Germans Aug. 1941–Sept. 1943.

Ros·lyn \'räz-lən\. 1 Residential village, Nassau co., SE New York, on Long I. ab. 4 m. N of Mineola; pop. (1970c) 2546; home and burial place of William Cullen Bryant. Adjacent villages are **Roslyn Harbor** and **Roslyn Estates,** of which **Roslyn Heights** is the post office.

2 Locality, Montgomery co., SE Pennsylvania, ab. 11 m. E of Norristown; pop. (1970c) 18,717.

Ros·ny–sous–Bois \rō-ˌnē-sü-'bwä\. Commune, Seine-St-Denis dept., N France, E suburb of Paris; pop. (1968c) 30,705.

Ro·so·li·ni \ˌrō-zə-'lē-nē\. Commune, Siracusa prov., SE Sicily, Italy, 25 m. SW of Syracuse; pop. (1968e) 18,768.

Ross \'rȯs\. 1 County in Ohio. See table at OHIO.

2 Residential town, Marin co., W California, 14 m. NW of San Francisco; pop. (1970c) 2742.

3 Urban township, Allegheny co., SW Pennsylvania N of Pittsburgh; pop. (1970c) 32,892.

Ross, Mount. Peak, Kerguelen I., in the Indian Ocean; 6430 ft.; highest point on the island.

Ross and Crom·ar·ty \-'kräm-ərt-ē\. County, N Scotland, including Lewis I. in the Outer Hebrides; 3089 sq. m.; pop. (1971p) 58,267; ⊗ Dingwall; a mountainous region with many lochs; livestock farming, fishing, tweed making, distilling.

Ros·sa·no \rə-'sän-(ˌ)ō\ *or anc.* **Ros·ci·a·num** \ˌräs-ē-'ā-nəm, -'an-əm\. Commune, Cosenza prov., Calabria, S Italy, near Gulf of Taranto 29 m. NE of Cosenza; pop. (1968e) 25,023; archiepiscopal see; valuable 6th cent. manuscript of gospels.

Ross·bach \'rȯs-ˌbäk\. Village, Halle dist., East Germany, 8 m. SW of Merseburg; scene of battle Nov. 5, 1757, during Seven Years' War, in which Frederick the Great defeated the French and Austrians.

Ross Barrier. See ROSS ICE SHELF.

Rossbodenhorn. See FLETSCHHORN.

Ross Dam. See UNITED STATES, *Dams and Reservoirs.*

Ross Dependency. Section of Antarctica lying S of 60°S lat. and bet. 160°E and 150°W long.; includes Balleny Is., Coulman I., Ross I., Scott I., and the shores of Ross Sea (Edward VII Penin. and part of Victoria Land), also Little America and Roosevelt I. in the Ross Ice Shelf area; ab. 165,000 sq. m. land and 130,000 sq. m. permanent ice shelf; by act of British Parliament placed under jurisdiction of New Zealand 1923.

Ros·seau Lake \ˌrō-sō-\. One of the Muskoka lakes in Muskoka dist., SE Ontario, Canada; connected with Lakes Joseph and Muskoka (*q.v.*).

Ros·sel \'rȯs-əl\. Island, easternmost of the Louisiade Archipelago, Papua New Guinea, in Solomon Sea 22 m. NE of Tagula I.; ab. 21 m. long by 7 m. wide; pop. (1969e) 1933.

Ross·ford \'rȯs-fərd\. Village, Wood co., NW Ohio, 3 m. S of Toledo; pop. (1970c) 5302; glass.

Ross Ice Shelf *or formerly* **Ross Barrier.** Ice wall bordering on S part of Ross Sea and extending from Ross I. to Edward VII Penin., Antarctica; its S edge lies along foot of Queen Maud Mountains and Queen Alexandra Range; 50 to 200 ft. high, 400 m. long; discovered 1841 by Capt. James Ross; crossed 1903–04 by Capt. Scott to 82°17′S; S end passed 1908 by Shackleton's expedition; region intensively explored since 1947 and made site of several permanent research stations.

Ros·sig·nol, Lake \-'räs-ig-ˌnäl\. Lake, SW Nova Scotia, Canada.

Ross Island. 1 Island, Weddell Sea, Antarctica. See JAMES ROSS ISLAND.

2 Island in Ross Sea, W Ross Dependency, Antarctica, at W end of Ross Ice Shelf; separated from Victoria Land by McMurdo Sound; highest point Mount Erebus 12,450 ft.; has also Mt. Terror 10,750 ft.

3 Island, Burma. See DAUNG ISLAND.

4 Three lakes, Kerry, Eire. See KILLARNEY, LAKES OF.

Rossiya. See RUSSIA.

Ross·land \'rós-ˌland, -lənd\. Residential city, SE British Columbia, Canada, near U.S. border 5 m. W of Trail; pop. (1971p) 3911; winter resort.

Ross·lau \'rós-ˌlau̇\. Manufacturing city, Halle dist., East Germany, on Elbe river N of Dessau; pop. (1970e) 17,246.

Ross of Mull. See MULL, ROSS OF.

Ross Quadrant. Formerly, the quarter section of Antarctica (*q.v.*) bet. 90°W and 180°W; now chiefly E part of Ross Dependency, Marie Byrd Land, and W part of Ellsworth Land.

Ross Sea. Arm of S Pacific Ocean bet. Victoria Land and Edward VII Penin., extending into Antarctica to ab. 85°S; on S borders an extensive area of Ross Ice Shelf. Discovered 1841 by Capt. James Ross.

Ross·ville \'rós-ˌvil\. City, Walker co., NW Georgia, on Tennessee border 23 m. WNW of Dalton; pop. (1970c) 3957; suburb of Chattanooga, Tenn.

Ros·tock \'räs-ˌtäk, 'ró-ˌstòk\. 1 District of East Germany. See table at GERMANY, EAST.

2 *also* **Rostock–War·ne·mün·de** \-ˌvär-nə-'myün-də\. Industrial city and seaport, its ✱, on the Warnow river 8 m. from the Baltic and 41 m. WSW of Stralsund; pop. (1970e) 198,396; produces diesel engines, chemicals, machinery; major shipbuilding and fishing center; 15th cent. brick church, 15th cent. town hall, 16th cent. tower; univ. (1419). Founded during 12th cent.; chartered 1218; member of Hanseatic League in 14th cent.; in World War II heavily damaged by Allied bombing but since substantially reconstructed.

Ros·tov \rə-'stóf, -'stòv\. 1 Principality, cen. Russia, c. 9th cent. to 13th cent.; united with Suzdal (*q.v.*) as Rostov-Suzdal (*q.v.*) principality; superseded by Vladimir and Moscow.

2 *or formerly* **Rostov–Ya·ro·slav·ski** \-ˌyär-ə-'släf-skē\ *or* **Rostov–Ve·li·ki** \-və-'lē-kē\. Town, S Yaroslavl Oblast, Russian S.F.S.R., U.S.S.R., on small lake 35 m. SW of Yaroslavl; pop. (1967e) 31,000; linen, handmade enamelware; 13th cent. cathedral, several 17th cent. churches. A very early Slavic town; ✱ of Rostov-Suzdal principality 10th–14th cents.; came under Moscow 1474.

Rostov–na–Do·nu \-nä-'dó-nü\ *or Eng.* **Rostov–on–Don** \-'dän\. City, ✱ of Rostov Oblast, SE Russian S.F.S.R., U.S.S.R., on N bank of the Don ab. 28 m. from its mouth on the Gulf of Taganrog (Sea of Azov); pop. (1970p) 789,000; an important industrial center, producing agricultural machinery, barges, electrical equipment, wire, road-making machinery, footwear, chemicals, glass, tobacco products, wine; univ. (1917). Founded as customs post 1749; fortified 1761 and made town 1797; in World War II occupied by Germans briefly in Nov. 1941 and again July 1942–Feb. 1943; suffered extensive damage.

Rostov Oblast \-'ó-bləst, -ˌblast\. Subdivision of SE Russian S.F.S.R., U.S.S.R., on the Lower Don; 38,919 sq. m.; pop. (1970p) 3,832,000; ✱ Rostov-na-Donu. Consists largely of low fertile plains along the Don and its tributaries; wheat, corn, melons, barley; vineyards; coal mining; considerable heavy industry. Chief towns Rostov-na-Donu, Taganrog, Shakhty, Novoshakhtinsk, Novocherkassk. Region of the lower Don held by Tatars c. 1237–1480; largely under Russian rule from mid-16th cent. except for S part which remained Turkish as part of Khanate of the Crimea until 1784; long inhabited by the Don Cossacks; in World War II occupied by the Germans during 1942.

Ro·stov–Suz·dal \-'süz-dəl\. Medieval Russian principality, in cen. part of Russia, NE of modern Moscow; ✱ Rostov; chief towns Rostov, Suzdal, Vladimir (*q.v.*), Tver, and Moscow; absorbed early in 14th cent. by rapidly growing Moscow principality.

Rostov–Veliki *or* **Rostov–Yaroslavski.** See ROSTOV 2.

Roşu. See TURNU ROŞU.

Røs·vatn \rə(r)s-ˌvät-ᵊn\. Lake, S Nordland co., N Norway.

Ros·well \'räz-ˌwel, -wəl\. 1 Residential city, Fulton co., NW cen. Georgia, 18 m. N of Atlanta; pop. (1970c) 5430.

2 City, ⊗ of Chavez co., SE New Mexico, 95 m. N of Texas border; pop. (1970c) 33,908; ships livestock, cotton, meat, fruit; winter resort; oil wells, potash mines; New Mexico Military Institute (1891); Walker Air Force Base (1941). Founded 1871, incorporated 1891.

Ro·syth \rō-'sīth\. Village, Fife, E Scotland, on N shore of Firth of Forth; site of naval base (opened 1916); base of Grand Fleet 1918; major repair base during World War II; in 1963 made base for nuclear-powered submarines.

Ro·ta \'rōt-ə\. Island, S end of Mariana Is., W Pacific, midway bet. Guam and Tinian; ab. 35 sq. m.; highest point 1612 ft.; Japanese base used in attack on Guam Dec. 11, 1941; severely bombed by U.S. during latter half of 1944 but not occupied until end of the war.

Ro·tan \rō-'tan\. City, Fisher co., NW cen. Texas, 28 m. N of Sweetwater; pop. (1970c) 2404.

Roterturm. See TURNU ROŞU.

Ro·then·burg ob der Tau·ber \'rōt-ᵊn-ˌbu̇(ə)rg-ˌop-dər-'tau̇-bər\. Commune, Bavaria, West Germany, on Tauber river 31 m. SSE of Würzburg; pop. (1969e) 11,786; soap, textiles; medieval walls; became free imperial city 1274; at height of its prosperity at end of 14th cent.

Roth·er \'räth-ər\. 1 River, Derbyshire and West Riding, Yorkshire, N England; 21 m. long; flows into the Don at Rotherham.

2 Either of two small streams in Sussex, S England: (1) in Hampshire and W Sussex; (2) in E Sussex, partly on boundary of Kent (see ROMNEY MARSH); flows into English Channel.

Roth·er·ham \'räth-ə-rəm\. County borough, West Riding, Yorkshire, N England, at confluence of Rother and Don rivers 6 m. NE of Sheffield; pop. (1971p) 84,646; steel, iron, and brass products, machinery, beer; incorporated 1871.

Roth·er·hithe \'räth-ər-ˌhith\ *or* **Red·riff** \'red-ˌrif\. Parish in Southwark metropolitan borough, London, England; terminus of Grand Surrey Canal; commercial dockyards.

Rothe·say \'räth-sē, -sā\. Manufacturing burgh, ⊗ of Bute co., on the island of Bute off SW coast of Scotland; pop. (1971p) 6524; naval base; resort; ruins of 11th cent. castle.

Roth·schild \'räths-ˌchīld\. Village, Marathon co., cen. Wisconsin, 6 m. S of Wausau; pop. (1970c) 3141.

Roth·well \'räth-ˌwel, -wəl\. Urban district, West Riding, Yorkshire, N England; pop. (1971p) 28,353; rope, chemicals; rhubarb.

Ro·ti \'rōt-ē\ *or* **Rot·ti** \'rót-ē\. Island, Indonesia, SW of Timor; 50 m. long by 14 m. wide; 467 sq. m.; chief village Baa.

Roti Strait. Channel bet. SW end of Timor I. and the island of Roti, Indonesia; connects Savu Sea with Timor Sea.

Ro·to·a·va \ˌrōt-ə-'wäv-ə\. Chief village of Fakarava atoll, 16°03'S, 145°37'W, Tuamotu Archipelago, S Pacific Ocean; former headquarters of French administrator.

Rotomagus. See ROUEN.

Ro·to·ma·ha·na \ˌrōt-ə-mə-'hän-ə\. Lake, N cen. North I., New Zealand, S of Lake Tarawera; 3½ sq. m., 4 m. long; famous for its sinter terraces ("pink" and "white" terraces) which were destroyed by an eruption of Mount Tarawera June 10, 1886.

Ro·ton·do, Mon·te \ˌmón-tē-rə-'tōn-(ˌ)dō\. Peak, in cen. part of the island of Corsica, France; 8612 ft.

Rotondo, Piz·zo \ˌpēt-(ˌ)sō-rə-ˈtōn-(ˌ)dō\. Peak, highest in the Saint Gotthard range of the Lepontine Alps, S cen. Switzerland; 10,472 ft.

Ro·to·rua \ˌrō-tə-ˈrü-ə\. City, N cen. North I., New Zealand, at SW end of **Rotorua Lake** (31 sq. m.) 120 m. SE of Auckland; pop. (1970e) 29,300; noted health resort with thermal springs; hunting and fishing.

Rot·ter·dam \ˈrät-ər-ˌdam\. 1 Industrial and commercial city and seaport, South Holland prov., W Netherlands, on both sides of the Nieuwe Maas ab. 15 m. from the North Sea; pop. (1970e) 686,586; center of an extensive system of canals connecting it with the Rhine and all parts of the Netherlands; site of the Europoort, a complex of industrial sites and harbor basins opp. the Hook of Holland, begun 1958; produces chemicals, paper, clothing, margarine, tobacco products, railway equipment; brewing, distilling, oil refining, shipbuilding, automobile assembly, heavy engineering; 15th cent. church, 17th cent. Schielandhaus, museum, public gardens.

History: Founded 13th cent. and a major commercial city from c. 1340; great prosperity during late 16th and 17th cent.; occupied by French 1795–1813; in World War II center of city destroyed by German bombing May 14, 1940; largely reconstructed to new plan 1946–mid 1960's. 2 Urban community (unincorporated), Schenectady co., E New York, NW of Schenectady; pop. (1970c) 25,123.

Rotti. See ROTI.

Rot·tum·er·oog \ˈrȯt-ə-mə-ˌrōg\. Island in the North Sea 4 m. SW of Borkum; easternmost of the Dutch West Frisian Is.

Rott·weil \ˈrȯt-ˌvī(ə)l\. City, Baden-Württemberg, West Germany, on Neckar river 49 m. SSW of Stuttgart; pop. (1969e) 20,019; silk.

Ro·tu·ma \rō-ˈtü-mə\. Chief island of small group of eight islands in SW Pacific Ocean, lat. 12°30′S and long. 177°5′E, 220 m. NNW of Fiji; ab. 8 m. long, area 14 sq. m.; administratively part of Fiji 1881. Chief village Motusa. Original Rotumans were pure Polynesians. Discovered 1791.

Rouad, Île. See ARWAD.

Rou·baix \rü-ˈbā\. Manufacturing and commercial city, Nord dept., N France, 7 m. NE of Lille; pop. (1968c) 114,547; major center of French textile industry; dyeing plants, rubber and plastics factories; chartered 1469; textile industry developed in 19th cent.; suffered under German occupation 1914–18.

Rou·en \rü-ˈä^{n}, -ˈän\ *or anc.* **Ro·tom·a·gus** \rō-ˈtäm-ə-gəs\. Commercial and industrial city, ✱ of Seine-Maritime dept., N France, on right bank of Seine river 71 m. NW of Paris; pop. (1968c) 120,471; ships wine, grain, livestock, sugar, petroleum products; produces textiles, chemicals, soap, paper, brandy; shipyards, oil refineries, railroad shops; the principal river port of France. Has an exceptional number of notable buildings, including the 13th cent. Gothic cathedral, restored after heavy damage in World War II; 14th cent. Abbey of Saint Ouen (where Joan of Arc was sentenced to death 1431), 15th cent. church, late Gothic palace of justice, museum, and several medieval houses; univ. (1967).

History: Founded in pre-Roman times; taken and burned by Normans 9th cent. A.D.; medieval capital of Normandy; occupied by English 1418–49; Joan of Arc burned here 1431 (in Place de la Pucelle, named for her); taken by Huguenots 1562; occupied by Germans 1870; in World War II suffered heavy damage from Allied bombing; taken by Allies Aug. 31, 1944.

Rou·ergue \rü-ˈe(ə)rg\. Ancient province (until 1789) of S France, in region now comprising Aveyron dept. and a small part of Tarn-et-Garonne dept.; ✱ Rodez; medieval countship came eventually to Armagnac family; passed to crown 1472.

Rouffaer. See TARIKU.

Roufiás. See ALPHEUS.

Rouge \ˈrüzh\. River, SW Quebec, Canada; ab. 120 m. long; flows S and empties into the Ottawa river in SW Argenteuil co.

Roulers. See ROESELARE.

Roum. See RUM.

Roumania. See ROMANIA.

Roumelia. See RUMELIA.

Round Butte Dam. See UNITED STATES, *Dams and Reservoirs.*

Round·house Rock \ˈrau̇nd-ˌhau̇s-\. Peak, Cheyenne co., W Nebraska; 4255 ft.

Round Lake Beach. Village, Lake co., NE Illinois, W of Waukegan; pop. (1970c) 5717.

Round Lake Park. Village, Lake co., of NE Illinois, 12 m. W of Waukegan; pop. (1970c) 3148.

Round Rock. Town, Williamson co., cen. Texas, 18 m. N of Austin; pop. (1970c) 2811; lime, cheese; diversified agriculture.

Round·top \ˈrau̇n(d)-ˌtäp\. 1 Mountain, Scotts Bluff co., W Nebraska; 4419 ft.
2 Elevation, Tioga co., N Pennsylvania; 2030 ft.

Round Top. Elevation comprising Little Round Top and Big Round Top, forming a granite spur at S end of Cemetery Ridge (*q.v.*), Gettysburg, Pennsylvania; vantage point held by Union forces on second and third days of battle of Gettysburg.

Round·up \ˈrau̇nd-ˌəp\. City, ⊗ of Musselshell co., cen. Montana, 45 m. N of Billings; pop. (1970c) 2116.

Round·way Down \ˌrau̇n-dwā-\. Hill near Devizes, Wiltshire, SW England; 796 ft.; Parliamentary forces under Sir William Waller defeated here by Royalists 1643.

Rour·ke·la *or* **Raur·ke·la** \rȯr-ˈkā-lə\. Town, Orissa, India, ab. 140 m. NW of Cuttack; pop. (1961c) 90,287; iron and steel plant.

Rou·say \ˈrau̇-zē\. One of the Orkney Is., off N coast of Scotland; 5¼ m. long by 4½ m. wide.

Rous·es Point \ˈrau̇s-əz-\. Village and port of entry, Clinton co., NE corner of New York, at the upper end of Lake Champlain at Canadian border 21 m. N of Plattsburg; pop. (1970c) 2250.

Rous·sil·lon \ˌrü-sē-ˈ(y)ō^{n}\. Historical region of S France, bounded anciently on N by Languedoc, on S by the Pyrenees, on W by Andorra, on NW by Countship of Foix; ✱ Perpignan (12th cent. ff.). Inhabited originally by Iberians; made part of Roman Gallia Narbonensis (see GAUL); began separate existence at beginning of 10th cent.; united to Aragon 1172; acquired by Louis XIV 1659 (Treaty of the Pyrenees); province of France under ancien régime.

Routt \ˈrau̇t\. County in Colorado. See table at COLORADO.

Rou·ville \ˈrü-ˌvil\. County, Quebec, Canada. See table at QUEBEC.

Rou·vroy \rü-ˈvrwä\. Commune, Pas-de-Calais dept., N France, 9 m. NE of Arras; pop. (1962c) 9653; coal mines.

Roux \ˈrü\. Commune, Hainaut prov., SW Belgium, NW suburb of Charleroi; pop. (1969e) 10,339.

Rou·yn \ˈrü-ən, rü-ˈwa^{n}\. Mining city, Timiskaming co., SW Quebec, Canada, 240 m. NW of Ottawa and on railroad N of Lake Timiskaming; pop. (1971p) 17,804; center of copper-mining and gold-mining district, Coll. Classique de Rouyn (1948); founded 1922, incorporated as a city 1948.

Ro·va·nie·mi \ˈrō-vən-ˌē-ə-mē\. City, ✱ of Lappi prov., Finland, ab. 100 m. N of Oulu; pop. (1970e) 27,774; founded 1929.

Ro·va·to \rō-ˈvä-tō\. Commune, Brescia prov., Lombardy, N Italy, 12 m. WNW of Brescia; pop. (1968e) 12,674.

Ro·ven·ki \ˈrȯv-ən-kē\. Town, Voroshilovgrad Oblast, Ukrainian S.S.R., U.S.S.R., ab. 34 m. S of Voroshilovgrad; pop. (1969e) 60,000.

Ro·ve·re·to \ˌrō-və-ˈrāt-(ˌ)ō\ *or Ger.* **Ro·freit** \ˈrō-ˌfrīt\. Commune, Trento prov., Trentino-Alto Adige, N Italy, on

ə abut; ᵊ kitten, Fr. table; ər further; a back; ā bake; ä cot, cart; å Fr. bac; au̇ out; ch chin; e less; ē easy; g gift
i trip; ī life; j joke; k̲ Ger. ich, Buch; ^{n} Fr. vin; ŋ sing; ō flow; ȯ flaw; œ Fr. bœuf; œ̄ Fr. feu; ȯi coin; th thin
t̲h̲ this; ü loot; u̇ foot; u̧e Ger. füllen; ue̅ Fr. rue; y yet; ^{y} Fr. digne \dēn^{y}\, nuit \nw^{y}ē\; yü few; yu̇ furious; zh vision

Adige river 13 m. SSW of Trent; pop. (1968e) 28,015; tourism; silk, wood products, paper; 14th cent. walls, art and historical collections; World War I museum. Scene of Napoleon's victory over the Austrians Aug. 15, 1796; scene of Austrian and Italian operations in World War I.

Rove Tunnel \'rōv-, 'rȯv-\ *or Fr.* **Sou·ter·rain du Rove** \sü-ter-aⁿ-dǖ-rȯv\. Tunnel, Bouches-du-Rhône dept., SE France, in the hills NW of Marseilles; 4½ m. long, 59 ft. wide, and 50 ft. high; provides a sea-level passageway for the Marseilles-Rhone canal.

Ro·vi·a·na \ˌrō-vē-'än-ə\. Lagoon. See NEW GEORGIA 2.

Ro·vi·go \rō-'vē-(ˌ)gō\. 1 Province of Veneto, NE Italy. See table at ITALY.

2 Commune, its ✻, 36 m. SW of Venice; pop. (1968e) 48,240; center of agricultural region; 16th cent. church, museum; first mentioned 838; came under Venice 1482; to Austria 1797; became part of Italy 1866.

Ro·vinj \'rō-ˌvēn-yə\; *Ital.* **Ro·vi·gno** \rō-'vēn-(ˌ)yō\ *or* **Rovigno d'I·stria** \-'dēs-trē-ə\. Manufacturing seaport commune, Istria Penin., Croatia, NW Yugoslavia, on Adriatic Sea 17 m. NNW of Pula; formerly in Italy.

Rov·no \'rȯv-nə\ *or Pol.* **Rów·ne** \'rüv-(ˌ)nā\ *or Ger.* **Row·no** \'rȯv-(ˌ)nō\. Industrial town, ✻ of Rovno Oblast, Ukrainian S.S.R., U.S.S.R., ab. 110 m. NE of Lvov; pop. (1970p) 116,000; railroad junction; produces machinery, building materials, leather goods, soap, canned meat. Formerly in Poland; occupied by Soviet troops in 1939 and by Germans 1941–44.

Rovno Oblast \-'ó-bləst, -ˌblast\. Subdivision of the Ukrainian S.S.R., U.S.S.R.; 7761 sq. m.; pop. (1970p) 1,048,000; ✻ Rovno; sugar beet; timber working.

Rovuma. See RUVUMA 1.

Row·an *Ky.* 'raů-ən, *N.C.* 'rō-ˌan\. Name of counties in two states of the U.S. See tables at KENTUCKY and NORTH CAROLINA.

Ro·way·ton \rō-'wāt-ᵊn\. Subdivision of town and city of Norwalk, Connecticut. See NORWALK 3.

Row·lett \'raů-lət\. City, Dallas co., NE Texas; pop. (1970c) 2579.

Row·ley \'raů-lē\. Town, Essex co., NE corner of Massachusetts, 22 m. ENE of Lowell; pop. (1970c) 3040; settled 1638; said to be site of first fulling mill in America.

Równe *or* **Rowno.** See ROVNO.

Row·ter, Mount \-'raů-tər\. Peak, Gunnison co., W cen. Colorado; 13,750 ft.

Ro·xas \'rō-ˌhäs\ *or formerly* **Ca·piz** \'kä-ˌpēs\. Chartered city, ✻ of Capiz prov., Panay I., Phil.; pop. (1970e) 69,400; trades in rice.

Rox·boro \'räks-ˌbər-ə, -ˌbə-rə\. 1 City, ⊗ of Person co., N North Carolina, 27 m. N of Durham; pop. (1970c) 5370; aluminum products; diversified agriculture.

2 Town, Montreal and Jesus Islands co., S Quebec, Canada, 8 m. W of Montreal; pop. (1971p) 7654.

Rox·burgh \'räks-ˌbər-ə, -ˌbə-rə, -b(ə-)rə\ *or* **Rox·burgh·shire** \-ˌshi(ə)r, -shər\. County, SE Scotland; 665 sq. m.; pop. (1971p) 41,942; ⊗ Jedburgh; rivers Teviot, Tweed; mountainous region; chief industry sheep raising; manufactures tweed cloth, woolen hosiery.

Rox·bury \'räks-ˌber-ē, -b(ə-)rē\. 1 Residential district, S Boston, Massachusetts; formerly a city, became part of Boston 1868; founded 1630.

2 Town, Delaware co., S New York, 18 m. E of Delhi; pop. (1970c) 2252; birthplace of John Burroughs and Jay Gould.

Rox·en, Lake \-'rȯk-sən\. Lake, SE Sweden, bet. Lake Vättern and the Baltic Sea; ab. 16 m. long; Linköping is near its S shore.

Ro·xo, Cape \-'rō-(ˌ)shü\. Point on W coast of Africa, at S end of coast of Senegal, 12°20'N, 16°43'W.

Roy \'rȯi\. 1 Village, Harding co., NE New Mexico, 58 m. NNW of Tucumcari; pop. (1970c) 476.

2 City, Weber co., NE Utah, SW of Ogden; pop. (1970c) 14,356; agriculture.

Roy·al, Mount \-'rȯi(-ə)l\ *or Fr.* **Mont Royal** \mōⁿ-rwä-yál\. A height in center of Montreal city, Quebec, Canada; 769 ft.

Roy·ale \rwä-'yal\. One of the Safety Is. (*q.v.*).

Royale, Isle. See ISLE ROYALE.

Royal Gorge. Scenic gorge in the Grand Canyon of the Arkansas river just W of Canon City, S cen. Colorado; 4½ m. long; its red granite walls rise sheerly more than 1000 ft. Railroad runs through bottom of gorge; gorge crossed by Royal Gorge Suspension Bridge 1053 ft. above the Arkansas river, completed 1929.

Royal Leamington Spa. Municipal borough, England. See LEAMINGTON.

Royal Oak. City, Oakland co., SE Michigan, 12 m. N of Detroit; pop. (1970c) 86,238; residential suburb of Detroit.

Royal Society Range. Mountain range, Antarctica, ab. 77°55'S, N Victoria Land.

Royal Tsavo National Park. See TSAVO NATIONAL PARK.

Roy·an \rwä-'yäⁿ\. Commune, Charente-Maritime dept., W France, on Atlantic Ocean at mouth of the Gironde; pop. (1968c) 17,292; seaside resort; in World War II largely destroyed by bombing 1945.

Roye \'rwä\. Town, Somme dept., N France, 18 m. N of Compiègne; pop. (1962c) 5106; battles Mar. 1917 and Aug. 27, 1918.

Roy·ers·ford \'rȯi-ərz-fərd\. Borough, Montgomery co., SE Pennsylvania, on Schuylkill river 27 m. NW of Philadelphia; pop. (1970c) 4235; tools, steel forgings.

Royes·ville *or* **Roys·ville** \'rȯiz-ˌvil\. Town, W Liberia, W Africa, just NW of Monrovia on the coast.

Roys·ton \'rȯi-stən\. 1 City, Franklin, Hart, and Madison cos., NE Georgia, NE of Athens; pop. (1970c) 2428.

2 Urban district, West Riding, Yorkshire, N England; pop. (1971p) 8839.

Roysville. See ROYESVILLE.

Roy·ton \'rȯit-ᵊn\. Urban district, Lancashire, NW England, 9 m. NE of Manchester; pop. (1971p) 20,319.

Ro·ze·wie, Cape \-rȯ-'zē-vyə\ *or Ger.* **Cape Rix·höft** \-'riks-ˌhə(r)ft\. Cape projecting into the Baltic Sea on coast of Poland just W of base of Hel Penin.

Rózsahegy. See RUŽOMBEROK.

Rrë·shen \'rə-shən\. Town, ✻ of Mirditë prov., N cen. Albania; pop. (1967e) 1146.

Ruacana Falls. See CUNENE.

Ruaha. See GREAT RUAHA.

Ru·a·ha National Park \rů-'ä-(ˌ)hä-\. National park, Tanzania; 5000 sq. m.; habitat for wildlife, incl. elephant, lion, ostrich, zebra; established 1964.

Ruanda. See RWANDA.

Ru·an·da–Urun·di \rü-än-də-ů-'rün-dē\ *also* **Belgian East Africa.** Former Belgian trust territory, cen. Africa; 20,916 sq. m.; ✻ Usumbura; comprised two districts, Ruanda (now Rwanda) in N, Urundi (now Burundi) in S; formerly part of German East Africa; ceded to Belgium 1919 as mandatory of the League of Nations; united administratively with Belgian Congo 1925–60; made a U.N. trust territory Dec. 1946; divided 1962 into two independent countries, Rwanda and Burundi. See RWANDA and BURUNDI.

Ru·a·pe·hu \ˌrü-ə-'pā-(ˌ)hü\. Volcano, S cen. North I., New Zealand, in Tongariro National Park; 9175 ft.

Ru·a·pu·ke \ˌrü-ə-'pü-kē\. Small island at E end of Foveaux Strait off S coast of South I., New Zealand.

Rub' al-Kha·li \ˌrůb-al-'käl-ē\ *or* **Ar Ri·mal** \ˌər-rə-'mal\ *or Eng.* **Great Sandy Desert.** Desert region, S Arabian Penin., extending S from Nejd (Saudi Arabia) to Hadhramaut (Yemen, ✻ Aden), and from NE border of Yemen (✻ San'a) to Oman; ab. 250,000 sq. m.; only partly explored. Sometimes also called **Dah·na** \'da-(hə-)nə\ *or* **Da·ha·na** \'da-hə-nə\, a name which is more correctly restricted to the area of red sand in NE Nejd which sends a narrow tongue down into the S desert.

Ru·bezh·no·ye \rů-'bezh-nə-yə\. Town, Voroshilovgrad Oblast, Ukrainian S.S.R., U.S.S.R., ab. 50 m. NW of Voroshilovgrad; pop. (1969e) 54,000.

Rubi. See RUVO DI PUGLIA.

Ru·bi·con \'rü-bi-ˌkän\ *or* **Ru·bi·co·ne** \ˌrü-bə-'kō-nə\. Small river, N cen. Italy; flows E into Adriatic Sea in lat. 44°10'N just N of Rimini; with the Apennines, formed boundary bet. Italy and Cisalpine Gaul in the time of the ancient Roman republic. Its crossing in 49 B.C. by Julius Caesar with his army began a civil war against Pompey and the senate.

Ru·bi·doux, Mount \-ˌrü-bi-'dü\. Rocky height, Riverside, Riverside co., SE California; has on its top a cross dedicated to memory of Junípero Serra, Spanish missionary to the Indians; Easter sunrise services.

Rub·tsovsk \'rüpt-ˌsófsk\. Town, Altai Krai, Russian S.F.S.R., U.S.S.R., ab. 80 m. NE of Semipalatinsk; pop. (1970p) 145,000.

Ru·by \'rü-bē\. Village, W cen. Alaska, on S bank of the Yukon, ab. 240 m. W of Fairbanks; pop. (1970c) 145; river port and gold mines.

Ruby Dome. See RUBY MOUNTAINS.

Ruby Lake. Lake in S Elko co. and N White Pine co., NE Nevada.

Ruby Mountains. Range chiefly in S Elko co., NE Nevada, extending S into White Pine co.; highest peak **Ruby Dome,** Elko co., 11,387 ft.

Rück·er, Mount \-'rů-kər\. Mountain, Antarctica, 78°11'S, 162°32'E; 12,520 ft.

Ruda. See RODA.

Ru·da Śląs·ka \ˌrü-də-'shlōⁿ-skə\. Mining commune, Katowice prov., S Poland, just E of Zabrze; pop. (1970p) 142,000.

Rud·kø·bing \'rü-ˌkə(r)-biŋ\. Town, Fyn co., on W coast of Langeland I., Denmark; pop. (1970e) 7069.

Rud·nik Mountains \ˌrüd-nik-\. Low mountain range in N Serbia, NE Yugoslavia; highest peak 3714 ft.; scene of battle in which Serbians defeated Austrians in the "Battle of the Ridges" Dec. 1914.

Rud·ny \'rüd-nē\. Town, Kustanai Oblast, Kazakh S.S.R., U.S.S.R., ab. 25 m. SW of Kustanai; pop. (1969e) 97,000.

Ru·dolf, Lake \-'rü-ˌdälf\. Lake, N Kenya, E Africa; 154 m. long and 10 to 20 m. wide; area 2473 sq. m.; N tip is bet. Ethiopia and SE Sudan.

Ru·dolph \'rü-ˌdälf\. Island, northernmost of Franz Josef Land, Russian S.F.S.R., U.S.S.R., in Arctic Ocean; Soviet base and meteorological station.

Ru·dol·stadt \'rüd-ᵊl-ˌs(h)tät\. Manufacturing city, Gera dist., East Germany, on Saale river 18 m. S of Weimar; pop. (1970e) 31,539; hardware, chemicals, porcelain.

Ru·eil–Mal·mai·son \rů-'ā-ˌmal-mā-'zōⁿ\. Industrial commune, Hauts-de-Seine dept., N France, on Seine river 8 m. W of Paris; pop. (1968c) 60,804; manufactures automobiles, chemical products, photographic supplies, foundry products; tombs of Empress Josephine and Queen Hortense.

Ru·fi·ji \rü-'fē-jē\. Navigable river, E Africa; ab. 175 m. long; rises in S cen. Tanzania; flows NE and E into Indian Ocean opp. island of Mafia.

Ru·fisque \rü-'fēsk\. Commune, W Senegal, W Africa, near Dakar and 10 m. E of Cape Vert; pop. (1967e) 60,000; leather goods, cement, vegetable oils; commercial fisheries, titanium mines.

Rug·by \'rəg-bē\. 1 City, ® of Pierce co., N cen. North Dakota, 65 m. E of Minot; pop. (1970c) 2889; diversified agriculture. Determined by the Geological Survey to be the geographic center of North America.

2 Municipal borough, Warwickshire, cen. England, on the Avon 28 m. ESE of Birmingham; pop. (1971p) 59,372; railroad junction and livestock market; machinery, electrical equipment; site of Rugby School, opened 1574 and chartered 1777.

Ruge·ley \'rüj-lē\. Urban district, Staffordshire, W cen. England, 9 m. SE of Stafford; pop. (1971p) 22,234; iron founding, coal mining.

Rü·gen \'rü-gən, 'rē-\. Island in the Baltic Sea, part of Rostock dist., East Germany, opp. Stralsund; largest island of East Germany; 358 sq. m.; chief town Bergen. Separated by the narrow Strelasund from the mainland and connected by ferry with Stralsund. Chief industry fishing. Seized by the Danes 1168; united with Pomerania 1325 and with Sweden 1648; became part of Prussia 1815.

Ruhr \'rů(ə)r\. River, West Germany; 146 m. long; flows NW and W and joins the Rhine at Ruhrort (a part of Duisburg); navigable to Witten, ab. 30 m. The **Ruhr·ge·biet** \'rür-gə-ˌbēt\, the valley of the Ruhr, is a mining region and includes many major industrial cities, as Essen, Bochum, Duisburg, Gelsenkirchen, Dortmund, etc. In World War I the district was of great military importance; at end of war occupied Jan. 1923 to July 1925 by France and Belgium because of Germany's default in reparations. In World War II bombed severely and continuously 1942–45; in Allied advance into Germany 1945 surrounded and cut off Mar.–Apr.; occupied and cleared by Apr. 18.

Ru–i–khaf. See KHUĀF.

Rui·vo, Pi·co \ˌpē-(ˌ)kü-rü-'ē-(ˌ)vü\. Volcanic peak on the island of Madeira; 6106 ft.; highest point in the Madeira Is.

Ruiz \rü-'ēz, -'ēs\. Peak in the Andes Mts., in Tolima dept., W cen. Colombia; 17,716 ft.

Ru·ki \'rü-kē\. River, NW Zaire, S cen. Africa; ab. 250 m. long; flows W into the Congo river at Mbandaka at the equator; has several long tributaries, esp. the Busira.

Ruk·wa, Lake \-'rək-wə\. Shallow lake, SW Tanzania, E Africa; ab. 20 m. long.

Rum \'rüm\ *or* **Roum** \'rüm\ *also* **Ico·ni·um** \ī-'kō-nē-əm\. Arabic name used indefinitely by Muslims for the people of the Byzantine Empire — from *Rōmaivi,* Romans, the name the Byzantine Greeks applied to themselves; hence: (1) That part of the Byzantine Empire in Asia Minor. (2) Later, the Seljuk sultanate ab. 1200, occupying most of Asia Minor. Its capital was Iconium.

Rum, Isle of *or* **Isle of Rhum** \-'rəm\. Island of the Inner Hebrides, off W coast of Scotland; 8 sq. m.; administratively a part of Inverness co.; chiefly a deer preserve.

Rum, Sound of. Channel bet. Isle of Rum and Eigg I. in the Inner Hebrides, off W coast of Scotland.

Ru·ma \'rü-mə\. Commune, Serbia, NE Yugoslavia, 35 m. NW of Belgrade; pop. (1965e) 21,000.

Rumadiya. See RAMADI.

Rumania. See ROMANIA.

Rum Cay \'rəm-'kē, -'kā\. One of the Bahama Is., in the Atlantic Ocean SSW of San Salvador (Watlings I.); 30 sq. m.; pop. (1963c) 77.

Ru·me·lange \ˌrüm-(ə-)'läⁿzh\ *or Ger.* **Rü·me·ling·en** \'rüm-ə-ˌliŋ-ən\. Commune, Grand Duchy of Luxembourg, in extreme S on French border SE of Esch.

Ru·me·lia *also* **Rou·me·lia** \rü-'mēl-yə, -'mē-lē-ə\. European division (*Turk.* Rumeli, the land of the Romans or Byzantines, sometimes called **Ro·ma·nia** \rō-'mā-nē-ə, -nyə\) of the old Turkish empire; included Albania, Macedonia, and Thrace. See EASTERN RUMELIA.

Ru·me·li Hi·sa·ri *or* **Ru·me·li·hi·sa·rı** \ˌrü-mə-'lē-ˌhis ə 'rē\. Village, W Turkey, on W bank of the Bosporus 7 m. NE of İstanbul of which it is a suburb; has fortifications with tower, built by Mohammed II 1452.

Rum·ford \'rəm(p)-fərd\. Town, Oxford co., W Maine, 35 m. NNW of Lewiston; pop. (1970c) 9363; paper.

Ru·mia \'rů-mē-ə, -myə\. Town, Gdańsk prov., N Poland, ab. 20 m. NNW of Gdańsk; pop. (1970p) 23,200.

Rummel. See KÉBIR, OUED AL-.

Ru·moi \rü-'mȯi\. Seaport, Hokkaidō prefecture, W coast of Hokkaidō, Japan, 65 m. N of Sapporo; pop. (1970c) 38,-691.

Rum·son \'rəm(p)-sən\. Borough and summer resort, Monmouth co., E cen. New Jersey, 16 m. SE of Perth Amboy; pop. (1970c) 7421; yachting center.

Run·a·way, Cape \-'rən-ə-ˌwā\. Cape on NE coast of North I., New Zealand, at E side of entrance to the Bay of Plenty.

Run·corn \'rəŋ-kərn\. Urban district, Cheshire, NW England, on the Mersey 10 m. ESE of Liverpool; pop. (1971p) 35,953; terminus of the Bridgewater Canal; boatbuilding, chemical manufacture; ironworks.

Rung·we \'rüŋ-(ˌ)wā\. Volcanic peak, SW Tanzania, E Africa, N of Lake Nyasa; 9713 ft.

Run·nels \'rən-əlz\. County in Texas. See table at TEXAS.

Run·ne·mede \'rən-ē-ˌmēd\. Residential borough, Camden co., SW New Jersey, 7 m. S of Camden; pop. (1970c) 10,475; settled by Quakers 1683.

Run·ny·mede \'rən-ē-ˌmēd\. Meadow on S bank of the Thames in Surrey, S England, near Egham, W of Staines; Magna Carta signed here by King John June 15, 1215; in the river off the meadow is Magna Charta I., popularly considered to be site of the signing.

Ru·pan·co, La·go \ˌläg-ō-rü-'päŋ-(ˌ)kō\. Lake, Osorno prov., S cen. Chile, N of Puerto Montt; 25 m. long by 4 m. wide.

Ru·pat *or Du.* **Roe·pat** \'rü-ˌpät\. Island of Indonesia, in the Strait of Malacca off E coast of Sumatra.

Ru·pel \rü-'pel\. Stream, N cen. Belgium; ab. 7 m. long; formed by confluence of the Dijle and Nethe rivers, flows NW into the Schelde 8 m. SW of Antwerp.

Rupella. See LA ROCHELLE.

Rupel Pass \'rü-pəl-\. Mountain pass, valley of Struma river, Macedonia, NE Greece; used by Germans in invasion of Greece Apr. 1941.

Ru·pert \'rü-pərt\. 1 City, ⊗ of Minidoka co., S Idaho, on Snake river 40 m. E of Twin Falls; pop. (1970c) 4563; in dairy and livestock farming region.
2 River, W Quebec, Canada; 380 m. long; flows out of Lake Mistassini W into James Bay at Rupert House.

Rupert's Land. See PRINCE RUPERT'S LAND.

Rup·pert Coast \ˌrü-pərt-, ˌrüp-ərt-\. Section of Antarctica on coast of Marie Byrd Land E of Edward VII Penin. ab. 75°45′S, extending 140°30′W to 147°W.

Ru·pu·nu·ni \ˌrü-pə-'nü-nē\. River, Guyana; ab. 250 m. long; rises in SW and flows N and E into Essequibo river.

Rur *or Du.* **Roer** \'rü(ə)r\. River, W Europe; 129 m. long; rises in the Hohe Venn Mts., Belgium, and flows through North Rhine-Westphalia, West Germany to the Meuse at Roermund in the Netherlands; fighting along its banks in World War II, esp. near Düren and Jülich; dam near source blown up Feb. 1945, delaying Allied advance.

Rurki. See ROORKEE.

Ru·ru·tu \rü-'rü-tü\. See TUBUAI ISLANDS.

Rusaddir. See MELILLA.

Ru·se \'rü-(ˌ)sā\; *Turk.* **Rus·chuk** *also* **Rus·tchuk** \'rüs-'chük\. 1 Province of N Bulgaria. See table at BULGARIA.
2 City, its ✱, on Danube river, ab. 155 m. NE of Sofia; pop. (1968e) 145,295; major industrial center producing textiles, rubber goods, agricultural machinery, electrical equipment, plastics; tanning, shipbuilding; founded as Roman fortress 2d cent. A.D.; destroyed in 7th cent.; developed industrially after 1878.

Rusein, Piz. See TÖDI.

Rusellae. See GROSSETO.

Rush \'rəsh\. Name of counties in two states of the U.S. See tables at INDIANA and KANSAS.

Rush·den \'rəsh-dən\. Urban district, Northamptonshire, cen. England, 14 m. ENE of Northampton; pop. (1971p) 20,136; footwear.

Rush·more, Mount \-'rəsh-ˌmō(ə)r, -ˌmȯ(ə)r\. Peak in Black Hills, W South Dakota, NE of Harney Peak; 5600 ft.; faces of Washington, Lincoln, Jefferson, and Theodore Roosevelt, carved 1927–41 under direction of Gutzon Borglum, constitute **Mount Rushmore National Memorial.**

Rush·ville \'rəsh-ˌvil\. 1 City, ⊗ of Schuyler co., W Illinois, 45 m. ENE of Quincy; pop. (1970c) 3300.
2 City, ⊗ of Rush co., E cen. Indiana, 40 m. ESE of Indianapolis; pop. (1970c) 6686; furniture, automobile parts, canned goods; hogs.
3 City, ⊗ of Sheridan co., NW Nebraska; pop. (1970c) 1137; grain, stock, and dairy farms.

Rusk \'rəsk\. 1 Name of counties in two states of the U.S. See tables at TEXAS and WISCONSIN.
2 Town, ⊗ of Cherokee co., E Texas, 28 m. E of Palestine; pop. (1970c) 4914; oil wells; truck farms.

Rusk, Mount. Peak in the Catskill Mts., Greene co., SE New York; 3680 ft.

Ruspina. See MONASTIR 1.

Russ. See NEMAN.

Rus·sell \'rəs-əl\. 1 Name of counties in four states of the U.S. See tables at ALABAMA, KANSAS, KENTUCKY, VIRGINIA.
2 City, ⊗ of Russell co., cen. Kansas, 37 m. N of Great Bend; pop. (1970c) 5371; oil wells; grain farms.
3 City, Greenup co., NE Kentucky, on Ohio river 5 m. NNW of Ashland; pop. (1970c) 1982.
4 County, Ontario, Canada. See table at ONTARIO.
5 Borough, N North I., New Zealand, on Bay of Islands 115 m. NNW of Auckland; old whaling port; has oldest buildings in New Zealand; site first chosen 1840 as future capital of colony but soon relinquished for Auckland.

Russell, Mount. Peak in Sierra Nevada in W Inyo co., E California; 14,086 ft.

Russell Cave National Monument. See UNITED STATES, *National Monuments.*

Russell Islands. Group of small islands 30 m. NW of Guadalcanal I., SE cen. Solomon Is., W Pacific Ocean; part of British Solomon Is. protectorate; occupied by U.S. troops Feb. 21, 1943.

Russell Springs. City, ⊗ of Logan co., W Kansas; pop. (1970c) 83.

Rus·sell·ville \'rəs-əl-ˌvil\. 1 City, ⊗ of Franklin co., NW Alabama, 20 m. S of Wilson Dam and Tennessee river; pop. (1970c) 7814; clothing, aluminum; cotton.
2 City, ⊗ of Pope co., NW cen. Arkansas, near Arkansas river 64 m. NW of Little Rock; pop. (1970c) 11,750; furniture, footwear; coal mines; Arkansas Polytechnic Coll. (1909).
3 City, ⊗ of Logan co., S Kentucky, 35 m. E of Hopkinsville; pop. (1970c) 6456; coal mines; tobacco, poultry, dairy farms.

Rüs·sels·heim \'rü-səls-ˌhīm\. City, Hesse, West Germany, on the Main river 7 m. E of Mainz; pop. (1969e) 55,373.

Rus·sia \'rəsh-ə\ *or Russ.* **Ros·si·ya** \rä-'sē-yə\. 1 Former empire, E Europe and N and W Asia; ✱ St. Petersburg (Leningrad); its territories (except for Finland and Kars) now comprise the Union of Soviet Socialist Republics (U.S.S.R.). For geographical description see UNION OF SOVIET SOCIALIST REPUBLICS.

History: Region settled by eastern Slavs 3d–8th cents. A.D.; entered from north in 9th cent. by Varangians (Scandinavians) who established Novgorod and Kiev (*qq.v.*) and traded from Baltic to Black Sea; Kiev lost supremacy to independent principalities, such as Suzdal and Vladimir; invaded 1224 and conquered 1237–40 by Mongols; Tatar Khanate of the Golden Horde, capital at Sarai, levied tribute on all Russia; in 14th–15th cents. princes of Moscow (*q.v.*) rose to lead and began defeat of Tatars and subjugation of rival principalities; under Ivan IV 1533–84, first tsar, Russia conquered Astrakhan and Kazan and pushed into Siberia; under Romanov dynasty 1613–1917; in war with Poland 1654–67 wrested part of Ukraine to middle Dnieper; in Great Northern War 1700–21, Peter I (the Great) secured "window" on Baltic (see BALTIC PROVINCES); annexed Lithuania and rest of Ukraine as share of partitions of Poland 1772–95; spread to northern coast of Black Sea bet. Dnieper and Dniester 1774 and 1792;

acquired Finland 1809; acquired Bessarabia 1812; invaded by French 1812; annexed Georgia, Dagestan, and other territory in Caucasus 1813; received most of grand duchy of Warsaw 1815; Russian southward advance against Ottoman Empire of key importance to Europe (see CRIMEAN OBLAST); Chinese cession of left bank of Amur and of Ussuri, 1858 and 1860, marked active policy in Far East; sold Alaska (*q.v.*) to U.S. 1867; in Central Asia advanced to borders of Afghanistan (*q.v.*); secured Sakhalin 1875, rights in Liaotung Penin. 1895 and Kwantung 1898; defeated in war with Japan 1904–05, Russia lost hold in Manchuria; unsuccessful revolution 1905; Russian foreign policy, dictated by its vital interest in Balkans and the Straits, brought her into World War I on side of Allies 1914–17; overthrew tsarist regime Mar. 1917; set up government of soviets Nov. 1917 after Bolshevist revolution. For history after 1917, see UNION OF SOVIET SOCIALIST REPUBLICS.

2 Popularly the name for the Union of Soviet Socialist Republics.

Rus·sian \ˈrəsh-ən\. River, NW California; ab. 100 m. long; rises in cen. Mendocino co. and flows S into Sonoma co. and then W into the Pacific Ocean.

Russian America. See ALASKA.

Russian Island. See RUSSKI.

Russian Poland. See POLAND 1.

Russian River. See RUSSIAN.

Russian So·vi·et Federated Socialist Republic \-ˈsōv-ē-ˌet-, -ˈsäv-, -ē-ət-\. The largest constituent republic of the U.S.S.R. (76% of the total area); extends from Baltic Sea to Pacific Ocean; 6,592,812 sq. m.; pop. (1970p) 130,090,-000; ✱ Moscow. *Physical features:* Its mountains include the entire Ural range and the various ranges of E Siberia, and its highest peaks are in Kamchatka; in Europe it contains the great plain of the Volga and Northern Dvina, in Asia the valleys of the Ob, Yenisei, Lena, and Amur; in the N in both continents is the belt of tundra, farther S extensive forests, steppes, and fertile areas. *Chief products:* Wheat, flax, sugar beet; livestock; coal, iron ore, copper, nickel, manganese, lead, zinc, platinum, oil; manufacturing: chemicals, textiles, motor vehicles, iron and steel; accounts for ab. 57% of Soviet industrial production. *Chief cities:* Moscow, Leningrad, Gorki, Novosibirsk, Kuibyshev, Sverdlovsk.

History: As the main part of former tsarist empire was first to come under control of Soviets Nov. 7, 1917; its first constitution adopted July 10, 1918; joined other soviet republics 1922 to form Union of Soviet Socialist Republics (*q.v.*). See also RUSSIA and SIBERIA.

Russian Turkistan. See TURKISTAN.

Rus·ski \ˈrüs-kē, ˈrəs-\ *or Eng.* **Rus·sian Island** \ˈrəsh-ən-\. Island bet. Amur Bay and Ussuri Bay, Russian S.F.S.R., U.S.S.R., just S of Vladivostok.

Russki Za·vo·rot \-ˌzä-və-ˈrōt\. Cape on NE coast of Arkhangelsk Oblast, Russian S.F.S.R., U.S.S.R.; 68°58′N, 54°34′E; on E shore of Barents Sea N of Pechora delta.

Rus·ta·vi \rü-ˈstä-vē\. Town, Georgian S.S.R., U.S.S.R., ab. 15 m. SE of Tbilisi; pop. (1969e) 102,000.

Rustchuk. See RUSE.

Rus·ten·burg \ˈrəs-tən-ˌbərg\. Town, SW cen. Transvaal, NE Rep. of South Africa, on branch of Limpopo river ab. 70 m. W of Pretoria; pop. (1967e) 32,500; grows fruit, tobacco, and cotton.

Rus·ton \ˈrəs-tən\. City, ⊗ of Lincoln parish, N Louisiana, 33 m. W of Monroe; pop. (1970c) 17,565; dairy products, lumber, chemicals, fertilizer; diversified agriculture; Louisiana Polytechnic Institute (1894).

Rut·ba \ˈrüt-bə\ *also* **Rutba Wells** *or* **Ar Ruṭ·bah** \är-ˈrüt-bə\. Town, W Iraq, on Wadi Hauran in the Syrian Desert; a junction of highways from the Euphrates to the Mediterranean coast; police and radio station.

Ru·te \ˈrü-tə\. Commune, Córdoba prov., S Spain, 45 m. SSE of Córdoba; pop. (1970p) 11,205; marble and jasper quarries.

Ruth \ˈrüth\. Town, White Pine co., E Nevada, ab. 3 m. W of Ely; pop. (1970c) 800.

Ru·the·nia \rü-ˈthē-nyə, -nē-ə\. Former autonomous region, later a province of Czechoslovakia, now constitutes Transcarpathian Oblast, Ukrainian S.S.R., U.S.S.R. See TRANSCARPATHIAN OBLAST.

Ruth·er·ford \ˈrət͟h-ə(r)-fərd, ˈrəth-\. 1 Name of counties in two states of the U.S. See tables at NORTH CAROLINA and TENNESSEE.

2 Borough, Bergen co., NE corner of New Jersey, 7 m. SSE of Paterson; pop. (1970c) 20,802; residential suburb of New York City; Fairleigh Dickinson Univ. (1942).

Ruth·er·ford·ton \ˈrət͟h-ə(r)-fərd-tən\. Town, ⊗ of Rutherford co., SW North Carolina, in Blue Ridge Mts. on edge of piedmont plateau 25 m. W of Shelby; pop. (1970c) 4180; textiles; fruit and truck farms.

Ruth·er·glen \ˈrət͟h-ər-ˌglen\. Burgh, Lanark co., S cen. Scotland, on the Clyde 3 m. SE of Glasgow; pop. (1971p) 24,728; paper, chemicals, textiles, furniture; made royal burgh 1126.

Ruth·in \ˈrüt͟h-ən, ˈrith-in\. Municipal borough, ⊗ of Denbighshire, N Wales; pop. (1971p) 4331; beverages; site of castle attacked by Owen Glendower 1400; 14th cent. church of St. Peter.

Ruth Mountain \ˈrüth-\. Peak, cen. Whatcom co., NW Washington; 6800 ft.

Ruth Siple, Mount. See SIPLE, MOUNT.

Ruthven. See KINGUSSIE.

Ruth·well \ˈrət͟h-ˌwel, -wəl\. Village, S Dumfries co., S Scotland, on Solway Firth; site of Ruthwell Cross, 18 ft. high, having runic inscriptions.

Ru·ti·glia·no \ˌrü-tə-ˈlyä-nō\. Commune, Bari prov., Apulia, SE Italy, 11 m. SE of Bari; pop. (1968e) 13,507; Norman church.

Rutlam. See RATLAM.

Rut·land \ˈrət-lənd\. 1 County in Vermont. See table at VERMONT.

2 Town, Worcester co., cen. Massachusetts, 12 m. NW of Worcester; pop. (1970c) 3198.

3 Industrial city, ⊗ of Rutland co., W Vermont, 22 m. E of Poultney river entrance on Lake Champlain; pop. (1970c) 19,293; commercial and transportation center in a summer and winter resort region; produces aircraft parts, plywood, gloves, machinery; marble quarries; Coll. of Saint Joseph the Provider (1957). Chartered by New Hampshire 1761; settled 1770; meeting place of Vermont legislature 1784–1804; made city 1892; suffered heavy damage in flood June 3, 1947.

4 Small island off S point of South Andaman I., Andaman Is., Bay of Bengal; separated from Little Andaman I. by Duncan Passage; part of the Indian territory of Andaman and Nicobar Is.

5 County in England. See RUTLANDSHIRE.

Rut·land·shire \ˈrət-lən(d)-ˌshi(ə)r, -shər\ *or* **Rutland.** County, E cen. England; 153 sq. m.; pop. (1971p) 27,463; ⊗ Oakham; Welland river flows along SE border; agriculture and livestock raising, iron mining.

Rut·ledge \ˈrət-lij\. Town, ⊗ of Grainger co., NE Tennessee; pop. (1970c) 863.

Rüt·li \ˈrüt-lē\ *or* **Grüt·li** \ˈgrüt-\. Meadow in Uri canton, cen. Switzerland, where the first League of the Three Forest Cantons (Uri, Schwyz, and Unterwalden) was formed 1291.

Rutupiae. See RICHBOROUGH.

Ru·vo di Pu·glia \ˌrü-vōd-i-ˈpül-yə\ *or anc.* **Ru·bi** \ˈrü-ˌbī\. Commune, Bari prov., Apulia, SE Italy, 9 m. W of Bari; pop. (1968e) 23,269; 13th cent. cathedral; ancient town noted for its ceramic art 5th–2d cents. B.C.

Ru·vu \ˈrü-(ˌ)vü\. River, Tanzania, E Africa; the lower course of the Pangani (*q.v.*).

Ru·vu·ma \rü-ˈvü-mə\. **1** *or Port.* **Ro·vu·ma** \rü-ˈvü-mə\. River, SE Africa; ab. 450 m. long; rises in S Tanzania, flows E, forming boundary bet. Tanzania and Mozambique; has important headstreams in both Tanzania and Mozambique; empties into Indian Ocean N of Cape Delgado.

2 Administrative region of S Tanzania. See table at TANZANIA.

Ru·wan·diz \rü-ˈwan-diz\ *or* **Ra·wan·dūz** \rə-ˈwän-dəz\. Town in mountains of Kurdistan, NE Iraq, 80 m. ENE of Mosul; on the highway from the Tigris to Tabrīz.

Ru·wen·zo·ri, Mount \-ˌrü-(w)ən-ˈzōr-ē, -ˈzȯr-\. Mountain group in cen. Africa, bet. Lake Albert and Lake Edward and on the boundary bet. Uganda and Zaire; central peak Mount Stanley (known in Zaire as **Mount Nga·li·e·ma** \-eŋ-ˌgäl-ē-ˈā-mə\), with two summits, Mt. Margherita 16,763 ft. and Mt. Alexandra 16,750 ft.; discovered by Stanley 1889; identified with Ptolemy's "Mountains of the Moon."

Ru·wer \ˈrü-vər\. Short stream, W Rhineland-Palatinate state, West Germany; ab. 25 m. long; flows into the Mosel below Trier; in wine-producing region.

Ru·žom·be·rok \ˌrüzh-ȯm-ˈber-ˌȯk\ *or Hung.* **Ró·zsa·hegy** \ˈrō-(ˌ)zhȯ-ˌhej\ *or Ger.* **Ro·sen·berg** \ˈrōz-ᵊn-ˌbe(ə)rg\. Town, Slovak S.R., E cen. Czechoslovakia, on the Váh 118 m. NE of Bratislava; pop. (1968e) 21,127.

Rwan·da *or formerly* **Ru·an·da** \rü-ˈän-də\. Republic, E cen. Africa, bounded on N by Uganda, on E by Tanzania, on S by Burundi, and on W and NW by Zaire; 10,169 sq. m.; pop. (1970e) 3,736,000; ✻ Kigali; most of country lies at an alt. of over 5000 ft.; highest peak Karisimbi 14,787 ft. *Chief products:* Sorghum, corn, beans, cassava, coffee; livestock; cassiterite, wolfram. Formerly part of the Belgian trust territory of Ruanda-Urundi (*q.v.*); achieved independence 1962.

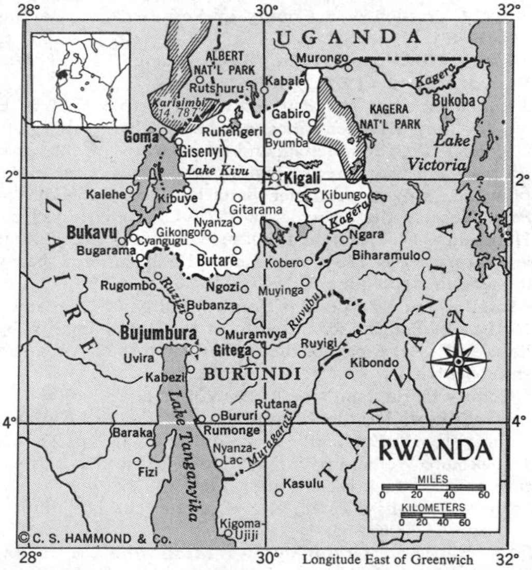

Ry·an, Loch \läk-ˈrī-ən, läk-\. Inlet, Wigtown co., Galloway, on SW coast of Scotland; extends S inland ab. 9 m. with the town of Stranraer at its head; fine harbor.

Ryan Peak. Mountain, S Custer co., cen. Idaho; 11,794 ft.

Rya·zan *also* **Ria·zan** \ˌrē-ə-ˈzan(-yə)\. **1** Medieval principality, cen. Russia, SE of Moscow; ✻ Old Ryazan; included Murom to the NE and Kolomna on the Moskva. A border state of warlike inhabitants, involved in almost continuous conflict; became subject to Moscow in 14th cent.

2 City, ✻ of Ryazan Oblast, Russian S.F.S.R., U.S.S.R., on right bank of Oka river 120 m. SE of Moscow; pop. (1970p) 357,000; produces agricultural machinery, radios, machine tools, leather goods; sawmills, oil refinery.

History: Town of **Old Ryazan,** capital of the principality, founded (11th cent.) on site ab. 30 m. SE; lost importance after destruction by Tatars 1237. Replaced as capital in 15th cent. by **Pe·re·ya·slav–Rya·zan·ski** \ˌper-ə-ye-ˈsläf-ryə-ˈzän-skē\, which came under Moscow 1521 and took present name 1778.

Ryazan Oblast \-ˈō-bləst, -ˌblast\. Subdivision of cen. Russian S.F.S.R., U.S.S.R., crossed by Oka river; 15,290 sq. m.; pop. (1970p) 1,412,000; ✻ Ryazan. Level, well-watered area, with many lakes and some forest areas, chiefly agricultural, growing grain, sugar beets, vegetables, flax, and tobacco; industries mainly concerned with food processing; only large town is Ryazan; established as oblast 1937.

Ry·bache \ri-ˈbach-(y)ə\. Town, N Kirgiz S.S.R., U.S.S.R., at W end of Issyk-Kul; pop. (1967e) 28,000.

Ry·ba·chi Peninsula \ri-ˌbäch-ē-\ *also* **Ri·ba·chi Peninsula** \rī-ˈbä-chē-\. Irregular land projection, extending into Barents Sea on NW coast of Murmansk Oblast, Russian S.F.S.R., U.S.S.R., N of Kola Bay and Murmansk and NE of Pechenga; ab. 17 m. wide; its base touches the former Finnish boundary line.

Ry·binsk \ˈrib-ən(t)sk\ *or formerly* **Shcher·ba·kov** \ˌsh(ch)er-bə-ˈkȯv\. City, Yaroslavl Oblast, Russian S.F.S.R., U.S.S.R., on right bank of Volga; pop. (1970p) 218,000; engineering industries.

Rybinsk Reservoir *also* **Sea of Rybinsk.** Large lake, N cen. Russian S.F.S.R., U.S.S.R., for the greater part in NW Yaroslavl Oblast; 1757 sq. m.; formed (completed in 1941) by damming waters of upper Volga; on N receives the Suda and Sheksna rivers; formerly the world's largest man-made lake.

Ryb·nik \ˈrib-nik\. Coal-mining and manufacturing commune, Katowice prov., S Poland, 20 m. SW of Katowice; pop. (1970p) 43,400; tools; iron foundries, coal mines.

Ry·dal \ˈrīd-ᵊl\. Village, Westmorland, NW England, on **Rydal Water,** a small lake just E of Grasmere; site of Rydal Mount, home of Wordsworth from 1813 to 1850; 2 m. NW of the village are the **Rydal Falls.**

Ryde \ˈrīd\. Municipal borough on Isle of Wight, S England, in English Channel 6 m. SW of Portsmouth; pop. (1971p) 23,171; seaside resort.

Rye \ˈrī\. **1** Town, Rockingham co., SE New Hampshire, on Atlantic Ocean 4 m. S of Portsmouth; pop. (1970c) 4083; includes summer resort of **Rye Beach.**

2 Residential city in town of Rye, Westchester co., SE New York, on Long Island Sound 24 m. NE of New York; pop. (1970c) 15,869 (city), 43,234 (town); founded 1660; organized as town of Connecticut before settlement of border line in 1700. **Rye Beach** nearby; home of John Jay.

3 Municipal borough, East Sussex, S England; pop. (1971p) 4434; tourism; market town; incorporated 1289; one of the Cinque Ports (*q.v.*).

Rye·gate \ˈrī-ˌgāt\. Town, ⊗ of Golden Valley co., cen. Montana; pop. (1970c) 261.

Rye House. Village, Hertfordshire, SE England, 2 m. from Ware; site of remains of the manor house (Rye House) at which a conspiracy to kill Charles II and James, Duke of York, is alleged to have been made. Lord William Russell and Algernon Sidney were implicated and executed.

Ryezhitsa. See REZEKNE.

Ry·ma·nów \ri-ˈmän-ˌüf\. Commune, Rzeszów prov., SE Poland, ab. 35 m. SW of Rzeszów; pop. (1966e) 3316; Greek Catholic episcopal see; spa and summer resort in foothills of Carpathian Mts.; produces petroleum; formerly in U.S.S.R.

Ryojun. See PORT ARTHUR.

Ryssel. See LILLE.

Ryswick. See RIJSWIJK.

Ry·sy \'ri-sē\. Peak in Carpathian Mountains, S Poland; 8197 ft.; highest mountain in Poland.

Ry·ton \'rīt-ᵊn\. Urban district, Durham, N England, on the Tyne 6 m. W of Newcastle upon Tyne; pop. (1971p) 14,831.

Ryu·kyu Islands *also* **Riu·kiu Islands** \rē-'(y)ü-(ˌ)k(y)ü-\ *or* **Nan·sei Islands** \ˌnän-ˌsā-\; *Jap.* **Ryukyu Ret·to** \-'re-(ˌ)tō\; *also* **Lu·chu Islands** *or* **Loo·choo Islands** \ˌlü-ˌchü-\. Island chain, W Pacific Ocean, extending in a 600-mile-long arc between Taiwan and Kyūshū, Japan; includes Sakishima, Okinawa, and Amami island groups; 848 sq. m.; pop. (1970c) 945,111; chief town Naha on Okinawa I.; highest point in N, a volcano 3215 ft. on Nakano Shima in Tokara Is. (part of Amami group).

History: Came under political influence of China 1372; became tributary to Japan as well as China 1451 and Japanese protectorate 1609; integral part of Japan by 1879; under the Japanese the Amami group belonged to Kagoshima prefecture and the Okinawa and Sakishima groups constituted Okinawa prefecture; after World War II placed under U.S. military government 1945; received native civil government 1951 but remained under U.S. occupation except for the Amami group, which was returned to Japan Dec. 1953; received local self-government 1966; returned to Japan 1972.

Rze·szów \'zhesh-ˌüf\. 1 Province of SE Poland. See table at POLAND.
2 Industrial commune, its ✱, ab. 95 m. E of Kraków; pop. (1970p) 82,200; textiles, metal goods, railway rolling stock, canned foods; made town mid-14th cent.; under Austrian rule 1772–1918.

Rzhev \ər-'zhef, rə-'zhef, -'zhev\. City, S Kalinin Oblast, Russian S.F.S.R., U.S.S.R., on both banks of upper Volga 125 m. WNW of Moscow; pop. (1969e) 59,000; railroad junction; lumber, dairy products, building materials; first mentioned 1216 and formerly ✱ of an independent princedom; came under rule of Moscow 1390; in World War II occupied by Germans Oct. 1941–Mar. 1943.

Sa·ad·a·bad \'säd-ə-ˌbäd, sä-'äd-ə-ˌbäd\. Suburb of Tehran, Iran; royal palace; nonaggression pact signed here July 9, 1937 by Turkey, Iran, Iraq, and Afghanistan.

Saadani. See SADANI.

Saa·le \'zäl-ə, 'säl-\. River, Europe; 265 m. long; rises in the Fichtelgebirge range, NE Bavaria, West Germany, and flows N into the Elbe river 18 m. SE of Magdeburg, East Germany.

Saale, Frän·ki·sche \ˌfreŋ-ki-shə-'zäl-ə\. River, Bavaria, West Germany; ab. 70 m. long; rises in the Rhön Mts., flows SW into Main river NW of Würzburg.

Saal·feld \'zäl-ˌfelt\ *also* **Saalfeld an der Saa·le** \-än-dər-'zäl-ə\. Manufacturing city, Gera dist., East Germany, on Saale river 29 m. SSE of Erfurt; pop. (1970e) 33,405; iron and steel, electrical equipment, paper products; present town founded c. 1200.

Saa·ne \'zän-ə\ *or Fr.* **Sa·rine** \sə-rēn\. River, SW Switzerland; 80 m. long; rises in Bernese Alps, flows N through Fribourg canton and into Aare river 10 m. WNW of Bern.

Saar \'sär, 'zär\ *or Fr.* **Sarre** \sår\. **1** River, Moselle dept., France, and Saarland and Rhineland-Palatinate, West Germany; 75 m. long; flows N and NNW across German border to the Mosel (Moselle) just above Trier. In World War II severe fighting on its banks Dec. 1944–Jan. 1945. **2** State, West Germany. See SAARLAND.

Saar·brück·en \zär-'bru̇k-ən, sär-, -'brik-\ *or Fr.* **Sar·re·bruck** \sår-ə-brüek\. Industrial city, ✱ of Saarland, West Germany, on Saar river on Franco-German frontier ab. 39 m. SE of Trier; pop. (1970c) 127,989; major center of iron and steel industry; also produces optical instruments, cement, sugar, beer, pottery; printing, coal mining; 18th cent. castle, 18th cent. town hall, 13th cent. Gothic church; univ. (1948).

History: First mentioned 999; received charter 1321; under Counts of Nassau-Saarbrücken 1381–1793; to France 1793–1815; to Prussia 1815. After World War I made capital of government of the Saar estab. by League of Nations; returned to Germany by plebiscite Mar. 1, 1935 and made capital of Saarland state; in World War II heavily bombed by Allies and scene of major fighting Feb.–Mar. 1945; largely rebuilt since war.

Saarburg. See SARREBOURG.

Saa·re·maa *or* **Sa·re·ma** \'sär-ə-ˌmä\ *or Ger.* **Oe·sel** \'ə-zəl\. Island in E Baltic Sea off W coast of Estonian S.S.R., U.S.S.R., and NW of Gulf of Riga; 1050 sq. m.; livestock raising, fishing. Conquered by Teutonic Knights of the Sword 1227, governed by its own bishops until 1561; held by the Danes, then passed to Sweden 1645; as part of Livonia was united to Russia 1721 and became part of Estonia 1918. In World War II seized by Germans 1941 but recovered in 1944.

Saargemünd. See SARREGUEMINES.

Saar·land \'sär-ˌland, 'zär-\ *or* **Saar·ge·biet** \-gə-ˌbēt\ *also* **Saar** \'sär, 'zär\ *or Fr.* **Sarre** \sår\. A state of West Germany; 991 sq. m.; pop. (1970e) 1,127,000; ✱ Saarbrücken; iron and steel, chemicals, glass; coal mining.

History: Became part of France 1766 but by Treaty of Paris 1815 divided between Prussia and Bavaria; by Treaty of Versailles 1919 coal mines assigned to France and territory placed under administration of the League of Nations; returned to Germany by plebiscite 1935; after World War II assigned to French occupation zone, became united economically to France; became a state of West Germany 1957.

Saar·lou·is \zär-'lü-ē, sär-; ˌsär-lə-'wē, -'lwē\ *or from 1936 to 1945* **Saar·lau·tern** \sär-'lau̇t-ərn, zär-\. Manufacturing commune, Saarland, West Germany, on left bank of the Saar 11 m. WNW of Saarbrücken; pop. (1969e) 36,312; founded 1681 by Louis XIV; birthplace of Marshal Ney; much bombed during World War II.

Saaz. See ŽATEC.

Sa·ba \'säb-ə\. Island, NE West Indies, in Leeward Is. 16 m. NW of St. Eustatius; 5 sq. m.; pop. (1969e) 972; ✱ Leverock (popularly, the Bottom); part of Netherlands Antilles; an extinct volcano, its coasts are sheer cliffs ab. 2800 ft. high; first occupied by Dutch 1632.

Ṣaba *or* **Saba'.** see SHEBA.

Ša·bac \'shäb-ˌäts\. Town, Serbia, Yugoslavia, 40 m. W of Belgrade on Sava river; pop. (1965e) 32,000; trade center and river port; founded in 15th cent.

Sa·ba·dell \ˌsäb-ə-'del(-yə)\. Manufacturing commune, Barcelona prov., NE Spain, 8 m. N by W of Barcelona; pop. (1970p) 159,408; ships agricultural products, wine, oil; manufactures cotton, wool, and silk textiles, iron, paper, leather, china.

Sa·bae \sə-'bä-ē\. City, Fukui prefecture, Honshū, Japan, 13 m. S of Fukui; pop. (1970c) 52,614.

Sa·bah \'säb-(ˌ)ä\; *formerly* **British North Bor·neo** \-'bȯr-nē-ˌō\ *also* **North Borneo.** A state of Malaysia, NE island of Borneo, SE Asia; 29,545 sq. m.; pop. (1970p) 655,622; ✱ Kota Kinabalu. Almost all mountainous with highest ranges parallel with W coast (highest mountain Kinabalu, 13,455 ft., highest on island of Borneo); cut by open river valleys, esp. the Kinabatangan and Labuk in the E; has coastline of 900 m. bordering on South China Sea, Sulu Sea, and Celebes Sea; much indented by bays, esp. on E coast; coconuts, rice, rubber, timber; chief towns: Sandakan, Kota Kinabalu, Kudat.

History: English attempts at settlement in 17th and 18th cents. unsuccessful; first concessions in North Borneo granted to Sir James Brooke (see SARAWAK 1) 1841; new concessions granted by Sultans of Brunei and Sulu to British North Borneo Company, chartered in 1881; territory proclaimed British protectorate 1888 but continued to be administered by company until World War II. Occupied by Japanese Dec. 17, 1941; recovered in part by British in last months of war. Became a British colony 1946 and a state of Malaysia 1963.

Sa·ba·ki \sə-'bäk-ē\. River, SE Kenya, E Africa; ab. 120 m. long; formed by confluence of Athi and Tsavo rivers, flows E into Indian Ocean.

Sa·ba·lān \ˌsä-bə-'län\ *or* **Sa·va·lan** \-və-\. Peak, East Azerbaijan prov., NW Iran, ab. 85 m. E of Tabrīz; 15,784 ft.

Sa·ba·na Archipelago \sə-ˌbän-ə-\. Group of islands off N coast of Las Villas prov., W cen. Cuba.

Sabana Gran·de \-'gränd-ē\. Town and municipality, SW Puerto Rico; pop. (1970p) 5556 (town), 16,031 (munic.); town is 24 m. WNW of Ponce.

Sa·ba·na·lar·ga \sə-ˌbän-ə-'lär-gə\. Town, Atlántico dept., N Colombia, 30 m. S of Barranquilla; munic. pop. (1968e) 38,452.

Sa·bang \'sä-ˌbäŋ\. Seaport on the island of We off N Sumatra, Indonesia; pop. (1960e) 10,000; good harbor, with considerable trade; held by Japanese 1942–45 but frequently bombed by Allies 1944–45.

Sabanilla *or* **Sabanilla del Encomendadoro.** See JUAN GUALBERTO GOMEZ.

Sa·ba·ri \'səb-ə-rē\. River, E cen. India; ab. 130 m. long; rises in S Orissa and flows SW along SE boundary of Madhya Pradesh into Godavari river in N Andhra Pradesh.

Sabaria. See SZOMBATHELY.

Sa·bar Kan·tha \ˌsəb-ər-'kən-tə\. Formerly a political agency of the Western India States Agency; 5408 sq. m.; was in N Gujarat and comprised the states of the former Banas Kantha and Mahi Kantha Agencies.

Sa·bar·ma·ti \ˌsäb-ər-'mət-ē\. River, W India; ab. 250 m. long; rises in the Aravalli Range in Rajasthan, flows S into the head of Gulf of Cambay, W of the mouth of Mahi river.

Sabastīyah. See SAMARIA 2.

Sabatinus. See BRACCIANO, LAKE.

Sa·bau·dia \sä-'bau̇d-yə\. Town, Latina prov., SW Latium, cen. Italy, on the coast N of Monte Circeo; pop. (1968e) 9917; built on reclaimed land in Agro Pontino.

Sabbioncello. See PELJESĂC.

Sa·be·ta Peak \sə-ˌbāt-ə-\. Mountain, Chaffee co., cen. Colorado; 13,600 ft.

Sa·betha \sə-'beth-ə\. City, Nemaha co., NE Kansas, 43 m. NW of Atchison; pop. (1970c) 2376.

Sabhah. See SEBHA.

Sa·bi Game Preserve \ˌsäb-ē-\. See KRUGER NATIONAL PARK.

Sa·bi·nal Cay \ˌsäb-ə-'näl-'kē, -'kā\. Island off NE coast of Camagüey prov., E cen. Cuba, in the Camagüey Archipelago.

Sa·bi·nas \sä-'bē-nəs\. 1 River, Mexico. See SALADO 2.
2 Town, Coahuila state, NE Mexico, on Sabinas river 70 m. SW of Piedras Negras; munic. pop. (1970p) 30,726.

Sabinas Hi·dal·go \-ē-'däl-(ˌ)gō\. Town, Nuevo León state, NE Mexico, 55 m. N of Monterrey; pop. (1960c) 11,592.

Sa·bine \sə-'bēn\. 1 Navigable river, E Texas and W Louisiana; 360 m. long; drains an area of 9733 sq. m.; formed by confluence of forks in Hunt co., NE Texas, flows SE to Louisiana border, forming S section of Texas-Louisiana boundary, and empties through Sabine Lake and Sabine Pass into the Gulf of Mexico; has two large reservoirs.
2 Parish in Louisiana and county in Texas. See tables at LOUISIANA and TEXAS.

Sabine, Cape. Point on E coast of Ellesmere I., N Canada, extending into Smith Sound; here part of Greely's expedition perished 1884.

Sabine, Mount. Peak in Admiralty Mts., Victoria Land, Antarctica, 71°55′S, 169°33′E; 12,198 ft.

Sabine Crossroads. Hamlet, DeSoto parish, Louisiana, ab. 40 m. S of Shreveport; battle Apr. 8, 1864 in which Union forces under Gen. Banks were defeated.

Sabine Lake. Lake bet. Louisiana and Texas, 5 m. from the Gulf of Mexico, formed by expansion of Sabine river, which flows through it and Sabine Pass to the Gulf of Mexico.

Sabine–Nech·es Waterway \-'nā-chəz-\. System of waterways at Port Arthur, Texas; includes the ship canal at Port Arthur, Sabine Pass, and the **Sabine–Neches Canal** which comprises the Neches river as far as Beaumont and the Sabine river as far as Orange; part of the Gulf Intracoastal Waterway.

Sabine Pass. Outlet for Sabine river extending from Sabine Lake to Gulf of Mexico on boundary bet. Louisiana and Texas.

Sabiya'. See SABYA, AṢ.

Sab·khat al–Kur·zī·yah \'säb-ˌkät-al-ku̇r-'zē-ə\ *or* **Seb·kret el Kour·zia** \'seb-ˌkret-el-'ku̇r-zē-ə\. Saline lake, N cen. Tunisia, W of Zaghouan; scene of fighting Apr. and May 1943.

Sabkhat Tāwurghā'. See SEBCHA DI TAUORGA.

Sa·ble, Cape \-'sā-bəl\. 1 Cape at SW tip of Florida penin. in Monroe co., enclosing Whitewater Bay, 25°12′N, 81°05′W.
2 Southern point of Cape Sable I., SW Nova Scotia, Canada, 43°25′N, 65°45′W.

Sable Island. Low, sandy island, Nova Scotia, Canada, in North Atlantic Ocean 115 m. SE of Cape Canso, 43°55′N, 59°50′W; ab. 20 m. long and 1 m. wide, the exposed part of a sand bar along W edge of Gulf Stream. Dangerous to navigation and the scene of more than 200 recorded wrecks; has been equipped with two lighthouses (one dismantled 1948), life-saving station, and radio.

Sables–d'Olonne, Les. See LES SABLES-D'OLONNE.

Sa·blé–sur–Sarthe \sa-'blā-sü(ə)r-'särt\. Commune, SW Sarthe dept., NW France, on the Sarthe; pop. (1962c) 7367; 14th–16th cent. castle, restored.

Sab·ra·ta \'sab-rə-tə\ *or* **Sab·ra·tha** \-thə\ *or* **Abrot·o·num** \ə-'brät-ᵊn-əm\. Ancient town, Roman Africa, on coast 48 m. W of Tripoli; founded 4th cent. B.C. by Carthaginians; one of three chief cities of Tripolis (see TRIPOLI 1); remains include Roman and Byzantine fortifications, temples, forum, theater, two Christian basilicas.

Sa·bra·ton \'sā-brə-tən\. Former industrial town, Monongalia co., West Virginia; annexed to Morgantown 1949; site of Thomas Decker's settlement (founded 1758, destroyed by Mingo Indians 1759).

Sabrina. See SEVERN 4.

Sa·bri·na Coast \sə-'brī-nə-, -'brē-\. Section of coast of Wilkes Land, Antarctica, on Indian Ocean at ab. 67°S, bet. 117° and 119°30′E; probably first seen 1839 by British navigator John Balleny.

Sab·tang \säb-'täŋ\. Island, most southerly of Batan Is., N Phil.; 13 sq. m.

Sa·bya, Aṣ \as-'sab-ē-ə, -'sab-yə\ *or* **Sa·bi·ya'** \'sab-ē-(y)ə\. City, Saudi Arabia, near Yemen (✱ San'a) border, at foot of mountain range ab. 40 m. inland from Red Sea.

Sab·za·war \ˌsab-zə-'vär\. Town, W Afghanistan, on highway 75 m. S of Herāt.

Sab·ze·vār \ˌsab-zə-'vär\. Town, Khorāsān prov., NE Iran, 110 m. W of Mashhad; pop. (1971e) 45,000; on the highway to Tehran.

Sac \'sȯk\. County in Iowa. See table at IOWA.

Sac·an·da·ga \ˌsak-ən-'dȯ-gə\. River, E New York; ab. 50 m. long; rises in Piseco Lake and flows SE through Great Sacandaga Reservoir into the Hudson river in N Saratoga co.

Sa·ca·te·pé·quez \ˌsäk-ə-tə-'pāk-es\. Department of S cen. Guatemala. See table at GUATEMALA.

Sac·ca·rel·lo \ˌsäk-ə-'rel-(ˌ)ō\. Mountain, NW Italy, on boundary bet. Liguria and Piedmont; 7216 ft.; highest point in the Ligurian Alps.

Sac City \'sȯk-\. City, ⊗ of Sac co., W Iowa, 43 m. W of Fort Dodge; pop. (1970c) 3268; livestock, dairy farms.

Sac·co \'säk-(ˌ)ō\. River, cen. Italy; flows SE, joins the Liri S of Frosinone.

Să·ce·le \'sə-che-le\. Town, Braşov co., cen. Romania, ab. 5 m. ESE of Braşov; pop. (1970e) 23,933.

Sach·seln \'zäk-səln\. Commune, Unterwalden canton, cen. Switzerland, near Sarnen; pop. (1970c) 3059; nearby is birthplace of Nicholas of Flüe.

Sachsen. See SAXONY.

Sachsen–Coburg und Gotha. See SAXE-COBURG-GOTHA.

Sächsische Schweiz. See SAXON SWITZERLAND.

Sa·ci·le \sä-'chē-lē\. Commune, Pordenone prov., Friuli-Venezia Giulia, NE Italy, 23 m. NE of Udine; pop. (1968e) 15,085; 15th cent. cathedral.

Sack·ets Harbor \ˌsak-əts-\. Village and summer resort, Jefferson co., N New York, on Lake Ontario 11 m. WSW of Watertown; pop. (1970c) 1202; settled 1801; during War of 1812, when it served as U.S. naval station, scene of several engagements.

Säck·ing·en \'zek-iŋ-ən\. Town, SW Baden-Württemberg, Germany, on the Rhine E of Basel; site of monastery founded by Saint Fridolin in 6th cent.; scene of Scheffel's poem *Der Trompeter von Säckingen* (1853).

Sack·ville \'sak-(ˌ)vil\. Industrial town, Westmorland co., SE New Brunswick, Canada, 25 m. SE of Moncton and near the Nova Scotia boundary; pop. (1971p) 3176; paper products, footwear; diversified agriculture; Mount Allison Univ. (1839).

Sa·co \'sȯ-(ˌ)kō\. 1 River, E cen. New Hampshire and SW Maine; 104 m. long; rises in White Mts. W of Mt. Washington, NE cen. New Hampshire, flows S and SE across Maine border and SE into Atlantic Ocean 6 m. below Saco, York co., SW Maine.
2 Residential city, York co., SW Maine, on Saco river just N of Biddeford; pop. (1970c) 11,678.

ST

Sacralias. See ZALLAKA.

Sac·ra·men·to \ˌsak-rə-ˈment-(ˌ)ō\. 1 River, NW California; ab. 320 m. long; rises near Mt. Shasta in Siskiyou co., and flows S into Suisun Bay, E extension of San Francisco Bay; navigable for 180 m.

2 County in California. See table at CALIFORNIA.

3 City, ✱ of California and ⊗ of Sacramento co., N cen. California, on Sacramento river at the head of navigation 72 m. NE of San Francisco; pop. (1970c) 257,105; transportation center; market and commercial center for important truck- and fruit-farming region; produces jet fuels, soaps, machinery, brick, furniture; flour mills, rice polishing plants, almond shellers; Sacramento City Coll. (1916), Sacramento State Coll. (1947), American River Coll. (1955); three U.S. Air Force bases. Site settled 1839 by John Sutter; in California Gold Rush of 1840's an important trading center; made state capital 1854; W terminus of Pony Express 1860.

Sacramento Mountains. Range in S New Mexico, in Otero co. and extending N into Lincoln co. and E into Chaves and Eddy cos.; in center of region between the Pecos river and the Rio Grande; name sometimes includes range to the S known as Guadalupe Mts.

Sa·cri·fi·cios \ˌsäk-rə-ˈfis-ē-ˌōs\. Small island in the Gulf of Mexico, 3 m. S of the city of Veracruz, Mexico; a place of sacrifice under the Aztecs; contains remains of ancient temples.

Sacrum Promontorium. See CORSE, CAPE.

Sac·sa·hua·man \ˌsäk-sə-wə-ˈmän\. Ancient fortress of early Inca construction on a hill just N of Cuzco, Peru.

Sada, Cape. See ASHIZURI, CAPE.

Sá da Ban·dei·ra \ˌsä-də-ban-ˈde(ə)r-ə\. Inland town, SW Angola, SW Africa, ab. 95 m. ENE of Moçâmedes; met. area pop. (1960c) 15,129.

Sa·da·ni *or* **Saa·da·ni** \sä-ˈdä-nē\. Seaport, Tanzania, E Africa, opp. Zanzibar I.

Sad·dle \ˈsad-ᵊl\ *or* **Va·lua** \və-ˈlü-ə\. Island, one of the Banks Is. in the New Hebrides, W Pacific Ocean, NE of Vanua Lava, at 13°40′S, 167°40′E.

Sad·dle·back \ˈsad-ᵊl-ˌbak\ *or* **Blen·cath·a·ra** \blen-ˈkath-ə-rə\. Mountain, Cumberland, NW England, in the Lake District 4¼ m. NE of Keswick; 2847 ft.

Saddleback Mountain. 1 Peak, Franklin co., W Maine, near Rangeley Lakes; 4116 ft.

2 Peak in the Adirondack Mts., Essex co., NE New York; 4530 ft.

Saddle Brook. Urban township, Bergen co., NE New Jersey, E of Paterson; pop. (1970c) 15,975.

Saddle Mountain. 1 Peak on E boundary of Idaho co., N cen. Idaho; 8225 ft.

2 Peak, Clatsop co., NW corner of Oregon; 3283 ft.

3 Peak, S cen. Klamath co., S Oregon; 6976 ft.

4 Peak, E Yellowstone National Park, NW Wyoming; 10,670 ft.

Saddle Mountains. Range in S Kittitas and S Grant cos., cen. Washington.

Sad·dle·worth \ˈsad-ᵊl-ˌwərth\. Urban district, West Riding, Yorkshire, N England; pop. (1970p) 20,525.

Sa·di·ya \ˈsəd-ē-ə, -ē-yä\. Town, Arunachal Pradesh, NE India, ab. 575 m. NE of Calcutta. In World War II after the loss of the Burma Road (1942) it became the supply base for road building and the starting point for two new transportation routes to China.

Sa·do \ˈsäd-(ˌ)ō\. Mountainous island in E Sea of Japan, off NW coast of island of Honshū, Japan; 331 sq. m.; pop. (1960c) 84,404. Rice growing, fishing, tourism; in early times, a place of exile.

Sado \ˈsat͟h-(ˌ)ü\. River, S Portugal; 110 m. long; flows NW into Atlantic Ocean at Setúbal; wide estuary.

Saena Julia. See SIENA 2.

Sa·fad \ˈsä-(ˌ)fad\ *or* **Sa·fed** \-(ˌ)fed\ *or Hebrew* **Ze·fat** \ˈzef-(ˌ)ät\. City, N Israel, 7 m. NNW of the Sea of Galilee; pop. (1970e) 13,100; tourism. One of the four Jewish holy cities of Palestine; fortified by Flavius Josephus and later by Crusaders; seat of important school of medieval Jewish mysticism (Kabbala).

Safaqis. See SFAX.

Sa·fed Koh \sə-ˌfed-ˈkō\. Mountain range, E Afghanistan, SE of Kabul on Pakistan border, an offshoot of the Hindu Kush; its remarkable evenness of height presents appearance of towering wall; highest peak Mt. Sikaram 15,619 ft. Peiwar Pass is at W end.

Safe·ty Harbor \ˈsāf-tē-\. City, Pinellas co., W cen. Florida peninsula, N of St. Petersburg; pop. (1970c) 3103.

Safety Islands *or Fr.* **Îles du Sa·lut** \ēl-dᵫ-sȧ-lᵫ\. French group of three islands, Royale, Joseph, and Devil's I., in the Atlantic Ocean 7 m. off the N coast of French Guiana; used by France for a penal settlement until 1938.

Saffi. See SAFI.

Saf·ford \ˈsaf-ərd\. City, ⊗ of Graham co., SE Arizona, on Gila river; pop. (1970c) 5333.

Saf·fron Wal·den \ˌsaf-rən-ˈwȯl-dən\. Municipal borough, Essex, SE England, 40 m. NNE of London; pop. (1971p) 9945; saffron cultivation was an important occupation from 14th to 18th cents.

Sa·fi *or* **Saf·fi** \ˈsaf-ē\. Seaport, W cen. Morocco, NW Africa, SW of Casablanca; pop. (1960c) 81,072; sardine canneries, large chemical complex; ships fertilizer; old Portuguese citadel. Allies landed here Nov. 8, 1942.

Sa·fid Rud \sa-ˈfēd-ˈrüd\ *or* **Se·fid Rud** \se-ˈfēd-\. The Qezel Owzan (*q.v.*) river in its lower course.

Sa·fo·no·vo \sə-ˈfō-nə-vō\. Town, Smolensk Oblast, Russian S.F.S.R., U.S.S.R., ab. 50 m. ENE of Smolensk; pop. (1967e) 41,000.

Sa·ga \ˈsäg-(ˌ)ä\. 1 Prefecture, NW Kyūshū, Japan; 929 sq. m.; pop. (1970c) 838,468; ✱ Saga.

2 City, its ✱, near coast of Shimabara Bay 43 m. NE of Nagasaki; pop. (1970c) 143,454; textiles, ceramics.

Sag·a·da·hoc \ˌsag-əd-ə-ˈhäk\. 1 Early name for the Kennebec river, Maine. See KENNEBEC 1.

2 County in Maine. See table at MAINE.

Sa·gaing \sə-ˈgīŋ\. 1 Division, NW Upper Burma. See table at BURMA.

2 District, S Sagaing division, Upper Burma; 968 sq. m.; pop. (1962e) 379,392; ✱ Sagaing.

3 Town, ✱ of division and of district, on right bank of the Irrawaddy opp. Ava 10 m. W of Mandalay; formerly a capital of Burma; terminus of railroad to Myitkyina and port of call for river steamers.

Sa·ga·mi Sea \sə-ˈgäm-ē-\ *or Jap.* **Sagami–na·da** \-ˈnäd-ə\. Widemouthed bay on SE coast of Honshū, Japan, in Kanagawa prefecture SSW of Tokyo; scene of U.S. naval attack July 1945.

Sagan. See ŻAGAŃ.

Sa·gan·thit Island \ˌsäg-ən-ˈthēt-\ *or formerly* **Sel·lore Island** \sə-ˈlō(ə)r-, -ˈlȯ(ə)r-\. Island in Mergui Archipelago (*q.v.*), Burma.

Sa·gar \ˈsäg-ər\. 1 Island at the mouth of the Hooghly river, S West Bengal, NE India.

2 Town, India. See SAUGOR.

Sagauli. See SEGAULI.

Sa·gay \sä-ˈgī\. Municipality, NE Negros Occidental, Negros, Phil., on Visayan Sea 37 m. NE of City of Bacolod; pop. (1969e) 97,300.

Saghalien. See SAKHALIN.

Sag Harbor \ˈsag-\. Village, Suffolk co., SE New York, at E end of Long I., S of Shelter I., on Gardiners Bay 25 m. W of Montauk Point; pop. (1970c) 2363; seaside resort and yachting center; in mid-19th cent. an important whaling port.

Sag·i·naw \ˈsag-ə-ˌnȯ\. 1 Navigable river, cen. Michigan; 20 m. long; formed by confluence of the Flint and Shiawassee rivers, flows N into Saginaw Bay.

2 County in cen. Michigan. See table at MICHIGAN.

3 City, its ⊗, on Saginaw river 32 m. NNW of Flint; pop. (1970c) 91,849; port of entry, commercial and transportation center; produces automobile parts, graphite, mobile homes, paper products, malleable iron; in sugar beet and

bean farming region. Settlement developed around fur trading post founded 1816; chartered 1870; combined with East Saginaw (chartered 1859) to form Saginaw 1889.

Saginaw Bay. Inlet of Lake Huron on coast of E cen. Michigan, SE of Arenac co., E of Bay co., NW of Tuscola co., and W of Huron co.

Sa·go·ne, Bay of \-sə-ˈgō-nē\ *or Fr.* **Anse de Sa·gone** \ä^{n}s-də-sȧ-gȯn\. Inlet on W coast of Corsica, France, N of Ajaccio.

Sagra, La. See LA SAGRA.

Sagres. See SAINT VINCENT, CAPE 2.

Sagrus. See SANGRO.

Sa·guache \sə-ˈwäch\. **1** County in S Colorado. See table at COLORADO.

2 Town, its ⊗; pop. (1970c) 642.

Sa·gua de Tá·na·mo \ˌsäg-wə-də-ˈtän-ə-ˌmō\. Municipality, Oriente prov., E Cuba, near N coast 33 m. N of Guantánamo; pop. (1967e) 70,320.

Sagua la Gran·de \-lə-ˈgränd-ē\. **1** River, N Las Villas prov., W cen. Cuba; flows N.

2 Town and municipality, Las Villas prov., W cen. Cuba; munic. pop. (1967e) 47,610; town is railroad center 30 m. NNW of Santa Clara.

Sa·gua·ro Lake \sə-ˈ(g)wär-(ˌ)ō-\. See STEWART MOUNTAIN DAM.

Saguaro National Monument. See UNITED STATES, *National Monuments.*

Sag·ue·nay \ˌsag-ə-ˈnā\. **1** River, S Quebec, Canada; 105 m. long; flows from Lake St. John E into St. Lawrence river at Tadoussac; including the Peribonca river, ab. 475 m. long. Leaves Lake St. John by two channels, Big Discharge and Little Discharge, which enclose the island of Alma (see ALMA 7). Its fall 314 ft. is a source of hydroelectric power and its shores are in many places high cliffs 1000 to 1800 ft. Noted for its scenery, its boating and fishing, and as a summer resort region.

2 County, Quebec, Canada. See NEW QUEBEC and table at QUEBEC.

Sa·gui·et el Ham·ra \sə-ˌgē-ə-ˌtel-ˈham-rə\ *or* **Sa·guia El Hamra** *also* **Se·kia el Hamra** \sə-ˌgē-ə-ˌel-\. River, Spanish Sahara, NW Africa.

Sa·gun·to \sə-ˈgün-(ˌ)tō\ *or formerly* **Mur·vie·dro** \mu̇r-ˈvyā-(ˌ)drō\ *or anc.* **Sa·gun·tum** \sə-ˈgən-təm\. Commune, Valencia prov., E Spain, near Mediterranean 15 m. NNE of Valencia; pop. (1970p) 47,026; agricultural products, oil, wine; manufactures linen, brandies; garrisoned castle; ancient Roman theater and other Roman and Greek remains.

History: Settled by Greeks 3d cent. B.C.; allied with Rome; made famous heroic resistance to siege by Carthaginian forces under Hannibal 219–218 B.C.; made Roman municipium; captured by Moors 713 A.D.; reconquered by James of Aragon 1238; captured by French under Suchet 1808; end of republic proclaimed here 1874 and Bourbons, in person of Alfonso XII, restored to throne; medieval name (Murviedro) discarded in favor of earlier name (Sagunto) 1877.

Sa·ha·gún \ˌsä-hə-ˈgün\. Commune, León prov., Spain; pop. (1970p) 2661; ruins of Benedictine monastery; scene of start of Sir John Moore's retreat before Napoleon Dec. 1808.

Sahama. See SAJAMA.

Sa·hand, Kūh–e \ˌkü-(h)ē-sə-ˈhand\. Mountain, NW Iran, E of Lake Urmia and just S of Tabrīz; 12,105 ft.

Sa·hara \sə-ˈhar-ə, -ˈher-, -ˈhär-\ *or Arab.* **Sah·ra** \ˈsä-(ˌ)hrä\. Vast region of deserts and oases, N Africa; ab. 3,500,000 sq. m.; of varied surface and irregular relief, ranging from 100 ft. below sea level to more than 11,000 ft. above (in Tibesti region); extends from Atlas Mts. and Atlantic coast of Spanish Sahara E to Red Sea.

Saharan Atlas. See ATLAS MOUNTAINS.

Sa·ha·ran·pur \sə-ˈhär-ən-ˌpu̇(ə)r\. City, NW Uttar Pradesh, N India, 100 m. NNE of Delhi; pop. (1970e) 228,053; paper, sugar, railroad shops; woodworking; founded c. 1340.

Sa·hi·wal \ˈsä-(h)ē-ˌwäl, -ˌväl\ *or formerly* **Mont·gom·ery** \(ˌ)mən(t)-ˈgəm-(ə-)rē, män(t)-, -ˈgäm-\. **1** District, Multan division, Punjab, Pakistan; 4224 sq. m.; pop. (1961c) 2,134,072.

2 Town, its ✱, on Bari Doab Canal 92 m. SW of Lahore; pop. (1961c) 75,180; founded 1864.

Sahra. See SAHARA.

Sa·hua·yo \sə-ˈ(h)wī-(ˌ)ō\ *or in full* **Sahuayo de Por·fi·rio Dí·az** \-ˌdā-pȯr-ˌfir-ē-ō-ˈdē-ˌäs\. Municipality, Michoacán state, Mexico, 62 m. NW of Uruapan; pop. (1970p) 42,513; livestock and poultry raising; diversified agriculture.

Sai·bai \ˈsī-ˌbī\. Australian island off S coast of New Guinea I., WSW of Daru and on N side of Torres Strait.

Sa·ï·da \ˈsīd-ə\. **1** Department of NW Algeria. See table at ALGERIA.

2 Town, its ✱; pop. (1966c) 33,497.

3 Seaport, Lebanon. See SIDON.

Saïda Mountains. Branch range of the Atlas Mts., in Maritime Atlas, Saïda dept., NW Algeria; highest peak ab. 3870 ft.

Sai·dor \ˈsī-(ˌ)dȯr\. Coastal town, E coast of New Guinea I., Papua New Guinea, on Vitiaz Strait ab. 55 m. ESE of Madang; has good harbor; occupied by Allied troops Jan. 2, 1944.

Said·pur \ˈsīd-ˌpu̇(ə)r\. Town, N Bangla Desh, ab. 165 m. NNW of Dacca; pop. (1961c) 60,628.

Sai·gō \ˈsī-(ˌ)gō\. See OKI ARCHIPELAGO.

Sai·gon *or* **Sai Gon** \sī-ˈgän, ˈsī-ˌ\ *or Fr.* **Sa·ï·gon** \sȧ-ē-gō^{n}\. City, ✱ of South Vietnam and its principal port and commercial center, on **Saigon River** (a branch of the Dong Nai); pop. (1970e) 1,761,335; formerly an important rice-exporting port; laid out in French style with wide streets and numerous notable parks and public buildings; Univ. of Saigon (1954).

History: Captured by French 1859 and came under French administration 1862; chosen capital of South Vietnam after Geneva Convention of 1954; in Vietnam War a major military headquarters with extensive base facilities for U.S. and South Vietnamese ground and air forces; has been scene of numerous political demonstrations and riots during 1960's and also of a continuous campaign of terrorist activity by Communist elements; in 1968 was object of a large-scale assault by organized Communist forces and suffered considerable damage in the fighting.

Saihun. See SYR DARYA.

Sai·jō \ˈsī-ˌjō\. City, Ehime prefecture, Shikoku, Japan, 30 m. ENE of Matsuyama; pop. (1970c) 51,127.

Sai·kai National Park \ˈsī-ˌkī-\. National park, Kyūshū, Japan; 94 sq. m.; subtropical forests, dendritic coastline; established 1955.

Sa·i·ki \sä-ˈē-kē\. City, Ōita prefecture, Kyūshū, Japan, 25 m. S of Ōita; pop. (1970c) 50,698.

Sai·la·na \sī-ˈlän-ə\. Former Indian state, W cen. India; 300 sq. m.; joined Union of Rajasthan June 26, 1947.

Sai–li–mu Hu \ˈsī-ˈlē-ˈmü-ˈhü\ *or* **Sai·ram Nor** \ˌsī-ˌräm-ˈnȯ(ə)r\ *or* **Zai·ram Nor** \ˌzī-\. Lake, NW Sinkiang Uighur, W China, S of the Dzungarian Ala Tau.

Sail·ly–Sail·li·sel \sa-ˌyē-sa-yē-ˈzel\. Village, Somme dept., N France, 6 m. N of Péronne; pop. (1962c) 393; severe fighting 1916 to 1918, esp. during battle of the Somme July to Nov. 1916.

Sai·maa, Lake \-ˈsī-ˌmä\. Lake, SE Finland; 680 sq. m.; drains E through Vuoksi river into Lake Ladoga.

Sain–ni \ˈsīn-ˈnē\. Town, ✱ of South P'yŏngan prov., North Korea.

Saint *Eng.* sānt, sənt; *Fr.* sa^{n}\. The following are foreign equivalents for the word "saint" often occurring in place-names: *Fr.,* Saint or Sainte; *Ital. and Span.,* San, Santa, Santo; *Port.,* São; *Ger. and Scandinavian,* Sankt; *Rom.,* Sfânta, Sfântul; *Du.,* Sint; *Slovak,* Svätý; *Serb.,* Sveti; *Bulg.,* Svetiya; *Russ.,* Svyatoi; *Hung.,* Szent; *Gk.,* Hagios, Hagion.

Saint Abb's Head \-'abz-\. Cape, SE coast of Scotland, near English border, projecting into North Sea; lighthouse.

Saint–Acheul \ˌsa^{n}(n)t-ə-'shə(r)l\. Hamlet and gravel pit near Amiens, Somme dept., N France; Paleolithic remains discovered here; type station of the *Acheulean* or third Paleolithic period.

Saint Ag·a·tha \-'ag-ə-thə\. Town, Aroostook co., N Maine, 14 m. E of Fort Kent; pop. (1970c) 868.

Saint Ag·nes Head \-'ag-nəs-\. Promontory, W coast of Cornwall, SW England, WNW of Truro.

Saint Aignan. See MISIMA.

Saint Al·bans \-'ȯl-bənz\. **1** City, ⊗ of Franklin co., NW Vermont, near Lake Champlain 25 m. N of Burlington; pop. (1970c) 8082; summer resort; chemicals, dairy products; railroad shops; incorporated as town 1788, as city 1897.

2 City, Kanawha co., W cen. West Virginia, on Kanawha river 12 m. W of Charleston; pop. (1970c) 14,356; machine shops; truck farms.

3 *or anc.* **Ver·u·la·mi·um** \ˌver-(y)ə-'lā-mē-əm\. Municipal borough, Hertfordshire, SE England, on the Ver 20 m. NNW of London; pop. (1971p) 52,057; electrical equipment, musical instruments, clothing; printing, horticulture; 11th–14th cent. cathedral (former abbey church) with longest Gothic nave in the world; abbey founded 793 and prominent in the Middle Ages, being the home of notable chroniclers including Roger of Wendover, Matthew Paris, and Thomas Walsingham; after dissolution of abbey, city received first charter 1553.

Saint Alban's Head \-ˌȯl-bənz-\. Headland on the coast of Dorsetshire, S England.

Saint Al·bert \-'al-bərt\. Town, Alberta, Canada, 5 m. NW of Edmonton; pop. (1971p) 11,800; agriculture.

Saint–Amand \ˌsa^{n}t-ə-'mä^{n}\ *also* **Saint–Amand–les–Eaux** \-lā-'zō\. Manufacturing city, Nord dept., N France, 22 m. SE of Lille; pop. (1968c) 17,190; manufactures machinery, hardware, textiles, foundry products; thermal springs; built around abbey founded 647 by Saint Amand; important center for production of faïence in 18th cent.

Saint–Amand–Mont–Rond \-mō^{n}-'rō^{n}\. Town, Cher dept., cen. France, ab. 23 m. SSE of Bourges; pop. (1968c) 11,-495.

Saint An·dré, Cape \-ˌsa^{n}n-tä^{n}-'drā\. Cape extending into Mozambique Channel on NW cen. coast of the Malagasy Republic.

Saint An·drews \-'an-(ˌ)drüz\. **1** Town, ⊗ of Charlotte co., SW New Brunswick, Canada, on Passamaquoddy Bay at mouth of St. Croix river; pop. (1971p) 1743; summer resort.

2 Seaport burgh, Fife co., E Scotland, on **Saint Andrews Bay** 13 m. SE of Dundee; pop. (1971p) 11,468; noted seaside and golfing resort; St. Andrews Univ. (1413, oldest univ. in Scotland); ruins of 12th–13th cent. cathedral, former seat of the primate of Scotland, 13th cent. castle; received charter 1160 and was one of the principal towns in Scotland during the Middle Ages.

Saint An·drew Sound \-ˌan-(ˌ)drü-\. Inlet of Atlantic Ocean on NE coast of Camden co., SE Georgia, receiving the Satilla river on the W.

Saint Ann \-'an\. City, St. Louis co., E Missouri, NW suburb of St. Louis; pop. (1970c) 18,215.

Saint Ann Bay. See SAINT ANN'S BAY 1.

Saint Anne \-'an\. Town, ✱ of Alderney I., Channel Is.

Saint Anne's on the Sea \-'anz-\. Former urban district, Lancashire, W England, on the coast S of Blackpool; since 1924 part of Lytham St. Anne's municipal borough.

Saint Ann's Bay. 1 *also* **Saint Ann Bay.** Inlet of Atlantic Ocean in NE Cape Breton I., Nova Scotia, Canada.

2 Town and bay on N coast of island of Jamaica, West Indies; pop. (1960c) 5087.

Saint Ann's Head. Cape on SW extremity of Wales, N of entrance to Milford Haven; lighthouse.

Saint An·tho·ny \-'an(t)-thə-nē\. **1** City, ⊗ of Fremont co., E Idaho, 40 m. NE of Idaho Falls; pop. (1970c) 2877; grain, stock, dairy farms.

2 Village, Hennepin and Ramsey cos., Minnesota, N suburb of Minneapolis; pop. (1970c) 9239.

3 Seaport, NE Newfoundland, Canada, on Atlantic Ocean 20 m. S of Cape Bauld; pop. (1971p) 2586.

Saint Anthony, Falls of. Waterfall in the Mississippi river in the center of the city of Minneapolis, Minnesota; ab. 50 ft. high; total fall including rapids above and below is ab. 85 ft.; furnishes industrial power. Discovered 1680 by Hennepin; center of first settlement in area 1837.

Saint An·toine des Lau·ren·tides \ˌsa^{n}-tä^{n}-ˌtwän-dā-ˌlȯ-rä^{n}-'tēd\. Village, Terrebonne co., S Quebec, Canada, 24 m. NW of Montreal; pop. (1966c) 4401.

Saint As·aph \-'ā-səf\. City, Flintshire, NE Wales; parish pop. (1961c) 1830; cathedral, one of smallest in Great Britain.

Saint Au·gus·tine \-'ȯ-gə-ˌstēn\. City, ⊗ of St. Johns co., NE Florida, on Atlantic Ocean 35 m. SE of Jacksonville; pop. (1970c) 12,352; port of entry; winter and summer resort; Florida Memorial Coll. (1892). Oldest permanent existing European settlement on continent of North America; founded by Pedro Menéndez de Avilés 1565; burned by Sir Francis Drake 1586; great stone fort of San Marcos (Fort Marion 1825–1942, renamed Castillo de San Marcos 1942) begun 1672, completed 1756; attacked by British in 18th cent. wars; a refuge of Tories during American Revolution (see FLORIDA).

Saint Augustine Inlet. Narrow strait leading from Atlantic Ocean through barrier reef opp. cen. St. Johns co., NE Florida.

Saint Aus·tell with Fow·ey \-'ȯst-ᵊl . . . 'fȯi, -'fō-ē\. Municipal borough, Cornwall, SW England, on **Saint Austell Bay** 28 m. W of Plymouth; pop. (1971p) 32,252; center of kaolin production in England.

Saint–Avold \ˌsa^{n}-ta-'vȯl\. Town, Moselle dept., NE France, 23 m. E of Metz; pop. (1968e) 16,820; United States military cemetery.

Saint Bar·thé·le·my *or* **Saint–Barthélemy** \sa^{n}-ˌbär-ˌtāl-'mē\. Island in Guadeloupe dept., West Indies, in Leeward Is.

Saint Bath·ans, Mount \-'bath-ənz\. Peak, S cen. South I., New Zealand; 6842 ft.

Saint Bees Head \-'bēz-\. Cape on NW coast of England, projecting into Irish Sea S of entrance to Solway Firth; lighthouse.

Saint–Be·noît \ˌsa^{n}-be-'nwä\. Town on E coast of the French island of Réunion in the Indian Ocean E of Malagasy Republic; pop. (1967c) 7731.

Saint Ber·nard \ˌsānt-bə(r)-'närd\. **1** Parish in Louisiana. See table at LOUISIANA.

2 City, Hamilton co., SW corner of Ohio, 5 m. N of Cincinnati; pop. (1970c) 6080; suburb of Cincinnati.

3 Two Alpine passes, Great Saint Bernard and Little Saint Bernard. See ALPS.

Saint Bonaventure. See ALLEGANY 2.

Saint Bon·i·face \-'bän-ə-ˌfās\. City, S Manitoba, Canada, on Red river across from Winnipeg; pop. (1971p) 46,661; stockyards, oil refineries, packing plants, flour mills; Coll. de Saint Boniface (1818); founded 1818, incorporated as city 1908. Largely French Canadian in population; Roman Catholic headquarters for NW Canada.

Saint Boniface de Sha·win·i·gan \-də-shə-'win-i-gən\. Village, Saint-Maurice co., S Quebec, Canada, 18 m. NW of Three Rivers; pop. (1971p) 2586.

Saint Botolph's Town. See BOSTON 3.

Saint Bride's Bay \-'brīdz-\. Inlet of St. George's Channel on the SW extremity of Wales.

Saint–Bri·euc \ˌsa^{n}-brē-ˈər\. Manufacturing and commercial city, ✱ of Côtes-du-Nord dept., NW France, on English Channel 70 m. NE of Quimper; pop. (1968c) 50,281; railroad junction, commercial center, coastal and fishing port, 13th cent. fortress-cathedral; founded 5th cent. A.D. by St. Brieuc, a Welsh monk; sacked by Spanish 1592.

Saint Bru·no de Mon·tar·ville \ˌsa^{n}-brü-ˈnō-də-ˌmō^{n}-tär-ˈvil\. Town, Chambly co., S Quebec, Canada, 10 m. E of Montreal; pop. (1971p) 15,822.

Saint Cath·a·rine, Lake *or* **Lake Cath·er·ine** \-ˈkath-(ə-)rən\. Lake in SW Rutland co., W Vermont.

Saint Cath·a·rines \-ˈkath-(ə-)rənz\. Industrial city, ⊗ of Lincoln co., SE Ontario, Canada, on Welland Ship Canal just S of Lake Ontario; pop. (1971p) 109,636; automobile parts, machinery, electrical equipment, hosiery; packs and ships fruit; Brock Univ. (1962); settled 1790; incorporated as town 1845, as city 1876.

Saint Cath·er·ine, Mount \-ˈkath-(ə-)rən\. Mountain, N Grenada I., Windward Is., West Indies; 2757 ft.; highest point on the island.

Saint Catherine Point. Cape on N extremity of Bermuda I., in the Bermuda Is.

Saint Cath·er·ines Island \-ˈkath-(ə-)rənz-\. Island in Atlantic Ocean, off E mainland of Liberty co., SE Georgia; 21 sq. m.

Saint Catherine's Point. Cape on S tip of Isle of Wight, off S coast of England; lighthouse.

Saint Catherines Sound. Inlet of Atlantic Ocean on E coast of Liberty co., SE Georgia.

Saint–Cha·mond \ˌsa^{n}-shə-ˈmō^{n}\. Manufacturing commune, Loire dept., SE cen. France, 7 m. NE of Saint-Étienne; pop. (1968c) 37,728; motor vehicles, bronze and copper products, steel, silk; coal mines.

Saint Charles \-ˈchär(ə)lz\. **1** Name of a parish in Louisiana and of a county in Missouri. See tables at LOUISIANA and MISSOURI.

2 City, Kane co., NE Illinois, 37 m. W of Chicago; pop. (1970c) 12,928; iron and steel products; agriculture; Saint Dominic Coll. (1963).

3 City, ⊗ of St. Charles co., E Missouri, on Missouri river 20 m. NW of St. Louis; pop. (1970c) 31,834; footwear, foundry products; coal mines; diversified agriculture; Lindenwood Coll. (1827); incorporated as city 1849; capital of Missouri Territory, and first capital of state 1821–26.

Saint Chris·to·pher \-ˈkris-tə-fər\ *or* **Saint Kitts** \-ˈkits\. Island, Leeward Is., West Indies; 68 sq. m.; pop. (1965e) 37,384; ✱ Basseterre; administratively united with Nevis (see SAINT CHRISTOPHER-NEVIS). Has long narrow point of land extending to SE, its tip separated by strait 2 m. wide from island of Nevis. Mountainous, of volcanic origin; fertile and well watered; highest point at NW end 4314 ft.; Mt. Misery 3792 ft. in center; besides Basseterre only other town is Old Road. Discovered by Columbus 1493; settled by British 1625, the first of the Leeward Is. to be colonized by British; sent colonies to Antigua and Montserrat 1632; held jointly by French and English 1628 to 1713, but returned to Great Britain by Treaty of Utrecht 1713; held by French 1782–83.

Saint Christopher–Ne·vis \-ˈnē-vəs, -ˈnev-əs\ *also* **Saint Kitts–Nevis** \-ˈkits-\. A self-governing state, Leeward Is., West Indies, consisting of Nevis, Saint Christopher, and Sombrero; 118 sq. m.; pop. (1965e) 52,020; ✱ Basseterre; became a self-governing state (in association with Great Britain) 1967; was constitutionally united with Anguilla (forming **Saint Christopher–Nevis–Anguilla**) 1967–71.

Saint Clair \-ˈkla(ə)r, -ˈkle(ə)r\. **1** Navigable river, SE Michigan; ab. 40 m. long; connects Lake Huron with Lake St. Clair; forms United States-Canada boundary.

2 Name of counties in four states of the U.S. See tables at ALABAMA, ILLINOIS, MICHIGAN, MISSOURI.

3 City, St. Clair co., SE Michigan, on St. Clair river 10 m. S of Port Huron; pop. (1970c) 4470.

4 Town, Franklin co., E Missouri, 50 m. SW of St. Louis; pop. (1970c) 2978; shoes; diversified agriculture.

5 Borough, Schuylkill co., E cen. Pennsylvania, 4 m. WNW of Pottsville; pop. (1970c) 4576; coal mines.

Saint Clair, Lake. **1** Lake bet. state of Michigan and Canadian province of Ontario; the U.S.-Canada boundary passes through it; ab. 30 m. long; area 432 sq. m., maximum depth 26 ft.; connects with Lake Huron by St. Clair river, and with Lake Erie by Detroit river.

2 Lake, E cen. Tasmania, Australia, source of Derwent river; 9 m. long; ab. 16 sq. m.; noted for its scenery and fishing.

Saint Clair Shores. City, Macomb co., SE Michigan, on Lake St. Clair 13 m. NE of Detroit; pop. (1970c) 88,093; residential; boating center.

Saint Clairs·ville \-ˈkla(ə)rz-ˌvil, -ˈkle(ə)rz-\. Village, ⊗ of Belmont co., E Ohio, 24 m. SSW of Steubenville; pop. (1970c) 4754; dairy products; oil and gas wells.

Saint–Claude \sa^{n}-ˈklōd\ *or anc.* **Con·da·te** \kän-ˈdā-tē\. Manufacturing commune, Jura dept., E France, 25 m. SE of Lons-le-Saunier; pop. (1968c) 12,486; gem-cutting, woodworking; 15th cent. cathedral. Founded in pre-Roman times.

Saint Clem·ent Bay \-ˌklem-ənt-\. Inlet of Potomac river on SW shore of St. Marys co., S Maryland.

Saint–Cloud \sa^{n}-ˈklü\. Commune, Hauts-de-Seine dept., N France, WSW suburb of Paris near Seine river; pop. (1968c) 28,162; national porcelain factory (formerly located at Sèvres); summer resort; formerly residence of French monarchs; scene of murder of Henry III 1589; royal castle built by Louis XIV 1658; scene of Napoleon's coup of the 18th Brumaire; Blücher's headquarters 1815.

Saint Cloud \-ˈklau̇d\. **1** City, Osceola co., cen. Florida penin., 23 m. S of Orlando; pop. (1970c) 5041.

2 City, Benton, Sherburne, and Stearns cos., ⊗ of Stearns co., cen. Minnesota, on Mississippi river 58 m. NW of Minneapolis; pop. (1970c) 39,691; optical goods, granite products, granite quarrying, metalworking; railroad shops; in dairy farming region; St. Cloud State Coll. (1866); settled 1851; incorporated as city 1889.

Saint Croix \-ˈkrȯi\. **1** River forming S section of boundary bet. Maine and the Canadian province of New Brunswick; 129 m. long; flows S from Chiputneticook Lakes into Passamaquoddy Bay.

2 River, NW Wisconsin and E Minnesota; 164 m. long; rises in Douglas co., NW Wisconsin, flows SW and forms part of Wisconsin-Minnesota boundary until it empties into the Mississippi below St. Paul; navigable ab. 54 m. to **The Dalles** \-ˈdalz\ in Interstate Park where a deep gorge has been cut.

3 County in Wisconsin. See table at WISCONSIN.

4 *or* **San·ta Cruz** \ˌsant-ə-ˈkrüz\. Largest and most populous of the Virgin Is. of the United States, in the West Indies, ab. 37 m. S of St. Thomas; 84 sq. m.; pop. (1970p) 31,892; chief town Christiansted; only other town is Frederiksted, at W end; tourism; sugar, rum. Discovered 1493 by Columbus; in turn became possession of Dutch, English, Spanish, and French; purchased by Denmark 1753; sold to U.S. 1917.

Saint Croix Island National Monument. See UNITED STATES, *National Monuments.*

Saint–Cyr–l'École \sa^{n}-ˌsi(ə)r-lā-ˈkȯl\. Commune, Yvelines, N France, 3 m. W of Versailles; pop. (1968c) 16,000; site of military school, established 1808.

Saint David. See MAPIA.

Saint Da·vid de l'Aube·ri·vière \ˌsa^{n}-dä-ˈvēd-də-ˌlōb-ri-ˈvyer\. Town, Levis co., S Quebec, Canada, on St. Lawrence river opposite Quebec; pop. (1971p) 3808.

ə abut; ᵊ kitten, Fr. table; ər further; a back; ā bake; ä cot, cart; å Fr. bac; au̇ out; ch chin; e less; ē easy; g gift
i trip; ī life; j joke; k Ger. ich, Buch; ^{n} Fr. vin; ŋ sing; ō flow; ȯ flaw; œ Fr. bœuf; œ̄ Fr. feu; ȯi coin; th thin
th this; ü loot; u̇ foot; ue Ger. füllen; ūē Fr. rue; y yet; ^{y} Fr. digne \dēn^{y}\, nuit \nw^{y}ē\; yü few; yu̇ furious; zh vision

Saint David Island \-ˌdā-vəd-\. Island, NE Bermuda Is., N of Castle Harbour.

Saint Da·vid's \-ˈdā-vədz\ *or anc.* **Me·ne·via** \mə-ˈnē-vē-ə\. Parish, Pembrokeshire, SW Wales; pop. (1961c) 1690; 12th–14th cent. cathedral; according to tradition, see of Menevia founded in 6th cent. by Saint David, patron saint of Wales.

Saint Da·vids Head \-ˈdā-vədz-\. Cape at E end of Saint David I., NE Bermuda Is.; easternmost point of the islands, 32°22′N, 64°38′W.

Saint David's Head. Cape, Pembrokeshire, SW coast of Wales, extending into St. George's Channel; cliffs ab. 100 ft. high; most western point of Wales, 51°55′N, 5°19′W.

Saint–De·nis \ˌsaⁿ(t)-də-ˈnē\. 1 Manufacturing commune, Seine-St-Denis dept., N France, 7 m. NNE of Paris; pop. (1968c) 99,268; chemicals, plastics, diesel engines, leather, pharmaceuticals, glue, fireworks; 12th cent. Gothic abbatial church containing tombs of French monarchs, among them Louis XII, Henry II, Catherine de Médicis, Louis of Orléans, Francis I, Claude of France, Louis XVI, Marie Antoinette, Louis XIII; abbey of Saint-Denis founded here 626 by the Merovingian king Dagobert I; Abelard resided here as monk in 12th cent.; the banner of Saint Denis, the oriflamme, served as royal standard until reign of Charles III; called **Fran·ciade** \fräⁿ-ˈsyäd\ during the Revolution.

2 City, ✱ of French island of Réunion in the Indian Ocean, on N coast; pop. (1971e) 94,104.

Saint–Denis–du–Sig. See SIG.

Saint–Denis–le–Gast \ˌsaⁿ(t)-də-ˈnē-lə-ˈgäst\. Commune, Manche dept., NW France, 12 m. N of Avranches; pop. (1962c) 807; scene of breakthrough of U.S. armored forces July 30, 1944.

Saint–Dié \ˌsaⁿ-dē-ˈā\. Manufacturing commune, Vosges dept., NE France, on Meurthe river 25 m. ENE of Épinal; pop. (1968c) 25,117; textiles, machinery; distilleries; 12th cent. cathedral, 17th cent. episcopal palace; built around a monastery founded by Saint Deodatus in the 7th cent.

Saint–Di·zier \ˌsaⁿ-dē-ˈzyā\ *or anc.* **Des·i·de·rii Fa·num** \ˌdes-ə-ˈdir-ē-ˌī-ˈfā-nəm\. Manufacturing commune, Haute-Marne dept., NE France, on Marne river 39 m. N of Chaumont; pop. (1968c) 36,616; iron, steel, copper, and bronze foundries. Besieged and taken 1544; battle nearby 1814.

Saint Do·mingue \ˌsaⁿ(n)d-ə-ˈmaŋ\. French form of Santo Domingo, early name of Dominican Republic, sometimes applied to entire island (see HISPANIOLA).

Sainte–Adresse \ˌsaⁿ-ta-ˈdres\. Commune, Seine-Maritime dept., N France, near Le Havre; pop. (1962c) 8193; seat of Belgian government Oct. 13, 1914 to Dec. 1918 during World War I.

Sainte Agathe des Monts \ˌsaⁿ-ta-ˌgät-dā-ˈmōⁿ\. Resort town, Terrebonne co., S Quebec, Canada, 52 m. NW of Montreal; pop. (1971p) 5525.

Sainte–Anne \saⁿ-ˈtan\. Commune and village, S coast of Grande Terre, Guadeloupe, West Indies.

Sainte Anne. 1 \sānt-ˈan, sənt-\. Fort, Vermont. See FORT SAINTE ANNE.

2 *Fr.* saⁿ-tan\. River, Charlevoix and Montmorency cos., S Quebec, Canada; ab. 50 m. long; flows S into the St. Lawrence at Sainte Anne de Beaupré.

Sainte Anne de Beau·pré \saⁿ-ˈtan-də-bō-ˈprā\. Village, Montmorency co., S Quebec, Canada, on St. Lawrence river 21 m. NE of Quebec; pop. (1971p) 1778; site of shrine (estab. 1620) and church to Saint Anne.

Sainte Anne de Belle·vue\saⁿ-ˈtan-də-bel-ˈvyü\.Town at SW end of Montreal I., S Quebec, Canada, on Lake St. Louis 21 m. WSW of Montreal; pop. (1971p) 4932; summer resort; Macdonald Coll. of Agriculture.

Sainte Anne des Monts \saⁿ-ˈtan-dā-ˈmōⁿ\. Town (unincorporated), ⊗ of Gaspé-Ouest co., on Gaspé Penin., SE Quebec, Canada, on St. Lawrence river at its mouth; pop. (1966c) 4827.

Sainte Anne's Point. See FREDERICTON.

Sainte–Baume \saⁿt-ˈbōm\. Mountain chain in Bouches-du-Rhône and Var depts., SE France; highest point 3260 ft.; site of grotto (La Grotte de Sainte Madeleine) where Mary Magdalene is supposed to have spent the end of her life; popular place of pilgrimage.

Sainte Croix \saⁿ-tə-ˈkrwä, sānt-ˈkrȯi\. Village, ⊗ of Lotbinière co., S Quebec, Canada, on S bank of the St. Lawrence river 28 m. SW of Quebec; pop. (1971p) 1559.

Sainte Fa·mille \ˌsaⁿt-fa-ˈmēʸ\. Village (unincorporated), ⊗ of Montmorency co., S Quebec, Canada, on N shore of Orleans I., 28 m. NE of Quebec; pop. (1966c) 1016.

Sainte Foy \saⁿt-ˈfwä\. City, Quebec co., S Quebec, Canada, 4 m. SW of Quebec; pop. (1971p) 67,834.

Sainte Gen·e·vieve \sānt-ˈjen-ə-ˌvēv, sənt-\. 1 County in E Missouri. See table at MISSOURI.

2 City, its ⊗, on Mississippi river 46 m. S of St. Louis; pop. (1970c) 4468; marble quarries; diversified agriculture; site of first settlement, by the French, in Missouri c. 1735.

Sainte Ge·ne·viève \ˌsaⁿt-ˌzhə-nə-ˈvyev\. Town, ⊗ of Champlain co., S Quebec, Canada, on Batiscan river near its mouth, 18 m. NE of Three Rivers; pop. (1971p) 2847.

Sainte–Geneviève–des–Bois \ˌsaⁿt-ˌzhə-nə-ˈvyev-dā-ˈbwä\. Commune, Essonne dept., N France, ab. 15 m. S of Paris; pop. (1968c) 23,684.

Sainte Hé·né·dine \ˌsaⁿ-tā-nā-ˈdēn\. Village (unincorporated), ⊗ of Dorchester co., S Quebec, Canada, 21 m. SSE of Quebec; pop. (1966c) 640.

Sainte Ju·lienne \ˌsaⁿt-zhül-ˈyen\. Village (unincorporated), ⊗ of Montcalm co., S Quebec, Canada, 32 m. N of Montreal; pop. (1966c) 848; agriculture.

Saint Eli·as, Cape \-ˌsānt-ᵊl-ˈī-əs\. Point, S end of Kayak I., off SE coast of Alaska.

Saint Elias, Mount. 1 Peak in the Saint Elias Mountains, on the boundary bet. SW Yukon Territory, Canada, and E Alaska; 18,008 ft.

2 Mountain peaks, Greece. See HAGIOS ELIAS, MOUNT.

Saint Elias Mountains *also* **Saint Elias Range.** Mountain range, SW Yukon Territory, Canada, and E Alaska, near the Pacific Ocean; ab. 250 m. long; highest peak Mt. Logan 19,850 ft. On its S slopes are the Malaspina and Guyot glaciers in Alaska.

Saint–Éloi. See SINT-ELOOIS-VIJVE.

Saint–Éloy–les–Mines \ˌsaⁿ-tāl-ˌwä-lā-ˈmēn\. Mining commune, Puy-de-Dôme dept., S cen. France, NNW of Clermont-Ferrand; pop. (1962c) 6898.

Sainte–Marguerite. See LÉRINS, ÎLES DE.

Sainte–Ma·rie \ˌsaⁿt-má-ˈrē, ˌsānt-mə-ˈrē\. Commune, NE coast of Martinique, West Indies; pop. (1967e) 19,515.

Sainte–Marie *or* **Île Sainte–Marie–de–Mad·a·gas·car** \ˌēl-ˌsānt-mə-ˈrē-də-ˌmad-ə-ˈgas-kər\. Island in the Indian Ocean off NE cen. coast of Malagasy Republic; 64 sq. m.

Sainte Marie \saⁿt-ˈma-rē, ˌsānt-mə-ˈrē\. Town, Beauce co., S Quebec, Canada, on Chaudière river 28 m. SSE of Quebec; pop. (1971p) 4308; dairy products, lumber.

Sainte–Marie, Cape \-ˌsānt-mə-ˈrē\. Extreme S tip of the Malagasy Republic.

Sainte–Marie–aux–Mines \ˌsaⁿt-má-ˌrē-ō-ˈmēn\ *or Ger.* **Mar·kirch** \ˈmär-(ˌ)kirk\. Commune, Haut-Rhin dept., NE France; pop. (1962c) 7923; silver, copper, and lead mines in the vicinity, worked 9th–19th cents.; weaving industry.

Sainte Mar·tine \ˌsaⁿt-mär-ˈtēn\. Village (unincorporated), ⊗ of Châteauguay co., S Quebec, Canada, 21 m. SSW of Montreal; pop. (1966c) 1786.

Sainte–Me·ne·hould \ˌsaⁿt-mə-ˈnü\. Commune, NE Marne dept., NE France, on the Aisne; pop. (1966e) 5050; on W border of the Argonne Forest; occupied by Germans Sept. 1914 but regained by French and became their headquarters for the Argonne sector.

Sainte–Mère–Église \ˌsaⁿt-ˌmar-ā-ˈglēz\. Commune, Manche dept., NW France, ab. 20 m. SE of Cherbourg; pop. (1962c) 1221; taken June 6–10, 1944 by U.S. paratroops in invasion of Normandy.

Sainte Phi·lo·mène \sa^{n}t-ˌfē-lō-ˈmen\. Town, Châteauguay co., S Quebec, Canada, 10 m. SW of Montreal; pop. (1966c) 3234.

Saintes \ˈsa^{n}t\ *or anc.* **Me·di·o·la·num** \ˌmed-ē-ə-ˈlā-nəm, -ˈlan-əm\. Industrial city, Charente-Maritime dept., W France, on Charente river 40 m. SE of La Rochelle; pop. (1968c) 26,507; market town; produces brandy, tile, pottery, iron goods; 15th–16th cent. church (cathedral until 1790), Roman amphitheater. Ancient capital of the Santones; formerly capital of province of Saintonge; scene of defeat of Henry III by Louis IX 1242.

Saintes, Les. See LES SAINTES.

Sainte–Sa·vine \ˌsa^{n}t-sa-ˈvēn\. Commune, Aube dept., NE France, suburb of Troyes; pop. (1968c) 11,622.

Sainte Scho·las·tique \ˌsa^{n}t-ˌskō-las-ˈtēk\. City, ⊗ of Two Mountains co., S Quebec, Canada, 27 m. WNW of Montreal; pop. (1971p) 14,778; dairy farms.

Saint–Es·tèphe \sa^{n}-tes-ˈtef\. Commune, Gironde dept., SW France, on the Gironde ab. 25 m. NNW of Bordeaux; pop. (1962c) 2120; in the Médoc; red wines from the Châteaux Cos d'Estournel and Montrose.

Sainte Thé·rèse \ˌsa^{n}t-tā-ˈrez, ˌsānt-tə-ˈrēz\. 1 Island, in the St. Lawrence at the foot of Montreal I., S Quebec, Canada; ab. 3 m. long.

2 Town, Terrebonne co., S Quebec, Canada, 18 m. NW of Montreal; pop. (1971p) 17,161; motor vehicles, chemicals, furniture.

Saint–Étienne \ˌsa^{n}-tā-ˈtyen\. Industrial city, ✱ of Loire dept., SE cen. France, 32 m. SW of Lyons; pop. (1968c) 213,468; important center of textile and dyeing industry; also produces alloy steels, chemicals, aircraft engines, hardware, small arms and ammunition; government armaments factory, coal mines. A center of metallurgical industry from 16th cent. and formerly one of the leading steel-producing centers of France.

Saint–Étienne–du–Rou·vray \-də-ˌrüv-ˈrā\. Commune, Seine-Maritime dept., N France, 3 m. S of Rouen; pop. (1968c) 34,713; textiles.

Saint Eus·tache \ˌsa^{n}-tyü-ˈstash\. Town, Two Mountains co., S Quebec, Canada, on Rivière des Mille Îles across from Jesus I.; pop. (1971p) 9464.

Saint Eu·sta·ti·us \ˌsānt-yu̇-ˈstā-sh(ə-)əs\. Small island of the Leeward Is., West Indies, NW of St. Christopher; 8 sq. m.; pop. (1969e) 1341; part of the Netherlands Antilles; settled by French 1625; became Dutch 1632; sacked by English 1781.

Saint Fé·li·cien \sa^{n}-ˌfā-lis-ˈya^{n}, ˌsānt-fə-ˈlish-ən\. Town, Lake St. John co., S Quebec, Canada, on Ashuapmuchuan river near its mouth, W of Lake St. John; pop. (1971p) 4955; lumber; potatoes, vegetables.

Saint–Flo·rent, Gulf of \-ˌsa^{n}-flō-ˈrä^{n}\. Inlet, NW coast of Corsica, France; the town of **Saint–Florent** is on it.

Saint–Flour \sa^{n}-ˈflu̇(ə)r\. Manufacturing commune, E Cantal dept., S cen. France; pop. (1968c) 6898; built on a steep rock; 14th–15th cent. cathedral.

Saint–Fons \sa^{n}-ˈfō^{n}\. Industrial commune, Rhône dept., E cen. France, near Rhône river 4 m. SSE of Lyons; pop. (1968c) 15,096.

Saint Fran·cis \sānt-ˈfran(t)-səs\. 1 River, N Maine; with **Lake Saint Francis** (actually an expansion of the river) forms a section of the extreme N boundary of Maine and flows into St. John river.

2 River, SE Missouri and E Arkansas; 425 m. long; rises in Iron co., SE Missouri, flows S and forms section of boundary bet. SE Missouri and NE Arkansas, continues S through E Arkansas into Mississippi river; navigable 125 m.

3 County in Arkansas. See table at ARKANSAS.

4 City, ⊗ of Cheyenne co., NW corner of Kansas; pop. (1970c) 1725; livestock, corn.

5 City, Milwaukee co., SE Wisconsin, SW of Milwaukee; pop. (1970c) 10,489.

6 *or Fr.* **Saint–Fran·çois** \sa^{n}-frä^{n}-swȧ\. River, S Quebec, Canada; 165 m. long; flows SW out of Lake Saint Francis in Frontenac co., then NW into Lake St. Peter in the St. Lawrence river below Sorel.

Saint Francis, Cape. 1 Cape, Canada. See FRANCIS, CAPE.

2 Cape on SE coast of Cape Province, Rep. of South Africa, W of St. Francis Bay.

Saint Francis, Lake. 1 Lake in N Maine. See SAINT FRANCIS 1.

2 Lake, S Quebec and SE Ontario, Canada, 35 m. SW of the city of Montreal, formed by a widening of the St. Lawrence river; 88 sq. m.

3 Lake, Frontenac co., S Quebec, Canada. See SAINT FRANCIS 6.

Saint Francis Bay. Bay, SE coast of Cape Province, Rep. of South Africa, E of Cape St. Francis.

Saint Fran·cis·ville \-ˈfran(t)-səs-ˌvil\. Town, ⊗ of West Feliciana parish, E cen. Louisiana; pop. (1970c) 1603; potatoes.

Saint–Fran·çois \ˌsa^{n}-frä^{n}-ˈswä; sānt-ˈfran(t)-səs, sənt-\. 1 River, Canada. See SAINT FRANCIS 6.

2 Commune, SE coast of Grande Terre, Guadeloupe, West Indies.

Saint Fran·cois \-ˈfran(t)-səs\. County in Missouri. See table at MISSOURI.

Saint Fran·çois du Lac \ˌsa^{n}-frä^{n}-ˌswä-də-ˈläk\. Village, ⊗ of Yamaska co., S Quebec, Canada, S of Lake St. Peter and ab. 25 m. SE of Three Rivers; pop. (1966c) 957.

Saint Ga·bri·el de Bran·don \sa^{n}-ˌgȧ-brē-ˈel-də-brä^{n}-ˈdō^{n}\. Village, Berthier co., S Quebec, Canada, 42 m. W of Three Rivers on S shore of Lake Maskinongé; pop. (1966c) 3464; summer resort; lumber.

Saint Gall \sānt-ˈgȯl, sənt-, -ˈgäl\ *or Ger.* **Sankt Gal·len** \zäŋ(k)t-ˈgäl-ən\ *or Fr.* **Saint–Gall** \sa^{n}-gȧl\. 1 Swiss canton, in Alps; includes Lake Wallen and part of Lake Constance; stone quarries; pastures; lumber; textile manufacturing. See table at SWITZERLAND.

2 Commune, its ✱, NE Switzerland, 39 m. E of Zurich; pop. (1968e) 78,600; lace and embroidery work, linen and cotton textiles, glass, metal goods; 18th cent. Baroque cathedral (formerly abbey church), notable library containing numerous manuscripts, public parks. Developed around Benedictine abbey founded in early 7th cent. by Saint Gall, an Irish missionary; became free imperial city 1206; joined Swiss Confederation 1454; abbey a notable center of learning in early Middle Ages.

Saint–Gau·dens \ˌsa^{n}-gō-ˈda^{n}s\. Town, Haute-Garonne dept., S France, ab. 50 m. SSW of Toulouse; pop. (1962c) 7945; 11th–12th cent. church; important in medieval times.

Saint George \-ˈjȯ(ə)rj\. 1 Town, Knox co., S Maine, on Atlantic Ocean inlet 36 m. ESE of Augusta; pop. (1970c) 1639; on the site of Fort St. George, built 1719–20 and frequently attacked by Indians during 18th cent.

2 Post office station, ⊗ of Richmond co., SE New York, N Staten I. on Upper New York Bay. See RICHMOND 8.

3 Town, ⊗ of Dorchester co., SE South Carolina, 28 m. SSE of Orangeburg; pop. (1970c) 1806; agriculture.

4 City, ⊗ of Washington co., SW corner of Utah, 50 m. SSW of Cedar City; pop. (1970c) 7097; resort; diversified agriculture; Dixie Junior Coll. (1911).

5 Town, S coast of St. George's I., N Bermuda Is.; pop. (1960c) 1335; founded 1612, first settlement in Bermuda, was capital until 1815.

Saint George, Cape. 1 Cape, S extremity of St. George Island, in Gulf of Mexico, off S coast of Franklin co., NW Florida.

2 Peninsula, SE New South Wales, SE Australia, S of Beecroft Head and with it encloses Jervis Bay.

3 Cape and peninsula, N of St. Georges Bay, SW Newfoundland, Canada.

4 Cape, S point of New Ireland, Bismarck Archipelago, Trust Territory of New Guinea, 4°52′N, 152°52′E, at N end of Solomon Sea.

Saint George, Point. Point on W coast of Del Norte co., NW California.

Saint George Channel *or* **Saint George's Channel.** Passage bet. S end of New Ireland on E and NE New Britain on W, Bismarck Archipelago; ab. 20 m. wide; connects Bismarck Sea with Solomon Sea.

Saint George Island. 1 Island off coast of Franklin co., NW Florida, bet. Gulf of Mexico on the S and St. George Sound and Apalachicola Bay on the N; 13 sq. m.

2 Island in Potomac river near its mouth, in St. Marys co., S Maryland.

3 Island, most southerly of Pribilof Is. (*q.v.*) in Bering Sea, Alaska; 10 m. long by ab. 4 m. wide; 27 sq. m.

4 Island, Azores. See SÃO JORGE.

5 Island in Danube delta. See SFÎNTU GHEORGHE.

Saint Georges \saⁿ-ˈzhȯrzh\. Town, E French Guiana, ab. 90 m. SE of Cayenne on Oyapock river.

Saint–Georges \saⁿ-ˈzhȯrzh\. Town, Beauce co., S Quebec, Canada, on E bank of Chaudière river 30 m. E of Thetford Mines; pop. (1971p) 7570; wood products; dairy farms.

Saint George's *or* **Saint Georges** \-ˈjȯr-jəz\. 1 Seaport town, SW Newfoundland, Canada, at E end of St. Georges Bay; pop. (1971p) 2085.

2 Town on Grenada I., Windward Is., West Indies; ✻ of Grenada; pop. (1969e) 8644.

Saint Georges Bay \-ˌjȯr-jəz-\. Inlet of Gulf of St. Lawrence in SW Newfoundland, Canada.

Saint Georges Cay \-ˈkē, -ˈkā\. Small island in Caribbean Sea off NE coast of British Honduras; resort; scene of defeat of Spaniards by British settlers Sept. 10, 1798.

Saint George's Channel. 1 Channel, Bismarck Archipelago. See SAINT GEORGE CHANNEL.

2 Strait bet. Wales on the E and Ireland on the W; joins Atlantic Ocean and Irish Sea, ab. 100 m. N to S and bet. 50 and 95 m. E to W.

Saint George's Island. An island in N Bermuda Is., on W side of Castle Harbour; first of the islands to be colonized by English 1612, settlement at St. George on S coast.

Saint George Sound. Inlet of Gulf of Mexico in S coast of Franklin co., NW Florida.

Saint Georges West *or Fr.* **Saint Georges Ouest** \saⁿ-zhȯrzh-west\. Town, Quebec, Canada; pop. (1971p) 6002.

Saint–Ger·main \ˌsaⁿ-zhər-ˈmaⁿ\ *or in full* **Saint–Germain–en–Laye** \-äⁿ-ˈlā\. Commune, Yvelines dept., N France, on Seine river 11 m. WNW of Paris; pop. (1968c) 38,808; summer resort; Parisian residential suburb; noted for extensive forest and park; terrace of St. Germain one of the most notable promenades in Europe; 14th cent. castle (birthplace of Charles IX, Margaret of Valois, Henry II, Louis XIV, now a museum); treaties signed here 1570, 1632, 1679, and, bet. Allied Powers and Austria, 1919.

Saint–Gilles \saⁿ-ˈzhē(ə)l\. 1 *or Flemish* **Sint–Gil·lis** \sənt-ˈgil-əs\. Commune, Brabant prov., cen. Belgium, a suburb of Brussels; pop. (1969e) 54,272.

2 Town, Gard dept., S France, ab. 12 m. SSE of Nîmes; pop. (1968c) 8785; medieval countship held by counts of Toulouse; site of first priory in Europe founded by the Knights of St. John of Jerusalem; of the 12th cent. church only the west front and the crypt remain, the rest being 17th cent.

Saint–Go·bain \ˌsaⁿ-gō-ˈbaⁿ\. Town, Aisne dept., N France, ab. 7 m. NW of Laon; pop. (1962c) 2070; in the **Fo·rêt de Saint–Gobain** \fō-ˌred-ˌsaⁿ-\; site of glass factories established 1685; during World War I, held by Germans until Oct. 1918 as a strongly fortified point on the Hindenburg Line.

Saint Gott·hard *or* **Saint Got·hard** \sānt-ˈgät-ərd, sənt-; ˌsaⁿ-gə-ˈtär\ *also Ger.* **Sankt Gotthard** \zäŋ(k)t-ˈgȯt-ˌhärt\. 1 Mountain range of the Lepontine Alps, mostly bet. Uri and Ticino cantons, SE cen. Switzerland; highest peak Pizzo Rotondo 10,472 ft.

2 Alpine pass and tunnel. See ALPS.

Saint Gotthard. See SZENTGOTTHÁRD.

Saint Gow·an's Head \-ˈgau̇-ənz-\. Cape, SW corner of Wales, S of Pembroke.

Saint He·le·na \ˌsānt-ᵊl-ˈē-nə, -hə-ˈlē-\. 1 Parish in Louisiana. See table at LOUISIANA.

2 City, Napa co., W cen. California, 22 m. N of San Pablo Bay; pop. (1970c) 3173; wine; quicksilver mines; fruit farms.

3 British island in South Atlantic Ocean, ab. 1200 m. from W coast of Africa, lat. 15°57′S and long. 5°42′W; 47 sq. m.; pop. (1969e) 4829; ✻ Jamestown; exports flax and cordage; with Ascension I. (since 1922) and the Tristan da Cunha Is. (since 1938) constitutes a British crown colony (119 sq. m.; pop. [1969e] 6356). The crater rim of a volcano long extinct; highest point 2704 ft.; marked by gorges and valleys, many springs, and plains in the NE. Discovered May 21, 1502 by a Portuguese navigator; first visited by English 1588; granted to British East India Company 1661; Napoleon's place of exile 1815–21; detention camp for Boer prisoners during Boer War 1899–1902.

Saint Hel·e·na Bay \-ˌhel-ə-nə-\. Bay, W coast of Cape Province, Rep. of South Africa.

Saint Hel·e·na Island \-ˈhel-ə-nə-\. Island, Beaufort co., S South Carolina; ab. 13 m. long.

Saint Helena Sound. Inlet on N coast of Saint Helena I., South Carolina.

Saint Hel·ens \-ˈhel-ənz\. 1 City and river port, ⊗ of Columbia co., NW Oregon, on Columbia river 25 m. N of Portland; pop. (1970c) 6212; paper products; salmon fisheries; dairy and truck farms.

2 County borough, Lancashire, NW England, 10 m. ENE of Liverpool; pop. (1971p) 104,173; important glassmaking center; textiles, pottery, iron and brass goods; incorporated 1868.

Saint Helens, Mount. Peak, NW Skamania co., S Washington; 9677 ft.

Saint Hel·ier \-ˈhel-yər\. Commercial town and civil parish on the island of Jersey, Channel Is., in the English Channel 122 m. SSW of Southampton; ✻ of Jersey bailiwick; pop. (1971p) 28,135; residential community and seaside resort; residence of Victor Hugo 1852–55; Victoria College (1852).

Saint–Honorat. See LÉRINS, ÎLES DE.

Saint Hu·bert \ˌsaⁿ-yü-ˈber\. Town, Chambly co., Quebec, E Canada, just E of Montreal; pop. (1971p) 21,753.

Saint Hy·a·cinthe \sānt-ˈhī-ə-(ˌ)sin(t)th, sənt-, ˌsant-yə-ˈsant\. 1 County, Quebec, Canada. See table at QUEBEC.

2 Industrial city, its ⊗, on Yamaska river 34 m. ENE of Montreal; pop. (1971p) 24,192; machinery, furniture, clothing, silk, maple-sugar products; Coll. de Saint-Maurice, Séminaire de Saint-Hyacinthe (1811), L'École de Médicine Vétérinaire (1886); settled 1760.

Saint Ig·nace \-ˈig-nəs\. City, ⊗ of Mackinac co., SE Michigan penin., on Straits of Mackinac; pop. (1970c) 2892; summer resort; diversified agriculture.

Saint Ignace Island. Island in N Lake Superior, W of Simpson I., SW Ontario, Canada.

Saint–Imier \ˌsaⁿ-tē-ˈmyā\. Manufacturing commune, Bern canton, Switzerland, ab. 12 m. W of Biel; pop. (1970c) 6740.

Saint Ives \-ˈīvz\. Municipal borough on NW coast of Cornwall, SW England, on **Saint Ives Bay** 60 m. W of Plymouth; pop. (1971p) 9710; seaside resort.

Saint Jacques \saⁿ-ˈzhäk\. Village, Montcalm co., S Quebec, Canada, 28 m. N of Montreal; pop. (1971p) 1973; tobacco farms.

Saint Jacques, Cape. See VUNG TAU.

Saint James \-ˈjāmz\. 1 Parish in Louisiana. See table at LOUISIANA.

2 City, ⊗ of Watonwan co., S Minnesota, 33 m. WSW of Mankato; pop. (1970c) 4027; agriculture.

3 City, Phelps co., S cen. Missouri, 10 m. E of Rolla; pop. (1970c) 2929; fruit and truck farms.
4 City, Manitoba, Canada, 3 m. SW of Winnipeg; pop. (1966c) 35,685; residential suburb of Winnipeg.

Saint James, Cape. Cape, S tip of Kunghit I., S Queen Charlotte Is., off W British Columbia, Canada; 51°56′N, 131°01′W.

Saint-Jean \sa^{n}-'zhä^{n}\. County and city, S Quebec, Canada. See SAINT JOHNS 1 and 2.

Saint-Jean, Île-. See PRINCE EDWARD ISLAND.

Saint-Jean, Lac. See SAINT JOHN, LAKE.

Saint-Jean-Cap-Fer·rat \sa^{n}-ˌzhä^{n}-ˌkap-fə-'rä\. Commune, Alpes-Maritimes dept., SE France, E of Nice; pop. (1962c) 2416; fishing port, resort.

Saint-Jean-d'Acre. See ACRE.

Saint-Jean-d'An·gé·ly \sa^{n}-ˌzhä^{n}-ˌdä^{n}-zhā-'lē\. Town, Charente-Maritime dept., W France, ab. 35 m. SE of La Rochelle; pop. (1962c) 7868; suffered during religious wars of 16th cent. when it was a strong Protestant center; finally taken by Louis XIII 1621.

Saint-Jean-de-Luz \sa^{n}-ˌzhä^{n}-də-'lüz\. Coast town, Pyrénées-Atlantiques dept., SW France, on the Bay of Biscay SW of Biarritz near Spanish border; pop. (1962c) 9056; a Basque town; important fishing and trading port 14th–17th cents.; now mainly a resort.

Saint-Jean-de-Mau·rienne \sa^{n}-ˌzhä^{n}d-mȯr-'yen\. Town, Savoie dept., E France, SE of Chambéry; pop. (1962c) 5231; ecclesiastical town dating from 6th cent.; cathedral mainly 15th cent.; Allied conference Apr. 19, 1917.

Saint Jean Eudes \sa^{n}-'zhä-'nəd\. Village, Quebec, Canada; pop. (1966c) 2721.

Saint Jean Port Jo·li \sa^{n}-ˌzhä^{n}-pȯr-zhȯ-'lē\. Town (unincorporated), ⊗ of L'Islet co., S Quebec, Canada, on S bank of St. Lawrence river 55 m. NE of Quebec; pop. (1966c) 3335.

Saint Jé·rôme \ˌsa^{n}-zhā-'rōm\. Industrial city, ⊗ of Terrebonne co., SW Quebec, Canada, 28 m. NW of Montreal; pop. (1971p) 26,131; textile mills, foundries; tourist center; settled 1818.

Saint John \-'jän\. 1 City, ⊗ of Stafford co., cen. Kansas, 47 m. W of Hutchinson; pop. (1970c) 1477; oil wells.
2 Village, St. Louis co., E Missouri, W suburb of St. Louis; pop. (1970c) 8690.
3 River, NE United States and SE Canada; 418 m. long; rises in NW Maine (Somerset co.), flows NE and for 70 m. forms a part of the boundary bet. Maine and New Brunswick, turns SE through W New Brunswick, then E and S to Bay of Fundy at St. John. Navigable to Fredericton (81 m.) for large vessels, Fredericton to Grand Falls and for ab. 65 m. above Grand Falls for smaller boats. At Grand Falls, ab. 220 m. from its mouth, is great cataract ab. 75 ft. high; at its mouth in St. John harbor narrowed to gorge 450 ft. wide with sides ab. 100 ft. high. Chief tributaries Allagash and Aroostook in Maine, Madawaska in Quebec, and Tobique and Nashwaak in New Brunswick.
4 County in New Brunswick, Canada. See table at NEW BRUNSWICK.
5 Seaport city, ⊗ of St. John co., S New Brunswick, Canada, on Bay of Fundy at mouth of St. John river; pop. (1971p) 87,910, met. area pop. 105,227; largest city in the province and its principal port, with a large ice-free harbor; commercial center; pulp and paper products, canned fish; oil refineries, shipyards, salmon fisheries, iron foundries, limestone quarries; summer resort.
History: Site first settled by French as fortified trading post 1635; refortified as Fort Frederick by English 1758; area settled by Loyalists 1783 and city chartered (first city charter in Canada) 1785; in mid-19th cent. a major lumber and shipbuilding center; suffered destructive fire 1877.
6 River, cen. Liberia; 120 m. long; rises on NE boundary, flows SW to Atlantic Ocean near Buchanan.

Saint John, Cape. Cape, N coast of Newfoundland, Canada, NW point of entrance to Notre Dame Bay.

Saint John, Isle. See PRINCE EDWARD ISLAND.

Saint John, Lake *or Fr.* **Lac Saint-Jean** \lȧk-sa^{n}-zhä^{n}\. Lake, Lake St. John co., S Quebec, Canada; 414 sq. m.; receives the Ashuapmuchuan, Mistassini, and Peribonca rivers on the N; its outlet is the Saguenay (*q.v.*) river to the E, leaving by two channels. Much frequented by sportsmen and fishermen.

Saint John, Mount. Peak, cen. Grand Teton National Park, NW Wyoming; 11,412 ft.

Saint John Island. 1 One of the Virgin Is. of the United States in the West Indies, 4 m. E of St. Thomas; 20 sq. m.; pop. (1968e) 1689; highest point 1286 ft.; produces bay leaves for bay rum industry of St. Thomas. See VIRGIN ISLANDS.
2 Island off Kwangtung prov., SE China. See SHANG-CH'UAN.

Saint John River. See SAINT JOHN 4.

Saint Johns \-'jänz\. 1 Navigable river, E Florida; 285 m. long; rises in Brevard co., E cen. Florida, flows N into Atlantic Ocean NE of Jacksonville.
2 County in Florida. See table at FLORIDA.
3 City, ⊗ of Apache co., E Arizona; pop. (1970c) 1320.
4 City, ⊗ of Clinton co., S cen. Michigan, 20 m. N of Lansing; pop. (1970c) 6672; agriculture.
5 Town, ✻ of Antigua, Leeward Is., West Indies; pop. (1960c) 21,396; tourism.

Saint Johns *or Fr.* **Saint-Jean** \sa^{n}-zhä^{n}\. 1 County, S Quebec, Canada. See table at QUEBEC.
2 City, its ⊗, on Richelieu river 21 m. SE of Montreal; pop. (1971p) 32,484; manufactures paper products, textiles, chemicals, furniture, metal goods, sewing machines; dairy, poultry farms. Founded 1666; an important fort in 17th and 18th cents.; British base in American Revolution.

Saint John's \-'jänz\. City, ✻ of Newfoundland, Canada, on Atlantic Ocean on the SE coast; pop. (1971p) 86,290, met. area pop. 129,304; commercial center and principal port of Newfoundland; good natural harbor; terminus of the railroad across the island; fishing and fish-processing, shipbuilding and repairing, iron founding; produces textiles, marine hardware, cordage, paper products; Queen's Coll. (1841), Memorial Univ. of Newfoundland (1949). An anchorage of fishing fleets from early 16th cent.; colonized by British under Sir Humphrey Gilbert 1583 but permanent settlement not established until early 17th cent.; twice destroyed by French and Indians; came permanently under British 1762.

Saint Johns·bury \-'jänz-ˌber-ē, -b(ə-)rē\. Town, ⊗ of Caledonia co., NE Vermont, 30 m. ENE of Montpelier; pop. (1970c) 8409; dairy and maple-sugar products, clothing; dairy farms; settled 1786.

Saint John's Point. Cape, NE coast of Northern Ireland, S of Strangford Lough and at N side of entrance to Dundrum Bay; lighthouse.

Saint Johns·ville \-'jänz-ˌvil\. Village, Montgomery co., E New York, on Mohawk river 30 m. E of Utica; pop. (1970c) 2089; clothing.

Saint John the Bap·tist \-'bap-təst\. Parish in Louisiana. See table at LOUISIANA.

Saint Jo·seph \-'jō-zəf, -səf\. 1 River, S Michigan and NW Indiana; 210 m. long; rises in Hillsdale co., S Michigan, flows W along S Michigan, curves S and W in NW Indiana, then NW into Lake Michigan at St. Joseph, W Berrien co., SW Michigan; navigable for a short distance.
2 River, S Michigan, NW Ohio, and NE Indiana; over 100 m. long; rises in S Michigan, flows SW across NW corner of Ohio and unites with St. Marys river at Fort Wayne in Allen co., NE Indiana, to form the Maumee river.
3 Name of counties in two states of the U.S. See tables at INDIANA and MICHIGAN.

4 Town, ⊗ of Tensas parish, NE Louisiana; pop. (1970c) 1864; cotton, livestock.

5 City, ⊗ of Berrien co., SW corner of Michigan, on Lake Michigan at mouth of St. Joseph river 49 m. WSW of Kalamazoo; pop. (1970c) 11,042; automobile parts; cans and ships fruit; summer resort; incorporated as city 1891.

6 Village, Stearns co., cen. Minnesota, 7 m. W of St. Cloud; pop. (1970c) 1786; College of Saint Benedict (1913).

7 City, ⊗ of Buchanan co., NW Missouri, on Missouri river 46 m. NNW of Kansas City; pop. (1970c) 72,691; grain, tobacco, and livestock market; meat-packing, flour milling; machine shops, foundries; Missouri Western Coll. (1915). Settled 1826 as fur-trapping station; town laid out 1843 and chartered as city 1851; eastern terminus of the Pony Express 1860.

Saint Joseph \ˌsa^{n}-zhō-ˈzef; sānt-ˈjō-zəf, -səf, sənt-\. Village, St. Hyacinthe co., S Quebec, Canada, just SE of St. Hyacinthe; pop. (1971p) 4944.

Saint Joseph, Lake \-ˈjō-zəf, -səf\. Lake, SW Ontario, Canada; 187 sq. m.; a source of the Albany river flowing into James Bay.

Saint Joseph Bay \-ˈjō-zəf-, -səf-\. Inlet of Gulf of Mexico on SW coast of Gulf co., NW Florida.

Saint Joseph d'Al·ma \ˌsa^{n}-zhō-ˈzef-dȧl-ˈmä\. City, ⊗ of East Lake St. John co., S Quebec, Canada, on S bank of Saguenay river 5 m. E of Lake St. John; pop. (1966c) 22,195; paper mills, aluminum plant; nearby **Isle Ma·ligne** \ˌēl-ma-ˈlēn^{y}\ is a major hydroelectric station on the Saguenay.

Saint Joseph de Beauce \ˌsa^{n}-zhō-ˈzef-də-ˈbōs\. Town, Beauce co., S Quebec, Canada, 38 m. SSE of Quebec; pop. (1971p) 2886; shoes, pine timber; diversified agriculture.

Saint Joseph de So·rel \ˌsa^{n}-zhō-ˈzef-də-sə-ˈrel\. Town, Richelieu co., S Quebec, Canada, 48 m. NE of Montreal; pop. (1971p) 3279.

Saint Joseph Island \-ˈjō-zəf-, -səf-\. 1 Island, Aransas co., S Texas, bet. Aransas Bay and Gulf of Mexico.

2 Island, N end of Lake Huron, just E of Chippewa co., Michigan; ab. 19 m. long; belongs to Ontario, Canada.

Saint Joseph Point. Point at N end of narrow peninsula extending from SW coast of Gulf co., NW Florida, into Gulf of Mexico.

Saint Joseph River. See SAINT JOSEPH 1.

Saint–Josse–ten–Noo·de \sa^{n}-ˌzhōs-tä^{n}-ˈnōd\ *or Flemish* **Sint–Joost–ten–Noode** \sint-ˌyōst-tə-ˈnōd-ə\. Commune, Brabant prov., cen. Belgium, a suburb of Brussels; pop. (1969e) 23,469.

Saint Jo·vite \ˌsa^{n}-zhō-ˈvēt\. Village, Terrebonne co., S Quebec, Canada, 65 m. NW of Montreal; pop. (1971p) 2844; diversified agriculture.

Saint–Ju·lien–Beyche·velle \ˌsa^{n}-zhül-ˈya^{n}-bāsh-ˈvel\ *or* **Saint–Julien.** Commune, Gironde dept., SW France, on the Gironde estuary near Pauillac; pop. (1962c) 1165; wine.

Saint–Ju·nien \ˌsa^{n}-zhü-ˈnya^{n}\. Industrial commune, Haute-Vienne dept., W cen. France, 18 m. WNW of Limoges; pop. (1962c) 11,424; hydroelectric power plant; produces paper, leather, woolens, machinery.

Saint Just \-ˈjəst\ *or* **Saint Just in Pen·with** \-pen-ˈwith\. Urban district, Cornwall, SW England, ab. 4 m. N of Land's End; pop. (1971p) 3573; amphitheater where miracle plays were produced in medieval times.

Saint Kil·da \-ˈkil-də\. 1 Municipality, S Victoria, SE Australia, SE suburb of Melbourne on Port Phillip Bay; pop. (1966c) 58,129; residential community and seaside resort.

2 Borough, SE South I., New Zealand, S suburb of Dunedin on Pacific coast; pop. (1970e) 6700.

3 An island of Scotland, westernmost of the Outer Hebrides, in the Atlantic Ocean W of the Sound of Harris, at 57°49′N, 8°36′W; pop. (1961c) 73; max. elev. 1220 ft.

Saint Kitts. See SAINT CHRISTOPHER.

Saint Kitts–Nevis. See SAINT CHRISTOPHER-NEVIS.

Saint Lam·bert \ˌsa^{n}-lä^{n}-ˈber; sānt-ˈlam-bərt, sənt-\. Residential city, Chambly co., S Quebec, Canada, on St. Lawrence river opp. Montreal; pop. (1971p) 18,590; yachting center; part of Greater Montreal.

Saint Lan·dry \-ˈlan-drē\. Parish in Louisiana. See table at LOUISIANA.

Saint Lau·rent \ˌsa^{n}-lə-ˈrä^{n}, ˌsant-lȯ-ˈrent\. 1 City, Montreal I., S Quebec, Canada, 6 m. W of Montreal; pop. (1971p) 63,067; chemicals, aircraft, woolens, stoves; Coll. de Saint-Laurent (1847), Seminaire Sainte Croix (1899), Coll. Basile Moreau (1929).

2 *or* **Saint Laurent du Ma·ro·ni** \-də-ˌmar-ō-ˈnē\. Seaport, N French Guiana, on the Maroni near its mouth; pop. (1967c) 3486.

Saint–Laurent–sur–Mer \ˌsa^{n}-lə-ˈrä^{n}-sü(ə)r-ˈma(ə)r\. Commune, Calvados dept., NW France, on the coast of the Bay of the Seine 8 m. NW of Bayeux. In invasion of Normandy in World War II an American beachhead June 6, 1944; large artificial harbor destroyed off this beach by gale June 19–22, 1944.

Saint Law·rence \-ˈlȯr-ən(t)s, -ˈlär-\. 1 County in New York. See table at NEW YORK.

2 Navigable river, S Quebec and SE Ontario provs., Canada; ab. 760 m. long; flows NE out of Lake Ontario into the Gulf of St. Lawrence; including the waterway provided by the Great Lakes, ab. 2000 m. long. Leaving Lake Ontario the St. Lawrence proper passes through the Thousand Is. (*q.v.*) and for ab. 120 m. forms the boundary bet. New York state and Ontario; on entering Quebec prov. it widens into Lake St. Francis, then passes through Lake St. Louis and the Lachine Rapids past Montreal I.; at Sorel passes through another expansion, Lake St. Peter, and below Quebec around Orleans I. into a wide stream fully 90 m. wide at its mouth in the Gulf of St. Lawrence. Its chief tributaries are the Ottawa, St. Maurice, and Saguenay on the N, and the Richelieu, Yamaska, St. Francis, and Chaudière on the S. Chief cities on it are Ogdensburg (New York), Kingston and Cornwall (Ontario), and Montreal, Sorel, Three Rivers, and Quebec (Quebec). The headstream of the greater St. Lawrence is the St. Louis river in Minnesota; then the waterway passes through Lake Superior, the St. Marys river (by the Sault Sainte Marie Canals, *q.v.*), Lake Huron, St. Clair river, Lake St. Clair, Detroit river, Lake Erie, Niagara river (by the Welland Ship Canal, *q.v.*), and Lake Ontario into the St. Lawrence proper. See SAINT LAWRENCE SEAWAY.

Saint Lawrence, Cape. Point, N coast of Cape Breton I., Canada, on Gulf of St. Lawrence, W of Cape North.

Saint Lawrence, Gulf of. Deep gulf of the Atlantic Ocean off E coast of Canada, bet. Newfoundland and the Canadian mainland (Quebec, New Brunswick, and Nova Scotia provs.); receives the St. Lawrence river in the NW; connected with the Atlantic Ocean through the Strait of Belle Isle on the NE (N of Newfoundland), Cabot Strait on the E (bet. Newfoundland and Cape Breton I.), and Strait of Canso on SE (bet. Nova Scotia mainland and Cape Breton I.). Has many islands, Anticosti, Prince Edward I. (province), Magdalen Is., and islands along the shores.

Saint Lawrence Island. Island, W Alaska, in the Bering Sea 150 m. S of Bering Strait and 118 m. from nearest Alaskan mainland; 95 m. long by ab. 10 to 35 m. wide; 1712 sq. m.; highest point 2204 ft. Chief settlements Gambell at NW point and Savoonga on N cen. coast; inhabited by Eskimos; discovered 1728. Extensive archaeological excavations conducted here by the University of Alaska, tracing development of Eskimo culture for 2000 years.

Saint Lawrence Islands National Park. See CANADA, *National Parks.*

Saint Lawrence Seaway. Waterway, Canada and U.S., along upper St. Lawrence river bet. Montreal and Lake Ontario, in Ontario, Quebec, and New York; permits passage of deep-draft vessels bet. Atlantic Ocean and Great Lakes; includes a system of canals, locks, and dams; hydroelectric power project; constructed 1955–59.

Saint Laz·a·rus, Islands of \-ˈlaz-(ə-)rəs\. Magellan's name for Philippine Islands.

Saint Lé·o·nard \ˌsa^{n}-ˌlā-ȯ-ˈnär; sānt-ˈlen-ərd, sənt-\. City, Montreal and Jesus Islands co., S Quebec, Canada, 4 m. N of Montreal; pop. (1971p) 52,013; residential suburb of Montreal.

Saint-Léonard-de-No·blat \ˌsa^{n}-ˌlā-ȯ-ˌnȧr-də-nȯ-ˈblä\. Town, Haute-Vienne dept., W cen. France, ab. 12 m. E of Limoges; pop. (1962c) 3810; 11th–12th cent. church.

Saint Li·boire \ˌsa^{n}-lē-ˈbwär\. Village, ⊗ of Bagot co., S Quebec, Canada, 12 m. E of St. Hyacinthe; pop. (1971p) 667.

Saint-Lô \sa^{n}-ˈlō; sānt-ˈlō, sənt-\; *anc.* **Bri·o·ve·ra** \ˌbrī-ə-ˈvi(ə)r-ə\ *or later* **Lau·dus** \ˈlȯ-dəs\. Commune, ✱ of Manche dept., NW France, 34 m. W of Caen; pop. (1968c) 18,615; market town; food processing.

History: Fortified by Charlemagne; pillaged by Normans 889, Geoffrey Plantagenet 1141, and Edward III of England 1346. In battle of Normandy in World War II an important German defense base; attacked by Allies July 7, 1944; its capture July 18 after severe fighting resulted in unhinging entire W end of German line and was followed by Allied breakthrough; town almost entirely destroyed in the fighting.

Saint-Lou·is \ˌsa^{n}-lü-ˈē\. **1** Commune, Haut-Rhin dept., NE France, on the Swiss frontier; pop. (1968c) 12,511.

2 Town on SW coast of the island of Réunion in the Indian Ocean; pop. (1962c) 7753.

3 City, Senegal, W Africa, on **Saint-Louis Island** at mouth of the Senegal river; pop. (1969e) 75,000; founded 1658; capital of Senegal until 1958 and of French West Africa 1895–1902.

Saint Louis \-ˈlü-əs\. **1** River, NE Minnesota; 160 m. long; rises near E border of St. Louis co., flows SW, then turns SE to empty into Lake Superior at Duluth; sometimes considered the ultimate source of the St. Lawrence river.

2 Name of counties in two states of the U.S. See tables at MINNESOTA and MISSOURI.

3 City, Gratiot co., cen. Michigan, 17 m. SSE of Mt. Pleasant; pop. (1970c) 4101; oil and gas wells.

4 City, Missouri, on Mississippi river ab. 10 m. below its confluence with the Missouri; pop. (1970c) 622,236; independent of St. Louis co.; largest city in the state; major river port; manufactures aircraft, chemicals, electrical equipment, iron and steel products, paints and varnishes, household appliances, soap, beer; oil refineries, automobile assembly plants. Saint Louis Univ. (1818), Concordia Seminary Coll. (1839), Maryville Coll. of the Sacred Heart (1846), Washington Univ. (1853), Harris Teachers Coll. (1857), Saint Louis Coll. of Pharmacy (1864), Notre Dame Coll. (1896), Cardinal Glennan Coll. (1900), Fontbonne Coll. (1923), Saint Louis Institute of Music (1924), Mercy Junior Coll. (1952), Marrilac Coll. (1955), Univ. of Missouri at St. Louis (1960), Junior Coll. of St. Louis (1963). Settled 1764 under direction of Pierre Laclède and Auguste Chouteau; under Spanish 1770–1800; ceded by France to U.S. 1804; chartered as city 1822; in Civil War a center of Unionist support in Missouri; scene of Louisiana Purchase Exposition 1904.

Saint Louis, Lake \-sa^{n}-ˈlü-ē\. Lake, S Quebec, Canada, SW of Montreal and below Ile Perrot, 57 sq. m.; formed by a widening of St. Lawrence river.

Saint-Louis Island. See SAINT-LOUIS 3.

Saint Louis Park \-ˌlü-əs-\. City, Hennepin co., SE cen. Minnesota, 6 m. WSW of Minneapolis; pop. (1970c) 48,-922; suburb of Minneapolis.

Saint Louis River. See SAINT LOUIS 1.

Saint Luc \sa^{n}-ˈlük, sānt-ˈlük\. Town, Quebec, Canada; pop. (1971p) 4852.

Saint Lu·cia \sānt-ˈlü-shə, sənt-; ˌsānt-lü-ˈsē-ə\. Island, a self-governing state of the Windward Is., E West Indies, S of Martinique and N of St. Vincent; 238 sq. m.; pop. (1970e) 101,100; ✱ Castries; high mountainous volcanic mass, Canaries Mountain 3145 ft., near the S and the Pitons (2619 ft. and 2461 ft.) on SW coast; has rich soil, exports sugar, cocoa, logwood, spices, and coconuts.

History: Probably discovered by Columbus 1502; first settlement by English 1605; contended for by French and English in 17th cent., regarded by both as neutral in 1748 but changed hands many times in wars of late 19th cent. and in Napoleonic Wars; finally became British 1814; in World War II naval base on Gros Islet Bay, N of Castries, leased by Great Britain to U.S. Sept. 3, 1940; became a self-governing state (in association with Great Britain) 1967.

Saint Lucia, Cape. Cape extending into Indian Ocean on E cen. coast of Natal, Rep. of South Africa.

Saint Lucia Bay *or* **Lake Saint Lucia.** Inlet of Indian Ocean, on E coast of Natal, Rep. of South Africa, N of Cape Saint Lucia.

Saint Lucia Channel. Channel bet. the islands of Martinique and Saint Lucia in the West Indies.

Saint Lu·cie \-ˈlü-sē\. County in Florida. See table at FLORIDA.

Saint Lucie Canal. Canal linking the Atlantic coast at Stuart, Florida, with Lake Okeechobee; part of the Cross-Florida Waterway (*q.v.*).

Saint Lucie Inlet. Narrow strait leading from Atlantic Ocean through barrier reef off NE coast of Martin co., SE Florida; E terminus of St. Lucie Canal.

Saint-Maix·ent-l'École \ˌsa^{n}-ˌmek-ˈsä^{n}-lā-ˈkȯl\. Town, Deux-Sèvres dept., W France, 15 m. NE of Niort by rail; pop. (1962c) 6744; abbey church, built 12th–15th cents., destroyed by Protestants 1568, rebuilt 17th cent.

Saint-Ma·lo \ˌsa^{n}-mə-ˈlō\. Commercial seaport, Ille-et-Vilaine dept., NW France, on rocky island in Atlantic Ocean at mouth of Rance river 40 m. NNW of Rennes; pop. (1968c) 42,297; fishing port, tourist resort and yachting center; ships fruit and vegetables; 15th cent. Gothic-Renaissance church (formerly cathedral), 14th cent. castle, town hall, customhouse. Site of a monastery in 6th cent.; became episcopal see in 12th cent.; headquarters of many privateers 17th and 18th cents.; episcopal see suppressed 1790. Birthplace of Jacques Cartier. German occupation forces surrendered to Allies Aug. 17, 1944.

Saint-Malo, Gulf of. Inlet of English Channel, NW coast of France, bet. peninsulas of Normandy and Brittany.

Saint-Man·dé \ˌsa^{n}-mä^{n}-ˈdā\. Commune, Val-de-Marne dept., N France, ESE suburb of Paris near the Bois de Vincennes; pop. (1968c) 23,044; chemicals, furniture.

Saint Marc \sānt-ˈmärk, sənt-; sa^{n}-ˈmȧrk\. Town, W Haiti, 44 m. NW of Port-au-Prince; pop. (1971e) 15,988.

Saint Marc des Car·rières \sa^{n}-ˈmȧrk-dā-kär-ˈya(ə)r\. Village, Portneuf co., S Quebec, Canada, 40 m. W of Quebec; pop. (1971p) 2664.

Saint Mar·ga·ret Bay \-ˌmär-g(ə-)rət-\. Inlet of Atlantic Ocean, S Nova Scotia, Canada, SW of Halifax.

Saint Mar·ies \-mə-ˈrēz\. City, ⊗ of Benewah co., NW Idaho, 30 m. SSE of Coeur d'Alene; pop. (1970c) 2571.

Saint Mark \-ˈmärk\. The island of San Marco, E part of Venice; used in name of Republic of Saint Mark formed by Manin 1848–49. See history at VENICE 3.

Saint Mar·tin \-ˈmärt-^{ə}n\. Parish in Louisiana. See table at LOUISIANA.

Saint Martin *or Du.* **Sint Maar·ten** \sint-ˈmärt-^{ə}n\. Island of E West Indies in Leeward Is. group E of British Virgin Is. and ab. 43 m. NNW of St. Christopher; 37 sq. m.; N section is a dependency of the French department of Guadeloupe and has area of 20 sq. m. and population (1961c) 4502; S section is administratively a part of Netherlands Antilles, and has area of 17 sq. m. and population (1969e) 6081, with ✱ Philipsburg. Produces salt and exports cotton and livestock. Occupied by French and

ə abut; ^{ə} kitten, Fr. table; ər further; a back; ā bake; ä cot, cart; ȧ Fr. bac; au̇ out; ch chin; e less; ē easy; g gift
i trip; ī life; j joke; k̲ Ger. ich, Buch; ^{n} Fr. vin; ŋ sing; ō flow; ȯ flaw; œ Fr. bœuf; œ̄ Fr. feu; ȯi coin; th thin
t̲h̲ this; ü loot; u̇ foot; u̵e Ger. füllen; ū̵e Fr. rue; y yet; ^{y} Fr. digne \dēn^{y}\, nuit \nw^{y}ē\; yü few; yu̇ furious; zh vision

Spanish bet. 1640 and 1648; divided 1648 bet. French and Dutch.

Saint Martin, Lake. Lake, S cen. Manitoba, Canada, E of N Lake Manitoba; 125 sq. m.; Dauphin river, connecting Lakes Manitoba and Winnipeg, passes through it.

Saint–Martin–Bou·logne \ˌsa^{n}-mär-ˈta^{n}-bü-ˈlōn^{y}\. Commune, Pas-de-Calais dept., N France, suburb of Boulogne; pop. (1968c) 12,032.

Saint–Martin d'Hères \ˌsa^{n}-mär-ˈta^{n}-ˈde(ə)r\. Town, Isère dept., SE France, just E of Grenoble; pop. (1968c) 33,605.

Saint Mar·tin·ville \-ˈmärt-ᵊn-ˌvil\. Town, ⊗ of St. Martin parish, S Louisiana, 13 m. ESE of Lafayette; pop. (1970c) 7153; place to which a number of Acadians were sent from Nova Scotia 1755 and later; the Evangeline Oak marks the reputed landing place of the Acadians, and the meeting place of Emmeline Labiche and Louis Arcenaux—the Evangeline and Gabriel of Longfellow's poem *Evangeline.*

Saint Mary \-ˌme(ə)r-ē, -ˈma(ə)r-ē\. 1 Parish in Louisiana. See table at LOUISIANA.

2 River, SW Alberta, Canada, and NW Montana; ab. 75 m. long; rises in Saint Mary lakes, Glacier National Park, NW Montana, and flows NNE to the Oldman river near Lethbridge, Alberta.

Saint Mary, Cape. Point of land, SE Canada, projecting W along W coast of Nova Scotia on S side of entrance to **Saint Mary Bay,** a narrow inlet of the Atlantic ab. 40 m. long, in Digby co.

Saint Mary, Island of *or* **Saint Mary's Island.** Island, Gambia, W Africa, in the Gambia river near its mouth; site of the town of Bathurst, ✱ of Gambia.

Saint Mary Peak. Highest peak in North Flinders Range, E South Australia, NNE of Port Augusta; 3825 ft.

Saint Mary River. See SAINT MARY 2.

Saint Mar·ys \-ˈme(ə)r-ēz, -ˈma(ə)r-ēz\. 1 River, SE Georgia and NE Florida; 175 m. long; rises in Okefenokee Swamp, SE Georgia, forms a section of E Georgia-Florida boundary, and empties into Cumberland Sound N of Amelia I. and NNE of Jacksonville.

2 River, E Michigan penin.; ab. 63 m. long; flows from Whitefish Bay on Lake Superior; forms boundary bet. U.S. and Canada; descending ab. 20 ft. in a mile at **Saint Marys Falls** where canals have been built (see SAULT SAINTE MARIE CANALS), then flows around Sugar I. and Neebish I., W of Saint Joseph I. (Canada) and through Detour Passage into N end of Lake Huron.

3 River, NW Ohio and NE Indiana; ab. 110 m. long; rises in Auglaize co., Ohio, flows N and NW to unite with St. Joseph river at Fort Wayne, Allen co., NE Indiana, and form the Maumee river.

4 County in Maryland. See table at MARYLAND.

5 City, Camden co., SE Georgia, 29 m. S of Brunswick; pop. (1970c) 3408; agriculture.

6 City, Pottawatomie co., NE Kansas, on Kansas river 24 m. WNW of Topeka; pop. (1970c) 1434; one of the oldest towns in Kansas, site of a Roman Catholic mission to the Potawatomi Indians 1847–48.

7 Village, Maryland. See SAINT MARYS CITY.

8 City, Auglaize co., W Ohio, on Lake St. Marys 20 m. SW of Lima; pop. (1970c) 7699; paper, tools and dies; poultry farms; settled 1823.

9 Industrial borough, Elk co., NW cen. Pennsylvania, 24 m. NNE of Du Bois; pop. (1970c) 7470; electronic components, wood and clay products, beer; agriculture.

10 City, ⊗ of Pleasants co., NW West Virginia, on Ohio river; pop. (1970c) 2348; oil and gas wells.

Saint Mary's. Town, Perth co., SE Ontario, Canada, on Thames river 20 m. N of London; pop. (1971p) 4569; farm machinery, hardware; diversified agriculture.

Saint Marys, Lake *also* **Grand Lake** *or* **Grand Reservoir.** Lake, Auglaize and Mercer cos., W Ohio, 9 m. long and 3 m. wide; formed by damming Wabash river.

Saint Mary's Bay. Inlet of Atlantic Ocean, SE Newfoundland, Canada; ab. 40 m. long.

Saint Marys City *or formerly* **Saint Marys.** Village, Saint Marys co., S Maryland; Saint Mary's Coll. of Maryland (1839); first settlement in Maryland made here Mar. 1634 by Leonard Calvert, arriving in the ships *Ark* and *Dove;* site purchased from the Indians; prospered as capital of Maryland until 1694; later declined rapidly until few traces of town remained; revived 1934 at Tercentenary Celebration and site now maintained by state of Maryland.

Saint Marys Falls. See SAINT MARYS 2.

Saint Mary's Island. See SAINT MARY, ISLAND OF.

Saint Mary's Loch. Lake, Selkirk co., SE Scotland; 3 m. long; max. depth 153 ft.

Saint Marys River. Name of three rivers in the U.S. See SAINT MARYS.

Saint–Ma·thieu, Pointe de \ˌpwa^{n}(n)t-də-ˌsa^{n}-mə-ˈtyər\. Cape on the NW coast of France, near Brest.

Saint Mat·thew Island \-ˌmath-yü-\. 1 Island, cen. Bering Sea, Alaska, 63°30'N, 170°30'W, 135 m. W of Nunivak I.; 123 sq. m.; includes Hall islet off NW; uninhabited.

2 Island, Mergui Archipelago. See ZADETSKYI ISLAND.

Saint Mat·thews \-ˈmath-(ˌ)yüz\. 1 City, Jefferson co., N cen. Kentucky, E suburb of Louisville; pop. (1970c) 13,152.

2 Town, ⊗ of Calhoun co., cen. South Carolina, 13 m. NNE of Orangeburg; pop. (1970c) 2403; lumber; livestock, cotton.

Saint Mat·thi·as Group \-mə-ˌthī-əs-\. Group of small islands in N Bismarck Archipelago, W Pacific Ocean, NNW of island of New Hanover; largest is Mussau; Emirau I. in S part of group occupied by U.S. Marines Mar. 19, 1944.

Saint–Maur–des–Fos·sés \ˌsa^{n}-ˌmȯr-dā-fō-ˈsā\. Industrial commune, Val-de-Marne dept., N France, SE suburb of Paris on Marne river; pop. (1968c) 77,251; residential; produces felt, cork, chemicals.

Saint–Mau·rice \ˌsa^{n}-mō-ˈrēs\ *or formerly* **Pe·tit–Cha·ren·ton** \pə-ˈtē-ˌsha-rä^{n}-ˈtō^{n}\. Commune, Val-de-Marne dept., N France, SE suburb of Paris; pop. (1968c) 10,477; Protestant stronghold 1606–85.

Saint–Maurice \ˌsa^{n}-mə-ˈrēs, ˌsānt-; sānt-ˈmȯr-əs, sənt-, -ˈmär-\. 1 River, S Quebec, Canada; 325 m. long; flows S from Gouin Reservoir into the St. Lawrence river at Three Rivers; chief tributary the Mattawin from the W. See SHAWINIGAN.

2 County, Quebec, Canada. See table at QUEBEC.

Saint Mi·chael \-ˈmī-kəl\. 1 Village, W Alaska, on S coast of Norton Sound and SW of Unalakleet; pop. (1970c) 207.

2 Island, Azores. See SÃO MIGUEL.

Saint Mi·chaels Bay \-ˈmī-kəlz-\. Bay, E coast of Labrador, Canada, 52°44'N.

Saint Michael's Mount. Lofty rock in Mounts Bay, Cornwall, SW England; seat of an ancient castle.

Saint Mi·chel \ˌsa^{n}-mē-ˈshel\. City, Montreal I., S Quebec, Canada, N of Montreal city; pop. (1966c) 71,446; suburb of Montreal.

Saint–Mi·hiel \ˌsa^{n}-mē-ˈyel\. Commune, Meuse dept., NE France; pop. (1962c) 5366; battle Sept. 12–14, 1918, one of the principal battles at the close of World War I; Germans driven from salient (held since 1914) in first major American offensive under Gen. Pershing.

Saint–Mo·ritz \ˌsānt-mə-ˈrits\ *or Ger.* **Sankt Moritz** \ˌzäŋ(k)t-\ *or Romansh* **San Mu·rez·zan** \ˌsän-mü-ˈret-ˌsän\. Commune, Graubünden canton, E Switzerland, on Inn river in upper Engadine 28 m. SSE of Chur; pop. (1970c) 5699; major winter resort; thermal springs; site of Winter Olympic Games 1928 and 1948.

Saint–Na·zaire \ˌsa^{n}-nə-ˈza(ə)r, -ˈze(ə)r\. Seaport and industrial commune, Loire-Atlantique dept., NW France, at mouth of Loire river 33 m. WNW of Nantes; pop. (1968c) 63,289; major shipbuilding center and fishing port; produces aircraft, chemicals, steel, canned fish, fertilizers.

History: Believed to occupy site of ancient **Car·bi·lo** \ˈkär-bə-ˌlō\ where Romans built a fleet 56 B.C.; developed as a port from mid-19th cent.; in World War I a major port of debarkation for American Expeditionary Force 1917–

18; in World War II a German submarine base 1940–44; in 1942 scene of British commando raid which destroyed principal dock; surrounded by Allied forces Aug. 1944 and surrendered May 1945; town almost entirely destroyed from Allied bombing but since rebuilt.

Saint Neots \-ˈnēts\. Urban district, Huntingdon and Peterborough co., England, ab. 50 m. N of London; pop. (1971p) 10,329; 15th cent. church and stone bridge.

Saint Nicholas. See SÃO NICOLAU.

Saint Nich·o·las, Mount \-ˈnik-(ə-)ləs\. Peak in Glacier National Park, NW Montana; 9380 ft.

Saint Nicholas Point. See PUDJUT, POINT.

Saint–Ni·co·las \ˌsa^{n}-ˌnē-kȯ-ˈlä\. 1 Commune, Belgium. See SINT-NIKLAAS.

2 Commune, Liège prov., E Belgium, W suburb of Liège; pop. (1969e) 10,023.

3 *or* **Saint Nicolas du Port** \-də-ˈpȯ(ə)r\. Commune, Meurthe-et-Moselle dept., NE France, ab. 8 m. SE of Nancy; pop. (1966e) 6551; 15th–16th cent. Gothic church; noted for its fairs in 16th and 17th cents.

Saint–Omer \ˌsa^{n}-tȯ-ˈme(ə)r\. Commune, Pas-de-Calais dept., N France, 40 m. NW of Arras; pop. (1962c) 18,205; ships fruit and vegetables; produces linen, paper, cement, glass; 13th–15th cent. church (cathedral 1563–1801), museums, library. Monastery founded on site by St. Omer 7th cent.; fortified settlement 9th cent.; prosperous center of wool trade with England 11th–13th cents.; in World War I one of the headquarters of the British Army.

Sain·tonge \sa^{n}-ˈtō^{n}zh\. Ancient province of France, on the Bay of Biscay N of the Gironde; comprised most of present department of Charente-Maritime and small part of Charente; ✻ Saintes; country of the Santones; ceded to England 1360, retaken by DuGuesclin 1371; passed to French crown 1375.

Saint–Ou·en \sa^{n}-ˈtwa^{n}\. Manufacturing and commercial commune, Seine-St-Denis dept., N suburb of Paris on Seine river, N France; pop. (1968c) 48,886; a center of metallurgical and automobile manufacturing industries.

Saint Pas·cal \ˌsa^{n}-pas-ˈkal\. Town, ⊗ of Kamouraska co., S Quebec, Canada, 85 m. ENE of Quebec, near right bank of St. Lawrence river and on highway to Gaspé Penin.; pop. (1971p) 2491.

Saint–Paul \sa^{n}-ˈpȯl\. Town on NW coast of Réunion I.; pop. (1971e) 47,861.

Saint Paul \-ˈpȯl\. 1 City, ✻ of Minnesota and ⊗ of Ramsey co., E Minnesota, on Mississippi river 10 m. E of Minneapolis; pop. (1970c) 309,828; transportation and commercial center; livestock market; produces automobiles, chemicals, electronic equipment, abrasives, paints and varnishes, steel; breweries, oil refineries, printing plants. Macalester Coll. (1853), Hamline Univ. (1854), Bethel Coll. (1871), Coll. of St. Thomas (1885), Concordia Coll. (1893), Saint Paul Seminary (1895), William Mitchell Coll. of Law (1900), Coll. of St. Catherine (1906), Saint Paul Bible Coll. (1916). First settlement on site 1838; made capital of Minnesota Territory 1849; incorporated 1854; made capital of the state 1858.

2 City, ⊗ of Howard co., E cen. Nebraska, 21 m. N of Grand Island; pop. (1970c) 2026; dairy, grain farms.

3 Town, Alberta, Canada, 90 m. ENE of Edmonton; pop. (1971p) 4171; diversified agriculture; lake resort; feed and flour mills.

4 River, Liberia, W Africa; ab. 125 m. long; flows into the Atlantic Ocean near Monrovia.

5 *Fr.* sa^{n}-pȯl\. Uninhabited island, S Indian Ocean, 38°43′S, 77°32′E, just S of Amsterdam I.; part of French Southern and Antarctic Lands.

Saint Paul, Cape. Cape extending into the Bight of Benin on SE coast of Ghana, W Africa, E of the mouth of the Volta river.

Saint Paul Island. 1 Island most northerly of Pribilof Is. (*q.v.*) in Bering Sea, Alaska; 35 sq. m.; 13 m. long by ab. 6 m. wide.

2 Island, Cabot Strait, ab. 14 m. off Cape North, N Cape Breton I., at entrance to Gulf of St. Lawrence, E Canada; lighthouse.

Saint Paul Park. Village, Washington co., E Minnesota, 9 m. SSE of St. Paul; pop. (1970c) 5587.

Saint Paul's Bay. See BAIE SAINT PAUL.

Saint Paul's Rocks *or Port.* **Pe·ne·dos de São Pe·dro e São Pau·lo** \pə-ˌnā-düs-də-sä(^{n})m-ˈpā-drü-e-sä(^{n})m-ˈpau̇-(ˌ)lü\. Group of volcanic rocks in the Atlantic Ocean, 0°56′N, 29°22′W, ab. 600 m. NE of Natal, Brazil.

Saint Pe·ter \-ˈpēt-ər\. City, ⊗ of Nicollet co., S Minnesota, on Minnesota river 12 m. N of Mankato; pop. (1970c) 8339; clothing; diversified agriculture; Gustavus Adolphus Coll. (1862).

Saint Peter, Lake. Lake, S Quebec, Canada, 60 m. NE of the city of Montreal; 142 sq. m.; formed by a widening of St. Lawrence river.

Saint Peter Port. Town and civil parish, Guernsey, Channel Is.; pop. (1961c) 15,804; ✻ of Guernsey bailiwick; house of Victor Hugo is preserved as he left it (his residence 1855–70).

Saint Pe·ters \-ˈpēt-ərz\. Town, NE suburb of Adelaide, SE South Australia; pop. (1966c) 11,334.

Saint Peter's. See BROADSTAIRS AND SAINT PETER'S.

Saint Pe·ters·burg \-ˈpēt-ərz-ˌbərg\. 1 City, Pinellas co., W cen. Florida penin., on W shore of Tampa Bay; pop. (1970c) 216,232; ships fruit and vegetables; winter resort, yachting and sport-fishing center; Saint Petersburg Junior Coll. (1927), Eckerd Coll. (1960); settled c. 1888; incorporated 1892.

2 Capital of Russia 1712–1917. See LENINGRAD.

Saint Petersburg Beach. City, Pinellas co., W cen. Florida; pop. (1970c) 8024.

Saint Phil·ip and Saint James Bay \-ˈfil-əp . . . ˈjāmz-\. Large inlet on N coast of Espíritu Santo I., New Hebrides Is., SW Pacific, bet. two peninsulas.

Saint–Pierre \sa^{n}-ˈpye(ə)r\. Town, SW coast of the island of Réunion, Indian Ocean; pop. (1971e) 43,808.

Saint Pierre \sānt-ˈpi(ə)r, sənt-; *Fr.* sa^{n}-pyer\. 1 Town, Montreal I., S Quebec, Canada, on N bank of Lachine Canal bet. Montreal and Lachine; pop. (1971p) 6762; glass.

2 *or Fr.* **Saint–Pierre** \sa^{n}-pyer\. Small island off S coast of Newfoundland, Canada, in Atlantic Ocean; part of French territory of Saint Pierre and Miquelon; 10 sq. m.; chief town Saint Pierre; rocky and of very irregular shape.

3 *or Fr.* **Saint–Pierre.** Town on Saint Pierre I. off Newfoundland, Canada; pop. (1967e) 4000; seat of government of territory of Saint Pierre and Miquelon; its harbor is port for fishing fleet.

4 Small island in the Indian Ocean 240 m. NNE of Malagasy Republic; ab. $^{1}/_{2}$ sq. m.; pop. (1960e) 45, belongs to British colony of Seychelles.

5 Island in Lake of Biel, W Switzerland; home of Rousseau 1765.

6 *or Fr.* **Saint–Pierre.** Town, Martinique I., West Indies; pop. (1961c) 5434; had pop. of 26,000 before its destruction by volcanic eruption of Mount Pelée 1902.

Saint Pierre and Miq·ue·lon \-ˈmik-ə-ˌlän\ *or Fr.* **Saint–Pierre et Mi·que·lon** \sa^{n}-pye(ə)r-ā-mē-klō^{n}\. French overseas territory consisting of two small islands, Saint Pierre and Miquelon, in the Atlantic Ocean just S of Newfoundland, Canada; 93 sq. m.; pop. (1971e) 5600; ✻ Saint Pierre. Chief occupation cod fishing; exports dried and frozen cod, fox and mink pelts; tourism.

History: Visited by French fishermen 16th and 17th cents., esp. Bretons and Basques; settlement increased by French expelled from Newfoundland 1713 and from

Acadia 1763. For the next century fishing rights of French on the islands and on the French Shore (*q.v.*) a source of international controversy, which was finally settled 1904. Classified as a territory 1946 by French Constitution of Fourth Republic.

Saint-Pierre-de-Chartreuse. See CHARTREUSE, LA GRANDE.

Saint-Pierre-Saint-Paul. See OULED MOUSSA.

Saint-Pol-de-Lé·on \saⁿ-ˌpòl-də-lā-'ōⁿ\. Town, Finistère dept., NW France, ab. 30 m. NE of Brest and ab. 1 m. from the coast; pop. (1962c) 6271; 13th-14th cent. cathedral.

Saint-Pol-sur-Mer \saⁿ-ˌpòl-sü(ə)r-'me(ə)r\. Commune, Nord dept., WSW suburb of Dunkerque, N France; pop. (1968c) 19,084; seaside resort.

Saint-Priest \saⁿ-'prēst\. Commune, NW Isère dept., SE France; pop. (1968c) 20,419; castle of the ancient countship.

Saint-Pri·vat-la-Mon·tagne \ˌsaⁿ-prē-'vä-lä-mōⁿ-'taⁿnʸ\ *or* **Saint-Privat.** Village, Moselle dept., NE France, 7 m. NW of Metz; pop. (1962c) 1124; scene of critical phase of battle of Gravelotte Aug. 18, 1870.

Saint-Quen·tin \ˌsaⁿ-käⁿ-'taⁿ; sānt-'kwent-ᵊn, sənt-\. Industrial commune, Aisne dept., N France, on Somme river 25 m. NW of Laon; pop. (1968c) 64,196; textiles, iron goods, chemicals, machinery; 12th-15th cent. church, 14th-16th cent. city hall; important center of woolen industry during Middle Ages; came under French crown 1191; ceded to Burgundians 1435-77; scene of Spanish victory over the French 1557; center of major battle in Franco-Prussian War Jan. 1871; in World War I scene of decisive British breakthrough, September-October 1918.

Saint-Ra·pha·ël \ˌsaⁿ-ˌraf-ə-'el\. Town, Var dept., SE France, on the Riviera ab. 18 m. SW of Cannes; pop. (1962c) 9470; scene of severe fighting Aug. 1944.

Saint Raphaël. Village, ⊗ of Bellechasse co., S Quebec, Canada, 24 m. E of Quebec; pop. (1971p) 1220; agriculture.

Saint Ray·mond \ˌsaⁿ-rā-'mōⁿ; sānt-'rā-mənd, sənt-\. Town, Portneuf co., S Quebec, Canada, on Ste. Anne river 28 m. W of Quebec; pop. (1971p) 4000.

Saint Re·gis Indian Reservation \-'rē-jəs-\. Settlement, partly in Franklin co., NE New York, and partly in Huntingdon co., Quebec, Canada, on right bank of St. Lawrence river ab. 20 m. NW of Malone, New York; ab. 9 m. long by 3 m. wide; farming, basketmaking, etc.; inhabited chiefly by descendants of Saint Regis tribe of Iroquois Indians.

Saint Ré·mi \ˌsaⁿ-rā-'mē\. Town, Napierville co., S Quebec, Canada, 17 m. S of Montreal; pop. (1971p) 2297.

Saint-Ré·my-de-Pro·vence \ˌsaⁿ-rā-ˌmē-də-prə-'väⁿs\ *or* **Saint-Rémy.** Town, Bouches-du-Rhône dept., SE France, ab. 15 m. NE of Arles; pop. (1962c) 4420.

Saint-Ri·quier \ˌsaⁿ-rē-'kā\. Town, Somme dept., N France, ab. 8 m. NE of Abbeville; pop. (1962c) 1129; abbey founded 7th cent.

Saint Ro·mu·ald \saⁿ-ˌròm-ü-'al\ *or* **Saint Romuald-d'Etch·e·min** \-dech-'maⁿ\. City, ⊗ of Levis co., S Quebec, Canada, ab. 6 m. SW of Levis; pop. (1971p) 8439; glass, clothing, metal goods.

Saint-Sau·veur-le-Vi·comte \ˌsaⁿ-sō-'vər-lə-vē-'kōⁿt\. Commune, Manche dept., NW France, 18 m. S of Cherbourg; pop. (1962c) 2239. An old Norman town, once a possession of Sir John Chandos; in World War II taken by U.S. forces June 18, 1944.

Saint Sé·bas·tien, Cape \-ˌsānt-sə-'bas-chən, -ˌsaⁿ-ˌsā-bäs-'tyaⁿ\. Cape projecting into N Mozambique Channel on extreme NW coast of the Malagasy Republic.

Saint Si·mon Island \-'sī-mən-\. Island, E coast of Glynn co., SE Georgia, in Atlantic Ocean S of entrance to Altamaha Sound; 36 sq. m.

Saint So·phia Ridge \-sə-ˌfī-ə-\. Peak, Ouray and San Miguel cos., SW Colorado; 13,100 ft.

Saint Ste·phen \-'stē-vən\. Town, Charlotte co., SW New Brunswick, Canada, on St. Croix river 15 m. NW of its mouth and at head of navigation; pop. (1966c) 3285; lumber; diversified agriculture.

Saint Tam·ma·ny \-'tam-ə-nē\. Parish in Louisiana. See table at LOUISIANA.

Saint Thom·as \-'täm-əs\. **1** City, ⊗ of Elgin co., SE Ontario, Canada, near Lake Erie 15 m. S of London; pop. (1971p) 25,062; electric motors, automobile and aircraft parts, bearings, tile; Alma Coll. (1878); founded 1810.

2 Island, Gulf of Guinea. See SÃO TOMÉ 1.

3 Island, U.S. Virgin Is., West Indies, ab. 40 m. E of Puerto Rico; separated from Culebra I. on W by Virgin Passage; 28 sq. m.; pop. (1968e) 31,867; ✱ Charlotte Amalie (also ✱ of U.S. Virgin Is.) on S coast; second in size and commercially the most important of the group; of volcanic origin, with range of hills traversing island E to W (highest point 1556 ft.). Coastline much indented, with **Saint Thomas Harbor,** the harbor of Charlotte Amalie, a good anchorage; has fueling and repair facilities. Produces bay oil and bay rum; tourism. Discovered and named by Columbus 1493; first settlement by Dutch 1657, who soon abandoned it; occupied by Danes 1666 and 1672; in 19th cent. twice held temporarily by English. See VIRGIN ISLANDS, WEST INDIES.

4 Town, Saint Thomas Island. See CHARLOTTE AMALIE.

Saint Tho·mé \ˌsānt-tə-'mā\ *or Port.* **São To·mé** \ˌsaù(ⁿ)n-tü-'mā\. Originally Portuguese fort (1615-69) on Coromandel Coast, India; now part of the city of Madras (*q.v.*). Occupied by English 1749; battle bet. French and English 1759.

Saint Tite \saⁿ-'tēt\. Town, Champlain co., S Quebec, Canada, 27 m. N of Three Rivers; pop. (1971p) 3136.

Saint-Trond. See SINT-TRUIDEN.

Saint-Tro·pez \ˌsaⁿ-trò-'pā\. Commune, Var dept., SE France, on Bay of St. Tropez, SSW of Fréjus; pop. (1962c) 5689; noted seaside resort.

Saint Ubes. See SETÚBAL 2.

Saint-Va·lé·ry-sur-Somme \ˌsaⁿ-ˌval-ā-ˌrē-sü(ə)r-'sòm\. Town, Somme dept., NE France, on S side of mouth of the Somme just NW of Abbeville; pop. (1962c) 3176; point of departure of William the Conqueror 1066 for invasion of England. See DIVES.

Saint-Ve·nant \saⁿ(n)v-'näⁿ\. Commune, Pas-de-Calais dept., N France, on the Lys river N of Béthune; pop. (1962c) 4076; as fortified place important in latter part of Thirty Years' War and in War of the Spanish Succession.

Saint Vin·cent \-'vin(t)-sənt\. **1** Island off SW coast of Franklin co., NW Florida, bet. Apalachicola Bay on E and Gulf of Mexico on W; 19 sq. m.

2 Island, Cape Verde Is. See SÃO VICENTE 2.

3 Self-governing state of the Windward Is., West Indies; comprises St. Vincent I. and the northern Grenadines (including Union and Bequia); 150 sq. m.; pop. (1970e) 89,129; ✱ Kingstown, on SW coast of St. Vincent I.

4 Principal island of the state, S of Saint Lucia and W of Barbados; ab. 18 m. long by 11 m. wide; area 133 sq. m.; ✱ Kingstown; volcanic, with many hills and valleys; highest point Soufrière volcano 4048 ft.; noted for its sea-island cotton; also produces arrowroot, copra, cocoa, sugar, molasses, spices; has botanical garden, established 1768.

History: One of the original homes of the Carib Indians; island supposed to have been sighted by Columbus 1498; granted 1627 by Charles I for English settlement and several times later by English sovereigns, but possession by English not confirmed until Treaty of Paris 1763; held by French 1779-83. Has suffered much from hurricanes (esp. 1898) and volcanic eruptions (Soufrière May 1902); became, with N Grenadines, a self-governing state (in association with Great Britain) 1969.

5 City, Brazil. See SÃO VICENTE 1.

Saint Vincent, Cape. **1** Cape on W coast of the Malagasy Republic, 21°57′S, 43°16′E.

2 *or Port.* **Ca·bo de São Vi·cen·te** \ˌkä-bü-də-ˌsaùⁿ-vē-'sā(ⁿ)n-tə\; *Roman name* **Pro·mon·to·ri·um Sa·crum**

\ˌpräm-ən-ˌtōr-ē-əm-'sā-krəm, -ˌtȯr-\. Cape, SW point of Portugal, ab. 118 m. S of Lisbon. Regarded by ancient geographers Marinus and Ptolemy as westernmost point of Europe. On the cape or nearby at **Sa·gres** \'sä-grĕsh\ 3 m. E, Prince Henry the Navigator established c. 1420 his school of navigation and observatory; lighthouse now on site of ruins. In naval battle fought 25 to 30 m. SW of cape English admiral Sir John Jervis (later Earl of St. Vincent) defeated Spanish fleet under Don José de Córdoba Feb. 14, 1797; other naval battles off the cape were: defeat of English and Dutch 1693 by French Admiral Tourville; defeat of Spanish 1780 by English Admiral Rodney; and defeat 1833 of fleet of Portuguese usurper Dom Miguel by fleet of Dom Pedro I.

Saint Vincent, Gulf of. Gulf, South Australia, E of Yorke Penin.; ab. 100 m. long; connected with Indian Ocean by Investigator Strait on SW and Backstairs Passage on S; Kangaroo I. across its entrance; Adelaide and Port Adelaide, its seaport, are on its E shore.

Saint Vi·tal \-və-'tal\. City, Manitoba, Canada; pop. (1971p) 32,613; residential suburb of Winnipeg.

Saint Vital, Point \-'vīt-əl\. Point in SE Chippewa co., E Michigan penin., extending into Lake Huron.

Saint–Vith \saⁿ-'vēt\ *or* **Sankt–Vith** \zäŋkt-'vēt\. Town, Liège prov., E Belgium, near Luxembourg border 35 m. SE of Liège; pop. (1969e) 2966; formerly German. In World War II in the Battle of the Bulge (E Belgium), taken by Germans Dec. 1944 and retaken by U.S. troops after severe fighting Jan. 23, 1945.

Saint–Yri·eix–la–Perche \ˌsaⁿ-ti(ə)r-ˌyā-lä-'persh\. Town, S Haute-Vienne dept., W cen. France; pop. (1962c) 3905; china-clay deposits.

Saint Yves. See SETÚBAL 2.

Sai·pan \sī-'pän, -'pan, 'sī-ˌ\. 1 Island, S cen. Mariana Is., W Pacific Ocean; 14 m. long and 2 to 5 m. wide; area 70 sq. m.; pop. (1971e) 10,458. Hilly with highest point 1551 ft.; at N end, Marpi Point, are high cliffs. On SE coast is wide inlet, Magicienne Bay; best anchorage is Tanapag Harbor on W coast just N of Garapan. Spanish possession 1565–1899; German 1899–1914; included in Japanese mandate 1919, and developed as naval base with several airfields; captured by U.S. troops after severe fighting June 15 to July 9, 1944; developed into major American air base, used Nov. 1944 to end of war.

2 Village, W coast of Angaur I., S Palau Is.

Sairam Nor. See SAI-LI-MU HU.

Sairussu. See SAYR USA.

Sa·ïs \'sā-əs\. Important city in ancient Egypt, ancient capital of Lower Egypt, in the Nile delta on the Canopic branch of the river; 30°57'N, 30°48'E.

Saishu. See CHEJU 2.

Saishu To. See CHEJU 1.

Sai·ta·ma \'sī-tə-(ˌ)mä, sī-'täm-ə\. Prefecture, Honshū, Japan; 1467 sq. m.; pop. (1970c) 3,866,472; ✱ Urawa; sericulture; textiles.

Sa·ja·ma \sə-'häm-ə\ *also* **Sa·ha·ma** \sə-'(h)äm-ə\. Peak, W Bolivia, near Chilean boundary; 21,391 ft.

Sa·jó \'shō-(ˌ)yō\. River, Czechoslovakia and Hungary; 125 m. long; rises in Slovak S.R., Czechoslovakia, flows S and SE to the Tisza.

Sa·kai \'säk-ˌī\. City, Ōsaka prefecture, W cen. Honshū, Japan, 6 m. S of Ōsaka on Ōsaka Bay; pop. (1970c) 594,367; machinery, hosiery, chemicals and dyes, fertilizer, automobile parts; numerous earthen tombs, including that of Emperor Nitoku; in 16th cent. a leading seaport but declined after silting up of harbor.

Sa·kai·de \sä-'kī-(ˌ)dā\. City, Kagawa prefecture, Shikoku, Japan, 12 m. W of Takamatsu; pop. (1970c) 64,147.

Sa·ka·ka *or* **Sa·kā·kā** \sə-'käk-ə\. Town, N Nejd, Saudi Arabia, ab. 35 m. ENE of Jauf.

Sakartvelo. See GEORGIAN SOVIET SOCIALIST REPUBLIC.

Sa·kar·ya \sə-'kär-yə\ *or anc.* **San·gar·i·us** \saŋ-'gar-ē-əs, -'ger-\. 1 River, NW Turkey; 510 m. long; rises in mountains N of Afyonkarahisar and flows in double curve E, W, and N into the Black Sea 80 m. E of the Bosporus. The Porsuk and Ankara are its chief tributaries; Adapazari is chief town on its banks.

2 Province of NW Turkey, Asia. See table at TURKEY.

Sa·ka·ta \sə-'kät-ə, 'säk-ə-ˌtä\. Seaport city, Yamagata prefecture, N Honshū, Japan, 85 m. N of Niigata; pop. (1970c) 96,072; Shinto shrine.

Sa·kha·lin \'sak-ə-ˌlēn, -lən\ *or formerly* **Sa·ghal·ien** \ˌsäg-əl-'yen\ *or Jap.* **Ka·ra·fu·to** \ˌkär-ə-'füt-(ˌ)ō\. Island, Sakhalin Oblast, Russian S.F.S.R., U.S.S.R., N of Japan in W part of Sea of Okhotsk; 28,597 sq. m.; 589 m. long, 16 to 100 m. wide, average width 62 m.; separated from Russian mainland on W by Tatar Strait and from Hokkaidō, Japan, on S by Sōya Strait; in SE are two large inlets Terpeniya Bay and Aniva Bay; covered with forests; in S mountainous, highest point 5277 ft.; fishing and fish canning, lumbering, coal mining; oil wells, ship-repairing yards.

History: In ancient times Chinese; first visited by Japanese c. 1630; explored by them ab. end of 18th cent.; disputed bet. Japan and Russia 1853–75; first settled by Russians 1853, came entirely under Russian control 1875 when Japan ceded it in exchange for Kuril Is.; occupied by Japanese 1905; S part below 50°N granted to Japan by Treaty of Portsmouth 1905, returned to U.S.S.R. 1946 after defeat of Japan by Allies in World War II.

Sakhalin, Gulf of. Inlet of Sea of Okhotsk bet. N end of Sakhalin I. and mainland of Khabarovsk Krai, U.S.S.R.; on S connects with Tatar Strait.

Sakhalin Oblast \-'ō-bləst, -ˌblast\. Subdivision of the Russian S.F.S.R., U.S.S.R., consisting of Sakhalin I. and the Kuril Is.; 33,629 sq. m.; pop. (1970p) 616,000; principal towns Yuzhno-Sakhalinsk, Korsakov, Kholmsk, and Okha. See KURIL ISLANDS and SAKHALIN.

Sakhar. See SUKKUR.

Sakhara. See SAQQARA.

Sakis–Adasi. See CHIOS.

Sa·ki·shi·ma Islands \ˌsäk-i-'shē-mə-\. Group of ab. 20 small islands in S section of Ryukyu Is. (*q.v.*), in W Pacific Ocean off E coast of N Taiwan; 343 sq. m.; all formed of coral reefs. Largest are Miyako, Ishigaki, and Iriomote. In World War II site of Japanese airfields, frequently bombed by British and U.S. carrier planes Apr. to June 1945.

Sakkara. See SAQQARA.

Sak·ma·ra \sək-'mär-ə\. River, E Russian S.F.S.R., U.S.S.R.; 440 m. long; rises in S Ural Mts. in Bashkir A.S.S.R. and flows S and W to the Ural river at Orenburg.

Sa·kon Na·khon \sə-'kȯn-nə-'kȯn\ *or* **Sa·kol Na·korn** \sə-'kȯn-nə-'kȯn—*sic*\. 1 Province, NE Thailand; 3683 sq. m.; pop. (1960c) 420,755; ✱ Sakon Nakhon.

2 Town, its ✱, on a small lake with outlet to the Mekong, 50 m. W of Nakhon Phanom; pop. (1960c) 15,997.

Sa·kon·net River \sə-ˌkän-ət-, -ˌkən-\. Inlet of Atlantic Ocean extending into Newport co., SE Rhode Island, E of Rhode I. (island).

Sakota. See SEKOTA.

Sak·ti \'sək-tē\. Former Indian state, now part of Madhya Pradesh, India, 45 m. E of Bilaspur; 137 sq. m.; ✱ Sakti.

Sa·ku \'säk-ˌü\. City, Nagano prefecture, Honshū, Japan, 27 m. E of Matsumoto; pop. (1970c) 55,214.

Sakurajima. See ON-TAKE.

Sal, Cay \'kē-'sal, 'kā-\. Lighthouse in W Bahama Is. See CAY SAL BANK.

Sala. See IJSSEL.

Salaberry de Valleyfield. See VALLEYFIELD.

Sa·la·di·llo \ˌsal-ə-'dē-(ˌ)(y)ō\. Name of several rivers in Argentina, esp.: (1) the upper course of the Dulce (*q.v.*); (2) river in N cen. part, in Córdoba prov., flowing E, joining

Tercero river to form the Carcarañá, a tributary of the Paraná.

Sa·la·do \sə-'läd-(,)ō\. 1 River, W cen. Oriente prov., E Cuba; 60 m. long; flows W into Cauto river.

2 River, Coahuila and Nuevo León states, NE Mexico; ab. 250 m. long; flows SE into the Rio Grande river; in upper course known as the **Sa·bi·nas** \sə-'bē-nəs\.

Salado, Río \'rē-(,)ō-sə-'läth-(,)ō, -'läd-\. 1 Three rivers in Argentina: (1) river in N part; more than 1100 m. long; rises in Andes Mts. and flows SE into the Paraná river at Santa Fe; (2) river in W part; ab. 850 m. long; flows S forming boundary bet. Mendoza and San Luis provs., turns SE and empties into Colorado river; known as **Des·a·gua·de·ro** \,des-,äg-wə-'de(ə)r-(,)ō\ in its upper course, and as **Cha·di·leo** \,chäd-ᵊl-'ā-(,)ō\ in its course through La Pampa prov.; (3) river in E part, in Buenos Aires prov.; ab. 400 m. long; flows W into Samborombón Bay.

2 Small river, Cádiz prov., S Spain near Tarifa; battle on its bank Oct. 30, 1340 in which Alfonso XI of Castile as ally of Alfonso IV of Portugal defeated the Moors.

Salado Bay \sə-'lad-(,)ō-, -'läd-\. Inlet of Pacific Ocean on W coast of Atacama prov., N cen. Chile.

Sa·la·ga \'säl-ə-gə\. Town, Ghana, W Africa, E of the Volta and ab. 60 m. SSE of Tamale; pop. (1970p) 6647.

Salahiyeh. See DURA-EUROPOS.

Sălaj \sə-'läzh\. County of NW Romania. See table at ROMANIA.

Salajar. See SELAJAR.

Salajar Strait. See SELAJAR STRAIT.

Sa·lak \'säl-,äk\. Volcano, W Java, Indonesia, SW of Bogor; 7252 ft.; tea and coffee plantations on its slopes. Severe eruptions 1669 and 1699.

Sa·la·lah \sə-'lal-ə\. Coastal town, Oman, ab. 80 m. E of Yemen (✱ Aden) border.

Sa·la·má \,säl-ə-'mä\. Town, ✱ of Baja Verapaz dept., cen. Guatemala; munic. pop. (1964p) 18,632.

Sal·a·man·ca \,sal-ə-'maŋ-kə\. City, Cattaraugus co., SW New York, on Allegheny river 13 m. WNW of Olean; pop. (1970c) 7877; within Allegany Indian Reservation, from whom ground is leased; furniture; dairy farms.

Salamanca \,sal-ə-'maŋ-kə, ,säl-ə-'mäŋ-\. 1 Town, Guanajuato state, cen. Mexico, 17 m. S of Guanajuato; munic. pop. (1970p) 103,740.

2 Province of W Spain. See table at SPAIN.

3 *anc.* **Sal·man·ti·ca** \sal-'mant-i-kə\ *or* **Hel·man·ti·ca** \hel-\. Commune, ✱ of Salamanca prov., W Spain, on Tormes river 107 m. WNW of Madrid; pop. (1970p) 125,220; center of an agricultural region; two cathedrals (12th cent. Romanesque and 16th cent. Gothic), Roman bridge, notable colonnaded square, the Plaza Mayor, lined with Renaissance buildings; Univ. of Salamanca (1218; one of the major universities of medieval Europe), Pontifical Univ. of Salamanca (1940).

History: Important city of the Vettones, conquered by Hannibal 220 B.C.; became Roman military station on the road from Augusta Emerita (Mérida) to Asturica Augusta (Astorga); captured by Moors early 8th cent.; reconquered by Christians 1095 but a disputed city between Moors and Christians until c. 1187; in Peninsular War occupied by the French, and scene of a victory of the British under Wellington over the French 1812.

Sal·a·maua \,sal-ə-'maü-ə\. Coastal town, New Guinea I., Papua New Guinea, on W shore of Huon Gulf ab. 19 m. S of Lae; has good harbor. Seized by Japanese Mar. 8, 1942; made a military base; scene of much fighting bet. Apr. 1942 and Sept. 1943; finally captured by Allied forces Sept. 11.

Salambria. See PINIÓS.

Sa·la·mi·na \,säl-ə-'mē-nə\. Town, Caldas dept., W cen. Colombia, NNW of Manizales; munic. pop. (1968e) 41,960.

Sal·a·mis \'sal-ə-məs\ *or* **Sal·a·mís** \,säl-ə-'mēs\. 1 Chief city of Cyprus in ancient times, on E coast; its site 3 m. N of Famagusta. Had active trade with Phoenicia, Egypt, and Cilicia. According to tradition founded by Teucer, a hero of the Trojan War, c. 1180 B.C.; was a major Hellenic center during struggle bet. Greece and Persia; scene of naval victory 449 B.C. for Greeks and again 306 B.C. when Demetrius I defeated Ptolemy I. Suffered often from earthquakes. Visited by Paul and Barnabas (*Acts* xiii. 4, 5). Under the Eastern Roman Empire known as **Con·stan·tia** \kən-'stan-ch(ē-)ə\, after Constantius II who rebuilt it 337–361; abandoned after destruction by Arabs 648.

2 *or* **Kou·lou·ri** \kü-'lü(ə)r-ē\. Island in the Saronic Gulf, Attica dept., Greece, near Piraeus; 37 sq. m.; pop. (1961c) 20,645; naval base; forms an irregular semicircle with large inlet on the W and is S boundary of Bay of Eleusis. Important naval battle fought 480 B.C. in narrow strait off NE coast, in which allied Greeks under Themistocles defeated Persians under Xerxes. See CYNOSURA.

3 *also* **Koulouri.** Commune on NE Salamis I., Greece, W of Piraeus.

Sal·a·mon·ie \'sal-ə-,mō-nē\. River, Indiana; ab. 100 m. long; flows NW from SE Jay co. to Wabash river in E Wabash co.

Salang. See PHUKET 1.

Sa·lar de Uyu·ni \sə-'lär-,dā-ə-'yü-nē\. Extensive salt marsh in SW Bolivia, near border of Chile.

Sa·lar·i·an Way \sə-,lar-ē-ən-, -,ler-\ *or Lat.* **Via Sa·lar·ia** \,vī-ə-sə-'lar-ē-ə, -'ler-\. Ancient Roman road from Rome NE through Reate (Rieti) and Asculum Picenum (Ascoli Piceno) to Adriatic coast; ab. 150 m. long; route by which the Sabines got their salt from the sea.

Sa·las \'säl-əs\. Commune, Oviedo prov., NW Spain, 24 m. WNW of Oviedo; pop. (1970p) 10,636.

Sa·la·sun·go Dan·da \,säl-ə-,süŋ-(,)gō-'dən-də\. Mountain in the Himalayas, on the China-Nepal boundary; 24,299 ft.

Sa·la·ti·ga \,säl-ə-'tē-gə\. Town, Central Java prov., Indonesia, ab. 25 m. S of Semarang; pop. (1961c) 58,135; health resort.

Sa·la·vat \sə-'läv-(,)ät\. Town, Bashkir A.S.S.R., Russian S.F.S.R., U.S.S.R., ab. 100 m. S of Ufa; pop. (1970p) 114,000.

Sa·la·wa·ti \,sal-ə-'wät-ē\. Island off W Doberai Penin., NW Irian Barat, Indonesia; roughly circular in shape with greatest diameter ab. 30 m.; separated by narrow channel from mainland of New Guinea.

Salayar. See SELAJAR.

Sa·la y Go·mez \,säl-ə-ē-'gō-,mās, -,mez\. Uninhabitable rocky island in S Pacific Ocean, 210 m. ENE of Easter I., 26°28′S, 105°28′W; belongs to Chile.

Sa·la·zar \,sal-ə-'zär, ,säl-\ *or* **Vi·la Salazar** \'vē-lə-\. Town, NW Angola, 160 m. ESE of Luanda; pop. (1968e) 22,079.

Sal·can·tay \,sal-kən-'tī\. Peak in Cordillera Oriental, Peru, NW of Cuzco; 20,574 ft.

Sal·ce·do \säl-'sā-(,)dō\. 1 Province, N cen. Dominican Republic. See table at DOMINICAN REPUBLIC.

2 Town, its ✱; pop. (1970p) 11,459.

Sal·chak·et \sal-'chak-ət\. Village on Tanana river and on Alaska Highway, E Alaska, 36 m. SE of Fairbanks.

Sal·combe \'sòl-kəm\. Urban district, Devonshire, SW England, on English Channel; pop. (1971p) 2471; resort; U.S. naval training base in World War II.

Saldae. See BEJAÏA.

Sal·da·nha Bay \sal-,dan-yə-\. Bay on SW coast of Cape Province, Rep. of South Africa, at 33°04′S, 18°E.

Salduba. See SARAGOSSA 2.

Sale \'sāl\. 1 Town, SE Victoria, SE Australia, 120 m. ESE of Melbourne; pop. (1966c) 8640; chief town of Gippsland in a fertile agricultural district.

2 Municipal borough, Cheshire, NW England, on the Mersey 5 m. SW of Manchester; pop. (1971p) 55,623; residential suburb of Manchester.

Sa·lé \sa-'lā\ *or Arab.* **Sla** \'slä\ *also* **Sal·lee** *or* **Sa·li** \'sal-ē\. Seaport, NW Morocco, NW Africa, at the mouth of the Bou Regreg opp. Rabat of which it is a suburb; pop. (1960c) 75,799; important esp. in Middle Ages; in 17th cent. an independent republic and a center of the Barbary pirates (sometimes called *Sallee rovers* or *salleemen*).

Sa·le·ba·bu *or* **Sa·le·ba·boe** \ˌsäl-ə-ˈbäb-(ˌ)ü\. One of the Talaud Is. (*q.v.*), Indonesia.

Sa·leh Bay \ˌsäl-ē-\. Large inlet of Flores Sea on N coast of Sumbawa I., Lesser Sunda Is., Indonesia, ab. 45 m. long by 22 m. wide. Nearly cuts the island into two parts; its entrance nearly closed by Mojo I.

Sa·lem \ˈsāl-əm\. **1** County in New Jersey. See table at NEW JERSEY.

2 City, ⊗ of Fulton co., N Arkansas; pop. (1970c) 1277.

3 City, ⊗ of Marion co., S cen. Illinois, 13 m. ENE of Centralia; pop. (1970c) 6187; clothing, ceramic fixtures, lumber; dairy and fruit farms; birthplace of William Jennings Bryan.

4 City, ⊗ of Washington co., S Indiana, 28 m. NW of New Albany; pop. (1970c) 5041; birthplace of John Hay.

5 City, a ⊗ of Essex co., NE Massachusetts, on Atlantic Ocean 14 m. NE of Boston; pop. (1970c) 40,556; produces parlor games and leather goods; residential suburb of Boston; Massachusetts State Coll. at Salem (1854). Salem Maritime National Historic Site, incorporating part of 18th cent. waterfront and several merchants' houses. Founded 1626; scene of witchcraft hysteria 1692, in which 20 persons were executed; from c. 1775 to 1807 a leading American port in the East Indies trade.

6 City, ⊗ of Dent co., SE cen. Missouri, 26 m. SSE of Rolla; pop. (1970c) 4363; footwear, dairy products; agriculture.

7 Town, Rockingham co., SE New Hampshire, 12 m. E of Nashua; pop. (1970c) 20,142. Part of Haverhill, Massachusetts until 1741; incorporated 1750.

8 City, ⊗ of Salem co., SW New Jersey, on Salem Creek near its confluence with Delaware river 16 m. WNW of Bridgeton; pop. (1970c) 7648; manufactures glass, linoleum, canned goods; English settlement founded 1675; made port of entry 1682; scene of fighting in American Revolution; incorporated as city 1858.

9 Former city, Forsyth co., North Carolina; now part of Winston-Salem (*q.v.*).

10 City, Columbiana co., E Ohio, 17 m. SW of Youngstown; pop. (1970c) 14,186; chemicals, machinery, tools and dies, furniture; coal mines; diversified agriculture; founded 1801.

11 City, ✱ of Oregon and ⊗ of Marion co., NW Oregon, on Willamette river 44 m. SSW of Portland; pop. (1970c) 68,296; marketing and distributing center of agricultural area (esp. fruit and vegetables, livestock); canneries, paper, linen, and woolen mills, packing houses, sawmills; Willamette Univ. (1842), Salem Technical Vocational Community Coll. (1954). Founded 1840; territorial capital 1851, continued as capital of state of Oregon 1859.

12 City, ⊗ of McCook co., SE South Dakota; pop. (1970c) 1391; agriculture.

13 Town, ⊗ of Roanoke co. but politically independent, W cen. Virginia, 8 m. W of Roanoke; 8 sq. m.; pop. (1970c) 21,982; summer resort; elevators, bricks, canned goods, leather; Roanoke Coll. (1853).

14 City, Harrison co., N West Virginia, 13 m. W of Clarksburg; pop. (1970c) 2597; Salem Coll. (1888).

15 City, cen. Tamil Nadu, S India, 175 m. SW of Madras; pop. (1970e) 302,935; trade center; handwoven cotton textiles.

Sa·le·mi \sä-ˈlā-mē, -ˈlem-ē\. Commune, Trapani prov., NW Sicily, Italy, 22 m. SE of Trapani; pop. (1968e) 13,778; Garibaldi declared himself dictator of Sicily here May 14, 1860.

Sa·len·ti·na Peninsula \ˌsäl-ən-ˈtēn-ə-\. Peninsula, Apulia, S Italy; from the ancient name, Sallentinum Promontorium, of Cape Santa Maria di Leuca at its tip.

Sa·ler·no \sə-ˈlər-(ˌ)nō, -ˈle(ə)r-\. **1** Province of Campania, S Italy. See table at ITALY.

2 *or anc.* **Sa·ler·num** \sə-ˈlər-nəm\. Seaport, its ✱, on Gulf of Salerno 29 m. ESE of Naples; pop. (1968e) 148,127; manufactures textiles, machinery, cement, ceramics, building materials, ironwork; 11th cent. cathedral said to contain tomb of St. Matthew and containing tomb of Gregory VII; Lombard and Roman remains.

History: Founded by Romans 197 B.C.; in Middle Ages under Goths, Lombards, Normans, and Kingdom of Naples; site of the first medical school of medieval Europe, founded 11th cent.; became part of kingdom of Italy 1860; in World War II scene of major U.S. troop landing Sept. 9, 1943, and occupied by U.S. troops Sept. 18 after severe fighting.

Salerno, Gulf of *or anc.* **Bay of Paes·tum** \-ˈpes-təm, -ˈpē-stəm\. Inlet of Tyrrhenian Sea on SW coast of Italy, S of the Bay of Naples.

Sal·ford \ˈsal-fərd\. County borough, Lancashire, NW England, on the Irwell adjacent to Manchester; pop. (1971p) 130,641; major port on Manchester Ship Canal; textiles, machinery, locomotives, lumber, beer, rubber goods, paper; Univ. of Salford (1967); received first charter 1230; incorporated as municipal borough 1844, city 1926.

Sal·gó·tar·ján \ˈshȯl-gō-ˌtȯ(ə)r-ˌyän\. City, ⊗ of Nógrád co., N Hungary, 52 m. NE of Budapest; pop. (1970p) 37,212.

Sal·hu·tu, Mount *or* **Mount Sal·hoe·toe** \-säl-ˈhü-tü\. Peak, Moluccas, Indonesia; 3360 ft.; highest point on Ambon I.

Sali. See SALÉ.

Sa·li·da \sə-ˈlī-də\. City, ⊗ of Chaffee co., cen. Colorado, on Arkansas river 65 m. WSW of Colorado Springs; pop. (1970c) 4355; sheet metal works; truck, dairy, livestock farms.

Sa·lies \sə-ˈlēs\. Town, Pyrénées-Atlantiques dept., SW France, ab. 27 m. E of Bayonne; pop. (1962c) 3451.

Sa·lih·li \ˈsä-lə-ˌlē\. Town, Manisa prov., W Turkey, ab. 40 m. E of Manisa; pop. (1965c) 28,909.

Sa·li·na \sə-ˈlī-nə\. City, ⊗ of Saline co., Kansas, on Smoky Hill river 58 m. NNE of Hutchinson; pop. (1970c) 37,714; trade center in wheat-farming area; produces aircraft, clothing, dairy products; grain elevators, foundries; Kansas Wesleyan Univ. (1886), Marymount Coll. (1922); founded 1858; incorporated 1870.

Salina \sə-ˈlē-nə\ *or anc.* **Did·y·me** \ˈdid-ə-(ˌ)mē\. One of the Lipari Is. (*q.v.*); 5 m. long; chief town Malfa.

Salina Cruz \-ˈkrüz\. Seaport, Oaxaca state, Mexico, on the Gulf of Tehuantepec; pop. (1960c) 14,897.

Sa·li·nas \sə-ˈlē-nəs\. **1** River, W California; 150 m. long; rises in S cen. San Luis Obispo co. and flows NW into Monterey Bay on NW coast of Monterey co.

2 City, ⊗ of Monterey co., W California, 10 m. E of Monterey Bay and 47 m. SSE of San Jose; pop. (1970c) 58,896; sugar refining; center of a major truck farming region; Hartnell Coll. (1920); settled c. 1856; incorporated 1874.

3 Seaport town and resort on Santa Elena Penin., W Guayas prov., W Ecuador, ab. 70 m. W of Guayaquil; pop. (1962c) 5460; in district producing salt, oil, and sulfur.

4 Town and municipality, S Puerto Rico; pop. (1970p) 4447 (town), 21,816 (munic.); town on coast 20 m. E of Ponce.

Salinas, Cape. Cape, S tip of the island of Majorca, W Mediterranean Sea.

Salinas, Point. Cape, NE coast of Puerto Rico, W of entrance to San Juan harbor.

Salinas Bay. Inlet of Pacific Ocean, extreme NW coast of Costa Rica.

Sa·line \sə-ˈlēn\. **1** River, S cen. Arkansas; ab. 175 m. long; navigable 100 m.; rises in Saline co., flows S into the Ouachita near the Louisiana boundary.

2 River, Kansas; ab. 200 m. long; rises in W Thomas co., NW Kansas, flows E into Smoky Hill river near Salina, Saline co., cen. Kansas.

3 Name of counties in five states of the U.S. See tables at ARKANSAS, ILLINOIS, KANSAS, MISSOURI, NEBRASKA.

4 City, Washtenaw co., SE Michigan, 9 m. S of Ann Arbor; pop. (1970c) 4811; diversified agriculture.

Saline di Barletta. See MARGHERITA DI SAVOIA.

Saline Lake. Lake, N cen. Louisiana, on boundary bet. Winn and Natchitoches parishes.

Salis·bury \'sȯlz-ˌber-ē, 'salz-, -b(ə-)rē\. 1 Resort town, NW Litchfield co., NW Connecticut, on New York and Massachusetts borders; pop. (1970c) 3573; settled 1719, incorporated 1741.

2 City, ⊗ of Wicomico co., SE Maryland, 50 m. ENE of mouth of Potomac river; pop. (1970c) 15,252; port; manufactures building materials, leather goods, clothing; seafood packing plant; truck, fruit farms; Salisbury State Coll. (1925).

3 Town, Essex co., NE corner of Massachusetts, 27 m. ENE of Lowell; pop. (1970c) 4179.

4 Industrial city, ⊗ of Rowan co., cen. North Carolina, in Piedmont section 37 m. NNE of Charlotte; pop. (1970c) 22,515; textiles, lumber, dairy products; grain and livestock farms; Catawba Coll. (1851), Livingstone Coll. (1879); settled 1753; incorporated 1755; in Civil War site of camp for Union prisoners.

5 City, ✱ of Rhodesia, also ✱ of South Mashonaland prov., 240 m. NE of Bulawayo; met. area pop. (1970e) 435,000; a commercial, industrial, and transportation center; gold mines, steel mills, textile plants; center of agricultural region (esp. tobacco); two cathedrals, library, museum, Univ. of Rhodesia (1957); founded 1890; chartered 1935.

6 *also* **New Sar·um** \-'sar-əm, -'ser-\. Municipal borough, ⊗ of Wiltshire, S England, on the Avon 22 m. NW of Southampton; pop. (1971p) 35,271; 13th cent. cathedral with the tallest spire (404 ft.) in England; tourist center; brewing, tanning, printing; livestock market. Present city developed around cathedral; chartered 1220.

Salisbury Island. Island, W end of Hudson Strait, SE Franklin dist., Northwest Territories, Canada, S of Foxe Penin.; 312 sq. m.

Salisbury Plain. Undulating tract of land, Wiltshire, S England, near the city of Salisbury; average elevation 400 ft.; highest point **West·bury Down** \ˌwest-ˌber-ē-, -b(ə-)rē-\ 775 ft.; contains Stonehenge (*q.v.*).

Salisbury Sound. Channel bet. S Chichagof I. and N Baranof I., SE Alaska.

Sal·ke·hatch·ie \ˌsȯl-kə-'hach-ē\. River, S South Carolina; 60 m. long; rises in W Barnwell co., flows SE to unite with Little Salkehatchie river and form Combahee river.

Sal·khad \'sal-ˌkȯd\. Town, Syria, ab. 16 m. SSE of Es Suweida.

Sal·lau·mines \ˌsal-ō-'mēn\. Commune, Pas-de-Calais dept., N France, 10 m. NNE of Arras; pop. (1968c) 14,768; coal mines.

Sallee. See SALÉ.

Sallentinum Promontorium. See SANTA MARIA DI LEUCA, CAPE.

Sal·li·saw \'sal-ə-ˌsȯ\. City, ⊗ of Sequoyah co., E Oklahoma, 39 m. SE of Muskogee; pop. (1970c) 4888; coal mines; agriculture; home of Sequoyah nearby.

Salmantica. See SALAMANCA 3.

Salm·on \'sam-ən\. 1 River, cen. Connecticut; rises in S Tolland co., flows SW into Connecticut river.

2 River, cen. Idaho; 420 m. long; rises in S Custer co., cen. Idaho, flows N, then W across Idaho, and again N to empty into Snake river at S extremity of Nez Perce co., W Idaho.

3 City, ⊗ of Lemhi co., E cen. Idaho, at confluence of Salmon and Lemhi rivers; pop. (1970c) 2910; gold mines; dairy and livestock farms.

Salmone, Cape. See PLÁKA, CAPE.

Salmon Falls Dam. Dam across Salmon Falls Creek, a S tributary of Snake river, Twin Falls co., SW Idaho; height 220 ft.; completed 1912; impounds water for irrigation. Dam also known as **Salmon River Dam;** reservoir variously known as **Salmon Falls Reservoir, Salmon Creek Reservoir,** *or* **Salmon River Reservoir.** See CEDAR CREEK DAM.

Salmon River Mountains. Group of mountain ranges, chiefly in Valley, Custer, and Lemhi cos., cen. Idaho; includes many peaks above 9000 ft., highest 9279 ft.; source of Salmon and Boise rivers and other tributaries of the Snake. See SAWTOOTH RANGE.

Sa·lo·ma·gue Harbor \ˌsäl-ə-'mäg-ə-\. Inlet and sheltered anchorage on N coast of Ilocos Sur prov., Luzon, Phil., 15 m. N of Vigan; 17°46′N, 120°24′E.

Sa·lo·na \sə-'lō-nə\. Roman colony on coast of Dalmatia; founded 78 B.C.; residence 305–313 A.D. of Diocletian (born 245 at Dioclea, a nearby village) who built palace and other buildings on site of Spalatum (see SPLIT) 3 m. S; captured several times by Goths and Huns and destroyed by Avars 639.

Sal·o·ni·ka \sə-'län-i-kə, ˌsal-ə-'nē-kə\ *also* **Thes·sa·lo·ní·ki** \ˌthes-ə-lō-'nē-kē\ *or* **Sal·o·ni·ki** \ˌsal-ə-'nēk-ē\ *or Turk.* **Se·la·nik** \ˌsel-ə-'nēk\; *before 315* B.C. *called* **Ther·ma** \'thər-mə\, *afterwards* **Thes·sa·lo·ni·ca** \ˌthes-ə-le-'nī-kə, -'län-i-\. Seaport city, ✱ of Thessalonike dept., W cen. Macedonia, NE Greece, at head of Gulf of Salonika; pop. (1971p) 339,496; railroad center; good harbor; exports grain, livestock, silk, tobacco, manganese; produces textiles, wines and spirits, beer, leather goods, building materials, soap; has some Roman remains and numerous Byzantine churches (5th–14th cents.); univ. (1926).

History: Founded 315 B.C. and Roman capital of Macedonia 148 B.C. ff.; important city under Roman Empire; Paul's epistles to the Thessalonians addressed to converts here; massacre of insurrectionists by Theodosius 390 A.D.; taken by Saracens 904 and by Normans 1185; capital of 13th cent. kingdom created 1204 out of remains of Byzantine Empire by Baldwin I for his rival Boniface III, Count of Montferrat; occupied by Turks 1430–1912; swept by fires 1890, 1917; headquarters of Young Turks 1908; seat of Greek provisional government 1916; important base for Allied operations in World War I; in World War II occupied by Germans Apr. 9, 1941–Oct. 30, 1944.

Salonika, Gulf of *or Gk.* **Ther·ma·ï·kós Kól·pos** \ther-ˌmä-i-ˌkȯs-'kȯl-(ˌ)pȯs\ *or anc.* **Ther·ma·i·cus Si·nus** \thər-ˌmā-ə-kə(s)-'sī-nəs\. Arm of the NW Aegean Sea, extending into NE coast of Greece, E of Thessaly and W of Chalcidice and Kassándra penins.

Sa·lon·ta \'säl-ȯn-(ˌ)tä\ *or Hung.* **Nagy·sza·lon·ta** \'näj-'sȯl-ən-ˌtȯ\. City, W Romania, near Hungarian border, 25 m. SSE of Oradea; pop. (1966c) 17,754; transferred to Hungary 1940–45.

Salop. County, W England. See SHROPSHIRE.

Sa·loum *or* **Sa·lum** \sə-'lüm\. River, Senegal, W Africa; 100 m. long; flows into Atlantic Ocean just N of Gambia; navigable for 60 m.; has wide mouth containing many islands; Kaolack is on it.

Sal Rei \säl-'rā\. One of the Cape Verde Is., N of Boa Vista; 83 sq. m.; pop. (1960c) 2626; manufactures salt.

Sal·sette \sal-'set\. Island, N of Bombay I., India; 18 m. long, 246 sq. m.; pop. (1961c) 186,449; principal town Thana. Taken by Portuguese from Marathas 1739 and from Portuguese by British 1774; has numerous Buddhist cave shrines.

Salsk \'salsk\. Town, S Rostov Oblast, Russian S.F.S.R., U.S.S.R.; pop. (1967e) 44,000; railroad junction point S of the Manych; taken by Germans in Caucasus drive July 31, 1942; retaken by U.S.S.R. early in 1943.

Sal·so \'säl-(ˌ)sō\. River, Sicily, Italy; 89 m. long; flows from Madonie Mts. into the Mediterranean Sea.

Sal·so·mag·gio·re Ter·me \ˌsäl-sō-mə-'jōr-ē-'ter-mē, -'jȯr-\. Commune, Parma prov., Emilia-Romagna, N Italy, 18 m. W of Parma; pop. (1968e) 17,589; mineral baths.

Salt \'sȯlt\. 1 River, Arizona; ab. 200 m. long; rises in Apache co., E Arizona, flows W into Gila river in Maricopa co. W of Phoenix; water utilized for irrigation and water-power through a system of dams forming a 60-mile chain of lakes including Roosevelt Dam and Roosevelt Lake, Horse Mesa Dam and Apache Lake, Mormon Flat Dam, and Stewart Mountain Dam and Saguaro Lake.

2 River, N cen. Kentucky; ab. 100 m. long; rises in Boyle co., cen. Kentucky, flows N, then W into Ohio river below Louisville.

3 River, NE Missouri; 200 m. long; rises in Schuyler co., N Missouri, flows SE into Mississippi river in E Pike co., E Missouri.

Sal·ta \'säl-tə\. 1 Province of NNW Argentina. See table at ARGENTINA.

2 City, its ✱, 140 m. NW of San Miguel de Tucumán; pop. (1960c) 117,400; produces tobacco products, leather, wine, flour, vegetable oils, sugar; cathedral; univ. (1960); founded 1582; scene of decisive defeat of Spanish royalist forces by Gen. Manuel Belgrano 1813.

Salt Block Mountain. Peak, Garrett co., NW corner of Maryland; 2768 ft.

Salt·burn and Marske–by–the–Sea \'sält-bərn . . . 'märsk-\. Urban district, North Riding, Yorkshire, NE England; pop. (1971p) 19,562.

Salt Cay \-'kē, -'kā\. One of Turks Is.; pop. (1960c) 414. See TURKS AND CAICOS ISLANDS.

Salt·coats \'sölt-ˌkōts\. Seaport burgh, Ayr co., SW Scotland, on the Firth of Clyde 30 m. SW of Glasgow; pop. (1971p) 14,901; formerly known for its salt mines and for shipbuilding.

Sal·tee Islands \ˌsȯl-tē-\. Two small islands, St. George's Channel, off SE coast of Ireland, E of Waterford.

Salt Fjord \'sȯlt-\. Inlet of Norwegian Sea, NW coast of Norway, extending E from SE entrance to Vest Fjord, in Nordland co.

Salt Fork. River, NW Texas; unites with Double Mountain Fork in Stonewall co. to form the Brazos river.

Salt·holm \'sält-ˌhəlm, 'sȯlt-\. Danish island in the Øresund, opp. Copenhagen, in the Sjælland group; 4½ m. long; 6 sq. m.; pop. (1965c) 13.

Sal·ti·llo \säl-'tē-(ˌ)(y)ō\. City, ✱ of Coahuila state, NE Mexico, ab. 660 m. N of Mexico City; munic. pop. (1970p) 191,879; alt. 5244 ft.; commercial center; produces textiles and flour; noted for serapes; gold, lead, silver, coal mines; summer resort; cathedral; univ. (1907); founded 1575.

Salt Island. One of the British Virgin Is., West Indies.

Salt Lake. County in Utah. See table at UTAH.

Salt Lake City. City, ✱ of Utah and ⊗ of Salt Lake co., N Utah, on Jordan river 13 m. E of Great Salt Lake; pop. (1970c) 175,885; alt. 4390 ft.; largest city in the state; produces textiles, canned foods, pottery, steel and iron products, electronic components; copper, silver, lead smelting, oil refining, printing and publishing; Univ. of Utah (1850), Westminster Coll. (1875), Latter-day Saints Business Coll. (1886), Stevens Henager Coll. (1907); several notable buildings, including Mormon Temple and Tabernacle, state capitol, and state cathedral. Headquarters of the Mormon Church since 1847.

History: Settled by Mormons under leadership of Brigham Young 1847; developed as station on route to California during gold rush of 1849 ff.; served successively as capital of Provisional State of Deseret (*q.v.*), Territory of Utah, and (except 1851–56 and 1858) state of Utah; prominent in "Utah War" of 1857–58 and as center of dispute bet. U.S. government and Mormon Church 1865 to ab. 1890.

Salt Lake Region. Extensive region, SW cen. Western Australia; contains many salt lakes; rich mining region, especially in gold.

Sal·to \'säl-(ˌ)tō\. 1 Town, Buenos Aires prov., E Argentina, 107 m. from Buenos Aires; pop. (1960c) 9979; fossil remains discovered nearby.

2 Department of NW Uruguay. See table at URUGUAY.

3 City and port, ✱ of Salto dept., NW Uruguay, at head of navigation on E bank of Uruguay river opp. Concordia, Argentina, 260 m. NW of Montevideo; pop. (1963c) 57,958; produces wines and nonalcoholic fruit drinks; shipyards; early shipping depot for hides.

Salto, El. See EL SALTO.

Sal·ton Sea \ˌsȯlt-ᵊn-\. Lake, Riverside and Imperial cos., SE California; 360 sq. m.; 235 ft. below sea level; formerly a depression 280 ft. below sea level; became a lake 1891 but later dried up; lake began to form again 1893; waters from Colorado river diverted into it 1905; break in river closed July 1907.

Salt·pond \'sȯlt-ˌpänd\. Seaport town, S Ghana, just E of Cape Coast; pop. (1970p) 10,047.

Salt Range. Mountain range bet. the Indus and Jhelum rivers, Punjab, Pakistan; highest peak 4074 ft.; salt beds.

Salt River. Name of three rivers in the U.S. See SALT.

Salt Sea. An occasional Biblical name for the Dead Sea (*Num.* xxxiv. 3; *Josh.* xv. 2).

Salt·ville \'sȯlt-ˌvil\. Town, Smyth and Washington cos., SW Virginia, 32 m. NE of Bristol; pop. (1970c) 2527; scene of engagement during Civil War 1864.

Sa·lu·a·fa·ta \ˌsal-ü-ə-'fät-ə\. Harbor, N coast of Upolu I., Western Samoa, SW cen. Pacific Ocean; formerly (1879–99) a German coaling station.

Saluces *or* **Saluciae.** See SALUZZO.

Salud, La. See LA SALUD.

Sa·lu·da \sə-'lüd-ə\. 1 River, W cen. South Carolina; rises in Blue Ridge Mts., NW South Carolina, flows SE through Lake Murray and unites near Columbia with Broad river to form Congaree river.

2 County in South Carolina. See table at SOUTH CAROLINA.

3 Town, ⊗ of Saluda co., W South Carolina, 27 m. ESE of Greenwood; pop. (1970c) 2442; agriculture.

4 Village, ⊗ of Middlesex co., E Virginia.

Salum. See SALOUM.

Sa·lūm \sə-'lüm\ *or* **Sol·lum** \sə-'lüm\ *also* **As–Sal·lūm** \ˌas-\ *or anc.* **Cat·a·bath·mus Mag·na** \ˌkat-ə-ˌbath-məs-'mag-nə\. Village, extreme NW Egypt, on the **Gulf of Salūm,** an inlet of the Mediterranean Sea, ab. 275 m. W of Alexandria. Several times taken in North African campaigns of World War II; by Italians Sept. 1940; by British Dec. 16, 1940; by Germans Apr. 1941; and finally by British Jan. 13, 1942.

Sa·luz·zo \sə-'lüt-(ˌ)sō\ *or Fr.* **Sa·luces** \sa-lüs\ *or anc.* **Sa·lu·ci·ae** \sə-'lü-s(h)ē-ˌē\. Commune, Cuneo prov., Piedmont, NW Italy, 18 m. N by W of Cuneo; pop. (1968e) 18,049; early 16th cent. cathedral; castle. Formed medieval margraviate from 11th cent.; to France 1548, Piedmont 1601.

Sal·va·dor \'sal-və-ˌdȯ(ə)r, ˌsal-və-'\; *formerly* **São Salvador** \saùⁿ-ˌsal-və-'dȯ(ə)r\ *or* **Ba·hia** \bä-'ē-ə\. Seaport city, ✱ of Bahia state, E Brazil, on All Saints Bay ab. 225 m. SSW of Recife; pop. (1970p) 1,000,647; on a peninsula with the modern part of the city on heights back of the harbor; modern port, shipping tobacco, sugar, hides, hardwoods, diamonds, oil; produces textiles, tobacco products, leather, metal goods, lumber; tourism; univ. (1946), Catholic univ. (1961); naval base and dockyard; 16th cent. cathedral and many other buildings dating from 16th and 17th cents.

History: Town (in early times usually called Bahia) founded by Thomé de Sousa 1549; made episcopal see 1552; captured by Dutch 1624; to Brazil 1823; declined after transfer of capital to Rio de Janeiro 1763.

Salvador, El. See EL SALVADOR.

Salvador, Lake \-'sal-və-ˌdȯ(ə)r\. Lake, St. Charles, Jefferson, and Lafourche parishes, SE Louisiana.

Sal·va·ges \säl-'vazh-ēsh\ *or* **Sel·va·gens** \sel-'vazh-āⁿsh\. Group of small uninhabited islands of the Madeiras, ab. 180 m. SSE of Madeira.

Sal·va·tie·rra \ˌsäl-və-ˈtyer-ə\. Town, Guanajuato state, cen. Mexico, on railroad near Lake Cuitzeo ab. 125 m. NW of Mexico City; munic. pop. (1970p) 80,531.

Sal·ween *or* **Sal·win** \ˈsal-ˌwēn\; *Chin.* **Nu Chiang** \ˈnü-jē-ˈäŋ\ *or Thai* **Mae Nam Khong** \ˈmī-ˈnäm-ˈkȯŋ\. River, SE Asia; ab. 1500 m. long; rises in Tibetan Plateau, E Tibet, China, flows E through S Szechwan, then S through W Yunnan prov. of SW China; continues S through Shan State, Burma, and on into Lower Burma, in its lower course forming a section of Thailand-Burma boundary; empties into Gulf of Martaban at Moulmein; has few tributaries; its lower course scene of fighting in early 1942; its middle course in N Burma scene of fighting in 1944, esp. in May.

Sal·ya·ny *or* **Sal·ya·ni** \səl-ˈyan-ē\. Town, SE Azerbaijan S.S.R., U.S.S.R., on the Kura in its delta 72 m. SW of Baku; pop. (1967e) 19,000.

Sal·yers·ville \ˈsal-yərz-ˌvil\. Town, ⊗ of Magoffin co., E Kentucky; pop. (1970c) 1196.

Sal·zach \ˈzält-ˌsäk\. River, W Austria; 139 m. long; rises in N slopes of Hohe Tauern, flows E and N through Salzburg state past Salzburg to the West German border; continues N, forming the boundary bet. Bavaria, West Germany, and Upper Austria; empties into Inn river ab. 30 m. N of Salzburg. See GOLLINGER.

Salz·burg \ˈsȯlz-ˌbərg, ˈsälz-, ˈsalz-, -ˌbu̇(ə)rg; *Ger.* ˈzälts-ˌbu̇rk\. 1 State of cen. Austria. See table at AUSTRIA.

2 *or anc.* **Ju·va·vum** \jü-ˈvā-vəm\. Industrial city, its ✱, on Salzach river 71 m. ESE of Munich, West Germany; pop. (1971p) 127,500; one of Austria's principal tourist centers and one of the major music centers of W Europe; two archiepiscopal palaces, notable 17th cent. cathedral, numerous notable churches and houses; univ. (founded 1622, reestablished 1964). Founded late 7th cent. A.D.; ruled by prince-archbishops for over 1000 years from 798; birthplace of Mozart.

Salz·git·ter \ˈzälts-ˌgit-ər\ *or formerly* **Wa·ten·stedt–Salz·gitter** \ˈvät-ᵊn-ˌs(h)tet-\. City, SE Lower Saxony, West Germany, SW of Brunswick; pop. (1969e) 117,306; major center of metallurgical industry; also produces automobiles, railroad cars, television sets, textiles, sugar, and pharmaceuticals; first mentioned c. 1000.

Salz·kam·mer·gut \ˈzälts-ˌkäm-ər-ˌgüt\. Region, Styria, Salzburg, and Upper Austria states of Austria; contains great salt deposits, used from prehistoric times. Now a tourist resort with lakes, mountains (Dachstein) in S part, and several small towns, esp. Hallstatt (*q.v.*), noted for its early cultural remains.

Salz·we·del \ˈzälts-ˌvād-ᵊl\. City, Magdeburg dist., East Germany, 55 m. NNW of Magdeburg; pop. (1970e) 19,960; machinery, pumps; brewing, printing; received charter 1233; a Hanse town 13th–16th cents.

Sa·ma \ˈsäm-ə\. River, Tacna dept., S Peru; ab. 250 m. long; flows into Pacific Ocean.

Sama de Lan·greo \ˌsäm-ə-dā-läŋ-ˈgrā-(ˌ)ō\ *or* **Langreo.** Commune, Oviedo prov., NW Spain, 14 m. SE of Oviedo; pop. (1970p) 58,864; corn, cattle.

Samakov. See SAMOKOV.

Sa·mal \ˈsäm-ˌäl\. Island, N end of Davao Gulf, Davao del Norte prov., Mindanao, Phil.; 96 sq. m.; pop. (1969e) 29,000; coextensive with municipality of Samal (village of Samal on W coast). Forms shelter for Davao harbor to the W.

Sa·ma·les \sə-ˈmäl-əs\. Group of islands, E Sulu Archipelago, Phil., E of Jolo and SW of Basilan; ab. 45 sq. m.; comprises ab. 20 small islands: largest, Tongquil I. (19 sq. m.) and most important, Balanguingui I. Chief town Tungkil, munic. pop. (1969e) 8100.

Sa·ma·ná \ˌsä-mə-ˈnä\. 1 Province of NE Dominican Republic. See table at DOMINICAN REPUBLIC.

2 *or formerly* **San·ta Bár·ba·ra de Samaná** \ˌsän-tə-ˈbär-bər-ə-dā-\. Commune, its ✱; pop. (1970e) 4892; cacao, coconuts, honey; tropical woods.

Samaná, Bay of. Inlet on NE coast of Dominican Republic; ab. 40 m. long; extends E and W, protected on N by **Cape Samaná** which extends E from coast.

Sa·ma·na Cay \sə-ˌmän-ə-ˈkē, -ˈkā\ *or* **At·wood Cay** \ˌat-wu̇d-\. Small island, cen. Bahama Is., 23°9′N, 73°54′W; formerly sometimes identified with Columbus' San Salvador.

Samanala. See ADAM'S PEAK.

Sa·mān·gan \ˌsäm-äŋ-ˈ(g)än\. Province of N Afghanistan. See table at AFGHANISTAN.

Samannud. See SEBENNYTUS.

Samanti. See YENICE.

Sa·mar \ˈsäm-ˌär\. Island, one of the Visayan Is., E Phil.; constitutes with several small adjacent islands three provinces: **Samar del Nor·te** \-del-ˈnȯrt-ē\ (1343 sq. m.; pop. [1970p] 305,337; ✱ Catarman), **Samar Oc·ci·den·tal** \-ˌōk-si-den-ˈtäl\ (2166 sq. m.; pop. 444,950; ✱ Catbalogan), **Samar Ori·en·tal** \-ˌōr-ē-en-ˈtäl, -ˌȯr-\ (1676 sq. m.; pop. 274,049; ✱ Borongan); irregular shape, having many inlets and offshore islands, 150 m. long from NW to SE and ab. 75 m. at widest point and third in size of the Philippines group. Touches San Bernardino Strait on NW, Pacific Ocean on N and E, Leyte Gulf on S, and Samar Sea on W; on SW separated from Leyte by very narrow San Juanico Strait. Has very rugged surface so that density of population is not large; mountains low, highest point 2789 ft. in N cen. part. Well watered, with many short navigable rivers on both coasts; experiences violent typhoons. Agriculture not extensively pursued; rice, coconuts, cacao, and abacá are raised. Inhabitants are mainly Visayans, with some Bikols and Tagalogs. Chief towns Catbalogan, Basey, Calbayog, Guiuan, and Borongan.

History: First island of archipelago discovered 1521 by Spaniards (first landing on Homonhon, *q.v.*); in early times under jurisdiction of Cebu; united with Leyte in separate province 1735 but after 1768 constituted a province by itself; until beginning of 19th cent. often attacked by Moro pirates; granted civil government June 1902; came under Japanese control 1942; retaken by U.S. Oct. 1944; subdivided into three provinces 1969.

Sa·ma·ra \sə-ˈmär-ə\. 1 River, Orenburg and Kuibyshev oblasts, SE Russian S.F.S.R., U.S.S.R.; ab. 360 m. long; flows W into the Volga river at Kuibyshev. Buzuluk is on it.

2 Region and city. See KUIBYSHEV 2.

Sa·ma·rai \ˌsäm-ə-ˈrī\. 1 Island, Papua New Guinea, ab. 3 m. off SE tip of New Guinea I., just SE of Milne Bay; ab. 60 acres.

2 Township on island; commercial center, shipping copra. Destroyed by Japanese Jan. 1942; since rebuilt.

Samarang. See SEMARANG.

Samar del Norte. See SAMAR.

Sa·mar·ia \sə-ˈmer-ē-ə, -ˈmar-\. 1 District, ancient Palestine, in cen. part, extending from the Mediterranean to the Jordan and lying S of Galilee and N of Judaea; in 6 A.D. made by Augustus a division of the province of Judaea.

2 *or modern* **Sa·bas·tī·yah** \sə-ˈbȯs-tē-(y)ə\. Ancient city, ✱ of Samaria, its ruins now in region of Jordan occupied by Israel 1967; the Holy City of the Samaritans; built on a hill 887 B.C. by Omri; strengthened by Ahab but its idolatry and corruption led to complete overthrow by Shalmaneser V and Sargon II 724–721 B.C. (*2 Kings* xvii. 3–6); inhabitants transported into captivity; taken by Alexander and in 107 B.C. by John Hyrcanus, who destroyed it.

Sam·a·rin·da \ˌsam-ə-ˈrin-də\. Coastal town, ✱ of East Kalimantan prov., E Borneo, Indonesia, on lower course of Mahakam river ab. 30 m. from its mouth; pop. (1961c) 69,715; important trading town for products of the river region, also for nearby coal and oil fields; univ. (1962).

Sam·ar·kand \ˈsam-ər-ˌkand\ *or* **Sa·mar·qand** \ˌsäm-ər-ˈkänd\. 1 Former province, Russian Turkistan, now part of Uzbek S.S.R., U.S.S.R.; ab. 26,620 sq. m.

2 City, ❋ of Samarkand Oblast, Uzbek S.S.R., U.S.S.R., in the fertile valley of the Zerayshan 180 m. SW of Tashkent, on W spur of Alai Mts.; pop. (1970p) 267,000; alt. 2330 ft.; has railroad connections with Orenburg and the S Caspian; produces motor vehicle parts, silk, canned fruit, textiles, wine, leather, footwear; has many medieval structures; has several Muslim educational institutions, tomb and palace of Tamerlane, numerous monuments, several mosques.

History: One of the oldest cities in the U.S.S.R.; as **Ma·ra·can·da** \ˌmar-ə-ˈkan-də\, capital of Sogdiana, destroyed by Alexander the Great 329 B.C.; important point on "Silk Route" from China to Europe 7th cent. A.D.; under Samanids (874–999) and successors a notable center of Arab culture; destroyed by Genghis Khan 1221 but made capital of Tamerlane's empire 1370. By 1700 almost uninhabited; came successively under the Chinese, the Emir of Bukhara, and the Russians, who took it 1868; in 1924 incorporated in Uzbek S.S.R. and its ❋ until 1930.

Samarkand Oblast \-ˈō-bləst, -ˌblast\. Subdivision of the Uzbek S.S.R., U.S.S.R.; area 11,274 sq. m.; pop. (1970p) 1,470,000; ❋ Samarkand; wheat, cotton, fruit; sheep, goats; sericulture; formed 1938.

Samarobriva. See AMIENS.

Samar Occidental. See SAMAR.

Samar Oriental. See SAMAR.

Samarqand. See SAMARKAND.

Sa·mar·ra \sə-ˈmər-ə\. Town, N cen. Iraq, 65 m. NNW of Baghdad, on the E bank of the Tigris river; head of navigation for small steamers. In 9th cent. residence of Abbasside rulers; sacred to Shiite Muslims; occupied by British Apr. 23, 1917.

Samar Sea \ˌsäm-är-\. Interisland body of water, E Phil., bounded by Luzon on N, Samar on E, Leyte on S, and Masbate on W; connects by San Bernardino Strait with the Pacific on N and joins Visayan Sea on SW.

Sa·ma·wa \sə-ˈma-wə, -ˈmä-\ *or* **As–Sa·mā·wah** \ˌas-\. Town, SE cen. Iraq, on the right bank of the Euphrates river near the lower junction of the Hindiya with the main stream; pop. (1965c) 33,473; trade and agricultural center.

Sam·bal·pur \ˈsəm-bəl-ˌpu̇(ə)r\. Town, N Orissa, E India, on N bank of Mahanadi river 140 m. NW of Cuttack; pop. (1961c) 38,915; ❋ of former Orissa Feudatory States.

Sam·bas \ˈsäm-bəs\. River, NW West Kalimantan prov., Borneo, Indonesia; ab. 90 m. long; flows W and SW into South China Sea.

Sam·bhal \ˈsəm-bəl\. Town, NW cen. Uttar Pradesh, N India, 80 m. E of Delhi; pop. (1961c) 68,940; sugar, calico; important Muslim capital in late 15th cent.

Sam·bo·dja \säm-ˈbō-jə\. Oil field near Balikpapan, E coast of Borneo, East Kalimantan prov., Indonesia; captured by Australians July 18, 1945.

Sam·bor \ˈsäm-bȯ(ə)r\. Manufacturing town, Lvov Oblast, W Ukrainian S.S.R., U.S.S.R., on Dniester river 50 m. WSW of Lvov; pop. (1967e) 27,000; formerly in Poland; a railroad junction town.

Sam·bo·rom·bón Bay \ˌsäm-bə-ˌrȯm-ˈbȯn-\. Inlet of Atlantic Ocean, S of the mouth of Río de la Plata on E coast of Buenos Aires prov., E Argentina.

Sambre \ˈsaⁿ(m)brᵊ\. River, N France and S cen. Belgium; ab. 120 m. long; rises in Aisne dept., N France, flows ENE across the Belgian border and into the Meuse river at Namur; scene of British victory Nov. 1918.

Sam·mam·ish Lake \sə-ˌmam-ish-\. Lake, King co., W cen. Washington; 9 m. long.

Samnan. See SEMNĀN.

Sam·ni·um \ˈsam-nē-əm\. Country in ancient cen. Italy, the modern Abruzzi region and part of Campania region. Its inhabitants, the Samnites, were enemies of the Romans until conquered c. 290 B.C.; they spoke Oscan.

Sa·moa \sə-ˈmō-ə\ *also* **Samoa Islands** *or formerly* **Nav·i·ga·tors Islands** \ˈnav-ə-ˌgāt-ərz-\. Group of islands, SW cen. Pacific Ocean, N of Tonga and NE of Fiji, bet. 13°26′ and 14°22′S lat. and 168° and 172°48′W long.; 1209 sq. m.; divided into **American Samoa,** islands E of 171°W long., 76 sq. m., pop. (1970p) 27,769, and **Western Samoa,** islands W of 171°W long., 1133 sq. m., pop. (1970e) 145,000. Islands are volcanic, with soil generally fertile; copra is chief commercial product; the island group was probably for centuries the cradle of Polynesian settlement.

History: Discovered 1722 by Jacob Roggeveen, a Dutchman; visited 1768 and named (Navigators Islands) by Louis de Bougainville; visited by U.S. naval officers Charles Wilkes 1839 and Richard Meade 1872, the latter visit ultimately resulting in securing Pago Pago (*q.v.*) as U.S. naval base; under native rulers until c. 1860; U.S., British, and German interest in islands produced period of international friction and internal dissension culminating in civil war and German intervention 1887; tense situation eased by destruction of U.S. and German naval forces (3 warships each; the single British warship escaped) in harbor of Apia by terrific hurricane of Mar. 15–16, 1889; neutrality and independence of islands under three-power supervision established by tripartite agreement 1889; difficulties in administration led to agreement 1899 by which, Britain having ceded her interests to Germany in exchange for territory elsewhere, the islands were divided bet. U.S. and Germany; German Samoa mandated to New Zealand 1919, achieved independence 1962. See AMERICAN SAMOA and WESTERN SAMOA.

Sam·o·gi·tia \ˌsam-ə-ˈjish-(ē-)ə\ *or Lith.* **Že·mai·ti·ja** \ˌzhe-mī-ˈtē-(y)ə\. Baltic region, coextensive with most of modern Lithuanian S.S.R., U.S.S.R., a lowland country N of the Neman; in 14th cent. held by Teutonic Knights; surrendered to Poland by Treaty of Thorn (Toruń) 1411.

Sa·mo·kov *also* **Sa·ma·kov** \ˈsäm-ə-ˌkȯf, -ˌkȯv\. Town, Sofia prov., W Bulgaria, 30 m. SSE of Sofia; pop. (1968e) 23,220.

Sa·mos \ˈsā-ˌmäs\. 1 *or Turk.* **Su·sam–Ada·si** \sü-ˌsäm-ˌäd-ə-ˈsē\. Island in the Aegean Sea off W coast of Turkey; 184 sq. m.; pop. (1961c) 41,124; with Ikaria I. and several other islets forms a department of Greece (see table at GREECE); by some considered an island of the Southern Sporades (see SPORADES). Produces olive oil, wine, silk, cotton, tobacco; boatbuilding, cigarette-making; mountainous, with highest point 4725 ft. at W end.

History: Settled by Ionians and by 7th cent. B.C. one of the principal commercial centers of Greece; under the tyrant Polycrates (late 6th cent. B.C.) a major cultural center, esp. in sculpture; notable Temple of Hera built. Birthplace of Pythagoras. Under Persia 522–479 B.C.; a member of Delian League and then subject variously to Athens, Sparta, Rome, Byzantium, and the Ottoman Empire; restored to Greece 1912; in World War II occupied by Axis 1941–44.

2 Ancient town on SE coast of Samos I., one of the 12 Ionian Cities; now in ruins.

Sa·mos·a·ta \sə-ˈmäs ət-ə\ *or* **Sam·sat** \säm-ˈsat\. Ruined city, ancient Syria, on right bank of Euphrates river ab. 30 m. NNW of Edessa (*mod.* Urfa); Kurdish village of Samsat, SE Turkey, on its site. In ancient times an important crossing of the river; long a frontier fort, linked with Edessa, and a caravan station. Capital of Hellenistic kingdom of Commagene under Seleucids 3d cent. B.C., and later, 72 A.D., of a Roman province.

Sa·mo·sir, Pu·lau \ˌpü-(ˌ)lau̇-ˌsäm-ə-ˈsi(ə)r\. Island in Lake Toba, N cen. Sumatra I., Indonesia; 30 m. long, ab. 10 m. wide.

Sam·o·thrace \ˈsam-ə-ˌthrās\ *or Gk.* **Sa·mo·thrá·ki** \ˌsäm-ə-ˈthräk-ē\; *anc.* **Sam·o·thra·ce** \ˌsam-ə-ˈthrā-(ˌ)sē\ *or* **Sam·o·thra·cia** \ˌsam-ə-ˈthrā-sh(ē-)ə\. 1 Greek island, NE Aegean Sea, 14 m. NNW of Turkish island of İmroz; part of Evros dept., Thrace, Greece; 69 sq. m.; pop. (1961c) 3830; sponge fisheries. Has prominent peak 5577 ft., the

highest point on any of the Aegean Is.; was not important politically in ancient times but here was erected by the Rhodians the famous sculpture known as Nike of Samothrace (now in the Louvre, Paris) to commemorate a naval victory at Cyprus c. 190 B.C. See AEGEAN ISLANDS.
2 Town on the island.

Sam·pa·loc Point \säm-ˌpäl-ȯk-\. Point at SW side of entrance to Subic Bay, S Zambales prov., Luzon, Phil.

Sam·pang \ˈsäm-ˌpäŋ\. Town near S coast of Madura I., East Java prov., Indonesia; pop. (1961c) 15,716.

Sampanmangio, Cape. See SEMPANG MANGAYAU.

Samp·son \ˈsam(p)-sən\. County in North Carolina. See table at NORTH CAROLINA.

Samsat. See SAMOSATA.

Samshui. See CHIU-SAN-SHUI.

Samsø \ˈsam(p)-sər\. Island in Sjælland group, forming a part of Denmark, lying bet. W tip of the island of Sjælland and the E coast of Jutland Penin.; 15 m. long; 44 sq. m.; pop. (1965e) 5852.

Sam·son \ˈsam(p)-sən\. City, Geneva co., SE Alabama, 8 m. N of Florida border and 40 m. WSW of Dothan; pop. (1970c) 2257; lumber; agriculture.

Sam's Point \ˈsamz-\. Peak, Ulster co., SE New York; 2289 ft.; highest peak in the Shawangunk Mts.

Sam·sun \säm-ˈsün\. 1 Province of N Turkey, Asia. See table at TURKEY.
2 *or anc.* **Ami·sus** \ə-ˈmī-səs\. Seaport city, its ✱, on **Samsun Bay,** an inlet of the Black Sea, ab. 200 m. NE of Ankara; pop. (1965c) 107,510; located between the deltas of the Kızıl Irmak and the Yeşil Irmak; ships tobacco, cereals, wool; produces cigarettes and textiles. Ancient Amisus one of the principal Greek cities on the Black Sea (Euxine); later prominent on the trade route from Central Asia and under Trebizond.

Sam·thar \ˈsəm(p)-tər\. 1 Former Indian state, now part of Uttar Pradesh, N India; 189 sq. m.
2 Town, its ✱, 55 m. SE of Gwalior; pop. (1961c) 9400.

Sa·mui \sä-ˈmü-ē\ *or* **Ko Samui** \ˈkō-\. Island (Siamese *ko*) in SW Gulf of Siam off E coast of Isthmus of Kra 65 m. N of Nakhon Si Thammarat.

Sa·mut Pra·kan \sä-ˌmu̇t-prä-ˈkän\ *or* **Pak·nam** \päk-ˈnäm\. 1 Province, S cen. Thailand; 361 sq. m.; pop. (1960c) 234,701; ✱ Samut Prakan.
2 Town, its ✱, lower port of Bangkok at the mouth of the Chao Phraya 12 m. SSE of the capital; pop. (1960c) 21,766.

Samut Sa·khon \-sä-ˈkȯn\ *or* **Tha Chin** \ˈtä-ˈchēn\ *also* **Ma·ha Chai** \ˌmä-ˌhä-ˈchī\. 1 Province, S cen. Thailand; 324 sq. m.; pop. (1960c) 165,712; ✱ Samut Sakhon.
2 Town, its ✱, at mouth of Tha Chin river on left bank, ab. 21 m. SW of Bangkok; pop. (1960c) 27,602.

Samut Song·khram \-ˌsəŋ-ˈkräm\ *or formerly* **Me·klong** \mə-ˈklȯŋ\. 1 Province, W Thailand; 154 sq. m.; pop. (1960c) 161,899; ✱ Samut Songkhram.
2 Seaport, its ✱, at mouth of Klong river 40 m. SW of Bangkok; pop. (1960c) 12,801.

San. See SAINT.

San \ˈsän\. River, SE Poland; 247 m. long; flows out of the Carpathian Mts. NNW into Vistula river 4 m. NE of Sandomierz; formerly formed part of boundary bet. W Ukraine and Poland; battle line in several battles May 1915.

San'a *also* **San·aa** \sä-ˈna\. City, ✱ of Yemen, SW Arabian Penin., SW Asia, ab. 40 m. from its port of Hodeida with which it is connected by road; pop. (1970e) 125,093; alt. 7250 ft.; commercial center; handicrafts (leather, jewelry, brass work, etc.); walled city with eight gates and numerous mosques. Founded before first cent. A.D.; continually subject to nomad raids from 8th cent.; became capital of Imam of Yemen 1918 and of Yemen Arab Republic 1962.

Sa·na·fi·ri \ˌsan-ə-ˈfi(ə)r-ē\. Island in Red Sea. See TĪRĀN.

Sa·na·ga \ˈsän-ə-gə\. River, Cameroon, W Africa; ab. 325 m. long; flows WSW into the Bight of Biafra opp. the island of Fernando Póo.

San Agus·tin, Cape \-ˌsan-ˌäg-ü-ˈstēn\. South extremity of long peninsula marking E side of Davao Gulf, Mindanao, Phil., 6°16′N, 126°11′E.

San Am·bro·sio \ˌsan-əm-ˈbrō-(ˌ)zhō, ˌsan-ˌam-\. Island in Pacific Ocean, ab. 550 m. off W cen. coast of Chile, close to San Félix I.; belongs to Chile.

Sa·na·na \sə-ˈnän-ə\. 1 *or formerly* **Su·la Be·si** \ˌsü-lə-bə-ˈsē\ *or* **Besi.** Island, smallest but most important of the three islands of the Sula Is., E of Celebes, Indonesia.
2 Chief village of Sula Is. at N end of Sanana I.; former residence of Dutch commissioner.

Sa·nan·daj \ˌsän-ən-ˈdäj\ *or* **Sin·neh** \si-ˈnä\. Town, ✱ of Kordestān prov., NW Iran, on highway to Mosul 100 m. NNW of Hamadān; pop. (1971e) 58,000.

Sa·nan·di·ta \ˌsän-ən-ˈdēt-ə\. Town, S Bolivia, near the Argentine border; pop. (1966c) 54,578; oil wells.

San An·dre·as \ˌsan-an-ˈdrā-əs\. Village, ⊗ of Calaveras co., cen. California.

San Andreas Fault. Zone of faults, extending along the coast of N California, through the San Francisco Penin., and SE toward the head of the Gulf of California; movement along part of this zone caused the San Francisco earthquake of 1906.

San An·drés \ˌsan-ən-ˈdres\. 1 Small island in Caribbean Sea, off E coast of Nicaragua; belongs to Colombia.
2 Town on island, ✱ of San Andrés y Providencia intendancy; munic. pop. (1968e) 14,413; ships oranges and copra.

San Andrés It·za·pa \-ēt-ˈsäp-ə\. Town, Chimaltenango dept., S cen. Guatemala; pop. (1964p) 7034.

San An·dres Mountains \ˌsan-ən-ˌdres-\. Range, chiefly in S Socorro and N Dona Ana cos., S cen. New Mexico, E of the Rio Grande.

San Andrés Tux·tla \-ˈtüs-(ˌ)tlä\ *also* **Tuxtla.** Town, Veracruz state, E Mexico, 80 m. SE of Veracruz; munic. pop. (1970p) 77,351; center of research of joint expedition of National Geographic Society and Smithsonian Institution, where carved objects of early Maya civilization were found.

San Andrés y Pro·vi·den·cia \-ē-ˌprō-və-ˈden(t)-sē-ə\. Intendancy of Colombia. See table at COLOMBIA.

San An·ge·lo \sa-ˈnan-jə-(ˌ)lō\. City, ⊗ of Tom Green co., W cen. Texas, 77 m. SSW of Abilene; pop. (1970c) 63,884; alt. 1845 ft.; wool market; produces leather goods, footwear, cottonseed oil, dairy products, printing and binding supplies; oil and gas wells; in a ranching and farming region; San Angelo State Coll. (1928); Goodfellow Air Force Base; founded 1867.

San An·sel·mo \ˌsan-ən-ˈsel-(ˌ)mō\. Residential town, Marin co., W California, 14 m. NW of San Francisco; pop. (1970c) 13,031; San Francisco Theological Seminary (1871).

San An·to·nio \ˌsan-ən-ˈtō-nē-ˌō\. 1 River, S Texas; 180 m. long; rises in city of San Antonio, receives waters of Medina river in Bexar co., flows SE through Wilson, Karnes, and Goliad cos., forms boundary line bet. Refugio and Victoria cos., and empties into San Antonio Bay.
2 Commercial and industrial city and port of entry, ⊗ of Bexar co., S cen. Texas, on San Antonio river 74 m. SW of Austin; pop. (1970c) 654,153; ships wool, mohair, petroleum products; produces soap, flour, beer, clothing, cottonseed oil; oil refineries; tourist center. St. Mary's Univ. of San Antonio (1852), Trinity Univ. (1869), Incarnate Word Coll. (1881), Our Lady of the Lake Coll. (1896), Saint Philip's Coll. (1898), San Antonio Coll. (1925). Military aviation center, with Kelly, Lackland, Randolph, and Brooks Air Force bases; Fort Sam Houston (1865).
History: Franciscan mission San Antonio de Valero (later the Alamo) and presidio of San Antonio de Bexar founded 1718; first civil municipality, San Fernando, founded 1731; all three consolidated into San Antonio de Bexar c. 1793, which became city 1809. Prominent in conflicts between Spanish and French, Mexicans and Indians, Mexican Revolution, and Texas Revolution; in

Texas Revolution a military base, captured by Mexicans in historic siege of the Alamo and recaptured by Texans after their victory at San Jacinto 1836.

3 Seaport and resort, Santiago prov., cen. Chile, 58 m. W of Santiago; pop. (1966e) 34,051.

4 Town, Central dept., cen. Paraguay, on Paraguay river SE of Asunción; pop. (1970e) 7012.

5 Municipality, Nueva Ecija prov., Luzon, Phil., near right bank of Pampanga river W of San Isidro and 14 m. SSW of Cabanatuan; pop. (1969e) 35,200.

6 Municipality, SW Zambales prov., Luzon, Phil., near coast ab. 65 m. NW of Manila; pop. (1969e) 15,900; U.S. troops landed on coast bet. here and San Narciso Jan. 29, 1945.

San Antonio, Cape. 1 Cape extending into Atlantic Ocean on E coast of Buenos Aires prov., E Argentina, S of Samborombón Bay.

2 Cape, W extremity of Cuba, projecting into Yucatán Channel.

3 Cape, N coast of Alicante prov., SE Spain.

San Antonio Bay. Inlet of Gulf of Mexico, S Calhoun co., S Texas, receiving San Antonio river on N.

San Antonio de Ca·be·zas \-ˌdā-kə-ˈbez-əs\. Municipality, Matanzas prov., W cen. Cuba; pop. (1967e) 10,530.

San Antonio de las Ve·gas \-ˌdā-ləs-ˈvā-gəs\. Municipality, La Habana prov., W Cuba, just S of Havana; pop. (1967e) 10,300.

San Antonio de las Vuel·tas \-ˌdā-ləs-ˈvwel-təs\. Municipality, Las Villas prov., W cen. Cuba, 16 m. ENE of Santa Clara; pop. (1967e) 37,850.

San Antonio de los Ba·ños \-ˌdā-lȯs-ˈbän-ˌyōs\. Municipality and town, La Habana prov., W Cuba; munic. pop. (1967e) 37,850; town 20 m. SW of Havana.

San Antonio de los Co·bres \-ˌdā-lȯs-ˈkō-brəs\. Town, Salta prov., NW Argentina, 75 m. NW of Salta; pop. (1960c) 1439.

San Antonio Peak. 1 *or formerly* **Mount Baldy** \-ˈbȯl-dē\. Mountain, Los Angeles co., S California; 10,080 ft.; highest peak in San Gabriel Mountains.

2 Mountain, NE Rio Arriba co., N New Mexico; 10,908 ft.

San Au·gus·tine \san-ˈȯ-gəs-ˌtēn\. 1 County in E Texas. See table at TEXAS.

2 Town, its ⊗, 37 m. ENE of Lufkin; pop. (1970c) 2539; livestock farms.

San Be·ne·det·to del Tron·to \ˌsan-ˌben-ə-ˈde-tō-del-ˈtrȯn-(ˌ)tō\. Seaport, Ascoli Piceno prov., Marches, cen. Italy, on Adriatic 16 m. ENE of Ascoli Piceno; pop. (1970c) 39,718.

San Be·ni·to \ˌsan-bə-ˈnēt-(ˌ)ō\. 1 County in California. See table at CALIFORNIA.

2 City, Cameron co., S Texas, 18 m. N of Brownsville; pop. (1970c) 15,176; packs and ships fruit and vegetables; citrus orchards, truck farms.

San Ber·nar·di·no \ˌsan-ˌbər-nə(r)-ˈdē-(ˌ)nō\. 1 County in SE California. See table at CALIFORNIA.

2 City, its ⊗, 55 m. E of Los Angeles; pop. (1970c) 104,783; manufactures steel, aircraft and missiles, cement; printing plants, foundries, railroad shops; San Bernardino Valley Coll. (1926), California State Coll. at San Bernardino (1960); Norton Air Force Base; site named 1810; city founded 1851, incorporated 1854.

3 Islet, Philippines. See SAN BERNARDINO STRAIT.

4 Mountain pass in Lepontine Alps, Graubünden canton, SE Switzerland; alt. 6773 ft.

San Bernardino Mountain. Peak in San Bernardino Mts., S California; 10,630 ft.

San Bernardino Mountains. Mountain range, SW San Bernardino co., extending SE into cen. Riverside co., S California; one of the series of ranges bordering the Mojave Desert on the SW; between the San Gabriel Mts. and the San Jacinto Mts.; highest point San Gorgonio Mt., 11,502 ft., located at SE end.

San Bernardino Strait. Strait bet. S Sorsogon prov., SE Luzon, and N end of Samar I., Phil.; ab. 27 m. long by 5 m. wide at narrowest point; by some extended to include Ticao Pass (*q.v.*). The main entrance to the Philippines from the E forming with the Sibuyan Sea and Verde Island Passage the main channel for ships from U.S. and the Pacific to Manila and the South China Sea. In Pacific at E end is **San Bernardino** rock, an islet 7 m. off Bulusan, on which is one of the major lighthouses in the archipelago. Scene of naval battle Oct. 24–25, 1944 in which part of Japanese fleet was defeated. Islands in it seized by U.S. forces Jan.–Mar. 1945.

San Ber·nar·do \ˌsan-bər-ˈnärd-(ˌ)ō\. 1 City, Santiago prov., cen. Chile, 10 m. S of Santiago; pop. (1966e) 58,798.

2 Group of small islands in the Caribbean Sea, off NW coast of Colombia, at entrance to Gulf of Morrosquillo.

San Blas \san-ˈblas\. Municipality, Nayarit state, Mexico, on Pacific Ocean 25 m. W of Tepic; pop. (1970p) 32,609; shellfishing; diversified agriculture.

San Blas, Cape. Low point of land projecting into Gulf of Mexico from SW coast of Gulf co., NW Florida.

San Blas, Cor·di·lle·ra de \ˈkȯrd-ᵊl-ˈ(y)er-ə-dā-san-ˈblas, kȯrd-ē-ˈer-\. Range, NE Panama, S of the Gulf of San Blas.

San Blas, Gulf of. Inlet of the Caribbean Sea on the N coast of Panama, E of the Panama Canal.

San Blas, Point. Cape, N coast of Panama, N of the Gulf of San Blas.

San·born \ˈsan-bərn\. County in South Dakota. See table at SOUTH DAKOTA.

San Bru·no \san-ˈbrü-(ˌ)nō\. City, San Mateo co., W California, S of San Francisco; pop. (1970c) 36,254; residential.

San Buenaventura. See VENTURA 2.

San Car·los \san-ˈkär-ləs\. 1 River, SE Arizona; forms part of NW boundary of Graham co.; flows in curve W to S and into San Carlos Reservoir formed by the Coolidge Dam.

2 Residential city, San Mateo co., W California, 17 m. SE of San Francisco; pop. (1970c) 25,924.

3 City, Ñuble prov., S cen. Chile, 15 m. NNE of Chillán; pop. (1960c) 13,598.

4 River, Costa Rica; 75 m. long; flows NE into the San Juan river.

5 Chartered city, Pangasinan prov., Luzon, Phil., 10 m. SE of Lingayen; pop. (1970e) 103,400; largest town in the province; on border of Agno delta.

6 Chartered city, NE Negros Occidental, Negros, Phil., near N end of Tanon Strait 33 m. ESE of Bacolod; pop. (1970e) 174,800; largest town in the province.

7 Town, Maldonado dept., S Uruguay, ab. 9 m. N of Maldonado and 65 m. E of Montevideo; pop. (1963c) 13,663.

8 Town, ✱ of Cojedes state, NW cen. Venezuela, ab. 130 m. SW of Caracas; pop. (1970p) 18,482.

San Carlos de Ancud. See ANCUD.

San Carlos de Bariloche. See BARILOCHE.

San Ca·scia·no in Val di Pe·sa \ˌsan-kə-ˈshän-(ˌ)ō-ēm-ˌväl-dē-ˈpā-zə\. Commune, Firenze prov., Tuscany, W Italy, 10 m. S by W of Florence; pop. (1970c) 14,149.

San Ca·tal·do \ˌsan-kə-ˈtäl-(ˌ)dō\. Commune, Caltanissetta prov., cen. Sicily, Italy, 4 m. W of Caltanissetta; pop. (1968e) 22,488; sulfur mining.

Sán·chez \ˈsän-chəz\. Seaport, Samaná prov., NE Dominican Republic, 24 m. from Samaná; munic. pop. (1970p) 23,103; produces cacao, coffee, rice, coconuts.

Sánchez Ra·mí·rez \-rə-ˈmir-əz\. Province, cen. Dominican Republic. See table at DOMINICAN REPUBLIC.

San·chi \ˈsän-chē\. Village, W Madhya Pradesh, N cen. India, ab. 23 m. NE of Bhopal. Site of several Buddhist topes or stupas, the oldest buildings now standing in India; erected either in the time of or before King Asoka c. 250 B.C. The Great Stupa (or Tope) is a memorial shrine in the shape of a solid dome of stone and brick, ab. 103 ft. in diameter and 42 ft. high.

San Ci·pri·a·no Bay \san-ˌsip-rē-ˈän-ō-\. Bay, SW coast of Spanish Sahara, NW Africa, 22°20′N, 16°35′W.

San Cle·men·te \ˌsan-klə-ˈment-ē\. City, Orange co., SW California, SE of Los Angeles; pop. (1970c) 17,063; vacation home of Richard M. Nixon, 37th president of the U.S.

San Clemente Island. Island, SW part of Santa Barbara group in Pacific Ocean, S of Santa Catalina I.; 57 sq. m.; part of Los Angeles co., SW California; U.S. naval base.

San·co Point \säŋ-ˈkō-\. Point, E coast of Mindanao, Phil., at S end of Surigao del Sur prov., 8°14′N, 126°25′E.

San Cris·to·bal \ˌsan-kris-ˈtō-bəl\. Mountain, SE border of Laguna prov., Luzon, Phil.; ab. 4900 ft.; an extinct volcano with fresh-water lake in its crater.

San Cris·tó·bal \ˌsan-kris-ˈtō-bəl\. 1 Municipality, Pinar del Río prov., W Cuba, on railroad 45 m. ENE of Pinar del Río; pop. (1967e) 31,960.

2 Province, E cen. Dominican Republic. See table at DOMINICAN REPUBLIC.

3 Municipality, ✱ of San Cristóbal prov., S Dominican Republic, 25 m. WSW of Santo Domingo; pop. (1970p) 105,904; in an area producing rice, sugar, coffee; founded 1575.

4 *also* **Chat·ham Island** \ˈchat-əm-\. One of the Galápagos Is. (*q.v.*); ab. 24 m. long, 8 m. wide; produces sugarcane, coffee.

5 Lake in the Valley of Mexico, cen. Mexico, 12 m. NNE of Mexico City.

6 *or in full* **San Cristóbal de las Ca·sas** \-də-lä-ˈskä-səs\. City, Chiapas state, SE Mexico, ab. 40 m. E of San Andrés Tuxtla; pop. (1970p) 32,110.

7 *or* **Ma·ki·ra** \mə-ˈkir-ə\ *also* **San Cris·to·val** \-vəl\. Island in S Solomon Is., W Pacific Ocean, 38 m. SE of Guadalcanal; 80 m. long and 22 m. wide at greatest width; 1270 sq. m.; pop. (1970p) 10,929; mountainous; most of its settlements, including Kira Kira, location of the government station, and Star Harbour, are along the N shore.

8 City, ✱ of Tachira state, W Venezuela, in mountains at SW end of Cordillera Mérida and S of Lake Maracaibo, near Colombian border; pop. (1970e) 156,618; elevation 2700 ft.; textiles, leather products, footwear, cigarettes, cement; ships coffee; founded 1561; heavily damaged by earthquake 1875.

Sanc·ti Spí·ri·tus \ˌsäŋ(k)-tē-ˈspir-ə-ˌtüs\. Town and municipality, E Las Villas prov., W cen. Cuba, 45 m. SE of Santa Clara; munic. pop. (1967e) 146,450; trading center for sugar and cattle; founded 1516, oldest inland city of Cuba.

San Cui·cuil·co \ˌsan-kwē-ˈkwil-(ˌ)kō\ *or* **Cuicuilco.** Hill, Mexico, ab. 12 m. S of Mexico City; artificial mound, 412 ft. in diameter, 52 ft. high; probably an ancient temple.

San·cy, Puy de \ˌpwēd-ə-ˌsäⁿ-ˈsē\. Peak, Puy-de-Dôme dept., S cen. France; 6186 ft.; highest peak of the Monts Dore in the Auvergne Mts.

San·da·kan \san-ˈdäk-ən\. Seaport town, Sabah, Malaysia, on island of Borneo, on **Sandakan Harbour,** an inlet of the Sulu Sea having a length of 15 m. and an entrance 1¼ m. wide; pop. (1960c) 28,806; ✱ of former British North Borneo, suffered much destruction during Japanese occupation 1942–45; capital transferred to Jesselton (now Kota Kinabalu) 1947.

Sandalwood Island. See SUMBA.

San·day \ˈsan-(ˌ)dā\. Island, NE part of the Orkney Is. off N coast of Scotland; 12 m. long; pop. (1961c) 1403.

Sand·bach \ˈsan(d)-ˌbach\. Urban district, Cheshire, NW England, 24 m. S of Manchester; pop. (1971p) 13,303.

San·de·fjord \ˈsän-ə-ˌfyü(ə)r\. Seaport, Vestfold co., SE Norway, SSW of Oslo near the mouth of Oslo Fjord; pop. (1970e) 31,723; base for whaling fleets operating in Arctic waters; shipbuilding yards, whale-oil refineries, chemical works.

San·ders \ˈsan-dərz\. County in Montana. See table at MONTANA.

San·der·son \ˈsan-dər-sən\. Unincorporated town, ⊗ of Terrell co., W Texas, 55 m. SSE of Fort Stockton; pop. (1970c) 1229; ships wool and livestock.

San·ders·ville \ˈsan-dərz-ˌvil\. City, ⊗ of Washington co., cen. Georgia, 58 m. SW of Augusta; pop. (1970c) 5546; lumber, paper; diversified agriculture.

Sand·gate \ˈsan(d)-ˌgāt\. Seaport town, SE Queensland, Australia, suburb of Brisbane; pop. (1966c) 22,621.

Sand·ham·mar, Cape \-ˈsand-ˌham-ər\. Cape, S extremity of Sweden, projecting into Baltic Sea at S side of Hanö Bay.

Sand·hurst \ˈsand-ˌhərst\. 1 City, Australia. See BENDIGO.

2 Civil parish in Berkshire, S England; pop. (1961c) 3802. Site of Royal Military College, founded 1799 and merged 1946 with Royal Military Academy at Woolwich.

San·dia Peak \san-ˈdē-ə-\. Mountain, SE Sandoval co., NW cen. New Mexico; 10,676 ft.

San Di·e·go \ˌsan-dē-ˈā-(ˌ)gō\. 1 County in California. See table at CALIFORNIA.

2 Commercial and industrial seaport city, and port of entry, its ⊗, on San Diego Bay ab. 12 m. N of the Mexican border; pop. (1970c) 697,027; a center of the electronics, aircraft, and missile industries; tuna fisheries; tourism; in a major truck and fruit farming area; numerous military and naval installations including a naval shipyard and a Naval Training Center. San Diego State Coll. (1897), Univ. of California at San Diego (1901), San Diego City Coll. (1914), United States International Univ. (1924), Univ. of San Diego Coll. for Men (1949), Univ. of San Diego Coll. for Women (1952); notable zoological park. Bay discovered by Cabrillo 1542 and settled as base for exploration of California by Gaspar de Portolá 1769; mission dedicated 1769; organized as pueblo 1834; captured by Commodore Stockton 1846; first incorporated 1850; new charter granted 1872.

3 City, ⊗ of Duval co., S Texas, 50 m. W of Corpus Christi; pop. (1970c) 4398; oil and gas wells.

San Diego, Cape. Cape, E end of Tierra del Fuego I., S Argentina.

San Diego Bay. Inlet of Pacific Ocean, San Diego co., SW corner of California; 12 m. long, 1–3 m. wide; 22 sq. m.; landlocked; forms harbor for the city of San Diego.

San Diego de la Uni·ón \-də-ˌlä-ün-ˈyōn\. Municipality, Guanajuato state, Mexico, 60 m. NE of León; pop. (1970p) 25,898.

San Diego del Va·lle \-del-ˈvī-(ˌ)ā\. Municipality, Las Villas prov., W cen. Cuba, 12 m. NW of Santa Clara; pop. (1967e) 19,120.

San Di·mas \san-ˈdē-məs\. City, Los Angeles co., SW California, 25 m. E of Los Angeles; pop. (1970c) 15,692; citrus fruit.

Sand Island \ˈsand-\. 1 Island, Lake Superior. See APOSTLE ISLANDS.

2 Island, Pacific Ocean. See MIDWAY.

Sandju. See SANG-CHU-PA-CHA.

Sand·nes \ˈsän-ˌnās\. Municipality, Rogaland co., SW Norway, ab. 9 m. S of Stavanger; pop. (1970e) 30,036.

Sandø \ˈsan-ˌər\. Island in S part of the Faeroes (*q.v.*); 48 sq. m.; pop. (1966c) 1684.

San·do·mierz \sän-ˈdō-myesh\ *or Russ.* **San·do·mir** \ˌsan-də-ˈm(y)ir\. Commune, Kielce prov., SE cen. Poland, on Vistula river 52 m. ESE of Kielce; pop. (1968e) 15,800; sulfur, glass products; Romanesque church, Gothic cathedral. Founded 11th cent. and capital of an independent principality; gained town rights 1286; to Austria 1795 and to Russia 1815–1918.

San Do·min·go \ˌsan-də-ˈmiŋ-(ˌ)gō\. Early name of Dominican Republic and name of earliest settlement on Hispaniola. See SANTO DOMINGO 3.

San Domino. See TREMITI ISLANDS.

San Do·nà di Pia·ve \ˌsan-də-ˈnä-dē-ˈpyäv-ē, -(ˌ)ā, -pē-ˈäv-\. Commune, Venezia prov., Veneto, NE Italy, on Piave river 19 m. NE of Venice; pop. (1968e) 27,336.

San·do·val \san-ˈdō-vəl\. County in New Mexico. See table at NEW MEXICO.

San·do·way \ˈsan-də-ˌwā\. 1 District, Arakan division, Lower Burma; 4149 sq. m.; pop. (1962e) 164,670; ✱ Sandoway.

2 Town, its ✱, near coast of Bay of Bengal 63 m. WSW of Prome; pop. (1962e) 69,924; seaside resort.

San·down Park \ˌsan-ˌdau̇n-\. Fashionable racecourse near Esher, Surrey, S England.

Sandown–Shank·lin \-ˈshaŋ-klən\. Urban district, E Isle of Wight, S England, on English Channel; pop. (1971p) 15,-807; seaside resort.

Sand·point \ˌsan(d)-ˈpȯint\. City, ⊗ of Bonner co., N Idaho, on Pend Oreille Lake, 45 m. N of Coeur d'Alene; pop. (1970c) 4144; ski resort; lumber; dairy, livestock farms.

San·dray \ˈsan-ˌdrā\. See BARRA.

San·dring·ham \ˈsan-driŋ-əm\. Village, Norfolk, E England, near E shore of the Wash; Sandringham House, royal residence.

Sands Point \ˈsandz-\. Village, Nassau co., SE New York, 5 m. W of Glen Cove; pop. (1970c) 2916.

Sand Springs. Industrial city, Tulsa co., NE Oklahoma, on Arkansas river 8 m. W of Tulsa; pop. (1970c) 10,565; textiles, glass; oil and gas wells.

San·dus·ky \sən-ˈdəs-kē, san-\. 1 River, N Ohio; ab. 150 m. long; rises in W Richland co., N cen. Ohio, flows W, then N into Sandusky Bay.

2 County in Ohio. See table at OHIO.

3 City, ⊗ of Sanilac co., E Michigan, 38 m. NNW of Port Huron; pop. (1970c) 2071.

4 Industrial city and port of entry, ⊗ of Erie co., N Ohio, on Lake Erie 50 m. W of Cleveland; pop. (1970c) 32,674; automobile parts, ball bearings, paper products, rubber goods, boats; ships coal and lumber; platted 1818, incorporated 1824.

Sandusky Bay. Inlet of Lake Erie on N coasts of Sandusky and Erie cos., N Ohio; the city of Sandusky lies S of the entrance to the bay.

Sand·vi·ken \ˈsan(d)-ˌvē-kən\. Town, Gävleborg co., Sweden, WSW of Gävle; pop. (1970e) 26,687.

Sand·wich \ˈsan(d)-wich\. 1 City, De Kalb and Kendall cos., N Illinois, 30 m. WNW of Joliet; pop. (1970c) 5056; electronic components, aluminum.

2 Town, Barnstable co., SE Massachusetts, just S of Cape Cod end of Cape Cod Canal; pop. (1970c) 5239; noted for glass made here c. 1827–88. Cape's oldest settlement, founded 1637.

3 Municipal borough, Kent, SE England; pop. (1971p) 4467; one of the Cinque Ports; noted golf links.

Sandwich Island. See EFATE.

Sandwich Islands. See HAWAII 2.

Sandwich Mountain. Mountain, Carroll and Grafton cos., New Hampshire, at W end of Sandwich Range; 3993 ft.

Sandwich Range. Southern range of the White Mts., New Hampshire; highest point Passaconaway 4060 ft.; includes Mt. Chocorua 3475 ft.

San·dwip \ˈsən-ˌdwēp\. Island, E mouth of the Ganges-Brahmaputra delta, Bangla Desh; 126 sq. m.

Sandy \ˈsan-dē\. 1 River, W Maine; 55 m. long; rises in W Franklin co., flows SE and E into Kennebec river in S Somerset co.

2 River, Kentucky and West Virginia. See BIG SANDY 2.

Sandy Cape. Cape, N point of Fraser I. off SE coast of Queensland, Australia, 24°42′S, 153°17′E.

Sandy City. City, Salt Lake co., N Utah, 13 m. S of Salt Lake City; pop. (1970c) 6438.

Sandy Hook. 1 Peninsula, NE Monmouth co., E cen. New Jersey, ab. 15 m. S of S tip of Manhattan I.; 6 m. long; encloses **Sandy Hook Bay** (inlet of Raritan Bay) on W; lighthouse.

2 Subdivision of town of Newtown, Connecticut. See NEWTOWN 1.

3 City, ⊗ of Elliott co., NE Kentucky; pop. (1970c) 192.

San Es·ta·nis·lao \ˌsan-ə-ˌstän-əs-ˈlau̇\. Town, San Pedro dept., cen. Paraguay, 90 m. NE of Asunción; pop. (1962c) 3569.

San Eugenio *also* **San Eugenio del Cuareim.** See ARTIGAS 2.

San Fa·bian \san-ˈfā-bē-ən, ˌsän-fä-ˈbyän\. Municipality, Pangasinan prov., Luzon, Phil., on SE shore of Lingayen Gulf 13 m. ENE of Lingayen; pop. (1969e) 40,700; important coast town, scene of severe fighting on landing of U.S. forces Jan. 1945.

San Fe·li·ce sul Pa·na·ro \ˌsan-fə-ˈlē-chā-ˌsül-pə-ˈnär-(ˌ)ō\. Commune, Modena prov., Emilia-Romagna, N Italy, 17 m. NE of Modena; pop. (1968e) 9281.

San Fe·li·pe \ˌsan-fə-ˈlē-(ˌ)pā\. 1 City, ✱ of Aconcagua prov., cen. Chile, ab. 48 m. N of Santiago; pop. (1966e) 21,979.

2 Town, ✱ of Guainía commissary, E Colombia; pop. (1968e) 212.

3 Mountain, cen. Oaxaca state, SE Mexico, N of Oaxaca; 10,207 ft.

4 Municipality, Guanajuato state, cen. Mexico, 33 m. N of Guanajuato; pop. (1970p) 56,021.

5 City, ✱ of Yaracuy state, NW Venezuela, 125 m. W of Caracas; pop. (1970e) 43,402.

San Felipe de Puerto Plata. See PUERTO PLATA 2.

San Fe·liu de Gui·xols \san-fā-ˌlē-ü-dā-gē-ˈhȯls\. Seaport, Gerona prov., Catalonia, NE Spain; pop. (1970p) 12,508.

San Fé·lix \san-ˈfā-liks\. Island in Pacific Ocean, ab. 600 m. off W cen. coast of Chile, close to San Ambrosio I.; belongs to Chile.

San Fer·di·nan·do di Pu·glia \ˌsan-fer-də-ˌnän-dō-dē-ˈpül-yə\. Commune, Foggia prov., Apulia, SE Italy, 29 m. SE of Foggia; pop. (1968e) 13,679.

San Fer·nan·do \ˌsan-fər-ˈnan-(ˌ)dō\. 1 City, Los Angeles co., SW California, enclave of Los Angeles; pop. (1970c) 16,571; San Fernando Rey de España mission nearby.

2 Seaport, Buenos Aires prov., E Argentina, on the Río de la Plata just N of Buenos Aires; pop. (1960c) 92,302; part of Greater Buenos Aires.

3 City, ✱ of Colchagua prov., cen. Chile, 80 m. S of Santiago; pop. (1966e) 25,271; founded by José Manso de Velasco 1742.

4 River, N Tamaulipas state, Mexico; ab. 170 m. long; rises in mountains S of Monterrey and flows E into Laguna Madre.

5 Municipality, E coast of Cebu I., Phil., on Bohol Strait 17 m. SW of City of Cebu; pop. (1969e) 25,900.

6 Municipality, ✱ of La Union prov., Luzon, Phil. on the coast 45 m. N of Dagupan; pop. (1969e) 51,700; fishing; has a harbor sheltered by San Fernando Point and coastal trade with Manila and other ports; on main W coast highway and terminus of railroad to Manila. Taken by Japanese Dec. 1941; fighting in U.S. invasion Jan. 1945.

7 Municipality, ✱ of Pampanga prov., cen. Luzon, Phil., 35 m. NNW of Manila; pop. (1969e) 78,200; sugar refining; ships rice; in reconquest of Philippines captured by U.S. forces Jan. 29–30, 1945.

8 *or formerly* **Is·la de Le·ón** \ˌēz-lə-dā-lā-ˈōn\. Seaport and naval base, Cádiz prov., SW Spain, 7 m. SE of Cádiz; pop. (1970p) 60,187; dockyard and arsenal; naval academy, observatory; produces salt.

9 Seaport, Trinidad and Tobago, West Indies, SW Trinidad; pop. (1970p) 37,313; founded 1786; made borough 1853.

10 *or in full* **San Fernando de Apu·re** \-dā-ə-ˈpu̇(ə)r-ē\. Town, ✱ of Apure state, W Venezuela, on Apure river 185 m. S of Caracas; pop. (1970e) 44,358; river port; livestock, hides.

San Fernando de Ata·ba·po \-ˌdā-ˌät-ə-ˈbäp-(ˌ)ō\. Town, former ✱ of Amazonas territory, S Venezuela, on the Atabapo and Orinoco rivers; pop. (1961c) 898.

San Fernando de Ca·ma·ro·nes \-dā-ˌkäm-ə-ˈrō-nəs\. Municipality, Las Villas prov., W cen. Cuba, 25 m. WSW of Santa Clara; pop. (1967e) 10,820.

San Fernando de Monte Cristi. See MONTECRISTI 2.

San Fernando Point. Point on coast of NW Luzon, Phil., La Union prov., 16°37′N, 120°16′E, just W of San Fernando and marking northeasternmost point of Lingayen Gulf.

San Fernando Valley. Valley, Los Angeles co., S California, NW of cen. Los Angeles; partly included in city of Los Angeles; farming area, many suburban residential communities.

San·ford \ˈsan-fərd\. 1 City, ⊗ of Seminole co., cen. Florida penin., 20 m. NNE of Orlando; pop. (1970c) 17,393; sawmills, railroad shops; citrus orchards, truck farms; Seminole Junior Coll. (1965).

2 Industrial town, York co., SW Maine, 15 m. W of Biddeford; pop. (1970c) 15,812; carpets, lumber; apples; Nasson Coll. at Springvale (1912).

3 City, ⊗ of Lee co., cen. North Carolina, 31 m. NNW of Fayetteville; pop. (1970c) 11,716; electronic equipment, furniture; agriculture.

Sanford, Mount. Mountain at W end of Wrangell Mts., S Alaska; 16,237 ft.

San Fran·cis·co \ˌsan-frən-ˈsis-(ˌ)kō, -fran-\. 1 River, W New Mexico and E Arizona; 105 m. long; rises in Catron co., W New Mexico, flows W across Arizona border and into the Gila river in Greenlee co., SE Arizona.

2 County in W California. See table at CALIFORNIA.

3 Seaport city, its ⊗, on W side of San Francisco Bay and on Pacific Ocean and Golden Gate; pop. (1970c) 715,674; exceptionally good harbor; connected with Marin co. to the N by Golden Gate bridge and with Yerba Buena I. and Oakland to the E by the Transbay bridge; commercial, financial, and industrial center; ships food products, fruit, cotton, mineral ores; produces aircraft and missile parts, canned goods, tools and dies, plastic and rubber products, paper, textiles, computers; printing and publishing, shipbuilding, fishing; important tourist and cultural center. Univ. of San Francisco (1855), Heald Engineering Coll. (1863), Univ. of California Medical Center (1864), San Francisco Art Institute Coll. (1874), San Francisco State Coll. (1899), Golden Gate Coll. (1901), California Podiatry Coll. (1914), San Francisco Conservatory of Music (1917), Simpson Bible Coll. (1921), San Francisco Coll. of Mortuary Science (1930), San Francisco Coll. for Women (1930), Cogswell Polytechnical Coll. (1930), City Coll. of San Francisco (1935), Holy Family Coll. (1945); several Army, Navy, and U.S. Marine facilities.

History: Bay entered 1769 by Don Gaspar de Portolá, Spanish governor of Baja California; mission and pueblo founded 1776; pueblo of Yerba Buena founded by Father Junípero Serra 1777; came under Mexican control after Mexican independence 1821; occupied by U.S. naval forces July 9, 1846; name changed to San Francisco 1848; city grew rapidly after discovery of gold in nearby areas; incorporated as city 1850; terminus of first transcontinental railroad 1869; developed as commercial and fishing port from 1860's; suffered extensive damage from earthquake and fire Apr. 18, 1906 (see SAN ANDREAS FAULT); scene of organization meeting of the United Nations Apr.–June 1945; U.S.-Japan peace treaty signed here 1951.

4 Town, Córdoba prov., N cen. Argentina, midway bet. Cordoba and Santa Fe; pop. (1960c) 38,000.

5 Island, river, municipality and town in Brazil. See SÃO FRANCISCO.

6 Town, ✱ of Morazán dept., NE El Salvador; pop. (1968e) 4515.

7 Municipality on SE coast of Pacijan I., Camotes Is., Cebu prov., Phil., ab. 41 m. NE of City of Cebu; pop. (1969e) 28,300; largest town of the Camotes.

San Francisco, Pa·so de \ˌpäs-ō-dā-\. Andean mountain pass on Argentina-Chile border, bet. NW Catamarca prov., NW Argentina, and E cen. Atacama prov., N cen. Chile; altitude 14,025 ft.

San Francisco Bay. Inlet of Pacific Ocean, W cen. California, connecting with the Pacific through the Golden Gate (*q.v.*); ab. 60 m. long (N-S; including San Pablo Bay) and 3–12 m. wide; the city of San Francisco is S of its Pacific entrance and the city of Oakland is on its E shore. See SAN PABLO BAY and SUISUN BAY.

San Francisco de la Selva. See COPIAPÓ.

San Francisco de Limache. See LIMACHE.

San Francisco del Oro \-del-ˈōr-ō\. Town, Chihuahua state, N Mexico; munic. pop. (1970p) 16,193.

San Francisco del Rin·cón \-ˌdel-riŋ-ˈkōn\. Town, Guanajuato state, cen. Mexico, 35 m. W of Guanajuato; munic. pop. (1970p) 43,271.

San Francisco de Ma·co·rís \-dā-ˌmäk-ə-ˈris\. Commune and city, ✱ of Duarte prov., N cen. Dominican Republic, ab. 60 m. NNW of Santo Domingo; commune pop. (1970p) 126,337; produces sugar, molasses, wax, timber.

San Francisco de Pau·la, Cape \-dā-ˈpau̇-lə\. Cape extending into Atlantic Ocean on E coast of Santa Cruz prov., S Argentina.

San Francisco Mountains. Mountain range, W Catron co., W New Mexico, extending across border into Arizona.

San Francisco Peaks *also* **San Francisco Mountain.** Three peaks in S cen. Coconino co., N Arizona: Humphreys (*also* **San Francisco Mountain**), 12,633 ft., highest point in Arizona; Agassiz 12,340 ft.; and Fremont 11,940 ft.

San Fra·tel·lo \ˌsan-frə-ˈtel-(ˌ)ō\. Commune, Messina prov., NE Sicily, Italy, 54 m. WSW of Messina; pop. (1970c) 11,607; destroyed 1754 and 1922 by landslides; founded by Lombards.

San Fructuoso. See TACUAREMBÓ 2.

Sanga. See SANGHA.

San Ga·bri·el \san-ˈgā-brē-əl\. 1 River, SW California; ab. 75 m. long; rises in San Gabriel Mts., flows SW across Los Angeles co. into Pacific Ocean near Long Beach.

2 Residential city, Los Angeles co., SW California, 8 m. ENE of Los Angeles; pop. (1970c) 29,336; San Gabriel Arcángel mission nearby; starting point for colonizers of Los Angeles 1781.

3 Town, Carchi prov., N Ecuador, ab. 80 m. NNE of Quito, in Andes Mts.

4 Cape, E cen. Baja California, NW Mexico, projecting into the Gulf of California.

San Gabriel Mountains. Mountain range, SW California, SW of Mojave Desert, between it and coastal plain in which Los Angeles is situated; chiefly in Los Angeles co.; highest point San Antonio Peak 10,080 ft.

San Gabriel No. 1 Dam. See UNITED STATES, *Dams and Reservoirs*.

San·ga·mon \ˈsaŋ-gə-mən\. 1 River, cen. Illinois; 225 m. long; rises in S McLean co., flows SW and W into Illinois river at NW extremity of Cass co.

2 County in Illinois. See table at ILLINOIS.

Sangarius. See SAKARYA.

Sanga Sanga \säŋ-ä-säŋ-ˈä\. Island, SW Sulu Archipelago, SW Phil., separated by narrow strait from W Tawitawi I.; 18 sq. m.; forms part of Banggaw municipality.

San·gay \säŋ-ˈgī\. Volcano, cen. Ecuador; 17,159 ft.

Sang–chu–pa–cha \ˈsäŋ-ˈchü-ˈpä-ˈchä\ *also* **San·ju** *or* **Sand·ju** \ˌsän-ˈjü\. Town, Sinkiang Uighur, W China, on N slope of Kunlun Shan.

Sang·er \ˈsaŋ-ər\. City, Fresno co., S cen. California, 14 m. ESE of Fresno; pop. (1970c) 10,088; wine, raisins, frozen foods; citrus fruit, truck farms.

Sang·er·hau·sen \ˈzäŋ-ər-ˌhau̇-zən\. City, Halle dist., East Germany, 37 m. NNE of Erfurt; pop. (1970e) 32,312; machinery, lumber, copper products; municipal rose garden; first mentioned 991; chartered 1230.

San Ger·mán \ˌsaŋ-her-ˈmän\. Town and municipality, SW Puerto Rico; pop. (1970p) 11,319 (town), 27,769 (munic.); in sugar and coffee farming region; Inter-American Univ. of Puerto Rico (1912); 16th cent. church; founded 1508, moved to present site 1573.

San Germano. See CASSINO.

Sang·er·ville \ˈsaŋ-ər-ˌvil\. Town, Piscataquis co., N cen. Maine, 8 m. W of Dover-Foxcroft; pop. (1970c) 1107; birthplace of Sir Hiram Maxim.

San·gha *or* **San·ga** \'saŋ-gə\. River, Congo, E equatorial Africa; ab. 400 m. long; flows S into the Congo river.

Sang·i·he Islands \säŋ-'gē-ə-\ *or* **Sangi Islands** \'säŋ-ē-\. Group of volcanic islands, Indonesia, bet. NE end of Celebes I. and S end of Mindanao I. and SW of the Talaud group; 314 sq. m.; main islands are Sangihe, Siau, Tahulandang, and Biaro. Largest of the group at N end, **Sangihe** *or formerly* **Great Sang·ir** \-'säŋ-ˌi(ə)r\, ab. 30 m. long by 8 to 17 m. wide, suffered from eruptions of volcano Gunung Awu (6102 ft.) in 1856 and 1892; has fertile soil; raises copra, hemp, and nutmegs; chief town Tahuna; first came under Dutch 1677.

San Gil \san-'hēl\. Town, Santander dept., N cen. Colombia, S of Bucaramanga; munic. pop. (1968e) 29,377.

San Gi·mi·gna·no \ˌsan-jē-mē-'nyä-(ˌ)nō\. Commune, Siena prov., Tuscany, cen. Italy, 19 m. NW of Siena; pop. (1968e) 8227; wine; tourism; numerous medieval towers, walls, gates, and several 13th cent. and 14th cent. palaces, 12th cent. former cathedral, and 13th cent. church of St. Augustine.

San Gior·gio a Cre·ma·no \ˌsan-ˌjōr-jō-ˌäk-rā-'män-(ˌ)ō, -ˌjor-\. Commune, Napoli prov., Campania, S Italy, on Bay of Naples 3 m. E by S of Naples; pop. (1968e) 30,569.

San Giorgio Mag·gio·re \-mä-'jōr-(ˌ)ā, -'jȯr-\. Island in the Lagoon of Venice, NE Italy.

San Gio·van·ni in Fio·re \ˌsan-jō-'vän-ē-ˌin-fē-'ō(ə)r-(ˌ)ā, -'ȯ(ə)r-\. Commune, Cosenza prov., Calabria, S Italy, 23 m. E by S of Cosenza; pop. (1968e) 20,012; 12th cent. convent.

San Giovanni in Per·si·ce·to \-in-ˌper-si-'chāt-(ˌ)ō\. Commune, Bologna prov., Emilia-Romagna, N Italy, 13 m. NNW of Bologna; pop. (1968e) 21,492.

San Giovanni Ro·ton·do \-rō-'tōn-(ˌ)dō\. Commune, Foggia prov., Apulia, SE Italy, 19 m. NNE of Foggia; pop. (1968e) 20,747.

San Giovanni Val·dar·no \-väl-'där-(ˌ)nō\. Commune, Arezzo prov., Tuscany, W Italy, 20 m. WNW of Arezzo; pop. (1968e) 18,777; lignite mining.

Sangir, Great. See SANGIHE ISLANDS.

San Giu·lia·no Ter·me \ˌsan-jül-ˌyän-(ˌ)ō-'ter-mē\ *or formerly* **Ba·gni San Giuliano** \ˌbän-yē-\. Commune, Pisa prov., Tuscany, cen. Italy, 6 m. NNE of Pisa; pop. (1968e) 22,717; warm radioactive mineral springs.

San Giu·sep·pe Ve·su·via·no \ˌsan-jü-'zep-ē-va-ˌzü-vē-'än-(ˌ)ō\. Commune, Napoli prov., Campania, S Italy, 12 m. E of Naples; pop. (1968e) 23,267.

San·gley Point \säŋ-'glā-\. Point, NE tip of Cavite Penin., NE Cavite prov., Luzon, Phil., on N side of entrance to Cañacao Bay; part of Cavite naval base.

San·gli \'säŋ-glē\. 1 Former Indian state, now part of Maharashtra state, India; 1146 sq. m.; a former Southern Maratha state; joined United Deccan State Aug. 26, 1947.

2 District of Maharashtra, India; 3229 sq. m.; pop. (1961c) 1,230,716.

3 Town, its ✱, on Krishna river 190 m. SE of Bombay; pop. (1961c) 73,828; trades in tobacco and peanuts; produces textiles, cigarettes, brass vessels.

San·gol·quí \ˌsaŋ-gȯl-'kē\. Town, Pichincha prov., N cen. Ecuador.

San Gor·go·nio Mountain \ˌsan-gȯr-ˌgō-nē-ō-\. Peak, San Bernardino co., S California; 11,502 ft.; highest of San Bernardino Mts.

San Gorgonio Pass. Mountain pass, SE end of San Bernardino Mts., San Bernardino co., S California; 1500 ft.; a gateway bet. San Gorgonio Mt. and San Jacinto Peak and connecting the San Bernardino Valley with the Coachella Valley.

San·gre de Cris·to Mountains \ˌsaŋ-grēd-ə-'kris-(ˌ)tō-\. A range of the Rocky Mts., extending from Chaffee co., cen. Colorado, to Santa Fe co., N cen. New Mexico; highest peak Blanca Peak 14,317 ft.

Sangre de Cristo Pass. Mountain pass, Costilla co., S Colorado, in the Sangre de Cristo Mts. of the Rocky Mts.; 9459 ft.; used before 1800; abandoned road.

Sangre Gran·de \-'gran-dē\. Town near E coast of island of Trinidad, Trinidad and Tobago, West Indies; pop. (1960c) 5087.

San·gro \'saŋ-(ˌ)grō\ *or anc.* **Sa·grus** \'sā-grəs\. River, SE cen. Italy; ab. 65 m. long; flows out of the Apennines NE into the Adriatic Sea 12 m. SE of Ortona.

San·grur \'səŋ-grů(ə)r\. Town, Punjab, NW India, in N part of state 58 m. W of Ambala; pop. (1961c) 28,344.

Sanhsing. See I-LAN 1.

San·i·bel Island \'san-ə-bəl-\. Island in Gulf of Mexico, off SW coast of Lee co., SW Florida; 16 sq. m.

San Ig·na·cio \ˌsan-ig-'näs-ē-ˌō\. 1 *or formerly* **El Ca·yo** \el-'kī-(ˌ)ō\ *or* **Cayo.** Town, ✱ of Cayo dist., W British Honduras; pop. (1967e) 2446.

2 Town, cen. Misiones dept., S Paraguay; pop. (1970e) 18,408.

San·i·lac \'san-ə-ˌlak\. County in Michigan. See table at MICHIGAN.

San Il·de·fon·so \ˌsan-ˌil-də-'fän(t)-(ˌ)sō\. 1 Municipality, Bulacan prov., Luzon, Phil., on E side of Candaba swamp near Pampanga border; pop. (1969e) 35,900.

2 *or* **La Gran·ja** \lä-'gräŋ-(ˌ)hä\. Commune, Segovia prov., cen. Spain, 7 m. SE of Segovia; pop. (1970p) 4164; seat of former summer palace of kings of Spain; scene of two treaties bet. Spain and France: Aug. 19, 1796, by which Spain joined France against England; and Oct. 1, 1800, by which France (Napoleon) secured Louisiana in exchange for Parma in Italy.

San Ildefonso, Cape. Point, E coast of Luzon, Quezon prov., Phil., SE of entrance to Casiguran Sound, 16°01′N, 122°E.

San–in Kai·gan National Park \ˌsän-ˌen-kī-'gän-\. National park, Honshū, Japan; 35 sq. m.; coastal region; established 1964.

San Isi·dro \ˌsan-ə-'sē-(ˌ)drō\. 1 Town, Buenos Aires prov., E cen. Argentina; pop. (1960c) 188,065; part of Greater Buenos Aires.

2 Municipality, Leyte prov., on NW coast of Leyte I., Phil., 45 m. WNW of Tacloban; pop. (1969e) 33,900; battle in **San Isidro Bay** Dec. 7, 1944 in which an entire Japanese convoy was sunk by U.S. planes.

3 Municipality, Nueva Ecija prov., Luzon, Phil., 13 m. S of Cabanatuan; pop. (1969e) 22,400; capital of the province 1852–1912.

Sanitary and Ship Canal. See ILLINOIS WATERWAY.

San Ja·cin·to \ˌsan-jə-'sint-ō\. 1 River, SE Texas; ab. 85 m. long; flows from Walker co. into Galveston Bay; battle near its mouth Apr. 21, 1836 in which Americans under Gen. Sam Houston decisively defeated Mexicans under Santa Anna.

2 County in Texas. See table at TEXAS.

3 City, Riverside co., SE California, 23 m. W of Palm Springs; pop. (1970c) 4385; health resort; agriculture.

4 Town, Bolívar dept., N Colombia, 48 m. SE of Cartagena; munic. pop. (1968c) 18,136.

5 Municipality, E coast of Ticao I., Masbate prov., Phil., port on Ticao Pass; pop. (1969e) 23,800.

San Jacinto Mountains. Range, chiefly in Riverside co., SW California, extending SE toward Salton Sea; generally considered as one of the Coast Ranges; highest peak **San Jacinto Peak** 10,801 ft.

San Ja·vier \ˌsan-hä-'vye(ə)r\ *also* **San Javier de Lon·co·mi·lla** \-dā-ˌlōŋ-kə-'mē-(y)ə\. City, Linares prov., S cen. Chile, 160 m. SW of Santiago; pop. (1960c) 8541.

San Jerónimo Ixtepec. See CIUDAD IXTEPEC.

San·jō \'sän-'jō\. City, Niigata prefecture, Honshū, Japan, 24 m. S of Niigata; pop. (1970c) 77,814.

San Joa·quin \ˌsan-wä-'kēn\. 1 River, cen. California; 350 m. long; formed by junction of forks in SE Madera co., flows W then NW into Sacramento river near its mouth; navigable 88 miles for ocean-going vessels. **Flor·ence Lake Dam** \ˈflȯr-ən(t)s-, ˈflär-\ (completed 1926; 166 ft. high) at upper end of its S fork in NE Fresno co. forms **Florence Lake,** from which water is diverted to **Hun·ting·ton Lake** \ˈhənt-iŋ-tən-\ 14 m. SW; where **Big Creek No. 2 and No. 3** (completed 1917; 120 and 152 ft. high, respectively) across Big Creek tributary impounds it for hydroelectric power; ab. 8 m. SSW of Huntington Lake is **Sha·ver Lake** \ˈshā-vər-\, another reservoir for water power, formed by **Shaver Lake Dam** (completed 1927; 198 ft. high) across Stevenson Creek tributary; lower in course bet. Fresno and Madera cos. is Friant Dam (completed 1942, 319 ft. high).

2 County in California. See table at CALIFORNIA.

3 Municipality, Iloilo prov., Panay, Phil., at W end of Iloilo Strait on Panay Gulf 31 m. WSW of City of Iloilo; pop. (1969e) 33,600.

San Joa·quín \ˌsan-wä-ˈkēn\. Town, Caaguazú dept., E Paraguay; munic. pop. (1970e) 18,309.

San Joaquin Ridge. Mountain, San Miguel co., SW Colorado; 13,446 ft.

San Jor·ge \saŋ-ˈhȯr-(ˌ)hā\. 1 River, N Colombia; ab. 250 m. long; flows NE into Cauca river; lower course through marshy region.

2 Lake port, W cen. shore of Lake Nicaragua, Rivas dept., SW Nicaragua; connected by rail with Rivas and the Pacific port of San Juan del Sur.

3 Small island, British Solomon Is. in W Pacific Ocean, off SE coast of Santa Isabel I., with which it forms Thousand Ships Bay.

San Jorge, Gulf of. 1 Widemouthed inlet of Atlantic Ocean on E coast of Chubut and Santa Cruz provs., S Argentina.

2 Inlet of Mediterranean Sea on E coast of Spain, S of Tarragona and N of Cape Tortosa.

San Jorge Bay. Inlet of NE Gulf of California, NW coast of the state of Sonora, Mexico.

San Jo·se \ˌsan-ə-ˈzā\. 1 Commercial and industrial city, ⊗ of Santa Clara co., W California, on Coyote and Guadalupe rivers, SE of San Francisco Bay and ab. 40 m. SE of San Francisco; pop. (1970c) 445,779; computers, rockets and missiles, electronic components, aluminum, plastics, wine and beer, paint, canned and dried fruit and vegetables; in truck and fruit farming region; San Jose State Coll. (1857), San Jose City Coll. (1921), San Jose Bible Coll. (1939). Founded 1777; first civil community in California; state capital Dec. 1849–Jan. 1852; incorporated 1850.

2 Municipality, Nueva Ecija prov., cen. Luzon, Phil., ab. 21 m. N of Cabanatuan; pop. (1969e) 51,700.

3 Municipality, Mindoro Occidental prov., SW coast of Mindoro I., Phil.; pop. (1969e) 50,200; harbor.

San Jo·sé \ˌsan-ə-ˈzā\. 1 Province of cen. Costa Rica. See table at COSTA RICA.

2 City, ✱ of Costa Rica and of San José prov.; pop. (1968e) 198,523; commercial and industrial center of the country; ships coffee and livestock; tourism; cathedral; Univ. of Costa Rica (estab. 1843, abolished 1888, reestablished 1940). Founded 1736; made capital 1823; developed during 19th cent. as center of coffee production.

3 Town, Bolívar prov., cen. Ecuador.

4 Seaport, Escuintla dept., S Guatemala; munic. pop. (1964p) 17,956; chief exports coffee, sugar, hides, forest products.

5 Island off SE coast of Baja California, Mexico, in the Gulf of California; 20 m. long.

6 Town, Caaguazú dept., cen. Paraguay; munic. pop. (1970e) 15,293.

7 One of Pearl Is., Gulf of Panama; ab. 25 sq. m.

8 Department of S Uruguay. See table at URUGUAY.

9 City, ✱ of San José dept., S Uruguay, on San José river, 55 m. NW of Montevideo; pop. (1963c) 27,478; livestock.

San José, Gulf of. Inlet of Gulf of San Matías, NE coast of Chubut prov., S Argentina; enclosed by Valdés Penin.

San Jose de Bue·na·vis·ta \-də-ˌbwā-nə-ˈvis-tə\. Municipality, ✱ of Antique prov., in S part, Panay, Phil.; port on coast of Sulu Sea; pop. (1969e) 23,400; has active coastal trade.

San José de Cúcuta. See CÚCUTA.

San José de Gua·ri·be \-də-gwə-ˈrē-bə\ *or* **San José de Gua·ni·na** \-gwə-ˈnē-nə\. Town, Anzoategui, N Venezuela, just E of El Tigre; pop. (1970e) 29,841.

San José de las La·jas \-dā-läz-ˈlä-ˌhäs\. Town and municipality, La Habana prov., W Cuba; town is railroad junction point 18 m. SE of Havana; munic. pop. (1967e) 31,750.

San José de los Ra·mos \-də-lōz-ˈräm-əs\. Municipality, Matanzas prov., W cen. Cuba, 33 m. ESE of Cárdenas; pop. (1967e) 11,630.

Sanju. See SANG-CHU-PA-CHA.

San Juan \san-ˈ(h)wän\. 1 River, Colorado, New Mexico, and Utah; 360 m. long; rises in Archuleta co., S Colorado, flows SW across New Mexico border, bends W then NW across SW Colorado into Utah, and empties into Colorado river in SW San Juan co., SE Utah; important in projects for development of the upper Colorado.

2 Name of counties in four states of the U.S. See tables at COLORADO, NEW MEXICO, UTAH, WASHINGTON.

3 City, Hidalgo co., S Texas, 6 m. E of McAllen; pop. (1970c) 4927; ships citrus fruit, vegetables.

4 River, W Argentina; ab. 160 m. long; main course ESE in San Juan prov., forming a headstream of the Desaguadero (Río Salado).

5 Province of W Argentina. See table at ARGENTINA.

6 City, ✱ of San Juan prov., W Argentina, 100 m. N of Mendoza; pop. (1960c) 106,564; commercial city with food-processing industries; founded 1562; moved to present site after 1593; largely destroyed by earthquake 1944; birthplace of Domingo Faustino Sarmiento, president of Argentina 1868–74.

7 River, W Colombia; ab. 200 m. long; flows S and W into the Pacific Ocean; the Calima is a tributary.

8 Peak, S Las Villas prov., W cen. Cuba; 3722 ft.

9 Province of W cen. Dominican Republic. See table at DOMINICAN REPUBLIC.

10 River, Nuevo León and Tamaulipas, NE Mexico; ab. 150 m. long; flows NE into Rio Grande.

11 River, S Nicaragua; 120 m. long; flows E out of Lake Nicaragua into the Caribbean Sea; forms E section of Nicaragua-Costa Rica boundary. See SAN JUAN DEL NORTE.

12 *or formerly* **Bol·bok** \bȯl-ˈbȯk\. Municipality, Batangas prov., Luzon, Phil., ab. 4 m. inland from Tayabas Bay; pop. (1969e) 49,400.

13 Seaport city and municipality, ✱ of Puerto Rico, on NE coast; pop. (1970p) 444,952 (city), 455,421 (munic.); oldest part of city built on an island in a large bay which has a narrow entrance, connected with mainland by a causeway and bridges; exports (chiefly to U.S.) sugar, tobacco, fruit, cacao; manufactures clothing, sugar, cigars and cigarettes; tourism; School of Tropical Medicine of the University of Puerto Rico.

History: Site first visited (1508) by Ponce de León who made a settlement 1509 on the mainland (see CAPARRA); in 1511 Caparra abandoned and site on island settled; fortifications begun 1533, El Morro castle built 1539–84; attacked by Drake and Hawkins 1595; held by the British under Lord Clifford for a short time 1598; sacked by the Dutch 1625; attacked again unsuccessfully by British 1797; occupied by Americans 1898.

14 *or in full* **San Juan de los Mo·rros** \-də-lōz-ˈmȯr-əs\. Town, ✱ of Guárico state, N cen. Venezuela, 50 m. SW of Caracas; pop. (1970e) 43,107.

San Juan, Cape. 1 Cape, extending into the Gulf of Guinea on the SW coast of Río Muni, Equatorial Guinea, W Africa, at N side of entrance to Corisco Bay.

2 Cape, NE tip of Puerto Rico; lighthouse.

3 Cape, E tip of Isla de los Estados, in South Atlantic Ocean off E point of Tierra del Fuego I.

San Juan, Point. Cape, S coast of Camagüey prov., E cen. Cuba, at N entrance to Guacanayabo Bay.

San Juan Bau·tis·ta \-bau̇-'tēs-tə\. 1 City, Mexico. See VILLAHERMOSA.

2 Town, ✻ of Misiones dept., S Paraguay, 240 m. SE of Asunción; munic. pop. (1970e) 13,595.

San Juan Bautista Tuxtepec. See TUXTEPEC.

San Juan Cap·is·tra·no \-ˌkap-əs-'trä-(ˌ)nō\. City, Orange co., SW California, SE of Los Angeles; pop. (1970c) 3781; site of Spanish mission founded 1776.

San Juan·ci·to \ˌsan-(h)wän-'sēt-(ˌ)ō\. Town, S cen. Honduras, 20 m. from Tegucigalpa; site of the Rosario mine (silver, gold).

San Juan de la Ma·gua·na \-del-ə-mə-'gwän-ə\. Municipality, ✻ of San Juan prov., Dominican Republic, 85 m. NW of Santo Domingo; pop. (1970p) 114,488.

San Juan del Mon·te \-del-'mȯnt-ē\. Municipality, W Rizal prov., Luzon, Phil., N of the Pasig; pop. (1969e) 77,700; borders on Manila to the W and on Quezon City to the N.

San Juan del Nor·te \-del-'nȯrt-ē\ *or formerly* **Grey·town** \'grā-ˌtau̇n\. Seaport, extreme SE coast of Nicaragua, at mouth of San Juan river; pop. (1963c) 599. The port (formerly called Greytown by the English) and region (Mosquito Coast) along the Caribbean coast N of the mouth of San Juan, claimed by Great Britain 1841–48, and port occupied 1848; river under consideration 1849–50 by U.S. for ship canal to Pacific via Lake Nicaragua; dispute settled by Clayton-Bulwer Treaty Apr. 19, 1850 whereby the two countries agreed to neutralization of any proposed interoceanic canal; control of coastal region finally given up by Great Britain by 1860.

San Juan de los La·gos \-də-lōz-'lä-gōs\. Town, Jalisco state, W cen. Mexico, 80 m. NE of Guadalajara; munic. pop. (1970p) 31,389.

San Juan de los Morros. See SAN JUAN 14.

San Juan de los Remedios. See REMEDIOS.

San Juan de los Ye·ras \-də-lōz-'yar-əs\. Municipality, Las Villas prov., W cen. Cuba; pop. (1967e) 14,420.

San Juan del Río \-del-'rē-(ˌ)ō\. Town, Querétaro state, cen. Mexico, 25 m. SE of Querétaro; munic. pop. (1970p) 53,-332.

San Juan del Sur \-del-'su̇(ə)r\. Seaport on SW coast of Rivas dept., SW Nicaragua; outlet for products of S and SW Nicaragua, esp. cacao, coffee, sugar, and woods.

San Juan de Sal·va·men·to \-dā-ˌsal-və-'men-(ˌ)tō\. See ESTADOS, ISLA DE LOS.

San Juan de Ulúa \-ˌdā-ə-'lü-ə\ *also* **San Juan de Ulloa** \-ˌdā-ə-'yō-ə\. Small island off Veracruz, Mexico, 19°12′N, 96°08′W; contains a fort defending the harbor.

San Juan Hill. Elevation near Santiago de Cuba, E Cuba; captured by Cubans and American troops in Spanish-American War July 1, 1898. See EL CANEY.

San Jua·ni·co Strait \ˌsan-(h)wä-ˌnē-kō-\. Narrow passage extending E and S bet. SW Samar and NE Leyte, Phil., from Samar Sea to San Pedro Bay; 25 m. long and from 1/5 to 3 m. wide. Noted for its scenery and navigable to medium-sized ships, but dangerous because of swift current and numerous islands. Has many pueblos on its banks; Tacloban at its S end. In occupation of Leyte secured on both sides by U.S. forces Oct. 30, 1944.

San Juan Islands. Group of islands, bet. Haro and Rosario straits, off NW Washington, including Orcas I. (59 sq. m.), San Juan I. (56 sq. m.; see *San Juan Island National Historical Park* at UNITED STATES, *National Historical Parks*), and Lopez I. (26 sq. m.), and constituting as a group San Juan co., Washington.

San Jua·ni·to \ˌsan-(h)wä-'nēt-(ˌ)ō\. Small island of the Tres Marías group (*q.v.*) in the Pacific Ocean off W cen. Mexico.

San Juan Ji·qui·pil·co \-ˌhē-ki-'pil-(ˌ)kō\ *or* **Jiquipilco.** Town, México state, cen. Mexico; munic. pop. (1970p) 67,682.

San Juan Mountains. A range of the Rocky Mts., SW Colorado, extending NW and SE through several counties and containing rugged and well-forested peaks, several above 14,000 ft.; highest are Uncompahgre Peak 14,309 ft., Mt. Wilson 14,246 ft., and Mt. Sneffels 14,150 ft.

San Juan Ne·po·mu·ce·no \-ˌnā-pō-ˌmü-'sā-(ˌ)nō\. Town, Caazapá dept., S Paraguay; munic. pop. (1970e) 19,013.

San Juan No·nual·co \-nō-'nwäl-(ˌ)kō\. Town, La Paz dept., S El Salvador.

San Juan Teotihuacán. See TEOTIHUACÁN.

San Juan y Mar·tí·nez \-ē-mär-'tēn-əs\. Municipality, Pinar del Río prov., W Cuba; pop. (1967e) 39,690; on railroad 15 m. SW of Pinar del Río.

San Ju·lián \ˌsan-hül-'yän\. Seaport, Santa Cruz prov., S Argentina, ab. 200 m. N of E entrance to Strait of Magellan; pop. (1960c) 3649; Magellan wintered here Mar. 1519–Aug. 1520 on his circumnavigation voyage.

San Jus·to \san-'hüs-(ˌ)tō\. Town, Buenos Aires prov., E cen. Argentina, ab. 10 m. WSW of Buenos Aires; pop. (1960c) 401,738; part of Greater Buenos Aires.

Sankt. See SAINT.

Sankt Andrä. See SZENTENDRE.

Sankt An·ton am Arl·berg \zäŋ(k)-'tän-ˌtōn-äm-'är(-ə)l-ˌbərg\. Village resort and winter sports center, Tirol, W Austria, at E end of Arlberg tunnel; alt. 4221 ft.

Sankt Beatenberg. See BEATENBERG.

Sankt Gallen. See SAINT GALL.

Sankt Go·ars·hau·sen \ˌzän(k)t-gō-'ärs-ˌhau̇-zən\ *or* **Sankt Go·ar** \-gō-'är\. Town, Rhineland-Palatinate, West Germany, on the Rhine river 24 m. WNW of Wiesbaden; Lorelei (*q.v.*) nearby.

Sankt Gotthard. See SAINT GOTTHARD.

Sankt Ing·bert \zäŋ(k)t-'iŋ-bərt, -ˌbe(ə)rt\. Town, Saarland, West Germany, ab. 7 m. NE of Saarbrücken; pop. (1969e) 28,818; iron and steel, glass, machinery, beer; coal mines.

Sankt Joachimsthal. See JÁCHYMOV.

Sankt Michel. See MIKKELI 2.

Sankt Moritz. See SAINT-MORITZ.

Sankt Pöl·ten \zäŋ(k)t-'pə(r)lt-ᵊn\. City, Lower Austria, 35 m. W of Vienna; pop. (1961c) 40,710; railroad junction; paper, machinery, furniture; cathedral; chartered 1159.

Sankt Veit am Flaum. See RIJEKA.

Sankt–Vith. See SAINT-VITH.

San·ku·ru \säŋ-'ku̇(ə)r-(ˌ)ü\. River, Zaire; 750 m. long; flows WNW and empties into Kasai river; upper course called the Lubilash (*q.v.*).

San Lá·za·ro, Cape \-san-'laz-ə-ˌrō\. Point, SW coast of Baja California, Mexico, extending into the Pacific Ocean W of Magdalena Bay.

San Le·an·dro \ˌsan-lē-'an-(ˌ)drō\. City, Alameda co., W California, 15 m. SE of Oakland; pop. (1970c) 68,698; residential; hosiery, paper products, household appliances; incorporated 1872.

San Lo·ren·zo \ˌsan-lə-'ren-(ˌ)zō\. 1 Unincorporated urban region, Alameda co., W California, SE of Oakland; pop. (1970c) 24,633.

2 Peak, NW Santa Cruz prov., S Argentina, on border of Chile; 12,136 ft.

3 Town, Santa Fe prov., N cen. Argentina, ab. 20 m. NNW of Rosario; pop. (1960c) 21,908.

4 Town, Valle dept., S Honduras, on an inlet of the Gulf of Fonseca 80 m. by road S of Tegucigalpa; pop. (1961c) 4400.

5 Town and municipality, E Puerto Rico; pop. (1970p) 7699 (town), 27,598 (munic.); town on railroad 20 m. SE of San Juan.

San Lorenzo, Cape. Cape extending into Pacific Ocean on W cen. coast of Ecuador.

San Lorenzo Island. Island, Pacific Ocean, off the city of Callao, Peru; ab. 5 m. long.

San·lú·car de Ba·rra·me·da \san-ˈlü-ˌkär-dā-ˌbär-ə-ˈmād-ə\. Seaport, Cádiz prov., SW Spain, at mouth of Guadalquivir river 18 m. NW of Cádiz; pop. (1970p) 41,072; produces wine, flour, salt; ships fruit and vegetables; fisheries; 14th cent. church, palace of dukes of Medina Sidonia; starting place of Columbus's 3d voyage 1498 and of Magellan's voyage of circumnavigation 1519.

San Lu·cas, Cape \-san-ˈlü-kəs\. Cape, south extremity of Baja California, Mexico, extending into the Pacific Ocean.

San Lu·is \san-ˈlü-əs\. City, ⊗ of Costilla co., S Colorado; pop. (1970c) 781.

San Lu·is \ˌsan-lu̇-ˈēs\. 1 Province of cen. Argentina. See table at ARGENTINA.

2 City, its ✱, 150 m. ESE of Mendoza; pop. (1960c) 40,420; hydroelectric power production; founded 1596.

3 Town and municipality, Oriente prov., E Cuba; town is on railroad just N of Santiago de Cuba; munic. pop. (1967e) 68,870.

4 Town and municipality, Pinar del Río prov., W Cuba; town is near S coast 11 m. S of Pinar del Río; munic. pop. (1967e) 24,990.

San Luis Dam. See UNITED STATES, *Dams and Reservoirs.*

San Luis d'Apra. See APRA HARBOR.

San Luis de la Paz \ˌsan-lu̇-ˈēs-də-lä-ˈpäz, -ˈpäs\. Municipality, Guanajuato state, Mexico, 75 m. ENE of León; pop. (1970p) 26,819; viticulture; alfalfa, corn.

San Luis Ji·lo·te·pe·que \ˌsan-lu̇-ˈēs-ˌhēl-ə-tā-ˈpek-ē\. Town, Jalapa dept., SE Guatemala, 30 m. E of Guatemala; pop. (1964p) 12,674.

San Luis Obis·po \san-ˌlü-ə-sə-ˈbis-(ˌ)pō\. 1 County in SW California. See table at CALIFORNIA.

2 City, its ⊗, 12 m. from Pacific Ocean and ab. 80 m. NW of Santa Barbara; pop. (1970c) 28,036; dairy products, furniture, building materials; diversified agriculture; Cuesta Coll. (1963). Founded 1772; incorporated as city 1856.

San Luis Park *or* **San Luis Valley** \san-ˌlü-əs-\. An area of irrigated land bet. mountain ranges in S Colorado; ab. 120 m. long, 60 m. wide; southernmost of a chain of high, grassy areas enclosed by snowcapped peaks (see NORTH PARK).

San Luis Peak \san-ˌlü-əs-\. Mountain, Saguache co., S Colorado; 14,014 ft.

San Luis Po·to·sí \ˌsan-lu̇-ˌē-ˌspōt-ə-ˈsē\. 1 State of cen. Mexico. See table at MEXICO.

2 City, its ✱, NE of León; munic. pop. (1970p) 274,320; major industrial center, producing rope, footwear, textiles, arsenic; large smelting and refining plants; silver mines; in agricultural region; cathedral, several notable churches; univ. (estab. 1859, received univ. status 1923). Founded as Franciscan mission 1583; seat of Juárez's government 1863; place where Francisco Madero drew up basic social and political program of Mexican revolution 1910.

San Luis Río Co·lo·ra·do \ˌsan-lu̇-ˈēs-ˈrē-ō-ˌkäl-ə-ˈräd-(ˌ)ō\. Municipality, Sonora state, Mexico, 45 m. ESE of Mexicali; pop. (1970p) 63,644; formed 1939.

San Luis Valley. See SAN LUIS PARK.

San Mar·co \san-ˈmär-(ˌ)kō\. One of the two large islands of Venice, Italy; in English often known as Saint Mark (*q.v.*).

San Marco in La·mis \-in-ˈläm-əs\. Commune, Foggia prov., Apulia, SE Italy, 17 m. N by E of Foggia; pop. (1968e) 17,903.

San Mar·cos \san-ˈmär-kəs\. 1 City, San Diego co., SW California, 22 m. NNW of San Diego; pop. (1970c) 3896; aircraft parts, optical devices; diversified agriculture.

2 City and resort, ⊗ of Hays co., S cen. Texas, 30 m. S of Austin; pop. (1970c) 18,860; cottonseed oil, woolens, building materials; agriculture; Southwest Texas State Coll. (1889).

3 Department of W Guatemala. See table at GUATEMALA.

4 Town, ✱ of San Marcos dept., Guatemala; pop. (1964p) 10,557; coffee trade.

5 Municipality, Guerrero state, Mexico, 35 m. E of Acapulco; pop. (1970p) 33,954; hammocks; wheat, avocados, mangoes.

San Marcos de Arica. See ARICA.

San Ma·ri·no \ˌsan-mə-ˈrē-(ˌ)nō\. 1 Suburban residential city, Los Angeles co., SW California, 11 m. NE of Los Angeles and E of Pasadena; pop. (1970c) 14,177.

2 Republic, cen. Italian penin. on Mount Titano, 11 m. SSW of Rimini (Italy); 24 sq. m.; pop. (1972e) 18,320; ✱ San Marino; smallest republic in the world and claims to be oldest state in Europe; legislative powers vested in grand council of 60 members elected by popular vote; executive powers vested in two regents appointed by grand council every six months; judicial powers vested in magistrates of Italian citizenship. Treaty of friendship with Italy June 28, 1897 (latest renewal Mar. 31, 1939); exports wine and building stone quarried on Mount Titano; agriculture; tourism.

History: Traditionally founded in 4th cent. by St. Marinus of Dalmatia; except for a few short periods has preserved its independence; protected by Montefeltro family of Urbino; its independence recognized by Papacy 1631. Entered by German troops Aug. 10, 1944; occupied by British Sept. 23, 1944; had a Communist government 1945–57.

3 City, its ✱; pop. (1970e) 4198; manufactures silk; built around hermitage dating from 441 A.D.; entered by one road; city walls, governor's palace, six churches, town hall and other public buildings.

San Mar·tín \ˌsan-mär-ˈtēn\. 1 Town, Buenos Aires prov., E Argentina. See GENERAL SAN MARTÍN.

2 Town, Mendoza prov., W Argentina, 30 m. SE of Mendoza; pop. (1960c) 20,466.

3 Department of NE Peru. See table at PERU.

San Martín, Lake. Lake, S Chile and S Argentina, on border bet. S Aysén prov. in Chile and SW Santa Cruz prov. in Argentina.

San Martín del Rey Au·re·lio \-del-ˌrā-au̇-ˈrā-lē-ˌō\. Commune, Oviedo prov., NW Spain, 7 m. SE of Oviedo; pop. (1970p) 27,329; agriculture and stock raising; coal mines; tomb of Aurelio, King of Oviedo.

San Martín Hi·dal·go \-hid-ˈal-(ˌ)gō, -ē-t͟häl-\. Municipality, Jalisco state, Mexico, 45 m. SW of Guadalajara; pop. (1970p) 29,258; corn, wheat, beans, fruit.

San Martín Tex·me·lu·cán \-ˌtās-mā-lu̇-ˈkän\. Town, Puebla state, SE cen. Mexico, NW of Puebla; munic. pop. (1970p) 50,571.

San Ma·teo \ˌsan-mə-ˈtā-(ˌ)ō\. 1 County in California. See table at CALIFORNIA.

2 Residential city, San Mateo co., W California, on SW shore of San Francisco Bay; pop. (1970c) 78,991; Coll. of San Mateo (1922); town site platted 1863.

San Ma·tías, Gulf of \-ˌsan-mə-ˈtē-əs\. Inlet of Atlantic Ocean in SE Río Negro prov., S cen. Argentina, enclosed on S by Valdés Penin. in Chubut prov.

San–men Bay \ˈsän-ˈmən-\. Bay on E coast of Chekiang prov., E China, S of Ning-po.

San Mi·che·le, Mon·te \ˈmȯn-tē-ˌsan-mi-ˈkā-lē, -ˈkel-ē\. Mountain, Friuli-Venezia Giulia, NE Italy, E of the Isonzo, dominating Gorizia to the NE and the Kras to the SE; scene of fighting Aug. 1916.

San Mi·guel \ˌsan-mə-ˈgil\. 1 River, SW Colorado; ab. 85 m. long; rises in San Juan Mts. in SE San Miguel co. and flows NW into the Dolores river in W Montrose co.

2 Name of counties in two states of the U.S. See tables at COLORADO and NEW MEXICO.

San Miguel \ˌsan-mi-ˈgel\. 1 River, E Bolivia; ab. 475 m. long; sometimes known as the **Ito·na·mas** \ˌē-tə-ˈnäm-əs\ in its lower course; flows NNW into Guaporé river on the Brazil-Bolivia boundary.

2 Town, Bolívar prov., W Ecuador, near Riobamba; pop. (1962c) 2410.

3 Mountain, El Salvador. See EL SALVADOR.

4 Department of E El Salvador. See table at EL SALVADOR.
5 City, ✱ of San Miguel dept., E El Salvador, ab. 65 m. E of San Salvador at foot of San Miguel volcano (6957 ft.); pop. (1970e) 52,060; commercial center; produces vegetable oil, leather goods, flour, clothing, pottery, tobacco products; founded 1530.
6 Town, Mexico. See SAN MIGUEL DE ALLENDE.
7 Town, N Misiones dept., S Paraguay; pop. (1970e) 6167.
8 Seaport town, N Isla del Rey, Pearl Is., Gulf of Panama.
9 Island, Albay prov., Luzon, Phil., smallest of group off E coast of Luzon bet. Lagonoy Gulf and Tabaco Bay NW of Cagraray I.; 8 sq. m.; forms part of Tabaco municipality. Has important fisheries.
10 Municipality, Bulacan prov., Luzon, Phil., 23 m. NNE of Malolos; pop. (1969e) 58,900; rice; iron mines, mineral springs.

San Miguel, Gulf of. Inlet of the Gulf of Panama, extending E into SE Panama.

San Miguel Bay. Large inlet of Pacific Ocean, N coast of SE Luzon, Phil., ab. 25 m. long by 12 to 17 m. wide; lies bet. Camarines Norte prov. on NW and Camarines Sur on S and E. Has large, safe anchorage.

San Miguel de Allen·de \-dā-ä(l)-'yen-dē\ *also* **Allende.** Municipality, Guanajuato state, cen. Mexico; pop. (1970p) 63,937.

San Miguel de Ibarra. See IBARRA.

San Miguel de la Palma. See LA PALMA 3.

San Miguel de Tu·cu·mán \-də-ˌtük-ə-'män\ *or* **Tucumán.** City, ✱ of Tucumán prov., N Argentina, at foot of E ranges of the Andes on a tributary of the Dulce river; pop. (1960c) 271,546; center of sugar industry; univ. (1914). Founded 1565; in 1776 became part of viceroyalty of La Plata; independence of Argentina was first proclaimed here at the first congress of the republic which met here July 1816. See *History* at ARGENTINA.

San Miguel el Al·to \-el-'äl-(ˌ)tō\. Town, Jalisco state, W cen. Mexico, 70 m. NE of Guadalajara; munic. pop. (1970p) 11,967.

San Miguel Island \ˌsan-mə-'gil-\. Island, NW end of Santa Barbara group in Pacific Ocean; part of Santa Barbara co., SW California, and separated from mainland by Santa Barbara Channel.

San Miguel Passage. Strait bet. Santa Rosa I. and San Miguel I., off S Santa Barbara co., SW California.

San Miguel Peak. Mountain, Dolores and San Miguel cos., SW Colorado; 13,700 ft.

San Mi·nia·to \ˌsan-mi-'nyät-(ˌ)ō\. Commune, Pisa prov., Tuscany, cen. Italy, 23 m. E by S of Pisa; pop. (1970c) 22,792; 10th cent. cathedral.

San Murezzan. See SAINT-MORITZ.

San Nar·ci·so \ˌsan-när-'sē-(ˌ)sō\. Municipality, Zambales prov., Luzon, Phil., on coast road ab. 75 m. NW of Manila; pop. (1969e) 20,700; founded 1849; U.S. troops landed near here Jan. 29, 1945.

San·ni·can·dro Gar·ga·ni·co \ˌsan-i-'kän-drō-gär-'gän-i-ˌkō\. Commune, Foggia prov., Apulia, SE Italy, 25 m. N of Foggia; pop. (1968e) 18,740.

San Ni·co·las \ˌsan-ˌnē-kə-'läs\. 1 Village, Netherlands Antilles. See SINT NICOLAAS.
2 Municipality, Pangasinan prov., Luzon, Phil., on E tributary of the Agno 105 m. NNW of Manila; pop. (1969e) 26,100.

San Ni·co·lás \ˌsan-ˌnē-kə-'läs\. 1 Town, Buenos Aires prov., E cen. Argentina, on Paraná river; pop. (1960c) 49,082; river port, exporting meat and wool; steel mill, electric power plant; founded 1748.
2 Municipality, La Habana prov., W Cuba, 35 m. SE of Havana; pop. (1967e) 16,930.

San Nicolás de los Gar·zas \-də-lōz-'gär-səs\. City, Nuevo León state, Mexico, 45 m. NW of Monterrey; munic. pop. (1970p) 111,502; barley, oranges.

San Nic·o·las Island \sa(n)-ˌnik-ə-ləs-\. Island, cen. Santa Barbara group in Pacific Ocean; part of Ventura co., SW California.

Sânnicolaul–Mare. See SÎNNICOLAU MARE.

San·nois \san-'wä\. Commune, Val-d'Oise, N France, NNW suburb of Paris; pop. (1968c) 19,060.

Sa·no \'sä-ˌnō\. City, Tochigi prefecture, Honshū, Japan, 49 m. N of Tokyo; pop. (1970c) 71,573.

Sa·nok \'sän-ˌȯk\. Commune, Rzeszów prov., SE Poland, on San river 35 m. S of Rzeszów; pop. (1970p) 21,600; manufactures vehicles.

San Pab·lo \san-'pab-(ˌ)lō\. City, Contra Costa co., W California, N of Berkeley; pop. (1970c) 21,461; Contra Costa Jr. Coll. (1948).

San Pa·blo \san-'päb-(ˌ)lō\. Chartered city, S Laguna prov., Luzon, Phil., 17 m. SW of Santa Cruz; pop. (1969e) 99,000; ships copra; largest town in the province, an important rail and highway center in a valley near several small crater lakes; created a city 1940.

San Pab·lo Bay \san-'pab-(ˌ)lō-\. North extension of San Francisco Bay (*q.v.*), W cen. California.

San Pa·blo del Mon·te \san-'päb-lō-del-'mȯnt-ē\. Town, Tlaxcala state, cen. Mexico; pop. (1970p) 20,170.

San Pas·qual *or* **San Pas·cual** \ˌsan-pə-'skwȯl\. Locality, San Diego co., SW California, ab. 40 m. NE of San Diego; site of battle Dec. 6, 1846 in which U.S. troops under Gen. Stephen W. Kearny suffered greater losses but were not prevented by Spanish-Californian troops from reaching San Diego.

San Pa·tri·cio \ˌsan-pə-'trish-ē-ˌō\. County in Texas. See table at TEXAS.

San Pe·dro \san-'pē-(ˌ)drō, -'pā-\. 1 River, SE Arizona; ab. 100 m. long; flows NW into the Gila river in Pinal co.
2 Former city, Los Angeles co., SW California; annexed to Los Angeles 1909; harbor; port of entry; U.S. military and naval base.

San Pedro \san-'pā-drō\. 1 Town, Buenos Aires prov., E cen. Argentina, port on the Paraná river 90 m. NW of Buenos Aires; pop. (1960c) 17,960.
2 River, S cen. Camagüey prov., E cen. Cuba; ab. 60 m. long; flows SW and W into Caribbean Sea; the city of Camagüey is situated on its upper course.
3 River, Durango and Nayarit states, W Mexico; ab. 250 m. long; flows S and W past Tuxpan to the Pacific.
4 *or in full* **San Pedro de las Co·lo·nias** \-ˌdā-ˌläs-kə-'lō-nyəs\. Municipality, Coahuila state, NE Mexico, 40 m. NE of Torreón; pop. (1970p) 70,407; wheat.
5 Department of cen. Paraguay. See table at PARAGUAY.
6 Town, ✱ of San Pedro dept., cen. Paraguay, on Jejui Guazú river ab. 90 m. N of Asunción; pop. (1970e) 26,797.

San Pedro, Point. 1 \-san-'pē-(ˌ)drō\. Point, NW coast of San Mateo co., W California.
2 \-san-'pā-drō\. Cape, SW Antofagasta prov., N Chile, S of Nuestra Señora Bay.

San Pedro Bay. 1 \san-ˌpē-drō-\. Inlet of San Pedro Channel, S Los Angeles co., California; the city of Long Beach is on it.
2 \san-ˌpā-drō-\. Inlet of Pacific Ocean, SW cen. coast of Chile, NW of Puerto Montt.
3 \san-ˌpā-drō-\. Inlet of Leyte Gulf, E Phil., bet. SW Samar and NE Leyte; connects by San Juanico Strait with Samar Sea. Tacloban is at its NW corner.

San Pedro Car·chá \san-ˌpā-drō-kär-'chä\. Town, Alta Verapaz dept., cen. Guatemala; pop. (1968e) 69,019.

San Pedro Channel \san-ˌpē-drō-\. Strait bet. S California mainland and Santa Catalina I., off W coast of Orange co., SW California.

San Pedro Cho·lu·la \san-ˌpā-drō-chō-'lü-lə\. Municipality, Puebla state, Mexico, 10 m. W of Puebla; pop. (1970p) 34,661.

San Pedro de las Colonias. See SAN PEDRO 4.

San Pedro del Durazno. See DURAZNO 2.

San Pedro de Lloc \san-ˌpā-drō-dā-ˈyōk\. Town, La Libertad dept., NW Peru, N of Trujillo; pop. (1961c) 7500.

San Pedro del Pa·ra·ná \san-ˌpā-drō-del-ˌpar-ə-ˈnä\. City, Itapúa dept., SE Paraguay; pop. (1962c) 19,150.

San Pedro de Ma·co·rís \san-ˌpā-drō-dā-ˌmäk-ə-ˈris\. 1 Province of SE Dominican Republic. See table at DOMINICAN REPUBLIC.
2 Municipality, its ✻, 40 m. E of Santo Domingo; pop. (1970p) 70,092; exports sugar, molasses, and livestock; manufactures clothing, soap, alcohol.

San Pedro Mountain \san-ˌpē-drō-\. Peak, SW Rio Arriba co., NW cen. New Mexico; 10,624 ft.

San Pedro Sa·ca·te·pé·quez \san-ˌpā-drō-ˌsäk-ə-tā-ˈpek-əs\. Town, San Marcos dept., W Guatemala, ab. 20 m. NW of Quezaltenango; munic. pop. (1964p) 24,054.

San Pedro Su·la \san-ˈpā-drō-ˈsü-lə\. Town, ✻ of Cortés dept., NW Honduras, ab. 100 m. NW of Tegucigalpa; pop. (1969e) 96,341; commercial center; ships bananas; produces foodstuffs, clothing, beverages, tobacco products, soap, building materials.

San Pedro y San Pab·lo Te·pos·co·lu·la \san-ˈpā-drō-ē-san-ˈpäb-lō-tā-ˌpō-skə-ˈlü-lə\. Municipality, Oaxaca state, Mexico, 60 m. NW of Oaxaca; pop. (1970p) 33,556; livestock and poultry raising; corn.

San·pete \ˈsan-ˌpēt\. County in Utah. See table at UTAH.

San Pie·tro \ˌsan-pē-ˈe-(ˌ)trō\. Island in Mediterranean Sea, off SW coast of the island of Sardinia; 20 sq. m.; attached to Cagliari prov., Italy; chief town Carloforte.

San Pitch \san-ˈpich\. River, cen Utah; ab. 60 m. long; flows SW through Sanpete co. into Sevier river.

San·quhar \ˈsaŋ-kər\. Burg, Dumfries, Scotland, 26 m. NW of Dumfries by rail; pop. (1971p) 1991; scene of publication by Richard Cameron 1680 and James Renwick 1685 of the Covenanters' declarations renouncing allegiance to Charles II and James VII; ruined castle.

San Quin·tín Glacier \san-kin-ˈtēn-\. Glacier in Andes, Chile; 35 m. long; ab. 4 m. wide near its terminus.

San Ra·fael \ˌsan-rə-ˈfel\. 1 River, E cen. Utah; ab. 90 m. long; flows SE through Emery co. into Green river.
2 Residential city, ⊗ of Marin co., W California, 13 m. NW of San Francisco; pop. (1970c) 38,977; aluminum products, boats, plastics, gloves; truck and dairy farms; Dominican Coll. of San Rafael (1890); Hamilton Air Force Base is 6 m. NNE of San Rafael.

San Ra·fa·el \ˌsan-ˌräf-ē-ˈel\. Town, Mendoza prov., W cen. Argentina, 120 m. S of Mendoza; pop. (1960c) 46,599; agricultural district.

San Rafael National Park. National park, Chile; 2278 sq. m.; rare animals; established 1945.

San Ra·món \ˌsan-rə-ˈmōn\. Town, Canelones dept., S Uruguay, 45 m. N of Montevideo.

San Re·mi·gio \ˌsan-rə-ˈmē-hē-ˌō\. Municipality, Cebu prov., on NW coast of Cebu I., Phil., at N end of Tanon Strait 56 m. N of City of Cebu; pop. (1969e) 32,700.

San Re·mo \san-ˈrē-(ˌ)mō\. Urban community (unincorporated), Suffolk co., SE New York, on Long Island E of New York; pop. (1970c) 8302.

San Remo \san-ˈrā-(ˌ)mō, -ˈrē-\. Seaport, Imperia prov., Liguria, NW Italy, on Ligurian Sea 12 m. WSW of Imperia; pop. (1968e) 63,735; important year-round resort; flower market; 12th cent. Romanesque cathedral. Site of international conference Apr. 19–26, 1920 of representatives of countries in World War I.

San Ro·mán, Cape \-ˌsan-rə-ˈmän\. Cape, N extremity of Paraguaná Penin., NW Venezuela.

San Ro·que \san-ˈrō-kē\. Commune, Cádiz prov., SW Spain, 54 m. SE of Cádiz; pop. (1970p) 17,727.

San Sa·ba \san-ˈsab-ə\. 1 River, Texas; 100 m. long; flows ENE from Schleicher co. to Colorado river on E boundary of San Saba co.
2 County in Texas. See table at TEXAS.
3 Town, its ⊗, cen. Texas, on San Saba river; pop. (1970c) 2555; pecans, watermelons.

San Sal·va·dor \san-ˈsal-və-ˌdȯ(ə)r\. 1 *or formerly* **Watlings Island** \ˌwät-liŋz-\. One of the Bahama Is., ESE of Cat I. (*q.v.*) at 24°0′N, 74°30′W; 60 sq. m.; pop. (1963c) 968; now generally identified (Cat I., formerly so identified) with the first landfall (Oct. 12, 1492) of Columbus in the New World, an island which Columbus says was called **Gua·na·ha·ni** \ˌgwän-ə-ˈhän-ē\ by the native Lucayans before he renamed it San Salvador; has lighthouse near NE end (estab. 1887).
2 Peak in SW El Salvador; 6187 ft.
3 Department of SW cen. El Salvador. See table at EL SALVADOR.
4 City, ✻ of El Salvador, also ✻ of San Salvador dept., 23 m. from the port of La Libertad; pop. (1970e) 358,913, met. area pop. 496,667; the republic's financial, commercial, and industrial center; produces textiles and clothing, leather and wood products, pottery, liquors, soap, cigars, cement; cathedral, national observatory, national library; Univ. of El Salvador (1841), José Simeón Cañas Univ. (1965). Founded 1524 and established on present site 1528; capital of El Salvador since 1841 except for the years 1854–59; destructive earthquakes 1854 and 1873.
5 Town, Angola, Africa. See SÃO SALVADOR 1.
6 *also* **James Island** \ˈjāmz-\ *or* **San·ti·a·go** \ˌsant-ē-ˈäg-(ˌ)ō, ˌsänt-\. One of the Galápagos Is. (*q.v.*).

San Salvador de Jujuy. See JUJUY 2.

San·sa·por \ˈsan(t)-sə-ˌpȯ(ə)r\. Village, NW coast of Doberai Penin., NW Irian Barat, Indonesia, opp. Waigeo I. and NE of Sorong. In World War II in advance of Allies toward the Philippines, seized in surprise landing by U.S. forces July 30, 1944; this led a little later to occupation of Morotai.

San Se·bas·tián \ˌsan-si-ˈbas-chən, -bas-ˈtyän\. 1 Settlement, E side of Gulf of Urabá, NW Colombia, made 1509 by Ojeda; unsuccessful and later removed to Darién (*q.v.*).
2 Town and municipality, NW Puerto Rico; pop. (1970p) 7039 (town), 29,892 (munic.); town is 12 m. SE of Aguadilla.
3 Chief town and port, Gomera I., Canary Is., Spain; pop. (1970p) 5321.
4 Commercial seaport, ✻ of Guipúzcoa prov., N Spain, on Bay of Biscay 48 m. E of Bilbao; pop. (1970p) 165,829; episcopal see; produces chemicals, cement, beer, chocolate, metal goods; commercial fisheries; 16th and 18th cent. churches; first mentioned 1014; received charter late 12th cent.; burned by Anglo-Portuguese army under Wellington 1813; former summer residence of Spanish court.

San Sebastián, Cape. Cape, NE coast of Tierra del Fuego I., Argentina, off S South America.

San Sebastián Bay. Bay, NE coast of Tierra del Fuego I., Argentina.

Sansego. See SUŠAK.

San·se·pol·cro \ˌsan-se-ˈpōl-(ˌ)krō\. Commune, Arezzo prov., Tuscany, W Italy, on Tiber river 15 m. ENE of Arezzo; pop. (1968e) 15,622; 11th cent. cathedral.

San Ser·vo·lo \san-ˈser-və-ˌlō\. Island in the Lagoon of Venice, NE Italy.

San Se·ve·ri·no Mar·che \san-ˌsev-ə-ˈrē-nō-ˈmär-kē\. Commune, Macerata prov., Marches, cen. Italy, near Potenza river 16 m. W by S of Macerata; pop. (1968e) 13,398; episcopal see.

San Se·ve·ro \ˌsan-sə-ˈver-(ˌ)ō\. Commune, Foggia prov., Apulia, SE Italy, 20 m. NNW of Foggia; pop. (1968e) 52,458; center of agricultural region; episcopal see.

Sansing. See I-LAN 1.

San·som Park Village \ˌsan-səm-\. City, Tarrant co., N Texas, 8 m. NW of Fort Worth; pop. (1970c) 4771.

San Stefano. See YEŞILKÖY.

Sant *or* **Santh** \ˈsənt\. Former Indian state, now part of Gujarat state, W India; 390 sq. m.

Santa. See SAINT.

San·ta \ˈsant-ə\. River, N cen. Peru; ab. 200 m. long; empties into Pacific Ocean at Chimbote ab. 75 m. SE of Trujillo; large hydroelectric plant on its banks.

Santa Ana \ˌsant-ə-ˈan-ə\. 1 Residential and commercial city, ⊗ of Orange co., SW California, 20 m. E of Long Beach; pop. (1970c) 156,601; feed, soft drinks, perfumes, electronic components, sugar, canned fruits and vegetables; in a rich agricultural area; Santa Ana Coll. (1915); founded 1869; incorporated as city 1886.

2 Municipality, Matanzas prov., W cen. Cuba, W of Matanzas; pop. (1967e) 6640.

3 Town, Manabí prov., W Ecuador, ab. 80 m. NW of Guayaquil; pop. (1962c) 3940.

4 Volcanic peak, El Salvador; 7724 ft. See IZALCO.

5 Department of NW El Salvador. See table at EL SALVADOR.

6 City, ✻ of Santa Ana dept., NW El Salvador, 50 m. NW of San Salvador; pop. (1970e) 104,962; important commercial and industrial center; ships coffee; produces textiles, leather and wood products, cigars, pottery; food processing, distilling.

7 Peak on Paraguaná Penin., NW Venezuela; 2625 ft.

Santa Ana Bay. Bay, SW coast of Spanish Sahara, NW Africa.

Santa Ana de Coro. See CORO.

Santa Ana Mountains. Range of mountains along border between Orange and Riverside cos., S California; highest point 5685 ft.

Santa An·na \ˌsant-ə-ˈan-ə\. Town, Coleman co., cen. Texas, 20 m. W of Brownwood; pop. (1970c) 1310.

Santa Bar·ba·ra \ˌsant-ə-ˈbär-b(ə-)rə\. 1 County in SW California. See table at CALIFORNIA.

2 Residential city, its ⊗, on Santa Barbara Channel ab. 80 m. NW of Los Angeles; pop. (1970c) 70,215; seaside resort; oil wells; citrus, nut, and livestock farms; Univ. of California at Santa Barbara (1891), Westmont Coll. (1940), Brooks Institute of Oceanography (1945), Santa Barbara City Coll. (1946), Center for the Study of Democratic Institutions; Vandenburg Air Force Base, important center for military space research and satellite launchings, is nearby. Founded 1782; incorporated as city 1850.

3 Municipality, cen. Pangasinan prov., Luzon, Phil., 12 m. E of Lingayen; pop. (1969e) 32,900.

4 Municipality, Iloilo prov., Panay, Phil., on Jaro river and on railroad 12 m. NNW of City of Iloilo; pop. (1969e) 32,100.

Santa Bár·ba·ra \ˌsan-tə-ˈbär-b(ə-)rə\. 1 Department of W Honduras. See table at HONDURAS.

2 Town, its ✻; pop. (1961c) 4915.

3 Mining town, Chihuahua state, near Hidalgo de Parral, N Mexico; munic. pop. (1970p) 20,117.

Santa Barbara Channel. Strait bet. S California mainland and the island chain of Santa Barbara Is., off coast of Santa Barbara and Ventura cos., SW California.

Santa Bárbara de Samaná. See SAMANÁ 2.

Santa Barbara Island. Island, cen. Santa Barbara group in Pacific Ocean, part of Santa Barbara co., SW California; part of island included in Channel Islands National Monument (see UNITED STATES, *National Monuments*).

Santa Barbara Islands. Chain of islands off S California coast, separated from mainland by Santa Barbara and San Pedro channels, in Santa Barbara, Ventura, and Los Angeles cos.; includes islands of San Miguel, Santa Rosa, Santa Cruz, Anacapa, Santa Barbara, San Nicolas, Santa Catalina, and San Clemente.

Santa Cat·a·li·na \ˌsant-ə-ˌkat-ᵊl-ˈē-nə\. 1 *or* **Catalina.** Island, SW Santa Barbara group in Pacific Ocean, part of Los Angeles co., SW California; 70 sq. m.; tourist resort.

2 Small island in lower Gulf of California, off SE coast of Baja California, Mexico.

Santa Catalina, Gulf of. Inlet of Pacific Ocean, W coast of Orange and San Diego cos., SW California.

Santa Catalina Mountains. Small range, NE corner of Pima co., S Arizona; highest point Mount Lemmon 9157 ft.

Santa Cat·a·ri·na \ˌsant-ə-ˌkat-ə-ˈrē-nə\. 1 Island in Atlantic Ocean, off the E cen. coast of Santa Catarina state, S Brazil.

2 State, S Brazil; 37,060 sq. m.; pop. (1970p) 2,911,479; ✻ Florianópolis; corn, wheat, tobacco, coal; meat processing.

3 City, Nuevo León, Mexico, 5 m. W of Monterrey; munic. pop. (1970p) 35,723; palm mats; livestock raising; agriculture.

Santa Clara \ˌsant-ə-ˈklar-ə, -ˈkler-\. 1 River, California; ab. 75 m. long; rises in Los Angeles co. and flows W through Ventura co. to Santa Barbara Channel near Ventura.

2 County in California. See table at CALIFORNIA.

3 City, Santa Clara co., W California, 5 m. NW of San Jose; pop. (1970c) 87,717; produces fiberglass, electrical equipment, chemicals, paper products; in fruit and truck farming area; Univ. of Santa Clara (1851), Santa Clara mission. Settled 1777 as Franciscan mission, incorporated as city 1852.

Santa Clara. 1 Former name of Las Villas prov., Cuba. See LAS VILLAS.

2 Municipality and city, ✻ of Las Villas prov., W cen. Cuba, ab. 165 m. ESE of Havana; munic. pop. (1967e) 202,120; railroad junction; sugar and tobacco; univ. (1949); founded 1689.

3 Island, Pacific Ocean. See JUAN FERNÁNDEZ.

4 Municipality, Michoacán state, Mexico, 35 m. NW of Uruapan; pop. (1970p) 25,940; livestock raising; corn, wheat, fruit.

Santa Clara Bay. Bay, N coast of Matanzas prov., W cen. Cuba, E of Cárdenas Bay.

Santa Co·lo·ma de Gra·ma·net \ˌsant-ə-kə-ˈlō mə-dā-ˌgräm-ə-ˈnet\. Commune, Barcelona prov., NE Spain, N suburb of Barcelona; pop. (1970p) 106,711.

Santa Cruz \ˌsant-ə-ˈkrüz\. 1 Island, NW end of Santa Barbara group in Pacific Ocean; part of Santa Barbara co., SW California; separated from mainland by Santa Barbara Channel.

2 River, S Arizona; ab. 150 m. long; rises in E Pima co. S of Tucson, flows NW into Gila river in NW Pinal co.

3 Name of counties in two states of the U.S. See tables at ARIZONA and CALIFORNIA.

4 City, ⊗ of Santa Cruz co., W California, at N end of Monterey Bay; pop. (1970c) 32,076; tourist center; commercial fisheries; truck and fruit farms; Univ. of California at Santa Cruz (1965); founded 1791; incorporated 1876.

5 Island, Virgin Islands, U.S. See SAINT CROIX 4.

Santa Cruz \ˌsant-ə-ˈkrüz, *Span.* ˌsän-tä-ˈkrüs\. 1 River, S Argentina; ab. 250 m. long; flows E out of Lake Argentino in W Santa Cruz prov. and empties into Atlantic Ocean at Santa Cruz.

2 Province of S Argentina. See table at ARGENTINA.

3 Port, E Santa Cruz prov., S Argentina, at mouth of Santa Cruz river; pop. (1960c) 1178.

4 Department of E Bolivia. See table at BOLIVIA.

5 City, ✻ of Santa Cruz dept., E Bolivia, on the Piray river ab. 180 m. NE of Sucre; pop. (1971e) 135,000; sugar, rum, furniture, leather goods, lumber; univ. (1880); founded 1560.

6 *also* **In·de·fat·i·ga·ble Island** \in-di-ˈfat-i-gə-bəl-\. One of the Galápagos Is. (*q.v.*).

7 Municipality, Ilocos Sur prov., Luzon, Phil., on coast highway 34 m. S of Vigan; pop. (1969e) 23,000.

8 Municipality, ✻ of Laguna prov., Luzon, Phil., on SE shore of Laguna de Bay 34 m. SE of Manila; pop. (1969e) 45,200; ships rice and sugar; connected by highway, railroad, and boat with Manila; made capital of province 1858.

9 Municipality, Zambales prov., W Luzon, Phil., on coast 30 m. N of Iba; pop. (1969e) 28,500.

10 Municipality, NE coast of Marinduque I., Phil., 18 m. E of Boac; pop. (1969e) 44,700.
11 Municipality, Davao del Sur prov., Mindanao, Phil., on W shore of Davao Gulf 21 m. SW of City of Davao; pop. (1969e) 33,500.
12 Chief island of Santa Cruz Is., SW Pacific Ocean. See NDENI.

Santa Cruz Bay. Inlet of Atlantic Ocean, E cen. coast of Santa Cruz prov., S Argentina; receives the Santa Cruz and Chico rivers from the W and NW.

Santa Cruz Channel. Strait bet. Santa Cruz I. and Santa Rosa I., off S coast of Santa Barbara co., SW California.

Santa Cruz da Gra·ci·o·sa \ˌsa(ⁿ)nt-ə-ˈkrüzh-də-ˌgras-ē-ˈō-zə\. Chief town of Graciosa I., cen. Azores.

Santa Cruz de Bravo. See FELIPE CARRILLO PUERTO.

Santa Cruz de Ju·ven·ti·no Ro·sas \ˌsant-ə-ˈkrüz-də-ˌhü-vən-ˌtē-nō-ˈrō-zəz, ˌsän-tä-ˈkrüs-\. Municipality, Guanajuato state, cen. Mexico; pop. (1970p) 31,834.

Santa Cruz de la Pal·ma \-də-lə-ˈpäl-mə\. Chief town, La Palma I., Canary Is., Spain; pop. (1970p) 13,163.

Santa Cruz del Nor·te \-del-ˈnȯrt-ē\. Town and municipality, La Habana prov., W Cuba; town pop. (1967e) 11,780.

Santa Cruz del Qui·ché \-del-kē-ˈchā\. Town, ✱ of Quiché dept., W cen. Guatemala, ab. 60 m. NW of Guatemala (city); pop. (1964p) 30,079.

Santa Cruz del Seibo *or* **Santa Cruz del Seybo.** See EL SEIBO 2.

Santa Cruz del Sur \-del-ˈsu̇(ə)r\. Municipality, Camagüey prov., E cen. Cuba, on S coast 50 m. S of Camagüey; pop. (1967e) 77,760.

Santa Cruz de Te·ne·ri·fe \-də-ˌten-ə-ˈrē-fē\. 1 Province of Spain. See table at SPAIN.
2 Seaport, its ✱, W Canary Is., Spain, on N coast 57 m. NW of Las Palmas; pop. (1970p) 151,361; principal city of Tenerife I.; ships bananas and tomatoes; manufactures wine, pottery, lime; oil refinery; 16th cent. church; founded 1494; attacked by British 1657 and 1797; developed rapidly after c. 1880.

Santa Cruz do Sul \ˌsa(ⁿ)nt-ə-ˌkrüzh-du̇-ˈsül\. City, E cen. Rio Grande do Sul state, S Brazil, 80 m. WNW of Pôrto Alegre; munic. pop. (1968e) 89,963.

Santa Cruz Islands \ˌsant-ə-ˌkrüz-\. Island group in SW Pacific Ocean N of the New Hebrides and 240 m. E of S part of the Solomon Is.; 362 sq. m.; chief island Ndeni; administratively attached to the British protectorate of Solomon Is. Other islands are Vanikoro, Utupua, and a number of islets, including Tinakula, an active volcano. Rarely visited; limited trade in copra. Discovered 1595 by Mendaña. In World War II site of naval engagement Oct. 26, 1942 in which U.S. vessels and carrier planes defeated the Japanese but suffered loss of the carrier *Hornet.*

Santa Ele·na \ˌsant-ə-ə-ˈlā-nə\. 1 Peninsula, W Guayas prov., W Ecuador, on N side of the Gulf of Guayaquil; its tip is La Puntilla and on its N side is **Santa Elena Bay;** site of Ecuador's principal oil field; seaside resort region.
2 Town, Santa Elena Penin., Guayas prov., W Ecuador, ab. 65 m. W of Guayaquil; pop. (1962c) 4241; oil wells.
3 Town, Usulután dept., SE El Salvador.
4 Town, Cordillera dept., cen. Paraguay; pop. (1970e) 10,456.

Santa Elena, Cape. Cape, NW coast of Costa Rica, extending into the Pacific Ocean.

Santa Elena Bay. Peninsula, Ecuador. See SANTA ELENA 1.

Santa Eugenia, Point. See EUGENIA, POINT.

Santa Fe \ˌsant-ə-ˈfā, ˈsant-ə-ˌ\. 1 River, N Florida penin.; ab. 70 m. long; flows from E Alachua co., N Florida penin., W into the Suwannee river.
2 County in New Mexico. See table at NEW MEXICO.
3 City, ✱ of New Mexico and ⊗ of Santa Fe co., N cen. New Mexico, ab. 40 m. W of Las Vegas, bet. the Pecos and Rio Grande rivers; pop. (1970c) 41,167; altitude 6950 ft.; major tourist center and health resort; noted for Indian and Mexican handicrafts; ships livestock, gold, silver, copper; Coll. of Santa Fe (1947). Notable buildings include Palace of the Governors (1610, museum since 1914), San Miguel Church (c. 1636), cathedral, Old Fort Marcy (1846). Has large Spanish-American population; Indian pueblos and Bandelier National Monument in vicinity.
History: Oldest capital in U.S., founded by Spanish c. 1609; a mission and exploration center in colonial era; occupied by Indians 1680–92; after Mexican independence 1821 became center of trade with U.S.; W terminus of Santa Fe Trail (*q.v.*); occupied by U.S. forces under Gen. Stephen W. Kearny 1846; made territorial capital 1851.
4 Province of N cen. Argentina. See table at ARGENTINA.
5 City, its ✱, on E bank of Salado river 90 m. N of Rosario; pop. (1960c) 208,900; ships grain, flax, and cotton; National Univ. of the Littoral (1889), Catholic Univ. (1960); founded 1573; here Argentine constitution adopted by convention 1853; port opened to oceangoing vessels 1911.
6 *also* **Santa Fe de Bo·go·tá** \-də-ˌbō-gə-ˈtȯ, -ˈtä\. City, Colombia. See BOGOTÁ 2.
7 Village, Nueva Vizcaya prov., Luzon, Phil., N of Balete Pass and ab. 25 m. SSW of Bayombong; in World War II scene of severe fighting in U.S. conquest of Luzon; taken May 27, 1945; opened route to Cagayan valley.

Santa Fe Bal·dy \-ˈbȯl-dē\ *or formerly* **Baldy Peak.** Mountain, Santa Fe co., New Mexico; 12,623 ft.

Santa Fe Peak. Mountain, Summit and Clear Creek cos., cen. Colorado; 13,146 ft.

Santa Fe Springs. City, Los Angeles co., SW California, N of Long Beach; pop. (1970c) 14,750.

Santa Fe Trail. Former commercial route to the West, starting in W Missouri (first at Franklin, now nonexistent, then at Independence, and later at Westport, now Kansas City); ab. 800 m. long; used esp. 1821–80; proceeded along the prairie divide bet. the tributaries of the Kansas and Arkansas rivers to the great bend of the Arkansas, followed the Arkansas almost to the mountains, then turned south to Santa Fe, here giving a choice of three routes: the westernmost branch, the Taos Trail, crossed the Sangre de Cristo Range at La Veta Pass, the middle branch went through Raton Pass (*q.v.*), and the shortest route, from present site of Cimarron, Kansas, went SW across Cimarron valley; trail first traced by William Becknell 1821; wagons used on his second trip 1822 and thereafter by many traders until 1880 when completion of railroad to Santa Fe reduced importance of the wagon road.

Sant'·Aga·ta de' Go·ti \sän-ˌtäg-ə-tə-də-ˈgō-tə\. Commune, Benevento prov., Campania, S Italy, 15 m. WSW of Benevento; pop. (1968e) 11,618; episcopal see.

Sant'Agata di Mi·li·tel·lo \-dē-ˌmēl-ə-ˈtel-(ˌ)ō\. Commune, Messina prov., NE Sicily, Italy, on Tyrrhenian Sea 52 m. WSW of Messina; pop. (1968e) 11,723.

Santa Ge·no·ve·va \ˌsänt-ə-ˌhā-nə-ˈvā-və\. Mountain, S Baja California, Mexico; 7894 ft.

Santa Inés \ˌsant-ə-ē-ˈnes\. Chilean island in Tierra del Fuego Archipelago (*q.v.*); separated from Brunswick Penin. on E by Strait of Magellan.

Santa Inés Za·ca·tel·co \-ˌsäk-ə-ˈtel-(ˌ)kō\. Town, Tlaxcala state, cen. Mexico; pop. (1960c) 11,303.

Santa Is·a·bel \ˌsant-ə-ˈiz-ə-ˌbel\. 1 Mountain on island of Fernando Póo, Equatorial Guinea, W Africa; 9865 ft.; highest peak in Equatorial Guinea.
2 Chief town on the island of Fernando Póo, ✱ of Equatorial Guinea; ab. 70 m. WSW of Donala, Cameroon; pop. (1965e) 37,152.
3 Town and municipality, S Puerto Rico; pop. (1970p) 4543 (town), 16,023 (munic.); town is on coast ab. 13 m. E of Ponce.
4 *or* **Isabel** *also Span.* **Ys·a·bel** \ˈiz-ə-ˌbel\. Island in E cen. Solomon Is., W Pacific Ocean, ab. 40 m. E of SE Choiseul I. and separated from it by Manning Strait; ab. 140 m. long; 1460 sq. m.; pop. (1970p) 8548. Part of British Solomon Islands protectorate. Has mountain chain the length of the island; highest peak Mt. Marescot ab. 3900 ft; coconut plantations; chief villages are Kia at N end and

Tunnibuli at S end. Under German control from 1886 to 1899. Rekata Bay on its NW coast was a Japanese base in 1942–43.

Santa Isabel de las La·jas \-də-läs-ˈlä-həs\. Municipality, Las Villas prov., W cen. Cuba, 22 m. W of Santa Clara; pop. (1967e) 17,100.

San·tal Par·ga·nas \ˈsən-ˌtäl-pər-ˈgən-əz, -ˈpər-gə-ˌnäz\. District, E Bihar, NE India; 5480 sq. m.; pop. (1961c) 2,675,-203; ✱ Dumka.

Santa Lu·cía \ˌsant-ə-lü-ˈsē-ə\. **1** River, Uruguay; ab. 125 m. long; flows into Río de la Plata 7 m. NW of Montevideo. **2** City, Canelones dept., S Uruguay, just N of Montevideo; pop. (1963c) 12,630.

Santa Lucia Range \ˌsant-ə-lü-ˌsē-ə-\. Mountain range, Monterey and San Luis Obispo cos., SW California; one of the Coast Ranges.

Santa Lu·zia \ˌsant-ə-lü-ˈzē-ə\. One of the Cape Verde Is.; 18 sq. m.; highest point 1296 ft.

Santa Mar·ga·ri·ta \ˌsant-ə-ˌmär-gə-ˈrēt-ə\. Island in Pacific Ocean off SW coast of Baja California, Mexico, at the entrance to Magdalena Bay.

Santa Mar·ghe·ri·ta Li·gu·re \ˌsant-ə-ˌmar-gə-ˈret-ə-ˈlē-gü-rē\. Commune, Genova prov., Liguria, NW Italy, on Ligurian Sea 16 m. ESE of Genoa; pop. (1968e) 12,691; lacemaking; winter health resort.

Santa Ma·ria \ˌsant-ə-mə-ˈrē-ə\. **1** River, W Arizona; ab. 45 m. long; rises in Yavapai co., flows W to join Big Sandy river and form Williams river.

2 City, Santa Barbara co., SW California, 52 m. NW of Santa Barbara; pop. (1970c) 32,749; dairy products, phonograph records; oil wells; truck farms.

3 Cape, SW cen. coast of Angola, SW Africa, N of Cape Santa Marta.

4 Island, SE Azores, in Ponta Delgada dist.; 42 sq. m.; highest point 1936 ft.; used by Allies in latter part of World War II as military and naval base.

5 City, cen. Rio Grande do Sul state, S Brazil, ab. 150 m. W of Porto Alegre and connected with it by rail; munic. pop. (1968e) 141,160; transportation center; ships livestock, grain, coal, fruit; railroad shops, packing plants, tanneries; univ. (1960).

6 Municipality, Bulacan prov., Luzon, Phil., 10 m. E of Malolos; pop. (1969e) 36,400; ships rice and fruit.

Santa Ma·ría \ˌsant-ə-mə-ˈrē-ə\. **1** Volcanic peak, SW Mendoza prov., W Argentina; 6200 ft.

2 Island in Pacific Ocean off W cen. coast of Chile, at entrance to Gulf of Arauco.

3 *also* **Charles Island** \ˈchär(-ə)lz-\. One of the Galápagos Is. (*q.v.*).

4 Volcano in Sierra Madre range near Quetzaltenango, Guatemala; 12,375 ft.; frequent eruptions bet. 1900 and 1930.

5 *or* **Gaua** \ˈgaú-ə\. One of the Banks Is., N New Hebrides Is., SW Pacific Ocean, ab. 12 m. long by 10 m. wide; has central peak 2300 ft.

Santa Maria, Cape. Cape on island off coast of Faro dist., S Portugal.

Santa María, Cape. Cape projecting from SE coast of Uruguay.

Santa Maria Bay. Bay, NW coast of St. Thomas I., Virgin Is. of the U.S., West Indies.

Santa Maria Ca·pua Ve·te·re \-ˌkäp-wə-ˈvet-ə-ˌrā\. Commune, Caserta prov., Campania, S Italy, 16 m. N of Naples; pop. (1968e) 31,483; 5th cent. cathedral; Roman ruins.

Santa María Cay \-ˈkē, -ˈkā\. Island off NE coast of Las Villas prov., W cen. Cuba.

Santa María de Je·sús \-də-hā-ˈsüs\. Town, Sacatepéquez dept., S cen. Guatemala; pop. (1964p) 5771.

Santa María del Buen Ai·re \-ˌdel-bwā-ˈnī(ə)r-ē\. See BUENOS AIRES 3.

Santa María del Río \-del-ˈrē-(ˌ)ō\. Municipality, San Luis Potosí state, Mexico, 30 m. SE of San Luis Potosí; pop. (1970p) 30,072; thermal springs; silver, slate, gypsum mines; bottling plant; diversified agriculture.

Santa María del Ro·sa·rio \-del-rō-ˈzär-ē-ˌō, -ˈsär-\. Municipality, La Habana prov., W Cuba, 8 m. ESE of Havana; pop. (1967e) 36,060.

Santa Maria di Le·u·ca, Cape \-dē-ˈleü-kə\ *or anc.* **Sal·len·ti·num Pro·mon·to·ri·um** \ˌsal-ən-ˈtī-nəm-ˌpräm-ən-ˈtōr-ē-əm, -ˈtȯr-\. Cape, SE coast of Apulia, SE Italy, on SE side of entrance to the Gulf of Taranto. See SALENTINA PENINSULA.

Santa María la Antigua del Darién. See DARIÉN 1.

Santa Mar·ta \ˌsant-ə-ˈmärt-ə\. Seaport, ✱ of Magdalena dept., N Colombia, on coast 50 m. E of Barranquilla; munic. pop. (1968e) 129,223; episcopal see; tourist resort; ships bananas; univ. (1958). Founded 1525, the oldest city in Colombia; became banana-shipping center late 19th cent.; connected with Bogotá by railroad 1961.

Santa Marta, Cape. Cape on SW cen. coast of Angola, SW Africa.

Santa Marta, Sierra Nevada de. See SIERRA NEVADA DE SANTA MARTA.

Santa Marta Gran·de, Cape \-ˈgrand-ē\. Cape on E coast of Santa Catarina state, S Brazil.

Santa Maura. See LEUKAS.

Santa Mon·i·ca \sant-ə-ˈmän-i-kə\. Residential city, Los Angeles co., SW California, on Santa Monica Bay 15 m. W of center of Los Angeles; pop. (1970c) 88,289; seaside resort; tools and dies, cosmetics; aircraft factories; Santa Monica City Coll. (1929); settled 1875 as terminus of projected railroad; incorporated 1885.

San·ta·na do Li·vra·men·to \san-ˈtan-ə-dü-ˌlē-vrə-ˈment-(ˌ)ō\ *or formerly* **Livramento.** City, Rio Grande do Sul state, S Brazil, on Uruguay border opp. Rivera; munic. pop. (1968e) 65,522; in livestock and fruit-growing region.

Sant'·Ana·sta·sia \san-ˌtan-ə-ˈstäz-ē-ə\. Commune, Napoli prov., Campania, S Italy, near Mt. Vesuvius 7 m. E of Naples; pop. (1968e) 19,511.

San·tan·der \ˌsän-ˌtän-ˈde(ə)r, ˌsan-ˌtan-\. **1** Department of N cen. Colombia. See table at COLOMBIA.

2 Province of N Spain. See table at SPAIN.

3 Industrial and commercial seaport, ✱ of Santander prov., N Spain, on Bay of Biscay 212 m. N of Madrid; pop. (1970p) 149,704; major seaport and summer resort; produces paper, glass, soap, textiles, chemicals; shipyards; fish processing; univ. (1890); caves of Altamira and Castillo nearby. Sacked by French under Soult 1808; in 1941 center of town destroyed by fire.

Sant'·An·ge·lo Lo·di·gia·no \san-ˈtan-jə-lō-ˌlōd-i-ˈjän-(ˌ)ō\. Commune, Milano prov., Lombardy, N Italy, 20 m. SE of Milan; pop. (1968e) 11,068.

San·ta·no·ni Peak \ˌsant-ə-ˌnō-nē-\. Mountain in the Adirondack Mts., Essex co., NE New York; 4621 ft.

Sant'·An·ti·mo \san-ˈtän-ti-ˌmō\. Commune, Napoli prov., Campania, S Italy, 6 m. N of Naples; pop. (1968e) 21,721.

Sant'·An·ti·o·co \ˌsan-tän-ˈtē-ə-ˌkō\. **1** Island in Mediterranean Sea off SW coast of the island of Sardinia, Italy; 41 sq. m.; attached to Cagliari prov., Italy; connected with Sardinia by a causeway.

2 *or anc.* **Sul·ci** \ˈsəl-ˌsī\. Town on the island; pop. (1968e) 11,346; founded by Carthaginians; antiquities include remains of ancient walls, tombs both Punic and Roman, and catacombs.

Santa Pau·la \ˌsant-ə-ˈpȯ-lə\. City, Ventura co., SW California, 33 m. E of Santa Barbara; pop. (1970c) 18,001; plastics; packs fruit and nuts; oil wells; citrus fruit.

Sant'·Ar·can·ge·lo di Ro·ma·gna \ˌsan-tär-ˈkän-jə-ˌlō-dē-rō-ˈmän-yə\. Commune, Forlì prov., Emilia-Romagna, N Italy, 23 m. ESE of Forlì; pop. (1968e) 14,333.

San·ta·rém \ˌsant-ə-ˈrem\. 1 City, W Pará state, N Brazil, on right bank of Amazon river at its juncture with the Tapajós; munic. pop. (1968e) 111,706; important river port, shipping rosewood oil, lumber, and rubber; center of an agricultural area; founded 1661, made city 1848.
2 District of W cen. Portugal. See table at PORTUGAL.
3 Commune, ✱ of Santarém dist., W cen. Portugal, on right bank of Tagus river 43 m. NE of Lisbon; pop. (1970p) 57,292; ships olive oil, fruit, wine; tourism; 17th cent. seminary, 13th cent. church; reconquered from Moors 1147.

San·ta·ren Channel \ˌsant-ə-ˈren-\ *also* **San·ta·rem Channel** \-ˈrem-\. Channel, W Bahama Is., bet. Great Bahama Bank on E and Cay Sal Bank on W, and N of cen. part of Cuba.

Santa Ri·ta \ˌsant-ə-ˈrēt-ə\. 1 Village, Grant co., SW New Mexico, ab. 12 m. NNE of Silver City; pop. (1970c) 300.
2 City, Paraíba state, E Brazil; munic. pop. (1968e) 48,052; a SW suburb of João Pessóa.

Santa Ro·sa \ˌsant-ə-ˈrō-zə\. 1 County in Florida. See table at FLORIDA.
2 City, ⊗ of Sonoma co., W California, 50 m. NNW of San Francisco; pop. (1970c) 50,006; canned fruit, footwear, chemicals; fruit and dairy farms; Santa Rosa Junior Coll. (1918); home and experimental gardens of Luther Burbank; nearby are geysers, petrified forest, and Armstrong Redwoods state park; settled 1868.
3 Town, ⊗ of Guadalupe co., E cen. New Mexico on Pecos river ab. 38 m. NE of Vaughn; pop. (1970c) 1813.
4 Town, ✱ of La Pampa prov., S cen. Argentina, ab. 180 m. NW of Bahia Blanca; pop. (1960c) 25,273; univ. (1958).
5 Town, El Oro prov., SW Ecuador, near SE shore of Gulf of Guayaquil; pop. (1962c) 8935.
6 Mining town, E El Salvador, NE of San Miguel; gold and silver mines.
7 Department of S Guatemala. See table at GUATEMALA.
8 *or in full* **Santa Rosa de Co·pán** \-ˌdā-kō-ˈpän\. Town, ✱ of Copán dept., W Honduras; pop. (1961c) 7946; a center of mining and cattle-raising area; 35 m. to the W is ruined city of Copán, southernmost point of the Old Empire of the Mayas, now largely buried under tropical vegetation and alluvial deposits; consists of courtyards, ball courts, stone columns, etc.
9 Town, Misiones dept., S Paraguay.
10 Municipality on W shore of Laguna de Bay, Laguna prov., Luzon, Phil.; pop. (1969e) 82,960.

Santa Rosa de Ca·bal \-dā-kə-ˈbäl\. Town, Risaralda dept., W cen. Colombia, on E slope of Cordillera Occidental 30 m. SW of Manizales; munic. pop. (1968e) 82,960.

Santa Rosa Island. 1 Island at NW end of Santa Barbara group in Pacific Ocean; part of Santa Barbara co., SW California; separated from mainland by Santa Barbara Channel.
2 Narrow island in Gulf of Mexico, lying along S coast of Santa Rosa and Okaloosa cos., NW Florida; belongs to Escambia co.

Santa Rosa Mountains. Small range, Humboldt co., N Nevada; highest peak 9731 ft.

Santa Tecla. See NUEVA SAN SALVADOR.

San·tee \san-ˈtē, ˈsan-ˌ\. River, SE cen. South Carolina; 143 m. long; formed by confluence of Congaree and Wateree rivers, flows SE into Atlantic Ocean.

Santee Dam. Dam across Santee river, bet. Clarendon and Berkeley cos., SE cen. South Carolina; 60 ft. high; completed 1941; provides power from water impounded in **Lake Mar·i·on** \-ˈmer-ē-ən, -ˈmar-\ (*or* **Santee Reservoir**), a broad lake 40 m. long extending back to junction of Congaree and Wateree rivers.

San·teet·lah, Lake \-san-ˈtēt-lə\. Lake, Graham co., W North Carolina, in resort area of Great Smoky Mts. SW of the national park; ab. 5 sq. m.

Sant·el·pi·dio a Ma·re \ˌsän-tāl-ˈpēd-yō-ä-ˈmär-ē\. Commune, Ascoli Piceno prov., Marches, cen. Italy, near Adriatic coast 22 m. NNE of Ascoli Piceno; pop. (1968e) 13,174; earthquake 1915.

Sant·e·ra·mo in Col·le \san-ˈter-ə-ˌmō-in-ˈkò-(ˌ)lā\. Commune, Bari prov., Apulia, SE Italy, 23 m. S by W of Bari; pop. (1968e) 20,826.

Sant'·Eu·fe·mia, Gulf of \-ˌsän-ˌteù-ˈfām-yə\ *or anc.* **Gulf of Hip·po·ni·a·tes** \-hi-ˌpō-nē-ˈā-ˌtēz\ *or* **Gulf of Vi·bo** \-ˈvī-(ˌ)bō\. Inlet of Tyrrhenian Sea, W coast of Calabria, S Italy.

Santh. See SANT.

San·ti·a·go \ˌsant-ē-ˈäg-(ˌ)ō, ˌsänt-; *Port.* ˌsa(^{n})n-ˈtyä-gü\. 1 City, W Rio Grande do Sul state, S Brazil, 70 m. NW of Santa Maria; munic. pop. (1968e) 40,291.
2 One of the Cape Verde Is. See SÃO TIAGO.
3 Province of cen. Chile. See table at CHILE.
4 *or* **San·tia·go de Chi·le** \-də-ˈchil-ē\. City, ✱ of Chile, also ✱ of Santiago prov., in cen. Chile, ab. 70 m. ESE of Valparaíso on the Mapocho river; met. area pop. (1970p) 2,661,920; on a plain at an altitude of 1706 ft. within view of the Andes to the E; economic and cultural center of Chile, archiepiscopal see, and the principal industrial city, producing textiles, footwear, foodstuffs, and beverages; numerous public buildings, including cathedral (destroyed by fire 1769 and rebuilt), national legislature, presidential palace, museums, libraries, and an extensive system of parks; Univ. of Chile (1843), Catholic Univ. (1888), Technical Univ. (1947), and military academy.
History: Founded by Pedro de Valdivia 1541; made city 1552 and episcopal see 1651; has suffered frequently from earthquakes, floods, and civil disorders; occupied by forces under San Martín 1817.
5 Seaport, Cuba. See SANTIAGO DE CUBA 2.
6 Province, N cen. Dominican Republic. See table at DOMINICAN REPUBLIC.
7 *or* **Santiago de los Ca·ba·lle·ros** \-ˌdā-lō-ˌskäb-ə-ˈle(ə)r-(ˌ)ōz, -ə(l)-ˈye(ə)r-\. Commune, ✱ of Santiago prov., N cen. Dominican Republic, on banks of the Río Yaque; pop. (1970p) 244,794; produces pharmaceuticals, tobacco products, coffee; univ. (1962); founded 1500; rebuilt after destruction by earthquake 1564.
8 River, SE Ecuador and NW Peru; ab. 130 m. long; formed by confluence of Paute and Zamora rivers in SE Ecuador, flows E across border of Peru, and S into Marañón river.
9 One of the Galápagos Islands. See SAN SALVADOR 6.
10 *also* **Río Gran·de de Santiago** \ˌrē-ō-ˈgrän-dē-dā-\. River, SW Mexico; length below Lake Chapala 340 m.; rises ab. 18 m. W of the city of Mexico, flows through Lake Chapala W into the Pacific Ocean; known as **Ler·ma** \ˈle(ə)r-mə\ river above Lake Chapala; length including Lerma river ab. 600 m. See JUANACATLÁN.
11 Town, ✱ of Veraguas prov., SW cen. Panama; pop. (1970p) 14,391.
12 Town, Misiones dept., S Paraguay; pop. (1970e) 6209.
13 Island marking NW corner of Lingayen Gulf, Pangasinan prov., Luzon, Phil., opp. Bolinao municipality; 8 sq. m.
14 Municipality, Isabela prov., Luzon, Phil., junction point on main highway N from cen. Phil. to Cagayan valley; pop. (1969e) 54,100. In World War II taken by U.S. troops June 15, 1945.
15 *or* **Santiago de Com·pos·te·la** \-də-ˌkäm-pə-ˈstel-ə\. Commune, La Coruña prov., NW Spain, 32 m. SW of La Coruña; pop. (1970p) 70,893; brandy, linen, paper, soap, silverwork, engraved wood; 12th cent. Romanesque cathedral said to be built on site of grave of the apostle St. James and to contain his remains; 16th cent. pilgrim hospice; univ. (founded 1495, received univ. status 1566). Alleged tomb of St. James discovered 9th cent. A.D.; since 11th cent. one of the principal places of pilgrimage in Europe.

Santiago, Cape. Point, SW coast of Batangas prov., Luzon, Phil., in Verde Island Passage on SW side of entrance to Balayan Bay.

Santiago, Mount *or Span.* **Ce·rro Santiago** \ˌser-(ˌ)ō-\. Mountain, W Panama; 9269 ft.; highest in Serranía de Tabasará.

Santiago Ati·tlán \-ä-tē-'tlän\ *or formerly* **Atitlán.** Town, Sololá dept., S Guatemala, on S shore of Lake Atitlán; munic. pop. (1964p) 12,833.

Santiago Bay. See SANTIAGO DE CUBA BAY.

Santiago de Chile. See SANTIAGO 4.

Santiago de Compostela. See SANTIAGO 15.

Santiago de Cu·ba \ˌsant-ē-ˌäg(ˌ)ōd-ə-'kyü-bə\. 1 Former name of Oriente prov., Cuba. See ORIENTE.

2 *abbr.* **Santiago.** Seaport, ✱ of Oriente prov., on S coast of Cuba; munic. pop. (1967e) 264,200; second largest city in Cuba; on a landlocked bay 6 m. long by 3 m. wide, connected with the Caribbean by a narrow channel passing beneath Morro Castle (alt. 200 ft.); ships iron, manganese and copper ore, sugar, rum, tobacco; textile mills, distilleries, oil refinery; univ. (1947).

History: Founded 1514 and moved to present site 1522; capital of Cuba until 1589; point of departure for the expedition of Cortés to Mexico 1518; in colonial period frequently attacked by pirates and damaged by earthquakes. In the Spanish-American War center of military activity (see EL CANEY and SAN JUAN HILL) and scene of destruction of Spanish fleet under Cervera July 3, 1898, final major event of the war; on July 26, 1953, scene of the attack of band of revolutionaries under Fidel Castro on Moncada army barracks which gave name to Castro's revolutionary movement during period 1956–59.

Santiago de Cuba Bay *or formerly* **Santiago Bay.** Bay, S coast of Oriente prov., E Cuba.

Santiago de Guayaquil. See GUAYAQUIL.

Santiago de las Ve·gas \-dā-läs-'vā-gəs\. Town and municipality, La Habana prov., W Cuba, 10 m. S of Havana; munic. pop. (1967e) 62,890.

Santiago del Es·te·ro \-ˌdel-ə-'ste(ə)r-(ˌ)ō\. 1 Province of N Argentina. See table at ARGENTINA.

2 City, its ✱, on the Dulce river 88 m. SE of San Miguel de Tucumán; pop. (1960c) 80,395; in a semi-arid region producing grain, cotton, and flax; founded 1553 and refounded on present site 1556; oldest continuous settlement in Argentina.

Santiago de los Caballeros. See SANTIAGO 7.

Santiago de Ma·ría \-ˌdā-mə-'rē-ə\. Town, Usulután dept., SE El Salvador; pop. (1961c) 7134.

Santiago Ix·cuin·tla \-ē-'skwēnt-lä\. Town, Nayarit state, W Mexico, on the Santiago river ab. 20 m. from its mouth; munic. pop. (1970p) 84,167; founded 1531.

Santiago Mountains. Range, W cen. Brewster co., W Texas, extending S to the Rio Grande river; across the river in Mexico the range is called Del Carmen Mts.

Santiago Pa·pa·squi·a·ro \-ˌpäp-ə-'skyär-(ˌ)ō\. Municipality, Durango state, Mexico, 95 m. NW of Durango; pop. (1970p) 35,828; important timber producer.

Santiago Peak. Mountain, W cen. Brewster co., W Texas; 6521 ft.

Santiago Ro·drí·guez \-rȯ-'drē-gəz, -gəs\. 1 Department, NW Dominican Republic. See table at DOMINICAN REPUBLIC.

2 Town, its ✱; pop. (1970p) 9637.

Santiago Tux·tla \-'tüst-lä\. Town, Veracruz state, E Mexico; munic. pop. (1970p) 33,471.

San·ti·am \ˌsan-tē-'am\. River, NW Oregon; length with longest branch ab. 75 m.; formed by confluence of branches (North Santiam and South Santiam) on SW boundary of Marion co., flows W into Willamette river.

San·ti·pur \'sänt-i-ˌpu̇(ə)r\. Town, West Bengal, NE India, on left bank of Hooghly river 45 m. N of Calcutta; pop. (1961c) 51,190.

Santi Quaranta. See SARANDË 2.

Sän·tis *or* **Sen·tis** \'zent-əs\. Peak, Appenzell canton, NE Switzerland; 8205 ft.; highest point in the canton.

Santo. See SAINT.

San·to \'sänt-ō\ *or formerly* **Lu·gan·ville** \lü-'gan-ˌvil\. Town, SE coast of Espíritu Santo I., New Hebrides Is., SW Pacific Ocean.

Santo, Mount \-'sant-(ˌ)ō\. Mountain, W coast of Espíritu Santo I., New Hebrides Is., SW Pacific; 5420 ft.

Santo Agos·ti·nho, Cape \-'sa(^{n})n-(ˌ)tü-ˌag-ə-'stē-(ˌ)nyü\. Cape extending into Atlantic Ocean on E coast of Pernambuco state, E Brazil, S of Recife.

Santo Ama·ro \ˌsa(^{n})n-(ˌ)tü-ə-'mär-(ˌ)ü\. City, E Bahia state, E Brazil, ab. 30 m. NW of Salvador; munic. pop. (1968e) 53,855.

Santo An·dré \ˌsa(^{n})n-(ˌ)tü-an-'drā\. City, São Paulo state, SE Brazil; munic. pop. (1968e) 289,442.

Santo An·ge·lo \ˌsa(^{n})n-(ˌ)tü-'a^n-zhə-ˌlü\. Municipality, Rio Grande do Sul, S Brazil, 220 m. NW of Pôrto Alegre; pop. (1968e) 74,825.

Santo An·tão \ˌsa(^{n})n-(ˌ)tü-an-'tau̇^{n}\. Island, ✱ Ribeira Grande, in extreme NW of the Cape Verde Is.; 30 sq. m.; pop. (1960c) 34,598; highest point 6493 ft.; mineral springs; produces coffee, sugar, and fruit.

Santo An·tô·nio \ˌsa(^{n})n-(ˌ)tü-an-'tōn-ˌyü\. Municipality, Rio Grande do Sul state, S Brazil, 40 m. NE of Pôrto Alegre; pop. (1968e) 64,075.

Santo Do·min·go \ˌsant-əd-ə-'min-(ˌ)gō\. 1 Municipality, Las Villas prov., W cen. Cuba, 20 m. NW of Santa Clara; pop. (1967e) 44,640; railroad junction and shipping point in sugar-raising district.

2 Former name of Dominican Republic. See DOMINICAN REPUBLIC.

3 *or formerly* **Ciu·dad Tru·ji·llo** \ˌsē-ü-ˌthä-trü-'hē-(ˌ)(y)ō, -ˌdäd-\. City, ✱ of the Dominican Republic; pop. (1970p) 671,402; constitutes with surrounding region the National District (533 sq. m.); commercial and cultural center of the republic and its principal seaport; exports sugar; steel foundry; tourism; two universities; cathedral (early 16th cent.) containing reputed tomb of Christopher Columbus.

History: Founded 1496 by Bartolomé Columbus; the oldest continuous European settlement in the Americas; repelled British attack 1655; largely destroyed by hurricane 1930; from 1936 to 1961 named Ciudad Trujillo after Pres. Rafael Leonidas Trujillo Molina; renamed after assassination of Trujillo 1961; scene of fighting during civil war and U.S. intervention 1965.

4 Early name of the island of Hispaniola. See HISPANIOLA.

Santo Domingo, Point. Cape on SW coast of Pinar del Río prov., W Cuba, on N side of Cortés Bay.

Santo Domingo de Basco. See BASCO.

Santo Domingo Tehuantepec. See TEHUANTEPEC.

San Tomé de Guayana. See SANTO TOMÉ DE GUAYANA.

Santorin. See THÍRA.

San·tos \'sant-əs\. Seaport, SE São Paulo state, SE Brazil, 45 m. SSE of São Paulo, of which it is the port, and ab. 200 m. WSW of Rio de Janeiro; munic. pop. (1968e) 313,771; on an island in a tidal inlet (sometimes called Santos river); one of the principal ports of Brazil and the largest coffee-exporting port in the world, with extensive modern dock and warehouse facilities; also exports bananas, beef, oranges, hides. Its suburb, Guarujá (munic. pop. 48,160), is one of the principal seaside resorts of Brazil; settled 1543; sacked by English privateer Thomas Cavendish 1591.

Santos, Los. See LOS SANTOS.

Santos Du·mont \ˌsant-əs-dü-'mänt, -'mo(^{n})nt\. City, Minas Gerais state, E Brazil; munic. pop. (1968e) 39,415.

Santo Sti·no di Li·ven·za \ˌsant-ō-'stē-nō-dē-lē-'vent-sə\. Commune, Venezia prov., Veneto, NE Italy, 22 m. NE of Venice; pop. (1968e) 10,319.

Santo To·mas \ˌsant-ō-tō-'mäs\. Municipality, Batangas prov., Luzon, Phil., NE of Lake Taal; pop. (1969e) 31,000.

Santo Tomas, Mount. Mountain, Benguet prov., Luzon, Phil., S of Baguio; 7406 ft.

Santo To·mé de Gua·ya·na \ˌsant-ō-tə-ˈmād-ə-gwə-ˈyän-ə\ *or* **San Tomé de Guayana** \ˌsan-tō-ˈmād-\ *or* **Ciu·dad Guayana** \ˌsē-ü-ˌthä-, -ˌdäd-\. City, NE Bolívar state, E Venezuela, at confluence of Orinoco and Caroní rivers; pop. (1970e) 140,319; a planned city, founded 1961.

San–tu–ao *or* **San·tu·ao** \ˈsän-ˈdü-ˈaù\. Seaport, N coast of Fukien prov., SE China, on San-tu I., ab. 48 m. NE of Foochow (70 m. by sea); opened to foreign trade 1899; formerly had large tea trade.

San Va·len·tín \ˌsan-ˌval-ən-ˈtēn\. Peak, S Chile, W of Lake Buenos Aires; 13,314 ft.

San Va·len·ti·no in Abruz·zo Ci·te·rio·re \san-ˌval-ən-ˈtēn-ō-in-ə-ˈbrüt-sō-chē-ˌtä-rē-ˈōr-ē\. Commune, Pescara prov., Abruzzi, cen. Italy, 20 m. SW of Pescara; pop. (1968e) 2264.

San Vi·cen·te \ˌsan-və-ˈsent-ē\. 1 Peak, El Salvador; 7426 ft.
2 Department of cen. El Salvador. See table at EL SALVADOR.
3 City, its ✱; pop. (1968e) 19,314; industrial and commercial center; trades in tobacco, indigo, coffee, sugarcane; damaged by earthquake 1937.

San Vicente de Al·cán·ta·ra \-dā-äl-ˈkän-tə-rə\. Commune, Badajoz prov., SW Spain, 35 m. NNW of Badajoz; pop. (1970p) 7940.

San Vi·to \san-ˈvē-(ˌ)tō\. Cape on NW coast of Sicily, Italy.

San Vito al Ta·glia·men·to \-äl-ˌtäl-yə-ˈmen-tō\. Commune, Pordenone prov., Friuli-Venezia Giulia, NE Italy, 22 m. WSW of Udine; pop. (1968e) 11,124.

San Vito dei Nor·man·ni \-ˌdā-nòr-ˈmän-ē\. Commune, Brindisi prov., Apulia, SE Italy, 13 m. WNW of Brindisi; pop. (1968e) 20,151.

San·ya·ti \sän-ˈyät-ē\. River, N cen. Rhodesia; ab. 260 m. long; flows NW into Zambezi river.

São. See SAINT.

São Ber·nar·do do Cam·po \saùⁿ(m)-ber-ˈnär-dü-dù-ˈkäm-(ˌ)pü\. Municipality, São Paulo state, SE Brazil, 13 m. SE of São Paulo; pop. (1968e) 97,301.

São Bor·ja \saùⁿ(m)-ˈbōr-zhə\. City, W Rio Grande do Sul state, S Brazil, on W bank of Uruguay river on Argentina border; munic. pop. (1968e) 46,544.

São Brás de Al·por·tel \saùⁿ(m)-ˈbrazh-dē-ˌäl-pòr-ˈtel\. Commune, Faro dist., S Portugal, 10 m. N of Faro; pop. (1970p) 7632.

São Ca·e·ta·no do Sul \ˌsaùⁿ(ŋ)-kī-ˈtä-nü-dù-ˈsül\. Municipality, São Paulo state, SE Brazil, 7 m. SE of São Paulo; pop. (1968e) 135,095.

São Car·los \saùⁿ(ŋ)-ˈkär-ləs\. City, E cen. São Paulo state, SE Brazil, on railroad 130 m. NW of São Paulo; pop. (1968e) 73,256.

São Fi·de·lis \saùⁿ(m)-fē-ˈde-lēs\. Municipality, Rio de Janeiro state, SE Brazil; pop. (1968e) 51,530.

São Fran·cis·co \ˌsaùⁿ(m)-frən-ˈsis-(ˌ)kō\ *also* **San Francisco.** 1 Island off NE coast of Santa Catarina state, Brazil; 20 m. long.
2 River, E Brazil; 1988 m. long; rises in S cen. Minas Gerais state, flows N, NE, and E into Atlantic Ocean S of Maceió.
3 Municipality, Minas Gerais state, E Brazil, 280 m. NNW of Belo Horizonte; pop. (1968e) 52,570.

São Francisco do Sul \-dù-ˈsül\ *or formerly* **São Francisco.** Seaport town, Santa Catarina state, S Brazil, on São Francisco I. 90 m. N of Florianópolis; munic. pop. (1968e) 22,489.

São Ga·bri·el \saùⁿ(ŋ)-ˌgab-rē-ˈel\. City, Rio Grande do Sul state, S Brazil, 60 m. SW of Santa Maria; munic. pop. (1968e) 54,202.

São Gon·ça·lo \ˌsaùⁿ(ŋ)-gōⁿ-ˈsal-(ˌ)ü\. City, Rio de Janeiro state, SE Brazil, on E side of Guanabara Bay opp. Rio de Janeiro; munic. pop. (1968e) 329,764.

São João \saùⁿ-ˈzhwaùⁿ\. Island off N coast of Maranhão state, NE Brazil, at entrance to Turiaçu Bay.

São João da Bar·ra \-də-ˈbä-rə\. Municipality, Rio de Janeiro state, SE Brazil, 160 m. NNE of Rio de Janeiro; pop. (1968e) 72,984.

São João da Boa Vis·ta \-də-ˌbō-ə-ˈvēsh-tə\. City, E São Paulo state, SE Brazil, 110 m. N of São Paulo; munic. pop. (1968e) 46,697.

São João del Rei \-del-ˈrā\. City, S Minas Gerais state, E Brazil, 82 m. S of Belo Horizonte; munic. pop. (1968e) 54,736.

São João de Me·ri·ti \-dē-mə-rē-ˈtē\. Municipality, Rio de Janeiro state, SE Brazil; pop. (1968e) 255,201.

São Jor·ge \saùⁿ-ˈzhòr-zhə\ *or Eng.* **Saint George** \sānt-ˈjò(ə)rj\. Island, cen. Azores, W of Terceira, in the district of Angra do Heroísmo; 85 sq. m.

São Jo·sé Bay \ˌsaùⁿ-zhù-ˌzā-\. Bay, in Maranhão state, on NE coast of Brazil, SE of Maranhão I.

São José do Rio Par·do \-dù-ˌrē-ü-ˈpär-(ˌ)dü\. City, E São Paulo state, SE Brazil, 135 m. N of São Paulo; munic. pop. (1968e) 37,051.

São José do Rio Prêto \-dù-ˌrē-ü-ˈpre-(ˌ)tü\. Municipality, São Paulo state, SE Brazil; pop. (1968e) 99,224.

São José dos Cam·pos \-düsh-ˈkam-pəs\. City, São Paulo state, SE Brazil, ab. 50 m. NNE of São Paulo; munic. pop. (1968e) 91,542; center of Brazilian aircraft industry, with aeronautical research institute and production facilities.

São Le·o·pol·do \saùⁿ-ˌlā-ə-ˈpōl-(ˌ)dü\. City, Rio Grande do Sul state, S Brazil; munic. pop. (1968e) 53,398; railroad center; N suburb of Pôrto Alegre.

São Lou·ren·ço \ˌsaùⁿ-lə-ˈrān-(ˌ)sü\. 1 River, Mato Grosso state, SW Brazil; ab. 300 m. long; flows SW through large marsh area (Pantanal de São Lourenço) into Paraguay river near Bolivian border; the Cuiabá is a tributary on the N.
2 Health resort, S Minas Gerais state, E Brazil, ab. equidistant from Rio de Janeiro and São Paulo; munic. pop. (1968e) 18,223; altitude ab. 2800 ft. on N slopes of Serra da Mantiqueira; mineral waters and baths.

São Luís \ˌsaùⁿ-lù-ˈēs\. 1 *or* **São Luis do Ma·ra·nhão** \-dù-ˌmar-ə-ˈnyaùⁿ\. Island, Brazil. See MARANHÃO 1.
2 Seaport city, ✱ of Maranhão state, NE Brazil, on the island of Maranhão; munic. pop. (1970p) 267,321; exports agricultural products, lumber, hides and skins, balsam; produces sugar, chocolate, brandy, canned fruit, and margarine; 17th cent. cathedral. Founded by French 1612; taken by Portuguese 1615; held by Dutch 1641–44; made bishopric 1679.

São Lu·ís Gon·za·ga \ˌsaùⁿ-lù-ˈēz-gən-ˈzäg-ə\. City, NW Rio Grande do Sul state, S Brazil, 95 m. NNW of Santa Maria; pop. (1968e) 40,611.

São Manuel. See TELES PIRES.

São Mar·cos Bay \saùⁿ-ˌmär-kəs-\. Inlet of Atlantic Ocean on NE coast of Brazil, in Maranhão state, W of Maranhão I.

São Mi·guel \ˌsaùⁿ-mi-ˈgel\ *or Eng.* **Saint Mi·chael** \sānt-ˈmī-kəl\. Island, E Azores, in the district of Ponta Delgada; 288 sq. m.; chief town Ponta Delgada; largest island of the group.

Sa·o·na Island \sä-ˌō-nə-\. Small island of the West Indies, in the N cen. Caribbean Sea off SE coast of the Dominican Republic; 13 m. long.

Saône \ˈsōn\ *or anc.* **Arar** \ˈā-ˌrär\. River, E France; 298 m. long; rises in Vosges dept., NE France, flows SSW into Rhone river at Lyons; receives the Doubs from the E; navigable for 233 m.

Saône, Haute– \ōt-ˈsōn\. Department of E France. See table at FRANCE.

Saône–et–Loire \ˈsōn-ā-lə-ˈwär\. Department of E cen. France. See table at FRANCE.

São Ni·co·lau \ˌsaùⁿ-ˌnē-kù-ˈlaù\ *or Eng.* **Saint Nich·o·las** \sānt-ˈnik-(ə-)ləs\. One of the Cape Verde Is.; 30 m. long; 132 sq. m.; pop. (1960c) 13,894; highest point 4278 ft. One of first of the group to be colonized; at height of its prosperity in middle of 18th cent.

São Pau·lo \saùⁿ(m)-ˈpaù-(ˌ)lü, -(ˌ)lō\. 1 State, SE Brazil; 95,713 sq. m.; pop. (1970p) 17,716,186; ✱ São Paulo; Brazil's most populous state; important industrial region; major crops incl. coffee, rice, corn, cotton.

2 City, its ✻, on the Tietê river 45 m. NNW of Santos, its port; munic. pop. (1970p) 5,901,533; largest city and principal industrial center of Brazil; transportation center; produces steel, motor vehicles, machine tools, and a wide range of consumer goods including textiles, household appliances, furniture, foodstuffs, pharmaceuticals; oil refineries, chemical plants; has an extensive complex of residential suburbs and a notable system of public parks, a large stadium, art museum, and libraries; important cultural and publishing center; three universities, including Univ. of São Paulo (1934).

History: Founded by Jesuits 1554; base for exploration in 17th cent.; became capital of captaincy 1681 and city 1711; in 1822 scene of declaration of Brazilian independence by Emperor Pedro I (site now marked by Ypiranga Museum); developed rapidly as industrial center after 1880, receiving a substantial influx of European immigrants.

São Paulo de Loanda. See LUANDA 2.

São Pedro do Rio Grande do Sul. See RIO GRANDE 2.

São Ro·que, Cape \-saùⁿ-'rò-kə\ *or* **Ca·bo de São Roque** \ˌkäb-ō-də-\. Cape, E coast of Rio Grande do Norte, NE Brazil, N of Natal.

Saorstat Eireann *or* **Saorstát Éireann.** See EIRE.

São Sal·va·dor \saùⁿ-'sal-və-ˌdò(ə)r, ˌsal-və-'\. **1** *or* **São Salvador do Con·go** \-dü-käŋ-ˌgü, -ˌgō\ *also* **San Salvador** \'san-\. Town, N Angola, SW Africa; munic. pop. (1960c) 12,691; capital of kingdom of Congo 16th to 18th cents.

2 Seaport, E Brazil. See SALVADOR.

São Se·bas·tião \ˌsaùⁿ-ˌsā-bə-'styaùⁿ\. Island in Atlantic Ocean off NE coast of São Paulo state, Brazil; belongs to Brazil.

São Sebastião, Cape. Cape, extending into Mozambique Channel on SE coast of Mozambique, SE Africa, N of Inhambane.

São Tia·go \ˌsaùⁿ(n)t-ē-'äg-(ˌ)ü, -(ˌ)ō\ *also* **San·ti·a·go** \ˌsant-ə-'äg-(ˌ)ō\. Largest of the Cape Verde Is.; 383 sq. m.; pop. (1960c) 88,940; chief town Praia, ✻ of the group; highest point 4562 ft.; mountainous, many ravines and streams; grows coffee, oranges, sugarcane.

São To·mé \ˌsaùⁿ(n)t-ə-'mā\. **1** *or* **São Tho·mé** *or Eng.* **Saint Thom·as** \sānt-'täm-əs\. Portuguese island in the Gulf of Guinea, on the equator, W Africa; 330 sq. m.; with Principe I. (*q.v.*), forms the Portuguese overseas province **São Tomé e Prin·ci·pe** \ ˌsaùⁿ(n)t-ə-'mā-ē-'prēⁿ(n)-si-pə\, 372 sq. m.; pop. (1970e) 61,000; exports cacao, coffee, coconuts, copra, palm oil.

2 Part of Madras city, India, originally a Portuguese port. See SAINT THOMÉ.

São Tomé, Cape. Cape extending into Atlantic Ocean on NE coast of Rio de Janeiro state, SE Brazil.

Saou·ra \saù-'rä\. Department of W Algeria. See table at ALGERIA.

São Vi·cen·te \ˌsaùⁿ(n)-vē-'sāⁿ(n)-tə\ *or Eng.* **Saint Vin·cent** \sānt-'vin(t)-sənt\. **1** City, São Paulo state, SE Brazil, on same island with Santos, SSE of São Paulo; munic. pop. (1968e) 82,189. First settlement 1532 on São Paulo coast; not successful at first and burned by Cavendish 1591.

2 One of the Cape Verde Is.; 88 sq. m.; pop. (1960c) 21,361; chief town Mindelo; highest point 2539 ft.; coaling station.

São Vicente, Cabo de. See SAINT VINCENT, CAPE 2.

Sa·pé \ˌsä-'pā\. Municipality, Paraíba state, E Brazil, just W of Joáo Pessoa; pop. (1968e) 53,438.

Sa·pe·le \sə-'pā-lē\. Port in Niger delta, Mid-Western State, Nigeria; pop. (1969e) 70,749; on the Benin river at the junction of its headstreams.

Sap·e·lo Island \ˌsap-ə-(ˌ)lō-\. Island in Atlantic Ocean, off E mainland of McIntosh co., SE Georgia; to the NW is **Sapelo Sound.**

Sa·pe Strait \ˌsäp-(ˌ)ā-\. Channel, bet. E end of Sumbawa I. and Komodo I. (part of Flores group), Lesser Sunda Is., Indonesia; ab. 13 m. wide; connects Flores Sea with Indian Ocean.

Sapoedi. See SAPUDI.

Sap·pa \'sap-ə\. River, NW Kansas and SW Nebraska; ab. 150 m. long; rises in Sherman co., NW Kansas, flows NE into Nebraska and joins Beaver creek 10 m. before emptying into Republican river in Harlan co.

Sap·phire Mountains \ˌsaf-ī(ə)r-\. A range of the Rocky Mts. in W Montana, extending along the boundary bet. Granite and Ravalli cos.; highest peak 8995 ft.

Sap·po·ro \sə-'pōr-(ˌ)ō, -'pòr-\. City, ✻ of Hokkaidō prefecture, Hokkaidō I., Japan, in W part near head of Ishikari Bay; pop. (1970c) 1,010,123; commercial center of Hokkaidō; manufactures flour, dairy products, lumber, beer; printing and publishing; winter sports center; Hokkaidō Univ. (1918). City founded 1871 by Japanese government as center for the development of the island; site of Winter Olympic Games 1972.

Sa·pu·caia \ˌsap-ə-'kā-ə\. Small island in Guanabara Bay, N of the city of Rio de Janeiro, Brazil, and S of Bom Jesús I.

Sa·pu·di *or Du.* **Sa·poe·di** \sə-'püd-ē\. Island, Malay Archipelago, E of Madura I., in East Java prov., Indonesia; area with adjacent small islands, 94 sq. m.

Sa·pul·pa \sə-'pəl-pə\. City, ⊗ of Creek co., E cen. Oklahoma, 13 m. SSW of Tulsa; pop. (1970c) 15,159; pottery, glassware; packing plant, oil wells; grain farms.

Saq·qa·ra *or* **Saq·qā·rah** *also* **Sak·ha·ra** *or* **Sak·ka·ra** \sə-'kär-ə\. Village, Lower Egypt, just SW of ruins of Saqqara; pop. (1966c) 12,700; Step Pyramid, the oldest Egyptian pyramid, built by Zoser, second king of the IIId dynasty; also pyramids of the Vth and VIth dynasties and many mastabas.

Sa·ra \'sä-rə\. Municipality, Iloilo prov., Panay, Phil., 48 m. NE of City of Iloilo; pop. (1969e) 24,300.

Sarabat. See GEDIZ.

Sarābīt al–Khadím. See SERABIT EL KHADIM.

Sa·ra Bu·ri *or* **Sa·ra·bu·ri** \ˌsär-ə-'bùr-ē\. **1** Province, S Thailand; 1144 sq. m.; pop. (1960c) 303,505; ✻ Sara Buri.

2 Town, its ✻, on right bank of the Sak river and on the railroad 20 m. NE of Phra Nakhon Si Ayutthaya and ab. 65 m. NE of Bangkok; pop. (1964e) 26,374.

Sarafand. See ZAREPHATH.

Sar·a·gos·sa \ˌsar-ə-'gäs-ə\ *or Span.* **Za·ra·go·za** \ˌzär-ə-'gō-zə\ *or anc.* **Sal·du·ba** \sal-'d(y)ü-bə\ *or later* **Cae·sar·au·gus·ta** \ˌsē-zə-rò-'gəs-tə, -rə-\. City, ✻ of Zaragoza prov., NE Spain, on Ebro river 170 m. NE of Madrid; pop. (1970p) 479,845; railroad and industrial center; manufactures agricultural machinery, cement, chemicals, textiles, soap, paper, glass, chocolate; two cathedrals, La Seo (12th–16th cent. Gothic) and El Pilar (17th cent.), two 14th cent. Gothic churches, La Lonja (the exchange, 16th cent. Gothic), several palaces; univ. (1474).

History: Celt-Iberian settlement of Salduba taken by Romans late 1st cent. B.C.; important city under Roman rule; made episcopal see 3d cent. A.D.; taken by Moors c. 713; reconquered by Alfonso I of Aragon 1118 and capital of Aragon until 15th cent.; French defeated by English nearby 1710; in 1808–09 underwent two sieges by French, commemorated in "The Maid of Saragossa" in Byron's *Childe Harold.*

Sa·ra·gu·ro \ˌsär-ə-'gù(ə)r-(ˌ)ō\. Town, Loja prov., SW Ecuador, in Andes Mountains 60 m. S of Cuenca; pop. (1962c) 1562.

Sa·rai \sä-'rī\. City, ancient ✻ of the Khanate of the Golden Horde, near modern Leninsk (*q.v.*), Volgograd Oblast, Russian S.F.S.R., U.S.S.R., E of lower Volga. Founded by Batu Khan 1241; for 200 years the Tatar (Kipchak) seat of government to which Russians paid tribute; seized by a vassal of Tamerlane 1382; declined after 1480 when Ivan III threw off Tatar yoke.

Sa·rai·ke·la \sə-ˈrī-kə-lə\. Former Indian state, now part of Orissa state, NE India; 446 sq. m.; ✱ Saraikela.

Sa·ra·je·vo \ˈsär-ə-ye-ˌvȯ, ˈser-\ *or* **Se·ra·je·vo** \ˈser-\. City, ✱ of Bosnia and Herzegovina, W cen. Yugoslavia, ab. 125 m. SW of Belgrade; pop. (1971p) 244,045; in valley of upper Bosna river at alt. 1800 ft.; produces steel, pottery, silk, railroad rolling stock, tobacco products, sugar, beer, embroidery, carpets; univ. (1946); notable 15th cent. mosque.

History: Site of a Roman military station; citadel near present town first mentioned 1415; sacked by Hungarians 1480; burned by Austrians 1697; came under Austrian rule 1878 and became a center of Serbian nationalist activity. In 1914 was scene of assassination of Archduke Francis Ferdinand (June 28), an act which precipitated World War I; joined to Yugoslavia 1918; in World War II occupied by Germans Apr. 1941–Apr. 1945.

Sa·rakhs \sə-ˈraks\. Fortified town, Khorāsān prov., NE Iran; on Hari Rud river at Turkmen S.S.R., U.S.S.R., border 90 m. ENE of Mashhad.

Sa·ra·land \ˈser-ə-ˌland, ˈsar-\. City, Mobile co., SW Alabama, 10 m. N of Mobile; pop. (1970c) 7840.

Sa·ra·mac·ca \ˌsar-ə-ˈmak-ə\. **1** River, cen. and N cen. Surinam; ab. 250 m. long; flows N into Atlantic Ocean.

2 District, Surinam.

Saramati. See ARAKAN YOMA.

Sa·ran \sä-ˈrän(-yə)\. Town, Karaganda Oblast, Kazakh S.S.R., U.S.S.R., ab 15 m. WSW of Karaganda; pop. (1969e) 54,000.

Sa·ra·na \sə-ˈrän-ə\. Valley and pass in mountains of NE Ahu I., W Aleutians, Alaska, leading from **Sarana Bay** on S to Chichagof Harbor to the N; severe fighting May 1942.

Sar·a·nac \ˈsar-ə-ˌnak\. River, NE New York; ab. 100 m. long; outlet of Saranac Lakes in Franklin co., flows NE into Lake Champlain at Plattsburg.

Saranac Lake. Village, Essex and Franklin cos., NE New York, near Lower Saranac Lake 36 m. S of Malone; pop. (1970c) 6086; in Adirondack region at alt. of 1600 ft.; summer and winter sports resort; health resort (orig. estab. for the tubercular in late 19th cent.); North Country Community Coll. (1967).

Saranac Lakes. Three lakes in S Franklin co., NE New York, **Upper Saranac Lake** ab. 8 m. long, **Middle Saranac Lake** ab. 2½ m. wide, and **Lower Saranac Lake** ab. 5 m. long; elevation 1540 ft.

Sa·ran·dë \sə-ˈrän-də\. **1** Province of S Albania. See table at ALBANIA.

2 *formerly* **San·ti Qua·ran·ta** \ˌsän-tē-kwə-ˈrän-tə\ *or* **Por·to Ed·da** \ˌpȯr-tō-ˈed-ə\. Seaport, its ✱, on the Adriatic NE of the island of Corfu; pop. (1967e) 8279; developed as commercial port under Italian occupation.

Sa·ran·dí del Yi \ˌsär-ən-ˌdē-del-ˈyē\. Town, Durazno dept., cen. Uruguay.

Sarandí Gran·de \-ˈgrän-dē\. Town, Florida dept., S cen. Uruguay.

Sa·ran·ga·ni Bay \ˌsär-ən-ˈgän-ē-\. Inlet of Celebes Sea, S Mindanao, in S part of Cotabato del Sur prov., Phil.; 19 m. long by 9 m. wide. Town of Buayan at its head.

Sarangani Islands. Island group, S Davao del Sur prov., Mindanao, Phil., 8 m. off Tinaca Point SW of entrance to Davao Gulf; 36 sq. m.; comprises two islands, Balut and **Sarangani** (smaller and easternmost of the two, ab. 14 sq. m.), and an islet.

Sarangani Strait. Passage bet. Sarangani Is. and S tip of Mindanao, Phil.

Sa·ran·garh \ˈsär-ən-ˌgär\. **1** Former Indian state, now part of Madhya Pradesh state, India; 541 sq. m.

2 Town, its ✱, 60 m. W of Sambalpur; pop. (1961c) 9500.

Sa·ransk \sə-ˈrän(t)sk, -ˈran(t)sk\. Town, ✱ of Mordovian A.S.S.R., Russian S.F.S.R., U.S.S.R., in cen. part, on a branch of the Moscow-Kuibyshev R.R., W of Ulyanovsk; pop. (1970p) 190,000; railroad junction; machinery, rope and cordage, pharmaceuticals, footwear, cables; univ. (1957); founded 1641.

Sa·ra·pi·quí \ˌsär-ə-pi-ˈkē\. River of Costa Rica; flows N into the San Juan river; link in waterway from cen. Costa Rica to the Caribbean Sea.

Sa·ra·pul \sə-ˈräp-əl\. Town on Kama river, SE Udmurt A.S.S.R., Russian S.F.S.R., U.S.S.R., 35 m. SE of Izhevsk; pop. (1969e) 94,000; center of an agricultural area.

Sa·ra·sa·ra \ˌsär-ə-ˈsär-ə\. Peak in Cordillera Occidental, Peru; 17,923 ft.

Sar·a·so·ta \ˌsar-ə-ˈsōt-ə\. **1** County in W cen. Florida. See table at FLORIDA.

2 City, its ⊗, on Gulf of Mexico 15 m. S of mouth of Tampa Bay; pop. (1970c) 40,237; winter resort; truck and livestock farms; New College (1960); John and Mable Ringling Museum of Art; incorporated 1914.

Sarasota Bay. Inlet of Gulf of Mexico on coast of NW Sarasota and SW Manatee cos., W Florida penin.

Sa·ras·wa·ti \ˈsär-əs-ˌwət-ē\ *or* **Sa·ras·va·ti** \-ˌvət-ē\. **1** A sacred river of Punjab (region now divided bet. India and Pakistan); frequently mentioned in the Vedas and identified by Hindus with the goddess Sarasvati. In early times held to be the Indus, later one of its tributaries; its modern equivalent, thought to be the **Sar·su·ti** \ˈsär-sət-ē\, loses itself in the sands of NW India.

2 River, W India; ab. 120 m. long; rises in S Rajasthan and flows SW to Little Rann of Kutch, Gujarat.

Sar·a·to·ga \ˌsar-ə-ˈtō-gə\. **1** County in New York. See table at NEW YORK.

2 City, Santa Clara co., W California, SW of San Jose; pop. (1970c) 27,110; residential; wine.

3 Former village, now Schuylerville (*q.v.*), on W bank of Hudson river, Saratoga co., E New York, ab. 10 m. E of Saratoga Springs; has given its name to two battles fought just to the S, near Stillwater, Sept. 19, 1777 and Oct. 7, 1777, that resulted in surrender of British forces under Gen. Burgoyne at Saratoga Oct. 17, 1777 to Americans under Gen. Gates; marked the turning point of the Revolutionary War in favor of the Americans. Actual fighting of the two battles occurred at Freeman's Farm and Bemis Heights (Gen. Gates's headquarters) ab. 3 m. N of Stillwater; site set apart June 22, 1948 as **Saratoga National Historical Park:** see UNITED STATES, *National Historical Parks.*

Saratoga Lake. Lake, Saratoga co., E New York, SE of Saratoga Springs; ab. 7 m. long by 2 m. wide; drains into Hudson river; summer resort.

Saratoga Passage. Strait bet. Camano I. and Whidbey I. in upper Puget Sound, Washington.

Saratoga Springs. City, Saratoga co., E New York, W of Hudson river in Adirondack foothills 33 m. N of Albany; pop. (1970c) 18,845; important health resort and horse racing center; Skidmore Coll. (1911); medicinal springs used for health purposes since late 18th cent.; in latter part of 19th cent. one of the principal resort communities of North America; incorporated as village 1826, as city 1815.

Sa·ra·tov \sə-ˈrät-əf\. City, ✱ of Saratov Oblast, SE Russian S.F.S.R., U.S.S.R., on W bank of the Volga 220 m. N of Volgograd; pop. (1970p) 758,000; important industrial center, producing agricultural machinery and parts, machine tools, precision instruments, cranes; flour mills, furniture factories, oil refineries, natural gas wells; univ. (1919); founded on site nearby 1590; reestablished on present site 1674; made capital of a province 1750; developed 1870 ff. after construction of railroad from Moscow.

Saratov Oblast \-ˈō-bləst, -ˌblast\. Subdivision of the Russian S.F.S.R., U.S.S.R., on both sides of the lower Volga; 38,687 sq. m.; pop. (1970c) 2,454,000; ✱ Saratov. Occupies E part of great cen. plateau; E of Volga is steppe region; well watered by Volga, which here has elevation of not more than 20 ft., and its tributaries. Almost entirely in steppe zone; fertile soil but suffers from droughts. Agriculture (esp. grains), food processing industries; natural gas, oil; chief towns Saratov, Engels, Balashov, Volsk.

History: Area has evidence (bronze articles in kurgans) that it was inhabited in prehistoric times; followed in ancient European history by Scythians, later by the Mordvinians and various Slavic peoples; came under the Khazars in 8th and 9th cents. and under the Russians in 18th cent.; under Russian S.F.S.R. included in the Lower Volga Area 1928; reorganized as a separate region 1934.

Sa·ra·via \sə-ˈrä-vē-ə\. Municipality, Negros Occidental, Negros, Phil., near coast 15 m. N of City of Bacolod; pop. (1969e) 44,600.

Sa·ra·wak \sə-ˈrä-(ˌ)wä(k), -ˌwak\. 1 A state of Malaysia, NW island of Borneo, SE Asia, bordering on Sabah (with which it constitutes East Malaysia), Brunei, and Indonesian Borneo; 48,342 sq. m.; pop. (1970p) 977,013; ✱ Kuching; coconuts, rice, rubber, oil; coastline of 450 m. extends along South China Sea on W and NW. Has several navigable rivers (Rajang, Baram, Limbang, and Batang Lupar); generally mountainous, esp. along E and S borders.

History: Brunei (*q.v.*) visited in 1839 and 1840 by Sir James Brooke who sought to quell piracy; S part of Brunei (originally ab. 7000 sq. m.) ceded 1841 to Brooke by sultan and became independent state of Sarawak; additional territory received 1861, 1882, 1884; by agreement of 1888 became a British protectorate and for three generations was governed by the Brooke family; occupied by Japanese 1941–45; became British crown colony 1946; joined Malaysia 1963; its inclusion in Malaysia disputed by Indonesia 1963–66.

2 Town, its ✱. See KUCHING.

Sar·bi·no·wo \ˌsär-bə-ˈnō-vō\ *or Ger.* **Zorn·dorf** \ˈtsorn-ˌdȯrf, ˈzȯrn-\. Village, Zielona Góra prov., W Poland; formerly in Prussia; scene of battle Aug. 25, 1758 during the Seven Years' War in which the Prussians under Frederick the Great defeated the Russians under Count William of Fermor.

Sar·celles \sär-ˈsel\. Commune, Val-d'Oise dept., N France, ab. 9 m. N of Paris; pop. (1968c) 51,674.

Sar·da \ˈsärd-ə\. River, N India; ab. 220 m. long; rises in N Uttar Pradesh, flows S (as Kali river) along border of W Nepal, then SE through Uttar Pradesh into Ghaghara river NE of Lucknow.

Sar·din·ia \sär-ˈdin-ē-ə, -ˈdin-yə\ *or Ital.* **Sar·de·gna** \sär-ˈdān-yə\. Island in the Mediterranean Sea, W of S Italian penin.; 9301 sq. m.; pop. (1968e) 1,488,008; ✱ Cagliari; politically, together with some minor islands, constitutes an autonomous region of Italy (see table at ITALY); mountainous, highest point 6017 ft. in E cen. part; chief rivers Tirso in center, Samassi in S, and Flumendosa in SE; separated on N from Corsica, France, by Strait of Bonifacio; more important inlets on its coast are Gulf of Asinara on NW, Oristano on W, and Cagliari on S. Chief towns Cagliari, Sassari, and Carbonia.

History: Settled by Phoenicians and Greeks before it came under control of Carthage during 6th cent. B.C.; taken by Romans 238 B.C.; in Vandal kingdom 5th cent. A.D.; reconquered by Byzantine Empire 533; from 8th cent., frequently raided by Muslims whose threat was eliminated by Pisa 1016; object of rivalry bet. Genoese and Pisans who were driven out by Aragonese 14th–15th cents.; held by Austria 1713–20; ceded to Savoy 1720 in exchange for Sicily, after which ruler of Savoy and Piedmont took title King of Sardinia (see SAVOY); during World War II used as air base by Germans until Italian surrender; Germans evacuated the island Sept. 1943.

Sar·dis \ˈsärd-əs\. 1 Town, a ⊗ of Panola co., NW Mississippi, 40 m. ENE of Clarksdale; pop. (1970c) 2391; lumber; site of a dam and reservoir designed to control flood waters in the Tallahatchie river basin.

2 *or* **Sar·des** \ˈsärd-(ˌ)ēz\. Ancient city in Asia Minor, in a strategic position in the Hermus valley ab. 50 m. E of Smyrna; chief city and capital of ancient kingdom of Lydia, and an important city in Roman and Byzantine times; captured by both Persians and Athenians in 6th and 5th cents. B.C., and by Antiochus the Great after a two-year siege in 213 B.C.; one of the Seven Churches of Asia Minor (*Rev.* i-iii); suffered from attacks of Seljuk Turks who took possession of it early in 14th cent.; surrendered to Ottoman power c. 1390 and destroyed 1402 by Tamerlane. Site has many ruins, esp. of a major Ionic temple; earliest known coins (700 B.C.) found here.

Sa·rek National Park \ˈsär-ˌek-\. National park, N Sweden; 735 sq. m.; one of the largest wilderness regions in W Europe; glaciers; established 1909.

Sa·rek·tjåk·ko \ˌsär-ek-ˈchȯ-(ˌ)kō\. Peak, N Sweden, in Kjølen Mts. near source of Luleålv river; 6854 ft.

Sarema. See SAAREMAA.

Sarepta. See ZAREPHATH.

Sa·re·ra Bay \sə-ˈre-rə-\ *or formerly* **Geel·vink Bay** \ˈkāl-viŋk-\. Bay on N coast of Irian Barat, Indonesia; ab. 250 m. wide at mouth, Cape Perkam to Manokwari, extends ab. 150 m. inland; contains the Schouten Is. and Japen and Numfoor Is.

Sar·gas·so Sea \sär-ˌgas-(ˌ)ō-\. The large tract of comparatively still water in the North Atlantic Ocean— so named from the floating seaweed there; may be considered to lie bet. the parallels 20°–35°N and the meridians 30°–70°W.

Sar·gent \ˈsär-jənt\. County in North Dakota. See table at NORTH DAKOTA.

Sar·go·dha \sər-ˈgōd-ə\. Town, Punjab, Pakistan, 106 m. WNW of Lahore; met. area pop. (1969e) 193,500; railroad junction and industrial center, producing textiles, soap, chemicals, flour, and vegetable oils; grain market; founded 1903.

Sā·rī \sä-ˈrē\. Town, ✱ of Māzanderān prov., N Iran, 17 m. E of Bābol; pop. (1971e) 50,000.

Sa·ria·ya \ˌsär-ˈyä-yə\. Municipality, Quezon prov., Luzon, Phil., 7 m. WNW of Lucena; pop. (1969e) 57,700.

Sa·ri Ba·ir \ˌsär-ē-bä-ˈ(y)i(ə)r\ *or Turk.* **Sa·rı Ba·yır** \-bä-ˈyi(ə)r\. Rugged hills in cen. Gallipoli Penin., Turkey, Europe; scene of unsuccessful attack of Anzac forces on Turkish position Aug. 6–10, 1915.

Sa·ri·gan \ˌsär-i-ˈgän\ *or* **Sa·ri·guan** \-ˈgwän\. Small island, cen. Mariana Is., 100 m. N of Saipan, 16°42′N, 145°47′E; highest point 1801 ft.

Sa·rı·ka·miş *or* **Sa·ri·ka·mish** \ˌsär-i-kə-ˈmish\. Town, SW Kars prov., NE Turkey, ab. 30 m. SW of Kars; pop. (1965c) 16,618; formerly included in Russian Armenia. Scene of battle Dec. 1914 in World War I in which Turks were decisively defeated by Russians.

Sarine. See SAANE.

Sar–i–Pul *or* **Sar·i·pul** \ˌsär-ē-ˈpül\. Town, N Afghanistan, 75 m. SW of Mazār-i-Sharīf; chief town of a former khanate of the same name.

Sarī Qūl. See ZORKUL, LAKE.

Sa·ri·ta \sə-ˈrē-tə\. Village, ⊗ of Kenedy co., S Texas; pop. (1969e) 196.

Sa·ri·wŏn \ˈsä-ˈrē-ˈwən\. Town, ✱ of North Hwanghae prov., North Korea, 36 m. S of P'yŏngyang.

Sar·ju \ˈsär-(ˌ)jü\. River, W Nepal and Uttar Pradesh, N India; ab. 150 m. long; flows NW and S into the Ghāghara river.

Sark \ˈsärk\. 1 *or Fr.* **Sercq** \serk\. One of the Channel Is., in the English Channel; 2 sq. m.; pop. (1961c) 560; comprises **Great Sark** and **Little Sark** connected by an isthmus; included in Guernsey bailiwick; chief landing place Creux.

2 Small stream of Dumfries, Scotland. See ESK 2.

Sar·kad \'shȯr-ˌkȯd\. Commune, Békés co., SE Hungary, 60 m. S of Debrecen, near Romanian border; pop. (1970p) 11,933.

Sar·lat \sär-'lä\ *or* **Sarlat–la–Ca·né·da**\-lə-kə-'nā-də\. Mining and commercial town, Dordogne dept., SW cen. France, ab. 32 m. SE of Périgueux; pop. (1962c) 8737; 11th–12th cent. church, numerous old houses (14th–16th cents.).

Sar·ma·tia \sär-'mā-sh(ē-)ə\. Land of Sarmatians (4th cent. B.C.), a people NE of Black Sea. Later, in time of Roman Empire, the region, without definite boundaries, bet. the Vistula and Volga, corresponding to S Russia in Europe and Poland and bordering on Germania and Dacia; divided by ancient Tanais (*mod.* Don) river; its peoples were probably ancestors of the Slavs.

Sar·mi \'sär-mē\. Village, N coast of Irian Barat, Indonesia, 125 m. W of Djajapura; taken by Allies May 17, 1944.

Sar·mien·to \ˌsär-mē-'en-(ˌ)tō\. 1 Peak, Chile, in SW Tierra del Fuego I.; 7218 ft.
2 Town, Argentina. See GENERAL SARMIENTO.

Sar·mi·zeg·e·tu·sa \'sär-mē-ˌzej-ə-'t(y)ü-sə\. Ancient town, SW cen. Dacia, ESE of modern Lugoj in W Romania; capital of Dacia; occupied by Trajan 102 A.D.

Sar·nath \sär-'nät\. Archaeological site, N India, 3½ m. N of Varanasi, Uttar Pradesh; here was the Deer Park in which Gautama Buddha first taught. Ruins consist of the court of the monastery, a great stupa of Asoka 130 ft. high, and remains of Asoka's memorial pillar.

Sar·nen \'zär-nən\. Commune, ✻ of Obwalden demicanton and of Unterwalden canton, cen. Switzerland, 37 m. E of Bern; pop. (1970c) 6952; health resort; manufactures straw hats.

Sarnen, Lake of *or Ger.* **Sar·ner See** \'zär-nər-ˌzā\. Lake, Unterwalden canton, cen. Switzerland; ab. 4 m. long and 1 m. wide; 3 sq. m.; max. depth 170 ft.

Sarner–Aa. See AA 2.

Sar·nia \'sär-nē-ə\. City, ⊗ of Lambton co., SE Ontario, Canada, on St. Clair river at S end of Lake Huron; pop. (1971p) 56,727; opp. Port Huron, Michigan, and connected with it by railroad tunnel and highway bridge; important lake port; lumber, steel products, sailboats, chemicals, plastics, automobile parts; oil refineries, salt works; truck farms. Settled 1807 by French and 1833 by English.

Sar·no \'sär-(ˌ)nō\. Manufacturing and commercial commune, Salerno prov., Campania, S Italy, 12 m. NW of Salerno; pop. (1968e) 31,357; episcopal see; manufactures textiles and preserves; iron, iodine, and sulfur springs.

Saron, Plain of. See SHARON, PLAIN OF.

Sa·ron·ic Gulf \sə-ˌrän-ik-\ *or* **Gulf of Ae·gi·na** \-ē-'jī-nə\ *or anc.* **Si·nus Sa·ron·i·cus** \ˌsī-nə(s)-sə-'rän-i-kəs\ *or Gk.* **Sa·ro·ni·kós Kól·pos** \sə-ˌrȯn-i-ˌkȯs-'kȯl-pȯs\. Inlet of Aegean Sea on SE coast of Greece, S of Attica dept.

Sa·ron·no \sə-'rȯn-(ˌ)ō\. Manufacturing commune, Varese prov., Lombardy, N Italy, 18 m. SE of Varese; pop. (1968e) 30,890; pilgrimage church (13th–17th cents.).

Sa·ros Gulf \'sar-ˌäs-, 'ser-\. Inlet of NE Aegean Sea extending E into SW coast of Turkey, Europe, at the base of Gallipoli Penin.

Sá·ros·pa·tak \'shä-rəsh-ˌpä-tək\. Commune, Barsod-Abaúj-Zemplén co., NE Hungary, 40 m. NE of Miskolc; pop. (1970p) 14,173.

Sarps·borg \'särps-ˌbȯ(ə)r\. City, Østfold co., SE Norway, on W bank of Glåma river; pop. (1970e) 13,165; hydroelectric power plant; chemical works, textile and paper mills, zinc smelters; city rebuilt 1838 on site of a ruined medieval town.

Sarps·foss \'särps-ˌfȯs\. Waterfall in the Glåma river near its mouth, Østfold co., SE Norway; 60 ft. high and 164 ft. wide.

Sar·py \'sär-pē\. County in Nebraska. See table at NEBRASKA.

Sarre. 1 River, France. See SAAR 1.
2 State, West Germany. See SAARLAND.

Sarre, La. See LA SARRE.

Sarre·bourg \'sär-'bü(ə)r\ *or Ger.* **Saar·burg** \'zär-ˌbu̇(ə)rg\. Commune, Moselle dept., NE France, 44 m. NW of Strasbourg; pop. (1968c) 11,413.

Sarrebruck. See SAARBRÜCKEN.

Sarre·gue·mines \ˌsär-gə-'mēn\ *or formerly* **Saar·ge·mund** \ˌzär-gə-'myünt\. Town, Moselle dept., NE France, on Sarre river at German border 42 m. E of Metz; pop. (1968c) 24,284; iron and copper foundries; manufactures faïence (since 1785).

Sa·rria \'sä-rē-ə, -ryə\. Commune, Lugo prov., NW Spain, 19 m. SSE of Lugo; pop. (1970p) 12,052; leather goods, dairy products; livestock farms.

Sars, Le. See LE SARS.

Sar·si·na \'särs-ᵊn-ə\. Ancient town in mountains of N Umbria, cen. Italy; birthplace of Plautus c. 254 B.C.

Sars·toon *or* **Sars·tún** \sär-'stün\. River, E cen. Guatemala; ab. 70 m. long; flows E into the Gulf of Amatique; forms S boundary of British Honduras.

Sarsuti. See SARASWATI 1.

Sar·tène \sär-'ten\. Town, S Corsica, France, 23 m. SSE of Ajaccio; pop. (1962c) 5935.

Sarthe \'särt\. 1 River, NW France; 177 m. long; rises in Orne dept., flows S to unite with Mayenne river near Angers and form Maine river.
2 Department of NW France. See table at FRANCE.

Sar·trou·ville \ˌsär-trü-'vēl\. Commune, Yvelines dept., N France, NW suburb of Paris on Seine river; pop. (1968c) 40,277.

Sarum, New. See SALISBURY 6.

Sarum, Old. See OLD SARUM.

Sarus. See SEYHAN.

Sa·ry·su \ˌsär-ē-'sü\. River, cen. Kazakh S.S.R., U.S.S.R.; ab. 520 m. long; flows S into the desert, not quite reaching the Syr Darya.

Sar·za·na \sär(d)-'zän-ə\. Commune, La Spezia prov., Liguria, NW Italy, 7 m. E of La Spezia; pop. (1968e) 18,203; 14th cent. cathedral.

Sa·sa·la·guan, Mount \-ˌsäs-ə-lə-'gwän\. Mountain at S end of Guam, Mariana Is.; 1120 ft.

Sa·sa·ram \'səs-ə-ˌräm\. Town, W Bihar, NE India, 90 m. WSW of Patna; pop. (1961c) 37,782; contains tomb of Emperor Sher Shah (1540–45), one of India's most notable examples of Pathan architecture, and tombs of Sher Shah's father and son.

Sasau. See SÁZAVA.

Sa·se·bo \'säs-ə-ˌbō\. Seaport city on large inlet of outer Omura Bay, Nagasaki prefecture, NW Kyūshū, Japan; pop. (1970c) 247,898; a commercial and fishing port; formerly site of a large naval base (estab. 1886), with a dockyard and arsenal; heavily bombed during World War II 1944–45 but town since rebuilt.

Saseno. See SAZAN.

Sa·ser Kan·gri \ˌsäs-ər-'käŋ-grē\. Mountain in the Karakoram Range, in part of Jammu and Kashmir controlled by India; 25,172 ft.

Sas·katch·e·wan \sə-'skach-ə-wən, sa-, -ˌwän\. 1 River, SW and S cen. Canada, flowing from the Rocky Mts. E into N Lake Winnipeg; upper part divided into 2 branches, **North Saskatchewan** (760 m.) and **South Saskatchewan** (865 m.); length of river after confluence of its branches, E of Prince Albert, 340 m. The South Saskatchewan and its tributary the Bow constitute the longest headstream of the Nelson river with a total length of 1205 m.; including the Nelson 1600 m. The main tributaries of the North Saskatchewan are the Battle, Brazeau, and Clearwater; of the South Saskatchewan the Red Deer, Bow, and Oldman.
2 Province, W Canada, cen. province of the Prairie Provinces, bounded on N by Mackenzie dist., on E by Manitoba, on S by U.S. (North Dakota and Montana), and on W by Alberta; 251,700 sq. m. (incl. 31,518 sq. m. of water); pop. (1970e) 942,000; ✻ Regina. *Physical features:* Entirely a plains region with prairie in S and wooded country containing many lakes and swamps in N. Highest point in SW corner 4546 ft.; average elevation 1000 to 2000 ft. Watered

in N by headstreams of the Mackenzie flowing into Lake Athabaska, in cen. part by the Churchill, in S cen. and SW by the Saskatchewan and branches, and in the SE by Assiniboine and tributaries. Lakes include Athabaska (E half), Reindeer, Wollaston, Churchill, Rouge, etc. It has one large national park, the Prince Albert, in cen. part and 14 provincial parks. *Chief products:* Wheat, oats, barley; livestock raising; potash, oil, natural gas, zinc, copper; manufacturing: cement, paper products, steel pipes. *Chief cities:* Regina, Saskatoon, Moose Jaw, Prince Albert.

History: For two centuries 1670–1869 region controlled by Hudson's Bay Company; S part explored by La Vérendrye c. 1743–49; part of Northwest Territory to 1869 with few settlements before that date; S half set up 1882 as districts of Saskatchewan and Assiniboia and N half made a part of district of Athabaska; established as a province 1905; commenced potash production 1958.

3 Former district, cen. Canada, formed 1882 out of Northwest Territories bet. Athabaska on N and Assiniboia on S, bet. 52° and 55°N; 101,000 sq. m.; ✱ Battleford; most of it included in Saskatchewan prov. 1905.

Sas·ka·toon \ˌsas-kə-ˈtün\. City, S cen. Saskatchewan, Canada, on South Saskatchewan river 150 m. NW of Regina; pop. (1971p) 125,079; center of an important grain and livestock-farming region; creameries, machine shops, meat-packing plants, grain elevators, flour mills, oil refineries, potash mines; Coll. of Emmanuel and Saint Chad (1879), Univ. of Saskatchewan (1907), Saint Andrew's Coll. (1912), Lutheran Theological Seminary (1913), Saint Thomas More Coll. (1936); founded 1883.

Saskatoon Mountain Reserve. Provincial park, W Alberta, Canada; 3000 acres; lookout point in hills near Grande Prairie.

Sason. See SAZAN.

Sas·sa·fras \ˈsas-(ə-)ˌfras\. River, NE Maryland; ab. 20 m. long; rises in NW Delaware, flows W into upper Chesapeake Bay.

Sassafras Mountain. Peak, Pickens co., NW South Carolina; 3560 ft.; highest point in the state.

Sas·san·dra \sə-ˈsan-drə\. 1 River, W Ivory Coast, W Africa; ab. 350 m. long; flows S into the Atlantic Ocean.

2 Seaport at mouth of the river, SW Ivory Coast, 145 m. W of Abidjan; pop. (1963e) 8367.

Sas·sa·ri \ˈsäs-ə-(ˌ)rē\. 1 Province of Sardinia, Italy. See table at ITALY.

2 Commune, its ✱, 110 m. NNW of Cagliari; pop. (1968e) 104,977; trades in agricultural produce; cathedral, two Romanesque churches; univ. (estab. 1562, univ. status 1612). In Middle Ages called Thatari; came under Genoa 1284; to Aragon 1323; to Piedmont (kingdom of Sardinia) 1718.

Sasseno. See SAZAN.

Sas·so·fer·ra·to \ˌsä-sō-fer-ˈä-tō\ *or anc.* **Sen·ti·num** \sen-ˈtī-nəm\. Commune, Ancona prov., Marches, cen. Italy, 37 m. WSW of Ancona; pop. (1968e) 7769; near ancient town Romans defeated allied Etruscan, Samnite, and Gaulish forces 295 B.C., thus establishing themselves in cen. Italy.

Sasstown. See SASTOWN.

Sas·suo·lo \sä-ˈswȯ-(ˌ)lō\. Commune, Modena prov., Emilia-Romagna, N Italy, 11 m. SW of Modena; pop. (1968c) 32,523.

Sas·town *or* **Sass·town** \ˈsas-ˌtau̇n\. Coastal town, SE Liberia, W Africa, 53 m. WNW of Cape Palmas.

Sa·ta, Cape \-ˈsä-tə\. Cape, S extremity of Kyūshū, Japan.

Sa·ta·ra \sə-ˈtär-ə\. Town, S Maharashtra, W India, near Krishna river 120 m. SE of Bombay; pop. (1961c) 48,709; 12th cent. fort; came under Muslim rule 14th cent.; under Marathas was at one time capital of the Maratha kingdom; came under British mid-19th cent.

Satara Ja·girs \-jə-ˈgi(ə)rz\. Five former Indian states—Akalkot, Aundh, Bhor, Jath, and Phaltan—once tributary to Satara, later in the Kolhapur and Deccan States Agency; area now in S Maharashtra state.

Sat·el·lite Beach \ˈsat-ᵊl-ˌīt-\. Town, Brevard co., E Florida, on Atlantic coast 15 m. SSE of Cocoa; pop. (1970c) 6558.

Sa·til·la \sə-ˈtil-ə\. River, S and SE Georgia; ab. 220 m. long; navigable at its mouth; rises in Irwin co., flows E, S, and again E into St. Andrew Sound.

Satit. See TEKEZE.

Sat·ka \ˈsät-kə\ *or formerly* **Sat·kin·ski Za·vod** \sät-ˌkin(t)-skē-zə-ˈvȯt, -ˈvȯd\. Town, Chelyabinsk Oblast, Russian S.F.S.R., U.S.S.R., ab. 100 m. W of Chelyabinsk; pop. (1967e) 45,000.

Sat·na *or* **Sut·na** \ˈsət-nə\. Town, NE Madhya Pradesh, NE India, 90 m. SW of Allahabad; pop. (1961c) 38,046.

Sá·tor·al·ja·új·hely \ˌshä-ˌtō(ə)r-ˌȯl-yȯ-ˈüi-(ˌ)hā\. City, Borsod-Abaúj-Zemplén co., NE Hungary, on a tributary of the Bodrog near Czechoslovakian border; pop. (1970p) 16,-853; in grape-growing region.

Sat·pu·ra Range \ˈsät-pə-rə-\. Range of hills, W cen. India, bet. the Narmada and Tapti rivers; average elevation ab. 3000 ft.; highest point 4429 ft.

Satrunjaya. See PALITANA 2.

Sa·tsu·ma \ˈsät-sə-ˌmä, sat-ˈsü-mə\. Former province, S Kyūshū, Japan, now in Kagoshima prefecture; noted for its pottery, dating from close of 16th cent., and the hard-glazed ware, a later production. Home of a powerful clan, at first much opposed to foreign influence 1858–68, but after Restoration (in 1869) offered their lands to the emperor as an aid to terminate feudalism.

Sattima. See LESATIMA.

Sa·tu–Mare \ˈsät-ü-ˈmär-ə\. 1 County of NW Romania. See table at ROMANIA.

2 *or Hung.* **Szat·már–Né·me·ti** \ˈsȯt-ˌmär-ˈnā-mət-ē\. City, its ✱, near Hungarian border on Someşul river; pop. (1970e) 78,812; commercial and industrial center, producing machinery, textiles, metal goods; palace; mentioned in 14th cent.

Sa·tun \sä-ˈtün\ *also* **Sa·tul** *or* **Se·tul** \sä-ˈtün—*sic*\. 1 Province, SW Thailand; 1031 sq. m.; pop. (1960c) 69,636; ✱ Satun; formerly one of the Malay States under Thai protection.

2 Town, its ✱, near W coast of Malay Penin., just NNW of Perlis state in Malaysia; pop. (1964e) 7202.

Sa·tur·ni·an \sə-ˈtər-nē-ən\. Original name of the Capitoline Hill. See SEVEN HILLS.

Sau. See SAVA 2.

Sau·ce \ˈsau̇-(ˌ)sā\ *or* **Puer·to Sauce** \ˌpwert-ō-\. Small port on La Plata estuary, Colonia dept., SW Uruguay, 78 m. WNW of Montevideo; port for Rosario.

Sau·ci·llo \sau̇-ˈsē-yō\. Municipality, Chihuahua state, N Mexico, 70 m. SE of Chihuahua; pop. (1970p) 30,781; cattle raising; cotton, barley.

Saud·hár·kró·kur \ˈsȯi-ˌ(th)au̇(ə)r-ˌkrō-kər\. Town, N Iceland, ab. 45 m. WNW of Akureyri; pop. (1970c) 1600.

Sa·u·di Arabia \ˌsau̇d-ē-, sä-ˌüd-ē-\; *officially* **Kingdom of Saudi Arabia** *or Arab.* **Al–Mam·la·kah al–ʻAra·bī·yah as–Suʻūdī·yah** \al-mem-ˈlek-ə-al-ar-ə-ˈbē-(y)ə-as-sü-ˈdē-yə\. Kingdom, Arabian Penin., SW Asia; 873,972 sq. m.; pop. (1969e) 7,200,000; ✱ Riyadh. *Physical features:* A plateau region, average elevation 2500 ft., with band of highlands having elevations of 7000 to 10,000 ft. in W near Red Sea coast in Hejaz; includes great deserts of An Nafud (in the N) and Rub ʻal Khali (in the S). *Chief export:* Oil (the kingdom is the world's fourth largest oil-producer); other products incl. natural gas, gypsum, sulfur, manganese; pastoralism. *Chief towns:* Riyadh, Jidda, Mecca, Hofuf.

History: A dual kingdom formed 1926 by ibn-Saud as king of Nejd and Hejaz (*qq.v.*) and as a single kingdom renamed Saudi Arabia 1932; absorbed Asir 1933; fought successful war against Yemen (✱ Sanʻa) but independence

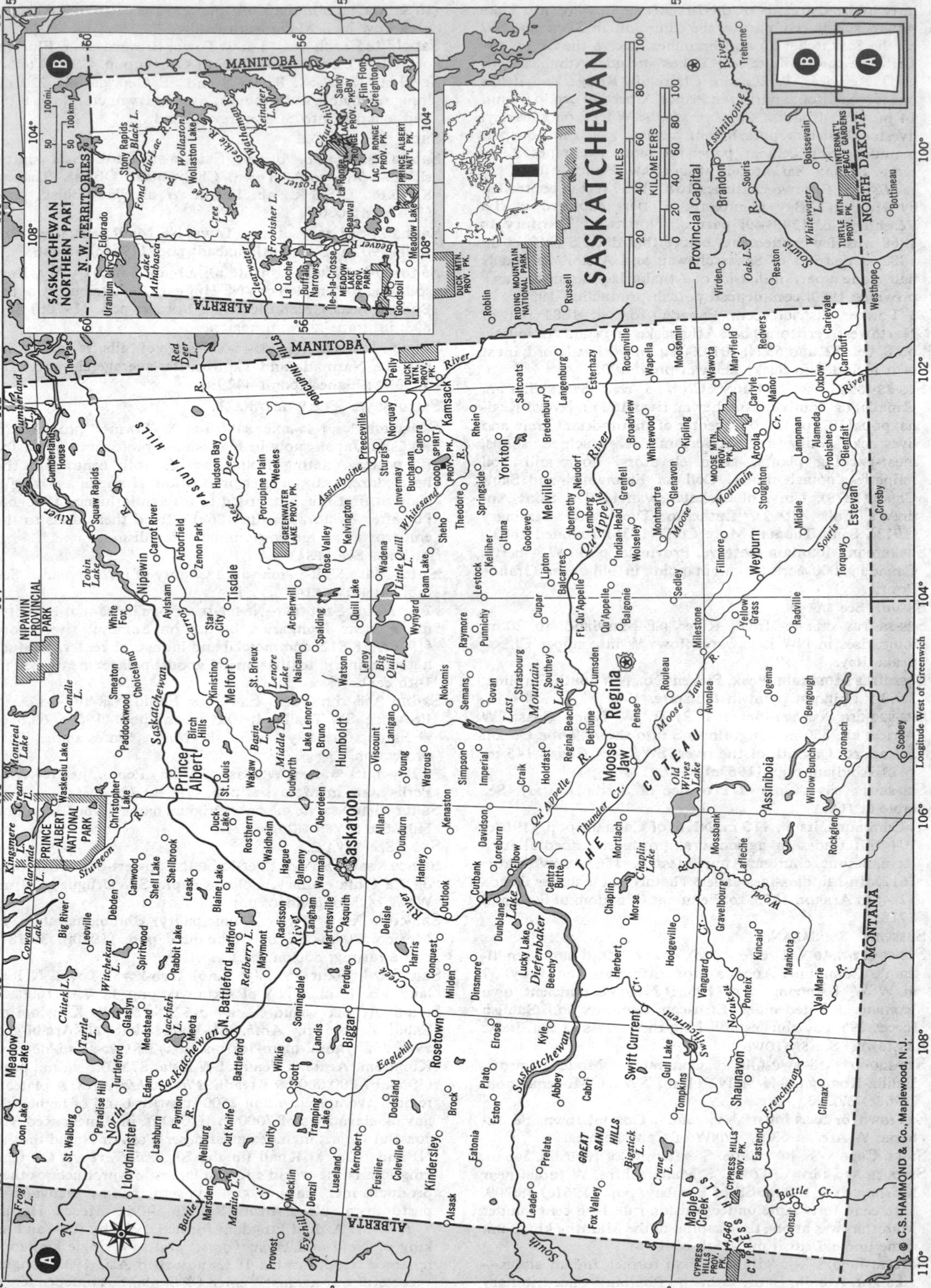
SASKATCHEWAN
MILES
KILOMETERS
Provincial Capital
SASKATCHEWAN NORTHERN PART
N. W. TERRITORIES
ALBERTA
MANITOBA
MONTANA
NORTH DAKOTA
Lake Athabasca
Uranium City
Eldorado
Stony Rapids
Black L.
Fond du Lac R.
Wollaston Lake
Reindeer L.
Cree L.
Churchill R.
Frobisher L.
Buffalo Narrows
La Loche
Île-à-la-Crosse
Beauval
La Ronge
LAC LA RONGE PROV. PK.
Flin Flon
Creighton
Sandy Bay
MEADOW LAKE PROV. PARK
Goodsoil
Meadow Lake
PRINCE ALBERT NAT'L PK.
DUCK MTN. PROV. PK.
RIDING MOUNTAIN NATIONAL PARK
Roblin
Russell
Brandon
Souris
Virden
Boissevain
TURTLE MTN. PROV. PK.
INTERNAT'L PEACE GARDENS
Bottineau
Westhope
Treherne
Assiniboine River
Lloydminster
Meadow Lake
St. Walburg
North Battleford
N. Battleford
Battleford
North Saskatchewan R.
Prince Albert
PRINCE ALBERT NATIONAL PARK
Waskesiu Lake
NIPAWIN PROVINCIAL PARK
Nipawin
Tisdale
Melfort
Humboldt
Saskatoon
Biggar
Rosetown
Kindersley
Kerrobert
Unity
Macklin
Outlook
Watrous
Wynyard
Big Quill L.
Little Quill L.
Last Mountain Lake
Yorkton
Melville
Kamsack
Canora
Hudson Bay
PASQUIA HILLS
Cumberland House
Cumberland L.
The Pas
Squaw Rapids
Tobin Lake
Red Deer R.
Qu'Appelle River
Regina
Moose Jaw
Weyburn
Estevan
Assiniboia
Swift Current
Maple Creek
Shaunavon
Gravelbourg
Lake Diefenbaker
South Saskatchewan
GREAT SAND HILLS
CYPRESS HILLS PROV. PK.
CYPRESS HILLS
4,546
THE COTEAU
Old Wives Lake
Chaplin Lake
Moose Mountain Cr.
MOOSE MTN. PROV. PK.
Souris R.
Frenchman R.
Battle Cr.
Leader
Eastend
Consul
Kipling
Carlyle
Oxbow
Carnduff
Moosomin
Esterhazy
Preeceville
GREENWATER LAKE PROV. PK.
GOOD SPIRIT PROV. PK.
PORCUPINE HILLS
Red Deer L.
Longitude West of Greenwich
© C.S.HAMMOND & Co., Maplewood, N.J.

of latter guaranteed by Great Britain 1934; entered treaty of nonaggression and brotherhood with Iraq 1936; formed agreement with Egypt 1937 by which recognition was obtained of its annexation of Hejaz; neutral in World War II; Saudi Arabia-Oman boundary dispute basis of friction with Great Britain during early 1950's; supported royalists in Yemen's (✱ San'a) civil war of 1960's; dispatched troops (though these remained inactive) to Jordan during Arab-Israeli War 1967.

Sau·er \'zaů(-ə)r\. River, Belgium, Grand Duchy of Luxembourg, and West Germany; 107 m. long; rises in Belgian province of Luxembourg, flows E across Grand Duchy of Luxembourg into the Moselle river 7 m. SW of Trier in Rhineland-Palatinate, West Germany; navigable for ab. 40 m.; scene of severe fighting in World War II in the Battle of the Bulge Dec. 1944–Jan. 1945.

Sau·ga·tuck \'sȯ-gə-ˌtək\. River, SW Connecticut; ab. 20 m. long; rises in cen. Fairfield co., flows S into Long Island Sound.

Saugeen Peninsula. See BRUCE PENINSULA.

Sau·ger·ties \'sȯ-gər-ˌtēz\. Village, Ulster co., SE New York, on W side of Hudson river 11 m. N of Kingston; pop. (1970c) 4190; clothing; cement and flagstone quarries; agriculture; former river port.

Sau·gor \'sȯ-gər\ *or* **Sa·gar** \'säg-ər\. Town, N Madhya Pradesh, India, 180 m. N of Nagpur; pop. (1967e) 97,556; flour, cigarettes; univ. (1946); Maratha fort.

Sau·gus \'sȯ-gəs\. 1 Residential town, Essex co., NE corner of Massachusetts, 8 m. NNE of Boston; pop. (1970c) 25,-110.

2 Former name of Lynn, Massachusetts. See LYNN 2.

Saujbulagh. See MAHĀBĀD.

Sauk \'sȯk\. 1 River, cen. Minnesota, 120 m. long; flows from Osakis Lake, SW Todd co., to Mississippi river above St. Cloud.

2 County in Wisconsin. See table at WISCONSIN.

3 Village, Cook co., NE Illinois, W of Chicago; pop. (1970c) 7479.

Sauk Centre. City, Stearns co., cen. Minnesota, on the Sauk river 39 m. WNW of St. Cloud; pop. (1970c) 3750; dairy farms; boyhood home of Sinclair Lewis and setting for several of his novels.

Sauk Rapids. Village, Benton co., cen. Minnesota, on Mississippi river 3 m. N of St. Cloud; pop. (1970c) 5051; dairy products; granite quarries.

Sault Sainte Ma·rie \ˌsü-ˌsānt-mə-'rē\. 1 City, ⊗ of Chippewa co., E Michigan penin., at the falls on Saint Marys river (*q.v.*) bet. Lakes Huron and Superior; pop. (1970c) 15,136; opp. Canadian city of the same name; dairy products, lumber, pulp and paper; center of a summer resort region; Lake Superior State Coll. (1946). Site first reached by Étienne Brulé c. 1618 and by Jean Nicolet 1634; first settled by Marquette 1668; ceded to U.S. 1783 by British but U.S. did not take possession until 1820; incorporated as village 1879, as city 1887.

2 City, ⊗ of Algoma dist., S Ontario, Canada, at the falls on St. Marys river opp. Sault Sainte Marie, Michigan; pop. (1971p) 78,175; iron and steel, coke, lumber, chemicals, beer; truck and dairy farms; in summer resort region; Algoma Coll. (1965). City developed 1887 ff. on site of mission founded by Marquette 1668; site of lock for small craft built 1798 and destroyed in War of 1812.

Sault Sainte Marie Canals *or* **Soo Canals** \ˌsü-\. Two U.S. ship canals and a Canadian ship canal, Saint Marys Falls on Saint Marys river (*q.v.*); first U.S. canal begun 1853, completed 1855; since then replaced and enlarged; now divided: the N canal (U.S.), completed 1919, is 1.61 m. long, 80 ft. wide and 24.5 ft. deep; the S canal (U.S.), completed 1896, is 1.56 m. long, 100 ft. wide and 18 ft. deep; the Canadian canal, completed 1895, is 1.38 m. long, 150 ft. wide and 22 ft. deep; there are five locks (one on the Canadian canal), one of the two largest, the Davis lock, being 1350 ft. long bet. the gates, 80 ft. wide and having a lift of 20.5 ft.

Sau·mur \sō-'m(y)ů(ə)r\. Industrial commune, Maine-et-Loire dept., W France, on Loire river 28 m. SE of Angers; pop. (1968c) 21,551; wines, mushrooms, canned fruits and vegetables; 14th–16th cent. chateau, 16th cent. town hall, 12th cent. church; site of Cavalry School (estab. 1768, now training center for French armored forces). Site inhabited from prehistoric times; local stronghold in 9th cent.; came under French crown 1480; in 16th–17th cents. a major center of French Protestantism and declined after revocation of Edict of Nantes 1685; in World War II heavily damaged in fighting 1940.

Sau·mu·rois \ˌsōm-yər-'wä\. Historical region of NW France; bounded on N by Anjou, E by Touraine, S and W by Poitou; now included in Maine-et-Loire and Vienne depts.; ✱ Saumur.

Saun·ders \'sȯn-dərz\. County in Nebraska. See table at NEBRASKA.

Saunders, Cape. Cape, SE coast of South I., New Zealand, S of entrance to Otago Harbor.

Sau·rash·tra \saů-'räsh-trə\. Former state, W India, in Kathiawar penin.; established 1948; in 1956 became part of Bombay state; since 1960 in Gujarat state.

Saur·bær \'sȯi-ər-ˌbī(-ə)r\. Town, NW Iceland, on NW shore of Breidha Fjord; pop. (1970c) 292.

Sau·sa·li·to \ˌsȯ-sə-'lēt-(ˌ)ō\. Suburban residential city, Marin co., W California, on San Francisco Bay 3 m. NW of San Francisco; pop. (1970c) 6158; fishing and yachting resort. Forts Barry and Baker.

Sau·ternes \sō-'te(ə)rn, sȯ-, -'tərn\. Commune, Gironde dept., SW France, on tributary of the Garonne ab. 20 m. SSE of Bordeaux; pop. (1962c) 640; center of a district including Barsac, Bommes, Preignac, and Fargues, noted for production of white wine.

Sa·va \'säv-ə\. 1 Commune, Taranto prov., Apulia, SE Italy, 17 m. ESE of Taranto; pop. (1968e) 16,177.

2 *or Fr.* **Save** \säv\ *or Ger.* **Sau** \'zaů\ *or Hung.* **Szá·va** \'säv-ˌȯ\; *anc.* **Sa·vus** \'säv-əs\. River, N Yugoslavia; 584 m. long; rises on Italian-Yugoslav border, flows E into Danube river at Belgrade; navigable for 362 m.

3 Former county, N Yugoslavia; ⊗ Zagreb; later Savska co.; now approx. coextensive with Croatia.

Sav·age \'sav-ij\. Village, Scott co., SE Minnesota, 9 m. E of Minneapolis; pop. (1970c) 3611.

Savage Island. See NIUE.

Sav·age's Station \ˌsav-ij-əz-\. Battlefield near Richmond, Virginia, where Confederates under Magruder made unsuccessful attack on Union troops under Sumner June 29, 1862, one of the Seven Days' Battles.

Sa·vai'i *or* **Sa·vaii** \sə-'vī-(ˌ)ē\. Island, Western Samoa, in SW Pacific Ocean; 700 sq. m.; largest island in Samoa group; has many rocky mountains, several of them semiactive volcanoes; highest point Mt. Mauga Sili 3503 ft.

Savalan. See SABALĀN.

Sa·van·na \sə-'van-ə\. City, Carroll co., NW Illinois, on Mississippi river 55 m. WSW of Rockford; pop. (1970c) 4942; livestock, dairy farms.

Sa·van·nah \sə-ˌvan-ə\. 1 Navigable river, E Georgia; 314 m. long; formed by confluence of Tugaloo and Seneca rivers in W Anderson co., NW South Carolina, flows SE forming Georgia-South Carolina boundary, and empties into Atlantic Ocean at Savannah.

2 City, ⊗ of Chatham co., SE Georgia, at mouth of Savannah river; pop. (1970c) 118,349; oldest city in Georgia and its principal seaport; cotton market; paper products, sugar, building materials, fertilizers, chemicals, paints; railroad shops, shipyards; Savannah State Coll. (1890), Armstrong State Coll. (1935). Original settlement in Georgia, founded by Oglethorpe 1733; capital of Georgia 1754–86; in Civil

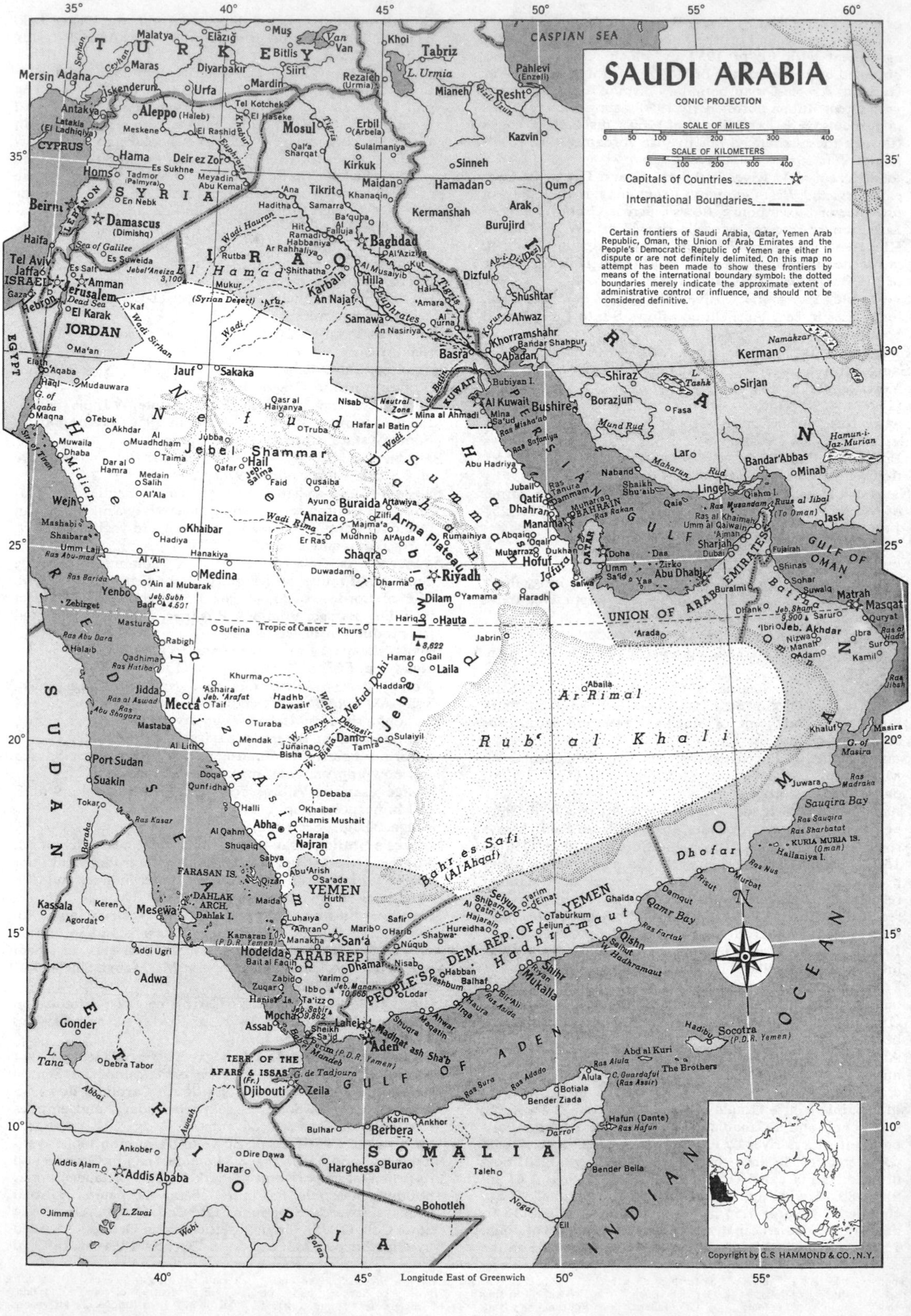
SAUDI ARABIA
CONIC PROJECTION
SCALE OF MILES
0 50 100 200 300 400
SCALE OF KILOMETERS
0 100 200 300 400
Capitals of Countries
International Boundaries
Certain frontiers of Saudi Arabia, Qatar, Yemen Arab Republic, Oman, the Union of Arab Emirates and the People's Democratic Republic of Yemen are either in dispute or are not definitely delimited. On this map no attempt has been made to show these frontiers by means of the international boundary symbol: the dotted boundaries merely indicate the approximate extent of administrative control or influence, and should not be considered definitive.
Copyright by C. S. HAMMOND & CO., N.Y.
Longitude East of Greenwich
35° 40° 45° 50° 55° 60°
TURKEY
SYRIA
IRAQ
IRAN
JORDAN
ISRAEL
LEBANON
CYPRUS
EGYPT
KUWAIT
BAHRAIN
QATAR
UNION OF ARAB EMIRATES
OMAN
YEMEN
ARAB REP.
PEOPLE'S DEM. REP. OF YEMEN
SUDAN
ETHIOPIA
SOMALIA
TERR. OF THE AFARS & ISSAS (Fr.)
CASPIAN SEA
RED SEA
PERSIAN GULF
GULF OF OMAN
GULF OF ADEN
INDIAN OCEAN
Nefud
Jebel Shammar
Dahana
Summan
Tuwaiq
Hejaz
Asir
Hadhramaut
Rub' al Khali
Ar Rimal
Tropic of Cancer
Riyadh
Mecca
Medina
Jidda
Taif
Hofuf
Dhahran
Al Kuwait
Baghdad
Damascus
Amman
Jerusalem
Beirut
San'a
Aden
Masqat
Abu Dhabi
Doha
Manama
Djibouti
Addis Ababa
Socotra
Dhofar

War captured by Union forces under Sherman Dec. 21, 1864.

3 City, ⊗ of Andrew co., NW Missouri, 14 m. N of St. Joseph; pop. (1970c) 3324; diversified agriculture.

4 Town, ⊗ of Hardin co., SW Tennessee, on Tennessee river 45 m. ESE of Jackson; pop. (1970c) 5576; lumber, clothing; hay, livestock.

Sa·van·na·khet \sə-ˌvän-ə-ˈket\. Town, S Laos, on Mekong river ab. 130 m. NW of Pakse; pop. (1967e) 35,682.

Savanna–la–Mar \sə-ˌvan-ə-lə-ˈmär\. Seaport on S coast at W end of Jamaica, West Indies; pop. (1960c) 9789; shipping point for region producing sugar, coffee, ginger, and logwood; destroyed by earthquake 1740 and rebuilt.

Sa·vant·va·di \ˌsäv-ənt-ˈväd-ē\ *or* **Sa·want·wa·di** \ˌsä-wənt-ˈwäd-ē\. 1 Former Indian state, now part of Maharashtra state, W India; 937 sq. m.; a Maratha state with history dating back to 6th cent.; suffered much from rivalry of Portuguese at Goa in 16th and 17th cents.

2 Town, its ✱, near coast 63 m. SSW of Kolhapur.

Savaria. See SZOMBATHELY.

Sa·ve \ˈsav-ə\ *or Eng.* **Sa·bi** \ˈsäb-ē\. River, SE Africa; ab. 400 m. long; rises in Rhodesia, flows ESE across border into Mozambique, continues E across S Mozambique into Mozambique Channel; its large tributary in Rhodesia is the **Lun·di** \ˈlən-dē\ river.

Save \ˈsȧv\. 1 River, S France; ab. 90 m. long; rises on the slopes of the Pyrenees, flows NE into Garonne river 15 m. NNW of Toulouse.

2 River, Yugoslavia. See SAVA 2.

Sa·verne \sə-ˈvern\ *or* **Za·bern** \ˈtsä-bərn\. Commune, Bas-Rhin dept., NE France, ab. 20 m. NW of Strasbourg; pop. (1962c) 9382; important in Roman times when it was called **Tres Ta·ber·nae** \ˌtrēz-tə-ˈbər-nē\; held by bishops of Metz under the Carolingians and by the bishops of Strasbourg 13th–18th cents.; several ruined castles in vicinity; scene of incident (Zabern affair) Nov. 1913 when a German officer insulted Alsatian civilians.

Sa·vi·glia·no \ˌsäv-ēl-ˈyän-(ˌ)ō\. Commune, Cuneo prov., Piedmont, NW Italy, 18 m. NE of Cuneo; pop. (1968e) 18,726; livestock market; textiles; Benedictine abbey.

Sa·vi·gny–sur–Orge \ˌsav-i-ˌnyē-su̇(ə)r-ˈȯ(ə)rzh\. Commune, Essonne dept., N France, 9 m. S of Paris; pop. (1968c) 32,075; manufactures shoes and gloves.

Sa·vi·ñao \ˌsä-vi-ˈnyau̇\. Commune, Lugo prov., NW Spain, 30 m. SSW of Lugo; pop. (1970p) 8534.

Sa·vo \ˈsäv-(ˌ)ō\. Small island, SE Solomon Is., part of British Solomon Islands protectorate, W Pacific Ocean, ab. 8 m. N of W end of Guadalcanal I. (Cape Esperance) and 18 m. W of Florida I.; highest point 1600 ft. Notable for naval and air battles in Guadalcanal campaign, esp. the night of Aug. 8–9, 1942 when Allied forces lost four cruisers, and Nov. 12–13, 1942 resulting in defeat of Japanese.

Savoia. See SAVOY.

Sa·voie \sa-ˈvwä\. 1 Departments of France: **Haute–Savoie** \ˌōt-sa-ˈvwä, ˌōt-sə-ˈvȯi\ and **Savoie.** See table at FRANCE.

2 Region, France and Italy. See SAVOY.

Sa·vo·na \sə-ˈvō-nə\. 1 Province of Liguria, NW Italy. See table at ITALY.

2 Seaport, its ✱, on Gulf of Genoa 23 m. WSW of Genoa; pop. (1968e) 17,168; iron and steel, machinery, electrical equipment, glass; tanning, shipbuilding, food processing; late 16th cent. cathedral. First mentioned c. 205 B.C.; destroyed by Lombards 641; under Genoese rule 1528 ff., under French 1805–15; to Savoy 1815; heavily bombed in World War II.

Sa·von·lin·na \ˈsav-(ˌ)ȯn-ˌlin-ə\. City, Mikkeli prov., S Finland; pop. (1970e) 17,942; built on a large island in the Lake Saimaa region; summer resort; founded 1639.

Sa·voon·ga \sə-ˈvüŋ-gə\. City on N coast of St. Lawrence I., Bering Sea, Alaska; pop. (1970c) 364.

Sa·voy \sə-ˈvȯi\ *or Fr.* **Sa·voie** \sȧ-vwȧ\ *or Ital.* **Sa·vo·ia** \sä-ˈvȯ-yä\. Historical region of SE France and NW Italy, of varying limits, now chiefly in French departments of Haute-Savoie and Savoie; chief city Chambéry.

History: From 11th cent., counts of Savoy ruled area in W Alp region as part of kingdom of Arles (*q.v.*); became virtually independent and expanded its territory to encircle Lake Geneva and to include plain of Piedmont in Italy; elevated to duchy 1416 by Emperor Sigismund; territory scene of fighting in many wars; at times allied with France, at times with Italy; involved in wars bet. France and Spain with alternating allegiances; under Charles Emmanuel I lost territories beyond the Rhone; joined Grand Alliance 1704; by Treaty of Utrecht 1713 received island of Sicily and held it until 1720 when it was exchanged for the island of Sardinia and the kingdom of Sardinia was formed (included Piedmont, Savoy, and island of Sardinia), the dukes of Savoy becoming kings of Sardinia. Kingdom of Sardinia sided with Royalists in French Revolution and as result lost territory of Savoy 1792 and Piedmont 1796; restored to Victor Emmanuel I by Congress of Vienna 1815 and Genoa added; in 1860 Sardinia, Genoa, and Piedmont joined other states of Italy to form kingdom of Italy with house of Savoy ruling, while territory of Savoy, with Nice (*q.v.*), was ceded to France.

Savoy Alps. See table at ALPS.

Sav·ska \ˈsäv-skə\. Former county, N and NW Yugoslavia; ⊗ Zagreb; formed 1929, dissolved 1945; approximately coextensive with Croatia.

Sa·vu *or* **Sa·wu** *or Du.* **Sa·woe** \ˈsä-vü\. Island of the Lesser Sunda Is., Indonesia, WSW of Timor and SE of Sumba; 23 m. long by 10 m. wide; with nearby islands 200 sq. m.; only port Seba on NW coast.

Savus. See SAVA 2.

Sa·vu·sa·vu Bay \ˌsäv-ü-ˌsäv-ü-\. Inlet of Pacific Ocean, S coast of Vanau Levu I., Fiji.

Savu Sea *or* **Sawu Sea** *or Du.* **Sawoe–Zee** \ˌsä-vü-ˈzā\. Part of Indian Ocean in Indonesia, lying S of Flores, Lomblen, and Pantar Is., W of Timor, N of Savu I., and E of Sumba I.; connected with Timor Sea by Roti Strait.

Sa·wah·lun·to *or Du.* **Sa·wah·loen·to** \ˌsä-wə-ˈlün-(ˌ)tō\. Town, W cen. Sumatra, Indonesia, ab. 45 m. ENE of Padang; pop. (1961c) 12,276.

Sa·wan·kha·lok \sä-ˌwän-kä-ˈlōk\ *or* **Swan·ka·lok** \ˌswän-kä-ˈlōk\. Village, W Thailand, on left bank of Yom river, 40 m. NW of Phitsanulok; pop. (1964e) 11,457; has one of three temples celebrated in Thailand for architecture.

Sawantwadi. See SAVANTVADI.

Sa·watch Range \sə-ˈwäch-\. A range of the Rocky Mts., cen. Colorado; highest peak Mount Elbert, 14,433 ft.

Sawfajjīn. See SOFEGGIN.

Saw Grass Lake \ˈsȯ-ˌgras-\. Lake in S Brevard co., E cen. Florida; outlet St. Johns river flowing N.

Saw·haj \ˈsau̇-ˌhäj\. 1 Governorate of Upper Egypt. See table at EGYPT.

2 Town, its ✱, on the W bank of the Nile 190 m. NNW of Aswān; pop. (1970e) 85,300; on main Cairo railroad; textile mills, cotton gins, limestone quarries; in an agricultural region.

Sawoe. See SAVU.

Sawoe–Zee. See SAVU SEA.

Saw·teeth \ˈsȯ-ˌtēth\. Mountain in Adirondack Mts., Essex co., NE New York; 4138 ft.

Saw·tooth Mountain \ˌsȯ-tüth-\. Peak, Jeff Davis co., W Texas; 7748 ft.

Sawtooth Range. Large group of mountain ranges, Custer, Blaine, and Camas cos., S cen. Idaho, just S of Salmon River Mts.; 40 m. long; contains a number of peaks above 10,000 ft., many alpine lakes, and the sources of Boise and Big Wood rivers; resort area and game reserves.

Sawtooth Ridge. Ridge in N cen. Washington, extending along the NE shore of Lake Chelan and along boundary bet. Okanogan and Chelan cos.

Sawu. See SAVU.

Sawu Sea. See SAVU SEA.

Saw·yer \'sȯ-yər\. County in Wisconsin. See table at WISCONSIN.

Saxa Ru·bra \ˌsak-sə-'rü-brə\. Town of ancient Etruria, Italy, on Flaminian Way ab. 9 m. N of Rome, just W of the Tiber; scene 312 A.D. of Constantine's victory over Maxentius who, in trying to escape to Rome over the Tiber, was drowned in crossing the **Mil·vi·an Bridge** \ˌmil-vē-ən-\ (*Lat.* **Pons Mul·vi·us** \'pänz-'məl-vē-əs\; *mod.* **Pon·te Mol·le** \ˌpon-tā-'mȯ-(ˌ)lā\) just N of Rome; the battle, usually called the "battle of Milvian Bridge," is associated with the legend of the flaming cross and the words, *in hoc signo vinces* ("by this sign thou shalt conquer"), which appeared in the heavens and led Constantine to accept Christianity.

Saxe \'säks\. French name of Saxony (*q.v.*) used in English chiefly in names of former duchies in Thuringia which from 1485 to 1547 was in the electorate of Saxony; in the 19th cent. these were **Saxe–Al·ten·burg** \-'äl-tᵊn-ˌbu̇(ə)rg\ in the E, **Saxe–Wei·mar–Ei·se·nach** \-'vī-ˌmär-'īz-ᵊn-ˌäk, -ˌäk\ in the N and W and SE (grand duchy after 1815), **Saxe–Mei·ning·en** \-'mī-niŋ-ən\ in the SW, and **Saxe–Go·tha** \-'gōt-ə, -'gō-thə\ in the NW, all made part of Thuringia 1920, and **Saxe–Co·burg** \-'kō-ˌbərg\ in the S, made part of Bavaria 1920.

Saxe–Co·burg–Go·tha \-'kō-ˌbərg-'gōt-ə, -'gō-thə\ *or Ger.* **Sach·sen–Co·burg und Go·tha** \'zäk-sən-'kō-ˌbu̇(ə)rg-u̇nt-'gō-(ˌ)tä\. Name of Saxe-Coburg after it acquired Gotha 1826.

Sax·on Switzerland \'sak-sən-\ *or Ger.* **Säch·si·sche Schweiz** \ˌzek-si-shə-'shfīts\. Mountainous region, Dresden dist., East Germany, SE of Dresden.

Sax·o·ny \'sak-s(ə-)nē\ *or Ger.* **Sach·sen** \'zäk-sən\. Former German state, now part of East Germany.

History: Occupied by the Saxons who controlled much of N Germany W of the Elbe until finally subdued by Charlemagne 772–804 A.D.; as duchy of East Frankish kingdom, repulsed Wends and incorporated Thuringia; its duke elected German emperor (Henry I, first of Saxon line 919); extended E of the Elbe by Henry the Lion from whom Frederick Barbarossa took duchy, splitting it up 1180; march of Meissen on lower Elbe the nucleus of new duchy of Saxony which became an electorate; in 15th cent., electoral and ducal Saxony (which broke into separate small duchies) belonged to two lines of rulers; elector an active participant, usually on Austrian side, in 18th cent. wars; became kingdom 1806; received rule of grand duchy of Warsaw 1807; lost N part of territory to Prussia (became Prussian province of Saxony) 1815; rest of kingdom free state in German Empire 1871–1918; republic 1918; lost status as free state 1933–35; part of Soviet-occupied sector of Germany 1945; divided 1952 bet. the East German districts of Cottbus, Dresden, Karl-Marx-Stadt, and Leipzig.

Say \'sā\. Town, W Niger, W Africa, on Niger river ab. 30 m. SE of Niamey; marked the boundary bet. British and French territory 1890–98; district ceded to France 1898.

Sa·yan Mountains \sə-'yän-\. Mountain range extending E and W bet. Tuva A.S.S.R. and the Krasnoyarsk Krai and Irkutsk Oblast of the Russian S.F.S.R., U.S.S.R.; average height 7000 to 9000 ft.; highest peak Munku-Sardyk 11,451 ft.; Siberian side is steep; at ab. 92°E pierced by the upper Yenisei.

Say·brook \'sā-ˌbru̇k\. 1 *or officially* **Old Saybrook.** Residential town, SE Middlesex co., S Connecticut, on Long Island Sound, on W bank of Connecticut river opp. Old Lyme; pop. (1970c) 8468; settled by Dutch 1623; fortified by Gov. Winthrop of Massachusetts Bay Colony 1635; incorporated 1854.

2 Subdivision of town of Old Saybrook (see 1, above), Connecticut.

3 Town, Connecticut. See DEEP RIVER 2.

Saydā. See SIDON.

Sayre \'sā-ər, 'se(ə)r\. 1 City, ⊗ of Beckham co., W Oklahoma, 43 m. WSW of Clinton; pop. (1970c) 2712; gas and oil wells; diversified agriculture; Sayre Junior Coll. (1938).

2 Borough, Bradford co., N Pennsylvania, on Susquehanna river at New York border; pop. (1970c) 7434; knit goods, hardware, lumber, dairy products.

Sayre·ville \'sā-ər-ˌvil, 'se(ə)r-\. Borough, Middlesex co., cen. New Jersey, on Raritan Bay inlet 5 m. ESE of New Brunswick; pop. (1970c) 32,508.

Sayr Usa \'sīr-'ü-sə\ *or* **Sair·us·su** \'sīr-'ü-sə\. Village, SE Mongolian People's Republic, on N edge of the Gobi.

Sa·yu·la \sə-'yü-lə\. Town, Jalisco state, W cen. Mexico, on **Lake Sayula,** SW of Lake Chapala; munic. pop. (1970p) 18,878.

Say·ville \'sā-ˌvil\. Unincorporated community, Suffolk co., SE New York, on Long I. and Great South Bay, ab. 5 m. SW of Patchogue; pop. (1970c) 11,680; summer resort; oyster fishery; truck and dairy farms.

Sa·zan \'säz-ˌän\ *or Ital.* **Sa·se·no** \'sə-'zā-(ˌ)nō\ *also* **Sas·se·no** \sä-'zā-(ˌ)nō, -'zen-(ˌ)ō\ *or anc.* **Sa·son** \'sā-sən\. Small island in N Strait of Otranto at the entrance to the harbor of Vlorë, Albania, opp. the heel of Italy; ab. 4 m. long; ab. 2 sq. m. Seized by Italy Oct. 31, 1914 and held as a naval base until its return by treaty Feb. 1947.

Sá·za·va \'sä-zə-və\ *or Ger.* **Sa·sau** \'zäz-ˌau̇\. River, cen. Czechoslovakia; 135 m. long; flows W into Vltava river 12 m. S of Prague.

Sbeït·la \'zbāt-lə\ *or anc.* **Su·fet·u·la** \sü-'fet-ə-lə\. Town, N cen. Tunisia, N Africa, ab. 100 m. WNW of the port of Sfax and on railroad leading NE to Sousse; pop. (1966c) 5800; ancient town flourished during time of Antoninus and Marcus Aurelius; ruins include the Forum, temples, baths. In World War II taken by Germans Feb. 17–18, 1943; retaken by U.S. forces Mar. 1.

Sca·fa·ti \skä-'fät-ē\. Manufacturing commune, Salerno prov., Campania, S Italy, 14 m. WNW of Salerno; pop. (1968e) 25,429.

Sca·fell \'skȯ-ˌfel\. Mountain, Cumberland, NW England, in the Lake District 11 m. SW of Keswick; 3162 ft.; second highest peak in England.

Scafell Pike. Peak, Cumberland, NW England, in Cumbrian Mts. 1 m. NE of Scafell; 3210 ft.; highest peak in England.

Sca·la Nuo·va, Gulf of \-ˌskäl-ə-nu̇-'ȯ-və\. Italian name of KUŞADASI GULF.

Scaldis. See SCHELDE.

Scald Law. See PENTLAND HILLS.

Scale Force \'skā(ə)l-'fō(ə)rs, -'fȯ(ə)rs\. Waterfall, Lake District, NW England, in Cumberland near Keswick; 125 ft. high.

Scamander. See MENDERES 2.

Scan·dia \'skan-dē-ə\. Ancient name of S Scandinavian peninsula.

Scan·dia·no \'skän-dē-'ä-(ˌ)nō, -'dyä-\. Commune, Reggio nell'Emilia prov., Emilia-Romagna, N Italy, 8 m. S by E of Reggio nell'Emilia; pop. (1968e) 15,848.

Scan·dic·ci \skän-'dē-chē\. Commune, Firenze prov., Tuscany, W Italy, ab. 3 m. SW of Florence; pop. (1968e) 40,-230.

Scan·di·na·via \ˌskan-də-'nā-vē-ə, -vyə\. 1 Ancient name of the country of the Norsemen.

2 Name of region encompassing Denmark, Norway, and Sweden; sometimes expanded to incl. Finland and Iceland.

Scania. See SKÅNE.

Scan·tic \'skant-ik\. River, N cen. Connecticut; rises in Hampden co., S Massachusetts, flows SW into Hartford co., N Connecticut, and into Connecticut river N of Windsor.

Scapa Flow \ˌskap-ə-'flō\. Sea basin in Orkney Is., off N coast of Scotland; 15 m. long and 8 m. wide; chief British naval base in World War I; in it Germans scuttled their fleet after the war June 21, 1919; in World War II again a major naval base which was closed 1956.

Scar·ba \'skär-bə\. Island in the Inner Hebrides, N of Jura, off W coast of Scotland; 9 sq. m.; height 1470 ft.

Scar·boro *or* **Scar·bor·ough** \'skär-ˌbər-ə, -ˌbə-rə, -b(ə-)rə\. Town, Cumberland co., SW Maine, 7 m. S of Portland; pop. (1970c) 7845.

Scar·bor·ough \'skär-ˌbər-ə, -ˌbə-rə, -b(ə-)rə\. 1 Town, Maine. See SCARBORO.
2 Municipal borough, North Riding, Yorkshire, N England on North Sea 37 m. N of Hull; pop. (1971p) 44,370; seaport and seaside resort; site of Bronze Age village and of ancient Roman watchtower. Chartered 1181; a seaside resort since the late 17th cent.
3 Town, Tobago. See TOBAGO.

Scardona. See SKRADIN.

Scarp \'skärp\. Small island of the Outer Hebrides, W of the island of Lewis with Harris, off NW coast of Scotland; 3 m. long; administratively a part of Inverness co.

Scarpanto. See KARPATHOS.

Scarpanto Strait. See KARPATHOS STRAIT.

Scarpe \'skärp\. River, Pas-de-Calais dept., N France; 62 m. long; flows into Schelde river.

Scars·dale \'skärz-ˌdāl\. Residential town, Westchester co., SE New York, 20 m. NNE of New York City; pop. (1970c) 19,229.

Scat·tery Island \'skat-ə-rē-\. See KILRUSH.

Sceaux \'sō\. Town, Hauts-de-Seine dept., N France, S of Paris; pop. (1968c) 19,913; site of castle, destroyed at the Revolution, which was scene during 17th cent. of literary court of the duchesse du Maine; present castle built 19th cent.

Schaan \'shän\. Town, W Liechtenstein, ab. 2 m. NNW of Vaduz; pop. (1970e) 3878.

Schaer·beek *or Flem.* **Schaar·beek** \'skär-ˌbāk\. Commune, Brabant prov., cen. Belgium, a NE suburb of Brussels; pop. (1969e) 119,810.

Scha·fer \'shā-fər\. Village, former ⊗ of McKenzie co., W North Dakota, near **Schafer Springs.**

Schaff·hau·sen \shäf-'hau̇z-ᵊn\. 1 Swiss canton. See table at SWITZERLAND.
2 Commune, its ✻, N cen. Switzerland, on Rhine river 23 m. N of Zurich; pop. (1970c) 37,035; textiles, watches; tourism; 11th cent. minster, town hall, gates and towers, castle; owes industrial development to power derived from Schaffhausen Falls in Rhine river.

Schaffhausen Falls *or* **Falls of the Rhine** *or Ger.* **Rhein·fall** \'rīn-ˌfäl\. Waterfall in Rhine river near Schaffhausen, Switzerland; 65 ft. high and 377 ft. wide.

Schar·hörn \'shär-ˌhərn\. Small island in Heligoland Bight, West Germany, at mouth of Elbe river.

Schässburg. See SIGHIŞOARA.

Schaulen. See SIAULIAI.

Schaum·burg \'shȯm-ˌbərg\. Village, Cook and Du Page cos., NE Illinois, 25 m. NW of Chicago; pop. (1970c) 18,-730.

Schaumburg–Lip·pe \'shau̇m-ˌbu̇(ə)rg-'lip-ə\. Former German state, now part of West Germany; 131 sq. m.; ✻ Bückeburg; former principality, founded 1613; divided 1640 into Brunswick-Lüneburg, Hesse-Cassel, Lippe; became republic 1918; lost sovereignty to Germany 1933–35; in 1946 made part of Lower Saxony state.

Schef·fer·ville \'shef-ər-ˌvil\. Town, Saguenay co., NE Quebec, Canada, 260 m. N of Chicoutimi; pop. (1971p) 3277; iron ore.

Scheggia Pass. See table at APENNINES.

Schei·degg \'shī-ˌdek\. Village, Bern canton, cen. Switzerland, E of Lauterbrunnen in the Bernese Alps; alt. 6762 ft.; resort and starting point of Jungfrau railway; lies on **Little Scheidegg** (*Ger.* **Klei·ne Scheidegg** \ˌklī-nə-\), pass N of the Jungfrau and leading from Lauterbrunnen to Grindelwald; noted for view; to NE is **Great Scheidegg** (*Ger.* **Gros·se Scheidegg** \ˌgrō-sə-\), pass at 6434 ft. leading from Grindelwald to the valley of the Aare; just NW of the Wetterhorn.

Schel·de \'skel-də\ *or* **Scheldt** \'skelt\ *or Fr.* **Es·caut** \es-kō\ *or anc.* **Scal·dis** \'skal-dəs\. Navigable river, W Europe; 270 m. long; rises in Aisne dept., N France, flows N and NE through W Belgium to the city of Antwerp, turns NW and empties into the North Sea through two estuaries, East Schelde and West Schelde, in Netherlands.

Sche·nec·ta·dy \skə-'nek-təd-ē\. 1 County in E New York. See table at NEW YORK.
2 City, its ⊗, on Mohawk river 13 m. NW of Albany; pop. (1970c) 77,958; a major center of the electrical industry, producing generators, radios, electronic equipment; also manufactures jet engines, wire, mica products, paint and varnish, plastics; locomotive works, meat-packing plants, printing and binding plants, atomic research facilities; Union Coll. and Univ. (1795). Settled 1661; village destroyed by Indians 1690; chartered as borough 1765, as city 1798; became center of locomotive building c. 1850 and of electrical industry late 19th cent.

Scher·er·ville \'shir-ər-ˌvil\. Town, Lake co., NW Indiana, 10 m. S of Hammond; pop. (1970c) 3663.

Schertz \'shərts\. Town, Bexar and Guadalupe cos., S cen. Texas, 17 m. NE of San Antonio; pop. (1970c) 4061; agriculture.

Sche·ve·ning·en \'skā-və-ˌniŋ-ə(n)\. Seaside resort, part of the Hague, South Holland prov., SW Netherlands; scene of British naval victory 1653 over the Dutch under Admiral Tromp.

Schie·dam \skē-'däm\. Commune, South Holland prov., SW Netherlands, 3 m. W of Rotterdam near the Meuse; pop. (1970e) 83,049; machinery, glass, anchors and chains; gin distilling, shipbuilding; chartered 1275.

Schie·hal·lion \shē-'hal-yən\. Peak, Perth co., cen. Scotland; 3547 ft.

Schier·mon·nik·oog \'ski(ə)r-ˌmȯ-ni-ˌkōk\. Island, Netherlands, easternmost of the West Frisian Is., 10 m. E of Ameland I.; 8 m. long, 12 sq. m.; lighthouse; administratively a part of Friesland prov.

Schif·fer·stadt \'shif-ər-ˌs(h)tät\. Agricultural commune, SE Rhineland-Palatinate, West Germany, in Rhine valley 7 m. SSW of Ludwigshafen; pop. (1968e) 16,991; prehistoric artifact (called the "Golden Hat") found nearby 1835.

Schildpad Islands. See PENJU ISLANDS.

Schil·ler Park \ˌshil-ər-\. Village, Cook co., NE Illinois, NW suburb of Chicago; pop. (1970c) 12,712.

Schil·tig·heim \'shil-tik-'hīm\. Industrial commune, Bas-Rhin dept., NE France, NW suburb of Strasbourg; pop. (1968c) 29,128; wines.

Schio \'skē-(ˌ)ō\. Manufacturing commune, Vicenza prov., Veneto, NE Italy, near Monti Lessini 16 m. NW of Vicenza; pop. (1968e) 32,176; cathedral.

Schlei \'shlī\ *or Dan.* **Sli** \'slē\. Inlet of the Baltic Sea in E Schleswig-Holstein, West Germany.

Schlei·cher \'s(h)lī-kər\. County in Texas. See table at TEXAS.

Schlesien. See SILESIA.

Schles·wig \'s(h)les-(ˌ)wig, -(ˌ)wik\ *or Dan.* **Sle·svig** \'slis-vē\. 1 Historical region of NW Germany; a former duchy of the Danish crown, now largely in Schleswig-Holstein, West Germany.

History: German mark of Schleswig attached to Holy Roman Empire 934–1027; in 1027 ceded to Denmark; in 14th cent., as Danish fief, came to be ruled by Holstein (*q.v.*), a part of German Empire; from 1460, in personal union with Holstein, ruled by Danish royal house of Oldenburg; its status as part of Schleswig-Holstein (*q.v.*) caused conflict bet. Germany and Denmark and later bet. Prussia and Austria; by agreement, administered by

Prussia 1865–66; northern Schleswig (*Dan.* Nord Slesvig) awarded to Denmark by plebiscite 1920 (see SOUTH JUTLAND).

2 Seaport city, Schleswig-Holstein, West Germany, at W end of Schlei inlet 70 m. NNW of Hamburg; pop. (1969e) 33,265; tanning, distilling, sugar refining, fishing; 13th cent. cathedral. Site of church 850; chartered 1200; Danish capital of Schleswig-Holstein 1721–1848; occupied by Austrians 1864; to Prussia 1865; capital of Prussian province of Schleswig-Holstein 1879–1917.

Schleswig–Hol·stein \-ˈhōl-ˌstīn\. A state of West Germany; 6046 sq. m.; pop. (1970e) 2,561,200; ✱ Kiel; oats, rye, potatoes, sugar beet, wheat; livestock; textiles; shipbuilding.

History: See HOLSTEIN and SCHLESWIG which were duchies held by king of Denmark, although Holstein was also a German state; in 1848–50 became issue of war bet. Germanic Confederation and Denmark because of Danish desire to incorporate Schleswig; in 1863 Danish annexation of Schleswig, contrary to previous agreement involving question of succession to Danish throne, brought war bet. Denmark and Austria and Prussia 1864; under joint administration of Austria and Prussia 1865 whose rivalry for domination of Germany (*q.v.*) was brought to head by Schleswig-Holstein issue in war of 1866; annexed to Prussia as province of Schleswig-Holstein 1866; N part of Schleswig to Denmark 1920, remainder being constituted a state of West Germany 1946.

Schlettstadt. See SÉLESTAT.

Schley \ˈslī\. County in Georgia. See table at GEORGIA.

Schlüsselburg. See PETROKREPOST.

Schmal·kal·den \ˈshmäl-ˌkäl-dən\; *Eng.* **Smal·kald** *or* **Smal·cald** \ˈsmȯl-ˌkȯld\. Manufacturing city, Suhl dist., East Germany, 30 m. SW of Erfurt; pop. (1970e) 14,103; iron goods, machinery; 15th cent. town hall, 16th cent. castle; mentioned 874 A.D.; became city 1227; League of Schmalkalden formed here 1531.

Schmölln \ˈshməln\. Industrial city, Leipzig dist., East Germany, 13 m. NNW of Zwickau; pop. (1970e) 13,866; paper, leather goods, buttons; 16th cent. town hall; chartered 1320.

Schnee·berg \ˈshnā-ˌbe(ə)rg\. 1 City, Karl-Marx-Stadt dist., East Germany, 22 m. SW of Karl-Marx-Stadt; pop. (1970e) 21,234; metalware, lace; 16th cent. church.

2 Highest peak in the Fichtelgebirge, NE Bavaria, West Germany, NE of Bayreuth; 3453 ft.

Schneekoppe. See SNĚŽKA.

Schneidemühl. See PIŁA.

Scho·field \ˈskō-ˌfēld\. City, Marathon co., cen. Wisconsin, on Wisconsin river 4 m. S of Wausau; pop. (1970c) 2577.

Schofield Barracks. City, Honolulu co., Hawaii, 18 m. NW of Honolulu; pop. (1970c) 13,516.

Scho·har·ie \skō-ˈhar-ē\. 1 County in E New York. See table at NEW YORK.

2 Village, its ⊗; pop. (1970c) 1125.

Schö·ne·beck \ˈshə(r)-nə-ˌbek\. City, Magdeburg dist., East Germany, on left bank of Elbe river 10 m. SSE of Magdeburg; pop. (1970e) 46,146; motor vehicles, paints and dyes, cement; salt mines.

Schön·hau·sen \ˌshə(r)n-ˈhau̇z-ᵊn\. Village, Magdeburg dist., East Germany, on the Elbe ab. 35 m. NNE of Magdeburg; Bismarck's birthplace.

Schoo·dic Lake \ˌsküd-ik-\. Lake, cen. Maine, in SE Piscataquis co.

Schoodic Point. Point, SE Hancock co., SE Maine.

School·craft \ˈskül-ˌkraft\. County in Michigan. See table at MICHIGAN.

Schoo·ne·veldt \ˈskō-nə-ˌvelt\. Locality on S shore of the mouth of the Schelde river, Zeeland, SW Netherlands; naval battle off here 1673 bet. the Dutch fleet under de Ruyter and the combined English and French fleets.

Schoo·ten \ˈskōt-ᵊn\ *or* **Scho·ten** \ˈskōt-ᵊn\. Commune, Antwerp prov., N Belgium, just NE of Antwerp; pop. (1969e) 29,464.

Schorn·dorf \ˈshȯrn-ˌdȯrf\. Town, Baden-Württemberg, West Germany, ab. 15 m. W of Stuttgart; pop. (1969e) 21,113.

Schou·ten Islands \ˈskau̇t-ᵊn-, ˈskau̇t-ə-\. 1 *or* **Mi·so·re Islands** \mi-ˌsȯ-rē-\. Island group in the Pacific Ocean across the entrance to Sarera Bay, off N coast of Irian Barat, Indonesia; 1231 sq. m.; chief islands Biak, Supiori, and Numfoor; chief settlement Bosnik on SE coast of Biak; Biak occupied by U.S. troops May 27, 1944, Numfoor on July 6.

2 Group of small islands off NE coast of island of New Guinea; part of Papua New Guinea.

Schou·wen \ˈskau̇-vən\. Island in Zeeland prov., SW Netherlands, in estuary of Schelde river; 88 sq. m.; chief town Zierikzee. See DUIVELAND.

Schram·berg \ˈshräm-ˌbe(ə)rg\. City, Baden-Württemberg, West Germany, 30 m. NE of Freiburg; pop. (1968e) 18,780; clock-making center; paper, furniture.

Schreck·horn, Gross \grōs-ˈshrek-ˌhȯ(ə)rn\. Peak in the Bernese Alps, SW cen. Switzerland, N of the Finsteraarhorn and S of the Wetterhorn; 13,379 ft.

Schroon \ˈskrün\. River, NE New York; ab. 50 m. long; rises in cen. Essex co., flows S through Schroon Lake into Hudson river in cen. Warren co.

Schroon Lake. Lake, Essex co., NE New York; 10 m. long by 1½ m. wide; the Schroon river flows through it.

Schroon Mountain. Peak in Adirondack Mts., Essex co., NE New York; 3200 ft.

Schu·len·burg \ˈshü-lən-ˌbərg\. City, Fayette co., SE cen. Texas, 46 m. SW of Brenham; pop. (1970c) 2294.

Schul·pfor·te *or* **Schul·pfor·ta** \shülp-ˈfȯrt-ə\ *or* **Pfor·ta** \ˈpfȯ(ə)r-tə\. Village, N Hesse, West Germany, 2 m. SW of Naumburg on the Saale; site of school (founded 1543 by Maurice, Duke of Saxony) which occupies a former Cistercian monastery founded 1140.

Schurz, Mount \-ˈshu̇(ə)rts\. Peak, W Park co., NW Wyoming; 11,139 ft.

Schütt, Great. See GREAT SCHÜTT.

Schütt, Little. See SZIGETKÖZ.

Schuy·ler \ˈskī-lər\. 1 Counties in three states of the U.S. See tables at ILLINOIS, MISSOURI, NEW YORK.

2 City, ⊗ of Colfax co., E Nebraska, on Platte river 30 m. W of Fremont; pop. (1970c) 3597; diversified agriculture.

Schuy·ler·ville \ˈskī-lər-ˌvil\. Village and tourist resort, Saratoga co., E New York, on W bank of Hudson river 32 m. N of Albany; pop. (1970c) 1402; settled 1689 and called Saratoga; for history, see SARATOGA 3.

Schuyl·kill \ˈskül-ˌkil, ˈskü-kəl\. 1 River, SE Pennsylvania; 130 m. long; rises in Schuylkill co., E cen. Pennsylvania, flows SE into Delaware river at Philadelphia.

2 County in Pennsylvania. See table at PENNSYLVANIA.

Schuylkill Haven. Borough, Schuylkill co., E cen. Pennsylvania, on Schuylkill river 5 m. S of Pottsville; pop. (1970c) 6125; clothing, footwear; dye works.

Schwa·bach \ˈshfäb-ˌäk\. City, N Bavaria, West Germany, 8 m. SSW of Nürnberg; pop. (1969e) 25,069; metalworking; 15th cent. church; chartered 1371.

Schwaben. See SWABIA.

Schwä·bisch–Gmünd \ˈshfā-bish-gᵊ-ˈmu̇nt\ *also* **Gmünd.** City, Baden-Württemberg, West Germany, 28 m. E of Stuttgart; pop. (1969e) 44,134; chartered as city 1162; free city until 1803 when it passed to Württemberg.

Schwäbisch–Hall \-ˈhäl\ *also* **Hall.** City, Baden-Württemberg, West Germany, 34 m. NE of Stuttgart; pop. (1969e) 23,856; salt mines.

Schwa·ner Mountains \ˌskfän-ər-\. Range in SW cen. Borneo, Indonesia, S of the Kapuas river; highest peak Raja 7474 ft.

Schwang·au \ˈshfäŋ-ˌau̇\. Village, SW Bavaria, West Germany, NE of Füssen; resort; two notable castles (Hohenschwangau and Neuschwanstein).

Schwarz·burg \ˈshfärts-ˌbu̇(ə)rg\. Village, Gera dist., East Germany; ab. 9 m. SW of Rudolstadt.

Schwarze Elster. See ELSTER 1.

Schwar·zen·berg \'shfärt-sən-ˌbe(ə)rg\. City, Karl-Marx-Stadt dist., East Germany, in the Erzgebirge 20 m. SE of Zwickau; pop. (1970e) 14,717; metalware.

Schwarzwald. See BLACK FOREST.

Schwe·chat \'shfä-ˌkät\. Town, Lower Austria, on the Leitha, SE suburb of Vienna; pop. (1961c) 13,403; scene of defeat 1848 of Hungarians by Prince Windisch-Graetz.

Schwedt an der Oder \'shfāt-än-der-'ōd-ər\. City, Frankfurt dist., East Germany, 50 m. NE of Berlin; pop. (1970e) 34,134; tobacco processing; sawmills; founded 1265; to Brandenburg 1469; largely destroyed in World War II.

Schweidnitz. See ŚWIDNICA.

Schwein·furt \'shfīn-ˌfu̇(ə)rt\. City, Bavaria, West Germany, on Main river 66 m. E of Frankfurt am Main; pop. (1969e) 59,402; chemicals; river port; 15th cent. church, 16th cent. town hall; first mentioned 791; made imperial city 1282; in World War II center of German ball-bearing production; heavily bombed by Allied planes 1942–45; taken by U.S. forces Apr. 12, 1945.

Schweiz *or* **Schweizerische Eidgenossenschaft.** See SWITZERLAND.

Schwelm \'shfelm\. Manufacturing city, North Rhine-Westphalia, West Germany, E of Wuppertal; pop. (1969e) 32,969; rubber and iron goods, paper, damask; chartered 1496.

Schwen·ning·en \'shfen-iŋ-ən\. City, Baden-Württemberg, West Germany, 34 m. E of Freiburg; pop. (1969e) 34,954; clock manufacturing center; machinery, footwear, beer.

Schwe·rin \shfā-'rēn\. 1 District of East Germany. See table at GERMANY, EAST.

2 City, its ✱, on SW shore of Lake Schwerin; pop. (1970e) 96,949; cigarettes, ceramics, pharmaceuticals; food processing, shipbuilding (fishing vessels); 13th cent. Gothic cathedral; mentioned 1018; chartered 1160; ✱ of former Mecklenburg state.

Schwerin, Lake *or Ger.* **Schwe·ri·ner See** \'shfā-rin-ər-ˌzā\. Lake, Schwerin dist., East Germany, 8 m. S of Wismar; 14 m. long; 24 sq. m.; max. depth 177 ft.; drains into the Elbe river.

Schwer·te \'shfert-ə\. Industrial city, North Rhine-Westphalia, West Germany, on Ruhr river 7 m. SSE of Dortmund; pop. (1969e) 24,342; iron and nickel ware, textiles; 15th cent. town hall; chartered 1397.

Schwiebus. See ŚWIEBODZIN.

Schwyz *also* **Schwiz** \'shfēts\. 1 Swiss canton. See history and table at SWITZERLAND.

2 Commune, its ✱, E cen. Switzerland, 22 m. E of Lucerne; pop. (1970c) 12,194; tourism.

Schyl. See JIUL.

Sciac·ca \'shäk-ə\. Seaport, Agrigento prov., SW Sicily, Italy, on Mediterranean Sea 30 m. NW of Agrigento; pop. (1968e) 33,524; hot sulfur and ferruginous springs nearby.

Sci·cli \'shē-klē\. Commune, Ragusa prov., SE Sicily, Italy, 9 m. S of Ragusa; pop. (1968e) 24,165.

Scil·la \'sil-ə, 'shē-lə\ *or anc.* **Scyl·la** \'sil-ə\. Headland projecting into the Strait of Messina from the coast of Reggio di Calabria prov., S Italy. See CHARYBDIS.

Scil·li·um \'sil-ē-əm\ *or* **Scil·la** \'sil-ə\. Ancient town, Byzacium, Roman province of Africa, near modern Sbeïtla in Tunisia; gives its name to the *Scillitan martyrs,* twelve Christians, seven men and five women, executed in Carthage July 17, 180 A.D., whose martyrdom is the earliest on record for the Roman province of Africa.

Scil·ly Isles \'sil-ē-\ *or* **Scilly Islands** *or* **Isles of Scilly.** 1 Group of 140 small islands off Lands End, SW England; 6 sq. m.; pop. (1971p) 2428; main town Hugh Town; administratively a part of Cornwall; tourism, market gardening, and flower growing; formerly a haunt of pirates, and later of smugglers.

2 *or Fr.* **Îles Scilly** \ēl-sē-lē\. Group of islets forming atoll, W Society Is., S Pacific Ocean, ab. 150 m. W of Bora Bora.

Scio. See CHIOS.

Sci·o·to \sī-'ōt-ə\. 1 River, cen. and S Ohio; ab. 237 m. long; rises in Auglaize co., W Ohio, flows E, then S through Columbus and Chillicothe to empty into Ohio river at Portsmouth, S Scioto co., S Ohio.

2 County in Ohio. See table at OHIO.

Scit·u·ate \'sich-(ə-)wət\. 1 Town, Plymouth co., SE Massachusetts, on Atlantic Ocean 16 m. ENE of Brockton; pop. (1970c) 16,973; summer resort; truck and fruit farms.

2 Town, Providence co., N Rhode Island, W of Cranston; pop. (1970c) 7489; settled 1710.

Scituate Dam *and* **Scituate Reservoir.** See GAINER MEMORIAL DAM.

Sco·bey \'skō-bē\. City, ⊗ of Daniels co., NE Montana; pop. (1970c) 1486; coal mines, oil wells; grain farms.

Scodra. See SHKODËR 2.

Sco·field Reservoir \'skō-ˌfēld-\. Reservoir in NW Carbon co., E cen. Utah.

Sco·glit·ti \ˌskȯl-'yē-tē\. Town on S coast of Sicily, Italy, SE of Gela; in World War II a beachhead in Allied invasion of Sicily, secured by U.S. forces July 11, 1943.

Scone \'skün\. Parish, Perth co., Scotland, just NE of Perth; pop. (1961c) 3713; New Scone is a modern village, Old Scone site of abbey founded 1115, destroyed 1559; Scottish kings crowned at Scone until 1651; the *Stone of Scone* or *Stone of Destiny* upon which early Scottish kings sat at coronation is said to have been brought to Scone by Kenneth MacAlpin (d. ?858 A.D.) from a castle on Loch Etive; it was taken to England by Edward I 1296 and is now in Westminster Abbey beneath the coronation chair.

Sconset. See SIASCONSET.

Sco·pus, Mount \-'skō-pəs\ *or Heb.* **Har HaZofim** \ˌhär-ˌhä-zə-'fēm\. Mountain, N extension of the Mount of Olives, NE of Jerusalem, Israel; 2694 ft. Site of old campus of Hebrew Univ., dedicated 1925; an Israeli exclave surrounded by Jordanian-held territory 1949–67; reunited with Israel after the 1967 Arab-Israeli war.

Scores·by Sound \ˌskō(ə)rz-bē-, ˌskȯ(ə)rz-\. Large inlet of Norwegian Sea on E coast of Greenland, in cen. part just N of 70°N; has many fjords and two large islands; length of NW fjord 280 m. On N side of entrance is Eskimo and Danish settlement of **Scores·by·sund** \-ˌsu̇n\, established 1925.

Scotch Plains \'skäch-\. Urban township, Union co., NE New Jersey, 10 m. W of Elizabeth; pop. (1970c) 22,279.

Sco·tia \'skō-shə\. 1 Village, Schenectady co., E New York, on Mohawk river 15 m. NW of Albany; pop. (1970c) 8224; residential suburb.

2 Medieval Latin name of Scotland, still sometimes used poetically and in the modern names Nova Scotia and Scotia Sea.

Scotia Sea. Part of South Atlantic SE of Falkland Is. and South America; bordered by South Sandwich Is., South Georgia I., and South Orkney Is.

Scot·land \'skät-lənd\. 1 North part of the island of Great Britain, a part of the United Kingdom of Great Britain and Northern Ireland, bounded on N by the Atlantic Ocean, on E by the North Sea, on S by England and the Irish Sea, and on W by the Atlantic Ocean; 29,797 sq. m.; pop. (1971p) 5,230,152; ✱ Edinburgh. *Physical features:* Greatest length of mainland 274 m., Mull of Galloway to Cape Wrath (see also DUNNET HEAD and JOHN O'GROAT'S HOUSE); greatest width 154 m. Divided physically into three regions: (1) Highlands (see NORTHERN HIGHLANDS), nearly two thirds of N part of country, comprising the Grampians and many smaller ranges; highest Ben Nevis 4406 ft.; noted for scenery; (2) Central Lowlands, valleys of the Clyde, Tay, and Forth; (3) Southern Uplands, in S, with ranges of hills in which highest points are 2600–2700 ft.; Cheviot Hills and Tweed river on English border. Includes three large island groups: Shetland Is. in N, Orkney Is., separated from mainland by Pentland Firth, and Hebrides (*qq.v.*), and many islands off W coast (largest Mull, Islay, Jura, Arran, Bute, Rum, etc.); has many deep inlets (firths): Forth, Clyde, Moray, Solway, Lorn. *Chief products:* Wheat, barley, oats, potatoes; livestock raising, fishing; coal; manufacturing: textiles, agricultural machinery, electrical apparatus, whisky; shipbuilding; tourism. *Chief cities:* Edinburgh, Glasgow, Dundee, Aberdeen, Paisley. Divided into the following 33 counties (for pronunciation of their names, see their individual entries):

NAME	AREA (sq. m.)	POP. (1971p)	CO. SEAT
Aberdeen	1,971	319,887	Aberdeen
Angus	874	279,396	Forfar
Argyll	3,110	59,909	Lochgilphead
Ayr	1,131	361,074	Ayr
Banff	630	43,501	Banff
Berwick	457	22,523	Duns
Bute	218	13,237	Rothesay
Caithness	686	27,754	Wick
Clackmannan	55	45,553	Alloa
Dumfries	1,075	88,215	Dumfries
Dunbarton	242	237,518	Dunbarton
East Lothian	267	55,891	Haddington
Fife	505	326,989	Cupar
Inverness	4,211	89,545	Inverness
Kincardine	382	26,050	Stonehaven
Kinross	82	6,422	Kinross
Kirkcudbright	897	27,450	Kirkcudbright
Lanark	897	1,524,848	Hamilton
Midlothian	366	595,631	Edinburgh
Moray	476	51,485	Elgin
Nairn	163	11,049	Nairn
Orkney	376	17,075	Kirkwall
Peebles	347	13,675	Peebles
Perth	2,493	127,138	Perth
Renfrew	225	362,144	Paisley
Ross and Cromarty	3,089	58,267	Dingwall
Roxburgh	665	41,942	Jedburgh
Selkirk	268	20,868	Selkirk
Stirling	451	208,956	Stirling
Sutherland	2,029	13,053	Dornoch
West Lothian	120	108,474	Linlithgow
Wigtown	487	27,335	Wigtown
Zetland	552	17,298	Lerwick

History: Occupied by Picts when invaded by Romans after 80 A.D.; area south of rampart from Firth of Forth to Clyde river held briefly by Romans (see GREAT BRITAIN); in 5th cent., included four kingdoms: of the Picts in highlands N of Forth, of Scots (of Irish extraction) in W highlands, of Strathclyde in S, and a part in SE belonging to Anglo-Saxon kingdom of Northumbria; Picts converted to Christianity by St. Columba c. 565; in 685 Picts broke Anglo-Saxon power on border; invaded by Norse from late 8th cent.; Picts conquered Scots in 9th cent. and Lothian and Strathclyde were added by Malcolm II (1005–34) to unite Scottish kingdom; from 11th cent., came under anglicizing influence; its ruler was forced to do homage to English crown 1174, the source of frequent future disputes; in war with England, defeated in 1304, but in 1314 won independence under Robert Bruce at Bannockburn; ruled by house of Stuart 1371–1688; acquired Orkneys and Shetlands 1472; in frequent intermittent conflict with England until accession of King James VI of Scotland as James I of England brought about personal union of two kingdoms 1603; united with England by Parliamentary act 1707 (see GREAT BRITAIN).

2 Counties in two states of the U.S. See tables at MISSOURI and NORTH CAROLINA.

Scotland Neck. Town, Halifax co., NE North Carolina, 25 m. ENE of Rocky Mount; pop. (1970c) 2869.

Scot·land·ville \ˈskät-lən(d)-ˌvil\. Unincorporated urban community, East Baton Rouge parish, Louisiana, 5 m. N of Baton Rouge; pop. (1970c) 22,557; Southern University and Agricultural and Mechanical Coll. (1880).

Scott \ˈskät\. 1 Name of counties in eleven states of the U.S. See tables at ARKANSAS, ILLINOIS, INDIANA, IOWA, KANSAS, KENTUCKY, MINNESOTA, MISSISSIPPI, MISSOURI, TENNESSEE, VIRGINIA.

2 *or formerly* **Scott Field.** United States Air Force base, 6 m. E of Belleville, St. Clair co., Illinois; U.S. Air Force Technical School, established 1917.

3 Urban township, Allegheny co., SW Pennsylvania, SW of Pittsburgh; pop. (1970c) 21,856.

Scott, Cape. Cape, NW tip of Vancouver I., off W British Columbia, Canada.

Scott, Mount. 1 Peak on S cen. boundary of Siskiyou co., N California; 7850 ft.

2 Peak, Wichita Mountains, SW Oklahoma; 2464 ft.; highest point in range.

3 Peak, W Klamath co., near E shore of Crater Lake, S Oregon; 8926 ft.

Scott City. City, ⊗ of Scott co., W Kansas, 72 m. NW of Dodge City; pop. (1970c) 4001; oil wells; dairy, grain, poultry farms.

Scott·dale \ˈskät-ˌdāl\. Borough, Westmoreland co., SW Pennsylvania, 17 m. NNE of Uniontown; pop. (1970c) 5818; castings, lumber, coke; coal mines; agriculture.

Scott Field. See SCOTT 2.

Scott Island. Small island N of Ross Sea, Ross Dependency, Antarctica, ab. 315 m. NE of Cape Adare, 67°24′S, 179°55′W.

Scott Islands. Group of small islands in Pacific Ocean off extreme NW tip of Vancouver I., British Columbia, Canada; meteorological station.

Scott Peak. Highest mountain in Bitterroot Range, E Idaho; 11,393 ft.

Scotts·bluff \ˈskäts-ˌbləf\. City, Scotts Bluff co., W Nebraska, on North Platte river 20 m. E of Wyoming border; pop. (1970c) 14,507; dairy products, flour, fertilizer; summer resort; diversified agriculture; Scotts Bluff County Junior Coll. (1926), Hiram Scott Coll. (1965).

Scotts Bluff. 1 Butte, Scotts Bluff co., W Nebraska; 4662 ft.; site of **Scotts Bluff National Monument** (see UNITED STATES, *National Monuments*).

2 County in Nebraska. See table at NEBRASKA.

Scotts·boro \ˈskäts-ˌbər-ə, -ˌbə-rə\. City, ⊗ of Jackson co., NE Alabama; pop. (1970c) 9324; lumber; center of agricultural region.

Scotts·burg \ˈskäts-ˌbərg\. Town, ⊗ of Scott co., SE Indiana, 27 m. N of New Albany; pop. (1970c) 4791.

Scotts·dale \ˈskäts-ˌdāl\. 1 City, Maricopa co., SW cen. Arizona, E suburb of Phoenix; pop. (1970c) 67,823; residential; ceramics, women's clothing.

2 Town, NE Tasmania, Australia, 28 m. NE of Launceston; pop. (1970e) 3820; in fruit-orchard and poultry district; tin and gold mined nearby.

Scotts·ville \ˈskäts-ˌvil\. Town, ⊗ of Allen co., S Kentucky, 23 m. SE of Bowling Green; pop. (1970c) 3584; tobacco, fruit, livestock farms.

Scran·ton \ˈskrant-ᵊn\. Commercial and industrial city, ⊗ of Lackawanna co., NE Pennsylvania, 20 m. W of Lake Wallenpaupack; pop. (1970c) 103,564; textiles, clothing, electronic equipment, furniture, plastic, canvas, and metal products, paints and varnishes, printing supplies; coal mines; Univ. of Scranton (1888), Lackawanna Junior Coll. (1894), Marywood Coll. (1915). Settled 1788; incorporated as borough 1853, as city 1866.

Screv·en \ˈskriv-ən\. County in Georgia. See table at GEORGIA.

Scroo·by \ˈskrü-bē\. Village, Nottinghamshire, cen. England, ab. 18 m. E of Sheffield; home of William Brewster and other Pilgrims who later founded Plymouth colony in New England.

Scru·ton Peak \ˌskrüt-ᵊn-\. Mountain, Pennington co., SW South Dakota; 5950 ft.

Scu·gog, Lake \-ˈskyü-ˌgäg\. Lake at junction of Ontario, Durham, and Victoria cos., SE Ontario, Canada; 39 sq. m.; connects with Trent Canal by Scugog river.

Scultenna. See PANARO.

Scun·thorpe \ˈskən-ˌthȯ(ə)rp\. Municipal borough, the Parts of Lindsey, Lincolnshire, E England, 18 m. WSW of

Hull; pop. (1971p) 70,880; iron and steel, tar, building materials, footwear, machinery.

Scupi. See SKOPJE.

Scur·dy Ness \ˌskərd-ē-ˈnes\. Headland on E coast of Scotland, S of Montrose; lighthouse.

Scur·ry \ˈskər-ē, ˈskə-rē\. County in Texas. See table at TEXAS.

Scu·ta·ri \ˈsküt-ə-rē\ *or Serb.* **Ska·dar** \ˈskä-ˌdär\. 1 Province and town, Albania. See SHKODËR.

2 Town, Turkey. See ÜSKÜDAR.

Scutari, Lake *or Albanian* **Li·qen i Shkod·rës** \ˌlēk-ən-ē-ˈshkȯd-rəs\ *or anc.* **Pa·lus La·be·a·tis** \ˌpā-ləs-ˌlā-bē-ˈāt-is\. Lake on boundary bet. Montenegro, SW Yugoslavia, and NW Albania; 143 sq. m.; receives Morača river on the N and drains into Bunë river in Albania; Shkodër is at its SE end.

Scylla. See SCILLA.

Scyros. See SKYROS.

Scyth·ia \ˈsith-ē-ə, ˈsith-\. Ancient name of sections of Europe and Asia now included in U.S.S.R.; the country had undefined boundaries, but the Scythians, a nomadic and savage people, dwelt chiefly in the steppes N and NE of the Black Sea and in the region E of Aral Sea. They are mentioned as early as the 7th cent. B.C. when they were driven out of Media; in 2d cent. B.C. they were conquered by the Sarmatians and a little later practically disappeared.

Scythopolis. See BET SHE'AN.

Sea Bright \ˈsē-ˌbrīt\. Borough, Monmouth co., New Jersey, on Atlantic Ocean; pop. (1970c) 1339; resort.

Sea·brook \ˈsē-ˌbru̇k\. 1 Town, Rockingham co., SE New Hampshire, on Atlantic Ocean 13 m. S of Portsmouth; pop. (1970c) 3053.

2 City, Harris co., SE Texas, on Galveston Bay 25 m. SE of Houston; pop. (1970c) 3811; boats, canvas products; truck farming.

Sea Cliff. Residential village, Nassau co., SE New York, on Long I., on Long Island Sound 21 m. ENE of New York City; pop. (1970c) 5890.

Sea·ford. 1 \ˈse-fərd\. City, Sussex co., Delaware, on Nanticoke river 15 m. W of Georgetown; pop. (1970c) 5587; nylon, feed; truck and fruit farms.

2 \ˈse-fərd\. Urban community (unincorporated), Nassau co., SE New York, on Long Island E of New York City; pop. (1970c) 17,379.

3 \ˈsē-fərd, sē-ˌfō(ə)rd\. Urban district, East Sussex, S England; pop. (1971p) 16,196; seaside resort.

Sea·forth \ˈsē-ˌfō(ə)rth, -ˌfō(ə)rth\. Town, Huron co., SE Ontario, Canada, 22 m. SE of Goderich; pop. (1971p) 2138.

Seaforth, Loch. Inlet of the Minch on E coast of island of Lewis with Harris in the Outer Hebrides, off NW coast of Scotland.

Sea Gardens. Eastern part of harbor of Nassau, New Providence I., Bahama Is.

Sea·go·ville \ˈsē-gō-ˌvil\. Town, Dallas co., NE Texas, 17 m. SE of Dallas; pop. (1970c) 4390.

Sea·ham \ˈsē-əm\ *or formerly* **Seaham Harbour.** Urban district, Durham, N England, 16 m. SE of Newcastle upon Tyne; pop. (1971p) 23,410.

Sea Islands. Chain of islands in Atlantic Ocean off coasts of South Carolina, Georgia, and Florida; noted for the production of sea-island cotton.

Seal \ˈsē(ə)l\. River, N Manitoba, Canada; ab. 240 m. long; flows E through a chain of lakes into Hudson Bay.

Seal, Cape. Cape, S cen. coast of Cape Province, Rep. of South Africa.

Sea·lark Channel \ˌsē-lärk-\. Channel, bet. Guadalcanal and Florida Is., SE Solomon Is., W Pacific Ocean; ab. 3 m. wide. See FLORIDA ISLAND.

Seal Beach. Resort city, Orange co., SW California, on Pacific Ocean 8 m. below Long Beach; pop. (1970c) 24,441; chemicals; truck farms.

Seale \ˈsē(ə)l\. Town, a ⊗ of Russel co. (see PHENIX CITY), E Alabama.

Seal Islands. See LOBOS ISLANDS.

Seal Rock. Island in Pacific Ocean, in Lincoln co., W Oregon.

Sea·ly \ˈsēl-ē\. City, Austin co., SE cen. Texas, ab. 48 m. W of Houston; pop. (1970c) 2685; agriculture.

Sea of Rybinsk. See RYBINSK RESERVOIR.

Sea Point. Town, Cape Province, S Rep. of South Africa, suburb (including Green Point) 4 m. W of Cape Town on Table Bay.

Sear·cy \ˈsər-sē\. 1 County in Arkansas. See table at ARKANSAS.

2 City, ⊗ of White co., NE cen. Arkansas, 48 m. NE of Little Rock; pop. (1970c) 9040; cotton gins, sawmills; strawberries; Harding Coll. (1924).

Searles Lake \ˈsər(-ə)lz-\. Lake, N San Bernardino co., SE California; extends a little way into Inyo co.; important source of potash and borates.

Sea·side \ˈsē-ˌsīd\. 1 City, Monterey co., W California, N of Monterey; pop. (1970c) 35,395; fruit.

2 City and seaside resort, Clatsop co., NW corner of Oregon, on Pacific Ocean 15 m. S of Astoria; pop. (1970c) 4402; summer resort; crab and clam fisheries.

Sea·ton Valley \ˈsēt-ᵊn-\. Urban district, Northumberland, N England, NE of Newcastle upon Tyne; pop. (1971p) 32,011; bricks, ceramics; extensive coal mines.

Seat Pleas·ant \sēt-ˈplez-ᵊnt\. Town, Prince Georges co., S cen. Maryland, 6 m. E of Washington; pop. (1970c) 7217.

Se·at·tle \sē-ˈat-ᵊl\. Commercial and industrial city, ⊗ of King co., W cen. Washington, bet. Elliott Bay of Puget Sound and Lake Washington (*q.v.*); pop. (1970c) 530,831; seaport; largest city in the state and the commercial, industrial, and financial center of the Pacific northwest; ships coal, grain, tallow; fish and timber market; supply center for fishing and lumbering industries; produces aircraft, aluminum products, iron and steel, clothing, lumber, flour; shipyards, railroad shops, fruit and vegetable canneries; tourist and yachting center. Univ. of Washington (1861), Seattle Pacific Coll. (1891), Seattle Univ. (1892), Shoreline Community Coll. (1964), Seattle Community Coll. (1966).

History: First settled 1851; platted and became ⊗ 1853; incorporated 1869; suffered from severe fire 1889; became important commercial center during Alaskan gold rush 1897 ff.; further expanded as seaport following opening of Panama Canal 1914 and during World War I; became a center of the aircraft industry during World War II. Site of Alaska-Yukon Pacific Exposition 1909 and of Century 21 International Exposition 1962.

Seaturo, Mount. See NAVOTUVOTU.

Se·ba·go Lake \sə-ˈbā-(ˌ)gō-\. Lake in cen. Cumberland co., SW Maine; ab. 13 m. long by 10 m. wide; resort.

Sebaste *or* **Sebastia.** See SIVAS 2.

Se·bas·tian \si-ˈbas-chən\. County in Arkansas. See table at ARKANSAS.

Sebastian, Cape. Cape on W coast of Curry co., SW corner of Oregon.

Se·bas·tián Viz·ca·í·no Bay \ˌseb-ə-ˈstyän-ˌvis-kä-ˌē-nō-\. Large inlet of Pacific Ocean on W coast of Baja California, Mexico.

Se·bas·ti·cook Lake \si-ˌbas-ti-ˌku̇k-\. Lake, S cen. Maine, near SW boundary of Penobscot co.

Se·bas·to·pol \sə-ˈbas-tə-ˌpül\. City, Sonoma co., W California, 7 m. SW of Santa Rosa; pop. (1970c) 3993.

Sebastopol. See SEVASTOPOL.

Seb·cha di Tau·or·ga \'seb-chə-ˌdē-taù-'ór-gə\ *or* **Sab·khat Tā·wur·ghā'** \'säb-ˌkät-tə-'wùr-gə\. Salt marsh, N Libya, N Africa, extending along W shore of the Gulf of Sidra.

Sebenico. See ŠIBENIK.

Se·ben·ny·tus \si-'ben-ə-təs\ *or mod.* **Sa·man·nud** \ˌsam-ə-'nüd\. City of ancient Egypt, in Nile delta on W bank of Damietta mouth; ruins are SW of Al-Mansūra.

Seb·ha *or* **Sab·hah** \'seb-ˌhä\. Oasis, SW Libya, N Africa; chief town Sebha.

Şe·bin·ka·ra·hi·sar \she-'bin-ˌkä-rə-hi-'sär\ *or anc.* **Ka·ra·his·sar** \ˌkä-rə-hi-'sär\. Town, Giresun prov., NE Turkey; pop. (1965c) 9764; alt. 4860 ft.; built around a citadel. In early days a Roman colony; later a Byzantine frontier station, taken by Turks 1465.

Sebkret el Kourzia. See SABKHAT AL-KURZĪYAH.

Seb·nitz \'zāp-nəts\. City, Dresden dist., East Germany, 24 m. ESE of Dresden; pop. (1970e) 14,181; paper, machinery, artificial flowers.

Se·boe·is Lake \si-ˌbō-əs-\. Lake, SE Piscataquis co., cen. Maine.

Seboekoe. See SEBUKU.

Se·boo·mook Lake \si-ˌbü-mək-\. Lake, cen. Somerset co., W Maine, an expansion of the West Branch of the Penobscot river just E of junction of its headstreams; ab. 12 m. long.

Se·bou *or* **Se·bu** \sə-'bü\. River, NW Morocco; ab. 180 m. long; flows N, then W into Atlantic Ocean N of Rabat; navigable up as far as Fès.

Seb·ra, Bay of \-'seb-rə\. See BIZERTE.

Se·bring \'sē-briŋ\. 1 City, ⊗ of Highlands co., cen. Florida penin., 50 m. SE of Lakeland; pop. (1970c) 7223; citrus orchards.

2 Village, Mahoning co., NE Ohio, 21 m. SW of Youngstown; pop. (1970c) 4954; pottery; dairy farms.

Sebu. See SEBOU.

Se·bu·ku *or Du.* **Se·boe·koe** \sā-'bü-(ˌ)kü\. Small island in SW Makasar Strait, E of Laut I., SE of Borneo, Indonesia.

Se·cau·cus \si-'kò-kəs\. Town, Hudson co., NE New Jersey, 5 m. NNW of Jersey City; pop. (1970c) 13,228; aluminum products, pharmaceuticals, frozen foods, coffee.

Sec·chia \'sek-ē-ə, -'sāk-\. River, N Italy; 97 m. long; rises in the Apennines, flows N into Po river 12 m. SE of Mantua.

Se·chu·ra Bay \sā-ˌchùr-ə-\. Inlet of Pacific Ocean on NW coast of Peru.

Sechura Desert. Desert, N coast of Peru; N–S extent ab. 65 m. long, E–W extent ab. 40 m. wide.

Sec·re·tary Island \ˌsek-rə-ˌter-ē-\. Island off SW coast of South I., New Zealand.

Se·cun·der·a·bad *or* **Si·kan·dar·a·bad** \si-'kən-də-rə-ˌbad, -ˌbäd\. Town and cantonment, N Andhra Pradesh, S cen. India, part of Hyderabad; pop. (1961c) 187,471. Formerly one of the largest of the British military stations in India, with infantry and cavalry posts.

Se·da·lia \si-'dāl-yə\. City, ⊗ of Pettis co., W cen. Missouri, 58 m. W of Jefferson City; pop. (1970c) 22,847; packs and ships agricultural produce; glass, flour, trailers; State Fair Community Coll. (1966); founded 1860.

Se·dan. 1 \si-'dan\. City, ⊗ of Chautauqua co., SE Kansas, 28 m. WSW of Independence; pop. (1970c) 1555; oil wells; grain farms.

2 \sə-'däⁿ, -'dan\. Manufacturing city, Ardennes dept., NE France, on Meuse river 11 m. ESE of Mézières; pop. (1968c) 23,037; woolens, steel pipe, chemicals. Scene of decisive battle of Franco-Prussian War, resulting in French defeat and surrender of Napoleon III with 80,000 men Sept. 2, 1870; occupied by Germany during World War I; taken by Germans in World War II May 1940 and held until retaken by U.S. forces Aug. 31, 1944.

Sedd el Bahr \'sed-al-'bä(ə)r\ *or Turk.* **Sedd·ül·ba·hir** \'sed-ül-bä-'hi(ə)r\. Village with adjacent forts on the S end of Gallipoli Penin., Turkey, Europe; just E of Cape İlyasbaba; one of the landing places of British forces Apr. 1915.

Sedge·moor \'sej-ˌmù(ə)r, -ˌmō(ə)r, -ˌmò(ə)r\. Tract of moorland in Somersetshire, SW England; scene of Duke of Monmouth's defeat July 6, 1685 by Feversham and Churchill.

Sedg·wick \'sej-(ˌ)wik\. Name of counties in two states of the U.S. See tables at COLORADO and KANSAS.

Sedlez. See SIEDLCE.

Sed·li·ce \'sed-lət-ˌsā\ *or Ger.* **Sed·litz** \'zed-ləts, 'sed-\. Town, SW Czech S.R., Czechoslovakia, 11 m. NW of Písek; mineral springs; gave name to Seidlitz powders.

Se·dro Wool·ley \ˌsēd-(ˌ)rō-'wùl-ē\. City, Skagit co., NW Washington, on Skagit river 20 m. SSE of Bellingham; pop. (1970c) 4598; lumbering, agriculture.

Sedunum. See SION.

See·heim \'sē-ˌhām\. Town, S South-West Africa, on Fish river; elev. 2300 ft.; railroad junction point.

See·konk \'sē-ˌkäŋk\. 1 Navigable river, NE Rhode Island; ab. 5 m. long; formed by the widened Blackstone river at Pawtucket; the most northerly point of Narragansett Bay tidewater, flows S into Providence river at Providence.

2 Town, Bristol co., SE Massachusetts, 10 m. NW of Fall River; pop. (1970c) 11,116.

Seeland. See SJÆLLAND.

Seeonee. See SEONI.

Sefid Rud. See SAFĪD RŪD.

Se·frou \sə-'frü\. Town, N cen. Morocco, NW Africa, ab. 20 m. SE of Fès; pop. (1960c) 21,478.

Sef·ton \'sef-tən\. Mountain range in the Southern Alps, W cen. South I., New Zealand; highest peak 10,359 ft.

Seg \'sek\ *or* **Seg Oze·ro** \-'ò-zə-rə\. Lake (*ozero*), Russian S.F.S.R., U.S.S.R.; 303 sq. m.; outlet is Vyg Lake and river to the White Sea.

Se·gau·li *or* **Sa·gau·li** \sə-'gaù-lē\. Town, NW Bihar, NE India, 85 m. N of Patna; former British military station; treaty signed here Mar. 3, 1816 that defined English relations with Nepal.

Se·ges·ta \si-'jes-tə\ *or* **Se·ges·te** \-(ˌ)tē\. Ancient city in NW Sicily; its ruins, near modern Alcamo, include a well-preserved theater. Often in disputes with Selinus; besieged by Dionysius; 10,000 of its men massacred 307 B.C. by Agathocles, tyrant of Syracuse; besieged by Carthaginians during First Punic War.

Segesvár. See SIGHIŞOARA.

Segodunum. See RODEZ.

Segontia. See SIGÜENZA.

Sé·gou \sā-'gü\ *also* **Se·gu** \sā-'gü\. Town on Niger river, S Mali, W Africa, 120 m. ENE of Bamako; met. area pop. (1970e) 300,627.

Se·go·via \si-'gō-vē-ə\. 1 River, Nicaragua. See COCO.

2 Province of cen. Spain. See table at SPAIN.

3 Commune, ✱ of Segovia prov., cen. Spain, 40 m. NNW of Madrid; pop. (1970p) 41,880; rubber and chemical products, cement, flour, fertilizers; a walled town with a restored 14th–15th cent. alcazar, 16th cent. Gothic cathedral, Roman aqueduct (2d cent. A.D., still in use), several Romanesque churches. Founded c. 700 B.C. and important under Romans; taken by Moors early 8th cent. A.D. and reconquered by Alfonso VI 1079; a medieval residence of kings of Castile and León; sacked by French 1808.

Seg Ozero. See SEG.

Se·gre \'sā-(ˌ)grā\. River, Catalonia, NE Spain; 162 m. long; rises in the Pyrenees, flows SW past Lérida into Ebro river.

Segu. See SÉGOU.

Se·guam \sā-'gwäm\. Island of the Andreanof group in the Aleutians, SW Alaska, separated on the E from Amukta I. by Amukta Pass and on the W from Amlia I. by **Seguam Pass.**

Se·guin \sə-'gēn\. City, ⊗ of Guadalupe co., S cen. Texas, 33 m. ENE of San Antonio; pop. (1970c) 15,934; fiberglass, cottonseed oil, flour; oil wells; livestock farms; Texas Lutheran Coll. (1891).

Se·gun·do \sā-'gùn-(ˌ)dō\. River, Córdoba prov., N cen. Argentina; ab. 200 m. long; flows ENE into Mar Chiquita.

Se·gu·ra \sā-ˈgu̇r-ə\. 1 Mountain range mostly in Jaén and Albacete provs., in SE Spain; highest peak 5935 ft.
2 River, SE Spain; 202 m. long; rises in the Segura Mts., flows E and SE into the Mediterranean Sea.

Se·hore \sə-ˈhō(ə)r, -ˈhȯ(ə)r\. Town, W Madhya Pradesh, cen. India, 20 m. WSW of Bhopal; pop. (1961c) 28,489; market town.

Seibo, El. See EL SEIBO.

Seibus. See SEYBOUSE.

Seiche·prey \sesh-ˈprā\. Village, Meurthe-et-Moselle dept., NE France, E of St-Mihiel; pop. (1962c) 107; battle Apr. 20, 1918 during U.S. advance in St-Mihiel sector.

Seierø. See SEJERØ.

Seierø Bight. See SEJERØ BIGHT.

Seihun. See SEYHAN.

Sei·land \ˈsā-ˌlän\. Island in Finnmark co., in Arctic Ocean off NW coast of Norway; 226 sq. m.

Seille \ˈsā(-yə)\. River, Lorraine, NE France; 80 m. long; flows W and NW to the Moselle at Metz; forms part of S boundary of Moselle dept.

Seim \ˈsām\. River, SW cen. U.S.S.R.; 460 m. long; flows through Kursk Oblast of the Russian S.F.S.R. and Sumy Oblast of the Ukrainian S.S.R. to the Desna river E of Chernigov.

Sei·nä·jo·ki \ˈsā-nə-ˌyȯ-kē\. Town, Vaasa prov., SW cen. Finland; pop. (1970e) 20,261; railroad junction point; founded 1931.

Seine \ˈsān, ˈsen\. 1 *or anc.* **Seq·ua·na** \ˈsek-wə-nə\. River, N France; 482 m. long; rises in Côte-d'Or dept., E France; flows NW through Paris and on into the English Channel near Le Havre; navigable for ab. 350 m.
2 Former department of France; officially abolished Jan. 1, 1968.

Seine, Bay of the *or Fr.* **Baie de la Seine** \bād-lä-sen\. Inlet of the English Channel, N coast of Normandy, NW France; along its curving coastline, from Cotentin Penin. on W to mouth of the Seine on E, are many popular spas.

Seine–et–Marne \-ā-ˈmärn\. Department of N France. See table at FRANCE.

Seine–et–Oise \-ā-ˈwäz\. Former department of France; officially abolished Jan. 1, 1968.

Seine–Ma·ri·time \-ˌmä-rē-ˈtēm\ *or formerly* **Seine–In·fé·ri·eure** \-aⁿ-ˌfer-ē-ˈər\. Department of N France. See table at FRANCE.

Seine–St–Denis \-saⁿ-də-ˈnē\. Department of N France. See table at FRANCE.

Se·ir \ˈsē-ər, ˈsi(ə)r\. 1 Country. See EDOM.
2 Mountain range of ancient Edom, along E side of Wadi al-ʻAraba; now in Jordan; highest point Mt. Hor 4367 ft.

Seis de Septiembre. See MORÓN 1.

Seishin. See CH'ŎNGJIN.

Seis·tan \sā-ˈstän\ *also* **Sis·tan** \sē-\. Former province, E Iran; ✱ Nasratabad (now Zābol); now divided bet. Iran and Afghanistan. A depression with much marshland including Lake Helmand; corresponds nearly with ancient Drangiana. Under the Safawids (1502–1736) played important part in Persian history; in 19th cent. was center of dispute bet. Persia and Afghanistan.

Se·je·rø \ˈsī-ər-ˌər\ *or formerly* **Sei·erø** \ˈsī-ər-ər\. Small island off NW coast of Sjælland I., Denmark, in Sejerø Bight; pop. (1965c) 620.

Sejerø Bight *or formerly* **Seierø Bight.** Bay on NW coast of Sjælland I., Denmark.

Sekia el Hamra. See SAGUIET EL HAMRA.

Se·ki·ga·ha·ra \ˌsek-ē-gə-ˈhär-ə\. Town, SW Gifu prefecture, cen. Honshū, Japan, ab. 16 m. WSW of Gifu; pop. (1970c) 10,788; site of battle in 1600 in which the shogun Iyeyasu gained complete control of the government.

Sek·ka, Ras ben \ˈräs-ben-sə-ˈkä\. Cape, N Tunisia; most northerly point of Africa, 37°21′N.

Se·kon·di–Ta·ko·ra·di \ˌsek-ən-ˈdē-ˌtäk-ə-ˈräd-ē\. Seaport and commercial city, ✱ of Western Region, SW Ghana, W Africa, 110 m. WSW of Accra; pop. (1970p) 89,686; connected by rail with Kumasi; has modern port facilities and boatbuilding, cigarette-making, and railway-repair industries. Site of Dutch and British forts in 17th cent.; area ceded to British by Dutch 1872 and became site of principal port of the Gold Coast; made city 1963.

Se·ko·ta *or* **Sa·ko·ta** \sə-ˈkō-tə\. Town, NW Ethiopia, ab. 100 m. NE of Lake Tana; pop. (1970e) 10,300.

Sela. City, ✱ of ancient Edom. See PETRA.

Se·lah \ˈsē-lə\. Town, Yakima co., S Washington, 8 m. NW of Yakima; pop. (1970c) 3070; beer, wine, fruit; fruit-packing plant.

Se·la·jar *or* **Sa·la·jar** *or* **Sa·la·yar** \sə-ˈlä-ˌyär\. Long narrow island in Flores Sea, 11 m. off S coast of SW peninsula of Celebes I., Indonesia, at entrance to the Gulf of Bone, Malay Archipelago; 51 m. long; 259 sq. m. Chief town Benteng, in cen. part of W coast. Chief crops copra, cotton, tobacco, and hemp.

Selajar Strait *or* **Salajar Strait.** Channel bet. Selajar I. and Celebes I. in the Malay Archipelago.

Se·lang·or \sə-ˈlaŋ-ər\. A state of Malaysia, W coast of S Malay Penin., bounded on N by Perak, on E by Pahang and Negri Sembilan, on S and W by Strait of Malacca; 3150 sq. m.; pop. (1970p) 1,629,386; ✱ Shah Alam; generally level with mountain range along E boundary; rubber, rice, pineapples, tin. Crossed by the main railroad line along W coast of peninsula and by the branch from Kuala Lumpur to Port Swettenham, Malaysia's second major port.

History: Overrun by the Dutch 1783–84; made commercial treaty with British 1818 who took control of the state 1874; became part of the Federated Malay States 1895 and of the independent Federation of Malaya 1957; became a state of Malaysia 1963.

Selanik. See SALONIKA.

Se·la·ru *or Du.* **Se·la·roe** \sā-ˈlär-(ˌ)ü\. Island of the Tanimbar group, in S Moluccas, Indonesia, E Malay Archipelago, off S end of Jamdena I.; ab. 32 m. long by 4 to 8 m. wide.

Se·la·tan \sā-ˈlä-ˌtän\ *or Du.* **Tan·djoeng Selatan** \ˈtän-ˌju̇ŋ-\. Cape, S coast of Borneo, Indonesia, projecting into Java Sea, 4°10′S, 114°38′E; southernmost point of the island of Borneo.

Selat Makasar. See MAKASAR STRAIT.

Selat Tebrau. See JOHORE STRAIT.

Selb \ˈzelp\. City, Bavaria, West Germany, 40 m. SSW of Zwickau; pop. (1968e) 18,142; important center of porcelain industry.

Sel·by \ˈsel-bē\. 1 City, ⊗ of Walworth co., N South Dakota; pop. (1970c) 957; agriculture.
2 Urban district, West Riding, Yorkshire, N England, on the Ouse river S of York; pop. (1971p) 10,164; traditional birthplace of King Henry I.

Sel·çuk \sel-ˈchük\ *or formerly* **Aya So·luk** \ˌä-yə-sō-ˈlük\. Village, S İzmir prov., W Turkey, Asia, near site of ancient Ephesus (*q.v.*).

Sel·do·via \sel-ˈdōv-ē-ə, -vyə\. Village near S tip of Kenai Penin., S Alaska, on Cook Inlet.

Se·le \ˈsā-lə\. Short stream, Campania, S Italy; ab. 20 m. long; flows W to Gulf of Salerno ab. 8 m. S of Salerno; divided the U.S. and British beaches in Allied landing at Salerno Sept. 9–10, 1943.

Se·lem·dzha \ˌsel-əm-ˈjä\. River, main tributary of the Zeya in S Khabarovsk Krai, Russian S.F.S.R., U.S.S.R.; 376 m. long; rises in SE spurs of Stanovoi Mts. and flows SW to the Zeya ab. 120 m. NE of Blagoveshchensk.

Se·len·ga \ˌsel-əŋ-ˈgä\. River, N cen. Asia; 620 m. long; rises near Uliastay in W Mongolian People's Republic and flows E; joined by the Orhon near U.S.S.R. border which it crosses just W of Kyakhta, flows N through Buryat A.S.S.R., turns W at Ulan-Ude to enter Lake Baikal on SE.

Sé·les·tat \sā-ləs-ˈtä\ *or Ger.* **Schlett·stadt** \ˈshlet-ˌs(h)tät\. Commune, Bas-Rhin dept., NE France, near Ill river 34 m. SW of Strasbourg; pop. (1970c) 14,635; manufactures cottons and paper. Became free city under the Hohenstaufens; taken by Swedes 1632; taken by French 1634; French rule confirmed by Peace of Westphalia; bombarded and besieged 1815; taken by Germans 1870; reverted to French rule after World War I.

Se·leu·cia \sə-ˈlü-sh(ē-)ə\. Name of several cities in ancient Syria and Asia Minor, esp.: (1) *or* **Seleucia Tra·che·o·tis** \-ˌtrā-kē-ˈōt-əs\. Ancient city, Cilicia, SE Asia Minor, SW of Tarsus, on the Calycadnus (*mod.* Göksu) near its mouth; site of modern Silifke. (2) City, now in ruins, on W bank of Tigris, cen. Iraq, opp. Ctesiphon and ab. 20 m. SSE of Baghdad. Founded by Seleucus Nicator c. 300 B.C. to become chief city of Seleucid Empire; developed extensive trade and at one time was said to have 600,000 inhabitants; superseded by Ctesiphon under the Persians; sacked by Romans c. 162 A.D. See PARTHIA. (3) *or* **Seleucia Pi·e·ria** \-pī-ˈir-ē-ə, -ˈer-\. Ancient port of Antioch, now seaport town, SW Hatay, S Turkey in Asia. See SÜVEYDIYE.

Sel·fridge Field \ˈself-ˌrij-\. United States Air Force base 3 m. NE of Mount Clemens, Macomb co., SE Michigan; built during World War I, much enlarged and improved 1934 and later; 3660 acres.

Seli. See ROKEL.

Se·li·ger \ˈsel-i-gər\. Lake, N Kalinin Oblast, Russian S.F.S.R., U.S.S.R.; 57 m. long; 104 sq. m.; discharges into headwaters of the Volga river.

Se·lins·grove \ˈsē-lənz-ˌgrōv\. Borough, Snyder co., cen. Pennsylvania, on Susquehanna river; pop. (1970c) 5116; mobile homes, furniture, flour; Susquehanna Univ. (1858).

Se·li·nus \si-ˈlī-nəs\. Greek city, S coast of ancient Sicily; its ruins are near Castelvetrano; founded 7th cent. B.C.; destroyed by Carthaginians 409 B.C.; partly rebuilt by Hermocrates 408 B.C.; inhabitants transferred to Lilybaeum 250 B.C.

Sel·kirk \ˈsel-ˌkərk\. **1** Resort town, SE Manitoba, Canada, on Red river 23 m. NNE of Winnipeg, near S end of Lake Winnipeg; pop. (1971p) 9158; lake port, boatbuilding, fishing; iron and steel foundries; truck farms. Established near the Red River Settlement of the earl of Selkirk.

2 *or* **Sel·kirk·shire** \-ˌshi(ə)r, -shər\. County, SE Scotland; area 268 sq. m.; pop. (1971p) 20,868; ⊗ Selkirk; hilly region; chief industry sheep raising. Sir Walter Scott was sheriff of Selkirk for 33 years.

3 Burgh, ⊗ of Selkirk co., SE Scotland, on Ettrick river 30 m. SE of Edinburgh; pop. (1971p) 5687; market town; woolens.

Selkirk Mountains *or* **Sel·kirks** \ˈsel-ˌkərks\. Range of the Rocky Mts., SE British Columbia, Canada, within the Big Bend of the Columbia river; ab. 200 m. long; highest peak Mt. Sir Sanford 11,591 ft. Crossed by the Canadian Pacific Railways at Rogers Pass near the Illecillewaet Glacier (*q.v.*), contains part of Glacier National Park and Mount Revelstoke National Park (see CANADA, *National Parks*).

Sel·la·sia \sə-ˈlā-zh(ē-)ə\. Town in ancient Laconia, SE Peloponnesus, S Greece, ab. 5 m. N of Sparta; scene of battle 222 or 221 B.C. in which Antigonus Doson, king of Macedonia, defeated the Spartans under Cleomenes III.

Selle \ˈsel\. Small river in Nord dept., N France, flowing into Schelde river; scene of fighting Oct. 1918.

Sel·lers·ville \ˈsel-ərz-ˌvil\. Borough, Bucks co., SE Pennsylvania, 19 m. SSE of Allentown; pop. (1970c) 2829; founded 1738.

Sel·lery, Mount \-ˈsel-ər-ē\. Peak, Antarctica, 84°58′S, 172°45′W; 12,779 ft.

Selling Tso. See ZILLING TSO.

Sellore Island. See SAGANTHIT ISLAND.

Selm \ˈzelm\. Industrial commune, North Rhine-Westphalia, West Germany, 20 m. S of Münster; pop. (1968e) 15,543; electrical equipment.

Sel·ma \ˈsel-mə\. **1** Industrial city, ⊗ of Dallas co., SW cen. Alabama, on Alabama river 40 m. W of Montgomery; pop. (1970c) 27,379; cotton, livestock, and pecan market; produces clothing, fertilizer, cigars, yarn, dairy products; meat-packing plants, cotton gins; Selma Univ. (1878); Craig Air Force Base with U.S. Air Force Special Staff School is ab. 5 m. SE of Selma; settled c. 1815, incorporated 1820; Confederate arsenal and supply depot in Civil War, captured by Union troops 1865; in 1965 scene of major non-violent civil rights demonstrations.

2 City, Fresno co., S cen. California, 15 m. SE of Fresno; pop. (1970c) 7459; wine; diversified agriculture.

3 Industrial town, Johnston co., E North Carolina, 27 m. SE of Raleigh; pop. (1970c) 4356; fertilizers, lumber, textiles; livestock, corn.

Sel·mer \ˈsel-mər\. Town, ⊗ of McNairy co., SW Tennessee; pop. (1970c) 3495; agriculture.

Sel·sey Bill \ˌsel-sē-ˈbil\. Headland on S coast of England, E of Portsmouth.

Se·luk·we \si-ˈlək-wē\. Town, cen. Rhodesia, ab. 20 m. SE of Gwelo; munic. pop. (1969p) 8410; center of mining, ranching, and agricultural region.

Selvagens. See SALVAGES.

Sel·vas \ˈsel-vəz\. Extensive forested region of the upper Amazon river basin in N cen. South America.

Selzaete. See ZELZATE.

Se·man \ˈse-ˌmän\ *or formerly* **Se·me·ni** \ˈsem-ə-nē\. River, cen. Albania, formed by confluence of two headstreams N of Berat; 157 m. long; flows W to Adriatic Sea.

Se·mang·ka Bay \sā-ˌmäŋ-kə-\. Bay on S end of Sumatra, Indonesia, W of Lampung Bay; opens on Sunda Strait.

Se·ma·rang *or* **Sa·ma·rang** \sə-ˈmär-ˌäŋ\. **1** Residency, Central Java prov., Indonesia; 2088 sq. m.; ✱ Semarang; mostly level but borders on high mountains in SW; has many short streams and is specially suitable for raising sugar and kapok; also produces coffee; part of early sultanate of Mataram.

2 Seaport city, its ✱, also ✱ of Central Java prov., Indonesia, on N coast railroad ab. 255 m. E of Djakarta; pop. (1961c) 503,153; third port of Java but unprotected against NW monsoon; manufactures machinery and textiles; shipbuilding, fishing; exports rubber, coffee, sugar; univ. (1957); came under Dutch control c. 1748; occupied by Japanese in World War II Feb. 1942–Sept. 1945.

Semendria. See SMEDEREVO.

Semeni. See SEMAN.

Se·me·nov \sə-ˈmyȯ-nəf\. Highest peak of Kirgiz Range, N Kirgiz S.S.R., U.S.S.R.; 15,994 ft.

Semenovka. See ARSENYEV.

Se·me·ru *or Du.* **Se·me·roe** \sə-ˈme(ə)r-(ˌ)ü\ *also* **Sme·roe** \ˈsmer-(ˌ)ü\. Active volcano, E Java I., Indonesia, SE of Malang; 12,060 ft.; highest mountain in Java; joins with Tengger Mts. to the N; erupted 1963.

Se·mi·chi Islands \sə-ˌmē-chē-\. Small island group at W end of Aleutian Is., SW Alaska, in the Near Is. ESE of Attu; includes Shemya (*q.v.*).

Se·mi·di Islands \sə-ˌmēd-ē-\. Group of eight islands off the S coast of Alaska, 56°07′N, 156°44′W.

Semien Mountains. See SIMYEN MOUNTAINS.

Se·mi·na·ra \ˌse-mə-ˈnä-rə\. Commune, Reggio di Calabria prov., Calabria, S Italy, on W coast N of Reggio di Calabria; pop. (1968e) 5551; scene of several battles, esp. that of 1503 in which the French were defeated by the Spanish under García de Paredes.

Sem·i·noe Dam \ˌsem-ə-nō-\. Dam across North Platte river, N Carbon co., S cen. Wyoming; height 295 ft.; completed 1939; impounds water, **Seminoe Reservoir,** for flood control, irrigation, and power.

Sem·i·nole \ˈsem-ə-ˌnōl\. **1** Name of counties in three states of the U.S. See tables at FLORIDA, GEORGIA, OKLAHOMA.

2 City, Seminole co., cen. Oklahoma, 13 m. ESE of Shawnee; pop. (1970c) 7878; carbon black; oil wells and refineries; agriculture.

3 City, ⊗ of Gaines co., NW Texas, 62 m. N of Odessa; pop. (1970c) 5007; oil wells; agriculture.

Se·mi·pa·la·tinsk \ˌsem-i-pə-ˈlä-ˌtin(t)sk\. City, ✱ of Semipalatinsk Oblast, NE Kazakh S.S.R., U.S.S.R., on right bank of Irtysh river 445 m. SE of Omsk; pop. (1970p) 236,000; center of food-processing and meat-packing industries; produces leather goods, textiles, lumber; founded 1718 and transferred to present site 1778.

Semipalatinsk Oblast \-ˈó-bləst, -ˌblast\. Subdivision of the Kazakh S.S.R., U.S.S.R., bounded on N by Altai Krai of Russian S.F.S.R., on NE by East Kazakhstan Oblast, on SE by Sinkiang Uighur, China, on S by Taldy-Kurgan Oblast, on W by Karaganda Oblast, and on NW by Pavlodar Oblast; 69,344 sq. m.; pop. (1970p) 712,000; ✱ Semipalatinsk. Economy predominantly agricultural (esp. grain); has manganese, graphite, copper, gold deposits.

Se·mi·ra·ra Islands \ˌsem-ə-ˌrär-ə-\. Island group bet. SE Mindoro I. and NW Panay I., cen. Phil.; ab. 50 sq. m.; marks S end of Tablas Strait; comprises three large islands, Semirara, Sibay, and Caluya, and several smaller ones.

Sem·i·so·poch·noi \ˌsem-i-sə-ˈpäch-ˌnȯi\. Small island in N part of Rat Is. group, Aleutians, SW Alaska, E of Kiska; sea-lion rookery.

Sem·li·ki \ˈsem-lə-kē\. River, E cen. Africa; ab. 110 m. long; connects Lake Edward and Lake Albert.

Semlin. See ZEMUN.

Sem·me·ring Pass \ˈzem-ə-riŋ-\. Mountain pass in E Alps, Austria, 23 m. SW of Wiener Neustadt, bet. Lower Austria and Styria; alt. 3232 ft.; railroad tunnel.

Sem·nān \sem-ˈnän\ *or* **Sam·nan** \sam-\. 1 Governorate of N cen. Iran. See table at IRAN.

2 Town, its ✱, on highway 110 m. E of Tehran, S of Elburz Mts.; pop. (1971c) 35,000; market town; textiles, carpets; an ancient town, mentioned by Ptolemy.

Se·mois \sə-ˈmwä\. River, SE Belgium and NE France; ab. 120 m. long; flows NW in Luxembourg prov., crosses French border and empties into Meuse 9 m. N of Mézières.

Sem·pach \ˈzem-ˌpäk\. Commune, Lucerne canton, cen. Switzerland, on Lake of Sempach 8 m. NW of Lucerne; pop. (1970c) 1619; scene of victory of Swiss confederates over Austrian army July 9, 1386; traditional scene of death of Arnold von Winkelried.

Sempach, Lake of *or Ger.* **Sem·pach·er See** \ˈzem-ˌpäk-ər-ˌzā\. Lake, N cen. Switzerland, NW of Lake of Lucerne; ab. 4 m. long by 1 m. wide; ab. 5½ sq. m.; max. depth 285 ft.; outlet to the N into Aare river.

Sem·pang Man·ga·yau, Cape \-səm-ˌpäŋ-ˈmäŋ-yō\ *or* **Cape Sam·pan·man·gio** \-ˌsäm-pən-ˈmän-jō\. North point of island of Borneo, Sabah, Malaysia, 7°02′N, 116°45′E.

Sempione. See ALPS.

Se·na \ˈsā-nə\. Town, Mozambique, SE Africa, on right bank of Zambezi river, ab. 125 m. SE of Tete; nearby is railroad bridge across the Zambezi; 18th cent. fort.

Sena Gallica. See SENIGALLIA.

Sen·a·to·bia \ˌsen-ə-ˈtōb-ē-ə, -ˈtō-byə\. Town, ⊗ of Tate co., NW Mississippi, 45 m. NE of Clarksdale; pop. (1970c) 4247.

Sen·dai \sen-ˈdī\. City, ✱ of Miyagi prefecture, N Honshū, Japan, near E coast 180 m. N of Tokyo; pop. (1970c) 545,065; local consumer goods industry; an important cultural center with univ. (1907) and several technical schools. Ruins of 16th cent. castle and memorial to Date Masamune, 16th cent. founder of daimiate controlling area for c. 270 years.

Sen·e·ca \ˈsen-i-kə\. 1 River, W cen. New York; ab. 65 m. long; flows from Seneca Lake at N end to Cayuga Lake (canalized, part of N.Y. State Barge Canal system) then N and E joining the Oneida river to form the Oswego river.

2 River, NW South Carolina; rises in Blue Ridge Mts. in W North Carolina, flows S across South Carolina border and unites with Tugaloo river W of Anderson to form the Savannah river; in its upper course called the **Ke·o·wee** \ˈkē-ə-ˌwē\.

3 Name of counties in two states of the U.S. See tables at NEW YORK and OHIO.

4 City, ⊗ of Nemaha co., NE Kansas, 50 m. NE of Manhattan; pop. (1970c) 2182; agriculture.

5 Town, Oconee co., NW South Carolina, 22 m. WNW of Anderson; pop. (1970c) 6382; textiles; agriculture.

Seneca Falls. Manufacturing village, Seneca co., W cen. New York, on Seneca river 11 m. W of Auburn; pop. (1970c) 7794; pumps, hosiery, television tubes; fruit farms; Eisenhower Coll. (1965); scene of first women's rights convention in U.S. 1848.

Seneca Lake. Lake, chiefly in Yates and Seneca cos., W New York; one of the Finger Lakes (*q.v.*); ab. 35 m. long, 67 sq. m.; max. depth ab. 600 ft.; connected at N end with Cayuga Lake by canalized Seneca river, part of the N.Y. State Barge Canal system.

Sen·e·gal \ˌsen-i-ˈgȯl\ *or Fr.* **Sé·né·gal** \sā-nā-gal\. 1 Republic, W Africa, bounded on N and NE by Mauritania, on E by Mali, on S by Guinea and Portuguese Guinea, and on W by the Atlantic Ocean; in S part Rep. of the Gambia extends as exclave ab. 200 m. on both sides of the Gambia river; 76,124 sq. m.; pop. (1970e) 3,930,000; ✱ Dakar. *Physical features:* Mostly low on coast and only slightly elevated in cen. part, with mountain region in SE; lower Senegal river and its chief tributary the Falémé form N and E boundary; other streams are the upper Gambia, the Casamance, and the wide estuary of the Saloum. Coastline extends ab. 120 m. S from mouth of Senegal river to Cape Vert (its W point) and Dakar, thence S for 190 m. (not including Gambia coast) to a point just SE of Cape Roxo. *Chief products:* Peanuts, cotton, rice, millet; livestock raising, fishing; salt, titanium, zircon. *Chief towns:* Dakar, Thiès, Kaolack, Rufisque, Saint-Louis.

History: First settlements were Portuguese (15th cent.); first French settlement at Saint-Louis (founded 1658); coastal region object of much rivalry and conflict in 18th and 19th cents. bet. French and Portuguese; French possession recognized 1814; after beginning of administration of Gen. Faidherbe 1854 great improvement in organization and development and hinterland explored; revolt 1899–1900 put down; status changed from protectorate to that of colony 1920; in World War II Dakar became important as naval and air base; became a territory within French Union 1946 and a republic within French Com-

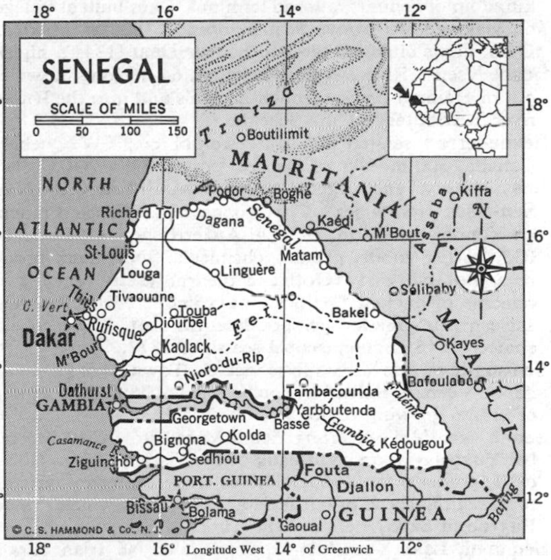

munity 1958; member of Mali Federation 1959–60; achieved independence 1960.

2 River, W Africa; 1015 m. long; rises in the Fouta Djallon highlands of Guinea near the border of Sierra Leone, flows N and NW, forming the N boundary of Senegal (1, above), empties into Atlantic Ocean at Saint-Louis; in its upper course, above its union at Bafoulabé with the Bakoy, known as Bafing river (*q.v.*); its chief tributary on the S is the Falémé, in E Senegal; navigable to the Bafing at high water.

Sen·e·gam·bia \ˌsen-i-ˈgam-bē-ə\. Region of the Senegal and Gambia rivers, W Africa, since 1904 mostly in Senegal and W Mali.

Sen·e·kal \ˈse-nə-ˌkäl\. Town, Orange Free State, Rep. of South Africa, ab. 100 m. NE of Bloemfontein; pop. (1967e) 7400.

Senf·ten·berg \ˈzenf-tən-ˌbe(ə)rg\. City, Cottbus dist., East Germany, on the Schwarze Elster 25 m. NNW of Bautzen; pop. (1970e) 24,301; glass, tile; lignite mines.

Senglea. See COSPICUA.

Seniavin Islands. See SENYAVIN ISLANDS.

Se·ni·gal·lia \ˌsā-ni-ˈgäl-yə\ *or anc.* **Se·na Gal·li·ca** \ˌsē-nə-ˈgal-i-kə\. Seaport, Ancona prov., Marches, cen. Italy, on Adriatic coast 18 m. NW of Ancona; pop. (1968e) 36,730; market town; 15th cent. castle, 18th cent. cathedral. An ancient capital of the Senones; captured by Romans c. 290 B.C.; became Roman military colony; Hasdrubal defeated by Romans nearby.

Se·nio \ˈsān-(ˌ)yō, ˈsen-\. River, Emilia-Romagna, N Italy; ab. 55 m. long; rises in Apennines and flows NE to the Adriatic S of Comacchio; fighting on its banks Apr. 1945.

Senj \ˈsen-yə\ *or Hung.* **Zengg** \ˈzeŋ\. Seaport, Croatia, N Yugoslavia; occupied by Italy during World War II.

Sen·ja \ˈsen-yə\. Island in Troms co., in Arctic Ocean off NW coast of Norway; 614 sq. m.

Sen·lac \ˈsen-ˌlak\. Hill in Sussex, S England, near Hastings; battle 1066 (generally called "Battle of Hastings").

Sen·lis \säⁿ-lēs\. Town, Oise dept., N France, ab. 28 m. NNE of Paris; pop. (1962c) 8717; ancient town, has remains of Gallo-Roman walls; early Gothic cathedral; by treaty signed here bet. Charles VIII and Emperor Maximilian I, May 23, 1493, Charles gave up Franche-Comté.

Sen·nar *or* **Sen·naar** \sə-ˈnär\. 1 Region and ancient kingdom, E Sudan, chiefly bet. the White Nile and Blue Nile.

2 Town, Blue Nile prov., E Sudan, on the Blue Nile river S of Wad Medani; pop. (1956c) 8093; capital of the ancient kingdom of Sennar; railroad terminus. Dam built at village of Makwar just above Sennar, opened 1925 as Makwar Dam; name changed later to **Sennar Dam** (134 ft. high).

Senne \ˈsen\. River, W cen. Belgium; 64 m. long; flows N out of Hainaut prov. through Brussels and into the Rupel river, a tributary of the Schelde.

Senne·terre \sen-ˈter\. Town, Abitibi co., SW Quebec, Canada, 300 m. NW of Quebec; pop. (1971p) 4305.

Sens \ˈsäⁿs\; *anc.* **Agen·di·cum** \ə-ˈjen-di-kəm\ *or later* **Sen·o·nes** \ˈsen-ə-ˌnēz\. City, Yonne dept., NE cen. France, on Yonne river 32 m. NNW of Auxerre; pop. (1968c) 23,-035; leather goods, plastics, chemicals, flour, dairy products; notable early Gothic cathedral (12th cent.) and remains of ancient fortifications. Conquered by Romans 1st cent. B.C.; made bishopric late 4th cent. A.D.; received charter 1146; archiepiscopal see since 1817.

Sen·sun·te·pe·que \ˌsen-sün-tə-ˈpek-ē\. Town, ✻ of Cabañas dept., N cen. El Salvador; pop. (1968e) 6006; former center of indigo-growing region.

Sen·ta \ˈsen-(ˌ)tä\ *or Hung.* **Zen·ta** \ˈzen-(ˌ)tȯ\. City, Serbia, NE Yugoslavia, on right bank of the Tisza ab 80 m. NNW of Belgrade; pop. (1965e) 22,000; trade center in agricultural region; scene of battle Sept. 11, 1697 in which Prince Eugene of Savoy defeated the Turks.

Sen·ta·ni, Lake \-sen-ˈtän-ē\. Small lake, NE Irian Barat, Indonesia, ab. 10 m. SW of Djajapura; site of Japanese airfields captured by forces of Allied Nations Apr. 26, 1944.

Sen·ti·nel, The \ˈsent-nəl, -ᵊn-əl\. Mountain, Glacier National Park, NW Montana; 8100 ft.

Sentinel Dome. Peak in the Sierra Nevada, E Fresno co., S cen. California; 9127 ft.

Sentinel Peak. Mountain in the Adirondack Mts., Essex co., NE New York; 3858 ft.

Sentinel Range *also* **Sentinel Mountains.** Group of high mountains, Ellsworth Land, Antarctica, bet. 77° and 78°S and bet. 86° and 92°30′W; highest peak Vinson Massif 16,860 ft.; discovered Nov. 1935 by Lincoln Ellsworth.

Sentinum. See SASSOFERRATO.

Sentis. See SÄNTIS.

Sen·ya·vin Islands *also* **Sen·ia·vin Islands** \sen-ˌyäv-ən-\. Island group, E part of the Caroline Is., 6°55′N, 158°E, W Pacific Ocean; chief island Ponape.

Seo de Urgel. See URGEL, SEO DE.

Se·o·nath \ˌsā-ə-ˈnät\. River, E India; ab. 200 m. long; flows N and E in E Madhya Pradesh to Mahanadi river.

Se·o·ni *also* **See·o·nee** \sā-ˈō-nē\. Town, S cen. Madhya Pradesh, E cen. India; pop. (1961c) 30,274.

Seoul \ˈsōl, ˈsül, se-ˈül\ *or* **Kyong·song** \ke-ˈöŋ-ˈsȯŋ\ *or Jap.* **Kei·jo** \ˈkā-(ˌ)jō\. City, ✻ of South Korea, also ✻ of Kyonggi prov., 40 m. E of Inch'ŏn, its port; 237 sq. m.; pop. (1970e) 5,536,377; commercial, cultural, and industrial center of South Korea, with textile, metallurgical, chemical, and food-processing industries; univ. (1945), Ducksoo Palace, Changduk Palace.

History: Capital of the Korean Yi dynasty 1392–1910; extensively modernized and developed under Japanese rule 1910–45; made capital of U.S. military government 1945 and capital of South Korea Aug. 15, 1948. In Korean War occupied by Communist forces June 28–Sept. 29, 1950 and Jan. 4–Mar. 14, 1951 and suffered extensive damage; has been largely rebuilt since 1953.

Sep·a·ra·tion Point *or* **Separation Head** \ˌsep-ə-ˈrā-shən-\. Cape, N coast of South I., New Zealand, forming SE side of Golden Bay and NW Point of Tasman Bay.

Se·pi \ˈsā-pē\. Village at SE tip of Santa Isabel I., Solomon Is.

Se·pik \ˈsā-pik\ *or Ger.* **Kai·se·rin Au·gus·ta** \ˌkī-zər-in-ȯ-ˈgüs-tə\. River, NE New Guinea I., Papua New Guinea; ab. 600 m. long; one of its headstreams is in Irian Barat, Indonesia; navigable for ab. 300 m.

Sepphoris. See ZIPPORI.

Sepsiszentgyörgy. See SFÎNTU-GHEORGHE.

Sept–Îles. See SEVEN ISLES.

Sept–Îles, Les \lā-set-ˈēl\. Group of islands off the coast of Côtes-du-Nord dept., Brittany, NW France.

Sep·ti·ma·nia \ˌsep-tə-ˈmā-nē-ə\. Ancient territory, S France, from mouth of the Rhone to the Pyrenees on the S, and extending NW to the Cévennes Mts.

Sep·ti·mer Pass \ˌzep-tə-mər-\. Mountain pass in the Rhaetian Alps, SE Switzerland, above Upper Engadine valley; 7577 ft.

Sequana. See SEINE 1.

Se·quatch·ie \si-ˈkwäch-ē\. 1 River, SE cen. Tennessee; rises in S Cumberland co., flows SW into Tennessee river in S Marion co.

2 County in Tennessee. See table at TENNESSEE.

Se·quoia–Kings Canyon National Park \si-ˈkwȯi-ə-\. Sequoia National Park and Kings Canyon National Park (see these names at UNITED STATES, *National Parks*) considered as one administrative unit.

Se·quoy·ah \si-ˈkwȯi-ə\. County in Oklahoma. See table at OKLAHOMA.

Se·ra·bit el Kha·dim *or* **Sa·rā·bīt al–Kha·dím** \sə-ˌrab-ət-al-ˈkäd-əm\. Mountain, SW Sinai Penin., NE Egypt, in territory occupied by Israel 1967; site of discovery of alphabetic inscriptions dating from c. 1900 B.C.

Se·ra·fi·mo·vich \ˌser-ə-fi-ˈmō-vich\. Town, Volgograd Oblast, SE Russian S.F.S.R., U.S.S.R., on the Don NW of Volgograd; first attack of Soviet forces in envelopment of Stalingrad (now Volgograd) Nov. 1942.

Se·raing \sə-ˈra^{n}\. Mining and manufacturing commune, Liège prov., E Belgium, on Meuse river SSW of Liège; pop. (1969e) 40,617; a center of the Belgian metallurgical industry; machinery, glass.

Serajevo. See SARAJEVO.

Seram. See CERAM.

Ser·am·pore \ˈser-əm-ˌpō(ə)r, -ˌpȯ(ə)r\. Town, West Bengal, NE India, on right bank of Hooghly river 13 m. N of Calcutta; pop. (1961c) 91,521; jute and textile industry. Occupied by Danes from 1755 to 1845, when it was known as **Fred·er·iks·na·gar** \ˈfred-(ə-)riks-ˌnəg-ər\.

Seram Sea. See CERAM SEA.

Se·rang \ˈsä-ˌräŋ\. **1** Island, Indonesia. See CERAM. **2** Town, West Java prov., Indonesia; pop. (1961c) 40,956; inland town on railroad to Djakarta and 5 m. S of old port of Banten.

Se·ra·vez·za \ˌse-rə-ˈvet-sə\. Commune, Lucca prov., Tuscany, cen. Italy, 17 m. NW of Lucca; pop. (1968e) 13,044; early 15th cent. cathedral; marble quarries, mercury and tin mines.

Ser·bia \ˈsər-bē-ə\ *or Serb.* **Sr·bi·ja** \ˈsər-bē-ˌ(y)ä\ *or formerly* **Ser·via** \-vē-ə\. A constituent republic of Yugoslavia; 34,115 sq. m. (including autonomous regions Vojvodina and Kosovo-Metohija); pop. (1971p) 8,436,547; ✱ Belgrade. Mountainous country with short ranges and spurs, running in various directions, highest on Bulgarian border; bordered on N by the Danube and traversed in E cen. part by the Morava and in cen. by its tributaries the Western Morava and Ibar. *Chief cities:* Belgrade, Niš, Subotica, Zrenjanin.

History: Settled by Serbs, a south Slavic people, who were pushed across Danube into Moesia (*q.v.*) by Avars in 7th cent. A.D.; nominally under Byzantine suzerainty, by 10th cent. were united and converted to eastern Christianity; became independent in 12th cent. but soon broken by dynastic struggles and loss of territory to Hungary and Bulgaria; became leading Slav kingdom under Stephen Dushan (1331–55) who ruled Serbs, Greeks, Bulgars, and Albanians; seat of Patriarchate of Serbs 1346–1766; defeated by Turks at battle of Kosovo (*q.v.*) 1389; after alternately resisting and cooperating with Turks, became part of Ottoman Empire 1459; northern Serbia held by Austria 1718–39; revolted against Turkey under leadership of Karageorge 1804–13, and again in 1815–17, led by Miloš Obrenović; guaranteed autonomy 1829 and ruled by hereditary prince 1830; secured withdrawal of Turkish garrisons 1867; made completely independent of Turkey 1878, but deprived of Bosnia and Herzegovina (*q.v.*); defeated by Bulgaria (*q.v.*) 1885; after 1903 and especially after "annexation crisis" of 1908–09 (see AUSTRIA-HUNGARY), pushed by extreme nationalists into anti-Austrian policy; disappointed at formation of Albania (*q.v.*) at end of First Balkan War; received territory in Macedonia after Second Balkan War 1913; blamed by Austria for assassination of Archduke Francis Ferdinand (1914) which Austria used as excuse for ultimatum and declaration of war on Serbia, ultimately precipitating World War I; utterly defeated by Central Powers; at collapse of Austro-Hungarian monarchy, proclaimed united Kingdom of Serbs, Croats, and Slovenes 1918 (see YUGOSLAVIA); at reorganization of Yugoslavia 1929 region divided into a number of counties; made a constituent republic of Yugoslavia in 1946 constitution.

Ser·bo·nis, Lake \-sər-ˈbō-nəs\. Former lake and marsh, now dry, Lower Egypt, near coast E of the Suez Canal; described by Herodotus as place in which whole armies were engulfed; called **Ser·bo·ni·an Bog** \ˌsər-ˌbō-nē-ən-\ by Milton (*Paradise Lost*).

Serbs, Croats and Slovenes, Kingdom of the. See YUGOSLAVIA.

Ser·chio \ˈser-(ˌ)kyō, -kē-ˌō\. River, Tuscany, NW Italy; ab. 60 m. long; flows SE, SW, and W into the Ligurian Sea.

Sercq. See SARK 1.

Serdica. See SOFIA 2.

Ser·do·bol \ˌserd-ə-ˈbȯl(-yə)\ *or Finn.* **Sor·ta·va·la** \ˈsȯrt-ə-ˌväl-ə\. Town, S Karelian A.S.S.R., U.S.S.R., on N shore of Lake Ladoga 120 m. N of Leningrad; pop. (1967e) 21,000; lake port; wood products; granite and marble quarries; under Finland 1917–40.

Se·re·gno \sə-ˈrān-(ˌ)yō\. Commune, Milano prov., Lombardy, N Italy, 13 m. N of Milan; pop. (1968e) 32,984.

Se·rem·ban \sə-ˈrem-bən\. Town, ✱ of Negri Sembilan state, Malaysia, in W part; pop. (1970p) 79,915; on coastal railroad ab. 42 m. NW of Malacca; connected with Port Dickson and Malacca by branch railroads.

Serena, La. See LA SERENA.

Se·ren·ge·ti National Park \ˌser-ən-ˈget-ē-\. National park, N Tanzania; 5600 sq. m.; noted for its wildlife.

Seres. See SERRAI 2.

Se·ret \ˈser-ət\. River, W Ukrainian S.S.R., U.S.S.R.; ab. 150 m. long; flows S and SE into Dniester river at Khotin; formerly in SE Galicia, Poland.

Sereth. See SIRETUL.

Sergiev. See ZAGORSK.

Sergiopol. See AYAGUZ 2.

Ser·gi·pe \ser-ˈzhē-pə\. State, E Brazil; 8492 sq. m.; pop. (1970p) 900,119; ✱ Aracaju; livestock raising; cotton, rice, tobacco.

Sergo. See KADIYEVKA.

Ser·gy \ser-ˈzhē\. Village, Aisne dept., N France, 3 m. SE of Fère-en-Tardenois; pop. (1962c) 150; fighting July 28–29, 1918.

Se·ria \sə-ˈrē-ə\. Town, W Brunei, ab. 45 m. SW of Bandar Seri Begawan; pop. (1971p) 20,801.

Ser·i·ca \ˈser-i-kə\. Name applied by ancient Greeks and Romans to a region of E Asia approx. equivalent to modern China; its people, the Seres, were said to have cultivated silkworms and made silken fabrics.

Ser·in·dia \sə-ˈrin-dē-ə\. Region of Asia bet. the Pamirs and the Pacific watershed, including Sinkiang Uighur, W China.

Se·rin·ga·pa·tam \sə-ˌriŋ-gə-pə-ˈtam\. Town, Mysore, S India, ab. 8 m. N of Mysore. Former capital of Mysore under Tipu Sahib whose fort and palace were here on an island in Cauvery river; treaty signed here with the British 1792; in Fourth Mysore War 1799 besieged and captured by the British and Tipu killed; contains his mausoleum and that of his son, Haidar Ali.

Seringes-et-Nesles. See FÈRE-EN-TARDENOIS.

Se·ri·phos \sə-ˈrī-fəs, ˈser-i-ˌfȯs\. Island in W Cyclades, Aegean Sea, in Cyclades dept., Greece, S of Kythnos; ab. 25 sq. m.; colonized by Ionians from Athens.

Ser·ma·ta \ser-ˈmät-ə\. Island, South West Is., Indonesia, NE of Timor.

Ser·mi·de \ˈser-mē-də\. Commune, Mantova prov., Lombardy, N Italy, on Po river 26 m. ESE of Mantua; pop. (1968e) 8014.

Sermione. See SIRMIONE.

Ser·mo·ne·ta \ˌser-mō-ˈnā-tə\. Town, Latina prov., Latium, cen. Italy, on edge of Agro Pontino NW of Latina; pop. (1968e) 5434.

Se·rov \ˈser-əf\ *or formerly* **Na·dezh·dinsk** \nə-ˈdezh-ˌdin(t)sk\. City, Sverdlovsk Oblast, Russian S.F.S.R., U.S.S.R., E of Ural Mts. on railroad ab. 200 m. N of Sverdlovsk; pop. (1970p) 100,000; steel mills; lignite, iron, bauxite, gold, and manganese mines.

Se·rowe \sə-ˈrō-ē\. Town, E Botswana, S Africa, ab. 160 m. NNE of Gaborone; pop. (1969c) 34,186.

Ser·pa \ˈser-pə\. Commune, Beja dist., S Portugal, near Guadiana river 17 m. ESE of Beja; pop. (1970p) 23,375.

Serpent Mound, Great. See GREAT SERPENT MOUND.

Ser·pent's Mouth \'sər-pən(t)s-ˌmau̇th\. Strait bet. NE Venezuela and the S coast of the island of Trinidad; ab. 10 m. wide; connects Gulf of Paria with the Atlantic Ocean. See DRAGON'S MOUTH.

Ser·pu·khov \ser-'pü-kəf\. City, Moscow Oblast, Russian S.F.S.R., U.S.S.R., on railroad and on navigable Oka river 56 m. S of Moscow; pop. (1970p) 124,000; textiles, synthetic silk, machine tools, pumps, concrete pipes, foodstuffs; founded 1374 and originally a fortified outpost of Moscow.

Se·rra Aca·raí *or* **Serra Aca·ra·hy** \ˌser-ə-ˌak-ə-rə-'(h)ē\. Mountain range forming boundary bet. S Guyana and Brazil; highest peak ab. 2000 ft.

Serra Cu·ru·pi·ra \-ˌku̇r-ə-pi-'rä\ *or Span.* **Sie·rra de Curupira** \sē-ˌer-ə-də-\. Mountain range, N South America, extending along a section of boundary bet. Venezuela and Brazil; highest peak 7675 ft.

Serra da Es·tre·la \-ˌdä-e-'strel-ə\. Mountain range, Portugal; contains highest peak in Portugal, 6532 ft.

Serra da Man·ti·quei·ra \-dä-ˌmant-i-'ker-ə\. Mountain range, SE Brazil, on border of São Paulo, Minas Gerais, and Rio de Janeiro states; highest peak Pico das Agulhas Negras 9141 ft.

Serra das Di·vi·sões \-dəz-ˌdē-vē-'zōiⁿs\. Mountain range, S cen. Brazil; highest point 2870 ft.

Serra de Amam·baí \-dē-ˌam-a(ⁿ)m-bə-'ē\; *in Paraguay* **Cor·di·lle·ra de Amam·bay** \ˌkȯrd-ᵊl-'(y)er-ə-dā-ˌäm-äm-'bī, ˌkȯrd-ē-'er-\. Mountain range, S Mato Grosso state, SW Brazil, extending along a section of Brazil-Paraguay boundary; average elevation ab. 1300 ft.

Ser·ra·di·fal·co \ˌser-ə-dē-'fal-kō\. Commune, Caltanissetta prov., cen. Sicily, Italy, WSW of Caltanissetta; pop. (1968e) 8178.

Serra do Es·tron·do \-ˌdü-ēsh-'trō(ⁿ)n-(ˌ)dü\. Mountain range, N Goiás state, NE cen. Brazil, bet. the Araguaia and Tocantins rivers.

Serra do Mar \-du̇-'mär\. Coastal mountain range, chiefly in Santa Catarina, Paraná, and São Paulo states, S Brazil; highest point 7423 ft. in the Serra dos Orgãos.

Serra do Mon·chi·que \-ˌdü-mō(ⁿ)n-'shē-kə\. Mountain range, S Portugal; highest point 2959 ft.

Serra do Piauí \-ˌdü-pyau̇-'ē\. Mountain range, NE Brazil, extending along boundary bet. Bahia and Piauí states.

Serra do Ron·ca·dor \-du̇-ˌrō(ⁿ)n-kə-'dȯ(ə)r\. Mountain range, NE Mato Grosso state, cen. Brazil.

Serra dos Ai·mo·rés \-du̇-ˌzī-mu̇-'res\. Region, E Brazil; formerly in dispute between Minas Gerais and Espírito Santo states; partitioned 1964 with 1515 sq. m. to Minas Gerais and 2405 sq. m. to Espírito Santo.

Serra dos Or·gãos \-du̇-'zȯ(ə)r-ˌgau̇ⁿs\ *or Eng.* **Or·gan Mountains** \ˌȯr-gən-\. Mountain range, Rio de Janeiro state, SE Brazil, ab. 30 m. from Rio de Janeiro; highest peak 7323 ft.; part of the Serra do Mar; part of region estab. as **Serra dos Orgãos National Park** 1939 (39 sq. m.).

Serra dos Pa·re·cis \-du̇s-ˌpar-ə-'sēs\. Range of mountains, Mato Grosso state, SW Brazil, E of, and parallel with, the NE border of Bolivia; highest peak 2194 ft.

Serra do Tom·ba·dor \-du̇-ˌtō(ⁿ)m-bə-'dȯ(ə)r\. Range of mountains, N cen. Mato Grosso state, SW Brazil.

Serra Ge·ral \-zhə-'räl\. Mountain range, E Santa Catarina state, S Brazil; highest peak 4133 ft.

Ser·rai *or Gk.* **Sér·rai** \'se(ə)r-(ˌ)ā\. 1 Department of Macedonia, Greece. See table at GREECE.
2 *also* **Ser·res** *or* **Ser·es** \'ser-əs\ *or anc.* **Si·ris** \'sī-rəs\. City, its ✱, near N end of Lake Akhinou and ab. 42 m. NE of Salonika; pop. (1971p) 41,124; ships rice, cotton, and hides; occupied by Serbians 1345–71, by Turks 1383–1913, by Bulgarians 1916–18; center of revolt 1935; again occupied by Bulgarians 1941–44 in World War II.

Se·rra·na Bank \sə-ˌrän-ə-\. Shoal in W Caribbean Sea off NE coast of Nicaragua; claimed by U.S.A. and Colombia.

Ser·ra·nía de Cuen·ca \ˌser-ə-ˌnē-əd-ə-'kweŋ-kə\. Mountain range, Cuenca and Guadalajara provs., E cen. Spain; highest peak 6084 ft.

Serranía de la Macarena. See MACARENA MOUNTAINS.

Serranía de Ta·ba·sa·rá \-dā-ˌtäb-ə-sə-'rä\. Mountain range, W Panama; highest point Mt. Santiago 9269 ft.

Serranía Ima·ta·ca \-ˌē-mə-'tä-kə\. Mountain range, E Venezuela, S of Orinoco delta.

Se·rra·no \sə-'rän-(ˌ)ō\. Island in Pacific Ocean off SW coast of Chile, N of Wellington I., 48°30′S, 74°43′W.

Serra Pa·ca·rai·ma \-ˌpak-ə-'rī-mə\ *or in Venezuela* **Sie·rra Pacaraima** \sē-ˌer-ə-\; *in Guyana* **Pacaraima Mountains** *also* **Pa·ka·rai·ma Mountains** \ˌpak-\. Mountain range, N South America, extending W to E along section of Brazil-Venezuela boundary; highest peak Roraima 9219 ft.

Serra Pa·ri·ma \-pə-'rē-mə\. Mountain range, N South America, extending N and S along a section of the Venezuela-Brazil boundary; ab. 200 m. long; highest peak ab. 5000 ft.; source of the Orinoco river.

Ser·rat, Cape \-sə-'rät\. Cape, N coast of Tunisia, W of Bizerte.

Serra Tumucumaque. See TUMUC-HUMAC MOUNTAINS.

Serra Ua·ça·ri \-wä-'sar-ē\ *or in Guyana* **Vas·sa·ri Mountains** \və-ˌsär-ē-\. Mountain range forming part of boundary bet. S Guyana and Brazil, a W extension of Serra Acaraí; source of Essequibo river and of several rivers of Brazil.

Serres. See SERRAI 2.

Sert. See SIIRT.

Servia. See SERBIA.

Se·sa·jap \sə-'sä-ˌyäp\. River, NE part of island of Borneo; ab. 200 m. long; rises in NE Sarawak (Malaysia) and flows E in the Indonesian prov. of East Kalimantan to the Celebes Sea; has large delta with many islands. See TARAKAN.

Se·sen·heim \'zā-zən-ˌhīm\. Village, N Alsace, France, ab. 18 m. NNE of Strasbourg near the Rhine; noted as home from 1760 of Frederike Brion, friend of Goethe.

Se·sia \'säz-ē-ə, 'sez-\. River, N Italy; 86 m. long; rises on slopes of Monte Rosa, flows S into Po river 5 m. E of Casale Monferrato.

Ses·sa Au·run·ca \ˌses-ə-au̇-'rüŋ-kə\ *or anc.* **Sues·sa Aurunca** \ˌswes-ə-ȯ-'rəŋ-kə\. Commune, Caserta prov., Campania, S Italy, 33 m. NNW of Naples; pop. (1968e) 30,212; ships fruit and wine; 13th cent. cathedral; Roman ruins; sulfur springs.

Ses·tao \sä-'stau̇\. Commune, Vizcaya prov., N Spain, 5 m. NW of Bilbao; pop. (1970p) 37,312; iron foundries.

Se·sto Fio·ren·ti·no \'ses-tō-fē-ˌōr-ən-'tē-(ˌ)nō, -ˌȯr-\. Commune, Firenze prov., Tuscany, cen. Italy, 5 m. NW of Florence; pop. (1968e) 36,295.

Ses·tos \'ses-təs\. Ruined town on the Dardanelles (Hellespont), Turkey, Europe; at narrowest point of the strait opp. Abydos; N terminus of bridge of boats built 481 B.C. by Xerxes for the crossing of his armies for invasion. Scene of legend of Hero and Leander.

Sesto San Gio·van·ni \'ses-tō-ˌsan-jə-'vän-ē\. Industrial commune, Milano prov., Lombardy, N Italy, NE suburb of Milan; pop. (1968e) 85,094.

Se·stri Le·van·te \ˌses-trē-lā-'vän-(ˌ)tā\. Commune, Genova prov., Liguria, NW Italy, on Ligurian Sea 21 m. ESE of Genoa; pop. (1968e) 20,786; winter and seaside resort.

Setabis. See JÁTIVA.

Sète *or formerly* **Cette** \'set\. Commercial and industrial town, Hérault dept., S France, 18 m. SSW of Montpellier on a strip of land which separates the Étang de Thau from the Mediterranean; pop. (1968c) 40,576; the principal seaport of S France after Marseilles; large export trade in wine; produces chemicals, phosphates, cement; distilleries, oil refineries, fisheries (incl. esp. cultivation of shellfish in the lagoon); seaside resort; founded 1666; birthplace of Paul Valéry.

Se·te La·go·as \ˌsāt-ə-lə-'gō-əs\. City, Minas Gerais state, E Brazil, just N of Belo Horizonte; munic. pop. (1968e) 47,727.

Sete Que·das \'sā-tə-'kā-t̲h̲əsh\; *formerly* **Guaí·ra** *or* **Guay·ra** \'gwī-(ˌ)rä\. Cataract, in the Paraná river on boundary bet. Brazil and Paraguay; formed by a narrowing of the river bed into a gorge ab. 200 ft. wide through which the water plunges 56 ft.; total descent 130 ft.

Se·ti \'sät-ē\. River, W Nepal; ab. 120 m. long; flows S into the Karnali river.

Setia. See SEZZE.

Sé·tif \sā-'tēf\. 1 Department of N Algeria. See table at ALGERIA.

2 Town, its ✻, on railroad 60 m. NW of Constantine; pop. (1966c) 98,000; center of a grain-producing region; important provincial capital under Romans and Byzantines.

Setit. See TEKEZE.

Se·to \'set-(,)ō\. City, Aichi prefecture, Honshū, Japan, 13 m. ENE of Nagoya; pop. (1970c) 92,681.

Seto–naikai *or* **Seto no Uchi.** See INLAND SEA.

Se·tú·bal \sə-'tü-bəl\. 1 District of SW Portugal. See table at PORTUGAL.

2 *or formerly called in English* **Saint Ubes** \-'yübz\ *or* **Saint Yves** \-'īvz\. Seaport, its ✻, on **Bay of Setúbal** (receives the Sado river) 19 m. SE of Lisbon; pop. (1970p) 64,531; good harbor; manufactures and trades in muscatel wine, corks, oranges, salt; shipbuilding; royal residence in time of John II.

Setul. See SATUN.

Seul, Lake \-'sül\ *or Fr.* **Lac Seul** \lák-sœl\. Lake, W Ontario, Canada; 539 sq. m.; outlet is English river (a headstream of the Winnipeg).

Seul Choix Point \sə-'shwä-\. Point on SE coast of Schoolcraft co., S Michigan penin., in Lake Michigan.

Se·van \sə-'vän\ *or* **Se·vang** \-'väŋ\ *or Turk.* **Gök·cha** \'gə(r)k-chə\ *or anc.* **Lych·ni·tis** \lik-'nīt-əs\. Lake, N Armenian S.S.R., U.S.S.R.; 547 sq. m.; altitude 6279 ft.; surrounded by high mountains; largest lake in Armenian S.S.R.; its outlet is the Razdan, a tributary of the Araks; fisheries.

Se·vas·to·pol *or formerly* **Se·bas·to·pol** \sə-'vas-tə-,pōl, -,pȯl; ,sev-ə-'stō-pəl, -'stō-\. Seaport city, SW Crimean Oblast, Ukrainian S.S.R., U.S.S.R., forming a peninsula 40 m. SW of Simferopol; pop. (1970p) 229,000; on an inlet of the Black Sea (Sevastopol Bay), which forms a good natural harbor. Principal base of the Russian Black Sea Fleet since early 19th cent., with extensive dockyard facilities and arsenals; has shipbuilding and food-processing industries; center of a region noted for health resorts.

History: Site of Greek colony founded late 6th cent. B.C. and absorbed c. 100 B.C. into kingdom of Cimmerian Bosporus; for subsequent changes of sovereignty see CRIMEAN OBLAST; Tatar settlement founded here late 13th cent. under name **Akh·tiar** \'ak-tē-,(y)är\. Came under Russia 1783 and made site of naval base 1784; commercial port opened 1808. Has undergone two notable sieges: (1) in the Crimean War, fell to Allies after 322 days Oct. 1854–Sept. 11, 1855 (see REDAN and MALAKHOV); (2) in World War II fell to Germans after 250 days (Oct. 1941–July 2, 1942) and intense and costly fighting; recaptured by Soviet troops May 10, 1944. In civil war 1918–21 headquarters of White army under Wrangel.

Seven Devils Mountains. Mountain range, W Idaho, E of Snake river in Adams and Idaho cos.; ab. 40 m. long; highest point ab. 7900 ft.

Seven Hills. Village, Cuyahoga co., N Ohio, S of Cleveland; pop. (1970c) 12,700; residential.

Seven Hills. The seven hills upon and about which was built the city of Rome (*q.v.*). According to tradition, the original city of Romulus was built upon the *Palatine* hill (later the site of the palaces of the Caesars), though later he united with his settlement those upon the *Capitoline* and *Quirinal*. The *Caelian* was said to have been added by Tullus Hostilius; the *Aventine,* by Ancus Marcius; the *Esquiline* and *Viminal,* by Servius Tullius, who built a wall (the *Servian Wall*) around the whole group. The Capitoline hill (originally called the *Saturnian*) anciently comprised two peaks, the *Capitolium,* which was earlier known as the *Tarpeian Rock,* and the *Arx.* In early times the hills, which are of volcanic origin, were very abrupt.

Seven Hunters. See FLANNAN ISLANDS.

Seven Isles *or Fr.* **Sept–Îles** \se-tēl\. City, Saguenay co., SE Quebec, 250 m. NE of Chicoutimi; pop. (1971p) 24,289; iron ore, salmon fisheries.

Seven Mile Beach. Island off E cen. Cape May co., S New Jersey.

Sev·en·oaks \'sev-(ə-),nōks\. Urban district, Kent, SE England, 20 m. SSE of London; pop. (1971p) 18,240; residential; Knole House.

Seven Pines. See FAIR OAKS.

Seven Sisters Falls *or* **Syv Sis·tre** \səv-'sis-trə, 'süv-\. Waterfall in a small stream emptying into Stor Fjord on W coast of Norway.

Seven Troughs Peak. Mountain, W Pershing co., NW Nevada; 7480 ft.

Sev·ern \'sev-ərn\. 1 Navigable inlet of Chesapeake Bay, E Anne Arundel co., cen. Maryland; ab. 10 m. long; Annapolis is located 2 m. from its mouth.

2 River, NW Ontario, Canada; 610 m. long; has source in several large lakes in W Ontario, flows NE into Hudson Bay.

3 River, SE Ontario, Canada. See SIMCOE, LAKE.

4 *or anc.* **Sa·bri·na** \sə-'brī-nə\. River, E Wales and W England; 180 m. long; rises in E cen. Wales, flows in a curve NE, E, and S, crossing English border near Shrewsbury and continuing S into Bristol Channel; the "Shakespeare" Avon is one of its chief tributaries; bridge (across Severn) linking S Wales with Bristol opened 1967.

Severnaya Dvina. See DVINA, NORTHERN.

Se·ver·na·ya Zem·lya \'sev-ər-nə-,yä-,zem-lē-'ä\; *Eng.* **Northern Land** *also* **North Land;** *formerly* **Nich·o·las II Land** \,nik-(ə-)ləs-thə-'sek-ənd-\. Island group in Arctic Ocean, Krasnoyarsk Krai, Russian S.F.S.R., U.S.S.R., dividing Laptev Sea from Kara Sea, N of Taimyr Penin.; 14,286 sq. m.; comprises three large islands, Bolshevik, Komsomolets, and October Revolution, and a number of smaller islands; separated from mainland by Vilkitski Strait; discovered 1913.

Se·ve·ro·do·netsk \,sev-(y)ir-ə-də-'netsk\. Town, Voroshilovgrad Oblast, Ukrainian S.S.R., U.S.S.R., ab. 45 m. NW of Voroshilovgrad; pop. (1969e) 80,000.

Se·ve·rod·vinsk \,sev-ər-əd-'vin(t)sk\ *or formerly* **Mo·lo·tovsk** \'mȯl-ə-təfsk\. Seaport town, NW Arkhangelsk Oblast, Russian S.F.S.R., U.S.S.R., on Dvina Gulf across the delta of the Northern Dvina from Arkhangelsk; pop. (1970p) 145,000; exports timber.

Se·ve·ro·morsk \,sev-(y)ir-ə-'mȯrsk\ *or formerly* **Va·yen·ga** \və-'yen-gə, -'yeŋ-\. Town, Murmansk Oblast, Russian S.F.S.R., U.S.S.R., ab. 10 m. NE of Murmansk; pop. (1967e) 44,000.

Se·vier \sə-'vi(ə)r\. 1 River, SW cen. Utah; 279 m. long; formed by confluence of forks in W Garfield co., S Utah, flows N, then turns SW in E Juab co., empties into Sevier Lake in cen. Millard co., W Utah.

2 Name of counties in three states of the U.S. See tables at ARKANSAS, TENNESSEE, UTAH.

Sevier Lake. Lake, Millard co., W Utah; ab. 25 m. long; waters strongly saline; receives Sevier river from N; no outlet.

Se·vier·ville \sə-'vi(ə)r-,vil\. Town, ⊗ of Sevier co., E Tennessee; pop. (1970c) 2661.

Se·vi·lla \sā-'vē-yä\. 1 Town, Valle dept., W Colombia; munic. pop. (1968e) 47,018.

2 Province of SW Spain. See table at SPAIN.

Se·ville \sə-'vil\ *or Span.* **Se·vi·lla** \sā-'vē(l)-yä\ *or anc.* **His·pa·lis** \'his-pə-ləs\. City, ✻ of Sevilla prov., SW Spain, on Guadalquivir river 62 m. NNE of Cádiz; pop. (1970p)

548,072; inland port with extensive facilities, exporting wine, citrus fruit, olives, mercury, iron and lead ores; hemp, jute, agricultural implements, tobacco and cigars, pottery, porcelain ware; major shipyards, iron foundries, butane gas deposits. One of the principal tourist centers of Spain, with walks (*paseos*), the medieval pattern of Old Seville, and numerous notable buildings, incl. the cathedral (15th cent. Gothic), the Giralda (tower of the Almohades), one of the most notable Moorish structures in Spain (late 12th cent.), and the 12th cent. Alcazar; univ. (1502). Birthplace of Velázquez and Murillo; noted for its processions and ceremonies during Holy Week.

History: Iberian settlement at early period; prosperous under Romans, chief city of Baetica; chief town of southern Spain under Vandals and Goths 5th–8th cents.; captured 712 A.D. by Moors under Musa; an important city in Moorish Western Caliphate 712–1248; captured 1248 by Ferdinand III of León and Castile; after 1492, center of Spanish colonial trade (Casa de Contratación, begun 1503); in 17th cent. declined in rivalry with Cádiz; occupied 1808–12 by French under Soult; site of Spanish-American Exhibition 1929.

Se·vli·e·vo \sāv-'lē-yə-ˌvō\. Town, Gabrovo prov., N cen. Bulgaria, ab. 15 m. NW of Gabrovo; pop. (1968e) 21,431.

Se·vran \səv-'rä^{n}\. Commune, Seine-St-Denis dept., N France, ENE suburb of Paris; pop. (1962c) 17,792; powder works; manufactures brakes.

Sè·vre Nan·taise \ˌsev-rə-nä^{n}-'tez, -'tāz\. River, W France; ab. 80 m. long; rises in Deux-Sèvres dept., flows NW into Loire river opp. Nantes.

Sèvre Nior·taise \-nyȯr-'tez, -'tāz\. River, W France; ab. 95 m. long; rises in Deux-Sèvres dept., flows W into Bay of Biscay.

Sè·vres \'sevr^{ə}\. Commune, Hauts-de-Seine dept., N France, on Seine river 6 m. SW of Paris; pop. (1968c) 20,083; manufactures ammunition; site of national porcelain factory (transferred from Vincennes 1756) and ceramics museum; treaty signed here bet. Allies and Turkey 1920.

Sèvres, Deux– \'də(r)-'sevr^{ə}\. Department of France. See table at FRANCE.

Se·wa·nee \sə-'wȯ-nē, -'wän-ē\. Unincorporated town and summer resort, Franklin co., S Tennessee, ab. 38 m. NW of Chattanooga; pop. (1970c) 1186; Univ. of the South (1857).

Sew·ard \'sü-ərd\. 1 Name of counties in two states of the U.S. See tables at KANSAS and NEBRASKA.

2 City, S Alaska, on Resurrection Bay, an inlet of Gulf of Alaska, on SE shore of Kenai Penin.; pop. (1970c) 1587; important port, open all the year, and S terminal of government-owned Alaska railroad running N to Fairbanks; badly damaged by earthquake 1964.

3 City, ⊗ of Seward co., SE Nebraska, 22 m. WNW of Lincoln; pop. (1970c) 5294; fertilizers, china; dairy farms; Concordia Teachers Coll. (1894).

Seward, Mount. 1 Peak, Glacier National Park, NW Montana; 8879 ft.

2 Peak in the Adirondack Mts., Franklin co., NE New York; 4404 ft.

Seward–Ma·las·pi·na Glacier \-mal-əs-'pē-nə-\. Glacier in St. Elias Mountains, SE Alaska and SW Yukon, Canada; 70 m. long, ab. 43 m. wide near its terminus.

Seward Peninsula. Peninsula, W Alaska, bet. Kotzebue Sound on N and Norton Sound on S; ab. 180 m. long by 130 m. wide; its W tip, Cape Prince of Wales on Bering Strait, is most westerly point of continent of North America; Nome is on its S coast.

Sew·ell \'sü-əl\. Town, O'Higgins prov., cen. Chile; pop. (1960c) 10,866; railroad terminus E of Rancagua and mining center at 8000 ft. for El Teniente copper mines at 10,000 ft.

Se·wick·ley \si-'wik-lē\. Residential borough, Allegheny co., SW Pennsylvania, on Ohio river 12 m. WNW of Pittsburgh; pop. (1970c) 5660.

Sexi. See ALMUÑÉCAR.

Seybo, El. See EL SEIBO.

Sey·bouse \sā-'büz\ *or* **Sei·bus** \'sā-ˌbu̇s\. Unnavigable river, NE Algeria, N Africa; 145 m. long; flows N into the Mediterranean at Annaba.

Sey·chelles \sā-'shel(z)\. British colony, consisting of a group of islands in the Indian Ocean, E of NE Tanzania, ab. lat. 4°S and long. 56°E; 107 sq. m.; pop. (1972e) 54,000; ✱ Victoria on Mahé; chief islands Mahé (58 sq. m.; pop. [1969e] 41,924), Praslin (7 sq. m.; pop. [1969e] 4867), and La Digue (6 sq. m.; pop. [1969e] 750); chief products coconuts, cinnamon, and essential oils. First claimed by French 1744; taken by English 1794 and made a dependency of Mauritius 1810; became a crown colony 1903.

Sey·dhis·fjör·dhur *or* **Sey·dis·fjör·dur** \'sā-t͟həs-ˌfyər-t͟hər\. Coastal town, NE Iceland; pop. (1970c) 884.

Sey·han \sā-'hän\ *or* **Sei·hun** \sā-'hün\ *also* **Si·hun** \si-'hün\. 1 *or anc.* **Sar·us** \'sar-əs, 'ser-\. River, S cen. Turkey; 748 m. long; rises in NE Anti-Taurus Mts., flows SSW into the Mediterranean Sea E of Içel; Adana is on left bank of its lower course; the Yenice is its chief tributary.

2 Province, Turkey. See ADANA 1.

3 City, Turkey. See ADANA 2.

Sey·mour \'sē-ˌmō(ə)r, -ˌmȯ(ə)r\. 1 Industrial town, W New Haven co., S Connecticut, on Housatonic river N of Ansonia; pop. (1970c) 12,776; textiles, paper, brass and rubber goods, wire; settled 1680; incorporated 1850; site of first successful woolen mill in U.S. (1806).

2 Industrial city, Jackson co., S Indiana, 38 m. ESE of Bloomington; pop. (1970c) 13,352; lumber, pharmaceuticals, fertilizers, plastics, automobile parts.

3 City, ⊗ of Baylor co., N Texas, 48 m. WSW of Wichita Falls; pop. (1970c) 3469; cotton gins, oil wells.

Seymour, Mount. Peak, Franklin co., NE New York; 4120 ft.

Seymour Island. Small island of Galápagos Is.; during World War II U.S. air base Dec. 1941 until evacuated by U.S. forces July 1, 1946.

Seymour Lake. Lake, E Orleans co., N Vermont.

Seyne–sur–Mer, La. See LA SEYNE-SUR-MER.

Sé·zanne \ˌsā-'zan\. Town, SW Marne dept., NE France; pop. (1962c) 5216; vicinity was scene of Foch's victory in the first battle of the Marne Sept. 9, 1914 when his forces drove the Germans under von Bülow into the Marshes of St-Gond to the NE.

Sez·ze \'sāt-sā, 'set-\ *or anc.* **Se·tia** \'sē-sh(ē-)ə\. Commune, Latina prov., Latium, cen. Italy; pop. (1968e) 18,424; episcopal see; ancient Roman amphitheater and temple of Saturn.

Sfânta *or* **Sfântul.** See SAINT.

Sfântu Gheorghe. See SFÎNTU GHEORGHE.

Sfântul–Gheorghe. See SFÎNTU-GHEORGHE.

Sfax \'sfaks\ *or* **Sā·faqis** \sə-'fäk-əs\. Seaport city, E Tunisia, N Africa, 78 m. S of Sousse on N shore of Gulf of Gabès; pop. (1966c) 70,472; exports phosphates, fruit, sponges, olive oil. Of little importance before 11th cent.; bombarded by French 1881; in World War II heavily damaged by Allied bombing 1942–43 and occupied by British troops Apr. 10, 1943.

Sfîn·tu Gheor·ghe \ˌsfin-tü-'gyȯr-ge\ *or* **Sfân·tu Gheorghe** \ˌsfän-tü-\ *or Eng.* **Saint George.** Large island in cen. part of Danube delta, E Romania.

Sfîn·tu–Gheorghe \ˌsfin-tü-'gyȯr-ge\ *or* **Sfân·tul–Gheorghe** \ˌsfän-tül-\ *or Hung.* **Sep·si·szent·györgy** \ˌshep-shi-ˌsent-'gyȯr-ge\. City, ⊗ of Covasna co., cen. Romania, in Transylvanian Alps on the upper Olt ab. 20 m. NNE of Braşov; pop. (1970e) 24,975.

's Gravenhage. See HAGUE, THE.

Sgurr nan Gil·lean \ˌskər-ˌnan-gə-'lēn\. Mountain, N Cuillin Hills, S Skye I., Inner Hebrides Is.; 3167 ft.

Sha·ba \'shäb-ə\; *formerly* **Ka·tan·ga** \kə-'täŋ-gə, -'taŋ-\ *also* **Elis·a·beth·ville** \i-'liz-ə-bəth-ˌvil\. Province, S Zaire; 191,878 sq. m.; pop. (1969e) 2,174,404; ✱ Lubumbashi; noted esp. for its rich deposits of copper, uranium, chrome, cobalt, tin, iron, gold, and other minerals; seceded from Congo (now Zaire) 1960–63 (secession suppressed with aid of U.N. intervention).

Sha·ba·ni \shə-'bän-ē\. Town, S cen. Rhodesia, S Africa, 90 m. SW of Salisbury; pop. (1970e) 17,000; asbestos mines.

Sha·ba·rakh Usu \'shäb-ə-ˌräk-'ü-(ˌ)sü\. Archaeological site, S Mongolian People's Republic, ab. 103°40′E, 44°N; dinosaur eggs discovered at Flaming Cliffs near here in 1925.

Shack·el·ford \'shak-əl-fərd\. County in Texas. See table at TEXAS.

Shack·le·ton Ice Shelf \ˌshak-əl-tən-, -əlt-ᵊn-\. Large field of shelf ice, Queen Mary Coast, Antarctica; ab. 165 m. long; extends E at ab. 66°S, 100°E, and out into Indian Ocean for more than 130 m.

Shackleton Inlet. Inlet, W side of Ross Ice Shelf, Antarctica, 82°21′S, 163°15′E; ab. 10 m. wide; occupied by glacier.

Shade's Mills. See GALT 2.

Sha·drinsk \'shad-(ˌ)rin(t)sk\. Town, NW Kurgan Oblast, Russian S.F.S.R., U.S.S.R., on a tributary of Tobol river; pop. (1969e) 69,000; on Sverdlovsk-Kurgan railroad.

Shad·well \'shad-ˌwel, -wəl\. Former estate, Albemarle co., Virginia, site ab. 5 m. E of Charlottesville; birthplace of Thomas Jefferson, 3d president of the U.S.

Sha·dy·side \'shād-ē-ˌsīd\. Village, Belmont co., E Ohio, on Ohio river 27 m. S of Steubenville; pop. (1970c) 5070.

Sha·fer Butte \ˌshā-fər-\. Mountain, Boise co., W cen. Idaho; 7580 ft.

Shafer Lake. Lake, NW Indiana, N of Freeman Lake (*q.v.*), formed in Tippecanoe river by Norway Dam (built 1935).

Shaf·ter \'shaf-tər\. City, Kern co., S California, 17 m. NW of Bakersfield; pop. (1970c) 5327; cement products, fertilizer, vegetable packing; diversified agriculture.

Sha·ga·mu \shə-'gäm-(ˌ)ü\. Town, Western State, Nigeria, 40 m. SSW of Ibadan; pop. (1969e) 59,574.

Shah·a·bad \'shä-hə-ˌbäd, 'shȯ-\. 1 District, W Bihar, NE India; 4408 sq. m.; pop. (1961c) 3,218,017; ✱ Arrah.

2 Town, S Haryana, NW India, 16 m. S of Ambala; pop. (1961c) 19,000.

3 Town, cen. Uttar Pradesh, N India, 80 m. NW of Lucknow; pop. (1961c) 28,399.

Shah Alam \'shä-'äl-əm, 'shȯ-\. Town, ✱ of Selangor state, Malaysia; residence of sultan.

Shah·da·ra \'shäd-ə-rə\. Suburb of Lahore, Punjab, Pakistan, ab. 5 m. NW across the Ravi river; contains tomb of the Mogul emperor Jahangir.

Shāh Dhar \'shä-'där\. Mountain in the Hindu Kush, Afghanistan; 23,082 ft.

Shāh Fu·lā·di \ˌshäf-ˌu̇l-ə-'dē, ˌshȯf-\. Highest peak in the Koh-i-Baba range, E cen. Afghanistan; 16,872 ft.

Shā·hī \shä-'hē\. 1 Lake, Iran. See URMIA, LAKE.

2 Island, N cen. part of Lake Urmia, NW Iran; highest point 7161 ft.

3 Town, Māzandarān prov., N Iran, ab. 94 m. NE of Tehran; pop. (1971e) 42,000.

Shahjahanabad. See DELHI 2.

Shah·ja·han·pur \ˌshäj-ə-'hän-ˌpu̇(ə)r, ˌshȯ-jə-\. City, cen. Uttar Pradesh, N India, on affluent of Ramganga river 100 m. NW of Lucknow; pop. (1970e) 122,381; sugar, carpets; military cantonment. Founded 1647 by Nawab Bahadur Khan, a Pathan leader, during the reign of Shah Jahan.

Sha Ho *or* **Sha·ho** \'shä-'hō\. Small river, a tributary of the Liao, and town, 15 m. S of Mukden, NE China; battle Oct. 1904, in which the Russians were defeated by the Japanese.

Shah·pur \'shäp-u̇(ə)r, 'shȯp \. Ancient city, Fārs prov., SW Iran, W of Shīrāz and N of Kāzerūn; notable ruins.

Shah·pu·ra \'shäp-ə-rə, 'shȯp-\. 1 Former Indian state, now part of Rajasthan state, NW India; 405 sq. m.

2 Town, its ✱, 60 m. SE of Ajmer; pop. (1961c) 12,200.

Shah·re·zā *or* **Shah·ri·za** \shär-i-'zä, ˌshȯr-\. City, Eşfahān prov., cen. Iran, 50 m. S of Eşfahān; pop. (1971e) 36,000.

Shahr–i–Zabul. See ZĀBOL.

Shahr Kord \'shär-'kō(ə)rd, -'kȯ(ə)rd\. Town, ✱ of Bakhtīarī va Chahār Mahāll gov., W cen. Iran; pop. (1966c) 23,757.

Shāh·rūd *or* **Shah Rud** \shä-'rüd, shȯ-\. 1 River, N Iran; ab. 100 m. long; flows W parallel with and S of the Elburz Mts. and empties into the Safīd Rūd 40 m. S of Rasht.

2 Town, Semnān gov., N Iran, ab. 210 m. ENE of Tehran; pop. (1971e) 32,000.

Shaikh 'Othman. See SHEIKH 'OTHMAN.

Shak·er Heights \ˌshā-kər-\. Residential city, Cuyahoga co., N Ohio, 8 m. E of Cleveland; pop. (1970c) 36,606.

Sha·khri·sabz \ˌshək-ri-'säps\. City, SE Uzbek S.S.R., U.S.S.R., 40 m. S of Samarkand; pop. (1970p) 22,000.

Shakh·tersk \shäk-'t(y)ȯrsk, -'tersk\. Town, Donetsk Oblast, Ukrainian S.S.R., U.S.S.R., 31 m. E of Donetsk; pop. (1969e) 73,000.

Shakh·ty \'shäk-tē\ *or formerly* **Ale·ksan·drovsk Gru·shev·ski** \ˌal-ik-'san-drefsk-gru̇-'shef-skē, -ig-'zan-, -'shev-\. City, SW Rostov Oblast, Russian S.F.S.R., U.S.S.R., on railroad ab. 35 m. NE of Rostov-na-Donu; pop. (1970p) 205,000; mining town in E part of Donets coal region; iron foundries, breweries.

Shaki \'shä-kē\. Town, Western State, Nigeria, 95 m. NNW of Ibadan; pop. (1969e) 88,473.

Shak·o·pee \'shak-ə-(ˌ)pē\. City, ⊗ of Scott co., SE Minnesota, on Minnesota river 18 m. SW of Minneapolis; pop. (1970c) 6876; soft drinks; agriculture.

Sha·la, Lake \-'shäl-ə\. Lake, cen. Ethiopia, ab. 110 m. S of Addis Ababa.

Sha·la·mar Gardens *or* **Sha·li·mar Gardens** \'shal-ə-ˌmär-\. Oriental gardens, Pakistan, 6 m. E of Lahore; laid out in 1637 by the Mogul emperor Shah Jahan.

Sha·ler \'shā-lər\. Urban township, Allegheny co., SW Pennsylvania, N of Pittsburgh; pop. (1970c) 33,369.

Sham, Jeb·el \ˌjeb-əl-'sham\. Mountain in the Jebel Akdar, Oman, Arabian Penin.; 9927 ft.; highest peak in Oman.

Sham·be \'sham-bē\. Town, Upper Nile prov., SE Sudan, on Bahr al-Jebel (Nile) NNW of Mongalla.

Sha·mien \'shä-'myen\ *or* **Sha·meen** \-'mēn\. Sandy island in Pearl river at Canton, China, in SW part of city; ab. $^1/_9$ of a sq. m. Set apart 1859 as foreign settlement quarter; improved and built up by British and French.

Shamo. See GOBI.

Sha·mo, Lake \-'shä-mō\ *also* **Lake Cha·mo** \-'chä-mō\. Lake, SW Ethiopia.

Sha·mo·kin \shə-'mō-kən\. City, Northumberland co., E cen. Pennsylvania, 21 m. WNW of Pottsville; pop. (1970c) 11,719; fertilizer, hosiery, footwear, beer, cigars; anthracite coal mines.

Sham·rock \'sham-ˌräk\. City, Wheeler co., NW Texas, in the Panhandle 44 m. ESE of Pampa; pop. (1970c) 2644; oil and gas wells; truck farms.

Shan·da·ken Tunnel \shan-ˌdā-kən-\. Tunnel, Greene co., SE New York; 18.1 m. long; built 1917–24; part of New York City's water-supply system.

Shandī. See SHENDI.

Shan·ga·ni \shaŋ-'gän-ē\. River, W cen. Rhodesia, S Africa; 270 m. long; flows WNW into Zambezi river near Victoria Falls.

Shang–ch'iu \'shäŋ-'jō\ *or* **Shang·kiu** \'shäŋ-'jō\. Town, Honan prov., E cen. China, ab. 115 m. ESE of Cheng-chou; pop. (1970e) 250,000.

Shang–ch'uan \'shäng-'chwän\ *also* **Chang·chuen** \'chäŋ-'chün\ *or Eng.* **Saint John Island.** Island, Kwangtung prov., S coast of China, SW of Macao.

Shang·hai *also* **Shang–hai** \shaŋ-'hī\. City and seaport, SE Kiangsu prov., E China, on Huang-p'u river 13 m. from its mouth, 150 m. SE of Nanking; 772 sq. m.; pop. (1968e) 11,000,000; constitutes a special administrative unit; one of China's leading ports, with extensive harbor facilities; a major commercial and manufacturing center, producing textiles, steel, agricultural and electrical machinery, leather and rubber goods, chemicals, cigarettes; food processing, publishing; several universities and colleges, incl. Shanghai Univ. (1895) and a medical coll. (1956).

History: Of small importance before 1840; opened 1842 as one of first five treaty ports; developed rapidly with increase of concession sections; attacked Jan.–Mar. 1932 by Japanese who withdrew in May; scene of severe fighting in Japanese-Chinese War Aug.–Nov. 1937; its foreign settlements occupied by Japanese 1941 and entire city under complete Japanese control after Dec. 7; restored to China Aug. 1945; taken by Communists May 1949.

Shang–jao \'shäŋ-'raů\. Town, Kiangsi prov., SE China, ab. 130 m. E of Nan-ch'ang; pop. (1970e) 100,000.

Shangkiu. See SHANG-CH'IU.

Shan–hai–kuan \'shän-'hī-'gwän\ *or* **Lin·yu** \'lin-'yü\. Town on Gulf of Liaotung, NE Hopeh prov., NE China, at E end of Great Wall; ab. halfway bet. Peking and Mukden (260 m. from either) and for centuries an important border town; first Chinese city occupied by the Manchus 1644 and scene of great activity in Boxer Rebellion 1900.

Shan·non \'shan-ən\. 1 Counties in two states of the U.S. See tables at MISSOURI and SOUTH DAKOTA.

2 Navigable river, N, cen., and SW Eire; 230 m. long; chief river in Ireland; rises in N co. Cavan in N Eire, flows S through a number of lakes (including Lough Ree and Lough Derg) to Limerick, where it turns W and empties into Atlantic Ocean through a long, deep estuary.

Shannon Dam. Dam across Baker river, tributary of Skagit river, NW Washington; height 263 ft.; completed 1927; impounds water for power, forming **Lake Shannon** in Skagit and Whatcom cos.

Shan·non·town \'shan-ən-ˌtaůn\. Unincorporated urban community, Sumter co., E cen. South Carolina, SE of Sumter; pop. (1970c) 7491.

Shan·si \'shän-'sē\. Province, NE China, bounded on N by Inner Mongolia, on E by Hopeh, on S and SE by Honan, and on W by Shensi; 60,656 sq. m.; pop. (1967e) 18,000,000; ✱ T'ai-yüan; a plateau forming an intermediate region bet. arid Inner Mongolia and the fertile plain of N China; its W and S boundaries are the Yellow river; a tributary, the Fen, traverses most of the province from NE to SW. Its N border is marked by a section of the Great Wall and further S is crossed by another section. Covered by great loess deposits, it was the home of early Chinese agriculture; in its NE part is the sacred mountain Wu-t'ai Shan 9261 ft., formerly visited by many pilgrims. *Chief products:* Wheat, millet, cotton, tobacco; livestock; coal, copper, iron ore. *Chief cities:* T'ai-yüan, Ta-t'ung.

History: For centuries has been an integral part of the various northern kingdoms of China; after the Revolution (1911) was a "model province" (1912–28) under its governor Yen Hsi-shan; in Chinese-Japanese War (1937–45) was in part occupied by Japanese forces and was the scene of much guerrilla warfare.

Shan State \'shän-\; *formerly* **Federated Shan States** *also* **Shan States.** State, E Burma; 61,090 sq. m.; pop. (1969e) 2,725,000; ✱ Taunggyi; original Shan States flourished 12th to 16th cents.; not brought under British control until 1887; states federated 1922, reconstituted as one administrative unit 1948.

Shan·tar·skie Islands \shən-ˌtär-skē-(y)ə-\. Island group, W Sea of Okhotsk, Khabarovsk Krai, Russian S.F.S.R., U.S.S.R.; crossed by 55°N.

Shan–t'ou. See SWATOW.

Shan·tung \'shan-'təŋ\. Coastal province, NE China, bounded on NW by Hopeh, on W by Hopeh and Honan and on S by Honan and Kiangsu; 59,189 sq. m.; pop. (1967e) 57,000,000; ✱ Tsinan; its E part is a peninsula separating Gulf of Chihli from the Yellow Sea. Bet. 1852 and 1938 and since 1947 traversed by lower course of the Yellow river; in the W crossed by the Grand Canal. Has two elevated regions: one in cen. part (highest point the sacred mountain of T'ai Shan 5048 ft.) and the other in E end of peninsula S of Chefoo (highest point above 5000 ft.). *Chief products:* Wheat, corn, millet; fishing; iron ore, gold. Has several good harbors, esp. Tsingtao, Chefoo, Wei-hai, and P'eng-lai; other towns Tsinan, Tsingtao, Po-shan.

History: Probably occupied by Chinese cultivators from very early times; became influential in Chinese history because it was the birthplace of Confucius (c. 551–479 B.C.) and of Mencius, and because of T'ai Shan (*q.v.*); made a province under the Ming dynasty (1368–1644); its chief port, Chefoo, opened 1863 as a treaty port; Wei-hai leased (1898; returned 1930) to Great Britain and Kiaochow dist. to Germany 1898. In World War I Tsingtao captured by Japanese army 1914 (returned 1922); was in part concerned in the secret demands on China by Japan in 1915; occupied 1937 by Japanese; restored to China 1945; in Chinese civil war came under control of the Communist forces with their capture of Tsinan Sept. 1948.

Shantung Peninsula. East section of Shantung prov., NE China, bet. the Gulf of Chihli and the Yellow Sea.

Shao–hsing *or* **Shao·hing** \'shaů-'shiŋ\. City, N Chekiang prov., E China, ab. 40 m. ESE of Hangchow on rich delta plain; pop. (1970e) 225,000; center for trade in cotton, rice, and distilled liquors. An old town, seat of government of a powerful king of Yüeh in 5th cent. B.C.

Shao–kuan \'shaů-'gwän\ *also* **Ku·kong** \'kü-'kòŋ\. City, N Kwangtung, SE China, 125 m. N of Canton; pop. (1970e) 125,000; trading and coal-mining center.

Shao–yang *or* **Shao·yang** \'shaů-'yäŋ\ *or formerly* **Pao·king** \'baů-'chiŋ\. Town, cen. Hunan prov., SE cen. China, ab. 120 m. SW of Ch'ang-sha; pop. (1970e) 275,000; Japanese base 1944–45.

Shap·in·say \'shap-ən-ˌsā\. One of the Orkney Is. off N coast of Scotland; ab. 5 m. long; pop. (1961c) 618; ancestral home of Washington Irving.

Shaq·ra \shək-'rä\ *or* **Ash–Shaqrā** \'ash-\. Town, cen. Nejd, Saudi Arabia, ab. 100 m. WNW of Riyadh.

Sha·raf·khā·neh \shə-ˌräf-kä-'nā\ *or* **Sha·rif·kha·neh** \ˌshä-rəf-kə-'nā\. Town, East Azerbaijan prov., NW Iran, on NE shore of Lake Urmia (*q.v.*).

Sha·ra·va·ti \shə-'rä-və-tē\. See GERSOPPA, FALLS OF.

Shar·ba·tat, Cape \-ˌshär-bə-'tat\ *or Arab.* **Ras ash–Shar·ba·tāt** \'räs-ash-\. Cape, SE coast of Oman, SE Arabian Penin., extending into the Arabian Sea, NE of Cape Nus.

Shari. See CHARI.

Sharifkhaneh. See SHARAFKHĀNEH.

Shar·jah \'shär-jə\. 1 Emirate. See UNITED ARAB EMIRATES.

2 Town, its ✱, on Persian Gulf; pop. (1968c) 19,198.

Shark Bay \'shärk-\ *or* **Sharks Bay** \'shärks-\. Large bay, inlet of Indian Ocean, W Western Australia, 25°30′S, 113°30′E; pearl fishing.

Shar·key \'shär-kē\. County in Mississippi. See table at MISSISSIPPI.

Sharm al–Sheikh \'shärm-al-'shēk, -'shāk\ *or* **Sharm ash–Shaykh** \shärm-ə-'shāk\ *or Heb.* **Mif·raz Shlo·mo** \mi-ˌfräz-shə-'lō-mō\. Bay, S end of Sinai Penin. (*q.v.*), opp. Tīrān I.; Israeli naval base; former Egyptian military base, captured by Israel 1956, restored to Egypt 1957; a United Nations Emergency Force was stationed there from 1957 until requested (1967) by Egypt to leave; captured by Israel during Arab-Israeli War 1967.

Shar·on \'shar-ən, 'sher-\. 1 Residential and resort town, W Litchfield co., NW Connecticut, S of Salisbury on New York border; pop. (1970c) 2491.

2 Residential town, Norfolk co., E Massachusetts, 9 m. WNW of Brockton; pop. (1970c) 12,367.

3 Industrial city, Mercer co., W Pennsylvania, on Ohio border 18 m. NNW of New Castle; pop. (1970c) 22,653; chains, steel castings, pipes.

Sharon, Plain of *also* **Plain of Sar·on** \'sär-ən, -'ser-\. Coastal plain, W Israel, extending from Mt. Carmel to Tel Aviv-Jaffa; ab. 50 m. long by 10 m. wide; very fertile.

Sharon Hill. Borough, Delaware co., SE Pennsylvania, 7 m. WSW of Philadelphia; pop. (1970c) 7464.

Sharon Springs. 1 City, ⊗ of Wallace co., W Kansas; pop. (1970c) 1012; agriculture.

2 Village and health resort, Schoharie co., E New York, ab. 34 m. W of Schenectady; pop. (1970c) 421.

Shar·on·ville \'shar-ən-ˌvil, 'sher-\. City, Hamilton co., SW Ohio, 14 m. NNE of Cincinnati; pop. (1970c) 10,985.

Sharp \'shärp\. County in Arkansas. See table at ARKANSAS.

Sharp Mountain. Ridge, Schuylkill co., E cen. Pennsylvania, forming the S boundary of the Pottsville coal basin.

Sharps·burg \'shärps-ˌbərg\. 1 Town, Washington co., N Maryland, on W side of Antietam Creek; pop. (1970c) 863; nearby is Antietam National Battlefield Site, commemorating battle (Sept. 16–17, 1862) of Antietam (sometimes called battle of Sharpsburg) when Union forces under McClellan met Lee's first invasion of the north in the Civil War, causing Lee's withdrawal from Maryland into Virginia.

2 Industrial borough, Allegheny co., SW Pennsylvania, on Allegheny river 6 m. NE of Pittsburgh; pop. (1970c) 5499; chemicals, hardware, beer; fruit and truck farms.

Sharps·ville \'shärps-ˌvil\. Industrial borough, Mercer co., W Pennsylvania, 19 m. NNW of New Castle; pop. (1970c) 5453.

Shar·qat \shär-'kät\ *or* **As Shar·qāṭ** \ˌas-shər-'kät\. Village, N Iraq, on right bank of Tigris river 60 m. S of Mosul at site of ancient Sumerian settlement of Ashur; scene of final battle of Mesopotamian campaign Oct. 1918 resulting in defeat of Turkish forces.

Shar·qī·ya \shər-'kē-(y)ə\. Governorate of NE Egypt. See table at EGYPT.

Sha–shih \'shä-'sē, -'shir\ *or* **Sha·si** \'shä-'sē, -'shir\. Port, S Hupeh prov., E cen. China, on N bank of Yangtze, 304 m. by river above Hankow and 83 m. below I-ch'ang; pop. (1970e) 125,000; chief river port of region during Taiping Rebellion.

Shas·ta \'shas-tə\. County in California. See table at CALIFORNIA.

Shasta, Mount. Peak, cone of an extinct volcano, in Cascade Range, Siskiyou co., N California; 14,162 ft.; covered with glaciers; discovered 1827, first climbed 1854.

Shasta Dam *and* **Shasta Lake.** See UNITED STATES, *Dams and Reservoirs.*

Shasukotan. See SHIASHKHOTAN.

Sha·to Plateau \ˌshä-(ˌ)tō-\. Tableland, Coconino and Navajo cos., N Arizona.

Shatt–al–Ar·ab \ˌshat-ˌal-'ar-əb\. Channel, formed by the confluence of the Tigris and Euphrates rivers, SE Iraq, flowing SE into Persian Gulf; ab. 120 m. long; it is generally considered to begin at Al-Qurna, flowing past Iraqi port of Basra, past Khorramshahr and Ābādān in Iran, and entering the gulf near the port of Fao in Iraq; forms in part the boundary bet. Iran and Iraq; for ab. 60 m. above Fao, the waterway lies entirely within Iraq; navigation above Ābādān is difficult because of bar at Fao and silt in the delta region. On E shore is Ābādān I. at N end of which it receives the Kārūn river. For the most part formed since ancient times because formerly Bassorah (Basra) was much nearer the sea.

Shatt al–Hodna. See HODNA, CHOTT EL.

Shatt al–Jerid. See DJERID, CHOTT.

Shatt al–Melghir. See MELRHIR, CHOTT.

Shatt al–Shergui. See CHERGUI, CHOTT ECH.

Shatt Dijla. See TIGRIS.

Shaulyai. See ŠIAULIAI.

Shau·na·von \'shȯ-nə-vən\. Town, SW Saskatchewan, Canada, 50 m. SW of Swift Current; pop. (1971p) 2253.

Sha·va·no Peak \ˌshav-ə-ˌnō-\. Mountain, Chaffee co., cen. Colorado; 14,229 ft.

Shaver Lake *and* **Shaver Lake Dam.** See SAN JOAQUIN 1.

Sha·vers Mountain \ˌshā-vərz-\. Ridge extending along boundary bet. Randolph and Pocahontas cos., E cen. West Virginia.

Shaw \'shȯ\. Town, Bolivar and Sunflower cos., NW Mississippi, 20 m. NE of Greenville; pop. (1970c) 2513; cotton.

Shaw·an·gunk Mountains \ˌshäŋ-gəm-\. Range, part of the Kittatinny Mt. (*q.v.*), SE New York; highest peak Sam's Point 2289 ft., in Ulster co.

Sha·wa·no \'shȯ-(ˌ)nō\. 1 County in E cen. Wisconsin. See table at WISCONSIN.

2 City, its ⊗, 34 m. WNW of Green Bay (city); pop. (1970c) 6488; paper, furniture, dairy products; diversified agriculture.

Shawano Lake. Lake, Shawano co., E cen. Wisconsin; ab. 6 m. long and 3 m. wide; drains into Wolf river.

Sha·win·i·gan \shə-'win-i-gən\ *or formerly* **Shawinigan Falls.** Manufacturing city, St-Maurice co., S Quebec, Canada, on St-Maurice river 18 m. NNW of Three Rivers; pop. (1971p) 27,502; aluminum, pulp and paper, chemicals, abrasives; Seminaire Sainte Marie (1947); founded 1901; ab. 2 m. S is town of **Shawinigan–Sud** \-'süd\, pop. 11,452. **Shawinigan Falls** (165 ft. high) furnishes power for local plants and light and power for Montreal 70 m. distant.

Shaw·nee \shȯ-'nē, shä-\. 1 County in Kansas. See table at KANSAS.

2 City, Johnson co., E Kansas, S suburb of Kansas City; pop. (1970c) 20,482.

3 City, ⊗ of Pottawatomie co., cen. Oklahoma, on North Canadian river 38 m. ESE of Oklahoma City; pop. (1970c) 25,075; flour, dairy products, aircraft parts, clothing; packing plants, oil wells; Oklahoma Baptist Univ. (1906), St. Gregory's Coll. (1915).

Shaw·nee·town \'shȯ-nē-ˌtau̇n, 'shän-\. City, ⊗ of Gallatin co., SE Illinois, near Ohio river 10 m. below its confluence with Wabash river; pop. (1970c) 1742; coal mines, oil wells; agriculture; prehistoric Indian mounds.

Shaykh, Jabal ash–. See HERMON, MOUNT.

Shaykh Sa'īd. See CHEIK-SAÏD.

Shaykh 'Uthman. See SHEIK 'UTHMĀN.

Shcha·ra \'shchär-ə\ *or Pol.* **Szcza·ra** \'shchär-ə\. River, W Belorussian S.S.R., U.S.S.R.; ab. 100 m. long; flows NNW from Polesye to Neman river.

Shche·ki·no \ˌshchek-i-'nȯ\. Town, Tula Oblast, Russian S.F.S.R., U.S.S.R., ab. 15 m. SSE of Tula; pop. (1969e) 58,000.

Shchel·ko·vo \'shchel-kō-ˌvȯ\. Town, Moscow Oblast, Russian S.F.S.R., U.S.S.R., ab. 20 m. NE of Moscow; pop. (1969e) 75,000.

Shcherbakov. See RYBINSK.

Shchu·chinsk \'shchü-ˌchinsk\ *or formerly* **Shchu·chye** \'shchü-chē\. Town, Kokchetav Oblast, Kazakh S.S.R., U.S.S.R., ab. 40 m. NW of Kokchetav; pop. (1967e) 44,000.

Shear, Mount \-'shi(ə)r\. Mountain, Antarctica, 78°21'S, 86°13'W; 13,100 ft.

She·ba \'shē-bə\ *also* **Sa·ba** \'sā-bə\ *or Arab.* **Sa·ba'** \'sab-ə\. Ancient country, S Arabian Penin., probably included Yemen (✱ Aden) and Yemen (✱ San'a). Its inhabitants were Sabaeans, a Semitic race of very ancient culture; its language was closely related to Ethiopic and its people were early colonizers of Ethiopia. Wealthy and commercially strong because of its position on the India-Africa trade route (cf. story of Queen of Sheba's visit to Solomon, *1 Kings* x). Its chief cities were San'a and Marib.

She·bel·le *also* **She·be·le** \shə-'bel-ē\. River, E Africa; 1250 m. long; rises in cen. Ethiopia, flows SE across border of Somalia, approaches the coast near Mogadisho, then turns SW and flows ab. 200 m. parallel with the coast to be lost in a swamp N of the Juba river.

She·boy·gan \shi-'bȯi-gən\. 1 County in E Wisconsin. See table at WISCONSIN.

2 City, its ⊗, on Lake Michigan 51 m. N of Milwaukee; pop. (1970c) 48,484; aluminum products, plastics, veneers, paints, beer, cheese; Lakeland Coll. (1862), Sheboygan County Teachers Coll. (1909).

Sheboygan Falls. City, Sheboygan co., E Wisconsin, 3 m. W of Sheboygan; pop. (1970c) 4771.

Shechem. See NABLUS 2.

Shed·i·ac \'shed-ē-ˌak\. Resort town, Westmorland co., SE New Brunswick, Canada, on Northumberland Strait 15 m. ENE of Moncton; pop. (1971p) 2201.

Shee·lin, Lough \läk-'shē-lən\. Lake, S co. Cavan, N Eire, ENE of Longford; ab. 5 m. long; drains SW through Inny river into Lough Ree.

Sheep Haven \'shēp-\. Bay of Atlantic Ocean, N coast of co. Donegal, N Eire, W of Lough Swilly.

Sheep Mountain. 1 Peak, Banner co., W Nebraska; 4507 ft.
2 Peak, Snohomish co., NW cen. Washington; 6120 ft.
3 Peak, Teton co., WSW Wyoming; 10,772 ft.

Sheep Rock. Peak, Baker co., E Oregon; 6017 ft.

Shef·field \'shef-ˌēld\. 1 Industrial city, Colbert co., NW Alabama, on Tennessee river near Wilson Dam; pop. (1970c) 13,115.
2 Town, Berkshire co., W Massachusetts, on Housatonic river 24 m. S of Pittsfield; pop. (1970c) 2734; resort.
3 Unincorporated community, in Sheffield township (pop. [1970c] 2793), Warren co., NW Pennsylvania, ab. 12 m. SSE of Warren; pop. (1970c) 1564.
4 City and county borough, West Riding, Yorkshire, N England, on the Don 68 m. NNE of Birmingham; pop. (1971p) 519,703; center of the English cutlery industry; also manufactures steel, plated ware, iron and brass goods, type, paints and varnishes, canned goods, optical instruments, chemicals; Univ. of Sheffield (1905); former site of Norman castle (destroyed 1644) where Mary, Queen of Scots, was prisoner during part of 1570–84. Developed as center of cutlery manufacture from early 18th cent. and of steel industry (incl. esp. armor plate and alloy steels) from mid-19th cent.; made city 1893.

Sheffield Lake. City, Lorain co., N Ohio, on Lake Erie W of Cleveland; pop. (1970c) 8734.

Shef·ford \'shef-ərd\. County, Quebec, Canada. See table at QUEBEC.

She–hsien *or* **Si·hsien** \'shē-'shen\ *or formerly* **Hwei·chow** \'hwā-'jō\. City, SE Anhwei, E China.

Sheikh 'Oth·man *or* **Shaikh 'Othman** \ˌshīk-ȯth-'man, ˌshāk-\ *or* **Shaykh 'Uth·mān** \-əth-\. Town, Yemen (✱ Aden), SW Arabian Penin., ab. 6 m. N of Aden; pop. (1960e) 35,000.

She·ki \'shek-ē\ *or formerly* **Nu·kha** \nu̇-'kä\. Town, N Azerbaijan S.S.R., U.S.S.R., at foot of Caucasus Mts. 55 m. NE of Kirovabad; pop. (1967e) 39,000; has several silk-spinning factories. Once the center of a Tatar khanate, was taken over by Russians in 1819.

Shek·sna \shek-'snä\. Navigable river, Vologda and Yaroslavl oblasts, Russian S.F.S.R., U.S.S.R.; ab. 280 m. long; flows S from Lake Beloye; near Cherepovets enters Rybinsk Reservoir (*q.v.*); before 1940 entered the Volga river just W of Shcherbakov (now Rybinsk). Forms important part of the Volga-Baltic Waterway (*q.v.*).

She·lag·ski, Cape \-shə-'läk-skē\. Point on N coast of Chukot National Okrug, Russian S.F.S.R., U.S.S.R., on East Siberian Sea, 70°06'N, 170°26'E.

Shel·bi·na \shel-'bīn-ə\. City, Shelby co., NE Missouri, 28 m. NE of Moberly; pop. (1970c) 2060.

Shel·burne \'shel-bərn\. 1 Town, Chittenden co., NW Vermont, 6 m. S of Burlington; pop. (1970c) 3728.
2 County, Nova Scotia, Canada. See table at NOVA SCOTIA.
3 Seaport town, ⊗ of Shelburne co., SW Nova Scotia, Canada, on inlet of Atlantic Ocean 43 m. E of Yarmouth; pop. (1971p) 2699; shipyards; fishing resort.

Shel·by \'shel-bē\. 1 Name of counties in nine states of the U.S. See tables at ALABAMA, ILLINOIS, INDIANA, IOWA, KENTUCKY, MISSOURI, OHIO, TENNESSEE, TEXAS.
2 City, Bolivar co., NW Mississippi, 20 m. SSW of Clarksdale; pop. (1970c) 2645; cotton.
3 City, ⊗ of Toole co., N Montana, 75 m. NNW of Great Falls; pop. (1970c) 3111; oil, gas wells.
4 City, ⊗ of Cleveland co., SW North Carolina, 21 m. W of Gastonia; pop. (1970c) 16,328; textiles, flour, lumber, rayon; agriculture.
5 City, Richland co., N cen. Ohio, 11 m. NW of Mansfield; pop. (1970c) 9847; automobile parts; grain farms.

Shel·by·ville \'shel-bē-ˌvil\. 1 City, ⊗ of Shelby co., cen. Illinois, 32 m. SSE of Decatur; pop. (1970c) 4597; dairy products; coal mines.
2 City, ⊗ of Shelby co., cen. Indiana, 27 m. SE of Indianapolis; pop. (1970c) 15,094; plastics, fiber glass, clothing, paper, dairy products.
3 City, ⊗ of Shelby co., N cen. Kentucky, 20 m. W of Frankfort; pop. (1970c) 4182; tobacco market; chemicals; oil wells.
4 City, ⊗ of Shelby co., NE Missouri; pop. (1970c) 601.
5 Town, ⊗ of Bedford co., S cen. Tennessee, 25 m. S of Murfreesboro; pop. (1970c) 12,262; clothing, lumber, dairy products.

Shel·don \'shel-dən\. City, O'Brien co., NW Iowa, 32 m. NW of Cherokee; pop. (1970c) 4535; soybeans.

Shelekova Gulf. See SHELIKHOV GULF.

Shelia, Jebel. See CHELIA, DJEBEL.

Sheliff. See CHÉLIFF.

She·li·khov Gulf \ˌshel-i-kȯf-\ *also* **She·le·ko·va Gulf** \-ə-ˌkō-və-, -ˌkȯ-və-\. Gulf, Khabarovsk Krai, Russian S.F.S.R., U.S.S.R.; ab. 200 m. wide; Penzhinskaya Bay is an extension on the NE; its E shore is the NW part of Kamchatka Penin.

She·li·kof Strait \ˌshel-i-kȯf-\. Strait bet. mainland (Alaska Penin.) on W and Kodiak and Afognak Is. on E; connects with Cook Inlet at N end; ab. 150 m. long and 25–30 m. wide.

Shell Creek Range \'shel-\. Range, E White Pine co., E Nevada.

Shel·ley \'shel-ē\. City, Bingham co., SE Idaho, 8 m. SW of Idaho Falls; pop. (1970c) 2614; potatoes.

Shell Lake. City, ⊗ of Washburn co., NW Wisconsin; pop. (1970c) 928; dairy products.

Shel·ter Island \'shel-tər-\. 1 Island bet. Little Peconic Bay and Gardiners Bay, E Long I., New York; 6 m. long; summer resort.
2 Town on Shelter I., Suffolk co., New York; pop. (1970c) 1644; resort.

Shel·ton \'shelt-ᵊn\. 1 Manufacturing city, Fairfield co., SW Connecticut, on Housatonic river opp. Derby 8 m. N of Long Island Sound; pop. (1970c) 27,165; wire, hardware; incorporated 1915; town (settled 1697, incorporated 1789) is coextensive with city.
2 City, ⊗ of Mason co., W Washington, on inlet of Puget Sound 17 m. NW of Olympia; pop. (1970c) 6515; lumber; dairy products, wine; diversified agriculture.

She·ma·kha \ˌshem-ə-'kä\. Town, E Azerbaijan S.S.R., U.S.S.R., 65 m. WNW of Baku on S slopes of E Caucasus Mts.; pop. (1967e) 17,000; silk manufacturing. An ancient trading town known to Ptolemy; former capital of Shirvan khanate, subject to Persia; taken and destroyed by Nadir Shah 1742; rebuilt but annexed by Russians. Declined after earthquake 1902 and damage in Civil War 1917.

Shem·ya \'shem-yə\. Small island, one of the Semichi Is., at W end of Aleutian Is., SW Alaska, E of Attu; location of a U.S. Air Force base.

Shen·an·do·ah \ˌshen-ən-'dō-ə, ˌshan-ə-'dō-ə\. 1 River, N Virginia; 55 m. long; formed by junction of north and south forks in Warren co., flows NE across NE tip of West Virginia and empties into Potomac river at Harpers Ferry.
2 County in Virginia. See table at VIRGINIA.
3 City, Page and Fremont cos., SW Iowa, 44 m. SE of Council Bluffs; pop. (1970c) 5968; seeds; railroad shops; poultry and grain farms.

4 Borough, Schuylkill co., E cen. Pennsylvania, 11 m. N of Pottsville; pop. (1970c) 8287; clothing, plastics, beer; coal mines; truck farms.

5 Town, Page co., N Virginia, 15 m. E of Harrisonburg; pop. (1970c) 1714.

Shenandoah National Park. See UNITED STATES, *National Parks.*

Shenandoah Valley. Valley, Virginia; ab. 110 m. long, 25 m. wide; drained by the Shenandoah river bet. the Allegheny and Blue Ridge mountains, and extending SW from Harpers Ferry; scene of important operations during Civil War, esp. at Cedar Creek, Harpers Ferry, Martinsburg, and Winchester, including Sheridan's ride from Winchester to Cedar Creek where his arrival turned a Union defeat into victory.

She·nan·go \shə-'naŋ-(,)gō\. River, W Pennsylvania; ab. 100 m. long; rises in Crawford co., flows S and joins Mahoning river 4 m. SW of New Castle, Lawrence co., to form Beaver river.

Shen·di \'shen-dē\ *or* **Shan·dī** \'shän-\. Town, Northern Province, NE Sudan, on right bank of Nile river 100 m. NNE of Khartoum; leather goods, coffee.

Shengking. See LIAONING.

Sheng–li Feng. See POBEDA PEAK.

She·nip·sit Lake \,snip-sik-\. Small lake, NW cen. Tolland co., N Connecticut, W of Tolland.

Shen·si \'shen-'sē\. Province, E cen. China, bounded on NW by Ningsia Hui, on N by Inner Mongolia, on E by Shansi, Honan, and Hupeh, on S by Szechwan, and on W by Kansu; 75,598 sq. m.; pop. (1968e) 21,000,000; ✱ Sian; separated from Shansi by the Yellow river; crossed in cen. part by the Wei and Ching rivers and in the S by the Han; bordered on N by the Great Wall; divided climatically N and S by the Ch'in Ling Shan (highest point 13,474 ft.) and bordered on S, separating it from Szechwan prov., by the Ho Pa Shan and Ta-pa Shan (highest point ab. 8884 ft.). Covered extensively by loess, which makes it agriculturally rich; chief crops incl. winter wheat, cotton, beans, corn, tobacco, fruit; coal, manganese, oil.

History: For centuries a region in which Chinese civilization has developed, its capital Sian, under various names, being chief city of the empire for long periods down to 12th cent. A.D.; suffered greatly during the Muslim rebellion 1861–76 and also from a severe famine early in 20th cent. Since beginning of Chinese-Japanese War 1937 has been headquarters (at Yen-an) of the Eighth Route (Communist) Army against the Japanese and later Communist headquarters in civil war with Nationalist forces.

Shen–yang. See MUKDEN.

She·paug \shə-'pȯg\. River, W Connecticut; ab. 35 m. long; rises in N cen. Litchfield co., flows S into Housatonic river.

She·pe·tov·ka \,shep-ə-'tȯf-kə\. Town, N Khmelnitski Oblast, Ukrainian S.S.R., U.S.S.R., 70 m. W of Berdichev; pop. (1967e) 36,000; railroad junction on main line to Kovel.

Shep·herds·town \'shep-ərdz-,taůn\. Town, Jefferson co., NE West Virginia, in E panhandle on Potomac river, ab. 15 m. SW of Hagerstown, Maryland; pop. (1970c) 1688; Shepherd Coll. (1871).

Shep·herds·ville \'shep-ərdz-,vil\. City, ⊗ of Bullitt co., cen. Kentucky; pop. (1970c) 2769.

Shep·par·ton \'shep-ərt-ᵊn\. Town, N Victoria, SE Australia, on Goulburn river 102 m. NNE of Melbourne; pop. (1968e) 18,250.

Shep·pey, Isle of \-'shep-ē\. Island in mouth of the Thames, SE England; 9 m. long; 35 sq. m.; pop. (1968e) 28,360; vegetables, sheep; bridge connections with Kentish mainland.

Shep·shed \'shep-,shed\. Urban district, Leicestershire, cen. England, 12 m. NW of Leicester; pop. (1971p) 8456.

Shep·ton Mal·let \,shep-tən-'mal-ət\. Urban district, Somersetshire, SW England, 22 m. SW of Bath; pop. (1971p) 5910; church has oak roof of 13th cent. with 350 panels each of different design; market cross 50 ft. high (1500).

She·qua·ga Falls \shə-,kwȯ-gə-\. Waterfall in Montour Falls, New York; 156 ft. high.

Sher·born \'shər-bərn\. Town, Middlesex co., NE Massachusetts, 16 m. SW of Boston; pop. (1970c) 3309.

Sher·borne \'shər-bərn\. Urban district, Dorsetshire, S England, 50 m. W of Southampton; pop. (1971p) 6774; trade center in agricultural section.

Sher·bro \'shər-(,)brō\. Estuary, SW coast of Sierra Leone, W Africa, opp. Sherbro I.

Sherbro Island. Island, SW coast of Sierra Leone, W Africa; town of Bonthe is on its E coast.

Sher·brooke \'shər-,brůk\. 1 County, Quebec, Canada. See table at QUEBEC.

2 Industrial city, its ⊗, at confluence of Magog and St. Francis rivers 85 m. E of Montreal; pop. (1971p) 80,457; in summer resort region; produces gloves, mining machinery, leather and rubber products, footwear, paper, textiles; railroad shops, hydroelectric power plants; Coll. de Sacré-Coeur, Séminaire de Sherbrooke (1875), Univ. de Sherbrooke (1954), École des Sciences Domestiques.

Sher·burne \'shər-bərn\. 1 County in Minnesota. See table at MINNESOTA.

2 Village, Chenango co., S cen. New York, 32 m. SSW of Utica; pop. (1970c) 1613; boyhood home of Brigham Young 1804 ff.

Sherburne Peak. Mountain, Glacier National Park, NW Montana; 8500 ft.

Shergui, Shatt al–. See CHERGUI, CHOTT ECH.

Sher·i·dan \'sher-əd-ᵊn\. 1 Name of counties in five states of the U.S. See tables at KANSAS, MONTANA, NEBRASKA, NORTH DAKOTA, WYOMING.

2 City, ⊗ of Grant co., S cen. Arkansas; pop. (1970c) 2480; cotton gins; peanuts.

3 City, Arapahoe co., NE cen. Colorado, 4 m. S of Denver; pop. (1970c) 4787.

4 Town, Hamilton co., cen. Indiana, 25 m. N of Indianapolis; pop. (1970c) 2137.

5 City, ⊗ of Sheridan co., N Wyoming, 13 m. S of Montana border; pop. (1970c) 10,586; tourist resort; iron goods, flour; railroad shops, sugar refineries; diversified agriculture; Northern Wyoming Community Coll. (1948).

Sheridan, Mount. 1 Peak, Lake and Park cos., cen. Colorado; 13,700 ft.

2 Peak, Yellowstone National Park, NW Wyoming; 10,308 ft.

Sher·iff Knob \,sher-əf-\. Peak, Union co., N Georgia; 3400 ft.

Sher·iff·muir \'sher-əf-,myů(ə)r, 'sher-ē-,myů(ə)r\. Battlefield, S Perth co., cen. Scotland, just W of the Ochil Hills; scene of battle Nov. 13, 1715 bet. Jacobites under John Erskine, Earl of Mar, and Royalists under Archibald Campbell in which the advance of the Jacobites was checked; battle gave its name to the whole rebellion (*Sherramoor* or *Sherrymoor*).

Sher·man \'shər-mən\. 1 Name of counties in four states of the U.S. See tables at KANSAS, NEBRASKA, OREGON, TEXAS.

2 Industrial city, ⊗ of Grayson co., NE Texas, 60 m. N of Dallas; pop. (1970c) 29,061; textiles, furniture, flour, margarine, cottonseed oil; railroad shops, marble works; agriculture; Austin Coll. (1849); Perrin Air Force base.

Sherman, Fort. See FORT SHERMAN.

Sherman, Mount. Peak, Park and Lake cos., cen. Colorado; 14,036 ft.

Sher·rill \'sher-əl\. City, Oneida co., cen. New York, 19 m. W of Utica; pop. (1970c) 2986.

Shershell. See CHERCHELL.

's Her·to·gen·bosch \'ser-ˌtō-gə(n)-ˌbȯs\ *or Fr.* **Bois–le–Duc** \bwäl-ə-d(y)ük\. Commune, ✱ of North Brabant prov., S Netherlands, at the confluence of Aa and Dommel rivers; pop. (1970e) 81,574; railroad junction, cattle market; cathedral of St. John; town hall with carillon; museum; received charter 1185; fortress until 1874.

Sher·wood \'shər-ˌwu̇d\. City, Pulaski co., cen. Arkansas, 5 m. NE of Little Rock; pop. (1970c) 2754.

Sherwood Forest. Ancient royal forest, chiefly in Nottinghamshire, cen. England; remains near Mansfield, Rotherham, and vicinity.

Shet·land \'shet-lənd\. 1 *or* **Zet·land** \'zet-\ *or* **Shetland Islands.** Archipelago off N Scotland, 50 m. NE of Orkney Is.; includes islands of Unst, Fetlar, Whalsay, Mainland, Foula, Papa Stour, Yell; 552 sq. m.; pop. (1971p) 17,298; ✱ Lerwick; constitutes Zetland co.; northernmost part of Great Britain; herring fisheries, sheep and cattle raising, native horses (Shetland ponies), woolens and knitwear. Long a Norse dependency; acquired by Scotland 1472.
2 County of Scotland. See ZETLAND.

She·tuck·et \shē-'tək-ət\. River, E Connecticut; ab. 20 m. long; formed by confluence of Willimantic and Natchaug rivers at Willimantic, flows SE to unite with the Quinebaug and form the Thames.

Shev·chen·ko \shəv-'cheŋ-(ˌ)kō, shev-\. Town, Kazakh S.S.R., U.S.S.R., on E coast of the Caspian Sea; pop. (1971e) 60,000; fast breeder reactor (completed 1972); in oil-producing region.

She·wa \'shā-wə\ *or* **Shoa** \'shō-ə\. Province of cen. Ethiopia. See table at ETHIOPIA.

Shey·enne \shī-'en, -'an\. River, cen. and SE North Dakota; ab. 325 m. long; rises in Sheridan co., cen. North Dakota, flows E, then S and again E into Red River of the North above Fargo.

Shi·ash·kho·tan \shi-'äsh-kə-tən\ *or formerly* **Sha·su·ko·tan** \'shä-'sü-'kō-'tän\. One of the Kuril Is. (*q.v.*), N part of chain, S of Onekotan; highest point 3097 ft.

Shi·a·was·see \ˌshī-ə-'wȯs-ē, -'wäs-\. 1 River, SE Michigan; ab. 100 m. long; flows from Oakland co. N to unite with Flint river to form Saginaw river in Saginaw co.
2 County in Michigan. See table at MICHIGAN.

Shi·bar·ghān \ˌshi-bər-'gän\. Town, ✱ of Jowzjan prov., N Afghanistan; pop. (1969e) 54,891.

Shi·bar Pass \ˌshē-bär-\. Mountain pass, E Afghanistan, NW of Kabul, on highway to N Afghanistan; alt. 9800 ft.

Shi·ba·ta \shē-'bät-ə\. City, Niigata prefecture, Honshū, Japan, 16 m. E of Niigata; pop. (1970c) 74,459.

Shibenik. See ŠIBENIK.

Shi·bīn al–Kōm \shi-ˌbēn-al-'kōm\. Town, ✱ of Minūfīya gov., Egypt, in Nile delta 40 m. NNW of Cairo; pop. (1970e) 75,600.

Shick·shock Mountains \ˌshik-shäk-\. Mountains, N Gaspé Penin., Quebec, Canada; highest point 4159 ft.

Shiel, Loch \läk-'shē(ə)l, läk-\. Lake, W Scotland, along the border bet. Argyll and Inverness cos., 16 m. W of Fort William; 16 m. long and 1 m. wide.

Shif·nal *or* **Shiff·nal** \'shif-nəl\. Parish, Shropshire, W England, 17 m. E of Shrewsbury; church of St. Andrew; pop. (1961c) 3137; market town; Tong (*q.v.*) is 3 m. to the E.

Shi·ga \'shē-gə\. Prefecture, Honshū, Japan; 1550 sq. m.; pop. (1970c) 889,768; ✱ Ōtsu; rice; textiles.

Shigatse. See JIH-K'A-TSE.

Shih–chia–chuang *or* **Shih·kia·chwang** \'shir-jē-'ä-jə-'wäŋ\. Town, ✱ of Hopeh prov., NE China, ab. 75 m. SW of Pao-ting; pop. (1970e) 1,500,000; transportation and industrial center.

Shi·kar·pur \shi-'kär-ˌpü(ə)r\. City, Sind, Pakistan, near right bank of Indus river 240 m. NNE of Karachi; pop. (1969e) 62,500; ships silk, indigo, grains, and spices.

Shi·ko·ku \shi-'kō-(ˌ)kü\. The smallest of the four principal islands of Japan, S of Honshū and E of Kyūshū; 7245 sq. m.; pop. (1970c) 3,904,014; separated from Honshū on E by Kii Channel and from Kyūshū on W by Bungo Strait. Divided into four prefectures (see table at JAPAN); has no good harbors; crossed by range of high mountains with many branches; highest Ishizuchino 6500 ft. Chief products tea, camphor, rice, fruit, tobacco. From early times held in turn by feudal families until subjugated (c. 1590) by Hideyoshi; subdivided by him; daimiate of Tosa (old province in S part) powerful until Restoration 1868.

Shi·ko·tan–tō \ˌshē-kō-'tän-tō\ *or* **Shikotan** \ˌshē-kō-'tän\. One of the Kuril Is. (*q.v.*), just E of Hokkaidō.

Shil·don \'shil-dən\. Urban district, Durham, N England, 25 m. S of Newcastle upon Tyne; pop. (1971p) 14,499.

Shil·ka \'shil-kə\. 1 River, SW cen. Chita Oblast, Russian S.F.S.R., U.S.S.R.; 345 m. long; formed by confluence of Ingoda and Onon rivers, flows NE to unite with the Argun to form the Amur river.
2 Town, N bank of the river, ab. 110 m. E of Chita, on Trans-Siberian R.R.; pop. (1967e) 16,000.

Shilla. See SILLA.

Shil·le·lagh \shə-'lā-lē\. Village, SW co. Wicklow, Eire; famous for its oaks, whence comes the name for a cudgel originally applied only to cudgels made of oak or blackthorn saplings.

Shil·ling·ton \'shil-iŋ-tən\. Borough, Berks co., SE Pennsylvania, 5 m. SSW of Reading; pop. (1970c) 6249.

Shil·long \shi-'lȯŋ\. Town, ✱ of Assam and of Meghalaya, NE India, in W cen. part 310 m. NE of Calcutta; met. area pop. (1967e) 130,195; military cantonment; resort center. Became important as headquarters of former Khasi and Jaintia Hills District 1864 and as capital of Assam 1874; destroyed by earthquake 1897 but rebuilt.

Shi·loh \'shī-(ˌ)lō\ *or Arab.* **Khir·bat Say·lūn** \kir-ˌbät-sī-'lün, -sā-\. Ruins of ancient village in Israeli-occupied part of Jordan, 15 m. W of Jordan river on E slope of Mt. Ephraim; meeting place and sanctuary of Israelites, where a tabernacle was set up (*Josh.* xviii. 1) and where the ark of the covenant was kept until captured by the Philistines.

Shiloh National Military Park. See UNITED STATES, *National Historical Parks.*

Shi·ma·ba·ra \shi-'mäb-ə-rə\. Peninsula, W Kyūshū, Japan, E of Nagasaki; site of early establishment of Christianity, its inhabitants and those on nearby island of Amakusa suffered persecution; they rebelled 1637–38 and ab. 37,000 of them were massacred 1638 in old castle by order of Iyemitsu.

Shimabara Bay. Inlet of East China Sea, W coast of Kyūshū, Japan, NE of Nagasaki.

Shi·ma·da \shē-'mäd-ə\. City, Shizuoka prefecture, Honshū, Japan, 15 m. SW of Shizuoka; pop. (1968e) 63,493.

Shi·ma·ne \shi-'män-ē\. Prefecture, Honshū, Japan; 2559 sq. m.; pop. (1970c) 773,575; ✱ Matsue; rice; livestock raising.

Shi·ma·nov·ski \ˌshim-ə-'nȯf-skē\. Town, S Amur Oblast, Russian S.F.S.R., U.S.S.R., on Trans-Siberian R.R., 115 m. N of Blagoveshchensk; pop. (1967e) 15,000.

Shi·mi·zu \shi-'mē-(ˌ)zü\. Seaport, Shizuoka prefecture, on S coast of cen. Honshū, Japan, on Suruga Bay; pop. (1970c) 234,966; exports tea.

Shi·mo·da \shi-'mōd-ə, -'mō-ˌdä\. Seaport, Shizuoka prefecture, S Honshū, Japan, on SE coast of Izu Penin.; pop. (1970c) 30,318; visited by Commodore Perry and opened to U.S. commerce 1854; place where Townsend Harris, first U.S. consul general to Japan, established his office 1857; closed 1859 to foreign trade and Yokohama opened instead. Suffered from severe earthquake 1856.

Shi·mo·da·te \ˌshē-mō-'dät-ē\. City, Ibaraki prefecture, Honshū, Japan, 47 m. NNE of Tokyo; pop. (1970c) 53,863.

Shi·mo·ga \shi-'mō-gə\. Town, cen. Mysore, S India, on Tunga river (upper tributary of the Tungabhadra) 150 m. WNW of Bangalore; pop. (1961c) 63,764; ships rice, pepper, coffee; textiles, vegetable oils.

Shi·mo·no·se·ki \ˌshim-ə-nō-'sek-ē\; *formerly* **Aka·ma·ga·se·ki** \ˌäk-ə-ˌmäg-ə-'sek-ē\ *or* **Ba·kan** \'bäk-ˌän\. Seaport city, Yamaguchi prefecture, SW extremity of Honshū, Japan, on Shimonoseki Strait opp. Kitakyūshū and connected with it by tunnels under the straits; pop. (1970c) 258,425; modern port facilities, shipyards, heavy industrial plants; controls W entrance of Inland Sea.

History: In 1185 scene of notable battle at Danno-ura (E end of town) in which Minamoto clan under Yoshitsune decisively defeated Taira clan. Bombarded Sept. 5–8, 1864, by British, Dutch, French, and U.S. warships in retaliation against Choshu daimio for firing on foreign ships; shogun paid indemnity (U.S. portion refunded 1883). Increased rapidly in prosperity after Meiji Restoration 1868; scene of signing of treaty of peace bet. Japan and China Apr. 17, 1895.

Shimonoseki Strait. Narrow strait separating extreme SW Honshu, and extreme N Kyūshū, Japan; only ¼ m. wide at its narrowest point; W outlet of Inland Sea, with strong tidal movements. Shimonoseki and Kitakyūshū are on opposite sides (1½ m. apart) but connected by tunnel under the strait.

Shi·mu·shir \shi-'mü-shir\ *or formerly* **Shi·mu·shi·ru** \-shi-ˌrü\. One of the Kuril Is. (*q.v.*), in cen. part of chain.

Shin, Loch \läk-'shin, läk-\. Lake, Sutherland co., N Scotland; 16½ m. long.

Shi·na·no \shi-'nän-(ˌ)ō\. River, W cen. Honshū, Japan; ab. 225 m. long; rises in Nagano prefecture, flows N into the Sea of Japan at Niigata; longest river in Japan.

Shi·nar \'shī-nər, -ˌnär\. A country known to the early Hebrews as a plain in Babylonia (*Gen.* xi. 2 & xiv. 1); probably equivalent to Sumer (*q.v.*).

Shin·bwi·yang \ˌshin-bwē-'yäŋ\. Town, N Burma, on the upper Chindwin at foot of Hukawng valley.

Shin·chi·ku \'shēn-'chē-'kü\. Seaport city, NW coast of Taiwan, 37 m. SW of Taipei; univ. (1964).

Shi·ner \'shī-nər\. Town, Lavaca co., SE cen. Texas, 46 m. N of Victoria, pop. (1970c) 2095; dairy farms.

Shingishu. See SINŬIJU.

Shin·gū \'shēn-ˌgü\. Town, Wakayama prefecture, S coast of W Honshū, Japan, 55 m. SE of Wakayama; pop. (1970c) 38,808; place of pilgrimage; Shinto shrine; has ruins of ancient castle.

Shinn, Mount \-'shin\. Mountain, Antarctica, 78°27′S, 85°46′W; 15,750 ft.

Shinn·ston \'shin(t)s-tən\. City, Harrison co., N West Virginia, 8 m. N of Clarksburg; pop. (1970c) 2576.

Shinshu. See CHINJU.

Shin·yan·ga \shēn-'yäŋ-gə\. 1 Administrative region of N Tanzania. See table at TANZANIA.
2 Town, its ✻; pop. (1967e) 5135.

Shi·o·ga·ma \'sh(y)ō-gə-mə\. City, Miyagi prefecture, Honshū, Japan, 15 m. NE of Sendai; pop. (1970c) 58,772.

Shi·o·no, Cape \-shē-'ō-(ˌ)nō\ *also* **Cape Shio** \-'shē-(ˌ)ō\. Cape on S extremity of Honshū, Japan, in Wakayama prefecture.

Ship Island \'ship-\. Island, Gulf of Mexico, off SE coast of Harrison co., SE Mississippi; ab. 7 m. long. In early part of 18th cent. harbor and base for French exploration of Gulf coast region; British naval base in War of 1812. Reserved for military purposes 1847 by U.S. government; point of contention in Civil War and in latter part a Confederate prison camp. Quarantine station established 1878 and lighthouse 1879.

Ship·ka Pass *or* **Šip·ka Pass** \ˌship-kə-\ *or Bulg.* **Ship·chen·ski Pro·khod** \shēp-ˌchen(t)-skē-prə-'kōd\. Mountain pass in the Balkan Mts., cen. Bulgaria, bet. Gabrovo on N and Kazanlŭk on S; 4376 ft.; scene of major battles 1877 during the Russo-Turkish War.

Ship·ley \'ship-lē\. Urban district, West Riding, Yorkshire, N England, on the Aire 10 m. WNW of Leeds; pop. (1971p) 28,444; residential; machinery.

Ship·pan Point \ˌship-ən-\. Point on SW coast, Fairfield co., Connecticut, S of Stamford.

Ship·pens·burg \'ship-ənz-ˌbərg\. Borough, Cumberland and Franklin cos., S Pennsylvania, 10 m. NE of Chambersburg; pop. (1970c) 6536; furniture, clothing, flour; Shippensburg State College (1871).

Ship·pi·gan Island \ˌship-i-gən-\. Island off NE tip of New Brunswick, SE Canada, S of Miscou I.

Ship·shaw \'ship-(ˌ)shȯ\. River, S Quebec, Canada; ab. 90 m. long; a N tributary of the Saguenay flowing into it below Lake St. John; large hydroelectric plant for aluminum production.

Shi·ra \'shir-ə\ *also* **Shi·ra·ka·wa** \ˌshir-ə-'kä-wə\. River, W cen. Kyūshū, Japan; flows W through Kumamoto into Shimabara Bay.

Shi·rai·to–no–ta·ki \shi-ˌrīt-ō-nō-'täk-ē\. Waterfall, S Honshū, Japan, near Fuji; 87 ft. high and 420 ft. wide.

Shi·ra·ka·mi \ˌshir-ə-'käm-ē, shi-'räk-ə-mē\. Cape at S extremity of Hokkaidō, Japan.

Shirakawa. See SHIRA.

Shi·ra·ki \'shir-ə-kē\. Steppe region, a semidesert plain in E Georgian S.S.R., U.S.S.R., bet. two N tributaries of the Kura SE of Tbilisi; extensive oil fields.

Shi·ra·ku·mo–no–ta·ki \shi-'räk-ə-ˌmō-nō-'täk-ē\. Waterfall, cen. Honshū, Japan, W of Nikkō, E of Lake Chuzenji, and near the waterfall Kegon-no-taki; ab. 300 ft. high.

Shi·ra·ne \shi-'rän-ē\. Name of three mountains in Japan: (1) mountain, S cen. Honshū, W of Kōfu; several summits, highest 10,470 ft.; (2) mountain, Nagano prefecture, on border E of Nagano; 6908 ft.; (3) mountain, Gumma prefecture, with 2 summits, in Nikkō Range W of Nikkō; 8456 ft.

Shī·rāz \shi-'räz\. Industrial and commercial city, ✻ of Fārs prov., SW cen. Iran, on highway from Tehran to Būshehr; pop. (1971e) 280,000; textiles, cement, sugar, fertilizers; handicrafts (gold and silver work, mosaics, carpets and brocades); univ. (1962); numerous notable mosques, tomb of Persian poet Hafiz; birthplace of the poet Saadi and the Bab (Mirza Ali Mohammed). Became important city after 11th cent. A.D.; often damaged by earthquakes. Ruins of ancient Persepolis (*q.v.*) lie ab. 30 m. NE.

Shi·re *or* **Shi·ré** \'shi(ə)r-(ˌ)ā\ *or Port.* **Chi·re** \'shi(ə)r-ə\. River, S Malawi and cen. Mozambique, SE Africa; ab. 250 m. long; flows from Lake Nyasa S into Zambezi river; in Malawi has several cataracts, esp. Murchison Falls.

Shire Highlands *or* **Shiré Highlands.** Hill country, E bank of Shire river, S Malawi; altitude ab. 3000 ft.; healthful climate.

Shi·re·to·ko, Cape \-ˌshir-ə-'tō-(ˌ)kō\. Cape, NE extremity of Hokkaidō, Japan.

Shiretoko National Park. National park, E Hokkaidō, Japan; 160 sq. m.; volcanic mountain ranges; established 1964.

Shi·ri·ya, Cape \-shi-'rē-yə\. Cape, NE extremity of Honshū, Japan.

Shir·ley \'shər-lē\. Town, Middlesex co., NE Massachusetts, 7 m. SE of Fitchburg; pop. (1970c) 4909.

Shirpurla. See LAGASH.

Shir·van \shi(ə)r-'vän\. Medieval khanate, W shore of Caspian Sea S of the E end of the Caucasus Mts.; ✻ Shemakha. Subject to Persia 15th–19th cents.; conquered by Russia 1805–06 and annexed 1813; now forms a part of NE Azerbaijan S.S.R., U.S.S.R.

Shirwa, Lake. See CHILWA, LAKE.

Shi·shal·din \shish-'al-dən\. Volcano, S Unimak I., SW Alaska; 9370 ft.; has had several eruptions; locally known as "Smoking Moses."

Shish·ma·ref \'shish-mə-ˌref\. City, **Shishmaref Inlet,** NW coast of Seward Penin., W Alaska; pop. (1970c) 267.

Shit·tim \'shit-əm\. Valley on W side of lower Jordan N of Dead Sea, in Israeli-occupied part of Jordan; usually dry.

Shi·ve·luch, Sop·ka \ˌsȯp-kə-ˌshiv-ə-ˈlüch\. Volcano (*sopka*), Kamchatka Penin., Kamchatka Oblast, Russian S.F.S.R., U.S.S.R.; N end of Eastern Range; 15,580 ft.

Shive·ly \ˈshīv-lē\. City, Jefferson co., N cen. Kentucky, S suburb of Louisville; pop. (1970c) 19,150.

Shiv·pu·ri National Park \shiv-ˈpu̇(ə)r-ē-\. National park, Madhya Pradesh, India; 61 sq. m.; wide variety of wildlife (bear, leopard, sambar, tiger).

Shi·zu·o·ka \ˌshiz-ə-ˈwō-kə, ˈshiz-ə-(ˌ)wō-ˌkä\. 1 Prefecture, Honshū, Japan; 300 sq. m.; pop. (1970c) 3,089,895; ❋ Shizuoka.
2 City, its ❋, 55 m. SW of Tokyo, near W shore of Suruga Bay; pop. (1970c) 416,378; important tea-processing center; its port is Shimizu; univ. (1949). Residence of Iyeyasu, founder of the Tokugawa shogunate, from 1607.

Shkha·ra \ˌshə-kä-ˈrä\ *also* **Shka·ra Tau** \ˌshə-kə-rə-ˈtau̇\. Mountain (*tau*), N spur of Caucasus Mts. SE of Elbrus, in S Kabardino-Balkarian A.S.S.R., U.S.S.R.; 17,063 ft.

Shko·dër \ˈshkōd-ər\ *or* **Shko·dra** \-rə\ *or Ital.* **Scu·ta·ri** \ˈsküt-ə-rē\. 1 Province of NW Albania. See table at ALBANIA.
2 *anc.* **Sco·dra** \ˈskōd-rə\. Town, its ❋, bet. Drin river and Lake Scutari; pop. (1967e) 49,830; market town; produces cement, textiles, glass, footwear, canned goods; 14th cent. citadel, cathedral; teacher training coll. (1957). Former capital of Albania; stronghold of Scanderbeg in 15th cent.; under Turkish rule 1479–1913; battlefield in World War I.

Shkodrës, Liqen i. See SCUTARI, LAKE.

Shkum·bin \ˈshküm-bēn\ *or* **Shkum·bi** \ˈshküm-bē\. River, cen. Albania, flowing into Adriatic Sea; ab. 50 m. long; approximately the ethnological division line bet. the Ghegs of the N and the Tosks of the S.

Shlisselburg. See PETROKREPOST.

Shoa. See SHEWA.

Shoals \ˈshōlz\. Town, ⊗ of Martin co., SW Indiana, 40 m. E of Vincennes; pop. (1970c) 1039.

Shoal·wa·ter, Cape \-ˈshōl-ˌwȯt-ər, -ˌwät-\. Cape, NW coast of Pacific co., SW Washington, at N entrance to Willapa Bay.

Shō·do \ˈshōd-(ˌ)ō\ *or Jap.* **Sho·do·shi·ma** \ˌshōd-ə-ˈshē-mə, shō-ˈdō-shə-mə\. Island on W side of Harima Sea, Japan, bet. the S coast of Honshū and the NE coast of Shikoku, W of Awaji I.

Shoe·bur·y·ness \ˈshü-b(ə-)rē-ˌnes\. 1 Cape on the coast of Essex co., SE England.
2 Village, Essex, SE England, at mouth of Thames estuary in Southend-on-Sea county borough; resort.

Sho·la·pur \ˈshō-lə-ˌpu̇(ə)r\. City, SE Maharashtra, W India, 170 m. W of Hyderabad; pop. (1970e) 406,349; trade center; textiles; has old fort prominent in Deccan wars; scene of British victory 1818 over the Marathas.

Shom·du \ˈshäm-ˌdü\. Town, Lagos State, SW Nigeria; pop. (1969e) 75,068.

Shonan. See SINGAPORE 3.

Shoot·ers Island \ˌshüt-ərz-\. Island, Newark Bay, close to N coast of Staten I., New York; part of Richmond borough; shipbuilding.

Shore·ham–by–Sea \ˌshōr-əm-, ˌshȯr-\. Urban district, West Sussex, S England; pop. (1971p) 18,804; shipbuilding.

Shore·view \ˈshō(ə)r-ˌvyü, ˈshȯ(ə)r-\. Village, Ramsey co., E Minnesota, N suburb of St. Paul; pop. (1970c) 10,995.

Shore·wood \ˈshō(ə)r-ˌwu̇d, ˈshȯ(ə)r-\. Village, Milwaukee co., SE Wisconsin, 4 m. N of Milwaukee; pop. (1970c) 15,576.

Short·land Islands \ˈshȯrt-lənd-\. Group of islands, comprising **Shortland Island,** Fauro I., and other small islands in Bougainville Strait off S end of Bougainville, NW Solomon Is., W Pacific Ocean; part of British Solomon Islands protectorate. Chief town Faisi, on Shortland I. Japanese base in World War II.

Sho·sho·ne \shə-ˈshō-nē\. 1 River, NW Wyoming; length with longest headstream ab. 120 m.; rises in Park co., flows NE into Bighorn river in N Big Horn co.; formed by uniting of two headstreams, North Fork and South Fork, in Buffalo Bill Reservoir near Cody.
2 County in Idaho. See table at IDAHO.
3 City, ⊗ of Lincoln co., S Idaho; pop. (1970c) 1233.

Shoshone Falls. Waterfall in the Snake river, near Twin Falls, S Idaho; 210 ft. high.

Shoshone Lake. Lake, Yellowstone National Park, NW Wyoming, W of Yellowstone Lake; ab. 12 m. long and 8 m. wide; alt. 7800 ft.; a source of Snake river.

Shost·ka \shəst-ˈka\. Town, Sumy Oblast, Ukrainian S.S.R., U.S.S.R., ab. 85 m. NW of Sumy; pop. (1969e) 57,000.

Shott al–Jerid. See DJERID, CHOTT.

Shot·tery \ˈshät-ə-rē\. Village, Warwickshire, cen. England, 1 m. W of Stratford-upon-Avon; birthplace of Anne Hathaway.

Shott Melghir. See MELRHIR, CHOTT.

Shqipni *or* **Shqipri** *or* **Shqipëri.** See ALBANIA.

Shreve·port \ˈshrēv-ˌpō(ə)rt, -ˌpȯ(ə)rt, ˈsrēv-\. City, ⊗ of Caddo parish, NW Louisiana, on Red river 18 m. E of Texas border; pop. (1970c) 182,064; commercial and industrial center, producing lumber, chemicals, fertilizer, feed, dairy products, iron and steel goods, paper; oil refineries, oil and gas wells, cottonseed-oil mills; Centenary Coll. of Louisiana (1825); Barksdale Air Force Base; founded 1835; developed notably after discovery of oil in region 1906.

Shrews·bury \ˈshrüz-ˌber-ē, -b(ə-)rē; ˈsrüz-\. 1 Town, Worcester co., cen. Massachusetts, 5 m. ENE of Worcester; pop. (1970c) 19,186.
2 City, St. Louis co., E Missouri, W suburb of St. Louis; pop. (1970c) 5896.
3 Borough, Monmouth co., E cen. New Jersey, 8 m. NW of Asbury Park; pop. (1970c) 3315.
4 *or* ˈshrōz-\. Municipal borough, ⊗ of Shropshire, W England, on the Severn (which surrounds it on three sides) 40 m. NNW of Birmingham; pop. (1971p) 56,140; livestock market; locomotives, machine tools, electrical equipment; malting.
History: Founded 5th cent. A.D., became part of Mercia at end of 8th cent. and named Scrobesbyrig (*mod.* Shrewsbury); became seat of one of oldest English earldoms, first granted 1071 to Roger de Montgomery who established an abbey; scene of much fighting with the Welsh; plain N of town scene of battle in which Sir Henry Percy (Hotspur) was defeated and killed by forces of Henry IV.

Shrewsbury River. See NAVESINK RIVER.

Shrivijaya. See SRIVIJAYA.

Shrop·shire \ˈshräp-ˌshi(ə)r, ˈsräp-, -shər\ *or* **Sal·op** \ˈsal-əp\. County, W England, on border of Wales; 1348 sq. m.; pop. (1971p) 336,934; ⊗ Shrewsbury; chief river Severn; wheat, barley, sugar beet, potatoes; livestock; metallurgical and engineering industries; main towns incl. Shrewsbury, Wenlock, Bridgnorth.

Shtip. See ŠTIP.

Shu \ˈshü\. Ancient kingdom, China; one of the three kingdoms formed at the breakup of the Chinese Empire on the fall of the Eastern Han dynasty 220 A.D.; comprised Szechwan and most of Kweichow and Yunnan and lasted until 264 A.D.

Shuang–liao \ˈshwäŋ-ˈlyau̇\ *or* **Liao·yuan** \lə-ˈyau̇-yə-ˈwän\ *or Jap.* **Cheng·chia·tun** \ˈjuŋ-ˈjyä-ˈdün\. Town, Kirin prov., NE China, on right bank of Liao river ab. 115 m. N of Mukden; formerly an important market city for E Mongolia; rapid growth in modern times began ab. 1876.

Shuang–ya–shan \ˈshwäŋ-ˈyä-ˈshän\. Town, Heilungkiang prov., NE China, ab. 240 m. ENE of Harbin; pop. (1970e) 150,000.

Shub·rā al–Khay·mah \shu̇-ˈbrä-al-ˈkām-ə\. City, Egypt, N suburb of Cairo; pop. (1970e) 252,000.

Shuk·san, Mount \-ˈshək-ˌsän\. Peak, cen. Whatcom co., NW Washington; 9125 ft.

Shu·ma·gin \'shü-mə-ˌgēn\. Island group off SE coast of Alaska Penin., SW Alaska, in Pacific Ocean; chief island and village is Unga.

Shu·men \'shü-ˌmen\. 1 Province of NE Bulgaria. See table at BULGARIA.
2 City, its ✱, ab. 50 m. W of Varna; pop. (1968e) 68,124; has trade in grain and wine; strategically important stronghold and often besieged in wars with Turks; surrendered to Russians June 22, 1878.

Shum·shu \'shu̇m-ˌshü\ *or formerly* **Shu·mu·shu** \'shüm-(ə-)ˌshü\. Small island of the Kurils (*q.v.*), off N point of Paramushir.

Shung·nak \'shəŋ-ˌnak\. Unincorporated community, NW Alaska, on N bank of upper Kobuk river; pop. (1970c) 56.

Shur, Wilderness of \-'shər\. Desert region, N Sinai Penin., NE Egypt, near the Mediterranean Sea, in territory occupied by Israel 1967; traversed for three days by the Israelites (*Exod.* xv. 22).

Shu·rup·pak \shə-'ru̇p-ˌak\. Ancient city of Sumer, now the village of **Fa·ra** \'fär-ə\, SE Iraq, ab. 55 m. NW of An Nasiriya; was probably subject to Lagash; disappeared from the records c. 2300 B.C.; its excavations have brought to light much information.

Shūsh *or* **Shushan.** See SUSA 1.

Shu·sha \shü-'shä\. Town, SW Azerbaijan S.S.R., U.S.S.R., just S of Stepanakert.

Shūsh·tar \shüsh-'tär\. Town, Khūzestān prov., SW Iran, 50 m. N of Ahvāz, on the Kārūn river at head of navigation; pop. (1966c) 21,999; has ruins of a large citadel and remains of an elaborate canal system; has been a stronghold of the Kharijites and of the Shiites.

Shu·swap Lake \ˌshü-swäp-\. Lake, SE British Columbia, Canada, ab. 35 m. W of Revelstoke; 120 sq. m., 42 m. long; outlet is the Thompson river.

Shu·tar·gar·dan \'shü-ˌtär-gər-'dän\. Mountain pass at W end of Safed Koh, E Afghanistan; altitude 10,800 ft.; important in SE approach to Kabul.

Shu·ya \'shü-yə\. Town, cen. Ivanovo Oblast, Russian S.F.S.R., U.S.S.R., ab. 20 m. SE of Ivanovo; pop. (1970p) 70,000; textiles.

Shwe·bo \'shwā-(ˌ)bō\. 1 District, Sagaing division, Upper Burma; 7605 sq. m.; pop. (1962e) 676,625; ✱ Shwebo.
2 Town, its ✱, 50 m. NNW of Mandalay; in rice-growing region. Birthplace and capital of Alompra, founder of last Burmese dynasty; in World War II captured by British Jan. 9, 1945.

Shwe·daung \'shwā-ˌdau̇ŋ\. Town, Lower Burma, on Irrawaddy river just S of Prome.

Shwe·li \'shwā-lē\. River, E Upper Burma; ab. 400 m. long; flows SW out of Yunnan prov. in SW China, crossing Burma-China boundary at Namhkam, continues SW, turns N and empties into Irrawaddy river below Katha.

Si. 1 River, China. See HSI.
2 River, Thailand. See CHI.

Sia·chen Glacier \'syä-chən-\. Glacier in Karakoram Range, in area controlled by Pakistan; 46 m. long, ab. 2 m. wide near its terminus.

Sia·han Range \sē-'ä-ˌhän-\. Mountain range, W cen. Baluchistan, Pakistan; highest point 6775 ft.

Si·al·kot \sē-'äl-ˌkōt\. 1 District, Lahore division, Punjab, Pakistan; 2067 sq. m.; pop. (1961c) 1,596,383; ✱ Sialkot.
2 City, its ✱, near left bank of Chenab river 70 m. N of Lahore; pop. (1961c) 164,346; rubber goods, ceramics, surgical instruments, cutlery; military cantonment. Site of ancient fort and mausoleum of Sikh apostle Nanak (d. 1538).

Siam. See THAILAND.

Si·am, Gulf of \-sī-'am\ *or* **Gulf of Thai·land** \-'tī-ˌland, -lənd\. Inlet of South China Sea, mostly in Thailand, but its SE shore formed by Cambodia and South Vietnam; ab. 385 m. from NW to SE and 385 m. wide at its widest part (in S); Chao Phraya and Tha Chin rivers enter at NW point.

Si·an \'shē-'än\ *or* **Chang·an** \'chäŋ-'än\ *also* **Si·king** \'shē-'jiŋ\ *or* **Si·ngan** \'shē-'än\ *or* **Si·gnan** \'shē-'än\. City, ✱ of Shensi prov., NE cen. China, in S cen. part of province, on S bank of Wei river ab. 80 m. above its junction with the Yellow river; pop. (1970e) 1,900,000; iron and steel, textiles, chemicals, steel tubes, cement; univ. (1937), and several colleges incl. technical coll. (1960). Surrounded by walls (30 ft. high); contains many notable temples, tombs, old fortified points; principal historical remains are at **Pei-lin** \'bā-'lin\, S of the city, a collection of ab. 1000 historical stone tablets or monuments incl. one giving history of city's Christian colony 7th and 8th cents. (discovered 1625).
History: Under the name **Hsien-yang** \shē-'en-'yäŋ\ was capital of first universal emperor, Shih Huang Ti (247–210 B.C.); under later dynasties frequently the capital of the empire (under Han dynasty as Changan—also its modern official name; under T'ang dynasty as Siking). Because of location on inland trade routes an important commercial center; visited by Marco Polo 13th cent. and known by him as **Ken-zan-fu** \'ken-'zän-'fü\. Original center of Buddhism, Judaism, Islam, and Nestorian Christianity in China. Successfully withstood a siege during the Muslim rebellion 1868–70; was refuge of Empress Dowager and Emperor Kuang Hsü after Boxer rebellion 1900–02; scene of Communist kidnapping of Chiang Kai-shek Dec. 1936; has developed network of industrial suburbs under Communist rule.

Siang \shē-'äŋ\. 1 River, SE cen. China. See HSIANG.
2 *or* **Si·yang** \shē-'äŋ\ *or formerly* **Yu** \'yü\. River, S China; ab. 400 m. long; a S tributary of the Hsi (*q.v.*); rises in SE Yunnan and flows generally E in Kwangsi Chuang to unite at Kuei-p'ing with the Hung-shui to form the Hsi proper; near Nan-ning receives the Li from the S.

Siangshan. See HSIANG-SHAN.

Siangtan. See HSIANG-T'AN.

Siangyang. See HSIANG-YANG.

Siangyun. See HSIANG-YÜN.

Sia·pa \sē-'äp-ə\. River, S Venezuela; ab. 200 m. long; flows W into Casiquiare river.

Siar·gao \sē-ˌär-'gau̇\. Island, part of Surigao del Norte prov., off NE coast of Mindanao, Phil.; 169 sq. m.; chief municipality Dapa. Separated from Dinagat I. on the W by Dinagat Sound.

Si·a·scon·set \ˌsī-əs-'kȯn-set\ *or locally* **Scon·set** \'skȯn-set\. Summer resort, originally a fishing hamlet, Nantucket I., Massachusetts; first wireless station in U.S., built 1901, dismantled 1918.

Sia·si \sē-'äs-ē\. Chief island of Tapul group, cen. Sulu Archipelago, Sulu prov., Phil.; 30 sq. m.; munic. pop. (1969e) 53,800.

Šiau \'shau̇\. See SANGIHE ISLANDS.

Šiau·liai \'shau̇-'lā\ *or Russ.* **Shau·lyai** \'shau̇-'lyī\ *or Ger.* **Schau·len** \'shau̇-lən\. City, N Lithuanian S.S.R., U.S.S.R., 75 m. NNW of Kaunas; pop. (1969e) 88,000; leather and footwear industries, flax processing; railroad shops. Battlefield Nov. 1919 where a combined force of Lithuanians and Letts defeated Germans; in World War II held by Germans 1941–44.

Si·ba·lom \ˌsē-bə-'lōm\. Municipality, Antique prov., Panay, Phil., interior town 10 m. NE of San Jose de Buenavista; pop. (1969e) 33,500.

Ši·be·nik \shē-'ben-ik\ *also* **Shi·be·nik** \shi-\ *or Ital.* **Se·be·ni·co** \ˌsā-bə-'nē-(ˌ)kō\. Seaport city, Croatia, Yugoslavia, 30 m. NW of Split; pop. (1965e) 29,000; ships bauxite and wine; woolens, calcium carbide, dyes; naval base, hydroelectric plant; 15th cent. cathedral, 16th cent. town hall.

Si·be·ria \sī-'bir-ē-ə\. Region, U.S.S.R., extending from the Ural Mountains to the Pacific Ocean, on N bounded by the

Arctic Ocean, approx. S limits cen. Kazakh S.S.R. and the boundaries of China and the Mongolian People's Republic; 5,330,896 sq. m.; pop. (1970p) 35,605,000; region lies almost entirely within the Russian S.F.S.R., except for a small part in the Kazakh S.S.R.; in an administrative sense, political subdivisions bordering on the Ural Mountains and the Pacific Ocean are not considered part of Siberia; constituent administrative units are: Altai Krai, Krasnoyarsk Krai, Chita, Irkutsk, Kemerovo, Novosibirsk, Omsk, and Tomsk oblasts, and the Buryat, Tuva, and Yakutsk A.S.S.Rs. *Physical features:* Bordered by Kara, Laptev, and East Siberian seas on N (parts of the Arctic Ocean) and by Bering Sea, Sea of Okhotsk, and Sea of Japan on E (parts of the Pacific). Has 3 large peninsulas, Taimyr, Chukotski, and Kamchatka; principal islands off its coasts are Severnaya Zemlya group, New Siberian Is., Wrangel, Komandorskiye Is., and Sakhalin. The N belt along the Arctic Ocean consists of open, frozen tundra, rich in fur-bearing animals; in the W are low plains, some with extensive marshland; in the S and cen. parts are several plateaus; in the E and SE numerous mountain ranges: Eastern Range on Kamchatka, containing highest peak in Siberia (Klyuchevskaya Sopka 15,580 ft.); Cherskogo and Chukot Ranges, and Verkhoyansk Kolyma, Stanovoi and Yablonovy mountains, and the Sikhote-Alin along the coast of the Sea of Japan; Sayan Mts. on the S border and Ural Mts. on the W. Its great rivers, the Ob, Yenisei, and Lena, flow N to the Arctic Ocean, and the Amur on its SE border flows E to Tatar Strait; other rivers are the Khatanga, Yana, Indigirka, Kolyma, and Anadyr. In the S is the large Lake Baikal. *Chief products:* Coal, iron ore, manganese, gold, copper, lead, zinc, tungsten; large oil fields in W brought into production 1966; spring wheat, oats, rye; lumbering, fishing. *Chief cities:* Novosibirsk, Omsk, Krasnoyarsk, Novokuznetsk, Irkutsk, Barnaul, Kemerovo, Tomsk, Ulan-Ude, Chita.

History: Tatar Khanate of Siberia conquered for Russia by Cossacks under Ermak Timofeev 1581 (Cossack name of region **Si·bir** \sə-'bi(ə)r\); region of Amur river (*q.v.*) reached by Russians in 1644 and partly abandoned by Treaty of Nerchinsk 1689; Maritime Province ceded to Russia by China 1860; connected with Russia by Trans-Siberian R.R., built 1891–1905. Eastern Siberia the scene of activities of anti-Bolshevist Admiral Kolchak and of Allied intervention 1918–19; reconquered by Bolsheviks and made part of Russian S.F.S.R. In World War II its W part, esp. the industrial and mining areas, played an important role in the Soviet war effort. Has undergone large-scale colonization and exploitation of its natural resources since World War II.

Si·be·rut *or Du.* **Si·be·roet** \ˌsē-bə-'rüt\. Island, Mentawai Is., off W coast of Sumatra opp. Padang, Indonesia; ab. 54 m. long.

Siberut Strait. Channel bet. Siberut I. on S and Buta Is. on N, Indonesia, off W coast of Sumatra; ab. 27 m. wide.

Si·bi \'sē-bē\. Town, NE Baluchistan, Pakistan, on railroad at S end of Bolan Pass, 73 m. SE of Quetta; pop. (1961c) 13,327.

Si·bil·li·ni Mountains \ˌsē-bə-ˌlē-nē-\. Range of the Roman Apennines, SW Marches, cen. Italy; includes Monte Vettare 8130 ft., highest point in the Roman Apennines.

Sibir. 1 Region, U.S.S.R. See SIBERIA.

2 Anc. town, W Siberia. See ISKER 2.

Si·biu \sē-'byü\. 1 County of cen. Romania. See table at ROMANIA.

2 City, its ⊗, N of the Transylvanian Alps; pop. (1970e) 120,118; commercial and industrial center producing machinery, chemicals, textiles, footwear, and building materials; cathedral, 14th cent. church, museum, art gallery. A Roman colony; refounded by German settlers from Saxony 12th cent. and destroyed by Tatars 1241; came under Austria 1699.

Sib·ley \'sib-lē\. 1 County in Minnesota. See table at MINNESOTA.

2 City, ⊗ of Osceola co., NW Iowa, 46 m. NNW of Cherokee; pop. (1970c) 2749; dairy farms.

Si·bol·ga \si-'bȯl-gə\. Coastal town, NW Sumatra, Indonesia, on Sibolga Bay; pop. (1961c) 38,655.

Sibolga Bay *or formerly* **Ta·pa·noe·li Bay** \ˌtäp-ə-'nü-lē-\. Inlet of the Indian Ocean, NW coast of Sumatra, Indonesia, opp. Nias I.; Sibolga is on its NE shore.

Si·bo·ney \ˌsē-bə-'nā\. Town, S coast of Cuba, just E of Santiago de Cuba; with Daiquirí to the E was landing place of U.S. forces June 20, 1898.

Si·bonga \sē-'bȯŋ-gə\. Municipality, Cebu prov., on E coast of Cebu I., Phil., 28 m. SW of City of Cebu; pop. (1969e) 26,100; has anchorage on Bohol Strait.

Sib·sa·gar \sib-'säg-ər\. Town, NE Assam, NE India, near left bank of Brahmaputra 85 m. SW of Sadiya; pop. (1961c) 15,100; center of tea cultivation.

Si·bu \'sē-(ˌ)bü\. Commercial town, W Sarawak, Malaysia, on island of Borneo, at head of delta of Rajang river 60 m. upstream, and 115 m. NE of Kuching; pop. (1960c) 29,630.

Si·bu·guey Bay \ˌsē-bə-ˌgā-\. Large inlet of Moro Gulf, SE coast of Zamboanga prov., Mindanao, Phil.; its mouth is ab. 35 m. wide from Olutanga I. on the E to SW peninsula on the W.

Si·bu·tu \ˌsē-bü-'tü\. Low, wooded island, westernmost of the Sulu Archipelago, Phil.; 39 sq. m.; SW of Tawitawi and separated from it by Sibutu Passage; ab. 25 m. SE of the NE point of Sabah, Malaysia. After conclusion of treaty with Spain Dec. 10, 1898, by which Philippine possessions were ceded to U.S., it was discovered that this island was omitted; by a supplementary convention concluded Nov. 7, 1900 and proclaimed Mar. 23, 1901 $100,000 was granted Spain for correction of the oversight.

Sibutu Passage. Channel, SW Sulu Archipelago, Phil., separating Sibutu I. on the SW from Tawitawi I.; ab. 12 m. wide; one of the main channels of navigation connecting Sulu Sea and Celebes Sea.

Si·bu·yan \ˌsē-bu-'yän\. Island, E part of Romblon prov., cen. Phil., in Sibuyan Sea; 173 sq. m.; chief municipality Cajidiocan. Mountainous with **Mount Sibuyan** in center 6745 ft., highest point in province.

Sibuyan Sea. Body of interisland water, cen. Phil., NW of Visayan Sea; bordering it are Marinduque I. and S coast of Luzon on the N and enclosing it on other sides are the Visayan islands of Burias, Masbate, Panay, and Tablas. Sibuyan I. and Romblon I. are within it. From this sea in Oct. 1944 part of the Japanese fleet emerged through San Bernadino Strait to engage U.S. fleet off Leyte.

Si·ca·poo, Mount \-ˌsē-kə-'pō\ *or* **Mount Pac·san** \-päk-'sän\. Mountain in Cordillera Central, NW Luzon, Phil.; highest point 7715 ft. in Ilocos Norte prov.

Sicca Veneria. See LE KEF.

Sichang. See HSI-CH'ANG.

Sic·i·lies, The Two \-'sis-(ə-)lēz\. Former kingdom consisting of S Italy and the island of Sicily (*q.v.*).

Sic·i·ly \'sis-(ə-)lē\; *Ital. and anc.* **Si·ci·lia** \si-'sil-yə, *Ital.* sē-'chēl-yä\; *anc. also* **Tri·nac·ria** \trə-'nak-rē-ə, trī-\. Largest island in the Mediterranean Sea, W of extreme S point of the Italian penin.; 9925 sq. m.; pop. (1968e) 4,867,650; ✱ Palermo; politically, an autonomous region of Italy (see table at ITALY); separated from Italian mainland by narrow Strait of Messina and from Africa (NE Tunisia) by a narrow part of the Mediterranean (ab. 90 m.). Volcano of Etna 10,902 ft. dominates its E end; entire island is mountainous with most of it a plateau having highest range along N coast (highest point 6467 ft.); rivers numerous but small, largest the Simeto. Coastline regular with several wide inlets, esp. Gulf of Castellammare on NW and Gulf of Catania on E; Cape Passero is SE point and chief islands are Lipari Is. off NE coast, Egadi Is. at W end, and Ustica I. farther out to NW in Tyrrhenian Sea. *Chief products:* Wheat, fruit, olives and olive oil, wines, vegetables; oil, sulfur; fishing. *Chief cities:* Palermo, Catania, Messina, Syracuse (Siracusa), Trapani, Caltanissetta.

History: Originally inhabited by Sicani; from 8th cent. B.C. colonized by Greeks who drove to W coast the earlier Phoenician settlements; Syracuse (*q.v.*) became leading city of ancient Sicily and, for a time, successfully resisted cities under Carthage; former Carthaginian territory in Sicily, conquered by Rome in 3d cent. B.C., became first Roman province; part of Vandal and Ostrogothic kingdoms and of Byzantine Empire; overrun by Muslims 9th cent. A.D.; Sicily and Naples conquered by Normans 1072–91 who founded kingdom of **The Two Sicilies,** consisting of S Italy and Sicily; became Hohenstaufen territory by marriage of its heiress to future Emperor Henry VI; under Emperor Frederick II (d. 1250), despite struggle with Papacy, kingdom of Two Sicilies eclipsed other European states in cultural brilliance and administration; conquered 1266 by Charles of Anjou whose harsh rule caused uprising and massacre (Sicilian Vespers) 1282, his expulsion from Sicily, and the introduction of the rule of the house of Aragon (finally established after war lasting until 1302); Naples (*q.v.*) remained Angevin; Sicily under separate Aragonese dynasty 1295–1409; reunited with Naples from 1442; under Spanish rule to 1713; held by Savoy 1713–20, by Austria 1720–35; see NAPLES for later years of its history in connection with Italy. In World War II invaded by U.S. troops July 9–10, 1943 and by British July 10; Allied conquest of island completed by Aug. 16 (38 days); received a degree of local autonomy 1948.

Si·cua·ni \si-ˈkwän-ē\. Town, Cuzco dept., SE Peru; alt. 11,650 ft.; pop. (1961c) 10,700; highway and railroad junction point on the Urubama river 70 m. SE of Cuzco.

Siculum Fretum. See MESSINA, STRAIT OF.

Si·cy·on \ˈsis(h)-ē-ˌän\ *or Gk.* **Sik·y·on** \ˈsik-ē-ˌȯn\. Ancient city, NE Peloponnesus, S Greece, ab. 10 m. NW of Corinth and near the S shore of the Gulf of Corinth; chief town of the district of Sicyonia. Influential in Greek history, esp. when it assumed leadership of Ionians under the tyrant Cleisthenes at beginning of 6th cent. B.C.; noted for its artists and art schools. After 500 B.C. generally followed Sparta or Corinth, but in 3d cent. B.C. was prominent under Aratus as a leader in the Achaean League; declined after 146 B.C.

Si·cy·o·nia \ˌsis(h)-ē-ˈō-nē-ə\. Small district, NE Peloponnesus, anc. Greece, comprising the territory immediately around the city of Sicyon; touched upon Corinth, Argolis, Arcadia, and Achaea.

Si·da·mo \si-ˈdäm-(ˌ)ō\. Province of S Ethiopia. See table at ETHIOPIA.

Siddhpur. See SIDHPUR.

Side·ling Hill \ˌsīd-liŋ-\. Ridge, S Pennsylvania, extending SW in Huntingdon and Bedford cos. to the Maryland border; highest point 2195 ft.

Si·der·no \si-ˈde(ə)r-(ˌ)nō\. Commune, Reggio di Calabria prov., Calabria, S Italy, 33 m. ENE of Reggio di Calabria; pop. (1968e) 15,191.

Si·de·ro, Cape \-ˈsē-t͟hə-ˌrō\ *or Gk.* **Sí·dhe·ros** \-ˌrōs\. Point, NE tip of Crete, Greece, projecting into Caso Strait.

Si·de·ro·kas·tron \ˌsē-t͟hi-ˈrō-kä-ˌstrȯn\ *or Gk.* **Ákra Si·dhi·ró·kas·tron** \ˌäk-rä-ˌsē-t͟hē-ˈrō-käs-ˌtrȯn\; *Turk.* **De·mir His·sár** *or* **Demir Hi·sar** \ˌdem-i(ə)r-hi-ˈsär\. Commune, Serrai dept., cen. Macedonia, Greece, on Struma river near Bulgarian frontier NNW of Serrai.

Sidh·pur *or* **Siddh·pur** \ˈsid-ˌpu̇(ə)r\. City, E Gujarat, W India, on Saraswati river 63 m. N of Ahmadabad; pop. (1961c) 33,850; very old town with ruins of ancient temple of Rudra Mala; a place of pilgrimage.

Si·di Abd·al·lah \ˌsē-dē-ab-ˈdu̇l-ə\. See BIZERTE.

Sī·dī al–Ha·ni \ˌsēd-ē-al-ˈhän-ē\. Salt depression, NE Tunisia, near coast.

Sīdī Bar·rā·ni \-bə-ˈrän-ē\. Coastal village, NW Egypt, E of Buqbuq and W of Marūh. In World War II scene of much fighting in North Africa campaign; captured by Italians Sept. 1940, by British Dec. 11, 1940; taken by Rommel's army 1941 but recaptured Nov. 10–11, 1942 in Rommel's retreat.

Sidi–bel–Ab·bès \ˌsē-dē-ˌbel-ə-ˈbes\. Commune, N cen. Oran dept., NW Algeria, 40 m. S of Oran; pop. (1966c) 86,581; alt. 1552 ft.; headquarters of the French Foreign Legion until Algerian independence (1962); founded 1843.

Sidi–bou–Zid \-bü-ˈzēd\. Town, cen. Tunisia, 10 m. WSW of Faïd Pass; pop. (1966c) 3700.

Sidi Ka·cem \-ˈkä-səm\ *or formerly* **Pe·tit·jean** \pə-ˌtē-ˈzhäⁿ\. Town, N Morocco, NW Africa, W of Fès.

Sid·law Hills \ˌsid-lȯ-\. Range of hills in Perth and Angus cos., cen. Scotland; highest point **Auch·ter·house Hill** \ȯk-tər-ˌhau̇s-\ 1399 ft.

Sid·ley, Mount \-ˈsid-lē\. Peak, Marie Byrd Land, Antarctica, 77°02′S, 126°05′W; 13,713 ft.; discovered 1934.

Sid·mouth \ˈsid-məth\. Urban district, Devonshire, SW England, on English Channel at the mouth of the Sid 13 m. ESE of Exeter; pop. (1971p) 12,039; seaside resort.

Sid·ney \ˈsid-nē\. 1 Town, ⊗ of Fremont co., SW corner of Iowa; pop. (1970c) 1061; agriculture.

2 City, ⊗ of Richland co., E Montana, on Yellowstone river 50 m. NE of Glendive; pop. (1970c) 4543; sugar refinery; livestock, grain farms.

3 City, ⊗ of Cheyenne co., W Nebraska, 61 m. SE of Scottsbluff; pop. (1970c) 6403; dairy products.

4 Village, Delaware co., S New York, on Susquehanna river 30 m. ENE of Binghamton; pop. (1970c) 4789; automobile parts; poultry farms.

5 Manufacturing city, ⊗ of Shelby co., W Ohio, 30 m. NW of Springfield; pop. (1970c) 16,332; engine lathes, refrigerator compressors, aluminum products; hogs, soybeans.

6 Village, British Columbia, Canada, on Vancouver I. 20 m. N of Victoria; pop. (1971p) 4859; fish- and fruit-canning; agriculture.

Si·do·ar·djo *or* **Si·do·ar·jo** \ˌsē-dō-ˈär-(ˌ)jō\.Town, East Java prov., Indonesia, near coast ab. 15 m. S of Surabaja; pop. (1961c) 33,414.

Si·don \ˈsīd-ᵊn\ *or* **Zi·don** \ˈzīd-ᵊn\ *or Fr.* **Saï·da** \sä-ē-dȧ\ *or Arab.* **Say·dā** \ˈsīd-ə\. Seaport, SW Lebanon, 22 m. N of Tyre; trade center in agricultural region; fishing port; Mediterranean terminus of oil pipeline from Saudi Arabian oil fields.

History: Ancient city founded 3d millenium B.C. and from 2d millenium a principal city of Phoenicia; noted for colonization and for its manufacture of glass and purple dyes. Ruled successively by the major powers of ancient times: Philistines, Assyria, Babylonia, Egypt (7th cent. B.C.), Alexander, Selucids, and Romans; greatly embellished by Herod the Great. Changed hands several times during the Crusades and destroyed by Mongols 1260; flourished under Turkish rule after 1517 but declined following expulsion of French traders 1791 and earthquake 1837.

Sid·ra, Gulf of \-ˈsid-rə\ *or Arab.* **Kha·līj Surt** \kä-ˈlēj-ˈsu̇(ə)rt\ *or anc.* **Syr·tis Ma·jor** \ˌsər-təs-ˈmā-jər\. Inlet of Mediterranean Sea, on N cen. coast of Libya, N Africa.

Siebenbürgen. See TRANSYLVANIA 2.

Sie·ben·ge·bir·ge \ˈzē-bən-gə-ˌbi(ə)r-gə\. Hills in the Westerwald, West Germany, on right bank of the Rhine 6 m. SSE of Bonn, including Drachenfels 1053 ft., Löwenburg 1506 ft., and Ölberg 1509 ft.

Siedl·ce \ˈshed-ᵊl-ˌtsā\ *also* **Syed·lets** \ˈshed-ləts\ *or Ger.* **Sed·lez** \ˈzed-lets\. Industrial commune, Warszawa prov., NE cen. Poland, ab. 55 m. ESE of Warsaw; pop. (1970p) 39,000; episcopal see; food processing, metalworking; received town rights c. 1557; to Austria 1795; part of Duchy of Warsaw 1809–15 and then to Russia until 1918; site of German concentration camps in World War II.

Sieg \ˈzēk\. River, West Germany; ab. 80 m. long; flows W into the Rhine 2 m. N of Bonn.

Sieg·burg \'zēk-ˌbərg, -ˌbu̇(ə)rg\. City, North Rhine-Westphalia, West Germany, on Sieg river 14 m. SE of Cologne; pop. (1969e) 33,940; synthetic fibers; 12th cent. church; made city 1182.

Sie·gen \'zē-gən\. Industrial city, North Rhine-Westphalia, West Germany, on Sieg river 49 m. E of Cologne; pop. (1969e) 57,946; metal goods, machinery; iron mines; 13th cent. church. Birthplace of the painter Rubens.

Siegfried Line. See WESTWALL.

Sieg·lar \'zēg-lər\. City, North Rhine-Westphalia, West Germany, 6 m. N of Bonn; pop. (1969e) 26,904; plastics, ceramics.

Sie·mia·no·wi·ce Śląskie \she-ˌmyän-ə-ˌvēt-sə-'shlōⁿ(n)-skē-ə\ *or formerly* **Siemianowice–Hu·ta Lau·ra** \-ˌhüt-ə-'lau̇-rə\. Industrial city, Katowice prov., S Poland; pop. (1970p) 67,300; iron and steel, machinery, hardware; coal mines.

Si·em Re·ap *or* **Si·em·ré·ap** \ˌsē-əm-'rē-əp\. Town, NW Cambodia, SE Asia, on highway just N of NW end of Tonle Sap; pop. (1962p) 10,230; official station for visitors to ruins of Angkor (*q.v.*).

Sie·na \sē-'en-ə\. 1 Province of Tuscany, W Italy. See table at ITALY.

2 *or anc.* **Sae·na Ju·lia** \ˌsē-nə-'jül-yə\. Commune, its ✱, 33 m. S of Florence; pop. (1968e) 65,966; produces fertilizer, chemicals, wine; tourist center. Retains an essentially medieval appearance, with medieval walls and numerous notable buildings, including the 13th cent. Gothic-Romanesque cathedral with 14th cent. campanile, church of San Giovanni (beneath the cathedral and serving as its crypt), 13th cent. Palazzo Pubblico, Palazzo Piccoloimini, Loggia del Nobilii, Palazzo Buonsignori, Accademia di Belle Arti, Accademia dei Fisiocritici (natural history museum); univ. (1240).

History: Founded by Etruscans, passing later to Romans and Lombards; at time of Frankish invasions, formed countship; became independent in 12th cent.; seat of Ghibelline faction and rival of Florence; conquered by Charles of Anjou 1270 and forced to join Guelph confederation; became seat of Sienese school of art, second in importance only to Florence and Rome, producing such artists as Duccio and Jacopo della Quercia; era of artistic splendor ended by Black Death 1348; under Visconti of Milan for short time; under Pandolfo Petrucci 1487 ff.; taken by Spaniards 1531, French, and later (1557) by Florence whose subsequent history it shared. In World War II occupied by Allies July 3, 1944.

Sienyang. See HSIEN-YANG.

Sie·radz \'sher-ˌäts\. Commune, Łódź prov., cen. Poland, on Warta river 35 m. WSW of Łódź; pop. (1968e) 17,000; manufactures leather, lumber; seat of independent medieval principality, later residence of voivode and meeting place of Polish national assembly.

Sie·ro \sē-'e(ə)r-(ˌ)ō\. Commune, Oviedo prov., NW Spain, 9 m. ENE of Oviedo; pop. (1970p) 35,896; leather, soap, linen; coal mines.

Sierpc \'sherpts\. Industrial commune, Warszawa prov., NE cen. Poland, 70 m. NW of Warsaw; pop. (1968e) 12,200.

Si·er·ra \sē-'er-ə\. Name of counties in two states of the U.S. See tables at CALIFORNIA and NEW MEXICO.

Sierra An·cha \-'an-chə\. Ridge, cen. Gila co., cen. Arizona, NE of Roosevelt Lake; highest point 7694 ft.

Sierra Blan·ca \-'blaŋ-kə\. 1 Range, S cen. New Mexico, chiefly in N Otero and S Lincoln cos.

2 Village, ⊗ of Hudspeth co., W Texas; pop. (1969e) 900.

Sierra Blanca Peak *or* **White Mountain.** Mountain, N Otero co., S New Mexico; 12,003 ft.

Sie·rra de Al·ca·raz \-dā-ˌäl-kə-'räz\. Mountain range, mostly in Albacete prov., SW cen. Spain.

Sierra de Curupira. See SERRA CURUPIRA.

Sierra de Fa·ma·ti·na \-dā-ˌfäm-ə-'tē-nə\ *or* **Ne·va·do de Famatina** \nā-ˌväd-ō-, -ˌväth-\. Mountain range in the Andes Mts., in La Rioja prov., NW Argentina; highest peak **Ge·ne·ral Man·uel Bel·gra·no** \ˌhā-nā-'räl-man-ˌwel-bel-'grän-(ˌ)ō\, 20,505 ft.

Sierra de Ga·ta \-dā-gät-ə\. Mountain range, W Spain and E Portugal, separating the basins of the Tagus and Douro rivers; highest peak 5690 ft.

Sierra de Gre·dos \-də-'grād-(ˌ)ōs\. Mountain range, W cen. Spain, W of Madrid; highest peak Plaza de Almanzor, 8501 ft.

Sierra de Guadalupe. See GUADALUPE MOUNTAINS 2.

Sierra de Gua·da·rra·ma \-də-ˌgwäd-ə-'räm-ə\. Mountain range, cen. Spain; highest peak Pico de Peñalara 7970 ft.

Sierra de Juá·rez \-dā-'hwär-ˌes, -'wär-əz\. Mountain range, N Baja California, Mexico; highest peak 6560 ft.

Sierra de la Gi·gan·ta \-də-ˌlä-hē-'gänt-ə\. Range, SE coast of Baja California, Mexico; highest peak 5760 ft.

Sierra de la Ma·ca·re·na National Park \-də-lə-ˌmä-kə-'rā-nə-\. National park, Colombia; 4366 sq. m.; established 1948.

Sierra de la Ven·ta·na \-ˌdā-lə-ven-'tän-ə\. Mountain range, S Buenos Aires prov., E cen. Argentina; highest peak 4077 ft.

Sierra de los Ór·ga·nos \-dā-lōz-'ȯr-gä-ˌnōs\. Mountain range, W Pinar del Río prov., W Cuba; highest point 1938 ft.

Sierra del Ro·sa·rio \-del-rō-'zär-ē-ˌō, -'sär-\. Mountain range, N Pinar del Río prov., W Cuba.

Sierra de Luquillo. See LUQUILLO MOUNTAINS.

Sierra de Mérida. See CORDILLERA MÉRIDA.

Sierra de Mi·sio·nes \-ˌdā-mēs-'yōn-es\. Mountain range, NE Argentina, extending NE into S Brazil.

Si·er·ra Gal·li·nas \-gə-'yē-nəs\. Mountain range, cen. New Mexico, chiefly in Torrance and Lincoln cos.

Sierra Le·one \sē-ˌer-ə-lē-'ōn, ˌsir-ə-\. 1 Republic, W Africa, bounded on N and E by Guinea, on SE by Liberia, on S by Liberia and the Atlantic Ocean, and on W by the Atlantic Ocean; 27,699 sq. m.; pop. (1972e) 2,627,000; ✱ Freetown. *Physical features:* Its coastal belt, ab. 350 m. long and 30–50 m. wide, characterized by mangrove swamps; N region consists of upland plateau, highest peak in Loma Mts. (Bintimane, 6390 ft.). *Chief products:* Palm kernels, coffee, cocoa, ginger; diamonds, iron ore, rutile; ab. 75% of labor force is engaged in agriculture. *Chief towns:* Freetown, Bo, Kenema.

History: Coast region first visited by Portuguese 1462; followed by English slave traders; settlements for runaway and freed slaves established on coast under sponsorship of English philanthropists 1787; Freetown first established 1788 on land purchased from Temne chief; settlement failed but reestablished 1794; coastal settlement became a British colony 1808. Hinterland gradually penetrated; after clash with French 1893 region acquired by treaty 1895 and proclaimed a protectorate 1896; achieved independence 1961; civilian government overthrown by armed forces 1967, restored 1968; became a republic 1971.

2 River, Sierra Leone (1 above), W Africa, the estuary of the Rokel river; flows into the Atlantic Ocean at Freetown.

Sierra Leone Peninsula. Peninsula extending into Atlantic Ocean on W coast of Sierra Leone; ab. 28 m. long and 9 m. wide.

Si·er·ra Mad·re \sē-'er-ə-ˌmäd-rē\. 1 Range, S Wyoming, extending S into N Colorado; part of the Continental Divide.

2 City, Los Angeles co., SW California, 13 m. NE of Los Angeles; pop. (1970c) 12,140; residential; plastics.

Sie·rra Ma·dre. 1 Range, SE Mexico, extending SE into N Guatemala; chiefly in S Chiapas state, Mexico.

2 Main mountain range of NE Luzon, Phil., extending ab. 215 m. along coast of Pacific Ocean, turning SW at its S end to join the Cordillera Central in N Nueva Vizcaya; averages 3500 to 5000 ft. with highest point 6068 ft.; sometimes applied also to continuation of range S into Bicol Penin.

Sierra Madre del Sur \-ˌdel-'su̇(ə)r\. Coastal range, S Mexico, along SW and S coasts of Guerrero and Oaxaca states.

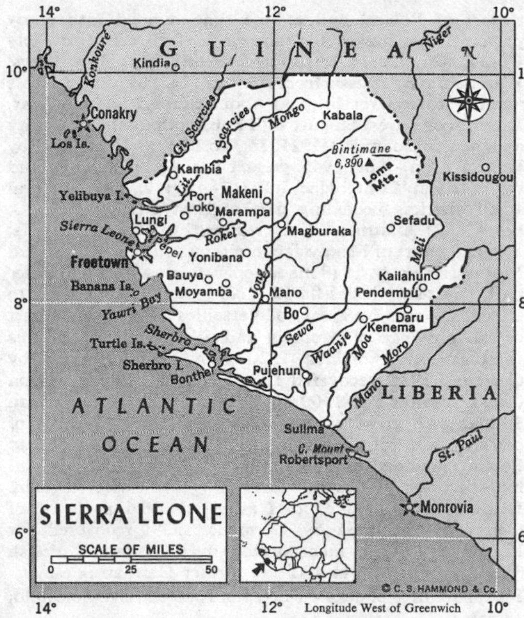

Sierra Madre Oc·ci·den·tal \-ˌäk-sə-ˌden-ˈtäl\ *also* **Western Sierra Madre.** Range of mountains, Mexico, running parallel to Pacific Ocean coast and bordering cen. Mexican plateau on the W; ab. 700 m. long N to S; several peaks above 10,000 ft.

Sierra Madre Orien·tal \-ˌōr-ē-en-ˈtäl, -ˌȯr-\ *also* **Eastern Sierra Madre.** Range of mountains, Mexico, running parallel to Gulf of Mexico coast and bordering cen. Mexican plateau on the E; average height ab. 7000 ft., with some peaks above 10,000 ft.

Sierra Ma·es·tra \-mä-ˈes-trə\. Mountain range, Oriente prov., E Cuba, extending W and E along the S coast; highest peak Pico Turquino 6540 ft.

Sierra Mo·re·na \-mə-ˈrā-nə\. Mountain range, SW Spain, bet. the Guadiana and Guadalquivir rivers; highest peak Estrella, 4339 ft.

Si·er·ra Ne·vada \-nə-ˈvad-ə, -ˈväd-\. Mountain range, E California, parallel to the Coast Ranges; ab. 400 m. long; highest peak Mount Whitney 14,494 ft. See CASCADE RANGE.

Sie·rra Ne·va·da \-nə-ˈvad-ə, -ˈväd-\. Mountain range, S Spain, mostly in Granada and Almería provs.; highest peak Mulhacén 11,408 ft.

Sierra Nevada de Co·cuy \-ˌdā-kō-ˈkwē\. Mountain ridge of the Cordillera Oriental, E Andes, in Colombia; highest point 18,021 ft.

Sierra Nevada de Mérida. See CORDILLERA MÉRIDA.

Sierra Nevada de San·ta Mar·ta \-də-ˌsant-ə-ˈmärt-ə\. Mountain range, N Colombia, on the Caribbean coast; highest peak 19,020 ft.

Sierra Pacaraima. See SERRA PACARAIMA.

Sierra San Pe·dro Már·tir \-san-ˌpā-drō-ˈmär-ˌti(ə)r\. Mountain range, N Baja California, Mexico.

Sie·rras de Cór·do·ba \sē-ˌer-əz-dā-ˈkȯrd-ə-bə, -ə-və\. Mountain range, San Luis and W Córdoba provs., cen. Argentina; highest peak Champaquí 9459 ft.

Si·er·ra Vis·ta \-ˈvis-tə\. City, Cochise co., SE Arizona, 50 m. SE of Tucson; pop. (1970c) 6689; ranching.

Sierre \syār\. Commune, cen. Valois canton, Switzerland, on the Rhone; pop. (1968e) 11,500; resort.

Sie·vers·hau·sen \ˈzē-fərs-ˌhau̇-zən, -vərs-\. Village, Lower Saxony, West Germany, ab. 15 m. E of Hannover; Maurice of Saxony defeated Albert Alcibiades here July 9, 1553 but was mortally wounded.

Sifnós. See SIPHNOS.

Sig \ˈsēg\ *or formerly* **Saint–De·nis–du–Sig** \ˌsaⁿ-də-ˈnē-də-ˈsēg\. Commune, Oran dept., NW Algeria, just SE of Oran; pop. (1966c) 32,000.

Sigeum. See YENIŞEHIR 2.

Si·ghet Mar·ma·ţiei \ˈsē-get-ˌmär-mä-ˈtyā\ *or Hung.* **Má·ra·ma·ros·szi·get** \ˈmär-ə-ˌmȯr-ōsh-ˈsig-ˌet\. City, Maramureş co., N Romania, 45 m. E of Satu-Mare near the U.S.S.R. border; pop. (1970e) 33,361; in Hungary 1940–45.

Si·ghi·şoa·ra \ˌsē-gi-ˈshwär-ə\ *or Hung.* **Se·ges·vár** \ˈsheg-(ˌ)esh-ˌvär\ *or Ger.* **Schäss·burg** \ˈshes-ˌbu̇(ə)rg\. City, Mureş co., cen. Romania, 45 m. NE of Sibiu; pop. (1970e) 29,090; an old city built around a castle on a hill; founded by German colonists 1280; battlefield 1849 where Russians defeated Hungarian insurrectionists.

Si·gir·i·ya \si-ˈgir-yə\ *or* **Si·giri** \si-ˈgi(ə)r-ē\. Fortress rock, N cen. Ceylon, N of Kandy; ruined ancient capital of Ceylon serving as refuge for King Kasyapa in 5th cent. A.D.

Si·gli \ˈsēg-lē\. Town, N coast of Sumatra, Indonesia, 45 m. ESE of Banda Atjeh; pop. (1961c) 4519.

Sig·lu·fjör·dhur *or* **Sig·lu·fjör·dur** \ˌsik-lü-ˈfyər-t͟hu̇r\. Town, N Iceland, in cen. part of N coast; pop. (1970c) 2161.

Sig·ma·ring·en \ˈzēk-mə-ˈriŋ-ən\. City, Baden-Württemberg, West Germany, on Danube river 30 m. S of Reutlingen; pop. (1968e) 10,674; site of a castle, the ancestral home of the Hohenzollerns; chartered in 13th cent.; became property of the Hohenzollerns 1535.

Sig·nal Butte \ˌsig-nəl-\. Elevation, Scotts Bluff co., W Nebraska; 4583 ft.

Signal Hill. 1 Peak, Custer co., SW South Dakota; 6500 ft. 2 City, Los Angeles co., SW California, 18 m. SSE of Los Angeles and E of Long Beach; pop. (1970c) 5582.
3 Elevation, cen. Saint Thomas I., Virgin Is., West Indies; 1504 ft.

Signal Hill National Historic Park. See CANADA, *National Historic Parks.*

Signan. See SIAN.

Sig·our·ney \ˈsig-ər-nē\. City, ⊗ of Keokuk co., SE cen. Iowa, 25 m. E of Oskaloosa; pop. (1970c) 2319.

Sigs·bee Deep \ˌsigz-bē-\. Deepest point in Gulf of Mexico, in SW cen. part; 12,425 ft.

Sig·sig \sēg-ˈsēg\. Town, Azuay prov., S Ecuador, just SE of Cuenca; pop. (1962c) 1228.

Si·gua·nea Bay \ˌsē-gwə-ˌnā-ə-\. Bay, W coast of Isle of Pines, Cuba, West Indies.

Si·güen·za \si-ˈgwān-sə\ *or anc.* **Se·gon·tia** \si-ˈgän-shē-ə\. Municipality, Guadalajara prov., cen. Spain, ab. 70 m. NE of Madrid; pop. (1970p) 6006.

Sihanoukville. See KOMPONG SOM.

Sihsien. See SHE-HSIEN.

Sihun. See SEYHAN.

Si·irt \si-ˈyi(ə)rt\ *or* **Sert** \ˈse(ə)rt\. 1 Province of SE Turkey. See table at TURKEY.
2 *or anc.* **Ti·gra·no·cer·ta** \tī-ˌgrā-nə-ˈsərt-ə\. Town, its ✱, on a tributary of the Tigris 85 m. E of Diyarbakır; pop. (1965c) 25,480; blankets. Tigranocerta was fortified capital of Armenia; here in 69 B.C. Lucullus defeated Tigranes and in 59 A.D. it was captured by Roman general Corbulo.

Si·kai·a·na \ˌsē-kī-ˈän-ə\. Chief island of the Stewart Is., E Solomon Is., 110 m. E of Malaita; has no entrance to its lagoon.

Si·kan·dar·a·bad \si-ˈkən-də-rə-ˌbäd\. 1 Town, W Uttar Pradesh, N India; pop. (1961c) 26,290.
2 Town, N Andhra Pradesh, India. See SECUNDERABAD.

Si·kan·dra \si-ˈkən-drə\. Village, Uttar Pradesh, N India, 6 m. NW of Agra; site of Tomb of Akbar, mausoleum of red sandstone.

Si·kang *also* **Hsi·kang** \'shē-'käŋ\. Former province, S China, now part of Tibet and Szechwan; region forms E part of Tibetan plateau with nearly all of it above 10,000 ft.; bordered on the S by the E end of the Himalayas with peaks as high as 25,000 ft.; E edge cut by the great gorges of three streams—Salween, Mekong, and Yangtze—all of which have their upper courses here; province formed 1928, dissolved 1955.

Si·kar \'sik-ər\. Town, NE Rajasthan, NW India, NW of Jaipur; pop. (1961c) 50,636.

Si·kas·so \si-'käs-(,)ō\. Town, S Mali, W Africa, ab. 190 m. SE of Bamako near Ivory Coast boundary; munic. pop. (1970e) 237,361.

Sikes·ton \'sīk-stən\. City, Scott and New Madrid cos., SE Missouri, 30 m. S of Cape Girardeau; pop. (1970c) 14,699; cotton market and processing center.

Si·kho·te–Alin \,sē-kə-,tā-ə-'lēn\. Mountain range, E coast of Primorski Krai, Russian S.F.S.R., U.S.S.R.; ab. 650 m. long; average height 4000 to 5000 ft.; highest point 6083 ft., at S end. Rich in minerals (coal, iron, graphite, manganese, gold, lead, zinc).

Siking. See SIAN.

Sik·i·nos \'sik-ə-,näs\. Island, S Cyclades, S Aegean Sea, E of Melos and W of Ios; ab. 17 sq. m.

Sik·kim \'sik-əm\. Kingdom, NE Indian subcontinent; bounded on N and E by China, on SE by Bhutan, on S by India, and on W by Nepal; 2744 sq. m.; pop. (1970e) 193,-020; ❋ Gangtok; located on S slope of the Himalayas, alt. of ranges from ab. 1000 ft. to Mt. Kanchenjunga 28,146 ft., third highest mountain in the world, on W border; chief river the Tista. Major crops incl. corn, millet, fruit, barley. Buddhism is the state religion. Relations with British began in 1816; ceded site of Darjeeling to Great Britain in 1839; in 1890 British protectorate recognized by China; became a protectorate of India 1949.

Siktivkar. See SYKTYVKAR.

Sikyon. See SICYON.

Sil \'sē(ə)l\. River, NW Spain; ab. 100 m. long; rises in NW León prov., flows SSW into Miño river.

Si·la·cay·oá·pan \,sil-ə-kī-'wä-pən\. Municipality, Oaxaca state, Mexico, 105 m. WNW of Oaxaca; pop. (1970p) 37,-346; rum; agriculture.

Silagian Mountains. See table at APENNINES.

Si·lang \si-'läŋ\. Municipality, Cavite prov., Luzon, Phil., ab. 30 m. S of Manila; pop. (1969e) 39,300; center of agricultural region.

Si·lao \si-'lau̇\. Town, Guanajuato state, cen. Mexico, just WSW of Guanajuato; munic. pop. (1970p) 69,886.

Si·lay \si-'lī\. Chartered city, Negros Occidental, Negros, Phil., on Guimaras Strait 10 m. N of City of Bacolod; pop. (1970e) 165,600; has coastwise trade.

Silay, Mount. Mountain, N Negros Occidental, Negros, Phil.; 5048 ft.

Sil·char \sil-'chär\. Town, NE India, on highway to Manipur; British supply base in Burma campaign in World War II.

Sil·ches·ter \'sil-,ches-tər, -chəs-\. Village, N Hampshire, S England; site of ancient Roman town **Cal·le·va Atreb·a·tum** \kə-,lē-və-ə-'treb-ə-,təm\, excavated 1889–1909; walls, earth banks of a Roman amphitheater, and ruins of forum, baths, etc., uncovered.

Si·ler City \,sī-lər-\. Town, Chatham co., cen. North Carolina, 28 m. SE of Greensboro; pop. (1970e) 4689; lumber, clothing; dairy farms.

Si·ler's Bald \,sī-lərz-\. Peak, Sevier co., E Tennessee, in Great Smoky Mountain National Park; 5607 ft.; a peak of the Great Smoky Mts. near the North Carolina border.

Si·le·sia \sī-'lē-zh(ē-)ə, sə-, -sh(ē-)ə\ *or Ger.* **Schle·si·en** \'shlā-zē-ən\. Region, E cen. Europe, lying mostly in SW Poland, with minor sections in Czechoslovakia and East Germany. The region comprised: (1) Former Prussian prov., subdivided into **Lower Silesia** (*Ger.* **Nie·der·schle·si·en** \,nē-dər-\) and **Upper Silesia** (*Ger.* **Ober·schle·si·en** \,ō-bər-\), located in valley of Upper Oder. For centuries a part of Poland and at one time divided into many principalities; passed to Bohemia in 14th cent., to Holy Roman Empire 1478; suffered greatly in Thirty Years' War. Seized by Prussia from Austria 1742; Maria Theresa's attempt to recover brought about Second Silesian War. After much unrest SE part with Polish population majority assigned to Poland in 1921. In World War II invaded by U.S.S.R. Jan.–Apr. 1945; greater part assigned to Poland by Potsdam Conference July 17–Aug. 2, 1945, several small districts becoming part of East Germany (see 3, below). (2) Austrian Silesia, region S of Prussian Silesia; originally part of Moravia, containing sources of Oder and Morava rivers; in 1849 made separate crownland. Greater part, **Slez·sko** \'sles-(,)kȯ\ (1719 sq. m.), passed to Czechoslovakia by Treaty of Versailles 1919; became part of the province of Moravia and Silesia; E strip of this (Teschen, *q.v.*) divided 1920 with Poland; seized by Germany 1938; recovered 1945. (3) Polish Silesia, region (**Śląsk** \'shlōⁿsk\), 1600 sq. m., at SE end of Prussian Silesia, with great wealth of coal and iron. Because of predominant Polish-speaking population assigned 1921 to Poland; included many large mining and industrial communities, as Katowice, Chorzów, Sosnowiec, Będzin. Disputes over coal exports adjusted 1926 in favor of Germany. Occupied by Germans 1939; recovered for Poland 1945 and incorporated in an enlarged Polish Silesia, comprising in addition former German Silesia.

Si·lex, Mount \-'sī-,leks\. Peak, San Juan co., SW Colorado; 13,650 ft.

Sil·hou·ette \,sil-ə-'wet\. One of the Seychelles (*q.v.*); ab. 6 sq. m.

Si·lif·ke \sə-lēf-'kē\. See SELEUCIA 1.

Si·li·gu·ri \sə-'lē-gu̇-,rē\. Town, West Bengal, India; pop. (1961c) 65,471; by direct line ab. 30 m. SSE of Darjeeling and connected with it by narrow-gauge (2 ft.) railroad of 50 m., ascending from 400 ft. to ab. 7000 ft. (average elevation of Darjeeling).

Si·lis·tra \si-'lis-trə, -'lēs-\. 1 Province of N Bulgaria. See table at BULGARIA.
2 *also* **Si·lis·tria** \si-'lis-trē-ə\ *or anc.* **Du·ros·to·rum** \d(y)u̇-'räs-tə-rəm\. City, its ❋, on Danube river 70 m. ENE of Ruse; pop. (1968e) 36,151; ships grain; bricks, furniture, cotton textiles. Founded as Roman camp 1st cent. A.D. and important town under Byzantines and Bulgars; under Turks 1420–1878; to Bulgaria 1878–1912; to Romania 1913–40.

Si·li·vri \sil-ə-'vrē\. Port on the Sea of Marmara, İstanbul prov., Turkey, ab. 35 m. W of İstanbul.

Sil·jan \'sil-,yän\. Lake, cen. Kopparberg co., cen. Sweden; 137 sq. m.; drains into Dal river.

Sil·ke·borg \'sil-kə-,bȯ(ə)rg\. City, Århus co., E Jutland Penin., Denmark, 27 m. W of Århus; pop. (1970e) 26,129; health resort in lake region.

Silk Road *or* **Silk Route.** Former trade route, extending from E China up the Wei valley through Kansu and Sinkiang Uighur to the W; at Tun-huang, oasis town in extreme W Kansu just WSW of An-hsi, divided into two ancient caravan routes that led westward: "South Road" (Chin. *Nan Lu*), along N Astin Tagh (now A-erh-chin Shan-Mo) and Kunlun mountain ranges S of the Takla Makan to Khotan and So-ch'e, thence W and S through high passes of Pamirs and Hindu Kush to the Oxus (now Amu Darya) and India; "North Road" (Chin. *Pei Lu*), along N edge of the Takla Makan through Kashgar, thence by way of Fergana to the Jaxartes (now Syr Darya) and towns of Turkistan; this "North Road" later became the "Middle Road" and was superseded by the true "North Road" from An-hsi via Ha-mi to its junction at K'u-erh-lo; routes were used for shipments of silk to W markets and for travel by ambassadors, pilgrims, and early missionaries.

Sill, Mount \-'sil\. Peak in Sierra Nevada, Fresno co., S cen. California; 14,162 ft.

Sil·la \'sil-ə\ *also* **Shil·la** \'shil-ə\. Early Korean kingdom, in SE part of Korean peninsula; established, probably in 3d cent. A.D.; after the elimination of Chinese influence, adopted Buddhism 528, drove out Japanese, and from 670 to 935 dominated all Korea.

Si·llaj·huay, Cor·di·lle·ra \ˌkȯrd-ᵊl-'(y)er-ə-ˌsē-yə-'kwī, ˌkȯrd-ē-'er-ə-\ *or* **Cordillera Si·llaj·guay** \-'gwī\. Range, W Bolivia, on the Chilean boundary NW of Salar de Uyuni; highest peak 19,669 ft.

Sillein. See ŽILINA.

Sil·le·ry \'sil-ə-rē, ˌsē-yə-'re\. 1 City, Quebec co., S Quebec, Canada, 3 m. SW of Quebec; pop. (1971p) 13,950.

2 Village, Marne dept., NE France, just SE of Reims; pop. (1962c) 736; noted for champagne.

Sil·li·man, Mount \-'sil-ə-mən\. Peak in Sierra Nevada, N Tulare co., S cen. California; 11,188 ft.

Si·loam Springs \ˌsī-lōm-, -ləm-\. City, Benton co., NW corner of Arkansas, in Ozarks 23 m. NW of Fayetteville; pop. (1970c) 6009; health resort; diversified agriculture; John Brown Coll. (1919).

Sil·pia \'sil-pē-ə\. Ancient town, Baetica, S Hispania, N of the Baetis (Guadalquivir); scene of defeat of Carthaginian general Mago 206 B.C. by Scipio Africanus.

Sils, Lake of \-'zils\ *or Ger.* **Sil·ser See** \'zil-zər-ˌzā\. Lake, Graubünden canton, E Switzerland, in SW part of Upper Engadine; 3 m. long by ab. 1 m. wide; 1.5 sq. m.; max. depth 232 ft.

Sils·bee \'silz-bē\. City, Hardin co., E Texas, 19 m. N of Beaumont; pop. (1970c) 7271; saw and paper mills, oil wells.

Sil·ver Bank \'sil-vər-\. Bank in Atlantic Ocean, off N coast of Hispaniola, West Indies.

Silver Bank Passage. Channel, N cen. West Indies, SE of Mouchoir Bank and NW of Silver Bank.

Silver Bay. Village, Lake co., NE Minnesota, on Lake Superior 50 m. NE of Duluth; pop. (1970c) 3504; diversified agriculture; resort.

Silver Bow \-'bō\. County in Montana. See table at MONTANA.

Silver City. 1 Town, ⊗ of Grant co., SW New Mexico, ab. 45 m. NW of Deming; pop. (1970c) 7751; health resort; ships livestock; Western New Mexico Teachers Coll. (1893); Gila Cliff Dwellings National Monument to NE. Founded 1870 as Spanish settlement; incorporated 1876.

2 Town, Canal Zone. See RAINBOW CITY 2.

Silver Creek. Village, Chautauqua co., SW corner of New York, on Lake Erie 28 m. S of Buffalo; pop. (1970c) 3182; lake resort; missiles, textiles, canned goods.

Sil·ver·heels, Mount \-'sil-vər-ˌhēlz\. Peak, Park co., cen. Colorado; 13,825 ft.

Silver Peak Mountains. Small range, W Esmeralda co., SW Nevada; highest peak ab. 9000 ft.

Silver Plume Mountain \-ˌplüm-\. Peak, Clear Creek co., N cen. Colorado; 13,500 ft.

Silver Run Peak. Mountain, Carbon co., S Montana; 12,-610 ft.

Silver Spring. Urban community (unincorporated), Montgomery co., cen. Maryland, N suburb of Washington; pop. (1970c) 77,496; Xaverian Coll. (1931).

Silver Springs. Village, Marion co., N Florida, near Ocala; site of 150 springs which form a pond ab. 35 ft. deep, source of **Silver River,** navigable tributary of the Oklawaha to the E.

Sil·ver·tip Peak \ˌsil-vər-ˌtip-\. Mountain, Park co., NW Wyoming; 10,400 ft.

Sil·ver·ton \'sil-vərt-ᵊn\. 1 Town, ⊗ of San Juan co., SW Colorado; pop. (1970c) 797.

2 Residential city, Hamilton co., SW corner of Ohio, 8 m. NE of Cincinnati; pop. (1970c) 6538.

3 City, Marion co., Oregon, ENE of Salem; pop. (1970c) 4301; cannery; fruit and grain farms.

4 City, ⊗ of Briscoe co., NW Texas; pop. (1970c) 1026.

Sil·ves \'sil-vēsh\. Town, S coast of Portugal, 18 m. NNW of Faro; pop. (1970p) 26,991; sacked by Ferdinand I of Castile; destroyed in earthquake 1755; small Gothic cathedral; Moorish castle.

Sil·vies \'sil-vēz\. River, E cen. Oregon; 75 m. long; rises in S Grant co., flows S into Malheur Lake, Harney co.

Sil·vis \'sil-vəs\. City, Rock Island co., NW Illinois, 9 m. E of Rock Island; pop. (1970c) 5907.

Sil·vret·ta \silv-'ret-ə\. Mountain group along border bet. E Switzerland and SW Tirol, Austria; heights **Piz Li·nard** \ˌpēts-li-'närt\ 11,188 ft., **Flucht·horn** \'flu̇kt-ˌhȯ(ə)rn\ 11,162 ft.

Sim, Cape \-'sim\. Cape, SW coast of Morocco, NW Africa, 31°23′N, 9°51′W.

Simalur. See SIMEULUE.

Si·man·cas \sē-'män-kəs\. Commune, Valladolid prov., N cen. Spain, 8 m. SW of Valladolid; pop. (1970p) 1408; national archives housed in the castle; very ancient city; scene of victory of Ramiro II over Caliph Abder-Rahman 934.

Si·mang·gang \sē-'mäŋ-ˌgäŋ\. Town, S Sarawak, Malaysia, NW Borneo, on Batang Lupar river 80 m. ESE of Kuching.

Si·mang·ge·la \si-məŋ-'gē-lə\; *formerly* **Door·man** \'dō(ə)r-mən, 'dȯ(ə)r-\ *or Du.* **Doorman Top** \-'tȯp\. Peak, N cen. part of Maoke Mts., cen. Irian Barat, Indonesia; 13,287 ft. high.

Si·ma·ra \sē-'mär-ə\. Island in Romblon group, Phil., N of Tablas I.; 8 sq. m.

Si·mav \sē-'mäv\. 1 River, NW Turkey; ab. 160 m. long; flows W and N.

2 Town on upper Simav river, Kütahya prov., 60 m. E of Akhisar.

Simbirsk. See ULYANOVSK.

Sim·coe \'sim-(ˌ)kō\. 1 County, Ontario, Canada. See table at ONTARIO.

2 Town, ⊗ of Norfolk co., SE Ontario, Canada, 20 m. S of Brantford; pop. (1971p) 10,800; textiles, canned goods, tobacco products; fruit farms.

Simcoe, Lake. Lake, SE Ontario, Canada, ab. 40 m. N of Toronto; 271 sq. m., 30 m. long by 20 m. wide; outlet is Severn river flowing N and W into Georgian Bay, ab. 45 m. Popular resort region; Barrie and Orillia are chief towns on it.

Si·me·to \sē-'mā-(ˌ)tō, -'me-\. River, E Sicily, Italy; rises W of Mt. Etna, flows E, S, and SE into Mediterranean S of Catania.

Si·meu·lue *or Du.* **Si·meu·loeë** \ˌsē-mə-'lü-ə\ *or* **Si·ma·lur** \sē-'mäl-u̇(ə)r\. Island, Indonesia, in the Indian Ocean off NW coast of Sumatra; ab. 54 m. long by 14 m. wide; 683 sq. m., with adjacent islands 712 sq. m.; chief settlement Sinabang, on SE coast; forest-covered with central ridge; highest point 1860 ft.; surrounded by reefs.

Sim·fer·o·pol \ˌsim(p)-fə-'rō-pəl, -'rō-\. City, ✱ of Crimean Oblast, Ukrainian S.S.R., U.S.S.R., in S part, on Sevastopol-Kharkov R.R.; pop. (1970p) 250,000; machine tools, power plant and chemical equipment, canned goods, knitwear, wine; in a fruit-growing region.

History: In first cent. B.C. a small Scythian town and fortress; settled by Tatars as **Ak Me·chet** \ˌäk-mi-'chet\ in 16th cent.; seized and destroyed by Russians 1736; refounded and fortified under present name by Russians 1784; in World War II occupied by Germans Nov. 1941–Apr. 1944.

Simi *or* **Sími.** See SYME.

Si·mi Valley \si-'mē-\. City, Ventura co., SW California, 30 m. NW of Los Angeles; pop. (1970c) 59,832; citrus fruit.

Sim·la \'sim-lə\. Town, ✱ of Himachal Pradesh, NW India, 53 m. NE of Ambala; pop. (1961c) 42,597; hill resort, situated on a ridge of the Himalayas at elevation of 6600–8000 ft. (highest point Mt. Jakko). Resort established by British 1819; formerly summer ✱ of British government of India.

Simla Hill States. Formerly a group of Indian states, now part of Himachal Pradesh state, NW India, around Simla; 4960 sq. m.; chief states were Bashahr, Jubbal, Keonthal, and Nalagarh.

Sim·me \'zim-ə\. River, SW cen. Switzerland; ab. 35 m. long; rises in S Bern canton, flows N and NE into Lake of Thun.

Sim·o·is \'sim-ə-wəs\ *or mod.* **Dom·brek** \də(r)m-'brek\. Small river near ancient Troy, Asia Minor; tributary of Scamander (*mod.* Menderes).

Si·mons·town \'sī-mənz-ˌtau̇n\. Town, SW Cape Province, S Rep. of South Africa, on W shore of False Bay 20 m. S of Cape Town; pop. (1967e) 8900; fishing; naval base and dockyard facilities. Naval base established by Dutch 1741; made base of British South Atlantic Naval Squadron 1814, transferred to Union (now Rep.) of South Africa 1957.

Simplon. See ALPS.

Simp·son \'sim(p)-sən\. 1 Name of counties in two states of the U.S. See tables at KENTUCKY and MISSISSIPPI.
2 Trading post, Canada. See FORT SIMPSON.
3 Island, Chonos Archipelago, in Pacific Ocean off SW coast of Chile.

Simpson Desert. Desert, cen. Australia, largely in SE Northern Territory, extending S into South Australia and E into Queensland; ab. 50,000 sq. m.; first land-crossing 1939.

Simpson Harbour. Harbor, inner landlocked part of Blanche Bay, NE coast of New Britain I., Bismarck Archipelago, W Pacific Ocean, forming the harbor of Rabaul.

Simpson Peninsula. Part of mainland of NE Keewatin dist., Northwest Territories, Canada, bet. Pelly Bay on W and Committee Bay on E; ab. 40 m. wide.

Simp·son·ville \'sim(p)-sən-ˌvil\. Town, Greenville co., NW South Carolina, 11 m. SE of Greenville; pop. (1970c) 3308.

Sims·bury \'simz-ˌber-ē, -b(ə-)rē\. Town, NW cen. Hartford co., N Connecticut, S of Granby; pop. (1970c) 17,475; machine tools, safety fuses; dairy farms; incorporated 1670; first colonial copper coins (Higley coppers) minted here 1737 and 1739.

Si·myen Mountains *or* **Se·mien Mountains** \si-'myān-\. Mountains, N Ethiopia, E Africa; highest peak Ras Dashan 15,158 ft.

Sin, Wilderness of \-'sin\. Arid region along SW coast of Sinai Penin., NE Egypt, on E side of Gulf of Suez, in territory occupied by Israel 1967; traversed by the Israelites during the Exodus (*Ex.* xvi. 1; xvii. 1).

Si·na \'sē-nə\. River, S cen. India, in SE Maharashtra; ab. 170 m. long; flows SE and empties into Bhima river.

Si·nai \'sī-ˌnī, 'sī-nē-ˌī\. Peninsula, NE Egypt, bet. Gulf of Suez on W and Gulf of 'Aqaba on E, at N end of Red Sea; constitutes a governorate of Egypt; 23,442 sq. m.; pop. (1970e) 140,000; ✱ Al-'Arish; very mountainous, contains plateaus of Al-Tih and Egma, and at S end Gebel Musa group. Majority of population except in extreme N are nomadic Bedouin; has oil fields and manganese deposits. Under Israeli occupation since Six-Day War, June 1967, in which it was the scene of the principal campaign of the war.

Sinai, Mount *or Arab.* **Ja·bal Mū·sā** \ˌjab-əl-'mü-sə\. A mountain of the Gebel Musa group, S Sinai Penin.; 7497 ft., thought to be the same as Biblical Mt. Horeb (*Ex.* iii. 1). See MUSA, GEBEL.

Si·na·ia \si-'nī-ə\. Town, SE Prahova co., Romania, 21 m. S of Braşov; pop. (1966c) 11,976; castle, former royal residence; monastery founded 1695, all there was to the town until ab. 1850.

Si·na·loa \ˌsē-nə-'lō-ə\. State of W Mexico. See table at MEXICO.

Si·na·lun·ga \ˌsē-nə-'lu̇ŋ-gə\ *or formerly* **Asi·na·lun·ga** \ə-\. Commune, Siena prov., Tuscany, W Italy, 23 m. ESE of Siena; pop. (1968e) 11,362.

Sin·cé \sin-'sā\. Town, Sucre dept., N Colombia; munic. pop. (1968e) 27,666.

Sin·ce·le·jo \ˌsin-sə-'le-(ˌ)hō\. Town, ✱ of Sucre dept., N Colombia, 80 m. S of Cartagena; munic. pop. (1968e) 62,968.

Sin·clair's Bay \ˌsin-kla(ə)rz-, ˌsiŋ-, -kle(ə)rz-\. Inlet of North Sea, extreme NE coast of Scotland, N of town of Wick.

Sind \'sind\. 1 *or* **Sindh** \'sind\. River, cen. India; 240 m. long; rises in Madhya Pradesh, flows NE through Gwalior into the Yamuna E of Gwalior.
2 Province, Pakistan, bounded on N by the provinces of Baluchistan and Punjab, on E and S by India, on SW by the Arabian Sea, and on W by Baluchistan; 58,983 sq. m.; pop. (1969e) 11,142,174; ✱ Karachi; region is generally flat, lying along both banks of the Indus; chief occupation agriculture and rice is chief crop; other exports wheat, cotton, barley, oilseeds. A large area under cultivation is irrigated by Sukkur (*q.v.*) barrage. Chief cities Karachi, important seaport in SW, Hyderabad in S cen. part, and Shikarpur and Sukkur in the N.

History: Important evidences of prehistoric culture in the region; invaded by Alexander 325 B.C.; later part of Ganges empire of Chandragupta. Since beginning of Christian era has often been crossed by invaders, but long remained semi-independent under local dynasties; under Akbar made part of the Delhi empire; conquered by Sir Charles Napier 1842–43 and annexed to British India as N part of Bombay presidency; transferred 1936 and constituted an autonomous province Apr. 1, 1937; became part of Pakistan Aug. 1947; provincial status abolished 1955, restored 1970.

Sin·dang·an \sin-'däŋ-ˌän\. Municipality, Zamboanga del Norte prov., Mindanao, Phil., on E shore of **Sindangan Bay** (inlet of Sulu Sea ab. 100 m. NNE of Zamboanga); pop. (1969e) 50,900.

Sin·dan·gla·ja \ˌsin-däŋ-'glī-ə\. Village and mountain health resort, W Java, Indonesia, on slope of Mt. Gede at 3500 ft. elevation, SE of Bogor.

Sin·del·fing·en \'zin-dəl-ˌfiŋ-ən\. Town, Baden-Württemberg, West Germany, ab. 9 m. SW of Stuttgart; pop. (1969e) 40,347.

Sinder. See ZINDER.

Sin·e·pux·ent Inlet \ˌsin-i-'pək-sənt-\. Narrow strait leading from Atlantic Ocean through barrier reefs, E Worcester co., SE Maryland.

Si·nes \'sē-nēsh\. Town, Setúbal dist., SW Portugal, on coast 35 m. SSE of Setúbal; pop. (1970p) 6996; birthplace of Vasco da Gama.

Si·ne·wit, Mount \-'sin-ə-ˌwit\. Mountain, New Britain I.; 7999 ft.; highest peak on island.

Sinfeng. See HSIN-FENG.

Sin·ga \'siŋ-gə\. Town, cen. Blue Nile prov., E Sudan, on the Blue Nile river, 190 m. SSE of Khartoum; pop. (1965e) 15,986.

Singan. See SIAN.

Sin·ga·pore \'siŋ-(g)ə-ˌpō(ə)r, -ˌpȯ(ə)r\. 1 Republic, SE Asia, S of the Malay Penin., comprising Singapore I. and several smaller adjacent islets; 225 sq. m.; pop. (1971e) 2,110,400; ✱ Singapore. For economy, see 2 and 3 below.

History: Established as part of the colony of Straits Settlements 1826; occupied by Japanese Feb. 1942–Sept. 1945; made a separate British colony 1946; a state of Malaysia 1963–65; became an independent republic 1965.
2 Island off S end of Malay Penin., SE Asia, comprising the main part of Singapore (see 1 above); 209 sq. m.; separated from the Malay Peninsula by Johore Strait (ab. ¾ of a mile wide) and from Batam and other islands of the Riau Archipelago on the S by Singapore Strait; 77 m. N of the equator. Hilly (highest point 581 ft.), well cultivated; vegetables, fruit, tobacco; livestock raising; crossed by railroad connecting by causeway over Johore Strait with Johore Bahru and towns of Malaysia; Singapore (city) on S coast.
3 Seaport city, ✱ of Singapore (see 1 above), on Singapore Strait; met. area pop. (1971e) 206,500; major entrepôt;

shipbuilding, food processing; electrical appliances, apparel, steel products, footwear, furniture; two universities.

History: A Malay city of importance in 13th cent.; destroyed by Javanese 1365 and remained a ruin until refounded by Sir Thomas Raffles Jan. 29, 1819; attached to British settlement of Benkoelen until 1823; became property of East India Company 1824, a part of the new colony of Straits Settlements 1826, and capital of the colony 1836. Developed as a great port and trade center and later as naval base, with docks, powerhouses, repair shops, etc. In World War II violently attacked by Japanese Dec. 1941 and Jan. 1942; captured Feb. 15, 1942 and renamed **Sho·nan** \shō-'nän\; bombed by Allied planes 1944 and 1945.

Singapore, Strait of. Channel bet. Singapore I. on the N and Batam, Bintan, and other islands of the Riau Archipelago on the S; ab. 50 m. long by 10 m. wide; connects South China Sea with Strait of Malacca.

Sin·ga·ra·dja \ˌsiŋ-gə-'räj-ə\. Town, N Bali I., Indonesia, chief town on Bali; pop. (1961c) 33,252; important market facilities.

Sing Bu·ri *or* **Sin·gha·bu·ri** \ˌsiŋ-bə-'rē—*sic*\. **1** Province, SW cen. Thailand; 325 sq. m.; pop. (1960c) 154,409.

2 Town, its ✱, on the Chao Phraya and on railroad 40 m. N of Phra Nakhon Si Ayutthaya; pop. (1960c) 8322.

Sing·en \'ziŋ-ən\. Industrial city, Baden-Württemberg, West Germany, 15 m. WNW of Konstanz; pop. (1969e) 38,950; aluminum products.

Singhasari. See SINGOSARI.

Singh·bhum \siŋ-'büm\. District, Chota Nagpur division, S Bihar, NE India; 1591 sq. m.; pop. (1961c) 2,049,911; ✱ Chaibasa.

Sin·ghi Kan·gri \ˌsiŋ-gē-'käŋ-grē\. Mountain in the Karakoram Range, Sinkiang Uighur, China; 25,431 ft.

Sin·gi·da \siŋ-'gē-də\. **1** Administrative region, cen. Tanzania. See table at TANZANIA.

2 Town, its ✱; pop. (1967c) 9478.

Singidunum. See BELGRADE 2.

Sin·git·ic Gulf \sin-ˌjit-ik-\ *or Gk.* **Sin·gi·ti·kós Kól·pos** \siŋ-ˌgē-ti-ˌkós-'kól-ˌpós\. Inlet of Aegean Sea, NE coast of Greece, S of Chalcidice and bet. the peninsulas of Acte and Sithonia.

Sing·ka·rak \ˌsiŋ-kə-'räk\. Mountain lake, W Sumatra, Indonesia, NE of Padang; ab. 12 m. long by 5 m. wide.

Sing·ka·wang \siŋ-'kä-ˌwäŋ\. Town, West Kalimantan prov., Borneo, Indonesia, on South China Sea coast 70 m. N of Pontianak; pop. (1961c) 35,169.

Sing·kep \'siŋ-ˌkep\. Island, SW Lingga Archipelago, Indonesia, SW of Lingga I. and separated from E coast of Sumatra by Berhala Strait; tin mines.

Sin·gle·shot Mountain \ˌsiŋ-gəl-ˌshät-\. Peak, Glacier National Park, NW Montana; 7700 ft.

Singora. See SONGKHLA.

Sin·go·sa·ri *or* **Sing·ha·sa·ri** \ˌsiŋ-ə-'sä-rē\. A powerful Malay kingdom of E Java in the 13th cent. (1222–92) with capital at Singosari, now a village just N of Malang; its story is the source of many Javanese legends.

Sing Peak \'siŋ-\. Mountain in Sierra Nevada, E Madera co., cen. California; 10,544 ft.

Sing Sing. See OSSINING.

Sining. See HSI-NING.

Sin·kiang Ui·ghur \'shin-jē-'äŋ-wē-'gů(ə)r\. Autonomous region, W China, bounded on NE by the Mongolian People's Republic, on E by Kansu prov., on SE by Tsinghai, on S by Tibet, on SW by Jammu and Kashmir (disputed bet. India and Pakistan), and Afghanistan, and on W and NW by U.S.S.R.; 635,829 sq. m.; pop. (1968e) 8,000,000; ✱ Urumchi. *Physical features:* Tableland above 2000 ft. surrounded on three sides by high mountain ranges: on S by Kunlun Mts., on SW by Pamirs, on W by Tien Shan (which extend E as N boundary of Takla Makan desert), on NW by the Ala Tau, and on the N and NE by the Altai Mts.; cen. part is extensive Takla Makan desert, which includes the Tarim basin (in places less than 1000 ft. alt.), watered seasonally by the Tarim river and its branches, the Yarkand, Ho-t'ien, etc.; in the S are other desert streams, the K'o-li-ya, Ch'e-erh-ch'en, etc.; in the N the headstreams of the Irtysh. Has many salt lakes, esp. Turfan depression (below sea level) and Bagrach Kol in center, Lop Nor in SE, and Ai-pi lake in NW. Inhabitants include various peoples speaking Turkic languages. Produces wheat, corn, sorghum, cotton; iron ore, coal, oil, molybdenum, tungsten. Politically, W and cen. parts correspond to Chinese Turkistan (or Eastern Turkistan); Dzungaria and Chuguchak are regions in N. Chief towns Urumchi, Kashgar, Kuldja, Asku.

History: Possibly the earliest home of the human race; inhabited since earliest times by nomad tribes. Important in Chinese history as the region traversed by the "Silk Road" by which China traded with the West. Controlled by Uigurs for centuries; later entered by Mongolians who fought for it against Chinese, Tibetans, and Muslims; conquered by Genghis Khan in 13th cent. and under his successor became E half of khanate of Jagatai. Came under Chinese control (vaguely 16th cent., definitely 1872); after 1917 under Soviet influence; established as a Chinese province, **Sinkiang,** 1942; revolt and civil war 1944–45; reconstituted as an autonomous region 1955.

Sink·ing Spring \'siŋk-iŋ-\. Borough, Berks co., SE Pennsylvania, 6 m. W of Reading; pop. (1970c) 2862.

Sin–le–No·ble \ˌsaⁿl-'nōblᵊ\. Commune, Nord dept., N France, 2 m. ESE of Rouen; pop. (1968c) 14,000; coal mines, iron foundries, textile mills.

Sinmin. See HSIN-MIN.

Sin·na·ma·ry *or* **Sin·na·ma·rie** \ˌsēn-ə-mə-'rē\. **1** River, N French Guiana; ab. 100 m. long; flows N into Atlantic Ocean 70 m. NW of Cayenne.

2 Coastal town, N French Guiana.

Sinneh. See SANANDAJ.

Sin·ni \'sēn-ē\ *or* **Sin·no** \'sēn-(ˌ)ō\ *or anc.* **Si·ris** \'sī-rəs\. River, S Italy; ab. 60 m. long; flows E into Gulf of Taranto 19 m. SW of the mouth of Bradano river.

Sîn·ni·co·lau Ma·re \sin-ˌnē-kə-lau̇-'mä-rə\ *or* **Sân·ni·co·la·ul–Ma·re** \sən-ˌnē-kə-'lau̇l-'mä-rə\ *or Hung.* **Nagy·szent·mi·klós** \'näzh-sent-'mi-klōsh\. Commune, Timiş co., SW Romania, on the Mureş river 25 m. SE of Szeged; pop. (1966c) 11,428; site of discovery in 1799 of remarkable gold ornamented utensils, probably of 10th cent. Turkish origin.

Sin·nū·ris \si-'nu̇(ə)r-əs\. Town, Faiyūm gov., Egypt, SE of Birket Qārūn; pop. (1966c) 34,900.

Sino. See GREENVILLE.

Si·nop \sə-'nóp\. **1** Province of N Turkey, Asia. See table at TURKEY.

2 *or anc.* **Si·no·pe** \sə-'nō-pē\. Seaport, its ✱, on narrow part of a peninsula extending into the Black Sea; pop. (1965c) 13,354; good natural harbor; ruins of Byzantine castle.

History: Founded c. 7th cent. B.C.; as seaport and terminus of caravan route became a major Greek trading city; capital of Pontic monarchy 183 B.C. ff.; taken and destroyed by Romans 70 B.C.; Roman colony; came under Ottoman Empire 1461; scene of Russian naval victory over Turks 1853, one of the precipitating incidents of the Crimean War. Birthplace of Diogenes and Mithridates the Great.

Sin·o·pah Mountain \ˌsin-ə-ˌpä-\. Peak, Glacier National Park, NW Montana; 8435 ft.

Sinope. See SINOP 2.

Sin·qu \'siŋ-kü\. River, Lesotho, S Africa; a headstream of the Orange river.

Sinsiang. See HSIN-HSIANG.

Sint. See SAINT.

Sint Amands·berg \sint-'a-mänts-ˌbe(ə)rg\ *or formerly* **Mont–Saint–Amand** \ˌmōⁿ-ˌsaⁿ-ta-'mäⁿ\. Commune, East Flanders prov., NW cen. Belgium; pop. (1969e) 23,141; NE suburb of Gent.

Sin·tang \'sin-ˌtäŋ\. Town, West Kalimantan prov., W Borneo, Indonesia, on left bank of Kapuas river 155 m. E of Pontianak; pop. (1961c) 9013.

Sint–Eloo·is–Vij·ve \ˌsint-ā-ˌlō-is-'vīv-ə\; *Fr.* **Vive–Saint–Éloi** \vēv-saⁿ-tāl-wä\ *also* **Saint–Éloi.** Village, West Flanders prov., NW Belgium, 3 m. S of Ieper (Ypres); pop. (1969e) 2814; in World War I scene of heavy engagements 1915, 1916, 1918.

Sint–Gillis. See SAINT-GILLES 1.

Sint–Joost–ten–Noode. See SAINT-JOSSE-TEN-NOODE.

Sint–Ka·te·lij·ne–Wa·ver \ˌsint-ˌkat-ə-ˌlī-nə-'vä-vər\ *or Fr.* **Wa·vre–Sainte–Ca·the·rine** \vä-vrə-saⁿt-ka-trēn\. Commune, Antwerp prov., Belgium; pop. (1969e) 13,273.

Sint–Lambrechts–Woluwe. See WOLUWE-SAINT-LAMBERT.

Sint Maarten. See SAINT MARTIN.

Sint Ni·co·laas \sint-'nē-kə-ˌläs\ *or* **San Ni·co·las** \sän-'nē-kə-ˌläs\. Village, SE coast of Aruba I., Netherlands Antilles; pop. (1965e) 16,714; oil refining.

Sint Nicolaas Punt. See PUDJUT, POINT.

Sint–Ni·klaas \sint-'nēk-ləs\ *or Fr.* **Saint–Ni·co·las** \saⁿ-nē-kə-lä\. Commercial and manufacturing commune, East Flanders prov., NW cen. Belgium, 14 m. ENE of Gent; pop. (1969e) 48,968; railroad junction, market town; textiles; chartered 1513.

Sin·ton \'sin-tᵊn\. Town, ⊗ of San Patricio co., S Texas, 20 m. N of Corpus Christi; pop. (1970c) 5563; oil wells; truck, cotton farms.

Sint–Pieters–Woluwe. See WOLUWE-SAINT-PIERRE.

Sin·tra *or formerly* **Cin·tra** \'sēn-trə, 'sin-\. Commune, Lisboa dist., W Portugal, 12 m. NW of Lisbon; pop. (1960c) 20,321; resort; Moorish castle, royal palace, convent; marble quarries; convention signed here 1808 by French, English, and Portuguese military leaders. Notable for scenery celebrated by Byron in *Childe Harold.*

Sint–Trui·den \sint-'tröid-ᵊn\ *or Fr.* **Saint–Trond** \saⁿ-trōⁿ\. Manufacturing commune, Limburg prov., NE Belgium, 20 m. NW of Liège; pop. (1969e) 21,364; captured by the Germans 1914.

Sin·ŭi·ju \'shin-ē-ˌjü\ *or Jap.* **Shin·gi·shu** \'shiŋ-gi-ˌshü\. City, ✱ of North P'yŏngan prov., North Korea, near mouth of Yalu river.

Si·nus \'sī-nəs\. Latin for "gulf or bay" in classical names, as Sinus Saronicus, see the second element or its anglicized form.

Sinus Aelaniticus. See 'AQABA, GULF OF.

Sinus Arabicus. See RED SEA 1.

Sinus Cantabricus. See BISCAY, BAY OF.

Sinus Gallicus. See LIONS, GULF OF.

Sinus Ligusticus. See LIGURIAN SEA.

Sinus Pagasaeus. See VOLOS, GULF OF.

Sinyang. See HSIN-YANG.

Sion. See ZION 2.

Sion \sē-'ōⁿ\ *or Ger.* **Sit·ten** \'zit-ᵊn, 'sit-\ *or anc.* **Se·du·num** \si-'d(y)ün-əm\. Commune, ✱ of Valais canton, SW cen. Switzerland, 50 m. S of Bern; pop. (1970c) 21,925; tourist resort; produces fruit, tobacco, wine; trades in cattle; pilgrimage church of 9th–13th cents., Gothic cathedral (with 9th cent. clock tower), 17th cent. town hall. Made episcopal see in 6th cent.; mentioned as city 1179.

Sioux \'sü\. Name of counties in three states of the U.S. See tables at IOWA, NEBRASKA, NORTH DAKOTA.

Sioux Center. City, Sioux co., NW Iowa, 40 m. N of Sioux City; pop. (1970c) 3450; Dordt Coll. (1955).

Sioux City. City, ⊗ of Woodbury co., W Iowa, on Missouri river at confluence of Big Sioux and Floyd rivers; pop. (1970c) 85,925; alt. 1110 ft.; feed, fertilizer, automobile parts, truck bodies, lumber, tools, flour; foundries, meat-packing plants; grain market and trade center; Morningside Coll. (1889), Briar Cliff Coll. (1930); platted 1854, incorporated 1857.

Sioux Falls. City, ⊗ of Minnehaha co., SE South Dakota, on Big Sioux river, ab. 75 m. N of Sioux City, Iowa; pop. (1970c) 72,488; alt. 1395 ft.; commercial center in a corn- and livestock-farming region; fertilizer, agricultural machinery, textiles, baked goods, dairy products; meat-packing plants, granite quarries; North American Baptist Seminary (1850), Augustana Coll. (1860), Sioux Falls Coll. (1860); Indian mounds nearby. First settled 1857; abandoned during Sioux uprising 1862; military post established 1865; permanent settlement begun 1870; incorporated as city 1883.

Sioux Lookout. Town, Kenora dist., W Ontario, Canada, 120 m. E of Kenora; pop. (1971p) 2495; diversified agriculture.

Si·par·ia \si-'par-ē-ə\. Town, SW Trinidad, Trinidad and Tobago, West Indies; pop. (1960c) 4174.

Siph·nos \'sif-nəs\ *or Gk.* **Sif·nós** \'sēf-ˌnòs\. 1 Greek island, W Cyclades, Aegean Sea, SE of Seriphos and NE of Melos; in Cyclades dept., Greece; 29 sq. m.
2 Town, E coast of island.

Šipka Pass. See SHIPKA PASS.

Si·ple, Mount \-'sī-pəl\ *or formerly* **Mount Ruth Siple** \-ˌrüth-\. Mountain on coast of Marie Byrd Land, Antarctica, extending into the South Pacific at 73°15′S, 126°06′N bet. Wrigley Gulf and Amundsen Sea; 10,168 ft.; discovered 1940.

Sipora. See SIPURA.

Sip·par \sip-'är\. City of ancient Babylonia on the right bank of the Euphrates river ab. 16 m. SSW of Baghdad. In the early period a center of the worship of the Sumerian sun-god, Shamash. Excavations, begun in 1882, have uncovered remains of a large temple and many thousands of religious and historic clay tablets.

Sip·sey \'sip-sē\. Navigable river, NW Alabama; ab. 85 m. long; rises in NW Alabama, flows S into the Tombigbee river in S Pickens co., W cen. Alabama.

Si·pu·ra *or Du.* **Si·po·ra** \si-'pu̇(ə)r-ə\. Central island, Mentawai Is., off W coast of Sumatra, Indonesia; ab. 27 m. long by 12 m. wide.

Si·quia \'sē-(ˌ)kyä\. River, S cen. Nicaragua; 95 m. long; flows E into the Escondido river.

Si·qui·jor \ˌsē-ki-'hō(ə)r\. 1 Island, one of the Visayan Is. and a part of Negros Oriental prov., Phil.; 130 sq. m.; chief municipality Siquijor. In NW part of Mindanao Sea, SE of Negros, S of Cebu, and SW of Bohol; ab. 12 m. from N to S and 17 m. E to W. Hilly (highest point 1394 ft.), fertile, and most densely populated island of the archipelago; has several good harbors. Chief products copra, rice, corn, abacá, and tobacco. Chief towns Siquijor, Lazi, and Maria.
2 Municipality, NW coast of Siquijor I., 16 m. SE of Dumaguete; pop. (1969e) 22,300; chief town of the island.

Si·ra·cu·sa \ˌsir-ə-'kü-zə\. 1 Province of Sicily, Italy. See table at ITALY.
2 City, Sicily. See SYRACUSE 3.

Si·raj·ganj \si-'räj-ˌgənj\. Town, Bangla Desh, on Jamuna river ab. 68 m. NW of Dacca; pop. (1961c) 47,152; river port, trading in jute cloth; founded early 19th cent.

Sir Darya. See SYR DARYA.

Sir Ed·ward Pel·lew Group \sər-ˌed-wərd-pəl-'yü-, -'pel-(ˌ)yü-\. Island group, SW part of Gulf of Carpentaria, Australia; belongs to Northern Territory.

Si·re·tul \'sir-ə-ˌtu̇l\ *or* **Si·ret** \sē-'ret\ *or Ger.* **Se·reth** \'zā-ˌret\. 1 River, NE Romania; ab. 280 m. long; rises in the Carpathian Mts. in Ukrainian S.S.R., U.S.S.R., flows SSE into Danube river above Galati; chief tributary the Bistriţa.
2 Town, Suceava co., N Romania, ab. 25 m. NNW of Suceava; pop. (1966c) 8018.

Sirguja. See SURGUJA.

Sir·han, Wa·di \ˌwäd-ē-si(ə)r-'han\ *or* **Wā·dī as Sir·ḥān** \-as-\. Region, NW Saudi Arabia; extends NW to SE just

E of Jordan; altitude ab. 1850 ft.; contains many pools of brackish water.

Si·rik, Cape \-'sir-ik\ *or Malay* **Tan·jong Sirik** \ˌtän-ˌjȯŋ-\. Cape, SW coast of Sarawak, E Malaysia, on an island in delta of Rajang river, projecting into South China Sea.

Siris. 1 City, Greece. See SERRAI 2.
2 River, Italy. See SINNI.

Sir·mio·ne *or formerly* **Ser·mio·ne** \sər-'myō-nē\ *or anc.* **Sir·mio** \'sir-mē-ˌō\. Port and village on Sirmione peninsula, Brescia prov., Lombardy, N Italy, on S shore of Lake Garda.

Sir·mi·um \'sər-mē-əm\. Important city, ancient Pannonia; its site is on the Sava river near modern Sremska Mitrovica, NE Yugoslavia.

Sir·mur *or* **Sir·moor** \sir-'mu̇(ə)r\ *also* **Na·han** \'nä-hən\. Former Indian state, now part of Himachal Pradesh state, N India; 1091 sq. m.; ✱ Nahan.

Si·ro·hi \si-'rō-hē\. 1 Former Indian state, now part of Rajasthan state, NW India; 1988 sq. m.; region contains Mount Abu (*q.v.*); hilly and covered with dense jungle.
2 Town, its ✱, 53 m. NW of Udaipur; pop. (1961c) 14,500; cutlery.

Síros. See SYROS.

Sirs al–Lai·ya·na \ˌsirs-ˌal-lə-'ya-nə\. Town, Minūfīya gov., Egypt; pop. (1966c) 22,900.

Sir San·ford, Mount *or* **Mount Sir Sand·ford** \-sər-ˌsanfərd\. Peak, highest in Selkirk Mts., SE British Columbia, Canada, ab. 50 m. N of Revelstoke; 11,591 ft.

Sir·te \'sir-ˌtā\. Town on coastal road, N Libya, N Africa, SE of Misurata on S shore of Gulf of Sidra; poor harbor; starting point of many caravan routes. In World War II taken by British Dec. 26, 1942.

Sir Wil·frid Lau·ri·er, Mount \-sər-ˌwil-frəd-'lȯr-ē-ˌā, -'lär-\. Mountain, SE British Columbia, Canada; 11,749 ft.

Si·sak \'sē-ˌsäk\ *or* **Si·sek** \-ˌsek\ *or Ger.* **Sis·sek** \'zis-ek\ *or Hung.* **Szi·szek** \'sis-ek\ *or anc.* **Si·scia** \'sish-ē-ə\. Town, Croatia, N Yugoslavia, on the Sava river 30 m. SE of Zagreb; pop. (1965e) 31,000; ancient town important in the Roman Empire; during 3d cent. had chief mint and treasury; Turks defeated here 1593 and 1641; part of Austria-Hungary 1641–1918.

Sisapon. See ALMADÉN.

Sis·ki·you \'sis-ki-ˌ(y)ü\. County in California. See table at CALIFORNIA.

Siskiyou Peak. Mountain, S Jackson co., SW Oregon, in **Siskiyou Mountains,** range in SW Oregon and N California; 7147 ft.

Sis·op·hon \'sis-ə-ˌpän\. Town, W Cambodia, SE Asia, ab. 40 m. NNW of Battambang and near Thailand border; in last few centuries has been several times transferred bet. Thailand and Cambodia.

Sissek. See SISAK.

Sis·se·ton \'sis-ə-tən\. City, ⊗ of Roberts co., NE corner of South Dakota, 53 m. N of Watertown; pop. (1970c) 3094; resort; dairy, poultry farms.

Sis·sonne \sē-'sȯn\. Town, Aisne dept., N France; pop. (1962c) 4439; military camps; German outpost during World War I until retaken Oct. 1918.

Sistan. See SEISTAN.

Sis·ters·ville \'sis-tərz-ˌvil\. City, Tyler co., NW West Virginia, on Ohio river 28 m. SSW of Moundsville; pop. (1970c) 2246.

Sistova. See SVISHTOV.

Si·ta·mau \si-'tä-ˌmau̇\. Former Indian state, now part of Madhya Pradesh state, cen. India; 191 sq. m.

Si·ta·pur \'sēt-ə-ˌpu̇(ə)r\. Town, cen. Uttar Pradesh, N India, 50 m. NNW of Lucknow; pop. (1961c) 53,884; grain market; manufactures plywood.

Si·tho·nia \si-'thōn-yə\ *or Gk.* **Si·tho·niá** \si-thō-'nyä\. Middle peninsula of Chalcidice, Macedonia, NE Greece, ab. 31 m. long, bet. Singitic Gulf on E and Toronaic Gulf on W; highest point 2470 ft. In early times inhabited by Thracians.

Sit·ka \'sit-kə\. City, ⊗ of Greater Sitka borough, SE Alaska, on W coast of Baranof I. 932 m. N of Seattle, Washington; pop. (1970c) 3370; lumber; salmon fisheries; tourism; Sheldon Jackson Junior Coll. (1878); U.S. naval air base. Founded as New Archangel by Aleksandr Baranov 1799; chief town of Russian America, continuing as capital of Alaska under U.S. rule 1867–1906 and principal commercial center of the territory; declined after transfer of capital to Juneau 1906.

Sitka National Monument. See UNITED STATES, *National Monuments.*

Sitoebondo. See SITUBONDO.

Si·tra \'si-trə\. Small island, Bahrain, Persian Gulf, off NW coast of Bahrain I.

Sitsang. See TIBET.

Sit·tang \'si-ˌtäŋ\. River, E cen. Burma; 260 m. long; flows S into the head of the Gulf of Martaban; Toungoo and Pyinmana are on its banks. Scene of severe fighting in early part of 1942 and in May 1945.

Sit·tard \'sit-ˌärt\. Commune, Limburg prov., SE Netherlands, 13 m. NNE of Maastricht on West German border; pop. (1970e) 33,887; railroad junction; chemicals, textiles, electronic components; coal mines; chartered 1243.

Sit·taung \'sit-ˌau̇ŋ\. Town, Sagaing div., W Burma, on right bank of Chindwin river near Manipur border.

Sitten. See SION.

Sit·ting·bourne and Mil·ton \'sit-iŋ-ˌbō(ə)rn . . . 'milt-ᵊn, -ˌbȯ(ə)rn-\. Urban district, Kent, SE England, on Milton Creek 39 m. ESE of London; pop. (1971p) 30,861; paper, bricks and cement; ships cherries; situated on the old route followed by pilgrims on their way to Canterbury.

Sit·twe \'sit-ˌwē\ *or formerly* **Ak·yab** \ak-'yab\. Town, ✱ of Arakan div., Burma, on Bay of Bengal, at mouth of Kaladan river; pop. (1962e) 86,451; rice mills.

Si·tu·bon·do *or Du.* **Si·toe·bon·do** \si-ˌtü-'bȯn-ˌdō\. Town, East Java prov., Indonesia, on railroad near coast of SE Madura Strait; pop. (1961c) 34,483.

Si·u·slaw \sī-'yü-(ˌ)slȯ\. River, W Oregon; ab. 60 m. long; rises in cen. Lane co., flows W into Pacific Ocean, W Lane co.; navigable 10 to 30 m.

Siut. See ASYŪT.

Si·vas \si-'väs\. 1 Province of E cen. Turkey. See table at TURKEY.
2 *anc.* **Se·bas·te** \sə-'bas-tē\ *or* **Se·bas·tia** \sə-'bas-ch(ē-)ə\ *or* **Ca·bi·ra** \kə-'bī(ə)r-ə\. City, its ✱, on right bank of upper Kızıl Irmak 225 m. E of Ankara; pop. (1965c) 108,-320; textiles, hosiery, cement. One of the principal cities of Asia Minor under Diocletian and Byzantine Empire; came under Muslim rule 1071; sacked by Tamerlane 1400; restored under Ottoman rule mid-15th cent. ff.

Si·va·sa·mu·dram \ˌsē-vəs-ə-'mü-drəm\. See CAUVERY.

Si·vash \si-'vash\ *or* **Pu·trid Sea** \ˌpyü-trəd-\. Salt lagoons and marshes, N and NE Crimean Oblast, Ukrainian S.S.R., U.S.S.R.; enclosed by the Arabat Penin.; contains valuable mineral salts.

Si·ve·rek \ˌsē-və-'rek\. Town, Urfa prov., SE Turkey, ab. 50 m. NE of Urfa; pop. (1965c) 27,527.

Siv·ri·hi·sar \ˌse-vri-hi-'sär\. Town, Eskişehir prov., W cen. Turkey, 58 m. ESE of Eskişehir; important as fortress town on Byzantine military road to the east.

Si·wa \'sē-wə\ *or anc.* **Am·mo·ni·um** \ə-'mō-nē-əm\. 1 Oasis, Matruh gov., NW Egypt, N of Libyan Desert; ancient seat of the oracle of Jupiter Ammon.
2 Town, in S part of the oasis; pop. (1966c) 3600.

Si·wa·lik Range *or* **Siwalik Hills** \si-ˌwäl-ik-\. Range of foothills, N India and Nepal, parallel with the main Himalayan system and extending more than 1000 m. SE from N Punjab, Pakistan, into Sikkim; notable for its geological formation, containing extensive paleontological remains.

Siyang. See SIANG 2.

Si·yeh, Mount \-ˌsī-(y)ə\. Peak, Glacier National Park, NW Montana; 10,014 ft.

Sjæl·land \ˈshel-ˌän\ *or Eng.* **Zea·land** \ˈzē-lənd\ *also* **See·land** \ˈzā-ˌlänt\. 1 Group of islands in Danish territorial waters; 2901 sq. m.; pop. (1965c) 2,055,040; includes Sjælland, Møn, Samsø, Amager, Saltholm, and smaller islands.

2 Largest of the islands of Denmark; 2709 sq. m.; pop. (1965c) 1,855,500; bounded on the N and NW by the Kattegat, on the W by the Great Belt, on the S by narrow channels separating it from smaller islands, and on the E by the Baltic Sea and Øresund.

Skadar. See SCUTARI.

Ska·ga Fjord \ˌskäg-ə-\. Inlet of the Arctic Ocean, N coast of Iceland.

Ska·gen \ˈskä-gən\. Town, Nordjylland co., NE Jutland Penin., Denmark, at the N extremity of Jutland on the Skaw; pop. (1970e) 11,699.

Skagen, Cape. See SKAW, THE.

Skag·er·rak *or* **Skag·e·rak** \ˈskag-ə-ˌrak\. Broad arm of the E cen. North Sea, extending bet. Norway on the N and Denmark on the S, connecting with the Kattegat on the E; ab. 130 m. long and more than 70 m. wide.

Skag·it \ˈskaj-ət\. 1 River, NW Washington; 163 m. long; rises in British Columbia, flows S across Washington border and W into Skagit Bay, SW Skagit co.

2 County in Washington. See table at WASHINGTON.

Skagit Bay. Inlet on boundary bet. Skagit and Snohomish cos., NW Washington.

Skag·way \ˈskag-(ˌ)wā\. City, SE Alaska, at head of Lynn Canal, 80 m. N of Juneau; pop. (1970c) 675; terminal of railroad N to Whitehorse in Yukon Territory, Canada. Founded 1897 and a boom town in the Klondike gold rush 1897–98 as starting point over White Pass to the Yukon goldfields.

Ska·ma·nia \skə-ˈmān-yə\. County in Washington. See table at WASHINGTON.

Skan·der·borg \ˈskän-ər-ˌbȯ(ə)rg\. Town, Århus co., E Jutland, Denmark; pop. (1970e) 11,227.

Skå·ne \ˈskō-nə\ *or* **Sca·nia** \ˈskān-yə\. Section of S Sweden, comprising counties of Kristianstad and Malmöhus; land area 4356 sq. m.; pop. (1970e) 973,095.

Skan·e·at·e·les \ˌskan-ē-ˈat-ləs, ˌskin-\. Village and resort, Onandaga co., cen. New York, at N end of Skaneateles Lake 8 m. E of Auburn; pop. (1970c) 3055; chemicals, paper; agriculture; center of abolitionist activities before Civil War.

Skaneateles Lake. Lake, chiefly in Onondaga and Cayuga cos., cen. New York; 14 sq. m.; one of the Finger Lakes (*q.v.*); ab. 16 m. long and 1½ m. wide; outlet from N end flows into Seneca river.

Skap·tar \ˈskäp-ˌtär\. Volcanic mountain, SE Iceland, N of Öraefajökull; violent eruption in 1783.

Ska·ra·borg \ˈskär-ə-ˌbȯ(ə)r\. County of S Sweden. See table at SWEDEN.

Skar·du \ˈskär-(ˌ)dü\ *or* **Skar·do** \ˈskär-(ˌ)dō\. Town with fort, in region of Jammu and Kashmir under Pakistani control, ab. 95 m. NNE of Srinagar; on left bank of the Indus above the great gorge, in the Himalayas at elevation of ab. 7500 ft.; chief town of Baltistan.

Skar·ży·sko–Ka·mien·na \ˌskär-zhi-skə-kə-ˈmyen-ə\. Commune, Kielce prov., Poland; pop. (1970p) 39,200.

Skaw, The \-ˈskȯ\ *or* **Cape Ska·gen** \-ˈskä-gən\. Cape on N extremity of Jutland, Denmark; extends into the Skagerrak.

Sked·smo \ˈshedz-(ˌ)mō\. Town, Akershus co., SE Norway; pop. (1970e) 30,519.

Skee·na \ˈskē-nə\. River, W British Columbia, Canada; 360 m. long; rises in N cen. British Columbia, flows S and then W into Hecate Strait.

Skeg·ness \ˈskeg-ˈnes\. Urban district, Parts of Lindsey, Lincolnshire, E England, on North Sea 48 m. SSE of Hull; pop. (1971p) 13,557; seaside resort.

Skei·dar·ar·jö·kull \ˈskā-dər-är-ˌyə-küt-ᵊl\. Glacier, Iceland; 37 m. long, ab. 11 m. wide near its terminus.

Skel·lef·te \she-ˈlef-tə\. River, Västerbotten and Norrbotten cos., N Sweden; 255 m. long; flows SE into the Gulf of Bothnia.

Skel·lef·teå \she-ˈlef-tə-ˌō\. Coastal town, Västerbotten co., N Sweden, at the mouth of Skellefte river; pop. (1970e) 61,895.

Skel·ligs \ˈskel-igz\. Three small islands off Bolus Head, co. Kerry, Eire, SW coast of Ireland: Great Skellig, Little Skellig, and Lemon Rock. Great Skellig has 2 lighthouses and the ruins of a monastery, said to be founded by St. Finan, once a place of pilgrimage.

Skel·mers·dale and Hol·land \ˈskel-mərz-ˌdāl . . . ˈhäl-ənd\. Urban district, Lancashire, NW England, 13 m. NE of Liverpool; pop. (1971p) 30,522.

Skel·ton and Brot·ton \ˈskelt-ᵊn . . . ˈbrät-ᵊn\. Urban district, North Riding, Yorkshire, N England; pop. (1971p) 15,083.

Sker·ries \ˈske(ə)r-ēz\. Group of islets, S Irish Sea, off NW extremity of the island of Anglesey, Wales; lighthouse.

Sker·row, Loch \läk-ˈsker-(ˌ)ō, läk-\. Lake, Kirkcudbright co., S Scotland; max. depth 33 ft.; noted for scenery.

Ski·a·thos \ˈskī-ə-ˌthäs\ *or Gk.* **Skí·a·thos** \ˈskē-ə-ˌthȯs\. Island, Northern Sporades (see SPORADES), in W end of the group, nearest the mainland; 16 sq. m.; belongs to Euboea dept., Greece.

Ski·a·took \ˌskī-(ə-)ˈtük, -ˈtu̇k\. Town, Tulsa and Osage cos., NE Oklahoma, N of Tulsa; pop. (1970c) 2930.

Skid·daw \ˈskid-ˌȯ\. Mountain, cen. Cumberland, NW England, in the Lake District E of Bassenthwaite Lake; 3053 ft.

Skid·e·gate Inlet \ˌskid-i-gət-\. Channel, Queen Charlotte Is., off W British Columbia, Canada, separating Graham I. from Moresby I.

Ski·en \ˈshā-ən, ˈshē-\. City, ⊗ of Telemark co., S Norway; pop. (1970e) 45,472; trade center in iron and copper mining area; exports ores, lumber, and paper.

Ski·ens·elva \ˈshā-ən-ˌselv, ˈshē-\. River, S Norway; 152 m. long; flows S into Skagerrak.

Skier·nie·wi·ce \ˌskyer-nyə-ˈvēt-sə\. Industrial commune, Łódź prov., cen. Poland, 42 m. SW of Warsaw; pop. (1970p) 25,600; railroad junction point. Scene of meeting bet. emperors of Germany, Austria, and Russia 1844.

Ski·hist, Mount \-ˈskē-ˌhist\. Peak, S British Columbia, Canada, W of Fraser river; 9960 ft.

Skik·da \ˈskēk-də\ *or formerly* **Phi·lippe·ville** \ˈfil-əp-ˌvil, fə-ˈlēp-\. Seaport, Constantine dept., NE Algeria; pop. (1966c) 60,535; exports cereals, wool, fruits; fishing; founded by French 1838.

Skip·ton \ˈskip-tən\. Urban district, West Riding, Yorkshire, N England; pop. (1971p) 26,308; textiles.

Skíros. See SKYROS.

Ski·ve \ˈskē-və\. Town, Viborg co., N cen. Jutland, Denmark, on inlet of Lim Fjord 16 m. WNW of Viborg; pop. (1970e) 17,980.

Skjál·fan·da \ˈskyau̇l-ˌvän-də\. River, NE cen. Iceland; flows N into Arctic Ocean W of Húsavík.

Skjeg·ge·dal \ˈsheg-ə-ˌdäl\. Waterfall, in a small stream E of Hardanger Fjord, Hordaland co., SW Norway; 525 ft. high.

Skjern \ˈskya(ə)rn, ˈskye(ə)rn\. River, W cen. Jutland, Denmark; flows W into Ringkøbing Fjord.

Skobelev. See FERGANA 2.

Sko·kie \ˈskō-kē\ *or formerly* **Niles Carter** \ˈnī(ə)lz-\. Village, Cook co., NE Illinois, 15 m. N of Chicago; pop. (1970c) 68,627; aluminum and plastic products, electronic components, sports equipment, pharmaceuticals; residential; Hebrew Theological Coll. (1922).

Sko·ko·mish \skō-ˈkō-mish\. River, W Washington; ab. 35 m. long; rises in Mason co., flows SW through Lake Cushman into Hood Canal. See CUSHMAN, LAKE.

Sko·mer \ˈskō-mər\. Island in St. George's Channel off SW coast of Wales, S of entrance to St. Bride's Bay.

Skop·e·los \ˈskäp-ə-ˌläs\ *or Gk.* **Skó·pe·los** \ˈskō-pā-lòs\. 1 Island, Northern Sporades (see SPORADES); 37 sq. m.; second largest island in the group; belongs to Euboea dept., Greece.
2 Town on E coast of Skopelos I.

Skop·je \ˈskäp-(ˌ)yā, ˈskōp-\ *or* **Skop·lje** \ˈskäp-lē-ˌā, ˈskōp-\ *or Turk.* **Üs·küb** \u̇-ˈsküb\ *also* **Üs·küp** \-ˈsküp\ *or anc.* **Scu·pi** \ˈskyü-ˌpī\. City, ✱ of Macedonia, S Yugoslavia, on Vardar river 200 m. SSE of Belgrade; pop. (1971p) 312,-091; road junction; iron and steel, chemicals, textiles, glass; handicrafts; univ. (1949). A capital of medieval Serbia; under Turkish rule 1392–1913; incorporated in Yugoslavia 1918; occupied by Germans in World War II; made ✱ of Macedonia 1945; almost entirely destroyed by earthquake 1963.

Skövde \ˈshəv-də\. Town, Skaraborg co., S Sweden, bet. lakes Vättern and Vänern; pop. (1970e) 29,147; military post.

Skow·he·gan \skau̇-ˈhē-gən\. Town, ⊗ of Somerset co., W Maine, on Kennebec river 15 m. NNW of Waterville; pop. (1970c) 7601; shoes, lumber; dairy, truck farms.

Skra·din \ˈskrä-(ˌ)dēn\ *or Ital.* **Scar·do·na** \skär-ˈdō-nə\. Commune, Croatia, Yugoslavia, 35 m. NW of Split; town is small port several miles from the Adriatic on the Krka.

Skra·par \skrə-ˈpär\. Province of S cen. Albania. See table at ALBANIA.

Skunk \ˈskəŋk\. River, SE Iowa; 264 m. long; rises in Hamilton co., N cen. Iowa, flows SE into the Mississippi below Burlington, Des Moines co., SE Iowa.

Skye \ˈskī\. Island of the Inner Hebrides off NW coast of Scotland; 48½ m. long, 670 sq. m.; pop. (1961c) 7478; administratively a part of Inverness co.; sheep and (West Highland) cattle raising; mining of diatomaceous earth, whisky distilling; noted for wild, mountainous scenery.

Sky·kje \ˈshü-hə, -kə\. Waterfall, Hordaland, SW Norway, near inner Hardanger Fjord; total drop 820 ft.

Sky·ko·mish \skī-ˈkō-mish\. River, NW cen. Washington; rises in Cascade Mts., flows W through S Snohomish co. and joins Snoqualmie river to form the Snohomish river.

Sky·light Mountain \ˈskī-ˌlīt-\. Peak in the Adirondack Mts., Essex co., NE New York; 4926 ft.

Sky·ring Water \ˈskī-ˌriŋ-\. Large salt-water lake, Chile, extreme S mainland, NW of Otway Water.

Sky·ros \ˈskī-rəs, -ˌräs\; *Gk.* **Skí·ros** \ˈskē-ˌròs\ *also* **Scy·ros** \ˈsī-rəs\. 1 Island, Northern Sporades (see SPORADES), N cen. Aegean Sea E of Euboea; 81 sq. m.; pop. (1961c) 2882; largest island in the group; belongs to Euboea dept., Greece. Important in the legends of Greece, esp. those connected with Theseus. Occupied by Athenians c. 475 B.C. Here the English poet, Rupert Brooke, died and was buried (1915)
2 Town on Skyros I., on NE coast; pop. (1961c) 2411.

Sla. See SALÉ.

Sla·gel·se \ˈslā-(g)əl-sə\. Town, Vestsjælland co., SW Sjælland, Denmark; pop. (1970e) 23,169.

Sla·ma·da·tang Bay \ˌsläm-ə-ˌdä-ˌtäŋ-\ *or Eng.* **Wel·come Bay** \ˌwel-kəm-\ *or Du.* **Wel·komst Baai** \ˌvel-kòmst-ˈbä-ə\. Inlet of Sunda Strait, W end of Java, Indonesia.

Sla·met \ˈsläm-ˌet\. Peak, W cen. Java I., Indonesia; 11,247 ft.

Sla·ney \ˈslā-nē\. River, SE Eire; ab. 60 m. long; rises in co. Wicklow, flows S through co. Wexford into Wexford Harbour; navigable as far as Enniscorthy.

Slankamen. See NOVI SLANKAMEN.

Śląsk. See SILESIA.

Śląsk Dolny. See WROCŁAW 1.

Slate Mountain \ˈslāt-\. Peak, cen. Coconino co., N cen. Arizona; 8209 ft.

Sla·ter \ˈslāt-ər\. City, Saline co., W cen. Missouri, 36 m. N of Sedalia; pop. (1970c) 2576.

Sla·ters·ville \ˈslāt-ərz-ˌvil\. Village, Providence co., N Rhode Island, ab. 4 m. W of Woonsocket; seat of government for North Smithfield.

Sla·ti·na \ˈslät-ᵊn-ə\. City, ⊗ of Olt co., S Romania, on railroad 30 m. E of Craiova; pop. (1970e) 24,872.

Slat·ing·ton \ˈslāt-iŋ-tən\. Borough, Lehigh co., E Pennsylvania, on Lehigh river 13 m. NNW of Allentown; pop. (1970c) 4687; clothing; slate quarries; fruit farms.

Sla·ton \ˈslāt-ᵊn\. City, Lubbock co., NW Texas, 18 m. SE of Lubbock; pop. (1970c) 6583; mattresses, cottonseed oil; railroad shops.

Slave \ˈslāv\ *also* **Great Slave.** River, W cen. Canada, bet. Lake Athabaska and Great Slave Lake; 258 m. long; receives Peace river just below its outlet from Lake Athabaska and enters Great Slave Lake at Fort Resolution.

Slave Coast. Coastal region, W Africa, along the Bight of Benin and bet. the Benin and Volta rivers, approximately from 1° to 5°E long.; along coasts of Nigeria, Dahomey, and Toga; from this region most of the slaves were taken during the three centuries bet. 1500 and 1800.

Slav·go·rod \ˈslav-gə-ˌräd\. Agricultural town, W Altai Krai, SW Russian S.F.S.R., U.S.S.R., on branch railroad 210 m. W of Barnaul; pop. (1967e) 31,000.

Slav·kov \ˈsläf-ˌkòf\ *or Ger.* **Aus·ter·litz** \ˈau̇s-tər-ˌlits, ˈòs-\. Commune, Czech S.R., Czechoslovakia, 12 m. ESE of Brno; has palace and church. Scene of battle Dec. 2, 1805 in which French under Napoleon defeated combined forces of Russians and Austrians led by Kutuzov, thus terminating Third Coalition against France.

Sla·vo·nia \slə-ˈvō-nē-ə, -nyə\ *or Serb.* **Sla·vo·ni·ja** \-ˈvō-nē-(y)ə\. Region, Croatia, N Yugoslavia, bet. the Sava river on the S and the Drava and Danube rivers on N and E; the E part of former Croatia and Slavonia crownland; region from early times a part of kingdom of Croatia (*q.v.*) with history of which it is closely connected.

Sla·von·ska Po·že·ga \slə-ˈvòn-skə-ˈpò-zhə-gə\ *or formerly* **Požega** *or Hung.* **Po·zse·ga** \ˈpō-zhe-(ˌ)gä\. Town, Croatia, N Yugoslavia, N of the Sava ab. 90 m. ESE of Zagreb; pop. (1965e) 16,000.

Sla·von·ski Brod \slə-ˈvòn-skē-ˈbròt\ *or formerly* **Brod.** Town, N cen. Yugoslavia, on Sava river 120 m. WNW of Belgrade; pop. (1965e) 32,000.

Sla·vyansk \sləv-ˈyan(t)sk\. Town, N Donetsk Oblast, E Ukrainian S.S.R., U.S.S.R., on tributary of the Donets 55 m. N of Donetsk; pop. (1970p) 124,000; health resort; chemicals, electrical equipment, pencils; founded 1676.

Slavyansk–na–Ku·ba·ni \-nä-kü-ˈbän-(y)ē\. Town, Krasnodar Krai, Russian S.F.S.R., U.S.S.R., ab. 45 m. NE of Krasnodar; pop. (1969e) 54,000.

Slay·ton \ˈslāt-ᵊn\. Village, ⊗ of Murray co., SW Minnesota, 27 m. NNW of Worthington; pop. (1970c) 2351.

Slea·ford \ˈslēf-ərd\. Urban district, ⊗ of Parts of Kesteven, Lincolnshire, E England, on the **Slea** \ˈslē\ 32 m. E of Nottingham; pop. (1971p) 7975; site of Roman and Saxon settlements; Norman castle.

Slea Head \ˈslā-\. Cape, SW coast of Eire, on N side of entrance to Dingle Bay.

Sleat, Point of \-ˈslāt\. Cape, S tip of Skye I. in the Inner Hebrides, off NW coast of Scotland.

Sleat, Sound of. Body of water off W coast of Scotland, bet. SE coast of the island of Skye and the Scottish mainland.

Sleep·ing Bear Point \ˈslēp-iŋ-ˌba(ə)r-, -ˌbe(ə)r-\. Point, W coast of Leelanau co., NW Michigan, extending into Lake Michigan.

Sleeping Deer Mountain \-ˌdi(ə)r-\. Peak, W cen. Lemhi co., E cen. Idaho; 9885 ft.

Sleepy Eye \'slēp-ē-,ī\. City, Brown co., S Minnesota, 37 m. WNW of Mankato; pop. (1970c) 3461; diversified agriculture.

Sleepy Hollow. Valley, near Tarrytown, New York, made famous by Washington Irving's *Legend of Sleepy Hollow;* Washington Irving buried here.

Slesvig. See SCHLESWIG.

Slezsko. See SILESIA.

Sli. See SCHLEI.

Sli·dell \slī-'del\. Town, St. Tammany parish, SE Louisiana, 30 m. NE of New Orleans; pop. (1970c) 16,101; lumber; strawberries.

Slide Mountain \'slīd-\. **1** Peak in Sierra Nevada, E Tuolumne co., cen. California; 11,902 ft.

2 Peak, N Clark co., E Idaho; 10,200 ft.; on the Montana boundary.

3 Highest peak in the Catskill Mts., Ulster co., SE New York; 4204 ft.

Slie·drecht \'slē-,drekt\. Commune, South Holland prov., SW Netherlands, on the lower Waal SE of Rotterdam; pop. (1970e) 19,868.

Slie·ma \'slē-mə\. Town, E Malta, across bay NW of Valletta; pop. (1969e) 21,983.

Slieve Bin·gian \slēv-'bin-yən\. Mountain in Mourne Mts., SE co. Down, SE Northern Ireland; 2449 ft.

Slieve Car \-'kär\. Mountain, NW co. Mayo, NW Eire; 2369 ft.

Slieve Com·me·dagh \-'käm-ə-,dä\. Mountain in Mourne Mts., SE co. Down, SE Northern Ireland; 2512 ft.

Slieve Don·ard \-'dän-ərd\. Highest peak in the Mourne Mts., co. Down, SE Northern Ireland; 2796 ft.

Slieve Mish \-'mish\. Mountain range, cen. co. Kerry, SW Eire; 14 m. long; highest peak 2796 ft.

Slieve Mis·kish \-'mis-kish\. Mountain range, SW co. Cork, S Eire, bet. Bantry Bay and Kenmare river; highest peak 2251 ft.

Slieve·more *or* **Slieve More** \slēv-'mō(ə)r, -'mȯ(ə)r\. Mountain, N coast of Achill I. off W coast of co. Mayo, W Eire; 2204 ft.

Slieve·na·man *or* **Slieve–na–Man** \,slēv-nə-'män\. Mountain, SE co. Tipperary, S Eire, NE of Clonmel; 2364 ft.

Slieve Snaght \-'snäkt\. Mountain, co. Donegal, N Eire; 2014 ft.

Sli·go \'slī-(,)gō\. **1** County, Connacht prov., N Eire; 693 sq. m.; pop. (1971p) 50,236; ⊗ Sligo; livestock raising, dairy farming, fishing.

2 Municipal borough and seaport, ⊗ of co. Sligo, N Eire, on **Sligo Bay** (inlet of Atlantic Ocean); pop. (1971p) 14,071; butter; brewing, grain milling; exports hogs and cattle. Ruins of 13th cent. Dominican abbey; site of 13th cent. castle. Nearby are megalithic remains and the traditional burial place of Queen Mab (identified with an early queen of Connacht).

Slip·pery Rock \,slip-(ə-)rē-\. Borough, Butler co., W Pennsylvania, 17 m. ENE of New Castle; pop. (1970c) 4949; Slippery Rock State Coll. (1889).

Sli·ven \'sliv-ən\. **1** Province of E cen. Bulgaria. See table at BULGARIA.

2 *or* **Sliv·no** \'slēv-(,)nō\. City, its ✱, 60 m. W of Burgas; pop. (1968e) 77,458; woolen textiles, silk; woodworking. Frequently a center of conflict, in medieval times between Bulgaria and Byzantine Empire and in 19th cent. between Russians and Turks.

Sliv·ni·ca *or* **Sliv·ni·tza** \'sliv-nit-,sä\. Commune, Sofia prov., W Bulgaria, 19 m. NW of Sofia; scene of battle Nov. 17–19, 1885 in which the Bulgarians defeated the Serbs.

Sloan \'slōn\. Village, Erie co., W New York, adjoining Buffalo; pop. (1970c) 5216.

Sloan Peak. Mountain, Snohomish co., NW cen. Washington; 7790 ft.

Sloats·burg \'slōts-,bərg\. Village, Rockland co., SE New York, near New Jersey state line 31 m. NNW of New York; pop. (1970c) 3134.

Slo·bo·zia \slō-'bȯz-yə\. Town, ⊗ of Ialomiţa co., SE Romania, ab. 65 m. ENE of Bucharest; pop. (1966c) 12,443.

Sloch·te·ren \'slȯk-tə-rə(n)\. Commune, Groningen prov., NE Netherlands, 8 m. E of Groningen; pop. (1970e) 12,901; gas wells.

Slo·nim \'slȯ-nyim\ *or Pol.* **Sło·nim** \'slȯ-(,)nēm\. Town, Grodno Oblast, W Belorussian S.S.R., U.S.S.R., on Shchara river 43 m. SSW of Novogrudok; pop. (1967e) 29,000; formerly in Poland; scene of battle Sept. 13–18, 1915 in which Russians were defeated by Germans.

Slope \'slōp\. County in North Dakota. See table at NORTH DAKOTA.

Slot, The \-'slät\. Long open-water passage, cen. Solomon Is., W Pacific Ocean, running NW and SE ab. 300 m. from the Shortland Is. to Florida I. and Savo I.—so named in World War II by Americans because it was the regular course followed by Japanese planes and vessels in their attempts to save Guadalcanal Aug. 1942–Jan. 1943.

Slough \'slaů\. Municipal borough, Buckinghamshire, SE cen. England, 20 m. W of London; pop. (1971p) 86,757; residential and industrial center.

Slo·vak Socialist Republic \'slō-,väk-, -,vak-\ *also* **Slo·va·kia** \slō-'väk-ē-ə, -'vak-\ *or Czech* **Slo·ven·sko** \slȯ-'ven(t)-skȯ\. Constituent republic, Czechoslovakia; 18,923 sq. m.; pop. (1970e) 4,563,460; ✱ Bratislava; rivers Váh and Hron; potatoes, sugar beet, wheat; livestock raising; iron ore, salt, gypsum; chief towns: Bratislava, Plzeň, Košice, Banská Bystrica.

History: Settled in 6th and 7th cents. A.D. by Slovaks, a Slavic people; part of Great Moravia in 9th cent., conquered by Magyars in 906, it remained in kingdom of Hungary (*q.v.*) until 1918; Slovak National Council joined Czechs in forming Czechoslovakia (*q.v.*) 1918; Slovakian autonomy, long the goal of Slovaks, granted in 1938 after dismemberment of Czechoslovak state; region along S border assigned to Hungary 1938–45; declared itself independent Mar. 14, 1939 but on Mar. 16 taken under the protection of the German Reich; an ally of the Axis powers during World War II; liberated bet. Oct. 1944 and May 1945 and ceased to be independent Slovak state Apr. 1945; established as a constituent republic in Czech federal constitution of 1968.

Slo·ve·nia \slō-'vēn-ē-ə, -'vēn-yə\ *or Serb.* **Slo·ve·ni·ja** \-'ven-ē-,(y)ä\. Constituent republic, Yugoslavia; 7819 sq. m.; pop. (1971p) 1,725,088; ✱ Ljubljana; textiles, steel, wood products; chief towns Ljubljana, Maribor, Celje, Kranj.

History: Region settled by Slovenes in 6th cent. A.D.; except for 1809–13 when it was part of Slavic Illyrian Provinces (*q.v.*) erected by Napoleon, most of territory inhabited by Slovenes belonged to Austria; when Dual Monarchy was established 1867, all Slovenes (including those in Hungary) were grouped under Austria where they remained, largely in provinces of Carniola and Styria, until 1918; becoming independent 1918, joined other S Slavs in proclaiming Kingdom of Serbs, Croats, and Slovenes 1918 (see YUGOSLAVIA); constituted approximately Dravska co. 1929–45; made a constituent republic in 1946 constitution.

Slo·win·ski National Park \slə-'win-skē-\. National park, Poland; 69 sq. m.; migratory birds, moving dunes; established 1966.

Sloy, Loch \läk-'slȯi, läk-\. Small lake, Dunbarton co., W Scotland, at NW end of Loch Lomond; ab. 1 m. long; its outlet flows SE to Loch Lomond; site of huge hydroelectric project 1948.

Słu·bi·ce \slü-'bēt-sə\. City, W Zielona Góra prov., W Poland, on E bank of the Oder opp. Frankfurt, East Germany; pop. (1968e) 11,500; before boundary revisions of 1945 part of Frankfurt.

Sluis *or* **Sluys** \'slȯis\ *or Fr.* **Écluse** \ā-klüz\. Commune, Zeeland prov., SW Netherlands; pop. (1970e) 2810; on the Belgian border and connected with sea by a canal; scene of naval battle June 24, 1340 in which Edward III of England almost completely destroyed the French fleet.

Sluis·kin \'slü-skən\. Waterfall, S side of Mt. Rainier, Pierce co., W cen. Washington; 300 ft. high.

Słu·pia \'slü-pē-ə\ *or Ger.* **Stol·pe** \s(h)tȯl-pə\. River, N Poland; 112 m. long; flows NW into the Baltic Sea.

Słupsk \'slüpsk\ *or Ger.* **Stolp** \'s(h)tȯlp\. City, Koszalin prov., N Poland, 39 m. ENE of Koszalin; pop. (1970p) 68,300; formerly in Germany; furniture, agricultural implements, machinery, dairy products. First mentioned 1180; became city 1310; member of Hanseatic League; captured by U.S.S.R. Mar. 9, 1945; assigned to Poland by Potsdam Conference 1945.

Slutsk \'slütsk\. 1 Town, Minsk Oblast, S cen. Belorussian S.S.R., U.S.S.R., 60 m. S of Minsk; pop. (1967e) 27,000; sawmills and flour mills; annexed to Russia 1795.
2 Town, Leningrad Oblast, Russian S.F.S.R., U.S.S.R. See PAVLOVSK.

Sluys. See SLUIS.

Slyne Head \'slīn-\. Cape, W coast of Eire, in W co. Galway, projecting into Atlantic Ocean; lighthouse.

Smaalenenes. See ØSTFOLD.

Små·land Highlands \'smō-(,)land-\. Plateau region, S Sweden, S of Lake Vättern.

Smalcald *or* **Smalkald.** See SCHMALKALDEN.

Şma·li Ana·do·lu Da·ğla·rı \shmä-'lē-,än-ə-dō-'lü-,dä(g)-lə-'rē\ *also* **Zi·ga·na Si·ra Dagları** \,zig-ə-'nä-sə-,rä-\. Mountain range (*dağları*), N Turkey, along Black Sea coast from ab. 33°E long. to the U.S.S.R. border at 42°E; ab. 520 m. long; has many peaks 9000 to 12,000 ft.

Smal·ling·er·land \'smäl-iŋ-ər-,länt\. Commune, Friesland prov., N Netherlands, on canal 12 m. NE of Heerenveen; pop. (1970e) 38,627.

Small Point. Point, SW Sagadahoc co., S Maine.

Sma·ra \'smär-ə\. Settlement, N Spanish Sahara, NW Africa; pop. (1967e) 1384; administrative post.

Sme·de·re·vo \'smed-ə-rə-,vō\ *or Ger.* **Se·men·dria** \zā-'men-drē-ə\. Town, Serbia, E Yugoslavia, 25 m. ESE of Belgrade on Danube river; pop. (1965e) 31,000; trade center in grape-growing region; shipbuilding yards; 15th cent. castle with 19 square towers; capital of Serbia 1430–59 when Belgrade was held by the Turks; occupied by Germans during World War II.

Sme·la \'smel-ə\. Town, Cherkassy Oblast, N cen. Ukrainian S.S.R., U.S.S.R., ab. 16 m. SW of Cherkassy; pop. (1969e) 52,000.

Smeroe. See SEMERU.

Smeth·port \'smeth-(,)pō(ə)rt, -(,)pȯ(ə)rt\. Borough, ⊗ of McKean co., N Pennsylvania, 15 m. SE of Bradford; pop. (1970c) 1883; chemicals; coal mines; agriculture.

Smi·ley Mountain \,smī-lē-\. Peak, S Custer co., cen. Idaho; 11,506 ft.

Smith \'smith\. Name of counties in four states of the U.S. See tables at KANSAS, MISSISSIPPI, TENNESSEE, TEXAS.

Smith Center. City, ⊗ of Smith co., N Kansas, 65 m. WNW of Concordia; pop. (1970c) 2389; grain farms.

Smith·ers \'smith-ərz\. 1 City, Fayette and Kanawha cos., S cen. West Virginia; pop. (1970c) 2020.
2 Village, British Columbia, Canada, 125 m. ENE of Prince Rupert; pop. (1971p) 3772; diversified agriculture.

Smith·field \'smith-,fēld\. 1 Town, ⊗ of Johnston co., E North Carolina, 26 m. SE of Raleigh; pop. (1970c) 6677; tobacco market; corn.
2 Town, Providence co., N Rhode Island, 10 m. NW of Providence; pop. (1970c) 13,468; incorporated 1731.
3 City, Cache co., N Utah, 8 m. N of Logan; pop. (1970c) 3342; livestock and dairy farms.
4 Town, Isle of Wight co., SE Virginia, on James river 13 m. W of Newport News; pop. (1970c) 2713; lumber, ham; peanuts.
5 *or* **West Smithfield.** Region in London, England; originally a scene of tournaments, later a trading center and place of executions; scene 1133–1840 of Bartholomew Fair, a great annual fair beginning on St. Bartholomew's Day, later, 1840–55, held at Islington; now site of chief London meat market.

Smith Island. 1 Marshy island, Lower Chesapeake Bay, SW Somerset co., SE Maryland, its S tip extending into Virginia.
2 Island in Atlantic Ocean at SE extremity of North Carolina; Cape Fear constitutes its S tip.
3 Island in Atlantic Ocean, S extremity of Northampton co., Virginia.

Smith·land \'smith-lənd\. City, ⊗ of Livingston co., W Kentucky; pop. (1970c) 514.

Smith Peak. Mountain, E Tuolumne co., cen. California; 7751 ft.

Smiths Falls \'smiths-\. Town, Lanark co., SE Ontario, Canada, on Rideau river 41 m. SSW of Ottawa; pop. (1971p) 9598; furniture, dairy products.

Smith Sound. Channel, separating NW Greenland from coast of SE Ellesmere I.; ab. 50 m. long by 35 m. wide; connects Kane Basin with Baffin Bay.

Smith·ville \'smith-,vil\. 1 Town, ⊗ of De Kalb co., cen. Tennessee; pop. (1970c) 2997.
2 City, Bastrop co., S cen. Texas, on Colorado river 38 m. ESE of Austin; pop. (1970c) 2959; furniture; cotton, fruit.

Smokies. See GREAT SMOKY MOUNTAINS.

Smoky \'smō-kē\. River, W Alberta, Canada; 245 m. long; rises in Rocky Mts. near British Columbia border and flows N into Peace river at Peace River town.

Smoky Cape. Cape, N New South Wales coast, SE Australia, 165 m. NE of Newcastle.

Smoky Hill. River, cen. Kansas; 540 m. long; rises in Cheyenne co., E Colorado, flows E through cen. Kansas to unite with the Republican river at Junction City in Geary co. and form the Kansas river.

Smoky Hill Buttes. Buttes, McPherson co., cen. Kansas; highest point 1580 ft.

Smoky Mountains. See GREAT SMOKY MOUNTAINS.

Smø·la \'smə(r)-lə\. Island in Norwegian Sea off W coast of Norway, WSW of Hitra I.

Smo·lensk \smō-'len(t)sk\. 1 Medieval principality, 12th–14th cents., in W Russia S of Novgorod and W of Rostov-Suzdal; ❋ Smolensk; at first covered wide area. Allied with princes of Kiev; overcome 1408 by Lithuanians.
2 City, ❋ of Smolensk Oblast, Russian S.F.S.R., U.S.S.R., on left bank of upper Dnieper; pop. (1970p) 211,000; railroad junction and commercial center; manufactures motor vehicle parts, textile machinery, flour, bricks, glass, footwear; cultural center with a cathedral, libraries and museums, and several educational institutions.
History: First mentioned 882; became important commercial center on trade route from Baltic Sea to Constantinople; capital of Smolensk principality 12th–14th cents.; sacked by Tatars c. 1240; taken by Lithuania 1408; disputed between Poland and Russia for over 250 years and finally ceded to Russia 1686; burned during French invasion of Russia 1812; in World War II scene of heavy fighting on several occasions; occupied by Germans Aug. 1941–Sept. 1943.

Smolensk Oblast \-'ȯ-bləst, -,blast\. Subdivision of W Russian S.F.S.R., U.S.S.R.; 19,228 sq. m.; pop. (1970p) 1,106,000; ❋ Smolensk; occupies part of W plateau of Russian S.F.S.R., containing source of the Dnieper river and of several headstreams of the Volga and Western Dvina; forest regions greatly reduced. Economy is largely agricultural: flax, grains, potatoes; dairy and livestock farming; lignite and peat extraction. Smolensk, Roslavl, and Vyazma are only large urban centers. Territory contested 15th–17th cents. between Poland and Russia and ceded to Russia 1686; scene of major fighting in Napoleonic invasion 1812, in civil war 1918–20, and in World War II 1941 and 1943.

Smo·lyan \smōl-'yän\. 1 Province of S Bulgaria. See table at BULGARIA.
2 Town, its ✻, ab. 40 m. S of Plovdiv in Rhodope Mts. near Greek border; pop. (1968e) 19,311.

Smooth·face Mountain \ˌsmüth-fās-\. Mountain, Yellowstone National Park, NW Wyoming; has two peaks, S 10,417 ft. and N 10,500 ft.

Smrčiny. See FICHTELGEBIRGE.

Smyr·na \'smər-nə\. 1 Short stream, N cen. Delaware; forms section of boundary bet. New Castle and Kent cos.; empties into Delaware river.
2 Town, Kent co., cen. Delaware, 10 m. N of Dover; pop. (1970c) 4243; poultry, fruit farms.
3 Town, Cobb co., NW Georgia, 9 m. NW of Atlanta; pop. (1970c) 19,157; residential suburb of Atlanta.
4 Town, Rutherford co., cen. Tennessee, 11 m. NW of Murfreesboro; pop. (1970c) 5698; diversified agriculture.
5 Province and seaport city, Turkey. See İZMİR.

Smyrna, Gulf of. See İZMİR, GULF OF.

Smyrnaeus, Sinus. See İZMİR, GULF OF.

Smyth \'smīth\. County in Virginia. See table at VIRGINIA.

Snae·fell \'snā-ˌfel\. Highest peak on the Isle of Man, in the Irish Sea off NW coast of England; 2034 ft.

Snae·fells·jö·kull \'snī-ˌfelz-ˌyər-ˌküt-ᵊl\. Mountain and glacier, W Iceland, NW of Reykjavík on peninsula on N side of Faxa Bay; mountain height 4744 ft.

Snaght, Slieve. See SLIEVE SNAGHT.

Snake \'snāk\. 1 River, NW United States; 1038 m. long; rises in Yellowstone National Park, NW Wyoming, flows S, then SW, W, and N across Idaho in a big arc; turns N and forms parts of Idaho-Oregon and Idaho-Washington boundaries; turns W at Lewiston, cuts across SE Washington and empties into the Columbia river in S Franklin co., SE Washington; on the Idaho-Oregon boundary has created a canyon more than 40 m. long and more than 7000 ft. deep at one point; has numerous notable springs; in section in S Idaho N of Twin Falls has several cascades, esp. Twin Falls and Shoshone Falls (*qq.v.*) and is used to irrigate the desert region to the S.
2 River, Minnesota; 135 m. long; rises in S Aitkin co. E of Mille Lacs, flows S and E into St. Croix river in Pine co.

Snake Creek. 1 Creek, N Nebraska; 80 m. long; rises in Sheridan co., flows E into Niobrara river in Cherry co.
2 River, NE cen. North Dakota; ab. 60 m. long; rises in W Faulk co., flows E into Dakota (James) river in W Spink co.

Snake Mountain. Peak, Rabun co., NE Georgia; 3365 ft.

Snake Range. Mountain range, E White Pine co., E Nevada; highest point Wheeler Peak 13,065 ft.; Lehman Caves National Monument is in it.

Snares Islands \'sna(ə)rz-, 'sne(ə)rz-\ *or* **The Snares.** Group of uninhabited islets, SW of New Zealand, in S Pacific Ocean at 48°00'S, 166°30'E; 15 sq. m.

Snee·berg \'snē-ˌbərg\ *or* **Sneeuw·berg** \'snē-ü-ˌbərg\. Mountain range and peak, cen. Cape Province, S Rep. of South Africa; 8215 ft.

Sneed·ville \'snēd-ˌvil, -vəl\. Village, ⊗ of Hancock co., NE Tennessee; pop. (1970c) 874.

Sneek \'snāk\. Commune, Friesland prov., N Netherlands, 14 m. SSW of Leeuwarden; pop. (1970e) 26,244; transportation center (canal and railroad) and market town.

Sneeuwberg. See SNEEBERG.

Sneeuw Gebergte. See MAOKE MOUNTAINS.

Snef·fels, Mount \-'snef-əlz\. Peak in the San Juan Mts., Ouray co., SW Colorado; 14,150 ft.

Snezh·no·ye \'sn(y)ezh-nə-yə\. Town, Donetsk Oblast, Ukrainian S.S.R., U.S.S.R., ab. 45 m. E of Donetsk; pop. (1969e) 72,000.

Sněž·ka \'snyesh-kə\ *or Ger.* **Schnee·kop·pe** \'shnā-ˌkȯp-ə\. Peak in Riesengebirge, on boundary bet. Czechoslovakia and Poland; 5256 ft.; highest peak in Riesengebirge.

Śniar·dwy \shnə-'ärd-vē\ *or Ger.* **Spir·ding** \'shpir-diŋ\. Lake, SE Olsztyn prov., N Poland; 10 m. long, 41 sq. m.; max. depth 82 ft.; largest lake in Poland; connected by canals with Lake Mamry and other smaller lakes. In German territory assigned to Poland by Potsdam Conference 1945.

Sni·zort, Loch \läk-'snē-ˌzȯ(ə)rt, läk-\. Inlet of the Little Minch, N Skye I. in the Inner Hebrides, NW of Scotland.

Snø·het·ta \'snər-ˌhet-ə\. Snow-capped peak in cen. Norway, in the Dovrefjell plateau; 7500 ft.

Sno·ho·mish \snō-'hō-mish\. 1 River, NW cen. Washington; 65 m. long; formed by junction of Skykomish and Snoqualmie rivers in SW Snohomish co., flows NW into Puget Sound.
2 County in Washington. See table at WASHINGTON.
3 City, Snohomish co., NW cen. Washington, 8 m. SE of Everett; pop. (1970c) 5174; lumber, dairy products; fruit and vegetable canning.

Sno·qual·mie \snō-'kwäl-mē\. River, W cen. Washington; ab. 70 m. long; flows W and N in King co., crosses into Snohomish co. and joins Skykomish river to form Snohomish river.

Snoqualmie Falls. Waterfall, Snoqualmie river, King co., W cen. Washington; 270 ft.

Snow·don \'snōd-ᵊn\. Massif in Caernarvonshire, NW Wales; has five peaks, the highest 3560 ft. being the highest mountain in Wales; region often called **Snow·do·nia** \snō-'dō-nē-ə, -nyə\.

Snow Hill \'snō-\. 1 Town, ⊗ of Worcester co., SE Maryland, 18 m. SSE of Salisbury; pop. (1970c) 2201.
2 Town, ⊗ of Greene co., E North Carolina; pop. (1970c) 1359; agriculture.

Snow·mass Mountain \ˌsnō-ˌmas-\. Peak, Pitkin and Gunnison cos., W cen. Colorado; 14,092 ft.

Snow Mountains. See MAOKE MOUNTAINS.

Snow Peak. Mountain in Sierra Nevada, in E Tuolumne co., cen. California; 10,933 ft.

Snow·slip Mountain \ˌsnō-ˌslip-\. Peak, Glacier National Park, NW Montana; 7290 ft.

Snow Water Lake. Lake, E cen. Elko co., NE Nevada.

Snowy \'snō-ē\. River, SE New South Wales and E Victoria, SE Australia; 278 m. long; flows S through Gippsland from Australian Alps to South Pacific Ocean; hydroelectric power project.

Snowy Mountain. Peak in the Adirondack Mts., Hamilton co., NE cen. New York; 3898 ft.

Snowy Mountains. Range of the Australian Alps (*q.v.*), E Victoria and SE New South Wales, Australia; site of important hydroelectric power project.

Sny·der \'snīd-ər\. 1 County in Pennsylvania. See table at PENNSYLVANIA.
2 City, ⊗ of Scurry co., NW cen. Texas, 33 m. NW of Sweetwater; pop. (1970c) 11,171; oil wells; agriculture.

So·an \ˌsō-'än\ *or* **So·han** \ˌsō-'hän\. River, Punjab, Pakistan; ab. 130 m. long; flows from the Himalayas SW into the Indus river.

Soap Lake \'sōp-\. City, Grant co., cen. Washington, at S end of the Grand Coulee; pop. (1970c) 1064; on **Soap Lake,** containing minerals and salts; health resort.

Soar \'sō(ə)r, 'sȯ(ə)r\. River, Leicestershire, cen. England; 40 m. long; flows N into the Trent 12 m. ESE of Derby.

Soa Salt Pan. See MAKARIKARI.

So·bat \'sō-ˌbat\. River, E cen. Africa; formed by confluence of Pibor and Baro rivers on extreme W border of Ethiopia; length from source of the Baro 460 m.; flows W into White Nile river SW of Malakal, Sudan.

So·bo \'sō-(ˌ)bō\ *or* **So·bo·zan** \-'zän\. Peak, E cen. Kyūshū, Japan, E of Mt. Aso; 5766 ft.

So·bral \sü-'bräl\. City, NW Ceará state, NE Brazil, 125 m. W of Fortaleza; munic. pop. (1968e) 78,135.

So·braon \sō-'braůn\. Village, Punjab, NW India, on right bank of the Sutlej; on opp. bank was site of battle Feb. 16, 1846 in which British under Sir Hugh Gough were victors over the Sikhs, ending First Sikh War.

Soča. See ISONZO.

So·cha·czew \sō-ˈhäch-ˌef, -ˈkach-\. Commune, Warszawa prov., cen. Poland, 32 m. W of Warsaw; pop. (1970p) 20,600.

So–ch'e \ˈswä-ˈchə\ *or Turki* **Yar·kend** \yär-ˈkend\. Town and oasis, SW Sinkiang Uighur, W China, on Yarkand river at edge of Takla Makan Desert 100 m. SE of Kashgar; altitude 3900 ft., at foot of N slope of Kunlun mountains: has for centuries been a trade center; irrigation highly developed; grows wheat, barley, beans, and oil plants. Visited by Marco Polo.

So·chi \ˈsō-chē\. Seaport town, S Krasnodar Krai, Russian S.F.S.R., U.S.S.R., on Black Sea near Georgian S.S.R. border 110 m. SSE of Krasnodar; pop. (1970p) 224,000; popular health resort with beaches, thermal and mineral springs; many sanatoria.

So·cial Circle \ˌsō-shəl-\. City, Walton co., N cen. Georgia, 38 m. ESE of Atlanta; pop. (1970c) 1961.

Socialist Federal Republic of Yugoslavia. See YUGOSLAVIA.

Socialist Republic of Romania. See ROMANIA.

So·ci·e·ty Islands \sə-ˈsī-ət-ē-\ *or Fr.* **Îles de la So·cié·té** \ēl-də-lȧ-sȯ-syā-tā\. Island group in W part of French Polynesia, S Pacific Ocean; 621 sq. m.; pop. (1967e) 81,-424; ✱ Papetee. Comprises two groups: Windward Is. (Tahiti, Mooréa, and several islets); and the Leeward Is. (*q.v.*); chief island Tahiti. Volcanic in origin and mountainous, with several high peaks; produce copra, pearl shell, vanilla, phosphate rock.

History: First discovered 1607 by Portuguese navigator Pedro Fernandes de Queirós; rediscovered and claimed for Great Britain 1767 by Samuel Wallis; claimed for France 1768 by Louis de Bougainville but claim not immediately sustained; visited 1768 by *Endeavour* expedition under James Cook; made French protectorate 1843.

Socijalisticka Federativna Republika Jugoslavija. See YUGOSLAVIA.

So·com·pa \sō-ˈkȯm-pə\. Volcanic peak, E Antofagasta prov., N Chile, near Argentina border; 19,786 ft.

So·co·nus·co \ˌsō-kə-ˈnü-(ˌ)skō\. Volcanic peak, SW Chiapas state, Mexico, ab. 26 m. SE of Tuxtla Gutiérrez; 7872 ft.

So·cor·ro \sə-ˈkȯr-(ˌ)ō\. **1** County in New Mexico. See table at NEW MEXICO.

2 City, ⊗ of Socorro co., cen. New Mexico, on the Rio Grande 70 m. S of Albuquerque; pop. (1970c) 5849; agriculture; New Mexico Inst. of Mining and Technology (1889).

3 Island off coast of Chile. See GUAMBLIN.

4 Peak, Colombia. See TRES MORROS.

5 Town, Santander dept., N cen. Colombia; munic. pop. (1968e) 19,551.

6 Island, Revilla Gigedo group (*q.v.*), Pacific Ocean off cen. Mexico.

So·co·tra *or* **So·ko·tra** \sə-ˈkō-trə\ *or Arab.* **Su·qu·trā**\sü-ˈküt-rə\. Island, part of Yemen (✱ Aden), Indian Ocean, S of Arabian Penin., ab. 160 m. ENE of Ras Asir, Somalia, E Africa; ab. 1200 sq. m., 70 m. long; ✱ Tamridah; mountainous interior, highest peak 4686 ft.; chief products dates, ghee, tobacco; fishing.

History: Known to the ancients; except for Portuguese occupancy (1507–11) was a possession of sultans of Qishn; subject of a treaty between sultan and Great Britain 1876; came under British protection 1886; became part of Yemen (✱ Aden) 1967.

So·da Lake \ˌsōd-ə-\. **1** Large dry sink, at times a lake, in Mojave Desert, NE cen. San Bernardino co., California.

2 Lake, Caddo parish, NW Louisiana, E of and connected with Caddo Lake.

So·dan·ky·lä \ˈsō-dan-ˌkü-lə\. Town, Lappi prov., N Finland, on tributary of Kemi river 55 m. NNW of Kemijärvi; pop. (1970e) 11,836.

Soda Springs. City, ⊗ of Caribou co., SE Idaho, 45 m. ESE of Pocatello; pop. (1970c) 2977; dairy products; phosphate mines.

Sod·dy–Dai·sy \ˌsäd-ē-ˈdāz-ē\. City, Hamilton co., SE Tennessee, 16 m. NE of Chattanooga; pop. (1970e) 7569.

Sö·der·hamn \ˌsəd-ər-ˈhäm-ən\. Seaport, Gävleborg co., E Sweden, on an inlet of the Gulf of Bothnia; pop. (1970e) 13,911; shipping point for timber, wood pulp, iron ore, and fish; burned by the Russians 1621.

Sö·der·man·land \ˈsəd-ər-man-ˌland\. County of SE Sweden. See table at SWEDEN.

Sö·der·täl·je \ˌsəd-ər-ˈtel-yə\. Town, Stockholm co., SE Sweden, a suburb of Stockholm; pop. (1970e) 58,873; motor vehicles, medicines, dairy machinery, concrete; 11th cent. church.

Sod·om \ˈsäd-əm\. City in the plain of the Jordan, anc. Palestine, notorious for its wickedness; destroyed, together with Gomorrah (*Gen.* x. 19; xviii. 20; xix. 24–28); sites of both cities unknown, possibly now beneath waters of Dead Sea.

So·dor \ˈsōd-ər\. Medieval diocese comprising the "Southern islands" (*Norse* **Suthr·ey·jar** \süth-ˈrā-ˌyär\), modern Hebrides and the Isle of Man; now, as Sodor and Man, includes only the Isle of Man.

So·dus \ˈsōd-əs\. Village, N Wayne co., W New York, in Sodus town near Lake Ontario 29 m. E of Rochester; pop. (1970c) 1813. The village resort of **Sodus Point** (pop. [1970c] 1172) is about 3 m. to the NE on **Sodus Bay,** inlet of Lake Ontario.

Soebang. See SUBANG.

Soekaboemi. See SUKABUMI.

Soela Islands. See SULA ISLANDS.

Soemba. See SUMBA.

Soembawa. See SUMBAWA.

Soembing. See SUMBING.

Soemedang. See SUMEDANG.

Soemenep. See SUMENEP.

Soenda Deep. See SUNDA DEEP.

Soenda Isles. See SUNDA ISLES.

Soenda Strait. See SUNDA STRAIT.

Soepiori. See SUPIORI.

Soerabaja. See SURABAJA.

Soerabaja Strait. See SURABAJA STRAIT.

Soerakarta. See SURAKARTA.

Soest. 1 \ˈsüst\. Commune, Utrecht prov., cen. Netherlands, 11 m. NE of Utrecht; pop. (1970e) 35,713; residential; founded 1029.

2 \ˈzōst\. City, North Rhine-Westphalia, West Germany, 33 m. N of Münster; pop. (1969e) 35,731; market town; sugar, wire, clothing; 12th cent. cathedral, early 18th cent. town hall; first mentioned 836; chartered 1144; important Hanse town.

So·fa·la \sō-ˈfäl-ə\. **1** Former district, SE Mozambique, SE Africa; now part of Manica and Sofala district (*q.v.*).

2 Seaport village, Mozambique. See NOVA SOFALA.

So·feg·gin \sō-ˈfej-ən\ *or* **Saw·faj·jīn** \sȯ-ˈfaj-ən\. Short river, dry at certain seasons, in N Libya, N Africa; flows NE into W Gulf of Sidra.

So·fia *also* **So·phia** \ˈsō-fē-ə, ˈsȯ-, sō-ˈ\ *or Bulg.* **So·fi·ya** \ˈsȯ-fē-(y)ə\. **1** Province of W Bulgaria. See table at BULGARIA.

2 City, ✱ of Bulgaria, also ✱ of Sofia prov.; constitutes a separate administrative unit, 400 sq. m.; pop. (1968e) 950,676; principal transportation center of Bulgaria; metallurgical, engineering, chemical, textile, and food-processing industries; cultural center of Bulgaria, with opera house, museums, 19th cent. cathedral, univ. (estab. 1888, received univ. status 1904) and several technical colleges.

History: Founded by Romans as **Ser·di·ca** \ˈsərd-i-kə\ 2d cent. A.D.; a favorite residence of Constantine the

Great; burned by Huns 447; established as Bulgarian town 809 but under Byzantine Empire 1018–1185; ruled by Ottoman Turks 1382–1878; made ❋ of Bulgaria 1879; suffered considerable damage from Allied bombing 1943–44; rebuilding completed since 1945.

So·ga·mo·so \ˌsō-gə-ˈmō-(ˌ)sō\. 1 River, N cen. Colombia; ab. 100 m. long; flows N and NW into the Magdalena river. 2 City, Boyacá dept., cen. Colombia, in the Cordillera Oriental 110 m. NE of Bogotá; munic. pop. (1968e) 55,276.

Sog·di·a·na \ˌsäg-dē-ˈan-ə, -ˈän-ə, -ˈā-nə\. Province of NE Persian Empire; ❋ Maracanda (*mod.* Samarkard); conquered by Cyrus the Great 525 B.C.; invaded by Alexander the Great 329–327 B.C.; conquered by Diodotus, satrap of Bactria (*q.v.*), later by the Parthians and Persians. For the later history, see BUKHARA 1.

Sog·ne Fjord \ˌsȯŋ-nə-\. Inlet of Norwegian Sea, W coast of Norway, 61°10′N, 7°03′E; extends E inland 127 m.

Sogn og Fjord·a·ne \ˌsȯŋ-ən-ō-ˈfyu̇r-ə-nə\. County of W Norway. See table at NORWAY.

So·god \ˈsō-ˌgȯd\. Municipality at head of Sogod Bay, Southern Leyte prov., Leyte I., Phil.; pop. (1969e) 24,200.

Sogod Bay. Inlet of Mindanao Sea, S Leyte I., Phil., ab. 35 m. long and 4 to 8 m. wide; Panaon I. forms part of its E shore and Limasawa I. is at its mouth.

Sohan. See SOAN.

So·har *or* **Ṣu·ḥār** \su̇-ˈhär\. Seaport town, Oman, SE Arabian Penin., on Gulf of Oman 140 m. NW of Masqat.

So·ho \sō-ˈhō\. A district in London, England, S of Oxford Street; since 1685 chiefly a foreign quarter; noted for its restaurants; in it is **Soho Square,** once a fashionable residential section.

Soi·gnies \swa-ˈnyē\. Commune, Hainaut prov., SW Belgium, 23 m. SSW of Brussels; pop. (1969e) 11,985; bluelimestone quarries.

Soi·roc·co·cha \ˌsȯi-rō-ˈkō-chä\. Peak, Cordillera Oriental, Peru; 18,600 ft.

Sois·sons \swä-ˈsōⁿ\; *anc.* **No·vi·o·du·num** \ˌnō-vē-ō-ˈd(y)ün-əm\ *or later* **Au·gus·ta Sues·si·o·num** \ȯ-ˈgəs-tə-ˌswes-ē-ˈō-nəm, ə-ˈgəs-\. Commune, Aisne dept., N France, on Aisne river 18 m. SW of Laon; pop. (1968c) 25,890; iron and copper goods, boilers, rubber products, glass, sugar; 12th–13th cent. cathedral (heavily damaged in World War I), remains of 11th cent. abbey.

History: In ancient times a principal town of Belgian Gaul; occupied by the Suessiones; here Clovis defeated Syagrius 486, Charles Martel defeated the Neustrians 716–717; chartered 1131; captured by Germans 1870, 1914, 1918; reduced to almost complete ruin by German bombardments in World War I; in World War II taken by Allies Aug. 27–28, 1944.

Sō·ka \ˈsō-kə\. City, Saitama prefecture, Honshū, Japan; pop. (1970e) 123,269.

Sö·ke \sə-ˈkā\. Town, Aydın prov., SW Turkey, near coast at mouth of Menderes; pop. (1965c) 27,558.

So·khon·do \sə-ˈkȯn-də\. Highest peak in the Yablonovy Mts., SW Chita Oblast, Russian S.F.S.R., U.S.S.R., near border with Mongolian People's Rep.; 7188 ft.

So·ko·dé \sō-ˈkō-dā\. Town, cen. Togo, W Africa; pop. (1970e) 29,623.

So·kol \ˈsȯ-kəl\. Town, Vologda Oblast, Russian S.F.S.R., U.S.S.R., ab. 20 m. NNE of Vologda; pop. (1967e) 50,000.

So·ko·lov \ˈsȯk-ə-ləf\; *formerly* **Falk·nov** \ˈfälk-ˌnȯf\ *or Ger.* **Fal·ke·nau** \ˈfäl-kə-ˌnau̇\. Town, Czech S.R., W Czechoslovakia, on Ohře river 11 m. WSW of Karlovy Vary; pop. (1968e) 19,689.

So·ko·to \ˈsō-kə-ˌtō\. 1 Sultanate, North-Western State, Nigeria; ab. 25,000 sq. m. With its dependencies, it once formed the Fulah Empire, with estimated area of 100,000 sq. m. Region was inhabited by Hausas and developed under Berber and Arab influences 12th to 18th cents.; had many small kingdoms under Muslim rulers; these subdued 1801–04 by Fulah tribes who established new sultanate of Sokoto; after decline in power its ruler made treaty 1885 with British who took over control 1903; religious uprising put down 1906.

2 Town, ❋ of North-Western State, Nigeria, 250 m. WNW of Kano; pop. (1969e) 104,160; commercial center; pottery, leather goods; sultan's palace; ❋ of former Fulah Empire.

Sokotra. See SOCOTRA.

So·la de Vega \ˈsō-lə-də-ˈvā-gə\. Municipality, Oaxaca state, Mexico, 47 m. SSW of Oaxaca; pop. (1970p) 42,401.

So·lai \sō-ˈlī\. Town, Rift Valley prov., W cen. Kenya, E Africa, ab. 25 m. N of Nakuru; terminus of railroad branch line.

Solana, La. See LA SOLANA.

So·la·no \sō-ˈlän-(ˌ)ō\. 1 County in California. See table at CALIFORNIA.

2 Municipality, Nueva Vizcaya prov., Luzon, Phil., on Magat river ab. 5 m. NE of Bayombong; pop. (1969e) 30,900; largest town in province.

Sol·dier Mountain \ˌsōl-jər-\. Peak, Glacier National Park, NW Montana; 7460 ft.

Sol·dot·na \säl-ˈdät-nə\. City, ⊗ of Kenai Peninsula borough, S cen. Alaska; pop. (1970c) 1202.

So·le, Mon·te \ˌmȯnt-ē-ˈsȯ-lə\ *or formerly* **Ec·no·mus** \ˈek-nə-məs\. Hill, near Licata, S Sicily, Italy; naval battle in nearby waters 256 B.C. in which Roman fleet defeated the Carthaginians.

Sole Bay. See SOUTHWOLD.

So·le·dad. 1 \ˈsäl-ə-ˌdad\. City, Monterey co., W California, 35 m. SE of Monterey; pop. (1970c) 4222; wineries, diversified agriculture.

2 \ˌsō-lə-ˈthä(th)\. Town, Atlántico dept., N Colombia, S suburb of Barranquilla; munic. pop. (1968e) 45,986.

3 \ˌsȯl-ə-ˈdäd\. Municipality, San Luis Potosí state, Mexico, 5 m. NE of San Luis Potosí; pop. (1970p) 60,976; fruit, dairy, and truck farming.

Solenhofen. See SOLNHOFEN.

So·lent, The \-ˈsō-lənt\. Channel extending bet. the Isle of Wight and the mainland of S England; varies in width bet. 2 and 5 m.

So·lesmes \sō-ˈlem\. 1 Town, Nord dept., N France, E of Cambrai on Selle river; pop. (1962c) 6369; scene of fighting during British retreat from Mons 1914.

2 Village, Sarthe dept., NW France, on Sarthe river ab. 23 m. SW of Le Mans; pop. (1962c) 818; Benedictine abbey noted for studies in plain chant.

Sol·fe·ri·no \ˌsäl-fə-ˈrē-(ˌ)nō\. Village, Mantova prov., SE Lombardy, N Italy, 5 m. W of the Mincio river; scene of indecisive battle June 24, 1859 bet. French and Sardinian troops under Napoleon III and Austrians under Emperor Francis Joseph.

So·li \ˈsō-ˌlī\ *or* **So·loi** \-ˌlȯi\. Ancient town, Cilicia, Asia Minor, on coast SW of Tarsus; founded by colonists from Argos and Rhodes; in Mithridatic War destroyed by Tigranes, rebuilt by Pompey. Source of the English word *solecism,* because of the bad Greek spoken there.

So·li·gny–la–Trappe \ˌsȯ-lə-ˈnyē-lə-ˈtrap\. Commune, Orne dept., NW France, NE of Alençon; pop. (1962c) 606; site of La Trappe, monastery (founded c. 1140) of the Trappist monks.

So·li·hull \ˌsōl-ə-ˈhəl\. County borough, Warwickshire, England, 8 m. SE of Birmingham; pop. (1971p) 106,968; light industries.

So·li·kamsk \sə-li-ˈkämsk\. Town, Perm Oblast, Russian S.F.S.R., U.S.S.R., on the Usolka river 125 m. N of Perm; pop. (1969e) 89,000; major salt-mining center; chemical and magnesium plants; founded in 15th cent.

Sol–Iletsk \ˌsȯl-ə-ˈletsk\; *formerly* **Ilet·ska·ya Zash·chi·ta** \ē-ˈl(y)et-skī-(y)ə-zäsh-ˈchē-tə\ *also* **Iletsk.** Town, Orenburg Oblast, Russian S.F.S.R., U.S.S.R.; pop. (1967e) 23,000; health resort.

So·li·ma·na \ˌsō-li-ˈmän-ə\. Peak in Cordillera Occidental, Arequipa dept., S Peru; 20,068 ft.

So·li·mões \ˌsü-lē-ˈmōiⁿsh\. Brazilian name of upper Amazon from Peruvian border to mouth of the Rio Negro.

So·ling·en \'zō-liŋ-ən, 'sō-\. Industrial city, North Rhine-Westphalia, West Germany, in the Ruhr valley 14 m. ESE of Düsseldorf; pop. (1969e) 175,167; major center of cutlery industry; machine tools, steel castings, chemicals; chartered 1374; severely damaged by bombing in World War II but since rebuilt.

Sol·i·tar·io, El \el-ˌsäl-ə-'tar-ē-ˌō\. Peak, Brewster and Presidio cos., W Texas; 5048 ft.

Sól·ler \sō(l)-'ye(ə)r\. Town, NW Majorca, Balearic Is.; pop. (1970p) 10,145; tourist resort.

Sollum. See SALŪM.

Sol·na \'sȯl-nə\. City, N suburb of Stockholm, Sweden; pop. (1970e) 56,607.

Soln·ho·fen \'zōln-ˌhō-fən\ *or* **So·len·ho·fen** \'zō-lən-\. Village, Bavaria, West Germany; remains of archaeopteryx discovered here 1739.

So·lo \'sō-(ˌ)lō\. 1 River, cen. and NE cen. Java, Indonesia; 335 m. long; rises in mountains near S coast, flows N then ENE into Java Sea opp. the W end of the island of Madura just N of Gresik; largest river in Java; navigable for small craft in much of its upper course; called **Beng·a·wan** \beŋ-'ä-wän\ in its lower course.

2 City, Indonesia. See SURAKARTA 2.

So·logne \sȯ-'lȯn(-yə), -'lōn\. Plateau region, cen. France; ab. 2000 sq. m.; a marshy district, now largely reclaimed and used for agriculture.

Soloi. See SOLI.

So·lo·lá \ˌsō-lō-'lä\. 1 Department of SW cen. Guatemala. See table at GUATEMALA.

2 Town, its ✱; munic. pop. (1964p) 21,382; altitude ab. 7000 ft.; market town; overlooks Lake Atitlán.

Sol·o·mon \'säl-ə-mən\. River, N cen. Kansas; 210 m. long; formed by confluence of North Fork and South Fork in W Mitchell co., flows SE into Smoky Hill river in W Dickinson co.

Solomon Islands. Group of islands, W Pacific Ocean, E of the island of New Guinea; 15,220 sq. m.; pop. (1970e) 204,186; Bougainville, Buka, and Green islands form part of Papua New Guinea, 3720 sq. m.; remaining islands, including Guadalcanal, Malaita, New Georgia, Choiseul, Santa Isabel, Florida, Savo, Gizo, San Jorge, Rendova, Russell Is., and many small islands, together with the Santa Cruz Is., form British Solomon Islands protectorate, 11,500 sq. m., pop. (1971e) 166,280, ✱ Honiara, on Guadalcanal; copra, gold.

History: First discovered by Álvaro de Mendaña 1567 and later explored by Mendaña and Pedro de Queirós; not seen by Europeans for 200 years; visited by Bougainville 1768, by D'Urville 1837–40, and by missionaries and traders 1845–93; in agreement of 1886 divided bet. Great Britain and Germany, the latter receiving the northern islands (Bougainville, Choiseul, Santa Isabel); islands in SW part came under British dominion 1893. Bougainville and Buka retained by Germany 1899; German group taken by Australian forces 1914 and became Australian mandate, as part of Trust Territory of New Guinea (*q.v.*) 1920. In World War II occupied (except for Malaita and San Cristóbal) 1942 by Japanese who developed harbors and established airfields, esp. around Buin, Munda, and Tulagi; invaded by Americans who landed on Guadalcanal Aug. 7, 1942, completely occupied it by Feb. 1943, made landings on New Georgia and Bougainville (*qq.v.*) 1943, but with development of campaign on New Guinea bypassed ab. 120,000 Japanese in the islands. For other facts about World War II in the islands, see SAVO, CORAL SEA, and SLOT, THE.

Sol·o·mons \'säl-ə-mənz\. Town, Calvert co., Maryland, on an island at N side of Patuxent river mouth; during World War II base for training men in use of amphibious craft.

Solomon Sea. Northern part of Coral Sea; enclosed on the W by New Guinea, on NW by New Britain, and on E by the Solomon Is.

So·lon \'sō-lən\. Village, Cuyahoga co., N Ohio, 13 m. ESE of Cleveland; pop. (1970c) 11,519.

So·lor \sō-'lō(ə)r\. Small mountainous island, Lesser Sunda Is., Indonesia, in Savu Sea, off E tip of Flores I. and W of Lomblen I.; 25 m. long by 3 or 4 m. wide; 114 sq. m.; copra, fishing. The islands of Solor, Adonara, and Lomblen are sometimes known as the **Solor Islands.**

So·lo·thurn \'zō-lə-ˌtu̇(ə)rn, 'sō-\. 1 Swiss canton. See table at SWITZERLAND.

2 Commune, ✱ of Solothurn canton, NW Switzerland, on Aare river 19 m. N of Bern; pop. (1970c) 17,708; tourism; watches, electrical equipment; 18th cent. cathedral, town hall, clock tower of 5th or 6th cent.; known in Roman times; free imperial city 1218.

So·lo·vets·ki Islands \ˌsäl-ə-ˌvet-skē-\ *or Russ.* **So·lo·vets·kiye Ostro·va** \ˌsäl-ə-ˌvet-skē-ə-'ȯs-trȯ-və\. Island group, SW White Sea, Arkhangelsk Oblast, Russian S.F.S.R., U.S.S.R., 30 m. E of Kem; 134 sq. m.; **Solovetski,** the largest, 100 sq. m., is site of a former monastery, built in 1429; in 16th and 17th cents. used as a fortress against Swedes; in recent times buildings made into a social center for development of local resources; in 1917 became a political prison and place of exile.

Solt \'shōlt\. Commune, Bács-Kiskun co., S Hungary, on the Danube ab. 50 m. S of Budapest; pop. (1970p) 6900.

Šol·ta \'shōl-tə\ *or Ital.* **Sol·ta** \'sȯl-tə\. Island, Adriatic Sea, opp. Split, Croatia, Yugoslavia; 14 m. long, 21 sq. m.

So·luch \sō-'lük\. Town, NE Libya, S of Benghazi.

So·lu·tré \ˌsȯl-ü-'trā\ *or in full* **Solutré–Pouil·ly** \-pü-'yē\. Village, Saône-et-Loire dept., E cen. France, near Mâcon; pop. (1962c) 387; site of rock shelter where prehistoric human remains have been found; type station of the Solutrean epoch of Paleolithic culture, distinguished by beautifully chipped stone implements.

Sol·vay \'säl-(ˌ)vā\. Village, Onondaga co., cen. New York, 5 m. W of Syracuse; pop. (1970c) 8280; chemicals.

Sol·way Firth \ˌsäl-wā-\. Inlet of Irish Sea, on the boundary bet. England and Scotland; extends inland 38 m.

Solway Moss \-'mȯs\. District, Cumberland, NW England, NW of Esk river near Scottish border; scene of battle Nov. 25, 1542 in which the English defeated the Scots under James V.

So·ma \sō-'mä\. Town, Manisa prov., W Turkey, on railroad 20 m. NNW of Akhisar; pop. (1965c) 18,633.

So·main \sȯ-'maⁿ\. Industrial commune, Nord dept., N France, 20 m. E of Arras; pop. (1968c) 15,261.

So·ma·lia \sō-'mäl-ē-ə, -'mäl-yə\ *or officially* **So·ma·li Democratic Republic** \sō-'mäl-ē-\. Republic, E Africa, bounded on N by the Gulf of Aden, on E and S by the Indian Ocean, and on W by Kenya, Ethiopia, and Afars and Issas; 246,154 sq. m.; pop. (1970e) 3,000,000; ✱ Mogadisho. *Physical features:* Much of country semidesert; cen. and S regions flat, N hilly with highest peak Surud Ad 7894 ft. *Chief products:* Sorghum, millet, cotton, bananas; pastoralism is important. *Chief towns:* Mogadisho, Hargeysa, Kismayu.

History: For early history, see BRITISH SOMALILAND and ITALIAN SOMALILAND. Independent republic constituted 1960 by union of British Somaliland with Trust Territory of Somalia (formerly Italian Somaliland); military clash with Ethiopia over boundary dispute 1964; boundary problems with Ethiopia and Kenya resolved 1967; dissolution of national assembly by army 1969.

Somalia Italiana. See ITALIAN SOMALILAND.

Somali Democratic Republic. See SOMALIA.

So·ma·li·land \sō-'mäl-ē-ˌland\. Region, E Africa, bet. the equator and the Gulf of Aden, including Somalia, Afars and Issas, and SE Ethiopia; ab. 300,000 sq. m.

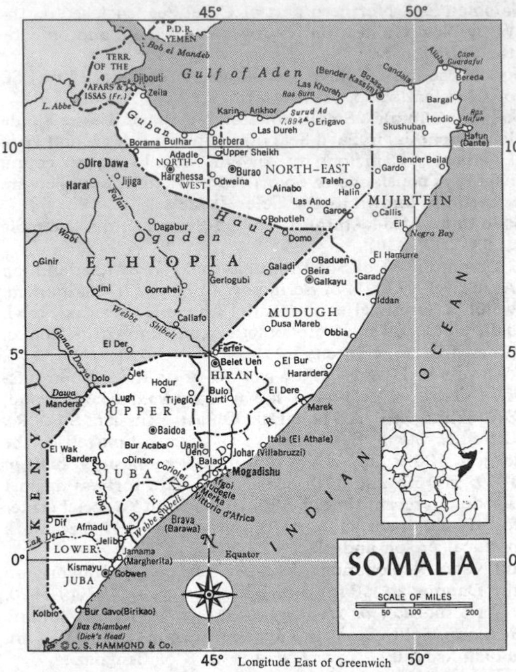

Somaliland Protectorate. See BRITISH SOMALILAND.

Som·bor \'sōm-ˌbō(ə)r, -ˌbȯ(ə)r\ *or Hung.* **Zom·bor** \'zōm-ˌbō(ə)r, -ˌbȯ(ə)r\. City, Vojvodina autonomous prov., NE Yugoslavia, near the Danube ab. 95 m. NW of Belgrade; pop. (1965e) 32,000; commercial center in agricultural and livestock-raising region.

Som·bre·re·te \ˌsȯm-brā-'rā-tā\. Municipality, Zacatecas state, cen. Mexico, 83 m. NW of Zacatecas; pop. (1970p) 48,411.

Som·bre·ro \səm-'bre(ə)r-(ˌ)ō, säm-\. Small island, West Indies, in Anegada Passage bet. Anegada and Anguilla Is.; a part of Saint Christopher-Nevis.

Sombrero Channel. Strait bet. Katchall I. and Little Nicobar I. in the Nicobar Is., Bay of Bengal.

Som·er·dale \'səm-ər-ˌdāl\. Borough, Camden co., SW New Jersey, 10 m. SE of Camden; pop. (1970c) 6510.

Som·ers \'səm-ərz\. Town, NW Tolland co., N Connecticut, E of Enfield on Massachusetts border; pop. (1970c) 6893; incorp. as town by Massachusetts 1734; annexed to Connecticut 1749.

Som·ers·by \'səm-ərz-bē\. Parish, the Parts of Lindsey, Lincolnshire, E England, near Louth; birthplace of Tennyson.

Som·er·set \'səm-ər-ˌset, -sət\. **1** Name of counties in four states of the U.S. See tables at MAINE, MARYLAND, NEW JERSEY, PENNSYLVANIA.

2 City, ⊗ of Pulaski co., SE cen. Kentucky, 40 m. S of Danville; pop. (1970c) 10,436; coal mines, poultry farms.

3 Town, Bristol co., SE Massachusetts, 4 m. N of Fall River; pop. (1970c) 18,088; residential.

4 Village, Perry co., SE cen. Ohio, 18 m. SW of Zanesville; pop. (1970c) 1417; boyhood home of Gen. Philip Sheridan.

5 Borough, ⊗ of Somerset co., S Pennsylvania, 25 m. SSW of Johnstown; pop. (1970c) 6269; concrete blocks, fertilizer; coal mines.

6 County in England. See SOMERSETSHIRE.

Somerset Dam. Dam across branch of Deerfield river, W Windham co., S Vermont; height 106 ft.; completed 1913; impounds water, **Somerset Reservoir,** for water power.

Somerset East. Town, SE Cape Province, S Rep. of South Africa, 83 m. N of Port Elizabeth, at E end of Great Karroo; pop. (1967e) 9800; center for raising sheep and angora goats. Founded 1825.

Somerset Island. Island, cen. Franklin dist., Northwest Territories, Canada, E of Prince of Wales I. and N of Boothia Penin.; 9370 sq. m.

Somerset Nile. See NILE.

Som·er·set·shire \'səm-ər-set-ˌshi(ə)r, -sət-, -shər\ *or* **Somerset.** County, SW England; area 1613 sq. m.; pop. (1971p) 681,974; ⊗ Taunton; chief rivers Avon, Parrett, Axe, Exe; livestock, fruit, and dairy farming, tourism; main towns: Bath, Weston-super-Mare, Taunton, Bridgwater, Glastonbury.

Somerset West. Town, SW Cape Province, S Rep. of South Africa, 30 m. ESE of Cape Town near NE shore of False Bay; pop. (1967e) 9500; in agricultural district; produces wine; manufactures chemicals and explosives; copper, tin, and bismuth deposits nearby. See STRAND.

Somers Islands. See BERMUDA.

Som·ers Point \ˌsəm-ərz-\. City, Atlantic co., SE New Jersey, on Great Egg Harbor 10 m. WSW of Atlantic City; pop. (1970c) 7919; known as Egg Harbor in Revolutionary days.

Som·ers·worth \'səm-ərz-ˌwərth\. City, Strafford co., SE New Hampshire, on Salmon Falls river 5 m. N of Dover; pop. (1970c) 9026; woolens, footwear, dairy farms; incorporated as city 1893.

Som·er·vell \'səm-ər-ˌvel\. County in Texas. See table at TEXAS.

Som·er·ville \'səm-ər-ˌvil\. **1** City, Middlesex co., NE Massachusetts, 3 m. NW of Boston; pop. (1970c) 88,779; tools and dies, paper products, tanning supplies, vehicle bodies, clothing, brooms; residential. Founded 1630 as part of Charlestown; launching place of first ship built in Massachusetts 1631; American base in 1775; incorporated as town 1842 and as city 1871.

2 Borough, ⊗ of Somerset co., N cen. New Jersey, 10 m. WNW of New Brunswick; pop. (1970c) 13,652; residential; electronic components, pharmaceuticals; Somerset County Coll. (1968); Washington's headquarters 1778–79.

3 Town, ⊗ of Fayette co., SW Tennessee, 43 m. E of Memphis; pop. (1970c) 1816.

So·me·şul \sō-ˌmesh-ül\ *or* **So·meş** \sō-'mesh\ *or Hung.* **Sza·mos** \'sȯm-ˌȯsh\. River, NE Hungary and NW Romania; 145 m. long; formed by junction of **Someşul Mare** \-'mär-ā\ (from Carpathians) and **Someşul Mic** \-'mēk\ (rises in Bihor Mts.); flows NW into Tisza river.

Somma, Monte. See VESUVIUS.

Som·ma Ve·su·via·na \'sō-mə-vā-ˌzü-vē-'än-ə\. Commune, Napoli prov., Campania, S Italy, near Mt. Vesuvius 9 m. NE of Naples; pop. (1968e) 19,740; damaged by volcanic eruption 1794.

Somme \'säm, 'səm\. **1** River, N France; 152 m. long; rises near St-Quentin in Aisne dept., flows W to Amiens and NW past Abbeville into the English Channel; scene of one of the great battles, July 1–Nov. 18, 1916, of World War I, a series of conflicts in which the Allies, chiefly British under Haig and Rawlinson, made minor gains against German lines. Its valley occupied by Germans May–June 1940 in World War II; recovered by Allies Aug. 1944.

2 Department of N France. See table at FRANCE.

Somme·py \sȯm-'pē\ *or* **Sommepy–Ta·hure** \-tä-'yu̇(ə)r\. Village, Marne dept., NE France, 23 m. E of Reims; pop. (1962c) 588; American memorial to U.S. and French soldiers who fought in the region during World War I.

Sommerfeld. See LUBSKO.

Som·nath \sōm-'nät\ *or* **Pa·tan Somnath** \ˌpət-ən-\. Port, S coast of Gujarat, W India, near Veraval; famous in Hindu legends as the spot where Krishna was shot by the Bhils. Has several ancient temples; one was looted by Mahmud of Ghazni in 1024 when the "Gates of Somnath" were carried off to his capital; in 1842 Lord Ellenborough brought back to Agra what was said to be these gates.

So·mogy \sə-'mōj\. County of SW Hungary. See table at HUNGARY.

So·mo·sie·rra Pass \ˌsō-mō-sē-ˌer-ə-\. Mountain pass in the Sierra de Guadarrama, cen. Spain; 4770 ft.

So·mo·to \sō-ˈmō-(ˌ)tō\. Town, ✱ of Madriz dept., NW Nicaragua, near the Honduras border; pop. (1970e) 16,-480.

Som·port, Col de \ˌkȯl-də-sōⁿ-ˈpȯ(ə)r\ *or anc.* **Sum·mus Por·tus** \ˌsəm-ə-ˈspōrt-əs, -ˈspȯrt-\. Mountain pass in W Pyrenees, N of Jaca, N Spain, on boundary bet. Huesca dept., Spain, and Pyrénées-Atlantiques dept., France; 5354 ft.; used by Saracens under Abd-er-Rahman 732.

Son \ˈsōn\ *or* **So·ne** \ˈsō-(ˌ)nā\. River, NE cen. India; 475 m. long; rises in E Madhya Pradesh, flows NW, then E and NE to the Ganges river near Dinapur; source of irrigation system for Bihar.

Søn·der·borg \ˈsə(r)n-dər-ˌbȯ(ə)rg\. 1 Former county of Denmark, comprising Als I. and part of SE Jutland penin.; under German rule 1864–1919; now forms part of Sønderjylland co.

2 Town, Sønderjylland co., SW Als I. off SE coast of Jutland, Denmark, 17 m. NE of Flensburg; pop. (1970e) 23,-069; seaside resort; trade center of Als I.

Søn·der·jyl·land \ˈsən-ə-ˌē-lan\. County, S Jutland, Denmark. See table at DENMARK.

Son·ders·hau·sen \ˌzȯn-dərs-ˈhau̇z-ᵊn\. Commune, Erfurt dist., East Germany, N of Erfurt; pop. (1970e) 22,880; former ✱ of Schwarzburg-Sondershausen; castle.

Son·drio \ˈsȯn-drē-ˌō\. 1 Province of Lombardy, Italy. See table at ITALY.

2 Commune, its ✱, on the Adda river 62 m. NE of Milan; pop. (1968e) 22,449; near Bernina Pass; produces wines and textiles.

Sone. See SON.

So·ne·que·ra \ˌsō-nə-ˈker-ə\. Peak, S Potosí dept., SW Bolivia; 18,652 ft.

Song Da. See BLACK 9.

Son·gea \sȯŋ-ˈgā-ə\. Town, ✱ of Ruvuma region, S Tanzania, E Africa, E of Lake Nyasa; pop. (1967c) 5430; road junction and trade center.

Song·hai Empire *or* **Song·hay Empire** \ˌsȯŋ-hī-\. Negro empire (10th–16th cents.), in the region of the bend of the Niger in W cen. Sudan, Africa; chief town Tombouctou; under Muslim influence; besides Sudanese, included many Moors and Fulah; destroyed by Spanish and Portuguese force 1591.

Songjin. See KIMCH'AEK.

Song·khla *or* **Song·kla** \səŋ-ˈklä-\ *or Malay* **Sin·go·ra** \siŋ-ˈgō(ə)r-ə\. 1 Province, SW Thailand; 2576 sq. m.; pop. (1960c) 500,285; ✱ Songkhda.

2 Seaport, its ✱, on E coast of Malay Penin. 50 m. NW of Pattani; pop. (1964e) 36,277; trade center and coastal port; fisheries; taken by Japanese Dec. 8–9, 1941.

Song·we \ˈsȯŋ-(ˌ)wā\. River, E Africa; ab. 100 m. long; flows into N end of Lake Nyasa; forms N boundary of Malawi.

Son·hat \ˈsōn-ˌhät\. Town, Madhya Pradesh, India. See KOREA.

Son·mi·a·ni Bay \ˌsōn-mē-ˌän-ē-\. Inlet of Arabian Sea, S coast of Pakistan.

Son·ne·berg \ˈzȯ-nə-ˌbe(ə)rg\. City, Suhl dist., East Germany, 44 m. S of Erfurt; pop. (1970e) 29,767; a center of toy-manufacturing industry; chartered 1317.

So·no·ma \sə-ˈnō-mə\. 1 County in California. See table at CALIFORNIA.

2 City, Sonoma co., W California, 13 m. S of Santa Rosa; pop. (1970c) 4112; wineries; automobile parts, plywood; diversified agriculture.

So·no·ra \sə-ˈnōr-ə, -ˈnȯr-\. 1 City, ⊗ of Tuolumne co., cen. California, 45 m. E of Stockton; pop. (1970c) 3100; wine, cheese; diversified agriculture.

2 City, ⊗ of Sutton co., SW cen. Texas, 65 m. S of San Angelo; pop. (1970c) 2149; tourism; ships wool, livestock.

3 River, Sonora state, NW Mexico; ab. 250 m. long; flows SW and W into upper Gulf of California near Tiburón I.

4 State of NW Mexico. See table at MEXICO.

Sonora Pass. Mountain pass, Mono, Alpine, and Tuolumne cos., E California; 9628 ft.; one of important passes through the Sierra Nevada Mts. used by early emigrants and explorers.

Sonora Peak. Mountain on boundary bet. Mono and Alpine cos., E cen. California; 11,429 ft.

Son·pur \ˈsōn-ˌpu̇(ə)r\. Former Indian state, now part of Orissa state, E India; 948 sq. m.

Son·so·na·te \ˌsȯn-sə-ˈnä-(ˌ)tā\. 1 Department of SW El Salvador. See table at EL SALVADOR.

2 City, its ✱; pop. (1968e) 31,435; center of rich agricultural region; founded 1524.

Son·tay \sōn-ˈtī\. Town, North Vietnam, on highway 25 m. WNW of Hanoi; on right bank of Red river just S of its junction with the Black.

Sont·ho·fen \ˈzȯnt-ˌhō-fən\. Town, S Bavaria, West Germany, on upper Iller river in mountains 25 m. E of Bregenz; pop. (1968e) 16,209.

Sontius. See ISONZO.

Soo Canals. See SAULT SAINTE MARIE CANALS.

Soochow. See SU-CHOU.

So·per·ton \ˈsōp-ərt-ᵊn\. City, ⊗ of Treutlen co., E cen. Georgia, 90 m. WNW of Savannah; pop. (1970c) 2596; clothing, turpentine; agriculture.

So·phe·ne \sō-ˈfē-nē\. District in SW ancient Armenia, E of the Euphrates, bordering on Mesopotamia on the S and on Cappadocia on the W; became Roman under Pompey ab. 63 B.C.

Sophia. See SOFIA.

Sopoctan. See SOPUTAN.

So·pot \ˈsȯ-ˌpȯt\ *or Ger.* **Zop·pot** \ˈtsȯp-ˌȯt\. Commune, Gdańsk prov., N Poland, on the Gulf of Danzig ab. 8 m. NNW of Gdańsk; pop. (1970p) 47,600; seaside resort; mentioned in 13th cent.; developed as resort from 1823.

Sop·ron \ˈshō-ˌprōn\ *or Ger.* **Öden·burg** \ˈərd-ᵊn-ˌbu̇(ə)rg\. City, Győr-Sopron co., NW Hungary, near the Austrian boundary; pop. (1970p) 47,100; preserved fruit, sugar, textiles; medieval church; a Roman settlement on a strategic road; the only part of Burgenland (*q.v.*) remaining in Hungary when rest of province transferred to Austria Feb. 1922.

So·pu·tan *or Du.* **So·poe·tan** \sō-ˈpü-(ˌ)tän\. Peak, NE Celebes I., Indonesia, just S of Manado; 5994 ft.

So·ra \ˈsȯr-ə\. Commune, Frosinone prov., Latium, cen. Italy, on Liri river 14 m. ENE of Frosinone; pop. (1968e) 25,319; 12th cent. cathedral; damaged by earthquake 1349, 1634, 1915.

So·rac·te \sə-ˈrak-te\ *or Ital.* **So·rat·te** \sō-ˈrät-ā\. Mountain, Italy, near the Tiber river 24 m. NE of Rome; 2267 ft.

So·ra·ta \sō-ˈrät-ə\. 1 Mountain, Bolivia, E of Lake Titicaca, consisting of the peaks Ancohuma and Illampu (*qq.v.*).

2 Village, La Paz dept., W Bolivia, E of Lake Titicaca and at foot of Mt. Illampu; health resort; scene of Indian massacre in revolt of 1781.

Soratte. See SORACTE.

Sorau *or* **Sorau in der Niederlausitz.** See ŻARY.

Sorbiodunum. See OLD SARUM.

So·rel \sə-ˈrel\. Industrial city, ⊗ of Richelieu co., S Quebec, Canada, on S bank of St. Lawrence river at mouth of Richelieu river 35 m. SW of Three Rivers; pop. (1971p) 19,317; ships grain; clothing, furniture, dairy products; shipbuilding; founded 1672 on site of earlier Fort Richelieu (erected 1665).

So·rell \sō-ˈrel\. Town, SE Tasmania, Australia, on Pitt Water 15 m. ENE of Hobart; munic. pop (1970e) 3560; in district devoted to dairying and general farming.

Sorell, Cape. Point, W coast of Tasmania, Australia, at entrance to Macquarie Harbour.

Sorell, Lake. Lake, E cen. Tasmania, Australia; 19 sq. m.; source of Clyde river, a tributary of the Derwent.

So·ria \'sōr-ē-ə, 'sȯr-\. 1 Province of N cen. Spain. See table at SPAIN.

2 Commune, its ✻, on Duero river 113 m. NE of Madrid; pop. (1970p) 25,030; lumber, tile, soap; food processing.

So·ria·no \ˌsōr-ē-'än-(ˌ)ō, sōr-'yä-nō, sȯr-\. 1 Department of SW Uruguay. See table at URUGUAY.

2 Town, Soriano dept., SW Uruguay, at mouth of the Río Negro 162 m. NW of Montevideo; settled 1624, said to be oldest settlement in Uruguay; transshipping point for Mercedes.

Sorø \'sōr-ˌər, 'sȯr-\. Town, Vestsjælland co., SW Sjælland, Denmark; pop. (1970e) 5591.

Soroca. See SOROKI.

So·ro·ca·ba \ˌsōr-ü-'kab-ə, ˌsȯr-\. City, SE São Paulo state, SE Brazil, 68 m. W of São Paulo; munic. pop. (1968e) 142,835; center of cotton-growing region; industrial and commercial center.

Soroka. See BELOMORSK.

So·ro·ki \sə-'rȯ-kē\ *or Rom.* **So·ro·ca** \sȯ-'rȯ-kə\. Town, NE Moldavian S.S.R., U.S.S.R., on right bank of Dniester 30 m. SE of Mogilev Podolski; pop. (1967e) 23,000; raises fruit, corn, tobacco. Originally a Genoese colony; here in 15th cent. Stephen the Great of Moldavia erected fortress and castle; often changed hands bet. Poles, Russians, and Turks; held by Axis powers 1941–44 in World War II.

So·rol \sȯ-'rōl\. Atoll island, W Caroline Is., W Pacific Ocean, SE of Yap, 8°08'N, 140°23'E.

So·ron \'sō-ˌrōn\. Town, W Uttar Pradesh, N India, 107 m. SE of Delhi near right bank of Ganges; pop. (1961c) 15,-300; place of pilgrimages.

So·rong \'sȯ-ˌrōŋ\. Port, Irian Barat, Indonesia, on Dampier Strait, opp. N end of Salawati I.; was Japanese base 1942–44.

Sør·øya \'sər-ˌȯi\. Island, off NW coast of Norway; 315 sq. m.

Sor·ren·to \sə-ren-(ˌ)tō\ *or anc.* **Sur·ren·tum** \sə-'rent-əm\. Seaport, Napoli prov., Campania, S Italy, on **Sorrento Peninsula** (*or* **Sur·ren·tine Peninsula** \ˌsər-en-ˌtēn-\) on S side of Bay of Naples 17 m. SE of Naples; pop. (1968e) 14,364; oranges and lemons; tourist center and summer resort; cathedral, several notable churches and palaces, Roman ruins. Birthplace of Torquato Tasso; occupied by Allied forces during Salerno campaign Sept. 1943.

Sor·so·gon \ˌsȯr-sə-'gȯn\. 1 Province, SE Luzon, Phil.; 827 sq. m.; pop. (1970p) 426,842; ✻ Sorsogon; comprises SE tip of Luzon; coastline irregular, its W coast being deeply indented by Sorsogon Bay. Mountainous, with Bulusan volcano its most noted peak; ranges are covered with excellent timber. Streams are short, but soil, of volcanic origin, is fertile. Hemp (abacá) is the main crop, but coconuts, corn, sugarcane, and pili nuts are also grown. Chief towns Sorsogon, Bulan, Gubat, and Pilar.

History: Under Spanish government a part of Albay prov.; early in 17th cent. visited by Spaniards who established mission at Casiguran; many of the galleons used in the Manila-Acapulco trade built here; civil government established Apr. 1901.

2 Municipality, its ✻, at head of Sorsogon Bay; pop. (1969e) 48,600; port of call for vessels from Manila; has export trade in hemp.

Sorsogon Bay *or* **Sorsogon Gulf.** Landlocked body of water, cen. Sorsogon prov., Luzon, Phil.; 19 m. long and from 3 to 8 m. wide; opens onto Ticao Pass, NW of San Bernardino Strait.

Sortavala. See SERDOBOL.

Sør–Trøn·de·lag \'sər-'trən-də-ˌläg\. County of cen. Norway. See table at NORWAY.

Sõr·ve \'sər-və\ *or Ger.* **Swor·be** \'svȯr-bə\. Peninsula, S Saaremaa I., Estonian S.S.R., U.S.S.R.

Sos \'sōs\ *or in full* **Sos del Rey Ca·tó·li·co** \-del-ˌrā-kä-'tō-li-(ˌ)kō\. Commune, Zaragoza prov., N Spain, 60 m. NNW of Saragossa; pop. (1970p) 1301; birthplace of Ferdinand V of Aragon.

Sos·na \sə-'snä\. River, Orel and Lipetsk oblasts, Russian S.F.S.R., U.S.S.R.; 188 m. long; flows E to join the Don E of Yelets.

Sos·no·wiec \sä-'snōv-ˌyets\ *or unofficially* **Sos·no·wi·ce** \ˌsȯs-nə-'vēt-sə\. Industrial city, Katowice prov., S Poland, 4 m. E of Katowice; pop. (1970p) 145,000; railroad junction; iron and steel, machinery, glass, textiles; coal mines; developed as industrial center c. 1877; received town rights 1902.

Sos·va \'sȯs-və\. River, chiefly in N Khanty-Mansi National Okrug, Tyumen Oblast, Russian S.F.S.R., U.S.S.R.; 556 m. long; flows S and E to the Ob in its lower course near the town of Berezovo.

So·ta·rá \ˌsō-tə-'rä\. Volcanic peak, SW Colombia, in the Cordillera Central S of Popayán; 14,550 ft.

So·to la Ma·ri·na \ˌsōt-ō-ˌläm-ə-'rē-nə\. River, cen. Tamaulipas state, Mexico; ab. 160 m. long; flows E into Gulf of Mexico.

Sot·ra \'sōt-(ˌ)rä\ *also* **Sto·re Sot·ra** \ˌstȯr-ə-\. Island off SW coast of Norway, near Bergen; 67 sq. m.

Sot·te·ville–lès–Rou·en \sȯt-ˌvē-le-rü-'äⁿ\. Industrial commune, Seine-Maritime dept., N France, S suburb of Rouen on left bank of Seine; pop. (1968c) 34,495; cotton textiles.

Sou·chez \sü-'shā\. Village, Pas-de-Calais dept., N France, 4 m. SW of Lens; pop. (1962c) 1652; battle Sept. 25, 1915 in which it was captured by the French.

Souda Bay. See SUDA BAY.

Soudan. See SUDAN.

Soudan français. See MALI.

Sou·der·ton \'saủd-ərt-ᵊn\. Borough, Montgomery co., SE Pennsylvania, 26 m. N of Philadelphia; pop. (1970c) 6366; clothing, silk, dairy products.

Soúdhas, Kolpos. See SUDA BAY.

Soueida. See ES SUWEIDA.

Soueidié. See SÜVEYDIYE.

Souflíon. See SOUPHLI.

Sou·fri·ère \ˌsü-frē-'e(ə)r\. 1 also **Grande Soufrière** \'graⁿd-\. Volcano, S Basse-Terre I., Guadeloupe, West Indies; 4813 ft.

2 Volcanic peak, S Montserrat, Leeward Is., West Indies; 3000 ft.; highest point on island.

3 Town, W coast of St. Lucia I., West Indies, near Canaries Mt.

4 *also* **La Soufrière** \lä-\. Volcano at N end of St. Vincent I., in the Windward Is., West Indies; 4048 ft.; violent eruption May 7, 1902, resulting in loss of 2000 lives; remained active until Mar. 1903.

Souil·lac \sü-'yäk\. Small town, S coast of the island of Mauritius, in Indian Ocean.

Souk–Ah·ras \sü-'ka(ə)r-ˌäs\ *also* **Suk–Ahras** \sük-'ar-äs\ *or anc.* **Ta·gas·te** \tə-'gas-tē\. Commune, Annaba dept., NE Algeria, ab. 40 m. S of Annaba; pop. (1966c) 34,397.

Sou·langes \sü-'läⁿzh\. County, Quebec, Canada. See table at QUEBEC.

Sound, The. See ØRESUND.

Sounds National Park. See FIORDLAND NATIONAL PARK.

Sounion, Cape. See COLONNA, CAPE.

Sou·phli \sü-'flē\ *also* **Suf·li** \sü-\ *or Gk.* **Sou·flí·on** \sü-'flē-ˌȯn\. Town, Evros dept., Western Thrace, NE Greece, ab. 32 m. NE of Alexandroúpolis.

Sour. See TYRE.

Sour al–Ghoz·lane \ˌsủr-al-'gäz-(ˌ)län\ *or formerly* **Au·male** \ō-'mäl\. Commune, Médéa dept., N Algeria, ab. 58 m. SE of Algiers.

Sou·ris \'sủr-əs\. River, S Canada; ab. 450 m. long; rises in S Saskatchewan, flows in curve SE, N, and NE through Saskatchewan, North Dakota, and Manitoba to the Assiniboine SE of Brandon. In North Dakota also called the **Mouse** \'maủs\ river.

Sousse \'süs\ *or* **Su·sa** \'sü-zə, -sə\ *or anc.* **Had·ru·me·tum** \ˌhad-rə-mēt-əm\. Coastal town, NE Tunisia, on S shore of the Gulf of Hammamet; pop. (1966c) 58,161; ships fish and oils; produces textiles, olive oil, plastics, canned foods. An ancient city founded by the Phoenicians and important under the Carthaginians and Romans; important Arab city 9th–11th cents.; developed greatly under French protectorate 1881 ff.

South \'saůth\. River, SE North Carolina; ab. 70 m. long; rises in E cen. North Carolina, flows S into Black river in E Bladen co.

South Africa, Republic of *or Afrikaans* **Re·pu·bliek van Suid–Afri·ka** \ˌrā-pü-'blēk-fän-ˌsòit-'äf-ri-kä\; *formerly* **Union of South Africa** *or Afrikaans* **Unie van Suid–Afrika** \'ü-nē\. Republic, S Africa, bounded on E, S, and W by the Indian and Atlantic oceans (conventional boundary bet. the oceans at 20°E), on NW by South-West Africa, on N by Botswana and Rhodesia, and on NE by Mozambique and Swaziland; the kingdom of Lesotho lies wholly within the republic; 471,445 sq. m.; pop. (1970e) 21,282,000, (1967e) 18,675,293; administrative ✱ Pretoria, legislative ✱ Cape Town, judicial ✱ Bloemfontein. *Physical features:* A plateau region with Drakensberg Mts. in E along boundary bet. Orange Free State and Natal; in Cape Province an inner plateau is bordered on S by an escarpment roughly parallel with the coast which contains many short ranges 6000 to 8000 ft. in height; S of this escarpment is the Great Karroo, 2000 to 3000 ft. high, separated by the Swartberg Mts. from the Little Karroo, 1000 to 2000 ft. high, along the S coast (see KARROO); has much grassland (veld)—bush veld in Cape Province bet. the Great Karroo and the Orange river, and grass veld in the Transvaal and Natal; desert or semidesert in much of the W and S part; bet. the Orange river and the Molopo is the S part of the Kalahari Desert. Chief river the Orange, which with its tributary the Vaal traverses whole cen. part, flowing W to the Atlantic Ocean; many short streams along S and SE coast. *Chief products:* Wheat, corn, citrus and deciduous fruit, sugarcane, sorghum, tobacco; livestock raising, fishing; gold, copper, coal, diamonds, asbestos, manganese, chrome; manufacturing: chemicals, textiles, wood pulp, automotive equipment. *Chief cities:* Johannesburg, Durban, Cape Town, Pretoria, Port Elizabeth, Germiston, Springs, East London. Divided into the following four provinces (for further details, see their individual entries):

NAME	AREA (sq. m.)	POP. (1967e)	CAPITAL
Cape Province	278,380	6,199,634	Cape Town
Natal	33,578	3,418,942	Pietermaritzburg
Orange Free State	49,866	1,661,756	Bloemfontein
Transvaal	109,621	7,394,961	Pretoria

History: Cape settlement ceded by Dutch to British 1814 (see CAPE PROVINCE); in 1836 Dutch settlers (Boers) left Cape in great trek N and E of Orange river; Orange Free State and Transvaal (*qq.v.*) founded by Boers; Natal (*q.v.*) annexed to Cape Colony 1844, given separate government 1845; in 1877 British annexed South African Republic which had been guaranteed its independence by Sand River Convention 1852; Kaffraria, Griqualand West, British Bechuanaland, Zululand, and Tongaland were annexed to provinces later in Union 1865–98; after Boers were defeated in South African (Boer) War 1899–1902, former Boer states met with Cape and Natal in constitutional convention 1908; federal union went into effect 1910; received mandate to former German Southwest Africa 1919; declared war on Germany 1939; became a republic and withdrew from the Commonwealth of Nations 1961; established the Transkei, a partly self-governing territory, 1963; rejected a United Nations resolution calling for termination of the republic's mandate over South-West Africa 1966.

South African Republic *or Du.* **Zuid Afri·kaans·che Re·pub·liek** \zòit-ˌäf-rē-'kän-sə-ˌrā-pü-'blēk\. The Dutch (Boer) republic 1856–77 and 1881–1902 coextensive with Transvaal (*q.v.*).

South Am·boy \-'am-(ˌ)bòi\. City, Middlesex co., cen. New Jersey, on Raritan Bay across from Perth Amboy; pop. (1970c) 9338; ships coal; uniforms, raincoats, cigars; truck farms.

South America. Continent (4th in size), W hemisphere, comprising greater part of Latin America; 6,880,706 sq. m.; ab. 4500 m. N to S and 3200 m. at max. width; pop. (1970e) 190,038,000. *Boundaries:* On N, Caribbean Sea; chief inlets: Gulf of Darien (Colombia), Gulf of Venezuela and Lake Maracaibo, Gulf of Paria (Venezuela); most N point, Point Gallinas in Colombia, 12°25′N; chief islands: Curaçao, Bonaire, and Aruba of Netherlands Antilles, Margarita (Venezuela), and Trinidad and Tobago. On NE and E, Atlantic Ocean; chief inlets: mouth of Amazon, estuary of Río de la Plata, and in Argentina, Bahía Blanca, and Gulfs of San Matías and San Jorge; most E point, Point Coqueiros, just N of Recife, Brazil, 7°38′S, 34°47′W; off Brazil E of Cape São Roque is Fernando de Noronha I. and E of S extremity of Argentina lie the Falkland Is. On S, Drake Passage; Strait of Magellan borders on extreme S of mainland; to the S is large island of Tierra del Fuego and many adjacent smaller islands, including Horn I. on which is Cape Horn, generally considered the most S point of South America, 56°S; most S point of mainland is Cape Froward, S point of Brunswick Penin., Chile, 53°54′S. On W, Pacific Ocean; chief inlets: Corcovado Gulf (Chile) and Gulf of Guayaquil (Ecuador); most W point, Point Pariñas, Peru, 81°20′W; islands: Galápagos Is., 600 m. off Ecuador coast. On NW, Panama, republic and isthmus, connecting with Central America.

Mountains: On W side bordering the Pacific for entire length of continent are the Andes (*q.v.*); highest point Aconcagua 23,834 ft. Other ranges: in N, chiefly in Venezuela and on border bet. Venezuela and the Guianas (on N) and Brazil (on S), the Serras Curupira, Parima, and Acaraí, and the Tumuc-Humac Mts.; in E, the highland of Brazil (Goiás, Minas Gerais, Bahia, São Paulo, and Paraná states) and the plateau of Mato Grosso; and in S the mountains in Córdoba prov., Argentina. Lowland regions are known as the *llanos* in the N, the *selvas* of the Amazon, and the *pampas* of the Paraná basin; the Chaco is the swamp region of the S cen. part. *Rivers:* Amazon in N Brazil with headstreams in Colombia, Peru, and Bolivia and many large tributaries; Orinoco in the N (Venezuela and Colombia), connecting with Rio Negro of the Amazon system through the Casiquiare; Magdalena in Colombia, Essequibo in Guyana; in E, Paranaíba and São Francisco in E Brazil; in S, Uruguay (bet. Uruguay, Argentina, and Brazil), the Paraná system, with its two large headstreams the Alto Paraná and the Paraguay, and many tributaries, and in cen. and S Argentina the Salado, Negro, and Chubut; in W, in the Andes many short streams. *Lakes:* Lake Titicaca (Peru and Bolivia), one of the highest large lakes in the world (alt. 12,500 ft.); Poopó in Bolivia, Lagõa dos Patos in S Brazil, Mirim in Uruguay and Brazil, Mar Chiquita in cen. Argentina; many resort lakes in S Andes, esp. Nahuel Huapí, Todos los Santos, Llanquihue.

Political divisions: Argentina, Bolivia, Brazil, Chile, Colombia, Ecuador, Falkland Is., French Guiana, Guyana, Netherlands Antilles (Aruba, Bonaire, Curaçao), Paraguay, Peru, Surinam, Trinidad and Tobago, Uruguay, and Venezuela.

South Am·herst \-'am-(ˌ)(h)ərst\. Village, Lorain co., N Ohio, 9 m. SW of Lorain; pop. (1970c) 2913.

South·amp·ton \saůth-'(h)am(p)-tən\. **1** County in Virginia. See table at VIRGINIA.

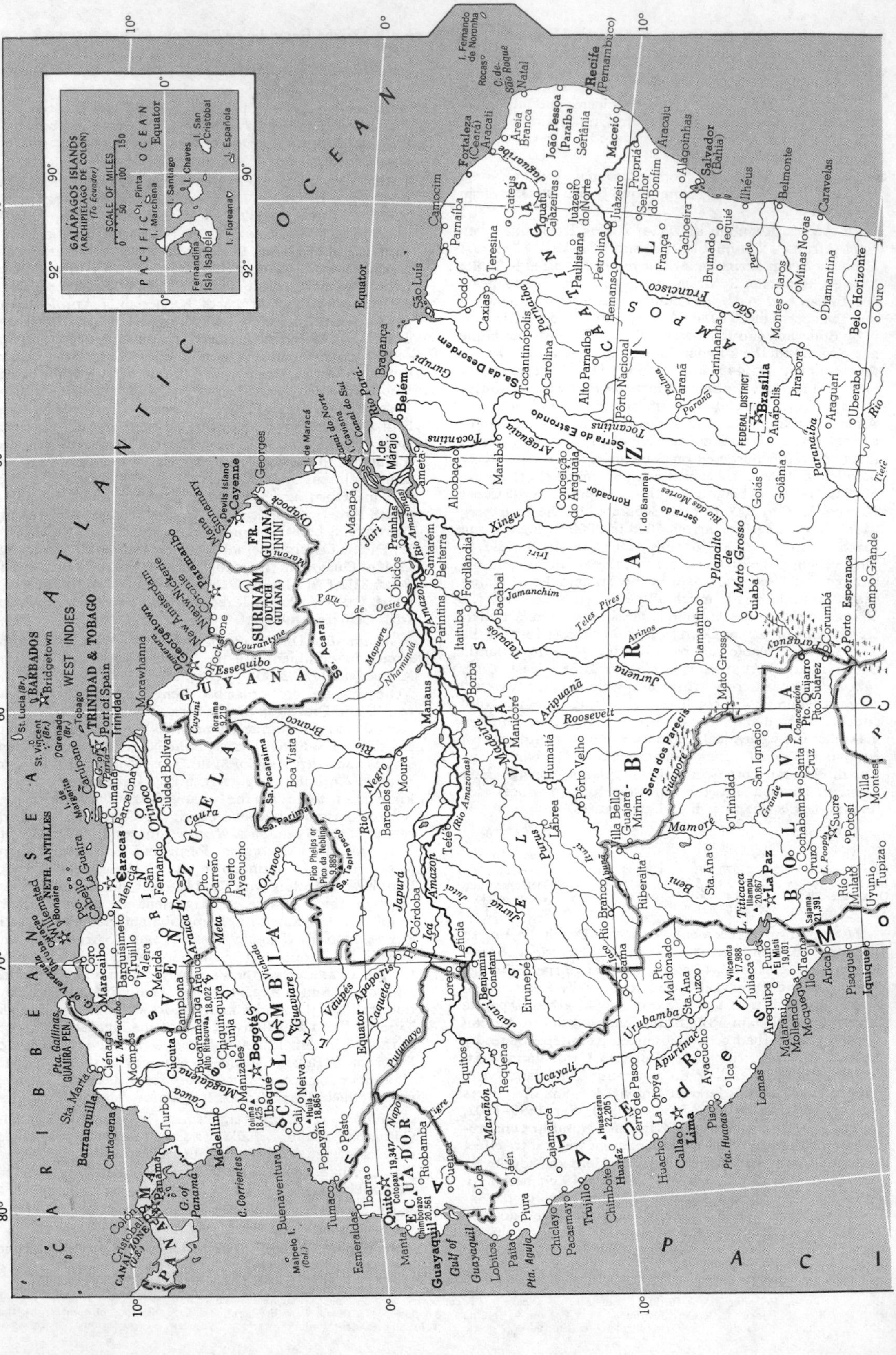

GALÁPAGOS ISLANDS
(ARCHIPIÉLAGO DE COLÓN)
(To Ecuador)
SCALE OF MILES
P A C I F I C
O C E A N
Equator
Isla Isabela
Fernandina
I. Marchena
I. Pinta
I. Santiago
I. Chaves
I. San Cristóbal
I. Floreana
I. Española
C A R I B B E A N   S E A
A T L A N T I C   O C E A N
P A C I F I C   O C E A N
WEST INDIES
BARBADOS
Bridgetown
TRINIDAD & TOBAGO
Port of Spain
Trinidad
Tobago
Grenada
St. Vincent
St. Lucia
NETH. ANTILLES
Willemstad
Bonaire
Curaçao
Aruba
PANAMA
Panamá
Colón
Cristóbal
CANAL ZONE
G. of Panama
V E N E Z U E L A
Caracas
Maracaibo
L. Maracaibo
Valencia
Barquisimeto
Mérida
Ciudad Bolívar
Barcelona
Cumaná
Orinoco
C O L O M B I A
Bogotá
Barranquilla
Cartagena
Medellín
Cali
Cúcuta
Magdalena
Cauca
G U Y A N A
Georgetown
Essequibo
SURINAM
(DUTCH GUIANA)
Paramaribo
FR. GUIANA
Cayenne
Devils Island
INÍNI
E C U A D O R
Quito
Guayaquil
Gulf of Guayaquil
Cuenca
Chimborazo 20,561
Cotopaxi 19,347
P E R U
Lima
Callao
Iquitos
Cuzco
Arequipa
Trujillo
Chiclayo
Huascarán 22,205
Ucayali
Marañón
Urubamba
Apurímac
B O L I V I A
La Paz
Sucre
Potosí
Cochabamba
Oruro
Santa Cruz
L. Titicaca
L. Poopó
Illimani 20,867
Beni
Mamoré
B R A Z I L
Brasília
FEDERAL DISTRICT
Manaus
Belém
Recife
(Pernambuco)
Salvador
(Bahia)
Fortaleza
(Ceará)
João Pessoa
(Paraíba)
Natal
Maceió
Aracaju
São Luís
Teresina
Belo Horizonte
Goiânia
Cuiabá
Corumbá
Pôrto Velho
Santarém
Óbidos
Macapá
I. de Marajó
Amazon
(Rio Amazonas)
Rio Negro
Rio Branco
Madeira
Purus
Juruá
Tapajós
Xingu
Tocantins
Araguaia
São Francisco
Paraná
Paranaíba
Mato Grosso
Planalto de Mato Grosso
Serra dos Parecis
Serra do Roncador
Serra do Estrondo
Sa. da Desordem
C A M P O S
C A A T I N G A S
S E L V A S
I. Fernando de Noronha
Rocas
C. de São Roque
Equator
0°
10°
20°
40°
50°
60°
70°
80°
90°
92°

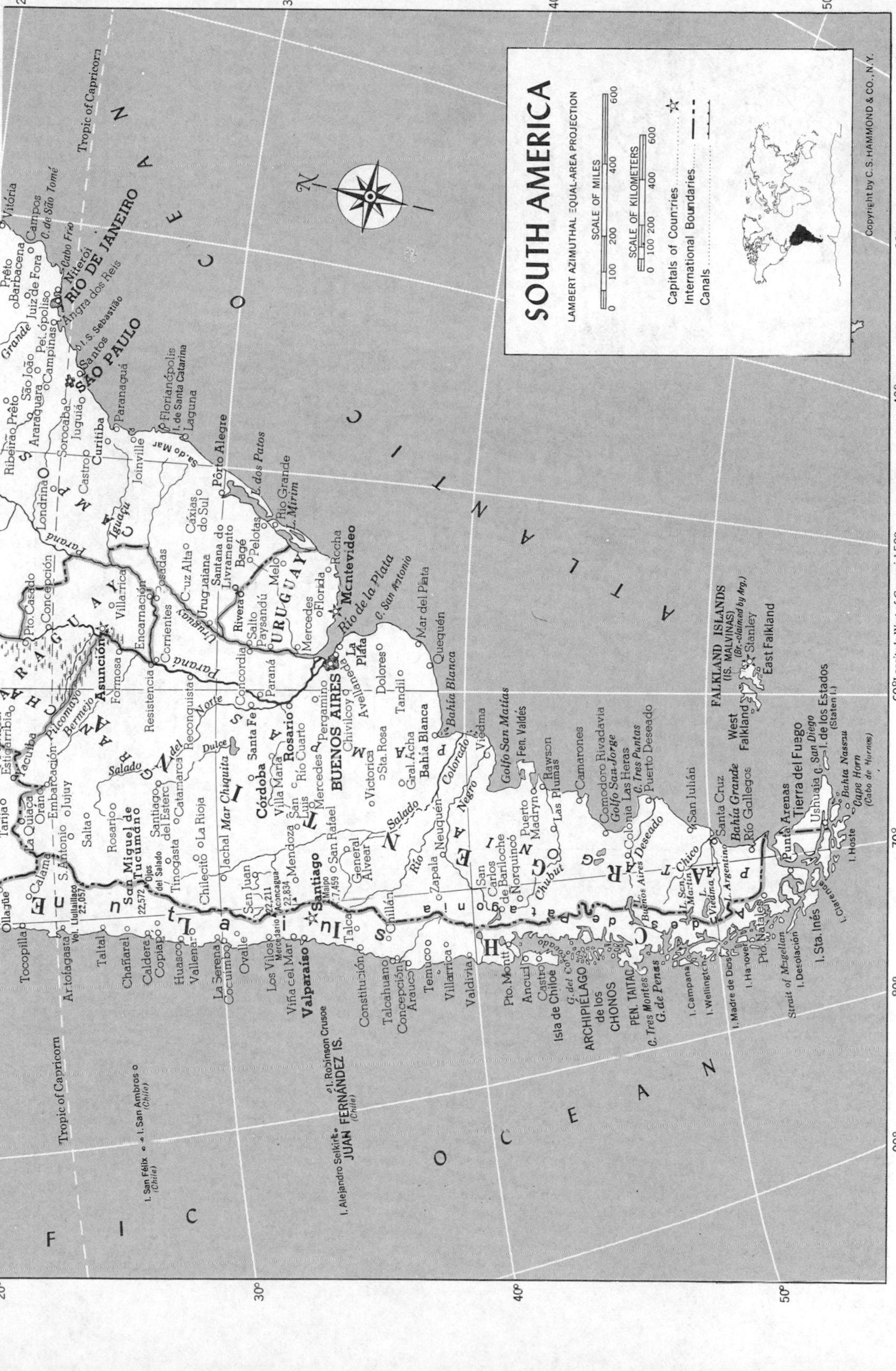
SOUTH AMERICA
LAMBERT AZIMUTHAL EQUAL-AREA PROJECTION
SCALE OF MILES
0 100 200 400 600
SCALE OF KILOMETERS
0 100 200 400 600
Capitals of Countries
International Boundaries
Canals
Copyright by C. S. HAMMOND & CO., N.Y.
60° Longitude West of Greenwich 50°
Tropic of Capricorn
ATLANTIC OCEAN
PACIFIC OCEAN
PARAGUAY
URUGUAY
ARGENTINA
CHILE
BUENOS AIRES
Montevideo
Asunción
Santiago
RIO DE JANEIRO
SÃO PAULO
Rio de la Plata
FALKLAND ISLANDS (IS. MALVINAS) (Br.-claimed by Arg.)
JUAN FERNÁNDEZ IS. (Chile)
Tierra del Fuego
Strait of Magellan
Cape Horn (Cabo de Hornos)

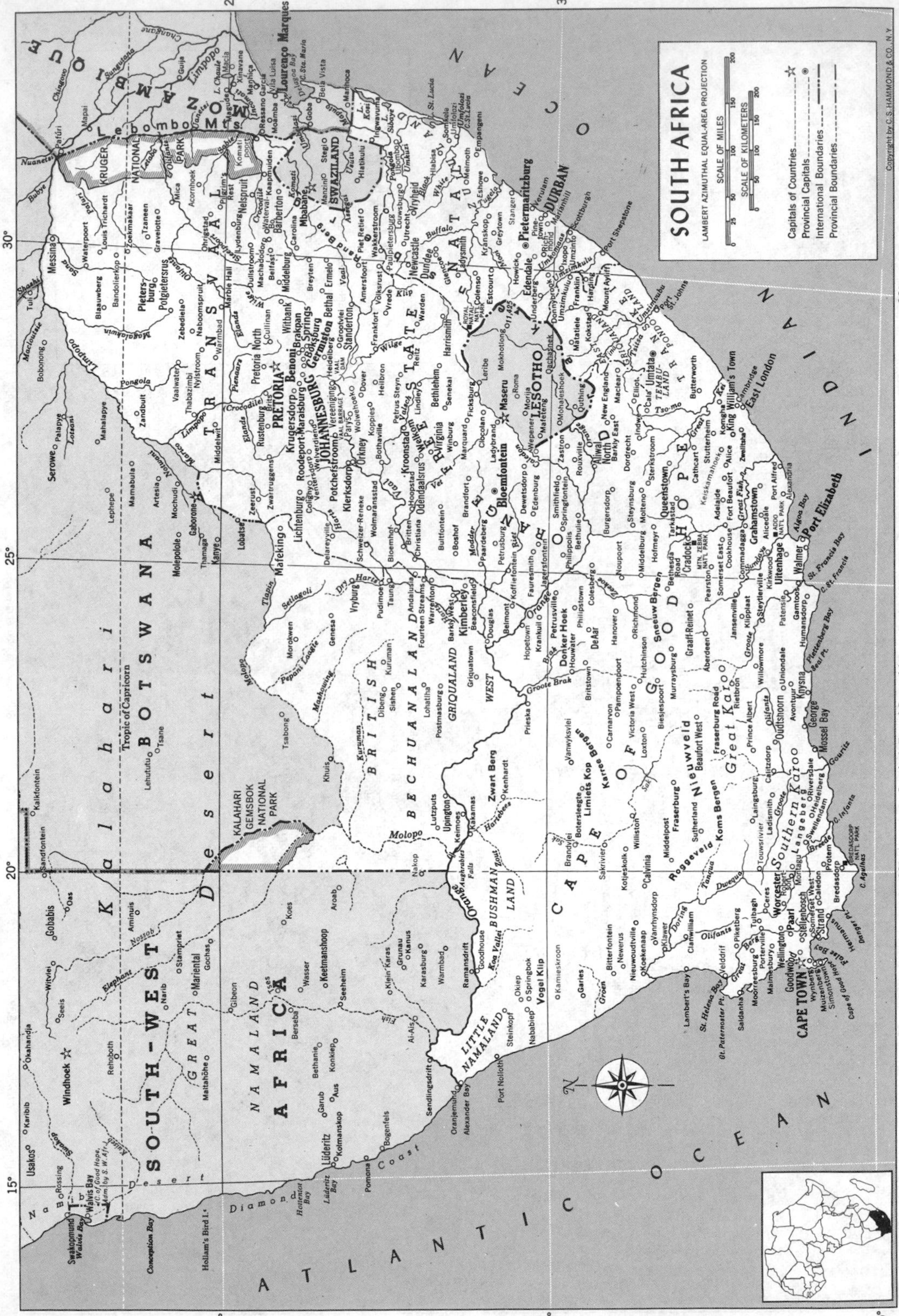
SOUTH AFRICA
LAMBERT AZIMUTHAL EQUAL-AREA PROJECTION
SCALE OF MILES
SCALE OF KILOMETERS
Capitals of Countries
Provincial Capitals
International Boundaries
Provincial Boundaries
Copyright by C.S. HAMMOND & CO., N.Y.
Longitude East of Greenwich
ATLANTIC OCEAN
INDIAN OCEAN
SOUTH-WEST AFRICA
BOTSWANA
Kalahari Desert
TRANSVAAL
NATAL
ORANGE FREE STATE
CAPE OF GOOD HOPE
LESOTHO
SWAZILAND
MOZAMBIQUE
BRITISH BECHUANALAND
GRIQUALAND WEST
NAMALAND
GREAT NAMALAND
LITTLE NAMALAND
BUSHMAN LAND
KALAHARI GEMSBOK NATIONAL PARK
KRUGER NATIONAL PARK
Tropic of Capricorn
Windhoek
PRETORIA
JOHANNESBURG
Bloemfontein
Pietermaritzburg
DURBAN
CAPE TOWN
Port Elizabeth
East London
Kimberley
Lourenço Marques
Maseru
Mbabane
Gaborone
Mafeking
Great Karoo
Southern Karoo
Walvis Bay
Lüderitz
Diamond Coast
Cape of Good Hope
C. Agulhas

2 Town, Hampshire co., W Massachusetts, 11 m. NW of Springfield; pop. (1970c) 3069.
3 Village and seaside resort, Suffolk co., SE New York, on S shore of Long I. 33 m. W of Montauk Point; pop. (1970c) 4904; truck farms; near Shinnecock Indian Reservation.
4 City and county borough, Hampshire, S England, at head of Southampton Water 70 m. WSW of London; pop. (1969e) 210,000; a major seaport, England's principal port for transatlantic passenger service, with extensive dock facilities; shipyards, marine engineering works, oil refineries; Univ. of Southampton (1952). Roman and Saxon settlements on the site; incorporated 1445; heavily damaged by German bombing in World War II, in which it was important U.S. naval base; made city 1964.

Southampton Island. Island, N Hudson Bay, Keewatin dist., Northwest Territories, Canada; 15,700 sq. m.

Southampton Water. Estuary of the Test river, Hampshire, S England.

South Andaman. One of the Andaman Is. (*q.v.*).

South An·na \-'an-ə\. River, E cen. Virginia; ab. 75 m. long; flows SE to unite with North Anna river in E Hanover co. and form Pamunkey river.

South Arabia, Federation of. Former federation, S Arabian Penin., consisting of territories controlled by native rulers in treaty relations with Great Britain; constituted 1959, dissolved and made part of Yemen (✱ Aden) 1967.

South Ar·gen·tine Peak \-ˌär-jən-ˌtēn-\. Mountain in Clear Creek and Summit cos., cen. Colorado; 13,600 ft.

South Atlantic Ocean. See ATLANTIC OCEAN.

South Australia. State, S cen. Australia; 380,070 sq. m.; pop. (1970e) 1,164,700; ✱ Adelaide. *Physical features:* Relatively little land above 2000 ft.; in NW is extension of W plateau; in NE is large section (including Lake Eyre) of Artesian Basin with many mud and marsh depressions. In S part varied physiographical region: Nullarbor Plain in W, salt lakes and North Flinders Range in E, Eyre and Yorke penins. and Kangaroo I. in S. In SE an extension of Murray river lowland. Shoreline generally low but several good harbors on Spencer Gulf and Gulf of St. Vincent, inlets of Indian Ocean. Chief river is lower course of Murray (ab. 500 m. in South Australia). *Chief products:* Wheat, barley, oats, grapes; iron ore, limestone, opal, salt; livestock rearing; manufacturing: mineral processing; automobiles, cement, electronic equipment. *Chief cities:* Adelaide, Whyalla, Mount Gambier, and Port Pirie.

History: Shore probably first visited by F. Thyssen 1627; discoveries by Flinders 1802 and Capt. Sturt 1830 opened up S part; formed into a British province 1836; first Constitution 1856; included Northern Territory (*q.v.*) 1863–1901; franchise extended to women 1894 who first voted in election of 1896; became a state of Commonwealth of Australia 1901.

South Bass Island. See BASS ISLAND.

South Bay. Town, Palm Beach co., SE Florida; pop. (1970c) 2958.

South Be·loit \-bə-'lȯit\. City, Winnebago co., N Illinois, on Wisconsin border 16 m. N of Rockford; pop. (1970c) 3804.

South Bend \-'bend\. 1 City, ⊗ of St. Joseph co., N Indiana, 68 m. NW of Fort Wayne; pop. (1970c) 125,580; automobile parts, missiles, agricultural machinery, tools and dies, wallpaper, surgical supplies; Univ. of Notre Dame (1842), Saint Mary's Coll. (1844), Holy Cross Junior Coll. (1966) at Notre Dame, suburb 2 m. N. Fur trading post established 1820; incorporated as town 1835, as city 1865.
2 City, ⊗ of Pacific co., SW Washington, on Willapa Bay; pop. (1970c) 1795; crab and oyster fisheries.

South Ber·wick \-'bər-wik\. Town, York co., SW Maine, on New Hampshire border 24 m. SW of Biddeford; pop. (1970c) 3488; birthplace of Sarah Orne Jewett.

South Beveland. See BEVELAND.

South·boro \'sau̇th-ˌbər-ə, -ˌbə-rə\. Town, Worcester co., cen. Massachusetts, 14 m. E of Worcester; pop. (1970c) 5798.

South·bor·ough \'sau̇th-ˌbər-ə, -ˌb(ə-)rə\. Urban district, Kent, SE England, 27 m. SSE of London; pop. (1971p) 3750.

South Bos·ton \-'bȯ-stən\. Town, S Virginia, 28 m. ENE of Danville, in Halifax co. but politically independent; 2 sq. m.; pop. (1970c) 6889; ships tobacco; flour, lumber.

South Bound Brook \-'bau̇n(d)-ˌbru̇k\. Industrial borough, Somerset co., N cen. New Jersey; pop. (1970c) 4525.

South Branch. See POTOMAC.

South·bridge \'sau̇th-(ˌ)brij\. Industrial town, Worcester co., cen. Massachusetts, 17 m. SW of Worcester; pop. (1970c) 17,057; optical goods, textiles; dairy farms; incorporated 1816.

South Bulgaria. See EASTERN RUMELIA.

South Bur·ling·ton \-'bər-liŋ-tən\. Town, Chittenden co., NW Vermont; pop. (1970c) 10,032.

South Bur·ro Mountain \-ˌbər-ō-, -ˌbu̇r-ō-, -ˌbə-rō-\. Peak, E Summit co., NE Utah; 12,746 ft.

South·bury \'sau̇th-ˌber-ē, -b(ə-)rē\. Town, NW New Haven co., S Connecticut, on Housatonic river; pop. (1970c) 7852; settled 1673, incorp. 1787.

South Can·on \-'kan-yən\. Locality, Fremont co., S cen. Colorado, on Arkansas river S of Canon City; includes Lincoln Park (unincorp.) and Brookside and Prospect Heights (towns); total pop. (1970c) 3195.

South Cape. 1 Cape, Hawaii I. See KA LAE.
2 Cape, S end of Stewart I., New Zealand.

South Car·o·li·na \-ˌkar-ə-'lī-nə\. Southeastern seaboard state of U.S.A., bounded on N by North Carolina, on E and SE by the Atlantic Ocean, on S, SW, and W by Georgia; 40th state in area, 31,055 sq. m. (land area 30,280 sq. m.); 26th state in population, (1970c) 2,590,516; ✱ Columbia; an original state of the Union, the 8th to ratify the Federal Constitution (May 23, 1788).

Nickname: Palmetto State. *State flower:* Yellow jasmine (Carolina jessamine). *Motto:* Dum Spiro, Spero (While I Breathe, I Hope). *Rivers:* Pee Dee, crossing border from S North Carolina and flowing SE into Winyah Bay; Wateree and Congaree uniting in cen. region to form the Santee flowing SE into the Atlantic; Edisto, in S region flowing SE into the Atlantic; Tugalos and Savannah, forming NW, W, and SW boundary. *Lakes:* No large natural lakes, but several artificial ones, incl. Lake Marion or Santee Reservoir (see SANTEE DAM), Pinopolis Reservoir (see PINOPOLIS DAM) and Wateree Pond, formed by a dam in the Wateree river. *Highest point:* Sassafras Mt. 3560 ft., in Pickens co. *Islands:* Has a number of islands off SE coast including Edisto, Hilton Head, and Parris I. and constituting the N part of the Sea Is. chain. *Chief products:* Tobacco, cotton, soybeans, corn; livestock; lumbering; manufacturing: textiles, chemicals, paper products. *Chief cities:* Columbia, Charleston, Greenville, Spartanburg, Rock Hill. See *Table of States* at UNITED STATES. Divided into the following 46 counties (for pronunciation of their names, see their individual entries):

NAME	LOCATION	AREA[1] (sq. m.)	POP. (1970c)	CO. SEAT
Abbeville	W	506	21,112	Abbeville
Aiken	W	1,100	91,023	Aiken
Allendale	SW	418	9,783	Allendale
Anderson	NW	775	105,474	Anderson
Bamberg	SW	395	15,950	Bamberg
Barnwell	SW	553	17,176	Barnwell
Beaufort	S; coastal[2]	579	51,136	Beaufort
Berkeley	SE	1,110	56,199	Moncks Corner
Calhoun	cen.	377	10,780	Saint Matthews
Charleston	SE; coastal[2]	939	247,650	Charleston
Cherokee	N	394	36,791	Gaffney
Chester	N	584	29,811	Chester
Chesterfield	NE	792	33,667	Chesterfield

NAME	LOCATION	AREA[1] (sq. m.)	POP. (1970c)	CO. SEAT
Clarendon	E cen.	599	25,604	Manning
Colleton	S; coastal[2]	1,049	27,622	Walterboro
Darlington	NE	544	53,442	Darlington
Dillon	NE	407	28,838	Dillon
Dorchester	SE	569	32,276	St. George
Edgefield	W	481	15,692	Edgefield
Fairfield	N cen.	696	19,999	Winnsboro
Florence	E	805	89,636	Florence
Georgetown	E; coastal	812	33,500	Georgetown
Greenville	NW	793	240,774	Greenville
Greenwood	W	446	49,686	Greenwood
Hampton	SW	562	15,878	Hampton
Horry	E; coastal	1,154	69,992	Conway
Jasper	S	652	11,885	Ridgeland
Kershaw	N cen.	781	34,727	Camden
Lancaster	N	502	43,328	Lancaster
Laurens	NW	711	49,713	Laurens
Lee	NE cen.	409	18,323	Bishopville
Lexington	cen.	717	89,012	Lexington
McCormick	W	306	7,955	McCormick
Marion	E	488	30,270	Marion
Marlboro	NE	483	27,151	Bennettsville
Newberry	NW cen.	635	29,273	Newberry
Oconee	NW	670	40,728	Walhalla
Orangeburg	S cen.	1,106	69,789	Orangeburg
Pickens	NW	501	58,956	Pickens
Richland	W cen.	748	233,868	Columbia
Saluda	W	444	14,528	Saluda
Spartanburg	NW	831	173,724	Spartanburg
Sumter	E cen.	672	79,425	Sumter
Union	NW	514	29,230	Union
Williamsburg	E	935	34,243	Kingstree
York	N	684	85,216	York

[1]Area = land area.
[2]Includes islands of the Sea Is. chain.

History: Reached by Spanish 1521; settled by French Huguenots at Port Royal 1562; region included in Carolina grant given 1663 by Charles II to eight noblemen of his court (see CAROLINA); Charleston (*q.v.*) founded 1680; became Royal Province 1729; scene of several engagements during American Revolution, notably Kings Mountain, Cowpens, Eutaw Springs, and Camden, and brought under American control by Gen. Greene's defeat of British under Cornwallis at battle of Guilford Courthouse 1781; ceded W lands to U.S. 1787; ratified Federal Constitution May 23, 1788; first state to secede from Union, passing ordinance of secession Dec. 20, 1860; Confederate forces attacked Fort Sumter Apr. 12, 1861, in the initial action of the Civil War; ordinance of secession repealed and slavery abolished 1865; readmitted to the Union June 25, 1868; adopted its present constitution 1895.

South Carpathians. See TRANSYLVANIAN ALPS.

South Car·ter \-'kärt-ər\. Mountain, Coos co., N New Hampshire, NE of Mt. Washington; 4645 ft.

South Channel. Southern part of entrance to Manila Bay, Luzon, Phil., bet. mainland of Cavite prov. and Corregidor I.; 6½ m. wide; called **Bo·ca Gran·de** \ˌbō-kə-'grän-dē\ by the Spaniards.

South Charleston. City, Kanawha co., W cen. West Virginia, on Kanawha river 4 m. W of Charleston; pop. (1970c) 16,333; chemicals.

South Chicago Heights. Village, Cook co., NE Illinois, 28 m. S of Chicago; pop. (1970c) 4923; residential suburb of Chicago Heights.

South China Sea. See CHINA SEA.

South Chŏl·la \-'chə-'lä\. Province of South Korea. See table at KOREA, SOUTH.

South Ch'ung·ch'ŏng \-'chüŋ-'chȯŋ\. Province of South Korea. See table at KOREA, SOUTH.

South Concho. River, Texas; 41 m. long; rises in Schleicher co., flows N and joins North Concho.

South Coventry. Subdivision (pop. [1970c] 3735) of town of Coventry, Connecticut. See COVENTRY 1.

South Da·ko·ta \-də-'kōt-ə\. Northwestern state of U.S.A., bounded on N by North Dakota, on E by Minnesota and Iowa, on S by Nebraska, and on W by Wyoming and Montana; 16th state in area, 77,047 sq. m. (land area 75,955 sq. m.); 44th state in population, (1970c) 666,257; ✱ Pierre; 40th state admitted to Union (1889).

Nicknames: Coyote State; Sunshine State. *State flower:* Pasqueflower. *Motto:* Under God the People Rule. *Rivers:* Missouri, bisecting state from N to S and receiving from the W the waters of the Moreau in the N cen. region, the Cheyenne in the cen. region, and the White in the S section. *Lakes:* Numerous small lakes in E, and on NE boundary are Big Stone Lake and Lake Traverse; in W in Butte co. is the Belle Fourche Reservoir formed by Belle Fourche Dam. *Highest point:* Harney Peak, 7242 ft., in Black Hills in SW. *Chief products:* Corn, wheat; livestock; gold, beryl, feldspar; manufacturing: food processing; lumber and wood products. *Chief cities:* Sioux Falls, Rapid City, Aberdeen, Brookings. See *Table of States* at UNITED STATES. Divided into the following 67 counties (for pronunciation of their names, see their individual entries):

NAME	LOCATION	AREA[1] (sq. m.)	POP. (1970c)	CO. SEAT
Aurora	SE cen.	709	4,183	Plankinton
Beadle	E cen.	1,260	20,877	Huron
Bennett	S	1,181	3,088	Martin
Bon Homme	SE	560	8,577	Tyndall
Brookings	E	800	22,158	Brookings
Brown	NE	1,674	36,920	Aberdeen
Brule	S	818	5,870	Chamberlain
Buffalo	S cen.	482	1,739	Gannvalley
Butte	W	2,250	7,825	Belle Fourche
Campbell	N	732	2,866	Mound City
Charles Mix	S	1,097	9,994	Lake Andes
Clark	NE	964	5,515	Clark
Clay	SE	405	12,923	Vermillion
Codington	NE	687	19,140	Watertown
Corson	N	2,470	4,994	McIntosh
Custer[3]	SW	1,557	4,698	Custer
Davison	SE	432	17,319	Mitchell
Day	NE	1,030	8,713	Webster
Deuel	E	639	5,686	Clear Lake
Dewey	N cen.	2,351	5,170	Timber Lake
Douglas	S	435	4,569	Armour
Edmunds	N	1,154	5,548	Ipswich
Fall River	SW corner	1,743	7,505	Hot Springs
Faulk	N cen.	996	3,893	Faulkton
Grant	NE	681	9,005	Milbank
Gregory	S	997	6,710	Burke
Haakon	W cen.	1,816	2,802	Philip
Hamlin	E	511	5,520	Hayti
Hand	E cen.	1,432	5,883	Miller
Hanson	SE	430	3,781	Alexandria
Harding	NW corner	2,682	1,855	Buffalo
Hughes	cen.	748	11,632	Pierre
Hutchinson	SE	815	10,379	Olivet
Hyde	cen.	863	2,515	Highmore
Jackson	SW cen.	808	1,531	Kadoka
Jerauld	SE cen.	527	3,310	Wessington Springs
Jones	S cen.	973	1,882	Murdo
Kingsbury	E	818	7,657	De Smet
Lake	E	567	11,456	Madison
Lawrence	W	800	17,453	Deadwood
Lincoln	SE	576	11,761	Canton
Lyman	S cen.	1,683	4,060	Kennebec
McCook	SE	575	7,246	Salem
McPherson	N	1,147	5,022	Leola
Marshall	NE	848	5,965	Britton
Meade	W	3,465	17,020	Sturgis
Mellette	S	1,306	2,420	White River
Miner	E	570	4,454	Howard
Minnehaha	SE	813	95,209	Sioux Falls
Moody	E	523	7,622	Flandreau
Pennington	SW	2,779	59,349	Rapid City
Perkins	NW	2,860	4,769	Bison
Potter	N cen.	869	4,449	Gettysburg
Roberts	NE corner	1,108	11,678	Sisseton
Sanborn	SE cen.	570	3,697	Woonsocket
Shannon[2]	SW	2,100	8,198	
Spink	NE cen.	1.505	10.595	Redfield
Stanley	cen.	1,414	2,457	Fort Pierre
Sully	cen.	1,004	2,362	Onida
Todd[2]	S	1,388	6,606	
Tripp	S	1,620	8,171	Winner
Turner	SE	612	9,872	Parker
Union	SE corner	452	9,643	Elk Point
Walworth	N	718	7,842	Selby
Washabaugh[2]	SW	1,061	1,389	
Yankton	SE	518	19,039	Yankton
Ziebach	NW cen.	1,981	2,221	Dupree

[1]Area = land area.
[2]Three counties (occupied by Indian reservations) remain unorganized, being attached for judicial purposes to adjacent counties, as follows: Shannon (attached to Fall River), Todd (to Tripp), Washabaugh (to Jackson). Washington county added to Shannon co., in 1943, Armstrong county to Dewey co. 1954.
[3]Contains (in S cen. part) Wind Cave National Park.

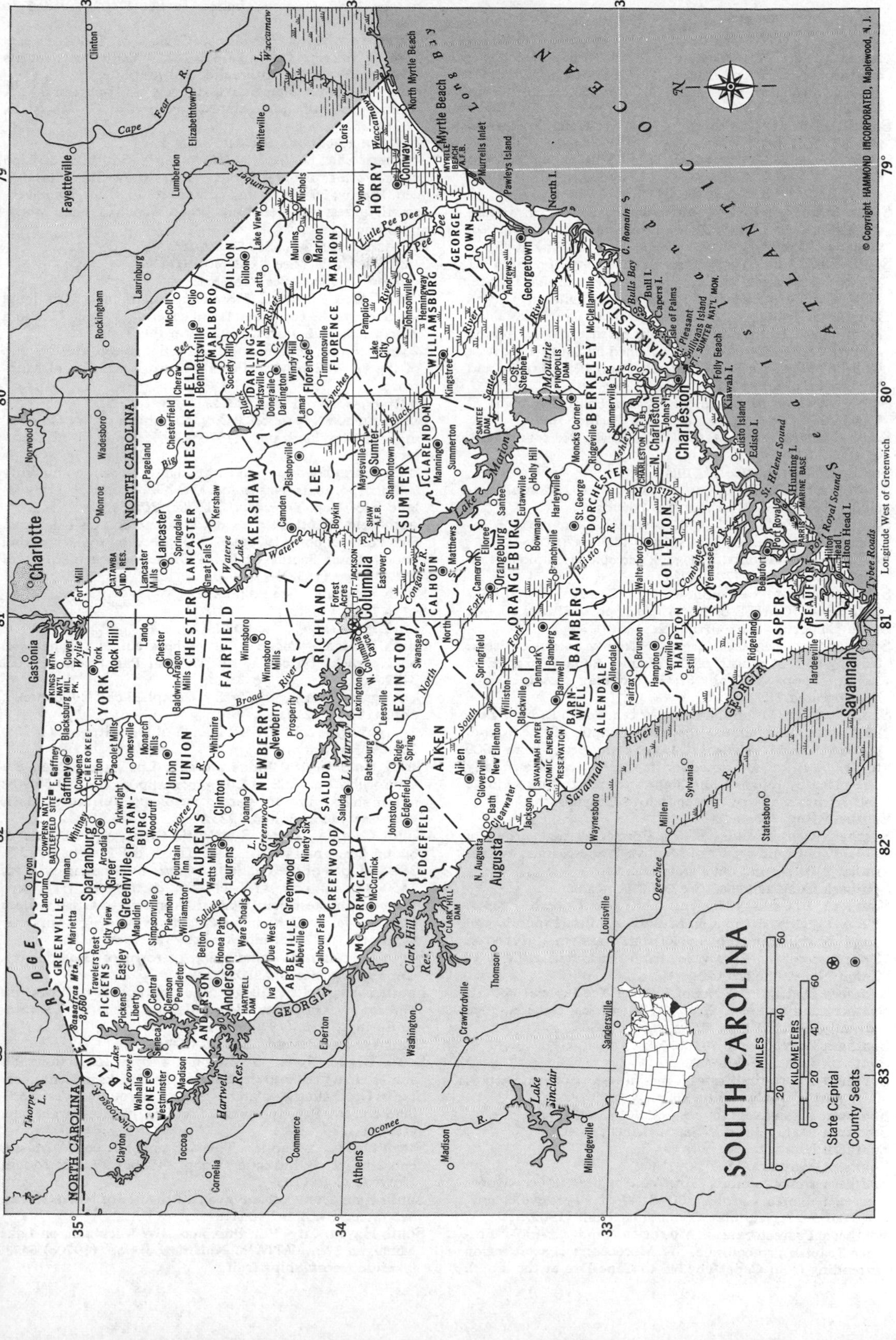
SOUTH CAROLINA
MILES
0 20 40 60
KILOMETERS
0 20 40 60
State Capital
County Seats
© Copyright HAMMOND INCORPORATED, Maplewood, N.J.
Longitude West of Greenwich
ATLANTIC OCEAN
NORTH CAROLINA
GEORGIA
BLUE RIDGE
Sassafras Mtn. 3,560
OCONEE
PICKENS
GREENVILLE
SPARTANBURG
CHEROKEE
YORK
LANCASTER
CHESTERFIELD
MARLBORO
DILLON
MARION
HORRY
ANDERSON
ABBEVILLE
GREENWOOD
LAURENS
UNION
CHESTER
FAIRFIELD
KERSHAW
LEE
DARLINGTON
FLORENCE
WILLIAMSBURG
GEORGETOWN
McCORMICK
EDGEFIELD
SALUDA
NEWBERRY
RICHLAND
SUMTER
CLARENDON
LEXINGTON
CALHOUN
AIKEN
ORANGEBURG
BERKELEY
CHARLESTON
BARNWELL
BAMBERG
DORCHESTER
ALLENDALE
COLLETON
HAMPTON
JASPER
BEAUFORT
Columbia
Charleston
Greenville
Spartanburg
Rock Hill
Anderson
Florence
Sumter
Aiken
Orangeburg
Myrtle Beach
Georgetown
Conway
Beaufort
Charlotte
Augusta
Savannah
Lake Marion
L. Moultrie
L. Murray
Clark Hill Res.
Hartwell Res.
Lake Keowee
Lake Wylie
Wateree Lake
SAVANNAH RIVER ATOMIC ENERGY RESERVATION
Savannah River
Santee R.
Pee Dee R.
Broad River
Saluda R.
Edisto R.
Long Bay
Bulls Bay
St. Helena Sound
Port Royal Sound
Hilton Head I.
Tybee Roads
FT. SUMTER NAT'L MON.
COWPENS NAT'L BATTLEFIELD SITE
KINGS MTN. NAT'L MIL. PK.
FT. JACKSON
SHAW A.F.B.
MYRTLE BEACH A.F.B.
CHARLESTON A.F.B.
PARRIS I. MARINE BASE
SANTEE DAM
PINOPOLIS DAM
CLARK HILL DAM
HARTWELL DAM
35°
34°
33°
83°
82°
81°
80°
79°

History: See DAKOTA TERRITORY. First settlement established within present state was at Fort Pierre 1817; constituted S part of Dakota Territory, organized 1861; gold discovered in the Black Hills area 1874; admitted to Union Nov. 2, 1889.

South Day·to·na \-dā-ˈtō-nə\. City, Volusia co., E Florida; pop. (1970c) 4979.

South Downs \-ˈdau̇nz\. Range of low hills, extending W to E from W Dorsetshire to E Sussex in S England; highest point **But·ser Hill** \ˌbət-sər-\ 889 ft.

South Drum·mond·ville \-ˈdrəm-ən-ˌ(d)vil\ *or Fr.* **Drummondville–Sud** \-süd\. Town, Drummond co., S Quebec, Canada, 30 m. S of Three Rivers; pop. (1971p) 9003.

South–East Asia Treaty Organization *or abbr.* **SEATO** \ˈsē-tō\. Military alliance, consisting of Australia, France, New Zealand, Pakistan, Philippines, Thailand, United Kingdom, United States; headquarters Bangkok, Thailand; purpose: to promote joint defense of the region against Communist attack; established by South-East Asia Collective Defense Treaty (Manila Pact) 1954; France and Pakistan not active since 1966–67.

Southeast Cape *or* **South–East Cape.** Southeast point of Tasmania, Australia, on the South Pacific Ocean.

South–Eastern State. State of SE Nigeria. See table at NIGERIA.

Southeast Island. See TAGULA ISLAND.

South East Islands. Group of islands, SE Indonesia; includes Tanimbar, Kai, and Aru islands.

South–East Su·la·we·si \-ˌsü-lə-ˈwā-sē\. Province of Indonesia, Celebes. See CELEBES and table at INDONESIA.

South El·gin \-ˈel-jən\. Village, Kane co., NE Illinois, 4 m. S of Elgin; pop. (1970c) 4289.

South El Mon·te \-el-ˈmȯnt-ē\. City, Los Angeles co., SW California, 10 m. SE of Los Angeles; pop. (1970c) 13,443.

South Emporia. See EMPORIA 2.

South·end–on–Sea \ˌsau̇-ˌthend-\. County borough, Essex, SE England, at mouth of the Thames estuary 36 m. E of London; pop. (1971p) 162,326; popular seaside resort; incorporated 1892.

Southern Alps. Mountain range, W cen. South I., New Zealand, extending almost the entire length of the island; highest peak Mt. Cook 12,349 ft.; many peaks from 8000 to 11,000 ft.; region noted for its scenery; crossed in only one place by railroad and highway through Otira Gorge and Arthur's Pass, Christchurch to Greymouth.

Southern Bug. See BUG 2.

Southern Central India States. Former agency, group of Indian states, now part of Madhya Pradesh state, W cen. India; 5101 sq. m.; chief state Dhar.

Southern Cook Islands. See COOK ISLANDS.

Southern Dec·can \-ˈdek-ən, -ˌan\ *also* **Deccan Proper.** Plateau region, S India, in Mysore, Andhra Pradesh, and Tamil Nadu; drained by the Krishna and Penner rivers; on S separated by a deep valley from the Nilgiri Hills in W Tamil Nadu. See DECCAN.

Southern District. District of S Israel. See table at ISRAEL.

Southern Indian Lake. Lake, NW Manitoba, Canada; 1060 sq. m.; Churchill river flows through it.

Southern Karroo. See KARROO.

Southern Leyte. See LEYTE.

Southern Ma·ra·tha States \-mə-ˈrät-ə-\. Former agency, now part of Maharashtra state, W India.

Southern Mashonaland. See MASHONALAND.

Southern Matabeleland. See MATABELELAND.

Southern Morava. See MORAVA 3.

Southern Moytura. See MOYTURA.

Southern Pines \-ˈpīnz\. Town and winter resort, Moore co., cen. North Carolina, 30 m. W of Fayetteville; pop. (1970c) 5937; Sandhills Community Coll. (1963).

Southern Protectorate of Mo·roc·co \-mə-ˈräk-(ˌ)ō\. Former Spanish protectorate, SW Morocco; a coastal region extending from Cape Juby NE to Cape Dra at the mouth of the Wad Dra and inland to ab. 8°40′W; ceded to Morocco 1958.

Southern Province. Province, S Ceylon, on Indian Ocean; 2146 sq. m.; pop. (1963c) 1,433,781; ✱ Galle; has deposits of precious stones, anthracite, and graphite.

Southern Raj·pu·ta·na States Agency \-ˌräj-pə-ˈtän-ə-\. A former group of Indian states, now part of Gujarat state, W India.

Southern Rhodesia. See RHODESIA 2.

Southern Shan States \-ˈshän-, -ˈshan-\. Southern division of the former Federated Shan States (now Shan State), E cen. Burma; 36,416 sq. m.; comprised 36 states, some very small; largest was Kengtung, others were Mongnai, Mongpan, and Lawksawk.

Southern Sporades. See SPORADES.

Southern Urals. See URAL MOUNTAINS.

Southern Yemen. See YEMEN 1.

South Esk. 1 River, NE Tasmania, Australia; 120 m. long; longest river in Tasmania; flows generally W then N to join North Esk at Launceston to form the Tamar.
2 River, E cen. Scotland; 48½ m. long; rises in the E slopes of the Grampian Mts., flows SE into North Sea at Montrose.
3 River, Scotland. See ESK 3.

South Eu·clid \-ˈyu-kləd\. City, Cuyahoga co., N Ohio, 10 m. E of Cleveland; pop. (1970c) 29,759; suburb of Cleveland.

South Farm·ing·dale \-ˈfär-miŋ-ˌdāl\. Urban community (unincorporated), Nassau co., SE New York, on Long Island E of New York; pop. (1970c) 20,464.

South·field \ˈsau̇th-ˌfēld\. City, Oakland co., SE Michigan, S of Pontiac; pop. (1970c) 69,285; precision tools, sporting goods; Duns Scotus Coll. (1930), Lawrence Institute of Technology (1932).

South Foreland. See FORELAND.

South Fork Edisto. See EDISTO.

South Fox Island. See FOX ISLANDS 1.

South Ful·ton \-ˈfu̇lt-ᵊn\. City, Obion co., NW Tennessee, on Kentucky border 35 m. WNW of Paris; pop. (1970c) 3122.

South·gate \ˈsau̇th-ˌgāt\. 1 City, Campbell co., N Kentucky; pop. (1970c) 3212.
2 City, Wayne co., SE Michigan, S of Detroit; pop. (1970c) 33,909; residential.

South Gate \-ˌgāt\. Industrial city, Los Angeles co., SW California, 7 m. SSE of Los Angeles; pop. (1970c) 56,909; automobiles, aircraft parts, chemicals, furniture, glass, knitwear; incorporated 1923.

South Georgia. Island, S Atlantic Ocean on N border of Scotia Sea, ab. 1100 m. E of Tierra del Fuego, 54°15′S, 36°45′W; one of the Falkland Islands Dependencies (*q.v.*); 1450 sq. m.; pop. (1964e) 499; chief town Grytviken Harbour; highest point 9625 ft. Annexed to Great Britain by Capt. James Cook in his circumnavigation of Antarctic Continent 1772–75; interior explored 1964–65.

South Glastonbury. Subdivision of town of Glastonbury, Connecticut. See GLASTONBURY.

South Glens Falls. Village, Saratoga co., New York, on Hudson river opposite Glens Falls and 17 m. NE of Saratoga Springs; pop. (1970c) 4013.

South Graham Island. See GRAHAM LAND.

South Grand. River, W Missouri; 140 m. long; flows SE across Henry co. into the Lake of the Ozarks in Benton co.

South Greens·burg \-ˈgrēnz-ˌbərg\. Borough, Westmoreland co., SW Pennsylvania, 26 m. ESE of Pittsburgh; pop. (1970c) 3288.

South Had·ley \-ˈhad-lē\. Town, Hampshire co., W Massachusetts, N of Springfield; pop. (1970c) 17,033; Mount Holyoke Coll. (1837).

South Ham·gyŏng \-ˈhäm-ˈgyəŋ\. Province of North Korea. See table at KOREA, NORTH.

South Haven. City, Van Buren co., SW Michigan, on Lake Michigan 37 m. WNW of Kalamazoo; pop. (1970c) 6471; lakeside resort; ships fruit.

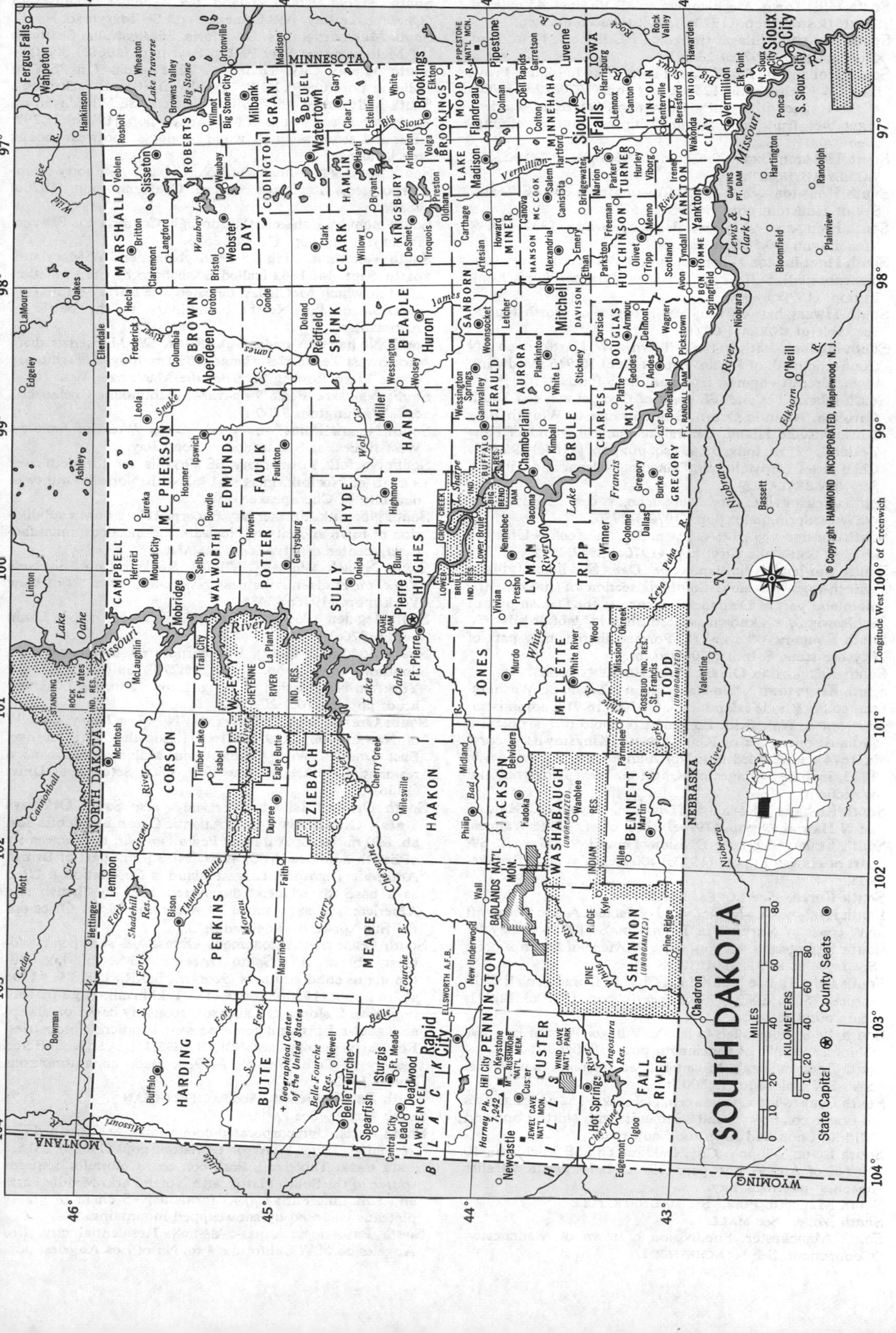
SOUTH DAKOTA
MILES
KILOMETERS
State Capital
County Seats
© Copyright HAMMOND INCORPORATED, Maplewood, N.J.
Longitude West 100° of Greenwich
NORTH DAKOTA
MINNESOTA
IOWA
NEBRASKA
MONTANA
WYOMING
+ Geographical Center of the United States
HARDING
PERKINS
CORSON
CAMPBELL
MC PHERSON
MARSHALL
ROBERTS
BROWN
EDMUNDS
WALWORTH
DEWEY
ZIEBACH
BUTTE
MEADE
LAWRENCE
PENNINGTON
CUSTER
FALL RIVER
SHANNON (UNORGANIZED)
WASHABAUGH (UNORGANIZED)
JACKSON
HAAKON
JONES
MELLETTE
TODD (UNORGANIZED)
BENNETT
TRIPP
LYMAN
STANLEY
HUGHES
SULLY
POTTER
FAULK
HYDE
HAND
SPINK
BEADLE
CLARK
DAY
CODINGTON
GRANT
DEUEL
HAMLIN
KINGSBURY
BROOKINGS
LAKE
MOODY
MINNEHAHA
MINER
SANBORN
JERAULD
BUFFALO
BRULE
AURORA
DAVISON
HANSON
MC COOK
TURNER
LINCOLN
UNION
CLAY
YANKTON
HUTCHINSON
DOUGLAS
CHARLES MIX
BON HOMME
GREGORY
Pierre
Rapid City
Sioux Falls
Aberdeen
Watertown
Huron
Mitchell
Brookings
Yankton
Missouri
Lake Oahe
Lewis & Clark L.

South Hill. Town, Mecklenburg co., S Virginia, 45 m. E of South Boston; pop. (1970c) 3858; tobacco market.

South Holland. Village, Cook co., NE Illinois, 17 m. S of Chicago; pop. (1970c) 23,391.

South Holland *or Du.* **Zuid·hol·land** \zȯit-ˈhȯl-änt\. Province, SW Netherlands; 1259 sq. m.; pop. (1970e) 2,968,700; ✱ the Hague; other cities Rotterdam, Schiedam, Leiden; vegetables, fruit; dairy farming; shipbuilding; oil refining, chemicals.

South Hol·ston Dam \-ˈhōl-stən-\. See table at TENNESSEE VALLEY AUTHORITY.

South Hous·ton \-ˈhyü-stən\. Town, Harris co., SE Texas, SW of Houston; pop. (1970c) 11,527.

South Hsing·an \-ˈshiŋ-ˈän\. Former province (1932–45), W Manchukuo; 30,502 sq. m.

South Hunt·ing·ton \-ˈhənt-iŋ-tən\. Urban community (unincorporated), Suffolk co., SE New York on W cen. Long I.; pop. (1970c) 8946.

South Hwang·hae \-ˈhwäŋ-ˈhī\. Province of North Korea. See table at KOREA, NORTH.

South·ing·ton \ˈsəth-iŋ-tən\. Town, SW Hartford co., N Connecticut, W of Berlin; pop. (1970c) 30,946; hardware, tools, aircraft engines; fruit and dairy farms.

South Island. 1 Island, SE coast of Georgetown co., South Carolina, Atlantic Ocean, S of entrance to Winyah Bay. 2 *also* **Middle Island.** Central and largest island of New Zealand; 525 m. long; 59,439 sq. m.; pop. (1968e) 798,681. Chief cities Christchurch, Dunedin, Nelson, and Timaru. See NEW ZEALAND.

South Jacksonville. City, Morgan co., W cen. Illinois, 30 m. WSW of Springfield; pop. (1970c) 2950.

South Jor·dan \-ˈjȯrd-ᵊn\. Town, Salt Lake co., N Utah, 14 m. S of Salt Lake City; pop. (1970c) 2942.

South Jut·land \-ˈjət-land\ *or Dan.* **Syd·li·ge Jyl·land** \ˌsüeth-li-gə-ˈyüe-ˌlän\. Southern section of Jutland, the mainland part of Denmark; constitutes the Danish part of Schleswig (*q.v.*), known as **Nord Sle·svig** \ˈnȯ(ə)r-ˈslis-vē\.

South Ka·na·ra \-ˈkä-nə-rə\. Former district, now part of Mysore state, S India; 4045 sq. m.

South Kazakhstan Oblast. See CHIMKENT OBLAST.

South Kings·town \-ˈkiŋ-stən, -ˌstau̇n\. Town, SE Washington co., S Rhode Island; pop. (1970c) 16,913; administrative center Wakefield. Former stronghold of Narraganset Indians; once part of Kings Towne (Kingstown), incorp. in 1674 and divided into North and South Kingstown in 1723; includes villages of Kingston, West Kingston, and Wakefield.

South Ko·ha·la \-kō-ˈhäl-ə\. Division, Hawaii co., Hawaii, on N Hawaii I.; pop. (1970c) 2310; chief village Waimea.

South Ko·na \-ˈkō-nə\. Division, Hawaii co., Hawaii, SW part of Hawaii I.; pop. (1970c) 4004; chief village Kealakekua.

South Korea. See KOREA, SOUTH.

South Kval·øy \-kə-ˈväl-ˌȯi, -ˈkfäl-\. Island, Arctic Ocean off NW coast of Norway, in Troms co., S of Ringvassøy I.

South Kyŏng·sang \-ˈkyəŋ-ˈsäŋ\. Province of South Korea. See table at KOREA, SOUTH.

South Lake Ta·hoe \-ˈtä-(ˌ)hō\. City, El Dorado co., E California, 75 m. ENE of Sacramento; pop. (1970c) 12,921; year-round resort.

South Le·ba·non \-ˈleb-(ə-)nən\. Village, Warren co., SW Ohio, 28 m. NE of Cincinnati; pop. (1970c) 3014.

South Lookout Peak. Mountain, San Juan and San Miguel cos., SW Colorado; 13,500 ft.

South Loup \-ˈlüp\. River, cen. Nebraska; 152 m. long; rises in Logan co., flows E and SE to unite with North Loup and Middle Loup and form the Loup river.

South Ly·on \-ˈlī-ən\. City, Oakland co., SE Michigan, 10 m. NE of Ann Arbor; pop. (1970c) 2675; plastics, trailer coaches; potatoes, hay.

South Magnetic Pole. See MAGNETIC POLE.

South Male. See MALE.

South Manchester. Subdivision of town of Manchester, Connecticut. See MANCHESTER 1.

South Marsh Island. Island bet. Tangier Sound and Chesapeake Bay, NW Somerset co., SE Maryland.

South Melbourne. City, S Victoria, SE Australia, S suburb of Melbourne on Port Phillip Bay; pop. (1966c) 30,200.

South Miami. City, Dade co., SE Florida, 7 m. SW of Miami; pop. (1970c) 19,571; ships fruit and truck crops.

South Milwaukee. City, Milwaukee co., SE Wisconsin, on Lake Michigan 9 m. S of Milwaukee; pop. (1970c) 23,297; iron and steel, castings, wood products, footwear; boats; truck farms.

South Mo·des·to \-mə-ˈdes-(ˌ)tō\. Urban community (unincorporated), Stanislaus co., cen. California; pop. (1970c) 7889.

South·mont \ˈsau̇th-ˌmänt\. Borough, Cambria co., SW cen. Pennsylvania; pop. (1970c) 2653.

South Mountain. Ridge, S Pennsylvania and W Maryland; battle Sept. 14, 1862 (called Boonsboro by the Confederates) in which McClellan defeated Lee's army on its first invasion of the North, preliminary to the battle of Antietam.

South Na·han·ni \-nə-ˈhan-ē\. River, SW Mackenzie dist., Northwest Territories, Canada; 350 m. long; a N tributary of the Liard flowing SE from the Mackenzie Mts.

South Na·varre Peak \-nə-ˌvär-\. Mountain, Chelan co., cen. Washington; 7800 ft.

South Ne·gril Point \-nə-ˈgril-\. Cape, W end of Jamaica, West Indies, at S entrance to Long Bay.

South Norfolk. Former city, SE Virginia, on Elizabeth river 3 m. S of Norfolk; merged 1963 with Norfolk county in new city of Chesapeake (*q.v.*).

South Norwalk. Former city (incorp. 1870), now a subdivision of town and city of Norwalk, Connecticut; manufacturing center of city. See NORWALK 3.

South Ny·ack \-ˈnī-ˌak\. Village, Rockland co., SE New York, on Hudson river near Nyack and 24 m. N of New York; pop. (1970c) 3435.

South Og·den \-ˈȯg-dən, -ˌäg-\. City, Weber co., N Utah; pop. (1970c) 9991.

South·old \ˈsau̇th-(ˌ)ōld\. Unincorporated summer resort in Southold town (pop. [1970] 15,770), Suffolk co., New York, on N extension of Long. I. ab. 18 m. NE of Riverhead; pop. (1970c) 2030.

South Orange. Village, Essex co., NE New Jersey, 5 m. W of Newark; pop. (1970c) 16,671; together with Orange, East Orange, West Orange, and Maplewood, forms a residential suburb of New York City; Seton Hall Univ. (1856).

South Ork·ney Islands \-ˈȯrk-nē-\ *also* **South Ork·neys** \-nēz\. Group of islands, S Atlantic Ocean S of Scotia Sea, ab. 850 m. NE of Antarctic Penin., and SE of S extremity of South America, 61°S, 45°W; 240 sq. m.; part of British Antarctic Territory. Largest island is Coronation I. Used as a base for whalers; discovered 1821 by British and American sealers; claimed by Argentina (*Span.* **Or·ca·das del Sur** \ȯr-ˌkäd-əs-del-ˈsu̇(ə)r\).

South Os·se·tian Autonomous Oblast \-ä-ˈsēn-shən . . . ˈō-bləst, -ˌblast\ *also* **South Os·se·tia** \-ä-ˈsē-sh(ē-)ə\. Autonomous subdivision, N Georgian S.S.R., U.S.S.R.; 1506 sq. m.; pop. (1970p) 100,000; ✱ Tskhinvali. High plateau region on S slopes of Caucasus; economy based on sheep- and goat-raising and some peasant handicraft industries. For early history, see NORTH OSSETIAN A.S.S.R. Suffered heavily in Civil War 1917–1920; made an autonomous oblast 1922.

South Pacific Ocean. See PACIFIC OCEAN.

South Pagai. See PAGAI.

South Paris. Unincorporated community, ⊗ of Oxford co., W Maine, 17 m. WNW of Lewiston; pop. (1970c) 2315.

South Park. Tableland, Park co., cen. Colorado; contains source of the South Platte; with North Park, Middle Park, and San Luis Park (*qq.v.*) forms a N–S chain of grassy plateaus enclosed by snowcapped mountains.

South Pas·a·de·na \-ˌpas-ə-ˈdē-nə\. Residential city, Los Angeles co., SW California, 4 m. NE of Los Angeles; pop.

(1970c) 22,979; electronic components, pharmaceuticals, canned goods.

South Pass. 1 One of the channels at the mouth of the Mississippi river (*q.v.*).
2 Pass, Fremont co., SW cen. Wyoming, at S end of Wind River Range; 7550 ft.; discovered 1824, used first for wagons 1832 by Capt. Benjamin Bonneville's exploring party. See OREGON TRAIL.

South Pitts·burg \-'pits-ˌbərg\. City, Marion co., S Tennessee, on Tennessee river 24 m. W of Chattanooga; pop. (1970c) 3613; cast iron goods, hosiery; coal mines; agriculture.

South Plain·field \-'plān-ˌfēld\. Borough, Middlesex co., cen. New Jersey, 6 m. NNE of New Brunswick; pop. (1970c) 21,142; chemicals, lamps; truck farms.

South Platte \-'plat\. River, Colorado and W Nebraska; 424 m. long; rises in NW Park co., cen. Colorado, flows SE then NE across Nebraska boundary to join the North Platte river in Lincoln co., SW cen. Nebraska, and form the Platte river.

South Point. 1 Cape, Hawaii I. See KA LAE.
2 Point, SE tip of Marsh I., off S coast of Louisiana.
3 Point, SE coast of Alpena co., NE Michigan, at S entrance to Thunder Bay.
4 Village, Lawrence co., S Ohio, on Ohio river 10 m. SE of Ironton; pop. (1970c) 2243.

South Pole. The S extremity of the earth's axis, at 90°S lat.; S center from which start all meridians of longitude; the point from which the only direction is N. The area around it (**South Polar Regions:** see POLAR REGIONS) is a lofty plateau (Polar Plateau) in W cen. part of Antarctica (*q.v.*). See MAGNETIC POLE.

South·port \'sau̇th-ˌpō(ə)rt, -ˌpȯ(ə)rt\ 1 Subdivision of town of Fairfield, Connecticut. See FAIRFIELD 4.
2 City, Marion co., cen. Indiana, 2 m. S of Indianapolis; pop. (1970c) 2317.
3 City and resort, ⊗ of Brunswick co., S North Carolina, at mouth of Cape Fear river 22 m. S of Wilmington; pop. (1970c) 2220.
4 Town, SE Queensland, Australia, on Pacific Ocean 45 m. SSE of Brisbane; seaside resort.
5 County borough, Lancashire, NW England, on Irish Sea 17 m. N of Liverpool; pop. (1971p) 84,348; seaside resort.

South Portland. Residential city, Cumberland co., SW Maine, SE suburb of Portland; pop. (1970c) 23,267.

South P'yŏng·an \-pē-'ȯŋ-'än, -'an\. Province of North Korea. See table at KOREA, NORTH.

South River. 1 River, North Carolina. See SOUTH.
2 Borough, Middlesex co., cen. New Jersey, 6 m. SE of New Brunswick; pop. (1970c) 15,428; clothing, brick, tile.

South Ron·ald·say \-'rän-ᵊl(d)-ˌsā\. One of the Orkney Is., off N coast of Scotland.

South Saint Paul. City, Dakota co., SE Minnesota, on Mississippi river 4 m. SSE of St. Paul; pop. (1970c) 25,016.

South Salt Lake. City, Salt Lake co., N Utah, ab. 4 m. S of Salt Lake City; pop. (1970c) 7810.

South Sand·wich Islands \-'san-(d)wich-\. Group of small volcanic islands, South Atlantic Ocean at E end of Scotia Sea ab. 1350 m. ESE of Cape Horn, South America; 120 sq. m.; part of the Falkland Islands Dependencies; discovered 1775.

South Sandwich Trench. See ATLANTIC OCEAN.

South San Francisco. Industrial city, San Mateo co., W California, 9 m. S of San Francisco; pop. (1970c) 46,646; chemicals, paints, magnesium products, aircraft parts, air conditioners; steel mills, meat-packing plants; adjacent to San Francisco International Airport.

South San Ga·bri·el \-san-'gā-brē-əl\. Urban community (unincorporated), Los Angeles co., SW California; pop. (1970c) 5051.

South Saskatchewan. See SASKATCHEWAN 1.

South·sea \'sau̇th-ˌsē\. Residential district and resort area in S part of Portsmouth, England, within the city limits on the Spithead; navy memorials.

South Sea *or Span.* **El Mar del Sur** \el-ˌmär-del-'su̇(ə)r\. The Pacific Ocean— so named by Balboa on his discovery of it 1513. In the plural, **South Seas,** the waters of the Southern Hemisphere, esp. the South Pacific Ocean.

South Sea Islands. Islands of the South Pacific Ocean; equivalent in general usage to Oceania.

South Sea Mandated Territories. Collective name of the Caroline, Marshall, and Mariana (excluding Guam) Is. (*qq.v.*), in W Pacific Ocean N of the equator; so called while they were under Japanese mandate 1914–45.

South Seas. See SOUTH SEA.

South Shet·land Islands \-'shet-lənd-\ *or* **South Shet·lands** \-lən(d)z\. Group of islands, British Antarctic Territory, N of the Antarctic Penin. and separated from its N tip by Bransfield Strait; S of Drake passage and ab. 550 m. SE of Cape Horn, bet. 61° and 63°S lat. and bet. 54° and 63°W long. Chief islands Livingston, King George (the largest, with harbor at Admiralty Bay), Deception (with harbor at Port Foster and with a submerged volcano), Elephant, Clarence, and Greenwich. Rocky and mountainous, has several summer harbors with fishing activities. Discovered 1819 by English navigator William Smith. In 1946–48, ownership a matter of dispute bet. Great Britain and the republics of Argentina and Chile.

South Shields \-'shē(ə)l(d)z\. County borough, Durham, N England, on North Sea at mouth of the Tyne 10 m. E of Newcastle upon Tyne; pop. (1971p) 100,513; ships coal and iron; shipyards and marine engineering works; founded in 13th cent.; incorporated 1850.

South Sioux City \-ˌsü-\. City, Dakota co., NE Nebraska, across Missouri river from Sioux City, Iowa; pop. (1970c) 7920; agricultural equipment; grain farms.

South Su·la·we·si \-ˌsü-lə-'wā-sē\. Province of Indonesia, Celebes. See CELEBES and table at INDONESIA.

South Ta·ra·na·ki Bight \-ˌtar-ə-ˌnäk-ē-\. Gulf, W coast of North I., New Zealand, ab. 75 m. NW of Palmerston North.

South Te·ton \-'tē-ˌtän\. Peak in cen. Grand Teton National Park, NW Wyoming; 12,505 ft.

South Thompson. See THOMPSON 2.

South Tirol. See ALTO ADIGE.

South Tuc·son \-'tü-ˌsän\. City, Pima co., S Arizona; pop. (1970c) 6220.

South Tyne. See TYNE 1.

South Uist \-'yü-əst\. Island of the Outer Hebrides, off NW coast of Scotland, separated by Little Minch from Skye I.; administratively part of Inverness co.

South Ump·qua \-'əm(p)-kwȯ\. River, SW Oregon; 85 m. long; rises in E Douglas co., flows E and then N uniting with North Umpqua river ab. 8 m. NW of Roseburg to form the Umpqua river.

South Victoria Land. See VICTORIA LAND.

South Vietnam. See VIETNAM, SOUTH.

South·wark \'sət͟h-ərk, 'sau̇th-wərk\. A borough of Greater London, SE England. See table at LONDON 4.

South Waziristan. See WAZIRISTAN.

South·well \'sau̇th-ˌwel, -wəl\. Parish, Nottinghamshire, N cen. England; cathedral; near place where Charles I surrendered himself to the Scots 1646.

South–West Africa *or Afrikaans* **Suid·wes–Afri·ka** \ˌsīt-ˌves-'äf-re-kə\; *United Nations name* **Na·mi·bia** \nə-'mib-ē-ə\; *formerly* **German Southwest Africa** *or Ger.* **Deutsch–Süd·west·a·fri·ka** \ˌdȯich-sūed-vest-'äf-ri-kä\. Territory, SW Africa, a mandate (not recognized by UN) of the Rep. of South Africa, bounded on N by Angola and Zambia, on E by Botswana and Rep. of South Africa, on S by Rep. of South Africa, and on W by the Atlantic Ocean; does not include Walvis Bay (*q.v.*); 317,887 sq. m.; pop. (1970p)

746,328; ✻ Windhoek. *Physical features:* Greater part is plateau 3000 to 4000 ft.; highest point 8153 ft. near Windhoek. Namib Desert extends along the coast; in N is extensive depression with salt pans, esp. Etosha Pan. The Cunene and Okavango rivers form part of boundary on N with Angola, and the Orange river forms boundary with Rep. of South Africa. *Chief products:* Diamonds, copper, zinc, lead, salt; karakul sheep; fishing. *Chief towns:* Windhoek, Tsumeb, Keetmanshoop.

History: Bartholomeu Dias landed at the harbor on which Lüderitz is situated 1486; region not much visited before middle of 19th cent.; annexed by Germany 1885; after the Hottentots were defeated by the Herreros, the latter were conquered 1904–08 by the Germans; captured in World War I by forces from Union (now Rep.) of South Africa, which received it as mandate 1919 from League of Nations. A 1966 UN resolution (rejected by the Rep. of South Africa) declared the mandate terminated.

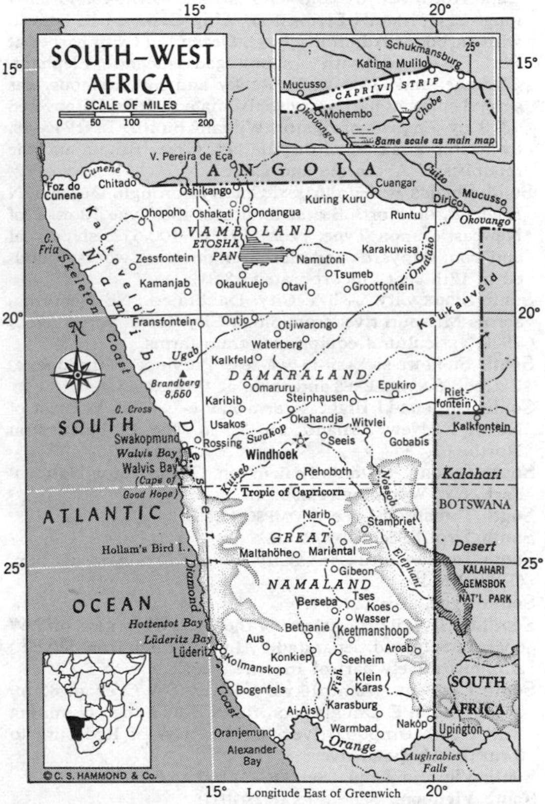

South West·bury \-ˈwest-ˌber-ē\. Urban community (incorporated), Nassau co., SE New York, on Long Island E of New York; pop. (1970c) 10,978.

South West Cape. Cape, SW point of Tasmania, Australia.

Southwest Greens·burg \-ˈgrēnz-ˌbərg\. Borough, Westmoreland co., SW Pennsylvania, 26 m. ESE of Pittsburgh; pop. (1970c) 3186.

South West Islands. Group of islands, SE part of Indonesia, on S edge of Banda Sea and NE of Timor; includes Wetar I., Kisar I., Damar Is., Moa I., and Sermata I.

South West Miramichi. See MIRAMICHI BAY.

Southwest Pass. 1 One of the channels at the mouth of the Mississippi river (*q.v.*).

2 Narrow strait, leading from Gulf of Mexico into Vermilion Bay, S Louisiana, bet. mainland of SE Vermilion parish and Marsh I.

Southwest Peak. See OTTER, PEAKS OF.

South·wick \ˈsau̇th-(ˌ)wik\. 1 Town, Hampden co., SW Massachusetts, 9 m. WSW of Springfield; pop. (1970c) 6330.

2 Urban district, West Sussex, S England; pop. (1971p) 11,850.

South Williamsport. Borough, Lycoming co., N cen. Pennsylvania, S suburb of Williamsport; pop. (1970c) 7153.

South Windsor. Town, E Hartford co., N Connecticut, NE of Hartford; pop. (1970c) 15,553.

South·wold \ˈsau̇th-ˌwōld\. Municipal borough, Suffolk, E England; pop. (1971p) 1992; seaside resort; 15th cent. church; on **Southwold Bay** *or* **Sole Bay** \ˈsōl-\, scene of naval battle in which the Dutch under De Ruyter were defeated by the English under James, Duke of York, May 28, 1672.

Sovereign State of Malta. See MALTA 1.

So·vetsk \səv-ˈyetsk\ *or Ger.* **Til·sit** \ˈtil-sət, -zət\. Industrial and commercial city, Kaliningrad Oblast, Russian S.F.S.R., U.S.S.R., on left bank of Neman river 37 m. NNW of Gusev; pop. (1967e) 36,000; trade center in agricultural region; produces lumber, iron, machinery, dairy products, beer; 18th cent. town hall.

History: Founded 1408; chartered 1552; treaty between France, Russia, and Prussia signed here 1807; in World War II occupied by Soviet troops 1944; in section of East Prussia assigned to U.S.S.R. by Potsdam Conference 1945.

So·vet·ska·ya Ga·van \sə-ˌv(y)et-skī-yə-ˈgä-vən\. Seaport town on Tatar Strait, N coast of Khabarovsk Krai, Russian S.F.S.R., U.S.S.R., 190 m. SE of Komsomolsk-na-Amure; pop. (1967e) 26,000; ships timber; major naval base.

Soviet Central Asia. See CENTRAL ASIA, SOVIET.

Soviet Union. See UNION OF SOVIET SOCIALIST REPUBLICS.

Sow·er·by Bridge \ˈsau̇(-ə)r-bē-\. Urban district, West Riding, Yorkshire, N England; pop. (1971p) 16,260.

Sō·ya, Cape \-ˈsō-(ˌ)yä\. Cape on N extremity of Hokkaidō, Japan.

Sōya Strait *or Jap.* **Sōya Mi·sa·ki** \-mi-ˈsäk-ē\ *also* **La Pé·rouse Strait** \ˈla-pᵊ-rüz-\. Channel bet. NW Hokkaidō, Japan, and S tip of Sakhalin I.; ab. 25 m. wide.

Sozh \ˈsȯsh\. Navigable river, W U.S.S.R., an E tributary of the Dnieper in W Russian S.F.S.R., U.S.S.R.; 402 m. long; rises near Smolensk and flows S in Smolensk Oblast and Belorussian S.S.R. to join the Dnieper below Gomel.

Sozopol. See APOLLONIA 2.

Spa \ˈspä, ˈspȯ\. Commune, Liège prov., E Belgium; pop. (1969e) 9487; medicinal mineral springs.

Spain \ˈspān\ *or Span.* **Es·pa·ña** \ä-ˈspän-yä\ *or anc.* **His·pa·nia** \his-ˈpān-ē-ə, -pān-yə, -ˈpan-\. A state (nominally a kingdom), SW Europe, occupying greater part of Iberian Penin. and including the Balearic and Canary Is.; 194,881 sq. m.; pop. (1970p) 33,823,918; ✻ Madrid. *Physical features:* On NE, separating Spain from France, the Pyrenees (highest Pico de Aneto 11,168 ft.); greater part of peninsula is plateau (*meseta*), averaging 2000 ft. alt. and rising in the N in the Cantabrian Mts., in the cen. part in the Sierra de Gredos and Sierra de Guadarrama (N of Madrid), and in the SW the Sierra Morena; near the SE coast along the Mediterranean is the range of the Sierra Nevada, containing the peak Mulhacén 11,407 ft., the highest point in Spain. Only lowlands besides the narrow strips along the E coast of the Mediterranean are the valleys of the Ebro, Tagus, and Guadiana, and esp. that of the Guadalquivir; other notable rivers are the Miño, Duero, Segura, and Jucár; no large lakes. Has few indentations and consequently few good harbors; on the Mediterranean are the Gulfs of Rosas and Almería and the harbors of Alicante and Málaga; at Strait of Gibraltar (separating Spain from Africa) is Bay of Gibraltar and on Atlantic the Gulf of Cádiz in S and harbors of La Coruña and Santander in N; its southernmost point, Point Tarifa, 36°N, is southernmost point of Europe. *Chief products:* Wheat, rice, barley, onions, olives, fruit (incl. citrus fruit and grapes); livestock raising, fishing; mercury, iron ore, coal, tin, lead, zinc, manganese; manufacturing: textiles, footwear, chemicals, electrical equipment; metallurgical industries; tourism. *Chief cities:* Madrid, Barcelona, Valencia, Seville, Saragossa, Bilbao, Málaga. Divided into the following 50 provinces (for pronunciation of their names, see their individual entries):

NAME	AREA (sq. m.)	POP. (1970p)	CAPITAL
Álava	1,176	204,323	Vitoria
Albacete	5,737	335,026	Albacete
Alicante	2,264	920,105	Alicante
Almería	3,388	375,004	Almería
Ávila	3,107	203,798	Ávila
Badajoz	8,362	687,599	Badajoz
Baleares[1]	1,936	558,287	Palma
Barcelona	2,986	3,929,194	Barcelona
Burgos	5,509	358,075	Burgos
Cáceres	7,701	457,777	Cáceres
Cádiz	2,851	885,433	Cádiz
Castellón de la Plana	2,579	385,823	Castellón de la Plana
Ciudad Real	7,625	507,650	Ciudad Real
Córdoba	5,297	724,116	Córdoba
Cuenca	6,587	247,158	Cuenca
Gerona	2,273	414,397	Gerona
Granada	4,838	733,375	Granada
Guadalajara	4,707	147,732	Guadalajara
Guipúzcoa	771	631,003	San Sebastián
Huelva	3,894	397,683	Huelva
Huesca	6,051	222,238	Huesca
Jaén	5,212	661,146	Jaén
La Coruña	3,041	1,004,188	La Coruña
Las Palmas[2]	1,569	579,710	Las Palmas de Gran Canaria
León	5,972	648,721	León
Lérida	4,644	347,015	Lérida
Logroño	1,944	235,713	Logroño
Lugo	3,785	415,052	Lugo
Madrid	3,087	3,792,561	Madrid
Málaga	2,809	867,330	Málaga
Murcia	4,369	832,313	Murcia
Navarra	4,024	464,867	Pamplona
Orense	2,810	413,733	Orense
Oviedo	4,079	1,045,635	Oviedo
Palencia	3,100	198,763	Palencia
Pontevedra	1,729	750,701	Pontevedra
Salamanca	4,763	371,607	Salamanca
Santa Cruz de Tenerife[3]	1,239	590,514	Santa Cruz de Tenerife
Santander	2,042	467,138	Santander
Segovia	2,683	162,770	Segovia
Sevilla	5,406	1,327,190	Seville
Soria	3,972	114,956	Soria
Tarragona	2,426	431,961	Tarragona
Teruel	5,715	170,284	Teruel
Toledo	5,934	468,925	Toledo
Valencia	4,156	1,767,327	Valencia
Valladolid	3,166	412,572	Valladolid
Vizcaya	853	1,043,310	Bilbao
Zamora	4,077	251,934	Zamora
Zaragoza	6,639	760,186	Saragossa

[1]Island group in W Mediterranean, comprising Majorca, Minorca, Ibiza, Formentera, and several smaller islands.

[2]E part of Canary Is. (*q.v.*), consisting principally of islands of Grand Canary, Lanzarote, and Fuerteventura.

[3]W part of Canary Is. (*q.v.*), consisting of islands of Tenerife, La Palma, Gomera, and Hierro.

History: Southern and eastern coasts colonized by Phoenicians and Greeks; Mediterranean coastal region ruled by Carthage which ceded it to Rome 201 B.C.; Tarraconensis (Hither Spain), Boetica (Farther Spain), and Lusitania were provinces of Roman Empire; invaded by Vandals 409 A.D.; Toledo the seat of Visigothic kingdom 534–712; conquered by Muslims from North Africa 711–719; most of Spain ruled by Ommiad dynasty of Córdoba (*q.v.*) 756–1031, except in north where there arose various small Christian states, such as Asturias, León, Galicia, Navarre, Barcelona; Moorish Spain, ruled by Almoravides after 1090 and by Almohades after 1147, gradually reconquered by Christian states of Castile and Aragon; Spain united in 1479 as result of marriage (1469) of Ferdinand II of Aragon and Isabella of Castile; conquered Granada, last kingdom of Moors 1492; annexed southern Navarre 1515; in 1516 Spanish throne ascended by Charles I, Hapsburg ruler who brought to Spain rule of Netherlands and was elected Holy Roman Emperor Charles V 1519; in 16th cent. Spanish acquired huge colonial empire in New World, Philippines, and in northern Africa; ceded to France forts in Artois and Flanders, Roussillon and Cerdagne 1659; lost Franche-Comté, rest of Artois and forts in Flanders 1678; accession of Philip V 1700, first Bourbon, brought on war through which Spain lost Gibraltar, Minorca, Sardinia, Sicily, Luxembourg, and Spanish Netherlands; gave up cen. Italian holdings for kingdom of Two Sicilies 1735–38; scene of Peninsular War 1808–13; restored Bourbon ruler 1814; set up first republic 1873–74; lost Cuba, Puerto Rico, Philippines, Guam to U.S. 1898; set up second republic 1931; gave autonomy to Catalonia (*q.v.*) 1932; scene of civil war 1936–39 which resulted in collapse of republican (Loyalist) government and victory for the Insurgents under Gen. Francisco Franco who thereupon became chief of state; nominally neutral during World War II; approved by referendum 1947 a law of succession to the head of state making possible the future restoration of the monarchy; joined United Nations 1955; adopted new constitution 1966; relinquished control over Spanish (now Equatorial) Guinea 1968, over Ifni 1969.

Spalato *or* **Spalatum.** See SPLIT.

Spal·ding \ˈspȯl-diŋ\. 1 County in Georgia. See table at GEORGIA.

2 Urban district, Parts of Holland, Lincolnshire, E England, on the Welland; pop. (1971p) 16,950.

Span·dau \ˈs(h)pän-ˌdau̇\. District, West Berlin, on the Spree; first mentioned 1197; received civic rights 1232; residence of electors of Brandenburg; captured several times in wars of 17th and 19th cents.; united with Berlin 1920; became part of West Berlin 1945.

Spang·ler \ˈspaŋ-glər\. Borough, Cambria co., SW cen. Pennsylvania, 22 m. WNW of Altoona; pop. (1970c) 3109; coal mines.

Span·ish America \ˌspan-ish-\. Those parts of America settled by Spaniards and now governed or occupied chiefly by their descendants; includes all of South America (except Brazil and the Guianas), Central America (except British Honduras), Mexico, Cuba, Puerto Rico, Dominican Republic, and some small islands in West Indies.

Spanish Fork. City, Utah co., N cen. Utah, 10 m. S of Provo; pop. (1970c) 7284; sugar, flour, lumber, canned goods, explosives; settled c. 1850.

Spanish Guinea. See EQUATORIAL GUINEA.

Spanish March. Region, NE Spain, a boundary (*march*) region bet. the Pyrenees and the Ebro, set up 795 by Charlemagne after his conquest of Catalonia 778. See history at CATALONIA.

Spanish Morocco. See MOROCCO 1.

Spanish Mountain. Peak in Sierra Nevada, E Fresno co., S cen. California; 10,044 ft.

Spanish Netherlands. Southern provinces of Netherlands; remained under Spain when seven northern provinces formed Union of Utrecht 1579; became independent kingdom of Belgium 1830. See BELGIUM and NETHERLANDS.

Spanish Peaks. Two mountains in Huerfano and Las Animas cos., S Colorado; E peak 12,683 ft. high, W peak 13,623 ft. high; landmarks for early explorers and traders.

Spanish Point. Cape, W cen. coast of Bermuda I., extending W bet. Grassy Bay and Great Sound.

Spanish Sahara. Spanish overseas province, NW Africa, bounded on N by Morocco, on NE by Algeria, on E and S by Mauritania, and on W by the Atlantic Ocean; 102,703 sq. m.; pop. (1970p) 76,425; ✱ Aaiún. *Chief products:* Barley; livestock raising, fishing; phosphates. *Chief towns:* Aaiún, Villa Cisneros, Smara.

History: Spanish trading post established on coast 1476, abandoned 1524; Spanish protectorate over region extend-

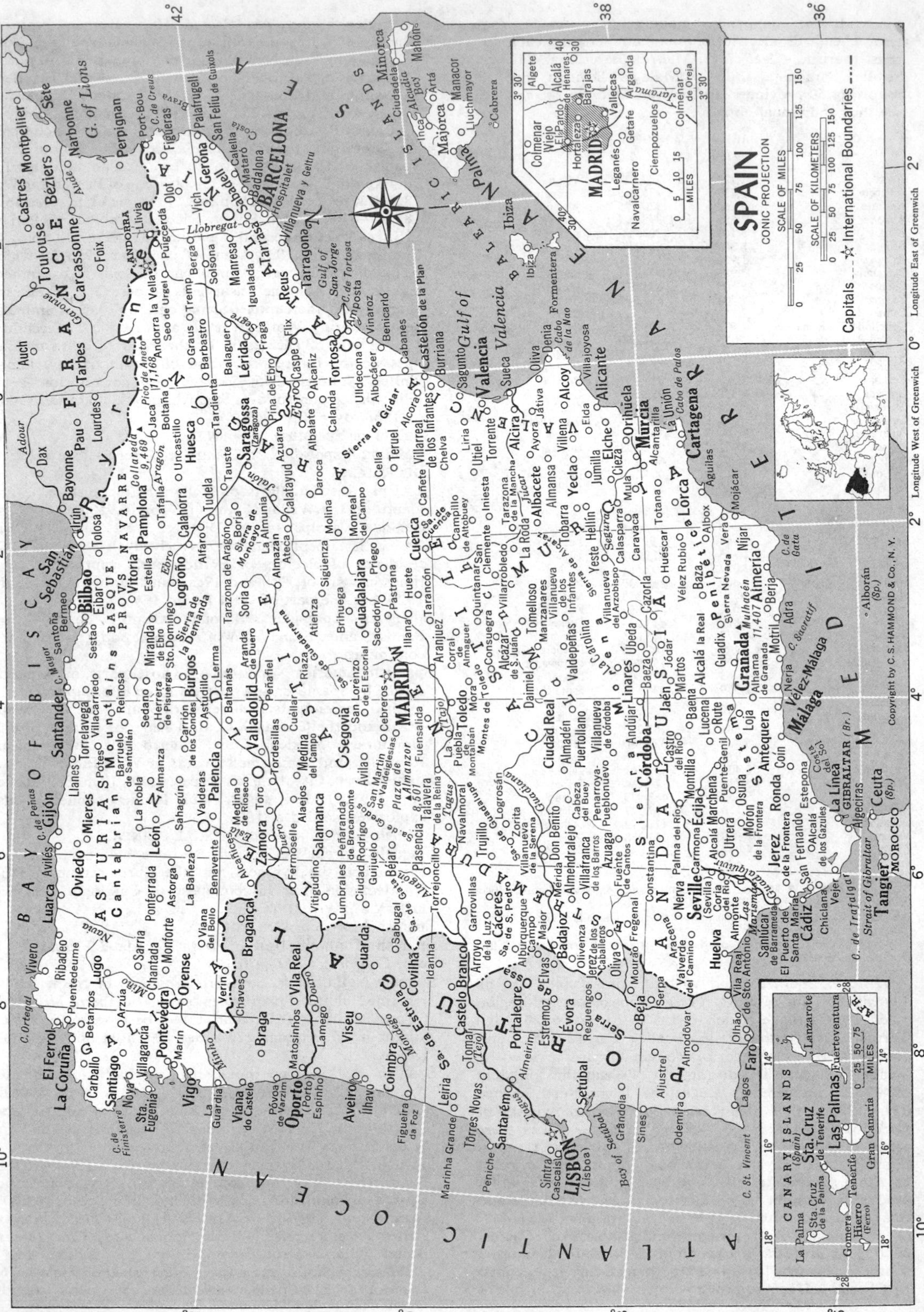
SPAIN
CONIC PROJECTION
SCALE OF MILES
0 25 50 75 100 125 150
SCALE OF KILOMETERS
0 25 50 75 100 125 150
Capitals ✫ International Boundaries
Longitude West of Greenwich
Longitude East of Greenwich
Copyright by C. S. HAMMOND & Co., N. Y.
BAY OF BISCAY
ATLANTIC OCEAN
MEDITERRANEAN SEA
FRANCE
PORTUGAL
G. of Lions
BALEARIC ISLANDS
Gulf of Valencia
Strait of Gibraltar
MOROCCO
Tangier
Ceuta (Sp.)
GIBRALTAR (Br.)
MADRID
LISBON (Lisboa)
Oporto (Porto)
BARCELONA
Valencia
Seville (Sevilla)
Málaga
Saragossa (Zaragoza)
Bilbao
Granada
Córdoba
Murcia
Cartagena
Alicante
Cádiz
Valladolid
Salamanca
Santander
Gijón
Oviedo
La Coruña
Vigo
Pamplona
San Sebastián
Toledo
Pyrenees
Sierra de Guadarrama
Sierra Nevada
Mulhacén 11,407
Cantabrian Mountains
ANDORRA
Mallorca
Minorca
Ibiza
Palma
CANARY ISLANDS (Spain)
Sta. Cruz de Tenerife
Las Palmas
Lanzarote
Fuerteventura
Gran Canaria
Tenerife
Gomera
Hierro (Ferro)
La Palma
0 25 50 75 MILES

ing from Cape Bojador to Cape Blanc proclaimed 1884; boundary agreements concluded with France 1900 and 1912; status changed from colony to overseas province 1958; partially elected assembly formed 1967.

Spanish Town. Town, SE cen. Jamaica I., West Indies, ab. 20 m. W of Kingston; pop. (1960c) 14,706; originally called St. Iago de la Vega; founded 1520–26; capital of Jamaica until 1872.

Spanish Wells. Island off N tip of Eleuthera I., Bahama Is.; 1 sq. m.; pop. (1963c) 849.

Sparks \'spärks\. City, Washoe co., NW corner of Nevada, on Truckee river 3 m. E of Reno; pop. (1970c) 24,187; railroad shops, silver mines; agriculture.

Sparnacum. See ÉPERNAY.

Spar·ta \'spärt-ə\. 1 City, ⊗ of Hancock co., cen. Georgia; pop. (1970c) 2172; lumber, clothing; agriculture.

2 City, Randolph co., SW Illinois, 45 m. SE of East St. Louis; pop. (1970c) 4307; aluminum castings, clothing; coal mines; diversified agriculture.

3 Village, Kent co., W Michigan, 13 m. N of Grand Rapids; pop. (1970c) 3094; dairy, fruit farms.

4 Town, ⊗ of Alleghany co., N North Carolina; pop. (1970c) 1304; lumber; grain farms.

5 Town, ⊗ of White co., cen. Tennessee, 17 m. S of Cookeville; pop. (1970c) 4930; rayon, silk, lumber; coal mines.

6 City, ⊗ of Monroe co., W cen. Wisconsin, 23 m. ENE of La Crosse; pop. (1970c) 6258; building materials, dairy products; tobacco, poultry.

7 *or* **Lac·e·dae·mon** \ˌlas-ə-'dē-mən\. Ancient city of Greece, ✱ of ancient Laconia and chief city of the Peloponnesus, in cen. part of Laconian plain on right bank of the Eurotas. A city-state of Dorian origin; conquered Messenia 736–716 B.C.; became leading state in Peloponnesus and founder of Peloponnesian League; after long contest with Athens (see ATHENS 10), known as Peloponnesian Wars 460–404 B.C., Sparta attained hegemony in Greece; Spartan power broken by Thebes at battle of Leuctra 371 B.C.; lost independence when it joined Achaean League 192 B.C.; made part of Roman province of Achaea (*q.v.*) 146 B.C.

8 *or Gk.* **Spár·ti** \'spär-tē\. Town, ✱ of Laconia dept., SE Peloponnesus, S Greece, S of the remains of ancient city (7 above); pop. (1971p) 11,981.

Spar·tan·burg \'spärt-ᵊn-ˌbərg\. 1 County in South Carolina. See table at SOUTH CAROLINA.

2 Commercial and industrial city, ⊗ of Spartanburg co., NW South Carolina, at foot of Blue Ridge Mts. 30 m. ENE of Greenville; pop. (1970c) 44,456; textiles, plumbing fixtures, lumber, sheet metal; flour mills, railroad shops; Wofford Coll. (1854), Converse Coll. (1889), Spartanburg Junior Coll. (1911); Cowpens and Kings Mountain battlefields in vicinity; settled c. 1785.

Spar·tel, Cape \-spär-'tel\. Cape, NW coast of Morocco, NW Africa, at the Strait of Gibraltar.

Spárti. See SPARTA 8.

Spar·ti·ven·to \ˌspärt-i-'ven-(ˌ)tō\. 1 Cape, the SE point of Reggio di Calabria prov., S extremity of mainland of Italy.

2 Cape, S extremity of the island of Sardinia, Italy, in the Mediterranean Sea W of Italy.

Spassk–Dal·ni \'späsk-'däl-n(y)ē\ *or* **Spassk.** Town, SW Primorski Krai, Russian S.F.S.R., U.S.S.R., on Trans-Siberian R.R. 120 m. N of Vladivostok; pop. (1967e) 41,-000.

Spa·tha, Cape \-'spä-thə\ *or Gk.* **Ák·ra Spatha** \ˌäk-rə-\. Point at tip of peninsula on NW coast of Crete, Greece, NW of Canea.

Spav·i·naw Creek \ˌspav-ə-ˌnȯ-\. Stream, NE cen. Oklahoma; dammed to form **Lake Spavinaw,** 6 m. long, impounding 20,000,000,000 gallons of water used as supply for the city of Tulsa.

Spear·fish \'spir-ˌfish\. City, Lawrence co., W South Dakota, 12 m. NNW of Lead; pop. (1970c) 4661; tourist resort; Black Hills State Coll. (1883).

Spearfish Peak. Mountain, Lawrence co., W South Dakota; 5976 ft.

Spear·man \'spi(ə)r-mən\. Town, ⊗ of Hansford co., NW Texas, in the Panhandle; pop. (1970c) 3435.

Spec·ta·cle Island \ˌspek-ti-kəl-\. Island, S area of the harbor of Boston, Massachusetts.

Speed·way \'spēd-ˌwā\. Town, Marion co., cen. Indiana, 5 m. W of Indianapolis; pop. (1970c) 15,056; site of the Indianapolis Motor Speedway, where the annual 500-mile International Sweepstakes races are held.

Speichern. See SPICHEREN.

Speights·town \'spīts-ˌtau̇n\. Town, NW Barbados I., Lesser Antilles, West Indies.

Spe·nard \spə-'närd\. Urban community (unincorporated), S cen. Alaska, S of Anchorage; pop. (1970c) 18,809.

Spen·bor·ough \'spen-b(ə-)rə\. Municipal borough, West Riding, Yorkshire, N England, 7 m. S of Leeds; pop. (1971p) 40,693; textiles, machinery, sheet metal.

Spen·cer \ˌspen(t)-sər\. 1 Name of counties in two states of the U.S. See tables at INDIANA and KENTUCKY.

2 Town, ⊗ of Owen co., SW cen. Indiana, 14 m. NW of Bloomington; pop. (1970c) 2553; birthplace of William Vaughn Moody (1869–1910), poet and playwright.

3 City, ⊗ of Clay co., NW Iowa; pop. (1970c) 10,278; leather goods, fertilizer; packing plant; grain farms.

4 Industrial town, Worcester co., cen. Massachusetts, 10 m. W of Worcester; pop. (1970c) 8779; chemicals, plastics, footwear; dairy farms.

5 City, Rowan co., cen. North Carolina, NE suburb of Salisbury; pop. (1970c) 3075.

6 Town, Oklahoma co., cen. Oklahoma, 7 m. E of Oklahoma City; pop. (1970c) 3714.

7 Town, ⊗ of Van Buren co., cen. Tennessee; pop. (1970c) 1179.

8 City, ⊗ of Roane co., W cen. West Virginia, 35 m. NNE of Charleston; pop. (1970c) 2271.

Spencer, Cape. 1 Point, mainland of SE Alaska, on N side of entrance to Cross Sound.

2 Cape, S tip of Yorke Penin., SE South Australia, on E side of entrance to Spencer Gulf.

Spencer, Mount. Peak, cen. Piscataquis co., N cen. Maine; 3135 ft.

Spencer Gulf *also* **Spen·cer's Gulf** \ˌspen(t)-sərz-\. Large inlet, South Australia, bet. Yorke and Eyre penins.; 200 m. long and ab. 90 m. at its widest part; its entrance bet. Capes Catastrophe and Spencer partly shut off by Thistle I. and Gambier Is.; discovered 1802.

Spen·cer·port \'spen(t)-sər-ˌpō(ə)rt, -ˌpȯ(ə)rt\. Village, Monroe co., W New York, 10 m. NW of Rochester; pop. (1970c) 2929; diversified agriculture.

Spen·ny·moor \'spen-i-ˌmu̇(ə)r\. Urban district, Durham, N England, 21 m. S of Newcastle upon Tyne; pop. (1971p) 19,063.

Spermunde Archipelago. See PABBIRING ARCHIPELAGO.

Sper·rin Mountains \ˌsper-ən-\. Mountain range, cos. Londonderry and Tyrone, Northern Ireland; highest peak 2240 ft.

Spe·su·tie Island \spə-ˌsü-shē-ə-\. Island, upper Chesapeake Bay, easternmost point of Harford co., NE Maryland.

Spe·tsai *or Gk.* **Spé·tsai** \'spet-(ˌ)sā\ *or Ital.* **Spez·zia** \'spet-sē-ə\. Island, Gulf of Argolis, Greece; 7 sq. m.

Spey \'spā\. River, Inverness, Banff, and Moray cos., NE Scotland; 107 m. long; flows NE into Moray Firth; noted for salmon fishing.

Spey·er \'s(h)pī(-ə)r\ *or angl.* **Spires** \'spī(ə)rz\; *anc.* **Civ·i·tas Ne·me·tum** \ˌsiv-ə-təs-ne-'mēt-əm, -'nem-ə-təm\ *or later* **Spi·ra** \'spī(ə)r-ə\. City, Rhineland-Palatinate,

West Germany, on the Rhine 22 m. N of Karlsruhe; pop. (1969e) 41,957; produces aircraft, electrical equipment, wood products, textiles, chemicals, footwear, building materials, beer and wine; notable 11th cent. Romanesque cathedral (restored in 18th and 20th cents.) containing remains of numerous German rulers; 18th cent. church.

History: Town developed under Romans but destroyed during barbarian invasions; became free imperial city 1111 and seat of numerous diets, including Diet of Spires 1592; destroyed by French 1689; part of French department of Donnersberg 1801–14; passed to Bavaria 1814.

Spe·zia, Gulf of \-'spet-sē-ə\. Small bay, inlet of Gulf of Genoa, on E coast of Genova prov., NW Italy; excellent harbor.

Spezia, La. See LA SPEZIA.

Spezzia. See SPETSAI.

Sphinx, Mount \-'sfiŋ(k)s\. Peak, SE cen. Madison co., SW Montana; 10,860 ft.

Spice Islands. See MOLUCCAS.

Spi·cer Islands \'spī-sər-\. Two small islands, center of Foxe Basin, Northwest Territories, Canada; discovered 1879; all trace of existence of islands lost until rediscovered Aug. 28, 1946.

Spi·che·ren *or* **Spick·e·ren** \spē-'kren\; *Ger.* **Spi·chern** \'s(h)pē-kərn\ *also* **Spei·chern** \'s(h)pī-kərn\. Village and heights, Moselle dept., France, E of Forbach; pop. (1962c) 2202; battle Aug. 6, 1870 in which Germans under Steinmetz defeated French under Frossard.

Spie·ker·oog \'s(h)pē-kə-ˌrōk\. Island, East Frisian Is., off NW coast of West Germany bet. Langeoog and Wangerooge; ab. 5½ sq. m.

Spij·ke·nis·se \'spī-kən-ˌis-ə\. Commune, South Holland prov., Netherlands; pop. (1970e) 24,735.

Spin·dale \'spin-ˌdāl\. Town, Rutherford co., SW North Carolina, 23 m. W of Shelby; pop. (1970c) 3848; Isothermal Community Coll. (1966).

Spink \'spink\. County in South Dakota. See table at SOUTH DAKOTA.

Spi·on Kop \'spī-ən-ˌkäp, 'spē-\. Hill, Natal, Rep. of South Africa, 24 m. WSW of Ladysmith; scene of battle Jan. 24, 1900 in which the Boers defeated the British under Sir Redvers Buller.

Spira. See SPEYER.

Spirding. See ŚNIARDWY.

Spire Point \'spī(ə)r-\. Peak, N cen. Washington, on boundary bet. Skagit and Chelan cos.; 8220 ft.

Spires. See SPEYER.

Spirit Lake \ˌspir-ət-\. 1 Lake on N boundary of Dickinson co., NW Iowa; ab. 10 m. long, 9 sq. m.

2 City, ⊗ of Dickinson co., NW Iowa, 51 m. NNE of Cherokee; pop. (1970c) 3014; lake resort.

Spiš·ská No·vá Ves \'spish-(s)kä-ˌnȯ-və-'ves\ *or Hung.* **Igló**\'ig-(ˌ)lō\ *or Ger.* **Zip·fer Neu·dorf** \ˌtsip-fər-'nȯi-ˌdȯrf\. Town, Slovak S.R., E cen. Czechoslovakia, ab. 35 m. NW of Košice; pop. (1968e) 22,025.

Spit·head \'spit-'hed\. Roadstead, S coast of England, off Portsmouth harbor bet. Portsea I. and the NE coast of the Isle of Wight; connects with the Solent on the W; formerly a frequent rendezvous of British fleet.

Spits·ber·gen \'spits-ˌbər-gən\. Norwegian archipelago, Arctic Ocean, 360 m. N of Norway; part of Svalbard; 23,641 sq. m.; chief settlement Green Harbor; extensive coal deposits; chief islands Spitsbergen (formerly West Spitsbergen; 15,075 sq. m.), North East Land, Edge I., Barents I.; highest point Mt. Newton 5617 ft., on Spitsbergen. Probably known to Vikings but discovered in modern times by William Barents in June 1596; became officially a part of Norway Aug. 14, 1925. Held by Allies during World War II but towns heavily damaged by German raids. See ARCTIC, THE.

Split \'split\ *or* **Spljet** \splē-'et\ *or Ital.* **Spa·la·to** \'späl-ə-ˌtō\ *or anc.* **Spal·a·tum** \'spal-ə-təm\. Seaport on the Adriatic Sea, Croatia, W Yugoslavia, ab. 105 m. WSW of Sarajevo; pop. (1971p) 151,875; good harbor; commercial center and naval base; one of Yugoslavia's leading resort centers; cathedral (former mausoleum of Diocletian, converted in 7th cent.), amphitheater, museum, art gallery.

History: Roman colony of Salona (*q.v.*) founded 78 B.C.; after its destruction by Avars 639 A.D. inhabitants established new town within walls of former palace of Diocletian (early 4th cent.); came under Byzantine rule 812–1069; after succession of rulers came under Venice 1420–1797; to Austria 1797, to Yugoslavia 1918; in World War II occupied by Axis troops 1941–45.

Split Mountain. Peak in Sierra Nevada, in Fresno and Inyo cos., SE cen. California; 14,058 ft.

Splügen *or Ital.* **Spluga.** Alpine pass. See ALPS.

Spo·kane \spō-'kan\. 1 River, E Washington; ab. 120 m. long; rises in Coeur d'Alene Lake, Kootenai co., N Idaho, flows W across Washington border and into Columbia river in N Lincoln co.

2 County in Washington. See table at WASHINGTON.

3 City, ⊗ of Spokane co., E Washington, on falls of Spokane river 18 m. W of Idaho border; pop. (1970c) 170,516; alt. 1890 ft.; center of an agricultural, lumbering, and mining region; produces aluminum, clay and cement products, machinery, paper, electrical equipment, feed, flour; railroad shops; gateway to extensive recreational region and national parks; Gonzaga Univ. (1887), Whitworth Coll. (1890), Fort Wright Coll. of the Holy Names (1907). Settled 1872; incorporated as village of **Spokane Falls** 1881; destroyed by fire 1889; reincorporated as city of Spokane 1891.

Spo·le·to \spə-'lāt-(ˌ)ō\ *or anc.* **Spo·le·ti·um** \spō-'lē-shē-əm\. Commune, Perugia prov., Umbria, cen. Italy, 30 m. SE of Perugia; pop. (1968e) 37,036; center of olive-growing region; phosphorus, textiles; Roman walls, 12th cent. cathedral, numerous notable churches of the 5th–14th cents.

History: Founded by Etruscans; came under Rome 241 B.C.; episcopal see from 4th cent. A.D.; capital of Lombard duchy and one of principal cities of Italy 570 ff.; declined after mid-8th cent. and came under church c. 1240; passed to kingdom of Italy 1860.

Spoon·er \'spün-ər\. City, Washburn co., NW Wisconsin, 25 m. N of Rice Lake (city); pop. (1970c) 2444.

Spor·a·des \'spȯr-ə-ˌdēz, 'spär-\. Two groups of islands, Aegean Sea: the **Northern Sporades** (*Gk.* **Vo·rí·ai Spo·rá·dhes** \vȯ-ˌrē-ā-spȯ-'rä-thās\) and the **Southern Sporades** (*Gk.* **Nó·ti·ai Sporádhes** \'nȯ-tē-e-\); administratively attached to Euboea and Magnesia depts., Greece. Chief islands of the Northern Sporades, off the mainland coast of Magnesia (Thessaly) and the island Euboea, are Skyros, Skopelos, Skiathos, and Iliodhrómia. Chief islands of the Southern Sporades are Rhodes and the Dodecanese, which belonged to Italy 1912–47; also included in the Southern Sporades by some geographers are the islands of Samos, Ikaria, Chios, and Lesbos.

Spot Mountain \'spät-\. Peak, Glacier National Park, NW Montana; 7800 ft.

Spots·wood \'späts-ˌwu̇d\. Borough, Middlesex co., cen. New Jersey, SE of New Brunswick; pop. (1970c) 7891.

Spot·syl·va·nia \ˌspät-səl-'vān-yə\. 1 County in NE Virginia. See table at VIRGINIA.

2 Village, its ⊗, 11 m. SW of Fredericksburg; battles of **Spotsylvania Court House** May 8–21, 1864, (result indecisive), bet. Union troops under Grant and Confederates under Lee included battle at the Bloody Angle May 12.

Spot·ted Range \ˌspät-əd-\. Small range, Clark, Lincoln, and S Nye cos., S Nevada.

Sprague \'sprāg\. 1 River, S Oregon; rises in SW Lake co., flows W across Klamath co., into the Williamson river near Upper Klamath Lake.

2 Town, N New London co., SE Connecticut, N of Norwich; pop. (1970c) 2912.

Sprat·ly Islands \'sprat-lē-\. Group of small islands, actually reefs, in cen. part of South China Sea, ab. 280 m. SE of Camranh Bay and 775 m. NE of Singapore; seized by Japan

June 1940 and made submarine base; rights to islands renounced by Japan 1951.

Spree \'s(h)prā\. River, East Germany; 247 m. long; rises in mountains near Czech border, flows N past Bautzen and Cottbus and through Berlin, where it joins the Havel river at Spandau; navigable for vessels of light draft.

Spree·wald \'s(h)prā-ˌvält\. Woody and marshy district, Cottbus dist., East Germany, in the Spree valley, NW of Cottbus.

Sprem·berg \'s(h)prem-ˌbe(ə)rg\. City, Cottbus dist., East Germany, on Spree river 14 m. S of Cottbus and 77 m. SE of Berlin; pop. (1970e) 22,629; manufactures textiles, machinery, and paper.

Sprend·ling·en \'s(h)prend-liŋ-ən\. City, Hesse, West Germany, 7 m. S of Frankfurt; pop. (1969e) 22,773; machine shops; furniture.

Spring \'spriŋ\. River, NE Arkansas; ab. 60 m. long; rises in S Missouri, crosses Arkansas border in Fulton co., flows SE into Black river.

Spring·bok \'spriŋ-ˌbäk\ *or* **Spring·bok·fon·tein** \-fön-'tān\. Village, NW Cape Province, S Rep. of South Africa; pop. (1967e) 4100.

Spring·bo·ro \'spriŋ-ˌbər-ə, -ˌbə-rə\. Village, Warren co., SW Ohio, 15 m. S of Dayton; pop. (1970c) 2799.

Spring City. Borough, Chester co., SE Pennsylvania, on Schuylkill river 28 m. NW of Philadelphia; pop. (1970c) 3578; transistors, machine tools, castings; agriculture.

Spring·dale \'spriŋ-ˌdāl\. **1** City, Washington co., NW Arkansas, 12 m. N of Fayetteville; pop. (1970c) 16,783; wineries and distilleries; ships fruit; poultry farms.

2 Subdivision of town of Stamford, Connecticut. See STAMFORD 1.

3 Borough, Allegheny co., SW Pennsylvania, on Allegheny river 14 m. NE of Pittsburgh; pop. (1970c) 5202.

4 Town, Lexington co., cen. South Carolina; pop. (1970c) 2638.

5 Town, Newfoundland, Canada, 90 m. E of Corner Brook; pop. (1971p) 3221.

Spring·er \'spriŋ-ər\. Town, Colfax co., N New Mexico, on Cimarron river 38 m. S of Raton; pop. (1970c) 1574.

Springer Mountain. Peak, Dawson co., N Georgia; 3782 ft.

Spring·field \'spriŋ-ˌfēld\. **1** Town, ⊗ of Baca co., SE corner of Colorado; pop. (1970c) 1660; stock, dairy farms.

2 City, Bay co., NW Florida; 2 m. E of Panama City; pop. (1970c) 5949.

3 City, ⊗ of Effingham co., E Georgia; pop. (1970c) 1001.

4 City, ✱ of Illinois and ⊗ of Sangamon co., cen. Illinois, on Sangamon river 185 m. SW of Chicago; pop. (1970c) 91,753; electronic equipment, automobile parts, boilers, footwear, paints, fertilizer, flour; center of agricultural area. Home (became a National Historic Site 1971) and burial place of Abraham Lincoln; Lincoln tomb and monument designed and executed by Larkin G. Meade, in Oak Ridge cemetery; house in which Lincoln lived 1844–61; Springfield Junior Coll. (1929), Lincoln Land Community Coll. (1967). Settled 1818; incorporated as town 1832; made ✱ of Illinois 1837; incorporated as city 1840.

5 City, ⊗ of Washington co., cen. Kentucky, 25 m. W of Danville; pop. (1970c) 2961; among records in the county courthouse are the marriage bond of Thomas Lincoln, father of Abraham Lincoln, and the certificate of marriage of Thomas Lincoln and Nancy Hanks. See HARRODSBURG.

6 City, ⊗ of Hampden co., SW Massachusetts, on Connecticut river 5 m. N of Connecticut border; pop. (1970c) 163,905; electrical equipment, chemicals, machine tools, firearms, hosiery, matches, brass goods, radios, plastics, clothing; home of Merriam-Webster *Dictionaries.* Springfield Coll. (1885), American International Coll. (1885), Western New England Coll. (1919), Springfield Technical Community Coll. (1965). Settled 1636; incorporated 1641; burned during King Philip's War 1675; scene of Shay's Rebellion 1786–87; site of United States Armory 1794–1968.

7 City, Calhoun co., S Michigan, 5 m. W of Battle Creek; pop. (1970c) 3994.

8 City, Brown co., S Minnesota; pop. (1970c) 2530.

9 City, ⊗ of Greene co., SW Missouri, ab. 150 m. SSE of Kansas City; pop. (1970c) 120,096; alt. 1300 ft.; center of agricultural region, shipping poultry, livestock, dairy products, fruit; produces typewriters, trailers, men's clothing, furniture; tourist center for Ozarks region; railroad shops, flour mills; Drury Coll. (1873), Southwest Missouri State Coll. (1905), Central Bible Coll. (1922), Evangel Coll. (1955); settled 1829.

10 Residential suburban township, Union co., NE New Jersey, ab. 6 m. NW of Elizabeth; pop. (1970c) 15,585; scene of battle in American Revolution June 23, 1780 in which Gen. Greene repulsed the British; Revolutionary cemetery.

11 Industrial city, ⊗ of Clark co., Ohio, 23 m. NE of Dayton; pop. (1970c) 81,941; electric motors, automobile parts, machine tools, diesel engines, castings, incubators; Wittenberg Univ. (1842); settled 1799; made ⊗ 1818; incorporated as town 1827, as city 1850.

12 City, Lane co., W Oregon, 5 m. E of Eugene; pop. (1970c) 27,047; lumber; diversified agriculture.

13 Urban township, Delaware co., SE Pennsylvania, ab. 5 m. NE of Chester; pop. (1970c) 29,006.

14 Urban township, Montgomery co., SE Pennsylvania, SW suburb of Philadelphia; pop. (1970c) 22,394.

15 City, Bon Homme co., SE South Dakota, on Missouri river ab. 28 m. W of Yankton; pop. (1970c) 1566; Southern State Coll. (1881).

16 City, ⊗ of Robertson co., N Tennessee, 23 m. N of Nashville; pop. (1970c) 9720; tobacco market; flour, stoves, footwear; agriculture.

17 Town, Windsor co., E Vermont, on Black river 33 m. SE of Rutland; pop. (1970c) 10,063.

18 Unincorporated urban area, Fairfax co., NE Virginia; pop. (1970c) 11,613.

Springfield, Lake. Artificial lake, Sangamon co., cen. Illinois; 15 m. long; shoreline 45 m.; completed 1935; source of water supply for Springfield.

Springfield Place. Unincorporated urban community, Calhoun co., S Michigan, W of Battle Creek; pop. (1970c) 4831.

Spring·fon·tein \ˌspriŋ-fön-'tān\. Town, S Orange Free State, E cen. Rep. of South Africa, 85 m. SSW of Bloemfontein.

Spring Garden. Urban township, York co., S Pennsylvania, S of York; pop. (1970c) 12,443.

Spring·hill \'spriŋ-ˌhil\. **1** City, Webster parish, NW Louisiana, 38 m. NNE of Shreveport; pop. (1970c) 6946.

2 Coal-mining town, Cumberland co., N Nova Scotia, Canada, 15 m. SE of Amherst; pop. (1971p) 5195.

Spring Lake. **1** Village, Ottawa co., W Michigan, 14 m. S of Muskegon; pop. (1970c) 3034.

2 Borough, Monmouth co., E cen. New Jersey, on Atlantic Ocean 6 m. S of Asbury Park; pop. (1970c) 3896; summer resort.

3 Town, Cumberland co., S cen. North Carolina; pop. (1970c) 3968.

Spring Lake Heights. Borough, Monmouth co., E cen. New Jersey, 6 m. SSW of Asbury Park; pop. (1970c) 4602.

Spring Lake Park. Village, Anoka and Ramsey cos., E Minnesota, 11 m. N of St. Paul; pop. (1970c) 6417.

Spring·lands \'spriŋ-lən(d)z, -ˌlan(d)z\. Town, NE Guyana, on W bank of Courantyne river near its mouth, 95 m. SE of Georgetown.

Spring Mountain Range. Mountain range, W cen. Clark co., SE Nevada.

Springs \'spriŋz\. City, S Transvaal, NE Rep. of South Africa, 29 m. E of Johannesburg; pop. (1968e) 143,117; gold- and uranium-mining center; glass, machine tools, paper, bicycles. Settled as coal-mining camp 1885; first gold mine opened 1908.

Spring Valley. 1 City, Bureau co., N Illinois, on Illinois river 18 m. W of Ottawa; pop. (1970c) 5605; clothing, automobile parts; sand pits.

2 Village, Fillmore co., SE Minnesota; pop. (1970c) 2572.

3 Village, Rockland co., SE New York; pop. (1970c) 18,112; residential; summer resort; fruit farms.

4 City, Harris co., SE Texas, 10 m. W of Houston; pop. (1970c) 3170.

Spring·view \'spriŋ-(ˌ)vyü\. Village, ⊗ of Keya Paha co., N Nebraska; pop. (1970c) 260.

Spring·ville \'spriŋ-ˌvil\. 1 Village, Erie co., W New York, 27 m. SSE of Buffalo; pop. (1970c) 4350.

2 City, Utah co., N cen. Utah, 5 m. S of Provo; pop. (1970c) 8790; steel mills; fruit and sugar beet farms.

Sprottau. See SZPROTAWA.

Spruce Hill \'sprüs-\. Peak, Berkshire co., W Massachusetts; 1974 ft. See HOOSAC MOUNTAINS.

Spruce Knob. Peak, Pendleton co., E West Virginia; 4862 ft.; highest point in the state.

Spruce Mountain. Peak, SE cen. Elko co., NE Nevada; 11,041 ft.

Spruce Pine. Town, Mitchell co., W North Carolina, in Blue Ridge Mts. 36 m. NE of Asheville; pop. (1970c) 2333; resort; feldspar mines; agriculture.

Spruce Ridge Top. Peak, W North Carolina; 6076 ft.

Spruce·top \'sprü-ˌstäp\. Peak in the Catskill Mts., Greene co., SE New York; 3620 ft.

Spurn Head \'spərn-\. Cape, E coast of England, in Yorkshire, at NE entrance to mouth of the Humber river; lighthouse.

Spurr, Mount \-'spər\. Mountain peak, W of head of Cook Inlet, SW Alaska; 11,070 ft.

Spuy·ten Duy·vil \'spīt-ᵊn-ˌdī-vəl\. District of N New York City, formerly a village, on Hudson river just N of Spuyten Duyvil Creek.

Spuyten Duyvil Creek. Narrow channel, N of Manhattan I., New York, separating the island from the mainland and connecting Hudson and Harlem rivers.

Spy \'spē, 'spī\. Commune, Namur prov., S Belgium, 6 m. W of Namur; pop. (1969e) 3320; cave in which two skeletons were found 1886 representing a type of Paleolithic man.

Squam Lake \'skwäm-\. Lake, cen. New Hampshire, on boundary bet. Grafton, Belknap, and Carroll cos.; ab. 6 m. long and 4 m. wide; resort.

Squa·pan Lake \ˌskwȯ-pan-\. Lake, E cen. Aroostook co., N Maine.

Squaw Peak \'skwȯ-\. 1 Mountain, E California, in Sierra Nevada W of Lake Tahoe; 8884 ft.

2 Mountain, SE Idaho co., N cen. Idaho; 8660 ft.

Squaw Valley. Valley, E California, in the Sierra Nevada on E slopes of Squaw Peak; ski resort; site of Winter Olympic Games 1960.

Squil·la·ce, Gulf of \-skwi-'läch-ē\. Inlet of Ionian Sea, S Italy.

Squin·za·no \skwēnt-'sä-nō\. Commune, Lecce prov., Apulia, SE Italy, 9 m. NW of Lecce; pop. (1970c) 14,729.

Squt·pans·berg \sküt-'päns-ˌbe(ə)rg\ *or* **Zout·pans·berg** \'sōt-ˌpän(t)s-ˌbe(ə)rg\. Mountain range, N Transvaal, NE Rep. of South Africa; highest peak ab. 6700 ft.; a continuation of the Drakensberg Mts.

Sra·gen \'srä-gən\. Town, cen. Java, Indonesia, on railroad ab. 17 m. NE of Surakarta; pop. (1961c) 22,685.

Srbija. See SERBIA.

Sredinny Khrebet. See CENTRAL RANGE.

Srem. See SYRMIA.

Srem·ska Mi·tro·vi·ca \'srem(p)-skä-'mē-trə-ˌvēt-sə\ *or formerly* **Mitrovica** *or Ger.* **Mi·tro·witz** \'mēt-rə-ˌvits\. Town, Serbia, N cen. Yugoslavia, on Sava river 42 m. WNW of Belgrade; pop. (1965e) 23,000; river port and commercial center; Roman ruins of Sirmium nearby; suffered much destruction in wars of Middle Ages.

Srem·ski Kar·lov·ci \ˌsrem(p)-skē-'kär-lōv-tsē\ *or Ger.* **Kar·lo·witz** *also* **Car·lo·witz** \'kär-lō-ˌvits\ *or Hung.* **Kar·ló·cza** \'kär-lōt-sə\. Town, N Serbia, NE Yugoslavia, on right bank of Danube river; pop. (1961c) 6383; trade center in grape-growing region; cathedral; palace; scene of signing of Treaty of Karlowitz Jan. 26, 1699 by Austria, Poland, Turkey, Venice, marking suppression of power of Turkey in Europe and cession of lands to Austria and Poland.

Sri·ha·ri·ko·ta Island \ˌsrē-ˌhär-ə-'kōt-ə-\. Island off SE coast of India, N of Madras; 30 m. long.

Sri Lanka. See CEYLON.

Sri·na·gar \sri-'nəg-ər\ *also* **Kash·mir South** \'kash-mir-, 'kazh-, kash-', kazh-'\. 1 District, Jammu and Kashmir, N India; pop. (1961c) 640,411.

2 City, summer ✱ of Jammu and Kashmir, also ✱ of the district, on Jhelum river 170 m. N of Amritsar; pop. (1970e) 327,076; alt. 5250 ft.; carpets, silk, silver, leather, and copper ware; woodcarving; tourism; numerous mosques and notable public gardens, palaces, museums, and fortress; Univ. of Jammu and Kashmir (1948). Dal Lake with noted floating gardens lies to NE. Scene of Thomas Moore's *Lalla Rookh.*

Sri·ran·gam \srē-'rəŋ-gəm\. Town, SE Tamil Nadu, S India, on island in Cauvery river 2 m. N of Tiruchchirappalli and 30 m. W of Thanjavur; pop. (1961c) 46,816; place of pilgrimage to notable 17th cent. temple, dedicated to Vishnu.

Sri·vi·ja·ya \ˌsrē-wi-'jō-yə\ *or* **Shri·vi·ja·ya** \ˌshrē-vi-\. Hindu-Malayan empire of wide extent, SE Asia, 12th cent. A.D. See MALAY ARCHIPELAGO.

Sri·vil·li·put·tur \ˌsrē-vi-li-pu̇-'tu̇(ə)r\. City, S Tamil Nadu, S India, 42 m. SW of Madurai; pop. (1961c) 46,816.

Ssu–p'ing \'sü-'piŋ\ *also* **Sze·ping·kai** \'sü-'piŋ-'gī\ *or* **Ssu-ping·chieh** \-chē-'e(r), -'ā\. Town, Kirin prov., NE China, 70 m. SSW of Ch'ang-ch'un; pop. (1970e) 180,000.

Stabiae. See CASTELLAMMARE DI STABIA.

Stablo. See STAVELOT.

Stabroek. See GEORGETOWN 17.

Stadacona. See QUEBEC 3.

Sta·de \'s(h)täd-ə\. Manufacturing city, Lower Saxony, West Germany, 22 m. W of Hamburg; pop. (1969e) 31,658; manufactures salt, tile, bricks, textiles, lumber; shipyards, oil refineries. First mentioned 988; member of Hanseatic League.

Städ·jan \'stād-ˌyan\. Peak, SW cen. Sweden, near the Norwegian border; 3710 ft.

Stads·ka·naal \ˌstäts-kə-'näl\. Commune, Groningen prov., Netherlands; pop. (1970e) 32,829.

Stadt·lohn \'s(h)tät-ˌlōn\. Town, North Rhine-Westphalia, West Germany, W of Münster near Netherlands border; pop. (1968e) 15,107; scene of victory Aug. 6, 1623 of Catholic League under Count of Tilly over Imperial forces under Christian of Brunswick.

Staf·fa \'staf-ə\. Small island, Inner Hebrides, Scotland, 7 m. W of Mull; location of **Fin·gal's Cave** \ˌfiŋ-gəlz-\, 227 ft. long, 117 ft. high.

Staf·ford \'staf-ərd\. 1 Name of counties in two states of the U.S. See tables at KANSAS and VIRGINIA.

2 Town, N Tolland co., N Connecticut, on Massachusetts border E of Somers; pop. (1970c) 8680; includes borough of Stafford Springs; founded 1719.

3 Town, Fort Bend and Harris cos., SE Texas, 18 m. SW of Houston; pop. (1970c) 2906.

4 Village, ⊗ of Stafford co., NE Virginia.

5 County in England. See STAFFORDSHIRE.

6 Municipal borough, ⊗ of Staffordshire, W cen. England, on the Sow 25 m. NNW of Birmingham; pop. (1971p) 54,890; market town; diesel engines, electrical equipment, footwear. Birthplace of Izaak Walton.

Staf·ford·shire \'staf-ərd-ˌshi(ə)r, -shər\ *or* **Staf·ford** \'staf-ərd\ *or* **Staffs** \'stafs\. County, W cen. England; 1157 sq.

m.; pop. (1971p) 1,856,890; ⊗ Stafford; rivers the Trent and its tributaries; dairy and livestock farming, coal mining, manufacturing (iron and steel products, pottery, glass, textiles, chemicals), brewing; contains much of the Black Country (*q.v.*); chief towns Wolverhampton, Stoke-on-Trent, Dudley.

Stafford Springs. Industrial borough in town of Stafford, Connecticut; pop. (1970c) 3339; tools and dies, chemicals, woolens, silk; incorporated 1873; formerly a health resort.

Stag Dome \ˈstag-\. Peak in Sierra Nevada, in E Fresno co., S cen. California; 7707 ft.

Sta·gi·ra \stə-ˈjī-rə\ *or* **Sta·gi·ros** \-rəs\. Town in ancient Macedonia, NE Greece, on E Chalcidice Penin., on Strymonic Gulf. Birthplace of Aristotle ("the Stagirite").

Staierdorf–Anina. See ANINA.

Staines \ˈstānz\. Urban district, Surrey, SE England, on the Thames 19 m. WSW of London; pop. (1971p) 56,386; residential.

Staked Plain. See LLANO ESTACADO.

Stakhonovo. See ZHUKOVSKI.

Stalin. 1 Seaport, Bulgaria. See VARNA 2.
2 City, Romania. See BRAŞOV 2.
3 City, U.S.S.R. See DONETSK.

Stalinabad. See DUSHANBE.

Stalingrad. See VOLGOGRAD.

Stalingrad Oblast. See VOLGOGRAD OBLAST.

Stalinir. See TSKHINVALI.

Stalino. See DONETSK.

Stalinogorsk. See NOVOMOSKOVSK.

Stalino Oblast. See DONETSK OBLAST.

Stalin Peak. 1 Peak, Czechoslovakia. See GERLACHOVKA.
2 Peak, U.S.S.R. See COMMUNISM PEAK.

Stalinsk. See NOVOKUZNETSK.

Sta·lo·wa Wo·la \stä-ˌlō-və-ˈvō-lə\. Town, Rzeszów prov., SE Poland, ab. 35 m. NNE of Rzeszów; pop. (1970p) 29,800.

Sta·ly·bridge \ˈstā-lē-ˌbrij\. Municipal borough, Cheshire, NW England, on the Tame 10 m. E of Manchester; pop. (1971p) 22,782; textiles, plastics.

Stam·baugh \ˈstam-ˌbȯ\. City, Iron co., SW Michigan penin., 32 m. WNW of Iron Mountain; pop. (1970c) 1458.

Stam·ford \ˈstäm(p)-fərd\. 1 City, Fairfield co., SW Connecticut, on Long Island Sound and New York border; pop. (1970c) 108,798; computers, electronic components, plastics, sheet metal, ball bearings; shipyards; Saint Basil's Coll. (1939). Settled 1641; annexed to Connecticut 1662; city government formed within town 1893; town and city government consolidated 1949.
2 City, Jones and Haskell cos., NW cen. Texas, 35 m. N of Abilene; pop. (1970c) 4558; clothing, cottonseed oil, dairy products; oil and gas wells.
3 Municipal borough, Parts of Kesteven, Lincolnshire, E England, on the Welland 35 m. SE of Nottingham; pop. (1971p) 14,485; site of Saxon, Danish, and Norman fortified settlements.

Stamford Bridge. Village, East Riding, Yorkshire, N England, 8 m. ENE of York; scene of battle Sept. 25, 1066 in which King Harold II defeated his brother Tostig and Harold Haardraade, King of Norway, Tostig's ally, just before Battle of Hastings.

Stampalia. See ASTYPALAIA.

Stam·pede Tunnel \ˌstam-ˌpēd-\. Railroad tunnel, King and Kittitas cos., W cen. Washington, in Cascade Range; 9850 ft. long.

Stan·ards·ville \ˈstan-ərdz-ˌvil\. Town, ⊗ of Greene co., N cen. Virginia; pop. (1970c) 296.

Stan·der·ton \ˈstan-dərt-ᵊn\. Town, SE Transvaal, NE Rep. of South Africa, on Vaal river 90 m. ESE of Johannesburg; pop. (1967e) 22,500; in agricultural region; scene of much action in first Boer War 1880–81.

Standing Indian. Mountain, Clay co., SW North Carolina; 5500 ft.

Stan·dish \ˈstan-dish\. 1 Town, Cumberland co., SW Maine, 15 m. NW of Portland; pop. (1970c) 3122.
2 City, ⊗ of Arenac co., E Michigan; pop. (1970c) 1184; agriculture.

Standish–with–Lang·tree \-ˈlaŋ-ˌtrē\. Urban district, Lancashire, NW England, NE of Liverpool; pop. (1971p) 11,450.

Stand·ley Lake Dam \ˈstan-dlē-\. Dam across branch of Big Dry Creek, Jefferson co., cen. Colorado; height 113 ft.; completed 1909; impounds water for irrigation, forming **Standley Lake.**

Stan·ford \ˈstan-fərd\. 1 Residential city, ⊗ of Lincoln co., E cen. Kentucky, 10 m. SE of Danville; pop. (1970c) 2474.
2 Town, ⊗ of Judith Basin co., cen. Montana; pop. (1970c) 505; coal mines; diversified agriculture.

Stang·er \ˈstaŋ-ər\. Town, E Natal, E Rep. of South Africa, near coast 40 m. NNE of Durban; pop. (1967e) 11,200; sugar; burial place of Chaka, Zulu warrior and chieftain.

Stan·hope \ˈstan-ˌhōp\. Borough, Sussex co., N New Jersey; pop. (1970c) 3040.

Stanimaka. See ASENOVGRAD.

Stanislau. See IVANO-FRANKOVSK.

Stan·is·laus \ˈstan-ə-ˌslȯ(s)\. 1 River, N cen. California; 95 m. long; rises in Alpine co. near Nevada border, flows SW into San Joaquin river bet. San Joaquin and Stanislaus cos. See MELONES DAM.
2 County in California. See table at CALIFORNIA.

Stanislaus Peak. Mountain, S Alpine co., E cen. California, in the Sierra Nevada; 11,202 ft.

Stanislav. See IVANO-FRANKOVSK.

Stanislav Oblast. See IVANO-FRANKOVSK OBLAST

Sta·ni·sla·wów \ˌstän-i-ˈsläv-ˌüf\. 1 Former department, SE Poland; now approx. coextensive with Ivano-Frankovsk Oblast, Ukrainian S.S.R., U.S.S.R.
2 City, its ✱. See IVANO-FRANKOVSK.

Stan·ke Di·mi·trov \ˌstän-kə-də-ˈmē-trȯv\. Town, Kyustendil prov., W Bulgaria, ab. 20 m. W of Kyustendil; pop. (1968e) 37,161.

Stan·ley \ˈstan-lē\. 1 County in South Dakota. See table at SOUTH DAKOTA.
2 City, ⊗ of Mountrail co., NW North Dakota; pop. (1970c) 1581; dairy products; flax, corn.
3 City, Chippewa co., W Wisconsin, 20 m. E of Chippewa Falls; pop. (1970c) 2049.
4 *or* **Circular Head.** Town, NW Tasmania, Australia, on peninsula in Bass Strait 37 m. WNW of Burnie; pop. (1970e) 8400; Tasmanian port nearest to Melbourne; a popular seaside resort at the foot of the headland Circular Head (*q.v.*).
5 Urban district, Durham, N England, 18 m. SSW of Newcastle upon Tyne; pop. (1971p) 41,940; clothing, dairy products; coal mines.
6 Urban district, West Riding, Yorkshire, N England; pop. (1971p) 20,776.
7 *or* **Port Stanley.** Town, ✱ of Falkland Is., South Atlantic Ocean, on E coast of East Falkland; pop. (1970e) 1080; principal town and harbor of the Falkland Is.

Stanley, Mount. See RUWENZORI, MOUNT.

Stanley Falls. Seven cataracts of the upper Congo river, in Zaire, S cen. Africa, on the equator, above Kisangani, extending ab. 60 m.

Stanley Pool; *in Zaire known as* **Ma·le·bo Pool** \mä-ˈlā-(ˌ)bō-\. Expansion of the Congo river, bet. Congo and Zaire, 4°15′S, 15°25′E; Brazzaville and Kinshasa are situated on its NW and SW shore, respectively.

Stanley Range. See MAIN BARRIER RANGE.

Stanleyville. See KISANGANI.

Stan·ly \ˈstan-lē\. County in North Carolina. See table at NORTH CAROLINA.

Stann Creek \'stan-\. 1 District, cen. British Honduras; 840 sq. m.; pop. (1967e) 14,091; ✱ Stann Creek.
2 Coastal town, its ✱, E cen. coast of British Honduras; pop. (1970p) 6961.
Stan·o·voi Range \'stan-ə-ˌvȯi-\ *or Russ.* **Sta·no·voi Khre·bet** \-kri-'b(y)et\. Mountain range, E Russian S.F.S.R., U.S.S.R., mostly bet. Yakutsk A.S.S.R. and Khabarovsk Krai; highest peak at E end 8268 ft.; watershed bet. Arctic and Pacific Ocean streams.
Stans \'s(h)täns\. Commune, ✱ of Nidwalden demicanton, Unterwalden canton, cen. Switzerland, 7 m. SSE of Lucerne; pop. (1970c) 5180; tourism; 17th cent. parish church with 12th cent. Romanesque tower, town hall, convents.
Stans·bury Island \ˌstanz-ˌber-ē-, -bə-rē-\. Peninsula, formerly an island, in SW Great Salt Lake, Utah; 11½ m. long and 5½ m. wide.
Stan·stead \'stan-(ˌ)sted\. County, Quebec, Canada. See table at QUEBEC.
Stan·thorpe \'stan-ˌthȯ(ə)rp\. Town, SE Queensland, Australia, 100 m. SW of Brisbane on New South Wales border at N end of New England Plateau; pop. (1966c) 3641; tin mines and uranium deposits.
Stan·ton \'stant-ᵊn\. 1 Name of counties in two states of the U.S. See tables at KANSAS and NEBRASKA.
2 City, Orange co., SW California, SW of Anaheim; pop. (1970c) 18,149.
3 City, ⊗ of Powell co., E Kentucky; pop. (1970c) 2037.
4 City, ⊗ of Montcalm co., cen. Michigan; pop. (1970c) 1089.
5 City, ⊗ of Stanton co., NE Nebraska, 12 m. ESE of Norfolk; pop. (1970c) 1363; ships livestock.
6 City, ⊗ of Mercer co., W cen. North Dakota; pop. (1970c) 317; dairy, poultry, wheat farms.
7 City, ⊗ of Martin co., NW Texas; pop. (1970c) 2117.
Stanton Peak. Mountain in Sierra Nevada, E Tuolumne co., cen. California; 11,666 ft.
Sta·ples \'stā-pəlz\. City, Todd co., cen. Minnesota, 26 m. W of Brainerd; pop. (1970c) 2657; diversified agriculture.
Staples, The. See FARNE ISLANDS.
Sta·ple·ton \'stā-pəlt-ᵊn\. 1 Village, ⊗ of Logan co., cen. Nebraska; pop. (1970c) 311.
2 Section of Richmond, borough of New York City. See RICHMOND 8.
Sta·ra·cho·wi·ce \ˌstar-ə-kə-'vēt-sə\. Town, Kielce prov., S Poland, ab. 25 m. NE of Kielce; pop. (1970p) 42,800.
Stara Planina. See BALKAN MOUNTAINS.
Starav, Ben. See BEN STARAV.
Sta·ra·ya Rus·sa \ˌstär-ə-yə-'rü-sə\. Town, cen. Novgorod Oblast, NW Russian S.F.S.R., U.S.S.R., 15 m. S of Lake Ilmen; pop. (1967e) 32,000; trades in grain and flax; resort, with mineral springs, salt lakes, parks. An old town under Novgorod, dating back at least to 12th cent.; suffered much in medieval wars; later belonged to Moscow. In World War II occupied by Germans 1941–44 and scene of heavy fighting 1944.
Sta·ra Za·go·ra \ˌstär-ə-zə-'gȯr-ə\. 1 Province of cen. Bulgaria. See table at BULGARIA.
2 City, its ✱, on S slope of Balkan Mts. 50 m. ENE of Plovdiv; pop. (1968e) 103,853; trade center in rose-growing region; produces attar of roses, chemical fertilizers; scene of Turkish victory over Russians 1877.
Star·buck \'stär-ˌbək\. Small island, Line Is., cen. Pacific Ocean, 5°37′S, 155°33′W; discovered 1823; in area claimed by both Great Britain and United States.
Star City \'stär-\. City, ⊗ of Lincoln co., SE Arkansas; pop. (1970c) 2032; agriculture.
Star·gard Szcze·ciń·ski \ˌstär-gärt-sh(ch)ə-'chin-skē\ *or formerly* **Stargard in Pom·mern** \-in-'pȯm-ərn\. City, W cen. Szczecin prov., NW Poland, ab. 20 m. ESE of Szczecin; pop. (1970p) 44,500; agricultural implements, beer, tobacco products; medieval walls and gates, 13th cent. church; an early Hanse town; destroyed in Thirty Years' War 1633; occupied by U.S.S.R. Mar. 5, 1945; assigned to Poland by Potsdam Conference 1945.

Star Harbour. Inlet and trading station, N coast at SE end of San Cristóbal I., SE British Solomon Is., W Pacific Ocean.
Sta·ri Grad \'stär-e-ˌgräd\ *or Ital.* **Cit·ta·vec·chia** \ˌchē-tə-'vek-ē-ə\. Seaport, NW coast of Hvar I., Bosnia and Herzegovina, W Yugoslavia.
Stark \'stärk\. Name of counties in three states of the U.S. See tables at ILLINOIS, NORTH DAKOTA, OHIO.
Starke \'stärk\. 1 County in Indiana. See table at INDIANA.
2 City, ⊗ of Bradford co., NE Florida; pop. (1970c) 4848; lumber; strawberries.
Stark·ville \'stärk-ˌvil, -vəl\. City, ⊗ of Oktibbeha co., NE cen. Mississippi, 23 m. W of Columbus; pop. (1970c) 11,369; dairy products, clothing; cotton; Mississippi State Univ. (1878).
Starn·berg \'s(h)tärn-ˌbərg, -ˌbe(ə)rg\. Village, Bavaria, West Germany, at N end of Lake of Starnberg, ab. 10 m. SSW of Munich; health resort.
Starnberg, Lake of *or Ger.* **Starn·ber·ger See** \'s(h)tärn-bər-gər-ˌzā, -ber-\; *formerly* **Würm·see** \'vūerm-ˌzā\ *or* **Würmer See** \'vūerm-ər-ˌzā\. Lake, Bavaria, West Germany, 15 m. SSW of Munich; 12 m. long, max. width 3 m.
Sta·ro·dub \ˌstär-ə-'düp\. Town, W Bryansk Oblast, Russian S.F.S.R., U.S.S.R., 80 m. SW of Bryansk. An old town, important in Russian medieval history; destroyed by Mongols in 13th cent., disputed among Russians, Lithuanians, and Poles down to 1686 when it became permanently Russian; in World War II behind German lines 1941–43.
Sta·ro·gard Gdań·ski \stə-'rō-gärt-gə-'dän(t)-skē\ *or formerly* **Preus·sisch–Star·gard** \'prȯi-sish-'s(h)tär-ˌgärt\. Commune, Gdańsk prov., N Poland, 64 m. N of Toruń; pop. (1970p) 33,400; chemicals, shoes, tobacco; suffered much destruction in World War II.
Sta·ro·kon·stan·ti·nov \ˌstär-ə-ˌkən-stən-'t(y)ē-nəf\. Town, Khmelnitski Oblast, W Ukrainian S.S.R., U.S.S.R., 160 m. SSW of Kiev; pop. (1967e) 22,000.
Star Peak. 1 Mountain, Gunnison and Pitkin cos., W cen. Colorado; 13,562 ft.
2 Mountain, Chelan co., cen. Washington; 8400 ft.
Starr \'stär\. County in Texas. See table at TEXAS.
Start Point \'stärt-\. 1 Cape, S coast of Devonshire, SW England; lighthouse; at S end of **Start Bay,** wide inlet of English Channel on Devonshire coast S of Dartmouth.
2 Cape, NE tip of Sanday I., Orkney Is., off N coast of Scotland; lighthouse.
Starved Rock \'stärvd-\. Locality, S bank of Illinois river, near Ottawa, La Salle co., N Illinois, 90 m. SW of Chicago; narrow strip of high bluff above river, highest point 140 ft., steep on all sides with flat top (½ acre); now part of **Starved Rock State Park,** oldest (opened 1912) of Illinois state parks, 900 acres; contains also springs, trails, bluffs, caves. Of historical interest; visited by Jolliet and Marquette 1673 on return from exploration of the Mississippi and by Marquette 1675 just before his death, also by La Salle and Tonti 1679; Fort St. Louis erected here on summit 1682, abandoned 1702, burned by Indians 1721. Story of Illinois Indians starving on rock (c. 1770) is purely legendary.
Sta·ry Os·kol \ˌstär-e-əs-'kōl\. Town, Belgorod Oblast, Russian S.F.S.R., U.S.S.R., ab. 70 m. NE of Belgorod; pop. (1967e) 45,000.
Stass·furt \'s(h)täs-ˌfu̇(ə)rt\. Salt-mining city, Magdeburg dist., East Germany, 21 m. S of Magdeburg; pop. (1970e) 25,695.
State College. 1 Post office for Mississippi State Univ., SE suburb of Starkville (*q.v.*), NE cen. Mississippi.
2 Suburb of Las Cruces, New Mexico. See LAS CRUCES.
3 Suburb of Fargo, North Dakota. See FARGO.
4 Borough, Centre co., cen. Pennsylvania, 22 m. NW of Lewistown; pop. (1970c) 33,778; Pennsylvania State Univ. (1855).
Stat·en Island \'stat-ᵊn-\. 1 Island, New York Bay, 5 m. S of Manhattan; 64 sq. m.; ab. 15½ m. long by 7 m. wide;

separated on E from Long I. by the Narrows and on W from New Jersey by narrow Arthur Kill connecting Newark Bay on N with Raritan Bay on S. Forms Richmond borough, New York City, and Richmond co., New York state; connected with Brooklyn by Verrazano-Narrows Bridge (1964). Part of island granted by Dutch West India Company to David Pietersen de Vries 1636; first settlement 1641. See RICHMOND 8.

2 Island, Argentina. See ESTADOS, ISLA DE LOS.

Sta·ten·ville \ˈstāt-ᵊn-ˌvil\. Town, ⊗ of Echols co., S Georgia, 20 m. ESE of Valdosta; pop. (1970c) 600.

State of Israel. See ISRAEL 2.

State of Vatican City. See VATICAN CITY.

States·boro \ˈstāts-ˌbər-ə, -ˌbə-rə\. City, ⊗ of Bulloch co., E Georgia, 47 m. WNW of Savannah; pop. (1970c) 14,616; lumber; peanuts, poultry, cotton; Georgia Southern Coll. (1908).

States of the Church *or* **Pa·pal States** \ˌpā-pəl-\ *or Ital.* **Lo Sta·to del·la Chie·sa** \lō-ˈstät-ō-ˌdel-ə-kē-ˈez-ə, -ˈāz-\. Temporal domain of the pope, cen. Italy, 754–1870; 16,000 sq. m.; ✱ Rome, during periods when actually under control of papacy.

History: Temporal power of medieval papacy based upon Donation of Pepin 754 A.D., by which king of Franks promised to pope lands in cen. Italy, conquered from Lombards but formerly Byzantine; acquired duchy of Benevento 1052; strengthened and expanded by Innocent III (d. 1216) who controlled Ravenna, Romagna, Spoleto, the Pentapolis, and for a time, much of Tuscany; from 1274 to 1791 included Comtat Venaissin in S France; during residence of pope at Avignon (*q.v.*) 1309–77, under rule of virtually independent lords; boundaries until 19th cent. were reestablished by Julius II (1503–13) who regained Romagna; annexed Ferrara by reversion 1598; invaded by French 1796; territorial status altered during Napoleonic Wars; established as Roman Republic 1798–99; divided between France and kingdom of Italy 1809; restored to papacy 1815; in 1860, Romagna, Marches, and Umbria joined Piedmont; Rome (*q.v.*) annexed to kingdom of Italy 1870; temporal authority in Vatican City (*q.v.*) granted to pope 1929.

States·ville \ˈstāts-ˌvil, -vəl\. City, ⊗ of Iredell co., cen. North Carolina, 37 m. N of Charlotte; pop. (1970c) 19,996; furniture, textiles, paper and plastic products, bricks, hosiery; Mitchell Coll. (1853); founded 1789; entire city made a bird sanctuary 1930.

Stato della Chiesa, Lo. See STATES OF THE CHURCH.

Statue of Liberty National Monument. See UNITED STATES, *National Monuments.*

Staub·bach Falls \ˌs(h)taůp-(ˌ)bäk-\. Waterfall near Lauterbrunnen, Switzerland; 984 ft. high; slight flow.

Staun·ton. 1 \ˈstȯnt-ᵊn, -ˈstänt-\. City, Macoupin co., SW cen. Illinois, 32 m. NE of East St. Louis; pop. (1970c) 4396; coal mines; dairy farms.

2 \ˈstant-ᵊn\. City, ⊗ of Augusta co., N cen. Virginia, 35 m. WNW of Charlottesville; politically independent; 9 sq. m.; pop. (1970c) 24,504; center of agricultural area of S Shenandoah Valley; produces flour, clothing, furniture, air conditioners; ships livestock and fruit; Mary Baldwin Coll. (1842). Birthplace of Woodrow Wilson, 28th president of the U.S. Founded 1736; briefly capital of Virginia 1781; in Civil War twice occupied by Union forces; incorporated as city 1871.

Sta·vang·er \stə-ˈväŋ-ər\. Seaport, ⊗ of Rogaland co., SW Norway, on **Stavanger Fjord,** a S branch of Bokn Fjord, 190 m. WSW of Oslo; pop. (1971e) 82,079; fish canning, shipbuilding; 12th cent. cathedral, two museums. Thought to have been founded in 8th cent.; made bishopric c. 1125 (see removed to Kristiansand 1682).

Stave·ley \ˈstāv-lē\. Urban district, Derbyshire, N cen. England; pop. (1971p) 17,644.

Sta·ve·lot \stav-ˈlō\ *or Flemish* **Sta·blo** \ˈstab-(ˌ)lō\. Commune, Liège prov., Belgium, on the Amblève river 21 m. SE of Liège; pop. (1969e) 4761; Romanesque tower of ancient Benedictine abbey founded 651. In World War II in the Battle of the Bulge Dec. 1944–Jan. 1945, reached by Germans Dec. 18 but held by Allies against further advance on Liège.

Stav·ro·pol \stav-ˈrō-pəl, -ˈrō-\. **1** *or bet. 1940 and 1944* **Vo·ro·shi·lovsk** \ˌvȯr-ə-ˈshē-ˌlȯfsk, ˌvär-\. City, ✱ of Stavropol Krai, Russian S.F.S.R., U.S.S.R., on tributary of upper Kalaus; pop. (1970p) 198,000; produces flour, dairy products, wine and fruit juice, leather goods, canned meat; founded 1777 as fortress by Suvorov. Briefly occupied by Germans 1942–43 during advance towards Caucasus.

2 Town, Kuibyshev Oblast, U.S.S.R. See TOLYATTI.

Stavropol Krai \-ˈkrī\ *or formerly* **Or·dzho·ni·kid·ze Krai** \ȯr-ˌjän-ə-ˈkid-zə-\. Territory, SE Russian S.F.S.R., U.S.S.R.; 31,120 sq. m.; pop. (1970p) 2,306,000; ✱ Stavropol. Contains high land in W part and plain in the E, watered by Kuma and Terek rivers, the latter mostly on S border. Economy is principally agricultural (grain, sunflowers, flax, potatoes, livestock); natural gas and oil fields. Chief towns Stavropol, Kislovodsk, Pyatigorsk.

History: In medieval times a part of the Khanate of the Golden Horde; came under Moscow in 16th cent.; E part home of the Terek Cossacks and in modern times whole region formed E half of North Caucasus region; krai formed 1924, reorganized and renamed 1944.

Stav·ros *or* **Stav·rós** \stäv-ˈrȯs\. Town, Chalcidice dept., S Macedonia, NE Greece, on NE coast of the Chalcidice Penin., on S shore of the Strymonic Gulf E of Salonika.

Staw·ell \ˈstȯ-əl\. Town, W Victoria, SE Australia, 130 m. WNW of Melbourne; pop. (1966c) 5909; mining town in center of gold district.

Stay·ton \ˈstāt-ᵊn\. City, Marion co., NW Oregon, 18 m. SE of Salem; pop. (1970c) 3170; diversified agriculture; sawmills.

Steam·boat Springs \ˌstēm-ˌbōt-\. Town, ⊗ of Routt co., NW Colorado, on Yampa river 38 m. E of Craig; pop. (1970c) 2340; Colorado Alpine Coll. (1961).

Stearns \ˈstərnz\. County in Minnesota. See table at MINNESOTA.

Stę·bark \ˈstenm-ˌbärk\ *or Ger.* **Tan·nen·berg** \ˈtän-ən-ˌbe(ə)rg\. Village, Olsztyn prov., N Poland, 15 m. SE of Ostróda; site of two battles: (1) 1410, in which Teutonic Knights were defeated by the Lithuanians and Poles; (2) Aug. 26–30, 1914, in which Germans under Hindenburg severely defeated Russians under Rennenkampf. Before 1945 in East Prussia, Germany.

Steele \ˈstē(ə)l\. **1** Name of counties in two states of the U.S. See tables at MINNESOTA and NORTH DAKOTA.

2 City, Pemiscot co., SE corner of Missouri, 12 m. WSW of Caruthersville; pop. (1970c) 2107.

3 City, ⊗ of Kidder co., S cen. North Dakota; pop. (1970c) 696; ships livestock, grain.

Steele, Mount. Peak in St. Elias Mountains, SW Yukon Territory, Canada, near Alaska border; 16,644 ft.

Steel Mountain \ˈstē(ə)l-\. Peak, N Elmore co., SW cen. Idaho; 9752 ft.

Steel·ton \ˈstē(ə)l-tən\. Borough, Dauphin co., SE cen. Pennsylvania, on Susquehanna river just S of Harrisburg; pop. (1970c) 8556; iron and steel mills.

Steel·ville \ˈstē(ə)l-ˌvil\. City, ⊗ of Crawford co., SE cen. Missouri; pop. (1970c) 1392; fruit farms.

Steen·ker·ke \ˈstān-ˌker-kə\ *or* **Steen·kerque** \sten-ˈkerk, stanⁿ-\ *also* **Stein·kirk** \ˈstēn-ˌkərk\. Village in Hainaut prov., SW Belgium; pop. (1969e) 360; scene of battle July 23–Aug. 3, 1692 in which the French under the duc de Luxembourg defeated the English under William III.

Steens Mountain \ˈstēnz-\. Mountain mass, SE Harney co., SE Oregon; highest point 9354 ft.

Steen·wijk \ˈstān-ˌvīk\. Commune, Overijssel prov., E Netherlands, ab. 7 m. NNW of Meppel; pop. (1970e) 12,512.

Stee·ple \ˈstē-pəl\. Mountain, Cumberland, NW England, in the Lake District; two peaks, 2746 ft. and 2687 ft.

Steep Point \ˈstēp-\. Extreme W point of mainland of Australia, 26°08′S, 113°08′E.

Stef·a·nie, Lake \-ˈstef-ə-nē\ *or* **Chew Ba·hir** \ˌchü-bä-ˈhi(ə)r\. Shallow saline lake, SW Ethiopia, E of N end of Lake Rudolf; ab. 37 m. long; elevation ab. 1900 ft.

Ste·fans·son Island \ˈstef-ən-sən-\. Island, Franklin dist., Northwest Territories, Canada, off NE coast of Victoria I.; 2890 sq. m.

Stefansson Strait. Strait, bet. E Antarctic Penin. and Hearst I., Antarctica; 40 m. long, 3 m. wide at narrowest point; filled with shelf ice.

Stef·fen \ˈstef-ən\. Peak, W Chubut prov., S Argentina, on Chile border; 6916 ft.

Stef·fis·burg \ˈs(h)tef-əs-ˌbu̇(ə)rg\. Commune, Bern canton, Switzerland, N of Thun; pop. (1970c) 12,621.

Ste·ge \ˈstā-gə\. Town, W coast of Møn I., Denmark; pop. (1965c) 2866.

Ste·ger \ˈstā-gər\. Village, Cook and Will cos., NE Illinois, 28 m. S of Chicago; pop. (1970c) 8104.

Steier. See STEYR.

Steierdorf–Anina. See ANINA.

Steiermark. See STYRIA.

Stei·la·coom \ˈstil-ə-kəm\. Town, Pierce co., W cen. Washington, 10 m. SW of Tacoma; pop. (1970c) 2856.

Steinamanger. See SZOMBATHELY.

Stein·bach \ˈstīn-ˌbak\. Town, Manitoba, Canada, 39 m. SE of Winnipeg; pop. (1971p) 5161; diversified agriculture.

Steinkirk. See STEENKERKE.

Stein·kjer \ˈstān-ˌka(ə)r\. Town, ⊗ of Nord-Trøndelag co., N cen. Norway, N of Levanger and at the head of Trondheim Fjord; pop. (1970e) 20,224; lumber port and railroad station; scene of fighting bet. Germans and British Apr. 1940.

Steinschönau. See KAMENICKY ŠENOV.

Steins·øy \ˈstān-ˌsœi\. Small island off Sogne Fjord, Norway, 58°59′N, 5°46′E; the most W point of Norway.

Stein·stück·en \ˈs(h)tīn-ˌs(h)t(y)ük-ən\. Exclave of West Berlin, ab. 3 m. E of Potsdam, East Germany; 31 acres; pop. (1970e) 200.

Stel·la·land \ˈstel-ə-ˌland\. Former Boer republic, S Africa; ab. 5000 sq. m.; ✱ Vryburg; established in W Transvaal 1882 as part of westward expansion of Boers (see GOSHEN 5); dissolved 1885; region now part of Cape Province, Rep. of South Africa.

Stel·lar·ton \ˈstel-ərt-ᵊn\. Town, Pictou co., N Nova Scotia, Canada, 7 m. S of New Glasgow; pop. (1971p) 5334; coal mines.

Stel·len·bosch \ˈstel-ən-ˌbȯs, -ˌbu̇sh\. Residential town, SW Cape Province, S Rep. of South Africa, 25 m. E of Cape Town; pop. (1969e) 29,900; produces wine and lumber; educational center, with Univ. of Stellenbosch (1918) and many schools; second-oldest town in Rep. of South Africa (after Cape Town), founded 1679.

Stel·ler, Mount \-ˈstel-ər\. Mountain in Chugach Mts., S Alaska; 10,617 ft.; Bering Glacier is on it.

Stel·vio National Park \ˌstel-vē-ˌō-\. National park, N Italy; 368 sq. m.; alpine region; established 1935.

Stelvio Pass. Mountain pass, Ortler Mts., bet. Italy and Switzerland; 9045 ft.

Ste·nay \stə-ˈnā\. Town, N Meuse dept., NE France, on Meuse river 26 m. NNW of Verdun; pop. (1962c) 3883; an old town, residence of the kings of Austrasia; held by Spanish in middle of 17th cent.; taken by siege by Marshall Fabert for Louis XIV in 1654; last town taken by U.S. forces in World War I, on morning of Armistice Day Nov. 11, 1918.

Sten·dal \ˈs(h)ten-ˌdäl\. Industrial city, Magdeburg dist., East Germany, 32 m. NNE of Magdeburg; pop. (1970e) 36,478; chemicals, metal goods; sugar refining; numerous Gothic buildings. Former capital of the Altmark; first mentioned 1022; chartered c. 1150; member of the Hanseatic League.

Ste·pa·na·kert \ˌstep-ə-nə-ˈk(y)ert\. Town, ✱ of Nagorno-Karabakh Autonomous Oblast, Azerbaijan S.S.R., U.S.S.R., in mountains at edge of Armenian plateau, 62 m. SSE of Kirovabad; pop. (1970p) 30,000.

Ste·phens \ˈstē-vənz\. Name of counties in three states of the U.S. See tables at GEORGIA, OKLAHOMA, TEXAS.

Ste·phen·son \ˈstē-vən-sən\. County in Illinois. See table at ILLINOIS.

Ste·phen·ville \ˈstē-vən-ˌvil\. 1 City, ⊗ of Erath co., N cen. Texas, 60 m. SW of Fort Worth; pop. (1970c) 9277; dairy products; pecans, peanuts, cotton; Tarleton State Coll. (1899).

2 Town on SW coast of Newfoundland, Canada, near head of St. Georges Bay; pop. (1971p) 7723.

Stepnoi. See ELISTA.

Steppes, The \-ˈsteps\. Region, W cen. Asia. See KIRGIZ STEPPE.

Ster·ling \ˈstər-liŋ\. 1 County in Texas. See table at TEXAS.

2 City, ⊗ of Logan co., NE Colorado, on South Platte river 40 m. NE of Fort Morgan; pop. (1970c) 10,636; sugar refining; sugar beets, beans; Northeastern Junior Coll. of Colorado (1941).

3 Industrial city, Whiteside co., NW Illinois, 48 m. SW of Rockford; pop. (1970c) 16,113; wire, builders' hardware, toys, electrical appliances; agriculture.

4 City, Rice co., cen. Kansas, on Arkansas river 20 m. NW of Hutchinson; pop. (1970c) 2312; Sterling Coll. (1887).

5 Town, Worcester co., cen. Massachusetts, 10 m. S of Fitchburg; pop. (1970c) 4247.

6 *or* **Sterling City.** City, ⊗ of Sterling co., W cen. Texas; pop. (1970c) 780; livestock.

Sterling, Mount. Peak, Haywood co., in E Great Smoky Mts., W North Carolina; 5835 ft.

Sterling Heights. City, Macomb co., SE Michigan, 19 m. N of Detroit; pop. (1970c) 61,365.

Sterling Peak. Mountain, S Jackson co., SW Oregon; 7377 ft.

Ster·li·ta·mak \ˌster-li-tə-ˈmak\. Town, S cen. Bashkir A.S.S.R., Russian S.F.S.R., U.S.S.R., on left bank of Belaya river 75 m. S of Ufa; pop. (1970p) 185,000; machinery, soda, cement, flour, leather goods; distilling, oil refining; formerly capital of republic 1919–22.

Štern·berk \ˈshtern-ˌberk\ *or Ger.* **Stern·berg** \ˈstərn-ˌbərg, ˈs(h)tern-ˌbe(ə)rg\. Town, Czech S.R., Czechoslovakia, 10 m. N of Olomouc; pop. (1968e) 12,396.

Stern Park Gardens. See LIDICE 1.

Sterzing. See VIPITENO.

Stettin. See SZCZECIN 2.

Stettiner Haff. See ZALEW SZCZECIŃSKI.

Stett·ler \ˈstet-lər\. Town, Alberta, Canada, 90 m. SSE of Edmonton; pop. (1971p) 4106; agriculture.

Steu·ben \ˈst(y)ü-bən\. Name of counties in two states of the U.S. See tables at INDIANA and NEW YORK.

Steu·ben·ville \ˈst(y)ü-bən-ˌvil\. Industrial city, ⊗ of Jefferson co., E Ohio, on Ohio river 50 m. S of Youngstown; pop. (1970c) 30,771; steel, chemicals, dinnerware, stoves, ferrous alloys; Coll. of Steubenville (1946). Fort Steuben built on site 1786 but abandoned 1790; permanent settlement begun 1797; incorporated 1805.

Ste·ven·age \ˈstē-və-nij\. Urban district, Hertfordshire, SE England, 28 m. N of London; pop. (1971p) 66,918; center of electronics industry.

Ste·vens \ˈstē-vənz\. Counties in three states of the U.S. See tables at KANSAS, MINNESOTA, WASHINGTON.

Stevens Dam. See UNITED STATES, *Dams and Reservoirs.*

Ste·ven·son \ˈstē-vən-sən\. Town, ⊗ of Skamania co., S Washington; pop. (1970c) 916.

Stevenson, Mount. Peak, Yellowstone National Park, NW Wyoming; 10,352 ft.

Stevens Point. City, ⊗ of Portage co., cen. Wisconsin, 30 m. S of Wausau; pop. (1970c) 23,479; paper, furniture, fishing tackle, dairy products; Wisconsin State Coll. at Stevens Point (1894).

Stew·art \'st(y)ü-ərt, 'st(y)u̇(-ə)rt\. 1 Name of counties in two states of the U.S. See tables at GEORGIA and TENNESSEE.

2 River, cen. Yukon Territory, Canada; 331 m. long; flows W in S Klondike region to Yukon river.

Stewart Island. Island, Pacific Ocean S of South I., New Zealand; 675 sq. m.; pop. (1968e) 320; mountainous, forested.

Stewart Islands. Atoll group, 110 m. E of N end of Malaita I., SE cen. Solomon Is., W Pacific Ocean; chief island Sikaiana; no harbor but there is some trade in copra. Scene of U.S. naval victory Oct. 30, 1942.

Stewart Mountain Dam. Dam across Salt river below Mormon Flat Dam, E Maricopa co., S cen. Arizona; height 207 ft.; completed 1936; impounds water for power, forming **Sa·gua·ro Lake** \sə-(ˌ)(g)wär-(ˌ)ō-\ 10 m. long.

Stewart Peak. Mountain, Saguache co., S Colorado; 13,980 ft.

Steyns·burg \'stānz-ˌbərg\. Town, E cen. Cape Province, Rep. of South Africa, 170 m. N of Port Elizabeth; pop. (1967e) 4300; sheep-raising center.

Steyr \'s(h)tī(ə)r\ *also* **Stei·er** \'s(h)tī-ər\. Industrial city, Upper Austria, on Steyr river at its confluence with the Enns 16 m. SSE of Linz; pop. (1961c) 38,306; motor vehicles, sporting firearms, tractors, iron goods; has a medieval center with 15th cent. church and 18th cent. town hall.

Stick·ney \'stik-nē\. Village, Cook co., NE Illinois, W suburb of Chicago; pop. (1970c) 6601.

Stieringen–Wendel. See STIRING-WENDEL.

Stig·ler \'stig-lər\. City, ⊗ of Haskell co., E Oklahoma, 38 m. SSE of Muskogee; pop. (1970c) 2347; coal mines, gas wells; agriculture.

Sti·kine \stik-'ēn\. River, NW British Columbia, Canada, and S Alaska; 335 m. long; rises in Stikine Mts. and flows W and SW through the Coast Mts. and across S Alaska to the Pacific Ocean.

Stikine Mountains. Range, S Yukon and N British Columbia, Canada; ab. 400 m. long; a range of the Rocky Mts.; highest peak Mt. Cushing 8676 ft. in N British Columbia.

Sti·kle·stad \'stik-lə-ˌstä\. Village, Nord-Trøndelag co., N cen. Norway, on Trondheim Fjord NE of Trondheim; scene of battle in which King Olaf II of Norway was killed 1030.

Stil·fon·tein \'stil-ˌfän-ˌtān\. Town, Transvaal, NE Rep. of South Africa, ab. 90 m. SW of Johannesburg; pop. (1967e) 29,800.

Still·wa·ter \'stil-ˌwȯt-ər, -ˌwät-\. 1 County in Montana. See table at MONTANA.

2 City, ⊗ of Washington co., E Minnesota, on St. Croix river 15 m. ENE of St. Paul; pop. (1970c) 10,191; footwear, clothing, flour, boats, plastics.

3 Village, Saratoga co., New York, on W bank of Hudson river ab. 21 m. N of Albany; pop. (1970c) 1428; battle fought ab. 3 m. N in Revolutionary War generally known as the battle of Saratoga. See SARATOGA 3.

4 City, ⊗ of Payne co., N cen. Oklahoma, 42 m. S of Ponca City; pop. (1970c) 31,126, flour, dairy products; packing plants, machine shops, gas wells; Oklahoma State Univ. (1891); founded 1889; incorporated as town 1891.

Stillwater Mountains. Range, cen. Churchill co., W Nevada.

Stil·ton \'stilt-ᵊn\. Parish, Huntingdon and Peterborough co., E cen. England; gives name to cheese now made chiefly in Leicestershire.

Stil·well \'stil-ˌwel, -wəl\. City, ⊗ of Adair co., E Oklahoma, 44 m. E of Muskogee; pop. (1970c) 2134.

Stilwell Road. Former military highway, connecting NE India with K'un-ming, Yunnan prov., China; 1044 m. long.

Stim·son, Mount \-'stim(p)-sən\. Peak, Glacier National Park, NW Montana; 10,182 ft.

Stin·nett \sti-'net\. Town, ⊗ of Hutchinson co., NW Texas; pop. (1970c) 1932; oil wells.

Štip *or* **Shtip** \'shtēp\ *or Turk.* **Ish·tib** *also* **Is·tib** *or* **Is·tip** \ish-'tēp\. Town, Macedonia, SE Yugoslavia, 40 m. SE of Skopje; pop. (1965e) 25,000; an old town, in early times belonging to the Byzantines, later to the Serbs, and Turkish from 1389 to 1913.

Sti·ring–Wen·del \stē-ˌraⁿg-väⁿ-'del\ *or Ger.* **Stie·ring·en–Wendel** \ˌshtir-iŋ-ən-'ven-dᵊl\. Commune, Moselle dept., NE France, 34 m. ENE of Metz; pop. (1968c) 13,757; coal mines.

Stir·ling \'stər-liŋ\. 1 *or* **Stir·ling·shire** \-ˌshi(ə)r, -shər\. County, cen. Scotland; 451 sq. m.; pop. (1971p) 208,956; ⊗ Stirling; rivers Forth, Avon, Endrick, Carron; coal mining, manufacturing (iron, brick, pharmaceuticals and dyes, aluminum; oil refinery), livestock farming; chief towns Stirling, Falkirk, Kilsyth, Grangemouth.

2 Burgh, its ⊗, on the Forth river 36 m. NW of Edinburgh; pop. (1971p) 29,769; food processing, coal mining; Univ. of Stirling (1964). Early medieval castle, birthplace of James II of Scotland; scene of the coronation of infant Mary, Queen of Scots, and James VI of Scotland; battle (also known as Stirling Bridge) Sept. 11, 1297 in which Wallace defeated English under earl of Surrey.

3 Island, one of the Treasury Is. group off S end of Bougainville, Solomon Is., W Pacific Ocean; landing of Americans Oct. 26–27, 1943.

Stirling Range. Mountain range, Papua New Guinea, SE New Guinea I., forming the SE extension of the Owen Stanley Range to the shores of Milne Bay.

Stirling Range National Park. National park, SW Western Australia; 445 sq. m.; mountain range; established 1957.

Stjer·nø·ya \'styar-nə-yə\. Island, Arctic Ocean off NW coast of Norway, in Finnmark co. S of Sørøya I.

Sto·bi \'stō-bē\. Ancient town of Paeonia (in Macedonia after 336 B.C.) dating probably from the 6th cent. B.C.; esp. prominent in Roman times when it was capital of Roman province of Macedonia; destroyed by earthquake 518 A.D. Its ruins not far from Bitola in Macedonia, Yugoslavia.

Stochód. See STOKHOD.

Stock·ach \'s(h)tȯk-ˌäk\. Commune, Baden-Württemberg, West Germany, NW of Konstanz; scene of two battles: Mar. 25, 1799 in which Charles Louis, Archduke of Austria, defeated French under General Jourdan, and May 3, 1800 in which General Moreau defeated the Austrians.

Stock·bridge \'stäk-ˌbrij\. Town, Berkshire co., W Massachusetts, 12 m. S of Pittsfield; pop (1970c) 2312; summer resort in the Berkshire Hills.

Stock·e·rau \'s(h)tȯk-ə-ˌrau̇\. City, Lower Austria, NNW of Vienna on arm of Danube river; pop. (1961c) 11,853; manufactures machinery, chemicals.

Stock·holm \'stäk-ˌhō(l)m\. 1 County of SE Sweden. See table at SWEDEN.

2 Seaport city, ✱ of Sweden, also ⊗ of Stockholm co., on the Baltic Sea; pop. (1970e) 747,490, met. area pop. 1,306,762; largest city in Sweden and its cultural, commercial, and financial center; textiles, paper, rubber, chemicals, beer; shipbuilding, printing, metalworking, food processing. Built on several islands and peninsulas and often called "The Venice of the North." Has numerous notable buildings, including the city hall, Olympic stadium, Ridarkyrka, burial place of the kings and notable men of Sweden, Nobel Institute, national museum, royal palace,

17th cent. cathedral; technical institute (1827), univ. (1877).

History: According to tradition, founded by Birger Jarl c. 1250; reported to have been important town as early as 1288; chief port of Sweden during Middle Ages and allied with Hanseatic League; developed rapidly during 17th cent. and was again extensively redeveloped during industrial growth of 19th cent.

Stock·port \ˈstäk-ˌpō(ə)rt, -ˌpȯ(ə)rt\. County borough, Cheshire, NW England, on the Mersey 6 m. S of Manchester; pop. (1971p) 139,633; textiles, hats, chemicals, machinery; granted first charter 1220.

Stocks·bridge \ˈstäks-ˌbrij\. Urban district, West Riding, Yorkshire, N England; pop. (1971p) 13,400.

Stock·ton \ˈstäk-tən\. 1 Commercial and industrial city, ⊗ of San Joaquin co., cen. California, on San Joaquin river 53 m. E of Oakland; pop. (1970c) 109,963; deepwater port and distributing center for agricultural produce of San Joaquin Valley; grain elevators, creameries, meat-packing plants, fruit and vegetable canneries, shipyards, iron and steel foundries; Univ. of the Pacific (1851), Humphreys Coll. (1896), San Joaquin Delta Coll. (1935). Settled 1848; developed during gold rush; made ⊗ 1850.

2 City, ⊗ of Rooks co., N Kansas; pop. (1970c) 1818.

3 City, ⊗ of Cedar co., W Missouri; pop. (1970c) 1063.

Stockton Islands. See APOSTLE ISLANDS.

Stock·ville \ˈstäk-ˌvil\. Village, ⊗ of Frontier co., S Nebraska; pop. (1970c) 61.

Stod·dard \ˈstäd-ərd\. County in Missouri. See table at MISSOURI.

Sto·er, Point of \-ˈstō(-ə)r\. Cape, NW coast of Scotland, at S entrance to Eddrachillis Bay; lighthouse.

Stoke, East \-ˈstōk\ *also* **Stoke.** Village, Nottinghamshire, N cen. England, near Newark; scene of battle June 16, 1487 in which Lambert Simnel the pretender was defeated by Henry VII.

Stoke–on–Trent \-ˈtrent\. City and county borough, Staffordshire, W cen. England, 38 m. N of Birmingham; pop. (1971p) 265,153; center of the Staffordshire pottery-making industry; coal mining, brick making. Home of several of the pioneers in the pottery industry: Josiah Wedgewood (see BURSLEM), Josiah Spode, Herbert Minton. See POTTERIES, THE.

Stoke Po·ges \stōk-ˈpō-jəs, -jəz\. Parish, Eton rural district, Buckinghamshire, SE cen. England; pop. (1961c) 3886; generally considered the scene of Gray's "Elegy."

Stokes \ˈstōks\. 1 County in North Carolina. See table at NORTH CAROLINA.

2 Peak in Andes Mts., S Chile, near Argentina border and E of Hanover I.; 7020 ft.

Sto·khod \ˈstȯ-kət\ *or Pol.* **Sto·chód** \-küt\. River, NW Ukrainian S.S.R., U.S.S.R.; ab. 90 m. long; flows into Pripyat river from the S; formerly in Poland; battles on its banks in 1916.

Stol·berg \ˈs(h)tȯl-ˌbe(ə)rg\ *also* **Stolberg im Rhein·land** \-im-ˈrīn-ˌlänt\. City, North Rhine-Westphalia, West Germany, on Belgian border 7 m. E of Aachen; pop. (1969e) 39,393; glass, textiles, chemicals, soap, furniture, beer; first mentioned 1118.

Stol·bo·vo *or* **Stol·bo·va** \stəl-ˈbȯ-və\. Village, Leningrad Oblast, NW Russian S.F.S.R., U.S.S.R., near S end of Lake Ladoga; by terms of treaty signed here June 1617, ending war bet. Russia and Sweden, Russia cut off from Baltic Sea.

Stoll·berg \ˈs(h)tȯl-ˌbe(ə)rg\ *also* **Stollberg im Erz·ge·bir·ge** \-im-ˈerts-gə-ˌbir-gə\. City, Karl-Marx-Stadt dist., East Germany, 10 m. SW of Karl-Marx-Stadt; pop. (1970e) 12,751.

Stolp. See SŁUPSK.

Stolpe. See SŁUPIA.

Stone \ˈstōn\. 1 Name of counties in three states of the U.S. See tables at ARKANSAS, MISSISSIPPI, MISSOURI.

2 Urban district, Staffordshire, W cen. England; pop. (1971p) 10,985.

Stone·ham \ˈstōn-əm\. Residential town, Middlesex co., NE Massachusetts, 9 m. N of Boston; pop. (1970c) 20,275.

Stone·ha·ven \ˈstōn-ˌhā-vən\. Seaport burgh, ⊗ of Kincardine co., E Scotland; pop. (1969e) 4573.

Stone·henge \ˈstōn-ˌhenj\. An assemblage of standing stones, Salisbury Plain, 7 m. N of Salisbury, England; originally in two concentric circles enclosing two rows of smaller stones. Much uncertainty exists as to its origin and purpose; probably dates back to the Bronze Age in Britain.

Stone Mountain. 1 Massive monadnock of gray granite, De Kalb co., NW cen. Georgia, near Atlanta; 1686 ft. high; Confederate memorial carved on the NE wall of the mountain; work began 1917 and continued 1923–25 by Gutzon Borglum; after Borglum's dismissal work taken up by Augustus Lukeman 1925; completed 1967.

2 Peak, Carter co., NE Tennessee; 3500 ft.

Stone Park. Village, Cook co., NE Illinois 15 m. W of Chicago; pop. (1970c) 4451.

Stones River \ˈstōnz-\. River, Tennessee; 60 m. long; formed by confluence of East Fork and West Fork in N Rutherford co., flows N into Cumberland river E of Nashville; on West Fork near Murfreesboro occurred battle (also known as battle of Murfreesboro, *q.v.*) Dec. 31, 1862–Jan. 2, 1863, a drawn contest but strategic victory for Union forces; site of battle has been set aside as **Stones River National Battlefield Site** (see UNITED STATES, *National Historical Parks*).

Stone·wall \ˈstōn-ˌwäl\. 1 County in Texas. See table at TEXAS.

2 Village, Gillespie co., cen. Texas, on Pedernales river; birthplace of Lyndon B. Johnson, 36th president of the U.S., nearby.

Ston·ey Creek \ˈstō-nē-\. Town, Wentworth co., SE Ontario, Canada, at W end of Lake Ontario; pop. (1971p) 8364; scene of battle June 6, 1813 in which the British under General Vincent defeated the Americans under Generals Chandler and Winder.

Ston·ing·ton \ˈstō-niŋ-tən\. Town, SE New London co., SE Connecticut, on Long Island Sound E of Groton; pop. (1970c) 15,940; precision tools, velvets, boats; agriculture; settled 1649; incorporated 1801. Includes (1) borough of Stonington; pop. (1970c) 1413; incorporated 1801 (first such incorporation in Connecticut); formerly important fishing port; attacked by British 1775 and 1812; (2) Mystic (*q.v.*).

Stony Creek \ˈstō-nē-\. River, S Pennsylvania; flows N from Somerset co. to unite with the Little Conemaugh river at Johnstown and form the Conemaugh.

Stony Man Mountain. Peak, Shenandoah National Park, Page co., N Virginia; 4011 ft.

Stony Mountain. Peak in the Catskill Mts., SE New York; 3844 ft.

Stony Point. 1 Point, W cen. coast of Jefferson co., N New York, extending into Lake Ontario SW of Sackets Harbor.

2 Village, Rockland co., SE New York; pop. (1970c) 8270; named from a rocky promontory on the Hudson; in Revolutionary War an American blockhouse 1776–79; taken by British May 31, 1779 and converted into a strong fort; taken by Gen. Anthony Wayne July 15–16, 1779; evacuated as untenable July 18.

Stony Tunguska. See TUNGUSKA.

Stor \ˈstȯ(ə)r\. River, NW cen. Jutland penin., Denmark; ab. 55 m. long; flows W into North Sea.

Sto·ra Sjö·fall·et \ˌstü(ə)r-ə-ˈshər-ˌfal-ət\. Waterfall, upper Luleålv river, N Sweden; 131 ft.

Stor·a·van \ˈstü(ə)r-ˌäv-ən\. Lake, Västerbotten co., N Sweden; 62 sq. m.; drained by Skellefte river.

Stord \ˈstü(ə)rd\. Island in Hordaland co., off SW coast of Norway, ab. 30 m. S of Bergen; 92 sq. m.

Store Sotra. See SOTRA.

Sto·rey \ˈstōr-ē, ˈstȯr-\. County in Nevada. See table at NEVADA.

Stor Fjord \'stu̇(ə)r-ˌfyu̇(ə)r\. 1 Fjord, Svalbard; separates the main island of Spitsbergen, Norway, from Barents I. and Edge I.

2 Inlet of the Norwegian Sea, W coast of Norway; extends inland over 70 m., E of Ålesund.

Stor·foss \'stu̇(ə)r-ˌfȯs\. Rapids in the Tana river, NE Norway, ab. 45 m. from its mouth.

Storm Bay \'stȯ(ə)rm-\. Large inlet of South Pacific Ocean, SE Tasmania, Australia, bet. Tasman Penin. and Bruny I.; receives Derwent river.

Storm·berg \'stȯ(ə)rm-ˌbərg\. 1 Mountain range, NE Cape Province, Rep. of South Africa.

2 Village, N Cape Province, Rep. of South Africa, S of Burgersdorp; scene of battle Dec. 10, 1899 in which the Boers defeated the English.

Storm King. Mountain in Highlands of the Hudson, SE New York, overlooking Hudson river on W bank N of West Point; 1355 ft.

Storm King Peak. Mountain, San Juan co., SW Colorado; 13,749 ft.

Storm Lake. 1 Lake, S Buena Vista co., NW Iowa.

2 City, ⊗ of Buena Vista co., NW Iowa, 20 m. ESE of Cherokee; pop. (1970c) 8591; canned goods, dairy products, plastics; Buena Vista Coll. (1891).

Stor·mont \'stȯ(ə)r-ˌmänt\. 1 County, SE Ontario, Canada. See table at ONTARIO.

2 Seat of government of Northern Ireland, 4 m. E of Belfast; parliament building (1928) situated in 300-acre estate.

Storms, Cape of. See GOOD HOPE, CAPE OF.

Stormy Mountain \'stȯr-mē-\. Peak, Chelan co., cen. Washington; 7219 ft.

Stor·no·way \'stȯr-nə-ˌwā\. Seaport burgh, Ross and Cromarty co., N Scotland, on Lewis with Harris I.; pop. (1971p) 5247; chief town of Lewis with Harris; manufactures tweed.

Storrs \'stȯ(ə)rz\. Subdivision (pop. [1970c] 10,691) of town of Mansfield, Connecticut; Univ. of Connecticut (1881). See MANSFIELD 1.

Stor·sjön \'stu̇(ə)r-ˌshərn\. Lake, Jämtland co., W Sweden; 176 sq. m.; Östersund is on its E shore.

Stor·strøm \'stȯr-strəm\. County, Denmark; incl. S part of Sjælland I., Lolland I., Falster I., and Møn I. See table at DENMARK.

Stor·strøm·me Glacier \'stȯr-ˌstrəm-ə-\. Glacier, Greenland; 81 m. long, ab. 18 m. wide near its terminus.

Stort \'stȯ(ə)rt\. River, Essex and Hertfordshire, SE England; 22 m. long; flows S and SW to the Lea at Hoddesdon.

Stor·u·man \'stu̇(ə)r-ˌü-mən\. Lake, Västerbotten co., N Sweden; 64 sq. m.; drained by Ume river.

Sto·ry \'stōr-ē, 'stȯr-ē\. County in Iowa. See table at IOWA.

Stouff·ville \'stō-ˌvil\. Village, York co., SE Ontario, Canada, 21 m. NE of Toronto; pop. (1968e) 3906; diversified agriculture; planing mills, fish hatcheries.

Stough·ton \'stōt-ᵊn\. 1 Town, Norfolk co., E Massachusetts, 5 m. NW of Brockton; pop. (1970c) 23,549; woolens, footwear, plastics, machine tools.

2 City, Dane co., S Wisconsin, 14 m. SSE of Madison; pop. (1970c) 6096; vehicle bodies, dairy products.

Stour \'stau̇(ə)r, 'stu̇(ə)r, 'stō(ə)r\. 1 River, SE England; 47 m. long; flows bet. Essex and Suffolk cos. and into North Sea at Harwich.

2 River, S England; 55 m. long; flows across Dorsetshire from NW to SE, enters Hampshire, and empties into the Avon at Christchurch.

3 River, Kent, SE England; 40 m. long; flows NE past Canterbury and empties into North Sea through two arms which cut off the island of Thanet; navigable as far as Canterbury.

4 River, cen. England; 20 m. long; rises in Oxfordshire and flows NW to the Avon $1^1/_2$ m. SW of Stratford-upon-Avon, Warwickshire.

5 River, W cen. England; 20 m. long; flows S in Staffordshire and Worcestershire past Kidderminster and into the Severn at Stourport.

Stour·bridge \'stau̇(ə)r-(ˌ)brij, 'stu̇(ə)r-, 'stō(ə)r-\. Municipal borough, Worcestershire, W cen. England, on the Stour 11 m. W of Birmingham; pop. (1971p) 54,331; glass, tools, leather goods.

Stour·port–on–Sev·ern \'stau̇(ə)r-ˌpō(ə)rt . . . 'sev-ərn; 'stu̇(ə)r-, 'stō(ə)r-, -'pȯ(ə)rt\. Urban district, Worcestershire, W cen. England; pop. (1971p) 17,913.

Stow \'stō\. 1 Town, Middlesex co., NE Massachusetts, 22 m. NW of Boston; pop. (1970c) 3984.

2 City, Summit co., NE Ohio, NE of Akron; pop. (1970c) 19,847.

Stowe \'stō\. Urban area, Montgomery co., SE Pennsylvania, NW of Philadelphia; pop. (1970c) 3596.

Stowey, Nether. See NETHER STOWEY.

Stra·bane \strə-'ban\. Urban district, N co. Tyrone, W cen. Northern Ireland, on Mourne and Finn rivers; pop. (1969e) 9040; linens.

Strad·broke \'strad-ˌbrōk\. Island off SE coast of Queensland, Australia; ab. 64 m. long; encloses part of Moreton Bay.

Straf·ford \'straf-ərd\. County in New Hampshire. See table at NEW HAMPSHIRE.

Stra·han \'strō-ən\. Town, W Tasmania, Australia, at N end of Macquarie Harbour; pop. (1970e) 430; in mining region.

Strahl·horn \'s(h)träl-ˌhȯ(ə)rn\. Peak in the Pennine Alps, Switzerland, N of Monte Rosa; 13,750 ft.

Straits, The \-'strāts\. 1 Name formerly used specifically to designate the Strait of Gibraltar (*q.v.*); later the Strait of Malacca.

2 The link bet. the Mediterranean and Black seas, including the Bosporus and Dardanelles (*qq.v.*), to which the name came to be applied when with Russian expansion to the Black Sea the "Straits Question," the issue of fortification by Ottoman Empire and of terms of passage bet. Black Sea and Mediterranean, became a problem in European diplomacy; opened to passage of Russian vessels 1774; by Straits Convention (1841), basic settlement of 19th cent., the five great powers agreed to principle of closing Straits to foreign war vessels; after closure to merchant vessels in World War I 1914, became object of Allies to reopen Straits in Dardanelles campaign 1915; occupied by Allies 1918 (see ZONE OF THE STRAITS); by terms of Treaty of Lausanne 1923, demilitarized and placed under supervision of international commission, actually controlled by Turkey; remilitarized by Turkey as provided by Convention of Montreux 1936; special rights in control demanded by U.S.S.R. 1946–47.

Straits Settlements. Former British crown colony, on S and W coast of Malay Penin., incl. adjacent islands, comprising Singapore, Penang, and Malacca settlements.

History: United 1826 under one government as a presidency of India with capital at Penang; incorporated under Bengal 1830; capital removed to Singapore 1836; taken from control of Indian government 1867 and placed under direct British control; after 1886 Cocos Is., Christmas I., and Labuan brought under control of Governor of Straits Settlements and later incorporated in the Colony, although Labuan was constituted a separate settlement 1912; under Japanese control 1941–45; Cocos Is. and Christmas I. ceded to Australia 1955 and 1958 respectively; Penang and Malacca made states of independent Federation of Malaya 1957, becoming states of Malaysia (*q.v.*) 1963; Singapore made a separate colony 1946, part of Malaysia 1963–65, independent republic 1965.

Stral·sund \'s(h)träl-ˌzu̇nt, -ˌsu̇nt\. Industrial city, Rostock dist., East Germany, on the Strelasund opp. Rügen I. in the Baltic; pop. (1970e) 71,551; beer, pipe, furniture, preserves; shipbuilding, fish-processing; 13th cent. church of St. Mary, 13th cent. town hall.

History: Chartered as city 1234; member of Hanseatic League; besieged by Wallenstein 1628; repeatedly changed hands (1678, 1715, 1720, 1807, 1814) until it passed to Prussia 1815; suffered considerable damage in World War II.

Strand \'strand\. Town, SW Cape Province, S Rep. of South Africa, on NE shore of False Bay adjoining Somerset West; pop. (1967e) 21,200; seaside resort.

Strang·ford Lough \ˌstraŋ-fərd-'läk, -'läk\. Inlet of Irish Sea, E coast of Northern Ireland; extends N inland ab. 19 m. in co. Down.

Stran·raer \stran-'rär\. Seaport burgh, Wigtown co., SW Scotland, at head of Loch Ryan; pop. (1971p) 9853; market town; flour mills, fisheries.

Stras·bourg \'sträs-ˌbu̇(ə)rg, 'sträz-\ *or Ger.* **Strass·burg** \'s(h)träs-ˌbu̇(ə)rg\ *or anc.* **Ar·gen·to·ra·tum** \är-ˌjen-tə-'rāt-əm\. Industrial and commercial city, ✱ of Bas-Rhin dept., NE France, on the Ill river ab. 2 m. W of its confluence with the Rhine, 83 m. SE of Metz; pop. (1968c) 249,396; important transportation center and major river port; produces pâté de foie gras, synthetic textiles, metal goods, beer, leather products; printing, food processing, oil refining; episcopal see; seat of Council of Europe. Numerous notable buildings, including 10th–14th cent. cathedral with noted 14th cent. astronomical clock, chamber of commerce, governor's palace, town hall, museums, former episcopal palace; univ. (founded 1537, univ. status 1621).

History: Important from ancient times because of strategic location; a Celtic settlement; passed to Romans; destroyed by Attila; in late 5th cent. restored by Franks; in 842 scene of Oath of Strasbourg; linked to Germany through homage of Duke of Lorraine to Henry I 923; attained status of free imperial city 1262; some work done here by Gutenberg on movable type c. 1436; occupied by French 1681 and formally ceded 1697; under German rule 1871–1918; in World War II occupied by Germans June 1940–Nov. 1944 and suffered considerable damage.

Strassburg. 1 City, France. See STRASBOURG.
2 Town, Romania. See AIUD.

Strata Flor·i·da \ˌstrat-ə-'flȯr-ə-də\ *or Welsh* **Ys·trad Fflur** \ˌəs-träd-'fli(ə)r\. Ruins of Cistercian abbey, Cardiganshire, W Wales, SE of Aberystwyth near the Teifi river; flourished 12th cent., destroyed by fire at end of 13th cent.; few ruins.

Stratfield. See BRIDGEPORT 3.

Strat·ford \'strat-fərd\. 1 Industrial and residential town, SE Fairfield co., SW Connecticut, on Long Island Sound at mouth of Housatonic river E of Bridgeport; pop. (1970c) 49,775; aircraft and helicopters, chemicals, rubber goods, hardware, forgings, boats, roofing materials; truck farms; Housatonic Community Coll. (1966); settled 1639.
2 Borough, Camden co. SW New Jersey, 9 m. SSE of Camden; pop. (1970c) 9801.
3 Town, ⊗ of Sherman co., NW Texas; pop. (1970c) 2139.
4 Estate, Westmoreland co., E Virginia, on Potomac river near George Washington Birthplace National Monument; birthplace of Robert E. Lee.
5 City, ⊗ of Perth co., SE Ontario, Canada, 28 m. W of Kitchener; pop. (1971p) 23,863; furniture, brass, leather and rubber goods; railroad shops; diversified agriculture; founded 1832.
6 Borough, W North I., New Zealand; pop. (1970e) 5510.

Stratford–upon–Avon \-'ā-vən\. Municipal borough, Warwickshire, cen. England, 21 m. SSE of Birmingham; pop. (1971p) 19,449; tourism; birthplace and burial place of William Shakespeare.

Strath·aird Point \ˌstrath-ˌa(ə)rd-, -ˌe(ə)rd-\. Cape, S coast of Skye I., Inner Hebrides, off NW coast of Scotland, projecting into Cuillin Sound.

Strath·clyde \strath-'klīd\. Medieval Celtic kingdom of Scotland, S of the Clyde river; ✱ Dumbarton; established 6th cent.; threatened and ravaged by Picts and Norsemen 8th and 9th cents.; suffered defeat by English at Brunanburh 937 and also in 945–946; added to Scottish kingdom by Malcolm II (king 1005–34); S part known as Cumbria (*q.v.*).

Strathcona. See EDMONTON 2.

Strath·co·na Park \strath-ˌkō-nə-\. Provincial park, cen. Vancouver I., British Columbia, Canada; 829 sq. m.; alpine area; a game sanctuary and fishing resort.

Strath·more \strath-'mō(ə)r, -'mȯ(ə)r\. Valley of cen. Scotland, S of the Grampian Mts.

Strath·roy \strath-'rȯi\. Town, Middlesex co., SE Ontario, Canada, 22 m. W of London; pop. (1971p) 6594; stoves, canned goods; potatoes, fruit.

Stratton and Bude. See BUDE-STRATTON.

Strat·ton Mountain \'strat-ən-\. Peak, W Windham co., SE Vermont; 3859 ft.

Stra·tus \'strāt-əs, 'strat-\. Chief town of ancient Acarnania, W Greece, on W bank of the Achelous river.

Strau·bing \'s(h)trau̇-biŋ\. Industrial city, Bavaria, West Germany, on the Danube river 23 m. ESE of Regensberg; pop. (1969e) 37,024; beer, hats, tiles, electrical equipment; 12th cent. church, two 15th cent. churches; Roman settlement on site; present town founded 1218.

Straus·berg \'strau̇s-ˌbərg, 's(h)trau̇s-ˌbe(ə)rg\. City, Frankfurt dist., East Germany, 33 m. NW of Frankfurt an der Oder; pop. (1970e) 19,507; shoes, furniture.

Straw·ber·ry \'strȯ-ˌber-ē, -b(ə-)rē\. River, N cen. Utah; ab. 60 m. long; rises in Wasatch co., flows E into Duchesne river in cen. Duchesne co.

Strawberry Mountain. Mountain, Grant co., E cen. Oregon; 9038 ft.

Strawberry Point. Northeast point of Plymouth co., E Massachusetts, E of Hingham; marks the S limit of Massachusetts Bay.

Stream·wood \'strēm-ˌwu̇d\. Village, Cook co., NE Illinois, 7 m. ESE of Elgin; pop. (1970c) 18,176.

Strea·tor \'strēt-ər\. City, La Salle and Livingston cos., N Illinois, 50 m. NE of Peoria; pop. (1970c) 15,600; building materials, canned goods; railroad shops.

Street Mountain \'strēt-\. Peak in the Adirondack Mts., Essex co., NE New York; 4216 ft.

Streets·ville \'strēts-ˌvil\. Town, Peel co., SE Ontario, Canada, 20 m. W of Toronto; pop. (1971p) 6833; radio parts, margarine; brickyards.

Streheln. See STRZELIN.

Stre·la·sund \'s(h)trā-lə-ˌzu̇nt\. Strait bet. Rügen I. and the mainland, Rostock dist., East Germany; ab. 1½ m. wide and 15–20 m. long; Stralsund is on its W shore.

Stre·sa \'strā-zə\. Town, W shore of Lake Maggiore, Novara prov., NE Piedmont, NW Italy; pop. (1968e) 5100; resort; scene of conference bet. representatives of 15 nations Sept. 5–20, 1932 during which recommendations for economic collaboration of European countries were decided upon and submitted to the Commission of Inquiry for European Union; scene of conference bet. representatives of France, Great Britain, and Italy Apr. 11–14, 1935 in effort to show united opposition to the rearmament of Germany.

Stret·ford \'stret-fərd\. Municipal borough, Lancashire, NW England, 4 m. SW of Manchester; pop. (1971p) 54,011; industrial community.

Strick·land \'strik-lənd\. River, main tributary of the Fly river, Papua New Guinea, New Guinea I.; ab. 225 m. long; rises in mountains of cen. part of the island and flows S and SW through large swamp area to join the Fly on E ab. in the middle of its course.

Striegau. See STRZEGOM.

Strip·ed Mountain \ˌstrī-pəd-, 'strīp(t)-\. Peak in Sierra Nevada, E Fresno co., S cen. California; 13,160 ft.

Strofádhes. See STROPHADES.

Strom·bo·li \'sträm-bə-(,)lē\. 1 *or anc.* **Stron·gy·le** \'strän-jə-,lē\. Island, Lipari Is. (*q.v.*).

2 Active volcano, Stromboli I.; 3038 ft.; erupted 1966.

Strom·lo, Mount \-'sträm-(,)lō\. Elevation, Australian Capital Territory, SE Australia, 7 m. W of Canberra; astronomical observatory (74-inch telescope) of Australian National Univ.

Strømø \'strər-,mər\. Largest island of the Faeroes (*q.v.*); 28 m. long; area 151 sq. m.; pop. (1966c) 14,078; chief town Thorshavn.

Strongs·ville \'strȯŋz-,vil\. Village, Cuyahoga co., N Ohio, 14 m. SSW of Cleveland; pop. (1970c) 15,182.

Strongyle. See STROMBOLI 1.

Stron·say \'strän-(,)sā\. One of the Orkney Is. off N coast of Scotland; 7¼ m. long; site of a well whose water was once believed to cure leprosy.

Stroph·a·des \'strȯf-ə-,dēz\ *or Gk.* **Stro·fá·dhes** \strȯ-'fä-thās\. Two small islands, Ionian Sea, S of Zante and ab. 30 m. W of Peloponnesus, Greece.

Stroud \'strau̇d\. 1 City, Lincoln co., cen. Oklahoma, 34 m. NNE of Shawnee; pop. (1970c) 2502.

2 Urban district, Gloucestershire, SW cen. England, on Thames and Severn canal 8 m. S of Gloucester; pop. (1971p) 19,125; textile weaving and dyeing.

Strouds·burg \'strau̇dz-,bərg\. Borough, ⊗ of Monroe co., E Pennsylvania, 30 m. NNE of Allentown; pop. (1970c) 5451; in Blue Mts. region near the Delaware Water Gap and the Pocono foothills; site of Fort Penn (1776).

Stru·ma \'strü-mə\ *or Gk.* **Stry·mon** \'strī-(,)mȯn, strē-'mȯn\. River, SW Bulgaria and N Greece; 215 m. long; rises SW of Sofia, flows S and SE through Lake Akhinou into the Strymonic Gulf (Aegean Sea).

Strum·ble Head \,strəm-bəl-\. Cape, N side of SW projection of Wales, NE of St. David's Head; lighthouse.

Stru·mi·ca \'strü-mət-,sä\ *or* **Stru·mi·tsa** \-mət-,sä\ *also* **Strum·ni·tza** \'strüm-nit-sä\. 1 River, SE Yugoslavia and SW Bulgaria; ab. 50 m. long; flows E into the Struma river.

2 Town, Macedonia, SE Yugoslavia, on Strumica river ab. 75 m. SE of Skopje; pop. (1965e) 18,000; passed from Turkish rule to Bulgarian 1913, and to Yugoslavia 1919; battlefield in the Balkan Wars and in World War I.

Strumnitza. See STRUMICA.

Struth·ers \'strəth-ərz\. City, Mahoning co., NE Ohio, on Mahoning river 5 m. SE of Youngstown; pop. (1970c) 15,543; iron and steel products.

Stry \'strē\ *or Pol.* **Stryj** \'strē\. 1 River, W Ukrainian S.S.R., U.S.S.R.; 143 m. long; flows from the Carpathian Mts. NE to the Dniester river S of Lvov.

2 City, Lvov Oblast, SW Ukrainian S.S.R., U.S.S.R., on Stry river 44 m. NW of Ivano-Frankovsk; pop. (1967e) 46,000; center of lumber industry; formerly in Poland; in World War I Russians driven back by Germans May–June 1915.

Strymon. See STRUMA.

Stry·mon·ic Gulf \strī-,män-ik-\ *or* **Gulf of Ren·di·na** \-ren-'dē-nə\ *or* **Gulf of Or·fa·ni** \-ȯr-'fän-ē\. Inlet of Aegean Sea, NE coast of Greece, NE of Chalcidice Penin.; receives the Struma river.

Stry·pa \'strip-ə\. River, SW Ukrainian S.S.R., U.S.S.R.; ab. 60 m. long; a tributary of the Dniester river bet. Ternopol and Ivano-Frankovsk; battle along its course July 1917. Formerly in SE Poland.

Strze·gom \'scheg-,ȯm\ *or Ger.* **Strie·gau** \'s(h)trē-(,)gau̇\. City, cen. Wrocław prov., SW Poland, 31 m. WSW of Wrocław; pop. (1968e) 14,100; granite quarrying; manufactures paper; formerly in Germany; assigned to Poland by Potsdam Conference 1945.

Strzel·ce Opol·skie \,schelt-sə-ȯ-'pȯl-skyə\ *or Ger.* **Gross Streh·litz** \'grōs-'s(h)trā-(,)lits\. Town, Opole prov., SW Poland, ab. 18 m. SE of Opole; pop. (1968e) 14,600.

Strze·lin \'schel-(,)ēn\ *or Ger.* **Streh·len** \'s(h)trā-lən\. City, SE Wrocław prov., SW Poland, 22 m. S of Wrocław; pop. (1966c) 9489; formerly in Germany; assigned to Poland by Potsdam Conference 1945.

Stu·art \'st(y)ü-ərt, 'st(y)u̇(-ə)rt\. 1 City, ⊗ of Martin co., SE Florida, on S end of Indian river 37 m. N of West Palm Beach; pop. (1970c) 4820; yachting and fishing resort.

2 Town, Adair and Guthrie cos., SW cen. Iowa, 40 m. W of Des Moines; pop. (1970c) 1354.

3 Town, ⊗ of Patrick co., S Virginia; pop. (1970c) 947.

4 Town, Australia. See ALICE SPRINGS.

5 River, British Columbia, Canada; 258 m. long; flows from Stuart Lake SE into Nechako river.

Stuart, Mount. Peak, SW Chelan co., cen. Washington; 9470 ft.

Stuart Lake. Lake, cen. British Columbia, Canada; 139 sq. m.; drains SE through Stuart river.

Stu·arts Range \'st(y)ü-ərts-, 'st(y)u̇(-ə)rts-\ *or* **Stuart Range.** Range of hills, N cen. South Australia, W of Lake Eyre and NW of Lake Torrens.

Stuhlweissenburg. See SZÉKESFEHÉRVÁR.

Stumpy Point \,stəm-pē-\. Cape, NW St. Thomas I., Virgin Is. of the U.S., at W entrance to Santa Maria Bay.

Stu·pi·no \'stü-pi-nə\ *or formerly* **Elek·tro·voz** \e-,l(y)ek-trə-'vȯz\. Town, Moscow Oblast, Russian S.F.S.R., U.S.S.R., ab. 60 m. SSE of Moscow; pop. (1969e) 54,000.

Stu·ra di De·mon·te \,stu̇r-ə-dē-dā-'mȯnt-ā\. River, Piedmont, NW Italy; 44 m. long; flows E and NE into Tanaro river.

Stur·bridge \'stər-(,)brij\. Industrial town, Worcester co., cen. Massachusetts, 18 m. SW of Worcester; pop. (1970c) 4878.

Stur·geon \'stər-jən\. River, SE Ontario, Canada; 110 m. long; rises in E Ontario, flows SSE into Lake Nipissing.

Sturgeon Bay. City, ⊗ of Door co., NE Wisconsin, on Sturgeon Bay, an inlet of Green Bay, 38 m. NE of Green Bay (city); pop. (1970c) 6776; canal connects Green Bay with Lake Michigan; vacation resort; shipyard, fruit packing plant; grows cherries.

Sturgeon Falls. Town, Nipissing dist., SE Ontario, Canada, on N shore of Lake Nipissing 25 m. W of North Bay; pop. (1971p) 6661.

Stur·gis \'stər-jəs\. 1 City, St. Joseph co., S Michigan, 35 m. S of Kalamazoo; pop. (1970c) 9295; furniture; lake resort.

2 City, ⊗ of Meade co., W South Dakota, in Black Hills 8 m. ENE of Lead; pop. (1970c) 4536; lumber, dairy products; grain farms.

Stur·te·vant \'stər-tə-vənt\. Village, Racine co., SE Wisconsin, 7 m. W of Racine; pop. (1970c) 3376.

Stuts·man \'stəts-mən\. County in North Dakota. See table at NORTH DAKOTA.

Stut·ter·heim \'stət-ər-,hīm\. Town, SE Cape Province, S Rep. of South Africa, ab. 40 m. NW of East London; pop. (1967e) 10,600.

Stutt·gart. 1 \'stət-,gärt, -gərt\. City, a ⊗ of Arkansas co., E Arkansas, 33 m. NE of Pine Bluff; pop. (1970c) 10,477; footwear; rice, oats.

2 \'s(h)tu̇t-,gärt, 'stət-\. Industrial city, ✻ of Baden-Württemberg, West Germany, on Neckar river 38 m. ESE of Karlsruhe; pop. (1970c) 633,158; transportation and industrial center, producing electrical equipment, motor vehicles, machinery, textiles, chemicals, footwear, paper, musical instruments, beer; publishing center; 12th–13th cent. church; two universities (1967). Residence of Hegel. Founded as fortified manor c. 950; developed into town c. 1254; became capital of dukes of Württemberg 1495 and of kingdom of Württemberg 1806; seat of Reichstag and National Assembly at time of Kapp putsch 1920; in World War II heavily bombed and occupied by French troops Apr. 22, 1945.

Stym·pha·lis \stim-ˈfā-ləs\; *Gk.* **Stym·fa·li·as** \ˌstēm-fäl-ˈyē-äs\ *also* **Za·ra·ka** \ˌzär-ə-ˈkä\. Lake, NE Peloponnesus, Greece; in ancient Arcadia; in Greek mythology the scene of the slaying by Hercules of the man-eating (Stymphalian) birds.

Styr \ˈsti(ə)r\. River, NW Ukrainian S.S.R., U.S.S.R.; 271 m. long; flows N into Pripyat river in the Polesye Marshes, W of the Goryn; battle line in World War I; formerly in E Poland.

Styr·ia \ˈstir-ē-ə\ *or Ger.* **Stei·er·mark** \ˈs(h)tī(ə)r-ˌmärk\. State, Austria; 6326 sq. m.; pop. (1971p) 1,191,000; ✱ Graz; mountainous part of cen. and SE Austria watered by the Mur, Mürz, and Enns rivers; chief towns Graz, Leoben, and Bruck. In 9th cent. a part of Carinthia under Charlemagne; became separate as a mark 1085; became a duchy 1180; came under the Hapsburgs 1246.

Styx \ˈstiks\. Short stream, Achaea and Elis depts., NW Peloponnesus, Greece; flows N to Gulf of Corinth; associated to some extent in Greek geography with the mythological Styx of the underworld.

Sua·kin \ˈswäk-ən\ *or* **Sua·kim** \-im\. Seaport on Red Sea, E Kassala prov., NE Sudan, S of Port Sudan.

Sual \ˈswäl\ *or* **Port Sual.** Municipality, NW Pangasinan prov., Luzon, Phil., port on small harbor at SW corner of Lingayen Gulf ab. 11 m. W of Lingayen; pop. (1969e) 12,900; at W end of U.S. troop landings Jan. 14, 1945.

Su·bang *or Du.* **Soe·bang** \ˈsü-ˌbäŋ\. Town, West Java prov., Indonesia, ab. 25 m. NNE of Bandung; pop. (1961c) 33,649.

Su·bar·na·re·kha \sủ-ˌbər-nə-ˈrāk-ə\. River, Bihar and West Bengal, NE India; ab. 290 m. long; flows SE into Bay of Bengal SW of the mouth of the Hooghly river and NE of Balasore.

Su·ba·sio, Mon·te \ˌmȯnt-ē-sü-ˈbäz-ē-ˌō\. Mountain in cen. Apennines, Umbria, cen. Italy; 4232 ft.; town of Assisi is located on S slope of a W spur.

Sub·han Dağ·la·rı \süp-ˌhän-ˌdä(g)-lä-ˈrē\. Mountain range, E Turkey, N of Lake Van; highest point 14,547 ft.

Su·bi·a·co \ˌsü-bē-ˈä-(ˌ)kō\. Municipality, SW Western Australia, W suburb of Perth; pop. (1966c) 16,600.

Su·bia·co \sủ-ˈbyä-(ˌ)kō\. Commune, Roma prov., W Latium, cen. Italy, 50 m. E of Rome; pop. (1968e) 8855; site of first monastery founded by St. Benedict c. 505; first printing press in Italy set up here 1464.

Su·bic \ˈsü-bik\ *or* **Su·big** \-big\. Municipality, S Zambales prov., Luzon, Phil., at head of Subic Bay (*q.v.*) 35 m. SSE of Iba; pop. (1969e) 17,900; one of the two harbors (see OLONGAPO) on Subic Bay.

Subic Bay *or* **Subig Bay.** Inlet of South China Sea, S Zambales prov., Luzon, Phil.; ab. 7 m. long; affords protected anchorage 35 m. N of entrance to Manila Bay. Its SE shore is part of Bataan prov.; mouth divided by small Grande I. U.S. naval base established here 1901; seized by Japanese Jan. 1942; retaken by U.S. forces Jan. 29, 1945.

Sub·lette \sə-ˈblet\. 1 County in Wyoming. See table at WYOMING.

2 City, ⊗ of Haskell co., SW Kansas; pop. (1970c) 1208.

Su·bo·ti·ca \ˈsü-bə-ˌtēt-sə\ *or* **Su·bo·ti·tsa** \-ˌtēt-sə\ *or Hung.* **Sza·bad·ka** \ˈsä-bäd-ˌkä\ *or Ger.* **Ma·ria–The·re·si·o·pel** \mä-ˌrē-ə-te-ˌrā-zē-ˈō-pəl\. City, Serbia, NE Yugoslavia, near Hungarian frontier ab. 100 m. NW of Belgrade; pop. (1971p) 88,787; iron goods, rolling stock, textiles, chemicals; first mentioned 1391; joined Yugoslavia 1918; occupied by Hungary 1941–45.

Suc·coth \ˈsək-äth, -ˌōth\. 1 Locality in Goshen, ancient Egypt, E of the Nile delta, probably the same as Pithom; first encampment of the Israelites in the Exodus (*Exod.* xii. 37; xiii. 20).

2 Town of ancient Palestine, E of the Jordan and near the N bank of the Jabbok (*Gen.* xxxiii. 17).

Su·cea·va *also* **Su·cza·wa** \sü-ˈchäv-ə\. 1 River, N Romania; ab. 110 m. long; flows into the Siretul river.

2 County of N Romania. See table at ROMANIA.

3 Town, its ⊗, on the Suceava river; pop. (1970e) 44,941; textiles, lumber; 14th cent. citadel; 16th cent. church; capital of Moldavia 1401–1565.

Su·chan \sü-ˈchan\. Town, S Primorski Krai, Russian S.F.S.R., U.S.S.R., near coast 60 m. E of Vladivostok; pop. (1967e) 50,000; coal mines.

Su·chia·te \sü-ˈchä-(ˌ)tā\. River, W Guatemala; flows S and SW into Pacific Ocean; forms section of Guatemala-Mexico boundary.

Su·chi·te·pé·quez \sủ-ˌchēt-ə-ˈpā-kəs\. Department of S Guatemala. See table at GUATEMALA.

Su·chi·to·to \ˌsü-chi-ˈtō-tō\. Town, Cuscatlán dept., cen. El Salvador.

Su–chou *or* **Soo·chow** \ˈsü-ˈjō, -ˈchaủ\ *or formerly* **Wuh·sien** \ˈwü-shē-ˈen\. City, S Kiangsu prov., E China, on the Grand Canal; pop. (1970e) 1,300,000; surrounded by rectangular walls (built 1662) ab. 15 m. in length, with six gates. Noted for its bridges, palaces, temples, etc., for its many pagodas, esp. the Great Pagoda, one of the largest in China (built c. 1131 A.D.).

History: One of the oldest Chinese cities; founded c. 525 B.C.; capital of Wu, ancient feudal kingdom, 513–473 B.C.; received its present name under Sui dynasty 6th cent. A.D.; partly destroyed by Mings 14th cent.; restored under Emperor K'ang-hsi 1662; destroyed 1853 in Taiping Rebellion but again rebuilt; opened as treaty port 1896; seized by Japanese Nov. 1937.

Suchow. 1 Town, Kansu prov., China. See CHIU-CH'ÜAN.

2 City, Szechwan prov., China. See I-PIN.

Sü·chow *or* **Hsü–chou** \ˈs(h)ü-ˈjō, ˈsü-ˈchaủ\ *or formerly* **T'ung–shan** \ˈtủŋ-ˈshän\. Town, Kiangsu prov., E China, ab. 180 m. NW of Nanking; pop. (1970e) 1,500,000; textiles, flour.

Süch·teln \ˈzük-təln\. City, North Rhine-Westphalia, West Germany, 20 m. WNW of Düsseldorf; pop. (1968e) 17,111.

Su·cia Bay \ˌsü-sē-ə-\. Bay, S shore of Puerto Rico, enclosed by Cape Rojo on the W.

Suck \ˈsək\. River, W cen. Eire; 60 m. long; flows SSE in Connacht prov. into the Shannon river N of Lough Derg.

Su·cre \ˈsü-(ˌ)krā\. 1 *or formerly* **Chu·qui·sa·ca** \ˌchü-kē-ˈsä-kə\. City, constitutional ✱ of Bolivia, also ✱ of Chuquisaca dept., ab. 260 m. SE of La Paz; pop. (1969e) 47,800; alt. 8530 ft.; food processing, oil refining; cement; seat of the national Supreme Court, the Univ. of San Francisco Xavier (1624), and the Archbishopric of La Plata; cathedral (1553). Founded as Chuquisaca 1538; scene of start of revolt against Spain May 1809; name changed 1840 to Sucre in honor of first president of Bolivia.

2 Department of N Colombia. See table at COLOMBIA.

3 State of N Venezuela. See table at VENEZUELA.

Sucro. See ALCIRA.

Suczawa. See SUCEAVA.

Sud, Mas·sif du \mä-ˈsēf-dü-ˈsüd\ *or formerly* **Massif de la Hotte** \-də-lä-ˈōt\. Highland, Tiburon Penin., SW Haiti, West Indies; highest point 7700 ft.

Su·da \ˌsüd-ə\. River, W Vologda Oblast, Russian S.F.S.R., U.S.S.R.; 130 m. long; flows SE and near Cherepovets enters the Rybinsk Reservoir (*q.v.*).

Suda Bay *also* **Sou·da Bay** \ˌsüd-ə-\ *or Gk.* **Kól·pos Soú·dhas** \ˌkȯl-pȯs-ˈsü-t͟häs\. Inlet, N coast of Crete, Greece, near W end, shut in on NW by Akroteri Penin.; just E of Canea, only good harbor on N coast; in World War II site of a British base which was captured by German airborne troops May 26–27, 1941.

Su·dan \sü-ˈdan, -ˈdän\ *or Fr.* **Sou·dan** \sü-dän\ *or Arab.* **Bi·lād–es–Sudan** \bi-ˌlad-as-sü-ˈdan\. 1 Region, N cen. Africa, S of the Sahara and Libyan deserts—not a political unit; extends across the African continent from W coast 4000 m. to mountains of Ethiopia, with widest part nearly 1000 m.; approximate area 2,000,000 sq. m. Includes major parts of republics of Senegal, Guinea, Mali, Niger, Chad, Sudan, Gambia, Upper Volta, and the N sections of the countries bordering on the Atlantic from Portuguese

Guinea to Cameroon; occupies the basin of the Senegal and cen. parts of the Niger and Nile basins and the Lake Chad region. Consists of desert, grassy steppes, and extensive plains; ethnologically that part of Africa N of the equator inhabited by Negro peoples under Muslim influence and in medieval times site of the Negro empires of Bornu, Songhai, and Fulah.

2 *officially* **Democratic Republic of the Sudan** *or Arab.* **Jum·hūr·ī·yat as–Sū·dān ad–Dī·mu·qra·tī·yah** \jəm-ˌhu̇r-ē-ˌ(y)at-as-sü-ˈdan-ad-ˌdē-mə-ˈkrat-ē-(y)ə\ *or formerly* **Anglo–Egyp·tian Sudan** \ˌaŋ-glō-i-ˈjip-shən-\. Republic, NE Africa, bounded on N by Egypt, on NE by the Red Sea, on E by Ethiopia, on S by Kenya, Uganda, and Zaire, on W by the Central African Republic and Chad, and on NW by Libya; 967,500 sq. m.; pop. (1971e) 15,675,000, (1969e) 14,797,000; ✻ Khartoum. *Physical features:* N region chiefly desert or semidesert; extreme S characterized by tropical rain forest; grassy plains in cen. region; Darfur prov. in W, and NE part of republic are hilly. *Chief exports:* Cotton, gum arabic; other products: millet, salt, sesame, wheat, peanuts; livestock raising. *Chief towns:* Khartoum, Omdurman, North Khartoum, Port Sudan, Wad Medani, Kassala. Divided into the following nine provinces (for pronunciation of their names, see their individual entries):

NAME	AREA (sq. m.)	POP. (1969e)	CAPITAL
Bahr al-Ghazal	82,530	1,421,000	Wau
Blue Nile	54,880	3,124,000	Wad Medani
Darfur	199,650	1,683,000	Al-Fashir
Equatoria	76,495	1,295,000	Juba
Kassala	131,528	1,620,000	Kassala
Khartoum	8,097	860,000	Khartoum
Kordofan	146,930	2,394,000	Al-Ubayyid
Northern	184,200	1,126,000	Ed Damer
Upper Nile	91,190	1,274,000	Malakal

History: Conquered by Egypt under Hussein, son of Mehemet Ali, 1820–22; under nominal Egyptian authority until 1882; ravaged by slave trade which Sir Samuel Baker and General Charles Gordon (1874–80) sought to suppress; after fanatical Sudanese revolt under the Mahdi 1883 in which the evacuating Egyptian forces were defeated and General Gordon killed (at Khartoum 1885), territory abandoned to rule of the dervishes until Kitchener's campaign 1896–98 defeated them and rescued upper Nile from threat of French advance from W; jointly administered after 1899 by Egypt and Great Britain; after assassination of governor-general in Cairo in 1924 saw withdrawal of Egyptian forces, who were excluded from the country until treaty of 1936 which reaffirmed condominium agreement; achieved independence 1956; civilian government overthrown by army 1958, reestablished 1964, and again overthrown 1969; carried out widespread purge of Communists 1971 following unsuccessful leftist coup; announced granting of limited autonomy to three S provinces (in sporadic rebellion against Sudan government since mid-1950's) 1972.

Sud·bury \ˈsəd-ˌber-ē, -b(ə-)rē\. 1 Town, Middlesex co., NE Massachusetts, 18 m. W of Boston; pop. (1970c) 13,506; fruit farms; settled 1638; important town at time of Revolutionary War. Wayside Inn (first building 1686 known as Howe Tavern) subject of Longfellow's *Tales of a Wayside Inn.*

2 District, Ontario, Canada. See table at ONTARIO.

3 Mining city, ⊗ of Sudbury dist., SE Ontario, Canada, 38 m. N of Georgian Bay and 165 m. E of Sault Ste. Marie; pop. (1971p) 89,898, met. area pop. 153,959; center of one of the world's richest nickel-mining regions; also produces copper, platinum, and palladium; ore smelting; lumbering and making of wood pulp; Laurentian Univ. of Sudbury (1960).

4 Municipal borough, West Suffolk, E England, on the Stour 52 m. NE of London; pop. (1971p) 8183; manufactures silk goods. Birthplace of Thomas Gainsborough.

Sud·die \ˈsəd-ē\. Town, N Guyana, on W bank of Essequibo river at its mouth 35 m. NW of Georgetown.

Su·derø \ˈsü-t͟hə-ˌrər\. Island, Faeroes (*q.v.*), southernmost island of the group; 64 sq. m.; pop. (1965e) 5734.

Sud–Est Island. See TAGULA ISLAND.

Sudeten. See SUDETIC MOUNTAINS.

Su·de·ten·land \sü-ˈdāt-ᵊn-ˌland, -ˌlänt\. Term originally used for the mountainous region comprising the Sudetic Mts. on N borders of Bohemia and Silesia, Czechoslovakia; after the crisis of 1938–39 applied also to all the borderlands of Bohemia and Moravia inhabited by German-speaking people; 8719 sq. m. These border regions seized by Germans Sept. 1938 (cession officially approved Nov. 21, 1938) and later (Mar. 1939) absorbed into the German Reich; restored to Czechoslovakia 1945.

Su·det·ic Mountains \sü-ˌdet-ik-\ *also* **Su·de·tes** \sü-ˈdēt-(ˌ)ēz\; *Czech and Polish* **Su·de·ty** *Czech* ˈsu̇-det-yē, *Polish* su̇-ˈdet-ē\ *or Ger.* **Su·de·ten** \sü-ˈdāt-ᵊn\. Mountain ranges along part of boundary bet. N Czechoslovakia and S Poland, WNW of the Carpathians; they consist of several smaller mountain groups or ranges, incl. the Riesengebirge and Eulengebirge; highest peak Sněžka 5256 ft.

Sudharam. See NOAKHALI.

Su·dir·man Range \su̇-ˈdi(ə)r-mən-\ *or formerly* **Nas·sau Range** \ˈnas-ˌȯ-\. Mountain range, cen. Irian Barat, Indonesia, forming W end of Maoke Mts.; highest point Mount Djaja 16,535 ft.; only 4°S of the equator but covered with ice and glaciers; has great precipices; not discovered until 1911 and N slopes not explored until 1926.

Sue·ca \su̇-ˈā-kə\. Commune, Valencia prov., E Spain, 22 m. S of Valencia; pop. (1970p) 21,500; produces rice.

Sue Peaks \ˈsü-\. Mountains, S Brewster co., W Texas; highest peak 5857 ft.

Suessa Aurunca. See SESSA AURUNCA.

Sues·su·la \ˈswes-yu̇-lə\. Ancient Samnite town, Campania, S Italy, N of modern Caserta, near the Caudine Forks; battle 343 B.C. in the first Samnite War.

Suez \sü-ˈez, *chiefly Brit.* ˈsü-iz\ *or Arab.* **As–Su·ways** \ˌas-su̇-ˈwās\. 1 Governorate of NE Egypt. See 2, below, and table at EGYPT.

2 City, constituting the governorate, at the N end of the Gulf of Suez and at the S terminus of the Suez Canal; pop. (1970e) 315,000; extensive port facilities; oil refineries and storage facilities, fertilizer plant. In 7th cent. A.D. terminal point of canal connecting Red Sea with the Nile; under Ottoman Empire (16th cent.) became naval and commercial port; later, a port of departure for pilgrims to Mecca.

Suez, Gulf of. Northwest arm of the Red Sea; joined to the Mediterranean Sea by the Suez Canal.

Suez, Isthmus of. Isthmus connecting NE Africa with Asia; 72 m. wide; Gulf of Suez and the Red Sea on the S, and the E Mediterranean Sea on the N.

Suez Canal. Ship canal across Isthmus of Suez, NE Africa, connecting the Red Sea with the E Mediterranean; 101 m. long from Suez to Port Said; nowhere less than 179 ft. wide; minimum depth of channel 40 ft. Passes along E edge of Lake Manzala and through Lake Timsah and the Bitter Lakes; Ismailia is principal town on its banks in cen. part.

History: Built 1859–69; chief engineer for its construction Ferdinand de Lesseps; opened Nov. 16, 1869; ownership originally vested in French company in which British acquired controlling interest 1875; effectively under British control after establishment of British protectorate in Egypt 1882; nationalized by Egyptian government 1956, precipitating Anglo-French intervention Nov. 1956; canal closed until Apr. 1957. Canal again closed June 1967 ff. as result of Arab-Israeli War; its banks scene of considerable fighting between Egyptian and Israeli forces 1967–70.

Sufetula. See SBEÏTLA.

Suf·fern \'səf-ərn\. Village, Rockland co., SE New York, 28 m. NNW of New York; pop. (1970c) 8273; residential suburb in summer-resort region; summer theater; Rockland Community Coll. (1959).

Suf·field \'sə-fēld\. Town, N Hartford co., N Connecticut, on Massachusetts border; pop. (1970c) 8634; agriculture; Saint Alphonsus Coll. (1963); settled 1670; incorporated by Massachusetts 1674; annexed to Connecticut 1749.

Suf·folk \'səf-ək, -ˌōk\. **1** Name of counties in two states of the U.S. See tables at MASSACHUSETTS and NEW YORK.

2 Independent city, ⊗ of Nansemond co., SE Virginia, on Nansemond river 18 m. WSW of Portsmouth; 2 sq. m.; pop. (1970c) 9858; peanut market; lumber, fertilizer, hosiery, building materials. Established 1742; incorp. as town 1808; burned by British in Revolution 1779 and occupied by Union forces in Civil War 1862; became independent city 1910.

3 County, E England; 1482 sq. m.; pop. (1971p) 544,725; divided into the administrative counties **East Suffolk** (871 sq. m.; pop. 380,524; ⊗ Ipswich) and **West Suffolk** (611 sq. m.; pop. 164,201; ⊗ Bury St. Edmunds); rivers Waveney, Stour, Deben, Orwell, Alde; agriculture, fishing, food processing; main towns Ipswich, Bury St. Edmunds, Lowestoft, Beccles, Newmarket, Sudbury, Felixstowe.

Suffolk Broads. See BROADS, THE.

Sufli. See SOUPHLI.

Sug·ar Creek \'shu̇g-ər-\. **1** City, Jackson and Clay cos., W Missouri, 9 m. E of Kansas City; pop. (1970c) 4755.

2 Borough, Venango co., NW Pennsylvania, 10 m. W of Oil City; pop. (1970c) 5944.

Sugar Hill. See LISBON 3.

Sugar Island. Island, Chippewa co., E and NE Michigan penin., in Saint Marys river N of Neebish I.

Sugar Land. City, Fort Bend co., SE Texas, 20 m. SW of Houston; pop. (1970c) 3318.

Sugar Loaf Hill \'shu̇g-ər-ˌlōf-\. Height, S Okinawa, Ryukyu Is., Japan, dominating approach to Shuri; scene of heavy fighting in May 1945, recaptured by U.S. five times.

Sug·ar·loaf Key \'shu̇g-ər-ˌlōf-\. See FLORIDA KEYS.

Sugarloaf Mountain. **1** Peak, SE Elko co., NE Nevada; 6164 ft.

2 Peak in Catskill Mts., Greene co., New York; 3647 ft.
3 Peak in Le Flore co., E Oklahoma; 2630 ft.
4 Peak, Brazil. See PÃO DE AÇÚCAR.

Sugbu. See CEBU.

Suğ·la, Lake \-'sü(g)-lə\ *or Turk.* **Sugla Gö·lü** \-gəl-'(y)ü\. Lake (*gölü*), SW Turkey, N of the Gulf of Antalya and SE of Lake Beyşehir; 48 sq. m.

Şuḥār. See SOHĀR.

Suhl \'zü(ə)l\. 1 District of East Germany. See table at GERMANY, EAST.
2 Industrial city, its ✱, 30 m. SSW of Erfurt; pop. (1970e) 31,445; produces motor vehicles, machinery, precision instruments, tools, sporting firearms; first mentioned 1239.

Sui–ch'uan *or* **Sui·chwan** \'swā-chə-'wän\. Town, W Kiangsi prov., SE China, 50 m. NW of Kan-chou; in World War II an U.S. airfield, captured by Japanese 1944 and recaptured 1945.

Suid–Afrika, Republiek van. See SOUTH AFRICA, REPUBLIC OF.

Suidwes–Afrika. See SOUTH-WEST AFRICA.

Suifu. See I-PIN.

Suir \'shu̇(ə)r\. River, SE Eire; 114 m. long; rises in N co. Tipperary, flows S and E into Waterford Harbour.

Suisse. See SWITZERLAND.

Sui·sun Bay \sə-ˌsün-\. Inlet of San Francisco Bay, W cen. California; lying on boundary bet. Contra Costa and Solano cos.; connected with San Pablo Bay by Carquinez Strait; crossed by Martinez Bridge, a vertical lift bridge with clearance of 291.5 ft.

Suisun City. City, Solano co., cen. California, 36 m. SW of Sacramento; pop. (1970c) 2917.

Su·i·ta \sü-'ēt-ə\. City, Ōsaka prefecture, Honshū, Japan; pop. (1970e) 259,619.

Suit·land–Silver Hill \'süt-lənd-\. Urban community (unincorp.), Prince Georges co., Maryland, E of Washington, D.C.; pop. (1970c) 30,335.

Sui·yuan \'swā-yü-'än\. Former province, Inner Mongolia, N China; 112,493 sq. m.; ✱ Hu-ho-hao-t'e.

Su·ka·bu·mi *or Du.* **Soe·ka·boe·mi** \ˌsük-ə-'bü-mē\. City, West Java prov., Indonesia, on railroad 28 m. SSE of Bogor; pop. (1961c) 80,438; health resort with sanatorium at S foot of Mt. Salak.

Suk–Ahras. See SOUK-AHRAS.

Sukarnapura. See DJAJAPURA.

Sukarno, Mount. See DJAJA, MOUNT.

Su·ket \'sü-'kāt\. Former Indian state, now part of Himachal Pradesh state, N India; 392 sq. m.; ✱ Suket.

Sukhan–Darya Oblast. See SURKHANDARYA OBLAST.

Su·kho·na \sü-'kȯ-nə\. River, chiefly in Vologda Oblast, N cen. Russian S.F.S.R., U.S.S.R.; 358 m. long; rises in Lake Kubenskoe and flows E to unite with the Yug river near Veliki Ustyug in NE part of the region and form the Northern Dvina river.

Su·kho·thai *also* **Su·ko·tai** \'sük-ə-'tī\. Village, W Thailand, 30 m. NW of Phitsanulok; has one of Thailand's best known temples; important formerly as the capital of a Tai-Khmer state of the same name that flourished 1256 to 1350.

Su·khu·mi \'sük-ə-mē\ *or formerly* **Su·khum** \sü-'küm\ *or anc.* **Di·os·cu·ri·as** \ˌdī-əs-'kyu̇r-ē-əs\. Seaport town, ✱ of Abkhazian A.S.S.R., Georgian S.S.R., U.S.S.R., on the Black Sea 100 m. NW of Kutaisi; pop. (1970p) 102,000; popular resort; produces wine, canned fruit, leather goods.

Suk·ker·top·pen \'sük-ər-ˌtō-pən\. Headland and settlement, on an island on SW coast of Greenland, 65°25'N, 52°53'W, N of Godthåb; pop. (1968e) 3660.

Suk·kur \'sük-ər\ *or* **Sa·khar** \'sək-ər\. 1 District, Pakistan; 5553 sq. m.; pop. (1961c) 836,867; ✱ Sukkur.
2 Town, its ✱, on right bank of Indus river ab. 225 m. NNE of Karachi; pop. (1961c) 130,600; textiles, vegetable oils, flour; center of irrigation system, known as the Lloyd or Sukkur barrage, built 1928–32. Height of dam 190 ft.

Sukotai. See SUKHOTHAI.

Su·la \'sü-lə\. River, N cen. Ukrainian S.S.R., U.S.S.R.; 250 m. long; rises near Konotop and flows S to the Dnieper above Kremenchug.

Sula Besi. See SANANA 1.

Su·lai·ma·ni·ya \ˌsu̇l-ā-mə-'nē-(y)ə, ˌsu̇-lī-\. Town, NE Iraq, in mountains 60 m. E of Kirkuk near Iranian border; pop. (1965c) 86,877; market town; founded 1781.

Su·lai·man Range \ˌsu̇l-ī-ˌmän-\. Mountain range, Pakistan, W of Indus river; highest, twin peaks at N end, Takht-i-Sulaiman ("throne of Solomon") 11,289 ft.

Sula Islands *also* **Soe·la Islands** \'sü-lə-\ *or formerly* **Xul·la Islands** \'shü-lə-\. Island group, Indonesia, S of Molucca Sea and bet. Celebes I. on the W and the Ceram Sea on the E; 1873 sq. m.; chief town Sanana on Sanana I. Comprises islands of Taliabu, Mangole, and Sanana, and several small islands. Mountainous and thickly forested; grows sago, rice, sugarcane; fishing.

Sulawesi. See CELEBES.

Sulci. See SANT'ANTIOCO 2.

Sul·grave \'səl-ˌgrāv\. Village, SW Northamptonshire, England, 7 m. NE of Banbury; site of Sulgrave Manor, an ancestral home of George Washington, now a museum.

Sulimov. See CHERKESSK.

Su·li·na \sü-'lē-nə\. Port, Tulcea co., E Romania, on the Black Sea at the cen. mouth of the Danube; pop. (1966c) 4005.

Su·li·tjel·ma \ˌsü-li-'tyel-mə\. Peak in the Kjølen Mts., N Norway, on the Swedish border; 6280 ft.

Su·lla·na \sü-'yän-ə\. City, Piura dept., NW Peru, 32 m. NE of Paita; pop. (1969e) 42,600; cinchona bark.

Sul·li·van \'səl-ə-vən\. 1 Name of counties in six states of the U.S. See tables at INDIANA, MISSOURI, NEW HAMPSHIRE, NEW YORK, PENNSYLVANIA, TENNESSEE.
2 City, ⊗ of Moultrie co., cen. Illinois, 25 m. SE of Decatur; pop. (1970c) 4112; footwear, concrete products; agriculture.
3 City, ⊗ of Sullivan co., SW Indiana, 25 m. S of Terre Haute; pop. (1970c) 4683; coal mines, oil wells.
4 City, Crawford and Franklin cos., SE cen. Missouri, 63 m. SW of St. Louis; pop. (1970c) 5111.

Sullivan Island. See LAMBI ISLAND.

Sul·ly \'səl-ē\. County in South Dakota. See table at SOUTH DAKOTA.

Sul·lys Hill \ˌsəl-ēz-\. National game preserve, Benson co., NE North Dakota, just S of Devils Lake; 1⅕ sq. m.; estab. 1914; has esp. bison, elk, deer, geese.

Sul·mo·na \sül-'mō-nə\ *or anc.* **Sul·mo** \'səl-(ˌ)mō\. Industrial commune, Aquila prov., Abruzzi, cen. Italy, 35 m. SE of Aquila; pop. (1968e) 21,439; market town; copper goods; cathedral; medieval remains.

Sul·phur \'səl-fər\. 1 *or* **Sulphur Fork of Red River.** River, NE Texas; 200 m. long; rises in Fannin co., flows E across Arkansas border and into Red river in SW Arkansas.
2 City, Calcasieu parish, SW Louisiana, 10 m. W of Lake Charles; pop. (1970c) 13,551; livestock farms.
3 City, ⊗ of Murray co., S Oklahoma, 24 m. NNE of Ardmore; pop. (1970c) 5158; health resort.

Sulphur Island. See IWO JIMA.

Sulphur Springs. City, ⊗ of Hopkins co., NE Texas, 27 m. E of Greenville; pop. (1970c) 10,642; clothing, fertilizer, dairy products; truck and livestock farms.

Sultanabad. See ARĀK and 'IRAQ-I-'AJAM.

Sul·tan Dağ·la·ri \sül-'tän-ˌdä(g)-lä-'rē\. Mountain range, extending NW and SE in W cen. Turkey, N of Lake Beyşehir; highest point 8304 ft.

Sul·tan·pur \sül-'tän-ˌpu̇(ə)r\. 1 Town, SE cen. Uttar Pradesh, N India, on right bank of Gomati river 60 m. N of Allahabad; pop. (1961c) 26,081.

2 Town, India. See KULU.

Sultan sa Ba·ron·gis \sül-ˌtän-sä-bə-ˈrȯŋ-ēs\ *or formerly* **Lam·bay·ong** \läm-ˈbī-ȯŋ\. Municipality, Cotabato prov., Mindanao, Phil., ab. 45 m. SE of Cotabato; pop. (1969e) 56,300.

Su·lu \ˈsü-(ˌ)lü\. 1 Province, SW Phil., coextensive with the Sulu Archipelago; 1038 sq. m.; pop. (1970p) 427,386; ✱ Jolo. Chain of islands extending 180 m. SW from Basilan I. to Borneo and separating the Sulu Sea from the Celebes Sea; comprises five groups: Samales, Pangutaran, Jolo and adjacent islands, Tapul, Tawitawi and adjacent islands, all together ab. 400 named islands, and more than 500 unnamed small islands. Many coral reefs around the island groups; fishing is most important industry.

History: Visited by foreign traders long before Legaspi colonized Cebu. Inhabitants converted to Islam ab. the end of 14th cent.; revolted against Spaniards 1578–1600 and did not come under Spanish control until 19th cent.; were ruled by Moro sultans; during these years, esp. in 17th and 18th cents., Moros conducted many destructive piratical raids against Spaniards and Filipinos of Visayan Is. and Luzon. The archipelago finally became Spanish protectorate in latter half of 19th cent.; suffered from civil war 1884–94; came under U.S. 1899 and made part of Moro Province 1903; civil government established 1914; sultanate terminated by treaty of Apr. 1940, in which ownership of Sulu Archipelago transferred to Philippines.

2 Chief island and municipality, Sulu, Phil. See JOLO.

Su·lu·an \sü-ˈlü-ˌän\. Small island, Phil., 10 m. E of Homonhon I. and ab. 13 m. S of S point of Samar, Phil.; ab. 2 sq. m. Landmark for ships approaching cen. Philippines (Leyte Gulf or Surigao Strait) from the Pacific. Sighted by Magellan Mar. 16, 1521; first landing (simultaneously with Homonhon) of U.S. forces on their return to the Philippines Oct. 19, 1944 in World War II.

Sulu Archipelago. Chain of islands, SW Phil., extending from Basilan I. to Borneo and constituting Sulu prov. (*q.v.*).

Sulu Sea. Large interisland sea, SW Phil., bordered on N by Cuyo Is., on E by islands of Panay, Negros, and W Mindanao, on SE by Sulu Archipelago, on SW by North Borneo, and on W and NW by Palawan I.; extends N and S ab. 350 m. bet. 5° and 10°N lat. and ab. 425 m. E and W from entrance to Mindanao Sea to Balabac Strait; open sea except for three small clusters of islands.

Sulz·bach \ˈzülts-ˌbäk\. Town, Saarland, West Germany, ab. 6 m. NNW of Saarbrücken; pop. (1969e) 22,815; coal mining.

Sulz·ber·ger Bay \ˌsəlz-ˌbər-gər-\. Large inlet of Ross Sea, NW Marie Byrd Land, Antarctica, E of Edward VII Penin. and Little America, 77°S, 152°W; ab. 100 m. wide; discovered 1929.

Sulzer Belchen. See GUEBWILLER, BALLON DE.

Su·ma·tra \sü-ˈmä-trə\. Island, W part of Indonesia, S of the Malay Penin.; 182,561 sq. m. (incl. small islands along its W and SE coasts); pop (1970e) 19,840,000; for administrative divisions, see table at INDONESIA. *Physical features:* Separated on NE from Malay Penin. by Strait of Malacca and at S end from Java by Sunda Strait. Divided into two almost equal parts by the equator; 1060 m. long, max. width ab. 248 m. Along its W coast extends for the length of the island the Barisan Mts. containing many peaks 6000 ft. to 12,000 ft.; highest Kerintji 12,483 ft.; many peaks of volcanic origin, some active today. Its E and SE parts are jungle lowlands with numerous rivers having many tributaries—chief are Hari, Inderagiri, Kampar, and Asahan; Lake Toba in the N is only large lake. *Chief products:* Rice, corn, root crops, coffee, copra, tobacco, pepper, rubber, peanuts; fishing. *Chief cities:* Palembang, Medan, Padang, Pematangsiantar.

History: Visited by Hindu emigrants, who established a kingdom in 7th cent.; invaded by Arabs in the 13th cent.; first known to Europeans in early part of 16th cent.; W coast settlements established by Dutch 1663–64, and elsewhere on island settlements also made by Portuguese and English; parts acquired from native sultans by treaty; was object of great rivalry with English, who held it for short periods bet. 1796 and 1814; last remaining British possession (Bengkulu) given up 1824; Atjeh (*q.v.*) in N not overcome until 20th cent.; has been developed agriculturally since c. 1850; occupied by Japanese 1942–45.

Sumatra, North. Province, Sumatra, Indonesia. See table at INDONESIA.

Sumatra, South. Province, Sumatra, Indonesia. See table at INDONESIA.

Sumatra, West. Province, Sumatra, Indonesia. See table at INDONESIA.

Sum·ba *or Du.* **Soem·ba** \ˈsüm-bə\ *or Eng.* **San·dal·wood Island** \ˌsan-dᵊl-ˌwu̇d-\. Island of the Lesser Sunda Is., Indonesia, S of Flores and SE of Sumbawa; 140 m. long; max. width 50 m.; 4306 sq. m.; pop. (1961c) 251,126; chief town Waingapu. Separated from Timor on the E by Savu Sea. Mainly a plateau of ab. 2000 ft. with highest point at 4019 ft.; has good harbors on N coast, esp. at Waingapu. Noted in 17th–19th cents. for its sandalwood trees, now found only in interior regions; produces rice, maize, tobacco, and exports copra; its chieftains made treaty with Dutch 1756, renewed and revised several times in 19th cent.; uprising in 1914; occupied by Japanese 1942–45.

Sum·ba·wa *or Du.* **Soem·ba·wa** \süm-ˈbä-wə\. Island, Lesser Sunda Is., Indonesia, E of Lombok I. and W of Flores I.; 175 m. long, max. width 55 m.; 5693 sq. m.; pop. (1961c) 407,596; chief town Raba. Separated on W from Lombok by Alas Strait and on E from Komodo I. (a dependency of Flores) by Sape Strait; has irregular coastline with deep indentation (Saleh Bay) in center of N coast; on NE coast is Bima Bay, one of best harbors in Indonesia. Mountainous throughout with highest point, the volcano Mt. Tambora, at tip of peninsula on N coast, 9350 ft. Not highly developed but has fertile soil and tropical products of many kinds can be raised; horse and cattle raising important. Originally divided into six native states whose condition of allegiance has often changed during last two centuries; relations with Dutch first began early in 18th cent.; final treaty of 1905 settled arrangements with various chieftains; occupied by Japanese 1942–45.

Sum·bing *or Du.* **Soem·bing** \ˈsüm-biŋ\. Volcanic peak, Central Java prov., Indonesia; 11,060 ft.; overlooks Magelang plain from the W.

Sum·burgh Head \ˈsəm-b(ə-)rə-\. Cape, S tip of Mainland I., Shetland Is., NNE of Scotland; lighthouse.

Su·me·dang *or Du.* **Soe·me·dang** \ˈsü-mə-ˌdäŋ\. Town, West Java prov., Indonesia, ab. 20 m. E of Bandung; pop. (1961c) 27,891.

Su·me·nep *or Du.* **Soe·me·nep** \ˈsü-mə-ˌnep\. Inland town, E end of Madura I., East Java prov., Indonesia; pop. (1961c) 26,823.

Su·mer \ˈsü-mər\. The southern division of ancient Babylonia; from ab. the 4th millennium B.C. a kingdom of non-Semitic people. Little is known about it but Sumerians thought to have invented cuneiform system of writing. About 2600–2400 B.C., esp. under Sargon I (c. 2637–2582 B.C.), united gradually with Akkadians; combined empire overcome c. 1950 B.C. by the Semitic Babylonian kingdom. Gudea was one of its great rulers; its chief cities were Nippur, Lagash, Larsa, Erech, and Ur—all near the lower Euphrates. Probably the same as the Biblical Shinar (*q.v.*) (*Gen.* x. 10).

Sum·ga·it \ˌsu̇m-gä-ˈēt\. Town, Azerbaijan S.S.R., U.S.S.R., ab. 15 m. NE of Baku; pop. (1970p) 124,000.

Su·mi·da \ˈsu̇-mēd-ə, su̇-ˈmēd-ə\. River, SE Honshū, Japan; ab. 180 m. long; flows S through the city of Tokyo into Tokyo Bay.

Sum·mer Island \ˌsəm-ər-\. Island, N Lake Michigan, at N entrance to Green Bay; belongs to Delta co., S Michigan penin.

Summer Lake. Lake, cen. Lake co., S Oregon; ab. 15 m. long.

Sum·mers \'səm-ərz\. County in West Virginia. See table at WEST VIRGINIA.

Sum·mer·side \'səm-ər-ˌsīd\. Town, ⊗ of Prince co., W Prince Edward I., Canada, on Northumberland Strait 35 m. W of Charlottetown; pop. (1971p) 9315; exports farm produce; summer resort; founded 1780 by Daniel Green, Quaker Loyalist from Pennsylvania.

Sum·mers·ville \'səm-ərz-ˌvil\. Town, ⊗ of Nicholas co., cen. West Virginia; pop. (1970c) 2429; ab. 6 m. SSW is Summersville Dam (see UNITED STATES, *Dams and Reservoirs*).

Sum·mer·ville \'səm-ər-ˌvil\. 1 City, ⊗ of Chattooga co., NW Georgia; pop. (1970c) 5043; sawmills, truck farms; incorp. 1839.

2 Town and resort, Dorchester co., SE South Carolina, 22 m. NW of Charleston; pop. (1970c) 3704; rayon fabrics, aluminum, lumber.

Sum·mit \'səm-ət\. 1 Elevation, McKean co., N Pennsylvania; 2252 ft.

2 Name of counties in three states of the U.S. See tables at COLORADO, OHIO, UTAH.

3 Village, Cook co., NE Illinois, 12 m. WSW of Chicago; pop. (1970c) 11,569.

4 Residential city, Union co., NE New Jersey, 10 m. W of Newark; pop. (1970c) 23,620; site used as sentry point in Revolutionary days.

Summit Hill. Borough, Carbon co., E Pennsylvania, 28 m. S of Wilkes-Barre; pop. (1970c) 3811; coal mining.

Summit Mountain. Peak, Glacier National Park, NW Montana; 8775 ft.

Summus Portus. See SOMPORT, COL DE.

Sum·ner \'səm-nər\. 1 Name of counties in two states of the U.S. See tables at KANSAS and TENNESSEE.

2 City, Bremer co., NE Iowa, 27 m. NE of Waterloo; pop. (1970c) 2174.

3 Town, a ⊗ of Tallahatchie co., NW Mississippi; pop. (1970c) 533.

4 City, Pierce co., W cen. Washington, 11 m. E of Tacoma; pop. (1970c) 4325; manufactures lumber and lumber products, yeast, vinegar; canneries, dairies.

Su·mo·to \sü-'mōt-(ˌ)ō\. Chief town of Awaji I. (*q.v.*), Hyōgo prefecture, Japan; pop. (1970c) 44,499.

Sum·pan·go \süm-'päŋ-(ˌ)gō\. Town, Sacatepéquez dept., S cen. Guatemala; pop. (1964c) 8054.

Šum·perk \'shüm-ˌpe(ə)rk\ *or Ger.* **Mäh·risch–Schön·berg** \ˌme(ə)r-ish-'shə(r)n-ˌbe(ə)rg\. Town, Czech S.R., cen. Czechoslovakia, on Morava river 28 m. NNW of Olomouc; pop. (1968e) 22,670.

Sum·pra·bum \ˌsüm-prə-'büm\. Town, N Burma, ab. 80 m. N of Myitkyina and SE of Chaukan Pass.

Sum·ter \'səm(p)-tər\. 1 Name of counties in four states of the U.S. See tables at ALABAMA, FLORIDA, GEORGIA, SOUTH CAROLINA.

2 Industrial city, ⊗ of Sumter co., E cen. South Carolina, 42 m. E of Columbia; pop. (1970c) 24,555; manufactures furniture, lumber, textiles, chemicals, foundry and machine-shop products; Shaw Air Force Base; Morris Coll. (1908); founded 1799.

Su·my \'sü-mē\. Town, ✻ of Sumy Oblast, Ukrainian S.S.R., U.S.S.R., near the Psel river 95 m. NW of Kharkov; pop. (1970p) 159,000; mining equipment; sugar refineries; founded 1652.

Sumy Oblast \-'ō-bləst, -ˌblast\. Subdivision of the Ukrainian S.S.R., U.S.S.R., on N and E borders on Bryansk and Kursk oblasts of the Russian S.F.S.R.; 9189 sq. m.; pop. (1970p) 1,505,000; ✻ Sumy; fertile black-earth region, crossed by the Seim, Psel, and Vorskla rivers; sugar beet, hemp, tobacco; livestock.

Sun \'sən\. River, NW cen. Montana; ab. 100 m. long; rises in W Teton co., flows S and E into Missouri river at Great Falls, Cascade co.

Sun·a·pee Lake \ˌsən-ə-ˌpē-\. Lake on boundary bet. Sullivan and Merrimack cos., SW cen. New Hampshire; ab. 9 m. long and from 1 to 3 m. wide; summer resort.

Su·nart, Loch \läk-'sü-nərt, läk-\. Inlet of the Atlantic Ocean, Argyll co., W Scotland, S of Loch Shiel and N of Loch Linnhe.

Sun·bury \'sən-ˌber-ē, -bə-rē\. 1 Village, Delaware co., cen. Ohio, 18 m. NNE of Columbus; pop. (1970c) 2512.

2 Commercial and industrial city, ⊗ of Northumberland co., E cen. Pennsylvania, on Susquehanna river 30 m. SSE of Williamsport; pop. (1970c) 13,025; ships coal; manufactures textiles, processed foods, machine parts; site of Fort Augusta (1756) nearby. Laid out 1772; in 1883 Thomas A. Edison set up and operated an incandescent electric lighting plant here.

3 County, New Brunswick, Canada. See table at NEW BRUNSWICK.

Sunbury–on–Thames \-'temz\. Urban district, Surrey, SE England, 15 m. WSW of London; pop. (1970e) 40,035; part of Greater London.

Sun·ch'ŏn \'sün-'chən\. Town, South Chŏlla prov., South Korea, ab. 19 m. NW of Yŏsu; pop. (1970e) 90,910.

Sun·cook \'sən-ˌkük\. 1 River, S cen. New Hampshire; rises in **Suncook Ponds,** SE Belknap co., flows S into Merrimack river in SE Merrimack co.

2 Industrial village (unincorp.), Merrimack co., S cen. New Hampshire in town of Pembroke, SE of Concord; pop. (1970c) 4320.

Sun·da Deep *also* **Soen·da Deep** \ˌsən-də-, ˌsün-də-\. One of the deepest parts of the Indian Ocean, off S coast of Java, Indonesia; 24,452 ft.

Sunda Isles *or* **Soenda Isles.** Islands, Malay Archipelago, divided into two groups: (1) **Greater Sunda Islands,** comprising Java, Sumatra, Borneo, Celebes (*qq.v.*), and adjacent islands, 514,953 sq. m., pop. (1970e) 112,138,626; (2) **Lesser Sunda Islands,** comprising chain of islands E from Bali to and including Alor and Timor, but not Wetar, 29,441 sq. m., pop. 6,999,000.

Sun·dance \'sən-ˌdans\. Town, ⊗ of Crook co., NE corner of Wyoming; pop. (1970c) 1056; Devils Tower National Monument is 20 m. to NW.

Sundarbans. See GANGES DELTA.

Sunda Strait *also* **Soenda Strait.** Channel bet. the islands of Sumatra and Java, Indonesia, connecting Java Sea with the Indian Ocean; 16 m. wide at its narrowest part. In its center is volcanic island of Krakatau (*q.v.*); on S side of entrance is Panaitan I.; on N side two large bays of S Sumatra—Lampung and Semangka—open into it.

Sun·day \'sən-dē\ *or* **Sun·days** \-dēz\. River, Cape Province, Rep. of South Africa; 250 m. long; flows into Algoa Bay.

Sunday Island. See RAOUL ISLAND.

Sunday Strait. Channel, the entrance to King Sound E of Cape Leveque, N Western Australia.

Sund·by·berg \ˌsən(d)-be-'be(ə)r\. City, Stockholm co., SE Sweden, a NW suburb of Stockholm; pop. (1970e) 27,666; manufactures cables.

Sunderbunds. See GANGES DELTA.

Sun·der·land \'sən-dər-lənd\. County borough, Durham, N England, on North Sea on S side of mouth of the Wear 12 m. SE of Newcastle upon Tyne; pop. (1971p) 216,892; shipbuilding center; shipping point, esp. for coal, steel, glassware; fisheries, coal mines; manufactures telecommunication equipment, furniture, pottery. A very old town, frequently called **Wear·mouth** \'wi(ə)r-məth\ in Saxon times. Monkwearmouth on N side of the mouth of the Wear was birthplace of Bede and contained the abbey where he was educated. **Bishop's Wearmouth,** an early settlement of the church on the S side of the river, is now within the borough of Sunderland but was long used as the name of the port.

Sund·gau \'zu̇nt-ˌgau̇\. Region, S Alsace, chiefly in Haut-Rhin dept., NE France.

Sunds·vall \'sən(t)s-ˌväl\. Seaport, Västernorrland co., E Sweden, on the Gulf of Bothnia; pop. (1970e) 63,939; trade center; exports lumber, wood pulp, cellulose.

Sun·flow·er \'sən-ˌflau̇(-ə)r\. 1 River, NW Mississippi; 240 m. long; flows S from Coahoma co., to Yazoo river on border bet. Yazoo and Sharkey cos.

2 County in Mississippi. See table at MISSISSIPPI.

Sunflower, Mount. Peak, Wallace co., Kansas; 4039 ft.; highest peak in Kansas.

Sung \'su̇ŋ\ *or* **Sung Shan** \-'shän\. Mountain (*shan*), N Honan prov., E cen. China, ab. 35 m. ESE of Lo-yang; 9200 ft.; one of the Five Sacred Mountains of China.

Sun·ga·ri \'su̇ŋ-gə-rē\ *or* **Sung–hua** \'su̇ŋ-'(h)wä\. River, NE China; 1150 m. long; chief tributary of the Amur; rises in Ch'ang-pai Shan on border of North Korea, flows NW past Yungki to join the Nen near Fu-yü, then turns sharply E and NE through a fertile plain to join the Amur at Tungkiang; navigable to Yungki.

Sungaria. See DZUNGARIA.

Sung–chiang *or* **Sung·kiang** \'su̇ŋ-jē-'äŋ\. 1 Former province, Manchuria, in cen. part; 30,703 sq. m.; ✱ Harbin.

2 Town, E China, 25 m. SW of Shanghai on the Huang-p'u river; burial place of Gen. Frederick T. Ward, leader of "Ever-Victorious Army" at time of Taiping Rebellion; also has temple erected by Chinese in his honor.

Sung·ei Pa·ta·ni \ˌsüŋ-ˌī-pə-'tän-ē\. Town, SW Kedah state, Malaysia, near coast ab. 15 m. N of Butterworth; pop. (1957c) 22,916.

Sungei Ujong \-'ü-ˌjȯŋ\. Former state, W Malay Penin.; became a part of Negri Sembilan state (*q.v.*) 1895.

Sung–hua. See SUNGARI.

Sungkiang. See SUNG-CHIANG.

Sung Shan. See SUNG.

Sunium Promontorium. See COLONNA, CAPE.

Su·ni·ya, Hor \hȯ(ə)r-'sü-nē-(y)ə\. Marshland region, SE Iraq, along W bank of lower Tigris; ab. 80 m. long, 10 m. wide.

Sunk Island \'səŋk-\. Parish in the estuary of the Humber, East Riding, Yorkshire, England; 7334 acres; formerly an islet.

Sun·light Peak \ˌsən-līt-\. 1 Mountain, La Plata co., SW Colorado; 14,059 ft.

2 Mountain, W Park co., NW Wyoming; 11,977 ft.

Sun·ny·side \'sən-ē-ˌsīd\. City, Yakima co., S Washington, 33 m. SE of Yakima; pop. (1970c) 6751; poultry packing; dairying.

Sun·ny·vale \'sən-ē-ˌvāl\. City, Santa Clara co., W California, 8 m. WNW of San Jose; pop. (1970c) 95,408; electronic equipment, cast iron products, chemicals; fruit and poultry farms; settled 1849, incorp. 1924.

Sun Prairie. City, Dane co., S Wisconsin, 11 m. NE of Madison; pop. (1970c) 9935; dairy farming.

Sun·rise Golf Village \'sən-ˌrīz-'gälf-, -'gȯlf-, -'gäf-, -'gȯf-\. City, Broward co., SE Florida; pop. (1970c) 7403.

Sun River. See SUN.

Sun·set \'sən-ˌset\. City, Davis co., N Utah, 7 m. SW of Ogden; pop. (1970c) 6268.

Sunset Crater. Volcanic crater, cen. Coconino co., N cen. Arizona, E of San Francisco Peaks and ab. 15 m. NE of Flagstaff; 5 sq. m.; central feature of **Sunset Crater National Monument:** see UNITED STATES, *National Monuments.*

Sunset Hills. City, St. Louis co., E Missouri; pop. (1970c) 4126.

Sun·shine Peak \ˌsən-shīn-\. Mountain, Hinsdale co., SW Colorado; 14,001 ft.

Sün·tel \'zün-tᵊl\ *or* **Sün·tel·berg** \-ˌbe(ə-)rg\. Elevation, Lower Saxony, West Germany, on N bank of Weser; 1433 ft.; here Wittekind destroyed Frankish army 782.

Sun Valley. Resort center, Sawtooth Range, Blaine co., cen. Idaho, just N of Ketchum; Sun Valley Lodge, built by Union Pacific R.R., opened Sept. 1936.

Sun·ya·ni \su̇n-'yä-nē\. Town, ✱ of Brong-Ahafo region, Ghana, W Africa, on Kumasi-Pamu motor road 80 m. NW of Kumasi; pop. (1970p) 23,872.

Suo·men·lin·na \'swȯ-mən-ˌlin-ə\ *or Swed.* **Sve·a·borg** \ˌsfā-ə-'bȯ(ə)rg, -'bȯ(ə)r(-yə)\. Fortress in the harbor of Helsinki, S Finland; built by the Swedes 1749; captured by Russians 1808; bombarded by French-British fleet 1855 in Crimean War.

Suomen Tasavalta. See FINLAND.

Suomi. See FINLAND.

Suo·mus·sal·mi \'swȯ-mu̇s-ˌsal-mē\. Town, Oulu prov., E Finland, near Karelian border 105 m. E of Oulu; pop. (1970e) 15,300.

Suō Sea *also* **Su·wo Sea** \'sü-(ˌ)(w)ō-\. The W part of the Inland Sea, Japan, bet. SW Honshū and NE Kyūshū.

Supanburi. See SUPHAN BURI.

Su·pe·ri·or \su̇-'pir-ē-ər\. 1 Town (unincorporated), Pinal co., S Arizona; pop. (1970c) 4975; formerly silver mines, now copper.

2 Town, ⊗ of Mineral co., W Montana; pop. (1970c) 993.

3 City, Nuckolls co., S Nebraska, on Kansas border 43 m. SSE of Hastings; pop. (1970c) 2779; cement products; farming.

4 City, ⊗ of Douglas co., NW corner of Wisconsin, at extreme W end of Lake Superior opposite Duluth, Minnesota; pop. (1970c) 32,237; port of entry; railroad center and lake transportation terminus; grain center and shipping point for iron and copper ore; manufactures flour, lumber products, engines, marine equipment; oil refining; Wisconsin State College (1896).

Superior, Lake. Lake, U.S. and Canada, bounded on N and E by province of Ontario, Canada, on S by Michigan and Wisconsin, on W by Minnesota, the U.S.-Canada boundary passing through it; northernmost and westernmost of the five Great Lakes; ab. 350 m. long; area 31,800 sq. m.; greatest depth 1333 ft.; elevation 600 ft.; area of drainage basin 80,100 sq. m.; largest body of fresh water in the world; at SE end connected by St. Marys river with Lake Huron.

Su·phan Bu·ri *or* **Su·pan·bu·ri** \ˌsü-ˌpän-bu̇-'rē\. 1 Province, SW Thailand; 2061 sq. m.; pop. (1960c) 491,252; ✱ Suphan Buri.

2 Town, its ✱, on left bank of the Tha Chin 30 m. WNW of Phra Nakhon Si Ayutthaya; pop. (1964e) 15,761.

Su·pi·o·ri *or* **Soe·pi·o·ri** \ˌsü-pē-'ȯr-ē\. Island, N Irian Barat, Indonesia, just W of Biak in the Schouten Is., N of Sarera Bay; ab. 17 m. long by 6 m. wide; very rugged surface with highest point 3392 ft.; occupied by Allies Sept. 7, 1944.

Suqutrā. See SOCOTRA.

Sur \'su̇(ə)r\. 1 Seaport town, E Oman, SE Arabian Penin., on the Gulf of Oman 70 m. SE of Masqat and near Cape Hadd.

2 Town, Lebanon. See TYRE.

Sur, Point \-'sər\. Point, NW coast of Monterey co., W California.

Su·ra \'su̇r-ə\. Ancient city of Babylonia, on the Euphrates just W of Thapsacus; in Roman times a border stronghold; site of famous Talmudic school 609 to 1038.

Sura \su̇-'rä\. River, E cen. Russian S.F.S.R., U.S.S.R.; 537 m. long; rises in E Penza Oblast and flows N through or on the border of Ulyanovsk Oblast and Chuvash A.S.S.R. to the Volga below Gorki; navigable to Penza.

Su·ra·ba·ja *or Du.* **Soe·ra·ba·ja** \ˌsu̇r-ə-'bī-ə\. 1 Former residency, now part of East Java prov., Indonesia; 1362 sq. m.; ✱ Surabaja. Before 17th cent. a small commercial kingdom, overcome 1625 by Mataram; came under Dutch control 1743; occupied by Japanese 1942–45.

2 Seaport city, ✱ of East Java prov., Indonesia, at mouth of Kali Mas river on Surabaja Strait, near W end of Madura Strait; pop. (1971e) 1,273,000; major seaport, exporting sugar, rubber, coffee, and spices; industrial center, producing textiles, glass, footwear, tobacco products; locomotive works, shipyards, oil refinery; principal Indonesian naval base, with dockyard facilities and naval college; large 19th

cent. mosque; univ. (1954). Before World War II the principal Dutch naval base in the East Indies; occupied by Japanese 1942–45 and suffered heavy damage.

Surabaja Strait *or formerly* **Soerabaja Strait.** Narrow passage bet. NE Java and Madura I., Indonesia; ab. 24 m. long; connects Java Sea with W end of Madura Strait.

Su·ra·kar·ta *or Du.* **Soe·ra·kar·ta** \ˌsu̇r-ə-ˈkärt-ə\. 1 Former protected native principality, S cen. Java, Indonesia; 2331 sq. m.; ❋ Surakarta. Constituted a government of the former Netherlands East Indies. Founded 1755 at the breakup of Mataram sultanate; its prince (Susuhunan) was under advice of Dutch resident from 1830; occupied by Japanese 1942–45; abolished after Indonesia became independent.

2 *also* **So·lo** \ˈsō-(ˌ)lō\. City, Central Java prov., Indonesia, 50 m. SE of Semarang; pop. (1961c) 367,626; market for tobacco, sugar, rice, fruits; produces batik cloth, cigarettes, furniture, textiles; handicrafts; palaces of former native rulers, Dutch fort; Islamic Univ. of Indonesia, with library and museum.

Su·ram Mountains \ˌsu̇(ə)r-ˌäm-\. Mountain range, cen. Georgian S.S.R., U.S.S.R., WNW of Tbilisi; ranges from 5000 to 6000 ft.; separates the Rioni and Kura river basins and forms a connecting link bet. the Caucasus Mts. on N and highlands of Armenia on S; lowest point is **Suram Pass** (3500 ft.); crossed by railroad (tunnel 2½ m. long) from Baku to Black Sea.

Su·rat \ˈsu̇r-ət, sə-ˈrat\. City, SE Gujarat, W India, on Tapti river near its mouth 150 m. N of Bombay; pop. (1970e) 393,915; has cotton, rice, and paper mills, and soap works; silk brocade, gold- and silverware, carpets, and inlaid work; several colleges.

History: Chief seaport and commercial city of India under Akbar, Jahangir and Shah Jahan; destroyed by Portuguese 1512, 1530, and 1531; conquered by Akbar 1573. English factory founded 1608, the first in India and beginning of British Empire in India; seat of British Indian government until 1687; began to decline at beginning of 19th cent.; population at one time reputed to have been 800,000.

Surat Agency. Former agency, W India; comprised three small Indian states Bansda, Dharampur, and Sachin; later part of Gujarat States Agency; the states became part of India 1947.

Surat Tha·ni *or* **Su·rat·dha·ni** \ˌsu̇r-ät-ˈän-ē\. 1 Province, SW Thailand; 4946 sq. m.; pop. (1960c) 324,784; ❋ Surat Thani.

2 Railroad town and port, its ❋, on Gulf of Siam 70 m. NW of Nakhon Si Thammarat; pop. (1964e) 30,413.

Su·resnes \sü-ˈrān, -ˈren\. Manufacturing commune, Hauts-de-Seine dept., N France, W suburb of Paris on Seine river; pop. (1968c) 40,616; machinery, automobiles, chemicals, perfumes; American military cemetery.

Surf·side \ˈsərf-ˌsīd\. Town, Dade co., SE Florida, on Atlantic coast 6 m. N of Miami Beach; pop. (1970c) 3614.

Sur·gu·ja \su̇r-ˈgü-jə\ *or* **Sir·gu·ja** \sir-\. Former Indian state, now part of E Madhya Pradesh state, India; 6067 sq. m.; ceded to British in 1818.

Sur·gut \su̇r-ˈgüt\. Town, S Khanty-Mansi National Okrug, Russian S.F.S.R., U.S.S.R., on right bank of Ob river in swamp region 270 m. NE of Tobolsk; pop. (1967e) 19,000; in oil-producing region.

Su·ri·ba·chi, Mount \-ˌsu̇r-ə-ˈbäch-ē\. Active volcano, S tip of Iwo Jima, in Volcano Is.; 548 ft.; taken by U.S. Marines Feb. 23, 1945 and flag raising on its summit provided one of the best known photographs relating to World War II; top of mountain leveled off by U.S. engineers after island established as base.

Su·ri·gao \ˌsu̇r-i-ˈgau̇\. 1 Former province, NE Mindanao, Phil., now consisting of **Surigao del Nor·te** \-del-ˈnȯrt-ē\ and **Surigao del Sur** \-del-ˈsu̇(ə)r\ (see table at PHILIPPINES).

History: Coast explored in middle of 16th cent. and missions established as early as 1597; settlement difficult because of Moro raids, esp. the destructive attack of 1752; made part of a province 1849 and given military government 1860; civil government set up by U.S. May 1901 and its present boundaries determined 1911; divided into two provinces 1960.

2 Municipality, ❋ of Surigao del Norte prov., at N tip of mainland on narrow strait opp. Dinagat I.; pop. (1969e) 51,100; one of oldest Spanish towns in the Philippines.

Surigao Strait. Channel, SE Phil., bet. Leyte I. on W and Dinagat I. on E and touching NE point of Mindanao on SE; 10 to 25 m. wide; connects Pacific Ocean with Mindanao Sea; in World War II on Oct. 23–25, 1944 S division of Japanese fleet defeated here by U.S. fleet.

Su·rin \su̇-ˈrin\. 1 Province, SE Thailand; 3392 sq. m.; pop. (1960c) 581,732; ❋ Surin.

2 Town, its ❋, on railroad 95 m. E of Nakhon Ratchasima; pop. (1964e) 16,520.

Su·ri·nam \ˈsu̇r-ə-ˌnam\ *or Du.* **Su·ri·na·me** \ˌsue̅-rē-ˈnäm-ə\. 1 *also* **Netherlands Gui·a·na** \-gē-ˈan-ə, -ˈän-ə; -gī-ˈan-ə\ *or* **Dutch Guiana.** Autonomous territory within the Netherlands realm, South America, bounded on N by the Atlantic Ocean, on E by French Guiana, on S by Brazil, and on W by Guyana; 63,251 sq. m.; pop. (1968e) 375,200; ❋ Paramaribo. *Physical features:* S and cen. parts consist of a forested plateau region and extensive savannas; mountain ranges in cen. part and S have peaks 3300 and 4200 ft. (Wilhelmina Mts.) and the Tumuc-Humac Mts. on Brazilian border reach 2700–3000 ft.; entire S part almost completely unexplored. Has many rivers, esp. the Courantyne (or Corantijn) on Guyana border, the Maroni (or Marowijne) and its headstream, the Itany, on French Guiana border, and the Suriname, Saramacca, Coppename, and Commewijne flowing N through cen. part. Agricultural areas along the coast and river courses. *Chief products:* Rice, citrus fruit, coffee, bananas, coconuts, corn; timber; bauxite. *Chief towns:* Paramaribo, Nieuw Nickerie.

History: First settled by the English; first permanent settlement set by Lord Willoughby of Parham 1650; capitulated to the Dutch and was ceded to them by Treaty of Breda 1667; held by the English 1799–1802 and 1804–16; became an autonomous territory under the Dutch crown 1954.

2 District of N Surinam.

Su·ri·na·me \ˌsu̇r-ə-ˈnäm-ə\. River, N Surinam; ab. 250 m. long; flows N into Atlantic Ocean at Paramaribo.

Sur·khan·dar·ya Oblast \ˌsu̇r-kən-dər-ˈyä-ˈō-bləst, -ˌblast\ *or formerly* **Su·khan–Dar·ya Oblast** \ˌsü-kən-dər-ˈyä-\. Subdivision of the Uzbek S.S.R., U.S.S.R., bet. Turkmen S.S.R. on W and Tadzhik S.S.R. on E and on the S bordering on Afghanistan; 8031 sq. m.; pop. (1970p) 662,000; ❋ Termez; cotton, wheat.

Sur·khob *or* **Surkh·ab** \su̇(ə)r-ˈkäb\. River, Tadzhik S.S.R., U.S.S.R.; ab. 400 m. long; a N tributary of the Amu Darya.

Sur·ma \ˈsu̇r-mə\. River, NE India; ab. 560 m. long; rises in Manipur state (where it is called the Barak, *q.v.*), flows W into Bangla Desh.

Surrentine Peninsula *and* **Surrentum.** See SORRENTO.

Sur·rey \ˈsər-ē, ˈsə-rē\. County, S England; area 654 sq. m.; pop. (1971p) 999,588; ⊗ Kingston on Thames; rivers Wey, Mole, both tributaries of the Thames; largely residential; market gardening, dairy farming; main towns Epsom and Ewell, Esher, Reigate, and Guildford.

Sur·ry \ˈsər-ē, ˈsə-rē\. 1 Name of counties in two states of the U.S. See tables at NORTH CAROLINA and VIRGINIA.

2 Town, ⊗ of Surry co., SE Virginia; pop. (1970c) 269.

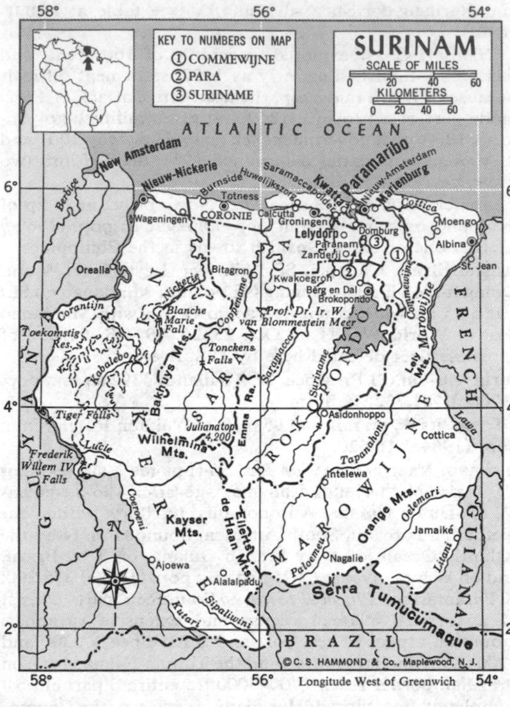

Surt·sey \'sərt-sē\. Island off S Iceland; ab. 1 sq. m.; formed by volcanic activity 1963; established as nature reserve 1965.

Su·rud Ad \'sùr-əd-'äd\. Mountain, N Somalia, ab. 240 m. NE of Hargeysa; 7894 ft.; highest peak in Somalia.

Su·ru·ga Bay \ˌsùr-ə-gə-\. Inlet of the Pacific Ocean, SE coast of Honshū, Japan, SW of Tokyo.

Su·sa \'sü-sə, -zə\. **1** *or Biblical* **Shu·shan** \'shü-shən, -ˌshan\. Ancient city, ✱ of Elam (*q.v.*), now ruins at the village of **Shūsh** \'shüsh\ on the railroad ab. 15 m. S of Dezfūl, SW Iran. Settled in very early times, it came to be the winter residence of Achaemenian kings (7th cent. to 331 B.C.); its palace and treasure house were in a strong citadel. Made Persian capital by Cyrus; scene of the story of Esther, the Jewish queen of the Persian king Ahasuerus.
2 Town, Tunisia. See SOUSSE.

Su·šak \'sü-ˌshäk\ *or Ital.* **San·se·go** \'sän-sā-(ˌ)gō\. Island, SW of Lošinj I., Croatia, NW Yugoslavia, in group SE of Istria Penin.; 1½ sq. m.; formerly belonged to Italy; by treaty of 1947 assigned to Yugoslavia.

Susam–Adasi. See SAMOS 1.

Su·san·ville \'süz-ᵊn-ˌvil\. City, ⊗ of Lassen co., NE California, at head of Honey Lake Valley 40 m. E of Lassen Peak; pop. (1970c) 6608; Lassen Coll. (1925).

Susiana. 1 Ancient kingdom, Iran. See ELAM.
2 Province, Iran. See KHŪZESTĀN.

Su·sit·na \sü-'sit-nə\. River, S Alaska; 300 m. long; flows W and S from E end of Alaska Range to Cook Inlet.

Sus·que·han·na \ˌsəs-kwə-'han-ə\. **1** River, cen. New York, Pennsylvania, and Maryland; 444 m. long; rises in Otsego Lake, Otsego co., cen. New York, flows S across Pennsylvania border and across E Pennsylvania and NE corner of Maryland to empty into N Chesapeake Bay. By the use of canals it has been made navigable for a short distance from its mouth. The **West Branch of Susquehanna River,** ab. 200 m. long, rises in SW cen. Pennsylvania and flows NE and E across cen. Pennsylvania to unite with the Susquehanna near Sunbury, Northumberland co.
2 County in Pennsylvania. See table at PENNSYLVANIA.

Sus·sex \'səs-iks\. **1** Name of counties in three states of the U.S. See tables at DELAWARE, NEW JERSEY, VIRGINIA.
2 Village, ⊗ of Sussex co., SE Virginia, S of Petersburg.
3 Village, Waukesha co., SE Wisconsin, 18 m. NW of Milwaukee; pop. (1970c) 2758.
4 Town, Kings co., S New Brunswick, Canada, 43 m. NE of St. John; pop. (1971p) 3840; poultry processing.
5 Anglo-Saxon kingdom, S England; traditionally founded 477 but little known about its early history; subject at times in 6th and 7th cents. to Kent and Mercia; in conflict with Wessex in 8th cent. and in 825 became part of it. See HEPTARCHY, THE.
6 County, S England, on the English Channel; 1457 sq. m.; pop. (1971p) 1,241,332; divided into two administrative counties, **East Sussex** (824 sq. m.; pop. 750,312; ⊗ Lewes) and **West Sussex** (633 sq. m.; pop. 491,020; ⊗ Chichester); rivers Arun, Ouse, Rother, Adur; dairy cattle, poultry; fisheries; largest towns Worthing, Brighton, Hastings, Eastbourne, Bexhill, Chichester.

Suth·er·land \'sət͟h-ər-lənd\ *or* **Suth·er·land·shire** \-lən(d)-ˌshi(ə)r, -shər\. County, N Scotland; area 2029 sq. m.; pop. (1971p) 13,053; ⊗ Dornoch; mountainous region; deer-hunting resort; fisheries.

Sutherland Falls. Waterfall, South I., New Zealand, near W coast 16 m. S of the head of Milford Sound; 1904 ft. high; one of the world's highest waterfalls, plunges down in three sections of 815, 751, and 338 ft.

Suth·er·lin \'sət͟h-ər-lən\. City, Douglas co., SW Oregon, 15 m. N of Roseburg; pop. (1970c) 3070; logging; diversified agriculture; sawmills.

Suthreyjar. See SODOR.

Sut·lej \'sət-ˌlej\. River, Asia; 850 m. long; one of the "Five Rivers" of the Punjab; rises in SW Tibet, China, flows W through the Himalayas across Himachal Pradesh and Punjab states, India, then SW across Punjab prov. of Pakistan, to join the Chenab and form the Panjnad (*q.v.*); in its middle course important for irrigation projects.

Sutna. See SATNA.

Su·tro Tunnel \ˌsü-(ˌ)trō-\. Drainage tunnel, near present site of Virginia City, Nevada; 4½ m. long; built (completed 1878) to drain the Comstock mine.

Sut·ter \'sət-ər\. County in California. See table at CALIFORNIA.

Sutter's Mill. See COLOMA.

Sut·ton \'sət-ᵊn\. **1** County in Texas. See table at TEXAS.
2 Town, Worcester co., cen. Massachusetts, 8 m. SSE of Worcester; pop. (1970c) 4590.
3 Town, ⊗ of Braxton co., cen. West Virginia; pop. (1970c) 1031.
4 A borough of Greater London, SE England. See table at LONDON 4.

Sutton Cold·field \ˌsət-ᵊn-'kōl(d)-ˌfēld\. Municipal borough, Warwickshire, cen. England, 8 m. NE of Birmingham; pop. (1971p) 83,130; residential suburb of Birmingham; holiday resort.

Sutton in Ash·field \-'ash-ˌfēld\. Urban district, Nottinghamshire, N cen. England, 13 m. N of Nottingham; pop. (1971p) 40,725; coal mines; lime works.

Sutton–on–the–Forest *also* **Sutton–in–the–Forest.** Village, North Riding, Yorkshire, England, 8 m. N of York; residence (1738–59) of Lawrence Sterne.

Suursaari. See HOGLAND.

Su·va \'sü-və\. Seaport town, ✱ of Fiji, on SE coast of Viti Levu I., SW Pacific Ocean; pop. (1971e) 63,200; food processing; tourism; Univ. of the South Pacific (1968); has one of best harbors in South Pacific Ocean.

Suvalkai *or* **Suvalki.** See SUWAŁKI.

Sü·vey·di·ye \sü-ˌvī-di-'yā\ *or Fr.* **Souei·dié** \swā-dyā\. Seaport town, S Turkey, just N of mouth of the Orontes river ab. 35 m. S of İskenderun; nearby is site of ancient **Se·leu·cia** \sə-'lü-sh(ē-)ə\ *or* **Seleucia Pi·e·ria** \-pī-'ir-ē-ə\, which was founded by Seleucus Nicator 300 B.C.; strongly fortified, it became a great city and seaport, the port of Antioch; held by Egyptians 246 to 219 B.C. but recovered by Antiochus the Great; became independent c. 108 B.C. and its freedom confirmed by Pompey; disappeared c. 6th cent. A.D.

Suvla Bay. See ANAFARTA BAY.

Su·vo·rov \sü-ˈvȯr-əf\ *or* **Su·war·row** \sü-ˈwär-ō\. Island, Pacific Ocean, NNW of Cook Is. and E of Samoa, 13°S and 163°W; has good anchorage but is uninhabited; administered by New Zealand.

Su·vo Ru·diš·te \ˌsü-vō-ˈrüd-ish-ˌtā\. Highest peak in Kopaonik range, Serbia, S cen. Yugoslavia; 7020 ft.

Su·wa \ˈsü-wə, sü-ˈwä\. Lake, W cen. Honshū, Japan, within sight of Fuji; ab. 10 m. in circumference; altitude 2600 ft.

Su·wał·ki \sü-ˈväl-kē\ *or Russ.* **Su·val·ki** \sü-ˈväl-kē\ *or Lith.* **Su·val·kai** \sü-ˈväl-kī\. 1 Region, NE Poland, E of the Masurian Lakes; scene of several battles in World War I from Feb. to July 1915, esp. Feb. 7–14. After 1919 divided, N part to Lithuania, S part to Poland; assigned to Germany 1939 and after outbreak of war with U.S.S.R. held until retaken by U.S.S.R. 1944; part of Belorussian S.S.R. 1944–45 but ceded back to Poland Aug. 1945 (see BIAŁYSTOK).

2 City, Białystok prov., NE Poland, 68 m. N of Białystok; pop. (1970p) 25,400; textiles; center of conflict 1915 in World War I.

Su·wan·nee \sə-ˈwän-ē\. 1 River, SE Georgia and N Florida penin.; ab. 250 m. long; rises in Ware co., SE Georgia, flows SW across Florida into Gulf of Mexico at Suwannee Sound.

2 County in Florida. See table at FLORIDA.

Suwannee Sound. Inlet of Gulf of Mexico, W coast of Levy co., NW Florida penin., receiving Suwannee river on N.

Suwarrow. See SUVOROV.

Suweida, Es. See ES SUWEIDA.

Su·wŏn \ˈsü-ˈwən\. Town, Kyŏnggi prov., South Korea, 18 m. S of Seoul; pop. (1970e) 170,518.

Suwo Sea. See SUŌ SEA.

Suz·dal \ˈsüz-dəl(-yə)\. Principality, cen. Russia, c. 9th cent. to 13th cent.; united with Rostov (Rostov-Suzdal principality); later, c. 1150, with Vladimir (*q.v.*); ultimately absorbed by it and by Moscow.

Su·zu·ka \sə-ˈzü-kə\. City, Mie prefecture, Honshū, Japan, ab. 28 m. SW of Nagoya; pop. (1970c) 131,185.

Sval·bard \ˈsfäl-ˌbär\. Island group, Arctic Ocean, bet. long. 10° and 35°E and lat. 74° and 81°N; 23,958 sq. m.; pop. (1970e) 2900; includes Spitsbergen (*q.v.*) group and Bear I. (*q.v.*); Norwegian possession.

Svart \ˈsfärt\. 1 Short river, S cen. Sweden; flows E into W end of Lake Hjälmaren at Örebro.

2 Short river, E Sweden; flows S into Lake Mälaren at Västerås.

Svart·i·sen *or* **Svart Isen** \ˈsfärt-ˌēs-ᵊn\. Ice field, N Norway, on the Arctic Circle; ab. 230 sq. m.; source of glaciers descending almost to sea level.

Svätý. See SAINT.

Sveaborg. See SUOMENLINNA.

Sve·a·land \ˈsvā-ə-ˌland\. Region, cen. Sweden; 33,126 sq. m.; pop. (1970e) 3,009,579; comprises the counties of Uppsala, Södermanland, Värmland, Örebro, Västmanland, and Kopparberg.

Svend·borg \ˈsfen-ˌbȯ(ə)r\. Seaport, Fyn I., Denmark; pop. (1970e) 23,149; shipbuilding yards; textile mills, breweries; tobacco processing.

Sverd·lovsk \sferd-ˈlȯfsk\. 1 *or before 1924* **Eka·te·rin·burg** \i-ˈkat-ə-rən-ˌbərg\ *also* **Ye·ka·te·rin·burg** \yi-\. City, ✻ of Sverdlovsk Oblast, Russian S.F.S.R., U.S.S.R.; pop. (1970p) 1,026,000; has long been a mining center with furnaces and factories processing wide range of minerals from mines in the Ural Mts.; chemicals, heavy machinery, electrical equipment, ball bearings, precision instruments; univ. (1920); railroad junction city and a W terminus of the Trans-Siberian R.R.

History: Founded 1721 by Peter the Great and named after his wife, (the Empress) Catherine I (Russ. *Ekaterina*); place where the Emperor Nicholas II and his family were held as prisoners by the Bolsheviks after the Revolution 1917 and all killed July 16, 1918; renamed 1924 after a Communist leader.

2 *or formerly* **Ime·ni Sverd·lo·va Rud·nik** \ˈē-mā-nyi-ˌsverd-ləv-ə-ˈrüd-nik\. Town, Voroshilovgrad Oblast, Ukrainian S.S.R., U.S.S.R., ab. 35 m. SSE of Voroshilovgrad; pop. (1969e) 72,000.

Sverdlovsk Oblast \-ˈō-bləst, -ˌblast\. Subdivision of the Russian S.F.S.R., U.S.S.R.; 75,212 sq. m.; pop. (1970p) 4,319,000; ✻ Sverdlovsk. Crossed from N to S by Ural Mts. (*q.v.*) where tributaries of both the Tobol and Kama rise; for the most part lies on the E slopes of the mountains and has rich soil. Has extensive mineral resources (iron ore, manganese, cobalt, nickel, asbestos, bauxite, copper). Chief cities Sverdlovsk, Nizhni Tagil, Kamensk-Uralski, Serov. Organized as a subdivision of the Russian S.F.S.R. 1934.

Sver·drup Islands \ˈsfer-drəp-\. Island group, W of Ellesmere I. in Arctic Archipelago, Franklin district, Northwest Territories, Canada; chief islands Axel Heiberg, Ellef Ringnes, and Amund Ringnes.

Sverige. See SWEDEN.

Sveti. See SAINT.

Svetiya. See SAINT.

Sve·to·za·re·vo \ˈsfe-tə-ˌzä-rə-(ˌ)vō\. Town, Serbia, Yugoslavia, ab. 70 m. SE of Belgrade; pop. (1965e) 24,000.

Svir \ˈsfi(ə)r\. Navigable river, NE Leningrad Oblast, Russian S.F.S.R., U.S.S.R.; 139 m. long; flows from Lake Onega to Lake Ladoga; has large hydroelectric power station on its banks. Its course forms part of the Volga-Baltic Waterway (*q.v.*). Formed battle line bet. Finns and Soviets 1941 and bet. Germans and Soviets 1944.

Svi·shtov *or* **Svi·štov** \sfi-ˈshtȯf\ *or angl.* **Sis·to·va** \ˈsis-ˌtō-və\. Town, Veliko Tŭrnovo prov., N Bulgaria, on the Danube; pop. (1968e) 22,456. Treaty of Sistova signed here Aug. 4, 1791 determining the boundary bet. Austria and Turkey.

Svi·ta·vy \ˈsfi-tə-vē\ *or Ger.* **Zwit·tau** \ˈtsfit-aü\. Town, Czech S.R., cen. Czechoslovakia, 38 m. N of Brno; pop. (1968e) 13,805.

Svi·ya·ga \sfē-ˈyäg-ə\. River, Russian S.F.S.R., U.S.S.R.; 245 m. long; rises in S Ulyanovsk Oblast, flows N into Volga river just W of Kazan; near Ulyanovsk it approaches within 4 m. of the Volga.

Svizzera. See SWITZERLAND.

Svo·bod·ny \sfə-ˈbȯd-nē\. Town, Amur Oblast, Russian S.F.S.R., U.S.S.R., on Zeya river and on Trans-Siberian R.R.; pop. (1969e) 64,000.

Svyatoi. See SAINT.

Swa·bia \ˈswā-bē-ə\ *or Ger.* **Schwa·ben** \ˈshfä-ben\. Duchy, medieval Germany, nearly coextensive with modern Baden-Württemberg, Hesse, and W Bavaria states, West Germany. Original inhabitants were Suevi (whence its name) and Alamanni; conquered by Franks in 5th cent. A.D. Duchy from 10th cent., a fief of Emperor Henry IV, and ruled by Hohenstaufen kings and emperors 1105–1254; divided in 1268. Leagues of Swabian cities formed esp. 1331 and 1488–1534. Chief cities of duchy Augsburg, Ulm, Freiburg, Konstanz.

Swad·lin·cote \ˈswäd-lin-ˌkōt\. Urban district, Derbyshire, N cen. England, 26 m. NE of Birmingham; pop. (1971p) 20,235.

Swain \ˈswān\. County in North Carolina. See table at NORTH CAROLINA.

Swain Reefs. Coral reefs, S end of Great Barrier Reef, Queensland, Australia.

Swains \ˈswānz\ *also* **Qui·ros** \ˈkē-ˌrōs\ *or formerly* **Gen·te Her·mo·sa** \ˌhān-tā-er-ˈmō-sə\. Island, American Samoa,

SW cen. Pacific Ocean, 200 m. NW of the island of Tutuila; lat. 11°S and long. 171°W; 1 sq. m.; formerly a part of the Tokelau Is. under the jurisdiction of Gilbert and Ellice Islands Colony; transferred to U.S. 1926.

Swains·boro \ˈswānz-ˌbər-ə, -ˌbə-rə\. City, ⊗ of Emanuel co., E cen. Georgia, 33 m. WNW of Statesboro; pop. (1970c) 7325; cotton gins, machine shops; corn, tobacco.

Swa·kop \ˈsfäk-ˌȯp\. River, South-West Africa; 250 m. long; flows into Atlantic Ocean N of Walvis Bay.

Swa·kop·mund \ˈsfäk-ˌȯp-ˌmənt\. Town, W South-West Africa, on Atlantic Ocean 175 m. W of Windhoek; pop. (1960c) 4660; formerly chief port of German Southwest Africa but now closed to shipping; vacation resort.

Swale \ˈswāl\. River, Yorkshire, N England; 60 m. long; flows S to unite with the Ure river and form the Ouse.

Swamp·scott \ˈswäm(p)-skət\. Town, Essex co., NE corner of Massachusetts, on Massachusetts Bay 11 m. NE of Boston; pop. (1970c) 13,578; summer resort.

Swan \ˈswän\. **1** River, SW Western Australia; flows W to Indian Ocean; ab. 240 m. long; called Avon in upper course. Perth situated on it near its mouth. Discovered and named 1697 by Willem de Vlamingh, Dutch navigator.
2 River, E Saskatchewan and W Manitoba, Canada; ab. 110 m. long; flows NE into Swan Lake.

Swan·age \ˈswän-ij\. Urban district, Dorsetshire, S England, on English Channel 33 m. SW of Southampton; pop. (1971p) 8550; seaside resort; stone quarrying.

Swan Islands. Two small islands, W Caribbean Sea, N of Honduras; total area 1 sq. m.

Swankalok. See SAWANKHALOK.

Swan Lake. **1** Lake, Nicollet co., S Minnesota.
2 Lake, W Manitoba, Canada; 118 sq. m.; receives Swan river from SW and drains N into Lake Winnipegosis.

Swan·land \ˈswän-ˌland, -lənd\. Region, SW Western Australia—the plateau to the E of the Upper Swan (Avon) river.

Swan Point. Point, SW shore of Kent co., NE Maryland, extending into upper Chesapeake Bay.

Swan Quarter. Town, ⊗ of Hyde co., E North Carolina.

Swan Range. A range of the Rocky Mts.; chiefly in Flathead and Powell cos., W Montana.

Swan River. **1** Rivers in Australia and Canada. See SWAN.
2 Town, W Manitoba, Canada, on Swan river 30 m. SW of Swan Lake; pop. (1971p) 3487; stock farms.

Swans·combe \ˈswänz-kəm\. Urban district, Kent, SE England, on the Thames 10 m. E of London; pop. (1971p) 9184.

Swan·sea \ˈswän-zē, ˈswän(t)-sē\. **1** Village, Saint Clair co., SW Illinois, 11 m. SE of East St. Louis; pop. (1970c) 5432.
2 Town, Bristol co., SE Massachusetts, 3 m. NW of Fall River; pop. (1970c) 12,640; settled 1632, incorp. 1668; scene of first bloodshed in King Philip's War 1675; in agricultural region.
3 Village, York co., SE Ontario, Canada, on Lake Ontario 6 m. W of Toronto; pop. (1966c) 9703.
4 County borough and seaport, Glamorganshire, S Wales; pop. (1971p) 172,566; steel works, oil refineries, smelters; center of tin-plate industry; shipbuilding yards; Univ. Coll. of Swansea (1920).

Swans Island \ˈswänz-\. Island, Atlantic Ocean, off S coast of SE Maine; part of Hancock co.

Swan·son Mountains \ˌswän(t)-sən-\. Mountain range, a subsidiary range of the Ford Ranges, Marie Byrd Land, Antarctica, ab. 77°S, 145°W; highest peak ab. 3000 ft.; discovered 1934.

Swan·ton \ˈswänt-ᵊn\. **1** Manufacturing village, Fulton co., NW Ohio, 19 m. W of Toledo; pop. (1970c) 2927.
2 Town, Franklin co., NW Vermont, on Missisquoi river 8 m. N of St. Albans; pop. (1970c) 4622.

Swan·zey \ˈswän-zē\. Town, Cheshire co., SW corner of New Hampshire, 4 m. S of Keene; pop. (1970c) 4254.

Swart·berg \ˈsvärt-ˌbərg, -ˌbe(ə)rg\ *or Afrikaans* **Zwaar·te·berg** \ˈsvärt-ə-ˌbərg, -ˌbe(ə)rg\. Mountains, S Cape Province, S Rep. of South Africa, separating Great Karroo from Little Karroo; contains the Cango Caves; traversed by a pass at alt. 5000 ft.

Swarth·more \ˈswȯ(ə)rth-ˌmō(ə)r; ˈswäth-, -ˌmȯ(ə)r\. Borough, Delaware co., SE Pennsylvania, 11 m. W of Philadelphia; pop. (1970c) 6156; residential suburb of Philadelphia; Swarthmore Coll. (1864).

Swartz Creek \ˈswȯrts-\. City, Genessee co., SE cen. Michigan, 10 m. WSW of Flint; pop. (1970c) 4928; diversified agriculture.

Swat \ˈswät\. **1** River, North-West Frontier Province, Pakistan; ab. 400 m. long; rises in N Swat dist., flows SW and SE into Kabul river NE of Peshawar.
2 District, Malakand division, Pakistan, in the valley of the Swat river, NNE of Peshawar; 2934 sq. m.; pop. (1961c) 614,395; emerald mines. The inhabitants, Swatis, are Afghans and Sunni Muslims; since 1947 a part of Pakistan; retained limited autonomy until 1969.

Swa·tow \ˈswä-ˈtau̇\ *or* **Shan–t'ou** \ˈshän-ˈtō\. Town, E Kwangtung prov., SE China, at mouth of Han Shui on S side ab. 170 m. NW of Hong Kong; pop. (1970e) 400,000; has excellent harbor; trades in tea, sugar, oranges, tobacco; has grown from small fishing village in latter half of 19th cent.; made a treaty port 1869; in World War II held by Japanese until 1945.

Swa·zi·land \ˈswäz-ē-ˌland\. Kingdom, S Africa, bordering on Mozambique and the Rep. of South Africa; 6705 sq. m.; pop. (1972e) 442,195; ✱ Mbabane. *Physical features:* W consists of high veld (elev. ranges from 4000 to 6000 ft.), cen. region consists of middle veld (max. elev. 4000 ft.), and E is characterized by low veld (mean elev. 1500 ft.); major rivers Komati, Umbeluzi, Usutu. *Chief products:* Corn, cotton, peanuts, pineapples, sugarcane; asbestos, iron ore, coal; lumber. *Chief towns:* Mbabane, Manzini.
History: Area settled by Swazi branch of Zulu nation during early 1880's; independence guaranteed by British and Transvaal governments 1881 and 1884; following Boer War (1899–1902) administered by British governor of Transvaal; governor's powers transferred to British High Commissioner 1906; Union (now Republic) of South Africa's request for control over Swaziland rejected by British government 1949; limited self-government introduced 1963; achieved independence 1968.

Swe·den \ˈswēd-ᵊn\ *or Swed.* **Sve·ri·ge** \ˈsfar-yə\. Kingdom, NW Europe, occupying the E and larger section of the Scandinavian penin.; bounded on the W by Norway, on the NE by Finland, on the E by the Gulf of Bothnia, on the E and S by the Baltic Sea, and on the SW by the Kattegat; 173,665 sq. m. (incl. 14,879 sq. m. of water); pop. (1970e)

8,013,696; ✻ Stockholm. *Physical features:* The N part of the boundary with Norway is marked by the Kjølen Mts. which include Sweden's highest peak, Kebnekaise 6965 ft. and which are source of many rivers in Norrland flowing SE to Gulf of Bothnia, esp. Ljusnan, Indal, Ångerman, Luleålv, and the Torne (Tornio) on the Finnish border; abundant waterpower, and many waterfalls and lakes. In S third of country (Svealand and Götaland) is lowland, including Dal river and several large lakes, the largest being Vänern, Vättern, Mälaren, and Hjälmaren. Separated from Sjælland I., Denmark, on S by narrow strait of the Øresund and from Jutland Penin., Denmark, by the Kattegat; has two large islands Gotland and Öland off SE in Baltic. Extreme N forms part of Lapland. *Chief products:* Wheat, oats, barley, sugar beet, potatoes; dairy products; lumbering, fishing; iron ore, copper, zinc, gold, silver; manufacturing: steel, electrical appliances, chemicals, office equipment, ball bearings; shipbuilding; tourism. *Chief cities:* Stockholm, Göteborg, Malmö, Västerås, Uppsala, Norrköping, Örebro. Divided into the following 24 counties (for pronunciation of their names, see their individual entries):

NAME	AREA (sq. m.)	POP. (1970e)	CAPITAL
Älvsborg	4,928	400,995	Vänersborg
Blekinge	1,173	152,702	Karlskrona
Gävleborg	7,615	293,377	Gävle
Göteborg and Bohus	1,986	699,395	Göteborg
Gotland	1,225	54,093	Visby
Halland	1,904	194,266	Halmstad
Jämtland	19,903	126,158	Östersund
Jönköping	4,436	305,045	Jönköping
Kalmar	4,487	242,150	Kalmar
Kopparberg	11,722	279,138	Falun
Kristianstad	2,478	265,772	Kristianstad
Kronoberg	3,827	166,105	Växjö
Malmöhus	1,878	707,323	Malmö
Norrbotten	40,879	256,750	Luleå
Örebro	3,493	275,243	Örebro
Östergötland	4,278	375,947	Linköping
Skaraborg	3,262	255,964	Mariestad
Södermanland	2,645	247,703	Nyköping
Stockholm	3,070	1,459,814	Stockholm
Uppsala	2,084	201,882	Uppsala
Värmland	7,497	284,930	Karlstad
Västerbotten	2,284	233,971	Umeå
Västernorrland	9,924	274,104	Härnösand
Västmanland	2,615	260,869	Västerås

History: Inhabitants of Sweden among Scandinavian (Viking) raiders of 9th cent. A.D.; united and converted to Christianity by 11th cent.; conquered Finns in 12th cent., united with Denmark and Norway 1397; broke away under house of Vasa (1523–1654) under which Swedes began territorial expansion; took Reval and Estonia 1561, E Karelia and Ingria 1617, and Livonia 1629; acquired Jämtland and Herjedalen and islands of Gotland and Sarema 1645; through participation in Thirty Years' War (Swedish phase 1630–35) won territory on German mainland, Hither Pomerania and Rügen, part of Farther Pomerania, Wismar, bishoprics of Bremen and Verden; leading Baltic power in 17th cent.; Danish territories in S Scandinavia were ceded to Sweden 1660; greatly weakened by defeat in Great Northern War 1700–21, as result of which Sweden lost most of German territories and Livonia, Estonia, Ingria, and Karelia; Finland (*q.v.*) and Åland Is. were gradually lost to Russia 1743–1809; received constitution 1809; gave up Swedish Pomerania in return for Norway which entered personal union with Sweden 1814; acknowledged independence of Norway 1905; neutral in both World War I and II; became a member of the United Nations 1946; joined the European Free Trade Association 1959; adopted unicameral parliament 1971.

Swedish Pomerania. See POMERANIA.

Swee·ney \ˈswē-nē\. Town, Brazoria co., SE Texas, 50 m. SSW of Houston; pop. (1970c) 3191.

Sweet Bri·ar \ˈswēt-ˌbrī-ər\. Village, Amherst co., cen. Virginia, ab. 12 m. N of Lynchburg; Sweet Briar Coll. (1901).

Sweet Grass. County in Montana. See table at MONTANA.

Sweet Home. City, Linn co., W Oregon, 32 m. NE of Eugene; pop. (1970c) 3799; agriculture; sawmills.

Sweet·wa·ter \ˈswēt-ˌwȯt-ər, -ˌwät-\. 1 River, cen. Wyoming; ab. 175 m. long; rises in SW Fremont co., flows E to Pathfinder Reservoir, which was formed by damming the North Platte river.

2 County in Wyoming. See table at WYOMING.

3 City, Dade co., SE Florida; pop. (1970c) 3357.

4 City, Monroe co., SE Tennessee, 41 m. SW of Knoxville; pop. (1970c) 4340; furniture.

5 Commercial and industrial city, ⊗ of Nolan co., NW Texas, 40 m. W of Abilene; pop. (1970c) 12,020; gypsum products, feeds, cottonseed oil, dairy products; meatpacking.

Sweetwater Lake. Lake, Ramsey co., NE North Dakota.

Swel·len·dam *also* **Zwel·len·dam** \ˈswel-ən-ˌdam\. Town, SW Cape Province, S Rep. of South Africa, 115 m. E of Cape Town in Bree river valley; pop. (1967e) 4900; in rich agricultural region. One of the oldest towns in South Africa, founded 1745; in 1795 rebelled against Dutch East India Company but surrendered to English in same year.

Swett Peninsula \ˈswet-\. Peninsula, extending W from SW coast in Chile, SSE of the Gulf of Penas.

Świd·ni·ca \shfid-ˈnēt-sə\ *or Ger.* **Schweid·nitz** \ˈshfīt-nits\. City, S cen. Wrocław prov., SW Poland, 33 m. SW of Wrocław; pop. (1970p) 47,500; chemicals, textiles; 14th cent. church; 13th cent. town hall; founded at beginning of 13th cent.; to Bohemia 1392, to Prussia 1742; suffered much in Hussite wars 15th cent., Thirty Years' War, and in Silesian Wars, esp. when besieged 1757–59 and 1761–62; assigned to Poland by Potsdam Conference 1945.

Świd·nik \ˈshfēd-nik\. Town, Lublin prov., E Poland, ab. 5 m. ESE of Lublin; pop. (1970p) 22,000.

Świe·bo·dzin \shf(y)e-ˈbȯ-ˌjēn\ *or Ger.* **Schwie·bus** \ˈshfē-ˌbüs\. Town, Zielona Góra prov., W Poland, ab. 25 m. N of Zielona Góra; pop. (1968e) 14,100; formerly in Brandenburg, Germany.

Swie·to·krzy·ski National Park \ˌshf(y)e-tȯk-ˈzhis-kē-\. National park, Poland; 23 sq. m.; mountain range; established 1950.

Swift \ˈswift\. 1 River, cen. Massachusetts; rises in Franklin co., flows S; 16 m. ENE of Springfield it is joined by Quaboag river to form Chicopee river.

2 County in Minnesota. See table at MINNESOTA.

Swift Current. City, SW Saskatchewan, Canada, 105 m. W of Moose Jaw; pop. (1971p) 15,048; railroad divisional point and trading center for large wheat district.

Swift·cur·rent Mountain \ˈswift-ˌkər-ənt-\. Peak, Glacier National Park, NW Montana; 8300 ft.

Swift Dam. See UNITED STATES, *Dams and Reservoirs.*

Swil·ly, Lough \läk-ˈswil-ē\. Inlet of Atlantic Ocean, N coast of Ireland in N co. Donegal, Eire; extends inland 24 m.

Świ·na \ˈshfē-nə\. River, NW Poland; ab. 10 m. long; main outlet of Zalew Szczeciński.

Swin·burne Island \ˌswin-bərn-\. Island off E coast of Staten I., New York, in Lower New York Bay; part of Richmond borough.

Swin·don \ˈswin-dən\. Municipal borough, Wiltshire, S England, 70 m. W of London; pop. (1971p) 90,830; locomotives and rolling stock.

Świ·no·ujś·cie \ˌshfē-nə-ˈü-ēsh-chə\ *or Ger.* **Swi·ne·mün·de** \ˌshfē-nə-ˈmün-də\. Seaport city, NW Szczecin prov., NW Poland, on Baltic Sea on N coast of Usedom I. at mouth of the Świna river 37 m. NNW of Szczecin; pop. (1970p) 27,900; resort; manufactures lumber, furniture; shipbuilding. Formerly in Prussia, Germany; bombed in World War

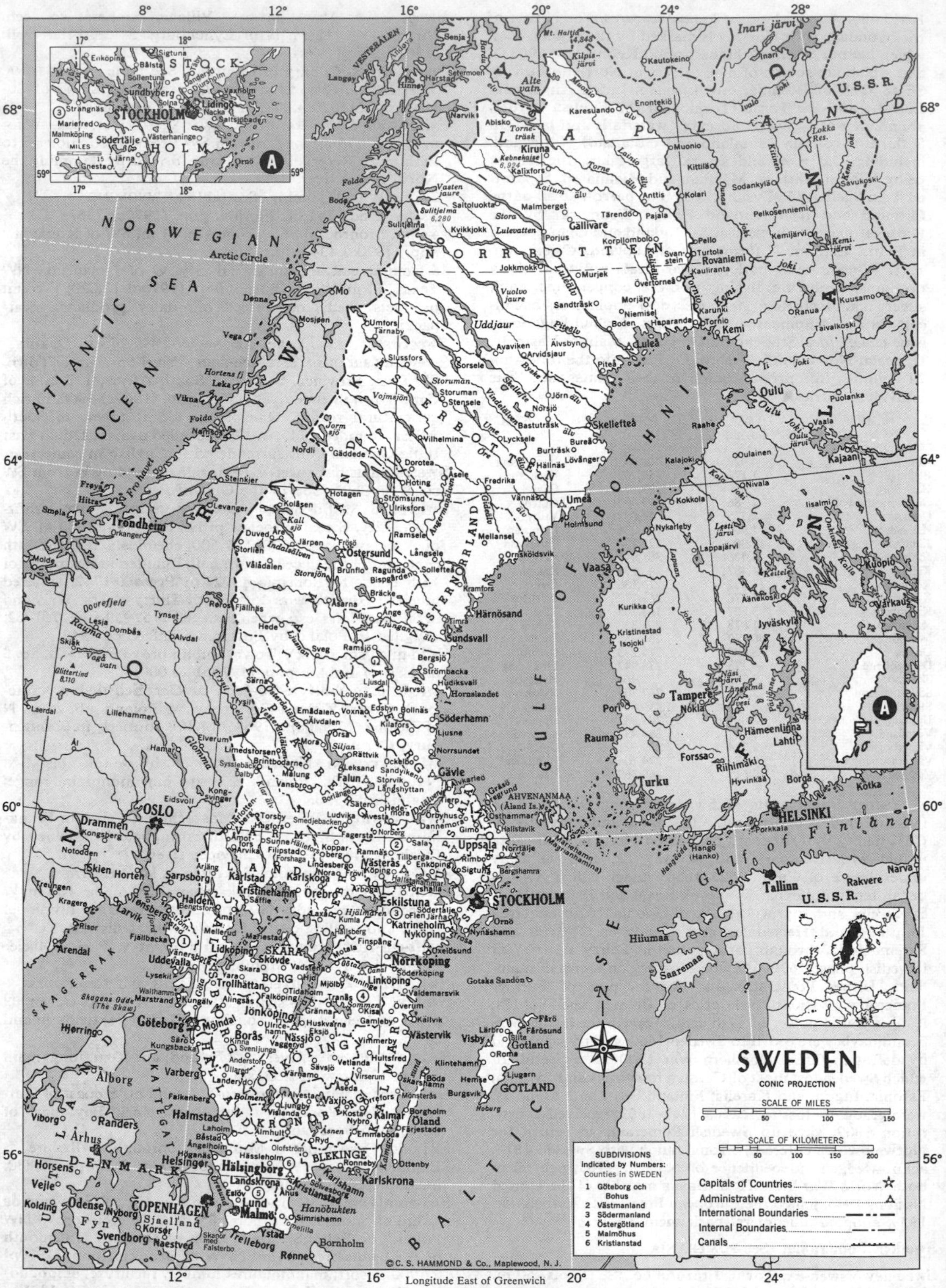
SWEDEN
CONIC PROJECTION
SCALE OF MILES
0 50 100 150
SCALE OF KILOMETERS
0 50 100 150 200
Capitals of Countries
Administrative Centers
International Boundaries
Internal Boundaries
Canals
SUBDIVISIONS indicated by Numbers: Counties in SWEDEN
1 Göteborg och Bohus
2 Västmanland
3 Södermanland
4 Östergötland
5 Malmöhus
6 Kristianstad
©C. S. HAMMOND & Co., Maplewood, N. J.
Longitude East of Greenwich
NORWEGIAN SEA
ATLANTIC OCEAN
GULF OF BOTHNIA
BALTIC SEA
Gulf of Finland
SKAGERRAK
KATTEGAT
LAPLAND
NORRBOTTEN
VÄSTERBOTTEN
VÄSTERNORRLAND
JÄMTLAND
KOPPARBERG
GÄVLEBORG
UPPSALA
STOCKHOLM
VÄRMLAND
ÖREBRO
SKARABORG
ÄLVSBORG
HALLAND
JÖNKÖPING
KALMAR
KRONOBERG
BLEKINGE
GOTLAND
ÖLAND
DENMARK
NORWAY
FINLAND
U.S.S.R.
AHVENANMAA (Åland Is.)
Arctic Circle
Stockholm
Oslo
Helsinki
Copenhagen
Tallinn
Göteborg
Malmö
Uppsala
Norrköping
Trondheim
Kiruna
Luleå
Umeå
Sundsvall
Gävle
Västerås
Örebro
Jönköping
Linköping
Karlstad
Hälsingborg
Visby
Kalmar
Karlskrona
Östersund
Turku
Tampere
Vaasa
Oulu
8° 12° 16° 20° 24° 28°
68° 64° 60° 56°
A
STOCKHOLM
Sundbyberg
Solna
Lidingö
Nacka
Södertälje
MILES

II; its harbor place where German battleship *Lützow* was sunk Apr. 1945; captured by U.S.S.R. May 5, 1945; assigned to Poland by Potsdam Conference 1945.

Swin·ton \'swint-ᵊn\. Urban district, West Riding, Yorkshire, N England, 10 m. NE of Sheffield; pop. (1971p) 14,897; potteries (formerly noted for Rockingham ware), iron foundries, glassworks.

Swinton and Pen·dle·bury \-'pen-dᵊl-ˌber-ē\. Urban district, Lancashire, NW England, 4 m. NW of Manchester; pop. (1971p) 40,114; cotton; coal mining.

Swish·er \'swish-ər\. County in Texas. See table at TEXAS.

Swiss·vale \'swis-ˌvāl\. Industrial borough, Allegheny co., SW Pennsylvania, 7 m. E of Pittsburgh; pop. (1970c) 13,819; manufactures switches and signals, glass products.

Swit·zer·land \'swit-sər-lənd\. 1 *or Fr.* **Suisse** \swʸēs\ *or Ger.* **Schweiz** \'shfīts\ *or Ital.* **Sviz·ze·ra** \'zvēt-tsä-rä\ *or Latin* **Hel·ve·tia** \hel-'vē-sh(ē-)ə\; *officially* **Swiss Confederation** *or Fr.* **Con·fé·dé·ra·tion Suisse** \kōⁿ-fā-der-ä-syōⁿ-swēs\ *or Ger.* **Schwei·ze·ris·che Eid·ge·nos·sen·schaft** \'shvīt-sər-ˌish-ə-'īd-gə-ˌnōs-ən-ˌshäft\ *or Ital.* **Con·fe·de·ra·zi·o·ne Sviz·ze·ra** \kȯn-ˌfād-ā-ˌrät-sē-'ōn-ā-svēt-'sär-ä\. Federal republic, cen. Europe, bounded on N by West Germany, on E by Austria and Liechtenstein, on SE and S by Italy, and on SW, W, and NW by France; 15,941 sq. m.; pop. (1970c) 6,269,783; ✱ Bern. *Physical features:* Jura Mts. in the W and the Swiss Alps in S and E including Bernese, Lepontine, Pennine, and the Rhaetian Alps (see ALPS); highest peak Monte Rosa 15,217 ft. *Chief rivers:* In S part the Rhone, which has its source in E Valais canton; in E and N, forming part of the N boundary, the Rhine; in cen. and NW part the Aare, the largest river completely within Switzerland. *Lakes:* In SW the Lake of Geneva on French border, in W Lake of Neuchâtel, on the N boundary Lake Constance, and in cen. part Lakes of Lucerne, Zurich, Wallen, Brienz, and Thun. *Chief products:* Wheat, rye, sugar beet, vegetables; dairy products, wines; salt, limestone; manufacturing: textiles, chemicals, watches and clocks, precision tools; abundant waterpower; tourism; international finance. *Chief cities:* Zurich, Basel, Bern, Geneva, Lausanne, Winterthur. Divided into the following 22 cantons (for pronunciation of their names, see their individual entries):

NAME	AREA (sq. m.)	POP. (1970c)	CAPITAL
Aargau	542	433,284	Aarau
Appenzell Inner Rhodes[1]	67	13,124	Appenzell
Appenzell Outer Rhodes[1]	94	49,023	Herisau
Basel-Land[2]	165	204,889	Liestal
Basel-Stadt[2]	14	234,945	Basel
Bern	2,659	983,296	Bern
Fribourg	645	180,309	Fribourg
Geneva	109	331,599	Geneva
Glarus	264	38,155	Glarus
Graubünden	2,745	162,086	Chur
Lucerne	577	289,641	Lucerne
Neuchâtel	308	169,173	Neuchâtel
Nidwalden[3]	106	25,634	Stans
Obwalden[3]	190	24,509	Sarnen
Saint Gall	778	384,475	Saint Gall
Schaffhausen	115	72,854	Schaffhausen
Schwyz	351	92,072	Schwyz
Solothurn	305	224,133	Solothurn
Thurgau	389	182,835	Frauenfeld
Ticino	1,085	245,458	Bellinzona
Uri	415	34,091	Altdorf
Valais	2,020	206,563	Sion
Vaud	1,240	511,851	Lausanne
Zug	92	67,996	Zug
Zurich	668	1,107,788	Zurich

[1]Appenzell Inner Rhodes and Appenzell Outer Rhodes are demicantons which together constitute the canton of Appenzell.
[2]Basel-Land and Basel-Stadt are demicantons which together constitute the canton of Basel.
[3]Nidwalden and Obwalden are demicantons which together constitute the canton of Unterwalden.

History: Occupied by Helvetians who were conquered by Romans; southwest invaded by Burgundians, northeast by Alamanni; made part of Frankish empire; part in kingdom of Arles (*q.v.*, see also BURGUNDY); region without political unity under Holy Roman Empire; in 1291 the Forest Cantons, Uri, Schwyz, and Unterwalden, formed anti-Hapsburg league which became nucleus of Swiss Confederation; added Lucerne, Zurich, Glarus, Bern, and Zug by 1353. Solothurn and Fribourg joined confederation 1481 and later, Basel and Appenzell; various cantons expanded their territories and won virtual independence in 15th cent. (not recognized until 1648); center of Protestant Reformation (see ZURICH and GENEVA 2) which divided cantons and inaugurated a period of political and religious rivalry; organized by French as Helvetic Republic 1798–1803; with new cantons added 1803 and 1815, restored as independent confederation of 22 cantons 1815; after war of Sonderbund (seven Roman Catholic cantons—Lucerne, Uri, Schwyz, Unterwalden, Zug, Fribourg, and Valais—against the Protestants) adopted new constitution 1848, present constitution 1874; perpetual neutrality guaranteed by international agreement 1815 (Congress of Vienna) and 1919 (Treaty of Versailles); remained neutral in World Wars I and II; became a member of the European Free Trade Association 1959.

2 County in Indiana. See table at INDIANA.

Sworbe. See SÕRVE.

Swoy·ers·ville \'swȯi-ərz-ˌvil\. Borough, Luzerne co., E Pennsylvania, 4 m. N of Wilkes-Barre; pop. (1970c) 6786; textiles; anthracite coal mines.

Syas \sē-'as(-yə)\. River, E Leningrad Oblast, Russian S.F.S.R., U.S.S.R.; 162 m. long; flows NW to S end of Lake Ladoga, just E of the Volkhov river. With its tributary, the Tikhvinka, forms part of a canal system connecting the lake with the Volga through the Mologa to Rybinsk.

Syb·a·ris \'sib-ə-rəs\. Ancient city, S Italy, on N side of mouth of Crathis river on the Gulf of Tarentum; site near modern **Ter·ra·no·va di Si·ba·ri** \ˌter-ə-'nō-və-dē-si-'bä-rē\, Cosenza prov., N Calabria, pop. (1968e) 4983. Founded c. 720 B.C. by Achaeans, the oldest city of Magna Graecia; became noted for its luxury; defeated in war with Crotona and was destroyed 510 B.C.

Sycaminum. See HAIFA 2.

Syc·a·more \'sik-ə-ˌmō(ə)r, -ˌmȯ(ə)r\. City, ⊗ of De Kalb co., N Illinois, 30 m. ESE of Elgin; pop. (1970c) 7843; canneries, wire factories, brassworks.

Sydlige Jylland. See SOUTH JUTLAND.

Syd·ney \'sid-nē\. 1 City, ✱ of New South Wales, Australia, in E part on Port Jackson (*q.v.*) on Pacific Ocean; pop. (1970e) 67,700, met. area pop. 2,780,310; largest city in Australia; has one of world's finest natural harbors, with extensive port facilities (incl. container terminal); a major commercial and manufacturing center; chemicals, electrical equipment; shipbuilding, oil refining, food processing; wool market; exports incl. wheat, wool, meat; Anglican cathedral (1888), Roman Catholic cathedral (1868); Univ. of Sydney (1850), Univ. of New South Wales (1949), Macquarie Univ. (1964); State Parliament House (1811–17), Old Mint Building (1811), Government House (1837–45), National Art Gallery (1871), Town Hall (1889), Opera House. First British settlement in Australia; founded 1788 by British officials in charge of group of convicts (penal settlement had been established on Botany Bay (*q.v.*).

2 Industrial and commercial city, ⊗ of Cape Breton co., E Nova Scotia, Canada, on **Sydney Harbor,** an inlet of Atlantic Ocean; pop. (1971p) 32,459; steel and coal center with many mills, foundries, and furnaces; fisheries; steamship connections with Montreal, Halifax, and Newfoundland. First English settlement 1784; capital of Cape Breton I. 1784–1820.

3 One of the smaller islands of the Phoenix Is. (*q.v.*), in SE part of group, S Pacific Ocean, S of Enderbury I.

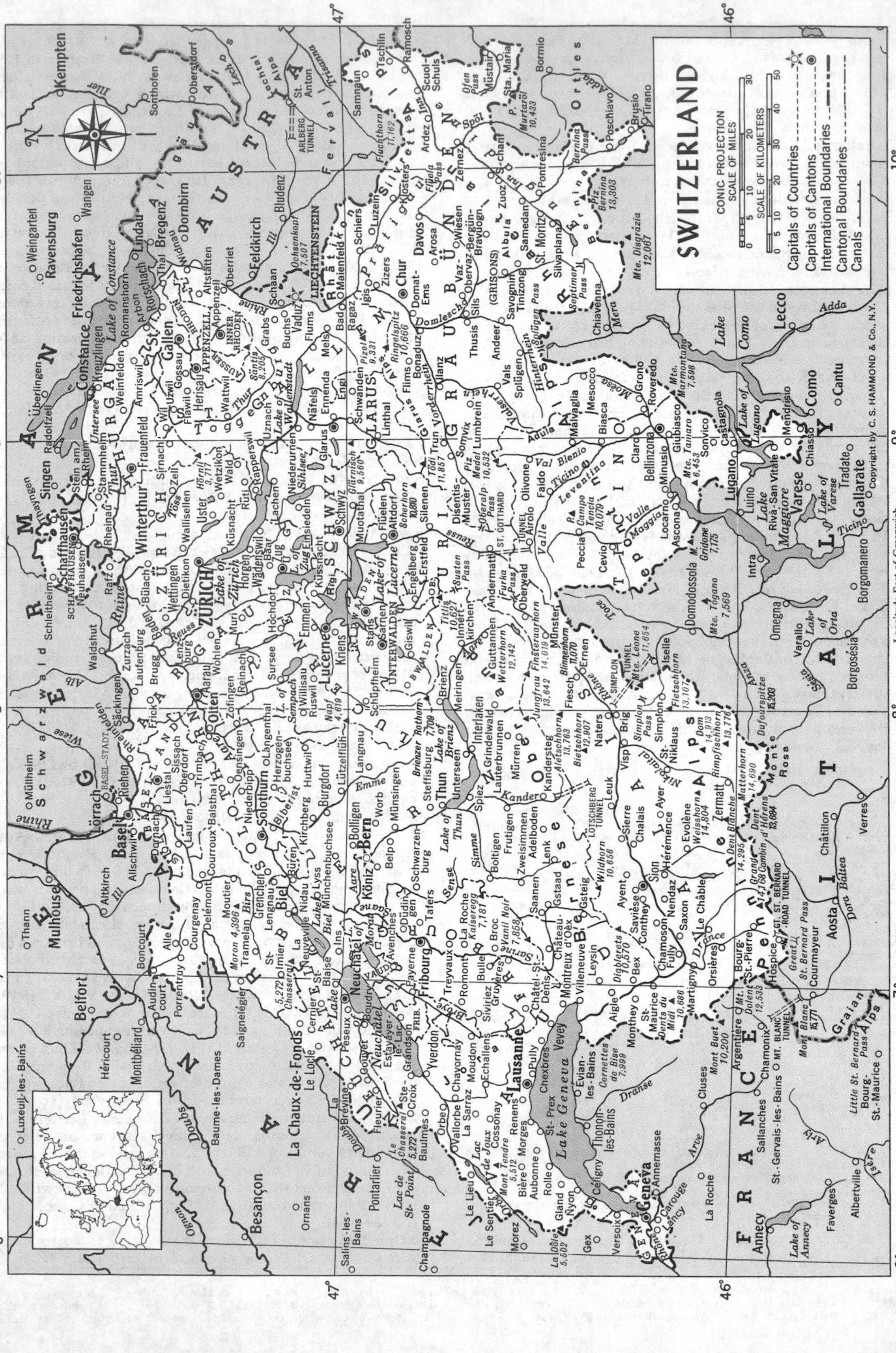
SWITZERLAND
CONIC PROJECTION
SCALE OF MILES
0 5 10 20 30
SCALE OF KILOMETERS
0 5 10 20 30 40 50
Capitals of Countries
Capitals of Cantons
International Boundaries
Cantonal Boundaries
Canals
Copyright by C. S. HAMMOND & Co., N.Y.
Longitude East of Greenwich
GERMANY
AUSTRIA
FRANCE
ITALY
LIECHTENSTEIN
Bern
Zürich
Basel
Geneva
Lausanne
Lucerne
Lake of Constance
Lake Geneva
Lake Maggiore
Lake Como
Lake of Lucerne

Sydney Mines \-'mīnz\. Town, Cape Breton co., E Nova Scotia, Canada, on Atlantic Ocean 10 m. N of Sydney; pop. (1971p) 8957; in coal-mining region; steel plant, foundries.

Syedlets. See SIEDLCE.

Syene. See ASWĀN 2.

Syk·tyv·kar *also* **Sik·tiv·kar** \sik-tif-'kär\ *or formerly* **Ust Sy·solsk** \'üst-si-'sólsk\. Town, ❋ of Komi A.S.S.R., Russian S.F.S.R., U.S.S.R., on the Sysola river just above its junction with the Vychegda, 220 m. N of Kirov; pop. (1970p) 125,000; lumber.

Syl·a·cau·ga \ˌsil-ə-'kò-gə\. City, Talladega co., E cen. Alabama, 42 m. SE of Birmingham; pop. (1970c) 12,255; marble quarries; textiles, cottonseed oil.

Sy·lar·na \'sü-lər-ˌnä\. Peak, W cen. Sweden, on the Norwegian border; 5781 ft.

Syl·het \sil-'het\. **1** District, E Bangla Desh; 4785 sq. m.; pop. (1961c) 3,489,589; ❋ Sylhet.

2 Town, its ❋, on Surma river 120 m. NE of Dacca; pop. (1961c) 37,740; tea; three colleges.

Sylt \'zilt, 'silt\. Island off W coast of Schleswig-Holstein, West Germany; 36 sq. m.; pop. (1967e) 23,603; chief island of North Frisian Is.; connected with mainland by causeway; summer resort.

Syl·va \'sil-və\. Town, ⊗ of Jackson co., SW North Carolina, 40 m. WSW of Asheville; pop. (1970c) 1561; paperboard plant; meat-packing.

Syl·va·nia \sil-'vā-nyə\. **1** City, ⊗ of Screven co., E Georgia, 55 m. NW of Savannah; pop. (1970c) 3199; lumber, cotton; fertilizer.

2 Village, Lucas co., NW Ohio, on Michigan border 10 m. WNW of Toledo; pop. (1970c) 12,031; cement and cement blocks; Lourdes Junior Coll. (1957).

Syl·ves·ter \sil-'ves-tər\. City, ⊗ of Worth co., S Georgia, 20 m. E of Albany; pop. (1970c) 4226.

Sylvia, Mount. See TZ'U-KAO.

Sy·mē *or* **Sí·mi** *or Ital.* **Si·mi** \'sī-mē, 'sē-\. **1** Island of the Dodecanese (*q.v.*), Greece, NW of Rhodes; 25 sq. m.

2 Town on the island.

Sym·me·try Spire \ˌsim-ə-trē-'spī(ə)r\. Peak, cen. Grand Teton National Park, NW Wyoming; 10,546 ft.

Syra. See SYROS.

Syr·a·cuse \'sir-ə-ˌkyüs, -ˌkyüz\. **1** City, ⊗ of Hamilton co., W Kansas; pop. (1970c) 1720.

2 Commercial and manufacturing city, ⊗ of Onondaga co., cen. New York, 12 m. S of W end of Oneida Lake; pop. (1970c) 197,297; electronic equipment, pharmaceuticals, chinaware, roller bearings, paper products; State Univ. of New York Upstate Medical Center (1834), Maria Regina Coll. (1934), Syracuse Univ. (1870), Le Moyne Coll. (1946), Onondaga Community Coll. (1962), Everson Museum of Art.

History: Territory visited by French 1620, subsequently by English; salt springs discovered 1654; trading post set up by whites c. 1786; saltworks established c. 1789 and flourished until after Civil War; salt settlements sprang up, including Salina (also called Salt Point, now N section of Syracuse) and site of present Syracuse, latter became important port on Erie Canal at junction with Oswego Canal (opened 1838); Salina incorporated as village 1824, Syracuse 1825; became ⊗ 1827; Syracuse and Salina, together with Lodi first incorporated as city of Syracuse 1847.

3 *or Ital.* **Si·ra·cu·sa** \ˌsē-rə-'kü-zə\ *or anc.* **Syr·a·cu·sae** \ˌsir-ə-'kyü-(ˌ)sē, -(ˌ)zē\. Seaport, ❋ of Siracusa prov., SE Sicily, Italy, on Ionian Sea 130 m. SE of Palermo; partly on Ortygia I. (separated from mainland by narrow canal); pop. (1968e) 101,542; salt processing, wine making; tourism; cathedral; castle; 14th cent. palaces; saltwater fountain (Fonte Aretusa); ruins include 5th cent. (B.C.) Greek temple and theater, parts of city walls and fortifications, aqueducts of the period of Hiero II, Roman amphitheater, and numerous catacombs.

History: Founded 734 B.C. by Corinthian colonists; became largest and most important city in Sicily, extending its influence throughout Sicily and S Italy; seized by tyrant of Gela 485 B.C.; ruled by despotic Hiero I 478–466; democratic government established 465; Athenians defeated by Syracusans in land and sea engagements 413; under Dionysius the Elder 405–367 and Dionysius the Younger 367–356 and 347–344; democracy reestablished 337; under Agathocles the Tyrant 317–289; Carthaginians repulsed by Pyrrhus 278; Hiero II made king 270; allied with Rome in First Punic War; fell to Romans 211 after three years of resistance; conquered by Byzantines 535 A.D. and made capital of Sicily; residence 663–668 of Emperor Constans II; conquered by Arabs 878 and by Normans 1085, becoming part of the kingdom of the Two Sicilies. Birthplace of Theocritus and Archimedes. Not important in medieval times. In World War II taken by British July 12, 1943.

Syr Dar·ya *or* **Sir Darya** \si(ə)r-'där-yə\ *or* **Sai·hun** \sī-'hün\ *or anc.* **Jax·ar·tes** \jak-'särt-(ˌ)ēz\. River, Kirgiz, Uzbek, and Kazakh S.S.Rs., U.S.S.R.; ab. 1370 m. long; formed by two headstreams in Kazakh S.S.R. rising in the Tien Shan; flows W and NW into the Aral Sea at its NE corner; flows through the fertile Fergana valley; its lower course on E edge of Kyzyl Kum Desert; part of its course in ancient times separated the Scythian tribes from Sogdiana; in recent times has often changed its course.

Syr·ia \'sir-ē-ə\. **1** *or Heb.* **Aram** \'ā-ˌram, 'er-əm\; *Arab.* **Ash Shām** *or* **Esh Shām** \ash-'sham\. Ancient country, Asia, at E end of Mediterranean Sea, incl. modern Syria, Lebanon, Israel, and Jordan.

History: Conquered by Egypt c. 1471 B.C.; part of Babylonian, Assyrian, and Persian empires; conquered by Alexander the Great; ruled by the Seleucidae who carried on war against Egypt in 3d cent B.C.; made a Roman province by Pompey 64 B.C.; invaded on several occasions by Persians before Khosrau II conquered it 611 A.D.; overrun by Muslim Arabs 635–636; seat of Ommiad dynasty with capital at Damascus (*q.v.*) 661–750; in hands of Seljuks and later, of Fatimids, during early Crusades; came under Ottoman Turks 1516; invaded by French 1798–99; occupied by Mehemet Ali, governor of Egypt, 1831–33 and 1839–40; scene of insurrection 1860–61; saw end of Turkish rule 1917.

2 *Fr.* **Sy·rie** \sē-rē\ *or* **La Syrie** \lȧ-\. Former French mandate, E end of Mediterranean Sea; consisted of Syria (see 3 below) and Lebanon (known as the **Le·vant States** \lə-'vant-\).

History: Became French mandate 1920; in 1925 Damascus and Aleppo were united to form state of Syria which became republic 1930; Lebanon formed 1926; Sanjak of Alexandretta (*q.v.*), previously autonomous, ceded to Turkey 1939; under control of Vichy forces 1940–41; taken over by British and Free French June–July 1941; ceased to be French mandate Sept. 27, 1941.

3 *officially* **Syr·i·an Arab Republic** \'sir-ē-ən-\ *or Arab.* **Al–Jum·hū·rī·yah al–'Ara·bī·yah as–Sū·rī·yah** \al-jum-hu-'rē-(y)ə-al-ˌär-ə-'bē-(y)ə-as-su-'rē-(y)ə\. Republic, SW Asia, at E end of Mediterranean Sea, bounded on N by Turkey, on E and SE by Iraq, on S by Jordan, on SW by Israel and Lebanon, and on W by Lebanon and the Mediterranean Sea; 71,498 sq. m.; pop. (1970c) 6,292,000; ❋ Damascus. *Physical features:* In the SE is the N part of the Syrian Desert; in cen. is a plateau region having elev. 1500–4500 ft.; in NE lies the upper part of the plain of Mesopotamia; in W are Anti-Lebanon and the N extension of the Lebanon mountain ranges; in SW is Jebel Druze 5907 ft.; in E cen. part is the Euphrates, flowing from NW to SE and receiving on the left the tributaries Balikh and Khabur. *Chief*

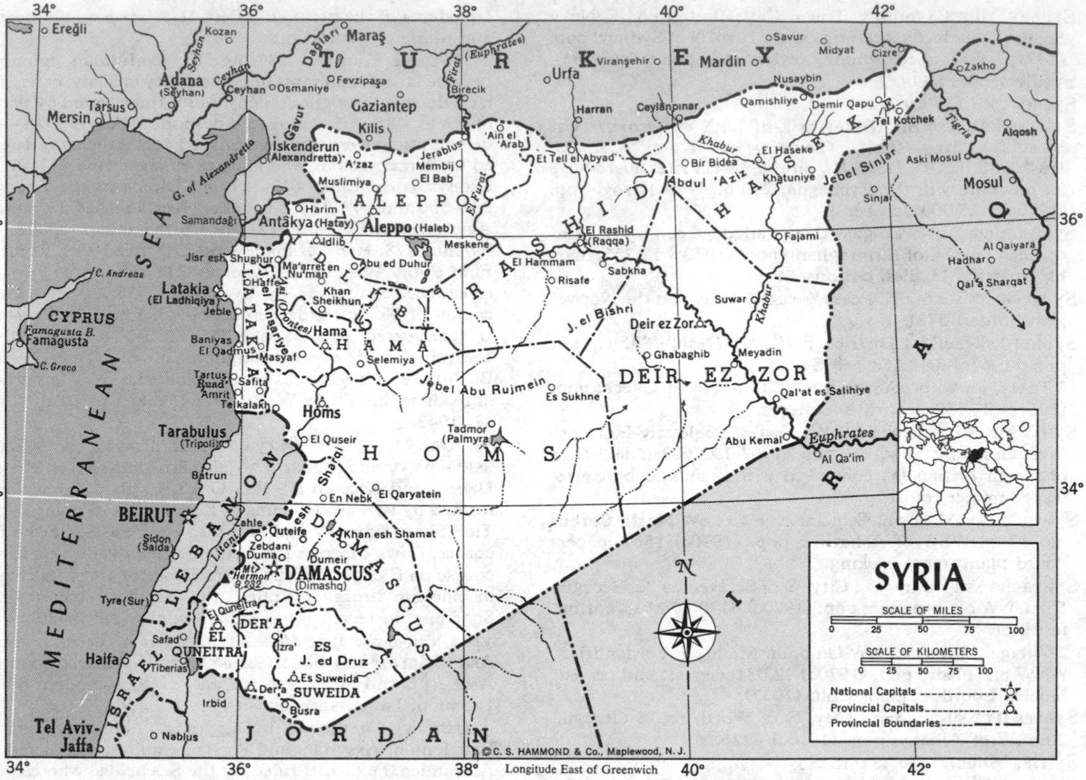

products: Wheat, cotton, barley, olives, grapes, tobacco; oil, salt; manufacturing: textiles, cement, glass. *Chief towns:* Damascus, Aleppo, Homs, Hama, Latakia.

History: For history before 1941, see 1 and 2 above. French mandate declared terminated 1941, but total independence not achieved until 1944; withdrawal of French and British troops completed 1946; united with Egypt 1958, forming United Arab Republic (union dissolved 1961); participated in Arab-Israeli War 1967 (see GOLAN HEIGHTS); formed federation with Egypt and Libya 1971.

Syr·dar·ya Oblast \si(ə)r-'där-yə-'ō-bləst, -ˌblast\. Subdivision of the Uzbek S.S.R., U.S.S.R.; 8919 sq. m.; pop. (1970p) 737,000; ✱ Gulistan; formed 1963.

Syriae Portae. See BAILAN.

Syr·i·am \'sir-ē-əm\. Town, Pegu div., Lower Burma, on Rangoon river opp. Rangoon; seaport.

Syr·i·an Desert \ˌsir-ē-ən-\. Extensive desert region, N Saudi Arabia, SE Syria, W Iraq, and NE Jordan, bet. lat. 30° and 34°N and long. 36° and 44°E; its W part known as **Al–Ha·mad** \ˌal-hə-'mad\, a name applied by some to the entire desert; crossed by pipelines connecting the oil fields of Kirkuk with Haifa and Tripoli.

Syrian Gates. See BAILAN.

Syrie. See SYRIA 2.

Syr·mia \'sər-mē-ə\ *or Serb.* **Srem** \'srem\ *or Hung.* **Sze·rém** \'ser-əm, -ˌām\. Region, N Yugoslavia; formerly the E division of Slavonia; since 1945 corresponds to E part of Croatia.

Sy·ros \'sī-ˌräs\ *or Gk.* **Sí·ros** \'sē-ˌrȯs\ *also* **Sy·ra** \'sī-rə\. 1 Island, cen. Cyclades, in Aegean Sea; 31 sq. m.; pop. (1961c) 19,750; chief town Hermoupolis, which is also capital of Cyclades dept., Greece. Haven of many Greek refugees during War of Independence; in 19th cent. of considerable commercial importance.

2 Seaport city, Cyclades Is., Greece. See HERMOUPOLIS.

Syrtica, Regio. See TRIPOLI 1.

Syrtis Major. See SIDRA, GULF OF.

Syrtis Minor. See GABÈS.

Syv Sistre. See SEVEN SISTERS FALLS.

Syz·ran \'siz-rən(-yə)\. City, SW Kuibyshev Oblast, Russian S.F.S.R., U.S.S.R., on right bank of the Volga 80 m. W of Kuibyshev; pop. (1970p) 174,000; on railroad from Moscow to Kuibyshev and Chelyabinsk which crosses the Volga here on long bridge; river port; oil refining; engineering industries; founded 1683.

Szabadka. See SUBOTICA.

Sza·bolcs–Szat·már \'sä-ˌbȯlch-'sät-ˌmär\. County of NE Hungary. See table at HUNGARY.

Szalánkemén. See NOVI SLANKAMEN.

Szamos. See SOMEȘUL.

Szar·vas \'sȯ(ə)r-ˌvȯsh\. Commune, Békés co., SE Hungary, on the Körös ab. 83 m. SE of Budapest; pop. (1970p) 19,478.

Szatmár–Németi. See SATU-MARE 2.

Száva. See SAVA 2.

Szczara. See SHCHARA.

Szcze·cin \'shchet-ˌsēn\. 1 *or formerly* **Po·mo·rze Za·chod·nie** \pȯ-ˌmȯ-zhe-zä-'kȯd-nye\. Province, NW Poland; formerly in Prussia, Germany. See table at POLAND.

2 *or Ger.* **Stet·tin** \s(h)te-'tēn\. Seaport, its ✱, near mouth of Oder river ab. 125 m. NE of Poznán; pop. (1970p) 337,200; chemicals; metallurgical industries; shipbuilding, fishing; one of Poland's chief ports; technical univ. (1945); agricultural coll. (1954).

History: Incorporated into Polish state by Mieszko I at end of 10th cent. A.D.; largest city in Pomerania 1124; joined Hanseatic League 1360; ducal residence 12th–17th cents.; peace of Stettin 1570 closed Northern Seven Years' War bet. Denmark and Sweden; to Sweden 1648 by Treaty of Westphalia; to Brandenburg 1637, Prussia 1720. In World War II frequently bombed 1944–45; taken Apr. 26, 1945 by Soviet troops after long siege and battle; assigned to Poland by Potsdam Conference 1945.

Szcze·ci·nek \shchet-'sē-ˌnek\ *or Ger.* **Neu·stet·tin** \ˌnòi-s(h)te-'tēn\. City, Koszalin prov., N Poland, 41 m. SE of Koszalin; pop. (1970p) 28,600; summer resort. Founded 1310 by duke of Pomerania; occupied by Soviet troops Jan. 1945; assigned to Poland by Potsdam Conference 1945.

Szczyt·no \'shchit-(ˌ)nō\ *or Ger.* **Or·tels·burg** \'ȯrt-ᵊls-ˌbu̇(ə)rg\. City, Olsztyn prov., N Poland, 27 m. SE of Olsztyn; pop. (1968e) 16,200; formerly in East Prussia, Germany; founded 13th cent.; became city 1616; occupied and burned by Russians 1914; in World War II taken by Soviets Jan. 1945; assigned to Poland by Potsdam Conference 1945.

Sze·chwan *or* **Sze·chuan** \'sech-'wän\. Province, S cen. China, bounded on N by Tsinghai, Kansu, and Shensi provs., on E by Hupeh and Hunan, on S by Kweichow and Yunnan, and on W by Tibet; 219,691 sq. m.; pop. (1968e) 70,000,000; ✻ Ch'eng-tu. Well-watered plateau province, heart of which is known as the Red Basin; crossed in S section by the Yangtze and in the cen. part by three of its tributaries, Min, To, and Chia-ling, flowing N to S. On NE bordered by Ta Pa Shan range and on W by mountains rising steeply to border of Tibetan plateau (edge of which is 10,000 to 20,000 ft.) In mountains in SE the Yangtze flows through the Yangtze Gorges (*q.v.*); rivers in the Red Basin are navigable and there is much junk traffic. *Chief products:* Rice, sweet potatoes, sugarcane, tobacco, cotton, wheat; coal, salt, gold, silver, copper. *Chief cities:* Chungking, Ch'eng-tu, I-pin, Wu-t'ung-ch'iao.

History: In early years of Chinese history its population entirely non-Chinese; incorporated (c. 3d cent. A.D.) in empire under Chin dynasty; although long isolated by its mountain barriers, now definitely Chinese. Wanhsien on the Yangtze opened 1917 to foreign trade. After outbreak 1937 of war with Japan, government removed from coast to Chungking establishing that city as capital of China; also its population and influence increased by migration of industries, government bureaus, schools, etc.; headquarters of military forces; bombed frequently by Japanese 1938–45.

Sze·chwan·ese Alps \ˌsech-wə-ˌnēz-'alps\. Mountain ranges, NW, W, and SW borders of Szechwan prov., S cen. China, the E scarp of the Tibetan plateau, from 10,000 to 24,900 ft.; Minya Konka is the highest peak.

Sze·ged \'seg-ˌed\ *or Ger.* **Sze·ge·din** \'sā-gā-(ˌ)dēn\. City, ⊗ of Csongrád co., S Hungary, on the Yugoslav border; 43 sq. m.; pop. (1970p) 118,490; timber, salt; univ. (1921); important port on the Tisza river; old town damaged by flood 1879; taken by Soviet troops Oct. 6, 1944.

Szé·kes·fe·hér·vár \'sā-ˌkesh-ˌfe-ər-ˌvär\ *or Ger.* **Stuhl·weis·sen·burg** \s(h)tül-'vīs-ən-ˌbərg, -ˌbu̇(ə)rg\. City, ⊗ of Fejér co., W cen. Hungary; pop. (1970p) 72,940; market center for wine and fruit; scene of crowning of kings of Hungary 1027–1527; many of its buildings destroyed 1686 at end of Turkish occupation.

Szek·szárd \'sek-ˌsärd\ *or formerly* **Szeg·szárd** \'seg-ˌzärd\. City, ⊗ of Tolna co., S Hungary, 85 m. S of Budapest; pop. (1970p) 24,201.

Szeming. See AMOY.

Szent. See SAINT.

Szent·en·dre \'sent-ən-drə\ *or Ger.* **Sankt An·drä** \zäŋkt-'än-drā\. City, Pest co., N Hungary, on a branch of the Danube ab. 12 m. N of Budapest; pop. (1970p) 12,744; metal industries.

Szent·es \'sent-ˌesh\. City, Csongrád co., SE Hungary, 30 m. N of Szeged; pop. (1970p) 32,492; food processing.

Szent·gott·hárd \'sent-gȯt-ˌhärd\ *or Eng.* **Saint Gott·hard** \sānt-'gät-ərd\. Commune, Vas co., W Hungary, on Rába river, on Austrian boundary; pop. (1970p) 8195; scene of battle Aug. 1, 1664 in which imperial forces under General Montecuccoli defeated the Turks. See VASVÁR.

Szepingkai. See SSU-P'ING.

Szerém. See SYRMIA.

Szi·get·köz \'sig-ət-ˌkə(r)z\ *also* **Little Schütt** \-'shüt\. Island in NW Hungary, formed by arms of the Danube river near Győr; ab. 28 m. long and 7 m. wide.

Szi·get·vár \'sig-ət-ˌvär\. Commune, Baranya co., S Hungary, W of Pécs; pop. (1970p) 10,409; object of siege Aug. 5–Sept. 7, 1566 in which Miklós Zrinyi with ab. 3000 men heroically defended the city against Suleiman I.

Sziszek. See SISAK.

Szol·nok \'sōl-ˌnōk\. **1** County of E cen. Hungary. See table at HUNGARY.

2 City, its ⊗, ab. 55 m. SE of Budapest; pop. (1970p) 61,418; industrial and commercial center; Franciscan convent.

Szom·bat·hely \'sōm-ˌbȯt-ˌhā\ *or Ger.* **Stein·am·ang·er** \ˌs(h)tīn-äm-'äŋ-ər\; *anc.* **Sa·bar·ia** \sə-'ber-ē-ə, -'bar-\ *or* **Sa·var·ia** \-'ver-, -'var-\. City, ⊗ of Vas co., W Hungary, near Austrian frontier; pop. (1970p) 64,745; commercial center in rich wine-producing region; cathedral; episcopal palace; ancient Sabaria was the Roman capital of Pannonia; in World War II taken by U.S.S.R. Mar. 29, 1945.

Szpro·ta·wa \shprō-'täv-ə\ *or Ger.* **Sprot·tau** \'s(h)prōt-ˌau̇\. Industrial town, Zielona Góra prov., SW Poland, on Bóbr river ab. 25 m. S of Zielona Góra; pop. (1968e) 10,900; formerly in Silesia, Germany; iron goods, textiles; assigned to Poland by Potsdam Conference 1945.

Ta·al \tä-'äl, 'täl\. 1 Volcano on Volcano I. (14 m. in circumference, 6 sq. m.), in center of Lake Taal, Batangas prov., Luzon, Phil.; its crater is 1¼ to 1⅓ m. in diameter. Has had 9 recorded eruptions since 1709, those of 1754, 1911, 1965, and 1968 especially severe.
2 Municipality, Batangas prov., Luzon, Phil., on Pansipit river near its mouth, SW of Lake Taal and near the NE coast of Balayan Bay; pop. (1969e) 31,400; named after older town destroyed by the eruption of Mt. Taal in 1754.

Taal, Lake *or formerly* **Lake Bom·bon** \-bȯm-'bȯn\. Lake, Batangas prov., Luzon, Phil., ab. 40 m. S of Manila; 17 m. long by 12 m. wide; 94 sq. m.; its outlet is the Pansipit river flowing S to Balayan Bay.

Ta·a·nach \'tā-ə-ˌnak\. Ancient city of Canaan, on S side of Plain of Esdraelon ab. 5 m. SE of Megiddo. Near here Sisera was defeated by Barak and Deborah (*Judges* v. 19); important during Solomon's reign.

Taasinge. See TÅSINGE.

Tab. See ZOHREH.

Ta·ba·co \tä-'bä-kō\. Municipality, E coast of Albay prov., Luzon, Phil., on Tabaco Bay, N of Mt. Mayon and ab. 15 m. N of Legaspi; pop. (1969e) 63,800.

Tabaco Bay. Inlet of Lagonoy Gulf, E coast of Albay prov., Luzon, Phil.; ab. 12 m. long; San Miguel I. and Cagraray I. enclose it on the E; it affords sheltered harbors for Tabaco and Bacacay.

Ta·bar·ca \tə-'bär-kə\. Town, NW Tunisia, N Africa, near Algerian border ab. 80 m. WSW of Bizerte; pop. (1966c) 2600.

Ta·bar Islands \tə-'bär-\. Group of small islands, NE part of the Bismarck Archipelago, W Pacific Ocean, off NE coast of island of New Ireland; comprise the three islands of Tabar, Tatau, and Simberi; practically unexplored until 1910.

Tabariya, Bahr. See GALILEE, SEA OF.

Ta·bas \tə-'bäs\. 1 Town, S Khorāsān prov., NE Iran, at N border of the Dasht-e-Lūt 180 m. NE of Yazd.
2 Town, SE Khorāsān prov., NE Iran, ESE of Bīrjand near Afghan border.

Ta·bas·co \tə-'bas-(ˌ)kō\. 1 State of SE Mexico. See table at MEXICO.
2 River, Mexico. See GRIJALVA.

Ta·ber \'tāb-ər\. Town, Alberta, Canada, 32 m. E of Lethbridge; pop. (1971p) 4790; sugar beets, canning; diversified agriculture; oil and gas wells.

Ta·be·ris Lagoon \tə-ˌber-əs-\ *or* **Tua·pi Lagoon** \ˌtwä-pē-\. Inlet of the Caribbean Sea, NE coast of Nicaragua.

Ta·bi·te·u·ea \ˌtäb-i-teu̇-'ā-ə\. Island (atoll), near S end of Gilbert Is., W Pacific Ocean, ab. 80 m. S of the equator; ab. 50 m. long.

Ta·blas \'täb-ləs\. Largest island of Romblon group, Romblon prov., cen. Phil., in W marking part of W border of Sibuyan Sea; 265 sq. m.; ab. 40 m. long; chief municipality Odioñgan. Long narrow island, separated from E Mindoro by Tablas Strait, and from Romblon I. at its N end by a channel 8 m. wide; has low mountain range through its center.

Tablas, Las. See LAS TABLAS.

Tablas Strait. Passage bet. Mindoro on the W and Tablas, Simara, and Banton Is. on the E, Phil.; ab. 35 m. wide; connects E end of Verde Island Passage with Sulu Sea.

Ta·ble Bay \ˌtā-bəl-\. Inlet forming the harbor of Cape Town, SW Cape Province, Rep. of South Africa; 6 m. wide.

Table Cape. 1 Cape, E cen. coast of North I., New Zealand, at the base of Mahia Penin. at 39°06'S, 178°E.
2 Cape, NW Tasmania, Australia, N of Wynyard.
3 Town, Tasmania. See WYNYARD.

Table Mountain. 1 Peak, cen. Churchill co., W Nevada; 8330 ft.
2 Peak in Catskill Mts., Ulster co., SE New York; 3847 ft.
3 Peak, Kittitas co., cen. Washington; 6243 ft.
4 Peak in Teton Range, W Teton co., NW Wyoming; 11,101 ft.
5 Peak, Yellowstone National Park, NW Wyoming; 10,063 ft.
6 Mountain, Cape Province, Rep. of South Africa, S of Cape Town; 3563 ft.

Table Rock. Peak, Scotts Bluff co., W Nebraska; 4139 ft.

Ta·ble·top Mountain \ˌtā-bəl-ˌtäp-\. Peak in the Adirondack Mts., Essex co., NE New York; 4440 ft.

Ta·bo·ga \tə-'bō-gə\. Small island, Gulf of Panama, 10 m. S of the city of Panama; part of Panama.

Ta·bo·gon \ˌtäb-ə-'gȯn\. Municipality, NE coast of Cebu I., Cebu prov., Phil., 47 m. N of City of Cebu; pop. (1969e) 27,400.

Tá·bor \'täb-ˌȯ(ə)r\. Town, Czech S.R., W Czechoslovakia, on Lužnice river 47 m. S of Prague; pop. (1961c) 20,142; manufactures textiles and tobacco products; founded 1420 by Jan Žižka, a Hussite; remained Protestant stronghold (of Taborites) during Hussite Wars; 15th cent. church.

Ta·bor, Mount \-'tā-bər\ *or Heb.* **Har Ta·vor** \'här-tə-'vȯr\. Mountain, N Israel, 6 m. E by S of Nazareth; 1929 ft.; notable in Biblical (*Ps.* lxxxix. 12) and Roman times.

Ta·bo·ra \tə-'bōr-ə, -'bȯr-\. 1 Administrative region of W Tanzania. See table at TANZANIA.
2 Town, its ✱, on railroad 430 m. WNW of Dar es Salaam; pop. (1967c) 21,012; trade center; modern town founded by Arabs 1820; in World War I taken by Belgian forces Sept. 19, 1916.

Ta·bou *or* **Ta·bu** \tə-'bü\. Seaport, SW Ivory Coast, W Africa, ab. 20 m. E of the Liberian border; pop. (1963e) 9300.

Ta·brīz \tə-'brēz\. Commercial city, ✱ of East Azerbaijan prov., NW Iran, ab. 38 m. E of Lake Urmia and N of Kūh-e Sahand; pop. (1971e) 420,000; alt. 4400 ft.; center of road and rail transportation, incl. a rail connection (80 m.) to Dzhulfa on the Araks in Azerbaijan S.S.R., U.S.S.R.; produces carpets, textiles, leather goods, soap, paint, dried fruits and nuts; restored 15th cent. mosque; univ. (1946). Has been subject to frequent destructive earthquakes and several times destroyed by invaders—Arabs, Turks, Mongols, and esp. Tamerlane in 1392. Became Persian 1618; occupied by Turks 1721–30 and by Russians 1827–28; object of conflict bet. Turks and Russians in World War I and of international dispute 1946.

Ta·buk \tə-'bük\. Municipality, ✱ of Kalinga-Apayao prov., N Luzon, Phil.; pop. (1970e) 31,600.

Tab·we·ma·sa·na, Mount \-ˌtab-wə-mə-'sä-nə\. Mountain, Espíritu Santo I., New Hebrides; 6167 ft.; highest peak on the island.

Ta·cám·bar·o \tə-'käm-bə-ˌrō\. Municipality, Michoacan state, Mexico, 45 m. SE of Uruapan; pop. (1970p) 33,690; sugar refining; wheat, sugarcane, oranges, mangoes.

Ta·ca·ná \ˌtäk-ə-'nä\. 1 Volcano, SW Guatemala, on the Guatemala-Mexico boundary in the Sierra Madre range; 13,428 ft.
2 Town, San Marios dept., SW Guatemala, NE of the volcano; munic. pop. (1964p) 27,874.

Tacape. See GABÈS.

Tacarigua. See VALENCIA 4.

T'a–ch'eng *or* **Tah·cheng** \'dä-'cheŋ\ *or formerly* **Chu·gu·chak** \'chü-'gü-'chäk\. Town, N Sinkiang Uighur, W China.

Ta·chi·ka·wa \tä-'chē-kə-wə, ˌtä-chē-'kä-wə\. Industrial town, Tokyo prefecture, SE Honshū, Japan, 19 m. W of Tokyo; pop. (1970c) 117,057.

Tá·chi·ra \'täch-i-ˌrä\. State of W Venezuela. See table at VENEZUELA.

Ta·clo·ban \tä-'klō-(ˌ)bän\. Chartered city, NE coast of Leyte I., ✱ of Leyte prov., Phil., at S end of San Juanico Strait and on NW shore of San Pedro Bay; pop. (1970e) 74,100; has good harbor with coastal trade; univ. (1946).

Made capital by Spanish in 19th cent. and as port opened to foreign trade 1874; seized by Japanese 1942 and retaken with its airport by U.S. forces Oct. 21, 1944.

Tac·na \'tak-nə\. 1 Department, extreme S Peru; 5701 sq. m.; pop. (1969e) 90,600; ✱ Tacna; mostly an arid region enclosed on E by foothills of the Andes. Part of **Tacna–Ari·ca** \-ə-'rē-kə\ region, which was occupied by Chile from 1884 (see ANCÓN for Treaty of Ancón 1883) to 1930 when region was divided bet. Peru (Tacna dept.) and Chile (Arica in Tarapaca prov.). See ARICA.

2 Town, its ✱, ab. 40 m. by rail N of Arica, Chile; pop. (1969e) 30,500; Peruvian and Bolivian forces defeated near here by Chileans 1880.

Ta·co·ma \tə-'kō-mə\. Seaport city, ⊗ of Pierce co., W cen. Washington, on Puget Sound 26 m. S of Seattle; pop. (1970c) 154,581; lumber and wood products, aluminum, copper products, candy, logging equipment; boat-building center, commercial fisheries, railroad shops, fish-canning plants; center of resort area; Univ. of Puget Sound (1888); McChord Air Force Base, Fort Lewis. First permanent settlement 1868; incorporated as city 1875.

Tacoma, Mount. See RAINIER, MOUNT.

Ta·con·ic Range \tə-'kän-ik-\. Ridge, extending along Massachusetts-New York boundary and into Vermont; highest peak Mount Equinox, 3816 ft. in Bennington co., SW Vermont.

Ta·co·ra \tə-'kōr-ə, -'kȯr-\. Peak, Tacna dept., S Peru; 19,522 ft.

Ta·cua·rem·bó \ˌtäk-wə-rem-'bō\. 1 Department of N cen. Uruguay. See table at URUGUAY.

2 *or* **San Fruc·tu·o·so** \ˌsan-frük-'twō-sō\. City, its ✱, 215 m. N of Montevideo; pop. (1963c) 29,058; trade center for wool, hides, and skins.

Ta·cua·rí \ˌtäk-wə-'rē\. River, E Uruguay; ab. 90 m. long; flows E into Lake Mirim.

Tacurupucú. See HERNANDARIAS.

Ta·cu·tu *or* **Ta·ku·tú** \ˌtäk-ə-'tü\. River, Guyana and N Brazil; 220 m. long; flows N, forming a section of the boundary bet. SW Guyana and Brazil, curves W into N Brazil and S to unite with the Uraricoera river and form the Rio Branco. See IRENG.

Ta·djou·ra *or* **Ta·ju·ra** \tə-jur-ə\. Seaport, Afars and Issas, E Africa, N side of the Gulf of Tadjoura; pop. (1968e) 2500.

Tadjoura, Gulf of *or* **Gulf of Tajura.** Inlet of the Gulf of Aden, E coast of Afars and and Issas, E Africa.

Tadmor. See PALMYRA 6.

Tad·ous·sac \'tad-ə-ˌsak\. Village, ⊗ of Saguenay co., SE Quebec, Canada, on N bank of St. Lawrence river at mouth of the Saguenay on its left bank, 117 m. NE of Quebec; pop. (1971p) 1004; popular summer resort. An Indian village at time of Jacques Cartier 1534–42; trading station for furs and fish; settlement made 1600, oldest in Canada.

Ta·dzhik Soviet Socialist Republic \tä-'jik-, -'jēk-, tə-\ *or* **Ta·dzhik·i·stan** \tä-ˌjik-i-'stan, tə-, -ˌjēk-, -'stän\ *also* **Tajik Soviet Socialist Republic** *or* **Ta·jik·i·stan.** Constituent republic of the U.S.S.R., bounded on N by Uzbek and Kirgiz S.S.Rs., on E by China, on S by Afghanistan, and on W by Uzbek S.S.R.; 55,251 sq. m.; pop. (1970p) 2,900,000; ✱ Dushanbe. *Physical features:* Very mountainous region, its E part containing the Pamirs (see PAMIR) and Trans Alai mountain systems; highest point Communism Peak 24,590 ft., highest point in the U.S.S.R.; W part also mountainous, marked by several valleys of N tributaries of the Amu Darya, which forms the S boundary with Afghanistan. *Chief products:* Cotton, wheat, barley; livestock; lead, zinc. *Chief towns:* Dushanbe, Leninabad, Ura-Tyube. Acquired as part of Russian Turkistan 1895; made part of the Russian S.F.S.R. 1924 and became a constituent republic 1929.

Tae·dong \ta-'dùŋ, tī-\ *or formerly* **Dai·do** \'dīd-(ˌ)ō\. River and inlet, North Korea; 245 m. long; river flows into Korea Bay at Namp'o.

Tae·gu \'tag-(ˌ)ü\ *or Jap.* **Tai·kyu** \'tī-(ˌ)kyü\. City, ✱ of North Kyŏngsang prov., South Korea, 56 m. NNW of Pusan; pop. (1970e) 1,082,750; important historically as far back as 8th cent. A.D.

Tae Han. See KOREA.

Tae Han Min'guk. See KOREA, SOUTH.

Tae·jŏn \'taj-'ȯn\ *or Jap.* **Tai·den** \'tī-'den\. City, ✱ of South Ch'ungch'ŏng prov., South Korea, on railroad 70 m. NW of Taegu; pop. (1970e) 414,598; food processing.

Taenarum. See TAÍNARON, CAPE.

Ta·enga \tä-'eŋ-ə\. Island, E cen. part of Tuamotu Archipelago, French Polynesia, S Pacific Ocean.

Ta·fa·hi \tä-'fä-(ˌ)hē\ *or formerly* **Bos·caw·en** \bä-'skō-ən, -'skȯ-\. Island, N part of Tonga, SW cen. Pacific Ocean, ab. 125 m. E of Niuafoo and 6 m. from Niuatoputapu (*q.v.*); 7 sq. m.

Ta·fel Berg \'taf-əl-ˌbe(ə)rg\. Hill, Curaçao I., Netherlands Antilles; 636 ft.; a source of calcium phosphate.

Ta·fel·berg National Park \'täf-əl-ˌbərg-, -ˌbe(ə)rg-\. National park, Surinam; 154 sq. m.; sandstone formations; established 1966.

Taff \'taf\. River, SE Wales; 40 m. long; flows SE through Glamorganshire into Bristol Channel at Cardiff.

Ta·fi·lalt \ˌtaf-i-'lalt\ *or* **Ta·fi·lelt** \-'lelt\ *or* **Ta·fi·let** \-'let\. Oasis, SE Morocco; ab. 533 sq. m.; chief town Bou-Am (Abuam); noted for its dates.

Ta·fí Vie·jo \tə-'fē-'vyā-hō\. Town, Tucuman prov., N Argentina; pop. (1960c) 21,197.

Taf·na \'taf-nə\. Unnavigable river, NW Algeria, N Africa, flowing N into Mediterranean Sea.

Taft \'taft\. 1 City, Kern co., S California, 28 m. SW of Bakersfield; pop. (1970c) 4285; oil and gas wells.

2 City, San Patricio co., S Texas, 15 m. N of Corpus Christi; pop. (1970c) 3274; aluminum.

Taf·tān, Kūh–e *or* **Kuh–i–Taf·tan** \ˌkü-(h)ē-taf-'tän\. Volcano, SE Iran, 65 m. SSE of Zāhedān; 13,261 ft.

Ta·fua, Mount \-tə-'fü-ə\. Peak, W Upolu I., Western Samoa, SW cen. Pacific; 2194 ft.; of volcanic origin.

Ta·gāb \tə-'gäb\. Town, ✱ of Kāpīsā prov., E Afghanistan, ab. 30 m. NE of Kabul; pop. (1969e) 70,590.

Ta·gan·rog \'tag-ən-ˌräg\. City, SW Rostov Oblast, Russian S.F.S.R., U.S.S.R., on N shore of Gulf of Taganrog 45 m. W of Rostov-na-Donu; pop. (1970p) 254,000; industrial center and seaport, shipping grain; shipyards, commercial fisheries. Pisan colony founded on site c. 13th cent. but destroyed by Mongols; site later settled by Turks; annexed to Russia 1769 and developed as naval base; in World War II occupied by Germans Aug. 1941–Aug. 1943. Birthplace of Anton Chekhov.

Taganrog, Gulf of *or Russ.* **Ta·gan·rog·skiy Za·liv** \tə-gən-'rȯg-ˌskē-zə-'lēf\. Northeast arm of the Sea of Azov, S U.S.S.R.; receives the Don river.

Tagaste. See SOUK-AHRAS.

Ta·gay·tay \tə-ˌgī-'tī\. Chartered city, S border of Cavite prov., Luzon, Phil.; pop. (1970e) 10,100; comprises **Tagaytay Ridge,** a mountain range, highest point ab. 2000 ft., running E and W along N Batangas boundary NW of Lake Taal.

Tag·bi·la·ran \ˌtäg-bi-'lär-ˌän\. Chartered city, ✱ of Bohol prov., Phil., in SW part on narrow strait opp. Panglao I.; pop. (1970e) 28,400; has shallow harbor.

Ta·gi·nae \tə-'jī-(ˌ)nē\. Ancient village, cen. Italy, in the Apennines near modern Gubbio; Totila, Gothic king, defeated and killed here 552 by the Byzantine general Narses.

Tag·ish Lake \'tag-ish-\. Lake, across boundary of S Yukon Territory and N British Columbia, Canada, W of Atlin Lake; 130 sq. m.; alt. 2152 ft.; discharges into Lewes river.

Ta·giu·ra \tä-'jü(ə)r-ə\ *or* **Ta·jū·rā'** \tä-'jü(ə)r-ə\. Seaport oasis, NW Libya, N Africa, E of Tripoli.

Ta·glia·coz·zo \ˌtäl-yə-'kòt-sō\. Commune, Aquila prov., Abruzzi, cen. Italy, 21 m. SSW of Aquila; pop. (1968e) 8751; 13th cent. Gothic church, 14th cent. castle; scene of battle Aug. 1268 in which Conradin was defeated by Charles I of Anjou.

Ta·glia·men·to \ˌtäl-yə-'men-(ˌ)tō\. River, N Italy; 106 m. long; flows S from the Carnic Alps into the head of the Gulf of Venice.

Ta·go \tə-'gō\. Municipality, Surigao del Sur prov., Mindanao, Phil., ab 70 m. SE of Surigao; pop. (1969e) 28,700.

Ta·go·lo Point \tə-ˌgō-lō-\. North point of Zamboanga del Norte prov., Mindanao, Phil., just NW of Dapitan; extends into W end of Mindanao Sea.

Ta·gu·din \ˌtä-gü-'dēn\. Municipality, Ilocos Sur prov., Luzon, Phil., on coast highway 43 m. S of Vigan and on N bank of Amburayan river; pop. (1969e) 24,600.

Ta·gu·la Island \'täg-ə-lə-\ *or* **Sud–Est Island** \sü-'dest-\ *or* **Southeast Island.** Island, S Louisiade Archipelago, Papua New Guinea, off SE point of New Guinea I., 50 m. SE of Misima I.; ab. 50 m. long and 15 m. max. width; 310 sq. m.; pop. (1969e) 1700; highest point 3000 ft.

Ta·gum \'tä-ˌgüm\. Municipality, ✱ of Davao del Norte prov., Mindanao, Phil., at head of Davao Gulf 27 m. NE of Davao; pop. (1969e) 39,000.

Ta·gus \'tā-gəs\ *or Span.* **Ta·jo** \'tä-(ˌ)hō\ *or Port.* **Te·jo** \'tā-(ˌ)zhü\. River, Spain and Portugal; 626 m. long; longest river in Iberian Penin.; rises in E cen. Spain ab. 80 m. E of Madrid, flows W across cen. Spain to Portuguese border; continues W forming a section (ab. 25 m.) of Spanish-Portuguese boundary, then turns SW and empties into Atlantic Ocean at Lisbon; ab. 10 m. above Lisbon expands into a lagoon ab. 7 m. wide which narrows at Lisbon to a channel ab. 2 m. wide and 8 m. long, partly blocked by a sand bar; navigable ab. 100 m.

Ta·haa \tə-'hä(-ˌä)\ *or* **Ta·hao** \tə-'haů\. One of the Leeward Is., Society Is., French Polynesia, S Pacific Ocean, just N of Raiatéa; 34 sq. m.; pop. (1967e) 3567.

Ta·han, Gu·nong \ˌgü-ˌnòŋ-'tä-ˌhän\. Mountain (*gunong*), N Pahang state on Kelantan boundary, Malaysia, S Malay Penin.; 7186 ft.; highest peak in the peninsula.

Tahcheng. See T'A-CH'ENG.

Taheiho. See AI-HUI.

Tahent, Djebel. See HILL 609.

Ta·hi·ti \tə-'hēt-ē\ *or Fr.* **Ta·ï·ti** \tȧ-ē-tē\ *or formerly* **Ota·hei·te** \ˌōt-ə-'hēt-ē, -'hāt-\. Island of E group (Windward Is.) of the Society Is., French Polynesia, S Pacific Ocean, 17°37'S, 149°27'W; 408 sq. m.; pop. (1967e) 61,519; ✱ Papeete. The largest and most important of the French islands of the S Pacific; the main part is nearly circular and very mountainous with several high peaks (highest Orohena, in the center, 7339 ft.) and fertile but narrow coastal strip; to the SE connected by narrow isthmus with broad peninsula; all villages are on the coast. Political as well as commercial center of French Polynesia; became a French colony 1880; in 1940 joined the Free French movement.

Tahlab. See TALAB.

Tah·le·quah \'tal-ə-ˌkwò\. City, ⊗ of Cherokee co., E Oklahoma, 26 m. ENE of Muskogee; pop. (1970c) 9254; canned goods, lumber; strawberries; Northeastern State Coll. (1846). Became permanent capital of the Cherokee Nation 1839.

Ta·hoe, Lake \-'tä-(ˌ)hō\. Lake on N cen. California-Nevada boundary; 22 m. long by 10 m. wide, 192 sq. m.; elevation 6229 ft.; greatest depth 1685 ft.; outlet Truckee river; tourist resort.

Tahoelandang. See TAHULANDANG.

Tahoena. See TAHUNA.

Ta·ho·ka \tə-'hō-kə\. City, ⊗ of Lynn co., NW Texas, 32 m. S of Lubbock; pop. (1970c) 2956.

Ta·houa \'taů-ə\. Town, SW Niger, ab. 225 m. NE of Niamey.

Tahpanhes. See DAPHNAE.

Ta–hsing–an–ling Shan–mo. See KHINGAN.

Tah·tā \'tät-ə, 'tä-hə-ˌtä\. Town, Asyūt gov., Egypt, on the Nile river SSE of Asyūt.

Ta·hua \'tä-wə\. Peak, W Bolivia, S of Lake Poopó; 17,547 ft.

Ta·hua·ta *also* **Ta·ua·ta** \tə-'wät-ə\. One of the Marquesas Is., French Polynesia, S Pacific Ocean, ab. 3 m. S of Hiva Oa.

Ta·hu·lan·dang *or* **Ta·hoe·lan·dang** \ˌtä-hů-'län-ˌdäŋ\. One of the main islands of the Sangihe Is. (*q.v.*).

Ta·hu·na *or* **Ta·hoe·na** \tə-'hü-nə\. Chief town, Sangihe I. (see SANGIHE ISLANDS).

Tahura. See KAULA.

Ta·hure \tä-'ür\. Village and hill in Marne dept., NE France, 30 m. ESE of Reims; battles Oct. 7, 1915, when taken by the Germans, and Sept. 25, 1918, when retaken by Allies.

T'ai–an *or* **Tai·an** \'tī-'än\. Town, W cen. Shantung prov., NE China, on railroad 37 m. S of Tsinan; noted as starting point of ascent of T'ai Shan mountain; a very old place, according to tradition, dating back to an emperor of the 23d cent. B.C.; has several large temples.

T'ai–chou \'tī-'jō, -'chaů\ *or* **Tai·chow** \'tī-'jō, -'chaů\. Town, Kiangsu prov., E China, ab. 80 m. ENE of Nanking; pop. (1970e) 275,000.

T'ai–chung *or* **Tai·chung** \'tī-'chůŋ\ *or Jap.* **Tai·chu** \'tī-(ˌ)chü\ *or formerly* **Tai·wan** \'tī-'wän\. City, W cen. Taiwan, on railroad along W coast; pop. (1971e) 456,719.

Taiden. See TAEJŎN.

Tai·e·ri \'tī-ə-rē\. River, SE South I., New Zealand; 179 m. long; flows SE into Pacific Ocean near Dunedin.

Ta·if \'tä-if\. Town, W Saudi Arabia, ab. 40 m. ESE of Mecca; pop. (1963e) 54,000; in mountains at over 5000 ft. altitude; produces great variety of fruit. Important town in time of Mohammed; resisted him 630 but finally capitulated; taken by Arabs from the Turks 1916 and captured by ibn-Saud 1924.

T'ai–hang Shan \'tī-'häŋ-'shän\ *or* **Tai·heng Shan** \'dī-'həŋ-'shän\. Mountain range on boundary bet. N Honan prov. and SE Shansi prov., NE China, N of the Yellow river.

Taihoku. See TAIPEI.

Taih·pa Ga \ˌtī-pə-'gä\. Village, N Burma, on the Chindwin river; taken by U.S. Feb. 1, 1944.

T'ai Hu *or* **Tai Hu** \'tī-'hü\. Lake (*hu*), Kiangsu and Chekiang provs., E China; 44 m. long; Huang-p'u is one of its outlets; large city of Su-chou is near its E shore.

Taikyu. See TAEGU.

Tai·ma *or* **Tay·mā** \'tī-mə, 'tā-\ *also* **Tei·ma** \'tām-ə\ *or Bib.* **Te·ma** \'tē-mə\. Oasis and ancient commercial town, NW Nejd, Saudi Arabia.

Tai·myr National Okrug *or* **Tai·mir National Okrug** \ˌtī-'mi(ə)r . . . ˌò-'krüg\. A national district, Russian S.F.S.R., U.S.S.R., approximately coextensive with the Taimyr Penin.; 332,857 sq. m.; pop. (1970p) 38,000; ✱ Dudinka; entirely within the Arctic Circle; has rich mineral deposits, esp. nickel, copper, platinum, and gold.

Taimyr Peninsula *or* **Taimir Peninsula.** Large peninsula, N Russian S.F.S.R., U.S.S.R., wholly within the Taimyr National Okrug, bet. the Yenisei and Khatanga rivers; includes Cape Chelyuskin, the northernmost point of Asia, 77°45'N, 104°20'E; crossed in cen. part by **Taimyr River,** 400 m. long, flowing E and N through the large, irregular-shaped **Taimyr Lake** to **Taimyr Bay,** 76°15'N, 98°E. To the W of the bay is **Taimyr Island.**

T'ai–nan \'tī-'nän\ *formerly* **Dai·nan** \'dī-'nän\. City, SW coast of Taiwan; pop. (1971e) 479,353; textiles, rubber products, plastics, aluminum, iron and steel products, electrical appliances; salt-refining plants; univ. (1956). One of the oldest cities on Taiwan, and from early 17th cent. to 1885 the capital, largest city, and economic center of the island.

Taí·na·ron, Cape \-'tä-nə-ˌrȯn\ *or formerly* **Cape Mat·a·pan** \-ˌmat-ə-'pan\ *or anc.* **Tae·na·rum** \'tēn-ə-ˌrəm\. Southernmost point of mainland of Greece, 36°22′N, 22°30′E, at tip of cen. peninsula of Peloponnesus. Naval battle nearby Mar. 28, 1941 in which British sank three Italian cruisers and two destroyers and damaged a battleship.

Taiohae *or* **Tai–o–hae.** See HAKAPEHI.

Tai·pa \'tī-pə\. See MACAO 1.

Tai·pei *or* **T'ai–pei** \'tī-'pā, -'bā\; *formerly* **Tai·ho·ku** \'tī-'hō-(ˌ)kü\ *or* **Dai·ho·ku** \'dī-'hō-(ˌ)kü\. City, ✱ of Taiwan, at N end of the island; pop. (1971e) 1,742,626; commercial, financial, industrial, and transportation center of Taiwan; produces textiles, rubber goods, chemicals, electrical equipment, machine tools, metal products; brewing, printing; railroad shops; National Taiwan Univ. (1928) and several other educational institutions. Founded 1708 and became important center of tea trade mid-19th cent.; under Japanese rule administrative capital of the island; became seat of Chinese Nationalist government 1949.

Tai·ping \'tī-'piŋ, -'biŋ\. 1 River, China and Upper Burma. See TA-YING.
2 City, Perak state, Malaysia, in NW part on railroad 50 m. SE of Penang; pop. (1957c) 48,200.

Tai·po \'tī-'pō\. Town, Hong Kong, China, at head of inlet of Mirs Bay on railroad to Canton.

Taira. See IWAKI 2.

Tai·ro·na National Park \ˌtī-'rō-nə-\. National park, Colombia; 442 sq. m.; established 1964.

T'ai Shan \'tī-'shän\ *or* **Tai Shan.** Mountain, Shantung prov., China, 32 m. S of Tsinan; 5048 ft.; many temples on the road and on the top; has been considered as sacred for several thousand years; formerly an important place of pilgrimage.

Tai·tao, Cape \-tī-'tau̇\. Cape, SW Chile, extending into Pacific Ocean on NW tip of Taitao Penin.

Taitao Peninsula. Peninsula, SW Chile, extending into Pacific Ocean, S of Chonos Archipelago and N of the Gulf of Penas.

Taïti. See TAHITI.

T'ai–tung \'tī-'du̇ŋ\ *or formerly* **Tai·to** \'tī-(ˌ)tō\. Coastal town, SE Taiwan.

Tai·vu Point \ˌtī-vü-\. Cape, NE coast of Guadalcanal I., in the Solomon Is. in the W Pacific Ocean; ab. 40 m. E of Cape Esperance; marks E limit of U.S. invasion coast 1942.

Tai·wan \'tī-'wän\. 1 *also* **For·mo·sa** \fȯr-'mo-sə, fər-, -zə\. Island, seat of Chinese Nationalist government, off Fukien prov., SE China; 13,807 sq. m., incl. its outlying islands 13,887 sq. m.; total pop. (1971e) 14,810,929; ✱ Taipei. *Physical features:* Has lofty mountain range extending through E cen. part, highest peaks Hsin-kao 13,-113 ft., and Tz'u-kao 12,743 ft.; no long rivers; its S point, O-luan, on Bashi Channel, which separates it from Batan Is. of the Philippines; minor dependencies incl. Pescadores (*q.v.*). *Chief products:* Rice, sugarcane, tea, peanuts, citrus fruit, soybeans; fishing; salt, sulfur; manufacturing: textiles, chemicals, glass, electrical equipment, rubber products, cement. *Chief cities:* Taipei, Kao-hsiung, T'ai-nan, T'ai-chung, Chi-lung.

History: Known to Chinese since early 7th cent. A.D.; visited by Portuguese 1590 (named Formosa by the Portuguese because of its beautiful scenery [Port. *formosa* beautiful]); settled by Chinese early 17th cent.; fort established 1624 by Dutch who were driven out by Manchus 1662; not open to Europeans again until two ports opened 1858 by Treaties of Tientsin; ceded to Japan 1895; in World War II made a strong military base by the Japanese; frequently bombed 1944–45 by U.S. planes; after defeat of Japan returned to China; became seat of Chinese Nationalist government 1949; concluded mutual security pact with U.S. 1955; lost its seat in the United Nations 1971.

2 City, Taiwan. See T'AI-CHUNG.

Taiwan Strait. See FORMOSA STRAIT.

Tai·ya Inlet \ˌtī-yə-\. Upper arm, Chilkoot Inlet, SE Alaska; ab. 15 m. long. See LYNN CANAL.

T'ai–yüan \'tī-yu̇-'än\ *or* **Yang·ku** \'yaŋ-'kü\. City, ✱ of Shansi prov., NE China, in center of province on the Fen 265 m. SW of Peking; pop. (1970e) 2,725,000; alt. 2600 ft.; railroad terminus; ships agricultural products; coal mines. Has historical museum; Shansi Univ. Known since 450 A.D.; a strategic center in time of Mongols; scene of massacre of missionaries in Boxer uprising; besieged by Communist forces 1948–49.

Ta·'izz \ta-'iz\. Town in highlands of S Yemen (✱ San'a), SW Arabian Penin., 32 m. E of Mocha; pop. (1970e) 48,-000; government offices; several mosques.

Tajamulco. See TAJUMULCO.

Tajikistan *or* **Tajik Soviet Socialist Republic.** See TADZHIK SOVIET SOCIALIST REPUBLIC.

Ta·ji·mi \tə-'jē-mē\. City, Gifu prefecture, Honshū, Japan, 17 m. NE of Nagoya; pop. (1970c) 63,522.

Tajo. See TAGUS.

Taj·rish \täj-'rēsh\. Town, Tehran prov., NW Iran, ab. 10 m. N of Tehran; pop. (1966c) 157,486.

Ta·ju·mul·co \ˌtä-hü-'mül-(ˌ)kō\ *or* **Ta·ja·mu·lco** \ˌtä-hə-\. Volcanic mountain, W Guatemala; 13,845 ft.; highest point in Central America.

Ta·ju·ña \tä-'hün-yə\. River, cen. Spain; ab. 150 m. long; flows SW through Guadalajara prov. and on into Jarama river ab. 7 m. NE of Aranjuez.

Tajūrā'. See TAGIURA.

Tajura. See TADJOURA.

Tajura, Gulf of. See TADJOURA, GULF OF.

Tak \'täk\ *or* **Ra·haeng** \'rä-'haŋ\. 1 Province, W Thailand; 6027 sq. m.; pop. (1960c) 167,992; ✱ Tak.
2 Town, its ✱, on left bank of Ping river 40 m. from Burma border and 70 m. W of Phitsanulok; pop. (1964e) 14,734.

Ta·ka·chi·ho·da·ke \tə-ˌkäch-i-hō-'däk-ē\. See KIRISHIMA.

Ta·ka·da \tä-'käd-ə\ *or* **Ta·ka·ta** \-'kät-\. City, Niigata prefecture, NW Honshū, Japan, 65 m. ENE of Toyama; pop. (1970c) 75,053.

Ta·ka·ma·tsu \ˌtäk-ə-'mät-(ˌ)sü\. City, ✱ of Kagawa prefecture, NE Shikoku I., Japan; pop. (1970c) 274,367; a major seaport on the Inland Sea; shipyards and warehouse facilities; notable public gardens.

Takao. See KAO-HSIUNG.

Ta·ka·o·ka \tə-'kaů-kə\. City, Toyama prefecture, Honshū, Japan, 15 m. W of Toyama; pop. (1970c) 159,664; ships rice; produces lacquer ware and brass articles, including inlaid ware.

Ta·ka·pu·na \ˌtäk-ə-'pü-nə\. City, N North I., New Zealand, N suburb of Auckland; pop. (1970e) 24,200.

Ta·ka·ra·zu·ka \tə-ˌkär-ə-'zü-kə\. City, Hyōgo prefecture, Honshū, Japan, ab. 13 m. NW of Ōsaka; pop. (1970c) 127,179.

Ta·ka·sa·go \ˌtä-kə-'sä-gō, tä-'kä-sä-(ˌ)gō\. City, Hyōgo prefecture, Honshū, Japan, 24 m. WNW of Kōbe; pop. (1970c) 68,900.

Ta·ka·sa·ki \ˌtäk-ə-'säk-ē\. Industrial city, Gumma prefecture, cen. Honshū, Japan, 10 m. SW of Maebashi; pop. (1970c) 193,072; important silk market.

Takata. See TAKADA.

Ta·kat·su·ki \tə-'kät-sů-(ˌ)kē\. City, Ōsaka prefecture, Honshū, Japan, ab. 13 m. NNE of Ōsaka; pop. (1970c) 231,129.

Ta·kaw \tə-'kȯ\. Town, Shan State, Burma, on right bank of Salween.

Ta·ka·wa \tə-'kä-wə\. City, Fukuoka prefecture, Kyūshū, Japan, 18 m. S of Kitakyūshū; pop. (1970c) 64,233.

Ta·ka·ya·ma \tə-'kä-yə-mə, ˌtäk-ə-'yäm-ə\. City, Gifu prefecture, Honshū, Japan, 71 m. NNE of Nagoya; pop. (1970c) 56,459.

Ta·ke·fu \tə-'kā-ˌfü\. City, Fukui prefecture, Honshū, Japan, 13 m. S of Fukui; pop. (1970c) 62,019.

Ta·khar \tə-'kär\. Province of NE Afghanistan. See table at AFGHANISTAN.

Takhino, Lake. See AKHINOU, LAKE.

Takh·mau \täk-'maů\. Town, S Cambodia, ab. 8 m. S of Pnompenh; pop. (1962p) 20,316.

Takht–i–Su·lai·man \ˌtak-tē-ˌsül-ī-'män\. 1 Twin peaks at N end of the Sulaiman Range, Pakistan; the higher peak, sometimes known as **Kai·sar·garh** \'kī-zər-ˌgär, -sər-\ 11,289 ft.
2 Town, Kirgiz S.S.R. See OSH.

Tak·ka·kaw \'tak-ə-ˌkȯ\. Waterfall, Yoho National Park, SE British Columbia, Canada; total drop 1650 ft., with highest single fall 1200 ft.; source is glacier in Rocky Mts.; its waters flow into Yoho river; highest waterfall in Canada.

Takkaze. See TEKEZE.

Ta·kla Ma·kan \ˌtäk-lə-mə-'kän\ *or Chin.* **T'a–k'o–la–ma–kan Shan–mo** \'tä-'kō-'lä-'mä-'kän-'shän-'mō\. Desert, forming greater part of Tarim basin, cen. Sinkiang Uighur, W China, bet. Tien Shan on N and Kunlun Mts. on S; ab. 38° to 41°N and 78° to 88°E; ab. 600 m. across, ab. 125,000 sq. m.; desert marked by shifting sand dunes.

Ta·ko·ma Park \tə-ˌkō-mə-\. City, Montgomery and Prince Georges cos., cen. Maryland, 6 m. N of Washington; pop. (1970c) 18,455; Columbia Union Coll. (1904).

Ta·ko·ra·di \ˌtä-kə-'räd-ē\. Seaport, SW Ghana; part of the joint municipality Sekondi-Takoradi (*q.v.*).

Takow. See KAO-HSIUNG.

Ta–ku *or* **Ta·ku** \'tä-'kü, 'dä-'gü\. Town, E Hopei prov., NE China, on right bank of mouth of Hai river 37 m. E of Tientsin; formerly site of forts guarding approach to Tientsin which were several times attacked by foreign forces, esp. in 1860 and in 1900 in the Boxer Rebellion, and finally demolished by terms of treaty of 1902.

Ta·ku Glacier \ˌtä-kü-\. Glacier in Coast Mountains, on Alaska-British Columbia border; 33 m. long, 3 m. wide near its terminus.

Takutú. See TACUTU.

Ta·la \'tä-lə\. Town, Jalisco state, W cen. Mexico, 20 m. W of Guadalajara; munic. pop. (1970p) 33,369.

Ta·lab *or* **Tah·lab** \tə-'läb\. River, SE Iran; ab. 175 m. long; rises near Zāhedān and flows SE to the border, then along the Iran-Pakistan boundary to Hammun-i-Mashkel.

Talabriga. 1 Seaport, Portugal. See AVEIRO 3.
2 Commune, Spain. See TALAVERA DE LA REINA.

Ta·la·gan·te \ˌtä-lə-'gän-tə\. City, Santiago prov., cen. Chile, SW of Santiago; pop. (1960c) 11,560.

Ta·la·kag \tə-'läk-ˌäg\. Municipality, Bukidnon prov., Mindanao, Phil.; pop. (1969e) 24,100.

Ta·lak·mau, Mount \-tə-'läk-ˌmaů\ *or formerly* **Mount Ophir** \-'ō-fər\. Peak in Barisan Mts., W Sumatra, Indonesia, NW of Bukittinggi; 9554 ft.

Talamanca, Cordillera de. See CORDILLERA DE TALAMANCA.

Ta·la·na Hill \tə-ˌlän-ə-\. See DUNDEE 3.

Ta·lang \'täl-ˌäŋ\. Volcanic peak in Barisan Mts., W Sumatra, Indonesia; 8517 ft.

Ta·la·ra \tə-'lär-ə\. Seaport, Piura dept., NW Peru, ab. 40 m. N of Paita and 610 m. NW of Lima; pop. (1969e) 38,200; oil refinery; export center for petroleum industry.

Ta·la·sea \ˌtäl-ə-'sā-ə\. Settlement, E side of Willaumez Penin. on Ncoast of New Britain, Bismarck Archipelago, WPacific Ocean; active trade in copra; occupied by U.S. Marines Mar. 6, 1944.

Talat. See MAHA SARAKHAM.

Ta·la·ta·koh \tə-ˌlät-ə-'kō\. See PENJU ISLANDS.

Ta·laud Islands \tə-'laůd-\ *or* **Ta·laur Islands** \tə-'laůr-\. Island group, Indonesia, NE of Celebes I. and SE of the island of Mindanao, Phil.; 494 sq. m.; chief town Beo. Comprises the main large island of Karakelong, two small islands S of it (Salebabu and Kaburuang), and the group of islets to the NE, Nanusa Is.; undeveloped; copra is only important product. First came under Dutch 1677.

Ta·la·ve·ra \ˌtäl-ə-'ver-ə\. Municipality, Nueva Ecija prov., Luzon, Phil., 8 m. N of Cabanatuan; pop. (1969e) 38,900.

Talavera de la Rei·na \-ˌdā-lä-'rā-nə\ *or anc.* **Tal·a·bri·ga** \ˌtal-ə-'brī-gə\. Commune, Toledo prov., cen. Spain, on Tagus river 41 m. WNW of Toledo; pop. (1970p) 45,327; olive oil, agricultural machinery, tobacco and dairy products; town walls with 18 medieval towers. Founded by Romans; conquered from Moors by Alfonso VI 1083; important center of woolen industry 16th–18th cents.; in 1809 scene of notable victory of British and Spanish forces under Wellington and Cuesta over French under Joseph Bonaparte.

Tal·bot \'tȯl-bət, 'tal-\. Name of counties in two states of the U.S. See tables at GEORGIA and MARYLAND.

Talbot, Cape. Point, N coast of Western Australia, W of Cape Londonderry; 13°48′S, 126°43′E.

Talbot Island \ˌtal-bət-\. Island off coast of Duval co., NE Florida, N of mouth of St. Johns river.

Tal·bot·ton \'tȯl-bət-ᵊn\. City, ⊗ of Talbot co., W Georgia; pop. (1970c) 1045; agriculture.

Tal·ca \'täl-kə\. 1 Province of cen. Chile. See table at CHILE.
2 City, its ✱, 155 m. S of Santiago on the Claro river; pop. (1966e) 80,777; commercial center and railroad junction; produces clothing, flour, food products; founded 1692.

Tal·ca·hua·no \ˌtäl-kə-'(h)wän-(ˌ)ō\. Seaport, Concepción prov., S cen. Chile, 9 m. NW of Concepción; pop. (1966e) 102,019; good anchorage; naval base.

Tal·dy–Kur·gan \ˌtal-dē-ků(ə)r-'gan\. Town, ✱ of Taldy-Kurgan Oblast, E Kazakh S.S.R., U.S.S.R., SE of Lake Balkhash and ab. 140 m. NE of Alma Ata; pop. (1970p) 61,000.

Taldy–Kurgan Oblast \-'ȯ-bləst, -ˌblast\. Subdivision of the Kazakh S.S.R., U.S.S.R.; 45,753 sq. m.; pop. (1970p)

610,000; ✱ Taldy-Kurgan. Lies between Semipalatinsk Oblast on N and Alma Ata Oblast on S and borders on E on Sinkiang Uighur, China.

Ta·lence \ta-'lä^{n}s\. Commune, Gironde dept., SW France, SW suburb of Bordeaux; pop. (1968c) 29,161; produces wine.

Ta–li *or* **Ta·li** \'tä-'lē\. 1 *or formerly* **Tung·chow** \'tu̇ŋ-'jō\. Town, E Shensi prov., NE cen. China, 60 m. ENE of Sian.

2 Commercial city, W cen. Yunnan prov., S China, on W shore of Erh Hai (Tali Lake) 180 m. W of K'un-ming; located at 6900 ft. above sea level bet. lake and high mountains; ancient city noted for its marble.

Ta·li·a·bu *or Du.* **Ta·li·a·boe** \ˌtäl-ē-'äb-(ˌ)ü\. Island, largest of the Sula Is., W Moluccas, Indonesia, E of Celebes I.; ab. 68 m. long by 26 m. at its greatest width; highest point 3796 ft.

Tal·ia·ferro \'täl-ə-vər\. County in Georgia. See table at GEORGIA.

Ta·li·bon \ˌtä-lə-'bōn\. Municipality, Bohol prov., N coast of Bohol I., Phil., 48 m. NE of Tagbilaran; pop. (1969e) 42,300.

Ta–lien. See DAIREN.

Ta·li·hi·na \ˌtal-ə-'hē-nə\. Town, Le Flore and Latimer cos., E Oklahoma, 34 m. SW of Poteau; pop. (1970c) 1227.

Ta·li·ko·ta \ˌtä-lē-'kō-tə\ *or* **Ta·li·kot** \'tä-lē-ˌkōt\. Town, N Mysore, W India; pop. (1961c) 12,800; scene in 1565 of major battle in which Muslim chieftains of the Deccan united in overthrowing the Hindu kingdom of Vijayanagar.

Tali Lake. See ERH HAI.

Ta·lim Island \tä-'lēm-\. Island in N cen. Laguna de Bay, cen. Luzon, Phil.; 10 m. long, ab. 11 sq. m.; belongs to Rizal prov.; has valuable stone quarries; its S point is **Talim Point,** 14°07′N, 121°14′E.

T'a–li–mu Ho. See TARIM.

Talin. See TALLINN.

Ta·li·qan \ˌtäl-i-'kän\. Town, ✱ of Takhar prov., NE Afghanistan; pop. (1969e) 66,654.

Ta·li·say \tä-'lē-ˌsī\. 1 Municipality, Cebu prov., E coast of Cebu I., Phil., at N end of Bohol Strait 6 m. SW of City of Cebu; pop. (1969e) 42,300.

2 Municipality, NW Negros Occidental, Negros, Phil., on Guimaras Strait 5 m. N of City of Bacolod; pop. (1969e) 62,200.

Tal·la·de·ga \ˌtal-ə-'dē-gə\. 1 County in E cen. Alabama. See table at ALABAMA.

2 City, its ⊗, 44 m. E of Birmingham; pop. (1970c) 17,662; cottonseed oil, lumber, woolen yarn, dairy products; marble and limestone quarries; Talladega Coll. (1867); incorporated 1835. Scene of battle Nov. 9, 1813, in which Andrew Jackson defeated Creek Indians.

Tal·la·has·see \ˌtal-ə-'has-ē\. City, ✱ of Florida and ⊗ of Leon co., N Florida, 25 m. N of Apalachee Bay; pop. (1970c) 72,586; tobacco market; lumber, turpentine, pecans; Florida State Univ. (1857), Florida Agricultural and Mechanical Univ. (1887), Tallahassee Junior Coll. (1963). Dates from era of Spanish colonial rule; made capital of Florida territory 1823; incorporated 1825; state capital 1845; scene of adoption of secession resolution 1861.

Tal·la·hatch·ie \ˌtal-ə-'hach-ē\. 1 River, N Mississippi; 301 m. long; rises in Tippah co., flows SW to unite with Yalobusha river in Leflore co. and form the Yazoo river; navigable for ab. 100 m.

2 County in Mississippi. See table at MISSISSIPPI.

Tall al–Dafana. See DAPHNAE.

Tall al–Ka·bīr, Al– \al-ˌtal-al-kə-'bir, a-ˌtel-\ *or* **Tell el–Ke·bir** \'tel-el-kə-'bēr\. Village, N Egypt, near Zagazig; scene of victory of British over Egyptians Sept. 13, 1882.

Tal·la·poo·sa \ˌtal-ə-'pü-sə\. 1 Navigable river, Alabama; 268 m. long; rises in Paulding co., NW Georgia, flows SW across Alabama border E of Heflin, S and then W to join the Coosa river in cen. Alabama and form the Alabama river.

2 County in Alabama. See table at ALABAMA.

3 City, Haralson co., W Georgia, 35 m. S of Rome; pop. (1970c) 2896; cotton gins, sawmills.

Tal·las·see \'tal-ə-ˌsē\. City, Elmore and Tallapoosa cos., E cen. Alabama; pop. (1970c) 4809.

Tal·linn \'tal-ən, 'täl-\ *or Russ.* **Ta·lin** \'tal-yin\; *formerly* **Re·vel** \'rā-vəl\ *or Ger.* **Re·val** \'rā-ˌväl\. Seaport city, ✱ of Estonian S.S.R., U.S.S.R., on the Gulf of Finland opp. Helsinki and ab. 200 m. W of Leningrad; pop. (1970p) 363,000; one of the principal Baltic ports of the U.S.S.R.; extensive port facilities; industrial center, producing paper, electrical equipment, textiles, furniture, cellulose; large shipyards; extensive naval and military installations; medieval city wall, remains of 13th cent. citadel.

History: Probably founded by Danish King Valdemar II 1219; developed as trading port and Hanse town 13th cent.; sold to Teutonic Knights 1346; on dissolution of order passed to Sweden 1561; taken by Russians 1710; capital of Estonia 1918–40; in World War II occupied by Germans 1941–44 and suffered heavy damage, substantially repaired since 1945.

Tall Kelakh. See TELKALAKH.

Tall·madge \'tal-mij\. City, Summit co., NE Ohio, 4 m. E of Akron; pop. (1970c) 15,274.

Tal·lu·lah \tə-'lü-lə\. 1 River, Georgia. See BURTON, LAKE.

2 Village, ⊗ of Madison parish, NE Louisiana, 57 m. E of Monroe; pop. (1970c) 9643; lumber, cottonseed oil; poultry.

Ta·lo·ga \tə-'lō-gə\. Town, ⊗ of Dewey co., W Oklahoma; pop. (1970c) 363; grain farms.

Tal·tal \täl-'täl\. Seaport, Antofagasta prov., N Chile; pop. (1960c) 5291; exports nitrates and ores.

Ta·lu·ti Bay *also* **Te·loe·ti Bay** \tə-'lü-tē-\. Inlet of Banda Sea, S coast of Ceram I., Indonesia.

Ta·ma \'tā-mə\. 1 County in Iowa. See table at IOWA.

2 City, Tama co., E cen. Iowa; pop. (1970c) 3000.

Tama \'täm-ə\. Peak, N Colombia, 20 m. ESE of Cúcuta; 13,126 ft.

Ta·ma·le \tə-'mäl-ē\. Town, ✱ of Northern Region, N Ghana, W Africa, in plain E of the Volta, ab. 270 m. N of Accra; pop. (1970p) 81,612; road junction and trade and educational center; ships agricultural products (rice, peanuts, butter, cotton).

Tamalipta. See TAMLUK.

Tam·al·pa·is, Mount \-ˌtam-əl-'pī-əs\. Peak, Marin co., W California, NW of San Francisco and overlooking the Pacific Ocean and San Francisco Bay; 2572 ft.; scenic resort.

Ta·man \tə-'män\. Peninsula and cape, E side of Kerch Strait, W Krasnodar Krai, Russian S.F.S.R., U.S.S.R.; ab. 25 m. long; oil field.

Taman Ne·ga·ra National Park \'tä-mə-nə-'gä-rə-\. National park, Malaysia; rain forest; varied wildlife; established 1938.

Ta·ma·no \tə-'mä-(ˌ)nō\. City, Okayama prefecture, Kyūshū, Japan, 15 m. NW of Kumamoto; pop. (1970c) 68,446.

Tam·an·ras·set \ˌtam-ən-'ras-ət\. Wadi, S Algeria, N of the Adrar des Iforas.

Ta·ma·qua \tə-'mäk-wə\. Borough, Schuylkill co., E cen. Pennsylvania, 15 m. ENE of Pottsville; pop. (1970c) 9246; explosives, women's clothing, canned goods; coal mines; diversified agriculture.

Ta·mar \'tā-mər\. 1 River, SW England; 60 m. long; rises in NW Devonshire, flows SSE, forming boundary bet. Devon and Cornwall, empties into the English Channel through Plymouth Sound.

2 Navigable river, N Tasmania, Australia; ab. 40 m. long; formed by confluence at Launceston of the North Esk and South Esk rivers; flows N to Bass Strait at Port Dalrymple.
3 Ancient city, Syria. See PALMYRA 6.

Ta·ma·ra \tə-'mär-ə\. Largest island of the Los Is. (*q.v.*).

Tam·a·rac \'tam-ə-ˌrak\. City, Broward co., SE Florida; pop. (1970c) 5078.

Tamarida. See TAMRIDAH.

Ta·ma·tave \ˌtam-ə-'täv, ˌtäm-\. Seaport, E coast of Malagasy Republic; pop. (1970e) 56,910; principal seaport of the republic; ships coffee, vanilla, graphite; sugar refining, rum distilling, meat-packing; terminus of railroad from Tananarive. Trading post founded by Portuguese 17th cent.; town ceded by English to French 1814; rebuilt after destruction by hurricane 1927.

Ta·mau·li·pas \ˌtäm-ˌaù-'lē-pəs\. State of E Mexico. See table at MEXICO.

Ta·ma·zu·la de Gor·dia·no \ˌtäm-ə-'zü-lē-dā-gȯr-'dyä-nō\. Town, Jalisco state, W cen. Mexico, 30 m. S of Lake Chapala; munic. pop. (1970p) 42,333.

Ta·ma·zun·cha·le \ˌtäm-ə-sən-'chä-lē\. Municipality, San Luis Potosí state, Mexico, 150 m. SE of San Luis Potosí; pop. (1970p) 60,976; rare woods; cattle raising; coffee, sugarcane.

Tam·bai·chi \täm-'bī-chē\. Town, Nara prefecture, W cen. Honshū, Japan, ab. 6 m. S of Nara; scene of pilgrimages.

Tam·be·lan Islands \ˌtäm-bə-ˌlän-\. Group of 17 small islands, Indonesia, in the South China Sea bet. the S tip of Malay Penin. and W coast of Borneo; administratively a part of Riau prov.

Tam·bo \'täm-(ˌ)bō\. 1 River, S Peru; ab. 150 m. long; flows SW into Pacific Ocean SE of Mollendo.
2 River, Peru. See APURÍMAC 1.

Tam·bo·pa·ta \ˌtäm-bō-'pät-ə\. River, SE Peru; 160 m. long; flows N into the Madre de Dios at Puerto Maldonado.

Tam·bo·ra \'täm-bə-rə\. Volcano, N coast of Sumbawa, Indonesia; 9350 ft.; had disastrous eruption in 1815 when it lost much of its top; was formerly ab. 13,000 ft. high.

Tam·bov \täm-'bȯf, -'bȯv\. City, ✱ of Tambov Oblast, cen. Russian S.F.S.R., U.S.S.R., on unnavigable Tsna 260 m. SE of Moscow; pop. (1970p) 229,000; railroad junction; flour mills, grain elevators, railroad shops, distilleries, brickworks. Founded 1636 as fort to defend Moscow against Tatar and Kalmuck raids; became ✱ of a province 1796.

Tambov Oblast \-'ō-bləst, -ˌblast\. Subdivision of cen. Russian S.F.S.R., U.S.S.R.; 13,243 sq. m.; pop. (1970p) 1,511,000; ✱ Tambov. A level black-earth region, with hills 400–800 ft. and valleys of the upper Tsna (unnavigable tributary of the Moksha) and in the S of the upper courses of Don tributaries. Economy principally agricultural: grain, sunflowers, potatoes; livestock. Chief towns Tambov, Michurinsk, Morshansk, Rasskazovo.
History: Part of Moscow principality from medieval period, but conflicts with Tatars limited colonization until Russian authority was consolidated in late 17th cent.; scene of fighting and famine 1917–20 during civil war; made a separate oblast 1937.

Tame \'tām\. 1 Small river, cen. England, flows past the city of Birmingham into the Trent in Staffordshire.
2 River, Yorkshire, Lancashire, and Cheshire, NW England; 18 m. long; flows SW to the Mersey at Stockport.

Tamesis *or* **Tamesa.** See THAMES.

Ta·met \'täm-ət\ *or* **Ta·med** \'täm-(ˌ)ed\ *or* **Thā·mit** \'täm-it\. Short river in W Libya, N Africa; flows N into Gulf of Sidra.

Ta·mia·hua, Lake of \-təm-'yä-wə\. Coastal lagoon, N Veracruz state, Mexico; ab. 60 m. long; at S end has outlet to Gulf of Mexico.

Ta·mil Na·du \ˌtam-əl-'nä-dü\ *or formerly* **Ma·dras** \mə-'dras, -'dräs\. State, SE India, on Coromandel Coast; 50,180 sq. m.; pop. (1971p) 41,103,125; ✱ Madras; formerly comprised a much larger area extending as far N as Orissa and including Laccadive Is. and part of Malabar Coast on W. Eastern Ghats extend from NE border to Nilgiri Hills in W; Cauvery river traverses the state. *Chief products:* Rice, millet, peanuts, sugarcane, cotton, timber. *Chief cities:* Madras, Madurai, Coimbatore, Salem.
History: In early times region occupied by Tamil kingdoms of Pandya, Chola, and Chera; then in the NE by the kings of Kalinga, and later in 14th cent. by Muslim invaders. South of the Kistna (now Krishna) the Hindu kingdom Vijayanagar existed 1336–1565; Vasco da Gama reached Calicut 1498; Portuguese driven out by Dutch in 16th cent.; English made first settlement in 1611 at Masulipatam (now Machilipatnam); after founding of Madras city 1640 English extended conquests; territory made a separate presidency 1653; captured by French 1746 but retroceded 1748 (Treaty of Aix-la-Chapelle); under the British received additional territory until early in 19th cent. Made autonomous province 1937; became part of Republic of India 1947; reorganized administratively 1956.

Ta·mines \ta-'mēn\. Commune, Namur prov., S Belgium; pop. (1969e) 7954; manufactures glass, mirrors, etc.

Tam·luk *also* **Tum·luk** \təm-'lük\. Town, West Bengal, NE India, ab. 30 m. SW of Calcutta; pop. (1961c) 18,000. In ancient times, as **Ta·ma·lip·ta** \ˌtäm-ə-'lip-tə\, a seaport at the mouth of the Ganges from which Chinese Buddhist pilgrims embarked; it is now 60 m. from the sea with temple; but most of its ancient remains are buried in the silt of the Hooghly.

Tam·ma·ny, Mount \-'tam-ə-nē\. Peak, New Jersey; ab. 1480 ft.; forms the E side of Delaware Water Gap.

Tammerfors. See TAMPERE.

Tam·pa \'tam-pə\. City, ⊗ of Hillsborough co., W cen. Florida penin., on NE end of Tampa Bay; pop. (1970c) 277,767; winter and fishing resort; ships citrus fruit and phosphates; produces cigars, fertilizer, chemicals, aluminum products, ceramics, pharmaceuticals; canning plants, boatyards; Univ. of Tampa (1931), Hillsborough Junior Coll. (1968). U.S. army fort established on site 1824; town incorporated 1855; developed as cigar-making center 1886 ff. and as major tourist center 1891 ff.

Tampa Bay. Inlet of Gulf of Mexico, W coast of Hillsborough co., W Florida penin.; the city of Tampa is at its NE end and St. Petersburg on W shore.

Tam·pe·re \'tam-pə-ˌrā, 'täm-\ *or Swed.* **Tam·mer·fors** \ˌtäm-ər-'fō(ə)rz, -'fōsh\. City, Häme prov., SW Finland, on Lake Näsijärvi; pop. (1970e) 157,697; second largest city of Finland; industrial, cultural, and transportation center; textiles, machinery, footwear, paper; hydroelectric power plants; has many notable public buildings in contemporary styles; technological institute (1965), univ. (1966); chartered 1779; developed as industrial center in 19th cent.

Tam·pi·co \tam-'pē-(ˌ)kō\. Seaport, S Tamaulipas state, E Mexico, ab. 6 m. from the Gulf of Mexico on the Panuco river; munic. pop. (1970p) 196,147; transportation center and one of the principal seaports of Mexico; modern port facilities; exports incl. oil, livestock, copper ore, agricultural products; boatyards, sawmills; tourist center and seaside resort. Developed around monastery founded 1532; abandoned 1683 after destruction by pirates; resettled 1823.

Tam·ri·dah \tam-'rēd-ə\ *also* **Ta·ma·ri·da** \ˌtam-ə-'rē-də\ *or formerly* **Ha·di·bu** \'had-i-ˌbü\. Chief town of Socotra I., Indian Ocean, S of Arabia; on NE coast.

Tam·worth \'tam-(ˌ)wərth\. 1 Town, E New South Wales, SE Australia, 190 m. N of Sydney; pop. (1968e) 22,480; ships eggs; flour, lumber, starch.
2 Municipal borough, Staffordshire, W cen. England, at confluence of Tame and Anker rivers 15 m. NE of Birmingham; pop. (1971p) 40,245; textiles, paper, bricks, aluminum ware; coal mines; Tamworth swine originally bred here.

Ta·na \'tän-ə\. 1 River, Kenya, E Africa; ab. 440 m. long; rises in S cen. region, flows in a curve NE, E, and S into Indian Ocean at Formosa Bay; longest river in Kenya.
2 *or* **Tan·na** \'tän-ə\. Island, S New Hebrides, SW Pacific Ocean, ab. 25 m. S of Eromanga; 22 m. long, 12 m. wide;

pop. (1967c) 10,476; highest point 3419 ft.; main agricultural products coconuts, sugar, taro, yams.

Tana \'tä-nə\ *or Finn.* **Te·no** \'te-nȯ\. River, NE Norway; 224 m. long; flows N and NE, forming a section of boundary bet. Norway and Finland, and empties into Tana Fjord.

Tana, Lake \-'tän-ə\ *or* **Lake Tsa·na** \-'(t)sän-ə\. Lake, N Ethiopia, E Africa; 47 m. long and 44 m. wide; ab. 1100 sq. m.; source of the Blue Nile.

Ta·na·be \tə-'näb-ē\. City, Wakayama prefecture, Honshū, Japan, 37 m. S of Wakayama; pop. (1970c) 63,368.

Tan·a·cross \'tan-ə-ˌkrȯs\ *or formerly* **Tan·a·na Crossing** \ˌtan-ə-ˌnȯ-\. Station, Alaska, on Alaska Highway and on Tanana river ab. 150 m. SE of Fairbanks; pop. (1970c) 84.

Tana Fjord \'tä-nə-\. Inlet of Arctic Ocean, NE coast of Norway; receives the Tana river from the S.

Ta·na·ga \tə-'näg-ə\. Island, W Andreanof Is., Aleutians, SW Alaska, 51°47'N, 177°57'W; 209 sq. m.; has active volcano. **Tanaga Bay** is on W coast; **Tanaga Pass** separates it from small islands on W.

Tan·a·gra \'tan-ə-grə, tə-'nag-rə\. Ancient town, E Boeotia, E cen. Greece, ab. 14 m. E of Thebes; scene of battle 457 B.C. in which the Spartans defeated the Athenians. Figurines (terra-cotta statuettes) were made here and exported to many Mediterranean countries; they are now valuable works of art.

Ta·nah·ba·la \ˌtän-ə-'bäl-ə\. See BATU.

Ta·nah·be·sar \ˌtän-ə-bə-'sär\. Large island, Aru Is. (*q.v.*), Indonesia; actually, five closely packed islands.

Ta·nah·ma·sa \ˌtän-ə-'mäs-ə\. See BATU.

Ta·nah·me·rah Bay \ˌtän-ə-ˌmer-ə-\. Inlet of Pacific Ocean, NE coast of Irian Barat, Indonesia, ab. 40 m. W of Djajapura. Landings made here by Allied forces at same time as at Hollandia (now Djajapura) Apr. 22, 1944.

Tanais. See DON 3.

Ta·nam·bo·go \ˌtän-äm-'bō-(ˌ)gō\. Small island, SE Solomon Is., W Pacific Ocean; attached to Gavutu I. by causeway and part of Japanese base; taken by U.S. Marines Aug. 7–8, 1942.

Tan·a·na \'tan-ə-ˌnȯ\. 1 River, chief S tributary of the Yukon, E and cen. Alaska; ab. 475 m. long; rises in glaciers of NE Wrangell Mts., flows NW to the Yukon at Tanana, 65°10'N, 152°05'W; navigable for ab. 225 m. and for smaller vessels nearly to its source. Fairbanks is on it and Alaska Highway follows it for nearly its entire course.

2 City, cen. Alaska, at junction of Tanana with Yukon; pop. (1970c) 120.

Tanana Crossing. See TANACROSS.

Ta·na·na·rive \tə-'nan-ə-ˌrēv\ *or Malagasy* **Ta·na·na·ri·vo** \tə-ˌnan-ə-'rē-(ˌ)vō\ *or Eng.* **An·ta·nan·a·ri·vo** \ˌan-tə-ˌnan-ə-'rē-(ˌ)vō\. City, * of the Malagasy Republic, in E cen. part; pop. (1970e) 343,670; built on a basaltic ridge at elevation of 4094 ft.; tobacco and food-processing industries; textiles, leather goods; univ. (1955, univ. status 1961).

Ta·nao Pass \tä-'naù-\. Channel, extending along N coast of Camarines Norte prov., Luzon, Phil., separating it from the Calagua Is.; ab. 10 m. wide.

Ta·na·pag Harbor \ˌtän-ə-ˌpäg-\. Anchorage, W coast of Saipan, Mariana Is., just N of Garapan; best harbor of the island.

Tana River. See TANA.

Ta·na·ro \'tän-ə-(ˌ)rō\ *or anc.* **Tan·a·rus** \'tan-ə-rəs\. River, N Italy; 171 m. long; rises in the Maritime Alps; flows N and NE into Po river 10 m. NE of Alessandria.

Ta·na·uan \tə-'nä-(ˌ)wän\. 1 Municipality, Leyte prov., E coast of Leyte I., Phil., on San Pedro Bay 9 m. S of Tacloban; pop. (1969e) 31,800; taken by U.S. forces Oct. 25, 1944.

2 Municipality, Batangas prov., Luzon, Phil., on railroad and highway from Batangas to Calamba; pop. (1969e) 61,700; NE of Lake Taal and ab. 24 m. N of Batangas; in center of sugar, tobacco, and fruit region; taken by U.S. Mar. 27, 1945.

Tan–chu \'dän-'jü\ *or* **Tan·chuk** \'dän-'jük\. Town, SE Kwangsi Chuang, SE China, on right bank of the Hsi river below Kuei-p'ing and ab. 60 m. W of Wu-chow; in World War II site of U.S. air base which was abandoned to Japanese Nov. 1, 1944 and retaken by Chinese July 9, 1945.

Tan·cí·ta·ro \tän-'sēt-ə-ˌrō\. Mountain, Michoacán state, SW Mexico, just W of Uruapan; 12,605 ft.

Tan·da \'tän-də\. Town, E Uttar Pradesh, N India, on Ghāgara river 85 m. NNW of Varanasi; pop. (1961c) 32,687.

Tan·dag \'tän-ˌdäg\. Municipality, * of Surigao del Sur prov., NE coast of Mindanao, Phil.; pop. (1969e) 14,200.

Tan·dil \tän-'dil\. City, Buenos Aires prov., E cen. Argentina, 190 m. S of Buenos Aires; pop. (1960c) 45,703; center of rich agricultural region; health and pleasure resort; univ. 1964.

Tandjoeng Poeting. See PUTING.

Tan·djung·ka·rang \ˌtän-ˌjůŋ-kə-'räŋ\. Town, * of Lampung prov., Sumatra, Indonesia; pop. (1961c) 133,091.

Tan·djung·pan·dan *or Du.* **Tan·djoeng·pan·dan** \ˌtän-jůŋ-pən-'dän\. Town, NW coast of Belitung I., Indonesia; pop. (1961c) 29,412.

Tan·djung·pi·nang *or Du.* **Tan·djoeng·pi·nang** \ˌtän-jůŋ-pi-'näŋ\. Town, Indonesia, on SW coast of Bintan I., Riau prov., E of Sumatra and ESE of Singapore; pop. (1961c) 37,638.

Tandjung Rangasa. See MANDAR, GULF OF.

Ta·ne·ga–shi·ma *or* **Ta·ne·ga·shi·ma** \tä-ˌneg-ə-'shē-mə, tä-'neg-i-shə-ˌmä\. Largest of the Osumi Is. (*q.v.*), off S end of Kyūshū, S Japan; ab. 25 m. long; ab. 176 sq. m.

Ta·ney \'tän-ē\. County in Missouri. See table at MISSOURI.

Tan·ga \'taŋ-gə\. 1 Administrative region of NE Tanzania. See table at TANZANIA.

2 Seaport, its *; pop. (1967c) 61,058.

Tanga Islands \ˌtaŋ-gə-\. Island group, E Bismarck Archipelago, W Pacific Ocean, ab. 55 m. off the E coast of New Ireland; comprises four islands, largest Malendok and Boang.

Tan·gan·cí·cua·ro \ˌtäŋ-gäŋ-'sē-kwä-(ˌ)rō\. Municipality, Michoacan state, Mexico, 40 m. NW of Uruapan; pop. (1970p) 30,224; spinning mills, bottling plant; livestock raising; wheat, alfalfa, sweet potatoes.

Tanganyika. See TANZANIA.

Tan·gan·yi·ka, Lake \-ˌtan-gən-'yē-kə, -ˌtaŋ-gən-, -gə-'nē-\. Lake, E cen. Africa, on boundary bet. W Tanzania and E Zaire; 420 m. long and bet. 30 and 45 m. wide; 12,700 sq. m.; max. depth 4710 ft.

T'ang–chia–huan \'täŋ-jyä-'(h)wän, -'gwän\ *also* **Chung·shan·kong** \'jůŋ-'shän-'kȯŋ\. Town, Kwangtung prov., SE China, on W side of estuary of Canton river N of Macao and opp. Hong Kong.

Tan·gier \tan-'ji(ə)r\ *also* **Tan·giers** \-'ji(ə)rz\ *or Fr. and Ger.* **Tan·ger** *Fr.* tänzhā; *Ger.* 'tän-jər, 'täŋ-ər\ *or Span.* **Tán·ger** \'täŋ-her\ *or anc.* **Tin·gis** \'tin-jəs\. Seaport, N Morocco, at W end of the Strait of Gibraltar; pop. (1960c) 141,714; with surrounding territory constituted until 1956 **Tangier Zone** or **International Zone** (225 sq. m.).

History: A Roman city (Tingis), later taken successively by Vandals, Byzantines, and Arabs; taken 1471 by Portuguese who lost it to Spain 1580 and regained it 1656; on marriage 1662 of Catherine of Braganza to Charles II came into possession of English who gave it up to Moors 1684. Zone established Dec. 18, 1923 and Feb. 7, 1924 by the Tangier Convention (revised 1928) bet. England, France, and Spain providing for permanent neutralization of the area and government by an international commission. During World War II controlled by Spain; international administration restored Oct. 11, 1945; international status abolished Oct. 29, 1956; became royal summer residence 1962. See MOROCCO.

Tangier, Bay of. Inlet of the Strait of Gibraltar, N coast of Africa; Tangier is on its W side.

Tangier Island. Island, lower Chesapeake Bay, belonging to Accomac co., E Virginia.

Tangier Sound. Inlet of Chesapeake Bay, W shore of Somerset co., SE Maryland.

Tangier Zone. See TANGIER.

Tan·gi·pa·hoa \ˌtan-jə-pə-ˈhō(-ə)\. Parish in Louisiana. See table at LOUISIANA.

Tang·ku·ban·pe·ra·hu \ˌtäŋ-ˌkü-bän-pə-ˈrä-(ˌ)hü\. Mountain, E Java, Indonesia, N of Bandung; 6809 ft.

T'ang–ku–la \ˈdäŋ-ˈkü-ˈlä\ *or* **Tang·lha** \ˈdäŋ-ˈlä\ *also* **Dang·la** *or* **Dang–la** \ˈdäŋ-ˈlä\. Mountain range, E Tibet, China, lat. 33°N and long. 88°–94°E; alt. ab. 20,000 ft.

T'ang–ku–la–yu–mu Hu \ˈtäŋ-ˈkü-ˈlä-ˈyü-ˈmü-ˈhü\ *also* **Tang·ra Tso** \ˈdäŋ-rä-ˈtsō\ *or* **Dang·ra Yum** \ˈdäŋ-rä-ˈyüm\. Lake, cen. Tibet, China, lat. 31°N, long. 86°22′E; ab. 45 m. long.

T'ang–la \ˈdäŋ-ˈlä\ *also* **Dang·la** *or* **Dang–la** \ˈdäŋ-ˈlä\. Pass in Himalayas, S Tibet, China, E of Sikkim; alt. ab. 15,200 ft.

Tanglha. See T'ANG-KU-LA.

Tangra Tso. See T'ANG-KU-LA-YU-MU HU.

T'ang–shan *or* **Tang·shan** \ˈtäŋ-ˈshän\. Town, Hopeh prov., NE China, ab. 100 m. ESE of Peking; pop. (1970e) 1,200,-000.

Tang·ub \täŋ-ˈüb\. Municipality, Misamis Occidental prov., Mindanao, Phil., on N shore of Panguil Bay 29 m. S of Oroquieta; pop. (1970e) 28,700.

Ta·nim·bar Islands \tə-ˈnim-ˌbär-, ˈtan-əm-\ *or* **Ti·mor·laut Islands** \ˈtē-ˌmȯr-ˌlau̇t-\ *also* **Te·nim·bar Islands** \tə-ˈnim-, ˈten-əm-\. Island group of ab. 30 islands, SE Moluccas, Indonesia, Malay Archipelago, ENE of Timor I.; 2096 sq. m.; pop. (1965e) 50,000; attached to Maluku province. Comprises the large island of Jamdena, the islands of Larat and Selaru, and many small islands. Mostly of coralline formation, but partly volcanic; has extensive swamps and few harbors. Produces corn, rice, coconut and sago palms; fishing; discovered by Dutch 1629.

Ta·nis \ˈtā-nəs\ *or Bib.* **Zo·an** \ˈzō-(ˌ)an\. Ruined city in the Nile delta, Lower Egypt, near Lake Manzala.

Tan·jay \täŋ-ˈhī\. Municipality, E Negros Oriental, Negros, Phil., near S end of Tanon Strait 17 m. NNW of Cumaguete; pop. (1969e) 54,100.

Tanjore. See THANJAVUR.

Tanna. See TANA 2.

Tannenberg. See STĘBARK.

Tannou Touva. See TUVA AUTONOMOUS SOVIET SOCIALIST REPUBLIC.

Tan·nu–Ola \ˌtan-ü-ˈō-lə\. Mountain range, running E and W bet. NW Mongolian People's Republic and S Tuva A.S.S.R., U.S.S.R.

Tannūrah, Ra's at. See RA'S AT TANNŪRAH.

Tannu Tuva. See TUVA AUTONOMOUS SOVIET SOCIALIST REPUBLIC.

Ta·non Strait \tä-ˈnyȯn-\. Strait bet. Cebu I. and Negros I., cen. Phil.; ab. 100 m. long and varying in width from 3 to 27 m.

Tan·qui·jo Reef \täŋ-ˌkē-hō-\. Reef, Gulf of Mexico, N of Tuxpan Reef, off coast of N Veracruz state, Mexico.

Tan–shui \ˈdän-ˈshwā\ *also* **Tan·sui** \ˈdän-ˈshwā, tän-ˈsü-ē\.
1 Stream, N Taiwan; ab. 50 m. long.
2 Seaport, N Taiwan.

Tan·ta \ˈtänt-ə\. City, ✱ of Gharbīya gov., Egypt, 51 m. N of Cairo; pop. (1970e) 253,600; transportation center; cotton, sugar.

Tan·ta·lus, Mount \-ˈtant-ᵊl-əs\. See HONOLULU 2.

Tan·to·yu·ca \ˌtän-tō-ˈyü-kə\. Municipality, Veracruz state, Mexico, 115 m. SSW of Tampico; pop. (1970p) 60,125; livestock and poultry raising; sugarcane, lemons.

Tan–tung \ˈtän-ˈdu̇ŋ, -ˈtu̇ŋ\ *or* **An·tung** \ˈän-ˈdu̇ŋ, -ˈtu̇ŋ\. City, Liaoning prov., NE China, on Yalu river; pop. (1970e) 450,000; chemicals, aluminum, paper; food processing; opened as a treaty port 1907.

Tantura. See DOR.

Tanura, Ras. See R'AS AT TANNŪRAH.

Tan·za·nia \ˌtan-zə-ˈnē-ə\ *or officially* **United Republic of Tanzania.** Republic, E Africa, bounded on N by Uganda and Kenya, on E by the Indian Ocean, on S by Mozambique and Malawi, on SW by Zambia, on W by Zaire, and on NW by Burundi and Rwanda; 364,943 sq. m. (incl. 22,805 sq. m. of water); pop. (1970e) 13,273,000, (1967c) 12,313,469; ✱ Dar es Salaam. *Physical features:* Greater part is high plateau with average alt. 3000 to 4000 ft.; has many heights 7000 to 10,400 ft., esp. in S cen. part and around N end of Lake Nyasa; in NE on the Kenya border are the Kilimanjaro peaks, the highest in Africa, 19,340 ft. Chief rivers are Rufiji (in S cen. part, flowing E to Indian Ocean), Ruvuma (on S border), Pangani (in NE), and the lower course of the Kagera (in NW). In W are a number of lakes and marshy regions (largest Lake Rukwa, in SW) and within its borders it includes S half of Lake Victoria, ab. 1/3 of Lake Tanganyika, and a section of NE Lake Nyasa; coastline is ab. 450 m. long. Major islands: Zanzibar, Pemba, Mafia. *Chief products:* Wheat, corn, sisal, cotton, coffee, sugar, tobacco, peanuts, cloves; livestock raising; diamonds, salt, mica, silver; manufacturing: textiles, leather goods, bricks and tiles; food processing. *Chief towns:* Dar es Salaam, Zanzibar, Tanga, Mwanza, Arusha, Moshi, Morogoro. Divided into the following 21 administrative regions (for pronunciation of their names, see their individual entries):

NAME	AREA (sq. m.)	POP. (1967c)	CAPITAL
Arusha	32,654	610,474	Arusha
Coast	13,020	784,327	Dar es Salaam
Dodoma	15,950	709,380	Dodoma
Iringa	22,750	689,905	Iringa
Kigoma	17,400	473,443	Kigoma
Kilimanjaro	5,100	652,722	Moshi
Mara	11,400	544,125	Musoma
Mbeya	34,799	969,053	Mbeya
Morogoro	28,199	685,104	Morogoro
Mtwara	31,881	1,041,146	Mtwara
Mwanza	13,850	1,055,883	Mwanza
Pemba	379	164,321	Wete
Ruvuma	24,800	393,043	Songea
Shinyanga	15,599	899,468	Shinyanga
Singida	19,051	457,938	Singida
Tabora	47,750	562,871	Tabora
Tanga	10,350	771,060	Tanga
West Lake	15,299	658,712	Bukoba
Zanzibar Mjini	97	95,047	Zanzibar
Zanzibar Shambani North	186	56,360	Mkokotoni
Zanzibar Shambani South	358	39,087	Koani

History: Coast dominated in turn by Arabs, Portuguese, and rulers of Oman and Zanzibar; under Karl Peters, Germans made treaties with natives 1884–85; German East Africa Company received charter 1887 and Germany declared region a protectorate (**German East Africa**) 1891; its boundaries with British territory (see KENYA) determined by agreements of 1886, 1890; Zanzibar declared a British protectorate 1890; put down native risings 1888, 1891–93, 1905; captured by British 1914–16; name changed to **Tan·gan·yi·ka** \ˌtan-gən-ˈyē-kə, ˌtaŋ-gən-, -gə-ˈnē-\ when it became a British mandate 1920 (Ruanda-Urandi not part of British mandate); a legislative council established 1926; made a United Nations trust territory under British administration 1946; achieved independence 1961; became a republic 1962; united with Zanzibar (*q.v.*) 1964 under new name of Tanzania.

Ta·or·mi·na \tau̇r-ˈmē-nə\ *or anc.* **Tau·ro·me·ni·um** \ˌtȯr-ə-ˈmē-nē-əm\. Commune, Messina prov., E coast of Sicily, Italy; pop. (1968e) 9274; church built into a 3d cent. temple; theater reconstructed from a Greek original; Roman remains; medieval castle. Occupied in 8th cent. B.C.; refounded by Carthaginians 397 B.C.; after death of Hiero II (215 B.C.) became allied to Rome; burned by the Saracens 902 A.D.

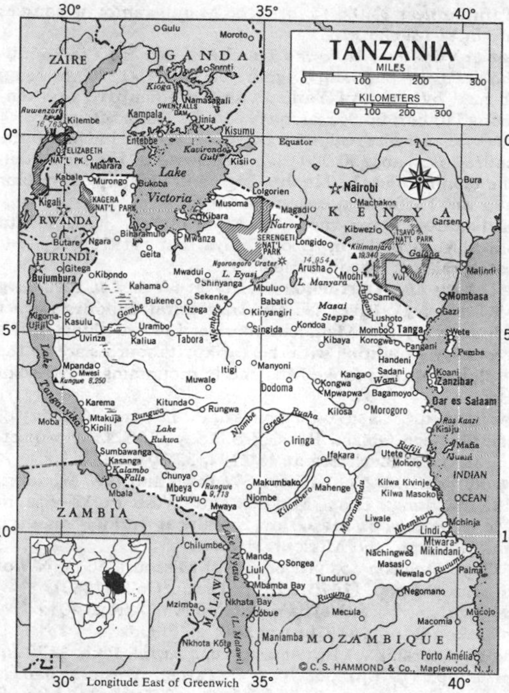

30° Longitude East of Greenwich 35° 40°

Taos \'taủs\. 1 County in N New Mexico. See table at NEW MEXICO.

2 Town and resort, its ⊗, 55 m. NNE of Santa Fe; pop. (1970c) 2475; legal name **Don Fer·nan·do de Taos** \ˌdän-fər-ˌnan-dō-dā-\; important commercial center in days of Sante Fe Trail; seat of art colony. Community includes also Taos Pueblo (to NE) and Ranchos de Taos (to SE).

Taos Trail. See SANTA FE TRAIL.

Taou·den·ni \ˌtaủ-de-'nē\. Oasis, Mali, W Africa, 425 m. NNW of Tombouctou.

Ta·pa·chu·la \ˌtäp-ə-'chü-lə\. Town, Chiapas state, SE Mexico, on railroad near Guatemalan border; munic. pop. (1970p) 108,464; chief product coffee.

Ta·pa·jós *or* **Ta·pa·joz** \ˌtap-ə-'zhȯs\. River, N Brazil; 807 m. long; formed by junction of Juruena (total length with Juruena ab. 1100 m.) and Teles Pires rivers on S end of the border bet. Amazonas and Pará states, flows NE into the Amazon river at Santarém; important rubber plantations along its banks.

Tapanoeli Bay. See SIBOLGA BAY.

Tapanshang. See PA-LIN-YU-CH'I.

Ta·pao Point \ti-ˌpaủ-\. Point, S tip of peninsula extending into Laguna de Bay, S Rizal prov., Phil.; is close to N end of Talim I.

Ta–pa Shan \'dä-'bä-'shän\. Mountain range, cen. China, on border bet. S Shensi and NE Szechwan provs.; highest peak 8884 ft.; its E end forms W edge of Hupeh basin and on S it is cut by the Yangtze Gorges (*q.v.*).

Taping. See TA-YING.

Ta·po·tchau *or* **Ta·po·cho** \ˌtäp-ə-'chō\. Mountain ridge, cen. Saipan I., Mariana Is., W Pacific Ocean; highest point 1552 ft.; severe fighting during U.S. conquest of island June 1944.

Tap·pa·han·nock \ˌtap-ə-'han-ək\. Town, ⊗ of Essex co., E Virginia; pop. (1970c) 1111.

Tap·pan \'tap-ən\. Unincorporated community, Rockland co., SE New York, near Haverstraw; pop. (1970c) 7424; scene of Major André's execution 1780.

Tappan Zee \-'zē\. Expansion of the Hudson river, bet. Westchester and Rockland cos., SE New York; 12 m. long by 2–3 m. wide.

Tap·ti \'täp-tē\. Unnavigable river, W cen. India; 436 m. long; flows W from mountains of SW Madhya Pradesh to Gulf of Cambay near Surat in Maharashtra.

Ta·pu·a·e·nu·ku, Mount \-ˌtäp-ˌü-ī-'nü-(ˌ)kü\. Highest peak in Kaikoura Range, NE South I., New Zealand; 9463 ft.

Ta·pul \tä-'pül\. 1 Island group, cen. Sulu Archipelago, Phil., bet. Jolo I. and Tawitawi I.; ab. 100 sq. m.; largest is Siasi. Includes also islands of Tapul, Lapac, and Lugus and ab. 70 other small islands and islets. See SULU 1.

2 Island, Tapul group, N of Siasi I. and S of Jolo; 11 sq. m.; forms part of Tapul municipality; pop. (1969e) 25,300.

Ta·qua·ri \ˌtak-wə-'rē\. River, S cen. Brazil; ab. 350 m. long; rises in S cen. Mato Grosso state, flows WSW into Paraguay river near Bolivian border; lower part traverses the Pantanal (marshes).

Tar \'tär\. River, NE North Carolina; 215 m. long, including Pamlico river; rises in Granville co., N North Carolina, flows SE into a wide estuary known as Pamlico river, Beaufort co., E North Carolina.

Tara \'tar-ə\. Parish, co. Meath, E Eire, 22 m. NW of Dublin; ancient capital (Hill of Tara) of Irish monarchs, abandoned c. 560; pre-Christian religious center.

Tarabulus al–Gharb. See TRIPOLI 4.

Tarabulus esh Sham. See TRIPOLI 3.

Taradie, Passage de. See POTERLA, COLLADO DE LA.

Taraika Bay. See TERPENIYA BAY.

Ta·ra·kan \ˌtär-ə-'kän\. 1 Island, Indonesia, in E Celebes Sea, off NE coast of Borneo; 117 sq. m.; in delta of Sesajap river; has large oil fields; taken by Japanese after battle Jan. 10–12, 1942 after destruction of wells by Dutch; retaken by Australians May 1–19, 1945.

2 Town on W side of island.

Taranaki. See EGMONT, MOUNT.

Tar·an·say \'tar-ən-ˌsā\. Island, Outer Hebrides, SW of island of Lewis with Harris, off NW coast of Scotland; ab. 4½ m. long.

Ta·ran·to \'tär-ən-ˌtō, tə-'rant-(ˌ)ō\. 1 Province of Apulia, SE Italy. See table at ITALY.

2 *or anc.* **Ta·ren·tum** \tə-'rent-əm\. Seaport and naval base, its ✱, on Gulf of Taranto 156 m. SE of Naples; pop. (1968e) 216,565; steel, chemicals, bricks, canned foods; shipyards, oyster and mussel fisheries; 11th cent. cathedral, castle, naval arsenal.

History: Founded by Greeks 8th cent. B.C. and a leading city of Magna Graecia; came under Rome 272 B.C. and made Roman colony 123 but declined; taken by Ostrogoths 494 A.D., Byzantines 540, Lombards 675, Arabs 856, Saracens 929, and Normans 1063; became part of kingdom of Naples. Joined kingdom of Italy 1860 and made major naval base; in World War II raided by British carrier aircraft Nov. 11–12, 1940, with considerable damage to Italian fleet; taken by British troops Sept. 9, 1943.

Taranto, Gulf of *or* **Gulf of Tarentum.** Inlet of Ionian Sea, SE coast of Italy; ab. 70 m. long.

Ta·ra·pa·ća \ˌtär-ə-pə-'kä\. 1 Province of N Chile. See table at CHILE.

2 Town, Amazonas commissary, SE corner of Colombia, on S bank of Putumayo river at Brazil frontier, N of Leticia.

Ta·ra·po·to \ˌtär-ə-'pōt-(ˌ)ō\. Town, San Martin dept., N Peru, on a tributary of the Huallaga river 90 m. E of Chachapoyas; pop. (1961c) 13,900.

Ta·rare \tə-'rär\. Manufacturing commune, Rhône dept., E cen. France, 22 m. NW of Lyons; pop. (1968c) 12,296; textiles.

Ta·ra·rua Range \ˌtar-ə-ˌrü-ə-\. Mountain range, SW North I., New Zealand; highest peak 5154 ft.

Ta·ras·con \ˌtar-ə-ˈskō^{n}\. Town, Bouches-du-Rhône dept., SE France, on left bank of the Rhone N of Arles; pop. (1962c) 8910; Romanesque-Gothic church, 15th cent. castle.

Ta·ra·wa \tə-ˈrä-wə, ˈtar-ə-ˌwä\. Island (atoll), N cen. Gilbert Is., ab. 90 m. N of the equator; comprises chain of islets in reef around lagoon ab. 18 m. long by 13 m. at widest point; pop. (1968c) 12,642. Chief islet and village is Betio at S end; occupied by Japanese 1942; seized by U.S. Marines after bitter and costly four-day battle Nov. 21–24, 1943; made ❋ of Gilbert and Ellice Is. after the war.

Ta·ra·we·ra \ˌtär-ə-ˈwer-ə\. River, N cen. North I., New Zealand; ab. 45 m. long; flows N out of **Lake Tarawera** (14 sq. m., 7 m. long, max. depth 285 ft.) into Bay of Plenty.

Tarawera, Mount. Volcanic peak, N cen. North I., New Zealand, ab. 90 m. NNW of Napier; 3645 ft.; an eruption June 10, 1886 destroyed the sinter ("pink" and "white") terraces of Rotomahana.

Tar·bat Ness \ˌtär-bət-ˈnes\. Headland, NE coast of Scotland, S of Dornoch Firth; lighthouse.

Tar·bert, Loch \läk-ˈtär-bərt, läḵ-\. Sea inlet, cen. Jura I., Inner Hebrides, off W Scotland; ab. 6 m. long; nearly cuts the island in two.

Tarbes \ˈtärb\ *or anc.* **Bi·gor·ra** \bi-ˈgȯr-ə, -ˈgär-\. City, ❋ of Hautes-Pyrénées dept., SW France, on Adour river 23 m. ESE of Pau; pop. (1968c) 55,375; market town; diesel engines, electrical equipment; 12th–14th cent. cathedral, archiepiscopal palace (now the prefecture). Ancient capital of province of Bigorre; scene of English victory over French 1814; birthplace of Marshal Foch and Théophile Gautier.

Tar·boro \ˈtär-ˌbər-ə, -ˌbə-rə\. Industrial town, ⊗ of Edgecombe co., NE North Carolina, 14 m. E of Rocky Mount; pop. (1970c) 9425; tobacco and peanut market; lumber and veneer, textiles, fertilizer, cottonseed oil.

Tar·cen·to \tär-ˈchen-tō\. Commune, Udine prov., Veneto, NE Italy, 12 m. N of Udine; pop. (1968e) 9574.

Ta·ree \tə-ˈrē\. Town, New South Wales, Australia, ab. 10 m. from coast, ab. 82 m. NE of Newcastle; pop. (1968e) 10,910; dairy products.

Ta·ren·tum \tə-ˈrent-əm\. **1** Borough, Allegheny co., SW Pennsylvania, on Allegheny river 17 m. NE of Pittsburgh; pop. (1970c) 7379; stainless steel products, paper, glass, chemicals, coal mines.
2 Seaport, Apulia, Italy. See TARANTO 2.

Tarentum, Gulf of. See TARANTO, GULF OF.

Tar·fa·ya \tär-ˈfī-(y)ə\; *formerly* **Ca·bo Yu·bi** \ˌkäb-(ˌ)ō-ˈyü-bē\ *or* **Cabo Ju·by** \-ˈhü-bē\ *also* **Vi·lla Bens** \ˌvil-ə-ˈbenz\. Town, SW Morocco, in former Spanish enclave on Cape Juby; pop. (1960c) 1532; former seat of administration of Spanish Sahara and Ifni.

Târgovişte. See TÎRGOVIŞTE.

Târgu–Jiu. See TÎRGU-JIU

Târgu–Mureş. See TÎRGU-MUREŞ.

Târgu–Neamţu *or* **Târgul–Neamţ.** See TÎRGU-NEAMŢ.

Târgu–Ocna. See TÎRGU-OCNA.

Ta·ri·fa \tə-ˈrēf-ə\; *anc.* **Ju·lia Jo·za** \ˌjül-yə-ˈjō-zə\ *or* **Julia Tra·duc·ta** \-trə-ˈdək-tə\. Seaport, Cádiz prov., SW Spain, on Point Marroquí 51 m. SE of Cádiz; pop. (1970p) 15,833; manufactures lime, brick, tile, cork, leather; fisheries and fish-salting works. Roman settlement; taken and fortified by Moors; reconquered by Sancho IV 1292; besieged by French 1812.

Tarifa, Point. Cape, S Spain, 36°01′N, 5°36′W; southernmost point in Europe.

Ta·ri·ja \tä-ˈrē-(ˌ)hä\. **1** Department of S Bolivia. See table at BOLIVIA.
2 City, its ❋, ab. 160 m. SSE of Potosí; pop. (1969e) 23,290; alt. 6398 ft.; commercial center; univ. (1966).

Tarikaikea. See MAMBERAMO.

Ta·ri·ku *also* **Ta·ri·koe** \tä-ˈrē-(ˌ)kü\ *or formerly* **Rouf·faer** \ˈraů-ˌfär\. Western upper tributary of the Mamberamo river, Irian Barat, Indonesia; ab. 150 m. long; joins the Taritatu near 3°10′S to form the Mamberamo; its sources are in W Maoke Mts.

Ta·rim \ˈdä-ˈrēm, ˈtä-\ *or Chin.* **T'a–li–mu Ho** \ˈtä-ˈlē-ˈmü-ˈhō\. River, Sinkiang Uighur, W China; 1250 m. long; formed by union of Yarkand and Ho-t'ien rivers, W Sinkiang Uighur; flows E along N edge of Takla Makan (*q.v.*), then SE into the region of Lop Nor; gives its name to the entire basin, ab. 350,000 sq. m., enclosed by the Tien Shan, the Pamirs, and the Kunlun Mts. and including Lop Nor and the Turfan depressions in the E.

Ta·ri·mo·ro \ˌtar-ə-ˈmȯr-ō\. Municipality, Guanajuato state, Mexico, 18 m. S of Celaya; pop. (1970p) 26,754; cattle raising; wheat, barley.

Ta·ri·ta·tu *also* **Ta·ri·ta·toe** \ˌtär-ē-ˈtät-ü\ *or Du.* **Iden·burg** \ˈēd-ᵊn-ˌbərg\. River, NE cen. Irian Barat, Indonesia, chief tributary of the Mamberamo river; 225 m. long; flows generally W, uniting with the Tariku; its sources are on the N slopes of the Maoke Mts. and in mountains of NE Irian Barat.

Tar·khan·kut, Cape \-ˌtär-kən-ˈküt\. Extreme W point of the Crimean Oblast, Russian S.F.S.R., U.S.S.R., projecting into the Black Sea at 45°21′N, 32°30′E.

Tar·kio \ˈtär-kē-ˌō\. **1** River, SW Iowa and NW Missouri; 125 m. long; East, Middle, and West Forks rise in Montgomery co., Iowa, flow S, unite at Tarkio, Missouri, and flow into the Missouri river.
2 City, Atchison co., NW corner of Missouri, 56 m. NW of St. Joseph; pop. (1970c) 2517; Tarkio Coll. (1883).

Tar·kwa \tä(r)-ˈkwä\. Town, W Ghana, W Africa, 40 m. NW of Sekondi; pop. (1970p) 11,000; goldfields.

Tar·lac \ˈtär-ˌläk\. **1** Province, N cen. Luzon, Phil.; 1179 sq. m.; pop. (1970p) 558,700; ❋ Tarlac. Western half is mountainous, comprising E slopes of Zambales Mts.; E part watered by tributaries of the Agno and Pampanga; produces rice, sugar, tobacco, vegetables, pineapples; chief towns Tarlac, Concepcion, and Camiling.
History: Through most of Spanish rule a part of Pampanga; part created as a military comandancia 1860 and extended 1873; joined revolt of 1896; civil government established Feb. 1901; came under control of Japanese Dec. 1941; recovered by U.S. Jan. 1945.
2 Municipality, its ❋, on a tributary of the Agno and on the Manila-Dagupan R.R. 65 m. NNW of Manila; pop. (1969e) 134,800; chief trade center of the province. Founded 1686; in World War II partly destroyed by Japanese before capture by U.S. Jan. 20, 1945.

Tar·ma \ˈtär-mə\. Town, Junín dept., cen. Peru, 95 m. NE of Lima; pop. (1961c) 15,500; alt. 10,000 ft.

Tarn \ˈtärn\. **1** River, S France; 233 m. long; rises in Lozère dept. on the slopes of Lozère Mts., flows W and SW into Garonne river.
2 Department of S France. See table at FRANCE.

Tarn–et–Ga·ronne \ˈtärn-ā-gə-ˈrän, -ˈrōn\. Department of S France. See table at FRANCE.

Tarnopol. See TERNOPOL.

Tar·nów \ˈtär-ˌnüf\. Industrial and commercial city, Kraków prov., S Poland, 45 m. E of Kraków; pop. (1970p) 85,500; textiles, machinery; iron foundries, sawmills, oil refinery; cathedral, Gothic town hall. An old town and a religious and cultural center in 15th and 16th cents.; occupied by Germans in World War I and II.

Tar·now·skie Gó·ry \tär-ˌnȯf-skē-ə-ˈgů(ə)r-ē\ *or unofficially* **Tar·no·wi·ce** \ˌtär-nə-ˈvēt-sə\ *or Ger.* **Tar·no·witz** \ˈtär-nə-ˌvits\. Mining commune, Katowice prov., S Poland, 16 m. NNW of Katowice; pop. (1970p) 34,300; coal deposits nearby; manufactures metal goods, lumber, cement.

Ta·ro \ˈtär-(ˌ)ō\. River, N Italy; 78 m. long; flows NE from the Apennines into Po river.

Ta·ro·ba National Park \tə-ˈrō-bə-\. National park, Maharashtra, India; 45 sq. m.; wildlife refuge (leopard, sambar, spotted deer, tiger).

Ta·rou·dant *also* **Ta·ru·dant** \ˌtar-ü-ˈdä^{n}\. Oasis, W Morocco, E of Agadir; pop. (1960c) 17,141.

Tar·pe·ian Rock \tär-ˌpē-(y)ən-\. See SEVEN HILLS.

Tar·pon Springs \ˌtär-pən-\. Resort city, Pinellas co., W cen. Florida penin., on Gulf of Mexico 28 m. N of St. Petersburg; pop. (1970c) 7118; sponge fisheries.

Tar·qui·nia \tär-ˈkwēn-yə\ *or anc.* **Tar·quin·ii** \tär-ˈkwin-ē-ˌī\; *in medieval times* **Cor·ne·to** \kȯr-ˈnā-(ˌ)tō\. Town, Viterbo prov., N Latium, cen. Italy, ab. 60 m. NW of Viterbo; pop. (1968e) 12,330; medieval fortifications (25 towers and a castle); government museum containing Etruscan antiquities in the 15th cent. Palazzo Vitelleschi; necropolis of archaeological interest with notable painted tombs. Chief of the 12 Etruscan cities; came under Rome probably in late 4th cent. B.C.; received Roman citizenship 90 B.C.; population transferred to present town 6th cent. A.D.

Tarracina. See TERRACINA.

Tarraco. See TARRAGONA 2.

Tar·ra·co·nen·sis \ˌtar-ə-kə-ˈnen(t)-səs\ *or* **His·pa·nia Tarraconensis** \his-ˌpā-nē-ə-\. Roman province comprising the greater part (N, cen., and SE) of ancient Spain (Hispania); ✱ Tarraco; other two provinces were Lusitania and Baetica.

Tar·ra·go·na \ˌtar-ə-ˈgō-nə\. 1 Province of NE Spain. See table at SPAIN.

2 *anc.* **Tar·ra·co** \ˈtar-ə-ˌkō\. Commune, its ✱, on Mediterranean Sea 54 m. WSW of Barcelona; pop. (1970p) 78,238; agricultural market town and seaport; archiepiscopal see; 12th–13th cent. cathedral, extensive Roman remains incl. walls, theater, circus, aqueduct, and triumphal arch. Captured by Romans 218 B.C. and as capital of Roman province of Tarraconensis one of the leading cities of Roman Spain; razed by Moors 714; reconquered early 12th cent. and restored under Aragonese rule 1119 ff.; captured by British 1705; sacked by French under Suchet 1811.

Tar·rant \ˈtar-ənt\. County in Texas. See table at TEXAS.

Tarrant City. City, Jefferson co., cen. Alabama, 10 m. NNE of Birmingham; pop. (1970c) 6835.

Ta·rra·sa \tə-ˈräs-ə\. Industrial commune, Barcelona prov., NE Spain, 14 m. NNW of Barcelona; pop. (1970p) 138,697; textiles, carpets, glass, machinery, electrical equipment; two 12th cent. churches; made episcopal see c. 450.

Tar River. See TAR.

Tar·ry·all Peak, North \-ˌtar-ē-ˌȯl-\. Peak in the Rocky Mts., Rio Grande co., cen. Colorado; 11,600 ft.

Tar·ry·town \ˈtar-ē-ˌtaůn\. Residential and resort village, Westchester co., SE New York, on Hudson river 24 m. N of New York; pop. (1970c) 11,115; automobiles, clothing, lumber; Marymount Coll. (1907); forms a single community with North Tarrytown, Elmsford, and Irvington. Dates from late 17th cent.; important center during American Revolution and scene of André's capture 1780; home of Washington Irving (described in his *Sketch Book*) to S near Irvington (Sunnyside) and burial place (Sleepy Hollow) to N of village.

Tarso Tieroko. See TIEROKO.

Tar·sus \ˈtär-səs\. Commercial town, İçel prov., S Turkey, on railroad 23 m. W of Adana; pop. (1965c) 57,737.

History: A very ancient city, with settlement on site from Neolithic times; city first mentioned 7th cent. B.C.; an essentially independent city after decline of Assyrians until annexation by Rome 67 B.C.; a leading industrial and cultural center of the Roman and early Byzantine empires and the principal city of Cilicia. Destroyed by Arabs c. 660 A.D.; rebuilt late 8th cent. and held successively by Arabs, Byzantines, Crusaders, Christian Kingdom of Little Armenia, Mamelukes; became Turkish 16th cent. Birthplace of Saint Paul. Considerable ruins of ancient city remain; modern city formerly malarial but swamps in vicinity drained c. 1930.

Tar·tes·sus *or* **Tar·tes·sos** \tär-ˈtes-əs\. Ancient kingdom and its chief port, SW coast of Hispania (Spain), near the mouth of the Guadalquivir in modern Andalusia; founded c. 1200 B.C.; prospered in trade of silver and tin and by some identified with the Biblical Tarshish. Later developed by Phoenicians and Greeks; destroyed by Carthaginians 480 B.C.

Tar·tu \ˈtär-(ˌ)tü\ *or Ger.* **Dor·pat** \ˈdȯ(ə)r-ˌpät\ *or Russ.* **Yur·ev** \ˈyůr-yəf\. City, E Estonian S.S.R., U.S.S.R., on Ema river W of Lake Peipus; pop. (1969e) 87,000; footwear, lumber, agricultural machinery; Univ. of Tartu (founded 1632 by Gustavus Adolphus of Sweden).

History: Founded 1030 as castle by Yaroslav I, grand prince of Kiev; captured by Teutonic Knights 1224; member of Hanseatic League; successively under Russian, Polish, and Swedish rule; became Russian 1704. Scene of considerable fighting during Russian Civil War 1918–19; scene of signing of peace treaty bet. U.S.S.R. and Estonia Feb. 2, 1920, and bet. U.S.S.R. and Finland Oct. 14, 1920; in World War II occupied by Germans 1941–44 and suffered considerable damage.

Tar·tūs \tär-ˈtüs\ *or anc.* **Tor·to·sa** \tȯr-ˈtō-sə\. Coastal town, W Syria, N of Tripoli and ab. 42 m. S of Latakia; fishing port.

Tarudant. See TAROUDANT.

Ta·ru·mae–san \ˌtär-ů-ˌmī-ˈsän\ *or* **Ta·ru·mai** \ˈtär-ů-ˌmī\. Active volcano, S Hokkaidō, Japan, S of Sapporo; 2969 ft.

Ta·ru·tao, Pu·lo \ˌpůl-ō-ˌtär-ə-ˈtaů\. Island (*pulo*), SW Thailand, off W coast of Malay Penin. at N end of Strait of Malacca, just N of Langkawi I.

Tarvisium. See TREVISO 2.

Täsch·horn \ˈtesh-ˌhȯ(ə)rn\. Peak, SW Switzerland, in the Pennine Alps; 14,733 ft.

Ta·shauz \tä-ˈshaůz, tə-\. Town, N Turkmen S.S.R., U.S.S.R., on the Karakalpak border 35 m. NW of Khiva; pop. (1969e) 64,000.

Tashi Chho Dzong. See THIMBU.

Tashihkiao. See YING-K'OU-HSIEN.

Tashilumpo. See JIH-K'A-TSE.

Tash·kent \tash-ˈkent, -ˈkend\. City, ✱ of Uzbek S.S.R., also ✱ of Tashkent Oblast, U.S.S.R., in NE part of Uzbek S.S.R., to E of the Syr Darya on a small tributary; pop. (1970p) 1,385,000; major industrial center, producing agricultural and mining machinery, textiles, electrical equipment, chemicals, furniture, pottery, foodstuffs; univ.; military headquarters and important center of Uzbek culture.

History: Founded c. 7th cent.; came under Arabs 8th cent. and under Timurid Empire 13th cent.; captured by Russians 1865 and new city built around old one; in 1966 scene of India-Pakistan conference on Kashmir dispute; suffered heavy damage from earthquake 1966.

Tashkent Oblast \-ˈō-bləst, -ˌblast\. Subdivision of the Uzbek S.S.R., U.S.S.R.; 6023 sq. m.; pop. (1970p) 2,865,000; ✱ Tashkent; cotton, melons; livestock raising; coal.

Tash·kur·ghān \ˌtäsh-kůr-ˈgän\ *or anc.* **Aor·nos** \ā-ˈȯr-nəs\. Town, Afghanistan, 30 m. E of Mazār-i-Sharīf; founded c. 1750 and became important trade center bet. India and Bukhara; 3 m. to the N are ruins of the ancient town of Khulm. Ancient Aornos in Bactria was on the line of march of Alexander the Great 330–329 B.C.

Ta·sik·ma·la·ja *or* **Ta·sik·ma·la·ya** \ˌtäs-ik-mə-ˈlī-ə\. Town, West Java prov., Indonesia, on railroad 50 m. SE of Bandung; pop. (1961c) 125,525; in fertile plain surrounded by high mountains.

Tå·singe *or* **Taa·singe** \ˈtȯ-ˌsiŋ-ə\. Danish island, Baltic Sea, S of Fyn I.; 27 sq. m.; pop. (1965c) 4956.

Ta·si·us·saq *or* **Ta·si·us·sak** \ˌtäs-ē-ˈü-ˌsək\. Settlement on an island in Baffin Bay, W coast of Greenland.

Tas·man, Mount \-ˈtaz-mən\. Peak in Southern Alps range, W cen. South I., New Zealand, NE of Mt. Cook; 11,475 ft.; 2d highest mountain in New Zealand; in Mount Cook National Park.

Tasman Bay. Inlet of Tasman Sea, on N coast of South I., New Zealand; Nelson is situated on its SE shore.

Tasman Glacier. Glacier, South I., New Zealand; 18 m. long, ab. 1¼ m. wide; largest glacier in New Zealand.

Tas·ma·nia \taz-ˈmā-nē-ə, -nyə\ *or formerly* **Van Die·men's Land** \van-ˈdē-mənz-\. Island, a state of Australia, South Pacific Ocean, ab. 150 m. S of state of Victoria; 26,383 sq. m.; pop. (1970e) 392,500; ✱ Hobart. *Physical features:* Includes Macquarie I. (89 sq. m.) to the SE in lat. 54°45′S, King I. 50 m. to the NW, Hunters Is. off the NW point, the Furneaux Is. off the NE point, and Bruny I. off the SE coast. Central part a highland including the Great Western Tiers and several mountains above 4000 ft. (highest Mt. Ossa 5305 ft.). Chief rivers Tamar in N, to which is joined the Esk and Macquarie river systems; Derwent in cen. and SE part; Gordon and Pieman rivers in W; and Arthur river in NW. Lakes are grouped in the center: Great Lake, Lake St. Clair, Lake Echo, and Lake Sorell. More important features of the coastline: on NE, Cape Portland; on E, Freycinet Penin.; on SE, Tasman Penin., Cape Pillar, Storm Bay, Southeast Cape; on SW, Southwest Cape; on W, Cape Sorell, Macquarie Harbour; on NW Cape Grim, and Circular Head on N coast. *Chief products:* Fruit, timber; copper, zinc, tin, tungsten; livestock raising; possesses ab. half of Australia's hydroelectric power potential. *Chief towns:* Hobart, Launceston, and Devonport.

History: Discovered and named Van Diemen's Land 1642 by Abel Tasman, Dutch navigator; renamed Tasmania 1853; taken over by Great Britain 1803 and for a time used as an auxiliary penal settlement; colony granted responsible government 1856; federated as state of Australian Commonwealth 1901. Aboriginal Tasmanians became extinct 1876.

Tasman Peninsula. Peninsula, SE coast of Tasmania, Australia, E of Storm Bay and Hobart; ab. 26 m. long by 20 m. wide; Capes Raoul and Pillar are at its S extremity. Port Arthur on its S coast near Cape Raoul was a penal settlement from 1833 to 1870.

Tasman Sea. The part of South Pacific Ocean bet. SE Australia and W New Zealand; ab. 1200 m. across.

Tas·so Island \ˌtas-ō-\. Small island, Sierra Leone river, Sierra Leone, W Africa, ENE of Freetown; the village of **Tasso** is on its NW coast.

Ta·ta·bán·ya \ˈtót-ó-ˌbän-(ˌ)yó\. Town, ⊗ of Komárom co., NW Hungary, ab. 35 m. W of Budapest; pop. (1970p) 65,130; aluminum, chemicals.

Ta·ta·houine \ˌtät-ə-ˈhwēn\. Town, SE Tunisia, N Africa, S of S end of Mareth Line (see MARETH); pop. (1966c) 4800.

Ta·ta·ko·to \ˌtät-ə-ˈkō-tō\. Atoll, E part of the Tuamoto Archipelago, S Pacific Ocean, 17°20′S, 138°23′W.

Tatanagar. See JAMSHEDPUR.

Ta·tar Autonomous Soviet Socialist Republic \ˈtät-ər-\ *or* **Ta·tar·stan** \ˌtät-ər-ˈstan, -ˈstän\. Autonomous republic of the Russian S.F.S.R., U.S.S.R., in E part at bend of the Middle Volga; 36,255 sq. m.; pop. (1970p) 3,131,000; ✱ Kazan. In level country on both sides of Volga and including lower course of Kama; both streams and their tributaries important for transportation and irrigation. Has a mixed economy: agriculture (fodder crops, legumes, truck crops), livestock farming; engineering, timberworking, tanning, and chemical industries; oil and natural gas fields. Crossed by two main rail lines from Moscow to Siberia; heavy freight traffic along rivers. Chief towns Kazan, Bugulma, Zelenodolsk, Chistopol, Almetyevsk.

History: In 5th cent. A.D. colonized by Bulgars, who established an important state; conquered by Mongols 13th cent.; in 15th cent. became Tatar khanate; conquered by Moscow under Ivan IV (the Terrible) 1552; autonomous republic established 1920.

Tatar Pass. See JABLONICA PASS.

Tatar Pazardzhik. See PAZARDZHIK 2.

Tatar Strait *or Russ.* **Ta·tar·ski Pro·liv** \tə-ˌtär-skē-prə-ˈl(y)ēf\. Wide strait, Russian S.F.S.R., U.S.S.R., bet. E coast of Primorski Krai and W coast of Sakhalin I.; forms the N end of the Sea of Japan.

Tate \ˈtāt\. County in Mississippi. See table at MISSISSIPPI.

Ta·te·ba·ya·shi \ˌtät-ə-bī-ˈyäsh-ē\. City, Gumma prefecture, Honshū, Japan, 41 m. NNW of Tokyo; pop. (1970c) 61,130.

Ta·te·ya·ma \ˌtät-ə-ˈyäm-ə\. 1 Volcanic peak, W cen. Honshū, Japan, SE of Toyama; 9892 ft.
2 City, Chiba prefecture, Honshū, Japan, 50 m. S of Tokyo; pop. (1970c) 55,236.

Tatoi *or* **Tatóï.** See DHEKÉLIA.

Ta·toosh Island \tə-ˌtüsh-\. Small island, NW Washington, off Cape Flattery; lighthouse; meteorological station.

Ta·tra Mountains \ˈtä-trə-\ *or* **High Tatra Mountains** *or Czech* **Vy·so·ké Ta·try** \ˌvis-ə-ˌkā-ˈtä-trē\. Chief mountain group of the cen. Carpathian Mts., Slovak S.R., Czechoslovakia; highest peak Gerlachovka 8711 ft.; many small lakes; resort region.

Tatra National Park. National park, S Poland; 84 sq. m.; highest part of Carpathian Mts.; established 1954.

Tatsienlu. See K'ANGTING.

Tatt·nall \ˈtat-nəl\. County in Georgia. See table at GEORGIA.

Ta-tu. See KHANBALIK.

Ta·tuí \tə-ˈtwē\. City, São Paulo state, SE Brazil, 75 m. W of São Paulo; munic. pop. (1968e) 37,430.

Ta-t'ung *or* **Ta·tung** \ˈdä-ˈtůŋ\. City, N Shansi prov., NE China, 180 m. W of Peking; pop. (1970e) 300,000; has rail connections with T'ai-yüan and has trade in livestock, coal, and furs; an ancient town, its fortress dating back to the Ch'in and Han dynasties. Nearby, ab. 10 m. distant, are the notable cave temples of Yunkang with stone Buddha images. Scene of fighting 1946 in Chinese civil war.

Tau \ˈtaů\. Largest of the Manua Is. (*q.v.*), American Samoa, in E part of group; 17 sq. m.; highest point 3056 ft.

Tauata. See TAHUATA.

Tau·ba·té \ˌtaů-bə-ˈtā\. City, São Paulo state, SE Brazil, 75 m. ENE of São Paulo on the Paraíba river; munic. pop. (1968e) 92,972.

Tau·ber \ˈtaů-bər\. River, Baden-Württemberg and Bavaria, West Germany; 75 m. long; rises W of Ansbach, flows NW to the Main at Wertheim.

Tau·ern \ˈtaů-ərn\. Railroad tunnel through the Hohe Tauern range of the Alps, Austria; 5.31 m. long; alt. 4021 ft.; connects the valley of the Gasteiner Ache in Salzburg with NW Carinthia.

Tauern, Hohe. See table at ALPS.

Tauern, Niedere. See NIEDERE TAUERN.

Tau·ghan·nock Falls \tə-ˌgan-ək-\. Waterfall in a small stream in Tompkins co., New York, 1 m. from Cayuga Lake and 10 m. NW of Ithaca; 215 ft. high.

Tau·hu·nu \taů-ˈhü-nü\. Village, W coast of island of Manahiki, Northern Cook Is., cen. Pacific Ocean.

Tau·ma·ru·nui \ˌtaů-mə-rů-ˈnü-ē\. Borough, W North I., New Zealand, on Wanganui river 170 m. N of Wellington; pop. (1970e) 6260; resort and starting point for tourists to Tongariro National Park.

Taum Sauk Mountain \ˌtäm-säk-\. Peak, Iron co., SE Missouri; 1772 ft.; highest point in the state.

Taung \ˈtaůŋ\ *or* **Taungs** \ˈtaůŋz\. Village, N Cape Province, S Rep. of South Africa, on an affluent of Vaal river 80 m. N of Kimberly; important tribal center. Taungs skull, a fossil skull of previously unknown anthropoid ape, found here.

Taung·gyi *also* **Tawng·gyi** \ˈtaůn-ˈjē\. Town, ✱ of Shan State, cen. Burma, 95 m. SE of Mandalay.

Taung·myo Range \ˌtaůn-ˌmyō-\. Mountain range, along the coast of Lower Burma, extending S from Moulmein; highest peak 3684 ft.

Taungs. See TAUNG.

Taun·ton \ˈtónt-ᵊn, ˈtänt-, ˈtant-\. 1 River, SE Massachusetts; rises in N cen. Plymouth co., flows S into Mount Hope Bay at Fall River; navigable as far as Taunton.

2 Industrial city, a ⊗ of Bristol co., SE Massachusetts, on Taunton river at head of navigation 13 m. N of Fall River; pop. (1970c) 43,756; silverware, electronic components, marine hardware, plastics, jewelry; founded c. 1639; center of ironworking industry 1656–1876.

3 Municipal borough, ⊗ of Somersetshire, SW England, on the Tone 38 m. SW of Bristol; pop. (1971p) 37,373; market town; produces clothing.

Tau·nus \'taů-nəs\. Mountain range, Hesse, West Germany, E of the Rhine river and N of the lower Main; highest peak Grosser Feldberg 2886 ft.

Tau·po \'taů-(ˌ)pō\. Borough, North I., New Zealand; pop. (1970e) 9480.

Taupo, Lake. Lake, cen. North I., New Zealand; 234 sq. m., 25 m. long; max. depth 522 ft.

Tau·ra·ge \ˌtaů-rə-'gā\ *or Ger.* **Tau·rog·gen** \'taů-ˌrō-gən\. Town, Lithuanian S.S.R., U.S.S.R., 65 m. WNW of Kaunas and NE of Sovetsk; pop. (1967e) 17,000. Meeting place of a convention 1812 to consider neutrality bet. Russia and neighboring states.

Tau·ranga \taů-'räŋ-ə\. City, N North I., New Zealand, on **Tauranga Harbor** (inlet of Bay of Plenty) 95 m. SE of Auckland; pop. (1970e) 26,800; an important seaport of New Zealand.

Taurasia. See TURIN.

Tau·ria·no·va \ˌtaů-rē-ə-'nō-və\. Commune, Reggio di Calabria prov., Calabria, S Italy, 28 m. NE of Reggio di Calabria; pop. (1968e) 17,130.

Tau·ric Cher·so·nese \ˌtȯr-ik-'kər-sə-ˌnēz, -ˌnēs\. The Crimea peninsula, part of the kingdom of the Cimmerian Bosporus acquired by Rome 47 B.C.

Tau·ri·da \'tȯr-ə-də\ *or Russ.* **Ta·vri·da** \təv-'rēd-ə\. Former Russian government, now included in Crimean Oblast, Russian S.F.S.R., U.S.S.R., and S Ukrainian S.S.R.

Tauroggen. See TAURAGE.

Tauromenium. See TAORMINA.

Tau·rus Mountains \ˌtȯr-əs-\ *or Turk.* **To·ros Dağ·la·rı** \tō-ˌrōs-ˌdä(g)-lä-'rē\. Mountain chain, S Turkey, running parallel to the Mediterranean coast; has many high peaks, highest above 12,000 ft.; crossed N of Tarsus by important pass of Cilician Gates; to the NE the extension of the range is the Anti-Taurus (*q.v.*).

Ta·var·es \tə-'var-ēz\. City, ⊗ of Lake co., cen. Florida penin., 28 m. NW of Orlando; pop. (1970c) 3261; fruit and truck farms.

Tavastehus. 1 Province, Finland. See HÄME.

2 City, Finland. See HÄMEENLINNA.

Tav·da \təf-'dä\. 1 River, U.S.S.R.; 450 m. long; chiefly in NE Sverdlovsk Oblast, Russian S.F.S.R.; flows SE from Ural Mts. to Tobol river SW of Tobolsk.

2 Town, E Sverdlovsk Oblast, Russian S.F.S.R., U.S.S.R., on lower Tavda river ab. 125 m. W of Tobolsk; pop. (1967e) 49,000.

Ta·ver·ny \ta-ver-'nē\. Commune, Val-d'Oise dept., France, just NNW of Paris; pop. (1966e) 11,484; 12th–13th cent. church.

Ta·ve·u·ni \ˌtäv-ē-'ü-nē\. Island, Fiji, SW Pacific Ocean, 2 m. SE of Vanua Levu; 28 m. long; 166 sq. m.; chief village Waiyevo; highest point 4071 ft. Grows coffee, sugar, cinchona, and tropical fruits and vegetables.

Ta·vi·gna·no \ˌtäv-ēn-'yän-(ˌ)ō\. River, cen. Corsica, France, flowing ESE to Tyrrhenian Sea.

Ta·vi·ra \tə-'vir-ə\. Municipality, Faro dist., S Portugal, on Atlantic Ocean 18 m. NE of Faro; pop. (1970p) 23,057; trades in white wines, mineral waters; tuna and sardine fisheries.

Ta·vo·la·ra \ˌtav-ə-'lär-ə\. Small island off NE coast of Sardinia, Italy, E of Olbia; ab. 2½ sq. m.; its settlement dates back to Roman times.

Tavor, Har. See TABOR, MOUNT.

Ta·voy \tə-'vȯi\. 1 River, Lower Burma; ab. 90 m. long; flows S into Andaman Sea E of Tavoy Penin. Its lower course for 30 m. forms a wide estuary.

2 District, Tenasserim division, Lower Burma; 5404 sq. m.; pop. (1962e) 297,871; ✱ Tavoy.

3 Town, its ✱, on left bank of Tavoy river ab. 30 m. from its mouth; pop. (1953c) 40,312; ships tin ore.

Tavoy Island. See MALI ISLAND.

Tavoy Point. Cape at S end of **Tavoy Peninsula,** on W coast of Lower Burma at the mouth of Tavoy river, 13°32′N, 98°10′E.

Tavrida. See TAURIDA.

Ta·vur·vur, Mount \-tə-'vůr-vůr\ *also* **Mount Ma·tu·pi** \-mə-'tüp-ē\. Volcano, one of a group nearly surrounding the town of Rabaul, on Blanche Bay, E New Britain I., Bismarck Archipelago; its sudden eruption May 29–30, 1937, together with that of the new volcano Mt. Vulcan, caused great destruction at Rabaul and on Gazelle Penin. See MOTHER, MOUNT.

Taw \'tȯ\. River, Devonshire, SW England; ab. 50 m. long; flows NW into Barnstaple Bay through an estuary at Barnstaple.

Ta·wa \'tä-wə\. Borough, North I., New Zealand; pop. (1970e) 11,000.

Ta·was City \ˌtȯ-(w)əs-\. City, ⊗ of Iosco co., NE Michigan; pop. (1970c) 1666.

Ta·wi \'tə-wē\. River, Jamma and Kashmir, N India; ab. 95 m. long; flows SW to Chenab river on the N Punjab border, Pakistan.

Ta·wi·ta·wi \ˌtä-wē-'tä-wē\. 1 Island group, SW Sulu Archipelago, Phil., comprising Tawitawi I., Sanga Sanga I., Simunul I., several smaller islands, and a number of clusters of small islands, totaling ab. 100; 360 sq. m. See SULU 1.

2 Large island of the group; ab. 34 m. long by 6 to 14 m. wide; 229 sq. m.; of volcanic origin, with rich soil and covered with tropical vegetation. Highest point 1751 ft. Occupied by U.S. troops Apr. 5, 1945.

Tawnggyi. See TAUNGGYI.

Tax·co \'täs-(ˌ)kō\. Town, Guerrero state, S Mexico, ab. 45 m. SSW of Mexico City; munic. pop. (1970p) 64,368; gold and silver mines; tourist resort; silverware manufacture.

Tax·i·la \'tak-sə-lə\. Ruins of ancient town, Pakistan, just E of Indus river SW of Rawalpindi; of archaeological interest; the town was in the Persian Empire, visited by Alexander the Great 326 B.C., and later an important Buddhist center.

Tay \'tā\. River, Scotland; 120 m. long; rises near W border of Perth co., flows NE through **Loch Tay** (15 m. long) and then SE into the Firth of Tay; longest river in Scotland.

Tay, Firth of. Estuary of the Tay river, E Scotland, N of the Firth of Forth; extends inland 24½ m.; empties into North Sea.

Ta·ya·bas \tə-'yäb-əs\. 1 Province, Phil. See QUEZON.

2 Municipality, Quezon prov., Luzon, Phil.; pop. (1969e) 35,200.

Tayabas Bay. Inlet, SW coast of Quezon prov., S Luzon, Phil.; W side borders on Batangas prov.; on SE connects with Mompog Pass; Lucena is on it.

Ta–ya Bay \ˌtä-ˌyä-\ *or formerly* **Bi·as Bay** \ˌbī-əs-\. Inlet of South China Sea, on coast of Kwangtung prov., SE China, E of Kowloon.

Ta–yeh *or* **Ta·yeh** \'dä-'ye\. Town, Hupeh prov., E cen. China, 60 m. SE of Han-yang near Yangtze river.

Ta·yg·e·tus \tā-'ij-ət-əs\. Mountain range, S Peloponnesus, Greece, forming border bet. Laconia and Messenia depts. and extending S in W Laconia along coast of Gulf of Messenia; highest point Hagios Elias 7904 ft.

Ta–ying \'tä-'yiŋ\ *or* **Tai·ping** \'tī-'piŋ\; *in Burmese* **Ta·ping** \'tä-'piŋ\. River, China and Upper Burma; ab. 170 m.

long; flows SW out of Yunnan prov., China, crosses Burmese border and empties into Irrawaddy river at Bhamo.

Tay·lor \'tā-lər\. 1 Name of counties in seven states of the U.S. See tables at FLORIDA, GEORGIA, IOWA, KENTUCKY, TEXAS, WEST VIRGINIA, WISCONSIN.
2 City, Wayne co., SE Michigan, 18 m. WSW of Detroit; pop. (1970c) 70,020.
3 Village, ⊗ of Loup co., cen. Nebraska; pop. (1970c) 240.
4 Borough, Lackawanna co., NE Pennsylvania, 3 m. WSW of Scranton; pop. (1970c) 6977; coal mines.
5 City, Williamson co., cen. Texas, 28 m. NE of Austin; pop. (1970c) 9616; clothing, fertilizer, iron goods, cottonseed oil; poultry, grain, onions.

Taylor, Mount. Peak, NE Valencia co., W New Mexico; 11,389 ft.

Taylor Mill. City, Kenton co., N Kentucky; pop. (1970c) 3194.

Taylor Mountain. 1 Peak, Chaffee co., cen. Colorado; 13,600 ft.
2 Peak, W cen. Lemhi co., E cen. Idaho; 9968 ft.

Taylor Park Dam. Dam across **Taylor River,** tributary of Gunnison river, E Gunnison co., W cen. Colorado; height 206 ft.; completed 1937; impounds water for irrigation, forming **Taylor Park Reservoir.**

Tay·lors·ville \'tā-lərz-ˌvil\. 1 City, ⊗ of Spencer co., cen. Kentucky; pop. (1970c) 897.
2 Town, ⊗ of Alexander co., W cen. North Carolina, in Blue Ridge foothills 18 m. WNW of Statesville; pop. (1970c) 1231; fruit farms.

Tay·lor·ville \'tā-lər-ˌvil\. City, ⊗ of Christian co., cen. Illinois, 25 m. SE of Springfield; pop. (1970c) 10,927; cigars, tools, paper, clothing; coal mines; dairy farms.

Taymā. See TAIMA.

Tay·tay \tī-'tī\. Town on coast at N end of Palawan I., Phil.; pop. (1969e) 11,900; established as a fort by Spaniards in early part of 18th cent.

Taz \'täz\. River, NE Russian S.F.S.R., U.S.S.R.; ab. 600 m. long; rises in W Krasnoyarsk Krai, flows N and NW through E Yamalo-Nenets National Okrug into **Taz Bay,** E arm of Gulf of Ob, 230 m. long, 35 m. at its widest part.

Ta·za \'täz-ə\. Town, N Morocco, NW Africa, E of Fès; pop. (1961c) 31,667.

Taze·well \'taz-ˌwel, -wəl\. 1 Name of counties in two states of the U.S. See tables at ILLINOIS and VIRGINIA.
2 Town, ⊗ of Claiborne co., NE Tennessee; pop. (1970c) 1860.
3 Town, ⊗ of Tazewell co., SW Virginia; pop. (1970c) 4168; coal mines; agriculture.

Ta·zoult \tä-'zült\; *formerly* **Lam·bes·sa** \lam-'bes-ə\ *or* **Lam·bèse** \läⁿ-'bez\; *anc.* **Lam·bae·sis** \lam-'bē-səs\. Commune, S Batna dept., Algeria, N Africa, SW of Batna; pop. (1966c) 6000; center of agricultural region and former site of French convict settlement (established 1852). Ancient Lambaesis an important Roman town of S Numidia; its numerous ruins of special interest as being the remains of great Roman camp.

Tbi·li·si \tə-'bil-ə-sē\ *or* **Tif·lis** \'tif-ləs, tə-'flēs\. City, ✱ of Georgian S.S.R., U.S.S.R., in SE part on both banks of the Kura river, 280 m. WNW of Baku; pop. (1970p) 889,000; machine tools, electrical equipment, locomotives, textiles, plastics, leather goods, furniture, wine, chocolate; hydroelectric power stations. Sion Cathedral (5th cent., restored), numerous parks and gardens; center of Georgian culture and education, with a university (1918), theaters, and research institutes.
History: Founded c. 455 A.D. as ✱ of ancient Georgian kingdom; for centuries an important center on trade routes between Europe and Asia and frequently sacked; has been under Persian, Byzantine, Arab, Mongol, Tatar, and Turkish rule; came under Russian rule 1801; center of rebellion against Russian government 1905; seat of new administration 1917; ✱ of Transcaucasian Federation 1921; made ✱ of Georgian S.S.R. 1936.

Tchad. See CHAD.

Tchongking. See CHUNGKING.

Tczew \'chef\ *or Ger.* **Dir·schau** \'dir-(ˌ)shaů\. Commune, E cen. Gdańsk prov., N Poland, on left bank of Vistula river 20 m. SSE of Gdańsk; pop. (1970p) 40,800; railroad junction and river port; shipyard, railroad shops; mentioned late 12th cent.; to Poland 1282, to Prussia 1772; returned to Poland 1919.

Teague \'tēg\. City, Freestone co., E cen. Texas, 45 m. E of Waco; pop. (1970c) 2867; livestock, cotton.

Te Anau Lake \tā-ˌä-naů-\. Lake, SW South I., New Zealand; 38 m. long; 133 sq. m.; max. depth 906 ft.; a source of the Waiau river.

Tea·neck \'tē-ˌnek\. Township, Bergen co., NE corner of New Jersey, 8 m. E of Paterson; pop. (1970c) 42,143; residential; Luther Coll. of the Bible and Liberal Arts (1948).

Te·a·no \tā-'ä-(ˌ)nō\ *or anc.* **Te·a·num Sid·i·ci·num** \tē-'ā-nəm-ˌsid-ə-'sī-nəm\. Commune, Caserta prov., Campania, S Italy, 29 m. N by W of Naples; pop. (1968e) 15,861; early 12th cent. cathedral, 8th cent. church of San Benedetto, 10th cent. church of Santa Maria de Foris.

Te Aro·ha \tā-'är-ō-ə\. Borough, N North I., New Zealand, on Waihou river 70 m. SE of Auckland; pop. (1970e) 3300; health resort with hot medicinal springs.

Teate. See CHIETI 2.

Teb, Al–. See AL-TEB.

Te·bes·sa \ti-'bes-ə\ *or anc.* **The·ves·te** \thi-'ves-tē\. Commune, E Annaba dept., NE Algeria, near Tunisia border; pop. (1966c) 40,521; trade center; as Theveste strategic town of Roman Africa, founded 1st cent. A.D.; site of extensive ruins.

Te·bi·cua·ry \ˌteb-i-kwä-'rē\. River, S Paraguay; ab. 250 m. long; flows W into Paraguay river.

Te·bing·ting·gi \tə-ˌbiŋ-'tiŋ-gē\. 1 *or* **Te·bing Ting·gi** \tə-ˌbiŋ-'tiŋ-gē\. Island off E coast of Sumatra, Indonesia, W of Singapore.
2 Town, NE Sumatra, Indonesia, on railroad ab. 35 m. SE of Medan; pop. (1961c) 26,228; center of tobacco cultivation.
3 Town, SE Sumatra, on S branch of Musi river ab. 60 m. ESE of Benkulu.

Té·bour·ba \tā-'bů(ə)r-bə\. Town, N Tunisia, N Africa, ab. 32 m. W of city of Tunis; pop. (1966c) 7700; battle May 4–8, 1943 in which British drove out the Germans.

Teche, Bayou \-'tesh\. Navigable stream in Louisiana; ab. 175 m. long; flows into Atchafalaya river; in Longfellow's "Evangeline Country."

Te–chou \'də-'chaů, -'jō\ *or* **Te·hsien** \'də-shē-'en\. Town, NW Shantung prov., NE China, on Grand Canal near Hopeh border 65 m. NW of Tsinan.

Tecolutla. See NECAXA.

Te·co·mán \ˌtā-kə-'män\. Municipality, Colima state, Mexico, 22 m. S of Colima; pop. (1970p) 43,933; cotton gins; cotton, coconuts, tropical fruits.

Tec·pan \'tek-ˌpän\. Municipality, Guerrero state, Mexico, 55 m. NW of Acapulco; pop. (1970p) 44,820; fishing, lumber; diversified agriculture.

Tec·pán Gua·te·ma·la \tek-ˌpän-ˌgwät-ə-'mäl-ə\. Town, Chimaltenango dept., S cen. Guatemala; munic. pop. (1964p) 21,150.

Te·cua·la \tā-'kwäl-ə\. Town, Nayarit state, W Mexico; munic. pop (1970e) 31,007.

Te·cu·ci \te-'küch(-ē)\. City, Galaţi co., E Romania, on a tributary of the Siretul ab. 30 m. SSW of Bîrlad; munic. pop. (1966) 28,454.

Te·cum·seh \tə-'kəm(p)-sə, -sē\. 1 City, Lenawee co., S Michigan, 22 m. SSW of Ann Arbor; pop. (1970c) 7120; automobile parts; truck farms.
2 City, ⊗ of Johnson co., SE Nebraska, 31 m. E of Beatrice; pop. (1970c) 2058; oil wells.
3 City, Pottawatomie co., cen. Oklahoma, 5 m. S of Shawnee; pop. (1970c) 4451; diversified agriculture.
4 Town, Essex co., SE Ontario, Canada, on Lake St. Clair 10 m. E of Windsor; pop. (1971p) 5157.

Te·dzhen \te-'jen\ *or formerly* **Te·jend** \-'jend\. Lower course of the Hari Rud (*q.v.*), S Turkmen S.S.R., U.S.S.R.; also the oasis near which the stream loses itself in sands of Kara Kum Desert.

Tees \'tēz\. River, N England; 70 m. long; flows E along boundary bet. Yorkshire and Durham, empties into North Sea at Middlesbrough; navigable up to Teeside.

Tee·side \'tē-ˌsīd\. County borough, North Riding, Yorkshire (N part in Durham), N England, on the Tees; 77 sq. m.; pop. (1971p) 395,477; extensive port facilities; steel, chemicals; shipbuilding; formed 1958.

Tee·wi·not, Mount \-'tē-wə-ˌnät\. Peak, cen. Grand Teton National Park, NW Wyoming; 12,317 ft.

Te·fé *or* **Tef·fé** \te-'fā\. River, Amazonas state, W Brazil; ab. 500 m. long; flows NE into Amazon river.

Te·gal \tā-'gäl\. Seaport, Central Java prov., Indonesia, on N coast railroad 50 m. W of Pekalongan; pop. (1961c) 89,016; exports sugar; has numerous sugar mills.

Te·gea \'tē-jē-ə\. Ancient city, SE Arcadia, cen. Peloponnesus, S Greece; the modern **Pi·a·li** \pyäl-'(y)ē\, in the department of Arcadia. Tegeans fought at Plataea and supported Sparta in Peloponnesian Wars; fought against Sparta at Leuctra. Had notable temple of Athena Alea with work by the sculptor Scopas. See ARCADIA 5.

Te·ge·len \'tā-gə-lən\. Commune, Limburg prov., SE Netherlands, just S of Venlo on German border; pop. (1970e) 18,168.

Te·gern·see \'tā-gərn-ˌzā\. 1 Lake in Bavaria, West Germany, 30 m. SSE of Munich, in foothills of Alps at 2382 ft. elevation; 4 m. long; popular resort.
2 Village on lake; 15th cent. church; castle.

Teg·na·pa·tam \ˌteg-nə-'pət-əm\. See FORT SAINT DAVID.

Te·gu·ci·gal·pa \tə-ˌgü-sə-'gal-pə\. 1 Department, Honduras. See FRANCISCO MORAZÁN.
2 City, ✱ of Honduras and of Francisco Morazán dept.; pop. (1969e) 218,510; alt. 3300 ft.; textiles, sugar, cigarettes; cathedral; univ. (1895), teacher training coll. (1956); one of the few capital cities in the world without a railroad. Founded as gold and silver mining center c. 1579; made ✱ of Honduras 1880.

Te·hach·a·pi \ti-'hach-ə-pē\. City, Kern co., SW California, ESE of Bakersfield; pop. (1970c) 4211; cement.

Tehachapi Mountains. Mountain range, S cen. California, running E-W bet. S end of the Sierra Nevada and the Coast Ranges; highest point Double Mountain 7988 ft.; at E end is **Tehachapi Pass,** 3799 ft., leading from Mojave Desert into the San Joaquin valley.

Te·ha·ma \ti-'hā-mə\. County in California. See table at CALIFORNIA.

Tehama. See TIHAMA.

Te·hip·i·te Dome \tə-ˌhip-ət-ē-\. Peak in Sierra Nevada in E Fresno co., S cen. California; 7713 ft.

Teh·ran *or* **Te·he·ran** \ˌtā-ə-'ran, -'rän\. 1 Province of N Iran. See table at IRAN.
2 City, ✱ of Iran, also ✱ of the prov., ab. 65 m. S of the Caspian Sea, at foot of S slope of Elburz Mts.; met. area pop. (1971e) 3,400,000; alt. 3800 ft.; transportation and industrial center, producing automobiles, cement, sugar, textiles, and firearms; two royal palaces, numerous public buildings and mosques, museum, opera house, stadiums, and parks and gardens; several universities and colleges, including Univ. of Tehran (1934); important cultural and tourist center.
History: Believed to have been originally a suburb of Ray, Iranian capital until Mongol invasion 1220; development as independent city began 16th cent.; made capital c. 1795; has undergone continuous and rapid modernization since 1925 and esp. since World War II; site of conference Nov. 26–Dec. 2, 1943 bet. Churchill, Roosevelt, and Stalin.

Teh·ri \'tar-ē\. 1 *or* **Tehri Garh·wal** \-gər-'wäl\. District, NW Uttar Pradesh, N India; 4516 sq. m.; ✱ Tehri. Lies entirely in the Himalayas with ranges 20,000 to 23,000 ft.; contains also the sources of both the Ganges and the Yamuna and hence has many places of pilgrimage; established 1815 as a state by the British after war with Nepal and formerly adminstered with Punjab States.
2 Town, its ✱, in the Himalayas on the Bhagirathi river 145 m. NE of Delhi.
3 Town, Madhya Pradesh, India. See TIKAMGARH.

Tehsien. See TE-CHOU.

Te–hua \'də-'hwä\. Town, S cen. Fukien prov., SE China, 75 m. SE of Foochow; noted for its white porcelain (*blanc de chine*).

Te·hua·cán \ˌtā-wə-'kän\. Town, Puebla state, SE cen. Mexico, 65 m. SE of Puebla; munic. pop. (1970p) 67,520; mineral springs.

Te·huan·te·pec \tə-'wänt-ə-ˌpek\ *or in full* **San·to Do·min·go Tehuantepec** \ˌsänt-əd-ə-'miŋ-gō-\. Town, Oaxaca state, S Mexico, on the **Tehuantepec River;** munic. pop. (1970p) 67,520; hot springs; fruits, sugar, and vegetables.

Tehuantepec, Gulf of. Widemouthed inlet of the Pacific Ocean, SE Mexico, bounded by states of Oaxaca and Chiapas.

Tehuantepec, Isthmus of. Isthmus, S Mexico, bet. the Bay of Campeche on the N and the Gulf of Tehuantepec on the S; 137 m. wide.

Tehuantepec River. See TEHUANTEPEC.

Tei·de, Pi·co de \ˌpē-kō-dā-'tā-dē\ *or* **Pico de Tey·de** \-'tā-dē\ *or* **Pico de Te·ne·ri·fe** \-dā-ˌtān-ə-'rēf-ə\ *or Eng.* **Peak of Ten·er·ife** \-ˌten-ə-'rif, -'rēf\. Volcanic mountain on the island of Tenerife, Canary Is. (*q.v.*); 12,198 ft.

Tei·fi \'tī-vē\. River, W Wales; ab. 50 m. long; flows SW and W into S Cardigan Bay.

Teign \'tin, 'tēn\. River, Devonshire, SW England; 30 m. long; rises in Dartmoor and flows SE into the English Channel at Teignmouth.

Teign·mouth \'tin-məth, 'tēn-\. Urban district, Devonshire, SW England, at mouth of the Teign 12 m. S of Exeter; pop. (1971p) 12,554; seaside resort and yachting center.

Teil, Le. See LE TEIL.

Teima. See TAIMA.

Tejend. See TEDZHEN.

Tejo. See TAGUS.

Te·ju·pil·ca de Hi·dal·go \ˌtā-hü-'pil-kə-ˌdā-ē-'thäl-(ˌ)gō\. Municipality, México state, Mexico, 70 m. SW of Mexico City; pop. (1970p) 92,183; lumber; agriculture; numerous Indian remains of archaeological interest.

Te·ka·mah \tə-'kā-mə\. City, ⊗ of Burt co., E Nebraska, 28 m. NE of Fremont; pop. (1970c) 1848.

Te·ka·po \tā-'käp-(ˌ)ō\. River, cen. South I., New Zealand; flows from S end of **Lake Tekapo** (32 sq. m.); one of the headstreams of the Waitaki river.

Te·kax \tā-'käs\ *or in full* **Tekax de Ál·va·ro Obre·gón** \-dā-'äl-və-ˌrō-ˌō-brā-'gōn\. Town, Yucatán state, on Yucatán penin., SE Mexico, ab. 60 m. SE of Mérida; munic. pop. (1970p) 16,370; Maya ruins.

Te·ke·ze \tə-'kəz-ā\ *also* **Tak·ka·ze** \tə-'kəz-ā\. River, E Africa; ab. 470 m. long; headstream of the Atbara; rises in N cen. Ethiopia and flows N and then W, crossing into Sudan where it is called the **Sa·tit** \'sä-tēt\ *or* **Se·tit** \'sā-tēt\.

Te·kir·dağ \te-'ki(ə)r-ˌdä(g)\. 1 Province of NW Turkey, Europe. See table at TURKEY.
2 *or Ital.* **Ro·do·sto** \rō-'dò-(ˌ)stō\; *anc.* **Bi·san·the** \bə-'san(t)-thē\ *or* **Rhae·des·tus** *also* **Rai·des·tos** \ri-'des-təs\. Seaport and market town, its ✱, on the Sea of Marmara 78 m. W of İstanbul; pop. (1965c) 27,069; former port for Edirne region but lost importance after completion of railroad to Dede Agach (Alexandroúpolis); ancient Bisanthe founded 7th cent. B.C.; came under Turks 1320.

Tekrit. See TIKRĪT.

Te Ku·i·ti \ˌtā-kü-ˈēt-ē\. Borough, NW North I., New Zealand, on Waipa river 105 m. S of Auckland; pop. (1970e) 4880; station for Waitomo Caves (*q.v.*).

Tel Aviv \ˌtel-ə-ˈvēv\. District of W cen. Israel. See table at ISRAEL.

Tel Aviv–Jaf·fa \-ˈjäf-ə, -ˈyaf-ə\ *also* **Tel Aviv–Ya·fo** \-ˈyä-(ˌ)fō\. Twin cities, Israel, on the Mediterranean Sea; pop. (1970e) 384,000; textiles, chemicals; food processing; banking and insurance; tourism; commercial port; Habima Theater (1945), univ. (1953, new status 1962), Temple of Culture (1957), botanical and zoological gardens; Tel Aviv founded 1909, ✽ of Israel 1948–50; Jaffa was incorporated with Tel Aviv 1950. See JAFFA.

Tel·de \ˈtel-(ˌ)dā\. Commune, Las Palmas prov. (E Canary Is.), Spain, on E Grand Canary I. 6 m. S of Las Palmas; pop. (1970p) 44,667.

Tel·e·mark \ˈtel-ə-ˌmärk\. 1 Mountain and lake region, Telemark co., S Norway; highest peak Gausta 6178 ft.
2 County of S Norway. See table at NORWAY.

Te·le·or·man \ˌtel-yȯr-ˈmän\. County of S Romania. See table at ROMANIA.

Tel·e·scope Peak \ˌtel-ə-ˌskōp-\. Mountain in Panamint Mts., SE Inyo co., E California; 11,049 ft.

Te·les Pi·res \ˌtel-ə-ˈspir-əs\ *or formerly* **São Ma·nuel** \ˌsaùⁿ-man-ˈwel\. River, cen. Brazil; ab. 600 m. long; flows NW out of Mato Grosso state, forming part of boundary bet. Mato Grosso and Pará states; joins with Juruena (*q.v.*) to form the Tapajós river.

Tel·fair \ˈtel-ˌfa(ə)r, -ˌfe(ə)r\. County in Georgia. See table at GEORGIA.

Tel·ford \ˈtel-fərd\. Borough, Bucks and Montgomery cos., SE Pennsylvania, 21 m. S of Allentown; pop. (1970c) 3409.

Tel·ka·lakh \ˌtel-kə-ˈlak\ *or* **Tall Ke·lakh** \ˌtal-\. Town, S Latakia, Syria, on Lebanon border and on railroad from Tripoli to Homs.

Tell al–ʻAmar·na \ˌtel-ˌel-ə-ˈmär-nə\. Former station on the Nile river, Egypt, midway bet. Thebes and Memphis, site of the capital of Amenhotep IV; in the ruins important documents (Tell al-ʻAmarna tablets and Tell al-ʻAmarna letters) were found 1887, providing an important source of modern knowledge of the period (Amarna Age) c. 1375–1360 B.C.

Tell Ar·pa·chi·ya \ˌtel-är-ˈpäch-ē-(y)ə\. Ancient Assyrian city, part of Nineveh; its site is just N of Mosul, N Iraq, bet. the sites of Nineveh and Dur Sharrukin (see KHORSABAD).

Tell As·mar \-ˈas-mər, -ˈaz-\ *or anc.* **Esh·nun·na** \esh-ˈnən-ə\. Locality, E Iraq, 33 m. ENE of Baghdad; archaeological site where numerous stone statuettes and copper objects of the Sumerians have been found, dating c. 3000 to 2700 B.C.

Tell Atlas. See ATLAS MOUNTAINS.

Tell Basta. See BUBASTIS.

Tell City \ˈtel-\. City, Perry co., S Indiana, on Ohio river 40 m. E of Evansville; pop. (1970c) 7933; boats, flour, electric motors; sawmills, oil refinery, coal mines.

Tell ed–Du·weir \ˌtel-ˌed-dü-ˈwa(ə)r\. See LACHISH.

Tell el–Kebir. See TALL AL-KABĪR, AL-.

Tel·ler \ˈtel-ər\. 1 County in Colorado. See table at COLORADO.
2 City, Port Clarence Inlet, W Seward Penin., W Alaska, ab. 60 m. NNW of Nome; pop. (1970c) 220.

Tel·li·cher·ry \ˌtel-ə-ˈcher-ē\. Town, NW Kerala, S India, on the Malabar Coast 168 m. WSW of Bangalore; pop. (1961c) 44,763; commercial seaport and distribution point; exports sandalwood, coffee, spices, cocoa, and coconuts. Factory established here by British East India Company 1683. Withstood two years' siege 1780–82.

Tel·li·co Dam \ˈtel-ə-ˌkō-\. See table at TENNESSEE VALLEY AUTHORITY.

Tell Je·zar \ˌtel-jə-ˈzär\. See GEZER.

Tel·lu·ride \ˈtel-ə-ˌrīd\. City, ⊗ of San Miguel co., SW Colorado, 40 m. S of Montrose; pop. (1970c) 553.

Teloeti Bay. See TALUTI BAY.

Te·lok An·son \ˌtel-ō-ˈan-sən\. Town, Perak state, Malaysia, on the Perak river, a commercial port near its mouth; pop. (1957c) 37,042.

Te·lo·lo·a·pan \ˌtā-lōl-ˈwä-(ˌ)pän\. Municipality, Guerrero state, Mexico, 24 m. W of Iguala; pop. (1970p) 48,458; lumber; agriculture.

Telo Martius. See TOULON.

Te·los \ˈtē-ˌläs\ *also* **Ti·los** \ˈtē-ˌlȯs\ *or Ital.* **Pi·sco·pi** \ˈpē-skə-pē\. An island of the Dodecanese (*q.v.*), bet. Nisyros and Khalkē and NW of Rhodes; 25 sq. m.

Tel·pos–iz *or* **Tel·pos Iz** \ˌtel-pȯ-ˈsiz\. Peak, N Ural Mts., Russian S.F.S.R., U.S.S.R., on boundary bet. Europe and Asia, 63°54′N, 59°10′E; 5558 ft.

Tel·town \ˈtel-ˌtaùn\. Village, co. Meath, Eire, 35 m. NW of Dublin; in early times scene of the great annual festival said to be instituted by the god Lug in honor of his foster mother Tailte and revived 1924 at Dublin as the Tailtean Games.

Te·luk·ba·jur \te-ˌlük-bä-ˈyü(ə)r\ *or formerly* **Em·ma·ha·ven** \ˌem-ə-ˈhä-vᵊn\. Port of Padang, W Sumatra, Indonesia, on NW shore of Bajur Bay 4 m. S of Padang.

Te·luk·be·tung \tə-ˌlük-bə-ˈtüŋ\. See LAMPUNG BAY.

Te·ma \ˈtā-mə\. Industrial city and seaport, SE Ghana, 20 m. ENE of Accra; pop. (1970p) 58,815; extensive harbor facilities completed 1961; steel, chemicals, aluminum; automobile assembly plants; chosen early 1950's as site for port and industrial park to serve Accra region.

Tema. See TAIMA.

Temagami, Lake. See TIMAGAMI, LAKE.

Te·mang·gung *or Du.* **Te·mang·goeng** \tə-ˈmäŋ-güŋ\. Town, Central Java prov., Indonesia, ab. 17 m. N of Mageland; pop. (1961c) 8107.

Te·ma·tangi \ˌtā-mə-ˈtäŋ-ē\. Atoll, Tuamotu Archipelago, in SW part 640 m. SE of Papeete, 21°41′S, 140°40′W.

Tem·be·ling \ˈtem-bə-ˌliŋ\. River, E headstream of the Pahang river, NE Pahang state, Malaysia; joins with the Jelai to form the Pahang.

Témbi. See TEMPE, VALE OF.

Tem·bu·land \ˈtem-(ˌ)bü-ˌland\. Region, Transkei, E Cape Province, Rep. of South Africa, bet. upper Great Kei river and the Umtata; 3339 sq. m.; includes Bomvanaland along the coast.

Teme \ˈtēm\. River, E Wales and W England; 60 m. long; rises in E Wales near the English border, flows S and E across the border, and curves S to join the Severn near Worcester.

Tem·er·loh \ˈtem-ər-ˌlō\. Village, SW Pahang state, Malaysia, on cen. peninsula railroad and on left bank of Pahang river. In fighting region during Japanese invasion of peninsula Dec. 1941–Jan. 1942.

Temeš. See TIMIS.

Temesvár. See TIMIŞOARA.

Te·me·tiu, Mount \-ˌtā-mə-ˈtē-(ˌ)ü\. Peak, Hiva Oa I., Marquesas Is., S Pacific Ocean; 4134 ft.; highest peak on Hiva Oa I.

Temir–Khan–Shura. See BUINAKSK.

Te·mir·tau \ˈtā-mir-ˌtaù\. Town, Karaganda Oblast, Kazakh S.S.R., U.S.S.R., ab. 20 m. NW of Karaganda; pop. (1970p) 167,000.

Témiscamingue. See TIMISKAMING.

Té·mis·coua·ta \ˌtem-ə-ˈskwat-ə\. 1 Lake, Témiscouata co., S Quebec, Canada; 24 m. long, 29 sq. m.; its outlet a tributary of St. John river.
2 County, Quebec, Canada. See table at QUEBEC.

Temiskaming. See TIMISKAMING.

Te·mo·aya \ˌtā-mō-ˈī-ə\. Municipality, México state, Mexico, 25 m. NW of Mexico City; pop. (1970p) 30,225; sheep, cattle raising; wheat.

Tem·pe \tem-ˈpē\. City, Maricopa co., SW cen. Arizona, on Salt river 9 m. E of Phoenix; pop. (1970c) 63,550; electronic equipment, steel, clothing; agriculture; Arizona State Univ. (1885).

Tempe, Vale of \-ˈtem-pē\ *or Gk.* **Tém·bi** \ˈtem-bē\. Valley, NE Thessaly, Greece; ab. 5 m. long; traversed by the Piniós (ancient Peneus) river in its lower course; lies bet. Mts. Olympus and Ossa.

Tem·ple \'tem-pəl\. City, Bell co., cen. Texas, 34 m. S of Waco; pop. (1970c) 33,431; furniture, plastics, footwear, dairy products; railroad shops.

Temple, Mount. Mountain, Banff National Park, Alberta, Canada, near British Columbia border; 11,626 ft.

Temple City. City, Los Angeles co., SW California, E suburb of Los Angeles; pop. (1970c) 31,040.

Temple Terrace. City, Hillsborough co., W cen. Florida, 7 m. NE of Tampa; pop. (1970c) 7347.

Tem·ple·ton \'tem-pəl-tən\. 1 Industrial town, Worcester co., cen. Massachusetts, 14 m. W of Fitchburg; pop. (1970c) 5863.

2 Village, Hull co., SW Quebec, Canada, 5 m. NE of Hull; pop. (1970p) 3696.

Tem·po·al \tem-'pwäl\. Municipality, Veracruz state, Mexico, 70 m. SW of Tampico; pop. (1970p) 36,551; oil wells; sugarcane, tobacco, citrus fruit.

Tem·ryuk \ˌtem-rē-'ük\. Town, W Krasnodar Krai, Russian S.F.S.R., U.S.S.R., on SE shore of Sea of Azov 75 m. W of Krasnodar; pop. (1967e) 29,673; fisheries.

Te·mu·co \tä-'mü-(ˌ)kō\. City, ✻ of Cautín prov., S cen. Chile, ab. 100 m. NNE of Valdivia on the Cautín river; pop. (1966e) 91,298; trade center, esp. in grains, fruit, and timber; founded 1881.

Te·na \'tān-ə\. Town, ✻ of Napo prov., E cen. Ecuador, 70 m. SE of Quito; pop. (1970e) 1500.

Ten·a·fly \'ten-ə-ˌflī\. Residential borough, Bergen co., NE corner of New Jersey, 11 m. E of Paterson; pop. (1970c) 14,827.

Ten·a·kee Inlet \ˌten-ə-(ˌ)kē-\. Inlet opening into Chatham Strait, E coast of Chichagof I., SE Alaska.

Te·na·li \tā-'näl-ē\. City, cen. Andhra Pradesh, E India, near Krishna river 160 m. ESE of Hyderabad; pop. (1961c) 78,525.

Te·nan·cin·go \ˌtā-nän-'sēŋ-(ˌ)gō\ *or in full* **Tenancingo de De·go·lla·do** \-də-ˌdā-gō(l)-'yäd-(ˌ)ō\. Town, México state, cen. Mexico, 40 m. SW of Mexico City E of Nevada de Toluca; pop. (1960c) 9320.

Te·nan·go \tā-'näŋ-(ˌ)gō\ *or in full* **Tenango de Aris·ta** \-dā-ə-'rē-stə\. Town, México state, cen. Mexico, SW of Mexico City; pop. (1960c) 7685.

Te·na·ru \tā-'när-(ˌ)ü\. Small river, N coast of Guadalcanal I., SE Solomon Is., W Pacific Ocean; battle Aug. 21, 1942.

Te·nas·ser·im \tə-'nas-ə-rəm\. 1 River, Tenasserim div., Lower Burma; ab. 250 m. long; flows S and empties into Andaman Sea.

2 Ancient region, later a province, along W coast of Indochina Penin. See YANDABU.

3 Division of S Lower Burma. See table at BURMA.

Ten·by \'ten-bē\. Municipal borough and seaport, Pembrokeshire, SW Wales, on Carmarthen Bay; pop. (1971p) 4985; seaside resort and fishing center.

Tenda. See BRIGA-TENDA.

Ten Degree Channel. See ANDAMAN ISLANDS.

Tène, La. See LA TÈNE.

Tenedos. See BOZCAADA.

Ten·er·ife \ˌten-ə-'rē-fē, -'rif, -'rēf\ *or formerly* **Ten·er·iffe** \ˌten-ə-'rif, -'rēf\ *or anc.* **Pin·tu·ar·ia** \ˌpin-chə-'war-ē-ə, -'wer-\. Largest of the Canary Is. (*q.v.*), Santa Cruz de Tenerife prov., Spain, in Atlantic Ocean 40 m. WNW of Grand Canary I.; 795 sq. m.; pop. (1970p) 500,381; chief city Santa Cruz de Tenerife; precipitous coast; its highest point, the volcanic Pico de Teide (called also Peak of Tenerife), 12,198 ft.; fertile soil, producing palms, dates, grapes, cotton, sugar, grain, and fruits; earthquake 1704.

Tenerife, Peak of. See TEIDE, PICO DE.

Tenerife, Pico de. See TEIDE, PICO DE.

Teneriffe. See TENERIFE.

Teng. See NAM TENG.

Tengchow. See P'ENG-LAI.

T'eng–ch'ung *or* **Teng·chung** \'təŋ-'chu̇ŋ\; *formerly* **Teng·yueh** \'təŋ-yü-'e(r)\ *or* **Mo·mein** \'mō-'mān\. Town, W Yunnan prov., S China, 105 m. SW of Ta-li; opened for trade 1886, esp. with Burma; taken by Chinese Sept. 1944 after being held by Japanese for two years.

Ten·ge \'teŋ-(ˌ)gā\ *also* **Ten·ke** \-(ˌ)kā\. Town, Shaba prov., S Zaire, 120 m. NW of Lubumbashi; railroad junction point.

Teng·ger Mountains \ˌteŋ-gər-\. Mountain group, E Java, Indonesia, S of Pasuruan; highest point 9088 ft. Contains the Bromo (7848 ft.) and on N slope is health resort of Tosari; on S joined with Semeru (*q.v.*).

Ten·giz, Lake \-teŋ-'gēz\ *or* **Lake Ten·iz** \-teŋ-'ēz\. Lake, Kazakh S.S.R., U.S.S.R., SW of Tselinograd; has no outlet.

Tengri Khan. See KHAN-TENGRI.

Tengri Nor. See NA-MU LAKE.

Tengyueh. See T'ENG-CH'UNG.

Tenimbar Islands. See TANIMBAR ISLANDS.

Ten·ka·si \teŋ-'kä-sē\. Town, S Tamil Nadu, S India, ab. 90 m. SW of Madurai; pop. (1961c) 34,403.

Tenke. See TENGE.

Ten·ley·town \'ten-lē-ˌtau̇n\. Locality, NW suburb of Washington, D.C.; highest point 420 ft., in District of Columbia.

Ten·nes·see \ˌten-ə-'sē, 'ten-ə-ˌ\. 1 Navigable river, Tennessee, N Alabama, and W Kentucky; 652 m. long; formed by confluence of Holston and French Broad rivers near Knoxville, E Tennessee, flows SW into N Alabama, W across N Alabama, then N across W Tennessee and W Kentucky and empties into Ohio river. Steady flow of water and sharp descent in certain areas have made river valuable for waterpower project and creation of storage reservoirs. Muscle Shoals, a series of rapids ab. 37 m. long on S border of Lauderdale co., NW Alabama, was by 1890 known to have great potential waterpower; Wilson Dam at its W end near Florence, Alabama, was begun during World War I and Wheeler Dam, at its E end, much later; both became part of the Tennessee Valley Authority (*q.v.*) 1933.

2 Southeast central state of U.S.A., bounded on N by Kentucky and Virginia, on E by North Carolina, on S by Georgia, Alabama, and Mississippi, and on W by Arkansas and Missouri; 34th state in area, 42,244 sq. m. (land area 41,367 sq. m.); 17th state in population, (1970c) 3,924,164; ✻ Nashville; 16th state admitted to Union (1796).

Nickname: Volunteer State. *State flower:* Iris. *Motto:* Agriculture, Commerce. *Rivers:* Mississippi, forming W boundary; Tennessee (see 1, above). *High point:* Clingmans Dome 6643 ft., in Sevier co. *Chief products:* Tobacco, soybeans, corn; livestock; coal, cement, phosphate rock; manufacturing: chemicals, textiles, electrical machinery. *Chief cities:* Memphis, Nashville, Knoxville, Chattanooga, Jackson. See *Table of States* at UNITED STATES. Divided into the following 95 counties (for pronunciation of their names, see their individual entries):

NAME	LOCATION	AREA[1] (sq. m.)	POP. (1970c)	CO. SEAT
Anderson	E	335	60,300	Clinton
Bedford	S cen.	482	25,039	Shelbyville
Benton	W	392	12,126	Camden
Bledsoe	SE cen.	404	7,643	Pikeville
Blount[2]	E	576	63,744	Maryville
Bradley	SE	334	50,686	Cleveland
Campbell	N	451	26,045	Jacksboro
Cannon	cen.	271	8,467	Woodbury
Carroll	W	596	25,741	Huntingdon
Carter	NE	348	43,259	Elizabethton
Cheatham	NW cen.	305	13,199	Ashland City
Chester	W	285	9,927	Henderson
Claiborne	NE	444	19,420	Tazewell
Clay	N	232	6,624	Celina
Cocke[2]	E	424	25,283	Newport
Coffee	S cen.	434	32,572	Manchester
Crockett	W	269	14,402	Alamo

NAME	LOCATION	AREA[1] (sq. m.)	POP. (1970c)	CO. SEAT
Cumberland	E cen.	678	20,733	Crossville
Davidson	N cen.	527	447,877	Nashville
Decatur	W	337	9,457	Decaturville
De Kalb	cen.	278	11,151	Smithville
Dickson	NW cen.	485	21,977	Charlotte
Dyer	NW	529	30,427	Dyersburg
Fayette	SW	704	22,692	Somerville
Fentress	N	498	12,593	Jamestown
Franklin	S	553	27,289	Winchester
Gibson	NW	607	47,871	Trenton
Giles	S	619	22,138	Pulaski
Grainger	NE	282	13,948	Rutledge
Greene	NE	613	47,630	Greeneville
Grundy	S cen.	358	10,631	Altamont
Hamblen	NE	155	38,696	Morristown
Hamilton	SE	550	254,236	Chattanooga
Hancock	NE	230	6,719	Sneedville
Hardeman	SW	656	22,435	Bolivar
Hardin[3]	SW	587	18,212	Savannah
Hawkins	NE	480	33,757	Rogersville
Haywood	W	519	19,596	Brownsville
Henderson	W	515	17,360	Lexington
Henry	NW	567	23,749	Paris
Hickman	W cen.	611	12,096	Centerville
Houston	NW	201	5,853	Erin
Humphreys	W	530	13,560	Waverly
Jackson	N	323	8,141	Gainesboro
Jefferson	E	274	24,940	Dandridge
Johnson	NE corner	293	11,569	Mountain City
Knox	E	508	276,293	Knoxville
Lake	NW corner	167	8,091	Tiptonville
Lauderdale	W	477	20,271	Ripley
Lawrence	S	634	29,097	Lawrenceburg
Lewis	SW cen.	285	6,761	Hohenwald
Lincoln	S	580	24,318	Fayetteville
Loudon	E	237	24,266	Loudon
McMinn	SE	432	35,462	Athens
McNairy	SW	569	18,369	Selmer
Macon	N	304	12,315	Lafayette
Madison	W	560	65,774	Jackson
Marion	S	506	20.577	Jasper
Marshall	S cen.	377	17,319	Lewisburg
Maury	W cen.	614	44,028	Columbia
Meigs	SE	191	5,219	Decatur
Monroe	SE	660	23,475	Madisonville
Montgomery	N	539	62,721	Clarksville
Moore	S	124	3,568	Lynchburg
Morgan	NE cen.	539	13,619	Wartburg
Obion	NW	556	29,936	Union City
Overton	N	441	14,866	Livingston
Perry	W	411	5,238	Linden
Pickett	N	158	3,774	Byrdstown
Polk	SE corner	435	11,669	Benton
Putnam	N cen.	405	35,487	Cookeville
Rhea	E cen.	312	17,202	Dayton
Roane	E	350	38,881	Kingston
Robertson	N	476	29,102	Springfield
Rutherford	cen.	630	59,428	Murfreesboro
Scott	N	544	14,762	Huntsville
Sequatchie	SE cen.	273	6,331	Dunlap
Sevier[2]	E	597	28,241	Sevierville
Shelby	SW corner	755	722,111	Memphis
Smith	N cen.	323	12,509	Carthage
Stewart	NW	470	7,319	Dover
Sullivan	NE	413	127.329	Blountville
Sumner	N	534	56,284	Gallatin
Tipton	W	459	28,001	Covington
Trousdale	N	114	5,155	Hartsville
Unicoi	NE	185	15,254	Erwin
Union	NE	212	9,072	Maynardville
Van Buren	cen.	254	3,758	Spencer
Warren	cen.	439	26,972	McMinnville
Washington	NE	324	73,924	Jonesboro
Wayne	S	739	12,365	Waynesboro
Weakley	NW	576	28.827	Dresden
White	cen.	382	16,355	Sparta
Williamson	cen.	593	34,423	Franklin
Wilson	N cen.	568	36,999	Lebanon

[1] Area = land area.
[2] Includes part of Great Smoky Mountains National Park.
[3] Shiloh National Military Park in SW part of county.

History: Originally a part of the French Louisiana claim; included in charter of Carolina 1663; claim to region ceded by France to Great Britain 1763; region explored by Daniel Boone 1769; acknowledged by Great Britain as a part of United States 1783; temporary state of Franklin (*q.v.*) formed 1784; North Carolina relinquished claims 1790; Territory South of the Ohio, coterminous with Tennessee, organized 1790; admitted to Union June 1, 1796; passed ordinance of secession May 6, 1861; scene of battles in Civil War, notably Shiloh, Chattanooga, Stone River, Nashville; slavery abolished and ordinance of secession declared null and void 1865; first of seceding states to be reorganized and readmitted to Union (July 24, 1866).

Tennessee Pass. Mountain pass, Lake and Eagle cos., NW cen. Colorado, in the Park Range of the Rocky Mts.; 10,426 ft.; used since c. 1873; railroad.

Tennessee Valley Authority *or abbr.* **TVA.** A United States Government Administrative Agency, created to develop the Tennessee river system in the interests of transportation, flood control, and national defense and to generate and sell surplus electricity to avoid waste of waterpower; the region of the system includes a large part of E and W Tennessee, a large area in N Alabama, and smaller areas in W Kentucky, NE Mississippi, N Georgia, W North Carolina, and SW Virginia, and extends from Paducah, Kentucky, to the sources of tributaries of the Tennessee river in Virginia, North Carolina, and Georgia; its jurisdiction covers an area of ab. 39,000 sq. m.; elevations range from 300 ft. above sea level at Paducah to more than 6000 ft. in mountains of E Tennessee. This multiple-purpose water-control project includes a number of dams (see table, p. 1194), hydroelectric power stations, aluminum and nitrate plants, and dehydrators; recreational facilities. Established by Congressional Act May 18, 1933; first dam completed as early as 1912 (and with others subsequently purchased by the TVA) but most have been constructed since 1936.

Teno. See TANA.

Te·noch·ti·tlán \tā-ˌnòch-tē-ˈtlän\. Ancient name of Mexico City, which with Texcoco and Tlacopán formed the Aztec confederacy and became the capital of the Aztec empire. Founded 1325 in the marshes of Lake Texcoco and at the time of the arrival of the Spaniards was a large and powerful city; occupied by Cortés Nov. 8, 1519 but evacuated with heavy losses July 7, 1520; destroyed by Spaniards 1521.

Te·nom \tə-ˈnüm\. Town, W cen. Sabah, Malaysia, 60 m. S of Kota Kinabalu.

Te·nos \ˈtē-ˌnäs\ *or Gk.* **Tí·nos** \ˈtē-ˌnòs\. **1** Island, NE Cyclades, part of Cyclades dept., Greece; 79 sq. m.; produces much wine.
2 Chief town of island, on S coast.

Ten·ri \ˌten-ˈrē\. City, Nara prefecture, Honshū, Japan, 21 m. ESE of Nagoya; pop. (1970c) 57,020.

Ten·ryū \ˈten-rē-ˌü\. River, S cen. Honshū, Japan, 134 m. long; rises in Nagano prefecture, flows S into Pacific Ocean W of Suruga Bay.

Ten·sas \ˈten-ˌsò\. **1** River in Alabama. See TENSAW.
2 Parish in Louisiana. See table at LOUISIANA.

Tensas River *or* **Tensas Bayou** *also* **Ten·saw River** \ˌten-ˌsò-\. River, NE Louisiana; 250 m. long; flows from East Carroll parish S, uniting with Ouachita river to form the Black river.

Ten·saw *or* **Ten·sas** \ˈten-ˌsò\. Navigable river, SW Alabama; ab. 40 m. long; formed (with the Mobile river) by confluence of Tombigbee and Alabama rivers, flows S into Mobile Bay at Mobile.

Ten·sift \ten-ˈsift\. River, W Morocco, NW Africa; ab. 124 m. long; flows W through city of Marrakech into Atlantic Ocean.

Ten Thousand Islands. Group of many small islands, Gulf of Mexico, off SW Collier co., SW Florida.

Ten Thousand Smokes, Valley of. See VALLEY OF TEN THOUSAND SMOKES.

Tentyra. See DENDERA.

Te·o·cal·ti·che \ˌtā-ə-käl-ˈtē-chē\. Town, Jalisco state, W cen. Mexico, 70 m. NE of Guadalajara; munic. pop. (1970p) 29,330.

Te·ó·fi·lo Oto·ni \tā-ˌò-fi-ˌlü-ə-ˈtō-nē\ *also* **The·o·phi·lo Ot·to·ni** \tē-ˌò-fi-lü-ə-ˈtōn-ē\. City, E cen. Minas Gerais state, E Brazil, 230 m. NE of Belo Horizonte; munic. pop. (1968e) 134,476.

Te·os \ˈtē-ˌäs\. Ancient city, on coast of Asia Minor, S shore of peninsula of Smyrna; one of the 12 Ionian Cities; birthplace of Anacreon.

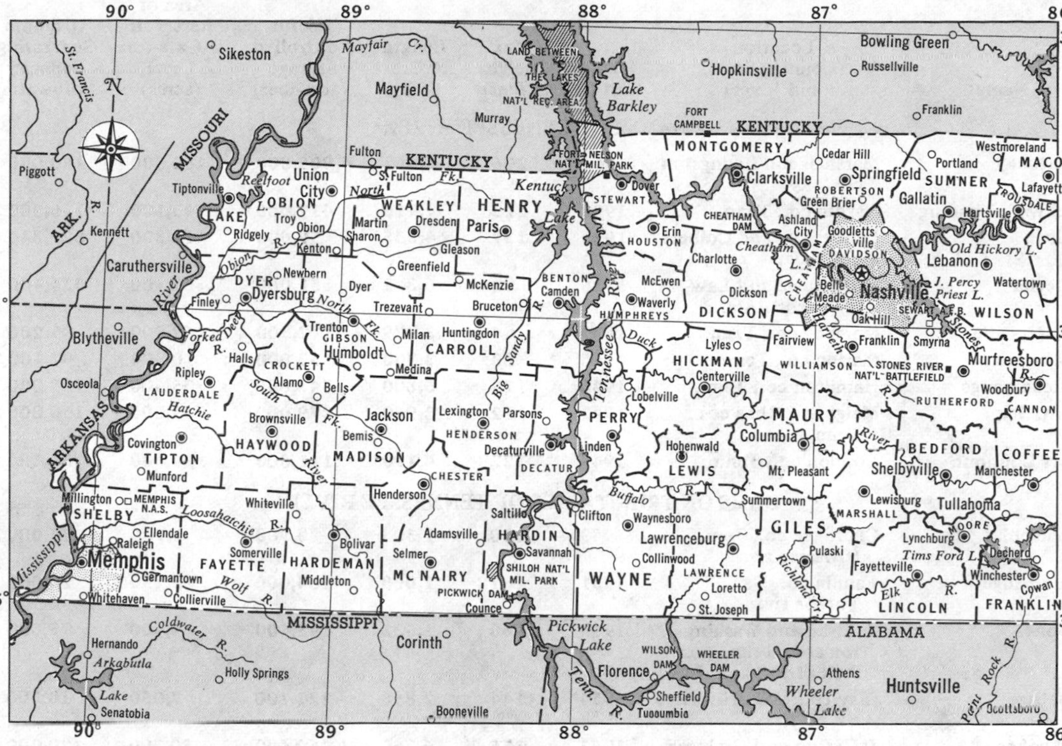
90°
89°
88°
87°
86°
37°
36°
35°
Sikeston
Mayfield
Mayfair Cr.
LAND BETWEEN THE LAKES NAT'L REC. AREA
Lake Barkley
Hopkinsville
Bowling Green
Russellville
Franklin
FORT CAMPBELL
KENTUCKY
MISSOURI
St. Francis
ARK.
Piggott
Kennett
Caruthersville
Blytheville
Osceola
Fulton
S. Fulton
Murray
FORT NELSON NAT'L MIL. PARK
Union City
Tiptonville
Reelfoot L.
LAKE
OBION
Troy
Obion
Ridgely
Kenton
WEAKLEY
Dresden
Martin
Sharon
Gleason
Greenfield
HENRY
Paris
Kentucky Lake
STEWART
Dover
MONTGOMERY
Clarksville
Cedar Hill
Springfield
ROBERTSON
Green Brier
Portland
SUMNER
Gallatin
Westmoreland
MACON
Lafayette
TROUSDALE
Hartsville
Old Hickory L.
Ashland City
Goodlettsville
DAVIDSON
CHEATHAM DAM
Cheatham L.
CHEATHAM
Nashville
Belle Meade
Oak Hill
Lebanon
J. Percy Priest L.
Watertown
WILSON
SEWART A.F.B.
Stones R.
Erin
HOUSTON
Charlotte
DICKSON
Dickson
McEwen
Waverly
HUMPHREYS
BENTON
Camden
McKenzie
Bruceton
DYER
Dyersburg
Newbern
Dyer
Trezevant
Obion R.
North Fk.
Finley
Forked Deer R.
River
Trenton
GIBSON
Humboldt
Milan
Huntingdon
CARROLL
Big Sandy R.
Tennessee River
Duck
Lyles
Fairview
Franklin
Smyrna
Murfreesboro
WILLIAMSON
STONES RIVER NAT'L BATTLEFIELD
HICKMAN
Centerville
RUTHERFORD
Woodbury
CANNON
Ripley
Halls
CROCKETT
Alamo
Bells
Medina
LAUDERDALE
South Fk.
Hatchie
Brownsville
HAYWOOD
Jackson
MADISON
Bemis
Lexington
Parsons
HENDERSON
Decaturville
PERRY
Lobelville
Linden
DECATUR
Hohenwald
LEWIS
Columbia
MAURY
Mt. Pleasant
BEDFORD
Shelbyville
COFFEE
Manchester
ARKANSAS
Covington
TIPTON
Munford
Millington
MEMPHIS N.A.S.
SHELBY
Loosahatchie R.
Whiteville
Ellendale
Raleigh
Memphis
Somerville
FAYETTE
Germantown
Collierville
Wolf R.
Whitehaven
Mississippi
HARDEMAN
Bolivar
Middleton
CHESTER
Henderson
Adamsville
Selmer
MC NAIRY
Saltillo
HARDIN
Savannah
SHILOH NAT'L MIL. PARK
PICKWICK DAM
Counce
Clifton
Buffalo
Waynesboro
WAYNE
Lawrenceburg
Collinwood
LAWRENCE
Loretto
St. Joseph
Summertown
GILES
Pulaski
Richland Cr.
MARSHALL
Lewisburg
Fayetteville
Elk R.
LINCOLN
Tullahoma
MOORE
Lynchburg
Tims Ford L.
Decherd
Winchester
Cowan
FRANKLIN
MISSISSIPPI
Hernando
Coldwater R.
Arkabutla Lake
Senatobia
Holly Springs
Corinth
Booneville
Pickwick Lake
Tenn. R.
Florence
WILSON DAM
WHEELER DAM
Sheffield
Tuscumbia
Athens
Wheeler Lake
ALABAMA
Huntsville
Paint Rock R.
Scottsboro

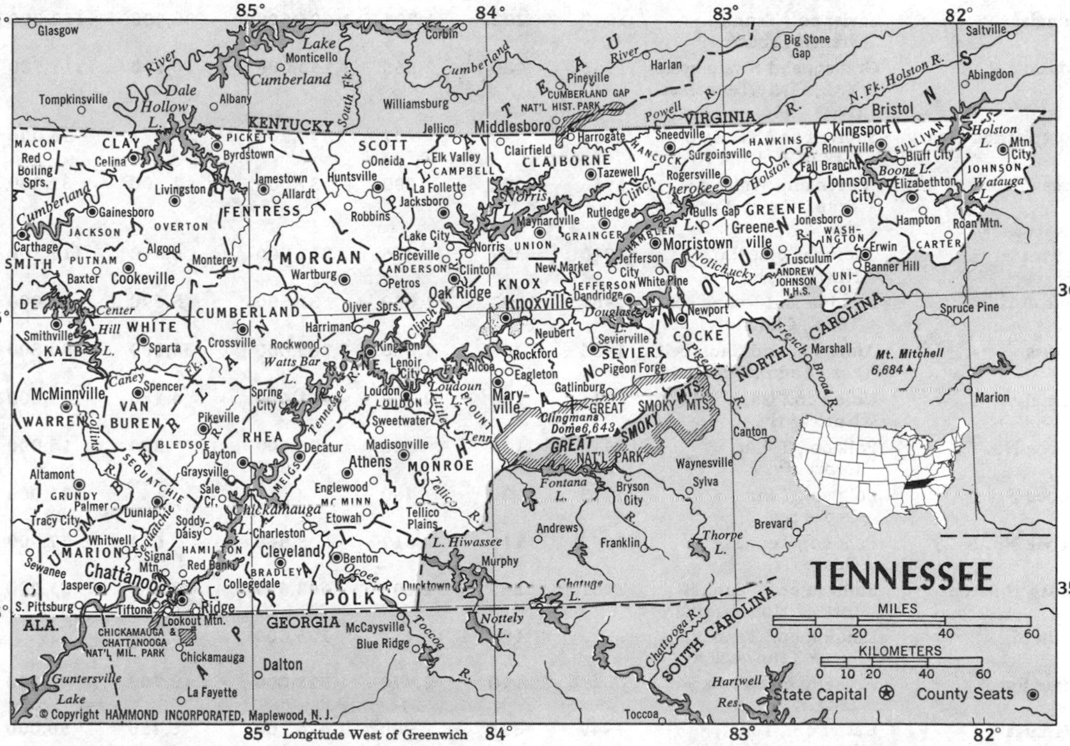
85°
84°
83°
82°
37°
36°
35°
Glasgow
Lake Cumberland
Monticello
Corbin
Saltville
Big Stone Gap
Harlan
Pineville
CUMBERLAND GAP NAT'L HIST. PARK
Abingdon
N. Fk. Holston R.
Tompkinsville
Dale Hollow L.
Albany
Williamsburg
Middlesboro
Powell R.
VIRGINIA
Bristol
Kingsport
KENTUCKY
Jellico
MACON
CLAY
PICKETT
Byrdstown
SCOTT
Oneida
Elk Valley
CAMPBELL
Clairfield
Harrogate
CLAIBORNE
HANCOCK
Sneedville
Surgoinsville
HAWKINS
Blountville
SULLIVAN
Bluff City
Holston L.
Mtn. City
JOHNSON
Red Boiling Sprs.
Celina
Jamestown
Allardt
Huntsville
La Follette
Jacksboro
Tazewell
Rogersville
Cherokee
Fall Branch
Boone L.
Johnson City
Elizabethton
Watauga L.
Livingston
Cumberland
Gainesboro
FENTRESS
Robbins
Norris L.
Maynardville
Rutledge
Clinch
Bulls Gap
GREENE
Greeneville
Jonesboro
WASHINGTON
Hampton
Roan Mtn.
JACKSON
OVERTON
Algood
Monterey
MORGAN
Lake City
Norris
UNION
GRAINGER
HAMBLEN
Morristown
Jefferson City
Tusculum
Erwin
CARTER
Carthage
SMITH
PUTNAM
Baxter
Cookeville
Wartburg
Briceville
ANDERSON
Petros
Clinton
KNOX
New Market
JEFFERSON
White Pine
Nolichucky
ANDREW JOHNSON N.H.S.
UNICOI
Banner Hill
Oliver Sprs.
Oak Ridge
Knoxville
Dandridge
Douglas L.
Newport
Spruce Pine
DE KALB
Center Hill L.
Smithville
WHITE
Sparta
CUMBERLAND
Crossville
Harriman
Rockwood
Kingston
ROANE
Lenoir City
Alcoa
Neubert
Rockford
Sevierville
SEVIER
Pigeon Forge
COCKE
Marshall
French Broad R.
NORTH CAROLINA
Mt. Mitchell 6,684
Caney Fk.
Watts Bar L.
Eagleton
Loudon
LOUDON
Maryville
BLOUNT
Gatlinburg
GREAT SMOKY MTS.
McMinnville
WARREN
Spencer
VAN BUREN
Spring City
Pikeville
RHEA
Sweetwater
Little Tenn.
Clingmans Dome 6,643
GREAT SMOKY NAT'L PARK
Canton
Marion
Collins R.
BLEDSOE
Dayton
MEIGS
Decatur
Madisonville
Athens
MONROE
Waynesville
Sylva
Altamont
GRUNDY
Palmer
SEQUATCHIE
Graysville
Sale Cr.
Englewood
MC MINN
Etowah
Tellico Plains
Tellico R.
Fontana L.
Bryson City
Tracy City
Dunlap
Soddy-Daisy
Chickamauga L.
Andrews
Franklin
Thorpe L.
Brevard
Whitwell
MARION
Sewanee
Signal Mtn.
HAMILTON
Charleston
Cleveland
BRADLEY
Red Bank
Benton
L. Hiwassee
Murphy
Jasper
Chattanooga
Collegedale
Ocoee R.
Ducktown
Chatuge L.
S. Pittsburg
Tiftona
Ridge
POLK
Nottely L.
ALA.
Lookout Mtn.
GEORGIA
McCaysville
Blue Ridge
Toccoa R.
Chattooga R.
SOUTH CAROLINA
CHICKAMAUGA & CHATTANOOGA NAT'L MIL. PARK
Chickamauga
Dalton
Guntersville Lake
La Fayette
Toccoa
Hartwell Res.
TENNESSEE
MILES
0
10
20
40
60
KILOMETERS
0
10
20
40
60
State Capital
County Seats
© Copyright HAMMOND INCORPORATED, Maplewood, N. J.
Longitude West of Greenwich

Name[1]	Location (County, State, and River)	Year of First Use	Max. Height (feet)	Length of Crest (feet)	Useful Controlled Storage (acre-feet)	Area of Reservoir at Gate-top Level (acres)	Ultimate Generating Capacity (kilowatts)
	DAMS ON TENNESSEE RIVER[2]						
Kentucky	Marshall and Livingston cos., Ky.	1944	206	8,422	4,008,000	160,300	160,000
Pickwick Landing	Hardin co., Tenn.	1938	113	7,715	417,000	43,100	216,000
Wilson	Lauderdale and Colbert cos., Ala.	1925	137	4,535	59,000	15,500	629,840
Wheeler	Lauderdale and Lawrence cos., Ala.	1936	72	6,342	351,000	67,100	356,400
Guntersville	Marshall co., Tenn.	1939	94	3,979	172,300	67,900	97,200
Nickajack	Marion co., Tenn.	1968	83	3,700	33,000	10,900	97,200
Chickamauga	Hamilton co., Tenn.	1940	129	5,800	347,000	35,400	108,000
Watts Bar	Meigs and Rhea cos., Tenn.	1942	112	2,960	379,000	39,000	150,000
Fort Loudoun	Loudon co., Tenn.	1943	122	4,190	111,000	14,600	131,190
	DAMS ON TRIBUTARIES OF TENNESSEE RIVER[3]						
Apalachia	Cherokee co., Tenn., Hiwassee riv.	1943	150	1,308	8,900	1,100	75,000
Blue Ridge	Fannin co., Ga., Toccoa riv.	1931	167	1,000	184,000	3,290	20,000
Boone	Sullivan and Washington cos., Tenn., S fork of Holston riv.	1953	160	1,532	148,400	4,400	75,000
Chatuge	Clay co., N.C., Hiwassee riv.	1954	144	2,850	222,100	7,050	10,000
Cherokee	Jeffersøn and Grainger cos., Tenn., Holston riv.	1942	175	6,760	1,460,400	30,300	120,000
Douglas	Sevier co., Tenn., French Broad riv.	1943	202	1,705	1,405,500	30,400	112,000
Fontana	Graham and Swain cos., N.C., Little Tennessee riv.	1945	480	2,365	1,153,000	10,640	211,500
Fort Patrick Henry	Sullivan co., Tenn., S fork of Holston riv.	1953	95	737	4,200	872	36,000
Great Falls	Warren and White cos., Tenn., Caney Fork riv.	1916	92	800	37,000	2,100	31,860
Hiwassee	Cherokee co., N.C., Hiwassee riv.	1940	307	1,376	362,200	6,090	117,100
Melton Hill	Loudon and Roane cos., Tenn., Clinch riv.	1964	103	1,020	31,500	5,690	72,000
Norris	Anderson and Campbell cos., Tenn., Clinch riv.	1936	265	1,860	2,265,000	34,200	100,800
Nottely	Union co., Ga., Nottely riv.	1956	184	2,300	161,600	4,180	15,000
Ocoee No. 1	Polk co., Tenn., Ocoee riv.	1912	135	840	33,800	1,890	18,000
Ocoee No. 2	Polk co., Tenn., Ocoee riv.	1913	30	450	....	....	21,000
Ocoee No. 3	Polk co., Tenn., Ocoee riv.	1943	110	612	3,860	621	27,000
South Holston	Sullivan co., Tenn., S fork of Holston riv.	1951	285	1,600	642,600	7,580	35,000
Tellico[4]	Loudon co., Tenn., Little Tennessee riv.	....	108	3,238	126,000	16,500	....
Tims Ford[4]	Franklin co., Tenn., Elk riv.	....	170	1,470	323,000	10,700	45,000
Watauga	Carter co., Tenn., Watauga riv.	1949	318	900	624,700	6,430	50,000

[1] The same name often applies to the reservoir or lake.
[2] Listed in the order of their location from the mouth of the Tennessee to its source near Knoxville.
[3] Listed in alphabetical order.
[4] Under construction.

Te·o·ti·hua·cán \ˌtā-ə-ˌtē-wä-ˈkän\ *or* **San Juan Teotihuacán** \san-ˌ(h)wän-\. Town, México state, cen. Mexico, 30 m. NE of Mexico City; munic. pop. (1970p) 15,704; site of famous Toltec ruins, including the Pyramid of the Sun (216 ft. high) with terraced sides and stairs leading to the summit, the Pyramid of the Moon (ab. 150 ft. high), the Temple of Tlaloc (rain-god) and of Quetzalcoatl (lord of the air and wind). See CHOLULA.

Te·o·ti·tlán del Ca·mi·no \ˌtā-ō-tē-ˌtlän-del-kə-ˈmē-(ˌ)nō\. Municipality, Oaxaca state, Mexico, 75 m. NNW of Oaxaca; pop. (1970p) 103,209; handwoven fabrics; cattle raising; wheat, beans, figs.

Te·pa·ti·tlán \ˌtep-ə-tē-ˈtlän\ *or in full* **Tepatitlán de Mo·re·los** \-dā-mə-ˈrel-əs\. Town, Jalisco state, W cen. Mexico, 43 m. ENE of Guadalajara; munic. pop. (1970p) 53,683.

Te·pe·a·ca \ˌtāp-ā-ˈäk-ə\. Municipality, Puebla state, Mexico, 25 m. ESE of Puebla; pop. (1970p) 26,334; marble quarries; agriculture.

Te·pe·a·pul·co \ˌtā-pā-ə-ˈpül-(ˌ)kō\. Municipality, Hidalgo state, Mexico, 30 m. SE of Pachuca; pop. (1970p) 26,254; 16th cent. church; settled by Franciscans 1530.

Te·pe·ji del Río \te-ˌpā-hē-del-ˈrē-(ˌ)ō\. Town, Hidalgo state, cen. Mexico; munic. pop. (1970p) 24,107.

Te·pe·le·në \ˌtāp-ə-ˈlā-nə\. 1 Province of S Albania. See table at ALBANIA.

2 Town, its ✱, on Vijosë river ab. 30 m. SE of Vlorë; pop. (1967e) 3410; scene of fighting 1940–41.

Te·pex·pán \ˌtep-i-ˈspän\. Village, NE México state, cen. Mexico; near Texcoco; site of discovery 1947 of 11,000–12,000-year-old skeleton ("Tepexpán man"), probably the oldest human remains found in Western Hemisphere.

Te·pic \tā-ˈpēk\. Town, ✱ of Nayarit state, W Mexico, near W coast 110 m. NW of Guadalajara; munic. pop. (1970p) 110,402.

Te·pli·ce–Ša·nov \ˌtep-lət-ˌsā-ˈshan-ˌóf\ *or Ger.* **Tep·litz–Schö·nau** \ˌtep-ləts-ˈshə(r)n-ˌau̇\. City, Czech S.R., W Czechoslovakia, in the Erzgebirge 56 m. NNW of Prague; pop. (1968e) 51,935; health resort with warm mineral springs; scene of formation (Treaty of Teplitz Sept. 9, 1813) of 6th coalition against Napoleon, including Prussia, Russia, Sweden, Great Britain, Austria.

Te·quen·da·ma Falls \ˌtā-kən-ˈdäm-ə-\. Waterfall in the Bogotá river (a tributary of the Magdalena) 10 m. S of the city of Bogotá, Colombia; 427 ft. high.

Teques, Los. See LOS TEQUES.

Te·ques·ta \tē-ˈkwes-tə\. Village, Palm Beach co., SE Florida; pop. (1970c) 2642.

Te·ra·mo \ˈter-ə-ˌmō\. 1 Province of Abruzzi, cen. Italy. See table at ITALY.

2 *or anc.* **In·ter·am·na** \ˌint-ə-ˈram-nə\. Commune, its ✱, 82 m. NE of Rome; pop. (1968e) 46,395; ships grain; ceramics; 12th–14th cent. cathedral, remains of Roman theater. Under Byzantines in early Middle Ages; came under Norman kingdom of Naples c. 1155.

Ter·cei·ra \tər-ˈsir-ə, -ˈser-\. Island, cen. Azores, in the district of Angra do Heroísmo; 153 sq. m.; pop. (1960c) 72,485; ✱ Angra do Heroísmo; site of Lajes Air Force Base (U.S.).

Ter·ce·ro \ter-ˈse(ə)r-(ˌ)ō\. River, Córdoba prov., cen. Argentina; unites with Saladillo river to form Carcarañá river.

Te·rek \ˈter-ək\. River, Russian S.F.S.R., U.S.S.R., N of Caucasus Mts.; 373 m. long; rises in Georgian S.S.R. at the base of Mt. Kazbek and flows N through Daryal Pass, turns E near Nalchik through steppe region to a wide delta on NW shore of Caspian Sea; some of its delta streams are dry during part of the year.

Terengganu. See TRENGGANU.

Te·re·si·na *also* **The·re·zi·na** \ˌter-ə-ˈzē-nə\. City, ✱ of Piauí state, NE Brazil, on Parnaíba river 170 m. WSW of Parnaíba; munic. pop. (1970p) 230,168; ships livestock, hides, rice; produces textiles, lumber, soap, sugar, rum; founded 1852.

Te·re·só·po·lis \ˌtā-rə-ˈzó-pu̇-ˌlēs\. City, Rio de Janeiro state, SE Brazil; munic. pop. (1968e) 69,636; a mountain resort (3000 ft.) near Petrópolis, N of Rio de Janeiro.

Te·res·sa \tə-ˈres-ə\. One of the Nicobar Is. (*q.v.*).

Terglou. See TRIGLAV.

Ter·liz·zi \ter-ˈlēt-sē\. Commune, Bari prov., Apulia, SE Italy, 16 m. W of Bari; pop. (1968e) 21,863.

Ter·mez \ter-ˈmez\. Town, ✱ of Surkhandarya Oblast, Uzbek S.S.R., U.S.S.R., on N bank of the Amu Darya, on the Afghan border 160 m. S of Samarkand; pop. (1970p) 35,000; cotton gins; dates from 10th cent.

Ter·mi·ni Ime·re·se \ˌter-mə-nē-ˌē-mə-ˈrā-sā\ *or anc.* **Thermae Him·er·en·ses** \ˌthər-mē-ˌhim-ə-ˈren-ˌsēz\. Seaport, Palermo prov., Sicily, Italy, on N coast 22 m. ESE of Palermo; pop. (1968e) 24,586; tourism; citrus fruit, olives; mineral springs; remains of ancient Roman theater; 17th cent. cathedral; convent; museum. Near ancient Himera (*q.v.*).

Tér·mi·nos, La·gu·na de \lə-ˌgü-nə-dā-ˈter-mi-ˌnōs\. Inlet, SE Bay of Campeche, on shore of state of Campeche, SE Mexico; enclosed by Carmen I.

Terminus. See ATLANTA 1.

Ter·mo·li \ˈter-mə-(ˌ)lē\. Port, Campobasso prov., S Molise, cen. Italy, on the Adriatic Sea; pop. (1968e) 13,506; 13th cent. cathedral, castle.

Termonde. See DENDERMONDE.

Ter·na·te \tər-ˈnät-ē\. 1 Small island, Moluccas, Indonesia, off the W coast of Halmahera I.; 41 sq. m.; pop. (1957e) 33,964. Consists mainly of a conical volcano 5627 ft. high, with three peaks; has suffered many eruptions in the last four centuries, the severest in 1763 and 1840; thickly forested; has fertile soil; produces spices, coffee, fruit. In 16th cent. a sultanate; settled by Portuguese 1521 who were expelled 1574; alliance bet. sultan and the Dutch 1607; sultan extended his territory by conquests in the Moluccas and Celebes, but conflicts with Dutch began 1635; finally completely subjected to Dutch 1683; occupied by Japanese 1942–45. See AMBON 3.

2 Town on S side of island at foot of volcano; pop. (1961c) 24,287; port of call for steamers.

3 Municipality, on NW coast of Cavite prov., Luzon, Phil., 15 m. SW of City of Cavite; pop. (1969e) 7500; terminus of coastal road.

Ter·neu·zen \ter-ˈnə-zən\ *also* **Neu·zen** \ˈnə-zən\. Commune, Zeeland prov., SW Netherlands, on S shore of Schelde estuary ab. 25 m. WNW of Antwerp; pop. (1970e) 22,014.

Ter·ni \ˈter-nē\. 1 Province of Umbria, cen. Italy. See table at ITALY.

2 *or anc.* **In·ter·am·na Na·hars** \ˌint-ər-ˌam-nə-ˈnā-ˌhärz\. Commune, its ✱, on Nera river 49 m. NE of Rome; pop. (1968e) 104,954; iron and steel, electrical equipment, machinery, textiles, soap, firearms, brandy, leather goods, pasta; 6th cent. cathedral (rebuilt 17th cent.) and other churches; waterfalls (Cascata delle Marmore 650 ft.) nearby furnish hydroelectric power. Destroyed by Totila 546 A.D., Narses 553, Lombards 755, Archbishop Christian of Mainz 1174; joined Papal States 14th cent.

Ter·no·pol \ter-ˈnō-pəl\ *also* **Tar·no·pol** \tär-ˈnó-ˌpól\. City, ✱ of Ternopol Oblast, Ukrainian S.S.R., U.S.S.R., 70 m. ESE of Lvov; pop. (1970p) 85,000; concrete and leather products, canned foods, footwear; founded 1540; passed to Austria 1772 and was annexed from Poland by U.S.S.R. 1939; largely destroyed in World War II.

Ternopol Oblast \-ˈō-bləst, -ˌblast\. Subdivision of the Ukrainian S.S.R., U.S.S.R., in W part N of the Dniester river; 5328 sq. m.; pop. (1970p) 1,153,000; ✱ Ternopol. Economy almost completely agricultural (grain, sugar beets, hops, tobacco, sunflowers, potatoes); formed 1939 from territory annexed from Poland.

Ter·pe·ni·ya Bay \tər-ˌpā-nē-(y)ə-\ *or formerly* **Ta·rai·ka Bay** \tə-ˌrī-kə-\. Large inlet, E coast of S Sakhalin I., E Russian S.F.S.R., U.S.S.R.

Ter·ra·ci·na \ˌter-ə-'chē-nə\; *anc.* **Anx·ur** \'aŋ(k)-sər\ *or later* **Tar·ra·ci·na** \ˌtar-ə-'sī-nə\. Seaport, Latina prov., Latium, cen. Italy, just SE of Agro Pontino and W of Gaeta; pop. (1968e) 32,729; ships grapes; fishing, food processing; 11th cent. cathedral, extensive Roman remains. A Volscian town which came under Rome c. 400 B.C.; important during 1st and 2d cents. A.D.

Terranova Bracciolini. See TERRANUOVA BRACCIOLINI.

Terranova di Sibari. See SYBARIS.

Terranova di Sicilia. See GELA.

Ter·ra No·va National Park \ˌter-ə-'nō-və-\. See CANADA, *National Parks.*

Terranova Pausania. See OLBIA 1.

Ter·ra·nuo·va Brac·cio·li·ni \ˌter-ə-'nwȯ-və-ˌbräch-ə-'lē-nē\ *also* **Ter·ra·no·va Bracciolini** \ˌter-ə-'nȯ-və-\. Commune, Arezzo prov., Tuscany, W Italy, 16 m. WNW of Arezzo; pop. (1968e) 9336.

Terre Adélie. See ADÉLIE COAST.

Terre·bonne \'ter-ə-ˌbän\. 1 Bayou, Terrebonne parish, SE Louisiana; flows S into Terrebonne Bay.

2 Parish in Louisiana. See table at LOUISIANA.

3 County, Quebec, Canada. See table at QUEBEC.

4 Town, Terrebonne co., Quebec, Canada, on left bank of the Rivière des Mille Îles 14 m. N of Montreal; pop. (1971p) 9208; Séminaire des Pères du Saint-Sacrement (1902); founded 1727.

Terrebonne Bay. Inlet of Gulf of Mexico, SE coast of Terrebonne parish, SE Louisiana.

Ter·re Haute \ˌter-ə-'hōt, ˌter-ē-, -'hət, -'hȯt\. City, ⊗ of Vigo co., W Indiana, on Wabash river 67 m. WSW of Indianapolis; pop. (1970c) 70,335; pharmaceuticals, plastics, glass, chemicals, clothing, foundry products; Saint Mary-of-the-Woods Coll. (1840), Indiana State Univ. (1865), Rose Polytechnic Institute (1874); platted 1816; incorporated as town 1832, as city 1853.

Ter·rel, Mount \-'ter-əl\. Peak, Sevier co., cen. Utah; 11,530 ft.

Ter·rell \'ter-əl\. 1 Name of counties in two states of the U.S. See tables at GEORGIA and TEXAS.

2 Industrial city, Kaufman co., NE Texas, 27 m. E of Dallas; pop. (1970c) 14,182; footwear, lumber, flour, cottonseed oil; agriculture.

Terrell Hills. City, Bexar co., S cen. Texas, NE of San Antonio; pop. (1970c) 5225.

Terre·noire \'ter-'nwär\. Town, Loire dept., SE cen. France, just E of Saint-Étienne; pop. (1962c) 7590.

Terres Australes et Antarctiques françaises. See FRENCH SOUTHERN AND ANTARCTIC TERRITORIES.

Terres Mauvaises. See BAD LANDS.

Territoire française des Afars et des Issas. See AFARS AND ISSAS.

Territorios Españoles del Golfo de Guinea. See EQUATORIAL GUINEA.

Territory of Papua. See PAPUA, TERRITORY OF.

Territory of Papua and New Guinea. See PAPUA NEW GUINEA.

Ter·ror, Mount \-'ter-ər\. 1 Peak, Skagit co., NW Washington; 8360 ft.

2 Extinct volcano, Ross I. in Ross Sea, Antarctica, at 77°31′S, 168°33′E; 10,750 ft.

Ter·ry \'ter-ē\. 1 County in Texas. See table at TEXAS.

2 City, ⊗ of Prairie co., E Montana; pop. (1970c) 870.

Terry Peak. Mountain, Lawrence co., W South Dakota; 7064 ft.

Ter·schel·ling \tər-'skel-iŋ\. Dutch island, one of the West Frisian Is., bet. Vlieland I. and Ameland I. off NW Friesland prov.; 16 m. long; 41 sq. m.; administratively part of North Holland prov.

Ter·try \te(ə)r-'trē\ *or formerly* **Tes·try** \tes-'trē\. Village, Somme dept., N France; pop. (1962c) 166; battle 687 by which Pepin of Herstal (Pepin II) became ruler of all the Franks.

Te·ruel \ˌter-ə-'wel\. 1 Province of E Spain. See table at SPAIN.

2 Commune, its ✱, 138 m. E of Madrid; pop. (1970p) 21,638; manufactures brandies, leather, soap, flour, woolens; 16th cent. Gothic cathedral, 16th cent. aqueduct. Conquered by Romans 196 B.C.; under Moorish rule; reconquered by Alfonso II of Aragon 1171; became city 1347; attacked by Carlists 1874.

Ter·vue·ren *or* **Ter·vu·ren** \ˌter-vyü-'ren\. Commune, Brabant prov., cen. Belgium, 10 m. E of Brussels; pop. (1969e) 10,595; royal park, 506 acres.

Te·schen \'tesh-ən\. 1 Former duchy, E Austrian Silesia; ab. 2820 sq. m.; founded 1290.

2 Region, part of former duchy; in dispute after World War I bet. Poland and Czechoslovakia; divided July 1920 ab. equally bet. the two; ab. 850 sq. m.; larger part including the E part of the city became Polish (see CIESZYN); smaller part on W bank of Olsa river (Český Těšín) remained in Czechoslovakia. During Czech crisis of 1938 S part demanded by Poland and occupied Oct. 2, adding 419 sq. m. to Poland. Overrun by German army Sept. 1939; Czech district and town restored after end of World War II.

3 Town, ✱ of former duchy, divided by Olsa river into (Czech) Český Těšín and (Polish) Cieszyn (*qq.v.*).

Te·shek·puk Lake \tə-'shek-ˌpük-\. Lake, N Alaska, ab. 80 m. SE of Point Barrow; 315 sq. m.

Teshi Lumpo. See JIH-K'A-TSE.

Te·shio \'tesh-ē-ˌō\. River, N Hokkaidō, Japan; 192 m. long; flows NW into the Sea of Japan.

Těšín. See CIESZYN.

Těšín Český. See ČESKÝ TĚŠÍN.

Te·sis·sat Falls \ˌtes-ə-ˌsät-\. Falls in Blue Nile, Ethiopia, ab. 20 m. SE of Lake Tana; 140 ft. high.

Tes·lin Lake \ˌtez-lən-\. Long, narrow lake, NW Canada, lying across the Yukon-British Columbia border; 142 sq. m.; alt. 2250 ft.; regarded as a source of the Yukon river; its outlet is **Teslin River,** ab. 100 m. long, a tributary of the Lewes.

Tessin. See TICINO 2.

Test \'test\. River, Hampshire, S England. See SOUTHAMPTON WATER.

Testa del Gargano. See GARGANO, MOUNT.

Teste, La. See LA TESTE.

Testigos, Los. See LOS TESTIGOS.

Testry. See TERTRY.

Te·te \'tāt-ə\. 1 District, W Mozambique, SE Africa; 38,886 sq. m.; pop. (1970p) 492,233; ✱ Tete.

2 Town, its ✱, on the Zambesi river, 270 m. NNW of Beira; pop. (1960p) 38,962.

Te·te·rev \'tet-ə-ˌref, -ˌrev\. River, W Ukrainian S.S.R., U.S.S.R.; ab. 220 m. long; rises W of Berdichev and flows NE to the Dnieper N of Kiev.

Te·ti·pa·ri \ˌtāt-ə-'pär-ē\. Small island, New Georgia Is., cen. Solomon Is., W Pacific, SE of Rendova.

Tet·nuld \'tet-nəld\. Mountain, W cen. Caucasus range, on the border of the Georgian S.S.R., U.S.S.R., near the source of the Inguri river; 15,920 ft.

Te·ton \'tē-ˌtän\. 1 River, NW cen. Montana; ab. 160 m. long; rises in W Teton co., flows E into Missouri river.

2 Name of counties in three states of the U.S. See tables at IDAHO, MONTANA, WYOMING.

Teton Range. Range, Teton co., NW Wyoming, extending N into Yellowstone National Park; S portion, which includes Grand Teton, highest peak (13,766 ft.) in the range, is in Grand Teton National Park.

Té·touan *or* **Te·tuán** \tā-'twän, tə-\. City, N Morocco, 25 m. S of Ceuta; pop. (1960c) 101,352; handicrafts, textiles, soap, building materials; ships livestock and agricultural products. Founded in 14th cent.; capital of former Spanish Morocco.

Te·to·vo \'tet-ə-(,)vō\ *or Turk.* **Kal·kan·de·len** \,käl-kän-də-'len\. City, Macedonia, S Yugoslavia, ab. 25 m. W of Skopje; pop. (1965e) 29,000.

Te·trar·chy \'te-,trär-kē, 'tē-\. The district or jurisdiction of a tetrarch; literally "the fourth part of a province"; in the Roman Empire esp.: (1) **Tetrarchy of He·rod An·ti·pas** \-,her-əd-'ant-ə-,pas\ (4 B.C.–40 A.D.), Galilee and Peraea; (2) **Tetrarchy of Phil·ip** \-'fil-əp\ (4 B.C.–34 A.D.), Ituraea, Trachonitis, Batanaea, etc.; these two tetrarchies reunited 41–44 A.D. under Herod Agrippa; (3) **Tetrarchy of Ly·sa·ni·as** \-lī-'sā-nē-əs\ (c. 29 A.D.), Abilene in SW Syria (*Luke* iii. 1).

Tetschen. See DĚČIN.

Tetuán. See TÉTOUAN.

Tetulia. See GANGES DELTA.

Teu·co \'tā-ü-(,)kō\. River, the middle course of the Bermejo, N Argentina; ab. 350 m. long; flows SE forming part of boundary bet. Formosa and Chaco provinces.

Teu·to·burg Forest \,t(y)üt-ə-,bərg-\ *or Ger.* **Teu·to·bur·ger Wald** \'tȯit-ə-,bu̇r-gər-,vält\. Range of hills, Lower Saxony and North Rhine-Westphalia, West Germany, S of Osnabrück; highest point ab. 1530 ft. Possibly scene of battle 9 A.D. in which Varus and Roman legions were defeated by Arminius and German tribes.

Tevere. See TIBER.

Teverone. See ANIENE.

Teverya. See TIBERIAS.

Te·vi·ot \'tē-vē-ət, 'tev-ē-\. River, Roxburgh co., SE Scotland; 37 m. long; flows NE into the Tweed; its valley is called **Te·vi·ot·dale** \-,dāl\.

Te Wae·wae Bay \ta-'wī-(,)wī-\. Bay, S coast of South I., New Zealand; receives Waiau river.

Tewkes·bury \'t(y)üks-,ber-ē, -b(ə-)rē\. Municipal borough, Gloucestershire, SW cen. England, at confluence of the Avon and the Severn; pop. (1971p) 8742; scene of battle May 3, 1471, during the Wars of the Roses, in which Edward IV's Yorkists defeated the Lancastrian forces of Queen Margaret.

Tewks·bury \'tu̇ks-b(ə-)rē\. Town, Middlesex co., NE Massachusetts, 5 m. SE of Lowell; pop. (1970c) 22,755.

Tex·ada Island \tek-,sad-ə-\. Island, cen. Strait of Georgia, bet. Vancouver I. and the British Columbia mainland, SW Canada; 30 m. long, 117 sq. m.

Tex·ar·kana \,tek-sär-'kan-ə, ,tek-sər-\. Twin cities on Arkansas-Texas border: (1) city, ⊗ of Miller co., SW corner of Arkansas, ab. 137 m. SW of Little Rock; pop. (1970c) 21,682; (2) city, Bowie co., NE Texas, 30 m. SE of Oklahoma border; pop. (1970c) 30,497. Twin cities produce lumber, railroad cars, missile components, dairy products, bricks; railroad shops, oil wells.

Tex·as \'tek-səs, -siz\. 1 A southwestern state of U.S.A., bounded on N by Oklahoma, on E by Arkansas and Louisiana, on SE and S by Gulf of Mexico and Mexican state of Tamaulipas, on SW and W by Mexican states of Coahuila and Chihuahua and by New Mexico; 2d state in area, 267,339 sq. m. (land area 262,970 sq. m.); 4th state in population, (1970c) 11,196,730; ✱ Austin; 28th state admitted to Union (1845). *Nickname:* Lone Star State. *State flower:* Bluebonnet. *Motto:* Friendship. *Rivers:* Red, forming N and NE boundary (with Oklahoma) and a boundary with Arkansas for a few miles; Trinity, in E region, flowing SE into Galveston Bay; Brazos, cen. region, flowing SE into Gulf of Mexico; Colorado, cen. region, flowing SE into Matagorda Bay; Rio Grande, forming S and SW boundaries. *Highest point:* Guadalupe Peak 8751 ft., in Culberson co. *Chief products:* Cotton, rice, sorghum grain, wheat; livestock; oil, natural gas, sulfur; manufacturing: chemicals, transportation equipment, primary metals; food processing. *Chief cities:* Houston, Dallas, San Antonio, Fort Worth, El Paso, Austin, Corpus Christi. See *Table of States* at UNITED STATES. Divided into the following 254 counties (for pronunciation of their names, see their individual entries):

NAME	LOCATION	AREA[1] (sq. m.)	POP. (1970c)	CO. SEAT
Anderson	E	1,072	27,789	Palestine
Andrews	NW	1,504	10,372	Andrews
Angelina	E	804	49,349	Lufkin
Aransas	S; coastal	271	8,902	Rockport
Archer	N	913	5,759	Archer City
Armstrong	NW	907	1,895	Claude
Atascosa	S	1,206	18,696	Jourdanton
Austin	SE cen.	663	13,831	Bellville
Bailey	NW	835	8,487	Muleshoe
Bandera	SW cen.	763	4,747	Bandera
Bastrop	S cen.	890	17,297	Bastrop
Baylor	N	875	5,221	Seymour
Bee	S	842	22,737	Beeville
Bell	cen.	1,066	124,483	Belton
Bexar	S cen.	1,246	830,460	San Antonio
Blanco	cen.	719	3,567	Johnson City
Borden	NW	907	888	Gail
Bosque	cen.	990	10,966	Meridian
Bowie	NE	891	67,813	Boston
Brazoria	SE; coastal	1,423	108,312	Angleton
Brazos	E cen.	586	57,978	Bryan
Brewster[2]	W	6,204	7,780	Alpine
Briscoe	NW	874	2,794	Silverton
Brooks	S	904	8,005	Falfurrias
Brown	cen.	950	25,877	Brownwood
Burleson	E cen.	683	9,999	Caldwell
Burnet	cen.	996	11,420	Burnet
Caldwell	S cen.	544	21,178	Lockhart
Calhoun	S; coastal	527	17,831	Port Lavaca
Callahan	N cen.	857	8,205	Baird
Cameron	S; coastal	896	140,368	Brownsville
Camp	NE	192	8,005	Pittsburg
Carson	NW	900	6,358	Panhandle
Cass	NE	941	24,133	Linden
Castro	NW	880	10,394	Dimmitt
Chambers	SE; on Galveston Bay	616	12,187	Anahuac
Cherokee	E	1,049	32,008	Rusk
Childress	NW	699	6,605	Childress
Clay	N	1,102	8,079	Henrietta
Cochran	NW	783	5,326	Morton
Coke	W cen.	911	3,087	Robert Lee
Coleman	cen.	1,279	10,288	Coleman
Collin	NE	867	66,920	McKinney
Collingsworth	NW	894	4,755	Wellington
Colorado	SE cen.	949	17,638	Columbus
Comal	S cen.	567	24,165	New Braunfels
Comanche	cen.	966	11,898	Comanche
Concho	W cen.	1,004	2,937	Paint Rock
Cooke	N	905	23,471	Gainesville
Coryell	cen.	1,043	35,311	Gatesville
Cottle	NW	900	3,204	Paducah
Crane	W	795	4,172	Crane
Crockett	W	2,794	3,885	Ozona
Crosby	NW	911	9,085	Crosbyton
Culberson[2]	W	3,851	3,429	Van Horn
Dallam	NW corner	1,494	6,012	Dalhart
Dallas	NE	875	1,327,321	Dallas
Dawson	NW	902	16,604	Lamesa
Deaf Smith	NW	1,510	18,999	Hereford
Delta	NE	276	4,927	Cooper
Denton	N	911	75,633	Denton
De Witt	S	910	18,660	Cuero
Dickens	NW	931	3,737	Dickens
Dimmit	S	1,344	9,039	Carrizo Springs
Donley	NW	905	3,641	Clarendon
Duval	S	1,814	11,722	San Diego
Eastland	N cen.	952	18,092	Eastland
Ector	W	907	91,805	Odessa
Edwards	SW cen.	2,076	2,107	Rocksprings
Ellis	NE cen.	950	46,638	Waxahachie
El Paso	W tip	1,058	359,291	El Paso
Erath	N cen.	1,085	18,141	Stephenville
Falls	cen.	764	17,300	Marlin
Fannin	NE	905	22,705	Bonham
Fayette	SE cen.	934	17,650	La Grange
Fisher	NW cen.	904	6,344	Roby
Floyd	NW	993	11,044	Floydada
Foard	N	676	2,211	Crowell
Fort Bend	SE	869	52,314	Richmond
Franklin	NE	293	5,291	Mount Vernon
Freestone	E cen.	865	11,116	Fairfield
Frio	S	1,116	11,159	Pearsall
Gaines	NW	1,489	11,593	Seminole
Galveston	SE; coastal	399	169,812	Galveston
Garza	NW	914	5,289	Post

ə abut; ᵊ kitten, Fr. table; ər further; a back; ā bake; ä cot, cart; ȧ Fr. bac; au̇ out; ch chin; e less; ē easy; g gift
i trip; ī life; j joke; k̲ Ger. ich, Buch; ⁿ Fr. vin; ŋ sing; ō flow; ȯ flaw; œ Fr. bœuf; œ̄ Fr. feu; ȯi coin; th thin
t̲h̲ this; ü loot; u̇ foot; ue Ger. füllen; ue̅ Fr. rue; y yet; ʸ Fr. digne \dēnʸ\, nuit \nwʸē\; yü few; yu̇ furious; zh vision

NAME	LOCATION	AREA[1] (sq. m.)	POP. (1970c)	CO. SEAT
Gillespie	cen.	1,055	10,553	Fredericksburg
Glasscock	W	863	1,155	Garden City
Goliad	S	871	4,869	Goliad
Gonzales	S cen.	1,056	16,375	Gonzales
Gray	NW	934	26,949	Pampa
Grayson	NE	940	83,225	Sherman
Gregg	NE	282	75,929	Longview
Grimes	E cen.	801	11,855	Anderson
Guadalupe	S cen.	714	33,554	Seguin
Hale	NW	979	34,137	Plainview
Hall	NW	885	6,015	Memphis
Hamilton	cen.	844	7,198	Hamilton
Hansford	NW	907	6,351	Spearman
Hardeman	N	687	6,795	Quanah
Hardin	E	895	29,996	Kountze
Harris	SE	1,723	1,741,912	Houston
Harrison	NE	894	44,841	Marshall
Hartley	NW	1,488	2,782	Channing
Haskell	N	877	8,512	Haskell
Hays	S cen.	670	27,642	San Marcos
Hemphill	NW	904	3,084	Canadian
Henderson	NE	943	26,466	Athens
Hidalgo	S	1,543	181,535	Edinburg
Hill	NE cen.	1,012	22,596	Hillsboro
Hockley	NW	908	20,396	Levelland
Hood	N cen.	426	6,368	Granbury
Hopkins	NE	793	20,710	Sulphur Springs
Houston	E	1,237	17,855	Crockett
Howard	NW	911	37,796	Big Spring
Hudspeth[3]	W	4,554	2,392	Sierra Blanca
Hunt	NE	869	47,948	Greenville
Hutchinson	NW	875	24,443	Stinnett
Irion	W cen.	1,073	1,070	Mertzon
Jack	N	945	6,711	Jacksboro
Jackson	SE	850	12,975	Edna
Jasper	E	927	24,692	Jasper
Jeff Davis	W	2,259	1,527	Fort Davis
Jefferson	SE; coastal	951	244,773	Beaumont
Jim Hogg	S	1,143	4,654	Hebbronville
Jim Wells	S	845	33,032	Alice
Johnson	N cen.	740	45,769	Cleburne
Jones	NW cen.	956	16,106	Anson
Karnes	S	758	13,462	Karnes City
Kaufman	NE	815	32,392	Kaufman
Kendall	S cen.	670	6,964	Boerne
Kenedy	S; coastal	1,394	678	Sarita
Kent	NW	880	1,434	Clairemont
Kerr	SW cen.	1,101	19,454	Kerrville
Kimble	W cen.	1,274	3,904	Junction
King	NW	944	464	Guthrie
Kinney	SW	1,393	2,006	Brackettville
Kleberg	S; coastal	851	33,166	Kingsville
Knox	N	851	5,972	Benjamin
Lamar	NE	906	36,062	Paris
Lamb	NW	1,022	17,770	Littlefield
Lampasas	cen.	726	9,323	Lampasas
La Salle	S	1,500	5,014	Cotulla
Lavaca	SE cen.	975	17,903	Hallettsville
Lee	cen.	644	8,048	Giddings
Leon	E cen.	1,102	8,738	Centerville
Liberty	E	1,182	33,014	Liberty
Limestone	E cen.	931	18,100	Groesbeck
Lipscomb	NW	934	3,486	Lipscomb
Live Oak	S	1,055	6,697	George West
Llano	cen.	941	6,979	Llano
Loving	W	648	164	Mentone
Lubbock	NW	893	179,295	Lubbock
Lynn	NW	915	9,107	Tahoka
McCulloch	cen.	1,066	8,571	Brady
McLennan	cen.	1,030	147,553	Waco
McMullen	S	1,159	1,095	Tilden
Madison	E cen.	480	7,693	Madisonville
Marion	NE	380	8,517	Jefferson
Martin	NW	911	4,774	Stanton
Mason	cen.	935	3,356	Mason
Matagorda	SE; coastal	1,157	27,913	Bay City
Maverick	SW	1,289	18,093	Eagle Pass
Medina	S cen.	1,352	20,249	Hondo
Menard	W cen.	914	2,646	Menard
Midland	W	939	65,433	Midland
Milam	cen.	1,028	20,028	Cameron
Mills	cen.	734	4,212	Goldthwaite
Mitchell	NW cen.	920	9,073	Colorado
Montague	N	934	15,326	Montague
Montgomery	E	1,090	49,479	Conroe
Moore	NW	909	14,060	Dumas
Morris	NE	260	12,310	Daingerfield
Motley	NW	980	2,178	Matador
Nacogdoches	E	943	36,362	Nacogdoches
Navarro	NE cen.	1,087	31,150	Corsicana
Newton	E	953	11,657	Newton
Nolan	NW	922	16,220	Sweetwater
Nueces	S; coastal	845	237,544	Corpus Christi
Ochiltree	NW	907	9,704	Perryton
Oldham	NW	1,478	2,258	Vega
Orange	E	359	71,170	Orange
Palo Pinto	N cen.	948	28,962	Palo Pinto
Panola	E	880	15,894	Carthage
Parker	N cen.	903	33,888	Weatherford
Parmer	NW	859	10,509	Farwell
Pecos	W	4,740	13,748	Fort Stockton
Polk	E	1,100	14,457	Livingston
Potter	NW	898	90,511	Amarillo
Presidio	W	3,892	4,842	Marfa
Rains	NE	219	3,752	Emory
Randall	NW	914	53,885	Canyon
Reagan	W	1,132	3,239	Big Lake
Real	SW cen.	622	2,013	Leakey
Red River	NE	1,033	14,298	Clarksville
Reeves	W	2,608	16,526	Pecos
Refugio	S; coastal	774	9,494	Refugio
Roberts	NW	899	967	Miami
Robertson	E cen.	877	14,389	Franklin
Rockwall	NE	147	7,046	Rockwall
Runnels	W cen.	1,058	12,108	Ballinger
Rusk	E	939	34,102	Henderson
Sabine	E	562	7,187	Hemphill
San Augustine	E	545	7,858	San Augustine
San Jacinto	E	624	6,702	Coldspring
San Patricio	S; coastal	686	47,288	Sinton
San Saba	cen.	1,120	5,540	San Saba
Schleicher	W cen.	1,331	2,277	Eldorado
Scurry	NW cen.	904	15,760	Snyder
Shackelford	N cen.	887	3,323	Albany
Shelby	E	820	19,672	Center
Sherman	NW	916	3,657	Stratford
Smith	NE	934	97,096	Tyler
Somervell	N cen.	197	2,793	Glen Rose
Starr	S	1,211	17,707	Rio Grande City
Stephens	N cen.	923	8,414	Breckenridge
Sterling	W cen.	914	1,056	Sterling City
Stonewall	NW	926	2,397	Aspermont
Sutton	SW cen.	1,493	3,175	Sonora
Swisher	NW	896	10,373	Tulia
Tarrant	N	868	716,317	Fort Worth
Taylor	NW cen.	913	97,853	Abilene
Terrell	W	2,391	1,940	Sanderson
Terry	NW	899	14,118	Brownfield
Throckmorton	N	920	2,205	Throckmorton
Titus	NE	418	16,702	Mount Pleasant
Tom Green	W cen.	1,535	71,047	San Angelo
Travis	cen.	1,012	295,516	Austin
Trinity	E	707	7,628	Groveton
Tyler	E	919	12,417	Woodville
Upshur	NE	584	20,976	Gilmer
Upton	W	1,312	4,697	Rankin
Uvalde	SW	1,588	17,348	Uvalde
Val Verde	SW	3,241	27,471	Del Rio
Van Zandt	NE	851	22,155	Canton
Victoria	S	892	53,766	Victoria
Walker	E	790	27,680	Huntsville
Waller	SE	508	14,285	Hempstead
Ward	W	827	13,019	Monahans
Washington	SE cen.	612	18,842	Brenham
Webb	S	3,306	72,859	Laredo
Wharton	SE	1,076	36,729	Wharton
Wheeler	NW	914	6,434	Wheeler
Wichita	N	611	120,563	Wichita Falls
Wilbarger	N	952	15,355	Vernon
Willacy	S; coastal	591	15,570	Raymondville
Williamson	cen.	1,126	37,305	Georgetown
Wilson	S cen.	802	13,041	Floresville
Winkler	W	887	9,640	Kermit
Wise	N	922	19,687	Decatur
Wood	NE	721	18,589	Quitman
Yoakum	NW	830	7,344	Plains
Young	N	888	15,400	Graham
Zapata	S	1,025	4,352	Zapata
Zavala	S	1,291	11,370	Crystal City

[1]Area = land area.
[2]Big Bend National Park on the Rio Grande (*q.v.*) in S part.
[3]Contains part of Guadalupe Mountains National Park.

History: Period of discovery and exploration by Spaniards 1519–1684; La Salle attempted French settlement at Matagorda Bay 1685, laying basis for French claim to region as part of Louisiana; effective Spanish occupation began 1715; United States acquired French claim in Louisiana Purchase 1803; United States claim to Texas relinquished by treaty with Spain 1819; Texas a province of Mexico; Declaration of Independence from Mexico Mar. 2, 1836; army under Sam Houston won decisive battle of San Jacinto 1836, gaining independence for the Republic of Texas; sought annexation to United States and was admitted to Union Dec. 29, 1845; boundary with Mexico along the Rio Grande river fixed after Mexican War by Treaty of Guadalupe Hidalgo 1848; passed

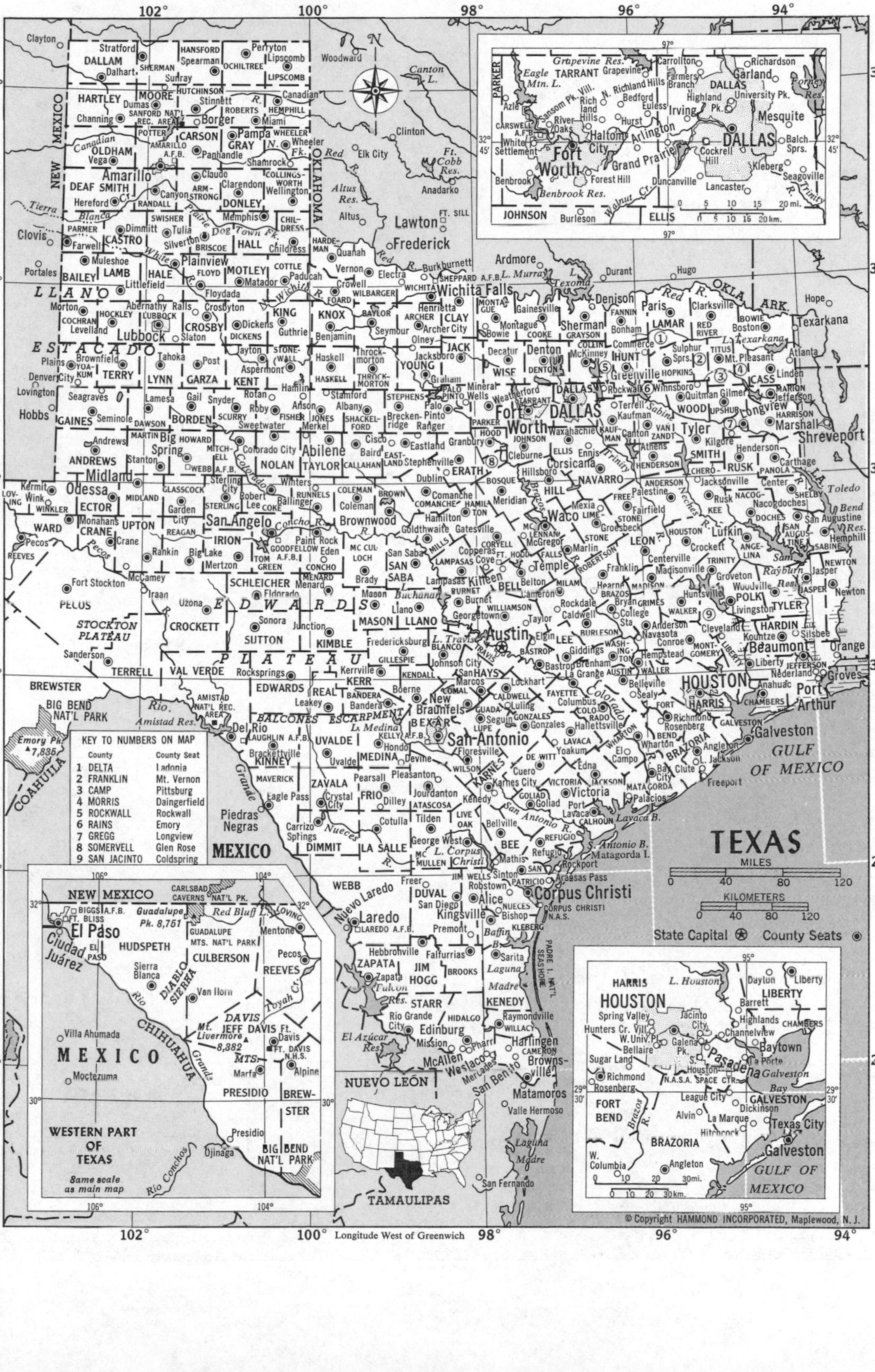
TEXAS
MILES
0 40 80 120
KILOMETERS
0 40 80 120
State Capital
County Seats
KEY TO NUMBERS ON MAP
County / County Seat
1 DELTA — Ladonia
2 FRANKLIN — Mt. Vernon
3 CAMP — Pittsburg
4 MORRIS — Daingerfield
5 ROCKWALL — Rockwall
6 RAINS — Emory
7 GREGG — Longview
8 SOMERVELL — Glen Rose
9 SAN JACINTO — Coldspring
WESTERN PART OF TEXAS
Same scale as main map
HOUSTON
DALLAS
Fort Worth
GULF OF MEXICO
MEXICO
NEW MEXICO
OKLAHOMA
Longitude West of Greenwich
© Copyright HAMMOND INCORPORATED, Maplewood, N. J.

THAILAND
SCALE OF MILES
0 50 100 150 200
SCALE OF KILOMETERS
0 50 100 150 200
Capitals of Countries
International Boundaries
© C. S. HAMMOND & Co., Maplewood, N. J.
Longitude East of Greenwich
96° 100° 104° 108°
20° 16° 12° 8°
CHINA
BURMA
LAOS
NORTH VIETNAM
CAMBODIA
SOUTH VIETNAM
MALAYSIA
MALAY PEN.
ANDAMAN SEA
GULF OF SIAM
GULF OF TONKIN
SOUTH CHINA SEA
Gulf of Martaban
HAINAN
Mandalay
Sagaing
Kehsi Mansam
Myingyan
Kyaukse
Taunggyi
Yamethin
Magwe
Pyinmana
Loikaw
Thayetmyo
Toungoo
Prome
Paungde
Papun
Shwegyin
Henzada
Tharrawaddy
Kyaikto
Thaton
Paan
Rangoon
Martaban
Myaungmya
Pyapon
Moulmein
Amherst
Ye
Heinze Bay
Tavoy
Moscos Is.
Amya
Tavoy Pt.
Mali Kyun
Kadan Kyun
Tenasserim I.
Thayawthadangyi Kyu
Daung Kyun
Mergui
Tenasserim
Bentincks I.
Letsôk-aw Kyun
Mergui Arch.
Lanbi Kyun
Maliwun
Zadetkyi Kyun
Victoria Point
Chance I.
Keng Tung
Yünkinghung
Chiang Saen
Doi Pha Hom Pok 7,532
Chiang Rai
Chiang Dao
Mae Hong Son
Chiang Mai
Doi Inthanon 8,512
Lamphun
Lampang
Phayao
Muang Lae
Ban Pua
Nan
Chae Hom
Na Noi
Phrae
Den Chai
Uttaradit
Thoen
Sawankhalok
Phichai
Tak
Rahaeng
Sukhothai
Phitsanulok
Kao Prawa 5,863
Kamphaeng Phet
Phichit
Khanu
Banphot Phisai
Khao Mukatu 5,925
Nakhon Sawan
Uthai Thani
Chainat
Sing Buri
Three Pagodas Pass
Lop Buri
Ang Thong
Suphan Buri
Sara Buri
Phra Nakhon Si Ayutthaya
Kanchanaburi
BANGKOK (Krung Thep)
Nakhon Pathom
Amya Pass
Samut Prakan
Rat Buri
Samut Songkhram
Thon Buri
Phet Buri
Hua Hin
Pran Buri
Khao Luang 4,040
Prachuap Khiri Khan
Bang Saphan
Pathiu
Kra Buri
Chumphon
Isthmus of Kra
Ranong
Lang Suan
Ko Tao
Ko Phangan
Ko Samui
Samui Str.
Chaiya
Surat Thani
Takua Pa
Sayer Is.
Kapong
Phangnga
Khao Luang 5,860
Nakhon Si Thammarat
Lem Kolam Puk
Pak Phanang
Lem Pak Phra
Ko Phuket
Phuket
Krabi
Trang
Phatthalung
Thale Luang
Kantang
Ko Lanta
Ko Libong
Songkhla (Singora)
Ban Hat Yai
Laem Pho
Pattani
Narathiwat
Pulo Tarutao
Satun
Ko Rawi
Yala
Pulau Langkawi
Kangar
Alor Setar
To Mo
Kuala Terengganu
Taiping
Ban Houei Sai
NamTha
Phong Saly
Luang Prabang
Sayaboury
Muong Hom
Xieng Khouang
Phu San 7,261
Vientiane
Chai Buri
Phon Phisai
Nong Khai
Chiang Khan
Loei
Udon Thani
Dan Sai
Kumphawap
Ban Tha Uthen
Nakhon Phanom
Nong Lahan
Sakon Nakhon
Thakhek
Lom Sak
Phetchabun
Khon Kaen
Kalasin
Mukdahan
Savannakhet
Maha Sarakham
Roi Et
Selaphum
Khemmarat
Chaiyaphum
Suwannaphum
Amnat
Phutthaisong
Ubon
Chai Badan
Nakhon Ratchasima (Khorat)
Buriram
Surin
Sisaket
M. Bua
Khu Khan
Nang Rong
Phanom Dang Raek
Nakhon Nayok
Prachin Buri
Kabin Buri
Ban Aranyaprathet
Chachoengsao
Phanat Nikhom
Chon Buri
Bang Lamung
Rayong
Sattahip
Chanthaburi
Trat
Ko Chang
Khlong Yai
Ko Kut
Koh Kong
Siem Reap
Battambang
Pailin
Tonle Sap
Kompong Thom
Pursat
Kompong Chhnang
Kompong Cham
Kratie
Stung Treng
Phnom Penh
Prey Veng
Kompong Speu
Kampot
Samit Pt.
Koh Rong
Koh Tang
Poulo Way
Phu Quoc
Is. Poulo Dama
Poulo Panjang
Pte. de Ca Mau
Poulo Obi
Les Deux Frères
Is. Poulo Condore (Con Dao)
Khong
Pakse
Muong May
Saravane
Kontum
An Khe
Ban Me Thuot
Dalat
Phan Thiet
Bien Hoa
Saigon
Tay Ninh
Soai Rieng
My Tho
Long Xuyen
Vinh Long
Can Tho
Soc Trang
Vinh Loi
Hue
Da Nang (Tourane)
Quang Nam
Quang Tri
Partition line July 1954
I. du Tigre
Dong Hoi
Ha Tinh
Vinh
Thanh Hoa
Ninh Binh
Nam Dinh
Sam Neua
Hanoi
Haiphong
Bac Ninh
Son La
Yen Bay
Thai Nguyen
Lang Son
Pingsiang
Bac Kan
Luc An Chau
Lao Kay
Lai Chau
Tsungshan
Mon Cay
Pakhoi
Weichow Tao
Bach Long Vi (Nightingale I.)
Aihsien
Mekong
Salween
Irrawaddy
Chindwin
Sittang
Red R.
Black R.
Nam Ou
Mae Nam Chao Phraya
Mae Nam Ping
Mae Nam Nan
Mae Nam Pa Sak
Mae Nam Mun
Chi
Tenasserim Range
Bilauktaung Ra.
Dawna Ra.

ordinance of secession Feb. 1, 1861; ordinance of secession declared null and void 1866; readmitted to Union Mar. 30, 1870.

2 Name of counties in two states of the U.S. See tables at MISSOURI and OKLAHOMA.

Texas City. City, Galveston co., SE Texas, on Galveston Bay 9 m. NW of Galveston; pop. (1970c) 38,908; ships phosphate; produces chemicals; oil wells and refineries; dairy and truck farms. On Apr. 16, 1947, explosion of shipload of ammonium nitrate in harbor and subsequent explosions and fires killed 561 persons and destroyed most of city.

Tex·co·co \tä-'skō-(ˌ)kō\ *or in full* **Texcoco de Mo·ra** \-də-'mȯr-ə\ *also* **Tez·cu·co** \tā-'skü-\. Town, México state, cen. Mexico, on E side of Lake Texcoco; munic. pop. (1970p) 67,220. In Aztec times an important town and seat of the Tezcucan kings; one of the three pueblos forming the Aztec confederation (see TENOCHTITLÁN); used by Cortés as base for operations against Mexico City.

Texcoco, Lake *or* **Lake Tezcuco.** Dry lake, México state, cen. Mexico, just E of Mexico City; 12 m. long; surface elevation above sea level 7340 ft.; in its W part Tenochtitlán, Aztec stronghold and capital, was built.

Tex·el \'tek-səl, 'tes-əl\. Dutch island, one of the West Frisian Is. in the North Sea off the N coast of North Holland prov.; 13 m. long; 71 sq. m.; pop. (1970e) 11,394; comprises a commune of North Holland prov.

Teyde, Pico de. See TEIDE, PICO DE.

Tezcuco. See TEXCOCO.

Tezcuco, Lake. See TEXCOCO, LAKE.

Te·ziu·tlán \ˌtes-ē-ü-'tlän\. Town, Puebla state, SE cen. Mexico, 100 m. NW of Veracruz; munic. pop. (1970p) 41,502; an old town near border of Veracruz state; copper mines.

Tez·pur \'tez-(ˌ)pu̇(ə)r\. Town, NE India, on Brahmaputra river 90 m. NE of Shillong; pop. (1961c) 24,200.

Tha·ba·na Ntlen·ya·na \tä-ˌbän-ə-ˌent-len-'yän-ə\. Mountain, E Lesotho; 11,425 ft.; highest peak in Drakensberg Mts., also highest peak in S Africa.

Tha·ba·zim·bi \ˌtäb-ə-'zim-bē\. Town, Transvaal, Rep. of South Africa, ab. 96 m. NW of Pretoria; pop. (1967e) 8800.

Tha·bor, Mont \ˌmōⁿ-ta-'bȯ(ə)r\. Mountain, on France-Italy border, SW of Modane and W of Col de Fréjus; 10,453 ft.; small area to S transferred from Italy to France 1947.

Tha Chin \'tä-'chēn\. 1 River, the W distributary of the main river system of W cen. Thailand, of which the Chao Phraya is E stream; ab. 135 m. long; flows S from Uthai Thani, where it leaves the Chao Phraya, to the Gulf of Siam at Samut Sakhon ab. 21 m. SW of Bangkok.

2 Town, Thailand. See SAMUT SAKHON.

Thai·land \'tī-ˌland, -lənd\ *or Thai* **Mu·ang Thai** \'mü-ˌäŋ-'tī\ *or formerly* **Si·am** \sī-'am\. Kingdom, SE Asia, lying to the N and W of the Gulf of Siam, bounded on N by Burma and Laos, on E by Laos and Cambodia, on extreme S by Malaysia, on SW by the Andaman Sea, and on W by Burma; 198,455 sq. m.; pop. (1970p) 34,152,000; ✻ Bangkok. *Physical features:* The kingdom's max. length is ab. 1024 m., its max. width ab. 485 m.; at its narrowest point (peninsular Thailand), lying bet. the Gulf of Siam and the Andaman Sea, width is ab. 30 m.; mountainous in NW with highest point Doi Inthanon 8512 ft., near Burma border; farther S along Burma border are Dawna Range and Bilauktaung Range and on the SE along the Cambodia border is the Phanom Dong Rak. Large cen. area is a plain lying in the basins of the Chao Phraya and its tributaries and in the E the tributaries of the Mekong. *Chief products:* Rice, corn, peanuts, rubber, soybeans, teak, jute; fishing; tin, tungsten, iron ore; manufacturing: textiles, cement, glass; food processing. *Chief towns:* Bangkok, Thon Buri, Chiang Mai, Nakhon Ratchasima.

History: In ancient times part of the Mon-Khmer kingdom; had no history of its own until c. 12th cent. A.D.; separate state formed by Thai people 1350; frequently overrun by Burmese in 15th and 16th cents. and Ayuthia destroyed 1767; lost Tenasserim to Burma. Visited by Portuguese and Dutch 16th and 17th cents. and later (18th cent.) by British and French who seized parts of Siamese territory. Renounced claim to Cambodia 1863 and ceded territory E of Mekong to French 1893. In early 20th cent. signed many treaties and conventions with European and Asiatic countries; yielded to British its rights over four Unfederated Malay States 1909. Became constitutional monarchy 1932; came under influence of Japan 1936–40; attacked Indochina 1940; seized by Japan Dec. 1941 and declared war on Great Britain and U.S.A. Jan. 25, 1942. By Japanese action received two Shan States from Burma and four of the Unfederated Malay States (Kedah, Kelantan, Perlis, and Trengganu) July 5, 1943; after defeat of Japan 1945 restored these states; participated in Korean War (1950–53) as member of United Nations force and allied with South Vietnam in Vietnam War (1965 ff.); abolished constitution 1971.

Thailand, Gulf of. See SIAM, GULF OF.

Thakhek. See MUANG KHAMMOUAN.

Tha·le \'täl-ə\. City, Halle dist., East Germany, 38 m. SW of Magdeburg; pop. (1970e) 17,596; mineral baths.

Tha·le Lu·ang \ˌtäl-ā-lu̇-'äŋ\ *or* **Thale Sap** \-'säp\. Lake, near Gulf of Siam on E coast of SW Thailand, on Malay Penin.

Thal·wil \'täl-ˌvēl\. Commune, Zurich canton, NE cen. Switzerland, on Lake of Zurich; pop. (1970c) 13,591; industrial center.

Thame \'tam\. Small river, Buckinghamshire and Oxfordshire, S cen. England; 30 m. long; flows into the Thames bet. Abingdon and Wallingford.

Thames. 1 \'temz, 'thāmz, 'tāmz\. River, SE Connecticut; 15 m. long; actually a tidal estuary formed by confluence of Shetucket and Yantic rivers at Norwich, flows S into Long Island Sound 3 m. below New London.

2 \'temz\. River, SE Ontario, Canada; 135 m. long; rises in Perth co., flows S and SW past London, St. Thomas, and Chatham to Lake St. Clair. In War of 1812, battle of the Thames fought on its banks just E of Thamesville Oct. 5, 1813, in which the Americans under Gen. William H. Harrison defeated the British and Indians; Indian leader, Tecumseh, killed.

3 \'temz\ *or anc.* **Tam·e·sis** \'tam-ə-səs\ *or* **Tam·e·sa** \-sə\. River, S England; 210 m. long; its headstreams, the Churn and Isis (Thames), rise on the slopes of the Cotswold Hills in Gloucestershire; flows E across S cen. England into a great estuary, through which it empties into the North Sea; London is situated on both its sides; navigable as far as London.

4 River, New Zealand. See WAIHOU.

5 \'temz\. Borough, N North I., New Zealand, on Firth of Thames 50 m. ESE of Auckland; pop. (1970e) 5180.

Thames, Firth of \-'temz\. Southern extension of Hauraki Gulf, N coast of North I., New Zealand; receives the Waihou river from the S.

Thames·ville \'temz-ˌvil\. Village, Kent co., SE Ontario, Canada, on Thames river; pop. (1971p) 1018. See THAMES 2.

Thāmit. See TAMET.

Thamugadi *or* **Thamugadis.** See TIMGAD.

Tha·na \'tän-ə\. Town, W Maharashtra, W India, on NE shore of Salsette I. 21 m. NNE of Bombay; pop. (1970e) 161,185; suburb of Bombay. In time of Marco Polo (13th cent.) a leading port of India; an early settlement of the Portuguese, who were driven out 1737 by the Marathas.

Than·et, Isle of \-'than-ət\. Area, NE end of Kent, SE England; 42 sq. m.; cut off from the mainland by arms of the river Stour, one of which roughly parallels course of an ancient channel, the Wantsum, once wide enough to make Thanet a true island; scene of many Norse invasions.

Thanh Hoa \'tän-(yə-)'hwä\. Town, North Vietnam, 90 m. S of Hanoi.

Than·ja·vur *also* **Tan·jore** \tan-'jō(ə)r, -'jó(ə)r\. 1 District, Tamil Nadu, S India; 3740 sq. m.; pop. (1961c) 3,245,927; ✱ Thanjavur.

2 City, its ✱, on right bank of Cauvery river 190 m. SSE of Madras; pop. (1970e) 121,831; produces jewelry, carpets, and embroidery; 11th cent. temple to Siva, with great tower (208 ft.); college (1955).

History: Capital from time to time since 10th cent. of Chola dynasty; independent state established here in 16th cent. by a governor of Vijayanagar; under Madura sovereignty in 1662; conquered by Marathas 1674 who held it to 1799; came into British possession 1855. Scene of activities of earliest Protestant missionaries in India.

Thann \'tän\. Town, Haut-Rhin dept., NE France, ab. 16 m. NW of Mulhouse; pop. (1962c) 7736; manufactures chemical products, machinery, textiles; 14th cent. church; ruins of castle nearby.

Thap·sa·cus \'thap-si-kəs\ *or mod.* **Dib·se** \'dib-sə\ *or Bib.* **Tiph·sah** \'tif-sə\ (*I Kings* iv. 24). Ancient city on the S bank of the middle Euphrates river, N Syria, ab. 60 m. ESE of Alep; location of a ford, much used in ancient times.

Thap·sus \'thap-səs\. Ancient town, N Africa; its site is on E coast of Tunisia SE of modern town of Sousse; battle 46 B.C. in which Julius Caesar defeated the Pompeians.

Thar Desert \'tär-, 'tər-\ *or* **Great Indian Desert.** Region of sandy desert, NW India and SE Pakistan, bet. Aravalli Range on E and Indus river on W, Sutlej river on N and Arabian Sea on S; ab. 400 m. long, ab. 225 m. wide; approx. 100,000 sq. m.; average alt. 250 ft. to 750 ft.; max. alt. ab. 1500 ft., on W slope of Aravalli Range. Annual rainfall less than 15 in.; has continuous high temperatures. Includes portions of Rajasthan and Gujarat states, India, and Punjab and Sind in Pakistan.

Thar·ra·wad·dy \ˌthar-ə-'wäd-ē\. 1 District, Pegu division, Burma; 2784 sq. m.; pop. (1962e) 823,459; ✱ Tharrawaddy.

2 Town, its ✱, 65 m. N of Rangoon; pop. (1953c) 8977.

Tha·sos \'thā-ˌsäs\ *or Gk.* **Thá·sos** \'thäs-ˌós\. 1 Island, N Aegean Sea, opp. the mouth of the Nestos; 146 sq. m.; pop. (1961c) 15,916; politically a part of Kavalla dept., NE Macedonia, Greece; mountainous, highest point 3428 ft. Early colonized by Phoenicians, later (in 8th cent. B.C.) by Parians; seized by Persians under Mardonius; later came under Athens, but revolted twice in 5th cent. B.C.; ruled successively by Romans, Byzantines, Latins, and Turks until ceded to Greece 1913.

2 Chief town of island, on N coast; now in ruins.

Thatch·er \'thach-ər\. Town, Graham co., SE Arizona, ab. 80 m. NE of Tucson; pop. (1970c) 2320; Eastern Arizona Coll. (1891).

Tha·ton \thə-'tōn\. 1 Coastal district of Tenasserim division, Burma; 1909 sq. m.; pop. (1962e) 435,410; ✱ Thaton.

2 Town, its ✱, near NE coast of Gulf of Martaban 35 m. NNW of Moulmein; pop. (1962e) 136,394.

Thau, Étang de \ā-ˌtäⁿ-də-'tō\. Salt lagoon, S France, on coast of Hérault dept.; ab. 40 sq. m.; separated from the Mediterranean (Gulf of Lions) by a narrow strip of sand on which Sète is located.

Thaun·gyin \'thaủn-'jin\. River, Burma; 150 m. long; flows NW into Salween river on the Burma-Thailand boundary; and in its own course forms a section of that boundary E of the Dawna Range.

Tha·yaw·tha·dang·yi Island \thä-ˌyó-thä-däŋ-'yē-\ *or formerly* **El·phin·stone Island** \ˌel-fən-ˌstōn-, -stən-\. Island, NW Mergui Archipelago (*q.v.*), Burma.

Thayer \'tha(ə)r, 'thā-ər\. County in Nebraska. See table at NEBRASKA.

Tha·yet·myo \thə-'yet-ˌmyō, 'thät-ˌmyō\. 1 District, Magwe division, Burma; 4626 sq. m.; pop. (1962c) 352,893; ✱ Thayetmyo.

2 Town, its ✱, on the Irrawaddy river opp. Allanmyo, 40 m. N of Prome; pop. (1962e) 59,035; oil wells; founded 1306.

Thebae. See THEBES 1.

The·ba·is \thē-'bā-əs\. Roman province of Upper Egypt.

Thebes \'thēbz\. 1 *classical* **The·bae** \'thē-(ˌ)bē\ *or later* **Di·os·po·lis** \dī-'äs-pə-ləs\ *also* **Diospolis Mag·na** \-'mag-nə\. Ancient ruined city, Egypt, on the left bank of the Nile, S of modern Qena; in early times included also Karnak and Luxor (*qq.v.*) on the right bank. Town of great antiquity preserving its importance because of the temple of Karnak; on decline of Memphis and after the brief rule of the Heracleopolitan dynasties, became capital of Upper Egypt giving its name to the XIth (2160–2000 B.C.), XIIth (2000–1788 B.C.), and XIIIth dynasties of the Middle Kingdom, although the Theban rulers continued to make their residence at Memphis until c. 1580 B.C. Obscured for two centuries under the Xoite dynasty and the Hyksos kings, rose again under the XVIIIth dynasty of the New Kingdom; its rulers (the Diospolite dynasties, XVIIIth to XXth) from c. 1580 B.C. to 1090 B.C. represent the great period of Egyptian power and achievement. Known as **No** \'nō\ in Biblical history (as in *Jer.* xlvi. 25, *Nahum* iii. 8) and to the Greeks through Homer's *Iliad* as the "hundred-gated" city; center of worship of Amen (or Amon) and famous for its vast temples, gateways, statues, sphinxes, tombs, obelisks, etc. Center of Egyptian civilization but declined after 10th cent. B.C. Sacked by Assyrians 671 B.C., later by Persians, and esp. by Romans 30–29 B.C. under Cornelius Gallus. Here in Valley of Kings near Luxor in 1922 tomb of Tutankhamen, ruler of the XVIIIth (Diospolite) dynasty, c. 1358 B.C., was discovered containing mummies and great wealth of jewels, objects of art, etc., in superb condition.

2 *or Gk.* **Thí·vai** \'thē-(ˌ)vā\. Commune, E Central Greece and Euboea region, Greece, 33 m. NNW of Athens; pop. (1961c) 15,779; market town; in low hilly country.

History: An ancient city, traditionally founded by Cadmus; closely identified with many of the early legends of Greece (as Dirce, Epigonus, Oedipus, the Sphinx, etc.). Historically, settled before 1500 B.C. by Boeotians; began struggles against Athens at end of the 6th cent. B.C.; headed Boeotian League c. 600–550 B.C. Sided with Persians against Greeks and was punished after defeat of Persians. Under Athenian rule 457–447 B.C.; joined Sparta against Athens in Peloponnesian War; left Sparta and joined Argos, Athens, and Corinth in the Corinthian War 395–387 B.C. Under Spartan rule 382–379 B.C.; regained freedom 379, destroyed Spartan supremacy at Leuctra 371 B.C. (the period of Theban leadership 371–362 B.C.); joined Athens against Philip of Macedon and shared defeat at Chaeronea 338 B.C.; almost totally destroyed by Alexander 336 B.C. Home of Pindar and produced the great generals Epaminondas and Pelopidas.

The Dalles. See DALLES, THE.

Thed·ford \'thed-fərd\. Village, ⊗ of Thomas co., cen. Nebraska; pop. (1970c) 303.

The Hague. See HAGUE, THE.

Theiss. See TISZA.

The·nia \tā-'nē-ə\ *or formerly* **Mé·ner·ville** \ˌmān-ər-'vēl\. Commune, N Algeria, on coastal railroad E of Algiers; pop. (1966c) 7903.

The·o·dore Roo·se·velt Island \ˌthē-ə-ˌdō(ə)r-'rō-zə-ˌvelt-\ *or formerly* **An·a·los·tan Island** \ˌan-ᵊl-ˌó-stən-\. Island in the Potomac river, District of Columbia; 90 acres; site of a memorial to President Theodore Roosevelt.

Theodosia. See FEODOSIYA.

Theophilo Ottoni. See TEOFILO OTONI.

The·ot·mal·li \'tā-ōt-ˌmäl-ē\. See DETMOLD.

The Pas. See PAS, THE.

Thera. See THÍRA.

Therezina. See TERESINA.

Therma. See SALONIKA.

Thermae Himerenses. See TERMINI IMERESE.

Thermaicus Sinus *or* **Thermaïkós Kólpos.** See SALONIKA, GULF OF.

Thermia. See KYTHNOS.

Ther·mop·o·lis \thər-ˈmäp-(ə-)ləs\. Town, ⊗ of Hot Springs co., NW cen. Wyoming; pop. (1970c) 3063; health resort with mineral springs; coal mines, oil wells; livestock.

Ther·mop·y·lae \(ˌ)thər-ˈmäp-ə-(ˌ)lē\ *or Gk.* **Ther·mo·pí·lai** \ˌther-mō-ˈpē-(ˌ)lā\. Locality, E Greece, bet. Mt. Oeta and S shore of Gulf of Maliakós 9 m. SSE of town of Lamia; in ancient times a narrow pass along the coast, now a rocky plain ab. 6 m. from the sea. Here the Spartans and Thespians under Leonidas met the Persian invaders in battle 480 B.C. Other battles here: (1) in 279 B.C. Brennus and Gauls checked for several months by the Greeks; (2) in 191 B.C. Antiochus III of Syria defeated by Romans; (3) Apr. 20–25, 1941 German army held in rearguard action by Anzacs.

Thé·rou·anne \ˌtā-rə-ˈwän\. Village, Pas-de-Calais dept., N France, S of St-Omer; pop. (1962c) 892; formerly a fortress; taken by the English in 1380 and 1513, and destroyed by the Emperor Charles V in 1553.

Thes·pi·ae \ˈthes-pē-ˌē\. Ancient town, S cen. Boeotia, E cen. Greece, E of Mt. Helicon and ab. 10 m. WSW of Thebes. Worshipped Eros and the Muses and possessed a famous statue of Eros made by Praxiteles; 700 of its inhabitants fought and died with Leonidas at Thermopylae and others were at Plataea 479 B.C.; town destroyed by Xerxes; friendly to Athens and suffered much in its opposition to Thebes.

Thes·pro·tia \thes-ˈprō-sh(ē-)ə\. 1 Department of Epirus, Greece. See table at GREECE.

2 Region of ancient Epirus, NW Greece, on W coast extending S from Thyamis river to Ambracian Gulf. The Thesprotians were the earliest inhabitants of Epirus; their oracle at Dodona was the great center of Pelasgic worship.

Thessalía. See THESSALY.

Thessalonica *or* **Thessaloníki.** See SALONIKA.

Thes·sa·lo·ni·ke \ˌthes-ə-lə-ˈnī-kē\ *or Gk.* **Thes·sa·lo·ní·ki** \-ˈnē-kē\. Department of Macedonia, Greece. See table at GREECE.

Thes·sa·ly \ˈthes-ə-lē\ *or Gk.* **Thes·sa·lía** \ˌthā-sə-ˈlē-ə\. Administrative region, Greece; includes E cen. portion of Greek penin.; 5382 sq. m.; pop. (1971p) 659,243; for subdivisions, see table at GREECE. Ancient Thessaly corresponds generally to modern division: an extensive plain region almost completely hemmed in by mountains—Pindus Mts. on W, Cambunian Mts. on N, Othrys Mts. along the S border, and Mts. Olympus, Ossa, and Pelion along the coast. Drained by Piniós river with many confluents, entering Aegean Sea through Vale of Tempe.

History: Land of many early migrations and cultures, esp. the Aeolic; figured prominently in many Greek legends (Argonauts, centaurs, Achilles); early inhabitants too isolated and disunited to play a prominent role in classical Greek history. Subject to Macedonia 4th to 2d cent. B.C.; scene of several great battles of ancient history; in Middle Ages had many Romanian inhabitants; ceded to modern Greece 1881; in World War II was a main area of conflict bet. Germans and forces of British and Greeks.

Thet·ford \ˈthet-fərd\. 1 Town, Orange co., E Vermont; pop. (1970c) 1422; comprises several villages along the Connecticut river N of White River Junction.

2 Municipal borough, Norfolk, E England, 27 m. SW of Norwich; pop. (1971p) 13,706; trade center; food canning, coffee milling.

Thetford Mines. City, Megantic co., S Quebec, Canada, 52 m. S of Quebec; pop. (1971p) 21,662; site of asbestos mines producing ab. one half the world's supply; founded 1802; developed rapidly after discovery of asbestos 1876.

Theux \ˈtə\. Commune, Liège prov., E Belgium, 12 m. SE of Liège; pop. (1969e) 5493.

Theveste. See TEBESSA.

The Village. See VILLAGE, THE.

Thiais \ˈtyā\. Commune, Val-de-Marne dept., N France, S of Paris; pop. (1968c) 22,476.

Thí·a·mis \ˈthē-ə-(ˌ)mēs\ *or formerly* **Ka·la·mas** \ˌkäl-ə-ˈmäs\. River, cen. Epirus, NW Greece; ab. 70 m. long; flows S and W to Ionian Sea opp. Corfu I.; marked N border of ancient Thesprotia.

Thian Shan. See TIEN SHAN.

Thiau·court \tyō-ˈkü(ə)r\. Village, Meurthe-et-Moselle dept., NE France, ab. 16 m. ENE of St-Mihiel; taken by U.S. troops Sept. 12, 1918; St-Mihiel U.S. military cemetery.

Thibet. See TIBET.

Thib·o·daux \ˈtib-ə-ˌdō\. City, ⊗ of Lafourche parish, SE Louisiana, on Bayou Lafourche 49 m. WSW of New Orleans; pop. (1970c) 15,028; agricultural equipment, brooms; sugar refineries, oil and gas wells; truck and dairy farms; Nicholls State Coll. (1948).

Thick·a·net·ley Bald \ˌthik-ə-ˈnet-lē-\. Peak, Gilmer co., N Georgia; 4054 ft.

Thief \ˈthēf\. River, NW Minnesota; 30 m. long; flows S out of **Thief Lake** in NE Marshall co. and empties into Red Lake river in N Pennington co.

Thief River Falls. City, ⊗ of Pennington co., NW Minnesota, 50 m. W of Upper Red Lake; pop. (1970c) 8618; trade center; dairy products.

Thiel·sen, Mount \-ˈt(h)ēl-sən\. Peak on boundary bet. Douglas and Klamath cos., S Oregon, N of Crater Lake; 9182 ft.

Thielt \ˈtēlt\ *or* **Tielt** \ˈtēlt\. Commune, West Flanders prov., NW Belgium, 15 m. SE of Brugge (Bruges); pop. (1969e) 14,067; market town; captured by the Germans 1914 and used for a long time as German headquarters on the Flanders front.

Thie·ne \tē-ˈā-nā\. Manufacturing commune, Vicenza prov., Veneto, NE Italy, 12 m. NNW of Vicenza; pop. (1968e) 16,256.

Thienen. See TIENEN.

Thiens·ville \ˈthēnz-ˌvil\. Village, Ozaukee co., E Wisconsin, 17 m. N of Milwaukee; pop. (1970c) 3182.

Thiep·val \tyep-ˈväl\. Village, Somme dept., N France, just N of Albert; pop. (1962c) 111; frequent fighting, esp. Sept. 1916 and Aug. 1918.

Thiers \tē-ˈe(ə)r\. Manufacturing commune, Puy-de-Dôme dept., S cen. France, 23 m. ENE of Clermont-Ferrand; pop. (1968c) 16,623; made barony 1569.

Thi·ès \ˈtyes\. Town, Senegal, W Africa, 40 m. E of Cape Vert; pop. (1970e) 91,000.

Thim·ble Islands \ˌthim-bəl-\. Group of islands, Long Island Sound off the S coast of New Haven co., Connecticut.

Thim·bu \thim-ˈbü\ *or* **Thim·phu** \-ˈpü\ *also* **Ta·shi Chho Dzong** \ˈtäsh-ē-ˈchō-ˈjȯŋ\. Town, ✱ of Bhutan; dist. pop. (1969c) 60,027.

Thing·val·la Water \ˌthēŋ(g)-ˌvät-lə-\. Lake, SW Iceland, E of Reykjavík; 32 sq. m.; largest lake in Iceland.

Thing·vel·lir \ˈthēŋ(g)-ˌvet-ˌli(ə)r\. Level plain with lava floor near Thingvalla Water, SW Iceland, ab. 25 m. E of Reykjavík; established as **Thingvellir National Park** 1928; meeting place from 930 A.D. to recent years of the *althing,* parliament of Iceland.

Thinis. See THIS.

Thio \ˈtē-(ˌ)ō\. Town, E coast of New Caledonia, SW Pacific Ocean, ab. 48 m. NNW of Nouméa; pop. (1969c) 3176.

Thion·ville \tyōⁿ-ˈvēl\ *or Ger.* **Die·den·ho·fen** \ˈdēd-ᵊn-ˌhō-fən\. Commune, Moselle dept., NE France, on Moselle river 16 m. N of Metz; pop. (1968c) 37,079; railroad center; center of iron-mining district; trades in agricultural products, lumber, wine. Taken by Germans after prolonged siege 1870; reverted to France 1919.

Thí·ra \'thir-ə\ *or formerly* **San·to·rin** \ˌsant-ə-'rēn\ *or anc.* **The·ra** \'thir-ə\. Volcanic island, S Cyclades, in the Aegean Sea on N side of Sea of Crete, in Cyclades dept., Greece; 29 sq. m.; pop. (1961c) 7751. Its surface has much tufa which is exported as a cement. Has had numerous volcanic eruptions; earliest recorded 196 B.C., latest 1866. Has prehistoric remains and is thought to have been settled early by Phoenicians and Spartans; c. 630 B.C. sent colonists to found Cyrene in Libya.

Thirl·mere \'thər(-ə)l-ˌmi(ə)r\. Lake, Lake District, Cumberland, NW England; 3¼ m. long; provides part of Manchester water supply.

This \'this\ *or* **Thi·nis** \'thī-nəs\. City of ancient Egypt, near the great bend of the Nile NW of Abydos and near the modern Girga; native city of Menes and capital of the Ist and IId dynasties, to which it gave its name (Thinite).

Thi·sted \'tē-steth\. Town, Viborg co., Denmark, NW Jutland penin.; pop. (1970e) 8730; textiles, beer.

This·til Fjord \ˌthis-tᵊl-\. Bay, NE Iceland, bet. Capes Rifstangi and Langanes; inlet of Arctic Ocean.

Thívai. See THEBES 2.

Thjórsá \'thyō(ə)r-ˌsaů, 'thȯ(ə)r-\. River, S cen. Iceland; 143 m. long; the longest river in Iceland; flows SW into Atlantic Ocean.

Tho·len \'tōl-ən\. Island, Zeeland prov., SW Netherlands; 46 sq. m.

Thom·as \'täm-əs\. Name of counties in three states of the U.S. See tables at GEORGIA, KANSAS, NEBRASKA.

Thomas Cole Mountain \-'kōl-\. Peak in the Catskill Mts., Greene co., SE New York; 3940 ft.

Thomas Peak. See BALDY PEAK 1.

Thom·as·ton \'täm-ə-stən\. 1 Industrial town, SE Litchfield co., NW Connecticut, on Naugatuck river; pop. (1970c) 6223; brass, glass; truck farms.

2 City, ⊗ of Upson co., W cen. Georgia, 38 m. W of Macon; pop. (1970c) 10,024; textiles, lumber; fruit farms.

3 Town, Knox co., S Maine, on inlet of Atlantic Ocean 35 m. ESE of Augusta; pop. (1970c) 2646.

Thom·as·ville \'täm-əs-ˌvil\. 1 Town, Clarke co., SW Alabama, 80 m. NNE of Mobile Bay; pop. (1970c) 3769; paper; agriculture.

2 City, ⊗ of Thomas co., S Georgia, 40 m. W of Valdosta; pop. (1970c) 18,155; cigars, fertilizer, lumber; agriculture.

3 City, Davidson co., cen. North Carolina, 7 m. SSW of High Point; pop. (1970c) 15,230; furniture, flour, clothing.

Tho·mond \'tü-mənd\. Medieval principality in N part of Munster prov., S Eire.

Thomp·son \'täm(p)-sən\. 1 Manufacturing town, NE Windham co., NE Connecticut, on Massachusetts and Rhode Island borders N of Putnam; pop. (1970c) 7580; incorporated 1785.

2 River, S British Columbia, Canada, main tributary of the Fraser river; length to head of North Thompson 304 m.; rises among the Rocky Mts. near E boundary of British Columbia, flows S (as **North Thompson River,** 210 m. long) and turns W and SW to the Fraser river. Joined at Kamloops by a branch (206 m. long) from Shuswap Lake usually known as the **South Thompson River.**

Thompson Falls. Town, ⊗ of Sanders co., NW Montana; pop. (1970c) 1356.

Thompson Glacier. Glacier, Axel Heiberg I., Northwest Territories, Canada; 24 m. long, ab. 1 m. wide near its terminus.

Thompson Island. Island, S area of the harbor of Boston, Massachusetts.

Thompson Peak. Mountain, N Santa Fe co., N cen. New Mexico; 10,456 ft.

Thomp·son·ville \'täm(p)-sən-ˌvil\. Subdivision of town of Enfield, Connecticut; paper, hardware; tobacco growing, truck farming. See ENFIELD 1.

Thom·son \'täm(p)-sən\. 1 City, ⊗ of McDuffie co., E Georgia, 30 m. W of Augusta; pop. (1970c) 6503; fertilizer, cottonseed oil; potatoes.

2 River, upper tributary of Cooper's Creek, cen. Queensland, Australia; 300 m. long; flows SW; dry bed part of the year.

Thon Bu·ri \tən-'bů(ə)r-ē\ *also* **Dhon·bu·ri** \tən-\. Province, Thailand, just SW of Bangkok; 174 sq. m.; pop. (1970p) 919,000; lumber; rice milling; national capital 1767–82.

Thong·wa \'thōn-'wä\. Town, Pegu div., S Burma, near W coast of Gulf of Martaban 23 m. E of Rangoon.

Tho·non–les–Bains \tō-ˌnōⁿ-lā-'baⁿ\. Commune, Haute-Savoie dept., E France, on Lake of Geneva 37 m. NNE of Annecy; pop. (1968e) 20,700; summer resort; mineral baths.

Thorn. See TORUN.

Thorn·ap·ple \'thȯr-ˌnap-əl\. River, S Michigan; ab. 100 m. long; flows from Eaton co. to Grand river.

Thorn·ton \'thȯrnt-ᵊn\. 1 Village, Adams co., NE cen. Colorado, N of Denver; pop. (1970c) 13,326.

2 Village, Cook co., NE Illinois, 20 m. S of Chicago; pop. (1970c) 3714.

3 Village, Providence co., N Rhode Island, ab. 4 m. SW of Providence; administrative center of Johnston.

Thornton Cleve·leys \-'klēv-lēz\. Urban district, Lancashire, NW England, on Irish Sea 7 m. N of Blackpool; pop. (1971p) 26,869; heavy machinery, wire; iron foundries, ship-breakers' yards.

Thor·o·fare Buttes \'thər-(ˌ)ō-ˌfa(ə)r-, -ˌe(ə)r-\. Mountain, SW Park co., NW Wyoming; 11,417 ft.

Thor·old \'thȯr-əld, 'thär-\. Industrial town, Welland co., SE Ontario, Canada, on Welland Ship Canal 3 m. SE of St. Catharines; pop. (1971p) 15,052; flour, textiles.

Thors·havn \tȯrs-'haůn\. Town, ✱ of the Faeroes, located on Strømø I.; pop. (1966c) 9738; occupied 1942–45 by the British as a defense measure.

Thórs·höfn \'thō(ə)rs-ˌhə(r)p-ən, 'thȯ(ə)rs-\. Town, NE Iceland, on Thistil Fjord; pop. (1967e) 400.

Thorvald Nilsen Mountains. See NILSEN PLATEAU.

Thospitis. See VAN 1.

Thou·ars \'twär\ *or anc.* **To·ar·ci·um** \tō-'är-shē-əm\. Commune, Deux-Sèvres dept., W France, 49 m. N of Niort; pop. (1968c) 11,787; market town; textiles, brandy. Taken by Pepin the Short 754 A.D.; made viscountship in 11th cent.; to France 1476; made duchy 1563; Protestant stronghold in wars of religion in 16th cent.

Thou·sand Islands \'thaůz-ᵊn(d)-\. 1 Group of ab. 1500 islands, in a widening of the upper St. Lawrence river, New York state, and Ontario, Canada, just below Kingston. Summer resort, with many hotels and villas. Some of the islands belong to Canada (see *Saint Lawrence Islands* at CANADA, *National Parks*) and some to the United States. The Thousand Islands International Bridge (five spans, bet. islands; total length 8½ m.; opened Aug. 18, 1938) connects Collins Landing, New York, ab. 3 m. SW of Alexandria Bay, with Ivy Lea, Ontario, below Gananoque.

2 Group of about 100 small islands, SW Java Sea; part of Indonesia.

Thousand Lake Mountain. Peak, W Wayne co., S cen. Utah; 11,295 ft.

Thousand Oaks \-'ōks\. City, Ventura co., SW California, 30 m. WNW of Los Angeles; pop. (1970c) 35,873; aircraft parts, plastics; citrus fruit.

Thousand Ships Bay. Bay, extreme SE end of Santa Isabel I., E cen. Solomon Is., W Pacific Ocean; formed partly by San Jorge I. on the W.

Thrace \'thrās\. Region, E Balkan Penin., SE Europe, varying in limits at different periods: (1) ancient **Thra·ce** \'thrā-sē\ *or* **Thra·cia** \'thrā-sh(ē-)ə\ bordered on Euxine (Black Sea) S of the Ister (Danube), on the Propontis (Sea of Marmara), on the N Aegean except for narrow strip of Greek settlements, and on the W on Macedonia. Drained by Hebrus (*mod.* Maritsa) and included Rhodope Mts.

Early Thracians a mixed race, akin to Illyrians. Country reduced to Roman province in time of Vespasian (69–79 A.D.); Lower Moesia formed out of its N part. Corresponded generally to cen. and S Bulgaria, Turkey in Europe, and NE Greece. Overrun by Goths, Huns, and other barbarian invaders; part of Eastern Roman Empire but part fell to Turks 1361 and all of it became Turkish after 1453; in 1878 N part separated as Eastern Rumelia; (2) modern Thrace is S part of ancient region, now divided by the Maritsa river into Western Thrace and Eastern Thrace. **Western Thrace** (*Gk.* **Dy·ti·kē Thra·kē** \ˌthē-ti-ˌkyē-ˈthräk-yē\), constitutes an administrative region of Greece, occupying the extreme NE corner of the country; 3312 sq. m.; pop. (1971p) 329,297 (for subdivisions, see table at GREECE); chief towns Alexandroúpolis, Komotinē, and Xanthe; **Eastern Thrace** constitutes Turkey in Europe (see TURKEY). A theater of the First Balkan War in which great battle of Lüleburgaz was fought; after Second Balkan War part assigned to Bulgaria, but by treaties of 1919 and 1920 boundaries changed and nearly all Thrace became Greek 1920–23.

Thra·cian Sea \ˌthrā-shən-\ *or Gk.* **Thrai·ki·kón Pé·la·gos** \ˌthra-ki-ˌkòn-ˈpel-ə-ˌgòs\. The NW part of the Aegean Sea, bordered on N by the peninsulas of Chalcidice, on S by the Northern Sporades, and on W by the mainland of Thessaly; its NW arm is the Gulf of Salonika.

Three Brothers. Mountain, Chelan co., cen. Washington; 7370 ft.

Three Fingers. Mountain, Snohomish co., NW cen. Washington; 6854 ft.

Three Forks. Town, Gallatin co., SW Montana, on Jefferson river ab. 4 m. SW of locality where it joins Madison and Gallatin rivers to form the Missouri; pop. (1970c) 1188.

Three Kings Islands. Three small islands, S Pacific Ocean NNW of N extremity of North I., New Zealand, 34°09′S, 172°09′E; 3 sq. m.

Three Pa·go·das Pass \-pə-ˈgōd-əz-\. Mountain pass; S end of Dawna Range, bet. SE Burma and W Thailand, at 15°18′N, 98°23′E and ab. 100 m. SSE of Moulmein; for centuries used as connecting highway bet. Burma and the plains of the lower Chao Phraya in Thailand.

Three Points, Cape. Cape extending into the Gulf of Guinea on SW coast of Ghana, W Africa, 4°45′N, 2°06′W.

Three Rivers. 1 City, St. Joseph co., S Michigan, 24 m. S of Kalamazoo; pop. (1970c) 7355; automobile parts, paper and dairy products, power tools.

2 *or Fr.* **Trois–Ri·vières** \trə-ˌwär-ēv-ˈye(ə)r, *Fr.* trwä-rē-vyer\. Industrial city, St-Maurice co., S Quebec, Canada, on N bank of St. Lawrence river at mouth of the St-Maurice river, 75 m. NE of Montreal; pop. (1971p) 55,240; paper, iron goods, textiles, electrical equipment; ships lumber, grain, asbestos. Séminaire Saint-Joseph (1663), Marie de l'Incarnation Univ. (1697), Séminaire de Trois-Rivières, Univ. of Quebec (1969). Founded by Champlain 1634; incorporated as city 1857.

Three Sisters. Adjacent peaks, Lane co., W Oregon; 10,430 ft., 10,094 ft., 10,053 ft.

Throck·mor·ton \ˈthräk-ˌmòrt-ᵊn\. 1 County in N Texas. See table at TEXAS.

2 Town, its ⊗; pop. (1970c) 1105.

Throgs Neck \ˈthrägz-\. Cape projecting into Long Island Sound from the coast of Bronx co., SE New York.

Throop \ˈtrüp\. Borough, Lackawanna co., NE Pennsylvania, 4 m. NE of Scranton; pop (1970c) 4307.

Throtmannia. See DORTMUND.

Thu·bur·bo Ma·jus \thə-ˌbər-bō-ˈmā-jəs\. Ancient city, Roman Africa, site SW of modern Tunis, Tunisia; founded by Octavian; ruins have been excavated.

Thug·ga \ˈthəg-ə\ *or mod.* **Doug·ga** \ˈdü-gə\. Ancient city, N Africa, SW of Carthage; ruins 68 m. SW of Tunis, Tunisia; important Punic city; most of ruins are of buildings constructed under the Romans, including a temple of Jupiter, Juno, and Minerva built by Marcus Aurelius (d. 180), the temple of Caelestis, forum, etc.

Thuile, La. See LA THUILE.

Thu·in \tü-ˈaⁿ\. Commune, Hainaut prov., SW Belgium, just SW of Charleroi; pop. (1969e) 6036.

Thu·le \ˈtü-lē\. Settlement, NW Greenland, on coast of Hayes Penin. N of Cape York; pop. (1966e) 600; Danish trading post founded 1910; its name has been given to a form of Eskimo culture found here but extending over all Arctic regions where Eskimos dwell. U.S. Air Force base nearby.

Thumb, The \-ˈthəm\. 1 Peak in Sierra Nevada, E Fresno co., S cen. California; 13,885 ft.

2 Peninsula, E Michigan, bet. Lake Huron and Saginaw Bay; chiefly Huron co.; its tip is Pointe Aux Barques.

Thun \ˈtün\. Commune, Bern canton, Switzerland, at head of Lake of Thun on Aare river 15 m. SSE of Bern; pop. (1970c) 36,523; machinery, pottery, dairy products; tourism; medieval castle, 16th cent. town hall; founded 12th cent.; to Bern 1323.

Thun, Lake of *or Ger.* **Thun·er See** \ˈtün-ər-ˌzā\. Lake, cen. Switzerland; 10 m. long, ab. 19 sq. m.; max. depth 712 ft.; formed by an expansion of the Aare river.

Thun·der Bay \ˈthən-dər-\. 1 Inlet of Lake Huron, E coast of Alpena co., NE Michigan; 12 m. long.

2 River, NE Michigan; ab. 50 m. long; flows into Thunder Bay at Alpena.

3 Inlet of NW Lake Superior, Ontario, Canada.

4 District, Ontario, Canada. See table at ONTARIO.

5 City, ⊗ of Thunder Bay dist., SW Ontario, Canada, on NW shore of Lake Superior; pop. (1971p) 107,805, met. area pop. 111,492; engineering shops, pulp and paper mills, coal docks, grain elevators; important transportation center in rich mining region; Lakehead Univ. (1965), Confederation Coll. (1967); formally established 1970 through the merging of Fort William with Port Arthur; Fort William a French trading post in 17th cent.; Port Arthur founded 1866.

Thunder Cape. Headland, SE of Thunder Bay, Ontario, Canada, projecting into Lake Superior.

Thun·der·er, The \-ˈthən-dər-ər\. Peak, NE Yellowstone National Park, NW Wyoming; 10,554 ft.

Thunder Mountain. Peak in Sierra Nevada, N Tulare co., S cen. California; 13,578 ft.

Thuner See. See THUN, LAKE OF.

Thur \ˈtu̇(ə)r\. River, NE Switzerland; 78 m. long; rises in cen. Saint Gallen canton, flows N to Thurgau canton (named for this river) and turns W; joins the Rhine in N Zurich canton.

Thur·gau \ˈtu̇(ə)r-ˌgau̇\ *or* **Thur·go·vie** \ˌtu̇r-gō-ˈvē\. Swiss canton. See table at SWITZERLAND.

Thu·rii \ˈth(y)u̇r-ē-ˌī\. Ancient Greek city, Lucania (now Basilicata), S Italy, near site of Sybaris; founded 443 B.C. by Greek colonists, among them Herodotus and Lysias. Important city until population removed by Hannibal 204 B.C.

Thu·rin·gia \th(y)u̇-ˈrin-j(e-)ə\ *or Ger.* **Thü·ring·en** \ˈtue̅-riŋ-ən\. Former German state, now part of East Germany, the land around the Thuringian Forest, approximately bet. Werra river on W and Weisse Elster on E; 4540 sq. m.; ✻ Weimar; crossed by the Saale; comprised former Thuringian States. See REUSS 2 and SAXE.

History: Region conquered by Franks in 6th cent. and generally under Frankish rule from 634 to 804 when Charlemagne founded the Thuringian Mark. In medieval period had many changes in rulers and political status; from 1485 to 1918 identified with duchy and kingdom of Saxony. States combined under Weimar republic 1919–33 but after 1934 under the Reich included in Saxony;

following partition of Germany (1945) became part of East Germany.

Thu·rin·gi·an Forest \th(y)u̇-ˌrin-j(ē-)ən-\ *or Ger.* **Thü·ring·er Wald** \ˈtue-riŋ-ər-ˌvält\. Wooded mountain range in Thuringia, East Germany; highest point ab. 3225 ft.

Thur·les \ˈthər-ləs\. Urban district, cen. co. Tipperary, S Eire; sporting center; remains of 12th cent. castle.

Thur·rock \ˈthər-ək, ˈthə-rək\. Urban district, Essex, SE England, on N bank of the Thames; pop. (1971p) 124,682; cement, soap; oil refining.

Thurs·day Island \ˌthərz-dē-\. Small island, N Queensland, Australia, in Torres Strait 30 m. NW of Cape York; has excellent harbor (Port Kennedy).

Thur·so \ˈthər-(ˌ)sō\. 1 Town, Papineau co., SW Quebec, Canada, 30 m. NE of Hull; pop. (1971p) 3243.

2 Burgh, Caithness co., N Scotland, at mouth of Thurso river; pop. (1971p) 9074; nuclear power station, naval training facilities; in 11th cent. principal Norse town in Scotland; most northerly town on mainland of Scotland.

Thurs·ton \ˈthər-stən\. Counties in two states of the U.S. See tables at NEBRASKA and WASHINGTON.

Thurston, Mount. See NDIKEVA, MOUNT.

Thurston Island *or formerly* **Thurston Peninsula.** Island, Antarctica, bet. Bellinghausen and Amundsen seas; before 1961 thought to be a peninsula of Marie Byrd Land.

Thyatira. See AKHISAR.

Thyland. See VENDSYSSEL-THY.

Thym·bra \ˈthim-brə\. Battlefield site, Asia Minor (today in Turkey), SE of ancient Troy; scene of battle 546 B.C. in which Cyrus the Great defeated Croesus, king of Lydia.

Tia·hua·na·co \ˌtē-ə-wə-ˈnäk-(ˌ)ō\ *or* **Tia·hua·na·cu** \-ˈnäk-(ˌ)ü\. Site of prehistoric ruins, W Bolivia, adjacent to mountain village of Tiahuanaco, near SE end of Lake Titicaca; ruins consist of statues, monoliths, pillars, carvings, remains of Temple of the Sun, etc., and are of great antiquity, preceding the Aymara and Inca civilizations.

Ti·a·hua·tlán \ˌtē-ə-wä-ˈtlän\. Municipality, Veracruz state, Mexico, 140 m. NW of Veracruz; pop. (1970p) 53,447.

Tian Shan. See TIEN SHAN.

Tia·ong \tyä-ˈȯŋ\. Municipality, SW Quezon prov., Luzon, Phil., 19 m. W of Lucena; pop. (1969e) 35,400.

Ti·a·ret \ˌtē-ə-ˈret\. 1 Department of N Algeria. See table at ALGERIA.

2 Commune, its ✱, ab. 110 m. E of Oran; pop. (1966c) 37,059; alt. 3350 ft.; on a pass in N Atlas Mts. Site occupied since Roman times; in medieval times seat of Muslim dynasty; came under Turks 16th cent. and under French 1843.

Ti·ber \ˈtī-bər\ *or Ital.* **Te·ve·re** \ˈtā-vā-rā\; *anc.* **Ti·ber·is** \ˈtī-bə-rəs\. River, cen. Italy; 252 m. long; rises in the Tuscan Apennines, flows S through Umbria and Latium; in Latium turns SW, flows through Rome which is 16 m. from its mouth at Ostia on the Tyrrhenian Sea; navigable at certain seasons to ab. 30 m. N of Rome.

Ti·be·ri·as \tī-ˈbir-ē-əs\ *or Heb.* **Te·ver·ya** \tə-ˈver-yə\. Town, Northern dist., Israel, on W shore of the Sea of Galilee 30 m. E of Haifa; pop. (1970e) 23,900; lake port and resort. Founded by Herod Antipas and named after Roman Emperor Tiberius; a center of Jewish learning 2d–6th cents. A.D.; seat of Sanhedrin and rabbinical schools; Talmud edited here; modern town refounded after 1922.

Tiberias, Sea of. See GALILEE, SEA OF.

Ti·bes·ti Mountains \tə-ˈbes-tē-\. Mountain group, NW Chad, N cen. Africa, in cen. Sahara region; highest peak Emi Koussi 11,204 ft.

Ti·bet *also* **Thi·bet** \tə-ˈbet\ *or Chin.* **Si·tsang** \ˈshēt-ˈsäŋ\. Autonomous region, China, cen. Asia, bounded on N by Sinkiang Uighur and Tsinghai, on E by Szechwan, on SE by Yunnan and Burma, on S by India, Nepal, Bhutan, and Sikkim, and on W by India; 471,660 sq. m.; pop. (1968e) 1,400,000; ✱ Lhasa. *Physical features:* A plateau, the highest region in the world, averaging ab. 16,000 ft.; its lowland regions and valleys are bet. 12,000 and 15,000 ft.; its mountain ranges rise to 20,000 and 24,000 ft.; the mountain passes are generally 14,000 to 18,000 ft. Bordered on N by the Kunlun Mts.; the S part, comprising valley or plain of Tsangpo (upper Brahmaputra) is separated from Nepal, India, and Bhutan by the Himalayas (containing highest peaks in the world); subsidiary ranges are the Kailas Range and A-ling Mts. Its N region (**Ch'iang-t'ang** \ˈjäŋ-ˈdäŋ\) has a terrain much broken up by mountain ranges, valleys, and lakes. The Salween river has its source in T'ang-ku-la range in E part and flows generally SE, crossing into Yunnan; the Indus and its tributary the Sutlej rise in the SW; plateau marked by numerous lakes; agricultural products incl. barley, wheat, peas, millet.

History: Buddhism introduced in 7th cent. A.D. First came under Chinese control during Manchu dynasty in 1720; generally closed to foreigners until late in 19th cent. when (1890, 1893) by Sikkim Convention boundaries and commercial relations bet. Tibet and India were determined; Anglo-Tibetan Convention signed 1904; invaded by Communist Chinese 1950; anti-Chinese rebellion (1959) crushed by Chinese forces; traditional religious institutions abolished under Chinese rule; made a nominally autonomous region within Communist China 1965.

Tibet, Little. See BALTISTAN.

Tibet, Nearer. An earlier name for E Tibet, region now included in Tibet and Tsinghai and Szechwan provs. of China.

Tibiscus. See TIMIŞ.

Tibur. See TIVOLI.

Tib·u·ron \ˈtib-ə-ˌrän\. 1 Peninsula, N of San Francisco, California, extending into San Francisco Bay.

2 City, Marin co., W California, on San Francisco Bay, 7 m. N of San Francisco; pop. (1970c) 6209; boat works.

Ti·bu·ron \ˌtē-bə-ˈrōⁿ\. 1 Peninsula, SW Haiti; ab. 140 m. long, 18 to 36 m. wide; mountainous, contains the Massif du Sud.

2 Cape, the SW point of Tiburon Penin., Haiti.

Ti·bu·rón \ˌtē-bə-ˈrōn\. Island off W cen. coast of Sonora state, Mexico, in Gulf of California; 34 m. long.

Tiburón, Cape. Cape on W coast of Colombia at the entrance to the Gulf of Urubá.

Ti·cao \ti-ˈkau̇\. Island, Masbate prov., Phil., off NE coast of Masbate I. and separated from Luzon (Sorsogon prov.) by Ticao Pass; 129 sq. m.; pop. (1969e) 41,900; coextensive with 2 municipalities of San Jacinto and San Fernando, both with population centers on E coast. Occupied by U.S. forces Mar. 1945.

Ticao Pass. Strait bet. SW Sorsogon prov., SE Luzon, Phil., and Ticao I.; ab. 37 m. long by 10 or 12 m. wide; sometimes considered as W part of San Bernardino Strait.

Tice \ˈtīs\. Urban community (unincorporated), Lee co., SW Florida, NE of Fort Myers; pop. (1970c) 7254.

Ti·ci·no \ti-ˈchē-(ˌ)nō\. 1 *or anc.* **Ti·ci·nus** \tis-ˈī-nəs\. River, Switzerland and Italy; 154 m. long; rises on the slopes of Saint Gotthard, flows SE and then SW in Ticino canton, traverses Lago Maggiore and continues S into Po river 3½ m. SSE of Pavia; navigable below Lake Maggiore; Hannibal defeated Romans on the banks of this river 218 B.C.

2 *or* **Tes·sin** \te-ˈsaⁿ\. Swiss canton in Lepontine Alps, watered by Ticino river; crossed by St. Gotthard railroad; wine; tourism; formed 1803. See table at SWITZERLAND.

Ticinum. See PAVIA 2.

Ti·con·der·o·ga \ˌtī-kän-dər-ˈō-gä\. Village, Essex co., NE New York, on N outlet of Lake George and near Lake Champlain; pop. (1970c) 3268; tourist center in resort region; incorporated 1889. Old Fort Carillon (restored as museum 1909) built at head of Lake Champlain by French 1755 and garrisoned by force under Montcalm 1758; defended from Abercrombie's attack 1758; taken by Gen. Amherst 1759, and renamed **Fort Ticonderoga;** captured by Ethan Allen 1775, retaken by Burgoyne 1777; held by British until Burgoyne's surrender.

Ti·cul \ti-'kül\. Town, Yucatán state, SE Mexico, 40 m. S of Mérida; munic. pop. (1970p) 16,537.

Tid·dim \'tid-ˌim\. Town, Chin Special Division, W Upper Burma, just E of Manipur river and S of Manipur border; a headquarters town of Japanese forces in campaign against India 1943–45.

Ti·do·re \ti-'dōr-ē, -'dȯr-\. 1 Island of the Moluccas, Indonesia, off W coast of Halmahera I. ab. 1 m. S of Ternate I.; ab. 45 sq. m.; pop. (1957e) 27,753. Has several volcanic peaks, highest 5676 ft.; fertile soil; raises tobacco, coffee, and fruits; formerly produced much spice. Former seat of an ancient and powerful sultanate; occupied 1521 by Portuguese, who built a fort 1571; deserted by Portuguese 1605 and occupied by Spanish 1606; conquered by Dutch 1654; occupied by Japanese 1942–45.

2 Town and port on E side of island; a walled town dating back to years before the coming of the Portuguese.

T'ieh–ling *or* **Tieh·ling** \tē-'ā-'liŋ\. Town, cen. Liaoning prov., NE China, on left bank of Liao river 40 m. NE of Mukden.

Tiel \'tē(ə)l\. Commune, Gelderland prov., E Netherlands, on the Waal 20 m. SE of Utrecht; pop. (1970e) 21,789.

Tielt. See THIELT.

Tien Ch'ih *or* **Tien Chih** \tē-'en-'chi(ə)r\. Lake, cen. Yunnan prov., S China, just S of K'un-ming.

Tie·nen *or* **Thie·nen** \'tē-nən\ *or Fr.* **Tir·le·mont** \ˌtir-lə-'mō^{n}\. Commercial and manufacturing commune, Brabant prov., cen. Belgium; pop. (1969e) 22,584; breweries; captured by the Germans 1914.

Tien Shan \tē-'en-'shän\ *or* **Tian Shan** *also* **Thian Shan** \tē-'än-\ *or Chin.* **T'ien Shan** \tē-'en-\ *or Russ.* **Tyan Shan** \tē-'än-\. Lofty mountain chain (*shan*), Kirgiz S.S.R., U.S.S.R., and in Sinkiang Uighur, W China; highest point Pobeda Peak 24,406 ft.

T'ien–shui *or* **Tien·shui** \tē-'en-'shwā\ *or formerly* **Tsin·chow** \'tsin-'jō\. Market city, SE Kansu prov., N cen. China; pop. (1970e) 100,000.

Tien·tsin \tē-'en(t)-'sin, 'tin(t)-\. City, ✱ of Hopei prov., NE China, at the junction of the Pai and Grand Canal where they form the Hai river, ab. 80 m. SE of Peking; met. area pop. (1970e) 4,500,000; major seaport and industrial center, producing textiles, chemicals, iron and steel, tobacco products, machinery; several colleges including Hopeh Univ. (1960); connected to Yangtze by Grand Canal.

History: Garrison town until 1782; became treaty port 1860 and developed rapidly with foreign concessions. Treaty signed here 1858 opened 11 Chinese ports to foreign trade; occupied by British and French 1858 and 1860; in Boxer Rebellion 1900 scene of siege and heavy fighting, after which city placed under control of international commission 1900–07 and walls razed; in Chinese Civil War occupied by Communist forces Jan. 1949; made ✱ of province 1958.

Tier·o·ko \ˌtyer-ə-'kō\ *or* **Tar·so Tieroko** \'tär-(ˌ)sō-\. Mountain peak, NW Chad, N cen. Africa; 9547 ft.; one of the highest peaks in the Tibesti Mts.

Ti·er·ra Am·a·ril·la \ˌtē-ˌer-ə-ˌam-ə-'ril-ə\. Village, ⊗ of Rio Arriba co., N New Mexico; pop. (1970c) 600.

Tierra Blan·ca \tē-ˌer-ə-'bläŋ-kə\. Town, Veracruz state, E Mexico; railroad junction point ab. 50 m. SSW of Veracruz; munic. pop. (1970p) 48,733; coffee raising.

Tierra Bom·ba \tē-ˌer-ə-'bäm-bə\. Small island, Caribbean Sea, off NW coast of Colombia, near city of Cartagena.

Tierra del Fu·e·go \tē-ˌer-ə-del-f(y)u̇-'ā-(ˌ)gō\. 1 Archipelago off S South America, comprising all islands S of Strait of Magellan; 28,434 sq. m.; separated from Antarctic Archipelago on S by Drake Passage. Its main island, Tierra del Fuego, is divided bet. Chile (W half) and Argentina (E half); of its groups of smaller islands the eastern (including Isla de los Estados) belongs to Argentina, and the southern (including Hoste I., Navarino I., Wollaston Is., and Diego Ramírez Is.) and western (including Desolación, Santa Inés, Clarence, and Dawson) belong to Chile.

2 *or* **Is·la Gran·de de Tierra del Fuego** \ēs-lə-'grand-ē-dā-\. Chief island of Tierra del Fuego archipelago; 18,530 sq. m.; W half belongs to Magallanes prov., Chile; E half and nearby Isla de los Estados constitute **Tierra del Fuego National Territory** of Argentina (see table at ARGENTINA).

Tie·tê \tyə-'tā\. River, São Paulo state, SE Brazil; 500 m. long; rises in mountains near Atlantic coast, flows NW through cen. São Paulo state and empties into Paraná river; São Paulo is on it.

Tiet·jerk·ste·ra·deel \tēt-'yerk-stə-rə-ˌdāl\. Commune, Friesland prov., N Netherlands; pop. (1970e) 23,416.

Ti·e·ton \'tī-ət-^{ə}n\. River, S Washington; 25 m. long; a tributary of Naches river; rises in W Yakima co., flows NE.

Tieton Dam. Dam across Tieton river, W Yakima co., S Washington; height 235 ft.; completed 1925; impounds water, **Tieton Reservoir,** for irrigation.

Tieton Peak. Mountain, Yakima co., S Washington; 7775 ft.

Tif·fa·ny Mountain \ˌtif-ə-nē-\. Peak, Okanogan co., N Washington; 8275 ft.

Tif·fin \'tif-ən\. Industrial city, ⊗ of Seneca co., N Ohio, 25 m. ENE of Findlay; pop. (1970c) 21,596; glass, pottery, drilling machinery, wire, automobile parts, furniture; diversified agriculture; Heidelberg Coll. (1850); settled 1817.

Tiflis. See TBILISI.

Tift \'tift\. County in Georgia. See table at GEORGIA.

Tif·ton \'tif-tən\. City, ⊗ of Tift co., S Georgia, 40 m. ESE of Albany; pop. (1970c) 12,179; textiles, plastics, lumber; tomatoes, peanuts; Abraham Baldwin Agricultural Coll. (1907).

Tigara. See HOPE, POINT.

Ti·gard \'tī-gərd\. City, Washington co., NW Oregon, 7 m. SSW of Portland; pop. (1970c) 5302; sawmill equipment, food processing; diversified agriculture.

Tig·ba·uan \tig-'bä-(ˌ)wän\. Municipality, Iloilo prov., Panay, Phil., on Iloilo Strait 15 m. W of City of Iloilo; pop. (1969e) 31,200; one of the oldest towns on Panay.

Tiger. See TYGER.

Ti·ger Bay \ˌtī-gər-\ *or Port.* **Ba·ia dos Ti·gres** \bə-ˌē-ə-du̇-'stē-grəsh\. Inlet of Atlantic Ocean, SW coast of Angola, SW Africa.

Tiger Hill. See DARJEELING 2.

Tigranocerta. See SIIRT 2.

Ti·gre \'tē-(ˌ)grā\. 1 *or formerly* **Las Con·chas** \läs-'kȯn-chəz\. Town, Buenos Aires prov., E Argentina, 20 m. N of Buenos Aires; pop. (1960c) 91,725; part of Greater Buenos Aires; seaside resort.

2 River, Ecuador and Peru; ab. 350 m. long; rises in cen. Ecuador, flows SE across border into Peru and empties into Marañón river, headstream of Amazon river.

Tigre \ti-'grā\. Province of N Ethiopia. See table at ETHIOPIA.

Tigre Island \'tē-grā-\. Island, Gulf of Fonseca, Honduras; chief town Amapala.

Tigres, Baia dos. See TIGER BAY.

Ti·gri \'tē-grē\. Town, ✱ of Laghmān prov., NE Afghanistan; pop. (1969e) 72,601.

Ti·gris \'tī-grəs\ *or Arab.* **Shatt Dij·la** \shät-'dij-lə\ *or Bib.* (*Gen.* ii. 14; *Dan.* x. 4) **Hid·de·kel** \'hid-ə-(ˌ)kel\. River, SE Turkey and Iraq; 1180 m. long; rises in a lake in the mountains of Kurdistan, S of Elâzığ, Turkey; flows SSE past Diyarbakır in Turkey and Mosul and Baghdad in Iraq, and unites in SE Iraq at Al-Qurna with the Euphrates river to form the Shatt-al-Arab. Has many tributaries on left bank, esp. the Great Zab, Little Zab, and Diyala in Iraq. Navigable for small steamers bet. Baghdad and a point just above Al-Qurna. Since ancient times, tributaries connected with Euphrates in their lower courses by irrigation canals; probably in Sumerian times its lower course was much more to the W. Sites of ruins of many ancient cities are on its banks, as Nineveh, Calah, Ashur, Ctesiphon, and Seleucia.

Tih, Al–. See AL-TIH.

Ti·ha·ma *or* **Te·ha·ma** \tē-'ham-ə\ *also* **Ha·ma** \'ham-ə\ *or* **'Asīr Ti·hā·mat** \a-ˌsi(ə)r-ti-'ham-ət\. Low coastal plain, W Saudi Arabia, along the Red Sea, from S Hejaz to Bab al-Mandab strait.

Ti·hany National Park \'ti-hän-yə-\. National park, Hungary; ab. 3 sq. m.; volcanic region; Bronze Age ramparts; established 1952.

Tihwa. See URUMCHI.

Ti·jua·na \ˌtē-ə-'wän-ə, tē-'wän-ə\. Town, Baja California, NW Mexico; pop. (1969e) 354,805; a popular tourist center and point of entry on U.S.-Mexico border.

Ti·ju·ca Peak \ti-ˌzhü-kə-\. Mountain, SW side of the city of Rio de Janeiro, SE Brazil; 3353 ft.

Ti·ju·cas Bay \ti-ˌzhü-kəs-\. Inlet of Atlantic Ocean, E coast of Santa Catarina state, S Brazil, N of Florianópolis.

Ti·kal \ti-'käl\. Ancient Mayan city, N Guatemala, NE of Petén Itza; ruins; excavation and restoration of ruins begun 1956; located in **Tikal National Park** (224 sq. m.).

Ti·kam·garh \ti-'kəm-ˌgär\ *or* **Teh·ri** \'te(ə)r-ē\. Town, Madhya Pradesh, India, ab. 100 m. SSE of Gwalior; pop. (1961c) 20,469; chosen as ✱ of Orchha state 1783.

Ti·kho·retsk \ˌtik-ə-'retsk\. Town, Krasnodar Krai, Russian S.F.S.R., U.S.S.R., ab. 100 m. S of Rostov-na-Donu; pop. (1969e) 58,000; key railroad junction point and scene of fighting Jan. and Feb. 1943.

Tikh·vin \'tik-vən\. Town, E Leningrad Oblast, Russian S.F.S.R., U.S.S.R., 110 m. ESE of Leningrad; pop. (1967e) 26,000; on S bank of the **Tikh·vin·ka** \'tik-vən-kə, -vin-ə\ tributary of the Syas, which forms part of canal system connecting Lake Ladoga with the Volga at Rybinsk via the Mologa river and Rybinsk Reservoir.

Ti·krīt *or* **Te·krit** \ti-'krēt\. Town, N cen. Iraq, on the W bank of the Tigris river ab. 100 m. NNW of Baghdad; birthplace of Saladin (1138). Battle Nov. 6, 1917 in World War I in which it was captured from the Turks.

Til·burg \'til-ˌbərg\. Commune, North Brabant prov., S Netherlands, 34 m. SE of Rotterdam; pop. (1970e) 152,589; a center of Dutch textile industry.

Til·bury \'til-ˌber-ē, -b(ə-)rē\. Town, Kent and Essex cos., SE Ontario, Canada, 17 m. SW of Chatham, near mouth of Thames river; pop. (1971p) 3626.

Til·den \'til-dən\. Village, ⊗ of McMullen co., S Texas; pop. (1969e) 466.

Till \'til\. Small river, Northumberland, N England; 32 m. long; flows N into the Tweed on the border of Scotland.

Til·la·mook \'til-ə-ˌmu̇k\. 1 County in NW Oregon. See table at OREGON.

2 City, its ⊗, on S end of **Tillamook Bay** (inlet of Pacific Ocean) 50 m. S of Astoria; pop. (1970c) 3968; veneer, dairy products; resort; salmon and oyster fisheries.

Til·leur \tē-'yər\. Commune, Liège prov., E Belgium; pop. (1969e) 5829; W suburb of Liège; blast furnaces, smelters.

Till·man \'til-mən\. County in Oklahoma. See table at OKLAHOMA.

Till·son·burg \'til-sən-ˌbərg\. Town, Oxford co., SE Ontario, Canada, 28 m. ESE of London; pop. (1971p) 6611.

Til·ly \tē-'yē\ *or officially* **Tilly–sur–Seulles** \-su̇(ə)r-'sə(r)l\. Village, Calvados dept., NW France, 7 m. SSE of Bayeux; pop. (1962c) 434; in World War II retaken from German occupation forces June 7–11, 1944.

Tilos. See TELOS.

Tilsit. See SOVETSK.

Til·till Mountain \ˌtil-til-\. Peak in Sierra Nevada, in E Tuolumne co., cen. California; 8951 ft.

Til·ton \'tilt-ᵊn\. 1 Village, Vermilion co., E Illinois, 3 m. SW of Danville; pop. (1970c) 2544.

2 Town, Belknap co., cen. New Hampshire, 7 m. SW of Laconia; pop. (1970c) 2579; united industrially, commercially, and residentially with Northfield, to the S, across Winnipesaukee river.

Ti·ma·ga·mi, Lake *or* **Lake Te·ma·ga·mi** \-ti-'mäg-ə-mē\. Lake, Ontario, Canada, N of Lake Nipissing and SW of Lake Timiskaming; 91 sq. m.; in forest reserve.

Tim·a·ru \'tim-ə-ˌrü\. Seaport, E South I., New Zealand, on Pacific Ocean 95 m. SW of Christchurch; pop. (1970e) 28,600; exports flour, wool, and frozen meat; seaside resort.

Tim·ba·lier Bay \'tam-bəl-ˌyā-\. Inlet of Gulf of Mexico, SW coast of Lafourche parish, SE Louisiana.

Timbalier Island. Island off SE Louisiana, in Lafourche parish, bet. Timbalier Island and the Gulf of Mexico.

Tim·ba·ú·ba \ˌtim-bə-'ü-bə\. City, Pernambuco state, E Brazil, near the coast ab. 40 m. NNW of Recife; munic. pop. (1968e) 54,055.

Tim·ber Crater \ˌtim-bər-\. Peak, W Klamath co., S Oregon, N of Crater Lake; 7403 ft.

Timber Lake. City, ⊗ of Dewey co., N cen. South Dakota; pop. (1970c) 625.

Timber Mountain. Peak, S Nye co., S Nevada; 7243 ft.

Tim·ber·wolf, Mount \-'tim-bər-ˌwu̇lf\. Peak, Yakima co., S Washington; 6435 ft.

Tim·bo \'tim-(ˌ)bō\. Town, Guinea, W Africa, in the Fouta Djallon region 140 m. NE of Conakry.

Timbuktu. See TOMBOUCTOU.

Tim·gad \'tim-ˌgad\; *anc.* **Tham·u·ga·di** \ˌtham-ə-'gād-ē\ *or* **Tham·u·ga·dis** \-'gād-əs\. Ruined city, NE Algeria, ESE of Batna; extensive ruins include the capitol, forum, theater (auditorium, almost complete, has capacity of 4000 people), several baths (well-preserved mosaic floors), and an arch of Trajan. Founded 100 A.D. by Trajan, declined after 5th cent.; revived for a time in 7th cent.; not mentioned in history since 647.

Ti·miş \'tē-ˌmēsh\ *or Serb.* **Te·meš** \'tem-ˌesh \ *or anc.* **Ti·bis·cus** \ti-'bis-kəs\. 1 River, W Romania; ab. 200 m. long; flows W and S to the Danube in Yugoslavia just below Belgrade.

2 County of W Romania. See table at ROMANIA.

Ti·mis·ka·ming *or* **Te·mis·ka·ming** \tə-'mis-kä-ˌmiŋ\ *or Fr.* **Té·mis·ca·mingue** \tā-mis-ka-maⁿg\. 1 Lake, SW Quebec and SE Ontario, Canada; 121 sq. m.; discharges SE into the Ottawa river.

2 District, Ontario, Canada. See table at ONTARIO.

3 County, Quebec, Canada. See table at QUEBEC.

4 Town, Timiskaming co., Quebec, Canada, on left bank of Timiskaming river, ab. 40 m. NNE of North Bay, Ontario; pop. (1966c) 2769.

Ti·mi·şoa·ra \ˌtē-mish-'wär-ə\ *or Hung.* **Te·mes·vár** \'tem-ˌesh-ˌvär\. City, ⊗ of Timiş co., W Romania, near the Timiş river and the Yugoslav border; pop. (1970e) 192,616; commercial and industrial center, producing electrical equipment, chemicals, footwear, textiles; cultural center, with univ. (1962), state theaters, libraries; 18th cent. cathedral, 15th cent. castle. First mentioned 1247; held by Turks 1552–1716 when it was captured by Austrians under Prince Eugene of Savoy; to Romania 1920.

Tim·mins \'tim-ənz\. Mining town, Cochrane dist., E Ontario, Canada, on Mattagami river 135 m. N of Sudbury; pop. (1971p) 28,252; principal gold-mining center of Canada; machine tools, beer; meat-packing plant; diversified agriculture; founded 1911.

Timms Hill \'timz-\. Peak, Price co., N Wisconsin; 1952 ft.; highest point in the state.

Ti·mok \'tē-ˌmōk\. River, E Yugoslavia; ab. 100 m. long; flows NE into Danube river 18 m. NNW of Vidin; in part forms boundary bet. Yugoslavia and Romania.

Ti·mor \'tē-ˌmō(ə)r, tē-'-\. Island, S Malay Archipelago, easternmost of the Lesser Sunda Is., bet. Savu Sea on the W and Timor Sea on the E; ab. 400 m. NW of Australia; ab. 300 m. long by 10 to 65 m. wide; 13,094 sq. m.; formerly divided bet. the Dutch and the Portuguese; see TIMOR, NETHERLANDS and TIMOR, PORTUGUESE.

Timor, Netherlands. Former Dutch-ruled sector of Timor, now (with adjacent islands) the Indonesian prov. East Nusa Tenggara (see table at INDONESIA). First occupied by Portuguese; Kupang and vicinity seized by Dutch 1618 and W half of island claimed by them after Napoleonic Wars; occupied by Japanese Feb. 1942; transferred to Indonesia by the Dutch 1949.

Timor, Portuguese. Portuguese overseas province, comprising the E half of Timor and an exclave Ocussi Ambeno on the N coast of Indonesian Timor; 5763 sq. m.; pop. (1970p) 610,541; ✱ Dili; coffee, sandalwood, copra.

History: Known to Portuguese in 16th cent.; scene of conflict with Dutch in 17th cent.; in 1618 Kupang and W end of island seized by Dutch; Dili made Portuguese capital; negotiations over boundary line conducted on several occasions: 1859, 1893, 1898; treaty made 1904 but not ratified until 1914; occupied by Japanese Feb. 1942.

Timor Sea. Arm of the Indian Ocean bet. Timor I. and the NW coast of Australia; ab. 300 m. wide.

Ti·mo·ta·kem \tē-ˌmüt-ə-ˈkäⁿ\. Peak, Tumuc-Humac Mts. in S French Guiana on Brazil border.

Tim·pah·ute Range \ˌtim-pə-ˈyüt-\. Small range, W Lincoln co., SE Nevada; highest peak 9380 ft.

Tim·pa·no·gos, Mount \-ˌtim-pə-ˈnō-gəs\. Peak, N cen. Utah; 12,008 ft.; highest peak in Wasatch Range.

Timpanogos Cave National Monument. See UNITED STATES, *National Monuments.*

Tim·sah \tim-ˈsä\ *or Arab.* **Bu·ḩay·rat at Tim·sāḩ** \bə-ˈhā-rət-ˌat-\. Lake, NE Egypt, at midpoint of Suez Canal; connected with the Nile river by the Ismailia Canal.

Tims Ford Dam \ˌtimz-ˌfō(ə)rd-, -ˌfȯ(ə)rd-\. See table at TENNESSEE VALLEY AUTHORITY.

Tin, Cape \-ˈtin\. Cape, N coast of Libya, N Africa, W of entrance to Gulf of Bomba.

Ti·na, Plain of \-ˈtē-nə\. Plain, NW Sinai Penin., NE Egypt, E of Suez Canal and near the Mediterranean; in it are ruins of Pelusium.

Ti·na·ca Point \ti-ˈnäk-ə-\. Most southerly point of Mindanao, Phil., in Davao del Sur prov.; 4°N, 125°20′E.

Ti·na·ga \ˌtē-nə-ˈgä\. Largest island of the Calagua group off N coast of Camarines Norte, SE Luzon, Phil., 14 m. NE of Paracale; 5 sq. m.

Tin·che·bray \taⁿsh-ˈbrā\. Town, NW Orne dept., NW France; pop. (1962c) 3238; scene Sept. 28, 1106 of victory of Henry Beauclerc over his brother Robert Curthose (Robert II of Normandy).

Ti·neo \ti-ˈnā-(ˌ)ō\. Commune, Oviedo prov., NW Spain, 32 m. W of Oviedo; pop. (1970p) 17,969; stock raising; lime; dairy products.

Tingchow. See CH'ANG-T'ING.

Ting–hai *or* **Ting·hai** \ˈdiŋ-ˈhī\. Commercial seaport, ✱ of Chou-shan archipelago, on S shore of Chou-shan I., Chekiang prov., E China.

Tingis. See TANGIER.

Tin·gi·ta·na \ˌtin-jə-ˈtān-ə, -ˈtan-, -ˈtän-\. Region, NW Africa; in Roman times, the W part of Mauretania; partly coextensive with Morocco.

Ti·ni·an \ˌtin-ē-ˈan\. Island, S Mariana Is., U.S. Trust Territory of the Pacific Islands, W Pacific Ocean, 3 m. SSW of Saipan; 10 m. long by ab. 5 m. wide; area 20 sq. m.; chief town Tinian on SW coast. Contains ruins of large columned tombs; in early times, Spanish, then German (see MARIANA ISLANDS), included in Japanese mandate 1919; occupied by U.S. forces July 23–Aug. 1, 1944

Tin·i·cum \ˈtin-i-kəm\. Small island, Delaware river just below Philadelphia; first settlement within Pennsylvania, made 1643 by Gov. Johan Printz of Swedish colony. See CHESTER 6.

Tin·ley Park \ˌtin-lē-\. Village, Cook and Will cos., NE Illinois, SW suburb of Chicago; pop. (1970c) 12,382.

Tínos. See TENOS.

Tin·ta·gel Head \tin-ˌtaj-əl-\. Cape, W coast of Cornwall, SW England; site of ruins of 12th cent. Tintagel Castle, reputed birthplace of King Arthur.

Tin·tern Abbey \ˌtint-ərn-\. Noted ruins, Monmouthshire, E Wales, 4½ m. N of Chepstow, on the river Wye. Founded 1131 by Walter de Clare for Cistercian monks; building in ruins dates from 13th cent.

Tin·to \ˈtin-(ˌ)tō, ˈtēn-\. River, Huelva prov., SW Spain; 58 m. long; flows into the Odiel river below Huelva; combined streams flow into the Mediterranean.

Ti·o·ga \tī-ˈō-gə\. 1 River, SW New York; 40 m. long; rises in N Pennsylvania near W boundary of Bradford co., flows N across New York border to unite with Cohocton river near Corning and form the Chemung river.

2 Name of counties in two states of the U.S. See tables at NEW YORK and PENNSYLVANIA.

Tio·man \tē-ˈō-ˌmän\. Island, South China Sea off SE Pahang, S Malay Penin.

Ti·o·nes·ta \ˌtī-ə-ˈnest-ə\. Borough, ⊗ of Forest co., NW Pennsylvania; pop. (1970c) 711.

Ti·o·ro Strait \tē-ˌōr-ə-, -ˌȯr-\. Channel bet. SE Celebes I. and the island of Muna, Indonesia.

Tiphsah. See THAPSACUS.

Ti·pi·ta·pa \ˌtē-pi-ˈtäp-ə\. River, W Nicaragua; 23 m. long; flows out of Lake Managua SE into Lake Nicaragua.

Tip·pah \ˈtip-ə\. County in Mississippi. See table at MISSISSIPPI.

Tipp City \ˈtip-\ *or formerly* **Tip·pe·ca·noe City** \ˌtip-ē-kə-ˈnü-\. Village, Miami co., W Ohio, 14 m. N of Dayton; pop. (1970c) 5090.

Tip·pe·ca·noe \ˌtip-ē-kə-ˈnü\. 1 River, N Indiana, ab. 200 m. long; rises in **Tippecanoe Lake** in NE cen. Kosciusko co., N Indiana, flows W and then S into Wabash river in W cen. Indiana. See FREEMAN LAKE, SHAFER LAKE. At the junction of the Tippecanoe with the Wabash near the Indian village of Prophetstown, Gen. William H. Harrison defeated the Indians under Tecumseh Nov. 7, 1811.

2 County in Indiana. See table at INDIANA.

Tip·pe·rary \ˌtip-ə-ˈre(ə)r-ē\. 1 County in Munster prov., S Eire; 1643 sq. m.; pop. (1971p) 123,196; ⊗ Clonmel; divided into North Riding and South Riding; livestock raising, food processing, tanning.

2 Urban district, SW co. Tipperary, S Eire, 24 m. SE of Limerick; pop. (1971p) 4592; market town; site of 13th cent. castle and abbey.

Tip·per·muir \ˈtip-ər-myu̇(ə)r\. Battlefield near Perth, Scotland; scene Sept. 1, 1644 of victory of Montrose over Covenanters under earl of Wemyss.

Tip·ton \ˈtip-tən\. 1 Name of counties in two states of the U.S. See tables at INDIANA and TENNESSEE.

2 City, ⊗ of Tipton co., cen. Indiana, 15 m. S of Kokomo; pop. (1970c) 5313; canned goods, furniture; dairy and livestock farms.

3 City, ⊗ of Cedar co., E Iowa, 23 m. ENE of Iowa City; pop. (1970c) 2877; cheese; corn.

Tipton, Mount. Peak, cen. Mohave co., NW Arizona; 7364 ft.

Tip·ton·ville \ˈtip-tən-ˌvil\. Town and resort, ⊗ of Lake co., NW Tennessee, 3 m. E of Mississippi river at SW end of Reelfoot Lake; pop. (1970c) 2424.

Tira. See TIRE.

Ti·rah \ˈtē-(ˌ)rä\. Mountainous region, Pakistan, WSW of Khyber Pass and Peshawar; scene of campaign 1897–98 in which British forces put down an uprising of Afridi and Orakzai tribes.

Tī·rān *or* **Ti·ran** \ti-ˈrän\. Island at N end of Red Sea; with Sanafiri I. lies across entrance to Gulf of ‘Aqaba; both belong to Saudi Arabia. Tīrān I. separated by **Strait of Tiran** from SE coast of Sinai Penin., Egypt.

Ti·ra·në *or* **Ti·ra·na** \ti-ˈrän-ə\. 1 Province of cen. Albania. See table at ALBANIA.

2 City, ✱ of Albania, also ✱ of Tiranë prov., 18 m. E of Durrës; pop. (1967e) 169,300; univ. (1957), national library, and various government buildings. Population largely Muslim. Founded by Turks early 17th cent.; made capital of Albania 1920; occupied by Axis forces Apr. 1939–Nov. 1944.

Ti·ra·no \ti-ˈrän-(ˌ)ō\. Commune, Sondrio prov., N Lombardy, N Italy, near the Swiss border; pop. (1968e) 8346; scene of massacre of Protestants July 11, 1620; church of Madonna di Tirano, object of many pilgrimages.

Ti·ras·pol \ti-ˈras-pəl\. City, Moldavian S.S.R., U.S.S.R., on the Dniester 55 m. NW of Odessa; pop. (1970p) 106,000; canned goods, wine, lumber, farm equipment, footwear; founded 1795; ✱ of Moldavian A.S.S.R. 1930–40; heavily damaged in World War II.

Tiravalur. See TIRUVARUR.

Ti·re \ti-ˈre\ *also* **Ti·ra** \-ˈrä\ *or anc.* **Tyr·rha** \ˈtir-ə\. Town, İzmir prov., W Turkey, on branch railroad 38 m. SE of İzmir; pop. (1965c) 27,243.

Ti·ree *or* **Ty·ree** \tī-ˈrē\. 1 Island, Inner Hebrides, off W coast of Scotland; 30 sq. m.; pop. (1961c) 1713; administratively a part of Argyll co.; horse breeding, marble quarrying.

2 Strait bet. the islands of Tiree and Mall, Inner Hebrides, off W coast of Scotland.

Tîr·go·vi·şte *or* **Târ·go·viş·te** \ˌtir-gə-ˈvēsh-tə\. City, ⊗ of Dîmboviţa co., S cen. Romania, on Ialomiţa river 45 m. NW of Bucharest; pop. (1970e) 33,359; commercial center; notable 16th cent. church; capital of Walachia 1383–1698; defended against Turks in 1597.

Tîr·gu–Jiu *or* **Târ·gu–Jiu** *also* **Tur·gu–Jiu** \ˌtir-gü-ˈzhü\. Town, ⊗ of Gorj co., SW Romania, on Jiul river ab. 50 m. NNW of Craiova; pop. (1970e) 42,935; trade center, esp. in lumber and petroleum.

Tîrgu–Mu·reş *or* **Târ·gu–Mureş** \ˌtir-gü-ˈmür-esh\ *also* **Osor·hei** \ˌó-sór-ˈhī\ *or Hung.* **Ma·ros–Vá·sár·hely** \ˈmär-ōsh-ˌvä-shär-ˈā\. City, ⊗ of Mureş co., N cen. Romania, ab. 50 m. ESE of Cluj; pop. (1970e) 98,201; 15th cent. Gothic church; palace, museum, library. In region ceded by Hungary to Romania 1918 but again, with the rest of northern Transylvania, was part of Hungary 1940–45.

Tîrgu–Neamţ \ˌtir-gü-ˈnyäm(p)ts\ *or* **Târ·gu–Neam·ţu** \-ˈnyäm(p)-tsü\ *or* **Târ·gul–Neamţ** \ˌtir-gül-ˈnyäm(p)ts\. Commercial town, NE Romania, 60 m. WNW of Iaşi; pop. (1966c) 12,877; founded 13th cent. by Teutonic Order; fortress and ancient monastery nearby.

Tîr·gu–Oc·na *or* **Târ·gu–Ocna** \ˌtir-gü-ˈók-nä\. Town, E Romania, in E Transylvanian Alps 45 m. W of Bîrlad; pop. (1966c) 11,647; salt mines.

Ti·rich Mir \ˌtir-ich-ˈmi(ə)r\. Mountain, Hindu Kush range, Pakistan, N of Chitral, on border of Afghanistan; 25,260 ft.; highest peak in the range.

Tirlemont. See TIENEN.

Tîr·nă·ve·ni \ˌtir-nə-ˈven(-ē)\. Town, Mureş co., cen. Romania, ab. 20 m. SW of Tîrgu-Mureş; pop. (1970e) 24,148.

Tírnavos. See TYRNAVOS.

Tirnovo. See VELIKO TŬRNOVO.

Ti·rol *or* **Ty·rol** \tə-ˈrōl; ˈtī-ˌrōl; tī-ˈ-; ˈtir-əl\ *or Ital.* **Ti·ro·lo** \tē-ˈró-(ˌ)lō\. State, W Austria, bet. the Vorarlberg on the W and Salzburg on the E; 4883 sq. m.; pop. (1971p) 539,000; ✱ Innsbruck. A very mountainous region with Bavarian Alps along N border and Ötztaler Alps in S cen. part (since 1919 when South Tirol was ceded to Italy, have marked S border). Traversed W to E by the Inn and in the NW by the Lech; before 1919 by the Adige in the S; wheat, rye, barley, corn; viticulture, livestock raising; salt, copper, magnesite.

History: Inhabited in early times by Celtic race; became part of Raetia in 1st cent. A.D.; under various counts and bishops until 14th cent.; passed to Hapsburgs 1363. Tirolese have been strongly independent people; their land scene of peasant uprising 1525 during Reformation, and after its cession to Napoleon 1805 by Treaty of Pressburg they carried on vigorous but unsuccessful revolt against French and Bavarians 1809–10; reunited with Austria 1814. Its S part (called Upper Adige by Italians) transferred to Italy by Treaty of St-Germain 1919.

Tirreno, Mare. See TYRRHENIAN SEA.

Tir·so \ˈti(ə)r-(ˌ)sō\. River, cen. Sardinia, Italy; ab. 90 m. long; flows SW into Gulf of Oristano.

Ti·ruch·chi·rap·pal·li \ˌtir-ə-chə-ˈräp-ə-lē\ *or* **Trich·i·nop·o·ly** \ˌtrich-ə-ˈnäp-ə-lē\. City, cen. Tamil Nadu, S India, on right bank of the Cauvery river 200 m. SSW of Madras; pop. (1967e) 269,457; railroad junction; cigars, silk; railroad shops; 17th cent. Dravidian temple, ruins of fort surrounding large rock (273 ft. high). Scene of fighting bet. English and French during Carnatic wars 1749; annexed by British 1801.

Ti·rup·pur \ˈtir-ə-ˌpů(ə)r\. Town, Tamil Nadu, India, ab. 25 m. E of Coimbatore; pop. (1961c) 79,773.

Ti·ru·van·na·ma·lai \ˌtir-ə-və-ˈnäm-ə-ˌlī\. Town, E Tamil Nadu, S India, 110 m. SW of Madras; pop. (1961c) 46,441; temple.

Ti·ru·va·rur \ˌtir-ə-ˈvär-ˌů(ə)r\ *or* **Ti·ra·va·lur** \-ˈvä-lů(ə)r\. Town, E Tamil Nadu, S India, 38 m. E of Thanjavur; pop. (1961c) 30,137.

Ti·ryns \ˈtir-ənz, ˈtī-rənz\. Prehistoric citadel N of Nauplia, Argolis, E Peloponnesus, S Greece. In legends connected with Perseus and Hercules; historically, a Dorian city, founded as early as 2000 B.C. under Cretan influence; declined, with Mycenae, as Argos grew in power; destroyed by Argives c. 468 B.C. Ruins of massive walls, palace, hall, etc., have been uncovered and give valuable information of pre-Homeric life in Greece.

Tir·zah \ˈtər-zə\. Ancient Canaanite town, its site thought to be just NE of Nablus, Jordan, in region occupied by Israel 1967; for a time (c. 911–887 B.C.) capital of the Northern Kingdom of Israel (*1 Kings* xv. 21, 33).

Tisa. See TISZA.

Tis·bury \ˈtiz-ˌber-ē, -b(ə-)rē\. Town, Dukes co., SE Massachusetts, on Martha's Vineyard; pop. (1970c) 2257; summer resort, including Vineyard Haven.

Tis·dale \ˈtiz-ˌdāl\. Town, Saskatchewan, Canada, 75 m. SE of Prince Albert; pop. (1971p) 2789; diversified agriculture.

Tish·o·min·go \ˌtish-ə-ˈmiŋ-(ˌ)gō\. 1 County in Mississippi. See table at MISSISSIPPI.

2 City, ⊗ of Johnston co., S Oklahoma, 28 m. E of Ardmore; pop. (1970c) 2663; ✱ of Chickasaw Nation 1856–1907; Murray State Coll. (1908).

Tisia *or* **Tissus.** See TISZA.

Tis·ta \ˈtis-tə\. River, India and Bangla Desh; ab. 300 m. long; rises on edge of Tibetan plateau, flows S through Sikkim and across both West Bengal, India, and Bangla Desh into the Brahmaputra.

Tis·te·dals·elva \ˈtis-tə-ˌdäls-ˌel-və\. River, S Norway; flows S through several long shallow lakes connected by rapids, and empties into Oslo Fjord.

Ti·sza \ˈtis-ˌó\ *or Ger.* **Theiss** \ˈtīs\ *or Serb.* **Ti·sa** \ˈtē-sə\; *anc.* **Tis·sus** \ˈtis-əs\ *or* **Ti·sia** \ˈtizh-(ē-)ə\. River in W Ukrainian S.S.R., U.S.S.R., E Hungary, and NE Yugoslavia; 600 m. long; rises in Carpathian Mts. in W Ukrainian S.S.R., flows W, forming a section of Russian-Romanian boundary; continues SW across Hungary and into NE Yugoslavia; empties into Danube river ab. 28 m. N of Belgrade; its largest tributaries are the Someşul and the Mureşul from Transylvania on the E; navigable for light-draft boats for ab. 450 m.

Tiszapolgár. See POLGÁR.

Ti·ta·garh \ti-ˈtäg-ər\. Town, West Bengal, India, on Hooghly river 13 m. N of Calcutta; pop. (1961c) 76,429.

Ti·ta·no, Mount \-ti-ˈtän-(ˌ)ō\. Mountain, San Marino; 2437 ft.; city of San Marino is built on it; notable for its three peaks.

Ti·ti·ca·ca, Lake \-ˌtit-i-ˈkäk-ə, -ˌtēt-\. Lake on Peru-Bolivia boundary; 122 m. long, 45 m. wide; 3200 sq. m.; max. depth 922 ft.; alt. 12,500 ft.; highest large navigable lake in the world; drains S through Desaguadero river into

Lake Poopó; traversed by steamboats bet. Puno in Peru and Guaqui in Bolivia. The Cordillera Real of the Andes is on its E shore. Was in center of early South American civilizations (see TIAHUANACO).

Titius. See KRKA.

Ti·to·grad \ˈtēt-(ˌ)ō-ˌgrad\; *formerly* **Pod·go·ri·ca** *or* **Pod·go·ri·tsa** \ˈpäd-gə-ˌrēt-sə\. City, ✱ of Montenegro, S Yugoslavia; pop. (1971p) 54,509; tobacco products; first mentioned 1330.

Ti·to·vo Uži·ce \ˌtēt-ə-vō-ˈü-zhit-se\. Town, Serbia, cen. Yugoslavia, ab. 75 m. SW of Belgrade; pop. (1965e) 28,000.

Ti·tov Ve·les \ˌtē-tōv-ˈvel-əs\ *or formerly* **Veles** *or Turk.* **Kö·pri·li** \ˌkə-prü-ˈlü\. Town, Macedonia, SE Yugoslavia, on the Vardar ab. 30 m. SE of Skopje; pop. (1965e) 31,000; commercial center, esp. for silks.

Tit·ta·ba·was·see \ˌtit-ə-bə-ˈwäs-ē\. River, E Michigan; ab. 65 m. long; flows from Ogemaw co. S into the Saginaw river in Saginaw co.

Titterstone Clee Hill. See CLEE HILLS.

Ti·tus \ˈtīt-əs\. County in Texas. See table at TEXAS.

Ti·tus·ville \ˈtīt-əs-ˌvil\. **1** City, ⊗ of Brevard co., E Florida, on Indian river 35 m. E of Orlando; pop. (1970c) 30,515; winter resort; citrus fruit.

2 City, Crawford co., NW Pennsylvania, on Oil Creek 14 m. N of Oil City; pop. (1970c) 7331; tool steel, forgings, dairy products, plastics; oil wells; founded 1796; site of first oil well drilled in U.S. 1859.

Tium·pan Head \ˌt(y)üm-ˌpän-\. Cape, NE coast of island of Lewis with Harris, Outer Hebrides, off NW coast of Scotland; lighthouse.

Tiv·er·ton \ˈtiv-ərt-ᵊn\. **1** Town and summer resort, Newport co., SE Rhode Island, on Sakonnet river 8 m. NE of Newport; pop. (1970c) 12,559; oyster fisheries. Incorp. as Massachusetts town 1692; annexed to Rhode Island 1746; prominent role in American Revolution.

2 Municipal borough, Devonshire, SW England, at confluence of Exe and Lowman rivers 48 m. NE of Plymouth; pop. (1971p) 15,548; lace and nylon; 12th cent. castle.

Ti·vo·li \ˈtiv-ə-lē\ *or anc.* **Ti·bur** \ˈtī-bər\. Commune, Roma prov., Latium, cen. Italy, 16 m. ENE of Rome; pop. (1968e) 40,501; paper; cathedral; Villa d'Este, with notable terraced gardens; extensive remains of ancient villas and temples, esp. villa of Emperor Hadrian. Received Roman citizenship 90 B.C.; a noted summer resort under the early empire.

Ti·zi·mín \ˌtē-zə-ˈmēn\. Town, Yucatán state, SE Mexico; munic. pop. (1970p) 29,895; railroad terminus ab. 65 m. E of Mérida.

Ti·zi–Ou·zou \tē-ˌzē-ü-ˈzü\. **1** Department of N Algeria. See table at ALGERIA.

2 Town, its ✱, ab. 65 m. E of Algiers; pop. (1966c) 25,852.

Tjareme. See TJIREMAJ.

Tje·pu *or Du.* **Tje·poe** \chə-ˈpü\. Town, Central Java prov., Indonesia, ab. 35 m. SE of Rembang.

Tji·a·mis \chē-ˈäm-əs\ *or* **Chi·a·mis** \chē-\. Town, West Java prov., Indonesia, just E of Tasikmalaja ab. 60 m. SE of Bandung; pop. (1961c) 35,189.

Tji·an·djur *or Du.* **Tji·an·djoer** \chē-ˈän-jü(ə)r\. Town, West Java prov., Indonesia, on railroad 35 m. SE of Bogor; pop. (1961c) 62,546; in plateau region E of Mt. Gede.

Tji·ku·raj *or* **Tji·koe·raj** \chi-ˈkür-ā\ *also* **Chi·ku·raj** \chi-\. Mountain, West Java prov., Indonesia, SSW of Garut; 9255 ft.; highest extinct volcano in the mountain groups around Garut.

Tji·la·tjap \chē-ˈlä-chäp\ *or* **Chi·la·chap** \chē-\. Seaport on SW coast of Central Java prov., Indonesia; pop. (1961c) 55,333; ships copra, rubber, tea; only harbor on S coast of Java. In World War II used as last port of Allied defense in Java.

Tji·le·dug *or Du.* **Tji·le·doeg** \ˈchē-lə-ˌdük\ *also* **Chi·le·dug** \ˈchē-\. Town, West Java prov., Indonesia, near coast just SE of Tjirebon.

Tjiliwong. See LIWUNG.

Tji·ma·hi \chi-ˈmä-hē\ *or* **Chi·ma·hi** \chi-\. Town, West Java prov., Indonesia, on railroad just NW of Bandung; pop. (1961c) 64,226.

Tjir·e·bon \ˌchir-ə-ˈbȯn\ *or formerly* **Cher·i·bon** \ˌcher-ə-\. Seaport, West Java prov., Indonesia; pop. (1961c) 158,299.

Tji·re·maj \chi-ˈrā-(ˌ)mī\ *also* **Tja·re·me** \chä-ˈrā-(ˌ)mā\. Volcano, West Java prov., Indonesia, SSW of Tjirebon; 10,098 ft.

Tla·co·lu·la de Ma·ta·mo·ros \ˌtlä-kə-ˈlü-lə-də-ˌmat-ə-ˈmōr-əs, -ˈmȯr-\. Municipality, Oaxaca state, Mexico, 25 m. SE of Oaxaca; pop. (1970p) 78,864; diversified agriculture.

Tla·co·pán \ˌtläk-ō-ˈpän\. See TENOCHTITLÁN.

Tlá·huac \ˈtlä-(ˌ)wäk\. Municipality, Federal District, Mexico, 14 m. SE of Mexico City; pop. (1970p) 62,087; livestock farming; wheat, alfalfa.

Tlal·ne·pan·tla \ˌtläl-nə-ˈpän-(ˌ)tlä\. City, México state, Mexico, 9 m. N of Mexico City; munic. pop. (1970p) 373,-657.

Tlal·pán \tläl-ˈpän\ *or* **Tlal·pam** \-ˈpän\. Town, Federal District, cen. Mexico, S of Mexico City; munic. pop. (1970p) 115,528; suburban and resort town. Founded by Spaniards soon after the conquest; has church begun in 1532. Residence of some of early Spanish viceroys.

Tlal·pu·ja·hua \ˌtläl-pü-ˈhä-wə\. Town, Michoacán state, SW Mexico, E of Lake Cuitzeo and 70 m. NW of Mexico City; munic. pop. (1970p) 16,499.

Tlal·til·co \tläl-ˈtēl-(ˌ)kō\. Town, Federal District, cen. Mexico; pop. (1960c) 10,423.

Tla·que·pa·que \ˌtlä-kā-ˈpä-kā\. Town, Jalisco state, W cen. Mexico; munic. pop. (1970p) 108,119.

Tla·tlau·qui·te·pec \ˌtlä-tlaù-ˌkēt-ə-ˈpek\. Municipality, Puebla state, Mexico, 75 m. NE of Puebla; pop. (1970p) 29,468; oil wells, coal mines; diversified agriculture.

Tlax·ca·la \tlä-ˈskäl-ə\. **1** State of cen. Mexico. See table at MEXICO.

2 *or in full* **Tlaxcala de Xi·coh·tén·catl** \-dā-ˌhē-kō-ˈteŋ-ˌkät-ᵊl\ *also* **Tlas·ca·la** \tlä-ˈskäl-ə\. Town, ✱ of Tlaxcala state, cen. Mexico; munic. pop. (1970p) 21,424; in mountainous region bet. Veracruz and Mexico City, alt. 7500 ft.; surrounded by hills and in sight of high peaks (Malinche, Popocatépetl, Iztaccíhuatl); has oldest church—Church of San Fernando—in North America, founded 1521. Home of a Nahua people, the Tlascalans, akin to Aztecs and Toltecs, who came here from the plains E of Lake Texcoco; they were enemies of the Aztecs in Tenochtitlán (Mexico City) and initially opposed Cortés on his march inland but were defeated 1519 and became his ally, aiding in his conquest of Montezuma. City (then with pop. ab. 30,000) was refuge for Spaniards when driven out of Mexico City June 1520.

Tla·xi·a·co \ˌtlä-hē-ˈä-(ˌ)kō\. Municipality, Oaxaca state, Mexico, 70 m. WNW of Oaxaca; pop. (1970p) 85,929.

Tlem·cen *or* **Tlem·sen** \tlem-ˈsen\. **1** Department of NW Algeria. See table at ALGERIA.

2 Town, its ✱, near the Morocco border 75 m. SW of Oran; pop. (1966c) 71,186; alt. 2500 ft.; flour, olive oil, handicrafts; numerous mosques and other medieval remains, incl. towers, walls, minarets. Capital of Arab sultanate 1282 ff.; prosperous town under Ottoman rule in 16th cent.; Abd-el-Kader's capital 1837–42; came under French 1842.

Tlemcen Mountains. Range of Little Atlas Mts., in NW Algeria.

Tmolus. See BOZ DAĞ.

To \ˈtō\ *or formerly* **Lu** \ˈlü\. River, tributary of the Yangtze in Szechwan prov., S cen. China; ab. 200 m. long; flows SSE bet. the Min and the Chia-ling.

Toa Al·ta \ˌtō-ə-ˈäl-tə\. Town and municipality NE cen. Puerto Rico, 10 m. SW of San Juan; pop. (1970p) 3154 (town), 18,537 (munic.).

Toa Ba·ja \-ˈbä-(ˌ)hä\. Town and municipality, NE Puerto Rico, W of San Juan; pop. (1970p) 2032 (town), 46,938 (munic.).

To·a·no Range \ˌtō-ə-ˌnō-\. Small range, Elko co., NE Nevada; crossed by a pass at 6940 ft.

Toarcium. See THOUARS.

To·ba, Lake \-ˈtō-bə\. Lake in the Barisan Mts., N cen. Sumatra I., Indonesia; 45 m. long, 502 sq. m.; elevation 2985 ft.; thought to occupy the crater of an extinct volcano. Drains E through the Asahan river into the Strait of Malacca; contains the large island of Samosir.

To·ba·go \tə-ˈbā-(ˌ)gō\. Island, West Indies, a constituent part of Trinidad and Tobago; 32 m. long; 116 sq. m.; pop. (1970p) 39,280; ✱ Scarborough. Chief products cacao, coconuts, and bananas.

History: Discovered by Columbus 1498; first settled by English 1616; has changed hands more often than any other island of the West Indies, having been at various times held by English, Dutch, and French; remained English after 1814. United with Trinidad by Order of Council 1898 and made part of the colony of Trinidad and Tobago Jan. 1, 1899; became part of independent state 1962.

To·bar·ra \tō-ˈbär-ə\. Commune, Albacete prov., SE Spain, 30 m. SSE of Albacete; pop. (1970p) 8707; health resort, with sulfur springs; iron peroxide seams nearby; center of agricultural section.

To·ba·ta \tō-ˈbät-ə\. See KITAKYŪSHŪ.

To·ba·tí \ˌtō-bə-ˈtē\. Town, Cordillera dept., cen. Paraguay, E of Asunción; dist. pop. (1962c) 9976.

To·bol \tə-ˈbȯl\. River, U.S.S.R.; 1042 m. long; rises in SE foothills of Ural Mts. in N Kazakh S.S.R. and flows NNE through E Chelyabinsk, Kurgan, and Tyumen oblasts to the Irtysh river at Tobolsk; navigable to Kurgan.

To·bolsk \tə-ˈbȯlsk\. City, N Tyumen Oblast, Russian S.F.S.R., U.S.S.R., on Irtysh river where it is joined by the Tobol, 300 m. NW of Omsk; pop. (1967e) 47,000; furniture; ivory carving. Founded by Cossacks 1587 and moved to present site 1610; in Tsarist times a frequent place of residence for political prisoners. See ISKER.

To·bruk \ˈtō-ˌbru̇k, tō-ˈ\ *or Ital.* **To·bruch** \ˈtō-ˌbrük\ *or Arab.* **Tu·bruq** \tu̇-ˈbrük\ *or anc.* **An·ti·pyr·gos** \ˌant-i-ˈpər-ˌgäs\. Port on coastal road, Libya, N Africa; pop. (1970e) 28,000; former Italian military post. Scene of much fighting in World War II; taken by British Dec. 1940; besieged by Germans for 8 months Mar.–Nov. 1941; surrendered to Rommel June 21, 1942; retaken by British Nov. 30, 1942.

To·can·tins \ˌtō-kən-ˈtēⁿs\. River, E cen. and NE Brazil; 1677 m. long; rises in S cen. Goiás state, flows N into Pará river.

Toc·coa \tə-ˈkō-ə\. 1 River, NE Georgia. See OCOEE.

2 City, ⊗ of Stephens co., NE Georgia, 33 m. NE of Gainesville; pop. (1970c) 6971; textiles, furniture, paint; truck farms.

To·ce \ˈtō-chā\. River, Piedmont, N Italy; contains **Toce Falls,** 470 ft. high.

Tochi. See WAZIRISTAN.

To·chi·gi \ˈtō-chə-(ˌ)gē\. 1 Prefecture, Honshū, Japan; 2479 sq. m.; pop. (1970c) 1,580,021; ✱ Utsunomiya.

2 Town, S Tochigi prefecture, Japan, 50 m. N of Tokyo; pop. (1970c) 78,345; lumber, silk.

To·cón Point \tō-ˈkōn-\. Cape, SW coast of Puerto Rico, E of Cape Rojo.

To·co·pi·lla \ˌtō-kō-ˈpē-(y)ə\. Seaport, Antofagasta prov., N Chile, 100 m. N of Antofagasta; pop. (1966e) 23,140; ships nitrates, sulfate, iodine, and copper ore.

To·cor·pu·ri, Ce·rros de \ˈser-ōz-dā-ˌtō-kȯr-ˈpu̇(ə)r-ē\. Mountain, SW Bolivia, near Chilean border; 19,137 ft.

To·cu·yo \tō-ˈkü-(ˌ)yō\. River, NW Venezuela; ab. 200 m. long; flows NE into Caribbean Sea ab. 50 m. N of Puerto Cabrillo.

Tocuyo, El. See EL TOCUYO.

Todd \ˈtäd\. Counties in three states of the U.S. See tables at KENTUCKY, MINNESOTA, SOUTH DAKOTA.

To·di \ˈtȯd-ē\ *or anc.* **Tu·der** \ˈt(y)üd-ər\. Commune, Perugia prov., Umbria, cen. Italy, on Tiber river 24 m. S of Perugia; pop. (1968e) 18,183; ancient and medieval walls; ancient Roman amphitheater; 11th cent. cathedral; 16th cent. church of Santa Maria della Consolazione.

Tö·di \ˈtərd-ē\ *or* **Piz Ru·sein** \ˌpēts-rü-ˈzīn\. Highest peak of the N Swiss Alps, Glarus canton, E cen. Switzerland; 11,857 ft.

Tod·mor·den \ˈtäd-ˌmȯrd-ᵊn, -mərd-ᵊn\. Municipal borough, West Riding, Yorkshire, N England, on the Calder 20 m. NNE of Manchester; pop. (1971p) 15,150.

To·dos los San·tos \ˌtōd-əs-lō-ˈsänt-əs\. Lake, Llanquihue prov., S cen. Chile, N of Puerto Montt; resort region.

Todos os Santos, Baía de. See ALL SAINTS BAY.

Toeban. See TUBAN.

Toe Head \ˈtō-\. Cape, extending NW into Atlantic Ocean from S part of island of Lewis with Harris, Outer Hebrides, off NW coast of Scotland.

Toekangbesi Islands. See TUKANGBESI ISLANDS.

Toeloengagoeng. See TULUNGAGUNG.

Tofo, El. See EL TOFO.

To·fua \tō-ˈfü-ə\. Volcanic island, W part of Haapai group, Tonga, SW cen. Pacific Ocean; 5 m. long by 4 m. wide; 21 sq. m.; uninhabited; large lake in crater.

Togara Islands. See TOKARA ISLANDS.

Tog·gen·burg \ˈtȯ-gən-ˌbərg, -ˌbu̇(ə)rg\. District, St. Gallen canton, NE Switzerland, in upper valley of the Thur; a rich pastoral and resort region; chief town Wattwil. Scene of almost continuous religious strife from 15th to 18th cent.; Toggenburg war ended 1712 in defeat of Catholic cantons by Protestants; to St. Gallen 1803.

To·gi·an \ˈtō-gē-ˌän\. See PENJU ISLANDS.

To·go \ˈtō-(ˌ)gō\. 1 *or formerly* **French Togo.** Republic, W Africa, bounded on N by Upper Volta, on E by Dahomey, on S by the Bight of Benin, and on W by Ghana; 21,853 sq. m.; pop. (1970c) 1,955,916; ✱ Lomé. *Physical features:* The republic consists of a strip of land (ab. 70 m. wide) extending ab. 340 m. inland from the Bight of Benin; coastal plain is swampy; N region characterized by savannah; in cen. is mountain range, with highest peak Mt. Agou 3937 ft. *Chief products:* Cotton, coffee, cocoa, cassava, rice, copra. *Chief towns:* Lomé, Palimé, Tsévie.

History: For history prior to 1914, see TOGOLAND. Territory constituted the E part of the German protectorate of Togoland, which was occupied by Anglo-French forces 1914; E part of Togoland assigned to France as mandate by League of Nations 1922; made a U.N. trust territory 1946; became an autonomous republic within the French Union 1956; achieved independence 1960; suspended constitution 1967.

2 Former British trust territory. See TOGOLAND.

To·go·land \ˈtō-gō-ˌland\. Former German protectorate, W Africa; the W section is now part of Ghana, the remainder constituting the independent republic of Togo (*q.v.*).

History: German protectorate proclaimed over coastal area 1884; hinterland and frontier boundaries not established until 1899; captured by Anglo-French forces 1914 and divided into two administrative zones; British zone (**Togo,** later **Trans–Vol·ta Togoland** \tran(t)s-ˈväl-tə, -ˈvōl-, -ˈvȯl-\) placed under control of Gold Coast (now Ghana), with which it merged 1956; French zone became independent republic of Togo 1960.

To·gu·chi \tō-ˈgü-chē, ˈtō-gə-(ˌ)chē\. Town on coast of NW Okinawa, Ryukyu Is., Japan.

To·ho·pe·ka·li·ga Lake \tə-ˌhō-pi-ˈkal-i-gə-\. Lake, NW Osceola co., cen. Florida penin.

Toi·ya·be Mountains \tȯi-ˌyäb-ē-\. Range, extending N and S in Lander and Nye cos., cen. Nevada; highest peak **Toiyabe Dome** 11,755 ft.

To·ka·chi \tō-ˈkäch-ē\. 1 Peak, Japan. See HOKKAIDŌ.

2 River, cen. Hokkaidō, Japan; 120 m. long.

Longitude West of Greenwich 0° Longitude East of Greenwich 2°

To·ka·ra Islands \tō-'kär-ə-\ *also* **To·ga·ra Islands** \tō-'gär-ə-\. Group of small islands, S of Kyūshū, in Kagoshima prefecture, Japan, northernmost part of Ryukyu chain. See RYUKYU ISLANDS.

To·ka·shi·ki \tō-'käsh-i-(ˌ)kē\. Largest of Kerama Is., Japan; 10 sq. m.

To·kat \tō-'kät\. 1 Province of N cen. Turkey, Asia. See table at TURKEY.

2 Town, its ✱, 50 m. NW of Sıvas; pop. (1965c) 37,368.

To·ke·lau Islands \'tō-kə-ˌlau̇-\ *or formerly* **Union Islands** \'yü-nyən-\. Group of islands, cen. Pacific Ocean, N of American Samoa; lat. 8° to 10°S and long. 171° to 173°W; 4 sq. m.; pop. (1970c) 1687; includes Atafu, Fakaofo, and Nukunonu; copra; placed under British protection 1877; part of Gilbert and Ellice Islands Colony 1916–25; administered by New Zealand 1925; made part of New Zealand 1948.

To·ke·wan·na Peak \ˌtō-kə-ˌwän-ə-\. Mountain, E Summit co., NE Utah; 13,173 ft.

To·ki \'tō-kē\. City, Gifu prefecture, Honshū, Japan, 22 m. N of Nagoya; pop. (1970c) 60,786.

Tokio. See TOKYO.

Tok·mak \tȯk-'mäk\. Town, N Kirgiz S.S.R., U.S.S.R., just E of Frunze on the Chu river; pop. (1967e) 38,000.

To·ko·na·me \tō-'kō-näm-ē, ˌtō-kō-'näm-ē\. City, Aichi prefecture, Honshū, Japan, 21 m. S of Nagoya; pop. (1970c) 54,168.

To·ko·ro·za·wa \ˌtō-kō-'rō-zä-wä\. City, Saitama prefecture, Honshū, Japan, NE suburb of Tokyo; pop. (1970c) 136,-611.

To·ku·no Shi·ma \tō-ˌku̇n-ō-'shē-mə\. Island, cen. Amami Is., Ryukyu Is., Japan.

To·ku·shi·ma \ˌtō-ku̇-'shē-mə, tō-'kü-shi-mə\. 1 Prefecture, Shikoku, Japan; 1600 sq. m.; pop. (1970c) 791,111; ✱ Tokushima.

2 Seaport city, its ✱, on E coast of Shikoku I. on Kii Channel, chief city on Shikoku I.; pop. (1970c) 223,451; univ. (1949); has close connection by water with Ōsaka and Hyōgo.

To·ku·ya·ma \ˌtō-ku̇-'yäm-ə\. Town, E Yamaguchi prefecture, SW Honshū, Japan, 50 m. E of Shimonoseki; pop. (1970c) 98,520; port at W end of Inland Sea.

To·kyo *also* **To·kio** \'tō-kē-ˌō\. 1 Prefecture, Honshū, Japan; 783 sq. m.; pop. (1970c) 11,408,071; ✱ Tokyo.

2 *formerly* **Edo** \'ed-(ˌ)ō\ *or* **Ye·do** *also* **Yeddo** \'yed-(ˌ)ō\. City, ✱ of Japan, also ✱ of Tokyo prefecture, on NW shore of Tokyo Bay, SE Honshū; pop. (1971e) 8,787,249; administrative, cultural, financial, commercial, and educational center of Japan; also center of an extensive complex of industrial suburbs producing metals, machinery, transportation and electronic equipment, chemicals, textiles and a wide variety of consumer goods; shipbuilding; one of the principal tourist centers of Japan. Sumida river flows through it, and city has extensive network of canals; site of Imperial Palace and gardens and numerous temples and shrines; ab. 150 institutions of higher learning, incl. Univ. of Tokyo (1877); its seaport is Yokohama.

History: Founded c. 1456; castle given to Tokugawa clan 1590 and under name of Edo became capital of Tokugawa Shogunate 1603; during 18th cent. one of the largest cities in the world, with a population exceeding 1,000,000; upon Restoration 1868 replaced Kyōto as Imperial capital and renamed Tokyo. Developed as cultural and industrial center in late 19th cent. with expansion of transportation facilities. City largely destroyed by earthquake and subsequent fire Sept. 1, 1923 with loss of over 100,000 lives; largely rebuilt by 1930. In World War II repeatedly bombed by U.S. aircraft 1944–45, and esp. after Mar. 1945; over two-thirds of total area of city destroyed with over 100,000 persons killed. City largely reconstructed since 1945, with large-scale modernization of transportation facilities; site of Summer Olympic Games 1964.

Tokyo Bay. Inlet of W Pacific Ocean, SE coast of Honshū, Japan; ab. 30 m. long by 23 m. wide, providing a spacious harbor for Tokyo, Yokohama, and Yokosuka. Connects with the Pacific by Uraga Strait.

Tol \'tōl\. Largest island in Truk Is. (*q.v.*), in W part.

To·la·go Bay \tə-ˌläg-ō-\. Inlet of Pacific Ocean, E coast of North I., New Zealand, ab. midway bet. East Cape and Poverty Bay.

To·la·ni Lakes \tō-ˌlän-ē-\. Small lakes, near E boundary of Coconino co., N cen. Arizona.

Tolbiacum. See ZÜLPICH.

Tol·bu·khin \tȯl-'bük-in\. 1 Province of NE Bulgaria. See table at BULGARIA.

2 *or Rom.* **Ba·zar·gic** \bə-'zär-jēk\ *or formerly* **Do·brich** \'dȯ-brich\. City, its ✱, ab. 25 m. N of Varna; pop. (1968e) 61,440; in Romania 1913–40.

To·le·do \tə-'lēd-(ˌ)ō, -'lēd-ə, *Span.* tō-'lā-t͟hō\. 1 Village, ⊗ of Cumberland co., SE cen. Illinois; pop. (1970c) 1068.

2 City, ⊗ of Tama co., E cen. Iowa, 17 m. E of Marshalltown; pop. (1970c) 2361; agriculture.

3 Industrial city and port of entry, ⊗ of Lucas co., NW Ohio, on Maumee river at SW corner of Lake Erie; pop. (1970c) 383,818; important lake port, shipping coal, automobiles, petroleum products, iron ore; considerable foreign commerce; produces automobiles, glass, machine tools, weighing machines; shipbuilding; Univ. of Toledo (1872) and Mary Manse Coll. (1873). Formed by union of two villages 1833; incorporated 1837; figured in "Toledo War" of 1835–36, dispute bet. Ohio and Michigan over location of their common boundary.

4 City, Lincoln co., W Oregon, 35 m. W of Corvalis; pop. (1970c) 2818; resort; salmon, oyster fisheries.

5 District, S British Honduras; 1795 sq. m.; pop. (1967e) 116,455; ✱ Punta Gorda.

6 Chartered city on W coast of Cebu I., Phil., in cen. part 19 m. W of City of Cebu; pop. (1970e) 89,000.

7 Province of Spain. See table at SPAIN.

8 *or anc.* **To·le·tum** \tə-ˈlēt-əm\. Commune, ✱ of Toledo prov., cen. Spain, on Tagus river 40 m. SSW of Madrid; pop. (1970p) 44,382; engraved metalwork, confectionary; archiepiscopal see and seat of primate of Spain; a great wealth of notable architecture (entire urban area is a national monument); Roman remains, 13th cent. Gothic cathedral, 15th cent. Franciscan monastery, 13th cent. synagogue, 16th cent. alcazar, city walls, and bridges. Home of Lope de Vega.

History: Stronghold of the Carpetani; conquered by Rome 193 B.C.; became Roman colony and capital of Roman Spain; Visigothic capital in Spain 534–712; center of conflict bet. Arianism and Roman Catholic orthodoxy; site of numerous church councils A.D. 396, 400, 589, etc.; conquered by Moors under Musa 712; a provincial capital in the caliphate of Córdoba 712–1031; under Moors, grew commercially and industrially, becoming noted for the manufacture of swords; center of Arabic and Hebrew culture; reconquered from Moors 1085 by the Cid and Alfonso VI of León and Castile; capital of New Castile and of the united kingdoms of León and Castile 1087–1560; noted for its tolerance of Jews and Arabs in 11th–15th cents.; occupied by French during Peninsular War 1808–14.

Toledo, Mon·tes de \ˌmȯn-tāz-ˌthā-tō-ˈlā-thō\. Mountain range, cen. Spain, WSW of Toledo; highest peak 4747 ft.

To·len·ti·no \ˌtäl-ən-ˈtē-(ˌ)nō\ *or anc.* **Tol·en·ti·num** \ˌtäl-ən-ˈtī-nəm\. Commune, Macerata prov., Marches, cen. Italy, 12 m. WSW of Macerata; pop. (1968e) 16,372; cathedral of 8th and 9th cents.; 15th cent. church of San Nicola. Treaty bet. Napoleon and Pope Pius VI signed here 1797; Murat defeated by Austrians here 1815.

Toletum. See TOLEDO 8.

To·li·ma \tə-ˈlē-mə\. 1 Volcano, Cordillera Central of the Andes, W cen. Colombia; 18,425 ft.

2 Department of W cen. Colombia. See table at COLOMBIA.

Tol·land \ˈtäl-ənd\. 1 County in Connecticut. See table at CONNECTICUT.

2 Agricultural town, Tolland co., N Connecticut, on Willimantic river; pop. (1970c) 7857.

Tol·le·son \ˈtäl-ə-sən\. Town, Maricopa co., SW cen. Arizona, 10 m. W of Phoenix; pop. (1970c) 3881.

Tol·me·ta \täl-ˈmāt-ə\ *or Arab.* **Tul·may·thah** \təl-ˈmāt-ə, -ˈmīt-\ *or anc.* **Ptol·e·ma·ïs** \ˌtal-ə-ˈmā-əs\. Town on the coast of NE Libya, 60 m. NE of Benghazi; ancient Ptolemaïs, port of Barka which it superseded during the time of the Ptolemies, was one of the cities of the Pentapolis.

Tolmin \ˈtȯl-min\ *or Ital.* **Tol·mi·no** \tōl-ˈmē-(ˌ)nō\ *or Ger.* **Tol·mein** \ˈtȯl-ˌmīn\. Commune, Slovenia, NW Yugoslavia, on Isonzo river in region that belonged to Italy before 1947.

Tol·na \ˈtōl-nə\. 1 County of S cen. Hungary. See table at HUNGARY.

2 Commune, its ⊗, 76 m. S of Budapest; pop. (1970p) 13,264; castle.

To·lo, Gulf of \-ˈtō-(ˌ)lō\. Inlet of Banda Sea, E cen. coast of Celebes I., Malay Archipelago; smallest of the three great gulfs of Celebes. Bordered on NE by the Banggai Archipelago and connected by Peleng Strait with the Molucca Sea.

To·lo·sa \tə-ˈlō-sə\. 1 City, France. See TOULOUSE.

2 Manufacturing commune, Guipúzcoa prov., N Spain, 11 m. SW of San Sebastián; pop. (1970p) 18,766; iron and copper founding; manufactures paper, metal products; occupied by French 1803–13.

To·lu·ca \tə-ˈlu-kə\. 1 Subdivision of the plateau of Anáhuac (*q.v.*), cen. Mexico; mean elevation 8570 ft.

2 *or in full* **Toluca de Ler·do** \-də-ˈler-(ˌ)dō\. City, ✱ of México state, cen. Mexico, ab. 35 m. SW of Mexico City; pop. (1969e) 108,602; alt. 8500 ft.; commercial center in livestock and agricultural region; textiles, beer, canned goods; founded 1530.

Toluca, Ne·va·do de \nə-ˌväth-(ˌ)ō-ˌthāt-ᵊl-ˈü-kə\ *or* **Zi·nan·te·ca·ti** \si-ˌnän-tə-ˈkät-ē\. Extinct volcanic peak, México state, Mexico, 27 m. SW of Toluca; 15,106 ft.; crater partly filled with a lake formed by melting snow.

T'o–lu–chia–erh–t'e Shan–k'ou. See TORUGART PASS.

To–lun *or* **To·lun** \ˈdō-ˈlün\ *or* **To·lun·no·erh** \-nō-ˈər\ *or formerly* **Do·lon** \ˈdō-lōn\. Town, Inner Mongolia, N China, near right bank of upper Luan river, ab. 120 m. NW of Ch'eng-te.

Tol·yat·ti \tȯl-ˈyät-ē\ *or formerly* **Sta·vro·pol** \stav-ˈrȯ-pəl, -ˈrō-\. Town, Kuibyshev Oblast, Russian S.F.S.R., U.S.S.R., on Volga; pop. (1970p) 251,000; automobile manufacturing.

Tom \ˈtäm, ˈtȯm\. River, SE Tomsk and cen. Kemerovo oblasts, Russian S.F.S.R., U.S.S.R.; ab. 450 m. long; rises in NW Altai Mts. and flows NNW into the Ob river near Tomsk; flows through the Kuznetsk Basin (*q.v.*).

Tom, Mount \-ˈtäm, -ˈtȯm\. Peak in **Mt. Tom Range,** Connecticut river valley, W Massachusetts; 1202 ft.

To·mah \ˈtō-mə\. City, Monroe co., W cen. Wisconsin, 15 m. E of Sparta; pop. (1970c) 5647; cranberries.

Tom·a·hawk \ˈtäm-ə-ˌhȯk\. City, Lincoln co., N Wisconsin, 20 m. N of Merrill; pop. (1970c) 3419; lake resort; paper, boats; agriculture.

To·ma·hu, Mount \-tō-ˈmä-(ˌ)hü\. Mountain, NW Buru I., Indonesia; 7969 ft.; highest point on island.

To·ma·ko·mai \tō-ˈmäk-ō-ˌmī, ˌtō-mə-ˈkō-(ˌ)mī\. City, Hokkaidō prefecture, Hokkaidō, Japan, 12 m. SE of Sapporo; pop. (1970c) 101,573.

To·ma·les Bay \tə-ˌmäl-əs-\. Inlet of Pacific Ocean, NW coast of Marin co., W California.

To·ma·nii·vi, Mount *or formerly* **Mount Vic·to·ria** \-vik-ˈtōr-ē-ə, -ˈtȯr-\. Mountain on Viti Levu, Fiji; 4341 ft.; highest peak in Fiji.

To·ma·ri \tō-ˈmär-ē\. Town on W coast of Sakhalin I., Russian S.F.S.R., U.S.S.R.

To·mar·us, Mount \-tō-ˈmar-əs\ *or Gk.* **Tó·ma·ros** \ˈtȯm-ə-ˌrȯs\. Mountain, S cen. Epirus, NW Greece; ab. 6100 ft.; was in ancient district of Thesprotia; oracle of Dodona (*q.v.*) was on its E slope.

Tom·a·saki, Mount \-ˌtäm-ə-ˈsäk-ē\. Peak, S Grand co., E Utah; 12,271 ft.

Tomaschow. 1 Commune, Łódź prov., Poland. See TOMASZÓW MAZOWIECKI.

2 Commune, Lublin prov., Poland. See TOMASZÓW LUBELSKI.

Tomaszów. See TOMASZÓW MAZOWIECKI.

To·ma·szów Lu·bel·ski \tȯ-ˈmä-shüf-lü-ˈbel-skē\ *or Ger.* **To·ma·schow** \tō-ˈmä-(ˌ)shō\. Commune, Lublin prov., E Poland, 67 m. SSE of Lublin; pop. (1968e) 11,700.

Tomaszów Ma·zo·wiec·ki \-ˌmä-zȯ-ˈvyet-skē\ *or formerly* **Tomaszów** *or Ger.* **To·ma·schow** \tō-ˈmä-(ˌ)shō\. Industrial commune, Łódź prov., cen. Poland, 30 m. SE of Łódź; pop. (1970p) 54,900; textiles, brick and tile.

Tombador, Serra do. See SERRA DO TOMBADOR.

Tom·ball \ˈtäm-ˈbȯl, ˈtȯm-\. Town, Harris co., SE Texas, 30 m. NW of Houston; pop. (1970c) 2734; oil wells; diversified agriculture.

Tom·big·bee \täm-ˈbig-bē\. River, Alabama; 409 m. long; navigable for 350 m.; formed by junction of E fork and W fork near Amory, Mississippi, crosses Alabama border W of Carrollton, flows S into the Alabama river to form the Mobile and Tensaw rivers flowing into Mobile Bay at Mobile.

Tom·bo Island \ˌtäm-(ˌ)bō-\. Small island off the coast of Guinea, W Africa; Conakry, ✱ of Guinea, is on it and is joined to the mainland by a bridge.

Tom·bouc·tou \ˌtōⁿ-bük-ˈtü\ *or* **Tim·buk·tu** \ˌtim-bək-ˈtü, tim-ˈbək-(ˌ)tü\. Town, Mali, W Africa, E of Lake Faguibine and near the Niger river; pop. (1960c) 6600; substantial trade in salt; large 14th cent. mosque; remains an important trade center on the Saharan camel caravan routes; extensive ruins.

History: Settled by Tuaregs c. 1000 A.D.; became important trade center 12th cent.; came under Mandingo kingdom 1310 and made center of Muslim culture; reached height of prosperity as commercial and cultural center under Songhai rule c. 1500, having as many as 1,000,000 people; declined rapidly in 16th–18th cents., being repeatedly plundered; came under French rule 1893.

Tomb·stone \ˈtüm-ˌstōn\. City, SW cen. Cochise co., SE corner of Arizona, 20 m. NNW of Bisbee; pop. (1970c) 1241; formerly (c. 1879–87) a mining center widely known for its rich mines and its lawlessness and crime.

To·mé \tō-ˈmā\. City, Concepción prov., S cen. Chile, ab. 20 m. N of Concepción; pop. (1966c) 34,968; port for Concepción.

To·me·llo·so \ˌtō-mə(l)-ˈyō-(ˌ)sō\. Commune, Ciudad Real prov., S cen. Spain, 51 m. ENE of Ciudad Real; pop. (1970p) 26,094; wine, cereals, vegetables; stock raising.

Tom Green \ˈtäm-ˈgrēn, ˈtȯm-\. County in Texas. See table at TEXAS.

Tomi *or* **Tomis.** See CONSTANȚA 2.

To·mi·ni, Gulf of \-tō-ˈmē-nē\ *or* **Gulf of Go·ron·ta·lo** \-ˌgȯr-ən-ˈtäl-(ˌ)ō\. Large inlet of Molucca Sea, extending deep into the coast of N Celebes I., Malay Archipelago; ab. 240 m. long; contains the Penju Is.

To·mi·ño \tō-ˈmēn-yō\. Commune, Pontevedra prov., NW Spain, 31 m. SSW of Pontevedra; pop. (1970p) 9865.

To·mo \ˈtō-(ˌ)mō\. River, E Colombia; ab. 260 m. long; flows E into Orinoco on Venezuelan border.

Tömös Pass. See PREDEAL PASS.

Tomp·kins \ˈtäm(p)-kənz\. County in New York. See table at NEW YORK.

Tomp·kins·ville \ˈtäm(p)-kənz-ˌvil\. **1** Section of Richmond borough, N.Y. See RICHMOND 8.

2 City, ⊗ of Monroe co., S Kentucky; pop. (1970c) 2207.

Toms \ˈtämz\. River, E New Jersey; ab. 25 m. long; rises in SW Monmouth co., flows SE into Barnegat Bay.

Tomsk \ˈtäm(p)sk, ˈtȯm(p)sk\. City, ✱ of Tomsk Oblast, SE Russian S.F.S.R., U.S.S.R., on right bank of Tom river near its junction with the Ob; pop. (1970p) 339,000; connected with main line of Trans-Siberian R.R.; produces electrical equipment, paints and dyes, rubber goods; educational center, with univ. (1888) and several technical institutes. Founded as fort 1604 and developed as regional administrative center, esp. after discovery of gold 1824.

Tomsk Oblast \-ˈó-bləst, -ˌblast\. Subdivision of SE Russian S.F.S.R., U.S.S.R.; 122,355 sq. m.; pop. (1970p) 786,000; ✱ Tomsk. Largely flat terrain in the basin of the Middle Ob; agriculture limited by severe climate and numerous swamps; economy based on forestry and fur-trapping; only major city Tomsk; formed 1944.

Toms River \ˈtämz-\. **1** River, New Jersey. See TOMS.

2 Unincorporated summer resort, ⊗ of Ocean co., E New Jersey, on inlet of Barnegat Bay 22 m. SSW of Asbury Park; pop. (1970c) 7303; boatyards, oyster and clam fisheries; agriculture. Settled before 1727; center for guerrilla fighting in American Revolution; burned by British 1782.

To·na·lá \ˌtōn-ᵊl-ˈä\. **1** River, E Veracruz state, E Mexico; ab. 90 m. long; flows NNW to Gulf of Mexico and in lower course forms boundary with Tabasco state; receives the Pedregal.

2 Municipality, Chiapas state, Mexico, 70 m. SW of Tuxtla Gutiérrez; pop. (1970p) 41,562; rum; cattle raising, dairy farming, fishing; corn, mangoes, sesame.

To·na·le Pass \tō-ˌnäl-ē-\. Mountain pass, Lombard Alps, NW of Trent, bet. Lombardy and Trentino-Alto Adige, NE Italy; alt. 6178 ft.

Ton·a·wan·da \ˌtän-ə-ˈwän-də\. **1** Manufacturing city, Erie co., W New York, 9 m. N of Buffalo; pop. (1970c) 21,898; lumber, paper, metal goods, boats; railroad shops. **North Tonawanda** (*q.v.*), its sister city, is on opp. side of **Tonawanda Creek.**

2 Urban community (unincorporated), Erie co., W New York, S of city of Tonawanda; pop. (1970c) 107,282.

Ton·bridge \ˈtən-brij\. Urban district, Kent, SE England, on the Medway 25 m. SSE of London; pop. (1971p) 31,003; lumber, plastics; printing.

Tøn·der \ˈtən-ər\. Town, Sønderjylland co., SW Jutland penin., Denmark, near the German border; pop. (1970e) 7489.

To·ne \ˈtō-(ˌ)nā\. River, E Honshū, Japan; 200 m. long; flows SE and E into Pacific Ocean E of Tokyo.

Tong \ˈtäŋ\. **1** Village, Kent, SE England, 2 m. E of Sittingbourne and Milton; site of Tong Castle, now a high mound encircled by a moat, a Saxon fortress.

2 Village, Shropshire, W England, 20 m. E of Shrewsbury; site of castle, originally medieval, rebuilt 18th cent.; nearby is Boscobel House where Charles II hid 1651 after the battle of Worcester.

Ton·ga \ˈtäŋ-(g)ə\ *also* **Tonga Islands** *or* **Friend·ly Islands** \ˌfrend-lē-\. Kingdom, SW Pacific Ocean; 270 sq. m.; pop. (1970e) 87,406; ✱ Nukualofa. *Physical features:* Comprises an archipelago of ab. 150 islands, divided into 3 groups, Tongatapu, Vavau, and Haapai, together with Niuafoo and Niuatobutabu further to the N; in the N the Vavau group, and Tofua of the Haapai group, are high and mountainous, of volcanic origin; the other islands are low-lying, of coral formation. *Chief products:* Corn, coconuts, sweet potatoes, bananas, citrus fruit, cassava. *Chief towns:* Nukualofa, Neiafu.

History: N islands discovered 1616 by Dutch navigator Jakob Lemaire, visited by Tasman 1643 and by Capt. Cook 1773 and 1777; modern kingdom estab. during reign (1845–93) of King George Tupou I; declared a neutral region in 1886; became British protectorate 1900; achieved independence 1970.

Ton·ga·land \ˈtäŋ-gə-ˌland\ *or* **Am·a·ton·ga·land** \ˌam-ə-\. Region on coast S of Mozambique, SE Africa; ab. 600 sq. m.; formerly a British protectorate, ruled by Zulu hereditary dynasty. Incorp. 1898 with Ingwavuma dist., N Zululand, as part of Natal, Union (now Rep.) of South Africa.

Tongareva. See PENRHYN 1.

Tong·a·ri·ro \ˌtäŋ-(g)ə-ˈri(ə)r-(ˌ)ō\. Volcano, cen. North I., New Zealand, in **Tongariro National Park** (260 sq. m.) which includes also Ruapehu and Ngauruhoe volcanoes; 6516 ft.

Tong·a·ta·pu \ˌtäŋ-(g)ə-ˈtä-(ˌ)pü\. **1** Island group, S Tonga, SW cen. Pacific Ocean, including islands of Tongatapu and Eua; ab. 133 sq. m.

2 Island, S Tonga, SW cen. Pacific Ocean; ab. 100 sq. m.; dist. pop. (1966c) 47,920; chief town Nukualofa, ✱ of Tonga; largest island in Tonga group.

Tong·e·ren \ˈtȯŋ-ə-rən\ *or Fr.* **Ton·gres** \tōⁿgrᵊ\. Commune, Limburg prov., NE Belgium, 12 m. NW of Liège; pop. (1969e) 17,224.

Tong·jo·sŏn \ˈtȯŋ-ˈjō-ˈsän\; *formerly* **East Cho·sen Bay** \-ˌchō-ˌsen-\ *or* **Brough·ton Bay** \ˌbrȯt-ᵊn-\. Inlet of the Sea of Japan, E coast of North Korea.

Tongking. See TONKIN.

Tong·quil \tȯŋ-ˈkē(ə)l\. Island, Samales group, Sulu Archipelago, Phil.; 19 sq. m. See SAMALES.

Tongue \ˈtəŋ\. River, SE Montana; 246 m. long; rises in Sheridan co., N Wyoming, flows N across Montana border into Yellowstone river in Custer co., SE Montana.

Tongue of the Ocean. Strait, Bahama Is., bet. Andros I. on the W and New Providence I. and Exuma Is. on the E.

Tonk \ˈtȯŋk\. **1** Former Indian state, now part of Rajasthan state, NW India; consisted of 6 separate regions; 2543 sq. m.; ruler was a Muslim of Afghan descent.

2 Town, its ✱, Rajasthan, near right bank of Banas river 60 m. S of Jaipur; pop. (1961c) 43,413.

Ton·ka·wa \ˈtäŋ-kə-ˌwä\. City, Kay co., N Oklahoma, 13 m. W of Ponca City; pop. (1970c) 3337; oil wells; Northern Oklahoma Coll. (1901).

Ton·kin \ˈtän-ˈkin, ˈtäŋ-\ *or* **Tong·king** \ˈtäŋ-ˈkiŋ\. Former French protectorate, SE Asia, now constituting the greater part of North Vietnam.

History: Formed part of China in early times; after 1801 united to Annam; first visited by French expedition 1866; Hanoi attacked 1873 and finally seized 1883; joined with other regions controlled by French to form French Indochina 1887; occupied by Japanese 1940–45; formed part of new state of Vietnam estab. 1945–46; part of North Vietnam 1954.

Tonkin, Gulf of. Arm of the South China Sea, E of North Vietnam and N and W of Hainan I., S China; ab. 300 m. long.

Ton·le Sap \ˌtän-lā-ˈsap\. 1 *or Fr.* **Grand Lac** \grän-läk\. Lake, W Cambodia, SE Asia; ab. 87 m. long; receives floodwaters of the Mekong river; area varies from 1000 to 9500 sq. m. according to season; abundance of fish; just N of its NW shore lie the ruins of Angkor (*q.v.*).
2 River, cen. Cambodia; ab. 75 m. long; flows SE to the Mekong river at Pnompenh; outlet of Tonle Sap lake.

To·no·ley Harbour \ˌtōn-ə-ˌlā-\. Large anchorage, Bougainville Strait, S end of Bougainville I., NW Solomon Is., W Pacific; Buin and Kahili are on it.

To·no·pah \ˈtōn-ə-ˌpä\. Unincorporated community, ⊗ of Nye co., cen. and S Nevada, 78 m. ESE of S end of Walker Lake; pop. (1970c) 1716; gold and silver mines.

Tøns·berg \ˈtə(r)nz-ˌba(ə)r\. Seaport, ⊗ of Vestfold co., SE Norway, located on N end of Nøtterøy I.; pop. (1970e) 11,260; oldest city in Norway; home port for whaling fleets; paper, wood products, dairy products; ships fish and lumber.

Ton·to \ˈtän-(ˌ)tō\. River, SE cen. Mexico; 135 m. long; flows E and NE across SE Veracruz state into the Bay of Campeche.

Tonto Basin. Region, N Gila co., cen. Arizona, alt. above 2000 ft.; shut in by Mogollan Rim on the N and by mountain ranges on E and W; traversed by **Tonto Creek,** 60 m. long, which flows S to the Salt river at Roosevelt Lake; fine forests and grazing land; just S of Roosevelt Lake is **Tonto National Monument:** see UNITED STATES, *National Monuments.*

Too·ele \tu̇-ˈel-ə\. 1 County in NW Utah. See table at UTAH.
2 City, its ⊗, 25 m. SW of Salt Lake City; pop. (1970c) 12,539; silver, copper, lead mines; sugar beets; settled 1849.

Toole \ˈtül\. County in Montana. See table at MONTANA.

Toombs \ˈtümz\. County in Georgia. See table at GEORGIA.

Too·woom·ba \tə-ˈwu̇m-bə\. City, SE Queensland, Australia, 65 m. W of Brisbane; pop. (1968e) 58,000; alt. 1920 ft.; trade center for extensive agricultural, timber, fruit, and pastoral hinterland; summer resort.

Top \ˈtȯp\. Large lake, N Karelian A.S.S.R., Russian S.F.S.R., U.S.S.R.; its outlet is Pongoma river flowing E to White Sea N of Kem.

To·pe·ka \tə-ˈpē-kə\. City, ✱ of Kansas and ⊗ of Shawnee co., NE Kansas, on Kansas river 55 m. W of Kansas City; pop. (1970c) 125,011; flour, tires, medicines, tents; meatpacking plants, railroad shops, foundry; Washburn Municipal Univ. of Topeka (1865); Forbes Air Force Base. Founded by antislavery colonists 1854 and prominent in political conflict bet. pro- and anti-slavery forces in Kansas before Civil War; became ✱ on admission of Kansas into Union 1861.

Topolia. See COPAIS.

To·po·lo·bam·po \tə-ˌpō-lō-ˈbäm-(ˌ)pō\. Village and port on coast of NW Sinaloa state, W Mexico, on Gulf of California; has good harbor.

Top·pe·nish \ˈtäp-ə-(ˌ)nish\. City, Yakima co., S Washington, 17 m. SSE of Yakima; pop. (1970c) 5744; dairy products, beet sugar.

Tops·field \ˈtäp-ˌsfēld\. Town, Essex co., NE Massachusetts, 20 m. NE of Boston; pop. (1970c) 5225.

Tops·ham \ˈtäp-səm\. Town, Sagadahoc co., S Maine, at mouth of Androscoggin river; pop. (1970c) 5022.

To·qui·ma Range \tō-ˌkē-mə-\. Range, N Nye co., cen. Nevada.

Tor·bat-e Hehy·da·rī·yeh \tȯr-ˌbat-i-ˌhād-ə-ˈrē-yə\ *or* **Turbat-i-Hai·da·ri** \tu̇r-ˌbat-i-ˌhī-də-ˈrē, -ˌhā-\. Town, Khorāsān prov., NE Iran; pop. (1966c) 30,106; on trade route 75 m. S of Mashhad; center of fertile agricultural region; chief trade is in grains.

Tor·bay \ˈtȯr-ˈbā, -ˌbā\. County borough, Devonshire, SW England, 28 m. ENE of Plymouth, on Tor Bay; pop. (1971p) 108,888; seaside resort; formed 1968, incorporating Torquay and several other centers.

Tor Bay \ˈtȯr-\. Inlet of the English Channel on the coast of Devonshire, SW England; landing place of William of Orange 1688.

Torda. See TURDA.

Tor·de·si·llas \ˌtȯrd-ə-ˈsē-(y)əs, -ˈsēl-yəs\. Village, cen. Valladolid prov., N Spain, on the Duero; pop. (1970p) 6604; church, convent; residence of Juana la Loca (Joanna the Mad) 1509–55. Treaty signed here June 7, 1494 bet. Spain and Portugal by which the line of demarcation bet. their respective discoveries in the New World (estab. 1493) was moved 270 leagues further west (to ab. 46°W), thus granting to Portugal the E part of Brazil.

To·rez \tō-ˈrāz\ *or formerly* **Chist·ya·kovo** \chist-ˈyä-kə-və\. Town, Donetsk Oblast, Ukrainian S.S.R., U.S.S.R., ab. 38 m. E of Donetsk; pop. (1969e) 94,000.

Tor·gau \ˈtȯ(ə)r-ˌgau̇\. Industrial city, Leipzig dist., East Germany, on Elbe river SE of Dessau; pop. (1970e) 21,688; railroad junction; agricultural machinery, glass, paper, ceramics; 16th cent. church, 17th cent. castle. First mentioned 973; chartered c. 1260; in World War II scene of first meeting between U.S. and Soviet troops during advance into Germany Apr. 27, 1945.

Torg·hat·ten \ˈtȯ(ə)rg-ˌhät-ᵊn\. Peak on a small island off W cen. coast of Norway; at a height of ab. 400 ft. from its base it is penetrated by a natural tunnel 553 ft. long, 200 to 250 ft. high, and 35 to 56 ft. wide.

To·ri·ña·na, Cape \-ˌtȯr-ēn-ˈyän-ə\. Cape, NW Spain, 43°03′N, 9°18′W; westernmost point of Spanish mainland.

To·ri·no \tō-ˈrē-(ˌ)nō\. 1 Province of Piedmont, Italy. See table at ITALY.
2 Commune, Italy. See TURIN.

Tor·ka·mān \ˌtȯr-kə-ˈmän\ *or formerly* **Turk·man·chai** \ˌtu̇rk-män-ˈchī\. Town, East Azerbaijan prov., NW Iran, ab. 70 m. SE of Tabrīz; treaty Feb. 22, 1828 bet. Persia (now Iran) and Russia.

Tor·ko·ro, Cape \-tȯr-ˈkōr-(ˌ)ō, -ˈkȯr-\. Point, N coast of New Britain I., Bismarck Archipelago, W Pacific Ocean, near its E end; extends into Bismarck Sea.

Tor·men·tine, Cape \-ˈtȯr-mən-ˌtīn\. Point, SE New Brunswick, Canada, extending into Northumberland Strait; most easterly point of New Brunswick.

Tormentoso, Cabo. See GOOD HOPE, CAPE OF.

Tor·mes \ˈtȯ(ə)r-ˌmās\. River, W Spain; 153 m. long; flows N and NW into Douro river on Portuguese border.

Tor·na·do Mountain \tȯr-ˌnād-ō-\. Peak in Rocky Mts., SW Canada, on border bet. SE British Columbia and Alberta; 10,170 ft.

Tor·ne \ˈtȯr-nə\ *or Finnish* **Tor·nio** \ˈtȯr-nē-ˌō\. River, N and NE Sweden; 354 m. long; issues from Torne Träsk in NW Sweden; flows SE and S, forming in its lower course a section of the Swedish-Finnish boundary, and empties into the head of the Gulf of Bothnia.

Torneå. See TORNIO 1.

Torne Träsk \-ˈtresk\. Lake (*träsk*), NW Sweden; 124 sq. m.; source of the Torne river.

Torn·gat Mountains \ˌtȯ(ə)rn-gat-\. Mountain range, extreme N tip of Labrador, Newfoundland, Canada; extends N to Cape Chidley; highest point Cirque Mt. 5160 ft., at S end.

Tor·nio \'tȯr-nē-ˌō\. 1 *or Swed.* **Tor·neå** \'tȯr-nē-ˌō\. Seaport, Lappi prov., W Finland; pop. (1970e) 7481; built on an island in the Torne river at its mouth, opp. the Swedish town of Haparanda; manufactures leather; founded 1621.

2 River, N Sweden. See TORNE.

To·ro \'tōr-(ˌ)ō, 'tȯr-\. 1 Town, Zamora prov., NW cen. Spain, on right bank of the Duero 35 m. W of Valladolid; pop. (1970p) 9768; an old town with fine bridge and 12th cent. cathedral. Seat of Spanish parliament 1371, 1442, and 1505; battle here in 1476 in which Ferdinand of Aragon defeated the Portuguese.

2 District, Uganda, E Africa, near Mt. Ruwenzori; 5233 sq. m.; pop. (1969p) 571,006; formerly a native kingdom.

To·ro, Ce·rro del \ˌser-(ˌ)ō-del-'tȯr-(ˌ)ō\. Peak, cen. Chile, near border of Argentina; 20,995 ft.

Tö·rök·szent·mi·klós \'tər-ˌək-sent-'mik-ˌlōsh\. Commune, 65 m. SE of Budapest, E Hungary; pop. (1970p) 24,229.

Tor·o·na·ic Gulf \ˌtȯr-ə-ˌnā-ik-, ˌtär-\ *or Gk.* **To·ro·naí·os Kól·pos** \ˌtȯr-ə-ˌnā-ȯs-'kȯl-ˌpȯs\ *also* **Gulf of Kas·san·dra** \-kə-'san-drə\. Inlet of N Aegean Sea, bet. the Sithonia and Kassándra penins. of Chalcidice, NE Greece. Ruins of ancient Olynthus are at its head.

To·ron·to \tə-'ränt-(ˌ)ō, -'ränt-ə\. 1 City, Jefferson co., E Ohio, on Ohio river 7 m. N of Steubenville; pop. (1970c) 7705; sheet steel, titanium alloys, paper, dairy products.

2 Commercial and industrial city, ❋ of Ontario, Canada, and ⊗ of York co., SE Ontario, at NW end of Lake Ontario; pop. (1971p) 698,634, met. area pop. 2,609,638; second largest city in Canada; major transportation center; lake port, shipping grain, meat, and livestock; produces electrical equipment, iron and steel products, agricultural machinery, aircraft; printing and publishing. Toronto Univ. (1827), Victoria Univ. (1836), Knox Coll. (1844), Univ. of Saint Michael's Coll. (1852), Univ. of Trinity Coll. (1852), Osgoode Hall Law School (1872), Wycliffe Coll. (1877), Pontifical Institute of Medieval Studies (1929), Regis Coll. (1930), Ontario Bible Coll. (1935), York Univ. (1959). Notable buildings include parliament buildings and Superior Court of Ontario, and City Hall (completed 1965). In Exhibition Park is held annually the Canadian National Exhibition.

History: Occupies the site of old French trading post, Fort Rouillé (founded c. 1750); city founded as **York** \'yȯ(ə)rk\ by British Loyalists 1793; succeeded Niagara-on-the-Lake as capital of Upper Canada 1797; twice sacked by American troops during the War of 1812; received city charter 1834 and changed name to Toronto; had as first mayor William Lyon Mackenzie, leader of abortive uprising of 1837; capital of Canada 1849–51 and 1855–59; lower part of city destroyed by fire 1904.

Toronto, Lake \-tə-'rōn-tō\. Lake in SE cen. Chihuahua state, N Mexico, produced by damming of the Conchos river; site of an airport.

Toros Dağları. See TAURUS MOUNTAINS.

Tor·quay \'tȯr-'kē\. See TORBAY.

Tor·rá \tȯ-'rä\. Peak in the Cordillera Occidental of the Andes, W Colombia; 11,660 ft.

Tor·rance \'tȯr-ən(t)s, 'tär-\. 1 County in New Mexico. See table at NEW MEXICO.

2 Industrial and residential city, Los Angeles co., SW California, 15 m. SSW of Los Angeles; pop. (1970c) 134,584; aircraft and missiles, electronic components, aluminum, plastics, synthetic rubber, chemicals, dairy products, paint, automobile parts; oil wells; founded 1912; incorporated 1921.

Tor·re An·nun·zia·ta \'tȯr-ē-ə-ˌnün(t)-sē-'ät-ə\. Commune, Napoli prov., Campania, S Italy, on Bay of Naples 12 m. SE of Naples; pop. (1969e) 63,070; port and seaside resort; ships fruit, macaroni.

Torre del Gre·co \'tȯr-ē-ˌdel-'grek-(ˌ)ō\. Commune, Napoli prov., Campania, S Italy, on Bay of Naples 7 m. SE of Naples; pop. (1969e) 91,439; fishing; seaside resort; damaged several times by earthquakes and volcanic eruptions.

To·rre·don·ji·me·no \ˌtȯr-ə-ˌthōn-hē-'mān-(ˌ)ō\. Commune, Jaén prov., S Spain, 12 m. W of Jaén; pop. (1970p) 14,276; agriculture, stock raising; oil, liquor, soap.

To·rre·la·ve·ga \ˌtȯr-ə-lä-'vā-gə\. Commune, Santander prov., N Spain, 14 m. SW of Santander; pop. (1970p) 42,-945; leather, flour, chocolates; salting works.

Tor·re·mag·gio·re \ˌtȯr-ā-mä-'jōr-(ˌ)ā, -'jȯr-\. Commune, Foggia prov., Apulia, SE Italy, 21 m. NW of Foggia; pop. (1968e) 16,274; castle.

Tor·rens \'tȯr-ənz, 'tär-\. 1 Shallow salt lake, E South Australia, N of Spencer Gulf; 130 m. long, 2230 sq. m.; 92 ft. above sea level.

2 River, South Australia; 50 m. long; flows W to Gulf of St. Vincent; Adelaide on it.

To·rren·te \tō-'ren-(ˌ)tā\. Commune, Valencia prov., E Spain, 8 m. SW of Valencia; pop. (1970p) 39,724.

To·rre·ón \ˌtȯr-ē-'ōn\. City, Coahuila state, NE Mexico, 150 m. W of Monterrey; munic. pop. (1970p) 257,045; railroad junction; textiles, flour, iron and steel; center of wheat- and cotton-growing district.

To·rres del Pai·ne National Park \ˌtȯr-ās-del-'pīn-ā-\. National park, Chile; 95 sq. m.; rare animals; established 1959.

Tor·res Islands \ˌtȯr-əs-\. Group of 4 small islands, not of volcanic origin, at N end of the New Hebrides, SW Pacific Ocean, 50 m. NW of Vanua Lava; largest is Hiu I.

Torres Strait. Strait bet. the island of New Guinea and the N tip of Cape York Penin. on the mainland of Australia; connects Arafura Sea and Coral Sea; ab. 80 m. wide; Australian boundary is ab. 3 m. from New Guinea shore. Has many reefs, shoals, and islands (**Torres Strait Islands**), and is dangerous to navigation; larger islands inhabited. Strait discovered by the Spanish navigator Torres in 1606; traversed by Cook in 1770.

To·rres Ve·dras \ˌtȯr-əs-'vā-drəs\. Commune, Lisboa dist., W Portugal, 26 m. N of Lisbon; pop. (1960c) 13,196; noted particularly for its 28-mile stretch of fortifications (begun 1809), extending to the Tagus river, from behind which Wellington hindered the French march against Lisbon 1810 (Peninsular War); sulfur baths; Moorish citadel.

Tor·reys Peak \'tȯr-ēz-, 'tär-\. Mountain, Clear Creek and Summit cos., cen. Colorado; 14,267 ft.

Tor·ridge \'tȯr-ij, 'tär-\. River, Devonshire, SW England; ab. 40 m. long; flows SE and then curves to the NW and empties into Barnstaple Bay through an estuary at Bideford.

Tor·ri·don, Loch \läk-'tȯr-əd-ᵊn, -'tär-, läk-\. Inlet, Ross and Cromarty co., on NW coast of Scotland; extends inland ab. 12 m.

Tor·ring·ton \'tȯr-iŋ-tən, 'tär-\. 1 Industrial city, E cen. Litchfield co., NW Connecticut, on Naugatuck river 18 m. NNW of Waterbury; pop. (1970c) 31,952; textiles, hardware, bearings, lumber, sporting goods; settled 1735; incorporated as city 1923. The town (incorp. 1740) is coextensive with the city.

2 Town, ⊗ of Goshen co., SE Wyoming, on North Platte river 7 m. W of Nebraska border; pop. (1970c) 4237; oil wells, uranium mines; sugar beet; livestock; Eastern Wyoming Coll. (1948).

Tortoise Islands. See GALÁPAGOS ISLANDS.

Tor·to·la \tȯr-'tō-lə\. Largest of the British Virgin Is., West Indies; 21 sq. m.; pop. (1969e) 9730; chief town Road Town; highest point Mount Sage 1710 ft.

Tor·to·li·ta Mountains \ˌtȯrt-ᵊl-ˌēt-ə-\. Small range, E Pinal co., S cen. Arizona.

Tor·to·na \tȯr-'tō-nə\ *or anc.* **Der·to·na** \dər-'tō-nə\. Manufacturing commune, Alessandria prov., Piedmont,

NW Italy, 13 m. E of Alessandria; pop. (1968e) 28,577; 16th cent. cathedral.

Tor·to·sa \tȯr-ˈtō-sə\. 1 *or anc.* **Der·to·sa** \dər-ˈtō-sə\. City, Tarragona prov., NE Spain, on Ebro river 40 m. SW of Tarragona; pop. (1970p) 46,376; olive oil, fertilizer, hats, soap, pharmaceuticals, flour, lumber; 14th cent. cathedral. Came under Rome 218 B.C.; episcopal see under Goths; captured by Moors 713 and capital of small independent Moorish kingdom; reconquered 1148 by Ramón Berenguer IV; occupied by French 1648, 1708, 1810; heavily damaged in Spanish Civil War.

2 Town, Syria. See TARTŪS.

Tortosa, Cape. Cape, E coast of Spain, E of Tortosa.

Tortuga, La. See LA TORTUGA.

Tor·tu·ga Island \tȯr-ˈtü-gə-\ *or Fr.* **Île de la Tor·tue** \ēl-də-lä-tȯr-tue\. Island, West Indies, off N coast of Haiti; 25 m. long; in 17th cent. a resort of pirates.

To·ru·gart Pass \ˈtȯr-ü-ˌgärt-\ *or* **Tu·ru·gart Pass** \ˈtu̇r-\ *or Chin.* **T'o–lu–chia–erh–t'e Shan–k'ou** \ˈtō-ˈlü-chē-ˈä-ˈe(ə)r-ˈtə-ˈshän-ˈkō\. Mountain pass through W end of Tien Shan range, cen. Asia, on highway from Kashgar in W Sinkiang Uighur, China, to Kirgiz S.S.R., U.S.S.R.; elev. 12,155 ft.

To·run \ˈtȯr-ˌün-(-yə)\ *or Ger.* **Thorn** \ˈtȯ(ə)rn\. Industrial and commercial city, Bydgoszcz prov., N Poland, on Vistula river 110 m. NW of Warsaw; pop. (1970p) 129,200; railroad junction and river port; chemicals, lumber, machinery; printing; Gothic town hall, three Gothic churches, remains of town walls; univ. (1945). Birthplace of the astronomer Copernicus.

History: Founded by Teutonic Knights 1231 and received town rights 1233; member of Hanseatic League; to kingdom of Poland 1454; two treaties signed here (1411, 1466) by which Poland gained territory; occupied by Charles XII of Sweden 1703; to Prussia 1793; part of grand duchy of Warsaw 1807–15; returned to Prussia 1815; to Poland 1919; in World War II occupied by Germans 1939–44.

To·ry \ˈtȯr-ē, ˈtȯr-\. Small island, Atlantic Ocean, off extreme NW coast of Ireland and administratively part of co. Donegal, Eire; pop. (1961c) 307; lighthouse; lobster fisheries. Ruins of churches, perhaps founded by St. Columba; a pirate stronghold of the legendary Fomorians.

Törz·bur·ger Pass \ˈtərts-ˌbu̇r-gər-\. Mountain pass in the Transylvanian Alps, Romania, 25 m. SW of Braşov; 4065 ft.

Tor·zhok \tər-ˈzhȯk\. Town, Kalinin Oblast, Russian S.F.S.R., U.S.S.R., ab. 35 m. WNW of Kalinin; pop. (1967e) 43,000.

To·sa \ˈtō-sə\. Old province in S Shikoku I., Japan, now Kōchi prefecture. Home of the Tosa clan, esp. influential at the time of the Restoration 1868.

Tosa Bay. Inlet of the Pacific Ocean on S coast of Shikoku I., Japan.

To·sa·ri \tō-ˈsär-ē\. Village on N slopes of Tengger Mts., E Java, Indonesia; alt. 5963 ft.; health resort.

Toscana. See TUSCANY.

Toscanella. See TUSCANIA.

Toscano *or* **Tosco–Emiliano, Appennino.** See table at APENNINES.

Toscano, Arcipelago. See TUSCAN ARCHIPELAGO.

To·sya \ˌtō-sē-ˈä\. Town, Kastamonu prov., N Turkey, on a tributary of the Kızıl Irmak; pop. (1965c) 14,119.

Tot·nes \ˈtät-nəs\. Municipal borough, Devonshire, SW England, 20 m. SSW of Exeter; pop. (1971p) 5771; brewing, flour milling; remains of ancient castle whose grounds are a public garden; an ancient town, important in Saxon times.

Totomi Sea. See ENSHŪ BIGHT.

To·to·ni·ca·pán \tə-ˌtō-nē-kə-ˈpän\. 1 Department of W cen. Guatemala. See table at GUATEMALA.

2 City, its ✱, on high plateau; munic. pop. (1964p) 42,335; flour, woolens, pottery.

To·to·wa \ˈtōt-ə-wə\. Residential borough, Passaic co., N New Jersey, 3 m. W of Paterson; pop. (1970c) 11,580; encampment of Washington and his men during Revolution.

Tot·ting·ton \ˈtät-iŋ-tən\. Urban district, Lancashire, NW England, 10 m. NNW of Manchester; pop. (1971p) 9740.

Tot·to·ri \tə-ˈtōr-ē, -ˈtȯr-\. 1 Prefecture, Honshū, Japan; 1347 sq. m.; pop. (1970c) 568,777; ✱ Tottori.

2 Seaport city, its ✱, 90 m. NW of Kyōto; pop. (1970c) 113,151; textiles, silk; univ. (1949). Formerly the castle town of a daimyo; became prosperous in recent times on the opening of the railroad.

Touamotou Archipelago. See TUAMOTU ARCHIPELAGO.

Toub·kal \ˈtüb-ˌkal\. Mountain peak, Grand Atlas range, Morocco, S of Marrakech; 13,671 ft.; highest peak in the Atlas Mts.

Toubkal National Park. National park, Morocco; 141 sq. m.; numerous high peaks incl. Mt. Toubkal; established 1942.

Toug·gourt *or* **Tug·gurt** \tu̇-ˈgu̇(ə)rt\. Town and oasis, Oasis dept., NE Algeria, 100 m. S of Biskra; pop. (1966c) 50,000.

Toul \ˈtül\ *or anc.* **Tul·lum** \ˈtəl-əm\. City, Meurthe-et-Moselle dept., NE France, on Moselle river 13 m. WSW of Nancy; pop. (1968c) 14,780; manufactures porcelain; trades in wine and brandy; 13th–15th cent. Gothic church (former cathedral).

History: Ancient capital of the Leuci; became episcopal see in 4th cent.; in Middle Ages an important city; with Metz and Verdun (*Les Trois Evêches,* the Three Bishoprics) occupied by France 1552 but French possession not confirmed until Treaty of Westphalia 1648; bishopric suppressed and united with Nancy 1777; occupied by Germans in Franco-Prussian War 1870.

Tou·lon \ˈtü-ˌlän\. City, ⊗ of Stark co., NW cen. Illinois; pop. (1970c) 1207.

Toulon \tü-ˈlōⁿ\ *or anc.* **Te·lo Mar·ti·us** \ˌtē-lō-ˈmär-sh(ē-)əs\. Seaport, Var dept., SE France, on Mediterranean 30 m. ESE of Marseilles; pop. (1968c) 174,746; principal base of French Mediterranean fleet, with docks, naval shipyard, and arsenal; shipbuilding, fishing, wine making; ships cork, figs, bauxite, almonds, vegetable oils; winter resort; episcopal see; 13th cent. cathedral, naval museum.

History: First mentioned 3d cent. A.D. as Roman naval station; frequently attacked by Saracens in 9th cent.; passed, with Provence, to French crown 1481; captured by Charles V in 1524 and 1536; naval arsenal founded by Henry IV; indecisive battle bet. English and French and Spanish fleets off Toulon 1744; scene of victory of Napoleon over English, Spanish, and French royalists 1793; important port of entry and naval station in World War I; in World War II large part of French Mediterranean fleet stationed at Toulon after French armistice of 1940; majority of ships scuttled by their crews Nov. 27, 1942, after German abrogation of armistice and occupation of Toulon; city entered by French troops Aug. 22, 1944.

Tou·louse \tu̇-ˈlüz\ *or anc.* **To·lo·sa** \tə-ˈlō-sə\. City, ✱ of Haute-Garonne dept., S France, on Garonne river 133 m. SE of Bordeaux; pop. (1968c) 370,796; railroad junction and canal port; a center of the French aviation industry; produces ammunition, fertilizer, paper, knit goods, footwear, tobacco; market for agricultural region and distribution center for textiles; numerous notable buildings, including 11th–17th cent. Gothic cathedral, 11th–13th cent. Romanesque basilica, town hall, courthouse, museum, observatory, botanical gardens, public library; univ. (1229), Catholic Institute of Toulouse (1877), several professional and technical schools and academies.

History: Founded c. 4th cent. B.C.; taken by Romans 106 B.C.; capital of Visigoths in 5th cent. A.D.; taken by Clovis 508; as seat of countship of Toulouse (founded 778) capital of a major feudal dynasty; center of resistance to Albigensian crusade early 13th cent.; received a *parlement* 1443; scene of massacre of Protestants 1562; in 1814 scene of British victory over French in last battle of Peninsular

Campaign; in World War II occupied by Germans Nov. 1942–Aug. 1944.

Toun·goo \'tau̇ŋ-ˌ(g)ü\. 1 District, Tenasserim division, Lower Burma; 6456 sq. m.; pop. (1962e) 506,840; ✱ Toungoo.

2 Town, its ✱, on Sittang river 150 m. N of Rangoon; pop. (1953c) 31,589; capital of an independent kingdom from 14th to 16th cents.; occupied by Japanese Mar. 1942–Apr. 1945.

Tou·raine \tə-'rān\. Historical region of NW cen. France; bounded anciently on N by Le Maine, NE by Orléanais, SE by Berry, S by Marche, SW by Poitou, W by Saumurois, NW by Anjou; ✱ Tours; watered by Indre, Cher, and Loire rivers; sometimes called the "Garden of France"; province under the ancien régime.

Tourane. See DA NANG.

Tour·coing \tu̇r-'kwaⁿ\. Manufacturing city, Nord dept., N France, on Belgian frontier 8 m. NE of Lille; pop. (1968c) 98,755; one of principal textile centers of France; soap works, sugar refineries. In World War I captured by Germans 1914 and seriously damaged.

Tour·nai *or* **Tour·nay** \tu̇(ə)r-'nā\ *or Flem.* **Door·nik** \'dōr-ˌnik, 'dȯr-\. Commercial and industrial commune, Hainaut prov., SW Belgium, on the Schelde 45 m. SW of Brussels; pop. (1969e) 33,625; hosiery, textiles, leather goods, cement; 11th–12th cent. cathedral, 12th cent. belfry. Made episcopal see 6th cent.; came under French rule and received charter 1187; frequently besieged in wars in Netherlands 16th–18th cents.; in World War I captured by Germans Aug. 1914 and held until 1918; severely damaged.

Tour·non \tu̇r-'nōⁿ\. Town, Ardèche dept., SE France, on Rhone river 58 m. by rail S of Lyons; pop. (1962c) 8127; remains of ancient fortifications.

Tour·nus \tu̇r-'nyü\. Town, Saône-et-Loire dept., E cen. France, on the Saône ab. 15 m. N of Mâcon; pop. (1962c) 6206; site of Benedictine abbey founded 7th or 8th cent.; notable abbey church. Birthplace of the painter Jean Baptiste Greuze.

Tours \'tu̇(ə)r\; *anc.* **Cae·sa·ro·du·num** \ˌsē-zər-ə-'d(y)ün-əm\ *or later* **Tu·ro·ni** \'t(y)u̇r-ə-ˌnī\. Industrial and commercial city, ✱ of Indre-et-Loire dept., NW cen. France, 129 m. SW of Paris; pop. (1968c) 128,120; silk, furniture, building materials, footwear, chemicals; ships wine and dried fruit; notable Gothic cathedral (12th–16th cents.), several other Gothic churches, two towers and cloister of old basilica of St. Martin of Tours.

History: A pre-Roman foundation; made episcopal see 3d cent.; in 732 scene of victory of Charles Martel over Saracens (also called battle of Poitiers); developed prosperous silk industry in 15th cent.; largely depopulated after revocation of Edict of Nantes 1685; seat of French government during siege of Paris 1870. Birthplace of Balzac.

Tou·si·dé \ˌtü-si-'dā\. Peak in Tibesti Mts., N Chad, N cen. Africa; 10,712 ft.

Tou·tle \'tüt-ᵊl\. River, SW Washington; ab. 40 m. long; flows W in N Cowlitz co. into Cowlitz river.

To·wa·da \tō-'wäd-ə\. Lake, N Honshū, Japan; 25 m. in circumference, elevation 1476 ft.; resort, ab. 25 m. S of Aomori.

Towada–Ha·chi·man·tai National Park \-ˌhä-chē-'män-ˌtī-\. National park, N Honshū, Japan; 322 sq. m.; consists of two sections; volcanoes; established 1936.

To·wan·da \tō 'wän-də\. Borough and summer resort, ⊗ of Bradford co., N Pennsylvania, on Susquehanna river 50 m. WNW of Scranton; pop. (1970c) 4224; resort; tungsten, silk; fruit farms.

Tow·ces·ter \'tōs-tər\. Parish, S Northamptonshire, cen. England; site of Roman camp on Watling Street; important in Saxon times.

Tow·er City \ˌtau̇-ər-\. Borough, Schuylkill co., E cen. Pennsylvania, 28 m. NE of Harrisburg; pop. (1970c) 1774.

Tower Falls. Waterfall, Yellowstone National Park, NW Wyoming; 132 ft. high.

Tower Hamlets. Borough of Greater London, SE England. See table at LONDON 4.

Tower Island. See GENOVESA.

Tower Peak. Mountain in Sierra Nevada, E Tuolumne co., cen. California; 11,704 ft.

Town and Country. Village, St. Louis co., E Missouri; pop. (1970c) 2645.

Tow·ner \'tau̇n-ər\. 1 County in North Dakota. See table at NORTH DAKOTA.

2 City, ⊗ of McHenry co., N cen. North Dakota; pop. (1970c) 870.

Towns \'tau̇nz\. County in Georgia. See table at GEORGIA.

Town·send \'tau̇n-zənd\. 1 Town, Middlesex co., NE Massachusetts, 7 m. NE of Fitchburg; pop. (1970c) 4281.

2 Town, ⊗ of Broadwater co., SW cen. Montana; pop. (1970c) 1371; gold mines; livestock.

Townsend Inlet. Narrow strait, leading from Atlantic Ocean through barrier reefs in E Cape May co., S New Jersey.

Towns·ville \'tau̇nz-ˌvil\. City, E Queensland, Australia, on Halifax Bay 380 m. NW of Rockhampton; pop. (1968e) 63,300; major seaport exporting meat, sugar, mineral concentrates, hides, wool; meat-packing, copper refining, sawmilling; James Cook Univ. of North Queensland (1970); founded 1864.

Tow·son \'tau̇s-ᵊn\. Unincorporated locality, ⊗ of Baltimore co., N Maryland, N of Baltimore; pop. (1970c) 77,809; Goucher Coll. (1885).

Tow·ton \'tau̇t-ᵊn\. Parish, West Riding, Yorkshire, N England; scene of battle Mar. 29, 1461 (the Wars of the Roses) in which Edward IV defeated the Lancastrians, a victory which confirmed his accession to the throne.

Towy \'tau̇-ē\. River, SW Wales; 65 m. long; flows SW to Carmarthen Bay.

To·ya·ma \tō-'yäm-ə\. 1 Prefecture, Honshū, Japan; 1642 sq. m.; pop. (1970c) 1,029,695; ✱ Toyama; rice; abundant hydroelectric power.

2 Seaport city, its ✱, near S shore of Toyama Bay 110 m. N of Nagoya; pop. (1970c) 269,276; cotton and synthetic textiles, pharmaceuticals, patent medicines; univ. (1949). From 16th cent. an important seat of daimios under Tokugawa Shogunate.

Toyama Bay. Inlet of the Sea of Japan on the W cen. coast of Honshū, Japan; enclosed on W by Noto Penin.

Toyohara. See YUZHNO-SAKHALINSK.

To·yo·ha·shi \ˌtȯ-yə-'häsh-ē\. City, Aichi prefecture, S Honshū, Japan, 38 m. SE of Nagoya and near E shore of inlet of E Ise Bay; pop. (1970c) 258,547; textiles.

To·yo·ka·wa \ˌtō-yō-'kä-wə\. City, Aichi prefecture, Honshū, Japan, 41 m. SE of Nagoya; pop. (1970c) 85,860.

To·yo·na·ka \ˌtō-yō-'näk-ə\. City, Ōsaka prefecture, Honshū, Japan; pop. (1970c) 368,498; suburb of Ōsaka.

To·zeur \tō-'zər\. Town and large oasis, W Tunisia, on W shore of Chott Djerid; pop. (1966c) 13,900.

Trab·zon \trab-'zän\ *or* **Treb·i·zond** \'treb-ə-ˌzänd\. 1 Province of NE Turkey. See table at TURKEY.

2 *or anc.* **Trap·e·zus** \'trap-i-zəs\. Seaport city, its ✱, on the SE coast of the Black Sea ab. 12 m. NW of Erzurum; pop. (1965c) 65,516; commercial center; technical univ. (1963). An ancient town, dating from the 7th cent. B.C. and for many centuries terminus of a trade route to Persia and Central Asia; held by Roman and Byzantine empires and ✱ of Greek Empire of Trebizond 1204–1478.

Trach·o·ni·tis \ˌtrak-ə-'nīt-əs\. District of anc. Palestine, beyond (E of) the Jordan, S of Damascus, and E of Gaulanitis; formed a part of the Tetrarchy of Philip 4 B.C.–34 A.D.

Tra·cy \ˈtrā-sē\. 1 Industrial city, San Joaquin co., cen. California, 18 m. SSW of Stockton; pop. (1970c) 14,724; packs fruit and vegetables; truck farms.
2 City, Lyon co., SW Minnesota, 18 m. SSE of Marshall; pop. (1970c) 2516; dairy farms.
3 Town, Richelieu co., S Quebec, Canada, 45 m. NE of Montreal; pop. (1971p) 11,845.

Tracy City. Town, Grundy co., S cen. Tennessee, ab. 30 m. NW of Chattanooga; pop. (1970c) 1388.

Tra·fal·gar, Cape \-trə-ˈfal-gər; *Span.* -ˌträ-fäl-ˈgär\. Cape, SW coast of Spain, SE of Cádiz and WNW of the Strait of Gibraltar; scene of decisive victory of British fleet under Lord Nelson over French and Spanish, and of Nelson's death Oct. 21, 1805.

Traf·ford \ˈtraf-ərd\. Borough, Allegheny and Westmoreland cos., SW Pennsylvania, 14 m. E of Pittsburgh; pop. (1970c) 4383.

Tragurium. See TROGIR.

Trai·guén \trī-ˈgen\. 1 Island in Chonos Archipelago, in Pacific Ocean off SW coast of Chile.
2 City, Malleco prov., S cen. Chile, ab. 45 m. S of Angol; pop. (1960c) 9990.

Trail \ˈtrā(ə)l\. Mining city, SE British Columbia, Canada, on Columbia river 7 m. N of U.S. border; pop. (1971p) 10,843; fertilizer; gold, lead, silver, zinc mines; dairy farms.

Trail Creek. Town, La Porte co., N Indiana, 1 m. S of Michigan City; pop. (1970c) 2697.

Traill \ˈtrā(ə)l\. County in North Dakota. See table at NORTH DAKOTA.

Trajani Portus. See CIVITAVECCHIA.

Tra·lee \trə-ˈlē\. Urban district and seaport, ⊗ of co. Kerry, SW Eire, at head of **Tralee Bay** (inlet of Atlantic Ocean N of Dingle Bay); pop. (1971p) 12,227; creamery; site of Norman castle, seat of earls of Desmond. At nearby Ardfert are the ruins of 13th cent. cathedral on site of earlier (6th cent.) foundation of St. Brendan.

Trälleborg. See TRELLEBORG.

Tralles. See AYDIN 2.

Tra·nent \trə-ˈnent\. Burgh, East Lothian, SE Scotland, ab. 9 m. E of Edinburgh near Prestonpans (*q.v.*); pop. (1971p) 6288.

Trang \ˈträŋ\. 1 Province, SW Thailand; 1909 sq. m.; pop. (1960c) 240,463; ✱ Trang.
2 Town, its ✱, on branch railroad 15 m. from the Strait of Malacca at Kantang and 85 m. ESE of Phuket; pop. (1960c) 17,158.

Trang·an \träŋ-ˈgän\. Island, S cen. part of Aru Is., Indonesia; ab. 50 m. long by 30 m. wide.

Tra·ni \ˈträn-ē\. Commercial seaport, Bari prov., Apulia, SE Italy, on the Adriatic Sea 26 m. WNW of Bari; pop. (1968e) 41,530; ships wine and marble; furniture; notable 12th cent. cathedral, 13th cent. castle.

Tran·que·bar \ˈtraŋ-kwə-ˌbär, ˈtraŋ-kə-\. Town, Tamil Nadu, S India, 50 m. NE of Tanjore; pop. (1961c) 14,800. Formerly a seaport of importance; Danish settlement established here 1616; taken by British 1801, restored 1814, but bought with other Danish settlements in India in 1845.

Trans Alai \ˌtran(t)s-ə-ˈlī, ˌtranz-\. Mountain range, NW Pamirs, extending E and W bet. Kirgiz S.S.R. and the Gorno-Badakhshan Autonomous Oblast, Tadzhik S.S.R., U.S.S.R.; highest point Lenin Peak 23,405 ft. See ALAI.

Transalpine Gaul. See GAUL 2.

Transantarctic Mountains. See ANTARCTICA.

Trans–Ap·pa·lach·ia \ˌtran(t)s-ˌap-ə-ˈlā-ch(ē-)ə, -ˈlach-(ē-)ə, tranz-\. Region, E cen. United States, W of the Appalachian Mts.; used historically, esp. of period of late 18th and early 19th cents., to designate region drained by Ohio river.

Trans·bai·ka·lia \ˌtran(t)s-bī-ˈkōl-yə, ˌtranz-, -ˈkal-\ *or* **Trans·bai·kal** \-bī-ˈkōl, -ˈkal\ *also* **Za·bai·kal** \ˌzä-bī-ˈkäl, -ˈkal\. Former Russian government, E of Lake Baikal, now included in Buryat A.S.S.R., Chita Oblast, and Khabarovsk Krai of the Russian S.F.S.R., U.S.S.R.

Trans·car·pa·thi·an Oblast \ˌtran(t)s-kär-ˈpā-thē-ən-ˈō-bləst, -ˌblast, ˌtranz-\ *or Russ.* **Za·kar·pat·ska·ya Oblast** \ˌzäk-ər-ˈpät-skə-yə-\; *formerly* **Car·pa·thi·an Ru·the·nia** \kär-ˈpā-thē-ən-rü-ˌthē-nyə, -nē-ə\ *or Czech* **Pod·kar·pat·ská Rus** \ˈpȯt-kär-ˌpät-skä-ˈrüs\. The extreme W subdivision of the Ukrainian S.S.R., U.S.S.R.; 4942 sq. m.; pop. (1970p) 1,057,000; ✱ Uzhgorod. Economy largely based on timber working; wheat, rye, oats, tobacco; principal towns Uzhgorod and Mukachevo. Organized from territory ceded to U.S.S.R. by Romania 1945.

Trans·cas·pi·an Region \tran(t)s-ˈkas-pē-ən-, tranz-\ *or* **Trans·cas·pia** \-pē-ə\. Former Russian government, E of the Caspian Sea, roughly equivalent to the present Turkmen S.S.R. and a part of SW Kazakh S.S.R. of the U.S.S.R.

Trans·cau·ca·sian Federation \ˌtran(t)s-kȯ-ˈkā-zhən-, ˌtranz-, -ˈkazh-ən-\ *also* **Trans·cau·ca·sia** \-ˈkāzh-(ē-)ə\ *or officially* **Transcaucasian Soviet Federated Socialist Republic.** Former federated union of what are now the three Soviet socialist republics of Armenia, Azerbaijan, and Georgia; ✱ Tbilisi.
History: First formed Sept. 20, 1917 after the Russian Revolution (prior to Revolution region divided into various Russian governments, provinces, and districts); soon dissolved into separate republics of Georgia, Azerbaijan, and Armenia; scene of fighting in 1919–21 when Turkish Nationalists struggled with the Bolsheviks for control of the region; reformed Mar. 12, 1922 and entered the U.S.S.R. July 6, 1923; separated again into three autonomous republics Dec. 1936 when the U.S.S.R. adopted a new constitution.

Trans·co·na \tran(t)s-ˈkō-nə, tranz-\. Industrial city, S Manitoba, Canada, 8 m. E of Winnipeg; pop. (1971p) 22,-085; fertilizer; railroad shops.

Trans–Dnies·tria \tran(t)s-ˈnēs-trē-ə, tranz-\. Region, bet. the Dniester and Bug rivers in SW Ukrainian S.S.R., U.S.S.R.; with Bessarabia was given 1941 to Romania by Germany; retaken by Soviet armies 1944–45.

Transilvania. See TRANSYLVANIA 2.

Transjordan. See JORDAN.

Trans–Juba. See JUBALAND.

Trans·kei \ˈtran(t)s-ˈkā, -ˈkī\. An internally self-governing Bantu territory, E Cape Province, Rep. of South Africa; 16,329 sq. m.; pop. (1960c) 1,439,195; ✱ Umtata. Different regions annexed to Cape Colony at various dates bet. 1879 and 1894; self-governing territory formed 1963; its laws subject to the approval of the government of the Rep. of South Africa.

Trans·ox·i·a·na \ˌtran(t)s-ˌäk-sē-ˈā-nə, ˌtranz-, -ˈan-ə\. Region, beyond (N of) the Oxus (*mod.* Amu Darya) and NE of Khorāsān, W Asia, including Bukhara and Samarkand. In ancient times known as Sogdiana (*q.v.*).

Transpadane Gaul. See GAUL.

Trans·pad·ane Republic \ˈtrans-pə-ˌdān-, trans-ˈpā-(ˌ)dān-, tranz-\. Provisionally organized republic, N Italy; created by Napoleon 1796–97 from lands N of Po around Milan, Bergamo, Brescia, and Cremona; incorporated into Cisalpine Republic 1797. See GAUL.

Trans·vaal \tran(t)s-ˈväl, tranz-\ *or formerly, as independent state,* **South African Republic.** Province, NE Rep. of South Africa; 109,621 sq. m.; pop. (1967e) 7,394,961; ✱ Pretoria; lies bet. Limpopo river (on N) and Vaal river (on S). Plateau land (high veld), averaging 5000 to 6400 ft. covers nearly one third of province in SE; drained by Komati, Pongolo, and other rivers flowing E to Indian Ocean. In W plateau slopes to ab. 4000 ft. average. Has abundant mineral resources, esp. gold in Witwatersrand near Johannesburg (richest goldfield in the world), and diamonds around Pretoria; also deposits of platinum, coal, iron, silver, etc. Agriculture second to mining in importance; livestock raising; corn, wheat, tobacco, citrus fruit. Chief towns Pretoria, Johannesburg with suburbs of Germiston, Boksburg, Springs, and Beroni.
History: About 1800 region was sparsely inhabited by Bantu Negroes, Bushmen, and Hottentots; later dominated by Zulus; few white persons crossed Vaal before 1836

when great trek of Boers began; first settlement at Potchefstroom 1838. Independence acknowledged by British in Sand River Convention 1852. South African Republic (*q.v.*) formed 1856; civil war, financial difficulties, discovery of diamonds 1867 led to loss of Griqualand West 1871 and annexation by British 1877–81; rebellion of Boers 1880–81 and restoration of republic 1881; discovery of gold 1886 brought in many foreigners (uitlanders); Jameson's Raid 1895; joined Orange Free State in war with Great Britain 1899–1900; as Transvaal annexed as British crown colony 1900; granted self-government 1906; joined Union (now Rep.) of South Africa 1910.

Trans–Volta Togoland. See TOGOLAND.

Tran·syl·va·nia \ˌtran-səl-ˈvān-yə, -ˈvān-ē-ə\. 1 County in North Carolina. See table at NORTH CAROLINA.

2 *or Rom.* **Tran·sil·va·nia** \ˌträn-sēl-ˈvän-yä\ *or Hung.* **Er·dély** \er-ˈdā\. Region, NW and cen. Romania; 21,297 sq. m.; a plateau (averaging 1000–1600 ft.) of triangular shape, shut in on N, E, and S by the Carpathian Mts. and Transylvanian Alps and drained chiefly by tributaries of the Tisza, esp. the Someşul and Mureşul.

History: In Roman times included in the province of Dacia; later overrun by various Germanic and other tribes; settled 9th cent. ff. by the Szeklers, Vlachs, and Saxons; called **Sie·ben·bür·gen** \ˌzē-bən-ˈb(y)ür-gən\ by the Saxons; conquered by Hungarians 1003; made a principality 1540; subject to Ottoman Empire in 17th cent.; scene of frequent religious and ethnic conflict; made a grand principality within the Austrian Empire 1765; scene of severe fighting in Revolution 1848; made integral part of Hungary 1867; annexed to Romania 1918; its N part assigned to Hungary 1940–45 (area ab. 17,000 sq. m.; pop. 2,500,000) but returned to Romania after the war.

Tran·syl·va·nian Alps \ˌtran-səl-ˌvān-yən-\ *also* **South Car·pa·thi·ans** \-kär-ˈpā-thē-ənz\. Mountain range, a continuation of the Carpathian Mts., extending E and W in cen. Romania, along the boundary bet. N Walachia and S Transylvania; ab. 230 m. long; highest point Moldoveanul 8343 ft.

Tra·pa·ni \ˈträp-ə-nē\. 1 Province of Sicily, Italy. See table at ITALY.

2 *or anc.* **Drep·a·num** \ˈdrep-ə-nəm\. Seaport, its ✱, on Mediterranean Sea at NW tip of the island, 48 m. SW of Palermo; pop. (1968e) 77,029; salt; marble working, fish canning; commercial fisheries; 17th cent. cathedral, notable 14th and 16th cent. churches, medieval walls, 17th cent. town hall.

History: Founded by Carthaginians and important naval base during First Punic War (264–241 B.C.) after which it was ceded to Rome; conquered by Vandals 440 A.D., Saracens 1077, and later by Normans who made it part of kingdom of the Two Sicilies.

Trapezus. See TRABZON 2.

Trappe, La. See SOLIGNY-LA-TRAPPE.

Trap·per Peak \ˌtrap-ər-\. 1 Mountain on SW border of Ravalli co., W Montana; 10,175 ft.

2 Mountain, Glacier National Park, NW Montana; 9675 ft.

Tra·ral·gon \trə-ˈral-gən\. Town, Victoria, Australia, 90 m. SE of Melbourne; pop. (1968e) 14,420.

Tras·i·mene \ˈtras-ə-ˌmēn\ *or* **Pe·ru·gia** \pə-ˈrü-j(ē-)ə\; *Ital.* **Tra·si·me·no** \ˌträ-zə-ˈmā-nō\ *or anc.* **Tras·i·me·nus** \ˌtras-ə-ˈmēn-əs\. Lake, Umbria, cen. Italy, 10 m. W of Perugia; scene of Hannibal's victory over the Romans 217 B.C., also of severe fighting June 28–July 3, 1944 in World War II bet. British and German armies.

Tras·te·ve·re \trä-ˈstā-vā-ˌrā\. Region across the Tiber from Rome, Italy.

Trat \ˈträt\ *or* **Bang Phra** \ˈbäŋ-ˈprä\. 1 Province, S Thailand; 1127 sq. m.; pop. (1960c) 66,638; ✱ Trat.

2 Town and port, its ✱, on NE coast of Gulf of Siam near Cambodia border; pop. (1960c) 3813; end of highway from Bangkok.

Traù *or* **Trau.** See TROGIR.

Traun \ˈtraủn\. 1 River, W cen. Austria; 95 m. long; rises in a series of lakes in the Salzkammergut and flows N out of Styria through the Hallstätter and Traun lakes in Upper Austria into Danube river 4 m. below Linz.

2 Town, N Austria; pop. (1961c) 16,026; paper, textiles.

Traun, Lake; *Ger.* **Traun See** \-ˌzā\ *also* **Gmund·ner See** \gə-ˈmủnt-nər-ˌzā\. Lake, S Upper Austria, formed by Traun river; 7 m. long by 2 m. wide; 9.4 sq. m.; max. depth 626 ft.

Traun·stein \ˈtraủn-ˌs(h)tīn\. Commune, Bavaria, West Germany; salt springs and baths.

Trautenau. See TRUTNOV.

Trav·an·core \ˈtrav-ən-ˌkō(ə)r, -ˌkȯ(ə)r\. Region, Kerala, SW India; Western Ghats reach height of 8000 ft.; rice.

Tra·ven·dal \ˈträ-vən-ˌdäl\. Village, Schleswig-Holstein, West Germany, 15 m. W of Lübeck; treaty signed here Aug. 18, 1700 by which Charles XII of Sweden forced a peace on the Danes.

Trav·erse \ˈtrav-ərs\. County in Minnesota. See table at MINNESOTA.

Traverse, Lake. Lake on boundary bet. Roberts co., NE South Dakota, and Traverse co., W Minnesota; 30 m. long; outlet on N is the Bois de Sioux river, headstream of Red River of the North.

Traverse City. City, ⊗ of Grand Traverse co., NW Michigan, at S end of W arm of Grand Traverse Bay; pop. (1970c) 18,048; center of a resort and boating region.

Trav·is \ˈtrav-əs\. County in Texas. See table at TEXAS.

Trav·nik \ˈträv-nēk\. Town, Bosnia and Herzegovina, W cen. Yugoslavia, 45 m. NW of Sarajevo; pop. (1965e) 13,000; stock-breeding center. Has Roman remains, a Turkish citadel; from 1686 to 1850 was capital of Bosnia.

Treas·ure \ˈtrezh-ər\. County in Montana. See table at MONTANA.

Treasure Island. 1 Man-made island, San Francisco Bay, California; site of Golden Gate International Exposition 1939, now a naval base.

2 City, Pinellas co., E Florida; pop. (1970c) 6120.

Treas·ury Islands \ˈtrezh-(ə-)rē-\. Group of small islands, off S end of Bougainville I. and SSW of Shortland Is., NW Solomon Is., W Pacific Ocean; includes Mono I. and Stirling I.; occupied by U.S. Oct. 26–30, 1943.

Treb·bia \ˈtreb-yä\ *or anc.* **Tre·bia** \ˈtrē-bē-ə\. River, NW Italy; 71 m. long; rises NE of Genoa, flows N into Po river 3 m. NW of Piacenza; scene of two battles: (1) 218 B.C. in which Hannibal defeated the Romans under Publius Scipio; (2) June 17–19, 1799 in which Suvorov defeated the French under Macdonald.

Tře·bíč \tər-ˈzheb-ēch\ *or Ger.* **Tre·bitsch** \ˈtrā-bich\. Town, Czech S.R., W cen. Czechoslovakia, 36 m. W of Brno; pop. (1968e) 21,294.

Treb·i·zond \ˈtreb-ə-ˌzänd\. 1 Greek empire, 1204–1461, founded by Alexius I (Comnenus) as an offshoot of Byzantine Empire; included at greatest extent Georgia, Crimea, and the entire S shore of Black Sea E of Sakarya river; ✱ Trebizond (*mod.* Trabzon); last Greek state to be conquered by Ottoman Turks 1461.

2 Province and city, Turkey. See TRABZON.

Tre·ca·te \trā-ˈkät-ā\. Commune, Novara prov., NE Piedmont, NW Italy, E of Novara; pop. (1968e) 13,252.

Tre·ce Mar·ti·res \ˌtrā-sā-mär-ˈtir-ās\. Chartered city, ✱ of Cavite prov., Luzon, Phil.; pop. (1970e) 6200.

Tre·de·gar \tri-ˈdē-gər\. Urban district, Monmouthshire, SE Wales, on the Sirhowy 33 m. WNW of Bristol; pop. (1971p) 17,976; iron and steel manufacturing; coal.

Tre·go \ˈtrē-(ˌ)gō\. County in Kansas. See table at KANSAS.

Tre·grosse Islets \tri-'grōs-\. Group of coral islets and reefs, Coral Sea, outside Great Barrier Reef, Queensland, Australia, 17°41'S, 150°43'E.

Tre·ia \'trā-(y)ä\. Commune, Macerata prov., Marches, cen. Italy, 7 m. W of Macerata; pop. (1968e) 9408; 15th cent. cathedral.

Trein·ta y Tres \ˌtrān-tä-ē-'trās\. 1 Department of E Uruguay. See table at URUGUAY.
2 Town, its ❋, 140 m. NE of Montevideo; pop. (1963c) 22,422.

Tré·la·tête, Ai·guille de \ā-ˌgwēd-ə-ˌtrā-lə-'tāt\. Peak in the French Alps, SW of Mont Blanc; 12,832 ft.

Tré·la·zé \ˌtrā-lə-'zā\. Commune, Maine-et-Loire dept., W France; pop. (1965e) 11,317; E suburb of Angers; slate quarries.

Tre·lew \trā-'leu̇\. Commercial town, NE Chubut prov., S Argentina, W of Rawson; pop. (1960c) 11,852; in sheep-raising district. Founded by Welshmen 1881.

Trel·le·borg *or* **Träl·le·borg** \ˌtrel-ə-'bȯr\. Seaport, Malmöhus co., SW Sweden, on the Baltic Sea; pop. (1970e) 36,021; shipping center; sugar refineries; machinery, rubber, and cement works.

Tre·mi·ti Islands \ˌtrem-ət-ē-, ˌtrām-\. Italian group of 5 small islands, Adriatic Sea, N of Mount Gargano; largest island **San Do·mi·no** \san-'dō-mi-ˌnō\, ab. 5 m. in circumference.

Tremonia. See DORTMUND.

Tre·mon·ton \'trē-ˌmänt-ᵊn\. City, Box Elder co., NW Utah, 38 m. NNW of Ogden; pop. (1970c) 2795.

Trem·pea·leau \'trem-pə-ˌlō\. 1 River, W Wisconsin; ab. 50 m. long; rises in W Jackson co., flows SW into Mississippi river on line bet. Buffalo and Trempealeau cos.
2 County in Wisconsin. See table at WISCONSIN.

Tren·čín \'tren-ˌchēn\ *or Hung.* **Tren·csén** \'tren-ˌchān\ *or Ger.* **Trent·schin** \'tren-chin\. Town, Slovak S.R., E cen. Czechoslovakia, on the Váh river ab. 70 m. NE of Bratislava; pop. (1968e) 28,011.

Treng·ga·nu \treŋ-'gä-(ˌ)nü\ *or* **Te·reng·ganu** \tə-reŋ-'gän-ü\. 1 River, Trengganu state, Malaysia, Malay Penin.; ab. 70 m. long; flows NE into South China Sea at Kuala Trengganu.
2 A state of Malaysia, Malay Penin., bounded on N and E by the South China Sea, on S by Pahang, on W by Pahang and Kelantan, and on NW by Kelantan; 5000 sq. m.; pop. (1970p) 405,751; ❋ Kuala Trengganu; has several small islands ab. 20 m. off the coast; rubber, copra, iron ore; fishing.
History: For several centuries disputed by Malacca and Siam (Thailand) until downfall of former; became British dependency 1909; under Japanese control 1941–45; became part of independent Federation of Malaya 1957; became a state of Malaysia 1963.

Trent \'trent\. 1 River, SE North Carolina; 40 m. long; flows W to E across Jones and Craven cos. into Neuse river at New Bern.
2 River, Victoria, Peterborough, and Northumberland cos., SE Ontario, Canada; ab. 150 m. long; has its source in the Kawartha chain of lakes, thence flows S (here called the Otonabee) past Peterborough to Rice Lake, from which it winds generally SE to Trenton on the Bay of Quinte. Its entire course either used or paralleled by the **Trent Canal** system (or **Trent Waterways**); in W part canal connects Kawartha Lakes with Lake Simcoe and thence by Severn river to Georgian Bay, total length 224 m. and 42 locks. Also it has branch S by way of Scugog river past Lindsay, ab. 35 m.
3 River, cen. England; 170 m. long; rises in Staffordshire, flows NNE and unites with the Ouse ab. 15 m. W of Hull to form the Humber; navigable as far as Gainsborough.
4 *or Ital.* **Tren·to** \'tren-(ˌ)tō\ *or Ger.* **Tri·ent** \trē-'ent\ *or anc.* **Tri·den·tum** \trī-'dent-əm\. Commune, ❋ of Trentino-Alto Adige, also ❋ of Trento prov., NE Italy, on Adige river 106 m. ENE of Milan; pop. (1968e) 88,544; furniture, leather goods; printing, truck farming; 12th–14th cent. Romanesque cathedral, 13th–16th cent. castle with palace.
History: Believed to date from 4th cent. B.C.; Roman military base; in Christian era came under Ostrogoths, Lombards, and Franks; became episcopal principality 1027; passed to Austria in 16th cent.; seat of Council of Trent 1545–63 at which was established basic doctrine of Counter-Reformation; part of Napoleonic kingdom of Italy 1810–14, then passed to Austria; to Italy by Treaty of St-Germain 1919.

Tren·ti·no–Al·to Adi·ge \tren-'tē-(ˌ)nō-ˌäl-(ˌ)tō-'äd-i-ˌjā\ *or formerly* **Ve·ne·zia Tri·den·ti·na** \və-'net-sē-ə-ˌtrē-den-'tēn-ə\. Autonomous region, NE Italy; 5256 sq. m.; pop. (1968e) 834,675; ❋ Trent; mountainous; corn, wheat, oats, vines; dairy farming; zinc, lead; hydroelectric power; tourism; annexed to Austria 1814; scene of much fighting throughout World War I; by Treaty of St-Germain 1919 ceded to Italy; administratively reorganized 1948.

Tren·to \'tren-(ˌ)tō\. 1 Province of Trentino-Alto Adige, Italy. See table at ITALY.
2 Commune, Italy. See TRENT 4.

Tren·ton \'trent-ᵊn\. 1 City, ⊗ of Gilchrist co., NW Florida penin.; pop. (1970c) 1074.
2 Town, ⊗ of Dade co., NW corner of Georgia; pop. (1970c) 1523; lumber, clothing.
3 City, Wayne co., SE Michigan, on Detroit river 15 m. SSW of Detroit; pop. (1970c) 25,196; steel, boats, chemicals, automobile engines; truck and dairy farms.
4 City, ⊗ of Grundy co., N Missouri, 22 m. N of Chillicothe; pop. (1970c) 6063; fertilizers; diversified agriculture; Trenton Junior Coll. (1925).
5 Village, ⊗ of Hitchcock co., S Nebraska; pop. (1970c) 770; livestock, dairy, grain farms.
6 Industrial city, ❋ of New Jersey and ⊗ of Mercer co., W cen. New Jersey, at head of navigation on Delaware river 28 m. NE of Philadelphia; pop. (1970c) 104,638; produces steel, steel cables, steam turbines, plastics, parachutes, cigars, paint, tile, woolens, dies, automobile parts; Trenton State Coll. (1855), Rider Coll. (1865), Mercer County Community Coll. (1947); battle monument (1893) marking spot where American forces under Washington opened fire on British 1776. Settled c. 1679 by English Quakers; incorporated as borough and town 1745; in American Revolution scene of American victory and capture of Hessian garrison in surprise attack Dec. 26, 1776; made state capital 1790; incorporated as city 1792.
7 Town, ⊗ of Jones co., SE North Carolina; pop. (1970c) 539; tobacco.
8 Village, Butler co., SW Ohio, 25 m. SW of Dayton; pop. (1970c) 5278.
9 City, ⊗ of Gibson co., NW Tennessee, 26 m. NNW of Jackson; pop. (1970c) 4226; cottonseed oil, footwear, lumber; strawberries.
10 Town, Pictou co., N Nova Scotia, Canada, on Pictou Harbor 3 m. N of New Glasgow; pop. (1971p) 3319.
11 Industrial town, Hastings co., SE Ontario, Canada, on Bay of Quinte 12 m. W of Belleville; pop. (1971p) 14,405; steel, textiles, flour; fruit and dairy farms; E terminus of Trent Canal system.

Trenton Falls. Cascades in West Canada Creek, cen. New York, 15 m. N of Utica; furnish waterpower for Utica; the creek cuts through limestone which was laid down in what geologists call the Trenton period, named after these formations.

Trentschin. See TRENČÍN.

Trent Waterways. See TRENT 2.

Tréport, Le. See LE TRÉPORT.

Tres Arro·yos \ˌtrā-sə-'rȯi-əs\. City, Buenos Aires prov., E cen. Argentina, ab. 70 m. NE of Bahía Blanca; pop. (1960c) 34,139; agricultural and cattle-raising center.

Tres Cru·ces \trā-'skrü-səs\. Mountain, N Chile, NE of Copiapó, on Argentine boundary; 20,853 ft.

Tres For·cas, Cape \-tras-'fȯr-kəs\. Cape, NE coast of Morocco; Melilla is on it.

Tres Ma·rí·as \ˌtrā-smə-ˈrē-əs\. Group of small islands, Pacific Ocean, off the state of Nayarit, W Mexico, comprising María Madre, María Magdalena, María Cleofás, and San Juanito.

Tres Mon·tes Gulf \trā-ˈsmòn-(ˌ)tās-\. Inlet of Gulf of Penas, S coast of Taitao Penin., SW Chile.

Tres Montes Peninsula. Peninsula, extending from SW Taitao Penin., SW Chile.

Tres Mo·rros \trā-smȯr-əs\ *or* **So·cor·ro** \sə-ˈkȯr-(ˌ)ō\. Peak, NW cen. Colombia, in the Cordillera Occidental; 11,155 ft.

Tres Pun·tas, Cape \-trā-ˈspün-təs\. 1 Cape on NE coast of Santa Cruz prov., S Argentina, at S side of entrance to the Gulf of San Jorge.

2 Cape, E Guatemala, extending into the Gulf of Honduras and enclosing Amatique Bay.

Três Ri·os \trās-ˈrē-üs\. Municipality, Rio de Janeiro state, SE Brazil, 50 m. N of Rio de Janeiro; pop. (1968e) 59,317.

Tres Tabernae. See SAVERNE.

Tres Za·po·tes \ˌtrās-sə-ˈpōt-əs\. Village, just W of San Andrés Tuxtla in E Veracruz state, E Mexico; colossal sculptured head of stone and inscribed monuments, chiefly of a pre-Mayan culture dating back nearly 300 years B.C.; discovered 1939.

Treut·len \ˈtrüt-lən\. County in Georgia. See table at GEORGIA.

Treves *or* **Trèves.** See TRIER.

Tre·vi·glio \trā-ˈvēl-(ˌ)yō\. Commune, Bergamo prov., Lombardy, N Italy, 12 m. SSW of Bergamo; pop. (1968e) 25,381.

Tre·vi·ño \trā-ˈvē-(ˌ)nyō\. Exclave of Burgos prov., in Álava prov., Spain.

Tre·vi·so \trə-ˈvē-(ˌ)zō\. 1 Province of Veneto, Italy. See table at ITALY.

2 *or anc.* **Tar·vi·si·um** \tär-ˈvizh-(ē-)əm\. Commune, its ❋, Veneto, NE Italy, 17 m. N by W of Venice; pop. (1968e) 88,148; rice refining; ceramics, fertilizers; surrounded by medieval ramparts; 11th cent. cathedral, 13th cent. palaces, 12th cent. Loggia dei Cavalieri.

History: Ancient Roman municipium; center of Lombard duchy; taken by Charlemagne 776 A.D. and made center of March of Treviso; independent from 1020; supported Lombard League against Emperor Frederick I 12th cent.; under the Ghibelline leader Ezzelino da Romano 1237 59; passed to Venice 1389, Austria 1797, kingdom of Naples 1805, Austria 1815, Italy 1866; severely damaged in World War II.

Tre·vose Head \trē-ˈvōs-\. Promontory, W coast of Cornwall, SW England; lighthouse.

Tré·voux \trā-ˈvü\. Commune, SW Ain dept., E France, on the Saône; pop. (1962c) 3866; capital of Dombes 11th–16th cents.; noted for Jesuit press 1801–30 which published a newspaper and a dictionary.

Trib·une \ˈtrib-ˌyün\. City, ⊗ of Greeley co., W Kansas; pop. (1970c) 1013.

Tricca. See TRIKKALA 2.

Trichinopoly. See TIRUCHCHIRAPPALLI.

Tri·cho·nis, Lake \-ˈtrik-ə-nəs, -ˌtrē-kə-ˈnēs\ *or Gk.* **Lím·ni Tri·kho·nís** \ˌlēm-nē-ˌtrē-kə-ˈnēs\. Lake, Greece, 125 m. WNW of Athens; ab. 37 sq. m.

Tri·chur \tri-ˈchu̇(ə)r\. Town, N Kerala, S India, 40 m. N of Cochin; pop. (1961c) 73,038; commercial center; textiles; site of one of India's oldest temples.

Tridentine Alps. See table at ALPS.

Tridentum. See TRENT 4.

Trient. See TRENT 4.

Trier \ˈtri(ə)r\ *or Eng.* **Treves** \ˈtrēvz\ *or Fr.* **Trèves** \trev\ *or anc.* **Au·gus·ta Tre·ve·ro·rum** \ȯ-ˌgəs-tə-ˌtrev-ə-ˈrōr-əm, ə-ˌgəs-, -ˈrȯr-\. Industrial city, Rhineland-Palatinate, West Germany, on Moselle river near Luxembourg border 58 m. SW of Koblenz; pop. (1969e) 104,093; beer, textiles, cigars, machinery; ships wine. Extensive Roman remains, including large amphitheater built by Trajan, Porta Nigra (a fortified gate), baths, imperial palace, piers of bridge across Moselle; 13th cent. Gothic church, cathedral (Romanesque and Gothic additions to a Roman core), 18th cent. Baroque church.

History: An ancient town, capital of the Treveri who were conquered by Julius Caesar; in 4th cent. A.D. frequently an imperial residence; seat of independent archbishops 5th–19th cents.; capital of French department of the Sarre under Napoleon; to Prussia 1815; in World War II suffered considerable damage and was captured by U.S. troops Mar. 1, 1945.

Tri·este \trē-ˈest, -ˈes-tē\. 1 Province of Friuli-Venezia Giulia, Italy. See table at ITALY.

2 Commercial seaport, ❋ of Friuli-Venezia Giulia, also ❋ of Trieste prov., NE Italy, at head of the Adriatic Sea on the **Gulf of Trieste,** on NW side of Istrian Penin.; pop. (1968e) 279,376; shipyards, steel mills, oil refineries; tourism; cathedral, 15th–17th cent. castle; univ. (1877, univ. status 1924).

History: Came under Rome c. 177 B.C.; fortified and expanded under Augustus; under episcopal rule 948–1202; under Austrian rule 1382 ff.; imperial free port 1719–1891; held by French 1809–14; made Austrian crownland 1867; ceded to Italy by Treaty of St. Germain 1919; in World War II occupied by Yugoslavs May 1945; returned to Italy 1954; made ❋ of Friuli-Venezia Giulia region 1963. See also 3, below.

3 *or in full* **Free Territory of Trieste.** Region on W side of Istrian Penin., surrounding and including city of Trieste; established 1947 as a free territory under the United Nations; divided for administrative purposes into two zones: Zone A in N, including city, 91 sq. m., under British and Americans; Zone B in S, 199 sq. m., under Yugoslavs; in 1954 Zone B incorporated into Yugoslavia; Zone A incorporated into Italy.

Trigarta. See JULLUNDUR 2.

Trigg \ˈtrig\. County in Kentucky. See table at KENTUCKY.

Trig·gia·no \trē-ˈjän-(ˌ)ō\. Commune, Bari prov., Apulia, SE Italy, near the Adriatic 5 m. ESE of Bari; pop. (1968e) 17,864.

Tri·glav \ˈtrē-(ˌ)gläv\ *or Ger.* **Ter·glou** \ˈter-(ˌ)glü\. Highest peak in the Julian Alps, NW Yugoslavia, near Italian border; 9395 ft.

Tri·gnac \trē-ˈnyak\. Commune, Loire-Atlantique dept., NW France, near Saint-Nazaire; pop. (1962c) 6917; iron foundries.

Trikhonís, Límni. See TRICHONIS, LAKE.

Trik·ka·la \ˈtrik-ə-lə, ˈtrē-kə-\. 1 Department of Thessaly, cen. Greece. See table at GREECE.

2 *or anc.* **Tric·ca** \ˈtrik-ə\. City, its ❋, N of Piníos river and ab. 35 m. W of Larissa; pop. (1971p) 38,150; trades in grain and tobacco. Temple of Asclepius anciently situated here.

Tri·ko·ra \trə-ˈkō-rə\ *or formerly* **Wil·hel·mi·na Top** \ˌvil-(h)el-ˈmēn-ə-ˈtäp\. Mountain, Djajawidjaja Range, Irian Barat, Indonesia; 15,585 ft.; highest peak in the range.

Tril·by \ˈtril-bē\. Village, Lucas co., NW Ohio, ab. 7 m. NW of Toledo; pop. (1970c) 5500.

Trim \ˈtrim\. Urban district, ⊗ of co. Meath, E Eire, on the Boyne; pop. (1971p) 1699; ruins of 12th cent. castle which housed several Irish parliaments (to 15th cent.) and a mint.

Trim·ble \ˈtrim-bəl\. County in Kentucky. See table at KENTUCKY.

Trinacria. See SICILY.

Trin·che·ra Peak \trin-ˌcher-ə-\. Mountain, Las Animas, Costilla, and Huerfano cos., S Colorado; 13,540 ft.

Trin·co·ma·lee *or* **Trin·ko·ma·li** \ˌtriŋ-kō-mə-ˈlē\. Seaport town, E Ceylon, on Bay of Bengal 110 m. SE of Jaffna, on a peninsula on N side of **Bay of Trincomalee;** pop. (1968e) 39,000; excellent natural harbor, with limited export trade in rice, timber, dried fish, coconuts; ruins of "Temple of a Thousand Columns."

History: One of the earliest Tamil settlements in Ceylon; taken by Portuguese 1622, Dutch 1639, French 1673; recovered by Dutch 1674; again taken by French 1782; taken by British 1795. Formerly an important British fleet anchorage and during World War II after loss of Singapore, principal British naval base in Far East; bombed by Japanese Apr. 1942; base ceded to Ceylon 1957.

Tři·nec \tər-'zhi-nets\. Town, Czech. S.R., N cen. Czechoslovakia, on border with Poland; pop. (1968e) 29,649.

Tring \'triŋ\. Urban district, Hertfordshire, SE England, 30 m. NW of London; pop. (1971p) 9155; natural-history museum, estab. by 2d Baron Rothschild.

Trin·i·dad \'trin-ə-ˌdad\. 1 Commercial city, ⊗ of Las Animas co., SE Colorado, on Purgatoire river 80 m. S of Pueblo; pop. (1970c) 9901; beer, dairy products; coal mines; diversified agriculture.

2 Island in Bahía Blanca, a bay on SE coast of Buenos Aires prov., Argentina.

3 Town, ✻ of El Beni dept., N Bolivia, ab. 6 m. E of the Mamoré river; pop. (1969e) 17,360; cattle market.

4 *or Port.* **Trin·da·de** \trē(ⁿ)n-'dad-ə\. Small rocky volcanic island, South Atlantic Ocean, 20°31'S, 29°19'W; belongs to Brazil.

5 Mountain range, S Las Villas prov., W cen. Cuba; highest peak 3724 ft.

6 Municipality and town, Las Villas prov., W cen. Cuba; town near S coast 40 m. S of Santa Clara; munic. pop. (1967e) 57,840; founded 1514.

7 Town, ✻ of Flores dept., SW Uruguay, 105 m. NNW of Montevideo; pop. (1963c) 15,460.

8 Island of the West Indies, Atlantic Ocean, off NE coast of Venezuela; 1864 sq. m.; pop. (1965e) 938,600; chief town Port of Spain, ✻ of Trinidad and Tobago (*q.v.*). *Physical features:* Nearly square in shape with two peninsulas extending from NW and SW corners enclosing the Gulf of Paria; the N peninsula and adjacent islands are separated by channel of Dragon's Mouth from Paria Penin. of Venezuela. Ranges of hills along N and S shores, several swamp regions on E and W. *Chief products:* Oil, asphalt, natural gas, limestone; sugarcane, coconuts, bananas, coffee.

History: Discovered by Columbus July 31, 1498; Spanish settlement made ab. 1577 but destroyed by Sir Walter Raleigh 1595; occupied by British 1797 and ceded to Great Britain by Treaty of Amiens 1802; in World War II in 1942 four regions leased to U.S. for seaplane base and naval station; two largest were on N shore of Gulf of Paria and in N cen. part; became part of independent state 1962, (see TRINIDAD AND TOBAGO); military facilities relinquished by U.S. 1971.

Trinidad, La. See LA TRINIDAD.

Trinidad and To·ba·go \-tə-'bā-(ˌ)gō\. Independent state, comprising the islands of Trinidad and Tobago, Atlantic Ocean, off NE coast of Venezuela; 1980 sq. m.; pop. (1970p) 945,210; ✻ Port of Spain.

History: By order in council 1898 union of the two islands authorized and British colony formally estab. Jan. 1, 1899; member of the West Indies Federation 1958–62; became an independent state 1962. See TRINIDAD 8 and TOBAGO.

Trinidad Gulf. Inlet of Pacific Ocean, SW of S Wellington I., off SW coast of Chile.

Tri·nil \'trē-(ˌ)nil\. Village, S cen. Java, Indonesia, on Solo river, at base of Mt. Lawu. Fossil skullcap found here 1891 and additional parts found 1936–37 of Java man or Trinil man (*Pithecanthropus erectus*).

Tri·ni·ta·po·li \ˌtrē-nə-'täp-ə-lē\. Commune, Foggia prov., Apulia, SE Italy, on S shore of Lake Salpi 29 m. ESE of Foggia; pop. (1968e) 13,694.

Trinité, La. See LA TRINITÉ.

Trin·i·ty \'trin-ət-ē\. 1 River, NW California; ab. 130 m. long; rises in NE Trinity co., flows SW and then NW into the Klamath river.

2 River, E Texas; 550 m. long; formed by confluence of West Fork and Elm Fork just NW of Dallas; flows SE into Trinity Bay.

3 Name of counties in two states of the U.S. See tables at CALIFORNIA and TEXAS.

4 City, Trinity co., E Texas, on Trinity river 45 m. SW of Lufkin; pop. (1970c) 2512.

Trinity, Cape. Promontory, Quebec, Canada, on S shore of Saguenay river ab. 40 m. from its mouth and opp. Cape Eternity (*q.v.*); 1700 ft. high.

Trinity Bay. 1 Northeast arm of Galveston Bay, Texas.

2 Inlet of Pacific Ocean, forming the harbor of Cairns, Queensland, NE Australia.

3 Inlet, SE Newfoundland, Canada; terminal of first Atlantic cable from Ireland 1866.

Trinity Dam. See UNITED STATES, *Dams and Reservoirs.*

Trinity Mountain. Mountain, N Elmore co., SW cen. Idaho; 9451 ft.

Trinity Peaks. Mountain, San Juan co., SW Colorado; 13,752 ft.

Trinkomali. See TRINCOMALEE.

Tri·phyl·ia \trī-'fil-ē-ə\. Southern district of ancient Elis (*q.v.*), W Peloponnesus, S Greece, S of the Alpheus river.

Triple Di·vide Peak \ˌtrip-əl-də-'vīd-\. 1 Mountain in Sierra Nevada, E Madera co., cen. California; 11,613 ft.

2 Peak in Sierra Nevada, N Tulare co., S cen. California, on border bet. Kings Canyon National Park and Sequoia National Park; 12,651 ft.

3 Mountain, Glacier National Park, NW Montana; 8011 ft. Water from the sides of this peak flows into three oceans, Pacific, Arctic, and Atlantic.

Trip·o·li \'trip-ə-(ˌ)lē\. 1 Region, N Africa; originally a Phoenician colony, **Trip·o·lis** \'trip-ə-ləs\(Greek *tripolis,* "with three cities") named for its three chief cities Oea (Tripoli), Leptis Magna, and Sabrata, founded on the coast bet. Syrtis Major and Syrtis Minor; the E part of Carthaginian territory; under Romans called **Re·gio Syr·ti·ca** \ˌrej-ē-ō-'sər-ti-kə\ until made a separate province, **Trip·o·li·ta·na** \ˌtrip-ə-lə-'tān-ə\, by Septimus Severus (193–211 A.D.); overrun by Vandals 5th cent.; recaptured 534 by Belisarius (see BYZANTINE EMPIRE); conquered by Islam in 7th cent.; ruled by successive Arab and Berber dynasties; the city of Tripoli captured by Ferdinand the Catholic 1510 and entrusted by Spanish to Knights of St. John (see MALTA 1) 1530–51; state became part of Ottoman Empire 1551 (Pashalik of Tripoli); achieved practical independence 1714; one of the Barbary States (see BARBARY), engaged in piracy; after war with United States 1801–05 and U.S. war with Algiers (*q.v.*) 1815, ceased to levy tribute on U.S. ships; became province under direct Turkish administration 1835; long the object of Italian aspirations, finally ceded to Italy by Turkey as result of Tripolitan War (1911–12); under Italians the entire W part of colony of Libya (*q.v.*) 1912–19 became known as **Trip·o·li·ta·nia** \trip-ˌäl-ə-'tān-yə, ˌtrip-ə-lə-, -'tān-ē-ə\; interior not conquered until after World War I; separated from Cyrenaica 1919, reunited 1929; in 1934 settled portion in N divided into four provinces for administrative purposes, one of which was Tripoli (see 2, below); from 1951–63 NW part of Libya administered as province (Tripolitania), which was dissolved 1963.

2 Former province, NW (Italian) Libya; 73,803 sq. m.

3 *or Arab.* **Ta·ra·bu·lus esh Sham** \tə-'räb-ə-ləs-esh-'sham\ *or anc.* **Trip·o·lis** \'trip-ə-ləs\. Commercial town and seaport, NW Lebanon, 43 m. NNE of Beirut; pop. (1964e) 127,611; ships oranges and cotton; sponge fishing, oil refining; fruit and tobacco farms; terminus of oil pipeline from Iraq.

History: Probably founded 7th cent. B.C.; capital of **Tripolis,** a Phoenician federation of three cities (Greek *tripolis,* "with three cities"): Sidon, Tyre, and Aradus; held by Seleucids and Romans and taken by Muslims 638 A.D.; taken by Crusaders after five-year siege and notable library destroyed; retaken by Mamelukes 1289 and destroyed; new town on present site occupied by British 1918 and by British and Free French 1941.

4 *or Arab.* **Ta·ra·bu·lus al–Gharb** \tə-'räb-ə-ləs-al-'gärb\ *or anc.* **Oea**\'e-ə\. Coastal city, ✱ of Libya, N Africa, on Mediterranean Sea 400 m. W of Benghazi; pop. (1971e) 162,200, met. area pop. 343,928; principal seaport of Libya; ships fruit, olive oil, fish; salt extraction, tunny and sponge fishing, carpet weaving; old city largely surrounded by Byzantine and 16th cent. walls; 16th cent. Spanish citadel, numerous mosques, Roman triumphal arch (163 A.D.). In World War II occupied by Axis forces 1941–42; taken by British Jan. 24, 1943. See also 1, above.

5 Medieval county, Syria, N of the kingdom of Jerusalem; ✱ Tripoli.

Trip·o·lis \'trip-ə-ləs\. 1 *also* **Tri·po·li·tsa** *or* **Tri·po·li·tza** \ˌtrē-pȯ-'lēt-sə\. City, ✱ of Arcadia dept., cen. Peloponnesus, S Greece; pop. (1971p) 20,327; manufactures leather goods, tapestries. Regional capital under Turks; taken by Greek insurgents 1821; retaken and destroyed by Ibrahim Pasha 1825.

2 Ancient Phoenician colony, N Africa. See TRIPOLI 1.

3 Ancient confederacy in Phoenicia comprising Sidon, Tyre, and Aradus; ✱ Tripolis. See TRIPOLI 3.

Tripolitana. See TRIPOLI 1.

Tripolitania. See TRIPOLI 1.

Tripolitsa *or* **Tripolitza.** See TRIPOLIS 1.

Tripp \'trip\. County in South Dakota. See table at SOUTH DAKOTA.

Tri·pu·ra \'trip-ə-rə\ *or formerly* **Hill Tip·pe·ra** \hil-'tip-ə-rə\. State, NE India; 4035 sq. m.; pop. (1971p) 1,556,822; ✱ Agartala; on N, W, and S borders on Bangla Desh; area comprises parallel ranges of hills (highest ab. 3200 ft.); rice, jute; conquered by Moguls in 1733; after 1808 in direct relations with British government; became a territory 1947; estab. as a state 1972.

Tris·tan da Cu·nha \ˌtris-tən-də-'kü-nə\. Island, South Atlantic Ocean; 38 sq. m.; pop. (1968e) 271; highest point 6760 ft. Chief of the **Tristan da Cunha Islands,** a group of five British volcanic islands at ab. 37°15′S, 12°30′W, including also Gough, Inaccessible, and Nightingale Is. (total area 52 sq. m.). Discovered 1506; annexed by Britain 1816; settled during 19th cent.; made a dependency of St. Helena I. Jan. 12, 1938; in 1961 volcanic eruption forced evacuation of population, most of which returned Apr.–Nov. 1963.

Tris·te, Gol·fo \ˌgȯl-fō-'trēs-tə\. Bay, N coast of Venezuela, bet. Carabobo and Falcón states, W of Caracas.

Tri·sul \tri-'sül\. Peak in the Himalayas, N India; 23,360 ft.

Tri·umph, Mount \-'trī-um(p)f\. Peak, Skagit co., NW Washington; 7150 ft.

Tri·van·drum \trə-'van-drəm\. Seaport city, ✱ of Kerala, SW India, on Arabian Sea 140 m. SW of Madurai; pop. (1970e) 359,580; produces rubber goods, chemicals, textiles, coconut oil; 18th cent. fort containing palaces and temples, observatory, zoological garden, museum; univ. (1937); made capital of kingdom of Travancore 1745.

Tr·na·va \'tər-nə-və\ *or Hung.* **Nagy·szom·bat** \'näzh-səm-ˌbät\ *or Ger.* **Tyr·nau** \'tür-ˌnau̇\. Town, Slovak S.R., E cen. Czechoslovakia, 23 m. NE of Bratislava; pop. (1968e) 37,474; market town; Gothic cathedral, dating from 14th cent.

Trnovo. See VELIKO TŬRNOVO.

Tro·as \'trō-ˌas\. 1 *or* **The Tro·ad** \-ˌad\. Territory surrounding the ancient city of Troy in NW Mysia, Asia Minor, extending along Aegean coast from the Sigeum promontory (*mod.* Yenişehir) S to Cape Lectum (*mod.* Baba) and eastward to include the Ida Mts. and plain of Scamander river (*mod.* Menderes).

2 *or later* **Al·ex·an·dria Troas** \ˌal-ig-'zan-drē-ə-, ˌel-\. Seaport of Mysia, in SW part of the ancient region of the Troas, and S of the site of Troy; visited by St. Paul on his second (*Acts* xvi. 8–11) and third journeys.

Tro·bri·and Islands \'trō-brē-ˌand-\. Group of small coral islands, Solomon Sea N of E end of New Guinea I. and N of D'Entrecasteaux Is.; 8°33′S, 151°05′E; largest Kiriwina I.; total area 170 sq. m.; chief town Losuia; administratively attached to Papua New Guinea; occupied by Allies June 30, 1943.

Troe·zen \'trē-zən\. Town, SE ancient Argolis, E Peloponnesus, S Greece, near the coast of the Saronic Gulf; celebrated in mythology as the home of Theseus.

Tro·gir \'trō-gi(ə)r\ *or Ital.* **Traù** \trä-'ü\ *or Ger.* **Trau** \'trau̇\ *or anc.* **Tra·gu·ri·um** \trə-'gyu̇r-ē-əm\. Seaport, W Yugoslavia, near Split; pop. (1961c) 5003; located on an island joined to mainland by a bridge; cathedral, dating in part from 13th cent., Dominican monastery, museum. Colonized by Greeks from Syracuse in 4th cent. B.C.; since medieval times has been held by many states (Venice, Hungary, Byzantium, Italy); since 1918 in Yugoslavia.

Troia. See TROY 8.

Tro·i·na \trȯ-'ē-nə\. Commune, Enna prov., cen. Sicily, Italy, 24 m. NE of Enna on W slope of Mt. Etna; pop. (1968e) 12,549; Capuchin convent. In World War II scene of severe fighting July 29–Aug. 5, 1943.

Trois–Évêchés, Les. See LES TROIS-ÉVÊCHÉS.

Trois Pis·toles \ˌtrwä-pi-'stōl\. Town, Rivière du Loup co., S Quebec, Canada, on right bank of St. Lawrence river 25 m. NE of Rivière du Loup; pop. (1971p) 4654; summer resort; agricultural center.

Trois–Ri·vières \ˌtrwä-rē-'vye(ə)r\. 1 City, Canada. See THREE RIVERS 2.

2 Maritime village, S Basse-Terre, Guadeloupe, E West Indies.

Trois–Rivières–Ouest. See WEST THREE RIVERS.

Tro·itsk \'trȯitsk\. City, S Chelyabinsk Oblast, Russian S.F.S.R., U.S.S.R., on a tributary of the upper Tobol river 75 m. S of Chelyabinsk; pop. (1969e) 87,000; railroad junction point; supply and trading center for the S Ural mining district.

Troja. See TROY 8.

Trold·tin·der \'trȯl-ˌtin-ər\. See ROMSDAL.

Troll·hät·tan \'trȯl-ˌhet-ən\. Town, Älvsborg co., SW Sweden, on Göta river near Lake Vänern; pop. (1970e) 43,566; falls in the river here which descends 108 ft. in ab. 1 m. provide water power for the hydroelectric power plant; produces locomotives, aircraft and aircraft engines, chrome alloys, turbines, plastics.

Troll·tin·da·ne \'trȯl-ˌtin-ən\. See ROMSDAL.

Trom·be·tas \trō(^{n})m-'bāt-əs\. River, NW Pará state, N Brazil; ab. 470 m. long; flows S from Guyana border into Amazon river.

Tro·me·lin \trȯm-'la^{n}\. Small French island, ab. 260 m. off NE Malagasy Republic, 15°52′S, 54°25′E.

Troms \'trüm(p)s\. County of N Norway. See table at NORWAY.

Tromsø \'träm-ˌsō, -ˌsə(r)\. Seaport, ⊗ of Troms co., N Norway, located on a small island bet. South Kvaløy and the mainland; pop. (1970e) 38,064; chief city in N Norway; founded c. 1870 esp. as a center for herring fisheries; shipbuilding yards; exports fish and furs; site of satellite telemetry station.

Tro·na·dor, Mon·te \ˌmänt-ē-ˌtrō-nə-'dȯ(ə)r\ *also* **El Tronador** \el-\. Volcano on Argentina-Chile boundary, near Lake Nahuel Huapí; 11,600 ft.

Trond·heim \'trän-ˌhām\; *formerly* **Trond·hjem** \'trän-ˌyem\ *also* **Ni·da·ros** \'nēd-ə-ˌrōs\. Seaport, ⊗ of Sør-Trøndelag co., cen. Norway; pop. (1971e) 127,699; major seaport and second largest city of Norway; hardware, building materials, canned goods, flour, soap; shipyards, breweries; notable 11th cent. cathedral (restored after several fires, coronation place of Norwegian kings), 18th cent. royal palace; Technical Univ. of Norway (1900). Founded by Olaf Trygvesson 997 and capital of Norway until 1380; in World War II occupied by Germans Apr. 1940–May 1945; one of the centers of the Norwegian resistance movement.

Trondheim Fjord. Inlet of Norwegian Sea, lower W cen. coast of Norway; extends inland 78 m.

Tron·to \'trän-ˌtō\. River, cen. Italy; ab. 50 m. long; flows N and E into Adriatic.

Troodos, Mount. See OLYMPUS, MOUNT 2.

Troon \'trün\. Burgh, Ayr co., SW Scotland; pop. (1971p) 11,315; seaside resort; ships coal; railroad shops, shipyards.

Trop·a·co Point \ˌträp-ə-ˌkō-\. Cape, N coast of St. Thomas I., Virgin Is. of the United States, West Indies, on W side of Magens Bay.

Tro·po·jë \trō-'pō-yə\. Province of N Albania. See table at ALBANIA.

Troppau. See OPAVA 2.

Tros·sachs \'träs-əks, -ˌaks\. Wooded valley, Perth co., cen. Scotland, bet. Loch Katrine and Loch Achray; immortalized by Scott's *Lady of the Lake* and *Rob Roy.*

Trotskoye. See GATCHINA.

Trot·wood \'trät-ˌwu̇d\. Village, Montgomery co., SW Ohio, 10 m. NW of Dayton; pop. (1970c) 6997; truck and bus bodies; diversified agriculture.

Troup \'trüp\. County in Georgia. See table at GEORGIA.

Trous·dale \'trüz-ˌdāl\. County in Tennessee. See table at TENNESSEE.

Trout Lake \'trau̇t-\. Name of several lakes, Canada, esp.: (1) a source of English river, SW Ontario, 156 sq. m.; (2) source of Mattawa river, SE Ontario, separated from Lake Nipissing to the W by watershed.

Trou·ville–sur–Mer \(ˌ)trü-ˌvē(ə)l-(ˌ)su̇r-'me(ə)r\. Seaport, Calvados dept., NW France, ab. 25 m. NE of Caen just NE of Deauville; pop. (1962c) 6822; popular resort; imports timber, coal, cement.

Trow·bridge \'trō-ˌbrij\. Urban district, Wiltshire, S England; pop. (1971p) 19,245; woolens, dairy products, gloves, beer.

Troy \'trȯi\. 1 Commercial city, ⊗ of Pike co., SE Alabama, 48 m. SSE of Montgomery; pop. (1970c) 11,482; lumber, vehicle bodies, fertilizer, peanut oil; cotton gins; agriculture; Troy State Coll. (1887).

2 City, ⊗ of Doniphan co., NE Kansas; pop. (1970c) 1047.

3 City, Oakland co., SE Michigan, SE of Pontiac; pop. (1970c) 39,149; residential.

4 City, ⊗ of Lincoln co., E Missouri; pop. (1970c) 2538.

5 Commercial and industrial city, ⊗ of Rensselaer co., E New York, on E bank of Hudson river 8 m. NE of Albany; pop. (1970c) 62,918; at head of tidewater navigation on Hudson river and opp. mouth of Mohawk river and outlet of N.Y. State Barge Canal; produces men's clothing, automobile parts, steel, paper, abrasives, precision instruments; Rensselaer Polytechnic Institute (1824), Russell Sage Coll. (1916), Hudson Valley Community Coll. (1953); settled in 1780s; incorporated as village 1794, as city 1816; major center of steel industry until after Civil War.

6 Town, ⊗ of Montgomery co., S cen. North Carolina, 40 m. S of High Point; pop. (1970c) 2429; furniture.

7 Industrial city, ⊗ of Miami co., W Ohio, 19 m. N of Dayton; pop. (1970c) 17,186; tobacco market; tools, paper; diversified agriculture; settled 1807.

8 *or* **Il·i·um** \'il-ē-əm\; *anc.* **Tro·ia** \'trȯi-ə, 'trō-yə\ *or* **Tro·ja** \'trō-jə, -yə\ *or* **Il·i·on** \'il-ē-ˌän, -ē-ən\. Ancient ruined city in Troas, NW Asia Minor, S of the Dardanelles; an archaeological site (*mod.* Hissarlik) on Menderes river, said to have nine cities built each on the ruins of its predecessor, Stone Age to Roman. In Greek legend besieged by the confederated Greek armies during a ten-year war (Trojan War), captured, and destroyed, c. 1200 B.C.; its story told in the *Iliad, Odyssey,* and *Aeneid,* by the cyclic poets, and in medieval romances.

Troyes \trə-'wä\ *or anc.* **Au·gus·tob·o·na Tri·cas·si·um** \ˌȯ-gə-'stäb-ə-nə-trī-'kas-ē-əm\. City, ✱ of Aube dept., NE France, on Seine river 92 m. SE of Paris; pop. (1968c) 74,898; center of French hosiery industry; textile machinery, needles, flour, automobile parts and tires; 13th–17th cent. cathedral, 13th cent. basilica of Saint-Urbain, several other notable churches, 17th cent. town hall, 12th cent. hospital.

History: Dates from pre-Roman times; sacked by Normans 889 A.D.; made capital of Champagne 1019; from 11th to 13th cents. a prosperous commercial town, site of the great Champagne fairs; gave name to system of measuring (*troy weights*) first used at the fairs; treaty bet. Charles VI and Henry V of England; English expelled by Joan of Arc 1429; a center of Protestantism and declined after revocation of Edict of Nantes 1685.

Tru·an·do \trü-'än-(ˌ)dō\. River, W Colombia; ab. 60 m. long; a W tributary of the Atrato flowing E.

Tru·chas Peak \'trü-chəs-\ *or* **North Truchas Peak.** Mountain peak, SE Rio Arriba co., N New Mexico, NE of Santa Fe; 13,110 ft.; the highest of three peaks forming **Truchas Peaks.**

Trucial Coast, Trucial Oman, Trucial States. See UNITED ARAB EMIRATES.

Truck·ee \'trək-ē\. River, W Nevada; 120 m. long; rises in Placer co., E California, flows E and NE into Pyramid Lake, S Washoe co., NW Nevada.

Trues·dell Heights \ˌtrüz-d^{ə}l-\. Elevation, Garrett co., NW corner of Maryland; 2809 ft.

Tru·ji·llo \trü-'hē-(ˌ)(y)ō\. 1 City, Dominican Republic. See SANTO DOMINGO.

2 Seaport, ✱ of Colón dept., Honduras, 58 m. NE of Tegucigalpa; pop. (1961c) 3491; founded c. 1525.

3 Coastal city, ✱ of La Libertad dept., NW Peru, 9 m. from its port Salaverry and ab. 315 m. NW of Lima; pop. (1969e) 149,000; ships sugar; produces textiles, machinery, foodstuffs, soap, leather; cathedral, univ. (1824); founded 1534;

4 m. to the W are the ruins of the pre-Incan city Chan-Chan.
4 Commune, Cáceres prov., W Spain, 25 m. ENE of Cáceres; pop. (1970p) 10,587; manufactures leather, chocolates, chinaware, pottery; stock raising, esp. for the bullring; birthplace of Francisco Pizarro.
5 State of W cen. Venezuela. See table at VENEZUELA.
6 Town, ✱ of Trujillo state, W cen. Venezuela, on W slope of the Cordillera Mérida ab. 60 m. E of Lake Maracaibo; pop. (1970e) 27,107; market town.

Trujillo, Monte. See DUARTE, PICO.

Trujillo Al·to \-'äl-ˌtō\. Town and municipality, NE Puerto Rico; pop. (1970p) 18,127 (town), 30,351 (munic.).

Truk Islands \'trək-, 'trủk-\ *or* **Ho·go·leu Islands** \ˌhō-gə-ˌlü-\. Island group, cen. Caroline Is., W Pacific Ocean, ab. 925 m. E of Yap I., 1500 m. W of Tarawa in the Gilbert Is., and 800 m. N of Rabaul; 45 sq. m.; pop. (1970e) 29,208; chief town Truk on SE coast of Dublon I. Group comprises ab. 11 major islands and many islets; chief islands Dublon, Moen, Tol, Udot, Fefan, and Uman; all within a lagoon ab. 38 m. in diameter, encircled by a reef which is pierced by 20 passes (only 4 navigable) allowing access to several fine harbors and anchorages within. Chief anchorage is enclosed by Dublon I., Fefan I., and Uman I. and was developed by Japanese into major naval base; airfield on Dublon. Strongly fortified by Japanese; in World War II raided and bombed by U.S. naval and air forces 1944–45 but not invaded by U.S. troops.

Tru·mann \'trü-mən\. City, Poinsett co., NE Arkansas, 15 m. S of Jonesboro; pop. (1970c) 6023; lumber.

Trum·bull \'trəm-bəl\. 1 County in Ohio. See table at OHIO.
2 Town, SE Fairfield co., SW Connecticut, N of Bridgeport; pop. (1970c) 31,394; electronic components; residential.

Trumbull, Mount. Peak, N Mohave co., NW Arizona; 8034 ft.

Tru·ro \'trủ(ə)r-ˌō\. 1 Town, ⊗ of Colchester co., cen. Nova Scotia, Canada, near head (E end) of Minas Basin; pop. (1971p) 12,968; lumber, clothing, carpets; truck, dairy farms; Nova Scotia Agricultural Coll. (1905). One of the principal Acadian settlements destroyed 1755 when the inhabitants were expelled by the British; resettled by New England colonists c. 1761.
2 Municpal borough, Cornwall, SW England, at head of Falmouth Harbor 40 m. W of Plymouth; pop. (1971p) 14,830; cathedral; tin smelting; pottery.

Truss·ville \'trəs-ˌvil\. Town, Jefferson co., cen. Alabama 10 m. NNE of Birmingham; pop. (1970c) 2985.

Trust Territory of Somalia. See ITALIAN SOMALILAND.

Trust Territory of the Pacific Islands. See PACIFIC ISLANDS, TRUST TERRITORY OF THE.

Truth or Con·se·quen·ces \ˌtrüth-ər-'kän(t)-sə-ˌkwen(t)-səz\ *or formerly* **Hot Springs.** Town, ⊗ of Sierra co., SW New Mexico, on the Rio Grande 60 m. NNW of Las Cruces; pop. (1970c) 4656; hot mineral springs.

Trut·nov \'trủt-ˌnȯf\ *or Ger.* **Trau·te·nau** \'traủt-ᵊn-ˌaủ\. Town, Czech S.R., W Czechoslovakia, 83 m. NE of Prague at foot of the Riesengebirge; pop. (1968e) 24,657; linen weaving; founded in 13th cent. by German colonists.

Try·on \'trī-ən\. Village, ⊗ of McPherson co., W cen. Nebraska.

Tsai·dam \'(t)sī-'däm\. Sandy swamp region with salt lakes, Tsinghai prov., W cen. China; in a depression (alt. 9000 ft.) bet. Nan Shan and A-erh-chin Shan-mo ranges on the N and the E end of Kunlun Mts. on the S.

Tsala Apop·ka \(tə-)'sal-ə-ə-'päp-kə\. Lake, E Citrus co., W Florida penin.; ab. 15 m. long; outlet through Withlacoochee river; has many islands.

Tsana, Lake. See TANA, LAKE.

Tsang·po \'(t)säŋ-'pō\ *or* **Tsan·po** \'(t)sän-'pō\. Name of the upper Brahmaputra river (*q.v.*) in S Tibet, China.

Tsan·gwu. See WU-CHOU.

Tsa·ra·ta·na·na Massif \ˌ(t)sär-ə-'tän-ə-ˌnä-\. Mountain group in N Malagasy Republic; highest peak 9436 ft., the highest point in the Malagasy Republic.

Tsargrad *or* **Tsarigrad.** See İSTANBUL 2.

Tsaritsyn. See VOLGOGRAD.

Tsarskoye Selo. See PUSHKIN.

Tsa·vo \'(t)säv-ˌō\. River, SE Kenya, E Africa; ab. 80 m. long; flows from Mt. Kilimanjaro into the Galana river.

Tsavo National Park *or formerly* **Royal Tsavo National Park.** National park, S Kenya; 8034 sq. m.; semiarid region; great variety of wildlife, incl. antelope, elephant, rhinoceros, hippopotamus, lion; established 1948.

Tschaslau. See ČÁSLAV.

Tscheliads. See CZELADŹ.

Tschenstochau. See CZĘSTOCHOWA.

Tse·lin·o·grad \(t)se-'lin-ə-ˌgräd\ *or formerly* **Ak·mo·linsk** \ˌäk-mə-'lin(t)sk\. Town, ✱ of Tselinograd Oblast, N cen. Kazakh S.S.R., U.S.S.R, on N bank of Ishim river near its source; pop. (1970p) 180,000; in center of a steppe region having copper, coal, and gold mines.

Tselinograd Oblast \-'ō-bləst, -ˌblast\ *or formerly* **Akmolinsk Oblast.** Subdivision of Kazakh S.S.R., U.S.S.R.; 59,884 sq. m.; pop. (1970p) 881,100; ✱ Tselinograd; wheat, oats; bauxite, coal; traversed by Ishim river and by two trunk railroads; Lake Tengiz in S.

Tsentralno–Chernozemny Rayon. See CENTRAL BLACK EARTH REGION.

Tsernagora. See MONTENEGRO.

Tsesis. See CĒSIS.

Tsé·vié \'(t)sā-ˌvyā\. Town, S Togo, W Africa, ab. 20 m. N of Lomé; pop. (1970c) 13,284.

Tshua·pa *or* **Chua·pa** \chə-'wap-ə\. River, S cen. Africa; ab. 420 m. long; flows W in N cen. Zaire and empties into Busira river.

Tsi. See TZU.

Tsien Tang. See FU-CH'UN.

Tsil·ma \'(t)sil-mə\. River, NW Komi A.S.S.R., Russian S.F.S.R., U.S.S.R.; ab. 125 m. long; a W tributary of the Pechora, flowing N and E to the Pechora at Ust Tsilma; navigable.

Tsi·nan *or* **Chi·nan** \'jē-'nän\. City, ✱ of Shantung prov., NE China, in NW part of province on former course of Yellow river ab. 225 m. S of Peking; pop. (1970e) 1,500,000; railroad junction and center of small-boat traffic on rivers of region; produces textiles, vegetable oils, flour, iron and steel, chemicals. Dates at least from classical (Chou) period; made capital of Shantung under Ming dynasty; opened to foreign commerce 1904 and became railroad junction 1912; occupied by Japanese 1937–45 and entered by Communist forces 1948.

Tsinchow. See TIENSHUI.

Tsing·hai *or* **Ch'ing–hai** \'chiŋ-'hī\ *also* **Ko·ko Nor** \'kō-'kō-'nōr\. Province, W cen. China, bounded on NW by Sinkiang Uighur, on N, NE, and E by Kansu, on SE by Szechwan, on S and SW by Tibet, and on W by Tibet and Sinkiang Uighur; 278,378 sq. m.; pop. (1967e) 2,000,000; ✱ Hsi-ning. *Physical features:* Forms NE part of Tibetan plateau with the greater part above 10,000 ft.; at the NW and in the center is Tsaidam swamp at an elevation of ab. 9000 ft. On the N border, partly in Kansu prov., is the Nan Shan range; in the W cen. part is the E end of the Kunlun Mts., the E extension of which is the Amne Machin Shan reaching heights from 18,000 ft. to 23,490 ft.; in this range the Yellow river has its source, winding in its upper course through E end of the province in tremendous gorges. *Chief products:* Millet, spring wheat, barley; coal, oil, salt.

Tsing Hai *or* **Ch'ing Hai** \'chiŋ-'hī\ *or* **Ko·ko Nor** \'kō-'kō-'nōr\. Lake (*hai, nor*), NE Tsinghai prov., China; 1625 sq. m.; 68 m. long; max. depth 125 ft.; lies at alt. 10,515 ft. bet. Nan Shan range on N and E end of Kunlun Mts. on S.

Tsing·tao \ˈchiŋ-ˈdau̇\ *or Ger.* **Tsing·tau** \ˈ(t)siŋ-ˈtau̇\. City on SE shore of Chia-Chou Bay, S coast of Shantung prov., NE China, equidistant (ab. 345 m.) from Peking and Shanghai; pop. (1970e) 1,900,000; textiles, flour, cottonseed oil; railroad shops, shipyards, tire plant, salt deposits; major fishing port; univ. (1926).

History: A fishing village until late 19th cent.; naval base established 1891; part of Kiaochow territory occupied by Germany 1897 in retaliation for murder of two German missionaries by Chinese; leased by treaty 1898 to Germany for 99 years; modern city constructed 1898–1914; besieged by Japanese and British forces Aug. 23–Nov. 7, 1914; occupied by Japanese until 1922; again occupied by Japanese 1938–45; U.S. naval headquarters in W Pacific after World War II; developed industrially under Communist rule after 1949.

Tsingyuan. See PAO-TING.

Tsinkiang. See CH'ÜAN-CHOU.

Tsinling Shan. See CH'IN LING SHAN.

Tsitsihar. See CH'I-CH'I-HA-ERH.

Tskhin·va·li \ˈ(t)skin-və-lē\ *or formerly* **Sta·li·nir** \ˌstä-lə-ˈnir\. Town, ✱ of South Ossetian Autonomous Oblast, Georgian S.S.R., U.S.S.R., 60 m. NW of Tbilisi; pop. (1970p) 30,000.

Tsna \ˈtsnä\. See TAMBOV OBLAST.

Tsu \ˈtsü\. Seaport city, ✱ of Mie prefecture, on W shore of Ise Bay in S Honshū, Japan, 37 m. SW of Nagoya; pop. (1970c) 125,203; bombed by U.S. planes July–Aug. 1945.

Tsu·chi·u·ra \(t)sü-ˈchē-u̇-rə\. City, Ibaraki prefecture, Honshū, Japan, 42 m. NE of Tokyo; pop. (1970c) 89,958.

Tsu·ga·ru Strait \(t)su̇-ˌgär-(ˌ)ü-\. Channel bet. islands of Honshū and Hokkaidō, Japan; 15 to 25 m. wide.

Tsu·kao \ˈ(d)zü-ˈgau̇\. Mountain, N cen. Taiwan; 12,743 ft.; 2d highest peak in Taiwan.

Tsu·meb \ˈ(t)sü-ˌmeb\. Town, N South-West Africa, 225 m. NNE of Windhoek; pop. (1970p) 12,338; chief copper-mining center in the territory; lead, silver, and vanadium also mined.

Tsun–i *or* **Tsun·yi** \ˈ(d)zü-ˈnē\. Town, N cen. Kweichow prov., S China, on highway ab. 75 m. NNE of Kuei-yang; pop. (1970e) 275,000.

Tsu·ru·ga \(t)su̇-ˈrü-gə\. Seaport, Fukui prefecture, W coast of Honshū, Japan, 60 m. NW of Nagoya; pop. (1970c) 56,445; fish processing; nuclear power plant.

Tsu·ru·o·ka \ˌ(t)su̇r-ə-ˈwō-kə\. City, Yamagata prefecture, N Honshū, Japan, near W coast S of Sakata; pop. (1970c) 95,136; produces silk and cotton fabrics.

Tsu·shi·ma \(t)sü-ˈshē-mə, ˈ(t)sü-shē-ˌmä\. Island, Korea Strait, part of Nagasaki prefecture, Japan; ab. 40 m. long; 271 sq. m.

Tsushima Strait. Channel bet. Tsushima I. and NW Kyūshū, Japan, connecting the Sea of Japan with the East China Sea and forming the SE part of Korea Strait; ab. 63 m. wide. Site of battle (called also "Battle of Sea of Japan") in the Russo-Japanese War in which the Russian fleet under Rozhdestvenski was destroyed or captured May 27–28, 1905 by Japanese fleet under Admiral Togo.

Tsu·ya·ma \(t)sü-ˈyäm-ə\. Inland town, Okayama prefecture, in center of W extension of Honshū, Japan, 30 m. N of Okayama; pop. (1970c) 76,368.

Tu·am \ˈtü-əm\. Town, N co. Galway, W Eire; pop. (1966c) 3624; seat of a Catholic archbishop and of a Church of Ireland bishop.

Tu·a·mo·tu Archipelago \ˌtü-ə-ˈmō-(ˌ)tü-\ *or Fr.* **Tou·a·mo·tou Archipelago** \twä-mō-tü̅-\ *or* **Pa·u·mo·tu Archipelago** \pau̇-ˈmō-tü-\ *or* **Low Archipelago** \ˈlō-\ *also* **Dan·ger·ous Islands** \ˈdānj-(ə-)rəs\. Group of ab. 80 small islands, French Polynesia, S Pacific Ocean, E of Society Is. and S of Marquesas; ab. lat. 14° to 23°S and long. 134° to 149°W; 331 sq. m.; pop. (1967e) 6148; mostly low coral atolls; chief islands Makatéa, Fakarava, Rangiroa, Anaa, Hao, and Reao; includes also the Gambier and Duke of Gloucester Is. Part of group first discovered by Spanish navigator Pedro Fernandes de Queirós 1606; occupied by France 1844 and annexed 1881; now form a part of Tahiti dependency.

Tuapi Lagoon. See TABERIS LAGOON.

Tu·ap·se \tu̇-ˌäp-ˈsā\ *or formerly* **Vel·ya·mi·nov·ski** \vel-ˌyä-mi-ˈnȯf-skē\. Seaport town, S Krasnodar Krai, Russian S.F.S.R., U.S.S.R., on Black Sea coast 62 m. S of Krasnodar; pop. (1969e) 51,000; terminus of oil pipelines from Grozny through Armavir and Maikop; oil refineries, shipyards, cement works; health resort; founded 1838.

Tu·ban *or Du.* **Toe·ban** \ˈtü-(ˌ)bän\. Seaport, N Java coast, East Java prov., Indonesia, 55 m. NW of Surabaja; pop. (1961c) 38,575.

Tu·bā·rao \ˌtü-bə-ˈrä(^{n})-(ˌ)ō\. Municipality, Santa Catarina state, S Brazil, 210 m. S of Curitiba; pop. (1968e) 59,210.

Tub·ber·gen \ˈtu̇-bər-kən\. Commune, Overijssel prov., E Netherlands, just NE of Almelo near German border; pop. (1970e) 16,135.

Tu·bi·gon \tü-ˈbē-ˌgōn\. Municipality, Bohol prov., on W coast of Bohol I., Phil., on Bohol Strait 22 m. NNE of Tagbilaran; pop. (1969e) 32,700.

Tü·bing·en \ˈt(y)ü-biŋ-ən\. Industrial city, Baden-Württemberg, West Germany, on Neckar river 17 m. S of Stuttgart; pop. (1969e) 55,795; machinery, textiles, paper, surgical instruments; publishing center; 16th cent. castle, 15th cent. church, 15th cent. town hall (restored); univ. (1477), one of the most noted German universities, with which the names of Melanchthon, Reuchlin, Baur, and others are associated. First mentioned 1078, as city 1231; sold to Württemberg 1342; captured by Swabian League 1519; occupied by French 1647, 1688.

Tubruq. See TOBRUK.

Tu·bu·ai Islands \ˌtü-bə-ˈwī-\ *or Fr.* **Îles Tubuai** \ēl-tü-bwī\ *or* **Aus·tral Islands** \ˈȯs-trəl-, ˈäs-\. Group of small volcanic islands, S French Polynesia, S Pacific Ocean, S of Society Is. and SW of Tuamotu Archipelago; form a chain ab. 850 m. long bet. lat. 21°50′ to 27°41′S and long. 144°22′ to 155°W; 54 sq. m.; pop. (1967e) 5053. The inhabited islands of the group, from NW to SE, are Rimatara, Rurutu, Tubuai, Raevavae, Rapa (*q.v.*). Islands are well-watered and fertile. Visited by Capt. Cook 1769 and 1777 and by Vancouver 1791; taken over by French bet. 1850 and 1889.

Tubuai Ma·nu \-ˈmän-(ˌ)ü\ *or* **Mai·ao** \mī-ˈau̇\. Small island of the Society Is., S Pacific Ocean, 45 m. W of Mooréa; ab. 3 sq. m.; most easterly of the Leeward Is.

Tu·bu·ran \tü-ˈbür-ˌän\. Municipality, NW coast of Cebu I., Phil.; pop. (1969e) 50,800; on Tanon Strait ab. 30 m. NNW of City of Cebu; has good port.

Tuch·kov \ˈtüch-kəf\. Former Russian name of Izmail (*q.v.*).

Tuck·a·hoe \ˈtək-ə-ˌhō\. 1 River, SE New Jersey; flows from W Atlantic co. S and E into Great Egg Harbor.

2 Village, Westchester co., SE New York, 18 m. NNE of New York; pop. (1970c) 6236; residential suburb of Yonkers and New York City; marble quarries; lime, stucco.

Tuck·a·sei·gee \ˌtək-ə-ˈsē-je\. River in SW North Carolina in which are located 2 dams, Thorpe 1 and Thorpe 2.

Tuck·er \ˈtək-ər\. County in West Virginia. See table at WEST VIRGINIA.

Tuck·er·man Ravine \ˈtək-ər-mən-\. Gorge, S side of Mt. Washington, Presidential Range, White Mts., New Hampshire; popular ski slopes; trail from Pinkham Notch to the summit of Mt. Washington.

Tuck·er·nuck Island \ˌtək-ər-ˌnək-\. Island in Atlantic Ocean, S of Cape Cod, Massachusetts, and a part of Nantucket co., Massachusetts.

Tu·co·pia \tü-ˈkō-pē-ə\. Small island, E Santa Cruz Is., SW Pacific Ocean, ESE of Vanikoro.

Tuc·son \ˈtü-ˌsän\. Commercial and residential city, ⊗ of Pima co., S Arizona, on Santa Cruz river 103 m. SE of Phoenix; pop. (1970c) 262,892; alt. 2390 ft.; railroad junction; aircraft parts, electronic components, guided missiles, plastics, optical goods, dairy products; railroad shops, meat-packing plants; tourist and health resort, with tuberculosis sanitariums; Univ. of Arizona (1885); Davis-Monthan Air Force Base.

History: San Xavier del Bac Indian mission founded 15 m. from site of modern city in 1700; Spanish established Presidio de San Augustín de Tuguison 1776; acquired by U.S. through Gadsden Purchase 1853; occupied by Confederate forces 1862; territorial capital 1867–77; incorporated as city 1883.

Tu·cu·mán \ˌtü-kə-ˈmän\. 1 Province of N Argentina. See table at ARGENTINA.

2 City, N Argentina. See SAN MIGUEL DE TUCUMÁN.

Tu·cum·cari \ˈtü-kəm-ˌkar-ē\. City, ⊗ of Quay co., E New Mexico, 60 m. NNW of Clovis; pop. (1970c) 7189; resort; ships livestock; grain farms.

Tu·cu·pi·ta \ˌtü-kə-ˈpēt-ə\. Town in the Orinoco delta, ✱ of Delta Amacuro territory, NE Venezuela; pop. (1970e) 12,119.

Tu·de·la \tü-ˈt͟hā-lə\ *or anc.* **Tu·te·la** \tu̇-ˈtē-lə\. Commune, Navarra prov., N Spain, on Ebro river 52 m. S of Pamplona; pop. (1970p) 20,942; stock raising, esp. for the bullring; 12th cent. Romanesque church. Conquered by Arabs 716; reconquered by Alfonso I of Aragon 1115; made episcopal see 1783; occupied by French 1808–13.

Tuder. See TODI.

Tug·a·loo *or* **Tug·a·lo** \ˈtu̇g-ə-ˌlō\. River, NE Georgia; forms section of NE Georgia boundary with South Carolina and unites with the Seneca river in W Anderson co., NW South Carolina, to form the Savannah river. Upper course known as Chattooga river.

Tu·ge·la \tü-ˈgā-lə\. River, cen. Natal, E Rep. of South Africa; 312 m. long; rises in Mont aux Sources, where it plunges through a gorge forming the **Tugela Falls** (total drop 3110 ft. in five falls, of which highest is 1350 ft.), and flows E to the Indian Ocean; not navigable; scene of battles of the Boer War Oct. 1899 to Feb. 1900, esp. at Colenso.

Tug Fork \ˈtəg-\. River, SW West Virginia; rises in McDowell co., flows NW and forms Kentucky-West Virginia boundary until it unites with Levisa Fork to form Big Sandy river (*q.v.*).

Tuggurt. See TOUGGOURT.

Tugh·lak·a·bad \tu̇g-ˈlək-ə-ˌbäd\. Ancient city, ab. 4 m. to the E of the site of Old Delhi, India; erected c. 1321 by Ghiyas-ud-din Tughlak, founder of the Tughlak dynasty. Only the ruins of its walls and fort remain. See DELHI 2.

Tu·gue·ga·rao \ˌtü-gā-gə-ˈrau̇\. Municipality, ✱ of Cagayan prov., Luzon, Phil., E side of Cagayan river, 240 m. NNE of Manila; pop. (1969e) 59,200. In World War II taken by Japanese Dec. 25, 1941 and held until retaken by Filipino guerrillas June 1945.

Tui·ra \tu̇-ˈir-ə\. River, Panama prov., E cen. Panama; ab. 90 m. long; rises near Colombian border, flows N and NW to Gulf of San Miguel.

Tu·kang·be·si Islands *also* **Toe·kang·be·si Islands** \ˌtü-kaŋ-ˈbā-sē-\. Group of ab. 16 islands, W Banda Sea, SE of Butung Is., Celebes, Indonesia; largest island Wangiwangi.

Tu·ko \ˈtü-ˌkō\. Village, N end of island of Manahiki, Northern Cook Is., cen. Pacific Ocean.

Tuk·uh·nik·i·vatz, Mount \-ˌtək-ə-ˈnik-ə-ˌväts\. Peak, N San Juan co., SE Utah; 12,004 ft.

Tu·ku·yu \tu̇-ˈkü-ˌyü\ *also* **Ntu·ku·yu** \ˌen-tu̇-\ *or formerly* **Neu–Lang·en·burg** \nȯi-ˈläŋ-ən-ˌbu̇(ə)rg\. Town, SW Tanzania, SE Africa, just NW of Lake Nyasa; pop. (1967c) 4100.

Tuk·wila \tək-ˈwil-ə\. City, King co., W cen. Washington, 9 m. SSE of Seattle; pop. (1970c) 3496.

Tu·la \ˈtü-lə\. 1 *or in full* **Tula de Allen·de** \-dā-ə-ˈlen-ˌdē, -ə-ˈyen-\. Town, SW Hidalgo state, cen. Mexico, 45 m. N of Mexico City; munic. pop. (1970p) 36,460. Excavations have revealed ruins of ancient capital of the Toltecs, dating back probably to 12th cent. A.D.

2 City, ✱ of Tula Oblast, Russian S.F.S.R., U.S.S.R., on a tributary of the Oka river 110 m. S of Moscow; pop. (1970p) 462,000; major industrial center producing armaments, agricultural machinery, hardware, chemicals, samovars, furniture, sporting firearms; 16th cent. citadel (restored).

History: First mentioned 1146; made important fortress on S approaches to Moscow in 16th cent.; developed in 17th cent. as center of Russian ironworking industry; made site of first Russian armament factory by Peter the Great 1712; in World War II scene of heavy fighting in Oct. 1941.

Tu·la·gi \tü-ˈläg-ē\. Small island, S cen. Solomon Is., W Pacific Ocean, off S coast of Florida I. and 22 m. N of Guadalcanal I.; chief town Tulagi, on SE coast, former ✱ of British Solomon Islands protectorate, has fine harbor. Seized by U.S. Marines Aug. 7–10, 1942.

Tu·la·in·yo Lake \ˌtü-lə-ˌin-yō-\. Lake, Tulare and Inyo cos., California, 1½ m. NE of Mt. Whitney; elev. 12,865 ft.; highest lake in the United States having an area of more than one tenth of a sq. m.

Tu·lan·cin·go \ˌtü-län-ˈsiŋ-(ˌ)gō\. Town, Hidalgo state, cen. Mexico, 65 m. NE of Mexico City; munic. pop. (1970p) 45,449.

Tula Oblast \-ˈō-bləst, -ˌblast\. Subdivision of the Russian S.F.S.R., U.S.S.R., S of Moscow; 9923 sq. m.; pop. (1970p) 1,953,000; ✱ Tula; traversed by upper Don and tributaries and by the Oka; has rich soil in S part; produces rye, oats, wheat and other grains, hemp, sugar beet, vegetables; has important chemical, metallurgical, and engineering industries. Chief cities Tula, Novomoskovsk, Uzlovaya, Aleksin. Became a part 1928 of Western Area, but reorganized 1936 as a separate region; again lost territory 1945 when Kaluga Oblast was formed from its W part; most of oblast briefly occupied by Germans in winter of 1941–42.

Tu·lare \tü-ˈla(ə)r(-ē), -ˈle(ə)r(-ē)\. 1 County in California. See table at CALIFORNIA.

2 City, Tulare co., S cen. California, 42 m. SE of Fresno; pop. (1970c) 16,235; wine, dairy products; diversified agriculture; founded 1872.

Tu·la·ro·sa \ˌtü-lə-ˈrō-sə, -zə\. Village, Otero co., S New Mexico, 65 m. NNE of Las Cruces; pop. (1970c) 2851.

Tul·cán \tül-ˈkän\. Town, ✱ of Carchi prov., N Ecuador, near Colombian frontier and 90 m. NE of Quito; pop. (1970e) 23,200.

Tul·cea \ˈtül-(ˌ)chä\. 1 County of SE Romania. See table at ROMANIA.

2 Town, its ⊗, in Danube delta near border with Ukrainian S.S.R., U.S.S.R., ab. 60 m. N of Constanta; pop. (1970e) 41,981.

Tu·lé·ar *or* **Tul·le·ar** \ˌtü-lā-ˈär\. Seaport, SW Malagasy Republic; pop. (1968e) 33,842.

Tu·le Lake \ˌtü-lē-\. Small lake, NE corner of Siskiyou co., N California; site of Japanese Relocation Camp in World War II.

Tu·lia \ˈtül-yə\. City, ⊗ of Swisher co., NW Texas, in the panhandle 25 m. N of Plainview; pop. (1970c) 5294; cotton gins; agriculture.

Tul·karm *or* **Tul Karm** \tül-ˈkärm\. Town, Central District, Israel, 24 m. NE of Tel Aviv-Jaffa; railroad junction point.

Tul·la·ho·ma \ˌtəl-ə-ˈhō-mə\. City and summer resort, Coffee and Franklin cos., S cen. Tennessee, 25 m. ENE of Fayetteville; pop. (1970c) 15,311; lumber, dairy products, plastic and leather goods, sporting equipment; tobacco; resort.

Tul·la·more \ˌtəl-ə-ˈmō(ə)r, -ˈmȯ(ə)r\. Urban district, ⊗ of co. Offaly, cen. Eire; pop. (1971p) 6810; brewing, distilling.

Tulle \ˈtül\. Industrial city, ✱ of Corrèze dept., S cen. France, 47 m. SSE of Limoges; pop. (1968c) 20,116; government small-arms factory; 12th cent. cathedral, 17th cent. church. Founded in 7th cent.; taken by English 1346,

1369; devastated by Black Death; retaken by Charles V 1370; taken by Protestants 1585.

Tullear. See TULÉAR.

Tullum. See TOUL.

Tully \'təl-ē\. Short river, NE Queensland, Australia; contains **Tully Falls,** 450 ft. high.

Tulmaythah. See TOLMETA.

Tu·lo·ma \ˌtu̇l-ə-'mä\. River, NW Murmansk Oblast, Russian S.F.S.R., U.S.S.R.; ab. 175 m. long; flows E to head of Kola Bay; its chief tributary is the Kola.

Tul·sa \'təl-sə\. 1 County in NE Oklahoma. See table at OKLAHOMA.

2 City, its ⊗, on Arkansas river ab. 15 m. NE of Sapulpa; pop. (1970c) 330,350; financial, commercial, and transportation center of major oil-producing region; produces aircraft, electronic components, oil-field equipment, machinery, cement, glass, canned goods; gas and oil wells, oil refineries, coal mines; Univ. of Tulsa (1894). Settled in 1830's as Creek Indian village; modern town founded 1882 and incorp. 1898; developed rapidly after discovery of oil in early 20th cent.

Tul·ti·tlán \ˌtül-ti-'tlän\. Municipality, México state, Mexico, 14 m. N of Mexico City; pop. (1970p) 50,084; cattle raising; alfalfa.

Tu·luá \ˌtü-lu̇-'ä\. Town, Valle dept., W Colombia, ab. 50 m. NNE of Cali; pop. (1968e) 84,386.

T'u-lu-fan. See TURFAN.

Tu·lun \tu̇-'lün\. Town, W Irkutsk Oblast, Russian S.F.S.R., U.S.S.R., on Trans-Siberian R.R. 225 m. NW of Irkutsk; pop. (1967e) 48,000.

Tu·lung·a·gung *or Du.* **Toe·loeng·a·goeng** \ˌtü-lu̇ŋ-'ä-gu̇ŋ\. City, East Java prov., Indonesia, 20 m. S of Malang; pop. (1961c) 62,069.

Tu·ma·ca·co·ri National Monument \ˌtü-mə-'kä-kə-rē-\. See UNITED STATES, *National Monuments.*

Tu·ma·co \tu̇-'mäk-(ˌ)ō\. Seaport, W Nariño dept., SW Colombia; munic. pop. (1968e) 80,279; located on an island; southernmost Pacific port of Colombia; exports ivory nuts, cacao, tobacco.

Tuman–gang. See TUMEN.

Tu·ma·tu·ma·ri Falls \ˌtü-mə-tu̇-ˌmär-ē-\. Waterfall in the Essequibo river, cen. Guyana.

Tum·ba, Lake \-'təm-bə\. Lake, Equator prov., W Zaire, SW of Mbandaka; 23 m. long, 8–12 m. wide; the Ubangi and Congo rivers meet just NW of the lake.

Tum·bes \'tüm-(ˌ)bās\. 1 Department of NW Peru. See table at PERU.

2 Town, its ✱, on Tumbes river ab. 645 m. NW of Lima, near Ecuador border; pop. (1969e) 34,600. Pizarro landed here for his invasion of Peru 1527.

Tu·men *or* **T'u–men** \'tü-'mən\ *or Russ.* **Tu·myn·tszy·an** \tu̇-'mēnt-syən\ *or Korean* **Tu·man–gang** \tü-'män-'gäŋ\. River, boundary bet. NE North Korea and NE China; 324 m. long; rises in Ch'ang-pai Shan, North Korea, flows generally N and NE but in its lower course turns sharply SE to the Sea of Japan; for ab. 11 m. from its mouth forms boundary of North Korea with Primorski Krai, Russian S.F.S.R., U.S.S.R.; navigable for light craft for ab. 30 m.

Tum·kur \tu̇m-'ku̇(ə)r\. 1 District, E Mysore state, S India; 4096 sq. m.; pop. (1961c) 1,367,402; ✱ Tumkur.

2 Town, its ✱, ab. 40 m. NW of Bangalore; pop. (1961c) 42,777; soap, tools; rice mill.

Tumluk. See TAMLUK.

Tum·mo \'tu̇m-(ˌ)ō\. Town and oasis, SW Libya, N Africa, SE of Gat, in the mountains on the border of Niger.

Tum·pat \'tu̇m-(ˌ)pät\. Coastal town, N Kelantan state, Malaysia; port of Kota Bharu.

Tu·muc–Hu·mac Mountains \tə-ˌmü-kə-'mäk-\ *or* **Se·rra Tu·mu·cu·ma·que** \'ser-ə-tu̇-ˌmük-ü-'mäk-ā\. Range, NE Brazil, extending W to E along the boundary bet. Surinam and French Guiana on the N, and Brazil on the S; averages 2000 to 3000 ft.

Tum·wa·ter \'təm-ˌwȯt-ər, -ˌwät-\. Town, Thurston co., Washington, SW of Olympia; pop. (1970c) 5373; first permanent settlement in state 1845.

Tumyntszyan. See TUMEN.

Tun. See FERDOWS.

Tu·na, Point \-'tü-nə\. Cape, SE Puerto Rico.

Tu·na·ri \tü-'nä-rē\. Peak, W Cochabamba dept., cen. Bolivia; 17,060 ft.

Tunari National Park. National park, Bolivia; 58 sq. m.; various species of flora; established 1962.

Tunas. See VICTORIA DE LAS TUNAS.

Tunb \'tün-əb\. Two small islands, **Greater Tunb** and **Lesser Tunb,** Persian Gulf, ab. 68 m. N of Dubai; claimed by Ras al-Khaimah and Iran; occupied by Iran 1971.

Tun·ce·li \ˌtün-jə-'lē\. Province of E cen. Turkey. See table at TURKEY.

Tun·dzha *or* **Tun·ja** \'tu̇n-(ˌ)jä\. River, SE Bulgaria; ab. 160 m. long; rises in Balkan Mts. W of Kazanlŭk, flows E then S into the Maritsa river at Edirne in Turkey.

Tu·ne·mah Peak \ˌtü-nə-ˌmä-\. Mountain in Sierra Nevada, E Fresno co., S cen. California; 11,873 ft.

Tunes. See TUNIS 2.

Tung \'du̇ŋ\. River, Kwangtung prov., SE China; ab. 280 m. long; rises in S Kiangsi and flows SW and W into upper Pearl river ab. 25 m. below Canton.

Tun·ga·bha·dra \ˌtu̇ŋ-gə-'bəd-rə\. River, S India; ab. 400 m. long; formed by confluence of Tunga and Bhadra rivers in W Mysore; flows NE along N border of Andhra Pradesh to the Krishna river.

Tungchow. 1 City, Kiangsu prov., China. See NAN-T'UNG.

2 Town, Shensi prov., China. See TA-LI 1.

3 City, Peking municipality, China. See T'UNG-HSIEN.

Tungchwan. See HUI-TSE.

T'ung–hsien *or* **Tung·hsien** \'tu̇ŋ-shē-'en\ *or formerly* **Tung·chow** \'tu̇ŋ-'jō\. City, Peking municipality, NE China, 12 m. E of Peking on Pai river; an old settlement known since the Earlier Han dynasty 202 B.C.

T'ung–hua *or* **Tung·hwa** \'tu̇ŋ-'(h)wä\. 1 Former province, SE Manchukuo; 12,216 sq. m.; formed 1932, dissolved 1945.

2 City, SE Liaoning prov., NE China, in mountainous region 140 m. E of Mukden; pop. (1970e) 275,000; ✱ of former T'ung-hua prov., SW Manchukuo; timber market.

T'ung-shan. See SÜCHOW.

Tung–t'ing Hu *or* **Tung·ting Hu** \'du̇ŋ-'tiŋ-'hü\. Shallow lake (*hu*), NE Hunan, SE cen. China; 1430 sq. m., but 3500 to 4000 sq. m. at high water in summer; ab. 75 m. long; receives the Hsiang, Yüan, Tzu, and Lin rivers; main outlet on NE at Yoyang to the Yangtze; also connects with the Yangtze on NW by the Sungtze river.

Tun·gu·ra·gua \ˌtu̇ŋ-gə-'räg-wə\. Volcano in the Andes Mts., Ecuador; 16,684 ft.

Tun·gu·ra·hua \ˌtu̇ŋ-gə-'rä-wə\. Province of cen. Ecuador. See table at ECUADOR.

Tun·gu·ska \tu̇ŋ-'gü-skə, 'təŋ-\. Name of three rivers in cen. Siberia, Russian S.F.S.R., U.S.S.R., tributaries of Yenisei river: (1) **Lower Tunguska** *or Russ.* **Nizh·nya·ya Tunguska** \ˌnish-nə-yə-\, ab. 2000 m. long, rises in N cen. Irkutsk Oblast and flows N, crossing into Evenki National Okrug at ab. 63°30'N, then flowing W to the Yenisei at Turukhansk; Tura, capital of Evenki, is on it. (2) **Stony Tunguska** *or Russ.* **Pod·ka·men·na·ya Tunguska** \pət-'kam-ə-nə-yə-\, ab. 1000 m. long, rises in SE corner of Evenki National Okrug and flows WNW into the Yenisei at ab. 61°30'N. (3) **Upper Tunguska.** See ANGARA 1.

Tun–huang *also* **Tun·hwang** \tu̇n-'hwäŋ\. Town, W Kansu prov., N cen. China.

Tu·ni·ca \'t(y)ü-nə-kə\. 1 County in NW Mississippi. See table at MISSISSIPPI.

2 Town, its ⊗; pop. (1970c) 1685.

Tu·nis \'t(y)ü-nəs\. 1 Former Barbary state, N Africa; the region S and W of the ancient city of Carthage (*q.v.*); Roman province of Africa from 2d cent. B.C. to 5th cent. A.D. when it was overrun by Vandals; reconquered by

Byzantine Empire 534; taken by Muslims 7th cent.; invaded by Louis IX of France on 7th Crusade 1270; attacked by Emperor Charles V as stronghold of Barbary Corsair, Barbarossa, 1535; conquered by Turks 1575; engaged in piracy (see BARBARY); in 1869, because of debts of its bey, accepted financial control by England, France, Italy; internal independence recognized by Turkey 1871; scene of rivalry bet. French and Italians 1879–81; forced by invasion to become French protectorate 1881. See TUNISIA.

2 *or anc.* **Tu·nes** \'t(y)ü-(,)nēz\. City, ✱ of Tunisia, in NE part; pop. (1966c) 468,997; produces textiles, carpets, olive oil, cement; railroad shops, lead smelter; Univ. of Tunis (1960). Situated on an isthmus bet. two lagoons; E lagoon is **Lake of Tunis,** at E end of which is Halq al-Wadi, port of the city of Tunis, with large trade. City divided into old town on the side of hills sloping down from the Kasbah (old fort) and including many mosques and markets, and new town on flat ground bet. old town and the lake.

History: Occupies site of ancient Carthage; existed as a small town under Carthaginian Empire but not important until Muslim conquest in 7th cent. A.D. Became capital of Tunisia in 9th cent. and under Hafsid dynasty (13th cent.) one of the leading cities of the Muslim world; held by Spanish 1535–69; ceded to Turks 1574 and later history that of Tunisia (*q.v.*).

Tunis, Gulf of. Inlet of Mediterranean Sea, NE coast of Tunisia; limited on E by Cape Bon Penin.; at its head is the seaport Halq al-Wadi, the Lake of Tunis, and the city of Tunis.

Tu·ni·sia \t(y)ü-'nē-zh(ē-)ə, -'nizh-(ē-)ə\ *or* **Tu·nis** \'t(y)ü-nəs\ *or Fr.* **Tu·ni·sie** \tue-nē-zē\. Republic, N Africa, bounded on N and E by Mediterranean Sea, on SE by Libya, and on SW and W by Algeria; 63,378 sq. m.; pop. (1972e) 5,238,000; ✱ Tunis. *Physical features:* Plateau region in W and W cen. parts with highest points ab. 4500 ft.; coastal region low in N and esp. along E; three indentations on E coast: Gulf of Tunis at N end, shut in on E by Cape Bon penin.; Gulf of Hammamet, S of the peninsula; and Gulf of Gabès in S. On SE side of Gulf of Gabès, is large island of Jerba. Chief river the Medjerda in N flowing E to Gulf of Tunis; has no other sizable streams. In S is large Chott Djerid; along E coast are several marshy lakes, esp. Sīdī al-Hani, and in N is Lake Bizerte. Long S tract of country extends into the Sahara. *Chief products:* Wheat, corn, citrus fruit, olives; phosphates, iron ore, salt; manufacturing: fertilizers, textiles; food processing. *Chief towns:* Tunis, Sfax, Sousse, Bizerte, and Kairouan.

History: Became French protectorate 1881 (see TUNIS 1); French occupation the cause of long-standing Franco-Italian enmity and Italian accession to Triple Alliance 1882; government reorganized 1922; cession demanded by Italy, esp. in 1938. Goal of Allied campaign in North Africa 1942–43; invaded by U.S. forces from the W Jan.–Feb. 1943 and by British from SE Mar. 1943; captured by May 12, 1943; recognized by France as independent 1956; abolished monarchy 1957; joined Arab League 1958; gained control over Bizerte naval facilities 1963; suffered major economic reverses due to severe flooding 1970.

Tun·ja. 1 \'tün-(,)jä\. River, Bulgaria. See TUNDZHA.

2 \'tüŋ-(,)hä\. Town, ✱ of Boyacá dept., cen. Colombia, in the Cordillera Oriental of the Andes on the Trans-Andean highway 85 m. NE of Bogotá; pop. (1968e) 72,661; technical univ. (1962).

Tunk, Mount \-'təŋk\. Peak, Okanogan co., N Washington; 6065 ft.

Tunk·han·nock \təŋk-'han-ək\. Borough, ⊗ of Wyoming co., NE Pennsylvania, on Susquehanna river 18 m. WNW of Scranton; pop. (1970c) 2251. A few miles to the NE, at Nicholson, is **Tunkhannock Viaduct** *or* **Nich·ol·son Via·duct** \'nik-əl-sən-\, one of the largest concrete railroad bridges in the world, 240 ft. high and 2375 ft. long, crossing **Tunkhannock Creek,** tributary of the Susquehanna.

Tun·stall \'tən-stᵊl\. See POTTERIES, THE.

Tu·nu·yán \,tü-nü-'yän\. River, W Argentina; ab. 200 m. long; rises in Andes Mts. E of Santiago, Chile, flows E, chiefly in Mendoza prov., to Salado river.

Tu·ol·um·ne \tù-'äl-ə-mē\. 1 River, cen. California; 155 m. long; rises in Yosemite National Park and flows W into San Joaquin river in Stanislaus co. W of Modesto; contains Hetch Hetchy and Don Pedro Reservoirs. The **Grand Canyon of the Tuolumne** is a scenic feature of Yosemite National Park.

2 County in California. See table at CALIFORNIA.

Tuolumne Peak. Mountain in Sierra Nevada, E Tuolumne co., cen. California; 10,875 ft.

Tu·pã \tü-'paⁿ\. Municipality, São Paulo state, SE Brazil, 270 m. WNW of São Paulo; pop. (1968e) 66,671.

Tu·pa·rro \tü-'pär-(,)ō\. River, NE Colombia; ab. 200 m. long; flows E into Orinoco river.

Tu·pe·lo \'t(y)üp-ə-,lō\. City, ⊗ of Lee co., NE Mississippi, 57 m. NNW of Columbus; pop. (1970c) 20,471; dairy products, power tools, clothing, fertilizer, furniture; scene of battle July 14, 1864 in Civil War in which Union forces under Gen. A. J. Smith defeated Confederate forces under Gen. Nathan Forrest.

Tupelo National Battlefield Site. See UNITED STATES, *National Historical Parks.*

Tu·pi·za \tù-'pē-zə, -sə\. Town, Potosí dept., SW Bolivia, 125 m. S of Potosí; alt. 9800 ft.; flour mills, and center of mining industries (silver, tin, bismuth, and lead); on railroad from La Paz to Argentina.

Tup·per Lake \,təp-ər-\. Village and resort, Franklin co., NE New York, 45 m. S of Malone; pop. (1970c) 4854; alt. 1569 ft.

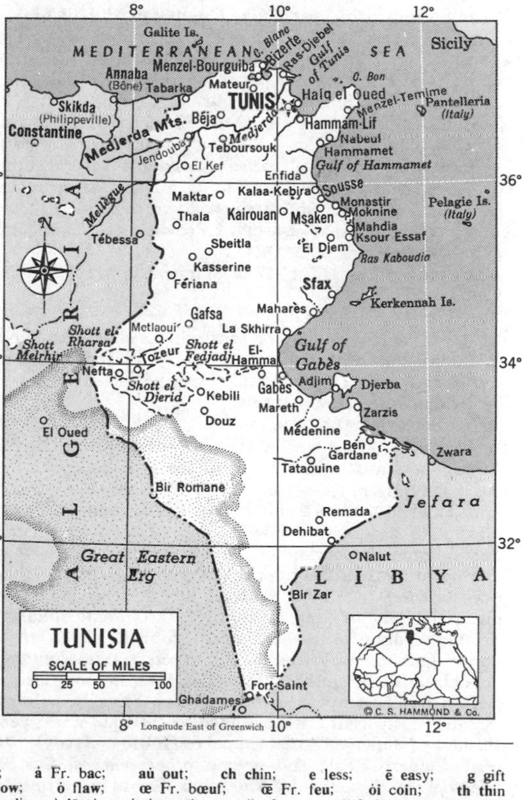

Tupper Lakes. Lakes, NE New York; **Great Tupper Lake** *or* **Big Tupper Lake** in S Franklin co., and **Little Tupper Lake** in N Hamilton co.; Great Tupper Lake is ab. 7 m. long; Little Tupper Lake, ab. 4 m. long; both are summer resorts.

Tu·pun·ga·to \ˌtü-pən-ˈgät-(ˌ)ō\. Peak in Andes Mts. on the Chile-Argentina boundary ab. 40 m. ENE of Santiago, Chile; 22,310 ft.

Tuque, La. See LA TUQUE.

Tur, Jebel at. See GERIZIM, MOUNT.

Tu·ra \tu̇-ˈrä\. 1 River, Sverdlovsk and Tyumen oblasts, Russian S.F.S.R., U.S.S.R.; ab. 400 m. long; a tributary of the Tobol; rises in the Ural Mts. and flows E past Tyumen; its valley much used by early Russian colonizers of Siberia for access to the region.

2 Town, ✱ of Evenki National Okrug, Russian S.F.S.R., U.S.S.R., on right bank of the Lower Tunguska river in cen. part of district.

Tu·ran \tu̇-ˈrän\. Ancient Persian name for the desert and steppe lands of central Asia N of Iran, roughly equivalent to the regions around the Syr Darya (Jaxartes) and Amu Darya (Oxus) in modern Uzbek and Kazakh S.S.Rs., U.S.S.R.; home of the Turanian peoples.

Tur·ba·co \tu̇r-ˈbäk-(ˌ)ō\. Town, Bolívar dept., N Colombia, just SE of Cartagena; pop. (1968e) 17,730.

Turbat-i-Haidari. See TORBAT-E HEHYDARĪYEH.

Tur·bo \ˈtu̇(ə)r-(ˌ)bō\. Municipality, Antioquia dept., NW Colombia, ab. 150 m. NW of Medellín, on the Gulf of Urabá; pop. (1968e) 55,763.

Turck·heim \tu̇r-ˈkem\ *or Ger.* **Türk·heim** \ˈtu̇rk-ˌhīm\. Village, Haut-Rhin dept., NE France, near Colmar; pop. (1962c) 3051; scene of battle Jan. 5, 1675 in which Turenne defeated the Imperial forces (Thirty Years' War).

Tur·da \ˈtu̇rd-ə\ *or Hung.* **Tor·da** \ˈtō(ə)r-(ˌ)dȯ, ˈtȯ(ə)r-\. City, Cluj co., NW cen. Romania, ab. 15 miles SSE of Cluj; munic. pop. (1970e) 50,113; chemicals, glass, bricks, cement.

Tur·fan \ˈtu̇(ə)r-ˈfän\ *or Chin.* **T'u-lu-fan** \ˈtü-ˈlü-ˈfän\. 1 *formerly* **Luk·chun** \ˈlu̇k-ˈchu̇n\. Depression, NE part of Tarim basin, E Sinkiang Uighur, W China; ab. 426 ft. below sea level at lowest point; partly filled with salt lakes.

2 Town, E cen. Sinkiang Uighur, W China, 30 m. N of Turfan depression and ab. 90 m. SE of Urumchi; at foot of Tien Shan range; in vicinity are many relics of early periods. As center of earlier kingdoms several times destroyed; ruled by the Uigurs in the 8th and 9th cents. but influences of Buddhism retained down to modern times.

Tŭr·go·vish·te \ˌtər-gə-ˈvēsh-tə\. 1 Province of NE cen. Bulgaria. See table at BULGARIA.

2 Town, its ✱, ab. 17 m. W of Shumen; pop. (1968e) 28,934.

Turgu-Jiu. See TÎRGU-JIU.

Tur·gut·lu \ˌtu̇r-(g)u̇t-ˈlü\ *or formerly* **Ka·sa·ba** \kə-ˈsäb-ə, ˌkäs-ə-ˈbä\. City, Manisa prov., Turkey, on railroad 32 m. E of İzmir; pop. (1965c) 35,674; casaba melons.

Turí, Point. See ZUMBI, POINT.

Turia. See GUADALAVIAR.

Tu·ria·çu Bay \ˌtu̇r-ē-ə-ˌsü-\. Bay, NE coast of Brazil, in NW Maranhão state, at the mouth of the Turiaçu river.

Tu·rin \ˈt(y)u̇r-ən, t(y)u̇-ˈrin\ *or Ital.* **To·ri·no** \tō-ˈrē-(ˌ)nō\; *anc.* **Tau·ra·sia** \tȯ-ˈrā-zh(ē-)ə\ *or later* **Au·gus·ta Tau·ri·no·rum** \ȯ-ˌgəs-tə-ˌtȯr-ə-ˈnōr-əm, ə-ˌgəs-, -ˈnȯr-\. Industrial and commercial commune, ✱ of Piedmont, also ✱ of Torino prov., NW Italy, on Po river 78 m. NW of Genoa; pop. (1970e) 1,190,688; railroad junction; second major industrial city of Italy; center of automobile industry; produces aircraft, leather goods, rubber, paper, metal goods, plastics, radio and television sets, pharmaceuticals, chocolate, wine, clothing; a leading international fashion center; archiepiscopal see; military base. Notable buildings include 15th cent. Renaissance cathedral, 18th cent. Basilica of Superga (burial chapel of House of Savoy), 17th cent. Palazzo Reale and several other palaces, Castello Medioevale, Castello del Valentino, Royal Albertine Library, national and municipal library, museums, town hall; univ. (1404), technical institute (1859).

History: Founded by the Taurini; destroyed by Hannibal 218 B.C.; made a Roman military colony under Augustus; seat of Lombard duchy 590–636 A.D.; seat of government under Charlemagne and remained capital until 1032; passed to House of Savoy 1045; occupied by French 1536–62; made capital of duchy 1563; scene of victory of Prince Eugene of Savoy over French 1706; made ✱ of Kingdom of Sardinia 1720; held by French as capital of department of the Po 1800–14; center of the Risorgimento in 19th cent. and first capital of kingdom of Italy (to 1865); in World War II heavily damaged by Allied air raids; occupied by U.S. troops Apr. 30, 1945.

Turiya *or* **Turja.** See TURYA.

Tur·ke·stan \ˌtər-kə-ˈstan, -ˈstän\. 1 Region, cen. Asia. See TURKISTAN.

2 Town, S Kazakh S.S.R., U.S.S.R., 140 m. NNW of Tashkent, ab. 20 m. E of the Syr Darya river; pop. (1967e) 47,000; notable mosque.

Tur·key \ˈtər-kē\. 1 *or Turk.* **Tür·ki·ye** \ˌtyu̇r-ki-ˈye\. Republic, SE Europe and SW Asia, bounded on N by the Black Sea, on NE by the U.S.S.R., on E by Iran, on SE by Iraq, on S by Syria and the Mediterranean Sea, on W by the Aegean Sea, and on NW by Greece and Bulgaria; 301,380 sq. m. (incl. 3568 sq. m. of water); pop. (1970p) 35,666,549; ✱ Ankara. *Physical features:* A mountainous country with extensive plateau covering cen. Asia Minor; highest ranges are in NE and E (highest peak Ararat 16,945 ft.); along N coast are the Şmali Anadolu Dağları and on S coast the Taurus Range. Its rivers comprise the upper courses of Tigris and Euphrates (Frat) in the E, the Kızıl Irmak in the N, Sakarya in NW and Menderes in W with many other smaller but important streams; its lakes are numerous, esp. Lake Van in the E and several large ones in cen. and W cen. Anatolia. Its long coastline has few islands except in the Aegean and there most of them belong to Greece. About 97% of the republic's area lies in Asia, the remainder in Europe. *Chief products:* Wheat, barley, corn, rye, rice, olives, vines, tobacco; pastoralism; coal, chrome, iron ore; manufacturing: iron and steel, textiles, cement, chemicals; food processing. *Chief cities:* İstanbul, Ankara, İzmir, Adana, Bursa, Eskişehir, Gaziantep, Konya. Divided into the following 67 provinces (for pronunciation of their names, see their individual entries):

NAME	AREA[1] (sq. m.)	POP. (1970p)	CAPITAL
Adana	6,661	1,035,373	Adana
Adıyaman	2,940	305,200	Adıyaman
Afyonkarahisar	5,494	542,752	Afyonkarahisar
Ağri	4,392	292,976	Karaköse
Amasya	2,131	309,777	Amasya
Ankara	11,859	2,023,031	Ankara
Antalya	7,950	576,828	Antalya
Artvin	2,871	225,751	Artvin
Aydın	3,092	567,360	Aydın
Balıkesir	5,518	752,595	Balıkesir
Bilecik	1,559	138,754	Bilecik
Bingöl	3,137	178,331	Bingöl
Bitlis	2,590	185,284	Bitlis
Bolu	4,267	402,774	Bolu
Burdur	2,659	210,515	Burdur
Bursa	4,268	847,605	Bursa
Çanakkale	3,759	360,337	Çanakkale
Çankırı	3,263	263,479	Çankırı
Çorum	4,950	521,277	Çorum
Denizli	4,582	511,804	Denizli
Diyarbakır	5,928	575,283	Diyarbakır
Edirne	2,419	318,318	Edirne
Elâzığ	3,533	378,349	Elâzığ
Erzincan	4,596	277,647	Erzincan
Erzurum	9,678	685,955	Erzurum
Eskişehir	5,271	463,458	Eskişehir
Gaziantep	2,951	604,756	Gaziantep
Giresun	2,677	447,266	Giresun
Gümüshane	3,949	282,466	Gümüşhane
Hakkâri	3,676	102,927	Cölemerik
Hatay	2,086	596,201	Antakya
İçel	6,121	596,324	Mersin
İsparta	3,449	300,391	İsparta
İstanbul	2,214	2,995,191	İstanbul
İzmir	4,623	1,430,368	İzmir

NAME	AREA[1] (sq. m.)	POP. (1970p)	CAPITAL
Kars	7,165	663,088	Kars
Kastamonu	5,061	446,864	Kastamonu
Kayseri	6,532	610,287	Kayseri
Kırklareli	2,529	257,477	Kırklareli
Kırşehir	2,537	212,083	Kırşehir
Kocaeli	1,539	383,552	İzmit
Konya	18,309	1,289,500	Konya
Kütahya	4,585	482,553	Kütahya
Malatya	4,754	515,003	Malatya
Manisa	5,332	793,366	Manisa
Maraş	5,532	523,153	Maraş
Mardin	4,927	457,693	Mardin
Muğla	5,150	372,089	Muğla
Muş	3,164	233,919	Muş
Nevşehir	2,111	231,873	Nevşehir
Niğde	5,519	408,684	Niğde
Ordu	2,317	607,319	Ordu
Rize	1,514	317,604	Rize
Sakarya	1,721	455,640	Adapazarı
Samsun	3,698	822,318	Samsun
Siirt	4,248	330,111	Siirt
Sinop	2,263	264,653	Sinop
Sivas	10,999	729,233	Sivas
Tekirdağ	2,401	296,898	Tekirdağ
Tokat	3,845	544,442	Tokat
Trabzon	1,809	662,412	Trabzon
Tunceli	3,002	159,672	Kalan
Urfa	7,175	542,128	Urfa
Uşak	2,062	208,388	Uşak
Van	7,363	326,069	Van
Yozgat	5,453	469,520	Yozgat
Zonguldak	3,332	742,255	Zonguldak

[1] Area = land area.

History: For earlier history, see OTTOMAN EMPIRE; beginning with Young Turk movement, which led revolt 1908, a nationalist group sought reform in Ottoman Empire; the nationalists, under Mustafa Kemal Pasha, later known as Kemal Atatürk, set up government at Ankara 1919, repudiated Sèvres treaty, defeated Greece (*q.v.*) 1920–22, adopted constitution 1921 (later amended), and formally proclaimed Turkish republic 1923; abolished caliphate 1924 and Islam as state religion 1928; joined Balkan Pact 1934 and nonaggression pact with Iraq, Iran, and Afghanistan 1937; remilitarized the Straits (*q.v.*) 1936; incorporated Republic of Hatay (see ALEXANDRETTA 1) 1939; remained neutral throughout World War II (1939–45); participated in Korean War (1950–53); became a member of NATO 1951; adopted new constitution 1961; relations with Greece strained (esp. 1964, 1967) over Cyprus issue. See *Eastern Thrace* at THRACE.

2 River, NE Iowa; 135 m. long; rises in Howard co., flows SE into Mississippi river in SE Clayton co.

Türkheim. See TURCKHEIM.

Turkish Armenia. See ARMENIA, TURKISH.

Turkish Empire. See OTTOMAN EMPIRE.

Tur·ki·stan *or* **Tur·ke·stan** \ˌtər-kə-ˈstan, -ˈstän\. Region of cen. Asia, in U.S.S.R., China, and Afghanistan. Its W part **(Russian Turkistan** *or* **Western Turkistan)**, a former Russian government-general; total area ab. 57,700 sq. m. Conquered by Russia 1859–65. Chief cities Tashkent, Samarkand, and Bukhara. Between 1920 and 1925 divided by Soviet government into the Turkmen, Uzbek, Tadzhik, Kirgiz, and S Kazakh S.S.Rs., U.S.S.R. Its E part **(Chinese Turkistan** *or* **Eastern Turkistan)** is now a part of Chinese province in Sinkiang Uighur. A small section of NE Afghanistan is sometimes included (see AFGHAN TURKISTAN).

Türkiye. See TURKEY.

Turkmanchai. See TORKAMĀN.

Turk·men Soviet Socialist Republic \ˌtərk-mən-\ *also* **Turk·me·ni·stan** \tərk-ˈmen-ə-ˌstan\. A constituent republic of the U.S.S.R., bounded on NW by Kazakh S.S.R., on N and NE by Uzbek S.S.R., on S by Afghanistan and Iran, and on W by Caspian Sea; 188,455 sq. m.; pop. (1970p) 2,158,000; ✱ Ashkhabad. Western and cen. parts are level and desert (Kara Kum); E part is plateau. Has Amu Darya along E border (in part as boundary with Uzbek S.S.R.) and the Murghab in SE. *Chief products:* Cotton, wheat, barley, fruit; sheep; silk; oil. *Chief towns:* Ashkhabad, Krasnovodsk, Mary, Nebit-Dag.

History: Since the 10th cent. the region has been inhabited by Turki tribes, of which the Tekke were most important; by their defeat 1881 the region became part of Russian Turkistan; organized as Soviet republic 1924, and in May 1925 became a constituent republic of the U.S.S.R.

Turks and Cai·cos Islands \ˈtərks . . . ˈkā-kəs-\. A British colony, consisting of two groups of islands in the SE part of the Bahama Is. and N of Hispaniola: **Turks Islands,** 2 islands, Grand Turk and Salt Cay, separated by Turks Island Passage from Caicos Is. to the W; **Caicos Islands,** a group of small islands comprising **South Caicos, East Caicos, Grand Caicos, North Caicos, Prov·i·den·ci·a·les** \ˌpräv-ə-ˌden-chē-ˈäl-əs\, **West Caicos,** and numerous small cays ENE of Great Inagua I. Total area 166 sq. m.; pop. (1970e) 5675; ✱ Grand Turk. Turks Is. are separated by Mouchoir Passage from Mouchoir Bank to the SE, and Caicos Is. by Caicos Passage from Mayaguana I. to the NW. Chief industries collecting sponges and salt production; chief exports sponges and shellfish. Discovered c. 1512; visited by traders after 1678; first permanent settlement c. 1781; at first under Bahamas government but a dependency of Jamaica 1848–62; adopted new constitution 1969.

Turks Island Passage. Channel, N cen. West Indies, SE of Caicos Is. and NW of Turks Is.

Turks Islands. See TURKS AND CAICOS ISLANDS.

Tur·ku \ˈtu̇(ə)r-(ˌ)kü\ *or Swed.* **Åbo** \ˈō-(ˌ)bü\. Seaport, ✱ of Turku ja Pori prov., SW Finland; pop. (1970p) 153,300; 3d largest city in Finland and one of its principal seaports; produces foodstuffs, textiles, pharmaceuticals, china; shipbuilding and repairing; Univ. of Åbo (1918), Univ. of Turku (1920); seat of archbishop of Finland. Established on present site early 13th cent.; scene of signing of Treaty of Åbo 1743; capital of Finland until 1812.

Turku ja Po·ri \-yä-ˈpȯr-ē\. Province of SW Finland. See table at FINLAND.

Tur·lock \ˈtər-ˌläk\. City, Stanislaus co., cen. California, 38 m. SE of Stockton; pop. (1970c) 13,992; dairy products; cans fruit; diversified agriculture.

Turn·a·gain, Cape \-ˈtər-nə-ˌgen, -gin\. Cape, SE coast of North I., New Zealand.

Turnagain Arm. Arm of Cook Inlet, S Alaska, SE of Anchorage and N of Kenai penin.; ab. 50 m. long.

Turnau. See TURNOV.

Turn·ber·ry Point \ˌtərn-ˌber-ē-, -b(ə-)re-\. Cape, W coast of Ayrshire, SW Scotland, on E side of entrance to Firth of Clyde; lighthouse.

Tur·neffe Islands \ˌtər-nəf-\. Island group, Caribbean Sea, off coast of E cen. British Honduras opp. Belize, comprising **Turneffe Island** and numerous islets.

Tur·ner \ˈtər-nər\. Name of counties in two states of the U.S. See tables at GEORGIA and SOUTH DAKOTA.

Tur·ners Falls \ˌtər-nərz-\. Village (unincorp.), Franklin co., NW Massachusetts; pop. (1970c) 5168; site of earliest dam on Connecticut river.

Tur·ner's Peninsula \ˌtər-nərz-\. Long narrow tongue of land, W Africa, SE of Sherbro I.; extending ab. 60 m. along the S shore of Sierra Leone.

Turn·hout \ˈtu̇rn-(ˌ)hau̇t\. Manufacturing commune, Antwerp prov., N Belgium, 26 m. NE of Antwerp near Netherlands border; pop. (1969e) 37,927; bricks, flour, leather goods, electrical equipment; diamond cutting, printing.

Tur·nov \ˈtu̇(ə)r-ˌnȯf\ *or Ger.* **Tur·nau** \ˈtu̇(ə)r-ˌnau̇\. Town, Czech S.R., NW Czechoslovakia, ab. 50 m. NE of Prague; pop. (1968e) 12,810; semiprecious stones.

Tŭrnovo. See VELIKO TURNOVO.

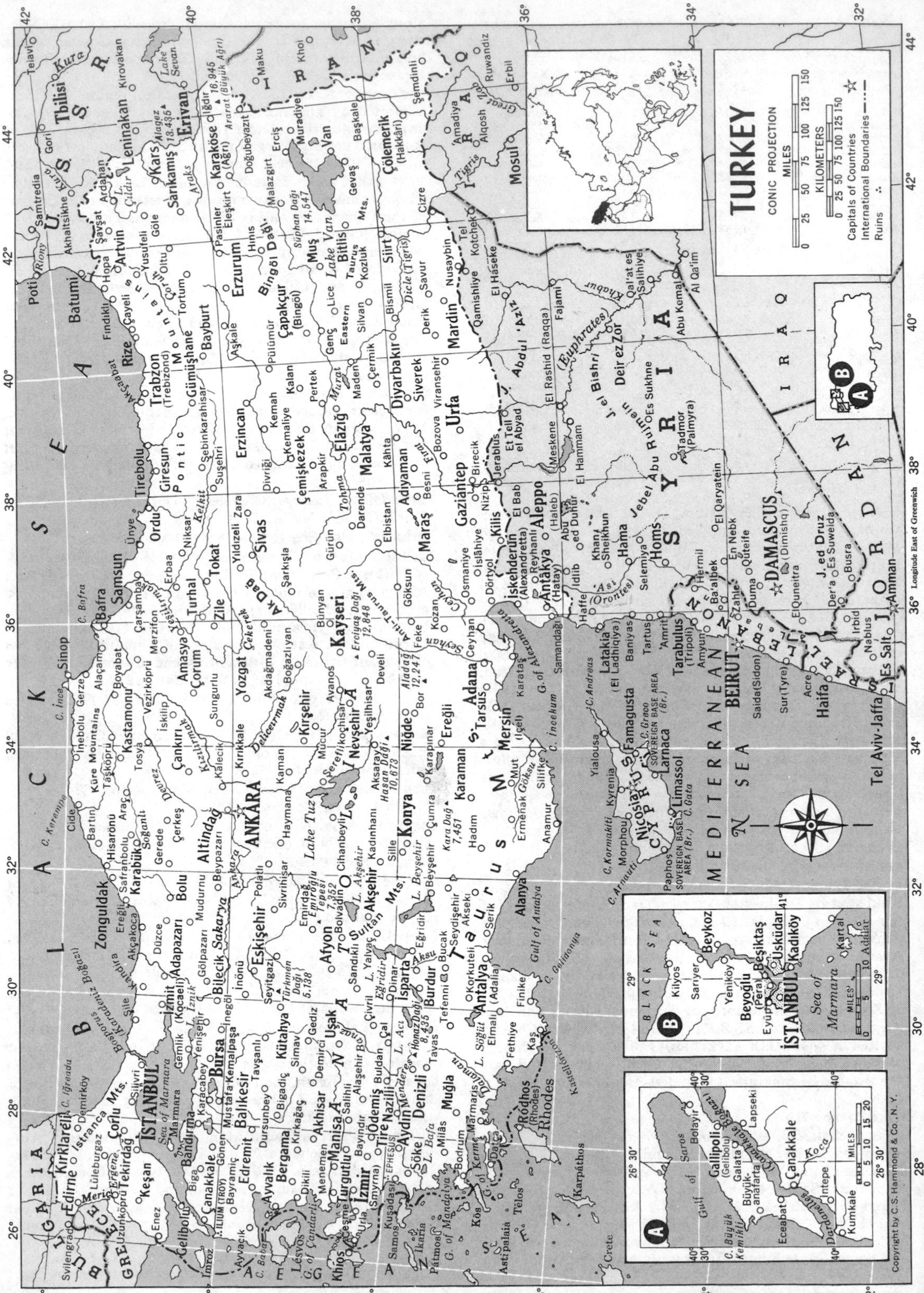
TURKEY
CONIC PROJECTION
MILES
0 25 50 75 100 125 150
KILOMETERS
0 25 50 75 100 125 150
Capitals of Countries
International Boundaries
Ruins
BLACK SEA
MEDITERRANEAN SEA
ANATOLIA
TAURUS MTS.
Pontic Mountains
U. S. S. R.
IRAN
IRAQ
SYRIA
JORDAN
ISRAEL
LEBANON
CYPRUS
BULGARIA
GREECE
AEGEAN SEA
ANKARA
İSTANBUL
İzmir (Smyrna)
Bursa
Adana
Konya
Kayseri
Eskişehir
Samsun
Trabzon (Trebizond)
Erzurum
Diyarbakır
Gaziantep
Aleppo
Antakya (Hatay)
İskenderun (Alexandretta)
Mersin (İçel)
Antalya (Adalia)
Sivas
Malatya
Van
Lake Van
Lake Tuz
Ararat (Büyük Ağrı) 16,945
Tbilisi
Leninakan
Erivan
Batumi
Mosul
DAMASCUS
BEIRUT
Nicosia
Famagusta
Limassol
Larnaca
Tel Aviv-Jaffa
Haifa
Amman
Homs
Hama
Latakia
Tarabulus (Tripoli)
Deir ez Zor
Euphrates
Tigris
Rhodes
Lesvos
Khios
Samos
Kos
Crete
Gallipoli (Gelibolu)
Çanakkale
Dardanelles
Sea of Marmara
Beyoğlu (Pera)
Üsküdar
Kadıköy
Beykoz
Beşiktaş
Longitude East of Greenwich
Copyright by C.S. Hammond & Co., N.Y.

Tur·nu–Mă·gu·re·le \'tu̇(ə)r-(ˌ)nü-mə-ˌgü-'rel-ē\. City, S Romania, on the Danube 80 m. SW of Bucharest opp. Nikopol in Bulgaria; pop. (1970e) 29,988.

Turnu Ro·şu \ˌtu̇r-nü-'rō-ˌshü\ *or* **Roşu** *or Ger.* **Ro·ter·turm** \'rō-tər-ˌtu̇(ə)rm\. Mountain pass in the Transylvanian Alps, cen. Romania, S of Sibiu; traversed by Olt river; battle Sept. 26–29, 1916.

Turnu–Se·ve·rin \'tu̇(ə)r-(ˌ)nü-ˌsev-ə-'rēn\ *or anc.* **Dro·be·ta** \drō-'bēt-ə\. City, ⊗ of Mehedinţi co., SW Romania, on Danube river near Iron Gate; pop. (1970e) 54,619; commercial center; shipbuilding, food processing. Ancient Roman town of Drobeta had commemorative tower (Turris Severi) built by the Emperor Severus; site of Trajan's bridge over the Danube, largest in the Roman Empire.

Turoni. See TOURS.

Tur·qui·no, Pi·co \ˌpē-kō-tu̇r-'kē-(ˌ)nō\. Peak in Sierra Maestra, E Cuba; 6560 ft.; highest mountain in Cuba.

Tur·ret Mountain \ˌtər-ət-, ˌtə-rət-\. Peak, Yellowstone National Park, NW Wyoming; 10,400 ft.

Turret Peak. Mountain, La Plata co., SW Colorado; 13,826 ft.

Tu·rri·al·ba \ˌtu̇r-ē-'äl-bə\. Volcano, Costa Rica, NE of Cartago; 10,650 ft.

Turris Libisonis. See PORTO TORRES.

Turt·kul \tu̇(ə)rt-'kül\ *or formerly* **Pe·tro·a·le·ksan·drovsk** \ˌpe-trō-ˌal-ik-'san-drəfsk, -ig-'zan-\. Town, W Uzbek S.S.R., U.S.S.R., just above Urgench, on right bank of lower Amu Darya; former ✱ of Karakalpak A.S.S.R.; originally a Russian fort.

Tur·tle Creek \'tərt-ᵊl-\. Borough, Allegheny co., SW Pennsylvania, 11 m. E of Pittsburgh; pop. (1970c) 8308; coal mines.

Turtle Islands. 1 Group of islands, Indonesia. See PENJU ISLANDS.

2 Group of islets, SW Sulu Sea off North Borneo coast, ab. 25 m. N of Sandakan; annexed by Philippines 1948.

3 Group of small islands off W point of Sherbo I., Sierra Leone, W Africa.

Turtle Mountains. Small range, Bottineau and Rolette cos., N North Dakota.

Tur·ton \'tərt-ᵊn\. Urban district, Lancashire, NW England, 13 m. NNW of Manchester; pop. (1971p) 21,500; cotton goods; stone quarrying.

Turugart Pass. See TORUGART PASS.

Tur·ya \'tu̇(ə)r-yə\ *or* **Tu·ri·ya** \'tu̇r-ē-(y)ə\ *or Pol.* **Tur·ja** \'tu̇(ə)r-(ˌ)yä\. River, NW Ukrainian S.S.R., U.S.S.R.; ab. 100 m. long; formerly in E Poland; flows N into the Pripyat river.

Tus·ca·loo·sa \ˌtəs-kə-'lü-sə\. 1 County in W cen. Alabama. See table at ALABAMA.

2 Commercial and industrial city, its ⊗, on Black Warrior river 50 m. SW of Birmingham; pop. (1970c) 65,773; cottonseed oil, chemicals, fertilizer, tires, veneer, paper; Univ. of Alabama (1831, in University, an E suburb), Stillman Coll. (1876). Settled 1816; incorporated 1819; state capital 1826–46; occupied by Union troops 1865.

Tuscan Apennines. See table at APENNINES.

Tus·can Archipelago \'təs-kən-\ *or Ital.* **Ar·ci·pe·la·go To·sca·no** \ˌär-chi-'pel-ə-ˌgō-tō-'skän-(ˌ)ō\. Group of small islands bet. Corsica, France and Italy; includes Elba, Pianosa, Montecristo, Giglio, and Giannutri.

Tus·ca·nia \təs-'kā-nē-ə\ *or formerly* **Tos·ca·nel·la** \ˌtäs-kə-'nel-ə, *Ital.* ˌtōs-kä-'nel-ə\. Commune, Viterbo prov., N Latium, cen. Italy, W of Viterbo; pop. (1968e) 7114; Etruscan tombs; medieval walls; four Romanesque churches; severely damaged by earthquake 1971.

Tus·ca·ny \'təs-kə-nē\ *or Ital.* **To·sca·na** \tō-'skän-ə\. Autonomous region, W Italy; 8876 sq. m.; pop. (1968e) 3,434,-618; ✱ Florence (for provincial divisions, see table at ITALY); on Tyrrhenian and Ligurian seas bet. Latium and Liguria; mountainous, with marshes in coastal areas; watered by Arno, Cecina, Serchio, and Ombrone rivers; considerable mineral wealth (lead, zinc, mercury, copper, lignite, marble); chemical, textile, metallurgical, shipbuilding, and handicraft industries; grain, livestock, olives, vines. Chief cities Florence, Leghorn, Apuania, Lucca, Pisa, Pistoia, and Arezzo.

History: A margravate in 9th cent. A.D.; elevated to duchy 10th cent.; in 12th and 13th cents. divided into several independent city-states, subsequently reunited under Medici dukes of Florence (see FLORENCE 9); passed to house of Lorraine, and subsequently to Sardinia and the kingdom of Italy. Tuscan dialect now standard Italian. Region suffered severe damage during fighting in World War II, esp. July–Sept. 1944, and in extensive floods 1966. Present region established 1948, received limited autonomy 1970.

Tus·ca·ra·was \ˌtəs-kə-'rō-(w)əs\. 1 River, NE Ohio; ab. 125 m. long; rises in Summit co., flows S and joins Walhonding river in Coshocton co. to form Muskingum river.

2 County in Ohio. See table at OHIO.

Tus·ca·ro·ra Mountain \ˌtəs-kə-ˌrōr-ə-, -ˌrȯr-\. Ridge, S Pennsylvania, extending along the boundary bet. Juniata, Huntingdon, and Fulton cos. on the NW, and Perry and Franklin cos. on the SE.

Tuscarora Mountains. Range in N Nevada, chiefly in Eureka and Elko cos.

Tus·co·la \təs-'kō-lə\. 1 County in Michigan. See table at MICHIGAN.

2 City, ⊗ of Douglas co., E cen. Illinois, 36 m. E of Decatur; pop. (1970c) 3917; chemicals, fertilizer, plastics.

Tus·cu·lum \'təs-k(y)ə-ləm\. Ancient town, Latium, Italy, ab. 12 m. SE of Rome and just N of Lake Albano and the Alban Hills; alt. ab. 2200 ft.; many ruins. In very early times a rival of Rome, by which it was made subject after battle of Lake Regillus 496 B.C.; furnished many prominent citizens of Rome in time of the Republic; home of Cicero.

Tus·cum·bia \tə-'skəm-bē-ə\. 1 Manufacturing city, ⊗ of Colbert co., NW Alabama, on Tennessee river 10 m. from Wilson Dam; pop. (1970c) 8828; lumber, fertilizer; founded 1817.

2 Town, ⊗ of Miller co., cen. Missouri; pop. (1970c) 256.

Tus·ke·gee \təs-'kē-gē\. City, ⊗ of Macon co., E Alabama, 38 m. E of Montgomery; pop. (1970c) 11,028; cottonseed oil and grist mills; Tuskegee Institute (1881); incorporated as city 1820.

Tus·sey Mountain \ˌtəs-ē-\. Peak, S Pennsylvania, on boundary bet. Blair, Bedford, and Huntingdon cos.; 2225 ft.

Tus·sum \tu̇-'süm\. Village, Egypt, on W bank of Suez Canal, near Ismailia; Turks defeated here 1915.

Tus·tin \'təs-tən\. City, Orange co., SW California, 20 m. E of Long Beach; pop. (1970c) 21,178; fruit juices, cement pipes; citrus fruit, beans.

Tutela. See TUDELA.

Tu·ti·co·rin \ˌtüt-i-kə-'rin\. Town, S Tamil Nadu, S India, on Gulf of Mannar 75 m. S of Madurai; pop. (1970e) 153,958; seaport; manufactures salt and cotton textiles; founded by Portuguese in 1540; taken by Dutch 1658; acquired by British 1825.

Tutt·ling·en \'tu̇t-liŋ-ən\. Manufacturing city, Baden-Württemberg, West Germany, on Danube river 45 m. E of Freiburg; pop. (1969e) 26,436; shoes, woolen goods, precision tools.

Tu·tu·i·la \ˌtüt-ə-'wē-lə\. Chief island of American Samoa, in SW cen. Pacific Ocean; 25 m. long by 2 to 6 m. wide; 52 sq. m.; pop. (1968e) 20,470; chief town Pago Pago, ✱ of American Samoa, at head of deep indentation on S coast, forming Pago Pago Harbor. Has mountain range running length of island; highest point Mt. Matafao 2141 ft.; is densely wooded; U.S. naval station on W coast of Pago Pago Harbor.

Tu·va Autonomous Soviet Socialist Republic \'tü-və-\; *formerly* **Tan·nu Tuva** *also* **Tan·nou Tou·va** \ˌtan-ü-\ *or* **Urian·khai** \ˌür-ē-äŋ-'kī\ *also* **Uriang·hai** \-aŋ-'hī\. Autonomous republic, Russian S.F.S.R., U.S.S.R., bet. Sayan and Tannu-Ola Mts.; 65,380 sq. m.; pop. (1970p) 231,000; ✱ Kyzyl. Mountainous and generally well-watered; crossed from E to W by the Bei Kem and Khua Kem, headstreams of the Yenisei. Economy based on livestock raising; deposits of gold, asbestos, cobalt, and coal, but their exploitation limited by poor communications.

History: Until 1911 a part (Uriankhai) of Outer Mongolia (now Mongolian People's Republic); nominally independent 1911–14; under Russian protection 1914–17, then under Chinese rule; independent from 1921; signed treaties of friendship with U.S.S.R. and Mongolian People's Republic 1926; annexed by U.S.S.R. 1944 as autonomous oblast; made autonomous republic 1961.

Tux·e·do Park \tək-ˌsēd-ō-\. Village and resort, Orange co., SE New York, bet. **Tuxedo Lake** and Palisades Interstate Park, on Ramapo river; pop. (1970c) 861.

Tux·pan \'tüs-ˌpän\. 1 Town, S Jalisco state, W cen. Mexico, 15 m. from Colima border; munic. pop. (1970p) 23,569.

2 Town, Nayarit state, W Mexico, 40 m. NW of Tepic on San Pedro river; munic. pop. (1970p) 28,345.

3 Town, Veracruz state, E Mexico, on coast 145 m. NW of Veracruz; munic. pop. (1970p) 65,211.

Tuxpan Reef. Reef, Gulf of Mexico, off the seaport town of Tuxpan in N Veracruz state, Mexico.

Tux·te·pec \ˌtüs-tə-'pek\ *or in full* **San Juan Bau·tis·ta Tuxtepec** \san-ˌ(h)wän-baü-'tēs-tə-\. Town, NE Oaxaca state, SE Mexico, 80 m. NNE of Oaxaca; munic. pop. (1970p) 184,757; Plan of Tuxtepec issued Jan. 1876 as statement against policies of Pres. Lerdo de Tejada.

Tux·tla \'tüst-lə\. 1 *or in full* **Tuxtla Gu·ti·é·rrez** \-gü-'tyer-əs\. Town, ✱ of Chiapas state, SE Mexico; munic. pop. (1970p) 69,326; altitude 1500 ft.; distributing center for sisal, tobacco, coffee, cattle.

2 Town, Veracruz state, E Mexico. See SAN ANDRÉS TUXTLA.

Túy \'tü-ē\. Commune, Pontevedra prov., NW Spain, 30 m. S of Pontevedra; pop. (1970p) 12,600; mineral baths; 9th cent. cathedral; captured several times by Portuguese, notably in 1388, 1397.

Tu·zi·goot National Monument \'tü-zi-ˌgüt-\. See UNITED STATES, *National Monuments.*

Tuz·la \'tüz-lä\ *or* **Dol·nja Tuzla** \ˌdōl-nyä-\. Town, Bosnia and Herzegovina, cen. Yugoslavia, 50 m. NNE of Sarajevo; pop. (1971p) 53,825; salt springs; salt mines.

Tuz Lake \'tüz-\ *or Turk.* **Tuz Gö·lü** \-gəl-'(y)ü\ *or anc.* **Pa·lus Tat·tae·us** \ˌpāl-əs-ta-'tē-əs\. Salt lake (*gölü*), W cen. Turkey; 624 sq. m.; alt. 2960 ft.; at times dried up.

Tver. See KALININ.

Tver·tsa \tver-'tsä\. River, Kalinin Oblast, Russian S.F.S.R., U.S.S.R.; ab. 110 m. long; flows SE to the Volga at Kalinin. Joined by canal with the Msta.

Tvin. See DWIN.

Tweed \'twēd\. River, SE Scotland and NE England; 97 m. long; rises in Peebles co., SE Scotland, flows E, forming a section of the boundary bet. Scotland and England; crosses the extreme NE border of England and empties into North Sea at Berwick.

Tweeddale. See PEEBLES 1.

Tweeds·muir Park \ˌtwēdz-myü(ə)r-\. Provincial park, British Columbia, Canada; 3788 sq. m.; in Rocky Mts. W of Fraser river and SE of the Skeena; has many lakes, rivers, and mountains; largest lake is Eutsuk Lake, highest point 8250 ft.

Twelve Apostles. See APOSTLE ISLANDS.

Twelve Bens of Bennebeola. See BENNEBEOLA, TWELVE BENS OF.

Twiggs \'twigz\. County in Georgia. See table at GEORGIA.

Twil·lin·gate \'twil-iŋ-ˌgāt\. Town, E Newfoundland, Canada, on island at entrance of Notre Dame Bay; pop. (1971p) 1438; harbor.

Twin Falls \ˌtwin-\. 1 County in S Idaho. See table at IDAHO.

2 City, its ⊗, 110 m. W of Pocatello; pop. (1970c) 21,914; produces beet sugar, dried fruit, dairy products, agricultural implements; founded 1904, incorporated as city 1907.

3 Falls, ab. 8 m. NE of the city in the Snake river, at a place where the river divides into two channels, to reunite after drop of ab. 200 ft.; S fall source of hydroelectric power.

Twin Lakes. Two lakes (Washinee and Washining), extreme NW Connecticut; resort.

Twin Lakes Reservoir. Reservoir, S Lake co., W cen. Colorado; formed from two small lakes, stores water for irrigation; on its SW shore is the village of **Twin Lakes,** resort.

Twin Mounds. Heights, Cheyenne co., W Nebraska; 4309 ft. and 4349 ft.

Twin Mountain. Peak in Blue Mts., NE Oregon; 8920 ft.

Twin Mountains. Two peaks in the Franconia Mts., N Grafton co., New Hampshire; North Twin 4769 ft. and South Twin 4926 ft.

Twin Peaks. Mountain on W cen. boundary of Lemhi co., E cen. Idaho; 10,328 ft.

Twins, The \-'twinz\. Two mountain peaks, S Jasper National Park, SW Alberta, Canada; N peak 12,085 ft. and S peak 11,675 ft.

Twins·burg \'twinz-ˌbərg\. Village, Summit co., NE Ohio, ab. 17 m. NNE of Akron; pop. (1970c) 6432.

Two·fold Bay \ˌtü-ˌfōld-\. Inlet of Tasman Sea, SE New South Wales, Australia; Eden on N shore has excellent harbor.

Two Harbors. City, ⊗ of Lake co., NE Minnesota, on Lake Superior 26 m. NE of Duluth; pop. (1970c) 4325; ships iron ore; resort; truck, dairy farms.

Two Med·i·cine Lake \-'med-ə-sən-\. Small lake, S Glacier National Park, NW Montana.

Two Mountains *or Fr.* **Deux–Mon·tagnes** \dœ̄-mōⁿ-'tanʸ\. 1 County, Quebec, Canada. See table at QUEBEC.

2 City, Two Mountains co., S Quebec, Canada; pop. (1971p) 8598; residential suburb of Montreal.

Two Mountains, Lake of *or Fr.* **Lac des Deux–Mon·tagnes** \ˌlák-dā-ˌdœ̄-mōⁿ-'tanʸ\. Expansion of the Ottawa river at its junction with the St. Lawrence, W of Montreal I., Quebec, Canada; bordered on SE by Île Perrot and has two outlets to the NE, the Rivière des Mille Îles and Rivière des Prairies.

Two Rivers. City, Manitowoc co., E Wisconsin, on Lake Michigan 7 m. NE of Manitowoc; pop. (1970c) 13,533; aluminum products, furniture, iron castings, knitwear, beer; resort; dairy farms.

Two Sicilies, The. See history at SICILY.

Ty·a·na \'tī-ə-nə\. Ancient city, SW Cappadocia, Asia Minor, on N slope of Taurus Mts.; birthplace of Apollonius, Greek philosopher.

Tyan Shan. See TIEN SHAN.

Ty·bee Island \ˌtī-(ˌ)bē-\. Island, Chatham co., SE Georgia, at mouth of the Savannah river; 6 m. long.

Ty·burn \'tī-bərn\. A former place of execution, near which is now the Marble Arch, Hyde Park, London, England.

Ty·chy \'ti-kē\. Town, Katowice prov., S Poland, ab. 10 m. S of Katowice; pop. (1970p) 71,400; breweries; site of large postwar resettlement community (1951) **No·we Tychy** \'nō-və-\.

Ty·ee, Mount \-'tī-ˌē\. Peak, Chelan co., cen. Washington; 6688 ft.

Ty·gart \'tī-gərt\. River, N West Virginia; ab. 160 m. long; rises in Randolph co., flows N and unites with West Fork of Monongahela river near Fairmont to form the Monongahela river.

Tygart River Dam. Dam across Tygart river, S of Grafton, Taylor co., N West Virginia; height 250 ft.; completed 1938; impounds water for flood control.

Ty·ger *also* **Ti·ger** \'tī-gər\. River, South Carolina; ab. 100 m. long; rises in NW in Greenville co., flows SE into the Broad river.

Tyldes·ley \'til(d)z-lē\. Urban district, Lancashire, NW England, 10 m. WNW of Manchester; pop. (1971p) 21,163; cotton mills; collieries.

Ty·ler \'tī-lər\. 1 Name of counties in two states of the U.S. See tables at TEXAS and WEST VIRGINIA.

2 Commercial and industrial city, ⊗ of Smith co., NE Texas, 85 m. ESE of Dallas; pop. (1970c) 57,700; metal products, prefabricated homes, ceramics, oil-field equipment; foundries, oil and gas wells, oil refineries; Texas. Coll. (1894); region settled c. 1840; incorporated as town 1846, as city 1907.

Ty·ler·town \'tī-lər-ˌtau̇n\. Town, ⊗ of Walthall co., S Mississippi; pop. (1970c) 1736.

Tý·lis·sos \'tē-li-ˌsȯs\. Archaeological site near N coast of cen. Crete, Greece, SW of Candia; relics of Late Minoan period.

Tylos. See BAHRAIN.

Tyn·dall \'tin-dᵊl\. City, ⊗ of Bon Homme co., SE South Dakota; pop. (1970c) 1245.

Tyndall, Mount. 1 Peak in Sierra Nevada, in Tulare co., S cen. California; 14,018 ft.

2 Mountain in Southern Alps, South I., New Zealand, NE of Mt. Cook; 8280 ft.

Tyne \'tīn\. 1 River, Northumberland, N England; 30 m. long; including North Tyne, 80 m. long; formed by confluence of **North Tyne** and **South Tyne;** flows E into North Sea bet. the cities of Tynemouth and South Shields.

2 River, SE Scotland; 28 m. long; rises in Midlothian co. and flows NE through East Lothian to the North Sea near Dunbar.

Tyne·mouth \'tīn-ˌmau̇th, -məth\. County borough, Northumberland, N England, on North Sea at mouth of the Tyne on its N bank 9 m. E of Newcastle upon Tyne; pop. (1971p) 68,861; shipbuilding and repair yards, commercial fisheries, oil storage depot; seaside resort. Abbey founded on site 7th cent. A.D.; town developed 14th cent.; incorporated 1849.

Tyras. 1 City, U.S.S.R. See BELGOROD-DNESTROVSKI.

2 River, U.S.S.R. See DNIESTER.

Tyre \'tī(ə)r\; *Fr.* **Tyr** \tir\ *or* **Sour** \'su̇(ə)r\; *Arab.* **Es Sur** \es-'su̇(ə)r\ *also* **Sur;** *Heb.* **Zor** \'tsȯ(ə)r, 'zȯ(ə)r\; *anc.* **Ty·rus** \'tī-rəs\. Town, S Lebanon, on the coast of the Mediterranean Sea; noted maritime city of antiquity; capital of Phoenicia from ab. 11th cent. to 573 B.C. In ancient times an island with two harbors; now a peninsula formed by the widening of the causeway or mole built by Alexander. Was for centuries a major commercial city, center of Phoenician civilization and dominant sea power; noted for its silken garments and Tyrian purple. Probably founded in 15th cent. B.C., a colony of Sidon. In Biblical history well known for its king, Hiram (*1 Kings* v. *2 Sam.* v). Withstood attacks from Assyrians and Babylonians but forced to pay tribute; successfully resisted in 6th cent. B.C. a siege of 13 years by Nebuchadnezzar II but was besieged and captured by Alexander 332 B.C.; under control of Seleucids and Romans and in 7th cent. A.D. passed over to Muslims; captured by Crusaders 1124 and became chief city of kingdom of Jerusalem; fell to Muslims 1291 and was destroyed.

Tyree. See TIREE.

Ty·ree, Mount \-ti-'rē\. Mountain, Sentinel Range, cen. Ellsworth Mts., Antarctica; 16,290 ft.; 2d highest peak in Antarctica; first scaled 1966.

Ty·ri·fjord \'tir-i-ˌfyu̇(ə)r\. Lake, SE Norway, 16 m. W of Oslo; 16 m. long by 7 m. wide; on the N receives the Begna, which issues from it on the SW as the Dramselva.

Tyrnau. See TRNAVA.

Tyr·na·vos *or Gk.* **Tír·na·vos** \'tir-nə-ˌvȯs\. Town, Larissa dept., E Thessaly, NE Greece, ab. 10 m. NW of Larissa.

Tyrol. See TIROL.

Ty·rone \'tī-ˌrōn\. Borough, Blair co., S cen. Pennsylvania, 15 m. NE of Altoona; pop. (1970c) 7072; boilers, mining machinery, paper, chemicals; limestone quarries.

Tyrone \tir-'ōn\. County, W cen. Northern Ireland; 1260 sq. m.; pop. (1971p) 137,997; ⊗ Omagh; barley, potatoes; livestock raising; whisky distilling, linen manufacturing; tourism.

Ty·ron·za Lake \tī-ˌrän-zə-\. Lake, cen. Mississippi co., NE Arkansas; outlet, **Tyronza River,** flowing S.

Tyros. See BAHRAIN.

Tyr·rell \'tir-əl\. County in North Carolina. See table at NORTH CAROLINA.

Tyrrha. See TIRE.

Tyr·rhe·ni·an Sea \tə-'rē-nē-ən-\ *or Ital.* **Ma·re Tir·re·no** \ˌmär-ē-ti-'ren-(ˌ)ō, -'rān-\ *or anc.* **Mare Tyr·rhe·num** \ˌmā-(ˌ)rē-tə-'rē-nəm, ˌmär-(ˌ)ā-\. The part of the Mediterranean Sea W of Italian mainland, N of Sicily, and E of Sardinia and Corsica.

Tyrus. See TYRE.

Tys Fjord \'tüs-\. Inlet, extending S from upper Vestfjorden on NW coast of Norway.

Tytärsaari. See BOLSHOI TYUTERS.

Tyu·men \tyü-'men\. City, ✱ of Tyumen Oblast, Russian S.F.S.R., U.S.S.R., in W part on Tura river 125 m. SW of Tobolsk and 190 m. E of Sverdlovsk; pop. (1970p) 269,000; sawmills, tanneries, breweries, distilleries, flour mills; founded 1585 and became first settled Russian town E of the Urals.

Tyumen Oblast \-'ō-bləst, -ˌblast\. Subdivision of the Russian S.F.S.R., U.S.S.R., in the basin of the Ob river; 554,208 sq. m.; pop. (1970p) 1,407,000; ✱ Tyumen. About 80% of area lies in Khanty-Mansi and Yamalo-Nenets national okrugs (*qq.v.*); economy predominantly agricultural; Tyumen only major town; established 1944.

Tzeliutsing. See TZU-KUNG.

Tzu *or* **Tze** \'(d)zə\ *also* **Tsi** \'chē, 'jē\. River, cen. Hunan prov., SE cen. China; ab. 375 m. long; flows into Tung-t'ing Hu (lake) just W of mouth of the Hsiang.

Tz'u–kao \'(d)zü-'gau̇\ *also* **Mount Syl·via** \-'sil-vē-ə\. Mountain, N cen. Taiwan; 12,743 ft.

Tzu–kung \'(d)zə-'gu̇ŋ\ *or* **Tze·liu·tsing** \'(d)zə-'lyü-'jiŋ\. City, S Szechwan prov., S cen. China, 110 m. W of Chungking; pop. (1970e) 350,000.

Ua Hu·ka \ˌü-ə-ˈhü-kə\. Small island of Marquesas Is., S Pacific Ocean, ab. 30 m. E of Nuku Hiva I.

Ualual. See WALWAL.

Uap. See YAP.

Ua Pu \ˌü-ə-ˈpü\ *or* **Ua Pau** \-ˈpau̇\. One of the Marquesas Is., French Polynesia, S Pacific Ocean, ab. 25 m. S of Nuku Hiva; has peak 4040 ft. high.

Uaso Nyiro. See EWASO NG'IRO.

Ua·tu·mã \ˌwät-ə-ˈmä\. River, N Brazil; 350 m. long; flows SE into the Amazon near E border of Amazonas state.

Uau·pés *also* **Wau·pés** \wau̇-ˈpes\. River, NW South America; 500 m. long; rises in S cen. Colombia where it is called the **Vau·pés** \vau̇-ˈpes\, flows ESE across Brazilian border into Rio Negro; forms small section of Colombia-Brazil boundary.

Ua·xac·tún \ˌwäsh-äk-ˈtün\. Ruins of an ancient town, N Guatemala, one of the oldest known centers of Maya civilization, founded probably in 1st cent. A.D.

Ubá \ü-ˈbä\. City, SE Minas Gerais state, E Brazil, 130 m. NNE of Rio de Janeiro; munic. pop. (1968e) 46,767.

Übach–Pa·len·berg \ˈü-bäk-ˈpäl-ən-ˌbərg, -ˌbe(ə)rg\. City, North Rhine-Westphalia, West Germany, 11 m. N of Aachen; pop. (1969e) 22,049; coal mines, gravel pits.

Uban·gi \(y)ü-ˈbaŋ-(g)ē\ *or Fr.* **Ou·ban·gui** \ü-bäⁿ-gē\. River, cen. Africa; 700 m. long, with longest headstream ab. 1400 m.; formed by confluence of Bomu and Uele rivers on N cen. border of Zaire; flows W and S, forming section of boundary bet. Zaire and Central African Republic; empties into Congo river W of Lake Tumba; sometimes called **Ma·kua** \ˈmä-ku̇-(w)ə\ in its upper course and **Mo·ban·gi** \ˌmō-ˈbaŋ-(g)ē\ in its lower course.

Ubangi–Shari *or* **Ubangi–Shari–Chad.** See CENTRAL AFRICAN REPUBLIC.

Ubay \ˈü-ˌbī\. Municipality, NE coast of Bohol I., Phil.; pop. (1969e) 46,700.

Ubayyid, Al–. See AL-UBAYYID.

Ube \ˈü-bē, -(ˌ)bā\. Seaport city, Yamaguchi prefecture, SW Honshū, Japan, at W end of Inland Sea 18 m. E of Shimonoseki; pop. (1970c) 152,935.

Ube·da \ˈü-bə-ˌdä\. Commercial commune, Jaén prov., S Spain, 22 m. NE of Jaén; pop. (1970p) 30,186; stock raising, esp. horses. Reconquered from Moors in 1212.

Ube·ra·ba \ˌü-bə-ˈrab-ə\. City, W Minas Gerais state, E Brazil, ab. 260 m. W of Belo Horizonte; munic. pop. (1968e) 100,634; altitude 2278 ft.; center of extensive cattle-raising district.

Uber·lân·dia \ˌü-bər-ˈlan-dē-ə\. City, Minas Gerais state, E Brazil, on railroad 60 m. NNW of Uberaba; munic. pop. (1968e) 101,149.

Ubi·na \ü-ˈbē-nə\. Peak, Potosí dept., SW Bolivia; 16,830 ft.

Ubi·nas \ü-ˈbē-nəs\. Peak, Moquegua dept., S Peru; 17,390 ft.

Ubon Rat·cha·tha·ni \ˌu̇-ˈbən-ˌräch-ə-ˈtän-ē\ *or* **Ubol Ra·ja·dha·ni** \ˌu̇-ˈbən-ˌräch-ə-ˈtän-ē—*sic*\. 1 Province, SE Thailand; 8787 sq. m.; pop. (1960c) 1,130,712; ✻ Ubon Ratchathani.

2 Town, its ✻, E terminal of railroad from Phra Nakhon Si Ayutthaya and ab. 40 m. W of the Laos border; pop. (1964e) 30,059; on left bank of Mun river just below its junction with the Chi.

Ub·su–Nur *or* **Ubsu Nur** \ˌu̇b-sü-ˈnu̇(ə)r\. Lake (*nur*), NW Mongolian People's Republic, on S border of Tuva A.S.S.R., U.S.S.R.; ab. 1293 sq. m.

Ubun·di \ü-ˈbu̇n-dē\ *or formerly* **Pon·thier·ville** \ˌpōⁿ-tyā-ˈvēl\. Town, S Haut-Zaïre prov., NE Zaire, on the Congo river ab. 70 m. S of Kinshasa.

Uca·ya·li \ˌük-ə-ˈyä-lē\. River, cen. and N Peru; chief headstream of Amazon river; ab. 1000 m. long; formed by confluence of Apurímac and Urubamba rivers in cen. Peru, flows N to unite with Marañón river and form Amazon river; navigable for 675 m.

Uccle. See UKKEL.

Uchi·u·ra Bay \u̇-ˌchē-ə-(ˌ)rä-\ *also* **Vol·ca·no Bay** \väl-ˌkā-(ˌ)nō-, vȯl-\. Inlet of W Pacific Ocean, E coast of S extension of Hokkaidō, Japan.

Uda. See CHUNA.

Udai·pur \ü-ˈdī-ˌpu̇(ə)r, ˌü-dī-ˈ\ *or* **Oo·dey·pore** \ü-ˈdī-ˌpō(ə)r, -ˌpȯ(ə)r, ˌü-dī-ˈ\. 1 Former Indian state, now part of Madhya Pradesh state, India; 1045 sq. m.

2 *also* **Me·war** \mā-ˈwär\. Former Indian state, now part of Rajasthan state, NW India; 13,170 sq. m.; offered strong resistance to Mogul emperors; in 18th cent. suffered from civil wars and attacks by Marathas.

3 City, ✻ of former Udaipur (Mewar) state, now in Rajasthan state, 210 m. SW of Jaipur; pop. (1970e) 136,045; altitude 2469 ft.; univ. (1962); numerous temples and palaces, including 16th cent. maharajah's palace.

Udayadhani. See UTHAI THANI.

Ud·de·val·la \ˌəd-ə-ˈval-ə\. Town, Göteborg and Bohus co., SW Sweden, near coast 45 m. N of Göteborg; pop. (1970e) 36,483; textile mills, match factories.

Udd·jaur \ˈəd-ˌyau̇(ə)r\. Lake, Västerbotten co., N Sweden, connecting Hornavan and Storavan lakes, and drained by the Skellefte river; 92 sq. m.

Uden \ˈü-dən\. Commune, North Brabant prov., Netherlands; pop. (1970e) 23,811.

Udi·ne \ˈüd-i-ˌnā\. 1 Province of Friuli-Venezia Giulia, Italy. See table at ITALY.

2 *or anc.* **Uti·na** \ˈyüt-ᵊn-ə\. Commune, its ✻, Friuli-Venezia Giulia, NE Italy, 61 m. NE of Venice; pop. (1968e) 95,675; railroad junction; iron goods, leather, textiles; 16th cent. castle, 15th cent. town hall (restored after fire 1876). In World War I headquarters of the Italian Supreme Command 1915–17.

Ud·murt Autonomous Soviet Socialist Republic \ˈu̇d-ˌmu̇(ə)rt-\ *or formerly* **Vot·ska·ya Autonomous Soviet Socialist Republic** \ˈvȯt-skä-yə-\. Autonomous republic, E Russian S.F.S.R., U.S.S.R.; 16,255 sq. m.; pop. (1970p) 1,417,000; ✻ Izhevsk. Economy based on metallurgical and engineering industries, exploitation of extensive forests, and agriculture (rye and flax, livestock). Crossed at the N and S by main E and W trunk railroads, with a branch to Izhevsk. Principal towns Izhevsk, Sarapul, Votkinsk, and Glazov.

History: Udmurts, also known as Votyaks, represent E branch of the Finno-Ugrian peoples, speaking a Finnish dialect similar to Permian. Russian penetration began c. 12th cent.; region came under Russian rule after fall of Kazan 1552; made autonomous oblast 1920; suffered heavily in famine 1921–22; elevated to autonomous republic 1934; underwent substantial industrial development as part of Ural Industrial Region during World War II.

Udon Tha·ni *or* **Udorn·dha·ni** \ˌu̇-ˈdȯn-ˈtän-ē\ *also* **Ban Mak Khaeng** \ˈbän-ˈmäk-ˈkaŋ\. 1 Province, NE Thailand; 6411 sq. m.; pop. (1960c) 744,174; ✻ Udon Thani.

2 Town, its ✻, 40 m. S of Laos border, and terminus of railroad from Nakhon Ratchasima; pop. (1964e) 36,088.

Udot \ˈü-ˌdȯt\. Island, cen. part of Truk Islands (*q.v.*).

Uea. See UVÉA.

Ue·da \ü-ˈed-ə, -ˈwād-ə\ *or* **Uye·da** \ü-ˈ(y)ed-ə\. Town, Nagano prefecture, cen. Honshū, Japan; pop. (1970c) 93,198; center of silkworm culture.

Ue·le *or* **Wel·le** \ˈwel-ē\. River, cen. Africa; ab. 700 m. long; flows W across N Zaire to unite with Bomu river and form Ubangi river.

Uel·zen *or* **Ül·zen** \ˈ(y)ült-sən\. City, Lower Saxony, West Germany, 21 m. SSE of Lüneburg; pop. (1969e) 23,759; became city 1270.

Ue·no \ˈwā-ˌnō\. City, Mie prefecture, Honshū, Japan, 36 m. E of Ōsaka; pop. (1970c) 57,666.

Ufa \ü-ˈfä\. 1 River, Bashkir A.S.S.R., Russian S.F.S.R., U.S.S.R.; 580 m. long; rises in W Chelyabinsk Oblast and

flows NW and SW through the Southern Ural Mts. to join the Belaya river at Ufa; partly navigable.
2 City, ✻ of Bashkir A.S.S.R., Russian S.F.S.R., U.S.S.R., at junction of Belaya and Ufa rivers 250 m. NE of Kuibyshev; pop. (1970p) 773,000; machine tools, electrical equipment, lumber and veneer, paper, typewriters; oil refining; Bashkir State Univ. (1957). Founded as fortress 1586; developed as industrial center from late 19th cent. and especially after World War II.

Ugan·da \(y)ü-ˈgan-də\. Republic, E Africa; bounded on N by Sudan, on E by Kenya, on S by Tanzania, on SW by Rwanda, and on W by Zaire; 91,134 sq. m. (including 16,386 sq. m. of water); pop. (1972e) 10,461,500; ✻ Kampala. *Physical features:* On E are high mountains along Kenya boundary, highest Mt. Elgon 14,178 ft.; high Ruwenzori Mts. on W, highest 16,763 ft.; plateau region (Ankole) in SW, dense forests in W part, and marshes on N shore of Lake Victoria and around Lake Kyoga in S cen. part. Traversed by the Nile which issues from Lake Victoria at Ripon Falls, flows through Lakes Kyoga and Albert on the W and then N in NW corner of Uganda into Sudan; Lakes Edward and George are in the SW. *Chief products:* Cotton, coffee, tea, sugar; livestock raising, fishing; copper, phosphates, salt; manufacturing: cement, textiles, tobacco products, fertilizer. *Chief towns:* Kampala, Jinja, Mbale, Entebbe.

History: Native kingdom crossed by explorers Grant and Speke 1862; soon after arrival of first group of missionaries 1877, religious factions developed which combined with political rivalry to produce civil strife; in 1890 agent of British East Africa Company arrived; formally proclaimed British protectorate 1894; achieved independence 1962; abolished federal system of government 1966; adopted republican constitution 1967; civilian government overthrown in coup 1971.

Uga·rit \ˌü-gə-ˈrēt\. Ancient city on site of modern Ras Shamra (*q.v.*), on E coast of the Mediterranean Sea N of Latakia, Syria; flourished c. 1450 to 1195 B.C., and mentioned in Egyptian inscriptions, in the Tell al-ʻAmarna letters, and in Hittite records. Its remains have contributed much to our knowledge of Western Semitic religion and language. Destroyed by an earthquake soon after 1200 B.C.

Ugernum. See BEAUCAIRE.

Ug·le·gorsk \ˌüg-lə-ˈgȯrsk\ *or Jap.* **Esu·to·ru** \ˌe-sə-ˈtō-rü\. Seaport town, NW coast of Sakhalin I., U.S.S.R., on Tatar Strait; pop. (1967e) 17,000; formerly Japanese.

Ugljan *or* **Uljan** \ˈül-yən\ *or Ital.* **Uglia·no** \u̇l-ˈyä-nō\. Island, Adriatic Sea, off coast of Bosnia and Herzegovina, Yugoslavia, opp. Zadar; 18 sq. m.

Uhar·ie \yü-ˈha(ə)r-ē, -ˈhe(ə)r-\ *or* **Uwhar·rie** \-ˈhwa(ə)r-, -ˈhwe(ə)r-\. River, cen. North Carolina; rises in NW Randolph co., flows S into Montgomery co., and joins Yadkin river 10 m. W of Troy to form Pee Dee river (*q.v.*).

Uh·richs·ville \ˈyu̇r-iks-ˌvil\. City, Tuscarawas co., E Ohio, 28 m. S of Canton; pop. (1970c) 5731; pottery, brick, cigars, gloves; coal mines; forms a single community with Dennison to the E.

Ui·ha \ü-ˈē-ə\. Island in E Haapai group, Tonga, SW cen. Pacific Ocean.

Uil·pa·ta \ü-ēl-ˈpät-ə\ *also* **Adai Khokh** \ə-ˈdī-ˈkōk\. Mountain, cen. Caucasus Mts., U.S.S.R., 42°46′N, 43°48′E; 15,239 ft.

Uin·ka·ret Plateau \ü-ˈ(w)iŋk-ə-ˌret-\. Tableland, N Mohave co., NW of Arizona, N of Colorado river; 5400 to 6100 ft.

Uin·ta \yü-ˈint-ə\. 1 River, NE Utah; 50 m. long; rises in Uinta Mts., flows SE into Duchesne river in W Uintah co.
2 County in Wyoming. See table at WYOMING.

Uin·tah \yü-ˈint-ə\. County in Utah. See table at UTAH.

Uinta Mountains. Range, chiefly in NE Utah, extending along the boundary bet. Summit and Daggett cos. on the N and Duchesne and Uintah cos. on the S; highest point Kings Peak 13,528 ft. (highest peak in Utah).

Uist \ˈyü-ist, ˈü-ist\. Two islands, Outer Hebrides off W coast of Scotland. See NORTH UIST and SOUTH UIST.

Ui·ten·hage \ˈyü-tən-ˌhāg, ˈȯit-ᵊn-ˌhäk-ə\. Town, S Cape Province, S Rep. of South Africa, 20 m. NW of Port Elizabeth; pop. (1967e) 63,400; textiles, motors, tires; railroad shops.

Ujae \ü-ˈjä-ə\. Atoll, Marshall Is., W Pacific Ocean, in the Ralik Chain W of Kwajalein.

Ujain. See UJJAIN.

Ujda. See OUJDA.

Új·fe·hér·tó \ˈüf-ə-har-ˌtō\. Commune, Szabolcs-Szatmor co., NE Hungary, 19 m. N of Debrecen; pop. (1970p) 14,445.

Uji \ˈü-jē\. 1 *or Jap.* **Uji·ga·wa** \ˌu̇j-ē-ˈgä-wə\. River, W cen. Honshū, Japan, immediate outlet of Lake Biwa; joins the Hozu to form the Yodo.
2 City, Kyōto prefecture, Honshū, Japan, 10 m. S of Kyōto; pop. (1970c) 103,497.

Uji·ji \ü-ˈjē-jē\. Town, Kigoma region, Tanzania, on E shore of Lake Tanganyika, 4 m. SE of Kigoma; formerly an important trading town, harbor now very shallow; place where Stanley found Livingstone Oct. 28, 1871.

Uji·na \ü-ˈjēn-ə\. Seaport, Hiroshima prefecture, SW Honshū, Japan, ab. 4 m. from Hiroshima; port for Hiroshima; greatly damaged Aug. 6, 1945 when Hiroshima was hit with atomic bomb.

Uji–yamada. See ISE 2.

Uj·jain *or* **Ujain** \ˈü-ˌjīn\. City, W Madhya Pradesh, W cen. India, ab. 200 m. E of Ahmadabad; pop. (1970e) 159,024; trades in grain; univ. (1957). One of the oldest cities of India and ranked as one of its seven holy cities; ancient capital of Avanti kingdom (6th to 4th cents. B.C.) and of legendary Hindu ruler, Vikramaditya; capital of Malwa c. 120 to c. 395 A.D., when it was a center of Sanskrit learning; also the seat of the Maratha dynasty of Sindhia in 18th cent. Possesses notable examples of Muslim and Hindu architecture—temples, mosques, palaces, mausoleums, and a notable old observatory.

Újvidék. See NOVI SAD.

Ukhrul \ü-ˈkru̇l\. Town, NE Manipur, NE India, ab. 38 m. NNE of Imphal near Burma border; in World War II used by Japanese as base in their invasion of India 1944; retaken by British July 1944.

Ukh·ta \u̇k-ˈtä\ *or formerly* **Chib·yu** \chib-ˈyü\. Town, Komi A.S.S.R., Russian S.F.S.R., U.S.S.R., ab. 160 m. NE of Syktyvkar; pop. (1969e) 57,000.

Uki·ah \yü-ˈkī-ə\. City, ⊗ of Mendocino co., W California, on Russian river 54 m. NNW of Santa Rosa; pop. (1970c) 10,095; sheet metal, wine; packs and ships fruit.

Uk·kel \ˈə(r)k-əl\ *or* **Uc·cle** \ˈ(y)üklᵊ\. Commune, Brabant prov., cen. Belgium, a suburb of Brussels; pop. (1969e) 78,070.

Uk·mer·gė \ˌu̇k-mer-ˈgā\ *or Russ.* **Vil·ko·mir** \ˌvil-kə-ˈmi(ə)r\ *or Ger.* **Wil·ko·mir** \ˈvil-kə-ˌmi(ə)r\. Town, E Lithuanian S.S.R., U.S.S.R., on tributary of Neman river 43 m. NE of Kaunas; pop. (1967e) 19,000.

Ukrai·ni·an Soviet Socialist Republic \yü-ˌkrā-nē-ən-\; *also* **Ukraine** \yü-ˈkrān, -ˈkrīn, ˈyü-ˌ\ *or Russ.* **Ukrai·na** \u̇-ˈkrī-nə\. A constituent republic of the U.S.S.R., bounded on N by the Belorussian S.S.R. and the Russian S.F.S.R., on E by the Russian S.F.S.R., on S by the Sea of Azov and the Black Sea, on SW by the Moldavian S.S.R., and on W by Hungary, Czechoslovakia, and Poland; 233,089 sq. m.; pop. (1970p) 47,136,000; ✱ Kiev. *Physical features:* Chiefly a wide extent of steppe land covered with fertile black earth (*chernozem*); its S border is a less fertile stretch of clayey soil and marshland along the Black Sea; in E and W are low hills. Traversed by three great rivers, Dnieper, Bug, and Donets, and is bordered on the SW by a fourth, the Dniester; in the S are two smaller streams, the Ingul and Ingulets (tributaries of the Bug and Dnieper); all others except the Donets (a tributary of the Don) flow into the Black Sea. *Chief products:* Wheat, corn, rye, barley, sunflower; livestock; coal, iron ore, manganese, natural gas; manufacturing: iron and steel, chemicals, agricultural machinery, transportation equipment; hydroelectric power plants. *Chief towns:* Kiev, Kharkov, Odessa, Donetsk, Dnepropetrovsk.

History: Early history dates back to 6th and 7th cents.: settled by Ukrainians (Little Russians) and Ruthenians; Kiev (*q.v.*), its chief town, was leading principality of Russia until Tatar conquest in 13th cent.; taken by Lithuania (see history at LITHUANIAN SOVIET SOCIALIST REPUBLIC); in 1667 by Treaty of Andrusovo, Russia acquired region E of middle Dnieper and in 1680 the region of the Cossacks; the rest acquired in partition of 1793; Ukrainian People's Republic, established 1917, declared its independence from U.S.S.R. 1918; part taken by Poland 1919–38; remainder reconquered by U.S.S.R., becoming a Soviet republic; entered U.S.S.R. 1923; a central theater of warfare in World War I and World War II; overrun by Axis armies in 1941; gradually rewon by Soviets Sept. 1943 to spring of 1944.

Uku \ˈü-ˌkü\. Island, Gotō Archipelago (*q.v.*), Japan.

Ulala. See GORNO-ALTAISK.

Ulan Ba·tor \ˌü-ˌlän-ˈbä-ˌto̊(ə)r\ *or Chin.* **Ku·lun** \ˈkü-ˈlün\ *or formerly* **Ur·ga** \ˈu̇(ə)r-gə\. City, ✱ of the Mongolian People's Republic, in N cen. part ab. 720 m. NW of Peking, China; pop. (1969e) 262,000; textiles; univ. (1942); junction point of principal Mongolian roads and caravan routes and on branch of Trans-Siberian R.R. from Kyakhta in U.S.S.R. to Peking, China.

History: Founded mid-17th cent. as residency of the Living Buddha (*bodgo-gegen*); in mid-18th cent. a trading center on caravan routes bet. Russia and China; center of Mongolian revolt 1911; occupied by U.S.S.R. 1921 and made capital of a secular Mongolian state 1924; renamed Ulan Bator ("Red Hero") and extensively rebuilt and developed; heavily damaged by floods 1966.

Ulan–Ude \ˌü-ˌlän-ü-ˈdā\ *or formerly* **Verkh·ne·u·dinsk** \ˌv(y)erk-nə-ˈü-ˌdin(t)sk\. City, ✱ of Buryat A.S.S.R., Russian S.F.S.R., U.S.S.R., on Selenga river ab. 70 m. SE of the S end of Lake Baikal; pop. (1970p) 254,000; important junction on Trans-Siberian R.R.; locomotives and railroad cars, lumber, glass, canned meat; railroad shops, boatyards. Founded as fort 1649; made town 1783; renamed 1934.

Ulasutai. See ULIASTAY.

Ulawun. See FATHER, THE.

Ul·cinj \ˈült-ˌsēn-yə\ *or Ital.* **Dul·ci·gno** \dül-ˈchēn-(ˌ)yō\ *or anc.* **Ol·cin·i·um** \äl-ˈsin-ē-əm\. Seaport, Montenegro, S Yugoslavia, on Adriatic Sea near Albanian border; cathedral. Captured by Romans 167 B.C.; pirate stronghold during the Middle Ages; taken from Venetians 1571 by the Turks and held by them until 1880.

Uleåborg. See OULU.

Ule·el·heue \ü-ˌlā-ə-ˈlü-ā, ü-lə-ˈlü-ā\ *or* **Oe·le·ë·heuë** \ü-lā-ə-ˈhü-ə\. Seaport town at N tip of Sumatra, Indonesia, opp. the island of We; port of Banda Atjeh.

Ul·has·na·gar \ˌül-həs-ˈnäg-ər\. Town, Maharashtra, India, ab. 25 m. NE of Bombay; pop. (1967e) 124,797.

Ulianovsk. See ULYANOVSK.

Uliarus. See OLÉRON, ÎLE D'.

Ulias·tay \ˈül-yə-ˌstī\ *or* **Ulias·su·tai** *or* **Ula·su·tai** \ˈül-yə-sə-ˌtī\ *or* **Dzhib·kha·lan·tu** \ˈjēb-kə-lən-ˌtü\. Town, W cen. Mongolian People's Republic, in mountainous district ab. 460 m. W of Ulan Bator; transport and trading center; square fortress built 1765.

Ulin·di \ü-ˈlin-dē\. River, S cen. Africa; ab. 100 m. long; rises in E cen. Zaire, flows WNW into the Lualaba river.

Uli·thi \ü-ˈlē-thē\. Islands (atoll group), W Caroline Is., W Pacific Ocean, 108 m. ENE of Yap, and 400 m. SW of Guam. Chief islands Falalop and Asor on the E and Mogmog on the N. Lagoon is 19 m. long by 5 to 10 m. wide and is excellent anchorage. Discovered 1791; in World War II taken by U.S. Sept. 20–21, 1944 and developed into major advance fleet base.

Uljan. See UGLJAN.

Ulloa. See ULÚA.

Ulls·wa·ter \ˈəlz-ˌwo̊t-ər, -ˌwät-\. Lake, Lake District, NW England, on border bet. Cumberland and Westmorland; 3½ sq. m.; 7½ m. long; max. depth 205 ft.

Ulm \ˈu̇lm\. Industrial and commercial city, Baden-Württemburg, West Germany, on Danube river near mouth of Iller 45 m. SE of Stuttgart; pop. (1969e) 91,852; motor vehicles, electrical equipment, furniture, leather goods, hats, beer, dairy products; notable 14th cent. cathedral with 528-ft. tower, 14th cent. town hall, 16th cent. corn exchange; univ. (1967).

History: First mentioned 854; chartered 1027; imperial city 1155–1802; accepted Reformation 1530 and was member of League of Schmalkalden; scene of battle October 17, 1805 in which Napoleon defeated the Austrians; to Württemburg 1810; in World War II occupied by French Apr. 24, 1945. Birthplace of Albert Einstein.

Ul·san \ˈül-ˈsän\. Town, South Kyŏngsang prov., South Korea, 33 m. NNE of Pu[illegible]; pop. (1970e) 159,340.

Ul·ster \ˈəl-stər\. **1** County [illegible] York. See table at NEW YORK.

2 Former province, N Ireland; 8331 sq. m., including water 8567 sq. m.; now forms Northern Ireland (6 counties) and Ulster prov. of Eire (3 counties).

History: Ancient Irish kingdom; a center of Irish missionary activity from 6th cent. A.D.; home of O'Neills (earls of Tyrone) who rebelled against English rule 1598–1603; most of land forfeited to English crown by James I and settled with Protestant Scots, Welsh, and English; further colonized after Cromwellian settlement; its Protestant majority made it oppose union of Northern Ireland (*q.v.*) with Eire (see IRELAND).

3 Province, N Eire, comprising counties of Cavan, Donegal, and Monaghan; 3093 sq. m.; pop. (1966c) 208,283.

Ulúa \ü-ˈlü-ə\ *also* **Ulloa** \ü-ˈyō-ə\. River, NW Honduras; ab. 200 m. long; flows NE into the Gulf of Honduras. See YOJOA, LAKE.

Ulu Dağ \ˌü-lə-ˈda(g)\ *or anc.* **Olym·pus** \ō-ˈlim-pəs\. Mountain, Bursa prov., NW Turkey, SE of Bursa; 8343 ft.

Ulugh Muztagh. See WU-LU-K'O-MU-SHIH.

Ulun·di \ü-ˈlün-dē\. Village (*kraal*), Natal, E Rep. of South Africa, ab. 115 m. NNE of Durban; formerly capital of

Zululand; nearby Lord Chelmsford defeated the Zulus July 4, 1879.

Ul·ver·ston \ˈəl-vər-stən\. Urban district, Lancashire, NW England, on Morecambe Bay 55 m. N of Liverpool; pop. (1971p) 11,888; leather, pharmaceuticals.

Ul·ya·novsk *or* **Ul·ia·novsk** \ül-ˈyän-əfsk\ *or formerly* **Sim·birsk** \sim-ˈbi(ə)rsk\. City, ✱ of Ulyanovsk Oblast, Russian S.F.S.R., U.S.S.R., on right bank of the Volga 485 m. ESE of Moscow; pop. (1970p) 351,000; river port and railroad junction; machinery, flour, beer, vodka; built along the river on top of a hill, with a major railroad bridge across the Volga. Founded 1648; birthplace of V. I. Lenin (V. I. Ulyanov); renamed in his honor 1924.

Ulyanovsk Oblast \-ˈō-bləst, -ˌblast\. Subdivision of E Russian S.F.S.R., U.S.S.R., on both sides of the middle Volga; 14,402 sq. m.; pop. (1970p) 1,225,000; ✱ Ulyanovsk. Predominantly agricultural, with Ulyanovsk the only major town. Formerly part of Kuibyshev Oblast; established as separate oblast 1943.

Ulys·ses \yu̇-ˈlis-(ˌ)ēz\. 1 City, ⊗ of Grant co., SW Kansas; pop. (1970c) 3779; carbon black; corn.
2 Town, Tomkins co., New York; pop. (1970c) 4500.

Ülzen. See UELZEN.

Uman \ü-ˈman(-yə)\. City, S Kiev Oblast, Ukrainian S.S.R., U.S.S.R., 125 m. S of Kiev; pop. (1969e) 64,000; center of a farming district. Formerly a Polish town; long fought over by Cossacks and Poles; in World War II held by Germans 1941–44.

Uman \ˈü-ˌmän\. Island, SE part of Truk Is. (*q.v.*).

Uma·nak \ˈü-mə-ˌnak\. Settlement, S shore of **Umanak Fjord** (inlet N of Nûgssuaq Penin.), W Greenland, 70°55′N, 53°W; pop. (1968e) 2348.

Uma·nan·da \ˌu̇m-ə-ˈnən-də\. See GAUHATI.

Umar·kot \ˈü-mär-ˌkōt\. Town, E Sind, Pakistan, in SW Thar Desert; birthplace of Akbar.

Uma·til·la \ˌyü-mə-ˈtil-ə\. 1 River, NE Oregon; ab. 80 m. long; rises in N Union co., flows W and N into Columbia river in NW Umatilla co.
2 County in Oregon. See table at OREGON.

Um·ba \ˈəm-bə\. River, Tanzania and Kenya, E Africa; flows E into the Indian Ocean in Kenya just N of Tanzania boundary.

Um·ba·gog Lake \əm-ˈbā-ˌgäg-\. Lake, part in Coos co., New Hampshire, and part in Oxford co., Maine; 10 m. long; source of the Androscoggin river.

Um·be·lu·zi \ˌəm-bə-ˈlü-zē\ *or* **Um·be·lo·si** \ˌəm-bə-ˈlō-zē\. River, Swaziland and S Mozambique, SE Africa, ab. 120 m. long; flows E into Delagoa Bay.

Um·boi \ˈüm-ˌbȯi\ *or* **Rooke** \ˈru̇k\. Island bet. W end of New Britain I., Bismarck Archipelago, and Huon Penin., E New Guinea; separated from New Britain by Dampier Strait and from New Guinea by Vitiaz Strait; ab. 25 m. long by 15 m. wide; highest point 5430 ft. Taken by Allies Feb. 12, 1944 to cover operations on New Britain I.

Um·brel·la Point \ˌəm-ˌbrel-ə-\. Cape, NW coast of Jamaica, West Indies.

Um·bria \ˈəm-brē-ə\. Autonomous region, cen. Italy; 3265 sq. m.; pop. (1968e) 783,274; ✱ Perugia (for provincial division, see table at ITALY); in Apennines; surrounded by Tuscany, Latium, and the Marches; agriculture (grain, sugar beet, grapes; pigs); chemical, textile, and electrical industries supported by hydroelectric power complex at Terni.
History: Inhabited by ancient Umbrians, known through the Eugubine tables found at Gubbio 1444 A.D.; conquered by Etruscans; came under Rome c. 300 B.C.; during Christian era became part of States of the Church (*q.v.*); seat of Umbrian school of painting in Middle Ages; home of St. Francis of Assisi and Jacopone da Todi. In World War II occupied by Allies June–July 1944.

Umbrian Apennines. See table at APENNINES.

Umbro. See OMBRONE.

Umbro, Appennino *or* **Umbro–Marchigiano, Appennino.** See table at APENNINES.

Ume \ˈü-mə\. River, Västerbotten co., N Sweden; 286 m. long; flows SE into upper Gulf of Bothnia.

Umeå \ˈü-mə-ˌō\. Seaport, ⊗ of Västerbotten co., N Sweden, on the Gulf of Bothnia at the mouth of Ume river; pop. (1970e) 54,530; manufactures wood pulp, machinery, furniture; exports tar; univ. (1963); burned by Russians 1720.

Um·fo·lo·zi National Park \ˌəm-fə-ˈlō-zē-\. Game reserve, NE Natal, Rep. of South Africa; 113 sq. m.; white rhinoceros; est. 1897.

Umgeni. See MGENI.

Uming·an \ü-ˈmēŋ-ˌän\. Municipality, Pangasinan prov., Luzon, Phil., 40 m. ESE of Lingayen; pop. (1969e) 41,800.

Um·ma \ˈəm-ə\. Important city of ancient Sumer, flourishing in the 3d millennium B.C.; its site is in S Mesopotamia, WNW of Lagash.

Umm al–Qai·wain \ˈüm-al-kī-ˈwīn\. 1 Emirate. See UNITED ARAB EMIRATES.
2 Coastal town, its ✱; pop. (1968c) 2828.

Umm Durmān. See OMDURMAN.

Um·nak \ˈüm-ˌnak\. Large island, W part of Fox Is. group, Aleutian Is., SW Alaska, separated from Unalaska I. on the NE by **Umnak Pass**; 70 m. long by 12 m. wide; 675 sq. m.; highest point 7050 ft.

Ump·qua \ˈəm(p)-ˌkwȯ\. River, SW Oregon; ab. 200 m. long; formed by union of two branches (North Umpqua and South Umpqua) in W cen. Douglas co., flows N and W into Pacific Ocean; navigable for 20 m.

Um·ta·li \u̇m-ˈtäl-ē\. Town, NE Rhodesia, S Africa, on Mozambique border 130 m. ESE of Salisbury; pop. (1970e) 18,000; distribution and trade center for mining and agricultural section; silver, lead, copper, iron, and especially gold found in region; soil particularly adapted to tobacco.

Um·tam·vu·na \ˌu̇m-ˌtam-ˈvü-nə\. River, E Rep. of South Africa; ab. 50 m. long; flows into Indian Ocean and marks part of boundary bet. Cape Province and Natal.

Um·ta·ta \u̇m-ˈtät-ə\. 1 River, E Rep. of South Africa; 50 m. long; divides Tembuland from Pondoland.
2 Town, ✱ of Transkei, E Cape Province, S Rep. of South Africa, on Umtata river 114 m. NNE of East London; pop. (1967e) 17,200.

Umua·ra·ma \ˌu̇m-wə-ˈrä-mə\. Municipality, Paraná state, S Brazil, 280 m. WNW of Curitiba; pop. (1968e) 63,462.

Umur·bro·gol \ˌü-mər-ˈbrō-ˌgȯl\. Mountain, Peleliu I., Palau Is. See BLOODY NOSE RIDGE.

Um·zim·ku·lu \ˌu̇m-zəm-ˈkü-(ˌ)lü\. River, S Natal, E Rep. of South Africa; ab. 125 m. long; flows SE into Indian Ocean at Port Shepstone.

Um·zim·vu·bu \ˌu̇m-zəm-ˈvü-(ˌ)bü\. River, Cape Province, S Rep. of South Africa; ab. 300 m. long; flows SE into Indian Ocean at Port St. Johns.

Una \ˈü-nə\. River, NW cen. Yugoslavia; 159 m. long; flows NW past Bihać, then turns NE and flows into Sava river; forms NW boundary of Bosnia and Herzegovina, separating it from Croatia.

Una, Mount \-ˈü-nə\. Peak, N South I., New Zealand; 7540 ft.

Una·ka Mountains \yu̇-ˌnā-kə-\. Range of the Appalachian Mts., Unicoi and Carter cos., NE Tennessee, along the Tennessee-North Carolina boundary; includes **Mount Unaka** 5258 ft. in Unicoi co.

Un·a·las·ka \ˌən-ə-ˈlas-kə\. 1 Large island, Aleutian Is., SW Alaska, in Fox Is. group; next to Unimak in size; 75 m. long, greatest width ab. 25 m.; 1064 sq. m. On it is Makushin volcano 6678 ft. and at E end on Amaknak I. in Unalaska Bay is the U.S. naval base of Dutch Harbor (*q.v.*).

2 City on Unalaska Bay, E end of island opp. Dutch Harbor; pop. (1970c) 178; oldest settlement of Aleutian Is., established by Russians 1760–65.

Unalaska Bay. Inlet, N coast at E end of Unalaska I., E Aleutian Is.; ab. 12 m. long and 9 m. wide at its mouth; Amaknak I. is in S cen. part. See DUTCH HARBOR.

Unao. See UNNAO.

Unayzah. See ANAIZA.

Unci. See ALMERÍA 2.

Un·com·pah·gre Peak \ˌən-kəm-ˌpäg-rē-\. Mountain, Hinsdale co., SW Colorado; 14,309 ft.; highest in the San Juan Mts.

Undavalle. See VIJAYAWADA.

Unfederated Malay States. Formerly, the Malay states of British Malaya on the Malay Penin. not federated: Johore, Kedah, Kelantan, Perlis, Trengganu; total area 22,276 sq. m. See MALAYSIA and names of individual states.

Un·ga \'ůŋ-gə\. 1 Island, Shumagin Is. group off S end of Alaska Penin.; ab. 20 m. long.

2 Village on island.

Ungarn. See HUNGARY.

Un·ga·va \ən-'gā-və, -'gäv-ə\. Region, Canada, E of Hudson Bay and N of Eastmain river, separated from Labrador on the E by the height of land. Organized 1895 as a part of Northwest Territories; transferred 1912 as New Quebec to province of Quebec; divided 1927 with larger part remaining as New Quebec (*q.v.*) and E part assigned to Newfoundland as part of Labrador. Covered with hills, lakes, and rivers; largely unexplored and sparsely inhabited (chiefly Eskimos). Has great mineral wealth.

Ungava Bay. Large inlet of S Hudson Strait, NE Quebec, E Canada; receives several large rivers, as the Koksoak, Leaf, and Payne.

Ungava Peninsula. The N part of New Quebec dist., Quebec, Canada.

Ung·gi \'üŋ-gē\ *or formerly* **Yu·ki** \'yü-kē\. Seaport, North Hamgyŏng prov., North Korea, N of Rashin close to U.S.S.R. border; occupied by Soviet troops Aug. 12, 1945.

Ungvár. See UZHGOROD.

Uni·ão dos Pal·ma·res \ü-'nyaů(ⁿ)n-düs-pəl-'mä-rəs\. City, Alagoas state, E Brazil, 40 m. NW of Maceió; munic. pop. (1968e) 50,166.

Uni·coi \'yü-nə-ˌkȯi\. County in Tennessee. See table at TENNESSEE.

Unicoi Mountains. Range of the Appalachian Mts., chiefly in Monroe co., SE Tennessee, along the Tennessee-North Carolina boundary.

Unieux \ü-'nyə\. Commune, Loire dept., SE cen. France; pop. (1962c) 7718; steelworks.

Unie van Suid–Afrika. See SOUTH AFRICA, REPUBLIC OF.

Uni·je \'ü-ni-ˌyā\ *or Ital.* **Unie** \'ü-nē-(ˌ)ā\. Small island, W of the island of Lošinj, NW Yugoslavia; formerly Italian.

Uni·mak \'yü-nə-ˌmak\. Largest island of the Aleutian Is., in Fox Is. group SW of tip of Alaska Penin.; 65 m. long by 25 m. wide; 1600 sq. m.; on it is Shishaldin volcano 9978 ft.

Unimak Pass \ˌyü-nə-ˌmak-\. Wide passage bet. Bering Sea and North Pacific Ocean, SW of Unimak I.

Un·ion \'yün-yən\. 1 River, Hancock co., SE Maine; ab. 50 m. long; flows S into Bluehill Bay.

2 Name of a parish in Louisiana and of counties in seventeen states of the U.S. See tables at ARKANSAS, FLORIDA, GEORGIA, ILLINOIS, INDIANA, IOWA, KENTUCKY, LOUISIANA, MISSISSIPPI, NEW JERSEY, NEW MEXICO, NORTH CAROLINA, OHIO, OREGON, PENNSYLVANIA, SOUTH CAROLINA, SOUTH DAKOTA, TENNESSEE.

3 City, ⊗ of Franklin co., E Missouri, 50 m. WSW of St. Louis; pop. (1970c) 5183; shoes; agriculture.

4 Township, Union co., NE New Jersey, 5 m. WNW of Elizabeth; pop. (1970c) 52,878; paint and lacquers, steel, metal goods; truck farms; Newark State Coll. (1855). Settled c. 1749 by colonists from Connecticut, hence its original name **Connecticut Farms;** figured in American Revolution (battle of Connecticut Farms 1780).

5 Village, Montgomery co., SW Ohio; pop. (1970c) 3654.

6 City, Union co., NE Oregon, 30 m. N of Baker; pop. (1970c) 1531.

7 City, ⊗ of Union co., NW South Carolina; pop. (1970c) 10,775; textiles, fertilizer; peaches.

8 Town, ⊗ of Monroe co., SE West Virginia; pop. (1970c) 566.

9 Islands, cen. Pacific Ocean. See TOKELAU ISLANDS.

Union, La. See LA UNION.

Unión, La. See LA UNIÓN.

Union, Mount. Peak in cen. Yavapai co., cen. Arizona; 7973 ft.

Union Beach. Borough and summer resort, Monmouth co., E cen. New Jersey, on Raritan Bay 7 m. SE of Perth Amboy; pop. (1970c) 6472.

Union City. 1 City, Alameda co., W California, S of Oakland; pop. (1970c) 14,724; sugar refinery, foundry; agriculture.

2 Subdivision of borough of Naugatuck, Connecticut. See NAUGATUCK 2.

3 City, Fulton co., NW cen. Georgia, 15 m. SW of Atlanta; pop. (1970c) 3031.

4 City, Randolph co., E Indiana, 30 m. E of Muncie on the Ohio border; pop. (1970c) 3995.

5 Industrial city, Hudson co., NE New Jersey, on Hudson river 3 m. N of and adjoining Jersey City; pop. (1970c) 58,537; embroidery, soap, toilet preparations and perfume, incandescent lamps; formed 1925 by merger of West Hoboken and Union Hill.

6 Borough, Erie co., NW corner of Pennsylvania, 20 m. SE of Erie; pop. (1970c) 3631; furniture; dairy, poultry farms.

7 Town, ⊗ of Obion co., NW Tennessee, 34 m. NNE of Dyersburg; pop. (1970c) 11,925; footwear, automobile parts, dairy products, clothing; packing plant; cotton, soybeans.

Union·dale \'yün-yən-ˌdāl\. Urban community (unincorporated), Nassau co., SE New York, on Long I.; pop. (1970c) 22,077.

Unión de Re·yes \ü-ˌnyȯn-də-'rā-əs\. Town, Matanzas prov., W cen. Cuba; pop. (1967e) 8120; junction point on railroad 17 m. S of Matanzas.

Union Grove. Village, Racine co., SE Wisconsin, 15 m. W of Racine; pop. (1970c) 2703.

Union Island. Island, one of the Grenadines, West Indies; 4 sq. m.; administratively a part of St. Vincent.

Union Islands. See TOKELAU ISLANDS.

Union Lake. Lake, cen. Cumberland co., SW New Jersey; ab. 3½ m. long; a widening of the Maurice river.

Union of Burma. See BURMA.

Union of India. See INDIA 2.

Union of South Africa. See SOUTH AFRICA, REPUBLIC OF.

Union of So·vi·et Socialist Republics \-'sōv-ē-'et-, -'säv-, -ē-ət-\; *commonly shortened to* **Soviet Union** *or* **U.S.S.R.;** *often popularly* **Rus·sia** \'rəsh-ə\. Republic, E Europe and N and cen. Asia; 8,649,512 sq. m. (exclusive of the Sea of Azov and the White Sea); pop. (1970p) 241,748,000; ✻ Moscow. *Physical features:* The largest country on the globe, having a max. E-W extent of ab. 6800 m. and a max. N-S extent of ab. 2800 m.; extends across 11 time zones; in Europe has common boundaries with: Finland, Poland, Czechoslovakia, Hungary, and Romania; in Asia has common boundaries with: Turkey, Iran, Afghanistan, China, Mongolian People's Republic, and North Korea; wide variety of physical features, incl. the fertile black-earth lands of the Ukrainian S.S.R., the deserts of Central Asia, the tundra of the north, and the high mountains of the Pamirs, Caucasus, Urals, and Kamchatka; contains some of the world's largest rivers: Volga, Ob, Yenisei, Lena, and many smaller but important streams, as the Dnieper, Don, Ural, Amur, etc. In the SW in Europe borders on the Black Sea and in the NW on the Baltic; its N coastline extends ab. 3000 m. on the Arctic Ocean and for more than 1000 m. along the Pacific. Most of the Caspian Sea lies within its borders; other large inland waters are the

Aral Sea and Lakes Baikal and Balkhash. Islands incl.: Novaya Zemlya, Franz Josef Land, Severnaya Zemlya, New Siberian Is., Wrangel I. (*qq.v.*). For further details, see entries for the constituent republics. *Chief products:* Wheat, corn, barley, sugar beet, cotton, flax, potatoes; livestock raising, fishing, lumbering; very extensive mineral resources incl. coal (ab. 50% of est. world reserves), oil (ab. 25% of est. world reserves), natural gas, iron ore, manganese, chromium, molybdenum, copper, lead, zinc, antimony, gold, salt, phosphates, asbestos; manufacturing: iron and steel, chemicals, textiles, transportation equipment, agricultural machinery, electrical apparatus. *Chief cities:* Moscow, Leningrad, Kiev, Tashkent, Baku, Kharkov, Gorki, Novosibirsk, Kuibyshev, Sverdlovsk, Minsk, Odessa. Comprises the following 15 constituent (Union) republics (for pronunciation of their names, see their individual entries):

NAME	AREA[1] (sq. m.)	POP. (1970p)	CAPITAL
Armenian S.S.R.	11,506	2,493,000	Yerevan
Azerbaijan S.S.R.	33,436	5,111,000	Baku
Belorussian S.S.R.	80,154	9,003,000	Minsk
Estonian S.S.R.	17,413	1,357,000	Tallinn
Georgian S.S.R.	26,911	4,688,000	Tbilisi
Kazakh S.S.R.	1,048,300	12,850,000	Alma-Ata
Kirgiz S.S.R.	76,641	2,933,000	Frunze
Latvian S.S.R.	24,595	2,365,000	Riga
Lithuanian S.S.R.	25,174	3,129,000	Vilnius
Moldavian S.S.R.	13,012	3,572,000	Kishinev
Russian S.F.S.R.	6,592,812	130,090,000	Moscow
Tadzhik S.S.R.	55,251	2,900,000	Dushanbe
Turkmen S.S.R.	188,455	2,158,000	Ashkhabad
Ukrainian S.S.R.	233,089	47,136,000	Kiev
Uzbek S.S.R.	173,591	11,963,000	Tashkent

[1]Exclusive of the Sea of Azov and the White Sea.

History: For earlier history, see RUSSIA. By treaty of Brest Litovsk (signed with Germany Mar. 3, 1918) the government of soviets gave up Finland, Poland, Estonia, Latvia, Lithuania, Moldavia, Ukraine, Transcaucasian Federation, but terms of this treaty abrogated by Treaty of Versailles June 28, 1919; period of unrest and civil war (1918–20) followed by severe famine 1921; state Communist methods modified 1921 by New Economic Policy; Union of Soviet Socialist Republics organized 1922 from soviet republics of Russian S.F.S.R. (*q.v.*), Ukrainian S.S.R., Belorussian S.S.R., and Transcaucasian Federation; with death of Lenin 1924 began struggle for power among leaders which ended with victory of Stalin 1926 and expulsion of Trotsky from the country 1929; by two Five-Year Plans (1928 and 1933) stimulated the industrial and agricultural development of the country; adopted new constitution 1936; purged country of "disloyal" persons 1936–39; launched third Five-Year Plan 1938. Signed nonaggression pact with Germany Aug. 1939; occupied E Poland 1939; took from Finland (*q.v.*) Karelian Isthmus and other territories 1939–40; in 1940 incorporated Bessarabia and N Bucovina and the Baltic countries; invaded June 22, 1941 by Germany, whose armies approached but did not take Moscow and Leningrad 1941–42; Kuibyshev temporary capital 1941–42; Ukrainian S.S.R. and Crimea (Crimean Oblast) overrun and Stalingrad (now Volgograd; farthest point reached) entered by Germans Sept. 16, 1942. First Soviet counteroffensive regained some ground Nov. 1941–June 1942; second begun Jan. 1943 and continued through 1943 to 1945; annexed Tannu Tuva (see TUVA A.S.S.R.) 1944; expelled last Germans from Soviet territory 1944 and Soviet troops reached Berlin Apr. 1945; one of the four powers occupying Germany after the end of the war; invaded Manchuria Aug. 8, 1945; annexed S part of Sakhalin I. 1946 (see KARAFUTO); started on fourth Five-Year Plan 1946. Founding member of the United Nations 1945; established the Communist Information Bureau (Cominform) 1947; brought about the establishment of Communist regimes throughout most of E Europe 1945–48; expelled Yugoslavia from the Cominform 1948; exploded its first atomic bomb 1949; signed treaty of alliance with China 1950 and supported North Korea and China during Korean War (1950–53) with large-scale military aid; adopted fifth Five-Year Plan (1951–55); death of Joseph Stalin Mar. 1953 followed by limited degree of political and cultural liberalization 1955 ff.; exploded its first hydrogen bomb 1953; restored relations with Yugoslavia and withdrew its forces from Austria 1955; established the Warsaw Treaty Organization 1955; intervened militarily in Hungary 1956, suppressing anti-Communist revolt; initiated sixth Five-Year Plan 1956 (cut short 1958 and replaced by a Seven-Year Plan 1959–65 which in 1966 was admitted to have been a failure); deterioration of Sino-Soviet relations 1959 ff.; during 21st Party Congress (1961) announced completion of the building of "Socialism" and declared new goal to be the building of "Communism" with emphasis on higher living standards; launched first manned orbital space flight 1961 (see table below); installed ballistic missiles in Cuba but forced to withdraw these under U.S. pressure 1962; signed nuclear test-ban treaty 1963; deposed Premier N.S. Khrushchev Oct. 1964, and began partial reversal of move towards liberalization; adopted new Five-Year Plan 1966–70 (plan retained emphasis on heavy industry but allotted greater proportion of investment capital to development of light industry); invaded Czechoslovakia 1968, suppressing that country's liberalization program; series of border clashes with China (the first of which believed to have taken place 1964) publicly acknowledged 1969.

Union Pass. Mountain pass, W Wyoming, crossing the Wind River Range; used 1807 by John Colter, trapper and explorer, member of Lewis and Clark Expedition.

Union Point. Town, Greene co., NE cen. Georgia, 30 m. SE of Athens; pop. (1970c) 1624.

Union Springs. City, ⊗ of Bullock co., SE Alabama; pop. (1970c) 4324; textiles, lumber.

Un·ion·town \ˈyün-yən-ˌtau̇n\. City, ⊗ of Fayette co., SW Pennsylvania, SSE of Pittsburgh; pop. (1970c) 16,282; glassware, steel scaffolds, lumber; dairy products; coal mines. Founded 1769; to SE is site of Fort Necessity (*q.v.*) built 1754.

Union Valley Dam. See UNITED STATES, *Dams and Reservoirs.*

Un·ion·ville \ˈyün-yən-ˌvil\. 1 Urban community (unincorporated) in the town of Farmington, Connecticut. See FARMINGTON 2.

2 City, ⊗ of Putnam co., N Missouri, 30 m. NW of Kirksville; pop. (1970c) 2075.

United Arab Emir·ates \-i-ˈmi(ə)r-əts, -ˌāts\; *formerly known as* **Tru·cial States** \ˈtrüsh-əl-\ *or* **Trucial Oman** \-ō-ˈmän, -ˈman\ *also* **Trucial Coast.** Federation of seven states, E Arabian Penin., extending from Qatar to Gulf of Oman; total length of coast ab. 400 m.; oil production (Abu Dhabi, Dubai), fishing, herding; dates, tobacco. The member states are listed in the following table (for pronunciation of their names, see their individual entries):

NAME	AREA (sq. m.)	POP. (1968c)	CAPITAL
Abu Dhabi	26,000	46,375	Abu Dhabi
Ajman	100	4,245	Ajman
Dubai	1,500	59,092	Dubai
Fujairah	450	9,724	Fujairah
Ras al-Khaimah	650	24,482	Ras al-Khaimah
Sharjah	1,000	31,480	Sharjah
Umm al-Qaiwain	300	3,740	Umm al-Qaiwain

History: Treaty of peace concluded between Great Britain and native rulers 1820; in further treaties (1839, 1853, 1892) rulers agreed to suppression of slave trade and restriction of foreign relations to Great Britain; establishment of Trucial Council 1952; defense treaties with Great

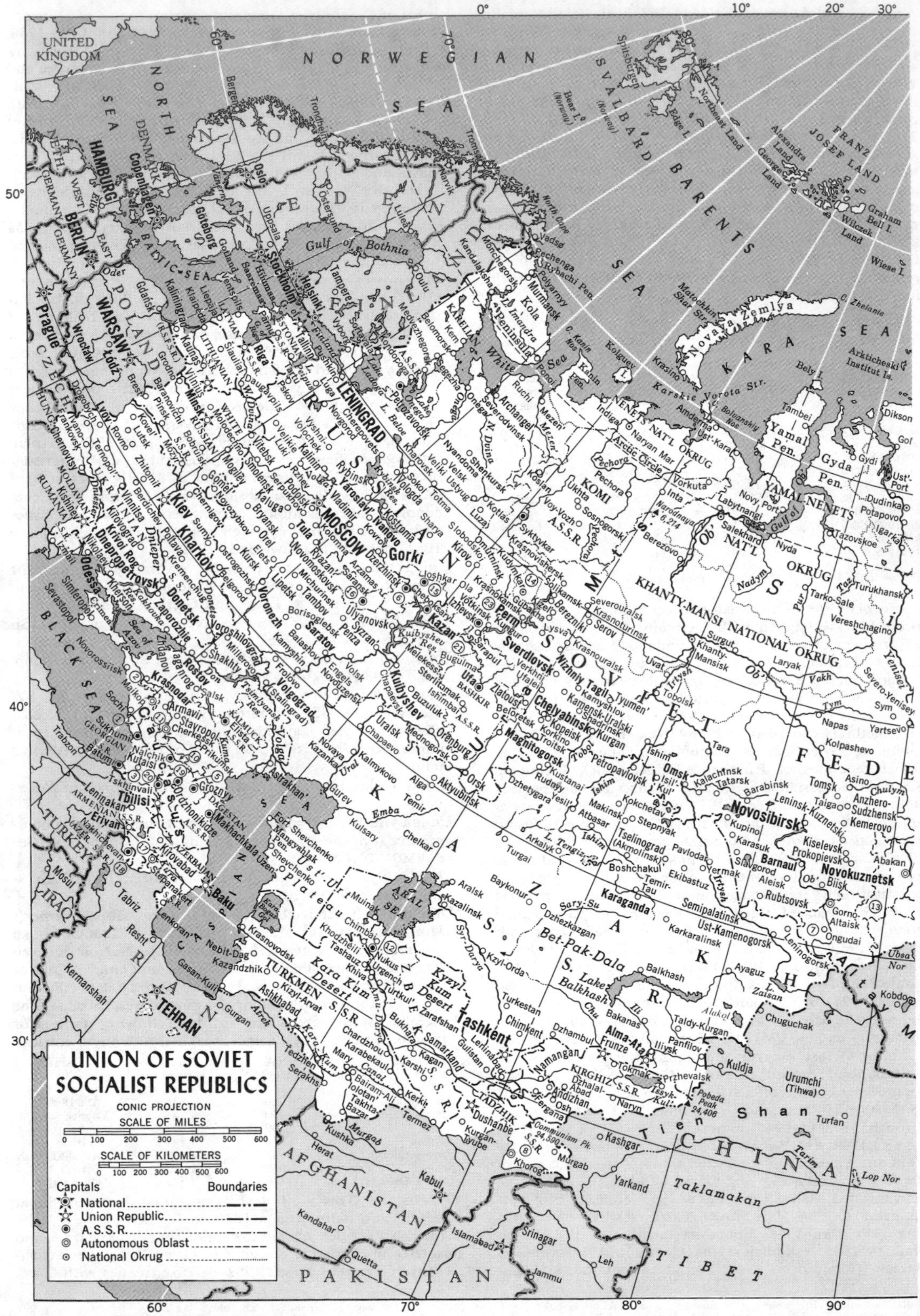
UNION OF SOVIET
SOCIALIST REPUBLICS
CONIC PROJECTION
SCALE OF MILES
0 100 200 300 400 500 600
SCALE OF KILOMETERS
0 100 200 300 400 500 600
Capitals
Boundaries
National
Union Republic
A.S.S.R.
Autonomous Oblast
National Okrug
NORWEGIAN SEA
NORTH SEA
BALTIC SEA
BARENTS SEA
KARA SEA
BLACK SEA
CASPIAN SEA
ARAL SEA
SVALBARD (Norway)
FRANZ JOSEF LAND
Novaya Zemlya
UNITED KINGDOM
DENMARK
NORWAY
SWEDEN
FINLAND
POLAND
CZECH.
HUNG.
RUMANIA
TURKEY
IRAQ
IRAN
AFGHANISTAN
PAKISTAN
CHINA
TIBET
RUSSIAN S.F.S.R.
KAZAKH S.S.R.
UZBEK S.S.R.
TURKMEN S.S.R.
TADZHIK S.S.R.
KIRGHIZ S.S.R.
UKRAINIAN S.S.R.
WHITE RUSSIAN S.S.R.
GEORGIAN S.S.R.
ARMENIAN S.S.R.
AZERBAIJAN S.S.R.
MOSCOW
LENINGRAD
Kiev
Kharkov
Gorki
Kuibyshev
Sverdlovsk
Novosibirsk
Tashkent
Alma-Ata
Frunze
Dushanbe
Ashkhabad
Baku
Tbilisi
Erivan
TEHRAN
Kabul
Stockholm
Helsinki
Oslo
Copenhagen
BERLIN
WARSAW
Prague
Tien Shan
Kara Kum Desert
Kyzyl Kum Desert
Bet-Pak-Dala
Taklamakan
Communism Pk. 24,590
Pobeda Peak 24,406
Narodnaya 6,214
Arctic Circle
50°
40°
30°
60°
70°
80°
90°
0°
10°
20°
30°

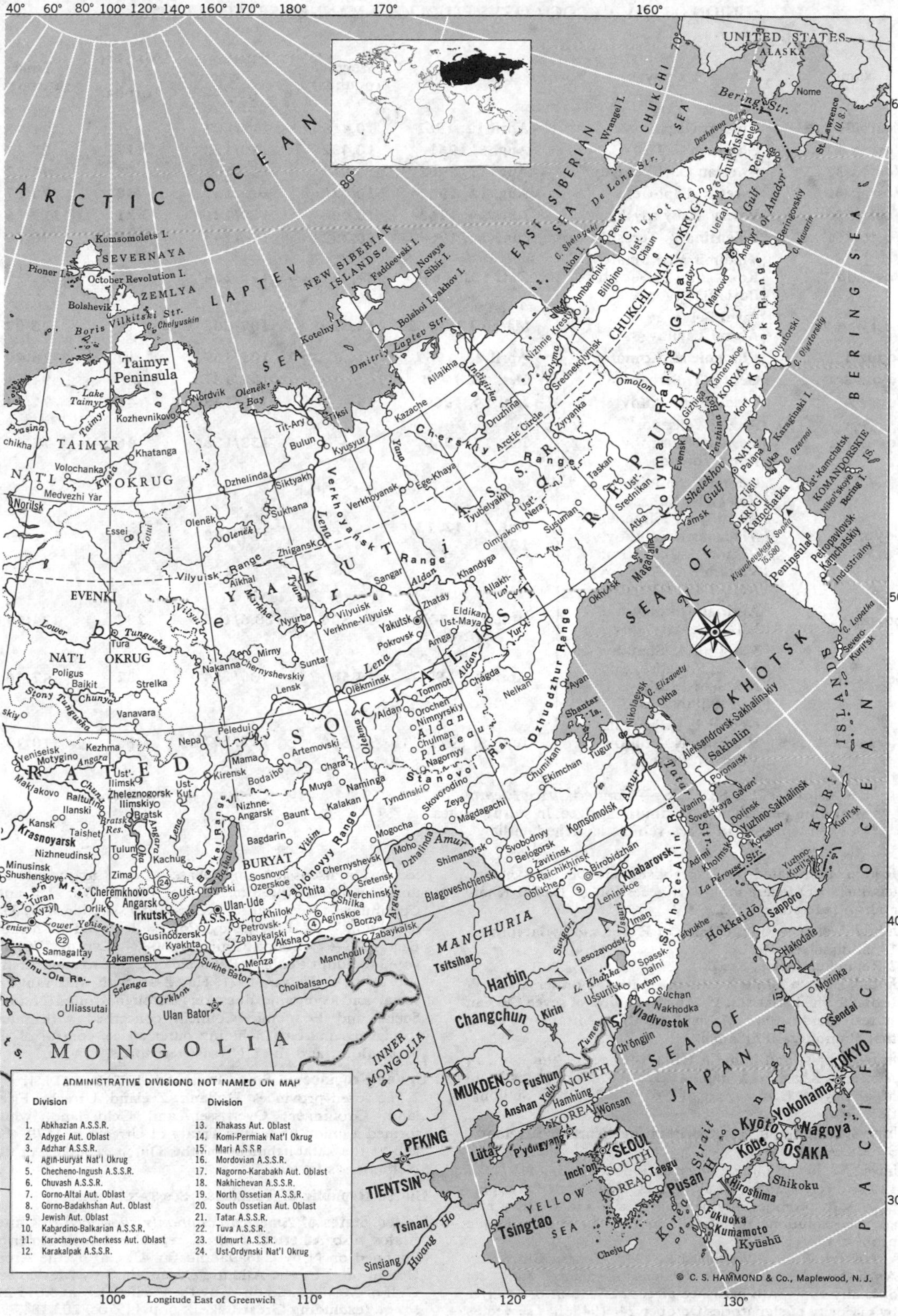
ARCTIC OCEAN
LAPTEV SEA
EAST SIBERIAN SEA
CHUKCHI SEA
BERING SEA
SEA OF OKHOTSK
SEA OF JAPAN
YELLOW SEA
PACIFIC OCEAN
UNITED STATES
ALASKA
Bering Str.
Nome
St. Lawrence I. (U.S.)
Wrangel I.
De Long Str.
Chukotski Pen.
Gulf of Anadyr'
Komsomolets I.
SEVERNAYA ZEMLYA
Pioner I.
October Revolution I.
Bolshevik I.
Boris Vilkitski Str.
C. Chelyuskin
NEW SIBERIAN ISLANDS
Faddeevski I.
Novaya Sibir I.
Kotelny I.
Bolshoi Lyakhov I.
Dmitriy Laptev Str.
Taimyr Peninsula
Lake Taimyr
TAIMYR NAT'L OKRUG
EVENKI NAT'L OKRUG
CHUKCHI NAT'L OKRUG
KORYAK NAT'L OKRUG
YAKUT A.S.S.R.
BURYAT A.S.S.R.
RUSSIAN SOVIET FEDERATED SOCIALIST REPUBLIC
Verkhoyansk Range
Cherskiy Range
Kolyma Range
Anadyr Range (Gydan)
Koryak Range
Chukot Range
Dzhugdzhur Range
Stanovoi Range
Yablonovy Range
Sikhote-Alin' Range
Aldan Plateau
Arctic Circle
Kamchatka Peninsula
Klyuchevskaya Sopka 15,580
Petropavlovsk-Kamchatskiy
KOMANDORSKIE IS.
Bering I.
KURIL ISLANDS
Sakhalin
Tatar Str.
La Pérouse Str.
Shelekhov Gulf
Magadan
Okhotsk
Yakutsk
Tiksi
Verkhoyansk
Norilsk
Khatanga
Mirny
Lensk
Olëkminsk
Vilyuisk
Kirensk
Bratsk
Irkutsk
Ulan-Ude
Chita
Krasnoyarsk
Kansk
Angarsk
Blagoveshchensk
Khabarovsk
Komsomolsk
Birobidzhan
Vladivostok
Nakhodka
Ussuriisk
Yuzhno-Sakhalinsk
Aleksandrovsk-Sakhalinskiy
Lake Baikal
MONGOLIA
Ulan Bator
Choibalsan
Uliassutai
MANCHURIA
INNER MONGOLIA
CHINA
Harbin
Changchun
Kirin
Mukden
Fushun
Anshan
PEKING
TIENTSIN
Tsinan
Tsingtao
Lüta
Tsitsihar
Manchouli
NORTH KOREA
P'yongyang
SEOUL
SOUTH KOREA
Inch'on
Taegu
Pusan
Cheju
Korea Strait
JAPAN
Hokkaidō
Sapporo
Hakodate
Honshu
Sendai
TOKYO
Yokohama
Nagoya
Kyōto
Kobe
ŌSAKA
Hiroshima
Shikoku
Fukuoka
Kumamoto
Kyūshū
Lena
Yenisei
Amur
Aldan
Kolyma
Indigirka
Yana
Lower Tunguska
Stony Tunguska
Vilyui
Angara
Ussuri
Sungari
ADMINISTRATIVE DIVISIONS NOT NAMED ON MAP
Division
1. Abkhazian A.S.S.R.
2. Adygei Aut. Oblast
3. Adzhar A.S.S.R.
4. Agin-Buryat Nat'l Okrug
5. Checheno-Ingush A.S.S.R.
6. Chuvash A.S.S.R.
7. Gorno-Altai Aut. Oblast
8. Gorno-Badakhshan Aut. Oblast
9. Jewish Aut. Oblast
10. Kabardino-Balkarian A.S.S.R.
11. Karachayevo-Cherkess Aut. Oblast
12. Karakalpak A.S.S.R.
Division
13. Khakass Aut. Oblast
14. Komi-Permiak Nat'l Okrug
15. Mari A.S.S.R
16. Mordovian A.S.S.R.
17. Nagorno-Karabakh Aut. Oblast
18. Nakhichevan A.S.S.R.
19. North Ossetian A.S.S.R.
20. South Ossetian Aut. Oblast
21. Tatar A.S.S.R.
22. Tuva A.S.S.R.
23. Udmurt A.S.S.R.
24. Ust-Ordynski Nat'l Okrug
100°
Longitude East of Greenwich
110°
120°
130°
© C. S. HAMMOND & Co., Maplewood, N. J.

UNION OF SOVIET SOCIALIST REPUBLICS—MANNED SPACE FLIGHTS[1]

Name	Crew	Launch date	Weight (pounds)	Perigee/ Apogee (m.)[2]	Number of orbits	Time (hr.:min.)
Vostok 1. . .	Yuri A. Gagarin	April 12, 1961	10,419	112/203	1	1:48
Vostok 2. . .	Gherman S. Titov	Aug. 6, 1961	10,432	110/152	17	25:11
Vostok 3. . .	Andrian G. Nikolayev	Aug. 11, 1962	10,412	113/146	64	94:22
Vostok 4. . .	Pavel R. Popovich	Aug. 12, 1962	10,425	112/147	48	70:57
Vostok 5. . .	Valery F. Bykovsky	June 14, 1963	10,408	109/146	81	119:06
Vostok 6. . .	Valentina V. Tereshkova	June 16, 1963	10,392	113/143	48	70:50
Voskhod 1. .	Vladimir M. Komarov Konstantin P. Feoktistov Boris B. Yegorov	Oct. 12, 1964	11,731	110/254	16	24:17
Voskhod 2. .	Pavel Belyayev Alexei Leonov	March 18, 1965	12,529	107/308	17	26:02
Soyuz 1 . . .	Vladimir M. Komarov	April 23, 1967	. . .	125/139	17	26:40
Soyuz 3 . . .	Georgi T. Beregovoi	Oct. 26, 1968	. . .	127/139	60	94:51
Soyuz 4 . . .	Vladimir Shatalov	Jan. 14, 1969	. . .	129/148	45	71:14
Soyuz 5 . . .	Alexei Yeliseyev Yevgeny Khrunov Boris Volynov	Jan. 15, 1969	. . .	132/158	46	72:46
Soyuz 6, 7, 8.	Georgi S. Shonin, Valery N. Kubasov; Anatoly V. Filipchenko, Vladislav N. Volkov, Viktor V. Gorbatko; Vladimir A. Shatalov, Alexei S. Yeliseyev	Oct. 11, 12, 13, 1969	. . .	124/140	79	121:19
Soyuz 9 . . .	Andrian Nikolayev Vitaly Sevastyanov	June 1, 1970	14,500	128.6/165.9	287	424:59
Soyuz 10[3] . .	Vladimir A. Shatalov Alexei S. Yeliseyev Nikolai N. Ruka-vishnikov	April 22, 1971	14,500	130/154	32	47:46
Soyuz 11. . .	Georgi T. Dobrovolsky Vladislav N. Volkov Viktor I. Patsayev	June 6, 1971	14,500	115/167	385	570:23

[1] See also UNITED STATES—*Manned Space Flights*.
[2] Minimum perigee and maximum apogee, in statute miles.
[3] Docked with Salyut space vehicle launched earlier.

Britain terminated and establishment of independent (six-member) federation 1971; accession of Ras al-Khaimah to federation 1972.

United Arab Republic. 1 Union of Egypt and Syria; formed 1958, dissolved 1961.
2 Republic, Africa. See EGYPT.

United Deccan State \-ˈdek-ən-, -ˌan-\. Former state, W India; formed Aug. 26, 1947 by the union of seven Deccan states: Aundh, Bhor, Kurundwad (Sr.), Miraj (Jr.), Phaltan, Ramdurg, and Sangli.

United Kha·si and Jain·tia Hills \-ˈkä-sē . . . ˈjīnt-ē-ə-\ *or formerly* **Khasi and Jaintia Hills.** District, mostly in Meghalaya, NE India; pop. (1961c) 462,152; ✱ Shillong; rice; coal.

United Kingdom of Great Britain and Northern Ireland. See GREAT BRITAIN.

United Nations. Political organization, consisting (1971) of 130 sovereign states; headquarters New York City; purpose is to promote international peace and security and advance solutions to international social and economic problems.
History: Formally established 1945; Charter (drawn up April–June 1945 at San Francisco), signed June 26; officially came into existence after ratification of Charter by majority of signatories October 24, 1945; has served as forum for discussion and debate on most major international political questions since World War II; anti-Communist forces sent to Korea 1950 sanctioned by UN resolution; UN Emergency Forces deployed in Middle East 1957–67, Congo (Zaire) 1960–64, Cyprus 1964 ff.; voted to admit People's Republic of China to membership and to expel Taiwan 1971. Has dealt with wide range of social and economic questions through United Nations Social and Economic Council; concerned with many specialized matters including outer space, control of the ocean floor, and the UN trust territories.

United Provinces. 1 State, India. See UTTAR PRADESH.
2 The seven provinces, Holland, Zeeland, Utrecht, Friesland, Groningen, Overijssel, and Gelderland, which formed a union under the Treaty of Utrecht in 1579, that led to the establishment of the Dutch republic, or the Netherlands (*q.v.*).

United Republic of Tanzania. See TANZANIA.

United States of America *commonly shortened to* **United States** *also* **America.** Federal republic, North America, bounded on N by Canada and (in Alaska) by the Arctic Ocean, on E by the Atlantic Ocean, on S by Mexico and Gulf of Mexico, and on W by the Pacific Ocean; 3,615,211 sq. m. (excluding Great Lakes); pop. (1970c) 203,184,772;

* Washington, D.C. *Physical features:* Easternmost point West Quoddy Head, Maine, 66°57'W; westernmost point (excluding Alaska and Hawaii) Cape Alava, Washington, 124°44'W; northernmost point (excluding Alaska) Northwest Angle, Minnesota, ab. 49°23'N; southernmost point East Cape, Florida (mainland), 25°07'N. *Chief rivers:* Mississippi system (including Missouri, Ohio, Platte, Red, Arkansas), Colorado, Columbia, Rio Grande. *Largest lakes:* Great Lakes in N (U.S.-Canada boundary runs through Ontario, Erie, Huron, and Superior; Michigan is wholly within boundary); Great Salt Lake in Utah and Okeechobee in Florida. *Mountains:* Appalachian system (including White Mts. and Green Mts. in New England, Adirondacks and Catskills in New York, Blue Ridge and Great Smoky Mts. in SE), Ozark Plateau in Missouri, Arkansas, and Oklahoma, Rocky Mts. across (N to S) the W (including Bitterroot Range in N, Wasatch, Uinta, and Front Ranges in cen. part), and ranges along Pacific coast (Cascade Range, Sierra Nevada, and Coast Ranges); highest point Mt. McKinley, Alaska, 20,320 ft.; lowest point Death Valley, California, 282 ft. below sea level; highest point (excluding Alaska) Mt. Whitney, California, 14,494 ft.; highest point E of Mississippi river Mt. Mitchell, North Carolina, 6684 ft. *Chief islands:* Hawaii, Kodiak, Prince of Wales, Chichagof, St. Lawrence, Admiralty, Nunivak, Unimak. *Chief products:* Corn, wheat, soybeans, cotton, tobacco, oats, barley, rice, sugar beet, fruit; dairy products; livestock raising, fishing, lumbering; iron ore, coal, oil, natural gas, copper, lead, zinc, uranium-radium ores, potash, sulfur, sand and gravel, phosphate rock; manufacturing: iron and steel, transportation equipment, construction and farm machinery, chemicals and pharmaceuticals, electronic and communications equipment, textiles, scientific instruments, rubber goods, paper; food processing, power production. *Largest cities:* New York, Chicago, Los Angeles, Philadelphia, Detroit, Houston, Baltimore, Dallas, Washington, Cleveland, Indianapolis, Milwaukee, San Francisco, San Diego (see also table *Population of Standard Metropolitan Statistical Areas,* below). *Principal ports:* New York, New Orleans, Houston, Philadelphia, Norfolk, Baltimore, Baton Rouge, Duluth, Beaumont, Tampa, Los Angeles. Divided into 50 states and Washington, D.C. (listed in the table *States, Territories, and Possessions;* for further details, see their individual entries).

History: Period of discovery: see NORTH AMERICA. Period of colonization: first permanent settlement, Spanish, at St. Augustine, Florida, 1565; English settlements in Virginia 1607, Massachusetts 1620, Maryland 1634, Pennsylvania 1681; English defeat of French in French and Indian War 1754–63 assured British political control over thirteen colonies along Atlantic seaboard. Period of political unrest caused by English colonial policy, and culminating in American Revolution 1775–83, and Declaration of Independence 1776. Period of political organization, first under the Articles of Confederation 1781–89 and finally under the Constitution, adopted 1787 and in effect 1789, and of increase of power as a nation; Louisiana Territory purchased from France 1803; War of 1812 with Great Britain; Florida purchased from Spain 1819; Monroe Doctrine announced 1823. Periods of westward expansion, initially into Middle West as result of acquisition of Louisiana Territory, and to Far West after discovery of gold in California 1848; Texas annexed 1845; NW boundary established by treaty with Great Britain 1846; New Mexico and California ceded by Mexico 1848 by Treaty of Guadalupe Hidalgo ending Mexican War; S Arizona acquired from Mexico by Gadsden Purchase 1853. Period of disunity, caused by development of slave cotton-growing plantation economy in South contrasted with free industrial and diversified agricultural economy in North, and culminating in War between the States 1861–65. *Territorial acquisition:* Alaska (1867: by purchase from Russia); Midway Is. (1867: by occupation); Hawaiian Is. (July 1898: by annexation); Philippine Is., Puerto Rico, and Guam (Dec. 1898: by treaty with Spain ending Spanish-American War); Wake I. (1898–99: by occupation); American Samoa (1899: by treaty with Germany); Panama Canal Zone (1903: by purchase from Panama); Virgin Is. of the United States (1917: by purchase from Denmark). Philippine Islands granted independence July 4, 1946; Puerto Rico became an autonomous commonwealth 1952; S Ryukyu Is. (occupied by U.S. 1945) returned to Japan 1972.

Period of reconstruction 1865–70. Period of rapid growth, urbanization, industrial development, and European immigration. Period of internationalism, caused by development of foreign trade and rapid communication and transportation, and marked by participation in foreign wars, Spanish-American War 1898, World War I 1914–18 (U.S. participation Apr. 6, 1917–Nov. 11, 1918), World War II 1939–45 (U.S. participation Dec. 8, 1941 Aug. 14, 1945); exploded first atomic bomb 1945; founding member of the United Nations 1945; undertook extensive program of economic and military assistance to nations of W Europe 1947 ff.; founding member of the North Atlantic Treaty Organization 1949; participated in Korean War (1950–53), U.S. troops constituting major component of United Nations forces; formally terminated state of war with Germany 1951; ratified peace treaty with Japan 1952; exploded first thermonuclear device 1952; racial segregation in public schools declared unconstitutional by Supreme Court 1954; intervened militarily in Lebanon 1958, in Dominican Republic 1965; Alaska and Hawaii made states 1959; began increased program of military assistance to anti-Communist government of South Vietnam 1961, subsequently expanding its role in Vietnam War (see history at VIETNAM, SOUTH); signed nuclear test-ban treaty 1963; President John F. Kennedy assassinated Nov. 22, 1963; 1960's marked by widespread civil disorders, esp. 1964, 1967, 1968; accomplished first manned lunar landing 1969.

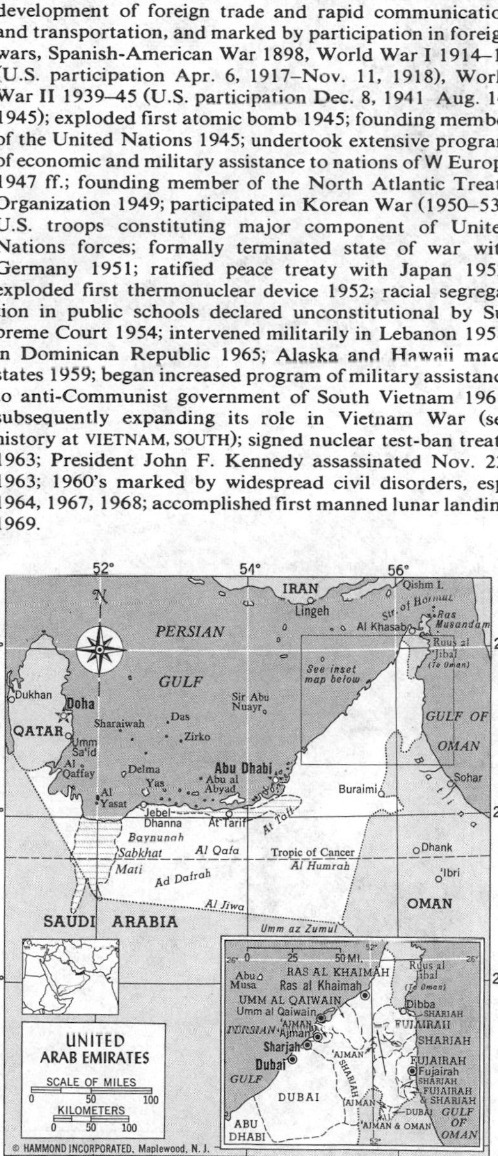

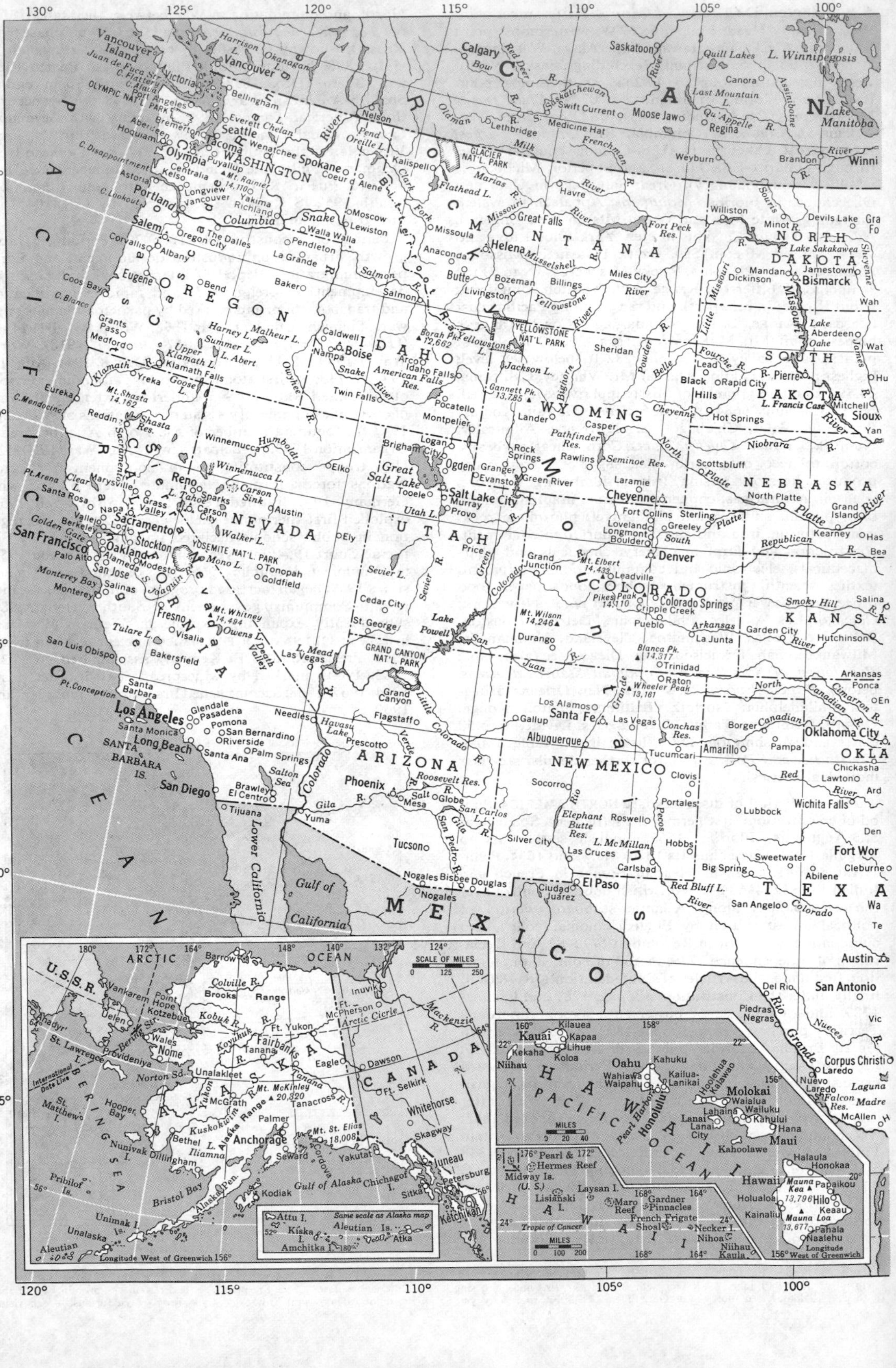
130°
125°
120°
115°
110°
105°
100°
45°
40°
35°
30°
25°
PACIFIC OCEAN
CANADA
ROCKY MOUNTAINS
Vancouver Island
Juan de Fuca Str.
C. Flattery
C. Alava
OLYMPIC NAT'L PARK
Victoria
Vancouver
Harrison L.
Okanagan L.
Bellingham
Port Angeles
Bremerton
Everett
Seattle
Tacoma
Aberdeen
Hoquiam
Olympia
WASHINGTON
Wenatchee
L. Chelan
Spokane
Coeur d Alene
Puyallup
Centralia
Mt. Rainier 14,410
C. Disappointment
Astoria
Kelso
Longview
Vancouver
Yakima
Richland
C. Lookout
Portland
Salem
Columbia
Snake
Walla Walla
Moscow
Lewiston
Pendleton
The Dalles
Oregon City
Corvallis
Albany
La Grande
Baker
OREGON
Bend
Eugene
Coos Bay
C. Blanco
Grants Pass
Medford
Harney L.
Malheur L.
Summer L.
L. Abert
Upper Klamath L.
Klamath Falls
Goose L.
Klamath
Eureka
C. Mendocino
Mt. Shasta 14,162
Yreka
Redding
Shasta Res.
Sacramento
Pt. Arena
Clear L.
Santa Rosa
Marysville
Grass Valley
Napa
Vallejo
Berkeley
Golden Gate
San Francisco
Oakland
Alameda
Palo Alto
San Jose
Monterey Bay
Monterey
Salinas
Sacramento
Lodi
Stockton
Modesto
San Joaquin
CALIFORNIA
Sierra Nevada
Fresno
Visalia
Tulare L.
Bakersfield
San Luis Obispo
Pt. Conception
Santa Barbara
Los Angeles
Glendale
Pasadena
Pomona
San Bernardino
Riverside
Santa Monica
Long Beach
Santa Ana
Palm Springs
SANTA BARBARA IS.
San Diego
Salton Sea
Brawley
El Centro
Tijuana
Lower California
Reno
Sparks
L. Tahoe
Carson City
Carson Sink
Winnemucca
Winnemucca L.
Humboldt
Elko
NEVADA
Austin
Walker L.
Ely
YOSEMITE NAT'L. PARK
Mono L.
Tonopah
Goldfield
Mt. Whitney 14,494
Owens L.
Death Valley
Las Vegas
L. Mead
Needles
Havasu Lake
Nelson
Pend Oreille L.
Kalispell
GLACIER NAT'L. PARK
Flathead L.
Clark Fork
Missoula
Bitterroot
Salmon
Marias R.
Havre
Great Falls
Missouri
Helena
MONTANA
Musselshell
Anaconda
Butte
Bozeman
Livingston
Billings
Yellowstone
Miles City
Fort Peck Res.
Milk
Calgary
Bow
Red Deer
Oldman
Lethbridge
Medicine Hat
Saskatchewan
Swift Current
Moose Jaw
Frenchman
Saskatoon
Quill Lakes
L. Winnipegosis
Canora
Last Mountain L.
Qu'Appelle R.
Regina
Assiniboine
Lake Manitoba
Weyburn
Brandon
Winni
Souris
Williston
Minot
Devils Lake
NORTH DAKOTA
Lake Sakakawea
Mandan
Dickinson
Jamestown
Bismarck
Sheyenne
Caldwell
Boise
Nampa
IDAHO
Borah Pk. 12,662
Arco
Idaho Falls
American Falls Res.
Snake
Twin Falls
Owyhee
Pocatello
Montpelier
YELLOWSTONE NAT'L. PARK
Jackson L.
Gannett Pk. 13,785
Sheridan
Powder R.
Bighorn
Little Missouri
Lake Oahe
Aberdeen
SOUTH DAKOTA
Pierre
Lead
Rapid City
Black Hills
Belle Fourche R.
Hot Springs
L. Francis Case
Mitchell
Sioux
James
WYOMING
Lander
Casper
Pathfinder Res.
Rawlins
Rock Springs
Seminoe Res.
Granger
Evanston
Green River
Cheyenne
North Platte
Laramie
Scottsbluff
Niobrara
NEBRASKA
Grand Island
Kearney
Logan
Brigham City
Ogden
Great Salt Lake
Salt Lake City
Tooele
Murray
Provo
Utah L.
UTAH
Price
Green
Sevier L.
Sevier R.
Cedar City
St. George
Lake Powell
San Juan
GRAND CANYON NAT'L. PARK
Grand Canyon
Little Colorado R.
Flagstaff
Prescott
Verde
ARIZONA
Roosevelt Res.
Phoenix
Salt
Mesa
Globe
San Carlos L.
Gila
Yuma
Tucson
San Pedro R.
Nogales
Bisbee
Douglas
Grand Junction
Mt. Elbert 14,433
Leadville
COLORADO
Pikes Peak 14,110
Cripple Creek
Colorado Springs
Mt. Wilson 14,246
Pueblo
Arkansas
La Junta
Durango
Blanca Pk. 14,317
Trinidad
Fort Collins
Loveland
Longmont
Boulder
Sterling
Greeley
South Platte
Denver
Republican
Smoky Hill
Salina
KANSAS
Garden City
Hutchinson
Raton
Wheeler Peak 13,161
Los Alamos
Santa Fe
Gallup
Las Vegas
Albuquerque
Conchas Res.
Tucumcari
NEW MEXICO
Socorro
Clovis
Portales
Elephant Butte Res.
Roswell
Pecos
L. McMillan
Silver City
Las Cruces
Hobbs
Carlsbad
El Paso
Ciudad Juárez
Rio Grande
Red Bluff L.
Arkansas
Ponca
Cimarron R.
Canadian
North Canadian R.
Borger
Amarillo
Pampa
Oklahoma City
OKLA
Chickasha
Lawton
Red River
Wichita Falls
Lubbock
Fort Wor
Sweetwater
Abilene
Big Spring
Cleburne
TEXA
San Angelo
Colorado
Austin
San Antonio
Del Rio
Piedras Negras
Nueces R.
Corpus Christi
Laredo
Nuevo Laredo
Laguna Madre
Falcon Res.
McAllen
Gulf of California
MEXICO
ARCTIC OCEAN
180°
172°
164°
156°
148°
140°
132°
124°
SCALE OF MILES
0 125 250
U.S.S.R.
Barrow
Colville R.
Brooks Range
Point Hope
Vankarem
Uelen
Kotzebue
Kobuk R.
Inuvik
Mackenzie R.
Ft. McPherson
Arctic Circle
Anadyr'
Bering Str.
Wales
Nome
St. Lawrence I.
Provideniya
Koyukuk R.
Ft. Yukon
Fairbanks
Tanana
ALASKA
Dawson
Eagle
CANADA
International Date Line
Norton Sd.
Unalakleet
Tanana R.
Ft. Selkirk
Mt. McKinley 20,320
Yukon
McGrath
Tanacross
Whitehorse
St. Matthews I.
Hooper Bay
Kuskokwim R.
Alaska Range
Palmer
Mt. St. Elias 18,008
Skagway
BERING SEA
Nunivak I.
Bethel
L. Iliamna
Anchorage
Seward
Cordova
Yakutat
Juneau
Dillingham
Gulf of Alaska
Chichagof I.
Petersburg
Sitka
Pribilof Is.
Bristol Bay
Alaska Pen.
Kodiak
Ketchikan
Unimak I.
Unalaska Is.
Aleutian
Longitude West of Greenwich 156°
Attu I.
Kiska I.
Amchitka I.
Aleutian Is.
Atka
Same scale as Alaska map
160°
158°
Kauai
Kilauea
Kapaa
Lihue
Kekaha
Koloa
Niihau
Oahu
Kahuku
Wahiawa
Waipahu
Kailua-Lanikai
Hoolehua
Kalawao
Pearl Harbor
Honolulu
Molokai
Waialua
Lahaina
Wailuku
Kahului
Lanai
Lanai City
Hana
Maui
Kahoolawe
HAWAII
PACIFIC OCEAN
MILES
0 20 40
176°
172°
Pearl & Hermes Reef
Midway Is. (U. S.)
Laysan I.
Lisianski I.
Maro Reef
Gardner Pinnacles
French Frigate Shoal
Necker I.
Nihoa
Niihau
Kaula
Tropic of Cancer
MILES
0 100 200
Hawaii
Halaula
Honokaa
Mauna Kea 13,796
Papaikou
Hilo
Keaau
Holualoa
Kainaliu
Mauna Loa 13,677
Pahala
Naalehu
Longitude West of Greenwich

UNITED STATES
POLYCONIC PROJECTION
SCALE OF MILES
0 50 100 200 300 400
SCALE OF KILOMETERS
0 100 200 300 400
Capitals of Countries
State Capitals
International Boundaries
Copyright by C. S. Hammond & Co., N. Y.
Longitude West of Greenwich
95° 90° 85° 80° 75° 70° 65°
45° 40° 35° 30° 25°
CANADA
Lake Winnipeg
Lake of the Woods
Lake Nipigon
James Bay
Lake Superior
Lake Michigan
Lake Huron
Georgian Bay
Lake Erie
Lake Ontario
St. Lawrence
Ottawa
Montréal
Québec
Toronto
Trois-Rivières
Sherbrooke
Fredericton
MINNESOTA
Minneapolis
St. Paul
Duluth
WISCONSIN
Milwaukee
Madison
Green Bay
MICHIGAN
Detroit
Lansing
Grand Rapids
Flint
IOWA
Des Moines
ILLINOIS
Chicago
Springfield
Peoria
INDIANA
Indianapolis
Fort Wayne
OHIO
Cleveland
Columbus
Cincinnati
Toledo
Akron
Dayton
PENNSYLVANIA
Pittsburgh
Philadelphia
Harrisburg
NEW YORK
Albany
Buffalo
Rochester
Syracuse
New York
MAINE
Augusta
Portland
N.H.
Concord
VT.
Montpelier
MASS.
Boston
RHODE ISLAND
Providence
CONN.
Hartford
New Haven
NEW JERSEY
Trenton
Newark
DEL.
Dover
MD.
Baltimore
Annapolis
Washington
D.C.
VIRGINIA
Richmond
Norfolk
WEST VIRGINIA
Charleston
KENTUCKY
Louisville
Frankfort
Lexington
TENNESSEE
Nashville
Memphis
Knoxville
Chattanooga
NORTH CAROLINA
Raleigh
Charlotte
Greensboro
SOUTH CAROLINA
Columbia
Charleston
GEORGIA
Atlanta
Savannah
Augusta
FLORIDA
Tallahassee
Jacksonville
Tampa
Miami
ALABAMA
Montgomery
Birmingham
Mobile
MISSISSIPPI
Jackson
LOUISIANA
Baton Rouge
New Orleans
Shreveport
ARKANSAS
Little Rock
MISSOURI
Jefferson City
St. Louis
Kansas City
KANSAS
Topeka
Wichita
OKLAHOMA
Tulsa
TEXAS
Dallas
Houston
Galveston
Omaha
Lincoln
Ozark Mts.
Mississippi River
Missouri
Ohio R.
Tennessee
Cumberland
Appalachian
ATLANTIC OCEAN
GULF OF MEXICO
Mississippi Delta
C. Hatteras
C. Lookout
C. Fear
C. Charles
C. Cod
Chesapeake Bay
Delaware Bay
Albemarle Sd.
Pamlico Sd.
C. Kennedy (C. Canaveral)
L. Okeechobee
The Everglades
C. Sable
Florida Bay
Key West
FLORIDA KEYS
Straits of Florida
BAHAMA ISLANDS (Br.)
Gt. Abaco
Gd. Bahama
Eleuthera
Nassau
Andros I.
Cat I.
Exuma Sound
Gt. Exuma
Long I.
Santaren Channel
Tropic of Cancer
Havana
CUBA

STATES

Name	Area[1] (sq. m.)	Rank in Area	Pop. (1970c)	Rank in Pop.	Date of Admission[2]	Rank of Admission	Capital	Nickname	Motto
Alabama	51,609	29th	3,444,165	21st	Dec. 14, 1819	22d	Montgomery	Cotton State	We Dare Defend Our Rights
Alaska[3]	586,400	1st	302,173	50th	Jan. 3, 1959	49th	Juneau		
Arizona	113,909	6th	1,772,482	33d	Feb. 14, 1912	48th	Phoenix	Grand Canyon State	Ditat Deus (God Enriches)
Arkansas	53,104	27th	1,923,295	32d	June 15, 1836	25th	Little Rock	Land of Opportunity	Regnat Populus (The People Rule)
California	158,693	3d	19,953,134	1st	Sept. 9, 1850	31st	Sacramento	Golden State	Eureka (I Have Found It)
Colorado	104,247	8th	2,207,259	30th	Aug. 1, 1876	38th	Denver	Centennial State	Nil Sine Numine (Nothing Without the Deity)
Connecticut[2]	5,009	48th	3,032,217	24th	Jan. 9, 1788	5th	Hartford	Constitution State	Qui Transtulit Sustinet (He Who Transplanted Sustains)
Delaware[2]	2,057	49th	548,104	46th	Dec. 7, 1787	1st	Dover	First State	Liberty and Independence
Florida	58,560	22d	6,789,443	9th	Mar. 3, 1845	27th	Tallahassee	Sunshine State	In God We Trust
Georgia[2]	58,876	21st	4,589,575	15th	Jan. 2, 1788	4th	Atlanta	Empire State of the South	Wisdom, Justice, Moderation
Hawaii[3]	6,450	47th	769,913	40th	Aug. 21, 1959	50th	Honolulu	Aloha State	Ua Mau Ke Ea O Ka Aina I Ka Pono (The Life of the Land is Perpetuated in Righteousness)
Idaho	83,557	13th	713,008	42d	July 3, 1890	43d	Boise	Gem State	Esto Perpetua (May She Endure Forever)
Illinois	56,400	24th	11,113,976	5th	Dec. 3, 1818	21st	Springfield	Prairie State	State Sovereignty—National Union
Indiana	36,291	38th	5,193,669	11th	Dec. 11, 1816	19th	Indianapolis	Hoosier State	The Crossroads of America
Iowa	56,290	25th	2,825,041	25th	Dec. 28, 1846	29th	Des Moines	Hawkeye State	Our Liberties We Prize and Our Rights We Will Maintain
Kansas	82,264	14th	2,249,071	28th	Jan. 29, 1861	34th	Topeka	Sunflower State	Ad Astra per Aspera (To the Stars Through Difficulties)
Kentucky	40,395	37th	3,219,311	23d	June 1, 1792	15th	Frankfort	Bluegrass State	United We Stand, Divided We Fall
Louisiana	48,523	31st	3,643,180	20th	Apr. 30, 1812	18th	Baton Rouge	Pelican State	Union, Justice, Confidence
Maine	33,215	39th	993,663	38th	Mar. 15, 1820	23d	Augusta	Pine Tree State	Dirigo (I Direct)
Maryland[2]	10,577	42d	3,922,399	18th	Apr. 28, 1788	7th	Annapolis	Old Line State	Fatti Maschii, Parole Femine (Manly Deeds, Feminine Words)
Massachusetts[2]	8,257	45th	5,689,170	10th	Feb. 6, 1788	6th	Boston	Bay State	Ense Petit Placidam Sub Libertate Quietem (By the Sword We Seek Peace, but Peace Only under Liberty)
Michigan	58,216	23d	8,875,083	7th	Jan. 26, 1837	26th	Lansing	Wolverine State	Si Quaeris Peninsulam Amoenam, Circumspice (If You Seek a Beautiful Peninsula, Look Around You)

Name	Area[1] (sq. m.)	Rank in Area	Pop. (1970c)	Rank in Pop.	Date of Admission[2]	Rank of Admission	Capital	Nickname	Motto
Minnesota	84,068	12th	3,805,069	19th	May 11, 1858	32d	St. Paul	Gopher State	L'étoile du Nord (Star of the North)
Mississippi	47,716	32d	2,216,912	29th	Dec. 10, 1817	20th	Jackson	Magnolia State	Virtute et Armis (By Valor and Arms)
Missouri	69,686	19th	4,677,399	13th	Aug. 10, 1821	24th	Jefferson City	Show Me State	Salus Populi Suprema Lex Esto (Let the Welfare of the People Be the Supreme Law)
Montana	147,138	4th	694,409	43d	Nov. 8, 1889	41st	Helena	Treasure State	Oro y Plata (Gold and Silver)
Nebraska	77,227	15th	1,483,791	35th	Mar. 1, 1867	37th	Lincoln	Cornhusker State	Equality Before the Law
Nevada	110,540	7th	488,738	47th	Oct. 31, 1864	36th	Carson City	Silver State	All for Our Country
New Hampshire[2]	9,304	44th	737,681	41st	June 21, 1788	9th	Concord	Granite State	Live Free or Die
New Jersey[2]	7,836	46th	7,168,164	8th	Dec. 18, 1787	3d	Trenton	Garden State	Liberty and Prosperity
New Mexico	121,666	5th	1,016,000	37th	Jan. 6, 1912	47th	Santa Fe	Land of Enchantment	Crescit Eundo (It Grows as It Goes
New York[2]	49,576	30th	18,241,266	2d	July 26, 1788	11th	Albany	Empire State	Excelsior (Ever Upward)
North Carolina[2]	52,712	28th	5,082,059	12th	Nov. 21, 1789	12th	Raleigh	Tar Heel State	To Be Rather Than to Seem
North Dakota	70,665	17th	617,761	45th	Nov. 2, 1889	39th	Bismarck	Flickertail State	Liberty and Union
Ohio	41,222	35th	10,652,017	6th	Feb. 19, 1803	17th	Columbus	Buckeye State	None
Oklahoma	69,919	18th	2,559,253	27th	Nov. 16, 1907	46th	Oklahoma City	Sooner State	Labor Omnia Vincit (Labor Conquers All)
Oregon	96,981	10th	2,091,385	31st	Feb. 14, 1859	33d	Salem	Sunset State	Alis Volat Propriis (She Flies with Her Own Wings)
Pennsylvania[2]	45,333	33d	11,793,909	3d	Dec. 12, 1787	2d	Harrisburg	Keystone State	Virtue, Liberty, and Independence
Rhode Island[2]	1,214	50th	949,723	39th	May 29, 1790	13th	Providence	Little Rhody	Hope
South Carolina[2]	31,055	40th	2,590,516	26th	May 23, 1788	8th	Columbia	Palmetto State	Dum Spiro, Spero (While I Breathe, I Hope)
South Dakota	77,047	16th	666,257	44th	Nov. 2, 1889	40th	Pierre	Coyote State	Under God the People Rule
Tennessee	42,244	34th	3,924,164	17th	June 1, 1796	16th	Nashville	Volunteer State	Agriculture, Commerce
Texas	267,339	2d	11,196,730	4th	Dec. 29, 1845	28th	Austin	Lone Star State	Friendship
Utah	84,916	11th	1,059,273	36th	Jan. 4, 1896	45th	Salt Lake City	Beehive State	Industry
Vermont	9,609	43d	444,732	48th	Mar. 4, 1791	14th	Montpelier	Green Mountain State	Freedom and Unity
Virginia[2]	40,817	36th	4,648,494	14th	June 25, 1788	10th	Richmond	Old Dominion	Sic Semper Tyrannis (Ever Thus to Tyrants)
Washington	68,192	20th	3,409,169	22d	Nov. 11, 1889	42d	Olympia	Evergreen State	Alki [*Chinook Jargon*] (By and By)
West Virginia	24,181	41st	1,744,237	34th	June 20, 1863	35th	Charleston	Mountain State	Montani Semper Liberi (Mountaineers Are Always Freemen)
Wisconsin	56,154	26th	4,417,933	16th	May 29, 1848	30th	Madison	Badger State	Forward
Wyoming	97,914	9th	332,416	49th	July 10, 1890	44th	Cheyenne	Equality State	Cedant Arma Togae (Let Arms Yield to the Toga)
District of Columbia[4]	69	. . .	756,510	. . .	. . .	. . .	Washington	. . .	E Pluribus Unum (One Out of Many)
	3,615,211[5]		203,184,772						

Name	Total Area (sq. m.)	Pop. (1970p)	Capital
American Samoa[6]	76	27,769	Pago Pago
Guam	209	86,926	Agana
Panama Canal Zone	557	44,650	Balboa Heights[7]
Puerto Rico[8]	3,435	2,689,932	San Juan
Virgin Islands of U.S.	133	63,200	Charlotte Amalie
Other (Trust Territory of the Pacific Islands, etc.)	8,516	102,250[9]	
	12,926	3,014,727	

[1] Total land and inland water.
[2] Date of admission of the 13 original colonies is that of ratification of the Constitution.
[3] The Alaska Statehood Act was signed by the President July 7, 1958; the Hawaii Statehood Act, Mar. 18, 1959.
[4] Coextensive with the city of Washington.
[5] Total land and inland water; does not include 74,364 sq. m. of Great Lakes and other primary bodies of water, of which total the state of Michigan has 38,575 sq. m.
[6] Including Swains I.
[7] Administrative center.
[8] Adopted constitution 1952 establishing it as a commonwealth with autonomy in internal affairs.
[9] Pop. (1970e) given only for Trust Territory of the Pacific Islands.

Shown in this table are the names of 45 major dams, with their location, year of completion, maximum height, and other important facts. Dams of the TENNESSEE VALLEY AUTHORITY are treated in a table at that entry.

Name of Dam	Year of Completion	Max. Height (feet)	Location	Purpose for which Water Impounded	Type
Anderson Ranch	1950	456	S fork of Boise riv., Elmore co., SW Idaho	flood control, irrigation, and power	earth fill
Auburn[2]		680	N fork of American riv., near Sacramento, California	irrigation, flood control, and recreation	cupola
Blue Mesa	1966	390	Gunnison riv., Gunnison co., W cen. Colorado	irrigation, power, and flood control	earth fill
Boulder	See Hoover Dam, below				
Brownlee	1959	395	Snake riv., Washington co., W Idaho	flood control, recreation, and public water supply	rock fill
Carters[2]		454	Coosawattee riv., NW Georgia	irrigation, power, and river regulation	rock fill
Cougar	1964	445	S fork McKenzie riv., Lane co., W Oregon	power and irrigation	gravity, earth fill
Detroit	1953	454	North Santiam riv., bet. Linn and Marion cos., W Oregon	flood control, navigation, power, and irrigation	gravity
Diablo	1929	389	Skagit riv., Whatcom co., NW Washington	power	arch-constant angle
Donnells	1957	484	Middle fork of Stanislaus riv., Tuolumne co., cen. California	irrigation and public water supply	arch
Dworshak[2]		717	N fork of Clearwater riv., near Orofino, NW Idaho	flood control, power, and navigation	gravity
Flaming Gorge	1964	502	Green riv., Daggett co., NE Utah	irrigation and power	cupola, rock fill
Glen Canyon	1964	710	Colorado riv., Coconino co., N Arizona	power and river regulation	cupola, rock fill
Grand Coulee	1942	550	Columbia riv., at junction of Douglas, Okanogan, and Lincoln cos., NE cen. Washington	flood control, irrigation, power, and river regulation	gravity
Green Peter	1967	365	Middle Santiam riv., Linn co., W Oregon	irrigation, power, flood control, and navigation	gravity
Hetch Hetchy	See O'Shaughnessy Dam, below				
Hoover (formerly Boulder)	1936	726	Colorado riv., bet. Clark Co., Nevada, and Mohave co., Arizona	flood control, irrigation, power, and river regulation	arch
Hungry Horse	1953	564	S fork of Flathead riv., Flathead co., NW Montana	irrigation, power, and navigation	arch
Jocassee[2]		390	Keowee riv., near Seneca, NW South Carolina	power	earth fill
Libby[2]		445	Kootenai riv., Lincoln co., NW Montana	flood control, power, and recreation	gravity
Lower Hell Hole	1966	410	Rubicon riv., Placer co., E California	power, irrigation, and river regulation	rock fill
Merriman	1949	370	Rondout creek, Ulster co., SE New York	power	earth fill
Morris	1935	375	San Gabriel riv., Los Angeles co., S California	water supply for Pasadena	multi-arch
Morrow Point	1968	468	Gunnison riv., Montrose co., W Colorado	power	arch-variable center

Name of Dam	Year of Completion	Max. Height (feet)	Location	Purpose for which Water Impounded	Type
Mossyrock	1968	605	Cowlitz riv., Lewis co., SW Washington	power	multi-arch
Mud Mountain (or Stevens)	1948	425	White riv., bet. Pierce and King cos., W cen. Washington	flood control	rock fill
Navajo	1963	402	San Juan riv., on boundary bet. San Juan and Rio Arriba cos., N New Mexico	irrigation and flood control	earth fill
New Bullards	1968	635	N Yuba riv., Yuba co., N cen. California	irrigation, power, and water supply	arch
New Don Pedro[2]		585	Tuolumne riv., Tuolumne co., cen. California	irrigation, power, and flood control	earth fill
New Exchequer	1966	490	Merced riv., Mariposa co., cen. California	irrigation, flood control, and power	rock fill
Oroville	1968	770	Feather riv., Butte co., N cen. California	flood control, recreation, and power	earth fill
O'Shaughnessy (or Hetch Hetchy)	1938	430	Tuolumne riv., in Yosemite National Park, E cen. California	power and public water supply	gravity
Owyhee	1932	417	Owyhee riv., Malheur co., SE Oregon	irrigation	gravity
Pacoima (or Reagan)	1929	372	Pacoima riv., Los Angeles co., S California NW of Los Angeles city	flood control	arch-constant angle
Pardee	1929	358	Mokelumne riv., bet. Amador and Calaveras cos., E cen. California	water supply	gravity
Pine Flat	1954	440	Kings riv., Fresno co., S cen. California	irrigation, flood control, power, and recreation	gravity
Reagan	See Pacoima, above				
Robert Moses	1962	389	Niagara riv. (off stream), Niagara co., W New York	power	gravity
Ross	1949	540	Skagit riv., NW Washington	power and flood control	arch-constant angle
Round Butte	1964	440	Deschutes riv., Jefferson co., N cen. Oregon	power and flood control	rock fill
San Gabriel No. 1	1939	337	San Gabriel riv., Los Angeles co., S California	irrigation and flood control	earth fill
San Luis	1967	382	San Luis Creek, Merced co., cen. California	irrigation and power	earth fill
Shasta	1945	602	Sacramento riv., Shasta co., N California	irrigation, power, navigation, and river regulation	gravity
Stevens	See Mud Mountain, above				
Summersville	1966	398	Gauley riv., Nicholas co., cen. West Virginia	flood control and river regulation	rock fill
Swift	1958	512	Lewis riv., Skamania co., S Washington	irrigation	earth fill
Trinity	1962	537	Trinity riv., Trinity co., NW California	irrigation and power	earth fill
Union Valley	1962	428	Silver Creek, El Dorado co., E California	power	earth fill
Yellowtail	1966	525	Bighorn riv., Big Horn co., S Montana	power, irrigation, and flood control	arch-variable center

[1] Dams arranged in alphabetical order. Dams and the lake or reservoir they create have the same name except for the following: Hoover Dam (Mead Reservoir), Glen Canyon Dam (Lake Powell Reservoir), Grand Coulee Dam (F. D. Roosevelt Lake), Merriman Dam (Rondout Reservoir), Morrow Point Dam (Blue Mesa Reservoir), New Exchequer Dam (Lake McClure), and O'Shaughnessy Dam (Hetch Hetchy Reservoir).

[2] Under construction.

Name	Established	Area (acres)	Location	Features and Facts of Interest
Agate Fossil Beds	1965[1]	2,995.19	Sioux co., W Nebraska	Miocene mammal fossils
Alibates Flint Quarries and Texas Panhandle Pueblo Culture	1965[1]	500.00	Potter co., NW Texas	Quarries worked by prehistoric Indians
Aztec Ruins	1923	27.14	San Juan co., NW New Mexico	Prehistoric pueblo
Badlands	1939	244,066.66	SW South Dakota	Eroded formations; fossils
Bandelier	1916	29,661.20	N cen. New Mexico	Cliff-dweller ruins
Biscayne	1968[1]	96,300.00	S Florida	Coral reef; wide variety of sea life
Black Canyon of the Gunnison	1933	13,689.72	W Colorado	Deep gorge formed by Gunnison river; see BLACK CANYON 2
Booker T. Washington	1956[1]	217.93	Franklin co., SW cen. Virginia	Booker T. Washington's birthplace and childhood home
Buck Island Reef	1961	850.00	St. Croix, Virgin Is.	Marine gardens
Cabrillo	1913	123.25	San Diego Bay, SW California	Land first sighted 1542 by Juan Rodriguez Cabrillo (d. 1543)
Canyon de Chelly	1931	83,840.00	NE Arizona	Cliff-dweller ruins
Capulin Mountain	1916	775.42	Union co., NE New Mexico	Site of ancient volcano, 8368 ft.
Casa Grande	1918	472.50	Pinal co., S Arizona	Prehistoric ruins, discovered 1694
Castillo de San Marcos	1924	20.36	St. Augustine, Florida	Old Spanish fort dating from 1672; see ST. AUGUSTINE
Castle Clinton	1950	1.00	New York City, New York	Structure built 1808–11; used for defense, later served as immigrant landing depot
Cedar Breaks	1933	6,154.60	SW Utah, N of Zion National Park	Canyons and cliffs, vast natural highly colored amphitheater
Chaco Canyon	1907	21,509.40	NW New Mexico	Cliff-dweller ruins
Channel Islands	1938	18,166.68	Anacapa Is. and Santa Barbara I., California	Fossils, examples of volcanic action, specimens of marine life
Chesapeake and Ohio Canal	1961	4,477.47	Maryland-West Virginia	Relatively unaltered 19th cent. canal
Chiricahua	1924	10,645.90	Cochise co., SE Arizona	Curious natural rock formations
Colorado	1911	17,362.26	Mesa co., W Colorado	Monoliths and eroded formations
Craters of the Moon	1924	53,545.05	Butte and Blaine cos., S Idaho	Lava flows in strange landscape effects
Custer Battlefield	1946	765.34	Big Horn co., S Montana, on Little Bighorn river	Site where Gen. Custer and his command were slain by Indians June 25–26, 1876; made national cemetery 1886
Death Valley	1933	1,907,760.00	E California	Ancient pictographs, curious geological formations; see DEATH VALLEY 1
Devils Postpile	1911	798.46	Madera co., cen. California	Peculiar hexagonal columns, like a pile of fence posts
Devils Tower	1906	1,346.91	On Belle Fourche river, Wyoming	Rock tower 865 ft. high, of volcanic origin
Dinosaur	1915	206,233.55	NE Utah and NW Colorado	Fossil remains of prehistoric animals
Effigy Mounds	1949	1,467.50	NE Iowa	Indian mounds
El Morro	1906	1,278.72	Valencia co., W New Mexico	Ruins of ancient pueblos; castellated sandstone with inscriptions by early Spanish explorers
Florissant Fossil Beds	1969[1]	5,992.32	Teller co., Colorado	Oligocene fossils
Fort Frederica	1945	250.00	W coast of Saint Simon I., Georgia	Site of fort built by Oglethorpe (1736–48) to protect against Spaniards from Florida

Name	Established	Area (acres)	Location	Features and Facts of Interest
Fort Jefferson	1935	47,125.00	Dry Tortugas (islands), W of Key West, Florida	Marine exhibit, remains of fortifications built in 1846
Fort McHenry	1925	43.26	Baltimore, Maryland	Bombardment by British 1814, occasion of writing of *Star Spangled Banner*
Fort Matanzas	1924	298.51	NE Florida, S of St. Augustine	Relics of Spanish occupation; see MATANZAS INLET
Fort Pulaski	1924	5,156.62	Island in mouth of Savannah river, Georgia	Fort built 1829–47 to replace Fort Greene. Fort bombarded 1862 by Union rifle cannon
Fort Sumter	1948	36.27	Charleston, South Carolina	Object of attack Apr. 12–13, 1861 which began Civil War
Fort Union	1956	720.60	Mora co., NE New Mexico	Ruins of Fort Union
George Washington Birthplace	1930	393.68	Frederick co., NE Virginia	Part of family plantation and site of house where George Washington was born
George Washington Carver	1951	210.00	Newton co., SW Missouri	Carver's birthplace and childhood home
Gila Cliff Dwellings	1907	533.13	SW New Mexico, 30 m. N of Silver City	Cliff dwellings
Glacier Bay	1925	2,803,840.00	SE Alaska, at S end of St. Elias Mts.	Large tidewater glaciers
Grand Canyon	1932	198,280.00	NW Arizona	Inner gorge of Grand Canyon, with Colorado river 3000 ft. below rim of canyon
Grand Portage	1958	770.00	NE Minnesota	Portage on route used by early settlers and explorers
Gran Quivira	1909	610.94	Torrance co., cen. New Mexico	Pueblo ruins and ruins of an early Spanish mission
Great Sand Dunes	1932	36,740.32	S cen. Colorado	Sand dunes of San Luis Park
Homestead	1939	162.73	Gage co., SE Nebraska	Site of first homestead entered under the General Homestead Act of 1862
Hovenweep	1923	505.43	SE Utah and SW Colorado	Prehistoric towers, pueblos, cliff dwellings
Jewel Cave	1908	1,274.56	SW South Dakota	Cave of limestone formation
Joshua Tree	1936	558,183.73	S California	Desert flora
Katmai	1918	2,792,137.00	S Alaska, on N end of Alaska Penin.	Katmai volcano (6715 ft.) and Valley of Ten Thousand Smokes
Lava Beds	1925	46,238.69	N California	Lava and ice caves; battleground of Modoc Wars 1873
Lehman Caves	1922	640.00	Whitepine co., E Nevada	Natural caves of limestone formation
Marble Canyon	1969	26,080.00	N Arizona	Canyon with 3000-ft. vertical walls
Montezuma Castle	1906	842.09	cen. Arizona	Prehistoric cliff dwellings
Mound City Group	1923	67.50	Ross co., S Ohio	Prehistoric mounds
Muir Woods	1908	502.90	12 m. NW of San Francisco, California	Fine redwood grove
Natural Bridges	1908	7,600.00	SE Utah	Three large natural bridges, largest 222 ft. high with span of 261 ft.
Navajo	1909	360.00	Navajo co., N Arizona	Cliff-dweller ruins
Ocmulgee	1936	683.48	Bibb co., cen. Georgia	Indian mounds
Oregon Caves	1909	480.00	Josephine co., SW Oregon	Caves of limestone formation
Organ Pipe Cactus	1937	330,874.25	S Arizona	Specimens of a species of cactus, the organ pipe cactus, and other plants
Pecos	1966	340.90	N cen. New Mexico	Ruins of 17th cent. Pecos Mission
Perry's Victory and International Peace Memorial	1936	21.44	N Ohio	Commemorates Perry's victory over British Sept. 10, 1813 at Put-in-Bay, Lake Erie, and the years of peace thereafter

Name	Estab-lished	Area (acres)	Location	Features and Facts of Interest
Pinnacles	1908	14,497.77	W cen. California	Spirelike rock formations
Pipe Spring	1923	40.00	Mohave co., NW Arizona	Old stone fort and a spring of pure water in a desert region
Pipestone	1937	282.58	SW Minnesota	Quarry from which Indians obtained material for ceremonial peace pipes
Rainbow Bridge	1910	160.00	San Juan co., S Utah	Natural bridge 309 ft. above creek, 235 ft. above top of inner canyon, span 278 ft.
Russell Cave	1961	310.45	NE Alabama	Cave containing valuable archaeological record of human habitation
Saguaro	1933	78,644.00	S Arizona	Giant cacti, or saguaro
Saint Croix Island	1949	56.50	Maine, on Canadian border	Commemorates French settlement of 1604
Scotts Bluff	1919	3,084.00	W Nebraska	Landmark on old Oregon Trail
Sitka	1910	54.33	Baranof I., SE Alaska	Eighteen totem poles; scene of a massacre of Russians by Tlingit Indians 1804
Statue of Liberty	1924	58.38	Liberty I., New York Harbor, N.Y.	Bartholdi's statue, Liberty Enlightening the World (unveiled 1886)
Sunset Crater	1930	3,040.00	N Arizona	Volcanic crater; lava flows, ice caves
Timpanogos Cave	1922	250.00	cen. Utah	Limestone cavern
Tonto	1907	1,120.00	Tonto co., E Arizona	Cliff-dweller ruins
Tumacacori	1908	15.00	Santa Cruz co., S Arizona	17th cent. Spanish mission ruins
Tuzigoot	1939	42.67	Yavapai co., cen. Arizona	Ruins of prehistoric pueblo
Walnut Canyon	1915	9.46	Coconino co., N cen. Arizona	Cliff dwellings in canyon
White Sands	1933	35.34	S cen. New Mexico	Dunes of gypsum sands
Wupatki	1924	32.84	Coconino co., N cen. Arizona	Prehistoric Indian dwellings
Yucca House	1919	9.60	Montezuma co., SW Colorado	Prehistoric ruins

[1] Year authorized.

UNITED STATES—NATIONAL HISTORICAL PARKS, NATIONAL MILITARY PARKS, AND NATIONAL BATTLEFIELD SITES

Name	Estab-lished	Area (acres)	Location	Features and Facts of Interest
Antietam National Battle-field Site	1890	783.63	Sharpsburg, Maryland	Site of battle Sept. 16–17, 1862, where Union army checked Lee's first invasion of the North in the Civil War; see SHARPSBURG 1
Appomattox Court House National Historical Park	1954	937.52	Appomattox, S cen. Virginia	Scene of surrender of Confederate army, April 9, 1865
Big Hole National Battle-field Site	1910	666.00	SW Montana	Site of battle Aug. 9, 1877 bet. U.S. troops and Nez Perce Indians under Chief Joseph
Brices Cross Roads National Battlefield Site	1929	1.00	Lee co., NE Mississippi	Battlefield 1864 of the Civil War
Chalmette National His-torical Park	1939	142.57	E of New Orleans, Louisiana	Commemorates battle of New Orleans Jan. 8, 1815
Chickamauga and Chatta-nooga National Military Park	1890	8,231.77	NW Georgia and SE Tennessee	Includes battlefields of Chickamauga and Missionary Ridge in the Civil War
City of Refuge National Historical Park	1961	180.78	W Hawaii I., Hawaii	Prior to 1819 place of refuge of Hawai-ian warriors; prehistoric house sites
Colonial National His-torical Park	1936	9,430.00	SE Virginia	Includes sites of Jamestown, Wil-liamsburg, and Yorktown
Cowpens National Battle-field Site	1929	1.24	Spartanburg co., NW South Carolina	Site of a battle Jan. 17, 1781 of Ameri-can Revolution; see COWPENS
Cumberland Gap National Historical Park	1940	20,176.49	Kentucky-Tennessee	Mountain pass explored by Daniel Boone; during Civil War held by Confederate forces (1861, 1861–63) and Union forces (1861, 1863–65)
Fort Donelson National Military Park	1928	600.00	NW Tennessee	Includes site of a Civil War fort, cap-tured by Gen. Grant 1862
Fort Necessity National Battlefield Site	1931	500.00	50 m. SE of Pittsburgh, Pennsylvania	Site of entrenchments thrown up by Major George Washington in the French and Indian War, finally sur-rendered by Washington July 3, 1754
Fredericksburg and Spotsyl-vania County Battlefields Memorial National Military Park	1927	3,672.15	Spotsylvania co., NE Virginia	Includes battlefields of Fredericks-burg, Chancellorsville, Spotsylvania Court House, and the Wilderness
George Rogers Clark Na-tional Historical Park	1966	17.00	Spencer co., S Indiana	Memorial near site of Fort Sackville, captured from British Feb. 25, 1779
Gettysburg National Mili-tary Park	1895	3,671.77	S Pennsylvania	Battlefield of Gettysburg
Guilford Courthouse National Military Park	1917	233.00	N cen. North Carolina	Site of battle Mar. 15, 1781 in which Americans defeated British and end-ed British control of the Carolinas
Harpers Ferry National Historical Park	1955	1,530.00	West Virginia-Maryland	Scene of John Brown raid 1859; changed hands many times during Civil War
Horseshoe Bend National Military Park	1959	2,040.00	Tallapoosa co., E Alabama	Site of battle between Gen. Andrew Jackson's forces and Creek Indian Confederacy, March 27, 1814
Independence National Historical Park	1956	21.84	Philadelphia, Pennsylvania	Several structures closely associated with the American Revolution and founding of the United States
Kennesaw Mountain National Battlefield Park	1947	3,682.62	25 m. NW of Atlanta, Georgia	Scene of fighting between Union forces under Sherman and Confeder-ates under Johnston, June 27, 1864
Kings Mountain National Military Park	1931	3,950.00	York co., N South Carolina	Includes site of battle Oct. 7, 1780 in which Americans defeated British in important battle of American Revolution
Manassas National Battle-field Park	1960	2,926.24	NE Virginia	Scene of battles of First and Second Manassas, July 21, 1861, and August 29–30, 1862
Minute Man National Historical Park	1959	750.00	13 m. NW of Boston, Massachusetts	Scene of first fighting of American Revolution, April 19, 1775

Name	Established	Area (acres)	Location	Features and Facts of Interest
Moores Creek National Military Park	1926	49.68	Pender co., SE North Carolina	Site of battle Feb. 27, 1776 of the American Revolution; the "Lexington and Concord" of the South
Morristown National Historical Park	1933	1,245.94	Morristown, New Jersey	Main campsite of American armies during winters of 1776–77 and 1779–80
Nez Perce National Historical Park	1965	3,000.00	Idaho co., N cen. Idaho	Commemorates culture and history of the Nez Perce Indian country
Pea Ridge National Military Park	1960	4,278.75	29 miles N of Fayetteville, NW Arkansas	Scene of a major engagement of the Civil War W of the Mississippi, March 7–8, 1862
Petersburg National Battlefield Site	1926	2,731.00	SE Virginia	Site of Civil War Battles 1864–65; see PETERSBURG 4, Virginia
Richmond National Battlefield Park	1936	746.56	8 m. ENE of Richmond, Virginia	Site of several battles to capture Richmond during Civil War
San Juan Island National Historical Park	1966	1,751.99	San Juan I., NW Washington	Commemorates the harmonious relations existing between the United States, United Kingdom, and Canada since 1872 border dispute in the region
Saratoga National Historical Park	1948	5,500.00	Saratoga co., E New York	Scene of victory of Americans over British Oct. 1777; turning point of American Revolution
Shiloh National Military Park	1894	3,515.46	Hardin co., SW Tennessee	Site of battle of Shiloh Apr. 1862 in Civil War; see PITTSBURG LANDING
Stones River National Battlefield Site	1927	330.86	cen. Tennessee, near Murfreesboro	Site of battle 1862–63 of Civil War; see MURFREESBORO
Tupelo National Battlefield Site	1929	1.50	Lee co., NE Mississippi	Site of battle July 13–14, 1864 during Civil War; see TUPELO
Vicksburg National Military Park	1899	1,740.00	W Mississippi	Includes site of siege of Vicksburg 1862–63 in Civil War
Wilson's Creek National Battlefield Park	1965	1,730.00	12 m. SW of Springfield, SW Missouri	Site of battle in Civil War, August 10, 1861

UNITED STATES—NATIONAL PARKS

Name	Established	Area (acres)	Location	Features and Facts of Interest
Acadia, formerly Lafayette (created 1919)	**1929**	**116.50**	**Maine coast**	**Granite peaks on Mount Desert I. and promontory on mainland across Frenchman Bay**
Arches	**1929**	**82,953.00**	**Grand co., E Utah**	**Wind-eroded natural arch formations**
Big Bend	**1944**	**708,221.20**	**W Texas, on Mexico border in big bend of Rio Grande**	**Mountain and desert scenery**
Bryce Canyon	**1928**	**36,010.38**	**S Utah**	**Canyon with curiously eroded pinnacles of various colors**
Canyonlands	**1964**	**337,258.00**	**SE Utah**	**Area of great geological interest**
Capitol Reef	**1937**	**254,241.72**	**S cen. Utah**	**Cliff dwellings, fossils, petrified trees, strange geologic formations**
Carlsbad Caverns	**1930**	**46,753.07**	**SE New Mexico**	**Huge natural caves; see CARLSBAD CAVERNS**
Crater Lake	**1902**	**160,290.33**	**S Oregon**	**Lake, maximum depth 2000 ft., in crater of extinct volcano in Cascade Range**
Everglades	**1947**	**1,400,533.00**	**S Florida penin.**	**See EVERGLADES, THE**
Glacier	**1910**	**1,013,129.12**	**NW Montana; U.S. part of Waterton-Glacier International Peace Park (*q.v.*)**	**Mountain region with many lakes and small glaciers**
Grand Canyon	**1919**	**673,575.00**	**NW Arizona**	**Canyon of the Colorado river; see GRAND CANYON**
Grand Teton	**1929**	**310,358.18**	**NW Wyoming**	**Most spectacular part of Teton Range including Grand Teton 13,766 ft.**
Great Smoky Mountains	**1930**	**516,626.02**	**Along S section of Tennessee-North Carolina boundary**	**Great Smoky Mts. (*q.v.*); dense forests, flowering shrubs and many varieties of flowers**
Guadalupe Mountains	**1966[1]**	**82,279.02**	**100 m. E of El Paso, Texas**	**Area of great geological interest; containing major Permian limestone fossil reef**
Haleakala	**1961**	**27,282.78**	**Hawaii**	**Large extinct volcanic crater in E Maui I.**
Hawaii Volcanoes	**1916**	**220,344.84**	**Hawaii**	**Volcanic area including active volcanoes Kilauea and Mauna Loa on Hawaii I.**
Hot Springs	**1921**	**3,535.24**	**W cen. Arkansas, in Ouachita Mts.**	**Forty-seven hot springs (147°F.)**
Isle Royale	**1940**	**539,341.01**	**Michigan, NW Lake Superior**	**Isle Royale (*q.v.*) and more than 100 surrounding islands; forested wilderness, cascades, inland lakes; old Indian copper pits**
Kings Canyon	**1940**	**460,330.90**	**S cen. California, in the Sierra Nevada**	**Canyon of middle and south branches of Kings river; snow-covered mountains, giant sequoias in General Grant Grove Section and Redwood Mountain**
Lassen Volcanic	**1916**	**160,933.78**	**N California, at S end of Cascade Range**	**Lassen Peak, active (1914–16) volcano; hot springs, mud geysers**
Mammoth Cave	**1941**	**51,354.40**	**SW cen. Kentucky**	**Series of huge caves; see MAMMOTH CAVE**
Mesa Verde	**1906**	**52,073.60**	**SW Colorado**	**Prehistoric cliff dwellings**
Mount McKinley	**1917**	**1,939,492.80**	**S cen. Alaska**	**Mount McKinley 20,320 ft., highest peak in North America; wildlife, esp. caribou and white Alaska mountain sheep**
Mount Rainier	**1899**	**241,781.09**	**W cen. Washington**	**Mount Rainier with extensive glacier systems; wild flowers in parks at it base**
North Cascades	**1968**	**505,000.00**	**NW Washington**	**Numerous glaciers and mountain lakes**
Olympic	**1938**	**896,599.00**	**NW Washington**	**Olympic Mts., virgin forests including temperate rain forests; glaciers**

Name	Established	Area (acres)	Location	Features and Facts of Interest
Petrified Forest	1962	94,189.33	E Arizona	Petrified wood; Indian ruins and petroglyphs
Platt	1906	911.97	S Oklahoma	Springs: 18 sulfur, 6 fresh water, 4 iron, 3 bromide, and several smaller ones
Redwood	1968	57,094.28	California	Groves of ancient trees, some of which are the world's tallest
Rocky Mountain	1915	262,324.22	N cen. Colorado	Heart of the Rockies; Longs Peak 14,256 ft. dominates region; interesting records of glacial period
Sequoia	1890	386,862.97	S cen. California, S of Kings Canyon National Park	Fine stands of sequoias; over 300 lakes; high mountains, Sierra Nevada, including Mount Whitney 14,494 ft.
Shenandoah	1935	193,538.56	N Virginia	Section of Blue Ridge; Hawksbill Mt. 4050 ft.; Skyline Drive part of Appalachian Trail (Maine to Georgia)
Virgin Islands	1956[1]	15,150.00	St. John, Virgin Is.	Interesting fauna and flora; prehistoric Caribbean Indian relics
Voyageurs	1971[1]	219,431.00	N Minnesota	Lakes, forests; area of geological interest
Wind Cave	1903	28,059.26	SW South Dakota	Cavern with intermittent air current; boxwork formations
Yellowstone	1872	2,221,772.61	NW Wyoming, S Montana and E Idaho	Geysers, hot springs; lakes and waterfalls; Grand Canyon of the Yellowstone, see YELLOWSTONE river, MAMMOTH HOT SPRINGS
Yosemite	1890	761,320.61	cen. California	Lofty cliffs; high waterfalls; groves of giant sequoias
Zion	1919	147,034.97	SW Utah	Zion Canyon cut by Virgin river, sandstone cliffs, remarkable for colors

[1] Year authorized.

UNITED STATES—MANNED SPACE FLIGHTS[1]

Name	Crew	Launch date	Weight (pounds)	Perigee/ Apogee (m.)*	Number of orbits	Time (hours: minutes)
"Freedom 7" . .	Alan B. Shepard, Jr.	May 5, 1961	2,855	116†	302‡	:15
"Liberty Bell 7".	Virgil I. Grissom	July 21, 1961	2,836	118†	303‡	:16
"Friendship 7".	John H. Glenn, Jr.	Feb. 20, 1962	2,987	100/162	3	4:55
"Aurora 7" . . .	M. Scott Carpenter	May 24, 1962	2,975	99/167	3	4:56
"Sigma 7"	Walter M. Schirra, Jr.	Oct. 3, 1962	3,029	100/176	6	9:13
"Faith 7" . . .	L. Gordon Cooper, Jr.	May 15, 1963	3,033	100/166	22	34:20
Gemini 3	Virgil I. Grissom John W. Young	March 23, 1965	7,111	99/139	3	4:53
Gemini 4	James A. McDivitt Edward H. White II	June 3, 1965	7,879	99/184	66	97:56
Gemini 5	L. Gordon Cooper, Jr. Charles Conrad, Jr.	Aug. 21, 1965	7,947	101/217	128	190:55
Gemini 7	Frank Borman James A. Lovell, Jr.	Dec. 4, 1965	8,076	100/204	220	330:35
Gemini 6	Walter M. Schirra, Jr. Thomas P. Stafford	Dec. 15, 1965	7,817	100/193	17	25:51
Gemini 8	Neil A. Armstrong David R. Scott	March 16, 1966	8,351	99/186	7	10:41
Gemini 9	Thomas P. Stafford Eugene A. Cernan	June 3, 1966	8,268	99/194	48	72:21
Gemini 10	John W. Young Michael Collins	July 18, 1966	8,295	99/474	46	70:47
Gemini 11	Charles Conrad, Jr. Richard F. Gordon, Jr.	Sept. 12, 1966	8,374	100/851	47	71:17
Gemini 12	James A. Lovell, Jr. Edwin E. Aldrin, Jr.	Nov. 11, 1966	8,296	100/187	62	94:35
Apollo 7	Walter M. Schirra, Jr. Donn F. Eisele R. Walter Cunningham	Oct. 11, 1968	32,560	138.4/177.9	163	260:07
Apollo 8	Frank Borman James Lovell, Jr. William Anders	Dec. 21, 1968	63,650		1½,10 §	147:11
Apollo 9	James A. McDivitt David R. Scott Russell L. Schweickart	March 3, 1969	91,702	‖	151	241:01
Apollo 10	Thomas P. Stafford Eugene A. Cernan John W. Young	May 18, 1969	94,320	¶	31 §	192:03
Apollo 11	Neil A. Armstrong Edwin E. Aldrin, Jr. Michael Collins	July 16, 1969	96,698	♀	31 §	195:18
Apollo 12	Charles Conrad, Jr. Alan L. Bean Richard F. Gordon, Jr.	Nov. 14, 1969	101,131	♁	45 §	244:36
Apollo 13	James A. Lovell, Jr. Fred W. Haise, Jr. John L. Swigert, Jr.	April 11, 1970	97,152	□	□	142:54
Apollo 14	Alan B. Shepard, Jr. Edgar D. Mitchell Stuart A. Roosa	Jan. 31, 1971	102,179	◇	34 §	216:02
Apollo 15	David R. Scott Alfred M. Worden James B. Irwin	July 26, 1971	107,155	⊕	74§	295:12
Apollo 16	John W. Young Chàrles M. Duke Thomas K. Mattingly	April 16, 1972	107,195	**	64	265:51

[1] See also UNION OF SOVIET SOCIALIST REPUBLICS, Manned Space Flights.
*Minimum perigee and maximum apogee, in statute miles. † Maximum altitude, statute miles (ballistic flight). ‡Range, statute miles. §Lunar orbits. ‖Checkout of Lunar Module in Earth orbit. ¶ Checkout of Lunar Module in lunar orbit. ♀Lunar Module on Moon, 21 hours 36 minutes. ♁Lunar Module on Moon, 31 hours 31 minutes. □Looped around Moon and returned to Earth. ◇ Lunar Module on Moon, 33 hours 31 minutes. ⊕Lunar Module on Moon, 66 hours 55 minutes. **Lunar Module on Moon, 71 hours 14 minutes.

1970 Rank	Name[1]	Pop. (1970c)	1960 Rank	Pop. (1960c)	Percent change 1960 to 1970
1	New York, N.Y.	11,571,899	1	10,694,633	8.2
2	Los Angeles-Long Beach, Calif.	7,032,075	3	6,038,771	16.4
3	Chicago, Ill.	6,978,947	2	6,220,913	12.2
4	Philadelphia, Pa.	4,817,914	4	4,342,897	10.9
5	Detroit, Mich.	4,199,931	5	3,762,360	11.6
6	San Francisco-Oakland, Calif.	3,109,519	6	2,648,762	17.4
7	Washington, D.C.-Md.-Va.	2,861,123	10	2,076,610	37.8
8	Boston, Mass.	2,753,700	7	2,595,481	6.1
9	Pittsburgh, Pa.	2,401,245	8	2,405,435	-0.2
10	St. Louis, Mo.-Ill.	2,363,017	9	2,104,669	12.3
11	Baltimore, Md.	2,070,670	12	1,803,745	14.8
12	Cleveland, Ohio	2,064,194	11	1,909,483	8.1
13	Houston, Texas	1,985,031	15	1,418,323	40.0
14	Newark, N.J.	1,856,556	13	1,689,420	9.9
15	Minneapolis-St. Paul, Minn.	1,813,647	14	1,482,030	22.4
16	Dallas, Texas	1,555,950	20	1,119,410	39.0
17	Seattle-Everett, Wash.	1,421,869	21	1,107,213	28.4
18	Anaheim-Santa Ana-Garden Grove, Calif.	1,420,386	39	703,925	101.8
19	Milwaukee, Wis.	1,403,688	17	1,278,850	9.8
20	Atlanta, Ga.	1,390,164	24	1,017,188	36.7
21	Cincinnati, Ohio	1,384,851	18	1,268,479	9.2
22	Paterson-Clifton-Passaic, N.J.	1,358,794	19	1,186,873	14.5
23	San Diego, Calif.	1,357,854	23	1,033,011	31.4
24	Buffalo, N.Y.	1,349,211	16	1,306,957	3.2
25	Miami, Fla.	1,267,792	26	935,047	35.6
26	Kansas City, Mo.-Kan.	1,253,916	22	1,092,545	14.8
27	Denver, Colo.	1,227,529	27	929,383	32.1
28	San Bernardino-Riverside-Ontario, Calif.	1,143,146	31	809,782	41.2
29	Indianapolis, Ind.	1,109,882	25	944,475	17.5
30	San Jose, Calif.	1,064,714	43	642,315	65.8
31	New Orleans, La.	1,045,809	28	907,123	15.3
32	Tampa-St. Petersburg, Fla.	1,012,594	32	772,453	31.1
33	Portland, Ore.-Wash.	1,009,129	29	821,897	22.8
34	Phoenix, Ariz.	967,522	41	663,510	45.8
35	Columbus, Ohio	916,228	33	754,885	21.4
36	Providence-Pawtucket-Warwick, R.I.-Mass.	910,781	30	821,101	11.3
37	Rochester, N.Y.	882,667	34	732,588	20.5
38	San Antonio, Texas	864,014	38	716,168	20.6
39	Dayton, Ohio	850,266	35	727,121	16.9
40	Louisville, Ky.-Ind.	826,553	36	725,139	14.0
41	Sacramento, Calif.	800,592	45	625,503	28.0
42	Memphis, Tenn.-Ark.	770,120	40	674,583	14.2
43	Fort Worth, Texas	762,086	50	573,215	32.9
44	Birmingham, Ala.	739,274	37	721,207	2.5
45	Albany-Schenectady-Troy, N.Y.	721,910	42	657,503	9.8
46	Toledo, Ohio-Mich.	692,571	44	630,647	9.8
47	Norfolk-Portsmouth, Va.	680,600	48	578,507	17.6
48	Akron, Ohio	679,239	47	605,367	12.2
49	Hartford, Conn.	663,891	52	549,249	20.9
50	Oklahoma City, Okla.	640,889	54	511,833	25.2
51	Syracuse, N.Y.	636,507	51	563,781	12.9
52	Gary-Hammond-East Chicago, Ind.	633,367	49	573,548	10.4
53	Honolulu, Hawaii	629,176	56	500,409	26.0
54	Ft. Lauderdale-Hollywood, Fla.	620,100	76	333,946	85.7
55	Jersey City, N.J.	609,266	46	610,734	-0.2
56	Greensboro-Winston-Salem-High Point, N.C.	603,895	53	520,249	16.1
57	Salt Lake City, Utah	557,635	63	447,795	24.5
58	Allentown-Bethlehem-Easton, Pa.-N.J.	543,551	58	492,168	10.4
59	Nashville, Tenn.	541,108	59	463,628	16.7
60	Omaha, Nebr.-Iowa	540,142	61	457,873	18.0
61	Grand Rapids, Mich.	539,225	60	461,906	16.7
62	Youngstown-Warren, Ohio	536,003	55	509,006	5.3
63	Springfield-Chicopee-Holyoke, Mass.	529,922	57	493,999	7.3
64	Jacksonville, Fla.	528,865	62	455,411	16.1
65	Richmond, Va.	518,319	64	436,044	18.9
66	Wilmington, Del.-N.J.-Md.	499,493	67	414,565	20.5
67	Flint, Mich.	496,658	66	416,239	19.3
68	Tulsa, Okla.	476,945	65	418,974	13.8
69	Orlando, Fla.	428,003	82	318,487	34.4
70	Fresno, Calif.	413,053	71	365,945	12.9
71	Tacoma, Wash.	411,027	79	321,590	27.8
72	Harrisburg, Pa.	410,626	69	371,653	10.5

1970 Rank	Name[1]	Pop. (1970c)	1960 Rank	Pop. (1960c)	Percent change 1960 to 1970
73	Charlotte, N.C.	409,370	83	316,781	29.2
74	Knoxville, Tenn.	400,337	70	368,080	8.8
75	Wichita, Kan.	389,352	68	381,626	2.0
76	Bridgeport, Conn.	389,153	75	337,983	15.1
77	Lansing, Mich.	378,423	87	298,949	26.6
78	Mobile, Ala.	376,690	72	363,389	3.7
79	Oxnard-Ventura, Calif.	376,430	129	199,138	89.0
80	Canton, Ohio	372,210	74	340,345	9.4
81	Davenport-Rock Island-Moline, Iowa-Ill.	362,638	81	319,375	13.5
82	El Paso, Texas	359,291	84	314,070	14.4
83	New Haven, Conn.	355,538	80	320,836	10.8
84	Tucson, Ariz.	351,667	103	265,660	32.4
85	West Palm Beach, Fla.	348,753	117	228,106	52.9
86	Worcester, Mass.	344,320	78	328,898	4.7
87	Wilkes-Barre-Hazleton, Pa.	342,301	73	346,972	-1.3
88	Peoria, Ill.	341,979	85	313,412	9.1
89	Utica-Rome, N.Y.	340,670	77	330,771	3.0
90	York, Pa.	329,540	89	290,242	13.5
91	Bakersfield, Calif.	329,162	88	291,984	12.7
92	Little Rock-North Little Rock, Ark.	323,296	98	271,936	18.9
93	Columbia, S.C.	322,880	105	260,828	23.8
94	Lancaster, Pa.	319,693	94	278,359	14.8
95	Beaumont-Port Arthur-Orange, Texas	315,943	86	306,016	3.2
96	Albuquerque, N.M.	315,774	104	262,199	20.4
97	Chattanooga, Tenn.-Ga.	304,927	91	283,169	7.7
98	Trenton, N.J.	303,968	101	266,392	14.1
99	Charleston, S.C.	303,849	108	254,578	19.4
100	Binghamton, N.Y.-Pa.	302,672	90	283,600	6.7
101	Greenville, S.C.	299,502	106	255,806	17.1
102	Reading, Pa.	296,382	97	275,414	7.6
103	Austin, Texas	295,516	125	212,136	39.3
104	Shreveport, La.	294,703	92	281,481	4.7
105	Newport News-Hampton, Va.	292,159	118	224,503	30.1
106	Madison, Wis.	290,272	120	222,095	30.7
107	Stockton, Calif.	290,208	111	249,989	16.1
108	Spokane, Wash.	287,487	95	278,333	3.3
109	Des Moines, Iowa	286,101	102	266,315	7.4
110	Baton Rouge, La.	285,167	116	230,058	24.0
111	Corpus Christi, Texas	284,832	100	266,594	6.8
112	Fort Wayne, Ind.	280,455	113	232,196	20.8
113	South Bend, Ind.	280,031	99	271,057	3.3
114	Appleton-Oshkosh, Wis.	276,891	114	231,990	19.4
115	Las Vegas, Nev.	273,288	184	127,016	115.2
116	Rockford, Ill.	272,063	115	230,091	18.2
117	Duluth-Superior, Minn.-Wis.	265,350	96	276,596	-4.1
118	Santa Barbara, Calif.	264,324	145	168,962	56.4
119	Erie, Pa.	263,654	110	250,682	5.2
120	Johnstown, Pa.	262,822	93	280,733	-6.4
121	Jackson, Miss.	258,906	121	221,367	17.0
122	Lorain-Elyria, Ohio	256,843	123	217,500	18.1
123	Huntington-Ashland, W. Va.-Ky.-Ohio	253,743	107	254,780	-0.4
124	Augusta, Ga.-S.C.	253,460	124	216,639	17.0
125	Salinas-Monterey, Calif.	250,071	132	198,351	26.1
126	Vallejo-Napa, Calif.	249,081	127	200,487	24.2
127	Pensacola, Fla.	243,075	126	203,376	19.5
128	Columbus, Ga.-Ala.	238,584	122	217,985	9.4
129	Colorado Springs, Col.	235,972	167	143,742	64.2
130	Scranton, Pa.	234,107	112	234,531	-0.2
131	Ann Arbor, Mich.	234,103	140	172,440	35.8
132	Evansville, Ind.-Ky.	232,775	119	222,890	4.4
133	Lawrence-Haverhill, Mass.-N.H.	232,415	130	199,136	16.7
134	Charleston, W.Va.	229,515	109	252,925	-9.3
135	Raleigh, N.C.	228,453	144	169,082	35.1
136	Huntsville, Ala.	228,239	156	153,861	48.3
137	Hamilton-Middletown, Ohio	226,207	131	199,076	13.6
138	Saginaw, Mich.	219,743	133	190,752	15.2
139	Eugene, Oregon	213,358	148	162,890	31.0
140	Lowell, Mass.	212,860	147	164,243	29.6
141	Fayetteville, N.C.	212,042	162	148,418	42.9
142	Waterbury, Conn.	208,956	136	185,548	12.6
143	New London-Groton-Norwich, Conn.	208,718	142	170,981	22.1
144	Stamford, Conn.	206,419	139	178,409	15.7
145	Macon, Ga.	206,342	138	180,403	14.4
146	Santa Rosa, Calif.	204,885	164	147,375	39.0

1970 Rank	Name[1]	Pop. (1970c)	1960 Rank	Pop. (1960c)	Percent change 1960 to 1970
147	Kalamazoo, Mich.	201,550	143	169,712	18.8
148	Montgomery, Ala.	201,325	128	199,734	0.8
149	Modesto, Calif.	194,506	152	157,294	23.7
150	Durham, N.C.	190,388	155	154,965	22.9
151	Brockton, Mass.	189,820	161	149,458	27.0
152	Savannah, Ga.	187,767	135	188,299	-0.3
153	Salem, Ore.	186,658	163	147,411	26.6
154	Wheeling, W.Va.-Ohio	182,712	134	190,342	-4.0
155	McAllen-Pharr-Edinburg, Texas	181,535	137	180,904	0.3
156	Roanoke, Va.	181,436	151	158,803	14.3
157	Lubbock, Texas	179,295	153	156,271	14.7
158	Terre Haute, Ind.	175,143	141	172,069	1.8
159	Atlantic City, N.J.	175,043	149	160,880	8.8
160	Lexington, Ky.	174,323	179	131,906	32.2
161	Lima, Ohio	171,472	150	160,862	6.6
162	Racine, Wis.	170,838	169	141,781	20.5
163	Galveston-Texas City, Texas	169,812	171	140,364	21.0
164	Lincoln, Nebr.	167,972	154	155,272	8.2
165	Steubenville-Weirton, Ohio-W.Va.	165,627	146	167,756	1.3
166	Champaign-Urbana, Ill.	163,281	177	132,436	23.3
167	Cedar Rapids, Iowa	163,213	175	136,899	19.2
168	Springfield, Ill.	161,335	165	146,539	10.1
169	Fort Smith, Ark.-Okla.	160,421	176	135,110	18.7
170	Green Bay, Wis.	158,244	187	125,082	26.5
171	Muskegon-Muskegon Heights, Mich.	157,426	159	149,943	5.0
172	Springfield, Ohio	157,115	180	131,440	19.5
173	Topeka, Kan.	155,322	170	141,286	9.9
174	Springfield, Mo.	152,929	185	126,276	21.1
175	New Bedford, Mass.	152,642	168	143,176	6.6
176	Fall River, Mass.-R.I.	149,976	173	138,156	8.6
177	Waco, Texas	147,553	158	150,091	-1.7
178	Lake Charles, La.	145,415	166	145,475	—
179	New Britain, Conn.	145,269	183	129,397	12.3
180	Asheville, N.C.	145,056	181	130,074	11.5
181	Amarillo, Texas	144,396	160	149,493	-3.4
182	Jackson, Mich.	143,274	178	131,994	8.5
183	Portland, Me.	141,625	172	139,122	1.8
184	Brownsville-Harlingen-San Benito, Texas	140,368	157	151,098	-7.1
185	Anderson, Ind.	138,451	186	125,819	10.0
186	Provo-Orem, Utah	137,776	200	106,991	28.8
187	Altoona, Pa.	135,356	174	137,270	-1.4
188	Biloxi-Gulfport, Miss.	134,582	191	119,489	12.6
189	Waterloo, Iowa	132,916	188	122,482	8.5
190	Mansfield, Ohio	129,997	194	117,761	10.4
191	Muncie, Ind.	129,219	195	110,938	16.5
192	Petersburg-Colonial Heights, Va.	128,809	202	106,685	20.7
193	Wichita Falls, Texas	127,621	182	129,638	-1.6
194	Ogden, Utah	126,278	196	110,744	14.0
195	Decatur, Ill.	125,010	193	118,257	5.7
196	Lynchburg, Va.	123,474	197	110,701	11.5
197	Vineland-Millville-Bridgeton, N.J.	121,374	201	106,850	13.6
198	Reno, Nev.	121,068	219	84,743	42.9
199	Fargo-Moorhead, N.D.-Minn.	120,238	203	106,027	13.4
200	Norwalk, Conn.	120,099	208	96,756	24.1
201	Pueblo, Colo.	118,238	192	118,707	-0.4
202	Kenosha, Wis.	117,917	206	100,615	17.2
203	Bay City, Mich.	117,339	199	107,042	9.6
204	Sioux City, Iowa	116,189	190	120,017	-3.2
205	Tuscaloosa, Ala.	116,029	198	109,047	6.4
206	Monroe, La.	115,387	205	101,663	13.5
207	Abilene, Texas	113,959	189	120,377	-5.3
208	Boise City, Idaho	112,230	209	93,460	20.1
209	Lafayette, La.	109,716	220	84,656	29.6
210	Lafayette-West Lafayette, Ind.	109,378	216	89,122	22.7
211	Manchester, N.H.	108,461	204	102,861	5.4
212	Lawton, Okla.	108,144	213	90,803	19.1
213	Wilmington, N.C.	107,219	210	92,020	16.5
214	Gainesville, Fla.	104,764	228	74,074	41.4
215	Bloomington-Normal, Ill.	104,389	221	83,877	24.5
216	Tallahassee, Fla.	103,047	227	74,225	38.8
217	Texarkana, Texas-Ark.	101,198	211	91,657	10.4
218	Fitchburg-Leominster, Mass.	97,164	215	90,158	7.8
219	Tyler, Texas	97,096	218	86,350	12.4

1970 Rank	Name[1]	Pop. (1970c)	1960 Rank	Pop. (1960c)	Percent change 1960 to 1970
220	Sioux Falls, S.D.	95,209	217	86,575	10.0
221	Gadsden, Ala.	94,144	207	96,980	-2.9
222	Odessa, Texas	91,805	212	90,995	0.9
223	Dubuque, Iowa	90,609	223	80,048	13.2
224	Albany, Ga.	89,639	226	75,680	18.4
225	Billings, Mont.	87,367	224	79,016	10.6
226	St. Joseph, Mo.	86,915	214	90,581	-4.0
227	Pine Bluff, Ark.	85,329	222	81,373	4.9
228	Rochester, Minn.	84,104	235	65,532	28.3
229	Sherman-Denison, Texas	83,225	230	73,043	13.9
230	Great Falls, Mont.	81,804	229	73,418	11.4
231	Columbia, Mo.	80,911	238	55,202	46.6
232	La Crosse, Wis.	80,468	231	72,465	11.0
233	Pittsfield, Mass.	79,727	225	76,772	3.8
234	Owensboro, Ky.	79,486	232	70,588	12.6
235	Danbury, Conn.	78,405	240	54,342	44.3
236	Laredo, Texas	72,859	236	64,791	12.5
237	Lewiston-Auburn, Me.	72,474	233	70,295	3.1
238	San Angelo, Texas	71,047	237	64,630	9.9
239	Nashua, N.H.	66,458	242	44,972	47.8
240	Bristol, Conn.	65,808	239	54,480	20.8
241	Midland, Texas	65,433	234	67,717	-3.4
242	Bryan-College Station, Texas	57,978	243	44,895	29.1
243	Meriden, Conn.	55,959	241	51,850	7.9

[1] **Located by state. For more detailed location, see entries of individual cities.**

United States of Brazil. See BRAZIL.

United States of Colombia. See history at COLOMBIA.

United States of Indonesia. See INDONESIA 2.

United States of Mexico. See MEXICO 1.

United States of Venezuela. See VENEZUELA.

United States Range. Mountain range, N Ellesmere I., NE Franklin dist., Northwest Territories, N Canada; highest point 9000 ft.

Uni·ver·sal City \ˌyü-nə-ˌvər-səl-\. 1 Suburb, NW of Los Angeles, California; motion-picture studios.

2 City, Bexar co., S cen. Texas, 17 m. NE of San Antonio; pop. (1970c) 7613.

Uni·ver·si·ty \ˌyü-nə-ˈver-sə-tē\. Suburb of Tuscaloosa, Alabama. See TUSCALOOSA 2.

University City. City, St. Louis co., E Missouri, 8 m. WNW of St. Louis; pop. (1970c) 46,309; suburb of St. Louis.

University Heights. Residential city, Cuyahoga co., N Ohio, 8 m. E of Cleveland; pop. (1970c) 17,055; John Carroll Univ. (1886).

University Park. 1 Town, Mahaska co., Iowa, adjacent to Oskaloosa; pop. (1970c) 534.

2 Town, Prince Georges co., S cen. Maryland, 7 m. NW of Washington, D.C.; pop. (1970c) 2926.

3 City, Dallas co., NE Texas, entirely within city of Dallas; pop. (1970c) 23,498.

University Peak. Mountain in Sierra Nevada, on NE boundary of Tulare co., S cen. California; 13,588 ft.

Un·ley \ˈən-lē\. City, SE South Australia, a S suburb of Adelaide; pop. (1966c) 39,700.

Un·na \ˈün-ə\. Industrial city, North Rhine-Westphalia, West Germany, 10 m. E of Dortmund; pop. (1969e) 49,470; coal mining; wire and machinery.

Un·nao *or* **Unao** \ü-ˈnaü\. Town, S cen. Uttar Pradesh, N India, 12 m. NE of Kanpur; pop. (1961c) 29,780.

Unst \ˈən(t)st\. One of the Shetland Is., NE of N Scotland; 38 sq. m. See MUCKLE FLUGGA.

Un·ter·wal·den \ˈünt-ər-ˌväl-dən\. Swiss canton; divided into two demicantons: **Nid·wal·den** \ˈnēd-ˌväl-dən\ and **Ob·wal·den** \ˈōp-ˌväl-dən\. See history and table at SWITZERLAND.

Unyam·we·zi \ˌü-ˌnyäm-ˈwā-zē\. Plateau region, W Tanzania, E Africa, around Tabora.

Un·zen \ˈün-ˌzen\. Active volcano, Nagasaki prefecture, NW Kyūshū, Japan, on peninsula at S end of Shimabara Bay and opp. Kumamoto; 4462 ft.

Un·zha \ˈün-zhə\. River, cen. Russian S.F.S.R., U.S.S.R.; 342 m. long; rises in Vologda Oblast, flows S through Kostroma and Ivanovo oblasts to the Volga below Kineshma; navigable for ab. 250 m.

Upem·ba National Park \ü-ˈpem-bə-\. National park, Shaba prov., Zaire; 4580 sq. m.; wide variety of wildlife; established 1939.

Uper·na·vik *or* **Uper·ni·vik** \ˈü-ˈpər-nə-ˌvēk\. Eskimo settlement, W coast of Greenland, N of Disko I., 72°47′N, 56°10′W; pop. (1968e) 1930.

Up·ing·ton \ˈəp-iŋ-tən\. Town, N Cape Province, S Rep. of South Africa, on N bank of Orange river ab. 405 m. NNE of Cape Town; pop. (1967e) 28,000; copper in region.

Up·land \ˈəp-lənd\. 1 City, San Bernardino co., SE California, 34 m. E of Los Angeles; pop. (1970c) 32,551; citrus fruits.

2 Town, Grant co., Indiana; pop. (1970c) 3202; Taylor Univ. (1846).

3 Borough, Delaware co., SE Pennsylvania, 15 m. WSW of Philadelphia; pop. (1970c) 3930.

Upo·lu \ü-ˈpō-(ˌ)lü\. Island, Western Samoa, in SW cen. Pacific Ocean, ab. 38 m. W by N of Tutuila; 46 m. long by ab. 16 m. wide; 403 sq. m.; chief town Apia on N coast. Has many mountains, highest peak Fito 3608 ft. Has fertile soil; chief product copra. Apia and Saluafata are chief harbors.

Upolu Point. Cape, N tip of Hawaii I., Hawaii, 20°16′N, 155°51′W.

Upper Andalusia. See ANDALUSIA 2.

Upper Angara. See ANGARA 2.

Upper Ar·ling·ton \-ˈär-liŋ-tən\. City, Franklin co., cen. Ohio, 8 m. NNW of Columbus; pop. (1970c) 38,630.

Upper Arrow Lake. See ARROW LAKE.

Upper Austria *or Ger.* **Ober·ö·ster·reich** \ˌō-bər-ˈœ-stər-ˌrīk\; *from 1938 to 1945* **Upper Danube** *or Ger.* **Ober·do·nau** \ˌō-bər-ˈdō-naü\. State, Austria, bet. Lower Austria and West Germany and mostly W of the Enns river; 4625 sq. m.; pop. (1971p) 1,244,000; ✱ Linz; crossed by the Danube. Chief industry agriculture. In Hohenstaufen period divided bet. duchies of Styria and Bavaria; later part of the duchy of Austria, then of the archduchy and empire.

Upper Avon. See AVON 8.

Upper Bann. See BANN.

Upper Burma. See BURMA.

Upper California. See ALTA CALIFORNIA.

Upper Canada. Former British province, North America, N of the Great Lakes and S of the watershed bet. the Great Lakes and Hudson Bay, equivalent to S part of modern province of Ontario, Canada. Established as separate province by act of 1791; its settlement by American Loyalists made its population predominantly English; after rebellion of 1837, reunited with Lower Canada (*q.v.*) 1841.

Upper Chateaugay Lake. See CHATEAUGAY LAKES.

Upper Danube. See UPPER AUSTRIA.

Upper Dar·by \-'där-bē\. Urban district (township), Delaware co., SE Pennsylvania; pop. (1970c) 45,000.

Upper Egypt. See EGYPT.

Upper Gastein. See GASTEINER ACHE.

Upper Guinea. See GUINEA 1.

Upper Hutt \-'hət\. City, North I., New Zealand; pop. (1970e) 20,300.

Upper Io·wa \-'ī-ə-wə\. River, NE Iowa; 135 m. long; rises in S Mower co., S Minnesota, flows E into Mississippi river in NE Allamakee co., NE Iowa.

Upper Ka·pu·as Mountains \-'käp-ü-äs-\. Mountain range in W cen. Borneo, extending E and W along the boundary between the Malaysian state of Sarawak and the Indonesian province of West Kalimantan; highest point ab. 2651 ft.

Upper Klamath Lake. See KLAMATH LAKES.

Upper Lorraine. See LORRAINE 2.

Upper Marl·boro \-'märl-bər-ə, -bə-rə\. Town, ⊗ of Prince Georges co., S cen. Maryland; pop. (1970c) 646.

Upper Mat·e·cum·be Key \-ˌmat-ə-'kəm-bē-\. See FLORIDA KEYS.

Upper More·land \-'mō(ə)r-lənd, -'mȯ(ə)r-\. Urban township, Montgomery co., SE Pennsylvania, N of Philadelphia; pop. (1970c) 24,866.

Upper New York Bay. See NEW YORK BAY.

Upper Nile. Province of SE Sudan. See table at SUDAN.

Upper Palatinate. See PALATINATE.

Upper Peninsula. North part of Michigan, bet. Lakes Superior and Michigan.

Upper Peru. Earlier name for region corresponding approximately to Bolivia; originally the audiencia of Charcas, a part (1559–1776) of the Spanish viceroyalty of Peru, capital Chuquisaca (modern Sucre); in 1776 became N part of new viceroyalty of La Plata; established as the independent state of Bolivia 1825.

Upper Red Lake. See RED LAKE 1.

Upper Region. Administrative region of N Ghana. See table at GHANA.

Upper Rhine *or Ger.* **Ober·rhein** \'ō-bə(r)-ˌrīn\. The section of the Rhine river bet. Basel and Mainz.

Upper Sad·dle River \-ˌsad-ᵊl-\. Borough, Bergen co., NE New Jersey, 10 m. NNE of Paterson; pop. (1970c) 7949.

Upper San·dus·ky \-sən-'dəs-kē, -san-\. Village, ⊗ of Wyandot co., NW cen. Ohio, 18 m. NNW of Marion; pop. (1970c) 5645.

Upper Saranac Lake. See SARANAC LAKES.

Upper Senegal–Niger. See history at MALI.

Upper Silesia. See SILESIA.

Upper Sind Frontier. See JACOBABAD 1.

Upper Tunguska. See ANGARA 1.

Upper Vol·ta \-'väl-tə, -'vōl-, -'vȯl-\ *or Fr.* **Haute–Volta** \ōt-vȯl-tà\; *sometimes* **Vol·ta·ic Republic** \väl-ˌtā-ik-, vōl-, vȯl-\. Republic, W Africa, bounded on W and N by Mali, on E by Niger, on SE by Dahomey, and on S by Togo, Ghana, and Ivory Coast; 105,869 sq. m.; pop. (1970e) 5,485,981; ✱ Ouagadougou. *Physical features:* Plateau region; characterized by savanna, grassy in N, sparsely forested in S. *Chief products:* Sorghum, corn, rice, cassava, sweet potatoes, peanuts; livestock raising. *Chief towns:* Ouagadougou, Bobo-Dioulasso.

History: French protectorate established over region 1895–97; S boundary demarcated through Anglo-French agreement 1898; part of Upper Senegal-Niger colony until 1919, when it became a separate colony; partitioned between other French possessions 1932, reconstituted as an overseas territory within the French Union 1947; became an autonomous republic within the French Community 1958; achieved total independence 1960; civilian government overthrown 1966; adopted new constitution 1970.

Upper Yukon. See LEWES 2.

Upp·sa·la \'əp-sə-ˌlä, -ˌsäl-ə, əp-'säl-ə\. 1 County of E Sweden. See table at SWEDEN.

2 City, its ⊗, 40 m. NNW of Stockholm; pop. (1970e) 101,696; railroad junction; produces building materials, machinery, ceramics; printing; military and air base; educational center, with univ. (1477) and many other academic institutions; 13th–15th cent. cathedral, episcopal palace (now museum), 16th cent. castle. Capital of the ancient pre-Christian kingdom of Svea; made archiepiscopal see 1164.

Up·sa·la Glacier \ùp-'säl-ə-\. Glacier in the Andes, Argentina; 37 m. long, ab. 2 m. wide near its terminus.

Up·shur \'əp-shər\. Name of counties in two states of the U.S. See tables at TEXAS and WEST VIRGINIA.

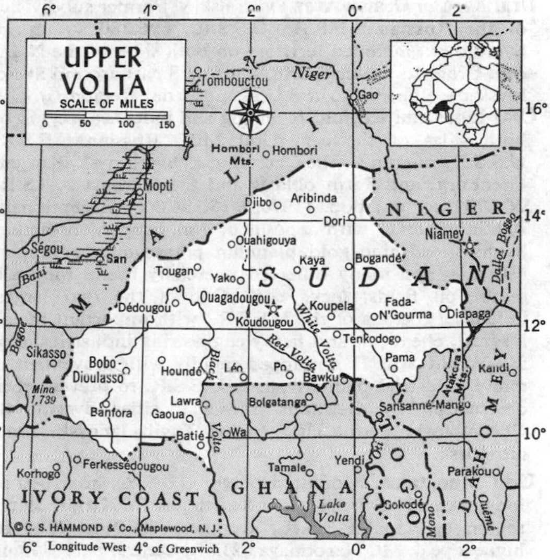

Up·son \'əp-sᵊn\. County in Georgia. See table at GEORGIA.

Up·ton \'əp-tən\. 1 County in Texas. See table at TEXAS.

2 Town, Worcester co., cen. Massachusetts, 12 m. ESE of Worcester; pop. (1970c) 5484.

3 *or formerly* **Camp Upton.** Former army camp, on Long I., Suffolk co., New York, ab. 10 m. WSW of Riverhead; estab. in World War I, rebuilt 1940 for use in World War II; site since 1947 of Brookhaven National Laboratory for Nuclear Research.

Uqsor, Al–. See LUXOR.

Ur \'ər, 'ù(ə)r\ *or Bib.* **Ur of the Chal·dees** \-'kal-ˌdēz\. City and district, ancient Sumer, S Babylonia, the modern **Mu-**

qai·yir \mu̇-ˈkī-yi(ə)r, -ˈkā-\, ab. 12 m. SW of An Nasiriya, S Iraq, on a former channel of the Euphrates river and near the Baghdad-Basra railroad. One of the oldest cities of Mesopotamia; its First Dynasty ruled c. 3000–c. 2600 B.C.; probably settled 1000 years earlier; seat of worship of Sin, the moon-god. Declined, but again important under a new dynasty, the Third, c. 2300–2200 B.C., founded by Ur-Engur. Birthplace of Abraham c. 2000 B.C. who led his family from it to Canaan (*Gen.* xi. 27–31, xii. 1–5). Suffered capture and destruction from Elamites, Babylonians, and others; restored by Nebuchadnezzar II in 6th cent. B.C.; known in records as late as 324 B.C. Site first visited in 17th cent.; excavations conducted since 1854 have uncovered remains of great archaeological value.

Ura·bá, Gulf of \-ˌu̇r-ə-ˈbä\. Bay, NW coast of Colombia, at the inner end of the Gulf of Darien (*q.v.*).

Urabá National Park. National park, Colombia; 112 sq. m.; established 1963.

Ura·ga \u̇-ˈräg-ə\. Seaport, Kanagawa prefecture, SE Honshū, Japan, 5 m. SE of Yokosuka on **Uraga Strait.** Port where first U.S. emissaries under Commodore Biddle attempted 1846 to establish relations with the Japanese; their repulse led to Commodore Perry's expedition; 1 m. to the S is Kurihama, where Perry's four ships anchored July 8, 1853.

Ural \ˈyu̇r-əl\. Unnavigable river, Russian S.F.S.R. and Kazakh S.S.R., U.S.S.R.; 1575 m. long; rises at the S end of the Ural Mts. on the E border of Bashkir A.S.S.R., flows S, then W through Orenburg Oblast, crossing its SW border to flow S through W Kazakh S.S.R. to the Caspian Sea at Gurev; Magnitogorsk, Orsk, Orenburg, and Uralsk are on its banks.

Ural Area *or* **Uralsk Area** \yu̇-ˈralsk-\. Former subdivision of the Russian S.F.S.R., U.S.S.R.; 696,380 sq. m.; ✱ Sverdlovsk; included territory on both sides of the N and cen. Ural Mts.; after World War I its S part around Sverdlovsk developed into the Ural Industrial Region (*q.v.*).

Ural Industrial Region. A mining and industrial region on both sides of the cen. Ural Mts., Russian S.F.S.R., U.S.S.R.; comprises the Chelyabinsk, Sverdlovsk, Kurgan, Orenburg, and Perm oblasts and the Udmurt A.S.S.R.; 262,702 sq. m.; pop. (1970p) 15,184,000. Exceptionally rich in minerals, with deposits of iron, copper, chromium, bauxite, lead, zinc, gold, platinum, potassium, magnesium, asbestos, and many other commercially useful minerals; major oil fields; lacks coal. One of the two largest industrial regions of the U.S.S.R., with important metallurgical, chemical, and heavy engineering industries; during World War II developed rapidly with movement of many industrial plants from W U.S.S.R. to prevent their destruction by Germans. Principal cities Sverdlovsk, Chelyabinsk, Perm, Ufa, Nizhni Tagil, Izhevsk, Magnitogorsk.

Ural Mountains. Mountain range, U.S.S.R.; ab. 1640 m. long; extends S from Kara Sea to the W Kirgiz Steppe region of Kazakh S.S.R., averaging 3000 to 4000 ft.; highest peak Mt. Narodnaya 6214 ft. Central part (**Middle Urals** \-ˈyu̇r-əlz\) is ab. 80 m. broad and lower in altitude, actually a plateau region 1000 to 2000 ft.; densely forested and very rich in minerals; this region now developed into the Ural Industrial Region (*q.v.*). **Southern Urals** have three parallel ranges, with rich pasture grounds; range constitutes the boundary bet. Europe and Asia.

Uralsk \yu̇-ˈralsk\. Town, ✱ of Uralsk Oblast, W Kazakh S.S.R., U.S.S.R., on Ural river at its lower bend near the Orenburg Oblast; pop. (1970p) 134,000; food processing; a trading center for cattle and grain.

Uralsk Area. See URAL AREA.

Uralsk Oblast \-ˈȯ-bləst, -ˌblast\. Subdivision of NW Kazakh S.S.R., U.S.S.R.; 58,378 sq. m.; pop. (1970p) 513,000; ✱ Uralsk.

Ura·ri·coe·ra *or* **Ura·ri·cue·ra** \u̇-ˌrar-i-ˈkwer-ə\. River, N Brazil; ab. 300 m. long; rises in Serra Parima near S Venezuelan border, flows E to unite with Tacutu river in N Amazonas and form Rio Branco.

Urar·tu \u̇-ˈrär-(ˌ)tü\ *or* **Van** \ˈvan\ *or Heb.* **Ar·a·rat** \ˈar-ə-ˌrat\. The Assyrian name for ancient kingdom around Lake Van (ancient Thospitis), N of Assyria. Kingdom lasted from c. 1270 to 612 B.C.; first inscriptions date from time of King Shalmaneser I (c. 1276–1257) of Assyria; repeatedly attacked by Assyrian kings and weakened so that in 7th cent. B.C. it ceased to exist after invasions by Scythians and Medes. Its peoples were of Hurrian and Vannic stock. See ARMENIA 1.

Ura–Tyu·be \ˌu̇r-ə-t(y)u̇-ˈbā\. Town, NW Tadzhik S.S.R., U.S.S.R., 40 m. WSW of Leninabad; pop. (1967e) 31,000.

Ura·wa \u̇-ˈrä-wə\. Town, ✱ of Saitama prefecture, SE cen. Honshū, Japan, 13 m. N of Tokyo; pop. (1970c) 269,397; univ. (1949); has an ancient Shinto shrine and groves of hinoki, cryptomeria, and cherry trees.

Ur·bana \ˌər-ˈban-ə\. **1** City, ⊗ of Champaign co., E cen. Illinois, 47 m. ENE of Decatur; pop. (1970c) 32,800; commercial center in agricultural region; Univ. of Illinois (1867); settled 1824, incorporated as town 1833, as city 1860. Adjoins city of Champaign (combination often known as **Cham·paign–Urbana** \sham-ˈpān-\).
2 City, ⊗ of Champaign co., W Ohio, 13 m. N of Springfield; pop. (1970c) 11,237; plastics, dies, machine tools, automobile parts; livestock; Urbana Coll. (1850).

Ur·ban·dale \ˈər-bən-ˌdāl\. Town, Polk co., S cen. Iowa, NW suburb of Des Moines; pop. (1970c) 14,434.

Ur·bi·no \u̇(ə)r-ˈbē-(ˌ)nō\; *anc.* **Ur·bi·num Hor·ten·se** \ər-ˌbī-nəm-hȯr-ˈten(t)-sē\ *or* **Ur·vi·num Met·au·ren·se** \ər-ˌvī-nəm-ˌmet-ȯ-ˈren(t)-ˈsē\. Commune, Pesaro e Urbino prov., Marches, cen. Italy, 19 m. SW of Pesaro; pop. (1968e) 16,720; tourism; cathedral (rebuilt after earthquake 1789), 15th cent. ducal palace; univ. (1506). Birthplace of Raphael. An Umbrian town which came under Rome 3d cent. B.C.; ruled by church 9th–13th cents. A.D.; as capital of Duchy of Urbino in 15th cent., a major political and cultural center; came under Papacy 1626; to kingdom of Italy 1860.

Urbino, Pesaro e. See PESARO E URBINO.

Urbinum Hortense. See URBINO.

Urbs Vetus. See ORVIETO.

Ur·cos \ˈu̇r-kōs\. Town, Cuzco dept., SE Peru, SE of Cuzco on railroad in upper Urubamba valley; pop. (1961c) 2700.

Ur·da·ne·ta \ˌu̇r-də-ˈnāt-ə\. Municipality, Pangasinan prov., Luzon, Phil., 20 m. ESE of Lingayen; pop. (1969e) 61,400.

Ure \ˈyu̇(ə)r\. River, Yorkshire, N England; ab. 50 m. long; unites with the Swale river to form the Ouse.

Ure·we·ra National Park \ˌu̇-rə-ˈwer-ə-\. National park, North I., New Zealand; 770 sq. m.; mountain ranges, forests; habitat of kiwi; established 1954.

Ur·fa \u̇r-ˈfä\. **1** Province of SE Turkey. See table at TURKEY.
2 *or anc.* **Edes·sa** \ē-ˈdes-ə\. City, its ✱, 75 m. E of Gaziantep; pop. (1965c) 73,498; trading town with remains of ancient walls and citadel.

History: Ancient Edessa had independent dynasty just before Christian Era, but its history is little known; an early center of Syriac-speaking Christianity until conquered by Arabs 639 A.D.; Bardesianism, a Gnostic sect, founded here in 2d cent. A.D.; conquered from Seljuk Turks by Baldwin I of Flanders who erected Christian county of Edessa 1098; reconquered by Muslims 1144; under Turkish rule from 1637; modern Urfa scene of massacres of Armenians 1895.

Urga. See ULAN BATOR.

Ur·gel, Seo de \ˌse-ō-dā-u̇r-ˈhel\. Commune, Lérida prov., Catalonia, NE Spain, on the Segre river 10 m. SSW of Andorra; pop. (1970p) 8007; episcopal see (Span. *seo*) founded 820; late Romanesque cathedral. Its bishop is co-prince (with French president) of Andorra (*q.v.*).

Ur·gench \u̇r-ˈgench\. **1** *or formerly* **No·vo Urgench** \ˌnō-və-\ *or Eng.* **New Urgench.** Industrial town, ✱ of Khorezm Oblast, W Uzbek S.S.R., U.S.S.R., on left bank of the Amu Darya (ancient Oxus); pop. (1970p) 76,000. **2** Ancient town, ab. 85 m. NW of Urgench; has some architectural remains; once dominated the lower Oxus region.

Uri \ˈu̇(ə)r-ē\. Swiss canton. See history and table at SWITZERLAND.

Uri, Bay of *or* **Lake of Uri** . Extension of Lake of Lucerne, cen. Switzerland; receives Reuss river at its S end.

Urian·ga·to \ˌu̇r-ē-äŋ-ˈgä-(ˌ)tō\. Town, Guanajuato state, cen. Mexico, just N of Lake Cuitzeo; munic. pop. (1970p) 23,333.

Uriang·hai *or* **Uriankhai.** See TUVA AUTONOMOUS SOVIET SOCIALIST REPUBLIC.

Uri·bia \ü-ˈrē-bē-ə\. Town, La Guajira dept., NE Colombia, 135 m. ENE of Santa Marta; munic. pop. (1968e) 73,301.

Uriburu, General J. F. See ZÁRATE.

Uriconium. See WROXETER.

Urmia. See REZĀ'ĪYEH.

Ur·mia, Lake \-ˈu̇r-mē-ə\; *Pers.* **Shā·hī** \shä-ˈhē\ *or* **Uru·mi·yeh** \ˌu̇r-ə-mē-ˈyäh\; *anc.* **Mat·i·a·nus** \ˌmat-ē-ˈā-nəs, -ˈan-əs\. Shallow saline lake, NW Iran, E of Rezā'īyeh and W of Tabrīz; area 1815 sq. m.; ab. 90 m. long; max. depth 49 ft. Shāhī I. is in N cen. part and a group of smaller islands in S cen. part; Sharafkhāneh on NE shore is only lake port; it is connected by branch railroad with Tabrīz and is operation center for fleet of Iranian motorboats.

Urm·ston \ˈərm(p)-stən\. Urban district, Lancashire, NW England, on the Mersey 5 m. WSW of Manchester; pop. (1971p) 44,523; asbestos, pipe, soap.

Ur of the Chaldees. See UR.

Urre Lau·quen \ˌu̇r-ē-lau̇-ˈken\. Lake, S La Pampa prov., S cen. Argentina.

Urseren. See ANDERMATT.

Urso. See OSUNA.

Ur·sus \ˈu̇r-süs\. Town, Warszawa prov., Poland, ab. 7 m. WSW of Warsaw; pop. (1970p) 30,300.

Urua·pan \u̇r-ˈwäp-ˌän\ *or in full* **Uruapan del Pro·gre·so** \-del-prə-ˈgres-(ˌ)ō\. City, Michoacán state, SW Mexico, 60 m. SW of Morelia; munic. pop. (1970p) 104,475; lacquerwork; in center of rich agricultural region and just E of Parícutin volcano. One of the chief towns of the Tarascan Indians; founded 1540.

Uru·bam·ba \ˌu̇r-ə-ˈbäm-bə\. **1** River, cen. Peru; 451 m. long; rises in Andes Mts. and flows NNW bet. parallel ranges of the Andes to unite with Apurímac river and form Ucayali river; Cuzco is on it.
2 Town, Cuzco dept., Peru, 20 m. NE of Cuzco; pop. (1961c) 3300; mining town.

Uru·gua·ia·na \ˌu̇r-ə-gwə-ˈyan-ə\. City, W Rio Grande do Sul state, S Brazil, on Argentine border; munic. pop. (1968e) 74,581; candles, soap, leather, tobacco products; meat-packing plants.

Uru·guay \ˈ(y)u̇r-ə-ˌgwī, -ˌgwā\. **1** *or officially* **Re·pú·bli·ca Ori·en·tal del Uru·guay** \rā-ˈpü-bli-(ˌ)kä-ˌōr-ē-en-ˈtäl-del-ˌu̇r-ə-ˈgwī, -ˌōr-ē-ˌen-\. Republic, SE cen. South America, E of the lower Uruguay river, bounded on N by Brazil, on E by Brazil and the Atlantic **Ocean,** on S by the La Plata river, and on W by Argentina; **68,536** sq. m.; pop. (1971e) 2,921,000, (1969e) 2,851,600; ✱ Montevideo. *Physical features:* Generally flat country (**pampas** region) with low range of Brazilian highlands in NE, less than 2000 ft. Traversed from NE to SW by the Río Negro. *Chief products:* Beef cattle; corn, oats, sunflower seeds, barley, rice; manufacturing: textiles, chemicals, cement; meat-packing. *Chief cities:* Montevideo, Paysandú, Salto, Rivera, Las Piedras, Melo, Mercedes, Minas. Divided into the following 19 departments (for pronunciation of their names, see their individual entries):

NAME	AREA (sq. m.)	POP. (1969e)	CAPITAL
Artigas	4,689	54,400	Artigas
Canelones	1,750	296,900	Canelones
Cerro Largo	5,348	74,300	Melo
Colonia	2,372	109,500	Colonia
Durazno	4,713	55,600	Durazno
Flores	1,982	24,500	Trinidad
Florida	4,009	66,500	Florida
Lavalleja	3,918	68,200	Minas
Maldonado	1,817	64,900	Maldonado
Montevideo	198	1,375,000	Montevideo
Paysandú	5,446	90,800	Paysandú
Río Negro	3,721	48,700	Fray Bentos
Rivera	3,513	80,700	Rivera
Rocha	4,244	57,800	Rocha
Salto	5,544	95,900	Salto
San José	1,928	80,500	San José
Soriano	3,442	81,400	Mercedes
Tacuarembó	6,166	80,600	Tacuarembó
Treinta y Tres	3,736	45,400	Treinta y Tres

History: Río de la Plata discovered by Solís 1516; Colonia founded by Portuguese 1680 and Montevideo (*q.v.*) in 1726; region (called Banda Oriental by the Spaniards) long in dispute bet. Portuguese and Spanish, the latter finally securing control; in Spanish viceroyalty of La Plata 1776; with Buenos Aires, obtained independence from Spain 1811–14; incorporated in Brazil as Cisplatine Province 1821; revolted from Brazil 1825 and was recognized as independent state 1828; in war against Paraguay (*q.v.*) 1865–70; broke off relations with Germany Oct. 7, 1917 and with the Axis powers in 1942; declared war on Germany and Japan Feb. 1945; abolished presidential office 1951, replacing it with a nine-man council; adopted new constitution and restored presidential system 1966.
2 River, SE South America; 1000 m. long; flows W in Santa Catarina state, S Brazil, forming section of boundary bet. Santa Catarina and Rio Grande do Sul states; turns SW and forms boundary bet. S Brazil and Argentina, and bet. Uruguay and Argentina; empties into Río de la Plata.

Uruk. See ERECH.

Uruk·tha·pel \ˌu̇r-ək-ˈtäp-el\. Second largest island of Palau Is. group, W Pacific Ocean, S of Babelthuap I.

Urum·chi *or* **Urum·tsi** \ü-ˈru̇m-chē\ *or* **Ti·hwa** \ˈdē-ˈ(h)wä\ *or Chin.* **Wu–lu–mu–ch'i** \ˈwü-ˈlü-ˈmü-ˈchē\. City, ✱ of Sinkiang Uighur, W China, in cen. part; pop. (1970e) 500,000; on N side of Tien Shan range at ab. 3000 ft. alt.; agricultural coll. (1952), univ. (1960).

Urumiyeh. See URMIA, LAKE.

Urundi. See BURUNDI.

Urup \ü-ˈrüp\. One of the Kuril Is. (*q.v.*), NE of Iturup.

Uruz·gān \u̇-ru̇z-ˈgän\. **1** Province of cen. Afghanistan. See table at AFGHANISTAN.
2 Town, its ✱; pop. (1969e) 46,818.

Urville, Cape d'. See PERKAM, CAPE.

Urvinum Metaurense. See URBINO.

Usa \ü-ˈsä, ˈüs-ˌä\. City, Ōita prefecture, Kyūshū, Japan, 25 m. NW of Ōita; pop. (1970c) 51,942.

Usa \ü-ˈsä\. River, NE Komi A.S.S.R., Russian S.F.S.R., U.S.S.R., an E tributary of the Pechora; 351 m. long; rises at N end of Ural Mts. and flows SW to Pechora at Ust Usa; navigable.

Usa·ga·ra \ˌü-sə-ˈgär-ə\. Hill region, E edge of the cen. plateau in Tanzania, E Africa; traversed by the Great Ruaha river.

Uşak \ü-ˈshäk\ *or* **Ushak** \ü-ˈshäk\. **1** Province of W Turkey. See table at TURKEY.
2 Industrial town, its ✱, on railroad 55 m. W of Afyonkarahisar; pop. (1965c) 35,517; carpets; sugar refining.

Usa·kos \ü-ˈsäk-əs\. Town, W cen. South-West Africa, 100 m. NW of Windhoek.

Usam·ba·ra \ˌü-səm-ˈbär-ə\. Highlands in NE Tanga region, NE Tanzania and SE Kenya, E Africa; highest peak 8428 ft.

URUGUAY
CONIC PROJECTION
SCALE OF MILES
0 20 40 60
SCALE OF KILOMETERS
0 20 40 60
Capitals of Countries
Department Capitals
International Boundaries
Department Boundaries
Copyright by C.S. Hammond & Co., N.Y.
Longitude West 56° of Greenwich
58° 57° 56° 55° 54°
31° 32° 33° 34° 35° 36°
BRAZIL
ARGENTINA
ATLANTIC OCEAN
ARTIGAS
SALTO
PAYSANDÚ
RÍO NEGRO
TACUAREMBÓ
RIVERA
CERRO LARGO
DURAZNO
TREINTA Y TRES
SORIANO
FLORES
FLORIDA
COLONIA
SAN JOSÉ
CANELONES
LAVALLEJA
MALDONADO
ROCHA
Cuchilla de Haedo
Cuchilla Grande
Cuchilla de Santa Ana
Cuchilla de Belén
Cuchilla del Dayman
Cuchilla Grande del Durazno
Cuchilla Grande Inferior
Embalse del Río Negro
RINCON DEL BONETE
Río de la Plata
Laguna Merim
Laguna Negra
Laguna de Castillos
Laguna de Rocha
Laguna Garzón
Laguna José Ignacio
Laguna del Sauce
Monte Caseros
Bella Unión
Artigas
Quaraí
Rosario-do-Sul
São Gabriel
Santana do Livramento
Rivera
Dom Pedrito
Bage
Concordia
Salto
Paysandú
Concepción del Uruguay
Tacuarembó
Melo
Jaguarão
Fray Bentos
Mercedes
Paso de los Toros
Durazno
Trinidad
Treinta y Tres
Dolores
Carmelo
Nueva Palmira
Colonia
Rosario
San José
Florida
Minas
Canelones
Rocha
San Carlos
Maldonado
Punta del Este
Piriápolis
Pando
Las Piedras
MONTEVIDEO
BUENOS AIRES
La Plata
Magdalena
Chuy
Lascano
Vergara
José Batlle y Ordóñez
Sarandí del Yi
Sarandí Grande
Carmen
Young
Tranqueras
Fraile Muerto
Sta. Vitória do Palmar
A
MILES
0 5 10 15
Santa Lucía
San Antonio
San Bautista
Santa Rosa
Sauce
Joaquín Suárez
Toledo
Soca
Atlántida
La Floresta
Santiago Vázquez
Carrasco

Us·borne \ˈəz-bərn\. Peak, East Falkland I., Falkland Is. (*q.v.*); 2312 ft.; highest peak in the Falkland Is.

Use·dom \ˈü-zə-ˌdȯm\ *or Pol.* **Uz·nam** \ˈüz-ˌnäm\. Island off the coast of NE East Germany, bet. Zalew Szczeciński and the Pomeranian Bay; 170 sq. m.; since 1945 divided bet. Poland and East Germany, chief town is port of Świnioujście in Polish section.

Useless Bay. See INÚTIL BAY.

U. S. Grant Peak \ˌyü-ˌes-ˈgrant-\. Mountain, San Juan and San Miguel cos., SW Colorado; 13,692 ft.

Ushak. See USAK.

Ushant. See ÎLE D'OUESSANT

Ush·ba \ˈu̇sh-ˌbä\. Peak, W cen. Caucasus Mts. in Georgian S.S.R., U.S.S.R., SE of Mt. Elbrus; 15,453 ft. high; glaciers.

Us·hua·ia \ü-ˈswā-yə\. Town, ❋ of Tierra del Fuego National Territory, S Argentina, on S Tierra del Fuego I., on Beagle Channel; pop. (1960c) 3398; farthest S city in the world, at 54°57′S, 68°20′W.

Usk \ˈəsk\. River, S Wales and W England; ab. 70 m. long; rises in S cen. Wales, flows E and S into the Severn estuary just below Newport in Monmouthshire.

Üsküb. See SKOPJE.

Üs·kü·dar \ˌu̇s-kə-ˈdär\ *or formerly* **Scu·ta·ri** \ˈsküt-ə-rē\ *or anc.* **Chry·sop·o·lis** \krə-ˈsäp-ə-ləs, krī-\. Town, İstanbul prov., Turkey, across the Bosporus from İstanbul; munic. pop. (1965c) 133,883; residential suburb of İstanbul. Base of British Army in Crimean War and site of hospital under charge of Florence Nightingale. Ancient Chrysopolis was port of Chalcedon.

Üsküp. See SKOPJE.

Usol·ye–Si·bir·sko·ye \u̇-ˈsȯl-yə-sē-ˈbir-skə-yə\ *or formerly* **Usolye.** Town, Irkutsk Oblast, Russian S.F.S.R., U.S.S.R., ab. 50 m. NW of Irkutsk; pop. (1969e) 81,000.

Us·pa·lla·ta Pass \ˌü-spə-ˈyät-ə-, -ˈzhät-\ *or* **La Cum·bre** \lə-ˈküm-brē\. Pass in the Andes Mts.; see ANDES.

Us·su·ri *also* **Usu·ri** \u̇-ˈsu̇(ə)r-ē\. River, Russian S.F.S.R., U.S.S.R., forming boundary bet. W Primorski Krai and NE China, N of Vladivostok; 365 m. long; rises in mountains at extreme S end of Primorski Krai and flows N to join the Amur near Khabarovsk; a W tributary of upper course is outlet for Lake Khanka. Chief Soviet town on its bank is Iman. Scene of clashes bet. Soviet and Chinese forces 1964 ff.

Ussuri Bay. Northeast extension of Peter the Great Bay, Primorski Krai, Russian S.F.S.R., U.S.S.R., just E of Vladivostok.

Us·su·risk \ˌü-su̇-ˈrēsk\ *or before 1957* **Vo·ro·shi·lov** \ˌvȯr-ə-ˈshē-ləf\ *or before 1935* **Ni·kolsk–Us·su·rii·ski** \ni-ˈkȯlsk-ˌü-su̇-ˈrēsk-ē\. City, SW Primorski Krai, Russian S.F.S.R., U.S.S.R., 50 m. N of Vladivostok; pop. (1970p) 128,000; brewing and distilling; rice mills, sugar refineries, railroad shops, coal mines; founded 1866.

Ust Dvinsk. See DAUGAVGRĪVA.

Uster \ˈu̇s-tər\. Manufacturing commune, Zurich canton, Switzerland, 8 m. ESE of Zurich; pop. (1970c) 21,819.

Ústí. See ÚSTÍ NAD LABEM.

Usti·ca \ˈü-sti-(ˌ)kä\. Small island, Tyrrhenian Sea, NW of Sicily, Italy.

Ústí nad La·bem \ˈü-st(y)ē-ˈnäd-lə-ˌbem\ *or* **Ústí** *or Ger.* **Aus·sig** \ˈau̇-sik\. City, Czech S.R., NW Czechoslovakia, on Elbe river; pop. (1968e) 73,897; chemicals, textiles, glass; Dominican monastery, dating from 10th cent.

Ust–Ka·me·no·gorsk \ˈüst-kə-ˌmen-ə-ˈgȯ(ə)rsk\. Town, ❋ of East Kazakhstan Oblast, E Kazakh S.S.R., U.S.S.R., on the Irtysh river 100 m. E of Semipalatinsk; on a branch of the Turkistan-Siberian R.R.; pop. (1970p) 230,000; zinc smelting, metalworking.

Ust–Kut \üst-ˈküt\. Town, N cen. Irkutsk Oblast, Russian S.F.S.R., U.S.S.R., ab. 310 m. N of Irkutsk.

Ust–Or·dyn·ski \ˌü-stȯr-ˈdēn-skē\ *or formerly* **Ust Or·da** \ü-stȯr-ˈdä\. Town, ❋ of Ust-Ordynski Buryat National Okrug, Russian S.F.S.R., U.S.S.R., 40 m. N of Irkutsk, W of Lake Baikal.

Ust–Ordynski Buryat National Okrug \-bu̇r-ˌyät . . . ˈō-ˌkrük\. National district, SE Irkutsk Oblast, Russian S.F.S.R., U.S.S.R., W of Lake Baikal; 8494 sq. m.; pop. (1970p) 146,000; ❋ Ust-Ordynski; has coalfield and important timber resources.

Ust Sysolsk. See SYKTYVKAR.

Ust Urt. See USTYURT.

Ustyug Veliki. See VELIKI USTYUG.

Ust·yurt \ü-ˈstyu̇(ə)rt\ *or* **Ust Urt** \ü-ˈstu̇(ə)rt\. Plateau, SW Kazakh S.S.R., U.S.S.R., extending bet. the Caspian Sea and Aral Sea; 77,220 sq. m.

Usu·ki \u̇-ˈsu̇k-ē\. Town, Ōita prefecture, NE Kyūshū, Japan, ab. 12 m. SE of Ōita; pop. (1970c) 39,890; has harbor in Bungo Strait.

Usu·lu·tán \ˌü-sü-lü-ˈtän\. 1 Department of SE El Salvador. See table at EL SALVADOR.

2 Town, its ❋, near coast 55 m. ESE of San Salvador; pop. (1968e) 17,041; produces tobacco, bananas, corn, beans.

Usu·ma·cin·ta \ˌü-sə-mə-ˈsint-ə\. River, N Guatemala and SE Mexico; ab. 270 m. long; rises in W Guatemala, flows NW forming section of Guatemala-Mexico (Chiapas state) boundary, empties into Grijalva river near its mouth in N Tabasco state, Mexico; navigable for a short distance; known as the **Chi·xoy** \chē-ˈhȯi\ river in its upper course.

Usumbura. See BUJUMBURA.

Usuri. See USSURI.

Usu·tu \u̇-ˈsüt-(ˌ)ü\. River, S Africa; 135 m. long; flows E in E Transvaal, Rep. of South Africa, and in Swaziland and unites with Pongolo river in Mozambique to form the Maputo river.

Utah \ˈyü-ˌtȯ, -ˌtä\. 1 Western state of U.S.A., bounded on N by Idaho and Wyoming, on E by Colorado, on S by Arizona, and on W by Nevada; 11th state in area, 84,916 sq. m. (land area 82,381 sq. m.); 36th state in population, (1970c) 1,059,273; ❋ Salt Lake City; 45th state admitted to Union (1896).

Nicknames: Beehive State; Mormon State. *State flower:* Sego lily. *Motto:* Industry. *Rivers:* Colorado flowing SW across SE region; Green in E region flowing S to join the Colorado; Sevier in SW cen. region, flowing N and SW to empty into Sevier Lake. *Highest point:* Kings Peak 13,528 ft., in Duchesne co. *Chief products:* Wheat, barley; livestock; copper, gold, silver, lead, molybdenum; manufacturing: metal processing; chemicals, lumber and wood products. *Chief cities:* Salt Lake City, Ogden, Provo, Bountiful. See *Table of States* at UNITED STATES. Divided into the following 29 counties (for pronunciation of their names, see their individual entries):

NAME	LOCATION	AREA[1] (sq. m.)	POP. (1970c)	CO. SEAT
Beaver	SW	2,584	3,800	Beaver
Box Elder[2]	NW corner	5,627	28,129	Brigham
Cache	N	1,174	42,331	Logan
Carbon	E cen.	1,476	15,647	Price
Daggett	NE	706	666	Manila
Davis[2]	N	297	99,028	Farmington
Duchesne	NE cen.	3,355	7,299	Duchesne
Emery	E cen.	4,439	5,137	Castle Dale
Garfield[3,4]	S	5,185	3,157	Panguitch
Grand	E	3,697	6,688	Moab
Iron[5]	SW	3,300	12,177	Parowan
Juab	W	3,412	4,574	Nephi
Kane[3,5]	S	4,016	2,421	Kanab
Millard[6]	W	6,793	6,988	Fillmore
Morgan	N	610	3,983	Morgan City
Piute	S cen.	754	1,164	Junction
Rich	N	1,023	1,615	Randolph
Salt Lake[2]	N	764	458,607	Salt Lake City
San Juan[4,7]	SE corner	7,799	9,606	Monticello
Sanpete	cen.	1,597	10,976	Manti
Sevier	cen.	1,929	10,103	Richfield

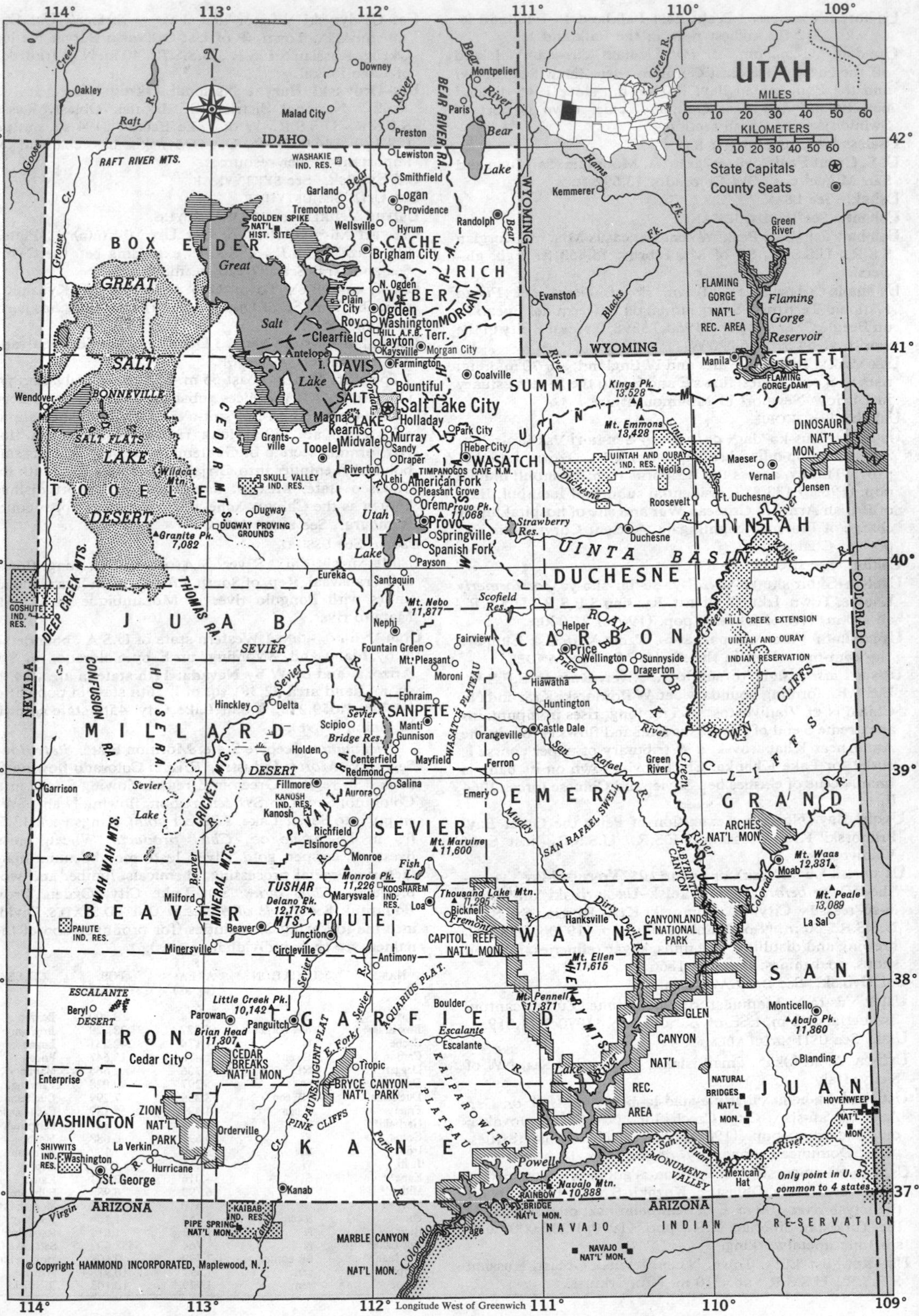

UTAH
MILES
0 10 20 30 40 50 60
KILOMETERS
0 10 20 30 40 50 60
State Capitals
County Seats
114°
113°
112°
111°
110°
109°
42°
41°
40°
39°
38°
37°
IDAHO
WYOMING
NEVADA
COLORADO
ARIZONA
BOX ELDER
CACHE
RICH
WEBER
MORGAN
DAVIS
SALT LAKE
SUMMIT
DAGGETT
TOOELE
WASATCH
UTAH
UINTAH
DUCHESNE
JUAB
CARBON
MILLARD
SANPETE
EMERY
GRAND
SEVIER
BEAVER
PIUTE
WAYNE
IRON
GARFIELD
SAN JUAN
WASHINGTON
KANE
GREAT SALT LAKE DESERT
Great Salt Lake
BONNEVILLE SALT FLATS
Salt Lake City
Ogden
Logan
Provo
Oakley
Downey
Malad City
Preston
Montpelier
Paris
Bear Lake
Lewiston
Smithfield
Hyrum
Providence
Wellsville
Garland
Tremonton
Brigham City
Randolph
Kemmerer
Green River
Evanston
N. Ogden
Plain City
Roy
Washington Terr.
Clearfield
Layton
HILL A.F.B.
Kaysville
Morgan City
Farmington
Bountiful
Coalville
Holladay
Magna
Kearns
Midvale
Murray
Sandy
Draper
Park City
Heber City
Grantsville
Tooele
Riverton
Lehi
American Fork
Pleasant Grove
Orem
Springville
Spanish Fork
Payson
Santaquin
Eureka
Wendover
Dugway
DUGWAY PROVING GROUNDS
SKULL VALLEY IND. RES.
WASHAKIE IND. RES.
GOLDEN SPIKE NAT'L HIST. SITE
TIMPANOGOS CAVE N.M.
Provo Pk. 11,068
Strawberry Res.
Kings Pk. 13,528
Mt. Emmons 13,428
UINTAH AND OURAY IND. RES.
Neola
Maeser
Vernal
Jensen
Roosevelt
Ft. Duchesne
Duchesne
UINTA BASIN
FLAMING GORGE NAT'L REC. AREA
Flaming Gorge Reservoir
Manila
FLAMING GORGE DAM
DINOSAUR NAT'L MON.
Antelope I.
Granite Pk. 7,082
Wildcat Mtn.
GOSHUTE IND. RES.
DEEP CREEK MTS.
THOMAS RA.
CEDAR MTS.
RAFT RIVER MTS.
BEAR RIVER RA.
UINTA MTS.
WASATCH RA.
Mt. Nebo 11,877
Nephi
Scofield Res.
Fountain Green
Mt. Pleasant
Moroni
Fairview
Helper
Price
Wellington
Sunnyside
Dragerton
ROAN OR BOOK CLIFFS
BROWN CLIFFS
HILL CREEK EXTENSION
UINTAH AND OURAY INDIAN RESERVATION
Hinckley
Delta
Ephraim
Manti
Gunnison
Scipio
Bridge Res.
Holden
Centerfield
Mayfield
Hiawatha
Huntington
Castle Dale
Orangeville
Ferron
Green River
Redmond
Salina
Fillmore
Garrison
Sevier Lake
CONFUSION RA.
HOUSE RA.
CRICKET MTS.
WAH WAH MTS.
MINERAL MTS.
PAVANT RA.
WASATCH PLATEAU
SAN RAFAEL SWELL
KANOSH IND. RES.
Kanosh
Aurora
Richfield
Elsinore
Monroe
Emery
ARCHES NAT'L MON.
Moab
Mt. Waas 12,331
Mt. Peale 13,089
La Sal
Mt. Marvine 11,600
Fish L.
Monroe Pk. 11,226
KOOSHAREM IND. RES.
Marysvale
TUSHAR MTS.
Delano Pk. 12,173
Thousand Lake Mtn. 11,295
Loa
Bicknell
Hanksville
CANYONLANDS NATIONAL PARK
LABYRINTH CANYON
Milford
Beaver
Junction
PAIUTE IND. RES.
Minersville
Circleville
Antimony
CAPITOL REEF NAT'L MON.
Mt. Ellen 11,615
HENRY MTS.
Mt. Pennell 11,371
Monticello
Abajo Pk. 11,360
Blanding
ESCALANTE DESERT
Beryl
Little Creek Pk. 10,142
Parowan
Panguitch
Brian Head 11,307
Cedar City
CEDAR BREAKS NAT'L MON.
AQUARIUS PLAT.
PAUNSAUGUNT PLAT
Boulder
Escalante
KAIPAROWITS PLATEAU
Tropic
BRYCE CANYON NAT'L PARK
GLEN CANYON NAT'L REC. AREA
Lake Powell
NATURAL BRIDGES NAT'L MON.
HOVENWEEP NAT'L MON.
Enterprise
ZION NAT'L PARK
Orderville
PINK CLIFFS
SHIVWITS IND. RES.
Washington
La Verkin
Hurricane
St. George
Kanab
MONUMENT VALLEY
Mexican Hat
Only point in U. S. common to 4 states.
Navajo Mtn. 10,388
RAINBOW BRIDGE NAT'L MON.
KAIBAB IND. RES.
PIPE SPRING NAT'L MON.
MARBLE CANYON NAT'L MON.
Page
NAVAJO INDIAN RESERVATION
NAVAJO NAT'L MON.
© Copyright HAMMOND INCORPORATED, Maplewood, N. J.
Longitude West of Greenwich

NAME	LOCATION	AREA[1] (sq. m.)	POP. (1970c)	CO. SEAT
Summit	NE	1,848	5,879	Coalville
Tooele[2]	NW	6,923	21,545	Tooele
Uintah	E	4,472	12,684	Vernal
Utah[8]	N cen.	2,014	137,776	Provo
Wasatch	N cen.	1,191	5,863	Heber
Washington[5]	SW corner	2,427	13,669	St. George
Wayne[4]	S cen.	2,486	1,483	Loa
Weber[2]	N	581	126,278	Ogden

[1]Area = land area.
[2]Upper part of Great Salt Lake in cen. and SE Box Elder co.; lower part in Weber, Davis, Salt Lake, and Tooele cos.
[3]Bryce Canyon National Park in SW Garfield co. and NW Kane co.
[4]Canyonlands National Park in NE Garfield co., NW San Juan co., and E Wayne co.
[5]Zion National Park in NE and E Washington co., with small regions in abutting S part of Iron co. and W part of Kane co.
[6]Includes Sevier Lake and several smaller lakes.
[7]SE point of county the only point in U.S. common to four states (Utah, Colorado, New Mexico, Arizona).
[8]Utah Lake in W cen. part.

History: First explored by Spaniards sent out by Coronado 1540; Great Salt Lake discovered by James Bridger 1824; acquired by United States from Mexico in Treaty of Guadalupe Hidalgo 1848; first permanent settlers were Mormons, led from Illinois and Missouri by Brigham Young 1847; Utah Territory organized 1850 (see DESERET); conflict bet. Mormon authorities and United States, known as Utah War (1857–58); admitted to Union Jan. 4, 1896.

2 County in Utah. See table at UTAH.

Utah Lake. Lake, Utah co., N cen. Utah; 150 sq. m.; 23 m. long by 8 m. wide; has outlet, Jordan river, flowing N into SE Great Salt Lake.

Utaidhani. See UTHAI THANI.

Utakamand. See OOTACAMUND.

Ute Pass \ˌyüt-\. Mountain pass, Teller co., cen. Colorado, near Pikes Peak; 7600 ft.; used by Indians before 1800; road.

Ute Peak. 1 Mountain, Grand and Summit cos., Colorado, S of Middle Park; 12,298 ft.

2 Mountain, Taos co., N New Mexico, on Colorado boundary; 10,151 ft.

Uthai Tha·ni *or* **Utai·dha·ni** *or* **Uda·ya·dha·ni** \ˌü-ˌtī-ˈtän-ē\. 1 Province, W cen. Thailand; 2499 sq. m.; pop. (1960c) 145,504; ✱ Uthai Thani.

2 Town, its ✱, on the Chao Phraya where the Tha Chin distributary leaves it, 25 m. S of Nakhon Sawan; pop. (1964e) 10,342.

Uti·ca \ˈyü-ti-kə\. 1 City, Macomb co., SE Michigan, 20 m. N of Detroit; pop. (1970c) 3504; automobile parts; diversified agriculture.

2 Industrial city and port of entry, a ⊗ of Oneida co., cen. New York, on Mohawk river and State Barge Canal, ab. 50 m. W of Syracuse; pop. (1970c) 91,611; produces automobile and aircraft parts, electronic components, sheet metal, magnesium castings, dairy products, rayon; Mohawk Valley Community Coll. (1946), Utica Coll. of Syracuse Univ. (1946). Settlement of region begun c. 1773; incorporated as village 1798, as city 1832; industrial development followed opening of Erie Canal 1825.

3 Ancient city on the coast of N Africa, 15 m. NW of ancient Carthage (and modern Tunis) and 10 m. SE of modern Ghār al-Milḩ; site now ab. 7 m. inland.

History: Founded c. 8th cent. B.C. and one of the principal Phoenician colonies in N Africa; capital of Roman province of Africa 1st cent. B.C. and scene of suicide of Cato the Younger after battle of Thapsus 46 B.C.; declined after revival of Carthage under Roman rule 44 B.C. ff.

Utiel \ü-ˈtyel\. Manufacturing commune, Valencia prov., E Spain, 42 m. NW of Valencia; pop. (1970p) 11,384; French defeated here 1812.

Uti·la Island \ü-ˌtē-lə-\. Island, Caribbean Sea, N of N Honduras, near S entrance to Gulf of Honduras.

Utina. See UDINE 2.

Utrecht \ˈyü-ˌtrekt\. 1 Province, cen. Netherlands; 538 sq. m.; pop. (1970e) 801,285; ✱ Utrecht; smallest province of Netherlands, traversed by branches of the Rhine river.

2 City, its ✱, on the Oude Rijn river 20 m. SSE of Amsterdam; pop. (1970e) 278,966; transportation center and residential city; 15th cent. Catholic cathedral and numerous other medieval churches, archiepiscopal museum; univ. (1636).

History: Fortified Roman settlement on site c. 48 A.D.; episcopal see established under St. Willibrord c. 690; ruled by bishops until 1527; in Middle Ages important center of commerce and of the weaving industry; ruled by Spain 1527–77 and then a center of Protestant resistance to Spanish rule. Scene of signing of Union of Utrecht 1579 (see NETHERLANDS) and of Treaty of Utrecht 1713 ending War of the Spanish Succession.

3 Village, NW Natal, E Rep. of South Africa; pop. (1967e) 7200; center of a district settled by Boers after the great trek of 1836 and declared by them a republic (see also LYDENBURG and VRYHEID); originally in Transvaal, ceded to Natal 1903.

Utre·ra \ü-ˈtrer-ə\. Commune, Sevilla prov., SW Spain, 19 m. SSE of Seville; pop. (1970p) 35,775; stock raising, esp. for the bullring; 14th cent. Gothic church, 13th cent. tower.

Utsu·no·mi·ya \ˌüt-sə-ˈnō-mē-(y)ə\. City, ✱ of Tochigi prefecture, cen. Honshū, Japan, 60 m. N of Tokyo; pop. (1970c) 301,231; just S of Nikkō and has view of Nikkō Range. Bombed by U.S. planes July 1945.

Ut·ta·ra·dit *or* **Uta·ra·dit** \ˌu̇-ˌtär-ə-ˈdit\. 1 Province, NW cen. Thailand; 2940 sq. m.; pop. (1960c) 259,919; ✱ Uttaradit.

2 Town, its ✱, on right bank of Nan river 55 m. N of Phitsanulok; pop. (1964e) 11,457.

Ut·tar Pra·desh \ˌu̇t-ər-prə-ˈdāsh, -ˈdesh\; *formerly* **United Provinces** *or in full* **United Provinces of Agra and Oudh** \-ˈäg-rə . . . ˈau̇d\. State, N India; 113,655 sq. m.; pop. (1971p) 88,299,453; ✱ Lucknow. *Physical features:* N part lies in the Himalayas (high peaks Nanda Devi, Trisul, Kedarnath) and the remainder, comprising most of the state, forms the plains of the Ganges and Yamuna and their tributaries (Ghaghara, Gomati, Rapti, etc.); a region corresponding roughly to the Hindustan of the early Muslim period. *Chief products:* Wheat, rice, sugarcane, cotton; textiles, leather goods. *Chief cities:* Kanpur, Lucknow, Agra, Varanasi, Allahabad.

History: Region of present Uttar Pradesh, nearly all of the Gangetic basin, was the scene (with Delhi on the W and Patna on the E) of much early Indian history. It was the country of the two great epics, the *Mahabharata* and *Ramayana,* of the rise of Buddhism, of Asoka's empire and the region ruled by the Guptas and Harsha, followed by the Moguls in the 16th cent. in which the city of Agra (*q.v.*) became a chief center. The British first came into the region (see OUDH) in the latter half of the 18th cent.; sovereignty of certain regions passed to them bet. 1798 and 1833; became 1835 the North-West Provinces, to which Oudh was annexed in 1856; placed under one administration 1877. United Provinces of Agra and Oudh formed 1902; placed under a governor 1921; was granted an autonomous government with a two-chamber legislature 1937; became a state of India 1947.

Ut·tox·e·ter \yu̇-ˈtäk-sət-ər, ə-ˈtäk-, ˈək-sət-ər\. Urban district, Staffordshire, W cen. England; pop. (1969e) 8980.

Utua·do \ü-ˈtwäd-(ˌ)ō\. Town and municipality, W cen. Puerto Rico; town 13 m. S of Arecibo; pop. (1970p) 11,475 (town), 35,504 (munic.).

Utu·pua \ˌüt-ə-ˈpü-ə\. Small island, Santa Cruz group, 62

m. SE of Ndeni I., SW Pacific Ocean; a circular island ab. 8 m. in diameter, with a large inlet, Basilisk Harbour, extending into its center.

Uu·si·kau·pun·ki \'ü-sē-'kau̇-pəŋ-kē\ *or Swedish* **Ny·stad** \'n(y)ü-ˌstä(d)\. Seaport town, Turku ja Pori prov., SW Finland, on the Baltic Sea; pop. (1970e) 7452; exports lumber and stone; founded 1617; scene of the signing of a treaty of peace (Treaty of Nystad) Aug. 30, 1721 bet. Russia and Sweden by which Russia restored Finland and Sweden ceded certain regions to Russia.

Uu·si·maa \'ü-si-ˌmä\ *or Swed.* **Ny·land** \'n(y)ü-ˌlan(d)\. Province of S Finland. See table at FINLAND.

Uva \'ü-və\. Province, SE Ceylon; 3277 sq. m.; pop. (1963c) 653,800; ✱ Badulla; high plain and mountains in the W part.

Uvá \ü-'vä\ *or* **Vua** \'vü-ə\. River, E Colombia; flows from **Lake Uvá** E into Guaviare river.

Uval·de \yu̇-'val-dē\. 1 County in SW Texas. See table at TEXAS.

2 City, its ⊗, 65 m. ESE of Del Rio; pop. (1970c) 10,764; feed, honey; ships livestock, mohair; asphalt mines; Southwest Texas Junior Coll. (1946); settled 1853.

Uvéa \ü-'vā-ə\ *or* **Uea** \ü-'ā-ə\. 1 Northernmost island of the chain of the Loyalty Is., E of New Caledonia and NW of Lifou; 51 sq. m.; pop. (1969c) 2001; low, narrow island ab. 30 m. long, with large lagoon on W side.

2 Main island of Wallis Is., SW Pacific Ocean; ab. 8 m. long by 3 m. wide; 29 sq. m.; pop. (1965c) 5711; enclosed by oval coral reef; chief village Mata-Utu.

Uwa·ji·ma \ˌü-wə-'jē-mə, u̇-'wäj-ə-mə\. Town, Ehime prefecture, NW Shikoku I., Japan; pop. (1970c) 64,262; on E side of Bungo Strait. Bombed by U.S. planes July–Aug. 1945.

'Uwaynāt, Jabal al *or* **Uweinat, Jebel.** See OWEINAT, JEBEL.

Uwharrie. See UHARIE.

Uxantis. See ÎLE D'OUESSANT.

Ux·bridge \'əks-(ˌ)brij\. 1 Industrial town, Worcester co., cen. Massachusetts, 15 m. SSE of Worcester; pop. (1970c) 8253.

2 Town, Ontario co., SE Ontario, Canada, 29 m. NE of Toronto; pop. (1971p) 3068; auto parts; diversified agriculture.

Uxellodunum. See ISSOUDUN.

Ux·mal \üz-'mäl\. Ancient city, Yucatán state, SE Mexico, ab. 50 m. S of Mérida; capital of the later Mayan empire; Mayan ruins.

Uyeda. See UEDA.

Uyu \'ü-(ˌ)yü\. River, Upper Burma, the most important tributary of the Chindwin river; ab. 140 m. long; rises in mountains S of Hukawng valley, flows SW to the Chindwin at ab. 25°N; navigable for small boats.

Uyu·ni \u̇-'yü-nē\. Town, Potosí dept., SW Bolivia; on railroad 191 m. S of Oruro; railroad junction and importing and exporting center bet. Antofagasta, Chile, and S Bolivia.

Uyuni, Salar de. See SALAR DE UYUNI.

Uz·bek Soviet Socialist Republic \'u̇z-ˌbek-, 'əz-\ *or* **Uz·bek·i·stan** \u̇z-ˌbek-i-'stan, əz-, -'stän\. A constituent republic of the U.S.S.R., bounded on N and W by Kazakh S.S.R., on E by Kirgiz and Tadzhik S.S.Rs., on S by Afghanistan and Turkmen S.S.R. In its NW part it includes the Karakalpak A.S.S.R. (*q.v.*); 173,591 sq. m.; pop. (1970p) 11,963,000; ✱ Tashkent. *Physical features:* For the most part plain and desert (Kyzyl Kum) regions but in SE bordering Tadzhik S.S.R. has plateau and high ranges. Includes S half of Aral Sea, the lower course and delta of the Amu Darya, and in S cen. part the Zeravshan river. *Chief products:* Cotton, silk, wool, fruit; natural gas, oil, iron ore, copper; agricultural machinery, chemicals; metallurgical industries. *Chief cities:* Tashkent, Samarkand, Andizhan, Namangan, Kokand.

History: Region once settled by Golden Horde, from one of whose chiefs, Uzbeg Khan (d. 1340), the Uzbeks, prevailing Muslim people of Turkish origin, received their name; from 8th to 19th cent. Muslim emirates flourished at Khiva, Bukhara, and Samarkand (*qq.v.*); see also KHWARIZM; in early 19th cent. visited by Russian geographers and scientists; Tashkent occupied by Russian forces 1865, Samarkand and Bukhara, 1868, but Khiva not overcome until 1873; as emirates these remained vassal states of Russian Empire until 1917; after the Revolution, Soviet governments set up but conditions unstable until organization 1924 of Uzbek S.S.R.

Uzès \ü-'zes\. Manufacturing town, Gard dept., S France, ab. 15 m. N of Nîmes; pop. (1962c) 6058; cathedral; ducal castle.

Uzh·go·rod \'üzh-gə-ˌräd\ *or Hung.* **Ung·vár** \'u̇ŋ-ˌvär\ *or Slovak* **Už·ho·rod** \'üzh-hȯ-ˌrȯt\. City, ✱ of Transcarpathian Oblast, SW Ukrainian S.S.R., U.S.S.R., on a headstream of the Tisza; pop. (1970p) 65,000; wine, brandy, wood products; lumber and cattle-trading center. Formerly a Hungarian city; from 1918 to 1939 chief town of Carpathian Ruthenia in Czechoslovakia; taken over by U.S.S.R. 1946.

Uzhok *or Czech* **Užok** \'üzh-ˌȯk\. Mountain pass, Transcarpathian Oblast, Ukrainian S.S.R., U.S.S.R., E Carpathian Mts., just N of Uzhok village and 36 m. NE of Uzhgorod; 2197 ft.

Uz·lo·va·ya \üz-'lə-vī-(y)ə\. Town, Tula Oblast, Russian S.F.S.R., U.S.S.R., ab. 30 m. SE of Tula; pop. (1969e) 54,000.

Uznam. See USEDOM.

Vaagö. See VÅGØ.

Vaal \'väl\. River, Rep. of South Africa; 720 m. long; rises in SE Transvaal, flows W, forming boundary bet. Transvaal and Orange Free State; empties into Orange river in N Cape Province.

Vaal Krantz *or* **Vaal·krantz** \'väl-'krän(t)s\. Village, W Natal, Rep. of South Africa, just SW of Ladysmith; scene of defeat of British by Boers Feb. 5, 1900.

Vaals \'väls\. Commune, Limburg prov., Netherlands, at the place where boundaries of Netherlands, Belgium, and Germany meet, just W of Aachen; pop. (1970e) 10,338; wool weaving.

Vaa·sa \'väs-ə\ *or Swed.* **Va·sa** \'väs-ə\. 1 Province of W Finland. See table at FINLAND.

2 *or formerly* **Ni·ko·lain·kau·pun·ki** \ˌnik-ə-līn-'kau̇-pu̇ŋ-kē\. Seaport city, its ✻, on the Gulf of Bothnia ab. 220 m. NW of Helsinki; pop. (1970p) 44,316; textiles, flour, baked goods, machinery, clothing; founded 1606; destroyed by fire 1852 but rebuilt on present site c. 1860.

Vác \'väts\ *or Ger.* **Wait·zen** \'vīt-sən\. City, N Hungary, on left bank of the Danube ab. 20 m. N of Budapest; pop. (1970p) 27,946; cathedral and episcopal palace.

Va·ca·ria \ˌvə-kə-'rē-ə\. Municipality, Rio Grande do Sul state, S Brazil, ab. 100 m. NNE of Pôrto Alegre; pop. (1968e) 57,060.

Vac·a·ville \'vak-ə-ˌvil\. City, Solano co., cen. California, 33 m. WSW of Sacramento; pop. (1970c) 21,690; packs fruit and vegetables; citrus orchards; founded 1850.

Vacca. See BÉJA.

Vache Island \'väsh-\. Island, Caribbean Sea, off S coast of W Hispaniola.

Va·co·as–Phoe·nix \və-ˌkō-əs-'fē-niks\. Town, W Mauritius, ab. 10 m. S of Port Louis; pop. (1969e) 48,480.

Väddö \'ved-ə(r)\. Island off the SE coast of Sweden, opp. Ahvenanmaa in W entrance to the Gulf of Bothnia.

Vad·nais Heights \ˌvad-nəs-, vad-ˌnā-\. Village, Ramsey co., E Minnesota; pop. (1970c) 3391.

Vadsø \'väd-sə(r)\. Seaport, ⊗ of Finnmark co., N Norway, on N shore of Varanger Fjord; pop. (1970e) 5625; ice-free harbor, trades in reindeer meat and hides, dried fish, guano.

Vad·ste·na \'väd-ˌstān-ə\. Town, Östergötland co., SE Sweden, on E shore of Lake Vättern 25 m. W of Linköping; pop. (1970e) 6915; site of convent founded by Saint Bridget, founder c. 1344 of the Brigittine order for men and women.

Va·duz \fä-'düts\. Commune, ✻ of Liechtenstein, on right bank of Upper Rhine ab. 50 m. SE of Zurich, Switzerland; pop. (1970c) 3921; tourism. Greatly damaged in 1499 in war bet. the Swiss and the emperor, rebuilt 1523–26; came into possession of Liechtenstein family 1712.

Vær·øy \'ver-ə-ˌü\. Island of the Lofoten, Norwegian Sea, off NW coast of Norway.

Vág. See VÁH.

Va·ga \'vä-gə\. 1 River, SW Arkhangelsk Oblast, Russian S.F.S.R., U.S.S.R.; 357 m. long; flows N to the Northern Dvina river.

2 Town, Tunisia. See BÉJA.

Vagarshapat. See ECHMIADZIN.

Vågø *also* **Vaagö** \'vȯg-ə(r)\. Island of W part of the Faeroes (*q.v.*); 69 sq. m.; pop. (1966c) 2500.

Váh \'vä(k̲)\ *or Hung.* **Vág** \'väg\ *or Ger.* **Waag** \'väk\. River, W Slovak S.R., Czechoslovakia; 245 m. long; rises in the Tatra Mts., flows W and S into the Danube at Komárno.

Vahalis. See WAAL.

Vai·den \'vä-dᵊn\. Town, a ⊗ of Carroll co., cen. Mississippi; pop. (1970c) 716.

Vai·gach \vī-'gäch\. Island, NE Nenets National Okrug, Russian S.F.S.R., U.S.S.R., bet. the mainland and Novaya Zemlya, SE of Kara Strait; 1306 sq. m.; 68 m. long.

Vai·gai \'vī-gī\. River, SE India; ab. 180 m. long; rises in the Cardamom Hills, flows NE and ESE in SE Tamil Nadu into Palk Strait.

Vai·li·ma \vī-'lē-mə\. Estate of Robert Louis Stevenson (1889–94), Upolu I., Western Samoa, ab. 4 m. S of Apia.

Vakh \'väk\. River, mostly in SE Khanty-Mansi National Okrug, Russian S.F.S.R., U.S.S.R.; 599 m. long; rises in W Krasnoyarsk Krai and flows W into Ob river.

Vakhsh *or* **Vaksh** \'väksh\. River, a N tributary of the Amu Darya, SW Tadzhik S.S.R., U.S.S.R.; 497 m. long; flows W and SW.

Va·la·am \'väl-ə-ˌäm\ *or Finnish* **Va·la·mo** \'väl-ə-ˌmȯ\. Island group, N Lake Ladoga, Karelian A.S.S.R., Russian S.F.S.R., U.S.S.R.; formerly belonged to Finland; site of Greek Orthodox monastery, founded in 10th cent.

Va·lais \va-'lā\ *or Ger.* **Wal·lis** \'väl-əs\. Swiss canton. See history and table at SWITZERLAND.

Val·cour Island \'val-ku̇r-\. Island, Lake Champlain, 5 m. SE of Plattsburgh, New York; battle 1776 (see PLATTSBURGH).

Val·da·gno \väl-'dän-ˌyō\. Commune, Vicenza prov., Veneto, NE Italy, in Alps 15 m. NW of Vicenza; pop. (1968e) 28,533; manufactures linen; lignite mining.

Val·dai Hills \väl-'dī-\. Hills and plateau, N Kalinin and S Novgorod oblasts, W Russian S.F.S.R., U.S.S.R.; average height 600 to 1000 ft.; highest point 1053 ft., highest in the interior of European U.S.S.R. Source of the Volga, Western Dvina, and Dnieper, and rivers flowing into Lake Ilmen; many lakes and marshes. In World War II overrun by Germans Oct. 1941 and controlled by them until winter of 1942–43.

Val d'Ajol, Le. See LE VAL D'AJOL.

Val–de–Marne \ˌväl-də-'märn\. Department of N France. See table at FRANCE.

Val·de·pe·ñas \ˌväl-də-'pān-yəs\. Commune, Ciudad Real prov., S cen. Spain, 33 m. SE of Ciudad Real; pop. (1970p) 24,397; red wines.

Valderaduey. See ARADUEY.

Val·dese \'val-ˌdēz\. Town, Burke co., W North Carolina, in foothills of Blue Ridge Mts. 12 m. S of Lenoir; pop. (1970c) 3182; yarn, hosiery; grapes.

Val·dés Peninsula *or* **Val·déz Peninsula** \väl-'des-\. Peninsula, extending into Atlantic Ocean from NE coast of Chubut prov., S Argentina, S of the Gulf of San Matías; encloses Gulf of San José on N.

Val·dez \val-'dēz\. Town and port at head of inlet on NE shore of Prince William Sound, S Alaska; pop. (1970c) 1005; military base in World War II; moved 4 m. to SW from original site after destruction by earthquake 1964.

Valdéz Peninsula. See VALDÉS PENINSULA.

Val di Gardena. See GARDENA, VAL DI.

Val·di·via \väl-'dēv-ē-ə\. 1 River, Valdivia prov., S cen. Chile; ab. 100 m. long; rises in Andes Mts., flows W into Pacific Ocean.

2 Province of S cen. Chile. See table at CHILE.

3 City, ✻ of Valdivia prov., S cen. Chile, on the Valdivia river 16 m. from its mouth; pop. (1966e) 80,035; lumber, metal goods, boats, foodstuffs; railroad shops; tourist center in lake region; univ. (1954). Founded 1552; developed after mid-19th cent. influx of German settlers; severely damaged by earthquake 1960.

Val·dob·bia·de·ne \ˌväl-dȯb-'yä-də-ˌnā\. Commune, Treviso prov., Veneto, NE Italy, 22 m. NW of Treviso; pop. (1968e) 11,006; ferruginous springs.

Val–d'Oise \väl-'dwäz\. Department of N France. See table at FRANCE.

Val d'Or \väl-'dȯr\. Town, Abitibi co., SW Quebec, Canada; pop. (1971p) 17,419; lumber; gold mines; diversified agriculture.

Val·dos·ta \val-'däs-tə\. City, ⊗ of Lowndes co., S Georgia, 57 m. WSW of Waycross; pop. (1970c) 32,303; feed, textiles, metal goods; tobacco, cotton, watermelons, livestock; Valdosta State Coll. (1906); settled 1859.

Vale \'vāl\. Town, ⊗ of Malheur co., SE Oregon, on Malheur river 62 m. SSE of Baker; pop. (1970c) 1448; diversified agriculture.

Va·len·ça \və-'lā(ⁿ)n-sə\. 1 City, Bahia state, E Brazil, on coast 50 m. SW of Salvador; munic. pop. (1968e) 45,145.
2 City, Rio de Janeiro state, SE Brazil, 40 m. NNW of Rio de Janeiro; munic. pop. (1968e) 56,930.

Va·lence \va-'läⁿs\; *anc.* **Ven·tia** \'ven-ch(ē-)ə\ *or later* **Va·len·tia** \və-'len-ch(ē-)ə\. Industrial commune, ✱ of Drôme dept., SE France, on left bank of Rhone river 116 m. NNW of Marseilles; pop. (1968c) 62,358; produces silk, furniture, footwear, walnut veneers; 11th cent. Romanesque cathedral; made episcopal see 4th cent. and site of univ. from 15th cent. until 1790.

Va·len·cia \və-'len-ch(ē-)ə\. County in New Mexico. See table at NEW MEXICO.

Valencia \və-'len-ch(ē-)ə, -len(t)-sē-ə\. 1 Region and ancient kingdom, E Spain, bounded on N by Aragon and Catalonia, on E by the Mediterranean, on S by Murcia, and on W by Murcia, New Castile, and Aragon; 8886 sq. m.; ✱ Valencia; comprises modern provinces of Alicante, Castellón de la Plana, and Valencia; watered by the Segura, Guadalaviar, Júcar, and Mijares rivers; generally mountainous, broken by coastal and inland plains; numerous salt lagoons on coast; wide variety of agricultural produce owing to wide variations in temperature and rainfall; sheep and goat raising; small deposits of lignite, iron, lead, zinc; well-developed industrially, having numerous textile mills, iron and copper foundries, distilleries, sugar mills, potteries, fisheries, and fish-preserving establishments.
History: Conquered successively by Romans, Visigoths, and Moors; part of Caliphate of Córdoba until its dissolution in early 11th cent.; became independent Moorish kingdom; held by the Cid 1094–99, but after his death again lost to Moors; reconquered 1238 by James I of Aragon.
2 Province of E Spain. See table at SPAIN.
3 *or anc.* **Va·len·tia** \və-'len-ch(ē-)ə\. Commune, ✱ of Valencia prov., E Spain, on Mediterranean at mouth of the Guadalaviar, 188 m. ESE of Madrid; pop. (1970p) 653,690; ships fruit, wine, textiles, ironwork; produces furniture, metal goods, ceramics, clothing, building materials, velvet, fans, linen; tourism; 13th–15th cent. cathedral, 14th cent. church, 15th cent. Gothic silk exchange, and several other notable buildings; univ. (1500).
History: First mentioned as Roman settlement 138 B.C.; taken by Visigoths 413 A.D. and Moors 714; made ✱ of independent Moorish kingdom of Valencia 1021; ruled by the Cid 1094–99; finally reconquered by James I of Aragon 1238; site of first Spanish printing press 1474; severely damaged in Peninsular War, Spanish Civil War, and by floods 1859 and 1957.
4 *or* **Ta·ca·ri·gua** \ˌtä-kə-'rē-gwə\. Lake, N Venezuela, SW of Caracas and ab. 20 m. S of coast of Caribbean Sea; 125 sq. m.
5 Commercial city, ✱ of Carabobo state, N Venezuela, 80 m. W of Caracas and near W end of Lake Valencia; pop. (1970e) 232,035; fourth largest city in Venezuela and one of its principal industrial and transportation centers; produces automobile parts, textiles, paper, cement, furniture, dairy products, soap, vegetable oils, pharmaceuticals, feed, fertilizer; automobile assembly plants; founded 1555.

Valencia *or* **Va·len·tia** \və-'len-sh(ē-)ə\. 1 Island off SW coast of Ireland, S of entrance to Dingle Bay; 7 m. long and 2 m. wide; 10 sq. m.; administratively part of co. Kerry, Eire; E terminus of the first transatlantic cable (to Newfoundland), laid by "Great Eastern" in 1866.
2 Town, SE Valencia I., the extreme W port of Europe.

Valencia, Gulf of. Widemouthed inlet of Mediterranean Sea, E coast of Spain bet. Cape Tortosa and Cape Nao.

Valencia de Al·cán·ta·ra \-al-'kän-tə-rə\. Commune, Cáceres prov., W Spain, near Portuguese border 47 m. W of Cáceres; pop. (1970p) 8315; cork; antimony and calcium phosphate mines.

Va·len·ci·ennes \və-ˌlen(t)-sē-'en(z)\. Industrial town, Nord dept., N France, on the Schelde 29 m. SE of Lille; pop. (1968c) 46,626; steel and steel products, motors, cement, paint, lace; coal mines, oil refinery; museum, library, several notable churches, 17th cent. town hall.
History: Held by Charlemagne 811; part of Holy Roman Empire; became capital of Hainaut; conquered by Louis XIV 1677; ceded to France 1678; besieged 1814; in World War I captured and occupied by Germans 1914–18; almost completely demolished 1918.

Valentia. 1 Commune, France. See VALENCE.
2 Island and town, Ireland. See VALENCIA 1 and 2.
3 Commune, Spain. See VALENCIA 3.

Val·en·tine \'val-ən-ˌtīn\. City, ⊗ of Cherry co., N Nebraska, on Niobrara river 10 m. S of South Dakota border; pop. (1970c) 2662; livestock.

Va·len·za \və-'len(t)-(ˌ)sä\. Manufacturing commune, Alessandria prov., Piedmont, NW Italy, on Po river 9 m. N of Alessandria; pop. (1968e) 22,148.

Va·len·zue·la \ˌväl-ən-'swā-lə\. Town, S Cordillera dept., cen. Paraguay; pop. (1970e) 9772.

Va·le·ra \və-'ler-ə\. Town, Trujillo state, W cen. Venezuela, 25 m. WSW of Trujillo; pop. (1970e) 71,223; trading center.

Va·le·ri·an Way \və-ˌlir-ē-ən-\ *or Lat,* **Via Va·le·ria** \ˌvī-ə-və-'lir-ē-ə\. Ancient Roman road, from Tibur (Tivoli) along the N bank of the Anio (Aniene) E and NE through the Apennines to Aternum (Pescara) on the Adriatic, then N along the coast.

Va·lé·rien, Mont \ˌmōⁿ-ˌva-ler-'yaⁿ\. Hill, W of Paris, France, near Suresnes; 531 ft.; site of a fort, built 1841–43, important defense in siege of Paris during Franco-Prussian War 1870–71.

Valetta. See VALLETTA.

Val·ga \'val-gə\. Town, S Estonian S.S.R., U.S.S.R., at boundary with Latvian S.S.R.; pop. (1967e) 15,000.

Valgrund. See VALLGRUND.

Va·lien·te, Cape \-väl-'yen-tē\. Cape, NW coast of Panama, enclosing Chiriquí Lagoon.

Va·li·ra \və-'lir-ə\ *or* **Gran Valira** \ˌgrän-\. River, Andorra, SW Europe; flows into the Segre river at Seo de Urgel in Spain.

Va·lje·vo \'väl-yə-ˌvō\ *also* **Val·ye·vo** \'väl-yə-ˌvō\. Town, Serbia, E cen. Yugoslavia, ab. 45 m. SW of Belgrade; pop. (1965e) 28,000; first open opposition to the Turks here 1804.

Val·kens·waard \'väl-kəns-ˌvärt\. Commune, North Brabant prov., Netherlands; pop. (1970e) 23,238.

Va·lla·do·lid \ˌval-əd-ə-'lid, -'lē(th)\. 1 Town, E Yucatán state, SE Mexico; munic. pop. (1970p) 25,367; E of the ruins of Chichén Itzá.
2 Municipality, Negros Occidental, Negros, Phil., on Guimaras Strait 16 m. SSW of Bacolod; pop. (1969e) 20,100.
3 Province of NW cen. Spain. See table at SPAIN.
4 Commune, ✱ of Valladolid prov., NW cen. Spain, on Pisuerga river 98 m. NNW of Madrid; pop. (1970p) 236,341; produces leather goods, textiles, chemicals, flour, canned goods, wine, bronze and iron work; 16th cent. cathedral, 12th cent. church of Santa María la Antigua, 17th cent. palace, house where Columbus died 1506; univ. (13th cent.). First mentioned 1074; seat of Castilian court 1454–1598; site of marriage of Isabella of Castile and Ferdinand of Aragon 1469; heavily damaged by fire 1561 and by French in Peninsular War.

Val·lau·ris \ˌval-ə-ˈrēs\. Commune, Alpes-Maritimes dept., SE France, 13 m. SW of Nice; pop. (1968c) 12,880; winter resort; manufactures faience, perfumes; site of Picasso's Museum of Peace.

Va·lle \ˈvä-(ˌ)yā\. 1 *or in full* **Valle del Cau·ca** \-del-ˈkau̇-kə\. Department of W Colombia. See table at COLOMBIA. 2 Department of S Honduras. See table at HONDURAS.

Val·le·ci·to Dam \ˌvī-sēt-ə-\. Dam across Pine (or Los Pinos) river, tributary of San Juan river, E La Plata co., SW Colorado; height 162 ft.; completed 1941; impounds water for irrigation, forming **Vallecito Reservoir.**

Val·le d'Aos·ta \ˌväl-ā-dä-ˈō-stə\. Autonomous region, NW Italy; 1260 sq. m.; pop. (1968e) 107,861; ✱ Aosta.

Va·lle de la Pas·cua \ˌvä-yā-də-lä-ˈpäs-kwə\. Town, Guárico, N cen. Venezuela, ab. 100 m. SE of San Juan de los Morros; pop. (1970e) 38,630.

Valle del Cauca. See VALLE 1.

Valle de San·tia·go \ˌvä-yā-də-ˌsant-ē-ˈäg-(ˌ)ō, -ˌsänt-\. Town, Guanajuato state, cen. Mexico, 40 m. S of Guanajuato; munic. pop. (1970p) 80,504; diversified agriculture.

Valle di Pompei. See POMPEI.

Va·lle·du·par \ˌvä-yā-du̇-ˈpär\. Town, ✱ of El Cesar dept., N Colombia; munic. pop. (1968e) 61,366.

Val·le·her·mo·so \ˌvä-yā-er-ˈmō-sə\. Municipality, Negros Oriental prov., Negros, Phil., on Tanon Strait 34 m. SE of city of Bacolod; pop. (1969e) 31,800.

Valle Her·mo·so \ˌvä-yā-er-ˈmō-so\. Municipality, Tamaulipas state, Mexico, 20 m. SW of Matamoros; pop. (1970p) 41,546; wheat, cotton.

Val·le·jo \və-ˈlā-(ˌ)ō\. Commercial city, Solano co., cen. California, on San Pablo Bay 20 m. N of Oakland; pop. (1970c) 71,710; ships wool and livestock, truck crops, nuts; flour, canned goods; California Maritime Academy (1929), Solano Coll. (1945); Mare Island Navy Yard (estab. 1854). Settled c. 1850; served briefly as state capital in 1852 and 1853; incorporated 1866.

Va·lle·nar \ˌvä-yā-ˈnär\. City, Atacama prov., N cen. Chile, ab. 80 m. SSW of Copiapó; pop. (1960c) 15,693.

Va·lles \ˈvä-(ˌ)yās\. 1 River, E cen. Mexico, a tributary of the Pánuco river.
2 *or officially* **Ciu·dad de Valles** \ˌsē-u̇-ˌt͟häd-ā-\. Town, San Luis Potosí state, cen. Mexico, ab. 125 m. E of San Luis Potosí; munic. pop. (1970p) 71,098.

Val·let·ta *also* **Va·let·ta** \və-ˈlet-ə\. Seaport city, ✱ of Malta, on the NE coast of island of Malta; pop. (1970e) 15,547; commercial center of the country; tourism. Located on a rocky promontory with harbors on either side; library, museum, two cathedrals, governor-general's residence; Royal Univ. of Malta (1769).

History: Built after siege of 1565; named for Jean Parisot de La Valette, grand master of the Knights of Malta, and made ✱ 1570; made principal base of British Mediterranean fleet after 1814 and remained important until after World War II, during which it suffered heavy damage from Axis bombing 1941–43.

Val·ley \ˈval-ē\. Name of counties in three states of the U.S. See tables at IDAHO, MONTANA, NEBRASKA.

Valley Brook. Town, Oklahoma co., cen. Oklahoma, 2 m. SE of Oklahoma City; pop. (1970c) 2869.

Valley Center. City, Sedgwick co., S cen. Kansas, 10 m. N of Wichita; pop. (1970c) 2551; agriculture; oil and gas wells.

Valley City. City, ⊗ of Barnes co., E North Dakota, 60 m. W of Fargo; pop. (1970c) 7843; dairy products; grain and livestock farms; Valley City State Coll. (1889); settled 1872.

Valley Falls. Industrial village, Providence co., N Rhode Island, 2 m. N of Central Falls; governmental center for Cumberland.

Val·ley·field \ˈval-ē-ˌfēld\ *or formerly* **Sal·a·ber·ry de Valleyfield** \ˌsal-ə-ˌber-ē-də-\. City, Beauharnois co., S Quebec, Canada, on S shore of Lake St. Francis on an island formed by St. Lawrence Seaway Canal, 35 m. SW of Montreal; pop. (1971p) 29,776; produces cotton and silk yarns, canned goods, wood pulp and paper, pharmaceuticals; Séminaire de Valleyfield (1893); founded c. 1840.

Valley Forge \-ˈfō(ə)rj, -ˈfȯ(ə)rj\. Locality, Chester co., SE Pennsylvania, on Schuylkill river ab. 4 m. SE of Phoenixville; winter headquarters of Washington and his army 1777–78; state park.

Valley Junction. See WEST DES MOINES.

Valley of Ten Thousand Smokes. Volcanic region, SW Alaska, in Katmai National Monument W of Mt. Katmai; formed at the eruption of Katmai in June 1912 when the valley—17 m. long by 4 m. wide—was covered by a flow of incandescent sand; later (1915), when discovered by an expedition of the National Geographic Society, its floor was found to have not 10,000, but actually millions of steam jets, large and small (largest 150 ft. in diameter), some of which had a temperature as high as 1200°F.

Valley Park. City, St. Louis co., E Missouri, 16 m. W of St. Louis; pop. (1970c) 3662.

Valleys of Andorra, The. See ANDORRA.

Valley Station. Unincorporated urban community, Jefferson co., N cen. Kentucky, S of Louisville; pop. (1970c) 24,471.

Valley Stream. Residential village, Nassau co., SE New York, on Long I. 16 m. ESE of New York; pop. (1970c) 40,413; incorporated 1925.

Vall·grund *or* **Val·grund** \ˈval-grənd\. Island, Gulf of Bothnia, Vaasa prov., Finland, opp. city of Vaasa.

Val·mi·era \ˈväl-(ˌ)mye(ə)r-ə\ *or Ger.* **Wol·mar** \ˈvȯl-(ˌ)mär\. Town, N Latvian S.S.R., U.S.S.R., 65 m. NE of Riga; pop. (1967e) 19,000.

Val·my \ˈval-mē, val-ˈmē\. Village, Marne dept., NE France; pop. (1962c) 354; scene of victory of French revolutionary army under Dumouriez and Kellermann over combined Austrian-Prussian force under the duke of Brunswick Sept. 20, 1792.

Va·lognes \va-ˈlōnʸ\. Commercial town, Manche dept., NW France, SSE of Cherbourg; pop. (1962c) 5743; church of 15th–17th cents.; a few Roman remains in vicinity.

Va·lois \ˈval-ˌwä\. Medieval county and duchy, NE Île-de-France, N France, now included in modern departments of Aisne and Oise; ✱ Crépy-en-Valois. County (10th to 12th cent.) united to crown by King Philip Augustus 1214, but soon detached; granted 1285 by Philip III to his son Charles (Charles de Valois), whose son Philip VI became first ruler of the House of Valois 1328; its last representative, Henry III, was succeeded 1589 by the House of Bourbon.

Valona. See VLORË.

Val·pa·rai \ˌväl-pə-ˈrī\. Town, Tamil Nadu, India, ab. 50 m. NW of Madurai; pop. (1961c) 80,023.

Val·pa·rai·so, 1 \ˌval-pə-ˈrī-(ˌ)zō\. City, Okaloosa co., NW Florida, on Choctawhatchee Bay; pop. (1970c) 6504; Okaloosa-Walton Junior Coll. (1963); Eglin Air Force Base, with air proving ground.
2 \ˌval-pə-ˈrā-(ˌ)zō\. Residential city, ⊗ of Porter co., NW Indiana, 12 m. S of Lake Michigan; pop. (1970c) 20,020; Valparaiso Univ. (1859); Valparaiso Technical Institute (1934).

Val·pa·ra·í·so \ˌväl-pä-rä-ˈē-sō\; *Eng.* **Val·pa·rai·so** \ˌval-pə-ˈrā-(ˌ)zō, -ˈrī-\. 1 Province of cen. Chile. See table at CHILE. 2 Seaport, its ✱, 75 m. WNW of Santiago on the **Bay of Valparaíso;** pop. (1970p) 238,557; principal seaport of Chile, handling the bulk of the country's imports; extensive modern dock facilities; produces chemicals, textiles, paint, leather goods, vegetable oils; foundries, ship repair facilities, naval base; Catholic univ. (1928), technical univ.

(1931), naval academy. Viña del Mar (*q.v.*) to NE is residential suburb. Founded 1536 and has been subject to frequent severe earthquakes, esp. in 1906–07 after which modern development began; bombarded by Spanish fleet Mar. 31, 1866; treaty signed here Apr. 4, 1884 by which Bolivia ceded to Chile coastal region containing principal nitrate deposits.

3 Municipality, Zacatecas state, Mexico, 65 m. W of Zacatecas; pop. (1970p) 43,410.

Vals, Cape \-'väls\ *or Du.* **Kaap Valsch** \kap-'väls\ *or Eng.* **False Cape.** Cape, SW tip of Dolak I., off S coast of Irian Barat, Indonesia.

Valua. See SADDLE.

Val·ver·de \val-'verd-ē\. 1 Province, Dominican Republic. See table at DOMINICAN REPUBLIC.

2 Chief town, Hierro I., Canary Is., Spain; pop. (1970p) 3190.

Val Ver·de \val-'vərd-ē\. County in Texas. See table at TEXAS.

Valyevo. See VALJEVO.

Vam·sa·dha·ra \,vəm-s(h)ə-'där-ə\. River, SW Orissa and NE Andhra Pradesh, India; 170 m. long; rises in Eastern Ghats and flows S to Bay of Bengal.

Van \'van\. 1 *or anc.* **Thos·pi·tis** \thäs-'pīt-əs\ *or Turk.* **Van Gö·lü** \,vän-gəl-'(y)ü\. Salt lake (*gölü*), E Turkey; 1419 sq. m.; 80 m. long; max. depth 82 ft.; alt. 5643 ft.; largest lake in Turkey; has no apparent outlet.

2 Ancient kingdom, N of Assyria. See URARTU and ARMENIA 1.

3 Province of E Turkey, Asia. See table at TURKEY.

4 Town, its ❋, on SE shore of Van lake; pop. (1965c) 31,431; ships hides, fruit, grain; ancient citadel.

History: Dates back to Vannic kingdom of Urartu (see ARMENIA 1 and URARTU) of which it was made capital c. 8th cent. A.D. and was also fortified; fell to Seljuk Turks after 1071 and to Ottoman Turks 1543.

Van Bu·ren \van-'byu̇r-ən\. 1 Name of counties in four states of the U.S. See tables at ARKANSAS, IOWA, MICHIGAN, TENNESSEE.

2 City, ⊗ of Crawford co., NW Arkansas, on Arkansas river 6 m. NE of Fort Smith; pop. (1970c) 8373; furniture; gas wells; peaches, strawberries.

3 Town, Aroostook co., N Maine, on St. John river 34 m. N of Presque Isle; pop. (1970c) 3971; lumber; potatoes.

4 Town, ⊗ of Carter co., SE Missouri; pop. (1970c) 714.

Vance \'van(t)s\. County in North Carolina. See table at NORTH CAROLINA.

Vance·burg \'van(t)s-,bərg\. City, ⊗ of Lewis co., NE Kentucky; pop. (1970c) 1773.

Van·cou·ver \van-'kü-vər\. 1 City, ⊗ of Clark co., SW Washington, on Columbia river ab. 8 m. N of Portland, Oregon; pop. (1970c) 42,493; ships grain; produces aluminum, chemicals, wood and paper products, beer, canned fruits; in dairy and poultry farming region; Clark Coll. (1933). Founded as Hudson's Bay Company Post 1824; taken over by U.S. government 1846 and made military reservation 1848; incorporated as city 1857.

2 City, S British Columbia, Canada, at mouth of Burrard Inlet on S side; pop. (1971p) 422,278, met. area pop. 1,071,081; principal Pacific seaport of Canada and the industrial and commercial center of British Columbia; ships forest products and grain; produces lumber, plywood, pulp and paper, iron and steel, chemicals; oil refining, food processing; commercial fisheries, shipyards, grain elevators, meat-packing plants; W terminus for transcontinental railroad. Univ. of British Columbia (1890, at Point Gray), Anglican Theological Coll. of British Columbia (1912), Saint Paul's Coll. (1926), Union Coll. of British Columbia (1927), Saint Mark's Coll. (1956), Saint Andrew's Hall (1957), Carey Hall (1960), Simon Fraser Univ. (1963, at Burnaby). First settlement in area estab. by 1865; founded 1881 and incorporated as city 1886; suffered major fire 1886 but rebuilt; development aided by completion of transcontinental railroad 1887 and of Panama Canal 1914.

Vancouver, Mount. Peak in St. Elias Mountains, SW Yukon Territory, Canada, near Alaska boundary SE of Mt. Logan; 15,700 ft.

Vancouver Island. Island off SW British Columbia, Canada; 12,408 sq. m.; largest island off W coast of Canada; chief city Victoria. On the S separated from Washington, U.S.A., by Juan de Fuca Strait and on E from Canadian mainland by Strait of Georgia, Johnstone Strait, and Queen Charlotte Sound. Has several fine harbors—Esquimalt in the S, Ladysmith and Nanaimo on the Strait of Georgia, Nootka Sound and Barkley Sound with Alberni Canal on the Pacific coast. Mountainous, averaging 2000 to 3000 ft.; highest peak Golden Hinde 7219 ft. Contains Strathcona Park (provincial); coal, iron ore, copper; lumbering, fishing; tourism. Visited by early Spanish and English explorers and at Nootka Sound by Capt. Cook 1778; made a British crown colony 1849 and united with British Columbia 1866.

Van·da·lia \van-'dāl-yə\. 1 City, ⊗ of Fayette co., S cen. Illinois, 30 m. N of Centralia; pop. (1970c) 5160; capital of Illinois 1820–39; Illinois State Penal Farm.

2 City, Audrain co., NE cen. Missouri, 29 m. SSW of Hannibal; pop. (1970c) 3160; clay pits; diversified agriculture.

3 City, Montgomery co., SW Ohio, N of Dayton; pop. (1970c) 10,756; automobile parts; truck farms.

Van·der·burgh \'van-dər-,bərg\. County in Indiana. See table at INDIANA.

Van·der·grift \'van-dər-,grift\. Industrial borough, Westmoreland co., SW Pennsylvania, on Kiskiminetas river 25 m. ENE of Pittsburgh; pop. (1970c) 7873.

Van Die·men, Cape \-van-'dē-mən\. Northwest point of Melville I., Northern Territory, Australia.

Van Diemen Gulf. Inlet of Arafura Sea, N Northern Territory, Australia, shut in by Melville I. and Cobourg Penin.; connected on the N by Dundas Strait with Arafura Sea and on the W by Clarence Strait with Timor Sea.

Van Diemen's Land. See TASMANIA.

Van Diemen Strait. See OSUMI ISLANDS.

Vä·nern \'vā-nərn\ *or* **Ve·ner** *also* **We·ner** *or* **Wen·ner** \'vā-nər\. Lake, SW Sweden; 2156 sq. m.; 91 m. long; 328 ft. max. depth; largest lake in Sweden; W section called **Dal·bo** \'däl-(,)bü\.

Vä·ners·borg \,vā-nərs-'bȯ(ə)rg, -'bȯ(ə)r(-yə)\. Town, ⊗ of Älvsborg co., SW Sweden, at S end of Lake Vänern; pop. (1970e) 20,280.

Van Gölü. See VAN 1.

Vang·u·nu \'väŋ-ü-(,)nü\. One of the New Georgia Is., cen. Solomon Is., W Pacific Ocean, off SE end of New Georgia. Mountainous, its highest point 3686 ft.; its N coast encloses Marovo lagoon (see NEW GEORGIA).

Van Horn \van-'hȯ(ə)rn\. Village, ⊗ of Culberson co., W Texas; pop. (1970c) 2889.

Van Horn Mountains. Range, SW Culberson co., W Texas; highest peak 5786 ft.

Va·nier \vaⁿ-'nyā, və-'ni(ə)r\. 1 *or formerly* **East·view** \'ēst-,vyü\. City, SE Ontario, Canada, on Ottawa river; pop. (1971p) 21,859.

2 *formerly* **Que·bec West** \kwi-'bek-'west\ *or Fr.* **Qué·bec-Ouest** \kā-bek-west\. Town, Quebec co., S Quebec prov., Canada, W suburb of Quebec city; pop. (1971p) 9716.

Va·ni·ko·ro \,vän-i-'kōr-(,)ō, -'kȯr-\ *or* **La Pé·rouse Island** \,läp-ə-'rüz-\. Island, S Santa Cruz Is., SW Pacific Ocean, 20 m. SE of Utupua I.; 11°37′S, 166°58′E; scene of the wreck of La Pérouse's fleet 1788.

Va·ni·yam·ba·di \,van-i-yəm-'bäd-ē\. Town, N Tamil Nadu, S India, on two islands in Palar river 118 m. WSW of Madras; pop. (1961c) 42,000.

Van Lear \van-'li(ə)r\. City, Johnson co., E Kentucky, 23 m. NNW of Pikeville; pop. (1970c) 1033.

Vannes \'van\ *or anc.* **Dar·i·or·i·gum** \,dar-ē-'ór-ə-gəm\. Industrial and commercial town, ❋ of Morbihan dept., NW France, 67 m. WNW of Nantes; pop. (1968c) 36,576;

tires, metal goods, feed; poultry farming, tourism; 14th–17th cent. fortifications, cathedral with 16th cent. chapel, museum of Celtic and Roman antiquities, public gardens. Ancient capital of the Veneti, for whom it is named; came under Brittany late 10th cent.

Vann·øy \ˈvän-ˌöi\. Island, Arctic Ocean, off NW coast of Norway.

Va·noise National Park \vä-ˈnwäz-\. National park, E France; 208 sq. m.; alpine fauna and flora; established 1963.

Va·nua La·va \və-ˌnü-ə-ˈläv-ə\. Largest of the Banks Is., N New Hebrides, SW Pacific Ocean; ab. 15 m. long and 12 m. wide. Of volcanic origin; highest point 3120 ft.; has excellent harbor, Port Patteson, on SE coast.

Vanua Le·vu \-ˈlev-(ˌ)ü\. Island, Fiji, 38 m. NE of Viti Levu; 2137 sq. m. Covered with mountains, highest Mt. Ndikeva 3134 ft. Its coastline irregular, esp. on E end where Natewa Bay makes deep indentation bet. mainland and Natewa Penin. (40 m. long). Chief river is the Ndreketi. Has many small coastal villages, most of them active in sugar industry; long reef and islets along its N shore.

Vanua Mba·la·vu \-ˌem-bə-ˈläv-(ˌ)ü\. Island, Fiji, largest of the Exploring Is. group; 14 m. long and from ½ to 2½ m. wide; chief town Lomaloma.

Vanves \ˈvänv\. Commune, Hauts-de-Seine dept., N France, SW suburb of Paris; pop. (1968c) 25,138; aluminum foundries; manufactures metal goods, chemical products; stone quarries.

Van Wert \van-ˈwərt\. 1 County in Ohio. See table at OHIO.
2 City, its ⊗, 26 m. WNW of Lima; pop. (1970c) 11,320; clothing, canned goods, dairy products; agriculture; settled 1835.

Van Zandt \van-ˈzant\. County in Texas. See table at TEXAS.

Vaph·io \ˈvaf-ē-ˌō, vä-ˈfyȯ\. Site of a beehive tomb, Laconia dept., SE Peloponnesus, S Greece, on Eurotas river 5 m. S of Sparta; tomb was excavated 1889 by Tsountas; among other important discoveries were two finely ornamented gold cups (the Vaphio cups), dating from c. 1500 B.C. (Late Minoan).

Vapincum. See GAP.

Var \ˈvär\. 1 *or Ital.* **Va·ro** \ˈvär-(ˌ)ō\ *or anc.* **Va·rus** \ˈvar-əs, ˈver-\. River, extreme SE France; 75 m. long; rises in the Alps, in Alpes-Maritimes dept., flows SE and S into Mediterranean Sea 4 m. SW of Nice.
2 Department of SE France. See table at FRANCE.

Va·ra·na·si \və-ˈrän-ə-(ˌ)sē\ *or* **Be·na·res** \bə-ˈnär-əs, -ēz\ *or* **Ba·na·ras** \-əs\. 1 Division, SE Uttar Pradesh, India; 10,378 sq. m.; pop. (1961c) 8,061,254; ✻ Varanasi; wheat, rice.
2 *earliest name* **Ka·si** \ˈkä-sē\. City, its ✻, on Ganges river 400 m. WNW of Calcutta; pop. (1970e) 637,612; silk fabrics, brass vessels, lacquered toys, chemicals; seed crushing, iron and steel rolling; Banaras Hindu Univ. (1916), Sanskrit Univ. (1957); one of India's most ancient cities. Holy City of the Hindus and the object of constant pilgrimages; also sacred to Jains, Sikhs, and Buddhists, and it is said that Buddha preached his first sermon here in the Deer Park. Has ab. 1500 temples and large mosques; among its most famous structures are the Bisheshwar or Golden Temple, the Mosque of Aurangzeb, and the Durga Kund, a Maratha temple.

Va·rang·er Fjord \vä-ˌräŋ-ər-\. Inlet of the Arctic Ocean, extreme NE coast of Norway, NW of Pechenga, Russian S.F.S.R., U.S.S.R.; ab. 42 m. long.

Va·ra·no, Lake \-və-ˈrän-(ˌ)ō\. Lagoon of Adriatic Sea, SE Italy, on N side of Mount Gargano.

Va·raž·din \və-ˈräzh-ˌdēn\ *or Hung.* **Va·rasd** \ˈvȯr-ˌȯsht\ *or Ger.* **Wa·ras·din** \ˈvär-äs-(ˌ)dēn\. Town, Croatia, NW Yugoslavia, on Drava river ab. 38 m. NE of Zagreb; pop. (1965e) 31,000; industrial and commercial center; radioactive springs nearby; occupied by Italians in World War II.

Var·berg \ˈvär-ˌbərg, -ˌber(-yə)\. Town, Halland co., SW Sweden, on the Kattegat ab. 45 m. S of Göteborg; pop. (1970e) 19,368; port; museum; fishing.

Var·dar \ˈvär-ˌdär\ *or anc.* **Ax·i·us** \ˈak-sē-əs\; *in Greece* **Var·da·res** \vär-ˈdär-əs\. River, SE Yugoslavia and N Greece; 241 m. long; rises in mountains on Albanian border, flows S into the Gulf of Salonika. Chief tributary the Crna in Yugoslavia. In World War II its valley used by German forces in conquest of Yugoslavia Apr. 1941 and invasion of Greece.

Var·dar·ska \ˈvärd-ər-ˌskä\. Former county, SE Yugoslavia, now mostly in Macedonia, with N section in Serbia; 15,007 sq. m.; ⊗ Skopje.

Var·de \ˈvär-də\. River, cen. Jutland, Denmark; ab. 45 m. long; flows SW into North Sea NW of Esbjerg.

Vardø \ˈvär-ˌdər\. Port on island off NE tip of Norway, N of entrance to Varanger Fjord.

Va·rennes \va-ˈren\ *or officially* **Varennes–en–Ar·gonne** \-äⁿ-när-ˈgän\. Commune, Meuse dept., NE France; pop. (1962c) 643; place where Louis XVI was arrested June 21, 1791 in his flight from Paris.

Va·re·se \və-ˈrā-sē\. 1 Province of Lombardy, N Italy. See table at ITALY.
2 Commune, its ✻, near Lake Varese 30 m. NW of Milan; pop. (1968e) 80,324; leather goods and footwear, paper, textiles; 18th cent. palace with public gardens, 16th cent. basilica, 12th cent. baptistry.

Var·gi·nha \vər-ˈzhē-nyə\. City, Minas Gerais state, E Brazil, 170 m. NW of Rio de Janeiro; munic. pop. (1968e) 38,473.

Värm·land \ˈvarm-ˌland\. County of SW Sweden. See table at SWEDEN.

Var·na \ˈvär-nə\. 1 Province of E Bulgaria. See table at BULGARIA.
2 *or from 1949 to 1957* **Sta·lin** \ˈstäl-ən, ˈstal-, -ˌēn\ *or anc.* **Odes·sus** \ō-ˈdes-əs\. Seaport, its ✻, on Black Sea ab. 182 m. NE of Plovdiv; pop. (1968e) 206,297; transportation center and principal seaport of Bulgaria; textiles, flour, wine, furniture, ceramics, electrical equipment, diesel engines; shipbuilding and repair facilities; naval base; technical institute (1963), naval school.
History: Founded 6th cent. B.C.; came under Turks 1391; scene of battle Nov. 10, 1444, in which Turks under Murad II defeated Hungarians under János Hunyadi and killed Ladislas, King of Poland and Hungary; ceded to Bulgaria by Treaty of Berlin 1878; harbor opened 1906.

Varns·dorf \ˈvärn(t)s-ˌdȯ(ə)rf\ *or Ger.* **Warns·dorf** \ˈvärn(t)s-\. City, Czech S.R., Czechoslovakia, 58 m. N of Prague near East German border; pop. (1968e) 13,912; textile-manufacturing center.

Varo. See VAR 1.

Vár·pa·lo·ta \ˈvär-pə-ˌlō-tə\. Town, W Hungary, ab. 50 m. SW of Budapest; pop. (1970p) 24,527.

Varus. See VAR 1.

Vary Karlovy. See KARLOVY VARY.

Vas \ˈväsh\. County of W Hungary. See table at HUNGARY.

Vasa. See VAASA.

Vasconia. See GASCONY.

Vash·on Island \ˌvash-ˌän-\. Island, Puget Sound, midway bet. Seattle and Tacoma, Washington; 14 m. long; belongs to King co.

Va·sil·kov \ˌvas-əl-ˈkȯf\. Town, Kiev Oblast, NW Ukrainian S.S.R., U.S.S.R., 19 m. S of Kiev; pop. (1967e) 24,000. Dates back to 10th cent.; destroyed by Mongols 1239–42; restored, but later taken by Lithuanians and Poles; became Russian 1686.

Vas·lui \väs-ˈlü-ē\. 1 County of E Romania. See table at ROMANIA.
2 City, its ⊗, 35 m. S of Iaşi; pop. (1970e) 22,739.

Vas·quez Peak \ˌvas-ˌkez-\. Mountain, Clear Creek and Grand cos., N Colorado; 12,800 ft.

Vas·sal·bor·ough \'vas-əl-ˌbər-ə, -ˌbə-rə\. Town, Kennebec co., SW Maine, on Kennebec river 6 m. S of Waterville; pop. (1970c) 2618.

Vas·sar \'vas-ər\. City, Tuscola co., E Michigan, 19 m. ESE of Saginaw; pop. (1970c) 2802.

Vassarí Mountains. See SERRA UAÇARI.

Vas·sou·ras \və-'sōr-əs, -'sȯr-\. City, Rio de Janeiro state, SE Brazil, 45 m. NW of Rio de Janeiro; munic. pop. (1968e) 54,339.

Väs·ter·ås \ˌves-tə-'rōs\. City, ⊗ of Västmanland co., E Sweden, at mouth of Svart river on Lake Mälaren; pop. (1970e) 113,389; major inland port, shipping iron ore, lumber, and iron goods; a center of the Swedish electrical industry; produces also machinery, glass, metalware; Gothic cathedral, 12th cent. castle; scene of parliament 1527 which formally introduced Reformation into Sweden.

Väs·ter·bot·ten \'ves-tər-ˌbȯ-tən\. County of N Sweden. See table at SWEDEN.

Väster Dal. See DAL.

Väs·ter·norr·land \'ves-tər-ˌnȯr-land\. County of E Sweden. See table at SWEDEN.

Väs·ter·vik \'ves-tər-ˌvēk\. Seaport, Kalmar co., SE Sweden, on Baltic Sea 73 m. N of Kalmar; pop. (1970e) 23,830; manufactures machinery, matches; stone quarries.

Väst·man·land \'vest-man-ˌland\. County of E Sweden. See table at SWEDEN.

Va·sto \'väs-(ˌ)tō\ *or anc.* **His·to·ni·um** \his-'tō-nē-əm\. Commune, Chieti prov., Abruzzi, cen. Italy, on Adriatic 32 m. ESE of Chieti; pop. (1968e) 24,474; 13th cent. castle; 11th cent. church; cathedral.

Vas·vár \'vȯsh-(ˌ)vär\ *or Ger.* **Ei·sen·burg** \'ī-zən-ˌbərg, -ˌbu̇(ə)rg\. Commune, Vas co., W Hungary, ab. 15 m. SE of Szombathely; pop. (1970p) 7187; treaty signed here Aug. 10, 1664 after battle of Saint Gotthard (see SZENTGOTTHÁRD) concluding by 20-year truce, war bet. Emperor Leopold I and the Turks.

Vaté. See EFATE.

Va·ter·nish Point \'wȯt-ər-nish-, 'wät-\. Cape, NW coast of the island of Skye, Inner Hebrides, off NW coast of Scotland; bet. Loch Dunvegan and Loch Snizort.

Va·ter·say \'vät-ər-ˌsā\. See BARRA.

Va·thy *or Gk.* **Va·thí** \vä-'thē\. Seaport city, ❋ of Samos dept., Aegean Is., Greece, on NE coast of Samos I.; pop. (1971p) 5472.

Vat·i·can City \ˌvat-i-kən-\ *or Ital.* **Cit·tà del Va·ti·ca·no** \chēt-'tä-del-ˌvä-tē-'kä-nō\ *also* **State of Vatican City.** Independent papal state, within commune of Rome, Italy, on right bank of Tiber river; 108.7 acres; pop. (1971e) 648; created Feb. 11, 1929 by the Lateran Pact as a settlement of the Roman question; extraterritoriality of the state extends to Castel Gandolfo and to 13 churches and palaces in Rome proper; under jurisdiction of the state are the Basilica of St. John Lateran (the cathedral church of Rome and highest ranking of all Roman Catholic churches), the Basilica of St. Peter (founded by Constantine on site of Circus of Caligula where St. Peter is said by tradition to have suffered martyrdom), the Vatican (collection of papal palaces, containing the Sistine Chapel, the Loggie, and the Stanze), papal gardens, Villa Pia, churches of Santa Maria Maggiore, San Paolo fuori le mura, San Lorenzo, and San Sebastiano, Pontifical Gregorian University (opened 1930), etc.; railroad station, radio station; independent postal and monetary systems; publishing. Holy See, or Apostolic See, designates Rome as the official seat of the Pope. For history of temporal domain of the Popes 755–1870, see STATES OF THE CHURCH.

Va·ti·ca·no, Cape \-ˌvät-i-'kän-(ˌ)ō\. Cape, SW coast of Calabria, the "toe" of Italy, extending into Tyrrhenian Sea S of Gulf of Sant'Eufemia.

Va·ti·lau \ˌvät-ᵊl-'au̇\ *or* **Bue·na Vis·ta** \ˌbwā-nə-'vēs-tə\. Small island, SE Solomon Is., in W Pacific Ocean, off NW coast of Florida I. beyond Olevuga I.

Vatiu. See ATIU.

Vat·na·jö·kull \'vät-nä-ˌyə-küt-ᵊl\ *or* **Klo·fa·jö·kull** \'klȯ-vä-\. Snowfield, SE Iceland; 3247 sq. m.; average elevation 2000 to 3000 ft.

Va·toa Island \və-ˌtō-ə-\. Small island, Fiji, S end of Lau group, 19°50'S, 178°13'W.

Vät·tern \'vet-ərn\ *or* **Vet·ter** *also* **Wet·ter** \'vet-ər\. Lake, S Sweden, E of Vänern lake; 738 sq. m.; connected with the Baltic by the Göta Canal; Jönköping is at its S end.

Vau·clin \vō-'klaⁿ\ *or* **Le Vauclin** \lə-\. Seaport commune, SE Martinique, West Indies.

Vau·cluse \vō-'klüz\. Department of SE France. See table at FRANCE.

Vaud \'vō\ *or Ger.* **Waadt** \'vät\. Swiss canton; 1240 sq. m.; pop. (1970c) 511,851; ❋ Lausanne; includes part of Lake of Geneva and Lake of Neuchâtel; watered by Rhone river; wine; tourism. Conquered by Romans 58 B.C.; taken by Franks; passed to Bern 1536 and forced to accept Reformation; former canton of Leman (1798–1803).

Vau–de–Vire. See VIRE 2.

Vau·dreuil \vō-'drə-yə, vō-'drȯi\. 1 County, S Quebec, Canada. See table at QUEBEC.

2 Town, its ⊗, on Ottawa river near its mouth ab. 24 m. WSW of Montreal; pop. (1971p) 3831.

Vaught, Mount \-'vȯt\. Peak, Glacier National Park, NW Montana; 8840 ft.

Vaulx–en–Ve·lin \ˌvō-äⁿ-və-'laⁿ\. Commune, Rhône dept., E cen. France, ab. 5 m. ENE of Lyons; pop. (1968c) 20,726.

Vau·pés \vau̇-'pās\. 1 River, South America. See UAUPÉS.

2 Commissary of SE Colombia. See table at COLOMBIA.

Vaux \'vō\. 1 Village, Aisne dept., N France, 4 m. W of Château-Thierry; captured by U.S. forces in battle of July 1, 1918.

2 Village, Meuse dept., NE France, 3 m. NE of Verdun; Fort de Vaux in vicinity; severe fighting Mar.–June, 1916; captured June 7 by Germans.

Va·vau \vä-'vau̇\. 1 Island group, N Tonga, SW cen. Pacific Ocean; includes island of Vavau and ab. 30 islets; ab. 60 sq. m.; mountainous, of volcanic origin.

2 Chief island of the Vavau group; 10 m. long; 44 sq. m.; pop. (1966c) 13,533; chief town is Neiafu; island noted for its caves.

Väx·jö \'vek-ˌshər\. Town, ⊗ of Kronoberg co., S Sweden, 60 m. WNW of Kalmar; pop. (1970e) 35,994; manufactures matches; cathedral, traditionally founded in 11th cent. by an English missionary, St. Siegfrid.

Vayenga. See SEVEROMORSK.

Vech·te \'fek-tə\ *or Du.* **Vecht** \'vekt\. River, West Germany and the Netherlands; ab. 125 m. long; flows NW through North Rhine-Westphalia, West Germany, and W through province of Overijssel, Netherlands, into IJsselmeer.

Vectis. See WIGHT, ISLE OF.

Ve·dea \'ved-ē-ˌä\. River, S Romania, E of the Olt; ab. 130 m. long; flows SE into the Danube near Giurgiu.

Veen·dam \vān-'däm, 'vān-ˌ\. Commune, Groningen prov., NE Netherlands, 14 m. SE of Groningen; pop. (1970e) 23,709.

Vee·nen·daal \'vā-nən-ˌdäl\. Commune, Utrecht prov., cen. Netherlands, just N of the Neder Rijn SE of Utrecht; pop. (1970e) 29,637.

Ve·ga \'vā-gə\. Town, ⊗ of Oldham co., NW Texas; pop. (1970c) 839.

Vega, La. See LA VEGA.

Vega Al·ta \ˌvā-gə-'äl-tə\. Town and municipality, N Puerto Rico; pop. (1970p) 8752 (town), 22,857 (munic.); town is 14 m. SW of San Juan.

Vega Ba·ja \-'bä-hə\. Town and municipality, N Puerto Rico; pop. (1970p) 17,014 (town), 35,237 (munic.); town is 18 m. WSW of San Juan.

Vega Re·al \-rā-'äl\. Valley, N Dominican Republic; formed by two streams flowing in opposite directions.

Veglia. See KRK.

Ve·go·ri·tis, Lake \-ˌveg-ə-'rēt-əs\ *or Gk.* **Lím·ni Ve·gor·rí·tis** \ˌlēm-nē-ˌveg-ə-'rēt-əs\. Lake, N Greece, near Yugoslavia border; ab. 25 sq. m.

Veg·re·ville \'veg-ər-ˌvil\. Town, E Alberta, Canada, on a tributary of the North Saskatchewan river 57 m. E of Edmonton; pop. (1971p) 3696.

Ve·ii \'vē-(y)ī, 'vā-(y)ē\. Ancient city of Etruria, ab. 12 m. N of Rome, Italy; an Etruscan stronghold, one of the twelve cities of the confederation; for 350 years almost continually at war with Rome; captured by Camillus 396 B.C. after a ten-year siege.

Vej·le \'vī-lə\. 1 County of SE Jutland, Denmark. See table at DENMARK.

2 Seaport, its ⊗, at the head of **Vejle Fjord** (inlet 15 m. long); pop. (1970e) 31,763; ships dairy products; shipbuilding yards, textile mills, ironworks, breweries; St. Nicholas Church, dating from 13th cent.

Ve·la·de·ro \ˌvel-ə-'de(ə)r-(ˌ)ō\ *or* **Ve·la·de·res** \-'der-əs\. Peak, NW La Rioja prov., NW Argentina, near border of Chile; 20,735 ft.

Vé·lan \vā-'läⁿ\. Mountain in the Pennine Alps, on the Swiss-Italian border; 12,353 ft.

Ve·la·nai Island \ˌvel-ə-ˌnī-\. Island, N Palk Bay, off N tip of Ceylon.

Ve·las, Cape \-'vel-əs\. Cape, NW coast of Costa Rica, extending into the Pacific Ocean.

Vel·bert \'fel-bərt\. Manufacturing city, North Rhine-Westphalia, West Germany, in the Ruhr valley 14 m. NE of Düsseldorf; pop. (1970e) 27,307; manufactures locks, iron goods.

Veld·ho·ven \'velt-ˌhō-vən\. Commune, North Brabant prov., Netherlands; pop. (1969e) 26,417.

Ve·le·bit \ve-'leb-it\. Mountain range, W Yugoslavia, extending from NW to SE along the Adriatic coast from ab. 44° to 45°N; greatest height 5768 ft.

Ve·leb·it·ski Ka·nal \ve-'leb-it-skē-kə-'näl\ *or formerly* **Mor·lac·ca** \mȯr-'läk-ə, -'lak-\. Channel along the coast of Croatia, N Yugoslavia, bet. Krk I. and the mainland.

Veles. See TITOV VELES.

Ve·le·ta, Pi·ca·cho de \pi-ˌkäch-ō-ˌdā-və-'lāt-ə\. Peak in the Sierra Nevada, Granada prov., S Spain, just WNW of Mulhacén; 11,125 ft.

Vé·lez–Má·la·ga \ˌvā-lez-'mal-ə-gə\. Commune, Málaga prov., S Spain, on Mediterranean 16 m. ENE of Málaga; pop. (1970p) 42,454; sugarcane, olives, grapes; ancient Moorish castle. Recaptured from Moors 1487 by Ferdinand the Catholic.

Velho. See PÔRTO VELHO.

Ve·lia \'vē-lē-ə\ *or* **Elea** \'ē-lē-ə\. Ancient town of Lucania, S Italy, its ruins near coast ab. halfway bet. Gulf of Salerno and Gulf of Policastro; remains of walls; founded c. 530 B.C. by Phocaeans; home of Parmenides and Zeno of the *Eleatic* school of philosophers, reputedly founded by Xenophanes.

Ve·li·ka·ya \və-'lē-kə-yə\. River, Pskov Oblast, Russian S.F.S.R., U.S.S.R.; 252 m. long; flows N into Lake Pskov.

Veliki Bečkerek. See ZRENJANIN.

Veliki Kvarner. See KVARNER 1.

Ve·li·ki Ustyug \və-ˌlē-kē-ü-'styük\. Town, NE Vologda Oblast, Russian S.F.S.R., U.S.S.R., on the left bank of the Northern Dvina river just below the junction of the Sukhona and the Yug; pop. (1967e) 35,000; manufactures leather and textiles; sawmills.

Ve·li·ki·ye Lu·ki \və-ˌlē-kē-(y)ə-'lü-kē\. Town, Pskov Oblast, Russian S.F.S.R., U.S.S.R., on right bank of upper Lovat river 200 m. W of Kalinin; pop. (1969e) 84,000; railroad junction; bricks, lumber, footwear, foodstuffs; railroad shops; first mentioned 1166; occupied by Germans Aug. 1941–Mar. 1943 and was scene of heavy fighting in 1943.

Ve·li·ko Tŭr·no·vo \ˌvel-i-ˌkō-'tər-nə-ˌvō\ *or* **Tŭrnovo** *or* **Tr·no·vo** \'tər-nə-ˌvō\ *or* **Tir·no·vo** \'tər-\. 1 Province of N Bulgaria. See table at BULGARIA.

2 City, its ✱, on the Yantra river 55 m. ESE of Pleven; pop. (1968e) 42,344; meat products, beer, furniture, textiles; cultural center. Situated on a deep gorge with two high promontories and a connecting ridge. Probably a Roman fortress; capital of second Bulgarian empire 1186–1394; under Turkish rule 1394–1877; independent kingdom of Bulgaria proclaimed here Oct. 5, 1908; destructive earthquake 1911.

Ve·lin·grad \'vel-ən-ˌgräd\. Town, Pazardzhik prov., SW Bulgaria; pop. (1968e) 20,892.

Ve·li·no \vā-'lē-(ˌ)nō\. River, cen. Italy; 54 m. long; flows out of the Apennines into Nera river; contains noted waterfall, **Cas·ca·ta del·le Mar·mo·re** \kä-ˌskät-ə-ˌdel-ē-'mär-mə-ˌrā\, in three separate cascades.

Vel'ký Žitný. See GREAT SCHÜTT.

Vel·la Gulf \ˌvel-ə-\. Open water area in Solomon Is., W Pacific Ocean, SE of Vella Lavella I. and NW of Kolombangara I.; partly closed on the W by Ganongga I.; scene of U.S. naval victory over Japanese Aug. 6, 1943, following battle in Kula Gulf.

Vella La·vel·la \-lə-'vel-ə\. Island in the New Georgia Is., cen. Solomon Is., W Pacific Ocean, NW of Kolombangara I. and separated from it by Vella Gulf; ab. 200 sq. m.; surrounded by coral reefs which prevent use of its many bays; copra. Highest point 3000 ft. Occupied Aug. 15, 1943 by U.S. troops.

Vel·le·tri \və-'le-trē, -'lā-\. Commune, Roma prov., W Latium, cen. Italy, 20 m. SE of Rome; pop. (1968e) 37,469; cathedral (probably from 4th cent.); 16th cent. town hall. In World War II taken by U.S. forces after severe fighting June 2, 1944.

Vel·lore \və-'lō(ə)r, -'lȯ(ə)r\. City, Tamil Nadu, S India, on Palar river 80 m. WSW of Madras; pop. (1970e) 121,465; ships grain; has temple to Siva, and a strong fortress noted for its role in Carnatic wars. Occupied by British in 1760; withstood two-year siege by Haidar Ali, 1780–82; after 1799 became residence of sons of Tipu Sahib who instigated Sepoy Mutiny here in 1806.

Vel·sen \'vel-sən\. Commune, North Holland prov., W Netherlands, at the mouth of the North Sea Canal; pop. (1970e) 67,580; serves as the outer port of Amsterdam; fishing port; produces iron and steel, chemical fertilizers, paper, cement.

Velsuna. See ORVIETO.

Vel·u·we \'vel-ˌyü-və\. Range of hills, Gelderland prov., E Netherlands, N of Arnhem; highest point 361 ft.

Velyaminovski. See TUAPSE.

Ven *or* **Hveen** *or* **Hven** \'vān\. Swedish island in Øresund, off SW coast of Sweden; home of Danish astronomer Tycho Brahe.

Ve·na·do Tuer·to \və-ˌnäd-ō-'twer-(ˌ)tō\. Town, Santa Fe prov., Argentina; pop. (1960c) 26,284.

Venaissin. See COMTAT VENAISSIN.

Ve·nan·go \vi-'naŋ-(ˌ)gō\. County in Pennsylvania. See table at PENNSYLVANIA.

Ve·na·ria Re·a·le \ˌven-ə-ˌrē-ə-rā-'äl-ē\. Commune, Torino prov., Piedmont, NW Italy, 5 m. NNW of Turin; pop. (1968e) 23,053.

Vence \'väⁿs\. Commune, Alpes-Maritimes dept., SE France, W of Nice; pop. (1962c) 9080; medieval walls; Romanesque cathedral dating from 12th cent.

Ven·dée \väⁿ(n)-'dā\. 1 River, Vendée dept., France; ab. 45 m. long; flows to the Sèvre Niortaise.

2 Department of W France. See table at FRANCE. Formed at the time of the Revolution out of the W part of the ancient region of Poitou (*q.v.*); became, with adjoining regions of Poitou, Anjou, and Brittany, the scene of the

Wars of the Vendée, a series of peasant insurrections against the Revolutionary government 1793–96.

Ven·dôme \vä^n-'dōm\. Manufacturing town, Loir-et-Cher dept., N cen. France; pop. (1962c) 14,176; ancient countship, in 1515 made duchy whose dukes included César de Bourbon, natural son of Henry IV, and Louis Joseph, marshal of France during time of Louis XIV; 11th cent. castle; abbey of the Trinity.

Vend·sys·sel–Thy \'ven-ˌsüs-əl-'tē\. Island, N of Lim Fjord, forming the N end of the peninsula of Jutland, Denmark; 1792 sq. m.; pop. (1965c) 286,401; chief town Hjørring. The E section is called **Vendsyssel,** the W section **Thy·land** \'tē-ˌlan\.

Venedig. See VENICE 3.

Vener. See VÄNERN.

Veneta, Laguna. See VENICE, LAGOON OF.

Venetae Alpes. See table at ALPS.

Ve·ne·tia \vi-'nē-sh(ē-)ə\. 1 Ancient Roman division of NE Italy, including the territory bet. the Po river and the Alps and including the Istrian Penin.; named for its ancient inhabitants, the Veneti; principal towns included Aquileia, Pola, Tergeste, Tarvisium, Patavium, Atria, Vicentia, Tridentum, Verona, Mantua, Brixia, Cremona; prosperous under Roman rule; overrun by N barbarians in early Christian era.

2 *or Ital.* **Ve·ne·zia** \və-'net-sē-ə\. Region, N Italy, E of Lombardy; approximately coextensive with anc. region (1 above); administratively divided into Friuli-Venezia Giulia, Trentino-Alto Adige, and Veneto (*qq.v.*); part of its territory ceded by Italy to Yugoslavia 1947.

3 Seaport, Italy. See VENICE 3.

Venetian Republic. See history at VENICE 3.

Ve·ne·to \'ven-ə-ˌtō, 'vā-nə-\ *also* **Ve·ne·zia Eu·ga·nea** \və-ˌnet-sē-ə-eu̇-'gän-ē-ə\. Autonomous region, N Italy; 7096 sq. m.; pop. (1968e) 4,054,017; ✱ Venice; wheat, sugar beet, hemp, corn; for administrative subdivisions, see table at ITALY.

Ve·ne·zia \və-'net-sē-ə\. 1 Region, Italy. See VENETIA 2.

2 Province of Veneto, Italy. See table at ITALY.

3 Seaport, Italy. See VENICE 3.

Venezia, Golfo di. See VENICE, GULF OF.

Venezia Euganea. See VENETO.

Venezia Giu·lia \-'jül-yə\. Narrow strip of territory, along the Isonzo, Friuli-Venezia Giulia, Italy; left to Italy after the formation of the Free Territory of Trieste and cession of the greater part of Istrian Penin. and the city of Zara (Zadar) to Yugoslavia by treaty of Feb. 1947.

Venezia Tridentina. See TRENTINO-ALTO ADIGE.

Ven·e·zu·e·la \ˌven-əz-(ə-)'wā-lə, -(ə-)'wē-\ *or formerly* **United States of Venezuela** *or Span.* **Es·ta·dos Uni·dos de Venezuela** \es-ˌtäd-əs-ü-'nēd-əs-dā-\. Republic, N South America, bounded on the N by the Caribbean Sea, on the E by Guyana, on the S by Brazil, and on the W by Colombia; 352,143 sq. m.; pop. (1970e) 10,398,907; ✱ Caracas. *Physical features:* In the W are the highest ranges, the Cordillera Mérida, a NE spur of the Andes E of Lake Maracaibo; highest point Pico Bolívar, 16,427 ft.; along Caribbean coast extends the Cordillera de Venezuela, ranging from 5000 to 8530 ft. Lower ranges are in the S, esp. along the Brazilian border (Serra Parima, Serra Pacaraima). In cen. part are the great plains (*llanos*) watered by the Orinoco and its many tributaries, a rich agricultural region. *Rivers:* The Orinoco system covers practically the entire country and has an extensive and thickly wooded delta; its main tributaries the Apure, Arauca, Meta, Guaviare, and Ventuari, some of which drain E Colombia; in the S the Casiquiare unites the Orinoco with the Amazon system through the Rio Negro. *Lakes:* In the W is the large Lake Maracaibo, noted for its wealth in petroleum products, and in N is Lake Valencia. *Coastline:* Coastline is long and irregular extending from the large Gulf of Venezuela and Paraguaná Penin. on the W to the Gulf of Paria and mouths of the Orinoco on the E. Chief Venezuelan island off the coast is Margarita. *Chief products:* Oil, iron ore, salt, diamonds; coffee, cacao; livestock raising; manufacturing: steel, chemicals, textiles, building materials; oil refining. *Chief cities:* Caracas, Maracaibo, Barquisimeto, Valencia, Maracay, San Cristóbal, Cabimas. Divided into the following administrative units (for pronunciation of their names, see their individual entries):

NAME	AREA (sq. m.)	POP. (1970e)	CAPITAL
Federal District	745	2,009,561	Caracas
States			
Anzoátegui	16,718	501,384	Barcelona
Apure	29,537	158,487	San Fernando
Aragua	2,708	429,344	Maracay
Barinas	13,591	193,914	Barinas
Bolívar	91,892	383,315	Ciudad Bolívar
Carabobo	1,795	512,173	Valencia
Cojedes	5,714	95,177	San Carlos
Falcón	9,575	408,051	Coro
Guárico	25,091	330,147	San Juan de los Morros
Lara	7,645	611,192	Barquisimeto
Mérida	4,363	335,428	Mérida
Miranda	3,069	702,603	Los Teques
Monagas	11,158	316,732	Maturín
Nueva Esparta[1]	444	112,611	La Asunción
Portuguesa	5,869	284,523	Guanare
Sucre	4,556	493,840	Cumaná
Táchira	4,286	525,840	San Cristóbal
Trujillo	2,857	382,441	Trujillo
Yaracuy	2,741	222,041	San Felipe
Zulia	24,363	1,342,994	Maracaibo
Territories			
Amazonas	67,857	12,831	Puerto Ayacucho
Delta Amacuro	15,521	34,278	Tacupita
Federal Dependencies	46	–	–

[1]Comprises island group in the Caribbean Sea; chief island Margarita.

History: Coast traced by Spanish navigators Ojeda and de la Cosa 1499; first settled by Las Casas at Cumaná 1520; granted to Augsburg banking firm of the Welsers 1528–46; Caracas founded 1567; included in viceroyalty of New Granada (see COLOMBIA) 1718; was made a captaincy-general 1731; Venezuelan independence from Spain, proclaimed 1811, not assured until battle of Carabobo 1821; part of Greater Colombia 1819–29; formally separated from Colombia 1830; lost territory to British Guiana (now Guyana; Venezuelan boundary dispute 1895–96), Brazil, and Colombia; neutral in World War I; in World War II severed relations with Axis powers Dec. 31, 1941; overthrew dictatorship of Pérez Jiménez 1958; adopted new constitution 1961; agreed (1970) to a 12-year moratorium on its claims to ab. ⅔ of Guyana.

Venezuela, Cordillera de. See CORDILLERA DE VENEZUELA.

Venezuela, Gulf of *also* **Gulf of Mar·a·cai·bo** \-ˌmar-ə-'kī-(ˌ)bō\. Inlet of Caribbean Sea, NW Venezuela, bet. La Guajira Penin., Colombia, and Paraguana Penin., Venezuela; extends S as Lake Maracaibo (*q.v.*).

Veng·e·tind·er \'veŋ-ə-ˌtin-ər\. See ROMSDAL.

Ven·gi \'veŋ-gē\. Hindu kingdom of the Andhras, (1st–3d cents. A.D.), E India, bet. lower Godavari and Krishna rivers; ✱ Amaravati (*q.v.*).

Ven·gur·la \ven-'gu̇r-lə, veŋ-\. Town, SW Maharashtra, W India, on Arabian Sea 220 m. S of Bombay; pop. (1961c) 12,100; seaport with varied trade.

Ven·ice \'ven-əs\. 1 City, Sarasota co., W cen. Florida, 18 m. S of Sarasota; pop. (1970c) 6648; resort.

2 City, Madison co., SW Illinois, on Mississippi river 5 m. N of East St. Louis; pop. (1970c) 4680.

3 *or Ital.* **Ve·ne·zia** \və-'net-sē-ə\ *or Ger.* **Ve·ne·dig** \vā-'nā-dik\ *or Lat.* **Ve·ne·tia** \vi-'nē-sh(ē-)ə\. Seaport, ✱ of Veneto, also ✱ of Venezia prov., NE Italy, on 118 islands in Lagoon of Venice 162 m. E of Milan; pop. (1968e) 367,832; glass, textiles; tourism; univ. (1969); site of several international festivals, incl. annual film festival and Biennale (music festival). Majority of islands separated only by narrow canals (Ital. *rio;* pl. *rii*) crossed by ab. 400 bridges; main part of city traversed by S-shaped Grand Canal crossed by famous Rialto bridge (marble arch lined with double row of shops with broad footway between; built 1588–91) connecting Rialto I. (site of the exchange and

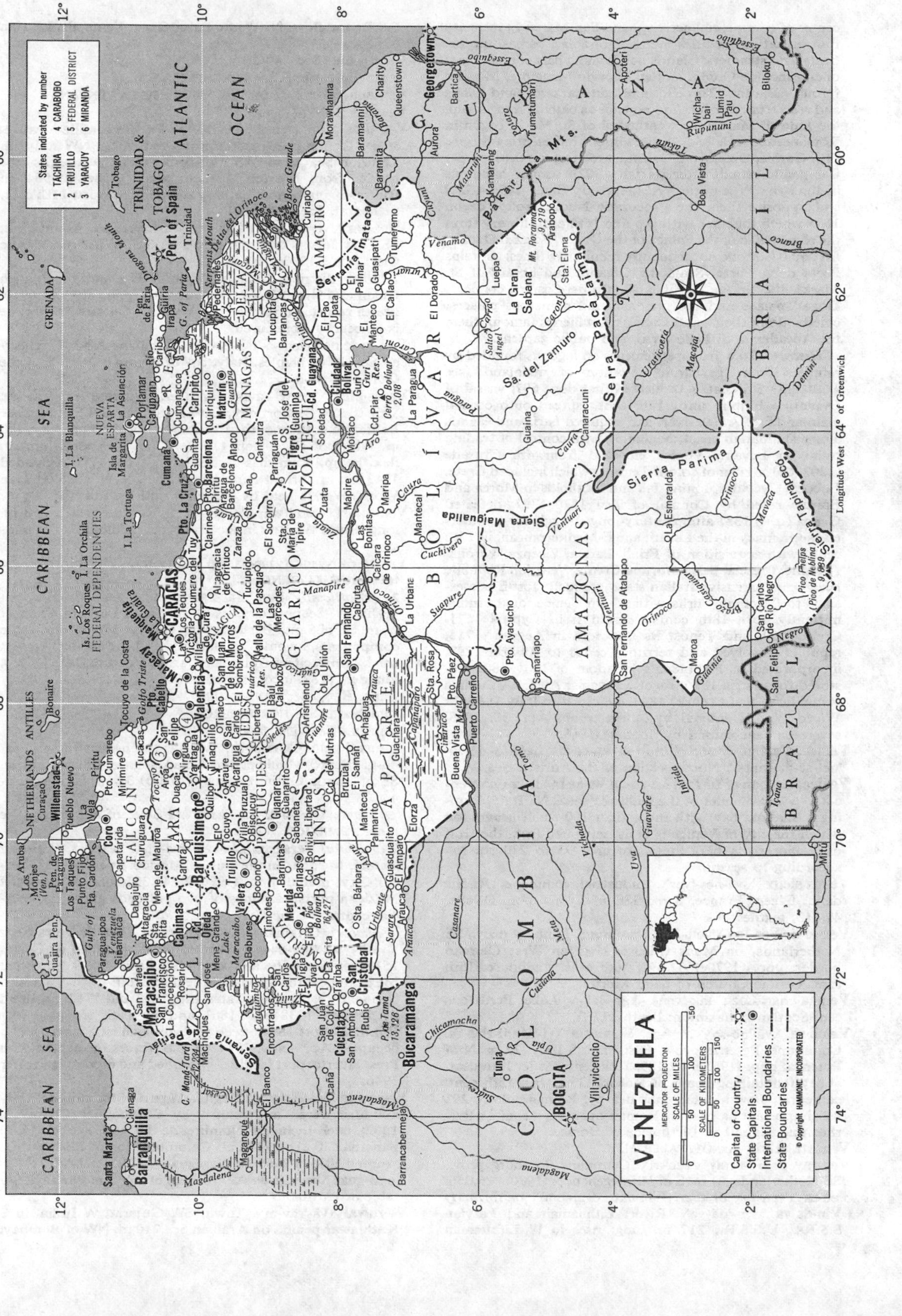
VENEZUELA
MERCATOR PROJECTION
SCALE OF MILES
SCALE OF KILOMETERS
Capital of Country
State Capitals
International Boundaries
State Boundaries
© Copyright HAMMOND INCORPORATED
States indicated by number
1 TÁCHIRA 4 CARABOBO
2 TRUJILLO 5 FEDERAL DISTRICT
3 YARACUY 6 MIRANDA
CARIBBEAN SEA
ATLANTIC OCEAN
NETHERLANDS ANTILLES
TRINIDAD & TOBAGO
GRENADA
GUYANA
BRAZIL
COLOMBIA
FEDERAL DEPENDENCIES
NUEVA ESPARTA
FALCÓN
LARA
ZULIA
MÉRIDA
TRUJILLO
PORTUGUESA
COJEDES
BARINAS
APURE
GUÁRICO
ARAGUA
ANZOÁTEGUI
MONAGAS
SUCRE
DELTA AMACURO
BOLÍVAR
AMAZONAS
CARACAS
Maracaibo
Barquisimeto
Valencia
Maracay
Cumaná
Barcelona
Cd. Bolívar
Cd. Guayana
Maturín
San Cristóbal
Mérida
Coro
San Fernando
Pto. Ayacucho
Tucupita
Georgetown
Port of Spain
Bogotá
Cúcuta
Bucaramanga
Barranquilla
Santa Marta
Willemstad
Lake Maracaibo
Gulf of Venezuela
G. of Paria
Orinoco
Sierra Parima
Sierra Pacaraima
Serranía Imataca
Sierra Maigualida
Mt. Roraima 9,219
Pico Bolívar 16,427
Pico Phelps (Pico de Neblina) 9,889
La Gran Sabana
Longitude West 64° of Greenwich

center of commercial activity) and San Marco I.; intracity transportation facilities include gondolas, barcas, motorboats, and steamers; islands not forming part of main mass of city include Giudecca, San Giorgio Maggiore, Murano (group), Burano, Torcello, and San Lazzaro; sand banks and reefs (Ital. *lido;* pl. *lidi*) popular as bathing resorts, esp. the Lido di Malamocco; cathedral of St. Mark (begun in Romanesque style 830, with additions representing Byzantine, Gothic, Greek, and Oriental architecture; the separate Campanile rebuilt after its fall 1902); secular buildings include the Procuratie Vecchie group (built 1496–1520) and opposite them the Procuratie Nuove group (begun 1584 which together with the fine 16th cent. library form the royal palace), the Palace of the Doges (Palazzo Ducale; first built 800 and subsequently rebuilt five times; contains Porta della Carta, Scala dei Giganti, and library of St. Mark), the Bridge of Sighs (Ponte dei Sospiri; connects Doges' palace and the prisons), and numerous palaces, chiefly along the Grand Canal; art galleries (among them the Accademia di Belle Arti), and public gardens.

History: Grew from settlements on lagoons founded by refugees from barbarian invasion of mainland (see AQUILEIA) 5th cent. A.D.; elected first doge 697; vassal of Byzantine Empire until 10th cent.; spread onto coastal mainland E of Adige river, and acquired Istria and islands along Dalmatian coast; beginning with control of trading route to Levant, Venice emerged from 4th Crusade (1202–04) as ruler of colonial empire which included Crete, Euboea, Cyclades, Ionian Is., and footholds in Morea and Epirus; ruled by Council of Ten 1310–1797; defeated Genoa (*q.v.*) 1381 after century-long struggle for commercial supremacy in the Levant and E Mediterranean; in 15th cent., with acquisition of Friuli, Padua, Vicenza, Verona, Polesine, Brescia, Bergamo, and Crema, Venetian Republic became an extensive Italian state; gradually lost E possessions to Ottoman Turks with whom Venice fought intermittently 15th–18th cents.; driven from Cyprus 1571, Crete 1669, and Tenos, its last hold in Aegean, 1715; republic dissolved and territory ceded to Austria 1797; incorporated in Napoleon's kingdom of Italy 1805; restored to Austria 1815; revolted against Austria (Manin's Republic of Saint Mark) 1848–49; ceded to Italy 1866. In World War II entered by Allied troops Apr. 30, 1945; severe damage caused by flooding 1966.

Venice, Gulf of *or Ital.* **Gol·fo di Ve·ne·zia** \ˌgōl-fō-ˌdē-və-ˈnet-sē-ə, -ˈnāt-\. North section of the Adriatic Sea.

Venice, Lagoon of *or Ital.* **La·gu·na Ve·ne·ta** \lə-ˌgü-nə-ˈven-ə-ˌtä, -ˈvā-nə-\. Inlet of the Gulf of Venice, NE Italy, forming a shallow bay with more than 100 small islands on which the city of Venice is built; separated from the Gulf of Venice by a bar, the Lido; area 95 to 210 sq. m., according to season.

Vé·nis·sieux \ˌvā-nēs-ˈyer\. Industrial commune, Rhône dept., E cen. France, 3 m. SSE of Lyons; pop. (1968c) 47,813; textiles.

Ven·lo *or* **Ven·loo** \ˈven-ˌlō\. Commune, Limburg prov., SE Netherlands, on Maas (Meuse) river on West German border; pop. (1970e) 62,694; 16th cent. stadhouse, 15th cent. Gothic Church of Saint Martin.

Ven·na·char, Loch \läk-ˈven-ə-ˌkär, läk-\. Lake, Perth co., cen. Scotland; maximum depth 111 ft.

Ve·no·sa \vā-ˈnō-sə\ *or anc.* **Ve·nu·sia** \vi-ˈn(y)ü-zhē-ə\. Commune, Potenza prov., Basilicata, S Italy, 22 m. N of Potenza; pop. (1968e) 12,129; 15th cent. castle; 11th cent. abbey (containing tomb of Robert Guiscard); 15th cent. cathedral; Jewish catacombs nearby. Roman colony 291 B.C.; important as base of Roman operations against Pyrrhus and Hannibal. Birthplace of Horace.

Venosti, Alpi. See ÖTZTALER ALPS.

Ven·ray *or* **Ven·raij** \ˈven-ˌrī\. Commune, Limburg prov., SE Netherlands, 21 m. S of Nijmegen; pop. (1970e) 26,056.

Ven·ta \ˈven-tə\ *or Ger.* **Win·dau** \ˈvin-ˌdau̇\ *or formerly* **Vin·da·va** \vin-ˈdä-və\. River, Lithuanian and Latvian S.S.Rs., U.S.S.R.; 217 m. long; rises in W Lithuanian S.S.R. and flows NNW into Baltic Sea at Ventspils, Latvian S.S.R.

Venta, La. See LA VENTA.

Venta Belgarum. See WINCHESTER 9.

Ventana, Sierra de la. See SIERRA DE LA VENTANA.

Ventia. See VALENCE.

Ven·ti·mi·glia \ˌvent-i-ˈmēl-yə\ *or Fr.* **Vin·ti·mille** \ˌvaⁿ-tē-ˈmēl\. Commune, Imperia prov., W Liguria, NW Italy, on Ligurian Sea 21 m. WSW of Imperia and just across the border from Menton, France; pop. (1968e) 25,564; in fruit-growing region; bathing and winter resort; 11th cent. cathedral. See GRIMALDI.

Vent·nor \ˈvent-nər\. 1 City and seaside resort, Atlantic co., SE New Jersey, on Atlantic Ocean 3 m. WSW of Atlantic City; pop. (1970c) 10,385.

2 Urban district, S Isle of Wight, S England, on English Channel 15 m. SSW of Portsmouth; pop. (1970e) 6910; health resort. Burial place of Algernon Charles Swinburne is at nearby Bonchurch.

Ven·to·te·ne \ˌvent-ə-ˈtān-ē, -ˈten-\. Italian island, Tyrrhenian Sea, W of Naples, Italy, SW of Ponza Is., and S of the Gulf of Gaeta.

Vents·pils \ˈven(t)-ˌspils\ *or Ger.* **Win·dau** *or* **Vin·dau** \ˈvin-ˌdau̇\. Seaport city, Latvian S.S.R., U.S.S.R., on the Baltic Sea at the mouth of Venta river N of Liepāja and 100 m. WNW of Riga; pop. (1967e) 37,000; exports lumber, flax, hemp, grain; has castle dating from 1290. Founded 1343; an important Russian port before World War I; in World War II held by Germans until end of war.

Ven·tua·ri \ven-ˈtwär-ē\. River, S Venezuela; ab. 350 m. long; flows W into Orinoco river near Colombian boundary.

Ven·tu·ra \ven-ˈt(y)u̇r-ə\. 1 County in SW California. See table at CALIFORNIA.

2 *or officially* **San Bue·na·ven·tu·ra** \san-ˌbwen-ə-ven-ˈt(y)u̇r-ə\. Seaport city, its ⊗, on Santa Barbara Channel 23 m. SE of Santa Barbara; pop. (1970c) 57,964; electronic components, women's clothing; oil-producing center; truck farms, citrus fruit, dairy farms; Ventura Coll. (1925); founded 1782, incorporated 1866.

Venue, Ben. See BEN VENUE.

Venusberg. See HÖRSELBERGE.

Venusia. See VENOSA.

Ve·nus·ti·a·no Ca·rran·za \və-ˌnüs-tē-ˌan-ō-kə-ˈran-zə, -ˌä-nō-kə-ˈrän-\. Municipality, Chiapas state, Mexico, 50 m. SE of Tuxtla Gutiérrez; pop. (1970p) 32,131; grain farming.

Ve·ra·cruz \ˌver-ə-ˈkrüz, -ˈkrüs\. 1 State of E Mexico. See table at MEXICO.

2 *or in full* **Veracruz Lla·ve** \-ˈyä-vā\. Seaport, Veracruz state, E Mexico, on the Gulf of Mexico, 264 m. from Mexico City; munic. pop. (1970p) 242,351; one of the chief Mexican ports; terminus of two railroads and a commercial center for the Gulf coast.

History: Original settlement (**Vi·lla Ri·ca de Ve·ra Cruz** \ˌvē(l)-yə-ˈrē-kə-də-ˌver-ə-ˈcrüz, -ˈcrüs\) founded by Cortés 1519; present city and port date from 1599; principal Mexican port for Spanish trade fleets 16th–18th cents. and frequently sacked by pirates, esp. 1653 and 1712; captured by French 1838 and 1861 and by U.S. troops under Winfield Scott 1847; scene of revolt against Madero 1912; occupied Apr.–Nov. 1914 by U.S. forces in dispute with Pres. Huerta; port facilities expanded and modernized after 1946.

Ve·ra·gua \və-ˈräg-wə\. Region, W part of Isthmus of Panama; discovered and named by Christopher Columbus 1502; later included Nombre de Dios, Portobelo, and Panama City. In 1537 Luis Columbus, son of Christopher, granted title of duke of Veragua by Charles I.

Ve·ra·guas \və-ˈräg-wəs\. Province of SW cen. Panama. See table at PANAMA.

Ve·ra·val \vā-ˈräv-əl\. Town, SW Gujarat, W India, in S Kathiawar penin., on Arabian Sea 210 m. NW of Bombay;

pop. (1961c) 46,900; seaport since ancient times; nearby is the old port of Somnath (*q.v.*).

Ver·ba·nia \vər-ˈbän-yə\. Commune, Novara prov., Piedmont, NW Italy, on W shore of Lake Maggiore 34 m. N of Novara; pop. (1968e) 34,184; summer resort; museum; 15th cent. church.

Verbanus Lacus. See MAGGIORE, LAKE.

Ver·cel·li \ver-ˈchel-ē\. 1 Province of Piedmont, NW Italy. See table at ITALY.

2 *or anc.* **Ver·cel·lae** \vər-ˈsel-ē\. Commune, its ✱, on Sesia river 39 m. WSW of Milan; pop. (1968e) 56,098; rice market; machinery, textiles, flour; cathedral (remodeled 1572), 13th cent. castle, 13th cent. basilica. Cimbri defeated by Marius 101 B.C. nearby; city-state in Middle Ages; under Visconti family of Milan 1335 ff. and dukes of Piedmont-Savoy 1427 ff.

Ver·chères \ver-ˈsha(ə)r\. 1 County, S Quebec, Canada. See table at QUEBEC.

2 Village, its ⊗, on S bank of St. Lawrence river 22 m. NE of Montreal; pop. (1971p) 1843.

Ver·de. 1 \ˈvərd-ē, ˈverd-ē\. River, cen. Arizona; ab. 190 m. long; formed by confluence of forks in N cen. Yavapai co., flows SE into Salt river ab. 20 m. E of Phoenix.

2 \ˈverd-ə\. River, S Mato Grosso state, SW Brazil; ab. 200 m. long; flows SE into Paraná river.

Verde, Cape. See VERT, CAPE.

Verde Island \ˌve(ə)r-(ˌ)dā-\. Island, center of Verde Island Passage S of Batangas, Luzon, Phil.; 7 sq. m.; 5 m. long; part of Batangas municipality; ab. 3 m. from mainland. Seized by U.S. forces Feb. 26, 1945.

Verde Island Passage. Channel bet. SW Luzon and N Mindoro, Phil., connecting waters S of Luzon with South China Sea; ab. 80 m. long and 9 to 22 m. wide; the W end of main interisland passage for ocean-going vessels from U.S. to Manila. See SAN BERNARDINO STRAIT.

Verde Islands, Cape. See CAPE VERDE ISLANDS.

Ver·den \ˈfe(ə)rd-ᵊn\ *or* **Verden an der Al·ler** \-än-dər-ˈäl-ər\. City, Lower Saxony, West Germany, on Aller river 57 m. SW of Hamburg; pop. (1968e) 16,669; furniture, tile, brandy. A bishopric founded c. 800; later became a duchy and was ceded 1648 to Sweden; passed to Hannover 1719.

Ver·di·gris \ˈvərd-ə-grəs\. River, SE Kansas and NE Oklahoma; 351 m. long; rises in SE Chase co., E cen. Kansas, flows S across Oklahoma border and into Arkansas river in N Muskogee co., E Oklahoma.

Ver·don \ver-ˈdōⁿ\. River, Alpes-de-Haute Provence dept., SE France; 110 m. long; flows into Durance river.

Ver·dun \vər-ˈdən\. 1 City, Montreal I., S Quebec, Canada, on St. Lawrence river SE of Montreal city; pop. (1971p) 74,520; residential suburb of Montreal; Jean-Jacques Olier Coll. (1951).

2 *or* **Verdun-sur-Meuse** \-syu̇r-ˈmyüz, -ˈmə(r)z\ *or anc.* **Ver·o·du·num** \ˌver-ə-ˈd(y)ün-əm\. City, Meuse dept., NE France, on Meuse river 29 m. NNE of Bar-le-Duc; pop. (1968c) 22,013; furniture; foundries; 11th–16th cent. Romanesque cathedral, 14th cent. castle, episcopal palace, citadel.

History: Treaty partitioning Charlemagne's empire among his three grandsons signed here 843 A.D.; with Metz and Toul (*Les Trois-Évêchés*, the three bishoprics) taken by Henry II of France 1552, and French possession confirmed by Treaty of Westphalia 1648; taken by Prussians 1792 and 1871. In World War I scene of one of the major battles on the Western Front, Feb.–Dec. 1916, in which French repelled a large-scale German offensive at great cost; total casualties ab. 750,000 and city practically destroyed. In World War II occupied by Germans June 1940–Aug. 3, 1944. Has numerous monuments and museums commemorating the battle; for further references, see DOUAUMONT, FLEURY, LE MORT HOMME, VAUX 2, WOËVRE.

Ve·ree·ni·ging \fə-ˈrēn-i-ˌkiŋ\. Town, S Transvaal, NE Rep. of South Africa, on Vaal river 35 m. S of Johannesburg; pop. (1967e) 94,500; industrial community in coal-mining district. Founded 1892; treaty ending Boer War signed here May 31, 1902.

Ver·en·drye National Monument \ˈver-ən-ˌdrī-\. Former national monument, South Dakota; abolished 1956; site now partly a state historical area, partly inundated by Garrison Reservoir.

Ver·ga, Cape \-ˈvər-gə\. Cape, extending into Atlantic Ocean on W coast of Guinea, W Africa, 10°12′N, 14°27′W.

Ver·ga·ra \ver-ˈgär-ə\. Commune, Guipúzcoa prov., N Spain; pop. (1970p) 15,148; Convention of Vergara Aug. 31, 1839 concluded Carlist war.

Ver·gennes \vər-ˈjenz\. City, Addison co., W Vermont, on Otter Creek near Lake Champlain; pop. (1970c) 2242; in War of 1812 U.S. fleet on Lake Champlain built here.

Verkhne–Saldinski Zavod. See VERKHNYAYA SALDA.

Verkhneudinsk. See ULAN-UDE.

Verkh·ni Ufa·lei \ˌv(y)erk-n(y)ē-ü-fəl-ˈ(y)ā\ *or formerly* **Ver·khne·ufa·lei·ski Za·vod** \ˌv(y)erk-n(y)ə-ˌü-fəl-ˈ(y)ās-kē-zə-ˈvȯd\. Town, Chelyabinsk Oblast, Russian S.F.S.R., U.S.S.R., ab. 80 m. NW of Chelyabinsk; pop. (1967e) 40,000.

Verkhnyaya Angara. See ANGARA 2.

Ver·khnya·ya Sal·da \ˌv(y)erk-n(y)ə-yə-ˈsäl-də\ *or formerly* **Ver·khne–Sal·din·ski Za·vod** \ˌv(y)erk-n(y)ə-säl-ˈdin(t)-skē-zə-ˈvȯd\. Town, Sverdlovsk Oblast, Russian S.F.S.R., U.S.S.R., ab. 80 m. N of Sverdlovsk; pop. (1967e) 43,000.

Ver·kho·yansk \ˌv(y)er-kə-ˈyan(t)sk\. Town, N cen. Yakutsk A.S.S.R., Russian S.F.S.R., U.S.S.R., on right bank of Yana river 385 m. NNE of Yakutsk, 67°35′N, 133°27′E; mining and fur-trading town; formerly a place of political exile. Has January mean of −59°, absolute mininum of −89.9°, and a range bet. Jan. and July means of 119°F. See OIMYAKON, FORT CONGER.

Ver·kho·yan·ski Khre·bet \ˌv(y)er-kə-ˈyan(t)-skē-kri-ˈbyet\ *or* **Verkhoyanski Mountains.** Mountain range, N cen. Yakutsk A.S.S.R., Russian S.F.S.R., U.S.S.R., extends for ab. 950 m. in a semicircle along right banks of the Lena and lower Aldan rivers; highest peak 7838 ft. Source of the headstreams of the Indigirka, Yana, and Omoloi rivers and of many short (eastern) tributaries of the Lena and Aldan.

Ver·man·dois \ˌver-mäⁿ-ˈdwä\. Ancient district, N France, in E Picardy; now included in the departments of Aisne, Somme, and Oise.

Vermejo. See BERMEJO.

Ver·mil·ion \vər-ˈmil-yən\. 1 River, N cen. Illinois; 50 m. long; formed by the junction of two forks in Livingston co., flows NW into Illinois river in La Salle co.

2 River, N Minnesota. See VERMILION LAKE.

3 River, SE South Dakota; ab. 100 m. long; rises in Lake co., flows S into Missouri river on S boundary of Clay co.

4 Name of a parish in Louisiana and of a county in Illinois. See tables at ILLINOIS and LOUISIANA.

5 City, Erie and Lorain cos., N Ohio, on Lake Erie E of Sandusky; pop. (1970c) 9872; summer resort; dairy, wheat farms.

6 Town, Alberta, Canada, 100 m. E of Edmonton; pop. (1971p) 2900; agriculture.

Vermilion Bay. Inlet of Gulf of Mexico, SW Iberia parish and SE Vermilion parish, S Louisiana.

Vermilion Lake. Lake, N Saint Louis co., NE Minnesota; ab. 35 m. long; 59 sq. m.; outlet, **Vermilion River** (ab. 50 m. long) flowing N into Crane Lake, at SE end of Rainy Lake.

Vermilion Peak. Mountain, San Juan and San Miguel cos., SW Colorado; 13,870 ft.

Vermilion Sea. See CALIFORNIA, GULF OF.

Ver·mil·lion \vər-ˈmil-yən\. 1 County in Indiana. See table at INDIANA.

2 City, ⊗ of Clay co., SE South Dakota, on Missouri river where the Vermilion unites with it, 27 m. ESE of Yankton; pop. (1970c) 9128; dairy products; diversified agriculture; Univ. of South Dakota (1862). Founded 1859 W of Fort Vermillion, an American Fur Company trading post (established 1835).

Ver·mont \vər-'mänt\. A northeastern state of U.S.A., bounded on N by Canadian province of Quebec, on E by New Hampshire (boundary line is W bank of Connecticut river), on S by Massachusetts, and on W by New York (boundary line goes through Lake Champlain); 43d state in area, 9609 sq. m. (land area 9274 sq. m.); 48th state in population, (1970c) 444,732; ❋ Montpelier; 14th state admitted to Union (1791).

Nickname: Green Mountain State. *State flower:* Red clover. *Motto:* Freedom and Unity. *Rivers:* Flowing into Lake Champlain on W boundary are the Lamoille and Winooski rivers, Otter Creek, and the Poultney river, which forms for a short distance the state boundary with New York; chief Vermont tributary of the Connecticut river is the White river in cen. part. *Highest point:* Mount Mansfield, 4393 ft., in Lamoille co. in N Green Mts. *Chief products:* Dairy products; marble, talc, asbestos; manufacturing: food processing, metalworking; textiles, furniture. *Chief cities:* Burlington, Rutland, Barre. See *Table of States* at UNITED STATES. Divided into the following 14 counties (for pronunciation of their names, see their individual entries):

NAME	LOCATION	AREA[1] (sq. m.)	POP. (1970c)	CO. SEAT
Addison	W[2]	784	24,266	Middlebury
Bennington	SW corner	672	29,282	Bennington and Manchester
Caledonia	NE	612	22,789	St. Johnsbury
Chittenden	NW[2]	533	99,131	Burlington
Essex	NE corner	663	5,416	Guildhall
Franklin	NW; borders Quebec[2]	660	31,282	St. Albans
Grand Isle	NW corner[3]	83	3,574	North Hero
Lamoille	N	474	13,309	Hyde Park
Orange	E	690	17,676	Chelsea
Orleans	N; borders Quebec	715	20,153	Newport
Rutland	W[4]	927	52,637	Rutland
Washington	N cen.	707	47,659	Montpelier
Windham	SE corner	787	33,074	Newfane
Windsor	E	965	44,082	Woodstock

[1] Area = land area.
[2] On W borders Lake Champlain.
[3] Major portion of county composed of islands in Lake Champlain (Grand Isle, North Hero, and Isle La Motte)
On W borders lower end of Lake Champlain and New York state.

History: Explored 1609 by Samuel de Champlain, who discovered the lake now bearing his name; temporary settlement by French at Fort Ste. Anne on Isle La Motte 1666; Massachusetts established Fort Dummer on site of present Brattleboro 1724; Bennington settled 1761; Green Mountain boys organized 1764 and under Ethan Allen captured Ticonderoga from the British May 10, 1775, and under Seth Warner captured Crown Point May 12, 1775; claims to the region relinquished by Massachusetts 1781, by New Hampshire 1782, and New York 1790; admitted to the Union Mar. 4, 1791.

Ver·nal \'vərn-^{ə}l\. City, ⊗ of Uintah co., E Utah, ab. 25 m. W of Colorado border; pop. (1970c) 3908; leather goods, dairy products, coal mines; livestock.

Vernal Falls. Waterfall, Yosemite National Park, E cen. California; 317 ft.

Ver·neuil \ver-'nə^{y}\. Town, S Eure dept., N France, ab. 25 m. SW of Évreux; pop. (1962c) 6031; 11th–17th cent. church; 12th cent. keep built by Henry I of England; scene of battle 1424 in which John of Lancaster, Duke of Bedford, defeated the French and Scots.

Vernoleninsk. See NIKOLAYEV.

Ver·non \'vər-nən\. 1 Name of a parish in Louisiana and of counties in two states of the U.S. See tables at LOUISIANA, MISSOURI, WISCONSIN.

2 Town, ⊗ of Lamar co., NW Alabama; pop. (1970c) 2190; clothing; cotton, potatoes.

3 Town, W Tolland co., N Connecticut, NE of Manchester; pop. (1970c) 27,237; electronic components, chemicals, silk; dairy, truck farms; incorporated 1808; includes city of Rockville (*q.v.*).

4 Town, ⊗ of Jennings co., SE Indiana; pop. (1970c) 440.

5 City, ⊗ of Wilbarger co., N Texas, 45 m. WNW of Wichita Falls; pop. (1970c) 11,454; mattresses, boilers, flour; oil wells, cotton gins; truck farms.

6 City, S British Columbia, Canada, 5 m. E of N end of Okanagan Lake; pop. (1971p) 12,921; lumber; cans and ships fruit; fruit, dairy, stock farms.

Vernon \ver-'nō^{n}\. Commune, Eure dept., N France, on Seine river 17 m. ENE of Évreux; pop. (1968c) 18,872; tourist resort; mineral springs; manufactures military equipment. Taken by king of France 1198; held by English 1419–49.

Vernon Valley \ˌvər-nən-\. Urban community (unincorporated), Suffolk co., SE New York, on Long I. ENE of Huntington; pop. (1970c) 7925.

Vernyi. See ALMA-ATA.

Ve·ro Beach \ˌvi(ə)r-(ˌ)ō-\. City, ⊗ of Indian River co., E Florida, on Indian river 70 m. NNW of West Palm Beach; pop. (1970c) 11,908; fishing resort; citrus fruit. In World War II site of naval air base.

Veröcze. See VIROVITICA.

Verodunum. See VERDUN 2.

Ve·roia *or* **Ver·roia** *or Gk.* **Vé·roia** \'ve(ə)r-yä\; *anc.* **Be·roea** *or* **Be·rea** \bə-'rē-ə\; *Turk.* **Ka·ra·fe·ri·eh** \ˌkär-ə-ˌfer-ē-'(y)ä\. Town, ❋ of Hematheia dept., W cen. Macedonia, Greece, 40 m. WSW of Salonika. According to *Acts* xvii. 10, Paul and Silas preached here.

Ve·ro·li \'ver-ə-lē\. Commune, Frosinone prov., Latium, cen. Italy, 4 m. NE of Frosinone; pop. (1968e) 17,464; 11th cent. church; cathedral.

Ve·ro·na \və-'rō-nə\. 1 Borough, Essex co., NE New Jersey, 7 m. SSW of Paterson; pop. (1970c) 15,067.

2 Borough, Allegheny co., SW Pennsylvania, on Allegheny river 10 m. ENE of Pittsburgh; pop. (1970c) 3757; glass, explosives.

3 Province of Veneto, NE Italy. See table at ITALY.

4 Commune, ❋ of Verona prov., NE Italy, on Adige river 92 m. E of Milan; pop. (1968e) 254,862; railroad junction; textiles, chemicals, leather goods, kitchen equipment, paper, furniture, wine; city walls flanked by bastions and towers; city gates; notable buildings include the ancient Roman amphitheater (1st cent. A.D.), ab. 50 churches, including the 15th cent. Gothic cathedral with 12th cent. Romanesque façade; 15th cent. Loggia del Consiglio, 5th cent. St. Zeno Maggiore (rebuilt 12th cent.), 12th cent. town hall, 14th cent. Gothic tombs of the Scaligeri (or della Scala) family, and the 14th cent. Castelvecchio (now a museum).

History: Came under Roman rule 89 B.C.; after fall of Roman Empire, captured by Goths; here Odoacer defeated by Theodoric 489; captured 774 A.D. by Charlemagne; became independent republic 1107; under della Scala family 1260–1387, the Visconti family of Milan 1387–1405, Venice 1405–1797; passed to Austria under whom it gained great strategic importance as a member of the Mantua-Verona-Peschiera-Legnago Quadrilateral; Congress of Verona held here 1822; became part of kingdom of Italy 1866.

Ve·ró·ni·ca \və-'rän-i-kə\. Peak in Andes, Peru, 30 m. NW of Cuzco; 19,342 ft.

Ver·sailles \vər-'sālz\. 1 Subdivision of town of Sprague, Connecticut. See SPRAGUE 2.

2 Town, ⊗ of Ripley co., SE Indiana; pop. (1970c) 1020.

3 City, ⊗ of Woodford co., E cen. Kentucky, 13 m. W of Lexington; pop. (1970c) 5679; feed, flour; dairy, poultry farms.

4 City, ⊗ of Morgan co., cen. Missouri; pop. (1970c) 2244.

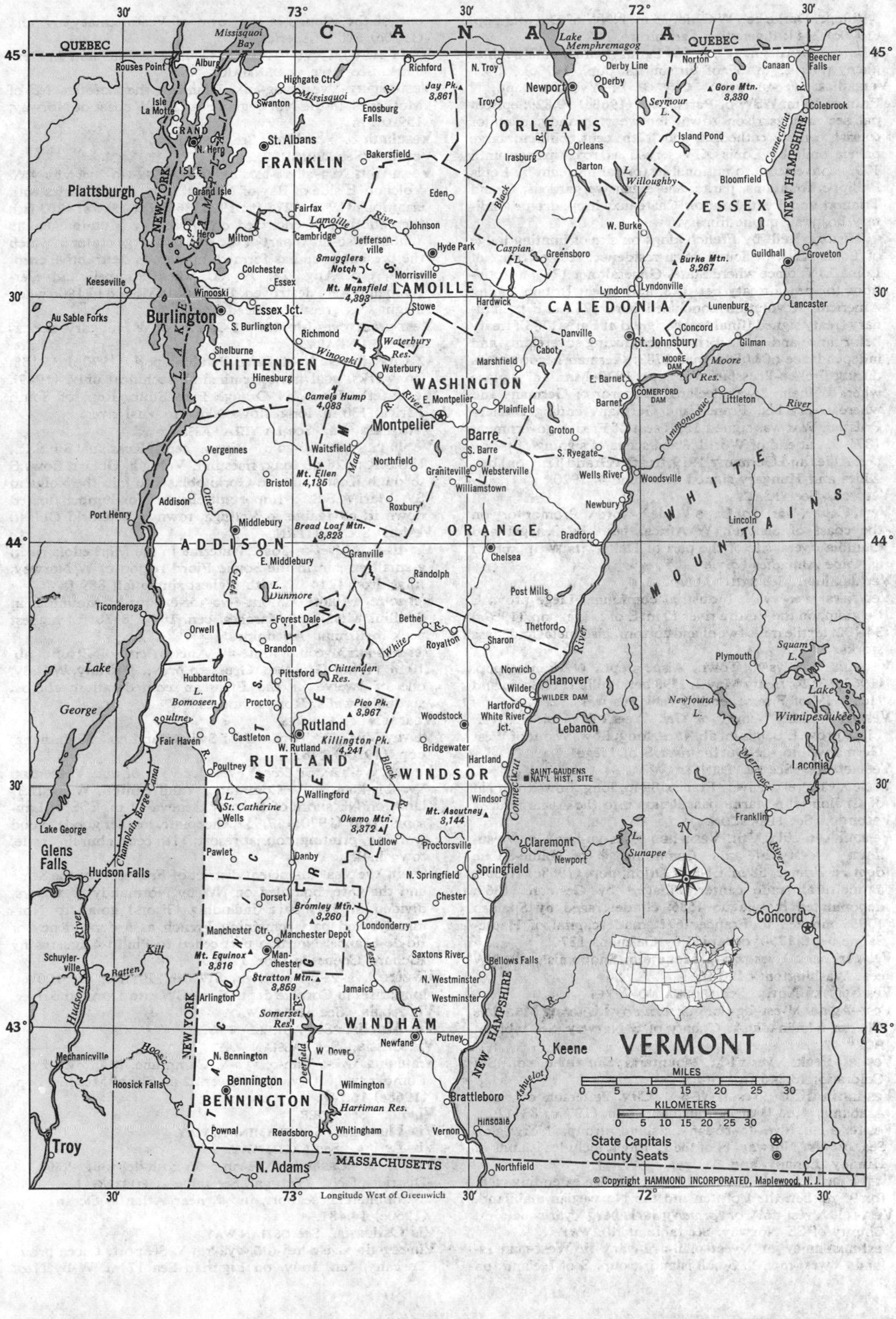
VERMONT
CANADA
QUEBEC
MASSACHUSETTS
NEW YORK
NEW HAMPSHIRE
FRANKLIN
ORLEANS
ESSEX
GRAND ISLE
LAMOILLE
CALEDONIA
CHITTENDEN
WASHINGTON
ORANGE
ADDISON
RUTLAND
WINDSOR
WINDHAM
BENNINGTON
GREEN MTS.
WHITE MOUNTAINS
Montpelier
Burlington
St. Albans
Newport
Hyde Park
St. Johnsbury
Guildhall
Chelsea
Middlebury
Rutland
Woodstock
Newfane
Manchester
Bennington
N. Hero
Jay Pk. 3,861
Gore Mtn. 3,330
Burke Mtn. 3,267
Mt. Mansfield 4,393
Camels Hump 4,083
Mt. Ellen 4,135
Bread Loaf Mtn. 3,823
Pico Pk. 3,967
Killington Pk. 4,241
Okemo Mtn. 3,372
Mt. Ascutney 3,144
Bromley Mtn. 3,260
Mt. Equinox 3,816
Stratton Mtn. 3,859
Smugglers Notch
Lake Memphremagog
Lake Champlain
Lake George
Missisquoi Bay
L. Willoughby
Seymour L.
Caspian L.
Waterbury Res.
Moore Res.
L. Dunmore
Chittenden Res.
L. Bomoseen
L. St. Catherine
Somerset Res.
Harriman Res.
Squam L.
Newfound L.
Lake Winnipesaukee
L. Sunapee
Connecticut River
Winooski River
Lamoille River
Missisquoi R.
White R.
Black R.
West R.
Otter Creek
Mad R.
Deerfield R.
Hoosic R.
Hudson River
Batten Kill
Poultney R.
Ammonoosuc R.
Merrimack River
Ashuelot R.
Champlain Barge Canal
COMERFORD DAM
MOORE DAM
WILDER DAM
SAINT-GAUDENS NAT'L HIST. SITE
Plattsburgh
Keeseville
Au Sable Forks
Port Henry
Ticonderoga
Glens Falls
Hudson Falls
Lake George
Schuylerville
Mechanicville
Hoosick Falls
Troy
N. Adams
Rouses Point
Alburg
Isle La Motte
Highgate Ctr.
Swanton
Richford
Enosburg Falls
N. Troy
Troy
Derby Line
Derby
Norton
Canaan
Beecher Falls
Colebrook
Island Pond
Orleans
Irasburg
Barton
Bakersfield
Bloomfield
Grand Isle
Eden
Fairfax
Johnson
S. Hero
Milton
Cambridge
Jeffersonville
W. Burke
Greensboro
Groveton
Colchester
Essex
Morrisville
Winooski
Essex Jct.
Lyndon
Lyndonville
Lunenburg
Lancaster
Stowe
Hardwick
S. Burlington
Richmond
Danville
Concord
Shelburne
Cabot
Gilman
Marshfield
Hinesburg
Waterbury
E. Barnet
Barnet
Littleton
E. Montpelier
Plainfield
Barre
Groton
Vergennes
Waitsfield
S. Barre
S. Ryegate
Northfield
Graniteville
Websterville
Wells River
Woodsville
Bristol
Williamstown
Addison
Roxbury
Newbury
Lincoln
Bradford
Granville
E. Middlebury
Randolph
Post Mills
Orwell
Forest Dale
Bethel
Thetford
Brandon
Royalton
Sharon
Plymouth
Hubbardton
Pittsford
Norwich
Hanover
Wilder
Proctor
Hartford
White River Jct.
Lebanon
Fair Haven
Castleton
W. Rutland
Bridgewater
Poultney
Hartland
Laconia
Wallingford
Windsor
Wells
Franklin
Claremont
Newport
Pawlet
Danby
Ludlow
Proctorsville
N. Springfield
Springfield
Dorset
Chester
Concord
Manchester Ctr.
Manchester Depot
Londonderry
Saxtons River
Bellows Falls
N. Westminster
Arlington
Jamaica
Westminster
Putney
Keene
N. Bennington
W. Dover
Wilmington
Brattleboro
Hinsdale
Pownal
Readsboro
Whitingham
Vernon
Northfield
MILES
0 5 10 15 20 25 30
KILOMETERS
0 5 10 15 20 25 30
State Capitals
County Seats
45°
44°
43°
30'
73°
72°
Longitude West of Greenwich
© Copyright HAMMOND INCORPORATED, Maplewood, N.J.

5 Village, Darke co., W Ohio, 35 m. NNW of Dayton; pop. (1970c) 2441; diversified agriculture.

6 Borough, Allegheny co., SW Pennsylvania, on Youghiogheny river 13 m. SE of Pittsburgh; pop. (1970c) 2754.

Versailles \vər-ˈsī, ver-\. City, ✱ of Yvelines dept., N France, 10 m. WSW of Paris; pop. (1968c) 90,829; episcopal see and garrison town; footwear, brandy; a major tourist center; cathedral and 17th cent. church; large palace built by Louis XIV served as royal palace until 1793, converted into national historical museum by Louis Philippe; fountains, parks, and extensive gardens; Grand Trianon and Petit Trianon Châteaux; hippodrome, military hospital, public library.

History: Built by French kings on site of hunting lodge of Louis XIII; principal royal residence; seat of court of Louis XIV; place where States-General met 1783; negotiations for peace treaty bet. U.S. and Great Britain ending American Revolution concluded here 1782 and preliminary treaty signed (final treaty signed at Paris 1783); treaty bet. France and Great Britain recognizing sovereignty and independence of U.S. signed 1783; German headquarters during Franco-Prussian War Sept. 1870–Mar. 1871; place where Wilhelm I was declared Emperor of Germany and where treaty bet. France and Germany ending Franco-Prussian War was signed 1871; seat of French government 1871–79; at end of World War I scene of signing of treaty bet. Allies and Germany 1919; treaty (Grand Trianon) bet. Allies and Hungary signed here June 4, 1920.

Versecz. See VRŠAC.

Vert, Cape \-ˈvərt\ *or* **Cape Verde** \-ˈvərd\. Promontory on the coast of Senegal, W Africa, bet. the Senegal and Gambia rivers; site of the port of Dakar; its W tip known as Cape Almadies (*q.v.*).

Verulamium. See SAINT ALBANS 3.

Ver·viers \ver-ˈvyā\. Industrial commune, Liège prov., E Belgium, on the Vesdre river 13 m. E of Liège; pop. (1969e) 34,402; textile mills (wool and cotton), also metal and glass works.

Ver·vins \ver-ˈvaⁿ\. Town, Aisne dept., N France; pop. (1962c) 3124; treaty May 2, 1598 bet. Philip II of Spain and Henry IV of France, ending religious wars.

Ves·dre \ˈvādrᵊ, ˈvedrᵊ\ *or Ger.* **We·ser** \ˈvā-zər\. River, Liège prov., E Belgium; ab. 45 m. long; flows W out of West Germany into the Ourthe river S of Liège.

Vésinet, Le. See LE VÉSINET.

Vesle \ˈväl, ˈvel\. River, France; 89 m. long; flows from NE of Châlons-sur-Marne past Reims into the Aisne river.

Vesontio. See BESANÇON.

Ve·soul \və-ˈzül\; *Lat.* **Ves·u·lum** \ˈves-yu̇-ləm\ *or* **Ve·su·li·um** \ve-ˈs(y)ü-lē-əm\. Commune, ✱ of Haute-Saône dept., E France, 58 m. ENE of Dijon; pop. (1968c) 16,352; agricultural trade center. Pillaged by Germans 1369; depopulated by plague 1586; citadel razed by Spanish 1595; annexed to France 1678; made capital of Haute-Saône dept. 1790; occupied by Germans 1870.

Ves·per Peak \ˌves-pər-\. Mountain, Snohomish co., NW cen. Washington; 6190 ft.

Ves Spišská Nová. See SPIŠSKÁ NOVÁ VES.

Vest–Ag·der \ˈvest-ˈäg-dər\ *or formerly* **Lis·ter og Man·dals** \ˈlis-tər-ȯ-ˈmän-ˌdäls\. County of S Norway. See table at NORWAY.

Ves·tal Peak \ˌves-tᵊl-\. Mountain, San Juan co., SW Colorado; 13,846 ft.

Ves·ta·via Hills \ves-ˌtā-vē-ə-\. City, Jefferson co., cen. Alabama, 4 m. S of Birmingham; pop. (1970c) 8311.

Ves·ter·å·len \ˈves-tə-ˌrō-lən\. Island group, Norwegian Sea, off NW Norway, N of the Lofoten; includes islands of Hinnøy, Langøy, and Andøya.

Vest Fjord \ˈvest-\. Inlet of Norwegian Sea extending NNE for 95 m. bet. the Lofoten and the Norwegian mainland.

Vest·fold \ˈvest-ˌfōl\ *or formerly* **Jarls·berg** \ˈyärls-ˌba(ə)r\. County of SE Norway. See table at NORWAY.

Vest·man·na·ey·jar \ˈvest-ˌmän-ə-ˈā-ˌyär\ *or* **West·man Islands** \ˌwest-mən-\. Small island group, S of Iceland; on one of the islands is the town of Vestmannaeyjar, pop. (1970c) 5183; fisheries.

Vests·jæl·land \ˈvests-ˌē-län\. County, W Sjælland I., Denmark. See table at DENMARK.

Vest·våg·øy \ˈvest-ˌvȯg-ˌȯi\. Island in the Lofoten, NE of Moskenes, in the Norwegian Sea off NW coast of Norway; 159 sq. m.

Vesulium *or* **Vesulum.** See VESOUL.

Vesuna. See PÉRIGUEUX.

Ve·su·vi·us \və-ˈsü-vē-əs\ *or Ital.* **Ve·su·vio** \vā-ˈzüv-yō\. Volcano, E side of Bay of Naples, Italy; height varies with eruptions (1900: 4275 ft.; 1906: 3668 ft.; 1960's: 4203 ft.); the cone is half encircled on N side by **Mon·te Som·ma** \ˌmȯnt-ē-ˈsō-mə\, part of the wall of a large crater in which the present cone has formed; numerous destructive eruptions, esp. Aug. 24, 79 A.D. when Pompeii and Herculaneum were destroyed, Dec. 16, 1631, and in 1906 when height was greatly reduced.

Vesz·prém \ˈves-(ˌ)prām\. 1 County of W Hungary. See table at HUNGARY.

2 City, its ⊗, N of Lake Balaton; pop. (1970p) 35,158; ironworks, coal mines; cathedral; technical univ. (1949).

Vet \ˈfet\. River, N Orange Free State, Rep. of South Africa; 130 m. long; flows NW into Vaal river.

Veta Pass, La. See LA VETA PASS.

Vet·lu·ga \vet-ˈlü-gə\. River, cen. Russian S.F.S.R., U.S.S.R.; 528 m. long; rises in E Vologda Oblast, flows S through Kostroma and Gorki oblasts to join the Volga in SW Mari A.S.S.R. Important channel for lumber floated down it; navigable to Vetluga, town in N Gorki Oblast.

Vetter. See VÄTTERN.

Vet·tis·foss \ˈvet-əs-ˌfȯs\. Waterfall in the Mörkedola river, a small stream in the Sogne Fjord region of W Norway; total drop 1214 ft., with highest single fall 889 ft.

Vet·to·re, Mon·te \ˌmȯnt-ē-və-ˈtōr-ē, -ˈtȯr-\. Mountain in Sibillini Mts., SW Marches, cen. Italy; 8130 ft.; highest peak in Roman Apennines.

Vet·u·lo·nia \ˌvech-ə-ˈlō-nē-ə\. Ancient city of Etruria, ab. 10 m. NW of Grosseto, Grosseto prov., Tuscany, W Italy; one of twelve in the Etruscan confederation; tombs, acropolis walls, Roman houses.

Veurne. See FURNES.

Ve·vay \ˈvē-vē\. Town, ⊗ of Switzerland co., SE Indiana; pop. (1970c) 1463.

Ve·vey \və-ˈvā\ *or Ger.* **Vi·vis** \ˈvē-vəs\ *or anc.* **Vi·bis·cum** \və-ˈbis-kəm, vī-\. Commune, Vaud canton, W Switzerland, on NE shore of Lake of Geneva 11 m. ESE of Lausanne; pop. (1970c) 17,957; chocolate, leather goods; wood working, printing; tourist resort; 11th cent. church, castle, town hall.

Vex·in \vek-ˈsaⁿ\. Ancient district of France, N of the Seine and the Oise, bounded on NW by Normandy; ✱ Gisors; divided in 911, part (including Gisors) going to Normandy, and part remaining French as a dependency of Île-de-France; Norman part ceded to Philip Augustus by Richard Coeur de Lion 1196.

Vé·zère \vā-ˈze(ə)r\. River, SW cen. France; ab. 120 m. long; rises in Corrèze dept., flows SW into Dordogne river.

Via Appia. See APPIAN WAY.

Via Aurelia. See AURELIAN WAY.

Via Cassia. See CASSIAN WAY.

Via·da·na \ˌvē-ə-ˈdän-ə, vyə-\. Commune, Mantova prov., Lombardy, N Italy, on Po river 22 m. SW of Mantua; pop. (1968e) 16,248.

Viadua. See ODER.

Via Flaminia. See FLAMINIAN WAY.

Via Latina. See LATIN WAY.

Via·na do Cas·te·lo \vē-ˌan-ə-du̇-kəsh-ˈtel-(ˌ)ü, -ˈtāl-\. 1 District of NW Portugal. See table at PORTUGAL.

2 Commercial seaport, its ✱, near Atlantic Ocean; pop. (1960c) 14,481.

Via Ostiensis. See OSTIAN WAY.

Via·reg·gio \ˌvē-ə-ˈrej-(ˌ)ō, vyä-ˈrej-\. Seaport, Lucca prov., Tuscany, cen. Italy, on Ligurian Sea 12 m. W by N of

Lucca; pop. (1968e) 54,549; seaside resort; monument to Shelley, whose body was cast ashore here; burial place of Puccini.

Via Salaria. See SALARIAN WAY.

Viatka. See VYATKA.

Via Valeria. See VALERIAN WAY.

Vibiscum. See VEVEY.

Vibo, Gulf of. See SANT'EUFEMIA, GULF OF.

Vi·borg \'vē-(,)bòrg, -bòr\. 1 County of N cen. Jutland, Denmark. See table at DENMARK.

2 City, its ⊗; pop. (1970e) 25,468; machinery, textiles; beer; Gothic cathedral founded c. 1130.

3 City, U.S.S.R. See VYBORG.

Vi·bo Va·len·tia \,vē-(,)bō-və-'lent-ē-ə\ *or formerly* **Mon·te·le·o·ne di Ca·la·bria** \,mònt-ē-lē-'ō-nē-dē-kə-'läb-rē-ə\ *or anc.* **Hip·po·ni·um** \hip-'ō-nē-əm\. Commune, Catanzaro prov., Calabria, S Italy, 30 m. SW of Catanzaro; pop. (1968e) 27,907; earthquakes 1783 and 1905.

Vi·cen·te, Point \-və-'sent-ē\. Point, SW coast of Los Angeles co., SW California, W of Long Beach.

Vicente Ló·pez \və-,sent-ē-'lō-,pez\. City, Buenos Aires prov., E cen. Argentina; pop. (1960c) 247,656; part of Greater Buenos Aires; incorporated 1905.

Vicente Pe·rez National Park \-'per-ez-\. National park, Chile; 522 sq. m.; volcanic activity; established 1926.

Vi·cen·za \vi-'chen(t)-sə\. 1 Province of Veneto, NE Italy. See table at ITALY.

2 *or anc.* **Vi·cen·tia** \vī-'sen-ch(ē-)ə\. Commune, its ✱, 40 m. W of Venice; pop. (1968e) 111,211; machinery, chemicals, lumber; food processing, tanning; numerous medieval remains; 12th cent. cathedral with 15th cent. façade (restored after World War II), 13th cent. churches of Santa Corona and San Lorenzo, 16th cent. Basilica Palladiana, Loggia del Capitanio, and Teatro Olimpico, and palaces of 14th, 15th, and 16th cents.; campanile in Piazza dei Signori; nearby is noted pilgrimage church, the Basilica di Monte Berico.

History: Founded c. 1st cent. B.C. by Ligurians; capital of Lombard duchy in early Middle Ages; gained independence 1164 and joined Lombard League; destroyed by Emperor Frederick II 1236; ruled by della Scala family of Verona 1311 ff., Visconti of Milan 1384 ff., Venetian Republic 1404 ff., Emperor Maximilian I 1509–16, Austria 1797 ff.; became part of kingdom of Italy 1866. Held by Axis powers throughout World War II; occupied by Allies Apr. 28–29, 1945.

Vich \'vēk\; *anc.* **Au·sa** \'ò-sə\ *or later* **Vi·cus Au·so·nen·sis** \,vī-kə-,sò-sə-'nen(t)-səs\. Commune, Barcelona prov., NE Spain, 38 m. NE of Barcelona; pop. (1970p) 25,906; manufactures textiles, hats, paper; 11th cent. cathedral.

Vi·cha·da \vi-'chä-də\. 1 River, cen. and E Colombia; ab. 400 m. long; flows ENE into Orinoco river on Venezuelan border.

2 Commissary of E Colombia. See table at COLOMBIA.

Vichegda. See VYCHEGDA.

Vi·chu·ga \vi-'chü-gə\. Town, Ivanovo Oblast, Russian S.F.S.R., U.S.S.R., ab. 40 m. NE of Ivanovo; pop. (1969e) 53,000.

Vi·chy \'vish-ē, 'vē-shē\. Commune, Allier dept., cen. France, on Allier river 200 m. SSE of Paris; pop. (1968c) 33,506; noted spa and health resort; many thermal alkaline springs used since Roman times; Vichy water and salts exported in large quantities. Taken by Charles VII 1440; as result of French armistice with Germany 1940, made capital, July 2, of unoccupied France; seat of French government until complete occupation of France by Germany Nov. 1942.

Vicks·burg \'viks-,bərg\. 1 Village, Kalamazoo co., SW Michigan, 7 m. S of Kalamazoo; pop. (1970c) 3139.

2 City, ⊗ of Warren co., W Mississippi, on Mississippi river 40 m. W of Jackson; pop. (1970c) 25,478; river port and railroad center; ships cotton and livestock; tourism. During Civil War besieged 1862–63; final siege operations Apr.–June 1863, captured July 4 by Union forces under Gen. Grant, securing Union control of the Mississippi river. See CHICKASAW BAYOU.

Vicksburg National Military Park. See UNITED STATES, *National Historical Parks.*

Vi·co Equen·se \,vē-kō-ā-'kwen-sē\. Commune, Napoli prov., Campania, S Italy, on Bay of Naples 15 m. SSE of Naples; pop. (1968e) 15,893; seaside resort; mineral baths.

Vi·ço·sa \vi-'sò-zə\. City, SE Minas Gerais state, E Brazil, 85 m. SE of Belo Horizonte; munic. pop. (1968e) 24,198; univ. (1948).

Vic·tor \'vik-tər\. City, Teller co., cen. Colorado, 18 m. SW of Colorado Springs; pop. (1970c) 258.

Vic·to·ria \vik-'tōr-ē-ə, -'tòr-\. 1 County in Texas. See table at TEXAS.

2 City, ⊗ of Victoria co., S Texas, 20 m. WNW of Matagorda Bay; pop. (1970c) 41,349; aluminum, chemicals, plastics, dairy products; oil and gas wells; Victoria Coll. (1925), Annunciation Coll. (1959); settled 1824.

3 Industrial town, Lunenburg co., S Virginia, 51 m. WSW of Petersburg; pop. (1970c) 1408.

4 City, Entre Ríos prov., E Argentina, ab. 40 m. NE of Rosario; pop. (1960c) 15,108.

5 River, NW Northern Territory, Australia; 350 m. long; flows N and NW to Queens Channel; navigable for ab. 100 m.

6 State, SE Australia; 87,884 sq. m.; pop. (1970e) 3,443,-800; ✱ Melbourne. *Physical features:* Separated on N from New South Wales by Murray river which forms almost entire boundary from its source in Australian Alps to point at 34°S where it crosses into South Australia. W and NW parts sandy desert and lowland; cen. and E parts are highlands forming S end of Great Dividing Range (here known as Australian Alps). Highest part is Darg Plateau with Mt. Bogong 6508 ft. SW coastal region known as Gippsland. In cen. part of S coast is spacious Port Phillip Bay, harbor of Melbourne; on coast SE of it is Wilson's Promontory, most S point of Australian mainland. Separated on S from Tasmania by Bass Strait. *Chief products:* Wheat, oats, barley, wool, dairy products; coal; manufacturing: chemicals, textiles, food processing; electrical engineering. *Chief cities:* Melbourne, Geelong, Ballarat, and Bendigo.

History: Discovered by Capt. Cook 1770, a few days before his arrival at Botany Bay to the N; Port Phillip Bay discovered 1802; first settled at Melbourne 1835 by immigrants from Tasmania; set off 1851 from New South Wales as separate colony; received many new settlers as result of discovery of gold in Ballarat region 1851; local self-government introduced 1853 and responsible government established 1855; became a state of Commonwealth of Australia 1901.

7 Seaport town, SW Cameroon, W Africa, on Bight of Biafra; port of Buea and chief trading town of former British Cameroons trust territory.

8 County, New Brunswick, Canada. See table at NEW BRUNSWICK.

9 County, Nova Scotia, Canada. See table at NOVA SCOTIA.

10 County, Ontario, Canada. See table at ONTARIO.

11 City, ✱ of British Columbia, Canada, on SE Vancouver I. and at E end of Juan de Fuca Strait; pop. (1971p) 60,897, met. area pop. 193,512; seaport; produces lumber, pulp and paper; salmon fishing, shipbuilding and repairing; Univ. of Victoria (1902, univ. status 1963), Royal Roads (United Services College, 1942); Pacific headquarters of Canadian Navy. Founded 1843; selected as capital 1868 when Vancouver I. united with British Columbia.

12 Town, Malleco prov., S cen. Chile, 110 m. SE of Concepción; pop. (1960c) 14,125.

13 *or* **Hong Kong** \'häŋ-ˌkäŋ, -'käŋ, 'hȯŋ-ˌkȯŋ, -'kȯŋ\. Seaport city, ✱ of Hong Kong colony, NW Hong Kong I.; pop. (1971p) 521,612; has extensive wharves; Univ. of Hong Kong (1911).
14 Town, on Labuan I., off NW coast of Borneo, Sabah, Malaysia; pop. (1960c) 3213.
15 Chief town, Gozo I., Malta; pop. (1961e) 6491.
16 *or* **Fort Victoria.** Town, Rhodesia, S Africa, 188 m. S of Salisbury; pop. (1970e) 13,000; goldfields; nearby are the Zimbabwe ruins.
17 Seaport and chief town on Mahé I., ✱ of Seychelles Is., Indian Ocean; pop. (1969e) 14,000.
Victoria. For cities in Brazil see VITÓRIA; in Sicily, VITTORIA; also see CIUDAD VICTORIA.
Victoria, La. See LA VICTORIA.
Victoria, Lake. 1 *or* **Victoria Ny·an·za** \-nē-'an-zə, -nī-\. Lake, E cen. Africa, S half in Tanzania and N half in Uganda, borders on Kenya in NE; 26,828 sq. m.; 2d largest freshwater body in the world; ab. 250 m. long (N to S) and 200 m. wide; max. depth 265 ft.; alt. ab. 3720 ft.; has indented coastline with deep gulfs, numerous islands; many tributaries (largest, Kagera) draining nearby uplands of E Africa, but chief source of water supply is rainfall; only outlet is Nile (*q.v.*).
History: Discovered 1858 by J. H. Speke in search of source of Nile; further explored 1862 by Speke and J. A. Grant and 1863 by Sir Samuel Baker; circumnavigated by H. M. Stanley 1875; ownership divided 1890 by England and Germany on E and W line 1°S; after 1920 entirely within British-controlled territory; became a reservoir with raised water level by completion of Owen Falls Dam 1954. Steamer service bet. chief ports (Kisumu, Entebbe, Bukoba, Mwansa).
2 Lake, U.S.S.R. See ZORKUL, LAKE.
Victoria, Mount. 1 Peak, W cen. Upper Burma at N end of Arakan Yoma and NE of Sittwe; 10,016 ft.
2 Peak on the boundary bet. Alberta and British Columbia, SW Canada, behind Lake Louise; 11,365 ft.
3 Peak, Fiji. See TOMANIIVI, MOUNT.
4 Peak, highest in the Owen Stanley Range, Papua New Guinea, New Guinea I., NE of Port Moresby; 13,363 ft.
Victoria de Durango. See DURANGO 3.
Victoria de las Tu·nas \-də-läs-'tü-nəs\ *also* **Tunas.** Municipality, Oriente prov., E Cuba, 100 m. NW of Santiago de Cuba; pop. (1967e) 172,060.
Victoria Falls. 1 Falls, Brazil. See IGUAÇU.
2 Falls in the Zambezi river, at a place where river is 5580 ft. wide, on the boundary bet. Zambia and Rhodesia, S Africa, near the town of Livingstone; broken by islands on precipice edge into four parts; height 355 ft.; volume varies with the seasons; water of falls drops into narrow chasm, hitting opp. wall 80 to 240 ft. above chasm floor. Railroad bridge (657 ft. long) crosses Zambezi just below falls. Surrounding land is Rhodesian public park. Falls discovered by Livingstone Nov. 17, 1855 who named them after Queen Victoria.
Victoria Falls National Park. National park, W Rhodesia; 205 sq. m.; contains Victoria Falls (*q.v.*); varied wildlife; established 1952.
Victoria Fjord. Fjord, N coast of Greenland, W of Peary Land; 140 m. long.
Victoria Island. 1 Third largest island of Arctic Archipelago, SW Franklin dist., Northwest Territories, Canada; 81,930 sq. m.; separated from mainland (Mackenzie dist.) by Dolphin and Union Strait, Coronation Gulf, and Dease Strait.
2 Island, Chonos Archipelago, in Pacific Ocean off SW coast of Chile.
Victoria Land *or formerly* **South Victoria Land.** Section of Antarctica, on W shore of Ross Sea and Ross Ice Shelf, lat. 70°–78°S and long. 164°E; largely included in Ross Dependency (*q.v.*); has mountain ranges, with highest peak ab. 13,000 ft.
Victoria Nile. See NILE.
Victoria Nyanza. See VICTORIA, LAKE 1.
Victoria Peak. 1 Mountain, N cen. Vancouver I., British Columbia, Canada; 7484 ft.
2 Hill above Victoria city, Hong Kong colony, NW Hong Kong I.; highest point on island, 1805 ft.; has view of Hong Kong harbor; last point surrendered to Japanese by British in fall of Hong Kong Dec. 25, 1941.
Victoria Point. Cape, extreme S of Burma, ab. 10°N, W of the mouth of Pakchan river.
Victoria Quadrant. Formerly the quarter section of Antarctica (*q.v.*), bet. 90°E and 180°E; now chiefly Wilkes Land and Victoria Land (W part of Ross Dependency).
Victoria River. See VICTORIA 5.
Victoria Strait. Channel bet. SE Victoria I. and King William I., off N Canada mainland, S Franklin dist., Northwest Territories.
Vic·to·ri·a·ville \vik-'tōr-ē-ə-ˌvil, -'tȯr-\. Manufacturing town, Arthabaska co., S Quebec, Canada, 36 m. SE of Three Rivers; pop. (1971p) 22,088; furniture, agricultural machinery, sporting goods, dairy products; Coll. de Victoriaville (1872); incorporated 1890.
Victoria West. Town, cen. Cape Province, S Rep. of South Africa, 230 m. NW of Port Elizabeth; pop. (1967e) 4100; sheep, Angora goats, and ostriches raised in vicinity.
Vic·tor·ville \'vik-tər-ˌvil\. City, San Bernardino co., SE California, N of San Bernardino; pop. (1970c) 10,845; Victor Valley Coll. (1961); site of U.S. Air Force base.
Vicus Ausonensis. See VICH.
Vicus Elbii. See VITERBO 2.
Vicus Julii. 1 Commune, France. See AIRE 3.
2 Commune, West Germany. See GERMERSHEIM.
Vid \'vit\. River, NW cen. Bulgaria; 117 m. long; flows from the Balkan Mts. NE into Danube river 8 m. W of Nikopol.
Vi·da·lia \və-'dāl-yə\. 1 City, Toombs and Montgomery cos., SE cen. Georgia, 76 m. W of Savannah; pop. (1970c) 9507; fertilizer, cottonseed oil, turpentine.
2 Town, ⊗ of Concordia parish, E cen. Louisiana; pop. (1970c) 5538.
Vi·din \'vēd-in\. 1 Province of NW Bulgaria. See table at BULGARIA.
2 *or anc.* **Bo·no·nia** \bə-'nō-nē-ə, -'nōn-yə\. City, its ✱, on Danube river near Yugoslav border; pop. (1968e) 42,495; river port in region producing wine, grain, olives; Celtic settlement on site 3d cent. B.C., then important Roman fortress; seat of independent state in 14th cent.; under Turks 1396–1807.
Vi·dor \'vī-ˌdȯr\. City, Orange co., E Texas, 7 m. NE of Beaumont; pop. (1970c) 9738; rice.
Vied·ma \'vyād-mä\. Town, ✱ of Río Negro prov., S cen. Argentina, on the Río Negro ab. 19 m. above its mouth; pop. (1960c) 7253.
Viedma, Lake. Lake, W Santa Cruz prov., S Argentina, S of Lake San Martín and N of Lake Argentino; 420 sq. m.; 53 m. long.
Viedma Glacier. Glacier in the Andes, Argentina; 27 m. long, ab. 3 m. wide near its terminus.
Viejo, El. See EL VIEJO.
Vi·en·na \vī-'en-ə\. 1 City, ⊗ of Dooly co., SW cen. Georgia, 40 m. NE of Albany; pop. (1970c) 2341; tobacco, peanuts, watermelons.
2 City, ⊗ of Johnson co., S Illinois; pop. (1970c) 1325.
Vienna \vē-'en-ə\. 1 Town, ⊗ of Maries co., S cen. Missouri; pop. (1970c) 505.
2 Town, Fairfax co., NE Virginia, NW of Alexandria; pop. (1970c) 17,152; fruit, grain farms.
3 City, Wood co., W West Virginia, on Ohio river 5 m. N of Parkersburg; pop. (1970c) 11,549; glass.
4 *or Ger.* **Wien** \'vēn\; *anc.* **Vin·dob·o·na** \vin-'däb-ə-nə\ *or* **Vin·dob·na** \-'däb-nə\. City, ✱ of Austria, also ✱ of Lower Austria state, NE Austria, on Danube river; 160 sq. m.; pop. (1971p) 1,603,000; commercial and industrial center of Austria; railroad junction and river port; produces textiles, machine tools, electrical equipment, motor vehicles, clothing, leather goods, building materials; food

processing, brewing; machine shops, railroad workshops, foundries; fruit and vegetable gardens; tourism. An important cultural center, with the Univ. of Vienna (1365), Vienna Technical Univ. (1815), several other higher educational institutions, opera, library, several museums, ten major theaters; headquarters of the International Atomic Energy Commission. Notable buildings include 14th–15th cent. Gothic St. Stephen's cathedral, Hofburg (former seat of the Hapsburgs), archiepiscopal palace, Rathaus, Schönbrunn Castle, the Winter Palace, Lichtenstein Palace; extensive system of public parks and gardens.

History: Founded by Celts; made Roman military station 1st cent. B.C.; came under Avars and in 6th cent. A.D. under Franks; to Magyars 907; to Leopold of Babenberg 976; became seat of dukes of Babenberg; important trade center during Crusades; taken and fortified by Ottokar of Bohemia 1251; taken by Rudolf of Hapsburg 1278 and remained seat of Hapsburgs until 1918; besieged by Turks 1529 and 1683; under Maria Theresa (reigned 1740–80) became one of leading cultural centers of Europe; under Francis I became seat of Austrian empire; occupied by French 1805–09; seat of Congress of Vienna 1814–15; scene of revolution 1848. Became capital of Austrian republic 1918; administrative center of German Austria 1938–45; in World War II frequently bombed by Allies 1943–45 and taken by Soviet troops Apr. 1945; suffered heavy damage. Under joint Soviet-Western Allied occupation 1945–55; has undergone considerable rebuilding since World War II. Site of Strategic Arms Limitations Talks bet. U.S. and U.S.S.R. 1970 ff.

5 City, France. See VIENNE 3.

Vienne \vē-'en\. 1 Navigable river, SW cen. France; 217 m. long; rises in Corrèze dept., flows NW through Limoges and Chinon into Loire river.

2 Department of W cen. France: **Haute–Vienne** \'ōt-vē-'en\ and **Vienne.** See table at FRANCE.

3 *or anc.* **Vi·en·na** \vē-'en-ə\. Manufacturing city, Isère dept., SE France, on the Rhone 47 m. NW of Grenoble; pop. (1968c) 29,057; river port; chemicals, plastics, footwear; wool combing; 12th cent. Romanesque-Gothic former cathedral; Roman remains include a Corinthian temple of Augustus and Livia, water conduits, theater, and obelisk.

History: In ancient times chief town of Allobroges and rival of Lyons; capital of Burgundy 413–534 and 879–933; formerly capital of Viennois; council held here 1311–12 in which Knights Templars were suppressed.

Vien·nois \ˌvē-ən-'wä, vyen-'wä\. Ancient county of SE France, in Dauphiné; now in Drôme and Isère depts.; ✱ Vienne.

Vien·tiane \vyen-'tyän\. City, administrative ✱ of Laos, SE Asia, near Thailand border ab. 5 m. N of Mekong river; pop. (1970e) 150,000; commercial center of the region; has road links to Luang Prabang and air connections with Saigon and Bangkok; teacher training coll. (1959); expanded rapidly after Laos became independent.

Vie·ques \vē-'ā-kəs\. 1 *or* **Crab Island** \'krab-\. Fertile island off E coast of Puerto Rico, 21 m. long by 6 m. wide; administratively a part of Puerto Rico, forming a municipality, pop. (1970p) 7817.

2 Chief town on Vieques I., on N coast; pop. (1970p) 2385; sugar.

Viern·heim \'fi(ə)rn-ˌhīm\. Agricultural commune, Hesse, West Germany, NE suburb of Mannheim; pop. (1969e) 27,406.

Vier·sen \'fi(ə)rz-ᵊn\. City, North Rhine-Westphalia, West Germany, 18 m. W of Düsseldorf; pop. (1969e) 42,576; textiles, machinery; church.

Vier·straat \'vir-ˌsträt\. Village, West Flanders prov., Belgium, S of Ieper (Ypres); monument to U.S. soldiers who fought in the region Aug. 18–Sept. 4, 1918.

Vier Waldstätter, Die. See FOREST CANTONS, THE FOUR.

Vierwaldstätter See. See LUCERNE, LAKE OF.

Vier·zon \vyer-'zōⁿ\. Town, Cher dept., cen. France, on the Cher river 18 m. NW of Bourges; pop. (1968c) 33,775; railroad junction; glass, porcelain, machinery.

Vie·ste \'vē-'es-tē\. Commune, Foggia prov., Apulia, SE Italy, 43 m. NE of Foggia; pop. (1968e) 13,085; castle.

Vi·et·nam *or* **Vi·et Nam** *or* **Viet–Nam** \vē-'et-'näm, vyet-, ˌvē-ət-, vēt-, -'nam\. Former state, SE Asia, now divided into North Vietnam and South Vietnam (see VIETNAM, NORTH and VIETNAM, SOUTH).

History: Region came under Chinese influence 221 B.C. ff.; N part made a province of Chinese Empire 111 B.C.; Vietnamese under continuous Chinese control until 939 A.D.; reimposition of Chinese rule 1407–28; region S of approx. lat. 13°N overrun by Vietnamese from N late 15th cent.; Cambodia conquered by Vietnamese 1698–1757; wall built by S Vietnamese at ab. lat. 18°N, dividing region into two parts 1613 (N part later known as Tonkin, S part as Cochin China); Vietnamese ports visited by Spanish and Portuguese traders early 16th cent., by Dutch and English traders 17th cent.; N and S parts of Vietnam unified under single dynasty 1802; Saigon captured by Franco-Spanish naval force (following several years of attempted French expansion in the region) 1859; three provinces of Cochin China ceded to France 1862; whole of Cochin China occupied by French 1867; French authority over Cochin China recognized by Vietnamese emperor 1874; appeal by emperor for Chinese support immediate cause of French military actions in N (Hanoi captured 1883); French protectorate established over Tonkin 1884, recognized by Chinese 1885; Vietnam occupied by Japanese (who declared it independent 1945) 1940–45; number of French troops in Vietnam increased to 50,000 Dec. 1945; period 1946–54 marked by war bet. French (supported by Nationalists under Emperor Bao Dai) and Viet Minh (Communist forces under Ho Chi Minh); major French defeat at Dien Bien Phu 1954; following international conference at Geneva (Switzerland) 1954, Vietnam partitioned along 17th parallel, with N part under Ho Chi Minh, and S part under Bao Dai (partition was to be temporary, and for purposes of reunification elections were to be held 1956); French troop withdrawal from Vietnam completed 1956. See also history at VIETNAM, NORTH and VIETNAM, SOUTH.

Vietnam, North; *officially* **Democratic Republic of Vietnam** *or Vietnamese* **Vi·et Nam Dan Chu Cong Hoa** \vē-'et-'näm-'dän-'chü-'kȯŋ-'hwä, 'vyet-\. Republic, SE Asia, bounded on N by China, on E by the Gulf of Tonkin, on S by Laos and South Vietnam, and on W by Laos; 63,360 sq. m.; pop. (1970e) 19,900,000; ✱ Hanoi. *Physical features:* Mountainous in N and NW (highest peak Fan-si-pan 10,306 ft.); E part consists of coastal plain; Red river delta is an important agricultural region. *Chief products:* Rice, sugarcane, corn, cotton, tobacco; coal, tin; manufacturing: textiles, cement, paper, fertilizers. *Chief towns:* Hanoi, Haiphong, Vinh, Thanh Hoa, Nam Dinh.

History: Communist republic set up in N part of Vietnam (*q.v.*) 1954, declaring at the outset its opposition to the existence of an anti-Communist government in S; suppressed peasant revolts 1956; intensified aid to Communist groups in South Vietnam 1959; adopted new constitution 1960; initiated large-scale troop infiltration into South Vietnam 1964; military targets in North Vietnam bombed by U.S. 1964 ff.; during latter part of 1960's expanded its military activities into Laos and Cambodia.

Vietnam, South; *officially* **Republic of Vietnam** *or Vietnamese* **Vi·et Nam Cong Hoa** \vē-'et-näm-'kȯŋ-'hwä, 'vyet-\. Republic, SE Asia, bounded on N by North Vietnam, on E and S by the South China Sea, on SW by the

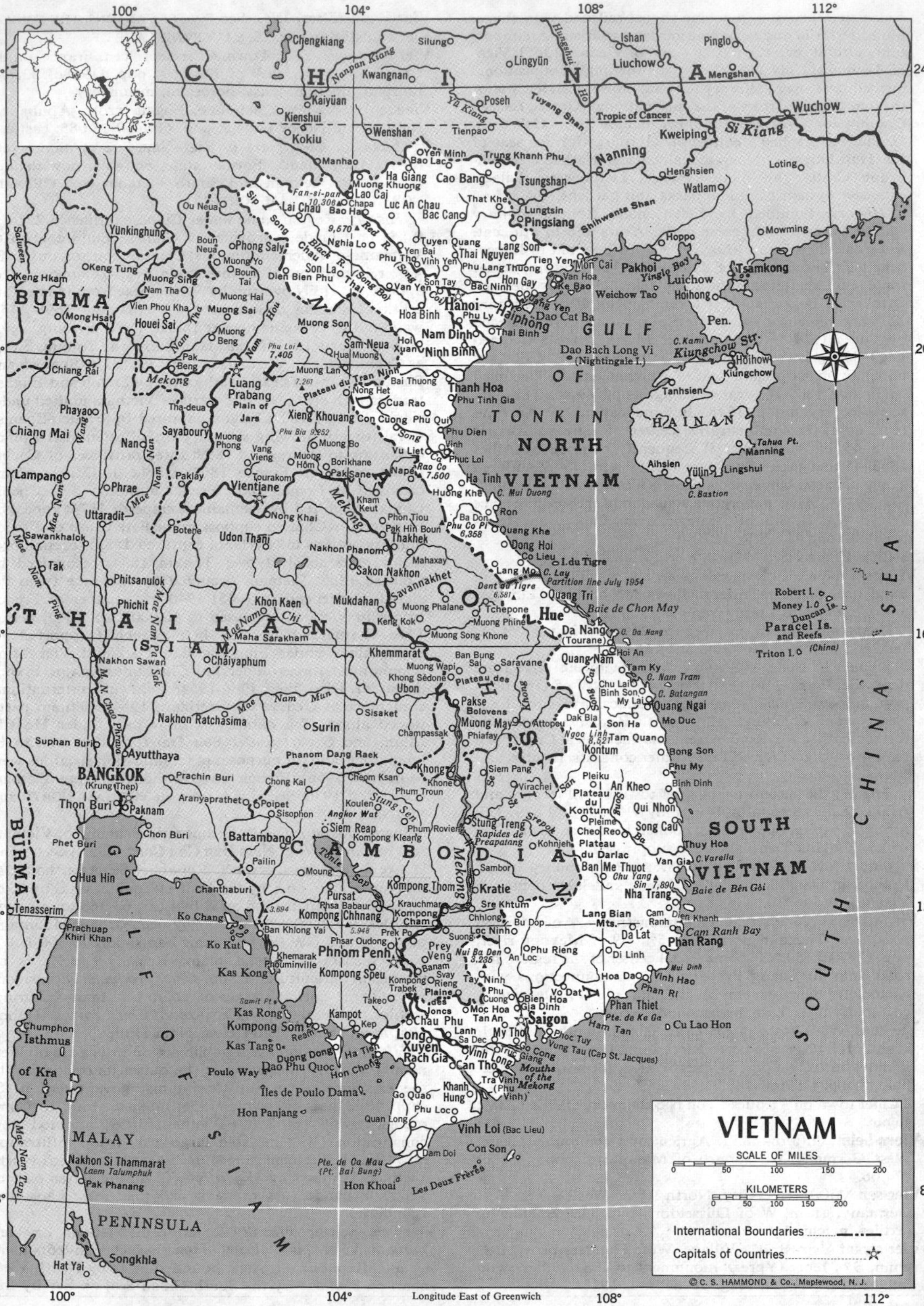
VIETNAM
SCALE OF MILES
0 50 100 150 200
KILOMETERS
0 50 100 150 200
International Boundaries
Capitals of Countries
© C. S. HAMMOND & Co., Maplewood, N. J.
Longitude East of Greenwich
100° 104° 108° 112°
24° 20° 16° 12° 8°
CHINA
BURMA
THAILAND (SIAM)
LAOS
CAMBODIA
NORTH VIETNAM
SOUTH VIETNAM
GULF OF TONKIN
SOUTH CHINA SEA
GULF OF SIAM
MALAY PENINSULA
HAINAN
Tropic of Cancer
Hanoi
Haiphong
Saigon
Hue
Da Nang (Tourane)
Vientiane
Luang Prabang
Phnom Penh
BANGKOK (Krung Thep)
Partition line July 1954
Paracel Is. and Reefs (China)
Mouths of the Mekong
Mekong
Red R.
Black R.
Fan-si-pan 10,308
Plain of Jars
Isthmus of Kra
Con Son
Cu Lao Hon
Cam Ranh Bay
Nha Trang
Da Lat
Kontum
Pleiku
Quang Tri
Dong Hoi
Vinh
Thanh Hoa
Nam Dinh
Dien Bien Phu
Lao Cai
Lang Son
Hon Gay
Nanning
Kunming
Tonle Sap
Angkor Wat
Battambang
Kampot
Chiang Mai
Udon Thani
Savannakhet
Pakse
Can Tho
My Tho
Vinh Long
Rach Gia
Long Xuyen
Ca Mau
Phan Thiet
Phan Rang
Qui Nhon
Quang Ngai
Tam Ky
Hoi An
Ban Me Thuot
Kratie
Stung Treng
Pte. de Ca Mau (Pt. Bai Bung)
Vung Tau (Cap St. Jacques)

Gulf of Siam, and on W by Cambodia and Laos; 67,108 sq. m.; pop. (1970e) 18,332,000; ❋ Saigon. *Physical features:* S part of country characterized by Mekong delta, a flat, frequently marshy region with rich soils suited esp. for rice production; N and cen. regions hilly (highest peak Ngoo Linh 8521 ft.) with narrow coastal plain. *Chief products:* Rice, yams, peanuts, corn, sweet potatoes, tea; manufacturing: textiles, paper, glass. *Chief towns:* Saigon, Da Nang, Hue, Gia Dinh, Qui Nhon.

History: Nationalist government under Emperor Bao Dai established in S part of Vietnam (*q.v.*) 1954; government offered economic aid (Oct. 1954) and military aid (Feb. 1955) by U.S.; abolished monarchy (Oct. 1955) and rejected Geneva formula (which called for reunification of Vietnam); latter part of 1950's characterized by increase in anti-government activity (initiated by South Vietnamese Communists and soon supported by infiltrators from North Vietnam); North Vietnam charged with complicity in attempts to overthrow the South Vietnam government in majority report of International Control Commission 1962; 1960's marked by massive U.S. military and economic assistance program in support of anti-Communist South Vietnam government; first U.S. ground combat troops deployed in South Vietnam 1965 (U.S. forces increased to 53,500 in mid-1965, 358,000 in Nov. 1966, and 542,500 in Feb. 1969); announcement of "Vietnamization" program by U.S. 1969 (program designed to lessen U.S. role in Vietnam War; U.S. forces decreased to ab. 80,000 by early 1972).

Viet Nam Dan Chu Cong Hoa. See VIETNAM, NORTH.

Vieux–Con·dé \ˌvyə(r)-kōⁿ-'dā\. Commune, Nord dept., N France, N of Valenciennes; pop. (1962c) 11,873.

Vieux Fort \ˌvyə(r)-'fō(ə)r\. 1 Point, S tip of Basse-Terre, Guadeloupe I., West Indies.

2 Town, S end of St. Lucia I., Windward Is., West Indies; first sugar works on the island established here 1765.

Vi·ga \'vē-gə\. Municipality, Catanduanes prov., Phil., ab. 3 m. from coast; pop. (1969e) 28,600.

Vi·gan \'vē-ˌgän\. Municipality, ❋ of Ilocos Sur prov., Luzon, Phil., just N of the mouth of the Abra; pop. (1969e) 35,200. Founded by Juan de Salcedo 1572; seized by Japanese Dec. 10, 1941.

Vi·ge·va·no \vē-'jev-ə-ˌnō\. Manufacturing commune, Pavia prov., Lombardy, N Italy, near Ticino river 18 m. NW of Pavia; pop. (1968e) 66,443; 10th cent. cathedral.

Vi·gia \vi-'zhē-ə\. City, E Pará state, N Brazil, at the mouth of Pará river on E bank; munic. pop. (1968e) 19,507.

Vigne·male, Pic de \ˌpēk-də-ˌvēn-yə-'mal\. Peak in the Pyrenees Mts., S France; 10,820 ft.; highest peak in the French Pyrenees.

Vi·go. 1 \'vē-ˌgō, 'vī-\. County in Indiana. See table at INDIANA.

2 \'vē-gō\. Seaport, Pontevedra prov., NW Spain, on the **Estuary of Vigo,** an inlet of Atlantic Ocean 17 m. S by W of Pontevedra; pop. (1970p) 197,144; lumber, leather, paper, flour, soap, brandy, machinery, tools; tunny and sardine fisheries. Under attack by Drake 1585, 1589; scene of French and Spanish naval defeat by English and Dutch 1702.

Vi·gon·za \vi-'gōn-tsə\. Commune, Padova prov., Veneto, NE Italy, NE of Padua; pop. (1968e) 13,136.

Vih·ren National Park \vi-'rān-\. National park, Bulgaria; 26 sq. m.; glacial valleys; established 1962.

Viipuri. See VYBORG.

Viipuri Bay. See VYBORG BAY.

Vi·ja·ya·na·gar \ˌvij-ə-yə-'nəg-ər\ *or* **Bi·ja·na·gar** \ˌbij-ə-'nəg-ər\. 1 Former Hindu kingdom, S India, S of the Krishna; established 1336 by two brothers of the Kanarese people; for more than two centuries formed defense of Hindu peoples against Muslim raiders from the N; was an important center of Brahman culture and Dravidian art. Finally overthrown at Talikota 1565 by confederacy (Bijapur, Ahmadnagar, and Golconda) of Deccan Muslim sultans.

2 City, its ❋ (destroyed 1565); its ruins now at modern Hampi on S bank of the Tungabhadra, SW Andhra Pradesh, India, ab. 30 m. WNW of Bellary.

Vi·ja·ya·pu·ri \ˌvij-ə-yə-'pu̇r-ē\. Town, Andhra Pradesh, India, ab. 80 m. SE of Hyderabad; pop. (1961c) 55,300.

Vi·ja·ya·wa·da \ˌvij-ə-yə-'wäd-ə\ *or formerly* **Bez·wa·da** \bez-'wäd-ə\. Town, Andhra Pradesh, SE India, on Krishna river at the head of its delta 155 m. ESE of Hyderabad; pop. (1970e) 322,717. Headquarters of Krishna irrigation canal system; active trade center and rail junction. Village of **Un·da·val·le** \'u̇n-də-ˌvəl-ā\ nearby has interesting rock temples and ruins.

Vi·jo·së \vē-'ō-sə\ *also* **Vi·o·sa** \vē-'ō-sə\ *or* **Vo·yu·tsa** \vō-'yüt-sə\ *or Gk.* **Aó·ös** \'au̇-(ˌ)ȯs\. River, NW Greece and S Albania; 148 m. long; rises in Pindus Mts., Greece, flows NW across Albania into Adriatic Sea 14 m. N of Vlorë.

Vík \'vēk\. Village, on most southerly point of Iceland, 63°25′N, 19°01′W; pop. (1970c) 379.

Vik·na \'vik-nə\. Small island, Norwegian Sea, off W cen. coast of Norway; 64°54′N, 11°E.

Vi·la \'vē-lə\. 1 Seaport, ❋ of New Hebrides Is., on Vila Harbor, SW Efate I., SW Pacific Ocean; pop. (1971e) 5000.

2 Village, SE coast of Kolombangara I., on Kula Gulf, cen. Solomon Is., W Pacific; in World War II a Japanese base, evacuated Oct. 1943.

Vila de Jo·ão Be·lo \ˌvē-ləd-ə-ˌzhwau̇ⁿ-'bā-ˌlü\. Seaport town, S Mozambique, SE Africa, at mouth of Limpopo river.

Vila de Ma·ni·ca \ˌvē-lə-də-mə-'nē-kə\; *formerly* **Ma·ce·que·ce** *or* **Ma·si·ke·si** \ˌmäs-ə-'kā-sē\. Town, W cen. Mozambique.

Vilafro, Lake. See VILLAFRO, LAKE.

Vi·laine \vi-'lān, -'len\. Navigable river, NW France; 140 m. long; rises in Mayenne dept., flows W to Rennes, and turns SW through Morbihan dept. into the Bay of Biscay.

Vila No·va de Ga·ia \ˌvē-lə-ˌnȯ-və-də-'gī-ə\. Town, Pôrto dist., NW Portugal, just S of Oporto; pop. (1960c) 46,298.

Vila Nova de Portimão. See PORTIMÃO.

Vila Re·al \ˌvē-lə-rē-'äl\. 1 District of N Portugal. See table at PORTUGAL.

2 *also* **Vila Ri·al** \-rē-'äl\. Commune, its ❋; munic. pop. (1970p) 44,286; episcopal see.

Vi·las \'vī-ləs\. County in Wisconsin. See table at WISCONSIN.

Vila Salazar. See SALAZAR.

Vil·ca·no·ta Knot \ˌvil-kə-ˌnōt-ə-\. Mountain mass in the Andes Mts., S Peru, NW of Lake Titicaca; highest point 17,988 ft.; junction point of ranges entering Peru from Bolivia and Chile.

Vîl·cea \vil-'chā-ə\. County of S cen. Romania. See table at ROMANIA.

Vildmose. See LILLE VILDMOSE.

Vilich. See BEUEL.

Viliya. See NERIS.

Vil·jan·di *or* **Vil·yan·di** \'vil-ˌyän-dē\ *also* **Wil·jan·di** \-ˌyän-\; *Ger.* **Fel·lin** \fe-'lēn\. Town, S cen. Estonian S.S.R., U.S.S.R., 42 m. E of Pärnu; pop. (1967e) 19,000.

Vil·kits·ki Strait \vil-ˌkit-skē-\. Channel, N coast of Taimyr Penin., Taimyr National Okrug, Russian S.F.S.R., U.S.S.R.; separates Bolshevik I. of the Severnaya Zemlya Is. from mainland and connects Laptev and Kara seas.

Vilkomir. See UKMERGE.

Villa Acuña. See CIUDAD ACUÑA.

Vi·lla Ale·ma·na \ˌvē-yə-ˌäl-ə-'män-ə\. City, Valparaíso prov., cen. Chile, just E of Valparaíso; pop. (1966e) 21,696.

Vi·lla Al·ta \ˌvē-yə-'äl-tə\. Municipality, Oaxaca state, Mexico, 45 m. NE of Oaxaca; pop. (1970p) 33,719.

Vi·lla Be·lla \ˌvē-yə-ˈbā-yə\. Frontier town, N Bolivia, at confluence of the Beni and Mamoré rivers; customs post and trading center.

Villa Bens. See TARFAYA.

Vi·lla·ca·rri·llo \ˌvē(l)-yə-kär-ˈē(l)-(ˌ)yō\. Commune, Jaén prov., S Spain, 41 m. NE of Jaén; pop. (1970p) 12,910; produces oil, wine, vegetables, woolens.

Villa Cecilia. See CIUDAD MADERO.

Vil·lach \ˈfil-ˌäk\ *or Slovenian* **Be·ljak** \ˈbel-ˌyäk\. City, Carinthia, Austria, on Drava river 21 m. W of Klagenfurt; pop. (1961c) 32,971; railroad junction; tourist resort; manufactures paper, beer; radioactive thermal springs nearby.

Vi·lla Cis·ne·ros \ˌvē(l)-yə-sis-ˈner-əs, ˌvē-(y)ə-\. Seaport on Río de Oro Bay, Spanish Sahara, NW Africa; pop. (1970p) 5570; military post; airport.

Villa Concepción. See CONCEPCIÓN 6.

Vi·lla Con·sti·tu·ción \ˌvē-yə-ˌkȯn(t)-sti-ˌtüs-ˈyȯn\ *also* **Constitución.** Port, Santa Fe prov., E cen. Argentina, on Paraná river 23 m. SE of Rosario; pop. (1960c) 18,720.

Vi·lla de Cu·ra \ˌvē-yəd-ə-ˈku̇r-ə\ *or* **Cura.** Town, Aragua state, N Venezuela, 50 m. SW of Caracas; pop. (1961c) 19,945.

Vi·lla Del·ga·do \ˌvē-yə-del-ˈgäd-(ˌ)ō\. Town, San Salvador dept., SW cen. El Salvador; pop. (1968e) 30,157.

Villa del Pilar. See PILAR 2.

Vi·lla Do·lo·res \ˌvē-yə-də-ˈlōr-əs, -ˈlȯr-\. Town, W Córdoba prov., N cen. Argentina, 75 m. SW of Córdoba; pop. (1960c) 16,730; resort.

Vi·lla Flo·res \ˌve-yə-ˈflȯr-ēz\. Municipality, Chiapas state, Mexico, 50 m. S of Tuxtla Gutiérrez; pop. (1970p) 38,946; cattle raising; coffee, sugarcane, cacao.

Vi·lla·fran·ca de los Ba·rros \ˌvē(l)-yə-ˈfräŋ-kə-ˌdā-lōz-ˈbär-(ˌ)ōs\. Commune, Badajoz prov., SW Spain, 37 m. SE of Badajoz; pop. (1970p) 12,908.

Vil·la·fran·ca di Ve·ro·na \ˌvēl-ə-ˈfräŋ-kə-ˌdē-və-ˈrōn-ə\. Commune, Verona prov., Veneto, NE Italy, 10 m. SW of Verona; pop. (1968e) 21,865; treaty bet. Austria and France signed here July 11, 1859.

Vi·lla·fro, Lake \-vē-ˈyäf-(ˌ)rō\ *or* **Lake Vi·la·fro** \-vē-ˈläf-\. Lake, N Arequipa dept., S Peru; regarded as remotest source of Amazon river through the Apurímac.

Vi·lla Fron·te·ra \ˌvē-yə-frȯn-ˈter-ə\. Town, Coahuila state, NE Mexico; munic. pop. (1970p) 31,055.

Vi·lla·gar·cía de Aro·sa \ˌvē(l)-yə-gär-ˈsē-ə-ˌdā-ə-ˈrō-sə\. Seaport, Pontevedra prov., NW Spain, on Atlantic Ocean 13 m. NNW of Pontevedra; pop. (1970p) 24,076; flour, soap, brick, tile.

Village, The. City, Oklahoma co., cen. Oklahoma, N suburb of Oklahoma City; pop. (1970c) 13,695.

Vil·la Giu·sti \ˌvē-lə-ˈjüs-tē\. Villa, near Padua, Padova prov., Veneto, NE Italy, where armistice bet. Italy and Austria-Hungary was signed Nov. 4, 1918.

Vil·la Grove \ˌvil-ə-\. City, Douglas co., E cen. Illinois, 20 m. S of Champaign; pop. (1970c) 2605.

Vi·lla·guay \ˌvē-yə-ˈgwī\. Town, Entre Ríos prov., E Argentina, 90 m. E of Paraná; pop. (1960c) 12,463.

Vi·lla Hayes \ˌvē-yə-ˈīs, -yə-ˈhāz\. Town, ✻ of Presidente Hayes dept., W cen. Paraguay, on right bank of the Paraguay river 9 m. N of Asunción; pop. (1968e) 2400; named for Rutherford B. Hayes, president of the U.S. who arbitrated Argentina-Paraguay boundary.

Vi·lla·her·mo·sa \ˌvē-yə-er-ˈmō-sə\ *or formerly* **San Juan Bau·tis·ta** \san-ˈ(h)wän-bau̇-ˈtis-tə\. City, ✻ of Tabasco state, SE Mexico, on the Grijalva river; pop. (1969e) 78,-034; ships tobacco, coffee, sugar, cacao, bananas, and rubber; univ. (1958).

Vi·lla·jo·yo·sa \ˌvē(l)-yə-hō-ˈyō-sə\. Seaport town and commune, Alicante prov., SE Spain, 20 m. NE of Alicante; pop. (1970p) 16,258.

Vi·llal·ba. 1 \vē-ˈyäl-bə\. Town and municipality, S cen. Puerto Rico; pop. (1970p) 4085 (town), 18,627 (munic.); town is in hilly region 9 m. NE of Ponce.

2 \vē(l)-ˈyäl-bə\. Commune, Lugo prov., NW Spain, 16 m. NNW of Lugo; pop. (1970p) 17,301; textiles.

Vi·lla Ma·ría \ˌvē-yə-mə-ˈrē-ə\. City, cen. Córdoba prov., N cen. Argentina, ab. 90 m. SE of Córdoba; pop. (1960c) 41,472.

Vil·la·no·va \vil-ə-ˈnō-və\. Locality, Delaware co., SE Pennsylvania, ab. 6 m. W of Philadelphia; Villanova Univ. (1824); Northeastern Junior Coll. (1956).

Vi·lla·nue·va \ˌvē-yə-ˈnu̇-ˈā-və\. Municipality, Zacatecas state, Mexico, 25 m. SW of Zacatecas; pop. (1970p) 35,553.

Villanueva de Cór·do·ba \ˌvē(l)-yə-ˌnu̇-ā-və-dā-ˈkȯrd-ə-bə, -ə-və\. Commune, Córdoba prov., S Spain, 31 m. NNE of Córdoba; pop. (1970p) 11,270; soap, flour, woolens.

Villanueva del Ar·zo·bis·po \-del-ˌär-sō-ˈbēs-(ˌ)pō\. Commune, Jaén prov., S Spain, 47 m. NE of Jaén; pop. (1970p) 10,320; produces wine, oil, flax; manufactures soap; stock raising.

Villanueva y Gel·trú \-ē-hel-ˈtrü\. Commune, Barcelona prov., NE Spain, on Mediterranean 26 m. WSW of Barcelona; pop. (1970p) 35,714; textiles, flour, preserves.

Vil·lány \ˈvil-än(-yə)\. Town, Baranya co., S Hungary, near Yugoslav border, ab. 18 m. SSE of Pécs; pop. (1970p) 3948; produces wine.

Vi·lla Oli·va \ˌvē-yə-ō-ˈlē-və\. Town, Neembucú dept., SW corner of Paraguay, on the Paraguay river 55 m. S of Asunción; pop. (1970e) 1959.

Villa Orotava. See LA OROTAVA.

Vil·la Park \ˌvil-ə-\. Village, Du Page co., NE Illinois, 25 m. W of Chicago; pop. (1970c) 25,891.

Vil·lard–Bon·not \vē-ˈlär-bȯ-ˈnō\. Commune, Isère dept., SE France, on the Isère; pop. (1962c) 6499.

Vi·lla·re·al \ˌvē-yə-rā-ˈäl\. Municipality, Samar Occidental prov., Phil., on S shore of **Villareal Bay** (ab. 12 m. wide and long) 13 m. S of Catbalogan.

Vil·la Rica \ˌvil-ə-ˈrik-ə\. City, Carroll and Douglas cos., W Georgia, 30 m. W of Atlanta; pop. (1970c) 3922; cottonseed oil; gold-mining center in early 19th cent.

Villa Rica de Vera Cruz. See VERACRUZ 2.

Vi·lla·rre·al \ˌvē(l)-yə-rā-ˈäl\ *or* **Villarreal de los In·fan·tes** \-dā-lōz-in-ˈfänt-ēz\. Commune, Castellón de la Plana prov., E Spain, 7 m. SSW of Castellón de la Plana; pop. (1970p) 33,215; manufactures liquors, paper.

Vi·lla·rri·ca \ˌvē-yə-ˈrē-kə\. 1 Volcanic peak, S cen. Chile, near Argentina border and bet. provinces of Cautín and Valdivia; 9318 ft.

2 City, ✻ of Guairá dept., S cen. Paraguay, 70 m. SE of Asunción; pop. (1970e) 38,052; sugar refineries, distilleries, sawmills, flour mills, brick and tile works; founded 1570.

Vi·lla·rro·ble·do \ˌvē(l)-yə-rō-ˈblād-(ˌ)ō\. Commune, Albacete prov., SE Spain, 42 m. WNW of Albacete; pop. (1970p) 19,963; iron products, earthenware.

Villas, Las. See LAS VILLAS.

Vi·lla·sis \vē-ˈyä-sēs\. Municipality, SE Pangasinan prov., Luzon, Phil., near right bank of Agno river 25 m. ESE of Lingayen; pop. (1969e) 37,100.

Vi·lla·vi·cen·cio \ˌvē-yə-vi-ˈsen(t)-sē-ˌō\. Town, ✻ of Meta dept., cen. Colombia, on Meta river ab. 45 m. SE of Bogotá; munic. pop. (1968e) 80,675.

Vi·lla·vi·cio·sa \ˌvē(l)-yə-ˌvē-sē-ˈō-sə\. Commune, Oviedo prov., NW Spain, on inlet of Bay of Biscay 21 m. ENE of Oviedo; pop. (1970p) 17,213; agricultural produce; fisheries.

Ville de Laval. See LAVAL 1.

Ville–de–Paris. See *Paris, Ville-de-* at table at FRANCE.

Ville·franche \ˌvēl-(ə-)ˈfräⁿsh\. 1 Seaport, Alpes-Maritimes dept., SE France, on coast E of Nice; pop. (1962c) 6735; resort.

2 *also* **Villefranche–sur–Saône** \-su̇r-ˈsōn\. Commune, Rhône dept., E cen. France, on Saône river 16 m. NNW of Lyons; pop. (1968c) 26,338; textiles; trades in wine.

Villefranche–de–Rou·ergue \-də-rü-ˈerg\. Commune, Aveyron dept., S France, ab. 26 m. W of Rodez; pop. (1962e) 10,461; 13th–16th cent. church, 15th–16th cent. Carthusian monastery; founded c. 1252.

Ville·juif \ˌvēl-zhə-ˈwēf\. Commune, Val-de-Marne dept., N France, S suburb of Paris; pop. (1968c) 51,120.

Ville Ma·rie \ˌvil-mə-ˈrē\. Town, ⊗ of Timiskaming co., SW Quebec, Canada, on E shore of Lake Timiskaming ab. 72 m. N of North Bay, Ontario; pop. (1971p) 1995.

Ville–Marie de Montréal. See MONTREAL 2.

Ville·mom·ble \vēl-ˈmōⁿblᵊ\. Commune, Seine-St-Denis dept., N France, ENE suburb of Paris; pop. (1968c) 28,756.

Vi·lle·na \vē(l)-ˈyā-nə\. Commune, Alicante prov., SE Spain, 26 m. NW of Alicante; pop. (1970p) 25,473; liquors, flour, soap.

Ville·nave–d'Or·non \vēl-ˌnav-dȯr-ˈnōⁿ\. Commune, Gironde dept., SW France, just S of Bordeaux in the Graves dist.; pop. (1968c) 21,263; wine (Château Carbonnieux).

Ville·neuve \vēl-ˈnə(r)v\. Town, Quebec co., S Quebec, Canada, 6 m. NE of Quebec; pop. (1971p) 4044.

Villeneuve–d'Agen. See VILLENEUVE-SUR-LOT.

Villeneuve–la–Ga·renne \vēl-ˌnə(r)v-lä-gə-ˈren\. Commune, Hauts-de-Seine dept., N France, ab. 5 m. NNW of Paris; pop. (1968c) 22,715.

Villeneuve–le–Roi \-lər-(ə-)ˈwä\. Commune, Val-de-Marne dept., N France, SSE suburb of Paris; pop. (1968c) 23,074.

Villeneuve–Saint–Georges \-saⁿ-ˈzhȯrzh\. Commune, Val-de-Marne dept., N France, on the Seine 7 m. SSE of Paris; pop. (1968c) 30,488; shipbuilding.

Villeneuve–sur–Lot \-su̇r-ˈlȯt\ *or sometimes* **Villeneuve–d'Agen** \-dä-ˈzhaⁿ\ *or early medieval* **Ga·jac** \ga-ˈzhäk\. Commune, Lot-et-Garonne dept., SW France, on Lot river 13 m. N of Agen; pop. (1968c) 21,682; paper, cloth, copper goods, table linen.

Ville Platte \vēl-ˈplat\. Town, ⊗ of Evangeline parish, S cen. Louisiana, 35 m. NNW of Lafayette; pop. (1970c) 9692; cotton gins; rice.

Vil·lers–Cot·te·rêts \ˌvē-ˌler-kȯ-ˈtre\. Town, Aisne dept., N France, 14 m. SW of Soissons; pop. (1962c) 5489; birthplace of Alexandre Dumas père; forest in vicinity was a battlefield in World War I; captured by Germans Aug. 1914; severe fighting June–July 1918 when it was the scene July 18 of the opening action of the great Allied offensive.

Ville·rupt \vēl-ˈrüp\. Industrial commune, Meurthe-et-Moselle dept., NE France, on Alzette river on Luxembourg border 36 m. N of Metz; pop. (1962c) 14,377; coal mines, steel mills; iron foundries.

Vi·lle·ta \vē-ˈyāt-ə\. Town, Central dept., S Paraguay, S of Asunción; pop. (1970e) 14,038.

Ville·ur·banne \ˌvē-lər-ˈban\. Industrial commune, Rhône dept., E cen. France, E suburb of Lyons; pop. (1968c) 119,879; electrical equipment, metal goods, textiles, chemicals.

Vil·ling·en \ˈfil-iŋ-ən\. Manufacturing city, Baden-Württemberg, West Germany, 30 m. ENE of Freiburg; pop. (1969e) 36,950; clocks, radios, meters, furniture, cutlery, electrical goods; founded 999.

Villmanstrand. See LAPPEENRANTA.

Vil·lu·pu·ram \ˌvil-ə-ˈpu̇r-əm\. Town, NE Tamil Nadu, SE India, 92 m. SSW of Madras; pop. (1961c) 43,500.

Vil·ni·us \ˈvil-nē-əs\ *or Pol.* **Wil·no** \ˈvil-(ˌ)nō\; *Russ.* **Vil·na** \ˈvil-nə\ *or* **Vil·no** \-(ˌ)nō\; *Ger.* **Wil·na** \ˈvil-nə\. Commercial city, ✱ of Lithuanian S.S.R., U.S.S.R., 57 m. ESE of Kaunas; pop. (1970p) 372,000; railroad junction; agricultural machinery, electrical equipment, foodstuffs, machine tools; seat of Roman Catholic and Orthodox archbishops; cathedral, twelve 17th cent. churches, ruins of castle; univ. (1578, abolished 1832, reestablished 1919).

History: Founded in 10th cent.; made capital of Lithuania 1323; destroyed by Teutonic Knights 1377; suffered frequently from plagues, fires, and invasions 15th–18th cents.; passed to Russia 1795. Occupied by Germans 1915–19; scene of fighting bet. Poland and U.S.S.R. during 1919–20; confirmed as Polish by League of Nations 1923; in World War II occupied by Soviet troops 1939 and by Germans June 1941–July 1944; restored to Lithuanian S.S.R. and made its ✱ 1944.

Vilp·pu·la \ˈvil-pə-ˌlä\. Town, Häme prov., SW Finland, on railroad 45 m. NNE of Tampere; pop. (1970e) 6498.

Vil·voor·de \ˈvil-ˌvȯrd-ə\ *or* **Vil·vorde** \vēl-ˈvȯrd\. Manufacturing commune, Brabant prov., cen. Belgium, on Senne river just N of Brussels; pop. (1969e) 34,148.

Vilyandi. See VILJANDI.

Vi·lyui \vil-ˈyü-ē\. River, W Yakutsk A.S.S.R., Russian S.F.S.R., U.S.S.R.; 1513 m. long; rises in E Evenki National Okrug, flows E into Lena river; as chief tributary on the W, it enters the Lena ab. 200 m. NW of Yakutsk; navigable for 900 m.

Vi·lyu·isk Range \vil-ˌyü-isk-\. Mountain range, W Yakutsk A.S.S.R., Russian S.F.S.R., U.S.S.R., W of Lena river and serving as watershed bet. Olenek and tributaries and the Vilyui tributaries; highest point ab. 3500 ft.

Vi·mei·ro \vē-ˈme(ə)r-ü\. Village, Lisboa dist., W Portugal, near Atlantic Ocean 32 m. NW of Lisbon; pop. (1970p) 945; important victory Aug. 21, 1808 (Peninsular War) of Wellington over French under Junot.

Vi·mer·ca·te \ˌvē-mer-ˈkät-ē\. Commune, Milano prov., Lombardy, N Italy, 14 m. NE of Milan; pop. (1968e) 17,110.

Vim·i·nal \ˈvim-ən-ᵊl\. One of the seven hills of Rome. See SEVEN HILLS.

Vi·mou·tiers \ˌvē-mü-ˈtyā\. Town, Orne dept., NW France, NE of Argentan; pop. (1962c) 3786; center for Camembert cheese, first made in village 3 m. SW (see CAMEMBERT).

Vi·my Ridge \ˈvim-ē-, ˈvē-mē-\. Ridge near **Vimy** commune, Pas-de-Calais dept., N France, 10 m. N of Arras; captured by Canadians Apr. 9–10, 1917.

Vi·ña del Mar \ˌvēn-yə-del-ˈmär\. City, a residential suburb 6 m. E of Valparaíso, Chile; pop. (1966e) 138,457; important seaside resort; textiles, paint, glass, beverages.

Vi·nai·gre, Mont \ˌmōⁿ-vē-ˈnagrᵊ, -ˈnegrᵊ\. Mountain, Var dept., S France; highest point 2020 ft. in the Estérel.

Vi·ña·les \vē-ˈnyäl-əs\. Municipality, Pinar del Río prov., W Cuba, 15 m. N of Pinar del Río; pop. (1967e) 18,710.

Vi·nal·ha·ven \ˈvīn-ᵊl-ˌhā-vən\. 1 Island at mouth of Penobscot Bay off S cen. Maine coast, part of Knox co.

2 Town on S end of Vinalhaven I.; pop. (1970c) 1135; summer resort and fishing center; granite quarries nearby.

Vin·cennes. 1 \vin-ˈsenz\. City, ⊗ of Knox co., SW Indiana, on Wabash river 55 m. S of Terre Haute; pop. (1970c) 19,867; paper products, footwear, glass; in wheat- and fruit-farming region; Vincennes Univ. (1804); site of memorial to George Rogers Clark.

History: Oldest town in Indiana. On site of a French mission; fortified 1732 by François Marie Bissot, Sieur de Vincennes and renamed after him 1736; ceded to Great Britain 1763; seized by George Rogers Clark 1779; capital of Indiana Territory 1800–13 (see NORTHWEST TERRITORY); incorporated 1856.

2 *Fr.* vaⁿ-sen\. Manufacturing commune, Val-de-Marne dept., N France, 5 m. E of Paris; pop. (1968c) 49,143; 14th cent. castle, once residence of French kings, later a state prison, and now an arsenal; extensive park (**Bois de Vin·cennes** \ˌbwäd-vaⁿ-ˈsen\); military school, hospital.

Vin·ces \ˈvin(t)-səs\. City, Los Ríos prov., W cen. Ecuador, just N of Guayaquil; pop. (1962c) 5901.

Vindau. See VENTSPILS.

Vindava. See VENTA.

Vin·del \ˈvin-dᵊl\. River, Västerbotten co., N Sweden; ab. 280 m. long; flows SE into Ume river.

Vin·de·li·cia \ˌvin-də-ˈlish-(ē-)ə\. Ancient Roman province, cen. Europe, S of the Danube river, including modern Baden-Württemberg and Bavaria, West Germany; later called **Rae·tia Se·cun·da** \ˌrē-sh(ē-)ə-si-ˈkən-də\.

Vin·dhya Mountains \ˌvin-dyə-, -dē-ə-\. Mountain range extending ENE across India from Gujarat to the Ganges valley, dividing the Ganges basin from the Deccan; greatest elevation 3651 ft. N of and parallel with the Narmada river.

Vindhya Pra·desh \-prə-ˈdäsh, -ˈdesh\. Former state, NE cen. India between Uttar Pradesh and Madhya Pradesh; merged 1956 in reorganized Madhya Pradesh.

Vindobona *or* **Vindobna.** See VIENNA 4.

Vin·e·gar Hill \ˌvin-i-gər-\. Hill, co. Wexford, SE Eire, E of Enniscorthy on the Slaney river; 398 ft.; scene of defeat of Irish rebels by General Lake June 21, 1798.

Vine Grove \ˌvīn-\. City, Hardin co., cen. Kentucky, 29 m. SW of Louisville; pop. (1970c) 2987.

Vine·land \ˈvīn-lənd\. 1 City, Cumberland co., SW New Jersey, 11 m. ENE of Bridgeton; pop. (1970c) 47,399; glassware, chemicals, clothing, foundry products; ships eggs; diversified agriculture; Vineland Training School (1888), Cumberland County Coll. (1964).
2 Coast, North America. See VINLAND.

Vineta. See JULIN.

Vine·yard Haven \ˌvin-yərd-\. Town, N Martha's Vineyard, SE Massachusetts, on W shore of **Vineyard Haven Harbor,** inlet of Nantucket Sound; summer resort. See TISBURY.

Vineyard Sound. Body of water, SE of Elizabeth Is. and NW of Martha's Vineyard, SE Massachusetts; connects with Nantucket Sound on the NE and the Atlantic Ocean on the SW.

Vinh \ˈvin(-yə)\. Town near coast, North Vietnam, ab. 160 m. S of Hanoi.

Vinh Long *or* **Vinh·long** \ˈvin-(yə-)ˈlȯŋ\. Town, South Vietnam, on right bank of the Mekong in the delta 65 m. SW of Saigon; pop. (1968e) 32,196; rice.

Vi·ni·ta \vi-ˈnēt-ə\. City, ⊗ of Craig co., NE Oklahoma; pop. (1970c) 5847; hosiery; diversified agriculture.

Vinita Park. City, St. Louis co., E Missouri; pop. (1970c) 3657.

Vin·ja·tin·da·ne \ˈvin-yə-ˌtin-də-nə\. See ROMSDAL.

Vin·kov·ci \ˈviŋ-ˌkȯft-sē\. Town, E Croatia, N Yugoslavia, ab. 85 m. NW of Belgrade; pop. (1965e) 27,000.

Vin·land \ˈvin-lənd\ *also* **Wine·land** \ˈwīn-\ *or* **Vine·land** \ˈvīn-\. A portion of the coast of North America visited and so-called by Norse voyagers, c. 1000 A.D., according to whose accounts it was well wooded and produced fruit, esp. grapes; has been variously located from Labrador, Canada, to New Jersey.

Vin·ni·tsa \ˈvin-ət-sə\. City, ✱ of Vinnitsa Oblast, Ukrainian S.S.R., U.S.S.R., on left bank of the upper Bug and on main railroad line 130 m. SW of Kiev; pop. (1970p) 211,000; fertilizer, machinery, footwear; sugar refining center; founded in 14th cent.; to Russia 1793; World War II held by Germans 1941–Mar. 30, 1944.

Vinnitsa Oblast \-ˈō-bləst, -ˌblast\. Subdivision of the Ukrainian S.S.R., U.S.S.R.; 10,232 sq. m.; pop. (1970p) 2,132,000; ✱ Vinnitsa; sugar beet, corn, wheat, tobacco; livestock raising.

Vin·son Massif \ˌvin(t)-sən-\. Mountain, Sentinel Range, cen. Ellsworth Mts., Antarctica; 16,860 ft.; highest peak in Antarctica; first scaled 1966.

Vintimille. See VENTIMIGLIA.

Vin·ton \ˈvint-ᵊn\. 1 County in Ohio. See table at OHIO.
2 City, ⊗ of Benton co., E cen. Iowa, 19 m. NW of Cedar Rapids; pop. (1970c) 4845; poultry processing.
3 Town, Calcasieu parish, SW Louisiana, 23 m. W of Lake Charles; pop. (1970c) 4845; sugarcane, livestock.
4 Town, Roanoke co., W cen. Virginia, 4 m. NE of Roanoke; pop. (1970c) 6347; motor vehicles; agriculture.

Vin·ton·dale \ˈvint-ᵊn-ˌdāl\. Borough, Cambria co., SW cen. Pennsylvania, 11 m. N of Johnstown; pop. (1970c) 812.

Vion·ville \vyōⁿ-ˈvēl\. Village, Moselle dept., NE France, near Metz and near Mars-la-Tour (*q.v.*).

Viosa. See VIJOSË.

Vi·pi·te·no \ˌvē-pə-ˈtān-(ˌ)ō\ *or Ger.* **Ster·zing** \ˈs(h)tert-siŋ\. Town, Bolzano prov., Trentino-Alto Adige, NE Italy, just S of the Brenner Pass; pop. (1968e) 4336. At end of World War II in Europe U.S. armies from N and S Italy met here May 4, 1945 and surrender of Germans in Italy May 5 ended fighting.

Vipuri. See VYBORG.

Vi·rac \vi-ˈräk\. Port city, ✱ of Catanduanes prov., Catanduanes I., Catanduanes I., Phil.; pop. (1969e) 47,400.

Vir·den \ˈvərd-ᵊn\. 1 City, Macoupin co., SW cen. Illinois, 23 m. SSW of Springfield; pop. (1970c) 3509.
2 Market town, SW Manitoba, Canada, 47 m. W of Brandon; pop. (1971p) 2778; oil wells.

Vire \ˈvir\. 1 River, Normandy, NW France; ab. 75 m. long; flows N past Vire and St-Lô to the Bay of the Seine near Isigny; its estuary in the invasion of June 1944 was the dividing point bet. the two U.S. landing beaches, Omaha Beach and Utah Beach.
2 Town, Calvados dept., NW France, on Vire river 32 m. SW of Caen; pop. (1962c) 10,309. Important Norman stronghold in Middle Ages. Nearby is the valley **Vau–de–Vire** \ˌvōd-ə-\ where Olivier Basselin lived in 15th cent. and supposedly composed the lively drinking songs by which the name of the valley became the source of the word *vaudeville.* In World War II occupied by Allies in Normandy invasion ab. July 29, 1944.

Vír·ge·nes \ˈvi(ə)r-hə-ˌnās\ *or angl.* **Vir·gins** \ˈvər-jənz\ *also* **Cape of the Eleven Thousand Virgins.** Headland on the N side of the E entrance to the Strait of Magellan, S Argentina; adjoins Point Dungeness.

Vir·gi·lio \vir-ˈjēl-yō\ *or formerly* **Pie·to·la** \ˈpyā-tə-lə\. Commune, Mantova prov., Lombardy, N Italy, ab. 3 m. S of Mantua; pop. (1968e) 6100; on site of ancient **An·des,** \ˈan-ˌdēz\, birthplace of Virgil.

Vir·gin \ˈvər-jen\. River, SW Utah and SE Nevada; 200 m. long; rises in W Kane co., S Utah, flows SW across NW corner of Arizona and across border of Nevada, then S into Lake Mead. In Utah portion is Zion Canyon, now included in Zion National Park (see UNITED STATES, *National Parks*).

Virgin Gor·da \-ˈgȯrd-ə\. 1 One of the British Virgin Is., West Indies; 8 sq. m.; pop. (1967e) 800.
2 Peak on the island; 1370 ft.

Vir·gin·ia \vər-ˈjin-yə, -ˈjin-ē-ə\. 1 Eastern state of U.S.A., bounded on N by West Virginia and Maryland, on E by Maryland, Chesapeake Bay, and Atlantic Ocean, on S by North Carolina and Tennessee, on W by Kentucky and West Virginia; 36th state in area, 40,817 sq. m. (land area 39,838 sq. m.); 14th state in population, (1970c) 4,648,494; ✱ Richmond; an original state of the Union, the 10th to ratify the Federal Constitution (June 25, 1788).

Nicknames: Old Dominion; Mother of Presidents; Mother of States. *State flower:* American dogwood. *Motto:* Sic Semper Tyrannis (Ever Thus to Tyrants). *Rivers:* Potomac, forming N cen., NE, and upper E boundary; Shenandoah, flowing NE to the Potomac in West Virginia; James, flowing from W cen. area E into Atlantic Ocean; Roanoke flowing from W area SE across North Carolina border. *Highest point:* Mount Rogers 5729 ft., in Grayson and Smyth cos. *Chief products:* Dairy products, tobacco, vegetables; coal; manufacturing: chemicals; food processing; tobacco products, textiles. *Chief cities:* Norfolk, Richmond, Virginia Beach, Newport News, Portsmouth. See *Table of States* at UNITED STATES. Divided into the following 96 counties and 38 independent cities (for pronunciation of their names, see their individual entries):

NAME	LOCATION	AREA[1] (sq. m.)	POP. (1970c)	CO. SEAT
Accomac	N part of E penin.; coastal	470	29,004	Accomac
Albemarle	cen.	739	37,780	Charlottesville
Alleghany	W	446	12,461	Covington
Amelia	SE cen.	366	7,592	Amelia Courthouse
Amherst	cen.	467	26,072	Amherst
Appomattox	cen.	343	9,784	Appomattox
Arlington	N	24	174,284	Arlington
Augusta	N cen.	986	44,220	Staunton

NAME	LOCATION	AREA[1] (sq. m.)	POP. (1970c)	CO. SEAT
Bath	W	540	5,192	Warm Springs
Bedford	SW cen.	770	26,728	Bedford
Bland	W	369	5,423	Bland
Botetourt	W cen.	548	18,193	Fincastle
Brunswick	S	579	16,172	Lawrenceville
Buchanan	SW	508	32,071	Grundy
Buckingham	cen.	576	10,597	Buckingham
Campbell	S cen.	524	43,319	Rustburg
Caroline	E	544	13,925	Bowling Green
Carroll	S	494	23,092	Hillsville
Charles City	E	184	6,158	Charles City
Charlotte	S	467	12,366	Charlotte Courthouse
Chesterfield	SE cen.	460	77,046	Chesterfield
Clarke	N	174	8,102	Berryville
Craig	W	336	3,524	New Castle
Culpeper	N	389	18,218	Culpeper
Cumberland	cen.	288	6,179	Cumberland
Dickenson	SW	335	16,077	Clintwood
Dinwiddie	SE	507	25,046	Dinwiddie
Essex	E	250	7,099	Tappahannock
Fairfax	NE	399	455,021	Fairfax
Fauquier	N	660	26,375	Warrenton
Floyd	SW	383	9,775	Floyd
Fluvanna	cen.	282	7,621	Palmyra
Franklin	SW cen.	718	28,163	Rocky Mount
Frederick	N	433	28,893	Winchester
Giles	W	356	16,741	Pearisburg
Gloucester	E	225	14,059	Gloucester
Goochland	E cen.	289	10,069	Goochland
Grayson	SW	450	15,439	Independence
Greene	N cen.	153	5,248	Standardsville
Greensville	S	301	9,604	Emporia
Halifax	S	800	30,076	Halifax
Hanover	E cen.	466	37,479	Hanover
Henrico	E cen.	232	154,364	Richmond
Henry	S	384	50,901	Martinsville
Highland	W	416	2,529	Monterey
Isle of Wight	SE	319	18,285	Isle of Wight
James City	E	148	17,853	Williamsburg
King and Queen	E	318	5,491	King and Queen Courthouse
King George	E	178	8,039	King George
King William	E	278	7,497	King William
Lancaster	E	142	9,126	Lancaster
Lee	SW tip	434	20,321	Jonesville
Loudoun	N	517	37,150	Leesburg
Louisa	cen.	514	14,004	Louisa
Lunenburg	S	443	11,687	Lunenburg
Madison	N	327	8,638	Madison
Mathews	E	87	7,168	Mathews
Mecklenburg	S	626	29,426	Boydton
Middlesex	E	132	6,295	Saluda
Montgomery	W	395	47,157	Christiansburg
Nansemond	SE	402	35,166	Suffolk
Nelson	cen.	468	11,702	Lovingston
New Kent	E	212	5,300	New Kent
Northampton	S part of E penin.	226	14,442	Eastville
Northumberland	E	200	9,239	Heathsville
Nottoway	S cen.	308	14,260	Nottoway
Orange	N cen.	354	13,792	Orange
Page	N	316	16,581	Luray
Patrick	S	469	15,282	Stuart
Pittsylvania	S	1,012	58,789	Chatham
Powhatan	E cen.	268	7,696	Powhatan
Prince Edward	S cen.	357	14,379	Farmville
Prince George	SE	281	29,092	Prince George
Prince William	NE	345	111,102	Manassas
Pulaski	SW	327	29,564	Pulaski
Rappahannock	N	267	5,199	Washington
Richmond	E	192	6,504	Warsaw
Roanoke	W cen.	277	67,339	Salem
Rockbridge	W cen.	604	16,637	Lexington
Rockingham	N	868	47,890	Harrisonburg
Russell	SW	483	24,533	Lebanon
Scott	SW	539	24,376	Gate City
Shenandoah	N	507	22,852	Woodstock
Smyth	SW	435	31,349	Marion
Southampton	SE	607	18,582	Courtland
Spotsylvania	NE	409	16,424	Spotsylvania
Stafford	NE	271	24,587	Stafford
Surry	SE	280	5,882	Surry
Sussex	SE	496	11,464	Sussex
Tazewell	SW	522	39,816	Tazewell
Warren	N	219	15,301	Front Royal
Washington	SW	579	40,835	Abingdon
Westmoreland	E	236	12,142	Montross
Wise	SW	411	35,947	Wise
Wythe	SW	460	22,139	Wytheville
York	SE	123	33,203	Yorktown

[1]Area = land area.

INDEPENDENT CITIES

NAME[1]	COUNTY	AREA[2] (sq. m.)	POP. (1970c)
Alexandria	Arlington	15	110,938
Bedford	Bedford	7	6,011
Bristol	Washington	4	14,857
Buena Vista	Rockbridge	3	6,425
Charlottesville	Albemarle	6	38,880
Chesapeake		344	89,580
Clifton Forge	Alleghany	2	5,501
Colonial Heights	Chesterfield	8	15,097
Covington	Alleghany	4	10,060
Danville	Pittsylvania	14	46,391
Emporia	Greensville	2	5,300
Fairfax	Fairfax	6	21,970
Falls Church	Fairfax	2	10,772
Franklin	Southampton	4	6,880
Fredericksburg	Spotslyvania	6	14,450
Galax	Carroll and Grayson	3	6,278
Hampton		57	120,779
Harrisonburg	Rockingham	3	14,605
Hopewell	Prince George	7	23,471
Lexington	Rockbridge	2	7,597
Lynchburg	Campbell	23	54,083
Martinsville	Henry	10	19,653
Newport News		75	138,177
Norfolk		50	307,951
Norton	Wise	3	4,172
Petersburg	Dinwiddie	8	36,103
Portsmouth		18	110,963
Radford	Montgomery	5	11,596
Richmond	Henrico	37	249,430
Roanoke	Roanoke	26	92,115
Salem	Roanoke	8	21,982
South Boston	Halifax	2	6,889
Staunton	Augusta	9	24,504
Suffolk	Nansemond	2	9,858
Virginia Beach		2	172,106
Waynesboro	Augusta	7	16,707
Williamsburg	James City and York	3	9,069
Winchester	Frederick	3	14,643

[1]These 38 cities have the status of counties. They are located geographically in the counties named, which do not include their area and population figures. Counties are not given for cities which have annexed their parent county.
[2]Area = land area.

History: Attempts made by Sir Walter Raleigh to found settlements 1584–87; 1st royal charter to London (Virginia) Company 1606, and 1st permanent settlement, made by colonists sent out by this company, at Jamestown 1607; first popular assembly in America convened 1619; one of the first colonies to express resistance to the Stamp Act and other British taxes 1765; active in movement for independence; scene of surrender of Lord Cornwallis at Yorktown 1781; NW part of western lands ceded to U.S. 1784, S part admitted to the Union as the state of Kentucky 1792; ratified the Federal Constitution June 25, 1788; passed ordinance of secession Apr. 17, 1861; W counties remained loyal to the Union, separated from Virginia 1861 and admitted to the Union as the state of West Virginia 1863; scene of many battles of the Civil War, notably Bull Run (first and second), Fair Oaks, Chancellorsville, Fredericksburg, Wilderness, Cold Harbor, and many engagements in Shenandoah Valley; readmitted to Union Jan. 26, 1870.

2 City, ⊗ of Cass co., W cen. Illinois, 30 m. NW of Springfield; pop. (1970c) 1789; agriculture.

3 City, St. Louis co., NE Minnesota, 20 m. E of Hibbing; pop. (1970c) 12,540; lumber, dairy products; lake resort; iron mines; Mesabi State Junior Coll. (1918).

4 Town, Orange Free State, Rep. of South Africa, ab. 80 m. NE of Bloemfontein; pop. (1967e) 48,400.

Virginia Beach. Independent city, SE Virginia, on Atlantic Ocean 18 m. E of Norfolk; 2 sq. m.; pop. (1970c) 172,106; summer resort and residential community.

Virginia City. 1 Town, ⊗ of Madison co., SW Montana; pop. (1970c) 149; founded 1863, after discovery of gold in Alder Gulch nearby; territorial capital 1865–75.

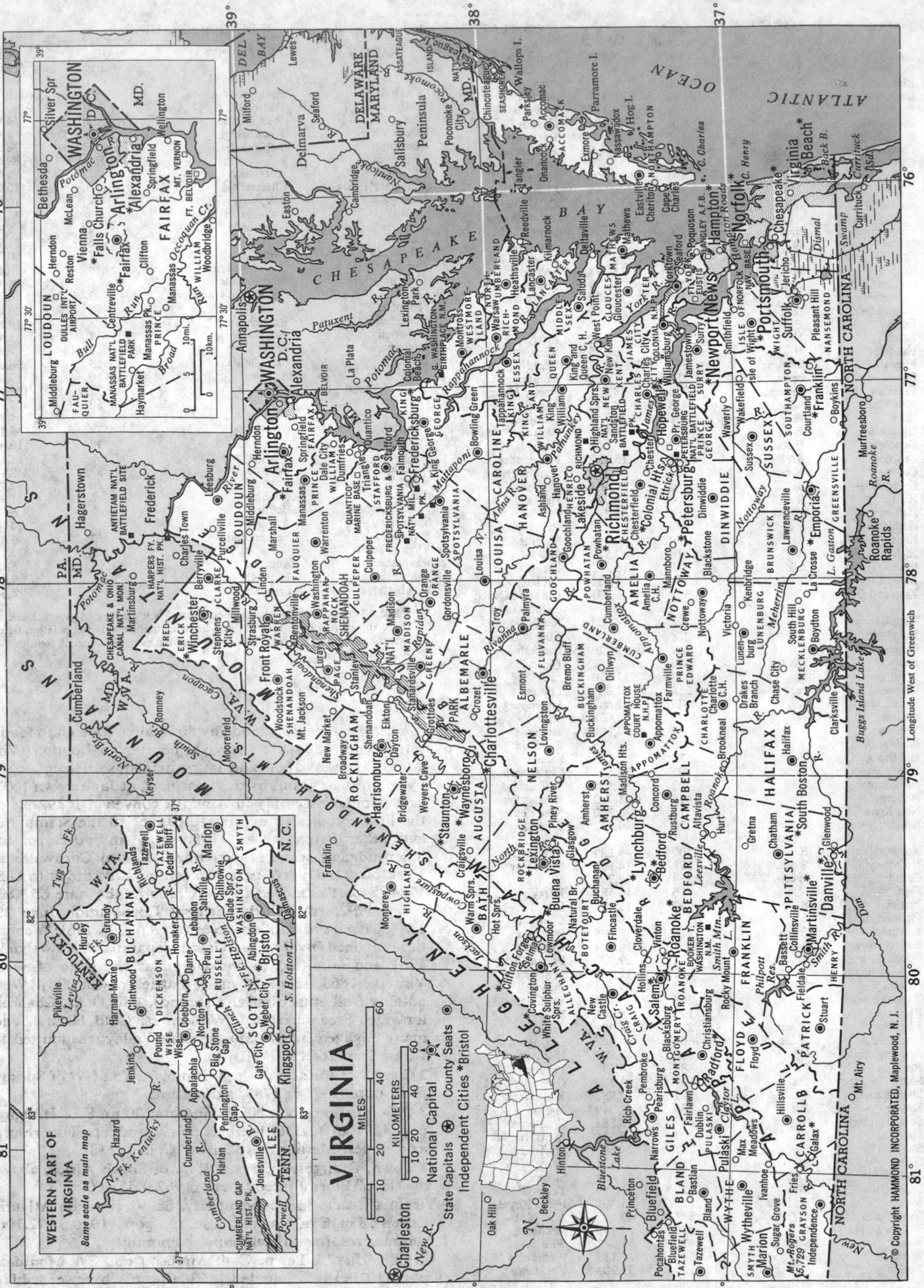
VIRGINIA
MILES
KILOMETERS
State Capitals
National Capital
County Seats
Independent Cities *Bristol
WESTERN PART OF VIRGINIA
Same scale as main map
WASHINGTON D.C.
ATLANTIC OCEAN
CHESAPEAKE BAY
NORTH CAROLINA
Richmond
Norfolk
Portsmouth
Newport News
Hampton
Virginia Beach
Chesapeake
Roanoke
Lynchburg
Charlottesville
Alexandria
Arlington
Petersburg
Danville
Longitude West of Greenwich
© Copyright HAMMOND INCORPORATED, Maplewood, N.J.

2 Village, ⊗ of Storey co., W Nevada, 16 m. SSE of Reno; settled 1859 at time of discovery on this site of the Comstock Lode, a gold and silver lode with many bonanzas, which until c. 1886 yielded half the silver output of the U.S.; now a ghost town.

Virginia Pass. Mountain pass, Tuolumne co., cen. California, at N end of Yosemite National Park; 10,500 ft.; one of passes most used by emigrants and explorers in crossing the Sierra Nevada Mts.

Virginia Range. Small range S of Pyramid Lake, W Nevada; highest point **Virginia Peak** 8366 ft.

Vir·gin Islands \ˌvər-jən-\. Group of islands, NE West Indies, westernmost of the Lesser Antilles, ab. 60 m. E of Puerto Rico. Divided bet. Great Britain and U.S.A.: (1) The **British Virgin Islands,** a British colony; 59 sq. m.; pop. (1967e) 8650; ✱ Road Town (on Tortola I.); chief islands Tortola, Virgin Gorda, Anegada, Jost Van Dyke, Peter, and Norman; includes also ab. 24 other small islands. Chief products fruit and tobacco. (2) *Officially,* the **Virgin Islands of the United States;** *before 1917* **Danish West Indies,** consisting of the islands St. Thomas, St. Croix, and St. John, and ab. 50 islets; 133 sq. m.; pop. (1970p) 63,200; ✱ Charlotte Amalie. **Virgin Islands National Park** is situated on St. John I. (see UNITED STATES, *National Parks*). Chief products sugar, bay oil, bay rum; cattle.

History: Discovered and named by Columbus 1493; St. Croix occupied by Dutch, English, Spanish; St. Thomas occupied by Denmark 1666 and 1672, St. John in 1684 and St. Croix in 1733 (the three islands estab. as a Danish colony 1754); British group, part of Leeward Islands colony until formation of West Indies Federation, of which the British Virgin Islands were not a member, acquired by England 1666. Danish group, known as Danish West Indies, subject of treaties of sale bet. U.S. and Denmark in 1867 and 1902, but finally acquired by U.S. by purchase 1917 and name changed to Virgin Islands; until 1931 administered by Navy Department; given Organic Act 1936 (revised 1954) and universal suffrage 1938.

Virgin Mountains. Range, NW Arizona, extending along E bank of Virgin river into SE Nevada; highest peak **Virgin Peak** 8075 ft.

Virgin Passage. Channel bet. W St. Thomas I. of the Virgin Is. of the United States and Culebra I.; off E end of Puerto Rico; ab. 9 m. wide.

Virgins. See VÍRGENES.

Viroconium. See WROXETER.

Vi·ro·flay \ˌvir-ə-ˈflā\. Commune, Yvelines dept., N France, near Versailles; pop. (1968c) 16,352.

Vi·ro·qua \vī-ˈrōk-wə\. City, ⊗ of Vernon co., SW Wisconsin, 25 m. SE of La Crosse; pop. (1970c) 3739; dairy, tobacco farms; Vernon County Teachers Coll. (1909).

Vi·ro·vi·ti·ca \ˌvir-ō-ˈvēt-ət-ˌsä\ *or Hung.* **Ve·rö·cze** \ˈver-ət-ˌsä\. Town, Croatia, N Yugoslavia, 65 m. E of Zagreb; pop. (1965e) 12,000.

Vir·rat \ˈvir-(ˌ)at\. Town, Häme prov., SW cen. Finland, at N end of Näsijärvi; pop. (1970e) 10,386.

Virts. See VĀRTS-JĀRV.

Vi·ru·du·na·gar *or* **Vi·ru·dhu·na·gar** \ˈvir-ə-ˌdən-ə-ˌgər\. Town, Tamil Nadu, India, ab. 25 m. SW of Madurai; pop. (1961c) 54,827.

Vi·ru Harbour \ˌvi(ə)r-(ˌ)ü-\. Harbor, W side of S end of New Georgia I., cen. Solomon Is., W Pacific Ocean; taken by U.S. Marines June 30, 1943.

Vi·run·ga Mountains \və-ˈrüŋ-gə-\ *or* **Mfum·bi·ro Mountains** \em-ˈfüm-bə-ˌrō-\ *also* **Mu·fum·bi·ro Mountains** \mü-ˌfüm-bə-(ˌ)rō-\. Range of volcanic mountains, E Zaire, SW Uganda, and Rwanda, E Africa, N of Lake Kivu; highest peak Karisimbi 14,187 ft.

Vi·ry–Cha·til·lon \vi-ˌrē-ˌshä-tē-ˈ(y)ōⁿ\. Commune, Essone dept., N France, S of Paris; pop. (1968c) 27,045.

Vis \ˈvēs\ *or Ital.* **Lis·sa** \ˈlis-ə, ˈlēs-\ *or anc.* **Is·sa** \ˈis-ə\. 1 Yugoslav island, Adriatic Sea, SSW of Split; 33 sq. m.; pop. (1961e) 6798; has fertile central plain; highest point 1926 ft. in SW; wine, citrus fruit; fishing.

History: Ruled by Venice from 996, held by French during Napoleonic Wars until British victory over Franco-Venetian squadron Mar. 13, 1811 in nearby waters; ceded to Austria 1815; nearby waters again scene of naval battle July 20, 1866 in which Austrians under Admiral Tegetthoff defeated Italians under Persano; island became Yugoslav after World War I; occupied by Italy in World War II.

2 Chief town on the island; palace of Venetian counts; ruins of ancient city of Issa.

Vi·sa·lia \vi-ˈsāl-yə\. City, ⊗ of Tulare co., S cen. California, 38 m. SE of Fresno; pop. (1970c) 27,268; electronic components, canned fruit, dairy products; Coll. of the Sequoias (1926); settled 1852.

Vi·sa·yan Islands \və-ˌsī-ən-\ *or* **Bi·sa·yas** \bə-ˈsī-əz\. Large group of islands, cen. Phil.; 23,944 sq. m.; pop. (1970p) 9,756,370; inhabited chiefly by the Visayan peoples; chief islands Panay, Samar, Leyte, Cebu, Negros, Bohol, Masbate, and the Romblon group; adjacent are many smaller islands.

Visayan Sea. Open body of interisland water, cen. Phil., bordered on N by Masbate, on E by Leyte and Cebu, on S by Negros, and on W by Panay; connects with Sibuyan Sea by Jintotolo Channel, with Mindanao Sea by Tanon Strait, and with Sulu Sea by Guimaras Strait.

Vis·by \ˈviz-bē\ *or Ger.* **Wis·by** \ˈviz-bē\. Seaport on Gotland I., in the Baltic Sea; ⊗ of Gotland co., Sweden; pop. (1970e) 19,319; seaside resort; a major commercial center of northern Europe from 10th to 14th cent.; member of Hanseatic League.

Vis·count Mel·ville Sound \ˌvī-kaůnt-ˈmel-ˌvil-, -vəl-\ *or formerly* **Melville Sound.** Body of water, Franklin dist., Northwest Territories, N Canada, bet. Melville I. on the N and N Victoria I.

Vi·sé \vē-ˈzā\. Commune, Liège prov., Belgium, NE of Liège; pop. (1969e) 6850; burned Aug. 1914; rebuilt.

Vi·seu *also* **Vi·zeu** \vi-ˈzeů\. 1 District of N cen. Portugal. See table at PORTUGAL.

2 Commune, its ✱, 41 m. NE of Coimbra; pop. (1960c) 17,365; 12th cent. cathedral; Roman, Visigothic, and Moorish ruins.

Vi·sha·kha·pat·nam \vi-ˌshäk-ə-ˈpət-nəm\ *or* **Vi·za·ga·pa·tam** \vi-ˌzäg-ə-ˈpət-əm\. City, NE Andhra Pradesh, E India, on Bay of Bengal 380 m. NE of Madras; pop. (1961c) 182,000; only protected harbor on the Coromandel Coast; exports sugar, manganese ore, peanuts; shipyard, oil refinery; univ. (1926; at N end of bay). English factory founded 1683; captured by French 1757 and recaptured 1758; harbor improved 1933.

Visla. See VISTULA.

Vis·lin·ski Za·liv \vis-ˌlin(t)-skē-ˈzä-lif\ *or Pol.* **Za·lew Wiś·la·ny** \ˌzä-lef-vēsh-ˈlän-ē\ *or Ger.* **Fri·sches Haff** \ˈfrish-əs-ˌhäf\. Lagoon on SW coast of Baltic Sea; 56 m. long, 4 to 12 m. wide; separated from Gulf of Danzig by long, narrow spit of land (**Bal·ti·ska·ya Ko·sa** \bäl-ˌtē-ski-ə-ˈkō-sə\ *or Pol.* **Mie·rze·ja Wiś·la·na** \mye-ˌzhe-yä-vēsh-ˈlän-ə\ *or Ger.* **Fri·sche Neh·rung** \ˌfrish-ə-ˈnar-ůŋ\) which has an opening at N end; receives the Pregolya at NE; formerly in East Prussia; divided 1945 bet. Poland and U.S.S.R.

Vi·so, Mount \-ˈvē-(ˌ)zō\ *or* **Mon·vi·so** \mōm-\. Peak, Torino prov., Piedmont, Italy, 40 m. SW of Turin near the French border; 12,602 ft.; highest peak in Cottian Alps.

Vis·ta \ˈvis-tə\. Urban community (unincorporated), San Diego co., SW California, N of San Diego; pop. (1970c) 24,688; truck farms.

Vi·stri·tsa \vi-'strēt-sə\ *or Gk.* **Ali·ák·mon** \äl-'yäk-(,)mōn\ *or anc.* **Hal·i·ac·mon** \,hal-ē-'ak-,män\. River, W Macedonia, N Greece; 195 m. long; rises near Florina and flows SE and NE into head of Gulf of Salonika.

Vis·tu·la \'vis(h)-chə-lə, 'vis-tə-\ *or Pol.* **Wis·ła** \'vē-(,)slä\ *or Russ.* **Vis·la** \'vē-slə\ *or Ger.* **Weich·sel** \'vīk-səl\. River, Poland; 675 m. long; rises on N slope of the Carpathian Mts. in SW Poland; flows in a great curve NE, N, and NW through Warsaw and Toruń, then N into the Baltic Sea at Gdańsk; navigable for most of its course; its chief tributaries on left are Bzura and Pilica; on right the Bug, San, Wisłoka, and Dunajec.

Visurgis. See WESER.

Vi·tebsk \'vē-,tepsk, -,tebsk, və-'\. City, ✱ of Vitebsk Oblast, NE Belorussian S.S.R., U.S.S.R., on both banks of the Western Dvina 140 m. NE of Minsk; pop. (1970p) 231,000; on the Riga-Moscow railroad; important industrial center, producing machine tools, furniture, radios, hosiery, alcohol; several medieval churches.

History: First mentioned 1021; trade center and chief town of an independent principality for ab. 200 years; came under Lithuania 1320 and under Poland in 16th cent.; held by Russia 1654–67 and finally came under Russia after First Partition of Poland 1772; in World War II occupied by Germans July 1941–June 1944; heavily damaged.

Vitebsk Oblast \-'ó-bləst, -,blast\. Subdivision of the Belorussian S.S.R., U.S.S.R.; 15,483 sq. m.; pop. (1970p) 1,370,000; ✱ Vitebsk; in basin of the Western Dvina with extensive forests and many swamp regions. Economy primarily agricultural (rye, flax, livestock, dairying); chief towns Vitebsk and Orsha; created 1938.

Vi·ter·bo \vi-'te(ə)r-(,)bō\. **1** Province of Latium, cen. Italy. See table at ITALY.

2 *or anc.* **Vi·cus El·bii** \,vī-kəs-'el-bē-,ī\. Commune, its ✱, 42 m. NNW of Rome; pop. (1968e) 52,522; center of an agricultural region; 12th cent. Gothic cathedral; 13th cent. episcopal palace; 13th cent. town hall; 15th cent. Farnese palace; churches of 9th, 11th, and 12th cents.; medieval walls and gates; sulfur baths nearby. Principal town in Countess Matilda's dominions bequeathed to pope at end of 11th cent., forming part of the Patrimony of St. Peter.

Vi·ti·az Strait \,vēt-ē-,az-\. Channel, separating island of New Guinea from Long I. and Umboi I. and connecting Bismarck Sea with Solomon Sea; ab. 150 m. long by 35 m. wide.

Vi·ti Le·vu \,vēt-ē-'lev-(,)ü\. Island, Fiji, SW Pacific Ocean; 90 m. from E to W and 50 m. from N to S; 4010 sq. m.; largest island in Fiji group; chief town Suva, ✱ of Fiji. Most of it mountainous; highest point Mt. Tomaniivi 4341 ft. Has several sizable streams; largest is the Rewa in the E. Most of its villages on the coast on a highway that encircles the island. Grows coffee, sugar, cinchona, coconuts, and tropical fruit and vegetables; exports copra and sugar.

Vi·tim \və-'tēm\. River, Russian S.F.S.R., U.S.S.R.; 1133 m. long; rises in cen. Buryat A.S.S.R., flows NE and N forming in part the NE boundary of the republic, then across NE Irkutsk Oblast to join the Lena on SW border of Yakutsk A.S.S.R.

Vi·to·cha National Park \'vē-tò-chä-\. National park, Bulgaria; 61 sq. m.; mountainous region; established 1933.

Vi·to·ria \vi-'tōr-ē-ə, -'tór-\. City, ✱ of Álava prov., N Spain, 50 m. W of Pamplona; pop. (1970p) 136,878; bicycles, agricultural machinery, furniture; sugar refining, tanning, distilling; 12th cent. fortress-cathedral; 13th cent. Franciscan monastery; scene of battle June 21, 1813 in which Wellington defeated the French, driving them from Spain (Peninsular War).

Vi·tó·ria \vi-'tōr-ē-ə, -'tór-\. Seaport, ✱ of Espírito Santo state, E Brazil, on Espírito Santo river ab. 250 m. NE of Rio de Janeiro; munic. pop. (1970p) 135,570; ships coffee; textiles; sugar refineries; univ. (1961); founded 1535; until 1960's leading iron-ore port of Brazil.

Vitória de San·to An·tão \-də-,sa(ⁿ)n-tō-a(ⁿ)n-'taùⁿ\. City, E Pernambuco state, E Brazil, on railroad just W of Recife; munic. pop. (1968e) 70,702.

Vi·to·ri·no Frei·re \,vi-tò-,rē-nō-'frer-ə\. Municipality, Maranhão state, NE Brazil; pop. (1968e) 88,215.

Vi·tré \vi-'trā\. Manufacturing and commercial town, Ille-et-Vilaine dept., NW France, 22 m. E of Rennes; pop. (1968c) 11,343; formerly a Huguenot stronghold.

Vi·try–le–Fran·çois \vi-,trē-lə-fräⁿ-'swä\. Town, Marne dept., NE France, on the Marne 20 m. SE of Châlons-sur-Marne; pop. (1968c) 16,879; built 1545 by Francis I; scene of fighting during battle of the Marne 1914; ab. 2½ m. to the NE is the village of **Vitry–en–Per·thois** \-äⁿ-per-'twä\ *or formerly* **Vitry–le–Brû·lé** \-lə-brü-'lā\, (pop. [1962c] 712), which suffered the burning of its church 1142 by Louis VII and destruction at hands of Charles V 1544.

Vitry–sur–Seine \-,sù(ə)r-'sān, -'sen\. Commune, Val-de-Marne dept., N France, SSE suburb of Paris; pop. (1968c) 77,846; chemicals, paper, boilers.

Vit·tel \vi-'tel\. Town, Vosges dept., NE France, ab. 30 m. W of Épinal; pop. (1962c) 5479; mineral waters; resort.

Vit·to·ria \vi-'tōr-ē-ə, -'tór-\. Commune, Ragusa prov., SE Sicily, Italy, 11 m. W of Ragusa; pop. (1968e) 46,938; wine, olive oil; 18th cent. cathedral.

Vittoriosa. See COSPICUA.

Vit·to·rio Ve·ne·to \vi-,tōr-ē-(,)ō-'ven-ə-,tō, -,tór-, -'vā-nə-\. Commune, Treviso prov., Veneto, NE Italy, 23 m. N of Treviso; pop. (1968e) 29,697; mineral baths; summer resort; cathedral; scene of last major battle in World War I bet. Austrian and Italian forces Oct. 24–Nov. 3, 1918, culminating in Italian victory and armistice of Villa Giusti Nov. 4, 1918.

Vi·tu Islands \,vē-(,)tü-\. Group of small islands, S Bismarck Sea, off the N coast of W end of New Britain I., Bismarck Archipelago, W Pacific; largest is Garove I.

Vitz·nau \'fits-,naù\. Village near Rigi Mt. in Lucerne canton, cen. Switzerland, on Lake of Lucerne; pop. (1970c) 930; resort.

Vi·va·rais \,vē-və-'rā\. Ancient district, SE France, now mostly in department of Ardèche; ✱ Viviers.

Vivario Cays. See VIVORILLO CAYS.

Vi·ve·ro \vi-'ve(ə)r-(,)ō\. Commune, Lugo prov., NW Spain, on Bay of Biscay 42 m. N of Lugo; pop. (1970p) 12,942; agricultural produce; commercial fishing; fish-salting works.

Vive–Saint–Éloi. See SINT-ELOOIS-VIJVE.

Viv·i·an \'viv-ē-ən\. Town, Caddo parish, NW corner of Louisiana, 28 m. NNW of Shreveport; pop. (1970c) 4096; oil wells and refineries.

Vi·viers \vē-'vyā\. Town, Ardèche dept., SE France, on the Rhone SSE of Privas; pop. (1962c) 3500; cathedral with six Gobelin tapestries; capital of ancient Vivarais.

Vivis. See VEVEY.

Vi·vo·ri·llo Cays \,vē-və-,rē-yō-'kēz, -'kāz\ *or* **Vi·va·rio Cays** \vi-,vär-ē-,ō-\. Group of small islands, Carribean Sea, E of NE coast of Honduras.

Vizagapatam. See VISHAKHAPATNAM.

Viz·ca·ya \vis-'kī-ə, vith-\ *or* **Bis·ca·ya** \bis-\ *or Eng.* **Bis·cay** \'bis-(,)kā, -kē\. Province of Spain. See table at SPAIN.

Vizeu. See VISEU.

Viz·i·a·nag·ram \,viz-ē-ə-'nəg-rəm\. Town, NE Andhra Pradesh, E India, 410 m. NNE of Madras and just NNE of Vishakhapatnam; pop. (1961c) 76,800; cotton textiles; 18th cent. fort and small military cantonment.

Vi·zille \vi-'zēl\. Town, Isère dept., SE France, S of Grenoble; pop. (1962c) 6729; Roman military post; château where the estates of Dauphiné met July 21, 1788 in the tennis court (a year before the Oath of the Tennis Court taken by the National Assembly) and made a protest which foreshadowed the Revolution.

Vlaanderen. See FLANDERS.

Vlaar·ding·en \'vlär-diŋ-ən\. Commune, South Holland prov., SW Netherlands, on the Nieuwe Maas river 6 m. W of Rotterdam; pop. (1970e) 79,085; metal goods, chemicals, lumber, dairy products; shipyards, commercial fisheries.

Vladikavkaz. See ORDZHONIKIDZE.

Vlad·i·mir \'vlad-ə-ˌmi(ə)r, vlə-'dē-\. 1 Former principality, cen. Russia; ✱ Vladimir; founded by Andrei Bogolyubski from Kiev c. 1150; later, with Suzdal and Rostov, a part of joint principality under princes of Vladimir; its last ruler, Ivan I (Kalita) removed court to Moscow; absorbed by Moscow in 15th cent.

2 City, ✱ of Vladimir Oblast, Russian S.F.S.R., U.S.S.R., on N bank of Klyazma river 110 m. E of Moscow; pop. (1970p) 234,000; textiles, tractors, plastics; two 12th cent. cathedrals (restored in 19th cent.).

History: An old town, founded possibly as early as 991; capital of Vladimir principality from 1157; sacked by Tatars 1238 and 1239; seat of Orthodox metropolitan 1300; court transferred to Moscow 1328 and city brought under authority of Moscow 15th cent.; made provincial capital 1796; developed industrially after Revolution.

Vladimir Oblast \-'ō-bləst, -ˌblast\. Subdivision of the Russian S.F.S.R., U.S.S.R.; 11,197 sq. m.; pop. (1970p) 1,512,000; ✱ Vladimir; rye, oats, potatoes; textiles, engineering goods, electronic equipment.

Vladimir–Vo·lyn·ski \-və-'lin(t)-skē\ *or Pol.* **Wło·dzi·mierz** \vló-'jē-ˌmyesh\. City, Volyn Oblast, Ukrainian S.S.R., U.S.S.R., 45 m. WNW of Lutsk; pop. (1967e) 23,000; food processing; 12th cent. cathedral; founded in 10th cent. and formerly capital of Volhynia, a principality known in the 12th and 13th cents. as Vladimir in Volhynia. Its name was Latinized as Lodomeria (*q.v.*).

Vla·di·vos·tok \ˌvlad-ə-və-'stäk, -'väs-ˌtäk\. Seaport city, ✱ of Primorski Krai, Russian S.F.S.R., U.S.S.R., at the S tip of a peninsula extending into Peter the Great Bay; pop. (1970p) 442,000; its harbor, the Golden Horn, is an inlet of Amur Bay; E terminus of Trans-Siberian R.R., principal Russian Pacific seaport, and main base of the Soviet Pacific fleet; extensive dock and storage facilities; produces lumber, flour, tea, beer, light machinery; shipyards; base for whaling and fishing fleets; univ. (1956). Harbor freezes in winter but can be kept open with icebreakers.

History: Founded 1860; made naval base 1872; connected with Europe by Chinese Eastern Railway (then under Russian lease 1897); became free commercial port 1904; scene of rebellion 1905–06; Trans-Siberian R.R. completed to Vladivostok 1908; major development as commercial center and military and naval base since the Russian Revolution.

Vlagt·wed·de \'flakt-ˌved-ə\. Commune, Groningen prov., NE Netherlands, 25 m. SE of Groningen near West German border; pop. (1970e) 16,622.

Vlie·land \'vlē-ˌlänt\. Island of the Netherlands, West Frisian Is., N of Texel I.; 10 m. long; administratively a part of North Holland prov.

Vlie Stroom *or* **Vlie·stroom** \'vlē-ˌstrōm\. Strait bet. Vlieland I. and Terschelling I. in the West Frisian Is., connecting the North Sea with Wadden Zee.

Vlis·sing·en \'vlis-iŋ-ən\ *or Eng.* **Flush·ing** \'fləsh-iŋ\. Commune and seaport, Walcheren I., Zeeland prov., SW Netherlands; pop. (1970e) 40,197; chief town on the island, on its S shore and on Schelde estuary; commercial and naval port and seaside resort; steamer line to Harwich, England. Birthplace of Admiral de Ruyter. Objective of Allied Walcheren expedition Oct.–Nov. 1944, to clear Schelde estuary for access to Antwerp.

Vlodava. See WŁODAWA.

Vlo·rë \'vlōr-ə, 'vlór-\ *or* **Vlo·na** \'vlō-nə\ *or Ital.* **Va·lo·na** \və-'lō-nə\. 1 Province of SW Albania. See table at ALBANIA.

2 *or formerly* **Av·lo·na** \av-'lō-nə\ *or anc.* **Au·lon** \'ó-ˌlän\. Seaport town, its ✱, on Bay of Vlorë; pop. (1967e) 50,351; olive oil, cement, alcohol, canned fish; commercial fisheries, rice mills; harbor protected by island of Sazan on W.

History: Important in wars bet. Normans and Byzantines 11th–12th cents.; under Turkish rule 1464–1912; independence of Albania proclaimed here Nov. 28, 1912; occupied by Italians 1914–20 and again in World War II 1939–44.

Vlorë, Bay of *or* **Bay of Vlona** *or Alb.* **Gji–i–Vlo·rës** \ˌgyē-ē-'vlōr-əs, -'vlór-\. Inlet of SE Adriatic Sea on SW coast of Albania; harbor for the city of Vlorë.

Vlotslavsk. See WŁOCŁAWEK.

Vl·ta·va \'vəl-tə-və\ *or Ger.* **Mol·dau** \'mōl-ˌdaů, 'mól-\. River, Czech S.R., Czechoslovakia; 267 m. long; flows SE, then N through České Budějovice and Prague into the Elbe river 20 m. N of Prague; navigable as far as České Budějovice.

Vluck Point \'vlək-\. Cape, NW coast of St. Thomas I., Virgin Is. of the U.S., West Indies, on E side of entrance to Santa Maria Bay.

Vly, Mount \-'vlī, -'flī\. Peak in the Catskill Mts., Greene co., SE New York; 3476 ft.

Vodena. See EDESSA 1.

Vod·njan \'vōd-(ˌ)nyän\ *or Ital.* **Di·gna·no d'Is·tria** \dēn-ˌyän-ō-'dis-trē-ə\ *or anc.* **At·tin·i·a·num** \ə-ˌtin-ē-'ā-nəm\. Commune, Istrian Penin., NW Yugoslavia, 8 m. N of Pula; before World War I belonged to Austria; in Italy 1918–47; to Yugoslavia 1947.

Voer·de \'fór-də, 'vór-\. City, North Rhine-Westphalia, West Germany, 15 m. NW of Essen; pop. (1969e) 27,420.

Vogelkop. See DOBERAI.

Vo·gels·berg \'fō-gəls-ˌbərg, -ˌbe(ə)rg\. Mountain range, Hesse, West Germany; highest point 2539 ft.

Vogesus. See VOSGES 1.

Vo·ghe·ra \vō-'ge(ə)r-ə\. Commune, Pavia prov., Lombardy, N Italy, 15 m. SSW of Pavia; pop. (1968e) 39,841; 14th cent. castle; churches of San Lorenzo (rebuilt 1605) and Sant'Ilario (remodeled 12th cent.).

Voi \'vói\. Town, Coast prov., SE Kenya, E Africa, 90 m. NW of Mombasa; railroad junction on the Mombasa-Nairobi line.

Voiotia. See BOEOTIA 2.

Voi·ron \vwa-'rōⁿ\. Industrial commune, Isère dept., SE France, 15 m. NNW of Grenoble; pop. (1962c) 18,395; manufactures textiles, paper, liqueurs, chemical products, lumber.

Voj·vo·dina *or* **Voi·vo·di·na** *also* **Voy·vo·di·na** \'vói-və-ˌdē-nə, -dē-ˌnä\. Autonomous province, N Serbia, Yugoslavia; pop. (1971p) 1,950,268; ✱ Novi Sad; formerly part of Hungary.

Volaterrae. See VOLTERRA.

Vol·cán \vōl-'kän\. Peak, E Coquimbo prov., cen. Chile, near Argentina border; 18,077 ft.

Volcán de Pu·ra·cé National Park \-dā-ˌpür-ə-'sā-\. National park, Colombia; 46 sq. m.; established 1961.

Volcano Bay. See UCHIURA BAY.

Vol·ca·no Island \väl-ˌkā-(ˌ)nō-, vól-\. Island in Lake Taal, Batangas, Phil. See TAAL 1.

Volcano Islands; *Jap.* **Ka·zan Ret·to** \ˌkäz-än-'ret-(ˌ)ō\ *also* **Iwo Retto** \ˌē-wō-\. Group of three small islands, W Pacific Ocean S of Bonin Is., 25°N, 141°E; comprise Iwo Jima (*q.v.*) or Naka Iwo, Kita Iwo, and Minami Iwo; administered by U.S. 1945–68; returned to Japan 1968.

Vol·chansk \vəl-'chän(t)sk\. Town, Kharkov Oblast, Ukrainian S.S.R., U.S.S.R., ab. 40 m. NE of Kharkov; pop. (1967e) 20,000.

Vol·ga \'väl-gə, 'vól-, 'vōl-\ *or anc.* **Rha** \'rā\. River, Russian S.F.S.R., U.S.S.R.; 2293 m. long; longest river in Europe; area of drainage basin 532,818 sq. m.; rises W of Lake Seliger in the Valdai Hills in N Kalinin Oblast, flows with greatly winding course E and SE to Kazan in Tatar A.S.S.R., then S in great bend at Kuibyshev, SW to Volgograd and SE to the Caspian Sea near Astrakhan; navigable for almost its entire course but in some sections too shallow for large vessels; subject to great floods. Has extensive delta ab. 75 m. wide. Fed by many tributaries; on left bank: Tvertsa, Mologa, Kostroma, Unzha, Vetluga, Kama, and Samara; on right bank: Oka, Sura. Chief cities on its banks are Kalinin, Rybinsk, Yaroslavl, Kostroma, Gorki, Kazan, Kuibyshev, Saratov, Volgograd, and Astrakhan. Fishing is important on its lower course; connects by canals in several places with Baltic rivers (see VOLGA-BALTIC WATERWAY) and in lower course near Volgograd with the Don. Important for power production, irrigation, flood control (see RYBINSK RESERVOIR), and transportation.

Volga–Bal·tic Waterway \\-'bȯl-tik-\\ *or formerly* **Ma·ri·insk Waterway** \\mə-r(y)i-'ēn(t)sk-\\. A series of navigable rivers and canals, U.S.S.R.; system links Volga river with the Baltic Sea; total length ab. 701 m. Its course is: (a) the Neva, (b) canal along S shore of Lake Ladoga, (c) the Svir (canalized in part), (d) canal along S shore of Lake Onega to Vytegra, (e) the Vytegra, a connecting canal (the **Beloye**), and the Kovzha, (f) canal along W and S shores of Beloye Ozero, and (g) the Sheksna past Cherepovets through the Rybinsk Reservoir on the Volga. Beloye canal constructed 1799–1810; system expanded and improved at various intervals, incl. major reconstruction during early 1960's.

Volga German Autonomous Soviet Socialist Republic *also* **German Volga Republic.** Former autonomous republic, Russian S.F.S.R., U.S.S.R., on E bank of Volga river except for a small area which was on W bank; 10,888 sq. m.; ✻ Engels. Region settled 1760–61 by 27,000 Germans invited by special decree of Empress Catherine II. At first granted special privileges, lost all autonomy by 1870; Revolution of 1917 prevented transfer of colonists to Siberia which had been ordered 1915. Organized as a district 1918 and in 1924 as an autonomous republic; suffered greatly in famine of 1921–22; republic abolished Sept. 24, 1941, its territory divided bet. Saratov and Volgograd oblasts.

Vol·go·grad \\'väl-gə-ˌgrad, 'vȯl-, 'vōl-\\; *formerly* **Sta·lin·grad** \\'stäl-ən-ˌgrad, 'stal-\\ *or earlier* **Tsa·ri·tsyn** \\tsə-'rēt-sən\\. City, ✻ of Volgograd Oblast, Russian S.F.S.R., U.S.S.R., in S part of oblast on the Volga ab. 280 m. from its mouth; pop. (1970p) 818,000; major river port and railroad junction; E terminus of Volga-Don Canal; produces steel, agricultural machinery, cable, chemicals, building materials, flour, clothing; shipbuilding, tanning, distilling, food processing; important hydroelectric power station.

History: Originated as a Russian fort 1589 as defense against Kalmuck, Cossack, and other raiders; captured by Stenka Razin 1670; importance increased rapidly with building of railroads; held by Bolsheviks 1917; a point of conflict during civil war 1919–20, for a time held by Denikin; renamed 1925 (in honor of Josef Stalin) and again in 1961. Suffered great destruction in World War II when it was the scene of severe fighting; German attack begun Aug. 20, 1942; entered, but not completely occupied, by German army during siege of 66 days Sept. 14 to Nov. 19, 1942; German forces cut off by Soviet counteroffensive begun in Nov.; finally recaptured, together with large German force, on surrender of Gen. Paulus Feb. 2, 1943.

Volgograd Oblast *or formerly* **Stalingrad Oblast** \\-'ō-bləst, -ˌblast\\. Subdivision of the Russian S.F.S.R., U.S.S.R., on the lower Volga; 44,054 sq. m.; pop. (1970p) 2,324,000; ✻ Volgograd. On the SE a long arm of the region extends along the Volga to the Caspian Sea; flat steppe land E of the Volga, fairly good brown soil bet. Volga and Don rivers, and rich black earth W of the Don. Besides the two main rivers, region is crossed by Don tributaries—Khoper and Medveditsa; also contains the Volga-Don canal. In E are Elton and other lakes which are productive sources of salt. Economy predominantly agricultural (wheat, millet, sunflowers, truck crops, dairy farming) with some heavy industry largely concentrated in Volgograd, the only major urban center.

History: Region in 5th cent. occupied by Bulgars, in 10th by Khazars; after Mongol invasion of Europe, Batu Khan fixed upon lands of the lower Volga as home of the Golden Horde and established Sarai (*q.v.*) as his capital; conquest of this Tatar territory begun in 15th cent. by Russians, who established Astrakhan 1557 and Tsaritsyn 1589 and in 17th and 18th cents. were in continual conflict with Nogai, Kirghiz, and Kalmuck tribesmen; in latter part of 18th cent. scene of Pugachev's rebellion; after Revolution of 1917 there was much disorder for several years. Suffered great famine 1921; became part of Lower Volga Area 1928; made a subdivision of the Russian S.F.S.R. 1936; in World War II its S part reached in farthest E advance of German armies 1942.

Vol·hyn·ia \\väl-'hin-ē-ə, väl-'in-\\; *Russ.* **Vo·lyn** \\və-'lin(-yə)\\ *or* **Vo·ly·nia** \\və-'lin-yə\\; *Pol.* **Wo·łyń** \\'vȯ-lin(-yə)\\. Region, E cen. Europe, around the headstreams of the Pripyat and Bug rivers; well forested, with marshlands and many lakes; originally a Russian medieval principality, SW of Polotsk and W of Pinsk and Kiev. In 14th cent. a smaller area in Lithuania; in 1569 to Poland; in 1796 became a government of Russia. Divided 1921 by Treaty of Riga bet. Poland (Wołyń) and U.S.S.R. (Volyn). Polish section taken by U.S.S.R. in partition of 1939 and retained as Volyn Oblast of NW Ukrainian S.S.R. after 1945.

Vol·khov \\'vȯl-kəf\\. **1** Navigable river, Leningrad Oblast, Russian S.F.S.R., U.S.S.R.; 142 m. long; area of drainage basin 30,977 sq. m.; outlet of Lake Ilmen; flows N to Lake Ladoga; bisects Novgorod and, at Volkhov near Lake Ladoga, forms rapids (fall nearly 30 ft.) that produce power at Lenin Hydroelectric Station, opened 1926 (first hydroelectric power station in U.S.S.R.). Area held by Germans in early part of World War II.

2 *or formerly* **Vol·khov·stroi** \\'vȯl-kəf-ˌstrȯi\\ *or* **Gos·ti·no·pol·ye** \\'gōs-ti-ˌnō-ˌpȯl-yə\\. Town, Leningrad Oblast, Russian S.F.S.R., U.S.S.R., ab. 70 m. E of Leningrad; pop. (1967e) 44,000.

Völk·ling·en \\'fəlk-liŋ-ən\\. Commune, Saarland, West Germany, on the Saar, just W of Saarbrücken; pop. (1969e) 40,128; ironworks.

Vol·ko·vysk \\vəl-'kō-visk\\ *or Pol.* **Woł·ko·wysk** \\vȯl-\\. Town, Grodno Oblast, W Belorussian S.S.R., U.S.S.R., 55 m. E of Belostok; pop. (1967e) 21,000; lumber, agricultural machinery; formerly in Poland.

Volks·rust \\'vōlks-(ˌ)rəst\\. Town, S Transvaal, NE Rep. of South Africa, 134 m. SE of Johannesburg on Natal border in Drakensburg Mts.; pop. (1967e) 9800; center of extensive pastoral region.

Vo·log·da \\'vȯ-ləg-də\\. City, ✻ of Vologda Oblast, N cen. Russian S.F.S.R., U.S.S.R., in S part of oblast on the **Vologda River** (tributary of upper Sukhona river) and SE of Lake Kubenskoye, ab. 330 m. E of Leningrad; pop. (1970p) 178,000; railroad junction and river port; lumber, furniture, pulp and paper, linen, cement, foodstuffs; shipyards, railroad shops. First mentioned 1147; disputed during 14th cent. bet. Moscow and Novgorod; came under Moscow 1478; important trading town until early 18th cent.; revived late 19th cent. as center of timber industry.

Vologda Oblast \\-'ō-bləst, -ˌblast\\. Subdivision of the Russian S.F.S.R., U.S.S.R.; 56,255 sq. m.; pop. (1970p) 1,296,000; ✻ Vologda. Level area with marshes, many lakes, and extensive forests. Beloye and Kubenskoye are largest lakes and chief rivers are the Sukhona and Sheksna; includes part of Volga-Baltic Waterway. Economy dominated by timber industry (lumbering, sawmilling, pulp and papermaking); some agriculture (flax, dairying). Chief towns Vologda, Cherepovets, Sokol, and Veliki Ustyug. In medieval times part of the Novgorod principality; came under Moscow 15th cent.; part of Leningrad Area 1918 until made separate oblast 1937.

Vo·lo·ko·lamsk \ˌvəl-ə-'kȯ-ləm(p)sk\. Town, Moscow Oblast, Russian S.F.S.R., U.S.S.R., ab. 65 m. WNW of Moscow; pop. (1967e) 15,000; reached by Germans Nov. 22, 1941 but retaken in winter campaign 1942–43.

Vo·los \'vō-ˌläs\; *Gk.* **Vó·los** \'vȯ-ˌlȯs\ *or* **Bo·los** \'vȯ-\. Seaport city, ✱ of Magnesia dept., E Thessaly, NE Greece, on Gulf of Volos; pop. (1971p) 51,340; ships grain, wine, tobacco, olives. Many ancient ruins found in vicinity; sites of ancient Iolcus and Demetrias nearby.

Volos, Gulf of *or Gk.* **Pa·ga·si·ti·kós Kól·pos** \ˌpäg-ə-'sē-ti-ˌkȯs-'kȯl-pȯs\ *or anc.* **Si·nus Pag·a·sae·us** \ˌsī-nəs-ˌpag-ə-'sē-əs\ *also* **Pag·a·sae·an Gulf** \ˌpag-ə-ˌsē-ən-\. Inlet of the Aegean Sea, E Thessaly, E coast of Greece; shut in on E by peninsula of Magnesia.

Volscian Mountains \ˌvȯl-shən-\. See LEPINI MOUNTAINS.

Vol·sin·ii \väl-'sin-ē-ˌī\. 1 Commune, Latium, cen. Italy. See BOLSENA.

2 Commune, Umbria, cen. Italy. See ORVIETO.

Volsk \'vȯlsk\. Town, cen. Saratov Oblast, Russian S.F.S.R., U.S.S.R., on W bank of the Volga 70 m. NE of Saratov; pop. (1969e) 71,000; important river port; cement and food processing industries; made town 1780.

Vol·ta \'väl-tə, 'vōl-, 'vȯl-\. 1 River, Ghana; incl. Lake Volta ab. 300 m. long, and Black Volta ab. 1000 m. long; flows S into Bight of Benin.

2 Administrative region of E Ghana. See table at GHANA.

Volta, Black *or Fr.* **Volta Noire** \vȯl-tà-nwär\. Chief headstream of Volta river, W Africa; rises in Upper Volta, flows S, forming section of W boundary of Ghana, turns E and flows into Lake Volta, Ghana.

Volta, Lake. Reservoir, Ghana; 3275 sq. m.; has inundated point of confluence of White Volta and Black Volta; hydroelectric power production.

Volta, Red *or Fr.* **Volta Rouge** \vȯl-tà-rüzh\. Tributary of the White Volta, N Ghana and Upper Volta.

Volta, Upper. See UPPER VOLTA.

Volta, White *or Fr.* **Volta Blanche** \vȯl-tà-bläⁿsh\. River, W Africa; ab. 550 m. long; rises in Upper Volta, flows SW and S into Lake Volta, Ghana.

Voltaic Republic. See UPPER VOLTA.

Volta Noire. See VOLTA, BLACK.

Volta Re·don·da \ˌväl-tə-ri-'dän-də, ˌvōl-, ˌvȯl-\. City, Rio de Janeiro state, E Brazil, on the Paraíba river ab. 50 m. NNW of Rio de Janeiro; munic. pop. (1968e) 118,114; center of Brazilian steel industry; founded 1941; steel plants constructed 1942–46.

Volta Rouge. See VOLTA, RED.

Vol·ter·ra \väl-'ter-ə, vōl-, vȯl-\ *or anc.* **Vol·a·ter·rae** \ˌvō-lə-'te(ə)r-ˌī, -(ˌ)ē\. Commune, Pisa prov., Tuscany, W Italy, 29 m. SE of Pisa; pop. (1968e) 16,558; produces salt, alabaster; tourism; notable buildings include the citadel, several palaces (13th–17th cents.), cathedral (13th–16th cents.), churches of 13th and 14th cents., and an old abbey; Etruscan antiquities; home of ancient Roman poet Persius. In World War II scene of severe fighting in Allied advance northward July 1944.

Vol·tur·no \väl-'tu̇(ə)r-(ˌ)nō, vōl-, vȯl-\. River, S cen. Italy; 109 m. long; flows S and SE out of the Apennines, then turns W through Capua into the Gulf of Gaeta, 20 m. SE of Gaeta; German line of defense in World War II; after severe fighting crossed by Allies Oct. 12–14, 1943.

Voltz·berg National Park \'vōlts-ˌbərg-\. National park, Surinam; 216 sq. m.; wildlife; established 1961.

Vo·lu·bi·lis \və-'l(y)ü-bi-ləs\. Ancient Roman town, W Mauretania; now ruins in N Morocco E of Rabat and ab. 19 m. N of Meknes; ruins extensive, esp. of walls; most notable Roman remains in Morocco.

Vo·lu·sia \və-'lü-shə\. County in Florida. See table at FLORIDA.

Vólvi, Límni. See BOLBE, LAKE.

Volyn *or* **Volynia.** See VOLHYNIA.

Vo·lyn Oblast \və-'lin(-yə)-'ō-bləst, -ˌblast\. Subdivision of the Ukrainian S.S.R., U.S.S.R.; 7799 sq. m.; pop. (1970p) 975,000; ✱ Lutsk; economy predominantly agricultural (grain, sugar beets, livestock); coal mines, chalk quarries. Formerly part of Volhynia (*q.v.*) and a province of Poland; formed 1939.

Volzhsk \'vȯlshsk\ *or formerly* **Lo·pa·ti·no** \lə-'pät-ə-nə\. Town, Mari A.S.S.R., Russian S.F.S.R., U.S.S.R., ab. 55 m. SSE of Yoshkar-Ola; pop. (1967e) 40,000.

Volzh·ski \'vȯlsh-shkē\. Town, Volgograd Oblast, Russian S.F.S.R., U.S.S.R., ab. 10 m. E of Volgograd; pop. (1970p) 142,000.

Voor·burg \'vō(ə)r-ˌbərg, 'vȯ(ə)r-\. Commune, South Holland prov., SW Netherlands; pop. (1970e) 45,011; E suburb of The Hague.

Voor·ne \'vō(ə)r-nə\. Island, South Holland prov., SW Netherlands, bet. the estuary of the Nieuwe Maas and the Haringvliet; chief town Brielle (*q.v.*).

Voorst \'vō(ə)rst\. Commune, Gelderland prov., E Netherlands, just NW of Zutphen; pop. (1970e) 21,379.

Vop·na Fjord \ˌvȯp-nə-\. Inlet of Norwegian Sea, NE Iceland, SE of Thistil Fjord.

Vor·arl·berg \'fō(ə)r-ˌärl-ˌbərg, 'fȯ(ə)r-\. State, Austria, in extreme W part; 1004 sq. m.; pop. (1971p) 274,000; ✱ Bregenz; a mountainous region, including source of the Lech and several upper tributaries of the Rhine, and noted for its Alpine scenery and glaciers; textile industry.

Vor·der·rhein *also* **Vor·der Rhein** \'fȯrd-ər-ˌrīn\. River, SE Switzerland; flows E to unite with the Hinterrhein and form the Rhine river.

Vor·ding·borg \ˌvȯrd-iŋ-'bȯ(ə)rg\. Town, Storstrøm co., SE Sjælland, Denmark, on coast opp. Falster I.; pop. (1970e) 11,640.

Voríai Sporádhes. See SPORADES.

Vø·ring·foss \'vər-iŋ-ˌfȯs\. Waterfall, Bjoreia river, a small stream in SW Norway E of Hardanger Fjord; total drop 597 ft.

Vor·ku·ta \vȯr-'küt-ə\. Town, Komi A.S.S.R., Russian S.F.S.R., U.S.S.R., at N end of the Ural Mts. on the **Vorkuta River;** pop. (1969e) 65,000; sawmills, coal mines; formerly site of one of largest penal camps in U.S.S.R.

Vorlich, Ben. See BEN VORLICH.

Vorm·si \'vȯ(ə)rm(p)-sē\ *or Ger.* **Worms** \'vȯ(ə)rm(p)s\. Small island, Baltic Sea, off W coast of Estonian S.S.R., U.S.S.R., bet. Hiiumaa and the mainland; 36 sq. m.

Vo·ro·na \və-'rō-nə\. River, Penza and Tambov oblasts, Russian S.F.S.R., U.S.S.R.; 282 m. long; flows S to the Khoper near Borisoglebsk in E Voronezh Oblast.

Vo·ro·nezh \və-'rȯ-nish\. 1 Navigable river, cen. Russian S.F.S.R., U.S.S.R.; 291 m. long; rises in S Ryazan Oblast, flows S to the Don just S of Voronezh.

2 City, ✱ of Voronezh Oblast, cen. Russian S.F.S.R., U.S.S.R., in W part of the oblast, on right bank of Voronezh river near its junction with the Don, 165 m. NE of Kharkov; pop. (1970p) 666,000; railroad junction; produces agricultural and construction machinery, chemicals, radios, tobacco products; food processing, distilling; nuclear power station; univ. (transferred from Tartu [now in Estonian S.S.R.] in 1918). Founded as fortress 1586; base for naval operations of Peter the Great against Turkish fortress of Azov late 17th cent.; in World War II occupied by Germans July 1942–Jan. 1943; largely destroyed but rebuilt since 1945.

Voronezh Oblast \-'ō-bləst, -ˌblast\. Subdivision of the Russian S.F.S.R., U.S.S.R.; 20,232 sq. m.; pop. (1970p) 2,527,000; ✱ Voronezh. Chiefly in the valley of the Don bet. the two plateau areas of cen. Russian S.F.S.R., but W part is hilly; wheat, rye, corn, sunflowers, potatoes; livestock raising. Chief towns Voronezh, Borisoglebsk, and Georgia-Dezh. In early times on the S border of Moscow principality; came entirely under Russian tsars in 16th cent.; oblast estab. 1934; part W of the Don taken by Germans in 1942 campaign but regained early in 1943.

Voroshilov. See USSURISK.

Vo·ro·shi·lov·grad \ˌvȯr-ə-ˈshē-ləf-ˌgrad\ *or formerly* **Lu·gansk** \lü-ˈgän(t)sk\. City, ✱ of Voroshilovgrad Oblast, E Ukrainian S.S.R., U.S.S.R., on a tributary of the Donets 100 m. N of Rostov-na-Donu; pop. (1970p) 382,000; center of coal-mining region in Donets Basin; steel tubes, coal-mining machinery, diesel locomotives. Founded c. 1795 when coal mines were opened; has grown rapidly since 1923; in World War II occupied by Germans 1942–43.

Voroshilovgrad Oblast \-ˈō-bləst, -ˌblast\. Subdivision of the Ukrainian S.S.R., U.S.S.R.; 10,309 sq. m.; pop. (1970p) 2,749,000; ✱ Voroshilovgrad; important industrial region (esp. heavy engineering, chemicals); wheat, barley.

Voroshilovsk. 1 City, U.S.S.R. See STAVROPOL 1.
2 City, Ukraine, U.S.S.R. See KOMMUNARSK.

Vorpommern. See POMERANIA.

Vor·skla \ˈvȯr-sklə\. River, cen. Ukrainian S.S.R., U.S.S.R.; rises in S Kursk Oblast and flows S past Poltava to the Dnieper above Dnepropetrovsk.

Vorst \ˈvȯrst\ *or Fr.* **Fo·rest** \fō-re\. Commune, Brabant prov., cen. Belgium, a suburb of Brussels; pop. (1969e) 55,145.

Võrts–Järv \ˈvərts-ˌyarv\ *or* **Virts** \ˈvirts\. Lake, S cen. Estonian S.S.R., U.S.S.R.; 95 sq. m.; largest lake in Estonian S.S.R.; its outlet is the Ema, flowing E to Lake Peipus.

Vosges \ˈvōzh\. 1 *anc.* **Vos·e·gus** \ˈväs-i-gəs\ *or* **Vog·e·sus** \ˈväj-i-səs\. Mountain range, extending bet. Haut-Rhin and Vosges depts., NE France; separated on S from Jura Mts. by Belfort Gap; highest point Ballon de Guebwiller 4672 ft.; has many rounded summits.
2 Department of NE France. See table at FRANCE.

Vos·kre·sensk \ˌvəs-kri-ˈshen(t)sk\. Town, Moscow Oblast, Russian S.F.S.R., U.S.S.R., ab. 50 m. SE of Moscow; pop. (1969e) 61,000.

Voss \ˈvȯs\. Town, Hordaland co., SW Norway, ab. 44 m. ENE of Bergen; pop. (1970e) 13,776.

Vos·tok \və-ˈstäk\. Small British uninhabited island, Line Is., cen. Pacific Ocean, ab. 100 m. SW of Caroline I.; discovered 1820.

Vot·kinsk \ˈvȯt-(ˌ)kin(t)sk\. Town, E Udmurt A.S.S.R., Russian S.F.S.R., U.S.S.R., on right bank of Kama river; pop. (1969e) 73,000; terminus of branch railroad 35 m. E of Izhevsk; produces metal goods, agricultural machinery. Birthplace of Tchaikovsky.

Votskaya Autonomous Soviet Socialist Republic. See UDMURT AUTONOMOUS SOVIET SOCIALIST REPUBLIC.

Voúxa, Ákra. See BUSA, CAPE.

Vou·ziers \vü-ˈzhā\. Commune, Ardennes dept., NE France, on Aisne river; pop. (1962c) 4706; fighting Oct. 1918.

Voya·geurs National Park \ˌvwä-ˌyä-ˈzhər-, ˌvȯi-ä-\. See UNITED STATES, *National Parks.*

Voyutsa. See VIJOSË.

Voyvodina. See VOIVODINA.

Voz·ne·sensk \ˌväz-nə-ˈsen(t)sk\. Town, Nikolayev Oblast, S Ukrainian S.S.R., U.S.S.R., at head of navigation of the Bug river 80 m. NNE of Odessa; pop. (1967e) 34,000.

Vraca. See VRATSA 2.

Vrakhori. See AGRINION.

Vran·cea \vrän-ˈchā-ə\. County of E Romania. See table at ROMANIA.

Vrangelya Ostrov. See WRANGEL ISLAND.

Vra·nje *also* **Vra·nja** \ˈvrän-yə\. Town, Serbia, SE Yugoslavia, ab. 45 m. NE of Skopje; pop. (1965e) 19,000; shoes, textiles, iron products.

Vra·tsa \ˈvrät-sə\. 1 Province of N Bulgaria. See table at BULGARIA.
2 *or* **Vra·ca** \ˈvrät-sə\. City, its ✱, 35 m. NNE of Sofia; pop. (1968e) 45,232; railroad junction; silk, textiles, chemicals, cement, ceramics; established on present site 15th cent.

Vr·bas \ˈvər-ˌbäs\. 1 River, W Yugoslavia; 149 m. long; flows N into Sava river.
2 Town, Serbia, E Yugoslavia, ab. 67 m. NW of Belgrade; pop. (1965e) 20,000.

Vr·bas·ka \ˈvər-bəs-kə\. Former county, NW cen. Yugoslavia; 7888 sq. m.; ⊗ Banja Luka; now forms NW part of Bosnia and Herzegovina.

Vre·de \ˈfrēd-ə, ˈvrēd\. Town, NE Orange Free State, E cen. Rep. of South Africa, 105 m. SE of Johannesburg; pop. (1967e) 7300; center of livestock-raising region.

Vries Island. See Ō-SHIMA.

Vriesland. See FRIESLAND.

Vrie·zen·veen \ˈvrē-zən-ˌvān\. Commune, Overijssel prov., Netherlands, just N of Almelo; pop. (1970e) 14,658.

Vrin·da·van \ˈvrin-də-vən\ *or formerly* **Brin·da·ban** \ˈbrin-\ *also* **Bind·ra·ban** \ˈbin-drə-bən\. Town, Uttar Pradesh, N India, on Yamuna river ab. 80 m. S of Delhi; pop. (1961c) 25,138; Hindu holy city.

Vr·šac \ˈvər-ˌshäts\ *or Hung.* **Ver·secz** \ˈve(ə)r-ˌshets\ *or Ger.* **Wer·schetz** \ˈve(ə)r-ˌshets\. City, Serbia, NE Yugoslavia, ab. 45 m. NW of Belgrade near Romanian frontier; pop. (1959e) 34,000; trade center in grape-growing region; produces red wines, brandy, and grains. Serbs defeated here by Hungarians during Revolution of 1848–49.

Vry·burg \ˈfrī-ˌbərg, ˈfrā-\. Town, N Cape Province, S Rep. of South Africa, on a tributary of Vaal river 125 m. N of Kimberly; pop. (1967e) 17,100; center of pastoral and grazing region. Occupied by Boers during Boer War. See STELLALAND.

Vry·heid \ˈfrī-ˌhāt, ˈfrā-\. Town, NW Natal, E Rep. of South Africa, 140 m. N of Durban; pop. (1967e) 14,300; large deposits of iron ore and coal nearby. Chief town of a district ceded to Boers by a Zulu chief 1884 and declared by them a republic (New Republic); in 1888 incorporated in Transvaal and after Boer War 1899–1902 transferred to Natal.

Vse·tín \fə-ˈset-(ˌ)yēn, və-\. Town, Czech S.R., cen. Czechoslovakia; pop. (1968e) 21,556.

Vua. See UVÁ.

Vught \ˈvə(r)kt\. Commune, North Brabant prov., S Netherlands; pop. (1970e) 22,633; S suburb of 's Hertogenbosch.

Vui·ma·sia \ˌvü-ē-ˈmäs-ē-ə\ *or* **Na·mo·si Peak** \nä-ˌmō-sē-\. Mountain, SE Viti Levu I., Fiji, SW Pacific Ocean; 3947 ft.

Vu·ko·var \ˈvü-kə-ˌvär\. Town, Croatia, N Yugoslavia, on the Danube ab. 83 m. NW of Belgrade; pop. (1965e) 28,000.

Vul·can \ˈvəl-kən\. Town, Hunedoara co., W cen. Romania, ab. 40 m. SE of Deva; pop. (1966c) 21,979.

Vulcan, Mount. Volcano, Blanche Bay, SSW of Rabaul and Mount Tavurvur (volcano), E New Britain I., Bismarck Archipelago; formed May 29–30, 1937, at time of eruption of Mount Tavurvur, by crater being built up on **Ma·nam Island** \mä-ˈnäm-\ in the bay (island formed by eruption of Mt. Mother 1878).

Vulcan Crest. Peak, Mineral and Saguache cos., S Colorado; 13,722 ft.

Vul·ca·no \vül-ˈkän-(ˌ)ō\ *or anc.* **Hi·era** \ˈhī-ə-rə\. Southernmost of the Lipari Is., Italy; erupted 1890.

Vulcan Pass \ˌvəl-kən-\. Mountain pass, W Transylvanian Alps, Romania; 5000 ft.

Vul·ture Peak \ˌvəl-chər-\. Mountain, Glacier National Park, NW Montana; 9621 ft.

Vung Tau \ˈvuŋ-ˈtau̇\ *or formerly* **Cape Saint Jacques** \-saⁿ-ˈzhäk\. Point on SE coast of South Vietnam, N of entrance to Saigon at 10°19′N, 107°05′E.

Vuok·si \ˈvü-ˌȯk-sē\ *or Russ.* **Vuok·sa** \və-ˈwȯk-sə\. River, SE Finland and Leningrad Oblast, Russian S.F.S.R., U.S.S.R.; flows out of Lake Saimaa E into Lake Ladoga.

Vyat·ka *or* **Viat·ka** \vē-ˈät-kə\. 1 River, Russian S.F.S.R., U.S.S.R.; 775 m. long; rises in N Udmurt A.S.S.R. and flows W, S, and SE into Kama river in N Tatar A.S.S.R.
2 City, U.S.S.R. See KIROV.

Vyaz·ma \vē-ˈäz-mə\. Town, E Smolensk Oblast, Russian S.F.S.R., U.S.S.R., 125 m. WSW of Moscow on a tributary of the Desna; pop. (1967e) 39,000; railroad junction. In 11th cent. a trading town; held alternately by Lithuania, Russia, and Poland, 15th–17th cents.; finally ceded to Russia 1634. In World War II occupied and fortified by Germans Oct. 1941–Mar. 1943.

Vyaz·ni·ki \vē-'äz-nē-kē\. Town, Vladimir Oblast, Russian S.F.S.R., U.S.S.R., ab. 70 m. E of Vladimir; pop. (1967e) 42,000.

Vy·borg \'vē-ˌbȯ(ə)rg\ *or Swed.* **Vi·borg** \'vē-ˌbȯ(ə)r\ *or Finn.* **Vii·pu·ri** *also* **Vi·pu·ri** \'vē-pə-rē\. Seaport city, NW Leningrad Oblast, Russian S.F.S.R., U.S.S.R., on Vyborg Bay 70 m. NW of Leningrad; pop. (1969e) 65,000; lumber, furniture; shipyards; fishing port. Founded as Swedish castle 1293; captured by Russians 1710; to Finland 1918; ceded back to U.S.S.R. 1940; occupied by Finnish and German forces Aug. 1941–June 1944; returned to U.S.S.R. 1944.

Vyborg Bay *or formerly* **Viipuri Bay.** Inlet of NE Gulf of Finland, Leningrad Oblast, Russian S.F.S.R., U.S.S.R.; at its head is the city of Vyborg.

Vy·cheg·da *or* **Vi·cheg·da** \'vi-chəg-də\. River, chiefly in Komi A.S.S.R., Russian S.F.S.R., U.S.S.R.; 702 m. long; flows W to the Northern Dvina river near Kotlas.

Vyernyi. See ALMA-ATA.

Vyk·sa \'vik-sə\. Town, Gorki Oblast, Russian S.F.S.R., U.S.S.R., ab. 100 m. SW of Gorki; pop. (1967e) 43,000.

Vyr·nwy \'vər-nü-ē\. River, N cen. and E Wales; 35 m. long; flows E into the Severn; **Lake Vyrnwy,** a reservoir ab. 5 m. long in N Montgomeryshire, was created 1880–90 by damming up the river, and is the largest lake in Wales. See BALA LAKE.

Vysh·ni Vo·lo·chek \ˌvish-n(y)ē-və-'lȯ-chək\. Town, N Kalinin Oblast, Russian S.F.S.R., U.S.S.R., 70 m. NW of Kalinin; pop. (1969e) 73,000; lumber, textiles, machinery.

Vy·so·ké Mý·to \ˌvi-sȯ-kā-'mēt-ō\ *or Ger.* **Ho·hen·mauth** \'hō-ən-ˌmau̇t\. Town, Czech S.R., W Czechoslovakia, on the upper Elbe river 75 m. E of Prague.

Vysoké Tatry. See TATRA MOUNTAINS.

Vy·te·gra \'vit-i-grə\. Town, NW Vologda Oblast, Russian S.F.S.R., U.S.S.R., near SE shore of Lake Onega on the **Vytegra River,** a short stream flowing into Lake Onega and forming part of the Volga-Baltic Waterway.

Wa \ˈwä\. 1 Group of states, Burma. See WA STATES.
2 Town, NW Upper Region, Ghana, W Africa, 120 m. NW of Tamale near Ivory Coast border; pop. (1970p) 21,155.

Waadt. See VAUD.

Waag. See VÁH.

Waal \ˈväl\ *or anc.* **Va·ha·lis** \ˈvä-(h)ə-lis\. River, Netherlands, the S branch of the Lower Rhine; unites with estuaries of the Meuse river at Gorinchem. Its course to the North Sea continues as the Merwede and its two branches, the Nieuwe Maas and the Oude Maas.

Waal·wijk \ˈväl-ˌvīk\. Commune, North Brabant prov., S Netherlands, N of Tilburg; pop. (1970e) 23,394.

Waas, Mount \-ˈwäs\. Peak, S Grand co., E Utah; 12,331 ft.

Wa·bana \wȯ-ˈban-ə\. Town, Newfoundland, Canada, on Bell I., ab. 11 m. WNW of St. John's; pop. (1971p) 5256.

Wa·bash \ˈwȯ-ˌbash\. 1 River, Indiana and Illinois; 475 m. long; rises in Darke co., W Ohio, flows W and SW across Indiana to form S section of Indiana-Illinois boundary, and empties into Ohio river at SW extremity of Indiana.
2 Name of counties in two states of the U.S. See tables at ILLINOIS and INDIANA.
3 City, ⊗ of Wabash co., N Indiana, 20 m. NNW of Marion; pop. (1970c) 13,379; tires, furniture, asbestos products; corn, hogs.

Wa·ba·sha \ˈwȯ-bə-ˌshȯ\. 1 County in SE Minnesota. See table at MINNESOTA.
2 City, its ⊗, on Mississippi river 30 m. NW of Winona; pop. (1970c) 2371; summer resort; flour.

Wa·baun·see \wä-ˈbȯn-(ˌ)sē\. County in Kansas. See table at KANSAS.

Wac·ca·maw \ˈwäk-ə-ˌmȯ\. River, S North Carolina and NE South Carolina; ab. 130 m. long; flows through **Waccamaw Lake,** in Columbus co., North Carolina, SW across South Carolina border into Pee Dee river near its mouth.

Wac·ca·sas·sa Bay \ˌwȯk-ə-ˌsas-ə-\. Inlet of Gulf of Mexico, SW coast of Levy co., NW Florida penin.

Wa·cho·via \wä-ˈchō-vē-ə\. Region, W cen. North Carolina, E of Yadkin river; settled and named by Moravians from Bethlehem, Pennsylvania, in 1752–53; Bethabara the first settlement (now a small village), and Salem, now part of Winston-Salem.

Wa·chu·sett Mountain \wä-ˌchü-sət-\. Isolated peak, Worcester co., cen. Massachusetts; 2006 ft.

Wachusett Reservoir. Reservoir, E cen. Worcester co., cen. Massachusetts; ab. 6 m. long; formed by **Wachusett Dam.** A rock tunnel 24½ m. long connected with Quabbin Reservoir furnishes constant water supply for Boston.

Wa·co \ˈwā-(ˌ)kō\. City, ⊗ of McLennan co., cen. Texas, on Brazos river 82 m. S of Fort Worth; pop. (1970c) 95,326; aircraft parts, glass, tires, hats, textiles, asbestos products; ships livestock and cotton; Baylor Univ. (1845), Paul Quinn Coll. (1881), McLennan Community Coll. (1966); settled 1849; incorporated 1856.

Wad, Al–. See AL-OUED.

Wadai. See OUADAÏ.

Wadan. See OUADANE.

Wad·den Zee \ˈväd-ᵊn-ˌzā\. Outer section of the former Zuider Zee, bet. the outer islands and the dike enclosing IJsselmer, Netherlands.

Wad·ding·ton \ˈwäd-iŋ-tən\. Parish, Lincolnshire, E England, just S of Lincoln.

Waddington, Mount. Peak, SW British Columbia, Canada, near head of Knight Inlet; 13,260 ft.; a peak of the Coast Mts. and highest point in British Columbia.

Wad Dra. See DRA, WAD.

Wade, Mount \-ˈwād\. Mountain, Antarctica, 84°51′S, 174°15′W; 13,399 ft.

Wa·de·na \wȯ-ˈdēn-ə\. 1 County in cen. Minnesota. See table at MINNESOTA.
2 Village, its ⊗, 43 m. WNW of Brainerd; pop. (1970c) 4640; butter; poultry farms.

Wä·dens·wil \ˈväd-ᵊn(t)s-ˌvēl\. Commune, Zurich canton, NE cen. Switzerland, on S shore of Lake of Zurich 12 m. SSE of Zurich; pop. (1970c) 15,695; manufactures woolen goods; produces wine, fruit.

Wades·boro \ˈwādz-ˌbər-ə, -ˌbə-rə\. Town, ⊗ of Anson co., S North Carolina, 46 m. ESE of Charlotte; pop. (1970c) 3977; lumber, textiles, feed.

Wadh·wan \wə-ˈdwän\. 1 Former state, W India, now part of Gujarat state; 242 sq. m.
2 Town, its ❋, railroad junction 65 m. WSW of Ahmadabad; pop. (1961c) 27,104.

Wa·di \ˈwäd-ē\. In the Near East and Northern Africa an Arabic term used in place names, meaning "valley, river, dry river bed," as Wadi al-Mawjib. For names beginning with this term, see the second element, as MAWJIB, etc.

Wadi al–Kebir. See GUADALQUIVIR.

Wadi Hal·fa \-ˈhal-fə\ *or* **Halfa.** Town, Northern prov., N Sudan, on E shore of Lake Nubia (S extension of Lake Nasser [*q.v.*]); N terminus of Khartoum railroad; site of old Wadi Halfa (just below 2d Cataract) now flooded.

Wādī Mūsa. See PETRA.

Wad Me·da·ni \wäd-ˈmed-ᵊn-ē\ *or* **Wad Ma·da·nī** \-mə-ˈdän-ē\. City, ❋ of Blue Nile prov., E Sudan, ab. 100 m. SSE of Khartoum; pop. (1969e) 71,030; center of irrigated agricultural region.

Wads·worth \ˈwädz-(ˌ)wərth\. Industrial city, Medina co., N Ohio, 11 m. WSW of Akron; pop. (1970c) 13,142; matches, dairy products, brick; coal mines; diversified agriculture; settled 1814.

Waereghem. See WAREGEM.

Waes \ˈvas\ *or* **Pays de Waes** \ˌpā-ˌēd-(ə-)-\. Ancient district, comprising part of the modern provinces of East Flanders in Belgium and Zeeland in the Netherlands.

Wagadugu. See OUAGADOUGOU.

Wa·ge·ning·en \ˈväg-ə-ˌniŋ-ən\. Commune, Gelderland prov., E Netherlands, on N bank of Neder Rijn 11 m. W of Arnhem; pop. (1970e) 26,572.

Wa·ger Bay \ˌwā-jər-\. Inlet, NE Keewatin dist., Northwest Territories, Canada, opening into Roes Welcome; 160 m. long, max. width 38 m.

Wag·ga Wag·ga \ˌwäg-ə-ˈwäg-ə\. Town, S New South Wales, SE Australia, on Murrumbidgee river 100 m. W of Canberra; pop. (1968e) 27,180; center of wheat, fruit, and grazing district (see RIVERINA).

Wa·gi·na \wä-ˈgin-ə\. Small island, W of Manning Strait and off SE end of Choiseul I., E Solomon Is., W Pacific Ocean.

Wag·on·er \ˈwag-(ə)n-ər\. 1 County in NE Oklahoma. See table at OKLAHOMA.
2 City, its ⊗, 14 m. N of Muskogee; pop. (1970c) 4959; gas, oil wells; cotton.

Wa·gram \ˈväg-ˌräm\. Village, Lower Austria, in the Marchfeld 11 m. NE of Vienna; battle July 5 and 6, 1809 in which Napoleon defeated the Austrians under Archduke Charles Louis.

Wa·ha Lake \ˌwȯ-(ˌ)hȯ-\. Lake, Nez Perce co., W Idaho, 18 m. SE of Lewiston; source of the Waha Lake trout (*Salmo bouvieri*).

Wa·hi·a·wa \ˌwä-hē-ə-ˈwä\. 1 Division, Honolulu co., cen. Oahu I., Hawaii; pop. (1970c) 37,329; pineapple plantations.
2 City in division on cen. plateau; pop. (1970c) 17,598; U.S. Army post of Schofield Barracks adjoins it.

Wahiawa Bay. Bay, S coast of Kauai I., Hawaii, bet. Lawai Bay and Hanapepe Bay.

Wa·hie Point \wä-ˌhē-ˌā-\. Cape, NE coast of Lanai I., Hawaii.

Wah·ki·a·kum \wȯ-ˈkī-ə-kəm\. County in Washington. See table at WASHINGTON.

Wahlstatt. See LEGNICKIE POLE.

Wa·hoo \'wä-ˌhü\. City, ⊗ of Saunders co., E Nebraska, 17 m. SSW of Fremont; pop. (1970c) 3835; agriculture; John F. Kennedy Coll. (1965).

Wah·pe·ton \'wȯ-pə-tən\. City, ⊗ of Richland co., SE corner of North Dakota, on Red river 44 m. S of Fargo; pop. (1970c) 7076; dairy products, sheet iron, pottery; North Dakota State School of Science (1889).

Wah Wah Mountains \ˌwä-wä-\. Range, S Millard and N Beaver cos., W Utah.

Wai·a·le·a·le \wī-ˌäl-ā-'äl-ā\. Mountain, cen. Kauai I., Hawaii; 5080 ft.

Wai·a·lua \ˌwī-ə-'lü-ə\. **1** Division, Honolulu co., N Oahu I., Hawaii; pop. (1970c) 9171.

2 *or* **Waialua Mill.** City in division near N coast of Oahu; pop. (1970c) 4047.

Waialua Bay. Bay, N coast of Oahu I., Hawaii, bet. Kaiaka Bay and Waimea Bay.

Wai·a·nae \ˌwī-ə-'nī\. **1** Division, Honolulu co., W Oahu I., Hawaii; pop. (1970c) 24,077.

2 City in division on W coast of Oahu; pop. (1970c) 3302.

Waianae Range *or* **Waianae Mountains.** Mountain range, extending along SW side of Oahu I., Hawaii; highest peak Kaala 4047 ft.

Wai·au \'wī-(ˌ)au̇\. River, S South I., New Zealand; 135 m. long from head of Clinton river; flows S from Te Anau Lake and Manapouri Lake into Te Waewae Bay on Foveaux Strait.

Wai·au–uha \ˌwī-au̇-'ü-hə\ *or* **Waiau** \'wī-(ˌ)au̇\. River, South I., New Zealand; 105 m. long; flows S and SE into Pacific Ocean N of Pegasus Bay.

Wai·bling·en \'vīp-liŋ-ən\. City, Baden-Württemberg, West Germany, 9 m. NE of Stuttgart; pop. (1969e) 24,328; orchid nurseries; leather, furniture, drugs; founded mid-13th cent.

Wai·geo \wī-'gā-(ˌ)ō\. Island, NE Moluccas, Indonesia, off NW end of Irian Barat; 80 m. long by 28 m. wide; highest point 3281 ft.; nearly divided in two parts by long inlet; covered with dense forests.

Wai·he·ke \'wī-ˌhā-kē\. Island, Hauraki Gulf, N coast of North I., New Zealand.

Wai·hi \wī-'hē\. Borough, N North I., New Zealand, 75 m. ESE of Auckland; pop. (1970e) 3180.

Wai·hou \'wī-(ˌ)hō-ü\ *or* **Thames** \'temz\. River, North I., New Zealand; 109 m. long; flows N into Firth of Thames.

Wai·ka·to \wī-'kät-ō\. River, NW North I., New Zealand; 264 m. long; flows N and W into Pacific Ocean S of Manukau Harbor; source of hydroelectric power.

Wai·ki·ki Beach \ˌwī-kə-ˌkē-\. Seaside resort, SE Oahu I., Hawaii, SE section of Honolulu, near Diamond Head; bathing and boating.

Wailangi Lala. See WELANGILALA.

Wai·lua Bay \wī-ˌlü-ə-\. Bay, E coast of Maui I., Hawaii.

Wai·lu·ku \wī-'lü-(ˌ)kü\. **1** Division, Maui co., Hawaii, W cen. Maui I.; pop. (1970c) 9084; sugar plantations.

2 City in division, ⊗ of Maui co., on N coast of Maui I.; pop. (1970c) 7979; an educational center since early days; schools established 1835–37.

Wailuku Valley. See IAO VALLEY.

Wai·ma·ka·ri·ri \(ˌ)wī-ˌmäk-ə-'ri(ə)r-ē\. River, NE cen. South I., New Zealand; ab. 100 m. long; flows SE into Pegasus Bay ab. 12 m. N of Port Lyttelton.

Wai·mea \wī-ˌmā-ə\. **1** Division, W Kauai I., Kauai co., Hawaii; pop. (with Kekaha, [1970c]) 4159; also includes Nuhau I. (to SW).

2 Village, South Kohala div., Hawaii co., Hawaii, in N part of Hawaii I.; pop. (1970c) 756; its post office is Kamuela; a place of importance in early wars of the kingdom.

3 Town, Waimea div., SW coast of Kauai I., Hawaii; pop. (1970c) 1569; canyon nearby 3000 ft. deep.

Waimea Bay. **1** Harbor of Waimea town, SW coast of Kauai I., Hawaii; first anchorage of Capt. Cook Jan. 1778; visited by Vancouver 1792.

2 Bay, N coast of Oahu I., Hawaii.

Wain·gan·ga \wīn-'gəŋ-gə\ *or* **Wain River** \'wīn-\. River (*ganga*), Madhya Pradesh and Maharashtra, cen. India; 360 m. long; rises S of Seoni, flows S to unite with Wardha and form the Pranhita river.

Wain·ga·pu *or Du.* **Wain·ga·poe** \wīn-'gäp-(ˌ)ü\. Seaport and chief town of Sumba I., Lesser Sunda Is., Indonesia, on N coast; pop. (1961c) 13,247.

Wai·ni \'wī-nē\. River, NW Guyana; ab. 140 m. long; flows NE, then curves to NW and empties into Atlantic Ocean near border of Venezuela.

Wain River. See WAINGANGA.

Wain·wright \'wān-(ˌ)rīt\. Town, Alberta, Canada, 120 m. SE of Edmonton; pop. (1971p) 3791.

Wai·pa \wī-'pä\. River, S tributary of Waikato river in SW North I., New Zealand; ab. 60 m. long.

Wai·pa·hu \wī-'pä-(ˌ)hü\. City, Honolulu co., S Oahu I., Hawaii, on NW shore of Pearl Harbor just W of Pearl City; pop. (1970c) 24,150; suffered damage in Japanese attack on Pearl Harbor Dec. 7, 1941.

Wai·pa·pa Point \ˌwī-'päp-ə-\. Cape, NE coast of South I., New Zealand, at mouth of Clarence river.

Wai·rau \'wī-ˌrau̇\. River, N South I., New Zealand; ab. 105 m. long; flows ENE into Cloudy Bay.

Wai·roa \wī-'rō-ə\. **1** River, E cen. North I., New Zealand; 85 m. long; flows S into N Hawke Bay.

2 River in N extension of North I., New Zealand; 82 m. long; flows S into Kaipara Harbor on W coast.

3 Seaport borough, E North I., New Zealand, on Hawke Bay at mouth of Wairoa river; pop. (1970e) 5490.

Wai·ta·ki \'wī-ˌtäk-ē\. River, SE cen. South I., New Zealand; 130 m. long; flows ESE into Pacific Ocean N of Oamaru; source of hydroelectric power.

Wai·tangi \'wī-ˌtäŋ-ē\. Village, N North I., New Zealand, on Bay of Islands 115 m. NNW of Auckland. In 1840 treaty signed here bet. Maori chiefs and Great Britain.

Wai·ta·ra \'wīt-ə-rə\. Borough on North Taranaki Bight, W North I., New Zealand, NE of New Plymouth; pop. (1970e) 4970.

Wai·te·ma·ta Harbor \ˌwīt-ə-ˌmät-ə-\. Inlet, SW corner of Hauraki Gulf, on N coast of North I., New Zealand; harbor for Auckland.

Wai·to·mo Caves \wī-ˌtō-mō-\. Underground caverns, W North I., New Zealand, near Te Kuiti; their Glowworm Grotto is illuminated by large numbers of glowworms.

Waitzen. See VÁC.

Waiyeung. See HUI-CHOU.

Wa·jir \wä-'ji(ə)r\. Town, ✱ of North-Eastern Province, NE Kenya; pop. (1969p) 1055.

Wa·ka·mat·su \ˌwäk-ə-'mät-(ˌ)sü\. See KITAKYŪSHŪ.

Wa·ka·sa Bay \wä-ˌkä-sə-\. Inlet of the Sea of Japan, W coast of Honshū, Japan, in Fukui prefecture.

Wa·ka·ti·pu Lake \ˌwäk-ə-ˌtē-pü-, ˌwäk-ə-ˌtip-\. Lake, SW South I., New Zealand; 48 m. long; 113 sq. m.; max. depth 1239 ft.

Wa·ka·ya·ma \ˌwäk-ə-'yäm-ə\. **1** Prefecture, SW Honshū, Japan; 1821 sq. m.; pop. (1970c) 1,042,736; ✱ Wakayama.

2 Seaport city, its ✱, 35 m. SSW of Ōsaka on Kii Channel; pop. (1970c) 365,267; textiles, lacquerware. Was seat of one of the Tokugawa branches; has large castle built in 16th cent. by Hideyoshi. Earthquake and tidal wave Dec. 21, 1946.

Wak·de \'wäk-də\. Group of small islands off NE coast of Irian Barat, Indonesia, halfway bet. Tanahmerah Bay and the mouth of the Mamberamo river; 1°57′S, 139°01′E; site of Japanese airdrome seized by Allies May 21, 1944.

Wake \'wāk\. County in North Carolina. See table at NORTH CAROLINA.

Wa Kee·ney \ˈwȯ-ˌkē-nē\. City, ⊗ of Trego co., W cen. Kansas, 78 m. NW of Great Bend; pop. (1970c) 2334.

Wake·field \ˈwāk-ˌfēld\. 1 Town, Middlesex co., NE Massachusetts, 10 m. N of Boston; pop. (1970c) 25,402; footwear, window screens, iron pipe, plastics.

2 City, Gogebic co., NW Michigan penin., 12 m. E of Ironwood; pop. (1970c) 2757.

3 Village and summer resort, Washington co., S Rhode Island, ab. 3 m. SSE of Kingston; pop. (1970c) 3570; administrative center of South Kingstown; Mount Saint Joseph Coll. (1953).

4 *or* **Bridg·es Creek** \ˈbrij-əz-\. Estate, Westmoreland co., Virginia, S bank of Potomac river and near mouth of Popes Creek; birthplace of George Washington. Estate acquired by Augustine Washington 1718; became property 1923 of Wakefield National Memorial Association which later conveyed its acres to the United States as the George Washington Birthplace National Monument (see UNITED STATES, *National Monuments*).

5 City and county borough, ⊗ of West Riding, Yorkshire, N England, on the Calder 10 m. S of Leeds; pop. (1971p) 59,650; textiles, chemicals, machinery; coal mining, brewing. Scene of battle (Wars of the Roses) at which Richard, Duke of York, was captured and beheaded by Lancastrians; possibly scene, ab. 15th cent., of presentation of the Towneley Mysteries or Wakefield Plays, one of the four collections of English miracle plays (see CHESTER 10, COVENTRY 3, YORK 12).

Wake Forest. Town, Wake co., E cen. North Carolina, 16 m. NNE of Raleigh; pop. (1970c) 3148.

Wake Island. Small sandy island, N Pacific Ocean, 480 m. N of N Marshall Is., 1180 m. W of Midway and 1500 m. ENE of Guam, 19°17′N, 166°36′E; total area 3 sq. m.; highest point 21 ft.; pop. (including Peale and Wilkes, [1970c]) 1978; actually three islets around a lagoon: Wake, the largest, on the E, Peale on the N, and Wilkes on the SW. Acquired by United States July 4, 1898, by expeditionary force on the way to Manila; became civil aviation station 1935 and naval and air station 1939–41. Captured by Japan Dec. 23, 1941, after resistance of 15 days by small contingent of U.S. Marines. Frequently raided 1942–44.

Wake·ly, Mount \-ˈwā-klē\. Peak in the Adirondack Mts., Hamilton co., NE cen. New York; 3617 ft.

Wa·ke·naam \ˌwäk-ə-ˈnäm\. Island at mouth of Essequibo river, off NE coast of Guyana.

Wa·khan \wä-ˈkän\. 1 High narrow valley in the Pamirs, NE Afghanistan, forming a district extending E to long. 75°E bet. Tadzhik S.S.R., U.S.S.R. and Pakistan.

2 *or* **Ab–i Wakhan** \ˌab-ē-\. River, flowing W through the valley, an upper tributary of the Ab-i-Pandj forming in part its NW boundary.

Wak·ka·nai \ˌwäk-ə-ˈnī\. Seaport town, Hokkaidō prefecture, N extremity of Hokkaidō, Japan, on S side of Sōya Strait; pop. (1970c) 54,493.

Wa·kul·la \wä-ˈkəl-ə\. 1 County in Florida. See table at FLORIDA.

2 Village, N Wakulla co., NW Florida, S of Tallahassee; nearby is **Wakulla Springs,** a pool (ab. 4 acres) out of which flows the **Wakulla River.**

Wa·la·chia *or* **Wal·la·chia** \wä-ˈlā-kē-ə\. Former principality bet. Danube river and Transylvanian Alps, now part of Romania; 29,575 sq. m.

History: Inhabited by a people which combines Slavic stock with strain possibly derived from Roman colonists of Dacia (*q.v.*); established as principality by Radul Negru (d. 1310), a vassal of Hungary; Târgoviște (Tîrgoviște) its capital 1383–1698; made tributary to Turks in 15th cent.; under Prince Michael the Bold (1593–1601) annexed Moldavia and Transylvania (*qq.v.*); from 1716 ruled by Phanariots from Constantinople instead of by dependent native princes; Little Walachia held by Austria 1713–39; occupied by Russia 1769; for history after 1774, see DANUBIAN PRINCIPALITIES.

Wał·brzych \ˈvälb-ˌzhik\; *Ger.* **Wal·den·burg** \ˈväl-dən-ˌbu̇(ə)rg\ *also* **Waldenburg in Schle·si·en** \-in-ˈshlā-zē-ən\. Industrial city, S Wrocław prov., SW Poland, on the Bóbr 42 m. SW of Wrocław; pop. (1970p) 125,000; chemicals, glass, ceramics; coal mines; assigned to Poland by Potsdam Conference 1945.

Wal·che·ren \ˈväl-kə-rən\. Island of the Netherlands, in Zeeland prov., in the North Sea off the SW coast; 11 m. in diameter; area 82 sq. m.; chief towns Vlissingen and Middelburg. Scene of earl of Chatham's unsuccessful expedition 1809 during Napoleonic Wars in attempt to capture Antwerp; in World War II strongly defended by German force but after Allied bombing of dikes occupied by British Nov. 1–3, 1944; drained again by Dec. 1945.

Wal·deck \ˈväl-(ˌ)dek\. Former German state, now part of Hesse, West Germany; 407 sq. m.; ✱ Arolsen. In Middle Ages a county; in 1712 raised to a principality; became part of Prussia 1867 and 1918–29 was a republic, forming a constituent state of the Weimar Republic; part of Hesse-Nassau prov., Prussia, 1929–45.

Wal·den \ˈwȯl-dən\. 1 Town, ⊗ of Jackson co., N Colorado; pop. (1970c) 907; coal mines, oil wells.

2 Village, Orange co., SE New York, 10 m. WNW of Newburgh; pop. (1970c) 5277; cutlery, furniture; diversified agriculture.

Waldenburg *or* **Waldenburg in Schlesien.** See WAŁBRZYCH.

Walden Pond. Pond, Middlesex co., NE Massachusetts, near Concord; on its shore Henry Thoreau lived 1845–47; results of his study and thought and observations of nature published 1854 as series of essays in *Walden, or Life in the Woods.*

Walden Ridge. Ridge extending from NE to SW in E cen. Tennessee.

Wald·heim \ˈvält-ˌhīm\. City, Leipzig dist., East Germany, 32 m. W of Dresden; pop. (1970e) 11,580; manufactures perfumes, wooden goods; serpentine quarrying.

Wal·do \ˈwȯl-(ˌ)dō, ˈwäl-\. County in Maine. See table at MAINE.

Wal·do·boro \ˈwȯl-dō-ˌbər-e, ˈwäl-, -ˌbə-rə\. Town, Lincoln co., S Maine, 26 m. ESE of Augusta; pop. (1970c) 3146.

Wal·dron \ˈwȯl-drən\. City, ⊗ of Scott co., W Arkansas; pop. (1970c) 2132; feed, dairy farms.

Waldstätter, Die Vier. See FOREST CANTONS, THE FOUR.

Wald·wick \ˈwȯl-(ˌ)dwik\. Residential borough, Bergen co., NE New Jersey, 7 m. N of Paterson; pop. (1970c) 12,313.

Walensee. See WALLEN, LAKE.

Wales \ˈwālz\. 1 Principality, forming wide peninsula on W of island of Great Britain; constitutes an integral part of the United Kingdom of Great Britain and Northern Ireland; 8016 sq. m.; pop. (1971p) 2,723,596; ✱ Cardiff.

Physical features: Bounded on N by Irish Sea, on E by England, on S by Bristol Channel, on W by St. George's Channel; St. David's Head, Pembrokeshire, its westernmost point, 5°19′W. Almost entirely an upland region, known generally as the Cambrian Mts.; highest mountains Snowdon massif in NW 3560 ft., highest point in England and Wales; Berwyn Mts. in NE and Brecon Beacons in SE. Its chief streams are the Dee in N, upper course of Severn in E, and Conway in N; numerous small lakes. Coastline irregular, indented by wide bays, esp. Cardigan Bay on W, enclosed on N by Lleyn Penin. and bounded on S by the large peninsula formed by counties of Pembroke, Cardigan, and Carmarthen. Only large island is Anglesey off NW coast, separated from mainland by narrow Menai Strait. *Chief industries:* Iron and steel, chemicals, paper; coal mining, ore smelting, oil refining; livestock raising; tourism. *Chief cities:* Cardiff, Swansea, Newport, Rhondda, Port Talbot. Divided into the following 13 counties (for pronunciation of their names, see their individual entries):

NAME[1]	AREA (sq. m.)	POP. (1971p)	CO. SEAT
Anglesey	276	59,705	Beaumaris
Brecknockshire	733	53,234	Brecknock
Caernarvonshire	569	122,852	Caernarvon

NAME[1]	AREA (sq. m.)	POP. (1971p)	CO. SEAT
Cardiganshire	693	54,844	Cardigan
Carmarthenshire	920	162,313	Carmarthen
Denbighshire	669	184,824	Ruthin
Flintshire	256	175,396	Mold
Glamorganshire	818	1,255,374	Cardiff
Merionethshire	660	35,277	Dolgellen
Monmouthshire[2]	542	461,459	Monmouth
Montgomeryshire	797	42,761	Welshpool
Pembrokeshire	614	97,295	Pembroke
Radnorshire	471	18,262	Presteigne

[1]For county names ending in -shire, the -shire is often omitted in informal use when there is no ambiguity. In legal use, county of Denbigh, Flint, etc., not Denbighshire, Flintshire, etc., is preferred. The redundant county of Denbighshire, etc. is regarded as incorrect.
[2]Monmouthshire (*q.v.*) is sometimes regarded as a part of England.

History: Inhabited in prehistoric times by the insular branch of the Celts, the Cymric, or Brythonic people, whose land covered much larger area than present Wales, extending into W and SW England; conquered by Romans in their occupation of Britain (see GREAT BRITAIN); remained Celtic during Anglo-Saxon invasions; in 12th cent. Normans established marches on Welsh border and in S Wales; N Wales conquered by Edward I 1277–84 and Wales made an English principality by Statute of Wales 1284; since 1301 the heir to the English throne has been Prince of Wales; incorporated with England by series of statutes drawn up in reign of Henry VIII; secretary of state for Wales, having seat in British cabinet, appointed 1964.

2 City on Cape Prince of Wales, W Alaska; westernmost point of mainland of North America, 168°05′W; pop. (1970c) 131.

Walfischbai. See WALVIS BAY 2.

Walfish Bay. See WALVIS BAY 1.

Wal·green Coast \ˌwȯl-grēn-\. Region on coast of Antarctica, W of Thurston Island (*q.v.*) and bordering on Amundsen Sea.

Wal·hal·la \wȯl-ˈhal-ə\. 1 City, Pembina co., NE corner of North Dakota, 80 m. NNW of Grand Forks; pop. (1970c) 1471; resort; ships potatoes.

2 Town, ⊗ of Oconee co., NW South Carolina, near Blue Ridge Mts. 31 m. WNW of Anderson; pop. (1970c) 3662; clothing, lumber, fertilizer; agriculture.

Wal·hon·ding \wȯl-ˈhän-diŋ\. River, Coshocton co., cen. Ohio, formed by junction of forks 16 m. NW of Coshocton; flows SE and joins Tuscarawas river to form Muskingum river.

Walk·er \ˈwȯ-kər\. 1 River, W cen. Nevada; ab. 50 m. long; formed in Lyon co. by branches which rise in California, flows N and then SE through Walker River Indian Reservation into Walker Lake.

2 Name of counties in three states of the U.S. See tables at ALABAMA, GEORGIA, TEXAS.

3 City, Kent co., W Michigan, 6 m. W of Grand Rapids; pop. (1970c) 11,492.

4 Village, ⊗ of Cass co., N cen. Minnesota; pop. (1970c) 1073.

Walker Lake. Lake, NW Mineral co., SW Nevada; ab. 28 m. long; no outlet.

Walker Pass. Mountain pass, Kern co., S California, in S end of the Sierra Nevada; 5250 ft.; named for the American trapper and guide, Joseph Walker, who explored this region 1834 ff.

Walk·er·ton \ˈwȯ-kər-tən\. Industrial town, ⊗ of Bruce co., SE Ontario, Canada, on Saugeen river 33 m. S of Owen Sound; pop. (1971p) 4364; lumber, flour; dairy, livestock farms.

Wall·a·bout Bay \ˌwȯ-lə-ˌbau̇t-\. Inlet of the East river, N shore of W end of Long I., New York, and opp. SE corner of Manhattan I.

Wal·lace \ˈwäl-əs\. 1 County in Kansas. See table at KANSAS.

2 City, ⊗ of Shoshone co., NE Idaho, 45 m. ESE of Coeur d'Alene; pop. (1970c) 2206; lead, silver, zinc mines.

Wal·lace·burg \ˈwäl-əs-ˌbərg\. Industrial town, Kent co., SE Ontario, Canada, 17 m. NW of Chatham; pop. (1971p) 10,553; glass, plastics, brass goods; cannery, sugar refinery; tomatoes.

Wallachia. See WALACHIA.

Wal·la·roo \ˈwäl-ə-ˌrü\. Seaport town, SE South Australia, on E shore of Spencer Gulf 90 m. NW of Adelaide; pop. (1966c) 2094; mining center; copper smelters.

Wal·la·sey \ˈwäl-ə-sē\. County borough, Cheshire, NW England, on Irish Sea 9 m. W of Liverpool; pop. (1971p) 97,061; residential suburb of Liverpool; incorporated 1910.

Wal·la Wal·la \ˌwäl-ə-ˈwäl-ə, ˈwäl-ə-ˌ\. 1 County in SE Washington. See table at WASHINGTON.

2 City, its ⊗, ab. 118 m. SW of Spokane near **Walla Walla River;** pop. (1970c) 23,619; lumber, dairy products; cans vegetables; livestock, alfalfa, peas; Whitman Coll. (1859), Walla Walla Coll. (1892, at College Place, a suburb), Walla Walla Community Coll. (1967). Settled around U.S. Army fort; founded 1856; incorporated 1862.

Walled Lake \ˈwȯld-\. City, Oakland co., SE Michigan, 28 m. NW of Detroit; pop. (1970c) 3759; summer resort.

Wal·len, Lake \-ˈväl-ən\; *Ger.* **Wa·len·see** *or* **Wal·len·see** \ˈväl-ən-ˌzā\. Lake, Saint Gallen canton, NE Switzerland; 9 sq. m.; receives the Linth river from the S; linked by canal (Linth Canal) with the Lake of Zurich to the W.

Wal·len·pau·pack, Lake \-ˌwäl-ən-ˈpȯ-ˌpak\. Lake on boundary bet. Wayne and Pike cos., NE Pennsylvania; 9 sq. m.; formed by dam in **Wallenpaupack Creek.**

Wal·ler \ˈwäl-ər\. County in Texas. See table at TEXAS.

Wall·face Mountain \ˌwȯl ˌfās-\. Peak in the Adirondack Mts., Essex co., NE New York; 3860 ft.

Wal·ling·ford \ˈwäl-iŋ-fərd, -ˌfō(ə)rd, -ˌfȯ(ə)rd\. 1 Town, NE New Haven co., S Connecticut, S of Meriden; pop. (1970c) 35,714; includes industrial borough of Wallingford on Quinnipiac river 12 m. NE of New Haven; chemicals, silverware, hardware, clothing, electronic components.

2 Municipal borough, Berkshire, S England; pop. (1971p) 6184; treaty 1153 (negotiated here but signed at Westminster) bet. King Stephen and Prince Henry, by which Stephen kept throne for his lifetime, and Henry succeeded him.

Wal·ling·ton \ˈwȯl-iŋ-tən\. Borough, Bergen co., NE corner of New Jersey, on Passaic river 6 m. SSE of Paterson; pop. (1969e) 10,284; paints, curtains.

Wallis. See VALAIS.

Wal·lis and Fu·tu·na Islands \ˈwäl-əs . . . fə-ˈtü-nə-\. French overseas territory, SW Pacific Ocean; 64 sq. m.; pop. (1969e) 8546; comprises the two groups of Wallis Is. and Futuna Is.; until 1959 a dependency of New Caledonia.

Wallis Islands. Island group, SW Pacific Ocean, a part of Wallis and Futuna Islands (*q.v.*); 35 sq. m.; pop. (1965e) 5711; comprises the main island of Uvéa and eight islets, all enclosed in one coral reef. Discovered by Samuel Wallis, English navigator, 1767; occupied by French 1842; joined with Futuna Is. 1887 and administratively attached to New Caledonia colony until 1959.

Wallo. See WELO.

Wal·lo·nia \wä-ˈlō-nē-ə\ *or Fr.* **Wal·lo·nie** \wä-lȯ-nē\. Name sometimes applied to the French-speaking part of Belgium, comprising provs. of Hainaut, Liège, Luxembourg, Namur, and S part of Brabant.

Wal·lops Island \ˈwäl-əps-\. Island, Accomac co., E Virginia, in Atlantic Ocean NE of Assawaman Inlet; 6 sq. m.; rocket-launching base.

Wal·lowa \wä-ˈlau̇-ə\. 1 River, NE Oregon; ab. 50 m. long; rises in Wallowa Lake, S Wallowa co., flows NW into Grande Ronde river on Wallowa co. boundary.

2 County in Oregon. See table at OREGON.

Wallowa Lake. Lake, S Wallowa co., NE corner of Oregon.

Wallowa Mountains. Range, S Wallowa, N Baker, and E Union cos., NE Oregon; highest peak 9832 ft.

Walls·end \'wȯl-ˌzend\. Municipal borough, Northumberland, N England, on the Tyne 4 m. ENE of Newcastle upon Tyne; pop. (1971p) 45,793; in coal-mining section (*Wallsend coal* takes its name from this place); shipyards. At eastern end of Hadrian's Wall, hence the name.

Wal·ney \'wȯl-nē\. Island off NW coast of England, N of entrance to Morecambe Bay; 8 m. long; pop. (1961c) 8013; bridge connects with Barrow in Furness, Lancashire.

Wal·nut \'wȯl-(ˌ)nət\. **1** River, SE Kansas; ab. 90 m. long; rises in N Butler co. flows S into Arkansas river at Arkansas City, S Cowley co., S Kansas.

2 City, Los Angeles co., SW California, 18 m. E of Los Angeles; pop. (1970c) 5992.

Walnut Canyon National Monument. See UNITED STATES, *National Monuments.*

Walnut Creek. City, Contra Costa co., W California, 10 m. S of Suisun Bay; pop. (1970c) 39,844; canned goods, power tools; processes walnuts; diversified agriculture.

Walnut Ridge. City, a ⊗ of Lawrence co., NE Arkansas; pop. (1970c) 3800; Southern Baptist Coll. (1941).

Wal·pole \'wȯl-ˌpōl, 'wäl-\. **1** Industrial town, Norfolk co., E Massachusetts, 18 m. SW of Boston; pop. (1970c) 18,149; textiles; state prison.

2 Town, Cheshire co., SW New Hampshire, on Connecticut river 13 m. NW of Keene; pop. (1970c) 2966; settled 1749.

Walpole Island. Island, New Caledonia, SW Pacific Ocean, ab. 154 m. SSE of Nouméa; ab. 310 acres; guano deposits.

Wal·sall \'wȯl-ˌsȯl\. County borough, Staffordshire, W cen. England, 10 m. NNW of Birmingham; pop. (1971p) 184,606; chemicals, aircraft parts, machine tools, leather goods; coal mines, limestone quarries.

Wal·sen·burg \'wȯl-sən-ˌbərg\. City, ⊗ of Huerfano co., S Colorado, 45 m. S of Pueblo; pop. (1970c) 4329; flour, dairy products; coal mines.

Walsh \'wȯlsh\. County in North Dakota. See table at NORTH DAKOTA.

Wal·sing·ham, Cape \-'wȯl-siŋ-ˌham\. Cape, E Baffin I., E Franklin dist., Northwest Territories, Canada, extending into Davis Strait.

Wal·sum \'väl-ˌzu̇m\. Industrial commune, North Rhine-Westphalia, West Germany, ab. 8 m. NNW of Duisburg, on the Rhine river; pop. (1969e) 48,262; manufactures paper, steel, tile.

Wal·ter·boro \'wȯl-tər-ˌbər-ə, -ˌbə-rə\. Town and winter resort, ⊗ of Colleton co., S South Carolina, 45 m. W of Charleston; pop. (1970c) 6257; lumber, cotton.

Wal·ters \'wȯl-tərz\. City, ⊗ of Cotton co., SW Oklahoma, 17 m. S of Lawton; pop. (1970c) 2611.

Wal·thall \'wȯl-(ˌ)thȯl\. **1** County in Mississippi. See table at MISSISSIPPI.

2 Village, ⊗ of Webster co., N cen. Mississippi; pop. (1970c) 161.

Wal·tham \'wȯl-ˌtham, *chiefly by outsiders* -thəm\. Industrial city, Middlesex co., NE Massachusetts, 9 m. W of Boston; pop. (1970c) 61,582; electronic components, precision instruments, clocks and watches, clothing, paint and varnish, iron castings; Bentley Coll. of Accounting and Finance (1917), Brandeis Univ. (1947). Settled 1636; incorporated as town 1738; first paper mill in U.S. founded here 1788 and first power loom for manufacture of cotton textiles 1814; incorporated as city 1884.

Waltham Forest \ˌwȯl-thəm-, -təm-\. A borough of Greater London, SE England. See table at LONDON 4.

Waltham Holy Cross *or* **Waltham Abbey.** Urban district, Essex, SE England, NE suburb of London; pop. (1971p) 14,585; plastics; greenhouses; remains of 11th cent. abbey church; part of Greater London.

Wal·ton \'wȯlt-ᵊn\. **1** Name of counties in two states of the U.S. See tables at FLORIDA and GEORGIA.

2 Village, Delaware co., S New York, on Delaware river 42 m. E of Binghamton; pop. (1970c) 3732.

Walton and Wey·bridge \-'wā-(ˌ)brij\. Urban district, Surrey, S England; pop. (1971p) 51,004.

Walton–le–Dale \-lə-'dāl\. Urban district, Lancashire, NW England, on the Ribble 26 m. NW of Manchester; pop. (1971p) 26,841; cotton mills, iron foundries.

Walton Mountain. Peak, Glacier National Park, NW Montana; 8931 ft.

Wal·trop \'väl-ˌtrȯp\. Commune, North Rhine-Westphalia, West Germany, NNW suburb of Dortmund; pop. (1969e) 25,122; coal mining; manufactures tile.

Wal·vis Bay \ˌwȯl-vəs-\. **1** *also* **Wal·fish Bay** \ˌwȯl-fish-\. Inlet of Atlantic Ocean, W cen. coast of South-West Africa, 22°59′S, 14°31′E.

2 *or Ger.* **Wal·fisch·bai** \'väl-fish-ˌbī\. Town, W South-West Africa, on Atlantic Ocean 170 m. W of Windhoek and 710 m. N of Cape Town by sea; town, harbor, and immediate vicinity (434 sq. m.; pop. [1965e] 17,877) an exclave of Cape Province; good harbor and railroad terminus; trades esp. in frozen meats; whaling and fishing industries.

Wal·wal *or* **Ual·ual** \'wȯl-ˌwȯl\. Settlement, SE Ethiopia, near Somalia border; scene of clash bet. Italian and Ethiopian forces Dec. 5, 1934. See ETHIOPIA.

Wal·worth \'wȯl-(ˌ)wərth\. Name of counties in two states of the U.S. See tables at SOUTH DAKOTA and WISCONSIN.

Wa·me·go \wä-'mē-(ˌ)gō\. City, Pottawatomie co., NE Kansas, on Kansas river E of Manhattan; pop. (1970c) 2507; snow plows, fertilizer; livestock.

Wamps·ville \'wämps-ˌvil\. Village, ⊗ of Madison co., cen. New York, 25 m. E of Syracuse; pop. (1970c) 586.

Wa·na \'wän-ə\. Village and frontier post, Pakistan, 85 m. WNW of Dera Ismail Khan, beyond Gumal Pass and near Afghanistan border; occupied 1894 by British expedition; later (1922) abandoned but reoccupied 1929. See WAZIRISTAN.

Wa·na·ka, Lake \-'wän-ə-kə\. Lake, SW cen. South I., New Zealand; 74 sq. m.; 28 m. long.

Wan·a·pi·tei Lake \ˌwän-ə-pə-'tā-\. Lake, S cen. Sudbury dist., SE Ontario, Canada; drains S through the **Wanapitei River** (ab. 60 m. long) into Georgian Bay.

Wan·a·que \wə-'näk-(w)ē; 'wän-ə-ˌkyü, -ə-kē\. Borough, Passaic co., N New Jersey, 10 m. NW of Paterson; pop. (1970c) 8636.

Wa·na·wa·na \ˌwän-ə-'wän-ə\. Small island off NW coast of New Georgia I., cen. Solomon Is., W Pacific Ocean, S of Arundel I.

Wan–ch'uan. See KALGAN.

Wan·damm·en Bay \wän-ˌdäm-ən-\. Inlet, W Sarera Bay, NW coast of Irian Barat, Indonesia, nearly opp. Berau Bay.

Wan·di·wash *or* **Wan·de·wash** \'wən-di-ˌwäsh\. Town, Tamil Nadu, S India, 60 m. SW of Madras; pop. (1961c) 12,500; scene of several conflicts bet. French and British 1752 to 1759, and especially of victory Jan. 22, 1760 of British under Col. (later Sir) Eyre Coote over the French under Lally.

Wan·dle \'wȯn-dᵊl\. River, Surrey co., S England; 9 m. long; flows NW into the Thames at Wandsworth.

Wands·worth \'wän(d)z-(ˌ)wərth\. A borough of Greater London, SE England. See table at LONDON 4.

Wang \'wäŋ\. River, N tributary of the Ping river, NW Thailand; ab. 150 m. long; flows S from hills S of Chiang Rai to the Ping above Tak.

Wang·a·nui \ˌwäŋ-(g)ə-'nü-ē\. **1** River, SW cen. North I., New Zealand; ab. 180 m. long; rises in Tongariro National Park, flows W and S into N part of Cook Strait; flows through region which was original home of Maoris.

2 Seaport city, W North I., New Zealand, at mouth of Wanganui river 95 m. N of Wellington; pop. (1970e) 36,600; has export trade in wool, meat, and dairy produce. Founded 1842; Maoris and British engaged in conflicts in this locality in 1847, 1864, and 1868.

Wan·ga·rat·ta \ˌwaŋ-gə-ˈrat-ə\. Town, N Victoria, SE Australia, 130 m. NE of Melbourne; pop. (1968e) 15,640.

Wang·er·oo·ge \ˌväŋ-ə-ˈrō-gə\. Island, most easterly of the East Frisian Is., in North Sea off NW coast of West Germany; 6 m. long.

Wang·i·wangi \ˌwäŋ-ē-ˈwäŋ-ē\. Island, Banda Sea, 25 m. off E coast of Butung I., and in NW part of the Tukangbesi Is.; lighthouse.

Wang Mai Khon. See SAWANKHALOK.

Wangyehmiao. See K'O-ERH-CH'IN-YU-I-CH'IEN-CH'I.

Wan·hsien \ˈwän-shē-ˈen\. City, E Szechwan prov., S cen. China, on left bank of Yangtze river 130 m. below Chungking in mountainous district at upper end of Yangtze Gorges; pop. (1970e) 175,000; important river port, opened to foreign trade 1917; has temple dedicated to Li Po, famous Chinese poet who resided here.

Wan·ka·ner \wäŋ-ˈkän-ər\. Former Indian state, W India, S of Morvi, now part of Gujarat state.

Wan·kie \ˈwäŋ-kē\. Town, W Rhodesia, near Victoria Falls; pop. (1970e) 21,000; coal mines.

Wankie National Park. National park, Rhodesia; 5600 sq. m.; wildlife reserve; established 1950.

Wan·ne–Eick·el \ˈvän-ə-ˈī-kəl\. Industrial city, North Rhine-Westphalia, West Germany, in Ruhr valley 8 m. NE of Essen; pop. (1969e) 100,263; railroad center; chemicals, beer; coal mines; formed 1926.

Wan–shan Islands \ˈwän-ˈshän-\ *or formerly* **La·drone Islands** \lə-ˈdrōn-\. Island group, China Sea, opp. entrance to the Pearl river.

Wan–shou–shan \ˈwän-ˈshō-ˈshän\. Park, N Hopeh prov., NE China, 8 m. NW of Peking; nearby was the Summer Palace, resort of imperial family, built by Emperor Yung Chêng in early 18th cent., original palaces destroyed 1860 by British under orders from Lord Elgin; rebuilt by Dowager Empress Tzu Hsi.

Wan·tage \ˈwänt-ij\. Urban district, cen. Berkshire, England, in the Vale of the White Horse (*q.v.*); pop. (1971p) 8007; birthplace of Alfred the Great.

Wan·tagh \ˈwän-ˌtȯ\. Urban community (unincorporated), Nassau co., SE New York, on Long I., SE of Hempstead; pop. (1970c) 21,873.

Wan–t'ing *or* **Wan·ting** \ˈwän-ˈtiŋ\. Frontier town on E bank of Shweli river, W Yunnan, S China, N of Namhkam; alt. 3200 ft.; held by Japanese during World War II; retaken by Chinese and U.S. forces Jan. 17–18, 1945.

Waoekara. See WAUKARA.

Wa·pa·ko·neta \ˌwȯ-pə-kə-ˈnet-ə\. City, ⊗ of Auglaize co., W Ohio, 13 m. S of Lima; pop. (1970c) 7324; plastics, furnaces, dairy products; diversified agriculture.

Wap·el·lo \ˈwäp-ə-ˌlō\. 1 County in Iowa. See table at IOWA.
2 City, ⊗ of Louisa co., SE Iowa, 19 m. SSW of Muscatine; pop. (1970c) 1873; agriculture; prehistoric Indian mounds nearby.

Wap·pin·gers Falls \ˌwäp-in-jərz-\. Village, Dutchess co., SE New York, near Hudson river 8 m. S of Poughkeepsie; pop. (1970c) 5607; foundries, agriculture; waterpower supplied by 75-ft. cascade in **Wap·pin·ger Creek** \ˈwäp-in-jər-\.

Wap·si·pin·i·con \ˌwäp-sə-ˈpin-ə-kən\. River, E Iowa and S Minnesota; 255 m. long; rises in S Mower co., S Minnesota, flows SE into Mississippi river forming most of boundary bet. Clinton and Scott cos., E Iowa.

Wa·quoit Bay \ˌwȯ-ˌkwȯit-\. Inlet of Nantucket Sound, S coast of W Barnstable co., SE Massachusetts.

Wa·ra·bi \wä-ˈräb-ē\. City, Saitama prefecture, Honshū, Japan, 12 m. NW of Tokyo; pop. (1970c) 77,225.

Wa·ra·maug, Lake \-ˈwȯr-ə-ˌmȯg\. Lake, W cen. Litchfield co., NW Connecticut; resort region.

Wa·ran·gal \ˈwȯr-əŋ-gəl\. City, N Andhra Pradesh, S cen. India, 86 m. ENE of Hyderabad; pop. (1970e) 181,255; textiles, silk, carpets; 12th cent. capital of Telugu Kingdom.

Warasdin. See VARAŽDIN.

War·burg \ˈwȯr-ˌbərg, ˈvär-ˌbu̇(ə)rg\. Town, North Rhine-Westphalia, West Germany; scene of battle July 31, 1760 in which Duke Ferdinand of Brunswick defeated the French (Seven Years' War).

War·bur·ton, The \-ˈwȯr-(ˌ)bərt-ᵊn\. River, NE South Australia; 275 m. long; flows SW into Lake Eyre.

Ward \ˈwȯ(ə)rd\. Name of counties in two states of the U.S. See tables at NORTH DAKOTA and TEXAS.

War·dak \ˈwär-ˌdäk\. Province of E cen. Afghanistan. See table at AFGHANISTAN.

Wardastalla. See GUASTALLA.

War·dha \ˈwȯrd-ə\. 1 River, E Maharashtra, cen. India; ab. 290 m. long; rises in NW, flows SE to unite on the S border with Wainganga river and form the Pranhita river; receives the Penganga from the W.
2 Town, E Maharashtra, cen. India, 45 m. SW of Nagpur; pop. (1961c) 49,113; occasional residence and retreat of Gandhi during his last years.

Ward Hunt, Cape \-ˈwȯ(ə)rd-ˈhənt\. Cape, Papua New Guinea, New Guinea I., on Solomon Sea, 8°05′S, 149°55′E.

Ward Hunt Strait. Passage bet. D'Entrecasteaux Is. and Papua New Guinea, New Guinea I., connecting Collingwood Bay and Solomon Sea on the NW with Goschen Strait on SE; 75 m. long, ab. 20 m. wide.

Ward's Island \ˈwȯ(ə)rdz-\. Island in East river, New York, part of Manhattan borough, just S of Randall's I.; 255 acres. Crossed by Triborough Bridge.

Ware \ˈwa(ə)r, ˈwe(ə)r\. 1 River, cen. Massachusetts; ab. 40 m. long; rises in Worcester co., flows SW into Swift river near N border of Hampden co.
2 County in Georgia. See table at GEORGIA.
3 Town, Hampshire co., W Massachusetts, 21 m. ENE of Springfield; pop. (1970c) 8187; textiles, iron castings.
4 Urban district, Hertfordshire, SE England, on the Lea 23 m. N of London; pop. (1971p) 14,666; market town; railroad cars, malt. The "great bed of Ware," mentioned in Shakespeare's *Twelfth Night*, formerly at the Saracen's Head inn here, was removed to Rye House (*q.v.*).

Wa·re·gem *or* **Wae·re·ghem** \ˈvär-ə-gəm\. Commune, West Flanders prov., NW Belgium, 43 m. W of Brussels; pop. (1969e) 17,664; site of Flanders Field Cemetery, the only U.S. military cemetery in Belgium for soldiers of World War I.

Ware·ham \ˈwar-əm, ˈwer-; ˈwa(ə)r-ˌham, ˈwe(ə)r-\. 1 Town, Plymouth co., SE Massachusetts, 13 m. ENE of New Bedford; pop. (1970c) 11,492; summer resort; oyster fisheries; cranberries.
2 Municipal borough, SE Dorsetshire, S England, on NW edge of the Isle of Purbeck; pop. (1971p) 4379; very old town, has remains of ancient earthworks.

Wa·ren \ˈvär-ən\. City, Neubrandenburg dist., East Germany, 60 m. E of Schwerin; pop. (1970e) 21,332; summer resort; dairy products, lumber.

Ware Shoals \ˈwa(ə)r-, we(ə)r-\. Village, Greenwood co., W South Carolina, on Saluda river ab. 17 m. N of Greenwood; pop. (1970c) 2480.

Wargla. See OUARGLA.

Warka. See ERECH.

Wark·worth \ˈwȯ(ə)rk-(ˌ)wərth\. Town, Northumberland, N England, ab. 1½ m. from the North Sea coast; pop. (1961c) 1246; Norman castle; hermitage and remains of Benedictine priory nearby.

War·ley \ˈwȯr-lē\. County borough, Worcestershire, W cen. England; pop. (1971p) 163,388; chemicals, steel tubes; glass works.

Warm·bad \ˈvärm-ˌbät\. Town, S South-West Africa, near Orange river 350 m. N of Cape Town; dist. pop. (1960c) 9907.

Warmia. See ERMELAND.

War·min·ster \'wȯr-ˌmin(t)-stər\. 1 Urban township, Bucks co., SE Pennsylvania; pop. (1969e) 12,710.
2 Urban district, Wiltshire, S England; pop. (1971p) 13,593; market town in agricultural region; several prehistoric barrows nearby.

Warm Springs \'wȯ(ə)rm-\. 1 City, S Meriwether co., W Georgia; pop. (1970c) 523; health resort; site of Warm Springs Foundation, estab. 1927 by Franklin D. Roosevelt for treatment of infantile-paralysis patients, and of Franklin D. Roosevelt Museum.
2 Village, ⊗ of Bath co., W Virginia, 23 m. NNE of Covington; warm sulfur springs.

Warm Springs Reservoir. Irrigation reservoir in middle fork of Malheur river, bet. Harney and Malheur cos., E Oregon; formed by **Warm Springs Dam.**

War·ner \'wȯr-nər\. Town, Muskogee co., E Oklahoma, ab. 18 m. S of Muskogee; pop. (1970c) 1217; Connors State Coll. (1908).

Warner Mountains. Range, E Modoc co., NE California, and S Lake co., S Oregon; called **Warner Range** in Oregon.

Warner Rob·ins \-'räb-ənz\. City, Houston co., cen. Georgia, S of Macon; pop. (1970c) 33,491; aircraft parts; fruit and nuts.

Warn·ham \'wȯr-nəm\. Village just N of Horsham, Sussex, S England; birthplace of Percy Bysshe Shelley.

War·now \'vär-(ˌ)nō\. Stream, East Germany; 80 m. long; flows N to Gulf of Mecklenburg; navigable for seagoing vessels to Rostock.

Warnsdorf. See VARNSDORF.

Warqla. See OUARGLA.

Warr Acres \'wȯ(ə)r-\. City, Oklahoma co., cen. Oklahoma, W suburb of Oklahoma City; pop. (1970c) 9887.

War·re·go \'wär-i-ˌgō\. River, Australia; 495 m. long; flows SSW from S cen. Queensland to the Darling in N New South Wales.

War·ren \'wȯr-ən, 'wär-\. 1 Name of counties of fourteen states of the U.S. See tables at GEORGIA, ILLINOIS, INDIANA, IOWA, KENTUCKY, MISSISSIPPI, MISSOURI, NEW JERSEY, NEW YORK, NORTH CAROLINA, OHIO, PENNSYLVANIA, TENNESSEE, VIRGINIA.
2 City, ⊗ of Bradley co., S Arkansas, 46 m. E of Camden; pop. (1970c) 6433; cottonseed oil, lumber; truck farms.
3 Town, Worcester co., cen. Massachusetts, 20 m. W of Worcester; pop. (1970c) 3633.
4 City, Macomb co., SE Michigan, NNE of Detroit; pop. (1970c) 179,260; suburb of Detroit, Macomb County Community Coll. (1953).
5 City, ⊗ of Marshall co., NW Minnesota, 27 m. WNW of Thief River Falls; pop. (1970c) 1999.
6 City, ⊗ of Trumbull co., NE Ohio, 13 m. NW of Youngstown; pop. (1970c) 63,494; fans, blowers, tools, paint, iron and steel products; automobile assembly plant; incorporated as city 1869.
7 Borough, ⊗ of Warren co., NW Pennsylvania, 30 m. WSW of Bradford; pop. (1970c) 12,998; furniture, valves, tools, patent medicines; oil refineries; dairy farms.
8 Town and summer resort, Bristol co., E Rhode Island, on Narragansett Bay 10 m. SE of Providence; pop. (1970c) 10,523; textiles, automobile parts, rubber goods; oyster fisheries. Settled 1632; originally part of Swansea, Massachusetts; annexed by Rhode Island and incorporated as town 1747; seat of Rhode Island Coll. (now Brown Univ.) 1764–70; pillaged and burned by British during American Revolution 1778.

War·rens·burg \'wȯr-ənz-ˌbərg, 'wär-\. City, ⊗ of Johnson co., W Missouri, 30 m. W of Sedalia; pop. (1970c) 13,125; footwear; coal mines; stock, dairy farms; Central Missouri State Coll. (1871).

War·ren·ton \'wȯr-ən-tən, 'wär-\. 1 City, ⊗ of Warren co., E cen. Georgia; pop. (1970c) 2073.
2 City, ⊗ of Warren co., E Missouri; pop. (1970c) 2057.
3 Town, ⊗ of Warren co., N North Carolina; pop. (1970c) 1035; lumber, flour; tobacco.
4 Town, ⊗ of Fauquier co., N Virginia, in foothills of Blue Ridge 35 m. NNW of Fredericksburg; pop. (1970c) 6069; feed; raises horses; dairy farms.

War·ren·ville \'wȯr-ən-ˌvil, 'wär-\. City, Du Page co., NE Illinois, 8 m. NE of Aurora; pop. (1970c) 3268.

War·ri \'wȯr-ē, 'wär-\. Town, Mid-Western State, Nigeria, 190 m. ESE of Lagos in Niger delta; pop. (1969e) 64,078.

War·rick \'wȯr-ik\. County in Indiana. See table at INDIANA.

War·ring·ton \'wȯr-iŋ-tən, 'wär-\. 1 Urban community, Escambia co., NW Florida, W of Pensacola; pop. (1970c) 15,848.
2 County borough, Lancashire, NW England, on the Mersey 14 m. E of Liverpool; pop. (1971p) 68,262; cotton, iron, and leather goods; chemicals.

Warr·nam·bool \'wȯr-nəm-ˌbül\. Seaport town, SW Victoria, SE Australia, 140 m. WSW of Melbourne; pop. (1968e) 17,980; trade center for dairying and farming region.

War·rum·bun·gle National Park \ˌwȯr-əm-'bəŋ-gəl-\. National park, New South Wales, Australia; 22 sq. m.; mountain range; established 1953.

War·saw \'wȯr-ˌsȯ\. 1 City, Hancock co., W Illinois, on Mississippi river 30 m. N of Quincy; pop. (1970c) 1758.
2 City, ⊗ of Kosciusko co., N Indiana, 36 m. SE of South Bend; pop. (1970c) 7506; dairy products, furniture, aircraft parts; lake resort.
3 City, ⊗ of Gallatin co., N Kentucky; pop. (1970c) 1232.
4 City, ⊗ of Benton co., W cen. Missouri; pop. (1970c) 1423.
5 Village, ⊗ of Wyoming co., W New York, 39 m. SW of Rochester; pop. (1970c) 3619; knit goods; agriculture.
6 Town, ⊗ of Richmond co., E Virginia; pop. (1970c) 511.

Warsaw *or Pol.* **War·sza·wa** \vär-'shäv-ə\. 1 Former grand duchy, E Europe. See history at POLAND.
2 Province of Poland. See WARSZAWA.
3 *or Ger.* **War·schau** \'vär-ˌshau̇\. City, ✱ of Poland, also ✱ of Warszawa prov., E cen. Poland, on both banks of Vistula river; pop. (1970p) 1,308,000; railroad junction; industrial center producing steel, motor vehicles, chemicals, electronic components, textiles, pharmaceuticals; food processing, brewing, distilling. Archiepiscopal see (seat of Roman Catholic primate of Poland) and cultural and educational center; univ. (1818), technical univ. (1826, univ. status 1915) and other institutions; notable buildings (largely rebuilt since World War II) include 14th cent. Gothic cathedral, medieval royal castle (Zamek), numerous 17th and 18th cent. palaces (most now housing various government agencies), national theater and museum, monuments, parks, zoological gardens; 17th cent. castle of John III Sobieski to S.
History: First settlement on site in 11th cent.; city founded c. 1300 and important trade center 14th–16th cents.; came under Poland 1526; made capital of Poland 1596; destroyed by Charles X Gustavus of Sweden 1656; expanded rapidly during late 18th cent.; city partly burned and ab. one half of population massacred by Russians 1794; made capital of Grand Duchy of Warsaw by Napoleon 1807; taken by Russians 1813 and made capital of kingdom under Russian rule 1815; center of Polish insurrection 1830–31; in World War I occupied by Germans 1916–1918; became capital of Polish republic Nov. 1918; in World War II occupied by Germans after severe bombing Sept. 27, 1939; retaken by U.S.S.R. Sept. 1944–Jan. 17, 1945. City almost entirely destroyed during the war, but has since been largely rebuilt. Treaty establishing Warsaw Treaty Organization signed here 1955.

Warsaw Treaty Organization *or commonly* **Warsaw Pact.** Military alliance, consisting of Bulgaria, Czechoslovakia, East Germany, Hungary, Poland, Romania, U.S.S.R.; headquarters Moscow, U.S.S.R.; purpose is to promote joint defense of the Soviet bloc nations; represents the Communist counterpart of NATO; established 1955; Albania withdrew 1968; forces of the Organization carried out invasion of Czechoslovakia 1968; Romania has resisted integration of her forces with those of other members of the alliance, and refused to participate in the invasion of Czechoslovakia.

Warschau. See WARSAW 3.

War·sop \'wȯr-səp\. Urban district, Nottinghamshire, N cen. England, on the Meden 18 m. N of Nottingham; pop. (1971p) 13,036.

War·sza·wa \vär-'shäv-ə\ *or Eng.* **War·saw** \'wȯr-ˌsȯ\. Province of NE cen. Poland. See table at POLAND.

War·ta *or Ger.* **War·the** \'värt-ə\. River, Poland; 502 m. long; rises 35 m. NW of Kraków, flows NW and W into the Oder at Kostrzyn; navigable for 250 m. Its lower course formerly in Germany, now in region assigned to Poland by Potsdam Conference 1945. Its chief tributaries are the Prosna and Notec.

Wart·burg \'wȯrt-ˌbərg\. Town, ⊗ of Morgan co., NE cen. Tennessee; pop. (1970c) 541.

War·wick \'wär-ik; *U.S. also* 'wȯr-ik, 'wȯ(ə)r-(ˌ)wik, 'wär-(ˌ)wik\. 1 Former county in Virginia, incorporated 1952 as independent city of Warwick and consolidated 1958 with city of Newport News.

2 Village, Orange co., SE New York, 40 m. NNW of New York; pop. (1970c) 3604; agriculture.

3 City and summer resort, Kent co., cen. Rhode Island, on Narragansett Bay 10 m. S of Providence; pop. (1970c) 83,694; aluminum products, clothing, electronic components; truck and dairy farms; Seminary of Our Lady of Providence (1939). Settled 1643; admitted to "Incorporation of Providence Plantations" 1647.

4 Former city, Virginia: see 1, above.

5 Town, SE Queensland, Australia, 80 m. WSW of Brisbane; pop. (1968e) 10,150; viticulture, agriculture, and grazing.

6 Town, Arthabaska co., S Quebec, Canada, 37 m. N of Sherbrooke; pop. (1971p) 2577.

7 County, England. See WARWICKSHIRE.

8 Municipal borough, ⊗ of Warwickshire, cen. England, on the Avon 20 m. SSE of Birmingham; pop. (1971p) 18,289; gelatin, vehicle bodies; Norman castle, with notable collection of pictures.

War·wick·shire \'wär-ik-ˌshi(ə)r, -shər\ *or* **War·wick** \'wär-ik\. County, cen. England; 973 sq. m.; pop. (1971p) 2,079,799; ⊗ Warwick; grain and dairy farming, coal mining, manufacturing: metal goods, motor vehicles, aircraft, textiles, electrical equipment; major towns Birmingham, Coventry, Solihull.

Wa·satch \'wȯ-ˌsach\. County in Utah. See table at UTAH.

Wasatch Mountain. Peak, San Miguel co., SW Colorado; 13,335 ft.

Wasatch Range. Range extending from Bannock co., SE Idaho, S along the E boundary of the Great Basin to Sanpete co., cen. Utah; highest peak Mount Timpanogos 12,008 ft.

Was·co \'wäs-(ˌ)kō\. 1 County in Oregon. See table at OREGON.

2 City, Kern co., S California, NW of Bakersfield; pop. (1970c) 8269; chemicals; oil wells; grapes.

Wa·se·ca \wä-'sē-kə\. 1 County in S Minnesota. See table at MINNESOTA.

2 City, its ⊗, 23 m. ESE of Mankato; pop. (1970c) 6789; boats, dairy products, sporting goods; lake resort.

Wash, The \-'wȯsh, -'wäsh\. Shallow bay, an inlet of the North Sea, on the E coast of Norfolk and Lincolnshire, E England; 22 m. long, 15 m. wide; includes the estuaries of several rivers, including the Witham, Welland, Nene, and Ouse.

Wash·a·baugh \'wäsh-ə-ˌbȯ\. County in South Dakota. See table at SOUTH DAKOTA.

Wash·a·kie \'wäsh-ə-kē\. County in Wyoming. See table at WYOMING.

Wash·burn \'wȯsh-bərn, 'wäsh-\. 1 County in Wisconsin. See table at WISCONSIN.

2 City, ⊗ of McLean co., W cen. North Dakota, on Missouri river 35 m. N of Bismarck; pop. (1970c) 804.

3 City, ⊗ of Bayfield co., NW Wisconsin, on Lake Superior 7 m. N of Ashland; pop. (1970c) 1957.

Washburn, Mount. Peak, N part of Yellowstone National Park, NW Wyoming, W of the Grand Canyon of the Yellowstone; 10,243 ft.

Wash·ing·ton \'wȯsh-iŋ-tən, 'wäsh-\. 1 A northwestern state of U.S.A., bounded on N by Canadian province of British Columbia, on E by Idaho, on S by Oregon, and on W by the Pacific Ocean, Juan de Fuca Strait, and Strait of Georgia; 20th state in area, 68,192 sq. m. (land area 66,663 sq. m.); 22d state in population, (1970c) 3,409,169; ✱ Olympia; 42d state admitted to Union (1889).

Nicknames: Evergreen State; Chinook State. *State flower:* Rhododendron. *Motto:* Alki (By and By). *Rivers:* Columbia, flowing from NE region to cen. region, then S to the border and W to form boundary bet. Washington and Oregon; its tributaries, Pend Oreille in NE, Snake in SE, and Yakima in S cen. region. *Highest point:* Mount Rainier, 14,410 ft., Pierce co. *Chief products:* Wheat, fruit, barley; dairy products; fishing; zinc, lead, gravel; manufacturing: transportation equipment, lumber, chemicals. *Chief cities:* Seattle, Spokane, Tacoma, Bellevue, Everett. See *Table of States* at UNITED STATES. Divided into the following 39 counties (for pronunciation of their names, see their individual entries):

NAME	LOCATION	AREA[1] (sq. m.)	POP. (1970c)	CO. SEAT
Adams	E	1,894	12,014	Ritzville
Asotin	SE corner	633	13,799	Asotin
Benton	S	1,722	67,540	Prosser
Chelan	cen.	2,926	41,355	Wenatchee
Clallam[2]	NW; coastal	1,753	34,770	Port Angeles
Clark	SW	627	128,454	Vancouver
Columbia	SE	860	4,439	Dayton
Cowlitz	SW	1,144	68,616	Kelso
Douglas	cen.	1,839	16,787	Waterville
Ferry	NE	2,202	3,655	Republic
Franklin	SE	1,260	25,816	Pasco
Garfield	SE	713	2,911	Pomeroy
Grant[3]	cen.	2,681	41,881	Ephrata
Grays Harbor	W; coastal	1,910	59,553	Montesano
Island[4]	NW	212	27,011	Coupeville
Jefferson[2]	W; coastal	1,805	10,661	Port Townsend
King	W cen.	2,131	1,156,633	Seattle
Kitsap	W[5]	393	101,732	Port Orchard
Kittitas	cen.	2,320	25,039	Ellensburg
Klickitat	S	1,908	12,138	Goldendale
Lewis[6]	SW	2,449	45,467	Chehalis
Lincoln	E	2,306	9,572	Davenport
Mason[2]	W	960	20,918	Shelton
Okanogan	N	5,301	25,867	Okanogan
Pacific	SW corner; coastal	908	15,796	South Bend
Pend Oreille	NE corner	1,402	6,025	Newport
Pierce[6]	W cen.	1,676	411,027	Tacoma
San Juan[7]	NW	179	3,856	Friday Harbor
Skagit[8]	NW	1,735	52,381	Mount Vernon
Skamania	S	1,672	5,845	Stevenson
Snohomish	NW cen.	2,098	265,236	Everett
Spokane	E	1,758	287,487	Spokane
Stevens	NE	2,481	17,405	Colville
Thurston	W	714	76,894	Olympia
Wahkiakum	SW	261	3,592	Cathlamet
Walla Walla	SE	1,267	42,176	Walla Walla
Whatcom	NW	2,126	81,950	Bellingham
Whitman	SE	2,166	37,900	Colfax
Yakima	S	4,271	144,971	Yakima

[1] Area = land area.

[2] Olympic National Park occupies adjoining areas in S Clallam co., cen. Jefferson co., and NW corner of Mason co.

[3] Grand Coulee Dam at NE corner.

[4] Composed of islands lying N of Puget Sound and E of Admiralty Inlet.

[5] Between Hood Canal (on its W) and Puget Sound.

[6] Mount Rainier National Park occupies SE corner of Pierce co. and adjoining smaller area in NE Lewis co.

[7] Composed of islands lying NE of Juan de Fuca Strait and S of Strait of Georgia.

[8] Includes islands separated from San Juan co. by Rosario Strait.

History: Region visited by Spanish, Russian, British, and French explorers 1543–1792 (short-lived settlement 1791 at Neah Bay, *q.v.*) and by Lewis and Clark, who sailed down Columbia river 1805; part of Oregon Country; occupied jointly by Great Britain and United States 1818–46; first permanent settlement at Tumwater 1845; by treaty with Great Britain 1846 N boundary set at 49th parallel; settlement at Seattle 1851, at Tacoma 1852; region organized as Washington Territory 1853, admitted to Union as state Nov. 11, 1889.

2 Name of a parish of Louisiana and of counties in thirty states of the U.S. See tables at ALABAMA, ARKANSAS, COLORADO, FLORIDA, GEORGIA, IDAHO, ILLINOIS, INDIANA, IOWA, KANSAS, KENTUCKY, LOUISIANA, MAINE, MARYLAND, MINNESOTA, MISSISSIPPI, MISSOURI, NEBRASKA, NEW YORK, NORTH CAROLINA, OHIO, OKLAHOMA, OREGON, PENNSYLVANIA, RHODE ISLAND, TENNESSEE, TEXAS, UTAH, VERMONT, VIRGINIA, WISCONSIN.

3 City, Hempstead co., SW Arkansas, 33 m. NE of Texarkana; pop. (1970c) 290; state capital 1863–65; ⊗ to 1939.

4 Residential town, S cen. Litchfield co., NW Connecticut, NE of New Milford; pop. (1970c) 3121; agriculture; incorporated 1779.

5 Capital city of the U.S.A., coextensive with the District of Columbia (area 69 sq. m., including 8 sq. m. of water), bet. Maryland and Virginia, on the E bank of the Potomac river at the head of navigation and at its confluence with the Anacostia river ab. 40 m. SW of Baltimore, Maryland; pop. (1970c) 756,510; a leading international political center; educational center; tourism and convention trade; scientific research.

Public buildings, monuments, etc.: Capitol (located on Capitol Hill, 88 ft. above the Potomac; cornerstone first laid Sept. 18, 1793; restored 1819; extensions built 1851), White House (the oldest government building in Washington; cornerstone laid 1792), Library of Congress (completed 1897; largest library in world) and the Annex Building of Georgia (1940), two Senate Office Buildings, three House Office Buildings, Treasury Building, State Department Building (begun 1871), Lincoln Memorial, Washington Monument (555 ft. $5^1/_8$ in. high; cornerstone laid 1848, opened to public 1888), Jefferson Memorial, National Bureau of Standards (1901), National Archives (1935), Supreme Court (1935), Federal Reserve Board (1937), Department of Justice (1934), Post Office Department, Department of Interior (1937), Department of Agriculture, Department of Commerce (1932), Bureau of Engraving and Printing, Government Printing Office (largest printing establishment in world), and the Pentagon Building (War Department; begun 1940; in Virginia 3 m. from White House), National Science Foundation (1950), National Aeronautics and Space Administration (1958), Taft Memorial (1959); among the outstanding nongovernment buildings are the Pan-American Union Building, Union R.R. Station, Constitution Hall, and Washington Cathedral (Episcopal Cathedral of Saint Peter and Saint Paul), National Shrine of the Immaculate Conception, John F. Kennedy Center for the Performing Arts (1971); institutions include St. Elizabeth's Hospital, Freedmen's Hospital, Walter Reed Hospital, U.S. Soldiers' Home, Home for the Aged and Infirm, National Training School for Boys, and many others. Parks include the Mall (oldest park in city), Potomac Park, Rock Creek Park, National Zoological Park, Anacostia Park (containing the National Arboretum), Palisades Park, and ab. 700 other public open spaces, including esp. Du Pont Circle, Mount Vernon Square, Lafayette Square, Fort Slocum Park, and Washington Circle.

Colleges, etc.: Georgetown Univ. (1789), George Washington Univ. (1821), District of Columbia Teachers Coll. (1851), Gallaudet Coll. (1857, for deaf, dumb, and blind), Howard Univ. (1867), Mount Vernon Junior Coll. (1875), Catholic Univ. of America (1887), Saint Paul's Coll. (1889), American Univ. (1893), Saint Joseph's Seminary (1892), Trinity Coll. (1897), Strayer Junior Coll. (1904), Oblate Coll. (1904), Immaculata Coll. of Washington (1905), Southeastern Univ. (1917), Washington Bible Coll. (1919), Marjorie Webster Junior Coll. (1920), Benjamin Franklin Univ. (1925), Dunbarton Coll. of the Holy Cross (1935), Capital Institute of Technology (1964), Federal City Coll. (1966), Washington Technical Institute (1966); other cultural agencies include the Smithsonian Institution, Washington Public Library, Folger Shakespeare Library, departmental government libraries, National Museum, Corcoran Gallery, old National Gallery of Art, Freer Gallery, Phillips Memorial Gallery, and new National Gallery of Art (opened 1941), Museum of History and Technology (1965; part of Smithsonian Institution); among the many institutes and societies with headquarters in Washington are: Carnegie Institute of Washington (physical sciences, 1902), Brookings Institution (social sciences, 1928), American Association for the Advancement of Science, National Geographic Society, American Political Science Association, American Historical Association, American Institute of Architects, Daughters of the American Revolution.

History: Site chosen by President Washington in 1790 and planned by French engineer Major L'Enfant; occupied by Federal government 1800; incorp. as city 1802; occupied by British troops and burned 1814; lost charter as city 1871 and, with annexation of Georgetown 1878, became coterminous with District of Columbia (*q.v.*); construction on subway system initiated 1970.

6 City, ⊗ of Wilkes co., NE Georgia, 40 m. ESE of Athens; pop. (1970c) 4131; lumber, fertilizer, dairy products; founded 1780.

7 City, Tazewell co., cen. Illinois, 10 m. E of Peoria; pop. (1970c) 6790; cans vegetables.

8 Industrial and commercial city, ⊗ of Daviess co., SW Indiana, 18 m. E of Vincennes; pop. (1970c) 11,358; railroad cars, refrigerators; coal mines, oil wells; apples.

9 City, ⊗ of Washington co., SE Iowa, 25 m. SSW of Iowa City; pop. (1970c) 6317; pearl buttons, dairy products, radio cabinets; soybean processing; agriculture.

10 City, ⊗ of Washington co., N Kansas, 52 m. NNW of Manhattan; pop. (1970c) 1584.

11 City, Franklin co., E Missouri, on Missouri river 50 m. E of St. Louis; pop. (1970c) 8499; footwear, plastics, dairy products.

12 Borough, Warren co., NW New Jersey, 12 m. ENE of Phillipsburg; pop. (1970c) 5943; hosiery, brass goods, electronic components; dairy farms.

13 City, ⊗ of Beaufort co., E North Carolina, on Pamlico river at head of navigation 30 m. N of New Bern; pop. (1970c) 8961; fertilizer, lumber, furniture, flour; tobacco market.

14 City, Ohio. See WASHINGTON COURT HOUSE.

15 Industrial city, ⊗ of Washington co., SW Pennsylvania, 25 m. SW of Pittsburgh; pop. (1970c) 19,827; steel, bricks, chemicals, glass containers, tires; coal mines; Washington and Jefferson Coll. (1780).

16 Village, Kent co., cen. Rhode Island; governmental seat of Coventry; textiles; settled c. 1750.

17 Town, ⊗ of Rappahannock co., N Virginia; pop. (1970c) 189.

18 Urban district, Durham, N England, $6^1/_4$ m. SSE of Newcastle upon Tyne; pop. (1971p) 24,105.

Washington, Lake. Lake, King co., W cen. Washington; ab. 20 m. long, 4 m. wide; max. depth 225 ft.; forms E boundary of city of Seattle; completion 1916 of ship canal 8 m. long, 100 ft. wide, and 30 ft. deep bet. the lake and Puget Sound gave Seattle a waterfront 140 m. long and a fresh-water, nontidal harbor; Lake Washington floating bridge, completed 1940, is largest concrete pontoon

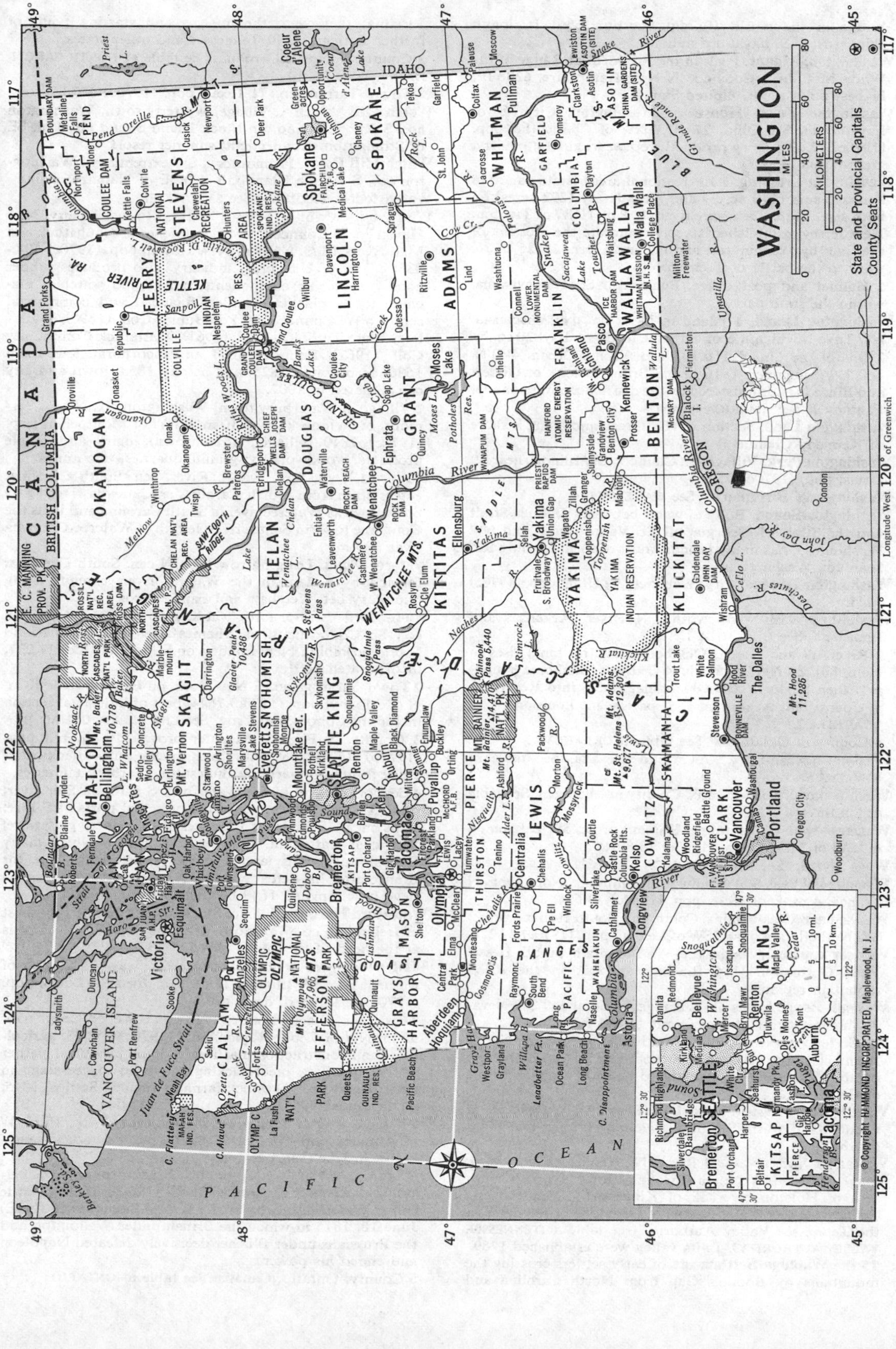
WASHINGTON
State and Provincial Capitals
County Seats
MILES
KILOMETERS
© Copyright HAMMOND INCORPORATED, Maplewood, N. J.
Longitude West 120° of Greenwich
C A N A D A
BRITISH COLUMBIA
IDAHO
OREGON
PACIFIC OCEAN
VANCOUVER ISLAND
Juan de Fuca Strait
WHATCOM
OKANOGAN
PEND OREILLE
STEVENS
FERRY
SPOKANE
LINCOLN
DOUGLAS
CHELAN
SKAGIT
SNOHOMISH
SAN JUAN
ISLAND
CLALLAM
JEFFERSON
KITSAP
MASON
GRAYS HARBOR
KING
KITTITAS
GRANT
ADAMS
WHITMAN
GARFIELD
ASOTIN
COLUMBIA
WALLA WALLA
FRANKLIN
BENTON
YAKIMA
KLICKITAT
SKAMANIA
CLARK
COWLITZ
LEWIS
PIERCE
THURSTON
PACIFIC
WAHKIAKUM
Olympia
Seattle
Tacoma
Spokane
Vancouver
Portland
Victoria
Bellingham
Everett
Yakima
Wenatchee
Walla Walla
Pasco
Kennewick
Aberdeen
Hoquiam
Bremerton
Port Angeles
Ellensburg
Pullman
Moses Lake
The Dalles
Columbia River
Snake R.
Mt. Rainier 14,410
Mt. St. Helens 9,677
Mt. Adams 12,307
Mt. Baker 10,778
Mt. Olympus 7,965
Mt. Hood 11,235
Glacier Peak 10,436
COULEE DAM NATIONAL RECREATION AREA
OLYMPIC NATIONAL PARK
RAINIER NAT'L PK.
NORTH CASCADES NAT'L PARK
YAKIMA INDIAN RESERVATION
COLVILLE INDIAN RES.
HANFORD ATOMIC ENERGY RESERVATION
CASCADE RANGE
WENATCHEE MTS.
SADDLE MTS.
BLUE MTS.
COAST RANGES
Puget Sound
Franklin D. Roosevelt L.
GRAND COULEE DAM
BONNEVILLE DAM
MCNARY DAM
JOHN DAY DAM
Bellevue
Kirkland
Renton
Auburn
Kent

bridge in the world (floating portion 6561 ft. long); shipyards; U.S. naval air station.

Washington, Mount. Peak in the Presidential Range of the White Mts., in S Coos co., N New Hampshire; 6288 ft.; highest point in NE United States.

Washington Court House *or* **Washington.** City, ⊗ of Fayette co., SW Ohio, 27 m. WNW of Chillicothe; pop. (1970c) 12,495; dairy products, footwear, gloves; poultry, grain farms.

Washington Crossing. 1 Recreational areas (state parks) in Pennsylvania (440 acres) and New Jersey (292 acres) on both sides of the Delaware river ab. 8 m. NNW of Trenton, New Jersey; established to commemorate the crossing of the river by Washington and his army Dec. 25–26, 1776, prior to the battle of Trenton.

2 Hamlet and post office, Bucks co., SE Pennsylvania, within the state park.

Washington Island. 1 Island in Door co., NE Wisconsin, NW Lake Michigan, S of entrance to Green Bay; 20 sq. m.

2 One of the Line Is. (*q.v.*), cen. Pacific Ocean, 4°43′N, 160°24′W; included 1916 in the British colony of Gilbert and Ellice Is.; administered by the district commissioner of Fanning I. See AMERICA ISLANDS.

Washington Land. Section of NW Greenland along E shore of Kennedy Channel.

Washington Park. Village, St. Clair co., SW Illinois, near St. Louis; pop. (1970c) 9524.

Washington's Birthplace. See WAKEFIELD 4.

Washington Sound. Body of water bet. Juan de Fuca Strait and the Strait of Georgia, off SE Vancouver I. and NW Washington; has many islands, most of them forming San Juan co., Washington.

Washington Terrace. City, Weber co., N Utah; pop. (1970c) 7241.

Wash·i·ta \ˈwäsh-ə-ˌtȯ, ˈwȯsh-\. 1 River, Arkansas and Louisiana. See OUACHITA 1.

2 River, W and S cen. Oklahoma; 500 m. long; rises in Hemphill co., NW Texas, flows E across Oklahoma boundary, then SE to S cen. Oklahoma, and S into Red river.

3 County in Arkansas and parish in Louisiana. See OUACHITA 2.

4 County in Oklahoma. See table at OKLAHOMA.

Wash·oe \ˈwäsh-(ˌ)ō\. County in Nevada. See table at NEVADA.

Wash·te·naw \ˈwäsh-tə-ˌnȯ\. County in Michigan. See table at MICHIGAN.

Wasmes \ˈväm\. Commune, Hainaut prov., SW Belgium, 6 m. SW of Mons; pop. (1969e) 13,802.

Waso Nyiro. See EWASO NG'IRO.

Was·que·hal \väs-ˈkäl\. Industrial commune, Nord dept., N France, 4 m. E of Lille; pop. (1962c) 13,634.

Was·se·naar \ˈväs-ə-ˌnär\. Commune, South Holland prov., SW Netherlands, just SSW of Leiden; pop. (1970e) 27,235.

Was·ser·kup·pe \ˈväs-ər-ˌku̇p-ə\. Mountain in SE Hesse, West Germany; 3116 ft.; highest peak in the Rhön mountain region.

Was·suk Range \ˌwäs-ək-\. Range, Mineral co., SW Nevada; highest point Mount Grant 11,245 ft.

Wa States \wä-\. A group of native states on E frontier of Burma, E of the Salween, a part of Shan State; 3332 sq. m.; inhabited by the Wa, thought to be an aboriginal people of the region.

Wast Water \ˈwäst-\. Lake, Lake District, NW England, in Cumberland 14 m. SW of Keswick; 3 m. long; maximum depth 258 ft.

Wa·tau·ga \wä-ˈtȯ-gə\. 1 River, NE Tennessee; ab. 60 m. long; rises in NW North Carolina, flows NW into south fork of Holston river SE of Kingsport, S Sullivan co., Tennessee. It contains **Watauga Dam,** one of the dams in the Tennessee Valley Authority (see table at TENNESSEE VALLEY AUTHORITY). In its valley were established 1769–75 the **Watauga Settlements** of early settlers crossing the mountains by Boone's Gap from North Carolina and Virginia; they were the nucleus and starting point of further settlements in Tennessee and other states.

2 County in North Carolina. See table at NORTH CAROLINA.

3 Town, Tarrant co., N Texas; pop. (1970c) 3778.

Watch Hill \ˈwäch-\. Village, Westerly town, Washington co., S Rhode Island, on Block Island Sound ab. 3 m. SE of Stonington, Connecticut; summer resort.

Watch Hill Point. Promontory, SW extremity of Washington co., S Rhode Island, ab. 1 m. E of Napatree Point.

Watenstedt–Salzgitter. See SALZGITTER.

Wa·ter·bury \ˈwȯt-ə(r)-ˌber-ē, ˈwät-\. 1 Industrial city, New Haven co., S Connecticut, at confluence of Naugatuck and Mad rivers 18 m. NNW of New Haven; pop. (1970c) 108,033; center of U.S. brass industry; also produces rubber goods, electronic components, clocks and watches, machine tools, plastics, textiles; financial and commercial center of W Connecticut; Post Junior Coll. (1890), Waterbury State Technical Coll. (1961), Mattatuck Community Coll. (1967). Founded 1677 and incorporated as town 1686, as borough 1825, and as city 1853; town and city consolidated in 1902.

2 Village in Waterbury town, Washington co., N cen. Vermont, on Winooski river 10 m. WNW of Montpelier; pop. (1970c) 2840 (village), 4614 (town); dairy and maple products, woodworking; granite quarries, talc mines.

Wa·ter·ee \ˈwȯt-ə-ˌrē, ˈwät-\. River, cen. South Carolina; enters state from North Carolina as Catawba river (*q.v.*) but known as Wateree river in South Carolina and joins the Congaree to form Santee river; length of Wateree-Catawba river 395 m.

Wateree Pond. Long narrow lake, N cen. South Carolina, formed by a dam in the Wateree river; extends along boundary bet. Kershaw and Fairfield cos.

Wa·ter·ford \ˈwȯt-ər-fərd, ˈwät-\. 1 Town, S New London co., SE Connecticut, on Thames river and Long Island Sound adjoining New London on E; pop. (1970c) 17,227; incorporated 1801.

2 Town, Saratoga co., E New York, on Hudson river 10 m. N of Albany; pop. (1970c) 7644; part of industrial section including Cohoes and Troy. See CHAMPLAIN CANAL.

3 County, S Eire, in Munster prov.; 710 sq. m.; pop. (1971p) 76,932; ⊗ Waterford; rivers Suir, Blackwater; dairy farming, quarrying (limestone, marble); tanneries.

4 Seaport city, ⊗ of co. Waterford, S Eire, on Suir river; pop. (1971p) 31,692; one of the principal ports of S Eire; ships meat, fish, fruit; produces beer, paper, glassware; 18th cent. cathedral. A historic seaport at which many English sovereigns landed; James II left from here for France after his defeat at the Boyne; successfully resisted siege by Cromwell 1649 but fell to Ireton 1650.

Waterford Harbour. Inlet of St. George's Channel, SE coast of Ireland, in co. Waterford, Eire; the city of Waterford is at the head of the inlet.

Wa·ter·loo \ˌwȯt-ər-ˈlü, ˈwȯt-ər-ˌ, ˌwät-, ˈwät-\. 1 City, ⊗ of Monroe co., SW Illinois, 22 m. S of East St. Louis; pop. (1970c) 4546; feed, dairy products.

2 City, ⊗ of Black Hawk co., NE cen. Iowa, on Cedar river 52 m. NW of Cedar Rapids; pop. (1970c) 75,533; agricultural and construction machinery, metal products, leather goods, textiles; meat-packing, soybean processing; in agricultural and livestock-farming region. Settled 1845; incorporated 1868.

3 Village, a ⊗ of Seneca co., W cen. New York, 15 m. W of Auburn; pop. (1970c) 5418; automobile bodies, sauerkraut; in lake resort region.

4 *Flem.* ˈvät-ər-ˌlō\. Commune, Brabant prov., cen. Belgium, ab. 12 m. S of Brussels; pop. (1969e) 16,924; battle called Waterloo nearby (at La Belle Alliance, 3 m. to SE) June 18, 1815 in which the British under Wellington and the Prussians under Blücher decisively defeated Napoleon and ended his power.

5 County, Ontario, Canada. See table at ONTARIO.

6 Town, Waterloo co., SE Ontario, Canada, adjoins Kitchener; pop. (1971p) 37,245; furniture, clothing, wood products, flour, beer; Univ. of St. Jerome's Coll. (1864), Waterloo Lutheran Univ. (1910), Univ. of Waterloo (1959), Renison Coll. (1959), Saint Paul's United Coll. (1961), Conrad Grebel Coll. (1961).
7 Town, ⊗ of Shefford co., S Quebec, Canada, 30 m. W of Sherbrooke; pop. (1971p) 4949; plastics, furniture, hardware; mushrooms.
8 Town on railroad in N cen. part of Sierra Leone Penin., Sierra Leone, W Africa, 14 m. SE of Freetown.

Wa·ter·mael–Boits·fort \'vät-ər-ˌmäl-bwä-'fō(ə)r\. Commune, Brabant prov., cen. Belgium, a suburb of Brussels; pop. (1969e) 25,047.

Wat·er·man, Mount \-'wȯt-ər-mən, -'wät-\. Mountain, Antarctica, 84°27′S, 175°24′E; 12,730 ft.

Water Rock Knob. Peak, Haywood co., W North Carolina; 6399 ft.

Wa·ter·ton–Gla·cier International Peace Park \ˌwȯt-ərt-ᵊn-'glā-shər-, ˌwät-\. International park, comprising Waterton Lakes National Park in S Alberta, Canada, and Glacier National Park in NW Montana; estab. 1932. See CANADA, *National Parks;* UNITED STATES, *National Parks.*

Waterton Lakes National Park. See CANADA, *National Parks.*

Wa·ter·town \'wȯt-ər-ˌtau̇n, 'wät-\. 1 Industrial town, SE Litchfield co., NW Connecticut, on W bank of Naugatuck river NW of Waterbury; pop. (1970c) 18,610; synthetic fabrics, wire, hardware, plastics; incorporated 1780.
2 Town, Middlesex co., NE Massachusetts, 7 m. W of Boston; pop. (1970c) 39,309; rubber goods, clothing, paint, precision instruments; Massachusetts Bay Community Coll. (1961); settled 1630.
3 Manufacturing city, ⊗ of Jefferson co., N New York, 10 m. E of Lake Ontario; pop. (1970c) 30,787; automobile parts, paper, snowplows, rubber and plastic products, paint, clothing; Jefferson Community Coll. (1963); settled 1800. Bisected by Black river, with 112 ft. falls within city.
4 City, ⊗ of Codington co., NE South Dakota, 70 m. ENE of Huron; pop. (1970c) 13,388; cement, flour, dairy products; grain elevators, seed mills, meat-packing plants; flax; incorporated 1885.
5 City, Dodge and Jefferson cos., SE Wisconsin, 32 m. E of Madison; pop. (1970c) 15,683; cutlery, furnaces, dairy products, rubber goods; agriculture; Northwestern Coll. (1865); home of Carl Schurz 1855–61; reputed site of first kindergarten in America, estab. by Mrs. Carl Schurz 1856.

Water Valley. City, a ⊗ of Yalobusha co., N Mississippi, 53 m. E of Clarksdale; pop. (1970c) 3285; clothing; ships watermelons.

Wa·ter·ville \'wȯt-ər-ˌvil, 'wät-\. 1 Subdivision of town and city of Waterbury, Connecticut. See WATERBURY 1.
2 City, Kennebec co., SW Maine, on Kennebec river 18 m. N of Augusta; pop. (1970c) 18,192; boats, wood pulp, clothing; railroad shops; diversified agriculture; Colby Coll. (1813), Thomas Coll. (1894).
3 City, Le Sueur co., S Minnesota, 20 m. E of Mankato; pop. (1970c) 1539; summer resort.
4 Village, Oneida co., cen. New York, 13 m. SW of Utica; pop. (1970c) 1808; birthplace of George Eastman.
5 Town, ⊗ of Douglas co., cen. Washington; pop. (1970c) 919; wheat, livestock.

Wa·ter·vliet \'wȯt-ərv-ˌlēt, 'wät-\. Industrial city, Albany co., E New York, on Hudson river opp. Troy near terminus of N.Y. State Barge Canal, 6 m. N of Albany; pop. (1970c) 12,404; steel castings, textiles, abrasives, bricks; agriculture. Seat of U.S. Arsenal, established 1813, producing arms for War of 1812 and all subsequent wars; specializes in heavy ordnance.

Wat·ford \'wät-fərd\. Municipal borough, Hertfordshire, SE England, on the Colne 17 m. NW of London; pop. (1971p) 78,117; commercial center; a small part lies within Greater London.

Watford City. City, ⊗ of McKenzie co., W North Dakota, 28 m. SE of Williston; pop. (1970c) 1768.

Wath upon Dearne \'wäth . . . 'dərn\. Urban district, West Riding, Yorkshire, N England, 8 m. SE of Barnsley; pop. (1971p) 15,022.

Wat·kins Glen \ˌwät-kinz-\. Village, ⊗ of Schuyler co., SW cen. New York, at S end of Seneca Lake 18 m. N of Elmira; pop. (1970c) 2716; summer resort; fruit farms; **Watkins Glen** nearby, a gorge 2 m. long, 100–300 ft. deep, the stream falling 1200 ft. in many cascades.

Wat·kins·ville \'wät-kinz-ˌvil\. Town, ⊗ of Oconee co., NE cen. Georgia; pop. (1970c) 986.

Watlings Island. See SAN SALVADOR 1.

Wat·ling Street \'wät-liŋ-\. Roman road in Britain, extending from London to Wroxeter (near Shrewsbury) in a general northwesterly direction; by some it is held to be the road that began at Richborough, or Dover, ran through Canterbury to London, and continued from Wroxeter to Chester. Southwest of Leicester it was intersected by Fosse Way. In 9th cent. divided Mercia (*q.v.*). See ERMINE STREET.

Watling Town. See WELLINGTON 6.

Wa·ton·ga \wə-'täŋ-gə\. City, ⊗ of Blaine co., W cen. Oklahoma, 50 m. SW of Enid; pop. (1970c) 3696; cotton gins, oil and gas wells; agriculture.

Wat·on·wan \'wät-ᵊn-ˌwän\. County in Minnesota. See table at MINNESOTA.

Wa·trous \'wō-trəs, 'wät-rəs\. Village, S Mora co., NE New Mexico; ruins of Fort Union nearby (see FORT UNION NATIONAL MONUMENT).

Wat·se·ka \wät-'sē-kə\. City, ⊗ of Iroquois co., E Illinois, 27 m. SSE of Kankakee; pop. (1970c) 5294; dairy products; diversified agriculture.

Wat·son, Mount \-'wät-sən\. Peak, S Summit co., NE Utah; 11,473 ft.

Watson Lake. Village, left bank of Liard river, S Yukon, Canada, 12 m. N of British Columbia border; station on the Alaska Highway.

Wat·son·town \'wät-sən-ˌtau̇n\. Borough, Northumberland co., E cen. Pennsylvania, 16 m. SSE of Williamsport; pop. (1970c) 2514.

Wat·son·ville \'wät-sən-ˌvil\. City, Santa Cruz co., W California, near Monterey Bay 30 m. S of San Jose; pop. (1970c) 14,569; pesticides, dairy products, vinegar; railroad shops; packs and ships fruit and vegetables; founded 1852.

Wat·tak·ka·nai \wä-ˌtäk-ə-'nī\. City, Hokkaidō prefecture, Hokkaidō, Japan, 164 m. N of Sapporo; pop. (1968e) 51,539.

Wat·ten·scheid \'vät-ᵊn-ˌshīt\. Industrial city, North Rhine-Westphalia, West Germany, in Ruhr valley, E suburb of Essen; pop. (1969e) 80,527; iron and steel, paper, textiles, glass, chemicals; first mentioned 900; chartered 1415.

Wat·ti·gnies \ˌvä-tēn-'yē\ *or in full* **Wattignies–la–Vic·toire** \-lä-vēk-'twär\. Village, Nord dept., N France; pop. (1962c) 209; battle Oct. 16, 1793 in which the French under Jourdan defeated the Austrians.

Wat·tre·los \ˌvä-trə-'lō\. Industrial commune, Nord dept., N France, 9 m. NE of Lille; pop. (1962c) 41,319; suburb of Roubaix; textile manufactures; oil refining.

Watts \'wäts\. Suburb of Los Angeles (*q.v.*), California; scene of severe racial violence 1965.

Watts Bar Dam. See table at TENNESSEE VALLEY AUTHORITY.

Watts Island. Island, lower Chesapeake Bay, W cen. coast of Accomac co., Virginia.

Watt·wil \'vät-ˌvēl\. Commune, St. Gallen canton, Switzerland; pop. (1970c) 8566; Capuchin convent; castle ruins.

Wau \'waů\. 1 Settlement, Papua New Guinea, E New Guinea I., 32 m. SW of Salamaua; alt. 3500 ft.; gold mining; settlement begun c. 1925; in World War II seized by Japanese but retaken by Australians and Americans bet. Feb. and Sept. 1943.
2 *or* **Wāw** \'wȯ\. Town, ✱ of Bahr al-Ghazal prov., S Sudan, on the Jur river.

Wau·bay Lake \wȯ-'bā-\. Lake, Day co., NE South Dakota.

Wau·be·sa, Lake \-wȯ-'bē-sə\. See FOUR LAKES.

Wau·chu·la \wȯ-'chü-lə\. City, ⊗ of Hardee co., cen. Florida penin., 37 m. S of Lakeland; pop. (1970c) 3007.

Wau·con·da \wȯ-'kän-də\. Village, Lake co., NE Illinois, 18 m. WSW of Waukegan; pop. (1970c) 5460; summer resort; dairy farming.

Waugh Mountain \'wȯ-\. Peak, SE Idaho co., N cen. Idaho; 8882 ft.

Wau·ka·ra *or Du.* **Waoe·ka·ra** \waů-'kär-ə\. Mountain, NW cen. Celebes, Indonesia; 10,259 ft.

Wau·ke·gan \wȯ-'kē-gən\. Residential city, ⊗ of Lake co., NE corner of Illinois, on Lake Michigan 40 m. N of Chicago; pop. (1970c) 65,269; wire, pharmaceuticals, outboard motors; lake port; settled 1835; incorporated as town 1849, as city 1859; Great Lakes Naval Training Center to S.

Wau·ke·sha \'wȯ-ki-ˌshȯ\. 1 County in SE Wisconsin. See table at WISCONSIN.
2 City, its ⊗, 15 m. W of Milwaukee; pop. (1970c) 40,274; ordnance, marine engines, wood products, castings; bottles mineral water; limestone quarries; Carroll Coll. (1840), Mount St. Paul Coll. (1962); settled 1835, incorporated as city 1896.

Wau·kon \wȯ-'kän\. City, ⊗ of Allamakee co., NE corner of Iowa, 17 m. E of Decorah; pop. (1970c) 3883; dairy products, ships livestock.

Waum·bek Mountain \ˌwȯm-bek-\. Peak, S Coos co., N New Hampshire; 4020 ft.

Wau·paca \wȯ-'pak-ə\. 1 County in E cen. Wisconsin. See table at WISCONSIN.
2 City, its ⊗, 32 m. WNW of Appleton; pop. (1970c) 4342; gloves; summer resort; potatoes.

Wau·pés. See UAUPÉS.

Wau·pun \wȯ-'pän—*sic*\. City, Dodge and Fond du Lac cos., SE cen. Wisconsin, 17 m. SW of Fond du Lac; pop. (1970c) 7946; shoes, canned vegetables; dairy farms.

Wau·ri·ka \wȯ-'rē-kə\. City, ⊗ of Jefferson co., S Oklahoma, 38 m. SSE of Lawton; pop. (1970c) 1833.

Wau·sau \'wȯ-ˌsȯ\. City, ⊗ of Marathon co., cen. Wisconsin, on Wisconsin river 84 m. WNW of Green Bay (city); pop. (1970c) 32,806; plastics, chemicals, aluminum products, electric motors, lumber, dairy products; incorporated 1872.

Wau·se·on \'wȯ-sē-ˌän\. Village, ⊗ of Fulton co., NW Ohio, 32 m. W of Toledo; pop. (1970c) 4932; automobile and aircraft parts, canned vegetables.

Wau·shara \wȯ-'sha(ə)r-ə, -'she(ə)r-\. County in Wisconsin. See table at WISCONSIN.

Wau·to·ma \wȯ-'tō-mə\. City, ⊗ of Waushara co., cen. Wisconsin; pop. (1970c) 1624; Waushara County Teachers Coll. (1911).

Wau·wa·to·sa \ˌwȯ-wə-'tō-sə\. City, Milwaukee co., SE Wisconsin, 5 m. W of Milwaukee; pop. (1970c) 58,676; suburb of Milwaukee.

Waveney. See BROADS, THE.

Wa·ver·ley \'wā-vər-lē\. Municipality, E New South Wales, SE Australia, E suburb of Sydney, on Pacific Ocean; pop. (1966c) 63,607.

Wa·ver·ly \'wā-vər-lē\. 1 City, ⊗ of Bremer co., NE Iowa, 15 m. NNW of Waterloo; pop. (1970c) 7205; condensed milk, automobile parts; livestock; Wartburg Coll. (1868).
2 Village, Tioga co., S New York, on Pennsylvania border 15 m. ESE of Elmira; pop. (1970c) 5261; dairy, truck farms.
3 Village, ⊗ of Pike co., S Ohio, 15 m. S of Chillicothe; pop. (1970c) 4858; lake resort; poultry farms.
4 Town, ⊗ of Humphreys co., W Tennessee; pop. (1970c) 3794; shirts; peanuts.

Wa·vre \'vävrᵊ\. Manufacturing commune, Brabant prov., cen. Belgium, 14 m. SE of Brussels; pop. (1969e) 11,858. Battle here June 18, 1815, a phase of Waterloo, in which French general, Grouchy, drove back part of Blücher's force but failed to aid Napoleon.

Wavre–Sainte–Catherine. See SINT-KATELIJNE-WAVER.

Wāw. See WAU 2.

Wa·wa \'wä-wä\. Village, Rizal prov., Luzon, Phil., NE of Manila; **Wawa Dam,** E of Montalban, in the Manila water system held by Japanese as defense point during fighting in 1945; taken by U.S. forces May 28, 1945.

Wa·wa·see Lake \ˌwä-wə-'sē-\. Lake, NE Kosciusko co., N Indiana; 4 sq. m.

Wax·a·hach·ie \ˌwȯk-sə-'hach-ē\. City, ⊗ of Ellis co., NE cen. Texas, 30 m. S of Dallas; pop. (1970c) 13,452; boats, fiber glass, clothing; pecan shelling; onions; Southwestern Assemblies of God Coll. (1927).

Wax·haw \'waks-ˌhȯ\. Village, Lancaster co., N South Carolina; birthplace of Andrew Jackson, 7th president of the U.S.

Way·ah Bald \ˌwī-ə-\. Peak, N Macon co., SW North Carolina; 5336 ft.

Way·cross \'wā-ˌkrȯs\. City, ⊗ of Ware co., SE Georgia, 50 m. W of Brunswick; pop. (1970c) 18,966; turpentine, honey, pecans; incorporated 1874.

Way·land \'wā-lənd\. 1 City, Floyd co., E Kentucky, 17 m. W of Pikeville; pop. (1970c) 384.
2 Town, Middlesex co., NE Massachusetts, 15 m. W of Boston; pop. (1970c) 13,461; fruit farms.
3 Village, Steuben co., S New York, 16 m. NNE of Hornell; pop. (1970c) 2022; agriculture.

Wayne \'wān\. 1 Name of counties in sixteen states of the U.S. See tables at GEORGIA, ILLINOIS, INDIANA, IOWA, KENTUCKY, MICHIGAN, MISSISSIPPI, MISSOURI, NEBRASKA, NEW YORK, NORTH CAROLINA, OHIO, PENNSYLVANIA, TENNESSEE, UTAH, WEST VIRGINIA.
2 Village, Wayne co., SE Michigan, 19 m. W of Detroit; pop. (1970c) 21,854.
3 City, ⊗ of Wayne co., NE Nebraska, 26 m. ENE of Norfolk; pop. (1970c) 5379; Wayne State Coll. (1891).
4 Urban township, Passaic co., N New Jersey, 6 m. W of Paterson; pop. (1970c) 48,778; machine tools, pharmaceuticals, electronic components; Patterson State Coll. (1855).
5 Residential locality, Delaware co., SE Pennsylvania, ab. 6 m. SSW of Norristown; pop. (1970c) 10,000; Valley Forge Military Junior Coll. (1928).
6 Town, ⊗ of Wayne co., SW West Virginia; pop. (1970c) 1385; potatoes, truck crops.

Waynes·boro \'wānz-ˌbər-ə, -ˌbə-rə\. 1 City, ⊗ of Burke co., E Georgia, 28 m. S of Augusta; pop. (1970c) 5530; steel, veneer, canned goods.
2 Town, ⊗ of Wayne co., SE Mississippi; pop. (1970c) 4368; cotton gins.
3 Borough and resort, Franklin co., S Pennsylvania, 14 m. S of Chambersburg; pop. (1970c) 10,011; ships fruit; pottery, prefabricated homes.
4 City, ⊗ of Wayne co., S Tennessee; pop. (1970c) 1983.
5 Independent city, Augusta co., N cen. Virginia, in Shenandoah Valley at foot of Blue Ridge Mts. 12 m. ESE of Staunton; 7 sq. m.; pop. (1970c) 16,707; stoves, plastics, flour, rayon, marine hardware, pencils; manganese mines; apples. Site first settled c. mid-18th cent.; scene of battle Mar. 2, 1865 in which Confederate forces under Gen. Early were defeated.

Waynes·burg \'wānz-ˌbərg\. Borough, ⊗ of Greene co., SW corner of Pennsylvania, 26 m. W of Uniontown; pop. (1970c) 5152; flour; coal mines; dairy, livestock farms; Waynesburg Coll. (1850).

Waynes·ville \'wānz-ˌvil\. 1 City, ⊗ of Pulaski co., S cen. Missouri; pop. (1970c) 3375.
2 Town, ⊗ of Haywood co., W North Carolina, 26 m. WSW of Asheville; pop. (1970c) 6488; summer resort; leather goods, paper; tobacco.

Way·no·ka \wā-'nōk-ə\. City, Woods co., NW Oklahoma, 32 m. ENE of Woodward; pop. (1970c) 1444.

Wazan. See OUEZZANE.

Wa·ziers \vä-'zhā\. Commune, Nord dept., N France; pop. (1962c) 10,507; ENE suburb of Douai.

Wa·zir·ā·bād \wə-'zir-ə-ˌbäd\. Ancient city, Bactria. See BALKH 2.

Wa·zir·a·bad \wə-'zir-ə-ˌbäd\. Town, Punjab, Pakistan, on Chenab river 60 m. N of Lahore; munic. pop. (1961c) 29,399; railroad junction with bridge over Chenab; boats, cutlery; founded by Shah Jahan.

Wa·zir·i·stan \wə-ˌzir-i-'stan, -'stän\. Mountain tract, SW North-West Frontier Province, Pakistan; 4373 sq. m.; pop. (1961c) 394,312; divided into **North Waziristan** (*formerly* **To·chi** \'tō-chē\), pop. (1961c) 159,470, and **South Waziristan** (*formerly* **Wa·na** \'wän-ə\), pop. (1961c) 235,442; lies along border of Afghanistan; inhabited by Wazirs, a Pathan tribe, divided into the Darwesh Khel and Mahsuds; their chief town is Kaniguram. Since 1860 there have been several uprisings in Waziristan (see WANA); most serious against the British, called Third Afghan War, was in 1919–22 when Mahsuds rose in revolt. Kaniguram and Wana subdued; last Mahsud tribes submitted Feb. 1922.

Wazzan. See OUEZZANE.

We *or* **Weh** \'wā\. Island ab. 14 m. off extreme NW tip of Sumatra, Indonesia, directly N of Banda Atjeh; 65 sq. m.; has irregular coastline with large bay on N coast, on which is Sabang, an important free port with fine harbor.

Weak·ley \'wēk-lē\. County in Tennessee. See table at TENNESSEE.

Weald, The \-'wē(ə)ld\. Wooded district, Kent, Surrey, and Sussex cos., SE England, lying bet. the North Downs and South Downs; formerly heavily forested; in 17th cent. covered ab. 325 sq. m.

Wear \'wi(ə)r\. River, Durham, N England; 67 m. long; flows E and NE into North Sea at Sunderland.

Wearmouth. See SUNDERLAND.

Weath·er·ford \'weth-ər-fərd\. 1 City, Custer co., W Oklahoma, 11 m. E of Clinton; pop. (1970c) 7959; agriculture; Southwestern State Coll. (1901).

2 City, ⊗ of Parker co., N cen. Texas, 25 m. W of Fort Worth; pop. (1970c) 11,750; oil drilling equipment, fertilizer; gas and oil wells; poultry, watermelons; Weatherford Coll. (1869).

Weath·er·ly \'weth-ər-lē\. Borough, Carbon co., E Pennsylvania, 21 m. S of Wilkes-Barre; pop. (1970c) 2554.

Wea·ver \'wē-vər\. River, Cheshire, NW England; ab. 45 m. long; rises near border of Shropshire, flows NE, and then NW into the Mersey; navigable as far as Winsford.

Wea·ver·ville \'wē-vər-ˌvil\. Village, ⊗ of Trinity co., NW California; pop. (1970c) 1489.

Web. See WEYIB.

Webb \'web\. County in Texas. See table at TEXAS.

Webb City. City, Jasper co., SW Missouri, 6 m. N of Joplin; pop. (1970c) 6923; machine tools, fertilizer, dairy products plastics.

Webbe. See WEYIB.

Webbe Mana. See MANA, WEBBE.

We·ber \'wē-bər\. 1 River, N Utah; ab. 100 m. long; rises in S Summit co., flows NW into Great Salt Lake.

2 County in Utah. See table at UTAH.

Web·ster \'web-stər\. 1 Name of a parish in Louisiana and of counties in seven states of the U.S. See tables at GEORGIA, IOWA, KENTUCKY, LOUISIANA, MISSISSIPPI, MISSOURI, NEBRASKA, WEST VIRGINIA.

2 Town, Worcester co., cen. Massachusetts, 15 m. S of Worcester; pop. (1970c) 14,917; lake resort; footwear; dairy farms.

3 Village, Monroe co., W New York, 10 m. ENE of Rochester; pop. (1970c) 5037; canned goods.

4 City, ⊗ of Day co., NE South Dakota, 37 m. NNW of Watertown; pop. (1970c) 2252.

Webster, Lake. See CHAUBUNAGUNGAMAUG, LAKE.

Webster, Mount. Peak, S Coos co., N New Hampshire; 3876 ft.

Webster City. Industrial city, ⊗ of Hamilton co., N cen. Iowa, 20 m. E of Fort Dodge; pop. (1970c) 8488; aluminum castings and boats, household appliances, feed; ships livestock.

Webster Groves. City, St. Louis co., E Missouri, 8 m. W of St. Louis; pop. (1970c) 27,455; Eden Theological Seminary (1850), Webster Coll. (1915).

Webster Springs. Town, ⊗ of Webster co., E cen. West Virginia, 43 m. SW of Elkins; pop. (1970c) 1132; incorporated 1892 as **Ad·di·son** \'ad-ə-sən\, but better known as Webster Springs, its post-office name.

Wed·dell Island \wə-'del-, 'wed-^{ə}l-\. One of the Falkland Is. (*q.v.*), W of West Falkland.

Weddell Quadrant. Former name of the quarter section of Antarctica bet. Greenwich meridian and 90°W; now chiefly W Queen Maud Land, Weddell Sea and Coats Land, and Palmer Archipelago and Antarctic Penin.

Weddell Sea. Arm of S Atlantic Ocean in Antarctica, SE of Antarctic Penin.; its W shore is along 60th meridian, W long.; its E shore is Coats Land (*q.v.*); Filchner Ice Shelf is at its S end; discovered 1823 by Capt. James Weddell. See FALKLAND ISLANDS DEPENDENCIES.

We·del \'väd-^{ə}l\. City, Schleswig-Holstein, West Germany, 12 m. W of Hamburg; pop. (1969e) 31,207; oil refining; textiles, furniture.

Wed·more \'wed-ˌmō(ə)r, -ˌmȯ(ə)r\. Village, N cen. Somerset, SW England; in 878 scene of signing of peace treaty bet. King Alfred and Guthrum, Danish king of East Anglia, by which Danes were restricted to territory (the Danelaw) in NE England, N of Watling Street.

Wednes·bury \'wenz-b(ə-)rē, 'wej-b(ə-)rē\. Municipal borough, Staffordshire, W cen. England, on the Tame 8 m. NW of Birmingham; pop. (1961c) 33,650; a center of the metallurgical industry, producing esp. tubes.

We·dow·ee \wē-'dau̇-ē\. Town, ⊗ of Randolph co., E Alabama; pop. (1970c) 842.

Weed \'wēd\. City, Siskiyou co., N California, 55 m. N of Redding; pop. (1970c) 2983; lumber, veneers; dairy farming.

Wee·haw·ken \wē-'hȯ-kən\. Township, Hudson co., NE New Jersey, on Hudson river opp. New York City (connected by Lincoln Tunnel), 5 m. N of Jersey City; pop. (1970c) 12,958; railroad shops; scene of Hamilton-Burr duel July 11, 1804.

Wee·nen \'vēn-ən\. Town, cen. Natal, E Rep. of South Africa, 85 m. NW of Durban; founded 1838, second oldest settlement in Natal; scene of massacre of Boer Voortrekkers by Zulus under Dingaan 1838—hence its name, literally "place of weeping."

Weert \'ve(ə)rt\. Commune, Limburg prov., SE Netherlands, near Belgian border 16 m. SE of Eindhoven; pop. (1970e) 35,190.

Weesp \'vāsp\. Commune, North Holland prov., W Netherlands, 7 m. SE of Amsterdam; pop. (1970e) 17,261.

Wę·go·rze·wo \ˌve^{n}(y)-gə-'zhev-(ˌ)ō\ *or Ger.* **Ang·er·burg** \'äŋ-ər-ˌbu̇(ə)rg\. Town, NE Olsztyn prov., N Poland, 60 m. N of Olsztyn; pop. (1966e) 7607; clay products; terminus on Angrapa river at N end of Lake Mamry for boat service on Masurian Lakes. Founded 1571 around monastery dating from 1328; scene of fighting 1914; assigned to Poland by Potsdam Conference 1945.

Weh. See WE.

Wehlau. See ZNAMENSK.

Wei \'wā\. 1 River rising in mountains of SE Kansu prov., N cen. China, and flowing E across Shensi to join the

Yellow river at T'ung-kuan, the point where it turns E; 537 m. long; on its S bank in Shensi is Sian.

2 Town, China. See WEI-FANG.

Wei–chou *or* **Wei·chow** \'wā-'jō\. Island in NE Gulf of Tonkin, Kwangtung prov., SE China, S of Pei-hai.

Weichsel. See VISTULA.

Wei·da \'vīd-ə\. City, Gera dist., East Germany, WNW of Zwickau; pop. (1970e) 11,912; footwear, textiles; 12th cent. Gothic church, 12th cent. castle.

Wei·de·nau \'vīd-ᵊn-ˌaů\ *or* **Weidenau an der Sieg** \-än-dər-'zēk\. Commune, North Rhine-Westphalia, West Germany, on Sieg river 48 m. E of Cologne; manufactures iron, steel, copper.

Wei·den in der Ober·pfalz \ˌvīd-ᵊn-ˌin-dər-'ō-bər-ˌ(p)fälts\. Manufacturing city, Bavaria, West Germany, on Naab river 31 m. SE of Bayreuth; pop. (1969e) 43,081; glass, porcelain; 16th cent. town hall, 17th cent. church.

Wei–fang \'wā-'fäŋ\ *also* **Wei·hsien** \'wā-shē-'en\ *or* **Wei** \'wā\. Commercial town, E cen. Shantung prov., NE China, on railroad 85 m. NW of Tsingtao; pop. (1970e) 260,000.

Wei–hai \'wā-'hī\ *or* **Wei·hai·wei** \'wā-'hī-'wā\. Seaport, NE Shantung prov., NE China, at E end of peninsula on N coast 40 m. E of Cheefoo and on S shore of Strait of Pohai; naval base, ship-repairing center, fishing port; good harbor protected by Liu-Kung I.

History: Chinese fleet destroyed here by Japanese 1895 and port occupied by Japanese 1895–98; leased to Great Britain 1898 and used as a naval base; returned to China 1930; occupied by Japanese 1938–45; occupied by Communist naval forces 1949.

Weihsien. See WEI-FANG.

Wei·mar \'vī-ˌmär, 'wī-\. City, Erfurt dist., East Germany, 13 m. E of Erfurt; pop. (1970e) 63,689; railroad junction; agricultural machinery, building materials, chemicals, furniture; Goethe National Museum, Liszt Museum, 18th cent. Belvedere Castle, Weimar Castle (housing literary research society), national observatory.

History: First mentioned 975; chartered 1348; ✱ of duchy of Saxe-Weimar 1547–1918; in latter part of 18th cent. residence of Goethe and Schiller and the most important cultural center of Germany. In 1919 German National Assembly met here and ratified Treaty of Versailles and established republican regime (often referred to as the "Weimar Republic") which lasted until 1933; in World War II occupied by U.S. forces Apr. 12, 1945.

Wein·heim \'vīn-ˌhīm\. City, Baden-Württemberg, West Germany, 10 m. NE of Mannheim; pop. (1969e) 29,199; leather and rubber goods, furniture, soap; health resort; 13th cent. Gothic chapel, 16th cent. Gothic town hall.

Weins·berg \'vīn(t)s-ˌbe(ə)rg\. Commune, Baden-Württemberg, West Germany, on a tributary of the Neckar just E of the Heilbronn; scene of defeat 1140 of Welf VI by Conrad III of Germany; free imperial city, in league of Swabian cities 1331–1440.

Weir·ton \'wi(ə)rt-ᵊn\. City, Brooke and Hancock cos., N West Virginia, on Ohio river ab. 26 m. NNE of Wheeling; pop. (1970c) 27,131; steel, chemicals, automobile parts; coal mines; steel mills estab. 1909; city incorporated 1947.

Wei·ser \'wē-sər\. City, ⊗ of Washington co., W Idaho, on Snake river 62 m. NW of Boise; pop. (1970c) 4108; dairy products; copper mines; potatoes, sugar beets.

Weissbad. See APPENZELL.

Weisse Elster. See ELSTER 1.

Weis·sen·burg \'vīs-ᵊn-ˌbů(ə)rg\. 1 Town, NE France. See WISSEMBOURG.

2 *or formerly* **Weissenburg–am–Sand** \-äm-'zänt\. Fortified town, Bavaria, West Germany, ab. 30 m. SW of Nürnberg; dates from 8th cent.; has old walls, Gothic town hall.

Weis·sen·fels \'vīs-ᵊn-ˌfels\. Manufacturing commune, Halle dist., East Germany; pop. (1970e) 46,120; railroad junction; footwear, leather goods; 17th cent. castle; first mentioned 1158; chartered 1254; to Prussia 1815.

Weisser Berg. See WHITE MOUNTAIN.

Weiss·horn \'vīs-ˌhȯ(ə)rn\. Peak, Valais canton, SW cen. Switzerland, in Pennine Alps; 14,782 ft.

Weisskirchen. See BELA CRKVA.

Weiss·ku·gel \'vīs-ˌkü-gəl\ *or Ital.* **Pa·la Bian·ca** \ˌpäl-ə-bē-'äŋ-kə\. Peak in the Ötztaler Alps, on the border bet. Austrian Tirol and Veneto, NE Italy; 12,257 ft.

Weiss·mies \'vī-ˌsmēs\. Mountain, SW cen. Switzerland, in E part of the Pennine Alps; 13,199 ft.

Weiss·was·ser \'vīs-ˌväs-ər\. Commune, Cottbus dist., East Germany, 25 m. NNE of Bautzen; pop. (1970e) 19,281; manufactures glass, porcelain, lumber, tile; lignite mining.

Wejh \'wāj\. Port on the Red Sea, W Saudi Arabia, 260 m. NW of Medina.

Wej·he·ro·wo \ˌvā-hə-'rò-vō\. Commune, Gdańsk prov., N Poland, 23 m. NW of Gdańsk; pop. (1970p) 33,700; on railroad from Gdynia to Szczecin.

We·lan·gi·la·la \wā-ˌläŋ-ē-'lä-lə\ *or* **Wai·langi La·la** \wī-\. Small island, NE Fiji, SW Pacific Ocean; site of lighthouse for ships passing through Nanuku Passage.

Welch \'welch, 'welsh\. City, ⊗ of McDowell co., S West Virginia, 24 m. WNW of Bluefield; pop. (1970c) 4149.

Welcome Bay. See SLAMADATANG BAY.

Weld \'weld\. County in Colorado. See table at COLORADO.

Wel·don \'wel-dən\. Town, Halifax co., NE North Carolina, on Roanoke river at head of navigation 34 m. NNE of Rocky Mount; pop. (1970c) 2304.

We·le·ga \we-'lā-gə\. Province of W Ethiopia. See table at ETHIOPIA.

Wel·fare Island \'wel-ˌfa(ə)r-, -ˌfe(ə)r-\. Island in East river, New York, 1½ m. long by ⅛ m. wide, part of Manhattan borough; municipal hospital, and formerly, a penal institution; known as **Black·wells Island** \ˌblak-ˌwelz-, -wəlz-\ until 1921.

Wel·kom \'vel-kəm\. Town, Orange Free State, Rep. of South Africa, ab. 85 m. NE of Bloemfontein; pop. (1967e) 137,400.

Welkomst Baai. See SLAMADATANG BAY.

Wel·land \'wel-ənd\. 1 County, SE Ontario, Canada. See table at ONTARIO.

2 Industrial city, its ⊗, on Welland Ship Canal 14 m. S of St. Catharines; pop. (1971p) 44,222; textiles, stainless steel, rubber goods, cordage, shoes, fertilizer, wine, dairy products; founded 1830; incorporated as city 1917.

3 River, E cen. England; 70 m. long; rises in Northamptonshire and flows NE into the Wash.

Welland Ship Canal *or formerly* **Welland Canal.** Canadian government-owned ship waterway, connecting Lake Erie with Lake Ontario in Welland and Lincoln cos., SE Ontario; 27.6 m. long and having 8 locks and minimum depth of 30 ft.; extends from Port Colborne on Lake Erie to Port Weller on Lake Ontario, with a rise of 326 ft. bet. the two. Old canal had 25 locks, was first built 1824–33; reconstructed 1872–87, and entirely rebuilt as a ship canal 1912–32.

Welle. See UELE.

Welles·ley \'welz-lē\. Residential town, Norfolk co., E Massachusetts, 12 m. WSW of Boston; pop. (1970c) 28,051; Wellesley Coll. (1870).

Wellesley, Province. See PROVINCE WELLESLEY.

Wellesley Islands. Group of islands off N coast of Queensland, Australia, at head of Gulf of Carpenteria.

Well·fleet \'wel-(ˌ)flēt\. Town, Barnstable co., SE Massachusetts, on Cape Cod Bay ab. 15 m. from Provincetown; pop. (1970c) 1743; inlet of the bay here called **Wellfleet Harbor.**

Wel·ling·bor·ough \'wel-iŋ-b(ə-)rə\. Urban district, Northamptonshire, cen. England, on the Nene 60 m. NNW of London; pop. (1971p) 37,500; leather goods, beer, plastics.

Wel·ling·ton \'wel-iŋ-tən\. 1 City, ⊗ of Sumner co., S Kansas, 30 m. S of Wichita; pop. (1970c) 8072; railroad shops, oil wells; grain farms.

2 Village, Lorain co., N Ohio, 35 m. SW of Cleveland; pop. (1970c) 4137; iron castings, warehouse trucks, foam-rubber products; dairy farms.

3 City, ⊗ of Collingsworth co., NW Texas, in the panhandle 87 m. ESE of Amarillo; pop. (1970c) 2884; cotton gin, slaughterhouse; wheat.

4 County, Ontario, Canada. See table at ONTARIO.

5 Island, S Pacific Ocean W of SW Chile, N of Madre de Dios Archipelago; 100 m. long by 15 to 25 m. wide.

6 *or formerly* **Wat·ling Town** \'wät-liŋ-\. Urban district, Shropshire, W England, 30 m. WNW of Birmingham; pop. (1971p) 17,154.

7 Urban district, Somersetshire, SW England, 44 m. SW of Bristol; pop. (1971p) 9343; textiles, dairy products.

8 Town and cantonment, SW Tamil Nadu, S India, 9 m. SE of Ootacamund; pop. (1961c) 12,100.

9 City, ✱ of New Zealand, in S part of North I. on Port Nicholson, an inlet of Cook Strait; pop. (1971p) 135,242; financial, commercial, and transportation center of New Zealand; exports frozen meat, wool, dairy products; produces motor vehicles, footwear, machinery, metal goods, textiles, chemicals. Site of the major government buildings and headquarters of many cultural, scientific, and agricultural organizations; museums, public parks; Victoria Univ. of Wellington (1962). Founded 1840; capital transferred from Auckland 1865.

10 Town, SW Cape Province, S Rep. of South Africa, 38 m. NE of Cape Town; pop. (1967e) 13,200; fruit orchards, stock raising.

Wellington, Mount. Mountain, S Tasmania, Australia, 4 m. WSW of Hobart; 4166 ft.

Wellington Harbour. PORT NICHOLSON.

Wells \'welz\. 1 Name of counties in two states of the U.S. See tables at INDIANA and NORTH DAKOTA.

2 Town, York co., SW Maine, 12 m. SSW of Biddeford; pop. (1970c) 4448; seaside resort.

3 Village, Faribault co., S Minnesota, 18 m. WNW of Albert Lea; pop. (1970c) 2791; grain, dairy farms.

4 City, Elko co., NE corner of Nevada, ab. 48 m. NE of Elko; pop. (1970c) 1081.

5 Municipal borough, Somersetshire, SW England, at foot of Mendip Hills 17 m. S of Bristol; pop. (1971p) 8586; printing; tourism; notable 12th cent. cathedral, 15th cent. deanery, 15th cent. church; an old town, important in ancient Wessex; its origin and development have been chiefly ecclesiastical; received first charter 1201.

Wells, Lake. Lake, cen. Western Australia, in region of salt lakes bordering Gibson Desert.

Wells·boro \'welz-ˌbər-ə, -ˌbə-rə\. Borough and resort, ⊗ of Tioga co., N Pennsylvania, 38 m. NNW of Williamsport; pop. (1970c) 4003; mountain resort; glass products.

Wells·burg \'welz-ˌbərg\. Industrial city, ⊗ of Brooke co., N West Virginia, in N panhandle on Ohio river 15 m. NNE of Wheeling; pop. (1970c) 4600; glassware, paper bags, flour; coal mines.

Wells Gray Park \ˌwelz-ˌgrā-\. Provincial park, S British Columbia, Canada, just N of Kamloops; 2036 sq. m.; big-game region.

Wells River. Industrial village, Orange co., E Vermont, at junction of Wells and Connecticut rivers ab. 19 m. S of St. Johnsbury; pop. (1970c) 1319; gateway bet. White Mts. and Green Mts.

Wells·ton \'wel-stən\. 1 City, St. Louis co., E Missouri, NW suburb of St. Louis; pop. (1970c) 7050.

2 Manufacturing city, Jackson co., S Ohio, 26 m. ESE of Chillicothe; pop. (1970c) 5815; machine tools, mining equipment; coal mines; apples, poultry.

Wells·ville \'welz-ˌvil\. 1 Village, Allegany co., SW New York, 20 m. SW of Hornell; pop. (1970c) 5815; oil wells; dairy farms.

2 City, Columbiana co., E Ohio, on Ohio river 16 m. N of Steubenville; pop. (1970c) 5891; pottery, bricks; dairy farms; settled 1797.

We·lo \'wā-lō\ *also* **Wal·lo** \'wȯl-ō\. Province of N cen. Ethiopia. See table at ETHIOPIA.

Wels \'vels\ *or anc.* **Ovi·la·va** \ˌō-və-'lā-və\. Manufacturing and commercial city, Upper Austria, on Traun river 26 m. SW of Linz; pop. (1961c) 41,060; agricultural machinery, textiles; gas wells; former imperial palace; site occupied since prehistoric times.

Welsh \'welsh\. Town, Jefferson Davis parish, SW Louisiana, 25 m. E of Lake Charles; pop. (1970c) 3203.

Welsh·pool \'welsh-ˌpül\. Municipal borough, ⊗ of Montgomeryshire, E Wales; pop. (1969e) 6820; market town; lumber; 12th cent. castle, residence of the earls of Powis (or Powys).

Wel·wyn Garden City \'wel-ən-\. Urban district, Hertfordshire, SE England, on tributary of the Lea 24 m. N of London; pop. (1971p) 40,369; residential; plastics, television sets; established as the second English garden city in 1920.

Wemyss \'wēmz\. Civil parish, Fife co., E Scotland, on N shore of Firth of Forth; pop. (1971p) 10,593; ships coal; produces fertilizer and building materials; Wemyss castle where Mary, Queen of Scots, met Darnley 1565; caves (*Scot.* weems) along the coast of the district.

We·natch·ee \wə-'nach-ē\. 1 River, cen. Washington; ab. 60 m. long; flows SE in Chelan co. into Columbia river at Wenatchee.

2 City, ⊗ of Chelan co., cen. Washington, at confluence of Columbia and Wenatchee rivers 30 m. S of Lake Chelan; pop. (1970c) 16,912; packs and ships apples; flour, lumber, dairy products; resort region (Wenatchee National Forest and Chelan National Forest nearby); Wenatchee Valley Coll. (1939).

Wenatchee Lake. Lake, cen. Chelan co., cen. Washington.

Wenatchee Mountains. Range, cen. Washington, extending along boundary bet. Chelan and Kittitas cos.; highest peak 9470 ft.

Wen–chou *also* **Wen·chow** \'wen-'jō\ *or formerly* **Yung·kia** \'yu̇ŋ-jē-'ä\. City, SE Chekiang prov., E China, at mouth of Wu; pop. (1970e) 250,000; former treaty port. Founded in 4th cent. A.D.; has many old buildings; opened to foreign trade 1876 by Chefoo Convention; in World War II occupied by Japanese; taken by Chinese June 1945.

Wenden. See CĒSIS.

Wen·do·ver \'wen-ˌdō-vər\. Town, Tooele co., W Utah, 12 m. W of Bonneville Salt Flats, on Nevada boundary; pop. (1970c) 781.

Wener *or* **Wenner.** See VÄNERN.

Wen·lock \'wen-ˌläk\. Municipal borough, Shropshire, W England, on the Severn 30 m. W of Birmingham; pop. (1969e) 14,149; clothing, metal goods, limestone quarries. It includes the market town of **Much Wenlock** \'məch-\, noted for its ruined Early English priory church.

Wen–su. See AKSU 2.

Went·worth \'went-wərth\. 1 Village, ⊗ of Rockingham co., N North Carolina; Rockingham Community Coll. (1964).

2 County, Ontario, Canada. See table at ONTARIO.

Wentworth Lake. Lake, S Carroll co., E New Hampshire; 4 m. long.

We·pe·ner \'vēp-ə-nər\. Town, S Orange Free State, E cen. Rep. of South Africa, near Caledon river 63 m. SE of Bloemfontein; pop. (1967e) 4200; trade center in agricultural and livestock-farming region.

Wer·dau \'ve(ə)r-ˌdau̇\. Manufacturing city, Karl-Marx-Stadt dist., East Germany, on Pleisse river 5 m. WNW of Zwickau; pop. (1970e) 23,023; textiles, furniture, trucks; 18th cent. church; chartered 1304.

Wer·dohl \ver-ˈdōl\. Industrial commune, North Rhine-Westphalia, West Germany, 41 m. E of Düsseldorf; pop. (1969e) 23,872; manufactures iron, steel, wire, metal goods.

Wer·mels·kir·chen \ˌver-məls-ˈki(ə)r-kən\. Industrial city, North Rhine-Westphalia, West Germany, 19 m. ESE of Düsseldorf; pop. (1969e) 26,381; iron goods, footwear; 11th cent. church.

Werne an der Lip·pe \ˈve(ə)r-nə-än-dər-ˈlip-ə\. Coal-mining city, North Rhine-Westphalia, West Germany, on Lippe river 22 m. S of Münster; pop. (1969e) 20,552.

Wer·ner Peak \ˌwər-nər-\. Mountain, W Flathead co., NW Montana; 7000 ft.

Wer·ners·ville \ˈwər-nərz-ˌvil\. Borough, Berks co., SE Pennsylvania, 10 m. W of Reading; pop. (1970c) 1761.

Wer·ni·ge·ro·de \ˌver-ni-gə-ˈrōd-ə\. City, Magdeburg dist., East Germany, 30 m. SSE of Brunswick; pop. (1970e) 32,662; health resort; electrical equipment, glass, pharmaceuticals; iron mines; 15th cent. town hall. Founded in middle of 9th cent.; became city 1229; member of Hanse 1267 ff.

Wer·ra \ˈver-ə\. River, East and West Germany; 181 m. long; rises in Suhl dist., East Germany, flows NW, N, and NE to unite with Fulda river at Münden, Lower Saxony, West Germany, and form the Weser river.

Werschetz. See VRŠAC.

Wert·heim \ˈve(ə)rt-ˌhīm\. Town, Baden-Württemberg, West Germany, at the confluence of the Tauber and the Main; Wertheim Bible published 1735.

Wer·wik *or* **Wer·vicq** \ver-ˈvēk\. Commune, West Flanders prov., W Belgium, 8 m. SE of Ieper; pop. (1969e) 12,668.

Wesel \ˈvā-zəl\. Industrial city, North Rhine-Westphalia, West Germany, on the Rhine at mouth of Lippe river, 49 m. WSW of Münster; pop. (1969e) 33,952; seaport and railroad junction; machinery, lumber, tile, marine hardware, soap, cement; chartered 1241; member of Hanseatic League 1407; to Brandenburg 1680; occupied by French 1808–14; almost completely destroyed in air raids during World War II and since rebuilt in modern style.

We·ser \ˈvā-zər, ˈwē-\ *or anc.* **Vi·sur·gis** \vī-ˈsər-jəs\. 1 River, Belgium. See VESDRE.

2 Navigable river, West Germany; 273 m. long; formed by confluence of Fulda and Werra rivers at Münden in SE Lower Saxony, flows NW into the North Sea through a large estuary; its chief tributary is the Aller from the E, joining it near Verden.

Wesermünde. See BREMERHAVEN.

Wes·la·co \ˈwes-lə-ˌkō\. City, Hidalgo co., S Texas, 17 m. E of McAllen; pop. (1970c) 15,313; cans and ships fruits and vegetables; cotton gins, gas wells.

Wes·ley·ville \ˈwes-lē-ˌvil\. Borough, Erie co., NW corner of Pennsylvania, on Lake Erie 5 m. E of Erie; pop. (1970c) 3920; electrical equipment.

Wes·se·ling \ˈves-ə-liŋ\. Town, North Rhine-Westphalia, West Germany, on left bank of Rhine just S of Cologne; pop. (1969e) 23,708.

Wes·sel Islands \ˌwes-əl-\. Island group, NW of Gulf of Carpentaria, off coast of N Northern Territory, Australia.

Wes·sex \ˈwes-iks\. Ancient Anglo-Saxon kingdom, S Britain; ✱ Winchester; also, the corresponding section of modern England, used esp. with reference to the novels of Thomas Hardy; approximately the counties of Berkshire, Dorsetshire, Hampshire, Somersetshire, and Wiltshire.

History: Kingdom founded, traditionally, by Saxon invaders of Britain; conquered Kent and Sussex (see KENT 7 and SUSSEX 5) and, in 9th cent. A.D., leader of the Anglo-Saxon Heptarchy (*q.v.*); under Alfred the Great 871–899, successfully kept Danes from conquest of England S of Danelaw; by c. 927 Wessex had reconquered the Danelaw and become ruler of all England; important Anglo-Saxon earldom.

Wes·sing·ton Springs \ˌwes-iŋ-tən-\. City, ⊗ of Jerauld co., SE cen. South Dakota; pop. (1970c) 1300.

West \ˈwest\. 1 River, Windham co., SE corner of Vermont; ab. 50 m. long; formed by confluence of forks in NW part of the county, flows SE into Connecticut river above Brattleboro.

2 City, McLennan co., cen. Texas, 19 m. N of Waco; pop. (1970c) 2406; ships livestock; truck farms.

West Al·lis \-ˈal-əs\. City, Milwaukee co., SE Wisconsin, 6 m. WSW of Milwaukee; pop. (1970c) 71,649; residential and industrial suburb of Milwaukee; manufactures trucks, tractors, construction machinery, gasoline engines, castings, air compressors; incorporated 1906.

West Antarctica. See ANTARCTICA.

West Australian Current. Warm ocean current, flowing N off W coast of Australia.

West Azerbaijan. See AZERBAIJAN 1.

West Ba·den Springs \-ˈbād-ᵊn-\. Town, Orange co., Indiana; pop. (1970c) 930.

West Bat·on Rouge \-ˌbat-ᵊn-ˈrüzh\. Parish in Louisiana. See table at LOUISIANA.

West Bel·mar \-ˈbel-ˌmär\. Village, E Monmouth co., E New Jersey; pop. (1970c) 2000.

West Bend. City, ⊗ of Washington co., SE Wisconsin, 29 m. NNW of Milwaukee; pop. (1970c) 16,555; aluminum, leather, and plastic products, tools, automobile parts; dairy farms.

West Ben·gal \-ben-ˈgȯl, -beŋ-\. State, NE India; 33,852 sq. m.; pop. (1971p) 44,440,095; ✱ Calcutta; rice, jute, coal; chief cities: Calcutta, Howrah, Bhatpara, Asansol; established 1947; comprises all of Burdwan division of Bengal, India; Calcutta, 24 Parganas, and Murshidabad dists. of Presidency division; Darjeeling dist. of Rajshahi division; parts of Nadia and Jessore dists. of Presidency division; and parts of Dinajpur, Jalpaiguri, and Malda dists. of Rajshahi division. For history see BENGAL.

West Berbice. See BERBICE 2.

West Berlin. See BERLIN, WEST.

West Beskids. See BESKIDS.

West Bloc·ton \-ˈbläk-tən\. Town, Bibb co., cen. Alabama, 30 m. SSW of Birmingham; pop. (1970c) 1172.

West·bor·ough *or* **West·boro** \ˈwest-ˌbər-ə, -ˌbə-rə\. Town, Worcester co., cen. Massachusetts, 9 m. E of Worcester; pop. (1970c) 12,594.

West Boyls·ton \-ˈbȯi(ə)l-stən\. Residential town, Worcester co., cen. Massachusetts, 7 m. N of Worcester; pop. (1970c) 6369.

West Branch. 1 Town, Cedar co., E Iowa, just E of Iowa City; pop. (1970c) 1322; birthplace of Herbert C. Hoover, 31st president of the U.S.

2 City, ⊗ of Ogemaw co., NE Michigan, 50 m. N of Bay City; pop. (1970c) 1912; lake resort; oil wells; diversified agriculture.

West Branch of Susquehanna River. See SUSQUEHANNA 1.

West Bridge·water \-ˈbrij-ˌwȯt-ər, -ˌwät-\. 1 Town, Plymouth co., SE Massachusetts, 4 m. S of Brockton; pop. (1970c) 7152.

2 Residential borough, Pennsylvania. See BRIDGEWATER 2.

West Bridg·ford \-ˈbrij-fərd\. Urban district, Nottinghamshire, N cen. England, SE suburb of Nottingham; pop. (1971p) 28,496; residential.

West Brom·wich \-ˈbrəm-ij, -ˈbräm-, -ich\. County borough, Staffordshire, W cen. England, 5 m. NW of Birmingham; pop. (1971p) 166,626; heavy machinery, hardware, chemicals, paint; coal mines, oil refineries; incorporated 1882.

West·brook \ˈwest-ˌbru̇k\. 1 Agricultural town, Middlesex co., S Connecticut, on Long Island Sound 4 m. W of mouth of Connecticut river; pop. (1970c) 3820.

2 Industrial city, Cumberland co., SW Maine, 7 m. W of Portland; pop. (1970c) 14,444; paper products, footwear, textiles; truck farms.

West Brook·field \-ˈbru̇k-ˌfēld\. Town, Worcester co., cen. Massachusetts, 18 m. W of Worcester; pop. (1970c) 2653.

West Bur·ling·ton \-ˈbər-liŋ-tən\. Town, Des Moines co., SE Iowa, W of Burlington; pop. (1970c) 3139; agriculture.

West·bury \'west-ˌber-ē, -bə-rē\. Residential village, Nassau co., SE New York, on Long I. 23 m. E of New York; pop. (1970c) 15,362; Meadowbrook polo fields.

Westbury Down. See SALISBURY PLAIN.

West·by \'west-bē\. City, Vernon co., SW Wisconsin, N of Viroqua; pop. (1970c) 1568.

West Cald·well \-'käld-ˌwel, -wəl\. Borough, Essex co., NE New Jersey, 9 m. SW of Paterson; pop. (1970c) 11,887.

West Canada Creek. Stream, cen. New York; ab. 55 m. long; flows S into Mohawk river at Herkimer; contains Trenton Falls (*q.v.*).

West Cape. Cape, W coast of Guadalcanal I., SE Solomon Is., W Pacific Ocean.

West Car·roll \-'kar-əl\. Parish in Louisiana. See table at LOUISIANA.

West Car·roll·ton \-'kar-əl-tən\. City, Montgomery co., SW Ohio, on Miami river 8 m. S of Dayton; pop. (1970c) 10,748.

West Carthage. Village, Jefferson co., N New York, 15 m. E of Watertown; pop. (1970c) 2047.

West Charlevoix. See CHARLEVOIX-OUEST.

West·ches·ter \'wes(t)-ˌches-tər\. **1** County in New York. See table at NEW YORK.

2 Village, Cook co., NE Illinois, W suburb of Chicago; pop. (1970c) 20,033.

West Chester. Borough, ⊗ of Chester county, SE Pennsylvania, 26 m. W of Philadelphia; pop. (1970c) 19,301; West Chester State Coll. (1812).

West Chicago. City, Du Page co., NE Illinois, 30 m. W of Chicago; pop. (1970c) 10,711; chemicals; railroad shops.

West·cliffe \'west-(ˌ)klif\. Town, ⊗ of Custer co., S cen. Colorado; pop. (1970c) 243.

West Columbia. **1** City, Lexington co., cen. South Carolina, on Congaree river W of Columbia; pop. (1970c) 7838. Known until 1938 as **Brook·land** \'brůk-lənd\.

2 City, Brazoria co., SE Texas, 19 m. ENE of Bay City; pop. (1970c) 3335; temporary capital of Republic of Texas in 1836.

West Concord. Urban community, Cabarrus co., SW North Carolina, NE of Charlotte; pop. (1970c) 5347.

West Co·vi·na \-kō-'vē-nə\. City, Los Angeles co., SW California, W of Los Angeles; pop. (1970c) 68,034; residential; incorporated 1923.

West Demerara. See DEMERARA 2.

West Des Moines. City, Polk co., S cen. Iowa, 7 m. W of Des Moines; pop. (1970c) 16,441; name changed from **Valley Junction** in 1938.

West Dinajpur. See DINAJPUR.

West Dun·dee \-dən-'dē\. Village, Kane co., Illinois, ab. 35 m. NW of Chicago; pop. (1970c) 3295.

West El·mi·ra \-el-'mī-rə\. Urban community (unincorporated), Chemung co., S New York; pop. (1970c) 5901.

West End. Town, W tip of Grand Bahama I., Bahama Is., 64 m. directly E of Palm Beach, Florida.

We·ster·land \'ves-tər-ˌlänt\. Town, NW West Germany, on the island of Sylt; resort.

Wes·ter·ly \'wes-tər-lē\. Town, Washington co., S Rhode Island, on Pawcatuck river and Connecticut state boundary 27 m. WSW of Newport; pop. (1970c) 17,248; printing presses, textiles, plastics, furniture; diversified agriculture; comprises several villages including Westerly village; settlement by whites 1648; involved in the boundary dispute bet. Rhode Island and Connecticut until 1728.

Western Australia. State, W Australia, W of 129°E long.; 975,920 sq. m.; pop. (1970e) 980,000; ✱ Perth. *Physical features:* Extensive interior region covered by three deserts, Great Sandy, Gibson, and Great Victoria; in W part is plateau and semidesert with numerous salt lakes. Coast along Timor Sea and Indian Ocean generally rugged with promontories, islands, and coral reefs with only a few good harbors; notable inlets are Joseph Bonaparte Gulf, King Sound, Exmouth Gulf, and Shark Bay. *Rivers:* Swan (with estuary forming excellent natural harbor of Fremantle), Murchison, Fortescue, and Fitzroy. *Mountains:* Highest point Mt. Bruce in NW, 4024 ft.; Darling Range along SW coast. Its great extent from N to S affords several distinct climatic regions. *Chief products:* Wheat, wool, meat, dairy products; gold, iron ore, coal, nickel. *Chief cities:* Perth, Fremantle, Kalgoorlie-Boulder, and Bunbury.

History: West coast first visited 1616 by Dirck Hartog; explored by Dampier 1688, 1699; Vancouver, English navigator, took formal possession 1791 of region about King George Sound; New South Wales formed small settlement there in 1826 but permanent colonization began in 1829 when Capt. Fremantle founded Swan River Settlement; made penal settlement 1850–88; became part of colonial government 1886; granted responsible government 1890; last state to ratify the federation 1900. Australia and U.S. reached agreement 1963 on establishment of a U.S. navy communications center in the state; important mineral discoveries made during the 1960's.

Western Bug. See BUG 1.

Western Carolines. The Palau Is. (*q.v.*).

Western Channel *or formerly* **Cho·sen Strait** \ˌchō-ˌsen-\. Channel bet. South Korea and island of Tsushima, connecting Sea of Japan with Yellow Sea and East China Sea; ab. 35 m. wide; NW part of Korea Strait (*q.v.*).

Western Desert. Desert, W cen. Egypt, approximately 25° to 30°N and 26° to 30°E; includes Siwa, Baharīya, and Farafa oases; actually a part of the greater Libyan Desert.

Western Dvina. See DVINA, WESTERN.

Western Empire *or* **Western Roman Empire.** The western part of the Roman Empire, first set apart 286 A.D. by Emperor Diocletian with the establishment of joint emperors of the East and West; later in 395 after the death of Theodosius I (the Great) and the actual division of the Empire (see BYZANTINE EMPIRE) the western part comprising Italy, Spain, Gaul, Britain, Illyricum, and Africa; it ceased to exist 476 on the death of Romulus Augustulus. By some considered to have been revived by Charlemagne 800 (see HOLY ROMAN EMPIRE).

Western Euphrates. See KARA SU 2.

Western Ghats. See GHATS.

Western India States. Formerly an agency, W India, comprising a group of states in Kathiawar and Gujarat; 37,894 sq. m.; ✱ Rajkot; formed 1924; comprised 17 salute states, 34 nonsalute states, and 84 talukas; some regions (Sabar Kantha) in N Gujarat were included in the former Banas Kantha and Mahi Kantha agencies. Among the more important salute states were Kutch, Idar, Junagadh, Navanagar, Bhaunagar, Porbandar. Since 1947 in Rep. of India.

Western Islands. See HEBRIDES.

Western Ka·thi·a·war \-ˌkät-ē-ə-'wär\. Former agency, forming a part of Western India States agency; 2552 sq. m.; chief town Jetpur.

Western Locris. See LOCRIS.

Western Manych. See MANYCH 3.

Western Morava. Branch of Morava river, Yugoslavia. See MORAVA 3.

West·ern·port \'wes-tərn-ˌpō(ə)rt, -ˌpȯ(ə)rt\. Town, Allegany co., NW Maryland, on Potomac river 20 m. SW of Cumberland; pop. (1970c) 3106; head of navigation on north branch of the Potomac river.

Western Province. **1** Province, SW Ceylon, on Indian Ocean; 1432 sq. m.; pop. (1963c) 2,839,110; ✱ Colombo. Other important towns are Dehiwala-Mount Lavinia, Moratuwa, Negombo, and Kalutara.

2 Province of W Kenya. See table at KENYA.

Western Punjab. See PUNJAB 4.

Western Raj·pu·ta·na States \-ˌräj-pə-ˈtän-ə-\. Western part of former Rajputana Agency, NW India, comprising Danta, Jaisalmer, Jodhpur, Palanpur, and Sirohi states.

Western Region. Administrative region of SW Ghana. See table at GHANA.

Western Reserve *also* **Connecticut Reserve.** Tract of land, NE corner of Ohio, on S shore of Lake Erie, forming the part of the western lands of Connecticut not included in region surrendered to Congress in 1786; extended southward to ab. 41°N and westward as far as Willard and Port Clinton; ab. 3,500,000 acres; sold in part to immigrants from Connecticut 1786–1800; ceded 1800 to Ohio to form Trumbull co., later divided into many counties. See NORTHWEST TERRITORY.

Western Roman Empire. See WESTERN EMPIRE.

Western Sa·moa \-sə-ˈmō-ə\. Independent state, a group of islands of Samoa (*q.v.*), SW cen. Pacific Ocean, 172°W; 1133 sq. m.; pop. (1971e) 148,565; ✱ Apia; copra, pineapples; fishing; chief islands Savai'i and Upolu. See AMERICAN SAMOA.

History: Apia granted to Germany by treaty with native ruler 1879; after period of joint administration of Samoan Is. (see SAMOA) by England, U.S., and Germany (1889–99), Savai'i and Upolu recognized as German 1899–1900; occupied by New Zealand expeditionary force 1914–20; surrendered by Germany as part of terms of Versailles Treaty 1919; became mandate of New Zealand 1920 and United Nations trust territory (administered by New Zealand) 1947; achieved independence 1962; suffered severe economic reverses due to hurricane damage 1966, 1968.

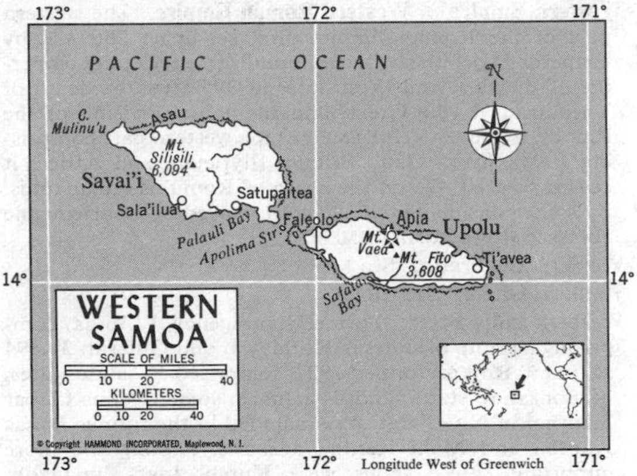

Western Sierra Madre. See SIERRA MADRE OCCIDENTAL.

Western Springs. Village, Cook co., NE Illinois, 15 m. W of Chicago; pop. (1970c) 13,029.

Western State. State of SW Nigeria. See table at NIGERIA.

Western Thrace. See THRACE.

Western Turkistan. See TURKISTAN.

Western Ukrai·nia \-yü-ˈkrān-ē-ə, -ˈkrīn-\. Republic, E Galicia, 1918–19; soon taken over by Poland; now in W Ukrainian S.S.R., U.S.S.R.

Wes·ter·ville \ˈwes-tər-ˌvil\. City, Franklin and Delaware cos., cen. Ohio, 12 m. N of Columbus; pop. (1970c) 12,530; Otterbein Coll. (1847).

We·ster·wald \ˈves-tər-ˌvält\. Mountainous region in West Germany, stretching NE from near Koblenz for ab. 70 m. bet. the rivers Rhine, Sieg, and Lahn; highest peak 2156 ft.

West Fair·view \-ˈfa(ə)r-(ˌ)vyü, -ˈfe(ə)r-\. Borough, Cumberland co., S Pennsylvania, on Susquehanna river 4 m. NW of Harrisburg; pop. (1970c) 1388.

West Falkland. See FALKLAND ISLANDS.

West Fargo. See FARGO.

West Fe·li·ci·ana \-fə-ˌlish-ē-ˈan-ə\. Parish in Louisiana. See table at LOUISIANA.

West·field \ˈwes(t)-ˌfēld\. 1 Unnavigable river, W Massachusetts; ab. 50 m. long; rises in NE Berkshire co., NW Massachusetts, flows SE into Connecticut river opp. Springfield.

2 City, Hampden co., SW Massachusetts, on Westfield river 8 m. W of Springfield; pop. (1970c) 31,433; residential suburb; paper, bicycles, machinery; Massachusetts State Coll. at Westfield (1839). Founded 1660 as trading post and established as separate town 1669; in 19th cent. important whip-manufacturing center; chartered as city 1920.

3 Residential town, Union co., NE New Jersey, 7 m. W of Elizabeth; pop. (1970c) 33,720; figured in American Revolution; incorporated 1903.

4 Village, Chautauqua co., SW corner of New York, on Lake Erie 23 m. WNW of Jamestown; pop. (1970c) 3651; canned fruit; grapes.

West Flanders *or Flem.* **West Vlaan·der·en** \-ˈvlän-dər-ən\. Province, NW Belgium; 1210 sq. m.; pop. (1970e) 1,056,855; ✱ Brugge (Bruges); wheat, sugar beet, potatoes, tobacco; livestock raising; tourism; chemical, shipbuilding, lace, and metallurgical industries.

West Florida. See history at FLORIDA.

West·ford \ˈwest-fərd\. Town, Middlesex co., NE Massachusetts, 8 m. SW of Lowell; pop. (1970c) 10,368; fruit farms.

West Frank·fort \-ˈfraŋk-fərt\. City, Franklin co., S Illinois, 33 m. S of Mount Vernon; pop. (1970c) 8854; clothing, boats; coal mines.

West Frisian Islands. See FRISIAN ISLANDS.

West Gaspé. See GASPÉ-OUEST.

West Germany. See GERMANY, WEST.

West Glacier *or formerly* **Bel·ton** \ˈbelt-ᵊn\. Village, Flathead co., NW Montana; W entrance to Glacier National Park.

West Grand Lake *or formerly* **Grand Lake.** Lake, E Maine, near W boundary of Washington co.

West Hartford. Suburban residential town, cen. Hartford co., N Connecticut, W of Hartford; pop. (1970c) 68,031; tools and dies, sheet metal products; St. Joseph Coll. (1925), Univ. of Hartford (1877); settled 1679; incorporated 1854; birthplace of Noah Webster.

West Haven. Suburban residential town, SW New Haven co., S Connecticut, separated from New Haven by West river; pop. (1970c) 52,851; aircraft parts, rubber products, tires, velvets, beer; New Haven Coll. (1920); incorporated 1921.

West Hav·er·straw \-ˈhav-ər-ˌstrȯ\. Village, Rockland co., SE New York, W of Hudson river 34 m. N of New York; pop. (1970c) 8558; site of Treason House, where Benedict Arnold and Major John André plotted betrayal of West Point to the British.

West Ha·zle·ton \-ˈhā-zəl-tən\. Borough, Luzerne co., E Pennsylvania, 20 m. SSW of Wilkes-Barre; pop. (1970c) 6059.

West Hel·e·na \-ˈhel-ə-nə\. City, Phillips co., E Arkansas, near Mississippi river 85 m. ENE of Pine Bluff; pop. (1970c) 11,007; wood products; founded 1909.

West Hemp·stead \-ˈhem(p)-ˌsted, -stəd\. Urban region, Nassau co., SE New York, on Long I.; pop. (1970c) 20,375 (with Lakeview).

West Hoboken. See UNION CITY 5.

West Hollywood. Urban region, Los Angeles co., SW California, NE of Beverly Hills; pop. (1970c) 29,448.

West Homestead. Borough, Allegheny co., SW Pennsylvania, on Monongahela river adjacent to Homestead and 5 m. ESE of Pittsburgh; pop. (1970c) 3789.

West·hough·ton \ˈwest-ˈhȯt-ᵊn, -ˈhau̇t-\. Urban district, Lancashire, NW England, 13 m. WNW of Manchester; pop. (1971p) 17,729.

West Hsing·an \-ˈshiŋ-ˈän\. Former province, W Manchukuo; 31,038 sq. m.; formed 1932, abolished 1945.

West Hungary. Name applied to Burgenland (*q.v.*) when it was part of Hungary.

West In·dies \-ˈin-(ˌ)dēz\. Islands lying bet. SE North America and N South America, enclosing the Caribbean Sea;

may be divided into the following groups: **(1) Greater An·til·les** \-an-'til-ēz\ including Cuba, Hispaniola (Haiti and Dominican Republic), Jamaica, and Puerto Rico; **(2) Lesser Antilles** *also* **Car·ib·bees** \'kar-ə-ˌbēz\ including Virgin Is., Windward Is., Leeward Is., and the islands in the S Caribbean Sea N of Venezuela (generally considered to include Trinidad and Tobago); **(3) Bahama Islands** (*q.v.*).

History: San Salvador (Watlings I.) in the Bahama Is. was first land in New World reached by Columbus Oct. 12, 1492; Cuba, Hispaniola, Dominica, Puerto Rico, Virgin Is., Jamaica, and Trinidad were among the islands discovered by Columbus during his voyages 1492–1504; Santo Domingo, founded 1496, was seat of Spanish rule in West Indies and base for expansion to American mainland; the English settled Barbados 1626, Dutch captured Curaçao 1634, and French occupied Guadeloupe and Martinique 1635; Jamaica was taken from Spanish by English 1655; St. Thomas in Virgin Is. came into Danish hands 1666; became a central theater of bitter Anglo-French colonial rivalry; by 1814 British had acquired the islands of Dominica, Grenada, Saint Lucia, and Tobago from France and Trinidad from Spain; Santo Domingo and Haiti became independent republics in 19th cent. (see DOMINICAN REPUBLIC and HAITI); Cuba and Puerto Rico (*qq.v.*), last of the Spanish colonies in America, became dependencies of U.S. 1898 (Cuba became a republic 1902); Virgin Is. purchased from Denmark by U.S. 1916–17. See INDIES.

West Indies Federation *also* **Federation of the West Indies.** Former federation, consisting of the British West Indian possessions with the exception of the Bahama Is. and the British Virgin Is.; ✱ Port of Spain; established 1958, dissolved 1962.

West Irian. See IRIAN BARAT.

West Java. Province of Java, Indonesia. See JAVA and table at INDONESIA.

West Jersey. Western and southern New Jersey, constituting a Quaker colony under William Penn from 1676 to 1702 when it was united with East Jersey to form the royal province of New Jersey (*q.v.*); ✱ (from 1681) Burlington.

West·ka·pel·le \ˌvest-kə-'pel-ə\. Town, Zeeland prov., SW Netherlands, at W tip of Walcheren I. NW of Vlissingen; pop. (1970e) 2478; lighthouse in church tower. Occupied by British commando units Nov. 1, 1944; with Vlissingen came under Allied control by Nov. 3, insuring free entry of the Schelde estuary.

West Kil·do·nan \-kil-'dō-nən\. City, Manitoba, Canada; pop. (1971p) 23,728; residential suburb of Winnipeg.

West Kill, Mount \-ˌkil\. Peak in the Catskill Mts., Greene co., SE New York; 3880 ft.

West Kingston. Village in South Kingstown town, ⊗ of Washington co., S Rhode Island; pop. (1970c) 900.

West La·fay·ette \-ˌläf-ē-'et, -ˌlaf-\. City, Tippecanoe co., W cen. Indiana, suburb of Lafayette across Wabash river; pop. (1970c) 19,157.

West·lake \'west-ˌlāk\ *or formerly* **Do·ver** \'dō-vər\. City, Cuyahoga co., N Ohio, W suburb of Cleveland; pop. (1970c) 15,689.

West Lake. Administrative region of N Tanzania. See table at TANZANIA.

West Lake St. John. See LAKE ST. JOHN, WEST.

West·land \'west-lənd\. City, Wayne co., SE Michigan, 20 m. W of Detroit; pop. (1970c) 86,749.

West Las Vegas. See LAS VEGAS 2.

West Liberty. 1 Town, Muscatine co., E Iowa, 17 m. NW of Muscatine; pop. (1970c) 2296.

2 City, ⊗ of Morgan co., E Kentucky; pop. (1970c) 1387.

3 Village, Ohio co., N West Virginia, ab. 9 m. NE of Wheeling; West Liberty State Coll. (1837).

West Linn \-'lin\. City, Clackamas co., NW Oregon, on Willamette river 10 m. S of Portland; pop. (1970c) 7091.

West·lock \'west-ˌläk\. Town, Alberta, Canada, 45 m. N of Edmonton; pop. (1971p) 3265; diversified agriculture; flour mill, creamery.

West Long Branch. Borough, Monmouth co., E cen. New Jersey, 4 m. N of Asbury Park; pop. (1970c) 6845; Monmouth Coll. (1933).

West Lo·thi·an \-'lō-t͟hē-ən\ *or formerly* **Lin·lith·gow** \lin-'lith-(ˌ)gō\ *or* **Lin·lith·gow·shire** \-ˌshi(ə)r, -shər\. County, SE Scotland; 120 sq. m.; pop. (1971p) 108,474; ⊗ Linlithgow; rivers Almond, Avon; dairy farming, coal and peat mining; motor vehicles, iron and steel products, electronic components, paper, rubber, furniture.

West Malaysia. See MALAYSIA.

Westman Islands. See VESTMANNAEYJAR.

West·meath \(')wes(t)-'mēt͟h\. County, N cen. Eire, in Leinster prov.; 681 sq. m.; pop. (1971p) 53,557; ⊗ Mullingar; rivers Shannon, Brosna; oats, wheat, potatoes.

West Memphis. City, Crittenden co., E Arkansas, 8 m. W of Memphis, Tennessee; pop. (1970c) 26,070; formerly Bragg's Spur; incorp. under present name 1927.

West Miami. Town, Dade co., SE Florida, N of Coral Gables; pop. (1970c) 5494.

West Miff·lin \-'mif-lən\. Borough, Allegheny co., SW Pennsylvania, SE suburb of Pittsburgh; pop. (1970c) 28,070.

West Milwaukee. Village, Milwaukee co., SE Wisconsin; pop. (1970c) 4405; suburb of Milwaukee.

West·min·ster \'wes(t)-ˌmin(t)-stər\. **1** City, Orange co., SW California, SE of Long Beach; pop. (1970c) 59,874; residential.

2 City, Adams co., NE cen. Colorado, NW of Denver; pop. (1970c) 19,432; residential.

3 City, ⊗ of Carroll co., N Maryland, 30 m. NW of Baltimore; pop. (1970c) 7143; Western Maryland Coll. (1867).

4 Town, Worcester co., cen. Massachusetts, 7 m. WSW of Fitchburg; pop. (1970c) 4273.

5 Town, Oconee co., NW South Carolina, 29 m. WNW of Anderson; pop. (1970c) 2521; agriculture.

6 *or in full* **City of Westminster** *or anc.* **West·mon·as·te·ri·um** \'west-ˌmän-ə-'stir-ē-əm\. A borough of Greater London, SE England. See table at LONDON 4.

West Mon·roe \-mən-'rō\. City, Ouachita parish, N Louisiana; pop. (1970c) 14,868; lumber, cottonseed oil, paper products; commercial fisheries, oil wells, truck farms.

West·mont \'west-ˌmänt\. **1** Village, Du Page co., NE Illinois, 20 m. W of Chicago; pop. (1970c) 8920.

2 Borough, Cambria co., SW cen. Pennsylvania, near Altoona; pop. (1970c) 6673.

West·more·land *Kans. and Pa.* wes(t)-'mō(ə)r-lənd, -'mȯ(ə)r-; *Va.* 'wes(t)-mər-lənd\. **1** Name of counties in two states of the U.S. See tables at PENNSYLVANIA and VIRGINIA.

2 City, ⊗ of Pottawatomie co., NE Kansas; pop. (1970c) 485; wheat, oats.

West·mor·land \'wes(t)-mər-lənd; *U.S. also* wes(t)-'mō(ə)r-, -'mȯ(ə)r-\. County, NW England; area 789 sq. m.; pop. (1969e) 71,710; ⊗ Appleby; lakes include Windermere, Hawes Water, Rydal Water; rivers include Eden and Kent; beef and dairy cattle; slate, marble quarries; paper; tourism; largest towns Kendal and Windermere.

West·mount \'wes(t)-ˌmau̇nt\. Residential city, Montreal I., S Quebec, Canada, part of Greater Montreal; pop. (1971p) 23,570.

West New Brigh·ton \-'brīt-ᵊn\. See RICHMOND.

West New·bury \-'n(y)ü-ˌber-ē\. Town, Essex co., NE corner of Massachusetts, 19 m. NE of Lowell; pop. (1970c) 2254.

West New Guinea. See IRIAN BARAT.

West Newton. 1 Village, Massachusetts. See NEWTON 6.

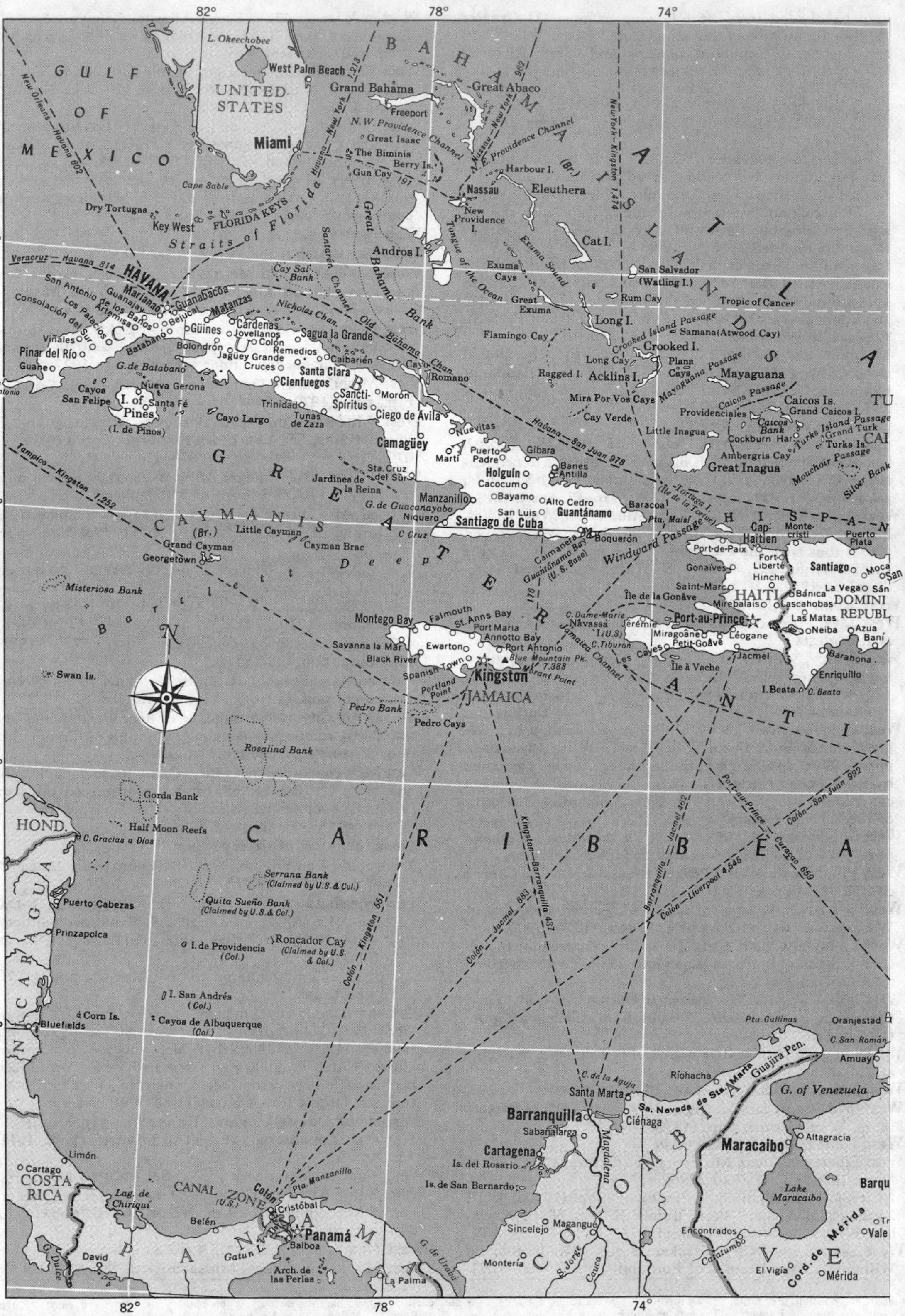
82°
78°
74°
24°
20°
16°
12°
L. Okeechobee
West Palm Beach
UNITED STATES
Miami
GULF OF MEXICO
New Orleans—Havana 602
Cape Sable
Dry Tortugas
Key West
FLORIDA KEYS
Straits of Florida
Veracruz—Havana 814
HAVANA
Mariano
Guanabacoa
Guanajay
San Antonio de los Baños
Artemisa
Bejucal
Matanzas
Los Palacios
Consolación del Sur
Viñales
Pinar del Río
Guane
C. de San Antonio
Batabanó
Güines
Cárdenas
Jovellanos
Colón
Bolondrón
Jagüey Grande
Sagua la Grande
Remedios
Caibarién
Cruces
Santa Clara
Cienfuegos
G. de Batabanó
Nueva Gerona
Cayos San Felipe
I. of Pines
Santa Fé
(I. de Pinos)
Cayo Largo
Trinidad
Tunas de Zaza
Sancti-Spíritus
Morón
Ciego de Avila
Cayo Romano
Nuevitas
Camagüey
Martí
Puerto Padre
Gibara
Banes
Antilla
Holguín
Cacocum
Bayamo
Alto Cedro
Manzanillo
Niquero
San Luis
Guantánamo
Baracoa
Pta. Maisí
Santiago de Cuba
Boquerón
Caimanera
Guantánamo Bay (U. S. Base)
Sta. Cruz del Sur
Jardines de la Reina
G. de Guacanayabo
C. Cruz
CUBA
BAHAMA ISLANDS
Grand Bahama
Freeport
Great Abaco
N.W. Providence Channel
Great Isaac
The Biminis
Berry Is.
Gun Cay
N.E. Providence Channel
Harbour I.
(Br.)
Nassau
Eleuthera
New Providence I.
Andros I.
Great Bahama Bank
Santarén Channel
Cay Sal Bank
Nicholas Chan.
Old Bahama Chan.
Tongue of the Ocean
Exuma Sound
Exuma Cays
Cat I.
Great Exuma
San Salvador (Watling I.)
Rum Cay
Long I.
Tropic of Cancer
Crooked Island Passage
Samana (Atwood Cay)
Crooked I.
Flamingo Cay
Long Cay
Acklins I.
Plana Cays
Mayaguana Passage
Mayaguana
Ragged I.
Mira Por Vos Cays
Cay Verde
Caicos Passage
Caicos Is.
Grand Caicos I.
Providenciales
Caicos Bank
Turks Island Passage
Grand Turk
Turks Is.
Cockburn Har.
Ambergris Cay
Mouchoir Passage
Silver Bank
Little Inagua
Great Inagua
Habana—San Juan 978
New York—Kingston 1,474
Nassau—New York 962
Havana—New York 1,213
Tortuga I. (Île de la Tortue)
Windward Passage
HISPANIOLA
Cap-Haïtien
Monte-cristi
Puerto Plata
Port-de-Paix
Fort-Liberté
Santiago
Moca
Gonaïves
Hinche
La Vega
HAITI
DOMINICAN REPUBLIC
Saint-Marc
Bánica
Île de la Gonâve
Mirebalais
Lascahobas
Port-au-Prince
Las Matas
Neiba
Azua
Baní
Jérémie
Miragoâne
Petit-Goâve
Léogane
C. Dame-Marie
Navassa I.(U.S.)
C. Tiburon
Les Cayes
Île à Vache
Jacmel
Barahona
Enriquillo
I. Beata
C. Beata
Jamaica Channel
GREATER ANTILLES
CAYMAN IS.
(Br.)
Little Cayman
Grand Cayman
Georgetown
Cayman Brac
Bartlett Deep
Misteriosa Bank
Tampico—Kingston 1,252
Montego Bay
Falmouth
St. Anns Bay
Port Maria
Annotto Bay
Savanna la Mar
Ewarton
Port Antonio
Black River
Spanish Town
Blue Mountain Pk. 7,388
Morant Point
Kingston
Portland Point
JAMAICA
Pedro Bank
Pedro Cays
Swan Is.
N
Rosalind Bank
Gorda Bank
HOND.
Half Moon Reefs
C. Gracias a Dios
CARIBBEAN SEA
Serrana Bank (Claimed by U.S. & Col.)
Quita Sueño Bank (Claimed by U.S. & Col.)
Puerto Cabezas
Prinzapolca
I. de Providencia (Col.)
Roncador Cay (Claimed by U.S. & Col.)
I. San Andrés (Col.)
Corn Is.
Cayos de Albuquerque (Col.)
Bluefields
NICARAGUA
Colón—Kingston 551
Colón—Jacmel 683
Kingston—Barranquilla 437
Barranquilla—Jacmel 452
Port-au-Prince—Curaçao 659
Colón—San Juan 992
Colón—Liverpool 4,545
Pta. Gallinas
Oranjestad
C. San Román
Guajira Pen.
Amuay
Ríohacha
C. de la Aguja
Santa Marta
Sa. Nevada de Sta. Marta
G. of Venezuela
Barranquilla
Ciénaga
Sabanalarga
Magdalena
Cartagena
Is. del Rosario
Maracaibo
Altagracia
Is. de San Bernardo
COLOMBIA
Lake Maracaibo
Barquisimeto
Encontrados
Catatumbo
Cord. de Mérida
El Vigía
Mérida
Valera
VENEZUELA
Limón
Cartago
COSTA RICA
Lag. de Chiriquí
CANAL ZONE (U.S.)
Colón
Pta. Manzanillo
Cristóbal
Belén
Gatun L.
Panamá
Balboa
Arch. de las Perlas
PANAMA
G. Dulce
David
G. de Urabá
La Palma
Sincelejo
Magangué
Montería
S. Jorge
Cauca

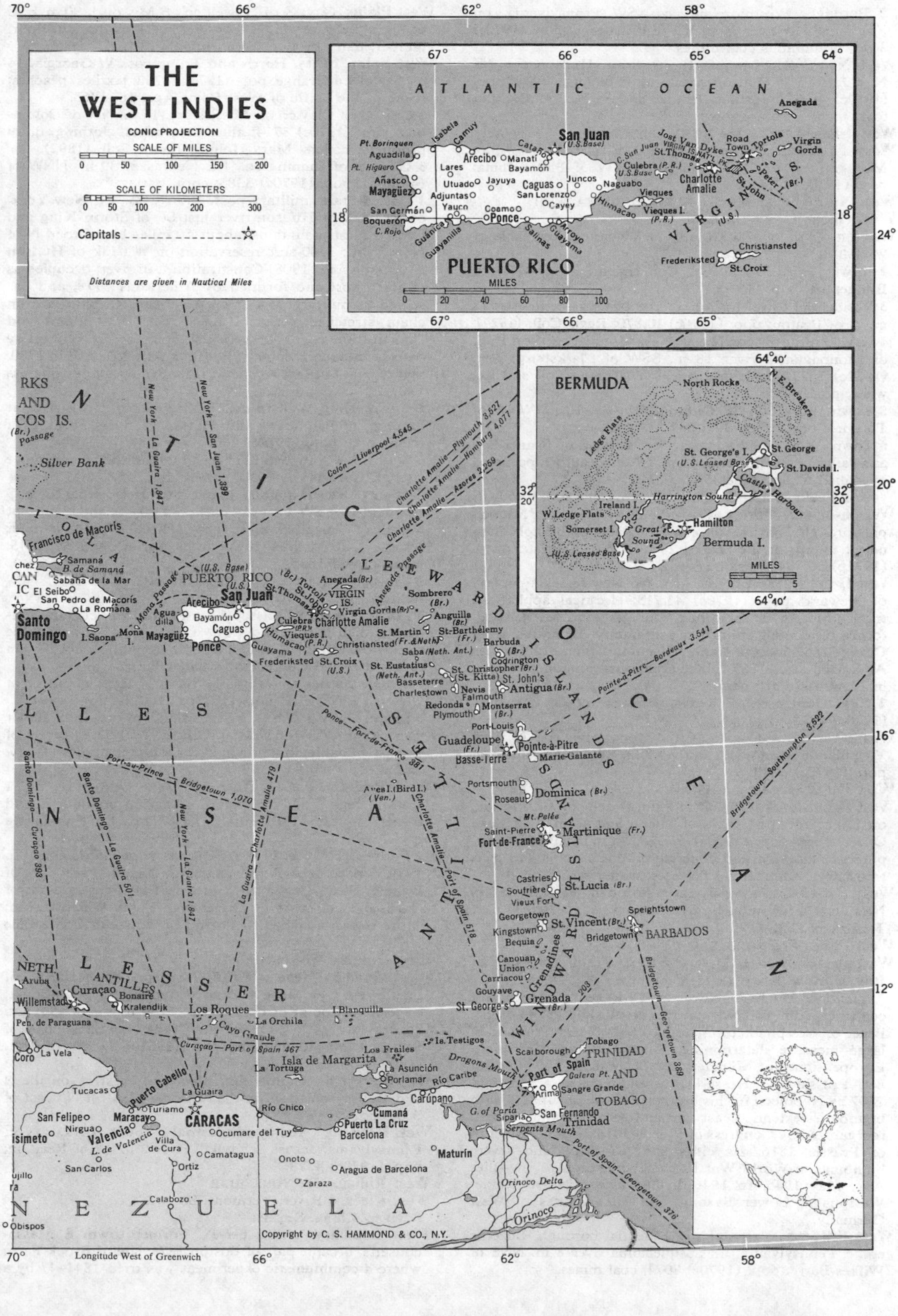
THE WEST INDIES
CONIC PROJECTION
SCALE OF MILES
0 50 100 150 200
SCALE OF KILOMETERS
0 50 100 200 300
Capitals
Distances are given in Nautical Miles
ATLANTIC OCEAN
PUERTO RICO
MILES
0 20 40 60 80 100
San Juan
(U.S.Base)
Pt. Borinquen
Aguadilla
Isabela
Camuy
Arecibo
Manatí
Cataño
Bayamón
Pt. Higüero
Lares
Añasco
Utuado
Jayuya
Caguas
Juncos
Mayagüez
Adjuntas
San Lorenzo
Naguabo
San Germán
Yauco
Coamo
Cayey
Boquerón
Ponce
C. Rojo
Guánica
Guayanilla
Salinas
Guayama
Arroyo
Humacao
Vieques
Vieques I.
(P.R.)
Culebra (P.R.)
(U.S.Base)
C. San Juan
St.Thomas
Charlotte Amalie
St. John
Jost Van Dyke
VIRGIN IS.NAT'L PK.
Road Town
Tortola
Peter I. (Br.)
Virgin Gorda
Anegada
VIRGIN IS. (U.S.)
Christiansted
Frederiksted
St. Croix
BERMUDA
North Rocks
N.E. Breakers
Ledge Flats
St. George's I.
(U.S. Leased Base)
St. George
St. Davids I.
Castle Harbour
Harrington Sound
Ireland I.
W. Ledge Flats
Somerset I.
Great Sound
(U.S. Leased Base)
Hamilton
Bermuda I.
MILES
0 5
TURKS AND CAICOS IS.
(Br.)
Passage
Silver Bank
Francisco de Macoris
Samaná
B. de Samaná
Sabana de la Mar
El Seibo
San Pedro de Macorís
La Romana
Santo Domingo
I. Saona
Mona I.
Mona Passage
Agua dilla
Mayagüez
Arecibo
Bayamón
Caguas
San Juan
Ponce
PUERTO RICO (U.S.)
(U.S. Base)
Humacao
Guayama
Frederiksted
St. Croix (U.S.)
Christiansted
Anegada (Br.)
Anegada Passage
VIRGIN IS.
Virgin Gorda (Br.)
Charlotte Amalie
Sombrero (Br.)
Anguilla (Br.)
St. Martin (Fr. & Neth.)
St-Barthélemy (Fr.)
Saba (Neth. Ant.)
Barbuda (Br.)
Codrington
St. Eustatius (Neth. Ant.)
St. Christopher (Br.)
(St. Kitts)
Basseterre
St. John's
Charlestown
Nevis
Antigua (Br.)
Falmouth
Redonda
Montserrat (Br.)
Plymouth
Port-Louis
Guadeloupe (Fr.)
Pointe-à-Pitre
Basse-Terre
Marie-Galante
Portsmouth
Roseau
Dominica (Br.)
Aves I. (Bird I.) (Ven.)
Mt. Pelée
Saint-Pierre
Martinique (Fr.)
Fort-de-France
Castries
Soufrière
St. Lucia (Br.)
Vieux Fort
Speightstown
Georgetown
St. Vincent (Br.)
Kingstown
Bridgetown
BARBADOS
Bequia
Grenadines
Canouan
Union
Carriacou
Gouyave
St. George's
Grenada (Br.)
LEEWARD ISLANDS
WINDWARD ISLANDS
ATLANTIC OCEAN
CARIBBEAN SEA
LESSER ANTILLES
Colón—Liverpool 4,545
Charlotte Amalie—Plymouth 3,527
Charlotte Amalie—Hamburg 4,077
Charlotte Amalie—Azores 2,259
New York—La Guaira 1,847
New York—San Juan 1,399
Pointe-à-Pitre—Bordeaux 3,541
Bridgetown—Southampton 3,622
Ponce—Fort-de-France 381
Port-au-Prince—Bridgetown 1,070
Santo Domingo—Curaçao 393
Santo Domingo—La Guaira 501
New York—La Guaira 1,847
La Guaira—Charlotte Amalie 479
Charlotte Amalie—Port of Spain 518
Bridgetown—Georgetown 369
Port of Spain—Georgetown 376
Curaçao—Port of Spain 467
NETH. ANTILLES
Aruba
Curaçao
Bonaire
Willemstad
Kralendijk
Los Roques
La Orchila
Cayo Grande
I. Blanquilla
Pen. de Paraguana
Coro
La Vela
Los Frailes
Is. Testigos
Isla de Margarita
La Asunción
Porlamar
La Tortuga
Tobago
Scarborough
TRINIDAD AND TOBAGO
Dragons Mouth
Port of Spain
Galera Pt.
Arima
Sangre Grande
Río Caribe
Carúpano
Tucacas
Puerto Cabello
La Guaira
Turiamo
Río Chico
Cumaná
Puerto La Cruz
Barcelona
San Felipe
Maracay
CARACAS
G. of Paria
Siparia
San Fernando
Trinidad
Serpents Mouth
Nirgua
Valencia
L. de Valencia
Villa de Cura
Ocumare del Tuy
Barquisimeto
San Carlos
Camatagua
Ortiz
Onoto
Aragua de Barcelona
Maturín
Orinoco Delta
Zaraza
Trujillo
Calabozo
Orinoco
Obispos
VENEZUELA
Copyright by C. S. HAMMOND & CO., N.Y.
Longitude West of Greenwich
70° 66° 62° 58°
24° 20° 16° 12°

2 Borough, Westmoreland co., SW Pennsylvania, on Youghiogheny river 20 m. SE of Pittsburgh; pop. (1970c) 3648; bituminous coal mines.

West New York. Manufacturing town, Hudson co., NE New Jersey, on Hudson river 4 m. N of Jersey City; pop. (1970c) 40,627; textiles, leather and rubber goods, silk, toys; made separate town 1898.

West Nishnabotna. See NISHNABOTNA.

West Nor·ri·ton \-ˈnȯr-ət-ᵊn, -ˈnär-\. Urban township, Montgomery co., SE Pennsylvania, W of Philadelphia; pop. (1970c) 12,456.

West Nusa Tenggara. See NUSA TENGGARA, WEST.

West Okoboji. See OKOBOJI.

Wes·ton \ˈwes-tən\. 1 County in Wyoming. See table at WYOMING.

2 Town, Fairfield co., SW Connecticut, 8 m. WNW of Bridgeport; pop. (1970c) 7417.

3 Residential town, Middlesex co., NE Massachusetts, 12 m. W of Boston; pop. (1970c) 10,870; Regis Coll. (1927).

4 City, ⊗ of Lewis co., N cen. West Virginia, on West Fork of Monongahela river 18 m. SSW of Clarksburg; pop. (1970c) 7323; glassware, bricks; coal mines, oil and gas wells; poultry.

5 Town, York co., SE Ontario, Canada, 10 m. WNW of Toronto; pop. (1966c) 11,047.

6 Town, W Sabah, Malaysia; port at head of Brunei Bay and railroad terminus ab. 15 m. SW of Beaufort; occupied by Allied troops June 19–21, 1945.

Weston Peak. Mountain, Park co., cen. Colorado; 13,500 ft.

Weston–su·per–Mare \-ˌsü-pər-ˈma(ə)r, -ˈme(ə)r\. Municipal borough, Somersetshire, SW England, on Bristol Channel at mouth of the Severn 20 m. WSW of Bristol; pop. (1971p) 50,794; seaside resort.

West Orange. 1 Town, Essex co., NE New Jersey, 5 m. NW of Newark; pop. (1970c) 43,715; electrical appliances; truck farms; with the other "Oranges" and Maplewood, forms residential suburban community; separated from Orange 1862; incorp. 1900; "Glenmont," home of Thomas A. Edison after 1887 (made a national monument 1961), in Llewellyn Park nearby.

2 City, Orange co., E Texas, 4 m. SW of Orange; pop. (1970c) 4820.

West·o·ver \ˈwes-ˌtō-vər\. City, Monongalia co., N West Virginia, on Monongahela river 3 m. SW of Morgantown; pop. (1970c) 5086.

West Pakistan. See PAKISTAN.

West Palm Beach. City, ⊗ of Palm Beach co., SE Florida, on Lake Worth 65 m. N of Miami and 40 m. E of Lake Okeechobee; pop. (1970c) 57,375; aircraft engines, computers, aluminum and concrete products, tools and dies, transistors; commercial fisheries; winter resort.

West Pat·er·son \-ˈpat-ər-sən\. Borough, Passaic co., N New Jersey, SW suburb of Paterson; pop. (1970c) 11,692; Tombrock Coll. (1956).

West Peak. See NAVOTUVOTU.

West·pha·lia \wes(t)-ˈfāl-yə, -ˈfā-lē-ə\. Former province of Prussia, now part of West Germany.

History: Duchy created in 12th cent.; for several centuries administered for the archbishop of Cologne. Peace of Westphalia terminating Thirty Years' War and in large measure determining political status of modern Europe, signed at Münster Oct. 24, 1648. In 1803 divided bet. Prussia and Hesse-Darmstadt; created a kingdom 1807 by Napoleon for his brother, Jérôme Bonaparte, with boundaries extended eastward and with capital at Kassel; reorganized by Congress of Vienna 1815; became province of Prussia 1816. Its cities suffered many and severe bombings in World War II; came under control of Allies Apr.–May 1945. In 1946 divided among North Rhine-Westphalia, Lower Saxony, and Hesse states of West Germany.

West Pitts·ton \-ˈpits-tən\. Residential borough, Luzerne co., E Pennsylvania, on Susquehanna river 8 m. NNE of Wilkes-Barre; pop. (1970c) 7074; coal mines.

West Plains. City, ⊗ of Howell co., S Missouri, 90 m. ESE of Springfield; pop. (1970c) 6893; livestock market; flour, lumber, dairy products; iron mines.

West Point. 1 City, Harris and Troup cos., W Georgia, 14 m. SW of La Grange; pop. (1970c) 4232; textiles, peaches; scene of the battle of West Point Apr. 16, 1865.

2 City, ⊗ of Clay co., E Mississippi, 16 m. NW of Columbus; pop. (1970c) 8714; aluminum boats, clothing, dairy products, boilers; Mary Holmes Junior Coll. (1892).

3 City, ⊗ of Cuming co., NE Nebraska, 30 m. NNW of Fremont; pop. (1970c) 3385; corn, barley.

4 United States military post, Orange co., SE New York, on W bank of Hudson river just SE of Storm King and Crow's Nest mountains; about 50 miles by railroad N of New York; 3500-acre reservation on W bank of Hudson river and (since 1908) Constitution I. in river; occupied as military post and fortified by Americans 1778, and has served as military post since American Revolution; iron chain stretched across Hudson bet. West Point and Constitution I. to block British ships as Revolutionary defense measure; center of Benedict Arnold's plot in 1780; seat of U.S. Military Academy (founded by act of Congress 1802).

5 Town, King William co., E Virginia, on York river at junction of Pamunkey and Mattaponi rivers 38 m. E of Richmond; pop. (1970c) 2600.

6 West tip of Anticosti I., at the mouth of the St. Lawrence river, E Canada.

West·port \ˈwes(t)-ˌpō(ə)rt, -ˌpȯ(ə)rt\. 1 Residential town, S Fairfield co., SW Connecticut, on Long Island Sound at mouth of Saugatuck river; pop. (1970c) 27,414; summer resort; soap, twine, toys; truck farms; settled 1645; incorporated 1835.

2 Town, Bristol co., SE Massachusetts, 8 m. W of New Bedford; pop. (1970c) 9791.

3 Former town, W Missouri, on Missouri river, now residential district of Kansas City (*q.v.*); scene of battle (see also INDEPENDENCE 6) Oct. 21–23, 1864 in which Union forces defeated Confederates under Price.

4 Urban district and seaport, SW co. Mayo, on shore of Clew Bay, NE Eire; pop. (1971p) 3100; fishing resort.

5 Seaport, NW South I., New Zealand, at mouth of Buller river 90 m. WSW of Nelson; pop. (1970e) 5200; center of extensive coal region; principal coal-shipping point of New Zealand.

West Prussia *or Ger.* **West·preus·sen** \ˈvest-ˌprȯis-ᵊn\. 1 Coastal region of Pomerania; of varying boundaries and ownership, 13th–18th cents.; after 1772 part of Prussia (see 2, below).

2 Former province, Prussia, Germany, on Baltic coast; in 1919 divided into Pomorze prov., Poland, Free City of Danzig, West Prussia govt. dist. in East Prussia prov. of Germany, and part of Grenzmark Posen-Westpreussen; entire region assigned to Poland by Potsdam Conference 1945.

West Punjab. See PUNJAB 4.

West Quod·dy Head \-ˈkwäd-ē-\. Cape, NE Maine, S of Eastport at S entrance to Passamaquoddy Bay; lighthouse; easternmost point of the U.S., 66°57′W long., 44°49′N lat.

Wes·tray \ˈwes-ˌtrā\. One of the Orkney Is., off N coast of Scotland; ab. 10 m. long; pop. (1961c) 872; 15th cent. castle.

Westray Firth. Channel bet. islands of Westray on the N and Rousay on the S in the N Orkney Is., off N coast of Scotland.

West Read·ing \-ˈred-iŋ\. Industrial borough, Berks co., SE Pennsylvania, across Schuylkill river 2 m. W of Reading; pop. (1970c) 4578.

West Riding. See YORKSHIRE.

West River. 1 River, Vermont. See WEST 1.

2 River, China. See HSI.

West Rox·bury \-ˈräks-ˌber-ē\. Former town, E Massachusetts, became part of Boston 1874; site of Brook Farm where a communistic experiment was tried 1841–47 by a group of noted Americans, including George Ripley (the leader), Hawthorne, George W. Curtis, Charles A. Dana, and Margaret Fuller; figures in Hawthorne's *Blithedale Romance* (1852).

West Rutland. Town, Rutland co., W Vermont; pop. (1970c) 2381; marble quarries.

West Saint Paul. City, Dakota co., SE Minnesota, 5 m. S of St. Paul; pop. (1970c) 18,799.

West Schelde Estuary \-'skel-də-\ *or* **Hon·te** \'hȯn-tə\. Inlet of the North Sea, SW coast of the Netherlands, at the mouth of the Schelde river, extending S of Walcheren I. and South Beveland I.

West Sen·e·ca \-'sen-ə-kə\. Urban community (unincorp.), Erie co., NW New York, SE suburb of Buffalo; pop. (1970c) 48,001.

West Side. The W part of Manhattan borough, New York City, New York, traversed at lower end by West Street, merging into West Side Highway and, above 72d Street, into the Henry Hudson Parkway; includes several miles of docks along E Hudson river waterfront.

West Smithfield. See SMITHFIELD 5.

West Spanish Peak. Mountain, Huerfano and Las Animas cos., S Colorado; 13,623 ft.

West Spitsbergen. See SPITSBERGEN.

West Springfield. Town, Hampden co., SW Massachusetts, on Connecticut river across from Springfield; pop. (1970c) 28,461; automobile parts, vehicle bodies, wire, paper, paint, cleaning fluids.

West·stel·ling·werf \ˌvest-ˌstel-iŋ-'ve(ə)rf\. Commune, Friesland prov., N Netherlands; pop. (1970e) 21,601.

West Suffolk. See SUFFOLK 3.

West Sussex. See SUSSEX 6.

West Terre Haute \-ˌter-ə-'hōt, -'hət, -'hȯt\. City, Vigo co., W Indiana, suburb of Terre Haute; pop. (1970c) 2704.

West Three Rivers *or Fr.* **Trois–Ri·vières–Ouest** \trwä-rē-vyer-west\. Town, St-Maurice co., S Quebec, Canada, 4 m. SW of Three Rivers; pop. (1971p) 8071.

West Union. 1 City, ⊗ of Fayette co., NE Iowa, 25 m. S of Decorah; pop. (1970c) 2624; livestock, dairy farms.

2 Village, ⊗ of Adams co., S Ohio; pop. (1970c) 1951.

3 Town, ⊗ of Doddridge co., N West Virginia; pop. (1970c) 1141; gas, oil wells; agriculture.

West University Place. City, Harris co., SE Texas, entirely within city of Houston; pop. (1970c) 13,317.

West View. Borough, Allegheny co., SW Pennsylvania, 6 m. N of Pittsburgh; pop. (1970c) 8312; residential suburb.

West·ville \'west-ˌvil\. **1** Village, Vermilion co., E Illinois, 6 m. S of Danville; pop. (1970c) 3655.

2 Borough, Gloucester co., SW New Jersey, 5 m. S of Camden; pop. (1970c) 5170.

3 Town, Pictou co., N Nova Scotia, Canada, ab. 5 m. W of New Glasgow; pop. (1971p) 3844; lumber, bricks; coal mines.

West Virginia. An east central state of U.S.A., bounded on N by Ohio, Pennsylvania, and Maryland, on E and S by Virginia, and on W by Kentucky and Ohio; 41st state in area, 24,181 sq. m. (land area 24,084 sq. m.); 34th state in population, (1970c) 1,744,237; ✱ Charleston; 35th state admitted to Union (1863).

Nickname: Mountain State. *State flower:* Rhododendron. *Motto:* Montani Semper Liberi (Mountaineers Are Always Free Men). *Rivers:* Ohio, forming large section of upper W boundary, and its tributaries Big Sandy, Guyandotte, Great Kanawha, Little Kanawha, Monongahela; Potomac, forming section of N boundary. *Highest point:* Spruce Knob 4862 ft., in Pendleton co. *Chief products:* Corn, tobacco, fruit; dairy products; coal; manufacturing: primary metals, chemicals, textiles. *Chief cities:* Huntington, Charleston, Wheeling, Parkersburg, Morgantown, Weirton. See *Table of States* at UNITED STATES. Divided into the following 55 counties (for pronunciation of their names, see their individual entries):

NAME	LOCATION	AREA[1] (sq. m.)	POP. (1970c)	CO. SEAT
Barbour	N	341	14,030	Philippi
Berkeley	NE	316	36,356	Martinsburg
Boone	SW	501	25,118	Madison
Braxton	cen.	517	12,666	Sutton
Brooke	N; in panhandle	88	29,685	Wellsburg
Cabell	W	279	106,918	Huntington
Calhoun	cen.	281	7,046	Grantsville
Clay	cen.	343	9,330	Clay
Doddridge	N	319	6,389	West Union
Fayette	S cen.	663	49,332	Fayetteville
Gilmer	cen.	339	7,782	Glenville
Grant	NE	478	8,607	Petersburg
Greenbrier	SE	1,026	32,090	Lewisburg
Hampshire	NE	639	11,710	Romney
Hancock	N tip of panhandle	83	39,749	New Cumberland
Hardy	NE	585	8,855	Moorefield
Harrison	N	418	73,028	Clarksburg
Jackson	W	461	20,903	Ripley
Jefferson	NE	211	21,280	Charles Town
Kanawha	W cen.	907	229,515	Charleston
Lewis	N cen.	392	17,847	Weston
Lincoln	W	438	18,912	Hamlin
Logan	SW	456	46,269	Logan
McDowell	S	533	50,666	Welch
Marion	N	311	61,356	Fairmont
Marshall	N; in panhandle	304	37,598	Moundsville
Mason	W	433	24,306	Point Pleasant
Mercer	S	417	63,206	Princeton
Mineral	NE	330	23,109	Keyser
Mingo	SW	423	32,780	Williamson
Monongalia	N	365	63,714	Morgantown
Monroe	SE	473	11,272	Union
Morgan	NE	233	8,547	Berkeley Springs
Nicholas	cen.	650	22,552	Summersville
Ohio	N; in panhandle	106	64,197	Wheeling
Pendleton	E	695	7,031	Franklin
Pleasants	NW	129	7,274	St. Marys
Pocahontas	E cen.	943	8,870	Marlinton
Preston	N	645	25,455	Kingwood
Putnam	W	348	27,625	Winfield
Raleigh	S	605	70,080	Beckley
Randolph	NE cen.	1,036	24,596	Elkins
Ritchie	NW	452	10,145	Harrisville
Roane	W cen.	486	14,111	Spencer
Summers	S	350	13,213	Hinton
Taylor	N	174	13,878	Grafton
Tucker	NE	421	7,447	Parsons
Tyler	NW	256	9,929	Middlebourne
Upshur	NE cen.	352	19,092	Buckhannon
Wayne	SW	513	37,581	Wayne
Webster	E cen.	551	9,809	Webster Springs
Wetzel	N	363	20,314	New Martinsville
Wirt	W	235	4,154	Elizabeth
Wood	W	368	86,818	Parkersburg
Wyoming	S	504	30,095	Pineville

[1]Area = land area.

History: A part of Virginia until the Civil War; voted against ordinance of secession May 23, 1861; loyal government organized at Wheeling June 11–25, 1861; admitted to Union June 20, 1863.

West Vlaanderen. See WEST FLANDERS.

West·wall \'west-ˌwȯl, 'vest-ˌväl\ *also often called, especially by the Germans,* **Sieg·fried Line** \'sēg-frēd-, 'zēk-frēt-\. In World War II the strong defense line in W Germany, prepared in great depth and extending from Swiss border on the S to Cleve on the N, generally parallel with the Rhine and in the S opposite to the French Maginot Line. Penetrated by Allied forces Sept. 1944–Feb. 1945.

West Warwick. Town, Kent co., cen. Rhode Island, 11 m. WSW of Providence; pop. (1970c) 24,323; textiles, lace; truck, dairy farms; governmental center River Point village; separated from Warwick and incorp. 1913.

West·we·go \west-'wē-(ˌ)gō\. City, Jefferson parish, SE Louisiana, 8 m. WSW of New Orleans; pop. (1970c) 11,402.

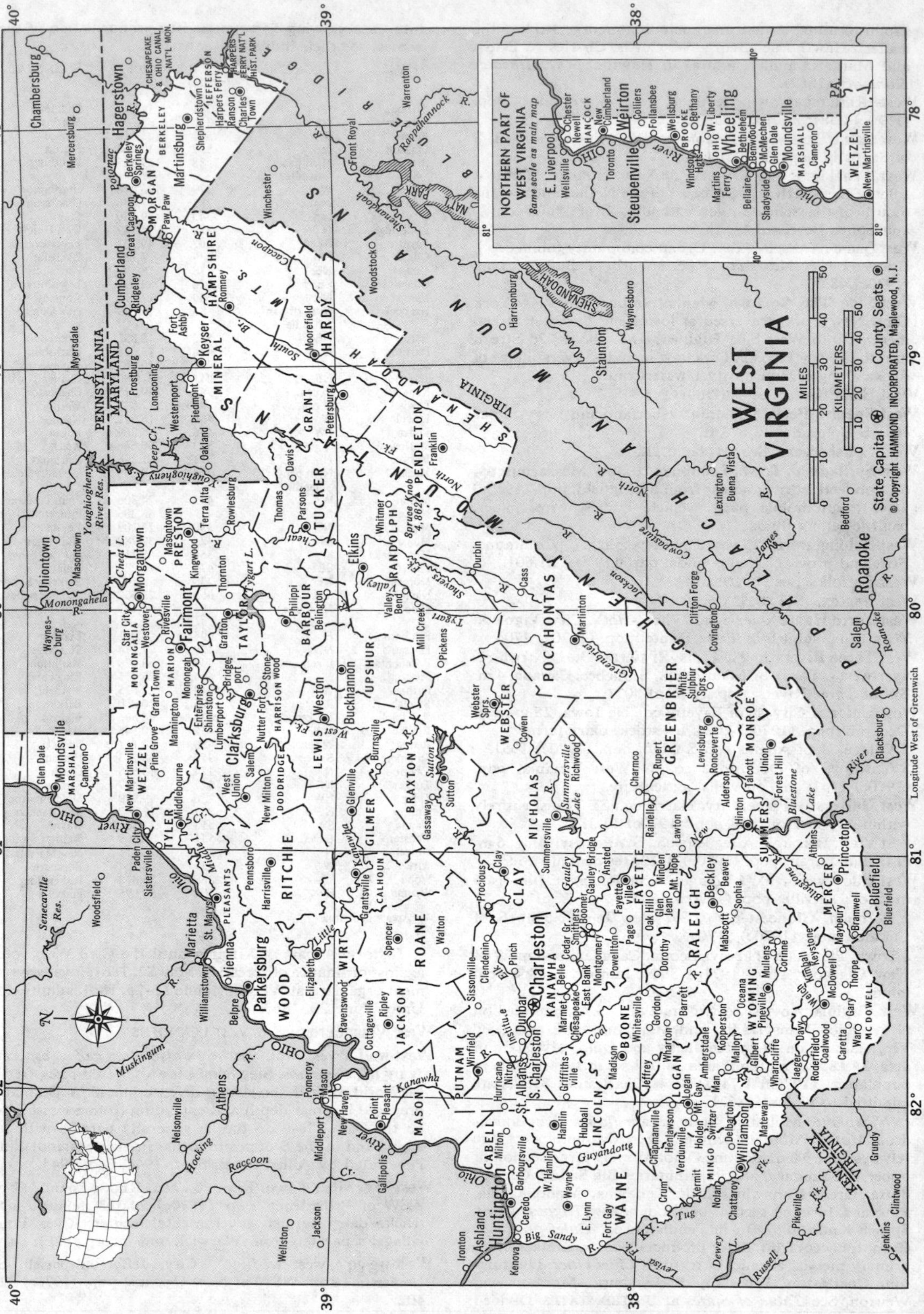
WEST VIRGINIA
NORTHERN PART OF WEST VIRGINIA
Same scale as main map
MILES
KILOMETERS
State Capital
County Seats
© Copyright HAMMOND INCORPORATED, Maplewood, N.J.
Longitude West of Greenwich
PENNSYLVANIA
MARYLAND
OHIO
KENTUCKY
VIRGINIA
KY.
PA.
BLUE RIDGE
SHENANDOAH MTS.
ALLEGHENY MOUNTAINS
APPALACHIAN
SHENANDOAH NAT'L PARK
CHESAPEAKE & OHIO CANAL NAT'L MON.
HARPERS FERRY NAT'L HIST. PARK
Spruce Knob 4,862
Ohio River
Kanawha
Monongahela R.
Potomac R.
Cheat L.
Youghiogheny River Res.
Sutton L.
Summersville Lake
Bluestone Lake
Big Sandy
Guyandotte
Tug Fk.
Greenbrier
New
Gauley
Coal
Elk
Little Kanawha
Middle I. Cr.
Senecaville Res.
Muskingum
Hocking
Raccoon Cr.
Rappahannock R.
Shenandoah
Cacapon
James R.
Roanoke R.
Jackson
Cowpasture
HANCOCK
BROOKE
OHIO
MARSHALL
WETZEL
TYLER
PLEASANTS
WOOD
WIRT
JACKSON
MASON
CABELL
WAYNE
LINCOLN
PUTNAM
KANAWHA
BOONE
LOGAN
MINGO
MCDOWELL
WYOMING
MERCER
RALEIGH
SUMMERS
MONROE
GREENBRIER
FAYETTE
NICHOLAS
CLAY
ROANE
CALHOUN
GILMER
RITCHIE
DODDRIDGE
HARRISON
LEWIS
BRAXTON
WEBSTER
POCAHONTAS
RANDOLPH
UPSHUR
BARBOUR
TAYLOR
MARION
MONONGALIA
PRESTON
TUCKER
GRANT
PENDLETON
HARDY
MINERAL
HAMPSHIRE
MORGAN
BERKELEY
JEFFERSON
Charleston
Huntington
Parkersburg
Wheeling
Weirton
Morgantown
Fairmont
Clarksburg
Martinsburg
Beckley
Bluefield
Princeton
Williamson
Logan
Elkins
Buckhannon
Weston
Keyser
Romney
Moorefield
Petersburg
Franklin
Marlinton
Lewisburg
Union
Hinton
Fayetteville
Summersville
Sutton
Webster Sprs.
Spencer
Ripley
Point Pleasant
Winfield
Hamlin
Wayne
Madison
Welch
Pineville
Glenville
Grantsville
Harrisville
West Union
Middlebourne
New Martinsville
Moundsville
St. Marys
Elizabeth
Philippi
Grafton
Kingwood
Parsons
Berkeley Springs
Charles Town
Hagerstown
Cumberland
Winchester
Front Royal
Harrisonburg
Staunton
Lexington
Covington
Roanoke
Salem
Blacksburg
Marietta
Athens
Gallipolis
Ashland
Ironton
Steubenville
Uniontown
Waynesburg
Chambersburg

West Winter Haven. Urban community (unincorporated), Polk co., cen. Florida, W of Lakeland; pop. (1970c) 7716.

West·wood \'west-ˌwu̇d\. 1 Town, Norfolk co., E Massachusetts, 12 m. SW of Boston; pop. (1970c) 12,750.
2 Residential borough, Bergen co., NE corner of New Jersey, 9 m. NE of Paterson; pop. (1970c) 11,105.

Westwood Lakes. Urban community (unincorporated), Dade co., SE Florida; pop. (1970c) 12,811.

West·worth \'west-(ˌ)wərth\. Village, Tarrant co., N Texas, 7 m. W of Fort Worth; pop. (1970c) 4578.

West Wyoming. Borough, Luzerne co., E Pennsylvania, 5 m. N of Wilkes-Barre; pop. (1970c) 3659.

West York. Borough, York co., S Pennsylvania, 2 m. W of York; pop. (1970c) 5314; pottery, furniture.

We·tar \'we-ˌtär\ *also* **Wet·ter** \'wet-ər\. Island, Indonesia, 30 m. N of E Portuguese Timor and WNW of the Leti group; ab. 80 m. long by 23 m. wide; ab. 1400 sq. m.; highest point 4633 ft.; chief settlement Ilwaki on SE coast.

Wetar Strait. Channel bet. NE Portuguese Timor and Wetar I., Malay Archipelago; ab. 30 m. wide.

We·tas·ki·win \wi-'tas-kə-ˌwin\. City, S cen. Alberta, Canada, 40 m. S of Edmonton; pop. (1971p) 6266; flour, fertilizer; oil refinery; dairy, grain farms.

We·te *or* **We·ti** \'wāt-ē\. Town, Pemba I., N of Zanzibar, off NE coast of Tanzania, E Africa; pop. (1967e) 8469.

Weth·ers·field \'weth-ərz-ˌfēld\. Suburban town, S cen. Hartford co., N Connecticut, on Connecticut river S of Hartford; pop. (1970c) 26,662; tools, structural tubing, sheet aluminum; Wethersfield state prison.

Weti. See WETE.

Wetter. See WETAR.

Wetter. See VÄTTERN.

Wet·te·ren \'vet-ə-rən\. Manufacturing commune, East Flanders prov., NW cen. Belgium, on Schelde river just ESE of Gent; pop. (1969e) 20,950.

Wet·ter·horn \'vet-ər-ˌhȯ(ə)rn\. Peak in the Bernese Alps, SW cen. Switzerland, N of the Finsteraarhorn; 12,142 ft.

Wetterhorn Peak \ˌwet-ər-ˌhȯ(ə)rn-\. Mountain, Hinsdale and Ouray cos., SW Colorado; 14,017 ft.

Wet·ter·stein Mountains \ˌvet-ər-ˌs(h)tīn-\ *or Ger.* **Wet·ter·stein·ge·bir·ge** \-gə-ˌbi(ə)r-gə\. Mountains, S Bavaria, West Germany; include Zugspitze, 9720 ft., highest peak in West Germany.

Wet·ting·en \'vet-iŋ-ən\. Commune, Aargau canton, Switzerland, ab. 10 m. NW of Zurich; pop. (1970c) 19,900; Cistercian abbey, now a school.

We·tum·ka \wi-'təm(p)-kə\. City, Hughes co., E cen. Oklahoma, 32 m. SSW of Okmulgee; pop. (1970c) 1687.

We·tump·ka \wi-'təm(p)-kə\. City, ⊗ of Elmore co., E cen. Alabama, on Coosa river 12 m. NE of Montgomery; pop. (1970c) 3912; lumber, textiles.

Wet·zel \'wet-səl\. County in West Virginia. See table at WEST VIRGINIA.

Wet·zi·kon \'vet-si-ˌkōn\. Commune, Zurich canton, Switzerland, ab. 12 m. ESE of Zurich; pop. (1970c) 13,469; railroad junction point near Lake of Pfäffikon (see PFÄFFIKON).

Wetz·lar \'vet-ˌslär\. City, Hesse, West Germany, on Lahn river 30 m. N of Frankfurt am Main; pop. (1969e) 36,871; manufactures optical goods, ironware; old Romanesque cathedral (founded in 12th cent.); became free city in 12th cent.

We·vel·gem \'vā-vəl-kəm\. Commune, West Flanders prov., NW Belgium, just W of Kortrijk; pop. (1969e) 13,737.

We·wa·hitch·ka \ˌwē-wə-'hich-kə\. Town, ⊗ of Gulf co., NW Florida; pop. (1970c) 1733.

We·wak \'wā-ˌwäk, 'wē-ˌwak\. Coastal town, Papua New Guinea, New Guinea I., ab. 75 m. W of the mouth of the Sepik river; pop. (1966c) 8945; good harbor. Japanese base in early part of World War II; severely bombed by U.S. planes Aug. 17, 1943; bypassed in Allied advance along N New Guinea coast.

We·wo·ka \wē-'wōk-ə\. City, ⊗ of Seminole co., cen. Oklahoma, 28 m. ESE of Shawnee; pop. (1970c) 5284; carbon black, chemicals, brick; machine shop, oil wells; cotton.

Wex·ford \'weks-fərd\. 1 County in Michigan. See table at MICHIGAN.
2 County, Leinster prov., SE Eire; 908 sq. m.; pop. (1971p) 85,892; ⊗ Wexford; chief river Slaney; wheat, turnips; livestock raising, dairy farming.
3 Municipal borough and seaport, ⊗ of co. Wexford, SE Eire; pop. (1971p) 11,744; ships livestock; agricultural implements, woolens, bacon, rugs, cheese; salmon and sea fisheries. An early settlement of Danish marauders and later of Anglo-Normans; sacked 1649 by Cromwell.

Wexford Harbour. Inlet of St. George's Channel, SE coast of Ireland, in co. Wexford; the city of Wexford is at the head of the inlet.

Wex·ler, Mount \-'weks-lər\. Mountain, Antarctica, 84°30'S, 175°01'E; 13,202 ft.

Wey \'wā\. River, S England; 35 m. long; flows NE in Hampshire and Surrey, S England, and empties into the Thames 2 m. SE of Chertsey.

Wey·burn \'wā-bərn\. City, SE Saskatchewan, Canada, on Souris river 65 m. SE of Regina; pop. (1971p) 8576; in grain-farming region.

Wey·ib \'wā-əb\ *or* **Web·be** \'web-ē\ *also* **Web** \'web\. River, SE Ethiopia; ab. 280 m. long; flows S to join the Genale and Dawa rivers, forming the Juba.

Wey·mouth \'wā-məth\. Town, Norfolk co., E Massachusetts, 11 m. SSE of Boston; pop. (1970c) 54,610; shoes, chemicals, electronic components.

Weymouth and Mel·combe Re·gis \-ˌmel-kəm-'rē-jəs\. Municipal borough, consisting of contiguous towns, Dorsetshire, S England, on Weymouth Bay of English Channel 53 m. WSW of Southampton; pop. (1971p) 42,332; port and seaside resort.

Weymouth Fore River. See FORE RIVER.

Wha·ka·ta·ne \ˌhwäk-ə-'tän-ē, ˌwäk-\. 1 River, N cen. North I., New Zealand; 65 m. long; flows N into Bay of Plenty.
2 Borough, N North I., New Zealand, on Bay of Plenty; pop. (1970e) 9830.

Whale Islands \ˌhwa(ə)l-, ˌwā(ə)l-\. See HVALER.

Whales, Bay of \-'hwā(ə)lz, -'wā(ə)lz\. Inlet of Ross Sea, Ross Ice Shelf, Ross Dependency, Antarctica, 78°30'S, 164°20'W; used since 1911 as a base for Antarctic exploring expeditions (see LITTLE AMERICA).

Whal·sey *or* **Whal·say** \'hwȯl-sē, 'wȯl-\. One of the Shetland Is., NE of N Scotland; 5½ m. long; pop. (1961c) 855; sea-fishing center.

Whampoa. See HUANG-PU.

Whang·a·ehu \ˌhwäŋ-ə-ā-'hü, ˌwäŋ-\. River, North I., New Zealand; 100 m. long; flows into Tasman Sea.

Whang·a·rei \ˌhwäŋ-ə-'rā, ˌwäŋ-\. City, N North I., New Zealand, on Whangarei Harbor 85 m. N of Auckland; pop. (1970e) 30,600.

Whangpoo. See HUANG-P'U.

Wharfe \'hwȯ(ə)rf, 'wȯ(ə)rf\. River, W Yorkshire, N cen. England; 7½ m. long; flows ESE into the Ouse.

Whar·ton \'hwȯrt-ᵊn, 'wȯrt-\. 1 County in Texas. See table at TEXAS.
2 Borough, Morris co., N New Jersey, 10 m. NNW of Morristown; pop. (1970c) 5535.
3 City, ⊗ of Wharton co., SE Texas, on Colorado river 28 m. N of Bay City; pop. (1970c) 7881; cottonseed oil; sulfur mines; diversified agriculture; Wharton County Junior Coll. (1946).

Wharton Peninsula. Peninsula extending from SW cen. Wellington I., off SW coast of Chile.

What·com \'hwät-kəm\. 1 County in Washington. See table at WASHINGTON.
2 Town, Washington. See BELLINGHAM 2.

Wheat·land \'hwēt-lənd, 'wēt-\. 1 County in Montana. See table at MONTANA.
2 Town, ⊗ of Platte co., SE Wyoming, 43 m. W of Torrington; pop. (1970c) 2498; dairy, stock farms.

Wheatland Reservoir. Reservoir in Laramie river, cen. Albany co., SE Wyoming.

Whea·ton \'hwēt-ᵊn, 'wēt-\. 1 City, ⊗ of Du Page co., NE Illinois, 25 m. W of Chicago; pop. (1970c) 31,138; residential community in agricultural region; Wheaton Coll. (1843).
2 Urban community (unincorporated), Montgomery co., cen. Maryland, SW of Baltimore; pop. (1970c) 66,247.
3 Village, ⊗ of Traverse co., W Minnesota, 39 m. SSW of Fergus Falls; pop. (1970c) 2011; hunting resort.

Wheat Ridge \'hwēt-, 'wēt-\. City, Jefferson co., cen. Colorado, WNW of Denver; pop. (1970c) 29,795.

Whee·ler \'hwē-lər, 'wē-\. 1 Counties in four states of the U.S. See table at GEORGIA, NEBRASKA, OREGON, TEXAS.
2 Town, ⊗ of Wheeler co., NW Texas; pop. (1970c) 1116.

Wheeler Dam. Dam across Tennessee river, NW Alabama, at head of Lake Wilson, forming **Wheeler Lake** 74 m. long. See table at TENNESSEE VALLEY AUTHORITY.

Wheeler Peak. 1 Mountain in Snake Range, SE White Pine co., E Nevada; 13,065 ft.
2 Mountain, Taos co., N New Mexico; 13,161 ft.; highest point in the state.

Whee·ling \'hwē-liŋ, 'wē-\. 1 Village, Cook co., NE Illinois, SW of Highland Park; pop. (1970c) 14,476.
2 Commercial and industrial city, ⊗ of Ohio co., N West Virginia, on Ohio river in N panhandle ab. 40 m. SW of Pittsburgh, Pennsylvania; pop. (1970c) 48,188; metal goods, textiles, tobacco products, pottery, glass, chemicals, enamelware, aluminum products; Wheeling Coll. (1954). Settled 1769; Fort Henry (built 1774) attacked by Indians 1777, 1781, 1782; incorporated as city 1836; important trading post on Cumberland Road until 1850's; center of Unionist activity in W Virginia 1861; capital of state of West Virginia 1863–70 and 1875–85.

Wheel·wright \'hwē(ə)l-ˌrīt, 'wē(ə)l-\. City, Floyd co., E Kentucky, 15 m. SW of Pikeville; pop. (1970c) 793.

Whern·side \'hwərn-ˌsīd, 'wərn-\. Mountain, Yorkshire, N England; 2414 ft.; a peak in the Pennine Chain.

Whet·stone \'hwet-ˌstōn, 'wet-\. Village, Middlesex, SE England, 10 m. N of London; residential suburb.

Whetstone Buttes. Isolated peaks, NW Adams co., SW North Dakota.

Whick·ham \'hwik-əm, 'wik-\. Urban district, Durham, N England, 6 m. SW of Newcastle upon Tyne; pop. (1971p) 28,704.

Whid·bey Island \'hwid-bē-, 'wid-\. Island, upper Puget Sound, E of Admiralty Inlet, Washington, a part of Island co.; ab. 45 m. long; chief town Coupeville.

Whid·dy Island \ˌhwid-ē-, ˌwid-\. Island, Bantry Bay, SW coast of Ireland; ruins of old castle.

Whirl·wind Peak \'hwər(-ə)l-ˌwind-, 'wər(-ə)l-\. Mountain, W Park co., NW Wyoming; 10,981 ft.

Whit·a·ker \'hwit-ə-kər, 'wit-\. Borough, Allegheny co., SW Pennsylvania, 7 m. E of Pittsburgh; pop. (1970c) 1697.

Whit·by \'hwit-bē, 'wit-\. 1 Town, ⊗ of Ontario co., SE Ontario, Canada, a port of entry on Lake Ontario 5 m. W of Oshawa; pop. (1971p) 25,291; paper products; iron foundries; dairy, livestock farms.
2 Urban district, North Riding, Yorkshire, N England, on the seacoast at mouth of the Esk river; pop. (1971p) 12,717; seaside resort and fishing port; potash deposits; site of an abbey founded by St. Hilda (657); meeting place of the Synod of Whitby 664, at which the English church allied itself to Rome in preference to Ireland; destroyed by the Danes 867, and founded again for the Benedictines in 1078; Anglo-Saxon poet Caedmon was a monk of Whitby. See NORTHUMBRIA.

White \'hwīt, 'wīt\. 1 River, Arkansas; 690 m. long; navigable for 260 m.; rises in Boston Mts., Madison co., NW Arkansas, bends N into Missouri, then SE across Arkansas to empty into the Mississippi on E boundary of Desha co., SE Arkansas.
2 River, NW Colorado and E Utah; 250 m. long; rises in NE Garfield co., Colorado, flows W across Utah border into Green river in cen. Uintah co., E Utah.
3 River, SW Indiana; 52 m. long; formed by confluence of West Fork 255 m. long rising in Randolph co., E Indiana, and East Fork 282 m. long rising in Henry co., E cen. Indiana; flows W into Wabash river in NW corner of Gibson co., SW Indiana. See BLUE 2.
4 River, SW and S cen. South Dakota; ab. 325 m. long; rises in NW Nebraska, flows NE across South Dakota border, then E into Missouri river on SE boundary of Lyman co.
5 River, NW Texas; 130 m. long; formed by confluence of Callahan Draw and Running Water Draw in N Hale co., flows SE into Salt Fork in Kent co.
6 River, E cen. Vermont; ab. 50 m. long; rises in E Addison co., flows S, then E and SE into Connecticut river at White River Junction.
7 River, W cen. Washington; ab. 60 m. long; rises in Mt. Rainier National Park, flows NW and unites with Green river in SW King co. to form Duwamish river.
8 Name of counties in five states of the U.S. See tables at ARKANSAS, GEORGIA, ILLINOIS, INDIANA, TENNESSEE.
9 River, SW Yukon Territory, Canada; 161 m. long; rises in Wrangell Mts. in Alaska, flows E, then N in Yukon to the Yukon river above Dawson. Its upper course crossed by Alaska Highway.
10 River, Iceland. See HVÍTÁ RIVER.

White Bay. Inlet of Atlantic Ocean, N coast of Newfoundland, Canada; ab. 60 m. long.

White Bear Lake. 1 Lake on border of Ramsey and Washington cos., E Minnesota; resort.
2 City, Ramsey and Washington cos., E Minnesota, 11 m. NNE of St. Paul; pop. (1970c) 23,313; summer resort; Lakewood State Junior Coll. (1967).

White Butte. Peak, Slope co., SW North Dakota; 3506 ft.; highest peak in the state.

White Car·pa·thi·an Mountains \-kär-'pā-thē-ən-\ *also* **White Car·pa·thi·ans** \-ənz\ *or Czech* **Bí·le Kar·pa·ty** \ˌbil-ə-'kär-pə-tē\. Mountain range, cen. Czechoslovakia, a SW spur of the Carpathian Mts. running NE and SW and forming boundary bet. Czech S.R. and Slovak S.R.; highest point 3514 ft.

White Castle. Town, Iberville parish, S Louisiana, on Mississippi river 20 m. S of Baton Rouge; pop. (1970c) 2206.

White·chap·el \'hwīt-ˌchap-əl, 'wīt-\. Parish, Tower Hamlets, London, England, E of the City of London and N of the Thames; Whitechapel Art Gallery, London Hospital.

White Cloud. City, ⊗ of Newaygo co., W Michigan; pop. (1970c) 1044.

White·cross Mountain \ˌhwīt-krȯs-, ˌwīt-\. Peak, Hinsdale co., SW Colorado; 13,550 ft.

White Dome. Peak, San Juan co., SW Colorado; 13,607 ft.

White Earth. River, NW North Dakota; ab. 60 m. long; rises in NE Williams co., flows S into Missouri river on SW boundary of Mountrail co.

White·face \'hwīt-ˌfās, 'wīt-\. River, NE Minnesota; ab. 60 m. long; rises in E cen. St. Louis co., flows SW into St. Louis river, SW St. Louis co.

Whiteface Mountain. Peak in the Adirondack Mts., Essex co., NE New York; 4867 ft.

White·field \'hwīt-ˌfēld, 'wīt-\. 1 Town, Coos co., N New Hampshire, 21 m. WSW of Berlin; pop. (1970c) 1538.
2 Urban district, Lancashire, NW England, 5 m. N of Manchester; pop. (1971p) 21,841.

White·fish \'hwīt-ˌfish, 'wīt-\. City, Flathead co., NW Montana, 15 m. N of Kalispell; pop. (1970c) 3349; lumber; lake resort.

Whitefish Bay. 1 Inlet of Lake Superior, N coast of Chippewa co., E Michigan penin.
2 Village, Milwaukee co., SE Wisconsin, on Lake Michigan 5 m. N of Milwaukee; pop. (1970c) 17,402; residential.

Whitefish Lake. Lake, N Crow Wing co., cen. Minnesota.

Whitefish Mountain. Peak, Glacier National Park, NW Montana; 8000 ft.

Whitefish Point. Point on extreme N coast of Chippewa co., E Michigan penin., at W entrance to Whitefish Bay.

Whitefish Range. A range of the Rocky Mts., NW Montana, extending along N section of boundary bet. Lincoln and Flathead cos.; highest peak 8107 ft.

White·fri·ars \ˈhwīt-ˌfrī(-ə)rz, ˈwīt-\. Section of London, England, in cen. part of the City; derived its name from a Carmelite monastery (c. 1241–1538) in Fleet Street, whose precincts were a sanctuary until 1697; became a refuge for lawless characters who gave the district the name Alsatia; now includes Whitefriars Street and has many journalistic offices.

White·hall \ˈhwīt-ˌhȯl, ˈwīt-\. 1 City, Muskegon co., W Michigan, 13 m. NNW of Muskegon; pop. (1970c) 3017; summer resort; diversified agriculture.
2 Industrial village, Washington co., E New York, on Vermont border at S end of Lake Champlain and N terminus of Champlain Canal, 10 m. E of Lake George; pop. (1970c) 3764; settled 1759.
3 City, Franklin co., cen. Ohio, E suburb of Columbus; pop. (1970c) 25,623.
4 Borough, Allegheny co., SW Pennsylvania, S suburb of Pittsburgh; pop. (1970c) 16,551.
5 City, ⊗ of Trempealeau co., W Wisconsin; pop. (1970c) 1486; dairy, poultry farms.
6 Wide thoroughfare, Westminster borough, London, England, running N and S bet. Trafalgar Square and the Houses of Parliament; lined with the chief government offices and hence frequently used figuratively for the British Government or its policies. Originally site of Whitehall Palace (from 1529 to 1698 when it was destroyed by fire), the chief residence of the Court of London.

White Hall \ˈhwīt-ˌhȯl, ˈwīt-\. City, Greene co., W Illinois, 48 m. WSW of Springfield; pop. (1970c) 2979.

White·ha·ven \ˈhwīt-ˌhā-ven, ˈwīt-\. Municipal borough, Cumberland, NW England, on Irish Sea SW of Carlisle; pop. (1971p) 26,720; ships coal; silk, chemicals; iron foundries, coal mines.

White Haven. Borough, Luzerne co., E Pennsylvania, on Lehigh river 14 m. S of Wilkes-Barre; pop. (1970c) 2134; explosives; health resort.

White·horse \ˈhwīt-ˌhȯ(ə)rs, ˈwīt-\. City, ✱ of Yukon, Canada, on left bank of Yukon river ab. 52 m. N of British Columbia border; pop. (1971p) 11,084; terminus of railroad from Skagway, Alaska, and one of most important stations on Alaska Highway; active trading town in Klondike gold-rush days; head of navigation on Yukon river.

White Horse, Vale of the. Valley, Berkshire, S England; named from the *White Horse,* a figure of a horse 374 ft. long, formed by cutting away the turf on the side of a chalk hill; many ancient earthworks in the valley which contains the town of Wantage (*q.v.*).

Whitehorse Rapids. Rapids on the Yukon river at the city of Whitehorse, Yukon, Canada.

White·house Mountain \ˌhwit-haủs-, ˌwīt-\. Peak, Ouray co., SW Colorado; 13,493 ft.

White Island. 1 Small island, Bay of Plenty, off NE cen. coast of North I., New Zealand.
2 Island, Spitzbergen archipelago. See KVITØYA.

White Lake. Lake, SW Vermilion parish, S Louisiana; connected by intracoastal canal with Vermilion Bay.

White·man Range \ˌhwīt-mən-, ˌwīt-\. Mountain range, New Britain I., W Pacific Ocean; highest peak 6650 ft.

White·marsh \ˈhwīt-ˌmärsh\. Village, Montgomery co., SE Pennsylvania, on Wissahickon Creek 14 m. N of Philadelphia; in American Revolution Washington's encampment 1777 during battle of Germantown and before retirement to Valley Forge.

White Mountain. 1 Peak in Sierra Nevada, on boundary bet. Alpine and Mono cos., E cen. California; 14,246 ft.
2 Mountain, New Mexico. See SIERRA BLANCA PEAK.
3 *or* **White Hill** *or Ger.* **Weis·ser Berg** \ˌvī-sər-ˈbe(ə)rg\ *or Czech* **Bi·lá Ho·ra** \ˌbil-ə-ˈhȯr-ə\. Hill, Czech S.R., Czechoslovakia, W of Prague; 1243 ft.; scene of battle Nov. 8, 1620 in which the Catholic forces (commanded by the count of Tilly) of Maximilian I, Duke of Bavaria, defeated the Bohemian Protestants under Frederick V (commander in the field, Christian of Anhalt); Bohemia lost its independence.

White Mountains. 1 Mountains, E California and SW Nevada, on boundary bet. Esmeralda co., Nevada, and Mono co., California; contain Boundary Peak 13,140 ft., highest peak in Nevada.
2 Mountains of the Appalachian range, N New Hampshire; highest point Mt. Washington 6288 ft. in Presidential Range (*q.v.*).

Whit·en Head \ˌhwīt-ᵊn-, ˌwīt-\. Cape, N coast of Scotland, in Sutherland co., 15 m. E of Cape Wrath.

White Nile. See NILE.

White Oak. 1 Locality, Montgomery and Prince Georges co., cen. Maryland, 12 m. NE of Washington, D.C.; pop. (1970c) 19,769; 938 acres here set aside 1944 for new naval ordnance laboratory; central unit dedicated Jan. 1949.
2 Borough, Allegheny co., SW Pennsylvania, SSE suburb of Pittsburgh; pop. (1970c) 9304.

White Pass. 1 Pass in mountains N of Skagway, SE Alaska; highest point 2890 ft.; superseded Chilkoot Pass ab. 1900 as easier route to Klondike goldfields; now traversed by railroad.
2 Post, Canadian border station ab. 14 m. N of Skagway.

White Peak. Mountain in Saguache co., S Colorado; 13,600 ft.

White Pine. County in Nevada. See table at NEVADA.

White Pine Mountains. Range in SW White Pine co., E Nevada; highest point is **Duck·water Peak** \ˌdək-ˌwȯt-ər-, -ˌwät-\ 11,513 ft.

White Plains. City, ⊗ of Westchester co., SE New York, 25 m. NNE of New York; pop. (1970c) 50,346; plastics, electronic components, precision machine parts; residential suburb of New York City; Good Counsel Coll. (1923). Settled 1683; meeting place of Provincial congress 1776, which ratified Declaration of Independence; scene of Washington's retreat from Manhattan and of British attack under Howe and battle at Chatterton Hill Oct. 28, 1776; incorp. as village 1866, as city 1916.

White River. 1 Name of several rivers of the U.S. and one of Canada. See WHITE.
2 Town, ⊗ of Mellette co., S South Dakota; pop. (1970c) 617; livestock, grain.
3 River, Iceland. See HVÍTÁ RIVER.

White River Junction. Unincorporated community, Windsor co., E Vermont, at junction of Connecticut and White rivers ab. 9 m. NNE of Woodstock; pop. (1970c) 2379.

White Rock. City, British Columbia, Canada, 25 m. S of Vancouver; pop. (1971p) 10,244; agriculture.

White Rock Mountain. Peak, Gunnison co., W cen. Colorado; 13,532 ft.

White Russia. See BELORUSSIAN SOVIET SOCIALIST REPUBLIC.

White Sands National Monument. See UNITED STATES, *National Monuments.*

White Sands Proving Ground. Region of white (gypsum) sand dunes, Dona Ana co., S New Mexico, SE of San Andres Mts. and SW of the White Sands National Monument; ab. 125 m. long; U.S. testing ground for rockets and guided missiles; Holloman Air Force Base adjacent, 11 m. SW of Alamogordo.

Whites·boro \'hwīts-ˌbər-ə, 'wīts-, -ˌbə-rə\. 1 Village, Oneida co., cen. New York, on Mohawk river 5 m. WNW of Utica; pop. (1970c) 4805; settled 1784.

2 Town, Grayson co., NE Texas, 18 m. W of Sherman; pop. (1970c) 2927; clothing, peanut oil; oil wells.

Whites·burg \'hwīts-ˌbərg, 'wīts-\. City, ⊗ of Letcher co., SE Kentucky, 30 m. SW of Pikeville; pop. (1970c) 1137.

White Sea *or Russ.* **Be·lo·ye Mo·re** \ˌbel-ə-yə-'mȯr-yə\. Large inlet of the Barents Sea, N coast of the Russian S.F.S.R., U.S.S.R.; ab. 34,700 sq. m.; enclosed on the N by Kola Penin.; chief port Arkhangelsk, on Dvina Gulf; on S borders on Arkhangelsk Oblast and on W on Karelian A.S.S.R.; receives the Northern Dvina and Onega rivers.

White Settlement. Town, Tarrant co., N Texas, W suburb of Fort Worth; pop. (1970c) 13,449.

White·shell Forest Reserve \'hwīt-ˌshel-, 'wīt-\. Provincial park, SE Manitoba, Canada, S of Winnipeg river; 1088 sq. m.; region of primitive forest with more than 200 lakes and rivers; characterized by volcanic rock cliffs.

White·side \'hwīt-ˌsīd, 'wīt-\. County in Illinois. See table at ILLINOIS.

White·stone \'hwīt-ˌstōn, 'wīt-\. Community on North Shore, N Queens co., New York, at W end of Long I. N of Flushing; terminus of bridge across East river to the Bronx; settled by Dutch farmers c. 1645.

White Sulphur Springs. 1 City, ⊗ of Meagher co., cen. Montana; pop. (1970c) 1200; gold, silver mines.

2 Residential city, Greenbrier co., SE West Virginia, near Virginia border 36 m. ENE of Hinton; pop. (1970c) 2869; resort; mineral springs; served as summer White House for U.S. presidents Van Buren, Tyler, Fillmore; Japanese diplomats interned here 1942.

White Top Mountain. Peak, Smyth co., SW Virginia; 5520 ft.

White·ville \'hwīt-ˌvil, 'wīt-\. Town, ⊗ of Columbus co., S North Carolina, 44 m. W of Wilmington; pop. (1970c) 4195; tobacco market; textiles, lumber; peanuts, strawberries.

White Volta. See VOLTA, WHITE.

White·wa·ter \'hwīt-ˌwȯt-ər, 'wīt-, -ˌwät-\. 1 River, E Indiana; 100 m. long; rises in E cen. Indiana, flows S, then E across Ohio border to empty into the Miami river just above its junction with the Ohio river, SW Ohio.

2 City, Walworth and Jefferson cos., S Wisconsin, 18 m. NE of Janesville; pop. (1970c) 12,038; Wisconsin State Univ. (1868).

Whitewater Baldy \-'bȯl-dē\. Mountain, S Catron co., W New Mexico; 10,892 ft.

Whitewater Bay. Inlet of Gulf of Mexico, Monroe co., SW Florida, bet. the mainland and Cape Sable.

Whitewater Lake. Lake, SW Manitoba, Canada, 42 m. SSW of Brandon; ab. 10 m. long.

White·wood Peak \ˌhwīt-ˌwu̇d-, ˌwīt-\. Mountain in Lawrence co., W South Dakota; 5140 ft.

White·wright \'hwīt-ˌrīt, 'wīt-\. Town, Grayson co., NE Texas, 15 m. SE of Sherman; pop. (1970c) 1742.

Whit·field \'hwit-ˌfēld, 'wit-\. County in Georgia. See table at GEORGIA.

Whit·horn \'hwit-ˌhȯ(ə)rn, 'wit-\. Burgh, Wigtown, SW Scotland, in S part near Burrow Head; pop. (1971p) 983; an old town, with first stone church in Scotland built 397 by St. Ninian; ruins of 12th cent. priory.

Whit·ing \'hwīt-iŋ, 'wīt-\. City, Lake co., NW corner of Indiana, on Lake Michigan 17 m. SE of Chicago; pop. (1970c) 7847; chemicals, soap; oil refinery; incorporated 1896.

Whit·ing·ham, Lake \-'hwīt-iŋ-ˌham, -'wīt-\. Reservoir in Deerfield river, SW Windham co., S Vermont, formed by 220 ft. earthen **Har·ri·man Dam** \ˌhar-ə-mən-\, completed 1924.

Whit·ins·ville \'hwīt-ᵊnz-ˌvil, 'wīt-\. Urban community (unincorporated), Worcester co., cen. Massachusetts, SE of Worcester; pop. (1970c) 5210.

Whit·ley \'hwit-lē, 'wit-\. Name of counties in two states of the U.S. See tables at INDIANA and KENTUCKY.

Whitley Bay *or formerly* **Whitley and Monks·ea·ton** \'məŋk-ˌsēt-ᵊn\. Municipal borough, Northumberland, N England, on North Sea 9 m. ENE of Newcastle upon Tyne; pop. (1971p) 37,775; summer resort.

Whitley City. Unincorporated community, ⊗ of McCreary co., SE Kentucky; pop. (1970c) 1060.

Whit·man \'hwit-mən, 'wit-\. 1 County in Washington. See table at WASHINGTON.

2 Town, Plymouth co., SE Massachusetts, 4 m. E of Brockton; pop. (1970c) 13,059; footwear, nails, plastics.

Whit·mire \'hwit-ˌmī(ə)r, 'wit-\. Town, Newberry co., NW cen. South Carolina, 35 m. SE of Spartanburg; pop. (1970c) 2226.

Whit·ney, Mount \-'hwit-nē, -'wit-\. Peak in Sierra Nevada, on boundary bet. Tulare and Inyo cos., SE cen. California, in Sequoia National Park; 14,494 ft.; highest point in the state, and in continental U.S. outside of Alaska. See DEATH VALLEY 1.

Whit·sta·ble \'hwit-stə-bəl, 'wit-\. Urban district, Kent, SE England, on North Sea 50 m. E of London; pop. (1971p) 25,404; seaside resort; oyster fisheries.

Whit·sun·day Island \ˌhwit-(ˌ)sən-dē-, ˌwit-, -sən-ˌdā-\. Island, N of Cumberland Is. off E coast of Queensland, Australia, SE of Townsville, 20°17′S, 148°59′E; 38 sq. m.

Whit·ti·er \'hwit-ē-ər, 'wit-\. 1 Seaport village on W shore of Prince William Sound, S Alaska; connected by rail with Fairbanks; pop. (1970c) 130.

2 Suburban residential city, Los Angeles co., SW California, 12 m. ESE of Los Angeles; pop. (1970c) 72,863; ships citrus fruit and walnuts; aircraft and automobile parts, alloy steels, plastics, chemicals, paper containers; Whittier Coll. (1901), Rio Hondo Junior Coll. (1963); founded 1887; incorporated as city 1898.

Whit·tle·sey *or formerly* **Whit·tle·sea** \'hwit-ᵊl-sē, 'wit-\. Urban district, Cambridgeshire and Isle of Ely co., E England, 43 m. E of Leicester; pop. (1971p) 10,451; bricks and tiles.

Whit·worth \'hwit-(ˌ)wərth, 'wit-\. Urban district, Lancashire, NW England, N of Manchester; pop. (1971p) 7417.

Why·al·la \hwī-'al-ə, wī-\. Port city, South Australia, on Spencer Gulf; pop. (1968e) 26,900; blast furnaces; shipbuilding.

Whydah. See OUIDAH.

Wiak. See BIAK.

Wi·ar·ton \'wī-ərt-ᵊn\. Town, Bruce co., SE Ontario, Canada, at head of an inlet of Georgian Bay 15 m. NW of Owen Sound; pop. (1971p) 2173.

Wia Wia National Park \ˌvē-ə-'vē-ə-\. National park, Surinam; 139 sq. m.; turtles; established 1961.

Wi·baux \'wē-(ˌ)bō\. 1 County in E Montana. See table at MONTANA.

2 Town, its ⊗; pop. (1970c) 644.

Wich·i·ta \'wich-ə-ˌtȯ\. 1 River, N Texas; 250 m. long; flows ENE into Red river; contains Wichita Falls Dam.

2 Name of counties in two states of the U.S. See tables at KANSAS and TEXAS.

3 City, ⊗ of Sedgwick co., S cen. Kansas, on Arkansas river 177 m. SW of Kansas City; pop. (1970c) 276,554; alt. 1290 ft.; important aircraft manufacturing center; precision tools, castings, chemicals, pharmaceuticals; flour mills, stockyards, printing plants, grain elevators; Wichita State Univ. (1892), Friends Univ. (1898), Sacred Heart Coll. (1933). Founded 1864; incorporated 1871; major cattle shipping center in early 1870's; developed as center of aircraft industry 1920 ff.

Wichita Falls. City, ⊗ of Wichita co., N Texas, 105 m. NNW of Fort Worth; pop. (1970c) 96,265; ships livestock; textiles, cottonseed and dairy products, electronic components, leather goods, oil field equipment; railroad shops, oil refineries, oil and gas wells; Midwestern Coll. (1922); founded 1876; incorporated 1889.

Wichita Falls Dam. See BIG WICHITA DAM.

Wichita Mountains. Range, SW Oklahoma, chiefly in Comanche and Kiowa cos.; highest peak Mount Scott 2464 ft.

Wick \ˈwik\. Burgh, ⊗ of Caithness co., N Scotland, at mouth of the Wick river; pop. (1971p) 7613; herring fisheries; creamery, distillery.

Wick·en·burg \ˈwik-ən-ˌbərg\. Town, Maricopa co., SW cen. Arizona; pop. (1970c) 2698.

Wick·ford \ˈwik-fərd\. Village, Washington co., S Rhode Island, on Narragansett Bay ab. 8 m. NE of Kingston; administrative center of North Kingstown.

Wick·liffe \ˈwik-ləf, -(ˌ)lif\. **1** City, ⊗ of Ballard co., W Kentucky; pop. (1970c) 1211; dairy farms.

2 City, Lake co., NE Ohio, on Lake Erie 13 m. NE of Cleveland; pop. (1970c) 21,354; Rabbinical Coll. of Telshe (1876), Borromeo Seminary of Ohio (1953).

Wick·low \ˈwik-(ˌ)lō\. **1** County, E Eire, in Leinster prov.; 782 sq. m.; pop. (1971p) 66,270; ⊗ Wicklow; stock raising; barley, wheat, oats; dairying.

2 Urban district and seaport, its ⊗; pop. (1971p) 3908; seaside resort; ruins of Franciscan abbey and 12th cent. castle.

Wicklow Head. Cape, E coast of Ireland, E of Wicklow; lighthouse.

Wicklow Mountains. Range extending along E coast of co. Wicklow, E Eire; highest peak **Lug·na·quil·la** \ˌləg-nə-ˈkwil-yə\ 3039 ft.

Wi·com·i·co \wī-ˈkäm-ə-ˌkō\. County in Maryland. See table at MARYLAND.

Wida. See OUIDAH.

Wid·nes \ˈwid-nəs\. Municipal borough, Lancashire, NW England, on the Mersey 10 m. E of Liverpool; pop. (1971p) 56,709; chemicals, machinery, asbestos goods, paper, clothing.

Wid·ows' Tears \ˈwid-ōz-ˌti(ə)rz\. Waterfall, Yosemite National Park, E cen. California; 1170 ft.

Wie·licz·ka \vye-ˈlēch-kə\. Commune, Kraków prov., S Poland, 8 m. SE of Kraków; pop. (1968e) 13,200; ancient rock-salt mines.

Wie·luń \ˈvye-lün-yə\. Commune, Łódź prov., cen. Poland, 61 m. SW of Łódź; pop. (1968e) 13,200; sugar products, beer.

Wien. See VIENNA 4.

Wie·ner Neu·stadt \ˌvē-nər-ˈnȯi-ˌs(h)tät\. Industrial city, Lower Austria, 24 m. SSW of Vienna; pop. (1961c) 33,845; railroad junction; textiles, leather goods, beer; 13th cent. cathedral, 13th cent. castle and three towers of medieval fortifications, 18th cent. Jesuit college (now museum). Burial place of Emperor Maximilian I. Founded 1194; at height of prosperity during 15th cent.; in World War II occupied by U.S.S.R. Apr. 3, 1945.

Wie·ner·wald \ˈvē-nər-ˌvält\. A spur of the Eastern Alps, Lower Austria, W and NW of Vienna and S of the Danube, covered with forests; in N part is the Kahlenberg.

Wieprz \ˈvyepsh\. River, cen. Poland; 194 m. long; rises in S Lublin prov., flows NW and W into the Vistula river.

Wier·den \ˈvi(ə)r-dən\. Commune, Overijssel prov., E Netherlands, just W of Almelo; pop. (1970e) 17,653.

Wie·ring·en \ˈvi(ə)r-iŋ-ən\. Commune, North Holland prov., W Netherlands, at W end of dike enclosing IJsselmeer; pop. (1970e) 7144; formerly an island in Zuider Zee, now constitutes N section of Wieringermeer.

Wie·ring·er·meer \ˈvē-riŋ-ər-ˌme(ə)r\. Polder, Netherlands; 77 sq. m.; NW part of former Zuider Zee; completed 1930; flooded by Germans Apr. 18, 1945, reclaimed again by May 1946.

Wies·ba·den \ˈvēs-ˌbäd-ᵊn, ˈvis-\. City, ✱ of Hesse, West Germany, on the Rhine 20 m. W of Frankfurt am Main; pop. (1970c) 250,122; metal goods, concrete products, plastics, chemicals, textiles, wine; printing, iron founding; noted for 27 hot springs known since Roman times; 17th cent. town hall, castle, remains of 4th cent. Roman wall. Fortified by Romans 12 B.C.; first mentioned under present name 829 A.D.; free imperial city c. 1242; capital of duchy of Nassau 1806–66; seat of Rhineland Commission under French and British occupation 1918–29; in World War II occupied by U.S. forces Mar. 1945.

Wig·an \ˈwig-ən\. County borough, Lancashire, NW England, on the Douglas 18 m. W of Manchester; pop. (1971p) 81,258; textiles, machinery, clothing, canned goods, plastics, paint, footwear, tar, rubber; coal-mining center since 14th cent.; chartered 1100.

Wig·gins \ˈwig-ənz\. Town, ⊗ of Stone co., SE Mississippi; pop. (1970c) 2995; lumber, pickles.

Wight, Isle of \-ˈwīt\ *or anc.* **Vec·tis** \ˈvek-təs\. Administrative county constituted by the Isle of Wight; 147 sq. m.; pop. (1971p) 109,284; ⊗ Newport; includes many seaside resorts, as Ryde, Ventnor, Cowes; other towns Shanklin, Sandown, Carisbrooke.

Wigs·ton Mag·na \ˌwig-stən-ˈmag-nə\. Urban district, Leicestershire, cen. England, 4 m. S of Leicester; pop. (1971p) 30,230.

Wig·town \ˈwig-tən, -ˌtau̇n\. **1** *or* **Wig·town·shire** \-ˌshi(ə)r, -shər\. County, SW Scotland; 487 sq. m.; pop. (1971p) 27,335; ⊗ Wigtown; hilly region; rivers Cree, Bladenoch; agriculture, livestock raising.

2 Burgh, its ⊗, on Wigtown Bay; pop. (1971p) 1118.

Wigtown Bay. Inlet of Irish Sea, S coast of Scotland; extends 15 m. inland in Wigtown co.

Wij·de·fjord·en \ˈvīd-ə-ˌfyȯ(ə)r-dən\ *or* **Wij·de Bay** \ˌvīd-ə-\. Fjord, N coast of the island of Spitsbergen, Svalbard, Norway; 70 m. long.

Wijm·brit·se·ra·deel *or* **Wym·brit·se·ra·deel** \vīm-ˈbrit-sər-ə-ˌdā(ə)l\. Commune, Friesland prov., N Netherlands; pop. (1970e) 10,641.

Wijnkoops–Baai. See PELABUHAN BAY.

Wil \ˈvē(ə)l\. Commune, NW Saint Gallen canton, NE Switzerland; pop. (1970c) 14,646; textiles.

Wil·bar·ger \ˈwil-ˌbär-gər\. County in Texas. See table at TEXAS.

Wil·ber \ˈwil-bər\. City, ⊗ of Saline co., SE Nebraska; pop. (1970c) 1483; diversified agriculture.

Wil·ber·force \ˈwil-bər-ˌfō(ə)rs, -ˌfȯ(ə)rs\. Village, Greene co., SW Ohio, ab. 3 m. NE of Xenia; pop. (1970c) 2800; Wilberforce University (1856); Central State College (1887).

Wilberforce, Cape. Point, N coast of Australia, Northern Territory, just NW of Cape Arnhem, 11°54′S, 136°35′E.

Wil·bra·ham \ˈwil-brə-ˌham\. Town, Hampden co., SW Massachusetts, 8 m. E of Springfield; pop. (1970c) 11,984; Wilbraham Academy (1817).

Wil·bur, Mount \-ˈwil-bər\. Peak, Glacier National Park, NW Montana; 9293 ft.

Wil·bur·ton \ˈwil-bərt-ᵊn\. City, ⊗ of Latimer co., E Oklahoma, 28 m. E of McAlester; pop. (1970c) 2504; Eastern Oklahoma Agricultural and Mechanical Coll. (1909).

Wil·cox \ˈwil-ˌkäks\. Name of counties in two states of the U.S. See tables at ALABAMA and GEORGIA.

Wil·czek Land \ˈvil-ˌchek-\. See FRANZ JOSEF LAND.

Wild·bad \ˈvilt-ˌbät\. Commune, Baden-Württemberg, West Germany; mineral springs; resort.

Wild·cat Mountain \ˌwīld-kat-\. Peak, Iron co., SE Missouri; 1757 ft.; connected with Taum Sauk by a saddle.

Wil·der·ness \ˈwil-dər-nəs\. Region, Orange and Spotsylvania cos., N Virginia, S of Rapidan river; battles 1863 (Chancellorsville) and May 5–7, 1864 bet. Union forces under Grant and Confederates under Lee, one of the bloodiest battles of the Civil War.

Wild·spit·ze \'vilt-ˌs(h)pit-sə\. Highest peak in Ötztaler Alps, Tirol, Austria; 12,382 ft.

Wild·wood \'wīl-(ˌ)dwu̇d\. City and seaside resort, Cape May co., S New Jersey, on Atlantic Ocean 33 m. SW of Atlantic City; pop. (1970c) 4110; plastics; commercial fisheries; truck farms.

Wil·helm, Mount \-'vil-ˌhelm\. Mountain, Bismarck Range, E New Guinea I., Papua New Guinea; 14,762 ft.; highest peak in Papua New Guinea.

Wil·hel·mi·na Mountains \ˌwil-hel-'mē-nə-, ˌwil-ə-'mē-nə-, ˌvil-\. Mountain range, cen. Surinam; highest peak 4200 ft.

Wilhelmina Top. See TRIKORA.

Wil·helm–Pieck–Stadt Gu·ben \ˌvil-helm-'pēk-ˌs(h)tät-'gü-bən\ *or from 1945 to 1961* **Guben.** City, Cottbus dist., East Germany, on Polish border; pop. (1970e) 29,521; textiles, machinery; became part of East Germany 1945, its historical section (see GUBIN) being assigned to Poland.

Wil·helms·ha·ven \ˌvil-helmz-'häf-ən\. Seaport city, Lower Saxony, West Germany, on W shore of Jade Bay 19 m. W of Bremerhaven; pop. (1969e) 102,682; textiles, typewriters, precision tools, cranes; principal North Sea base of the West German navy; seaside resort; oil storage facilities. Founded 1853; named 1869; principal base of German High Seas Fleet in World War I and major naval base in World War II, during which it was heavily damaged by Allied bombing 1939–45; largely rebuilt since the war.

Wilhelm II Coast \ˌvil-helm-t͟hə-'sek-ənd-\ *or formerly* **Kai·ser Wilhelm II Land** \ˌkī-zər-\. Section of coast of Antarctica ab. 67°S, 90°E; formerly claimed by Germany; now lies within region claimed by Great Britain.

Wi·lis \'vē-ləs\. Mountain group, E cen. Java, Indonesia; highest point Mt. Liman 8409 ft.

Wilja. See NERIS.

Wiljandi. See VILJANDI.

Wilkes \'wilks\. Name of counties in two states of the U.S. See tables at GEORGIA and NORTH CAROLINA.

Wilkes–Bar·re \'wilks-ˌbar-ə, -ˌbar-ē, -ˌba(ə)r\. Commercial and industrial city, ⊗ of Luzerne co., E Pennsylvania, on Susquehanna river 18 m. SW of Scranton; pop. (1970c) 58,856; clothing, footwear, pencils, tobacco products, electronic components, power tools; anthracite coal mines; Wilkes Coll. (1933), King's Coll. (1946), Luzerne County Community Coll. (1966). Settled 1769; burned by British and Indians 1778 and 1784.

Wilkes·boro \'wilks-ˌbər-ə, -ˌbə-rə\. Town, ⊗ of Wilkes co., NW cen. North Carolina; pop. (1970c) 1974; Wilkes Community Coll. (1965).

Wilkes Land. Coastal region of Antarctica, extending approximately through lat. 66° to 70°S and long. 102° to 142°E along the Indian Ocean from Queen Mary Coast to George V Coast; max. ice thickness ab. 9000 ft.; includes French Claim of Adélie Coast (*q.v.*).

History: Discovered 1839 by Charles Wilkes, U.S. naval officer, who coasted along this part of Antarctic barrier from ab. 150°E to 108°E. As result of explorations of T.W.E. David and Douglas Mawson, British explorers, region (coastal area and interior extending to South Pole) claimed 1908 by Great Britain. Except for Adélie Coast, part of the Australian claim as established 1933 and 1936, with concurrence of Great Britain.

Wil·kin \'wil-kən\. County in Minnesota. See table at MINNESOTA.

Wil·kins \'wil-kənz\. Township, Allegheny co., SW Pennsylvania, E suburb of Pittsburgh; pop. (1970c) 8749.

Wil·kins·burg \'wil-kənz-ˌbərg\. Residential borough, Allegheny co., SW Pennsylvania, 7 m. E of Pittsburgh; pop. (1970c) 26,780; machine tools, bricks; residential suburb of Pittsburgh.

Wil·kin·son \'wil-kən-sən\. Name of counties in two states of the U.S. See tables at GEORGIA and MISSISSIPPI.

Wilkomir. See UKMERGE.

Will \'wil\. County in Illinois. See table at ILLINOIS.

Wil·la·cy \'wil-ə-sē\. County in Texas. See table at TEXAS.

Wil·lam·ette \wə-'lam-ət\. River, NW Oregon; ab. 300 m. long; formed by junction of forks in cen. Lane co., flows N into Columbia river near Portland.

Wil·la·pa Bay \ˌwil-ə-ˌpȯ-, -ˌpä-\. Inlet of Pacific Ocean, W coast of Pacific co., SW Washington.

Wil·lard \'wil-ərd\. City, Huron co., N Ohio, 26 m. S of Sandusky; pop. (1970c) 5510; steel, rubber products; railroad shops; diversified agriculture.

Wil·lau·mez Peninsula \ˌvē-yō-'mez-\. Long point of land, extending from cen. part of N coast of New Britain I. into Bismarck Sea, Bismarck Archipelago, W Pacific Ocean; Cape Hollman is at N extremity, Kimbe Bay to the E, and Talasea on its E shore.

Wil·le·broeck \'vil-ə-ˌbru̇k\. Manufacturing commune, Antwerp prov., N Belgium, halfway bet. Antwerp and Brussels; pop. (1969e) 15,830.

Wil·lem·stad \'vil-əm-ˌstät\. City, ✱ of the Netherlands Antilles, on Curaçao island, at S end; pop. (1960c) 43,547; oil refineries, shipyards; tourism; handles crude oil from the Lake Maracaibo district of Venezuela. Founded 1634; became major oil-refining center after 1918.

Wil·len·dorf \'vil-ən-ˌdȯ(ə)rf\. Village, Lower Austria, on the Danube near Krems; site of Paleolithic station where the Venus of Willendorf (a limestone statuette ab. $4^1/_2$ inches tall representing a female, assigned to the Aurignacian period) was discovered.

Willes·den \'wilz-dən\. See BRENT.

Wil·ley, Mount \-'wil-ē\. Peak on W side of Crawford Notch, White Mts., New Hampshire, in NE Grafton co.; 4261 ft.

Wil·liam, Mount \-'wil-yəm\. See GRAMPIANS, THE 1.

Wil·liams \'wil-yəmz\. 1 River, W cen. Arizona; ab. 50 m. long; formed by confluence of Big Sandy and Santa Maria rivers on SE boundary of Mohave co., flows W into Colorado river.

2 Name of counties in two states of the U.S. See tables at NORTH DAKOTA and OHIO.

3 Town, Coconino co., N Arizona, 28 m. W of Flagstaff; pop. (1970c) 2386.

Williams Bay. Village, Walworth co., S Wisconsin, 24 m. ESE of Janesville; pop. (1970c) 1554; site of Yerkes Observatory (founded 1892; belongs to Univ. of Chicago).

Wil·liams·burg \'wil-yəmz-ˌbərg\. 1 County in South Carolina. See table at SOUTH CAROLINA.

2 City, ⊗ of Whitley co., SE Kentucky, 28 m. WNW of Middlesborough; pop. (1970c) 3687; coal mines, gas wells; corn; Cumberland Coll. (1888).

3 Town, Hampshire co., W Massachusetts, 15 m. SSW of Greenfield; pop. (1970c) 2342.

4 District, Brooklyn, New York. See BROOKLYN 3.

5 Independent city, ⊗ of James City co., James City and York cos., SE Virginia; on peninsula bet. James and York rivers 27 m. NNW of Newport News; 3 sq. m.; pop. (1970c) 9069; Coll. of William and Mary (1693). Site of a large-scale restoration project, Colonial Williamsburg (financed by Rockefeller Foundation), in which 700 modern buildings were removed, 83 original existing buildings renovated, and 413 buildings reconstructed on original sites, 1926 ff.; made part of Colonial National Historical Park 1936.

History: Settled 1633; made new capital of Virginia 1699; incorporated as city 1722 (first incorporated municipality in Virginia); political and social center of Virginia during 18th cent. until capital removed to Richmond 1780; in Civil War scene of battle May 5, 1862.

Williams Lake. Town, British Columbia, Canada, 125 m. NW of Kamloops; pop. (1971p) 4071; sawmills; agriculture.

Wil·liam·son \'wil-yəm-sən\. 1 River, Klamath co., S Oregon; ab. 70 m. long; flows NW then S to N end of Upper Klamath Lake; receives the Sprague near its mouth.

2 Name of counties in three states of the U.S. See tables at ILLINOIS, TENNESSEE, TEXAS.

3 Village in Williamson town, Wayne co., W New York, ab. 22 m. NE of Rochester; pop. (1970c) 1991.
4 City, ⊗ of Mingo co., SW West Virginia, 52 m. S of Huntington; pop. (1970c) 5831; furniture; railroad shops, coal mines.

Williamson, Mount. Peak in Sierra Nevada, W Inyo co., SE cen. California; 14,375 ft.

Williamson Head. Headland on Oates Coast, Antarctica, W of Ross Sea, 69°11′S, 157°57′E.

Wil·liams·port \ˈwil-yəmz-ˌpō(ə)rt, -ˌpȯ(ə)rt\. 1 Town, ⊗ of Warren co., W Indiana; pop. (1970c) 1661.
2 Town, Washington co., N Maryland, on Potomac river 7 m. WSW of Hagerstown; pop. (1970c) 2270.
3 Industrial city, ⊗ of Lycoming co., N cen. Pennsylvania, on W branch of Susquehanna river 70 m. N of Harrisburg; pop. (1970c) 37,918; textiles, leather goods, furniture, marine engines, wire rope, valves, silk; Williamsport Area Community Coll. (1920). Founded 1795; incorporated as city 1866; in 1860's a major lumbering center.

Wil·liams·ton \ˈwil-yəm-stən\. 1 City, Ingham co., S Michigan, 13 m. E of Lansing; pop. (1970c) 2600.
2 Town, ⊗ of Martin co., E North Carolina, on Roanoke river 42 m. E of Rocky Mount; pop. (1970c) 6570; lumber, peanut products; tobacco.
3 Town, Anderson co., NW South Carolina, 13 m. NE of Anderson; pop. (1970c) 3991; textiles; grain.

Wil·liams·town \ˈwil-yəmz-ˌtau̇n\. 1 City, ⊗ of Grant co., N Kentucky; pop. (1970c) 2063.
2 Town, Berkshire co., W Massachusetts, 19 m. N of Pittsfield; pop. (1970c) 8454; Williams Coll. (1785).
3 Unincorporated community, Gloucester co., SW New Jersey, ab. 14 m. SE of Woodbury; pop. (1970c) 4075; clothing; foundry; truck farms.
4 Borough, Dauphin co., SE cen. Pennsylvania, 26 m. NE of Harrisburg; pop. (1970c) 1919.
5 Town, Wood co., W West Virginia, on Ohio river across from Marietta, Ohio; pop. (1970c) 2743.
6 City, E Victoria, SE Australia, SW suburb of Melbourne on Port Phillip Bay; pop. (1966c) 30,449; seaport with floating decks, shipbuilding yards, and a navy depot; oil refinery, flour mills, cannery, railroad shops.

Wil·liams·ville \ˈwil-yəmz-ˌvil\. Residential village, Erie co., W New York, 10 m. NE of Buffalo; pop. (1970c) 6835; Saint Clare Coll. (1957).

Willimansett. See CHICOPEE 2.

Wil·li·man·tic \ˌwil-ə-ˈmant-ik\. 1 River, NE Connecticut; ab. 30 m. long; rises in S Massachusetts, flows S across cen. Tolland co. and unites with the Natchaug river at Willimantic to form the Shetucket river.
2 Industrial city in town of Windham, Windham co., NE Connecticut, at junction of Natchaug and Willimantic rivers; pop. (1970c) 14,402; synthetic textiles, silk, building materials, foundry products, radio parts; truck farms; Eastern Connecticut State Coll. (1889); incorporated as borough 1833, as city 1893.

Wil·ling·bo·ro \ˈwil-iŋ-ˌbər-ə, -ˌbə-rə\ *or formerly* **Lev·it·town** \ˈlev-ət-ˌtau̇n\. Urban township, Burlington co., S cen. New Jersey, NE of Camden; pop. (1970c) 43,386.

Wil·ling·ton \ˈwil-iŋ-tən\. 1 Town, NW cen. Tolland co., N Connecticut, on E bank of Willimantic river opp. Tolland; pop. (1970c) 3755; incorporated 1727.
2 City, N Delaware. See WILMINGTON 1.

Wil·lis Islets *or* **Willis Islands** \ˌwil-əs-\. Group of coral islets and reefs, Coral Sea, outside Great Barrier Reef, Queensland, Australia, 16°18′S, 150°E.

Wil·lis·ton \ˈwil-ə-stən\. City, ⊗ of Williams co., NW North Dakota, on Missouri river 20 m. E of Montana border; pop. (1970c) 11,280; flour, dairy products; coal mines, oil wells, railroad shops; agriculture.

Williston Park. Residential village, Nassau co., SE New York, on Long I. 18 m. E of New York; pop. (1970c) 9154.

Wil·lits \ˈwil-əts\. City, Mendocino co., N California, 73 m. NNW of Santa Rosa; pop. (1970c) 3091; lumber, furniture.

Will·mar \ˈwil-ˌmär, -mər\. City, ⊗ of Kandiyohi co., SW cen. Minnesota, 52 m. SW of St. Cloud; pop. (1970c) 12,869; poultry processing; foundry, machine shops; dairy farms; Willmar State Junior Coll. (1961).

Wil·lough·by \ˈwil-ə-bē\. City, Lake co., NE Ohio, on Lake Erie 18 m. NE of Cleveland; pop. (1970c) 18,634.

Willoughby Lake. Lake, E Orleans co., N Vermont; ab. 6 m. long by 2 m. wide; summer resort.

Wil·low Grove \ˌwil-ō-\. Locality, Montgomery co., SE Pennsylvania, 13 m. N of Philadelphia; pop. (1970c) 16,494; machine tools; truck, dairy farms.

Wil·lo·wick \ˈwil-ə-ˌwik\. City, Lake co., NE Ohio, E suburb of Cleveland; pop. (1970c) 21,237.

Wil·low·more \ˈwil-ə-ˌmō(ə)r, -ˌmȯ(ə)r\. Town, S Cape Province, S Rep. of South Africa, 130 m. WNW of Port Elizabeth; pop. (1967e) 4200; in E part of the Great Karroo; mohair, wool, and ostrich feathers produced in this region.

Willow Mountain. Peak, SW Brewster co., W Texas; 3080 ft.

Wil·lows \ˈwil-ōz\. City, ⊗ of Glenn co., N California, 42 m. NE of Clear Lake; pop. (1970c) 4085; dairy products; rice.

Willow Springs. 1 Village, Cook co., NE Illinois, 16 m. SW of Chicago; pop. (1970c) 3318.
2 City, Howell co., S Missouri, 18 m. N of West Plains; pop. (1970c) 2045.

Wills·boro \ˈwilz-ˌbər-ə, -ˌbə-rə\. Village in Willsboro town, (pop. [1970c] 1688), Essex co., NE New York, ab. 25 m. S of Plattsburg; settled 1765; scene of Burgoyne's encampment 1777.

Wills Point \ˌwilz-\. City, Van Zandt co., NE Texas, 40 m. E of Dallas; pop. (1970c) 2636; cottonseed oil; ships fruit; livestock.

Willyama. See BROKEN HILL 1.

Wil·mer·ding \ˈwil-mər-diŋ\. Borough, Allegheny co., SW Pennsylvania, 11 m. E of Pittsburgh; pop. (1970c) 3218.

Wil·mette \wil-ˈmet\. Residential village, Cook co., NE Illinois, 15 m. N of Chicago; pop. (1970c) 32,134; Mallinckrodt Coll. (1918).

Wil·ming·ton \ˈwil-miŋ-tən\. 1 Commercial and industrial city, ⊗ of New Castle co., N Delaware, at junction of Delaware and Christina rivers and Brandywine Creek; pop. (1970c) 80,386; seaport and transportation center; chemicals, textiles, rubber and leather products, explosives, tile, floor coverings, cork products, railroad cars; shipyards, copper smelter; Goldey Beacom Junior Coll. (1886), Brandywine Junior Coll. (1967); several 18th cent. churches.
History: Fort Christina (*q.v.*) founded by Swedes 1638; capital of New Sweden until 1643 and again in 1654; held by Dutch 1655–64 and then captured by English; renamed **Wil·ling·ton** \ˈwil-iŋ-tən\ 1731; chartered as borough and renamed Wilmington 1739; battle of Brandywine fought just N of city 1777; captured by British; Du Pont powder mills established 1802; chartered as city 1832.
2 City, Will co., NE Illinois, 15 m. S of Joliet; pop. (1970c) 4335; coal mines; agriculture.
3 Town, Middlesex co., NE Massachusetts, 9 m. SE of Lowell; pop. (1970c) 17,102; machinery; truck farms.
4 City, ⊗ of New Hanover co., SE North Carolina, on Cape Fear river 30 m. N of its mouth; pop. (1970c) 46,169; principal seaport of the state, shipping wood pulp and scrap metal; produces textiles, wood products, boilers, clothing, fertilizer; sport-fishing resort; truck farms, tobacco; Wilmington Coll. (1947).
History: Settled c. 1730; incorporated as town 1740; scene of armed resistance to Stamp Act 1765–66; occupied by British under Cornwallis 1781; a major port of entry for Confederate blockade runners during the Civil War until

closed by capture of Fort Fisher by Union forces Jan. 15, 1865; incorporated as city 1866.

5 City, ⊗ of Clinton co., SW Ohio, 29 m. SE of Dayton; pop. (1970c) 10,051; automobile parts, air compressors, castings; ships hogs; Wilmington Coll. (1863); Clinton County Air Force Base; founded 1810.

Wil·more \'wil-ˌmō(ə)r, -ˌmȯ(ə)r\. City, Jessamine co., E cen. Kentucky, 17 m. SW of Lexington; pop. (1970c) 3466; flour; tobacco; Asbury Coll. (1890).

Wilms·low \'wi(l)mz-(ˌ)lō\. Urban district, Cheshire, NW England, on the Bollin 12 m. S of Manchester; pop. (1971p) 28,982.

Wilna. See VILNIUS.

Wil·no \'vil-(ˌ)nō\. 1 Former Polish department, now part of U.S.S.R.; 11,196 sq. m.; area for several centuries scene of conflict bet. Lithuanians, Poles, and White Russians; in 1922 in region ceded by plebiscite to Poland; part ceded to Lithuania by U.S.S.R. 1939.

2 City, U.S.S.R. See VILNIUS.

Wil·pat·tu National Park \wil-'pät-(ˌ)ü-\. National park, Ceylon; 252 sq. m.; elephant, leopard, sambar; established 1938.

Wil·ryck \'vil-ˌrīk\. Commune, Antwerp prov., N Belgium; pop. (1969e) 43,382; S suburb of Antwerp.

Wil·son \'wil-sən\. 1 Name of counties in four states of the U.S. See tables at KANSAS, NORTH CAROLINA, TENNESSEE, TEXAS.

2 Subdivision of town of Windsor, Connecticut. See WINDSOR 3.

3 City, ⊗ of Wilson co., E North Carolina, 18 m. SSW of Rocky Mount; pop. (1970c) 29,347; tobacco market; truck bodies, fiber glass, cottonseed oil, clothing, fertilizer, feed; meat-packing plant; Atlantic Christian Coll. (1902); incorporated 1849.

4 City, Carter co., S Oklahoma, 20 m. W of Ardmore; pop. (1970c) 1569; dairy, poultry farms.

5 Borough, Northampton co., E Pennsylvania, 14 m. ENE of Allentown; pop. (1970c) 8482; woolens, paper products.

Wilson, Mount. 1 Peak in San Gabriel Mts., Los Angeles co., SW California, just NE of Pasadena; 5710 ft.; Mount Wilson Observatory operated by the Carnegie Institution and possessing a 100-inch telescope.

2 Peak in San Juan Mts., Dolores co., SW Colorado; 14,-246 ft.

Wilson Dam. Dam across Tennessee river, NW Alabama, forming **Lake Wilson** 15½ m. long submerging Muscle Shoals. See TENNESSEE 1; table at TENNESSEE VALLEY AUTHORITY.

Wilson Peak. 1 Peak in San Miguel co., SW Colorado; 14,-246 ft.

2 Mountain in E Summit co., NE Utah; 13,095 ft.

Wil·son's Creek \'wil-sənz-\. Small stream near Springfield, Greene co., SW Missouri; battle Aug. 10, 1861 in which Confederates under Price defeated Union forces under Lyon.

Wilson's Creek National Battlefield Park. See UNITED STATES, *National Historical Parks*.

Wilson's Promontory. Cape, S Victoria, Australia, 38°55'S, 146°20'E.

Wil·ton \'wilt-ᵊn\. 1 Residential and agricultural town, W Fairfield co., SW Connecticut, on New York border N of Norwalk; pop. (1970c) 13,572; Coll. of Notre Dame de Wilton; settled 1701.

2 Town, Franklin co., W Maine, 29 m. NW of Augusta; pop. (1970c) 3802; footwear; agriculture.

3 Town, Hillsborough co., S New Hampshire, 15 m. WNW of Nashua; pop. (1970c) 2276; summer resort.

4 Town, Saratoga co., E New York; pop. (1970c) 2984.

5 Municipal borough, Wiltshire, S England; pop. (1971p) 3815; Wilton rugs first manufactured here; former seat of kings of Wessex; battle 871 bet. Alfred the Great and the Danes.

Wilton Manors. City, Broward co., SE Florida, N of Fort Lauderdale; pop. (1970c) 10,948.

Wilt·shire \'wilt-ˌshi(ə)r, -shər\ *or* **Wilts** \'wilts\. County, S England; area 1344 sq. m.; pop. (1971p) 486,048; ⊗ Salisbury; rivers Avon, Kennet; livestock and dairy farming, manufacturing (railroad rolling stock, textiles and carpets; food processing); largest towns Swindon, Salisbury, Trowbridge, Chippenham.

Wim·ble·don \'wim-bəl-dən\. Former municipal borough, S England, part of Greater London; known for its sports facilities, esp. for cricket and lawn tennis ("All-England" championships); see BRENT.

Wim·borne Minster \ˌwim-bərn-\. Urban district, Dorsetshire, S England, ab. 7 m. NNW of Bournemouth; pop. (1971p) 5000; 12th cent. church; important in Anglo-Saxon times.

Wim·mera \'wim-ə-rə\. River, W Victoria, SE Australia; 228 m. long; flows N into Lake Hindmarsh.

Win·a·mac \'win-ə-ˌmak\. Town, ⊗ of Pulaski co., NW Indiana, 23 m. NW of Logansport; pop. (1970c) 2341.

Win·burg \'win-ˌbərg\. Town, cen. Orange Free State, E cen. Rep. of South Africa, 65 m. NE of Bloemfontein; pop. (1967e) 5000; founded 1836.

Win·chell, Mount \-'win-chəl\. Peak in the Sierra Nevada, California, on boundary bet. Fresno and Inyo cos.; 13,479 ft.

Win·chel·sea \'win-chəl-sē\. Village, East Sussex, S England, near coast just SW of Rye and ab. 8 m. NE of Hastings; major seaport 13th–15th cents., one of the Cinque Ports (*q.v.*); remains of Church of St. Thomas à Becket include chancel and aisles in Decorated style.

Win·chen·don \'win-chən-dən\. Town, Worcester co., cen. Massachusetts, 14 m. WNW of Fitchburg; pop. (1970c) 6635; plastics, toys, woodenware.

Win·ches·ter \'win-ˌches-tər, -chə-stər\. 1 Town, NE Litchfield co., NW Connecticut, N of Torrington; pop. (1970c) 11,106; incorporated 1771; includes city of Winsted (*q.v.*).

2 City, ⊗ of Scott co., W Illinois, 45 m. WSW of Springfield; pop. (1970c) 1788; agriculture.

3 City, ⊗ of Randolph co., E Indiana, 20 m. E of Muncie; pop. (1970c) 5493; glass, gloves; dairy farms.

4 City, ⊗ of Clark co., E cen. Kentucky, 20 m. E of Lexington; pop. (1970c) 13,402; clothing, fertilizer; limestone quarries; tobacco, livestock; Southeastern Christian Coll. (1949).

5 Residential town, Middlesex co., NE Massachusetts, 8 m. NW of Boston; pop. (1970c) 22,269.

6 Town, Cheshire co., SW corner of New Hampshire, on Ashuelot river 12 m. SSW of Keene; pop. (1970c) 2869.

7 Town, ⊗ of Franklin co., S Tennessee, 25 m. E of Fayetteville; pop. (1970c) 5256; silk, canned goods, dairy products, flour; diversified agriculture.

8 City, ⊗ of Frederick co., N Virginia, in Shenandoah Valley 70 m. WNW of Alexandria; 3 sq. m.; pop. (1970c) 14,463; politically independent; ships apples; cider, plastics, rubber goods, tin cans, woolens; Shenandoah Coll. and Shenandoah Conservatory of Music (1875).

History: Founded 1744; George Washington began career as surveyor here 1748; Fort Loudoun built here by Washington after defeat of Braddock 1755; incorporated as town 1779; military base and headquarters during Civil War and scene of battles May 25, 1862 and Sept. 19, 1864; incorporated as city 1874.

9 *or anc.* **Ven·ta Bel·ga·rum** \ˌvent-ə-bel-'gar-əm, -'ger-\. Municipal borough, ⊗ of Hampshire co., S England, on the Itchin 21 m. NNW of Portsmouth; pop. (1971p) 31,041; notable 11th–14th cent. cathedral (the longest in Britain), 15th cent. hospital, 13th cent. gate, ruins of castle and episcopal palace; Winchester Coll. (founded 1387 by William of Wykeham).

History: Important trade and cloth-making center under Romans; capital of Wessex and seat of government under Alfred the Great and Canute (buried here); remained important under Norman kings until emergence of London as sole capital of England late 12th cent.

Wind \ˈwind\. River, W cen. Wyoming; ab. 120 m. long; rises in NW Fremont co., flows SE along E slopes of Wind River Range and unites with Popo Agie river in cen. Fremont co. to form Big Horn river.

Windau. 1 River, U.S.S.R. See VENTA.

2 City, Latvian S.S.R., U.S.S.R. See VENTSPILS.

Wind·ber \ˈwin(d)-bər\. Borough, Somerset co., S Pennsylvania, 8 m. SE of Johnstown; pop. (1970c) 6332.

Wind Cave National Park \ˈwind-\. See UNITED STATES, *National Parks.*

Wind·crest \ˈwin(d)-ˌkrest\. Town, Bexar co., S cen. Texas; pop. (1970c) 3371.

Win·der \ˈwīn-dər\. City, ⊗ of Barrow co., N Georgia, 20 m. W of Athens; pop. (1970c) 6605; textiles, fertilizer, cottonseed oil; potatoes; scene of a skirmish Aug. 3, 1864 during the Civil War.

Win·der·mere \ˈwin-də(r)-ˌmi(ə)r\. 1 Lake in the Lake District, NW England, on border bet. Westmorland and Lancashire; 10½ m. long; maximum depth 219 ft.; largest lake in England.

2 Urban district, Westmorland, NW England, on Lake Windermere 33 m. S of Carlisle; pop. (1971p) 8063.

Wind·ham \ˈwin-dəm\. 1 Name of counties in two states of the U.S. See tables at CONNECTICUT and VERMONT.

2 Town, SW Windham co., NE Connecticut; pop. (1970c) 19,626; agriculture; incorporated 1692; includes industrial city of Willimantic. See WILLIMANTIC 2.

3 Town, Cumberland co., SW Maine, 15 m. NW of Portland; pop. (1970c) 6593.

4 Town, Rockingham co., SE New Hampshire, 20 m. SSE of Manchester; pop. (1970c) 3008.

Wind·hoek \ˈvint-ˌhu̇k\. Town, ❋ of South-West Africa, in cen. part 400 m. N of mouth of Orange river; pop. (1970p) 61,260; commercial and transportation center; ships Persian lamb skins; clothing, canned meat, bone meal. Originally settled by Germans; captured by South African troops 1915.

Win·dom \ˈwin-dəm\. City, ⊗ of Cottonwood co., SW Minnesota, 30 m. NE of Worthington; pop. (1970c) 3922; dairy products, honey.

Windom Peak. Mountain in La Plata co., SW Colorado; 14,087 ft.

Wind River. See WIND.

Wind River Range \ˌwind-\. Range of the Rocky Mts., W cen. Wyoming, extending along the boundary bet. Sublette and Fremont cos.; highest point Gannett Peak 13,785 ft.

Wind·sor \ˈwin-zər\. 1 County in Vermont. See table at VERMONT.

2 Town, Weld co., N Colorado; pop. (1970c) 1564.

3 Town, N cen. Hartford co., N Connecticut, on Connecticut river N of Hartford; pop. (1970c) 22,502; bricks; machine shops; in tobacco and truck-farming region. Settled 1635 by colonists from Massachusetts Bay Colony; named in 1637.

4 City, Henry co., W Missouri; pop. (1970c) 2734.

5 Town, ⊗ of Bertie co., NE North Carolina, 15 m. W of Albemarle Sound; pop. (1970c) 2199; barrels, agricultural machinery; cotton, peanuts.

6 Village in Windsor town (pop. [1970c] 4158), Windsor co., E Vermont, on Connecticut river 13 m. N of Springfield; settled 1764.

7 Town, cen. Newfoundland, Canada, near Grand Falls; pop. (1971p) 6651.

8 Town, ⊗ of Hants co., cen. Nova Scotia, Canada, on inlet of Minas Basin 37 m. NW of Halifax; pop. (1971p) 3626; gypsum quarries; apples, truck crops. Former site of King's Coll., oldest (1789) English college in Canada, now part of Dalhousie Univ. in Halifax. Founded by French 1710; came under English 1750.

9 Industrial city, ⊗ of Essex co., SE Ontario, Canada, on Detroit river opp. Detroit, Michigan; pop. (1971p) 199,784, met. area pop. 255,167; transportation center; automobiles, machine tools, pharmaceuticals, chemicals; salt mining, distilling and brewing; center of agricultural region; Assumption Univ. (1857), Holy Names Coll. (1934), Holy Redeemer Coll. (1956), Canterbury Coll. (1957), Univ. of Windsor (1963), Iona Coll. (1964). Connected with Detroit by Ambassador Bridge and by vehicular and railroad tunnels. French settlement of region begun after foundation of Detroit 1701; occupied by U.S. forces during War of 1812; incorporated as village 1854, as city 1892.

10 Town, Richmond co., S Quebec, Canada, on St. Francis river 12 m. N of Sherbrooke; pop. (1971p) 6047; paper; settled c. 1800.

11 *or officially* **New Windsor.** Municipal borough, Berkshire, S England, on the Thames 20 m. W of London; pop. (1971p) 16,447; seat of Windsor Castle, principal residence of England's sovereigns since the time of William the Conqueror; St. George's Chapel, burial place of many English kings; to the S is a park ab. 1500 acres.

Windsor Heights. Town, Polk co., S cen. Iowa, W of Des Moines; pop. (1970c) 6303.

Windsor Locks. Industrial town, NE Hartford co., N Connecticut, on Connecticut river S of Suffield; pop. (1970c) 15,080; paper, hand trucks; potatoes, truck crops; settled c. 1663; incorporated 1854. Named for locks in canal (1828) to bypass rapids in Connecticut river and provide waterpower.

Wind·ward Islands \ˈwin-dwərd-\. 1 Island group, forming the S chain of the Lesser Antilles, West Indies, extending from Martinique S to 12°N; they do not include Barbados, Trinidad, and Tobago. See LEEWARD ISLANDS.

2 *or Fr.* **Îles du Vent** \ēl-dü-väⁿ\. Eastern group in the Society Is., French Polynesia, S Pacific Ocean; chief islands Tahiti and Mooréa; 467 sq. m.; pop. (1967e) 66,150.

Windward Passage. Channel bet. the E end of Cuba and the NW tip of Hispaniola.

Windy Butte \ˌwin-dē-\. Isolated peak, Fall River co., SW corner of South Dakota; 3563 ft.

Windy·gate Hill \ˌwin-dē-ˌgāt-\. Peak in the Cheviot Hills along border bet. England and Scotland; 2034 ft.

Wineland. See VINLAND.

Win·field \ˈwin-ˌfēld\. 1 Village, Du Page co., NE Illinois, 27 m. W of Chicago; pop. (1970c) 4285.

2 City, ⊗ of Cowley co., S Kansas, 13 m. N of Arkansas City; pop. (1970c) 11,385; flour, feed, dairy products; foundries, oil and gas wells; grain farms; Southwestern Coll. (1885), Saint John's Coll. (1893).

3 Town, ⊗ of Putnam co., W West Virginia; pop. (1970c) 328.

Wing·ham \ˈwiŋ-əm\. Industrial town, Huron co., SE Ontario, Canada, 24 m. ENE of Goderich; pop. (1971p) 2910; gloves, wood products; agriculture.

Win·isk \ˈwin-(ˌ)isk\. River, N cen. Ontario, Canada; 295 m. long; flows N and NW into Hudson Bay.

Wink \ˈwiŋk\. City, Winkler co., W Texas, 33 m. NNE of Pecos; pop. (1970c) 1023; oil wells.

Wink·ler \ˈwiŋk-lər\. 1 County in Texas. See table at TEXAS.

2 Town, Manitoba, Canada, 58 m. SW of Winnipeg; pop. (1971p) 2942; grains, sugar beets.

Winn \ˈwin\. Parish in Louisiana. See table at LOUISIANA.

Win·ne·ba \win-ˈā-bə\. Coastal town, S Ghana, W Africa, ab. 35 m. WSW of Accra; pop. (1970p) 30,800.

Win·ne·ba·go \ˌwin-ə-ˈbā-(ˌ)gō\. Name of counties in three states of the U.S. See tables at ILLINOIS, IOWA, WISCONSIN.

Winnebago, Lake. Lake, E Wisconsin, bounded by Winnebago, Calumet, and Fond du Lac cos.; ab. 30 m. long and 10 m. wide at its greatest extent; 215 sq. m.; the Fox river enters from the W and flows out in the N; the cities of Menasha, Oshkosh, Fond du Lac, and Neenah are on its shores.

ə abut; ᵊ kitten, Fr. table; ər further; a back; ā bake; ä cot, cart; å Fr. bac; au̇ out; ch chin; e less; ē easy; g gift
i trip; ī life; j joke; k̲ Ger. ich, Buch; ⁿ Fr. vin; ŋ sing; ō flow; ȯ flaw; œ Fr. bœuf; œ̄ Fr. feu; ȯi coin; th thin
t̲h̲ this; ü loot; u̇ foot; ue Ger. füllen; ue̅ Fr. rue; y yet; ʸ Fr. digne \dēnʸ\, nuit \nwʸē\; yü few; yu̇ furious; zh vision

Win·ne·muc·ca \ˌwin-ə-'mək-ə\. City, ⊗ of Humboldt co., NW Nevada, on Humboldt river 77 m. NE of Humboldt Lake; pop. (1970c) 3587; ships livestock.

Winnemucca Lake. Lake, NW Nevada, ab. 6 m. E of Pyramid Lake; ab. 20 m. long; often dry.

Winnepesaukee. See WINNIPESAUKEE.

Winnepesaukee, Lake. See WINNIPESAUKEE, LAKE.

Win·ner \'win-ər\. City, ⊗ of Tripp co., S South Dakota, 33 m. SW of confluence of White and Missouri rivers; pop. (1970c) 3789; diversified agriculture.

Win·ne·sheik \'win-ə-ˌshēk\. County in Iowa. See table at IOWA.

Win·net·ka \wə-'net-kə\. Residential village, Cook co., NE Illinois, 19 m. N of Chicago; pop. (1970c) 14,131.

Win·nett \'win-ət\. Town, ⊗ of Petroleum co., cen. Montana; pop. (1970c) 271; oil wells.

Winn·field \'win-ˌfēld\. City, ⊗ of Winn parish, N cen. Louisiana, 45 m. N of Alexandria; pop. (1970c) 7142; lumber, creosote; salt mines; truck farms.

Win·ni·bi·go·shish Lake \ˌwin-ə-bə-'gō-shish-\. Lake on boundary of Itasca and Cass cos., N cen. Minnesota; ab. 14 m. long.

Win·ni·peg \'win-ə-ˌpeg\. 1 River, SW Ontario and SE Manitoba, Canada; 475 m. long; outlet of Lake of the Woods flowing NW to SE part of Lake Winnipeg; near Ontario border receives tributary, English river, outlet of a number of large lakes in SW Ontario.

2 City, ✱ of Manitoba, Canada, at confluence of Assiniboine and Red rivers and 45 m. S of Lake Winnipeg; pop. (1971p) 243,208, met. area pop. 543,685; fourth largest city in Canada; major grain market and distribution center; railroad junction; flour, clothing, beer, baked goods; food processing; slaughterhouses, railroad shops; Univ. of Winnipeg (1871, univ. status 1967), Univ. of Manitoba (1877). Fur-trading post established on site 1738; Scottish colony founded by Lord Selkirk; village of Winnipeg developed late 1860's and incorporated 1873.

Winnipeg, Lake. Lake, S cen. Manitoba, Canada; 9465 sq. m.; 266 m. long; max. depth 60 ft.; receives the Red and Winnipeg rivers in the S and the Saskatchewan in the N; outlet is the Nelson; remnant of Lake Agassiz, ancient Pleistocene lake. Summer resort region; discovered by Pierre de la Vérendrye in 1733.

Win·ni·peg·o·sis, Lake \-ˌwin-ə-pə-'gō-səs\. Lake, W Manitoba, Canada, W of Lake Winnipeg; 2103 sq. m.; 141 m. long; max. depth 38 ft.; connects with Lake Manitoba.

Win·ni·pe·sau·kee *or formerly* **Win·ne·pe·sau·kee** \win-ə-pə-'sȯ-kē\. Short river, cen. New Hampshire; flows SW out of Lake Winnipesaukee to unite with the Pemigewasset river at Franklin and form the Merrimack river.

Winnipesaukee, Lake *or formerly* **Lake Winnepesaukee.** Lake, Carroll and Belknap cos., cen. New Hampshire; 71 sq. m.; 25 m. long; largest lake in New Hampshire; summer resort.

Win·nis·quam Lake \ˌwin-ə-ˌskwäm-\. Lake, Belknap co., cen. New Hampshire, W of Lake Winnipesaukee; 72 sq. m.

Winns·boro \'winz-ˌbər-ə, -ˌbə-rə\. 1 Town, ⊗ of Franklin parish, NE Louisiana, 33 m. SE of Monroe; pop. (1970c) 5349; cotton gins, oil and gas wells; livestock, yams.

2 City, ⊗ of Fairfield co., N cen. South Carolina, 27 m. N of Columbia; pop. (1970c) 3411; textiles; granite works; corn, livestock.

3 City, Franklin and Wood cos., NE Texas, 40 m. N of Tyler; pop. (1970c) 3064; lumber; oil wells; cotton, strawberries.

Wi·no·na \wə-'nō-nə\. 1 County in SE Minnesota. See table at MINNESOTA.

2 City, its ⊗, on Mississippi river 40 m. E of Rochester; pop. (1970c) 26,438; river port; flour, pharmaceuticals, cosmetics, fertilizers, metal goods; Winona State Coll. (1858), Coll. of St. Teresa (1907), St. Mary's Coll. (1912); settled 1851; incorporated 1857; formerly a major wheat and lumber-shipping center.

3 City, ⊗ of Montgomery co., N cen. Mississippi, 25 m. E of Greenwood; pop. (1970c) 5521; cottonseed oil, dairy products, automobile parts; livestock, poultry farms.

Wi·noos·ki \wə-'nü-skē\. 1 *or* **On·ion** \'ən-yən\. River, N cen. Vermont; ab. 100 m. long; rises in NE Vermont, flows S to Montpelier, turns NW into Lake Champlain in W Chittenden co.

2 Industrial city, Chittenden co., NW Vermont, on Winooski river 3 m. NE of Burlington; pop. (1970c) 7309; woolens, lime, dairy products; fruit farms; St. Michael's Coll. (1904); settled 1787.

Win·scho·ten \'vin-ˌskōt-ᵊn\. Commune, Groningen prov., NE Netherlands, 19 m. ESE of Groningen, near German border; pop. (1970e) 18,043.

Winschoten Canal. Canal, NE Netherlands; 18 m. long; joins the city of Groningen with the Dollart.

Wins·ford \'winz-fərd\. Urban district, Cheshire, NW England, on the Weaver river 23 m. SE of Liverpool; pop. (1971p) 24,791.

Wins·low \'winz-(ˌ)lō\. 1 City, Navajo co., NE Arizona, near Little Colorado river 58 m. E of Flagstaff; pop. (1970c) 8066; lumber, clothing; railroad shops; livestock; settled 1882.

2 Town, Kennebec co., SW Maine, SE suburb of Waterville; pop. (1970c) 7299.

Win·sted \'win-stəd\. Manufacturing city in town of Winchester, Connecticut (see WINCHESTER 1); pop. (1970c) 8954; lake resort; tape, felt, electrical appliances, fishing tackle; truck farms; settled 1758; incorporated as city 1917.

Win·ston \'win(t)-stən\. Name of counties in two states of the U.S. See tables at ALABAMA and MISSISSIPPI.

Winston–Sa·lem \-'sā-ləm\. Industrial city, ⊗ of Forsyth co., N cen. North Carolina, 68 m. NNE of Charlotte; pop. (1970c) 132,913; tobacco market; produces tobacco products (esp. cigarettes), hosiery, clothing, electrical equipment, furniture, textiles, dairy products. Salem Coll. (1772), Wake Forest Univ. (1834), Winston-Salem State Coll. (1892), Piedmont Bible Coll. (1945), Forsyth Technical Institute (1969). Salem founded 1766, incorporated 1856; Winston founded 1849, incorporated 1859; two towns consolidated as Winston-Salem 1913.

Win·ter·berge \'wint-ər-ˌbərg\. Range, SE Cape Province, Rep. of South Africa; highest peak 7779 ft.

Winter Garden. City, Orange co., cen. Florida penin., 12 m. W of Orlando; pop. (1970c) 5153; ships citrus fruit.

Winter Haven. City, Polk co., cen. Florida penin., 15 m. E of Lakeland; pop. (1970c) 16,136; winter resort; alcohol; molasses, cigars, sheet metal; grows, packs, and ships citrus fruit; Polk Junior Coll. (1964).

Winter Park. Resort city, Orange co., cen. Florida penin., 5 m. NE of Orlando; pop. (1970c) 21,895; fertilizer; citrus fruit; Rollins Coll. (1885); founded 1858.

Win·ter·port \'wint-ər-ˌpō(ə)rt, -ˌpȯ(ə)rt\. Town, Waldo co., S Maine, on Penobscot river 12 m. S of Bangor; pop. (1970c) 1963.

Win·ters \'wint-ərz\. City, Runnels co., W cen. Texas, 37 m. S of Abilene; pop. (1970c) 2907; oil wells.

Win·ter·set \'wint-ər-ˌset\. City, ⊗ of Madison co., S cen. Iowa, 30 m. SW of Des Moines; pop. (1970c) 3654; ships grain, livestock.

Win·ters·wijk \'vint-ərs-ˌvīk\. Commune, Gelderland prov., E Netherlands, ab. 33 m. E of Arnhem near German border; pop. (1970e) 26,230.

Win·ter·thur \'vint-ər-ˌtu̇(ə)r\. Industrial commune, Zurich canton, NE cen. Switzerland, 12 m. NE of Zurich; pop. (1970c) 92,722; important railroad junction; 16th cent. late-Gothic church; old town hall; founded 1175; passed to Hapsburg family 1264; made imperial city 1415; reverted to Hapsburgs 1442; to Zurich 1467.

Win·throp \'win(t)-thrəp\. 1 Town, Kennebec co., SW Maine, 10 m. W of Augusta; pop. (1970c) 4355; coated fabrics; potatoes.

2 Town, Suffolk co., E Massachusetts, 4 m. ENE of Boston; pop. (1970c) 20,335; residential and yachting community.

Winthrop Harbor. Village, Lake co., NE Illinois, on Lake Michigan 9 m. N of Waukegan; pop. (1970c) 4794.

Win·ton \'wint-ᵊn\. **1** Town, ⊗ of Hertford co., NE North Carolina, 43 m. W of Elizabeth City; pop. (1970c) 917. **2** Borough, Lackawanna co., NE Pennsylvania, 9 m. NE of Scranton; coal mining, silk manufactures.

Win·yah Bay \ˌwin-yȯ-\. Inlet of Atlantic Ocean, SE coast of Georgetown co., E South Carolina, receiving the Black river on the NW and the Pee Dee river on the N.

Wir·ral \'wər-əl\. Urban district, Cheshire, NW England; pop. (1971p) 26,834.

Wirt \'wərt\. County in West Virginia. See table at WEST VIRGINIA.

Wis·bech \'wiz-ˌbēch\. Municipal borough, Cambridgeshire and Isle of Ely co., E England, on the Nene 83 m. N of London; pop. (1971p) 17,002; agricultural center; seaport.

Wisby. See VISBY.

Wis·cas·set \wis-'kas-ət\. Seaport town, ⊗ of Lincoln co., S Maine; pop. (1970c) 2244.

Wisch \'vis\. Commune, Gelderland prov., E Netherlands, E of Arnhem near German border; pop. (1969e) 17,349.

Wis·con·sin \wis-'kän(t)-sən\. **1** River, cen. and SW Wisconsin; 430 m. long; rises in Lac Vieux Desert in N Vilas co., flows S through cen. Wisconsin, turns W and enters Mississippi river on boundary line bet. Crawford and Grant cos.; navigation, difficult because of shifting sandbars, is possible for small craft for ab. 200 m. See FOX 2. **2** A northern state of U.S.A., bounded on N by Lakes Superior and Michigan, on E by Lake Michigan, on S by Illinois, and on W by Iowa and Minnesota; 26th state in area, 56,154 sq. m. (land area 54,464 sq. m.), in addition to this Wisconsin has 10,062 sq. m. of water of Lake Michigan; 16th state in population, (1970c) 4,417,933; ✱ Madison; 30th state admitted to Union (1848).

Nickname: Badger State. *State flower:* Violet. *Motto:* Forward. *Rivers:* Mississippi, forming lower W boundary; St. Croix (forming section of upper W boundary), Wisconsin (see 1, above), Black, and Chippewa rivers flowing into the Mississippi; Menominee, forming NE boundary. *Lakes:* Winnebago in E; Mendota in S. *Highest point:* Timms Hill, 1952 ft., Price co. *Chief products:* Dairy products; corn, oats, potatoes; granite, dolomite; manufacturing: machinery, paper products, transportation equipment. *Chief cities:* Milwaukee, Madison, Racine, Green Bay, Kenosha. See *Table of States* at UNITED STATES. Divided into the following 72 counties (for their pronunciations, see individual entries):

NAME	LOCATION	AREA[1] (sq. m.)	POP. (1970c)	CO. SEAT
Adams	cen.	645	9,234	Friendship
Ashland	N	1,038[2]	16,743	Ashland
Barron	NW	864	33,955	Barron
Bayfield	NW	1,460[2]	11,683	Washburn
Brown	E	524	158,244	Green Bay.
Buffalo	W	711	13,743	Alma
Burnett	NW	840	9,276	Grantsburg
Calumet	E[3]	322	27,604	Chilton
Chippewa	W	1,018	47,717	Chippewa Falls
Clark	W cen.	1,221	30,361	Neillsville
Columbia	S cen.	776	40,150	Portage
Crawford	SW	568	15,252	Prairie du Chien
Dane	S	1,199	290,272	Madison
Dodge	SE cen.	889	69,004	Juneau
Door	NE	492	20,106	Sturgeon Bay
Douglas	NW corner	1,313	44,657	Superior
Dunn	W	853	29,154	Menomonie
Eau Claire	W	647	67,219	Eau Claire
Florence	NE	487	3,298	Florence
Fond du Lac	E[3]	725	84,567	Fond du Lac
Forest	NE	1,007	7,691	Crandon
Grant	SW corner	1,147	48,398	Lancaster
Green	S	585	26,714	Monroe
Green Lake	cen.	354	16,878	Green Lake
Iowa	SW	762	19,306	Dodgeville
Iron	N	747	6,533	Hurley
Jackson	W cen.	999	15,325	Black River Falls
Jefferson	SE	564	60,060	Jefferson
Juneau	cen.	774	18,455	Mauston
Kenosha	SE corner	272	117,917	Kenosha
Kewaunee	E	330	18,961	Kewaunee
La Crosse	W	451	80,468	La Crosse
Lafayette	S	643	17,456	Darlington
Langlade	NE	856	19,220	Antigo
Lincoln	N	892	23,499	Merrill
Manitowoc	E	590	82,294	Manitowoc
Marathon	cen.	1,586	97,457	Wausau
Marinette	NE	1,378	35,810	Marinette
Marquette	cen.	455	8,865	Montello
Menominee	E cen.	256	2,607	Keshena
Milwaukee	SE	237	1,054,249	Milwaukee
Monroe	W cen.	915	31,610	Sparta
Oconto	NE	1,106	25,553	Oconto
Oneida	N	1,097	24,427	Rhinelander
Outagamie	E	634	119,356	Appleton
Ozaukee	E	236	54,461	Port Washington
Pepin	W	235	7,319	Durand
Pierce	W	590	26,652	Ellsworth
Polk	NW	931	26,666	Balsam Lake
Portage	cen.	806	47,541	Stevens Point
Price	N	1,261	14,520	Phillips
Racine	SE	337	170,838	Racine
Richland	SW	583	17,079	Richland Center
Rock	S	721	131,970	Janesville
Rusk	NW	906	14,238	Ladysmith
Saint Croix	W	735	34,354	Hudson
Sauk	S cen.	841	39,057	Baraboo
Sawyer	NW	1,259	9,670	Hayward
Shawano	E cen.	919	32,650	Shawano
Sheboygan	E	505	96,660	Sheboygan
Taylor	N	975	16,958	Medford
Trempealeau	W	735	23,344	Whitehall
Vernon	SW	802	24,557	Viroqua
Vilas	N	867	10,958	Eagle River
Walworth	S	557	63,444	Elkhorn
Washburn	NW	817	10,601	Shell Lake
Washington	SE	428	63,839	West Bend
Waukesha	SE	555	231,338	Waukesha
Waupaca	E cen.	751	37,780	Waupaca
Waushara	cen.	627	14,795	Wautoma
Winnebago	E[3]	448	129,934	Oshkosh
Wood	cen.	807	65,362	Wisconsin Rapids

[1] Area = land area.
[2] Most of Apostle Is. in Ashland co., rest in Bayfield co.
[3] Upper (larger) part of Lake Winnebago in Winnebago and Calumet cos., lower part in Fond du Lac co.

History: Area visited by Jean Nicolet 1634; first permanent settlement 1717; French settlement at Green Bay 1745; French claim ceded to Great Britain 1763; recognized by Great Britain as part of United States 1783; claims relinquished by Virginia 1784, Massachusetts 1785, Connecticut 1786; part of Northwest Territory 1787 and of Indiana Territory 1800; Wisconsin Territory organized 1836; admitted to Union May 29, 1848.

Wisconsin Dells. City, Columbia and Sauk cos., S cen. Wisconsin, on Wisconsin river; pop. (1970c) 2401.

Wisconsin Rapids. City, ⊗ of Wood co., cen. Wisconsin, on Wisconsin Rapids 40 m. S of Wausau; pop. (1970c) 18,587; paper and dairy products, paint, plastics, kitchen appliances; ships cranberries; livestock.

Wise \'wīz\. **1** Name of counties in two states of the U.S. See tables at TEXAS and VIRGINIA. **2** Town, ⊗ of Wise co., SW Virginia; pop. (1970c) 2891.

Wish·ek \'wish-ik\. City, McIntosh co., S North Dakota, 63 m. SW of Jamestown; pop. (1970c) 1275.

Wish·kah \'wish-kə\ *or* **Wy·noo·che** \wī-'nü-chē\. River, W Washington; 40 m. long; flows S in Grays Harbor co. into Chehalis river near its mouth.

Wisła. See VISTULA.

Wis·ło·ka \vē-'slò-kə\. River, Rzeszów prov., SE Poland; ab. 125 m. long; flows N from Carpathian Mts. to the Vistula.

Wis·mar \'viz-(ˌ)mär\. **1** Seaport and industrial city, Rostock dist., East Germany, on **Wismar Bay** (arm of Bay of Mecklenburg) 19 m. N of Schwerin; pop. (1970e) 56,057; sugar refining, shipbuilding, commercial fishing. First mentioned 1167; chartered 1229; member of Hanseatic League 1266; to Sweden 1649; to Denmark 1675; to

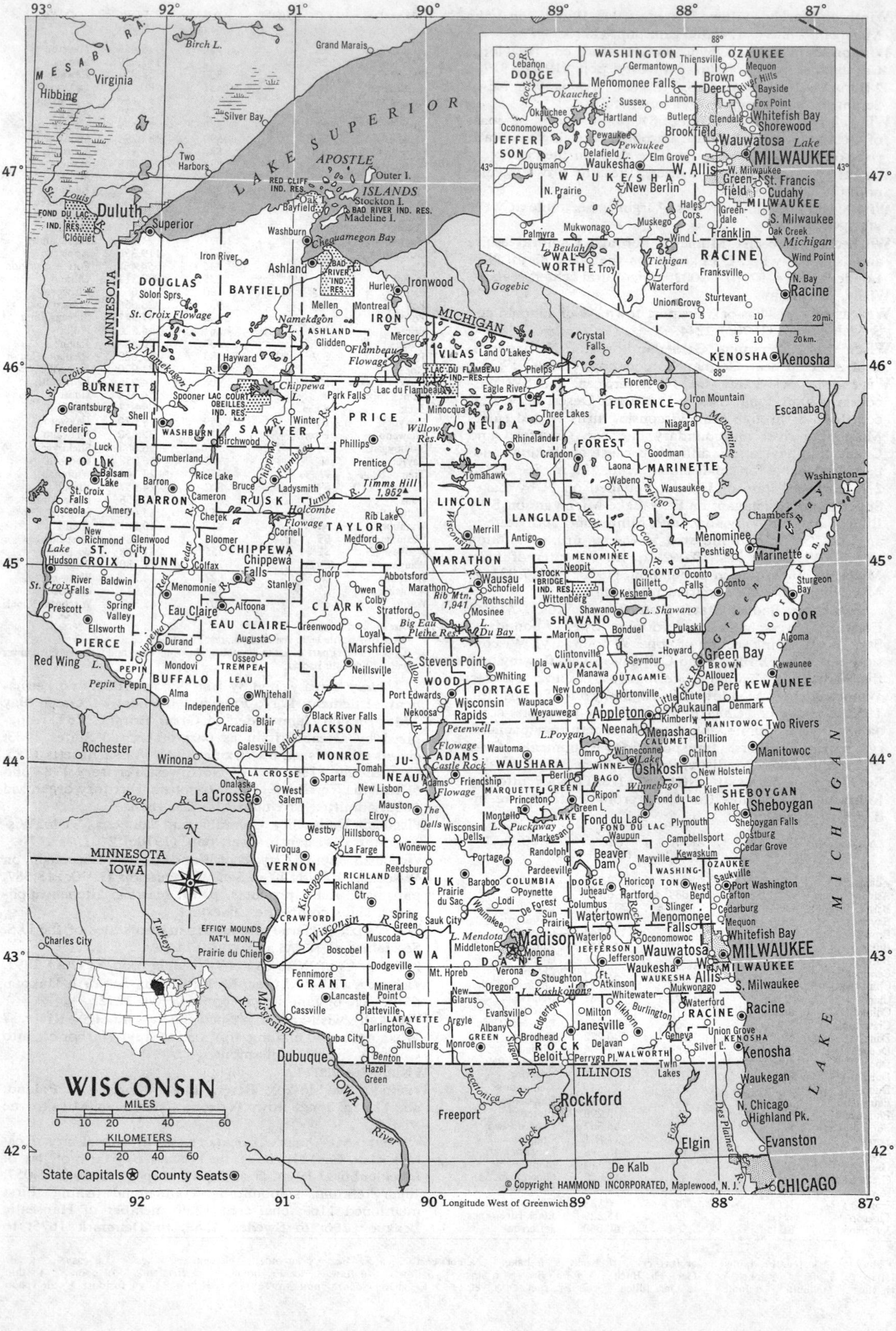
WISCONSIN
MILES
0 10 20 40 60
KILOMETERS
0 20 40 60
State Capitals
County Seats
© Copyright HAMMOND INCORPORATED, Maplewood, N. J.
Longitude West of Greenwich
93° 92° 91° 90° 89° 88° 87°
47° 46° 45° 44° 43° 42°
MESABI RA.
Hibbing
Virginia
Birch L.
Grand Marais
Silver Bay
LAKE SUPERIOR
Two Harbors
APOSTLE ISLANDS
RED CLIFF IND. RES.
Outer I.
Stockton I.
Oak I.
Bayfield
BAD RIVER IND. RES.
Madeline I.
St. Louis R.
FOND DU LAC IND. RES.
Duluth
Superior
Cloquet
Washburn
Chequamegon Bay
Iron River
Ashland
BAD RIVER IND. RES.
Hurley
Ironwood
MINNESOTA
DOUGLAS
Solon Sprs.
BAYFIELD
Mellen
Montreal
IRON
Gogebic L.
St. Croix Flowage
Namekagon L.
ASHLAND
Glidden
Mercer
MICHIGAN
Crystal Falls
Namekagon R.
Hayward
Flambeau Flowage
VILAS
Land O'Lakes
LAC DU FLAMBEAU IND. RES.
Phelps
St. Croix R.
BURNETT
Spooner
LAC COURT OREILLES IND. RES.
Chippewa L.
Park Falls
Lac du Flambeau
Eagle River
Florence
Iron Mountain
Grantsburg
Shell L.
WASHBURN
SAWYER
Winter
PRICE
Minocqua
ONEIDA
Three Lakes
FLORENCE
Escanaba
Frederic
Birchwood
Willow Res.
Rhinelander
Niagara
Menominee R.
Luck
POLK
Balsam Lake
Cumberland
Phillips
Prentice
FOREST
Crandon
Goodman
St. Croix Falls
Barron
Rice Lake
Chippewa R.
Flambeau R.
Timms Hill 1,952
Tomahawk
Laona
Wabeno
MARINETTE
Wausaukee
Washington I.
Osceola
BARRON
Amery
Cameron
Bruce
RUSK
Ladysmith
Jump R.
LINCOLN
LANGLADE
Peshtigo R.
Chetek
Holcombe Flowage
Rib Lake
Merrill
Wolf R.
Oconto R.
Chambers I.
Green Bay
New Richmond
Glenwood City
Bloomer
Cornell
TAYLOR
Medford
Antigo
MENOMINEE
Menominee
Peshtigo
Marinette
Lake
Hudson
ST. CROIX
DUNN
Cedar R.
CHIPPEWA
Chippewa Falls
Colfax
MARATHON
Wisconsin R.
STOCKBRIDGE IND. RES.
Neopit
OCONTO
Oconto Falls
Oconto
Gillett
Door Pen.
Sturgeon Bay
River Falls
Baldwin
Red R.
Menomonie
Thorp
Stanley
Abbotsford
Wausau
Schofield
Rothschild
Keshena
Wittenberg
St. Croix R.
Prescott
Spring Valley
Eau Claire
Altoona
Owen
Colby
CLARK
Marathon
Rib Mtn. 1,941
Mosinee
Shawano
L. Shawano
DOOR
Ellsworth
EAU CLAIRE
Greenwood
Stratford
Big Eau Pleine Res.
Du Bay L.
SHAWANO
Pulaski
Algoma
PIERCE
Chippewa R.
Durand
Augusta
Loyal
Marion
Bonduel
Red Wing
Pepin L.
Mondovi
Marshfield
Stevens Point
Clintonville
Seymour
Howard
Green Bay
Kewaunee
PEPIN
Pepin
BUFFALO
Osseo
TREMPEALEAU
Neillsville
Yellow R.
WOOD
Whiting
Iola
WAUPACA
Manawa
OUTAGAMIE
BROWN
Allouez
De Pere
KEWAUNEE
Alma
Whitehall
Port Edwards
PORTAGE
New London
Hortonville
Little Chute
Kaukauna
Independence
Black R.
Wisconsin Rapids
Waupaca
Weyauwega
Appleton
Kimberly
Denmark
Arcadia
Blair
Black River Falls
JACKSON
Nekoosa
Petenwell Flowage
L. Poygan
Neenah
Menasha
MANITOWOC
Two Rivers
Rochester
Galesville
Wisconsin R.
CALUMET
Brillion
Winona
MONROE
ADAMS
Castle Rock Flowage
Wautoma
Omro
Winneconne
Chilton
Manitowoc
WAUSHARA
WINNEBAGO
Lake Winnebago
Oshkosh
New Holstein
LA CROSSE
Tomah
JUNEAU
Friendship
Berlin
Onalaska
Sparta
Adams
Ripon
Kiel
SHEBOYGAN
Root R.
La Crosse
West Salem
New Lisbon
MARQUETTE
GREEN LAKE
Princeton
Green L.
N. Fond du Lac
Kohler
Sheboygan
Mauston
Elroy
The Dells
Montello
Puckaway L.
Fond du Lac
Plymouth
Sheboygan Falls
Wisconsin Dells
Markesan
FOND DU LAC
Westby
Hillsboro
Wonewoc
Waupun
Campbellsport
Oostburg
Cedar Grove
MINNESOTA
IOWA
Viroqua
La Farge
Portage
Randolph
Beaver Dam
Mayville
Kewaskum
OZAUKEE
VERNON
RICHLAND
Reedsburg
Pardeeville
WASHINGTON
Saukville
Kickapoo R.
Richland Ctr.
SAUK
Baraboo
COLUMBIA
Poynette
DODGE
Juneau
Horicon
Hartford
West Bend
Port Washington
Grafton
Turkey R.
Prairie du Sac
Waunakee
Lodi
De Forest
Columbus
Slinger
Cedarburg
CRAWFORD
Wisconsin R.
Spring Green
Sauk City
Sun Prairie
Watertown
Rock R.
Menomonee Falls
Mequon
EFFIGY MOUNDS NAT'L MON.
Muscoda
L. Mendota
Madison
Waterloo
Oconomowoc
Whitefish Bay
Charles City
Prairie du Chien
Boscobel
Middleton
Monona
JEFFERSON
Jefferson
Wauwatosa
MILWAUKEE
Dodgeville
IOWA
DANE
Waukesha
W. Allis
Fennimore
GRANT
Mt. Horeb
Verona
Stoughton
Ft. Atkinson
WAUKESHA
MILWAUKEE
S. Milwaukee
Mississippi R.
Lancaster
Mineral Point
New Glarus
Oregon
L. Koshkonong
Whitewater
Mukwonago
Waterford
Cassville
Platteville
Evansville
Edgerton
Milton
Elkhorn
Burlington
RACINE
Racine
LAFAYETTE
Darlington
Argyle
Albany
GREEN
Janesville
Union Grove
KENOSHA
Cuba City
Shullsburg
Monroe
Sugar R.
Brodhead
ROCK
Delavan
WALWORTH
L. Geneva
Silver L.
Kenosha
Dubuque
Benton
Hazel Green
Beloit
Perrygo Pl.
Twin Lakes
ILLINOIS
IOWA River
Pecatonica R.
Waukegan
Rockford
N. Chicago
Highland Pk.
Freeport
Rock R.
Fox R.
Des Plaines R.
Evanston
Elgin
De Kalb
CHICAGO
LAKE MICHIGAN
Green Bay
88°
WASHINGTON
OZAUKEE
Lebanon
Germantown
Thiensville
Mequon
DODGE
Brown Deer
River Hills
Bayside
Menomonee Falls
Okauchee L.
Sussex
Lannon
Fox Point
Okauchee
Hartland
Butler
Glendale
Whitefish Bay
Oconomowoc
Pewaukee
Pewaukee L.
Brookfield
Shorewood
JEFFERSON
Delafield
Wauwatosa
Lake
Dousman
Waukesha
Elm Grove
MILWAUKEE
43°
WAUKESHA
W. Allis
W. Milwaukee
Greenfield
St. Francis
N. Prairie
New Berlin
Cudahy
Fox R.
Hales Cors.
MILWAUKEE
Greendale
S. Milwaukee
Mukwonago
Muskego
Palmyra
Wind L.
Franklin
Oak Creek
Michigan
L. Beulah
WALWORTH
E. Troy
Tichigan L.
RACINE
Franksville
Wind Point
Waterford
N. Bay
Racine
Sturtevant
Union Grove
0 5 10 20 mi.
0 5 10 20 km.
KENOSHA
Kenosha
88°

Mecklenberg-Schwerin 1828; in World War II suffered considerable damage and occupied by British forces May 4, 1945.

2 Town, N Guyana, on Demerara river ab. 50 m. S of Georgetown.

Wis·sa·hick·on Creek \ˌwis-ə-ˈhik-ən-\. Short stream, SE Pennsylvania; flows SE through Whitemarsh to Schuylkill river in Philadelphia; furnished power for mills before the American Revolution, esp. first paper mill in America 1690.

Wis·sem·bourg \ˌvē-säⁿ-ˈbu̇(ə)r\ *or* **Weis·sen·burg** \ˈvīs-ən-ˌbərg, -ˌbu̇(ə)rg\. Town, Bas-Rhin dept., NE France, ab. 40 m. NE of Strasbourg; pop. (1962c) 5298; 13th cent. church of the Benedictine abbey founded 7th cent. by Dagobert II; place where Otfrid completed his Old High German poetical version of the life of Jesus c. 868; scene of two battles: (1) Oct. 1793 in which Count Wurmser was defeated by the French; (2) Aug. 4, 1870 in which Prussians defeated the French under MacMahon.

Wis·so·ta, Lake \-wis-ˈōt-ə\. Lake, S Chippewa co., W Wisconsin.

Wis·ter, Mount \-ˈwis-tər\. Peak, cen. Grand Teton National Park, NW Wyoming; 11,480 ft.

Wit·bank \ˈwit-ˌbaŋk\. Town, S cen. Transvaal, NE Rep. of South Africa, 60 m. E of Pretoria; pop. (1967e) 37,800; carbide; coal mines.

With·am \ˈwith-əm\. 1 River, E England; 80 m. long; rises in Rutlandshire, flows N into Lincolnshire, passing Grantham and Lincoln, turns SE and continues past Boston into the Wash.

2 Urban district, Essex, SE England; pop. (1971p) 17,306.

With·la·coo·chee \ˌwith-lə-ˈkü-chē\. 1 River, W Florida penin.; ab. 120 m. long; forms boundary bet. Levy and Citrus cos. and empties into Gulf of Mexico; outlet for Lake Tsala Apopka in Citrus co.

2 River, N Florida; ab. 110 m. long; rises in S Georgia, flows S across state border forming Madison-Hamilton co. boundary and empties into Suwannee river.

Wit·ney \ˈwit-nē\. Urban district, Oxfordshire, cen. England, ab. 60 m. WNW of London; pop. (1971p) 12,535; blankets.

Wit·tels·heim \ˈvit-ᵊlz-ˌhīm\. Commune, Haut-Rhin dept., NE France, pop. (1962c) 9782; potash mines.

Wit·ten \ˈvit-ᵊn\. Industrial city, North Rhine-Westphalia, West Germany, on Ruhr river 9 m. SW of Dortmund; pop. (1969e) 97,472; steel, glass, chemicals; chartered 1825; heavily damaged in World War II.

Wit·ten·berg \ˈvit-ᵊn-ˌbərg, -ˌbe(ə)rg\. Industrial city, Halle dist., East Germany, on the right bank of the Elbe river 19 m. E of Dessau; pop. (1970e) 47,151; railroad junction; chemicals, cellulose, rubber, machinery, soap. Starting point of the Reformation (1517) and residence of Luther; has several historical structures associated with the Reformation: 15th cent. Schlosskirche (restored 1892) to the doors of which Luther nailed his 95 theses; Stadtkirche in which Luther preached; ruins of 16th cent. Augustinian monastery in which Luther lived; home of Melanchthon; univ. (merged with Univ. of Halle 1817) at which Luther taught. First mentioned 1180; chartered 1293; residence of dukes and electors of Saxe-Wittenberg to 1547; to Prussia 1814.

Wittenberg, Mount \-ˈwit-ᵊn-ˌbərg\. Peak in the Catskill Mts., Ulster co., SE New York; 3802 ft.

Wit·ten·ber·ge \ˌvit-ᵊn-ˈbe(ə)r-gə\. Industrial city, Schwerin dist., East Germany, on Elbe river 80 m. SE of Hamburg and 78 m. NW of Berlin; pop. (1970e) 33,028; river port.

Wit·ten·heim \ˌvēt-en-ˈnem\. Commune, Haut-Rhin dept., NE France, ab. 10 m. N of Mulhouse; pop. (1968c) 10,055; potash mines.

Witt·stock \ˈwit-ˌstäk, ˈvit-ˌs(h)tȯk\. Town, Potsdam dist., East Germany, 58 m. NW of Berlin; pop. (1970e) 10,606; scene of battle Oct. 4, 1636 in which Swedes under Banér defeated imperial and Saxon forces.

Wi·tu \ˈwē-(ˌ)tü\. 1 Former sultanate, now part of Kenya, E Africa; ab. 1200 sq. m.; proclaimed German protectorate 1885, but given up to British in agreement of 1890.

2 Town, its ✱, near the mouth of the Tana river.

Wit·wa·ters·rand \ˈwit-ˌwȯt-ərz-ˌränd, -ˌwät-, -ˌrand\ *or popularly* **The Rand** \-ˈrand\. Ridge of auriferous rock, S Transvaal, NE Rep. of South Africa; ab. 62 m. long, 23 m. wide; Johannesburg located nearly at its center. Watershed for streams on N to Olifants river and on S to Vaal; exceptionally rich goldfields; gold first discovered 1886.

Wlingi \ˈvliŋ-ē\. Town, East Java prov., Indonesia, ab. 20 m. W of Malang.

Wło·cła·wek \vlȯt-ˈslä-vek\ *or Russ.* **Vlo·tslavsk** \vlət-ˈsläfsk\. Commune, Bydgoszcz prov., N cen. Poland, on Vistula river 87 m. WNW of Warsaw; pop. (1970p) 77,200; machinery, building materials, beer; 14th cent. cathedral; founded at end of 11th cent.; Russians defeated here 1914; held by Germans 1941–45.

Wło·da·wa \vlȯ-ˈdäv-ə\ *or Russ.* **Vlo·da·va** \vlə-ˈdäv-ə\. Commune, Lublin prov., E Poland, on W bank of the Bug ab. 50 m. NE of Lublin; battle Aug. 15, 1915.

Włodzimierz. See VLADIMIR-VOLYNSKI.

Wo·burn. 1 \ˈwō-bərn, ˈwü-\. City, Middlesex co., NE Massachusetts, 10 m. NNW of Boston; pop. (1970c) 37,406; chemicals, leather goods, canned foods, pharmaceuticals; incorporated as town 1642, as city 1888.

2 \ˈwü-bern\. Parish, Bedfordshire, SE cen. England; estate of duke of Bedford.

Wo·dzi·sław Śląski \vȯ-ˌjē-släf-ˈshlōⁿ-skē\. Town, Katowice prov., S Poland, ab. 30 m. SW of Katowice; pop. (1970p) 25,500.

Woer·den \ˈvu̇(ə)r-dən\. Commune, South Holland prov., SW Netherlands, just W of Utrecht; pop. (1970e) 18,448.

Woë·vre \ˈvwävrᵊ\. Plateau, E of Verdun, NE France, extending N and S parallel with the Meuse for 15 to 20 m.; scene of heavy fighting in World War I 1914–18.

Woh·len \ˈvōl-ən\. Commune, Aargau canton, Switzerland; pop. (1970c) 12,024.

Wo·kam \ˈwō-ˌkäm\. Island, N cen. Aru Is., Indonesia, N of Kobroor I.; ab. 35 m. long by 30 m. wide.

Wo·king \ˈwō-kiŋ\. Urban district, Surrey, S England, on the Wey 22 m. WSW of London; pop. (1971p) 75,771; residential suburb.

Wo·king·ham \ˈwō-kiŋ-əm\. Municipal borough, Berkshire, S England, 32 m. WSW of London; pop. (1971p) 21,058.

Wol·cott \ˈwu̇l-kət\. Town, N New Haven co., S Connecticut, NE of Waterbury; pop. (1970c) 12,495; incorp. 1796.

Wolds, The \-ˈwōldz\. Highland plain district, NE England, esp. in E Yorkshire and NE Lincolnshire, on both sides of the Humber.

Wo·le·ai \ˌwō-lē-ˈī\. Island (atoll), W Caroline Is., W Pacific Ocean, 7°21′N, 143°52′E; attacked by U.S. task force Mar. 31, 1944 and Japanese ships destroyed.

Wolf \ˈwu̇lf\. 1 River, Mississippi and Tennessee; 100 m. long; flows WNW from Benton co., Mississippi, to Mississippi river just above Memphis, Tennessee.

2 River, E Wisconsin; ab. 200 m. long; rises in N Langlade co., flows S into Lake Poygan, and then E into Fox river near Oshkosh.

Wolf Creek. River, N Texas and NW Oklahoma; ab. 110 m. long; rises in N Texas, flows E and NE into Oklahoma, joining Beaver river to form the North Canadian river.

Wolfe \ˈwu̇lf\. 1 County in Kentucky. See table at KENTUCKY.

2 County, Quebec, Canada. See table at QUEBEC.

Wolfe·boro \ˈwu̇lf-ˌbər-ə, -(ˌ)bə-rə\. Town, Carroll co., E New Hampshire, on Lake Winnipesaukee 13 m. ENE of Laconia; pop. (1970c) 3036; summer resort.

Wolfe Island. Island, NE end of Lake Ontario, Ontario, Canada; 18 m. long; divides head of St. Lawrence river, S of Kingston, but channel most used is on S or U.S. side.

Wol·fen \'vȯl-fən\. Town, Halle dist., East Germany, 17 m. NE of Halle; pop. (1970e) 26,941.

Wol·fen·büt·tel \'vȯl-fən-ˌbyüt-ᵊl\. Manufacturing city, Lower Saxony, West Germany, on Oker river S of Brunswick; pop. (1969e) 40,902; canned goods, chemicals, musical instruments; late 16th cent. town hall, 17th cent. castle, 17th cent. armory; first mentioned 1118; chartered 1540; to Brunswick 1753.

Wolf Jaws \-ˌjȯz\. Mountain in the Adirondack Mts., Essex co., NE New York; 4225 ft.

Wolf·pin Ridge \ˌwu̇lf-ˌpin-\. Ridge, Towns co., N Georgia; 4251 ft.

Wolf Point. City, ⊗ of Roosevelt co., NE Montana, on Missouri river 48 m. E of Glasgow; pop. (1970c) 3095.

Wolf River. 1 Two rivers in the United States. See WOLF.
2 *or Fr.* **Ri·vière du Loup** \rē-vyer-dᵫ-lü\. City, S Quebec, Canada. See RIVIÈRE DU LOUP 2.

Wolf Rock. Elevation, Allegany co., NW corner of Maryland; 2976 ft.

Wolfs·berg \'wu̇lfs-ˌbərg, -(ˌ)be(ə)rg\. Manufacturing commune, Carinthia, S Austria; pop. (1961c) 10,927; summer resort.

Wolfs·burg \'wu̇lfs-ˌbərg, -ˌbu̇(ə)rg\. City, Lower Saxony, West Germany, 15 m. NE of Brunswick; pop. (1969e) 88,024; automobiles (site of Volkswagen plant); founded 1938.

Wolf·ville \'wu̇lf-ˌvil\. Town, Kings co., W Nova Scotia, Canada, on Minas Basin 15 m. NW of Windsor; pop. (1971p) 2831; Acadia Univ. (1838). Center of land of Evangeline near the original settlement of Grand Pré (*q.v.*); founded by the English in 1760.

Wo·lin \'vȯ-(ˌ)lēn\ *or Ger.* **Wol·lin** \vȯ-'lēn\. 1 Island off the NW coast of Szczecin prov., NW Poland, bet. Zalew Szczeciński and the Baltic Sea; 95 sq. m.; assigned to Poland by Potsdam Conference 1945.
2 Commune, SE point of Wolin I.; pop. (1966e) 2867. See JULIN.

Wo·lin·ski National Park \vȯ-'lin(t)-skē-\. National park, NW Poland, on Wolin I.; 18 sq. m.; rare bird species; established 1960.

Wołkowysk. See VOLKOVYSK.

Wol·las·ton, Mount \-'wu̇l-ə-stən, -'wäl-\. See QUINCY 4.

Wollaston Islands. Chilean island group, S Tierra del Fuego Archipelago (*q.v.*); largest islands are Wollaston, Hermite, Grévy; includes also, at S extremity, Horn I. on which is Cape Horn.

Wollaston Lake. Lake, NE Saskatchewan, Canada; 796 sq. m.; connected through its outlet with Reindeer Lake and Churchill river.

Wollaston Peninsula. Peninsula, SW part of Victoria I., Franklin dist., Northwest Territories, N Canada; bet. Prince Albert Sound, and Dolphin and Union Strait.

Wollin. See WOLIN.

Wol·lon·gong \'wu̇l-ən-ˌgäŋ, -ˌgȯŋ\. Seaport, E New South Wales, SE Australia, on Pacific Ocean 40 m. S of Sydney; pop. (**Greater Wollongong;** 1969e) 160,630; center of Illawarra dairy and farm district.

Wolmar. See VALMIERA.

Wo·ło·min \vȯ-'lȯ-ˌmēn\. Commune, Warszawa prov., NE cen. Poland, 15 m. ENE of Warsaw; pop. (1970p) 24,000.

Wo·lu·we–Saint–Lam·bert \ˌvȯ-lə-'vā-saⁿ-läⁿ-'be(ə)r\ *or Flemish* **Sint–Lam·brechts–Woluwe** \sint-'läm-ˌbrekts-'vō-lə-və\. Commune, Brabant prov., cen. Belgium, a suburb of Brussels; pop. (1969e) 46,340.

Woluwe–Saint–Pierre \ˌvȯ-lə-ˌvā-saⁿ-'pye(ə)r\ *or Flemish* **Sint–Pie·ters–Woluwe** \sint-ˌpēt-ərs-'vōl-ü-və\. Commune, Brabant prov., cen. Belgium; pop. (1969e) 39,394.

Wol·ver·hamp·ton \'wu̇l-vər-ˌham(p)-tən\. County borough, Staffordshire, W cen. England, 12 m. NW of Birmingham; pop. (1970e) 268,847; iron and steel, motor vehicles, railroad cars, chemicals, paint, enamelware; incorporated 1848.

Wol·ver·ine Lake \ˌwu̇l-və-ˌrēn-\. Village, Oakland co., SE Michigan, 26 m. NW of Detroit; pop. (1970c) 4301.

Wol·ver·ton \'wu̇l-vər-tən\. Urban district, Buckinghamshire, SE cen. England, on the Ouse 48 m. NW of London; pop. (1971p) 13,819; railroad rolling stock.

Wo·łyń \'vȯ-ˌlin(-yə)\. 1 Region, cen. Europe. See VOLHYNIA.
2 Former Polish department; 13,780 sq. m.; now in U.S.S.R. See LUTSK.

Wom·an Bay \ˌwu̇m-ən-\. Inlet of Gulf of Alaska, E coast of Kodiak I., S Alaska, ab. 8 m. SW of Kodiak.

Womb·well \'wu̇m-(b)əl, 'wu̇m-wəl\. Urban district, West Riding, Yorkshire, N England; pop. (1971p) 17,933.

Wŏn·ju \'wən-'jü\. Town, Kangwŏn prov., South Korea, ab. 53 m. ESE of Seoul; pop. (1970e) 111,972.

Wo·no·so·bo \ˌwō-nə-'sō-(ˌ)bō\. Town, Central Java prov., Indonesia, 45 m. WNW of Magelang; pop. (1961c) 16,170.

Wŏn·san \'wən-ˌsän\ *or Jap.* **Gen·zan** \'gen-ˌsän\. City, ✱ of Kangwŏn prov., North Korea, on Sea of Japan; pop. (1967e) 300,000; engineering industries; former treaty port.

Won·se·ra·deel \'vȯn-sər-ə-ˌdā(ə)l\. Commune, Friesland prov., N Netherlands, on NE coast of IJsselmeer S of Harlingen; pop. (1970e) 11,656.

Won·thag·gi \wän-'thag-ē\. Town on coast of S Victoria, SE Australia, 65 m. SE of Melbourne; pop. (1966c) 4675.

Wood \'wu̇d\. Name of counties in four states of the U.S. See tables at OHIO, TEXAS, WEST VIRGINIA, WISCONSIN.

Wood, Mount. Peak in St. Elias Mountains, SW Yukon Territory, Canada, N of Mt. Logan; 15,885 ft.

Wood·all Mountain \ˌwu̇d-ˌȯl-\. Peak, Tishomingo co., NE Mississippi; 806 ft.; highest peak in the state.

Wood·bine \'wu̇d-ˌbīn\. 1 City, ⊗ of Camden co., SE corner of Georgia; pop. (1970c) 1002.
2 Borough, Cape May co., S New Jersey, 22 m. WSW of Atlantic City; pop. (1970c) 2625.
3 Urban community (unincorporated), Davidson co., N cen. Tennessee, SSW suburb of Nashville.

Wood·bridge \'wu̇d-(ˌ)brij\. 1 Suburban residential town, SW New Haven co., S Connecticut, NW of New Haven; pop. (1970c) 7673; incorporated 1784.
2 City, Middlesex co., cen. New Jersey, 4 m. N of Perth Amboy; pop. (1970c) 97,773; ceramics, chemicals, electronic components; settled 1665.
3 Urban district, East Suffolk, SE England, just ENE of Ipswich at head of wide inlet; pop. (1971p) 7272; residence of Edward FitzGerald and Bernard Barton.

Wood Buffalo Park. See CANADA, *National Parks.*

Wood·burn \'wu̇d-bərn\. City, Marion co., NW Oregon; pop. (1970c) 7495; canned vegetables, fertilizer, sausage; fruit, nuts.

Wood·bury \'wu̇d-ˌber-ē, -bə-rē\. 1 County in Iowa. See table at IOWA.
2 Agricultural and manufacturing town, S Litchfield co., NW Connecticut; pop. (1970c) 5869; settled 1672.
3 Residential city, ⊗ of Gloucester co., SW New Jersey, 8 m. S of Camden; pop. (1970c) 12,048; truck, dairy farms; settled c. 1665.
4 Town, ⊗ of Cannon co., cen. Tennessee; pop. (1970c) 1725; dairy products; livestock.

Wood Dale. Village, Du Page co., NE Illinois, 19 m. NW of Chicago; pop. (1970c) 8831.

Wood·ford \'wu̇d-fərd\. Counties in two states of the U.S. See tables at ILLINOIS and KENTUCKY.

Wood·haven \'wu̇d-ˌhā-vən\. City, Wayne co., SE Michigan; pop. (1970c) 3566.

Wood·lake \'wu̇d-ˌlāk\. City, Tulare co., S cen. California, 38 m. SE of Fresno; pop. (1970c) 3371; fruit and vegetable packing; diversified agriculture.

Wood·land \'wu̇d-lənd\. City, ⊗ of Yolo co., N cen. California, 15 m. WNW of Sacramento; pop. (1970c) 20,677; wine, olive oil, fertilizer, dairy products; rice, sugar beets; founded 1855.

Wood·lark \'wu̇d-ˌlärk\ *or* **Mu·rua** \'mu̇r-ə-wə\. Island in Solomon Sea, NE of SE end of New Guinea I., part of Papua New Guinea; ab. 38 m. long, 12 m. wide; ab. 400 sq. m.; pop. (1969e) 2379. Together with small island groups surrounding it, known as **Woodlark Islands** group and sometimes considered a part of the Trobriand Is. Low and hilly with good harbor; gold mining 1934–38; produces ebony. Used by Japanese as an air base 1942–43 but seized by Allied forces June 30, 1943.

Wood·lawn–Wood·moor \'wu̇d-ˌlȯn-'wu̇d-ˌmu̇(ə)r\. Urban community (unincorporated), Baltimore co., N Maryland, W of Baltimore; pop. (1970c) 28,811.

Wood–Lynne \'wu̇d-ˌlin\. Borough, Camden co., SW New Jersey, 2 m. SSE of Camden; pop. (1970c) 3101.

Wood·mere \'wu̇d-ˌmi(ə)r\. Urban community (unincorporated), Nassau co., SE New York, on Long I. SW of Hempstead; pop. (1970c) 19,831.

Wood Mountain. Peak, Hinsdale and San Juan cos., SW Colorado; 13,640 ft.

Wood·ridge \'wu̇d-(ˌ)rij\. Village, Du Page co., NE Illinois, 24 m. SW of Chicago; pop. (1970c) 11,028.

Wood–Ridge \'wu̇d-(ˌ)rij\. Residential borough, Bergen co., NE New Jersey, 7 m. SSE of Paterson; pop. (1970c) 8311; chemicals; residential.

Wood River. City, Madison co., SW Illinois, 15 m. N of East St. Louis; pop. (1970c) 13,186; plastics; oil refinery.

Wood·roffe, Mount \-'wu̇d-rəf\. Mountain in Musgrave Range, South Australia, near boundary bet. SW Northern Territory and NW South Australia; 4724 ft.

Wood·ruff \'wu̇d-rəf\. **1** County in Arkansas. See table at ARKANSAS.

2 Town, Spartanburg co., NW South Carolina, 17 m. SSW of Spartanburg; pop. (1970c) 4483.

Woods \'wu̇dz\. County in Oklahoma. See table at OKLAHOMA.

Woods, Lake of the. See LAKE OF THE WOODS.

Woods·field \'wu̇dz-(ˌ)fēld\. Village, ⊗ of Monroe co., SE Ohio, 30 m. NE of Marietta; pop. (1970c) 3239.

Woods Hole. See FALMOUTH 3.

Wood·side \'wu̇d-ˌsīd\. Town, San Mateo co., W California, 27 m. S of San Francisco; pop. (1970c) 4734.

Woodside National Historic Park. See CANADA, *National Historic Parks.*

Wood·son \'wu̇d-sən\. County in Kansas. See table at KANSAS.

Woodson Terrace. City, St. Louis co., E Missouri, NW of St. Louis; pop. (1970c) 5936.

Wood·stock \'wu̇d-ˌstäk\. **1** Town, NE Windham co., NE Connecticut, NW of Putnam; pop. (1970c) 4311; Annhurst Coll. (1941).

2 City, ⊗ of McHenry co., N Illinois, 33 m. W of Waukegan; pop. (1970c) 10,226; typewriters, dairy products; agriculture.

3 Village in Woodstock town, ⊗ of Windsor co. E Vermont, 23 m. E of Rutland; pop. (1970c) 1154 (village), 2608 (town).

4 Town, ⊗ of Shenandoah co., N Virginia, 30 m. SW of Winchester; pop. (1970c) 2338.

5 Market town, ⊗ of Carleton co., W New Brunswick, Canada, on St. John river 48 m. WNW of Fredericton; pop. (1971p) 4775; lumber; hunting resort; diversified agriculture.

6 City, ⊗ of Oxford co., SE Ontario, Canada, on Thames river 26 m. ENE of London; pop. (1971p) 25,559; rubber, cement, footwear, hosiery, veneers; dairy, fruit farms.

7 Municipal borough, Oxfordshire, cen. England, 8 m. NW of Oxford; pop. (1971p) 1940; medieval royal residence.

8 *or formerly* **Pa·pen·dorp** \'päp-ən-ˌdȯ(ə)rp\. Town, SW Cape Province, S Rep. of South Africa, E suburb of Cape Town.

Woods·town \'wu̇dz-ˌtau̇n\. Borough, Salem co., SW New Jersey, 16 m. NNW of Bridgeton; pop. (1970c) 3137; Quaker center since early 1700's.

Woods·ville \'wu̇dz-ˌvil\. Town, ⊗ of Grafton co., W New Hampshire, on Connecticut river 17 m. SW of Littleton; pop. (1970c) 1336; a section of Haverhill (*q.v.*).

Wood·ville \'wu̇d-ˌvil, -vəl\. **1** Town, ⊗ of Wilkinson co., SW corner of Mississippi; pop. (1970c) 1734; truck and livestock farms.

2 Town, ⊗ of Tyler co., E Texas; pop. (1970c) 2662.

3 Borough, E North I., New Zealand; pop. (1970e) 1520.

Wood·ward \'wu̇d-(w)ərd\. **1** County in NW Oklahoma. See table at OKLAHOMA.

2 City, its ⊗, 35 m. E of Oklahoma panhandle; pop. (1970c) 9412; meat-packing plant; grain, sorghum; U.S. Great Plains Field and Experiment Station.

Wood·way \'wu̇d-ˌwā\. Village, McLennan co., cen. Texas, 5 m. SW of Waco; pop. (1970c) 4819.

Woody Mountain \ˌwu̇d-ē-\. Peak, S cen. Coconino co., Arizona, near Flagstaff; 8064 ft.

Wool·lah·ra \wu̇-'lär-ə\. City, E New South Wales, SE Australia, E suburb of Sydney on S shore of Port Jackson; pop. (1966c) 47,326.

Woo·mera \'wu̇m-ə-rə\. Township, SE cen. South Australia, 100 m. NNW of Port Augusta; rocket range and satellite-tracking base, estab. 1945.

Woon·sock·et \wün-'säk-ət, 'wün-ˌ\. **1** Industrial city, Providence co., N Rhode Island, 13 m. NNW of Providence; pop. (1970c) 46,820; woolens and textiles, electronic components, plastics, paper, machine tools, clothing, rubber products; settled 1666; made separate town 1871; incorporated as city 1888.

2 City, ⊗ of Sanborn co., South Dakota; pop. (1970c) 852; dairy, poultry farms.

Woos·ter \'wu̇s-tər\. City, ⊗ of Wayne co., NE cen. Ohio, 27 m. W of Canton; pop. (1970c) 18,703; rubber products, pumps, truck bodies; oil and gas wells; Coll. of Wooster (1866); settled 1807.

Worces·ter \'wu̇s-tər\. **1** Counties in two states of the U.S. See tables at MARYLAND and MASSACHUSETTS.

2 City, a ⊗ of Worcester co., cen. Massachusetts, 37 m. W of Boston; pop. (1970c) 176,572; machine tools, wire, tools and dies, castings, abrasives, leather goods, textiles; Coll. of the Holy Cross (1843), Worcester Polytechnic Institute (1865), Massachusetts State Coll. (1871), Clark Univ. (1887), Becker Junior Coll. (1887), Assumption Coll. (1904), Worcester Junior Coll. (1905), Quinsigamond Community Coll. (1963). First permanent settlement made 1713; industrial development begun after opening of Blackstone canal 1828; incorporated as city 1848.

3 County, England. See WORCESTERSHIRE.

4 County borough, ⊗ of Worcestershire, W cen. England, on the Severn 25 m. SSW of Birmingham; pop. (1971p) 73,445; gloves, machine tools, porcelain, hardware; 11th–14th cent. cathedral. Battle Sept. 3, 1651 in which Charles II and his Scottish army were routed by Cromwell and Parliamentarian army.

5 Town, SW Cape Province, S Rep. of South Africa, on Bree river 60 m. ENE of Cape Town; pop. (1967e) 37,000; textiles, canned goods, wine; in agricultural region.

Worces·ter·shire \'wu̇s-tə(r)-ˌshi(ə)r, -shər\ *or* **Worcester.** County, W cen. England; area 704 sq. m.; pop. (1971p) 692,605; ⊗ Worcester; rivers Severn, Avon, Stour, Teme; wheat, oats, potatoes, barley, fruit; grazing; metallurgical, chemical, woolen, and porcelain industries; largest towns Warley, Worcester, Stourbridge, Halesowen.

Wor·dens Pond \'wər-dənz-\. Small lake, S cen. Washington co., S Rhode Island.

Wor·king·ton \'wər-kiŋ-tən\. Municipal borough, Cumberland, NW England, on Irish Sea at mouth of the Derwent

32 m. SW of Carlisle; pop. (1971p) 28,414; steel, machinery, textiles, carpets; coal mines; incorporated 1888.

Work·sop \'wərk-səp\. Urban district, Nottinghamshire, N cen. England, on the Ryton 17 m. ESE of Sheffield; pop. (1971p) 36,034; coal mines.

Wor·land \'wər-lənd\. Town, ⊗ of Washakie co., N cen. Wyoming, on Big Horn river 78 m. SW of Sheridan; pop. (1970c) 5055; sulfur deposits, oil wells; sugar beets, beans.

World's View. Height, in the Matopo Hills, S Rhodesia, S Africa, 23 m. SW of Bulawayo; burial place of Cecil Rhodes.

Wormatia. See WORMS 2.

Wor·mer·veer \ˌvȯr-mər-'ve(ə)r\. Commune, North Holland prov., W Netherlands, just N of Amsterdam; pop. (1970e) 14,804.

Worm·leys·burg \'wərm-lēz-ˌbərg\. Borough, Cumberland co., S Pennsylvania; pop. (1970c) 3192.

Worms. 1 \'vōrm(p)s\. Island, Baltic Sea. See VORMSI.

2 \'wərmz, 'vȯrm(p)s\; *anc.* **Bor·be·tom·a·gus** \ˌbȯr-bə-'täm-ə-gəs\ *or later* **Au·gus·ta Van·gi·o·num** \ȯ-ˌgəs-tə-ˌvan-jē-'ō-nəm, ə-ˌges-\ *also* **Wor·ma·tia** \wȯr-'mā-sh(ē-)ə\. City, Rhineland-Palatinate, West Germany, on the Rhine 10 m. NNW of Mannheim; pop. (1969e) 77,642; trades in wine; river port; leather, machinery, chemicals, paints, ceramics; notable 11th–14th cent. cathedral.

History: Destroyed by Huns 436 and rebuilt by Clovis I 486; episcopal see to 1806; Concordat of Worms, ending investiture controversy, concluded here 1122; free imperial city from early 13th cent.; member of Rhenish Confederation in 1255; seat of numerous imperial diets, including esp. the Diet of Worms 1521 convoked by Charles V at which Luther made his defense; destroyed by French 1689, 1792; to France by Peace of Lunéville 1801, to Hesse-Darmstadt 1815; occupied by French 1918–30; taken by Allied forces Mar. 20, 1945; severe war damage largely repaired since 1945.

Worm's Head \'wərmz-\. Cape, SW Gower Penin., off S coast of Wales.

Wors·bor·ough \'wərz-ˌbər-ə, -ˌbə-rə, -b(ə-)rə\. Urban district, West Riding, Yorkshire, N England; pop. (1971p) 15,433.

Wors·ley \'wər-slē\. Urban district, Lancashire, NW England, 6 m. WNW of Manchester; pop. (1971p) 49,573; textiles, stainless steel; coal mines.

Wor·stead \'wu̇s-təd\. Parish and village, Norfolk, E England; 14th cent. church; settled 12th cent. by Flemish weavers who manufactured wool fabric.

Worth \'wərth\. 1 Name of counties in three states of the U.S. See tables at GEORGIA, IOWA, MISSOURI.

2 Village, Cook co., NE Illinois, SW of Chicago; pop. (1970c) 11,999.

Wörth \'vərt\. Commune, Bas-Rhin dept., NE France; scene of battle Aug. 6, 1870 in which French under Marshal MacMahon were defeated by Crown Prince Frederick of Prussia; by the French called the battle of **Frösch·wil·ler** \ˌfresh-vi-'lär\.

Worth, Lake \-'wərth\. Lagoon, SE Florida, in Palm Beach co. bet. mainland and coastal island; 22 m. long.

Wör·ther See \'vər-tər-ˌzā\. Lake (*see*), largest in Carinthia, S Austria, in valley of the Drava just W of Klagenfurt; 7 ½ sq. m.; 11 m. long; max. depth 279 ft.; health resort.

Wor·thing \wər-t͟hiŋ\. Municipal borough, West Sussex, S England, on English Channel 47 m. S of London; pop. (1971p) 88,210; seaside resort and residential suburb.

Wor·thing·ton \'wər-t͟hiŋ-tən\. 1 Town, Greene co., SW Indiana, 24 m. WSW of Bloomington; pop. (1970c) 1691.

2 City, ⊗ of Nobles co., SW Minnesota, 55 m. W of Fairmont; pop. (1970c) 9916; lake resort; dairy, poultry, grain farms; Worthington State Junior Coll. (1936).

3 City, Franklin co., cen. Ohio, 9 m. N of Columbus; pop. (1970c) 15,326; Pontifical Coll. Josephinum (1888).

Worthington Peak. Mountain, NW Lincoln co., E Nevada; 8400 ft.

Wot·ho \'wät-(ˌ)hō\. Island (atoll), N cen. part of Ralik Chain, W Marshall Is., W Pacific Ocean, 10°06′N, 165°59′E; occupied by U.S. forces Mar. 1944.

Wot·je \'wät-jə\. Island (atoll), cen. part of Ratak Chain, E Marshall Is., W Pacific, 9°27′N, 170°02′E; has 65 islets; bombed by U.S. forces 1943–44 but bypassed in attack on Japan.

Wo·wo·ni \wō-'wō-nē\. Island, W Banda Sea, off SE coast of Celebes I., Indonesia, N of Butung I., at 4°08′S, 123°06′E.

Wran·gel Island \'raŋ-gəl-\ *or Russ.* **Ostrov Vran·ge·lya** \ȯ-strəf-'vraŋ-gəl-yə\. Island, Arctic Ocean, ab. 100 m. off N coast of Chukot National Okrug, Russian S.F.S.R., U.S.S.R.; ab. 2000 sq. m.; crossed by the 180th meridian; sought by Baron Wrangel 1823 but not found; discovered 1867 by Long, a U.S. whaler, and named for Wrangel by him.

Wran·gell \'raŋ-gəl\. 1 Island, SE Alaska, NE of Prince of Wales Island; 217 sq. m.

2 City, N tip of Wrangell I. and just S of mouth of Stikine river; pop. (1970c) 2029; fur market; fishing; sawmills, fish canneries, marble quarries.

Wrangell, Mount. Mountain in cen. part of Wrangell Mts., S Alaska; 14,163 ft.

Wrangell Mountains. Range, S Alaska, near Canadian border; highest peaks Mt. Bona 16,500 ft., Mt. Blackburn 16,390 ft., and Mt. Sanford 16,237 ft.

Wrath, Cape \-'rath\. Extreme NW point of Scotland, 58°37′N, 5°01′W; lighthouse.

Wray \'rā\. Town, ⊗ of Yuma co., NE Colorado, 65 m. SE of Sterling; pop. (1970c) 1953.

Wreake \'rēk\. River, Leicestershire, cen. England; 18 m. long; flows SW to the Soar.

Wreck Island \'rek-\. Island, Atlantic Ocean, E coast of Northampton co., Virginia.

Wreck Point. Cape, extreme NW coast of Cape Province, Rep. of South Africa, S of Alexander Bay.

Wreck Reef. Coral reef, South Pacific, 300 m. off E coast of Queensland, Australia, 22°13′S, 155°17′E.

Wre·kin, The \-'rē-kən\. A sugarloaf hill, an extinct volcano, in Shropshire, W England; 1335 ft.

Wren·tham \'ren-thəm\. Town, Norfolk co., E Massachusetts, 15 m. W of Brockton; pop. (1970c) 7315; settled 1669; burned during King Philip's War 1675.

Wrex·ham \'rek-səm\. Manufacturing and commercial municipal borough, Denbighshire, N Wales; pop. (1971p) 38,955; steel, chemicals, plastics, building materials; coal mines; burial place of Elihu Yale.

Wright \'rīt\. 1 Name of counties in three states of the U.S. See tables at IOWA, MINNESOTA, MISSOURI.

2 Municipality, Samar Occidental prov., W Samar, Phil., at head of an inlet of Villareal Bay ab. 9 m. E of Catbalogan; pop. (1969e) 22,400.

Wrights·town \'rīts-ˌtau̇n\. Borough, Burlington co., S cen. New Jersey, ab. 10 m. NNE of Mount Holly; pop. (1970c) 2719.

Wrights·ville \'rīts-ˌvil\. 1 City, ⊗ of Johnson co., cen. Georgia, 53 m. E of Macon; pop. (1970c) 2106; diversified agriculture.

2 Industrial borough, York co., S Pennsylvania, on Susquehanna river 12 m. ENE of York; pop. (1970c) 2668; hosiery; settled 1736.

Wrig·ley Gulf \ˌrig-lē-\. Inlet, South Pacific Ocean, E of Hobbs Coast in Marie Byrd Land, Antarctica, 74°S, 129°W; separated from Amundsen Sea by Mt. Siple.

Wro·cław \'vrȯt-ˌsläf\. 1 Province of SW Poland. See table at POLAND. Formed after 1945 from former German Lower Silesia and part of Brandenburg and at first called **Śląsk Dol·ny** \'shlōⁿsk-'dȯl-nē\.

2 *or Ger.* **Bres·lau** \'bres-ˌlau̇\. Commercial city, its ✱, on Oder (Odra) river ab. 190 m. SW of Warsaw; pop. (1970p) 523,000; railroad junction; major industrial center, producing railroad rolling stock, heavy machinery, electrical equipment, chemicals, textiles, flour, canned goods; 13th–

14th cent. cathedral (rebuilt 1945–51), three 13th cent. churches, Gothic town hall, 18th cent. palace, museums, theaters, public parks and gardens; univ. (1702, univ. status 1811), technical univ. (1945).

History: First settlement dates from 10th cent.; destroyed by Tatars 1241 and new town (chartered 1261) absorbed old town 1327; passed to Bohemia 1335 and with Bohemia to Hapsburgs 1526; passed to Prussia 1741; occupied by French 1807 (when medieval fortifications demolished) and 1813; in World War II besieged by U.S.S.R. Feb.–May 1945 and suffered heavy damage; assigned to Poland by Potsdam Conference 1945; largely rebuilt since the war.

Wrox·e·ter \'räk-sət-ər\. Village on the Severn river, Shropshire, W England, just below Shrewsbury, on the site of an ancient Roman town **Uri·co·ni·um** \ˌyu̇r-ə-'kō-nē-əm\ *or* **Vir·o·co·ni·um** \ˌvir-ə-\ of which the public baths, town hall, and market have been excavated.

Wu \'wü\. **1** River, cen. China; 700 m. long; rises in W Kweichow, flows NE, N, and NW through Szechwan into Yangtze river ab. 50 m. below Chungking; navigable for much of its course.

2 Two rivers, China. See LI.

3 River, Chekiang prov., E China; 285 m. long; rises on SW border of province and flows E to East China Sea at Wenchou.

Wu–ch'ang *or* **Wu·chang** \'wü-'chäŋ\. City, ✱ of Hupeh prov., E cen. China, part of the city of Wu-han in SE Hupeh on S bank of the Yangtze, 425 m. W of Shanghai; univ. (1913). See WU-HAN.

History: Oldest of the Han Cities, dating from several centuries B.C. as an important town; capital of kingdom of Chu 300 B.C. and of Wu 300 A.D.; important cultural center; under Yüan dynasty (1206–1368) capital of Hukwang prov. and upon establishment of Hupeh prov. continued as its capital; in 1911 was starting point of revolution against Imperial regime; occupied by Japanese 1938–45; fell to Communists 1949.

Wu–chou \'wü-'jō\ *or formerly* **Tsang·wu** \'tsäŋ-'wü\. City, E Kwangsi Chuang, SE China, on N bank of Hsi river at confluence with the Kuei, 130 m. W of Canton (220 m. by river); pop. (1970e) 150,000; on border of W Kwangtung and distributing center for Kwangsi Chuang and Kweichow for goods from Canton; situated in Hsi river gorge and at times subject to disastrous floods when water rises 50 to 60 ft. Made treaty port 1897; important U.S. air base in World War II, which, because of Japanese advance in S China, was destroyed by U.S. Air Force Sept. 22, 1944.

Wu–han *or* **Wu·han** \'wü-'hän\. Tri-city conurbation, SE Hupeh prov., E cen. China, at the junction of the Han with the Yangtze; pop. (1970e) 4,250,000; the principal industrial, commercial, and transportation center of central China; ships tea, cotton, silk, hides, tung oil, timber; steel plants, textile, rice, and oil mills, soap factories, distilleries. Formed 1950 by the consolidation under a single administration of the so-called Han Cities—Hankow, Han-yang, and Wu-ch'ang (*qq.v.* for historical data).

Wu–hsi *or* **Wu·sih** \'wü-'shē\. City, S Kiangsu prov., E China, on Grand Canal 70 m. WNW of Shanghai; pop. (1970e) 900,000; intersected by many canals.

Wuhsien. See SU-CHOU.

Wu–hsing \'wü-'shiŋ\ *or* **Wu·hing** \-'hiŋ\ *or formerly* **Hu·chow** \'hü-'jō\. City, N Chekiang prov., E China, 40 m. N of Hangchow.

Wuhu. See WU-NA-MU.

Wu·lar Lake \ˌwu̇l-ər-\. Lake in course of the Jhelum, Jammu and Kashmir, N India, 25 m. NW of Srinagar; ab. 10 m. long by 12 m. wide; largest natural fresh-water body in India.

Wülf·rath \'vu̇l-ˌfrät\. Industrial city, North Rhine-Westphalia, West Germany, NE suburb of Düsseldorf; pop. (1969e) 23,157; textiles, leather, iron goods.

Wul·sten Peak \ˌwu̇l-stən-\. Mountain, Custer co., S cen. Colorado; 13,659 ft.

Wu–lu–k'o–mu–shih \ˌwü-lə-ˌkō-mə-'shē\ *or* **Ulugh Muztagh** \ˌü-lə-məz-'tä(g)\. Mountain peak, W China, highest in Kunlun Shan, on border bet. S Sinkiang Uighur, and N Tibet, 36°25'N, 87°25'E; 25,348 ft.

Wu–lu–mu–ch'i. See URUMCHI.

Wu–na–mu \'wü-'nä-'mü\ *or* **Wu·hu** \'wü-'hü\. City, E Anhwei, E China, on right bank of the Yangtze 50 m. SSW of Nanking and 260 m. by river above Shanghai; pop. (1970e) 300,000; connected by canals with neighboring towns; former treaty port; opened to foreign trade 1877.

Wu·pat·ki National Monument \wu̇-'pat-kē-\. See UNITED STATES, *National Monuments.*

Wup·per \'vu̇p-ər\. River, S edge of the Ruhrgebiet, West Germany; ab. 65 m. long; with many windings flows generally W and SW past Wuppertal to the Rhine just N of Cologne.

Wup·per·tal \'vu̇p-ər-ˌtäl\. Industrial city, North Rhine-Westphalia, West Germany, on Wupper river in Ruhr valley 16 m. ENE of Düsseldorf; pop. (1969e) 413,042; major center of rubber and pharmaceutical industries; also produces motor vehicles, machine tools, electrical equipment, textiles; brewing, printing and publishing.

Würmer See *or* **Würmsee.** See STARNBERG, LAKE OF.

Wür·se·len \'vu̇r-zə-lən\. Industrial city, North Rhine-Westphalia, West Germany, N suburb of Aachen; pop. (1969e) 20,164; coal mining.

Würt·tem·berg \'wərt-əm-ˌbərg, 'wu̇rt-; 'virt-əm-ˌbe(ə)rg\. Former German state, now part of Baden-Württemberg, West Germany; 7530 sq. m.; ✱ Stuttgart.

History: Originally inhabited by Celts; later occupied successively by Suevi, Romans, Alamanni; became part of duchy of Swabia; ruled by counts 11th–15th cents.; became duchy 1495; suffered in wars of 17th and 18th cents.; became electorate 1803, kingdom 1806; constitutional monarchy 1819–1918; republic 1918–34; lost sovereignty to Reich 1934; in World War II overrun by Allies Apr.–May 1945; made part of Baden-Württemberg 1952. See BADEN-WÜRTTEMBERG.

Würz·burg \'wərts-ˌbərg, 'wu̇rts-, 'virts-ˌbu̇(ə)rg\. Industrial city, Bavaria, West Germany, on Main river 60 m. ESE of Frankfurt am Main; pop. (1969e) 120,145; ships wine; machinery, railroad equipment, tobacco products, beer, musical instruments, bricks, chocolate; 11th–12th cent. Romanesque cathedral, former episcopal castle, 14th cent. chapel, 15th cent. bridge, 18th cent. palace; univ. (1582). Bishopric established here 742 A.D.; bishops gained secular authority by 12th cent.; bishopric secularized 1801 (revived 1817); to Bavaria 1815; heavily damaged in World War II but largely restored by 1960's.

Wur·zen \'vu̇rt-sən\. City, Leipzig dist., East Germany, on Mulde river 16 m. E of Leipzig; pop. (1970e) 24,164; agricultural machinery, carpets, furniture; 12th cent. cathedral (remodeled 1932), 15th cent. episcopal palace. First mentioned 961 A.D.

Wusih. See WU-HSI.

Wu·ster·hau·sen \ˌvü-stər-'hau̇z-ᵊn\. Town, Potsdam dist., East Germany, on a tributary of the Havel river 50 m. NW of West Berlin; treaty signed here 1726 bet. Austria and Prussia.

Wu–t'ai Shan *or* **Wu Tai Shan** \'wü-'tī-'shän\. Mountain, NE Shansi prov., NE China, ab. 100 m. N of Tai-yüan; 9261 ft.; one of the four mountains of China sacred to Buddhism; formerly visited by many pilgrims. Its top and slopes covered with temples, monasteries, lamaseries—some said to date back to 1st cent. A.D.

Wu·ti·vi, Mount \-wu̇-ˈtē-vē\. Mountain, N Liberia, W Africa; 4528 ft.; highest peak in Liberia.

Wutsin. See CH'ANG-CHOU.

Wy·a·lu·sing \ˌwī-ə-ˈlü-siŋ\. Town, NW Grant co., SW Wisconsin, on the Mississippi river; pop. (1970c) 396; nearby is Elephant Mound (*q.v.*).

Wy·an·dot \ˈwī-ən-ˌdät, ˈwīn-ˌdät\. County in Ohio. See table at OHIO.

Wy·an·dotte \ˈwī-ən-ˌdät, ˈwīn-ˌdät\. **1** County in Kansas. See table at KANSAS.

2 City, Wayne co., SE Michigan, on Detroit river 11 m. SW of Detroit; pop. (1970c) 41,061; chemicals, magnesium, pharmaceuticals, paints, cement, hardware, detergents; shipyards, large salt mines; settled 1820; first Bessemer steel plant in U.S. established here 1864; incorporated as city 1867.

Wyck·off \ˈwī-ˌkȯf\. Town, Bergen co., NE corner of New Jersey, 7 m. N of Paterson; pop. (1970c) 16,025.

Wye \ˈwī\. **1** River, E Wales and W England; 130 m. long; rises in Montgomeryshire, cen. Wales, flows SE across English border W of Hereford, and continues S into the Severn estuary 2 m. S of Chepstow; the ruins of Tintern Abbey are on its banks a few miles N of Chepstow.

2 Small stream, tributary of the Thames, Buckinghamshire, SE cen. England.

3 River, Derbyshire, N cen. England; 20 m. long; flows E to the Derwent.

Wy·lie \ˈwī-lē\. City, Collin co., NE Texas, SE of McKinney; pop. (1970c) 2675; onions, pecans.

Wy·man Dam \ˌwī-mən-\. Dam across Upper Kennebec river, cen. Maine, NW of Bingham; height 263 ft.; completed 1930; impounds water for waterpower, forming **Wyman Lake.**

Wymbritseradeel. See WIJMBRITSERADEEL.

Wy·more \ˈwī-ˌmō(ə)r, -ˌmȯ(ə)r\. City, Gage co., SE Nebraska, 12 m. S of Beatrice; pop. (1970c) 1784; flour.

Wyncoops Bay. See PELABUHAN BAY.

Wynd·ham \ˈwin-dəm\. Town, NE Western Australia, near mouth of the Ord river; has a port; meat-packing industry.

Wynne \ˈwin\. City, ⊗ of Cross co., E Arkansas, 46 m. W of Memphis, Tennessee; pop. (1970c) 6696; cotton gins; ships fruit; peaches, cucumbers.

Wyn·ne·wood \ˈwin-i-ˌwu̇d\. City, Garvin co., S cen. Oklahoma, on Washita river 33 m. N of Ardmore; pop. (1970c) 2374; oil refinery; cotton, fruit.

Wynooche. See WISHKAH.

Wyn·yard \ˈwin-yərd\ *or formerly* **Ta·ble Cape** \ˈtā-bəl-\. Town, NW coast of Tasmania, Australia, 12 m. W of Burnie; pop. (1970e) 10,680; agricultural center and tourist resort.

Wy·o·ming \wī-ˈō-miŋ\. **1** A western state of U.S.A., bounded on N by Montana, on E by South Dakota and Nebraska, on S by Colorado and Utah, and on W by Utah and Idaho; 9th state in area, 97,914 sq. m. (land area 97,281 sq. m.); 49th state in population, (1970c) 332,416; ✱ Cheyenne; 44th state admitted to Union (1890).

Nickname: Equality State. *State flower:* Indian paintbrush. *Motto:* Equal Rights. *Rivers:* Green, with its tributaries, draining SW corner of state and flowing S across border into Utah; Bighorn, flowing from cen. region N into Montana; Yellowstone, rising in NW region and flowing N into Montana; Powder, flowing from cen. region E of the Bighorn, N into Montana; North Platte, flowing from S section N and then SW across border into Nebraska, receiving waters of the Laramie near the border; Snake, rising in NW corner of state and flowing S then NW across border into Idaho. *Highest point:* Gannett Peak, 13,785 ft., Fremont co. *Chief products:* Sugar beets, beans, barley; livestock; oil, natural gas, uranium; manufacturing: oil refining, food processing; tourism. *Chief cities:* Cheyenne, Casper, Laramie, Rock Springs. See *Table of States* at UNITED STATES. Divided into the following 23 counties (for pronunciation of their names, see their individual entries):

NAME	LOCATION	AREA[1] (sq. m.)	POP. (1970c)	CO. SEAT
Albany	SE	4,248	26,431	Laramie
Big Horn	N	3,177	10,202	Basin
Campbell	NE	4,756	12,957	Gillette
Carbon	S	7,905	13,354	Rawlins
Converse	E	4,282	5.938	Douglas
Crook	NE corner	2,882	4,535	Sundance
Fremont	cen.	9,196	28,352	Lander
Goshen	SE	2,228	10,885	Torrington
Hot Springs	NW cen.	2,122	4,952	Thermopolis
Johnson	N	4,175	5,587	Buffalo
Laramie	SE corner	2,703	56,360	Cheyenne
Lincoln	SW	4,098	8,640	Kemmerer
Natrona	cen.	5,342	51,264	Casper
Niobrara	E	2,614	2,924	Lusk
Park[2]	NW	6,958	17,752	Cody
Platte	SE	2,086	6,486	Wheatland
Sheridan	N	2,532	17,852	Sheridan
Sublette	W	4,851	3,755	Pinedale
Sweetwater	SW	10,473	18,391	Green River
Teton[3]	NW	3,999	4,823	Jackson
Uinta	SW corner	2,086	7,100	Evanston
Washakie	N cen.	2,262	7,569	Worland
Weston	NE	2,407	6,307	Newcastle

[1]Area = land area.
[2]Main part of Yellowstone National Park (its area is included in Park and Teton cos.) is within Wyoming state boundaries (2930.8 sq. m.), with adjacent strips in Montana (268.9 sq. m.) and Idaho (57.6 sq. m.). Total area with inland waters 3419 sq. m.
[3]Contains Grand Teton National Park in W and NW part, also part of Yellowstone National Park.

History: Originally a part of Louisiana region claimed by France; greater part acquired from France by United States under Louisiana Purchase 1803; part of region under joint British-American occupation 1818–46; Great Britain relinquished claim 1846 and Texas transferred its claim to United States 1850; Wyoming Territory organized 1868; adopted women's suffrage, first instance in United States, 1868; admitted to Union July 10, 1890; Mrs. Nellie Tayloe Ross governor 1925–27, first woman governor of a U.S. state.

2 Name of counties in three states of the U.S. See tables at NEW YORK, PENNSYLVANIA, WEST VIRGINIA.

3 City, Kent co., W Michigan, SW of Grand Rapids; pop. (1970c) 56,650; residential.

4 City, Hamilton co., SW corner of Ohio, 8 m. N of Cincinnati; pop. (1970c) 9089.

5 Borough, Luzerne co., E Pennsylvania, in Wyoming Valley on Susquehanna river 6 m. NNE of Wilkes-Barre; pop. (1970c) 4195; coal mines. See WYOMING VALLEY.

Wyoming Mountain. Ridge, Luzerne co., E Pennsylvania, extending along SE bank of Susquehanna river and bordering Wyoming Valley; ab. 18 m. long.

Wyoming Peak. Mountain, N Lincoln co., W Wyoming, at S end of Wyoming Range; 11,418 ft.

Wyoming Range. Range, W Wyoming, extending along boundary bet. Sublette and N Lincoln cos.

Wyoming Valley. Valley, Luzerne co., E Pennsylvania, along Susquehanna river; ab. 20 m. long, 3 m. wide; noted for scenery; old Forty Fort, near borough of Wyoming, was scene of an Indian and British attack on the settlers, the "Wyoming Massacre," July 3, 1778. Valley was settled from Connecticut and from 1753 to 1800 was subject of controversy bet. Connecticut and Pennsylvania.

Wy·o·mis·sing \ˌwī-ō-ˈmis-iŋ\. Borough, Berks co., SE Pennsylvania, 3 m. W of Reading; pop. (1970c) 7136; hosiery, building materials.

Wysz·ków \ˈvish-ˌküf\. Commune, Warszawa prov., NE cen. Poland, on Bug river 33 m. NE of Warsaw; pop. (1968e) 11,000.

Wythe \ˈwith\. County in Virginia. See table at VIRGINIA.

Wythe·ville \ˈwith-ˌvil, -vəl\. Town, ⊗ of Wythe co., SW Virginia, 19 m. WSW of Pulaski; pop. (1970c) 6069; clothing, lumber; meat-packing plant; grain, livestock farms.

Wyt·schae·te \ˈvit-ˌskät-ə\. Village in West Flanders prov., NW Belgium, S of Ieper (Ypres); scene of battles during 1914, 1917, and 1918, esp. as phase of the battle of Messines Ridge June 7, 1917.

Wyvis, Ben. See BEN WYVIS.

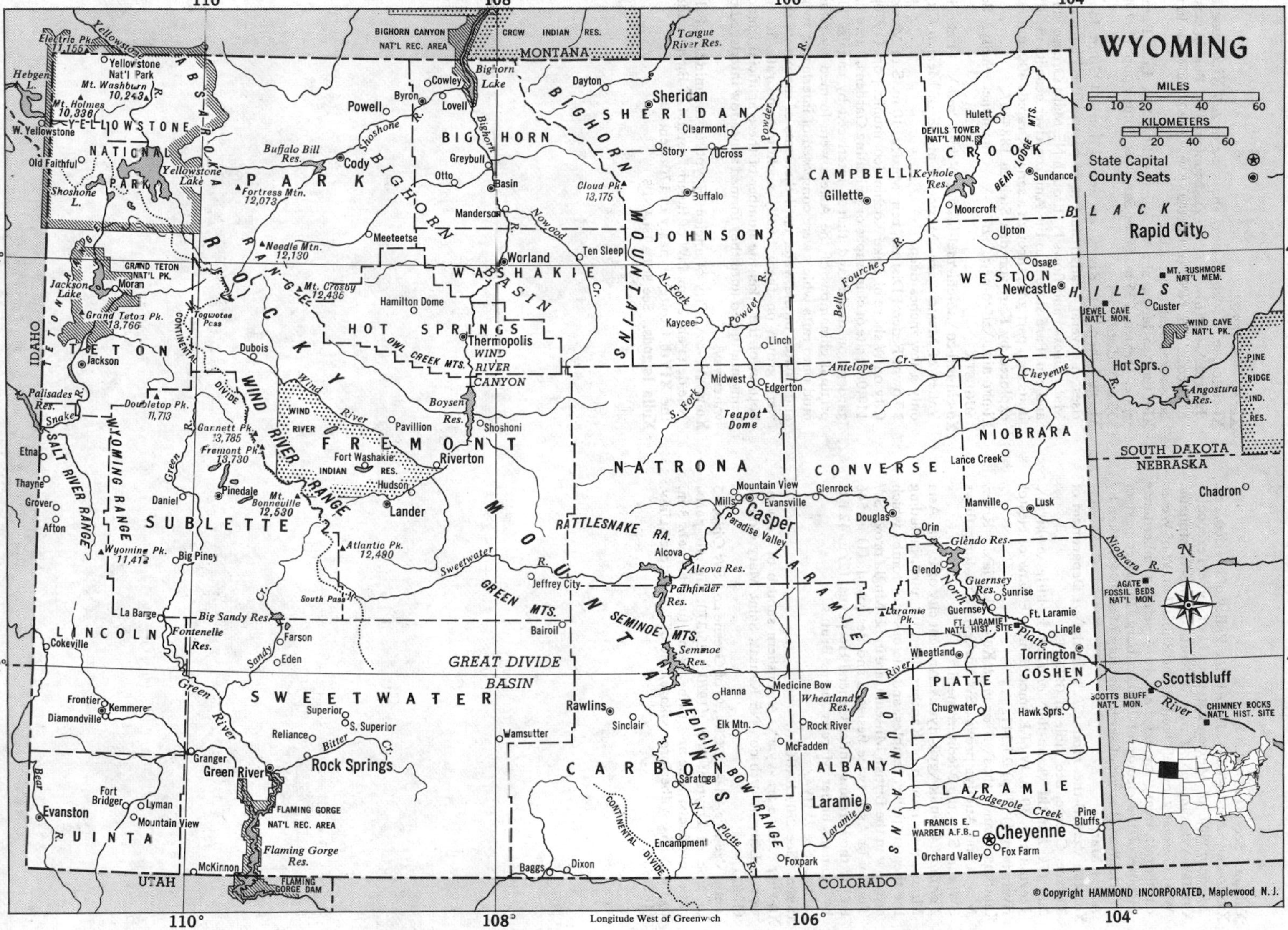
WYOMING
MILES
0 10 20 40 60
KILOMETERS
0 20 40 60
State Capital
County Seats
110°
108°
106°
104°
44°
42°
Longitude West of Greenwich
© Copyright HAMMOND INCORPORATED, Maplewood N. J.
MONTANA
IDAHO
UTAH
COLORADO
SOUTH DAKOTA
NEBRASKA
BIGHORN CANYON NAT'L REC. AREA
CROW INDIAN RES.
YELLOWSTONE NATIONAL PARK
Yellowstone Nat'l Park
Mt. Washburn 10,243
Mt. Holmes 10,336
Electric Pk. 11,155
Hebgen L.
W. Yellowstone
Old Faithful
Yellowstone Lake
Shoshone L.
ABSAROKA
GRAND TETON NAT'L PK.
Moran
Jackson Lake
Grand Teton Pk. 13,766
TETON RA.
TETON
Jackson
Togwotee Pass
CONTINENTAL DIVIDE
Palisades Res.
Snake
Etna
Thayne
Grover
Afton
SALT RIVER RANGE
WYOMING RANGE
Wyoming Pk. 11,412
Doubletop Pk. 11,713
SUBLETTE
Daniel
Pinedale
Big Piney
La Barge
LINCOLN
Cokeville
Fontenelle Res.
Frontier
Kemmerer
Diamondville
Fort Bridger
Lyman
Mountain View
Evanston
UINTA
Bear R.
Green R.
Granger
Green River
FLAMING GORGE NAT'L REC. AREA
Flaming Gorge Res.
FLAMING GORGE DAM
McKinnon
Rock Springs
Bitter Cr.
Reliance
Superior
S. Superior
SWEETWATER
Big Sandy Res.
Farson
Eden
Sandy
South Pass
Atlantic Pk. 12,490
Sweetwater R.
WIND RIVER RANGE
Garnett Pk. 13,785
Fremont Pk. 13,730
Mt. Bonneville 12,530
WIND RIVER INDIAN RES.
Fort Washakie
Hudson
Lander
Riverton
Pavillion
Shoshoni
Boysen Res.
Wind River
FREMONT
Dubois
ROCKY MOUNTAINS
PARK
Powell
Cody
Buffalo Bill Res.
Shoshone R.
Fortress Mtn. 12,073
Needle Mtn. 12,130
Mt. Crosby 12,435
Meeteetse
BIGHORN
Byron
Cowley
Lovell
Bighorn Lake
BIG HORN
Greybull
Otto
Basin
Manderson
Bighorn R.
Nowood R.
Worland
WASHAKIE
BIGHORN BASIN
Hamilton Dome
HOT SPRINGS
OWL CREEK MTS.
Thermopolis
WIND RIVER CANYON
Ten Sleep
Cloud Pk. 13,175
BIGHORN MOUNTAINS
Dayton
Sheridan
SHERIDAN
Tongue River Res.
Clearmont
Story
Ucross
Buffalo
JOHNSON
Kaycee
N. Fork
Powder R.
S. Fork
Midwest
Edgerton
Linch
Teapot Dome
NATRONA
Mountain View
Mills
Evansville
Casper
Paradise Valley
RATTLESNAKE RA.
Alcova
Alcova Res.
Pathfinder Res.
Jeffrey City
GREEN MTS.
Bairoil
SEMINOE MTS.
Seminoe Res.
GREAT DIVIDE BASIN
Rawlins
Sinclair
Wamsutter
CARBON
Hanna
Medicine Bow
Elk Mtn.
Saratoga
MEDICINE BOW RANGE
Encampment
Baggs
Dixon
Foxpark
McFadden
Rock River
Wheatland Res.
ALBANY
Laramie
Laramie R.
LARAMIE MOUNTAINS
Laramie Pk.
CONVERSE
Glenrock
Douglas
Orin
Glendo Res.
Glendo
North Platte R.
Guernsey Res.
Guernsey
Sunrise
FT. LARAMIE NAT'L HIST. SITE
Ft. Laramie
Lingle
Torrington
GOSHEN
PLATTE
Wheatland
Chugwater
Hawk Sprs.
LARAMIE
Lodgepole Creek
Pine Bluffs
FRANCIS E. WARREN A.F.B.
Cheyenne
Fox Farm
Orchard Valley
CAMPBELL
Gillette
Belle Fourche R.
Antelope Cr.
Cheyenne R.
CROOK
Hulett
DEVILS TOWER NAT'L MON.
BEAR LODGE MTS.
Keyhole Res.
Sundance
Moorcroft
Upton
Osage
WESTON
Newcastle
NIOBRARA
Lance Creek
Manville
Lusk
Niobrara R.
BLACK HILLS
Rapid City
MT. RUSHMORE NAT'L MEM.
JEWEL CAVE NAT'L MON.
Custer
WIND CAVE NAT'L PK.
Hot Sprs.
Angostura Res.
PINE RIDGE IND. RES.
Chadron
AGATE FOSSIL BEDS NAT'L MON.
N
Scottsbluff
SCOTTS BLUFF NAT'L MON.
CHIMNEY ROCKS NAT'L HIST. SITE
River

X

Xalapa. See JALAPA 3.

Xal·to·cán \ˌhäl-tə-'kän\. Lake in the Valley of Mexico, cen. Mexico, NNE of Mexico City and N of Lake Texcoco.

Xan·ten \'(k)sänt-ᵊn\. Town, W North Rhine-Westphalia, West Germany, on left bank of the Rhine 7 m. W of Wesel; cathedral; treaty signed here 1614 settling inheritance dispute of the elector of Brandenburg. In latter part of World War II scene of severe fighting Mar. 1945; taken by Allies Mar. 9.

Xan·the \'zan(t)-thē; *mod. Gk.* 'ksän-thē\. **1** Department of Thrace, Greece. See table at GREECE.

2 *or Gk.* **Xán·thi** \'ksän-thē\ *or Turk.* **Es·ki·je** \es-ki-'jä\. Town, its ✱, 30 m. W of Komotinē, near E bank of Nestos river; pop. (1971p) 25,341.

Xan·thus \'zan(t)-thəs\. **1** *or mod.* **Ko·ca** \kō-'jä\. River, Muğla and Antalya provs., SW Turkey; 78 m. long; flows SW and S to the Mediterranean.

2 *or mod.* **Gü·nük** \gyü-'nyük\. Ancient city of Lycia, Asia Minor, near mouth of Xanthus river; its ruins, including the theater, pillar, temples, and the bases of tombs which are now in the British Museum, are in SE Muğla prov., SW Turkey in Asia; twice besieged and destroyed: (1) in 546 B.C. by the Persians under General Harpagus; (2) in 42 B.C. by Romans under Marcus Junius Brutus.

Xátiva. See JÁTIVA.

Xauen. See CHECHAOUÈN.

Xa·vi·er \'zā-vē-ər, -vyər\. A southern suburb of Leavenworth, Leavenworth co., NE Kansas; Saint Mary College (1882).

Xe·nia \'zē-nyə, -nē-ə\. City, ⊗ of Greene co., SW Ohio, 15 m. ESE of Dayton; pop. (1970c) 25,373; aircraft parts, paper products, rope and twine, paint, furniture; ab. 3 m. to the NE is Wilberforce village, site of Wilberforce Univ. (1856).

Xeres. See JEREZ.

Xi·co·te·pec \sə-'kō-tə-ˌpek, shə-\ *or in full* **Xicotepec de Juá·rez** \-də-'(h)wä-res, -rez\. Municipality, Puebla state, Mexico, 90 m. NNE of Puebla; pop. (1970p) 27,372; lumber; corn, beans, tobacco.

Xi·li·tla \sə-'lēt-lə, shə-\. Municipality, San Luis Potosí state, Mexico, 135 m. SE of San Luis Potosí; pop. (1970p) 33,685; distilleries.

Xin·gu \shēŋ-'gü\. River, cen. and N Brazil; 1230 m. long; rises in several headstreams in N part of the Plateau of Mato Grosso and flows N through NE Mato Grosso state and cen. Pará state into the Amazon river near its mouth; in its cen. part goes through a series of rapids 400 m. long; explored by Karl von den Steinen 1884–87.

Xi·pho·nia \zif-'ō-nē-ə, zī-'fō-\. Commune, Sicily. See AUGUSTA.

Xo·chi·mil·co \ˌsō-chi-'mēl-(ˌ)kō, ˌsō-shi-, -'mil-\. **1** Lake in Valley of Mexico, cen. Mexico, 7 m. SE of Mexico City; only a few inches deep.

2 Town, Federal District, cen. Mexico, 10 m. S of Mexico City on W shore of Lake Xochimilco; munic. pop. (1970p) 117,083; site of chinampas or "Floating Gardens," actually gardens on made land that is interlaced by canals. The original chinampas of the Aztecs were formed by piling mud onto rafts which were composed of interlacing twigs and floated in the water until the roots of the plants that were grown on them finally anchored the rafts to the bottom of the lake, the number of these artificial islands being multiplied until they formed a meadow interlaced by waterways.

Xo·ïs \'zō-əs\. City of ancient Egypt, in the middle of the Nile delta ab. 20 m. NW of Busiris; capital of Egypt under the XIVth (Xoite) dynasty c. 17th cent. B.C.

Xulla Islands. See SULA ISLANDS.

Y. See IJ.

Ya–an *or* **Ya·an** \'yä-'än\ *or formerly* **Ya·chow** \'yä-'jō\. Town, Szechwan, S China, on tributary of Min river 70 m. SW of Ch'eng-tu; pop. (1970e) 100,000; center for tea trade.

Yablonitski, Pereval. See JABLONICA PASS.

Ya·blo·no·vy Mountains \ˌyäb-lə-nə-'vē-\ *or formerly* **Ya·blo·noi Mountains** \ˌyäb-lə-'nī-\. Range, U.S.S.R., along border bet. W Chita Oblast, Russian S.F.S.R., and E Buryat A.S.S.R.; highest peak Sokhondo 7188 ft., at its S end near border with Mongolian People's Republic; forms watershed for rivers flowing to Arctic and Pacific Oceans.

Ya·bu·coa \ˌyäb-ə-'kō-ə\. Town and municipality, SE Puerto Rico; town is 16 m. ENE of Guayama; pop. (1970p) 5071 (town), 29,947 (munic.).

Yachow. See YA-AN.

Ya·cui·ba \yä-'kwēb-ə\. Town, Tarija dept., S Bolivia, on Argentine frontier; port of entry and trading center for Chaco region.

Ya·cu·ma \yä-'kü-mə\. River, NW Bolivia; ab. 200 m. long; flows NE into Mamoré river.

Yad·kin \'yad-kən\. **1** River, cen. North Carolina; 202 m. long; rises in Watauga co., flows E, then S, and joins Uharie river to form Pee Dee river (*q.v.*). See also NARROWS DAM and HIGH ROCK LAKE.

2 County in North Carolina. See table at NORTH CAROLINA.

Yadkin Dam. See NARROWS DAM.

Yad·kin·ville \'yad-kən-ˌvil\. Town, ⊗ of Yadkin co., NW cen. North Carolina; pop. (1970c) 2232.

Ya·e·ju Hill \ˌyī-(ˌ)jü-\. Elevation, S Okinawa, Ryukyu Is., S Japan; highest point in S Okinawa, ab. 1840 ft.; captured by U.S. forces June 14, 1945.

Ya·e·ya·ma Islands \yī-ˌyäm-ə-\. Group of islands, S Ryukyu Is., part of Sakishima Is.; 247 sq. m.; chief islands Iriomote and Ishigaki.

Yafa *or* **Yafo.** See JAFFA.

Ya·gua·chi \yä-'gwäch-e\. Town, Guayas prov., W Ecuador; just ENE of Guayaquil; pop. (1962c) 2996.

Ya·gua·jay \ˌyäg-wə-'hī\. Municipality, Las Villas prov., W cen. Cuba, 45 m. E of Santa Clara; pop. (1967c) 42,380.

Ya·gua·rón \ˌyäg-wə-'rȯn\. **1** River, South America. See JAGUARÃO 1.

2 Town, E Central dept., S Paraguay, 20 m. SE of Asunción; noted for its old Jesuit church San Roque.

Yaila Range. See YALTINSKAYA YAILA.

Yai·nax Butte \'yī-ˌnaks-\. Mountain, SE Klamath co., S Oregon; 7277 ft.

Yai·zu \'yī-(ˌ)zü\. City, Shizuoka prefecture, Honshū, Japan, 9 m. SW of Shizuoka; pop. (1970c) 82,737.

Yak·i·ma \'yak-ə-ˌmȯ\. **1** River, S cen. Washington; 203 m. long; flows SE through Kittitas and Yakima cos. into Columbia river in Benton co.

2 County in S Washington. See table at WASHINGTON.

3 City, its ⊗, on Yakima river 5 m. N of Yakima Indian Reservation; pop. (1970c) 45,588; fruit juice, canned goods, agricultural machinery; in irrigated region producing fruit, livestock, sugar beets, hops; Yakima Valley Coll. (1928); incorporated 1886.

Ya·ku–shi·ma \ˌyäk-ů-'shē-mə, 'yäk-ů-shi-ˌmä\ *also* **Yaku** \'yäk-(ˌ)ü\. One of the Osumi Is. (*q.v.*), off S tip of Kyūshū, Japan; with adjacent small island, 208 sq. m.

Yak·u·tat \'yak-ə-ˌtat\. City at Ocean Cape on S shore of Yakutat Bay, SE Alaska; pop. (1970c) 190.

Yakutat Bay. Inlet of Gulf of Alaska, SE Alaska, 59°45′N, 140°45′W.

Ya·kutsk \yə-'kütsk\. Town, ✱ of Yakutsk A.S.S.R., U.S.S.R., on Lena river; pop. (1970p) 108,000; river port and a center for fur trade.

Yakutsk Autonomous Soviet Socialist Republic *or* **Ya·kut Autonomous Soviet Socialist Republic** \yə-'küt-\ *also* **Ya·ku·tia** \yə-'k(y)ü-sh(ē-)ə\. An autonomous republic of the Russian S.F.S.R., U.S.S.R., E cen. Siberia; 1,198,146 sq. m.; pop. (1970p) 664,000; ✱ Yakutsk.

Physical features: In area the largest administrative unit of the U.S.S.R. other than the Russian S.F.S.R., bounded on the N by the Arctic Ocean (Laptev and East Siberian seas), on the E by Khabarovsk Krai, on S by Chita and Irkutsk oblasts, and on W by Krasnoyarsk Krai (Evenki and Taimyr national okrugs). Includes nearly the whole great basin of the Lena (*q.v.*), as well as the valleys of the Olenek, Yana, Indigirka, and Kolyma; largely plain, with tundra in the N and mountain ranges (Verkhoyansk and Cherskogo) in the E; highest peaks 8000 to 10,200 ft. Includes New Siberian and Lyakhov Is. in the Arctic. Extremely severe climate, the towns of Verkhoyansk and Oimyakon being two of the coldest places on the globe. *Chief products:* Economic activity includes reindeer herding, fur trapping, and fishing; substantial timber resources; gold and diamonds, also tin, salt, and coal. No railroads but highway system has expanded substantially since World War II. *Chief towns:* Yakutsk and Aldan. Fort at Yakutsk founded 1632 and first gold mines worked 1850; organized as autonomous republic 1922; has been increasingly explored and surveyed since World War II.

Ya·la \'yäl-ə\. **1** Province of SW Thailand; 1821 sq. m.; pop. (1960c) 149,348, ✱ Yala.

2 Town, its ✱, 22 m. S of Pattani; pop. (1964e) 25,271.

Yala National Park \'yä-lə-\. National park, Ceylon; 91 sq. m.; ancient ruins; established 1938.

Yale, Mount \-'yā(ə)l\. Peak in Sawatch Range, Chaffee co., cen. Colorado; 14,196 ft.

Yales·ville \'yā(ə)lz-ˌvil\. Subdivision of town of Wallingford, Connecticut. See WALLINGFORD 1.

Ya·lias \yäl-'yäs\ *or anc.* **Ida·lia** \ī-'dāl-yə\. River, Cyprus; 45 m. long; flows E into Famagusta Bay.

Yal·o·busha \ˌyal-ə-'bůsh-ə\. **1** River, N cen. Mississippi; ab. 80 m. long; rises in Chickasaw co., flows W and SW to unite with Tallahatchie river in Leflore co. and form the Yazoo river.

2 County in Mississippi. See table at MISSISSIPPI.

Yal·pukh \'yal-ˌpůk\ *or Rom.* **Ial·pug** \'yäl-ˌpüg\. Lake, Odessa Oblast, SW Ukrainian S.S.R., U.S.S.R.; 58 sq. m.; outlet is into Danube river near the delta.

Yal·ta \'yȯl-tə\. Town, S Crimean Oblast, Ukrainian S.S.R., U.S.S.R., 30 m. E of Sevastopol; pop. (1969e) 57,000; resort; site of palace of former tsars. Held by Germans 1941–44; scene of "Big Three Conference" (President Roosevelt, Prime Minister Churchill and Premier Stalin) Feb. 3–11, 1945.

Yal·tins·ka·ya Yai·la \yəl-'tin-skə-yə-'yī-lə\ *or* **Yaila Range** \ˌyī-lə-\. Mountain range along SE coast of Crimea Penin., Crimean Oblast, Ukrainian S.S.R., U.S.S.R.; highest peak ab. 5000 ft.

Ya·lu *or* **Ya–lü** \'yäl-(ˌ)ü\ *or* **Am·nok** \'am-ˌnäk\ *or Jap.* **Oryok·ko** \ōr-'yō-(ˌ)kō, ȯr-\. River, bet. NE China and North Korea; 501 m. long; rises in Ch'ang-pai Shan on N border of North Korea, flows N, W, and SW to Korea Bay. Near its mouth is Tan-tung, important city of Liaoning prov., China; crossed here by railroad bridge 3000 ft. long. Has many tributaries, esp. in NE China; navigable for most of its course for smaller vessels. Naval battle off its mouth (Hai-yang I.) 1894 in which Japanese defeated the Chinese;

land battle May 1, 1904, first in Russo-Japanese War, in which Russians were defeated.

Ya–lung *or* **Ya·lung** \'yä-'lůŋ\. River, Szechwan prov., S China; 822 m. long; rises in Amne Machin Shan in Tsinghai prov. and flows S into the Yangtze on the Yunnan border W of Hui-li; unnavigable.

Ya·lu·to·rovsk \yə-'lüt-ə-ˌrəfsk\. Town, SW Tyumen Oblast, Russian S.F.S.R., U.S.S.R., on left bank of the Tobal river 50 m. SE of Tyumen; pop. (1967e) 23,000.

Yal·vaç \yäl-'väch\. Town, N İsparta prov., SW Turkey, 48 m. NE of İsparta; pop. (1965c) 10,912. Ruins of ancient city of Pisidian Antioch lie nearby; founded c. 290 B.C. by Seleucus Nicator and made free city by the Romans 189 B.C.; established as a colony by Augustus and became important Roman administrative center in S Galatia; visited by Saint Paul on first missionary journey c. 46 A.D.; source of many inscriptions.

Yama. See KINGISEPP.

Ya·ma·chiche \ˌya-mə-'shēsh\. Village, ⊗ of Saint-Maurice co., S Quebec, Canada, on N shore of Lake St. Peter; pop. (1971p) 1135.

Ya·ma·ga·ta \'yäm-ə-gə-ˌtä, yä-'mäg-ə-\. 1 Prefecture, N Honshū, Japan; 3600 sq. m.; pop. (1970c) 1,225,618; rice, fruit; fishing; oil, natural gas.

2 City, its ✱, on Mogami river 30 m. W of Sendai; pop. (1970c) 204,127; ships rice, silk; large metal casting industry; univ. (1949). Residence of daimyos from early 17th cent. to 1868.

Ya·ma·gu·chi \yä-'mäg-ə-chē, ˌyäm-ə-'gü-chē\. 1 Prefecture, W Honshū, Japan; 2347 sq. m.; pop. (1970c) 1,511,448; ✱ Yamaguchi; rice; fishing; coal, limestone.

2 City, its ✱, 35 m. NE of Shimonoseki; pop. (1970c) 101,-041; ships coal; commercial fisheries; several temples. From 14th to 16th cents. under the Ouchi family one of the leading cities of feudal Japan; visited c. 1550 by the Jesuit missionary Francis Xavier; important during Restoration period 1862–68.

Ya·mal \yə-'mäl\. Peninsula bet. Kara Sea and Gulf of Ob, N Yamalo-Nenets National Okrug, Russian S.F.S.R., U.S.S.R.; 434 m. long by 93 to 149 m. wide.

Ya·ma·lo–Ne·nets National Okrug \yə-ˌmal-ə-nə-'nets . . . 'ȯ-ˌkrük\. National district, Tyumen Oblast, Russian S.F.S.R., U.S.S.R.; 289,691 sq. m.; pop. (1970p) 80,000; ✱ Salekhard; includes Yamal Penin., region on E coast of Gulf of Ob, and the tundra along the lower Ob river and to the E of it; estab. 1930.

Ya·ma·na·ka \ˌyäm-ə-'näk-ə\. Lake, S Honshū, Japan; highest of lakes on slopes of Fuji; alt. 3270 ft.

Ya·ma·na·shi \ˌyäm-ə-'näsh-ē\. Prefecture, Honshū, Japan; 1723 sq. m.; pop. (1970c) 762,029; ✱ Kōfu; fruit; tourism.

Ya·mas·ka \yə-'mas-kə\. 1 River, S Quebec, Canada; ab. 75 m. long; flows N to Lake St. Peter.

2 County, Quebec, Canada. See table at QUEBEC.

Ya·ma·to \yä-'mä-(ˌ)tō\. Old province, W cen. Honshū, Japan, now Nara prefecture; in legendary Japan, the region of the original settlement of the imperial clan; here Jimmu Tenno first ruled 660 B.C.; in early centuries Japanese were called "people of Yamato."

Yamato–kō·ri·ya·ma \yə-'mä-tō-ˌkȯ-rē-'yä-mə\. Town, Nara prefecture, Honshū, Japan; pop. (1970c) 57,456.

Yam·bol *also* **Jam·bol** \'yäm-ˌbōl\. 1 Province of SE Bulgaria. See table at BULGARIA.

2 *or Turk.* **Yan·bo·li** \ˌyän-bə-'lē\. City, its ✱, on Tundzha river, 45 m. E of Stara Zagora; pop. (1968e) 67,941; ships wool and wine. First mentioned in 11th cent.; at one time under Byzantine rule.

Yamburg. See KINGISEPP.

Yamdena. See JAMDENA.

Yamdrok Tso. See YANG-CHO-YUNG.

Ya·me·thin \yə-'mā-t͟hən\. 1 District, Mandalay division, Upper Burma; 4196 sq. m.

2 Town, its ✱, on Rangoon-Mandalay railroad 105 m. S of Mandalay.

Yam·hill \'yam-ˌhil\. County in Oregon. See table at OREGON.

Y'A·mi \'yäm-ē\. Islet, N Batan Is., N Phil., 21°07'N, 121°57'E; 1 sq. m.; the northernmost point in Phil.

Yam·pa \'yam-pə\. River, NW Colorado; ab. 250 m. long; rises in S Routt co., flows N then W into the Green river near Utah boundary.

Yam·say Peak \ˌyam-zē-\. Mountain, E Klamath co., S Oregon; 8242 ft.

Ya·mu·na \'yä-mə-nə\ *also* **Jum·na** \'jəm-nə\ *or anc.* **Jom·a·nes** \'jäm-ə-ˌnēz\. River, N cen. India; ab. 860 m. long; rises in the Himalayas, flows S and SE into the Ganges at Allahabad, in its upper course forming long section of W boundary of Uttar Pradesh; flows just E of Delhi and past Mathura and Agra; connects with numerous canals; navigable for most of its course for barges and small vessels; chief tributaries, all from S, the Chambal, Sind, Betwa, and Ken.

Yamundá. See NHAMUNDÁ.

Ya·na \'yän-ə\. River, N cen. Yakutsk A.S.S.R., Russian S.F.S.R., U.S.S.R.; 546 m. long; rises in Verkhoyansk Mts. and flows N into Laptev Sea.

Ya·nam \yə-'näm\ *or* **Ya·na·on** \yə-'naůn\. Town and seaport, Pondicherry territory, E India, on the N mouth of Godavari delta 290 m. NNE of Madras; pop. (1961c) 7000; founded by French 1750; captured by British and returned to French in 1817; to India 1954.

Yanboli. See YAMBOL 2.

Yanbu'. See YENBO'.

Yan·cey \'yan-sē\. County in North Carolina. See table at NORTH CAROLINA.

Yan·cey·ville \'yan-sē-ˌvil\. Unincorporated community, ⊗ of Caswell co., N North Carolina; pop. (1970c) 1274.

Yan·da·bu \ˌyän-də-'bü\. Town on the Irrawaddy river, 40 m. W of Mandalay, Upper Burma; treaty signed here Feb. 24, 1826, by which the king of Ava abandoned his claim to Assam and ceded to the British the provinces of Arakan and Tenasserim.

Yang–chou \'yäŋ-'jō\ *or formerly* **Kiang·tu** \jē-'äŋ-'dü\. City, cen. Kiangsu, E China, on Grand Canal 15 m. N of Chen-chiang and the Yangtze; pop. (1970e) 210,000; old walled city, capital of China under Sui dynasty (589–618 A.D.); noted for its wealth; a literary and cultural center; Marco Polo appointed as its governor 1282–85 by Kublai Khan.

Yang–cho–yung \'yäŋ-'jō-'yůŋ\ *or* **Yam·drok Tso** \'yäm-'drȯk-'tsȯ\ *or* **Pal·ti** \'päl-tē\. Lake (Tibetan *tso*), SE Tibet, China, ab. 45 m. S of Lhasa; alt. 13,800 ft.

Yang·gang \'yäŋ-'gäŋ\. Province of North Korea. See table at KOREA, NORTH.

Yan·gi·yul \yəŋ-ˌgē-'yůl\. Town, Tashkent Oblast, Uzbek S.S.R., U.S.S.R., ab. 20 m. SW of Tashkent; pop. (1969e) 56,000.

Yangku. See T'AI-YÜAN.

Yang–p'i *or* **Yang·pi** \'yäŋ-'pē\. River, W Yunnan, S China, 170 m. long; flows S to the Mekong; outlet of the lake Erh Hai.

Yang–shuo \'yäŋ-'shwō\ *or* **Yang·so** \'yäŋ-'sō\. Town, NE Kwangsi Chuang, SE China, just S of Kuei-lin; U.S. air base in World War II; captured by Japanese Sept. 1944; retaken by Chinese July 27, 1945.

Yang·tze \'yaŋ-'sē, 'yaŋ(k)t-'sē\ *or* **Yangtze Kiang** \-kē-'aŋ\. Principal river (*kiang*) of China; 3434 m. long; rises in E Kunlun Shan in SW Tsinghai, flows SE through deep gorges marking boundary bet. Tibet and Szechwan, then E across the plateau of Yunnan and finally ENE across the entire width of China Proper to the East China Sea near Shanghai. Known as the Kinsha (*q.v.*) in its upper course. Navigable for vessels of large draft 585 m. to Hankow; above I-ch'ang navigation difficult and dangerous because of rapids in the Yangtze Gorges (*q.v.*); on some sections above the gorges navigable for smaller vessels. Its chief tributaries on the N are the Ya-lung, Min, Chia-ling, and Han Shui; on the S the Wu and the outlets of (lakes)

Tung-t'ing Hu and P'o-yang Hu. In its upper course 8000 to 10,000 ft. above sea level, at Pa-t'ang 8540 ft., at Chungking 650 ft., at I-ch'ang (below the gorges) 131 ft. and for the last 200 m. of its course practically at sea level.

Yangtze Gorges. Series of gorges in the Yangtze river, Hupeh and Szechwan provs., cen. China, bet. the cities of Chungking (at 650 ft. above sea level) and I-ch'ang (at 131 ft.), caused by the river forcing its passage through the Ta-Pa Shan. Most notable of the gorges are bet. I-ch'ang and Feng-chieh (120 m.).

Yang·tze·poo \'yäŋ-'dzə-'pō, 'yaŋ-'(t)sē-'pō\. The northern district of the city of Shanghai, China; from 1932 to 1945 held by the Japanese.

Ya·nis·yar·vi \'yan-əs-ˌya(ə)r-vē\ *or Finnish* **Jä·nis·jär·vi** \'yan-əs-ˌya(ə)r-vē\. Lake, SW Karelian A.S.S.R., Russian S.F.S.R., U.S.S.R., near Finnish border; formerly in Finland.

Yank·ton \'yaŋ(k)-tən\. 1 County in SE South Dakota. See table at SOUTH DAKOTA.

2 City, its ⊗, on Missouri river 60 m. SW of Sioux Falls; pop. (1970c) 11,919; electronic components, sheet metal products; agriculture; Yankton Coll. (1881), Mount Marty Coll. (1922). Settled 1858; capital of Dakota Territory 1861–83; scene of Indian uprising 1862.

Yannina. See IOANNINA 2.

Yannitsá. See GENITSA.

Yan·tic \'yan-tik\. River, SE Connecticut; ab. 20 m. long; formed by confluence of forks in W cen. New London co., flows E to join the Shetucket river at Norwich and form the Thames river.

Yan·tra \'yän-trə\. River, NE cen. Bulgaria; 178 m. long; flows N into Danube river E of Nikopol.

Ya·oun·dé \yaůn-'dā\ *or* **Yaun·de** \yaůn-'dā\. Town, ✱ of Cameroon, W Africa, 125 m. E of coast of the Gulf of Guinea; pop. (1970e) 178,000; univ. (1962).

Yap \'yap, 'yäp\ *or* **Uap** \'wäp\. Island group, W Caroline Is., in W Pacific Ocean ab. 225 m. NE of Palau Is.; 9°31′N, 138°06′E; 85 sq. m.; pop. (1970e) 7247; comprises four islands close together, of which Yap is largest. One of most fertile of the Carolines; covered with hills and notable for its numerous remains of an early people, esp. ancient stone platforms and large pieces of circular stone money (hence, often called "Island of Stone Money").

History: Seized by Germany 1885 (see CAROLINE ISLANDS); after World War I became subject of dispute 1920–21 bet. Japan and U.S.; settled at Washington Conference by inclusion in Japanese mandate but with cable and radio rights secured to U.S.; raided and bombed by U.S. naval and air forces 1944–45; bypassed in advance on Japan; became part of U.S. Trust Territory of the Pacific Islands 1947.

Yap·hank \'yap-ˌhaŋk\. Unincorporated community, Suffolk co., SE New York, on Long I. ab. 7 m. NE of Patchogue. Camp Upton was located nearby (see UPTON 3).

Yapurá. See JAPURÁ.

Ya·qui \yä-'kē\. River, Sonora, NW Mexico; ab. 420 m. long; rises near U.S. border, flows S and SW into the Gulf of California.

Ya·ra·cuy \ˌyär-ə-'kwē\. State of Venezuela. See table at VENEZUELA.

Yard·ley \'yärd-lē\. Borough, Bucks co., SE Pennsylvania; pop. (1970c) 2616; textiles, chemicals; truck farming.

Yare. See BROADS, THE.

Ya·ri \'yär-ē\ *or* **Ya·ri·ga·ta·ke** \ˌyär-i-gə-'täk-ē\. Peak, cen. Honshū, Japan, on W border of Nagano prefecture; 10,433 ft.

Yar·kand \yär-'kand\. River, W Sinkiang Uighur, W China; ab. 600 m. long; rises on N slopes of Karakoram Range; flows N and W forming part of border bet. Jammu and Kashmir, India, and Sinkiang-Uighur, China; then N around W end of Kunlun Shan, then N and NE to join the Ho-t'ien at ab. 41°N, 81°E and form the Tarim river.

Yarkend. See SO-CH'E.

Yar·mouth \'yär-məth\. 1 Seaport town, Cumberland co., SW Maine, on Casco Bay 10 m. N of Portland; pop. (1970c) 4854; commercial fisheries.

2 Town, Barnstable co., SE Massachusetts, 4 m. E of Barnstable; pop. (1970c) 12,033; summer resort; cranberries.

3 County, Nova Scotia, Canada. See table at NOVA SCOTIA.

4 Town, ⊗ of Yarmouth co., SW Nova Scotia, Canada, on Atlantic Ocean; pop. (1971p) 8291; resort; lumber, canvas, dairy products; fish curing; agriculture; founded 1759.

5 *or* **Great Yarmouth.** County borough, Norfolk, E England, on North Sea at mouth of the Yare 110 m. NE of London; pop. (1971p) 50,152; seaside resort and major herring fishing port. Settled as a fishing village before the Conquest; Church of St. Nicholas, founded 1101, destroyed by bombs.

Yar·muk \yär-'mük\. River, NW Jordan; ab. 50 m. long; flows W into the Jordan just S of the Sea of Galilee and in its course forms a section of the boundary bet. Syria and Jordan; in Biblical times separated Gilead on S from Bashan and Gaulanitis on N.

Yaroslav. See JAROSŁAW.

Ya·ro·slavl \ˌyär-ə-'släv-əl\. Industrial city, ✱ of Yaroslavl Oblast, Russian S.F.S.R., U.S.S.R., on the Volga ab. 160 m. NE of Moscow; pop. (1970p) 517,000; linen, diesel engines, construction equipment, dyes, footwear; oil refining; 12th cent. monastery, 17th cent. cathedral, 18th cent. theater; univ. Founded probably c. 1010 by Yaroslavl the Great; burned by Tatars 1238 and 1332; important textile manufacturing center from early 18th cent.

Yaroslavl Oblast \-'ó-bləst, -ˌblast\. Subdivision of the Russian S.F.S.R., U.S.S.R., part of level plain traversed by upper Volga; 14,015 sq. m.; pop. (1970p) 1,400,000; ✱ Yaroslavl. In NW is Rybinsk Reservoir (*q.v.*); in S part is Lake Pleshcheyevo. Extensive marshes and considerable forest areas. Produces fodder crops and potatoes; dairying; cheese. Chief towns Yaroslavl and Rybinsk. In early times part of Rostov-Suzdal principality; in early 15th cent. came under Moscow principality; made separate oblast 1936.

Yar·ra \'yar-ə\ *or formerly* **Yarra Yarra** \ˌyar-ə-'yar-ə\. River, Victoria, SE Australia; 115 m. long; flows W to Port Phillip Bay at Melbourne.

Yar·row \'yar-(ˌ)ō\ *or* **Yarrow Water.** Small river, Selkirk co., SE Scotland; flows into the Ettrick and on into the Tweed; celebrated by Wordsworth in his verse.

Yar·tse·vo \'yärt-sə-və\. Town, W cen. Smolensk Oblast, Russian S.F.S.R., U.S.S.R., on Moscow-Smolensk R.R. ab. 35 m. ENE of Smolensk; pop. (1967e) 34,000; textiles. Held by Germans 1941–43.

Ya·ru·mal \ˌyär-ə-'mäl\. Town, Antioquia dept., NW Colombia, 50 m. N of Medellín; pop. (1968e) 42,089.

Yar·vi·co·ya \ˌyär-vi-'kō-yə\. Peak, E Tarapacá prov., N Chile; 16,994 ft.

Ya·sa·wa Islands \yä-'sä-wə-\. Chain of islands and rocky islets extending NNE and SSW for 45 m. NW of Viti Levu I., W Fiji, SW Pacific Ocean.

Ya·sel·da \yə-'sel-də\ *or Pol.* **Ja·sioł·da** \yä-'shól-də\. River, SW Belorussian S.S.R., U.S.S.R.; 134 m. long; flows SE into the Pripyat river.

Yas·na·ya Po·lya·na \ˌyas-nə-yə-pəl-'yan-ə\. Village, cen. Tula Oblast, Russian S.F.S.R., U.S.S.R., ab. 13 m. S of Tula; birthplace and residence of Count Leo Tolstoi. Tolstoi Museum, national shrine, destroyed by Germans in World War II, restored 1946 ff.

Ya·soof \yə-'süf\. Town, ✱ of Boyer Ahmadī-ye Sardīr va Kohkīlūyeh gov., W cen. Iran; pop. (1966c) 931.

Yass \'yas\. Town, SE New South Wales, SE Australia, on tributary of Murrumbidgee river 32 m. N of Canberra; pop. (1965e) 3970; located in **Yass–Can·ber·ra** \-'kan-b(ə-)rə\

district, a part of which (Canberra) was set aside 1911 as the Federal Capital Territory (now Australian Capital Territory). See CANBERRA.

Yassy. See IAŞI.

Ya·sun, Cape \-yä-'sün\ *or Turk.* **Yasun Bur·nu** \-bur-'nü\. Cape on Black Sea, N coast of Turkey, bet. Samsun and Giresun.

Ya·te·ras \yä-'ter-əs\. Municipality, Oriente prov., E Cuba, just N of Guantánamo; pop. (1967e) 59,150.

Yates \'yāts\. County in New York. See table at NEW YORK.

Yates Center. City, ⊗ of Woodson co., SE Kansas, NW of Chanute; pop. (1970c) 1967; oil wells.

Yath·ky·ed Lake \,yath-kī-'ed-\. Lake, S cen. Keewatin dist., Northwest Territories, Canada; 860 sq. m.; in course of Kazan river.

Yathrib. See MEDINA 6.

Ya·tsu·shi·ro \'yäts-(ü-)shi-,rō, yät-'sü-shi-\. Town, Kumamoto prefecture, W cen. Kyūshū, Japan, on NE coast of Yatsushiro Bay 25 m. S of Kumamoto; pop. (1970c) 101,866.

Yatsushiro Bay. Inlet of East China Sea, W coast of Kyūshū, Japan; ab. 50 m. long by 5 to 15 m. wide; shut in on W by Amakusa Is.

Yauapery. See JAUAPERI.

Yau·co \'yaù-,kō\. Town and municipality, SW Puerto Rico; pop. (1970p) 12,880 (town), 35,090 (munic.); town is in sugar-growing section 15 m. W of Ponce, near the coast.

Yaunde. See YAOUNDÉ.

Yau·te·pec \,yaù-tə-'pek\. Municipality, Morelos state, Mexico, 35 m. S of Mexico City; pop. (1970p) 26,182; tourist center; rice, wheat, sugarcane, tropical fruits.

Yav·a·pai \'yav-ə-,pī\. County in Arizona. See table at ARIZONA.

Yavari. See JAVARI.

Yavero River. See PAUCARTAMBO.

Ya·wa·ta \yə-'wät-ə\. See KITAKYŪSHŪ.

Ya·wa·ta·ha·ma \yə-,wät-ə-'häm-ə\. Seaport town, Ehime prefecture, NW Shikoku I., Japan, on Bungo Strait; pop. (1965c) 50,005; trades esp. with Kyūshū.

Yawng·hwe \'yaùŋ-'(h)wā\. 1 Former state, Burma, now part of Shan State; 1389 sq. m.
2 Town, its ✱, 110 m. SE of Mandalay.

Yazd \'yazd\ *or* **Yezd** \'yezd\. 1 Governorship of cen. Iran. See table at IRAN.
2 Industrial city, its ✱, 170 m. SE of Eşfahān; pop. (1971e) 98,000; on main highway from Tehran and Qom to Kermān; produces silk and carpets; numerous mosques; dates from 5th cent.

Yaz·oo \ya-'zü\. 1 Navigable river, W cen. Mississippi; 189 m. long; formed by confluence of Tallahatchie and Yalobusha rivers in Leflore co., flows SW into Mississippi river above Vicksburg; in W part of the 35,000,000 acres sold for $500,000 (the Yazoo Fraud) by Act of the State of Georgia Jan. 7, 1795 to four land companies whose shareholders were discovered to include members of the Georgia legislature.
2 County in Mississippi. See table at MISSISSIPPI.

Yazoo City. City, ⊗ of Yazoo co., W cen. Mississippi, 42 m. N of Jackson; pop. (1970c) 10,796; cotton market; feed, lumber; oil refinery; hogs.

Ybbs \'ips\. River in W Lower Austria; 83 m. long; flows N into Danube river 25 m. W of Sankt Pölten.

Yby·cuí *also* **Iby·cuí** *or* **Ibi·cuí** \,ē-bi-'kwē\. Town, Paraguarí dept., S Paraguay; pop. (1970e) 28,006.

Yby·ty·mí \,ē-bi-ti-'mē\. Town, Paraguarí dept., S Paraguay; pop. (1970e) 8291.

Yea·don \'yād-ᵊn\. Borough, Delaware co., SE Pennsylvania, 5 m. W of Philadelphia; pop. (1970c) 12,136.

Yea·ger·town \'yā-gər-,taùn\. Locality, Mifflin co., cen. Pennsylvania, ab. 3 m. N of Lewistown; pop. (1970c) 1363.

Ye·ba·la \yə-'bäl-ə, jə-\ *or* **Ge·ba·la** \hā-, jə-\. Mountainous region, N Morocco, NW Africa, S of Tangier.

Ye·cla \'yā-klə\. Commune, Murcia prov., SE Spain, 43 m. N by E of Murcia; pop. (1970p) 20,724; produces oil, esparto, and, esp., wines; manufactures soap, leather.

Yeddo *or* **Yedo.** See TOKYO 2.

Ye·fre·mov \,yə-frə-'mòf\. Town, Tula Oblast, Russian S.F.S.R., U.S.S.R., ab. 75 m. SSE of Tula; pop. (1967e) 44,000.

Ye·gor·yevsk \yə-'gòr-(y)əfsk\ *or* **Egor·evsk** \yə-\. City, Moscow Oblast, Russian S.F.S.R., U.S.S.R., on branch railroad 60 m. SE of Moscow; pop. (1969e) 65,000; textile mills, dye works.

Ye·gros \'ya-(,)grōs\. Town, Caazapá dept., S Paraguay; pop. (1970e) 7964.

Ye·guas, Point \-'yā-(,)gwäs\. Cape, SE Puerto Rico.

Yehcheng. See KARGHALIK.

Yehsien. See I-HSIEN.

Yeisk *or* **Eisk** \'yāsk\ *also* **Eysk** \'yā-ēsk\. Seaport town, NW Krasnodar Krai, Russian S.F.S.R., U.S.S.R., on Gulf of Taganrog; pop. (1969e) 71,000; terminus of branch railroad 80 m. WSW of Rostov-na-Donu; important fisheries; resort.

Ye·ji \'yā-jē\. Town, SE Northern Region, Ghana, W Africa, on the Volta ab. 130 m. NE of Kumasi; pop. (1970p) 5739.

Yekaterinburg. See SVERDLOVSK 1.

Yekaterinenshtadt. See MARKS.

Yekaterinodar. See KRASNODAR.

Ye·la·bu·ga \ye-'läb-ə-gə\ *or* **Ela·bu·ga** \ye-\. Town, N Tatar A.S.S.R., Russian S.F.S.R., U.S.S.R., on Kama river 100 m. E of Kazan; pop. (1967e) 32,000; ships grain; on the Kama 3 m. above the town, notable ancient burial mound discovered 1858, in which were found skeletons, urns, weapons, bronze decorations, and other artifacts of Stone, Bronze, and Iron ages.

Ye·lets \yə-'lets\ *or* **Elets** \yə-\. City, Lipetsk Oblast, Russian S.F.S.R., U.S.S.R., on the Sosna river ab. 100 m. E of Orel; pop. (1970p) 101,000; railroad junction bet. Tula and Voronezh; ships grain and livestock. Mentioned in 12th cent. when it was an outlying fort of Ryazan principality; destroyed by Mongols 1239 and 1305 and plundered by Tatars 15th cent. when for a time it was entirely abandoned; its modern prosperity dates from 17th cent.; in World War II twice taken by Germans 1941 and 1942.

Yelgava. See JELGAVA.

Yelizavetgrad. See KIROVOGRAD.

Yelizavetpol. See KIROVABAD.

Yelizavety, Cape. See ELIZABETH, CAPE 2.

Yell \'yel\. 1 County in Arkansas. See table at ARKANSAS.
2 One of the Shetland Is., NE of N Scotland; 55 sq. m.; pop. (1961c) 1155.

Yel·low \'yel-(,)ō, -ə(-w)\. 1 River, Alabama and Florida; ab. 90 m. long; flows SW across border from S Alabama into NW Florida; empties into NE Pensacola Bay.
2 River, cen. Wisconsin; ab. 75 m. long; rises in E Clark co., flows S into Wisconsin river in E cen. Juneau co.
3 River, NW cen. Wisconsin; ab. 70 m. long; rises in cen. Taylor co., flows SW into Lake Wissota near Chippewa Falls.
4 *or Chin.* **Hwang Ho** \'hwäŋ-'hō\. River (*ho*), N cen. and E China; 2903 m. long; navigable as far as Lan-chou; rises in Amne Machin Shan, SE Tsinghai, at ab. 14,000 ft.; flows E and NE across Kansu, then N as E boundary of Ningsia Hui; at 40°N makes a great bend flowing E across Hu-ho-hao-t'e, Inner Mongolia, then S bet. Shensi and Shansi, receiving the Fen tributary from the E; at T'ung-kuan in E Shensi receives the Wei and turns directly E through gorges along N Honan border. Its lower course across the Great Plains has shifted many times through the centuries, vitally affecting 35,000,000 acres of rich farmland; for more than 500 years before 1852 its outlet was Yellow Sea in Kiangsu; from 1852 to 1938 its course NE from near K'ai-feng across Shantung past Tsinan to Gulf of Chihli; in 1938 again diverted, this time by Chinese military action against the

Japanese invaders, from near Cheng-chou in Honan SE across Honan and Anhwei to unite with the Huai, passing through Hung-tse Hu (lake) to its old bed in Kiangsu and its new mouth 250 m. farther S; in 1947 turned back to its old bed through Shantung. Large-scale construction of dam and reservoir system for flood control and power production begun 1955.

Yel·low·head Pass \ˌyel-ə-ˌhed-\. Mountain pass, Canadian Rocky Mts., on border bet. Jasper National Park, Alberta, and Mount Robson Provincial Park, British Columbia; 3717 ft.; railroad.

Yel·low·knife \ˈyel-ə-ˌnīf\. Town, ✱ of Northwest Territories, in S Mackenzie dist., Canada, on NW shore of Great Slave Lake at mouth of **Yellowknife River;** pop. (1971p) 5867; gold mining; became ✱ 1967.

Yellowknife Preserve. Extensive region, cen. Mackenzie dist., Northwest Territories, Canada, bet. Great Bear and Great Slave lakes; set aside as reservation for Yellowknife Indians.

Yellow Med·i·cine \-ˈmed-ə-sən\. County in Minnesota. See table at MINNESOTA.

Yellow Mountain. Peak, Glacier National Park, NW Montana; 8900 ft.

Yellow River. 1 Name of several rivers in the U.S. See YELLOW.

2 Name of river in China. See YELLOW 4.

Yellow Sea *or Chin.* **Hwang Hai** \ˈhwäŋ-ˈhī\. Large inlet of Pacific Ocean, bet. NE China and Korean penin.; ab. 180,000 sq. m.; average depth 121 ft., max. depth 250 ft.; N inlets are Gulf of Chihli and Korea Bay; connects with East China Sea on the S; Shantung Penin. extends into it from W.

Yellow Springs. Residential village, Greene co., SW Ohio, 8 m. S of Springfield; pop. (1970c) 4624; Antioch Coll. (1852).

Yel·low·stone \ˈyel-ə-ˌstōn\. 1 River, NW Wyoming and S and E Montana; 671 m. long; navigable for 300 m. during high water; rises in Park co., Wyoming, flows N through Yellowstone Lake and Yellowstone National Park, continues N across Montana border, then flows E and NE into Missouri river on boundary bet. Montana and North Dakota; the Grand Canyon of the Yellowstone is the valley, 2000 ft. wide and 1200 ft. deep, of this river in Yellowstone National Park; the park also includes **Yellowstone Falls,** upper fall 109 ft., lower fall 308 ft.

2 County in Montana. See table at MONTANA.

Yellowstone Lake. Lake, Yellowstone National Park, NW Wyoming; 137 sq. m.; ab. 20 m. long; alt. 7735 ft.; largest body of water in North America at so great an altitude. Yellowstone river flows through the lake from S to N.

Yellowstone National Park. See UNITED STATES, *National Parks.*

Yel·low·tail Dam \ˈyel-ə-ˌtāl-\. Dam in Bighorn river, S Montana; 525 ft. high; completed 1966; forms **Yellowtail Reservoir** (71 m. long) in Montana and Wyoming. See UNITED STATES, *Dams and Reservoirs.*

Yell·ville \ˈyel-ˌvil\. City, ⊗ of Marion co., N Arkansas; pop. (1970c) 860; agriculture.

Yel·mo \ˈyel-(ˌ)mō\. Highest peak in Segura Mts., SE Spain; 5935 ft.

Yem·en \ˈyem-ən, ˈyā-mən\. 1 *or officially* **People's Democratic Republic of Yemen** *or formerly* **Southern Yemen.** Republic, S Arabian Penin., SW Asia, bounded on N by Saudi Arabia, on E by Oman, on S by the Indian Ocean and the Gulf of Aden, and on W by Yemen (2 below); 112,075 sq. m.; pop. (1970e) 1,436,000; national ✱ Aden, administrative ✱ Madinat ash Sha'b. Includes islands of Kamaran, Perim, Socotra (*qq.v.*). *Chief products:* Millet, dates, tobacco, honey; fishing. *Chief towns:* Aden, Mukalla. Formed 1967. For further details, see ADEN 1 and 2 and HADHRAMAUT.

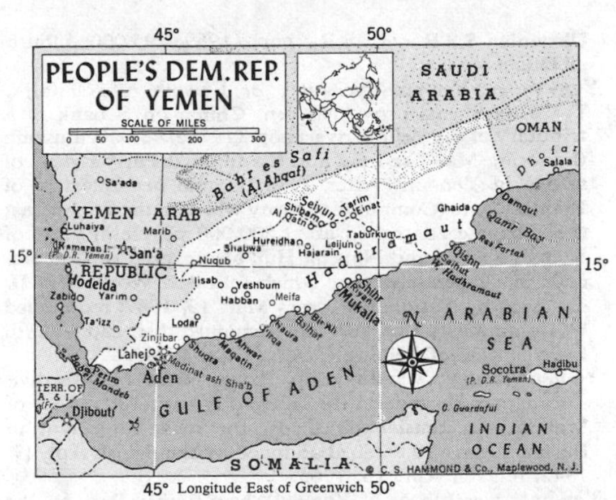

2 *or officially* **Yemen Arab Republic.** Republic, SW Arabian Penin., SW Asia, bounded on N and NE by Saudi Arabia, on E and S by Yemen (1 above), and on W by the Red Sea; 75,290 sq. m.; pop. (1970e) 6,500,000; ✱ San'a. *Physical features:* Crossed from N to S by a mountain range, with highest peak ab. 12,000 ft.; coastal plain varies in width from 20 to 30 m.; numerous fertile valleys and oases. *Chief products:* Sorghum, corn, barley, coffee, dates. *Chief towns:* San'a, Hodeida, Ta'izz, Mocha.

History: Seat of ancient Minaean kingdom; conquered by Egypt c. 1600 B.C.; invaded by Ethiopians and Romans; converted to Islam 628 A.D., ruled under caliphate; under Turkish control 16th cent.; practically independent until establishment of Egyptian control along coast by Mehemet Ali 1819; autonomy guaranteed by Porte 1913 following serious revolts; successful maintenance of independence by its imam following World War I; reached boundary agreement with Great Britain 1934; overthrew monarchy 1962; period 1962–70 marked by civil war between royalist and republican forces.

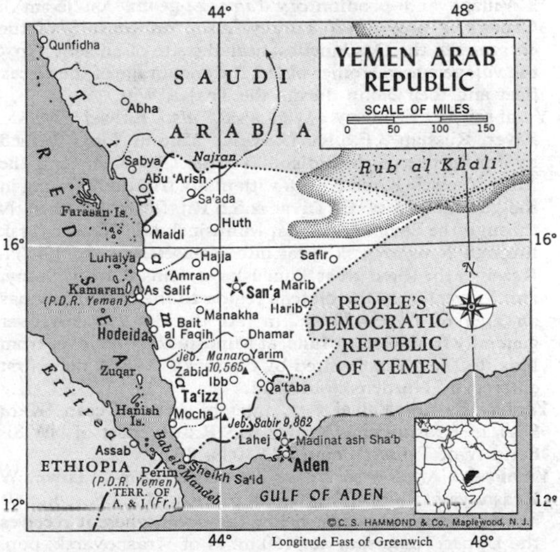

Yen \ˈyen\. Feudal state of early China under the Chou dynasty (1122–255 B.C.), in the extreme NE. Also so called under the Latter Han and Wei dynasties.

Ye·na·ki·ye·vo \ˌyen-ə-ˈkē-yi-və\ *or formerly* **Or·dzho·ni·kid·ze** \ˌȯr-ˌjän-ə-ˈkid-zə\. City, Donetsk Oblast, E

ə abut; ᵊ kitten, Fr. table; ər further; a back; ā bake; ä cot, cart; á Fr. bac; aù out; ch chin; e less; ē easy; g gift
i trip; ī life, j joke; k̲ Ger. ich, Buch; ⁿ Fr. vin; ŋ sing; ō flow; ȯ flaw; œ Fr. bœuf; œ̄ Fr. feu; ȯi coin; th thin
t̲h̲ this; ü loot; u̇ foot; ue Ger. füllen; ue̅ Fr. rue; y yet; ʸ Fr. digne \dēnʸ\, nuit \nwʸē\; yü few; yu̇ furious; zh vision

Ukrainian S.S.R., U.S.S.R.; pop. (1969e) 95,000; suburb of Donetsk.

Yen–an *or* **Yen·an** \'yen-'än\ *or* **Fu·shih** \'fü-'shi(ə)r\. Town, N Shensi prov., NE cen. China, on S bank of a tributary of the Yellow river; pop. (1971e) 45,000; museum (honoring Mao Tse-tung and Communist Party's years of refuge in Yen-an). After 1938 became headquarters of Eighth Route (Communist) Army which in the war against the Japanese controlled ab. 1,500,000 people in parts of Shensi, Kansu, and Ningsia Hui; also capital of Communists in Chinese civil war which followed World War II; captured by Nationalist forces Mar. 19, 1947; reoccupied by Communists Apr. 1948 and remained their capital until their capture of Peiping (Peking) Jan. 1949.

Ye·nan·gyaung \'yen-än-'jaủŋ\. Town, ✱ of Magwe division, Upper Burma, on the Irrawaddy river 130 m. SW of Mandalay; extensive oil fields, the most important in Burma; destroyed when abandoned by the British Apr. 17, 1942; retaken Apr. 16, 1945.

Yen·bo' \'yen-(,)bō\ *or* **Yan·bu'** \'yan-(,)bü\. Port on the Red Sea, Hejaz, W Saudi Arabia, 185 m. NNW of Jidda; seaport of Medina.

Yen–ch'eng *or* **Yen·cheng** \'yen-'chəŋ\. City, N cen. Kiangsu prov., E China, near coast 125 m. NE of Nanking.

Yen–chi \'yen-'jē\ *or* **Yen·ki** \'yen-'jē\. Town, SE Kirin prov., NE China, ab. 225 m. ESE of Ch'ang-ch'un; pop. (1970e) 130,000; ✱ of former Chientao prov., SE Manchukuo.

Yen–chi–hsien \'yen-'chē-shē-'en\ *or formerly* **Lung·ching–tsun** \'lủŋ-'jiŋ-'tsün\. Town and port, S Kirin prov., NE China, just S of Yen-chi near North Korea border.

Yen·di \'yen-dē\. Town, NE Ghana, W Africa, ab. 60 m. E of Tamale; pop. (1970p) 18,754.

Ye·ni·ce \,yə-nə-'je\ *or* **Sa·man·ti** \,sä-mən-'tē\. River, the W headstream of the Seyhan river in E cen. Turkey; ab. 100 m. long; rises at N end of Anti-Taurus Mts. and flows S into the Seyhan at ab. 37°30'N.

Yenifoça. See FOÇA 1.

Ye·ni·şe·hir \,yen-i-she-'hi(ə)r\ *or* **Ye·ni·shehr** \-'she(ə)r\. 1 Town, Bursa prov., NW Turkey, 30 m. E of Bursa; pop. (1965c) 11,352.

2 Village and promontory (*anc.* **Si·ge·um** \sī-'jē-əm\), Çanakkale prov., NW Turkey, Asia, on coast S of the entrance to the Dardanelles; near the site of ancient Troy; the village where Homer places the anchorage of the Greek fleet and their camp during the Trojan War.

Ye·ni·sei *or* **Ye·ni·sey** \,yen-ə-'sā\ *also* **Eni·sei** \,yen-\. River, Russian S.F.S.R., U.S.S.R.; 2566 m. long; formed by confluence of the Bolshoi Yenisei (Bei Kem) and the Maly Yenisei (Khua Kem), with many tributaries rising in the mountains of E Tuva A.S.S.R.; flows W, then N through the Sayan Mts. past Minusinsk and Krasnoyarsk through Krasnoyarsk Krai into Yenisei Bay at 71°45'N. Receives the three great Tunguska streams (Upper, Stony, and Lower) from the plateau region to the E; its basin has an area of 1,003,474 sq. m. At the delta frozen over generally from Oct. to June, at Minusinsk frozen over from Nov. to May. First visited by Cossacks c. 1618; delta first entered by Nordenskjöld 1875.

Yenisei Bay *or* **Enisei Bay.** Inlet of Arctic Ocean (Kara Sea), in Krasnoyarsk Krai, U.S.S.R.; on coast of NW Siberia W of Taimyr Penin., 72°30'N, 80°E.

Ye·ni·seisk \,yen-ə-'sāsk\ *or* **Eni·seisk** \,yen-\. Town, W Krasnoyarsk Krai, Russian S.F.S.R., U.S.S.R., on left bank of the Yenisei just below the point where it receives the Upper Tunguska, ab. 150 m. N of Krasnoyarsk; pop. (1967e) 19,000; has steamer connection with Krasnoyarsk; center for fur trade and gold mining. Founded 1618.

Yenisey. See YENISEI.

Yenishehr. See YENIŞEHIR.

Yenki. 1 Town, Kirin prov., China. See YEN-CHI.

2 Town, Sinkiang Uighur, China. See KARASHAHR.

Yen–man \'yen-'män\. See GREAT WALL.

Yenping. See NAN-P'ING.

Yen–t'ai. See CHEFOO.

Ye·ot·mal \yā-'ōt-mäl\. Town, E Maharashtra, E cen. India, 85 m. SW of Nagpur; pop. (1961c) 45,600; trade center; cotton gins.

Yeo·vil \'yō-,vil\. Municipal borough, Somersetshire, SW England, on the Yeo 36 m. S of Bristol; pop. (1971p) 25,492; helicopters, gloves.

Yer·ba Bue·na Island \,yər-bə-'bwā-nə-\ *or formerly* **Goat Island** \'gōt-\. Island, San Francisco Bay, California.

Ye·re·van \,yer-ə-'vän\ *or* **Ere·van** *or* **Eri·van** \(,)(y)er-ə-'vän\. City, ✱ of Armenian S.S.R., U.S.S.R., in W part on Razdan river, 110 m. S of Tbilisi; pop. (1970p) 767,000; chemicals, plastics, generators, turbines, machine tools, textiles, footwear, wine; hydroelectric power plants. Ruins of 16th cent. Turkish fort; Armenian state museum and theaters, Armenian State Univ. (1920), Armenian Academy of Sciences (1943), and various other educational and cultural institutions.

History: Site fortified since 8th cent. B.C. and part of Armenian kingdom since 6th cent.; a center of caravan trade across Transcaucasia since ancient times; successively under Romans, Parthians, Arabs, Mongols, Turks, Persians, Georgians, and Russians; fell to Russians 1827; made capital of Armenian S.S.R. 1920.

Yer·ing·ton \'yer-iŋ-tən\. City, ⊗ of Lyon co., W Nevada, 30 m. ESE of Carson City; pop. (1970c) 2010.

Yerushalayim. See JERUSALEM 2.

Yer·wa \'yer-wə\. See MAIDUGURI.

Ye·şil Ir·mak \yə-'shē(ə)-lir-'mäk\ *or anc.* **Iris** \'ī-rəs\. River, chiefly in Tokat and Amasya provs., N Turkey; 291 m. long; rises in Akdağ range W of Sivas, flows generally N into Black Sea, with wide delta just E of Samsun. Receives the Kelkit from the E.

Ye·şil·köy \,yesh-ēl-'kȯi\ *or Ital.* **San Ste·fa·no** \san-'stef-ə-,nō\. Village, İstanbul prov., Turkey, on the Sea of Marmara ab. 7 m. W of İstanbul. Treaty signed here Mar. 3, 1878 ending the Russo-Turkish War; its terms were: Romania, Serbia, and Montenegro recognized as independent; Bulgaria made a principality; part of Armenia ceded to Russia by the Porte, an indemnity paid, and reforms promised; modified by Treaty of Berlin July 13, 1878.

Yeso. See HOKKAIDŌ.

Yes·sen·tu·ki \,yə-sən-tủ-'kē\ *also* **Es·sen·tu·ki** \,yə-\. Town, Stavropol Krai, Russian S.F.S.R., U.S.S.R., on N slopes of Caucasus Mts. 10 m. W of Pyatigorsk; pop. (1967e) 53,000.

Yes·te \'yās-tə\. Commune, Albacete prov., SE Spain, 48 m. SE of Albacete; pop. (1970p) 7787.

Yetorofu. See ITURUP.

Yeu, Île d' \ēl-'dyər\. Island in Bay of Biscay off coast of Vendée dept., W France; 6 m. long by 2 m. wide; pop. (1962c) 4739; Pétain imprisoned here Nov. 1945.

Yev·pa·to·ri·ya \,yef-pə-'tōr-ē-(y)ə, -'tȯr-\ *or* **Ev·pa·to·ria** \,yef-\ *or* **Eu·pa·to·ria** \,ef-\. Town and seaport, W coast of Crimean Oblast, Ukrainian S.S.R., U.S.S.R., ab. 45 m. NW of Simferopol; pop. (1969e) 75,000; fishing port and health resort; taken from Turks by Russians 1783; landing place for Allied armies in Crimean War Sept. 1854.

Yezd. See YAZD.

Yezhovo–Cherkessk. See CHERKESSK.

Yezo. See HOKKAIDŌ.

Yhú *or* **Ihú** \ē-'(h)ü\. Town, Caaguazú dept., E cen. Paraguay, ab. 105 m. ENE of Asunción; pop. (1970e) 11,564.

Yi \'yē\. River, cen. Uruguay; 120 m. long; flows W into Río Negro.

Yin–ch'uan \'yin-'chwän, -chə-'wän\. Town, ✱ of Ningsia Hui, N cen. China.

Ying–k'ou *or* **Ying·kow** \'yiŋ-'kaủ, -'kō\ *or* **New·chwang** \'n(y)ü-chü-'äŋ, -chə-'wäŋ, -jü-'äŋ\ *also* **Niu·chwang** \'n(y)ü-\. City, SW Liaoning prov., NE China, on left bank of Liao ab. 13 m. from its mouth, 120 m. N of Dairen; pop. (1970e) 215,000; textiles. Formerly only the port of inland Newchwang but in 1858 became the trading port opened by treaty because of its superior location; only open port of Manchuria until 1907, was main export town for soybeans, bean cake, bean oil, cotton; in 20th cent. has lost trade in competition with Dairen and Tan-tung.

Ying–k'ou–hsien \'yiŋ-'kō-'shen\ *or formerly* **Ta·shih·kiao** \'dä-'shi(ə)r-chē-'au̇\. Town, S Liaoning prov., NE China, ab. 95 m. SSW of Mukden; railroad junction point for Ying-k'ou, 14 m. distant.

Yioúra. See GYAROS.

Yir·ga Alem \'yər-gə-ə-'lem\. Town, ✱ of Sidamo prov., S cen. Ethiopia; pop. (1970e) 13,715.

Yizréel. See JEZREEL.

Yizre'el, 'Emeq. See ESDRAELON, PLAIN OF.

Yngaví. See INGAVÍ.

Yoa·kum \'yō-kəm\. 1 County in Texas. See table at TEXAS.
2 City, De Witt and Lavaca cos., S Texas, 36 m. N of Victoria; pop. (1970c) 5755; leather goods; oil wells; truck, livestock farms.

Yo·be \'yō-(,)bā\. River, NE Nigeria; ab. 100 m. long; formed by confluence of Hadejia and another headstream; flows E to NW Lake Chad.

Yo·do \'yōd-(,)ō\. 1 Lake, Kyōto prefecture, W cen. Honshū, Japan, just S of Kyōto, near junction of Uji and Hozu rivers which form the Yodo river.
2 *or Jap.* **Yo·do·ga·wa** \,yōd-ə-'gä-wə\. River, W cen. Honshū, Japan; formed by the Uji and Hozu in S Kyōto prefecture S of Kyōto, flows S into Ōsaka Bay at Ōsaka through two mouths, the Ajikawa and the Kizugawa. See UJI 1.

Yog Point \'yōg-\. Point, N Catanduanes I., E Phil., 14°06'N, 124°12'E.

Yo·ho \'yō-(,)hō\. River and scenic valley, Yoho National Park, SE British Columbia; contains Takkakaw waterfall; joins Kicking Horse river to flow into the Columbia.

Yoho National Park. See CANADA, *National Parks.*

Yo·joa, Lake \-yō-'hō-ə\. Lake, W cen. Honduras; 25 m. long, ab. 6 m. wide; affords water communication via the Blanco river and the Ulúa river with the seaport town of Puerto Cortés.

Yok·kai·chi \yō-'kī-chē\. City, Mie prefecture, S Honshū, Japan, on NW shore of Ise Bay 25 m. SW of Nagoya; pop. (1970c) 229,234; ships textiles; bombed by U.S. forces 1945.

Yo·ko·ha·ma \,yō-kə-'häm-ə\. Seaport city, ✱ of Kanagawa prefecture, SE Honshū, Japan, on W shore of Tokyo Bay, 18 m. S of Tokyo; pop. (1971e) 2,279,483; one of the principal Japanese seaports and part of the Tokyo urban-industrial region, producing textiles (including silk), machinery, chemicals, steel; motor vehicles, electrical equipment; shipyards, oil refineries; Yokohama National Univ. (1949), Yokohama Municipal Univ. (1949).
History: In feudal era a fishing village; visited by Commodore Perry 1854; chosen as site of foreign settlement after 1859; harbor completed 1896; extraterritorial rights of foreign settlement abolished 1899; absorbed Kanagawa (*q.v.*) 1901; almost entirely destroyed by earthquake and fire 1923; rebuilt and modernized. Again largely destroyed by U.S. bombing in 1945 and afterwards rebuilt.

Yo·ko·su·ka \yō-'kȯ-s(ə-)kə\. Seaport city, Kanagawa prefecture, SE Honshū, Japan, on Tokyo Bay, 12 m. S of Yokohama; pop. (1970c) 347,576; shipbuilding and fishing center and base for a whaling fleet; has facilities of U.S. Navy and Japanese Maritime Self-Defense Force. Before 1865 a fishing village; made a naval base 1884 and through World War II one of the principal Japanese naval bases and shipyards; largely destroyed by U.S. bombing in 1945 but since rebuilt.

Yo·la \'yō-lə\. Town, E Nigeria, on the upper Benue river near Cameroon border; ab. 480 m. by river above Lokoja and reached by steamers of light draft in flood season; a former Fulah capital.

Yo·lo \'yō-,lō\. County in California. See table at CALIFORNIA.

Yom \'yəm, 'yäm\. River, NW Thailand; 345 m. long; flows S from mountains on N border to join the Nan just above its confluence with the Ping.

Yo·me–shi·ma \,yō-mē-'shē-mə, 'yō-mi-shē-,mä\. One of the Bonin Is., Japan.

Yo·na·ba·ru \,yō-nə-'bär-(,)ü\. Locality on E coast of Okinawa I., Ryukyu Is., Japan, at S end across from Naha on S shore of Nakagusuku Bay; airfield; severe fighting May 1945; airfield captured May 14.

Yo·na·go \yō-'näg-(,)ō\. Town, Tottori prefecture, W Honshū, Japan; pop. (1970c) 109,096; a rail and shipping center N of Okayama, with good harbor on Sea of Japan.

Yo·ne·za·wa \yō-'nā-zə-,wä, 'yō-nā-'zä-wə\. City, Yamagata prefecture, N Honshū, Japan, 55 m. E of Niigata; pop. (1970c) 92,764; its chief industry for 150 years has been the weaving of silken fabrics.

Yon·kers \'yäŋ-kərz\. City, Westchester co., SE New York, on Hudson river adjoining Greater New York on the N; center of city is ab. 15 m. N of S end of Manhattan I.; pop. (1970c) 204,370; residential suburb of New York City; elevators, copper cable, sugar, tools, dairy and paper products; St. Joseph's Seminary and Coll. (1839), Elizabeth Seton Coll. (1961). Part of purchase made by Dutch West India Company from Indians 1639; included in grant of land made 1646 to "Jonker" or "Jonkheer" Van der Donck; became part of Philipse Manor after 1672; was disputed territory in Revolutionary War; incorp. as village 1855, chartered as city 1872.

Yonne \'yän\. 1 River, cen. France; 182 m. long; flows N out of Nièvre dept. into Seine river at Montereau-faut-Yonne.
2 Department of NE cen. France. See table at FRANCE.

Yo·no \'yō-,nō\. City, Saitama prefecture, Honshū, Japan, 17 m. NNW of Tokyo; pop. (1970c) 62,802.

Yor·ba Lin·da \,yȯr-bə-'lin-də, ,yȯr-\. City, Orange co., SW California, 25 m. SE of Los Angeles; pop. (1970c) 11,856; oil wells; citrus fruit.

York \'yȯ(ə)rk\. 1 Estuary, E Virginia; ab. 40 m. long; formed by confluence of Pamunkey and Mattaponi rivers at West Point, flows SE into Chesapeake Bay.
2 Name of counties in five states of the U.S. See tables at MAINE, NEBRASKA, PENNSYLVANIA, SOUTH CAROLINA, VIRGINIA.
3 Town, Sumter co., W Alabama, 5 m. E of Mississippi border and 18 m. W of Tombigbee river; pop. (1970c) 3044.
4 Town, York co., SW Maine, on Atlantic Ocean 25 m. SSW of Biddeford; pop. (1970c) 5690. Includes **York Beach** and **York Harbor,** summer resorts.
5 City, ⊗ of York co., SE Nebraska, 41 m. E of Grand Island; pop. (1970c) 13,449; hog processing; grain farms; York Coll. (1890).
6 Industrial city, ⊗ of York co., S Pennsylvania, 23 m. S of Harrisburg; pop. (1970c) 50,335; refrigerators, turbines, agricultural equipment, building materials, stoves; York Coll. of Pennsylvania (1941). Settled 1735; capital of American colonies during British occupation of Philadelphia 1777–78; chartered as borough 1787; briefly occupied June 1863 by Confederate forces under Jubal Early; incorporated as city 1887.
7 Town, ⊗ of York co., N South Carolina, 13 m. WNW of Rock Hill; pop. (1970c) 5081; textiles, lumber, cottonseed oil; peaches.
8 County, New Brunswick, Canada. See table at NEW BRUNSWICK.
9 County, Ontario, Canada. See table at ONTARIO.
10 City, Ontario, Canada. See TORONTO 2.
11 County in England. See YORKSHIRE.

12 *anc.* **Eb·o·ra·cum** \i-ˈbȯr-ə-kəm, -ˈbär-\ *or* **Eb·u·ra·cum** \i-ˈb(y)ůr-ə-kəm\. City and county borough, Yorkshire, N England, at confluence of Foss and Ouse rivers 20 m. ENE of Leeds; pop. (1971p) 104,513; railroad center and livestock market; produces chocolate products, scientific instruments, glass, furniture, hydraulic pumps; railroad shops; printing, brewing; 13th–15th cent. cathedral (York Minster) with notable stained glass, 14th cent. walls, 13th cent. tower, 14th cent. Merchant Taylors' Hall, Railway Museum; Univ. of York (1963).

History: Successively a Celtic, Roman, Angle, Danish, and Norman settlement; Constantine the Great proclaimed Roman emperor here 306 A.D.; prosperous wool-trading town in Middle Ages and meeting place of several Parliaments 1175 ff.; in 15th and 16th cents. scene of presentation of the 48 plays of the York Cycle, one of four collections of English mystery plays (see CHESTER 10, COVENTRY 3, WAKEFIELD 5).

York, Cape. 1 Northern point of Cape York Penin., Queensland, Australia, on E side of Gulf of Carpentaria, 10°42′S, 142°31′E; extends into Torres Strait.

2 Point, SW Hayes Penin., NW Greenland, on N shore of Baffin Bay, 75°53′N, 66°12′W. Station here used by Peary and Bartlett on Polar expeditions. Noted for its large iron meteorites, one of which (weighing 100 tons) was brought by Peary to American National History Museum in New York. Monument erected here 1932 to Peary.

Yorke Peninsula \ˈyȯ(ə)rk-\ *or* **Yorke's Peninsula** \ˈyȯ(ə)rks-\. Peninsula, SE South Australia, bet. Spencer Gulf on W and Gulf of St. Vincent on E; ab. 100 m. long.

York·shire \ˈyȯ(ə)rk-ˌshi(ə)r, -shər\ *or* **York.** County, N England; 6123 sq. m.; pop. (1971p) 5,047,567; includes three administrative counties, North Riding (⊗ Northallerton), East Riding (⊗ Beverly), West Riding (⊗ Wakefield), and the City of York, which is a county of itself, outside the ridings; see table at ENGLAND. Rivers include Ouse, Swale, Wharfe, Aire, Derwent; agriculture, livestock raising, fisheries, coal mining, iron and steel manufacturing, manufacturing of wool and cotton textiles, leather goods, chemicals, shipbuilding. Towns include Leeds, Sheffield, Hull, Bradford, Wakefield, Middlesbrough, Rotherham.

York·ton \ˈyȯ(ə)rk-tən\. City, SE Saskatchewan, Canada, 110 m. ENE of Regina; pop. (1971p) 13,149; flour, dairy products, leather; grain, livestock farms; Saint Joseph's Coll. (1919).

York·town \ˈyȯ(ə)rk-ˌtaůn\. 1 Town, De Witt co., S Texas, 30 m. WNW of Victoria; pop. (1970c) 2411.

2 Town, ⊗ of York co., SE Virginia, on York river 20 m. N of Newport News; in Colonial National Historical Park; scene in 1781 of siege of British forces under Cornwallis by Washington and Rochambeau in Revolution and of surrender of Cornwallis; besieged by Union forces under McClellan in Civil War and evacuated 1862; U.S. naval base established 1917.

York·ville \ˈyȯ(ə)rk-ˌvil\. 1 City, ⊗ of Kendall co., NE Illinois; pop. (1970c) 2049; livestock, soybeans.

2 Village, Oneida co., cen. New York, on Mohawk river 3 m. WNW of Utica; pop. (1970c) 3425; residential suburb.

3 Village, Belmont and Jefferson cos., E Ohio, on Ohio river 15 m. S of Steubenville; pop. (1970c) 1656.

Yo·ro \ˈyōr-(ˌ)ō, ˈyȯr-\. 1 Department of N Honduras. See table at HONDURAS.

2 Town, its ✱; pop. (1961c) 2916.

Yor·tan Te·pe \ˌyȯr-ˌtän-te-ˈpä\. Locality, W Turkey; archaeological site, ruins of ancient city of W Lydia, ESE of Pergamum.

Yor·u·ba·land \ˈyȯr-ə-bə-ˌland\. Former kingdom, now part of Nigeria; ab. 35,000 sq. m.; country of the Yorubas.

Yo·sem·i·te Falls \yō-ˌsem-ət-ē-\. Two falls, Yosemite National Park, E cen. California; upper 1430 ft., lower 320 ft., total drop including a series of cascades 2425 ft.

Yosemite National Park. See UNITED STATES, *National Parks.*

Yosemite Valley. Valley of the upper Merced river, cen. California, in S Yosemite National Park; ab. 7 m. long; valley floor ab. 4000 ft. above sea level, walls 3000–4000 ft. high; many waterfalls.

Yo·shi·no \ˈyō-shi-ˌnō\. River, NE Shikoku, Japan; 146 m. long; flows E into Kii Channel at Tokushima.

Yosh·kar–Ola *also* **Iosh·kar Ola** \yəsh-ˈkär-ə-ˈlä\. Town, ✱ of Mari A.S.S.R., Russian S.F.S.R., U.S.S.R., ab. 80 m. NW of Kazan; pop. (1970p) 166,000.

Yŏ·su \ˈyə-ˈsü\. Town, South Chŏlla prov., South Korea, ab. 52 m. SE of Kwangju; pop. (1970e) 113,651.

Youghal \ˈyȯl\. Urban district and commercial seaport, E co. Cork, SW Eire, on **Youghal Bay,** estuary of Blackwater river; pop. (1966c) 5108; resort. A Norse settlement in 9th cent.; site of first Franciscan monastery in Ireland (1224); Sir Walter Raleigh was mayor 1588–89 and is said to have planted the first potato here.

Yough·io·ghe·ny \ˌyäk-ə-ˈgā-nē\. River, NW Maryland and SW Pennsylvania; ab. 150 m. long; flows N through NW Maryland into Pennsylvania, and NW into Monongahela river at McKeesport. Navigable for 9 m.

Young \ˈyəŋ\. County in Texas. See table at TEXAS.

Young Island. One of the Balleny Is., Antarctica; ab. 19 m. long by 5 m. wide; rises to a plateau ab. 4000 ft.

Youngs·town \ˈyəŋ(k)-ˌstaůn\. City, ⊗ of Mahoning co., Mahoning and Trumbull cos., NE Ohio, on Mahoning river 43 m. E of Akron; pop. (1970c) 139,788; center of iron and steel industry; also produces plastics, paper products, aluminum extrusions, automobile and aircraft parts, castings, rubber tubing; limestone quarries; Youngstown Univ. (1908). Platted 1802; iron manufacturing begun 1805 and progressively expanded throughout 19th and early 20th cents.; incorporated 1859.

Youngs·ville \ˈyəŋz-ˌvil\. Borough, Warren co., NW Pennsylvania, 36 m. NNE of Oil City; pop. (1970c) 2158.

Young·wood \ˈyəŋ-ˌwůd\. Industrial borough, Westmoreland co., SW Pennsylvania, 27 m. ESE of Pittsburgh; pop. (1970c) 3057.

Yous·sou·fia \yů-ˈsüf-ē-ə\ *or formerly* **Lou·is Gen·til** \lə-ˌwē-zhäⁿ-ˈtē\. Town, W cen. Morocco, ENE of Safi; junction point on railroad connecting the port of Safi with Casablanca and Marrakech; phosphate mines in region.

Yoz·gat \yȯz-ˈgät\. 1 Province of cen. Turkey, Asia. See table at TURKEY.

2 Town, its ✱, 100 m. E of Ankara; pop. (1965c) 23,081.

Ypa·ca·raí \ˌē-pə-ˌkär-ä-ˈē\ *or* **Ypa·ca·ray** \-kä-ˈrī\. 1 Lake, S cen. Paraguay, near Asunción; pleasure resort.

2 Town, Central dept., S Paraguay, ab. 160 m. ESE of Asunción; pop. (1970e) 11,926.

Ypa·né \ˌē-pə-ˈnā\. Town, Central dept., S Paraguay, ab. 80 m. SE of Asunción; pop. (1970e) 5741.

Ypi·ran·ga *or* **Ipi·ran·ga** \ˌē-pi-ˈraŋ-gə\. Plain, São Paulo state, SE Brazil, near São Paulo; site where independence of Brazil from Portugal was declared Sept. 7, 1822 by Prince Pedro.

Ypoá, Lake \-ˌē-pə-ˈwä\. Lake, S Paraguay; ab. 100 sq. m.; navigable for small boats.

Ypres. See IEPER.

Yp·si·lan·ti \ˌip-sə-ˈlant-ē\. Industrial city, Washtenaw co., SE Michigan, 8 m. SE of Ann Arbor; pop. (1970c) 29,538; automobile parts, paper, ladders; agriculture; Eastern Michigan Univ. (1849), Cleary Coll. (1883).

Yp·si·lon Mountain \ˈip-sə-ˌlän-\. Peak, Larimer co., N Colorado; 13,507 ft.

Yre·ka \wī-ˈrē-kə\ *or* **Yreka City.** Town, ⊗ of Siskiyou co., N California, 100 m. NE of Eureka; pop. (1970c) 5394; dairy products, furniture; gold mines; diversified agriculture.

Ysabel. See SANTA ISABEL 4.

Ysa·bel Channel \ˌiz-ə-ˌbel-\. Passage bet. New Hanover I. and the Saint Matthias Group, N Bismarck Archipelago, connecting Pacific Ocean with Bismarck Sea.

Yser \ē-ˈze(ə)r\. River, N France and Belgium; 48 m. long; flows into North Sea; battles 1914–18.

Yssel. See IJSSEL.

Yssel, Lake. See IJSSELMEER.

Ystad \'ü-stəd\. Seaport, Malmöhus co., SW Sweden, on the Baltic Sea; pop. (1970e) 14,211; iron foundries, steelworks, dairies.

Ystrad Fflur. See STRATA FLORIDA.

Ystradyfodwg. See RHONDDA.

Yst·wyth\'ist-with, 'əst-\. Small river, cen. Wales; flows W into cen. Cardigan Bay at Aberystwyth.

Ythan \'ī-thən\. River, NE Scotland; 35 m. long; flows SE in Aberdeen co. and empties into North Sea ab. 12 m. N of Aberdeen.

Yu. See SIANG 2.

Yüan *or* **Yuan** \yü-'än, -'an\. 1 River, China. See RED 4.

2 *or* **Yuen** \yü-'än, -'an, -'en\. River, SE cen. China; 537 m. long; rises in cen. Kweichow near Kuei-yang, flows NE in Hunan prov. to Tung-t'ing Hu (lake); navigable for most of its course.

Yüan Chiang. See RED 4.

Yuanchow. See CHIH-CHIANG.

Yu·ba \'yü-bə\. 1 River, N cen. California; its branches from Sierra and Nevada cos. join in Yuba co., then flow SW into Sacramento river N of Sacramento. See BULLARD'S BAR DAM and LAKE SPAULDING DAM.

2 County in California. See table at CALIFORNIA.

Yuba City. City, ⊗ of Sutter co., N cen. California, on Feather river 42 m. N of Sacramento; pop. (1970c) 13,986; packs and ships fruit and nuts; frozen food, dairy products; fruit, rice.

Yū·ba·ri \'yü-bə-(,)rē\. City, Hokkaidō prefecture, Hokkaidō, Japan, 35 m. E of Sapporo; pop. (1971p) 69,871.

Yubi, Cape. See JUBY, CAPE.

Yu·ca·ma·ni \,yü-kə-'män-ē\. Peak in the Andes Mts. in Moquegua dept., S Peru; 17,860 ft.

Yu·ca·tán \,yü-kə-'tan, -'tän\. 1 Peninsula, comprising the states of Campeche, Yucatán, and the territory of Quintana Roo in SE Mexico, and British Honduras and the N section of Guatemala in Central America; separates Gulf of Mexico from Caribbean Sea; its NE point, Cape Catoche, extends into Yucatán Channel; Bay of Campeche to the W and Cozumel I. off NE coast. Rich in historical associations; seat of Maya civilization (1st empire 100 B.C. to 630 A.D.; transitional period 630 to 930; 2d empire 960–1200) and of Toltecs 1200 to 1450. Many notable ruins of cities, temples, pyramids, esp. Chichén Itzá, Uaxactún, Uxmal (*qq.v.*).

2 State, N Yucatán penin., SE Mexico. See table at MEXICO.

Yucatán Channel. Channel bet. W end of Cuba and Yucatán penin., Mexico, connecting the Caribbean Sea with the Gulf of Mexico.

Yuc·ca House National Monument \'yək-ə-\. See UNITED STATES, *National Monuments.*

Yuen. See YÜAN 2.

Yug \'yük\. River, E Vologda Oblast, Russian S.F.S.R., U.S.S.R.; 305 m. long; flows N to unite with the Sukhona and form the Northern Dvina just above Veliki Ustyug.

Yu·gor·ski \yü-'gȯr-skē\ *or formerly* **Pai Khoi** \'pī-'kȯi\. Peninsula, E Nenets National Okrug, Russian S.F.S.R., U.S.S.R., bet. Kara Sea and Barents Sea; off its NW point is Vaigach I.

Yu·go·sla·via \,yü-gō-'släv-e-ə\ *or* **Ju·go·sla·via** \,yü-gō-\ *or Serb.* **Ju·go·sla·vi·ja** \-'släv-ē-ə\; *officially* **Socialist Federal Republic of Yugoslavia** *or Serbo-Croat.* **So·ci·ja·lis·tič·ka Fe·de·ra·tiv·na Re·pu·bli·ka Jugoslavija** \sō-tsē-yä-'lēs-tich-kə-,fed-ər-ə-'tēv-nə-rä-'püb-lē-kə\, *or formerly* **Kingdom of the Serbs, Cro·ats, and Slo·venes** \-'sərbz, 'krōtz . . . 'slō-,vēnz; -'krō-,ats-\ *or Serbo-Croat.* **Kral·je·vi·na Srba, Hrva·ta i Slo·ve·na·ca** \,kräl-yə-'vē-nə-'sər-bə, 'kr̥ə-və-tə-ē-,slō-vən-'ät-sə\. Republic, SE Europe, bounded on N by Austria and Hungary, on E by Romania and Bulgaria, on S by Greece and Albania, on W by the Adriatic Sea, and on NW by Italy; 98,766 sq. m.; pop. (1971p) 20,504,516; ✱ Belgrade.

Physical features: Has almost no coastal plain, the coastal region being a white limestone plateau (karst) including the Dinaric Alps and the Velebit range; in NW are the Karawanken Alps on Austrian border and the Julian Alps (highest point Triglav 9395 ft.) on Italian border; in S is a part of the North Albanian Alps; in cen. part is plateau (Slavic *planina,* "mountain pasture") region 2000 to 8200 ft. In E is a section of the Danube which in Yugoslavia receives the Tisza and the Drava rivers from the N, the Sava (its chief tributaries the Una, Vrbas, Drina) from the W, and the Morava (its chief tributary the Ibar) from the S; in SE flowing through Greece into Gulf of Salonika is the Vardar. *Lakes:* Parts of Scutari, Ohrid, and Prespa on SW border. *Chief products:* Corn, wheat, sugar beet, oats, fruit; tobacco; livestock; coal, iron ore, lead, bauxite; manufacturing: chemicals, steel, textiles; tourism. *Chief towns:* Belgrade, Zagreb, Skopje, Sarajevo, Ljubljana, Novi Sad. Consists of the following six republics (for further details, see their individual entries):

NAME	AREA (sq. m.)	POP. (1971p)	CAPITAL
Bosnia and Herzegovina	19,741	3,742,852	Sarajevo
Croatia	21,829	4,422,564	Zagreb
Macedonia	9,928	1,647,104	Skopje
Montenegro	5,333	530,361	Titograd
Slovenia	7,819	1,725,088	Ljubljana
Serbia[1]	34,115	8,436,547	Belgrade

[1]Includes the autonomous oblast of Kosovo-Metohija and the autonomous province of Vojvodina.

History: At collapse of Austria-Hungary proclaimed Kingdom of Serbs, Croats, and Slovenes, 1918 (see AUSTRIA-HUNGARY, SERBIA, CROATIA, BOSNIA, MONTENEGRO, DALMATIA, and SLOVENIA for earlier history of component parts); engaged in dispute with Italy over Fiume 1919–24; signed treaties with Czechoslovakia 1920, with Romania 1921, the beginning of Little Entente; ruled by absolute monarchy from 1929–31, at which time name was changed officially to Yugoslavia and the country was divided into 9 counties not based on racial lines; tried to end struggle bet. federalist minorities (Croats, Slovenes) and the predominantly Serbian government by providing for greater autonomy of Croatia and Slovenia in federalized constitution 1939; overthrew the government which had signed Axis pact Mar. 1941; invaded by German forces Apr. 6, 1941 and during rest of war was occupied by German, Italian, Hungarian, and Bulgarian troops; established a Communist republic 1945; its insistence on developing a national form of Communism precipitated friction with the U.S.S.R. and led to Yugoslavia's expulsion from the Cominform 1948; settled Trieste dispute with Italy 1954; partial reconciliation with U.S.S.R. 1955; adopted new constitution 1963; Soviet position (of 1955) *vis-à-vis* Yugoslavia reaffirmed 1971.

Yuki. See UNGGI.

Yu·kon \'yü-,kän\. 1 City, Canadian co., cen. Oklahoma, 13 m. W of Oklahoma City; pop. (1970c) 8411; flour and feed mills; grain, livestock.

2 River, NW North America; formed by confluence of Lewes and Pelly rivers in SW Yukon Territory, Canada; 1979 m. long from the headwaters of the Lewes; flows NW across Yukon border into Alaska, then SW from its junction with the Porcupine across cen. Alaska to Bering Sea S of Norton Sound. Receives Stewart and Klondike tributaries from the E in Yukon Territory, the Porcupine (*q.v.*) from the NE, the Koyukuk from the N, and the Tanana from the S, in Alaska; has delta 80 to 90 m. wide with only one mouth navigable. Third longest river highway in North America; its entire course of 1265 m. in Alaska is navigable, also as far as Dawson and to Whitehorse for

YUGOSLAVIA is a federation of six republics. The Serbian republic includes an autonomous province (Vojvodina), and an autonomous oblast (Kosovo-Metohija).

smaller vessels. Frozen over Oct. to June. Its lower course is broad and muddy flowing through a marshy plain. At its bend in NE Alaska it widens into the **Yukon Flats** (10 to 20 m. wide for ab. 200 m.).

3 Territory, NW Canada, bounded on N by Arctic Ocean, E by Northwest Territories, on S by British Columbia, and on W by Alaska; 207,076 sq. m.; pop. (1970e) 16,000; ✱ Whitehorse. *Physical features:* A plateau region with several mountain ranges: St. Elias Mts., across SW corner (containing Mt. Logan, highest mountain in Canada, 19,850 ft.); N end of Rocky Mts. in S, including Stikine Mts.; the Mackenzie Mts. along Mackenzie dist. border; and the Ogilvie Mts. in cen. part. Chief river the upper Yukon, with its tributaries and headstreams, the Porcupine, Klondike, White, Lewes, and Pelly; in the N is the Peel, a tributary of the Mackenzie and in the S the upper Liard. No large lakes (largest Kluane 184 sq. m.), but many small ones. Whitehorse is head of navigation of the Yukon and also terminus of only railroad, running S through White Pass to Skagway in Alaska. Many river valleys have extensive forests; mineral resources are very great, esp. silver, lead, gold, cadmium. *Chief towns:* Whitehorse, Dawson, Mayo. Formed from Northwest Territories in 1898, soon after the Klondike gold rush.

Yu·ma \ˈyü-mə\. **1** Name of counties in two states of the U.S. See tables at ARIZONA and COLORADO.

2 City, ⊗ of Yuma co., SW corner of Arizona, on Colorado river 20 m. N of Mexican border; pop. (1970c) 29,007; ships fruit and vegetables; fertilizer; gold mines; agriculture; Arizona Western Coll. (1963); incorporated 1871.

3 Town, Yuma co., NE Colorado, 43 m. SE of Sterling; pop. (1970c) 2259; grain farms.

Yü–men \ˈyü-ˈmən\ *or* **Lao–chün–miao** \ˈlau̇-ˈchu̇n-ˈmyau̇\. Town, Kansu prov., N cen. China, ab. 430 m. NW of Lan-chou; pop. (1970e) 325,000.

Yun·gay \ˈyüŋ-ˈgī\. City, Ancash dept., NW Peru, W of Mt. Huascarán; scene of a battle in which Chilean troops under Manuel Bulnes overthrew the Peruvian-Bolivian confederation Jan. 20, 1839; largely destroyed by earthquake 1970.

Yungchang. See PAOSHAN.

Yungki. See KIRIN 4.

Yungkia. See WEN-CHOU.

Yung–ning. See NAN-NING.

Yung–ting *or* **Yung·ting** \ˈyu̇ŋ-ˈdiŋ\ *or* **Hun** \ˈhu̇n\. River, China; ab. 300 m. long; rises in N Shansi prov., NE China, flows generally E and SE to the Pai at Tientsin.

Yün Ho. See GRAND CANAL 1.

Yunkang. See TA-T'UNG.

Yun·nan \yü-ˈnän\. **1** *also* **Yün·nan** \yü-ˈnän\. Province, S China, bounded on N by Tibet and Szechwan, on E by Kweichow and Kwangsi Chuang, on S by North Vietnam, Laos, and Burma, and on W by Burma; 168,417 sq. m.; pop. (1968e) 23,000,000; ✱ K'un-ming. Very mountainous esp. in N and W; its cen. part a plateau averaging 6500 ft. and sloping to SE. Has many small lakes; crossed by 3 major river systems—the Yangtze (here known as the Kinsha), the Mekong and Salween—and the source of two others—the Hsi (Hung-shui) and the Yüan; the N courses of the first three flow through great gorges. *Chief products:* Rice, corn, sweet potatoes, wheat, tea, sugar; coal, iron, tin, copper, lead, zinc, precious stones. A large part of its population consists of Miaos, Lolos, Shans, and other non-Chinese elements. *Chief cities:* K'un-ming, Ko-chiu, Meng-tzu. Long independent (because of its isolation) during the historical development of China; overrun by Kublai Khan in 13th cent., completely conquered 1382, and became part of empire in 17th cent.; scene of great Panthay (Muslim) revolt 1855–73; part of S section of province seized by Japanese 1942.

2 City, China. See K'UN-MING.

Yunque, El. See EL YUNQUE.

Yura Strait. See KITAN STRAIT.

Yu·ré·cua·ro \yə-ˈrā-kwə-(ˌ)rō\. Town, Michoacán state, SW Mexico, 65 m. N of Uruapan; munic. pop. (1970p) 20,042.

Yurev. See TARTU.

Yur·ga \ˈyu̇r-gə\. Town, Kemerovo Oblast, Russian S.F.S.R., U.S.S.R., ab. 55 m. S of Tomsk; pop. (1969e) 56,000.

Yu·ri·ma·guas \ˌyu̇r-i-ˈmäg-wəs\. Town, Loreto prov., NE Peru, on Huallaga river; pop. (1961c) 11,700.

Yu·ri·ria \yə-ˈrē-rē-ə\. Town, Guanajuato state, cen. Mexico, W of Salvatierra; munic. pop. (1970p) 53,228.

Yus·ca·rán \ˌyü-skə-ˈrän\. Town, ✱ of El Paraíso dept., Honduras, 35 m. SE of Tegucigalpa; pop. (1961c) 1608; cereals, fruit, coffee, silver.

Yu·sef, Bahr \ˌba-hər-ˈyü-səf\. Dry bed of the Nile, Egypt, on its W side, used as an artificial irrigation channel; extends ab. 270 m. from near Asyūt to Al-Faiyūm governorate.

Yu·ty \ˈyüt-ē\. Town, S Caazapá dept., S Paraguay; dist. pop. (1970e) 23,788.

Yu·zhno–Sa·kha·linsk \ˌyüzh-nə-sə-kə-ˈlin(t)sk\ *or formerly* **To·yo·ha·ra** \ˌtō-yə-ˈhär-ə\. Town, ✱ of Sakhalin Oblast, Russian S.F.S.R., U.S.S.R.; pop. (1970p) 106,000; pulp and paper; formerly Japanese.

Yuzovka. See DONETSK.

Yve·lines \ēv-ˈlēn\. Department of N France. See table at FRANCE.

Yver·don \ē-ver-ˈdōⁿ\ *or* **Yver·dun** \-ˈdœ̄ⁿ\ *or Ger.* **Ifer·ten** \ˈē-fərt-ᵊn\ *or anc.* **Eb·u·ro·du·num** \ˌeb-yə-rō-ˈd(y)ü-nəm\. Commune, Vaud canton, W Switzerland, 18 m. N of Lausanne; pop. (1970c) 20,538; tourist resort; manufactures locomotives and railroad cars, cigars; 12th cent. castle; 18th cent. church.

Yve·tot \ēv-ˈtō\. Town, Seine-Maritime dept., N France, 20 m. NW of Rouen; pop. (1962c) 8294; a small monarchy 15th–16th cents., the title of king being applied to its lords who became subject of one of Béranger's most famous songs, *Le Roi d'Yvetot* (1813).

Yzabal, Lake. See IZABAL, LAKE.

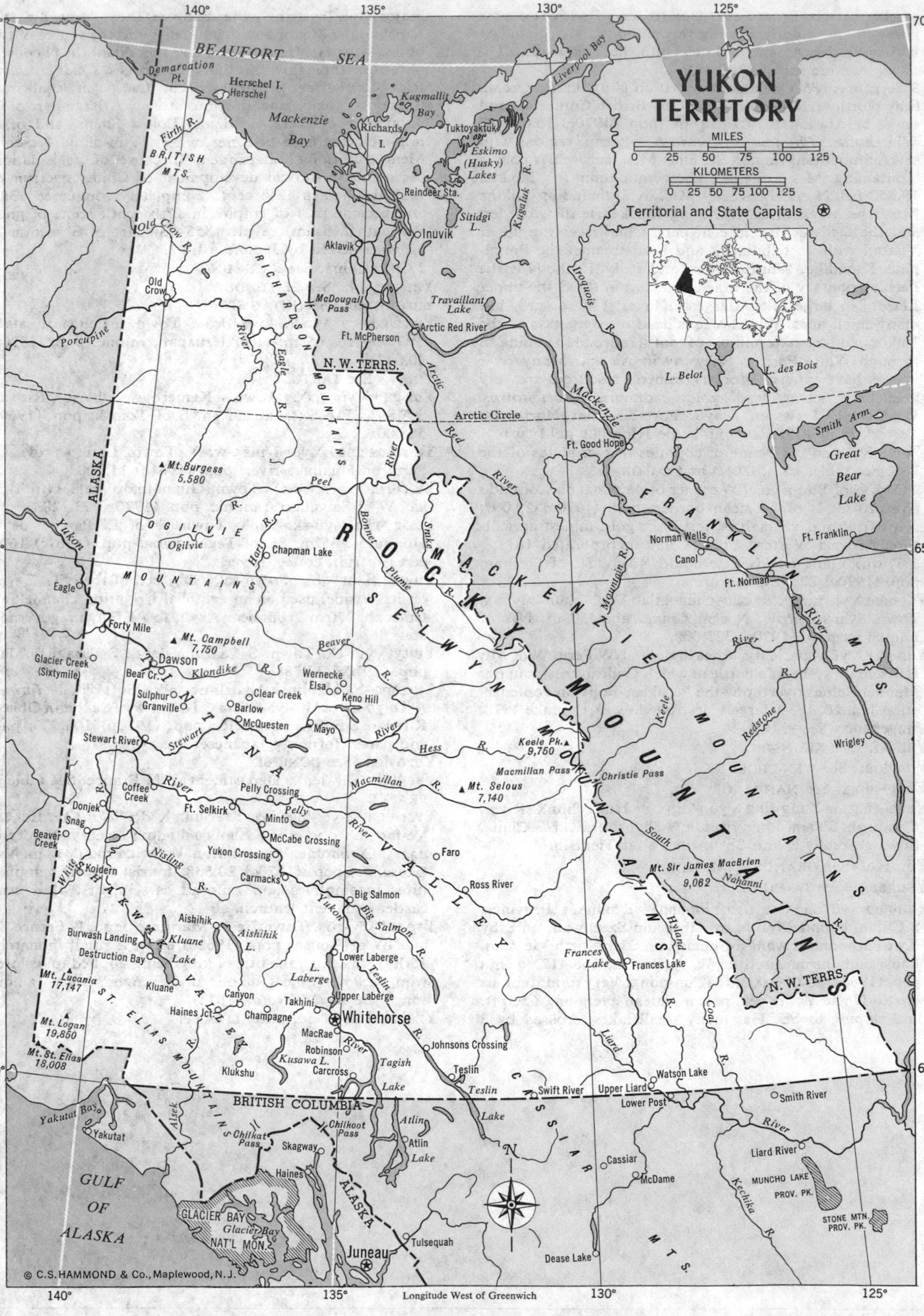
YUKON TERRITORY
MILES
0 25 50 75 100 125
KILOMETERS
0 25 50 75 100 125
Territorial and State Capitals
BEAUFORT SEA
Demarcation Pt.
Herschel I.
Herschel
Mackenzie Bay
Kugmallit Bay
Richards I.
Tuktoyaktuk
Eskimo (Husky) Lakes
Liverpool Bay
Reindeer Sta.
Inuvik
Aklavik
Sitidgi L.
Kugaluk R.
Firth R.
BRITISH MTS.
Old Crow R.
Old Crow
RICHARDSON MOUNTAINS
Porcupine
McDougall Pass
Ft. McPherson
Travaillant Lake
Arctic Red River
Iroquois R.
L. Belot
L. des Bois
N. W. TERRS.
Eagle R.
Arctic Circle
Smith Arm
Great Bear Lake
Ft. Good Hope
Mackenzie
Mt. Burgess 5,580
ALASKA
Peel
OGILVIE MOUNTAINS
Ogilvie
Hart R.
Chapman Lake
Bonnet Plume R.
Snake R.
ROCKY
MACKENZIE MOUNTAINS
SELWYN MOUNTAINS
FRANKLIN MTS.
Norman Wells
Canol
Ft. Franklin
Ft. Norman
Yukon
Eagle
Forty Mile
Mt. Campbell 7,750
Glacier Creek (Sixtymile)
Dawson
Bear Cr.
Klondike
Beaver R.
Wernecke
Elsa
Keno Hill
Clear Creek
Sulphur
Granville
Barlow
McQuesten
Mayo
TINTINA
Stewart River
Stewart
River
Hess R.
Keele Pk. 9,750
Keele
Redstone
Wrigley
Macmillan Pass
Christie Pass
Macmillan
Mt. Selous 7,140
Coffee Creek
Pelly Crossing
Ft. Selkirk
Pelly
Minto
Donjek
Snag
Beaver Creek
McCabe Crossing
Yukon Crossing
Nisling
Koidern
White
Carmacks
Faro
VALLEY
Ross River
South Nahanni
Mt. Sir James MacBrien 9,062
Big Salmon
Big Salmon R.
Aishihik
Aishihik L.
Burwash Landing
Kluane Lake
Destruction Bay
SHAKWAK VALLEY
Mt. Lucania 17,147
Kluane
Lower Laberge
L. Laberge
Teslin R.
Frances Lake
Hyland R.
Coal R.
N. W. TERRS.
Canyon
Upper Laberge
Takhini
Haines Jct.
Champagne
Whitehorse
ST. ELIAS MOUNTAINS
Mt. Logan 19,850
Mt. St. Elias 18,008
MacRae
Robinson
Kusawa L.
Tagish
Johnsons Crossing
Liard
Klukshu
Carcross
Lake
Teslin
Teslin
Swift River
Upper Liard
Watson Lake
Lower Post
Smith River
BRITISH COLUMBIA
Yakutat Bay
Yakutat
Alsek R.
Chilkat Pass
Chilkoot Pass
Atlin
Atlin Lake
CASSIAR MTS.
Liard River
Skagway
Haines
Cassiar
McDame
MUNCHO LAKE PROV. PK.
Kechika R.
GULF OF ALASKA
GLACIER BAY NAT'L MON.
Glacier Bay
ALASKA
STONE MTN. PROV. PK.
Tulsequah
Juneau
Dease Lake
© C.S.HAMMOND & Co., Maplewood, N.J.
Longitude West of Greenwich
70°
65°
60°
140°
135°
130°
125°

Z

Zaan·dam \zän-ˈdam, -ˈdäm\. Commune, North Holland prov., W Netherlands; pop. (1970e) 63,535; lumber center; many windmills; place where Peter the Great of Russia lived while he studied shipbuilding 1697.

Zab, Great \-ˈzab\ *or Arab.* **Zab al–Ka·bir** \-ˌal-kə-ˈbi(ə)r\. River, SE Turkey and N Iraq; ab. 260 m. long; rises in mountains of Kurdistan and flows S and SW into the Tigris river below Mosul.

Zab, Little *or Arab.* **Zab al–As·fal** \-al-ˈas-ˌfal\. River, NW Iran and N Iraq; ab. 230 m. long; flows SW into the Tigris river ab. 50 m. below the Great Zab.

Zabaikal. See TRANSBAIKALIA.

Zabern. See SAVERNE.

Ząb·ko·wi·ce \ˌzō^{n}(m)p-kə-ˈvēt-sə\ *or in full* **Ząbkowice Śląs·kie** \-ˈshlō^{n}s-kyə\; *Ger.* **Fran·ken·stein** \ˈfräŋ-kən-ˌs(h)tīn\ *or in full* **Frankenstein in Schle·si·en** \-in-ˈshlā-zē-ən\. City, S Wrocław prov., SW Poland, 39 m. SSW of Wrocław; pop. (1968e) 13,600; formerly in Prussia, Germany; late-Gothic church. Founded 13th cent.; sold to Prussia 1791; assigned to Poland by Potsdam Conference 1945.

Zab Mountains \ˈzab-\. Range of the Atlas Mts., N Algeria; highest peak ab. 4300 ft.

Zā·bol \zə-ˈbōl\ *or* **Shahr–i–Za·bul** \ˌshär-ē-zə-ˈbōl\ *or formerly* **Nas·rat·a·bad** \nas-ˈrat-ə-ˌbad\. Town, E Iran, 275 m. ENE of Kermān, in cen. part of Lake Helmand depression; pop. (1966c) 18,806.

Zab·rze \ˈzäb-(ˌ)zhä\; *Ger.* **Hin·den·burg** \ˈhin-dən-ˌbərg, -ˌbu̇(ə)rg\ *or in full* **Hindenburg in Ober·schle·si·en** \-in-ˌō-bər-ˈshlā-zē-ən\. Industrial city, Katowice prov., S Poland, WNW of Katowice; pop. (1970p) 197,200; coal mining; iron foundries, rolling mills, steelworks, glassworks; chemicals. Founded c. 1300; an obscure village until end of 19th cent. when it grew rapidly; became German 1915; increased 1927 by consolidation of several towns; in World War II taken by U.S.S.R. Jan. 1945; assigned to Poland by Potsdam Conference 1945.

Za·bul \zə-ˈbōl\. Province of SE Afghanistan. See table at AFGHANISTAN.

Za·ca·pa \zə-ˈkäp-ə\. 1 Department of E Guatemala. See table at GUATEMALA.
2 Town, its ✱; pop. (1964p) 30,187; sulfur springs; in tobacco-growing region.

Za·ca·poax·tla \ˌzä-kə-ˈpwä-slə\. Municipality, Puebla state, Mexico, 70 m. NE of Puebla; pop. (1970p) 25,479; beans, coffee, sugarcane, vanilla, tobacco, medicinal herbs.

Za·ca·pu \zə-ˈkäp-u\. Municipality, Michoacán state, Mexico, 40 m. W of Morelia; pop. (1970p) 52,649; wood pulp; livestock raising; diversified agriculture.

Za·ca·te·cas \ˌzak-ə-ˈtā-kəs, -ˈtek-əs\. 1 State of cen. Mexico. See table at MEXICO.
2 City, its ✱, 65 m. NNW of Aguascalientes; munic. pop. (1970p) 56,829; altitude 8075 ft.; cathedral; large mines and smelters.

Za·ca·te·co·lu·ca \ˌzäk-ə-ˌtek-ə-ˈlü-ka\. City, ✱ of La Paz dept., S El Salvador; pop. (1968e) 15,776; commercial and industrial center.

Za·ca·tlán \ˌzä-kət-ˈlän\. Municipality, Puebla state, Mexico, 65 m. NNE of Puebla; pop. (1970p) 37,261; wheat, sugarcane, coffee, tobacco, bananas.

Za·co·al·co \ˌzä-kə-ˈäl-(ˌ)kō\ *or in full* **Zacoalco de To·rres** \-də-ˈtȯr-əs\. Town, Jalisco state, W cen. Mexico, 35 m. SSW of Guadalajara; munic. pop. (1970p) 21,929.

Zacynthus. See ZANTE.

Za·dar \ˈzäd-ˌär\ *or Ital.* **Za·ra** \ˈzär-ə\ *or anc.* **Iad·era** \ī-ˈad-ə-rə\. Port on the Adriatic, Croatia, W Yugoslavia, 72 m. NW of Split; pop. (1965e) 31,000; shipbuilding; seaside resort; fortified until 1873; ancient Roman triumphal arch; 13th cent. Lombardesque cathedral, 8th to 13th cent. churches; became Roman colony under Augustus; captured by Venice 1202 A.D.; taken by Hungary; purchased by Venice 1409; taken by Austria 1797; held by Napoleon 1805–13, Austria 1813 ff.; ceded to Italy by Treaty of Rapallo 1920; made free port 1923; returned to Yugoslavia by treaty of Feb. 10, 1947.

Za·det·skyi Island \ˌzä-det-ˈskyē-\ *or formerly* **Saint Matthew Island** \-ˈmath-(ˌ)yü-, -ˈmath-(ˌ)ü-\. Island in Mergui Archipelago (*q.v.*), Burma.

Zafarin Islands. See CHAFARINAS ISLANDS.

Ża·gań *also* **Że·gań** \ˈzhäg-ˌän(-yə)\ *or Ger.* **Sa·gan** \ˈzäg-ˌän\. City, Zielona Góra prov., SW Poland, on Bóbr river, ab. 25 m. SSW of Zielona Góra; pop. (1970p) 21,500; formerly in Prussia, Germany; first mentioned 1202; site of prison camp in World War II.

Zag·a·zig \ˈzag-ə-ˌzig\ *or Arab.* **Az–Za·qā·zīq** \ˌaz-zə-ˌkä-ˈzēk\. City, ✱ of Sharqīya gov., Lower Egypt; pop. (1970e) 173,000; trades in cotton and grain; ruins of ancient Bubastis (*q.v.*) are at Tell Basta nearby.

Zagh·ouan \ˌzag-ˈwän\. Town, N Tunisia, N Africa, ab. 25 m. W of Hammamet; pop. (1966c) 5700; railroad terminus and road junction; battles 1943.

Za·gorsk \zə-ˈgȯ(ə)rsk\ *or before 1930* **Ser·gi·ev** \ˈser-gē-(y)əf\. Town, Moscow Oblast, Russian S.F.S.R., U.S.S.R., on railroad 45 m. NE of Moscow; pop. (1969e) 87,000; chemicals, agricultural machinery, furniture. Site of early Troitsko-Sergievskaya monastery, architecturally important and long venerated as a place of pilgrimage; original wooden church, built by monk Sergius, was destroyed by Tatars 1391; two cathedrals built in monastery 1422 and 1585; also had famous bell tower.

Za·greb \ˈzag-ˌreb\ *or Hung.* **Zá·gráb** \ˈzäg-ˌräb\ *or Ger.* **Agram** \ˈäg-ˌräm\ *or anc.* **Za·gra·bia** \zə-ˈgrā-bē-ə\. City, ✱ of Croatia, NW Yugoslavia, on Sava river; 2d largest city in Yugoslavia; pop. (1971p) 566,084; machinery, chemicals, textiles, leather goods; Yugoslav Academy of Science and Arts, univ. (1874), botanical gardens, nuclear energy institute; first mentioned 1093.

Zag·ros Mountains \ˈzag-rəs-\. Mountain system in many parallel ranges, S and SW Iran, extending along and across the Iran-Iraq border; many peaks above 9000 ft., highest Zardeh Kuh 14,921 ft.

Zagy·va \ˈzȯj-(ˌ)vȯ\. River, E cen. Hungary; ab. 100 m. long; flows S into Tisza river at Szolnok.

Zā·he·dān *or* **Za·hi·dan** \ˌzä-hi-ˈdän\ *or formerly* **Duz·dab** \du̇z-ˈdäb\. Town, ✱ of Bāluchestān va Sīstān prov., E Iran; pop. (1971e) 42,000.

Zah·le \ˈza-hə-ˌlā\ *or Fr.* **Zah·lé** \zȧ-lā\. Town, cen. Lebanon, on railroad 23 m. E of Beirut; pop. (1964e) 57,589; at foot of E slope of Lebanon Mts. in Bika valley.

Zairam Nor. See SAI-LI-MU HU.

Za·i·re \zə-ˈir-ə\ *or Fr.* **Za·ï·re** \zȧ-i(ə)r\. 1 *or formerly* **Con·go** \ˈkäŋ-(ˌ)gō\ *or officially* **Democratic Republic of the Congo;** *from 1908 to 1960* **Bel·gian Congo** \ˌbel-jən-\ *or Fr.* **Congo belge** \kō^{n}-gō-belzh\ *or Flem.* **Bel·gisch Congo** \ˌbel-gəs-ˈkȯŋ-gō\; *from 1885 to 1908* **Congo Free State.** Republic, equatorial Africa, bounded on NW and N by Central African Republic, on NE by Sudan and Uganda, on E by Rwanda, Burundi, and Tanzania, on SE by Zambia, on S by Zambia and Angola, on SW by Angola, and on W by Congo; its W extremity forms narrow corridor along lower Congo river with less than 25 m. of coastline on the Atlantic Ocean; 905,063 sq. m.; pop. (1969e) 16,585,944; ✱ Kinshasa. *Physical features:* A tropical country, crossed by the equator in N cen. part; occupies greater part of Congo river basin. *Chief tributaries of the Congo* (upper course known as the Lualaba): Ubangi (on NW and N border), Aruwimi, Lindi, Lomami, Lukuga (outlet of Lake Tanganyika), Lulonga, Ruki, and Kasai. *Lakes:* Tanganyika and Mweru on E and SE borders, Kivu in E, Edward and Albert on NE border, Mai-Ndomde in W and Stanley Pool. Mostly low plateau, with marshes along Congo in NW. *Mountains:* Ranges in SE with several peaks ab. 6000 ft., higher ranges along W shore of Lake Tanganyika, and high mountains on E (highest point of Virunga group 14,786 ft., of Ruwenzori 16,791 ft.). *Chief products:* Corn, palm oil, cassava, bananas, rubber; copper, industrial diamonds, tin, zinc, manganese. *Chief towns:* Kinshasa, Lubumbashi, Kisangani, Mbuji-Mayi, Bukavu. Divided into a Federal District and 8 provinces (for pronunciation of their names, see their individual entries):

NAME	AREA (sq. m.)	POP. (1969e)	CAPITAL
Federal District	763	1,052,520	Kinshasa
Provinces			
Bandundu	115,455	2,359,694	Bandundu
Bas-Zaïre	22,644	957,448	Matadi
Équateur	155,259	2,138,787	Mbandaka
Haut-Zaïre	194,300	2,603,075	Kisangani
Kasai-Occidental	55,500	1,435,515	Kananga
Kasai-Oriental	69,235	1,143,437	Mbuji-Mayi
Kivu	100,030	2,721,064	Bukavu
Shaba	191,878	2,174,404	Lubumbashi

History: Territory developed by International Association of the Congo (1878) which was controlled by Leopold II of Belgium; Congo Free State, with Leopold autonomous sovereign, established and recognized by Berlin Conference 1885; boundaries determined by Berlin Conference, treaties with Great Britain (1894 and 1914), and with France, Germany, and Portugal (see FRENCH EQUATORIAL AFRICA and ANGOLA 1); after international criticism of treatment of natives, annexed to Belgium 1908; divided into four provinces 1914; by negotiations with Great Britain and League of Nations (1919–23), granted mandate of Ruanda-Urundi (*q.v.*) which had been taken from Germany 1916; exchanged small piece of territory in SW Portugal 1927; achieved independence June 30, 1960; immediate post-independence period marked by internal unrest, including the secession of Katanga (now Shaba) 1960–63; adopted new constitution 1967.

2 *or formerly* **Congo.** District, N Angola, SW Africa; 15,-494 sq. m.; pop. (1970p) 41,766; ✱ São Salvador; site of native kingdom (Kongo) 16th–18th cents.

3 *or* **Rio Zaire.** River, Africa. See CONGO 4.

Zai·san \'zī-ˌsän\. Lake, NE Kazakh S.S.R., U.S.S.R., in the Ala Tau; 695 sq. m.; traversed by Irtysh river.

Zai·tun \zī-'tün\. See CH'ÜAN-CHOU.

Zakarpatskaya Oblast. See TRANSCARPATHIAN OBLAST.

Zakinthos. See ZANTE.

Za·ko·pa·ne \ˌzäk-ə-'pän-ē\. Commune, Kraków prov., S Poland, in Tatra Mts. 52 m. S of Kraków; pop. (1970p) 27,000; chief summer resort and winter sports center in Poland; alt. ab. 3300 ft.; founded in 16th cent.

Za·kou·ma National Park \zə-'kü-mə-\. National park, S Chad; 1145 sq. m.; wildlife refuge (elephant, lion, panther, rhinoceros); established 1963.

Za·la \'zä-lə\. County of W Hungary. See table at HUNGARY.

Zalaca. See ZALLAKA.

Za·la·e·ger·szeg \'zò-(ˌ)lò-ˌeg-ər-ˌseg\. City, ⊗ of Zala co., W Hungary, W of Lake Balaton; pop. (1970p) 39,176.

Za·lău \zə-'lə-ō, -'laů\ *or Hung.* **Zi·lah** \'zil-(ˌ)ō\. Commune, Romania, ab. 55 m. ENE of Oradea; pop. (1966c) 15,144.

Za·lew Szcze·ciń·ski \'zä-ləf-shə-'chēn-skē\ *or Ger.* **Stet·ti·ner Haff** \s(h)te-'tē-nər-ˌhäf\ *also* **Pom·mer·sche Haff** \'pò-mər-shə-ˌhäf\. Large lagoon on coast bet. Neubrandenburg dist., East Germany, and Szczecin prov., NW Poland, opening into Pomeranian Bay bet. the islands of Usedom (*Pol.* Uznam) and Wolin, which shut it off from the Baltic Sea; receives the Oder river.

Zalew Wiślany. See VISLINSKI ZALIV.

Zal·la·ka *or* **Za·la·ca** \zə-'läk-ə\ *or Arab.* **Al–Zal·lā·qah** \ˌal-\ *or Span.* **Sa·cra·lias** \sä-'kräl-yəs\. Ancient town, SW Spain, N of Badajoz; scene of battle Oct. 23, 1086 in which Yusuf ibn-Tashfin defeated Alfonso VI of León and Castile.

Za·ma \'zā-mə\. Ancient town, N Africa, SW of Carthage; scene of decisive defeat of the Carthaginians under Hannibal by the Romans under Scipio Africanus 202 B.C.

Zam·ba·les \zäm-'bäl-əs\. Province, W Luzon, Phil.; 1434 sq. m.; pop. (1970p) 339,816; ✱ Iba. In NE are the Zambales Mts., consisting of more or less isolated volcanic cones; highest points High Peak 6683 ft. in N cen. part and Pinatubo 5770 ft. on Pampanga border. Coast irregular with sheltered anchorage of Subic Bay in S. Lumbering and stock raising important industries; chromite and uranium ore. Chief towns Iba, Olongapo, Santa Cruz.

History: Coast explored by Juan de Salcedo 1572 and region organized as a province immediately; of slow growth at first but progressed rapidly in 19th cent.; civil government established by Americans Aug. 1901; U.S. force landed near San Narciso Jan. 1945.

Zambales Mountains. Mountain range, W Luzon, Phil., running from Lingayen Gulf in N to entrance to Manila Bay in S; many peaks from 2500 to 5000 ft.; highest point High Peak 6683 ft. in N cen. Zambales; Mt. Mariveles 4444 ft. is highest in Bataan.

Zam·be·zi *or* **Zam·be·si** \zam-'bē-zē\ *or Port.* **Zam·be·ze** \zam-'bā-zə\. River, S cen. and SE Africa; ab. 1700 m. long; rises in NW Zambia, flows S across E Angola and W Zambia to the border of Botswana; turns E and forms boundary bet. Zambia and Rhodesia; crosses cen. Mozambique and empties into Mozambique Channel at Chinde; navigable in three long stretches, separated by rapids and by the Victoria Falls (*q.v.*). Has many headstreams in the marshlands of SE Angola and W Zambia; its chief tributaries on the N are the Kafue and Luangwa in Zambia and the Shire, outlet of Lake Nyasa; on the S the Chobe bet. Caprivi Strip and Botswana and the Sanyati in Rhodesia. First visited by Livingstone 1851–53 and later 1858–60 by Dr. John Kirk; little additional information gained about it before end of 19th cent.

Zam·bé·zia \zam-'bē-zē-ə\. District, Mozambique, SE Africa; 39,322 sq. m.; pop. (1970p) 1,756,864; ✱ Quelimane.

Zam·bia \'zam-bē-ə\ *or formerly* **Northern Rho·de·sia** \-rō-'dēzh(ē-)ə\. Republic, S cen. Africa, bounded on N by Zaire and Tanzania, on E by Malawi, on SE by Mozambique, on S by Rhodesia and South-West Africa, and on the W by Angola; 290,585 sq. m.; pop. (1971e) 4,396,000; ✱ Lusaka. *Physical features:* Consists of tableland (3000 to 4500 ft.) through which flow three main streams, Zambezi (also forming boundary with Rhodesia), Kafue, and Luangwa. Victoria Falls (*q.v.*) are in the Zambezi near Livingstone in SW; Lake Bangweulu is in N and Lake Mweru on Zaire boundary in N ; S end of Lake Tanganyika touches N boundary. *Chief products:* Corn, tobacco, peanuts, cotton, cassava; livestock raising; copper, lead, zinc, cobalt; manufacturing: iron and steel, cement, tiles. *Chief towns:* Lusaka, Kitwe, Ndola, Chingola, Mulfuria, Luanshya.

History: Under jurisdiction of British South Africa Company 1889 to 1924; became a British protectorate 1924; part of Federation of Rhodesia and Nyasaland 1953–63; became an independent republic 1964; announced acceptance (1967) of Chinese aid in construction of major railroad, enabling it to reroute its exports through Tanzania.

Zam·bo·an·ga \ˌzam-bə-'wäŋ-gə\. 1 Former province, W Mindanao, Phil., now divided into **Zamboanga del Nor·te** \-del-'nò(ə)r-(ˌ)tā\ (2346 sq. m.; pop. [1970p] 411,897; ✱ Dipolog) and **Zamboanga del Sur** \-del-'sù(ə)r\ (3831 sq. m.; pop. [1970p] 1,032,198; ✱ Pagadian). Very mountainous region, with range through cen. part; highest is Mt. Dapiak in NE Zamboanga del Sur, 8416 ft. Coastline has many bays, largest being Sindangan and Sibuguey. Forest resources are large; chief products hemp (abacá), copra, and rice.

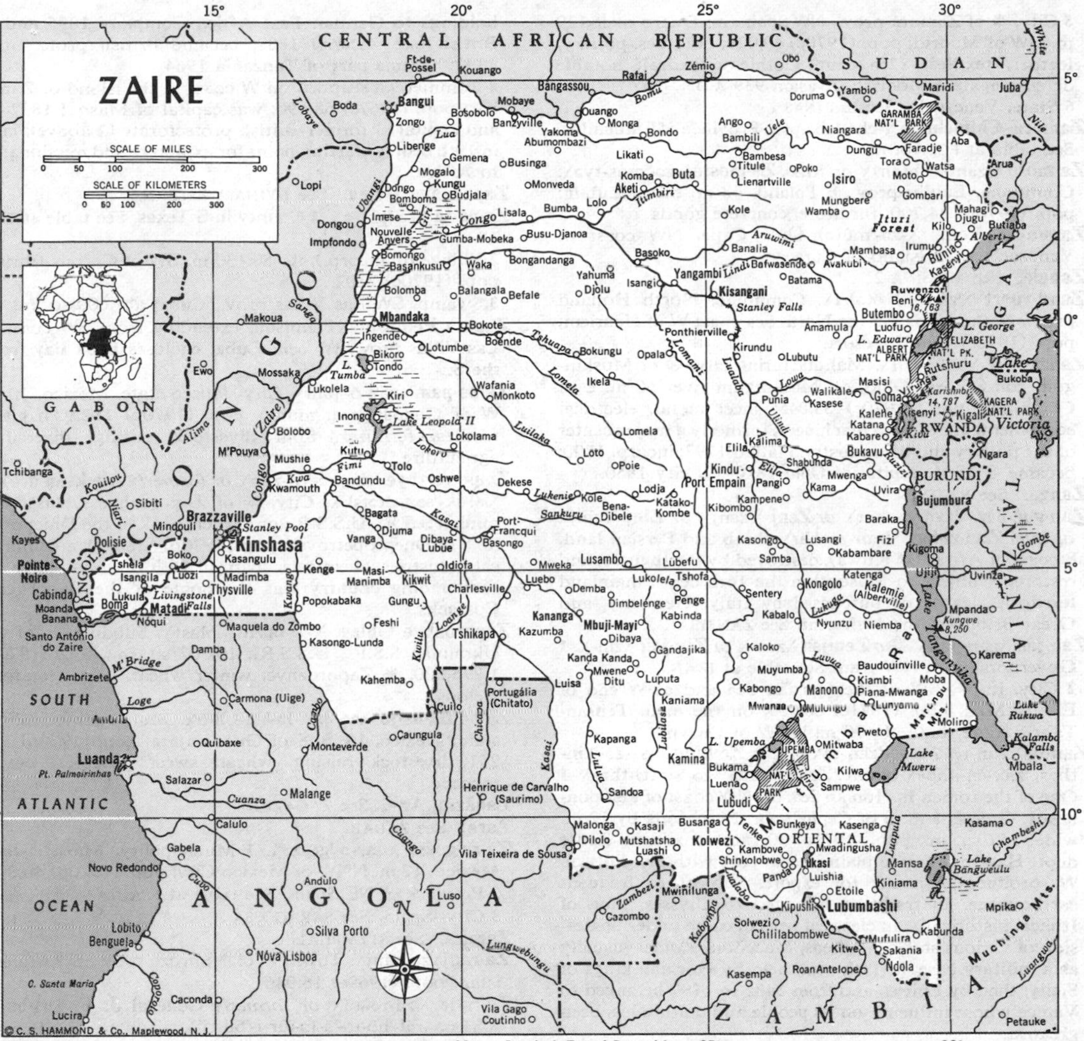

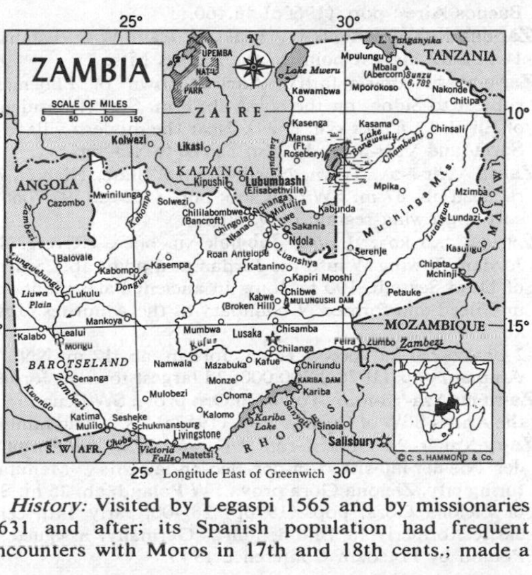

History: Visited by Legaspi 1565 and by missionaries 1631 and after; its Spanish population had frequent encounters with Moros in 17th and 18th cents.; made a military government 1837 and became part of Moro prov. 1903; civil government established 1914; divided into two provinces 1952.

2 *officially* **City of Zamboanga.** Chartered city, Zamboanga del Sur prov., Mindanao, Phil.; pop. (1970e) 188,300; exports copra and timber; port of call 600 m. S of Manila; has good roadstead but not a safe anchorage in SW monsoon. Founded 1635 as a fort for protection of Christian settlers; during U.S. possession was rebuilt into a fine town and the chief market of S Philippines. The City of Zamboanga was created c. 1940; in World War II a Japanese defense headquarters, taken by U.S. troops Mar. 10, 1945.

Zámky Nové. See NOVÉ ZÁMKY.

Za·mo·ra \zə-ˈmōr-ə, -ˈmȯr-\. 1 River, S and SE Ecuador; 190 m. long; flows E and N to join Paute river and form Santiago river, a tributary of the Marañón.

2 Town, ✱ of Zamora-Chinchipe prov., S Ecuador; pop. (1970e) 1800.

3 Town, Michoacán state, SW Mexico, 80 m. SE of Guadalajara; munic. pop. (1970p) 82,712; in center of rich agricultural region; founded 1540.

4 Province of NW Spain. See table at SPAIN.

5 City, ✱ of Zamora prov., NW Spain, on Duero river 129 m. NW of Madrid; pop. (1970p) 49,029; brandies, pottery, leather, textiles; 12th cent. Gothic cathedral; notable defense against Moorish invasion 939 A.D.
6 State, Venezuela. See BARINAS 1.

Zamora–Chin·chi·pe \-chə-'chē-pə\. Province of E Ecuador. See table at ECUADOR.

Za·mość \'zäm-ˌósh(ch)\ *or Russ.* **Za·moste** \zə-'mós-tyə\. Commune, Lublin prov., E Poland, 48 m. SE of Lublin; pop. (1970p) 34,700; furniture, concrete goods.

Za·mu·ro, Point \-zə-'mu̇(ə)r-(ˌ)ō\. Cape, NW coast of Venezuela, S of island of Curaçao.

Zancle. See MESSINA 2.

Zand·voort \'zänt-(ˌ)vō(ə)rt\. Commune, North Holland prov., Netherlands, on the North Sea coast W of Haarlem; pop. (1970e) 15,451; resort.

Zanes·ville \'zānz-ˌvil\. Manufacturing city, ⊗ of Muskingum co., SE cen. Ohio, on Muskingum river 50 m. E of Columbus; pop. (1970c) 33,045; sheet metal, electrical equipment, glass, farm machinery; formerly a major center of the pottery and tile industry. Platted 1797; incorp. 1800; became ⊗ 1804, capital of Ohio 1810–12, city 1850.

Zanga. See RAZDAN.

Zan·gue·bar \'zaŋ-gə-ˌbär\ *or* **Zenj** \'zenj\ *or* **Zinj** \'zinj\ *or later* **Zan·zi·bar** \'zan-zə-ˌbär\. Arab and Persian land, E coast of Africa (✱ Kilwa), destroyed by Portuguese, and restored (subject to Masqat) in the 16th cent.; mainland territories leased or purchased by Italy, Germany, and Great Britain in the 19th cent. See ZANZIBAR 3.

Zan·jān \zan-'jän\ *also* **Zen·jan** \zen-\ *or* **Zin·jan** \zin-\. 1 Governorship of NW Iran. See table at IRAN.
2 City, its ✱, SW of the Caspian Sea and at W end of Elburz Mts.; pop. (1971e) 60,000; on the main Tehran-Tabrīz trade route ab. 90 m. WNW of Qazvīn.

Zan·te \'zan-tē; *Ital.* 'dzän-tā\ *or Gk.* **Zá·kin·thos** \zə-'kin-thəs, 'zäk-ēn-ˌthós\ *or anc.* **Za·cyn·thus** \zə-'sin(t)-thəs\. 1 One of the Ionian Is., Ionian Sea, off NW coast of Peloponnesus, Greece, 8 m. S of Cephalonia; 25 m. long by 12 m. wide; 157 sq. m.; pop. (1971p) 30,156; constitutes Zante dept. Has wide fertile plain in cen. part with low hills on W; produces currants for export. Subject to frequent earthquakes. In tradition belonged to Ulysses, king of Ithaca; historically, in classical period, came under possession of various states—Athens, Macedon, Rome—usually as a military base; in 11th cent. held by Norman kings of Sicily; then by Epirus, and from 1482 to 1797 belonged to Venice whose influence on its people and culture has been greatest.
2 Department, Greece. See 1, above.
3 Town, ✱ of Zante dept., Ionian Is., Greece, on E coast of Zante I.; pop. (1971p) 9281; traditionally said to have been founded by Zacynthus, son of the Arcadian chief Dardanus.

Zan·zi·bar \'zan-zə-ˌbär\. 1 Former sultanate, E Africa, comprising Zanzibar (2 below) and Kenya; included also Mafia I., the coast of Tanzania, and the coast of Somalia S of lat. 3°N.
2 Former British protectorate, comprising Zanzibar I., Pemba I., and adjacent small islands; 1020 sq. m.; ✱ Zanzibar; became an independent sultanate Dec. 10, 1963 and a republic Jan. 12, 1964; united with Tanganyika 1964 to form Tanzania. See TANZANIA.
3 Chief island of Tanzania, E Africa, in the Indian Ocean off NE coast of Tanzania; 641 sq. m.; pop. (1967c) 190,494; subdivided into **Zanzibar Mji·ni** \-em-'jē-nē\, **Zanzibar Sham·ba·ni North** \-shəm-'bä-nē-\ and **Zanzibar Shambani South** (see table at TANZANIA); world's chief source of cloves; also produces copra, coconut oil, mangrove bark.
History: Formerly under Arab rulers, became dominated by Portuguese c. 1505; conquered by ruler of Oman (*q.v.*) in 18th cent.; came under Masqat when in 1832 the town of Zanzibar became capital of the sayid of Masqat whose successor received European recognition of his independence from Oman; granted part of mainland holdings to German East Africa Company 1895 and to British (see KENYA) 1887; became British protectorate 1890; became part of Tanzania 1964.
4 Commercial seaport, on W coast of the island of Zanzibar; pop. (1967c) 68,490; was capital of Masqat 1832–56 and capital of former British protectorate (2 above); later in 19th cent. a starting point for explorers and missionaries to Africa.

Zapadnaya Dvina. See DVINA, WESTERN.

Za·pa·ta \zə-'pät-ə\. 1 County in S Texas. See table at TEXAS.
2 Village (unincorp.), its ⊗, 130 m. SW of Corpus Christi; pop. (1970c) 2102.
3 Swamp, SW Las Villas prov., Cuba; ab. 600 sq. m.

Zapata Peninsula. Peninsula extending from SW coast of Las Villas prov., W cen. Cuba; encloses Broa Bay from the S.

Za·po·pan \ˌzäp-ō-'pän\. City, Jalisco state, Mexico, 10 m. W of Guadalajara; munic. pop. (1970p) 182,934; glass, textiles, fertilizer, flour; livestock raising; diversified agriculture.

Za·po·ro·zhye \ˌzäp-ə-'rò-zhə\ *or formerly* **Ale·ksan·drovsk** \ˌal-ik-'san-drəfsk\. City, ✱ of Zaporozhye Oblast, Ukrainian S.S.R., U.S.S.R., on the left bank of the Dnieper 45 m. S of Dnepropetrovsk; pop. (1970p) 658,000; metallurgical industries; chemicals, soap. In 16th cent. and later the surrounding country was the home of the Zaporogian Cossacks.

Zaporozhye Oblast \-'ò-bləst, -ˌblast\. Subdivision of the Ukrainian S.S.R., U.S.S.R.; 10,502 sq. m.; pop. (1970p) 1,775,000; ✱ Zaporozhye; winter wheat, corn, potatoes, melons.

Za·po·tla·ne·jo \zə-ˌpòt-lə-'nā-(ˌ)hō\. Municipality, Jalisco state, Mexico, 18 m. E of Guadalajara; pop. (1970p) 32,251; livestock raising; wheat, sweet potatoes, beans, tobacco.

Zaqāzīq, Az–. See ZAGAZIG.

Zara. See ZADAR.

Za·ra·go·za \ˌzar-ə-'gō-zə\. 1 Municipality, México state, Mexico, 12 m. NNW of Mexico City; pop. (1970p) 46,806.
2 Province of NE Spain. See table at SPAIN.
3 City, Spain. See SARAGOSSA.

Zaraka. See STYMPHALIS.

Za·ranj\zə-'ränj\. Town, ✱ of Nimroze prov., SW Afghanistan; pop. (1969e) 16,946.

Zá·ra·te \'zä-rə-ˌtā\ *or formerly* **General J. F. Uri·bu·ru** \ˌhā-nā-ˌräl-'hō-tə-'ā-fə-ˌu̇r-i-'bü-rü\. Town, N Buenos Aires prov., E Argentina, on Paraná river 56 m. NW of Buenos Aires; pop. (1960c) 46,460.

Zar·deh Kuh \ˌzärd-ə-'kü\. Peak, W Iran, W of Eşfahān; 14,921 ft.; highest point in the Zagros Mts.

Zar·e·phath \'zar-ə-ˌfath\. Ancient town of Phoenicia, subject to Sidon, on the coast ab. 8 m. S of it; residence of Elijah (*1 Kings* xvii. 8–24). Near the modern village of **Sar·a·fand** \'sär-ə-ˌfand\ *also* **Sa·rep·ta** \sə-'rep-tə\.

Za·ria \'zär-ē-ə\. Town, North-Central State, Nigeria, on railroad ab. 87 m. SW of Kano; pop. (1969e) 192,706; in cotton-growing region; univ. (1962).

Zar·qa \'zär-kə\. 1 *also* **Jab·bok** \jə-'bòk\. River, NW Jordan, flowing W into the Jordan at a point ab. 25 m. N of Dead Sea; ab. 100 m. long; in ancient Palestine it was in Gilead and formed N boundary of the Amorites (*Josh.* xii. 2).
2 *or* **Az–Zar·qā'** \az-\. Town, Jordan, ab. 12 m. NNE of Amman; pop. (1970e) 200,000; 2d largest town in Jordan.

Za·ru·ma \zä-'rü-mə\. Town, El Oro prov., SW Ecuador, in the Andes SSW of Cuenca; pop. (1962c) 9000; gold mining.

Ża·ry \'zhär-ē\; *Ger.* **So·rau** \'zō-ˌrau̇\ *or in full* **Sorau in der Nie·der·lau·sitz** \-in-dər-ˌnēd-ər-'lau̇-ˌzits\. Manufacturing city, Zielona Góra prov., SW Poland, ab. 25 m. SW of Zielona Góra; pop. (1970p) 28,400; early 14th cent. castle; formerly in Brandenburg, Germany; assigned to Poland by Potsdam Conference 1945.

Zas·tron \ˈzas-trən\. Town, S Orange Free State, E cen. Rep. of South Africa, bet. Caledon and Orange rivers 95 m. SSE of Bloemfontein; pop. (1967e) 4800; agriculture.

Ža·tec \ˈzha-ˌtets\ *or Ger.* **Saaz** \ˈzäts\. Town, Czech S.R., W Czechoslovakia, on Ohře river, ab. 45 m. WNW of Prague; pop. (1968e) 16,258; in hop-growing region.

Za·va·la \zə-ˈvä-lə\. County in Texas. See table at TEXAS.

Za·wia \ˈzä-wē-ə\ *or* **Az–Zā·wi·yah** \az-\. Coastal town, NW Libya, ab. 30 m. WSW of Tripoli; pop. (1970e) 37,000.

Za·wier·cie \zä-ˈvye(ə)r-(ˌ)chā\. Industrial commune, Katowice prov., S Poland, ab. 25 m. NW of Katowice; pop. (1970p) 39,400; coal and iron mining; glass, textiles.

Zay·ton \zā-ˈtōn\. See CH'ÜAN-CHOU.

Zba·razh \zə-ˈbär-əsh\ *or Pol.* **Zba·raż** \zə-ˈbär-ˌäsh\. Town, W Ukrainian S.S.R., U.S.S.R., just NE of Ternopol; formerly in Poland; famous in Polish wars in 17th cent.

Zbruch \zə-ˈbrüch\ *or Pol.* **Zbrucz** \zə-ˈbrüch\. River, bet. Ternopol and Khmelnitski oblasts, W Ukrainian S.S.R., U.S.S.R.; 152 m. long; flows S into the Dniester.

Zduń·ska Wo·la \zə-ˌdün-skə-ˈvȯ-lə\. Commune, Łódź prov., cen. Poland, 28 m. WSW of Łódź; pop. (1970p) 29,100; textiles, leather.

Zealand. See SJÆLLAND.

Zeb·u·lon \ˈzeb-yə-lən\. City, ⊗ of Pike co., W Georgia; pop. (1970c) 776.

Zee·brug·ge \ˈzā-ˌbrəg-ə\. Seaport, West Flanders prov., NW Belgium, port of the city of Brugge (Bruges) with which it is connected by canal; occupied by the Germans 1914 and used as a submarine base; raided by British naval contingents 1918, who succeeded in destroying the mole and blocking the harbor by sinking vessels at its mouth.

Zee·han \ˈzē-ən\. Mining town, W Tasmania, Australia, 18 m. N of upper end of Macquarie Harbour; pop. (1970c) 4000.

Zee·land. 1 \ˈzē-lənd\. City, Ottawa co., W Michigan, 21 m. WSW of Grand Rapids; pop. (1970c) 4734; poultry center.
2 \ˈzē-lənd, ˈzā-, ˈzā-ˌlänt\. Province, SW Netherlands, composed of several islands (esp. Walcheren, North and South Beveland, Schouwen, and Tholen) on the North Sea coast, and a part of the mainland S of the Schelde estuary; 1043 sq. m.; pop. (1970e) 305,754; ✱ Middelburg, on Walcheren I.; largely below sea level, protected by dikes; wheat, oats, potatoes, flax, fruit. United with Holland and Hainaut in 14th cent.

Zee·rust \ˈzā-(ˌ)rəst\. Town, W Transvaal, NE Rep. of South Africa, 135 m. W of Pretoria; pop. (1967e) 9300; center of fertile Marico valley producing citrus fruit, wheat, oats, and cotton; district is rich in various minerals.

Zefat. See SAFAD.

Żegań. See ŻAGAŃ.

Zeist \ˈzīst\. Commune, Utrecht prov., cen. Netherlands, 6 m. E of Utrecht; pop. (1970e) 55,619.

Zeitz \ˈ(t)sīts, ˈzīts\. Manufacturing city, Halle dist., East Germany, on Weisse Elster river 21 m. SSW of Leipzig; pop. (1970e) 46,736; machinery, chocolate, sugar, textiles.

Zela. See ZILE.

Ze·la·ya \zə-ˈlī-ə\. Department of E Nicaragua. See table at NICARAGUA.

Ze·le \ˈzā-lə\. Commune, East Flanders prov., NW cen. Belgium, E of Gent; pop. (1969e) 18,551.

Ze·lee, Cape \-zā-ˈlā\. Cape, S end of Maramasike I., SE Solomon Is., W Pacific Ocean.

Ze·le·no·dolsk \zə-ˌle-nə-ˈdȯlsk\ *or formerly* **Ze·le·ny Dol** \zə-ˈlyȯ-nē-ˈdȯl\. Town, Tatar A.S.S.R., U.S.S.R., ab. 25 m. E of Kazan; pop. (1969e) 76,000.

Ze·li·e·no·ple \ˌzēl-yə-ˈnō-pəl\. Borough, Butler co., W Pennsylvania, 18 m. SE of New Castle; pop. (1970c) 3602; lumber; manufactures metal products.

Zel·la–Meh·lis \ˌ(t)sel-ə-ˈmā-ləs, ˌzel-\. City, Suhl dist., East Germany, 28 m. SW of Erfurt; pop. (1970e) 17,286.

Zelle. See CELLE.

Zel·za·te \zel-ˈzä-tə\ *or* **Sel·zae·te** \sel-ˈzä-tə\. Commune, East Flanders prov., NW cen. Belgium, ab. 27 m. W of Antwerp near the Netherlands boundary; pop. (1969e) 12,538.

Žemaitija. See SAMOGITIA.

Zem·po·al·te·pec \ˌzem-pə-ˈwäl-tə-ˌpek\ *or* **Zem·po·al·te·petl** \-ˌwäl-ˈtā-ˌpet-ᵊl\. Mountain, SE Mexico, 55 m. E of the city of Oaxaca; 11,138 ft.; stands at the convergence of the Sierra Madre Occidental and the Sierra Madre Oriental.

Ze·mun \ˈzem-ˌün\ *or Ger.* **Sem·lin** \zem-ˈlēn\. City, S Vojvodina autonomous region, Serbia, NE Yugoslavia, on Danube river WNW of Belgrade; commercial center and shipping point.

Zengg. See SENJ.

Ze·ni·ca \ˈze-nət-sə\. Town, Bosnia and Herzegovina, W cen. Yugoslavia, ab. 35 m. NW of Sarajevo; pop. (1965e) 54,000; steel.

Zenj. See ZANGUEBAR.

Zenjan. See ZANJĀN.

Zenta. See SENTA.

Zen·tsu·ji \zent-ˈsü-jē, ˈzen(t)-sə-ˌjē\. Town, Kagawa prefecture, NE Shikoku I., Japan, SW of Takamatsu; pop. (1970c) 35,254; birthplace of the founder (Kobo Daishi) of the Buddhist sect Shingon-shu; has large temple; camp for U.S. war prisoners in World War II.

Ze·rav·shan \ˌzer-af-ˈshän\. River, U.S.S.R.; 460 m. long; rises at W end of Alai Mts., flows W through NW Tadzhik S.S.R. and the oasis region of Samarkand in SE Uzbek S.S.R. to the desert near Bukhara.

Zerbst \ˈ(t)se(ə)rpst, ˈze(ə)rpst\. City, Magdeburg dist., East Germany, NW of Dessau; pop. (1970e) 19,589; 13th cent. church, 17th cent. castle.

Zeria. See CYLLENE.

Zer·matt \(t)ser-ˈmät\. Village in Valais canton, SW cen. Switzerland; pop. (1970c) 3101; elevation 5315 ft., in the Pennine Alps; tourism; surrounded by meadows (*Matten*) forming a valley from which can be seen the Matterhorn to the SW.

Zet·land \ˈzet-lənd\ *or* **Shet·land** \ˈshet-\. Scottish county comprising the Shetland Is. (*q.v.*); 552 sq. m.; pop. (1971p) 17,298; ✱ Lerwick; agriculture, herring fisheries, livestock raising (Shetland ponies), knitted goods, tweeds.

Zeu·len·ro·da \ˌ(t)sȯi-lən-ˈrōd-ə, ˌzȯi-\. Industrial city, Gera dist., East Germany, WSW of Zwickau; pop. (1970e) 13,571; 15th cent. town hall; textiles, hosiery, woven goods.

Ze·ven \ˈ(t)sā-fən, ˈzā-\. Town, Lower Saxony, West Germany, 24 m. NE of Bremen; scene Sept. 8, 1757 during the Seven Years' War of duke of Cumberland's capitulation to the French (the Convention of Kloster-Zeven) by which Hannover was abandoned.

Ze·ve·naar \ˌzā-və-ˈnär\. Town, Gelderland prov., Netherlands, SE of Arnhem near the West German border on the Rhine; pop. (1970e) 18,433; customs station.

Ze·ya \ˈzā-yə\. River, Russian S.F.S.R., U.S.S.R.; 751 m. long; rises in Stanovoi Mts. in E Chita Oblast and flows S and SE into the Amur river in Khabarovsk Krai; joined by the Selemdzha in its lower course.

Ze·ze·re \ˈzez-ə-rə, ˈzāz-\. River, cen. Portugal; ab. 130 m. long; rises near Spanish border and flows SW to the Tagus below Abrantes; waterpower development.

Zgierz \zə-ˈgyesh\ *or Russ.* **Zgerzh** \zə-ˈgersh\. Town, Łódź prov., cen. Poland, 4 m. N of Łódź; pop. (1970p) 42,800; textiles.

Zgorzelec. See GÖRLITZ.

Zhda·nov \ˈzhdän-əf, zhə-ˈdän-\ *or formerly* **Ma·ri·u·pol** \ˌmar-ē-ˈü-ˌpȯl\. City, Donetsk Oblast, Ukrainian S.S.R., U.S.S.R., on N shore of Sea of Azov 60 m. W of Taganrog, at mouth of the Kalmius; pop. (1970p) 419,000; iron and steel works; a major Soviet port; exports incl. steel, coal, machinery; fishing. Probable site of ancient Greek colony, but modern town founded 1779; in World War II held by Germans Oct. 7, 1941–Aug. 30, 1943.

Zhe·lez·no·do·ro·zhny \zhə-ˌlez-nə-də-ˈrȯzh-nē\ *or formerly* **Obi·ra·lov·ka** \ˌə-bər-ə-ˈləf-kə\. Town, Moscow Oblast, Russian S.F.S.R., U.S.S.R., 16 m. E of Moscow; pop. (1969e) 52,000.

Zhel·ty·ye Vo·dy \ˈzhȯl-tē-yə-ˈvȯd-ē\ *or formerly* **Zhel·ta·ya Re·ka** \ˌzhȯl-tə-yə-rə-ˈkä\. Town, Dnepropetrovsk Oblast, Ukrainian S.S.R., U.S.S.R., ab. 70 m. W of Dnepropetrovsk; pop. (1967e) 41,000.

Zhi·gu·levsk \ˌzhə-gül-ˈyȯfsk\ *or formerly* **Ot·vazh·ny** \ət-ˈväzh-nē\. Town, Kuibyshev Oblast, Russian S.F.S.R., U.S.S.R., ab. 30 m. WNW of Kuibyshev; pop. (1969e) 51,000.

Zhi·to·mir \zhi-ˈtō-ˌmi(ə)r\ *also* **Ji·to·mir** \zhi-\. Industrial city, ✻ of Zhitomir Oblast, Ukrainian S.S.R., U.S.S.R., on the Teterev river 85 m. W of Kiev; pop. (1970p) 161,000; machinery; breweries, lumber mills.

History: An old town on the early trade route from Scandinavia to Constantinople and on the direct route W from Kiev; plundered by Tatars in medieval times; belonged to Lithuania after 1320, then to Poland, and was sacked by the Cossacks in 1648; incorporated in Russia 1778; occupied by Axis forces Aug. 2, 1941 in World War II; retaken by Soviets after much severe fighting Dec. 31, 1943.

Zhitomir Oblast \-ˈō-bləst, -ˌblast\. Subdivision of the Ukrainian S.S.R., U.S.S.R.; 11,544 sq. m.; pop. (1970p) 1,626,000; ✻ Zhitomir; winter wheat, corn, hops, sugar beets, flax.

Zhlo·bin \zhlō-ˈbyin\. Town, Gomel Oblast, Belorussian S.S.R., U.S.S.R., on right bank of the Dnieper ab. 75 m. S of Mogilev; pop. (1967e) 23,000; bitterly contested point in Soviet campaign of 1944; retaken by Soviets in June.

Zhme·rin·ka \zhmə-ˈriŋ-kə\. Town, W Vinnitsa Oblast, W cen. Ukrainian S.S.R., U.S.S.R., 20 m. SW of Vinnitsa; pop. (1967e) 31,000; railroad junction point, a key communication center in World War II campaigns of 1944; taken by Soviets Mar. 30, 1944.

Zhob \ˈzhōb\. District, NE Baluchistan, Pakistan; 10,478 sq. m.; pop. (1961c) 87,686; ✻ Fort Sandeman. Occupies extensive valley of the **Zhob River** (a tributary of the Gumal) which is direct route bet. North-West Frontier Province and Quetta in Pakistan. First opened up in 1884 by Zhob Valley Expedition; formed into a political agency 1890; scene of several frontier disturbances (1884, 1890, 1919).

Zhu·kov·ski \zhü-ˈkȯf-skē\; *formerly* **Ot·dykh** \ȯt-ˈdik\ *or* **Sta·kho·no·vo** \stə-ˈkȯn-ə-və\. Town, Moscow Oblast, Russian S.F.S.R., U.S.S.R., 23 m. SE of Moscow; pop. (1969e) 68,000.

Zidon. See SIDON.

Zie·bach \ˈzē-ˌbäk, -ˈbä, -ˈbȯ\. County in South Dakota. See table at SOUTH DAKOTA.

Ziel, Mount \-ˈzē(ə)l\. Mountain, Macdonnell Ranges, Northern Territory, Australia; 4955 ft.; highest peak in Northern Territory.

Zie·lo·na Gó·ra \zhe-ˌlō-nə-ˈgür-ə\. 1 Province of W cen. Poland. See table at POLAND.

2 *or Ger.* **Grün·berg** \ˈgrün-ˌbe(ə)rg\ *also* **Grünberg in Schle·si·en** \-in-ˈshlā-zē-ən\. Industrial city, its ✻; pop. (1970p) 73,200; wine, textiles, machinery, vehicles; coal mining; metal foundries; engineering coll. (1965); formerly in Germany; assigned to Poland by Potsdam Conference 1945.

Zie·rik·zee \ˈzir-ik-ˌzā\. Commune, Zeeland prov., SW Netherlands, on S shore of Schouwen I.; pop. (1970e) 7842.

Zigana Sira Dağları. See ŞMALİ ANADOLU DAĞLARI.

Zi·ghout You·cef \zē-ˌgüt-yü-ˈsef\ *or formerly* **Con·dé–Smen·dou** \kōⁿ-ˈdā-smäⁿ-ˈdü\. Commune, NE Algeria; pop. (1966c) 5260.

Zi·guin·chor \ˌzē-ˌgaⁿ-ˈshȯ(ə)r\. River port, ✻ of Casamance region, SW Senegal, on Casamance river 45 m. from its mouth; pop. (1967e) 46,333.

Zilah. See ZĂLĂU.

Zi·le \zi-ˈlā\ *or anc.* **Ze·la** \ˈzē-lə\. Town, Tokat prov., N cen. Turkey, on tributary of Yeşil Irmak; pop. (1965c) 26,113. In a battle here 47 B.C. Pharnaces II, king of Pontus, was defeated by Caesar who announced his victory to the senate at Rome by his famous laconic message: *Veni, Vidi, Vici.*

Ži·li·na \ˈzhil-ə-ˌnä\ *or Hung.* **Zsol·na** \ˈzhōl-ˌnȯ\ *or Ger.* **Sil·lein** \zil-ˈīn\. Town, E cen. Czechoslovakia, on Váh river, ab. 45 m. SE of Ostrava; pop. (1968e) 40,726.

Zil·le·be·ke \ˈzil-ə-ˌbā-kə\. Commune, West Flanders prov., NW Belgium, near Ieper (Ypres); pop. (1969e) 1830; held by the British in World War I.

Zil·ler·ta·ler Alps \ˌ(t)sil-ər-ˌtäl-ər-, ˌzil-\. Subsidiary range of the E Alps, along boundary bet. NE Italy and the Tirol, Austria, at W end of the Hohe Tauern; highest peak Hochfeiler 11,513 ft.

Zil·ling Tso \ˈzil-iŋ-ˈtsō\ *or* **Sel·ling Tso** \ˈsel-iŋ-\. Lake, E cen. Tibet, China; alt. 15,120 ft.

Zi·ma \ˈzē-mə\. Town, Irkutsk Oblast, Russian S.F.S.R., U.S.S.R., ab. 150 m. NW of Irkutsk; pop. (1967e) 42,000.

Zi·ma·tlán de Al·va·rez \ˌzē-mət-ˈlän-də-ˈäl-və-ˌrez\. Municipality, Oaxaca state, Mexico, 15 m. S of Oaxaca; pop. (1970p) 40,302; handwoven fabrics, ceramics; lumber; wheat, coffee, sugarcane, fruit.

Zim·ba·bwe \zim-ˈbäb-wē\. Site of ruins, Rhodesia, 17 m. SE of Victoria. Distinguished as **Great Zimbabwe** from a smaller and more recent group of ruins 8 m. distant (**Little Zimbabwe**). Ruins comprise a probable citadel or acropolis, a temple, and huge walls of granite monoliths fitted without mortar. Discovered by Adam Benders in 1868; origin a subject of controversy; recent excavations (late 1950's, early 1960's) have yielded iron tools, gold objects, pottery; radiocarbon dates indicate initial settlement by Iron Age people 3d cent. A.D. Similar ruins found in other parts of Rhodesia, also in Botswana and the Rep. of South Africa.

Zim·ni·cea \ˈzēm-ni-ˌchä\. Town, Teleorman co., S Romania, on the Danube ab. 27 m. SW of Bucharest; pop. (1966c) 13,231.

Zin, Wilderness of \-ˈzin\ *or Heb.* **Mid·bar Zin** \ˌmid-bär-\. Desert region, SW of the Dead Sea, S Israel; in Biblical times the region bet. W Edom and SE Judaea, traversed by the Israelites on their journey to Canaan (*Num.* xx. 1).

Zi·nal Rot·horn \(t)sē-ˈnäl-ˈrōt-ˌhȯ(ə)rn, zi-\ *also* **Mo·ming** \ˈmō-miŋ\. Peak, SW cen. Switzerland, in the Pennine Alps near Zermatt; 13,849 ft.

Zinantecati. See TOLUCA, NEVADO DE.

Zi·na·pé·cua·ro \ˌzē-nə-ˈpā-kwə-ˌrō\. Municipality, Michoacán state, Mexico, 32 m. NE of Morelia; pop. (1970p) 32,826; livestock raising; diversified agriculture.

Zin·der \ˈzin-dər\ *also* **Sin·der** \ˈsin-dər\. Commercial town and military headquarters, S Niger, N Africa, ab. 65 m. N of the Nigeria border; pop. (1969e) 32,905; since latter part of 19th cent. an administrative and trading town and center for exploration.

Zinj. See ZANGUEBAR.

Zinjan. See ZANJĀN.

Zinovievsk. See KIROVOGRAD.

Zi·on \ˈzī-ən\. 1 City, Lake co., NE corner of Illinois, on Lake Michigan 5 m. N of Waukegan; pop. (1970c) 17,268; founded as Zion City by John Alexander Dowie, head of the Christian Catholic Church, 1901; incorp. 1902; developed and industrialized by Dowie's successor, Wilbur Glenn Voliva, 1907–39.

2 *or* **Si·on** \ˈsī-ən, ˈzī-\. Height, E part of the city of Jerusalem (*q.v.*), Israel; originally the Jebusite stronghold captured by David (*2 Sam.* v). On it was built the Temple, residence of David, and other buildings so that it became the center of Jewish spiritual life and came to be used as synonym for the Jewish people as a whole.

Zion National Park. See UNITED STATES, *National Parks.*

Zi·pa·qui·rá \ˌzē-pə-ki-ˈrä\. Town, Cundinamarca dept., cen. Colombia, N of Bogotá; pop. (1968e) 28,812; center of salt-mining, cattle-raising district; site of underground Salt Cathedral, carved in a salt mountain.

Zipfer Neudorf. See SPIŠSKÁ NOVÁ VES.

Zip·po·ri \zə-ˈpȯr-ē\ *or anc.* **Sep·pho·ris** \sə-ˈfȯr-əs\. Village, N Israel, ab. 3 m. NNW of Nazareth; chief city of Galilee 1st cen. A.D.; in early centuries of Christian Era a rival of Tiberias.

Ziria. See CYLLENE.

Zi·ro \ˈzi(ə)r-(ˌ)ō\. Town, ✱ of Arunachal Pradesh, NE India, ab. 185 m. NE of Shillong.

Zi·sters·dorf \ˈ(t)sis-tərz-ˌdȯrf, ˈzis-\. Town, Lower Austria, ab. 27 m. NE of Vienna; pop. (1961c) 3008; extensive oil fields; in 1946–48 in Soviet zone.

Zi·tá·cua·ro \zə-ˈtä-kwə-ˌrō\. City, Michoacán state, Mexico, 60 m. SE of Morelia; munic. pop. (1970p) 67,173; commercial and tourist center; flour mills; livestock raising; wheat, barley, sugarcane, melons, coffee; early center of Mexican War of Independence, 1811 ff.; Junta of Zitácuaro the first central directing body of the independence movement; scene of fighting 1864–65; burned 1865.

Zit·tau \ˈ(t)zi-taů\. Manufacturing city, Dresden dist., East Germany, on left bank of Neisse river 46 m. ESE of Dresden; pop. (1970e) 43,087; textiles, electrical equipment, chemicals; promenades on site of old fortifications. Became city 1255; to Saxony 1635; important medieval textile-manufacturing center.

Zituni. See LAMIA.

Zla·to·ust \ˌzlät-ə-ˈüst\. City, W Chelyabinsk Oblast, Russian S.F.S.R., U.S.S.R., in S part of Ural Mts. 75 m. W of Chelyabinsk; pop. (1970p) 181,000; metallurgical industries; since middle of 18th cent. has been a center of the ironworking industry; founded 1865.

Zlín. See GOTTWALDOV.

Zna·men·ka \ˈznä-myen-kə\. Town, cen. Kirovograd Oblast, Ukrainian S.S.R., U.S.S.R., 20 m. NNE of Kirovograd; pop. (1967e) 26,000.

Zna·mensk \ˈznä-mənsk\ *or formerly* **Weh·lau** \ˈvā-laů, ˈwā-\. Town, Kaliningrad Oblast, Russian S.F.S.R., U.S.S.R., on S bank of the Pregolya at the mouth of the Lava; has late-Gothic church of 16th cent. and several other earlier structures; in part of Prussia assigned to the U.S.S.R. 1945. Treaty signed here Sept. 19, 1657 bet. Brandenburg and Poland by which Poland renounced sovereignty over duchy of Prussia and Brandenburg restored territory seized from Poland.

Znoj·mo \ˈznȯi-(ˌ)mō, ˈsnȯi-\ *or Ger.* **Zna·im** \ˈ(t)snä-ˌim, ˈ(t)snīm\. City, Czech S.R., cen. Czechoslovakia; pop. (1968e) 25,732; food processing; armistice signed here July 12, 1809 after Napoleon's victory in the battle of Wagram.

Zoan. See TANIS.

Zoar \ˈzō(ə)r\. Village, Tuscarawas co., E Ohio, N of Dover; pop. (1970c) 228; site of Separatist community founded 1817 by group of German Protestant peasants, disbanded 1898.

Zo·fing·en \ˈ(t)sō-fiŋ-ən, ˈzō-\. Commune, Aargau canton, Switzerland; pop. (1970c) 9292; textiles.

Zoh·reh *or* **Zuh·reh** \zə-ˈrä\ *or formerly* **Tab** \ˈtäb\. River, SW Iran; 200 m. long; flows W and SW into the head of the Persian Gulf along the boundary bet. Khūzestān and Fārs provs.

Zol·lern \ˈ(t)sȯl-ərn, ˈzȯ-\. Mountain, Baden-Württemberg, West Germany, near Hechingen; 2805 ft.; site of castle Hohenzollern.

Zolotoi Rog. See GOLDEN HORN 3.

Zólyom. See ZVOLEN.

Zom·ba \ˈzäm-bə\. Town, Malawi, SE Africa, in Shire Highlands, ab. 70 m. S of Lake Nyasa; pop. (1971e) 20,000.

Zombor. See SOMBOR.

Zone of the Straits. Demilitarized zone around the Bosporus, the Dardanelles, and the Sea of Marmara, administered 1920–22 by the League of Nations; mostly returned to Turkey 1923. See STRAITS, THE 2.

Zon·gul·dak \ˌzȯŋ-gəl-ˈdäk\. **1** Province of NW Turkey, Asia. See table at TURKEY.

2 Seaport city, its ✱, on the Black Sea 140 m. E of the Bosporus; pop. (1965c) 55,404; coal mining.

Zon·ne·be·ke \ˈzȯn-ə-ˌbāk-ə\. Commune, West Flanders prov., NW Belgium; pop. (1969e) 3525; battlefield 1915 and 1917 in World War I.

Zoppot. See SOPOT.

Zor. **1** \ˈtsȯ(ə)r, ˈzȯ(ə)r\. Town, Lebanon. See TYRE.

2 \ˈzȯ(ə)r\. Former region, Turkey, Asia, extending on both sides of Euphrates river; ✱ Deir-ez-Zor; now divided bet. Turkey and Syria.

Zor·kul, Lake \-zȯr-ˈkül\ *or in Afghanistan* **Sa·rī Qūl** \ˌsär-i-ˈkül\ *or Eng.* **Lake Vic·to·ria** \-vik-ˈtōr-ē-ə, -ˈtȯr-\. Small lake in high Pamirs, Tadzhik S.S.R., U.S.S.R., on NE border of Afghanistan; alt. 13,400 ft.

Zorndorf. See SARBINOWO.

Zoutpansberg. See SOUTPANSBERG.

Zren·ja·nin \ˈzren-yə-nin, zə-ˈren-\; *formerly* **Pe·trov·grad** \ˈpe-trəv-ˌgräd\ *or* **Ve·li·ki Beč·ke·rek** \ˌvel-ə-kē-bech-ˈker-ək\ *or Hung.* **Nagy·becs·ke·rek** \ˈnäj-ˈbech-kə-ˌrek\. City, Vojvodina autonomous prov., NE Yugoslavia, ab. 30 m. NE of Novi Sad; pop. (1971p) 59,580; commercial center for grain-producing region; sugar refineries, breweries, distilleries.

Zsolna. See ZILINA.

Zsombolya. See JIMBOLIA.

Zuetina, Ez. See EZ ZUETINA.

Zufar. See DHOFAR.

Zug \ˈ(t)sük, ˈzüg\. **1** Swiss canton; 92 sq. m.; pop. (1970c) 67,996; ✱ Zug; fruit growing; victory of Confederates over Habsburgs 1315.

2 Commune, its ✱, N cen. Switzerland, on Lake of Zug 15 m. S of Zurich; pop. (1970c) 22,972; electrical equipment, textiles; cattle market; tourism; clock tower (1480), town hall (1505); purchased by Rudolf I 1273; entered Swiss Confederation mid-14th cent.

Zug, Lake of *or Ger.* **Zu·ger See** \ˈ(t)sü-gər-ˌzā, ˈzü-\. Lake, N cen. Switzerland, N of Lake of Lucerne; ab. 15 sq. m.; max. depth 650 ft.; alt. 1368 ft.

Zug·spit·ze \ˈ(t)sük-ˌs(h)pit-sə\. Peak in Wetterstein Mts. of the Bavarian Alps, S Bavaria, West Germany, on border of the Tirol 54 m. SSW of Munich; 9720 ft.; highest peak in West Germany.

Zugur. See ZUQAR.

Zuhreh. See ZOHREH.

Zuid Afrikaansche Republiek. See SOUTH AFRICAN REPUBLIC.

Zui·der Zee *also* **Zuy·der Zee** \ˌzīd-ər-ˈzā, -ˈzē\ *or anc.* **Fle·vo La·cus** \ˌflē-(ˌ)vō-ˈlā-kəs\. Formerly a landlocked inlet of the North Sea, N coast of Netherlands; extended inland ab. 80 m.; originally a lake, but was joined to the North Sea by inundations; now again separated from the North Sea by a dike (completed 1932), and is called IJsselmeer (*q.v.*); partly drained, three polders already having been formed, the Noordoostpolder (completed 1942), the Wieringermeer (*q.v.*), and the Eastern Flevoland (completed 1957), of the five which are planned. See WADDEN ZEE.

Zuidholland. See SOUTH HOLLAND.

Zú·jar \ˈzü-ˌhär\. River, Badajoz prov., SW Spain; 100 m. long; flows into Guadiana river.

Zu·la \ˈzü-lə\. Seaport town, Ethiopia, on Gulf of Zula; ancient ruins nearby; became Italian protectorate 1888, part of Eritrea 1890.

ə abut; ə kitten, Fr. table; ər further; a back; ā bake; ä cot, cart; à Fr. bac; aů out; ch chin; e less; ē easy; g gift
i trip; ī life; j joke; k Ger. ich, Buch; ⁿ Fr. vin; ŋ sing; ō flow; ȯ flaw; œ Fr. bœuf; œ̄ Fr. feu; ȯi coin; th thin
th this; ü loot; ů foot; ue Ger. füllen; ue̅ Fr. rue; y yet; ʸ Fr. digne \dēnʸ\, nuit \nwʸē\; yü few; yů furious; zh vision

Zula, Gulf of *or* **Annes·ley Bay** \ˌanz-lē-\. Inlet of the Red Sea, Ethiopia.

Zu·lia \ˈzül-yə\. State of Venezuela. See table at VENEZUELA.

Zül·pich \ˈ(t)sül-pik, ˈzül-\ *or anc.* **Tol·bi·a·cum** \täl-ˈbī-ə-kəm\. Commune, North Rhine-Westphalia, West Germany, SW of Cologne; at Tolbiacum Clovis I, king of the Franks, defeated the Alamanni 496.

Zu·lue·ta \ˌzü-lə-ˈwāt-ə\. Town and municipality, Las Villas prov., W cen. Cuba; pop. (1967e) 13,770 (town).

Zu·lu·land \ˈzü-(ˌ)lü-ˌland\. Region, NE Natal, E Rep. of South Africa; 10,362 sq. m.; pop. (1960c) 570,160; chief cash crop sugarcane. Consists of native reserves of Zulus, a Bantu nation that first came into prominence in early part of 19th cent. Chiefs Chaka and Dingaan noted for their cruelty and for the fighting efficiency of their *impis* (regiments); under both Dingaan and Cetewayo fought with Boers and British; Cetewayo defeated in battle 1879 and finally overcome 1883; land of Zulus taken under British control 1887 and annexed to Natal 1897; known as "Province of Zululand" 1898–1910.

Zu·mar·ra·ga \zü-ˈmär-ə-gə\. Municipality, W coast of Buad I. off W Samar, Phil., 9 m. S of Catbalogan; pop. (1969e) 15,800; includes barrios on Daram I.

Zum·bi, Point \-ˈzüm-bē\ *or* **Point Tu·rí** \-ˈtür-ē\. Cape, N coast of Maranhão state, NE Brazil.

Zum·bo \ˈzům-bō, ˈzəm-\. Westernmost town of Mozambique, SE Africa, 600 m. up the Zambezi river.

Zum·pan·go \züm-ˈpäŋ-(ˌ)gō\. 1 Lake in the Valley of Mexico, cen. Mexico, ab. 30 m. N of the city of Mexico. 2 Town, México state, cen. Mexico; munic. pop. (1970p) 35,035.

Zungaria. See DZUNGARIA.

Zu·ni \ˈzü-n(y)ē\. 1 River, New Mexico and Arizona; ab. 90 m. long; rises in W New Mexico and flows W into the Little Colorado river in Arizona.
2 *or* **Zu·ñi** \ˈzü-nyē\. Indian pueblo and village, McKinley co., NW New Mexico, in Zuni Indian Reservation, on Zuni river ab. 32 m. S of Gallup; pop. (1970c) 3958; inhabited by descendants of people of Cibola, reported in 1539 by the Spaniards; agriculture, weaving, pottery.

Zuni Mountains. Range, McKinley and Valencia cos., W New Mexico; highest peak 8110 ft.

Zu·po, Piz \pēts-ˈ(t)sü-(ˌ)pō\. Mountain, second highest of the Bernina Mts. of the Rhaetian Alps, on the Swiss-Italian border; 13,120 ft.; its peak is hidden (*zupò*).

Zu·qar \ˈzü-ˌkär\ *or* **Zu·gur** \ˈzü-gər\. Island at S end of Red Sea, bet. Yemen (✻ San'a) and Ethiopia; belongs to Ethiopia.

Zu·rich \ˈzů(ə)r-ik\ *or Ger.* **Zü·rich** \ˈtsü̅e-ri<u>k</u>\. 1 Swiss canton. See table at SWITZERLAND.
2 City, its ✻, at foot of Alps on Limmat river at NW end of Lake of Zurich 60 m. NE of Bern; pop. (1970c) 422,640; largest city in Switzerland; machine tools, turbines, textiles; banking and insurance; publishing; tourism; railway center; among its buildings are an 11th–13th cent. Byzantine cathedral, 12th cent. Fraumünster, town hall, and museums; univ. (founded 1833), and the Swiss Federal Institute of Technology (founded 1860); botanical and zoological gardens.
History: Occupied by lake dwellers before Roman occupation 58 B.C.; became free imperial city 1219; joined Swiss Confederation 1351; Swiss defeated Austrians here 1443; center of Swiss Reformation; residence of Zwingli; scene of French victory over Russians 1799; place where treaty ending Franco-Italian war was concluded 1859.

Zurich, Lake of; *Ger.* **Zü·rich·see** \ˈtsü̅e-rik-ˌzā\ *or* **Zü·ri·cher See** \ˈtsü̅e-rik-ər-ˌzā\. Lake, N cen. Switzerland, for the most part in Zurich canton; 34 sq. m.; 25 m. long; max. depth 469 ft.

Zu·shi \ˈzü-shē\. Town, Kanagawa prefecture, SE Honshū, Japan, ab. 30 m. SW of Tokyo near Kamakura; pop. (1970c) 48,242; bathing resort.

Zus·mars·hau·sen \ˈ(t)sůs-ˌmärs-ˌhaůz-ᵊn, ˈzůs-\. Village, Bavaria, West Germany, ab. 14 m. W of Augsburg; battle May 17, 1648 in which Count Wrangel and Turenne defeated the Imperialists and Bavarians.

Zut·phen \ˈzət-fən\. Manufacturing commune, Gelderland prov., E Netherlands, on IJssel river; pop. (1970e) 27,610; formerly a fortified town; Church of St. Walpurgis, 12th cent. Gothic structure; battlefield on which Sir Philip Sidney was mortally wounded Sept. 1586.

Zuyder Zee. See ZUIDER ZEE.

Zvo·len \ˈzvȯ-ˌlen, ˈsfȯ-\ *or Hung.* **Zó·lyom** \ˈzō-ˌlyōm\ *or Ger.* **Alt·sohl** \ˈält-ˌzōl\. Town, Slovak S.R., E cen. Czechoslovakia, on the Hron river 100 m. NE of Bratislava; pop. (1968e) 24,769.

Zwaarteberg. See SWARTBERG.

Zwai, Lake \-ˈzwī\. Lake, cen. Ethiopia, ab. 65 m. S of Addis Ababa.

Zwei·brück·en \(t)sfī-ˈbrük-ən\ *or Fr.* **Deux·ponts** \dər-pōⁿ\ *or Lat.* **Bi·pon·ti·um**\bī-ˈpän-ch(ē-)əm\. Manufacturing city, Rhineland-Palatinate, West Germany, 53 m. WSW of Mannheim; pop. (1969e) 32,914; textiles, machinery, footwear; received charter 1352; known to scholars for its early editions of Greek and Latin classics; under Swedish crown 1697–1718; over 80 percent of city destroyed in World War II, since largely rebuilt.

Zwellendam. See SWELLENDAM.

Zwick·au \ˈtsfik-aů, ˈzwik-\. Manufacturing and mining city, Karl-Marx-Stadt dist., East Germany, on the Mulde river 42 m. S of Leipzig; pop. (1970e) 127,000; automobiles, chemicals, wire; coal mines; 14th and 15th cent. churches, 16th cent. town hall, old castle. Birthplace of composer Robert Schumann; Schumann Museum (1956). First mentioned 1118; became city 1220; free imperial city 1290–1323; prominent in rise of Anabaptists 1524; occupied by Allies Apr. 1945.

Zwijn·drecht \ˈzvīn-ˌdrekt, ˈsfīn-\. 1 Commune, Belgium. See ZWYNDRECHT.
2 Commune, South Holland prov., Netherlands; pop. (1970e) 31,761; suburb of Dordrecht.

Zwil·linge \ˈtsvil-iŋ-ə, ˈzvil-\. Two peaks in Pennine Alps. See CASTOR.

Zwittau. See SVITAVY.

Zwol·le. 1 \ˈzwäl-ē\. Town, Sabine parish, W Louisiana, 61 m. S of Shreveport; pop. (1970c) 2169.
2 \ˈzvȯl-ə, ˈsfȯl-\. Commune, ✻ of Overijssel prov., E Netherlands, on IJssel river; pop. (1970e) 76,167; shipbuilding yards, iron foundries; railroad junction; Church of St. Michael, dating from 15th cent.; provincial museum; Church of our Lady, 15th cent. Gothic building; Stadhuis. Thomas à Kempis lived for 64 years in a monastery on Agnietenberg, 3 m. from Zwolle.

Zwyn·drecht *or* **Zwijn·drecht** \ˈzvīn-ˌdrekt, ˈsfīn-\. Commune, Antwerp prov., Belgium; pop. (1969e) 9515; W suburb of Antwerp.

Ży·rar·dów \zhi-ˈrär-ˌdüf\. Commune, Warszawa prov., cen. Poland, 25 m. WSW of Warsaw; pop. (1970p) 33,200; textiles.

Zyrian Autonomous Area. See KOMI AUTONOMOUS SOVIET SOCIALIST REPUBLIC.

Zyr·ya·novsk \zər-ˈyä-nəfsk\. Town, East Kazakhstan Oblast, Kazakh S.S.R., U.S.S.R., ab. 80 m. ESE of Ust-Kamenogorsk; pop. (1969e) 56,000.

Ży·wiec \ˈzhi-vəts\. Town, Kraków prov., S Poland, ab. 40 m. SW of Kraków; pop. (1970p) 22,500.

GARY LIBRARY
VERMONT COLLEGE
MONTPELIER, VT.

VERMONT COLLEGE
MONTPELIER, VERMONT

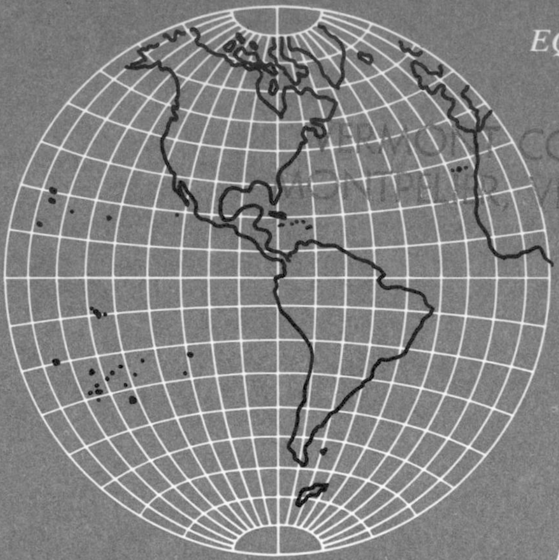

EQUAL-AREA

Lambert's Azimuthal Equal-Area represents square mileage correctly, showing areas of continental size to best advantage.

VERMONT COLLEGE
MONTPELIER, VERMONT

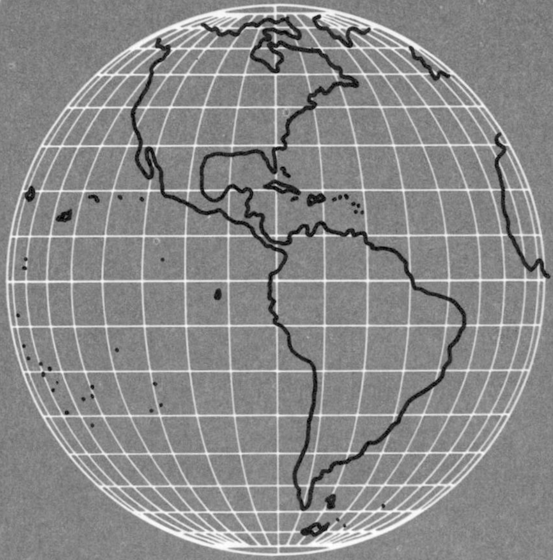

ORTHOGRAPHIC

Shows true scale in central area, viewed as if mapped from a very great height; distortions increase away from center in areas near edges.

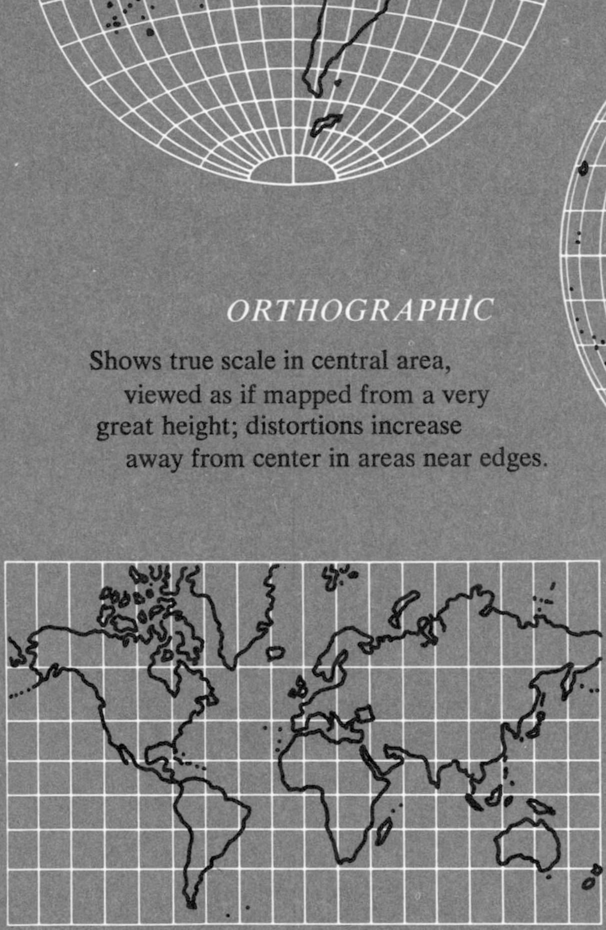

MERCATOR

Starts with central cylindrical projection; both meridians and parallels are straight lines and at true distance apart at equator.

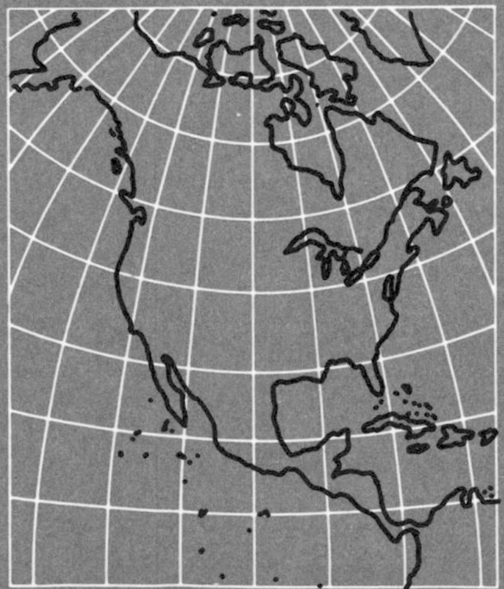

POLYCONIC

Based on conic projection with its central meridian a straight line and latitude circles marked on it true to scale.